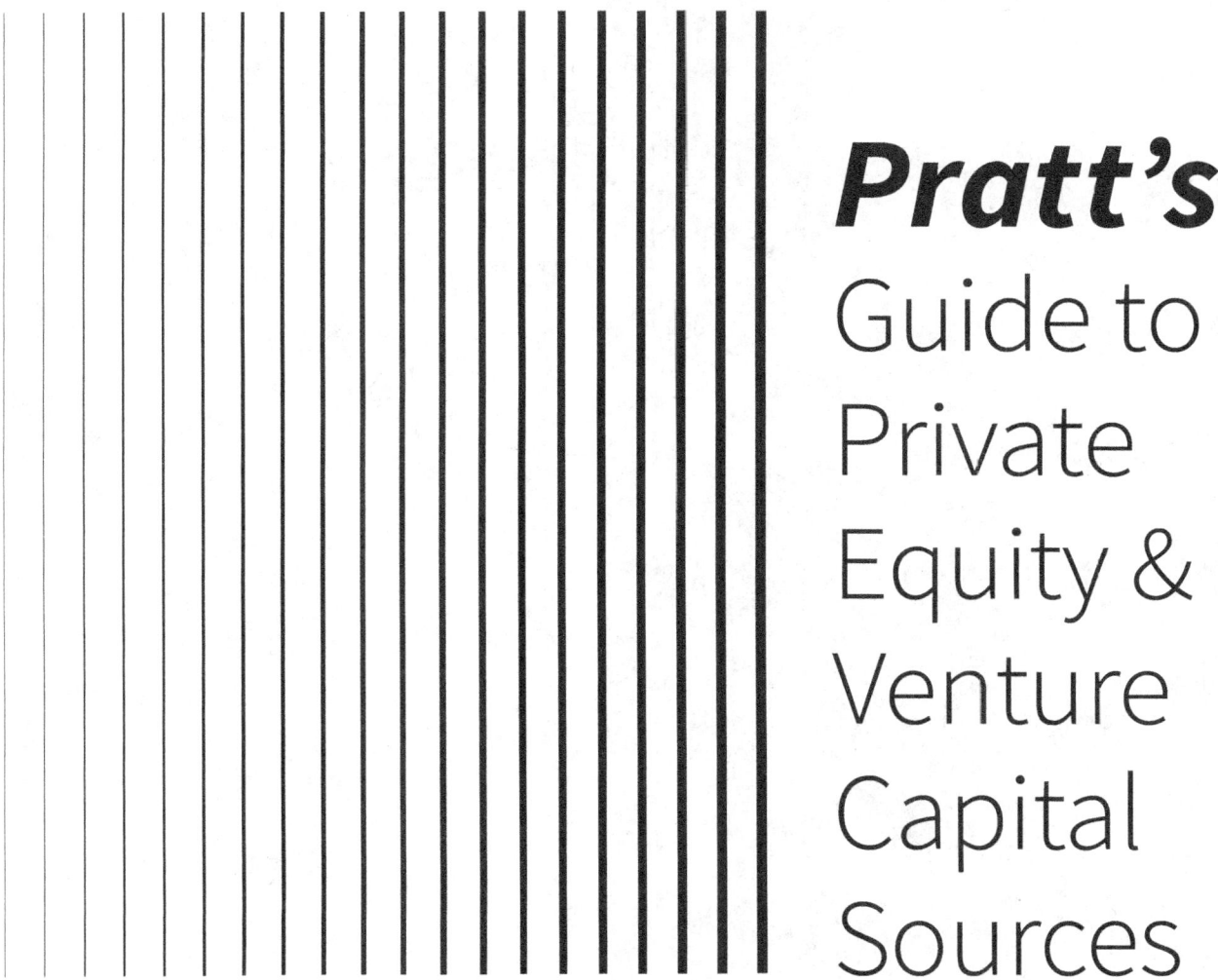

Pratt's Guide to Private Equity & Venture Capital Sources

2018 Edition

Buyouts Insider
9 East 38th Street
11th Floor
New York, NY 10016
Fax: (301) 287-2887
Customer Service: (800) 455-5844

For book orders, call (800) 455-5844

For access to *Pratt's Guide Online*,
call David Korn at (646) 356-4513
or email customerservice@buyoutsinsider.com

Paul Centopani .... Research Editor
Allison Brown .... Associate Art Director
David Toll .... Executive Editor
Jim Beecher .... President

Pratt's Guide to Private Equity & Venture Capital Sources

2018 Edition

Copyright 1970-2018 by Buyouts Insider, a division of Simplify Compliance LLC.

All Rights Reserved.
Photocopying or other reproduction without written permission of Buyouts Insider is strictly forbidden.
Printed in the United States of America

ISNN 2329-5791
ISBN 978-0-9912789-9-2

Library of Congress Catalog Card Number 85-644764
Buyouts Insider

Preface

Worldwide, private equity thrived on principles of entrepreneurship and individual and collective risk-taking. In myriad ways, its development sprung from the willingness to assume the risks involved in new business development. The imagination, boldness and energy of entrepreneurs and small business owners combined with the involvement and persistence of experienced private equity investors helped create new industries and new technologies. In turn, these have significantly increased the productivity of many economies and the workers involved in them.

This publication is dedicated all the people willing to take on the challenges of building new businesses, and to those private equity investors with the skills, fortitude and foresight to identify and participate in new business development. The contributions of the world's entrepreneurs are as important as ever as we seek to create new jobs and broaden our economic activities. With globalization increasing, this has become even more significant.

An important element in successful private equity financing is a good relationship between the entrepreneur and the investor. Understanding this partnership is a necessary initial step for the prospective entrepreneur. The entrepreneur brings fresh ideas, management skills, and personal commitments to this relationship, while the private equity investor adds financial backing and valuable new business development experience.

Although the entrepreneur and the management team are usually the most crucial elements in the relationship (especially since private equity investors cannot perform their roles without entrepreneurs), the collaboration of entrepreneurial management and private equity investors usually enables a developing business to achieve its objectives faster and more efficiently. In today's dynamic and competitive marketplace, such an investor/management partnership is often vital to the survival and success of new business development. Private equity has acted as a catalyst for economies worldwide by igniting the flames of expansion.

The amount of private equity raised internationally remains a fraction of the asset base of entities such as commercial banks and insurance companies. In the United States, certain state pension funds control more money than the entire domestic private equity industry. As a result, the private equity process involves a personal relationship, which can either grow and endure or end in frustration and disappointment. In the future, companies that receive private equity financing will require continuous financial support to fuel their growth. These follow-on investments – which constitute a large part of current private equity activity and the commitments to new investment opportunities – will absorb the capital currently available in the industry. This includes any "dry powder", or capital raised, but not yet invested. As these commitments are made, the demand for private equity will intensify.

This book was conceived and has grown over roughly the last four decades by helping to increase the entrepreneur's chances of success in receiving funding. It provides the most thorough analysis of what each private equity firm can and will supply to fledgling businesses. It is our hope that by organizing and simplifying this process, we can help you get the right financing for your business idea.

Table of Contents

Pratt's Guide to Private Equity & Venture Capital Sources

INTRODUCTION	11
FIRM STATISTICS REPORT	13
Buyout firms	15
Venture firms	23
Mezzanine firms	31
DIRECTORY OF PRIVATE EQUITY & VENTURE CAPITAL FIRMS	
Firm Listings	39

INDEX	
U.S. Firm Cross Reference by State	2359
Buyout Firms	2360
Fund of Funds	2372
Mezzanine	2373
Other Private Equity (OPE)	2374
Real	2375
Venture Firms	2375
Non-U.S. Firm Cross Reference by Nation	2390
Buyout Firms	2391
Fund of Funds	2410
Mezzanine Firms	2412
Other Private Equity (OPE)	2412
Real	2412
Venture Firms	2413
Executive Cross Reference by Firm Name	2436

Table of Contents

INTRODUCTION	17
FIRM STATISTICS REPORT	
Buyout firms	19
Venture firms	23
Mezzanine firms	27
DIRECTORY OF PRIVATE EQUITY & VENTURE CAPITAL FIRMS	
Firm Listings	29

INDEX	
U.S. Firm Cross Reference by State	2336
Buyout Firms	2360
Fund of Funds	2370
Mezzanine	2373
Other Private Equity (OPE)	2375
Real	2378
Venture Firms	2379
Non-U.S. Firm Cross Reference by Location	2390
Buyout Firms	2397
Fund of Funds	2410
Mezzanine Funds	2412
Other Private Equity (OPE)	2412
Real	2412
Venture Firms	2413
Alphabetic Cross Reference by Firm Name	2423

Introduction

This is the 42nd edition of Pratt's Guide to Private Equity & Venture Capital Sources, a directory long considered to be the industry benchmark. The goal of this publication is to incorporate the most current information on individual private equity and venture capital firms as well as the private equity investment process. This current edition contains over 5,500 listings, including firms from around the world. Our collection of data continues to increase with the inclusion of the research efforts of PricewaterhouseCoopers, with which in 2002 one of Buyouts Insider's predecessors, Thomson Financial, together with the National Venture Capital Association, jointly conducted the quarterly MoneyTree data collection report. Pratt's Guide was created as a practical tool to help entrepreneurs and small-business managers understand the process of raising capital and locating compatible private equity investors. Since various terms are mentioned in the directories, it is important that these terms are clearly defined.

Early-Stage Financing
- Seed Financing is generally a relatively small amount of capital provided to an inventor or entrepreneur to prove a concept and to qualify for start-up capital. This may involve product development and market research as well as building a management team and developing a business plan, if the initial steps are successful.
- Research and Development Financing is a tax advantaged partnership set up to finance product development for start-ups as well as more mature companies. Investors secure tax write-offs for the investments as well as a later share of the profits if the product development is successful.
- Start-up Financing is provided to companies completing product development and initial marketing. Companies may be in the process of organizing or they may already be in business for one year or less but have not sold their product commercially. Usually such firms will have made market studies, assembled the key management, developed a business plan and are ready to do business.
- First-Stage Financing is provided to companies that have expended their initial capital (often in developing and market testing a prototype), and require funds to initate full-scale manufacturing and sales.

Expansion Financing
- Second-Stage Financing is working capital for the initial expansion of a company that is producing and shipping, and has growing accounts receivable and inventories. Although the company has made progress, it may not yet be showing a profit.
- Third-Stage or Mezzanine Financing is provided for major expansion of a company whose sales volume is increasing and that is breaking even or profitable. These funds are used for further plant expansion, marketing, working capital, or development of an improved product.
- Bridge Financing is needed at times when a company plans to go public within six months to a year. Often bridge financing is structured so that it can be repaid from the proceeds of a public underwriting. It can also involve restructuring of major stockholder positions through secondary transactions. Restructuring is undertaken if there are early investors who want to reduce or liquidate their positions, or if management has changed and the stockholdings of the former management their relatives and associates are being bought out to relieve a potential oversupply of stock when public.
- Balanced is a venture strategy in which a variety of venture stages of development are invested in or there is no stated venture focus.

Acquisition/Buyout Financing
- Acquisition Financing provides funds to finance an acquisition of another company.
- Management/Leveraged Buyout funds enable an operating management group to acquire a product line or business (which may be at any stage of development) from either a public or private company; often these companies are closely held or family owned. Management/

leveraged buyouts usually involve revitalizing an operation, with entrepreneurial management acquiring a significant equity interest.
- Industry Rollups are financings that are involved in acquiring companies within the same industry category.
- Control-block Purchases are investments in which at least 50% of company's outstanding shares are acquired.

Other Financings
- Generalist PE refers to either a stated focus of investing in all stages of private equity investment (not just venture) or a fund considered to be a generalist by its investment record when it has no one investment focus.
- Fund of funds have direct investments that consist of investments in other private equity funds.
- Recapitalizations consist of financing provided for turnaround situations, particularly for distressed companies.
- Special Situations is a catchall category consisting of financings that do not apply to more specific categories.
- Private Placement financings consist of acquiring shares of publicly traded companies in privately placed issuances, as opposed to acquiring them on the open market.
- Public Companies are financings of publicly traded companies that occur in the open market.
- Distressed Debt financings consist of investing in the debt of companies that have either filed for bankruptcy or are likely to do so in the future.
- Turnaround financings involve investing in companies at a time of operational or financial difficult with the intention of improving the company's performance.

Each company seeking financing and its advisors must determine the type of private equity firm best suited for their specific investment situation. Each private equity firm has particular preferences, methods of investing and selecting investments, and its own type of legal investment agreements. Since no two private equity firms operate exactly in the same way, it is essential that entrepreneurs and business managers analyze their needs and attempt to match these requirements with the skills and interests of an appropriate private equity firm.

While the private equity firms included in Pratt's Guide have been selected because they are devoted primarily to private equity financing, there is no assurance that a specific group will be receptive to an approach or will have immediately available funds. At present, however, most private equity investors are actively seeking new investment opportunities. Even with the current availability of investment capital, the majority of new investment proposals are not financed. Convincing private equity investors that a potential development is an important investment opportunity is truly new company's first major sale. Further, a good working relationship must be established and maintained to optimize the benefits of a private equity investment.

The private equity firms in this directory have different capacities for servicing client companies and it is critical for the entrepreneur or business management to understand these capabilities. Some firms can provide a range of financial and managerial services while others may have specialized talents that would be valuable to some new businesses, but less important to others.

Both the nature and extent of active involvement private equity investors put into their investments vary. For the most part, the most successful investors need to be actively involved in the companies they finance. While the directories in Pratt's Guide attempt to delineate preferences as well as levels of activity and involvement, the entrepreneur and management team must develop a means of evaluating the ongoing role of the private equity investor.

Generally, private equity firms are not interested in reviewing situations that are clearly not going to meet their stated preferences. Consequently, a careful review of the information in the text and in the directories should help capital seekers begin to develop a productive investment relationship with the firms.

Pratt's Guide to Private Equity & Venture Capital Sources

Firm Statistics Report

Firm Statistics Report

Pratt's Guide to Private Equity & Venture Capital Sources

Firm Statistics Reported
Ranked Firms (by assets under management)
Buyout Firms
Data as of: January 1, 2018

Rank	Firm Name	Firm Capital Under Management (USD Mil)	No. of Companies Invested In	No. of Funds Managed by Firm
1	Carlyle Group LP	97,700.00	315	146
2	Blackstone Group LP	84,300.00	96	103
3	KKR & Co LP	80,379.50	151	62
4	Goldman Sachs & Co LLC	79,000.00	248	125
5	Apollo Global Management LLC	73,993.95	83	34
6	TPG Capital Management LP	57,600.00	102	44
7	Partners Group Holding AG	57,000.00	2	58
8	Ardian France SA	49,270.10	54	78
9	CVC Capital Partners Ltd	41,941.00	160	16
10	Oaktree Capital Management LP	40,281.00	1	69
11	Providence Equity Partners LLC	40,000.00	79	27
12	Apax Partners LLP	35,800.00	103	70
13	HarbourVest Partners LLC	35,551.00	78	98
14	Hermes Gpe Llp	33,943.50	5	9
15	Permira Advisers LLP	33,860.00	128	23
16	Letterone Holdings SA	29,000.00	2	1
17	Csfb Private Equity Advisers	28,000.00	66	27
18	Bain Capital Inc	27,000.00	142	55
19	Adams Street Partners LLC	26,800.00	2	85
20	Pliant Corp	25,000.00	3	42
21	Pantheon Ventures (UK) LLP	24,500.00	-	42
22	IFM Investors Pty Ltd	23,662.10	9	12
23	LGT Capital Partners AG	23,370.90	-	16
24	AG BD LLC	23,000.00	2	42
25	Fortress Investment Group LLC	22,000.00	9	41
26	3i Group PLC	21,667.10	868	34
27	Clayton Dubilier & Rice LLC	21,000.00	46	15

Pratt's Guide to Private Equity & Venture Capital Sources

Rank	Firm Name	Firm Capital Under Management (USD Mil)	No. of Companies Invested In	No. of Funds Managed by Firm
28	Ascribe Capital, LLC	21,000.00	14	15
29	Thomas H Lee Partners LP	20,000.00	97	20
30	Acas LLC	20,000.00	176	7
31	Capital Dynamics Sdn Bhd	20,000.00	-	81
32	Avenue Capital Group LLC	19,600.00	-	21
33	BlackRock Inc	17,200.00	4	21
34	Charterhouse Capital Partners LLP	16,870.50	44	16
35	Neuberger Berman LLC	16,732.87	-	17
36	Terra Firma Capital Partners Ltd	16,711.30	31	12
37	Cinven Group Ltd	16,679.50	70	9
38	BC Partners LLP	15,484.00	58	14
39	Hm Capital Partners LLC	15,000.00	64	10
40	Summit Partners LP	15,000.00	3	43
41	Hamilton Lane Advisors LLC	15,000.00	-	37
42	Madison Dearborn Partners LLC	14,000.00	54	24
43	Warburg Pincus LLC	14,000.00	64	23
44	EQT Funds Management Ltd	13,522.20	146	26
45	Insight Venture Partners LLC	13,211.40	56	17
46	Candover Investments PLC	13,017.40	43	8
47	Nordic Capital	12,851.20	83	10
48	PineBridge Investments LLC	12,700.00	3	32
49	Welsh Carson Anderson & Stowe	12,000.00	140	19
50	Golden Gate Capital Inc	12,000.00	18	24
51	Vista Equity Partners LLC	11,500.00	22	14
52	Pamplona Capital Management LLP	11,144.04	17	7
53	Berkshire Partners LLC	11,000.00	52	12
54	Siguler Guff & Company LP	10,964.70	6	37
55	TA Associates Management LP	10,792.00	62	49
56	GoldPoint Partners LLC	10,047.00	2	19
57	Advent International Corp	10,000.00	188	82
58	Lindsay Goldberg & Bessemer LP	10,000.00	12	7
59	Abraaj Capital Ltd	10,000.00	40	45

Pratt's Guide to Private Equity & Venture Capital Sources

Rank	Firm Name	Firm Capital Under Management (USD Mil)	No. of Companies Invested In	No. of Funds Managed by Firm
60	Stone Point Capital LLC	9,730.38	65	13
61	Gsc Partners	9,200.00	15	12
62	Leonard Green & Partners LP	9,000.00	25	10
63	Qalaa Holdings SAE	9,000.00	-	4
64	Db Capital Partners	8,943.00	7	13
65	Citigroup Venture Capital International Brazil LP	8,820.00	2	3
66	Equistone Partners Europe Ltd	8,779.60	200	15
67	Centerbridge Partners LP	8,627.95	11	8
68	Arle Heritage LLP	8,539.10	31	6
69	New Mountain Capital I LLC	8,500.00	12	8
70	HIG Capital LLC	8,500.00	39	19
71	BDT Capital Partners LLC	8,206.00	7	3
72	Hellman & Friedman LLC	8,000.00	56	11
73	Bridgepoint Advisers Ltd	8,000.00	166	32
74	GTCR Golder Rauner LLC	8,000.00	217	22
75	Sun Capital Partners Inc	8,000.00	45	11
76	Oak Hill Capital Management Inc	8,000.00	40	6
77	Mount Kellett Capital Hong Kong Ltd	7,443.59	8	4
78	Doughty Hanson and Co.	7,362.00	51	18
79	Waterland Private Equity Investments BV	7,073.30	55	9
80	KSL Capital Partners LLC	7,036.62	1	11
81	Cerberus Capital Management LP	7,000.00	-	18
82	IK Investment Partners Ltd	6,991.20	109	11
83	CVC Asia Pacific Ltd	6,845.00	44	5
84	Actis LLP	6,773.00	10	37
85	Veritas Capital Fund Management LLC	6,650.00	12	7
86	Hubei Province Changjiang Industry Investment Group Co Ltd	6,623.15	-	3
87	RRJ Capital Fund	6,562.00	16	4
88	Pacific Equity Partners Pty Ltd	6,404.60	27	15
89	Towerbrook Capital Partners LP	6,390.23	62	11
90	Morgan Stanley Private Equity	6,371.40	91	43
91	MBK Partners Inc	6,300.00	17	5

Pratt's Guide to Private Equity & Venture Capital Sources

Rank	Firm Name	Firm Capital Under Management (USD Mil)	No. of Companies Invested In	No. of Funds Managed by Firm
92	Wilshire Private Markets	6,242.20	-	21
93	Riverside Co	6,200.00	171	22
94	Platinum Equity LLC	6,050.00	8	5
95	Crestview Advisors, LLC	6,000.00	3	11
96	J.H. Whitney & Co LLC	6,000.00	81	22
97	Pomona Management LLC	6,000.00	-	19
98	Teachers Insurance and Annuity Association of America	6,000.00	1	5
99	Montagu Private Equity LLP	5,960.00	80	7
100	Silver Lake Partners LP	5,900.00	53	12
101	Jafco Co Ltd	5,889.30	8	73
102	Solidarity Fund QFL	5,631.20	-	12
103	Lion Capital LLP	5,321.90	9	6
104	Altor Equity Partners AB	5,084.30	51	4
105	Citic Private Equity Funds Management Co Ltd	5,067.46	13	9
106	Trilantic Capital Management LP	5,005.80	51	36
107	Jordan Company LP	5,000.00	39	5
108	Baring Private Equity Asia Ltd	5,000.00	41	38
109	Audax Group, Inc.	5,000.00	36	12
110	Levine Leichtman Capital Partners Inc	5,000.00	27	14
111	Capital Z Partners Ltd	4,840.00	25	7
112	Francisco Partners LP	4,831.90	26	9
113	Vitruvian Partners LLP	4,830.65	5	5
114	CapMan Oyj	4,747.30	126	47
115	Norwest Equity Partners	4,600.00	88	8
116	Acon Investments LLC	4,600.00	27	8
117	LBO France Gestion SAS	4,536.00	9	27
118	Hope Investments Management Co Ltd	4,500.00	4	5
119	One Equity Partners LLC	4,500.00	-	4
120	Allied Capital Corp	4,471.00	3	10
121	HGGC LLC	4,355.80	12	6
122	CCMP Capital Advisors LP	4,350.00	5	5
123	Vestar Capital Partners Inc	4,318.00	53	11

Rank	Firm Name	Firm Capital Under Management (USD Mil)	No. of Companies Invested In	No. of Funds Managed by Firm
124	Mid Europa Partners LLP	4,253.60	27	5
125	UBS Capital Corp	4,237.20	6	4
126	Allianz Capital Partners GmbH	4,200.00	6	9
127	Spectrum Equity Investors LP	4,019.10	17	9
128	Thoma Bravo LLC	4,000.00	12	9
129	JLL Partners Inc	4,000.00	19	10
130	Unitas Capital Pte, Ltd.	4,000.00	36	4
131	Sterling Partners GP LLC	4,000.00	9	8
132	GP Investimentos Ltda	4,000.00	11	7
133	Tianjin Venture Capital Management Co Ltd	4,000.00	-	15
134	Kohlberg & Co LLC	3,946.70	44	15
135	Archer Capital Pty Ltd	3,931.20	43	8
136	Brookfield Asset Management Inc	3,918.50	16	31
137	GI Partners	3,900.70	23	10
138	Trimaran Capital LLC	3,900.00	17	7
139	PAI Partners SAS	3,892.64	65	10
140	Avista Capital Holdings LP	3,833.26	12	7
141	HgCapital Trust PLC	3,816.00	68	13
142	TSG Consumer Partners, L.P.	3,800.00	26	8
143	Kayne Anderson Capital Advisors LP	3,783.00	3	16
144	Catalyst Capital Group Inc	3,601.19	5	6
145	AEA Investors LLC	3,600.00	35	18
146	Friedman Fleischer & Lowe Cap Ptnrs L P	3,500.00	18	7
147	Sycamore Partners LP	3,500.00	13	3
148	Metalmark Capital Holdings LLC	3,500.00	10	7
149	SAIF Partners	3,500.00	9	21
150	Canaan Partners	3,500.00	2	16
151	TDR Capital LLP	3,433.70	1	7
152	Cypress Advisors, L.P.	3,426.00	18	3
153	Eurazeo SA	3,387.30	21	7
154	Kelso & Company LP	3,378.40	50	12
155	Irving Place Capital LLC	3,300.00	25	11

Pratt's Guide to Private Equity & Venture Capital Sources

Rank	Firm Name	Firm Capital Under Management (USD Mil)	No. of Companies Invested In	No. of Funds Managed by Firm
156	Castle Harlan Inc	3,200.00	41	9
157	Newbridge Capital Ltd	3,200.00	8	5
158	IL & FS Investment Managers Ltd	3,200.00	7	23
159	Behrman Capital	3,100.00	30	6
150	JMI Management Inc	3,100.00	5	10
151	Bregal Investments LLP	3,048.40	28	7
152	Exponent Private Equity LLP	3,047.00	18	4
163	Marlin Equity Partners LLC	3,000.00	22	10
164	Roark Capital Group Inc	3,000.00	2	8
165	Olympus Partners	3,000.00	34	8
166	Lightyear Capital LLC	3,000.00	14	5
167	Veronis Suhler Stevenson LLC	3,000.00	33	11
168	Castle Harlan Aus Mezzanine	3,000.00	50	8
169	Mid-Ocean Partners LP	3,000.00	5	8
170	Morgenthaler Ventures	3,000.00	5	15
171	BancBoston Capital/BancBoston Ventures	2,996.00	77	9
172	Willis Stein & Partners LP	2,983.00	27	5
173	American Industrial Partners	2,905.51	23	7
174	Frazier Management LLC	2,900.00		19
175	Arsenal Capital Partners LP	2,886.30	18	5
176	LJ2 & Co LLC	2,800.00	29	6
177	KRG Capital Management LP	2,800.00	43	10
178	Calera Capital Management Inc	2,800.00	30	13
179	Investcorp Bank BSC	2,800.00	1	6
180	Unison Capital, Inc.	2,761.00	18	10
181	Electra Private Equity Plc	2,725.00	66	21
182	Sailing Capital Management Co Ltd	2,706.90	9	3
183	Arc Financial Corp.	2,700.00	2	15
184	Paine Schwartz Partners LLC	2,700.00	13	4
185	CLSA Capital Partners HK Ltd	2,700.00	5	20
186	H&Q Asia Pacific, Ltd.	2,691.00	5	23
187	Great Hill Equity Partners LLC	2,671.00	3	7

Rank	Firm Name	Firm Capital Under Management (USD Mil)	No. of Companies Invested In	No. of Funds Managed by Firm
188	WL Ross & Co LLC	2,657.68		13
189	Clearlake Capital Group LP	2,601.74	9	6
190	Boston Ventures	2,600.00	92	13
191	CITIC Capital Partners Ltd	2,600.00	37	16
192	Centre Partners Management LLC	2,600.00	34	7
193	KPS Capital Partners LP	2,600.00	1	10
194	Farallon Capital Management LLC	2,595.72	1	8
195	White Deer Energy LP	2,545.93	-	4
196	Riverwood Capital Group LLC	2,542.94	5	7
197	Court Square Capital Partners LP	2,534.04	3	6
198	Primavera Capital	2,520.37	9	4
199	Catterton Partners Corp	2,500.00	28	17
200	Nautic Partners LLC	2,500.00	54	19
201	Wind Point Advisors LLC	2,500.00	27	15
202	Chequers Capital Partners SA	2,464.59	18	5
203	Banco BTG Pactual SA	2,460.00		10
204	International Finance Corp	2,450.00	27	13
205	Alpha Group	2,426.80	96	12
206	Motion Equity Partners LLP	2,424.20	29	6
207	HPEF Capital Partners Ltd	2,400.00	55	13
208	Pacific Alliance Group Ltd	2,400.00	5	4
209	Henderson Global Investors Ltd	2,400.00	10	20
210	Vision Capital LLP	2,332.50	26	16
211	CHS Capital LLC	2,300.00	65	9
212	Bayou Steel Corp	2,300.00	5	4
213	UNITED FINANCIAL GROUP ASSET MANAGEMENT	2,300.00	5	4
214	Siris Capital Group LLC	2,291.07	1	4
215	ACG Capital SA	2,279.10	29	16
216	Herkules Capital AS	2,275.50	45	5
217	Water Street Healthcare Partners LLC	2,250.00	22	5
218	Baml Capital Partners	2,220.00	34	4
219	Parthenon Capital LLC	2,200.00	22	8

Pratt's Guide to Private Equity & Venture Capital Sources

Rank	Firm Name	Firm Capital Under Management (USD Mil)	No. of Companies Invested In	No. of Funds Managed by Firm
220	Southern Cross Capital Management SA	2,195.81	17	6
221	Yucaipa Cos	2,185.89	7	9
222	Silverfleet Capital Partners LLP	2,183.60	41	8
223	Access Capital Partners SA	2,179.20	-	11
224	Perella Weinberg Partners LP	2,128.01	10	5
225	Fenway Partners LLC	2,100.00	44	4
226	Proterra Investment Partners LP	2,100.00	3	1
227	Apax Partners SA	2,098.12	5	12
228	BRZ Investimentos SA	2,097.00	1	3
229	Ridgemont Partners Management LLC	2,050.00	2	4
230	Integrated Partners	2,043.45	1	10
231	Freeman Spogli & Co LLC	2,010.90	44	12
232	Odyssey Investment Partners LLC	2,000.00	26	9
233	Accel-KKR	2,000.00	14	12
234	Aurora Capital Group Ltd	2,000.00	15	7
235	Brown Brothers Harriman & Co	2,000.00	30	20
236	Vector Capital Management LP	2,000.00	2	8
237	Edgewater Funds	2,000.00	11	11
238	Peak Rock Capital LLC	2,000.00	15	2
239	Cartesian Capital Group LLC	2,000.00	4	4
240	CI Capital Partners LLC	2,000.00	1	3
241	Windjammer Capital Investors LLC	2,000.00	7	7
242	Saratoga Capital (Singapore) Pte Ltd	2,000.00	-	2
243	ICICI Venture Funds Management Company Ltd	2,000.00	3	29
244	Shamrock Holdings Of California Inc	2,000.00	10	10
245	Gilde Investment Management BV	1,979.90	23	8
246	Mercapital SL	1,977.10	54	8
247	Hahn & Company Eye Holdings Co Ltd	1,950.00	4	3
248	Banque Lombard Odier & Cie SA	1,947.10	-	11
249	SwanCap Investment Management SA	1,946.83		3
250	Northstar Advisors Pte Ltd	1,919.90		4

Firm Statistics Reported
Ranked Firms (by assets under management)
Venture Firms
Data as of: January 1, 2018

Rank	Firm Name	Firm Capital Under Management (USD Mil)	No. of Companies Invested In	No. of Funds Managed by Firm
1	Carlyle Group LP	97,700.00	197	146
2	Advanced Technology Ventures	81,550.00	225	10
3	Goldman Sachs & Co LLC	79,000.00	58	125
4	OrbiMed Advisors LLC	75,000.00	94	16
5	Partners Group Holding AG	57,000.00	8	58
6	Ardian France SA	49,270.10	38	78
7	Mutual Capital Partners	40,263.90	9	4
8	Schroders PLC	36,000.00	132	13
9	Apax Partners LLP	35,800.00	423	70
10	HarbourVest Partners LLC	35,551.00	145	98
11	Hermes Gpe Llp	33,943.50	5	9
12	Permira Advisers LLP	33,860.00	2	23
13	Prudential Capital Group LP	31,000.00	40	12
14	Csfb Private Equity Advisers	28,000.00	15	27
15	Bain Capital Inc	27,000.00	47	55
16	Adams Street Partners LLC	26,800.00	44	85
17	Pliant Corp	25,000.00	66	42
18	3i Group PLC	21,667.10	13	34
19	Pivotal Investments LLC	17,250.00	5	1
20	BlackRock Inc	17,200.00	4	21
21	Coller Capital Ltd	17,000.00	175	20
22	Charterhouse Capital Partners LLP	16,870.50	3	16
23	Neuberger Berman LLC	16,732.87	3	17
24	Terra Firma Capital Partners Ltd	16,711.30	-	12
25	Shanghai Talent Power Equity Investment Fund Management Co	16,000.00	2	1
26	China Reform Fund Management Co Ltd	15,909.54	2	2
27	China Venture Capital Fund Corp Ltd	15,083.60	2	1

Pratt's Guide to Private Equity & Venture Capital Sources

Rank	Firm Name	Firm Capital Under Management (USD Mil)	No. of Companies Invested In	No. of Funds Managed by Firm
28	Summit Partners LP	15,000.00	258	43
29	Hamilton Lane Advisors LLC	15,000.00	1	37
30	Pacific Corporate Group LLC	15,000.00	-	11
31	TL Ventures Inc	14,368.00	192	8
32	Sino IC Capital Co Ltd	14,231.97	2	1
33	New Enterprise Associates Inc	14,000.00	1005	25
34	Warburg Pincus LLC	14,000.00	509	23
35	EQT Funds Management Ltd	13,522.20	15	26
36	PineBridge Investments LLC	12,700.00	24	32
37	Golden Gate Capital Inc	12,000.00	3	24
38	Welsh Carson Anderson & Stowe	12,000.00	123	19
39	Siguler Guff & Company LP	10,964.70	12	37
40	TA Associates Management LP	10,792.00	392	49
41	Fortune Venture Capital Co Ltd	10,500.00	50	23
42	Tiger Global Management LLC	10,472.50	10	9
43	GoldPoint Partners LLC	10,047.00	5	19
44	Technology Crossover Ventures LP	10,000.00	216	15
45	Advent International Corp	10,000.00	215	82
46	Abraaj Capital Ltd	10,000.00	25	45
47	Beijing Holch Investment Management, Ltd.	10,000.00	8	2
48	Stone Point Capital LLC	9,730.88	6	13
49	Db Capital Partners	8,943.00	2	13
50	Equistone Partners Europe Ltd	8,779.60	7	15
51	HIG Capital LLC	8,500.00	48	19
52	Oak Investment Partners	8,400.00	524	24
53	Golub Capital Master Funding LLC	8,000.00	2	23
54	Bridgepoint Advisers Ltd	8,000.00	23	32
55	Sun Capital Partners Inc	8,000.00	2	11
56	Doughty Hanson and Co.	7,362.00	25	18
57	Paul Capital Partners LP	7,300.00	5	20
58	Shenzhen Oriental Fortune Capital Co Ltd	7,000.00	63	13
59	MCG Capital Corp	7,000.00	2	2

Rank	Firm Name	Firm Capital Under Management (USD Mil)	No. of Companies Invested In	No. of Funds Managed by Firm
60	Actis LLP	6,773.30	69	37
61	Center For Innovative Technology	6,500.00	118	6
62	Towerbrook Capital Partners LP	6,390.23	16	11
63	Morgan Stanley Private Equity	6,371.40	43	43
64	J.H. Whitney & Co LLC	6,000.00	177	22
65	Liberty Ridge Capital LLC	6,000.00	152	4
66	Jafco Co Ltd	5,889.30	18	73
67	Emerging Markets Partnership LP	5,700.00	69	6
68	Solidarity Fund QFL	5,631.20	30	12
69	China Science & Merchants Investment Management Group Co Ltd	5,458.08	26	39
70	Institutional Venture Partners	5,400.00	313	20
71	Citic Private Equity Funds Management Co Ltd	5,067.46	5	9
72	Trilantic Capital Management LP	5,005.80	32	36
73	Norwest Venture Partners	5,000.00	186	16
74	Draper Fisher Jurvetson	5,000.00	323	31
75	Baring Private Equity Asia Ltd	5,000.00	39	38
76	PineBridge Investments Asia Ltd	5,000.00	18	4
77	Audax Group, Inc.	5,000.00	13	12
78	CapMan Oyj	4,747.30	33	47
79	Battery Ventures LP	4,700.00	363	19
80	Acon Investments LLC	4,600.00	5	8
81	Andreessen Horowitz LLC	4,500.00	77	12
82	Vantagepoint Management Inc	4,500.00	156	13
83	ePlanet Capital	4,500.00	49	5
84	Allied Capital Corp	4,471.00	71	10
85	China Internet Investment Fund Mnagement Co Ltd	4,364.97	-	1
86	Vestar Capital Partners Inc	4,338.00	8	11
87	UBS Capital Corp	4,237.20	12	4
88	Allianz Capital Partners GmbH	4,200.00	25	9
89	Spectrum Equity Investors LP	4,019.10	93	9
90	Sequoia Capital Operations LLC	4,000.00	568	66

Pratt's Guide to Private Equity & Venture Capital Sources

Rank	Firm Name	Firm Capital Under Management (USD Mil)	No. of Companies Invested In	No. of Funds Managed by Firm
91	China Development Bank	4,000.00	1	3
92	Intel Capital Corp	4,000.00	263	20
93	Tpg Growth LLC	4,000.00	33	10
94	Ignition Ventures Management LLC	4,000.00	142	9
95	GP Investimentos Ltda	4,000.00	10	7
96	Sterling Partners GP LLC	4,000.00	20	8
97	Tianjin Venture Capital Management Co Ltd	4,000.00	16	15
98	Weston Presidio Capital	3,991.00	93	6
99	Brookfield Asset Management Inc	3,918.50	6	31
100	Menlo Ventures	3,900.00	321	21
101	Trimaran Capital LLC	3,900.00	2	7
102	HgCapital Trust PLC	3,816.00	17	13
103	IDG Capital Partners Inc	3,800.00	180	23
104	GGV Capital	3,800.00	94	14
105	China Everbright Ltd	3,634.06	10	16
106	European Investment Fund	3,619.80	-	13
107	Canaan Partners	3,500.00	342	16
108	SAIF Partners	3,500.00	88	21
109	Polaris Venture Partners	3,500.00	277	15
110	SV Health Investors LLP	3,500.00	191	12
111	Sprout Group	3,500.00	290	15
112	Natixis Private Equity SA	3,460.00	13	8
113	Accel Partners & Co Inc	3,432.00	359	42
114	Kleiner Perkins Caufield & Byers LLC	3,400.00	435	40
115	SEED Capital Management I/S	3,350.10	53	5
116	Softbank Capital Partners L P	3,300.00	102	10
117	Irving Place Capital LLC	3,300.00	18	11
118	U.S. Venture Partners	3,250.00	353	15
119	Guidepost Growth Equity	3,200.00	186	15
120	Bain Capital Venture Partners LLC	3,200.00	98	11
121	IL & FS Investment Managers Ltd	3,200.00	56	23
122	Gavea Investimentos Ltda	3,109.90	3	5

Pratt's Guide to Private Equity & Venture Capital Sources

Rank	Firm Name	Firm Capital Under Management (USD Mil)	No. of Companies Invested In	No. of Funds Managed by Firm
123	JMI Management Inc	3,100.00	3	10
124	Highland Capital Partners LLC	3,085.00	279	14
125	Mayfield Fund	3,000.00	536	29
126	General Catalyst Partners LLC	3,000.00	105	14
127	Doll Capital Management Inc	3,000.00	198	19
128	Morgenthaler Ventures	3,000.00	277	15
129	St Paul Venture Capital Inc	3,000.00	210	6
130	Shanghai Fosun Capital Investment Management Co Ltd	3,000.00	18	8
131	BancBoston Capital/BancBoston Ventures	2,996.00	267	9
132	Baidu Capital	2,977.08	5	2
133	Beijing Clutural Center Construction Dvlpmt Fund Mgmt Co Ltd	2,965.64	2	1
134	Deerfield Management Company LP	2,941.75	2	4
135	Frazier Management LLC	2,900.00	174	19
136	Austin Ventures	2,878.00	256	15
137	InterWest Partners LLC	2,800.00	313	20
138	Calera Capital Management Inc	2,800.00	9	13
139	Investcorp Bank BSC	2,800.00	1	6
140	Benchmark Capital Management Gesellschaft MBH In Liqu	2,730.40	209	21
141	Electra Private Equity Plc	2,725.00	4	21
142	CLSA Capital Partners HK Ltd	2,700.00	33	20
143	Arc Financial Corp.	2,700.00	14	15
144	H&Q Asia Pacific, Ltd.	2,691.00	79	23
145	Great Hill Equity Partners LLC	2,671.00	29	7
146	Domain Associates LLC	2,600.40	275	17
147	Meritech Capital Partners	2,600.00	142	6
148	CITIC Capital Partners Ltd	2,600.00	9	16
149	MPM Capital LLC	2,581.00	147	16
150	Atlas Venture Advisors Inc	2,580.00	401	16
151	EW Healthcare Partners	2,500.00	154	17
152	ABS Capital Partners, Inc.	2,500.00	104	11
153	Qiming Venture Partners Ii LP	2,500.00	39	11

Pratt's Guide to Private Equity & Venture Capital Sources

Rank	Firm Name	Firm Capital Under Management (USD Mil)	No. of Companies Invested In	No. of Funds Managed by Firm
154	Rho Capital Partners Inc	2,500.00	138	13
155	Wind Point Advisors LLC	2,500.00	71	15
156	Nautic Partners LLC	2,500.00	72	19
157	Columbia Capital LP	2,482.00	95	15
158	Banco BTG Pactual SA	2,460.00	-	10
159	Foundation Capital LLC	2,400.00	200	11
160	Henderson Global Investors Ltd	2,400.00	7	20
161	HPEF Capital Partners Ltd	2,400.00	17	13
162	Amundi Private Equity Funds SA	2,370.30	74	58
163	Vision Capital LLP	2,332.50	3	16
164	Lightspeed Management Company LLC	2,300.00	112	14
165	Venrock Inc	2,300.00	419	18
166	UNITED FINANCIAL GROUP ASSET MANAGEMENT	2,300.00	13	4
167	ChrysCapital Management Co	2,250.00	32	8
168	Sigma Partners	2,229.00	166	12
169	Challenger Group Holdings Ltd	2,226.40	2	1
170	Third Rock Ventures LLC	2,222.00	41	5
171	Greylock Partners LLC	2,200.00	397	23
172	Walden International	2,200.00	152	42
173	Khosla Ventures LLC	2,120.00	7	11
174	Apax Partners SA	2,098.12	26	12
175	Bright Stone Investment Management (Hong Kong) Ltd	2,007.40	8	11
176	Bessemer Venture Partners	2,000.00	311	27
177	Redpoint Ventures	2,000.00	117	14
178	Charles River Ventures LLC	2,000.00	310	22
179	FirstMark Capital LLC	2,000.00	135	14
180	Clarus Ventures LLC	2,000.00	47	5
181	Mohr Davidow Ventures	2,000.00	232	17
182	Crosspoint Venture Partners 2001 LP	2,000.00	158	15
183	Alta Partners	2,000.00	174	11
184	Bluerun Ventures LP	2,000.00	138	12
185	ICICI Venture Funds Management Company Ltd	2,000.00	124	29
186	Edgewater Funds	2,000.00	18	11

Pratt's Guide to Private Equity & Venture Capital Sources

Rank	Firm Name	Firm Capital Under Management (USD Mil)	No. of Companies Invested In	No. of Funds Managed by Firm
187	Goff Capital Partners, L.P.	2,000.00	6	2
188	Chemical Venture Partners	2,000.00	115	4
189	Shamrock Holdings Of California Inc	2,000.00	1	10
190	Zhiying Capital	2,000.00	7	1
191	Pequot Capital Management Inc	1,987.50	-	9
192	Gilde Investment Management BV	1,979.90	87	8
193	New Horizon Capital	1,946.00	12	6
194	AllianceBernstein LP	1,915.53	9	8
195	Arch Venture Partners LLC	1,900.00	172	13
196	Versant Venture Management, LLC	1,900.00	158	21
197	Balderton Capital LLP	1,900.00	21	5
198	Export Development Canada	1,896.00	26	3
199	Mail.Ru Group Ltd	1,872.05	20	3
200	Sydney Seed Fund Management Pty Ltd	1,805.95	2	1
201	Investor Growth Capital Inc	1,800.00	23	7
202	Darby Overseas Investments, Ltd.	1,800.00	18	32
203	Rcf Management LLC	1,800.00	6	7
204	Shanghai Trustbridge Partners Investment Management Co Ltd	1,791.74	12	5
205	Apollo Aviation Group LLC	1,789.00	-	4
206	Deutsche Beteiligungs AG	1,780.30	25	9
207	F&C Equity Partners PLC	1,737.60	64	17
208	Energy Investors Fund LP	1,713.00		12
209	Crosslink Capital Inc	1,700.00	97	20
210	Bowman Capital Management LP	1,700.00	36	3
211	Cornerstone Advisors Inc	1,700.00		2
212	Idinvest Partners SA	1,684.90	60	76
213	Vinacapital Investment Management Ltd	1,663.00	4	5
214	Everstone Capital Management, Ltd.	1,640.00	23	7
215	KTB Investment & Securities Co Ltd	1,636.50	5	41
216	Engelsberg	1,635.60	-	1
217	Sofinnova Partners SAS	1,624.80	216	19
218	Aisling Capital LLC	1,600.00	93	5

Pratt's Guide to Private Equity & Venture Capital Sources

Rank	Firm Name	Firm Capital Under Management (USD Mil)	No. of Companies Invested In	No. of Funds Managed by Firm
219	Bay City Capital LLC	1,600.00	61	8
220	Invesco Private Capital Inc	1,600.00	89	22
221	Climate Change Capital Ltd	1,600.00	3	5
222	Sierra Ventures	1,590.00	245	17
223	Shunwei Capital Partners	1,567.89	39	7
224	Everbright Capital Investment Co Ltd	1,567.75	6	3
225	Baker Bros Advisors LP	1,560.00	14	1
226	Alchemy Partners LLP	1,547.90	-	12
227	TVM Capital GmbH	1,542.90	181	24
228	Sevin Rosen Funds	1,535.00	253	17
229	Beijing Redstone International Capital Management Co Ltd	1,533.56	1	2
230	Tencent Collaboration Fund	1,531.23	42	1
231	Alta Communications Inc	1,518.90	291	11
232	Guochen Industry Capital Fund Management Co Ltd	1,517.45	1	1
233	Industrial and Commercial Bank of China Ltd	1,517.45	-	2
234	SBI Investment Co Ltd	1,513.70	28	25
235	Raine Group LLC, The	1,507.68	38	4
236	Baker Capital Corp	1,500.00	39	4
237	Fuse Capital	1,500.00	133	10
238	F-Prime Capital Partners	1,500.00	41	9
239	inventages venture capital GmbH	1,500.00	23	3
240	Frontenac Company LLC	1,500.00	125	21
241	Korea Venture Investment Inc	1,500.00	6	8
242	Undisclosed Firm	1,500.00	3	5
243	Acorn Ventures, Inc.	1,500.00	29	9
244	Evercore Inc	1,500.00	14	7
245	Poalim Cap Mark Tech, Ltd.	1,500.00	11	6
246	CIRCLE VENTURES INC	1,500.00	1	1
247	Industrialiseringsfonden for Udviklingslandene IFU	1,471.70	92	4
248	Pama Group Hong Kong Ltd	1,455.00	90	4
249	Qualium Investissement SAS	1,455.00	11	12
250	Healthcare Ventures LLC	1,409.10	97	11

Firm Statistics Reported
Ranked Firms (by assets under management)
Mezzanine Firms
Data as of: January 1, 2018

Rank	Firm Name	Firm Capital Under Management (USD Mil)	No. of Companies Invested In	No. of Funds Managed by Firm
1	Carlyle Group LP	97,700.00	41	146
2	Blackstone Group LP	84,300.00	27	103
3	KKR & Co LP	80,379.50	1	62
4	Goldman Sachs & Co LLC	79,000.00	10	125
5	Apollo Global Management LLC	73,993.95	2	34
6	Partners Group Holding AG	57,000.00	2	58
7	Ardian France SA	49,270.10	36	78
8	Oaktree Capital Management LP	40,281.00	1	69
9	Providence Equity Partners LLC	40,000.00	-	27
10	HarbourVest Partners LLC	35,551.00	5	98
11	Prudential Capital Group LP	31,000.00	11	12
12	Bain Capital Inc	27,000.00	25	55
13	JP Morgan Investment Management Inc	22,000.00	-	26
14	Thomas H Lee Partners LP	20,000.00	23	20
15	Neuberger Berman LLC	16,732.87	-	17
16	Summit Partners LP	15,000.00	30	43
17	Hamilton Lane Advisors LLC	15,000.00	1	37
18	EQT Funds Management Ltd	13,522.20	10	26
19	Welsh Carson Anderson & Stowe	12,000.00	60	19
20	Siguler Guff & Company LP	10,964.70	2	37
21	TA Associates Management LP	10,792.00	41	49
22	GoldPoint Partners LLC	10,047.00	-	19
23	Gsc Partners	9,200.00	1	12
24	Db Capital Partners	8,943.00	-	13
25	Equistone Partners Europe Ltd	8,779.60	-	15
26	Citigroup Private Equity LP	8,300.00	1	28
27	Crescent Capital Group LP	8,000.00	10	2

Pratt's Guide to Private Equity & Venture Capital Sources

Rank	Firm Name	Firm Capital Under Management (USD Mil)	No. of Companies Invested In	No. of Funds Managed by Firm
28	Golub Capital Master Funding LLC	8,000.00	2	23
29	GTCR Golder Rauner LLC	8,000.00	11	22
30	KSL Capital Partners LLC	7,038.62	-	11
31	Tennenbaum Capital Partners LLC	7,000.00	2	8
32	Morgan Stanley Private Equity	6,371.40	5	43
33	J.H. Whitney & Co LLC	6,000.00	6	22
34	Ares Management LLC	6,000.00		15
35	Solidarity Fund QFL	5,631.20	-	12
36	Citic Private Equity Funds Management Co Ltd	5,067.46		9
37	Trilantic Capital Management LP	5,005.80	1	36
38	Audax Group, Inc.	5,000.00	28	12
39	CapMan Oyj	4,747.30	37	47
40	Capvest Ltd	4,689.00	2	6
41	Vestar Capital Partners Inc	4,318.00	10	11
42	AREA Property Partners	4,108.00		15
43	Kayne Anderson Capital Advisors LP	3,783.00	4	16
44	China Everbright Ltd	3,634.06	1	16
45	AEA Investors LLC	3,600.00	4	18
46	Permira Debt Managers Ltd	3,593.05	1	3
47	Natixis Private Equity SA	3,460.00		8
48	Kelso & Company LP	3,378.40	-	12
49	Veronis Suhler Stevenson LLC	3,000.00	19	11
50	Asia Mezzanine Capital Advisers Ltd	3,000.00	1	2
51	CLSA Capital Partners HK Ltd	2,700.00	3	20
52	Benefit Street Partners LLC	2,550.00		2
53	CapitalSource Holdings Inc	2,500.00	25	1
54	Integrated Partners	2,043.45	2	10
55	Windjammer Capital Investors LLC	2,000.00	14	7
56	Brown Brothers Harriman & Co	2,000.00	25	20
57	Euromezzanine Gestion SaS	1,939.20	39	9
58	Darby Overseas Investments, Ltd.	1,800.00	27	32
59	ABRY Partners LLC	1,700.00	12	19

Pratt's Guide to Private Equity & Venture Capital Sources

Rank	Firm Name	Firm Capital Under Management (USD Mil)	No. of Companies Invested In	No. of Funds Managed by Firm
60	Merit Capital Partners IV LLC	1,700.00	69	8
61	Idinvest Partners SA	1,684.90	2	76
62	Roundtable Healthcare Partners LP	1,675.26	4	11
63	Monroe Capital LLC	1,569.66	-	5
64	Frontenac Company LLC	1,500.00	5	21
65	Sandler Capital Management	1,500.00	4	11
66	HillStreet Capital Inc	1,500.00	-	4
67	Norwest Mezzanine Partners	1,400.00	21	5
68	Kb Investment Co Ltd	1,400.00	3	34
69	European Capital	1,306.80	-	7
70	Comvest Partners	1,300.00	7	10
71	Atalante SAS	1,276.50	15	7
72	Capital Royalty LP	1,250.00	-	2
73	MML Capital Partners LLP	1,250.00	22	8
74	Peninsula Capital Partners LLC	1,200.00	93	7
75	Yukon Partners Management LLC	1,196.74	5	5
76	Argos Soditic SA	1,156.40	5	12
77	Gryphon Investors Inc	1,153.00	-	12
78	Gulf Capital Pvt JSC	1,140.00	5	5
79	Siparex Group	1,113.10	5	52
80	Friedbergmilstein LLC	1,100.00	2	3
81	Capital Resource Partners	1,100.00	61	10
82	CSFC Management Co, LLC	1,045.94	-	3
83	Penfund Partners Inc	1,012.08	25	9
84	Falcon Investment Advisors LLC	1,000.00	9	6
85	LBC Credit Partners Inc	1,000.00	5	4
86	Caltius Mezzanine	1,000.00	34	9
87	Morgan Stanley Credit Partners LP	1,000.00	13	5
88	Desai Capital Management Inc	1,000.00	22	7
89	Newspring Capital	1,000.00	43	12
90	CMS Mezzanine Fund	1,000.00	3	2
91	ONSET Ventures	1,000.00	-	15

Pratt's Guide to Private Equity & Venture Capital Sources

Rank	Firm Name	Firm Capital Under Management (USD Mil)	No. of Companies Invested In	No. of Funds Managed by Firm
92	PNC Equity Management Corp	972.00	21	7
93	Pamlico Capital Management LP	900.00	4	8
94	NBK Capital Partners Ltd	875.00	9	6
95	RSTW Partners	870.00	42	5
96	Cyprium Investment Partners LLC	813.00	7	5
97	BOC International Holdings Ltd	806.00	11	1
98	Rbc Capital Partners	800.00	6	20
99	Skyline Ventures Inc	800.00	-	10
100	Fulcrum Capital Partners Inc	782.00	20	7
101	Global Investment House KSCC	766.00	14	10
102	Tcw Capital	750.00	6	21
103	Bb&T Capital Partners LLC	725.00	17	9
104	Nordic Mezzanine Ltd	709.80	13	6
105	Harbour Group Ltd	706.50	1	7
106	VR Equitypartner GmbH	698.00	5	6
107	Edmond de Rothschild Investment Partners SAS	693.50	-	43
108	Medley Capital LLC	692.82	3	2
109	Stonehenge Growth Capital LLC	677.00	6	33
110	Energy Capital Partners LLC	673.90	5	8
111	HPS Investment Partners LLC	650.00	-	8
112	PPM America Capital Partners LLC	620.50	2	8
113	Hancock Capital Management LLC	619.00	4	6
114	Beringea LLC	617.00	3	13
115	First Israel Mezzanine Investors Ltd	600.00	20	4
116	Mckenna Gale Capital Inc	600.00	24	5
117	CDH China Management Co., Ltd.	600.00	-	23
118	Indigo Capital LLP	589.80	40	6
119	Omnes Capital SAS	586.40	18	59
120	MB Rahastot Oy	571.50	2	7
121	Churchill Equity Inc	558.00	27	9
122	Maranon Capital LP	557.00	7	4
123	Mezzanine Management Finanz und UnternehmensberatungsgmbH	534.50	27	4

Pratt's Guide to Private Equity & Venture Capital Sources

Rank	Firm Name	Firm Capital Under Management (USD Mil)	No. of Companies Invested In	No. of Funds Managed by Firm
124	Northwestern Mutual Capital LLC	530.00	-	13
125	MFC Capital Funding Inc	500.00	-	2
126	Fifth Street Capital LLC	500.00	13	4
127	Calvert Street Capital Partners Inc	500.00	4	5
128	Dominion Ventures Inc	500.00	25	7
129	Beechbrook Capital LLP	499.44	7	3
130	Multiplier Capital LP	497.31	2	3
131	Greyrock Capital Group	492.30	38	4
132	August Equity Llp	487.30	22	10
133	Amerra Capital Management LLC	486.78	-	3
134	Petra Capital Partners LLC	456.00	16	7
135	Green Mountain Advisors Inc	432.00	27	8
136	RLJ Equity Partners LLC	424.00	4	4
137	Eqvitec Partners Oy	412.00	7	4
138	Ife Mezzanine SARL	408.90	24	3
139	Beijing Huinong Capital Management Co Ltd	407.09	-	2
140	Oquendo Capital SL	406.45	1	3
141	Canterbury Capital Partners	400.00	17	4
142	Ep Power Finance LLC	400.00	-	1
143	Endeavour Capital Inc	400.00	-	13
144	Europa Capital LLP	392.53	-	7
145	Prairie Capital, L.P.	390.00	7	8
146	Mizuho Capital Partners Co Ltd	389.54	-	8
147	Cerea Partenaire SAS	381.15	21	6
148	LGV Capital Ltd	365.30	17	22
149	Boathouse Capital	350.00	23	2
150	Trust Company of the West	335.30	27	35
151	China Venture Management Inc	329.00	7	8
152	Cm Cic Mezzanine Sas	319.49	-	4
153	Caixa Capital BV	316.70	-	9
154	Northstar Capital LLC	300.30	47	7
155	Ironwood Investment Management LLC	300.00	9	6

Pratt's Guide to Private Equity & Venture Capital Sources

Rank	Firm Name	Firm Capital Under Management (USD Mil)	No. of Companies Invested In	No. of Funds Managed by Firm
156	Wellington Financial Lp	300.00	82	6
157	Seacoast Capital	300.00	30	5
158	Eastward Capital Partners LLC	300.00	11	5
159	Capital Trust Ltd	300.00	8	4
160	BCI Partners	300.00	54	8
161	Sand Hill Capital	300.00	3	8
162	Brookside International	295.24	17	4
163	Aju IB Investment Co Ltd	293.60	4	46
164	I-Cap Partners Ltd	286.70	1	4
165	Southfield Capital Advisors LLC	283.35	3	5
166	Business Development Bank of Canada	283.00	4251	15
167	Lakeside Capital Management LLC	279.20	9	3
168	Visium Asset Management LP	275.00	1	1
169	Banyantree Finance Pvt Ltd	275.00	10	2
170	Saskatchewan Government Growth Fund Management Corp	275.00	-	3
171	La Financiere Patrimoniale d'Investissement SAS	272.04	-	4
172	MMF Capital Management LLC	270.00	15	7
173	DIF Capital Partners Ltd	266.60	6	3
174	Maven Capital Partners UK LLP	264.70	16	24
175	Barings LLC	260.80	11	9
176	Centerfield Capital Partners LP	260.00	22	8
177	C3 Capital LLC	260.00	39	4
178	Westlb Europa Holding AG	251.40	8	9
179	Citicorp Venture Capital Ltd	250.00	3	18
180	Darby Asia Investors Ltd	250.00	18	2
181	Eagle Private Capital LLC	250.00	29	4
182	Insight Equity Holdings LLC	250.00	-	5
183	STIC Investment Inc	247.90	5	37
184	MCI Capital SA	245.20	-	6
185	Hawkesbridge Capital	238.60	1	6
186	LNC Partners	236.00	3	1
187	ESCALATE CAPITAL I L P	235.00	13	2

Pratt's Guide to Private Equity & Venture Capital Sources

Rank	Firm Name	Firm Capital Under Management (USD Mil)	No. of Companies Invested In	No. of Funds Managed by Firm
188	Bank of New York Mellon Corp	234.87	4	7
189	Nomura Principal Finance Co Ltd	233.72	-	2
190	Freeport Financial Partners LLC	230.00	-	2
191	Enlightenment Capital	227.00	-	3
192	CAPX PARTNERS III L L C	225.00	6	4
193	Banc One Mezzanine Corp	225.00	2	2
194	Certus Capital Partners	225.00	-	1
195	Batavia Investment Management	224.50	1	3
196	Main Street Capital Corp	213.00	7	3
197	Rocky Mountain Capital	210.00	39	5
198	Armada Mezzanine Capital Oy	208.90	10	3
199	Prospect Street Ventures	206.00	49	6
200	Japan Asia Investment Co Ltd	204.30	-	84
201	Northleaf Capital Partners Ltd	200.00	-	11
202	CIT Mezzanine Partners of Canada Ltd	200.00	14	4
203	Brooks, Houghton & Company Inc	200.00	2	4
204	Merion Investment Partners LP	200.00	16	4
205	St Cloud Capital LLC	200.00	4	3
206	Fidus Capital LLC	200.00	3	2
207	Tecum Capital Partners	191.00	17	4
208	Prism Capital Corporation	190.00	23	4
209	Spring Capital Partners	187.00	3	4
210	Needham Capital Partners	181.70	79	6
211	Tree Line Capital Partners LLC	181.38	1	3
212	Equinox Investment Partners LLC	181.00	11	3
213	Merrill Lynch Capital Partners Inc	180.00	1	23
214	BioMedPartners AG	179.38	-	4
215	Argosy Partners, Inc.	175.00	4	2
216	Validus Partners LLC	175.00	4	3
217	Hickory Venture Capital Corp	175.00	5	3
218	New Canaan Funding	172.08	1	4
219	Marquette Capital Partners Inc	170.80	28	2

Pratt's Guide to Private Equity & Venture Capital Sources

Rank	Firm Name	Firm Capital Under Management (USD Mil)	No. of Companies Invested In	No. of Funds Managed by Firm
220	Huntington Capital I	170.65	21	5
221	Marlborough Capital Advisors LP	170.00	20	4
222	Greycliff Group LLC	168.40		2
223	ZheShang Venture Capital Co Ltd	165.22	10	11
224	Samho Green Investment Inc	163.20		7
225	Great American Capital Partners LLC	155.00		2
226	Arrowhead Mezzanine LLC	152.00	4	4
227	Kendall Court Capital Partners Ltd	152.00	2	2
228	Crown Capital Partners Inc	150.00	18	6
229	Patriot Capital Funding Inc	150.00	34	4
230	Chatham Capital	150.00	12	4
231	AMI Advisory Pte Ltd	150.00		1
232	Webster Capital Mezzanine	150.00		1
233	EQUUS Total Return Inc	150.00	46	7
234	Kian Capital Partners LLC	150.00	14	2
235	Cdib Venture Management	150.00	8	3
236	ASC Group	150.00		3
237	SeaView Capital Advisors LLC	150.00	1	1
238	Breakaway Capital Partners LLC	147.27	-	2
239	Resolute Capital Partners Fund IV LP	140.78	5	2
240	Nel Fund Managers Ltd	140.50	1	11
241	Exeter Capital Partners	135.00	18	6
242	Independent Bankers Capital Funds	133.00	8	4
243	Small Enterprise Assistance Funds	130.00	1	30
244	Cimb Private Equity Sdn Bhd	130.00		5
245	Smith Whiley & Co	128.00	6	6
246	Capital Solutions Inc	125.00		18
247	Oxer Capital Inc	122.00	1	1
248	Barings (UK) Ltd	121.11	2	3
249	Stratford Capital Partners LP	121.00	21	3
250	TD Capital Group Ltd	120.00	15	15

Pratt's Guide to Private Equity & Venture Capital Sources

Firm Listings

- A -

@VENTURES

1601 Trapelo Road
Suite 170
North Waltham, MA USA 02451
E-mail: info@ventures.com
Website: www.ventures.com

Other Offices
Foermer HQ: 1100 Winter Street
Suite 4600
North Waltham, MA USA 02451
Phone: 7816635152

Management and Staff
Peter Mills, Founder

Type of Firm
Corporate PE/Venture

Project Preferences

Role in Financing:
Will function either as deal originator or investor in deals created by others

Type of Financing Preferred:
Early Stage

Geographical Preferences

United States Preferences:
North America

Industry Preferences

In Computer Software prefer:
Software

In Industrial/Energy prefer:
Energy
Alternative Energy
Advanced Materials
Environmental Related

Additional Information
Year Founded: 1995
Capital Under Management: $700,000,000
Current Activity Level : Actively seeking new investments
Method of Compensation: Return on investment is of primary concern, do not charge fees

A CAPITAL ASIA LTD

118 Connaught Road West
Suite 3603
Hong Kong, Hong Kong
E-mail: contact@acapital.hk
Website: www.acapital.hk

Other Offices
No.2 Gongti North Road
1109, Twr A, Yingke Center
Beijing, China 100027
Phone: 861065393229

32-46A Avenue Louise
Box 4
Brussels, Belgium 1050

Type of Firm
Private Equity Firm

Project Preferences

Type of Financing Preferred:
Leveraged Buyout
Acquisition

Geographical Preferences

International Preferences:
Europe
China

Industry Preferences

In Medical/Health prefer:
Medical/Health

In Consumer Related prefer:
Entertainment and Leisure
Retail
Consumer Products

In Industrial/Energy prefer:
Energy
Industrial Products
Environmental Related

In Transportation prefer:
Transportation
Aerospace

Additional Information
Year Founded: 2010
Current Activity Level : Actively seeking new investments

A HEIFETZ TECHNOLOGIES LTD

Wings of eagles 22nd Street
Jerusalem, Israel
Phone: 026527712
Website: www.heifetz.co.il

Type of Firm
Bank Affiliated

Project Preferences

Type of Financing Preferred:
Seed
Startup

Geographical Preferences

International Preferences:
Israel

Industry Preferences

In Communications prefer:
Commercial Communications

In Computer Software prefer:
Software

In Internet Specific prefer:
Internet

In Computer Other prefer:
Computer Related

In Medical/Health prefer:
Medical/Health
Pharmaceuticals

Additional Information
Year Founded: 1996
Current Activity Level : Actively seeking new investments

A PLUS FINANCE SASU

8, rue Bellini
Paris, France 75116
Phone: 33140080340
Fax: 33140080350
E-mail: infos@aplusfinance.com
Website: www.aplusfinance.com

Management and Staff
Danielle Kadeyan, Partner
Vanina Lanfranchi, Managing Director

Type of Firm
Private Equity Firm

Association Membership
French Venture Capital Association (AFIC)

Project Preferences

Type of Financing Preferred:
Fund of Funds
Leveraged Buyout
Mezzanine
Generalist PE
Early Stage
Seed
Later Stage
Management Buyouts
Acquisition
Startup

Size of Investments Considered:
Min Size of Investment Considered (000s): $1,252
Max Size of Investment Considered (000s): $6,263

Geographical Preferences

International Preferences:
Europe
France

Industry Preferences

In Communications prefer:
Telecommunications
Media and Entertainment

In Internet Specific prefer:
E-Commerce Technology

In Semiconductor/Electr prefer:
Electronic Components

In Medical/Health prefer:
Medical/Health
Health Services

In Industrial/Energy prefer:
Energy
Environmental Related

In Business Serv. prefer:
Media

In Other prefer:
Environment Responsible

Additional Information
Year Founded: 1998
Capital Under Management: $17,194,000
Current Activity Level : Actively seeking new investments

A&M CAPITAL ADVISORS LLC

289 Greenwich Avenue
Second Floor
Greenwich, CT USA 06830
Phone: 2037425880
Website: www.a-mcapital.com

Management and Staff
Alex Nivelle, Vice President
David Perskie, Principal
Jack McCarthy, Managing Director
Kurtis Kaull, Managing Director

Type of Firm
Private Equity Firm

Project Preferences

Type of Financing Preferred:
Leveraged Buyout
Turnaround
Acquisition
Recapitalizations

Geographical Preferences

United States Preferences:
North America
All U.S.

International Preferences:
Europe

Industry Preferences

In Medical/Health prefer:
Medical/Health
Health Services

In Consumer Related prefer:
Consumer
Retail

In Industrial/Energy prefer:
Industrial Products

In Financial Services prefer:
Financial Services

In Manufact. prefer:
Manufacturing

Additional Information
Name of Most Recent Fund: Alvarez & Marsal Partners Fund, L.P.
Most Recent Fund Was Raised: 02/04/2014
Year Founded: 2012
Capital Under Management: $917,254,000
Current Activity Level : Actively seeking new investments

A1 INVESTMENTS & RESOURCES LTD

Ste. 101, 12 Thomas St.
Chatswood
New South Wales, Australia 2067
Phone: 61-2-94118803
Fax: 61-2-94118882
E-mail: info@chinacenturycapital.com.au
Website: www.a1investments.com.au

Management and Staff
Charlie Nakamura, Chief Executive Officer
Peter Kao, Chief Operating Officer

Type of Firm
Private Equity Firm

Additional Information
Year Founded: 2007
Current Activity Level : Actively seeking new investments

A5 CAPITAL

8-1815 Ironstone Manor
Pickering, Canada L1W 3W9
Phone: 19054922813
Website: www.a5capital.co

Type of Firm
Private Equity Firm

Project Preferences

Type of Financing Preferred:
Leveraged Buyout
Management Buyouts

Additional Information
Year Founded: 2017
Current Activity Level : Actively seeking new investments

A5 INTERNET INVESTMENTS LTD

Av Brigadeiro Faria Lima
1478-15 First Floor - Jd
Sao Paulo, Brazil 01451-001
Phone: 551130343703
E-mail: contato@a5.com.br
Website: www.a5.com.br

Type of Firm
Investment Management Firm

Project Preferences

Type of Financing Preferred:
Early Stage
Seed
Startup

Geographical Preferences

International Preferences:
Brazil

Industry Preferences

In Communications prefer:
Media and Entertainment

In Internet Specific prefer:
Internet
Ecommerce

In Financial Services prefer:
Financial Services

In Business Serv. prefer:
Media

Additional Information
Year Founded: 2013
Current Activity Level : Actively seeking new investments

A>M VENTURES

65 Union Avenue
Memphis, TN USA 38103
Phone: 9015232000
Website: www.amventures.co

Type of Firm
Private Equity Firm

Project Preferences

Type of Financing Preferred:
Early Stage

Additional Information

Year Founded: 2014
Current Activity Level : Actively seeking new investments

AAA CAPITAL MANAGEMENT CO LTD

Jih-Nan Road, Section Two
Seventh Floor, Suite 39
Taipei, Taiwan
Phone: 886223567087
Fax: 886223567187
Website: www.aaacapital.com.tw

Management and Staff

Leo Liang, Partner

Type of Firm

Private Equity Firm

Association Membership

Taiwan Venture Capital Association(TVCA)

Project Preferences

Type of Financing Preferred:
Expansion
Balanced

Geographical Preferences

International Preferences:
Macau
Taiwan
Hong Kong
China

Industry Preferences

In Communications prefer:
Telecommunications

In Semiconductor/Electr prefer:
Electronics

In Biotechnology prefer:
Biotechnology

In Consumer Related prefer:
Retail

In Financial Services prefer:
Financial Services

In Business Serv. prefer:
Media

Additional Information

Year Founded: 2002
Current Activity Level : Actively seeking new investments

AAC CAPITAL PARTNERS

Gustav Mahlerplein 106
ITO Tower 21st floor
Amsterdam, Netherlands 1082 MA
Phone: 31203331300
E-mail: info@aaccapitalpartners.com

Other Offices

Birger Jarlsgatan 12
1st Floor
Stockholm, Sweden 10041
Phone: 46-8-407-4440

1 Carey Lane
London, United Kingdom EC2V 8AE
Phone: 44-20-7187-3000

Management and Staff

Andrew Moye, Partner
Bert-Jan Rozenstraten, Chief Financial Officer
Frank Trijbels, Partner
Johan Bjurstrom, Partner
Jonathan Bourn, Partner
Kristofer Runnquinst, Partner
Marc Staal, Managing Partner
Maurice Bronckers, Managing Partner
Olaf Tensen, Partner
Patrick Bulmer, Partner
Paul Van Steijn, Partner
Paul Southwell, Managing Partner
Paul Hugenholtz, Managing Partner
Simon Angeldorff, Partner
Tommy Wikstrom, Partner

Type of Firm

Private Equity Firm

Association Membership

British Venture Capital Association (BVCA)
Hong Kong Venture Capital Association (HKVCA)
Hungarian Venture Capital Association (HVCA)
Dutch Venture Capital Associaton (NVP)

Project Preferences

Role in Financing:
Prefer role as deal originator

Type of Financing Preferred:
Second Stage Financing
Leveraged Buyout
Mezzanine
Research and Development
Generalist PE
Early Stage
Balanced
Start-up Financing
Turnaround
Later Stage
Management Buyouts
Recapitalizations

Size of Investments Considered:
Min Size of Investment Considered (000s): $4,708
Max Size of Investment Considered (000s): $94,160

Geographical Preferences

United States Preferences:

International Preferences:
Hungary
Central Europe
Europe
No Preference
Netherlands
Switzerland
Austria
Eastern Europe
Brazil
Croatia
Australia
Belgium
Asia
Germany
All International
France

Industry Focus

(% based on actual investment)

Consumer Related	26.1%
Other Products	25.2%
Biotechnology	12.8%
Industrial/Energy	9.9%
Semiconductors/Other Elect.	7.8%
Medical/Health	6.1%
Communications and Media	4.9%
Internet Specific	3.5%
Computer Software and Services	2.4%
Computer Hardware	1.2%

Additional Information

Year Founded: 1980
Capital Under Management: $2,900,000
Current Activity Level : Actively seeking new investments
Method of Compensation: Return on investment is of primary concern, do not charge fees

AARIN ASSET ADVISORS LLP

70, Millers Road
Grace Towers, Second Floor
Bangalore, India 560 052
Phone: 918030789100
Website: www.aarincapital.com

Management and Staff

Deepak Natraj, Managing Director

Type of Firm

Private Equity Firm

Project Preferences

Pratt's Guide to Private Equity & Venture Capital Sources

Type of Financing Preferred:
Early Stage
Expansion
Startup

Geographical Preferences

International Preferences:
Asia
All International

Industry Preferences

In Medical/Health prefer:
Health Services

In Consumer Related prefer:
Education Related

Additional Information
Year Founded: 2010
Current Activity Level : Actively seeking new investments

AAVIN EQUITY ADVISORS LLC

118 Third Avenue South East
Suite 630
Cedar Rapids, IA USA 52401
Phone: 3192471072
Fax: 3193639519
E-mail: inquiries@aavin.com
Website: www.aavin.com

Management and Staff
James Thorp, Managing Partner
Thies Kolln, Partner

Type of Firm
Private Equity Firm

Association Membership
Natl Assoc of Small Bus. Inv. Co (NASBIC)

Project Preferences

Role in Financing:
Prefer role as deal originator but will also invest in deals created by others

Type of Financing Preferred:
Leveraged Buyout
Mezzanine
Expansion
Balanced
Later Stage
Management Buyouts
Acquisition
Startup
Recapitalizations

Size of Investments Considered:
Min Size of Investment Considered (000s): $5,000
Max Size of Investment Considered (000s): $10,000

Geographical Preferences

United States Preferences:
Midwest

Industry Preferences

In Communications prefer:
Telecommunications

In Computer Hardware prefer:
Computers

In Computer Software prefer:
Software

In Medical/Health prefer:
Medical Products
Health Services

In Consumer Related prefer:
Consumer

In Industrial/Energy prefer:
Industrial Products

In Transportation prefer:
Transportation

In Financial Services prefer:
Financial Services

In Business Serv. prefer:
Services
Distribution

In Manufact. prefer:
Manufacturing

Additional Information
Name of Most Recent Fund: Aavin Equity Partners I, LP
Most Recent Fund Was Raised: 01/20/2000
Year Founded: 1999
Capital Under Management: $47,000,000
Current Activity Level : Actively seeking new investments
Method of Compensation: Return on invest. most important, but chg. closing fees, service fees, etc.

AAVISHKAAR VENTURE MANAGEMENT SERVICES PVT LTD

Link Road, Malad (West)
516, Fifth Floor, Palm Spring
Mumbai, India 400064
Phone: 912242005757
Fax: 912242005777
E-mail: info@aavishkaar.org
Website: www.aavishkaar.org

Other Offices
57, Grange Road
Suite 16-02, Lucky Tower
Singapore, Singapore 249569

Century Plaza, 2C, 560-562
Anna Salai, Teynampet
Chennai, India 600 018
Phone: 91-44-4354-6937

125 Bay Street, Suite Eight
San Francisco, CA USA 94133
Phone: 650-207-0880

Management and Staff
Wim van der Beek, Managing Partner

Type of Firm
Private Equity Firm

Association Membership
Emerging Markets Private Equity Association
Indian Venture Capital Association (IVCA)

Project Preferences

Type of Financing Preferred:
Early Stage
Expansion
Balanced
Later Stage
Startup

Size of Investments Considered:
Min Size of Investment Considered (000s): $20
Max Size of Investment Considered (000s): $2,000

Geographical Preferences

United States Preferences:
Southeast

International Preferences:
Bangladesh
Indonesia
Pakistan
India
Sri Lanka
Burma

Industry Preferences

In Communications prefer:
Communications and Media

In Medical/Health prefer:
Medical/Health
Health Services

In Consumer Related prefer:
Education Related

In Industrial/Energy prefer:
Energy
Energy Conservation Relat
Environmental Related

In Financial Services prefer:
Financial Services

In Agr/Forestr/Fish prefer:
Agriculture related

AB CAPITAL AND INVESTMENT CORP

8th Floor, Phinma Plaza
39 Plaza Drive, Rockwell Ctr.
Makati City, Philippines 1200
Phone: 632-898-7555
Fax: 632-898-7597
Website: www.abcapitalonline.com

Management and Staff
Ericson Wee, Vice President
Lamberto Santos, President

Type of Firm
Bank Affiliated

Project Preferences

Type of Financing Preferred:
Leveraged Buyout
Early Stage
Expansion
Mezzanine
Startup

Size of Investments Considered:
Min Size of Investment Considered (000s): $579
Max Size of Investment Considered (000s): $3,589

Geographical Preferences

International Preferences:
Philippines

Industry Preferences

In Communications prefer:
Communications and Media

In Computer Other prefer:
Computer Related

In Semiconductor/Electr prefer:
Electronics

In Consumer Related prefer:
Consumer

In Industrial/Energy prefer:
Energy
Industrial Products

In Transportation prefer:
Transportation

In Financial Services prefer:
Financial Services

In Business Serv. prefer:
Services

In Manufact. prefer:
Manufacturing

Additional Information
Year Founded: 1980
Current Activity Level : Actively seeking new investments

AB2 SAS

22 Rue Des Capucines
Paris, France 75002
Phone: 33153459045
Fax: 33153459046

Type of Firm
Private Equity Firm

Project Preferences

Type of Financing Preferred:
Leveraged Buyout
Generalist PE
Later Stage
Management Buyouts
Acquisition
Recapitalizations

Size of Investments Considered:
Min Size of Investment Considered (000s): $1,193
Max Size of Investment Considered (000s): $8,353

Geographical Preferences

International Preferences:
Europe
France

Industry Preferences

In Communications prefer:
Communications and Media

In Computer Software prefer:
Software

In Internet Specific prefer:
E-Commerce Technology

In Medical/Health prefer:
Medical/Health

In Consumer Related prefer:
Consumer
Retail
Other Restaurants
Hotels and Resorts

Additional Information
Year Founded: 1932
Current Activity Level : Actively seeking new investments

ABAC CAPITAL SL

Avenida Diagonal 535
Barcelona, Spain 08029
Phone: 34935456500

Additional Information
Year Founded: 2002
Capital Under Management: $6,000,000
Current Activity Level : Actively seeking new investments

E-mail: enquiries@abaccapital.com
Website: www.abaccapital.com

Other Offices
40, Avenue Monterey
Luxembourg, Luxembourg L 2163

Management and Staff
Borja de la Rosa, Co-Founder
Javier Rigau, Co-Founder
Oriol Pinya, Chief Executive Officer
Saul de Marcos, Co-Founder

Type of Firm
Private Equity Firm

Project Preferences

Type of Financing Preferred:
Leveraged Buyout
Acquisition

Geographical Preferences

International Preferences:
Spain

Industry Preferences

In Consumer Related prefer:
Consumer

In Industrial/Energy prefer:
Energy
Industrial Products

Additional Information
Year Founded: 2014
Capital Under Management: $358,860,000
Current Activity Level : Actively seeking new investments

ABACUS ALPHA GMBH

Johann-Klein-Strasse 45
Frankenthal, Germany 67227
Phone: 496233326044
Fax: 496233326046
E-mail: info@ab-alpha.de
Website: www.ab-alpha.de

Type of Firm
Private Equity Firm

Project Preferences

Type of Financing Preferred:
Leveraged Buyout
Early Stage
Expansion
Generalist PE
Later Stage
Seed
Acquisition
Startup

Industry Preferences

In Medical/Health prefer:
Medical/Health

In Consumer Related prefer:
Retail

In Industrial/Energy prefer:
Industrial Products

In Business Serv. prefer:
Services

In Other prefer:
Environment Responsible

Additional Information
Year Founded: 2006
Current Activity Level : Actively seeking new investments

ABACUS PRIVATE EQUITY LTD

161 Bay Street
Suite 2430
Toronto, Canada M5J 2S1
Phone: 4168618711
Fax: 4168619979
E-mail: info@AbacusPE.com
Website: www.abacuspe.com

Other Offices

1095 West Pender Street
Suiet 1305
Vancouver, Canada V6E 2M6
Phone: 604-696-9995
Fax: 604-696-9935

Rene Levesque Boulevard West
Suite 2200
Montreal, Canada H3B 4W8
Phone: 514-841-1315
Fax: 514-841-1318

550 Burrard Street, Bentall Tower Five
Suite 2578
Vancouver, Canada V7X 1A6
Phone: 6046969995
Fax: 6046969935

140 Oxford Street
Suite 203
London, Canada N6A 5R9
Phone: 519-679-0880
Fax: 519-679-6556

Management and Staff
Bruce Wong, Vice President
Gene Gomes, Managing Director
Greg Tedesco, Chief Financial Officer
Jean-Marc Bougie, Chief Executive Officer
Kulwant Chauhan, Vice President
Michael Doner, Chief Operating Officer
Shams Tejani, Vice President
Tony Leone, Vice President

Type of Firm
Private Equity Firm

Project Preferences

Type of Financing Preferred:
Leveraged Buyout
Balanced
Acquisition

Geographical Preferences

United States Preferences:

Canadian Preferences:
All Canada

Industry Preferences

In Communications prefer:
Communications and Media

In Consumer Related prefer:
Consumer Products

In Industrial/Energy prefer:
Energy
Industrial Products
Machinery

In Financial Services prefer:
Financial Services
Real Estate

In Business Serv. prefer:
Services

In Manufact. prefer:
Manufacturing

In Agr/Forestr/Fish prefer:
Agriculture related

Additional Information
Year Founded: 1996
Current Activity Level : Actively seeking new investments

ABATIS CAPITAL LLC

1221 Avenue of the Americas
42nd Floor
New York, NY USA 10020
Phone: 212-906-4400
Fax: 212-906-4401
E-mail: info@abatiscapitalus.com
Website: www.abatiscapitalus.com

Management and Staff
Andrew Blevin, Managing Director
Grant Davis, Managing Director
Howard Kosel, Managing Director
Jennifer Katz, Vice President
John DaCosta, Managing Director

Type of Firm
Investment Management Firm

Project Preferences

Type of Financing Preferred:
Leveraged Buyout
Management Buyouts
Acquisition

Geographical Preferences

United States Preferences:

Industry Preferences

In Industrial/Energy prefer:
Energy

Additional Information
Year Founded: 2010
Current Activity Level : Actively seeking new investments

ABBEY ROAD VENTURE LTD

Ten Noble Street
Fifth Floor, Alder Castle
London, United Kingdom EC2V 7QJ

Management and Staff
Paul Harvey, Partner

Type of Firm
Private Equity Firm

Project Preferences

Type of Financing Preferred:
Balanced

Geographical Preferences

International Preferences:
United Kingdom
Europe

Additional Information
Year Founded: 2004
Current Activity Level : Actively seeking new investments

ABBOTT CAPITAL MANAGEMENT LLC

1290 Avenue of the Americas
Ninth Floor
New York, NY USA 10104
Phone: 2127572700
Fax: 2127570835
Website: www.abbottcapital.com

Other Offices

53 Davies Street
London, United Kingdom W1K 5JH
Phone: 442031782613

Management and Staff

Charles van Horne, Managing Director
Lauren Massey, Managing Director
Mary Hornby, Managing Director
Matthew Smith, Managing Director
Meredith Rerisi, Managing Director
Paolo Parziale, Managing Director
Raymond Held, Co-Founder
Stanley Pratt, Co-Founder
Timothy Maloney, Managing Director

Type of Firm

Private Equity Advisor or Fund of Funds

Association Membership

National Venture Capital Association - USA (NVCA)

Project Preferences

Type of Financing Preferred:
Fund of Funds

Industry Preferences

In Communications prefer:
Communications and Media
Telecommunications

In Computer Software prefer:
Software

In Biotechnology prefer:
Biotechnology

In Medical/Health prefer:
Medical/Health
Medical Products
Health Services

In Consumer Related prefer:
Consumer
Retail
Consumer Products

In Financial Services prefer:
Financial Services

In Business Serv. prefer:
Media

Additional Information

Name of Most Recent Fund: Abbott Capital Private Equity Investors 2012, L.P.
Most Recent Fund Was Raised: 05/24/2012
Year Founded: 1986
Capital Under Management: $7,344,300,000
Current Activity Level : Actively seeking new investments

ABC CAPITAL MANAGEMENT CO LTD

2558 West Yan An Road
Building 1
Shanghai, China 201103
Phone: 862162959001
Fax: 862162958055
E-mail: asia@abccapital.cn
Website: www.abccapital.cn

Management and Staff

Changhong Liao, Managing Partner
Cheng Ding, Managing Partner
Haitong Zhu, Managing Partner
Jianping Wei, Partner
Joan Zhang, Chief Executive Officer
Qiwei Chen, Partner

Type of Firm

Corporate PE/Venture

Project Preferences

Type of Financing Preferred:
Early Stage
Expansion
Balanced

Geographical Preferences

International Preferences:
China

Industry Preferences

In Biotechnology prefer:
Biotechnology

In Medical/Health prefer:
Medical/Health
Disposable Med. Products

In Consumer Related prefer:
Entertainment and Leisure

In Industrial/Energy prefer:
Energy
Environmental Related

In Manufact. prefer:
Manufacturing

Additional Information

Year Founded: 1988
Capital Under Management: $987,600,000
Current Activity Level : Actively seeking new investments

ABELL VENTURE FUND

111 South Calvert Street
Suite 2300
Baltimore, MD USA 21202
Phone: 4105471300
Fax: 4105396579
E-mail: abell@abell.org
Website: www.abell.org

Management and Staff

Anne La Culman, Vice President
Robert Embry, President

Type of Firm

Private Equity Firm

Project Preferences

Role in Financing:
Will function either as deal originator or investor in deals created by others

Type of Financing Preferred:
Early Stage
Balanced
Later Stage

Geographical Preferences

United States Preferences:
Maryland

Industry Focus

(% based on actual investment)
Industrial/Energy	39.0%
Internet Specific	24.3%
Medical/Health	9.2%
Semiconductors/Other Elect.	9.0%
Communications and Media	7.8%
Biotechnology	5.6%
Computer Software and Services	5.2%

Additional Information

Name of Most Recent Fund: Abell Venture Fund
Most Recent Fund Was Raised: 06/01/1998
Year Founded: 1998
Capital Under Management: $25,000,000
Current Activity Level : Actively seeking new investments
Method of Compensation: Return on investment is of primary concern, do not charge fees

---

ABENEX CAPITAL SAS

9 Avenue Matignon
Paris, France 75008
Phone: 33153936900
Fax: 33153936925
E-mail: contacts@abenexcapital.com
Website: www.abenex.fr

Management and Staff

Florent Rey, Partner
Laurent Kid, Chief Financial Officer
Olivier Moatti, Managing Partner
Patrice Verrier, Managing Partner

Type of Firm

Private Equity Firm

Association Membership

French Venture Capital Association (AFIC)
European Private Equity and Venture Capital Assoc.

Project Preferences

Type of Financing Preferred:
Leveraged Buyout
Management Buyouts
Acquisition

Geographical Preferences

International Preferences:
Europe
France

Industry Preferences

In Medical/Health prefer:
Medical/Health

In Consumer Related prefer:
Retail
Food/Beverage

In Industrial/Energy prefer:
Industrial Products

In Business Serv. prefer:
Services

Additional Information
Year Founded: 1998
Capital Under Management: $662,800,000
Current Activity Level : Actively seeking new investments

ABERDARE VENTURES

235 Montgomery Street
Suite 1230
San Francisco, CA USA 94111
Phone: 4153927442
Fax: 4153924264
Website: www.aberdare.com

Management and Staff
Darren Hite, Partner
Mohit Kaushal, Partner
Sami Hamade, Partner
Sigrid Van Bladel, Venture Partner

Type of Firm
Private Equity Firm

Project Preferences

Role in Financing:
Will function either as deal originator or investor in deals created by others

Type of Financing Preferred:
Early Stage
Expansion

Size of Investments Considered:
Min Size of Investment Considered (000s): $1,000
Max Size of Investment Considered (000s): $15,000

Geographical Preferences

United States Preferences:

Industry Preferences

In Medical/Health prefer:
Medical/Health
Medical Diagnostics
Medical Therapeutics
Drug/Equipmt Delivery
Health Services

Additional Information
Name of Most Recent Fund: Aberdare Ventures IV, L.P.
Most Recent Fund Was Raised: 04/09/2008
Year Founded: 1999
Capital Under Management: $400,000,000
Current Activity Level : Actively seeking new investments
Method of Compensation: Return on investment is of primary concern, do not charge fees

ABERDEEN ASSET MANAGEMENT PLC

Ten Queen's Terrace
Aberdeen
Scotland, United Kingdom AB10 1YG
Phone: 441224631999
Fax: 441224647010
Website: www.aberdeen-asset.com

Other Offices
One Bread Street
Bow Bells House
London, United Kingdom EC4M 9HH
Phone: 442074636000
Fax: 442074636001

Management and Staff
Andrew Laing, Chief Executive Officer
Bever Hendry, Chief Financial Officer
Hugh Young, Managing Director
Martin Gilbert, Chief Executive Officer

Type of Firm
Investment Management Firm

Project Preferences

Type of Financing Preferred:
Fund of Funds
Expansion
Balanced
Later Stage
Other

Geographical Preferences

United States Preferences:
North America
Alaska

International Preferences:
India
Europe
China
Australia
Asia
Japan

Industry Preferences

In Medical/Health prefer:
Medical/Health

In Consumer Related prefer:
Education Related

In Transportation prefer:
Transportation

In Financial Services prefer:
Real Estate

In Business Serv. prefer:
Services

In Other prefer:
Socially Responsible

Additional Information
Name of Most Recent Fund: Aberdeen Asia III Fund of Funds
Most Recent Fund Was Raised: 04/13/2012
Year Founded: 1983
Capital Under Management: $261,200,000
Current Activity Level : Actively seeking new investments

ABERDEEN GOULD CAPITAL MARKETS LTD

55 Street Claire Avenue West
Suite 401
Toronto, Canada M4V 2Y7
Phone: 416-488-2887
Fax: 416-488-1233
E-mail: info@aberdeengould.com

Management and Staff
Roger Rosmus, President, Founder
Sam Ho, Co-Founder

Type of Firm
Investment Management Firm

Project Preferences

Type of Financing Preferred:
Leveraged Buyout

Industry Preferences

In Industrial/Energy prefer:
Energy
Oil & Gas Drilling,Explor

In Manufact. prefer:
Manufacturing

Additional Information
Year Founded: 2009
Current Activity Level : Actively seeking new investments

ABINGWORTH MANAGEMENT LTD

38 Jermyn Street
London, United Kingdom SW1Y 6DN
Phone: 442075341500
Fax: 442072870480
E-mail: info@abingworth.com

Other Offices

890 Winter Street
Suite 150
Waltham, MA USA 02451
Phone: 781-466-8800
Fax: 781-466-8813

3000 Sand Hill Road
Building Four, Suite 135
Menlo Park, CA USA 94025
Phone: 650-926-0600
Fax: 650-926-9782

Management and Staff

Alex Asquith, Principal
David Leathers, Partner
David Mayer, Partner
Genghis Lloyd-Harris, Partner
Joe Anderson, Partner
John Shields, Principal
Jonathan MacQuitty, Partner
Ken Haas, Venture Partner
Kurt von Emster, Managing Partner
Michael Bigham, Partner
Michelle Doig, Principal
Sarah Shackelton, Principal
Shelley Chu, Partner
Timothy Haines, Managing Partner
Victoria Stewart, Principal
Vincent Miles, Venture Partner

Type of Firm

Private Equity Firm

Association Membership

British Venture Capital Association (BVCA)
Western Association of Venture Capitalists (WAVC)
European Private Equity and Venture Capital Assoc.

Project Preferences

Role in Financing:
Prefer role as deal originator but will also invest in deals created by others

Type of Financing Preferred:
Leveraged Buyout
Early Stage
Expansion
Generalist PE
Balanced
Later Stage
Seed
Acquisition
Recapitalizations

Size of Investments Considered:
Min Size of Investment Considered (000s): $5,000
Max Size of Investment Considered (000s): $20,000

Geographical Preferences

United States Preferences:

International Preferences:
United Kingdom
Europe

Industry Focus

(% based on actual investment)
Biotechnology	55.6%
Medical/Health	27.6%
Computer Software and Services	9.9%
Computer Hardware	1.7%
Communications and Media	1.6%
Other Products	1.2%
Consumer Related	1.1%
Industrial/Energy	0.6%
Semiconductors/Other Elect.	0.6%

Additional Information

Name of Most Recent Fund: Abingworth Bioventures VI, L.P.
Most Recent Fund Was Raised: 10/08/2013
Year Founded: 1973
Capital Under Management: $700,000,000
Current Activity Level : Actively seeking new investments
Method of Compensation: Return on investment is of primary concern, do not charge fees

---

ABLE CAPITAL MANAGEMENT LLC

745 Boylston Street
Suite 504
Boston, MA USA 02116
Website: www.ablecapitalmanagement.com

Management and Staff

Brooke Ablon, Partner
Christina Pai, Partner
Jamey Spencer, Partner
Paul Lipson, Partner

Type of Firm

Private Equity Firm

Project Preferences

Type of Financing Preferred:
Leveraged Buyout
Acquisition

Industry Preferences

In Computer Software prefer:
Software

In Medical/Health prefer:
Medical/Health

In Consumer Related prefer:
Consumer

In Business Serv. prefer:
Services

Additional Information

Name of Most Recent Fund: FPC Small Cap Fund I
Most Recent Fund Was Raised: 02/28/2012
Year Founded: 2009
Capital Under Management: $92,738,000
Current Activity Level : Actively seeking new investments

ABN AMRO PARTICIPATIES BV

Gustav Mahlerplein 106
ITO Tower, 21st floor
Amsterdam, Netherlands 1082 MA
Phone: 31206281276
Fax: 31203832697
Website: www.abnamroparticipaties.nl

Type of Firm

Private Equity Firm

Association Membership

Dutch Venture Capital Associaton (NVP)

Project Preferences

Type of Financing Preferred:
Leveraged Buyout

Geographical Preferences

International Preferences:
Netherlands

Industry Preferences

In Medical/Health prefer:
Medical/Health

In Business Serv. prefer:
Services
Distribution

In Manufact. prefer:
Manufacturing

Additional Information

Year Founded: 1959
Current Activity Level : Actively seeking new investments

ABOSS BV

Zekeringstraat 13A
Amsterdam, Netherlands 1014 BM
Phone: 31884747202
Website: www.a-boss.net

Type of Firm

University Program

Pratt's Guide to Private Equity & Venture Capital Sources

Project Preferences

Type of Financing Preferred:
Early Stage
Seed

Geographical Preferences

International Preferences:
Netherlands

Additional Information

Year Founded: 2016
Current Activity Level : Actively seeking new investments

ABP CAPITAL LLC

820 2nd Street
Encinitas, CA USA 92024
E-mail: info@abpcapital.com
Website: abpcapital.com

Management and Staff

Brian Profancik, Chief Financial Officer
Evert Alsenz, Founder
Jim Norum, Vice President
Paul Becker, Founder
Phillip Broderick, Chief Operating Officer

Type of Firm

Investment Management Firm

Project Preferences

Type of Financing Preferred:
Generalist PE

Size of Investments Considered:
Min Size of Investment Considered (000s): $1,000
Max Size of Investment Considered (000s): $100,000

Industry Preferences

In Financial Services prefer:
Real Estate

Additional Information

Year Founded: 2015
Capital Under Management: $1,290,000
Current Activity Level : Actively seeking new investments

ABRAAJ CAPITAL LTD

Dubai Int. Financial Center,
Gate Village 8, 3rd Floor
Dubai, Utd. Arab Em.
Phone: 97145064400
Fax: 97145064600
E-mail: info@abraaj.com
Website: www.abraaj.com

Other Offices

Kingdom Tower, 25th Floor, PO Box 301052
Riyadh, Saudi Arabia 11372
Phone: 966-1211-3044
Fax: 966-1211-3043

Jl. Jendral Sudriman Kav.21
Chase Plaza 2nd Floor Podium
Jakarta, Indonesia 12920
Phone: 62215208380
Fax: 622129669558

One Grafton Street
London, United Kingdom W1S 4FE
Phone: 442035401500
Fax: 442035401501

Seven Al Farabi Avenue
Nurly Tau 4A, Office 14
Almaty, Kazakhstan 050059
Phone: 77273110287
Fax: 77273110288

1701 Pennsylvania Avenue
Suite 300
WASHINGTON, DC USA 20006
Phone: 2025806540
Fax: 2025806559

510 Madison Avenue
MANHATTAN, NY USA 10022

Dr. Annie Besant Road
405, Ceejay House
Mumbai, India 400 018
Phone: 912267874500
Fax: 912267872828

68 Kijabe Street
Second Floor, Norfolk Towers
Nairobi, Kenya
Phone: 254202228870
Fax: 25420310355

158 Al Hijaz Towers, 8th Floor, Suite D,
Mecca Street, PO Box 3349
Amman, Jordan 11953
Phone: 962-6534-7254
Fax: 962-6552-2978

Ten Hong Kong Middle Road
Room 1601, Site A, Yihe
Shandong Province, China 266071
Phone: 8653266777161
Fax: 8653266777160

No. Two La By Pass
Regimanuel Gray Head Office
Accra, Ghana
Phone: 233302770212
Fax: 233302765118

Nile City Towers, North Tower, 17th Fl
Corniche El Nil, Ramlet Beaulac
Cairo, Egypt
Phone: 202-2461-9930
Fax: 202-2461-9931

Visnezade Mahallesi
No 32/2, Sleyman Seba Cad
Istanbul, Turkey 34357
Phone: 902-1238-14800
Fax: 902-1238-14810

Azarieh Building, 5th Floor, Block 3
Azarieh Street, PO Box 11-503
Beirut, Lebanon
Phone: 961-196-4570
Fax: 961-196-4501

Dolmen City, Executive Tower, 6th Floor
Office 6A, Clifton, Block 4
Karachi, Pakistan 75600
Phone: 922-1352-97556
Fax: 922-1352-97549

Eight First Avenue
Unit T3-6, KPMG Tower
Kuala Lumpur, Malaysia 47800
Phone: 60377100388
Fax: 60377106268

One Sandton Drive
First Floor, The Place
Johannesburg, South Africa
Phone: 27118842066

Cra. 9 No.113-52 Oficina 1404
Edificio Torres Unidas 2
Bogota, Colombia
Phone: 5716372500
Fax: 5716372500

Management and Staff

Adel Goucha, Principal
Alexandre Hamadouche, Principal
Aman Lakhaney, Principal
Anas Guennoun, Principal
Ashish Dave, Chief Financial Officer
Ayman Arekat, Partner
Elie Habib, Principal
Fabrice Callet, Principal
Fayez Husseini, Principal
Huda Ali Redha, Principal
Mark Bourgeois, Partner
Rafik Dalala, Principal
Saqib Rashid, Principal
Seifallah Sami Zoghbi, Principal
Tarek Kabrit, Principal
Walid Bakr, Principal

Type of Firm

Private Equity Firm

Association Membership
South African Venture Capital Association (SAVCA)
Gulf Venture Capital Association
Emerging Markets Private Equity Association
African Venture Capital Association (AVCA)
Indian Venture Capital Association (IVCA)

Project Preferences

Type of Financing Preferred:
Leveraged Buyout
Balanced
Acquisition
Private Placement

Geographical Preferences

International Preferences:
Malta
Mali
Jersey
Middle East
Asia
Africa

Industry Preferences

In Communications prefer:
Communications and Media
Satellite Microwave Comm.
Media and Entertainment
Entertainment

In Computer Hardware prefer:
Integrated Turnkey System

In Semiconductor/Electr prefer:
Fiber Optics

In Medical/Health prefer:
Medical/Health
Disposable Med. Products
Health Services
Hospitals/Clinics/Primary
Hospital/Other Instit.

In Consumer Related prefer:
Publishing-Retail

In Industrial/Energy prefer:
Energy

In Transportation prefer:
Transportation

In Agr/Forestr/Fish prefer:
Mining and Minerals

In Utilities prefer:
Utilities

Additional Information
Year Founded: 2002
Capital Under Management: $10,000,000,000
Current Activity Level : Actively seeking new investments

ABRIS CAPITAL PARTNERS SP ZOO

Grzybowska 5A
Grzybowska Park, Floor 6
Warsaw, Poland 00-132
Phone: 48225645858
Fax: 48225645859
E-mail: Warsaw@Abris-Capital.com
Website: www.abris-capital.com

Other Offices
Herastrau Office Building
15 Ghetarilor, 3rd Floor, 1st District
Bucharest, Romania 014106
Phone: 40314322988
Fax: 40314322987

Management and Staff
Cezar Scarlat, Partner
George Swirski, Co-Founder
Milorad Andjelic, Partner
Monika Nachyla, Partner
Neil Milne, Co-Founder
Paulina Pietkiewicz, Chief Operating Officer
Pawel Boksa, Partner
Wojciech Jezierski, Partner
Wojciech Lukawski, Partner

Type of Firm
Private Equity Firm

Association Membership
Emerging Markets Private Equity Association
Polish Venture Capital Association (PSIC/PPEA)

Project Preferences

Type of Financing Preferred:
Leveraged Buyout
Management Buyouts

Geographical Preferences

International Preferences:
Central Europe
Eastern Europe

Industry Preferences

In Communications prefer:
Telecommunications

In Medical/Health prefer:
Medical/Health
Health Services

In Consumer Related prefer:
Retail
Education Related

In Industrial/Energy prefer:
Alternative Energy
Environmental Related

In Financial Services prefer:
Financial Services

In Business Serv. prefer:
Media

In Manufact. prefer:
Manufacturing

Additional Information
Name of Most Recent Fund: Abris CEE Mid-Market Fund II, L.P.
Most Recent Fund Was Raised: 10/14/2011
Year Founded: 2007
Capital Under Management: $724,600,000
Current Activity Level - Actively seeking new investments

ABRT VENCHURNYI FOND

Five Bersenevskaya Embankment
Building Four, Golden Island
Moscow, Russia 119072
Phone: 78123355545
E-mail: project@abrtfund.com
Website: www.abrtfund.com

Other Offices
15/3 Kondratyevsky
"Kondratyevsky" Business Centre
Saint-Petersburg Russia 195197
Phone: 78123355545
Fax: 78123355546

Type of Firm
Private Equity Firm

Project Preferences

Type of Financing Preferred:
Early Stage
Expansion
Seed
Startup

Geographical Preferences

United States Preferences:
All U.S.

International Preferences:
Europe
Russia

Industry Preferences

In Computer Software prefer:
Software
Systems Software
Applications Software

In Internet Specific prefer:
Internet

Additional Information
Year Founded: 2005
Current Activity Level : Actively seeking new investments

Pratt's Guide to Private Equity & Venture Capital Sources

ABRUZZOCAPITAL SPA

Via Silvio Pellico 28/1
Pescara, Italy 65123
Phone: 39-85-421-7674
Fax: 39-85-422-1186

Type of Firm
Private Equity Firm

Project Preferences

Type of Financing Preferred:
Early Stage
Expansion
Seed
Startup

Geographical Preferences

International Preferences:
Italy

Additional Information
Year Founded: 2000
Capital Under Management: $3,300,000
Current Activity Level : Actively seeking new investments

ABRY PARTNERS LLC

888 Boylston
Suite 1600
Boston, MA USA 02199
Phone: 6178592959
Fax: 6178598797
E-mail: information@abry.com
Website: www.abry.com

Management and Staff
Andrew Banks, Co-Founder
Azra Kanji, Partner
Blake Battaglia, Partner
Bob Pan, Principal
Brent Stone, Partner
Brian St. Jean, Partner
C. J. Brucato, Managing Partner
Debbie Johnson, Chief Financial Officer
Erik Brooks, Managing Partner
James Scola, Principal
John Connor, Partner
John Hunt, Managing Partner
Matthew Lapides, Partner
Michael Yirilli, Principal
Michael Ashton, Partner
Nathan Ott, Principal
Nicolas Massard, Partner
Rob Nicewicz, Principal
Robert MacInnis, Partner
Royce Yudkoff, Co-Founder
T.J. Rose, Principal
Timothy Nickel, Partner
Tomer Yosef-Or, Partner
Tyler Wick, Principal

Type of Firm
Private Equity Firm

Project Preferences

Type of Financing Preferred:
Leveraged Buyout
Expansion
Mezzanine
Later Stage
Acquisition
Industry Rollups
Distressed Debt
Recapitalizations

Geographical Preferences

United States Preferences:
North America

Industry Focus
(% based on actual investment)
Internet Specific   33.2%
Communications and Media   24.3%
Computer Hardware   16.6%
Consumer Related   6.7%
Computer Software and Services 5.5%
Other Products   5.5%
Medical/Health   5.2%
Semiconductors/Other Elect. 3.1%

Additional Information
Year Founded: 1989
Capital Under Management: $1,700,000,000
Current Activity Level : Actively seeking new investments

ABS CAPITAL PARTNERS, INC.

400 East Pratt Street
Suite 910
Baltimore, MD USA 21202
Phone: 4102465600
Fax: 4102465606
E-mail: abscapital@abscapital.com
Website: www.abscapital.com

Management and Staff
Andrew Boyd, Vice President
Bobby Goswami, General Partner
Calbraith Wheaton, General Partner
Cass Gilmore, Principal
James Stevenson, Chief Financial Officer
John Stobo, Managing Partner
Kimberly Kile, Principal
Laura Witt, General Partner
Michael Avon, Venture Partner
Paul Mariani, General Partner
Ralph Terkowitz, General Partner
Robyn Lehman, Principal
Stephanie Carter, General Partner
Tim Zahrobsky, Vice President

Type of Firm
Private Equity Firm

Association Membership
Mid-Atlantic Venture Association
National Venture Capital Association - USA (NVCA)

Project Preferences

Role in Financing:
Prefer role as deal originator but will also invest in deals created by others

Type of Financing Preferred:
Leveraged Buyout
Later Stage

Size of Investments Considered:
Min Size of Investment Considered (000s): $10,000
Max Size of Investment Considered (000s): $50,000

Industry Focus
(% based on actual investment)
Internet Specific   27.9%
Computer Software and Services 26.1%
Medical/Health   14.0%
Other Products   13.8%
Communications and Media   4.5%
Industrial/Energy   4.4%
Computer Hardware   4.0%
Consumer Related   3.6%
Biotechnology   1.7%

Additional Information
Name of Most Recent Fund: ABS Capital Partners VII, L.P.
Most Recent Fund Was Raised: 10/27/2011
Year Founded: 1990
Capital Under Management: $2,500,000,000
Current Activity Level : Actively seeking new investments
Method of Compensation: Return on invest. most important, but chg. closing fees, service fees, etc.

ABS VENTURES

950 Winter Street
Suite 2600
Waltham, MA USA 02451
Phone: 7812500400
Fax: 7812500345
E-mail: abs@absventures.com
Website: www.absventures.com

Management and Staff
Bill Burgess, Managing Partner
Bruns Grayson, Managing Partner
Susan Adams, Chief Financial Officer

Type of Firm
Private Equity Firm

Association Membership
New England Venture Capital Association

Project Preferences

Role in Financing:
Will function either as deal originator or investor in deals created by others

Type of Financing Preferred:
Expansion
Balanced
Later Stage
Fund of Funds of Second

Geographical Preferences

United States Preferences:

Industry Focus

(% based on actual investment)
Computer Software and Services	32.0%
Medical/Health	18.7%
Communications and Media	15.2%
Internet Specific	12.2%
Computer Hardware	10.0%
Biotechnology	4.7%
Other Products	2.3%
Industrial/Energy	2.2%
Consumer Related	1.5%
Semiconductors/Other Elect.	1.0%

Additional Information

Year Founded: 1982
Capital Under Management: $200,000,000
Current Activity Level : Actively seeking new investments
Method of Compensation: Return on investment is of primary concern, do not charge fees

ABU DHABI CAPITAL MANAGEMENT LLC

Bainunah Street, Al Bateen
C2, Suite 204
Abu Dhabi, Utd. Arab Em.
Phone: 97126390099
Fax: 97126390700
E-mail: info@adcm.ae
Website: www.adcm.ae

Management and Staff

Jassim Mohammed RMS Alseddiqi Alansaari, Chief Executive Officer
Mustafa Ghazi Kheriba, Chief Operating Officer

Type of Firm

Private Equity Advisor or Fund of Funds

Project Preferences

Type of Financing Preferred:
Fund of Funds
Fund of Funds of Second

Geographical Preferences

United States Preferences:
All U.S.

International Preferences:
Europe
Middle East
Africa

Additional Information

Name of Most Recent Fund: ADCM Secondary Private Equity Fund
Most Recent Fund Was Raised: 03/29/2011
Year Founded: 2011
Capital Under Management: $45,000,000
Current Activity Level : Actively seeking new investments

ABU DHABI FINANCIAL GROUP LLC

Bainuna Street
C2 Tower, Albateen Towers
Abu Dhabi, Utd. Arab Em.
Website: www.adfg.ae

Type of Firm

Investment Management Firm

Project Preferences

Type of Financing Preferred:
Core
Leveraged Buyout
Value-Add
Early Stage
Expansion
Opportunistic
Later Stage
Management Buyouts
Acquisition

Industry Preferences

In Financial Services prefer:
Real Estate

Additional Information

Year Founded: 2011
Current Activity Level : Actively seeking new investments

ABU DHABI INVESTMENT AUTHORITY

211 Corniche
Abu Dhabi, Utd. Arab Em. 3600
Phone: 97124150000
Fax: 97124151000
Website: www.adia.ae

Management and Staff

Hamed Al Nehayan, Managing Director

Type of Firm

Government Affiliated Program

Geographical Preferences

United States Preferences:
North America

International Preferences:
Europe
Asia

Industry Preferences

In Financial Services prefer:
Real Estate
Financial Services

Additional Information

Year Founded: 1976
Current Activity Level : Actively seeking new investments

ABUNDANCE PARTNERS LLC

55 Fifth Avenue
18th Floor
New York, NY USA 10003
Phone: 6464967323
Fax: 2122083043
Website: abundancepartnersllc.com

Management and Staff

Alex Pinchev, Managing Partner
David Katona, Managing Partner
Dennis Shaya, Managing Partner
James Dascoli, Chief Operating Officer

Type of Firm

Private Equity Firm

Project Preferences

Type of Financing Preferred:
Early Stage
Startup

Industry Preferences

In Communications prefer:
Communications and Media

In Computer Software prefer:
Systems Software
Applications Software

In Semiconductor/Electr prefer:
Analytic/Scientific

Additional Information

Year Founded: 2003
Capital Under Management: $7,880,000
Current Activity Level : Actively seeking new investments

ABUNDANCE VENTURE CAPITAL SDN BHD

Petaling Jaya
Nine, Jalan 12/21A
Selangor, Malaysia 46200
Phone: 60379562151
E-mail: info@abundancevc.com
Website: www.abundancevc.com

Management and Staff
Gurmit Sidhu, Founder

Type of Firm
Private Equity Firm

Project Preferences

Type of Financing Preferred:
Expansion
Balanced

Size of Investments Considered:
Min Size of Investment Considered (000s): $250
Max Size of Investment Considered (000s): $5,000

Geographical Preferences

International Preferences:
India
Asia
Singapore
Malaysia

Industry Preferences

In Computer Software prefer:
Software

In Internet Specific prefer:
Internet

In Biotechnology prefer:
Biotechnology

In Medical/Health prefer:
Health Services

In Industrial/Energy prefer:
Energy
Alternative Energy
Energy Conservation Relat
Environmental Related

In Other prefer:
Environment Responsible

Additional Information
Year Founded: 1993
Capital Under Management: $250,000,000
Current Activity Level: Actively seeking new investments

ABUNDANT VENTURE PARTNERS LLC

111 E. Wacker Drive
Suite 300
Chicago, IL USA 60601
Website: www.abundantventurepartners.com

Management and Staff
Andrew Swinand, Co-Founder
Bryan Stuart, Chief Financial Officer
Eric Langshur, Co-Founder
Eric Jensen, Chief Operating Officer

Type of Firm
Incubator/Development Program

Project Preferences

Type of Financing Preferred:
Early Stage

Geographical Preferences

United States Preferences:

Industry Preferences

In Medical/Health prefer:
Health Services

In Business Serv. prefer:
Media

Additional Information
Year Founded: 2011
Current Activity Level: Actively seeking new investments

ACA VENTURES LLC

1575 Deming Drive
Orlando, FL USA 32825
Phone: 415-241-3501

Type of Firm
Private Equity Firm

Project Preferences

Type of Financing Preferred:
Balanced

Additional Information
Year Founded: 2009
Current Activity Level: Actively seeking new investments

ACACIA PARTNERS LLC

4330 Gaines Ranch Loop
Suite 100
Austin, TX USA 78735
Phone: 5128527458
Website: www.acaciapartnersllc.com

Type of Firm
Private Equity Firm

Project Preferences

Type of Financing Preferred:
Leveraged Buyout
Later Stage
Management Buyouts
Acquisition
Special Situation
Recapitalizations

Geographical Preferences

United States Preferences:
All U.S.

Additional Information
Year Founded: 2011
Current Activity Level: Actively seeking new investments

ACAS LLC

Two Bethesda Metro Center
14th Floor
Bethesda, MD USA 20814
Phone: 3019516122
Fax: 3016546714
E-mail: Info@AmericanCapital.com
Website: www.americancapital.com

Other Offices

155 North Wacker Drive
Suite 4250
Chicago, IL USA 60606
Phone: 312-681-7400
Fax: 312-454-0600

180 Main Street
Second Floor
Annapolis, MD USA 21401
Phone: 443-214-7070
Fax: 443-214-7071

161 Worcester Road
Suite 606
Framingham, MA USA 01701
Phone: 508-598-1100
Fax: 508-598-1101

2200 Ross Avenue
Suite 4500W
Dallas, TX USA 75201
Phone: 214-273-6630
Fax: 214-273-6635

505 Fifth Avenue
26th Floor
New York, NY USA 10017
Phone: 212-213-2009
Fax: 212-213-2060

Management and Staff

Adam Spence, Managing Director
Adam Stern, Principal
Amie Wright, Vice President
Andrew Flesch, Vice President
Bill Weiss, Vice President
Bowen Diehl, Managing Director
Bret Bero, Principal
Chris McCormack, Vice President
Christian Toro, Vice President
Craig Moore, Managing Director
Cydonii Fairfax, Vice President
Dan Cohn-Sfetcu, Principal
Dana Dratch, Vice President
David Malcarney, Vice President
Derek Walton, Vice President
Didier Lefevre, Managing Director
Douglas Cooper, Managing Director
Douglas Kelley, Principal
Dustin Smith, Principal
Elizabeth Masciopinto, Vice President
Erin Soule, Vice President
Eugene Krichevsky, Principal
Evan Kurtz, Vice President
Fernando Ruiz, Vice President
George Branca, Principal
Heather French, Vice President
Helen Yang, Principal
Jack Shields, Principal
James Shevlin, Principal
James Griffin, Vice President
Jeffrey MacDowell, Managing Director
Jennifer Vaughn, Principal
Jim Gregory, Vice President
Jimmy Byun, Vice President
John Rhoades, Vice President
Jon Isaacson, Managing Director
Jon Lindberg, Vice President
Joseph Romic, Principal
Juan Miguel Estela, Vice President
Justin DuFour, Vice President
Justin Cressall, Vice President
Kenneth Pollack, Vice President
Kevin Kuykendall, Managing Director
Kyle Bradford, Principal
Lucia Marin, Vice President
Lynn JangJan, Vice President
Mark Pelletier, Managing Director
Marshall White, Vice President
Melissa Smith, Vice President
Michael Sarner, Vice President
Michael Cerullo, Principal
Michael Shin, Principal
Michael Messersmith, Vice President
Michael Meretta, Vice President
Miles Arnone, Managing Director
Myung Yi, Managing Director
Nathalie Beaulieu, Managing Director
Pankaj Gupta, Managing Director
Peter Dahms, Vice President
Rob Carraway, Vice President
Robert Klein, Managing Director
Robert Sacks, Principal
Rustey Emmet, Vice President
Ryan Brauns, Principal
Ryan Nagim, Vice President
Scott Kauffman, Vice President
Sean Reid, Vice President
Sean Eagle, Principal
Steven Stubitz, Principal
Thomas Nathanson, Managing Director
Thomas Evans, Vice President
Todd Friant, Principal
Tristan Parisot, Managing Director
Wil Garland, Principal
William Rudat, Vice President
Yaniv Zief, Vice President

Type of Firm
Private Equity Firm

Project Preferences

Role in Financing:
Will function either as deal originator or investor in deals created by others

Type of Financing Preferred:
Leveraged Buyout
Mezzanine
Generalist PE
Other
Acquisition
Special Situation
Recapitalizations

Geographical Preferences

United States Preferences:
North America

International Preferences:
Europe

Industry Preferences

In Computer Software prefer:
Software

In Medical/Health prefer:
Medical Products
Health Services

In Consumer Related prefer:
Consumer Services
Education Related

In Industrial/Energy prefer:
Energy
Industrial Products

In Financial Services prefer:
Real Estate

In Business Serv. prefer:
Services
Distribution

In Manufact. prefer:
Manufacturing

Additional Information
Year Founded: 1986
Capital Under Management: $20,000,000,000
Current Activity Level: Actively seeking new investments
Method of Compensation: Return on invest. most important, but chg. closing fees, service fees, etc.

ACCEL INDIA VENTURE FUND

Cunningham Road
Suite 21/1-1, Nawab Towers
Bangalore, India 560 052
Phone: 918041232551
Fax: 918041238853
E-mail: bangalore@accel.com
Website: www.accel.com

Management and Staff

Anand Daniel, Principal
Mahendran Balachandran, Partner
Neeraj Bharadwaj, Partner
Prashanth Prakash, Partner
Prateek Dhawan, Partner
Shekhar Kirani, Partner
Subrata Mitra, Partner

Type of Firm
Private Equity Firm

Project Preferences

Type of Financing Preferred:
Early Stage
Seed

Geographical Preferences

International Preferences:
India

Industry Preferences

In Communications prefer:
Wireless Communications

Additional Information
Year Founded: 1983
Current Activity Level: Actively seeking new investments

ACCEL PARTNERS & CO INC

428 University Avenue
Palo Alto, CA USA 94301
Phone: 6506144800
Fax: 6506144880
E-mail: siliconvalley@accel.com
Website: www.accel.com

Other Offices

Level 2, Elegance Tower
Jasola, Mathura Road
New Delhi, India 110 025
Phone: 91-11-4060-1153

Pratt's Guide to Private Equity & Venture Capital Sources

16 St. James's Street
London, United Kingdom SW1A 1ER
Phone: 44-20-7170-1000
Fax: 44-20-7170-1099

111 Eighth Avenue
16th Floor
New York, NY USA 10011
Phone: 2127761912

Room 616 Tower A, COFCO Plaza
8 Jianguomen nei Daije
Beijing, China 100005
Phone: 86-10-6526-2400
Fax: 86-10-6526-0700

Room 1105, Aetna Tower
Number 107 Zunyi Road
Shanghai, China 200051
Phone: 86-21-6237-5899
Fax: 86-21-6237-5899

17th E Main, Sixth Block
Suite 885 A
Bangalore, India 560 095
Phone: 918041232551
Fax: 918041238853

Management and Staff

Anand Daniel, Principal
Arthur Patterson, Partner
Bruce Golden, General Partner
Bud Colligan, Partner
Gregory Waldorf, Chief Executive Officer
J. Peter Wagner, Managing Partner
James Breyer, Managing Partner
James Flach, Partner
James Swartz, General Partner
Jonathan Siegel, Venture Partner
Jonathan Biggs, Chief Financial Officer
Joseph Schoendorf, Partner
Judy Gibbons, Venture Partner
Kevin Efrusy, General Partner
Kevin Comolli, Managing Partner
Luciana Lixandru, Partner
Neeraj Bharadwaj, Managing Director
Nir Blumberger, Venture Partner
Richard Wong, Partner
Rob Glaser, Venture Partner
Ryan Sweeney, Partner
Sameer Gandhi, Partner
Sonali De Rycker, Partner
Stephanie Ichinose, Partner
Sven Schmidt, Venture Partner
Theresia Ranzetta, General Partner

Type of Firm
Private Equity Firm

Association Membership
China Venture Capital Association
Western Association of Venture Capitalists (WAVC)
National Venture Capital Association - USA (NVCA)
Indian Venture Capital Association (IVCA)

Project Preferences

Role in Financing:
Will function either as deal originator or investor in deals created by others

Type of Financing Preferred:
Early Stage
Expansion
Balanced
Later Stage
Seed
Startup

Size of Investments Considered:
Min Size of Investment Considered (000s): $1,000
Max Size of Investment Considered: No Limit

Geographical Preferences

United States Preferences:

International Preferences:
Italy
India
United Kingdom
Luxembourg
Europe
Netherlands
Belgium
Germany
All International
France

Industry Focus
(% based on actual investment)

Internet Specific	39.9%
Computer Software and Services	37.2%
Communications and Media	9.5%
Computer Hardware	3.4%
Semiconductors/Other Elect.	2.8%
Other Products	2.1%
Industrial/Energy	1.6%
Medical/Health	1.3%
Consumer Related	1.3%
Biotechnology	0.8%

Additional Information
Name of Most Recent Fund: Accel Growth Fund III, L.P.
Most Recent Fund Was Raised: 03/17/2014
Year Founded: 1983
Capital Under Management: $3,432,000,000
Current Activity Level : Actively seeking new investments
Method of Compensation: Return on investment is of primary concern, do not charge fees

ACCEL-KKR

2500 Sand Hill Road
Suite 300
Menlo Park, CA USA 94025
Phone: 6502892460
Fax: 6502892461
Website: www.accel-kkr.com

Other Offices

3284 Northside Parkway NW
Suite 475
Atlanta, GA USA 30339
Phone: 6788095989
Fax: 6789056809

33 Saint James Square
London, United Kingdom SW1Y 4JS
Phone: 442077696736

Management and Staff

Ben Bisconti, Managing Director
David Cusimano, Vice President
Dean Jacobson, Principal
Greg Williams, Managing Director
Jason Klein, Managing Director
Joe Savig, Principal
Maurice Hernandez, Vice President
Max Thoene, Chief Operating Officer
Park Durrett, Vice President
Robert Palumbo, Managing Director
Thomas Barnds, Partner

Type of Firm
Private Equity Firm

Project Preferences

Role in Financing:
Prefer role as deal originator

Type of Financing Preferred:
Leveraged Buyout
Expansion
Mezzanine
Management Buyouts
Acquisition
Recapitalizations

Geographical Preferences

International Preferences:
Ireland
United Kingdom
Netherlands
Australia

Industry Preferences

In Computer Software prefer:
Software

In Internet Specific prefer:
E-Commerce Technology

Additional Information
Name of Most Recent Fund: Accel-KKR Structured Capital Partners II, LP
Most Recent Fund Was Raised: 03/31/2014
Year Founded: 2000
Capital Under Management: $2,000,000,000
Current Activity Level : Actively seeking new investments
Method of Compensation: Return on investment is of primary concern, do not charge fees

ACCELE BIOPHARMA INC

865 Research Parkway
Suite 400, PHF Research Park
Oklahoma City, OK USA 73104
Phone: 4053198165
E-mail: info@accelebio.com
Website: accelebio.com

Management and Staff

Richard Gammans, President

Type of Firm

Private Equity Firm

Project Preferences

Type of Financing Preferred:
Early Stage
Seed

Industry Preferences

In Biotechnology prefer:
Biotechnology

Additional Information

Name of Most Recent Fund: Accele Venture Partners I, L.P.
Most Recent Fund Was Raised: 08/01/2012
Year Founded: 2011
Capital Under Management: $10,000,000
Current Activity Level : Actively seeking new investments

ACCELEPRISE LLC

1519 Connecticut Avenue NW
Suite 201
Washington, DC USA 20036
Phone: 7329395270
Website: www.acceleprise.vc

Other Offices

1538 Filbert Street
Suite 10
San Francisco, CA USA 94123
Phone: 5187277129

Management and Staff

Allen Gannett, Partner
Collin Gutman, Partner
Sean Glass, Managing Partner
Whitney Sales, General Partner

Type of Firm

Incubator/Development Program

Project Preferences

Type of Financing Preferred:
Expansion
Seed
Startup

Geographical Preferences

United States Preferences:
California

Industry Preferences

In Computer Software prefer:
Software
Systems Software

Additional Information

Name of Most Recent Fund: Acceleprise Venture Capital Fund I, L.P.
Most Recent Fund Was Raised: 06/07/2012
Year Founded: 2012
Capital Under Management: $10,900,000
Current Activity Level : Actively seeking new investments

ACCELERACE INVEST K/S

Fruebjergvej 3
Copenhagen O, Denmark 2100
Phone: 453917940
Website: www.accelerace.dk

Type of Firm

Incubator/Development Program

Project Preferences

Type of Financing Preferred:
Early Stage
Seed
Startup

Geographical Preferences

International Preferences:
All International
Denmark

Additional Information

Year Founded: 2009
Capital Under Management: $14,030,000
Current Activity Level : Actively seeking new investments

ACCELERANT EQUITY LLC

4364 Classic Links Court
Marietta, GA USA 30067
Website: www.accelerantdigital.com

Management and Staff

Paul Iaffaldano, Principal

Type of Firm

Private Equity Firm

Project Preferences

Type of Financing Preferred:
Early Stage

Additional Information

Year Founded: 2016
Current Activity Level : Actively seeking new investments

ACCELERANT FUND I LP

40 North Main Street
Suite 900
Dayton, OH USA 45423
Phone: 9372224422
E-mail: information@accelerantdayton.com
Website: www.accelerantdayton.com

Management and Staff

Joel Ivers, Vice President

Type of Firm

Private Equity Firm

Project Preferences

Type of Financing Preferred:
Seed

Geographical Preferences

United States Preferences:
Ohio

Additional Information

Year Founded: 2014
Capital Under Management: $9,500,000
Current Activity Level : Actively seeking new investments

ACCELERATE LONG ISLAND INC

300 Broadhollow Road
Suite 110W
Melville, NY USA 11747
Phone: 6314933024
Website: www.accelerateli.org

Type of Firm

Incubator/Development Program

Project Preferences

Type of Financing Preferred:
Early Stage
Startup

Geographical Preferences

United States Preferences:
New York

Additional Information

Year Founded: 2011
Current Activity Level : Actively seeking new investments

Pratt's Guide to Private Equity & Venture Capital Sources

ACCELERATE-IT VENTURES MANAGEMENT LLC

325 Pacific Avenue
San Francisco, CA USA 94111
Phone: 4159645102
E-mail: contact@aitv.co
Website: www.aitv.co

Management and Staff

Adam Bain, Partner
Andy Bair, Partner
Arnaud Wyck, Partner
Bill Malloy, General Partner
Brian Nugent, General Partner
John Vigouroux, Venture Partner
Jon Lonsdale, Partner
Karl Karlsson, General Partner
Ken Denman, Venture Partner
Lari Nguyen, Partner
Najib Khouri-Haddad, General Partner
Patrick ONeill, Partner
Scott Arnold, Chief Financial Officer

Type of Firm
Private Equity Firm

Project Preferences

Type of Financing Preferred:
Early Stage
Expansion
Startup

Geographical Preferences

United States Preferences:

International Preferences:
Europe

Industry Preferences

In Computer Software prefer:
Software
Systems Software
Applications Software

In Internet Specific prefer:
Internet
Ecommerce
Web Aggregration/Portals

Additional Information
Year Founded: 2013
Capital Under Management: $48,100,000
Current Activity Level : Actively seeking new investments

ACCELERATED GROWTH PARTNERS

5621 Cary Street Road #1
Richmond, VA USA 23226
Phone: 7578805262

Type of Firm
Private Equity Firm

Additional Information
Year Founded: 2002
Current Activity Level : Actively seeking new investments

ACCELERATOR ACADEMY

123A BOROUGH HIGH STREET
LONDON, United Kingdom SE1 1NP
Phone: 02032803705
E-mail: infor@acceleratoracademy.com
Website: acceleratoracademy.com

Management and Staff
Ian Merricks, Founder

Type of Firm
Incubator/Development Program

Project Preferences

Type of Financing Preferred:
Early Stage
Expansion
Startup

Geographical Preferences

International Preferences:
United Kingdom

Industry Preferences

In Communications prefer:
Telecommunications

In Business Serv. prefer:
Media

Additional Information
Year Founded: 2013
Current Activity Level : Actively seeking new investments

ACCELERATOR CENTRE

295 Hagey Boulevard
1st Floor, West Entrance
Waterloo, Canada
Phone: 5193422400
Fax: 5195132421
E-mail: info@acceleratorcentre.comc
Website: www.acceleratorcentre.com

Type of Firm
Incubator/Development Program

Project Preferences

Type of Financing Preferred:
Seed
Startup

Geographical Preferences

Canadian Preferences:
All Canada

Additional Information
Year Founded: 2006
Current Activity Level : Actively seeking new investments

ACCELERATOR CORP

1616 Eastlake Avenue East
Suite 200
Seattle, WA USA 98102
Phone: 2069577300
Fax: 2069577399
Website: www.acceleratorcorp.com

Type of Firm
Incubator/Development Program

Project Preferences

Type of Financing Preferred:
Early Stage
Seed
Startup

Industry Preferences

In Biotechnology prefer:
Biotechnology
Biotech Related Research

Additional Information
Year Founded: 2003
Capital Under Management: $64,050,000
Current Activity Level : Actively seeking new investments

ACCELERATOR VENTURES

480 Second Street
Suite 301
San Francisco, CA USA 94107
E-mail: info@acceleratorventures.com
Website: www.acceleratorventures.com

Management and Staff
Benjamin Smith, Venture Partner

Type of Firm
Private Equity Firm

Project Preferences

Type of Financing Preferred:
Early Stage
Seed
Startup

Geographical Preferences

United States Preferences:
California

Industry Preferences

In Internet Specific prefer:
Ecommerce

In Consumer Related prefer:
Consumer

Additional Information

Name of Most Recent Fund: Accelerator Venture Capital I, L.P.
Most Recent Fund Was Raised: 08/12/2008
Year Founded: 2008
Current Activity Level : Actively seeking new investments

ACCELFOODS LLC

205 East 42nd Street
New York, NY USA 10017
E-mail: info@accelfoods.com
Website: www.accelfoods.com

Management and Staff

Jordan Gaspar, Managing Partner
Lauren Jupiter, Managing Partner

Type of Firm

Incubator/Development Program

Project Preferences

Type of Financing Preferred:
Early Stage

Industry Preferences

In Consumer Related prefer:
Food/Beverage

Additional Information

Year Founded: 2013
Capital Under Management: $35,000,000
Current Activity Level : Actively seeking new investments

ACCENT EQUITY PARTNERS AB

Engelbrektsgatan 7
Stockholm, Sweden 114 87
Phone: 46854507300
Fax: 46854507329
E-mail: info@accentequity.se
Website: accentequitypartners.se

Management and Staff

Emmanuel Ergul, Partner
Niklas Sloutski, Chief Executive Officer

Type of Firm

Private Equity Firm

Association Membership

Swedish Venture Capital Association (SVCA)
European Private Equity and Venture Capital Assoc.

Project Preferences

Type of Financing Preferred:
Leveraged Buyout
Research and Development
Balanced
Turnaround
Later Stage

Size of Investments Considered:
Min Size of Investment Considered (000s): $6,814
Max Size of Investment Considered (000s): $68,138

Geographical Preferences

International Preferences:
Scandanavia/Nordic Region

Industry Preferences

In Medical/Health prefer:
Medical/Health
Medical Products

In Consumer Related prefer:
Consumer Products
Hotels and Resorts

In Industrial/Energy prefer:
Industrial Products

In Transportation prefer:
Transportation

In Manufact. prefer:
Manufacturing

In Agr/Forestr/Fish prefer:
Mining and Minerals

Additional Information

Name of Most Recent Fund: Accent Equity 2012
Most Recent Fund Was Raised: 12/15/2011
Year Founded: 1994
Capital Under Management: $843,700,000
Current Activity Level : Actively seeking new investments

ACCES CAPITAL QUEBEC

1000 Route de L'eglise
Sainte-Foy, Canada G1V3V9
Phone: 418-650-9199
Fax: 418-650-7666

Management and Staff

Lise Lapierre, General Partner
Serge Olivier, General Partner

Type of Firm

Private Equity Firm

Project Preferences

Type of Financing Preferred:
Leveraged Buyout
Generalist PE
Balanced

Geographical Preferences

Canadian Preferences:
All Canada

Additional Information

Year Founded: 1997
Current Activity Level : Actively seeking new investments

ACCESS ASSET MANAGERS PVT LTD

Bandra Kurla Complex
Level 1, Trade Centre Building
Mumbai, India 400 051
Phone: 912265154700
Website: www.accespe.in

Type of Firm

Private Equity Firm

Project Preferences

Type of Financing Preferred:
Expansion

Geographical Preferences

International Preferences:
India

Industry Preferences

In Consumer Related prefer:
Consumer Services

In Business Serv. prefer:
Services

In Manufact. prefer:
Manufacturing

Additional Information

Year Founded: 2012
Current Activity Level : Actively seeking new investments

ACCESS CAPITAL PARTNERS SA

121 avenue des Champs-Elysees
Paris, France 75008
Phone: 3315643 100
Fax: 3315643610
E-mail: acp@accesscp.com
Website: www.access-capital-partners.com

Other Offices

P.O. Box 431 13-15 Victoria Road
St Peter Port Guernsey
Channel Islands, United Kingdom GY1 3ZD
Phone: 441481713843

Ludwig-Ganghofer-Strasse 6
Grunwald, Germany 82031
Phone: 4989693862280
Fax: 4989693862289

PO Box 66856
London, United Kingdom E1W9DW
Phone: 442035861021

IT Tower- Avenue Louise 480
Brussels, Belgium 1050
Phone: 3222908720
Fax: 3222908721

Management and Staff

Agnes Nahum, Managing Partner
Alexandre Delos, Partner
Alison Ridge, Partner
Bernhard Fink, Partner
Daniel Lippera, Partner
Dominique Peninon, Managing Director
Louis Trincano, Partner
Mikko Moilanen, Partner
Philippe Poggioli, Managing Partner
Pierre Sorel, Chief Financial Officer
Thomas Kohlmeyer, Partner

Type of Firm

Private Equity Advisor or Fund of Funds

Association Membership

Finnish Venture Capital Association (FVCA)
French Venture Capital Association (AFIC)
European Private Equity and Venture Capital Assoc.

Project Preferences

Type of Financing Preferred:
Fund of Funds
Leveraged Buyout
Early Stage
Mezzanine
Turnaround
Later Stage
Management Buyouts

Geographical Preferences

International Preferences:
Europe
Eastern Europe
France

Industry Focus

(% based on actual investment)
Other Products 100.0%

Additional Information

Name of Most Recent Fund: Access Capital Fund V
LP Growth Buy-out Europe
Most Recent Fund Was Raised: 01/06/2012
Year Founded: 1998
Capital Under Management: $2,179,200,000
Current Activity Level : Actively seeking new investments

ACCESS HOLDINGS MANAGEMENT COMPANY LLC

Two East Read Street
Suite 300
Baltimore, MD USA 21202
Phone: 4432004819
Fax: 4439736108
Website: www.accessholdings.com

Type of Firm

Private Equity Firm

Project Preferences

Type of Financing Preferred:
Leveraged Buyout
Acquisition

Geographical Preferences

United States Preferences:

Canadian Preferences:
All Canada

Additional Information

Year Founded: 2014
Current Activity Level : Actively seeking new investments

ACCESS VENTURE PARTNERS

8787 Turnpike Drive
Suite 260
Westminster, CO USA 80031
Phone: 3034268899
Fax: 3034268828
E-mail: mail@accessvp.com

Management and Staff

Brian Wallace, Managing Director
David Gold, Partner
Jay Campion, Managing Director
Kirk Holland, Venture Partner
V. Frank Mendicino, Managing Director

Type of Firm

Private Equity Firm

Project Preferences

Role in Financing:
Will function either as deal originator or investor in deals created by others

Type of Financing Preferred:
Early Stage
Seed

Geographical Preferences

United States Preferences:
North America

Industry Focus

(% based on actual investment)
Computer Software and Services 35.5%
Internet Specific 33.5%
Semiconductors/Other Elect. 13.4%
Biotechnology 4.8%
Communications and Media 4.7%
Consumer Related 3.0%
Computer Hardware 2.6%
Other Products 1.5%
Industrial/Energy 1.1%

Additional Information

Name of Most Recent Fund: Access Venture Partners II, L.P.
Most Recent Fund Was Raised: 10/30/2006
Year Founded: 1999
Capital Under Management: $33,400,000
Current Activity Level : Actively seeking new investments
Method of Compensation: Return on investment is of primary concern, do not charge fees

ACCESS VENTURES

1229 South Shelby Street
Louisville, KY USA 40203
E-mail: info@accessventures.org
Website: accessventures.org

Type of Firm

SBIC

Project Preferences

Type of Financing Preferred:
Balanced

Industry Preferences

In Other prefer:
Socially Responsible

Additional Information

Year Founded: 2013
Current Activity Level : Actively seeking new investments

ACCION INTERNATIONAL

10 Fawcett Street
Suite 204
Cambridge, MA USA 02138
Phone: 6176257080
Fax: 6176257020
E-mail: info@accion.org
Website: www.accion.org

Other Offices

Carrera 45 A Numero 128 B 41 Local 14
Centro Comercial Rosetta
Bogota, Colombia
Phone: 5717480707
Fax: 5715203373

No. 9/3, Kaiser-E-Hind
Third Floor, Richmond Road
Bangalore, India 560 025
Phone: 918041120008
Fax: 918041120009

1401 New York Avenue, Northwest
Suite 500
WASHINGTON, DC USA 20005
Phone: 2023935113
Fax: 2023935115

No. 46 Fifth Norla Link North
Accion Africa Hub and Training Center
Labone, Ghana PMB KD.61
Phone: 23321769860
Fax: 23321782170

Av. Djalma Batista 946, sala 8
Nossa Senhora das Gracas
Manaus, Brazil 69053-110
Phone: 55923307455

No. 93 Jianguo Road Room 606, Building 3
Wan Da Plaza, Chaoyang District
Beijing, China
Phone: 861058208757
Fax: 861058208830

Management and Staff
Esteban Altschul, Chief Operating Officer
Livingston Parsons, Chief Financial Officer

Type of Firm
Incubator/Development Program

Association Membership
Emerging Markets Private Equity Association

Project Preferences

Type of Financing Preferred:
Early Stage
Mezzanine
Later Stage
Seed
Startup

Size of Investments Considered:
Min Size of Investment Considered (000s): $100
Max Size of Investment Considered (000s): $500

Geographical Preferences

United States Preferences:
Southeast

International Preferences:
Latin America
India
Asia
Africa

Industry Preferences

In Communications prefer:
Wireless Communications

In Internet Specific prefer:
Internet

In Financial Services prefer:
Financial Services

In Business Serv. prefer:
Distribution
Media

Additional Information
Year Founded: 1961
Current Activity Level : Actively seeking new investments

ACCOLADE CAPITAL MANAGEMENT LLC

2001 M Street NorthWest
Suite 801
Washington, DC USA 20036
Phone: 2027755595
Fax: 2027755599
E-mail: info@accoladepartners.com
Website: www.accoladepartners.com

Management and Staff
Andrew Salembier, Principal
Atul Rustgi, Partner
Atul Rustgi, Partner
Joelle Kayden, Founder
Joelle Kayden, Founder

Type of Firm
Private Equity Advisor or Fund of Funds

Project Preferences

Type of Financing Preferred:
Fund of Funds

Additional Information
Name of Most Recent Fund: Accolade Partners IV, L.P.
Most Recent Fund Was Raised: 05/17/2012
Year Founded: 2000
Capital Under Management: $719,000,000
Current Activity Level : Actively seeking new investments

ACCOMPLICE LLC

25 First Street
Suite 303
Cambridge, MA USA 02141
Phone: 6175882600
Website: accomplice.co

Management and Staff
Barry Fidelman, Venture Partner
Christopher Lynch, Co-Founder
Cort Johnson, Venture Partner
Dustin Dolginow, Venture Partner
Jeff Fagnan, Co-Founder
Ryan Moore, Co-Founder
Sarah Downey, Principal
TJ Mahony, Venture Partner

Type of Firm
Private Equity Firm

Project Preferences

Type of Financing Preferred:
Balanced

Additional Information
Year Founded: 2015
Capital Under Management: $235,000,000
Current Activity Level : Actively seeking new investments

ACCORD CAPITAL INVESTORS PTY LTD

Level 5
60 Pitt Street
Sydney, Australia 2000
Phone: 612-9241-2496
Fax: 612-9241-2750

Management and Staff
Glenn Goodacre, Managing Director

Type of Firm
Private Equity Firm

Project Preferences

Type of Financing Preferred:
Leveraged Buyout

Geographical Preferences

International Preferences:
Pacific

Additional Information
Year Founded: 1993
Current Activity Level : Actively seeking new investments

ACCORD VENTURES INC

153-0063, Meguro-ku
Meguro 2-11-3
Tokyo, Japan
Website: accordventures.co.jp

Type of Firm
Private Equity Firm

Project Preferences

Type of Financing Preferred:
Balanced

Industry Preferences

In Internet Specific prefer:
Internet

Additional Information
Year Founded: 2015
Current Activity Level : Actively seeking new investments

ACCRETIA CAPITAL LLC

Two Penn Center Plaza
Suite 200
Philadelphia, PA USA 19102
Phone: 2158546409
Website: www.accretiacapital.com

Management and Staff

Barry Reynolds, Partner
Bob Dahl, Partner
Brandon Cope, Partner
Christopher Sekula, Partner
Dan Peterson, Partner
Dave Carver, Partner
Dave Lazier, Partner
Gerald Risk, Partner
Jamie Turner, Partner
Jay Madsen, Managing Partner
Jeff Stevens, Partner
Jim Ellis, Partner
Jim Edmunds, Partner
Jose Stella, Partner
Joseph Niehaus, Partner
Kent Weaver, Partner
Kevin Taweel, Partner
Lew Davies, Partner
Mark Hilderbrand, Partner
Michael O Connell, Partner
Michael-Kevin O Connell, Partner
Rafael Somoza, Partner
Rene Lajous, Partner
Rich Kelley, Partner
Richard Augustyn, Partner
Scott Asen, Partner
Tim Ludwig, Partner
Tom Cassutt, Partner
William Egan, Partner
William Thorndike, Partner

Type of Firm
Private Equity Firm

Project Preferences

Type of Financing Preferred:
Leveraged Buyout
Management Buyouts
Acquisition

Additional Information
Name of Most Recent Fund: Accretia Capital LLC
Most Recent Fund Was Raised: 04/20/2012
Year Founded: 2012
Capital Under Management: $5,800,000
Current Activity Level : Actively seeking new investments

ACCRETIVE LLC

51 Madison Avenue
31st Floor
New York, NY USA 10010
Phone: 6462821920
Fax: 6462823138
E-mail: info@accretivellc.com
Website: www.accretivellc.com

Management and Staff

Arun Gupta, Vice President
Edgar Bronfman, General Partner
J. Michael Cline, Managing Partner
Mitch Slodowitz, Chief Financial Officer

Type of Firm
Private Equity Firm

Project Preferences

Type of Financing Preferred:
Balanced

Geographical Preferences

United States Preferences:

Industry Preferences

In Computer Software prefer:
Software

Additional Information
Year Founded: 1999
Current Activity Level : Actively seeking new investments

ACCRETIVE SOLUTIONS INC

105 Maxess Road
Suite 107
Melville, NY USA 11747
Phone: 631-348-9100
Fax: 631-348-7788
Website: www.accretivesolutions.com

Management and Staff

Frank Mack, Senior Managing Director
Kerry Barrett, President

Type of Firm
Private Equity Firm

Project Preferences

Type of Financing Preferred:
Turnaround
Special Situation

Geographical Preferences

United States Preferences:
All U.S.

Canadian Preferences:
All Canada

Additional Information
Year Founded: 2010
Current Activity Level : Actively seeking new investments

ACCUITIVE MEDICAL VENTURES LLC

2905 Premiere Parkway
Suite 150
Duluth, GA USA 30097
Phone: 6788121101
Website: www.amvpartners.com

Management and Staff

Anthony Lando, Partner
Charles Larsen, Co-Founder
Cory Anderson, Principal
Gordon Wyatt, Chief Financial Officer

Type of Firm
Private Equity Firm

Project Preferences

Role in Financing:
Will function either as deal originator or investor in deals created by others

Type of Financing Preferred:
Early Stage
Balanced
Later Stage
Seed

Additional Information
Name of Most Recent Fund: AMV Partners II, L.P.
Most Recent Fund Was Raised: 02/15/2006
Year Founded: 2003
Capital Under Management: $230,000,000
Current Activity Level : Actively seeking new investments

ACE & COMPANY SA

Tue du Rhone 42
Geneva, Switzerland 1204
Phone: 41223113333
Fax: 41223116666
Website: www.aceandcompany.com

Type of Firm
Private Equity Firm

Project Preferences

Type of Financing Preferred:
Fund of Funds
Leveraged Buyout
Later Stage
Management Buyouts
Acquisition

Geographical Preferences

United States Preferences:

International Preferences:
United Kingdom
Switzerland
Brazil
Belgium

Industry Preferences

In Consumer Related prefer:
Consumer

In Industrial/Energy prefer:
Oil and Gas Exploration

In Business Serv. prefer:
Services

In Agr/Forestr/Fish prefer:
Agriculture related

Additional Information
Year Founded: 2005
Current Activity Level : Actively seeking new investments

ACE MANAGEMENT SA

48, Rue De Lisbonne
Paris, France 75008
Phone: 33158562562
E-mail: ace@acemanagement.fr
Website: www.acemanagement.fr

Other Offices
7, Rue de la Republique
Lyon, France 69001
Phone: 33-4-7200-1141

255, Rue Saint Jacques
Montreal, Canada H2Y 1M6
Phone: 514-845-2746

4, Rue des Potiers
Tolouse, France 31400
Phone: 33-5-6155-3265

Management and Staff
Corinne d Agrain, Partner
Gilles Daguet, Partner
Jocelyne Le Gal, Chief Financial Officer
Xavier Herrmann, Partner

Type of Firm
Private Equity Firm

Association Membership
French Venture Capital Association (AFIC)

Project Preferences

Type of Financing Preferred:
Leveraged Buyout
Early Stage
Generalist PE
Turnaround
Later Stage
Seed
Acquisition
Startup

Geographical Preferences

International Preferences:
Europe
Switzerland
Germany
France

Industry Preferences

In Communications prefer:
Communications and Media
Telecommunications

In Internet Specific prefer:
Internet

In Semiconductor/Electr prefer:
Electronics

In Industrial/Energy prefer:
Industrial Products

In Transportation prefer:
Transportation
Aerospace

In Business Serv. prefer:
Services

Additional Information
Name of Most Recent Fund: Aerofund III
Most Recent Fund Was Raised: 01/25/2013
Year Founded: 1993
Capital Under Management: $300,000,000
Current Activity Level : Actively seeking new investments

ACE PARTNERS BV

Vrieseweg 80
Dordrecht, Netherlands 3311 NX
Phone: 31786314090
E-mail: info@acepartners.nl
Website: www.acepartners.nl

Type of Firm
Private Equity Firm

Project Preferences

Type of Financing Preferred:
Leveraged Buyout
Expansion
Later Stage
Management Buyouts
Acquisition

Geographical Preferences

International Preferences:
Luxembourg
Netherlands
Belgium
Germany

Additional Information
Year Founded: 2010
Current Activity Level : Actively seeking new investments

ACER TECHNOLOGY VENTURES ASIA PACIFIC

5201 Great America Parkway
Suite 270
Santa Clara, CA USA 95054
Phone: 4088947900
Fax: 4088947939
E-mail: info@idsoftcapital.com

Other Offices
7/F, No. 122
Dun Hwa N. Road
Taipei, Taiwan 105
Phone: 886-2-8712-9090
Fax: 886-2-8712-9091

Room 9C, Zhong Hai Building
398 Huai Hai Zhong Road
Shanghai, China 200020
Phone: 86-21-6386-8708
Fax: 86-21-6386-8709

Management and Staff
Ed Yang, Partner

Type of Firm
Corporate PE/Venture

Association Membership
Taiwan Venture Capital Association(TVCA)

Project Preferences

Role in Financing:
Prefer role as deal originator but will also invest in deals created by others

Type of Financing Preferred:
Early Stage
Expansion
Balanced
Later Stage
Seed

Size of Investments Considered:
Min Size of Investment Considered (000s): $500
Max Size of Investment Considered (000s): $3,000

Geographical Preferences

United States Preferences:

Canadian Preferences:
All Canada

Industry Preferences

In Communications prefer:
Commercial Communications

In Computer Software prefer:
Applications Software

In Semiconductor/Electr prefer:
Semiconductor

In Medical/Health prefer:
Medical/Health

Additional Information
Year Founded: 1998
Capital Under Management: $340,000,000
Current Activity Level : Actively seeking new investments
Method of Compensation: Return on investment is of primary concern, do not charge fees

---

ACERO CAPITAL, L.P.
2440 Sand Hill Road
Suite 101
Menlo Park, CA USA 94025
Phone: 6502337100
Fax: 6502337112
E-mail: info@acerovc.com
Website: www.acerovc.com

Management and Staff
Antonio Alvarez, Venture Partner
Debra Schilling, Venture Partner
Rami Elkhatib, General Partner

Type of Firm
Private Equity Firm

Association Membership
National Venture Capital Association - USA (NVCA)

Project Preferences

Type of Financing Preferred:
Balanced
Later Stage

Industry Preferences

In Industrial/Energy prefer:
Alternative Energy

Additional Information
Year Founded: 2009
Current Activity Level : Actively seeking new investments

ACG CAPITAL SA
49, avenue d'Iena
Paris, France 75116
Phone: 33153935151
Fax: 33153935152
E-mail: info@acg-capital.com
Website: www.acg-capital.com

Other Offices
26 Avenue de l'Opera
Paris, France 75001
Phone: 33184171600

Management and Staff
Didier Levy-Rueff, Chief Operating Officer
Pierre-Michel Deleglise, Chief Executive Officer
Stephane D agostino, Chief Financial Officer

Type of Firm
Insurance Firm Affiliate

Association Membership
French Venture Capital Association (AFIC)
European Private Equity and Venture Capital Assoc.

Project Preferences

Type of Financing Preferred:
Fund of Funds
Leveraged Buyout
Mezzanine
Generalist PE
Later Stage
Acquisition
Fund of Funds of Second
Recapitalizations

Size of Investments Considered:
Min Size of Investment Considered (000s): $6,642
Max Size of Investment Considered (000s): $33,214

Geographical Preferences

United States Preferences:
All U.S.

International Preferences:
Europe
Eastern Europe
France

Industry Preferences

In Communications prefer:
Entertainment

In Medical/Health prefer:
Medical/Health
Health Services
Pharmaceuticals

In Consumer Related prefer:
Entertainment and Leisure

In Industrial/Energy prefer:
Industrial Products

In Business Serv. prefer:
Services

Additional Information
Year Founded: 1988
Capital Under Management: $2,279,100,000
Current Activity Level : Actively seeking new investments

ACG MANAGEMENT SA
6, allees Turcat Mery
Marseille, France 13008
Phone: 33491294150
Fax: 33491294151
Website: www.acg-management.fr

Other Offices
Rue du Lac Victoria
Immeuble Yosr, appart 9-10
Les berges du lac, Tunisia 1053
Phone: 21671965770
Fax: 21671962638

10, rue Jean Jaures
Immeuble le Grand Theatre
Noumea, France 98800
Phone: 687283600
Fax: 687283601

Type of Firm
Bank Affiliated

Association Membership
French Venture Capital Association (AFIC)

Project Preferences

Size of Investments Considered:
Min Size of Investment Considered (000s): $668
Max Size of Investment Considered (000s): $6,687

Geographical Preferences

International Preferences:
Asia Pacific
Tunisia
Fr Polynesia
Europe
Morocco
Africa

Industry Preferences

In Consumer Related prefer:
Consumer Services

In Industrial/Energy prefer:
Environmental Related

In Business Serv. prefer:
Services

In Other prefer:
Environment Responsible

Additional Information
Year Founded: 2000
Capital Under Management: $109,920,000
Current Activity Level : Actively seeking new investments

ACG PRIVATE EQUITY SA

84 Avenue D'Iena
Paris, France 75116
Phone: 33156895900
Fax: 33156895915
E-mail: info@acg-pe.com
Website: www.acg-private-equity.com

Other Offices
Via Della Spiga 26
Milan, Italy 20121
Phone: 39-2-7601-7340
Fax: 39-2-7602-0155

Possartstrasse 13
Munich, Germany 81679
Phone: 49-89-4131-20
Fax: 49-89-4131-2513

7 Stratigi Street
154 51 Neo Psychiko
Athens, Greece
Phone: 30-210-677-2281
Fax: 30-210-672-8624

Dufourstrasse 60
Zollikon
Zurich, Switzerland CH-8702
Phone: 41-43-499-4343
Fax: 41-43-499-4344

30 St James's Square
London, United Kingdom SW1Y 4AL
Phone: 44-20-7484-4040
Fax: 44-20-7484-4010

5 Ralli Courts
West Riverside
Manchester, United Kingdom M3 5FT
Phone: 44-161-831-9133
Fax: 44-161-831-9144

Conference House
152 Morrison Street
Edinburgh, United Kingdom EH3 8EB
Phone: 44-131-200-6054
Fax: 44-131-200-6200

C/ Velazquez, 10 - 3 Izq.
Madrid, Spain 28001
Phone: 34-91-761-8800
Fax: 34-91-761-8820

Management and Staff
Gilles Michat, Managing Director
Mathieu Bourdie, Chief Financial Officer

Type of Firm
Private Equity Advisor or Fund of Funds

Association Membership
French Venture Capital Association (AFIC)

Project Preferences

Type of Financing Preferred:
Fund of Funds
Later Stage
Fund of Funds of Second

Geographical Preferences

International Preferences:
Italy
United Kingdom
Luxembourg
Central Europe
Europe
Netherlands
Western Europe
Scandanavia/Nordic Region
Spain
Belgium
Germany
France

Additional Information
Year Founded: 1998
Current Activity Level : Actively seeking new investments

ACKRA INVEST AB

Backgatan 1
Expolaris Center
Skelleftea, Sweden 93178
Phone: 46703497316
E-mail: info@ackrainvest.se
Website: www.ackrainvest.se

Management and Staff
Arne Moren, Chief Executive Officer
Nils-Gunnar Larsson, Managing Director

Type of Firm
Private Equity Firm

Project Preferences

Type of Financing Preferred:
Seed
Acquisition
Startup

Size of Investments Considered:
Min Size of Investment Considered (000s): $150
Max Size of Investment Considered (000s): $1,000

Geographical Preferences

International Preferences:
Sweden

Industry Preferences

In Communications prefer:
Wireless Communications

In Computer Software prefer:
Software

In Internet Specific prefer:
Internet

In Industrial/Energy prefer:
Alternative Energy
Energy Conservation Relat

In Other prefer:
Environment Responsible

Additional Information
Year Founded: 1999
Capital Under Management: $4,500,000
Current Activity Level : Actively seeking new investments

ACM LTD

Centennial Place East 3110-520
3rd Avenue Southwest
Calgary, Canada T2P 0R3
Phone: 4035171500
Fax: 4035171515
E-mail: info@kernpartners.com
Website: www.navigatingenergy.com

Management and Staff
Chris Hooper, Managing Director
D. Jeff van Steenbergen, Co-Founder
David Pearce, Managing Partner
Francesco Mele, Partner
Jason Montemurro, Partner
Jim Nieuwenburg, Partner
Kim Proctor, Chief Financial Officer
Nathan Kunec, Principal
Pentti Karkkainen, Co-Founder
Travis Smith, Principal

Type of Firm
Private Equity Firm

Association Membership
Canadian Venture Capital Association

Project Preferences

Type of Financing Preferred:
Other

Geographical Preferences

United States Preferences:

Canadian Preferences:
All Canada

International Preferences:
All International

Industry Preferences

In Industrial/Energy prefer:
Energy

Additional Information

Name of Most Recent Fund: Azimuth Energy Partners III Fund
Most Recent Fund Was Raised: 03/31/2008
Year Founded: 2000
Capital Under Management: $1,563,000,000
Current Activity Level : Actively seeking new investments

ACOFI GESTION SA

5 Boulevard De La Madeleine
Paris, France 75001
Phone: 33153769999
Fax: 33153769998
E-mail: contact@acofi.com
Website: www.acofi.com

Management and Staff

De Saint Priest Thibault, Chief Executive Officer

Type of Firm

Private Equity Firm

Association Membership

French Venture Capital Association (AFIC)

Project Preferences

Type of Financing Preferred:
Leveraged Buyout
Generalist PE
Later Stage
Acquisition

Geographical Preferences

International Preferences:
Europe
France

Additional Information

Year Founded: 1990
Capital Under Management: $228,110,000
Current Activity Level : Actively seeking new investments

ACONCAGUA VENTURES

Humboldt 1967
Second Floor
Buenos Aires, Argentina 5722
Phone: 541155562673
E-mail: contactus@aconcaguaventures.com
Website: www.aconcaguaventures.com

Management and Staff

Carlos Adamo, Partner
Emiliano Kargieman, Managing Partner
Gabriel Rozman, Partner
Gustavo Herrero, Partner
Jonatan Altszul, Managing Partner
Pablo Garfinkel, Partner

Type of Firm

Private Equity Firm

Project Preferences

Type of Financing Preferred:
Early Stage

Geographical Preferences

International Preferences:
Latin America
Argentina

Industry Preferences

In Communications prefer:
Communications and Media

In Computer Software prefer:
Software

In Internet Specific prefer:
Internet

In Medical/Health prefer:
Medical Products

Additional Information

Year Founded: 2011
Current Activity Level : Actively seeking new investments

ACORN CAMPUS VENTURES

1237 East Arques Avenue
Sunnyvale, CA USA 94085
Phone: 4085984200
Fax: 4085984201
E-mail: info@acorncampus.com
Website: www.acorncampus.com

Management and Staff

David Tsang, Co-Founder
Hsing Kung, Managing Partner
Ray Jamp, Venture Partner
Rueiming Jamp, Venture Partner
T. Chester Wang, Co-Founder
Tien-Lai Hwang, Venture Partner

Type of Firm

Private Equity Firm

Project Preferences

Role in Financing:
Prefer role as deal originator but will also invest in deals created by others

Type of Financing Preferred:
Early Stage
Balanced
Later Stage

Industry Preferences

In Communications prefer:
Telecommunications
Wireless Communications

In Internet Specific prefer:
Internet

In Semiconductor/Electr prefer:
Semiconductor

Additional Information

Name of Most Recent Fund: Acorn Campus Venture Fund III LLC
Most Recent Fund Was Raised: 05/30/2006
Year Founded: 2000
Capital Under Management: $100,000,000
Current Activity Level : Actively seeking new investments
Method of Compensation: Return on investment is of primary concern, do not charge fees

ACORN GROWTH COMPANIES

316 Northwest 61st Street
Oklahoma City, OK USA 73118
Phone: 4057372676
Fax: 4057324141
Website: www.acorngrowthcompanies.com

Management and Staff

Darryl Wilkerson, Vice President
Jeff Davis, Partner
Kendra Clements, Vice President
Rick Nagel, Partner
Robert Hinaman, Managing Director

Type of Firm

Private Equity Firm

Project Preferences

Type of Financing Preferred:
Leveraged Buyout
Management Buyouts
Acquisition

Geographical Preferences

United States Preferences:

International Preferences:
Europe

Industry Preferences

In Transportation prefer:
Aerospace

Additional Information

Name of Most Recent Fund: Acorn Growth Capital Fund III LLC
Most Recent Fund Was Raised: 08/31/2007
Year Founded: 2000
Capital Under Management: $17,720,000
Current Activity Level : Actively seeking new investments

ACORN INNOVESTMENTS LLC

334 Blackwell Street
Suite B011
Durham, NC USA 27701
Phone: 9196978162
Website: www.acorninnovestments.com

Management and Staff
Michael Noel, Founder
Robert O Reilly, Partner

Type of Firm
Private Equity Firm

Project Preferences

Type of Financing Preferred:
Early Stage
Startup

Geographical Preferences

United States Preferences:
All U.S.

Industry Preferences

In Industrial/Energy prefer:
Energy Conservation Relat
Industrial Products
Advanced Materials

In Manufact. prefer:
Manufacturing

Additional Information
Name of Most Recent Fund: White Oak Innovestment Fund, L.P.
Most Recent Fund Was Raised: 01/22/2014
Year Founded: 2010
Capital Under Management: $5,025,000
Current Activity Level : Actively seeking new investments

ACORN PACIFIC VENTURES

235 Kifer Road
Suite 260
Santa Clara, CA USA 95051
E-mail: contact@acornpacific.ventures
Website: www.acornpacific.ventures

Type of Firm
Private Equity Firm

Project Preferences

Type of Financing Preferred:
Early Stage

Geographical Preferences

United States Preferences:

Industry Preferences

In Financial Services prefer:
Investment Groups

Additional Information
Year Founded: 2017
Current Activity Level : Actively seeking new investments

ACORN PRIVATE EQUITY

10 Niblick Way
Unit A3 The Beach Head
Somerset West, South Africa 7130
Phone: 27218522887
Fax: 27218523161
E-mail: info@acornequity.com
Website: www.acornprivateequity.com

Management and Staff
Carl Neethling, Managing Director

Type of Firm
Private Equity Firm

Association Membership
South African Venture Capital Association (SAVCA)
Emerging Markets Private Equity Association

Project Preferences

Type of Financing Preferred:
Early Stage
Expansion
Later Stage
Startup

Size of Investments Considered:
Min Size of Investment Considered (000s): $12,114
Max Size of Investment Considered (000s): $12,157

Geographical Preferences

International Preferences:
South Africa
Africa

Industry Preferences

In Medical/Health prefer:
Health Services

In Industrial/Energy prefer:
Energy

In Financial Services prefer:
Real Estate

In Business Serv. prefer:
Services

In Agr/Forestr/Fish prefer:
Agriculture related

In Utilities prefer:
Utilities

In Other prefer:
Environment Responsible

Additional Information
Name of Most Recent Fund: Acron Venture Technology Fund One
Most Recent Fund Was Raised: 12/04/2009
Year Founded: 2009
Capital Under Management: $10,270,000
Current Activity Level : Actively seeking new investments

ACORN VENTURES, INC.

2635 North First Street
Suite 148
San Jose, CA USA 95131
Phone: 5104596500
Fax: 9252491748
E-mail: Partners@Acorn-Ventures.com
Website: www.acorn-ventures.com

Management and Staff
Cliff Girard, Chief Executive Officer

Type of Firm
Private Equity Firm

Project Preferences

Role in Financing:
Will function either as deal originator or investor in deals created by others

Type of Financing Preferred:
Early Stage
Expansion
Balanced
Seed
Startup

Size of Investments Considered:
Min Size of Investment Considered (000s): $1,000
Max Size of Investment Considered (000s): $5,000

Geographical Preferences

United States Preferences:
West Coast

Industry Focus

(% based on actual investment)

Computer Software and Services	25.6%
Computer Hardware	16.0%
Internet Specific	14.1%
Communications and Media	13.4%
Semiconductors/Other Elect.	11.8%
Industrial/Energy	10.8%
Biotechnology	3.5%
Medical/Health	2.2%
Other Products	2.2%
Consumer Related	0.3%

Additional Information
Name of Most Recent Fund: Acorn Ventures VI
Most Recent Fund Was Raised: 06/01/2003
Year Founded: 1986
Capital Under Management: $1,500,000,000
Current Activity Level : Reducing investment activity
Method of Compensation: Return on investment is of primary concern, do not charge fees

ACP INC
400 Hamilton Avenue
Suite 230
Palo Alto, CA USA 94301
Phone: 6502647750
E-mail: ACP-Info@altamontcapital.com
Website: www.altamontcapital.com

Other Offices
Former HQ: Two Palo Alto Square
Tenth Floor
Palo Alto, CA USA 94306
Phone: 650-264-7750

Management and Staff
Alex Rolfe, Managing Director
Carol Pereira, Chief Financial Officer
Casey Lynch, Managing Director
Chris Nicholson, Partner
Greg Corkran, Vice President
Gregory Ruiz, Vice President
Iain Bridges, Vice President
Jesse Rogers, Co-Founder
Jonathan Altman, Principal
Keoni Schwartz, Co-Founder
Kevin Mason, Principal
Kristin Johnson, Managing Director
Melissa Kennedy, Vice President
Melissa Francis, Principal
Randall Eason, Co-Founder
Sam Gaynor, Principal
Steve Brownlie, Managing Director

Type of Firm
Private Equity Firm

Project Preferences

Type of Financing Preferred:
Leveraged Buyout
Turnaround
Management Buyouts
Private Placement
Distressed Debt

Industry Preferences

In Medical/Health prefer:
Medical/Health

In Consumer Related prefer:
Consumer
Retail

In Transportation prefer:
Aerospace

In Financial Services prefer:
Financial Services

In Business Serv. prefer:
Services

Additional Information
Name of Most Recent Fund: ACP Investment Fund II, L.P.
Most Recent Fund Was Raised: 12/23/2013
Year Founded: 2010
Capital Under Management: $500,000,000
Current Activity Level : Actively seeking new investments

ACPE ADVISORS SA
Luis A. de Herrera 1248
Office 369
Montevideo, Uruguay
Phone: 541147781003
Fax: 541147781003

Type of Firm
Private Equity Firm

Project Preferences

Type of Financing Preferred:
Balanced

Geographical Preferences

International Preferences:
Uruguay
Argentina
Paraguay
Brazil
Chile

Industry Preferences

In Consumer Related prefer:
Food/Beverage

In Agr/Forestr/Fish prefer:
Agribusiness

Additional Information
Year Founded: 2011
Capital Under Management: $64,000,000
Current Activity Level : Actively seeking new investments

ACQUISITION SEARCH CORP
5555 Glenridge Connector
Suite 200
Atlanta, GA USA 30342
Phone: 404-459-2777
E-mail: info@acquisitionsearch.com
Website: www.acquisitionsearch.com

Type of Firm
Service Provider

Project Preferences

Role in Financing:
Prefer role as deal originator

Type of Financing Preferred:
Second Stage Financing
Leveraged Buyout
Control-block Purchases
First Stage Financing
Special Situation

Size of Investments Considered:
Min Size of Investment Considered (000s): $1,000
Max Size of Investment Considered: No Limit

Geographical Preferences

International Preferences:
No Preference

Additional Information
Year Founded: 1992
Current Activity Level : Actively seeking new investments
Method of Compensation: Function primarily in service area, receive contingent fee in cash or equity

ACREWOOD HOLDINGS LLC
40 Morris Avenue
Suite 230
Bryn Mawr, PA USA 19010
Phone: 6105184903
E-mail: info@acrewoodholdings.com
Website: www.acrewoodholdings.com

Management and Staff
Jamie Barrett, Vice President
Stephen Chang, Managing Director

Type of Firm
Investment Management Firm

Project Preferences

Type of Financing Preferred:
Fund of Funds
Leveraged Buyout
Mezzanine
Generalist PE
Balanced
Acquisition
Special Situation
Distressed Debt
Fund of Funds of Second

Size of Investments Considered:
Min Size of Investment Considered (000s): $1,000
Max Size of Investment Considered (000s): $15,000

Industry Preferences

In Consumer Related prefer:
Consumer Services

In Industrial/Energy prefer:
Alternative Energy

In Business Serv. prefer:
Services
Media

In Manufact. prefer:
Manufacturing

Additional Information
Name of Most Recent Fund: Acrewood 2011, L.P.
Most Recent Fund Was Raised: 06/27/2012
Year Founded: 2012
Capital Under Management: $28,301,000
Current Activity Level : Actively seeking new investments

ACROSS WEALTH MANAGEMENT OCP AS

Apollo Business Centrum
Mlynske nivy 45
Bratislava, Slovakia 821 09
Phone: 421-2-58240300
Fax: 421-2-58240311
Website: www.across.sk

Type of Firm
Investment Management Firm

Project Preferences

Type of Financing Preferred:
Generalist PE

Geographical Preferences

International Preferences:
Central Europe
Eastern Europe

Industry Preferences

In Medical/Health prefer:
Health Services

In Financial Services prefer:
Financial Services

Additional Information
Year Founded: 2005
Current Activity Level : Actively seeking new investments

ACT ONE VENTURES LP

1541 Ocen Avenue
Suite 200
Santa Monica, CA USA 90401

Management and Staff
Michael Silton, Managing Director

Type of Firm
Private Equity Firm

Project Preferences

Type of Financing Preferred:
Early Stage

Geographical Preferences

United States Preferences:
California

Industry Preferences

In Business Serv. prefer:
Media

Additional Information
Year Founded: 2016
Current Activity Level : Actively seeking new investments

ACT VENTURE CAPITAL LTD

Clonskeagh
Richview Office Park
Dublin, Ireland
Phone: 35312600966
Fax: 35312600538
E-mail: info@actvc.ie
Website: www.actventure.com

Other Offices
58 Howard Street
Windsor Business Center
Belfast, Ireland BT1 6PJ
Phone: 442890500880
Fax: 442890500888

Management and Staff
Charlie Glass, Venture Partner
John Flynn, Managing Director

Type of Firm
Private Equity Firm

Association Membership
Irish Venture Capital Association
British Venture Capital Association (BVCA)

Project Preferences

Role in Financing:
Prefer role as deal originator but will also invest in deals created by others

Type of Financing Preferred:
Early Stage
Expansion
Balanced
Later Stage
Seed
Startup

Size of Investments Considered:
Min Size of Investment Considered (000s): $257
Max Size of Investment Considered (000s): $38,620

Geographical Preferences

International Preferences:
Ireland
United Kingdom

Industry Focus
(% based on actual investment)
Semiconductors/Other Elect.	26.1%
Computer Software and Services	22.1%
Internet Specific	16.4%
Medical/Health	13.0%
Communications and Media	6.4%
Computer Hardware	6.0%
Consumer Related	5.4%
Other Products	2.7%
Industrial/Energy	1.7%
Biotechnology	0.3%

Additional Information
Year Founded: 1994
Capital Under Management: $455,100,000
Current Activity Level : Actively seeking new investments

ACTINIC VENTURES LLC

240 East 39th Street
New York, NY USA 10016
Phone: 8458939208
Website: www.actinicventures.com

Management and Staff
John Alvino, President, Founder

Type of Firm
Private Equity Firm

Project Preferences

Type of Financing Preferred:
Early Stage
Seed
Startup

Size of Investments Considered:
Min Size of Investment Considered (000s): $20
Max Size of Investment Considered (000s): $30

Industry Preferences

In Internet Specific prefer:
Internet

In Business Serv. prefer:
Services

Additional Information
Year Founded: 2011
Current Activity Level : Actively seeking new investments

ACTINVER SECURITIES INC

5075 Westheimer
Suite 650
Houston, TX USA 77056
Website: www.actinversecurities.com

Management and Staff
Richard Nunn, Chief Financial Officer

Type of Firm
Investment Management Firm

Project Preferences

Type of Financing Preferred:
Balanced

Geographical Preferences

International Preferences:
Mexico

Industry Preferences

In Medical/Health prefer:
Medical/Health

In Consumer Related prefer:
Retail

In Transportation prefer:
Transportation

Additional Information
Year Founded: 1993
Capital Under Management: $62,300,000
Current Activity Level : Actively seeking new investments

ACTION GROUP HOLDINGS KSCC

Rakan Tower, 27th Floor
Al Shohada Street
Safat, Kuwait
Phone: 96522247500
Fax: 96522247544
Website: www.actionkuwait.com

Type of Firm
Private Equity Firm

Project Preferences

Type of Financing Preferred:
Generalist PE

Geographical Preferences

United States Preferences:
All U.S.

International Preferences:
Europe
Middle East
Australia
Kuwait
Africa

Additional Information
Year Founded: 1998
Current Activity Level : Actively seeking new investments

ACTIS LLP

Two More London Riverside
London, United Kingdom SE1 2JT
Phone: 442072345000
Fax: 442072345010
E-mail: fundsadmin@act.is
Website: www.act.is

Other Offices

1st Floor, Cradock Heights 21
Cradock Avenue corner
Johannesburg, South Africa 2196
Phone: 27-11-778-5900
Fax: 27-11-327-7407

Norfolk Towers, 1st Floor
Kijabe Street
Nairobi, Kenya 43233-0010
Phone: 254-20-2219-952
Fax: 254-20-2219-744

1 Royal Plaza
St. Peter Port
GUERNSEY, United Kingdom GY1 2HL
Phone: 44-1481-713843

No. 1 Jianguomenwai Avenue
713 China World Tower 2
Beijing, China 100004
Phone: 861065354800
Fax: 861065058111

4th Floor Thapar House
Dr. Annie Besant Road Worli
Mumbai, India 400 030
Phone: 91-22-6146-7900
Fax: 91-22-2423-1549

Rua Sao Tome, 86 Cj.171
Vila Olimpia
Sao Paolo, Brazil 04551-080
Phone: 55-11-3844-6300
Fax: 55-11-3844-6301

Avenida Paulista 111
2Nd Floor, Bela Vista
Sao Paulo, Brazil 01311920

140 Broadway
Suite 2250
New York, NY USA 10005
Phone: 16468228070

16 Collyer Quay
#29-01, Hitachi Tower
Singapore, Singapore 049318
Phone: 65-6416-6400
Fax: 65-6227-1004

9th Floor, Garden City
20 Aisha El Taymoria St.
Cairo, Egypt
Phone: 202-2792-9220
Fax: 202-2792-9092

Maersk House, 121 Louis Solomon Close
Victoria Island
Lagos, Nigeria
Phone: 234-1-448-5700
Fax: 234-1-279-3944

1 & 2 Ishwar Nagar, Mathura Road
The Mira Corporate Suites, D Block, G/F
New Delhi, India 110 025
Phone: 91-11-6615-7200
Fax: 91-11-6615-7201

Management and Staff
Chris Coles, Partner
Chu Kong, Partner
David Morley, Partner
David Grylls, Partner
Dong Zhong, Partner
G Rathinam, Partner
J M Trivedi, Partner
Jiansheng Wang, Partner
Joe Sinyor, Partner
John van Wyk, Partner
Jonathon Bond, Partner
Mahesh Chhabria, Partner
Mark Richards, Partner
Meng Ann Lim, Partner
Michael Till, Partner
Mikael Karlsson, Partner
Murray Grant, Partner
Natalie Kolbe, Partner
Nick Luckock, Partner
Patrick Ledoux, Partner
Peter Schmid, Partner
Rick Phillips, Partner
Ron Bell, Chief Operating Officer
Sanjiv Aggarwal, Partner
Shomik Mukherjee, Partner
Simon Harford, Partner
Torbjorn Caesar, Partner

Type of Firm
Private Equity Firm

Association Membership
South African Venture Capital Association (SAVCA)
Brazilian Venture Capital Association (ABCR)
Emerging Markets Private Equity Association
China Venture Capital Association
Singapore Venture Capital Association (SVCA)

Project Preferences

Type of Financing Preferred:
Generalist PE
Balanced
Opportunistic
Acquisition

Geographical Preferences

International Preferences:
Nigeria
Uganda
Zambia
Tanzania
Kenya
South Africa

Industry Preferences

In Medical/Health prefer:
Medical/Health

In Consumer Related prefer:
Consumer

In Industrial/Energy prefer:
Energy
Oil and Gas Exploration
Industrial Products

In Transportation prefer:
Transportation

In Financial Services prefer:
Financial Services
Real Estate

In Agr/Forestr/Fish prefer:
Agribusiness

Additional Information

Name of Most Recent Fund: 57 Stars Actis 4 Investment Vehicle, L.P.
Most Recent Fund Was Raised: 01/15/2013
Year Founded: 2004
Capital Under Management: $6,773,000,000
Current Activity Level : Actively seeking new investments

ACTIVA CAPITAL SAS

203, rue du Faubourg
Saint-Honore
Paris, France 75008
Phone: 33143125012
Fax: 33143125013
E-mail: infos@activacapital.com
Website: www.activacapital.com

Management and Staff

Charles Diehl, Partner
Christophe Parier, Partner
Michael Diehl, Partner
Olivier Nemsguern, Partner
Philippe Latorre, Partner
, Chief Financial Officer

Type of Firm
Private Equity Firm

Association Membership
French Venture Capital Association (AFIC)
European Private Equity and Venture Capital Assoc.

Project Preferences

Type of Financing Preferred:
Leveraged Buyout
Early Stage
Expansion
Later Stage
Management Buyouts
Acquisition

Size of Investments Considered:
Min Size of Investment Considered (000s): $18,608
Max Size of Investment Considered (000s): $93,041

Geographical Preferences

International Preferences:
France

Industry Preferences

In Communications prefer:
Communications and Media

In Computer Software prefer:
Software

In Medical/Health prefer:
Medical/Health
Medical Diagnostics
Medical Therapeutics
Medical Products
Health Services
Pharmaceuticals

In Consumer Related prefer:
Consumer
Food/Beverage
Consumer Products
Consumer Services

In Industrial/Energy prefer:
Industrial Products
Environmental Related

In Business Serv. prefer:
Services
Distribution
Media

Additional Information

Name of Most Recent Fund: Activa Capital II
Most Recent Fund Was Raised: 04/18/2007
Year Founded: 2000
Capital Under Management: $721,600,000
Current Activity Level : Actively seeking new investments

ACTIVANT CAPITAL GROUP LLC

323 Railroad Avenue
Greenwich, CT USA 06830
Phone: 2033402880
Website: activantcapital.com

Management and Staff
Steven Sarracino, Founder

Type of Firm
Private Equity Firm

Project Preferences

Type of Financing Preferred:
Expansion
Generalist PE
Balanced
Later Stage
Acquisition

Industry Preferences

In Computer Software prefer:
Software

In Consumer Related prefer:
Consumer

Additional Information

Year Founded: 1969
Capital Under Management: $138,110,000
Current Activity Level : Actively seeking new investments

ACTIVATE VENTURE PARTNERS

551 Madison Avenue
Seventh Floor
New York, NY USA 10022
Phone: 2122237400
Fax: 2122230315
Website: www.activevp.com

Management and Staff
Edwin Goodman, General Partner
F. Morgan Rodd, General Partner
Richard Dumler, General Partner
Todd Pietri, General Partner

Type of Firm
Private Equity Firm

Association Membership
National Venture Capital Association - USA (NVCA)

Project Preferences

Role in Financing:
Will function either as deal originator or investor in deals created by others

Type of Financing Preferred:
Early Stage

Geographical Preferences

United States Preferences:
Mid Atlantic
Northeast
Connecticut
New Jersey
New York

Industry Preferences

In Computer Software prefer:
Software

In Business Serv. prefer:
Services

Additional Information
Name of Most Recent Fund: Milestone Venture Partners IV, L.P.
Most Recent Fund Was Raised: 05/10/2012
Year Founded: 1999
Capital Under Management: $100,000,000
Current Activity Level : Actively seeking new investments
Method of Compensation: Return on investment is of primary concern, do not charge fees

ACTIVE CAPITAL CO BV

Dam 7C
Amsterdam, Netherlands 1012 JS
Phone: 31202620275
E-mail: info@activecapitalcompany.com
Website: www.activecapitalcompany.com

Type of Firm
Private Equity Firm

Project Preferences

Type of Financing Preferred:
Leveraged Buyout

Size of Investments Considered:
Min Size of Investment Considered (000s): $1,356
Max Size of Investment Considered (000s): $5,425

Geographical Preferences

International Preferences:
Europe
Netherlands

Industry Preferences

In Consumer Related prefer:
Retail
Consumer Products
Consumer Services

Additional Information
Year Founded: 2009
Current Activity Level : Actively seeking new investments

ACTIVE CAPITAL LLC

119 Nueces Street
Austin, TX USA 78701
Phone: 7033383600

Type of Firm
Private Equity Firm

Project Preferences

Type of Financing Preferred:
Early Stage
Seed

Industry Preferences

In Computer Software prefer:
Computer Services

Additional Information
Year Founded: 2017
Capital Under Management: $13,080,000
Current Activity Level : Actively seeking new investments

ACTIVE CAPITAL PARTNERS SA

Paseo de Gracia 35, atico
Barcelona, Spain 08007
Phone: 34931786868
Fax: 34932722436
E-mail: info@acpvc.com
Website: www.active-vp.com

Management and Staff
Blair MacLaren, Partner
Christopher Pommerening, Partner
Philipp Schroeder, Partner
Ricard Soderberg, Partner

Type of Firm
Private Equity Firm

Association Membership
European Private Equity and Venture Capital Assoc.
Spanish Venture Capital Association (ASCRI)

Project Preferences

Type of Financing Preferred:
Early Stage
Balanced
Later Stage
Seed

Size of Investments Considered:
Min Size of Investment Considered (000s): $634
Max Size of Investment Considered (000s): $5,072

Geographical Preferences

International Preferences:
Sweden
Switzerland
Austria
Spain
Finland
Norway
Germany

Industry Preferences

In Communications prefer:
Telecommunications

In Computer Software prefer:
Software

In Internet Specific prefer:
Internet

Additional Information
Year Founded: 2002
Capital Under Management: $13,400,000
Current Activity Level : Actively seeking new investments

ACTIVE INVESTMENT PARTNERS

2-2-1 Marunouchi, Chiyoda-ku
Kishimoto Building, 5th Floor
Tokyo, Japan 100-0005
Phone: 81332018603

Management and Staff
Hideo Aomatsu, Chief Executive Officer
Hiroshi Sakai, Managing Director
Mayumi Takei, Principal
Naoto Mizoguchi, Managing Director

Type of Firm
Private Equity Firm

Project Preferences

Type of Financing Preferred:
Leveraged Buyout
Turnaround
Management Buyouts
Recapitalizations

Geographical Preferences

International Preferences:
Japan

Industry Focus
(% based on actual investment)
   Consumer Related   73.9%
   Other Products   26.1%

Additional Information
Year Founded: 2005
Current Activity Level : Actively seeking new investments

ACTIVE PRIVATE EQUITY

6 Burnsall Street
Second Floor
London, United Kingdom SW3 3ST
Phone: 442070428200
Fax: 442073519169
E-mail: enquiries@apeq.co.uk
Website: www.apeq.co.uk

Management and Staff
Gavyn Davies, Co-Founder
Nick Evans, Partner
Spencer Skinner, Co-Founder

Type of Firm
Private Equity Firm

Association Membership
British Venture Capital Association (BVCA)

Project Preferences

Type of Financing Preferred:
Leveraged Buyout
Management Buyouts
Acquisition

Size of Investments Considered:
Min Size of Investment Considered (000s): $790
Max Size of Investment Considered (000s): $23,703

Geographical Preferences

International Preferences:
United Kingdom

Industry Preferences

In Communications prefer:
Media and Entertainment

In Internet Specific prefer:
E-Commerce Technology

In Consumer Related prefer:
Entertainment and Leisure
Food/Beverage
Consumer Products
Consumer Services

In Business Serv. prefer:
Media

Additional Information
Year Founded: 2004
Current Activity Level : Actively seeking new investments

ACTIVE VENTURE PARTNERS LLC

119 Nueces Street
Austin, TX USA 78701
E-mail: info@activecapital.com
Website: www.activecapital.com

Type of Firm
Private Equity Firm

Project Preferences

Type of Financing Preferred:
Seed

Industry Preferences

In Computer Software prefer:
Software

Additional Information
Year Founded: 2017
Current Activity Level : Actively seeking new investments

ACTIVE-M

Grosvenor Business Tower
Office 1507
Dubai, Utd. Arab Em. 450167
Phone: 97144327522
Fax: 97144327521
Website: www.activemgroup.com

Management and Staff
Salam Saadeh, Chief Executive Officer

Type of Firm
Private Equity Firm

Project Preferences

Type of Financing Preferred:
Early Stage
Seed

Geographical Preferences

International Preferences:
Utd. Arab Em.

Industry Preferences

In Medical/Health prefer:
Medical/Health

Additional Information
Year Founded: 1969
Current Activity Level : Actively seeking new investments

ACTON CAPITAL PARTNERS GMBH

Widenmayerstrasse 29
Munich, Germany 80538
Phone: 498924218870
Fax: 4989242188759
E-mail: info@actoncapital.de
Website: www.actoncapital.de

Management and Staff
Boris Wertz, Venture Partner
Christoph Braun, Managing Partner
Frank Seehaus, Managing Partner
Jan-Gisbert Schultze, Managing Partner
Paul-Bernhard Kallen, Managing Partner
Sebastian Wossagk, Partner

Type of Firm
Private Equity Firm

Project Preferences

Type of Financing Preferred:
Early Stage
Later Stage
Seed
Startup

Geographical Preferences

United States Preferences:
All U.S.

International Preferences:
Europe

Industry Preferences

In Communications prefer:
Wireless Communications
Media and Entertainment

In Internet Specific prefer:
E-Commerce Technology
Internet
Ecommerce

In Industrial/Energy prefer:
Industrial Products

Additional Information
Name of Most Recent Fund: Heureka II
Most Recent Fund Was Raised: 01/15/2014
Year Founded: 2008
Capital Under Management: $391,816,000
Current Activity Level : Actively seeking new investments

ACTUA CORP

555 East Lancaster Avenue, Suite 640
Wayne, PA USA 19087
Phone: 6107276900
Fax: 6107276901
E-mail: ir@icg.com
Website: www.actua.com

Management and Staff
Darren Sandberg, Managing Director
Douglas Alexander, President
John Loftus, Managing Director
Kamal Advani, Managing Director
Matthew Safaii, Managing Director
Philip Rooney, Vice President
Raymond Morgan, Chief Financial Officer
Vincent Menichelli, Managing Director

Type of Firm
Corporate PE/Venture

Project Preferences

Type of Financing Preferred:
Leveraged Buyout
Acquisition

Industry Preferences

In Computer Software prefer:
Software

In Internet Specific prefer:
Internet

Additional Information
Year Founded: 1996
Current Activity Level : Actively seeking new investments

ACUMEN FUND INC

40 Worth Street
Suite 303
New York, NY USA 10011
Phone: 2125668821
Fax: 2125668817
Website: acumen.org

Other Offices
203 Dheeraj Plaza, Hill Road
Bandra West
Mumbai, India 400050
Phone: 912267589365
Fax: 912267589373

1st Commercial Lane, Shahbaz Commercial
11-C, Fourth Floor, Phase VI
Karachi, Pakistan
Phone: 92215846430-2
Fax: 92215846490

1st Floor, Cape Office Park
Ring Road, Kilimani
Nairobi, Kenya
Phone: 254-20-386-1559

Management and Staff
Carlyle Singer, President
Jacqueline Woo, Chief Financial Officer
Michael Greenberg, Chief Financial Officer

Type of Firm
Private Equity Firm

Project Preferences

Type of Financing Preferred:
Early Stage
Balanced

Size of Investments Considered:
Min Size of Investment Considered (000s): $300
Max Size of Investment Considered (000s): $2,500

Geographical Preferences

International Preferences:
Pakistan
India
South Africa

Industry Preferences

In Medical/Health prefer:
Medical/Health

In Consumer Related prefer:
Education Related

In Industrial/Energy prefer:
Energy
Environmental Related

In Business Serv. prefer:
Services

In Agr/Forestr/Fish prefer:
Agriculture related

In Other prefer:
Socially Responsible
Environment Responsible

Additional Information
Year Founded: 2001
Current Activity Level : Actively seeking new investments

ADAM SMITH CAPITAL LTD

8 Queens Road
18/F Central
Hong Kong, Hong Kong
Phone: 852-6187-9138

Type of Firm
Private Equity Firm

Project Preferences

Type of Financing Preferred:
Leveraged Buyout
Acquisition

Geographical Preferences

International Preferences:
Asia Pacific
Hong Kong

Industry Preferences

In Financial Services prefer:
Financial Services

Additional Information
Year Founded: 2011
Current Activity Level : Actively seeking new investments

ADAMS AND REESE LLP

340 East Parker Boulevard
Louisiana State University
Baton Rouge, LA USA 70803
Phone: 2256158905
Fax: 2256158910
Website: www.adamsandreese.com

Other Offices
451 Florida Street
19F Bank One Centre
Baton Rouge, LA USA 70801
Phone: 2253365200
P.O. Box 25128
Baton Rouge, LA USA 70894

Management and Staff
Charles Adams, Managing Partner
Joseph Lovett, Managing Director
Paul Lassalle, Chief Operating Officer

Type of Firm
Incubator/Development Program

Project Preferences

Type of Financing Preferred:
Early Stage
Seed
Startup

Geographical Preferences

United States Preferences:
Southeast
Louisiana
Southwest

Industry Preferences

In Biotechnology prefer:
Biotechnology

In Medical/Health prefer:
Medical/Health
Pharmaceuticals

In Agr/Forestr/Fish prefer:
Agriculture related

Additional Information
Name of Most Recent Fund: Louisiana Fund II, L.P.
Most Recent Fund Was Raised: 03/04/2014
Year Founded: 1993
Capital Under Management: $16,900,000
Current Activity Level : Actively seeking new investments

ADAMS CAPITAL MANAGEMENT, INC.

500 Blackburn Avenue
Sewickley, PA USA 15143
Phone: 4127499454
Fax: 4127499459

E-mail: info@acm.com
Website: www.acm.com

Other Offices

398 Columbus Avenue
Suite 502
BOSTON, MA USA 02116
Phone: 6174175916

525 University Avenue
Suite 230
PALO ALTO, CA USA 94301
Phone: 650-473-0700
Fax: 6504730712

Management and Staff

Jennifer Parulo, Chief Financial Officer
Martin Neath, General Partner
N. George Ugras, General Partner
Nikhil Sinha, Venture Partner
William Frezza, Venture Partner

Type of Firm

Private Equity Firm

Association Membership

National Venture Capital Association - USA (NVCA)

Project Preferences

Role in Financing:
Prefer role as deal originator but will also invest in deals created by others

Type of Financing Preferred:
Early Stage
Balanced

Size of Investments Considered:
Min Size of Investment Considered (000s): $1,000
Max Size of Investment Considered (000s): $5,000

Geographical Preferences

United States Preferences:

Industry Focus

(% based on actual investment)
Internet Specific	30.7%
Semiconductors/Other Elect.	24.3%
Computer Software and Services	21.4%
Communications and Media	8.1%
Computer Hardware	5.4%
Industrial/Energy	4.9%
Medical/Health	4.9%
Biotechnology	0.4%

Additional Information

Name of Most Recent Fund: Adams Capital Management IV, L.P.
Most Recent Fund Was Raised: 03/09/2009
Year Founded: 1994
Capital Under Management: $815,000,000
Current Activity Level : Actively seeking new investments
Method of Compensation: Return on investment is of primary concern, do not charge fees

ADAMS STREET PARTNERS LLC

One North Wacker Drive
Suite 2200
Chicago, IL USA 60606
Phone: 3125537890
Fax: 3125537891
E-mail: info@adamsstreetpartners.com
Website: www.adamsstreetpartners.com

Other Offices

1-7-2 Otemachi Chiyoda-Ku
Level 27 Tokyo Sankei Building
Tokyo, Japan 100-0004
Phone: 81332423242
Fax: 81332423246

2500 Sand Hill Road
Suite 100
MENLO PARK, CA USA 94025
Phone: 650-331-4860
Fax: 650-331-4861

77 Jianguo Road, Chaoyang District
Level 24, Tower 3, China Central Place
Beijing, China 100025
Phone: 861085872312
Fax: 861085880110

250 North Bridge Road
#14-02, Raffles City Tower
Singapore, Singapore 179101
Phone: 65-6303-8730
Fax: 65-6303-8740

Management and Staff

Adam Chenoweth, Vice President
Alex Kessel, Principal
Alicia Pando, Partner
Christopher Larson, Partner
Dominic Maier, Vice President
Fred Wang, Partner
Gary Fencik, Partner
Gregory Holden, Partner
James Korczak, Partner
Jeffrey Burgis, Partner
Jeffrey Akers, Partner
Justin Lawrence, Principal
Martin Gawne, Partner
Megan Heneghan, Partner
Michael Taylor, Vice President
Philipp Bohren, Partner
Raymond Chan, Partner
Rebecca Boyer, Principal
Sara Cushing, Partner
Sarah Bass, Partner
Sarah Finneran, Vice President
Stephen Baranowski, Partner
Terry Gould, Partner
Thomas Petty, Vice President
Thomas Bremner, Partner
Troy Barnett, Partner

Type of Firm

Private Equity Firm

Association Membership

Australian Venture Capital Association (AVCAL)
British Venture Capital Association (BVCA)
Illinois Venture Capital Association
National Venture Capital Association - USA (NVCA)
European Private Equity and Venture Capital Assoc.
Singapore Venture Capital Association (SVCA)

Project Preferences

Role in Financing:
Prefer role as deal originator but will also invest in deals created by others

Type of Financing Preferred:
Fund of Funds
Leveraged Buyout
Early Stage
Generalist PE
Balanced
Other
Fund of Funds of Second

Size of Investments Considered:
Min Size of Investment Considered (000s): $5,000
Max Size of Investment Considered (000s): $20,000

Geographical Preferences

United States Preferences:
North America

International Preferences:
Europe
Asia

Industry Focus

(% based on actual investment)
Other Products	70.6%
Computer Software and Services	11.5%
Internet Specific	5.7%
Biotechnology	3.5%
Medical/Health	3.4%
Consumer Related	1.6%
Communications and Media	1.6%
Semiconductors/Other Elect.	1.2%
Computer Hardware	0.9%
Industrial/Energy	0.2%

Additional Information

Name of Most Recent Fund: Adams Street 2013 US Fund, L.P.
Most Recent Fund Was Raised: 12/19/2012
Year Founded: 1972
Capital Under Management: $26,800,000,000
Current Activity Level : Actively seeking new investments
Method of Compensation: Return on investment is of primary concern, do not charge fees

ADAPTIVE HEALTHCARE LLC

11835 West Olympic Blvd
Suite 900
Los Angeles, CA USA 90064
Phone: 3102032820
E-mail: info@adaptivehealthcare.com
Website: adaptivehealthcare.com

Type of Firm
Private Equity Firm

Project Preferences

Type of Financing Preferred:
Early Stage

Industry Preferences

In Medical/Health prefer:
Health Services

Additional Information
Year Founded: 2015
Current Activity Level : Actively seeking new investments

ADARA VENTURE PARTNERS

Calle Jose Abascal 58
Madrid, Spain 28003
Phone: 34914517070
Fax: 34914517090
E-mail: info@adaravp.com
Website: www.adaravp.com

Management and Staff
Alberto Gomez, Managing Partner
Nicolas Goulet, Managing Partner
Roberto De Saint-Malo, General Partner

Type of Firm
Private Equity Firm

Association Membership
Spanish Venture Capital Association (ASCRI)

Project Preferences

Role in Financing:
Will function either as deal originator or investor in deals created by others

Type of Financing Preferred:
Early Stage
Startup

Geographical Preferences

International Preferences:
Portugal
Spain

Industry Preferences

In Communications prefer:
Telecommunications
Wireless Communications

In Computer Software prefer:
Software

In Semiconductor/Electr prefer:
Semiconductor

In Industrial/Energy prefer:
Alternative Energy
Energy Conservation Relat

Additional Information
Year Founded: 2005
Capital Under Management: $78,800,000
Current Activity Level : Actively seeking new investments

ADAXTRA CAPITAL

18 Quai De La Rapee
Paris, France 75012

Type of Firm
Bank Affiliated

Project Preferences

Type of Financing Preferred:
Leveraged Buyout
Early Stage
Expansion
Later Stage
Management Buyouts
Acquisition

Size of Investments Considered:
Min Size of Investment Considered (000s): $1,172
Max Size of Investment Considered (000s): $9,372

Geographical Preferences

International Preferences:
France

Additional Information
Year Founded: 2006
Current Activity Level : Actively seeking new investments

ADCURAM GROUP AG

Theatinerstrasse 7
Arco Palais
Munich, Germany 80333
Phone: 498920209590
Fax: 498920209599
E-mail: welcom@adcuram.com
Website: www.adcuram.de

Other Offices
Theatinerstrasse 7
Arco Palais
Munich, Germany 80333
Phone: 49-89-2020-9590
Fax: 49-89-2020-9099

Management and Staff
Florian Meise, Managing Partner
Matthias Meise, Managing Partner
Thomas Probst, Managing Partner
Ulf Lange, Managing Partner

Type of Firm
Private Equity Firm

Association Membership
German Venture Capital Association (BVK)

Project Preferences

Type of Financing Preferred:
Leveraged Buyout
Turnaround
Acquisition
Distressed Debt
Recapitalizations

Geographical Preferences

International Preferences:
Europe
Switzerland
Austria
Germany

Industry Preferences

In Biotechnology prefer:
Biotechnology

In Medical/Health prefer:
Medical/Health
Pharmaceuticals

In Consumer Related prefer:
Retail

In Industrial/Energy prefer:
Industrial Products
Materials
Machinery

In Business Serv. prefer:
Services

In Manufact. prefer:
Manufacturing

Additional Information
Name of Most Recent Fund: ADCURAM Fund I
Most Recent Fund Was Raised: 10/01/2012
Year Founded: 2003
Capital Under Management: $193,324,000
Current Activity Level : Actively seeking new investments

ADDISON CAPITAL PARTNERS LLC

319 Clematis Street
Suite 211
West Palm Beach, FL USA 33401
Phone: 5648354041
Website: www.addisoncapitalpartners.com

Management and Staff
Brian Miller, Principal

Type of Firm
Private Equity Firm

Project Preferences

Type of Financing Preferred:
Balanced
Management Buyouts
Acquisition
Recapitalizations

Industry Preferences

In Business Serv. prefer:
Services
Distribution

In Manufact. prefer:
Manufacturing

Additional Information
Year Founded: 2008
Current Activity Level : Actively seeking new investments

ADDISON CLARK MANAGEMENT LLC

2960 Post Road
Suite 200
Southport, CT USA 06890
Phone: 203-254-8700

Type of Firm
Private Equity Firm

Project Preferences

Type of Financing Preferred:
Other

Geographical Preferences

United States Preferences:

Additional Information
Year Founded: 2002
Capital Under Management: $3,200,000
Current Activity Level : Actively seeking new investments

ADDQUITY GROWTH CAPITAL SA

Alcala 119
3 Derecha
Madrid, Spain 28009
Phone: 34911250856
Website: www.addquity.com

Type of Firm
Private Equity Firm

Project Preferences

Type of Financing Preferred:
Expansion
Balanced

Geographical Preferences

International Preferences:
Europe
Spain

Industry Preferences

In Computer Software prefer:
Software

In Consumer Related prefer:
Consumer

In Industrial/Energy prefer:
Alternative Energy

Additional Information
Year Founded: 2011
Current Activity Level : Actively seeking new investments

ADELIS EQUITY PARTNERS AB

Biblioteksgatan 9
Stockholm, Sweden 111 46
Phone: 46852520000
Website: adelisequity.com

Management and Staff
Gustav Bard, Co-Founder
Jan Akesson, Co-Founder
Johan Seger, Chief Financial Officer

Type of Firm
Private Equity Firm

Association Membership
Danish Venture Capital Association (DVCA)
Swedish Venture Capital Association (SVCA)

Project Preferences

Type of Financing Preferred:
Leveraged Buyout

Geographical Preferences

International Preferences:
Scandanavia/Nordic Region

Additional Information
Name of Most Recent Fund: Adelis Equity Partners Fund I AB
Most Recent Fund Was Raised: 08/29/2013
Year Founded: 2013
Capital Under Management: $303,400,000
Current Activity Level : Actively seeking new investments

ADENA VENTURES

20 East Circle Drive
Suite 143
Athens, OH USA 45701
Phone: 7405971470
Fax: 7405971399
E-mail: info@adenaventures.com
Website: www.adenaventures.com

Management and Staff
David Wilhelm, Founder
Jakki Haussler, Partner
Jeff Doose, Partner
Lynn Gellermann, President
Thomas Parkinson, Partner

Type of Firm
Private Equity Firm

Association Membership
Community Development Venture Capital Alliance

Project Preferences

Role in Financing:
Will function either as deal originator or investor in deals created by others

Type of Financing Preferred:
Early Stage
Expansion
Balanced

Size of Investments Considered:
Min Size of Investment Considered (000s): $500
Max Size of Investment Considered (000s): $2,500

Geographical Preferences

United States Preferences:
East Coast

Industry Preferences

In Consumer Related prefer:
Food/Beverage

In Business Serv. prefer:
Services

In Manufact. prefer:
Manufacturing

Pratt's Guide to Private Equity & Venture Capital Sources

Additional Information

Name of Most Recent Fund: Adena Ventures, L.P.
Most Recent Fund Was Raised: 04/24/2002
Year Founded: 2002
Capital Under Management: $34,000,000
Current Activity Level : Actively seeking new investments
Method of Compensation: Return on investment is of primary concern, do not charge fees

ADENIA PARTNERS LTD

4th floor, Harbour Front Bldg
President John Kennedy Street
Port Louis, Mauritius
Phone: 2302138190
Fax: 2302138191
Website: www.adenia.com

Other Offices

4th floor, Harbour Front Bldg
President John Kennedy Street
Port Louis, Mauritius
Phone: 2302138190
Fax: 2302138191

Type of Firm

Private Equity Firm

Project Preferences

Type of Financing Preferred:
Generalist PE

Geographical Preferences

International Preferences:
India
Mauritius
Comoros
Ghana
Madagascar
Asia
Africa

Industry Preferences

In Communications prefer:
Telecommunications

In Computer Software prefer:
Systems Software

In Medical/Health prefer:
Hospitals/Clinics/Primary

In Consumer Related prefer:
Food/Beverage
Hotels and Resorts

In Financial Services prefer:
Insurance
Financial Services

In Business Serv. prefer:
Services

In Manufact. prefer:
Manufacturing

In Agr/Forestr/Fish prefer:
Agribusiness

Additional Information

Year Founded: 2002
Capital Under Management: $235,576,000
Current Activity Level : Actively seeking new investments

ADFISCO

22 Adam & Eve Mews
London, United Kingdom W8 6UJ
Phone: 442079376690
Fax: 442079376689
Website: www.adfisco.com

Type of Firm

Private Equity Firm

Industry Preferences

In Financial Services prefer:
Financial Services

Additional Information

Year Founded: 2017
Current Activity Level : Actively seeking new investments

ADINVEST AG

Rigistrasse 25
Zumikon, Switzerland 8126
Phone: 41442022155
Fax: 41442021942
E-mail: n.sunderland@adinvest.ch

Management and Staff

Neil Sunderland, Chief Executive Officer

Type of Firm

Private Equity Firm

Association Membership

Swiss Venture Capital Association (SECA)

Project Preferences

Type of Financing Preferred:
Leveraged Buyout
Turnaround
Later Stage
Seed
Management Buyouts

Size of Investments Considered:
Min Size of Investment Considered (000s): $669
Max Size of Investment Considered (000s): $6,689

Geographical Preferences

United States Preferences:

International Preferences:
United Kingdom
Europe
Switzerland
Australia
Germany

Industry Preferences

In Computer Software prefer:
Software

In Internet Specific prefer:
Internet

In Computer Other prefer:
Computer Related

In Semiconductor/Electr prefer:
Sensors

In Business Serv. prefer:
Services

In Manufact. prefer:
Manufacturing

Additional Information

Year Founded: 1986
Current Activity Level : Actively seeking new investments

ADITYA BIRLA CAPITAL ADVISORS PVT LTD

S. K. Ahire Marg, Worli
Aditya Birla Ctr, Thrid Floor
Mumbai, India 400 030
Phone: 912226655160
Fax: 912266525741
E-mail: abg.pe@adityabirla.com
Website: www.adityabirla.com

Management and Staff

Achin Bhardwaj, Principal
Bharat Banka, Chief Executive Officer
Mehul Maroo, Principal
Sailesh Shenoi, Principal
Sandeep Bhat, Chief Financial Officer
Shamik Moitra, Principal
Sunil Jain, Principal

Type of Firm

Investment Management Firm

Association Membership

Emerging Markets Private Equity Association
Indian Venture Capital Association (IVCA)

Project Preferences

Type of Financing Preferred:
Leveraged Buyout
Expansion
Acquisition

Geographical Preferences

International Preferences:
India

Industry Preferences

In Communications prefer:
Media and Entertainment

In Biotechnology prefer:
Biotechnology

In Medical/Health prefer:
Medical/Health
Health Services

In Consumer Related prefer:
Entertainment and Leisure
Education Related

In Financial Services prefer:
Financial Services

In Business Serv. prefer:
Services
Distribution

In Manufact. prefer:
Manufacturing

Additional Information

Year Founded: 2008
Capital Under Management: $250,000,000
Current Activity Level : Actively seeking new investments

ADIUVA CAPITAL GMBH

Messberg 1
Hamburg, Germany 20095
Phone: 494030191670
Fax: 494030191675
E-mail: info@adiuvacapital.de
Website: www.adiuvacapital.de

Management and Staff

Tobias Wollenhaupt, Partner
Tobias Osing, Partner

Type of Firm

Private Equity Firm

Project Preferences

Type of Financing Preferred:
Leveraged Buyout
Management Buyouts
Acquisition

Geographical Preferences

International Preferences:
Switzerland
Austria
Germany

Industry Preferences

In Biotechnology prefer:
Biotechnology

Additional Information

Year Founded: 2011
Current Activity Level : Actively seeking new investments

ADM CAPITAL

Three Garden Road
1008 ICBC Tower
Central, Hong Kong
Phone: 85225364567
Fax: 85221472813
E-mail: adminfo@admcap.com
Website: www.admcap.com

Other Offices

Cevdetpasa Cd. Germencik Sk.
Irtibat Burosu
Istanbul, Turkey
Phone: 902122635511
Fax: 902122573288

25B, Sagaydachnogo Street
Regus Podil Business Center
Kyiv, Ukraine 04070
Phone: 380444985161
Fax: 380444985100

Furmanov Street 240 V
Business Centre CDC2
Almaty, Kazakhstan 050059
Phone: 77273344400
Fax: 77273340444

4th floor, Maker Chambers VI
Nariman Point
Mumbai, India 400021
Phone: 912266102300
Fax: 912266102307

39 Sloane Street
London, United Kingdom SW1X 9LP
Phone: 442075292008
Fax: 442075295070

6 Wudinghou Street, Excel Centre
12/F, Suite 1256, Xicheng District
Beijing, China 100032

Management and Staff

Anthony Stalker, Partner
Baris Sivri, Partner
Florian Huth, Partner
Jeremy Alun-Jones, Chief Operating Officer
Mei Li, Partner
Orinbasar Kuatov, Managing Director
Robert Appleby, Co-Founder
Susheel Kak, Managing Director

Type of Firm

Bank Affiliated

Association Membership

Emerging Markets Private Equity Association

Project Preferences

Type of Financing Preferred:
Leveraged Buyout
Public Companies
Turnaround
Acquisition
Special Situation
Distressed Debt
Recapitalizations

Geographical Preferences

International Preferences:
Kazakhstan
Turkey
Central Europe
Europe
Eastern Europe
Ukraine
Bulgaria
Asia
Russia

Industry Preferences

In Medical/Health prefer:
Medical/Health

In Industrial/Energy prefer:
Oil and Gas Exploration

In Transportation prefer:
Transportation

In Financial Services prefer:
Real Estate

Additional Information

Year Founded: 1998
Capital Under Management: $1,700,000,000
Current Activity Level : Actively seeking new investments

ADMIRAL CAPITAL GROUP

52 Vanderbilt Avenue, Suite 1000
New York, NY USA 10017
Phone: 6464054808
E-mail: info@admiralcapitalgroup.com
Website: www.admiralcapitalgroup.com

Pratt's Guide to Private Equity & Venture Capital Sources

Other Offices
1150 North Loop 1604 West
Suite 108-505
San Antonio, TX USA 78248
Phone: 6464054808

Management and Staff
Daniel Bassichis, Founder
David Robinson, Co-Founder

Type of Firm
Private Equity Firm

Project Preferences

Type of Financing Preferred:
Leveraged Buyout
Value-Add
Generalist PE
Acquisition

Geographical Preferences

United States Preferences:
North America

Industry Preferences

In Communications prefer:
Entertainment

In Financial Services prefer:
Real Estate

Additional Information
Name of Most Recent Fund: Admiral Capital Real Estate Fund, L.P.
Most Recent Fund Was Raised: 06/01/2011
Year Founded: 2008
Capital Under Management: $238,000,000
Current Activity Level : Actively seeking new investments

ADMIRALTY PARTNERS INC

11111 Santa Monica Boulevard
Suite 1650
Los Angeles, CA USA 90025
Phone: 3104713772
Fax: 3104726601
E-mail: info@admiraltypartners.com
Website: www.admiraltypartners.com

Type of Firm
Private Equity Firm

Project Preferences

Type of Financing Preferred:
Leveraged Buyout
Turnaround
Acquisition
Recapitalizations

Industry Preferences

In Transportation prefer:
Aerospace

In Business Serv. prefer:
Services

Additional Information
Year Founded: 1992
Current Activity Level : Actively seeking new investments

ADOBE CAPITAL

Corina 59,
Colonia del Carmen
Mexico City, Mexico 04100
Phone: 525556045555
E-mail: contact@adobecapital.org
Website: www.adobecapital.org

Management and Staff
Erik Wallsten, Co-Founder
Rodrigo Villar, Co-Founder

Type of Firm
Private Equity Firm

Project Preferences

Type of Financing Preferred:
Early Stage
Expansion
Mezzanine
Generalist PE
Acquisition

Geographical Preferences

International Preferences:
Mexico

Industry Preferences

In Medical/Health prefer:
Medical/Health

In Consumer Related prefer:
Entertainment and Leisure
Education Related

In Industrial/Energy prefer:
Alternative Energy
Environmental Related

In Financial Services prefer:
Financial Services

In Agr/Forestr/Fish prefer:
Agribusiness

In Other prefer:
Environment Responsible

Additional Information
Name of Most Recent Fund: Adobe Social Mezzanine Fund I, L.P.
Most Recent Fund Was Raised: 11/30/2012
Year Founded: 2012
Capital Under Management: $36,000,000
Current Activity Level : Actively seeking new investments

ADVANCE VENTURE PARTNERS LLC

170 Grant Avenue
Fourth Floor
San Francisco, CA USA 94108
Phone: 4155946000
Website: www.avpgrowth.com

Type of Firm
Private Equity Firm

Project Preferences

Type of Financing Preferred:
Early Stage
Expansion
Later Stage

Geographical Preferences

United States Preferences:

Industry Preferences

In Communications prefer:
Media and Entertainment
Entertainment

In Business Serv. prefer:
Media

Additional Information
Year Founded: 2014
Current Activity Level : Actively seeking new investments

ADVANCED CAPITAL LTD

18 Hysan Avenue
1802B
Causeway Bay, Hong Kong
Phone: 85226778921
Fax: 85226778728
Website: www.acg188.com

Type of Firm
Private Equity Firm

Project Preferences

Type of Financing Preferred:
Leveraged Buyout

Geographical Preferences

International Preferences:
China

Additional Information
Year Founded: 2007
Current Activity Level : Actively seeking new investments

ADVANCED CAPITAL SGR SPA
Via Brera 5
Milano, Italy 20121
Phone: 39-02-799-555
Fax: 39-02-794-999
E-mail: segretaria@advancedcapital.com
Website: www.advancedcapital.com

Other Offices
14 Dover Street - 2nd piano
London, United Kingdom W1S 4LW
Phone: 44-207-499-4342

Via Magatti 3
Lugano, Switzerland 6900
Phone: 41-91-924-9240

6, Rue Guillaume Schneider
Luxembourg, Luxembourg L-2522
Phone: 352-26948-601
Fax: 352-26948-620

Management and Staff
Federico Braguglia, Vice President

Type of Firm
Private Equity Advisor or Fund of Funds

Association Membership
Italian Venture Capital Association (AIFI)
European Private Equity and Venture Capital Assoc.

Project Preferences
Type of Financing Preferred:
Fund of Funds
Balanced

Geographical Preferences
International Preferences:
Italy
All International

Additional Information
Year Founded: 2000
Current Activity Level : Actively seeking new investments

ADVANCED FINANCE AND INVESTMENT GROUP LLC
s/c Multiconsult Ltd
Rogers House 5
Port Louis, Mauritius
Phone: 230-405-2000
Fax: 230-212-5265
E-mail: info@afigfunds.com
Website: www.afigfunds.com

Other Offices
Nelson Mandela Square Maude Street
West Tower 2nd Floor
Sandton, South Africa 2196
Phone: 27-11-881-5685
Fax: 27-11-881-5611

83, Boulevard de la Republique
Immeuble Horizons
Dakar, Senegal
Phone: 221-33-865-0515
Fax: 221-33-825-4848

1776 I Street North West
Ninth Floor
Washington, DC USA 20006
Phone: 202-756-4782
Fax: 202-318-2276

Management and Staff
Papa Madiaw Ndiaye, Chief Executive Officer
Patrice Backer, Chief Operating Officer

Type of Firm
Private Equity Firm

Association Membership
Emerging Markets Private Equity Association

Project Preferences
Type of Financing Preferred:
Early Stage
Expansion
Generalist PE
Balanced
Later Stage
Acquisition

Geographical Preferences
International Preferences:
Angola
Nigeria
Gabon
Senegal
Ghana
Cameroon
Morocco
Congo, Dem Rep
Africa

Industry Preferences
In Communications prefer:
Telecommunications

In Industrial/Energy prefer:
Industrial Products

In Transportation prefer:
Transportation

In Financial Services prefer:
Financial Services

In Agr/Forestr/Fish prefer:
Mining and Minerals

Additional Information
Year Founded: 2005
Capital Under Management: $90,000,000
Current Activity Level : Actively seeking new investments

ADVANCED SCIENCE AND TECHNOLOGY ENTERPRISE CORP
2-3-11 Hirakawacho, Chiyoda-ku
4F Hanabishi-Hirakawacho Bldg
Tokyo, Japan 102-0093
Phone: 81332430870
Fax: 81332430875
Website: www.ut-astec.com

Type of Firm
Private Equity Firm

Project Preferences
Role in Financing:
Prefer role as deal originator but will also invest in deals created by others

Type of Financing Preferred:
Seed
Startup

Geographical Preferences
International Preferences:
Japan

Industry Preferences
In Communications prefer:
Telecommunications

In Computer Hardware prefer:
Computers

In Computer Software prefer:
Software

In Internet Specific prefer:
Internet

In Semiconductor/Electr prefer:
Electronics
Semiconductor
Optoelectronics

In Biotechnology prefer:
Human Biotechnology

In Industrial/Energy prefer:
Energy

Additional Information
Year Founded: 2001
Capital Under Management: $100,000
Current Activity Level : Actively seeking new investments

ADVANCED TECHNOLOGY VENTURES

485 Ramona Street
Palo Alto, CA USA 94301
Phone: 6503218601
Fax: 6503210934
E-mail: info@atvcapital.com
Website: www.atvcapital.com

Management and Staff

Adam Bruce, Chief Financial Officer
Edward Frank, Partner
Jean George, General Partner
Ken Noonan, Venture Partner
Michael Carusi, General Partner
Richard Popp, Venture Partner
Robert Hower, General Partner
Robert Finocchio, Venture Partner
Stephen Shapiro, Venture Partner
Steven Baloff, General Partner
William Wiberg, General Partner

Type of Firm

Private Equity Firm

Association Membership

New England Venture Capital Association

Project Preferences

Role in Financing:
Prefer role as deal originator but will also invest in deals created by others

Type of Financing Preferred:
Early Stage
Balanced
Later Stage

Geographical Preferences

United States Preferences:

International Preferences:
Europe
Israel

Industry Focus

(% based on actual investment)

Medical/Health	21.3%
Computer Software and Services	19.4%
Internet Specific	12.7%
Communications and Media	11.9%
Biotechnology	11.5%
Semiconductors/Other Elect.	9.9%
Industrial/Energy	8.1%
Computer Hardware	4.6%
Other Products	0.7%

Additional Information

Name of Most Recent Fund: Advanced Technology Ventures VIII, L.P.
Most Recent Fund Was Raised: 07/09/2007
Year Founded: 1979
Capital Under Management: $81,550,000,000
Current Activity Level : Actively seeking new investments
Method of Compensation: Return on investment is of primary concern, do not charge fees

ADVANCIT CAPITAL LLC

846 University Avenue
Norwood, MA USA 02062
Phone: 7812682640
E-mail: info@advancitcap.com
Website: www.advancitcapital.com

Management and Staff

Jason Ostheimer, Partner
Shari Redstone, Managing Partner

Type of Firm

Private Equity Firm

Project Preferences

Type of Financing Preferred:
Early Stage

Industry Preferences

In Communications prefer:
Media and Entertainment

In Business Serv. prefer:
Media

Additional Information

Name of Most Recent Fund: Advancit Capital I, L.P.
Most Recent Fund Was Raised: 08/12/2011
Year Founded: 2011
Capital Under Management: $36,500,000
Current Activity Level : Actively seeking new investments

ADVANS SA

69, route d'Esch
Luxembourg, Luxembourg 2953
E-mail: contact@advansgroup.com
Website: www.advansgroup.com

Type of Firm

Bank Affiliated

Project Preferences

Type of Financing Preferred:
Early Stage
Seed
Startup

Geographical Preferences

International Preferences:
Asia
Africa

Industry Preferences

In Financial Services prefer:
Financial Services

Additional Information

Year Founded: 2005
Capital Under Management: $59,300,000
Current Activity Level : Actively seeking new investments

ADVANTAGE CAPITAL

35 New Bridge Street
London, United Kingdom EC4V 6BW
Phone: 442074366022
Fax: 448453899366
E-mail: info@advantagecapital.co.uk
Website: www.advantagecapital.co.uk

Management and Staff

Martin Bodenham, Co-Founder
Trevor Jones, Co-Founder

Type of Firm

Private Equity Firm

Association Membership

British Venture Capital Association (BVCA)

Project Preferences

Role in Financing:
Prefer role as deal originator

Type of Financing Preferred:
Leveraged Buyout
Management Buyouts

Geographical Preferences

International Preferences:
United Kingdom
Europe

Industry Preferences

In Financial Services prefer:
Financial Services

Additional Information

Year Founded: 2001
Current Activity Level : Actively seeking new investments
Method of Compensation: Return on invest. most important, but chg. closing fees, service fees, etc.

ADVANTAGE CAPITAL PARTNERS

909 Poydras Street
Suite 2230
New Orleans, LA USA 70112
Phone: 5045224850
Fax: 5045224950
Website: www.advantagecap.com

Other Offices

174 West Comstock Avenue
Suite 209
WINTER PARK, FL USA 32789

Phone: 4074546184
Fax: 4077408091

5000 Plaza on the Lake
Suite 195
WEST LAKE HILLS, TX USA 78746
Phone: 5123801168
Fax: 5122411186

1911 Elmore Avenue
DOWNERS GROVE, IL USA 60515
Phone: 6302411848
Fax: 630241836

c/o Eastside Partners
207 East Side Square, Suite 200
HUNTSVILLE, AL USA 35801
Phone: 6084412700
Fax: 6084412727

Five Warren Street
Suite 204
WEST GLENS FALLS, NY USA 12801
Phone: 5187430060
Fax: 5187431787

6293 Silverado Trail
FAIRFIELD, CA USA 94558
Phone: 7079442310
Fax: 7079450161

2445 M Street, Northwest
Suite 234
WASHINGTON, DC USA 20037
Phone: 2024574190
Fax: 2024574191

c/o Venture Investors
505 South Rosa Road., Suite 100
FITCHBURG, WI USA 53719
Phone: 6084412700
Fax: 6084412727

c/o Wolf Asset Management Corporation
5690 DTC Boulevard, Suite 285 West
GREENWOOD VILLAGE, CO USA 80111
Phone: 3033214800
Fax: 3034689586

Management and Staff
Alyson Appleton, Vice President
Cara Schiffman, Vice President
Charles Booker, Principal
Damon Rawie, Managing Director
James O Rourke, Managing Director
Jeffrey Craver, Principal
Jeffrey Gentsch, Venture Partner
Jonathan Goldstein, Managing Director
Justin Obletz, Principal
Louis Dubuque, Managing Director
Maurice Doyle, Managing Director
Philip Ruppel, Vice President
Ryan Dressler, Vice President
Ryan Brennan, Vice President
Steven Stull, President, Founder

Stuart Noel, Vice President
Thomas Bitting, Vice President

Type of Firm
Private Equity Firm

Association Membership
Community Development Venture Capital Alliance
National Venture Capital Association - USA (NVCA)

Project Preferences
Role in Financing:
Will function either as deal originator or investor in deals created by others

Type of Financing Preferred:
Leveraged Buyout
Early Stage
Expansion
Mezzanine
Balanced
Later Stage

Size of Investments Considered:
Min Size of Investment Considered (000s): $500
Max Size of Investment Considered (000s): $10,000

Geographical Preferences
United States Preferences:
Illinois
Mississippi
Nebraska
Alabama
Oregon
Wisconsin
Colorado
Connecticut
Florida
Louisiana
Missouri
Washington
Arkansas
Kentucky
Maine
New York
Texas

Industry Focus
(% based on actual investment)
Other Products	24.4%
Industrial/Energy	13.6%
Medical/Health	11.3%
Consumer Related	11.1%
Internet Specific	9.1%
Biotechnology	8.2%
Communications and Media	7.2%
Computer Software and Services	6.1%
Computer Hardware	4.8%
Semiconductors/Other Elect.	4.2%

Additional Information
Name of Most Recent Fund: Advantage Capital Connecticut Partners I, L.P.
Most Recent Fund Was Raised: 12/20/2010
Year Founded: 1992
Capital Under Management: $650,000,000
Current Activity Level : Actively seeking new investments
Method of Compensation: Return on invest. most important, but chg. closing fees, service fees, etc.

ADVANTAGE PARTNERS LLP

4-1-28 Toranomon, Minato-ku
17F, Toranomon Towers Office
Tokyo, Japan 105-0001
Phone: 81354258202
Website: www.advantagepartners.com

Other Offices
No. 8 Queen's Road
13/F
Central, Hong Kong

Type of Firm
Private Equity Firm

Project Preferences
Type of Financing Preferred:
Leveraged Buyout
Expansion
Turnaround
Management Buyouts
Acquisition

Geographical Preferences
International Preferences:
Japan

Industry Focus
(% based on actual investment)
Other Products	28.9%
Computer Software and Services	24.1%
Consumer Related	19.4%
Communications and Media	19.4%
Medical/Health	6.4%
Internet Specific	1.8%

Additional Information
Year Founded: 1992
Capital Under Management: $535,000,000
Current Activity Level : Actively seeking new investments

ADVANTEC UNTERNEH-MENSBETEIL

Grunewaldstrasse 22
Berlin, Germany 12165
Phone: 49302190880
Fax: 493021908890
E-mail: berlin@advantec.net
Website: www.advantec-ag.com

Management and Staff
Bernd Henke, Managing Director

Type of Firm
Private Equity Firm

Project Preferences

Type of Financing Preferred:
Early Stage
Seed
Startup

Geographical Preferences

International Preferences:
Germany

Industry Preferences

In Communications prefer:
Telecommunications

In Internet Specific prefer:
Internet

In Biotechnology prefer:
Biotechnology

In Medical/Health prefer:
Medical/Health
Medical Diagnostics

In Business Serv. prefer:
Services

Additional Information
Year Founded: 1998
Current Activity Level : Actively seeking new investments

ADVANTUM INVESTMENTS SP Z O O

Plac Narutowicza 1/6
Plock, Poland 09-400
Phone: 48242627205
E-mail: poczta@advantum.pl
Website: advantum.pl

Type of Firm
Private Equity Firm

Project Preferences

Type of Financing Preferred:
Leveraged Buyout
Generalist PE
Later Stage
Acquisition

Geographical Preferences

International Preferences:
Central Europe
Europe
Eastern Europe

Industry Preferences

In Consumer Related prefer:
Food/Beverage

In Financial Services prefer:
Financial Services
Real Estate

Additional Information
Year Founded: 2010
Current Activity Level : Actively seeking new investments

ADVANTUS CAPITAL MANAGEMENT INC

400 Robert Street North
Saint Paul, MN USA 55101
Website: www.advantuscapital.com

Management and Staff
David Kuplic, President
Robert Senkler, President

Type of Firm
Insurance Firm Affiliate

Project Preferences

Type of Financing Preferred:
Fund of Funds

Additional Information
Year Founded: 2002
Current Activity Level : Actively seeking new investments

ADVENGYS ADVANCED ENERGY SYSTEMS AG

Passauer Platz 2
Wien, Austria 1010
Phone: 4315336013
Fax: 431533601313
E-mail: office@advengys.com
Website: www.advengys.com

Type of Firm
Private Equity Firm

Additional Information
Year Founded: 2008
Current Activity Level : Actively seeking new investments

ADVENT CAPITAL AND FINANCE CORP

105 Paseo De Roxas
6th Floor SSHG Law Center
Makati City, Philippines 1200
Phone: 63-2-813-0188
Fax: 63-2-817-1728
Website: www.allasiacapital.com.ph

Type of Firm
Bank Affiliated

Project Preferences

Type of Financing Preferred:
Expansion
Later Stage

Geographical Preferences

International Preferences:
Philippines

Industry Preferences

In Consumer Related prefer:
Consumer Products
Consumer Services

Additional Information
Year Founded: 1995
Current Activity Level : Actively seeking new investments

ADVENT INTERNATIONAL CORP

75 State Street, 29th Floor
Boston, MA USA 02109
Phone: 6179519400
Fax: 6179510566
Website: www.adventinternational.com

Other Offices
Via Sant' Andrea 19
Milan, Italy 20121
Phone: 3927712981
Fax: 39277129888

8-10 rue Lamennais
Paris, France 75008
Phone: 33155372900
Fax: 33155372929

Strawinskylaan 3145
Amsterdam, Netherlands 1077 ZX
Phone: 31203012530
Fax: 31203012539

Av. Del Libertador 498 Floor 13 North
Buenos Aires, Argentina
Phone: 541150778900
Fax: 541150778910

111 Buckingham Palace Road
London, United Kingdom SW1W 0SR
Phone: 442073330800
Fax: 442073330801

Dr. Annie Besant Road, Worli
#406, 4th Floor, Ceejay House
Mumbai, India 400018
Phone: 912240573000
Fax: 912240573001

No.1601 Nanjing West Road
Unit 3601, Park Place
Shanghai, China
Phone: 862161706322

Av. Brig. Faria Lima 3311
Sao Paulo, Brazil 04538-133
Phone: 551130146800
Fax: 551130146820

Warsaw Financial Center
ul. Emilii Plater 53
Warsaw, Poland 00-113
Phone: 48226275141
Fax: 48226275140

Serrano, n 57-2
Madrid, Spain 28006
Phone: 34917454860
Fax: 34917454861

Buyukdere Caddesi no.191
Apa Giz Plaza, Kat 12
Istanbul, Turkey 34394
Phone: 902123860600
Fax: 902123860601

Edificio Omega
Campos Eliseos 345-7 piso
Col Polanco, Mexico 11560
Phone: 525552810303
Fax: 525552810999

19-21 Bohdana Khmelnitskogo Street
10th Floor, Leonardo Business Center - 2
Kiev, Ukraine 01030
Phone: 38442204010
Fax: 38442204011

375 Park Avenue
New York, NY USA 10152
Phone: 12128138300
Fax: 12124516503

Avenida Calle 82 10 Avenue
Suite 33, Oficina 902
Bogota, Colombia
Phone: 5712544747

Westhafenplatz 1
Frankfurt am Main, Germany 60327
Phone: 49699552700
Fax: 496995527020

Na Porici 3a
Palladium
Prague, Czech Republic 110 00
Phone: 420234749750
Fax: 420234749759

89-97 Grigore Alexandrescu Street
Third Floor
Bucharest, Romania 010624
Phone: 40212111602
Fax: 40212111602

Management and Staff

Albena Vassileva, Managing Director
Alfredo Alfaro, Managing Partner
Andrew Crawford, Principal
Antonio Moya-Angeler, Managing Director
Carmine Petrone, Vice President
Cedric Chateau, Managing Director
Christian Mruck, Managing Partner
Christopher Ives, Vice President
Christopher Egan, Managing Director
Christopher Pike, Managing Director
David Mussafer, Managing Partner
David McKenna, Managing Partner
Diego Serebrisky, Managing Director
Emma Popa-Radu, Managing Director
Eric Wei, Principal
Eric Adjoubel, Managing Director
Filippo De Vecchi, Managing Director
Francesco De Giglio, Managing Director
Fred Wakeman, Managing Partner
Gabriel Gomez, Principal
Georg Stratenwerth, Managing Director
Guillaume Darbon, Managing Director
Gurinder Grewal, Principal
Humphrey Battcock, Managing Partner
Jaime Carvajal Urquijo, Managing Director
James Westra, Managing Director
James Brocklebank, Managing Director
Jeff Case, Principal
Jim McGee, Managing Director
Joanna James, Managing Partner
John Singer, Managing Partner
John Maldonado, Managing Director
Juan Diaz-Laviada, Managing Director
Juan Torres, Managing Partner
Juan Pablo Zucchini, Managing Director
Kevin Feinblum, Principal
Lauren Bouffard, Vice President
Luis Camilleri, Managing Director
Luis Solorzano, Managing Director
Mauricio Salgar, Managing Director
Mohammed Anjarwala, Principal
Monika Morali-Efinowicz, Managing Director
Pascal Stefani, Managing Director
Patrice Etlin, Managing Partner
Paul Ferrari, Managing Director
Robert Taylor, Managing Partner
Robert Brown, Managing Director
Ronald Sheldon, Managing Director
Rory Pope, Managing Director
Santiago Castillo, Managing Director
Sarah Smith, Vice President
Stephen Hoffmeister, Managing Director
Steven Collins, Managing Director
Tamas Nagy, Managing Director
Timothy Franks, Managing Director
Tom Lauer, Managing Partner
Tricia Patrick, Managing Director
Will Schmidt, Managing Partner

Type of Firm

Private Equity Firm

Association Membership

Brazilian Venture Capital Association (ABCR)
British Venture Capital Association (BVCA)
Hong Kong Venture Capital Association (HKVCA)
French Venture Capital Association (AFIC)
Hungarian Venture Capital Association (HVCA)
Danish Venture Capital Association (DVCA)
German Venture Capital Association (BVK)
Czech Venture Capital Association (CVCA)
Polish Venture Capital Association (PSIC/PPEA)
Swedish Venture Capital Association (SVCA)
European Private Equity and Venture Capital Assoc.
Dutch Venture Capital Associaton (NVP)
Spanish Venture Capital Association (ASCRI)

Project Preferences

Role in Financing:
Prefer role as deal originator but will also invest in deals created by others

Type of Financing Preferred:
Leveraged Buyout
Generalist PE
Balanced
Management Buyouts
Acquisition

Size of Investments Considered:
Min Size of Investment Considered (000s): $20,000
Max Size of Investment Considered (000s): $60,000

Geographical Preferences

United States Preferences:
North America
All U.S.

Canadian Preferences:
All Canada

International Preferences:
Latin America
Central Europe
Europe
Argentina
Western Europe
Mexico
Eastern Europe
Brazil
Ukraine
Asia
Colombia
All International

Industry Focus

(% based on actual investment)

Consumer Related	27.6%
Other Products	22.1%
Medical/Health	21.2%
Computer Software and Services	9.6%
Communications and Media	6.0%
Internet Specific	4.1%
Industrial/Energy	3.5%
Computer Hardware	2.4%
Biotechnology	2.2%
Semiconductors/Other Elect.	1.5%

Additional Information
Year Founded: 1984
Capital Under Management: $10,000,000,000
Current Activity Level: Actively seeking new investments
Method of Compensation: Return on investment is of primary concern, do not charge fees

ADVENT MORRO EQUITY PARTNERS INC

206 Tetuan Street
Banco Popular Bldg. Suite 903
Viejo San Juan, PR USA 00902
Phone: 7877255285
Fax: 7877211735
Website: www.adventmorro.com

Management and Staff
Cyril Meduna, President
Mariel Lama, Principal

Type of Firm
Private Equity Firm

Project Preferences

Role in Financing:
Will function either as deal originator or investor in deals created by others

Type of Financing Preferred:
Second Stage Financing
Leveraged Buyout
Early Stage
Expansion
Generalist PE
Balanced
Turnaround
Later Stage
Management Buyouts
First Stage Financing
Acquisition
Recapitalizations

Size of Investments Considered:
Min Size of Investment Considered (000s): $2,500
Max Size of Investment Considered (000s): $10,000

Geographical Preferences

International Preferences:
Puerto Rico

Industry Preferences

In Communications prefer:
Commercial Communications
Telecommunications
Wireless Communications
Data Communications

In Computer Hardware prefer:
Integrated Turnkey System

In Computer Software prefer:
Computer Services
Systems Software
Applications Software

In Internet Specific prefer:
E-Commerce Technology
Internet
Web Aggregation/Portals

In Medical/Health prefer:
Health Services

In Consumer Related prefer:
Consumer
Retail
Food/Beverage
Hotels and Resorts
Education Related

In Financial Services prefer:
Financial Services

In Business Serv. prefer:
Distribution

In Manufact. prefer:
Manufacturing

Additional Information
Name of Most Recent Fund: Guayacon Private Equity Fund L.P. II-A
Most Recent Fund Was Raised: 05/02/2007
Year Founded: 1989
Capital Under Management: $52,000,000
Current Activity Level: Actively seeking new investments
Method of Compensation: Return on invest. most important, but chg. closing fees, service fees, etc.

ADVENT PRIVATE CAPITAL PTY LTD

40 City Road
Level 17, HWT Tower
Southbank, Australia 3006
Phone: 61396909566
Fax: 61396909466
E-mail: enquiry@adventpc.com.au
Website: www.adventprivatecapital.com.au

Management and Staff
Rupert Harrington, Managing Director

Type of Firm
Private Equity Firm

Association Membership
Australian Venture Capital Association (AVCAL)

Project Preferences

Role in Financing:
Prefer role as deal originator but will also invest in deals created by others

Type of Financing Preferred:
Leveraged Buyout
Expansion
Generalist PE
Later Stage
Management Buyouts
Acquisition
Industry Rollups

Geographical Preferences

International Preferences:
Australia
New Zealand

Industry Preferences

In Computer Software prefer:
Software

In Medical/Health prefer:
Medical/Health

In Consumer Related prefer:
Entertainment and Leisure
Consumer Services

Additional Information
Name of Most Recent Fund: Advent 6
Most Recent Fund Was Raised: 11/30/2011
Year Founded: 1984
Capital Under Management: $571,100,000
Current Activity Level: Actively seeking new investments
Method of Compensation: Return on investment is of primary concern, do not charge fees

ADVENT VENTURE PARTNERS LLP

158-160 North Gower Street
London, United Kingdom NW1 2ND
Phone: 44279322100
Fax: 44279322174
E-mail: info@adventventures.com
Website: www.adventventures.com

Other Offices
25 Buckingham Gate
London, United Kingdom SW1E 6LD
Phone: 44279322100
Fax: 44278281474

Management and Staff
Alain Huriez, Venture Partner
Andrew Wood, Venture Partner
Dale Pfost, General Partner
Donald Drakeman, Venture Partner
Frederic Court, General Partner
Kaasim Mahmood, Partner
Les Gabb, Partner
Michael Chalfen, General Partner
Peter Baines, General Partner
Rajesh Parekh, General Partner
Shahzad Malik, General Partner
Stephan Gueorguiev, Principal

Type of Firm
Private Equity Firm

Association Membership
British Venture Capital Association (BVCA)
European Private Equity and Venture Capital Assoc.

Project Preferences

Role in Financing:
Prefer role as deal originator but will also invest in deals created by others

Type of Financing Preferred:
Leveraged Buyout
Early Stage
Balanced
Later Stage

Geographical Preferences

United States Preferences:

International Preferences:
United Kingdom
Europe

Industry Focus
(% based on actual investment)
Biotechnology	32.0%
Medical/Health	25.4%
Internet Specific	12.6%
Computer Software and Services	10.3%
Communications and Media	7.0%
Semiconductors/Other Elect.	5.0%
Computer Hardware	2.9%
Other Products	2.3%
Industrial/Energy	1.6%
Consumer Related	0.9%

Additional Information
Name of Most Recent Fund: Advent Life Sciences Fund I
Most Recent Fund Was Raised: 11/24/2010
Year Founded: 1981
Capital Under Management: $940,600,000
Current Activity Level : Actively seeking new investments

ADVEQ MANAGEMENT AG
Affolternstrasse 56
Zurich, Switzerland 8050
Phone: 41584455555
E-mail: info@adveq.com
Website: www.adveq.com

Other Offices
An der Welle 4
Frankfurt am Main, Germany 60322
Phone: 49-69-7593-8586
Fax: 49-69-7593-8319

8 Century Avenue, Pudong
Shanghai International Finance Center
Shanghai, China 200120
Phone: 86 (0)21 6062 7191
Fax: 86 (0)21 6062 7288

100 Park Avenue
Suite 2800
NEW YORK, NY USA 10017
Phone: 212-488-5330
Fax: 212-297-1743

42 Brook Street
London, United Kingdom W1K 5DB
Phone: 44203 008 7179

1206K-1206L, 12th Floor, Beijing Excel
6 Wudinghou Street, Xicheng District
Beijing, China 100032
Phone: 86-10-8800-3758
Fax: 86-10-8800-3868

Management and Staff
Berry Polmann, Vice President
Bruno Raschle, Managing Director
Lee Gardella, Managing Director
Markus Emberger, Vice President
Nils Rode, Managing Director
Philippe Bucher, Managing Director
Rainer Ender, Managing Director
Ron Li, Managing Director
Sanjay Gupta, Vice President
Steven Yang, Vice President
Tim Creed, Managing Director

Type of Firm
Private Equity Advisor or Fund of Funds

Association Membership
Swiss Venture Capital Association (SECA)
European Private Equity and Venture Capital Assoc.

Project Preferences

Type of Financing Preferred:
Fund of Funds
Fund of Funds of Second

Geographical Preferences

United States Preferences:
All U.S.

International Preferences:
Europe
Australia
Asia

Additional Information
Name of Most Recent Fund: Adveq Secondaries II
Most Recent Fund Was Raised: 09/30/2013
Year Founded: 1997
Capital Under Management: $5,457,800,000
Current Activity Level : Actively seeking new investments

ADVISUM GMBH
Wilmersdorfer Strasse 98/99
Berlin, Germany 10629
Phone: 49-30-688-3040
Fax: 49-30-688304199
E-mail: info@advisum.de
Website: www.advisum.de

Other Offices
Maximilianstrasse 47
Munich, Germany 80538
Phone: 49-89-210-2000
Fax: 49-89-2102-0099

Management and Staff
Jan Widenhaupt, Managing Director
Manfred Gabriel, Partner

Type of Firm
Investment Management Firm

Project Preferences

Type of Financing Preferred:
Balanced
Turnaround

Geographical Preferences

International Preferences:
Switzerland
Austria
Germany

Industry Preferences

In Communications prefer:
Telecommunications

In Consumer Related prefer:
Retail

In Financial Services prefer:
Real Estate

In Business Serv. prefer:
Services
Media

Additional Information
Year Founded: 2001
Capital Under Management: $698,234,000
Current Activity Level : Actively seeking new investments

AEA INVESTORS LLC
666 Fifth Avenue
36th Floor
New York, NY USA 10103
Phone: 2126445900
Fax: 2128881459
E-mail: info@aeainvestors.com
Website: www.aeainvestors.com

Other Offices

78 Brook Street
London, United Kingdom W1K 5EF
Phone: 44-20-7659-7800
Fax: 44-20-7491-2155

Widenmayerstr 3
Munchen, Germany 80538
Phone: 49-89-244-1730
Fax: 49-89-244-173860

288 Nanjing Road West
Suite 1901, 19th Floor
Shanghai, China 200003
Phone: 862123087888
Fax: 862123087880

AIA Central
Suite 2909, 29th Floor
Central, Hong Kong
Phone: 852-3556-8888
Fax: 852-3556-8808

Two Stamford Plaza
281 Tresser Boulevard, 15th FL
Stamford, CT USA 06901
Phone: 203-564-2660
Fax: 203-564-2661

Management and Staff

A. David Manzano, Managing Director
Alan Wilkinson, Managing Director
Alex Mehfar, Vice President
Alexander Hoffman, Vice President
Axel Holtrup, Managing Director
Baron Carlson, Managing Director
Brian Hoesterey, Managing Director
Cheri Fraiman, Vice President
Christian Johnson, Principal
Damon Ball, Managing Director
Dan Schorr, Vice President
J. Louis Sharpe, Managing Director
James Villa, Vice President
James Ho, Principal
Jessica Hodgkinson, Vice President
John Smith, Vice President
John Cozzi, Managing Director
Joseph Carrabino, Managing Director
Justin de la Chapelle, Vice President
Leo Fang, Vice President
Martin Eltrich, Managing Director
Michael Maechling, Vice President
Nannette McNally, Managing Director
Oliver Frey, Managing Director
Philipp Meyer, Vice President
Rahul Goyal, Principal
Robin Chiang, Vice President
Scott Zoellner, Managing Director
Shivanandan Dalvie, Managing Director
Stephen Elia, Principal
Susan Shui-Shien Lin, Managing Director
Thomas Pryma, Managing Director
Thomas Groves, Managing Director
Tim Whelan, Vice President
Todd Welsch, Vice President

Vinay Kumar, Vice President

Type of Firm
Private Equity Firm

Association Membership
China Venture Capital Association

Project Preferences

Type of Financing Preferred:
Leveraged Buyout
Mezzanine
Later Stage
Management Buyouts
Acquisition
Recapitalizations

Geographical Preferences

United States Preferences:
All U.S.

International Preferences:
Europe
Asia

Industry Focus

(% based on actual investment)
Consumer Related	32.8%
Medical/Health	18.0%
Industrial/Energy	15.1%
Computer Software and Services	12.5%
Communications and Media	11.8%
Other Products	8.4%
Biotechnology	1.5%
Semiconductors/Other Elect.	0.1%

Additional Information
Name of Most Recent Fund: AEA Mezzanine Fund III, L.P.
Most Recent Fund Was Raised: 03/27/2013
Year Founded: 1968
Capital Under Management: $3,600,000,000
Current Activity Level : Actively seeking new investments

AEGIS LLC

1760 Old Meadow Road
Suite 400
Stamford, CT USA 06901
Phone: 5714821260
E-mail: info@aegisworld.us
Website: www.aegisworld.us

Type of Firm
Private Equity Firm

Project Preferences

Type of Financing Preferred:
Balanced

Additional Information
Year Founded: 2015
Current Activity Level : Actively seeking new investments

AEQUITAS CAPITAL MANAGEMENT INC

5300 Meadows Road
Suite 400
Lake Oswego, OR USA 97035
Phone: 5034193500
Fax: 5034193530
E-mail: info@aequitascapital.com
Website: www.aequitascapital.com

Other Offices

Bellevue Way Center
800 Bellevue Way Northeast, Suite 400
Bellevue, WA USA 98004
Phone: 425-462-4041
Fax: 425-462-4046

1250 Prospect Street
Suite 101
La Jolla, CA USA 92037
Phone: 5034193500
Fax: 5034193530

50 Osgood Place
Suite 320
San Francisco, CA USA 94133
Phone: 5034193500
Fax: 5034193530

455 Park Avenue
Suite 900
New York, NY USA 10022
Phone: 5034193500
Fax: 5034193530

Management and Staff
Thomas Goila, Senior Managing Director

Type of Firm
Investment Management Firm

Project Preferences

Type of Financing Preferred:
Acquisition

Industry Preferences

In Consumer Related prefer:
Education Related

In Industrial/Energy prefer:
Alternative Energy

In Manufact. prefer:
Manufacturing

Additional Information
Year Founded: 1993
Capital Under Management: $102,071,000
Current Activity Level : Actively seeking new investments

AEQUITOS CAPITAL MANAGEMENT LLC

600 Six Flags Drive
Suite 418
Arlington, TX USA 76011
Phone: 8177517167
E-mail: contact@aequitosmgmt.com
Website: www.aequitosmgmt.com

Management and Staff
David Groce, Chief Operating Officer
Larry Sackett, Managing Director

Type of Firm
Private Equity Firm

Project Preferences

Type of Financing Preferred:
Leveraged Buyout
Mezzanine
Turnaround
Management Buyouts
Distressed Debt
Recapitalizations

Industry Preferences

In Financial Services prefer:
Real Estate

Additional Information
Year Founded: 2011
Current Activity Level : Actively seeking new investments

AEROEQUITY PARTNERS LLC

15 Lake Street
Suite 235
Savannah, GA USA 31411
Phone: 9125983102
Fax: 4047592448
Website: www.aeroequity.com

Other Offices

39 Locust Avenue
Suite 204
New Canaan, CT USA 06840
Phone: 203-594-1490
Fax: 404-759-2448

One Royal Palm Place
1877 S. Federal Hwy., Ste. 206
Boca Raton, FL USA 33432
Phone: 561-392-6910
Fax: 404-759-2448

Management and Staff
David Howe, Partner
Dennis Walsh, General Partner
Jon Nemo, Partner
Michael Greene, Managing Partner
Thomas Brew, General Partner
Thomas Churbuck, Managing Partner
Wayne Garrett, General Partner

Type of Firm
Private Equity Firm

Project Preferences

Type of Financing Preferred:
Leveraged Buyout
Acquisition

Geographical Preferences

United States Preferences:
North America

Industry Preferences

In Transportation prefer:
Aerospace

In Business Serv. prefer:
Distribution

In Manufact. prefer:
Manufacturing

Additional Information
Year Founded: 2004
Capital Under Management: $680,000,000
Current Activity Level : Actively seeking new investments

AESCAP VENTURE I BV

Strawinskylaan 1525
WTC World Trade Center
Amsterdam, Netherlands 1077 XX
Phone: 31205702940
Fax: 31206737846
E-mail: info@aescap.com

Management and Staff
Domenico Valerio, General Partner
Hakan Goker, Partner
Michiel de Haan, General Partner
Patrick Krol, General Partner
Rene Beukema, Partner

Type of Firm
Private Equity Firm

Association Membership
European Private Equity and Venture Capital Assoc.
Dutch Venture Capital Associaton (NVP)

Project Preferences

Type of Financing Preferred:
Early Stage
Balanced
Seed
Startup

Size of Investments Considered:
Min Size of Investment Considered (000s): $2,761
Max Size of Investment Considered (000s): $6,903

Geographical Preferences

International Preferences:
Europe

Industry Preferences

In Biotechnology prefer:
Biotechnology

In Medical/Health prefer:
Medical/Health
Medical Diagnostics
Medical Therapeutics
Pharmaceuticals

Additional Information
Year Founded: 2006
Capital Under Management: $6,600,000
Current Activity Level : Actively seeking new investments

AETERNAM STELLA FINANCIAL HOLDINGS CO LTD

Room 201, Building A
No. 1, Qianwan First Road
Shenzhen, China 518000
Phone: 862164668700
Website: www.as-fh.com

Type of Firm
Private Equity Firm

Project Preferences

Type of Financing Preferred:
Balanced

Geographical Preferences

International Preferences:
China

Industry Preferences

In Medical/Health prefer:
Medical/Health

In Consumer Related prefer:
Consumer
Education Related

In Industrial/Energy prefer:
Robotics

AETHER INVESTMENT PARTNERS LLC

1900 Sixteenth Street
Suite 825
Denver, CO USA 80202
Phone: 7209614190
Fax: 7209201690
E-mail: info@aetherip.com
Website: aetherip.com

Other Offices
1515 Wynkoop Street
Suite 310
Denver, CO USA 80202

Management and Staff
David Rhoades, Chief Operating Officer
Sean Goodrich, Co-Founder
Troy Schell, Co-Founder

Type of Firm
Private Equity Advisor or Fund of Funds

Project Preferences

Type of Financing Preferred:
Fund of Funds

Industry Preferences

In Industrial/Energy prefer:
Energy
Oil and Gas Exploration
Oil & Gas Drilling, Explor

In Agr/Forestr/Fish prefer:
Agriculture related
Mining and Minerals

Additional Information
Name of Most Recent Fund: Aether Real Assets III, L.P.
Most Recent Fund Was Raised: 12/09/2013
Year Founded: 2008
Capital Under Management: $799,500,000
Current Activity Level : Actively seeking new investments

AETIUS CAPITAL PTE LTD

Level 25 North Tower
One Raffles Quay, Singapore 048583
Website: aetiuscapital.com

Management and Staff
Eugene Goh, Managing Partner

Type of Firm
Private Equity Firm

Project Preferences

Type of Financing Preferred:
Early Stage
Expansion
Later Stage

Additional Information
Year Founded: 1969
Current Activity Level : Actively seeking new investments

AFFENTRANGER ASSOCIATES SA

Uraniastrasse 26
Zurich, Switzerland 8001
Phone: 41445752828
Fax: 41445752827
E-mail: info@aasa.com
Website: www.aasa.com

Other Offices
Kappelergasse 14
Zurich, Switzerland 8001
Phone: 41-442-215-053
Fax: 41-442-215-055

Management and Staff
Lukas Andre, Managing Partner
Nicolas Fulpius, Partner

Type of Firm
Private Equity Firm

Association Membership
Swiss Venture Capital Association (SECA)

Project Preferences

Type of Financing Preferred:
Leveraged Buyout
Early Stage
Turnaround
Later Stage
Seed
Startup
Recapitalizations

Geographical Preferences

International Preferences:
Europe
Switzerland
Germany

Industry Preferences

In Biotechnology prefer:
Biotechnology

In Medical/Health prefer:
Medical/Health
Medical Therapeutics

In Consumer Related prefer:
Entertainment and Leisure

Additional Information
Year Founded: 2002
Capital Under Management: $200,000,000
Current Activity Level : Actively seeking new investments

AFFINITY CAPITAL MANAGEMENT CO

901 Marquette Avenue
Suite 2820
Minneapolis, MN USA 55402
Phone: 6122529900
Fax: 6122529911
Website: www.affinitycapitalmanagement.com

Management and Staff
B. Kristine Johnson, President
Gregory Glarner, Venture Partner
Robin Dowdle, Chief Financial Officer

Type of Firm
Private Equity Firm

Project Preferences

Role in Financing:
Will function either as deal originator or investor in deals created by others

Type of Financing Preferred:
Early Stage
Expansion
Seed
Startup

Geographical Preferences

United States Preferences:
Midwest

Industry Focus
(% based on actual investment)

Medical/Health	60.2%
Internet Specific	12.3%
Computer Hardware	10.8%
Biotechnology	8.0%
Computer Software and Services	6.8%
Consumer Related	1.7%
Semiconductors/Other Elect.	0.1%
Communications and Media	0.0%

Additional Information
Name of Most Recent Fund: Affinity Ventures V, L.P.
Most Recent Fund Was Raised: 03/31/2008
Year Founded: 1993
Capital Under Management: $165,000,000
Current Activity Level : Actively seeking new investments
Method of Compensation: Return on investment is of primary concern, do not charge fees

AFFINITY EQUITY PARTNERS HK LTD

Eight Connaught Place
One Exchange Square, 40/F
Central, Hong Kong
Phone: 85231028329
Fax: 85231028321

Other Offices

9 Temasek Boulevard
#27-03 Suntec Tower Two
Singapore, Singapore 038989
Phone: 65-6238-2260
Fax: 65-6238-7765

No. 5 Jia, ShuGuangXiLi
Room 1506, Tower H, Phoenix Place
Beijing, China 100028
Phone: 861056383380
Fax: 861056383398

10F, The Energy Bldg, SCBD Lot 11A
Jl. Jend. Sudirman Kav., 52-53
Jakarta, Indonesia 12190
Phone: 6221-2995-1665
Fax: 6221-2995-1666

5th Floor, Young Poong Bldg
33 Seorin-Dong, Chongro-ku
Seoul, South Korea 110-752
Phone: 822-399-7773
Fax: 822-399-7771

61 York Street
Level 7
Sydney, Australia 2000
Phone: 612-9299-0889
Fax: 612-9299-0809

Management and Staff

Brett Sutton, Partner
Chul-Joo Lee, Partner
Weng-Sun Mok, Partner
Young-Taeg Park, Managing Partner

Type of Firm

Private Equity Firm

Association Membership

Australian Venture Capital Association (AVCAL)
Singapore Venture Capital Association (SVCA)

Project Preferences

Role in Financing:
Prefer role as deal originator but will also invest in deals created by others

Type of Financing Preferred:
Leveraged Buyout
Management Buyouts
Acquisition

Geographical Preferences

International Preferences:
Asia Pacific
Taiwan
Hong Kong
China
Australia
Singapore
Korea, South
Japan

Industry Preferences

In Medical/Health prefer:
Medical/Health
Health Services

In Consumer Related prefer:
Retail
Food/Beverage
Consumer Products
Consumer Services

In Industrial/Energy prefer:
Industrial Products

In Financial Services prefer:
Financial Services
Insurance

In Business Serv. prefer:
Services

In Manufact. prefer:
Manufacturing

Additional Information

Year Founded: 2004
Capital Under Management: $700,000,000
Current Activity Level : Actively seeking new investments
Method of Compensation: Return on invest. most important, but chg. closing fees, service fees, etc.

AFINUM MANAGEMENT GMBH

Theatinerstrasse 7
Munich, Germany 80333
Phone: 498925543301
Fax: 498925543399
E-mail: info@afinum.de
Website: www.afinum.de

Other Offices

Dufourstrasse 48
Zurich, Switzerland 8024
Phone: 41435003300
Fax: 41435003301

Schottenring 16
Vienna, Austria 1010
Phone: 4319971846
Fax: 4319971846

2F, Loks Industrial Building
204 Tsat Tsz Mui Road
Hongkong, Hong Kong
Phone: 85238568588
Fax: 85281470183

Management and Staff

Berthold Schmidt-Forger, Partner
Gernot Eisinger, Founder
Jochen Klemmer, Partner
Michael Bonisch, Managing Director
Michael Hildisch, Partner
Robert Greitl, Chief Financial Officer
Thomas Buhler, Founder
Tobias Fauser, Partner

Type of Firm

Private Equity Firm

Association Membership

Swiss Venture Capital Association (SECA)

Project Preferences

Type of Financing Preferred:
Leveraged Buyout
Later Stage
Management Buyouts
Acquisition

Geographical Preferences

International Preferences:
Luxembourg

Industry Preferences

In Consumer Related prefer:
Consumer Products

In Industrial/Energy prefer:
Machinery

In Transportation prefer:
Transportation

In Manufact. prefer:
Manufacturing

Additional Information

Name of Most Recent Fund: AFINUM Siebte Beteiligungsgesellschaft mbH & Co. KG
Most Recent Fund Was Raised: 04/23/2013
Year Founded: 2000
Capital Under Management: $64,700,000
Current Activity Level : Actively seeking new investments

AFLAC CORPORATE VENTURES

1932 Wynnton Road
Columbus, GA USA 31999
Phone: 8009923522
Fax: 8774423522
Website: www.aflac.com

Type of Firm
Private Equity Firm

Project Preferences

Type of Financing Preferred:
Early Stage
Startup

Geographical Preferences

United States Preferences:

International Preferences:
Japan

Additional Information
Year Founded: 2017
Current Activity Level: Actively seeking new investments

AFORE CAPITAL LP
25 Taylor Street
San Francisco, CA USA 94102

Type of Firm
Private Equity Firm

Project Preferences

Type of Financing Preferred:
Early Stage
Expansion
Later Stage

Additional Information
Year Founded: 2016
Capital Under Management: $47,000,000
Current Activity Level: Actively seeking new investments

AFRICA GROUP LLC
3028 Cambridge Place NorthWest
Washington, DC USA 20007
Website: www.theafricagroup.com

Management and Staff
Elias Schulze, Managing Partner

Type of Firm
Private Equity Firm

Project Preferences

Type of Financing Preferred:
Balanced

Geographical Preferences

International Preferences:
Africa

Additional Information
Year Founded: 2009
Current Activity Level: Actively seeking new investments

AFRICAN AGRICULTURAL CAPITAL LTD
UMA Showground
Plot M697, 2nd Floor
Lugogo, Uganda
Phone: 2563122649834
Fax: 256312264985
E-mail: info@pearlcapital.net
Website: www.pearlcapital.net

Management and Staff
Tom Adlam, CEO & Managing Director

Type of Firm
Investment Management Firm

Project Preferences

Type of Financing Preferred:
Early Stage
Expansion
Balanced
Later Stage

Geographical Preferences

International Preferences:
Uganda
Tanzania
Kenya
Africa

Industry Preferences

In Agr/Forestr/Fish prefer:
Agribusiness
Agriculture related

Additional Information
Name of Most Recent Fund: Africa Seed Investment Fund
Most Recent Fund Was Raised: 12/31/2010
Year Founded: 2005
Current Activity Level: Actively seeking new investments

AFRICAN ALLIANCE PRIVATE EQUITY
African Alliance House
Fairgrounds Office Park
Gaborone, Botswana
Phone: 2673643900
Fax: 2304670050
E-mail: info@africanalliance.com
Website: www.africanalliance.com

Other Offices
Moshoeshoe Rd, Suite 4
SA Trust Building
Maseru, Lesotho
Phone: 266-22-314-678
Fax: 266-22-313-637

32 Cyber City Ebene
First Floor
Ebene, Mauritius
Phone: 230-404-7400
Fax: 230-467-7050

Ridge Ambassadorial Enclave
2nd Floor Heritage Tower
Accra, Ghana
Phone: 233-21-679-761
Fax: 233-21-679-698

Kenya Re Towers Upper Hill
4th Floor
Nairobi, Kenya 00506
Phone: 254-20-273-5154
Fax: 254-20-271-0247

Sir Glyn Jones Rd
Livingston Towers, 4th Floor
Blantyre, Malawi
Phone: 265-183-1995
Fax: 265-831-1859

23 Melrose Boulevard
Nedbank Building, 4th Floor
Melrose Arch, South Africa
Phone: 24-11-214-8300
Fax: 27-11-684-1052

Hotel Intercontinental, 3rd Floor
Rooms 346 and 348
Lusaka, Zambia 10101
Phone: 260-21-184-0512
Fax: 260-21-184-0513

Cnr Sishayi and Sozisa Roads
Nedbank Centre, 2nd Floor
Mbabane, Swaziland
Phone: 268-404-2002
Fax: 268-404-8391

Pilkington Street, Worker's House
1st Floor
Kampala, Uganda
Phone: 256-41-423-5577
Fax: 256-41-423-5575

12 Love Street
Windhoek, Namibia
Phone: 264-613-865-10
Fax: 264-613-046-71

Type of Firm
Bank Affiliated

Project Preferences

Type of Financing Preferred:
Leveraged Buyout
Early Stage
Expansion
Mezzanine
Generalist PE
Later Stage
Management Buyouts
Acquisition

Geographical Preferences

International Preferences:
Uganda
Africa

Industry Preferences

In Financial Services prefer:
Financial Services

In Business Serv. prefer:
Services

In Manufact. prefer:
Manufacturing

Additional Information
Year Founded: 2009
Current Activity Level : Actively seeking new investments

AFRICAN CAPITAL ALLIANCE

C&C Towers, Sanusi Fafunwa St.
Victoria Island
Lagos, Nigeria
Phone: 23412777000
Fax: 23412706908
E-mail: info@aca-web.com
Website: www.acagp.com

Other Offices
320, Park Avenue
28th Floor
New York, NY USA 10022
Phone: 212-508-9400
Fax: 212-508-9494

Management and Staff
Afolabi Oladele, Partner
Bunmi Adeoye, Vice President
Chief Ernest Shonekan, Partner
Emmanuel Assiak, Vice President
Gbenga Adetoro, Vice President
Kikelomo Longe, Vice President
Nkem Odibeli, Vice President
Obi Nwogugu, Principal
Okechukwu Enelamah, Chief Executive Officer
Olumide Obayomi, Vice President
Pascal Dozie, Partner
Paul Kokoricha, Partner
Sam Oniovosa, Chief Financial Officer
Tony Egbuna, Vice President

Type of Firm
Private Equity Firm

Association Membership
Emerging Markets Private Equity Association
Nigerian Venture Capital Association
African Venture Capital Association (AVCA)

Project Preferences

Type of Financing Preferred:
Value-Add
Early Stage
Expansion
Generalist PE
Balanced
Opportunistic

Size of Investments Considered:
Min Size of Investment Considered (000s): $2,000
Max Size of Investment Considered (000s): $7,000

Geographical Preferences

International Preferences:
Nigeria
Africa

Industry Preferences

In Communications prefer:
Communications and Media
Telecommunications
Data Communications

In Internet Specific prefer:
E-Commerce Technology
Internet

In Medical/Health prefer:
Medical/Health

In Industrial/Energy prefer:
Energy
Oil and Gas Exploration

In Transportation prefer:
Transportation

In Financial Services prefer:
Real Estate
Financial Services

In Business Serv. prefer:
Services

In Manufact. prefer:
Manufacturing

Additional Information
Year Founded: 1997
Capital Under Management: $83,400,000
Current Activity Level : Actively seeking new investments

AFRICAN FRONTIER CAPITAL PARTNERS LLP

19-21 Crawford Street
London, United Kingdom W1H 1PJ
E-mail: info@africanfrontiercapital.com
Website: www.africanfrontiercapital.com

Type of Firm
Investment Management Firm

Project Preferences

Type of Financing Preferred:
Leveraged Buyout
Expansion
Generalist PE
Turnaround
Acquisition

Geographical Preferences

International Preferences:
Uganda
Ghana
Mozambique
South Africa
Burundi

Industry Preferences

In Communications prefer:
Telecommunications

In Internet Specific prefer:
E-Commerce Technology

In Industrial/Energy prefer:
Energy
Oil and Gas Exploration

In Transportation prefer:
Transportation

Additional Information
Year Founded: 2015
Current Activity Level : Actively seeking new investments

AFRICAN LION MANAGEMENT LTD

15 Queen Street
Level Four
Melbourne, Australia 3000
Phone: 61396143980
Fax: 61396148009
Website: www.afl.co.za

Type of Firm
Private Equity Firm

Project Preferences

Pratt's Guide to Private Equity & Venture Capital Sources

Type of Financing Preferred:
Early Stage
Balanced

Geographical Preferences

International Preferences:
Africa

Industry Preferences

In Industrial/Energy prefer:
Coal Related

In Agr/Forestr/Fish prefer:
Mining and Minerals

Additional Information

Year Founded: 1999
Capital Under Management: $27,000,000
Current Activity Level : Actively seeking new investments

AFRICINVEST TUNISIA SARL

Centre urbain Nord
Integra Building
Tunis, Tunisia 1082
Phone: 21671189800
Fax: 21671189850
E-mail: tfg.mail@tuninvest.com
Website: www.africinvest.com

Other Offices

18, Avenue Docteur Crozet
5th Floor, Azur Building
Abidjan, Ivory Coast
Phone: 22520310080
Fax: 22520210045

12, Owena Street
Victoria Court, Parkview Estate
Lagos, Nigeria
Phone: 234-1-7406-535
Fax: 234-1-7386-487

16 Bis, Avenue de la Motte Piquet
Paris, France 75007

Chiromo Road
8th Floor, Tower 3, Mirage Building
Nairobi, Kenya 00202
Phone: 254-20-3861-965
Fax: 254-20-386-1967

Villa la Falaise
07 lot
Rais-Algiers, Algeria
Phone: 213770333683
Fax: 213770129916

Rue Bab Chellah
les Champs d'Anfa D
Casablanca, Morocco
Phone: 212-522-363-736
Fax: 212-522-393-959

Management and Staff

Fethi Mestiri, Managing Director

Type of Firm

Private Equity Firm

Association Membership

Tunisian Venture Capital Association
Gulf Venture Capital Association
Emerging Markets Private Equity Association
African Venture Capital Association (AVCA)

Project Preferences

Type of Financing Preferred:
Leveraged Buyout
Early Stage
Expansion
Later Stage
Management Buyouts
Acquisition

Size of Investments Considered:
Min Size of Investment Considered (000s): $200
Max Size of Investment Considered (000s): $2,500

Geographical Preferences

International Preferences:
Tunisia
Nigeria
Zambia
Egypt
Algeria
Ivory Coast
Kenya
Madagascar
Morocco
Libya
Africa
Venezuela

Industry Preferences

In Communications prefer:
Telecommunications
Wireless Communications

In Medical/Health prefer:
Pharmaceuticals

In Consumer Related prefer:
Entertainment and Leisure
Education Related

In Industrial/Energy prefer:
Energy
Industrial Products

In Transportation prefer:
Transportation
Aerospace

In Financial Services prefer:
Financial Services
Financial Services

In Manufact. prefer:
Manufacturing

In Agr/Forestr/Fish prefer:
Agribusiness
Agriculture related

Additional Information

Name of Most Recent Fund: Maghreb Private Equity Fund III LLC
Most Recent Fund Was Raised: 09/06/2011
Year Founded: 1994
Capital Under Management: $61,100,000
Current Activity Level : Actively seeking new investments

AFTVINNUPROUNARS-JOOUR SUOURLANDS

Austurvegi 56
Selfoss, Iceland 800
Phone: 3544822419
Fax: 3544822921
Website: www.sudur.is

Type of Firm

Private Equity Firm

Project Preferences

Type of Financing Preferred:
Generalist PE

Geographical Preferences

International Preferences:
Iceland

Additional Information

Year Founded: 1980
Current Activity Level : Actively seeking new investments

AG BD LLC

245 Park Avenue
New York, NY USA 10167
Phone: 2126922000
Fax: 2128679328
E-mail: information@angelogordon.com

Other Offices

19-29 Martin Place
Level 56, MLC Centre
Sydney, Australia NSW 2000

2000 Avenue of the Stars
Suite 1020
Los Angeles, CA USA 90067
Phone: 310-777-5440
Fax: 310-246-0796

25 Hanover Square
London, United Kingdom W1S 1JF
Phone: 44-207-758-5300
Fax: 44-207-758-5420

6-10-1, Roppongi Minato-ku
Roppongi Hills Mori Tower 17th Floor
Tokyo, Japan 106-6117
Phone: 81-35-474-5610
Fax: 81-35-474-5620

101 Burr Ridge Parkway
Suite 204
Burr Ridge, IL USA 60527

Herengracht 478
2nd Floor, Unit 9
Amsterdam, Netherlands 1017 CB
Phone: 31-20-262-0660
Fax: 31-20-262-0664

One Exchange Square
Suite 1604
Central, Hong Kong
Phone: 852-3416-7300
Fax: 852-3416-7500

9th Floor, Youngpoong Building
33 Seorin-Dong, Chongno-Gu
Seoul, South Korea 110-752
Phone: 822-733-9200
Fax: 822-733-9339

Management and Staff
Adam Schwartz, Managing Director
Aliana Spungen, Managing Director
Arthur Peponis, Managing Director
Christopher Williams, Managing Director
Colleen Casey, Managing Director
David Roberts, Senior Managing Director
Gareth Henry, Managing Director
Garrett Walls, Managing Director
Garrett Ryan, Partner
Gordon Whiting, Managing Director
Jenny Morton, Managing Director
Jonathan Lieberman, Managing Director
Joseph Wekselblatt, Chief Financial Officer
Joshua Baumgarten, Senior Managing Director
Linda Eichenbaum, Managing Director
Louise Wasso-Jonikas, Managing Director
M. Gordon, Co-Founder
Mark Maduras, Managing Director
Marsha Roth, Senior Managing Director
Matthew Brody, Managing Director
Michael Flynn, Managing Director
Phillip Filippelis, Managing Director
Richard Leonard, Managing Director
Rick Finger, Managing Director
Ruth Gitlin, Managing Director
Teddy Kaplan, Managing Director
Terri Herubin, Managing Director
Thomas Fuller, Senior Managing Director
Trevor Clark, Managing Director
Victoria Aston-Duff, Managing Director
Wilson Leung, Managing Director

Type of Firm
Private Equity Firm

Project Preferences

Type of Financing Preferred:
Leveraged Buyout
Value-Add
Generalist PE
Turnaround
Opportunistic
Other
Management Buyouts
Acquisition
Distressed Debt
Recapitalizations

Geographical Preferences

United States Preferences:
North America

International Preferences:
Europe
Asia
All International

Industry Focus
(% based on actual investment)

Other Products	62.0%
Consumer Related	35.2%
Internet Specific	1.2%
Computer Hardware	0.8%
Computer Software and Services	0.7%

Additional Information
Name of Most Recent Fund: AG Energy Partners, L.P.
Most Recent Fund Was Raised: 02/07/2014
Year Founded: 1988
Capital Under Management: $23,000,000,000
Current Activity Level : Actively seeking new investments

AG VENTURES ALLIANCE

2023 South Federal
Mason City, IA USA 50401
Website: www.agventuresalliance.com

Type of Firm
Private Equity Firm

Project Preferences

Type of Financing Preferred:
Early Stage
Expansion
Later Stage
Seed

Industry Preferences

In Consumer Related prefer:
Food/Beverage

In Agr/Forestr/Fish prefer:
Agriculture related

Additional Information
Year Founded: 1969
Current Activity Level : Actively seeking new investments

AGATE MEDICAL INVESTMENTS LP

37 Menachem Begin Road
Beit Rubinstein, 29th Floor
Tel Aviv, Israel 67134
Phone: 97235652285
Fax: 97235652284
E-mail: agate@agate-invest.com
Website: www.agate-invest.com

Management and Staff
Chanan Schneider, Managing Partner
Dan Naveh, Managing Partner
Michel Habib, Venture Partner
Rony Davidoff, Managing Partner

Type of Firm
Private Equity Firm

Project Preferences

Type of Financing Preferred:
Generalist PE

Geographical Preferences

International Preferences:
Israel
Asia

Industry Preferences

In Medical/Health prefer:
Medical/Health
Medical Therapeutics
Medical Products
Health Services

Additional Information
Name of Most Recent Fund: Agate Medical Investments, L.P.
Most Recent Fund Was Raised: 12/31/2007
Year Founded: 2007
Current Activity Level : Actively seeking new investments

AGDEVCO UK

8-14 Verulam Street
Peer House
London, United Kingdom WC1X 8LZ
Phone: 2075392650
Website: www.agdevco.com

Type of Firm
Private Equity Firm

Pratt's Guide to Private Equity & Venture Capital Sources

Project Preferences

Type of Financing Preferred:
Generalist PE
Balanced
Acquisition

Geographical Preferences

International Preferences:
South Africa
Africa

Industry Preferences

In Biotechnology prefer:
Agricultural/Animal Bio.

In Agr/Forestr/Fish prefer:
Agribusiness

Additional Information

Year Founded: 2009
Capital Under Management: $23,000,000
Current Activity Level : Actively seeking new investments

AGENCE FRANCAISE DE DEVELOPPEMENT EPIC

5, rue Roland Barthes
Paris, France 75012
Phone: 33153443131
Fax: 33144879939
Website: www.afd.fr

Type of Firm
Government Affiliated Program

Project Preferences

Type of Financing Preferred:
Generalist PE

Geographical Preferences

International Preferences:
Latin America
Middle East
Africa

Industry Preferences

In Agr/Forestr/Fish prefer:
Agribusiness

Additional Information

Year Founded: 1941
Capital Under Management: $57,315,000
Current Activity Level : Actively seeking new investments

AGENT CAPITAL LLC

810 Memorial Drive
Mezzanine Floor, Suite 107
Cambridge, MA USA 02139
Website: www.agentcapital.com

Type of Firm
Private Equity Firm

Project Preferences

Type of Financing Preferred:
Early Stage

Industry Preferences

In Biotechnology prefer:
Biotechnology

Additional Information

Year Founded: 1969
Capital Under Management: $52,000,000
Current Activity Level : Actively seeking new investments

AGGREGATE STOCKHOLM AB

Humlegardsgatan 5, 3 tr
Stockholm, Sweden 10240
Phone: 4686605580
Website: www.aggregatemedia.com

Type of Firm
Private Equity Firm

Project Preferences

Type of Financing Preferred:
Expansion

Geographical Preferences

International Preferences:
Sweden
Norway

Industry Preferences

In Communications prefer:
Communications and Media
Media and Entertainment

In Internet Specific prefer:
E-Commerce Technology
Ecommerce

In Business Serv. prefer:
Media

Additional Information

Year Founded: 2002
Current Activity Level : Actively seeking new investments

AGIC PARTNERS GMBH

Odeonsplatz 18
Munich, Germany 80539
Phone: 4989235135620
Fax: 4989235135629
E-mail: munich@agic-group.com
Website: www.agic-group.com

Type of Firm
Private Equity Firm

Project Preferences

Type of Financing Preferred:
Leveraged Buyout
Acquisition

Geographical Preferences

International Preferences:
Europe

Additional Information

Year Founded: 2015
Current Activity Level : Actively seeking new investments

AGILE CAPITAL PARTNERS

1808 Lagoon View Drive
Tiburon, CA USA 94920
Phone: 4157890186
E-mail: info@agilecapitalpartners.com
Website: www.agilecapitalpartners.com

Management and Staff
Jason Goldberg, Managing Partner
Mark Allen, Managing Partner

Type of Firm
Private Equity Firm

Project Preferences

Type of Financing Preferred:
Leveraged Buyout
Acquisition

Industry Preferences

In Computer Software prefer:
Software

In Internet Specific prefer:
Ecommerce

In Consumer Related prefer:
Consumer Services

Additional Information

Year Founded: 1969
Current Activity Level : Actively seeking new investments

AGILE VENTURE CAPITAL LLC

414 Brannan Street
San Francisco, CA USA 94101
Website: www.agileventurecapital.com

Management and Staff
Sheffield Wang, Co-Founder
Shuonan Chen, Co-Founder

Type of Firm
Private Equity Firm

Project Preferences

Type of Financing Preferred:
Balanced

Additional Information
Year Founded: 2016
Current Activity Level : Actively seeking new investments

AGILITAS PARTNERS LLP

14, Buckingham Gate
London, United Kingdom SW1E6LB
Phone: 442033841111
E-mail: info@agilitaspartners.com
Website: www.agilitaspartners.com

Type of Firm
Private Equity Firm

Project Preferences

Type of Financing Preferred:
Leveraged Buyout
Management Buyouts
Acquisition

Geographical Preferences

International Preferences:
United Kingdom
Europe

Industry Preferences

In Communications prefer:
Telecommunications
Other Communication Prod.

In Computer Software prefer:
Data Processing

In Semiconductor/Electr prefer:
Analytic/Scientific

In Medical/Health prefer:
Health Services

In Consumer Related prefer:
Education Related

In Industrial/Energy prefer:
Energy

In Transportation prefer:
Transportation

In Financial Services prefer:
Financial Services

In Business Serv. prefer:
Media

Additional Information
Year Founded: 2010
Current Activity Level : Actively seeking new investments

AGIRE INVEST SA

Via Cantonale 2A
Manno, Switzerland 6928
Phone: 41-91-610-2710
E-mail: info@agire.ch
Website: www.agireinvest.ch

Management and Staff
Lorenzo Leoni, Managing Partner
Paolo Orsatti, Managing Partner

Type of Firm
Government Affiliated Program

Association Membership
Swiss Venture Capital Association (SECA)

Project Preferences

Type of Financing Preferred:
Early Stage
Seed
Startup

Geographical Preferences

International Preferences:
Switzerland
Western Europe

Industry Preferences

In Internet Specific prefer:
E-Commerce Technology

Additional Information
Year Founded: 2011
Capital Under Management: $7,800,000
Current Activity Level : Actively seeking new investments

AGNUS CAPITAL LLP

Number one Serenity Park
Sarjapur road, Kaikondranahall
Bangalore, India 560035

Type of Firm
Private Equity Firm

Project Preferences

Type of Financing Preferred:
Early Stage

Industry Preferences

In Communications prefer:
Wireless Communications

In Other prefer:
Environment Responsible

Additional Information
Year Founded: 2010
Current Activity Level : Actively seeking new investments

AGRIBUSINESS INVESTMENT & CONSULTATION LTD

1-1-12 Uchikanda, Chiyoda-ku
3/F Coop Building
Tokyo, Japan 104-0047
Phone: 81352836688
Fax: 81352836689
Website: www.agri-invest.co.jp

Type of Firm
Private Equity Firm

Project Preferences

Type of Financing Preferred:
Balanced

Geographical Preferences

International Preferences:
Japan

Industry Preferences

In Agr/Forestr/Fish prefer:
Agribusiness

Additional Information
Year Founded: 2002
Current Activity Level : Actively seeking new investments

AGRICULTURAL BANK OF CHINA LTD

No. 8, Finance No. 1 Street
Wuxi, China 214000
Website: www.abchina.com

Type of Firm
Bank Affiliated

Project Preferences

Type of Financing Preferred:
Leveraged Buyout
Acquisition
Recapitalizations

Geographical Preferences

International Preferences:
China

Industry Preferences

In Computer Software prefer:
Software

In Internet Specific prefer:
Internet

In Biotechnology prefer:
Biotechnology

In Medical/Health prefer:
Pharmaceuticals

In Consumer Related prefer:
Consumer

In Industrial/Energy prefer:
Energy Conservation Relat
Environmental Related

In Business Serv. prefer:
Services

In Other prefer:
Environment Responsible

Additional Information
Year Founded: 2009
Capital Under Management: $789,045,000
Current Activity Level : Actively seeking new investments

AGRO INVEST SAS

11 rue de Monceau
Paris, France 75378
Phone: 33140694815
Fax: 33140694845
E-mail: agroinvest@prolea.com
Website: zao-agroinvest.ru

Management and Staff
Jean Louis Ruatti, President

Type of Firm
Private Equity Firm

Association Membership
French Venture Capital Association (AFIC)

Project Preferences

Type of Financing Preferred:
Leveraged Buyout
Early Stage
Later Stage

Size of Investments Considered:
Min Size of Investment Considered (000s): $2,889
Max Size of Investment Considered (000s): $21,673

Geographical Preferences

International Preferences:
Europe
France

Industry Preferences

In Biotechnology prefer:
Agricultural/Animal Bio.

In Business Serv. prefer:
Services

In Agr/Forestr/Fish prefer:
Agribusiness
Agriculture related

Additional Information
Name of Most Recent Fund: Agro Invest
Most Recent Fund Was Raised: 05/29/2007
Year Founded: 2007
Current Activity Level : Actively seeking new investments

AGTECH ACCELERATOR CORP

Six Davis Drive
Durham, NC USA 27709
E-mail: info@agtechaccelerator.com
Website: www.agtechaccelerator.com

Type of Firm
Incubator/Development Program

Project Preferences

Type of Financing Preferred:
Early Stage
Seed

Industry Preferences

In Agr/Forestr/Fish prefer:
Agribusiness
Agriculture related

Additional Information
Year Founded: 2017
Current Activity Level : Actively seeking new investments

AH VENTURES

99 High Street
Boston, MA USA 02110
Phone: 6177881670
Fax: 6177881663
E-mail: info@ahventures.com

Other Offices
One Liberty Square
Boston, MA USA 02109
Phone: 617-423-6688
Fax: 617-426-8399

Management and Staff
Jay Corscadden, General Partner
Thomas Palmer, General Partner

Type of Firm
Bank Affiliated

Project Preferences

Role in Financing:
Prefer role as deal originator

Type of Financing Preferred:
Second Stage Financing
Expansion
Later Stage

Size of Investments Considered:
Min Size of Investment Considered (000s): $500
Max Size of Investment Considered (000s): $2,000

Geographical Preferences

United States Preferences:

Industry Preferences

In Computer Hardware prefer:
Computer Graphics and Dig

In Computer Software prefer:
Computer Services
Software
Systems Software
Applications Software
Artificial Intelligence

In Internet Specific prefer:
Internet
Ecommerce
Web Aggregation/Portals

In Semiconductor/Electr prefer:
Electronic Components
Semiconductor
Micro-Processing
Controllers and Sensors
Sensors
Circuit Boards
Component Testing Equipmt
Laser Related
Optoelectronics

Additional Information
Year Founded: 1969
Capital Under Management: $18,000,000
Current Activity Level : Actively seeking new investments
Method of Compensation: Return on investment is of primary concern, do not charge fees

AHEIM CAPITAL GMBH

Schlossbergstrasse 1
Starnberg, Germany 82319
Phone: 498151655980
Fax: 4981516559898
E-mail: info@aheim.com
Website: www.aheim.com

Management and Staff
Frank Henkelmann, Partner
Herbert Seggewiss, Partner
Peter Blumenwitz, Partner

Type of Firm
Bank Affiliated

Association Membership
German Venture Capital Association (BVK)

Project Preferences

Type of Financing Preferred:
Leveraged Buyout
Acquisition

Geographical Preferences

International Preferences:
Liechtenstein
Luxembourg
Switzerland
Austria
Germany

Industry Preferences

In Industrial/Energy prefer:
Advanced Materials

Additional Information
Name of Most Recent Fund: Buchanan Unternehmer-Fonds I
Most Recent Fund Was Raised: 03/27/2006
Year Founded: 2004
Current Activity Level : Actively seeking new investments

AHLSTROM CAPITAL OY

Etelaesplanadi 14
Helsinki, Finland 00131
Phone: 3581088818
Fax: 358108884769
E-mail: info@ahlstromcapital.com
Website: www.ahlstromcapital.com

Management and Staff
Sebastian Burmeister, Founder

Type of Firm
Private Equity Firm

Association Membership
Finnish Venture Capital Association (FVCA)
European Private Equity and Venture Capital Assoc.

Project Preferences

Type of Financing Preferred:
Leveraged Buyout
Turnaround

Size of Investments Considered:
Min Size of Investment Considered (000s): $6,785
Max Size of Investment Considered (000s): $33,926

Geographical Preferences

International Preferences:
Europe
Scandanavia/Nordic Region
Estonia
Finland
Latvia
Lithuania
Russia

Industry Focus
(% based on actual investment)
  Semiconductors/Other Elect.   74.8%
  Industrial/Energy   14.3%
  Computer Hardware   10.9%

Additional Information
Year Founded: 2001
Capital Under Management: $223,500,000
Current Activity Level : Actively seeking new investments

AHV HOLDING COMPANY LLC

101 South Hanley Road
Suite 200
Clayton, MO USA 63105
Phone: 3147338100
Fax: 3147338678
E-mail: info@ascensionventures.org
Website: ascensionhealth.org

Management and Staff
Matthew Hermann, Senior Managing Director
Ryan Schuler, Managing Director
Tara Butler, Managing Director
Victor Kats, Managing Director

Type of Firm
Corporate PE/Venture

Association Membership
National Venture Capital Association - USA (NVCA)

Project Preferences

Role in Financing:
Will function either as deal originator or investor in deals created by others

Type of Financing Preferred:
Early Stage
Balanced
Later Stage

Size of Investments Considered:
Min Size of Investment Considered (000s): $5,000
Max Size of Investment Considered (000s): $15,000

Geographical Preferences

United States Preferences:

Industry Preferences

In Medical/Health prefer:
Medical/Health
Medical Diagnostics
Diagnostic Services

Additional Information
Name of Most Recent Fund: CHV III, L.P.
Most Recent Fund Was Raised: 05/01/2012
Year Founded: 2001
Capital Under Management: $805,000,000
Current Activity Level : Actively seeking new investments
Method of Compensation: Return on investment is of primary concern, do not charge fees

AI SEED

69 Wilson Street
IDEALondon
London, United Kingdom EC2A 2BB
Website: aiseed.co

Type of Firm
Private Equity Firm

Project Preferences

Type of Financing Preferred:
Later Stage

Geographical Preferences

International Preferences:
United Kingdom

Industry Preferences

In Computer Software prefer:
Artificial Intelligence

Additional Information
Year Founded: 2017
Current Activity Level : Actively seeking new investments

AI8 VENTURES, L.P.

201 Spear Street
Suite 1100
San Francisco, CA USA 94105
Phone: 4159699007
Website: www.ai8ventures.com

Type of Firm
Private Equity Firm

Project Preferences

Type of Financing Preferred:
Early Stage

Industry Preferences

In Computer Software prefer:
Artificial Intelligence

Additional Information

Year Founded: 2017
Capital Under Management: $250,000
Current Activity Level : Actively seeking new investments

AID PARTNERS CAPITAL LTD

18 Middle Road, Tsim Sha Tsui
The Peninsula Office Tower,
Kowloon, Hong Kong
Phone: 85231876000
Fax: 85231876088
E-mail: apcl@aidpartners.com
Website: www.aidpartners.com

Other Offices

Jintian Road S., Futian District
1802, Great China Int'l Exchange Square
Shenzhen, China
Phone: 8675583133590

Management and Staff

Joel Chang, Co-Founder
Kelvin Wu, Co-Founder

Type of Firm

Private Equity Firm

Project Preferences

Type of Financing Preferred:
Leveraged Buyout
Early Stage
Expansion
Later Stage
Acquisition

Geographical Preferences

International Preferences:
China

Industry Preferences

In Communications prefer:
Entertainment

In Consumer Related prefer:
Retail
Food/Beverage

Additional Information

Year Founded: 2007
Current Activity Level : Actively seeking new investments

AID PARTNERS TECHNOLOGY HOLDINGS LTD

151 Gloucestor Road
Unit 502, 5th Floor, AXA Centr
Wan Chai, Hong Kong
Phone: 85234762700
Fax: 85221690008
E-mail: info@crosby.com
Website: www.aid8088.com

Other Offices

6 Battery Road
#13-01/02
Singapore, Singapore 049909
Phone: 65-6325-1960
Fax: 65-6223-0451

4 Old Park Lane
London, United Kingdom W1K 1QW
Phone: 44-0203-291-2863

Kav. 29, Jl. Jend. Sudirman
Wisma Metropolitan 1, 10th Floor
Jakarta, Indonesia 12920
Phone: 62-21-526-1794
Fax: 62-21-526-4101

I.I Chundrigar Road
10th Floor, Trade Center
Karachi, Pakistan 74000
Phone: 92-21-3262-8846
Fax: 92-21-3262-8845

Type of Firm

Bank Affiliated

Association Membership

Hong Kong Venture Capital Association (HKVCA)

Project Preferences

Role in Financing:
Will function either as deal originator or investor in deals created by others

Type of Financing Preferred:
Early Stage
Expansion
Balanced
Startup

Geographical Preferences

International Preferences:
Vietnam
Indonesia
India
Hong Kong
China
Thailand
Philippines
Asia
Singapore
Korea, South
Malaysia

Industry Preferences

In Communications prefer:
Media and Entertainment
Entertainment

In Consumer Related prefer:
Entertainment and Leisure

Additional Information

Year Founded: 1984
Capital Under Management: $98,000,000
Current Activity Level : Actively seeking new investments
Method of Compensation: Professional fee required whether or not deal closes

AIF CAPITAL ASIA III LP

One Connaught Place
Suite 3401, Jardine House
Central, Hong Kong
Phone: 85229127888
Fax: 85228450786
E-mail: info@aifcapital.com
Website: www.aifcapital.com

Other Offices

Ten Collyer Quay
Unit 4020, Ocean Financial Centre
, Singapore 049315
Phone: 6566225628

Exit 8, NH 8, Sector 30
6/F Park Centra
Gurgaon, India 122 001
Phone: 91-124-444-7888
Fax: 91-124-444-7898

2 Jianguomenwai Avenue
Unit 1509, 15/F, Yintai Office Tower C
Beijing, China 100022
Phone: 86-10-6535-0200
Fax: 86-10-6535-0119

Management and Staff
Ajay Lal, Managing Director
Andy Tse, Managing Director
Daniel Hui, Managing Director
Doris Ng, Managing Director
Lim Lek Suan, Managing Director
Peter Amour, Chief Executive Officer
Stephen Lee, Managing Director
Theresa Chung, Managing Director
Xiangming Fang, Managing Director

Type of Firm
Private Equity Firm

Association Membership
China Venture Capital Association
Emerging Markets Private Equity Association

Project Preferences

Type of Financing Preferred:
Leveraged Buyout
Expansion
Generalist PE
Special Situation

Geographical Preferences

International Preferences:
Asia

Industry Preferences

In Communications prefer:
Telecommunications

In Medical/Health prefer:
Medical/Health
Pharmaceuticals

In Consumer Related prefer:
Retail
Consumer Products

In Industrial/Energy prefer:
Energy

In Transportation prefer:
Transportation

In Financial Services prefer:
Financial Services

In Business Serv. prefer:
Services
Distribution
Media

In Manufact. prefer:
Manufacturing

In Agr/Forestr/Fish prefer:
Agriculture related

Additional Information
Year Founded: 1994
Capital Under Management: $1,700,000,000
Current Activity Level : Actively seeking new investments

Method of Compensation: Professional fee required whether or not deal closes

AIG CAPITAL PARTNERS INC

399 Park Avenue
4th Floor
New York, NY USA 10022

Management and Staff
Christopher Liu, Vice President
Conradin Schneider, Vice President
David Pinkerton, Managing Director
John Casale, Chief Financial Officer
Kevin Clowe, Managing Director
Klaus Hermann, Partner
Marc Kasher, Vice President
Patrick McGinnis, Vice President
Pierre Mellinger, Partner
Robert Howe, Managing Director
Scott Foushee, Managing Director

Type of Firm
Private Equity Firm

Project Preferences

Type of Financing Preferred:
Fund of Funds
Leveraged Buyout
Early Stage
Expansion
Mezzanine
Generalist PE
Balanced
Other
Management Buyouts
Special Situation
Recapitalizations

Geographical Preferences

United States Preferences:

International Preferences:
Latin America
India
Europe
China
Israel
Asia
Korea, South
Japan
Africa
France

Industry Focus
(% based on actual investment)
Consumer Related	29.1%
Communications and Media	20.0%
Medical/Health	13.6%
Other Products	12.2%
Internet Specific	9.8%
Biotechnology	5.7%
Computer Software and Services	4.2%
Computer Hardware	3.2%
Industrial/Energy	2.1%
Semiconductors/Other Elect.	0.0%

Additional Information
Name of Most Recent Fund: AIG Healthcare Partners, L.P.
Most Recent Fund Was Raised: 11/19/2004
Year Founded: 1996
Current Activity Level : Actively seeking new investments

AIGLE PRIVATE EQUITY FUND MANAGEMENT CO LTD

166 Lujiazui Ring Road
Suite 26A Mirae Asset Tower
Shanghai, China 200120
Phone: 862161605336
Fax: 862161605332
E-mail: acg@aiglecapital.com
Website: www.aiglecapital.com

Type of Firm
Private Equity Firm

Project Preferences

Type of Financing Preferred:
Expansion
Later Stage

Geographical Preferences

International Preferences:
China

Additional Information
Year Founded: 2011
Capital Under Management: $2,449,300,000
Current Activity Level : Actively seeking new investments

AIP PRIVATE CAPITAL

77 King Street West
Suite 4140, TD North Tower
Toronto, Canada M5K 1E7
Phone: 4166010808
Fax: 8889004123
E-mail: info@aipprivatecapital.com
Website: www.aipprivatecapital.com

Other Offices

Ninth Floor Korea Teachers Pension
Yeouido-dong, Yeongdeungpo-Gu
Seoul, South Korea 150-742

Tenth Floor Dubai Trade
Limitless Galleries, Building Four
Jabal Ali Downtown, Utd. Arab Em.

Management and Staff

Alex Kanayev, Principal

Type of Firm

Private Equity Firm

Association Membership

Canadian Venture Capital Association

Project Preferences

Type of Financing Preferred:
Expansion
Mezzanine
Turnaround
Management Buyouts
Acquisition
Special Situation
Recapitalizations

Size of Investments Considered:
Min Size of Investment Considered (000s): $92
Max Size of Investment Considered (000s): $2,302

Geographical Preferences

United States Preferences:
North America

Industry Preferences

In Financial Services prefer:
Financial Services

Additional Information

Year Founded: 2010
Capital Under Management: $100,000,000
Current Activity Level : Actively seeking new investments

AIRBUS GROUP SE

Mendelweg 30
Leiden, Netherlands 2333 CS
Website: www.airbusgroup.com

Type of Firm

Investment Management Firm

Geographical Preferences

International Preferences:
All International

Additional Information

Year Founded: 2015
Capital Under Management: $150,000,000
Current Activity Level : Actively seeking new investments

AIRBUS VENTURES

3000 Sand Hill Road
Unit 1-120
West Menlo Park, CA USA 94025
Phone: 7038890535
E-mail: Ventures@airbusventures.vc
Website: www.airbusventures.vc

Type of Firm

Private Equity Firm

Project Preferences

Type of Financing Preferred:
Early Stage

Industry Preferences

In Transportation prefer:
Aerospace

Additional Information

Year Founded: 2017
Current Activity Level : Actively seeking new investments

AIRTEK CAPITAL GROUP SA

Av Louise 480
Bte 5C
Brussels, Belgium 1050
E-mail: info@acgeu.com
Website: www.acgeu.com

Type of Firm

Private Equity Firm

Project Preferences

Type of Financing Preferred:
Early Stage
Seed
Startup

Geographical Preferences

United States Preferences:
All U.S.

International Preferences:
Europe

Industry Preferences

In Communications prefer:
Telecommunications

In Internet Specific prefer:
Internet

In Semiconductor/Electr prefer:
Electronics

Additional Information

Year Founded: 2013
Current Activity Level : Actively seeking new investments

AIRTREE VENTURES

120B Underwood Street
Paddington, Australia NSW 2021
Website: airtreevc.com

Type of Firm

Private Equity Firm

Association Membership

Australian Venture Capital Association (AVCAL)

Project Preferences

Type of Financing Preferred:
Early Stage
Expansion
Balanced
Later Stage

Size of Investments Considered:
Min Size of Investment Considered (000s): $357
Max Size of Investment Considered (000s): $4,282

Geographical Preferences

International Preferences:
Australia

Additional Information

Year Founded: 2014
Capital Under Management: $60,000,000
Current Activity Level : Actively seeking new investments

AISLING CAPITAL LLC

888 Seventh Avenue, 30th Floor
New York, NY USA 10106
Phone: 2126516380
Fax: 2126516379
Website: www.aislingcapital.com

Management and Staff

Andrew Schiff, Managing Partner
Anthony Sun, Partner
Brett Zbar, Partner
Dov Goldstein, Partner
Josh Bilenker, Principal
Lloyd Appel, Chief Financial Officer
Stacey Seltzer, Principal
Steven Elms, Managing Partner

Type of Firm

Private Equity Firm

Project Preferences

Role in Financing:
Prefer role as deal originator but will also invest in deals created by others

Type of Financing Preferred:
Balanced
Public Companies
Later Stage

Size of Investments Considered:
Min Size of Investment Considered (000s): $20,000
Max Size of Investment Considered (000s): $50,000

Industry Preferences

In Biotechnology prefer:
Biotechnology

In Medical/Health prefer:
Medical/Health
Medical Therapeutics
Medical Products
Health Services
Pharmaceuticals

Additional Information
Name of Most Recent Fund: Aisling Capital III, L.P.
Most Recent Fund Was Raised: 09/02/2008
Year Founded: 2000
Capital Under Management: $1,600,000,000
Current Activity Level : Actively seeking new investments

AITEC SGPS SA

Avenida Duque de Avila, 23
Lisbon, Portugal 1000138
Phone: 351213100013
Fax: 351213526314
E-mail: info@aitec.pt
Website: www.aitec.pt

Type of Firm
Private Equity Firm

Project Preferences

Type of Financing Preferred:
Balanced

Geographical Preferences

International Preferences:
Portugal

Industry Preferences

In Business Serv. prefer:
Consulting Services

Additional Information
Year Founded: 1987
Current Activity Level : Actively seeking new investments

AJANTA OY

Pohjoisranta 4 A 1
Helsinki, Finland 00170
Website: www.ajanta.fi

Type of Firm
Private Equity Firm

Project Preferences

Type of Financing Preferred:
Generalist PE

Geographical Preferences

International Preferences:
Finland
All International

Industry Preferences

In Communications prefer:
Communications and Media

In Financial Services prefer:
Real Estate

In Business Serv. prefer:
Media

Additional Information
Year Founded: 1989
Current Activity Level : Actively seeking new investments

AJU IB INVESTMENT CO LTD

201, Teheranro, Kangnam-Gu
4-5F, AJU Building
Seoul, South Korea 135916
Phone: 82234519200
Fax: 82234529805
Website: www.ajuib.co.kr

Management and Staff
Ji-Won Kim, Chief Executive Officer

Type of Firm
Private Equity Firm

Association Membership
Korean Venture Capital Association (KVCA)

Project Preferences

Type of Financing Preferred:
Leveraged Buyout
Early Stage
Expansion
Mezzanine
Balanced
Startup

Geographical Preferences

International Preferences:
North Korea
Asia
Korea, South

Industry Preferences

In Semiconductor/Electr prefer:
Semiconductor

In Industrial/Energy prefer:
Energy
Alternative Energy
Energy Conservation Relat

Additional Information
Year Founded: 1991
Capital Under Management: $293,600,000
Current Activity Level : Actively seeking new investments

AK GANGWON INVESTMENT CO LTD

Yulmun-ri, Sinbuk-eup
100 Gangwon Techno Park
Chuncheon-si, South Korea
Phone: 82262953000
Fax: 82262953015

Management and Staff
Kyung Oh Roh, Chief Executive Officer

Type of Firm
Private Equity Firm

Association Membership
Korean Venture Capital Association (KVCA)

Project Preferences

Type of Financing Preferred:
Balanced

Additional Information
Year Founded: 2009
Capital Under Management: $26,687,000
Current Activity Level : Actively seeking new investments

AKAYI CAPITAL PARTNERS LLC

1230 Avenue of the Americas
7/F Rockefeller Center Plaza
New York, NY USA 10020
Website: www.akayicapitalpartnersllc.com

Management and Staff
Anita Goel, Principal
Basil Smikle, Principal
Lunga Saki, Managing Director
William Ntsoana, Managing Director
Yogesh Chadha, Principal

Type of Firm
Private Equity Firm

Project Preferences

Type of Financing Preferred:
Leveraged Buyout
Mezzanine
Generalist PE
Balanced
Management Buyouts
Acquisition
Distressed Debt
Recapitalizations

Industry Preferences

In Industrial/Energy prefer:
Energy
Alternative Energy
Environmental Related

In Other prefer:
Environment Responsible

Additional Information
Name of Most Recent Fund: Akayi Capital Partners LLC
Most Recent Fund Was Raised: 08/29/2012
Year Founded: 2010
Capital Under Management: $500,000
Current Activity Level : Actively seeking new investments

AKG INVESTMENT

100 Kangwon Techno Park
946 Yulmun-ri Shinbook-eup
Kangwon, South Korea 200-821
Phone: 02-713-3138
Fax: 02-713-3138

Type of Firm
Private Equity Firm

Project Preferences

Type of Financing Preferred:
Balanced

Geographical Preferences

International Preferences:
Asia

Additional Information
Year Founded: 2009
Current Activity Level : Actively seeking new investments

AKKADIAN VENTURES LLC

Two Mint Plaza
Suite 307
San Francisco, CA USA 94114
Phone: 4156150130
Fax: 4153733828
E-mail: info@akkadianventures.com

Other Offices
50 East Serene Avenue
Suite 405
Las Vegas, NV USA 89123
Phone: 4152156666
Fax: 7025770096

Management and Staff
Josh Becker, Venture Partner
Michael Tanne, Partner
Mike Gridley, Managing Director
Peter Smith, Managing Director
Robert Bailey, Venture Partner

Type of Firm
Private Equity Advisor or Fund of Funds

Project Preferences

Type of Financing Preferred:
Fund of Funds

Industry Preferences

In Communications prefer:
Communications and Media
Wireless Communications
Media and Entertainment

In Computer Software prefer:
Software

In Internet Specific prefer:
Internet
Ecommerce
Web Aggregation/Portals

In Semiconductor/Electr prefer:
Electronics

In Other prefer:
Environment Responsible

Additional Information
Name of Most Recent Fund: Akkadian Ventures II, L.P.
Most Recent Fund Was Raised: 06/14/2012
Year Founded: 2011
Capital Under Management: $214,315,000
Current Activity Level : Actively seeking new investments

AKN HOLDINGS LLC

10250 Constellation Boulevard
17th Floor
Los Angeles, CA USA 90067
Phone: 3104327000
Fax: 3106912119
E-mail: admin@opengatecapital.com
Website: www.opengatecapital.com

Other Offices
215 rue du Faubourg Saint Honore
Paris, France 75008
Phone: 33-1-40-06-0158

Management and Staff
Andrew Nikou, Chief Executive Officer
Inbal Salzstein, Vice President
Jay Yook, Partner
Jonny Leppin, Principal
Julien Lagreze, Partner
Robert Lezec, Partner

Type of Firm
Private Equity Firm

Project Preferences

Type of Financing Preferred:
Leveraged Buyout
Management Buyouts
Special Situation

Geographical Preferences

International Preferences:
All International

Additional Information
Year Founded: 2005
Capital Under Management: $305,000,000
Current Activity Level : Actively seeking new investments

AKOYA CAPITAL PARTNERS LLC

625 North Michigan Avenue, Suite 2450
Chicago, IL USA 60611
Website: www.akoyacapital.com

Management and Staff
Carr Preston, Managing Director
Dennis Chandler, Managing Director
Jim Appleton, Managing Partner
John Regazzi, Managing Director
Luis Nieto, Managing Director
Mark Breckheimer, Managing Director
Max DeZara, Founder
Pat Riley, Vice President
Tim Gardner, Managing Director

Type of Firm
Private Equity Firm

Project Preferences

Type of Financing Preferred:
Leveraged Buyout
Expansion
Management Buyouts
Acquisition

Industry Preferences

In Consumer Related prefer:
Consumer

In Industrial/Energy prefer:
Industrial Products
Environmental Related

In Business Serv. prefer:
Services

Additional Information
Year Founded: 2005
Current Activity Level : Actively seeking new investments

AKSARBEN INNOVATION INITIATIVE

6825 Pine Street
Suite 120
Omaha, NE USA 68106
Website: www.aksarbeninnovation.org

Type of Firm
Incubator/Development Program

Project Preferences

Type of Financing Preferred:
Early Stage
Seed
Startup

Geographical Preferences

United States Preferences:
Nebraska

Additional Information
Year Founded: 2014
Current Activity Level : Actively seeking new investments

AKSIA GROUP SPA

Piazza Del Liberty 2
Milano, Italy 20121
Phone: 3928904631
Fax: 3928904635
E-mail: info@aksiagroup.com
Website: www.aksiagroup.com

Other Offices
Via des Am,brois, 3
Turin, Italy 10123
Phone: 39-11-812-9611
Fax: 39-11-569-0840

Management and Staff
Fausto Gallazzi, Chief Financial Officer

Type of Firm
Private Equity Firm

Association Membership
Italian Venture Capital Association (AIFI)

Project Preferences

Type of Financing Preferred:
Leveraged Buyout
Early Stage
Expansion
Generalist PE
Balanced

Size of Investments Considered:
Min Size of Investment Considered (000s): $863
Max Size of Investment Considered (000s): $5,179

Geographical Preferences

International Preferences:
Italy

Industry Preferences

In Communications prefer:
Telecommunications

In Consumer Related prefer:
Consumer Products

In Industrial/Energy prefer:
Industrial Products

In Business Serv. prefer:
Media

In Manufact. prefer:
Manufacturing

Additional Information
Year Founded: 2001
Capital Under Management: $25,900,000
Current Activity Level : Actively seeking new investments

AKT IP VENTURES

1300 I Street Northwest
Washington, DC USA 20017
Phone: 6463611063
E-mail: info@akt.ventures
Website: www.akt.fund

Type of Firm
Incubator/Development Program

Project Preferences

Type of Financing Preferred:
Balanced

Industry Preferences

In Computer Software prefer:
Software

In Consumer Related prefer:
Consumer
Entertainment and Leisure
Retail
Education Related

In Transportation prefer:
Transportation

In Financial Services prefer:
Real Estate
Financial Services

In Business Serv. prefer:
Services

Additional Information
Year Founded: 2015
Current Activity Level : Actively seeking new investments

AKTIS CAPITAL GROUP

8 Wyndham Street
18th Floor Asia Pacific Centre
Central, Hong Kong
Phone: 85221670600
Fax: 85221670699
E-mail: info.acal@aktiscapital.com
Website: www.aktiscapital.com

Other Offices
491-B River Valley Road
#03-01 Valley Point
Singapore, Singapore 248373
Phone: 6568360350
Fax: 6568361532

38 Qingnian Road
38F International Trade Centre
Chongqing PRC, China 400010
Phone: 862363845797
Fax: 862363103106

Management and Staff
Danny Yee, Managing Director
Eric Slighton, Managing Director
Teik Seng Cheah, Managing Director

Type of Firm
Private Equity Firm

Project Preferences

Type of Financing Preferred:
Leveraged Buyout
Balanced
Management Buyouts
Acquisition

Geographical Preferences

International Preferences:
China
Asia

Industry Preferences

In Medical/Health prefer:
Pharmaceuticals

In Consumer Related prefer:
Entertainment and Leisure

In Industrial/Energy prefer:
Materials

In Financial Services prefer:
Financial Services
Real Estate

In Business Serv. prefer:
Services
Consulting Services

In Manufact. prefer:
Manufacturing

Additional Information
Year Founded: 2003
Capital Under Management: $1,400,000
Current Activity Level : Actively seeking new investments

AKTIVFINANSMENEDZH-MENT OOO

Chkanova
43 A Building, 7th Floor
Orenburg, Russia 460001
Phone: 73532372303
E-mail: inbox@afmg.ru
Website: www.afmg.ru

Type of Firm
Government Affiliated Program

Project Preferences

Type of Financing Preferred:
Early Stage
Later Stage

Geographical Preferences

International Preferences:
Russia

Industry Preferences

In Communications prefer:
Communications and Media

In Internet Specific prefer:
E-Commerce Technology

In Computer Other prefer:
Computer Related

In Industrial/Energy prefer:
Alternative Energy

In Transportation prefer:
Transportation

In Financial Services prefer:
Real Estate

Additional Information
Year Founded: 2012
Current Activity Level : Actively seeking new investments

AL AMAN INVESTMENT COMPANY KPSC

Sharq, Khalid Bin Al Waleed St
Al Dhou Tower, Floor 11,12,13
Kuwait, Kuwait 26972.
Phone: 965822626
Fax: 9652497962
E-mail: info@alaman.com.kw
Website: www.alaman.com.kw

Management and Staff
Moamen Zahran, Chief Financial Officer

Type of Firm
Investment Management Firm

Project Preferences

Type of Financing Preferred:
Generalist PE

Geographical Preferences

International Preferences:
Kuwait
All International

Additional Information
Year Founded: 1974
Current Activity Level : Actively seeking new investments

AL BAWADER

One Paul VI Street
Third Floor,Henry Banna's Bldg
Nazareth, Israel 16071
Phone: 972737057070
Fax: 972737057075
Website: www.al-bawader.com

Management and Staff
Habib Hazzan, Managing Partner
Jimmy Levy, Managing Partner

Type of Firm
Private Equity Firm

Association Membership
Israel Venture Association

Project Preferences

Type of Financing Preferred:
Early Stage
Expansion
Later Stage

Geographical Preferences

International Preferences:
Utd. Arab Em.
Israel

Industry Preferences

In Business Serv. prefer:
Services

In Manufact. prefer:
Manufacturing

Additional Information
Year Founded: 2010
Current Activity Level : Actively seeking new investments

AL CAPITAL HOLDINGS 2016 LTD

Habarzel Street 38
Tel Aviv, Israel 69710
Phone: 97236849333
Fax: 97236853393
E-mail: info@dfjtamirfishman.com

Other Offices
2882 Sand Hill Road
Suite 150
Menlo Park, CA USA 94025
Phone: 6502339000
Fax: 6502339233

Management and Staff
Benny Zeevi, Managing General Partner
Moshe Levin, Managing General Partner
Ran Giladi, Venture Partner
Shai Saul, Managing General Partner

Type of Firm
Bank Affiliated

Association Membership
Israel Venture Association

Project Preferences

Type of Financing Preferred:
Early Stage
Balanced
Later Stage
Seed
Startup

Geographical Preferences

International Preferences:
Israel

Industry Focus
(% based on actual investment)

Communications and Media	31.6%
Computer Software and Services	21.0%
Internet Specific	16.7%
Biotechnology	12.9%
Semiconductors/Other Elect.	9.5%
Industrial/Energy	3.1%
Medical/Health	3.1%
Other Products	2.0%

Additional Information
Year Founded: 1997
Current Activity Level : Actively seeking new investments

AL FAWARES HOLDING CO KSCC

Wahran Street
Villa No. 7, Block 10
Shamiya, Kuwait 13023
Phone: 9654817332
Fax: 9654817300
E-mail: alfawares@alfawares.com.kw
Website: www.alfawares.com.kw

Type of Firm
Private Equity Firm

Project Preferences

Type of Financing Preferred:
Generalist PE

Geographical Preferences

United States Preferences:
All U.S.

International Preferences:
Bahrain
Ireland
Egypt
Middle East
Germany
Kuwait

Industry Preferences

In Communications prefer:
Radio & TV Broadcasting
Telecommunications
Publishing

In Computer Software prefer:
Software

In Industrial/Energy prefer:
Oil & Gas Drilling,Explor

In Transportation prefer:
Aerospace

In Financial Services prefer:
Real Estate
Financial Services

In Manufact. prefer:
Manufacturing

Additional Information
Year Founded: 1982
Current Activity Level : Actively seeking new investments

AL JAWHARA INVEST HOLDING GROUP CO KSCC

PO Box 4432
Sharq- Ahmad Al Jaber St
Safat, Kuwait 13045
Phone: 96522925911
Fax: 96522925912
E-mail: info@jihgroup.com
Website: www.jihgroup.com

Type of Firm
Private Equity Firm

Project Preferences

Type of Financing Preferred:
Early Stage
Expansion
Later Stage
Seed
Startup

Geographical Preferences

International Preferences:
Middle East
Africa

Industry Preferences

In Industrial/Energy prefer:
Energy
Oil and Gas Exploration
Oil & Gas Drilling,Explor
Alternative Energy

In Financial Services prefer:
Real Estate
Investment Groups

In Manufact. prefer:
Manufacturing

In Other prefer:
Environment Responsible

Additional Information
Year Founded: 2006
Current Activity Level : Actively seeking new investments

AL KHABEER CAPITAL CO

P.O. Box 128289
Madinah Road
Jeddah, Saudi Arabia 21362
Phone: 966126588888
Fax: 966126586663
E-mail: info@alkhabeer.com
Website: www.alkhabeer.com

Other Offices
Madinah Road
P.O. Box 128289
Jeddah, Saudi Arabia 21362
Phone: 966126588888
Fax: 966126586663

Management and Staff
Ahmad Ghouth, Chief Executive Officer
Ammar Shata, Chief Executive Officer
Tamer Abdul Rahim, Chief Financial Officer

Type of Firm
Investment Management Firm

Project Preferences

Type of Financing Preferred:
Leveraged Buyout
Early Stage
Expansion
Generalist PE
Turnaround
Later Stage
Seed
Strategic Alliances
Acquisition
Startup

Geographical Preferences

International Preferences:
Middle East
Saudi Arabia
Africa

Industry Preferences

In Medical/Health prefer:
Health Services

Additional Information
Year Founded: 2008
Capital Under Management: $500,000,000
Current Activity Level : Actively seeking new investments

AL MASAH PAPER INDUSTRIES LLC

Walker House,
87 Mary Street
George Town, Cayman Islands KY1-9005

Management and Staff
Amitava Ghosal, Partner

Type of Firm
Private Equity Firm

Association Membership
Gulf Venture Capital Association
Emerging Markets Private Equity Association

Project Preferences

Type of Financing Preferred:
Leveraged Buyout
Early Stage
Generalist PE
Balanced
Later Stage
Management Buyouts
Acquisition
Special Situation

Geographical Preferences

International Preferences:
Utd. Arab Em.
Middle East
Asia
Africa

Industry Preferences

In Medical/Health prefer:
Medical/Health
Health Services

In Consumer Related prefer:
Retail
Education Related

Additional Information
Year Founded: 2010
Capital Under Management: $1,000,000
Current Activity Level : Actively seeking new investments

AL ROUYAH INVESTMENT AND LEASING COMPANY

Darwaza Tower
Suite 51, Floor 13
Kuwait, Kuwait
Phone: 96522913000
Fax: 96522913016
Website: www.alrouyah.com

Type of Firm
Private Equity Firm

Project Preferences

Type of Financing Preferred:
Generalist PE

Geographical Preferences

International Preferences:
Middle East

Industry Preferences

In Communications prefer:
Telecommunications

In Financial Services prefer:
Financial Services

In Business Serv. prefer:
Media

Additional Information
Year Founded: 2006
Current Activity Level : Actively seeking new investments

AL SALAM ASIA-PACIFIC PTE LTD

80 Raffles Place
Suite 17-23 UOB Plaza Two
Singapore, Singapore 048624

Type of Firm
Bank Affiliated

Association Membership
Singapore Venture Capital Association (SVCA)

Project Preferences

Type of Financing Preferred:
Balanced

Geographical Preferences

International Preferences:
Asia Pacific

Additional Information
Year Founded: 2008
Current Activity Level : Actively seeking new investments

ALACON VENTURES LLC

101 California Street
Suite 2940
San Francisco, CA USA 94111
Phone: 415-392-9020
Fax: 415-392-9026
Website: www.alaconventures.com

Management and Staff
David Williams, Managing Partner
Scott McCarthy, Managing Partner

Type of Firm
Private Equity Firm

Project Preferences

Type of Financing Preferred:
Early Stage
Expansion
Balanced
Later Stage

Geographical Preferences

International Preferences:
Albania
China
Utd. Arab Em.

Industry Preferences

In Communications prefer:
Communications and Media

In Internet Specific prefer:
Internet

In Consumer Related prefer:
Consumer Services

Additional Information
Year Founded: 2007
Capital Under Management: $100,000,000
Current Activity Level : Actively seeking new investments

ALAFI CAPITAL CO LLC

P.O. Box 7338
Berkeley, CA USA 94707
Phone: 5106537425
Fax: 5106536231
Website: www.alafi.com

Management and Staff
Christopher Alafi, General Partner

Type of Firm
Private Equity Firm

Project Preferences

Role in Financing:
Will function either as deal originator or investor in deals created by others

Type of Financing Preferred:
Early Stage
Research and Development
Start-up Financing
Seed
First Stage Financing

Size of Investments Considered:
Min Size of Investment Considered (000s): $500
Max Size of Investment Considered (000s): $2,000

Geographical Preferences

International Preferences:
No Preference

Industry Preferences

In Semiconductor/Electr prefer:
Analytic/Scientific

In Biotechnology prefer:
Biotechnology
Genetic Engineering

In Medical/Health prefer:
Diagnostic Services
Drug/Equipmt Delivery

Additional Information
Name of Most Recent Fund: Alafi Capital Company
Most Recent Fund Was Raised: 12/31/1984
Year Founded: 1984
Capital Under Management: $60,000,000
Current Activity Level : Reducing investment activity
Method of Compensation: Return on investment is of primary concern, do not charge fees

ALANTRA

Calle Padilla 17
Madrid, Spain 28006
Phone: 34917458484
Fax: 34914313812
E-mail: info@nmas1.com
Website: www.alantra.com

Other Offices
One Bartholomew Lane
London, United Kingdom EC2N 2AX
Phone: 44 (0) 20 7496 300

14 Via Borgonuovo
Milan, Italy 20121
Phone: 39 02 303 061

Paseo de Gracia 110
Barcelona, Spain 08008
Phone: 34 93 218 15 40

Trinova Real Estate
Level 5 120 Moorgate
London, United Kingdom EC2M 6UR
Phone: 44 (0) 207 776 500

35 Alameda de Recalde
Bilbao, Spain 48011
Phone: 34 94 443 63 51

Schaumainkai 69
Frankfurt, Germany 60596
Phone: 69 69 665 758 720

25, rue de Berri
Paris, France 75008
Phone: 33 1 53 89 05 00

Buyukdere Cad. Maya Akar
Center No:100 Floor: 27
Esentepe Istanbul, Turkey 34394
Phone: 90 212 370 60 60

Management and Staff
Cristobal Rodriguez, Chief Financial Officer
Eduardo Munoz, Founder
Frederico Pastor, Chief Executive Officer
Guillermo Arboli, Managing Director
Lorenzo Astolfi, Managing Partner
Miguel Salis, Managing Director
Oscar Garcia, Founder
Roberto Leon, Founder

Type of Firm
Investment Management Firm

Association Membership
Spanish Venture Capital Association (ASCRI)

Project Preferences

Type of Financing Preferred:
Leveraged Buyout
Expansion
Management Buyouts
Acquisition

Geographical Preferences

International Preferences:
Latin America
Portugal
Mexico
Brazil
Chile
Spain

Industry Focus
(% based on actual investment)

Consumer Related	51.8%
Other Products	16.4%
Industrial/Energy	11.6%
Semiconductors/Other Elect.	11.1%
Communications and Media	6.9%
Medical/Health	1.7%
Computer Software and Services	0.5%

Additional Information
Name of Most Recent Fund: QMC II Iberian Capital Fund
Most Recent Fund Was Raised: 07/23/2013
Year Founded: 1990
Capital Under Management: $963,600,000
Current Activity Level : Actively seeking new investments

ALARA CAPITAL PARTNERS LLC

5001 Plaza on the Lake Dr.
Suite 103
Austin, TX USA 78746
Phone: 5127955893
E-mail: businessplans@alaracorp.com
Website: www.alaracap.com

Other Offices
135 East
57th Street
New York, NY USA 10022
Phone: 2129188811
Fax: 6104829169

1045 First Avenue
King of Prussia, PA USA 19406
Phone: 6102331014
Fax: 6104829169

Management and Staff
Andrew Maunder, Venture Partner
Darren Wallis, Partner
David Jannetta, Venture Partner
Eric Rothfus, Managing Partner
Joseph Thompson, Partner
Kenyon Hayward, Venture Partner
Lutz Henckels, Venture Partner
Michael Falcon, Partner
Michael Burns, Managing Partner

Type of Firm
Private Equity Firm

Project Preferences

Type of Financing Preferred:
Early Stage
Generalist PE
Later Stage
Startup
Distressed Debt

Geographical Preferences

United States Preferences:

Industry Preferences

In Communications prefer:
Communications and Media
Commercial Communications
Telecommunications
Wireless Communications

In Computer Software prefer:
Software
Systems Software

In Semiconductor/Electr prefer:
Electronics
Semiconductor

In Industrial/Energy prefer:
Energy
Environmental Related

In Business Serv. prefer:
Media

Additional Information
Year Founded: 2006
Capital Under Management: $65,000,000
Current Activity Level : Actively seeking new investments

ALARIS ROYALTY CORP

333 24th Avenue Southwest
Suite 250
Alberta, Canada T2S 3E6
Phone: 4032280873
Fax: 4032280906
Website: www.alarisroyalty.com

Other Offices
2031 33rd Avenue Southwest
Suite 232
Calgary, Canada T2T 1Z5
Phone: 4032217304

Management and Staff
Amanda Frazer, Vice President
Dan Bertram, Vice President
Darren Driscoll, Chief Financial Officer
Elizabeth McCarthy, Vice President

Type of Firm
Private Equity Firm

Project Preferences

Type of Financing Preferred:
Generalist PE

Geographical Preferences

United States Preferences:
All U.S.

Canadian Preferences:
All Canada

Additional Information
Year Founded: 2006
Current Activity Level : Actively seeking new investments

ALASKA PERMANENT FUND CORP

801 West 10th Street
Suite 302
Juneau, AK USA 99801
Phone: 9077961500
Website: www.apfc.org

Management and Staff
Julie Hamilton, Chief Financial Officer

Type of Firm
Government Affiliated Program

Project Preferences

Type of Financing Preferred:
Fund of Funds

Geographical Preferences

United States Preferences:
Alaska

Additional Information
Year Founded: 1977
Current Activity Level : Actively seeking new investments

ALBATROSS INVERSTMENT CO LTD

943-27 Daechi-Dong, Gangnam-gu
9F, Sindo Ricoh Bldg
Seoul, South Korea 121-807
Phone: 8227030231
Fax: 8227030233

Management and Staff
Young Min Lee, Chief Executive Officer

Type of Firm
Private Equity Firm

Association Membership
Korean Venture Capital Association (KVCA)

Project Preferences

Type of Financing Preferred:
Early Stage
Balanced
Startup

Geographical Preferences

International Preferences:
Korea, South

Additional Information
Year Founded: 2008
Capital Under Management: $20,790,000
Current Activity Level : Actively seeking new investments

ALBERTA ENTERPRISE CORP

10830 Jasper Avenue
Suite 1100
Edmonton, Canada T5J 2B3
Phone: 7803923901
Fax: 7803923908
E-mail: info@alberta-enterprise.ca
Website: www.alberta-enterprise.ca

Management and Staff
Rod Charko, Chief Executive Officer

Type of Firm
Private Equity Advisor or Fund of Funds

Association Membership
Canadian Venture Capital Association

Project Preferences

Type of Financing Preferred:
Fund of Funds
Early Stage
Expansion
Seed
Startup

Geographical Preferences

Canadian Preferences:
Alberta
All Canada

Industry Preferences

In Communications prefer:
Communications and Media

In Industrial/Energy prefer:
Alternative Energy

Additional Information
Year Founded: 2008
Capital Under Management: $100,000,000
Current Activity Level : Actively seeking new investments

ALBERTA INVESTMENT MANAGEMENT CORP

1100-10830 Jasper Avenue
Edmonton, Canada T5J 2B3
Phone: 7803923600
Fax: 7803923909
Website: www.aimco.alberta.ca

Other Offices
One Berkeley Street
London, United Kingdom W1J 8DJ

Type of Firm
Government Affiliated Program

Association Membership
Canadian Venture Capital Association

Additional Information
Year Founded: 2008
Current Activity Level : Actively seeking new investments

ALBERTA REV PPTY CORP

331 Terrace Building
9515-107 Street
Edmonton, Canada T5K2C3
Phone: 780-422-5620
Fax: 780-422-0257
Website: www.finance.gov.ab.ca

Type of Firm
Government Affiliated Program

Project Preferences

Type of Financing Preferred:
Leveraged Buyout

Additional Information
Year Founded: 2009
Current Activity Level : Actively seeking new investments

ALBION CAPITAL GROUP LLP

1 King's Arms Yard
London, United Kingdom EC2R 7AF
Phone: 44-20-7601-1850
E-mail: info@albion-ventures.co.uk
Website: www.albion-ventures.co.uk

Management and Staff
Andrew Elder, Partner
David Gudgin, Partner
Edward Lascelles, Partner
Emil Gigov, Partner
Henry Stanford, Partner
Isabel Dolan, Partner
Michael Kaplan, Partner
Patrick Reeve, Managing Partner
Robert Whitby-Smith, Partner
William Fraser-Allen, Managing Partner

Type of Firm
Bank Affiliated

Association Membership
British Venture Capital Association (BVCA)

Project Preferences

Type of Financing Preferred:
Early Stage
Expansion
Research and Development
Balanced
Start-up Financing
Management Buyouts

Size of Investments Considered:
Min Size of Investment Considered (000s): $319
Max Size of Investment Considered (000s): $15,305

Geographical Preferences

International Preferences:
United Kingdom
Europe

Industry Preferences

In Medical/Health prefer:
Health Services

In Consumer Related prefer:
Entertainment and Leisure
Other Restaurants
Hotels and Resorts

Additional Information
Year Founded: 1996
Capital Under Management: $312,300,000
Current Activity Level: Actively seeking new investments

ALBION INVESTORS LLC

75 Rockefeller Plaza
15th Floor
New York, NY USA 10019
Phone: 2122777520
Website: www.albioninvestors.com

Other Offices
2000 North Racine
Suite 2184
Chicago, IL USA 60614

Management and Staff
Alastair Tedford, Managing Partner
Basil Livanos, Managing Director
Charles Gonzalez, Managing Director
Christine Vogt, Vice President
James Pendergast, Managing Director
Mark Arnold, Managing Partner

Type of Firm
Private Equity Firm

Project Preferences

Type of Financing Preferred:
Fund of Funds
Leveraged Buyout
Mezzanine
Acquisition
Recapitalizations

Geographical Preferences

United States Preferences:
Mid Atlantic
Southeast
Northeast

Canadian Preferences:
All Canada

Industry Preferences

In Consumer Related prefer:
Consumer Products

In Business Serv. prefer:
Services
Distribution

In Manufact. prefer:
Manufacturing

Additional Information
Name of Most Recent Fund: Albion Alliance Mezzanine Fund II
Most Recent Fund Was Raised: 10/12/1999
Year Founded: 1995
Current Activity Level: Actively seeking new investments

ALCATEL-LUCENT VENTURES

600-700 Mountain Avenue
Murray Hill, NJ USA 07974
Phone: 9085088080
Fax: 9085826069
E-mail: venturescomms@alcatel-lucent.com

Management and Staff
Barton Shigemura, Vice President
Sudhir Ahuja, Vice President

Type of Firm
Corporate PE/Venture

Association Membership
Israel Venture Association

Project Preferences

Role in Financing:
Will function either as deal originator or investor in deals created by others

Type of Financing Preferred:
Balanced

Industry Focus
(% based on actual investment)
Communications and Media 28.3%
Semiconductors/Other Elect. 23.8%
Computer Software and Services 21.0%
Internet Specific 20.7%
Computer Hardware 6.3%

Additional Information
Name of Most Recent Fund: lucent Venture Partners III
Most Recent Fund Was Raised: 06/20/2001
Year Founded: 1998
Capital Under Management: $300,000,000
Current Activity Level: Making few, if any, new investments
Method of Compensation: Return on investment is of primary concern, do not charge fees

ALCEDO SOCIETA DI GESTIONE DEL RISPARMIO SPA

Vicolo XX Settembre, 11
Treviso, Italy 31100
Phone: 39422559111
Fax: 39422580000
E-mail: info@alcedo.it
Website: www.alcedo.it

Management and Staff
Franco Valvasori, Partner
Marco Guidolin, Partner
Maurizio Masetti, Chief Executive Officer
Maurizio Tiveron, Co-Founder
Michele Gallo, Partner
Sonia Lorenzet, Partner

Type of Firm
Private Equity Firm

Association Membership
Italian Venture Capital Association (AIFI)

Project Preferences

Type of Financing Preferred:
Leveraged Buyout
Turnaround
Management Buyouts
Acquisition

Geographical Preferences

International Preferences:
Italy

Additional Information
Year Founded: 2001
Capital Under Management: $222,420,000
Current Activity Level : Actively seeking new investments

ALCHEMY PARTNERS LLP

21 Palmer Street
London, United Kingdom SW1H 0AD
Phone: 442072409596
Fax: 442072409594
E-mail: info@alchemypartners.com
Website: www.alchemypartners.co.uk

Management and Staff
Alex Leicester, Partner
Dominic Slade, Managing Partner
Frits Prakke, Partner
Gavin Loughrey, Partner
Ian Cash, Partner
John Rowland, Partner
Martin Bolland, Co-Founder
Robert Barnes, Co-Founder

Type of Firm
Private Equity Firm

Association Membership
British Venture Capital Association (BVCA)

Project Preferences

Role in Financing:
Prefer role as deal originator

Type of Financing Preferred:
Leveraged Buyout
Balanced
Turnaround
Acquisition
Special Situation
Distressed Debt

Geographical Preferences

International Preferences:
Europe

Industry Focus
(% based on actual investment)

Consumer Related	38.0%
Other Products	23.9%
Industrial/Energy	10.0%
Communications and Media	9.0%
Computer Hardware	8.2%
Computer Software and Services	8.0%
Medical/Health	2.4%
Internet Specific	0.5%

Additional Information
Name of Most Recent Fund: AA Development Capital India Fund
Most Recent Fund Was Raised: 09/28/2007
Year Founded: 1997
Capital Under Management: $1,547,900,000
Current Activity Level : Actively seeking new investments
Method of Compensation: Return on invest. most important, but chg. closing fees, service fees, etc.

ALCUIN CAPITAL PARTNERS LLP

65 Sloane Street
London, United Kingdom SW1X 9SH
Phone: 442031784089
Fax: 442031784090
E-mail: info@alcuincapital.com
Website: www.alcuincapital.com

Management and Staff
Ian Henderson-Londono, Co-Founder
Mark Storey, Managing Director

Type of Firm
Private Equity Firm

Project Preferences

Type of Financing Preferred:
Expansion
Later Stage
Management Buyouts
Recapitalizations

Size of Investments Considered:
Min Size of Investment Considered (000s): $1,679
Max Size of Investment Considered (000s): $6,716

Geographical Preferences

International Preferences:
United Kingdom
Europe

Additional Information
Name of Most Recent Fund: Alcuin Capital Partners LLP III
Most Recent Fund Was Raised: 01/19/2011
Year Founded: 2007
Capital Under Management: $338,573,000
Current Activity Level : Actively seeking new investments

ALDER

Kungsgatan 30
9th Floor
Stockholm, Sweden 111 35
Phone: 4686797050
E-mail: info@alder.se
Website: www.alder.se

Management and Staff
Carl Hall, Partner
Dag Broman, Partner
Henrik Flygar, Partner
Jonas Frick, Partner
Thomas Nilsson, Partner

Type of Firm
Private Equity Firm

Association Membership
Swedish Venture Capital Association (SVCA)

Project Preferences

Type of Financing Preferred:
Leveraged Buyout

Geographical Preferences

International Preferences:
Sweden
Germany

Industry Preferences

In Industrial/Energy prefer:
Alternative Energy
Energy Conservation Relat
Environmental Related

In Other prefer:
Environment Responsible

Additional Information
Year Founded: 2010
Capital Under Management: $159,000,000
Current Activity Level : Actively seeking new investments

ALDINE CAPITAL PARTNERS INC

30 West Monroe Street
Suite 1310
Chicago, IL USA 60603
Phone: 3123463950
Fax: 3123463930
Website: www.aldinecapital.com

Management and Staff
Bert Brahm, Partner
Greg Gibson, Managing Director
Michael Revord, Managing Partner

Type of Firm
Private Equity Firm

Association Membership
Natl Assoc of Small Bus. Inv. Co (NASBIC)

Project Preferences

Type of Financing Preferred:
Leveraged Buyout
Mezzanine
Acquisition
Recapitalizations

Geographical Preferences

United States Preferences:
Midwest

Additional Information
Name of Most Recent Fund: Aldine Capital Fund II, L.P.
Most Recent Fund Was Raised: 03/25/2013
Year Founded: 2006
Capital Under Management: $108,000,000
Current Activity Level : Actively seeking new investments

ALDRICH CAPITAL PARTNERS

6430 Rockledge Drive
Suite 503
Bethesda, MD USA 20817
E-mail: info@aldrichcap.com
Website: www.aldrichcap.com

Type of Firm
Private Equity Firm

Project Preferences

Type of Financing Preferred:
Later Stage
Acquisition

Geographical Preferences

United States Preferences:
Southeast
North America

Industry Preferences

In Computer Software prefer:
Software

In Internet Specific prefer:
Internet

In Medical/Health prefer:
Medical/Health

In Financial Services prefer:
Financial Services

In Business Serv. prefer:
Services

Additional Information
Year Founded: 2014
Capital Under Management: $50,000,000
Current Activity Level : Actively seeking new investments

ALDUS EQUITY

2651 North Harwood Street
Suite 210
Dallas, PA USA 18612
Phone: 2142343995
Fax: 2142343772
Website: www.aldusequity.com

Type of Firm
Investment Management Firm

Project Preferences

Type of Financing Preferred:
Leveraged Buyout

Industry Preferences

In Other prefer:
Women/Minority-Owned Bus.

Additional Information
Year Founded: 2004
Current Activity Level : Actively seeking new investments

ALEPH CAPITAL PARTNERS LLP

14 Saint George Street
London, United Kingdom W1S 1FE
Phone: 4402035406
E-mail: info@aleph.com
Website: www.aleph.com

Management and Staff
Ben Freeman, Chief Financial Officer
Justine Dobbs-Higginson, Managing Director
Pietro Cinquegrana, Managing Director

Type of Firm
Private Equity Firm

Project Preferences

Type of Financing Preferred:
Leveraged Buyout
Management Buyouts
Acquisition
Private Placement
Distressed Debt

Additional Information
Year Founded: 2013
Current Activity Level : Actively seeking new investments

ALEPH CAPITAL SA

Calle Serrano 38
Madrid, Spain 28001
Phone: 34914261648
Fax: 34914356280

Management and Staff
Alfonso Botin, Managing Director

Type of Firm
Private Equity Firm

Project Preferences

Type of Financing Preferred:
Early Stage
Expansion
Seed
Startup

Geographical Preferences

International Preferences:
Europe
Spain

Industry Preferences

In Internet Specific prefer:
E-Commerce Technology
Internet
Ecommerce

In Business Serv. prefer:
Services

Additional Information
Year Founded: 2000
Current Activity Level : Actively seeking new investments

ALEPH VENTURE CAPITAL

Rothschild 32
Tel Aviv, Israel
Website: aleph.vc

Other Offices
Rothschild 32
Tel Aviv, Israel

Type of Firm
Private Equity Firm

Project Preferences

Type of Financing Preferred:
Early Stage
Balanced
Seed

Size of Investments Considered:
Min Size of Investment Considered (000s): $2,000
Max Size of Investment Considered (000s): $5,000

Geographical Preferences

International Preferences:
Israel

Industry Preferences

In Other prefer:
Environment Responsible

Additional Information
Name of Most Recent Fund: Aleph, L.P.
Most Recent Fund Was Raised: 07/03/2013
Year Founded: 2013
Capital Under Management: $320,000,000
Current Activity Level : Actively seeking new investments

ALERION PARTNERS LLC

23 Old Kings Highway South
Darien, CT USA 06820
Phone: 2032029900
Fax: 2032029906
E-mail: info@alerionpartners.com
Website: www.alerionpartners.com

Management and Staff
Bruce Failing, Partner
Michael Persky, Partner
Robert Cioffi, Venture Partner
Virginia Cargill, Venture Partner

Type of Firm
Private Equity Firm

Project Preferences

Type of Financing Preferred:
Early Stage
Balanced
Recapitalizations

Size of Investments Considered:
Min Size of Investment Considered (000s): $3,000
Max Size of Investment Considered (000s): $10,000

Geographical Preferences

United States Preferences:
All U.S.

Industry Preferences

In Consumer Related prefer:
Consumer Products
Consumer Services

In Business Serv. prefer:
Services
Media

Additional Information
Name of Most Recent Fund: Alerion Investment Partners II, L.P.
Most Recent Fund Was Raised: 05/27/2009
Year Founded: 2004
Capital Under Management: $40,000,000
Current Activity Level : Actively seeking new investments

ALERION VENTURES LLC

105 Broad Street
Charleston, SC USA 29401
Website: alerion.ventures

Management and Staff
Wiley Becker, Partner

Type of Firm
Private Equity Firm

Project Preferences

Type of Financing Preferred:
Early Stage

Geographical Preferences

United States Preferences:
North Carolina
South Carolina
Georgia

Industry Preferences

In Computer Software prefer:
Software

In Medical/Health prefer:
Medical/Health

In Consumer Related prefer:
Consumer

Additional Information
Year Founded: 2014
Current Activity Level : Actively seeking new investments

ALESTA GIRISIM SERMAYESI YATIRIM ORTAKLIGI AS

Mecidiyekoy Mah. Atakan Sokak
No: 14 Sisli
Istanbul, Turkey 34837
Phone: 902123406417
Fax: 902122120762
Website: www.alestagirisim.com

Type of Firm
Private Equity Firm

Project Preferences

Type of Financing Preferred:
Balanced

Geographical Preferences

International Preferences:
Turkey

Industry Preferences

In Communications prefer:
Telecommunications

In Industrial/Energy prefer:
Energy

Additional Information
Year Founded: 2012
Current Activity Level : Actively seeking new investments

ALETHEIA PARTNERS LTD

37 Upper Grosvenor Street
London, United Kingdom W1K 2NE
Phone: 44-20-7663-6666
E-mail: info@aletheiapartners.com
Website: www.aletheiapartners.com

Management and Staff
Robert Tchenguiz, Co-Founder
Scott Lanphere, Managing Partner

Type of Firm
Private Equity Firm

Project Preferences

Type of Financing Preferred:
Leveraged Buyout

Geographical Preferences

International Preferences:
United Kingdom
Germany
France

Additional Information
Year Founded: 2002
Current Activity Level : Actively seeking new investments

ALEXANDRIA REAL ESTATE EQUITIES, LLC

385 East Colorado Boulevard
Suite 299
Pasadena, CA USA 91101
Phone: 6265780777
Fax: 6265780896
E-mail: corporateinformation@are.com
Website: www.labspace.com

Management and Staff
Etsuko Mason, Vice President

Type of Firm
Corporate PE/Venture

Additional Information
Year Founded: 1994
Current Activity Level : Actively seeking new investments

ALFRED WIEDER AG

Muenchener Strasse 52
Pullach im Isartal, Germany 82049
Phone: 4989122281200
Fax: 4989122281299
E-mail: info@alfred-wieder.ag
Website: www.alfred-wieder.ag

Other Offices
Ergoldinger Strasse 2 a
Landshut, Germany 84030
Phone: 49-871-9746790
Fax: 49-871-87467918

Management and Staff
Alfred Wieder, Managing Director
Matthias Hallweger, Managing Director
Michael Motschmann, Managing Director

Type of Firm
Private Equity Firm

Project Preferences

Type of Financing Preferred:
Early Stage
Later Stage
Startup

Geographical Preferences

International Preferences:
Switzerland
Austria
Germany

Industry Preferences

In Biotechnology prefer:
Biotechnology

In Medical/Health prefer:
Medical/Health
Pharmaceuticals

Additional Information
Year Founded: 2002
Current Activity Level : Actively seeking new investments

ALGEBRA CAPITAL LTD

DIFC, Building 3, 7th Floor
P.O. Box 506558
Dubai, Utd. Arab Em.
Phone: 97144250999
Fax: 97144250998
E-mail: info@algebra-capital.com
Website: www.algebra-capital.com

Management and Staff
Alain Antoniades, Chief Operating Office
Daniel Smaller, Managing Director
Joe Kawkabani, Managing Director
Julia Ward, Vice President
Mohieddine Kronfol, Managing Director
Omar Farooqui, Vice President
Ziad Abou Sahyoun, Chief Financial Officer

Type of Firm
Private Equity Firm

Project Preferences

Type of Financing Preferred:
Early Stage
Balanced
Later Stage
Seed
Startup

Geographical Preferences

International Preferences:
Middle East
Asia
Africa

Additional Information
Year Founded: 2006
Current Activity Level : Actively seeking new investments

ALGEBRA VENTURES

6 Mohamed Mazhar St, Zamalek
Cairo, Egypt 11211
E-mail: info@algebraventures.com
Website: algebraventures.com

Other Offices
6 Mohamed Mazhar St, Zamalek
Cairo, Egypt 11211

Type of Firm
Private Equity Firm

Project Preferences

Type of Financing Preferred:
Early Stage
Seed
Startup

Geographical Preferences

International Preferences:
Egypt
Middle East
Africa

Industry Preferences

In Computer Software prefer:
Software

In Internet Specific prefer:
E-Commerce Technology
Internet

In Financial Services prefer:
Financial Services

Additional Information
Year Founded: 2015
Capital Under Management: $40,000,000
Current Activity Level : Actively seeking new investments

ALGONQUIN ADVISORS LLC

2 Greenwich Office Park
Building 2, Floor 2
Greenwich, CT USA 06831
Phone: 2036292114
Fax: 2036297074
Website: www.algonquinadvisors.com

Management and Staff
C. Thayer Walker, Managing Director
George Hubbard, Founder
Jessica Nelson, Vice President
John Hyman, Chief Executive Officer
Laura Sousa, Vice President
Michael Devine, Senior Managing Director
Michaela Barnum, Vice President

Type of Firm
Investment Management Firm

Project Preferences

Type of Financing Preferred:
Fund of Funds
Leveraged Buyout
Mezzanine
Generalist PE
Balanced

Additional Information
Year Founded: 2013
Capital Under Management: $31,000,000
Current Activity Level : Actively seeking new investments

ALIANTE PARTNERS SRL

Via dei Piatti 9
Milan, Italy 20123
Phone: 39-2-3651-5130
Fax: 39-2-3651-5138
E-mail: info@aliantepartners.com
Website: www.aliantepartners.com

Other Offices
Viale Trento 23
Vicenza, Italy 36100
Phone: 39-444-544-299
Fax: 39-444-321-744

Management and Staff
Niccolo Fischer, Partner
Paolo Righetto, Partner

Type of Firm
Private Equity Firm

Association Membership
Italian Venture Capital Association (AIFI)

Project Preferences

Type of Financing Preferred:
Leveraged Buyout

Geographical Preferences

International Preferences:
Italy
Europe

Industry Preferences

In Consumer Related prefer:
Consumer
Food/Beverage

Additional Information
Year Founded: 2006
Capital Under Management: $219,585,000
Current Activity Level : Actively seeking new investments

ALIGN CAPITAL LLC

1011 San Jacinto Boulevard
Suite 303
Austin, TX USA 78701
Phone: 5125224939
E-mail: InvestorRelations@AlignCapital.com
Website: www.aligncapital.com

Management and Staff
Brian Garsson, Managing Director
David Osborn, Co-Founder
Lisa Harris, Co-Founder
Ross Brown, Managing Director
William Hall, CEO & Managing Director

Type of Firm
Private Equity Firm

Project Preferences

Type of Financing Preferred:
Early Stage
Expansion
Later Stage
Seed

Additional Information
Year Founded: 1969
Current Activity Level : Actively seeking new investments

ALIGN CAPITAL PARTNERS LP

3811 Turtle Creek Boulevard
Suite 250
Dallas, TX USA 75219
Website: aligncp.com

Type of Firm
Private Equity Firm

Project Preferences

Type of Financing Preferred:
Generalist PE

Industry Preferences

In Medical/Health prefer:
Medical Products
Pharmaceuticals

In Industrial/Energy prefer:
Oil & Gas Drilling,Explor

In Transportation prefer:
Transportation
Aerospace

Additional Information
Year Founded: 2016
Capital Under Management: $325,000,000
Current Activity Level : Actively seeking new investments

ALIGNED PARTNERS LLC

2882 Sand Hill Road
Suite 100
Menlo Park, CA USA 94025
E-mail: info@alignedvc.com
Website: alignedvc.com

Management and Staff
Jodi Jahic, Co-Founder
Susan Mason, Co-Founder

Type of Firm
Private Equity Firm

Project Preferences

Type of Financing Preferred:
Early Stage

Industry Preferences

In Communications prefer:
Wireless Communications

In Computer Software prefer:
Software

Additional Information
Name of Most Recent Fund: Aligned Partners Fund II, L.P.
Most Recent Fund Was Raised: 11/14/2014
Year Founded: 2013
Capital Under Management: $75,939,000
Current Activity Level : Actively seeking new investments

ALIGNVEST CAPITAL MANAGEMENT INC

100 King Street West
70F First Canadian Place
Toronto, Canada M5X 1C7
Phone: 4163606390
Website: www.alignvestcapital.com

Type of Firm
Private Equity Firm

Project Preferences

Type of Financing Preferred:
Leveraged Buyout
Acquisition

Geographical Preferences

United States Preferences:
North America

Industry Preferences

In Medical/Health prefer:
Medical/Health

In Financial Services prefer:
Financial Services

Additional Information
Year Founded: 2010
Current Activity Level : Actively seeking new investments

ALIGO INNOVATION SOCIETE EN COMMANDITE

355 Rue Peel
Suite 503
Montreal, Canada H3C 2G9
Phone: 5148401226
E-mail: INFO@ALIGOINNOVATION.COM
Website: www.aligo.ca

Type of Firm
University Program

Project Preferences

Type of Financing Preferred:
Balanced

Geographical Preferences

Canadian Preferences:
All Canada

Additional Information

Year Founded: 2014
Current Activity Level : Actively seeking new investments

ALIUM CAPITAL MANAGEMENT PTY LTD

13 Leura Road
Double Bay, Australia NSW 2028
E-mail: corporate@aliumcap.com
Website: www.aliumcap.com

Type of Firm

Private Equity Firm

Project Preferences

Type of Financing Preferred:
Generalist PE
Later Stage
Recapitalizations

Geographical Preferences

United States Preferences:

International Preferences:
Australia

Additional Information

Year Founded: 2017
Current Activity Level : Actively seeking new investments

ALL MOBILE FUND

44 Tehama Street
San Francisco, CA USA 94105
Website: www.allmobilefund.com

Type of Firm

Private Equity Firm

Project Preferences

Type of Financing Preferred:
Seed
Startup

Industry Preferences

In Computer Software prefer:
Artificial Intelligence

Additional Information

Year Founded: 2015
Current Activity Level : Actively seeking new investments

ALL-AMERICAN HOLDINGS LLC

4200 Northside Parkway
Building Five, Suite 508
Atlanta, GA USA 30327
Website: www.allamericanholdings.com

Other Offices

358 Elmington Ave
Nashville, TN USA 37205
Phone: 6159693411

Management and Staff

Marshall Hunt, Co-Founder
Robert Shuler, Co-Founder
Sheryl Lyles, Chief Financial Officer
Thomas Joseph Guzik, Chief Financial Officer

Type of Firm

Private Equity Firm

Project Preferences

Type of Financing Preferred:
Turnaround
Acquisition
Distressed Debt

Geographical Preferences

United States Preferences:

International Preferences:
Europe

Industry Preferences

In Manufact. prefer:
Manufacturing

Additional Information

Year Founded: 2007
Current Activity Level : Actively seeking new investments

ALLEGISCYBER

525 University Avenue
Suite 220
Palo Alto, CA USA 94301
Phone: 6506870500
Fax: 6506870234
E-mail: vc@allegiscapital.com
Website: www.allegiscapital.com

Other Offices

Two Harrison Street
Suite 180
SAN FRANCISCO, CA USA 94105
Phone: 4153488868
Fax: 4152789794

Management and Staff

Barry Weinman, Managing Director
David DeWalt, Managing Director
Hossein Eslambolchi, Venture Partner
Jean-Louis Gassee, Venture Partner
Jeffrey Williams, Venture Partner
Joe Levy, Venture Partner
John Stewart, Venture Partner
Jonathan Funk, Managing Director
Kendall Cooper, Chief Financial Officer
Nawaf Bitar, Venture Partner
Peter Bodine, Managing Director
Robert Ackerman, Founder
Spencer Tall, Managing Director
Steve Simonian, Chief Financial Officer
Tom Gillis, Venture Partner

Type of Firm

Private Equity Firm

Association Membership

National Venture Capital Association - USA (NVCA)

Project Preferences

Type of Financing Preferred:
Early Stage
Seed
Startup

Size of Investments Considered:

Min Size of Investment Considered (000s): $3,000
Max Size of Investment Considered (000s): $5,000

Industry Focus

(% based on actual investment)
Internet Specific	37.6%
Computer Software and Services	35.5%
Communications and Media	10.7%
Semiconductors/Other Elect.	8.9%
Computer Hardware	6.3%
Other Products	1.1%

Additional Information

Name of Most Recent Fund: Allegis Capital VI, L.P.
Most Recent Fund Was Raised: 07/01/2015
Year Founded: 1996
Capital Under Management: $700,000,000
Current Activity Level : Actively seeking new investments
Method of Compensation: Return on investment is of primary concern, do not charge fees

ALLEGORY VENTURES MANAGEMENT LLC

610 Southwest Alder Street
Suite 210
Portland, OR USA 97205
Phone: 9713039335
Website: www.allegoryventurepartners.com

Other Offices
2450 Holcombe Boulevard
Houston, TX USA 77201

Type of Firm
Private Equity Firm

Project Preferences

Type of Financing Preferred:
Early Stage
Expansion
Later Stage
Seed

Industry Preferences

In Medical/Health prefer:
Medical Diagnostics

Additional Information
Year Founded: 2015
Current Activity Level : Actively seeking new investments

ALLEGRA CAPITAL GMBH

Pachmayrplatz 11
Munich, Germany 81927
Phone: 498999536755
Fax: 498992091518
E-mail: info@allegracapital.com
Website: www.allegracapital.com

Management and Staff
Hendrik Heinze, Chief Executive Officer

Type of Firm
Private Equity Firm

Association Membership
German Venture Capital Association (BVK)

Project Preferences

Type of Financing Preferred:
Leveraged Buyout
Turnaround
Acquisition
Special Situation

Geographical Preferences

International Preferences:
Europe
Germany

Industry Preferences

In Semiconductor/Electr prefer:
Electronics
Fiber Optics

In Medical/Health prefer:
Medical/Health

In Consumer Related prefer:
Retail

In Industrial/Energy prefer:
Factory Automation
Environmental Related

In Business Serv. prefer:
Services

In Manufact. prefer:
Manufacturing

Additional Information
Year Founded: 2000
Current Activity Level : Actively seeking new investments

ALLEGRO FUNDS PTY LTD

95 Pitt Street
Level Two
Sydney, Australia 2000
Phone: 61282288700
Fax: 61292518028
E-mail: enquiries@allegrofunds.com.au
Website: www.allegrofunds.com.au

Management and Staff
Adrian Loader, Co-Founder
Chester Moynihan, Co-Founder

Type of Firm
Private Equity Firm

Association Membership
New Zealand Venture Capital Association
Australian Venture Capital Association (AVCAL)

Project Preferences

Type of Financing Preferred:
Leveraged Buyout
Balanced
Turnaround
Management Buyouts
Recapitalizations

Size of Investments Considered:
Min Size of Investment Considered (000s): $13,685
Max Size of Investment Considered (000s): $31,931

Geographical Preferences

International Preferences:
New Zealand

Additional Information
Name of Most Recent Fund: Allegro Private Equity Fund I
Most Recent Fund Was Raised: 03/31/2006
Year Founded: 2006
Capital Under Management: $500,000,000
Current Activity Level : Actively seeking new investments

ALLEGRO INVESTMENT FUND NV

Romeinse Straat 18
Research Park Haasrode
Heverlee, Belgium B-3001
Phone: 32485664650
E-mail: info@allegroinvestmentfund.com
Website: www.allegroinvestmentfund.com

Management and Staff
Geert Everaert, Managing Partner

Type of Firm
Private Equity Firm

Project Preferences

Type of Financing Preferred:
Early Stage
Seed
Startup

Size of Investments Considered:
Min Size of Investment Considered (000s): $135
Max Size of Investment Considered (000s): $1,359

Geographical Preferences

International Preferences:
Europe
Belgium

Additional Information
Year Founded: 2005
Current Activity Level : Actively seeking new investments

ALLELE FUND

P.O. Box 60519
London, United Kingdom W2 7JU
Phone: 442072248499
Fax: 442072249405
E-mail: info@allelefund.com
Website: www.allelefund.com

Management and Staff
Cherie Blair, Founder

Type of Firm
Private Equity Firm

Project Preferences

Type of Financing Preferred:
Early Stage
Expansion
Balanced
Later Stage

Geographical Preferences

International Preferences:
United Kingdom
Europe

Industry Preferences

In Medical/Health prefer:
Medical/Health
Health Services

Additional Information

Year Founded: 2011
Current Activity Level : Actively seeking new investments

ALLEN & COMPANY INC

711 Fifth Avenue
Ninth Floor
Manhattan, NY USA 10022
Phone: 2128328000
Fax: 2128328023

Management and Staff

Fred Lopez, Vice President

Type of Firm

Investment Management Firm

Project Preferences

Type of Financing Preferred:
Generalist PE

Additional Information

Year Founded: 1922
Current Activity Level : Actively seeking new investments

ALLEN & COMPANY OF FLORIDA, INC.

1401 South Florida Avenue
Lakeland, FL USA 33803
Phone: 2128328300
Fax: 8636166354
Website: www.alleninvestments.com

Management and Staff

Enrique Senior, Managing Director
Eugene Protash, Vice President
Harold Wit, Managing Director
John Josephson, Managing Director
John Schneiorr, Managing Director
Paul Gould, Managing Director
Philip Scaturro, Managing Director
Robert Coseriff, Managing Director
Stanley Shuman, Managing Director
Walter O Hara, Managing Director
William Bradley, Managing Director

Type of Firm

Bank Affiliated

Project Preferences

Type of Financing Preferred:
Balanced

Geographical Preferences

United States Preferences:
All U.S.

Industry Focus

(% based on actual investment)
Internet Specific	49.1%
Computer Software and Services	15.5%
Communications and Media	10.3%
Medical/Health	6.2%
Computer Hardware	5.0%
Biotechnology	4.4%
Industrial/Energy	3.9%
Other Products	3.4%
Consumer Related	1.3%
Semiconductors/Other Elect.	0.8%

Additional Information

Name of Most Recent Fund: Allen Value Partners, L.P.
Most Recent Fund Was Raised: 12/31/1988
Year Founded: 1932
Current Activity Level : Actively seeking new investments

ALLEN CAPITAL GROUP LLC

800 Westchester Avenue
Port Chester, NY USA 10573
Phone: 9144818000
Fax: 9144818001
E-mail: inquiries@acptrs.com
Website: www.acptrs.com

Type of Firm

Investment Management Firm

Project Preferences

Type of Financing Preferred:
Special Situation
Distressed Debt
Fund of Funds of Second

Additional Information

Year Founded: 2000
Current Activity Level : Actively seeking new investments

ALLIANCE CONSUMER GROWTH LLC

655 Madison Avenue
20th Floor
New York, NY USA 10017
Phone: 2129409630
E-mail: info@acginvestors.com
Website: acginvestors.com

Management and Staff

Josh Goldin, Managing Partner
Julian Steinberg, Managing Partner
Trevor Nelson, Managing Partner

Type of Firm

Private Equity Firm

Project Preferences

Type of Financing Preferred:
Balanced

Size of Investments Considered:
Min Size of Investment Considered (000s): $2,000
Max Size of Investment Considered (000s): $10,000

Industry Preferences

In Consumer Related prefer:
Consumer
Retail
Food/Beverage
Consumer Products
Consumer Services
Other Restaurants

Additional Information

Name of Most Recent Fund: Alliance Consumer Growth Fund, L.P.
Most Recent Fund Was Raised: 09/12/2011
Year Founded: 2011
Capital Under Management: $344,655,000
Current Activity Level : Actively seeking new investments

ALLIANCE ENTREPRENDRE SAS

5-7 rue de Monttessuy
Paris, France 75007
Phone: 33158193208
Fax: 33158192856
E-mail: contact@allianceentreprendre.com
Website: www.allianceentreprendre.com

Type of Firm

Bank Affiliated

Association Membership

French Venture Capital Association (AFIC)

Project Preferences

Type of Financing Preferred:
Leveraged Buyout
Early Stage
Generalist PE
Balanced
Later Stage
Management Buyouts

Size of Investments Considered:
Min Size of Investment Considered (000s): $274
Max Size of Investment Considered (000s): $2,058

Geographical Preferences

International Preferences:
Europe
France

Industry Preferences

In Industrial/Energy prefer:
Industrial Products

In Business Serv. prefer:
Services
Distribution
Media

Additional Information

Year Founded: 1994
Capital Under Management: $40,000,000
Current Activity Level : Actively seeking new investments

ALLIANCE FUND MANAGERS LTD

One Dale Street
Second Floor, Exchange Court
Liverpool, United Kingdom L2 2PP
Phone: 441512364040
Fax: 441512363060

Type of Firm
Bank Affiliated

Association Membership
British Venture Capital Association (BVCA)

Project Preferences

Type of Financing Preferred:
Leveraged Buyout
Generalist PE
Balanced

Geographical Preferences

International Preferences:
United Kingdom
Europe

Additional Information

Year Founded: 1996
Capital Under Management: $104,400,000
Current Activity Level : Actively seeking new investments

ALLIANCE HEALTHCARE PARTNERS

6900 East Camelback Road
Suite 860
Scottsdale, AZ USA 85251
Phone: 6027735806
Fax: 6024193100
E-mail: info@alliancehcpartners.com
Website: test.alliancehcpartners.com

Type of Firm
Private Equity Firm

Project Preferences

Type of Financing Preferred:
Leveraged Buyout
Early Stage
Expansion
Balanced
Acquisition

Geographical Preferences

United States Preferences:

Industry Preferences

In Communications prefer:
Communications and Media

In Medical/Health prefer:
Medical/Health
Medical Products
Health Services

In Business Serv. prefer:
Services

Additional Information

Name of Most Recent Fund: Alliance Healthcare Investment Fund, L.P.
Most Recent Fund Was Raised: 09/10/2012
Year Founded: 2013
Capital Under Management: $3,200,000
Current Activity Level : Actively seeking new investments

ALLIANCE MANGEMENT CONSULTING CO LTD (TAIWAN BRANCH)

Eight DuenHua North Road
11th Floor
Taipei, Taiwan
Phone: 886-2-8771-9922
Fax: 886-2-2771-2321
E-mail: info@amcc.com.tw

Type of Firm
Private Equity Firm

Project Preferences

Type of Financing Preferred:
Early Stage
Generalist PE

Geographical Preferences

United States Preferences:

International Preferences:
Taiwan
China

Industry Preferences

In Communications prefer:
Communications and Media

In Computer Software prefer:
Software
Applications Software

In Semiconductor/Electr prefer:
Semiconductor
Optoelectronics

In Biotechnology prefer:
Biotechnology

Additional Information

Year Founded: 2000
Current Activity Level : Actively seeking new investments

ALLIANCE VENTURE AS

Stranden 57, Aker Brygge
Oslo, Norway 0250
Phone: 4722944020
Fax: 4722471221
E-mail: info@allianceventure.com
Website: www.allianceventure.com

Management and Staff

Arne Tonning, Partner
Bjorn Christensen, Partner
Erling Maartman-Moe, Partner
Jan-Erik Hareid, Managing Partner

Type of Firm
Private Equity Firm

Association Membership
Norwegian Venture Capital Association

Project Preferences

Type of Financing Preferred:
Early Stage
Seed
Startup

Geographical Preferences

International Preferences:
Scandanavia/Nordic Region
Norway

Industry Preferences

In Communications prefer:
Commercial Communications
Wireless Communications

In Computer Software prefer:
Software

In Internet Specific prefer:
Internet

In Medical/Health prefer:
Medical/Health
Medical Therapeutics

In Consumer Related prefer:
Education Related

In Industrial/Energy prefer:
Energy
Oil and Gas Exploration

Additional Information
Year Founded: 2001
Capital Under Management: $75,000,000
Current Activity Level : Actively seeking new investments

ALLIANCEBERNSTEIN LP

1345 Avenue of the Americas
New York, NY USA 10105
Phone: 2129691000
E-mail: ir@alliancebernstein.com
Website: www.abglobal.com

Management and Staff
David Steyn, Chief Operating Officer
James Gingrich, Chief Operating Officer

Type of Firm
Investment Management Firm

Project Preferences

Type of Financing Preferred:
Value-Add
Generalist PE
Balanced

Industry Focus
(% based on actual investment)

Computer Software and Services	36.7%
Other Products	23.9%
Consumer Related	15.2%
Internet Specific	6.2%
Computer Hardware	5.2%
Biotechnology	4.7%
Industrial/Energy	3.0%
Semiconductors/Other Elect.	2.5%
Communications and Media	2.0%
Medical/Health	0.6%

Additional Information
Name of Most Recent Fund: AllianceBernstein U.S. Real Estate Partners, L.P.
Most Recent Fund Was Raised: 01/19/2011
Year Founded: 1999
Capital Under Management: $1,200,000,000
Current Activity Level : Actively seeking new investments

ALLIANSYS SAS

2, avenue de Kaarst
Euralille, France 59777
Phone: 33359312004
Fax: 33320271804

Management and Staff
Eric Grimonprez, Chief Executive Officer

Type of Firm
Private Equity Firm

Project Preferences

Role in Financing:
Prefer role as deal originator but will also invest in deals created by others

Type of Financing Preferred:
Early Stage
Seed
Startup

Size of Investments Considered:
Min Size of Investment Considered (000s): $66
Max Size of Investment Considered (000s): $264

Geographical Preferences

International Preferences:
France

Industry Preferences

In Communications prefer:
Telecommunications

In Computer Hardware prefer:
Computer Graphics and Dig

In Biotechnology prefer:
Industrial Biotechnology

In Medical/Health prefer:
Medical Therapeutics
Hospitals/Clinics/Primary

In Consumer Related prefer:
Food/Beverage

In Industrial/Energy prefer:
Environmental Related

Additional Information
Year Founded: 1991
Capital Under Management: $5,000,000
Current Activity Level : Actively seeking new investments
Method of Compensation: Return on investment is of primary concern, do not charge fees

ALLIANZ CAPITAL PARTNERS GMBH

Theresienstrasse 6-8
Munich, Germany 80333
Phone: 498938007010
Fax: 498938007586
E-mail: contact@allianzcapitalpartners.com
Website: www.allianzcapitalpartners.com

Other Offices
6 Battery Road, #28-01
, Singapore 049909
Phone: 65-6311-8000
Fax: 65-6311-8906

Management and Staff
Adam Lichtenstein, Partner
Andress Goh, Partner
Christian Mayert, Managing Director
Claus Zellner, Chief Financial Officer
Elliot Royce, Managing Director

Type of Firm
Insurance Firm Affiliate

Association Membership
German Venture Capital Association (BVK)
European Private Equity and Venture Capital Assoc.

Project Preferences

Type of Financing Preferred:
Fund of Funds
Leveraged Buyout
Mezzanine
Generalist PE
Later Stage
Acquisition

Geographical Preferences

International Preferences:
All International

Industry Focus
(% based on actual investment)

Industrial/Energy	63.0%
Computer Software and Services	19.9%
Other Products	8.5%
Internet Specific	4.4%
Consumer Related	1.7%
Communications and Media	1.3%
Biotechnology	0.6%
Computer Hardware	0.4%
Medical/Health	0.1%

Additional Information
Year Founded: 2006
Capital Under Management: $4,200,000,000
Current Activity Level : Actively seeking new investments

ALLIANZ GLOBAL INVESTORS ITALIA SGR SPA

23 , Corso Italia
Milan, Italy 20122
Phone: 39-02721-64099
Fax: 39-02725-48905
E-mail: infoweb@rasfin.it
Website: secure.allianz.it

Type of Firm
Private Equity Firm

Project Preferences

Type of Financing Preferred:
Fund of Funds
Leveraged Buyout
Expansion

Pratt's Guide to Private Equity & Venture Capital Sources

Size of Investments Considered:
Min Size of Investment Considered (000s): $3,811
Max Size of Investment Considered (000s): $15,242

Geographical Preferences

International Preferences:
Italy
Europe

Additional Information

Year Founded: 1981
Capital Under Management: $249,000,000
Current Activity Level: Actively seeking new investments

ALLIED GROWTH STRATEGIES & MANAGEMENT LLC

1981 Pine Hall Road
State College, PA USA 16801
Phone: 8142725400
Website: www.agsm.biz

Management and Staff

Allen Potter, Founder
Donald Belt, Senior Managing Director
Peter O Donnell, Managing Director
Robert Delach, Managing Director
Robert Culhane, Managing Director

Type of Firm

Private Equity Firm

Project Preferences

Type of Financing Preferred:
Leveraged Buyout
Acquisition
Recapitalizations

Geographical Preferences

United States Preferences:
Mid Atlantic
Pennsylvania
Delaware
Maryland
Virginia
New Jersey
Washington
New York

Additional Information

Year Founded: 2010
Capital Under Management: $11,600,000,000
Current Activity Level: Actively seeking new investments

ALLIED MINDS LLC

33 Arch Street, 32nd Floor
Boston, MA USA 02110
Phone: 6174191800
Fax: 6174191813
Website: www.alliedminds.com

Management and Staff

Christopher Silva, Chief Executive Officer
Joseph Pignato, Chief Financial Officer
Marc Eichenberger, Chief Operating Officer
Omar Amirana, Managing Director
Vincent Chun, Vice President

Type of Firm

Private Equity Firm

Project Preferences

Type of Financing Preferred:
Early Stage
Seed
Startup

Geographical Preferences

United States Preferences:

Industry Preferences

In Medical/Health prefer:
Medical/Health
Medical Therapeutics

Additional Information

Year Founded: 2004
Current Activity Level: Actively seeking new investments

ALLON THERAPEUTICS INC

506-1168 Hamilton Street
Vancouver, Canada V6B 2S2
Phone: 6047333609
Fax: 6047361616
E-mail: info@ndicapital.com
Website: www.allontherapeutics.com

Management and Staff

Alistair Stewart, Vice President
Bruce Morimoto, Vice President
James Miller, Chairman & CEO
Matthew Carlyle, Chief Financial Officer

Type of Firm

Private Equity Firm

Project Preferences

Role in Financing:
Will function either as deal originator or investor in deals created by others

Type of Financing Preferred:
Balanced

Geographical Preferences

United States Preferences:

Canadian Preferences:
All Canada

Industry Preferences

In Biotechnology prefer:
Biotechnology

Additional Information

Year Founded: 2003
Capital Under Management: $23,900,000
Current Activity Level: Actively seeking new investments
Method of Compensation: Return on invest. most important, but chg. closing fees, service fees, etc.

ALLOS VENTURES LLC

11611 North Meridian Street, Suite 310
Carmel, IN USA 46032
Phone: 3172756800
Website: www.allosventures.com

Other Offices

312 Walnut Street
Suite 1120
Cincinnati, OH USA 45202
Phone: 5134561001

Management and Staff

Don Aquilano, Managing Director
John McIlwraith, Managing Director

Type of Firm

Private Equity Firm

Project Preferences

Type of Financing Preferred:
Early Stage

Size of Investments Considered:
Min Size of Investment Considered (000s): $1,500
Max Size of Investment Considered (000s): $5,000

Geographical Preferences

United States Preferences:
Ohio
Indiana

Industry Preferences

In Computer Software prefer:
Software

In Medical/Health prefer:
Medical Diagnostics
Diagnostic Test Products
Medical Products

In Manufact. prefer:
Manufacturing

Additional Information

Name of Most Recent Fund: Allos II, L.P.
Most Recent Fund Was Raised: 03/17/2012
Year Founded: 2010
Capital Under Management: $40,000,000
Current Activity Level: Actively seeking new investments

ALLOY VENTURES INC

400 Hamilton Avenue
Fourth Floor
Palo Alto, CA USA 94301
Phone: 6506875000
Fax: 6506875010
E-mail: info@alloyventures.com

Management and Staff

Ammar Hanafi, General Partner
Craig Taylor, General Partner
Daniel Rubin, General Partner
David Pidwell, Venture Partner
Douglas Kelly, General Partner
J. Leighton Read, Venture Partner
John Shoch, General Partner
Michael Hunkapiller, General Partner

Type of Firm

Private Equity Firm

Association Membership

Western Association of Venture Capitalists (WAVC)
National Venture Capital Association - USA (NVCA)

Project Preferences

Type of Financing Preferred:
Early Stage
Seed
Startup

Size of Investments Considered:
Min Size of Investment Considered (000s): $1,000
Max Size of Investment Considered (000s): $5,000

Geographical Preferences

United States Preferences:

Industry Focus

(% based on actual investment)
Biotechnology	24.5%
Internet Specific	18.6%
Computer Software and Services	16.2%
Medical/Health	15.5%
Communications and Media	9.8%
Semiconductors/Other Elect.	7.0%
Industrial/Energy	5.5%
Other Products	1.6%
Computer Hardware	1.4%

Additional Information

Name of Most Recent Fund: Alloy Ventures 2005, L.P.
Most Recent Fund Was Raised: 06/28/2005
Year Founded: 1996
Capital Under Management: $1,000,000,000
Current Activity Level : Actively seeking new investments

ALLSHARE CAPITAL

Dongsanhuan Road
Rm.1604, Landmark Tower 1
Beijing, China 100004
Phone: 861065907815
Fax: 861065900866
E-mail: info@allsharecapital.com
Website: www.allsharecapital.com

Management and Staff

Dustin Wen, Managing Partner
Lawrence Zhang, Partner

Type of Firm

Private Equity Firm

Project Preferences

Type of Financing Preferred:
Balanced

Geographical Preferences

International Preferences:
China

Industry Preferences

In Communications prefer:
Telecommunications

In Medical/Health prefer:
Medical/Health

In Consumer Related prefer:
Consumer Products
Education Related

In Industrial/Energy prefer:
Environmental Related

In Financial Services prefer:
Financial Services

In Business Serv. prefer:
Media

In Agr/Forestr/Fish prefer:
Agriculture related

Additional Information

Year Founded: 2010
Current Activity Level : Actively seeking new investments

ALLSTATE PRIVATE EQUITY

3075 Sanders Road
Suite G5D
Northbrook, IL USA 60062
Phone: 847-402-8247
Fax: 847-402-0880
Website: www.allstateinvestments.com

Other Offices

One Angel Court
Suite 1300
London, United Kingdom EC2R 7HJ

Management and Staff

Elliot Stultz, Senior Managing Director
Jerry Zinkula, Managing Director
Mark Cloghessy, Senior Managing Director
Peruvemba Satish, Managing Director
Sam Davis, Senior Managing Director
Steve Shebik, Chief Financial Officer

Type of Firm

Investment Management Firm

Project Preferences

Role in Financing:
Prefer role as deal originator but will also invest in deals created by others

Type of Financing Preferred:
Fund of Funds
Leveraged Buyout
Expansion
Mezzanine
Generalist PE
Turnaround
Later Stage
Distressed Debt

Size of Investments Considered:
Min Size of Investment Considered (000s): $15,000
Max Size of Investment Considered (000s): $50,000

Additional Information

Name of Most Recent Fund: Allstate Private Equity Fund I
Most Recent Fund Was Raised: 01/01/1997
Year Founded: 1958
Capital Under Management: $700,000,000
Current Activity Level : Actively seeking new investments
Method of Compensation: Return on investment is of primary concern, do not charge fees

ALLURE CAPITAL INC

2637 East Atlantic Boulevard
13640
Pompano Beach, FL USA 33062

Type of Firm

Private Equity Firm

Project Preferences

Type of Financing Preferred:
Early Stage

Geographical Preferences

United States Preferences:

International Preferences:
Australia

Industry Preferences

In Computer Software prefer:
Software

In Semiconductor/Electr prefer:
Electronics

In Medical/Health prefer:
Medical/Health

Additional Information

Year Founded: 2011
Current Activity Level : Actively seeking new investments

ALLY BRIDGE GROUP CAPITAL PARTNERS II LP

Abg Management Ltd, 1814-1816
HONG KONG, Hong Kong
Phone: 85228017336

Type of Firm
Private Equity Firm

Project Preferences

Type of Financing Preferred:
Leveraged Buyout
Early Stage
Balanced
Later Stage

Geographical Preferences

United States Preferences:

International Preferences:
Europe
China

Industry Preferences

In Medical/Health prefer:
Medical/Health
Pharmaceuticals

Additional Information

Year Founded: 2014
Current Activity Level : Actively seeking new investments

ALMA MUNDI VENTURES SGEIC SA

Plaza Santa Brbara 2
Madrid, Spain 28004
E-mail: INFO@MUNDIVENTURES.COM
Website: mundiventures.com

Type of Firm
Private Equity Firm

Project Preferences

Type of Financing Preferred:
Balanced

Geographical Preferences

International Preferences:
Spain

Additional Information

Year Founded: 2015
Current Activity Level : Actively seeking new investments

ALMAMED

8 Rue Ali Abderrazak
Casablanca, Morocco 20100
Phone: 212522257928
Fax: 212522996484
E-mail: contact@almamed.com
Website: www.almamed.com

Management and Staff
El Houssine Sahib, Founding Partner

Type of Firm
Investment Management Firm

Project Preferences

Type of Financing Preferred:
Leveraged Buyout
Expansion
Management Buyouts
Acquisition

Geographical Preferences

International Preferences:
Europe
Morocco
Africa

Additional Information

Name of Most Recent Fund: Massinissa Fund
Most Recent Fund Was Raised: 12/31/2011
Year Founded: 2008
Current Activity Level : Actively seeking new investments

ALMAZ CAPITAL PARTNERS

Vspolny Pereulok, 19/20
Building One
Moscow, Russia 123001
Phone: 74959848370
E-mail: info@almazcapital.com
Website: www.almazcapital.com

Other Offices
3274 Alpine Road
Portola Valley, CA USA 94028
Phone: 6506444530

Management and Staff
Charles Ryan, Venture Partner
Irina Goryacheva, General Director
Lyubov Simonova, Principal
Pavel Bogdanov, Partner
Serguei Beloussov, Venture Partner

Type of Firm
Private Equity Firm

Association Membership
Western Association of Venture Capitalists (WAVC)
Russian Venture Capital Association (RVCA)

Project Preferences

Type of Financing Preferred:
Early Stage
Expansion
Balanced
Later Stage
Seed
Startup

Geographical Preferences

United States Preferences:

International Preferences:
Armenia
Belarus
Kazakhstan
Kyrgyzstan
Eastern Europe
Tajikistan
Turkmenistan
Azerbaijan
Moldova
Ukraine
Uzbekistan
Russia

Industry Preferences

In Communications prefer:
Communications and Media

In Computer Software prefer:
Software
Systems Software

In Internet Specific prefer:
E-Commerce Technology
Internet
Ecommerce

In Semiconductor/Electr prefer:
Semiconductor
Optoelectronics

Additional Information

Name of Most Recent Fund: Almaz Capital Fund II
Most Recent Fund Was Raised: 07/25/2013
Year Founded: 2008
Capital Under Management: $102,000,000
Current Activity Level : Actively seeking new investments

ALMI INVEST AB

Vasagatan 11
P.O. Box 70407
Stockholm, Sweden 107 25
Phone: 46857891920
E-mail: info@innovationsbron.se
Website: www.almi.se

Other Offices

Ole Romers vag 12
Ideon Innovation
Lund, Sweden 223 70
Phone: 46-46-2868-500
Fax: 46-46-123-472

Aurorum 1 C
Lulea, Sweden 977 75
Phone: 46-920-751-30
Fax: 46-920-751-33

Tvistevagen 47, Uminova Science Park
PO Box 7984
Umea, Sweden 907 19
Phone: 46-90-154-832
Fax: 46-90-154-833

Lindholmspiren 5
PO Box 8077
Gothenburg, Sweden 402 78
Phone: 46-31-7647-101
Fax: 46-31-410-255

Dag Hammarskjolds Vag 36b
Uppsala Science Park
Uppsala, Sweden 751 83
Phone: 46-18-510-590

Platensgatan 29
PO Box 1224,
Linkoping, Sweden 581 12
Phone: 46-13-203-290

Type of Firm
Government Affiliated Program

Project Preferences

Type of Financing Preferred:
Early Stage
Seed
Startup

Geographical Preferences

International Preferences:
Sweden

Additional Information
Year Founded: 1994
Current Activity Level : Actively seeking new investments

ALMOND TREE CAPITAL MANAGEMENT CO LLC

502 Mace Boulevard
Davis, CA USA 95618

Type of Firm
Private Equity Firm

Project Preferences

Type of Financing Preferred:
Startup

Additional Information
Year Founded: 2014
Capital Under Management: $1,010,000
Current Activity Level : Actively seeking new investments

ALOTHON GROUP LLC

Rua Joaquim Floriano
1052 - 14 floor - Conj. 142
Sao Paulo, Brazil 04534
Phone: 551130740340
Fax: 551130740349
E-mail: info@alothon.com
Website: www.alothon.com

Other Offices

10 East 53rd Street
36th Floor
New York, NY USA 10022
Phone: 2128102726
Fax: 2127500191

Management and Staff
Ana Paula Bannwart, Partner
Juan Maguire, Managing Director

Type of Firm
Private Equity Firm

Association Membership
Emerging Markets Private Equity Association

Project Preferences

Type of Financing Preferred:
Leveraged Buyout
Expansion
Acquisition

Geographical Preferences

International Preferences:
Albania
Argentina
Mexico
Brazil

Additional Information
Name of Most Recent Fund: Alothon Fund III, L.P.
Most Recent Fund Was Raised: 01/30/2014
Year Founded: 2004
Capital Under Management: $139,900,000
Current Activity Level : Actively seeking new investments

ALP CAPITAL SAS

9 rue Daru
Paris, France 75008
Phone: 33146059230
E-mail: contact@alpcapital.com
Website: www.alpcapital.com

Type of Firm
Private Equity Firm

Association Membership
French Venture Capital Association (AFIC)

Project Preferences

Type of Financing Preferred:
Leveraged Buyout
Generalist PE
Later Stage
Management Buyouts
Acquisition

Geographical Preferences

International Preferences:
Europe
France

Industry Preferences

In Communications prefer:
Telecommunications

In Computer Software prefer:
Software

In Internet Specific prefer:
Internet

Additional Information
Year Founded: 2007
Current Activity Level : Actively seeking new investments

ALPES CAPITAL INNOVATION SASU

2, Avenue du Gresivaudan
Corenc, France 38700
Website: www.expansinvest.fr

Type of Firm
Bank Affiliated

Project Preferences

125

Type of Financing Preferred:
Early Stage
Expansion
Later Stage
Seed

Size of Investments Considered:
Min Size of Investment Considered (000s): $114
Max Size of Investment Considered (000s): $456

Geographical Preferences

International Preferences:
Europe
France

Industry Preferences

In Biotechnology prefer:
Biotechnology

In Industrial/Energy prefer:
Environmental Related

In Business Serv. prefer:
Media

Additional Information
Year Founded: 2009
Current Activity Level : Actively seeking new investments

ALPES DEVELOPPEMENT DURABLE INVESTISSEMENT SAS

2, Avenue du Gresivaudan
Corenc, France 38700
Website: www.a2dinvest.fr

Type of Firm
Bank Affiliated

Project Preferences

Type of Financing Preferred:
Leveraged Buyout
Early Stage
Generalist PE
Seed
Acquisition

Geographical Preferences

International Preferences:
France

Industry Preferences

In Industrial/Energy prefer:
Energy
Alternative Energy
Environmental Related

In Other prefer:
Environment Responsible

Additional Information
Year Founded: 2009
Current Activity Level : Actively seeking new investments

ALPHA CAPITAL PARTNERS, LTD.

122 South Michigan Avenue
Suite 1700
Chicago, IL USA 60603
Phone: 3123229800
Fax: 3123229808
E-mail: info@alphacapital.com
Website: www.alphacapital.com

Other Offices

3155 Research Boulevard
Dayton, OH USA 45402
Phone: 937-252-9580
Fax: 937-253-2634

2083 Bedford Road
Columbus, OH USA 43212
Phone: 614-487-8780

2593 Walnut Road
Ann Arbor, MI USA 48103
Phone: 734-994-1003
Fax: 734-994-0044

Management and Staff
Andrew Kalnow, President
Gary Stark, Managing Director
John Rose, Principal

Type of Firm
Private Equity Firm

Project Preferences

Role in Financing:
Prefer role as deal originator but will also invest in deals created by others

Type of Financing Preferred:
Leveraged Buyout
Expansion
Generalist PE
Turnaround
Later Stage
Acquisition
Recapitalizations

Size of Investments Considered:
Min Size of Investment Considered (000s): $500
Max Size of Investment Considered (000s): $5,000

Geographical Preferences

United States Preferences:
Midwest

Industry Focus
(% based on actual investment)

Computer Software and Services	40.0%
Consumer Related	17.1%
Industrial/Energy	15.9%
Other Products	8.3%
Communications and Media	6.2%
Medical/Health	4.4%
Internet Specific	3.4%
Biotechnology	3.0%
Semiconductors/Other Elect.	1.5%
Computer Hardware	0.2%

Additional Information
Name of Most Recent Fund: Alpha Capital Fund III, L.P.
Most Recent Fund Was Raised: 01/11/2001
Year Founded: 1984
Capital Under Management: $135,000,000
Current Activity Level : Actively seeking new investments
Method of Compensation: Return on investment is of primary concern, do not charge fees

ALPHA EDISON PARTNERS LLC

8163 Melrose Avenue
Los Angeles, CA USA 90046

Type of Firm
Private Equity Firm

Project Preferences

Type of Financing Preferred:
Early Stage

Additional Information
Year Founded: 2016
Current Activity Level : Actively seeking new investments

ALPHA FOUNDERS

Sukhumvit 63 (Thonglor 10)
2nd floor, North-Klongton
Bangkok, Thailand
Phone: 6623093490
Fax: 6623093489
E-mail: info@alphafounders.com
Website: www.alphafounders.com

Management and Staff
Andre Prenzlow, Venture Partner
Johannes Von Rohr, Founder
Marc Dassler, Venture Partner
Michael Steibl, Venture Partner
Nagarjun Srivastava, Venture Partner
Nigel Donald Thomas, Venture Partner
Pongpaichayont Thongchua, Venture Partner
Rahul Sethi, Venture Partner
Suneet Manchanda, Venture Partner

Type of Firm
Incubator/Development Program

Project Preferences

Type of Financing Preferred:
Early Stage
Balanced
Seed

Geographical Preferences

International Preferences:
Vietnam
Indonesia
Pakistan
India
Thailand
Philippines
Sri Lanka
Singapore
Malaysia

Industry Preferences

In Internet Specific prefer:
Internet

Additional Information
Year Founded: 1969
Current Activity Level : Actively seeking new investments

ALPHA GROUP

22 Grenville Street
Saint Helier
Jersey, Channel Islands JE4 8PX
Phone: 441534609000
Fax: 441534609333
E-mail: info@alphape.com
Website: www.groupealpha.com

Other Offices

916, Gildo Pastor Center
7 rue du Gabian
Monaco, Monaco 98000
Phone: 377-9350-4727
Fax: 377-9350-4730

49 Avenue Hoche
Paris, France F - 75008
Phone: 33-1-5660-2020
Fax: 33-1-5660-1022

Alfred Escher Strasse 10
Zurich, Switzerland 8002
Phone: 41433449963
Fax: 41433449965

Via Verdi, 6
Milan, Italy 20121
Phone: 39-2-0064-0064
Fax: 39-2-0064-0090

Ter Buken
Haachttraat
Herent, Belgium 3020
Phone: 32-0-473-578-890
Fax: 32-0-16-609-938

Het Neppelenbroek
Neppelenbroekerdijk
Broekland, Netherlands 8107
Phone: 31-0-6-5539-6697
Fax: 31-0-570-530-985

8-10 Avenue de la Gare
Luxembourg, Luxembourg L1610
Phone: 352274707
Fax: 44153460933

Management and Staff
Herve Hautin, Chief Financial Officer
Nicolas Ver Hulst, Managing Director
Nicolas Macquin, Partner
Olaf Kordes, Managing Director

Type of Firm
Private Equity Firm

Project Preferences

Role in Financing:
Prefer role as deal originator but will also invest in deals created by others

Type of Financing Preferred:
Leveraged Buyout
Management Buyouts
Acquisition

Geographical Preferences

International Preferences:
Italy
Luxembourg
Netherlands
Switzerland
Belgium
Germany
France

Industry Focus
(% based on actual investment)

Other Products	50.6%
Communications and Media	15.8%
Consumer Related	12.1%
Semiconductors/Other Elect.	8.4%
Internet Specific	6.4%
Computer Software and Services	3.2%
Biotechnology	2.3%
Industrial/Energy	0.6%
Medical/Health	0.5%

Additional Information
Name of Most Recent Fund: Alpha Private Equity Fund 5
Most Recent Fund Was Raised: 02/17/2006
Year Founded: 1985
Capital Under Management: $2,426,800,000
Current Activity Level: Actively seeking new investments

Method of Compensation: Return on investment is of primary concern, do not charge fees

---

ALPHA VENTURE PARTNERS

1 Pennsylvania Plaza
Suite 3905
New York, NY USA 10019
Website: www.alphavp.com

Type of Firm
Private Equity Firm

Project Preferences

Type of Financing Preferred:
Balanced

Additional Information
Name of Most Recent Fund: Alpha Venture Partners Fund, L.P.
Most Recent Fund Was Raised: 11/29/2013
Year Founded: 2012
Capital Under Management: $35,270,000
Current Activity Level : Actively seeking new investments

ALPHACODE PTY LTD

Cnr Fredman Dr & Rivonia Rd
Third Floor, 2 Merchant Place
Johannesburg, South Africa 2196
E-mail: info@alphacode.club
Website: www.alphacode.club

Type of Firm
Incubator/Development Program

Project Preferences

Type of Financing Preferred:
Balanced

Industry Preferences

In Financial Services prefer:
Financial Services

Additional Information
Year Founded: 1969
Current Activity Level : Actively seeking new investments

ALPHANORTH ASSET MANAGEMENT

333 Bay Street
Suite 630
Toronto, Canada M5H 2R2
Phone: 4165060776
E-mail: Info@AlphaNorthAsset.com
Website: www.alphanorthasset.com

Management and Staff
Joey Javier, Managing Partner
Ken Choi, Chief Financial Officer
Skye Collyer, Vice President

Type of Firm
Investment Management Firm

Project Preferences

Type of Financing Preferred:
Balanced

Geographical Preferences

Canadian Preferences:
All Canada

Additional Information
Year Founded: 2007
Current Activity Level : Actively seeking new investments

ALPHAPRIME VENTURES

540 Madison Avenue
30th Floor
New York, NY USA 10022
Phone: 2127105234
E-mail: info@alphaprime.com
Website: alphaprime.com

Type of Firm
Private Equity Firm

Project Preferences

Type of Financing Preferred:
Early Stage
Startup

Geographical Preferences

United States Preferences:
California
New York

Industry Preferences

In Computer Software prefer:
Software

Additional Information
Year Founded: 2013
Current Activity Level : Actively seeking new investments

ALPINA CAPITAL PARTNERS LLP

Two Fitzhardinge Street
London, United Kingdom W1H 6EE
Phone: 442032193441
Fax: 442032193451
E-mail: info@whebgroup.com
Website: www.whebpartners.com

Other Offices
Maximilianstrasse 36
Munich, Germany 80539
Phone: 4989122280820
Fax: 4989122280811

Management and Staff
Alexander Domin, Partner
Benjamin Goldsmith, Co-Founder
Clare Brook, Co-Founder
George Latham, Managing Partner
James McNaught-Davis, Managing Partner
Javier Guerra, Partner
Joerg Sperling, Partner
Michael Pearson, Partner
Pam Darchiville, Principal
Seb Beloe, Partner
Ted Franks, Partner
Timothy Dieppe, Partner

Type of Firm
Private Equity Firm

Association Membership
British Venture Capital Association (BVCA)
European Private Equity and Venture Capital Assoc.

Project Preferences

Type of Financing Preferred:
Later Stage

Geographical Preferences

International Preferences:
Ireland
Sweden
United Kingdom
Netherlands
Switzerland
Austria
Finland
Norway

Industry Preferences

In Industrial/Energy prefer:
Advanced Materials

Additional Information
Name of Most Recent Fund: WHEB Ventures Private Equity 2, L.P.
Most Recent Fund Was Raised: 09/08/2008
Year Founded: 1995
Capital Under Management: $209,500,000
Current Activity Level : Actively seeking new investments

ALPINE BIOVENTURES GP LLC

600 Stewart Street
Suite 1503
Seattle, WA USA 98101
Phone: 2064415064
Website: alpinebioventures.com

Type of Firm
Private Equity Firm

Project Preferences

Type of Financing Preferred:
Balanced

Industry Preferences

In Biotechnology prefer:
Biotech Related Research

In Medical/Health prefer:
Medical/Health
Health Services

Additional Information
Year Founded: 2013
Current Activity Level : Actively seeking new investments

ALPINE GROWTH PARTNERS

123 Edward Street
Suite 1112
Toronto, Canada M5G 1E2
Phone: 6475573450
Fax: 6475573505
E-mail: info@alpinegp.ca
Website: www.alpinegp.ca

Type of Firm
Private Equity Firm

Geographical Preferences

United States Preferences:

Canadian Preferences:
All Canada

Additional Information
Year Founded: 2017
Current Activity Level : Actively seeking new investments

ALPINE INVESTORS LP

Three Embarcadero Center
Suite 2330
San Francisco, CA USA 94111
Phone: 4153929100
Fax: 4153929101
Website: www.alpine-investors.com

Management and Staff
Billy Maguy, Partner
Dan Sanner, Partner
Graham Weaver, Founder
Mark Strauch, Partner
Will Adams, Partner

Type of Firm
Private Equity Firm

Association Membership
Natl Assoc of Small Bus. Inv. Co (NASBIC)

Project Preferences

Type of Financing Preferred:
Expansion

Industry Preferences

In Computer Software prefer:
Software
Applications Software

In Internet Specific prefer:
Ecommerce

In Semiconductor/Electr prefer:
Controllers and Sensors

In Consumer Related prefer:
Retail
Consumer Products
Consumer Services
Education Related

In Financial Services prefer:
Financial Services
Insurance

In Business Serv. prefer:
Services
Media

Additional Information
Name of Most Recent Fund: Alpine Investors V, L.P.
Most Recent Fund Was Raised: 10/18/2013
Year Founded: 2001
Capital Under Management: $500,000,000
Current Activity Level : Actively seeking new investments

ALPINE MERIDIAN INC

641 Lexington Avenue
New York, NY USA 10022
Website: www.alpinemeridian.com

Type of Firm
Investment Management Firm

Project Preferences

Type of Financing Preferred:
Balanced

Industry Preferences

In Computer Software prefer:
Software

Additional Information
Name of Most Recent Fund: Alpine Meridian Ventures, L.P.
Most Recent Fund Was Raised: 02/11/2014
Year Founded: 1987
Capital Under Management: $13,500,000
Current Activity Level : Actively seeking new investments

ALPINE TECHNOLOGY INVESTMENT CO LTD

7/F, 779-10, Daelim 3 dong
Youngdeungpo-gu
Seoul, South Korea 150-816
Phone: 8228362053
Fax: 8228362087

Management and Staff
Jinwoo Nam, President

Type of Firm
Corporate PE/Venture

Project Preferences

Type of Financing Preferred:
Balanced
Later Stage
Seed

Geographical Preferences

International Preferences:
Korea, South

Additional Information
Year Founded: 1999
Capital Under Management: $12,100,000
Current Activity Level : Actively seeking new investments

ALPINVEST PARTNERS BV

Jachthavenweg 118
Amsterdam, Netherlands 1081 KJ
Phone: 31205407575
Fax: 31205407500
E-mail: info@alpinvest.com
Website: www.alpinvest.com

Other Offices
3 Garden Road
701 Citibank Tower
Hong Kong, Hong Kong
Phone: 852-2878-7099
Fax: 852-2878-7009

201 North Illinois Street
Indianapolis, IN USA 46204
Phone: 3173614436

630 Fifth Avenue
28th Floor
New York, NY USA 10111
Phone: 212-332-6240
Fax: 212-332-6241

Management and Staff
Ashley Johansen, Principal
Christopher Perriello, Partner
Erik Thyssen, Managing Partner
George Westerkamp, Managing Partner
Jonathan Shimmin, Principal
Ken Bloomberg, Principal
Maarten Vervoort, Managing Partner
Marek Herchel, Partner
Nadim Barakat, Managing Partner
Neal Costello, Principal
Paul de Klerk, Chief Financial Officer
Philip Viergutz, Principal
Richard Dunne, Principal
Rob de Jong, Partner
Sander van Maanen, Managing Partner
Scott Hamner, Partner
Tatiana Chopova, Partner
Thomas Spoto, Partner
Tjarko Hektor, Managing Partner
Wendy Zhu, Partner
Wouter Moerel, Managing Partner
Youn Hong, Principal

Type of Firm
Private Equity Firm

Association Membership
Dutch Venture Capital Associaton (NVP)
European Private Equity and Venture Capital Assoc.

Project Preferences

Role in Financing:
Prefer role as deal originator but will also invest in deals created by others

Type of Financing Preferred:
Second Stage Financing
Leveraged Buyout
Mezzanine
Generalist PE
Balanced
Later Stage

Size of Investments Considered:
Min Size of Investment Considered (000s): $5,000
Max Size of Investment Considered: No Limit

Geographical Preferences

United States Preferences:
All U.S.

International Preferences:
Italy
United Kingdom
Europe
Netherlands
Bermuda
Spain
Asia
Germany
France

Industry Focus
(% based on actual investment)
Other Products	35.4%
Computer Software and Services	20.9%
Medical/Health	20.1%
Consumer Related	9.5%
Industrial/Energy	9.0%
Biotechnology	3.8%
Internet Specific	0.7%
Communications and Media	0.6%
Semiconductors/Other Elect.	0.1%

Additional Information
Name of Most Recent Fund: AlpInvest Secondaries Fund V
Most Recent Fund Was Raised: 10/14/2013
Year Founded: 1999
Capital Under Management: $750,000,000
Current Activity Level : Actively seeking new investments
Method of Compensation: Return on invest. most important, but chg. closing fees, service fees, etc.

ALPS VENTURE CAPITAL GMBH
Stumpergasse 65
Vienna, Austria 1060
E-mail: office@alpsventure.com
Website: www.alpsventures.com

Management and Staff
Dirk Van Quaquebeke, Co-Founder
Markus Pichler, Co-Founder
Max Scheichenost, Co-Founder
Michael Taufner, Partner

Type of Firm
Private Equity Firm

Project Preferences
Type of Financing Preferred:
Early Stage
Balanced
Later Stage
Seed
Startup

Geographical Preferences
International Preferences:
Europe
Asia

Additional Information
Year Founded: 2011
Current Activity Level : Actively seeking new investments

ALSOP LOUIE PARTNERS
50 Pacific Avenue
San Francisco, CA USA 94111
Website: www.alsop-louie.com

Management and Staff
Bill Coleman, Partner
Gilman Louie, Partner
Jim Whims, Partner
Jim Ward, Venture Partner
Joe Alsop, Venture Partner
Joe Addiego, Partner
Nancy Lee, Chief Financial Officer
Steve Mendel, Venture Partner
Stewart Alsop, Partner
Tom Kalinske, Venture Partner
William Crowell, Partner

Type of Firm
Private Equity Firm

Association Membership
National Venture Capital Association - USA (NVCA)

Project Preferences
Type of Financing Preferred:
Balanced

Industry Preferences
In Communications prefer:
Wireless Communications

In Computer Software prefer:
Software
Applications Software

In Business Serv. prefer:
Media

Additional Information
Year Founded: 2006
Capital Under Management: $75,000,000
Current Activity Level : Actively seeking new investments

ALSTON CAPITAL PARTNERS LLC
551 Fifth Avenue, 14th Floor
New York, NY USA 10176
Website: alstoncapital.com

Management and Staff
Donald Hofmann, Partner
Richard Cross, Partner
Robert Egan, Partner
Rodney Eshelman, Partner

Type of Firm
Private Equity Firm

Project Preferences
Type of Financing Preferred:
Leveraged Buyout
Turnaround
Management Buyouts
Acquisition
Recapitalizations

Geographical Preferences
United States Preferences:
Canadian Preferences:
All Canada

Industry Preferences
In Industrial/Energy prefer:
Environmental Related

In Manufact. prefer:
Manufacturing

In Other prefer:
Environment Responsible

Additional Information
Year Founded: 2012
Current Activity Level : Actively seeking new investments

ALTA BERKELEY VENTURE PARTNERS
42 Berkeley Square
London, United Kingdom W1J 5AW
Phone: 442033931107
Fax: 442030700797
E-mail: info@altaberkeley.com
Website: www.altaberkeley.com

Other Offices
17A rue de la Croix d'Or
Geneva, Switzerland 1204
Phone: 4122-310-2721
Fax: 4122-311-5536

Management and Staff
Barundeb Dutta, Partner
Kevin Fielding, Partner
Peter Magowan, Partner
Pini Lozowick, Partner

Type of Firm
Private Equity Firm

Project Preferences
Role in Financing:
Prefer role as deal originator but will also invest in deals created by others

Type of Financing Preferred:
Early Stage
Balanced
Startup

Geographical Preferences
International Preferences:
Europe
Israel

Industry Focus

(% based on actual investment)
Communications and Media	24.5%
Biotechnology	17.8%
Semiconductors/Other Elect.	13.5%
Medical/Health	12.6%
Computer Software and Services	11.3%
Computer Hardware	10.2%
Other Products	4.5%
Internet Specific	3.6%
Industrial/Energy	1.6%
Consumer Related	0.3%

Additional Information

Name of Most Recent Fund: Alta Berkeley VI, C.V.
Most Recent Fund Was Raised: 09/30/2000
Year Founded: 1982
Capital Under Management: $178,300,000
Current Activity Level: Actively seeking new investments
Method of Compensation: Return on investment is of primary concern, do not charge fees

ALTA CAPITAL

Avenida de la Innovacion s/n
Planta 5 Modulo E
Sevilla, Spain 41020
Phone: 34954944277
E-mail: info@altacapital.es
Website: www.altacapital.es

Other Offices

Avenida Diagonal 467 Planta 1
Barcelona, Spain

Type of Firm

Private Equity Firm

Project Preferences

Type of Financing Preferred:
Leveraged Buyout
Expansion
Mezzanine
Acquisition

Geographical Preferences

International Preferences:
Spain

Industry Preferences

In Business Serv. prefer:
Services

Additional Information

Year Founded: 2000
Capital Under Management: $14,272,000
Current Activity Level: Actively seeking new investments

ALTA COMMUNICATIONS INC

1000 Winter Street
Suite 3500
North Waltham, MA USA 02451
Phone: 6172627770
Website: www.altacomm.com

Other Offices

One Embarcadero Center
Suite 4050
San Francisco, CA USA 94111
Phone: 415-362-4022
Fax: 415-362-6178

Former: 28 State Street
Suite 1801
Boston, MA USA 02109

Management and Staff

Chris Dias, Vice President
Jessica Barry-Reed, Vice President
Philip Thompson, General Partner
William Egan, General Partner

Type of Firm

Private Equity Firm

Project Preferences

Role in Financing:
Prefer role as deal originator but will also invest in deals created by others

Type of Financing Preferred:
Leveraged Buyout
Expansion
Generalist PE
Balanced
Turnaround
Later Stage
Management Buyouts
Acquisition
Special Situation

Size of Investments Considered:
Min Size of Investment Considered (000s): $2,000
Max Size of Investment Considered (000s): $20,000

Geographical Preferences

United States Preferences:
North America

Canadian Preferences:
All Canada

Industry Focus

(% based on actual investment)
Communications and Media	55.3%
Internet Specific	14.8%
Other Products	10.2%
Computer Software and Services	4.6%
Medical/Health	3.9%
Consumer Related	2.8%
Computer Hardware	2.6%
Biotechnology	2.3%
Semiconductors/Other Elect.	2.3%
Industrial/Energy	1.0%

Additional Information

Year Founded: 1996
Capital Under Management: $1,518,900,000
Current Activity Level: Actively seeking new investments
Method of Compensation: Return on investment is of primary concern, do not charge fees

ALTA GROWTH CAPITAL SC

Bosque de Duraznos 127
Fourth Floor
Mexico DF, Mexico 11700
Phone: 5255525432830
E-mail: info@agcmexico.com
Website: www.agcmexico.com

Other Offices

Former HQ: Homero 440
Ninth Floor
Mexico DF, Mexico 11560

Management and Staff

Erik Carlberg, Founder
Javier Garcia-Teruel, Managing Director
Rafael Payro, Founder
Scott McDonough, Founder

Type of Firm

Private Equity Firm

Project Preferences

Type of Financing Preferred:
Leveraged Buyout
Expansion
Generalist PE
Later Stage
Acquisition

Size of Investments Considered:
Min Size of Investment Considered (000s): $10,000
Max Size of Investment Considered (000s): $20,000

Geographical Preferences

International Preferences:
Mexico

Industry Preferences

In Communications prefer:
Entertainment

131

In Medical/Health prefer:
Medical/Health
Health Services

In Consumer Related prefer:
Entertainment and Leisure
Consumer Products
Consumer Services
Education Related

In Industrial/Energy prefer:
Industrial Products

In Financial Services prefer:
Financial Services
Financial Services

In Manufact. prefer:
Manufacturing

Additional Information
Name of Most Recent Fund: Alta Growth Capital, Mexico Fund II, L.P.
Most Recent Fund Was Raised: 07/12/2012
Year Founded: 2008
Capital Under Management: $142,000,000
Current Activity Level : Actively seeking new investments

ALTA PARTNERS

One Embarcadero Center
37th Floor
San Francisco, CA USA 94111
Phone: 4153624022
Fax: 4153626178
E-mail: alta@altapartners.com
Website: www.altapartners.com

Management and Staff
Daniel Janney, Managing Director
Farah Champsi, Managing Director
Guy Nohra, Co-Founder
Larry Randall, Chief Financial Officer
Peter Hudson, Managing Director
Robert More, Managing Director

Type of Firm
Private Equity Firm

Project Preferences

Role in Financing:
Prefer role as deal originator but will also invest in deals created by others

Type of Financing Preferred:
Early Stage
Balanced
Public Companies
Later Stage

Industry Focus
(% based on actual investment)
Biotechnology	57.9%
Medical/Health	26.8%
Internet Specific	6.2%
Semiconductors/Other Elect.	3.0%
Communications and Media	2.7%
Computer Software and Services	2.3%
Consumer Related	0.5%
Computer Hardware	0.4%
Other Products	0.2%
Industrial/Energy	0.0%

Additional Information
Year Founded: 1996
Capital Under Management: $2,000,000,000
Current Activity Level : Actively seeking new investments

ALTA PARTNERS CAPITAL

Avenida Diagonal 399
Barcelona, Spain 08008
Phone: 34932387230
Fax: 34932380356
E-mail: info@altap.com
Website: www.altapartners.es

Management and Staff
Rafael Sunol, President
Roberto Gili, Partner

Type of Firm
Private Equity Firm

Project Preferences

Type of Financing Preferred:
Early Stage
Expansion
Startup

Size of Investments Considered:
Min Size of Investment Considered (000s): $2,825
Max Size of Investment Considered (000s): $22,598

Geographical Preferences

International Preferences:
Europe
Spain

Additional Information
Year Founded: 2000
Current Activity Level : Actively seeking new investments

ALTA VENTURES MEXICO

Av. Gomez Morin 955 Sur
Suite 315
Nuevo Leon, Mexico CP 66267
Phone: 528114779014
E-mail: info@altaventures.com
Website: altaventures.com

Management and Staff
Paul Ahlstrom, Co-Founder
Rogelio De los Santos, Managing Director

Type of Firm
Private Equity Firm

Project Preferences

Type of Financing Preferred:
Early Stage
Seed
Startup

Size of Investments Considered:
Min Size of Investment Considered (000s): $50
Max Size of Investment Considered (000s): $10,000

Geographical Preferences

International Preferences:
Mexico

Industry Preferences

In Communications prefer:
Communications and Media
Wireless Communications

In Computer Software prefer:
Software

In Internet Specific prefer:
Internet

In Medical/Health prefer:
Medical/Health

In Consumer Related prefer:
Consumer

In Business Serv. prefer:
Services

Additional Information
Name of Most Recent Fund: Alta Ventures Mexico Fund I, L.P.
Most Recent Fund Was Raised: 06/02/2010
Year Founded: 2010
Capital Under Management: $74,800,000
Current Activity Level : Actively seeking new investments

ALTAIR CAPITAL MANAGEMENT GMBH

Mooslackengasse 17
Vienna, Austria 1190
Website: www.altair.vc

Type of Firm
Private Equity Firm

Project Preferences

Type of Financing Preferred:
Early Stage
Start-up Financing
Seed
First Stage Financing
Startup

Geographical Preferences

United States Preferences:
All U.S.

International Preferences:
Europe
China
Russia

Industry Preferences

In Communications prefer:
Telecommunications

In Internet Specific prefer:
Internet

Additional Information
Year Founded: 2005
Current Activity Level : Actively seeking new investments

ALTALINK CAPITAL LLC

288 West Center Street
Provo, UT USA 84601
Phone: 8014712542
E-mail: Info@AltaLinkCapital.com
Website: altalinkcapital.com

Type of Firm
Private Equity Firm

Project Preferences

Type of Financing Preferred:
Leveraged Buyout
Acquisition

Geographical Preferences

United States Preferences:

Canadian Preferences:
All Canada

Additional Information
Year Founded: 1969
Current Activity Level : Actively seeking new investments

ALTAMAR PRIVATE EQUITY SGIIC SAU

Paseo de la Castellana, 31
Madrid, Spain 28046
Phone: 34913107230
Fax: 34913107231
E-mail: altamarcapital@altamarcapital.com
Website: www.altamarcapital.com

Other Offices
Av. El Bosque Norte 0177
Floor 17
Santiago, Chile 755-0100
Phone: 56223320010

Management and Staff
Alvaro Gonzalez, Partner
Claudio Aguirre Peman, Partner
Ines Andrade, Managing Partner
Joaquin Diaz-Reganon, Managing Director
Jose Luis Molina, Partner
Manuel Silvestre, Chief Financial Officer
Mariano Olaso, Co-Founder
Miguel Echenique, Managing Director
Miguel Zurita, Managing Partner
Miguel Rona, Partner
Paloma Ybarra, Partner
Rocio Fernandez, Chief Financial Officer

Type of Firm
Private Equity Advisor or Fund of Funds

Association Membership
European Private Equity and Venture Capital Assoc.
Spanish Venture Capital Association (ASCRI)

Project Preferences

Type of Financing Preferred:
Fund of Funds

Geographical Preferences

International Preferences:
Latin America
Europe
Spain

Additional Information
Name of Most Recent Fund: Altamar VII
Most Recent Fund Was Raised: 09/23/2013
Year Founded: 2004
Capital Under Management: $1,000,000,000
Current Activity Level : Actively seeking new investments

ALTARIS CAPITAL PARTNERS LLC

600 Lexington Avenue
Eleventh Floor
New York, NY USA 10022
Phone: 2129310250
E-mail: info@altariscap.com
Website: www.altariscap.com

Management and Staff
Daniel Tully, Managing Director
David Ellison, Vice President
George Aitken-Davies, Managing Director
Michael Kluger, Partner
Scott Freishtat, Vice President

Type of Firm
Private Equity Firm

Project Preferences

Type of Financing Preferred:
Leveraged Buyout
Expansion
Acquisition
Recapitalizations

Geographical Preferences

United States Preferences:
North America

International Preferences:
Western Europe

Industry Preferences

In Medical/Health prefer:
Medical/Health
Medical Products
Health Services
Pharmaceuticals

Additional Information
Name of Most Recent Fund: AIG Altaris Health Partners II, L.P.
Most Recent Fund Was Raised: 05/11/2007
Year Founded: 2003
Capital Under Management: $775,000,000
Current Activity Level : Actively seeking new investments

ALTAS PARTNERS LP

181 Bay Street
Suite 2300
Toronto, Canada M5J2T3
Phone: 4163069800
E-mail: contact@altaspartners.com
Website: altaspartners.com

Management and Staff
Andrew Sheiner, Co-Founder
Christopher McElhone, Co-Founder
Damon Conway, Principal
Scott Werry, Co-Founder

Type of Firm
Private Equity Firm

Project Preferences

Type of Financing Preferred:
Leveraged Buyout

Additional Information

Year Founded: 2012
Capital Under Management: $1,000,000,000
Current Activity Level : Actively seeking new investments

ALTEGRIS INVESTMENTS LLC

1200 Prospect Street
Suite 400
La Jolla, CA USA 92037
Phone: 8885249441
Website: www.altegris.com

Type of Firm

Investment Management Firm

Project Preferences

Type of Financing Preferred:
Fund of Funds of Second

Geographical Preferences

United States Preferences:
North America

International Preferences:
Europe
Asia

Additional Information

Year Founded: 2014
Current Activity Level : Actively seeking new investments

ALTER DANISMANLIK HIZMETLERI TICARET AS

Tesvikiye Caddesi 23/7
Nisantasi
Istanbul, Turkey
Phone: 902122596704
E-mail: info@crescent.com.tr
Website: www.crescent.com.tr

Type of Firm

Private Equity Firm

Project Preferences

Type of Financing Preferred:
Leveraged Buyout
Early Stage
Expansion
Mezzanine
Generalist PE
Later Stage
Management Buyouts
Acquisition

Geographical Preferences

International Preferences:
Armenia
Mongolia
Albania
Kazakhstan
Turkey
Europe
Macedonia
Kyrgyzstan
Croatia
Tajikistan
Turkmenistan
Azerbaijan
Moldova
Bulgaria
Uzbekistan
Bosnia
Romania
Georgia

Industry Preferences

In Industrial/Energy prefer:
Alternative Energy

Additional Information

Year Founded: 2011
Capital Under Management: $129,584,000
Current Activity Level : Actively seeking new investments

ALTER EQUITY SAS

9 rue Sebastien Bottin
Paris, France 75007
Website: alter-equity.com

Management and Staff

Anne-Valerie Bach, Chief Executive Officer

Type of Firm

Private Equity Firm

Association Membership

French Venture Capital Association (AFIC)

Project Preferences

Type of Financing Preferred:
Leveraged Buyout
Generalist PE
Later Stage
Acquisition

Geographical Preferences

International Preferences:
Europe
France

Industry Preferences

In Other prefer:
Socially Responsible
Environment Responsible

Additional Information

Year Founded: 2006
Current Activity Level : Actively seeking new investments

ALTERNATIVE INVESTMENT CAPITAL LTD

9-1 Marunouchi 1-chome
10/F, Marunouchi Central Bldg
Tokyo, Japan 100-0005
Phone: 81-3-52185230
Fax: 81-3-52185254
E-mail: info@aicapital.co.jp
Website: www.aicapital.co.jp

Type of Firm

Private Equity Advisor or Fund of Funds

Project Preferences

Type of Financing Preferred:
Fund of Funds

Geographical Preferences

United States Preferences:

International Preferences:
India
Europe
China
Australia
Asia
Japan

Additional Information
Name of Most Recent Fund: AIC Asia Opportunity Fund, L.P.
Most Recent Fund Was Raised: 07/08/2011
Year Founded: 2002
Capital Under Management: $150,000,000
Current Activity Level : Actively seeking new investments

ALTERNATIVE STRATEGIC INVESTMENT GMBH

Maximilianstrasse 34
Munich, Germany 80539
Phone: 4989255437250
Fax: 4989255437299
E-mail: info@alstin.de
Website: www.alstin.de

Management and Staff
Jorg Goschin, CEO & Managing Director

Type of Firm
Private Equity Firm

Project Preferences

Type of Financing Preferred:
Leveraged Buyout
Early Stage
Expansion
Public Companies
Later Stage
Management Buyouts
Acquisition

Geographical Preferences

International Preferences:
Europe
Switzerland
Austria
Germany

Industry Preferences

In Internet Specific prefer:
Internet

In Medical/Health prefer:
Medical/Health

In Industrial/Energy prefer:
Alternative Energy

In Business Serv. prefer:
Services

Additional Information
Year Founded: 2011
Current Activity Level : Actively seeking new investments

ALTEZZA VENTURES

360 Queen Street
Level 6
Brisbane, Australia QLD 4001
Website: www.altezzaventures.com

Type of Firm
Private Equity Firm

Project Preferences

Type of Financing Preferred:
Early Stage

Geographical Preferences

International Preferences:
Australia

Additional Information
Year Founded: 2015
Current Activity Level : Actively seeking new investments

ALTIEN VENTURES LLC

1331 Northwest Lovejoy Street
Suite 850
Portland, OR USA 97209
Phone: 503-226-8642

Management and Staff
John Miner, Co-Founder

Type of Firm
Private Equity Firm

Project Preferences

Type of Financing Preferred:
Start-up Financing
Startup

Geographical Preferences

United States Preferences:
Oregon

Industry Preferences

In Computer Software prefer:
Software

In Semiconductor/Electr prefer:
Semiconductor

Additional Information
Name of Most Recent Fund: Altien Investors I LLC
Most Recent Fund Was Raised: 08/30/2007
Year Founded: 2007
Current Activity Level : Actively seeking new investments

ALTIMETER CAPITAL MANAGEMENT LP

One International Place
Suite 2400
Boston, MA USA 02110
Website: www.altimetercapital.com

Management and Staff
Arpan Shah, Vice President
John Kiernan, Chief Financial Officer
Kevin Wang, Principal
Michael Chapman, Vice President

Type of Firm
Private Equity Firm

Project Preferences

Type of Financing Preferred:
Balanced

Industry Preferences

In Internet Specific prefer:
Internet

In Consumer Related prefer:
Entertainment and Leisure

In Transportation prefer:
Transportation

In Business Serv. prefer:
Media

Additional Information
Year Founded: 2008
Capital Under Management: $75,000,000
Current Activity Level : Actively seeking new investments

ALTIRA GROUP LLC

1675 Broadway
Suite 2400
Denver, CO USA 80202
Phone: 3035925500
Fax: 3035925519
E-mail: info@altiragroup.com
Website: www.altiragroup.com

Management and Staff
Dirk McDermott, Managing Partner
Hull McKinnon, Partner
J.P. Bauman, Principal
Marc Gulley, Chief Financial Officer
Sean Ebert, Principal

Type of Firm
Private Equity Firm

Association Membership
National Venture Capital Association - USA (NVCA)

Project Preferences

Role in Financing:
Prefer role as deal originator but will also invest in deals created by others

Type of Financing Preferred:
Early Stage
Expansion
Balanced
Later Stage

Size of Investments Considered:
Min Size of Investment Considered (000s): $5,000
Max Size of Investment Considered (000s): $30,000

Geographical Preferences

United States Preferences:
North America

Canadian Preferences:
All Canada

Industry Preferences

In Industrial/Energy prefer:
Energy
Oil and Gas Exploration
Alternative Energy

In Business Serv. prefer:
Services

Additional Information

Name of Most Recent Fund: Altira Technology Fund VI, L.P.
Most Recent Fund Was Raised: 06/30/2013
Year Founded: 1996
Capital Under Management: $275,000,000
Current Activity Level : Actively seeking new investments
Method of Compensation: Return on investment is of primary concern, do not charge fees

---

ALTITUDE FUNDS LLC

701 Fifth Avenue
Suite 5400
Seattle, WA USA 98101
Website: www.altitudefunds.com

Other Offices

Former HQ: 175 Mercado Street
Durango, CO USA 81301
Phone: 9707646300

Type of Firm

Private Equity Firm

Project Preferences

Type of Financing Preferred:
Early Stage
Balanced

Industry Preferences

In Biotechnology prefer:
Biotechnology

In Medical/Health prefer:
Medical Diagnostics
Diagnostic Services
Medical Products

Additional Information

Name of Most Recent Fund: Altitude Life Science Ventures, L.P.
Most Recent Fund Was Raised: 12/13/2005
Year Founded: 2005
Capital Under Management: $24,000,000
Current Activity Level : Actively seeking new investments

ALTITUDE PARTNERS LLP

George Curl Way
International House
Southampton, United Kingdom SO18 2RZ
Phone: 442380302006
E-mail: enquiries@altitudepartners.co.uk
Website: www.altitudepartners.co.uk

Management and Staff

Jonathan Simm, Co-Founder
Simon White, Co-Founder

Type of Firm

Private Equity Firm

Project Preferences

Type of Financing Preferred:
Expansion
Generalist PE
Balanced
Management Buyouts
Acquisition

Geographical Preferences

International Preferences:
United Kingdom
Europe

Additional Information

Name of Most Recent Fund: Altitude One LP
Most Recent Fund Was Raised: 08/04/2010
Year Founded: 2010
Capital Under Management: $11,121,000
Current Activity Level : Actively seeking new investments

ALTO INVEST SA

65 rue du Marechal Foch
Versailles, France 78000
Phone: 33139543567
Fax: 33139545376
E-mail: contact@altoinvest.fr
Website: www.altoinvest.fr

Management and Staff

Antoine Valdes, President, Founder
Didier Baneat, Managing Director
Jean-Francois Paumelle, Managing Director
Stefan Berger, Venture Partner

Type of Firm

Private Equity Firm

Association Membership

French Venture Capital Association (AFIC)

Project Preferences

Type of Financing Preferred:
Fund of Funds
Early Stage
Later Stage
Seed
Startup

Geographical Preferences

International Preferences:
Italy
Sweden
United Kingdom
Europe
Western Europe
Spain
Germany
France

Industry Preferences

In Communications prefer:
Telecommunications

In Computer Software prefer:
Software

In Internet Specific prefer:
Internet

In Semiconductor/Electr prefer:
Electronics

In Medical/Health prefer:
Medical/Health
Medical Diagnostics
Medical Products

In Consumer Related prefer:
Consumer Products
Consumer Services

In Industrial/Energy prefer:
Industrial Products
Materials
Environmental Related

In Business Serv. prefer:
Services
Distribution
Media

In Manufact. prefer:
Manufacturing

In Agr/Forestr/Fish prefer:
Agriculture related

In Other prefer:
Environment Responsible

Additional Information

Year Founded: 2001
Current Activity Level : Actively seeking new investments

ALTO PARTNERS SRL

Via Monte di Pieta 1/A
Milan, Italy 20121
Phone: 390272095041
Fax: 390272095012
E-mail: info@altopartners.it
Website: www.altopartners.it

Other Offices

Piazza Galvani, 3
Bologna, Italy 40124
Phone: 39-051-234-931

Management and Staff

Mario Visioni, Partner
Raffaele De Courten, Founder
Roberto Torazzi, Founder
Stefano Scarpis, Founder

Type of Firm

Private Equity Advisor or Fund of Funds

Association Membership

European Private Equity and Venture Capital Assoc.

Project Preferences

Type of Financing Preferred:
Leveraged Buyout
Early Stage
Expansion
Generalist PE
Later Stage
Management Buyouts
Acquisition

Size of Investments Considered:
Min Size of Investment Considered (000s): $437
Max Size of Investment Considered (000s): $30,597

Geographical Preferences

International Preferences:
Italy
Europe

Industry Preferences

In Consumer Related prefer:
Consumer
Entertainment and Leisure
Food/Beverage

In Industrial/Energy prefer:
Machinery

In Business Serv. prefer:
Services

Additional Information

Name of Most Recent Fund: Alto Capital II
Most Recent Fund Was Raised: 11/24/2005
Year Founded: 1997
Capital Under Management: $270,600,000
Current Activity Level : Actively seeking new investments

ALTOR EQUITY PARTNERS AB

Jakobsgatan 6
Stockholm, Sweden 111 52
Phone: 4686789100
Fax: 4686789101
E-mail: info@altor.com
Website: www.altor.com

Other Offices

Pohjoisesplanadi 25 B
5th floor
Helsinki, Finland 00130
Phone: 35896829470
Fax: 358968294750

Karenslyst Alle 4
Oslo, Norway 0278
Phone: 4722128383
Fax: 4722128384

Bredgade 29, III
Copenhagen, Denmark 1260
Phone: 4533367300
Fax: 4533367301

Management and Staff

Bengt Maunsbach, Partner
Claes Ekstrom, Partner
Fredrik Stromholm, Partner
Harald Mix, Partner
Hugo Maurstad, Partner
Jaakko Kivinen, Partner
Jesper Eliasson, Chief Financial Officer
Reynir Indahl, Partner
Soren Johansen, Partner
Stefan Linder, Partner

Type of Firm

Private Equity Firm

Association Membership

Danish Venture Capital Association (DVCA)
Norwegian Venture Capital Association
Swedish Venture Capital Association (SVCA)
European Private Equity and Venture Capital Assoc.

Project Preferences

Type of Financing Preferred:
Leveraged Buyout
Public Companies
Turnaround
Management Buyouts
Distressed Debt

Size of Investments Considered:
Min Size of Investment Considered (000s): $31,662
Max Size of Investment Considered (000s): $189,970

Geographical Preferences

International Preferences:
Scandanavia/Nordic Region

Industry Preferences

In Computer Software prefer:
Computer Services
Software

In Internet Specific prefer:
Ecommerce

In Semiconductor/Electr prefer:
Electronics

In Medical/Health prefer:
Medical/Health
Medical Products

In Consumer Related prefer:
Consumer Products
Consumer Services

In Industrial/Energy prefer:
Energy
Industrial Products

In Financial Services prefer:
Financial Services
Insurance

Additional Information

Name of Most Recent Fund: Altor Fund III
Most Recent Fund Was Raised: 08/22/2008
Year Founded: 2003
Capital Under Management: $5,084,300,000
Current Activity Level : Actively seeking new investments

ALTOS CAPITAL PARTNERS LLC

PO Box 1987
Los Altos, CA USA 94023
E-mail: hello@altos-capital.com
Website: www.altos-capital.com

Management and Staff

Ajay Shah, Principal
Romesh Wadhwani, Principal

Type of Firm

Private Equity Firm

Project Preferences

Type of Financing Preferred:
Leveraged Buyout
Value-Add
Generalist PE
Balanced
Acquisition

Geographical Preferences

United States Preferences:

Industry Preferences

In Financial Services prefer:
Real Estate

Additional Information
Year Founded: 2016
Current Activity Level : Actively seeking new investments

ALTOS VENTURES

2882 Sand Hill Road
Suite 100
Menlo Park, CA USA 94025
Phone: 6502349771
Fax: 6502339821
Website: www.altosventures.com

Other Offices
96-1 Cheongdam-dong
Fourth Floor, Gangnam-gu
Seoul, South Korea 135-517

Management and Staff
Alan Beringsmith, Chief Financial Officer
Anthony Lee, General Partner
Han Kim, General Partner
Hodong Nam, General Partner

Type of Firm
Private Equity Firm

Association Membership
Natl Assoc of Investment Cos. (NAIC)
Western Association of Venture Capitalists (WAVC)
National Venture Capital Association - USA (NVCA)

Project Preferences

Role in Financing:
Will function either as deal originator or investor in deals created by others

Type of Financing Preferred:
Early Stage
Later Stage
Startup

Size of Investments Considered:
Min Size of Investment Considered (000s): $1,000
Max Size of Investment Considered (000s): $10,000

Geographical Preferences

United States Preferences:
Northern California

Canadian Preferences:
All Canada

International Preferences:
Korea, South

Industry Focus
(% based on actual investment)
Internet Specific	49.9%
Computer Software and Services	42.8%
Communications and Media	4.3%
Biotechnology	0.8%
Semiconductors/Other Elect.	0.7%
Consumer Related	0.6%
Other Products	0.6%
Medical/Health	0.4%

Additional Information
Name of Most Recent Fund: Altos Ventures IV, L.P.
Most Recent Fund Was Raised: 09/17/2008
Year Founded: 1996
Capital Under Management: $215,000,000
Current Activity Level : Actively seeking new investments

ALTOUQ GROUP

PO Box 27483
Riyadh, Saudi Arabia 11417
E-mail: ADMIN@ALTOUQ.COM
Website: www.altouq.com

Management and Staff
AbdulMohsen AlTouq, Chief Executive Officer

Type of Firm
Private Equity Firm

Project Preferences

Type of Financing Preferred:
Leveraged Buyout
Early Stage
Generalist PE
Balanced
Later Stage
Acquisition

Geographical Preferences

International Preferences:
Middle East

Industry Preferences

In Communications prefer:
Telecommunications
Wireless Communications

In Industrial/Energy prefer:
Energy

In Financial Services prefer:
Financial Services
Real Estate
Financial Services

Additional Information
Year Founded: 1970
Current Activity Level : Actively seeking new investments

ALTPOINT CAPITAL PARTNERS LLC

712 Fifth Avenue
50th Floor
New York, NY USA 10019
Phone: 12124971100
Fax: 16468053976
E-mail: info@altpointcapital.com
Website: www.altpoint.com

Other Offices
1001 Fanning Street
38th Fl
Houston, TX USA 77002
Phone: 7139694700
Fax: 6468053976

Management and Staff
Anish Sheth, Principal
Brett Pertuz, Managing Director
Eric Chan, Chief Financial Officer
Kevin Hogan, Vice President
Steven Song, Vice President
Yuki Narula, Managing Director

Type of Firm
Private Equity Firm

Project Preferences

Type of Financing Preferred:
Early Stage
Expansion

Size of Investments Considered:
Min Size of Investment Considered (000s): $25,000
Max Size of Investment Considered (000s): $100,000

Geographical Preferences

United States Preferences:
All U.S.

Industry Preferences

In Medical/Health prefer:
Medical/Health

In Consumer Related prefer:
Consumer

In Industrial/Energy prefer:
Energy
Industrial Products

In Financial Services prefer:
Financial Services

Additional Information
Year Founded: 2006
Current Activity Level : Actively seeking new investments

ALTPOINT VENTURES LP

712 Fifth Avenue
50th Floor
New York, NY USA 10019
Phone: 2124971100
Fax: 6468053976
E-mail: info@altpointventures.com
Website: www.altpointventures.com

Management and Staff
Alexey Likuev, Principal
Andrew Grapkowski, Managing Director
Anton Pertsel, Vice President
Brett Pertuz, Managing Director
Vadim Tarasov, Managing Director
Yuki Narula, Co-Founder

Type of Firm
Private Equity Firm

Project Preferences

Type of Financing Preferred:
Early Stage
Expansion
Balanced

Geographical Preferences

United States Preferences:

Industry Preferences

In Communications prefer:
Communications and Media

In Computer Software prefer:
Data Processing
Software

In Internet Specific prefer:
E-Commerce Technology
Internet

Additional Information
Year Founded: 2015
Current Activity Level : Actively seeking new investments

ALTRA INVESTMENTS

Calle 116 No. 7-15
Calle 116 No. 7-15
Bogota, Colombia
Phone: 5712758340
E-mail: info@altrainv.com
Website: www.altrainvestments.com

Other Offices
Av. La Encalada 1388 Of. 605
Santiago de Surco, Peru
Phone: 5114342098
Fax: 5114342103

Management and Staff
Dario Duran, Co-Founder
Juan Pablo Gomez, Vice President
Laura Londono, Vice President
Mauricio Camargo, Co-Founder

Type of Firm
Private Equity Firm

Project Preferences

Type of Financing Preferred:
Leveraged Buyout
Acquisition

Geographical Preferences

International Preferences:
Latin America
Peru
Colombia

Additional Information
Name of Most Recent Fund: Altra Private Equity Fund II, L.P.
Most Recent Fund Was Raised: 08/20/2012
Year Founded: 2005
Capital Under Management: $80,000,000
Current Activity Level : Actively seeking new investments

ALTUR INVESTISSEMENT SCA

9, Rue de Teheran
Paris, France 75008
Phone: 33153430303
Fax: 33153430304
Website: www.altur-investissement.com

Management and Staff
Francois Lombard, Chief Executive Officer

Type of Firm
Private Equity Firm

Project Preferences

Type of Financing Preferred:
Leveraged Buyout
Early Stage
Expansion
Later Stage
Management Buyouts
Acquisition

Industry Preferences

In Medical/Health prefer:
Medical/Health

In Consumer Related prefer:
Hotels and Resorts

In Industrial/Energy prefer:
Industrial Products

In Business Serv. prefer:
Services
Distribution

Additional Information
Year Founded: 2006
Current Activity Level Actively seeking new investments

ALTURA MGMT INC

1095 West Pender Street
Suite 1120
Vancouver, Canada V6E 2M6
Phone: 604-689-0305
Fax: 604-872-2977
E-mail: info@bcmif.com

Management and Staff
Tony Flynn, President

Type of Firm
Private Equity Firm

Project Preferences

Type of Financing Preferred:
Balanced

Geographical Preferences

Canadian Preferences:
All Canada

Additional Information
Year Founded: 2003
Current Activity Level : Actively seeking new investments

ALTUS CAPITAL PARTNERS INC

Ten Westport Road
Suite C204
Wilton, CT USA 06897
Phone: 2034292000
Fax: 2034292010
Website: www.altuscapitalpartners.com

Management and Staff
Elizabeth Burgess, Co-Founder
Gregory Greenberg, Co-Founder
Heidi Goldstein, Partner
Kim VanCleef, Vice President
Nick DeMarco, Vice President
Peter Polimino, Chief Financial Officer
Russell Greenberg, Co-Founder

Type of Firm
Private Equity Firm

Project Preferences

Role in Financing:
Will function either as deal originator or investor in deals created by others

Type of Financing Preferred:
Leveraged Buyout
Acquisition
Recapitalizations

Geographical Preferences

United States Preferences:
Rocky Mountain

Canadian Preferences:
All Canada

Industry Preferences

In Medical/Health prefer:
Health Services

In Consumer Related prefer:
Food/Beverage
Consumer Products

In Industrial/Energy prefer:
Energy
Materials

In Transportation prefer:
Transportation
Aerospace

Additional Information

Name of Most Recent Fund: Altus Capital Partners II, L.P.
Most Recent Fund Was Raised: 10/13/2011
Year Founded: 2003
Capital Under Management: $242,600,000
Current Activity Level : Actively seeking new investments
Method of Compensation: Return on invest. most important, but chg. closing fees, service fees, etc.

ALTUS VENTURES LLC

120 West Broadway
Altus, OK USA 73521
Phone: 580-480-1319
Fax: 580-477-2983
Website: www.altusventuresok.com

Type of Firm

Bank Affiliated

Project Preferences

Type of Financing Preferred:
Early Stage
Expansion
Startup

Geographical Preferences

United States Preferences:
Oklahoma

Additional Information

Name of Most Recent Fund: Altus Venture Capital Fund V, LLC
Most Recent Fund Was Raised: 02/01/2006
Year Founded: 2002
Capital Under Management: $14,400,000
Current Activity Level : Actively seeking new investments

ALUMINA PARTNERS LLC

838 Sixth Avenue
Fifth Floor
New York, NY USA 10001
Phone: 6468631000
Fax: 6468631001
E-mail: info@aluminapartners.com
Website: www.aluminapartners.com

Type of Firm

Private Equity Firm

Project Preferences

Type of Financing Preferred:
Leveraged Buyout
Acquisition

Additional Information

Year Founded: 2015
Current Activity Level : Actively seeking new investments

ALUMNI CAPITAL NETWORK MANAGEMENT CO LLC

51 East 42nd Street
Suite 1100
New York, NY USA 10017
Phone: 2127925510
Fax: 2129220522
Website: www.alumnicapitalnetwork.com

Management and Staff

A. William Kapler, Managing Director
Arthur Sinensky, Managing Director
Denis Kelly, Managing Director
James Honohan, CEO & Managing Director
Jeffrey Miller, Managing Director
Kevin Jones, Managing Director
Richard Golden, Managing Director
Thomas Fox, Managing Director
Thomas Donahue, Managing Director
Walter Nollmann, Managing Director

Type of Firm

Private Equity Firm

Project Preferences

Type of Financing Preferred:
Leveraged Buyout
Management Buyouts
Acquisition

Industry Preferences

In Medical/Health prefer:
Medical/Health

In Consumer Related prefer:
Consumer
Retail

In Industrial/Energy prefer:
Industrial Products

In Transportation prefer:
Transportation

In Financial Services prefer:
Financial Services

In Business Serv. prefer:
Services
Distribution
Consulting Services

Additional Information

Year Founded: 2007
Current Activity Level : Actively seeking new investments

ALVEN CAPITAL PARTNERS SA

1 Place Andre Malraux
Paris, France 75001
Phone: 33155343838
Fax: 33155343839
E-mail: contact@alvencapital.com
Website: www.alven.co

Management and Staff

Charles Letourneur, Co-Founder
Guillaume Aubin, Co-Founder
Julie Barchilon, Chief Financial Officer
Nicolas Celier, Partner

Type of Firm

Private Equity Firm

Association Membership

French Venture Capital Association (AFIC)

Project Preferences

Type of Financing Preferred:
Early Stage
Balanced
Seed
Startup

Size of Investments Considered:
Min Size of Investment Considered (000s): $259
Max Size of Investment Considered (000s): $6,468

Geographical Preferences

International Preferences:
France

Industry Preferences

In Communications prefer:
Media and Entertainment

In Internet Specific prefer:
Internet

In Business Serv. prefer:
Services

Additional Information
Name of Most Recent Fund: Alven Capital III FCPR
Most Recent Fund Was Raised: 09/06/2007
Year Founded: 2000
Capital Under Management: $13,700,000
Current Activity Level : Actively seeking new investments

AM VENTURES HOLDING GMBH

Robert-Stirling-Ring 1
Krailling, Germany D-82152
Phone: 89 81059169-0
Website: www.amv.ventures

Management and Staff
Thomas Koehler, Chief Financial Officer
Uli Langer, Partner

Type of Firm
Private Equity Firm

Industry Preferences

In Computer Software prefer:
Software

In Computer Other prefer:
Computer Related

In Industrial/Energy prefer:
Materials
Advanced Materials

In Manufact. prefer:
Manufacturing

Additional Information
Year Founded: 2015
Current Activity Level : Actively seeking new investments

AMADEUS CAPITAL PARTNERS LTD

16 St. James's Street
Cambridge, United Kingdom SW1A 1ER
Phone: 442070246900
Fax: 442070246999
E-mail: info@amadeuscapital.com
Website: www.amadeuscapital.com

Other Offices
333 Bush Street
Suite 2250
SAN FRANCISCO, CA USA 94105
Phone: 4153912474

Management and Staff
Alex van Someren, Managing Partner
Andrea Traversone, Partner
Bhavani Rana, Partner
Hermann Hauser, Co-Founder
Jason Pinto, Partner
Mikael Johnsson, Venture Partner
Perry Blacher, Venture Partner
Richard Anton, Partner

Type of Firm
Private Equity Firm

Association Membership
British Venture Capital Association (BVCA)
European Private Equity and Venture Capital Assoc.

Project Preferences

Role in Financing:
Prefer role as deal originator but will also invest in deals created by others

Type of Financing Preferred:
Balanced
Seed
Startup

Geographical Preferences

International Preferences:
United Kingdom
Europe

Industry Focus
(% based on actual investment)

Computer Software and Services	24.3%
Semiconductors/Other Elect.	21.9%
Internet Specific	20.6%
Communications and Media	14.8%
Computer Hardware	10.2%
Biotechnology	3.8%
Other Products	1.9%
Consumer Related	1.1%
Medical/Health	0.8%
Industrial/Energy	0.6%

Additional Information
Name of Most Recent Fund: Amadeus IV Early Stage Funds
Most Recent Fund Was Raised: 01/16/2014
Year Founded: 1997
Capital Under Management: $968,000,000
Current Activity Level : Actively seeking new investments
Method of Compensation: Return on investment is of primary concern, do not charge fees

---

AMB PRIVATE EQUITY PARTNERS LTD

18 Fricker Road
Illovo, South Africa
Phone: 27-11-215-2099
Fax: 27-11-268-6889
E-mail: queries@amb.co.za
Website: www.ambpartners.co.za

Type of Firm
Private Equity Firm

Project Preferences

Type of Financing Preferred:
Leveraged Buyout
Early Stage
Expansion
Seed
Acquisition
Startup

Geographical Preferences

International Preferences:
South Africa

Additional Information
Year Founded: 1999
Current Activity Level : Actively seeking new investments

AMBER CAPITAL ITALIA SGR SPA

Piazza del Carmine 4
Milan, Italy 20121
Phone: 390200688006
E-mail: info.italia@ambercapital.com

Management and Staff
Edoardo Bounous, Managing Director

Type of Firm
Private Equity Firm

Association Membership
Italian Venture Capital Association (AIFI)

Project Preferences

Type of Financing Preferred:
Generalist PE

AMBIENTA SGR SPA

Piazza Fontana, 6
Milan, Italy 20122
Phone: 39027217461
Fax: 390272174646
E-mail: info@ambientasgr.com
Website: www.ambientasgr.com

Management and Staff
Mauro Roversi, Partner
Nino Provera, Chief Executive Officer
Rolando Polli, Partner

Type of Firm
Private Equity Firm

Association Membership
Italian Venture Capital Association (AIFI)
European Private Equity and Venture Capital Assoc.

Project Preferences

Type of Financing Preferred:
Leveraged Buyout
Later Stage
Management Buyouts
Acquisition

Geographical Preferences

International Preferences:
Europe

Industry Preferences

In Industrial/Energy prefer:
Energy
Energy Conservation Relat

In Other prefer:
Environment Responsible

Additional Information
Year Founded: 2007
Capital Under Management: $408,202,000
Current Activity Level : Actively seeking new investments

AMBINA PARTNERS LLC

1001 Brickell Bay Drive
Suite 2700
Miami, FL USA 33131
E-mail: Info@Ambina.com
Website: ambina.com

Management and Staff
Christine Blehle, Co-Founder
Gregory Share, Co-Founder

Type of Firm
Private Equity Firm

Project Preferences

Type of Financing Preferred:
Leveraged Buyout
Acquisition
Recapitalizations

Industry Preferences

In Financial Services prefer:
Financial Services

Additional Information
Year Founded: 2017
Current Activity Level : Actively seeking new investments

AMBIT PRAGMA VENTURES PVT LTD

449, Senapati Bapat Marg
Lower Parel
Mumbai, India 400 013
Phone: 91-22-3003-8400
Fax: 91-22-3003-8410
E-mail: info@ambitpragma.com

Management and Staff
Mangesh Pathak, Partner

Type of Firm
Private Equity Firm

Association Membership
Indian Venture Capital Association (IVCA)

Project Preferences

Type of Financing Preferred:
Early Stage
Expansion
Later Stage
Seed

Size of Investments Considered:
Min Size of Investment Considered (000s): $5,000
Max Size of Investment Considered (000s): $20,000

Geographical Preferences

International Preferences:
India

Industry Preferences

In Communications prefer:
Media and Entertainment
Entertainment

In Medical/Health prefer:
Health Services

In Consumer Related prefer:
Consumer
Entertainment and Leisure
Food/Beverage
Consumer Products

In Transportation prefer:
Transportation

In Financial Services prefer:
Real Estate

In Business Serv. prefer:
Services

Additional Information
Year Founded: 2007
Capital Under Management: $77,000,000
Current Activity Level : Actively seeking new investments

AMBRIAN RESOURCES AG

Bahnhofstrasse 23
Zug, Switzerland 6300

Management and Staff
Jean-Pierre Conrad, Partner
Kilian Cararrini, Partner
Nicolas Rouveyre, Partner

Type of Firm
Investment Management Firm

Project Preferences

Type of Financing Preferred:
Generalist PE

Geographical Preferences

International Preferences:
All International

Industry Preferences

In Agr/Forestr/Fish prefer:
Mining and Minerals

Additional Information
Year Founded: 2010
Current Activity Level : Actively seeking new investments

AME CLOUD VENTURES LLC

720 University Avenue
Suite 200
Los Gatos, CA USA 95032
Website: www.amecloudventures.com

Management and Staff
Chih-Yuan Yang, Founder
Nick Adams, Managing Director

Type of Firm
Private Equity Firm

Project Preferences

Type of Financing Preferred:
Balanced
Later Stage
Seed

Industry Preferences

In Communications prefer:
Wireless Communications
Data Communications

In Computer Software prefer:
Applications Software

Additional Information
Year Founded: 2012
Current Activity Level : Actively seeking new investments

AME VENTURES SRL

Galleria San Babila, 4b
Milan, Italy 20122
Phone: 39-2762-1241
Fax: 39-027621-2450
E-mail: info@ameventures.it
Website: www.ameventures.it

Type of Firm
Private Equity Firm

Project Preferences

Type of Financing Preferred:
Expansion

Size of Investments Considered:
Min Size of Investment Considered (000s): $121
Max Size of Investment Considered (000s): $1,817

Geographical Preferences

International Preferences:
Italy
Europe

Industry Preferences

In Industrial/Energy prefer:
Energy

In Business Serv. prefer:
Services

In Utilities prefer:
Utilities

Additional Information
Year Founded: 2005
Current Activity Level : Actively seeking new investments

AMERICAN BEACON ADVISORS INC

220 East Las Colinas Blvd
Suite 1200
Fort Worth, TX USA 76155
Phone: 8173916100
Fax: 8173916131
E-mail: American AAdvantage.Funds@aa.com
Website: www.americanbeaconfunds.com

Management and Staff
Brian Brett, Vice President
Erica Duncan, Vice President
Jeffrey Ringdahl, Chief Operating Officer
Rosemary Behan, Vice President
Samuel Silver, Vice President
Terri McKinney, Vice President

Type of Firm
Investment Management Firm

Project Preferences

Type of Financing Preferred:
Fund of Funds

Geographical Preferences

United States Preferences:

Additional Information
Name of Most Recent Fund: American Private Equity Partners II, L.P.
Most Recent Fund Was Raised: 06/09/2005
Year Founded: 1986
Capital Under Management: $117,400,000
Current Activity Level : Actively seeking new investments

AMERICAN DISCOVERY CAPITAL LLC

11150 Santa Monica Boulevard
Suite 1425
Los Angeles, CA USA 90025
Phone: 3104818706
E-mail: info@americandiscoverycapital.com
Website: americandiscoverycapital.com

Management and Staff
Brian Webber, Partner
Frank McMahon, Partner
Jeffrey Gelles, Partner
John Joliet, Partner
Kyle Madan, Managing Director
Laurent Degryse, Partner
Michael Denbeau, Partner

Type of Firm
Investment Management Firm

Industry Preferences

In Computer Software prefer:
Software

In Medical/Health prefer:
Health Services

In Financial Services prefer:
Financial Services

Additional Information
Year Founded: 1969
Current Activity Level : Actively seeking new investments

AMERICAN FAMILY VENTURES

111 North Fairchild Street
Suite 400
Madison, WI USA 53703
Website: www.amfamventures.com

Type of Firm
Private Equity Firm

Project Preferences

Type of Financing Preferred:
Early Stage
Expansion
Startup

Geographical Preferences

United States Preferences:

Additional Information
Year Founded: 2010
Current Activity Level : Actively seeking new investments

AMERICAN INDUSTRIAL ACQUISITION CORP

1465 East Putnam Avenue
229
Greenwich, CT USA 06830
Phone: 2036989595
E-mail: info@aiacgroup.com
Website: www.aiacgroup.com

Type of Firm
Private Equity Firm

Project Preferences

Type of Financing Preferred:
Leveraged Buyout
Acquisition

Industry Preferences

In Communications prefer:
Wireless Communications

In Industrial/Energy prefer:
Industrial Products

In Transportation prefer:
Transportation

In Business Serv. prefer:
Distribution

In Manufact. prefer:
Manufacturing

Additional Information
Year Founded: 1996
Current Activity Level : Actively seeking new investments

AMERICAN INDUSTRIAL PARTNERS

535 Fifth Avenue
32nd Floor
New York, NY USA 10017
Phone: 2126272360
Fax: 2126272372
Website: www.aipartners.com

Management and Staff
Ben DeRosa, Partner
Daryl Yap, Partner
Derek Leck, Partner
Dino Cusumano, Partner
Eric Baroyan, Partner
Graham Sullivan, Partner
John Becker, Partner
Kim Marvin, Partner
Ryan Hodgson, Partner

Type of Firm
Private Equity Firm

Project Preferences

Type of Financing Preferred:
Leveraged Buyout

Geographical Preferences

United States Preferences:
North America
All U.S.

Industry Focus
(% based on actual investment)
Industrial/Energy	69.4%
Other Products	25.7%
Computer Hardware	4.9%

Additional Information
Name of Most Recent Fund: American Industrial Partners Capital Fund V, L.P.
Most Recent Fund Was Raised: 12/15/2011
Year Founded: 1989
Capital Under Management: $2,500,000,000
Current Activity Level : Actively seeking new investments

AMERICAN WORLD TRADE FUND INC

3319 North San Gabriel
Rosemead, CA USA 91770
Phone: 86-10-85289
Fax: 86-10-85289

Type of Firm
Private Equity Firm

Additional Information
Year Founded: 2012
Current Activity Level : Actively seeking new investments

AMERICORP VENTURES LTD

1005 Maker Chambers V
Nariman Point
Mumbai, India 400 021
Phone: 912256324477
Fax: 912222027573
E-mail: india@americorpfund.com
Website: www.americorpfund.com

Type of Firm
Private Equity Advisor or Fund of Funds

Project Preferences

Type of Financing Preferred:
Early Stage
Expansion
Mezzanine
Turnaround
Later Stage
Seed
Startup

Size of Investments Considered:
Min Size of Investment Considered (000s): $2,000
Max Size of Investment Considered (000s): $10,000

Geographical Preferences

International Preferences:
India

Industry Preferences

In Communications prefer:
Telecommunications

In Consumer Related prefer:
Consumer
Consumer Products
Consumer Services

In Financial Services prefer:
Financial Services
Insurance
Real Estate
Financial Services

In Business Serv. prefer:
Media

Additional Information
Year Founded: 1996
Capital Under Management: $47,000,000
Current Activity Level : Actively seeking new investments

AMERRA CAPITAL MANAGEMENT LLC

1185 Avenue of the Americas
17th Floor
New York, NY USA 10036

Type of Firm
Investment Management Firm

Project Preferences

Type of Financing Preferred:
Generalist PE

Industry Preferences

In Agr/Forestr/Fish prefer:
Agriculture related

Additional Information
Year Founded: 2009
Capital Under Management: $486,770,000
Current Activity Level : Actively seeking new investments

AMERY CAPITAL

25 Camperdown Street
Level Three
London, United Kingdom E1 8DZ
Website: www.amerycap.com

Type of Firm
Private Equity Firm

Project Preferences

Type of Financing Preferred:
Leveraged Buyout
Acquisition

Industry Preferences

In Consumer Related prefer:
Consumer
Retail

Additional Information
Year Founded: 2004
Current Activity Level : Actively seeking new investments

AMETHIS ADVISORY SAS

18 rue de Tilsitt
Paris, France 75017
Phone: 33156688560
E-mail: info@amethisfinance.com
Website: www.amethisfinance.com

Management and Staff
Eric Ouedraogo, Chief Financial Officer

Type of Firm
Private Equity Firm

Association Membership
Emerging Markets Private Equity Association
African Venture Capital Association (AVCA)

Project Preferences

Type of Financing Preferred:
Mezzanine
Acquisition

Geographical Preferences

International Preferences:
Africa

Industry Preferences

In Consumer Related prefer:
Consumer

In Industrial/Energy prefer:
Energy

In Financial Services prefer:
Financial Services

In Agr/Forestr/Fish prefer:
Agribusiness

Additional Information
Year Founded: 2011
Capital Under Management: $530,000,000
Current Activity Level : Actively seeking new investments

AMG PRIVATE CAPITAL GROUP

6501 East Belleview Avenue
Suite 400
Englewood, CO USA 80111
Phone: 8009992190
Fax: 3036949242
Website: www.amgnational.com

Management and Staff
Michael Bergmann, Co-Founder

Type of Firm
Bank Affiliated

Project Preferences

Type of Financing Preferred:
Leveraged Buyout
Value-Add
Early Stage
Expansion
Mezzanine
Balanced
Later Stage
Seed
Special Situation

Industry Preferences

In Industrial/Energy prefer:
Energy
Oil and Gas Exploration

In Financial Services prefer:
Real Estate

Additional Information
Name of Most Recent Fund: AMGIC Venture Fund VIII LLLP
Most Recent Fund Was Raised: 09/12/2012
Year Founded: 2007
Capital Under Management: $11,010,000
Current Activity Level : Actively seeking new investments

AMGEN INC

One Amgen Center Drive
Thousand Oaks, CA USA 91320
Phone: 8054471000
Fax: 8054471010
E-mail: investor.relations@amgen.com
Website: www.amgen.com

Type of Firm
Corporate PE/Venture

Association Membership
National Venture Capital Association - USA (NVCA)

Project Preferences

Type of Financing Preferred:
Early Stage
Balanced
Later Stage

Size of Investments Considered:
Min Size of Investment Considered (000s): $2,000
Max Size of Investment Considered (000s): $10,000

Geographical Preferences

United States Preferences:
North America

International Preferences:
United Kingdom
Europe

Industry Preferences

In Biotechnology prefer:
Biotechnology

Additional Information
Year Founded: 1986
Capital Under Management: $100,000,000
Current Activity Level : Actively seeking new investments

AMHERST FUND LLC

401 E. Stadium
Ann Arbor, MI USA 48104
Phone: 17346622102
E-mail: info@amherstfund.com
Website: www.amherstfund.com

Management and Staff
Amherst Turner, Founder

Type of Firm
Private Equity Firm

Project Preferences

Type of Financing Preferred:
Early Stage
Later Stage

Industry Preferences

In Internet Specific prefer:
Web Aggregation/Portals

In Medical/Health prefer:
Drug/Equipmt Delivery
Medical Products

In Consumer Related prefer:
Consumer

In Manufact. prefer:
Manufacturing

Additional Information
Year Founded: 1998
Current Activity Level : Actively seeking new investments

AMICUS CAPITAL LLC

1045 Sansome Street
Suite 326
San Francisco, CA USA 94111
Phone: 4156460120
Fax: 4152764755
E-mail: ideas@amicuscapital.com
Website: www.amicuscapital.com

Management and Staff
Bob Zipp, Co-Founder

Type of Firm
Private Equity Firm

Project Preferences

Type of Financing Preferred:
Early Stage
Seed

Industry Preferences

In Internet Specific prefer:
Internet
Ecommerce

In Business Serv. prefer:
Media

Additional Information

Year Founded: 1998
Current Activity Level : Actively seeking new investments

AMICUS PARTNERS

12-16 Bridge Street
Arnott House
Belfast, Ireland BT1 1LS
Phone: 442890393852
E-mail: info@amicus-capital.com
Website: www.amicuspartners.co.uk

Other Offices

Monticello, Loudwater Lane, Rickmansworth
Hertfordshire
England, United Kingdom WD3 4HX

Stone Lodge, Clare Road
Ballycastle, Ireland BT1 1LS

Management and Staff

Bob Dutnall, Partner
Carl Francis, Co-Founder
John Beddows, Co-Founder
Lawson McDonald, Partner
Peter David, Partner
Terry McCartney, Co-Founder
Tony Smith, Partner

Type of Firm

Private Equity Firm

Project Preferences

Type of Financing Preferred:
Early Stage
Expansion
Turnaround
Management Buyouts

Geographical Preferences

International Preferences:
United Kingdom

Industry Preferences

In Medical/Health prefer:
Medical/Health

In Consumer Related prefer:
Retail

In Industrial/Energy prefer:
Industrial Products

In Business Serv. prefer:
Media

Additional Information

Year Founded: 2001
Current Activity Level : Actively seeking new investments

AMIDZAD PARTNERS, CO.

370 Convention Way
Redwood City, CA USA 94063
Phone: 6502162360
E-mail: info@amidzad.com
Website: www.amidzad.com

Other Offices

Colon, 18 - 7A
Valencia, Spain 46004

Management and Staff

Rahim Amidi, General Partner
Saeed Amidi, General Partner

Type of Firm

Private Equity Firm

Project Preferences

Type of Financing Preferred:
Early Stage
Balanced
Seed
Startup

Geographical Preferences

United States Preferences:
West Coast

Additional Information

Year Founded: 2000
Capital Under Management: $3,000,000
Current Activity Level : Actively seeking new investments

AMINO CAPITAL MANAGEMENT COMPANY LLC

119 University Avenue
Palo Alto, CA USA 94301
Website: www.aminocapital.com

Management and Staff

David Wei, Partner
Haitao Zheng, Partner
Huican Zhu, Partner
Jun Wu, Partner
Sue Xu, Partner

Type of Firm

Private Equity Firm

Project Preferences

Type of Financing Preferred:
Early Stage

Industry Preferences

In Communications prefer:
Communications and Media
Data Communications

In Computer Software prefer:
Data Processing

In Internet Specific prefer:
Internet

In Medical/Health prefer:
Medical/Health

In Consumer Related prefer:
Entertainment and Leisure

Additional Information

Year Founded: 2012
Capital Under Management: $50,000,000
Current Activity Level : Actively seeking new investments

AMITI VENTURES LLC

33 South State Street
Suite 400
Chicago, IL USA 60603
E-mail: info@amitiventures.com
Website: www.amitiventures.com

Management and Staff

Ben Rabinowitz, Managing Partner

Type of Firm

Private Equity Firm

Project Preferences

Role in Financing:
Prefer role in deals created by others

Type of Financing Preferred:
Early Stage
Expansion
Balanced
Later Stage

Geographical Preferences

International Preferences:
Israel

Industry Preferences

In Communications prefer:
Wireless Communications

In Computer Software prefer:
Software

In Internet Specific prefer:
Internet

In Computer Other prefer:
Computer Related

In Semiconductor/Electr prefer:
Semiconductor
Analytic/Scientific

Additional Information
Name of Most Recent Fund: Amiti Ventures I, L.P.
Most Recent Fund Was Raised: 12/08/2009
Year Founded: 2010
Capital Under Management: $37,780,000
Current Activity Level : Actively seeking new investments

AMKEY VENTURES LLC

44370 Old Warm Springs Blvd.
Fremont, CA USA 94538
Phone: 5106681816
Fax: 5106681017
E-mail: info@amkeyvc.com
Website: www.amkeyvc.com

Management and Staff
George Lee, Co-Founder
Woody Sing-Wood Yeh, Co-Founder

Type of Firm
Private Equity Firm

Project Preferences

Type of Financing Preferred:
Balanced

Geographical Preferences

United States Preferences:

Industry Preferences

In Medical/Health prefer:
Medical/Health
Medical Products

Additional Information
Year Founded: 2001
Current Activity Level : Actively seeking new investments

AMP CAPITAL INVESTORS LTD

50 Bridge Street
Level 12
Sydney, Australia 2000
Phone: 61292578020
Fax: 61292571234
E-mail: AMPCI_Investment_Research@amp.com.au
Website: www.ampcapital.com.au

Other Offices
Berkeley Square
Level Four, Berkeley Square House
London, United Kingdom W1J6BX
Phone: 44-20-7659-9252
Fax: 44-20-7659-9251

113-119 The Terrace
Ground Floor
Wellington, New Zealand 6140
Phone: 64-4494-2200
Fax: 64-4494-2123

Two-Four-One, Marunouchi
32nd Floor, Marunouchi Bldg., Chiyoda-ku
Tokyo, Japan 100-6332
Phone: 81-3-3212-7170
Fax: 81-3-3212-7191

23rd Flr. One Island East, 18 Westlands
Unit 33 Quary Bay
Island East, Hong Kong
Phone: 852-3750-7601
Fax: 852-3750-7602

18-20 Rue Edward Steichen
L-2540
, Luxembourg
Phone: 352-2784-8035
Fax: 352-2784-8034

612-A Embassy Centre
Nariman Point
Mumbai, India 400021
Phone: 91-22-6615-8898
Fax: 91-22-6615-8899

80 Raffles Place
Suite 18-20, UOB Plaza 2
Singapore, Singapore 048624
Phone: 65-6511-1850
Fax: 65-6511-1899

Number Seven Jian Guo Nei Avenue
Suite 322C Tower 2 Bright China Chang An
Beijing, China 100005
Phone: 86-10-6518-6158
Fax: 86-10-6518-6696

Management and Staff
Jim Dawson, Founder
Stephen Dunne, Managing Director

Type of Firm
Investment Management Firm

Association Membership
New Zealand Venture Capital Association

Project Preferences

Role in Financing:
Prefer role as deal originator

Type of Financing Preferred:
Leveraged Buyout
Value-Add
Early Stage
Expansion
Generalist PE
Balanced
Later Stage
Other
Management Buyouts
Acquisition

Geographical Preferences

United States Preferences:
North America

International Preferences:
Asia Pacific
Ireland
Europe
Pacific
Australia
New Zealand
Asia
Japan

Industry Focus
(% based on actual investment)
Other Products	85.0%
Consumer Related	6.5%
Industrial/Energy	3.3%
Medical/Health	2.7%
Internet Specific	1.8%
Computer Software and Services	0.6%

Additional Information
Name of Most Recent Fund: Global Infrastructure Fund
Most Recent Fund Was Raised: 12/17/2014
Year Founded: 1979
Capital Under Management: $201,000,000
Current Activity Level : Actively seeking new investments
Method of Compensation: Return on invest. most important, but chg. closing fees, service fees, etc.

AMPERSAND CAPITAL PARTNERS

55 William Street
Suite 240
Wellesley, MA USA 02481
Phone: 7812390700
Fax: 7812390824
E-mail: info@ampersandcapital.com
Website: www.ampersandventures.com

Management and Staff
Charles Yie, General Partner
Dana Niles, Chief Financial Officer
David Anderson, Partner
David Parker, General Partner
Eric Lev, Partner
Herbert Hooper, Managing Partner
Jared Bartok, General Partner
Stuart Auerbach, General Partner
Suzanne MacCormack, Partner
Timothy Tuff, Venture Partner

Type of Firm
Private Equity Firm

Association Membership
New England Venture Capital Association
Natl Assoc of Small Bus. Inv. Co (NASBIC)

Project Preferences

Role in Financing:
Prefer role as deal originator but will also invest in deals created by others

Type of Financing Preferred:
Leveraged Buyout
Generalist PE
Balanced

Size of Investments Considered:
Min Size of Investment Considered (000s): $10,000
Max Size of Investment Considered (000s): $50,000

Industry Focus
(% based on actual investment)

Industry	%
Medical/Health	21.2%
Biotechnology	16.4%
Semiconductors/Other Elect.	12.2%
Other Products	10.7%
Computer Software and Services	9.9%
Internet Specific	8.9%
Industrial/Energy	8.7%
Communications and Media	5.1%
Consumer Related	3.7%
Computer Hardware	3.3%

Additional Information
Name of Most Recent Fund: Ampersand 2014, L.P.
Most Recent Fund Was Raised: 02/03/2014
Year Founded: 1988
Capital Under Management: $600,000,000
Current Activity Level : Actively seeking new investments
Method of Compensation: Return on invest. most important, but chg. closing fees, service fees, etc.

AMPLE LUCK INTERNATIONAL CAPITAL GROUP LTD

Wool Hutong, Xicheng District
51 North Gate
Beijing, China 100031
Phone: 861085911016
Fax: 861085911015
E-mail: info@ampleluck.com
Website: www.ampleluck.com

Other Offices
Room 5012, North block 1
Dongguang Tower, No.78 West Ring road
Xi'An, China
Phone: 8602988639566

RM1001Da Biao International Ctr
Jiangnan Road
Guangzhou, China
Phone: 8602084427351
Fax: 8602034313782

Room 302,Block Feng 1
Unit 1, No.88 Guangheerjie, Gaoxin
Cheng Du, China
Phone: 8602861558259
Fax: 8602861558259

Management and Staff
Bing Liao, Partner
Changcai Li, Partner
Chunlin Zhao, Partner
Dajun Wang, Partner
Qiang Bai, Partner
Wei Li, Partner

Type of Firm
Investment Management Firm

Project Preferences

Type of Financing Preferred:
Generalist PE
Balanced

Geographical Preferences

International Preferences:
China

Industry Preferences

In Communications prefer:
Telecommunications

In Industrial/Energy prefer:
Energy
Oil and Gas Exploration
Oil & Gas Drilling,Explor
Environmental Related

In Financial Services prefer:
Real Estate

In Business Serv. prefer:
Services
Media

In Manufact. prefer:
Manufacturing

Additional Information
Year Founded: 2011
Capital Under Management: $188,900,000
Current Activity Level : Actively seeking new investments

AMPLIFIER MANAGEMENT LLC

1614 Brookside Road
McLean, VA USA 22101
Phone: 7036352655
Fax: 7037820222
Website: www.amplifierventures.com

Management and Staff
Edward Bersoff, Managing Director

Type of Firm
Private Equity Firm

Project Preferences

Type of Financing Preferred:
Early Stage
Seed
Startup

Size of Investments Considered:
Min Size of Investment Considered (000s): $500
Max Size of Investment Considered (000s): $1,000

Geographical Preferences

United States Preferences:
Washington

Industry Preferences

In Communications prefer:
Communications and Media
Media and Entertainment

In Computer Software prefer:
Software
Systems Software
Applications Software

In Internet Specific prefer:
E-Commerce Technology

In Industrial/Energy prefer:
Alternative Energy

In Business Serv. prefer:
Distribution

Additional Information
Year Founded: 2005
Capital Under Management: $15,000,000
Current Activity Level : Actively seeking new investments

AMPLIFY PARTNERS LP

1050 Doyle Street
Menlo Park, CA USA 94025
Phone: 6504450800
E-mail: info@amplifypartners.com
Website: www.amplifypartners.com

Other Offices

1050 Doyle Street
MENLO PARK, CA USA 94025
Phone: 6504450800

Management and Staff

David Beyer, Partner
Lenny Pruss, Partner
Mike Dauber, General Partner
Sarah Catanzaro, Principal

Type of Firm

Private Equity Firm

Project Preferences

Type of Financing Preferred:
Early Stage
Startup

Size of Investments Considered:
Min Size of Investment Considered (000s): $50
Max Size of Investment Considered (000s): $1,500

Industry Preferences

In Computer Software prefer:
Software
Applications Software

Additional Information

Name of Most Recent Fund: Amplify Partners, L.P.
Most Recent Fund Was Raised: 01/30/2013
Year Founded: 2012
Capital Under Management: $174,100,000
Current Activity Level : Actively seeking new investments

AMPLIFY.LA

1600 Main Street
Venice, CA USA 90292
Phone: 8587037794
Website: www.amplify.la

Management and Staff

Paul Bricault, Managing Director
Richard Wolpert, Managing Director

Type of Firm

Incubator/Development Program

Project Preferences

Type of Financing Preferred:
Seed
Startup

Geographical Preferences

United States Preferences:
California

Industry Preferences

In Communications prefer:
Media and Entertainment

Additional Information

Year Founded: 2011
Capital Under Management: $20,630,000
Current Activity Level : Actively seeking new investments

AMULET CAPITAL PARTNERS LLC

55 Railroad Avenue
Suite 302
Greenwich, CT USA 06830
Phone: 6465616650
Fax: 2129831234
E-mail: admin@amuletcapital.com
Website: www.amuletcapital.com

Type of Firm

Private Equity Firm

Project Preferences

Type of Financing Preferred:
Leveraged Buyout
Expansion

Industry Preferences

In Medical/Health prefer:
Medical/Health
Medical Products
Health Services
Pharmaceuticals

Additional Information

Year Founded: 1969
Capital Under Management: $145,000,000
Current Activity Level : Actively seeking new investments

AMUNDI PRIVATE EQUITY FUNDS SA

90 Boulevard Pasteur
Paris, France 75015
Phone: 33
Fax: 33
E-mail: privatequity@sgam.com

Other Offices

32-A Pictor Negulici St.
Bd Ion Mihalache Nr 1-7
Bucharest, Romania 71289
Phone: 40-21-301-4150
Fax: 40-21-301-4159

ul. Wspolna 47/49
Warsaw, Poland 00-584
Phone: 48-22-627-4000
Fax: 48-22-627-4001

5-1, Kabuto-Cho Nihonbashi Chuo-ku
Tokyo, Japan 103-0026
Phone: 81-3-3660-5185
Fax: 81-3-3669-8269

9th Floor-Exchange House
Primrose Street
London, United Kingdom EC2A 2EF
Phone: 44-20-7090-2500
Fax: 44-20-7329-5602

Mainzer Landstrasse 36
Frankfurt, Germany 60325
Phone: 49-69-71042-80812
Fax: 49-69-717-4249

Management and Staff

Olivier Leclerc, Chief Executive Officer
Philippe Collas, President

Type of Firm

Bank Affiliated

Association Membership

French Venture Capital Association (AFIC)

Project Preferences

Type of Financing Preferred:
Fund of Funds
Leveraged Buyout
Early Stage
Expansion
Generalist PE
Balanced
Turnaround
Later Stage
Seed
Acquisition
Startup

Geographical Preferences

United States Preferences:

International Preferences:
Europe
Western Europe
Eastern Europe
Asia
Romania
France

Industry Preferences

In Communications prefer:
Communications and Media
Telecommunications

In Computer Software prefer:
Computer Services
Software
Applications Software

In Internet Specific prefer:
Internet

In Computer Other prefer:
Computer Related

In Semiconductor/Electr prefer:
Semiconductor

In Biotechnology prefer:
Biotechnology

In Medical/Health prefer:
Medical/Health
Medical Therapeutics
Medical Products
Health Services
Pharmaceuticals

In Consumer Related prefer:
Consumer
Entertainment and Leisure
Retail
Consumer Products
Consumer Services

In Industrial/Energy prefer:
Energy
Alternative Energy
Energy Conservation Relat
Industrial Products
Materials
Environmental Related

In Financial Services prefer:
Financial Services
Financial Services

In Business Serv. prefer:
Services
Media

In Manufact. prefer:
Manufacturing

In Agr/Forestr/Fish prefer:
Agribusiness
Agriculture related

In Other prefer:
Environment Responsible

Additional Information
Name of Most Recent Fund: SGAM AI Kantara Fund, L.P.
Most Recent Fund Was Raised: 07/04/2008
Year Founded: 1999
Capital Under Management: $2,370,300,000
Current Activity Level : Actively seeking new investments

AMUNDI PRIVATE EQUITY FUNDS SA

90 Boulevard Pasteur
Paris, France 75730
Phone: 33176333030
E-mail: contact-pef@amundi.com
Website: www.amundi.com

Other Offices
2 rue Ahmad Ragheb
7eme etage, Garden City
Cairo, Egypt

1-7 boulevard Ion Mihalache
Corilius Advisor Srl, tour BRD
Bucharest, Romania 75015
Phone: 33176333030

3 rue Abou Zaid Eddaboussi
Casablanca, Morocco 20100

13 rue de Rhodes, Mutuelle Ville
Belvedere
Tunis, Tunisia 1002

ul Wspolna 47/49
Warsaw, Poland 00684

Management and Staff
Jean Daumet, Partner

Type of Firm
Private Equity Advisor or Fund of Funds

Association Membership
French Venture Capital Association (AFIC)
Czech Venture Capital Association (CVCA)
European Private Equity and Venture Capital Assoc.

Project Preferences
Type of Financing Preferred:
Fund of Funds
Early Stage
Expansion
Later Stage

Size of Investments Considered:
Min Size of Investment Considered (000s): $1,371
Max Size of Investment Considered (000s): $13,709

Geographical Preferences
United States Preferences:

Canadian Preferences:
All Canada

International Preferences:
Asia Pacific
Italy
Greece
Latin America
India
Tunisia
United Kingdom
Luxembourg
Europe
Czech Republic
Hong Kong
Brunei
China
Poland
Utd. Arab Em.
Monaco
Eastern Europe
Middle East
Brazil
Saudi Arabia
Chile
Spain
Australia
Belgium
Morocco
Romania
Singapore
Korea, South
Germany
Japan
Malaysia
Africa
All International
France

Industry Preferences

In Communications prefer:
Communications and Media

In Computer Software prefer:
Software

In Industrial/Energy prefer:
Industrial Products
Advanced Materials
Factory Automation
Machinery

Additional Information
Year Founded: 1996
Capital Under Management: $20,500,000
Current Activity Level : Actively seeking new investments

AMVENSYS CAPITAL GROUP LLC

1330 Capital Parkway
Carrollton, TX USA 75006
Phone: 9723371536
E-mail: info@amvensys.com
Website: www.amvensys.com

Other Offices

15 Walton Circle, Lavelle Road
Bangalore, India 560001
Phone: 8065396993

26 York Street
Suite 11835
London, United Kingdom W1U 6PZ
Phone: 2033718765

Management and Staff

Z. Ed Lateef, Chief Executive Officer

Type of Firm

Private Equity Firm

Project Preferences

Type of Financing Preferred:
Leveraged Buyout
Expansion
Later Stage
Management Buyouts
Acquisition
Recapitalizations

Geographical Preferences

United States Preferences:

International Preferences:
India
United Kingdom

Industry Preferences

In Communications prefer:
Telecommunications

In Computer Software prefer:
Software

In Industrial/Energy prefer:
Energy

In Business Serv. prefer:
Services

Additional Information

Year Founded: 1969
Current Activity Level : Actively seeking new investments

AMWAL INTERNATIONAL INVESTMENT COMPANY KSCP

10/F, Sahab Tower, Salhiya
P.O.Box 4871
Safat, Kuwait 13049
Phone: 96522971000
Fax: 96522403573
E-mail: info@smwal-invest.com
Website: www.amwal-invest.com

Management and Staff

Anmar Ahmadi, Chief Financial Officer

Type of Firm

Private Equity Firm

Project Preferences

Type of Financing Preferred:
Generalist PE

Geographical Preferences

International Preferences:
Kuwait

Additional Information

Year Founded: 2005
Current Activity Level : Actively seeking new investments

AMWAL INVEST COMPANY PSC

P.O.Box 940988
Amman, Jordan 11194
Phone: 96265000360
Fax: 96265000364
Website: www.amwalinvest.com

Type of Firm

Private Equity Firm

Project Preferences

Type of Financing Preferred:
Early Stage
Expansion
Public Companies
Later Stage
Seed
Startup

Geographical Preferences

International Preferences:
Middle East

Additional Information

Year Founded: 2005
Current Activity Level : Actively seeking new investments

AMWAL QSCC

PO Box 494
Amwal Tower West Bay
Doha, Qatar
Phone: 97444527777
Fax: 97444117426
E-mail: info@amwalqa.com
Website: www.amwal.qa

Management and Staff

George Shehade, Chief Executive Officer

Type of Firm

Investment Management Firm

Project Preferences

Type of Financing Preferred:
Balanced

Geographical Preferences

International Preferences:
Qatar

Additional Information

Year Founded: 1998
Current Activity Level : Actively seeking new investments

AMWIN MANAGEMENT PTY LTD

Level 4 Customs House
31 Alfred Street
Sydney, Australia 2000
Phone: 612-9251-9655
Fax: 612-9251-7655
E-mail: partners@amwin.com.au
Website: www.amwin.com.au

Management and Staff

Stuart Wardman-Browne, Chief Operating Officer

Type of Firm

Private Equity Firm

Project Preferences

Type of Financing Preferred:
Early Stage
Seed
Startup

Size of Investments Considered:
Min Size of Investment Considered (000s): $564
Max Size of Investment Considered (000s): $2,254

Geographical Preferences

International Preferences:
Pacific

Additional Information

Year Founded: 1998
Capital Under Management: $16,200,000
Current Activity Level : Actively seeking new investments

AMX CAPITAL LTD

60 State Street
Boston, MA USA 02109
Phone: 617-860-3400
Fax: 617-860-3450
E-mail: info@amxcapital.com
Website: www.amxcapital.com

Type of Firm
Private Equity Firm

Project Preferences

Type of Financing Preferred:
Generalist PE
Balanced
Acquisition
Recapitalizations

Size of Investments Considered:
Min Size of Investment Considered (000s): $50,000
Max Size of Investment Considered (000s): $200,000

Industry Preferences

In Industrial/Energy prefer:
Alternative Energy
Environmental Related

Additional Information
Year Founded: 2010
Current Activity Level : Actively seeking new investments

AMZAK CAPITAL MANAGEMENT LLC

980 North Federal Highway
Suite 315
Boca Raton, FL USA 33432
Website: amzak.com

Management and Staff
Billy Alejandro, Chief Financial Officer
Scot Fischer, Managing Partner

Type of Firm
Private Equity Firm

Project Preferences

Type of Financing Preferred:
Leveraged Buyout
Mezzanine
Acquisition
Distressed Debt

Geographical Preferences

United States Preferences:
All U.S.

Industry Preferences

In Communications prefer:
Telecommunications

In Medical/Health prefer:
Medical/Health

In Consumer Related prefer:
Entertainment and Leisure
Retail
Education Related

In Financial Services prefer:
Financial Services
Real Estate

Additional Information
Year Founded: 2006
Current Activity Level : Actively seeking new investments

ANACACIA CAPITAL PTY LTD

53 Cross Street
Level Two
Sydney, Australia 2028
Phone: 61293631222
Fax: 61285804600
E-mail: contact@anacacia.com.au
Website: www.anacacia.com.au

Management and Staff
Jeremy Samuel, Founder

Type of Firm
Private Equity Firm

Association Membership
Australian Venture Capital Association (AVCAL)

Project Preferences

Role in Financing:
Prefer role as deal originator but will also invest in deals created by others

Type of Financing Preferred:
Leveraged Buyout
Generalist PE
Balanced
Acquisition

Geographical Preferences

International Preferences:
Australia
New Zealand

Additional Information
Name of Most Recent Fund: Anacacia Partnership II, L.P.
Most Recent Fund Was Raised: 07/02/2012
Year Founded: 2007
Capital Under Management: $177,400,000
Current Activity Level : Actively seeking new investments

ANACAP FINANCIAL PARTNERS LLP

25 Bedford Street
Covent Garden
London, United Kingdom WC2E 9ES
Phone: 442070705250
Fax: 442070705290
E-mail: contact@anacapfp.com
Website: www.anacapfp.com

Management and Staff
Amber Hilkene, Partner
Chris Patrick, Partner
Fabrizio Cesario, Partner
Joe Giannamore, Managing Partner
Justin Sulger, Managing Director
Peter Cartwright, Managing Partner

Type of Firm
Private Equity Firm

Association Membership
European Private Equity and Venture Capital Assoc.

Project Preferences

Type of Financing Preferred:
Expansion
Generalist PE
Balanced
Turnaround
Later Stage
Acquisition
Recapitalizations

Industry Preferences

In Financial Services prefer:
Financial Services

Additional Information
Year Founded: 2005
Capital Under Management: $428,300,000
Current Activity Level : Actively seeking new investments

ANACAPA PARTNERS, L.P.

160 Bovet Road
Suite 405
San Mateo, CA USA 94402
Phone: 6503186881
Fax: 6507266057
E-mail: info@anacapapartners.com
Website: www.anacapapartners.com

Management and Staff
Jeff Stevens, Managing Partner

Type of Firm
Private Equity Firm

Project Preferences

Type of Financing Preferred:
Leveraged Buyout
Expansion
Acquisition

Industry Preferences

In Business Serv. prefer:
Services

Additional Information
Name of Most Recent Fund: Anacapa Partners, L.P.
Most Recent Fund Was Raised: 12/13/2010
Year Founded: 2010
Capital Under Management: $36,691,000
Current Activity Level : Actively seeking new investments

ANALYTICS VENTURES
P.O. Box 3170
Rancho Santa Fe, CA USA 92067
Phone: 8582205158
Website: www.analytics-ventures.com

Management and Staff
Blaise Barrelet, Founder
Michael Christian, Managing Director
Navid Alipour, Managing Partner

Type of Firm
Private Equity Firm

Project Preferences

Type of Financing Preferred:
Early Stage

Geographical Preferences

United States Preferences:
California

Industry Preferences

In Computer Software prefer:
Applications Software

Additional Information
Year Founded: 1969
Current Activity Level : Actively seeking new investments

ANAN HOLDING
Prince Sultan Street
Level 1, Office 7, Al-Saad Ctr
Jeddah, Saudi Arabia 21352
Phone: 96626165590
Fax: 96626165758
E-mail: info@ananholding.com
Website: www.ananholding.com

Type of Firm
Private Equity Firm

Project Preferences

Type of Financing Preferred:
Expansion
Later Stage
Acquisition

Industry Preferences

In Financial Services prefer:
Real Estate

Additional Information
Year Founded: 1969
Current Activity Level : Actively seeking new investments

ANANDA VENTURES GMBH
Isarwinkel 6
Munich, Germany 81379
Phone: 072213600
Website: www.socialventurefund.com

Management and Staff
Florian Erber, Managing Partner
Johannes Weber, Co-Founder
Monika Roell, Co-Founder
Sylvie Mutschler, Co-Founder

Type of Firm
Private Equity Firm

Association Membership
European Private Equity and Venture Capital Assoc.

Project Preferences

Type of Financing Preferred:
Early Stage
Mezzanine
Balanced
Later Stage
Seed
Startup

Geographical Preferences

International Preferences:
Western Europe
Germany

Industry Preferences

In Consumer Related prefer:
Consumer Services

Additional Information
Year Founded: 2010
Current Activity Level : Actively seeking new investments

ANANIA & ASSOCIATES INVESTMENT COMPANY LLC
765 Roosevelt Trail
Suite 9
Windham, ME USA 04062
Website: anania.biz

Management and Staff
David Hiatt, Chief Financial Officer
Scott Knoll, Partner

Type of Firm
Private Equity Firm

Project Preferences

Type of Financing Preferred:
Leveraged Buyout
Management Buyouts
Acquisition

Industry Preferences

In Computer Software prefer:
Software
Systems Software
Applications Software

In Medical/Health prefer:
Medical Products

In Industrial/Energy prefer:
Environmental Related

In Manufact. prefer:
Manufacturing

In Agr/Forestr/Fish prefer:
Mining and Minerals

Additional Information
Year Founded: 2008
Current Activity Level : Actively seeking new investments

ANANTA CAPITAL
Bestech Park View City 2
Sohna Road
Gurgaon, India 122 001
Phone: 91-124-426-5570
Website: www.ananta-capital.com

Management and Staff
Jaganath Swamy, Partner
NV Ramanan, Partner
Vikram Kuriyan, Partner

Type of Firm
Private Equity Firm

Project Preferences

Type of Financing Preferred:
Leveraged Buyout
Acquisition

Geographical Preferences

International Preferences:
India

Industry Preferences

In Industrial/Energy prefer:
Alternative Energy
Advanced Materials
Environmental Related

In Manufact. prefer:
Manufacturing

Additional Information
Year Founded: 2009
Current Activity Level : Actively seeking new investments

ANCHOR CAPITAL MANAGEMENT LTD

Coombe Bury Cottage
Kingston Hill
Surrey, United Kingdom KT2 7JG
Phone: 442085471454
Fax: 442085472191
Website: www.anchorcapital.co.uk

Other Offices
Linnegatan 6
PO Box 5712
Stockholm, Sweden SW-II487
Phone: 46-8-701-0900
Fax: 46-8-611-3088

Parkveien 57
Oslo, Norway N-0257
Phone: 47-22-562-252
Fax: 47-22-562-253

Management and Staff
Jens A. Wilhelmsen, Founder
Stein Wessel-Aas, Partner
Thomas Berg, Partner

Type of Firm
Private Equity Advisor or Fund of Funds

Association Membership
Swedish Venture Capital Association (SVCA)

Project Preferences

Type of Financing Preferred:
Fund of Funds

Geographical Preferences

International Preferences:
Scandanavia/Nordic Region

Additional Information
Year Founded: 2000
Capital Under Management: $160,400,000
Current Activity Level : Actively seeking new investments

ANCHORAGE CAPITAL PARTNERS LTD

Level 39, 259 George Street
Level Four
Sydney, Australia 2000
Phone: 61282597777
Fax: 61282597778
E-mail: anchorage@anchoragecapital.com.au

Management and Staff
Dani Sher, Chief Financial Officer
Daniel Wong, Partner
Michael Briggs, Partner
Phillip Cave, Partner

Type of Firm
Private Equity Firm

Association Membership
New Zealand Venture Capital Association
Australian Venture Capital Association (AVCAL)

Project Preferences

Role in Financing:
Will function either as deal originator or investor in deals created by others

Type of Financing Preferred:
Leveraged Buyout
Turnaround
Special Situation

Geographical Preferences

International Preferences:
Pacific
Australia
New Zealand
Asia

Industry Preferences

In Business Serv. prefer:
Services
Media

In Manufact. prefer:
Manufacturing

Additional Information
Name of Most Recent Fund: Anchorage Capital Partners II
Most Recent Fund Was Raised: 02/28/2013
Year Founded: 2007
Capital Under Management: $450,000,000
Current Activity Level : Actively seeking new investments

ANCOR CAPITAL PARTNERS

100 Throckmorton, 2 City Place, Suite 1600
Fort Worth, TX USA 76102
Phone: 8178774458
Fax: 8178774909
Website: www.ancorcapital.com

Management and Staff
Austin Henderson, Principal
Brian Brunett, Vice President
Brook Smith, Partner
Eric Gilchrest, Partner
J. Randall Keene, Partner
Michael Evans, Partner
Mitchell Green, Principal
Raymond Kingsbury, Partner
Timothy McKibben, Partner

Type of Firm
Private Equity Firm

Project Preferences

Type of Financing Preferred:
Leveraged Buyout
Acquisition
Recapitalizations

Geographical Preferences

United States Preferences:
All U.S.

Industry Preferences

In Medical/Health prefer:
Medical/Health

In Consumer Related prefer:
Consumer Products
Consumer Services

In Business Serv. prefer:
Distribution

In Manufact. prefer:
Manufacturing

Additional Information
Year Founded: 1994
Current Activity Level : Actively seeking new investments

ANDERSON GROUP LLC, THE

121 West Long Lake Road
Third Floor
Bloomfield Hills, MI USA 48304
Phone: 2486458000
Fax: 2486458001
Website: www.andersongroup.com

Management and Staff
Barry Shapiro, Co-Founder
Cory Gaffney, Partner
Eileen Garvey, Partner
Joe Maddox, Partner
Justin Flood, Partner
Marc Schechter, Partner
Scott Hukari, Partner
Thomas Gaffney, Co-Founder

Type of Firm
Private Equity Firm

Project Preferences

Type of Financing Preferred:
Leveraged Buyout
Turnaround
Management Buyouts
Acquisition
Recapitalizations

Geographical Preferences

United States Preferences:
All U.S.

International Preferences:
All International

Additional Information

Year Founded: 1985
Current Activity Level : Actively seeking new investments

ANDLINGER & CO INC

520 White Plains Road
Suite 500
Tarrytown, NY USA 10591
Phone: 9143324900
Fax: 4138321965
E-mail: info@andlinger.net
Website: www.andlinger.com

Other Offices

4445 North A1A
Suite 235
Vero Beach, FL USA 32963
Phone: 772-234-4998
Fax: 772-234-4952

Sieveringer Strasse 36/9
Vienna, Austria 1190
Phone: 43-1-328-7145
Fax: 43-1-328-7145-20

Avenue Louise 326
Brussels, Belgium 1050
Phone: 32-2-647-8070
Fax: 32-2-648-2105

Management and Staff

Charles Ball, Managing Director
George Doomany, Managing Director
Ivar Mitchell, Managing Director
Jim Russel, Vice President
Mark Callaghan, Managing Director
Merrick Andlinger, President
Stephen Magida, Managing Director

Type of Firm

Private Equity Firm

Project Preferences

Type of Financing Preferred:
Leveraged Buyout
Management Buyouts
Recapitalizations

Size of Investments Considered:
Min Size of Investment Considered (000s): $5,000
Max Size of Investment Considered (000s): $25,000

Geographical Preferences

United States Preferences:

Canadian Preferences:
All Canada

International Preferences:
Europe

Industry Preferences

In Communications prefer:
Telecommunications

In Computer Software prefer:
Software

In Medical/Health prefer:
Medical Products
Pharmaceuticals

In Industrial/Energy prefer:
Industrial Products

In Manufact. prefer:
Manufacturing

Additional Information

Year Founded: 1976
Current Activity Level : Actively seeking new investments

ANDOVER CAPITAL CORP

30 St. Clair Avenue West
Suite 1500
Toronto, Canada M4V 3A1
E-mail: info@andovercapital.ca
Website: www.andovercapital.ca

Type of Firm

Private Equity Firm

Project Preferences

Type of Financing Preferred:
Acquisition

Geographical Preferences

United States Preferences:
North America

Additional Information

Year Founded: 2017
Current Activity Level : Actively seeking new investments

ANDREESSEN HOROWITZ LLC

2865 Sand Hill Road
Suite 101
Menlo Park, CA USA 94025
Phone: 6503212400
E-mail: businessplans@a16z.com
Website: a16z.com

Management and Staff

Ashvin Bachireddy, Partner
Balaji Srinivasan, General Partner
Benjamin Horowitz, Co-Founder
Frank Chen, Partner
Jeff Jordan, General Partner
Jeffrey Stump, Partner
Kiersten Hollars, Partner
Lars Dalgaard, General Partner
Marc Andreessen, Co-Founder
Margit Wennmachers, Partner
Mark Cranney, Partner
Peter Levine, Venture Partner
Ramu Arunachalam, Partner
Ronway Conway, Partner
Scott Kupor, Chief Operating Officer
Shannon Callahan, Partner

Type of Firm

Private Equity Firm

Association Membership

National Venture Capital Association - USA (NVCA)

Project Preferences

Type of Financing Preferred:
Early Stage
Expansion
Balanced
Seed
Startup

Industry Preferences

In Communications prefer:
Wireless Communications

In Internet Specific prefer:
Internet

Additional Information

Name of Most Recent Fund: Andreessen Horowitz Fund IV, L.P.
Most Recent Fund Was Raised: 03/27/2014
Year Founded: 2009
Capital Under Management: $4,500,000,000
Current Activity Level : Actively seeking new investments

ANDREW W BYRD & CO LLC

201 Fourth Avenue North, Suite 1250
Nashville, TN USA 37219
Phone: 6152568061
Fax: 6152567057
E-mail: info@tvvcapital.com
Website: tvvcapital.com

Management and Staff

Andrew Byrd, President, Founder
Charles Sell, Principal
Frederic Reisner, Principal
Lon Johnson, Principal
Stephen Cook, Principal

Type of Firm
Private Equity Firm

Project Preferences

Role in Financing:
Prefer role as deal originator

Type of Financing Preferred:
Leveraged Buyout

Geographical Preferences

United States Preferences:
Southeast

Industry Focus
(% based on actual investment)
Communications and Media   100.0%

Additional Information
Name of Most Recent Fund: Tennessee Valley Ventures III, L.P.
Most Recent Fund Was Raised: 07/20/2012
Year Founded: 1997
Capital Under Management: $50,000,000
Current Activity Level : Actively seeking new investments
Method of Compensation: Return on invest. most important, but chg. closing fees, service fees, etc.

ANDROMEDA CAPITAL

One Alfred Place
London, United Kingdom WC1E 7EB
Phone: 447747773370
E-mail: info@andromedacapital.co.uk
Website: www.andromedacapital.co.uk

Type of Firm
Investment Management Firm

Project Preferences

Type of Financing Preferred:
Early Stage

Industry Preferences

In Communications prefer:
Media and Entertainment

In Industrial/Energy prefer:
Energy

In Financial Services prefer:
Financial Services

Additional Information
Year Founded: 2011
Current Activity Level : Actively seeking new investments

ANDURANCE VENTURES LLP

100 Brompton Road
London , United Kingdom SW3 1ER
E-mail: info@anduranceventures.com

Management and Staff
Damien Henault, Co-Founder
Nicolas Granatino, Co-Founder

Type of Firm
Private Equity Firm

Project Preferences

Type of Financing Preferred:
Early Stage

Additional Information
Year Founded: 2012
Current Activity Level : Actively seeking new investments

ANFAAL CAPITAL CO CJSC

Villa 47, Tujjar Jeddah
Al khaldiyah District
Jeddah, Saudi Arabia 21352
Phone: 96626068686
Fax: 96626068787
Website: www.anfaalcapital.com

Management and Staff
Ahmad Bin Mohammed, Chief Executive Officer

Type of Firm
Private Equity Firm

Project Preferences

Type of Financing Preferred:
Leveraged Buyout
Early Stage
Generalist PE
Later Stage
Acquisition

Geographical Preferences

International Preferences:
Middle East
Asia

Additional Information
Year Founded: 2010
Current Activity Level : Actively seeking new investments

ANGEL CAPITAL CO LTD

1-1-3-1000 Umeda, Kita-ku
10/F, #3 Building, Osakaekimae
Kita-Ku, Osaka, Japan 530-0001
Phone: 81664563604
Fax: 81663456288
E-mail: info@angelsec.co.jp
Website: www.angelcapital.jp

Type of Firm
Service Provider

Association Membership
Japan Venture Capital Association

Project Preferences

Type of Financing Preferred:
Balanced

Geographical Preferences

International Preferences:
Japan

Additional Information
Year Founded: 2001
Current Activity Level : Actively seeking new investments

ANGEL CAPITAL NETWORK INC

One Harbor Drive
Suite 112
Sausalito, CA USA 94965
Phone: 415-289-8701
Fax: 415-331-3978
Website: www.angelcapitalnetwork.com

Management and Staff
James Zappa, Chief Financial Officer
Osamu Tagaya, Chief Executive Officer

Type of Firm
Bank Affiliated

Project Preferences

Type of Financing Preferred:
Early Stage
Seed

Geographical Preferences

United States Preferences:

Industry Preferences

In Biotechnology prefer:
Biotechnology

Additional Information
Year Founded: 1999
Current Activity Level : Actively seeking new investments

ANGEL INVESTORS, LP

817 Orange Blossom Way
Danville, CA USA 94526
Phone: 6508147075

Fax: 2089758550
E-mail: webmaster@svangel.com

Management and Staff
Casey McGlynn, General Partner
Robert Bozeman, General Partner
Ronald Conway, General Partner

Type of Firm
Private Equity Firm

Project Preferences

Type of Financing Preferred:
Early Stage

Geographical Preferences

United States Preferences:
Northern California
California

Industry Focus

(% based on actual investment)
Internet Specific	53.6%
Computer Software and Services	33.6%
Other Products	4.9%
Communications and Media	4.0%
Computer Hardware	2.6%
Consumer Related	1.5%

Additional Information
Year Founded: 1998
Capital Under Management: $150,000,000
Current Activity Level : Making few, if any, new investments

ANGELENO GROUP INVESTORS LLC

2029 Century Park East
Suite 2980
Los Angeles, CA USA 90067
Phone: 3105522790
Fax: 3105522727
E-mail: info@angelenogroup.com

Management and Staff
Anil Tammineed, Vice President
Daniel Weiss, Managing Partner
Danny Jaffe, Vice President
Paula Robins, Chief Financial Officer
Prakesh Patel, Vice President
William Miller, Chief Operating Officer
Yaniv Tepper, Managing Partner
Zeb Rice, Managing Partner

Type of Firm
Private Equity Firm

Project Preferences

Type of Financing Preferred:
Expansion
Balanced
Later Stage

Geographical Preferences

United States Preferences:

International Preferences:
Australia
Asia

Industry Preferences

In Industrial/Energy prefer:
Alternative Energy
Environmental Related

Additional Information
Name of Most Recent Fund: Angeleno Investors III, L.P.
Most Recent Fund Was Raised: 03/27/2009
Year Founded: 2001
Current Activity Level : Actively seeking new investments

ANGELES EQUITY PARTNERS LLC

11661 SAN VICENTE BOULEVARD
SUITE 808
Los Angeles, CA USA 90049
Phone: 3108449200
E-mail: info@angelesequity.com
Website: www.angelesequity.com

Management and Staff
Jordan Katz, Co-Founder
Sam Heischuber, Vice President
Sameer Patel, Vice President
Timothy Meyer, Co-Founder

Type of Firm
Private Equity Firm

Project Preferences

Type of Financing Preferred:
Leveraged Buyout

Additional Information
Year Founded: 2014
Capital Under Management: $360,000,000
Current Activity Level : Actively seeking new investments

ANGELMD INC

918 South Horton Street
Suite 801
Seattle, WA USA 98134
Phone: 6503899595
E-mail: info@angelmd.co
Website: www.angelmd.co

Type of Firm
Private Equity Firm

Project Preferences

Type of Financing Preferred:
Seed
Startup

Size of Investments Considered:
Min Size of Investment Considered (000s): $500
Max Size of Investment Considered (000s): $5,000

Industry Preferences

In Medical/Health prefer:
Medical/Health

Additional Information
Year Founded: 2014
Current Activity Level : Actively seeking new investments

ANGELS' FORUM & THE HALO FUND

2665 Marine Way
Suite 1150
Mountain View, CA USA 94043
Phone: 6508570700
Fax: 6508570773
Website: www.angelsforum.com

Management and Staff
Leif Langensand, Chief Financial Officer

Type of Firm
Angel Group

Project Preferences

Role in Financing:
Will function either as deal originator or investor in deals created by others

Type of Financing Preferred:
Second Stage Financing
Early Stage
Expansion
Balanced
Seed
First Stage Financing
Startup

Size of Investments Considered:
Min Size of Investment Considered (000s): $100
Max Size of Investment Considered (000s): $1,000

Geographical Preferences

United States Preferences:
Northern California
California
All U.S.

Industry Preferences

In Communications prefer:
Telecommunications
Wireless Communications
Data Communications

In Computer Software prefer:
Software
Systems Software
Applications Software
Artificial Intelligence

In Internet Specific prefer:
Internet
Ecommerce

In Computer Other prefer:
Computer Related

In Semiconductor/Electr prefer:
Electronic Components
Semiconductor
Micro-Processing
Controllers and Sensors
Sensors
Component Testing Equipmt
Laser Related
Analytic/Scientific

In Biotechnology prefer:
Biotechnology
Human Biotechnology
Agricultural/Animal Bio.
Industrial Biotechnology
Biosensors
Biotech Related Research
Biotech Related Research

In Medical/Health prefer:
Medical/Health
Medical Diagnostics
Diagnostic Services
Diagnostic Test Products
Medical Therapeutics
Drug/Equipmt Delivery
Other Therapeutic
Medical Products
Disposable Med. Products
Health Services
Pharmaceuticals

In Consumer Related prefer:
Consumer
Entertainment and Leisure
Retail

In Industrial/Energy prefer:
Energy
Alternative Energy
Industrial Products
Superconductivity
Factory Automation
Process Control

In Transportation prefer:
Transportation

In Financial Services prefer:
Financial Services

In Business Serv. prefer:
Services

In Manufact. prefer:
Manufacturing

In Other prefer:
Socially Responsible
Environment Responsible
Women/Minority-Owned Bus.

Additional Information
Name of Most Recent Fund: Halo Fund III, L.P., The
Most Recent Fund Was Raised: 03/18/2008
Year Founded: 1997
Capital Under Management: $58,000,000
Current Activity Level : Actively seeking new investments
Method of Compensation: Return on investment is of primary concern, do not charge fees

ANGLER CAPITAL MANAGEMENT LLC

630 Fifth Avenue
Suite 2950
New York, NY USA 10111
Phone: 646-234-7745
Website: www.anglercap.com

Type of Firm
Private Equity Firm

Project Preferences

Type of Financing Preferred:
Leveraged Buyout
Acquisition
Recapitalizations

Geographical Preferences

United States Preferences:

Industry Preferences

In Consumer Related prefer:
Consumer Products

In Industrial/Energy prefer:
Energy
Industrial Products
Environmental Related

In Financial Services prefer:
Financial Services

In Business Serv. prefer:
Consulting Services
Media

Additional Information
Year Founded: 2008
Current Activity Level : Actively seeking new investments

ANGLO SCIENTIFIC LTD

The Elms Courtyard
Bromesberrow
Ledbury, United Kingdom HR8 1RZ
Phone: 44-1531-651-230
E-mail: info@angloscientific.com
Website: www.angloscientific.com

Management and Staff
Douglas Dundonald, Founder
Henry Hyde-Thomson, Partner
Jonathan Moulton, Managing Partner

Type of Firm
Corporate PE/Venture

Project Preferences

Type of Financing Preferred:
Early Stage
Seed
Startup

Size of Investments Considered:
Min Size of Investment Considered (000s): $400
Max Size of Investment Considered (000s): $400,000

Geographical Preferences

International Preferences:
United Kingdom
Europe

Additional Information
Year Founded: 2000
Current Activity Level : Actively seeking new investments

ANGOLA CAPITAL PARTNERS

Avenida Rei Katyavala 45
Avencas Plaza Bldg., 10th Flr.
Luanda, Angola
Phone: 244-22-269-3800
E-mail: contacto@angolacapitalpartners.com
Website: www.angolacapitalpartners.com

Management and Staff
Raquel Serra, Chief Financial Officer
Tiago Laranjeiro, Managing Director

Type of Firm
Bank Affiliated

Project Preferences

Type of Financing Preferred:
Early Stage
Expansion
Generalist PE
Management Buyouts
Private Placement
Startup

Size of Investments Considered:
Min Size of Investment Considered (000s): $500
Max Size of Investment Considered (000s): $10,000

Geographical Preferences

International Preferences:
Africa

Additional Information

Year Founded: 2009
Capital Under Management: $28,000,000
Current Activity Level : Actively seeking new investments

ANHOLT (USA) LLC

61 Wilton Road
Second Floor
Westport, CT USA 06880
Phone: 2032211703
Fax: 2032218253
E-mail: info@compassgroupmanagement.com
Website: www.compassequity.com

Other Offices

2010 Main Street
Suite 1020
Irvine, CA USA 92614
Phone: 9493335033
Fax: 9493335043

Management and Staff

Alan Offenberg, Partner
David Swanson, Partner
Demetrios Dounis, Principal
Elias Sabo, Partner
Gabe LePera, Vice President
I. Joseph Massoud, Managing Partner
James Ferrara, Vice President
Kenneth Terry, Vice President
Mark Langer, Vice President
Patrick Maciariello, Partner
Rudolph Krediet, Principal
Ryan Faulkingham, Founder
Tim Chiodo, Principal

Type of Firm

Private Equity Firm

Project Preferences

Role in Financing:
Prefer role as deal originator

Type of Financing Preferred:
Leveraged Buyout
Management Buyouts
Recapitalizations

Geographical Preferences

United States Preferences:
All U.S.

Canadian Preferences:
All Canada

International Preferences:
Latin America
Europe
Middle East
Africa

Industry Focus

(% based on actual investment)
Internet Specific 36.8%
Consumer Related 34.7%
Other Products 28.5%

Additional Information

Year Founded: 1998
Capital Under Management: $140,000,000
Current Activity Level : Actively seeking new investments
Method of Compensation: Return on investment is of primary concern, do not charge fees

ANHUI GUOFU PROPERTY INVESTMENT FUND MANAGEMENT LTD

Minsheng Road, Pudong New Area
2303, No.1, Lane 1199
Shanghai, China 210000
Phone: 862138751386
Fax: 862138973168
Website: http://zdb.pedaily.cn/company/%E5%9B%BD%E5%AF%8C%E
ny/%E5%9B%BD%E5%AF%8C%E

Type of Firm

Private Equity Firm

Project Preferences

Type of Financing Preferred:
Leveraged Buyout
Generalist PE
Balanced

Geographical Preferences

International Preferences:
China

Additional Information

Year Founded: 2009
Current Activity Level : Actively seeking new investments

ANHUI HONGTU VENTURE CAPITAL MANAGEMENT CO LTD

No.287, Suixi Rd, Luyang Dist
Rm 1206, C, Caifu Plaza
Hefei, China 230041
Phone: 865515773590
Fax: 865515666025

Type of Firm

Private Equity Firm

Project Preferences

Type of Financing Preferred:
Balanced

Geographical Preferences

International Preferences:
China

Industry Preferences

In Semiconductor/Electr prefer:
Electronics

In Biotechnology prefer:
Biotechnology
Agricultural/Animal Bio.

In Industrial/Energy prefer:
Energy
Energy Conservation Relat
Materials

Additional Information

Year Founded: 2010
Capital Under Management: $58,600,000
Current Activity Level : Actively seeking new investments

ANHUI PROVINCE VENTURE INVESTMENT LTD

c/o Anhui Investment Group
No. 46, Wangjiang Road
Hefei, China 230022
Phone: 865513677067
Fax: 865513677066

Management and Staff

Yonghua Chen, President

Type of Firm

Investment Management Firm

Project Preferences

Type of Financing Preferred:
Balanced

Geographical Preferences

International Preferences:
China

Industry Preferences

In Semiconductor/Electr prefer:
Electronics
Electronic Components

In Industrial/Energy prefer:
Industrial Products

In Transportation prefer:
Transportation

In Business Serv. prefer:
Services

In Other prefer:
Socially Responsible

Additional Information
Year Founded: 2008
Capital Under Management: $36,744,000
Current Activity Level : Actively seeking new investments

ANKAR CAPITAL MANAGEMENT LLC

41 West 57th Street
New York, NY USA 10019
Phone: 212-688-6410
Fax: 212-688-6497
E-mail: susan@anchorithaca.com
Website: www.ankarcapital.com

Type of Firm
Private Equity Advisor or Fund of Funds

Additional Information
Year Founded: 1999
Current Activity Level : Actively seeking new investments

ANKUR CAPITAL ADVISORS

300, Sai Sampanna Vikroli East
Mumbai, India
Website: www.ankurcapital.com

Type of Firm
Private Equity Firm

Project Preferences

Type of Financing Preferred:
Seed
Startup

Geographical Preferences

International Preferences:
India

Additional Information
Year Founded: 2014
Capital Under Management: $6,462,000
Current Activity Level : Actively seeking new investments

ANN ARBOR SPARK FOUNDATION

201 South Division
Suite 430
Ann Arbor, MI USA 48104
Phone: 7347619337
Website: www.annarborusa.org

Management and Staff
Greg Fronizer, Managing Director

Type of Firm
Government Affiliated Program

Project Preferences

Role in Financing:
Prefer role in deals created by others

Type of Financing Preferred:
Early Stage
Seed
Startup

Size of Investments Considered:
Min Size of Investment Considered (000s): $50
Max Size of Investment Considered (000s): $250

Geographical Preferences

United States Preferences:
Michigan

Industry Preferences

In Biotechnology prefer:
Human Biotechnology

In Medical/Health prefer:
Medical Therapeutics
Health Services

In Industrial/Energy prefer:
Alternative Energy
Advanced Materials

In Transportation prefer:
Transportation

In Manufact. prefer:
Manufacturing

Additional Information
Year Founded: 2007
Capital Under Management: $25,400,000
Current Activity Level : Actively seeking new investments
Method of Compensation: Other

ANNAPURNA CAPITAL MANAGEMENT LLC

65 Orchard Place
Suite One
Greenwich, CT USA 06830
E-mail: info@annapurnafunds.com
Website: www.annapurnafunds.com

Type of Firm
Private Equity Firm

Project Preferences

Type of Financing Preferred:
Leveraged Buyout

Geographical Preferences

United States Preferences:
All U.S.

Industry Preferences

In Industrial/Energy prefer:
Energy
Materials

In Transportation prefer:
Transportation

In Manufact. prefer:
Manufacturing

Additional Information
Year Founded: 2014
Current Activity Level : Actively seeking new investments

ANNEX CAPITAL MANAGEMENT LLC

126 East 56th Street
28th Floor
New York, NY USA 10022
Phone: 212-644-3510
Fax: 212-554-5808
E-mail: mail@annexcapital.com
Website: www.annexcapital.com

Management and Staff
Alexander Coleman, Managing Partner
Amant Dewan, Principal
Dale Cheney, Principal
Robert Fowler, Managing Partner

Type of Firm
Private Equity Firm

Project Preferences

Type of Financing Preferred:
Leveraged Buyout
Mezzanine
Acquisition
Special Situation
Distressed Debt
Recapitalizations

Geographical Preferences

United States Preferences:
North America

Industry Preferences

In Communications prefer:
Telecommunications

In Consumer Related prefer:
Food/Beverage
Consumer Products

In Business Serv. prefer:
Services
Media

In Manufact. prefer:
Manufacturing

Additional Information
Year Founded: 2004
Current Activity Level : Actively seeking new investments

ANNEX, THE

Shockoe Valley Innovation Vill
27 North 17th Street
Richmond, VA USA 23218
E-mail: contact@annexrva.com
Website: www.annexrva.com

Type of Firm
Incubator/Development Program

Project Preferences

Type of Financing Preferred:
Early Stage

Additional Information
Year Founded: 2016
Current Activity Level : Actively seeking new investments

ANNISON CAPITAL PARTNERS LLC

401 North Michigan Avenue
Suite1200
Chicago, IL USA 60611
Phone: 3126361656
Website: www.annisoncap.com

Type of Firm
Private Equity Firm

Project Preferences

Type of Financing Preferred:
Leveraged Buyout
Management Buyouts
Acquisition

Industry Preferences

In Communications prefer:
Wireless Communications

In Medical/Health prefer:
Medical/Health

In Business Serv. prefer:
Services

Additional Information
Year Founded: 2014
Current Activity Level : Actively seeking new investments

ANNOX CAPITAL

40701 Woodward Avenue, Suite 101
Bloomfield, MI USA 48304
Phone: 2487121086
E-mail: info@annoxcapital.com
Website: www.annoxcapital.com

Type of Firm
Private Equity Firm

Project Preferences

Type of Financing Preferred:
Leveraged Buyout
Generalist PE
Later Stage
Startup

Size of Investments Considered:
Min Size of Investment Considered (000s): $100
Max Size of Investment Considered (000s): $5,000

Industry Preferences

In Medical/Health prefer:
Health Services

In Financial Services prefer:
Financial Services
Real Estate

In Manufact. prefer:
Manufacturing

Additional Information
Year Founded: 1969
Current Activity Level : Actively seeking new investments

ANORAK VENTURES INC.

1770 PINE
Suite 506
San Francisco, CA USA 94101
Website: www.anorak.vc

Type of Firm
Private Equity Firm

Project Preferences

Type of Financing Preferred:
Early Stage

Additional Information
Year Founded: 2016
Capital Under Management: $13,000,000
Current Activity Level : Actively seeking new investments

ANSERA VENTURES LTD

47 Ingram Drive
North York, Canada M6M2L6
Phone: 416-241-0224

Type of Firm
Private Equity Firm

Additional Information
Year Founded: 2004
Current Activity Level : Actively seeking new investments

ANSLEY EQUITY PARTNERS

25 West Jefferson Avenue, Suite 200
Naperville, IL USA 60540
Phone: 8283334200
Website: www.acgequitypartners.com

Management and Staff
Donald Carson, Co-Founder
Orlo Dietrich, Managing Director
Russell Burks, Co-Founder

Type of Firm
Private Equity Firm

Project Preferences

Type of Financing Preferred:
Early Stage
Expansion
Balanced
Seed
Startup

Industry Preferences

In Medical/Health prefer:
Medical/Health
Diagnostic Services
Health Services
Pharmaceuticals

Additional Information
Year Founded: 1999
Current Activity Level : Actively seeking new investments

ANT CAPITAL PARTNERS CO LTD

1-2-1 Marunouchi, Chiyoda-ku
5/F Tokio Marine Nichido Bldg.
Tokyo, Japan 100-0005
Phone: 81332841711
Fax: 81332841885
Website: www.antcapital.jp

Management and Staff
Kenichi Ueda, Managing Partner
Reijiro Samura, Managing Partner
Ryosuke Iinuma, Managing Partner
Shunsa Hayashi, Managing Partner
Tadashi Takashina, Managing Partner
Takao Akaogi, Managing Partner
Takato Ogi, Managing Partner
Tomoyuki Imaizumi, Managing Partner
Toru Tanimoto, Managing Partner

Type of Firm
Private Equity Firm

Association Membership
Japan Venture Capital Association

Project Preferences

Type of Financing Preferred:
Leveraged Buyout
Early Stage
Expansion
Generalist PE
Balanced
Public Companies
Turnaround
Later Stage
Management Buyouts
Fund of Funds of Second

Geographical Preferences

International Preferences:
Asia
Japan

Industry Preferences

In Communications prefer:
Communications and Media
Wireless Communications
Data Communications

In Internet Specific prefer:
Internet

In Semiconductor/Electr prefer:
Semiconductor

In Industrial/Energy prefer:
Environmental Related

In Financial Services prefer:
Financial Services

Additional Information
Year Founded: 2000
Capital Under Management: $40,200,000
Current Activity Level : Actively seeking new investments

ANTARCTICA CAPITAL LLC

405 Lexington Avenue
Suite 5500
New York, NY USA 10174
Phone: 2129831602
Fax: 2129831609
E-mail: info@antarcticacapital.com
Website: www.antarcticacapital.com

Type of Firm
Private Equity Firm

Project Preferences

Type of Financing Preferred:
Value-Add
Generalist PE
Other

Geographical Preferences

United States Preferences:

International Preferences:
India

Industry Preferences

In Financial Services prefer:
Real Estate

In Utilities prefer:
Utilities

Additional Information
Year Founded: 2014
Current Activity Level : Actively seeking new investments

ANTARES CAPITAL CORP

500 West Monroe Street
Chicago, IL USA 60661
Phone: 3126973999

Other Offices
100 California Street
San Francisco, CA USA 94111
Phone: 415-277-7400

125 Summer Street
Suite 1230
Boston, MA USA 02110
Phone: 617-378-4778

201 Merritt 7 PO Box 5201
Norwalk, CT USA 06851
Phone: 866-243-5537

299 Park Avenue
New York, NY USA 10001
Phone: 212-370-8000

350 South Beverly Drive
Beverly Hills, CA USA 90212
Phone: 310-203-0335

Management and Staff
Alfredo Wang, Vice President
Amy Krebs, Vice President
Andrew Eversfield, Vice President
Andrew Crain, Vice President
Ankur Gupta, Vice President
Ashley Medio, Vice President
Barry Giarraputo, Chief Financial Officer
Ben Chapin, Vice President
Beth Troyer, Vice President
Bill Haffner, Managing Director
Bill Pescatello, Vice President
Brad Hamner, Vice President
Brian Keil, Managing Director
Chester Zara, Senior Managing Director
Cynthia Rogers, Managing Director
Daniel Landis, Vice President
Daniel Glickman, Managing Director
Daniel Barry, Senior Managing Director
Danielle Katz, Vice President
Darryl Jacobson, Vice President
Dave Rous, Vice President
David Schmuck, Chief Financial Officer
David Swanson, Managing Director
David Mahon, Managing Director
David Brackett, Senior Managing Director
Dean Jeffe, Vice President
Diane Burton, Managing Director
Doug Cannaliato, Managing Director
Eric Hansen, Managing Director
Erik Van Vuren, Vice President
Ethan Miller, Managing Director
Geoff Hall, Vice President
Graham Manley, Vice President
Greg Lawton, Managing Director
Heidi Rinehart, Vice President
Jack Steidle, Managing Director
James Kenefick, Managing Director
Jeff Bottcher, Vice President
Jennifer Pricco, Vice President
Jim Clayton, Senior Managing Director
Jim Wehrfritz, Vice President
John Goodwin, Managing Director
Joseph Angel, Vice President
Karen Dahlquist, Vice President
Kathleen Ramirez, Vice President
Laura Spence DeAngelis, Vice President
Laurent Paris, Managing Director
Lisa Jablonski, Managing Director
Lofton Spencer, Vice President
Marcus Meyer, Vice President
Mark Bernier, Managing Director
Mark Birkett, Vice President
Mary Beth O Keefe, Vice President
Matt Liepert, Managing Director
Matthew Bandini, Vice President
Matthew Kane, Vice President
Michael Rhea, Vice President
Michael Chirillo, Senior Managing Director
Michele Kovatchis, Managing Director
Pat Henahan, Managing Director
Patrick Koehl, Vice President
Patty Weitzman, Managing Director
Pete Foley, Senior Managing Director
Peter Nolan, Senior Managing Director
Ray Shu, Managing Director
Scott Garlinghouse, Vice President
Scott Lorimer, Managing Director
Sean Sullivan, Vice President
Seth Meier, Vice President
Stephanie Krebs, Vice President
Steven Rubinstein, Vice President
Steven Robinson, Managing Director
Tim Huban, Managing Director
Timothy Lyne, Senior Managing Director
Tom Byrne, Managing Director
Tom Regan, Managing Director
Tony McCord, Managing Director
Troy Unell, Vice President

Tyler Lindblad, Managing Director
Vivek Mathew, Managing Director
William Kane, Vice President

Type of Firm
Private Equity Firm

Project Preferences

Role in Financing:
Prefer role as deal originator but will also invest in deals created by others

Type of Financing Preferred:
Leveraged Buyout
Mezzanine
Turnaround
Distressed Debt
Recapitalizations

Geographical Preferences

International Preferences:
Latin America
Europe
Asia

Industry Preferences

In Medical/Health prefer:
Medical/Health

In Consumer Related prefer:
Consumer Products
Education Related

In Business Serv. prefer:
Services

In Manufact. prefer:
Manufacturing

Additional Information
Name of Most Recent Fund: Mariner CDO 2002 Ltd. Fund
Most Recent Fund Was Raised: 07/01/2002
Year Founded: 1996
Capital Under Management: $1,500,000,000
Current Activity Level : Actively seeking new investments
Method of Compensation: Return on investment is of primary concern, do not charge fees

ANTARES CAPITAL CORPORATION

9999 Northeast Second Avenue
Suite 306
Miami, FL USA 33138
Phone: 3058942888
Fax: 3058943227
E-mail: info@antarescapital.com
Website: www.antarescapital.com

Management and Staff
Randall Poliner, Founding Partner

Type of Firm
Private Equity Firm

Project Preferences

Role in Financing:
Prefer role as deal originator but will also invest in deals created by others

Type of Financing Preferred:
Expansion
Later Stage
Management Buyouts
Special Situation

Size of Investments Considered:
Min Size of Investment Considered (000s): $500
Max Size of Investment Considered (000s): $5,000

Geographical Preferences

United States Preferences:
Southeast
Texas

Industry Focus
(% based on actual investment)
Other Products	29.1%
Consumer Related	20.7%
Medical/Health	19.5%
Internet Specific	16.3%
Computer Software and Services	6.3%
Semiconductors/Other Elect.	4.6%
Communications and Media	1.9%
Industrial/Energy	1.5%
Computer Hardware	0.1%

Additional Information
Name of Most Recent Fund: Antares Capital Fund IV, L.P.
Most Recent Fund Was Raised: 06/21/2007
Year Founded: 1993
Capital Under Management: $48,000,000
Current Activity Level : Actively seeking new investments
Method of Compensation: Return on investment is of primary concern, do not charge fees

ANTEA PARTICIPATIES MANAGEMENT BV

Stadhouderslaan 100
Den Haag, Netherlands 2517 JC
Phone: 31703115959
Fax: 31703115950
E-mail: info@antea.nl
Website: antea.nl

Management and Staff
A.Th. Harmsen, President
H.J. Van den Bosch, President
H.J.M. Berden, President
P.F.C. Van Es, President
Robert De Boeck, Managing Director

Type of Firm
Private Equity Firm

Association Membership
Dutch Venture Capital Associaton (NVP)

Project Preferences

Type of Financing Preferred:
Leveraged Buyout
Generalist PE
Balanced
Turnaround
Later Stage
Management Buyouts

Geographical Preferences

International Preferences:
Europe
Netherlands

Industry Focus
(% based on actual investment)
Other Products	49.0%
Internet Specific	20.0%
Computer Software and Services	16.8%
Consumer Related	12.2%
Semiconductors/Other Elect.	2.0%

Additional Information
Year Founded: 1993
Capital Under Management: $51,800,000
Current Activity Level : Actively seeking new investments

ANTERRA CAPITAL BV

Herengracht 450
Amsterdam, Netherlands 1017 CA
Phone: 31202051034
E-mail: office@anterracapital.com
Website: www.anterracapital.com

Other Offices
One Broadway
CAMBRIDGE, MA USA 02142

Management and Staff
Adam Anders, Managing Partner
Dudley Hawes, Partner
Maarten Goossens, Principal
Philip Austin, Partner

Type of Firm
Private Equity Firm

Project Preferences

Type of Financing Preferred:
Early Stage
Expansion
Balanced

Industry Preferences

In Agr/Forestr/Fish prefer:
Agriculture related

Additional Information

Year Founded: 2013
Capital Under Management: $125,000,000
Current Activity Level : Actively seeking new investments

ANTHEM ASIA

608 Merchant Road
Floor Three
Yangon, Burma
Phone: 9514413410
Fax: 959425326228
E-mail: info@anthemasia.com
Website: anthemasia.com

Type of Firm

Investment Management Firm

Project Preferences

Type of Financing Preferred:
Generalist PE

Geographical Preferences

International Preferences:
Burma

Additional Information

Year Founded: 2015
Current Activity Level : Actively seeking new investments

ANTHEM CAPITAL MANAGEMENT INC

1448 South Rolling Road
Suite 200
Baltimore, MD USA 21227
Phone: 4106251510

Other Offices

Radnor Court, 259 Radnor-Chester Road
Suite 210
Radnor, PA USA 19087
Phone: 610-687-9773
Fax: 610-971-2154

Management and Staff

Ed Spiva, Partner
Gerry Schaafsma, Partner
Xander Perry, Partner

Type of Firm

Private Equity Firm

Project Preferences

Role in Financing:
Prefer role as deal originator

Type of Financing Preferred:
Early Stage
Expansion
Seed

Size of Investments Considered:

Min Size of Investment Considered (000s): $1,000
Max Size of Investment Considered (000s): $5,000

Geographical Preferences

United States Preferences:
Mid Atlantic

Industry Focus

(% based on actual investment)
    Computer Software and Services   31.7%
    Biotechnology   25.4%
    Medical/Health   25.4%
    Internet Specific   16.5%
    Other Products   0.6%
    Industrial/Energy   0.5%

Additional Information

Year Founded: 1994
Capital Under Management: $58,000,000
Current Activity Level : Actively seeking new investments
Method of Compensation: Return on investment is of primary concern, do not charge fees

ANTHEM VENTURE PARTNERS

225 Arizona Avenue
Suite 200
Santa Monica, CA USA 90401
Phone: 3108996225
Fax: 3108996234
E-mail: info@anthemvp.com
Website: www.anthemvp.com

Management and Staff

Brian Mesic, Partner
Claudia Llanos, Chief Financial Officer
Samit Varma, Partner
William Woodward, Partner

Type of Firm

Private Equity Firm

Project Preferences

Role in Financing:
Prefer role as deal originator but will also invest in deals created by others

Type of Financing Preferred:
Early Stage
Seed
Startup

Size of Investments Considered:

Min Size of Investment Considered (000s): $500
Max Size of Investment Considered (000s): $4,000

Geographical Preferences

United States Preferences:
Southern California
Northern California
California

Industry Preferences

In Communications prefer:
Wireless Communications

In Computer Software prefer:
Software
Systems Software

In Internet Specific prefer:
Internet

In Semiconductor/Electr prefer:
Semiconductor

In Business Serv. prefer:
Media

Additional Information

Year Founded: 2000
Capital Under Management: $170,000,000
Current Activity Level : Actively seeking new investments

ANTHEMIS GROUP SA

5, Rue Guillaume Kroll
Luxembourg, Luxembourg 1882
Phone: 442070879050
E-mail: info@anthemis.com
Website: www.anthemis.com

Other Offices

44 Great Marlborough
5th Floor
London, United Kingdom W1F 7JL
Phone: 442070879054

Management and Staff

Amy Nauiokas, President, Founder
Udayan Goyal, Founder

Type of Firm

Investment Management Firm

Project Preferences

Type of Financing Preferred:
Early Stage
Later Stage

Geographical Preferences

International Preferences:
Europe

Industry Preferences

In Internet Specific prefer:
Ecommerce

In Financial Services prefer:
Financial Services

Additional Information
Year Founded: 2010
Capital Under Management: $60,000,000
Current Activity Level : Actively seeking new investments

ANTHILIA CAPITAL PARTNERS SGR SPA

Corso di Porta Romana, 68
Milan, Italy 20122
Phone: 390297386101
Fax: 390297386100
Website: www.anthilia.it

Type of Firm
Private Equity Firm

Project Preferences

Type of Financing Preferred:
Generalist PE

Geographical Preferences

International Preferences:
Italy

Additional Information
Year Founded: 2008
Capital Under Management: $137,100,000
Current Activity Level : Actively seeking new investments

ANTHOS CAPITAL LP

707 Menlo Avenue
Suite 210
Menlo Park, CA USA 94025
Phone: 6502124100
Fax: 6502122798
E-mail: info@anthoscapital.com
Website: www.anthoscapital.com

Management and Staff
Bryan Kelly, Managing Partner
Byron Adams, Partner
Eff Martin, Partner
Gavyn Davies, Partner
Howard Behar, Partner
John Hagerty, Partner
Paul Farr, Managing Partner
Thomas Healey, Partner
Timothy Corriero, Partner
Wallace Hawley, Partner

Type of Firm
Private Equity Firm

Project Preferences

Type of Financing Preferred:
Leveraged Buyout
Expansion
Mezzanine
Generalist PE
Balanced
Later Stage
Management Buyouts
Acquisition

Industry Preferences

In Internet Specific prefer:
Internet

In Medical/Health prefer:
Medical/Health
Health Services

In Consumer Related prefer:
Consumer
Consumer Products
Consumer Services

In Financial Services prefer:
Financial Services

In Business Serv. prefer:
Services
Media

Additional Information
Year Founded: 2008
Capital Under Management: $300,000,000
Current Activity Level : Actively seeking new investments

ANTONI & LELO DE LARREA VENTURE PARTNERS

Sierra Mojada 447 PB
Lomas de Chapultepec
Mexico Distrito Federal, Mexico 11000
Phone: 525552495100
Website: www.allvp.vc

Type of Firm
Private Equity Firm

Industry Preferences

In Internet Specific prefer:
Ecommerce

In Medical/Health prefer:
Medical/Health

In Transportation prefer:
Transportation

In Financial Services prefer:
Financial Services
Financial Services

Additional Information
Year Founded: 2012
Current Activity Level : Actively seeking new investments

ANTS ASSETS MANAGEMENT CO LTD

A-9 Jinrong Avenue
Xicheng District
Beijing, China
Website: www.antscapital.com

Type of Firm
Investment Management Firm

Project Preferences

Type of Financing Preferred:
Generalist PE

Geographical Preferences

International Preferences:
China

Industry Preferences

In Communications prefer:
Media and Entertainment

In Internet Specific prefer:
Internet

In Financial Services prefer:
Financial Services

Additional Information
Year Founded: 2014
Current Activity Level : Actively seeking new investments

ANTS CAPITAL

Loushanguan Road No. 523
Jinhongqiao Center
Shanghai, China
Website: www.ants-vc.com

Type of Firm
Private Equity Firm

Project Preferences

Type of Financing Preferred:
Early Stage
Start-up Financing
Seed

Geographical Preferences

International Preferences:
China

Industry Preferences

In Communications prefer:
Telecommunications
Entertainment

In Medical/Health prefer:
Medical/Health

In Consumer Related prefer:
Consumer
Retail

In Industrial/Energy prefer:
Energy Conservation Relat

In Business Serv. prefer:
Media

Additional Information
Year Founded: 2015
Current Activity Level : Actively seeking new investments

ANTSON CAPITAL PARTNERS LLC

509 South Exeter Street
Suite 505
Baltimore, MD USA 21202
Phone: 4105613390
Fax: 4109284722
Website: antsoncapital.com

Management and Staff
Anthony Rodgers, Co-Founder
Jason Pappas, Co-Founder

Type of Firm
Private Equity Firm

Project Preferences

Type of Financing Preferred:
Leveraged Buyout
Acquisition

Geographical Preferences

United States Preferences:
Maryland

Industry Preferences

In Consumer Related prefer:
Retail

In Financial Services prefer:
Real Estate

In Business Serv. prefer:
Distribution

In Manufact. prefer:
Manufacturing

Additional Information
Year Founded: 2013
Current Activity Level : Actively seeking new investments

ANU CONNECT VENTURES PTY LTD

121 Marcus Clarke Street
Level Six
Canberra, Australia 2601
Phone: 61262477000
Fax: 61261251900
E-mail: info@anuconnectventures.com.au

Management and Staff
Michael Cardew-Hall, Chief Executive Officer

Type of Firm
University Program

Association Membership
Australian Venture Capital Association (AVCAL)

Project Preferences

Type of Financing Preferred:
Early Stage
Seed

Size of Investments Considered:
Min Size of Investment Considered (000s): $1
Max Size of Investment Considered (000s): $1,037

Geographical Preferences

International Preferences:
Australia

Industry Preferences

In Biotechnology prefer:
Biotechnology

In Medical/Health prefer:
Health Services

In Industrial/Energy prefer:
Energy
Advanced Materials

In Transportation prefer:
Aerospace

Additional Information
Year Founded: 2005
Capital Under Management: $33,400,000
Current Activity Level : Actively seeking new investments

ANVIL CAPITAL LLC

60 State Street
Suite 700
Boston, MA USA 02109
Phone: 6173712920
Fax: 6173712950
Website: anvilcap.com

Management and Staff
Benjamin Giess, Co-Founder
Robert Fortunato, Co-Founder

Type of Firm
Private Equity Firm

Project Preferences

Type of Financing Preferred:
Leveraged Buyout
Mezzanine
Acquisition
Recapitalizations

Geographical Preferences

United States Preferences:
Northeast

Industry Preferences

In Business Serv. prefer:
Services

In Manufact. prefer:
Manufacturing

Additional Information
Year Founded: 2003
Current Activity Level : Actively seeking new investments

ANZU PARTNERS

1399 New York Avenue
Suite 601
Washington, DC USA 20005
Phone: 2027425870
E-mail: info@anzupartners.com
Website: www.anzupartners.com

Type of Firm
Private Equity Firm

Project Preferences

Type of Financing Preferred:
Early Stage

Industry Preferences

In Industrial/Energy prefer:
Industrial Products

In Business Serv. prefer:
Consulting Services

In Agr/Forestr/Fish prefer:
Mining and Minerals

Additional Information
Year Founded: 2015
Capital Under Management: $128,400,000
Current Activity Level : Actively seeking new investments

AO INVEST AG

Clavadelerstrasse 8
Davos, Switzerland 7270
E-mail: info@ao-invest.com
Website: www.ao-invest.com

Type of Firm
Private Equity Firm

Project Preferences

Type of Financing Preferred:
Early Stage
Seed

Geographical Preferences

International Preferences:
Europe
Switzerland

Industry Preferences

In Biotechnology prefer:
Biotechnology

In Medical/Health prefer:
Medical/Health
Medical Therapeutics
Medical Products
Health Services

Additional Information
Year Founded: 2017
Current Activity Level : Actively seeking new investments

AP CAPITAL INVESTMENTS LP

149 South Barrington Avenue
Suite 815
Los Angeles, CA USA 90049
Phone: 3105934985
Fax: 3105642008
E-mail: info@apcinvest.com

Management and Staff
Bulend Corbacioglu, Partner

Type of Firm
Private Equity Firm

Project Preferences

Type of Financing Preferred:
Leveraged Buyout
Expansion
Management Buyouts
Acquisition
Recapitalizations

Size of Investments Considered:
Min Size of Investment Considered (000s): $5,000
Max Size of Investment Considered (000s): $100,000

Geographical Preferences

United States Preferences:

International Preferences:
Europe

Industry Preferences

In Medical/Health prefer:
Medical/Health

In Industrial/Energy prefer:
Industrial Products
Factory Automation
Environmental Related

In Financial Services prefer:
Financial Services

In Business Serv. prefer:
Services
Distribution

In Manufact. prefer:
Manufacturing

Additional Information
Year Founded: 2007
Current Activity Level : Actively seeking new investments

APAX PARTNERS DEVELOPMENT SA

11/13 avenue de Friedland
Paris, France 75008
Phone: 33156436520
Fax: 33158192190
E-mail: contact@epf-partners.com
Website: www.epf-partners.com

Management and Staff
Christian d Argoubet, Managing Director
Raphael Delmarre, Founder

Type of Firm
Private Equity Firm

Association Membership
French Venture Capital Association (AFIC)

Project Preferences

Type of Financing Preferred:
Leveraged Buyout
Early Stage
Expansion
Generalist PE
Later Stage
Management Buyouts
Acquisition

Geographical Preferences

International Preferences:
Europe
France

Industry Preferences

In Communications prefer:
Communications and Media
Commercial Communications
Wireless Communications

In Computer Software prefer:
Systems Software

In Medical/Health prefer:
Medical/Health

In Industrial/Energy prefer:
Industrial Products

In Business Serv. prefer:
Services
Distribution

Additional Information
Name of Most Recent Fund: European Pre-Flotation Fund III
Most Recent Fund Was Raised: 04/30/2006
Year Founded: 1996
Current Activity Level : Actively seeking new investments

APAX PARTNERS LLP

33 Jermyn Street
London, United Kingdom SW1Y 6DN
Phone: 442078726300
Fax: 442076666441
Website: www.apax.com

Other Offices
601 Lexington Avenue
53rd Floor
MANHATTAN, NY USA 10022
Phone: 212-753-6300
Fax: 212-319-6155

100 Century Avenue, Pudong New District
65th floor, Shanghai World Financial Cen
Shanghai, China 200120
Phone: 862151985656
Fax: 862151985000

Possartstrasse 11
Kopernikusstrasse
Munich, Germany 81679
Phone: 49899989090
Fax: 498999890933

Dr Annie Besant Road, Shivsagar Estate
2nd Floor, Devchand House, Worli
Mumbai, India 400 018
Phone: 912240508400
Fax: 912240508444

1 Glategny Esplanade
Third Floor, Royal Bank Place
St. Peter Port, Channel Islands GY1 2HJ
Phone: 441481810000
Fax: 441481810099

Av. Brigadeiro Faria Lima
2277 cj
, Brazil
Phone: 551149493700
Fax: 551149493799

Diagonal, 640, 5 F
Barcelona, Spain 08017
Phone: 34-93-545-6500
Fax: 34-93-545-6510

41 Connaught Road
16th Floor, Nexxus Building
Central, Hong Kong
Phone: 85222005813
Fax: 85222005820

Management and Staff

Adil Haque, Principal
Alex Pellegrini, Partner
Alex Satchcroft, Principal
Amedeo Carassai, Partner
Ameya Agge, Principal
Andrew Sillitoe, Partner
Arthur Brothag, Principal
Ashish Karandikar, Principal
Borja Martinez, Partner
Buddy Gumina, Partner
Christian Stahl, Partner
David Issott, Principal
David Kim, Partner
Dimitri Rodionov, Principal
Emilio Voli, Partner
Frank Ehmer, Partner
Gabriele Cipparrone, Partner
Gautam Narayan, Principal
Giancarlo Aliberti, Partner
Ian Jones, Partner
Irene Liu, Principal
Irina Hemmers, Partner
Isabelle Probstel, Founder
James Ruane, Principal
Jason Wright, Partner
Javier Rigau, Principal
John Megrue, Partner
Magnus Mattsson, Principal
Marcelo Gigliani, Partner
Mark Zubko, Principal
Massimiliano Belingheri, Partner
Michael Phillips, Partner
Mitch Truwit, Partner
Nico Hansen, Partner
Norberto Arrate, Principal
Oriol Pinya, Partner
Richard Zhang, Partner
Richard Wilson, Partner
Robert Whipple, Principal
Robin Murer, Principal
Rohan Haldea, Principal

Roy Mackenzie, Partner
Salim Nathoo, Partner
Sandeep Naik, Partner
Savvas Savvides, Principal
Seth Brody, Partner
Shantanu Rastogi, Principal
Shashank Singh, Partner
Shay Aba, Principal
Steve Hare, Partner
Steven Dyson, Partner
Thomas Clark, Principal
Tom Hall, Partner
Tripp Lane, Principal
Vivek Vyas, Principal
William Chen, Principal
Yasemin Arik, Principal
Zehavit Cohen, Managing Partner

Type of Firm
Private Equity Firm

Association Membership
British Venture Capital Association (BVCA)
China Venture Capital Association
German Venture Capital Association (BVK)
European Private Equity and Venture Capital Assoc.
Indian Venture Capital Association (IVCA)

Project Preferences

Type of Financing Preferred:
Leveraged Buyout
Early Stage
Generalist PE
Balanced
Later Stage
Management Buyouts
Acquisition
Recapitalizations

Geographical Preferences

United States Preferences:

International Preferences:
Europe
Israel
Japan

Industry Focus
(% based on actual investment)

Other Products	23.4%
Medical/Health	17.1%
Computer Software and Services	15.7%
Internet Specific	15.5%
Consumer Related	8.6%
Communications and Media	8.4%
Industrial/Energy	5.5%
Semiconductors/Other Elect.	2.5%
Biotechnology	2.2%
Computer Hardware	1.1%

Additional Information
Year Founded: 1969
Capital Under Management: $35,800,000,000
Current Activity Level: Actively seeking new investments

APAX PARTNERS SA

45 Av Kleber
Paris, France 75784
Phone: 33153650100
E-mail: partners@apax.fr
Website: www.apax.fr

Type of Firm
Private Equity Firm

Association Membership
French Venture Capital Association (AFIC)

Project Preferences

Type of Financing Preferred:
Leveraged Buyout
Generalist PE
Later Stage
Management Buyouts
Acquisition

Geographical Preferences

International Preferences:
Luxembourg
Europe
Netherlands
Belgium
France

Industry Preferences

In Communications prefer:
Telecommunications
Media and Entertainment

In Medical/Health prefer:
Medical/Health

In Consumer Related prefer:
Consumer Products
Consumer Services

In Financial Services prefer:
Financial Services

In Business Serv. prefer:
Services

Additional Information
Name of Most Recent Fund: Apax France VII
Most Recent Fund Was Raised: 09/30/2006
Year Founded: 1972
Capital Under Management: $2,098,122,000
Current Activity Level: Actively seeking new investments

APERTURE VENTURE PARTNERS LLC

645 Madison Avenue, 20th Floor
New York, NY USA 10022
Phone: 2127587325
Fax: 2123198779

E-mail: info@aperturevp.com

Management and Staff
Matthew Tierney, General Partner

Type of Firm
Private Equity Firm

Association Membership
National Venture Capital Association - USA (NVCA)

Project Preferences

Role in Financing:
Will function either as deal originator or investor in deals created by others

Type of Financing Preferred:
Early Stage

Industry Preferences

In Biotechnology prefer:
Biotech Related Research

In Medical/Health prefer:
Medical/Health
Medical Diagnostics
Medical Products
Pharmaceuticals

In Business Serv. prefer:
Services

Additional Information
Name of Most Recent Fund: Aperture Capital II, L.P.
Most Recent Fund Was Raised: 11/14/2005
Year Founded: 2002
Capital Under Management: $5,000,000
Current Activity Level : Actively seeking new investments
Method of Compensation: Return on investment is of primary concern, do not charge fees

---

APEX ONE EQUITY LLC

2704 West
Suite 550
Crawfordsville, IN USA 47933
Phone: 7654182122
Fax: 7658660091
Website: www.apexoneequity.com

Management and Staff
Steve Gerrish, Managing Partner

Type of Firm
Private Equity Firm

Project Preferences

Type of Financing Preferred:
Early Stage
Startup

Additional Information
Name of Most Recent Fund: Apex One Equity Fund 3 LLC
Most Recent Fund Was Raised: 07/09/2012
Year Founded: 2012
Capital Under Management: $500,000
Current Activity Level : Actively seeking new investments

APEX VENTURE PARTNERS LLC

225 West Washington Street
Suite 1500
Chicago, IL USA 60606
Phone: 3128572800
Fax: 3128571800
E-mail: apex@apexvc.com
Website: www.apexvc.com

Management and Staff
Armando Pauker, General Partner
George Middlemas, General Partner
James Johnson, Founder
Lon Chow, General Partner
Nancy Corrie, Chief Financial Officer
Wayne Boulais, General Partner

Type of Firm
Private Equity Firm

Association Membership
Illinois Venture Capital Association

Project Preferences

Role in Financing:
Prefer role as deal originator but will also invest in deals created by others

Type of Financing Preferred:
Early Stage
Expansion
Balanced
Later Stage
Seed
Startup

Size of Investments Considered:
Min Size of Investment Considered (000s): $200
Max Size of Investment Considered (000s): $6,000

Geographical Preferences

United States Preferences:
North America

Industry Focus
(% based on actual investment)

Industry	%
Internet Specific	24.1%
Computer Software and Services	22.4%
Industrial/Energy	17.9%
Other Products	11.0%
Semiconductors/Other Elect.	9.4%
Communications and Media	7.7%
Computer Hardware	4.8%
Consumer Related	1.8%
Medical/Health	0.8%
Biotechnology	0.2%

Additional Information
Name of Most Recent Fund: Apex Investment Fund VI, L.P.
Most Recent Fund Was Raised: 03/31/2008
Year Founded: 1987
Capital Under Management: $620,000,000
Current Activity Level : Actively seeking new investments
Method of Compensation: Return on investment is of primary concern, do not charge fees

---

APEX VENTURES BV

Liessentstraat 9A
Uden, Netherlands 5405 AH
Phone: 31413243480
Fax: 31413255738
E-mail: ventures@apex.nl

Management and Staff
Bas Horck, Co-Founder

Type of Firm
Incubator/Development Program

Project Preferences

Type of Financing Preferred:
Early Stage
Seed
Startup

Geographical Preferences

International Preferences:
Western Europe

Industry Preferences

In Communications prefer:
Communications and Media

In Computer Software prefer:
Software

In Internet Specific prefer:
Internet

In Computer Other prefer:
Computer Related

Additional Information
Year Founded: 2000
Capital Under Management: $8,400,000
Current Activity Level : Actively seeking new investments

APHELION CAPITAL LLC

100 Tiburon Boulevard
Suite 215
Mill Valley, CA USA 94941
Phone: 4159448123
E-mail: venture@aphelioncap.com
Website: www.aphelioncapital.net

Pratt's Guide to Private Equity & Venture Capital Sources

Management and Staff
Ned Scheetz, Managing Director

Type of Firm
Private Equity Firm

Project Preferences

Type of Financing Preferred:
Early Stage
Balanced
Later Stage
Seed

Geographical Preferences

United States Preferences:

Industry Preferences

In Medical/Health prefer:
Medical/Health
Medical Therapeutics

Additional Information
Name of Most Recent Fund: Aphelion Medical Fund II, L.P.
Most Recent Fund Was Raised: 03/01/2013
Year Founded: 2005
Capital Under Management: $23,000,000
Current Activity Level : Actively seeking new investments

APICAP SAS

79, rue La Boetie
Paris, France 75008
Phone: 33182281800
Fax: 33182281801
E-mail: infos@otcam.com
Website: otcagregator.com

Type of Firm
Private Equity Firm

Association Membership
French Venture Capital Association (AFIC)

Project Preferences

Type of Financing Preferred:
Leveraged Buyout
Early Stage
Generalist PE
Later Stage
Acquisition
Startup

Size of Investments Considered:
Min Size of Investment Considered (000s): $6
Max Size of Investment Considered (000s): $4,180

Geographical Preferences

International Preferences:
Europe
Western Europe
Eastern Europe
France

Industry Preferences

In Communications prefer:
Telecommunications

In Computer Software prefer:
Software

In Internet Specific prefer:
Internet

In Biotechnology prefer:
Biotechnology

In Consumer Related prefer:
Entertainment and Leisure
Other Restaurants
Hotels and Resorts

In Business Serv. prefer:
Services
Distribution

In Utilities prefer:
Utilities

Additional Information
Year Founded: 2002
Current Activity Level : Actively seeking new investments

APICIL GESTION

38 rue Francois Peissel
BP99
Caluire et Cuire, France 69300
Phone: 33472277328
Fax: 33472277388
Website: www.apicil.com

Type of Firm
Insurance Firm Affiliate

Association Membership
French Venture Capital Association (AFIC)

Project Preferences

Type of Financing Preferred:
Early Stage

Geographical Preferences

International Preferences:
Europe
France

Industry Preferences

In Financial Services prefer:
Insurance

Additional Information
Year Founded: 1998
Current Activity Level : Actively seeking new investments

APIS PARTNERS LLP

44 Great Marlborough Street
Sixth Floor
London, United Kingdom W1F 7JL
Phone: 442036530500
E-mail: info@apis.pe
Website: apis.pe

Management and Staff
Matteo Stefanel, Managing Director

Type of Firm
Private Equity Firm

Project Preferences

Type of Financing Preferred:
Leveraged Buyout
Early Stage
Balanced
Acquisition

Geographical Preferences

United States Preferences:
All U.S.

International Preferences:
India
United Kingdom
Nigeria
Utd. Arab Em.
Kenya
South Africa
Africa

Industry Preferences

In Financial Services prefer:
Financial Services
Financial Services

Additional Information
Year Founded: 2014
Capital Under Management: $287,000,000
Current Activity Level : Actively seeking new investments

APJOHN VENTURES LLC

350 East Michigan Avenue
Suite 500
Kalamazoo, MI USA 49007
Phone: 2693498999
Fax: 2693498993
Website: www.apjohnventures.com

Type of Firm
Private Equity Firm

Project Preferences

Type of Financing Preferred:
Early Stage
Balanced

Geographical Preferences

United States Preferences:
Midwest
Michigan

Industry Preferences

In Biotechnology prefer:
Biotechnology

In Medical/Health prefer:
Diagnostic Services
Medical Products
Health Services
Pharmaceuticals

Additional Information

Year Founded: 2003
Capital Under Management: $15,000,000
Current Activity Level : Actively seeking new investments

APL PARTNERS CO., LTD.

Jam Sil Dong, Song Pa Gu
175 Apple Tower 17F
Seoul, South Korea
Phone: 82221445000
Fax: 82221445006

Type of Firm

Private Equity Firm

Association Membership

Korean Venture Capital Association (KVCA)

Project Preferences

Type of Financing Preferred:
Balanced

Additional Information

Year Founded: 1998
Current Activity Level : Actively seeking new investments

APOLLO GLOBAL MANAGEMENT LLC

Nine West 57th Street, 43rd Floor
New York, NY USA 10019
Phone: 2125153200
Website: www.agm.com

Other Offices

Neue Mainzer Strasse 46-50
Garden Towers
Frankfurt, Germany
Phone: 4969789887000

2000 Avenue of the Stars
Suite 510
LOS ANGELES, CA USA 90067
Phone: 3108431900

730 Fifth Avenue
NEW YORK, NY USA 10019
Phone: 2125153200

25 St. George Street
London, United Kingdom W1S 1FS
Phone: 442070165000

Avenue J.F. Kennedy 44
Fifth Floor Axento Building
Luxembourg, Luxembourg 1855
Phone: 35220881300

61 Robinson Road
Level 11 Suite 1, Robinson Centre
Singapore, Singapore 68893
Phone: 6563725440

1200 Smith Street
Suite 1600
HOUSTON, TX USA 77002
Phone: 7139362420

One Manhattanville Road
Suite 201
PURCHASE, NY USA 10577
Phone: 9146948000

3A Chater Road, Central
The Hong Kong Club Building
Hong Kong, Hong Kong
Phone: 85235886300

Management and Staff

Eugene Donnelly, Chief Financial Officer
Joshua Harris, Senior Managing Director
Marc Rowan, Senior Managing Director
Martin Kelly, Chief Financial Officer

Type of Firm

Investment Management Firm

Association Membership

French Venture Capital Association (AFIC)
Private Equity Council (PEC)
European Private Equity and Venture Capital Assoc.
Indian Venture Capital Association (IVCA)

Project Preferences

Type of Financing Preferred:
Leveraged Buyout
Value-Add
Mezzanine
Acquisition

Geographical Preferences

United States Preferences:
North America

International Preferences:
Europe

Industry Focus

(% based on actual investment)
Other Products	30.1%
Industrial/Energy	26.2%
Consumer Related	20.9%
Communications and Media	16.5%
Internet Specific	2.7%
Computer Software and Services	2.5%
Medical/Health	1.1%
Semiconductors/Other Elect.	0.0%

Additional Information

Name of Most Recent Fund: Apollo Credit Opportunity Fund III, L.P.
Most Recent Fund Was Raised: 12/23/2013
Year Founded: 1990
Capital Under Management: $54,872,862,000
Current Activity Level : Actively seeking new investments

APPIAN VENTURES, INC.

4201 E Yale Avenue
Suite 230
Denver, CO USA 80220
Phone: 3038302450
Website: www.appianvc.com

Management and Staff

Christopher Onan, Managing Director
Donald Parsons, Managing Director
Mark Soane, Managing Director
Stacey McKittrick, Chief Financial Officer

Type of Firm

Private Equity Firm

Project Preferences

Role in Financing:
Prefer role as deal originator

Type of Financing Preferred:
Early Stage
Expansion
Balanced
Later Stage
Seed

Geographical Preferences

United States Preferences:
West Coast

Industry Preferences

In Communications prefer:
Communications and Media

In Computer Software prefer:
Software

Additional Information
Year Founded: 2002
Capital Under Management: $80,000,000
Current Activity Level : Actively seeking new investments

APPLE TREE PARTNERS

230 Park Avenue
Suite 2800
New York, NY USA 10169
Phone: 2124685800
Fax: 2124685849
E-mail: info@appletreepartners.com
Website: www.appletreepartners.com

Management and Staff
Aaron Kantoff, Vice President
Behshad Sheldon, Venture Partner
David McIntyre, Partner
Diane Daych, Partner
Frank Young, Venture Partner
Jonathan Waldstreicher, Principal
Julie Gionfriddo, Principal
Lauren Farrell, Chief Financial Officer
Mark Pruzansky, General Partner
Mayukh Sukhatme, Partner
Preston Brice, Vice President
Sami Hamade, Partner
Samuel Hall, Principal
Seth Harrison, Managing Partner

Type of Firm
Private Equity Firm

Geographical Preferences

United States Preferences:
New York

Industry Preferences

In Medical/Health prefer:
Medical/Health

Additional Information
Name of Most Recent Fund: Apple Tree Partners II, L.P.
Most Recent Fund Was Raised: 06/11/2001
Year Founded: 1999
Current Activity Level : Actively seeking new investments

APPLIED VENTURES LLC

3050 Bowers Avenue
P.O. Box 58039
Santa Clara, CA USA 95054
Phone: 4087275555
Fax: 4087489943
Website: www.appliedventures.com

Other Offices
974 East Arques Avenue
SUNNYVALE, CA USA 94085
Phone: 408-727-5555

Management and Staff
Omkaram Nalamasu, President

Type of Firm
Corporate PE/Venture

Association Membership
National Venture Capital Association - USA (NVCA)

Project Preferences

Role in Financing:
Prefer role as deal originator but will also invest in deals created by others

Type of Financing Preferred:
Early Stage

Size of Investments Considered:
Min Size of Investment Considered (000s): $500
Max Size of Investment Considered (000s): $3,000

Industry Preferences

In Communications prefer:
Communications and Media

In Computer Software prefer:
Software

In Medical/Health prefer:
Medical Diagnostics

In Industrial/Energy prefer:
Energy Conservation Relat
Advanced Materials

In Utilities prefer:
Utilities

Additional Information
Year Founded: 2000
Capital Under Management: $240,000,000
Current Activity Level : Actively seeking new investments

APPOSITE CAPITAL LLP

One Friday Street
Bracken House
London, United Kingdom EC4M 9JA
Phone: 442070906190
Fax: 442070906022
E-mail: enquiry@apposite-capital.com
Website: www.appositecapital.com

Management and Staff
Allan Marchington, Partner
David Porter, Co-Founder
Rory Pope, Partner
Samuel Gray, Partner
Steve Adkin, Partner

Type of Firm
Private Equity Firm

Association Membership
British Venture Capital Association (BVCA)

Project Preferences

Type of Financing Preferred:
Leveraged Buyout
Early Stage
Expansion
Generalist PE
Seed
Management Buyouts
Startup

Geographical Preferences

United States Preferences:

International Preferences:
Europe
Japan

Industry Preferences

In Biotechnology prefer:
Biotechnology

In Medical/Health prefer:
Medical/Health
Medical Therapeutics
Medical Products
Health Services
Pharmaceuticals

Additional Information
Name of Most Recent Fund: Apposite Healthcare Fund, L.P.
Most Recent Fund Was Raised: 04/14/2006
Year Founded: 2006
Capital Under Management: $200,000,000
Current Activity Level : Actively seeking new investments

APRIORI BETEILIGUNGEN GMBH

ABC-Strasse 35
Hamburg, Germany 20354
Phone: 494034914162
Fax: 494034914149
Website: www.apriori-beteiligungen.de

Type of Firm
Private Equity Firm

Project Preferences

Type of Financing Preferred:
Leveraged Buyout
Management Buyouts

Geographical Preferences

International Preferences:
Germany

Industry Preferences

In Financial Services prefer:
Real Estate

APSARA CAPITAL LLP

29 St Jame's Place
London, United Kingdom SW1A 1NR

Type of Firm
Private Equity Firm

Association Membership
British Venture Capital Association (BVCA)

Project Preferences

Type of Financing Preferred:
Early Stage
Expansion

Industry Preferences

In Industrial/Energy prefer:
Environmental Related

In Agr/Forestr/Fish prefer:
Agribusiness

Additional Information
Year Founded: 1969
Current Activity Level : Actively seeking new investments

AQUA ALTA SA

Lombardstraat 47
rue du Lombard
Brussels, Belgium 1000
Phone: 3227903499
Fax: 3227903488

Management and Staff
Brent Wilkey, Managing Director

Type of Firm
Private Equity Firm

Project Preferences

Type of Financing Preferred:
Early Stage
Start-up Financing
Later Stage
Seed

Geographical Preferences

United States Preferences:
All U.S.

International Preferences:
Europe

Industry Preferences

In Communications prefer:
Media and Entertainment

In Medical/Health prefer:
Medical/Health

In Industrial/Energy prefer:
Industrial Products

Additional Information
Year Founded: 2004
Capital Under Management: $2,100,000
Current Activity Level : Actively seeking new investments

AQUA ASSET MANAGEMENT SAS

5 Quai Jayr
Lyon, France 69009
Phone: 0033481073580
Fax: 0033481073581
E-mail: contact@promelys.com
Website: www.aqua-am.com

Other Offices
57 rue de Saint Cyr
Lyon, France 69009
Phone: 33-4-7864-6060
Fax: 33-4-7847-1172

Management and Staff
Herve Letoublon, Vice President

Type of Firm
Private Equity Firm

Association Membership
French Venture Capital Association (AFIC)

Project Preferences

Type of Financing Preferred:
Early Stage
Balanced
Later Stage
Startup

Size of Investments Considered:
Min Size of Investment Considered (000s): $138
Max Size of Investment Considered (000s): $1,376

Geographical Preferences

International Preferences:
Europe
France

Industry Preferences

In Communications prefer:
Communications and Media
Telecommunications

In Semiconductor/Electr prefer:
Electronics
Electronic Components

In Biotechnology prefer:
Biotechnology

In Medical/Health prefer:
Medical/Health

In Consumer Related prefer:
Consumer

In Industrial/Energy prefer:
Industrial Products

In Business Serv. prefer:
Services
Distribution

Additional Information
Name of Most Recent Fund: Atout PME 2 FIP
Most Recent Fund Was Raised: 06/30/2009
Year Founded: 2000
Current Activity Level : Actively seeking new investments

AQUA CAPITAL CONSULTORIA LTDA

Avenida Cidade Jardim 803
6th floor
Sao Paulo, Brazil 01453000
Phone: 551137075820
E-mail: info@aquacapitalpartners.com
Website: aquacapital.net

Type of Firm
Private Equity Firm

Association Membership
Brazilian Venture Capital Association (ABCR)

Project Preferences

Type of Financing Preferred:
Leveraged Buyout
Turnaround
Management Buyouts
Acquisition
Recapitalizations

Geographical Preferences

International Preferences:
Uruguay
Latin America
Brazil
Chile

Industry Preferences

In Consumer Related prefer:
Food/Beverage

In Transportation prefer:
Transportation

Additional Information (top)
Year Founded: 2009
Current Activity Level : Actively seeking new investments

In Agr/Forestr/Fish prefer:
Agribusiness
Agriculture related

Additional Information
Name of Most Recent Fund: Agribusiness & Food Fund
Most Recent Fund Was Raised: 10/02/2013
Year Founded: 2012
Capital Under Management: $173,400,000
Current Activity Level: Actively seeking new investments

AQUA SPARK BV

Achter Sint Pieter 5
Utrecht, Netherlands 3512 HP
Phone: 31308200369
Website: www.aqua-spark.nl

Management and Staff
Amy Novogratz, Managing Partner

Type of Firm
Private Equity Firm

Project Preferences

Type of Financing Preferred:
Early Stage
Expansion
Later Stage

Industry Preferences

In Biotechnology prefer:
Agricultural/Animal Bio.

Additional Information
Year Founded: 2014
Current Activity Level: Actively seeking new investments

AQUASOURCA FRANCE SAS

131 Bd Bataille de Stalingrad
Le Premium
Villeurbanne, France 69624
Phone: 33472690890
Fax: 33472690895
E-mail: invest@aquasourca.com
Website: www.aquasourca.com

Other Offices
1, Rue du Fort Rheinsheim
Luxembourg, Luxembourg L-2419
Phone: 35226258251
Fax: 35226458235

Management and Staff
Sophie Defforey-Crepet, Chief Executive Officer

Type of Firm
Private Equity Firm

Association Membership
French Venture Capital Association (AFIC)

Project Preferences

Type of Financing Preferred:
Leveraged Buyout
Early Stage
Generalist PE
Later Stage
Management Buyouts
Acquisition

Size of Investments Considered:
Min Size of Investment Considered (000s): $2,889
Max Size of Investment Considered (000s): $14,445

Geographical Preferences

United States Preferences:
All U.S.

International Preferences:
Tunisia
Czech Republic
Cambodia
Germany
France

Additional Information
Year Founded: 1996
Current Activity Level: Actively seeking new investments

AQUILINE CAPITAL PARTNERS LLC

535 Madison Avenue
24th Floor
New York, NY USA 10022
Phone: 2126249500
Fax: 2126249510
E-mail: contact@aquiline-llc.com
Website: www.aquiline-llc.com

Management and Staff
Bruce MacFarlane, Principal
Christopher Watson, Principal
Geoffrey Kalish, Principal
Ian Smith, Principal
Jeffrey Greenberg, Chief Executive Officer
Laurent Bouyoux, Principal
Matthew Grayson, Principal

Type of Firm
Private Equity Firm

Project Preferences

Type of Financing Preferred:
Leveraged Buyout
Early Stage
Start-up Financing
Turnaround
Seed
Acquisition

Geographical Preferences

United States Preferences:
All U.S.

International Preferences:
Europe

Industry Preferences

In Financial Services prefer:
Financial Services
Insurance
Financial Services

Additional Information
Name of Most Recent Fund: Aquiline Financial Services Fund II, L.P.
Most Recent Fund Was Raised: 04/29/2010
Year Founded: 2005
Capital Under Management: $143,200,000
Current Activity Level: Actively seeking new investments

AQUILLIAN INVESTMENTS LLC

275 Sacramento Street
Suite 800
San Francisco, CA USA 94111
Website: www.aquillian.com

Type of Firm
Investment Management Firm

Project Preferences

Type of Financing Preferred:
Early Stage
Later Stage

Industry Preferences

In Industrial/Energy prefer:
Energy Conservation Relat
Environmental Related

In Other prefer:
Environment Responsible

Additional Information
Current Activity Level: Actively seeking new investments

AQUITAINE CREATION INVESTISSEMENT SAS

162, av du Dr A. Schweitzer
Centre Condorcet
Pessac, France 33600
Phone: 33556151190
Fax: 33556151197
E-mail: contact@aquiti.fr
Website: www.aquiti.fr

Management and Staff
Alain Ricros, President

Type of Firm
Private Equity Firm

Project Preferences

Type of Financing Preferred:
Leveraged Buyout
Early Stage
Mezzanine
Generalist PE
Seed
Acquisition
Startup

Size of Investments Considered:
Min Size of Investment Considered (000s): $20
Max Size of Investment Considered (000s): $401

Geographical Preferences

International Preferences:
France

Industry Preferences

In Semiconductor/Electr prefer:
Electronics
Laser Related

In Biotechnology prefer:
Biotechnology
Industrial Biotechnology

In Medical/Health prefer:
Medical/Health

In Industrial/Energy prefer:
Energy
Industrial Products
Environmental Related

In Transportation prefer:
Aerospace

In Business Serv. prefer:
Services
Distribution

In Agr/Forestr/Fish prefer:
Agriculture related

Additional Information
Year Founded: 1998
Capital Under Management: $388,000
Current Activity Level : Actively seeking new investments

AQUITAINE INVESTMENT ADVISORS LTD

308 Des Voeux Road Central
Suite 1905, ING Tower
Central, Hong Kong
Phone: 852-2528-1600
Fax: 852-2528-1900
E-mail: info@aquitaine.com.hk
Website: www.aquitaine.com.hk

Other Offices
5/F Izumi Shibkoen Building
1-6-8 Shiba Koen, Minato-ku
Tokyo, Japan 105-0011
Phone: 813-5401-3002
Fax: 813-5401-3004

Management and Staff
Arthur Yama, Managing Director
Marlene Wittman, Managing Director

Type of Firm
Private Equity Advisor or Fund of Funds

Project Preferences

Type of Financing Preferred:
Early Stage
Expansion
Later Stage

Geographical Preferences

International Preferences:
Taiwan
Hong Kong
China
Thailand
Philippines
Asia
Singapore
Japan
Malaysia

Industry Preferences

In Medical/Health prefer:
Medical/Health
Pharmaceuticals

In Consumer Related prefer:
Entertainment and Leisure

In Financial Services prefer:
Financial Services

Additional Information
Year Founded: 1999
Current Activity Level : Actively seeking new investments

ARAB ANGEL FUND

4112 Lee Highway
Arlington, VA USA 22207
Website: www.arabangel.vc

Type of Firm
Private Equity Firm

Project Preferences

Type of Financing Preferred:
Early Stage

Geographical Preferences

International Preferences:
Middle East

Additional Information
Year Founded: 2016
Capital Under Management: $10,000,000
Current Activity Level : Actively seeking new investments

ARABIAN GULF FUND

Dubai International Financial
Centre Gate Predinct Building
Dubai, Utd. Arab Em.
Phone: 97143637456
Fax: 97143637457
E-mail: info@ArabianGulfFund.com
Website: www.arabiangulffund.com

Type of Firm
Private Equity Firm

Project Preferences

Type of Financing Preferred:
Early Stage
Balanced
Later Stage
Startup

Geographical Preferences

International Preferences:
Asia

Industry Preferences

In Medical/Health prefer:
Medical/Health

In Consumer Related prefer:
Education Related

In Industrial/Energy prefer:
Energy

In Transportation prefer:
Transportation

Additional Information
Year Founded: 2013
Current Activity Level : Actively seeking new investments

ARAFURA VENTURES INC

555 Bryant Street
Palo Alto, CA USA 94301
Phone: 6505300895
Website: www.arafuraventures.com

Management and Staff
Joe Kennedy, Managing Director
Marc Philips, Managing Director

Type of Firm
Private Equity Firm

Project Preferences

Type of Financing Preferred:
Early Stage

Geographical Preferences

United States Preferences:

Industry Preferences

In Computer Software prefer:
Software

Additional Information
Year Founded: 2017
Current Activity Level : Actively seeking new investments

ARALON AG

Churerstrasse 135
Pfaeffikon, Switzerland 8808
Phone: 41554162630
Fax: 41554162633
E-mail: info@aralon.ch
Website: www.aralon.ch

Management and Staff
Peter Dreher, Managing Partner
Werner Hane, Managing Partner
Werner Schwendimann, Chief Financial Officer

Type of Firm
Investment Management Firm

Association Membership
Swiss Venture Capital Association (SECA)

Project Preferences

Type of Financing Preferred:
Leveraged Buyout
Early Stage
Turnaround
Later Stage
Seed
Acquisition
Startup

Size of Investments Considered:
Min Size of Investment Considered (000s): $4,170
Max Size of Investment Considered (000s): $27,801

Geographical Preferences

International Preferences:
Belarus
Turkey
Central Europe
Europe
Switzerland
Austria
Eastern Europe
Ukraine
Bulgaria
Romania
Germany
Russia

Industry Preferences

In Medical/Health prefer:
Medical/Health

In Consumer Related prefer:
Consumer

In Industrial/Energy prefer:
Energy
Industrial Products
Environmental Related

In Financial Services prefer:
Real Estate

Additional Information
Year Founded: 2005
Current Activity Level : Actively seeking new investments

ARAVAIPA VENTURES LLC

319 Foxtail Court
Boulder, CO USA 80305
Phone: 3033235661

Management and Staff
Robert Fenwick-Smith, Senior Managing Director
Timothy Reeser, Managing Director

Type of Firm
Private Equity Firm

Project Preferences

Type of Financing Preferred:
Early Stage

Size of Investments Considered:
Min Size of Investment Considered (000s): $150
Max Size of Investment Considered (000s): $500

Geographical Preferences

United States Preferences:
Colorado

Industry Preferences

In Industrial/Energy prefer:
Environmental Related

In Transportation prefer:
Transportation

In Other prefer:
Environment Responsible

Additional Information
Name of Most Recent Fund: Aravaipa Venture Fund LLC
Most Recent Fund Was Raised: 06/13/2012
Year Founded: 2008
Capital Under Management: $7,913,000
Current Activity Level : Actively seeking new investments

ARAVIS SA

Merkurstrasse 70
Zurich, Switzerland 8032
Phone: 41434992000
Fax: 41434992001
E-mail: info@aravis.ch
Website: www.aravis.ch

Management and Staff
Bernard Mach, Partner
Fatt Kah Foo, Venture Partner
Francois L Eplattenier, Partner
Gerald Mazzalovo, Managing Partner
Hans-Joachim Boehm, Partner
Jacques Essinger, Venture Partner
Jean-Christophe Vilain, Venture Partner
Johanna Holldack, Venture Partner
Marc Krattinger, Partner
Martin Meiler, Partner
Oliver Thalmann, Partner
Richard Ulevitch, Partner
Rolf Zinkernagel, Venture Partner
Simon Nebel, Managing Partner
Tak Mak, Partner
Wylinn Boey, Venture Partner

Type of Firm
Private Equity Firm

Association Membership
Swiss Venture Capital Association (SECA)

Project Preferences

Role in Financing:
Prefer role as deal originator

Type of Financing Preferred:
Early Stage
Expansion
Other
Seed
Startup

Size of Investments Considered:
Min Size of Investment Considered (000s): $7,310
Max Size of Investment Considered (000s): $10,443

Geographical Preferences

United States Preferences:
All U.S.

International Preferences:
Italy
Europe
Switzerland
Western Europe
Asia
Singapore

Industry Preferences

In Biotechnology prefer:
Biotechnology

In Medical/Health prefer:
Medical/Health
Medical Therapeutics
Pharmaceuticals

In Industrial/Energy prefer:
Alternative Energy

In Other prefer:
Environment Responsible

Additional Information
Year Founded: 2001
Capital Under Management: $307,800,000
Current Activity Level : Actively seeking new investments

ARAX CAPITAL PARTNERS GMBH

Handelskai 94-96
Vienna, Austria 1200
Phone: 43137074740
Fax: 431370747422
E-mail: office@arax.at
Website: www.arax.at

Management and Staff
Christian Tiringer, Managing Director
Daniel Cesky, Managing Director
Michael Stranz, Managing Director

Type of Firm
Private Equity Firm

Association Membership
Austrian PE and Venture Capital Association (AVCO)

Project Preferences

Type of Financing Preferred:
Early Stage
Later Stage
Seed
Startup

Geographical Preferences

International Preferences:
Europe
Austria

Additional Information
Year Founded: 2009
Current Activity Level : Actively seeking new investments

ARB INVESTMENTS PTE LTD

7 Temasek Boulevard
#15-02 Suntec Tower 1
Singapore, Singapore 038987
Phone: 6566903360
E-mail: contact@rbworld.com

Type of Firm
Private Equity Firm

Project Preferences

Type of Financing Preferred:
Balanced
Seed

Additional Information
Year Founded: 2012
Current Activity Level : Actively seeking new investments

ARBOR PRIVATE INVESTMENT CO LLC

676 North Michigan Avenue
Suite 3410
Chicago, IL USA 60611
Phone: 3129813770
Fax: 3129813771
Website: www.arborpic.com

Other Offices
5135 Riverlake Drive
Duluth, GA USA 30097

Management and Staff
Alan Weed, Partner
Brody Lynn, Partner
Christopher Harned, Partner
Gregory Purcell, Chief Executive Officer
J. David Foster, Chief Financial Officer
Jerry Cronin, Vice President
John Camp, Managing Director
Joseph Campolo, President
Richard Boos, Partner
Ryan McKenzie, Partner

Type of Firm
Private Equity Firm

Association Membership
Illinois Venture Capital Association

Project Preferences

Role in Financing:
Prefer role as deal originator

Type of Financing Preferred:
Leveraged Buyout
Management Buyouts
Acquisition
Recapitalizations

Size of Investments Considered:
Min Size of Investment Considered (000s): $10,000
Max Size of Investment Considered (000s): $75,000

Geographical Preferences

United States Preferences:
North America
All U.S.

Canadian Preferences:
All Canada

Industry Focus
(% based on actual investment)
Internet Specific   100.0%

Additional Information
Name of Most Recent Fund: Arbor Investments III, L.P.
Most Recent Fund Was Raised: 07/27/2011
Year Founded: 1999
Capital Under Management: $700,000,000
Current Activity Level : Actively seeking new investments
Method of Compensation: Return on invest. most important, but chc. closing fees, service fees, etc.

ARBORETUM VENTURES INC

303 Detroit Street
Suite 301, Market Place Bldg.
Ann Arbor, MI USA 48104
Phone: 7349983638
Fax: 7349983689
E-mail: info@arboretumvc.com
Website: www.arboretumvc.com

Management and Staff
Dan Kidle, Principal
Jan Garfinkle, Co-Founder
Marcy Marshall, Chief Financial Officer
Paul McCreadie, Managing Director
Thomas Shehab, Managing Director
Timothy Petersen, Managing Director

Type of Firm
Private Equity Firm

Association Membership
National Venture Capital Association - USA (NVCA)

Project Preferences

Role in Financing:
Will function either as deal originator or investor in deals created by others

Type of Financing Preferred:
Early Stage
Seed

Size of Investments Considered:
Min Size of Investment Considered (000s): $5,000
Max Size of Investment Considered (000s): $15,000

Geographical Preferences

United States Preferences:
Midwest

Industry Preferences

In Medical/Health prefer:
Medical Diagnostics
Medical Products
Health Services

Additional Information

Name of Most Recent Fund: Arboretum Ventures III, L.P.
Most Recent Fund Was Raised: 02/08/2011
Year Founded: 2002
Capital Under Management: $450,000,000
Current Activity Level : Actively seeking new investments
Method of Compensation: Return on investment is of primary concern, do not charge fees

ARC FINANCIAL CORP.

400 - 3rd Avenue SouthWest
Suite 4300
Calgary, Canada T2P 4H2
Phone: 4032920680
Fax: 4032920693
E-mail: genfeedback@arcfinancial.com
Website: www.arcfinancial.com

Management and Staff

Carl Landry, Vice President
Duane Schellenberg, Vice President
James Major, Vice President
Jeff Prentice, Vice President
Jeremy Gackle, Vice President
John Stewart, Co-Founder
Kent Foster, Vice President
Nancy Smith, Managing Director
Nancy Lever, Managing Director
Peter Tertzakian, Managing Director
Wendy Liu, Vice President
William Slavin, Managing Director

Type of Firm

Private Equity Firm

Association Membership

Canadian Venture Capital Association

Project Preferences

Role in Financing:
Will function either as deal originator or investor in deals created by others

Type of Financing Preferred:
Early Stage
Balanced
Other

Size of Investments Considered:
Min Size of Investment Considered (000s): $25,000
Max Size of Investment Considered (000s): $100,000

Geographical Preferences

Canadian Preferences:
All Canada

Industry Focus

(% based on actual investment)
Industrial/Energy   100.0%

Additional Information

Year Founded: 1989
Capital Under Management: $2,700,000,000
Current Activity Level : Actively seeking new investments
Method of Compensation: Return on invest. most important, but chg. closing fees, service fees, etc.

ARCADIA SGR SPA

Foro Buonaparte, 12
Milan, Italy
Phone: 39236579510
Fax: 3928715234
Website: www.arcadiasgr.it

Management and Staff

Alberto Frausin, Partner
Giorgio Mancarella, Partner
Giorgio Pucci, Partner
Simone Arnaboldi, Chief Executive Officer
Walter Benati, Partner

Type of Firm

Private Equity Firm

Project Preferences

Type of Financing Preferred:
Leveraged Buyout

Geographical Preferences

International Preferences:
Italy

Additional Information

Year Founded: 2009
Capital Under Management: $84,600,000
Current Activity Level : Actively seeking new investments

ARCADY CAPITAL COMPANY

1223 North Rock Road
Suite E100
Wichita, KS USA 67206
Phone: 3168692864
Website: www.arcadycapital.com

Other Offices

10333 East 21st Street
Remington Place, Suite 303D
WICHITA, KS USA 67206

Management and Staff

Jared Sprole, Partner
Ronald Stier, Managing Director

Type of Firm

Private Equity Firm

Project Preferences

Type of Financing Preferred:
Expansion

Geographical Preferences

United States Preferences:
Midwest

Industry Preferences

In Medical/Health prefer:
Medical/Health
Medical Products
Health Services

In Consumer Related prefer:
Food/Beverage

In Financial Services prefer:
Financial Services

In Business Serv. prefer:
Services
Distribution
Consulting Services

In Manufact. prefer:
Manufacturing

Additional Information

Year Founded: 2011
Capital Under Management: $5,550,000
Current Activity Level : Actively seeking new investments

ARCAPITA INC

1180 Peachtree Street Northeast, Suite 3000
Atlanta, GA USA 30309
Phone: 4049209000
Fax: 4049209001
E-mail: info@arcapita.com
Website: www.arcapita.com

Other Offices

Nine Raffles Place
Level 44 Republic Plaza
Singapore, Singapore 048619
Phone: 6564999888
Fax: 6564999800

P.O. Box 1406
Manama, Bahrain
Phone: 97317218333
Fax: 97317217555

15 Sloane Square
Second Floor
London, United Kingdom SW1W 8ER
Phone: 442078245600
Fax: 442078245601

Management and Staff

Adrian Peck, Principal
Ahmed Al Zayani, Principal
Amin Jawad, Principal
Amy Doshi, Principal
Anthony Nambiar, Principal
Essa Zainal, Managing Director
Gana Balaratnam, Principal
Hafedh Al Najem, Principal
Hassan Shujaie, Principal
Hisham Al Raee, Chief Operating Officer
Kevin Keough, Managing Director
Mishal Al Hellow, Principal
Mohamed Sharif, Principal
Muhannad Buhindi, Principal
Osama Al Tamimi, Principal
Osama Al Haram, Principal
Pik Sian Sim, Principal

Type of Firm

Bank Affiliated

Association Membership

British Venture Capital Association (BVCA)

Project Preferences

Role in Financing:
Will function either as deal originator or investor in deals created by others

Type of Financing Preferred:
Leveraged Buyout
Early Stage
Expansion
Generalist PE
Acquisition

Size of Investments Considered:
Min Size of Investment Considered (000s): $4,000
Max Size of Investment Considered (000s): $8,000

Geographical Preferences

United States Preferences:

Canadian Preferences:
All Canada

International Preferences:
India
United Kingdom
Europe
Western Europe
China
Mexico
Eastern Europe
Middle East
Asia
Russia

Industry Focus

(% based on actual investment)
Other Products	33.0%
Consumer Related	30.1%
Industrial/Energy	13.7%
Computer Software and Services	9.7%
Communications and Media	7.0%
Medical/Health	5.4%
Semiconductors/Other Elect.	1.0%
Internet Specific	0.2%

Additional Information

Year Founded: 1997
Capital Under Management: $200,000,000
Current Activity Level: Actively seeking new investments

ARCARIS MANAGEMENT GMBH

Oststrasse 49
Dusseldorf, Germany 40211
Phone: 4921153818592
E-mail: info@arcaris.de
Website: arcaris.de

Type of Firm

Private Equity Firm

Project Preferences

Type of Financing Preferred:
Leveraged Buyout
Management Buyouts

Geographical Preferences

International Preferences:
Germany

Additional Information

Year Founded: 2013
Current Activity Level: Actively seeking new investments

ARCH DEVELOPMENT PARTNERS LLC

20 North Wacker Drive, Suite 2200
Chicago, IL USA 60606
Phone: 3124424400
Fax: 3122630724
E-mail: info@archdp.com
Website: www.archdp.com

Other Offices

241 Falcon Court
West Lafayette, IN USA 47906

346 West Michigan Avenue
Kalamazoo, MI USA 49007

Management and Staff

Caralynn Nowinski-Chenoweth, Principal
Elizabeth Long, Chief Financial Officer
Teri Willey, Managing Partner
Thomas Churchwell, Managing Partner

Type of Firm

University Program

Project Preferences

Type of Financing Preferred:
Early Stage
Seed
Startup

Geographical Preferences

United States Preferences:
Midwest
Illinois
Michigan
Ohio
Indiana

Industry Preferences

In Computer Software prefer:
Software

In Biotechnology prefer:
Biotechnology

In Consumer Related prefer:
Education Related

Additional Information

Name of Most Recent Fund: ARCH Development Fund I (ADF I)
Most Recent Fund Was Raised: 07/01/2006
Year Founded: 2001
Capital Under Management: $31,500,000
Current Activity Level: Actively seeking new investments

ARCH VENTURE PARTNERS LLC

8725 West Higgins Road
Suite 290
Chicago, IL USA 60631
Phone: 7733806600
Fax: 7733806306
E-mail: EUInquiries@ARCHventure.com

Other Offices

6300 Bridgepoint Parkway
Building One, Suite 500
Austin, TX USA 78730
Phone: 512-795-5830
Fax: 512-795-5849

1000 Second Avenue
Suite 3700
Seattle, WA USA 98104
Phone: 206-674-3028
Fax: 206-674-3026

1700 Owens Street
Suite 535
San Francisco, CA USA 94158
Phone: 415-565-7103
Fax: 415-565-7107

Management and Staff

Ajit Medhekar, Venture Partner
Alex Rives, Venture Partner
Clinton Bybee, Managing Director
Edgar Hotard, Venture Partner
George Kadifa, Venture Partner
Hong Hou, Venture Partner
Keith Crandell, Managing Director
Ken Bradley, Venture Partner
Kristina Burow, Managing Director
Mark McDonnell, Chief Financial Officer
Michael Knapp, Venture Partner
Nathaniel David, Venture Partner
Paul Thurk, Managing Director
Robert Nelsen, Managing Director
Scott Minick, Venture Partner
Steven Lazarus, Managing Director
Steven Gillis, Managing Director
T. Brennan, Venture Partner

Type of Firm
Private Equity Firm

Association Membership
Illinois Venture Capital Association
National Venture Capital Association - USA (NVCA)

Project Preferences

Role in Financing:
Prefer role as deal originator but will also invest in deals created by others

Type of Financing Preferred:
Early Stage
Seed

Geographical Preferences

United States Preferences:
Illinois
California
Washington
Texas

Industry Focus
(% based on actual investment)

Biotechnology	48.5%
Medical/Health	12.3%
Semiconductors/Other Elect.	11.5%
Industrial/Energy	11.0%
Internet Specific	6.3%
Computer Software and Services	4.7%
Communications and Media	3.8%
Computer Hardware	1.2%
Other Products	0.6%
Consumer Related	0.0%

Additional Information
Year Founded: 1986
Capital Under Management: $1,900,000,000
Current Activity Level : Actively seeking new investments
Method of Compensation: Return on investment is of primary concern, do not charge fees

---

ARCHANGEL INFORMAL INVESTMENT LTD

20 Rutland Square
Edinburgh, United Kingdom EH1 2BB
Phone: 441312219876
Fax: 441312291956
E-mail: enquiries@archangelsonline.com

Management and Staff
John Waddell, Chief Executive Officer

Type of Firm
Angel Group

Project Preferences

Type of Financing Preferred:
Early Stage
Later Stage
Seed
Management Buyouts
Startup

Size of Investments Considered:
Min Size of Investment Considered (000s): $398
Max Size of Investment Considered (000s): $797

Geographical Preferences

International Preferences:
United Kingdom

Industry Preferences

In Biotechnology prefer:
Biotechnology

In Medical/Health prefer:
Medical/Health

Additional Information
Year Founded: 1992
Current Activity Level : Actively seeking new investments

ARCHEAN CAPITAL PARTNERS I LP

6022 West Chester Pike
Newtown Square, PA USA 19073

Type of Firm
Investment Management Firm

Project Preferences

Type of Financing Preferred:
Fund of Funds
Leveraged Buyout
Value-Add
Turnaround
Opportunistic
Recapitalizations

Industry Preferences

In Financial Services prefer:
Real Estate

Additional Information
Year Founded: 2016
Capital Under Management: $100,000,000
Current Activity Level : Actively seeking new investments

ARCHER CAPITAL PTY LTD

13 Hickson Road
Suite 7, Pier 2/3, Dawes Point
Sydney, Australia 2000
Phone: 61282433333
Fax: 61292413151
Website: www.archercapital.com.au

Management and Staff
Andrew Gray, Managing Director
Ben Frewin, Partner
Craig Cartner, Managing Director
David Bull, Chief Financial Officer
Greg Minton, Managing Director
Peter Gold, Managing Director
Peter Wiggs, Managing Director
Scott Greck, Managing Director
Timothy Spencer, Managing Director

Type of Firm
Private Equity Firm

Association Membership
New Zealand Venture Capital Association
Australian Venture Capital Association (AVCAL)

Project Preferences

Role in Financing:
Prefer role as deal originator

Type of Financing Preferred:
Leveraged Buyout
Management Buyouts
Acquisition

Geographical Preferences

International Preferences:
Australia
New Zealand

Industry Focus

(% based on actual investment)
Consumer Related	29.4%
Medical/Health	28.5%
Computer Software and Services	18.0%
Industrial/Energy	10.4%
Other Products	7.6%
Internet Specific	3.0%
Computer Hardware	1.9%
Semiconductors/Other Elect.	1.1%

Additional Information

Name of Most Recent Fund: Archer Capital Growth Fund 2
Most Recent Fund Was Raised: 01/09/2011
Year Founded: 1997
Capital Under Management: $3,931,200,000
Current Activity Level : Actively seeking new investments
Method of Compensation: Return on investment is of primary concern, do not charge fees

ARCHER VENTURE CAPITAL LLC

2045 S. Barrington Avenue
Suite A
Los Angeles, CA USA 90025
Phone: 3109169599
E-mail: info@archervc.com
Website: www.archervc.com

Management and Staff

Greg Martin, Founder

Type of Firm

Private Equity Firm

Project Preferences

Type of Financing Preferred:
Balanced
Later Stage
Seed

Additional Information

Year Founded: 2015
Capital Under Management: $80,000,000
Current Activity Level : Actively seeking new investments

ARCHETYPE CORP

4-1-8, Azabujuban
4F, Sanwa 1 Bldg, Minato-Ku
Tokyo, Japan 106-0045
Phone: 81337983700
E-mail: info@archetype.co.jp
Website: www.archetype.co.jp

Management and Staff

Hirotaka Fukuoka, Partner
Osamu Higuchi, Co-Founder

Type of Firm

Incubator/Development Program

Project Preferences

Type of Financing Preferred:
Early Stage
Seed

Geographical Preferences

International Preferences:
Japan

Additional Information

Year Founded: 2006
Current Activity Level : Actively seeking new investments

ARCHIMED SA

2, place de Francfort
Lyon, France 69003
E-mail: contact@archimed-group.eu
Website: www.archimed-group.eu

Management and Staff

Denis Ribon, Co-Founder
Sandrine Laporte, Chief Financial Officer
Vincent Guillaumot, Co-Founder

Type of Firm

Private Equity Firm

Association Membership

French Venture Capital Association (AFIC)

Project Preferences

Type of Financing Preferred:
Leveraged Buyout

Geographical Preferences

International Preferences:
Europe
Switzerland
France

Industry Preferences

In Medical/Health prefer:
Medical/Health

Additional Information

Year Founded: 2014
Capital Under Management: $570,236,000
Current Activity Level : Actively seeking new investments

ARCHIMEDES HEALTH INVESTORS

250 Park Avenue
Suite 1105
New York, NY USA 10177

Type of Firm

Private Equity Firm

Industry Preferences

In Medical/Health prefer:
Health Services

Additional Information

Year Founded: 2017
Current Activity Level : Actively seeking new investments

ARCHIPEL CAPITAL LLC

701 Ellicott Street
Buffalo, NY USA 14203
Phone: 3129334522
Fax: 3128933849
Website: archipelcapital.com

Management and Staff

Bradford La Salle, Vice President
Gregory Gray, Founder
James Timlin, Vice President

Type of Firm

Private Equity Firm

Project Preferences

Type of Financing Preferred:
Later Stage

Geographical Preferences

United States Preferences:

Additional Information

Year Founded: 2005
Current Activity Level : Actively seeking new investments

ARCHYTAS VENTURES LLC

1880 Century Park East
Suite 300
Los Angeles, CA USA 90067
Phone: 4243341199
E-mail: info@archytasventures.com
Website: archytasventures.com

Type of Firm
Private Equity Firm

Project Preferences

Type of Financing Preferred:
Leveraged Buyout
Acquisition

Industry Preferences

In Medical/Health prefer:
Medical Therapeutics

Additional Information
Year Founded: 2017
Current Activity Level : Actively seeking new investments

ARCIS FINANCE SA

30 rue Galilee
Paris, France 75116
Phone: 33147238862
Fax: 33147238855
E-mail: mail@arcisgroup.com
Website: www.arcisgroup.com

Other Offices
509, Madison Avenue
New York, NY USA
Phone: 12128380136

170-173, Picadilly
London, United Kingdom
Phone: 442074942110

Management and Staff
Anne Rousseau, Chief Financial Officer
Arnaud Isnard, Co-Founder
Henri Isnard, Co-Founder
Mark Burch, Managing Partner
Pierre Nollet, Partner

Type of Firm
Private Equity Advisor or Fund of Funds

Association Membership
British Venture Capital Association (BVCA)
French Venture Capital Association (AFIC)
European Private Equity and Venture Capital Assoc.

Project Preferences

Type of Financing Preferred:
Fund of Funds
Fund of Funds of Second
Recapitalizations

Geographical Preferences

United States Preferences:
All U.S.

International Preferences:
Asia Pacific
Europe
Switzerland
Western Europe
Asia
Norway
France

Additional Information
Year Founded: 1993
Capital Under Management: $500,000,000
Current Activity Level : Actively seeking new investments

ARCLIGHT CAPITAL HOLDINGS LLC

200 Clarendon Street
55th Floor
Boston, MA USA 02116
Phone: 6175316300
Fax: 6178674698
E-mail: info@arclightcapital.com
Website: www.arclightcapital.com

Other Offices
152 West 57th Street
53rd Floor
New York, NY USA 10019
Phone: 212-901-1500
Fax: 212-888-9275

Eight Boulevard Royal
, Luxembourg L 2449

08960 Sant Just Desvern
Frederic Mompou 5, 3rd Floor
Barcelona, Spain
Phone: 34-93-480-3131

Management and Staff
Andrew Kapp, Vice President
Andy Gupta, Vice President
Carter Ward, Managing Director
Christopher Picotte, Managing Director
Daniel Revers, Managing Partner
Eric Lammers, Managing Director
Heidi Milne, Principal
James Steggall, Principal
John Erhard, Managing Director
Kevin Crosby, Managing Director
Laurence Molke, Managing Director
Lucius Taylor, Principal
Mark Bisso, Principal
Mark Tarini, Managing Director
Matthew Runkle, Principal
Matthew LeBlanc, Principal
Michael Christopher, Principal
Michael Chechelnitsky, Principal
Patricia Winton, Managing Director
Philip Messina, Principal
Robert McGaughey, Managing Director
Robert Howard, Vice President
Robert Trevisani, Chief Financial Officer

Ross Murphy, Vice President
Thomas Teich, Vice President
Timothy Evans, Principal
Winston Eaton, Vice President

Type of Firm
Private Equity Firm

Association Membership
Private Equity Council (PEC)

Project Preferences

Type of Financing Preferred:
Early Stage
Other

Geographical Preferences

United States Preferences:
North America

Industry Preferences

In Industrial/Energy prefer:
Energy
Oil and Gas Exploration
Oil & Gas Drilling,Explor
Alternative Energy

In Business Serv. prefer:
Distribution

Additional Information
Name of Most Recent Fund: ArcLight Energy Partners Fund V, L.P.
Most Recent Fund Was Raised: 10/14/2010
Year Founded: 2001
Capital Under Management: $4,685,000,000
Current Activity Level : Actively seeking new investments

ARCTERN VENTURES

101 College Street
Suite 420
Toronto, Canada M5G 1L7
Website: www.arcternventures.com

Management and Staff
Murray McCaig, Managing Partner
Tom Rand, Managing Partner

Type of Firm
Private Equity Firm

Project Preferences

Type of Financing Preferred:
Early Stage

Geographical Preferences

United States Preferences:

Canadian Preferences:
All Canada

Industry Preferences

In Computer Software prefer:
Artificial Intelligence

In Consumer Related prefer:
Food/Beverage

In Industrial/Energy prefer:
Advanced Materials
Environmental Related

Additional Information

Name of Most Recent Fund: ArcTern Ventures
Most Recent Fund Was Raised: 03/26/2012
Year Founded: 2012
Capital Under Management: $29,110,000
Current Activity Level : Actively seeking new investments

ARCTIC CAPITAL LLC

227 Walker Avenue North
Wayzata, MN USA 55391
Phone: 6123862948
Website: www.arcticcapital.com

Type of Firm
Private Equity Firm

Project Preferences

Type of Financing Preferred:
Leveraged Buyout
Recapitalizations

Additional Information
Year Founded: 2007
Capital Under Management: $1,100,000
Current Activity Level : Actively seeking new investments

ARCUS CAPITAL AG

Theatinerstrasse 7
Munich, Germany 80333
Phone: 498920061610
Fax: 498920061612
E-mail: info@arcus-muc.de
Website: www.arcus-muc.de

Type of Firm
Private Equity Firm

Project Preferences

Type of Financing Preferred:
Leveraged Buyout
Turnaround
Acquisition

Geographical Preferences

International Preferences:
Germany

Industry Preferences

In Industrial/Energy prefer:
Machinery
Environmental Related

Additional Information
Year Founded: 1994
Current Activity Level : Actively seeking new investments

ARCUS VENTURES

60 East 42nd Street
Ste 1610, 1 Grand Central Pl
New York, NY USA 10165
Phone: 2127852236
Fax: 2127852237
Website: www.arcusventures.com

Other Offices
Former HQ: 55 Broad Street
Suite 1840
New York, NY USA 10004

Management and Staff
James Dougherty, General Partner
Steven Soignet, General Partner

Type of Firm
Private Equity Firm

Project Preferences

Type of Financing Preferred:
Early Stage
Expansion
Balanced
Later Stage

Industry Preferences

In Biotechnology prefer:
Biotechnology

In Medical/Health prefer:
Medical Diagnostics
Diagnostic Services
Diagnostic Test Products
Medical Therapeutics
Drug/Equipmt Delivery
Medical Products
Health Services
Pharmaceuticals

Additional Information
Name of Most Recent Fund: Arcus Ventures Fund II, L.P.
Most Recent Fund Was Raised: 03/06/2013
Year Founded: 2007
Capital Under Management: $35,628,000
Current Activity Level : Actively seeking new investments

ARDENS & ASSOCIES SAS

28, Rue Boissy d'Anglas
Paris, France 75008
Phone: 33147424426
Fax: 33147424423
E-mail: ardens@ardens.fr
Website: www.ardens.fr

Management and Staff
Bernard Gervais, Managing Partner
Frederic Ruppli, Managing Partner
Louis Renaudin, Managing Partner

Type of Firm
Private Equity Firm

Association Membership
French Venture Capital Association (AFIC)

Project Preferences

Type of Financing Preferred:
Leveraged Buyout
Management Buyouts
Acquisition

Size of Investments Considered:
Min Size of Investment Considered (000s): $6,841
Max Size of Investment Considered (000s): $41,045

Geographical Preferences

International Preferences:
Europe
France

Additional Information
Year Founded: 2003
Current Activity Level : Actively seeking new investments

ARDENT CAPITAL LTD

Rama IV Road, Silom
4/F, 946 Dusit Thani Building
Bangkok, Thailand 10500
Phone: 6626363133
Fax: 6626363138
Website: www.ardentcapital.com

Management and Staff
John Srivorakul, Partner
Piers Bennett, Partner
Tom Srivorakul, Partner

Type of Firm
Private Equity Firm

Project Preferences

Type of Financing Preferred:
Early Stage

Geographical Preferences

United States Preferences:
Southeast

International Preferences:
Asia

Industry Preferences

In Internet Specific prefer:
Internet
Ecommerce

Additional Information
Year Founded: 2012
Current Activity Level : Actively seeking new investments

ARDENTON CAPITAL CORP

1021 West Hastings Street
9th floor
Vancouver, Canada V6E 0C3
Phone: 16045585206
Website: ardenton.com

Management and Staff
James Livingstone, Chief Executive Officer
Michael Walsh, Vice President
Thomas Green, Vice President

Type of Firm
Private Equity Firm

Additional Information
Year Founded: 2016
Current Activity Level : Actively seeking new investments

ARDIAN FRANCE SA

20 Place Vendome
Paris, France 75001
Phone: 33141719200
Fax: 33141719300
E-mail: cil-ardian@ardian-investment.com
Website: www.ardian.com

Other Offices

Via Priavata Fratelli Gabba n 1/A
Milan, Italy 20122
Phone: 39-02-5844-2401
Fax: 39-02-5844-2450

55 Grosvenor Street
London, United Kingdom W1K 3HY
Phone: 44-20-7003-1350
Fax: 44-20-7575-8309

Wipplingerstrasse 35
Vienna, Austria A-1010
Phone: 43-1-537-537-00
Fax: 43-1-537-537-07

1 Temasek Avenue
Unit 20-02A Millenia Tower
Singapore, Singapore 039192
Phone: 65-6513-3410
Fax: 65-6513-3426

Affolternstrasse 42
P.O. Box 6961
Zurich, Switzerland CH-8050
Phone: 41-43-299-1199
Fax: 41-43-299-1120

24 avenue Emile Reuter
Luxembourg, Luxembourg 2420
Phone: 352274448201
Fax: 352274448222

An der Welle 4
Frankfurt, Germany D-60322
Phone: 49-69-5050-41500
Fax: 49-69-5050-41550

No.1 Jian Guo Men Wai Avenue
Unit 20-22, Level 47
Beijing, China 100004
Phone: 861065809000
Fax: 861085351848

1370 Avenue of the Americas
NEW YORK, NY USA 10019
Phone: 212-641-8604
Fax: 212-641-8616

Management and Staff
Alexandre Motte, Managing Director
Amir Sharifi, President
Baudouin D Herouville, Managing Director
Bernd Haggenmuller, Managing Director
Cecile Levi, Managing Director
Dominique Senequier, President, Founder
Juan Angoitia, Managing Director
Laurent Foata, Managing Director
Philippe Poletti, Senior Managing Director
Rodolfo Petrosino, Managing Director
Stephanie Bensimon, Managing Director

Type of Firm
Private Equity Firm

Association Membership
French Venture Capital Association (AFIC)
Swiss Venture Capital Association (SECA)
German Venture Capital Association (BVK)
European Private Equity and Venture Capital Assoc.
Singapore Venture Capital Association (SVCA)

Project Preferences

Type of Financing Preferred:
Fund of Funds
Leveraged Buyout
Early Stage
Expansion
Mezzanine
Generalist PE
Balanced

Start-up Financing
Turnaround
Other
Seed
Management Buyouts
Acquisition
Startup
Fund of Funds of Second
Recapitalizations

Size of Investments Considered:
Min Size of Investment Considered (000s): $900
Max Size of Investment Considered (000s): $13,437

Geographical Preferences

United States Preferences:
All U.S.

International Preferences:
Italy
India
Europe
Western Europe
China
Australia
Asia
Korea, South
Germany
Japan
All International
France

Industry Preferences

In Communications prefer:
Communications and Media
Telecommunications

In Computer Hardware prefer:
Computers

In Computer Software prefer:
Software

In Semiconductor/Electr prefer:
Electronics
Semiconductor

In Biotechnology prefer:
Biotechnology

In Medical/Health prefer:
Health Services
Pharmaceuticals

In Industrial/Energy prefer:
Energy
Oil and Gas Exploration
Alternative Energy

In Financial Services prefer:
Financial Services
Insurance

In Business Serv. prefer:
Services

Additional Information

Year Founded: 1996
Capital Under Management: $49,270,100,000
Current Activity Level : Actively seeking new investments

ARENA VENTURES GP LLC

1720 Abbot Kinney Boulevard
21st Floor
Venice, CA USA 90291
Phone: 6463394666
Website: www.arenavc.com

Type of Firm

Private Equity Firm

Project Preferences

Size of Investments Considered:
Min Size of Investment Considered (000s): $500
Max Size of Investment Considered (000s): $100,000

Geographical Preferences

United States Preferences:
California

Industry Preferences

In Internet Specific prefer:
Internet

In Consumer Related prefer:
Consumer
Education Related

Additional Information

Year Founded: 2015
Capital Under Management: $27,125,000
Current Activity Level : Actively seeking new investments

ARENAL CAPITAL MANAGEMENT

277 Park Avenue
Suite 410
New York, NY USA 10172
Phone: 9179229848
Fax: 9175918130
E-mail: info@ArenalCM.com
Website: www.arenalcm.com

Type of Firm

Private Equity Firm

Project Preferences

Type of Financing Preferred:
Leveraged Buyout
Recapitalizations

Additional Information

Name of Most Recent Fund: Arenal Capital Fund, L.P.
Most Recent Fund Was Raised: 11/18/2011

Year Founded: 2011
Capital Under Management: $18,050,000
Current Activity Level : Actively seeking new investments

ARES CAPITAL CORP

245 Park Avenue
44th Floor
New York, NY USA 10167
Phone: 2127102100
E-mail: IRARCC@aresmgmt.com
Website: www.arescapitalcorp.com

Other Offices

One North Wacker Drive
48th Floor
Chicago, IL USA 60606
Phone: 3122527500
Fax: 3122527501

3340 Peachtree Road, North East
Suite 1800
Atlanta, GA USA 30326
Phone: 4048145204
Fax: 4048145299

2000 Avenue of the Stars
12th Floor
Los Angeles, CA USA 90067
Phone: 3102014200

220 Pennsylvania Avenue, North West
Suite 600-W
Washington, DC USA 20037
Phone: 2027216100

200 Crescent Court
Suite 1425
Dallas, TX USA 75201
Phone: 2143020100
Fax: 2147544700

Management and Staff

Daniel Nguyen, Vice President
Joshua Bloomstein, Vice President
Michael McFerran, Vice President
Michael Weiner, Vice President
Penelope Roll, Chief Financial Officer

Type of Firm

Private Equity Firm

Project Preferences

Type of Financing Preferred:
Leveraged Buyout
Early Stage
Expansion
Later Stage
Acquisition
Recapitalizations

Size of Investments Considered:
Min Size of Investment Considered (000s): $1,000
Max Size of Investment Considered (000s): $25,000

Geographical Preferences

United States Preferences:
Mid Atlantic
Midwest
Southeast
Northeast
West Coast
Southwest
New York

Canadian Preferences:
All Canada

Industry Preferences

In Communications prefer:
Telecommunications

In Semiconductor/Electr prefer:
Electronics
Semiconductor

In Medical/Health prefer:
Health Services

In Consumer Related prefer:
Retail
Food/Beverage
Consumer Services
Other Restaurants
Education Related

In Industrial/Energy prefer:
Energy
Oil and Gas Exploration
Alternative Energy
Energy Conservation Relat

In Business Serv. prefer:
Distribution

In Manufact. prefer:
Manufacturing

Additional Information

Year Founded: 1997
Current Activity Level : Actively seeking new investments

ARES MANAGEMENT LLC

2000 Avenue of the Stars
12th Floor
Los Angeles, CA USA 90067
Phone: 3102014100
Fax: 3102014170

Other Offices

1601 West Nan Jing Road
Unit 3701, Park Place Office Building
Shanghai, China 200040

19-29 Martin Place
Level 56, MLC Centre
Sydney, Australia 2000

13760 Noel Road
Suite 1100
Dallas, TX USA 75240
Phone: 2143020100
Fax: 2148660115

2200 Pennsylvania Avenue, Northwest
Suite 600-W
Washington, DC USA 20037
Phone: 2027216100

Taunusanlage 18
Frankfurt, Germany 60325
Phone: 4969970863400
Fax: 4969970863490

895 Dove Street
Suite 351
Newport Beach, CA USA 92660
Phone: 949-581-4625

41 Connaught Road
Level 15, Nexxus Building
Central, Hong Kong

65, boulevard Grande-Duchesse Charlotte
L-1331, R.C.S. Luxembourg B
, Luxembourg 35825

30 St. Mary Axe
Level 30
London, United Kingdom EC3A 8EP
Phone: 442071534600
Fax: 442071534601

3340 Peachtree Street
Suite 1800
Atlanta, GA USA 30326
Phone: 4048145204
Fax: 4048148299

227 West Monroe Street
Suite 3920
Chicago, IL USA 60606
Phone: 3122373100
Fax: 3122373150

Strandvagen 7A
4th Floor
Stockholm, Sweden 114 56
Phone: 4684503969

245 Park Avenue
44th Floor
New York, NY USA 10167
Phone: 212-750-7300
Fax: 212-750-1777

25 rue Balzac
Paris, France F-75008
Phone: 33170394150

Two North LaSalle Stree
Suite 925
Chicago, IL USA 60602
Phone: 312-324-5900

Management and Staff
Alex Dashiell, Principal

Type of Firm
Investment Management Firm

Project Preferences

Type of Financing Preferred:
Leveraged Buyout
Mezzanine
Turnaround
Management Buyouts
Special Situation
Distressed Debt
Recapitalizations

Geographical Preferences

United States Preferences:
North America

International Preferences:
Western Europe

Additional Information
Name of Most Recent Fund: Ares US Real Estate Fund VIII, L.P.
Most Recent Fund Was Raised: 09/27/2013
Year Founded: 1997
Capital Under Management: $6,000,000,000
Current Activity Level : Actively seeking new investments

ARETE CORP

P.O. Box 1299
Center Harbor, NH USA 03226
Phone: 6032539797
Fax: 6032539799
E-mail: aretecorp@roadrunner.com
Website: www.arete-microgen.com

Management and Staff
Robert Shaw, President

Type of Firm
Private Equity Firm

Association Membership
National Venture Capital Association - USA (NVCA)

Project Preferences

Role in Financing:
Prefer role as deal originator but will also invest in deals created by others

Type of Financing Preferred:
Early Stage
Balanced

Industry Preferences

In Industrial/Energy prefer:
Energy
Alternative Energy
Environmental Related

In Utilities prefer:
Utilities

Additional Information
Name of Most Recent Fund: Micro-Generation Technology Fund
Most Recent Fund Was Raised: 09/15/1997
Year Founded: 1983
Capital Under Management: $5,000,000
Current Activity Level : Actively seeking new investments

ARGAN CAPITAL

15-17 Grosvenor Gardens
London, United Kingdom SW1W 0BD
Phone: 442076476970
Fax: 442076476999
Website: www.argancapital.com

Other Offices

Al Szucha 13/15
Lokal Nr. 6
Warsaw, Poland 02-670
Phone: 48-226-271-272
Fax: 48-226-271-274

Via degli Omenoni 2
Third Floor
Milan, Italy 20121
Phone: 39-2-720-2571
Fax: 39-2-7202-5780

Management and Staff
Carlo Mammola, Managing Director
Giovanni Revoltella, Partner
Jeremy Paul, Partner
Lloyd Perry, Managing Partner
Wojciech Goc, Managing Partner

Type of Firm
Private Equity Firm

Project Preferences

Type of Financing Preferred:
Leveraged Buyout
Generalist PE
Balanced
Acquisition

Geographical Preferences

International Preferences:
Italy
Central Europe
Europe
Western Europe
Scandanavia/Nordic Region
France

Industry Preferences

In Consumer Related prefer:
Consumer

In Industrial/Energy prefer:
Industrial Products

In Business Serv. prefer:
Services

Additional Information

Year Founded: 1996
Current Activity Level : Actively seeking new investments

ARGAND PARTNERS LLC

1120 Avenue of the Americas
4th floor
New York, NY USA 10036
Phone: 2125886470
E-mail: inquiry@argandequity.com
Website: www.argandequity.com

Type of Firm

Private Equity Firm

Project Preferences

Type of Financing Preferred:
Leveraged Buyout
Management Buyouts

Geographical Preferences

United States Preferences:
North America

Additional Information

Year Founded: 2015
Capital Under Management: $206,000,000
Current Activity Level : Actively seeking new investments

ARGENTA PARTNERS, L.P.

1845 Woodall Rodgers Frwy
Suite 1600, LB-16
Dallas, TX USA 75201
Phone: 2148712400
Fax: 2148710075
Website: www.argentalp.com

Management and Staff

Harry Lynch, Founder
John Benefield, Partner
Michael Prentiss, Vice President
Peter Lynch, Vice President

Type of Firm

Private Equity Firm

Project Preferences

Type of Financing Preferred:
Leveraged Buyout
Acquisition
Recapitalizations

Additional Information

Year Founded: 1969
Current Activity Level : Actively seeking new investments

ARGENTUM GROUP LLC

60 Madison Avenue
Suite 701
New York, NY USA 10010
Phone: 2129496262
Fax: 2129498294
Website: www.argentumgroup.com

Management and Staff

Chris Leong, Principal
Daniel Raynor, Co-Founder
Daniel Tessler, Partner
James Hale, Partner
Walter Barandiaran, Co-Founder

Type of Firm

Private Equity Firm

Association Membership

Natl Assoc of Small Bus. Inv. Co (NASBIC)

Project Preferences

Role in Financing:
Prefer role as deal originator but will also invest in deals created by others

Type of Financing Preferred:
Leveraged Buyout
Expansion
Generalist PE
Turnaround
Later Stage
Acquisition

Geographical Preferences

United States Preferences:

Industry Focus

(% based on actual investment)
Computer Software and Services	26.9%
Other Products	25.9%
Computer Hardware	14.3%
Internet Specific	11.2%
Industrial/Energy	8.5%
Medical/Health	8.3%
Communications and Media	3.6%
Semiconductors/Other Elect.	1.2%

Additional Information

Name of Most Recent Fund: Argentum Capital Partners III, L.P.
Most Recent Fund Was Raised: 12/11/2013
Year Founded: 1988
Capital Under Management: $250,000,000
Current Activity Level : Actively seeking new investments
Method of Compensation: Return on invest. most important, but chg. closing fees, service fees, etc.

ARGIL VENTURE CAPITAL PTY LTD

Wanderers Office Park
52 Corlett Drive
Illovo, South Africa 2128
Phone: 27-11-783-7219
Fax: 27-11-783-7355

Type of Firm

Private Equity Firm

Project Preferences

Type of Financing Preferred:
Second Stage Financing
Expansion

Geographical Preferences

International Preferences:
Africa

Additional Information

Year Founded: 2000
Capital Under Management: $6,200,000
Current Activity Level : Actively seeking new investments

ARGON VENTURE PARTNERS

303 Twin Dolphin Drive
Sixth Floor
Redwood City, CA USA 94065
E-mail: info@argoncap.com
Website: www.argoncap.com

Other Offices

3553 31 Street NorthWest
Calgary, Canada T2L2K7

Management and Staff

Jason Bross, General Partner
Juan-Antonio Carballo, General Partner
Randy Thompson, General Partner

Type of Firm

Private Equity Firm

Project Preferences

Type of Financing Preferred:
Early Stage
Seed
Startup

Geographical Preferences

United States Preferences:
North America

Canadian Preferences:
All Canada

Additional Information
Year Founded: 2007
Current Activity Level : Actively seeking new investments

ARGONAUT PARTNERS LLC

390 Commonwealth Avenue
Suite 610
Boston, MA USA 02215
Phone: 5085842224
Fax: 5085599046
Website: www.argollc.com

Type of Firm
Private Equity Firm

Project Preferences

Type of Financing Preferred:
Leveraged Buyout
Turnaround
Management Buyouts
Acquisition

Geographical Preferences

United States Preferences:

Industry Preferences

In Consumer Related prefer:
Publishing-Retail

Additional Information
Year Founded: 1998
Current Activity Level : Actively seeking new investments

ARGONAUT PRIVATE EQUITY LLC

6733 South Yale
Tulsa, OK USA 74136
Phone: 9184914538

Management and Staff
Anil Khatod, Managing Director
Gagan Kapur, Vice President
Jason Martin, Managing Director
Steven Mitchell, Managing Director

Type of Firm
Private Equity Firm

Project Preferences

Type of Financing Preferred:
Leveraged Buyout
Generalist PE
Balanced

Size of Investments Considered:
Min Size of Investment Considered (000s): $1,000
Max Size of Investment Considered (000s): $200,000

Geographical Preferences

United States Preferences:
All U.S.

Industry Preferences

In Communications prefer:
Telecommunications

In Semiconductor/Electr prefer:
Electronics

In Biotechnology prefer:
Biotech Related Research

In Medical/Health prefer:
Drug/Equipmt Delivery
Medical Products
Health Services
Pharmaceuticals

In Industrial/Energy prefer:
Advanced Materials

In Transportation prefer:
Aerospace

In Financial Services prefer:
Financial Services

In Manufact. prefer:
Manufacturing

Additional Information
Year Founded: 2002
Current Activity Level : Actively seeking new investments

ARGONAUTIC VENTURES SPC

Willow House
Cricket Square
Grand Cayman, Cayman Islands KY1-1103
E-mail: info@argonauticventures.com
Website: argonauticventures.com

Type of Firm
Private Equity Firm

Project Preferences

Type of Financing Preferred:
Early Stage
Seed

Industry Preferences

In Computer Software prefer:
Applications Software

In Internet Specific prefer:
E-Commerce Technology
Internet
Ecommerce

Additional Information
Year Founded: 2017
Current Activity Level : Actively seeking new investments

ARGONNE CAPITAL GROUP LLC

One Buckhead Plaza
Suite 400
Atlanta, GA USA 30305
Phone: 4043642984
Fax: 4043642985
Website: argonnecapital.com

Management and Staff
Karl Jaeger, Managing Director
Michael Klump, President, Founder

Type of Firm
Private Equity Firm

Project Preferences

Type of Financing Preferred:
Leveraged Buyout
Acquisition

Industry Preferences

In Medical/Health prefer:
Medical/Health

In Consumer Related prefer:
Retail

In Industrial/Energy prefer:
Energy

In Financial Services prefer:
Real Estate

In Business Serv. prefer:
Distribution

In Manufact. prefer:
Manufacturing

Additional Information
Year Founded: 2003
Current Activity Level : Actively seeking new investments

ARGOS SODITIC SA

Rue de Rhone 118
Geneva, Switzerland 1204
Phone: 41228496633
Fax: 41228496627
E-mail: contact@argos-soditic.com
Website: www.argos-soditic.com

Management and Staff
Cedric Bruix, Partner
Gilles Lorang, Partner
Gilles Mougenot, Partner
Guy Semmens, Partner
Jean-Pierre di Benedetto, Partner
Karel Kroupa, Partner
Louis Godron, Partner
Mirco Dilda, Partner

Type of Firm
Private Equity Firm

Association Membership
Italian Venture Capital Association (AIFI)
Swiss Venture Capital Association (SECA)
French Venture Capital Association (AFIC)
Belgium Venturing Association
European Private Equity and Venture Capital Assoc.

Project Preferences

Role in Financing:
Prefer role as deal originator but will also invest in deals created by others

Type of Financing Preferred:
Leveraged Buyout
Mezzanine
Turnaround
Management Buyouts
Special Situation
Recapitalizations

Geographical Preferences

International Preferences:
Italy
Europe
Switzerland
France

Industry Focus
(% based on actual investment)

Other Products	36.2%
Consumer Related	27.9%
Industrial/Energy	20.3%
Medical/Health	7.1%
Computer Software and Services	4.1%
Internet Specific	2.9%
Communications and Media	1.0%
Semiconductors/Other Elect.	0.6%

Additional Information
Name of Most Recent Fund: Euroknights VI
Most Recent Fund Was Raised: 12/22/2010
Year Founded: 1989
Capital Under Management: $1,156,400,000
Current Activity Level : Actively seeking new investments
Method of Compensation: Return on invest. most important, but chg. closing fees, service fees, etc.

ARGOSY CAPITAL GROUP INC

950 West Valley Road
Suite 2900
Wayne, PA USA 19087
Phone: 6109719685
Fax: 6109649524
Website: www.argosycapital.com

Management and Staff
Gerald Mahoney, Partner
John Nevin, Partner
John Nugent, Principal
John Paul Kirwin, Co-Founder
Keven Shanahan, Principal
Kirk Griswold, Co-Founder
Melanie Lyren, Vice President
Michael Bailey, Partner
Richard Schwenk, Chief Financial Officer
Sarah Busch, Vice President

Type of Firm
Private Equity Firm

Association Membership
Natl Assoc of Small Bus. Inv. Co (NASBIC)

Project Preferences

Role in Financing:
Will function either as deal originator or investor in deals created by others

Type of Financing Preferred:
Leveraged Buyout
Mezzanine
Generalist PE
Opportunistic
Later Stage
Management Buyouts
Acquisition
Recapitalizations

Geographical Preferences

United States Preferences:

Industry Preferences

In Financial Services prefer:
Real Estate

In Business Serv. prefer:
Services
Distribution

Additional Information
Name of Most Recent Fund: Argosy Real Estate Partners III, L.P.
Most Recent Fund Was Raised: 04/18/2013
Year Founded: 1990
Capital Under Management: $500,000,000
Current Activity Level : Actively seeking new investments
Method of Compensation: Return on investment is of primary concern, do not charge fees

ARGOSY PARTNERS, INC.

8/F, Pacific Star Building
Makati Avenue
Makati City, Philippines
Phone: 63-2-811-5551
Fax: 63-2-886-0145

Management and Staff
Aloysius Colayco, Founder
Eduardo Cuyegkeng, Managing Director
Gloria Tan Climaco, Founder
Rufo Colayco, Founder

Type of Firm
Private Equity Firm

Project Preferences

Type of Financing Preferred:
Leveraged Buyout
Expansion
Mezzanine

Size of Investments Considered:
Min Size of Investment Considered (000s): $10,000
Max Size of Investment Considered (000s): $100,000

Geographical Preferences

International Preferences:
Philippines

Additional Information
Year Founded: 1998
Capital Under Management: $175,000,000
Current Activity Level : Actively seeking new investments

ARGUS CAPITAL LTD

26-28 Hammersmith Grove
London, United Kingdom W6 7BA
Phone: 442071824620
Fax: 442071824150
Website: www.arguscapitalgroup.com

Other Offices
Nagy Jeno utca 12
Hu-1126
Budapest, Hungary 1118
Phone: 361-309-00-90
Fax: 361-391-00-91

Krakovska 9
Prague, Czech Republic 110 00
Phone: 420-296-370-270
Fax: 420-296-370-271

Str. Facliei, nr. 6.,
Sfntu Gheorghe, Romania 520060
Phone: 40367802555

Management and Staff
Ali Artunkal, Managing Director
Mallindi Baldassarro, Chief Financial Officer

Type of Firm
Private Equity Firm

Association Membership
Czech Venture Capital Association (CVCA)

Project Preferences

Type of Financing Preferred:
Leveraged Buyout
Expansion
Generalist PE
Turnaround
Later Stage
Management Buyouts
Acquisition
Industry Rollups
Recapitalizations

Size of Investments Considered:
Min Size of Investment Considered (000s): $12,637
Max Size of Investment Considered (000s): $50,550

Geographical Preferences

International Preferences:
Central Europe
Europe
Eastern Europe

Additional Information
Name of Most Recent Fund: Argus Capital Partners Fund II
Most Recent Fund Was Raised: 12/31/2005
Year Founded: 1998
Capital Under Management: $569,100,000
Current Activity Level : Actively seeking new investments

ARGY VENTURE CAPITAL SRL

Via dei Pellegrini, 14
Milan, Italy 20122
Phone: 39-2-5843-0900
Fax: 39-2-5843-0489
E-mail: info@argy.it
Website: www.argyventurecapital.it

Type of Firm
Private Equity Firm

Association Membership
Italian Venture Capital Association (AIFI)

Project Preferences

Type of Financing Preferred:
Early Stage
Balanced
Later Stage

Geographical Preferences

International Preferences:
Europe

Additional Information
Year Founded: 1999
Current Activity Level : Actively seeking new investments

ARIADNE CAPITAL LTD

17-19 Cockspur Street
London, United Kingdom SW1Y 5BL
Phone: 442033569690
Fax: 442033569690
E-mail: info@ariadnecapital.com
Website: www.ariadnecapital.com

Management and Staff
David Scholtz, Principal

Type of Firm
Private Equity Firm

Project Preferences

Role in Financing:
Will function either as deal originator or investor in deals created by others

Type of Financing Preferred:
Later Stage

Size of Investments Considered:
Min Size of Investment Considered (000s): $235
Max Size of Investment Considered (000s): $1,563

Industry Preferences

In Communications prefer:
Wireless Communications
Satellite Microwave Comm.

In Internet Specific prefer:
Internet

In Medical/Health prefer:
Medical/Health

In Consumer Related prefer:
Consumer
Retail

In Transportation prefer:
Transportation

In Financial Services prefer:
Financial Services

Additional Information
Year Founded: 2000
Capital Under Management: $1,400,000
Current Activity Level : Actively seeking new investments
Method of Compensation: Return on invest. most important, but chg. closing fees, service fees, etc.

ARIAS RESOURCE CAPITAL MANAGEMENT LP

14 Wall Street
Third Floor
New York, NY USA 10005
Phone: 2122668600
Fax: 2122668615
E-mail: info@arc-fund.com
Website: www.arc-fund.com

Type of Firm
Private Equity Firm

Project Preferences

Type of Financing Preferred:
Expansion
Management Buyouts
Special Situation

Geographical Preferences

International Preferences:
Latin America

Industry Preferences

In Agr/Forestr/Fish prefer:
Mining and Minerals

Additional Information
Name of Most Recent Fund: Arias Resource Capital Fund II, L.P.
Most Recent Fund Was Raised: 11/14/2011
Year Founded: 2007
Capital Under Management: $69,120,000
Current Activity Level : Actively seeking new investments

ARIE CAPITAL LTD

115 Eastbourne Mews
London, United Kingdom W2 6LQ
Phone: 02070873570
E-mail: info@ariecapital.com
Website: www.ariecapital.com

Management and Staff
Donglai Lou, Vice President
Simon Tobelem, Chief Executive Officer

Type of Firm
Private Equity Firm

Project Preferences

Type of Financing Preferred:
Later Stage
Startup

Geographical Preferences

International Preferences:
Europe
Israel

Additional Information
Year Founded: 2015
Current Activity Level : Actively seeking new investments

ARIES CAPITAL PARTNERS LLC

6510 South Millrock Dr
Suite 425
Salt Lake City, UT USA 84121
Phone: 8014531000
Fax: 8014531020
Website: ariescapitalpartners.com

Management and Staff
Andrew Dent, Partner
Jason Reading, Partner

Type of Firm
Private Equity Firm

Project Preferences

Type of Financing Preferred:
Generalist PE

Additional Information
Year Founded: 2016
Current Activity Level : Actively seeking new investments

ARISTOS VENTURES

8226 Douglas Ave
Ste 355
Dallas, TX USA 75225
Phone: 2143069554
Website: www.aristosventures.com

Management and Staff
Felipe Mendoza, Managing Director

Type of Firm
Private Equity Firm

Project Preferences

Role in Financing:
Prefer role as deal originator but will also invest in deals created by others

Type of Financing Preferred:
Early Stage
Seed

Size of Investments Considered:
Min Size of Investment Considered (000s): $750
Max Size of Investment Considered (000s): $1,000

Geographical Preferences

United States Preferences:
Texas

Industry Preferences

In Communications prefer:
Wireless Communications

In Computer Software prefer:
Software
Applications Software

In Internet Specific prefer:
Web Aggregation/Portals

Additional Information
Name of Most Recent Fund: Aristos Ventures I, L.P.
Most Recent Fund Was Raised: 07/12/2013
Year Founded: 2013
Capital Under Management: $9,000,000
Current Activity Level : Actively seeking new investments

ARIX BIOSCIENCE PLC

20 Berkeley Square
London, United Kingdom W1J 6EQ
Phone: 442072901050
E-mail: info@arixbioscience.com
Website: arixbioscience.com

Management and Staff
James Rawlingson, Chief Financial Officer
Joseph Anderson, Chief Executive Officer

Type of Firm
Private Equity Firm

Project Preferences

Type of Financing Preferred:
Generalist PE

Additional Information
Year Founded: 2015
Current Activity Level : Actively seeking new investments

ARIYA CAPITAL GROUP LTD

4 Park Place
London, United Kingdom SW1A 1LP
Phone: 44-203-170-8065
Fax: 44-207-898-9101
E-mail: info@ariyacapital.com
Website: www.ariyacapital.com

Other Offices
The Square, Plot 54381
First Floor, Wing A
Gaborone, Botswana
Phone: 267-397-5846
Fax: 267-391-2582

Green Street
Channel House
Jersey, Channel Islands JE2 4UH
Phone: 44-153-4834600

Type of Firm
Private Equity Firm

Project Preferences

Type of Financing Preferred:
Early Stage
Balanced

Geographical Preferences

International Preferences:
Zambia
Botswana
Mozambique

Industry Preferences

In Communications prefer:
Telecommunications

In Industrial/Energy prefer:
Alternative Energy
Energy Conservation Relat

In Financial Services prefer:
Financial Services

Additional Information
Year Founded: 2009
Current Activity Level : Actively seeking new investments

ARIZONA FOUNDERS FUND LLC

2398 East Camelback Road
Suite 1020
Phoenix, AZ USA 85016
E-mail: founders@azff.co
Website: www.azff.co

Management and Staff
Romi Dhillon, Founder

Type of Firm
Private Equity Firm

Project Preferences

Type of Financing Preferred:
Early Stage
Seed

Size of Investments Considered:
Min Size of Investment Considered (000s): $50
Max Size of Investment Considered (000s): $400

Geographical Preferences

United States Preferences:
Arizona

Additional Information
Year Founded: 2016
Capital Under Management: $750,000
Current Activity Level : Actively seeking new investments

ARK APPLICATIONS LLC

16204 N Florida Avenue
Lutz, FL USA 33549
Website: arkapps.com

Management and Staff
Daniel Greco, Partner
Justin Smith, Partner
R. Bob Smith, Partner

Type of Firm
Private Equity Firm

Project Preferences

Type of Financing Preferred:
Leveraged Buyout

Industry Preferences

In Medical/Health prefer:
Medical/Health

In Consumer Related prefer:
Consumer

In Business Serv. prefer:
Distribution

In Manufact. prefer:
Manufacturing

Additional Information
Year Founded: 2009
Current Activity Level : Actively seeking new investments

ARKEA CAPITAL INVES-TISSEMENT SA

1 rue Louis Lichou
Le Relecq-Kerhuon, France 29480
Phone: 33298003296
E-mail: capital-investissement.contacts@arkea.com

Other Offices
168, route de Saint-Joseph
Nantes, France 44000
Phone: 33240682214
Fax: 33240582270

Management and Staff
Marc Briere, Chief Executive Officer

Type of Firm
Bank Affiliated

Association Membership
French Venture Capital Association (AFIC)

Project Preferences

Type of Financing Preferred:
Leveraged Buyout
Mezzanine
Generalist PE
Later Stage
Acquisition

Size of Investments Considered:
Min Size of Investment Considered (000s): $654
Max Size of Investment Considered (000s): $13,083

Geographical Preferences

International Preferences:
Europe
France

Industry Preferences

In Communications prefer:
Communications and Media
Commercial Communications
Publishing

In Biotechnology prefer:
Agricultural/Animal Bio.

In Medical/Health prefer:
Medical/Health

In Consumer Related prefer:
Consumer

In Business Serv. prefer:
Services
Distribution

Additional Information
Year Founded: 1982
Capital Under Management: $205,600,000
Current Activity Level : Actively seeking new investments

ARKEA CAPITAL PARTE-NAIRE SAS

1, Rue Louis Lichou
Le Relecq Kerhuon, France 29480
Website: www.arkea-capital-investissement.com

Type of Firm
Bank Affiliated

Project Preferences

Type of Financing Preferred:
Later Stage

Geographical Preferences

International Preferences:
France

Additional Information
Year Founded: 2001
Current Activity Level : Actively seeking new investments

ARKEON GESTION SAS

27 Rue de Berri
Paris, France 75008
Phone: 330153705040
Website: www.arkeongestion.com

Type of Firm
Private Equity Firm

Project Preferences

Type of Financing Preferred:
Leveraged Buyout
Acquisition

Geographical Preferences

International Preferences:
Europe
Eastern Europe
All International
France

Industry Preferences

In Biotechnology prefer:
Biotechnology

In Medical/Health prefer:
Medical/Health

In Other prefer:
Environment Responsible

Additional Information
Year Founded: 2002
Current Activity Level : Actively seeking new investments

ARKIMEDES MANAGEMENT NV

Oude Graanmarkt 63
Brussel, Belgium 1000
Phone: 3222295250
Fax: 3222295251
E-mail: arkimedes@pmv.eu

Management and Staff
Thomas Fiers, Chief Executive Officer

Type of Firm
Private Equity Advisor or Fund of Funds

Association Membership
Belgium Venturing Association

Project Preferences

Type of Financing Preferred:
Fund of Funds

Geographical Preferences

International Preferences:
Europe
Belgium

Additional Information
Year Founded: 2004
Capital Under Management: $143,287,000
Current Activity Level : Actively seeking new investments

ARKLEY VENTURE CAPITAL SP Z O O

Kopernika 11/23
Warsaw, Poland 00-359
Website: www.arkley.vc

Type of Firm
Private Equity Firm

Project Preferences

Type of Financing Preferred:
Early Stage
Expansion
Later Stage
Seed
Startup

Size of Investments Considered:
Min Size of Investment Considered (000s): $26
Max Size of Investment Considered (000s): $258

Industry Preferences

In Communications prefer:
Wireless Communications

In Computer Software prefer:
Software

In Internet Specific prefer:
Internet
Ecommerce
Web Aggregation/Portals

Additional Information
Year Founded: 2015
Current Activity Level : Actively seeking new investments

ARLE HERITAGE LLP

12 Charles Two Street
London, United Kingdom SW1Y 4QU
Phone: 442079790000
Fax: 442079791001
E-mail: info@arle.com
Website: www.arle.com

Management and Staff
Anders Pettersson, Partner
Frederik Arp, Partner
Javier Abad, Partner
Johnathan Arney, Managing Partner
Mark Dickinson, Partner
Nils Stoesser, Partner
Peter Goode, Partner
Philip Price, Chief Operating Officer

Type of Firm
Private Equity Firm

Project Preferences

Type of Financing Preferred:
Leveraged Buyout
Acquisition

Geographical Preferences

International Preferences:
United Kingdom
Europe

Industry Preferences

In Industrial/Energy prefer:
Energy
Oil and Gas Exploration
Industrial Products

In Business Serv. prefer:
Services

Additional Information
Name of Most Recent Fund: Candover 2008 Fund
Most Recent Fund Was Raised: 08/31/2008
Year Founded: 1980
Capital Under Management: $8,539,100,000
Current Activity Level : Actively seeking new investments

ARLINGTON CAPITAL PARTNERS

5425 Wisconsin Avenue
Suite 200
Chevy Chase, MD USA 20815
Phone: 2023377500
Fax: 2023377525
E-mail: requestinfo@arlingtoncap.com
Website: www.arlingtoncap.com

Management and Staff
David Wodlinger, Principal
David Wodlinger, Vice President
Edward Weklar, Vice President
Jeffrey Freed, Co-Founder
Jesse Liu, Principal
Matthew Rich, Vice President
Matthew Altman, Partner
Matthew Buckley, Chief Financial Officer
Michael Lustbader, Partner
Perry Steiner, Managing Partner
Peter Manos, Managing Partner
Robert Knibb, Co-Founder

Type of Firm
Private Equity Firm

Project Preferences

Role in Financing:
Prefer role as deal originator but will also invest in deals created by others

Type of Financing Preferred:
Leveraged Buyout
Management Buyouts
Acquisition
Recapitalizations

Geographical Preferences

United States Preferences:

Industry Focus

(% based on actual investment)
Computer Software and Services	33.2%
Other Products	32.1%
Communications and Media	29.1%
Internet Specific	5.6%

Additional Information
Name of Most Recent Fund: Arlington Capital Partners II, L.P.
Most Recent Fund Was Raised: 09/30/2005
Year Founded: 1999
Capital Under Management: $1,000,000,000
Current Activity Level : Actively seeking new investments
Method of Compensation: Return on invest. most important, but chg. closing fees, service fees, etc.

ARLON GROUP LLC

277 Park Avenue
New York, NY USA 10172
Phone: 2122075200
E-mail: ArlonCapitalPartners@ArlonGroup.com
Website: www.arlongroup.com

Management and Staff
Alexander Bernstein, Vice President
Brian Anderson, Principal
Charles Conner, Vice President
David Tanner, Managing Director
Sergio Suchodolski, Vice President

Type of Firm
Investment Management Firm

Project Preferences

Size of Investments Considered:
Min Size of Investment Considered (000s): $20,000
Max Size of Investment Considered (000s): $40,000

Geographical Preferences

United States Preferences:
North America

International Preferences:
Latin America
Europe
China

Industry Preferences

In Communications prefer:
Communications and Media

In Consumer Related prefer:
Food/Beverage
Consumer Products

In Financial Services prefer:
Financial Services

Additional Information
Name of Most Recent Fund: Arlon Food & Agriculture Partners, L.P.
Most Recent Fund Was Raised: 03/01/2010
Year Founded: 2008
Capital Under Management: $854,000,000
Current Activity Level : Actively seeking new investments

ARM CAPITAL PARTNERS

One Mekunwen Road
Off Oyinkan Abayomi
Lagos, Nigeria 55765
Phone: 2342701653
Fax: 2342701097
E-mail: info@arm.com.ng
Website: www.arm.com.ng

Management and Staff
Chioma Okigbo, Managing Director
Deji Alli, Chief Executive Officer
Deji Omotoso, Chief Financial Officer
Jumoke Ogundare, Chief Executive Officer
Sadiq Mohammed, Chief Executive Officer
Wale Odutola, Managing Director

Type of Firm
Private Equity Firm

Project Preferences

Type of Financing Preferred:
Leveraged Buyout
Expansion
Mezzanine
Generalist PE
Balanced
Management Buyouts

Geographical Preferences

International Preferences:
Nigeria
Africa

Additional Information
Year Founded: 1994
Current Activity Level : Actively seeking new investments

ARMADA INVESTMENT AG

Seestrasse 39
Kuesnacht, Switzerland 8700
Phone: 41449149000
Fax: 41449149001
E-mail: office@armada.com
Website: armada.com

Management and Staff
Simon Koenig, Managing Director

Type of Firm
Private Equity Firm

Project Preferences

Role in Financing:
Will function either as deal originator or investor in deals created by others

Type of Financing Preferred:
Early Stage
Later Stage
Special Situation

Geographical Preferences

United States Preferences:
All U.S.

International Preferences:
United Kingdom
Switzerland
Austria
Germany

Industry Preferences

In Internet Specific prefer:
Internet
Ecommerce

In Financial Services prefer:
Real Estate
Financial Services

In Business Serv. prefer:
Services

Additional Information
Year Founded: 2000
Capital Under Management: $120,000,000
Current Activity Level : Actively seeking new investments
Method of Compensation: Return on investment is of primary concern, do not charge fees

ARMAT GROUP SA

48 Boulevard Grande Duchesse
Charlotte, Luxembourg 1330
Website: www.armatgroup.com

Type of Firm
Private Equity Firm

Project Preferences

Type of Financing Preferred:
Leveraged Buyout
Mezzanine
Generalist PE
Balanced
Later Stage
Management Buyouts
Acquisition

Geographical Preferences

United States Preferences:

International Preferences:
Latin America
Europe
Middle East
Asia
Africa

Industry Preferences

In Communications prefer:
Communications and Media

In Computer Software prefer:
Software

In Internet Specific prefer:
Ecommerce

In Industrial/Energy prefer:
Energy
Environmental Related

In Transportation prefer:
Transportation
Aerospace

In Business Serv. prefer:
Services
Distribution

Additional Information
Year Founded: 1969
Current Activity Level : Actively seeking new investments

ARMILAR VENTURE PARTNERS SOCIEDADE DE CAPITAL DE RISCO SA

Rua Alexandre Herculano 38
5th Floor
Lisbon, Portugal 1250011
Phone: 351213106490
Fax: 351213106425
E-mail: info@es-ventures.com

Management and Staff
Duarte Mineiro, Principal
Jose Guerreiro de Sousa, Principal
Pedro Ribeiro Santos, Principal

Type of Firm
Bank Affiliated

Association Membership
Portuguese Venture Capital Association (APCRI)

Project Preferences

Type of Financing Preferred:
Seed
Startup

Size of Investments Considered:
Min Size of Investment Considered (000s): $1,301
Max Size of Investment Considered (000s): $13,011

Geographical Preferences

International Preferences:
Brazil

Industry Preferences

In Communications prefer:
Telecommunications

In Industrial/Energy prefer:
Environmental Related

In Financial Services prefer:
Financial Services

In Agr/Forestr/Fish prefer:
Agriculture related

In Other prefer:
Environment Responsible

Additional Information
Name of Most Recent Fund: Brasil Aceleradora de Start-ups Fundo de Investimento
Most Recent Fund Was Raised: 03/13/2014
Year Founded: 2000
Capital Under Management: $201,800,000
Current Activity Level : Actively seeking new investments

ARMORY CAPITAL LLC

100 West University Avenue
Suite 401
Champaign, IL USA 61820
Phone: 2173784205
Website: www.armorycap.com

Type of Firm
Private Equity Firm

Project Preferences

Type of Financing Preferred:
Leveraged Buyout
Acquisition

Industry Preferences

In Medical/Health prefer:
Health Services

In Consumer Related prefer:
Consumer Products

In Transportation prefer:
Transportation

In Financial Services prefer:
Financial Services

In Business Serv. prefer:
Services
Media

In Manufact. prefer:
Manufacturing

In Agr/Forestr/Fish prefer:
Agribusiness

Additional Information
Year Founded: 1969
Current Activity Level : Actively seeking new investments

ARMORY SQUARE VENTURES MANAGER LLC

32 Onondaga Street
Skaneateles, NY USA 13152
Phone: 3152219016

Type of Firm
Private Equity Firm

Project Preferences

Type of Financing Preferred:
Early Stage
Balanced
Later Stage
Seed
Startup

Size of Investments Considered:
Min Size of Investment Considered (000s): $500
Max Size of Investment Considered (000s): $750

Geographical Preferences

United States Preferences:
New York

Industry Preferences

In Communications prefer:
Communications and Media

In Computer Software prefer:
Software

In Medical/Health prefer:
Medical/Health

In Consumer Related prefer:
Education Related

In Business Serv. prefer:
Media

In Manufact. prefer:
Manufacturing

Additional Information
Name of Most Recent Fund: Armory Square Ventures, L.P.
Most Recent Fund Was Raised: 10/10/2013
Year Founded: 2013
Capital Under Management: $15,500,000
Current Activity Level : Actively seeking new investments

ARRAY VENTURES LP

One Cosco Avenue
San Francisco, CA USA 94110
Phone: 4083322743

Management and Staff
Shruti Gandhi, Managing Partner

Type of Firm
Private Equity Firm

Additional Information
Year Founded: 2016
Capital Under Management: $2,830,000
Current Activity Level : Actively seeking new investments

ARRIS VENTURES LLC

13835 North Tatum Boulevard
Suite 9-607
Phoenix, AZ USA 85032
Phone: 602-650-0176
Fax: 480-451-2789
E-mail: info@arrisventures.com

Pratt's Guide to Private Equity & Venture Capital Sources

Management and Staff
Charlie Lewis, Managing Director
Kent Petzold, Principal
Mike Stowell, Principal
Shawn Boskie, Principal

Type of Firm
Private Equity Firm

Project Preferences

Role in Financing:
Prefer role as deal originator but will also invest in deals created by others

Type of Financing Preferred:
Expansion
Later Stage

Size of Investments Considered:
Min Size of Investment Considered (000s): $500
Max Size of Investment Considered (000s): $6,000

Geographical Preferences

United States Preferences:
Southwest

Industry Preferences

In Internet Specific prefer:
Ecommerce

In Biotechnology prefer:
Human Biotechnology

Additional Information
Year Founded: 2001
Current Activity Level : Actively seeking new investments

ARROW VENTURE GP LLC

100 W
31st Street
New York, NY USA 10001
Phone: 7185145442

Type of Firm
Private Equity Firm

Geographical Preferences

United States Preferences:
New York

Additional Information
Year Founded: 2017
Capital Under Management: $100,000
Current Activity Level : Actively seeking new investments

ARROWHEAD MEZZANINE LLC

55 Railroad Avenue
Greenwich, CT USA 06830
Phone: 2034850700
Fax: 2032953771
E-mail: info@arrowmezz.com
Website: www.arrowheadmezzanine.com

Management and Staff
Andrew Stewart, Vice President
Craig Pisani, Managing Director
Elliott Jones, Senior Managing Director
Mary Gay, Managing Director
Paul Horton, Managing Director
Phillip Krall, Managing Director

Type of Firm
Private Equity Firm

Project Preferences

Type of Financing Preferred:
Mezzanine

Industry Preferences

In Medical/Health prefer:
Medical/Health

In Consumer Related prefer:
Consumer Products

In Industrial/Energy prefer:
Industrial Products
Materials

In Business Serv. prefer:
Services
Distribution

In Manufact. prefer:
Manufacturing

Additional Information
Name of Most Recent Fund: Gleacher Mezzanine Partners II, L.P.
Most Recent Fund Was Raised: 11/17/2006
Year Founded: 1996
Capital Under Management: $152,000,000
Current Activity Level : Actively seeking new investments

ARROWMARK PARTNERS

100 Fillmore Street
Suite 325
Denver, CO USA 80206
Phone: 3033982929
Website: arrowmarkpartners.com

Type of Firm
Private Equity Firm

Project Preferences

Type of Financing Preferred:
Early Stage
Expansion
Later Stage
Seed

Additional Information
Year Founded: 1995
Current Activity Level : Actively seeking new investments

ARROWPATH VENTURE CAPITAL

303 Twin Dolphin Drive
Sixth Floor
Redwood City, CA USA 94065
Phone: 6505516460
E-mail: vc@arrowpathvc.com
Website: www.arrowpathvc.com

Other Offices
1230 Avenue of the Americas
Seventh Floor
New York, NY USA 10020
Phone: 917-639-4152
Fax: 917-639-4005

30 Montgomery Street
Suite 1020
Jersey City, NJ USA 07302
Phone: 4159997058
Fax: 2015361444

Management and Staff
Daniel Brown, Partner
F. Morgan Rodd, Managing Partner
Teresa McDaniel, Chief Financial Officer
Thomas Bevilacqua, Managing Partner

Type of Firm
Private Equity Firm

Project Preferences

Role in Financing:
Will function either as deal originator or investor in deals created by others

Type of Financing Preferred:
Early Stage
Expansion
Balanced

Size of Investments Considered:
Min Size of Investment Considered (000s): $1,000
Max Size of Investment Considered (000s): $10,000

Geographical Preferences

United States Preferences:

Industry Preferences

In Communications prefer:
Wireless Communications
Data Communications

In Computer Software prefer:
Data Processing
Software
Systems Software
Applications Software
Artificial Intelligence

In Internet Specific prefer:
E-Commerce Technology
Internet
Ecommerce
Web Aggregation/Portals

In Financial Services prefer:
Financial Services

Additional Information
Year Founded: 1997
Capital Under Management: $325,000,000
Current Activity Level : Actively seeking new investments
Method of Compensation: Return on investment is of primary concern, do not charge fees

ARROWROOT CAPITAL LP

100 Wilshire Boulevard, Suite 1830
Santa Monica, CA USA 90401
Phone: 3105665966
E-mail: contact@arrowrootcapital.com
Website: www.arrowrootcapital.com

Type of Firm
Private Equity Firm

Project Preferences

Type of Financing Preferred:
Expansion
Later Stage
Acquisition

Size of Investments Considered:
Min Size of Investment Considered (000s): $5,000
Max Size of Investment Considered (000s): $250,000

Industry Preferences

In Computer Software prefer:
Software

In Internet Specific prefer:
Internet

Additional Information
Year Founded: 2014
Capital Under Management: $177,000,000
Current Activity Level : Actively seeking new investments

ARSENAL

750 South Orlando Ave, Suite 200
Winter Park, FL USA 32789
Phone: 4078381439
E-mail: info@arsenalvp.com
Website: arsenalgrowth.com

Other Offices
6701 Carnegie Avenue
Suite 100
CLEVELAND, OH USA 44103
Phone: 2163633428

350 North Old Woodward Avenue
Suite 100
BIRMINGHAM, MI USA 48009
Phone: 3132818188

385 Homer Avenue
PALO ALTO, CA USA 94301
Phone: 650-838-9200

Management and Staff
Christopher Fountas, General Partner
David Odom, Principal
Denny Behm, Principal
Henry Huey, Principal
Jason Rottenberg, General Partner
John Trbovich, General Partner
Kerri Breen, Principal
Patricia Glaza, Principal

Type of Firm
Private Equity Firm

Project Preferences

Type of Financing Preferred:
Early Stage
Seed

Industry Preferences

In Communications prefer:
Communications and Media

In Computer Software prefer:
Software

In Industrial/Energy prefer:
Energy

Additional Information
Name of Most Recent Fund: Arsenal Venture Partners II, L.P.
Most Recent Fund Was Raised: 08/04/2010
Year Founded: 1997
Current Activity Level : Actively seeking new investments

ARSENAL CAPITAL MANAGEMENT LLC

3870 S. Lindbergh Blvd
Suite 155
Saint Louis, MO USA 63127
Phone: 3142709048
Fax: 3147222211

Management and Staff
Eugene Gorbach, Principal
Frank Scrudato, Chief Financial Officer
Grace Kim, Principal
Jeffrey Kovach, Partner
Joelle Marquis, Partner
John Televantos, Partner
Joseph Rooney, Vice President
Roy Seroussi, Principal
Stephen McLean, Partner
Terrence Mullen, Partner
Timothy Zappala, Partner

Type of Firm
Private Equity Firm

Project Preferences

Type of Financing Preferred:
Early Stage

Geographical Preferences

United States Preferences:
Missouri

Additional Information
Year Founded: 2012
Current Activity Level : Actively seeking new investments

ARSENAL CAPITAL PARTNERS LP

100 Park Avenue
31st Floor
New York, NY USA 10017
Phone: 2127711717
Fax: 2127711718
Website: www.arsenalcapital.com

Other Offices
No. 1515 Nanjing West Road
Room 1805 Kerry Center
Shanghai, China 200040
Phone: 862152985858
Fax: 862152985878

Management and Staff
Carty Chock, Partner
Chee We Ng, Vice President
Eugene Gorbach, Principal
Frank Scrudato, Chief Financial Officer
Grace Kim, Principal
Jeffrey Kovach, Partner
Joelle Marquis, Partner
John Televantos, Partner
Joseph Rooney, Vice President
Patricia Grad, Senior Managing Director
Roy Seroussi, Principal
Stephen McLean, Partner
Terrence Mullen, Partner
Timothy Zappala, Partner
Yoonmo Yang, Vice President

Type of Firm
Private Equity Firm

Project Preferences

Type of Financing Preferred:
Leveraged Buyout
Expansion
Later Stage
Management Buyouts
Acquisition
Recapitalizations

Industry Preferences

In Communications prefer:
Satellite Microwave Comm.

In Medical/Health prefer:
Medical/Health
Medical Diagnostics
Medical Products
Health Services
Pharmaceuticals

In Industrial/Energy prefer:
Industrial Products
Materials
Advanced Materials
Environmental Related

In Transportation prefer:
Transportation

In Financial Services prefer:
Financial Services
Insurance

In Business Serv. prefer:
Services
Distribution

In Manufact. prefer:
Manufacturing

Additional Information
Year Founded: 2000
Capital Under Management: $2,886,300,000
Current Activity Level: Actively seeking new investments

ARTA CAPITAL SGEIC SA

Plaza del Marques de Salamanca
10- 4 DERECHA
Madrid, Spain 28006
Phone: 3491781788
Fax: 3491781932
E-mail: contacto@artacapital.com
Website: www.artacapital.com

Type of Firm
Private Equity Firm

Association Membership
Spanish Venture Capital Association (ASCRI)

Project Preferences

Role in Financing:
Prefer role as deal originator

Type of Financing Preferred:
Balanced
Later Stage

Size of Investments Considered:
Min Size of Investment Considered (000s): $42,337
Max Size of Investment Considered (000s): $84,674

Geographical Preferences

International Preferences:
Portugal
Spain

Additional Information
Year Founded: 2007
Capital Under Management: $573,100,000
Current Activity Level: Actively seeking new investments

ARTEMIS CAPITAL PARTNERS

84 State Street, Suite 320
Boston, MA USA 02109
Phone: 6178301117
Fax: 6172274128
E-mail: info@artemislp.com
Website: www.artemislp.com

Management and Staff
Peter Hunter, Managing Director

Type of Firm
Private Equity Firm

Project Preferences

Type of Financing Preferred:
Leveraged Buyout
Acquisition

Industry Preferences

In Computer Software prefer:
Software

In Semiconductor/Electr prefer:
Electronic Components
Controllers and Sensors
Sensors

In Medical/Health prefer:
Medical Products

In Industrial/Energy prefer:
Energy
Alternative Energy
Industrial Products
Factory Automation
Robotics
Machinery
Environmental Related

In Business Serv. prefer:
Services

Additional Information
Name of Most Recent Fund: Artemis Capital Partners I, L.P.
Most Recent Fund Was Raised: 04/29/2010
Year Founded: 2010
Capital Under Management: $49,380,000
Current Activity Level: Actively seeking new investments

ARTEMIS HOLDINGS GROUP LLC

2028 Allen Place NW
Washington, DC USA 20009
Website: www.artemisholdings.com

Type of Firm
Private Equity Firm

Project Preferences

Type of Financing Preferred:
Leveraged Buyout
Acquisition

Industry Preferences

In Biotechnology prefer:
Biotechnology

In Medical/Health prefer:
Pharmaceuticals

In Industrial/Energy prefer:
Industrial Products

In Transportation prefer:
Aerospace

In Manufact. prefer:
Manufacturing

Additional Information
Year Founded: 2010
Current Activity Level: Actively seeking new investments

ARTEMIS INVESTMENT MANAGEMENT LLP

57 St James's Street
Cassini House
London, United Kingdom SW1A 1LD
Phone: 442073996000
Website: www.artemis.co.uk

Management and Staff
Lesley Cairney, Chief Operating Officer
Mark Tyndall, Partner

Type of Firm
Investment Management Firm

Project Preferences

Type of Financing Preferred:
Balanced

Geographical Preferences

International Preferences:
United Kingdom

Additional Information

Year Founded: 2016
Current Activity Level : Actively seeking new investments

ARTEMIS INVESTMENT MANAGEMENT LTD

Five Hazelton Avenue
Suite 200
Toronto, Canada M5R 2E1
Phone: 4169347455
Fax: 4169347459
E-mail: info@artemisfunds.ca
Website: www.artemisfunds.ca

Management and Staff

Trevor Maunder, Chief Financial Officer

Type of Firm

Investment Management Firm

Project Preferences

Type of Financing Preferred:
Leveraged Buyout

Additional Information

Year Founded: 2004
Current Activity Level : Actively seeking new investments

ARTESIAN CAPITAL MANAGEMENT AUSTRALIA PTY LTD

281 Brunswick Street, Fitzroy
Studio Four, Level One
Melbourne, Australia 3065
Phone: 61392889444
E-mail: admin@artesianinvest.com
Website: www.artesianinvest.com

Other Offices

1515 Nanjing West Road
Unit 801, Eighth Floor
Shanghai, China 200040
Phone: 8613636610534

78 Duxton Road
, Singapore 089537
Phone: 6563279094

Four Park Place
London, United Kingdom SW1A LP
Phone: 442078989350

770 Broadway
Leve Two
New York, NY USA 10003
Phone: 6464956018

Management and Staff

Felix Zhang, Partner
John McCartney, Managing Partner
Kurt Tan, Managing Director
Matthew Clunies-Ross, Managing Partner
Pankaj Khanna, Chief Financial Officer
Tim Heasley, Chief Operating Officer
Yubin Meng, Managing Director

Type of Firm

Private Equity Firm

Project Preferences

Type of Financing Preferred:
Fund of Funds
Early Stage
Seed
Startup

Geographical Preferences

International Preferences:
China
Australia

Additional Information

Year Founded: 1969
Capital Under Management: $18,658,000
Current Activity Level : Actively seeking new investments

ARTHUR VENTURES LLC

210 N Broadway
Suite 301
Fargo, ND USA 58102
Phone: 7012323521
Fax: 7012323530
E-mail: info@arthurventures.com
Website: www.arthurventures.com

Management and Staff

James Burgum, Co-Founder
Ryan Kruizenga, Partner

Type of Firm

Private Equity Firm

Project Preferences

Type of Financing Preferred:
Early Stage
Balanced
Later Stage
Seed
Startup

Size of Investments Considered:
Min Size of Investment Considered (000s): $250
Max Size of Investment Considered (000s): $3,000

Geographical Preferences

United States Preferences:
Midwest
South Dakota
North Dakota

Industry Preferences

In Computer Software prefer:
Software

In Industrial/Energy prefer:
Energy
Environmental Related

Additional Information

Name of Most Recent Fund: Arthur Ventures Growth Fund II, L.P.
Most Recent Fund Was Raised: 07/16/2013
Year Founded: 2008
Capital Under Management: $13,200,000
Current Activity Level : Actively seeking new investments

ARTHVEDA FUND MANAGEMENT PVT LTD

Anand Kanekar Road, Bandra (E)
6th Floor, Dheeraj Arma
Mumbai, India 400051
Phone: 91-22-2658-3333
Fax: 91-22-2658-3344
E-mail: response@dhfl.com
Website: arthveda.co.in

Other Offices

53-55 Uxbridge Road
London, United Kingdom W5 5SA
Phone: 44-20-8579-1711
Fax: 44-20-8579-1712

Office No.211, Khalid Bin Al Waleed Road
2nd Floor, Atrium Centre
Dubai, Utd. Arab Em.
Phone: 971-4352-4905
Fax: 971-4352-5906

Management and Staff

Anil Sachidanand, Chief Executive Officer
Rajeev Sathe, Chief Operating Officer

Type of Firm

Bank Affiliated

Project Preferences

Type of Financing Preferred:
Core
Balanced
Other
Special Situation

Pratt's Guide to Private Equity & Venture Capital Sources

Geographical Preferences

International Preferences:
India

Industry Preferences

In Transportation prefer:
Transportation

In Financial Services prefer:
Real Estate

In Utilities prefer:
Utilities

Additional Information
Year Founded: 2006
Current Activity Level : Actively seeking new investments

ARTIMAN MANAGEMENT LLC

2000 University Avenue
Suite 602
East Palo Alto, CA USA 94303
Phone: 6508452020
Fax: 6508452019
E-mail: info@artiman.com
Website: www.artiman.com

Other Offices
Lavelle Road, Near Bangalore Club
Brigade Hulkul Centre, Ground Flr 82
Bangalore, India 560 001
Phone: 918061769400
Fax: 918025591454

Management and Staff
Ajit Singh, Managing Director
Akhil Saklecha, Managing Director
Amit Shah, Founder
Brian Wilcove, Managing Director
MJ Aravind, Managing Director
Ramesh Radhakrishnan, Managing Director
Tim Wilson, Managing Director
Tom Dennedy, Managing Director
Yatin Mundkur, Partner

Type of Firm
Private Equity Firm

Association Membership
National Venture Capital Association - USA (NVCA)

Project Preferences

Role in Financing:
Will function either as deal originator or investor in deals created by others

Type of Financing Preferred:
Early Stage
Balanced
Later Stage

Additional Information
Name of Most Recent Fund: Artiman Ventures Special Opportunities Fund, L.P.
Most Recent Fund Was Raised: 09/13/2011
Year Founded: 2000
Capital Under Management: $685,000,000
Current Activity Level : Actively seeking new investments

ARTIS VENTURES

988 Market Street
San Francisco, CA USA 94105
Phone: 4153446200
E-mail: contact@artisventures.com
Website: www.artisventures.com

Type of Firm
Private Equity Firm

Project Preferences

Type of Financing Preferred:
Early Stage
Balanced
Later Stage

Industry Preferences

In Communications prefer:
Telecommunications

In Computer Software prefer:
Software

In Internet Specific prefer:
Internet

In Semiconductor/Electr prefer:
Semiconductor

In Medical/Health prefer:
Medical/Health

In Consumer Related prefer:
Consumer

In Industrial/Energy prefer:
Energy
Alternative Energy
Energy Conservation Relat

In Business Serv. prefer:
Media

Additional Information
Name of Most Recent Fund: Artis Ventures Fund LLC
Most Recent Fund Was Raised: 01/12/2012
Year Founded: 2001
Capital Under Management: $65,000,000
Current Activity Level : Actively seeking new investments

ARTS ALLIANCE ADVISORS

5 Young Street
London, United Kingdom W8 5EH
Phone: 442073617720
Fax: 442073617766
E-mail: info@artsalliance.co.uk
Website: www.artsalliance.co.uk

Type of Firm
Private Equity Firm

Project Preferences

Type of Financing Preferred:
Early Stage
Balanced
Startup

Size of Investments Considered:
Min Size of Investment Considered (000s): $500
Max Size of Investment Considered (000s): $5,000

Geographical Preferences

United States Preferences:
All U.S.

International Preferences:
Europe
No Preference
Western Europe

Industry Focus
(% based on actual investment)
Internet Specific 45.9%
Computer Software and Services 28.7%
Consumer Related 13.0%
Communications and Media 6.5%
Other Products 5.8%

Additional Information
Name of Most Recent Fund: Digital Venture III
Most Recent Fund Was Raised: 03/06/2001
Year Founded: 1996
Capital Under Management: $80,200,000
Current Activity Level : Actively seeking new investments

ARX EQUITY PARTNERS SP Z O O

Al. Jana Pawla II 12
Eighth Floor
Warsaw, Poland 00-124
Phone: 48228509960
Fax: 48228509961
E-mail: warszawa@arxequity.com
Website: www.arxequity.com

Other Offices
Romniceanu Grigore dr. 3A
Bucharest, Romania 050574
Phone: 40-21-410-0123
Fax: 40-21-410-5284

Management and Staff
Bela Lendvai-Lintner, Partner
Brian Wardrop, Managing Partner
Jacek Korpala, Managing Partner

Type of Firm
Private Equity Firm

Association Membership
Hungarian Venture Capital Association (HVCA)
Czech Venture Capital Association (CVCA)
Polish Venture Capital Association (PSIC/PPEA)
European Private Equity and Venture Capital Assoc.

Project Preferences

Role in Financing:
Prefer role as deal originator

Size of Investments Considered:
Min Size of Investment Considered (000s): $4,237
Max Size of Investment Considered (000s): $16,947

Geographical Preferences

International Preferences:
Hungary
Romania

Industry Preferences

In Semiconductor/Electr prefer:
Optoelectronics

In Consumer Related prefer:
Entertainment and Leisure
Retail
Publishing-Retail
Food/Beverage
Consumer Services

In Industrial/Energy prefer:
Materials

In Financial Services prefer:
Financial Services

In Manufact. prefer:
Manufacturing

Additional Information
Year Founded: 1997
Capital Under Management: $320,600,000
Current Activity Level : Actively seeking new investments

ARZAN VENTURE CAPITAL

Ahmad Al Jaber Street
Kuwait City, Kuwait 13125
Phone: 9651820200
E-mail: info@arzanvc.com
Website: arzanvc.com

Other Offices
Unit 206, Gate Village # 7
DIFC
Dubai, Utd. Arab Em.

Type of Firm
Private Equity Firm

Project Preferences

Type of Financing Preferred:
Early Stage
Balanced
Start-up Financing
Later Stage
Seed

Geographical Preferences

United States Preferences:

International Preferences:
Jordan
Utd. Arab Em.
Middle East
Kuwait
Russia

Industry Preferences

In Computer Software prefer:
Software
Applications Software

In Internet Specific prefer:
E-Commerce Technology
Ecommerce
Web Aggregation/Portals

In Industrial/Energy prefer:
Environmental Related

In Financial Services prefer:
Real Estate

Additional Information
Year Founded: 2014
Capital Under Management: $5,000,000
Current Activity Level : Actively seeking new investments

ASAHI GIN JIGYOU TOUSHI

1-10-5 Nihonbashi Kayabacho
SF Kayabacho Building
Tokyo, Japan 103-0025
Phone: 81356413311

Other Offices
ResonaBnak Osakahonbu bldg
2-2-1 Bigocho, Chuo-ku
Osaka-shi, Japan 541-0051

Type of Firm
Bank Affiliated

Project Preferences

Type of Financing Preferred:
Balanced

Geographical Preferences

International Preferences:
Japan

Additional Information
Year Founded: 1988
Current Activity Level : Actively seeking new investments

ASCEND CAPITAL PARTNERS

No. 89, Jianguo Road
Bldg. 16, China Central Place
Beijing, China 100025
Phone: 861065305663
Fax: 861065305653
E-mail: admin@ascendvp.com.cn
Website: www.ascendvp.com.cn

Other Offices
Room 1903, Fortress Tower
250 King's Road
North Point, Hong Kong
Phone: 852-2312-0966
Fax: 852-2369-8484

Road No. 111
Room 309
Great Neck, NY USA 11021
Phone: 5167736688
Fax: 5167736699

Management and Staff
Keddy Wang, Partner
Monita Mo, Chief Executive Officer

Type of Firm
Bank Affiliated

Project Preferences

Type of Financing Preferred:
Expansion
Balanced

Geographical Preferences

International Preferences:
No Preference
China

Additional Information
Year Founded: 2002
Current Activity Level : Actively seeking new investments

ASCEND GLOBAL INVESTMENTS LLC

575 Madison Avenue, Sixth Floor
New York, NY USA 10022
Website: agi-llc.com

Management and Staff
Calvin Wells, Principal
David Acharya, Partner
Matt Robinson, Partner
Robert Kennedy, Partner

Type of Firm
Private Equity Firm

Project Preferences

Type of Financing Preferred:
Leveraged Buyout
Expansion
Management Buyouts
Recapitalizations

Geographical Preferences

United States Preferences:
North America

Industry Preferences

In Communications prefer:
Telecommunications

In Medical/Health prefer:
Medical/Health
Health Services

In Consumer Related prefer:
Retail
Food/Beverage
Consumer Products

In Industrial/Energy prefer:
Energy

In Financial Services prefer:
Financial Services

In Business Serv. prefer:
Media

In Manufact. prefer:
Manufacturing

Additional Information
Year Founded: 1998
Current Activity Level : Actively seeking new investments

ASCENDENT CAPITAL PARTNERS ASIA LTD

One Connaught Place
Suite 1609 16/F Jardine House
Central, Hong Kong
Website: www.ascendentcp.com

Type of Firm
Private Equity Firm

Association Membership
Hong Kong Venture Capital Association (HKVCA)

Project Preferences

Type of Financing Preferred:
Leveraged Buyout
Acquisition

Geographical Preferences

International Preferences:
China

Industry Preferences

In Consumer Related prefer:
Retail

In Industrial/Energy prefer:
Energy

In Financial Services prefer:
Real Estate

In Manufact. prefer:
Manufacturing

Additional Information
Year Founded: 1969
Current Activity Level : Actively seeking new investments

ASCENSION VENTURES LTD

Floral Street, Covent Garden
Amadeus House
London, United Kingdom WC2E 9DP
Phone: 442034285200
E-mail: info@ascensionventures.com
Website: www.ascensionventures.com

Management and Staff
Jaime Renvoize, Chief Financial Officer

Type of Firm
Private Equity Firm

Project Preferences

Type of Financing Preferred:
Early Stage
Expansion
Seed

Geographical Preferences

International Preferences:
United Kingdom

Industry Preferences

In Computer Software prefer:
Software

In Internet Specific prefer:
Ecommerce

In Consumer Related prefer:
Entertainment and Leisure

In Manufact. prefer:
Publishing

Additional Information
Year Founded: 2012
Current Activity Level : Actively seeking new investments

ASCENT BIOMEDICAL VENTURES

142 West 57th Street
Suite 4A
New York, NY USA 10019
Phone: 2123031680
Fax: 2127523633
E-mail: info@abvlp.com
Website: www.abvlp.com

Management and Staff
Avi Kometz, Partner
Geoffrey Smith, Managing Partner
Jonathan Edelson, Venture Partner
Steve Hochberg, Managing Partner

Type of Firm
Private Equity Firm

Project Preferences

Type of Financing Preferred:
Early Stage
Balanced
Seed

Geographical Preferences

United States Preferences:
All U.S.

Industry Preferences

In Biotechnology prefer:
Biotechnology

In Medical/Health prefer:
Medical/Health

Additional Information
Year Founded: 2005
Current Activity Level : Actively seeking new investments

ASCENT CAPITAL ADVISORS INDIA PVT LTD

24 Vittal Mallya Road
16F UB City, Concorde Block
Bangalore, India 5600 001
Phone: 918030551230
Fax: 918030551234
E-mail: info@ascentcapital.in
Website: www.ascentcapital.in

Type of Firm
Private Equity Firm

Association Membership
Indian Venture Capital Association (IVCA)

Project Preferences

Type of Financing Preferred:
Expansion
Balanced
Later Stage
Startup
Special Situation

Size of Investments Considered:
Min Size of Investment Considered (000s): $15,000
Max Size of Investment Considered (000s): $40,000

Geographical Preferences

International Preferences:
India

Industry Preferences

In Communications prefer:
Telecommunications

In Internet Specific prefer:
Internet

In Semiconductor/Electr prefer:
Semiconductor

In Biotechnology prefer:
Biotechnology

In Medical/Health prefer:
Health Services
Pharmaceuticals

In Consumer Related prefer:
Consumer
Entertainment and Leisure
Retail
Consumer Products

In Business Serv. prefer:
Services
Consulting Services
Media

In Manufact. prefer:
Manufacturing

Additional Information

Year Founded: 2000
Capital Under Management: $600,000,000
Current Activity Level : Actively seeking new investments

ASCENT CAPITAL AFRICA LTD

PwC Tower, Westlands
7th Floor
Nairobi, Kenya 0000
Phone: 254730112000
Website: www.ascent-africa.com

Other Offices

Abyssinia Mall
11th Floor
Addis Adaba, Ethiopia
Phone: 251911340034

Plot 1 Garuga Close, Mbuya
Kampala, Uganda
Phone: 256414500969

Type of Firm

Private Equity Firm

Project Preferences

Type of Financing Preferred:
Balanced

Size of Investments Considered:
Min Size of Investment Considered (000s): $1,000
Max Size of Investment Considered (000s): $10,000

Geographical Preferences

International Preferences:
Rwanda
Uganda
Tanzania
Kenya
Burundi
Sudan

Additional Information

Year Founded: 2014
Capital Under Management: $80,000,000
Current Activity Level : Actively seeking new investments

ASCENT EQUITY GROUP LLC

3131 Turtle Creek Boulevard
Suite 1001
Dallas, TX USA 75219
Phone: 2148656070
Fax: 2148656035
Website: www.ascentequity.com

Management and Staff

Daniel Williams, Co-Founder
Joseph Saliba, Co-Founder

Type of Firm

Private Equity Firm

Project Preferences

Type of Financing Preferred:
Leveraged Buyout
Acquisition

Geographical Preferences

United States Preferences:
Southwest
Texas

Industry Preferences

In Medical/Health prefer:
Health Services

In Consumer Related prefer:
Consumer Products
Education Related

In Financial Services prefer:
Financial Services

In Business Serv. prefer:
Distribution

Additional Information

Year Founded: 2013
Current Activity Level : Actively seeking new investments

ASCENT VENTURE MANAGEMENT INC

255 State Street
Fifth Floor
Boston, MA USA 02109
Phone: 6177209400
Fax: 6177209401
Website: www.ascentvp.com

Management and Staff

Brian Girvan, General Partner
Chane Graziano, Venture Partner
Christopher Dick, Co-Founder
Christopher Lynch, Co-Founder
Christopher Dick, General Partner
Edward Schmid, Venture Partner
Eric Schultz, Venture Partner
Geoffrey Oblak, General Partner
Hugh Kelly, Venture Partner
John Blaeser, Venture Partner
Luke Burns, Partner
Matt Fates, Partner
Michael D Amelio, Venture Partner
Nick Grewal, Venture Partner
Robert Mazzarella, Venture Partner

Type of Firm

Private Equity Firm

Association Membership

New England Venture Capital Association
National Venture Capital Association - USA (NVCA)
Indian Venture Capital Association (IVCA)

Project Preferences

Role in Financing:
Prefer role as deal originator but will also invest in deals created by others

Type of Financing Preferred:
Early Stage
Expansion
Balanced

Size of Investments Considered:
Min Size of Investment Considered (000s): $2,000
Max Size of Investment Considered (000s): $5,000

Geographical Preferences

United States Preferences:
All U.S.
East Coast

Industry Focus

(% based on actual investment)
Computer Software and Services	47.8%
Internet Specific	23.5%
Communications and Media	9.7%
Other Products	4.8%
Medical/Health	4.1%
Computer Hardware	4.0%
Industrial/Energy	3.1%
Consumer Related	2.2%
Semiconductors/Other Elect.	0.8%

Additional Information
Name of Most Recent Fund: Ascent Venture Partners V, L.P.
Most Recent Fund Was Raised: 08/27/2008
Year Founded: 1981
Capital Under Management: $544,000,000
Current Activity Level : Actively seeking new investments
Method of Compensation: Return on investment is of primary concern, do not charge fees

ASCET INVESTIMENTOS LTDA

Rua Taques Alvim, 172
Cidade Jardim
Sao Paulo, Brazil 05671-030
Phone: 551130381308
Fax: 551130381318
Website: www.ascet.com.br

Type of Firm
Private Equity Firm

Project Preferences

Type of Financing Preferred:
Balanced

Geographical Preferences

International Preferences:
Brazil

Industry Preferences

In Communications prefer:
Communications and Media
Commercial Communications

In Business Serv. prefer:
Media

Additional Information
Year Founded: 2006
Current Activity Level : Actively seeking new investments

ASCLEPIOS BIORESEARCH (UK) LTD

10, Philpot Lane
Fifth Floor
London, United Kingdom EC3M 8AA
Phone: 442073985680
Fax: 442073985681
E-mail: enquiries@abioresearch.com
Website: www.abioresearch.com

Management and Staff
Nigel Watts, Founder
Simon Conder, Managing Director
Tajinder Bhalla, Vice President

Type of Firm
Private Equity Firm

Project Preferences

Type of Financing Preferred:
Early Stage
Expansion
Seed

Geographical Preferences

International Preferences:
United Kingdom
Europe

Industry Preferences

In Biotechnology prefer:
Biotechnology
Human Biotechnology

In Medical/Health prefer:
Pharmaceuticals

Additional Information
Year Founded: 2009
Current Activity Level : Actively seeking new investments

ASCRIBE CAPITAL, LLC

299 Park Avenue
34th Floor
New York, NY USA 10171
Phone: 2124768000
Fax: 2126975524
Website: www.ascribecapital.com

Other Offices
989 Changle Road
Suite 3310, The Center
Shanghai, China 200031
Phone: 86-21-5419-1100
Fax: 86-21-5419-7003

Management and Staff
Aaron Maeng, Vice President
Alanna Hynes, Vice President
Benjamin Dickson, Principal
Bill Wiedman, Vice President
Bill Fry, Managing Director
Charles Klein, Managing Director
David Musicant, Managing Director
David Bard, Vice President
David Horing, Managing Director
David Xu, Vice President
Helen Chiang, Principal
Jamie Rossen, Vice President
Joseph Domonkos, Chief Financial Officer
Julian Hinderling, Vice President
Kevin Penn, Managing Director
Lee Dranikoff, Managing Director
Loren Easton, Managing Director
Marc Saiontz, Managing Director
Mark Lovett, Vice President
Matthew LeBaron, Managing Director
Michael Sand, Principal
Paul Rossetti, Managing Director
Raj Kanodia, Vice President
Scott Wolff, Managing Director
Vicky Qiu, Vice President

Type of Firm
Private Equity Firm

Association Membership
Private Equity Council (PEC)

Project Preferences

Role in Financing:
Prefer role as deal originator but will also invest in deals created by others

Type of Financing Preferred:
Leveraged Buyout
Turnaround
Acquisition
Recapitalizations

Geographical Preferences

United States Preferences:
North America

Industry Focus

(% based on actual investment)
Industrial/Energy	55.2%
Other Products	23.5%
Consumer Related	10.2%
Computer Hardware	6.0%
Communications and Media	2.8%
Internet Specific	2.2%
Medical/Health	0.1%

Additional Information
Name of Most Recent Fund: Ascribe Opportunities Fund III
Most Recent Fund Was Raised: 08/14/2013
Year Founded: 1947
Capital Under Management: $21,000,000,000

Current Activity Level : Actively seeking new investments
Method of Compensation: Return on invest. most important, but chg. closing fees, service fees, etc.

ASER CAPITAL SCR SA

Calle Urgell
Barcelona, Spain

Management and Staff
Daniel Gomez Garcia, President

Type of Firm
Private Equity Firm

Project Preferences

Type of Financing Preferred:
Balanced

Geographical Preferences

International Preferences:
Spain

Additional Information
Year Founded: 2008
Current Activity Level : Actively seeking new investments

ASGARD CAPITAL VERWALTUNG GMBH

Geschwister-Scholl-Strasse 54
Potsdam, Germany 14471
E-mail: contact@asgard.vc

Type of Firm
Private Equity Firm

Project Preferences

Type of Financing Preferred:
Early Stage
Expansion
Balanced
Later Stage
Seed
Startup

Industry Preferences

In Industrial/Energy prefer:
Robotics

Additional Information
Year Founded: 2015
Current Activity Level : Actively seeking new investments

ASHBY POINT CAPITAL

1240 Ashby Court
Arnold, MD USA 21012
Phone: 4105446250
Fax: 4105443264

Management and Staff
James Leroux, Partner
William Westervelt, Partner

Type of Firm
Private Equity Advisor or Fund of Funds

Project Preferences

Type of Financing Preferred:
Early Stage
Balanced
Later Stage

Size of Investments Considered:
Min Size of Investment Considered (000s): $100
Max Size of Investment Considered (000s): $5,000

Industry Preferences

In Financial Services prefer:
Financial Services

Additional Information
Year Founded: 2007
Current Activity Level : Actively seeking new investments

ASHHILL PHARMACEUTICAL INVESTMENTS LLC

20 North Grand Avenue
Suite 7
Fort Thomas, KY USA 41075
Phone: 8593096224
Website: www.ashhillpharma.com

Management and Staff
David Buffenbarger, Chief Financial Officer

Type of Firm
Private Equity Firm

Project Preferences

Type of Financing Preferred:
Expansion
Balanced
Later Stage
Seed

Industry Preferences

In Medical/Health prefer:
Medical/Health
Medical Products
Pharmaceuticals

Additional Information
Year Founded: 2011
Current Activity Level : Actively seeking new investments

ASHLAND CAPITAL PARTNERS

233 S. Wacker Drive
Suite 8400
Chicago, IL USA 60606
Website: www.ashlandcap.com

Type of Firm
Private Equity Firm

Project Preferences

Type of Financing Preferred:
Leveraged Buyout

Additional Information
Year Founded: 2016
Current Activity Level : Actively seeking new investments

ASHMORE INVESTMENT MANAGEMENT LTD

61 Aldwych
London, United Kingdom WC2B 4AE
Phone: 442030776000
Fax: 442030776001
E-mail: ashmail@ashmoregroup.com
Website: www.ashmoregroup.com

Other Offices
Calle 73, Piso Eight
Suite 7 - 06
Bogota, Colombia
Phone: 5713470649
Fax: 5713179937

Type of Firm
Private Equity Firm

Project Preferences

Type of Financing Preferred:
Leveraged Buyout
Turnaround
Other

Geographical Preferences

International Preferences:
Colombia

Industry Preferences

In Communications prefer:
Telecommunications

In Transportation prefer:
Transportation

Additional Information
Name of Most Recent Fund: Colombia Infrastructure Fund Ashmore I FCP
Most Recent Fund Was Raised: 06/24/2010
Year Founded: 1992
Capital Under Management: $230,000,000
Current Activity Level : Actively seeking new investments

ASI CAPITAL LLC
9475 Briar Village Point
Unit 220
Colorado Springs, CO USA 80920
Phone: 7192254003
Website: asicapital.com

Type of Firm
Private Equity Firm

Project Preferences

Type of Financing Preferred:
Generalist PE

Industry Preferences

In Medical/Health prefer:
Health Services

In Financial Services prefer:
Real Estate
Investment Groups

Additional Information
Year Founded: 2015
Capital Under Management: $10,360,000
Current Activity Level : Actively seeking new investments

ASIA ALTERNATIVES MANAGEMENT LLC
41 Connaught Road
10/F Nexxus Bldg, Room 1001
Central, Hong Kong
Phone: 852-2588-7575
Fax: 852-2588-7300
E-mail: info@asiaalt.com
Website: www.asiaalt.com

Other Offices
1421-1422, 14/F, South Tower
1 Guanghua Rd, Chaoyang Dist
Beijing, China 100020
Phone: 86-10-8529-9828
Fax: 86-10-8529-7090

One Maritime Plaza
Suite 1000
San Francisco, CA USA 94111
Phone: 415-723-8100
Fax: 415-399-1713

Management and Staff
Akihiko Yasuda, Managing Director
Jin Gu, Principal
Laure Wang, Co-Founder
Melissa Ma, Managing Partner
Praneet Garg, Principal
Rebecca Xu, Managing Director
William LaFayette, Chief Financial Officer

Type of Firm
Private Equity Advisor or Fund of Funds

Association Membership
Emerging Markets Private Equity Association
China Venture Capital Association

Project Preferences

Type of Financing Preferred:
Fund of Funds
Leveraged Buyout
Expansion
Generalist PE
Balanced
Management Buyouts
Special Situation
Fund of Funds of Second

Geographical Preferences

United States Preferences:
Southeast
California

International Preferences:
Asia Pacific
Indonesia
India
Taiwan
Hong Kong
China
Mexico
Australia
Asia
Korea, South
Japan

Industry Preferences

In Communications prefer:
Communications and Media

In Medical/Health prefer:
Health Services

In Transportation prefer:
Transportation

In Financial Services prefer:
Financial Services
Real Estate

In Business Serv. prefer:
Services

Additional Information
Name of Most Recent Fund: SBS Asia I Investors, L.P.
Most Recent Fund Was Raised: 11/08/2012
Year Founded: 2006
Capital Under Management: $6,817,225,000
Current Activity Level : Actively seeking new investments

ASIA BRIDGE CAPITAL LTD
No.19A East 3rd Ring Rd North
10F, SOHO Nexus Center
Beijing, China
Phone: 861085569033
Website: www.asiabridgegroup.com

Type of Firm
Private Equity Firm

Project Preferences

Type of Financing Preferred:
Generalist PE

Geographical Preferences

International Preferences:
China

Industry Preferences

In Medical/Health prefer:
Health Services

In Financial Services prefer:
Financial Services

Additional Information
Year Founded: 2012
Current Activity Level : Actively seeking new investments

ASIA CAPITAL MANAGEMENT LTD
8-12 Hennessy Road
17/F, China Hong Kong Tower
Wanchai, Hong Kong
Phone: 85225258151
Fax: 85228105590
E-mail: info@acmhk.com
Website: www.acmhk.com

Other Offices
16/F New Century Trade Center
No. 50 Hu Qiu Road
Shanghai, China
Phone: 86-21-6329-8979
Fax: 86-21-6323-5366

1100 Louisiana
Suite 5005
Houston, TX USA 77002
Phone: 713-655-8500
Fax: 713-655-8503

Longbao Mansion, Suite 312
36 Maizidian Jie, Chaoyang Qu
Beijing, China 100026
Phone: 86-10-6591-6491
Fax: 86-10-6591-6460

5th Floor PTC Building
105 Aguirre Street, Legazpi Village
Makati City, Philippines
Phone: 63-2-840-3020
Fax: 63-2-813-1278

2nd Industrial Zone
Yulu Gong Ming Town, Baoan County
Shenzhen City, China
Phone: 86-755-717-2931
Fax: 86-755-717-2930

Management and Staff
Louis Bowen, Managing Director

Type of Firm
Private Equity Firm

Association Membership
Hong Kong Venture Capital Association (HKVCA)

Project Preferences

Role in Financing:
Prefer role as deal originator but will also invest in deals created by others

Type of Financing Preferred:
Mezzanine
Balanced
Later Stage

Geographical Preferences

United States Preferences:
Southeast

International Preferences:
Hong Kong
China
Asia
Singapore

Industry Preferences

In Communications prefer:
Telecommunications

In Medical/Health prefer:
Health Services
Pharmaceuticals

In Consumer Related prefer:
Consumer Products

In Industrial/Energy prefer:
Environmental Related

In Financial Services prefer:
Insurance

In Business Serv. prefer:
Distribution

In Manufact. prefer:
Manufacturing

Additional Information
Year Founded: 1994
Capital Under Management: $198,000,000
Current Activity Level: Actively seeking new investments
Method of Compensation: Return on investment is of primary concern, do not charge fees

ASIA CULTURE TECHNOLOGY INVESTMENT

703-7, Yeonsan-dong, Yeonje-gu
2F, Gijeong Bldg.,
Busan, South Korea 611-080
Phone: 82518689333
Fax: 82518689332

Other Offices
2F, Hwanyoong Building
52-1, Nonheon-Dong, Gangnam-Gu
Seoul, South Korea 121-839

Management and Staff
Intack Yu, President

Type of Firm
Bank Affiliated

Association Membership
Korean Venture Capital Association (KVCA)

Project Preferences

Type of Financing Preferred:
Balanced

Geographical Preferences

International Preferences:
Korea, South

Additional Information
Year Founded: 2007
Capital Under Management: $31,400,000
Current Activity Level: Actively seeking new investments

ASIA FRONTIER INVESTMENTS LTD

7B, Hong Kong Jewellery Bldg
178-180 Queen's Road
Central, Hong Kong
Phone: 85239041015
Fax: 85239041017
E-mail: info@leopardcapital.com

Other Offices
75 Rue Faubert
Petion - Ville, Haiti

1748 National Road Five
P.O. Box 1141
Phnom Penh, Cambodia 12101
Phone: 85523723050
Fax: 85523723051

Level 4, No. 48 A Sunethradevi Road
Kohuwala
Colombo, Sri Lanka 10250
Phone: 94-77-7722-555
Fax: 94-11-552-3552

Thadeua Road
Suite 094, Unit Four
Thaphalanxay, Sisattanak, Cambodia
Phone: 85621315886
Fax: 85621315887

Management and Staff
Joseph Lovell, Chief Operating Officer
Lawrence Mackhoul, Partner
Reshma Alva, Partner
Thomas Hugger, Chief Financial Officer

Type of Firm
Private Equity Firm

Association Membership
Emerging Markets Private Equity Association

Project Preferences

Role in Financing:
Will function either as deal originator or investor in deals created by others

Type of Financing Preferred:
Core
Leveraged Buyout
Early Stage
Expansion
Generalist PE
Balanced
Later Stage
Management Buyouts
Acquisition
Startup

Geographical Preferences

International Preferences:
Hong Kong
Haiti
Cambodia
Sri Lanka
Asia
Burma

Industry Preferences

In Biotechnology prefer:
Agricultural/Animal Bio.

In Medical/Health prefer:
Medical/Health

In Consumer Related prefer:
Consumer
Retail
Food/Beverage
Consumer Services

In Industrial/Energy prefer:
Alternative Energy
Materials
Environmental Related

In Financial Services prefer:
Financial Services
Real Estate

In Business Serv. prefer:
Services

In Agr/Forestr/Fish prefer:
Agribusiness

In Other prefer:
Socially Responsible
Environment Responsible

Additional Information
Name of Most Recent Fund: Leopard Haiti Fund, L.P.
Most Recent Fund Was Raised: 07/16/2012
Year Founded: 2007
Capital Under Management: $20,000,000
Current Activity Level : Actively seeking new investments

ASIA GROWTH CAPITAL ADVISORS, LTD.

40, Ocean Financial Centre
10, Collyer Quay
Singapore, Singapore 049315
Phone: 6568086155

Type of Firm
Private Equity Firm

Project Preferences

Type of Financing Preferred:
Leveraged Buyout
Early Stage
Expansion
Generalist PE
Balanced
Later Stage
Acquisition

Geographical Preferences

International Preferences:
Vietnam
Indonesia
India
Philippines
Asia
Singapore
Malaysia

Industry Preferences

In Medical/Health prefer:
Health Services
Pharmaceuticals

In Consumer Related prefer:
Food/Beverage

In Industrial/Energy prefer:
Energy

In Business Serv. prefer:
Distribution

Additional Information
Year Founded: 2010
Current Activity Level : Actively seeking new investments

ASIA INVESTMENT PARTNERS INC

4350 South Monaco Street
Fifth Floor
Denver, CO USA 80237
Phone: 3035652416
E-mail: enquiries@aipjapan.com
Website: www.asiainvestmentpartners.com

Other Offices
Shiroyama Trust Tower
33/F, 3-1 Toranomon 4-chome
Tokyo, Japan
Phone: 81364356010

Type of Firm
Private Equity Firm

Project Preferences

Type of Financing Preferred:
Generalist PE
Balanced
Acquisition

Geographical Preferences

International Preferences:
Japan

Industry Preferences

In Medical/Health prefer:
Medical/Health

In Financial Services prefer:
Real Estate

Additional Information
Year Founded: 1998
Capital Under Management: $26,447,000
Current Activity Level : Actively seeking new investments

ASIA MEZZANINE CAPITAL ADVISERS LTD

10th Floor, Central Building
1 Peder Street
Hong Kong, Hong Kong
Phone: 85239752624
Website: www.asiamezzanine.com

Management and Staff
David Bussman, Partner
Jianjun Sun, Principal
Joseph Ferrigno, Managing Partner
Stephen Temple, Partner
Vernon Francis Moore, Partner

Type of Firm
Private Equity Firm

Association Membership
China Venture Capital Association

Project Preferences

Type of Financing Preferred:
Leveraged Buyout
Expansion
Mezzanine
Management Buyouts
Acquisition
Recapitalizations

Size of Investments Considered:
Min Size of Investment Considered (000s): $20,000
Max Size of Investment Considered (000s): $100,000

Geographical Preferences

United States Preferences:
Southeast

International Preferences:
India
China
Asia
Korea, South
Japan

Additional Information
Year Founded: 2003
Capital Under Management: $3,000,000,000
Current Activity Level : Actively seeking new investments

ASIA PACIFIC CAPITAL (HK) LTD

2607 Nine Queen's Road
Central, Hong Kong
Phone: 852-2801-5993
Fax: 852-2530-5527
E-mail: info@geapctechfund.com
Website: www.apcinvestors.com

Other Offices
Suite 67, Regent Chambers
208 Nariman Point
Mumbai, India 400 021

Management and Staff
Ashok Kothari, Managing Director
W. Gage McAffee, Managing Director

Type of Firm
Investment Management Firm

Project Preferences

Type of Financing Preferred:
Leveraged Buyout
Mezzanine
Generalist PE
Balanced
Later Stage

Size of Investments Considered:
Min Size of Investment Considered (000s): $3,000
Max Size of Investment Considered (000s): $20,000

Geographical Preferences

International Preferences:
Vietnam
Indonesia
India
Taiwan
Hong Kong
China
Thailand
Philippines
Asia
Singapore
Korea, South
Japan

Industry Preferences

In Communications prefer:
Telecommunications

In Internet Specific prefer:
Internet

In Medical/Health prefer:
Pharmaceuticals

In Consumer Related prefer:
Consumer
Retail
Consumer Products

In Financial Services prefer:
Real Estate

In Business Serv. prefer:
Media

In Manufact. prefer:
Manufacturing

Additional Information
Year Founded: 1992
Current Activity Level : Actively seeking new investments

ASIA PACIFIC HEALTHCARE ADVISORS PVT LTD

3, Factory Road
Near Safdarjung Hospital
New Delhi, India 110029
Phone: 911130611504
Website: www.asianhealthcarefund.com

Management and Staff
Mario Gobbo, Venture Partner
Preet Thakur, Vice President
Sameer Wagle, Managing Director
Sanuj Ravindran, Venture Partner
Shailendra Tandon, Chief Financial Officer

Type of Firm
Private Equity Firm

Association Membership
Indian Venture Capital Association (IVCA)

Project Preferences

Type of Financing Preferred:
Leveraged Buyout
Early Stage
Expansion
Generalist PE
Balanced
Later Stage
Management Buyouts
Acquisition

Size of Investments Considered:
Min Size of Investment Considered (000s): $5,000
Max Size of Investment Considered (000s): $20,000

Geographical Preferences

International Preferences:
India

Industry Preferences

In Medical/Health prefer:
Medical Products
Health Services
Hospitals/Clinics/Primary
Pharmaceuticals

Additional Information
Year Founded: 2010
Current Activity Level : Actively seeking new investments

ASIA PACIFIC INVESTMENT PARTNERS

16 Olympic Street
Ulaanbaatar, Mongolia
E-mail: info@apipcorp.com

Other Offices
11th Floor
New York, NY USA 10005
Phone: 212-724-0150

Suite 503, St. Georges Building
2 Ice House Street
Central, Hong Kong
Phone: 852-2868-0696
Fax: 852-2868-0696

52-54 Gracechurch Street
Oxford, United Kingdom EC3V 0EH

Management and Staff
Lee Cashell, Chief Executive Officer

Type of Firm
Private Equity Firm

Project Preferences

Type of Financing Preferred:
Balanced

Geographical Preferences

International Preferences:
Mongolia
Asia

Industry Preferences

In Consumer Related prefer:
Consumer Products

In Financial Services prefer:
Financial Services
Real Estate

In Agr/Forestr/Fish prefer:
Mining and Minerals

Additional Information
Year Founded: 2001
Current Activity Level : Actively seeking new investments

ASIA PACIFIC VENTURES

2370 Watson Court
Suite 200
Palo Alto, CA USA 94303
Phone: 650-354-3250
Fax: 650-813-1244
Website: www.apvtp.com

Management and Staff
David Duimich, President
David McQuilkin, Managing Director
Mitchell Nelson, Vice President
Will Stewart, Founder

Type of Firm
Private Equity Firm

Project Preferences

Type of Financing Preferred:
Expansion

Additional Information
Year Founded: 2009
Current Activity Level : Actively seeking new investments

ASIA VENTURES CORP

228 Queen's Road East
11th Floor Jonsim Place
Hong Kong, Hong Kong
Phone: 85231165075
Fax: 85228936881

Type of Firm
Private Equity Firm

Project Preferences

Type of Financing Preferred:
Early Stage
Expansion
Balanced
Public Companies
Later Stage

Geographical Preferences

International Preferences:
Hong Kong
China

Industry Preferences

In Communications prefer:
Communications and Media
Commercial Communications
Data Communications

In Computer Hardware prefer:
Computers

In Computer Software prefer:
Software

In Biotechnology prefer:
Biotechnology
Human Biotechnology

In Medical/Health prefer:
Medical/Health

In Industrial/Energy prefer:
Energy
Materials
Environmental Related

In Other prefer:
Environment Responsible

Additional Information
Year Founded: 2009
Current Activity Level : Actively seeking new investments

ASIA WEST LLC

20 Francesca Drive
Oyster Bay, NY USA 11771
Phone: 2034343005
Fax: 5169222705
E-mail: info@asiawestfunds.com
Website: www.asiawestfunds.com

Management and Staff
Sanford Selman, Managing Director

Type of Firm
Private Equity Firm

Project Preferences

Type of Financing Preferred:
Early Stage
Later Stage

Geographical Preferences

United States Preferences:
North America

Canadian Preferences:
All Canada

International Preferences:
Europe

Industry Preferences

In Other prefer:
Environment Responsible

Additional Information
Year Founded: 2002
Current Activity Level : Actively seeking new investments

ASIAN DEVELOPMENT BANK

Six ADB Avenue
Mandaluyong City, Philippines 1550
Phone: 6326324444
Fax: 6326362444
Website: www.adb.org

Management and Staff
Bindu Lohani, Vice President
Bruce Davis, Vice President
Lakshmi Venkatachalam, Vice President
Thierry de Longuemar, Vice President

Type of Firm
Bank Affiliated

Association Membership
Emerging Markets Private Equity Association

Project Preferences

Type of Financing Preferred:
Balanced

Geographical Preferences

International Preferences:
China
Philippines
Asia

Industry Preferences

In Industrial/Energy prefer:
Environmental Related

Additional Information
Year Founded: 1966
Current Activity Level : Actively seeking new investments

ASIAN TIGER CAPITAL PARTNERS LTD

UTC Building, Level 16
8 Panthapath
Dhaka, Bangladesh 1215
Phone: 880-2-815-5144
Fax: 880-2-911-8582
E-mail: info@at-capital.com
Website: www.at-capital.com

Management and Staff
Ifty Islam, Managing Partner
Syeed Khan, Partner

Type of Firm
Private Equity Firm

Project Preferences

Type of Financing Preferred:
Leveraged Buyout
Early Stage
Expansion
Generalist PE
Acquisition

Geographical Preferences

International Preferences:
Asia

Industry Preferences

In Medical/Health prefer:
Pharmaceuticals

In Consumer Related prefer:
Consumer
Retail
Consumer Products

In Industrial/Energy prefer:
Energy
Industrial Products

In Financial Services prefer:
Financial Services
Real Estate

In Business Serv. prefer:
Services

In Manufact. prefer:
Manufacturing

In Agr/Forestr/Fish prefer:
Agribusiness

Additional Information
Year Founded: 2008
Current Activity Level : Actively seeking new investments

ASIATECH MANAGEMENT LLC

20450 Stevens Creek Boulevard
Suite 200
Santa Clara, CA USA 95054
Phone: 4083309366
Fax: 4083309365

Other Offices
Rm. 0106, Bldg. C, Dragon Century Plaza
No. 3, Hangda Road
Hangzhou, China 31007
Phone: 86-571-2893-5296
Fax: 56-571-2893-5295

Rm. 1606, International Trade Bldg.
333 Keelung Road., Sec 1
Taipei, Taiwan 110
Phone: 886-2-2758-5828
Fax: 886-2-2758-1607

Management and Staff
Bill Chen, Principal
CK Cheng, Principal
Daniel Liu, Partner
Elise Huang, Principal
Katherine Jen, Managing Partner
Louie Liu, General Partner

Type of Firm
Private Equity Firm

Project Preferences

Type of Financing Preferred:
Early Stage
Balanced

Geographical Preferences

International Preferences:
Asia
All International

Additional Information
Year Founded: 1997
Current Activity Level : Actively seeking new investments

ASIMOV VENTURES MANAGEMENT LLC

85 Fifth Avenue
7th Floor
New York, NY USA 10003
E-mail: info@asimovventures.com
Website: asimovventures.com

Management and Staff
Alan Meckler, Co-Founder
Tyler Benster, General Partner

Type of Firm
Private Equity Firm

Project Preferences

Type of Financing Preferred:
Early Stage

Industry Preferences

In Industrial/Energy prefer:
Robotics

Additional Information
Year Founded: 2015
Current Activity Level : Actively seeking new investments

ASIYA CAPITAL INVESTMENTS COMPANY KSCP

Khalid Bin Al Waleed Street
KIPCO Tower, 31st Floor
Sharq, Kuwait
Phone: 96522971300
Fax: 96522971310
E-mail: info@asiyainvestments.com
Website: www.asiyainvestments.com

Management and Staff
Ahmad Al Hamad, Chief Executive Officer
Tokyou Lee, Chief Financial Officer

Type of Firm
Private Equity Firm

Project Preferences

Type of Financing Preferred:
Leveraged Buyout
Early Stage
Generalist PE

Geographical Preferences

International Preferences:
Asia

Additional Information
Year Founded: 2005
Current Activity Level : Actively seeking new investments

ASK PRAVI CAPITAL ADVISORS PVT LTD

Dr. Annie Besant Road, Worli
701-A, Poonam Chambers, A Wing
Mumbai, India 400 018
Phone: 912242258100
Fax: 912242258110
E-mail: info@askpravi.com
Website: www.askpravi.com

Management and Staff
Ajitabh Banerji, Vice President
Anand Vyas, Managing Partner
Jayanta Banerjee, Managing Partner
Sunay Mathure, Managing Partner
Tapan Gandhi, Principal

Type of Firm
Private Equity Firm

Association Membership
Indian Venture Capital Association (IVCA)

Project Preferences

Type of Financing Preferred:
Generalist PE

Geographical Preferences

International Preferences:
India
Asia

Industry Preferences

In Consumer Related prefer:
Consumer

In Industrial/Energy prefer:
Industrial Products

In Financial Services prefer:
Financial Services

In Business Serv. prefer:
Services

Additional Information
Year Founded: 2011
Current Activity Level : Actively seeking new investments

ASK PROPERTY INVESTMENT ADVISORS PVT LTD

Dr. Annie Besant Road, Worli
Bandbox House, 1/F, 254 - D
Mumbai, India 400025
Phone: 912266460000
Fax: 912224920163

Pratt's Guide to Private Equity & Venture Capital Sources

Other Offices

100 Feet Road, HAL 2nd Stage
Nc. 2002, 3rd Floor, Salarpuria Land Mrk
Bangalore, India 560 038
Phone: 91-80-4074-6600
Fax: 91-80-7074-6699

1195/1, F.C. Road
102 Nandadeep, 1st Floor
Shivajinagar, India 4111 005
Phone: 91-20-6604-2800
Fax: 91-20-6604-2811

Barakhamba Road
M-4, Kanchenjunga Building 18
New Delhi, India 110 001
Phone: 91-11-4369-9999
Fax: 91-11-4369-9900

The Residency, Avinashi Road
Coimbatore, India 641 018
Phone: 91-22-2241414

Nowroji Road, Sri Dasapalla Towers
D. #14-1-15/5, Flat 5
Visakhapatnam, India 530 002
Phone: 91-891-6465664
Fax: 91-891-6636640

80, Cathedral Road
Chennai, India 600 086
Phone: 91-44-4393-1700
Fax: 91-44-7393-1717

Govardhan Business Centre
510, Fifth Floor
Ernakulam, India 682 035
Phone: 91-484-2366686
Fax: 91-484-238232

Khalid Bin Walid Road
Opp. Askot Hotel, 703, Mohd Noor Bldg.
Dubai, Utd. Arab Em.
Phone: 9714-355-4770
Fax: 9714-355-6476

Tolstoy Road
108-109, Prakashdeep Building
New Delhi, India 110 001
Phone: 91-11-43689900

Rajbhavean Road, Somajiguda
6-3-927/A&B, 1st Floor, Shobhan
Hyderabad, India 500 082
Phone: 91-40-4432-7000
Fax: 91-40-4432-7010

Type of Firm
Investment Management Firm

Project Preferences

Type of Financing Preferred:
Value-Add
Opportunistic

Geographical Preferences

International Preferences:
Asia Pacific
India

Industry Preferences

In Financial Services prefer:
Real Estate

Additional Information
Name of Most Recent Fund: Offshore Realty Fund I
Most Recent Fund Was Raised: 01/04/2014
Year Founded: 1983
Capital Under Management: $492,075,000
Current Activity Level : Actively seeking new investments

ASLANOBA CAPITAL

Saray Mah. Dr Adnan Buyukdeniz
Cad. Ofis Park 3
Istanbul, Turkey
E-mail: contact@aslanobacapital.com
Website: www.aslanobacapital.com

Type of Firm
Private Equity Firm

Project Preferences

Type of Financing Preferred:
Early Stage
Seed

Geographical Preferences

International Preferences:
Turkey
Europe

Industry Preferences

In Computer Software prefer:
Software

In Internet Specific prefer:
E-Commerce Technology

Additional Information
Year Founded: 2013
Current Activity Level : Actively seeking new investments

ASML VENTURES

77 Danbury Road
Wilton, CT USA 06897
Phone: 203-761-4000
Fax: 646-822-6072
Website: www.asml.com

Type of Firm
Corporate PE/Venture

Project Preferences

Type of Financing Preferred:
Early Stage
Research and Development

Industry Preferences

In Semiconductor/Electr prefer:
Semiconductor

Additional Information
Year Founded: 2007
Current Activity Level : Actively seeking new investments

ASP CONSULTING GE-SELLSCHAFT MBH

Graben 10
Vienna, Austria 1010
Phone: 4315125000
Fax: 431512500050
E-mail: vienna@asp-consulting.com
Website: www.asp-consulting.com

Type of Firm
Investment Management Firm

Project Preferences

Type of Financing Preferred:
Early Stage
Turnaround
Later Stage
Seed
Special Situation

Geographical Preferences

International Preferences:
India
Austria

Additional Information
Year Founded: 1992
Current Activity Level : Actively seeking new investments

ASPADA ADVISORS

2 Walton Road
Bangalore, India 560001
E-mail: info@aspadainvestments.com
Website: www.aspadaadvisors.com

Type of Firm
Private Equity Firm

Project Preferences

Type of Financing Preferred:
Early Stage

Size of Investments Considered:
Min Size of Investment Considered (000s): $500
Max Size of Investment Considered (000s): $5,000

Geographical Preferences

International Preferences:
India

Industry Preferences

In Medical/Health prefer:
Medical/Health

In Consumer Related prefer:
Education Related

In Agr/Forestr/Fish prefer:
Agribusiness
Agriculture related

In Utilities prefer:
Utilities

Additional Information

Year Founded: 2013
Current Activity Level : Actively seeking new investments

ASPECT VENTURES LP

560 Brannan Street
San Francisco, CA USA 94107
E-mail: info@aspectventures.com
Website: aspectventures.com

Management and Staff

Jennifer Fonstad, Co-Founder
Lauren Kolodny, Partner
Theresia Gouw, Co-Founder

Type of Firm

Private Equity Firm

Project Preferences

Type of Financing Preferred:
Early Stage
Seed

Size of Investments Considered:

Min Size of Investment Considered (000s): $500
Max Size of Investment Considered (000s): $2,000

Industry Preferences

In Communications prefer:
Telecommunications
Wireless Communications
Data Communications

In Computer Software prefer:
Software
Applications Software

In Internet Specific prefer:
Internet

In Medical/Health prefer:
Medical/Health
Health Services

Additional Information

Year Founded: 2014
Current Activity Level : Actively seeking new investments

ASSEMBLEVC FUND I LP

53 State Street
10th Floor
Boston, MA USA 02109
Website: assemble.vc

Management and Staff

C.A. Webb, Co-Founder
John Pearce, Co-Founder
Michael Skok, Co-Founder
Richard Dulude, Principal

Type of Firm

Private Equity Firm

Project Preferences

Type of Financing Preferred:
Balanced

Additional Information

Year Founded: 2016
Current Activity Level : Actively seeking new investments

ASSET ALLOCATION & MANAGEMENT COMPANY LLC

30 North LaSalle
Suite 3500
Chicago, IL USA 60602
Phone: 312-263-2900
Fax: 312-263-1196
Website: www.aamcompany.com

Type of Firm

Insurance Firm Affiliate

Project Preferences

Type of Financing Preferred:
Leveraged Buyout

Additional Information

Year Founded: 1982
Current Activity Level : Actively seeking new investments

ASSET MANAGEMENT CO

2100 Geng Road
Suite 200
Palo Alto, CA USA 94303
Phone: 6506218808
Fax: 6508561826
Website: www.assetman.com

Management and Staff

Jialu Chen, Principal
Lisa Potocsnak, Chief Financial Officer
Louis Lange, Partner
Luke Lee, Principal
Richard Simoni, Partner
Skip Fleshman, Partner

Type of Firm

Private Equity Firm

Association Membership

Western Association of Venture Capitalists (WAVC)
National Venture Capital Association - USA (NVCA)

Project Preferences

Role in Financing:
Prefer role as deal originator but will also invest in deals created by others

Type of Financing Preferred:
Early Stage
Seed
Startup

Geographical Preferences

United States Preferences:
California

International Preferences:
Europe
Asia

Industry Focus

(% based on actual investment)

Biotechnology	27.2%
Medical/Health	22.3%
Computer Software and Services	17.5%
Internet Specific	9.3%
Semiconductors/Other Elect.	7.9%
Computer Hardware	7.3%
Communications and Media	5.4%
Consumer Related	1.5%
Industrial/Energy	0.8%
Other Products	0.8%

Additional Information

Year Founded: 1965
Capital Under Management: $180,000,000
Current Activity Level : Actively seeking new investments
Method of Compensation: Return on investment is of primary concern, do not charge fees

---

ASSOCIES MAGNUM CAPITAL PARTNERS

1290 Avenue Van Horne
Suite 218
Montreal, Canada H2V 4S2
Website: magnumcp.com

Management and Staff
Enrico Magnani, Co-Founder
Patricia Riopel, Co-Founder

Type of Firm
Private Equity Firm

Project Preferences

Type of Financing Preferred:
Leveraged Buyout
Acquisition

Geographical Preferences

Canadian Preferences:
All Canada

Additional Information
Year Founded: 2015
Current Activity Level : Actively seeking new investments

ASSSURANCE MEZZANINE FUND

509 W Colonial Drive
Suite 100
Orlando, FL USA 32804
Phone: 4079062467
Website: assurancemezz.com

Management and Staff
Alex Brown, Vice President
Anthony Yanni, Co-Founder
David Ellis, Co-Founder
Robert Whittel, Chief Financial Officer

Type of Firm
Private Equity Firm

Project Preferences

Type of Financing Preferred:
Management Buyouts
Acquisition
Recapitalizations

Geographical Preferences

United States Preferences:

Additional Information
Year Founded: 2017
Capital Under Management: $74,650,000
Current Activity Level : Actively seeking new investments

ASTELLA INVESTIMENTOS

Rua Gomes De Carvalho 1666
19th Floor
Sao Paulo, Brazil 04547006
E-mail: site@astellainvest.com
Website: astellainvest.com

Management and Staff
Edson Rigonatti, Partner
Laura Mello De Andrea Costantini, Partner
Martino Bagini, Partner

Type of Firm
Private Equity Firm

Association Membership
Brazilian Venture Capital Association (ABCR)

Project Preferences

Type of Financing Preferred:
Early Stage
Balanced
Seed

Geographical Preferences

International Preferences:
Brazil

Additional Information
Year Founded: 2008
Current Activity Level : Actively seeking new investments

ASTELLAS VENTURE MANAGEMENT LLC

P.O. Box 7585
Menlo Park, CA USA 94026
Phone: 6509260731
Fax: 6509260740
Website: www.astellasventure.com

Type of Firm
Corporate PE/Venture

Project Preferences

Role in Financing:
Prefer role in deals created by others

Type of Financing Preferred:
Early Stage
Later Stage

Size of Investments Considered:
Min Size of Investment Considered (000s): $500
Max Size of Investment Considered (000s): $3,000

Geographical Preferences

United States Preferences:

International Preferences:
Western Europe
All International

Industry Preferences

In Biotechnology prefer:
Biotechnology
Human Biotechnology

In Medical/Health prefer:
Medical Therapeutics
Pharmaceuticals

Additional Information
Year Founded: 1999
Capital Under Management: $210,000,000
Current Activity Level : Actively seeking new investments
Method of Compensation: Other

ASTER CAPITAL PARTNERS SAS

Seven Bd Malesherbes
Fourth Floor
Paris, France 75008
Phone: 33145613095
Fax: 33145613450
Website: www.aster.com

Other Offices
daVinci Shiba Park B-13
2-3-1 Shibakoen Minato- Ku
Tokyo, Japan 103-0011
Phone: 81-3-64022403

1751 S 4800W
Salt Lake City, UT USA UT84104
Phone: 1-801-990-1223
Fax: 1-801-665-3136

15Fth floor Innovation Building,
No. 1009 Yi Shan Road
Shanghai, China 200233
Phone: 86-21-2401-2507
Fax: 86-21-6485-7831

Management and Staff
Alexander Schlaepfer, Partner
Jean-Marc Bally, Managing Partner
Pascal Siegwart, Partner
Todd Dauphinais, Partner

Type of Firm
Corporate PE/Venture

Association Membership
French Venture Capital Association (AFIC)

Project Preferences

Type of Financing Preferred:
Early Stage
Seed
Startup

Geographical Preferences

United States Preferences:
All U.S.

International Preferences:
Europe
Asia

Industry Preferences

In Communications prefer:
Communications and Media

In Internet Specific prefer:
Internet

In Semiconductor/Electr prefer:
Electronics

In Industrial/Energy prefer:
Energy
Alternative Energy
Industrial Products
Materials
Factory Automation

In Other prefer:
Socially Responsible
Environment Responsible

Additional Information

Name of Most Recent Fund: Aster Capital II
Most Recent Fund Was Raised: 01/14/2010
Year Founded: 2000
Capital Under Management: $46,900,000
Current Activity Level : Actively seeking new investments

ASTOR CAPITAL GROUP, INC

10, Presnenskaya Naberezhnaya
Naberezhnaya Twr,B/C,4F,Of 404
Moscow, Russia 123317
Phone: 74959267314
Fax: 74959267315
E-mail: info@astorcg.com
Website: www.astorcg.com

Other Offices

Brestskaya 46, 1
Moscow, Russia 125047
Phone: 4952760777

Management and Staff

Will Andrich, President

Type of Firm

Investment Management Firm

Project Preferences

Type of Financing Preferred:
Generalist PE
Turnaround
Special Situation

Geographical Preferences

International Preferences:
Europe
Eastern Europe
Russia

Industry Preferences

In Consumer Related prefer:
Retail

In Industrial/Energy prefer:
Oil & Gas Drilling,Explor
Materials

In Transportation prefer:
Transportation

In Financial Services prefer:
Real Estate
Financial Services

In Manufact. prefer:
Manufacturing

In Agr/Forestr/Fish prefer:
Agribusiness
Agriculture related
Mining and Minerals

Additional Information

Year Founded: 2009
Current Activity Level : Actively seeking new investments

ASTOR PARTICIPATIES BV

Bezuidenhoutseweg 161
Postbus 93380
The Hague, Netherlands 2509 AJ
Phone: 31704278001
Fax: 31703657155
E-mail: info@astorparticipaties.nl

Type of Firm

Private Equity Firm

Association Membership

Dutch Venture Capital Associaton (NVP)

Project Preferences

Type of Financing Preferred:
Leveraged Buyout
Generalist PE
Turnaround
Later Stage
Management Buyouts
Acquisition

Size of Investments Considered:
Min Size of Investment Considered (000s): $1,400
Max Size of Investment Considered (000s): $10,500

Geographical Preferences

International Preferences:
Netherlands

Industry Preferences

In Medical/Health prefer:
Medical/Health

In Consumer Related prefer:
Consumer
Food/Beverage

In Industrial/Energy prefer:
Industrial Products

In Business Serv. prefer:
Consulting Services

Additional Information

Name of Most Recent Fund: Astor Participaties II BV
Most Recent Fund Was Raised: 12/31/2007
Year Founded: 2001
Capital Under Management: $26,400,000
Current Activity Level : Actively seeking new investments

ASTORG PARTNERS SAS

68 rue du Faubourg
Saint-Honore
Paris, France 75008
Phone: 33153054050
Fax: 33153054057
E-mail: info@astorg-partners.com
Website: www.astorg.com

Management and Staff

Catherine Couet, Chief Financial Officer
Christian Couturier, Partner
Joel Lacourte, Managing Partner
Thibault Surer, Partner
Thierry Timsit, Managing Partner

Type of Firm

Private Equity Firm

Association Membership

French Venture Capital Association (AFIC)
European Private Equity and Venture Capital Assoc.

Project Preferences

Role in Financing:
Will function either as deal originator or investor in deals created by others

Type of Financing Preferred:
Leveraged Buyout
Later Stage
Acquisition

Size of Investments Considered:
Min Size of Investment Considered (000s): $2,700
Max Size of Investment Considered: No Limit

Geographical Preferences

United States Preferences:

International Preferences:
United Kingdom
Europe
Switzerland
Germany
France

215

Industry Focus
(% based on actual investment)
Semiconductors/Other Elect.	64.7%
Internet Specific	11.8%
Consumer Related	11.1%
Industrial/Energy	10.2%
Biotechnology	2.3%

Additional Information
Name of Most Recent Fund: Astorg V FCPR
Most Recent Fund Was Raised: 02/03/2011
Year Founded: 1983
Capital Under Management: $680,600,000
Current Activity Level : Actively seeking new investments

ASTORIUS CAPITAL GMBH

Alsterarkaden 12
Hamburg, Germany 20354
Phone: 494046899130
Fax: 4940468991399
E-mail: mail@astoriuscapital.com
Website: www.astoriuscapital.com

Management and Staff
Frank Rohwedder, Managing Director
Juergen Breuer, Managing Director
Julien Zornig, Managing Director
Thomas Weinmann, Co-Founder

Type of Firm
Private Equity Advisor or Fund of Funds

Association Membership
German Venture Capital Association (BVK)

Geographical Preferences

International Preferences:
Ireland
Sweden
United Kingdom
Western Europe
Finland
Germany
Denmark

Additional Information
Year Founded: 2012
Capital Under Management: $14,241,000
Current Activity Level : Actively seeking new investments

ASTRA CAPITAL MANAGEMENT

1725 I Street NW
Suite 900
Washington, DC USA 20006
Phone: 2029307431
E-mail: info@astracapitalmgmt.com
Website: www.astracapitalmgmt.com

Type of Firm
Private Equity Firm

Project Preferences

Type of Financing Preferred:
Leveraged Buyout
Acquisition

Industry Preferences

In Communications prefer:
Communications and Media

Additional Information
Year Founded: 2017
Capital Under Management: $138,000,000
Current Activity Level : Actively seeking new investments

ASTUTIA VENTURES GMBH

Maximilianstrasse 45
Munich, Germany 80538
Phone: 4989189083880
Fax: 49891890838888
E-mail: astutia@astutia.de
Website: www.astutia.de

Management and Staff
Bernd Schruefer, Partner

Type of Firm
Private Equity Firm

Project Preferences

Type of Financing Preferred:
Early Stage
Later Stage
Startup

Geographical Preferences

International Preferences:
Europe
Switzerland
Austria
Germany

Industry Preferences

In Communications prefer:
Communications and Media

In Computer Software prefer:
Software

In Internet Specific prefer:
Internet
Ecommerce

In Consumer Related prefer:
Entertainment and Leisure
Retail
Education Related

In Financial Services prefer:
Financial Services

In Business Serv. prefer:
Media

Additional Information
Year Founded: 2006
Current Activity Level : Actively seeking new investments

ATA VENTURES

4300 El Camino Real
Suite 205
Los Altos, CA USA 94022
Phone: 6505940189
Fax: 6505940257
E-mail: contact@ataventures.com
Website: www.ataventures.com

Management and Staff
Hatch Graham, Co-Founder
John Loiacono, Venture Partner
Michael Hodges, Managing Director
Nancy McCroskey, Chief Financial Officer
T. Peter Thomas, Co-Founder

Type of Firm
Private Equity Firm

Association Membership
National Venture Capital Association - USA (NVCA)

Project Preferences

Type of Financing Preferred:
Early Stage
Seed

Industry Preferences

In Medical/Health prefer:
Medical/Health

In Consumer Related prefer:
Entertainment and Leisure
Retail
Food/Beverage

In Business Serv. prefer:
Media

Additional Information
Year Founded: 2003
Capital Under Management: $450,000,000
Current Activity Level : Actively seeking new investments

ATAIROS MANAGEMENT LP

40 Morris Avenue
3rd Floor
Bryn Mawr, PA USA 19010
Phone: 4843814144
E-mail: info@atairos.com
Website: www.atairos.com

Management and Staff
Alexander Evans, Partner
Clare McGrory, Chief Financial Officer
Jackson Phillips, Managing Director
Rachael Wagner, Managing Director
Robert Slinkard, Managing Director

Type of Firm
Private Equity Firm

Additional Information
Year Founded: 2016
Current Activity Level : Actively seeking new investments

ATALANTE SAS

242, rue de Rivoli
Paris, France 75001
Phone: 33142603805
Fax: 33142601433
E-mail: contact@capzanine.com
Website: www.capzanine.com

Management and Staff
Benedicte de Tissot, Chief Financial Officer
Christophe Karvelis, Partner
Christophe Karvelis, Co-Founder
David Hoppenot, Co-Founder
Laurent Benard, Partner

Type of Firm
Private Equity Firm

Association Membership
French Venture Capital Association (AFIC)

Project Preferences

Type of Financing Preferred:
Leveraged Buyout
Mezzanine
Generalist PE
Later Stage
Management Buyouts
Acquisition

Geographical Preferences

International Preferences:
Europe
France

Additional Information
Name of Most Recent Fund: Capzanine 3 FCPR
Most Recent Fund Was Raised: 09/06/2012
Year Founded: 2004
Capital Under Management: $1,276,500,000
Current Activity Level : Actively seeking new investments

ATALAYA CAPITAL MANAGEMENT LP

780 Third Avenue
27th Floor
New York, NY USA 10017
Phone: 2122011910
E-mail: IR@atalayacap.com
Website: www.atalayacap.com

Management and Staff
Michael Bogdan, Partner
Raymond Chan, Partner
Robert Flowers, Partner

Type of Firm
Investment Management Firm

Project Preferences

Type of Financing Preferred:
Mezzanine

Industry Preferences

In Communications prefer:
Communications and Media
Telecommunications

In Computer Software prefer:
Software

In Consumer Related prefer:
Other Restaurants

In Financial Services prefer:
Real Estate
Financial Services

In Business Serv. prefer:
Services

In Manufact. prefer:
Manufacturing

Additional Information
Name of Most Recent Fund: Atalaya Principal Finance Fund L.P.
Most Recent Fund Was Raised: 07/10/2012
Year Founded: 2006
Capital Under Management: $75,000,000
Current Activity Level : Actively seeking new investments

ATAMI CAPITAL

14 Albert Street
Isle of Man, United Kingdom IM1 2QA
E-mail: info@atamicapital.co.uk
Website: atamicapital.co.uk/

Type of Firm
Private Equity Firm

Project Preferences

Type of Financing Preferred:
Acquisition

Additional Information
Year Founded: 2017
Current Activity Level : Actively seeking new investments

ATAR CAPITAL LLC

1999 Avenue of the Stars
Suite 2810
Los Angeles, CA USA 90067
Phone: 3108700808
E-mail: info@atarcapital.com
Website: www.atarcapital.com

Management and Staff
Robert Lezec, Senior Managing Director
Stanley Huang, Managing Director
T. McCaffrey, Vice President
Vijay Mony, Managing Director

Type of Firm
Private Equity Firm

Project Preferences

Type of Financing Preferred:
Leveraged Buyout

Geographical Preferences

United States Preferences:
North America

International Preferences:
Western Europe

Industry Preferences

In Medical/Health prefer:
Health Services

In Consumer Related prefer:
Retail

In Industrial/Energy prefer:
Energy
Industrial Products

Additional Information
Year Founded: 1974
Current Activity Level : Actively seeking new investments

ATEL VENTURES INC

600 Montgomery Street
9th Floor
San Francisco, CA USA 94111
Phone: 4156163436
Fax: 4159893796
Website: www.atel.com

Management and Staff
Steven Rea, Vice President

Type of Firm
Corporate PE/Venture

Association Membership
National Venture Capital Association - USA (NVCA)

Project Preferences

Type of Financing Preferred:
Early Stage
Balanced
Later Stage

Geographical Preferences

United States Preferences:

Additional Information
Name of Most Recent Fund: ATEL Growth Capital Fund V LLC
Most Recent Fund Was Raised: 05/13/2009
Year Founded: 1998
Capital Under Management: $100,000,000
Current Activity Level : Actively seeking new investments

ATERIAN INVESTMENT MANAGEMENT LP

1700 Broadway
38th Floor
New York, NY USA 10019
Phone: 2125472806
Fax: 2125472868
E-mail: info@aterianpartners.com
Website: www.aterianpartners.com

Management and Staff
Brandon Bethea, Partner
Christopher Thomas, Partner
Michael Fieldstone, Partner

Type of Firm
Private Equity Firm

Project Preferences

Type of Financing Preferred:
Leveraged Buyout
Turnaround
Management Buyouts
Acquisition

Geographical Preferences

United States Preferences:
North America

Industry Preferences

In Medical/Health prefer:
Health Services

In Consumer Related prefer:
Retail
Food/Beverage
Consumer Products
Other Restaurants

In Industrial/Energy prefer:
Industrial Products

In Business Serv. prefer:
Distribution

In Manufact. prefer:
Manufacturing

In Agr/Forestr/Fish prefer:
Mining and Minerals

Additional Information
Name of Most Recent Fund: Aterian Investment Partners II. L.P.
Most Recent Fund Was Raised: 12/24/2013
Year Founded: 2013
Capital Under Management: $256,800,000
Current Activity Level : Actively seeking new investments

ATHENA CAPITAL PARTNERS LLC

8840 Wilshire Boulevard
Second Floor
Beverly Hills, CA USA 90211
Phone: 3106525900
Fax: 3103583285
Website: www.athenacapital.net

Type of Firm
Private Equity Firm

Project Preferences

Role in Financing:
Will function either as deal originator or investor in deals created by others

Type of Financing Preferred:
Acquisition
Startup
Special Situation

Geographical Preferences

United States Preferences:
Southern California

Additional Information
Year Founded: 2000
Current Activity Level : Actively seeking new investments

ATHENIAN FUND MANAGEMENT INC

340 West State Street
Unit #29/Suite 137D
Athens, OH USA 45701
Phone: 6143601155
Fax: 7405939311
E-mail: info@athenianvp.com
Website: www.athenianvp.com

Other Offices
2881 East Oakland Park Boulevard
FORT LAUDERDALE, FL USA 33306
Phone: 954-315-2091
Fax: 954-315-2092

Management and Staff
Daniel Kosoy, Partner
David Scholl, Partner
Mary Strother, Managing Director
Mitchell Cohen, Chief Financial Officer
Mitchell Rosich, Partner
William Tanner, Chief Financial Officer

Type of Firm
Private Equity Firm

Project Preferences

Role in Financing:
Will function either as deal originator or investor in deals created by others

Type of Financing Preferred:
Early Stage
Later Stage

Geographical Preferences

United States Preferences:
Midwest
Northwest
Rocky Mountain
West Coast
East Coast

Industry Preferences

In Communications prefer:
Communications and Media

In Computer Software prefer:
Software

In Semiconductor/Electr prefer:
Semiconductor

In Biotechnology prefer:
Biotechnology
Human Biotechnology

Additional Information
Year Founded: 1997
Capital Under Management: $105,100,000
Current Activity Level : Actively seeking new investments

ATHLONE INTERNATIONAL LTD

200 Brook Drive
Green Park
Reading, United Kingdom RG2 6UB
Phone: 44-870-351-9312
Fax: 44-870-351-9313
E-mail: info@athloneinternational.com
Website: www.athlonegroup.co.uk

Other Offices

Dubai Media City
Business Central Towers
Dubai, Utd. Arab Em.

Copthall
Roseay Valley, Dominica 00152

Erlenstrasse 81
Wollerau, Switzerland CH - 8832

5 Depovskaya
Karizma Building
Uralsk, Kazakhstan 0090006

P.O. Box 321
Baytown, TX USA 77522

4 Robert Speck Parkway
Mississauga, Canada L4Z 1S1

Management and Staff

Alex Miller, Chief Operating Officer
Jojar Singh Dhinsa, Chief Executive Officer

Type of Firm
Service Provider

Project Preferences

Type of Financing Preferred:
Public Companies
Turnaround

Geographical Preferences

International Preferences:
United Kingdom

Industry Preferences

In Communications prefer:
Telecommunications

In Business Serv. prefer:
Media

Additional Information
Year Founded: 2002
Current Activity Level : Actively seeking new investments

ATHYRIUM CAPITAL MANAGEMENT LLC

530 Fifth Avenue
25th Floor
New York, NY USA 10036
Phone: 2124026925
E-mail: info@athyrium.com
Website: www.athyrium.com

Type of Firm
Private Equity Firm

Project Preferences

Type of Financing Preferred:
Generalist PE
Balanced

Industry Preferences

In Medical/Health prefer:
Medical Therapeutics
Drug/Equipmt Delivery
Medical Products
Health Services
Pharmaceuticals

Additional Information
Year Founded: 2008
Capital Under Management: $3,225,000,000
Current Activity Level : Actively seeking new investments

ATINUM INVESTMENT CO LTD

Samsung-Dong Gangnam-Gu
5F, Cheil Building 168-26
Seoul, South Korea 135-882
Phone: 8225550781
Fax: 8225572570
Website: www.atinuminvest.co.kr

Other Offices

1133-10 Ingue-dong
Suwon
Kyonggi-do, South Korea
Phone: 82-331-38-1761
Fax: 82-331-36-1637

Management and Staff

Chang Seok Hwang, Managing Director
Kicheon Shin, President
Seung Yong Lee, Managing Director

Type of Firm
Corporate PE/Venture

Association Membership
Korean Venture Capital Association (KVCA)

Project Preferences

Type of Financing Preferred:
Balanced

Geographical Preferences

International Preferences:
Korea, South

Industry Preferences

In Communications prefer:
Communications and Media

In Industrial/Energy prefer:
Alternative Energy

Additional Information
Year Founded: 1988
Capital Under Management: $87,300,000
Current Activity Level : Actively seeking new investments

ATITLAN SA

27 Planta Quinta
Plaza Ayuntamiento
Valencia, Spain 46002

Management and Staff
Roberto Centeno, President

Type of Firm
Private Equity Firm

Project Preferences

Type of Financing Preferred:
Early Stage
Balanced
Seed
Startup

Geographical Preferences

International Preferences:
Europe
Spain

Industry Preferences

In Medical/Health prefer:
Medical/Health

In Consumer Related prefer:
Food/Beverage
Consumer Products

In Agr/Forestr/Fish prefer:
Agribusiness

Additional Information
Year Founded: 2007
Current Activity Level : Actively seeking new investments

ATL PARTNERS

320 Park Avenue
Suite 1600
New York, NY USA 10022
Phone: 6469265841
E-mail: contact@atlpartners.com
Website: www.atlpartners.com

Type of Firm
Private Equity Firm

Project Preferences

Type of Financing Preferred:
Leveraged Buyout
Acquisition

Geographical Preferences

United States Preferences:
North America

Industry Preferences

In Transportation prefer:
Transportation
Aerospace

Additional Information
Year Founded: 2014
Capital Under Management: $516,800,000
Current Activity Level : Actively seeking new investments

ATLANTA CAPITAL PARTNERS LLC

3455 Peachtree Road North East
Fifth Floor
Atlanta, GA USA 30326
Phone: 4048569157
Fax: 4043937074
E-mail: info@atlcp.com

Management and Staff
David Kugelman, President

Type of Firm
Private Equity Firm

Project Preferences

Type of Financing Preferred:
Leveraged Buyout
Mezzanine
Management Buyouts
Acquisition
Recapitalizations

Geographical Preferences

United States Preferences:

Additional Information
Year Founded: 2007
Current Activity Level : Actively seeking new investments

ATLANTA EQUITY INVESTORS LLC

191 Peachtree Street Northeast
Suite 4050
Atlanta, GA USA 30303
Phone: 4044786770
Fax: 4044786771
Website: www.atlantaeq.com

Management and Staff
David Crosland, Co-Founder
Gerald Benjamin, Co-Founder
William McCaleb, Principal

Type of Firm
Private Equity Firm

Project Preferences

Type of Financing Preferred:
Leveraged Buyout
Expansion
Acquisition
Recapitalizations

Geographical Preferences

United States Preferences:
Southeast

Industry Preferences

In Medical/Health prefer:
Health Services

In Consumer Related prefer:
Retail
Consumer Products
Consumer Services

In Business Serv. prefer:
Services

In Manufact. prefer:
Manufacturing

Additional Information
Year Founded: 2007
Capital Under Management: $109,000,000
Current Activity Level : Actively seeking new investments

ATLANTA TECHNOLOGY ANGELS

75 Fifth Street Northwest, Suite 311
Atlanta, GA USA 30308
Phone: 4045266039
Fax: 4045266035
Website: www.angelatlanta.com

Type of Firm
Angel Group

Project Preferences

Type of Financing Preferred:
Early Stage
Startup

Geographical Preferences

United States Preferences:
Georgia

Additional Information
Year Founded: 1999
Capital Under Management: $20,000,000
Current Activity Level : Actively seeking new investments

ATLANTA VENTURES

3423 Piedmont Road
Atlanta Tech Village
Atlanta, GA USA 30305
Website: www.atlantaventures.com

Type of Firm
Private Equity Firm

Project Preferences

Type of Financing Preferred:
Balanced

Additional Information
Year Founded: 2017
Capital Under Management: $20,000,000
Current Activity Level : Actively seeking new investments

ATLANTIC ASSET MANAGEMENT LLC

2187 Atlantic Street
Cearwater House
Stamford, CT USA 06902
Phone: 2033512800
Fax: 2033512866
Website: www.atlanticasset.com

Other Offices
9300 West 110th Street,
Suite 460
Overland Park, KS USA 66210
Phone: 9133451114
Fax: 9133450224

Management and Staff
Donald Trotter, Co-Founder
Elaine Hunt, Co-Founder
Gerald Thunelius, Managing Director
Jamie Pratt, Vice President
Sara Roche, Vice President
Steven Arnone, Vice President

Type of Firm
Investment Management Firm

Project Preferences

Type of Financing Preferred:
Other

Additional Information
Year Founded: 1992
Capital Under Management: $122,500,000
Current Activity Level : Actively seeking new investments

ATLANTIC BRIDGE

31 Kildare Street
Dublin 2, Ireland
Phone: 35316034450
Fax: 35316425661
Website: www.abven.com

Management and Staff
Brian Long, Partner
Elaine Coughlan, Partner
Gerry Maguire, Partner
Kevin Dillon, Partner
Larry Quinn, Venture Partner
Mark Horgan, Partner

Type of Firm
Private Equity Firm

Association Membership
Irish Venture Capital Association
European Private Equity and Venture Capital Assoc.

Project Preferences

Type of Financing Preferred:
Leveraged Buyout
Early Stage
Expansion
Generalist PE
Balanced
Later Stage

Geographical Preferences

International Preferences:
Ireland
Europe
China

Industry Preferences

In Communications prefer:
Wireless Communications

In Computer Software prefer:
Software

In Semiconductor/Electr prefer:
Semiconductor

Additional Information
Name of Most Recent Fund: Atlantic Bridge II
Most Recent Fund Was Raised: 11/15/2010
Year Founded: 1969
Capital Under Management: $509,300,000
Current Activity Level : Actively seeking new investments

ATLANTIC CANADA OPPORTUNITIES AGENCY

644 Main Street
Blue Cross Center, Third Floor
Moncton, Canada E1C9J8
Phone: 5068512271
Fax: 5068571301
Website: www.acoa-apeca.gc.ca

Management and Staff
Janet Gagnon, Vice President
Monique Colette, President
Patrick Dorsey, Vice President
Paul LeBlanc, President
Paul Mills, Vice President
Peter Hogan, Vice President

Type of Firm
Government Affiliated Program

Project Preferences

Type of Financing Preferred:
Balanced

Additional Information
Year Founded: 2007
Current Activity Level : Actively seeking new investments

ATLANTIC CAPITAL BV

Takkebijsters 37 B
Breda, Netherlands 4817 BL
Phone: 31765780066
Fax: 31765780065
E-mail: info@atlanticcapital.nl
Website: www.atlanticcapital.nl

Management and Staff
Kenneth Broos, Founder

Type of Firm
Private Equity Firm

Association Membership
Dutch Venture Capital Associaton (NVP)

Project Preferences

Type of Financing Preferred:
Leveraged Buyout
Generalist PE
Later Stage
Management Buyouts
Acquisition

Geographical Preferences

International Preferences:
Netherlands

Industry Preferences

In Computer Software prefer:
Software

In Medical/Health prefer:
Medical/Health

In Consumer Related prefer:
Consumer

In Industrial/Energy prefer:
Industrial Products

Additional Information
Year Founded: 1991
Capital Under Management: $3,200,000
Current Activity Level : Actively seeking new investments

ATLANTIC CAPITAL PARTNERS GMBH

Seestrasse 8
Munich, Germany 80802
E-mail: info@atlanticcp.com
Website: www.atlanticcp.com

Management and Staff
Alexander Bruehl, General Partner
Fred Van Den Bosch, Venture Partner
Marcus Englert, General Partner
Moshe Bar, General Partner
Raffaele Jerusalmi, Venture Partner

Type of Firm
Private Equity Firm

Association Membership
German Venture Capital Association (BVK)

Project Preferences

Type of Financing Preferred:
Early Stage
Seed
Startup

Geographical Preferences

United States Preferences:
All U.S.

International Preferences:
United Kingdom
Europe
Israel
Germany

Industry Preferences

In Communications prefer:
Media and Entertainment

In Computer Software prefer:
Data Processing
Software

Additional Information

Name of Most Recent Fund: Atlantic Capital Partners
Most Recent Fund Was Raised: 01/30/2011
Year Founded: 2010
Capital Under Management: $100,000,000
Current Activity Level : Actively seeking new investments

ATLANTIC INTERNET GMBH

Rosenthaler Strasse 13
Berlin, Germany 10119
E-mail: imprint@atlanticinternet.de
Website: www.atlanticlabs.de

Management and Staff

Dario Alborghetti, Venture Partner
Jens-Philipp Klein, Chief Financial Officer
Marc-Olivier Lucke, Venture Partner

Type of Firm

Private Equity Firm

Project Preferences

Type of Financing Preferred:
Early Stage
Seed
Startup

Geographical Preferences

International Preferences:
Germany

Industry Preferences

In Computer Software prefer:
Software

Additional Information

Year Founded: 2008
Current Activity Level : Actively seeking new investments

ATLANTIC STREET CAPITAL MANAGEMENT LLC

281 Tresser Boulevard
Sixth Floor Suite 601
Stamford, CT USA 06901
Phone: 2034283158
Fax: 2033888044
Website: atlanticstreetcapital.com

Management and Staff

Andrew Wilkins, Partner
Andy Wilkins, Managing Partner
George Parry, Principal
Grant Marcks, Vice President
Iris Rosken, Chief Financial Officer
M. Kurt Lentz, Principal
Peter Shabecoff, Founder
Phillip Druce, Principal
Stephanie James, Vice President
Timothy Lewis, Partner

Type of Firm

Private Equity Firm

Project Preferences

Type of Financing Preferred:
Leveraged Buyout
Turnaround
Acquisition
Recapitalizations

Geographical Preferences

United States Preferences:

Canadian Preferences:
All Canada

Industry Preferences

In Consumer Related prefer:
Consumer Products
Consumer Services

In Transportation prefer:
Transportation

In Business Serv. prefer:
Services

In Manufact. prefer:
Manufacturing

Additional Information

Year Founded: 2006
Capital Under Management: $100,000,000
Current Activity Level : Actively seeking new investments

ATLANTIC VENTURES GMBH

Habsburgerstrasse 12
Luzern, Switzerland 6002
E-mail: info@atlanticventures.com
Website: atlanticventures.yolasite.com

Management and Staff

Christophe Maire, Partner
Jens-Philipp Klein, Venture Partner
Olivier Kobel, Partner
Simon Fabich, Venture Partner

Type of Firm

Private Equity Firm

Project Preferences

Type of Financing Preferred:
Early Stage
Seed
Startup

Geographical Preferences

International Preferences:
Switzerland
Austria
Germany

Industry Preferences

In Communications prefer:
Communications and Media
Commercial Communications

In Internet Specific prefer:
Internet

Additional Information

Year Founded: 2006
Current Activity Level : Actively seeking new investments

ATLANTIC-PACIFIC CAPITAL INC

400 Madison Avenue
Suite 11A
New York, NY USA 10017
Phone: 2129810630
E-mail: info@apcap.com
Website: www.apcap.com

Other Offices

50 California Street
Suite 1500
San Francisco, CA USA 94111
Phone: 415-291-8199
Fax: 415-291-8198

40th Floor
118 Connaught Road West
Hong Kong, Hong Kong
Phone: 852-3579-2205
Fax: 852-3579-2691

102 Greenwich Avenue
Second Floor
Greenwich, CT USA 06830
Phone: 2038629182

800 Riverview Square
Suite 101
Brielle, NJ USA 08730
Phone: 732-292-0363
Fax: 732-292-0365

22 West Washington Street
Suite 1475
Chicago, IL USA 60602
Phone: 3122361157

2100 McKinney Avenue
Suite 700
Dallas, TX USA 75201
Phone: 214-661-8390
Fax: 214-661-8395

52 Jermyn Street
6th Floor
London, United Kingdom SW1Y 6LX
Phone: 44-20-7290-3080
Fax: 44-20-7290-3089

Management and Staff
Alexander Leykikh, Partner
Alexander Mejia, Principal
Bailey Puntereri, Vice President
Brendan Edmonds, Partner
Brian Wade, Partner
Donna Toth, Chief Financial Officer
James Weidner, Partner
Jennifer Tedesko, Partner
John Chase, Partner
John Pilson, Principal
Joshua Vogelhut, Partner
Kevin Imhoff, Principal
Mark Olexy, Partner
Michael Pilson, Partner
Peter Larsen, Principal
Richard Awbery, Principal
Sarah Sandstrom, Partner
Shierly Porbo, Vice President
Tanguy Cotton, Managing Partner
Victor Manuel, Partner
Vincent Ng, Partner
William Riedlinger, Principal

Type of Firm
Service Provider

Project Preferences

Type of Financing Preferred:
Leveraged Buyout
Early Stage
Generalist PE
Turnaround
Private Placement
Special Situation
Distressed Debt

Geographical Preferences

United States Preferences:

Canadian Preferences:
All Canada

International Preferences:
Latin America
Europe
Middle East
Pacific
Asia
Africa
All International

Additional Information
Year Founded: 1995
Current Activity Level : Actively seeking new investments
Method of Compensation: Function primarily in service area, receive contingent fee in cash or equity

ATLANTIS CAPITAL MARKETS NA LLC

Piazza del Carmine, 4
Milan, Italy 20121
Phone: 39245475210
Fax: 39245475206
E-mail: contact@atlantispartners.it

Management and Staff
Luciano Anzanello, Partner
Raffaele Legnani, Co-Founder

Type of Firm
Private Equity Firm

Project Preferences

Type of Financing Preferred:
Generalist PE
Turnaround

Size of Investments Considered:
Min Size of Investment Considered (000s): $1,270
Max Size of Investment Considered (000s): $38,106

Geographical Preferences

International Preferences:
Italy

Additional Information
Year Founded: 2005
Capital Under Management: $79,300,000
Current Activity Level : Actively seeking new investments

ATLANTIS INVESTMENT MANAGEMENT HONG KONG LTD

Rm 3501 The Centrium
60 Wyndham Street
Central, Hong Kong
Phone: 86-852-2110-63
Fax: 86-852-2110-98
Website: www.atlantis-investment.com

Type of Firm
Investment Management Firm

Project Preferences

Type of Financing Preferred:
Later Stage

Geographical Preferences

International Preferences:
China
Asia

Additional Information
Year Founded: 1994
Current Activity Level : Actively seeking new investments

ATLAS HOLDINGS FRM LLC

One Sound Shore Drive
Suite 203
Greenwich, CT USA 06830
Phone: 2036229138
Fax: 2036220151
Website: www.atlasholdingsllc.com

Management and Staff
Daniel Cromie, Partner
Edward Fletcher, Partner
Jacob Hudson, Principal
Jeffrey Nathan, Vice President
Philip Schuch, Partner
Sam Astor, Vice President
Timothy Fazio, Managing Partner
Zachary Sufrin, Principal

Type of Firm
Private Equity Firm

Project Preferences

Type of Financing Preferred:
Leveraged Buyout
Turnaround
Management Buyouts
Acquisition
Special Situation
Distressed Debt
Recapitalizations

Geographical Preferences

United States Preferences:
North America

Industry Preferences

In Biotechnology prefer:
Industrial Biotechnology

In Medical/Health prefer:
Medical/Health

In Consumer Related prefer:
Food/Beverage

In Industrial/Energy prefer:
Industrial Products

In Financial Services prefer:
Financial Services
Financial Services

In Business Serv. prefer:
Services
Consulting Services

In Agr/Forestr/Fish prefer:
Agribusiness

Additional Information
Name of Most Recent Fund: Atlas Capital Resources II, L.P.
Most Recent Fund Was Raised: 12/16/2013
Year Founded: 2002
Capital Under Management: $900,000,000
Current Activity Level : Actively seeking new investments

ATLAS PEAK CAPITAL

400 Montgomery Street
Suite 900
San Francisco, CA USA 94104
Phone: 4159670485
E-mail: info@atlaspeakcap.com
Website: www.atlaspeakcap.com

Management and Staff
Brian DiLaura, Co-Founder
Josh Blachman, Co-Founder

Type of Firm
Private Equity Firm

Project Preferences

Type of Financing Preferred:
Expansion
Balanced

Geographical Preferences

International Preferences:
Rest of World

Industry Preferences

In Communications prefer:
Communications and Media

In Computer Software prefer:
Software

In Internet Specific prefer:
Internet

In Financial Services prefer:
Financial Services

In Business Serv. prefer:
Services
Media

Additional Information
Name of Most Recent Fund: Atlas Peak Capital I, L.P.
Most Recent Fund Was Raised: 04/10/2013
Year Founded: 2013
Capital Under Management: $28,905,000
Current Activity Level : Actively seeking new investments

ATLAS VENTURE ADVISORS INC

400 Technology Square
10th Floor
Cambridge, MA USA 02139
Phone: 8572012700
Website: www.atlasventure.com

Management and Staff
Bruce Booth, Partner
David Grayzel, Partner
Jason Rhodes, Partner
Jean-Francois Formela, Partner
Kevin Bitterman, Partner
Michael Fizzell, Principal
Michael Gladstone, Principal
Ommer Chohan, Chief Financial Officer
Peter Barrett, Partner
Saurabh Saha, Venture Partner

Type of Firm
Private Equity Firm

Association Membership
British Venture Capital Association (BVCA)
New England Venture Capital Association
National Venture Capital Association - USA (NVCA)

Project Preferences

Role in Financing:
Will function either as deal originator or investor in deals created by others

Type of Financing Preferred:
Early Stage
Later Stage
Seed

Size of Investments Considered:
Min Size of Investment Considered (000s): $500
Max Size of Investment Considered (000s): $5,000

Geographical Preferences

United States Preferences:
Massachusetts

International Preferences:
Europe

Industry Focus
(% based on actual investment)

Biotechnology	25.9%
Computer Software and Services	22.7%
Internet Specific	21.5%
Medical/Health	11.7%
Semiconductors/Other Elect.	7.1%
Communications and Media	6.6%
Computer Hardware	3.1%
Other Products	0.6%
Consumer Related	0.5%
Industrial/Energy	0.4%

Additional Information
Name of Most Recent Fund: Atlas Venture Fund IX, L.P.
Most Recent Fund Was Raised: 04/26/2013
Year Founded: 1980
Capital Under Management: $2,580,000,000
Current Activity Level : Actively seeking new investments
Method of Compensation: Return on investment is of primary concern, do not charge fees

ATOMIC MANAGEMENT LLC

1 Letterman
Building C, Suite 3500
San Francisco, CA USA 94129
Phone: 4156121900
Website: atomic.vc

Type of Firm
Private Equity Firm

Project Preferences

Type of Financing Preferred:
Early Stage
Seed

Additional Information
Year Founded: 1969
Current Activity Level : Actively seeking new investments

ATOMICO VENTURES

50, New Bond Street
London, United Kingdom W1S 1BJ
E-mail: contact@atomico.com

Other Offices
15/F, China World Tower 3
1, Jianguomenwai Avenue
Beijing, China 100020

Buyukdere cad
Ecza Sok, No:4/1 Polcenter
Istanbul, Turkey

Av. Brigadeiro Faria Lima
Sao Paulo, Brazil 04538905

RoP 6fl. 5-11-1
Toranomon, Minato-ku
Tokyo, Japan 105-0001

Management and Staff
Andrew Crankshaw, Founder
Geoffrey Prentice, Partner
Hiro Tamura, Partner
Mattias Ljungman, Partner
Wouter Wort, Principal

Type of Firm
Private Equity Firm

Project Preferences

Type of Financing Preferred:
Early Stage
Expansion
Balanced
Later Stage

Geographical Preferences

International Preferences:
United Kingdom
Europe

Industry Preferences

In Computer Software prefer:
Software

In Internet Specific prefer:
Internet

Additional Information

Name of Most Recent Fund: Atomico Ventures III, L.P.
Most Recent Fund Was Raised: 12/21/2012
Year Founded: 2006
Capital Under Management: $1,241,630,000
Current Activity Level : Actively seeking new investments

ATP MANAGEMENT COMPANY LLC

1108 Lavaca Street
Suite 110-115
Austin, TX USA 78701
Phone: 5125883878

Type of Firm
Private Equity Firm

Project Preferences

Type of Financing Preferred:
Early Stage
Start-up Financing

Geographical Preferences

United States Preferences:
Texas

Industry Preferences

In Communications prefer:
Media and Entertainment

In Computer Software prefer:
Software
Systems Software

In Medical/Health prefer:
Medical Products

Additional Information
Year Founded: 2014

Current Activity Level : Actively seeking new investments

ATP PRIVATE EQUITY PARTNERS

Sjaeleboderne 2
1st Floor
Copenhagen, Denmark 1122
Phone: 4533193070
Fax: 4533193071
E-mail: info@atp-pep.com
Website: www.atp-pep.com

Other Offices
515 Madison Avenue
Suite 3700
New York, NY USA 10022
Phone: 2126445020
Fax: 2126441458

Management and Staff
Adam Saunte, Vice President
Christian Raaby Bronden, Vice President
Claudio Demontis, Vice President
Kent Kjaergaard, Chief Financial Officer
Klaus Ruehne, Partner
Rune Ulbak, Vice President
Soren Andersen, Partner
Susanne Forsingdal, Partner
Torben Vangstrup, Managing Partner

Type of Firm
Private Equity Advisor or Fund of Funds

Association Membership
Danish Venture Capital Association (DVCA)
European Private Equity and Venture Capital Assoc.

Project Preferences

Role in Financing:
Other

Type of Financing Preferred:
Fund of Funds
Fund of Funds of Second

Size of Investments Considered:
Min Size of Investment Considered (000s): $8,000
Max Size of Investment Considered (000s): $150,000

Geographical Preferences

United States Preferences:
North America
All U.S.

International Preferences:
Europe
Eastern Europe
Pacific
Scandanavia/Nordic Region
Asia
All International

Industry Focus
(% based on actual investment)
Other Products	85.9%
Medical/Health	13.7%
Internet Specific	0.3%
Biotechnology	0.0%

Additional Information
Name of Most Recent Fund: ATP Private Equity Partners V K/S
Most Recent Fund Was Raised: 03/31/2014
Year Founded: 2001
Capital Under Management: $8,480,700,000
Current Activity Level : Actively seeking new investments

ATTRACTOR INVESTMENT MANAGEMENT INC

1325 Fourth Avenue
Suite 1425
Seattle, WA USA 98101
Phone: 2064623980
Fax: 2064623985
Website: www.attractor.com

Management and Staff
Harvey Allison, President
Lysun Seto, Chief Financial Officer

Type of Firm
Private Equity Firm

Industry Focus
(% based on actual investment)
Internet Specific	70.2%
Computer Software and Services	16.0%
Computer Hardware	5.9%
Other Products	3.4%
Industrial/Energy	2.1%
Communications and Media	1.4%
Medical/Health	1.2%

Additional Information
Year Founded: 1996
Current Activity Level : Actively seeking new investments

ATW PARTNERS LLC

1600, 17 State Street
New York, NY USA 10004
Website: www.atwpartners.com

Type of Firm
Investment Management Firm

Project Preferences

Type of Financing Preferred:
Balanced

Additional Information
Year Founded: 2016
Current Activity Level : Actively seeking new investments

ATX SEED VENTURES

1011 San Jacinto Blvd
3rd Floor
Austin, TX USA 78746
Phone: 5127317674
E-mail: info@atxseedventures.com
Website: www.atxseedventures.com

Management and Staff
Brad Bentz, Principal
Christopher Shonk, General Partner

Type of Firm
Private Equity Firm

Project Preferences

Type of Financing Preferred:
Early Stage
Seed

Additional Information
Year Founded: 2014
Capital Under Management: $25,000,000
Current Activity Level : Actively seeking new investments

AUA PRIVATE EQUITY PARTNERS LLC

14 Penn Plaza
Suite 1305
New York, NY USA 10122
Phone: 2122318680
Fax: 2122318601
E-mail: info@auaequity.com
Website: www.auaequity.com

Management and Staff
David Benyaminy, Partner
Kyce Chihi, Vice President
Steven Flyer, Partner

Type of Firm
Private Equity Firm

Association Membership
Natl Assoc of Investment Cos. (NAIC)

Project Preferences

Type of Financing Preferred:
Leveraged Buyout
Expansion
Management Buyouts
Industry Rollups
Recapitalizations

Geographical Preferences

United States Preferences:

Industry Preferences

In Medical/Health prefer:
Medical/Health

In Consumer Related prefer:
Consumer
Retail
Consumer Products
Consumer Services
Other Restaurants

In Transportation prefer:
Transportation

In Business Serv. prefer:
Services
Distribution
Media

Additional Information
Name of Most Recent Fund: AUA Private Equity Fund I, L.P.
Most Recent Fund Was Raised: 01/07/2014
Year Founded: 2012
Capital Under Management: $64,000,000
Current Activity Level : Actively seeking new investments

AUCTUS CAPITAL PARTNERS AG

Prinzregentenstrasse 18
Munich, Germany 80538
Phone: 4989159070000
Fax: 4989159070049
E-mail: info@auctus.com
Website: www.auctus.com

Management and Staff
Ingo Krocke, Chief Executive Officer

Type of Firm
Private Equity Firm

Project Preferences

Type of Financing Preferred:
Leveraged Buyout
Balanced
Management Buyouts
Acquisition
Private Placement

Geographical Preferences

International Preferences:
Switzerland
Austria
Germany

Industry Preferences

In Computer Software prefer:
Software

In Medical/Health prefer:
Medical/Health
Pharmaceuticals

In Consumer Related prefer:
Food/Beverage
Education Related

In Industrial/Energy prefer:
Energy
Materials
Factory Automation
Machinery

In Business Serv. prefer:
Consulting Services

Additional Information
Year Founded: 2001
Capital Under Management: $300,000,000
Current Activity Level : Actively seeking new investments

AUDACIA SAS

6 Rue de Teheran
Paris, France 75008
Phone: 33156434800
Fax: 33156434808
E-mail: contact@audacia.fr
Website: www.audacia.fr

Type of Firm
Private Equity Firm

Association Membership
French Venture Capital Association (AFIC)

Project Preferences

Type of Financing Preferred:
Early Stage
Later Stage
Distressed Debt

Geographical Preferences

International Preferences:
Europe
France

Industry Preferences

In Internet Specific prefer:
Ecommerce

In Computer Other prefer:
Computer Related

In Semiconductor/Electr prefer:
Electronics

In Medical/Health prefer:
Health Services

In Consumer Related prefer:
Consumer
Consumer Services

In Industrial/Energy prefer:
Industrial Products

In Business Serv. prefer:
Services
Distribution

Additional Information
Year Founded: 2006
Current Activity Level : Actively seeking new investments

AUDAX GROUP, INC.

101 Huntington Avenue
24th Floor
Boston, MA USA 02199
Phone: 6178591500
Fax: 6178591600
Website: www.audaxgroup.com

Other Offices

2440 Sand Hill Road
Suite 100
Menlo Park, CA USA 94025
Phone: 6502520600

280 Park Avenue
20th Floor
New York, NY USA 10017
Phone: 212-703-2700
Fax: 212-703-2719

Management and Staff
Adam Abramson, Managing Director
Alexander Casale, Vice President
Andrew Hopkin, Vice President
Asheesh Gupta, Vice President
David Wong, Principal
Donald Bramley, Managing Director
Edgar Soule, Managing Director
Eric Brown, Vice President
Franklin Foster, Principal
Hiren Mankodi, Managing Director
Jason Ellis, Vice President
Jay Jester, Managing Director
John Mitchell, Managing Director
Joseph Rogers, Principal
Keith Palumbo, Managing Director
Kenneth Collins, Vice President
Matthew Rudnick, Vice President
Nicholas Romano, Principal
Oliver Ewald, Managing Director
Pamela Martin, Principal
Pascal Denis, Vice President
Scott Van Houten, Vice President
Timothy Porter, Vice President
Timothy Mack, Principal
Youn Lee, Managing Director

Type of Firm
Private Equity Firm

Project Preferences

Role in Financing:
Prefer role as deal originator

Type of Financing Preferred:
Leveraged Buyout
Mezzanine
Generalist PE
Balanced
Acquisition

Size of Investments Considered:
Min Size of Investment Considered (000s): $15,000
Max Size of Investment Considered (000s): $100,000

Geographical Preferences

United States Preferences:

Canadian Preferences:
All Canada

Industry Focus
(% based on actual investment)
Computer Software and Services	30.3%
Other Products	26.2%
Consumer Related	14.1%
Industrial/Energy	10.1%
Medical/Health	6.9%
Internet Specific	5.4%
Biotechnology	4.1%
Semiconductors/Other Elect.	1.8%
Communications and Media	1.3%

Additional Information
Year Founded: 1999
Capital Under Management: $5,000,000,000
Current Activity Level : Actively seeking new investments

AUDEN AG

Am Kupfergraben 6
Berlin, Germany 10117
Phone: 493080494800
Fax: 493080494809
E-mail: info@auden.com
Website: auden.com

Management and Staff
Reyke Schult, Chief Executive Officer

Type of Firm
Private Equity Firm

Additional Information
Year Founded: 2015
Current Activity Level : Actively seeking new investments

AUDERE CAPITAL LTD

Ensign House
Admirals Way
London, United Kingdom E14 9XQ
Phone: 442071483861
Website: auderecapital.co.uk

Type of Firm
Private Equity Firm

Project Preferences

Type of Financing Preferred:
Early Stage
Expansion
Later Stage
Seed

Geographical Preferences

International Preferences:
United Kingdom
Europe

Industry Preferences

In Consumer Related prefer:
Consumer Products

In Business Serv. prefer:
Media

Additional Information
Year Founded: 2008
Current Activity Level : Actively seeking new investments

AUGMENT VENTURES FUND I LP

206 South 4th Avenue
Ann Arbor, MI USA 48104
E-mail: info@augmentventures.com

Management and Staff
Becky Davenport, Principal
Eric Halverson, Principal
Sonali Vijayavargiya, Managing Director

Type of Firm
Private Equity Firm

Project Preferences

Type of Financing Preferred:
Early Stage

Industry Preferences

In Industrial/Energy prefer:
Energy
Advanced Materials

In Business Serv. prefer:
Distribution

In Manufact. prefer:
Manufacturing

In Other prefer:
Environment Responsible

Additional Information
Name of Most Recent Fund: Augment Ventures Fund I, L.P.
Most Recent Fund Was Raised: 07/25/2011
Year Founded: 2011
Capital Under Management: $1,000,000
Current Activity Level : Actively seeking new investments

AUGMENTUM CAPITAL LLP

27 Saint James's Place
London, United Kingdom SW1A 1NR
Phone: 442075141998
E-mail: info@augmentumcapital.com
Website: www.augmentumcapital.com

Management and Staff
Richard Matthews, Co-Founder
Tim Levene, Co-Founder

Type of Firm
Private Equity Firm

Project Preferences

Type of Financing Preferred:
Expansion
Later Stage

Size of Investments Considered:
Min Size of Investment Considered (000s): $4,916
Max Size of Investment Considered (000s): $16,388

Geographical Preferences

International Preferences:
United Kingdom
Europe

Industry Preferences

In Internet Specific prefer:
Internet
Ecommerce

Additional Information
Year Founded: 2009
Current Activity Level : Actively seeking new investments

AUGURY CAPITAL PARTNERS

8025 Forsyth Boulevard
Second Floor
Saint Louis, MO USA 63105
Phone: 3144481316
Fax: 3143357637
Website: www.augurycapital.com

Management and Staff
David Truetzel, Managing Partner
Robert Wetzel, General Partner

Type of Firm
Private Equity Firm

Project Preferences

Type of Financing Preferred:
Balanced
Later Stage

Industry Preferences

In Biotechnology prefer:
Biotechnology

In Medical/Health prefer:
Pharmaceuticals

In Financial Services prefer:
Financial Services

Additional Information
Year Founded: 2006
Current Activity Level : Actively seeking new investments

AUGUST CAPITAL MANAGEMENT LLC

2480 Sand Hill Road
Suite 101
Menlo Park, CA USA 94025
Phone: 6502349900
Fax: 6502349910
Website: www.augustcap.com

Management and Staff
Andrew Rappaport, Partner
David Marquardt, Co-Founder
John Johnston, Co-Founder
W. Eric Carlborg, General Partner

Type of Firm
Private Equity Firm

Association Membership
Western Association of Venture Capitalists (WAVC)
National Venture Capital Association - USA (NVCA)
Canadian Venture Capital Association

Project Preferences

Role in Financing:
Prefer role as deal originator but will also invest in deals created by others

Type of Financing Preferred:
Early Stage
Balanced
Later Stage
Seed
Startup

Geographical Preferences

United States Preferences:
Northwest
Rocky Mountain
California
West Coast
Southwest

Industry Focus
(% based on actual investment)
Internet Specific	46.7%
Computer Software and Services	24.9%
Semiconductors/Other Elect.	13.6%
Communications and Media	6.9%
Computer Hardware	4.8%
Consumer Related	1.9%
Industrial/Energy	0.9%
Other Products	0.2%

Additional Information
Year Founded: 1995
Capital Under Management: $1,300,000,000
Current Activity Level : Actively seeking new investments
Method of Compensation: Return on investment is of primary concern, do not charge fees

AUGUST CAPITAL PARTNERS

DDA Commercial Complex
Suite 2, 1st Floor, Niti Bagh
New Delhi, India 110049
Phone: 918040254555
E-mail: admin@augustcp.com
Website: www.augustcp.com

Other Offices
9, Venkat Swami Naidu Street
Taskar Town, Shivaji Nagar
Bangalore, India
Phone: 918040254555

Management and Staff
B. V. R. Mohan Reddy, Partner
Kapil Chadha, Partner
Sameer Narula, Partner

Type of Firm
Private Equity Firm

Project Preferences

Type of Financing Preferred:
Early Stage
Expansion
Seed

Geographical Preferences

International Preferences:
India
Asia

Industry Preferences

In Communications prefer:
Communications and Media

In Medical/Health prefer:
Health Services

In Consumer Related prefer:
Consumer
Food/Beverage
Consumer Products
Consumer Services
Education Related

In Financial Services prefer:
Financial Services

In Business Serv. prefer:
Media

Additional Information

Year Founded: 2011
Current Activity Level : Actively seeking new investments

AUGUST EQUITY LLP

10 Slingsby Place
St. Martin's Courtyard
London, United Kingdom WC2E 9AB
Phone: 442076328200
Fax: 442076328201
E-mail: info@augustequity.com
Website: www.augustequity.com

Management and Staff

Aatif Hassan, Partner
David Lonsdale, Partner
Ian Grant, Co-Founder
Philip Rattle, Managing Partner
Richard Green, Co-Founder
Timothy Clarke, Co-Founder

Type of Firm

Private Equity Firm

Association Membership

British Venture Capital Association (BVCA)

Project Preferences

Role in Financing:
Prefer role as deal originator but will also invest in deals created by others

Type of Financing Preferred:
Leveraged Buyout
Management Buyouts
Acquisition

Geographical Preferences

International Preferences:
United Kingdom
Europe

Industry Focus

(% based on actual investment)
Other Products	17.6%
Internet Specific	16.9%
Consumer Related	16.2%
Computer Software and Services	15.1%
Medical/Health	15.0%
Computer Hardware	8.7%
Biotechnology	7.3%
Industrial/Energy	1.9%
Communications and Media	1.0%
Semiconductors/Other Elect.	0.3%

Additional Information

Name of Most Recent Fund: August Equity Partners III, L.P.
Most Recent Fund Was Raised: 06/05/2013
Year Founded: 2001
Capital Under Management: $487,300,000
Current Activity Level : Actively seeking new investments

AULDBRASS PARTNERS LP

410 Park Avenue
15th Floor
New York, NY USA 10022
Phone: 2122130243
E-mail: general@aulbrasspartners.com
Website: www.auldbrasspartners.com

Management and Staff

Ahmad Ali, Partner
Christopher Salley, Managing Director
Howard Sanders, Founder
Riyadh Mohammed, Principal

Type of Firm

Private Equity Advisor or Fund of Funds

Association Membership

Natl Assoc of Investment Cos. (NAIC)

Project Preferences

Type of Financing Preferred:
Fund of Funds of Second

Geographical Preferences

United States Preferences:

International Preferences:
Europe

Industry Preferences

In Industrial/Energy prefer:
Energy

In Financial Services prefer:
Real Estate

Additional Information

Name of Most Recent Fund: Auldbrass Partners Secondary Opportunity Fund, L.P.
Most Recent Fund Was Raised: 11/18/2011
Year Founded: 2011
Capital Under Management: $15,000,000
Current Activity Level : Actively seeking new investments

AUMENTA GMBH

Cecilienallee 17
Duesseldorf, German D-40474
Phone: 4921154475410
Website: www.aumenta.eu

Type of Firm

Private Equity Firm

Project Preferences

Type of Financing Preferred:
Early Stage
Expansion
Balanced
Later Stage
Seed
Startup

Geographical Preferences

International Preferences:
Germany

Industry Preferences

In Medical/Health prefer:
Health Services
Pharmaceuticals

Additional Information

Year Founded: 2013
Current Activity Level : Actively seeking new investments

AURA CAPITAL GROUP

74 Castlereagh Street
Level 14
Sydney, Australia NSW 2000
Phone: 612 9248 6988
Fax: 612 9248 6989
E-mail: info@auracapital.com.au
Website: auracapita .com.au

Other Offices

585 Victoria Street
Level Two
Melbourne, Australia VIC 3067
Phone: 61292486988
Fax: 61280783872

Nine Battery Road
11/F & 12/F Straits Trading Building
Singapore, Singapore 049910
Phone: 6596818368
Fax: 61292486869

Type of Firm

Investment Management Firm

Project Preferences

Type of Financing Preferred:
Early Stage
Expansion
Management Buyouts

Geographical Preferences

International Preferences:
Australia
New Zealand

Additional Information
Year Founded: 2010
Current Activity Level : Actively seeking new investments

AURA CAPITAL MANAGEMENT GMBH

Neuer Wall 13
Hamburg, Germany 20354
Phone: 494022630770
Fax: 4940226307799
E-mail: info@auragroup.de
Website: www.auragroup.de

Type of Firm
Private Equity Firm

Project Preferences

Type of Financing Preferred:
Early Stage
Expansion
Balanced
Later Stage
Seed
Startup

Geographical Preferences

International Preferences:
Europe
Eastern Europe
Germany

Additional Information
Year Founded: 2012
Current Activity Level : Actively seeking new investments

AURELIA PRIVATE EQUITY GMBH

Kurhessenstrasse 1-3
Frankfurt, Germany 60431
Phone: 496980900
Fax: 49698090109
E-mail: info@aurelia-pe.de
Website: www.aurelia-pe.de

Management and Staff
Juergen Leschke, Managing Partner
Wolfgang Posselt, Managing Partner

Type of Firm
Private Equity Firm

Project Preferences

Type of Financing Preferred:
Early Stage
Later Stage
Seed
Startup

Size of Investments Considered:
Min Size of Investment Considered (000s): $679
Max Size of Investment Considered (000s): $4,074

Geographical Preferences

International Preferences:
Germany

Industry Preferences

In Communications prefer:
Communications and Media
Telecommunications

In Computer Other prefer:
Computer Related

In Industrial/Energy prefer:
Alternative Energy
Industrial Products
Environmental Related

In Other prefer:
Environment Responsible

Additional Information
Name of Most Recent Fund: Aurelia Technologie-Fonds I GmbH & Co. Beteiligungen KG
Most Recent Fund Was Raised: 12/31/2001
Year Founded: 2002
Capital Under Management: $44,300,000
Current Activity Level : Actively seeking new investments

AURELIUS AG

Ludwig-Ganghofer-Strasse 6
Gruenwald, Germany 82031
Phone: 49895447990
Fax: 498954479955
E-mail: info@aureliusinvest.de
Website: www.aureliusinvest.de

Management and Staff
Gert Purkert, Chief Operating Officer

Type of Firm
Private Equity Firm

Project Preferences

Type of Financing Preferred:
Leveraged Buyout
Management Buyouts
Acquisition
Recapitalizations

Geographical Preferences

International Preferences:
Europe

Industry Preferences

In Communications prefer:
CATV & Pay TV Systems

In Consumer Related prefer:
Retail
Publishing-Retail
Food/Beverage
Hotels and Resorts

In Industrial/Energy prefer:
Industrial Products
Factory Automation
Environmental Related

In Transportation prefer:
Transportation

In Financial Services prefer:
Financial Services

Additional Information
Year Founded: 2006
Current Activity Level : Actively seeking new investments

AURIGA PARTNERS SA

18 Avenue De Matignon
Paris, France 75008
Phone: 33153300707
Fax: 33153300700
E-mail: investisseur@aurigapartners.com
Website: www.auriga.vc

Management and Staff
Franck Lescure, Partner
Jacques Chatain, Co-Founder
Nicholas Tcherdakoff, Partner
P Peltier, Partner
Patrick Bamas, Co-Founder
Philippe Granger, Partner
Sebastien Descarpentries, Partner

Type of Firm
Private Equity Firm

Association Membership
French Venture Capital Association (AFIC)
European Private Equity and Venture Capital Assoc.

Project Preferences

Type of Financing Preferred:
Early Stage
Seed
Startup

Size of Investments Considered:
Min Size of Investment Considered (000s): $471
Max Size of Investment Considered (000s): $4,708

Geographical Preferences

United States Preferences:
All U.S.

International Preferences:
Europe
Israel
France

Industry Preferences

In Communications prefer:
Communications and Media

In Computer Software prefer:
Software
Systems Software

In Computer Other prefer:
Computer Related

In Biotechnology prefer:
Biotechnology
Biotech Related Research
Biotech Related Research

In Medical/Health prefer:
Medical/Health

In Industrial/Energy prefer:
Factory Automation

In Other prefer:
Socially Responsible
Environment Responsible

Additional Information

Name of Most Recent Fund: Auriga IV Bioseeds
Most Recent Fund Was Raised: 11/18/2013
Year Founded: 1998
Capital Under Management: $224,200,000
Current Activity Level : Actively seeking new investments

AURIK INVESTMENT HOLDINGS (PTY) LTD

132 Jan Smuts Avenue, Rosebank
Third Floor
Johannesburg, South Africa 2196
Phone: 27114475575
Fax: 27865177809
E-mail: enquiries@aurik.co.za
Website: www.aurik.co.za

Management and Staff

Carien Engelbrecht, Chief Operating Officer

Type of Firm

Private Equity Firm

Project Preferences

Type of Financing Preferred:
Early Stage
Expansion
Seed

Geographical Preferences

International Preferences:
South Africa

Additional Information

Year Founded: 2003
Current Activity Level : Actively seeking new investments

AURINVEST SAS

11bis rue Portalis
Paris, France 75008
Phone: 33144907320
Fax: 33144907324
E-mail: contact@aurinvest.com
Website: aurinvest.com

Management and Staff

Michel Demont, President

Type of Firm

Private Equity Firm

Association Membership

French Venture Capital Association (AFIC)

Project Preferences

Type of Financing Preferred:
Leveraged Buyout
Early Stage
Generalist PE
Later Stage
Acquisition

Geographical Preferences

International Preferences:
Europe
France

Industry Preferences

In Computer Software prefer:
Software

In Internet Specific prefer:
Ecommerce

Additional Information

Year Founded: 2001
Current Activity Level : Actively seeking new investments

AURORA CAPITAL GROUP LTD

10877 Wilshire Boulevard, Suite 2100
Westwood, CA USA 90024
Phone: 3105510101
Fax: 3102775591
Website: www.auroracap.com

Management and Staff

Andre Fohrer, Vice President
Ayush Singhania, Vice President
John Mapes, Partner
Josh Klinefelter, Partner
M. Randy Moser, Vice President
Mark Rosenbaum, Partner
Matthew Laylock, Principal
Michael Marino, Partner
Robert West, Chief Financial Officer
Robert Fraser, Vice President
Ryan McCarthy, Partner
Sean Ozbolt, Partner
Steven Smith, Partner
Zach Mager, Vice President

Type of Firm

Private Equity Firm

Project Preferences

Role in Financing:
Prefer role as deal originator

Type of Financing Preferred:
Leveraged Buyout

Geographical Preferences

United States Preferences:

Industry Preferences

In Computer Software prefer:
Software

In Medical/Health prefer:
Medical/Health

In Industrial/Energy prefer:
Energy
Industrial Products

In Transportation prefer:
Transportation
Aerospace

In Business Serv. prefer:
Services
Distribution

In Manufact. prefer:
Manufacturing

Additional Information

Year Founded: 1991
Capital Under Management: $2,000,000,000
Current Activity Level : Actively seeking new investments

AURORA FUNDS INC

790 SE Cary Parkway
Suite 204
Cary, NC USA 27511
Phone: 919484040
Fax: 919594670
Website: www.aurorafunds.com

Management and Staff
B. Jefferson Clark, Managing General Partner
Christopher Kroeger, Partner
Jan Bouten, Venture Partner
Richard Holcomb, Venture Partner
Scott Albert, Venture Partner

Type of Firm
Private Equity Firm

Project Preferences

Role in Financing:
Will function either as deal originator or investor in deals created by others

Type of Financing Preferred:
Early Stage
Seed

Geographical Preferences

United States Preferences:
Mid Atlantic
Southeast

Industry Focus
(% based on actual investment)

Medical/Health	30.7%
Computer Software and Services	22.9%
Biotechnology	21.8%
Internet Specific	8.7%
Semiconductors/Other Elect.	7.9%
Communications and Media	4.3%
Other Products	2.9%
Consumer Related	0.7%
Industrial/Energy	0.1%

Additional Information
Name of Most Recent Fund: Aurora Ventures V, LP
Most Recent Fund Was Raised: 08/26/2005
Year Founded: 1994
Capital Under Management: $75,600,000
Current Activity Level : Actively seeking new investments
Method of Compensation: Return on investment is of primary concern, do not charge fees

AURORA RESURGENCE MANAGEMENT PARTNERS LLC

10877 Wilshire Boulevard
Suite 2250
Los Angeles, CA USA 90024
Phone: 3105510101
Fax: 3102775591
Website: www.aurorares.com

Management and Staff
Bob West, Chief Financial Officer
Gerald Parsky, Partner
Joshua Phillips, Partner
Matthew Homme, Principal
Ryan McCarthy, Partner
Steven Smith, Partner

Type of Firm
Private Equity Firm

Project Preferences

Type of Financing Preferred:
Leveraged Buyout
Mezzanine
Turnaround
Special Situation
Distressed Debt

Geographical Preferences

United States Preferences:
All U.S.

International Preferences:
Europe

Industry Preferences

In Medical/Health prefer:
Medical/Health

In Consumer Related prefer:
Consumer

In Industrial/Energy prefer:
Energy

In Business Serv. prefer:
Services
Distribution
Media

In Manufact. prefer:
Manufacturing

Additional Information
Name of Most Recent Fund: Aurora Resurgence Fund II, L.P.
Most Recent Fund Was Raised: 10/18/2013
Year Founded: 2009
Capital Under Management: $1,188,560,000
Current Activity Level : Actively seeking new investments

AURUM VENTURES MKI

16 Abba Hillel Silver St
Aurec House
Ramat Gan, Israel 52506
Phone: 97235762420
Fax: 97235762605
E-mail: info@aurum.co.il
Website: www.aurum.co.il

Type of Firm
Private Equity Firm

Additional Information
Year Founded: 2009
Current Activity Level : Actively seeking new investments

AURUS GESTION DE INVERSIONES SPA

Avenue La Dehesa 1844
Office 801, Lo Barnechea
Santiago, Chile
Phone: 5624981300
Fax: 5624981301
E-mail: info@aurus.cl
Website: www.aurus.com

Management and Staff
Alejandro Furman, Partner
Alexander Seelenberger, Managing Director
Antonio Cruz, President
Jose Miguel Musalem, Partner
Juan Carlos Delano-Valenzuela, Partner
Raimundo Cerda-Lecaros, Managing Director
Roberto Koifman, Partner
Sergio Furman, Partner

Type of Firm
Investment Management Firm

Project Preferences

Type of Financing Preferred:
Early Stage

Geographical Preferences

International Preferences:
Latin America
Chile

Industry Preferences

In Biotechnology prefer:
Biotechnology

In Medical/Health prefer:
Medical Diagnostics
Medical Products
Pharmaceuticals

Additional Information
Year Founded: 2008
Current Activity Level : Actively seeking new investments

AUSTER CAPITAL PARTNERS LLC

30 Montgomery Street
Suite 660
Jersey City, NJ USA 07302

Other Offices
Stanmore House
29/30 Saint James's Street
London, United Kingdom SW1A IHB

Management and Staff
Charles Auster, Managing Partner
Peter Hase, Managing Director

Type of Firm
Private Equity Firm

Project Preferences

Type of Financing Preferred:
Balanced
Seed

Industry Preferences

In Communications prefer:
Telecommunications

In Computer Software prefer:
Software

In Business Serv. prefer:
Services

Additional Information
Year Founded: 2008
Current Activity Level : Actively seeking new investments

AUSTIN VENTURES

300 West Sixth Street
Suite 2300
Austin, TX USA 78701
Phone: 5124851900
Fax: 5126518500
Website: www.austinventures.com

Management and Staff
Adam Dell, Venture Partner
Andrew Busey, Venture Partner
Blaine Wesner, Partner
C. Thomas Ball, Partner
Christopher Pacitti, General Partner
Clark Jernigan, Venture Partner
Dave Benton, Vice President
David Lack, Partner
Jaime Aguirre, Principal
Jeff Garvey, Founder
Jeff Browning, Partner
John Thornton, General Partner
Joseph Aragona, Founder
Joseph Marengi, Venture Partner
Kenneth DeAngelis, Founder
Kevin Kunz, Chief Financial Officer
Matt Bowman, Principal
Michael Dodd, Partner
Phillip Siegel, General Partner
Scott Donaldson, Principal
Vernon Bryant, Venture Partner

Type of Firm
Private Equity Firm

Association Membership
Norwegian Venture Capital Association
National Venture Capital Association - USA (NVCA)

Project Preferences

Role in Financing:
Prefer role as deal originator but will also invest in deals created by others

Type of Financing Preferred:
Leveraged Buyout
Early Stage
Expansion
Generalist PE
Balanced
Later Stage
Seed
Management Buyouts
Acquisition

Size of Investments Considered:
Min Size of Investment Considered (000s): $500
Max Size of Investment Considered (000s): $80,000

Geographical Preferences

United States Preferences:
Texas

Industry Focus
(% based on actual investment)

Computer Software and Services	29.4%
Internet Specific	22.8%
Communications and Media	11.6%
Other Products	9.8%
Semiconductors/Other Elect.	9.1%
Computer Hardware	5.4%
Industrial/Energy	4.5%
Medical/Health	3.8%
Consumer Related	3.1%
Biotechnology	0.6%

Additional Information
Name of Most Recent Fund: Austin Ventures X, L.P.
Most Recent Fund Was Raised: 09/22/2008
Year Founded: 1979
Capital Under Management: $2,878,000,000
Current Activity Level : Actively seeking new investments
Method of Compensation: Return on investment is of primary concern, do not charge fees

AUSTRAL CAPITAL

El Bosque Norte 0123
Suite 601
Santiago, Chile
Phone: 5622460808
Fax: 5622460809
E-mail: info@australcap.com
Website: www.australcap.com

Other Offices
228 Hamilton Avenue, Third Floor
Palo Alto, CA USA 94301
Phone: 650-265-7322

Management and Staff
Felipe Camposano, General Partner
Gonzalo Miranda, Founding Partner
Hiroshi Wald, Managing Director

Type of Firm
Private Equity Firm

Project Preferences

Type of Financing Preferred:
Early Stage
Expansion
Later Stage
Seed
Startup

Geographical Preferences

United States Preferences:

International Preferences:
Latin America

Industry Preferences

In Biotechnology prefer:
Biotechnology

In Consumer Related prefer:
Consumer Services

Additional Information
Year Founded: 2007
Current Activity Level : Actively seeking new investments

AUSTRALIS PARTNERS

675 Third Avenue
Eight Floor
New York, NY USA 10017
Phone: 6468850417
Website: www.australispartners.com

Type of Firm
Private Equity Firm

Project Preferences

Type of Financing Preferred:
Leveraged Buyout

Geographical Preferences

International Preferences:
Peru
Mexico
Chile
Colombia

Additional Information
Year Founded: 2015
Capital Under Management: $379,000,000
Current Activity Level : Actively seeking new investments

AUSTRIA WIRTSCHAFTS-SERVICE GMBH

Ungargasse 37
Vienna, Austria 1030
Phone: 4350175100
Fax: 43150175900
E-mail: office@awsg.at
Website: www.awsg.at

Type of Firm
Government Affiliated Program

Association Membership
Belgium Venturing Association
European Private Equity and Venture Capital Assoc.

Project Preferences

Role in Financing:
Prefer role as deal originator

Type of Financing Preferred:
Early Stage
Later Stage
Seed
Startup

Geographical Preferences

International Preferences:
Austria

Industry Preferences

In Biotechnology prefer:
Biotechnology

In Medical/Health prefer:
Medical/Health

In Industrial/Energy prefer:
Industrial Products

Additional Information
Year Founded: 1954
Capital Under Management: $48,200,000
Current Activity Level : Actively seeking new investments

AUSTRO GESTAO DE RECURSOS LTDA

Av das Americas 7935
Bl 2-sala 359, Barra da Tijuca
Rio de Janeiro, Brazil 22793081
Phone: 552134313831
E-mail: norte@norteinvestimentos.com.br

Type of Firm
Private Equity Firm

Association Membership
Brazilian Venture Capital Association (ABCR)

Project Preferences

Type of Financing Preferred:
Early Stage
Balanced
Later Stage
Seed
Startup

Geographical Preferences

International Preferences:
Brazil

Industry Preferences

In Financial Services prefer:
Real Estate

Additional Information
Year Founded: 2008
Current Activity Level : Actively seeking new investments

AUTHENTIC VENTURES, L.P.

7955 Skyline Boulevard
Oakland, CA USA 94611
Website: www.authentic-ventures.com

Type of Firm
Private Equity Firm

Additional Information
Year Founded: 2016
Capital Under Management: $4,720,000
Current Activity Level : Actively seeking new investments

AUTOCHROME VENTURES LLC

15260 Ventura Boulevard
Suite 2000
Sherman Oaks, CA USA 91403
Website: www.autochrome.vc

Type of Firm
Private Equity Firm

Project Preferences

Type of Financing Preferred:
Seed

Additional Information
Year Founded: 2016
Capital Under Management: $1,000,000
Current Activity Level : Actively seeking new investments

AUTONOMIE & SOLIDARITE

146 Rue Nationale
Lille, France 59000
Phone: 33320143062
Fax: 33320546842
E-mail: info@autonomieetsolidarite.fr
Website: www.autonomieetsolidarite.fr

Management and Staff
Jean-Marie Didier, Managing Director

Type of Firm
Private Equity Firm

Project Preferences

Type of Financing Preferred:
Leveraged Buyout
Early Stage
Generalist PE
Later Stage
Seed
Acquisition

Geographical Preferences

International Preferences:
Europe
France

Industry Preferences

In Industrial/Energy prefer:
Industrial Products

In Business Serv. prefer:
Services

In Other prefer:
Environment Responsible

Additional Information
Year Founded: 1990
Current Activity Level : Actively seeking new investments

AUTOTECH MANAGEMENT LLC

101 Miramonte Avenue
Palo Alto, CA USA 94306
Phone: 6505156940
E-mail: info@autotechvc.com
Website: autotechvc.com

Management and Staff
Alexei Andreev, Managing Director
John Stockton, Venture Partner
Masahiro Suzuki, Partner
Quin Garcia, Managing Director
Tony Bona, Chief Financial Officer

Type of Firm
Private Equity Firm

Project Preferences

Type of Financing Preferred:
Early Stage
Startup

Industry Preferences

In Transportation prefer:
Transportation

Additional Information

Year Founded: 2016
Capital Under Management: $120,000,000
Current Activity Level : Actively seeking new investments

AUVEN THERAPEUTICS MANAGEMENT LLLP

1325 Avenue of Americas
Twelfth Floor
New York, NY USA 10019
Phone: 2126164000
Fax: 2126164099
E-mail: info@celtictherapeutics.com
Website: www.auventx.com

Other Offices

663 Fifth Avenue
New York, NY USA 10022
Phone: 212-616-4061

Management and Staff

Alexandre L Heureux, Chief Financial Officer
Beth Hecht, Partner
James Sipple, Vice President
Michael Forer, Managing Director
Patrick O Connor, Managing Director
Peter Corr, Co-Founder
Reinaldo Diaz, Managing Director
Richard Warburg, Managing Director
Solomon Babani, Vice President
Stephen Evans-Freke, Co-Founder
Tomasz Sablinski, Managing Director

Type of Firm
Private Equity Firm

Project Preferences

Type of Financing Preferred:
Leveraged Buyout
Acquisition

Industry Preferences

In Medical/Health prefer:
Medical/Health
Medical Therapeutics

Additional Information

Year Founded: 2007
Current Activity Level : Actively seeking new investments

AUVEST MARKETS FZ LLC

1504, Grosvenor Business Tower
TECOM
Duba, Utd. Arab Em.
Phone: 97144327135
Fax: 97144327136
E-mail: info@auvest.com
Website: www.auvest.com

Management and Staff

Ahamed Abdul Wahid, Managing Director

Type of Firm
Private Equity Firm

Project Preferences

Type of Financing Preferred:
Generalist PE

Additional Information

Year Founded: 2014
Current Activity Level : Actively seeking new investments

AUXITEX SA

4 cours de Gourgue
Bordeaux, France 33000
Phone: 33556817104
Fax: 33556817104
E-mail: gls@comborn.fr

Other Offices

24, rue du 4 Septembre
Paris, France 75002
Phone: 33153649639
Fax: 33153649630

Management and Staff

Bertrand Roux, President

Type of Firm
Private Equity Firm

Association Membership
French Venture Capital Association (AFIC)

Project Preferences

Type of Financing Preferred:
Early Stage
Later Stage

Geographical Preferences

International Preferences:
France

Additional Information

Year Founded: 2005
Current Activity Level : Making few, if any, new investments

AUXO MANAGEMENT LP

6441 Northam Drive
Mississauga, Canada L4V 1J2
Website: www.auxomanagement.com

Other Offices

6441 Northam Drive
Mississauga, Canada L4V 1J2

Management and Staff

Erik Mikkelsen, Managing Partner
Robert Cherun, Managing Partner

Type of Firm
Private Equity Firm

Project Preferences

Type of Financing Preferred:
Leveraged Buyout
Acquisition

Geographical Preferences

United States Preferences:
All U.S.

Canadian Preferences:
All Canada

Additional Information

Year Founded: 2010
Current Activity Level : Actively seeking new investments

AV CAPITAL HOLDINGS, LLC

300 West 6th street
Suite 2300
Austin, TX USA 78701
Website: av.capital

Type of Firm
Private Equity Firm

Project Preferences

Type of Financing Preferred:
Leveraged Buyout
Acquisition
Recapitalizations

Industry Preferences

In Medical/Health prefer:
Health Services

In Industrial/Energy prefer:
Energy

In Business Serv. prefer:
Distribution

In Manufact. prefer:
Manufacturing

Additional Information
Year Founded: 2015
Current Activity Level : Actively seeking new investments

AVALLON SP Z O O

AL. Kosciuszki 17
Lodz, Poland 90-418
Phone: 48426309771
Fax: 48426309775
E-mail: avallon@avallon.pl
Website: www.avallon.pl

Management and Staff
Michal Zawisza, Partner
Piotr Miller, Partner
Robert Wieclawski, Partner

Type of Firm
Private Equity Firm

Association Membership
Polish Venture Capital Association (PSIC/PPEA)

Project Preferences

Role in Financing:
Prefer role as deal originator

Type of Financing Preferred:
Leveraged Buyout
Management Buyouts
Acquisition

Geographical Preferences

International Preferences:
Central Europe
Poland
Eastern Europe

Additional Information
Year Founded: 2001
Capital Under Management: $81,267,000
Current Activity Level : Actively seeking new investments

AVALON VENTURES, LLC

1134 Kline Street
La Jolla, CA USA 92037
Phone: 8583482180
Fax: 8583482183
E-mail: info@avalon-ventures.com
Website: www.avalon-ventures.com

Other Offices
55 Cambridge Parkway
Suite 103
Cambridge, MA USA 02142

Management and Staff
Brady Bohrmann, Managing Director
Court Turner, Venture Partner
Doug Downs, Managing Director
Jay Lichter, Managing Director
Kevin Kinsella, Managing Director
Richard Levandov, Managing Director
Stephen Tomlin, Managing Director

Type of Firm
Private Equity Firm

Association Membership
National Venture Capital Association – USA (NVCA)

Project Preferences

Role in Financing:
Prefer role as deal originator

Type of Financing Preferred:
Early Stage
Seed
Startup

Geographical Preferences

United States Preferences:

Industry Preferences

In Communications prefer:
Wireless Communications

In Internet Specific prefer:
Internet

Additional Information
Name of Most Recent Fund: Avalon Ventures X, L.P.
Most Recent Fund Was Raised: 08/30/2012
Year Founded: 1983
Capital Under Management: $250,000,000
Current Activity Level : Actively seeking new investments
Method of Compensation: Return on invest. most important, but chg. closing fees, service fees, etc.

AVALT LLC

79 Newbury Street
Boston, MA USA 02116
Website: www.avalt.com

Management and Staff
Ian Reynolds, Partner
Jim McQuade, Vice President
Mark Verdi, Partner
Marko Kivisto, Principal

Type of Firm
Private Equity Firm

Project Preferences

Type of Financing Preferred:
Generalist PE

Additional Information
Year Founded: 2016
Current Activity Level : Actively seeking new investments

AVANTA INVESTMENT MANAGEMENT LTD

Unit 1001, Tower Two
Lippo Centre 89 Queensway
Central, Hong Kong
Phone: 852-2160-2880
Fax: 852-2801-7485

Type of Firm
Private Equity Firm

Project Preferences

Type of Financing Preferred:
Balanced

Geographical Preferences

International Preferences:
No Preference
Hong Kong

Additional Information
Year Founded: 2005
Current Activity Level : Actively seeking new investments

AVANTAGE VENTURES CAPITAL LLC

No.8 Dongdaqiao Road, Chaoyang
A-1005The Spaces Int'l Ctr
Beijing, China 100020
E-mail: info@avantageventures.com
Website: www.avantageventures.com

Other Offices
No. 111 Leighton Rd, Causeway Bay
Suite 1201
Hong Kong, Hong Kong 100020
Phone: 85231517877

Management and Staff
Dongxiang Wang, Partner
William Wang, Partner
Yiran Li, Chief Executive Officer

Type of Firm
Investment Management Firm

Project Preferences

Type of Financing Preferred:
Leveraged Buyout
Expansion
Seed

Geographical Preferences

International Preferences:
China

Industry Preferences

In Biotechnology prefer:
Biotechnology

In Medical/Health prefer:
Medical/Health

In Industrial/Energy prefer:
Energy
Energy Conservation Relat

In Agr/Forestr/Fish prefer:
Agribusiness

In Other prefer:
Environment Responsible

Additional Information

Year Founded: 2008
Current Activity Level : Actively seeking new investments

AVANTALION LLC

1600 Old Country Road
Plainview, NY USA 11803
Phone: 516-501-6724
Fax: 516-501-6729

Management and Staff

Charles B. Wang, Founder

Type of Firm

Private Equity Firm

Project Preferences

Type of Financing Preferred:
Balanced

Geographical Preferences

International Preferences:
China

Industry Preferences

In Business Serv. prefer:
Media

Additional Information

Year Founded: 2008
Current Activity Level : Actively seeking new investments

AVANTE CAPITAL PART-NERS LTD

13A, A.J. Marinho Drive
10th Floor, The Octagon
Victoria Island, Lagos, Nigeria
Phone: 234014603370
Fax: 23414616221
E-mail: info@argentilcp.com
Website: www.argentilcp.com

Type of Firm

Investment Management Firm

Project Preferences

Type of Financing Preferred:
Leveraged Buyout
Expansion
Acquisition
Recapitalizations

Geographical Preferences

International Preferences:
Nigeria
Africa

Industry Preferences

In Industrial/Energy prefer:
Energy
Oil and Gas Exploration

In Financial Services prefer:
Financial Services
Real Estate

Additional Information

Year Founded: 2002
Current Activity Level : Actively seeking new investments

AVANTE MEZZANINE INC

11150 Santa Monica Boulevard
Suite 1470
Los Angeles, CA USA 90025
Phone: 3106679242
Fax: 3107281762
E-mail: info@avantemezzanine.com
Website: www.avantemezzanine.com

Other Offices

75 Arlington Street
Suite 500
Boston, MA USA 02116
Phone: 6172741280

Management and Staff

Aaron DiCenzo, Vice President
Clifford Lyon, Chief Financial Officer
Dan Moss, Principal
Ivelisse Rodriguez Simon, Vice President
Jeri Harman, Partner
Natasha Fox, Partner
Paul Hayama, Vice President
Stephen Adamson, Partner

Type of Firm

Private Equity Firm

Association Membership

Natl Assoc of Small Bus. Inv. Co (NASBIC)

Project Preferences

Type of Financing Preferred:
Leveraged Buyout
Mezzanine
Management Buyouts
Acquisition
Recapitalizations

Industry Preferences

In Medical/Health prefer:
Medical/Health

In Consumer Related prefer:
Consumer Products
Consumer Services

In Industrial/Energy prefer:
Industrial Products

In Transportation prefer:
Aerospace

In Business Serv. prefer:
Services

In Other prefer:
Women/Minority-Owned Bus.

Additional Information

Year Founded: 2009
Current Activity Level : Actively seeking new investments

AVANZ CAPITAL PARTNERS LTD

Three Bethesda Metro Center
Suite 700
Bethesda, MD USA 20814
Phone: 2025362410
E-mail: contact@avanzcapital.com
Website: avanzcapital.com

Management and Staff

Hany Assaad, Co-Founder
Jorge Celaya, Co-Founder

Type of Firm

Private Equity Advisor or Fund of Funds

Association Membership

African Venture Capital Association (AVCA)

Project Preferences

Type of Financing Preferred:
Fund of Funds
Fund of Funds of Second

Geographical Preferences

International Preferences:
Latin America
Europe
Middle East
Asia
Africa

Additional Information

Year Founded: 2012
Current Activity Level : Actively seeking new investments

AVC SA

32 Aigialeias
Maroussi, Greece 15125
Phone: 302108170000
Fax: 302108171969

Type of Firm

Bank Affiliated

Project Preferences

Type of Financing Preferred:
Early Stage
Balanced
Startup

Geographical Preferences

International Preferences:
Greece
Europe

Additional Information

Year Founded: 1999
Current Activity Level : Actively seeking new investments

AVEDON CAPITAL PARTNERS BV

Apollolaan 153
Amsterdam, Netherlands 1077 AS
Phone: 310208002350
Fax: 31
E-mail: info@avedoncapital.com
Website: www.avedoncapital.com

Other Offices

Duesseldorfer Strasse 132
Duesseldorf, Germany 40545
Phone: 492115988902
Fax: 4921159889020

Management and Staff

Arjo Stammes, Partner
Gerard Burgers, Managing Partner
Hannes Hinteregger, Partner
Rikkert Beerekamp, Chief Financial Officer

Type of Firm

Private Equity Firm

Association Membership

European Private Equity and Venture Capital Assoc.
Dutch Venture Capital Associaton (NVP)

Project Preferences

Type of Financing Preferred:
Leveraged Buyout
Early Stage
Balanced
Later Stage
Management Buyouts
Acquisition

Geographical Preferences

International Preferences:
Luxembourg
Netherlands
Belgium
Germany

Industry Preferences

In Consumer Related prefer:
Consumer Products

In Industrial/Energy prefer:
Industrial Products

In Transportation prefer:
Transportation

In Financial Services prefer:
Financial Services

Additional Information

Name of Most Recent Fund: NIBC Growth Capital Fund II
Most Recent Fund Was Raised: 09/30/2011
Year Founded: 2011
Capital Under Management: $135,336,000
Current Activity Level : Actively seeking new investments

AVENIR SICAR

70-72 Avenue Habib Bourguiba
Tunis, Tunisia 1000
Phone: 216-71-142-851
Fax: 216-71-342-862
Website: www.sicaravenir.com

Management and Staff

Nejib Moalla, President

Type of Firm

Private Equity Firm

Project Preferences

Type of Financing Preferred:
Balanced

Geographical Preferences

International Preferences:
Tunisia

Additional Information

Year Founded: 2004
Current Activity Level : Making few, if any, new investments

AVENTIC PARTNERS AG

Schweizergasse 10
Zurich, Switzerland 8001
Phone: 41442851585
Fax: 41442851586
E-mail: info@aventicpartners.ch
Website: www.aventicpartners.ch

Management and Staff

Alan Frei, Partner
Jean-Claude Rebetez, Partner
Marc Kappeler, Partner
Peter Balsiger, Partner

Type of Firm

Bank Affiliated

Association Membership

Swiss Venture Capital Association (SECA)

Project Preferences

Type of Financing Preferred:
Early Stage
Later Stage
Management Buyouts
Acquisition

Size of Investments Considered:
Min Size of Investment Considered (000s): $564
Max Size of Investment Considered (000s): $5,643

Geographical Preferences

International Preferences:
Europe
Switzerland

Industry Preferences

In Communications prefer:
Communications and Media

In Internet Specific prefer:
Internet

In Semiconductor/Electr prefer:
Sensors

In Biotechnology prefer:
Biotechnology

In Medical/Health prefer:
Medical/Health

In Industrial/Energy prefer:
Industrial Products
Factory Automation
Robotics

AVENTURES CAPITAL MANAGEMENT PTE LTD

#16-03, 1 Shenton Way
Singapore, Singapore
Phone: 65-6220-8968
Website: www.aventures-capital.com

Management and Staff
Eng Hong Koh, Founder
Wan That Tan, Founder

Type of Firm
Private Equity Firm

Geographical Preferences

International Preferences:
Indonesia
Thailand
Philippines
Singapore
Malaysia

Additional Information
Year Founded: 2001
Current Activity Level : Actively seeking new investments

AVENTURES CAPITAL TOV

10 Geroyev Sevastopolya Street
Kiev, Ukraine 03065
Phone: 380445858282
Fax: 380445858282
E-mail: info@aventurescapital.com
Website: www.aventurescapital.com

Management and Staff
Andrey Kolodyuk, Managing Partner
Yevgen Sysoyev, Managing Partner

Type of Firm
Private Equity Firm

Project Preferences

Type of Financing Preferred:
Early Stage
Seed
Startup

Geographical Preferences

International Preferences:
Eastern Europe
Ukraine
Russia

Additional Information
Year Founded: 1999
Capital Under Management: $169,500,000
Current Activity Level : Actively seeking new investments

Industry Preferences

In Communications prefer:
Communications and Media
Telecommunications
Wireless Communications
Media and Entertainment
Entertainment

In Computer Hardware prefer:
Computer Graphics and Dig
Terminals

In Computer Software prefer:
Software
Systems Software
Applications Software

In Internet Specific prefer:
E-Commerce Technology
Internet
Web Aggregation/Portals

In Consumer Related prefer:
Entertainment and Leisure

In Financial Services prefer:
Real Estate

In Manufact. prefer:
Publishing

Additional Information
Year Founded: 1994
Current Activity Level : Actively seeking new investments

AVENUE CAPITAL GROUP LLC

399 Park Avenue
Sixth Floor
New York, NY USA 10022
Phone: 2128783500
Fax: 2128783559
E-mail: investorrelations@avenuecapital.com
Website: www.avenuecapital.com

Management and Staff
Alexander Wolfman, Senior Managing Director
Campbell Korff, Managing Director
Jennifer Tang, Senior Managing Director
John Larkin, Senior Managing Director
Julie Baumann, Senior Managing Director
Mark Harris, Senior Managing Director
Randy Takian, Senior Managing Director
Robert Ollwerther, Chief Operating Officer
Sonia Gardner, President
Stephen Trevor, Senior Managing Director
Stuart Sarnoff, Senior Managing Director
Thomas Larkin, Chief Financial Officer
Todd Greenbarg, Senior Managing Director

Type of Firm
Private Equity Firm

Project Preferences

Type of Financing Preferred:
Leveraged Buyout
Mezzanine
Generalist PE
Turnaround
Opportunistic
Management Buyouts
Distressed Debt
Recapitalizations

Geographical Preferences

United States Preferences:

International Preferences:
Italy
Ireland
United Kingdom
Europe
Netherlands
Spain
Asia
Germany
France

Industry Focus
(% based on actual investment)
Other Products	52.9%
Consumer Related	35.7%
Medical/Health	6.7%
Industrial/Energy	4.7%

Additional Information
Name of Most Recent Fund: Avenue Europe Private Opportunities Fund, L.P.
Most Recent Fund Was Raised: 06/05/2013
Year Founded: 1995
Capital Under Management: $19,600,000,000
Current Activity Level : Actively seeking new investments

AVENUE VENTURES LLC

501 Olympic Boulevard
Los Angeles, CA USA 90015
Phone: 2136228378
Website: www.aveventures.com

Type of Firm
Private Equity Firm

Project Preferences

Type of Financing Preferred:
Early Stage
Balanced
Seed

Additional Information
Year Founded: 2011
Current Activity Level : Actively seeking new investments

AVERY BUSINESS DEVELOPMENT SERVICES

2506 St. Michel Court
Ponte Vedra, FL USA 32082
Phone: 904-285-6033
Fax: 904-280-8840

Management and Staff
Henry Avery, President

Type of Firm
Angel Group

Project Preferences

Role in Financing:
Will function either as deal originator or investor in deals created by others

Type of Financing Preferred:
Early Stage
Turnaround
Later Stage
Seed
Management Buyouts
Acquisition
Startup
Special Situation

Geographical Preferences

United States Preferences:
Southeast

Industry Preferences

In Communications prefer:
Radio & TV Broadcasting

In Computer Software prefer:
Artificial Intelligence

In Biotechnology prefer:
Industrial Biotechnology
Biosensors
Biotech Related Research

In Medical/Health prefer:
Drug/Equipmt Delivery
Medical Products
Pharmaceuticals

In Consumer Related prefer:
Retail
Franchises(NEC)

In Industrial/Energy prefer:
Oil and Gas Exploration
Oil & Gas Drilling,Explor
Alternative Energy
Coal Related
Industrial Products
Materials
Robotics
Environmental Related

In Business Serv. prefer:
Consulting Services

In Agr/Forestr/Fish prefer:
Mining and Minerals

Additional Information
Year Founded: 1981
Current Activity Level : Actively seeking new investments
Method of Compensation: Function primarily in service area, receive contingent fee in cash or equity

---

AVIATION INVESTMENT MANAGEMENT CO LTD

No.9, Siwei Road, Shunyi Dist
4F, Block B, China Service Man
Beijing, China 100621
Phone: 861064557210

Type of Firm
Private Equity Firm

Project Preferences

Type of Financing Preferred:
Balanced

Geographical Preferences

International Preferences:
China

Additional Information
Year Founded: 2014
Current Activity Level : Actively seeking new investments

AVINDIA SGECR CAPITAL SA

C / La Paz, 28 - entlo.2
Valencia, Spain 46003
Phone: 34902060004
Fax: 34902071971
E-mail: info@avindia.es
Website: www.avindia.es

Other Offices
C/ Velzquez, 18 - 6 dcha
, Spain 28001
Phone: 34902060004
Fax: 34902071971

Management and Staff
Emilio Giner Hernandez, Chief Executive Officer

Type of Firm
Private Equity Firm

Project Preferences

Type of Financing Preferred:
Balanced
Acquisition

Geographical Preferences

International Preferences:
Spain

Industry Preferences

In Biotechnology prefer:
Biotechnology

In Industrial/Energy prefer:
Alternative Energy

Additional Information
Year Founded: 2012
Capital Under Management: $13,219,000
Current Activity Level : Actively seeking new investments

AVISTA CAPITAL HOLDINGS LP

65 East 55th Street
18th Floor
New York, NY USA 10022
Phone: 2125936900
Fax: 2125936901
E-mail: info@avistacap.com
Website: www.avistacap.com

Other Offices
14 Clifford Street
4th Floor, Bond Street House
London, United Kingdom W1S 4JU
Phone: 44-207290-2550
Fax: 44-2074999258

1000 Louisiana Street
Suite 1200
HOUSTON, TX USA 77002
Phone: 713-328-1099
Fax: 713-328-1097

Management and Staff
Amanda Heravi, Principal
Brendan Scollans, Partner
Carolyn Janiak Earthy, Vice President
Chandler Quisenberry, Vice President
David Burgstahler, President, Founder
David Durkin, Partner
Greg Evans, Principal
Jackson Phillips, Vice President
Jeff Gunst, Principal
John Cafasso, Chief Financial Officer
Kunal Pandit, Principal
Malcolm Little, Vice President
Newton Aguiar, Partner
OhSang Kwon, Partner
Robert Cabes, Partner
Robert Girardi, Vice President
Sriram Venkataraman, Partner

Type of Firm
Private Equity Firm

Project Preferences

Role in Financing:
Prefer role as deal originator

Type of Financing Preferred:
Leveraged Buyout
Expansion

Industry Preferences

In Communications prefer:
Communications and Media

In Medical/Health prefer:
Medical/Health

In Consumer Related prefer:
Consumer

In Industrial/Energy prefer:
Energy
Industrial Products

In Business Serv. prefer:
Media

Additional Information

Name of Most Recent Fund: Avista Capital Partners III, L.P.
Most Recent Fund Was Raised: 07/23/2012
Year Founded: 2005
Capital Under Management: $950,270,000
Current Activity Level : Actively seeking new investments

AVIV VENTURE CAPITAL, LTD.

32 Shacham Street,
Amargad Building, 4th floor
Petach Tikva, Israel 4951727
Phone: 97239761111
Fax: 97239199300
E-mail: info@avivvc.com
Website: www.avivvc.com

Management and Staff

Amir Guttman, Managing Partner
Gideon Ben-Zvi, Venture Partner
Sophie Caspi, Chief Financial Officer
Yoav Chelouche, Managing Partner

Type of Firm

Private Equity Firm

Association Membership

Israel Venture Association

Project Preferences

Type of Financing Preferred:
Early Stage
Expansion
Later Stage
Seed

Geographical Preferences

International Preferences:
Israel

Industry Preferences

In Medical/Health prefer:
Medical Products

In Consumer Related prefer:
Consumer Services

In Manufact. prefer:
Manufacturing

Additional Information

Year Founded: 1997
Current Activity Level : Actively seeking new investments

AVRIO CAPITAL MANAGEMENT CORP

400 Crowfoot Crescent N.W.
Suite 500
Calgary, Canada T3G 5H6
Phone: 4032155492
Fax: 4032155495
E-mail: info@avrioventures.com

Other Offices

600 Crowfoot Crescent N.W.
Suite 235
Calgary, Canada T3G 0B4
Phone: 4032155492
Fax: 4032155495

Management and Staff

Aki Georgacacos, Co-Founder
Daniel McCrimmon, Chief Financial Officer
Michael McGee, Managing Director
Steven Leakos, Managing Director

Type of Firm

Private Equity Firm

Association Membership

Canadian Venture Capital Association

Project Preferences

Type of Financing Preferred:
Expansion
Later Stage

Size of Investments Considered:
Min Size of Investment Considered (000s): $3,000
Max Size of Investment Considered (000s): $5,000

Geographical Preferences

United States Preferences:

Canadian Preferences:
Alberta
All Canada

Industry Preferences

In Biotechnology prefer:
Industrial Biotechnology

In Medical/Health prefer:
Health Services

In Consumer Related prefer:
Food/Beverage

In Agr/Forestr/Fish prefer:
Agribusiness
Agriculture related

Additional Information

Name of Most Recent Fund: Avrio Ventures, L.P. II
Most Recent Fund Was Raised: 09/20/2011
Year Founded: 2006
Capital Under Management: $239,200,000
Current Activity Level : Actively seeking new investments

AWAL BANK BSCC

Government Avenue
The Manama Ctr, Ent. 3, Lev. 1
Manama, Bahrain
Phone: 97317203333
Fax: 97317203355
E-mail: info@awal-bank.com

Management and Staff

Alistair Macleod, Chief Executive Officer
Anthony James, Chief Operating Officer
Christoph Gruninger, Managing Director

Type of Firm

Private Equity Firm

Project Preferences

Type of Financing Preferred:
Generalist PE

Industry Preferences

In Biotechnology prefer:
Biotechnology

In Medical/Health prefer:
Medical/Health
Health Services

In Financial Services prefer:
Real Estate

In Agr/Forestr/Fish prefer:
Mining and Minerals

Additional Information

Year Founded: 2004
Current Activity Level : Actively seeking new investments

AWEIDA VENTURE PARTNERS

500 Discovery Parkway
Suite 300
Superior, CO USA 80027
Phone: 3036649520
Fax: 3036649530
E-mail: info@aweida.com
Website: www.aweida.com

Management and Staff
Daniel Aweida, Managing Partner
Jesse Aweida, Managing Partner

Type of Firm
Private Equity Firm

Project Preferences

Role in Financing:
Prefer role as deal originator but will also invest in deals created by others

Type of Financing Preferred:
Early Stage
Mezzanine
Balanced

Industry Preferences

In Computer Software prefer:
Data Processing
Software

Additional Information
Year Founded: 1988
Capital Under Management: $100,000,000
Current Activity Level : Actively seeking new investments
Method of Compensation: Return on invest. most important, but chg. closing fees, service fees, etc.

AWESOME INC

348 East Main Street
Lexington, KY USA 40507
Phone: 5022099960
E-mail: founders@awesomeinc.org
Website: www.awesomeinc.org

Type of Firm
Incubator/Development Program

Project Preferences

Type of Financing Preferred:
Seed
Startup

Geographical Preferences

United States Preferences:
Kentucky

Additional Information
Year Founded: 2009
Current Activity Level : Actively seeking new investments

AXA INVESTMENT MANAGERS INC

One Fawcett Place
Suite 100
Greenwich, CT USA 06830
Phone: 2038638900
Fax: 2038638901
Website: www.axa-im.com

Other Offices

18 Westlands Road
57/F, One Island East
Quarry Bay, Hong Kong

Innere Kanalstr. 95
Koln
Deutschland, Austria D-50823

38/F Shanghai Central Plaza
Shanghai, China 200020

215 Schiphol Boulevard
Tower F1118 BHSchiphol
Airport, Netherlands

88 Phillip Street
RBS Tower
Sydney, Australia 2000
Phone: 61-2-8211-0621
Fax: 61-2-8211-0609

Corso di Porta Romana, 68
Milan, Italy 20122
Phone: 39-02-582-990-23
Fax: 39-02-582-990-60

Kalpataru Synergy Opp Grand Hyatt hotel
51, East Wing, vokola, Santacruz (E)
Mumbai, India 400 055

21, Bld Grande Duchesse
Charlotte, Luxembourg 1331

P.O. Box 22415, 15th Floor
Ministry of Economy & Commerce building
DOHA, Qatar
Phone: 974-496-7200
Fax: 974-496-7205

Nuschelerstrasse 31, CH
Zurich, Switzerland 8001

14 Rue du Rhone
Geneva, Switzerland 1204

1-17-3 Shirokane Minato-ku
NBF Platinum Tower 14F
Tokyo, Japan 108-0072

100 esplanade du General de Gaulle
Coeur Defense Tour B
Paris, France 92932

7 Newgate Street
London, United Kingdom ECIA7NY
Phone: 44-20-7003-123
Fax: 44-20-7003-231

Pr Marques de Pombal 14
2/F
Lisbon, Portugal 1250
Phone: 351-21-350-6220
Fax: 351-21-356-6164

Boulevard du Souverain 36
Brussels, Belgium 1170
Phone: 32-2-679-6372
Fax: 32-2-679-6399

Bleichstrasse 2-4
Frankfurt, Germany 60313
Phone: 49-69-900-250
Fax: 49-69-900-251-5990

Paseo de la Castellana, 93
6 Planta
Madrid, Spain 28046
Phone: 34-91-538-5555
Fax: 34-91-555-5030

Management and Staff
Amaury De Warenghien, Chief Financial Officer
Christophe Coquema, Chief Operating Officer
Dominique Carrel-Billiard, Chief Executive Officer

Type of Firm
Private Equity Advisor or Fund of Funds

Project Preferences

Role in Financing:
Prefer role as deal originator

Type of Financing Preferred:
Fund of Funds
Leveraged Buyout

Geographical Preferences

United States Preferences:
North America

Canadian Preferences:
All Canada

International Preferences:
Latin America
Europe
Asia

Additional Information
Name of Most Recent Fund: Europe Select Private Equity Partners II
Most Recent Fund Was Raised: 12/31/2000
Year Founded: 1999
Capital Under Management: $855,000,000

Current Activity Level : Actively seeking new investments
Method of Compensation: Return on investment is of primary concern, do not charge fees

AXA STRATEGIC VENTURES US LLC

9, Place de la Madeleine
Paris, France 75008

Type of Firm
Insurance Firm Affiliate

Project Preferences

Type of Financing Preferred:
Early Stage
Expansion
Later Stage
Seed
Startup

Geographical Preferences

United States Preferences:

International Preferences:
Europe

Industry Preferences

In Medical/Health prefer:
Medical/Health

In Industrial/Energy prefer:
Industrial Products

In Financial Services prefer:
Insurance
Financial Services

In Business Serv. prefer:
Services

Additional Information
Year Founded: 2015
Capital Under Management: $385,180,000
Current Activity Level : Actively seeking new investments

AXCEL INDUSTRIINVESTOR A/S

Sankt Annae Plads 10
Copenhagen, Denmark 1250
Phone: 4533366999
Fax: 4533366998
E-mail: axcel@axcel.dk

Other Offices
Strandvagen 5B, 5tr
Stockholm, Sweden 114 51
Phone: 46-8-442-5390

Management and Staff
Casper Lykke Pedersen, Partner
Jacob Thygesen, Partner
Jesper Rasmussen, Founder
Lars Thomassen, Chief Financial Officer
Nikolaj Vejlsgaard, Partner
Per Christensen, Partner
Povl Lutken Frigast, Managing Partner
Sigurd Lilienfeldt, Partner
Soren Lindberg, Partner
Vilhelm Sundstrom, Partner

Type of Firm
Private Equity Firm

Association Membership
Danish Venture Capital Association (DVCA)
Swedish Venture Capital Association (SVCA)

Project Preferences

Role in Financing:
Prefer role as deal originator

Type of Financing Preferred:
Leveraged Buyout
Turnaround
Acquisition
Recapitalizations

Geographical Preferences

International Preferences:
Sweden
Denmark

Industry Preferences

In Computer Software prefer:
Software

In Semiconductor/Electr prefer:
Electronics

In Medical/Health prefer:
Medical Diagnostics

In Consumer Related prefer:
Retail
Consumer Products

In Industrial/Energy prefer:
Industrial Products

In Transportation prefer:
Transportation

In Financial Services prefer:
Real Estate

In Business Serv. prefer:
Services

Additional Information
Name of Most Recent Fund: Axcel IV
Most Recent Fund Was Raised: 11/10/2010
Year Founded: 1994
Capital Under Management: $1,836,000,000
Current Activity Level : Actively seeking new investments

AXE INVESTMENTS NV

Noorderlaan 139
Antwerp, Belgium 2030
Phone: 3235437311
Fax: 3235419110
Website: www.axe-investments.com

Type of Firm
Investment Management Firm

Project Preferences

Type of Financing Preferred:
Early Stage
Later Stage
Startup

Geographical Preferences

International Preferences:
Belgium
Singapore
Germany

Industry Preferences

In Communications prefer:
Wireless Communications

In Transportation prefer:
Transportation

In Financial Services prefer:
Real Estate

In Business Serv. prefer:
Services

Additional Information
Year Founded: 1999
Capital Under Management: $22,600,000
Current Activity Level : Actively seeking new investments

AXELEO SAS

73, Rue de la Republique
Lyon, France 69002
Website: axeleo.com

Type of Firm
Incubator/Development Program

Project Preferences

Type of Financing Preferred:
Early Stage

Geographical Preferences

International Preferences:
France

Industry Preferences

In Communications prefer:
Data Communications

In Computer Software prefer:
Software

In Internet Specific prefer:
Internet

Additional Information
Year Founded: 2013
Current Activity Level : Actively seeking new investments

AXIAL GROUP OF COMPANIES

3004 Ogden Road South East
Calgary, Canada T2G 4N5
Phone: 4032650955
Website: axialcompanies.com

Management and Staff
Rod Orsten, President

Type of Firm
Private Equity Firm

Project Preferences

Type of Financing Preferred:
Leveraged Buyout
Acquisition

Industry Preferences

In Industrial/Energy prefer:
Oil and Gas Exploration
Industrial Products
Factory Automation

In Manufact. prefer:
Office Automation Equipmt

Additional Information
Year Founded: 2011
Current Activity Level : Actively seeking new investments

AXILOR VENTURE CAPITAL

No. 739, 15th Cross
Sarakki, India 560078
Phone: 91 800 49252401
E-mail: accelerator@axilor.com
Website: www.axilor.com

Type of Firm
Private Equity Firm

Additional Information
Year Founded: 2015
Current Activity Level : Actively seeking new investments

AXIO CAPITAL SAS

3, rue Chauveau Lagarde
Paris, France 75008
Phone: 33140604380
Website: www.axio.fr

Type of Firm
Private Equity Firm

Project Preferences

Type of Financing Preferred:
Leveraged Buyout
Management Buyouts
Acquisition

Geographical Preferences

International Preferences:
Europe
France

Additional Information
Year Founded: 2014
Current Activity Level : Actively seeking new investments

AXIOM ASIA PRIVATE CAPITAL PTE LTD

16 Collyer Quay
#11-02, Hitachi Tower
Singapore, Singapore 049318
Phone: 6563368886
Fax: 6563368868
E-mail: info@axiomasia.com
Website: www.axiomasia.com

Management and Staff
Chihtsung Lam, Managing Director
Edmond Chi-Man Ng, Managing Director
Yewhong Goh, Managing Director

Type of Firm
Private Equity Advisor or Fund of Funds

Association Membership
Singapore Venture Capital Association (SVCA)

Project Preferences

Type of Financing Preferred:
Fund of Funds
Distressed Debt
Fund of Funds of Second

Geographical Preferences

United States Preferences:
Southeast

International Preferences:
India
China
Pacific
Australia
Asia
Korea, South
Japan

Additional Information
Year Founded: 2006
Capital Under Management: $1,904,770,000
Current Activity Level : Actively seeking new investments

AXIOM VENTURE PARTNERS LP

185 Asylum Street
CityPlace II-17th Floor
Hartford, CT USA 06103
Phone: 8605487799
Fax: 8605487797
Website: www.axiomventures.com

Management and Staff
Alan Mendelson, Co-Founder
John Wieczorek, Chief Financial Officer
Samuel McKay, Co-Founder

Type of Firm
Private Equity Firm

Project Preferences

Role in Financing:
Will function either as deal originator or investor in deals created by others

Type of Financing Preferred:
Early Stage
Balanced
Later Stage

Geographical Preferences

United States Preferences:

Industry Focus

(% based on actual investment)

Communications and Media	22.3%
Medical/Health	21.2%
Computer Software and Services	19.6%
Biotechnology	16.6%
Semiconductors/Other Elect.	6.6%
Computer Hardware	4.7%
Industrial/Energy	3.0%
Internet Specific	2.9%
Other Products	1.6%
Consumer Related	1.4%

Additional Information
Name of Most Recent Fund: Axiom Venture Partners III, L.P.
Most Recent Fund Was Raised: 04/28/2000
Year Founded: 1994

Capital Under Management: $200,000,000
Current Activity Level : Actively seeking new investments
Method of Compensation: Return on investment is of primary concern, do not charge fees

AXIOMA VENTURES LLC

601 South Boulevard
Tampa, FL USA 33606

Management and Staff

Bill Morokoff, Managing Director
Chris Canova, Senior Managing Director
Christopher Woida, Managing Director
Greg Fenton, Managing Director
Ian Webster, Chief Operating Officer
Jacqueline Gaillard, Managing Director
Nico Kicillof, Managing Director
Pamela Vance, Managing Director
Stefan Schmieta, Managing Director
Sunil Rajan, Managing Director

Type of Firm

Private Equity Firm

Project Preferences

Type of Financing Preferred:
Balanced

Additional Information

Year Founded: 2017
Current Activity Level : Actively seeking new investments

AXIS CAPITAL CORP

105 Murray Street
Ottawa, Canada K1N 5M5
Phone: 6132366006
Fax: 6132366336
E-mail: info@axisfunds.com
Website: www.axiscapital.com

Management and Staff

Doug Hewson, Managing Partner
Kevin Goheen, Partner
Peter Low, Managing Partner

Type of Firm

Private Equity Firm

Project Preferences

Role in Financing:
Prefer role as deal originator

Type of Financing Preferred:
Early Stage
Expansion
Balanced
Seed
First Stage Financing
Startup

Size of Investments Considered:
Min Size of Investment Considered (000s): $500
Max Size of Investment Considered (000s): $1,000

Geographical Preferences

United States Preferences:

Canadian Preferences:
All Canada
Ontario

Industry Preferences

In Communications prefer:
Telecommunications
Wireless Communications

In Internet Specific prefer:
Internet

Additional Information

Year Founded: 2000
Current Activity Level : Actively seeking new investments

AXIS CAPITAL MANAGEMENT

Javier Barros Sierra 540
Oficina 103 Park Plaza Torre 1
Mexico, Mexico 01210
Phone: 525559928300
E-mail: contacto@daxis.com.mx
Website: axiscapital.com.mx

Management and Staff

Carlos Williamson, Co-Founder
Gonzalo Gil, Co-Founder
Jose Antonio Canedo, Co-Founder

Type of Firm

Investment Management Firm

Project Preferences

Type of Financing Preferred:
Generalist PE

Additional Information

Year Founded: 1990
Current Activity Level : Actively seeking new investments

AXIS PARTICIPACIONES EMPRESARIALES SGEIC SAU

C/ Los Madrazo 38 2
Madrid, Spain 28014
Phone: 34915231654
Fax: 34915321933
E-mail: axis@axispart.com
Website: www.axispart.com

Type of Firm

Private Equity Firm

Association Membership

European Private Equity and Venture Capital Assoc.
Spanish Venture Capital Association (ASCRI)

Project Preferences

Type of Financing Preferred:
Fund of Funds
Generalist PE
Balanced
Later Stage

Geographical Preferences

International Preferences:
Europe
Spain

Additional Information

Name of Most Recent Fund: FOND-ICO Global
Most Recent Fund Was Raised: 03/22/2013
Year Founded: 1993
Capital Under Management: $85,500,000
Current Activity Level : Actively seeking new investments

AXIVATE CAPITAL BV

Willem Fenengastraat 4B
Kauwgomballenfabriek Lab
Amsterdam, Netherlands 1096 BN
Phone: 31206724
Fax: 31206724
E-mail: info@axivate.com
Website: www.axivate.com

Type of Firm

Private Equity Firm

Project Preferences

Type of Financing Preferred:
Leveraged Buyout
Early Stage
Generalist PE

Industry Preferences

In Internet Specific prefer:
E-Commerce Technology
Internet

In Consumer Related prefer:
Entertainment and Leisure

Additional Information

Year Founded: 2015
Current Activity Level : Actively seeking new investments

AXM VENTURE CAPITAL LTD

57g Randolph Avenue
London, United Kingdom W9 1BQ
Phone: 442032398099
Fax: 442070228757
E-mail: corpfin@axmvc.co.uk
Website: www.axmvc.co.uk

Other Offices
259-269 Old Marylebone Road
Second Floor, Winchester House
London, United Kingdom NW1 5RA

Type of Firm
Private Equity Firm

Project Preferences

Type of Financing Preferred:
Early Stage
Expansion
Balanced
Seed
Acquisition
Startup

Size of Investments Considered:
Min Size of Investment Considered (000s): $119
Max Size of Investment Considered (000s): $1,027

Geographical Preferences

International Preferences:
United Kingdom
Europe

Industry Preferences

In Communications prefer:
Communications and Media
Media and Entertainment

In Computer Software prefer:
Software

In Internet Specific prefer:
Ecommerce

In Consumer Related prefer:
Consumer Products

Additional Information
Year Founded: 2005
Capital Under Management: $10,300,000
Current Activity Level : Actively seeking new investments

AXON PARTNERS GROUP INVESTMENT

Jos Ortega y Gasset, 25
Madrid, Spain 28006
Phone: 34913102894
Fax: 34911412540
Website: www.axonpartnersgroup.com

Other Offices
Fourm Synergies (India) PE Fund Managers
Suite No VI, A1-Epsilon ,
Bangalore, India 560037
Phone: 91 80 4000 6400

Calle 87
No. 10-93 of 701
Bogota, Colombia
Phone: 5716353007

801 Brickell Avenue
9th floor
Miami, FL USA 33131
Phone: 17865033847

Management and Staff
Alfonso Leon, Partner
Allan Majotra, Partner
Dimitri Kallinis, Partner
Hamchandra Javeri, Partner
Ishwar Subramanian, Partner
Julio Villalobos, Partner
Pierluigi Paracchi, Partner
Prashant Goyal, Partner
Samir Inamdar, Partner
Stefano Peroncini, Partner

Type of Firm
Private Equity Firm

Association Membership
Spanish Venture Capital Association (ASCRI)
Indian Venture Capital Association (IVCA)

Project Preferences

Type of Financing Preferred:
Early Stage
Expansion
Balanced
Seed
Startup

Size of Investments Considered:
Min Size of Investment Considered (000s): $100
Max Size of Investment Considered (000s): $25,000

Geographical Preferences

International Preferences:
Latin America
India
Peru
Mexico
Spain
Colombia

Industry Preferences

In Communications prefer:
Communications and Media
Media and Entertainment

In Internet Specific prefer:
Internet
Ecommerce

In Medical/Health prefer:
Medical/Health
Health Services

In Consumer Related prefer:
Education Related

In Industrial/Energy prefer:
Energy
Advanced Materials
Environmental Related

In Business Serv. prefer:
Media

In Manufact. prefer:
Manufacturing

Additional Information
Year Founded: 2007
Capital Under Management: $113,879,000
Current Activity Level : Actively seeking new investments

AXUM CAPITAL PARTNERS LLC

6100 Fairview Road
Suite 1156
Charlotte, NC USA 28210
Phone: 7043343334
Fax: 9802729045
E-mail: info@axum-partners.com
Website: axum-partners.com

Management and Staff
Cheryl Moynihan, Managing Director
Denis Ackah-Yensu, Managing Director
Edna Morris, Managing Director
Mak Kazimi, Vice President
Muhsin Muhammad, Managing Director
Raymond Groth, Managing Director

Type of Firm
Private Equity Firm

Project Preferences

Type of Financing Preferred:
Leveraged Buyout

Industry Preferences

In Consumer Related prefer:
Consumer
Food/Beverage
Consumer Services
Education Related

In Financial Services prefer:
Financial Services

Additional Information
Name of Most Recent Fund: Axum Capital Partners Fund I, L.P.
Most Recent Fund Was Raised: 11/29/2011
Year Founded: 2011
Capital Under Management: $15,000,000
Current Activity Level : Actively seeking new investments

AXXESS CAPITAL PARTNERS SA

33 Aviatorilor Boulevard
Bucharest, Romania 011853
Phone: 40212077100
Fax: 40212228503
E-mail: office@axxesscapital.net
Website: www.axxesscapital.net

Other Offices

545 Fifth Avenue
Suite 300
New York, NY USA 10017
Phone: 212-697-5766
Fax: 212-818-0445

36 Oborishe Street
Floor 1
Sofia, Bulgaria 1504
Phone: 359-2-819-4570
Fax: 359-2-944-1475

Management and Staff

Cristina Mogoroase, Partner
Daniela Toader, Chief Financial Officer
Horia Manda, Managing Partner
Neculai Sandu, Partner
Valentin Tabus, Partner

Type of Firm

Private Equity Firm

Association Membership

South Eastern Europes Private Equity Association
European Private Equity and Venture Capital Assoc.

Project Preferences

Type of Financing Preferred:
Leveraged Buyout
Generalist PE
Management Buyouts

Size of Investments Considered:
Min Size of Investment Considered (000s): $3,810
Max Size of Investment Considered (000s): $8,891

Geographical Preferences

International Preferences:
Albania
Turkey
Moldova
Ukraine
Bulgaria
Romania

Industry Preferences

In Communications prefer:
Communications and Media
Commercial Communications

In Medical/Health prefer:
Medical/Health
Health Services

In Consumer Related prefer:
Consumer
Consumer Products

In Industrial/Energy prefer:
Energy
Industrial Products
Materials

In Transportation prefer:
Transportation

In Financial Services prefer:
Financial Services

In Manufact. prefer:
Manufacturing

Additional Information

Year Founded: 2006
Capital Under Management: $265,000,000
Current Activity Level : Actively seeking new investments

AXXON GROUP SERVICOS DE CONSULTORIA E ASSESSORIA LTDA

Ladeira de Nossa Senhora 311
Gloria
Rio de Janeiro, Brazil 22211100
Phone: 552132350770
Fax: 552132350772
E-mail: axxon@axxongroup.com.br
Website: www.axxongroup.com.br

Other Offices

Avenida del Libertador, 7400
1st Floor
Buenos Aires, Argentina C1429BMT
Phone: 5411-4703-1112
Fax: 5411-4703-1112

Rua Iguatemi 192/Cj.
191, Itaim Bibi
Sao Paulo, Brazil 01451-010
Phone: 551130740920
Fax: 551130740923

Management and Staff

Fabio Maranhao, Partner
Jose Augusto de Carvalho, Partner
Nick Wollak, Managing Partner
Paulo Mordehachvili, Partner

Type of Firm

Private Equity Firm

Association Membership

Brazilian Venture Capital Association (ABCR)

Project Preferences

Type of Financing Preferred:
Leveraged Buyout
Early Stage
Generalist PE
Balanced
Later Stage
Management Buyouts
Acquisition

Size of Investments Considered:
Min Size of Investment Considered (000s): $15,000
Max Size of Investment Considered (000s): $50,000

Geographical Preferences

International Preferences:
Latin America
Brazil

Industry Preferences

In Consumer Related prefer:
Retail

In Transportation prefer:
Transportation

Additional Information

Year Founded: 1993
Capital Under Management: $250,000,000
Current Activity Level : Actively seeking new investments

AZ DIGITAL FARM LLC

3200 North Hayden Road, Suite 300
Scottsdale, AZ USA 85251
Phone: 4806090922
E-mail: info@AZDigitalFarm.com
Website: www.azdigitalfarm.com

Type of Firm
Private Equity Firm

Project Preferences

Type of Financing Preferred:
Early Stage

Industry Preferences

In Communications prefer:
Wireless Communications

In Internet Specific prefer:
E-Commerce Technology

In Consumer Related prefer:
Education Related

Additional Information
Year Founded: 2010
Current Activity Level : Actively seeking new investments

AZALEA CAPITAL LLC

One Liberty Square
Suite 1500, 55 Beattie Place
Greenville, SC USA 29601
Phone: 8642350201
Fax: 8642351155
Website: www.azaleacapital.com

Management and Staff
Ben Wallace, Vice President
Benny LaRussa, Partner
Patrick Duncan, Managing Partner
R. Patrick Weston, Managing Partner

Type of Firm
Private Equity Firm

Project Preferences

Role in Financing:
Prefer role as deal originator

Type of Financing Preferred:
Leveraged Buyout
Mezzanine
Management Buyouts
Acquisition
Recapitalizations

Size of Investments Considered:
Min Size of Investment Considered (000s): $2,000
Max Size of Investment Considered (000s): $20,000

Industry Preferences

In Consumer Related prefer:
Consumer Products

Additional Information
Year Founded: 1995
Capital Under Management: $60,215,000
Current Activity Level : Actively seeking new investments

AZINI CAPITAL PARTNERS LLP

29 Farm Street
London, United Kingdom W1J 5RL
Phone: 442031783388
Website: www.azini.com

Type of Firm
Private Equity Firm

Project Preferences

Type of Financing Preferred:
Leveraged Buyout
Acquisition

Industry Preferences

In Computer Software prefer:
Software

In Industrial/Energy prefer:
Materials

In Manufact. prefer:
Manufacturing

Additional Information
Name of Most Recent Fund: Azini 3 LLP
Most Recent Fund Was Raised: 12/19/2013
Year Founded: 2004
Capital Under Management: $100,000,000
Current Activity Level : Actively seeking new investments

AZKA CAPITAL SDN BHD

M-2-20 Plaza Damas
60, Jalan Sri Hartamas
Kuala Lumpur, Malaysia 50480
Phone: 60362031025
Fax: 60362034072
E-mail: info@azkacapital.com
Website: www.azkacapital.com

Type of Firm
Private Equity Firm

Project Preferences

Type of Financing Preferred:
Leveraged Buyout
Early Stage
Expansion
Generalist PE
Balanced
Later Stage
Management Buyouts
Acquisition

Geographical Preferences

International Preferences:
Asia
Malaysia

Industry Preferences

In Consumer Related prefer:
Food/Beverage

Additional Information
Year Founded: 2013
Current Activity Level : Actively seeking new investments

AZOIC VENTURES INC

17001 Collins Avenue
Suite 4608
North Miami, FL USA 33160

Management and Staff
Kurt Holstein, President, Founder

Type of Firm
Private Equity Firm

Project Preferences

Type of Financing Preferred:
Early Stage
Startup

Industry Preferences

In Computer Software prefer:
Software

In Medical/Health prefer:
Medical/Health

In Consumer Related prefer:
Consumer

Additional Information
Year Founded: 2011
Current Activity Level : Actively seeking new investments

AZTEC EQUITY PARTNERS LLC

One Gateway Center
Suite 2600
Newark, NJ USA 07102
Phone: 888-774-2983
E-mail: info@aztecpartners.com
Website: www.aztecpartners.com

Management and Staff
Alex Garcia, Managing Director
Alex Luis Pupo, Chief Financial Officer
Ali Akansu, Managing Director

Type of Firm
Private Equity Firm

Project Preferences

Type of Financing Preferred:
Early Stage
Mezzanine
Generalist PE
Seed
Startup

Geographical Preferences

United States Preferences:

Industry Preferences

In Industrial/Energy prefer:
Environmental Related

In Other prefer:
Environment Responsible

Additional Information
Year Founded: 2005
Current Activity Level : Actively seeking new investments

AZULIS CAPITAL SA

21 Boulevard De La Madeleine
Paris, France 75001
Phone: 33142987020
Fax: 33142987021
E-mail: info@azuliscapital.fr
Website: www.azuliscapital.fr

Management and Staff
Andre Belard, Partner
Bruno Lavolle, Partner
Christine Mariette, Partner
Donatien Noyelle, Chief Financial Officer
Franck Boget, Managing Partner
Gilles Perony, Partner
Michel Rowan, Managing Partner
Nicolas Cosson, Partner
Pierre Jourdain, Partner
Yann Collignon, Partner

Type of Firm
Bank Affiliated

Association Membership
French Venture Capital Association (AFIC)
European Private Equity and Venture Capital Assoc.

Project Preferences

Type of Financing Preferred:
Leveraged Buyout
Management Buyouts
Acquisition

Size of Investments Considered:
Min Size of Investment Considered (000s): $6,832
Max Size of Investment Considered (000s): $20,495

Geographical Preferences

International Preferences:
Europe
France

Industry Preferences

In Medical/Health prefer:
Medical/Health

In Consumer Related prefer:
Consumer
Food/Beverage

In Industrial/Energy prefer:
Energy
Industrial Products
Materials

In Business Serv. prefer:
Services

In Manufact. prefer:
Manufacturing

In Other prefer:
Socially Responsible

Additional Information
Year Founded: 2001
Capital Under Management: $890,700,000
Current Activity Level : Actively seeking new investments

AZURE CAPITAL PARTNERS, L.P.

1050 Battery Street
Suite 100
San Francisco, CA USA 94111
Phone: 4152765500
Fax: 4152765590
E-mail: info@azurecap.com
Website: www.azurecap.com

Other Offices
400, 1333 - Eighth Street SW
Calgary, Canada T2R 1M6

3000 Sand Hill Road
Bldg. 3, Suite 245
MENLO PARK, CA USA 94025

Management and Staff
Ali Wasti, Vice President
Cameron Lester, Co-Founder
Dan Park, Vice President
Larry Augustin, Venture Partner
Michael Kwatinetz, Co-Founder
Paul Ferris, Co-Founder
Paul Weinstein, Co-Founder
Ray Carey, Venture Partner
Steve Gillan, Chief Financial Officer

Type of Firm
Private Equity Firm

Association Membership
National Venture Capital Association - USA (NVCA)

Project Preferences

Role in Financing:
Prefer role as deal originator but will also invest in deals created by others

Type of Financing Preferred:
Early Stage

Geographical Preferences

United States Preferences:
North America
California

Canadian Preferences:
All Canada

Industry Preferences

In Communications prefer:
Communications and Media

In Internet Specific prefer:
Internet

In Consumer Related prefer:
Consumer

Additional Information
Name of Most Recent Fund: Azure Capital Partners III, L.P.
Most Recent Fund Was Raised: 08/29/2011
Year Founded: 2000
Capital Under Management: $750,000,000
Current Activity Level : Actively seeking new investments
Method of Compensation: Return on investment is of primary concern, do not charge fees

- B -

B CAPITAL GROUP

1240 Rosecrans Ave
Manhattan Beach, CA USA 90266
Phone: 3109555840
E-mail: info@bcapgroup.com
Website: www.bcapgroup.com

Type of Firm
Private Equity Firm

Project Preferences

Type of Financing Preferred:
Startup

Industry Preferences

In Internet Specific prefer:
Ecommerce

In Medical/Health prefer:
Health Services

In Consumer Related prefer:
Consumer

In Transportation prefer:
Transportation

In Financial Services prefer:
Financial Services

Additional Information
Year Founded: 2016
Capital Under Management: $181,010,000
Current Activity Level : Actively seeking new investments

B DASH VENTURES INC

11 5-Chome,Toranomon,Minato-ku
Holland Hills Mori Tower No. 2
Tokyo, Japan
E-mail: infobdashventures.com
Website: bdashventures.com

Type of Firm
Private Equity Firm

Project Preferences

Type of Financing Preferred:
Seed
Startup

Geographical Preferences

International Preferences:
Japan

Industry Preferences

In Computer Software prefer:
Applications Software

In Internet Specific prefer:
Internet
Ecommerce

Additional Information
Year Founded: 2011
Current Activity Level : Actively seeking new investments

B TO V PARTNERS AG

Blumenaustrasse 36
P.O. Box 142
St. Gallen, Switzerland 9004
Phone: 41712422000
Fax: 41712422001
E-mail: info@b-to-v.com
Website: www.b-to-v.com

Management and Staff
Christian Schuetz, Partner
Dirk Roesing, Partner
Florian Schweitzer, Partner
Jan Bomholt, Partner
Tetyana Astashkina, Vice President

Type of Firm
Angel Group

Association Membership
Swiss Venture Capital Association (SECA)

Project Preferences

Type of Financing Preferred:
Leveraged Buyout
Early Stage
Turnaround
Later Stage
Seed
Management Buyouts
Startup

Size of Investments Considered:
Min Size of Investment Considered (000s): $297
Max Size of Investment Considered (000s): $14,828

Geographical Preferences

United States Preferences:
All U.S.

International Preferences:
India
Sweden
United Kingdom
Turkey
Europe
Netherlands
Switzerland
Malta
China
Austria
Spain
Asia
Norway
Germany
All International

Industry Preferences

In Communications prefer:
Wireless Communications

In Internet Specific prefer:
Internet

In Medical/Health prefer:
Medical/Health

In Consumer Related prefer:
Retail

In Industrial/Energy prefer:
Environmental Related

In Business Serv. prefer:
Services

Additional Information
Name of Most Recent Fund: b-to-v Entrepreneurial Growth II
Most Recent Fund Was Raised: 04/18/2011
Year Founded: 2000
Capital Under Management: $98,161,000
Current Activity Level : Actively seeking new investments

B&Y VENTURE PARTNERS

BDD1243, 2nd Floor, Nassif El
Yazji Street, El Bachoura
Beirut, Lebanon
Website: byvp.com

Type of Firm
Private Equity Firm

Project Preferences

Type of Financing Preferred:
Early Stage
Seed

Geographical Preferences

International Preferences:
Lebanon

Industry Preferences

In Computer Software prefer:
Applications Software

Additional Information

Year Founded: 2016
Current Activity Level : Actively seeking new investments

B&Y VENTURE PARTNERS

6th Floor Nassif El Yajzi St
El Bachoura
Beirut, Lebanon BDD1243
Phone: 9611661830
E-mail: info@yventurepartners.com
Website: www.byvp.com

Other Offices

6th Floor Nassif El Yajzi St
El Bachoura
Beirut, Lebanon
Phone: 9611661830

Type of Firm

Private Equity Firm

Project Preferences

Type of Financing Preferred:
Early Stage
Seed
Startup

Size of Investments Considered:
Min Size of Investment Considered (000s): $30
Max Size of Investment Considered (000s): $300

Geographical Preferences

United States Preferences:
North America

International Preferences:
Europe
Middle East

Industry Preferences

In Computer Software prefer:
Software

In Internet Specific prefer:
Internet
Ecommerce

In Business Serv. prefer:
Consulting Services

Additional Information

Year Founded: 2015
Current Activity Level : Actively seeking new investments

B-29 INVESTMENTS, L.P.

201 West California Street
P.O. Box 170
Gainesville, TX USA 76241
Phone: 9406654373
E-mail: info@b29investments.com
Website: www.b29investments.com

Type of Firm

Private Equity Firm

Project Preferences

Type of Financing Preferred:
Leveraged Buyout
Value-Add
Mezzanine
Generalist PE
Other

Geographical Preferences

United States Preferences:

Industry Preferences

In Industrial/Energy prefer:
Energy
Oil and Gas Exploration

In Financial Services prefer:
Real Estate

Additional Information

Year Founded: 1997
Current Activity Level : Actively seeking new investments

B.P. MARSH & PARTNERS PLC

36 Broadway
Second Floor
London, United Kingdom SW1H 0BH
Phone: 442072333112
Fax: 442072220294
E-mail: enquiries@bpmarsh.co.uk
Website: www.bpmarsh.co.uk

Management and Staff

Rupert Marsh, Chief Executive Officer

Type of Firm

Private Equity Firm

Project Preferences

Type of Financing Preferred:
Early Stage

Geographical Preferences

United States Preferences:
All U.S.

International Preferences:
United Kingdom
Europe

Industry Preferences

In Financial Services prefer:
Financial Services

Additional Information

Year Founded: 1990
Current Activity Level : Actively seeking new investments

B12 CAPITAL PARTNERS LLC

4900 Main Street
Suite 950
Kansas City, MO USA 64112
Phone: 8169948631
Fax: 8169948633

Management and Staff

Daniel Schulte, Partner
Gregory Gaeddert, Managing Partner
Michael Wedel, Managing Partner

Type of Firm

Private Equity Firm

Project Preferences

Type of Financing Preferred:
Leveraged Buyout
Expansion
Generalist PE
Management Buyouts
Acquisition

Geographical Preferences

United States Preferences:
Midwest
Southeast

Industry Preferences

In Medical/Health prefer:
Medical Products

In Consumer Related prefer:
Entertainment and Leisure
Food/Beverage
Consumer Products
Consumer Services
Education Related

In Industrial/Energy prefer:
Energy
Industrial Products
Materials
Environmental Related

In Transportation prefer:
Transportation
Aerospace

In Business Serv. prefer:
Distribution

In Manufact. prefer:
Manufacturing
Publishing

Additional Information
Year Founded: 2007
Current Activity Level : Actively seeking new investments

B37 VENTURES LLC

201 Spear Street
Suite 1100
Cupertino, CA USA 95014
Website: b37.vc

Other Offices
201 Spear Streett
SAN FRANCISCO, CA USA 94105
Phone: 4157573431

Management and Staff
David Hite, Managing Partner
Rodrigo Servitje, Managing Partner

Type of Firm
Private Equity Firm

Project Preferences

Type of Financing Preferred:
Balanced

Additional Information
Year Founded: 2013
Current Activity Level : Actively seeking new investments

B4 VENTURES LLC

P.O. Box 703852
Dallas, TX USA 75370
Phone: 2148499882
Website: www.b4ventures.com

Management and Staff
Carl Karnes, Principal
Scott Pollock, Principal

Type of Firm
Private Equity Firm

Project Preferences

Role in Financing:
Prefer role as deal originator but will also invest in deals created by others

Type of Financing Preferred:
Later Stage

Size of Investments Considered:
Min Size of Investment Considered (000s): $250
Max Size of Investment Considered (000s): $5,000

Additional Information
Year Founded: 2002
Current Activity Level : Actively seeking new investments

BA PRIVATE EQUITY GMBH

Operngasse 6
Vienna, Austria 1010
Phone: 431513220181
Fax: 431513220125
E-mail: office@privateequity.at
Website: www.privateequity.at

Type of Firm
Bank Affiliated

Project Preferences

Type of Financing Preferred:
Leveraged Buyout
Mezzanine
Later Stage
Management Buyouts

Geographical Preferences

International Preferences:
Europe

Additional Information
Year Founded: 2001
Current Activity Level : Actively seeking new investments

BACCHUS CAPITAL MANAGEMENT LLC

601 California Street
Suite 810
San Francisco, CA USA 94108
Phone: 8667509463
Fax: 6465308365
Website: www.bacchuswinefund.com

Other Offices
4225 Solano Avenue
Suite 668
Napa, CA USA 94558
Phone: 4158288898
Fax: 6465308365

950 Third Avenue
17th Floor
New York, NY USA 10022
Phone: 8667509463
Fax: 2124863616

Management and Staff
Henry Owsley, Co-Founder
Peter Kaufman, Co-Founder
Quinton Jay, Managing Director
Robert Rupe, Managing Director
Samuel Bronfman, Co-Founder

Type of Firm
Private Equity Firm

Project Preferences

Type of Financing Preferred:
Leveraged Buyout
Mezzanine
Generalist PE
Balanced

Geographical Preferences

United States Preferences:
West Coast

Industry Preferences

In Consumer Related prefer:
Food/Beverage

Additional Information
Year Founded: 2007
Current Activity Level : Actively seeking new investments

BACHLEDA GRUPA IN-WESTYCYJNA SP Z O O

Ul. Krupowki 29
Second Floor
Zakopane, Poland 34-500
Phone: 48182020880
Fax: 48182020890
Website: www.bachleda.pl

Management and Staff
Adam Bachleda-Curus, Managing Partner
Adam Bachleda-Curus, Co-Founder
Bernadetta Bachleda-Curus, Managing Partner
Malgorzata Bachleda-Curus, Managing Partner
Malgorzata Stankiewicz, Managing Director
Wojciech Wyszynski, Managing Director

Type of Firm
Private Equity Firm

Project Preferences

Type of Financing Preferred:
Value-Add
Generalist PE

Geographical Preferences

International Preferences:
Poland

Industry Preferences

In Consumer Related prefer:
Food/Beverage
Consumer Products
Consumer Services
Hotels and Resorts

In Financial Services prefer:
Real Estate

In Business Serv. prefer:
Distribution

Additional Information
Year Founded: 2012
Capital Under Management: $129,600,000
Current Activity Level : Actively seeking new investments

BACKCAST PARTNERS LLC

825 Third Avenue
40th Floor
New York, NY USA 10022
E-mail: information@backcastpartners.com.
Website: www.backcastpartners.com

Type of Firm
Private Equity Firm

Project Preferences

Type of Financing Preferred:
Acquisition

Additional Information
Year Founded: 2016
Current Activity Level : Actively seeking new investments

BACKED VC

8 Warner Yard
London, United Kingdom EC1R 5EY
E-mail: info@backed.vc
Website: backed.vc

Type of Firm
Private Equity Firm

Project Preferences

Type of Financing Preferred:
Early Stage

Geographical Preferences

International Preferences:
Europe

Industry Preferences

In Computer Software prefer:
Artificial Intelligence

In Semiconductor/Electr prefer:
Analytic/Scientific

Additional Information
Year Founded: 2016
Current Activity Level : Actively seeking new investments

BACKLOG CAPITAL LLC

1730 Main Street
Suite 200
Weston, FL USA 33326
Phone: 9542175155
Fax: 9543373289
E-mail: info@backlogcapital.com

Management and Staff
Arhtur Cote, Vice President
JW Ray, Managing Director

Type of Firm
Investment Management Firm

Project Preferences

Type of Financing Preferred:
Early Stage
Balanced
Later Stage

Geographical Preferences

United States Preferences:

Industry Preferences

In Medical/Health prefer:
Medical/Health

Additional Information
Name of Most Recent Fund: Backlog Capital Fund
Most Recent Fund Was Raised: 04/27/2011
Year Founded: 2011
Capital Under Management: $20,000,000
Current Activity Level : Actively seeking new investments

BACKSTAGE INVEST AB

Engelbrektsgatan 28
Box 3097
Gothenburg, Sweden 400 10
Phone: 4631815710
Fax: 4631201891
Website: www.backstage.se

Management and Staff
Fredrik Tilander, President

Type of Firm
Private Equity Firm

Association Membership
Swedish Venture Capital Association (SVCA)

Project Preferences

Type of Financing Preferred:
Early Stage

Geographical Preferences

International Preferences:
Scandanavia/Nordic Region

Industry Preferences

In Communications prefer:
Media and Entertainment

In Consumer Related prefer:
Consumer
Retail
Consumer Products

Additional Information
Year Founded: 1996
Current Activity Level : Actively seeking new investments

BADER YOUNG ENTREPRE-NEURS PROGRAM

Berytech Building 5th Floor
Damascus Road Mathaf
Beirut, Lebanon
Phone: 9611612500
Fax: 9611611005
E-mail: info@baderlebanon.com
Website: www.baderlebanon.com

Management and Staff
Nader El Hariri, Vice President
Robert Fadel, President

Type of Firm
Incubator/Development Program

Project Preferences

Type of Financing Preferred:
Early Stage
Expansion
Balanced
Later Stage
Seed
Startup

Geographical Preferences

International Preferences:
Lebanon
Asia

Industry Preferences

In Consumer Related prefer:
Food/Beverage
Consumer Products

In Business Serv. prefer:
Services

Additional Information
Year Founded: 2005
Current Activity Level : Actively seeking new investments

BAGAN CAPITAL LTD

3A Chater Road
The HK Club Bldg., Suite 901
Central, Hong Kong
Phone: 85231257657
E-mail: enquiries@bagancapital.com
Website: www.bagancapital.com

Other Offices

204, Junction Hotel Nay Pyi Taw
Hotel Zone, Delkhina Thiri
Nay Pyi Taw, Burma
Phone: 9567422001

Mandalay Swan Hotel
68th Street
Mandalay, Burma

43/2, Thiri Mingalar Street
Ward, Kamayut Township
Yangon, Burma
Phone: 9512304064

Type of Firm
Private Equity Firm

Association Membership
Emerging Markets Private Equity Association

Project Preferences

Type of Financing Preferred:
Leveraged Buyout
Early Stage
Expansion
Balanced
Acquisition

Geographical Preferences

International Preferences:
Hong Kong
Asia
Burma

Industry Preferences

In Communications prefer:
Wireless Communications

In Medical/Health prefer:
Health Services

In Consumer Related prefer:
Retail
Consumer Services
Education Related

In Industrial/Energy prefer:
Energy

In Financial Services prefer:
Financial Services
Real Estate

In Manufact. prefer:
Manufacturing

In Agr/Forestr/Fish prefer:
Agribusiness

Additional Information
Year Founded: 2012
Current Activity Level : Actively seeking new investments

BAHRAIN DEVELOPMENT BANK BSCC

P. O. Box 20501
Manama, Bahrain
Phone: 97317511111
Fax: 97317530116
E-mail: info@bdb-bh.com
Website: www.bdb-bh.com

Management and Staff
Hassan Al Bin Mohammed, Vice President
Nedhal Saleh Al Aujan, Chief Executive Officer
Tawfeeq Al Qattan, Vice President

Type of Firm
Bank Affiliated

Project Preferences

Type of Financing Preferred:
Early Stage
Balanced
Later Stage
Startup

Geographical Preferences

International Preferences:
Bahrain
Asia

Industry Preferences

In Computer Hardware prefer:
Integrated Turnkey System

In Medical/Health prefer:
Medical/Health

In Consumer Related prefer:
Education Related

In Agr/Forestr/Fish prefer:
Agriculture related

Additional Information
Year Founded: 1992
Current Activity Level : Actively seeking new investments

BAILADOR INVESTMENT MANAGEMENT PTY LTD

37 Bligh Street
Suite 908, Level 9
Sydney, Australia 2000
Phone: 61292232344
E-mail: investorservices@bailador.com.au
Website: bailador.com.au

Management and Staff
David Kirk, Co-Founder
Paul Wilson, Co-Founder

Type of Firm
Private Equity Firm

Project Preferences

Type of Financing Preferred:
Early Stage
Expansion

Industry Preferences

In Computer Software prefer:
Software

Additional Information
Year Founded: 2010
Current Activity Level : Actively seeking new investments

BAIN CAPITAL INC

200 Clarendon Street
John Hancock Tower
Boston, MA USA 02116
Phone: 6175162000
Fax: 6175162010
Website: www.baincapital.com

Other Offices

Maximilianstrasse 11
Munich, Germany 80539
Phone: 498924441070
Fax: 4989244410731

590 Madison Avenue
42nd Floor
New York, NY USA 10022
Phone: 2123269420
Fax: 2124212225

8 Century Boulevard
46/F Two IFC
Shanghai, China 200120
Phone: 862161632000
Fax: 862161632088

6th Floor, Devonshire House
Mayfair Place
London, United Kingdom W1J 8AJ
Phone: 442075145252
Fax: 442075145250

9a Rue Gabriel Lippmann
L-5365
Mnsbach, Luxembourg
Phone: 3522678601
Fax: 35226786060

2 Queen's Road Central
51/F Cheung Kong Center
Central, Hong Kong
Phone: 85236566800
Fax: 85236566801

5F, Palace Building
1-1-1 Marunouchi, Chiyoda-ku
Tokyo, Japan 100-0005
Phone: 81362127070
Fax: 81362127071

2nd Floor, Free Press House
Nariman Point
Mumbai, India 400 021
Phone: 912267528000
Fax: 912267528010

335 Bryant Street
Palo Alto, CA USA 94301
Phone: 6507982500
Fax: 6507982501

Management and Staff

Adam Nebesar, Vice President
Adam Koppel, Managing Director
Ajay Agarwal, Managing Director
Alex Band, Vice President
Alexander Ripley, Principal
Alon Avner, Managing Director
Amanda Eisel, Vice President
Amit Chandra, Managing Director
Anand More, Managing Director
Andrew Carlino, Managing Director
Atsuhiko Sakamoto, Principal
Atsushi Yokoyama, Principal
Bear Albright, Managing Director
Ben Holzman, Partner
Benjamin Nye, Managing Director
Beth Clymer, Vice President
Blair Hendrix, Managing Director
Cecile Belaman, Managing Director
Chris Gordon, Managing Director
Christophe Jacobs van Merlen, Principal
Craig Boyce, Managing Director
Danny Lee, Managing Director
Darren Abrahamson, Vice President
David Humphrey, Principal
David Gross-Loh, Managing Director
David McCarthy, Managing Director
Deepak Sindwani, Partner
Dennis Goldstein, Managing Director
Devin O Reilly, Principal
Dewey Awad, Managing Director
Drew Chen, Principal
Dwight Poler, Managing Director
Edward Han, Managing Director
Eric Erb, Vice President
Felipe Merry del Val, Managing Director
Felix Hauser, Principal
Graham Blackwell, Vice President
Greg Moore, Managing Director
Ian Loring, Managing Director
Ian Andrew Reynolds, Managing Director
Ivano Sessa, Principal
Jack Zhu, Vice President
James Hildebrandt, Managing Director
James Nahirny, Managing Director
James Kellogg, Managing Director
Jared Kesselheim, Principal
Jay Corrigan, Chief Financial Officer
Jeffrey Robinson, Managing Director
Jeffrey Schwartz, Managing Director
Jeffrey Crisan, Managing Director
Jeffrey Woolbert, Managing Director
Jeffrey Glass, Managing Director
Jennifer Hoh, Vice President
Jerome Bertrand, Principal
John Connaughton, Managing Director
John Connolly, Managing Director
John Kilgallon, Managing Director
John Belitsos, Vice President
John Toussaint, Managing Director
Jonathan Greene, Vice President
Jonathan DeSimone, Managing Director
Jonathan Goodman, Managing Director
Jonathan Lavine, Managing Director
Jonathan Jia Zhu, Managing Director
Jordan Hitch, Managing Director
Joseph Robbins, Vice President
Joshua Bekenstein, Managing Director
Junya Ishikawa, Principal
Kate Gulliver, Vice President
Kaustuv Sen, Principal
Keith Harris, Managing Director
Kristin Mugford, Managing Director
Laki Nomicos, Managing Director
Lew Klessel, Managing Director
Lihong Wang, Managing Director
Lisa Claussen, Vice President
Lisa Hersch, Vice President
Luca Bassi, Managing Director
Marc Valentiny, Managing Director
Mark Midle, Principal
Mark Moore, Managing Director
Marko Kivisto, Principal
Marlene Reynolds, Chief Financial Officer
Martin Gilkes, Vice President
Matthew McPherron, Managing Director
Matthew Levin, Managing Director
Melissa Bethell, Managing Director
Michael Ewald, Managing Director
Michael Goss, Managing Director & CFO
Michael Bevacqua, Managing Director
Michael Krupka, Managing Director
Michael Siefke, Managing Director
Michel Plantevin, Managing Director
Nancy Lotane, Managing Director
Nikhil Raghavan, Principal
Patrick Dooling, Vice President
Paul Edgerley, Managing Director
Pavninder Singh, Principal
Peter Riehl, Managing Director
Peter Spring, Vice President
Petr Nosek, Principal
Rob Quandt, Principal
Robert Ehrhart, Managing Director
Robert Weiss, Managing Director
Robert Cunjak, Managing Director
Robin Marshall, Managing Director
Ryan Cotton, Principal
Sally Fassler, Chief Financial Officer
Samonnoi Banerjee, Principal
Sanjay Banker, Principal
Scott Friend, Managing Director
Sean Doherty, Managing Director
Seth Meisel, Managing Director
Stephen Thomas, Principal
Stephen Zide, Managing Director
Stephen Pagliuca, Managing Director
Steven Barnes, Managing Director
Stuart Gent, Managing Director
Stuart Davies, Managing Director
Susan Lynch, Managing Director
Ted Berk, Managing Director
Thomas De Waen, Principal
Tim Barns, Managing Director
Todd Cook, Managing Director
Tricia Patrick, Principal
Walid Sarkis, Managing Director
Warren Valdmanis, Principal
William Pappendick, Managing Director
Yuji Sugimoto, Managing Director
Zhao Frank Su, Principal

Type of Firm

Private Equity Firm

Association Membership

Australian Venture Capital Association (AVCAL)
British Venture Capital Association (BVCA)
China Venture Capital Association
German Venture Capital Association (BVK)
European Private Equity and Venture Capital Assoc.
Indian Venture Capital Association (IVCA)

Project Preferences

Type of Financing Preferred:
Leveraged Buyout
Generalist PE
Turnaround
Open Market

Geographical Preferences

United States Preferences:
North America

International Preferences:
India
Europe
Asia
Japan

Industry Focus
(% based on actual investment)

Other Products	17.2%
Computer Software and Services	17.1%
Consumer Related	15.5%
Semiconductors/Other Elect.	14.7%
Internet Specific	12.3%
Medical/Health	9.4%
Biotechnology	8.4%
Communications and Media	2.8%
Industrial/Energy	2.3%
Computer Hardware	0.3%

Additional Information
Name of Most Recent Fund: Sankaty Middle Market Opportunities Fund II, L.P.
Most Recent Fund Was Raised: 08/15/2013
Year Founded: 1984
Capital Under Management: $27,000,000,000
Current Activity Level : Actively seeking new investments

BAIN CAPITAL VENTURE PARTNERS LLC

200 Clarendon Street
Boston, MA USA 02116
Phone: 6175162000
Fax: 6175162010
E-mail: VentureDealLog@baincapital.com
Website: www.baincapitalventures.com

Other Offices
335 Bryant Street
PALO ALTO, CA USA 94301
Phone: 6507982500
Fax: 6507982501

632 Broadway
NEW YORK, NY USA 10012
Phone: 2128222900
Fax: 6464399100

Management and Staff
Ajay Agarwal, Managing Director
Ben Holzman, Managing Director
Brian Goldsmith, Principal
David Friend, Principal
Enrique Salem, Managing Director
Indranil Guha, Partner
J. Benjamin Nye, Managing Director
Jared Kesselheim, Partner
Kristen Deftos, Vice President
Matthew Harris, Managing Director
Michael Krupka, Managing Director
Salil Deshpande, Managing Director
Scott Friend, Managing Director
Yumin Choi, Managing Director

Type of Firm
Private Equity Firm

Association Membership
New England Venture Capital Association

Project Preferences

Type of Financing Preferred:
Early Stage
Expansion
Balanced
Later Stage
Seed

Size of Investments Considered:
Min Size of Investment Considered (000s): $100
Max Size of Investment Considered (000s): $50,000

Industry Preferences

In Communications prefer:
Wireless Communications

In Computer Software prefer:
Software

In Internet Specific prefer:
Internet

In Medical/Health prefer:
Medical/Health

In Consumer Related prefer:
Consumer

In Business Serv. prefer:
Services

Additional Information
Name of Most Recent Fund: Bain Capital Venture Fund 2012, L.P.
Most Recent Fund Was Raised: 01/30/2012
Year Founded: 2001
Capital Under Management: $3,200,000,000
Current Activity Level : Actively seeking new investments

BAIRD CAPITAL

777 East Wisconsin Avenue
Milwaukee, WI USA 53202
Phone: 8007922473
Website: www.bairdcapital.com

Other Offices
No. 1000 Lujiazui Ring Road
Room 42-022, 42/F
Shanghai, China 200120
Phone: 862161820980

227 West Monroe Street
Suite 1900
CHICAGO, IL USA 60606
Phone: 8887920477

Management and Staff
Aaron Rudberg, Partner
Alex Kessel, Principal
Andrew Ferguson, Partner
Andy Tse, Partner
Bonnie Chen, Vice President
C. Andrew Brickman, Partner
Christopher Harper, Partner
Gordon Pan, President
Huaming Gu, Partner
James Pavlik, Partner
James Benfield, Partner
Joanna Arras, Vice President
John DiGiovanni, Principal
Macie House, Managing Director
Martin Beck, Partner
Mathias Schirmer, Partner
Melissa Mounce, Principal
Michael Liang, Partner
Michael Bernstein, Partner
Nicole Walker, Partner
Rob Ospalik, Partner
Scott Skie, Chief Operating Officer
Tom Costello, Principal
Tom Smith, Principal

Type of Firm
Private Equity Firm

Association Membership
British Venture Capital Association (BVCA)
National Venture Capital Association - USA (NVCA)
Illinois Venture Capital Association

Project Preferences

Role in Financing:
Prefer role as deal originator but will also invest in deals created by others

Type of Financing Preferred:
Fund of Funds
Leveraged Buyout
Early Stage
Expansion
Generalist PE
Balanced
Acquisition

Geographical Preferences

United States Preferences:
All U.S.

International Preferences:
United Kingdom
Europe
China

Industry Focus

(% based on actual investment)
Computer Software and Services	22.0%
Other Products	19.1%
Medical/Health	18.4%
Industrial/Energy	13.1%
Internet Specific	11.0%
Consumer Related	10.4%
Computer Hardware	3.3%
Biotechnology	1.6%
Semiconductors/Other Elect.	1.0%
Communications and Media	0.2%

Additional Information

Name of Most Recent Fund: Baird Venture Partners III, L.P.
Most Recent Fund Was Raised: 08/18/2008
Year Founded: 1983
Capital Under Management: $880,000,000
Current Activity Level : Actively seeking new investments
Method of Compensation: Return on invest. most important, but chg. closing fees, service fees, etc.

BAKER & EASTLACK VENTURES

11281 Caramel Creek Road
San Diego, CA USA 92130
Phone: 6504683264
E-mail: bakerandeastlack@gmail.com
Website: www.bakerandeastlackventures.com

Type of Firm
Private Equity Firm

Project Preferences

Type of Financing Preferred:
Early Stage

Industry Preferences

In Medical/Health prefer:
Medical Diagnostics
Medical Therapeutics

Additional Information

Year Founded: 2016
Capital Under Management: $3,100,000
Current Activity Level : Actively seeking new investments

BAKER & MCKENZIE LLP

300 East Randolph Street
Suite 5000
Chicago, IL USA 60601
Phone: 3128618000
Fax: 3128612899
Website: www.bakermckenzie.com

Other Offices

14th Floor, Hutchison House
10 Harcourt Road
Hong Kong, China
Phone: 852-2846-1888
Fax: 852-2845-0476

#27-01 Millenia Tower
1 Temasek Avenue
Singapore, China 039192
Phone: 65-338-1888
Fax: 65-337-5100

Level 39 Rialto
525 Collins Street
Melbourne, Victoria, China 3000
Phone: 613-9617-4200
Fax: 613-9614-2103

Management and Staff

Beatriz de Araujo, Partner
Bruce Hambrett, Partner
Daniel Goelzer, Partner
Greg Walters, Chief Operating Officer
Jim Holloway, Partner
Jorge Adell, Managing Director
Juan Manuel de la Rosa, Partner
Koen Vanhaerents, Partner
Kuif Wassink, Partner
Marco Marazzi, Partner
Philip Suse, Partner
Raymundo Enriquez, Partner
Robert Spencer, Chief Financial Officer
Seong Soo Kim, Partner
William Linklater, Partner

Type of Firm
Investment Management Firm

Association Membership
Australian Venture Capital Association (AVCAL)
Canadian Venture Capital Association

Project Preferences

Type of Financing Preferred:
Leveraged Buyout

Additional Information

Year Founded: 1949
Current Activity Level : Actively seeking new investments

BAKER BROS ADVISORS LP

667 Madison Avenue
New York, NY USA 10021
Phone: 2123395600

Management and Staff

Felix Baker, Managing Director
Julian Baker, Managing Director

Type of Firm
Private Equity Firm

Project Preferences

Type of Financing Preferred:
Balanced

Geographical Preferences

United States Preferences:

Additional Information

Year Founded: 2000
Capital Under Management: $1,560,000,000
Current Activity Level : Actively seeking new investments

BALANCE POINT CAPITAL PARTNERS, L.P.

Eight Church Lane
Suite 200
Westport, CT USA 06880
Phone: 2036528250
Fax: 2037169828
E-mail: info@balancepointcapital.com
Website: www.balancepointcapital.com

Other Offices

Eight Church Lane
Westport, CT USA 06880
Phone: 2033419243
Fax: 860293338

Management and Staff

B. Lance Sauerteig, Partner
John Ritter, Co-Founder
Joseph Nardecchia, Chief Financial Officer
Justin Kaplan, Partner
Nathan Elliott, Vice President
Richard Klaffky, Co-Founder
Seth Alvord, Co-Founder

Type of Firm
SBIC

Project Preferences

Role in Financing:
Will function either as deal originator or investor in deals created by others

Type of Financing Preferred:
Leveraged Buyout
Mezzanine
Later Stage
Management Buyouts
Private Placement
Industry Rollups
Recapitalizations

Size of Investments Considered:
Min Size of Investment Considered (000s): $1,000
Max Size of Investment Considered (000s): $4,500

Industry Focus
(% based on actual investment)

Industrial/Energy	35.3%
Medical/Health	25.4%
Communications and Media	16.8%
Computer Software and Services	8.5%
Consumer Related	7.2%
Other Products	4.4%
Computer Hardware	1.7%
Internet Specific	0.8%

Additional Information
Name of Most Recent Fund: Balance Point Capital Partners, L.P.
Most Recent Fund Was Raised: 08/15/2011
Year Founded: 1988
Capital Under Management: $75,000,000
Current Activity Level : Actively seeking new investments
Method of Compensation: Return on invest. most important, but chg. closing fees, service fees, etc.

BALDERTON CAPITAL LLP

28 Britannia street
The Stables
London, United Kingdom W1K 6TL
Phone: 442070166800
Fax: 442070166810
E-mail: information@balderton.com
Website: www.balderton.com

Management and Staff
Alison Brownhill, Chief Financial Officer
Bernard Liautaud, Managing Partner
Daniel Waterhouse, Partner
James Wise, Partner
Lars Fjeldsoe-Nielsen, Partner
Nicolas Debock, Principal
Rob Moffat, Partner
Sam Myers, Principal
Suranga Chandratillake, Partner
Tim Bunting, Partner

Type of Firm
Private Equity Firm

Association Membership
British Venture Capital Association (BVCA)

Project Preferences

Type of Financing Preferred:
Early Stage
Expansion
Balanced
Later Stage
Startup

Size of Investments Considered:
Min Size of Investment Considered (000s): $1,000
Max Size of Investment Considered (000s): $20,000

Geographical Preferences

United States Preferences:
All U.S.

International Preferences:
Europe
Asia

Industry Preferences

In Communications prefer:
Wireless Communications

In Computer Software prefer:
Software

In Internet Specific prefer:
E-Commerce Technology
Internet

In Semiconductor/Electr prefer:
Semiconductor

In Medical/Health prefer:
Medical/Health

In Consumer Related prefer:
Consumer

In Industrial/Energy prefer:
Alternative Energy

Additional Information
Name of Most Recent Fund: Balderton Capital V, L.P.
Most Recent Fund Was Raised: 04/01/2014
Year Founded: 2000
Capital Under Management: $1,900,000,000
Current Activity Level : Actively seeking new investments

BALDWIN BEACH CAPITAL LLC

4010 West Boy Scout Boulevard
Suite 200
Tampa, FL USA 33607
Phone: 8139843200
Fax: 8139843211
E-mail: info@bbc-ventures.com
Website: bbc-ventures.com

Type of Firm
Private Equity Firm

Project Preferences

Type of Financing Preferred:
Balanced

Additional Information
Year Founded: 2011
Current Activity Level : Actively seeking new investments

BALLAST POINT VENTURE PARTNERS LLC

880 Carillon Parkway
Saint Petersburg, FL USA 33716
Phone: 7275671500
Fax: 7275671515
Website: www.ballastpointventures.com

Management and Staff
Donald Burton, Venture Partner
Drew Graham, Co-Founder
Matt Rice, Partner
O. Gene Gabbard, Venture Partner
Paul Johan, Co-Founder
Richard Brandewie, Co-Founder
Robert Faber, Principal
Sean Barkman, Vice President

Type of Firm
Private Equity Firm

Project Preferences

Role in Financing:
Prefer role as deal originator but will also invest in deals created by others

Type of Financing Preferred:
Expansion
Later Stage
Management Buyouts
Acquisition
Recapitalizations

Size of Investments Considered:
Min Size of Investment Considered (000s): $3,000
Max Size of Investment Considered (000s): $10,000

Geographical Preferences

United States Preferences:
Southeast
Florida
Texas

Industry Preferences

In Communications prefer:
Communications and Media
Wireless Communications
Media and Entertainment

In Computer Software prefer:
Software

In Internet Specific prefer:
Internet
Ecommerce

In Semiconductor/Electr prefer:
Electronics

In Medical/Health prefer:
Medical/Health
Medical Products
Health Services
Pharmaceuticals

In Consumer Related prefer:
Consumer
Retail
Consumer Products
Education Related

In Financial Services prefer:
Financial Services
Financial Services

In Business Serv. prefer:
Services

In Manufact. prefer:
Manufacturing

Additional Information
Name of Most Recent Fund: Ballast Point Ventures II, L.P.
Most Recent Fund Was Raised: 12/21/2007
Year Founded: 2001
Capital Under Management: $364,000,000
Current Activity Level : Actively seeking new investments

BALMORAL ADVISORS LLC

11150 Santa Monica Boulevard
Suite 825
Los Angeles, CA USA 90025
Phone: 3104733065
Fax: 3104791740
E-mail: info@balmoralfunds.com
Website: www.balmoralfunds.com

Management and Staff
Jonathan Victor, Managing Director
Stan Koss, Managing Director

Type of Firm
Private Equity Firm

Project Preferences

Type of Financing Preferred:
Leveraged Buyout
Turnaround
Management Buyouts
Acquisition
Special Situation
Recapitalizations

Geographical Preferences

United States Preferences:
North America
All U.S.

Canadian Preferences:
All Canada

Industry Preferences

In Consumer Related prefer:
Consumer
Retail

In Business Serv. prefer:
Services
Distribution

In Manufact. prefer:
Manufacturing

Additional Information
Year Founded: 2005
Capital Under Management: $118,650,000
Current Activity Level : Actively seeking new investments

BALMORAL PARTNERS LTD

165 University Avenue
Suite 200
Toronto, Canada
Phone: 416-350-3741
Fax: 416-366-0257

Type of Firm
Private Equity Firm

Additional Information
Year Founded: 1994
Current Activity Level : Actively seeking new investments

BALMORAL WOOD LITIGATION FINANCE

1255 Bay Street
Suite 700
Toronto, Canada M5R 2A9
Website: www.balmoralwood.com

Management and Staff
David Sedgwick, Managing Director
Edward Truant, Managing Director
John Fisher, Managing Director

Type of Firm
Private Equity Firm

Additional Information
Year Founded: 2017
Capital Under Management: $25,000,000
Current Activity Level : Actively seeking new investments

BALTCAP MANAGEMENT ESTONIA OU

Tartu Mnt. 2
Tallinn, Estonia 10145
Phone: 3726650280
Fax: 3726650281

Other Offices
Ulmana gatve 86F
Riga, Latvia LV-1046
Phone: 37167214225
Fax: 37167356395

J. Jasinskio 16B
Vilnius, Lithuania 01112
Phone: 37052546713
Fax: 37052546978

Management and Staff
Dagnis Dreimanis, Partner
Matts Andersson, Partner
Peeter Saks, Managing Partner
Simonas Gustainis, Partner

Type of Firm
Private Equity Firm

Association Membership
Latvian Private Equity and Venture Capital Assoc
Estonian Private Equity and Venture Capital Assoc
European Private Equity and Venture Capital Assoc.
Lithuanian Venture Capital Association

Project Preferences

Type of Financing Preferred:
Leveraged Buyout
Early Stage
Mezzanine
Generalist PE
Start-up Financing
Later Stage
Acquisition
Startup

Size of Investments Considered:
Min Size of Investment Considered (000s): $500
Max Size of Investment Considered (000s): $500,000

Geographical Preferences

International Preferences:
Central Europe
Eastern Europe
Scandanavia/Nordic Region
Estonia
Latvia
Lithuania

Industry Preferences

In Communications prefer:
Commercial Communications

In Computer Software prefer:
Data Processing

In Consumer Related prefer:
Consumer Products

In Business Serv. prefer:
Distribution

In Manufact. prefer:
Manufacturing

Additional Information

Name of Most Recent Fund: BaltCap Private Equity Fund II
Most Recent Fund Was Raised: 02/05/2014
Year Founded: 1995
Capital Under Management: $196,800,000
Current Activity Level : Actively seeking new investments

BALTIC BRIDGE SA

Prosta 32
Warsaw, Poland 00838
Phone: 48221166666
Fax: 48221166661
E-mail: biuro@igroup.pl
Website: balticbridge.com.pl

Type of Firm
Private Equity Firm

Project Preferences

Type of Financing Preferred:
Balanced

Geographical Preferences

International Preferences:
Poland

Industry Preferences

In Communications prefer:
Telecommunications

In Industrial/Energy prefer:
Energy
Alternative Energy
Energy Conservation Relat

In Financial Services prefer:
Real Estate
Financial Services

In Other prefer:
Environment Responsible

Additional Information

Name of Most Recent Fund: WI EEC Ventures
Most Recent Fund Was Raised: 07/30/2013
Year Founded: 2001
Capital Under Management: $18,831,000
Current Activity Level : Actively seeking new investments

BALTISSE NV

Pauline Van
Pottelsberghelaan 10
Gent, Belgium
E-mail: info@baltisse.com
Website: www.baltisse.com

Type of Firm
Private Equity Firm

Project Preferences

Type of Financing Preferred:
Generalist PE

Additional Information

Year Founded: 2006
Current Activity Level : Actively seeking new investments

BALYASNY ASSET MANAGEMENT LP

181 West Madison Street
Suite 3600
Chicago, IL USA 60602
Phone: 3124992999
Fax: 3124992998
E-mail: investorrelations@bamfunds.com
Website: www.bamfund.com

Other Offices

135 East 57th Street, 27th Floor
New York, NY USA 10022
Phone: 212-808-2300
Fax: 212-808-2301

73 Arch Street
Greenwich, CT USA 06830
Phone: 203-863-5400
Fax: 203-863-5433

Berkeley Square House
First Floor
London, United Kingdom W1J 6BD
Phone: 442078876403
Fax: 442071490001

1007, Embassy Center
Nariman Point
Mumbai, India 400021

Eight Queen's Road, Central
Tenth Floor
, Hong Kong
Phone: 85239652688
Fax: 85239652788

Type of Firm
Private Equity Firm

Project Preferences

Type of Financing Preferred:
Balanced

Geographical Preferences

International Preferences:
All International

Industry Preferences

In Financial Services prefer:
Investment Groups
Financial Services

Additional Information

Year Founded: 2001
Current Activity Level : Actively seeking new investments

BAM VENTURES GP LLC

12181 Bluff Creek Drive
5th Floor
Los Angeles, CA USA 90094
Website: www.bam.vc

Management and Staff

Brian Lee, Co-Founder
Richard Jun, Co-Founder

Type of Firm
Private Equity Firm

Project Preferences

Type of Financing Preferred:
Early Stage

Geographical Preferences

United States Preferences:
California

Additional Information

Year Founded: 2014
Capital Under Management: $4,035,000
Current Activity Level : Actively seeking new investments

BAMBOO FINANCE SA

37C, Avenue John F. Kennedy
Office 479
Luxembourg, Luxembourg 1855
Phone: 352260957
E-mail: info@bamboofinance.com
Website: www.bamboofinance.com

Other Offices

Westlands Road
7th Floor, Purshottam Place
Nairobi, Kenya
Phone: 254203601803

Type of Firm
Private Equity Firm

Project Preferences

Type of Financing Preferred:
Leveraged Buyout
Early Stage
Generalist PE
Later Stage
Acquisition

Geographical Preferences

International Preferences:
Latin America
Middle East
Asia
Africa

Industry Preferences

In Biotechnology prefer:
Agricultural/Animal Bio.

In Medical/Health prefer:
Health Services

In Consumer Related prefer:
Education Related

In Industrial/Energy prefer:
Energy

In Financial Services prefer:
Investment Groups
Financial Services

Additional Information

Year Founded: 2007
Capital Under Management: $31,000,000
Current Activity Level : Actively seeking new investments

BAMBOO SAS

2, impasse Josephine Baker
Saint-Herblain, France 44800
E-mail: contact@bamboo.eu
Website: www.bamboo.eu

Management and Staff

Louis-Marie Guillet, President
Pierre Voillet, President

Type of Firm

Angel Group

Project Preferences

Type of Financing Preferred:
Early Stage
Expansion
Later Stage
Seed

Geographical Preferences

International Preferences:
France

Industry Preferences

In Communications prefer:
Communications and Media

In Computer Software prefer:
Software

In Internet Specific prefer:
Internet

In Business Serv. prefer:
Services

Additional Information

Year Founded: 2005
Current Activity Level : Actively seeking new investments

BAML CAPITAL ACCESS FUNDS MANAGEMENT LLC

135 South LaSalle Street
Chicago, IL USA 60603
Phone: 3128282278
Fax: 3128288213
E-mail: BA_Capital_Access_Funds@bankofamerica.com

Management and Staff

Aris Hatch, Managing Director
Brett Gordon, Managing Director
Carolina Espinal, Managing Director
Corentin Du Roy, Managing Director
David Atterbury, Managing Director
George Anson, Managing Director
Gregory Stento, Managing Director
Hemal Mirani, Managing Director
Ian Lane, Managing Director
James Kase, Managing Director
Jeffrey Keay, Managing Director
John Morris, Managing Director
John Toomey, Managing Director
Kathleen Bacon, Managing Director
Nathan Bishop, Managing Director
Olav Konig, Managing Director
Peter Wilson, Managing Director
Peter Lipson, Managing Director
Robert Wadsworth, Managing Director
Sanjiv Shah, Managing Director
Tatsuya Kubo, Managing Director
Tim Flower, Managing Director

Type of Firm

Private Equity Advisor or Fund of Funds

Association Membership

Natl Assoc of Investment Cos. (NAIC)
Natl Assoc of Small Bus. Inv. Co (NASBIC)

Project Preferences

Type of Financing Preferred:
Fund of Funds

Size of Investments Considered:
Min Size of Investment Considered (000s): $5,000
Max Size of Investment Considered (000s): $25,000

Additional Information

Year Founded: 1997
Capital Under Management: $201,000,000
Current Activity Level : Actively seeking new investments

BANCA PROFILO SPA

Corso Italia 49
Milan, Italy 20122
Phone: 39-02-58408
Fax: 39-02-58316057
E-mail: info@bancaprofilo.it
Website: www.bancaprofilo.it

Management and Staff

Fabio Candeli, Chief Executive Officer

Type of Firm

Bank Affiliated

Additional Information

Year Founded: 2003
Current Activity Level : Actively seeking new investments

BANCO BTG PACTUAL SA

Av. Brigadeiro Faria Lima
N3.729, 9o Andar-Itaim Bibi
Sao Paulo, Brazil 04538-133
Phone: 551133832000
Website: www.btgpactual.com

Other Offices

Av. Brigadeiro Faria Lima, 3729
8,9,10 andares - parte Jardim Paulista
Sao Paulo, Brazil
Phone: 55-11-3046-2100
Fax: 55-11-3046-2001

Rua Antonio Lumack do Monte 128
salas 604-605 Boa Viagem
Recife, Brazil 51020-350
Phone: 55-81-3463-0203
Fax: 55-81-3463-0208

Av. Alvares Cabral 1741
7o andar
Belo Horizonte, Brazil 30170-001
Phone: 55-31-3339-3373
Fax: 55-31-3339-3399

780 Third Avenue
28th Floor
New York, NY USA 10017
Phone: 212-702-4104
Fax: 212-702-4114

Management and Staff

Joao Marcello Dantas Leite, Chief Financial Officer

Type of Firm

Bank Affiliated

Association Membership

Brazilian Venture Capital Association (ABCR)

Project Preferences

Type of Financing Preferred:
Leveraged Buyout
Generalist PE
Balanced
Later Stage
Management Buyouts
Acquisition
Startup

Geographical Preferences

International Preferences:
Brazil

Industry Focus

(% based on actual investment)
Consumer Related	74.7%
Other Products	20.1%
Internet Specific	4.1%
Medical/Health	0.6%
Computer Software and Services	0.5%

Additional Information

Year Founded: 1983
Capital Under Management: $2,460,000,000
Current Activity Level : Actively seeking new investments

BANCO NACIONAL DE DESENVOLVIMENTO ECONOMICO E SOCIAL BNDES

Avenida Republica do Chile 100
Centro
Rio de Janeiro, Brazil 20031917
Phone: 552121727447
Website: www.bndes.gov.br

Other Offices

One Cornhill
Third Floor
London, United Kingdom EC3V 3ND
Phone: 442030086741
Fax: 442030086742

Avenida Luiz Alberto de Herrera 1248
Torre II - 3 piso, World Trade Center
Montevideo, Uruguay 11300
Phone: 59826228875

Management and Staff

Fernando Marques dos Santos, Managing Director
Guilherme Narciso de Lacerda, Managing Director
Joao Carlos Ferraz, Managing Director
Julio Cesar Maciel Ramundo, Managing Director
Luiz Eduardo Melin de Carvalho e Silva, Managing Director
Mauricio Borges Lemos, Managing Director
Roberto Machado, Managing Director

Type of Firm

Bank Affiliated

Project Preferences

Type of Financing Preferred:
Leveraged Buyout
Early Stage
Generalist PE
Balanced
Later Stage
Management Buyouts
Acquisition

Geographical Preferences

International Preferences:
Brazil

Industry Preferences

In Medical/Health prefer:
Medical/Health

In Consumer Related prefer:
Education Related

In Industrial/Energy prefer:
Environmental Related

In Business Serv. prefer:
Services

In Agr/Forestr/Fish prefer:
Agriculture related

Additional Information

Year Founded: 1952
Current Activity Level : Actively seeking new investments

BANCO SANTANDER BRASIL SA

Rua Amador Bueno, 474
Sao Paulo, Brazil 04752-005
Phone: 551130395817
Fax: 551130395866
Website: www.santander.com.br

Management and Staff

Angel Santodomingo Martell, Chief Financial Officer
Sergio Agapito Lires Rial, Chief Executive Officer

Type of Firm

Bank Affiliated

Association Membership

Spanish Venture Capital Association (ASCRI)

Project Preferences

Type of Financing Preferred:
Balanced

Geographical Preferences

International Preferences:
Brazil

Industry Focus

(% based on actual investment)
Internet Specific	81.3%
Computer Software and Services	11.1%
Industrial/Energy	7.7%

Additional Information

Year Founded: 1985
Capital Under Management: $3,300,000
Current Activity Level : Actively seeking new investments

BANCO SANTANDER SA

Plaza De Canalejas, 1
Madrid, Spain 28014
Phone: 34-91-558-1571
Fax: 34-91-521-3387
Website: www.santander.com

Other Offices

Two Triton Square
Regent's Place
London, United Kingdom NW1 3AN
Phone: 8706076000

Management and Staff

Jacques Ripoll, Managing Director
Jose Alvarez Alvarez, Chief Executive Officer
Jose Garcia Cantera, Chief Financial Officer

Type of Firm

Bank Affiliated

Association Membership

Spanish Venture Capital Association (ASCRI)

Project Preferences

Type of Financing Preferred:
Balanced

Geographical Preferences

International Preferences:
Europe
Spain

Industry Preferences

In Computer Software prefer:
Software

In Internet Specific prefer:
E-Commerce Technology
Ecommerce

In Industrial/Energy prefer:
Alternative Energy
Environmental Related

In Financial Services prefer:
Financial Services

In Other prefer:
Environment Responsible

Additional Information
Year Founded: 1875
Capital Under Management: $200,000,000
Current Activity Level : Actively seeking new investments

BANCROFT GROUP LTD

195 Brompton Road
London, United Kingdom SW3 1NE
Phone: 442078239222
Fax: 442075893442
E-mail: theoffice@bancroftgroup.com

Other Offices

1. Damian Gruev Str.
Sofia, Bulgaria 1606
Phone: 359-2-950-3055
Fax: 359-2-954-9892

Parizska 22
Praha 1, Czech Republic 110 00
Phone: 420-224-238-505
Fax: 420-224-238-506

Csorszu. 45
Budapest , Hungary 1123
Phone: 36-1-487-6210
Fax: 36-1-487-6205

607 Fourteenth Street N.W.
Suite 800
Washington, DC USA 20005
Phone: 1-202-654-1780
Fax: 1-202-654-9680

Management and Staff
Hana Chrastecka, Partner
Krisztina Havas, Partner
Levent Aydinoglu, Partner
Monika Lukacs, Partner
Tamas Szalai, Partner
Valeri Petrov, Partner

Type of Firm
Private Equity Firm

Project Preferences

Type of Financing Preferred:
Leveraged Buyout
Expansion
Generalist PE
Later Stage
Management Buyouts
Acquisition

Geographical Preferences

International Preferences:
Hungary
Greece
United Kingdom
Turkey
Central Europe
Europe
Czech Republic
Eastern Europe
Croatia

Industry Preferences

In Communications prefer:
Telecommunications

In Industrial/Energy prefer:
Advanced Materials

In Business Serv. prefer:
Media

In Manufact. prefer:
Manufacturing

Additional Information
Name of Most Recent Fund: Bancroft II
Most Recent Fund Was Raised: 11/30/2002
Year Founded: 1989
Capital Under Management: $100,000,000
Current Activity Level : Actively seeking new investments

BAND OF ANGELS VENTURE FUND LP

535 Middlefield Road
Suite 190
Menlo Park, CA USA 94025
Phone: 6503210854
Fax: 6503211968
E-mail: contact@bandangels.com

Management and Staff
Ed Canty, Chief Financial Officer
Ian Sobieski, Founder
Tim Massey, Principal

Type of Firm
Angel Group

Project Preferences

Role in Financing:
Prefer role as deal originator but will also invest in deals created by others

Type of Financing Preferred:
Early Stage
Seed
Startup

Size of Investments Considered:
Min Size of Investment Considered (000s): $300
Max Size of Investment Considered (000s): $2,500

Geographical Preferences

United States Preferences:
Northern California
California

Industry Preferences

In Communications prefer:
Communications and Media
Telecommunications

In Computer Software prefer:
Software

In Internet Specific prefer:
Internet

In Semiconductor/Electr prefer:
Electronics
Semiconductor

In Biotechnology prefer:
Biotechnology

In Medical/Health prefer:
Medical/Health
Pharmaceuticals

In Industrial/Energy prefer:
Energy
Industrial Products

Additional Information
Name of Most Recent Fund: Band of Angels Acorn Fund LLC
Most Recent Fund Was Raised: 09/20/2009
Year Founded: 1994
Capital Under Management: $229,500,000
Current Activity Level : Actively seeking new investments

BANDGAP VENTURES LLC

5001 Plaza on the Lake Drive
Suite 103
Austin, TX USA 78746
Phone: 512-795-5822
E-mail: info@bandgapventures.com
Website: bandgapventures.com

Management and Staff
Michael Falcon, Managing Partner
Samuel Kim, Managing Partner

Type of Firm
Private Equity Firm

Project Preferences

Type of Financing Preferred:
Early Stage

Industry Preferences

In Semiconductor/Electr prefer:
Electronics

Pratt's Guide to Private Equity & Venture Capital Sources

In Industrial/Energy prefer:
Energy
Materials

In Manufact. prefer:
Manufacturing

Additional Information
Year Founded: 2014
Capital Under Management: $4,050,000
Current Activity Level: Actively seeking new investments

BANEXI VENTURES PARTNERS SA

13-15 Rue Taitbout
Paris, France 75009
Phone: 33173028969
E-mail: contact@banexiventures.com
Website: www.banexiventures.com

Management and Staff
Philippe Herbert, Partner
Philippe Mere, General Partner
Sophie Pierrin-Lepinard, General Partner

Type of Firm
Private Equity Firm

Association Membership
French Venture Capital Association (AFIC)
European Private Equity and Venture Capital Assoc.

Project Preferences

Role in Financing:
Prefer role as deal originator but will also invest in deals created by others

Type of Financing Preferred:
Early Stage
Balanced
Seed
Startup

Size of Investments Considered:
Min Size of Investment Considered (000s): $700
Max Size of Investment Considered (000s): $3,700

Geographical Preferences

International Preferences:
Europe
Switzerland
France

Industry Preferences

In Internet Specific prefer:
Internet

In Semiconductor/Electr prefer:
Electronics
Semiconductor

In Biotechnology prefer:
Biotech Related Research

In Medical/Health prefer:
Medical/Health

Additional Information
Name of Most Recent Fund: Banexi Ventures 5
Most Recent Fund Was Raised: 10/14/2011
Year Founded: 1983
Capital Under Management: $94,200,000
Current Activity Level: Actively seeking new investments
Method of Compensation: Return on investment is of primary concern, do not charge fees

BANK OF AMERICA CAPITAL ADVISORS (BACA)

100 Federal Street
Boston, MA USA 02110
Phone: 888-786-9977

Management and Staff
Joe Price, Chief Financial Officer
Lawrence Morgenthal, President

Type of Firm
Bank Affiliated

Project Preferences

Type of Financing Preferred:
Generalist PE

Additional Information
Year Founded: 2006
Current Activity Level: Actively seeking new investments

BANK OF CHINA FINANCE EQUITY INVESTMENT FUND MANAGEMENT

c/o Guangdong Finance Invest
No. 481 Fengzhong Road
Guangzhou, China
Phone: 862083063888

Type of Firm
Investment Management Firm

Project Preferences

Type of Financing Preferred:
Balanced

Geographical Preferences

International Preferences:
China

Additional Information
Year Founded: 2011
Capital Under Management: $762,115,000
Current Activity Level: Actively seeking new investments

BANK OF NEW YORK MELLON CORP

One Wall Street
New York, NY USA 10286
Phone: 2124951784
Website: www.bnymellon.com

Management and Staff
Michael Santomassimo, Chief Financial Officer
Michelle Neal, Managing Director

Type of Firm
Bank Affiliated

Association Membership
Natl Assoc of Small Bus. Inv. Co (NASBIC)

Project Preferences

Type of Financing Preferred:
Fund of Funds
Leveraged Buyout
Mezzanine
Generalist PE
Balanced
Distressed Debt
Fund of Funds of Second

Additional Information
Name of Most Recent Fund: BNY Mellon Private Equity Fund VIII, L.P.
Most Recent Fund Was Raised: 01/30/2014
Year Founded: 2007
Capital Under Management: $223,251,000
Current Activity Level: Actively seeking new investments

BANK SANKT-PETERBURG PAO

Prospekt Malookhtinskii, 64A
Saint Petersburg, Russia 195112
Phone: 78123295000
Fax: 78123327808
Website: www.bspb.ru

Management and Staff
Maris Mancinskis, Chief Executive Officer
Vyacheslav Ermolin, Vice President

Type of Firm
Bank Affiliated

Project Preferences

Type of Financing Preferred:
Leveraged Buyout
Early Stage
Expansion
Later Stage
Management Buyouts
Acquisition
Startup

Geographical Preferences

International Preferences:
Russia

Additional Information

Year Founded: 1990
Current Activity Level : Actively seeking new investments

BANKCAP PARTNERS FUND I LP

2100 McKinney Avenue
Suite 1225
Dallas, TX USA 75201
Phone: 2147406100
Fax: 2147406101
E-mail: contact@bankcap.com
Website: www.bankcap.com

Other Offices

623 Fifth Avenue
Suite 2302
New York, NY USA 10022
Phone: 2125377171

Management and Staff

Brian Jones, Co-Founder
James Graves, Partner
Joseph Grant, Co-Founder
Scott Reed, Co-Founder
Steven Reed, Principal

Type of Firm

Private Equity Firm

Project Preferences

Type of Financing Preferred:
Leveraged Buyout
Acquisition
Recapitalizations

Geographical Preferences

United States Preferences:

Industry Preferences

In Financial Services prefer:
Financial Services

Additional Information

Name of Most Recent Fund: BankCap Partners Fund I, L.P.
Most Recent Fund Was Raised: 06/14/2006
Year Founded: 2005
Current Activity Level : Actively seeking new investments

BANKHAUS LAMPE KG

Alter Markt 3
Bielefeld, Germany 33602
Phone: 4921149520
Fax: 492114952111
E-mail: info-allgemein@bankhaus-lampe.de
Website: www.bankhaus-lampe.de

Other Offices

Jaegerhofstrasse 10
Duesseldorf, Germany 40479
Phone: 49-221-495-20
Fax: 49-221-495-2111

Buechsenstrasse 28
Stuttgart, Germany 70174
Phone: 49-711-933-0080
Fax: 49-711-9330-0899

Brienner Strasse 29
Munich, Germany
Phone: 49-89-2903-5600
Fax: 49-89-2903-5799

Ballindamm 11
Hamburg, Germany 20095
Phone: 49-40-302-9040
Fax: 49-40-3029-0418

Domplatz 41
Muenster, Germany 48143
Phone: 49-251-418-330
Fax: 49-251-418-3350

Alter Markt 3
Bielefeld, Germany 33602
Phone: 4905215820
Fax: 4905215821195

Altenwall 21
Bremen, Germany 28195
Phone: 49-421-985-3880
Fax: 49-421-9853-8899

Kaethe-Kollwitz-Ufer 82
Dresden, Germany 01309
Phone: 49-351-2078-1510
Fax: 49-351-2078-1529

Schlossstrasse 28/30
Osnabrueck, Germany 49074
Phone: 49-541-580-5370
Fax: 49-541-5805-3799

Heinrich-Bruening-Strasse 16
Bonn, Germany 53113
Phone: 49-228-850-2620
Fax: 49-228-850-262-099

Freiherr-vom-Stein-Strasse 65
Frankfurt/Main, Germany 60323
Phone: 49-69-971-190
Fax: 49-69-9711-9119

Carmerstrasse 13
Berlin, Germany 10623
Phone: 49-30-319-0020
Fax: 49-30-319-0020-324

Type of Firm

Bank Affiliated

Project Preferences

Type of Financing Preferred:
Mezzanine
Later Stage
Management Buyouts
Recapitalizations

Geographical Preferences

International Preferences:
Germany

Additional Information

Year Founded: 1852
Current Activity Level : Actively seeking new investments

BANKINTER CAPITAL RIESGO SGECR SA

Paseo de la Castellara 29
Madrid, Spain 28046
Phone: 34913397500
Fax: 34913398323
E-mail: ofiaccionista@bankinter.es
Website: www.bankinter.com

Management and Staff

Gloria Ortiz Portero, Chief Financial Officer
Javier Rivero Garcia-Norena, Chief Executive Officer
Maria Dolores Dancausa Trevino, Chief Executive Officer

Type of Firm

Bank Affiliated

Association Membership

Spanish Venture Capital Association (ASCRI)

Project Preferences

Type of Financing Preferred:
Leveraged Buyout
Early Stage
Generalist PE
Balanced
Acquisition

Geographical Preferences

International Preferences:
Europe
Spain

Industry Preferences

In Internet Specific prefer:
Internet

Additional Information
Year Founded: 1965
Current Activity Level : Actively seeking new investments

BANKSIA CAPITAL

Seven Havelock Street
Level Two
West Perth, Australia 6005
Phone: 61893650200

Type of Firm
Private Equity Firm

Project Preferences

Type of Financing Preferred:
Leveraged Buyout
Expansion
Acquisition

Geographical Preferences

International Preferences:
Australia

Additional Information
Name of Most Recent Fund: Banksia Capital Fund II
Most Recent Fund Was Raised: 01/01/2012
Year Founded: 2008
Capital Under Management: $41,000,000
Current Activity Level : Actively seeking new investments

BANNEKER PARTNERS

Four Embarcadero Center
34th Floor
San Francisco, CA USA 94111
Phone: 4154390602
E-mail: info@BannekerPartners.com
Website: www.bannekerpartners.com

Type of Firm
Private Equity Firm

Project Preferences

Type of Financing Preferred:
Leveraged Buyout
Acquisition

Industry Preferences

In Computer Software prefer:
Software

In Internet Specific prefer:
Internet

In Business Serv. prefer:
Services

Additional Information
Year Founded: 2010
Current Activity Level : Actively seeking new investments

BANQUE DEGROOF PETERCAM SA

Rue de l'Industrie 44
Brussels, Belgium 1040
Phone: 3222879111
Fax: 3222306700
E-mail: pbbru@degroof.be
Website: www.degroofpetercam.com

Other Offices
Zoutelaan 134
Knokke-Heist, Belgium 8300
Phone: 32-50-632-370
Fax: 32-50-621-887

Avenue de la Plante 20
Namur, Belgium 5000
Phone: 32-81-420-020
Fax: 32-81-65-95-83

Van Putlei 33
Antwerpen, Belgium 2018
Phone: 32-3-225-1486

Square des Conduites d'Eau 7-8
Parc d'affaires Znobe Gramme
Liege, Belgium 4020
Phone: 32-4-252-0028
Fax: 32-4-252-6004

Fleurusstraat 2
Gent, Belgium 9000
Phone: 32-9-266-1366
Fax: 32-9-225-4481

Quai de Brabant 15
Charleroi, Belgium 6000
Phone: 32-71-321-825
Fax: 32-71-310-360

Avenue Einstein 12
Les Collines de Wavre
Wavre, Belgium 1300
Phone: 32-10-241-222
Fax: 32-10-241-631

Runkstersteenweg 356
Hasselt, Belgium 3500
Phone: 32-11-771-460
Fax: 32-11-771-1469

President Kennedypark 8
Kortrijk, Belgium 8500
Phone: 32-56-265-400
Fax: 32-56-306-362

Management and Staff
Alain Schockert, Managing Director
Etienne De Callatay, Managing Director
Gautier Bataille de Longprey, Managing Director
Jan Longeval, Managing Director
Patrick Keusters, Managing Director
Pierre-Paul De Schrevel, Managing Director

Type of Firm
Bank Affiliated

Association Membership
Belgium Venturing Association

Project Preferences

Type of Financing Preferred:
Balanced

Geographical Preferences

International Preferences:
Europe

Additional Information
Year Founded: 1871
Current Activity Level : Actively seeking new investments

BANQUE LOMBARD ODIER & CIE SA

Sihlstrasse 20
Zurich, Switzerland 8021
Phone: 41442201600
Fax: 41227092911
E-mail: private.equity@akinapartners.com
Website: www.lombardodier.com

Other Offices
40 AVENUE MONTEREY
Luxembourg, Luxembourg 2163
Phone: 35227867660

Management and Staff
Anne-Marie De Weck, Managing Partner
Christophe Hentsch, Managing Partner
Frederic Rochat, Managing Partner
Hubert Keller, Managing Partner
Hugo Baenziger, Managing Partner

Type of Firm
Private Equity Firm

Association Membership
Swiss Venture Capital Association (SECA)
European Private Equity and Venture Capital Assoc.

Project Preferences

Type of Financing Preferred:
Fund of Funds
Leveraged Buyout
Early Stage
Later Stage
Seed
Management Buyouts
Startup
Fund of Funds of Second

Geographical Preferences

International Preferences:
Italy
Sweden
United Kingdom
Albania
Luxembourg
Europe
Netherlands
Puerto Rico
Switzerland
Austria
Eastern Europe
Spain
Belgium
Finland
Norway
Germany
Denmark
France

Industry Preferences

In Communications prefer:
Communications and Media

In Semiconductor/Electr prefer:
Electronics
Electronic Components

In Medical/Health prefer:
Medical/Health

In Consumer Related prefer:
Consumer
Food/Beverage
Consumer Products
Consumer Services

In Industrial/Energy prefer:
Industrial Products
Materials

Additional Information
Name of Most Recent Fund: Euro Choice V
Most Recent Fund Was Raised: 07/20/2012
Year Founded: 1998
Capital Under Management: $1,947,100,000
Current Activity Level : Actively seeking new investments

BANQUE PICTET & CIE SA

Route des Acacias 60
Geneva, Switzerland 1211
Phone: 41583232323
Fax: 41583232324
Website: www.group.pictet

Other Offices
Sheikh Zayed Road
Park Place, 12th Floor
Dubai, Utd. Arab Em.
Phone: 971-4-308-5830
Fax: 971-4-308-5800

Freigutstrasse 12
Zurich, Switzerland 8002
Phone: 41-58-323-7777
Fax: 41-58-323-7778

15 Queen's Road Central
Suite 3901, Edinburgh Tower
, Hong Kong
Phone: 852-3191-1805
Fax: 852-3191-1808

34, avenue de Messine (VIIIe)
Paris, France F-75008
Phone: 33-1-5688-7100
Fax: 33-1-5688-7101

2-2-1 Marunouchi, Chiyoda-ku
Kishimoto Building 7F
Tokyo, Japan 100-0005
Phone: 813-3212-3411
Fax: 813-3211-6339

1000, de la Gauchetire Ouest
Suite 3100
Montreal, Quebec, Canada H3B 4W5
Phone: 514-288-0253
Fax: 514-288-5473

120 London Wall
Moor House, Level 11
London, United Kingdom EC2Y 5ET
Phone: 44-20-7847-5000
Fax: 44-20-7847-5300

Via Fratelli Gabba 1/A
Milan, Italy 20121
Phone: 39-02-631-1951
Fax: 39-02-631-195-125

Calle Hermosilla 11
Madrid, Spain 28001
Phone: 34-91-538-2550
Fax: 34-91-538-6521

Neue Mainzer Strasse 1
Frankfurt-am-Main, Germany 60311
Phone: 49-69-795-0090
Fax: 49-69-7950-0999

Management and Staff
Renaud de Planta, Managing Partner
Stephen Barber, Managing Director

Type of Firm
Bank Affiliated

Project Preferences

Type of Financing Preferred:
Leveraged Buyout
Early Stage
Later Stage
Special Situation

Geographical Preferences

International Preferences:
Switzerland
All International
France

Industry Preferences

In Computer Software prefer:
Software

In Internet Specific prefer:
Internet

In Semiconductor/Electr prefer:
Semiconductor

In Medical/Health prefer:
Medical/Health
Medical Therapeutics
Pharmaceuticals

Additional Information
Year Founded: 1805
Current Activity Level : Actively seeking new investments

BANYAN CAPITAL

Ping An Intl Financial
Block A
Beijing, China
Website: www.banyanvc.com

Type of Firm
Private Equity Firm

Project Preferences

Type of Financing Preferred:
Early Stage
Balanced
Seed
Startup

Geographical Preferences

International Preferences:
China

Industry Preferences

In Communications prefer:
Telecommunications

In Business Serv. prefer:
Media

BANYAN CAPITAL ADVISORS LLC

150 Southeast 2nd Avenue
Suite 712
Miami, FL USA 33131
Phone: 3052504681
Fax: 3053713422
Website: www.banyaninvestors.com

Management and Staff
James Davidson, Managing Director
John Miller, Managing Director
Richard Starke, Managing Director
Stephen Smith, Managing Director

Type of Firm
Private Equity Firm

Association Membership
Natl Assoc of Small Bus. Inv. Co (NASBIC)

Project Preferences

Type of Financing Preferred:
Mezzanine
Management Buyouts
Acquisition
Recapitalizations

Size of Investments Considered:
Min Size of Investment Considered (000s): $1,000
Max Size of Investment Considered (000s): $5,000

Geographical Preferences

United States Preferences:
Southeast
Alabama
South Carolina
Florida
Georgia

Additional Information
Year Founded: 2003
Capital Under Management: $9,900,000
Current Activity Level : Actively seeking new investments

BANYAN CAPITAL PARTNERS LP

1111 West Georgia Street
Suite 2200
Vancouver, Canada V6E 4M3
Phone: 6046080858
Fax: 6046432010
E-mail: info@banyancp.com

Additional Information
Year Founded: 2014
Capital Under Management: $1,106,563,000
Current Activity Level : Actively seeking new investments

Other Offices
800 5th Avenue
Suite 101-503
SEATTLE, WA USA 98104
Phone: 206-621-1623

181 University Avenue
Suite 300
Toronto, Canada M5H 3M7
Phone: 4168622020
Fax: 4163632089

350 7th Avenue S.W.
Suite 2800
Calgary, Canada T2P 3N9
Phone: 403-537-6713

Management and Staff
David Eisler, Managing Director
Jeff Wigle, Managing Director
Michael Martin, Managing Director

Type of Firm
Private Equity Firm

Project Preferences

Type of Financing Preferred:
Leveraged Buyout
Expansion
Mezzanine
Balanced
Management Buyouts
Acquisition
Recapitalizations

Geographical Preferences

United States Preferences:

Canadian Preferences:
All Canada

Industry Focus
(% based on actual investment)

Consumer Related	28.9%
Computer Software and Services	13.9%
Other Products	13.8%
Industrial/Energy	13.7%
Internet Specific	10.2%
Medical/Health	10.1%
Semiconductors/Other Elect.	9.3%

Additional Information
Year Founded: 1999
Current Activity Level : Actively seeking new investments

BANYAN VENTURES SDN BHD

Suite 13-17, Plaza Mont Kiara
Two Jalan 1/70C, Mont Kiara
Kuala Lumpur, Malaysia
Phone: 603-6203-4205
Fax: 603-6203-4204
E-mail: tzekai@pd.jaring.my
Website: www.banyanvc.com

Management and Staff
Tze Kai Wong, Principal

Type of Firm
Bank Affiliated

Project Preferences

Type of Financing Preferred:
Mezzanine
Balanced
Seed
Startup

Geographical Preferences

International Preferences:
Asia
Malaysia

Industry Preferences

In Communications prefer:
Communications and Media
Telecommunications

In Internet Specific prefer:
Internet

In Computer Other prefer:
Computer Related

In Consumer Related prefer:
Entertainment and Leisure
Education Related

In Business Serv. prefer:
Media

Additional Information
Year Founded: 2001
Current Activity Level : Actively seeking new investments

BANYANTREE FINANCE PVT LTD

1418, Maker Chambers V
Nariman Point
Mumbai, India 400021
Phone: 912266235555
Website: www.banyantreefinance.com

Management and Staff
Abhishek Poddar, Vice President
Arvind Jain, Vice President
Mitin Jain, Vice President
Sanjiv Singhal, Managing Director

Type of Firm
Private Equity Firm

Project Preferences

Type of Financing Preferred:
Expansion
Mezzanine
Balanced
Turnaround
Later Stage
Distressed Debt

Geographical Preferences

International Preferences:
India

Industry Preferences

In Manufact. prefer:
Manufacturing

Additional Information
Year Founded: 2009
Capital Under Management: $150,000,000
Current Activity Level : Actively seeking new investments

BAOLONG KANGDE INVESTMENT MANAGEMENT CO LTD

Qianhai Shengang Zone
Shenzhen, China

Type of Firm
Investment Management Firm

Project Preferences

Type of Financing Preferred:
Leveraged Buyout

Geographical Preferences

International Preferences:
China

Industry Preferences

In Industrial/Energy prefer:
Energy
Advanced Materials

Additional Information
Year Founded: 2014
Current Activity Level : Actively seeking new investments

BARCELONA NUMA

Palau de Mar
Placa de Pau Vila
Barcelona, Spain 08003
Website: barcelona.numa.co

Type of Firm
Incubator/Development Program

Project Preferences

Type of Financing Preferred:
Startup

Additional Information
Year Founded: 2016
Current Activity Level : Actively seeking new investments

BARCLAYS CAPITAL INC

200 Park Avenue
New York, NY USA 10166
Phone: 2124124000
Fax: 2124127300

Other Offices
Two Queen's Road Central
41st Floor Cheung Kong Center
Hong Kong, Hong Kong
Phone: 852-2903-2000
Fax: 852-2903-2999

Management and Staff
Andrew Richards, Managing Director
Benoit De Vitry, Chief Operating Officer
Edward King, Managing Director
Michael Evans, Managing Director
Patrick Clackson, Chief Financial Officer
Trace McCreary, Managing Director

Type of Firm
SBIC

Project Preferences

Role in Financing:
Will function either as deal originator or investor in deals created by others

Type of Financing Preferred:
Second Stage Financing
Leveraged Buyout

Size of Investments Considered:
Min Size of Investment Considered (000s): $1,000
Max Size of Investment Considered (000s): $5,000

Geographical Preferences

International Preferences:
No Preference

Additional Information
Year Founded: 1990
Capital Under Management: $50,000,000
Current Activity Level : Actively seeking new investments
Method of Compensation: Return on investment is of primary concern, do not charge fees

BARCLAYS VENTURES LTD

1 Churchill Place
London, United Kingdom E14 5HP
Phone: 44201606563191
Website: www.barclaysventures.com

Other Offices
One Snowhill, Snow Hill Queensway
5th Floor
Birmingham, United Kingdom B4 6GN
Phone: 44-121-480-5435
Fax: 44-121-480-5450

Management and Staff
Stuart Knuckey, Founder

Type of Firm
Bank Affiliated

Association Membership
British Venture Capital Association (BVCA)

Project Preferences

Type of Financing Preferred:
Leveraged Buyout
Expansion
Management Buyouts
Recapitalizations

Size of Investments Considered:
Min Size of Investment Considered (000s): $3,764
Max Size of Investment Considered (000s): $18,818

Geographical Preferences

International Preferences:
United Kingdom

Industry Focus
(% based on actual investment)
Other Products	30.0%
Consumer Related	24.3%
Industrial/Energy	15.3%
Internet Specific	14.6%
Computer Software and Services	7.2%
Computer Hardware	4.7%
Communications and Media	3.9%

Additional Information
Year Founded: 1997
Capital Under Management: $65,300,000
Current Activity Level : Actively seeking new investments

BARING PRIVATE EQUITY ASIA LTD

Eight Finance Street
Suite 3801, Two Intl. Finance
Central, Hong Kong
Phone: 85228439300
Fax: 85228439372
E-mail: hongkong@bpeasia.com
Website: www.bpeasia.com

Other Offices

2 Battery Road
#23-01 Maybank Tower
Singapore, Singapore 049907
Phone: 65-6232-6300
Fax: 65-6532-0660

1-12-32 Akasaka, Minato-ku
22/F, Ark Mori Building
Tokyo, Japan 107-6022
Phone: 81-3-5545-7200
Fax: 81-3-5545-7201

Unit 2903-05A, Tower 3
China Central Place, No.77 Jian Guo Road
Beijing, China 100025
Phone: 86-10-5904-7300
Fax: 86-10-5904-7333

GK Marg, Lower Parel (W)
BWP Towers
Mumbai, India 400013
Phone: 91-22-6132-2800
Fax: 91-22-6132-2806

28/F, Mirae Asset Tower
166 Lujiazui Ring Road
Shanghai, China 200120
Phone: 86-21-3135-9500
Fax: 86-21-3135-9499

Management and Staff

Amit Chander, Partner
Caroline Wee, Principal
Charles Lam, Managing Director
Dar Chen, Principal
David Huckfield, Chief Operating Officer
Dick Kwan, Managing Director
Edward Yang, Partner
Felix Fong, Partner
Gilbert Chalk, Partner
Gordon Shaw, Partner
Hedley Mayor, Partner
Jean Eric Salata, Chief Executive Officer
Joanna Lei, Partner
Joji Thomas, Partner
Jose Argel Sarasa, Managing Partner
Jun Chen, Partner
Keshav Misra, Partner
Leo Gherghina, Partner
Marcio Souza, Partner
N. Subramaniam, Partner
Peter Chan, Managing Partner
Posner Dirk, Partner
Wai San Loke, Principal

Type of Firm
Private Equity Firm

Association Membership
Venture Capital Association of Beijing (VCAB)
Hong Kong Venture Capital Association (HKVCA)
British Venture Capital Association (BVCA)
China Venture Capital Association
Emerging Markets Private Equity Association
European Private Equity and Venture Capital Assoc.
Singapore Venture Capital Association (SVCA)
Spanish Venture Capital Association (ASCRI)
Indian Venture Capital Association (IVCA)

Project Preferences

Role in Financing:
Will function either as deal originator or investor in deals created by others

Type of Financing Preferred:
Core
Leveraged Buyout
Expansion
Generalist PE
Balanced
Acquisition
Recapitalizations

Geographical Preferences

International Preferences:
India
Hong Kong
China
Asia
Singapore
Korea, South
Japan

Industry Focus
(% based on actual investment)

Other Products	33.2%
Internet Specific	26.2%
Consumer Related	15.2%
Industrial/Energy	9.1%
Computer Software and Services	5.4%
Computer Hardware	4.3%
Semiconductors/Other Elect.	3.0%
Communications and Media	1.4%
Biotechnology	1.3%
Medical/Health	1.0%

Additional Information
Name of Most Recent Fund: BPE Asia Real Estate Fund, L.P.
Most Recent Fund Was Raised: 07/12/2013
Year Founded: 1997
Capital Under Management: $5,000,000,000
Current Activity Level : Actively seeking new investments
Method of Compensation: Return on investment is of primary concern, do not charge fees

BARING VOSTOK CAPITAL PARTNERS LTD

7 Gasheka Street, Building 1
Ducat Place II, Suite 750
Moscow, Russia 123056
Phone: 74959671307
Fax: 74959671308
E-mail: info@bvcp.ru
Website: www.baring-vostok.com

Management and Staff

Anatoliy Karyakin, Partner
Gabbas Kazhimuratov, Chief Financial Officer
Konstantin Povstyanoy, Partner
Konstantin Smirnov, Partner
Michael Lomtadze, Partner
Mikhail Ivanov, Partner
Sergey Abramov, Partner
Vagan Abgaryan, Partner

Type of Firm
Bank Affiliated

Association Membership
Emerging Markets Private Equity Association
Russian Venture Capital Association (RVCA)

Project Preferences

Type of Financing Preferred:
Leveraged Buyout
Early Stage
Generalist PE
Turnaround
Later Stage
Acquisition

Geographical Preferences

International Preferences:
Armenia
Mongolia
Latin America
Belarus
Kazakhstan
Central Europe
Kyrgyzstan
Eastern Europe
Tajikistan
Turkmenistan
Azerbaijan
Moldova
Ukraine
Estonia
Uzbekistan
Asia
Latvia
Lithuania
Russia
Georgia

Industry Preferences

In Communications prefer:
Telecommunications
Media and Entertainment

In Medical/Health prefer:
Pharmaceuticals

In Consumer Related prefer:
Consumer

In Industrial/Energy prefer:
Energy
Oil & Gas Drilling,Explor

In Transportation prefer:
Transportation

In Financial Services prefer:
Financial Services

Additional Information
Name of Most Recent Fund: Baring Vostok Private Equity Fund V LP
Most Recent Fund Was Raised: 10/01/2012
Year Founded: 1994
Capital Under Management: $765,000,000
Current Activity Level : Actively seeking new investments

BARINGS (UK) LTD

61 Aldwych
London, United Kingdom WC2B 4AE
Phone: 442032064500
Fax: 442032064591
Website: www.barings.com

Other Offices

1500 Main Street
Springfield, MA USA 01115
Phone: 413-226-1000

Independence Wharf
470 Atlantic Avenue
Boston, MA USA 02210
Phone: 617-225-3800

340 Madison Avenue
18th Floor
New York, NY USA 10017
Phone: 917-542-8300

Suite 2400
Charlotte, NC USA 28244
Phone: 704-805-7200

Management and Staff

Andrew Wilson, Managing Director
David Hirschmann, Managing Director
Kamaljit Tugnait, Managing Director
Mark Wilton, Managing Director
Martin Horne, Managing Director
Neil Godfrey, Managing Director
Oliver Burgel, Chief Operating Officer
Stuart Mathieson, Managing Director

Type of Firm
Investment Management Firm

Project Preferences

Type of Financing Preferred:
Leveraged Buyout
Mezzanine
Recapitalizations

Geographical Preferences

International Preferences:
United Kingdom
Europe
Western Europe

Additional Information
Name of Most Recent Fund: Almack Mezzanine III, L.P.
Most Recent Fund Was Raised: 11/30/2010
Year Founded: 2000
Capital Under Management: $121,110,000
Current Activity Level : Actively seeking new investments

BARINGS CORPORATE INVESTORS

1500 Main Street
Suite 600
Springfield, MA USA 01115
Phone: 4132261516

Management and Staff

Janice Bishop, Vice President
Robert Shettle, President
Sean Feeley, Vice President

Type of Firm
Insurance Firm Affiliate

Project Preferences

Type of Financing Preferred:
Balanced

Additional Information
Year Founded: 1971
Current Activity Level : Actively seeking new investments

BARINGS LLC

1500 Main Street
Springfield, MA USA 01115
Phone: 4132261000
Website: www.barings.com

Other Offices

201 South College Street
Suite 2400
CHARLOTTE, NC USA 28244
Phone: 704-805-7200

340 Madison Avenue, 18th Floor
NEW YORK, NY USA 10017
Phone: 917-542-8300

Suite 22.06, Level 22
Grosvenor Place
Sydney, Australia NSW 2000
Phone: 612-8272-5000

2029 Century Park East
Suite 1130
LOS ANGELES, CA USA 90067
Phone: 310-407-2900

Independence Whar
470 Atlantic Avenue
BOSTON, MA USA 02210
Phone: 617-225-3800

Management and Staff

Brian C. Baldwin, Managing Director
Dave Acampora, Managing Director
Glenn Weiner, Managing Director
Lan M. Fowler, Managing Director
Mark J. Flessner, Managing Director
Thomas Finke, Chief Executive Officer

Type of Firm
Bank Affiliated

Project Preferences

Type of Financing Preferred:
Leveraged Buyout
Mezzanine
Private Placement

Geographica Preferences

United States Preferences:

International Preferences:
Asia Pacific
Europe
Hong Kong
Western Europe
Australia
New Zealand
Singapore
Japan

Additional Information
Year Founded: 1992
Capital Under Management: $260,800,000
Current Activity Level : Actively seeking new investments

BARNARD ASSOCIATES, INC.

20 North Meridian Street
Guaranty Building Suite 801
Indianapolis, IN USA 46204
Phone: 3176849106
Fax: 3176849195
E-mail: info@barnardassociates.com
Website: www.barnardassociates.com

Management and Staff
John Barnard, Founder
Timothy Tichenor, Managing Director

Type of Firm
Private Equity Advisor or Fund of Funds

Project Preferences

Type of Financing Preferred:
Early Stage
Balanced

Industry Preferences

In Biotechnology prefer:
Biotechnology

In Medical/Health prefer:
Medical Products
Pharmaceuticals

In Business Serv. prefer:
Services

In Agr/Forestr/Fish prefer:
Agriculture related

Additional Information
Name of Most Recent Fund: Pearl Street Venture Fund, L.P.
Most Recent Fund Was Raised: 05/28/2004
Year Founded: 1994
Current Activity Level: Actively seeking new investments

BARODA VENTURES LLC

245 South Beverly Drive, Suite 2151
Beverly Hills, CA USA 90212
Phone: 3102760005
Fax: 3102760007
E-mail: info@barodaventures.com
Website: www.barodaventures.com

Management and Staff
David Bohnett, Founder
Peter Lee, Partner

Type of Firm
Private Equity Firm

Project Preferences

Type of Financing Preferred:
Early Stage
Balanced

Geographical Preferences

United States Preferences:
California

Industry Preferences

In Internet Specific prefer:
E-Commerce Technology
Internet

In Business Serv. prefer:
Media

Additional Information
Year Founded: 1998
Current Activity Level: Actively seeking new investments

BASE VENTURES

3030 Ashby Avenue
Suite 100
Berkeley, CA USA 94705
E-mail: hello@base.ventures
Website: base.ventures

Type of Firm
Private Equity Firm

Project Preferences

Type of Financing Preferred:
Seed

Industry Preferences

In Computer Software prefer:
Software

Additional Information
Year Founded: 2013
Capital Under Management: $8,590,000
Current Activity Level: Actively seeking new investments

BASE10 PARTNERS

727 Sansome Street
Suite 300
San Francisco, CA USA 94111
Website: base10.vc

Type of Firm
Private Equity Firm

Project Preferences

Type of Financing Preferred:
Early Stage

Industry Preferences

In Computer Software prefer:
Software

Additional Information
Year Founded: 2017
Capital Under Management: $83,780,000
Current Activity Level: Actively seeking new investments

BASELINE VENTURES LLC

3101 Clay Street
Suite Three
San Francisco, CA USA 94115
Phone: 2067994389

Management and Staff
Ronald Conway, Partner
Steve Anderson, Founder

Type of Firm
Private Equity Firm

Project Preferences

Type of Financing Preferred:
Early Stage
Seed

Industry Preferences

In Internet Specific prefer:
Internet
Web Aggregation/Portals

Additional Information
Year Founded: 2006
Current Activity Level: Actively seeking new investments

BASF NEW BUSINESS GMBH

4, Gartenweg Z 25
Ludwigshafen, Germany 67063
Phone: 496216076811
Fax: 496216076818
Website: www.basf.com

Other Offices
Klybeckstrasse 141
Basel, Switzerland 4002

39 Veronica Avenue
Somerset, NJ USA 08873

45th Floor Jardine House
No 1 Connaught Place
Hong Kong, Central, Hong Kong

Management and Staff
Andreas Riehemann, Managing Director
Carla Seidel, Vice President
Joachim Rosch, Vice President
Stefan Blank, Managing Director

Type of Firm
Corporate PE/Venture

Project Preferences

Type of Financing Preferred:
Leveraged Buyout
Early Stage
Generalist PE
Acquisition
Startup

Geographical Preferences

International Preferences:
Europe
All International

Industry Preferences

In Semiconductor/Electr prefer:
Electronics
Analytic/Scientific

In Biotechnology prefer:
Biotechnology

In Medical/Health prefer:
Medical/Health

In Industrial/Energy prefer:
Energy
Materials
Environmental Related

Additional Information
Year Founded: 2001
Current Activity Level : Actively seeking new investments

BASF VENTURE CAPITAL GMBH

4 Gartenweg
Gebaeude Z 025
Ludwigshafen, Germany 67063
Phone: 496216076801
Fax: 496216076819
E-mail: info@basf-vc.de
Website: www.basf-vc.de

Other Offices
Kioicho, Chiyoda-ku
BASF Japan Nanbu-Bldg, 3-3
Tokyo, Japan 102-8750
Phone: 81-3-3238-2274
Fax: 81-3-3238-2413

46820 Fremont Boulevard
Fremont, CA USA 94538
Phone: 510-445-6141

45th Floor, Jardine House
No. 1 Connaught Place
Hong Kong, Hong Kong
Phone: 852-2731-3755

Management and Staff
Daniela Proske, Principal
Sven Harmsen, Principal

Type of Firm
Corporate PE/Venture

Association Membership
German Venture Capital Association (BVK)
European Private Equity and Venture Capital Assoc.

Project Preferences

Type of Financing Preferred:
Fund of Funds
Early Stage
Seed
Startup

Geographical Preferences

United States Preferences:

International Preferences:
Europe
Asia

Industry Preferences

In Semiconductor/Electr prefer:
Analytic/Scientific

In Biotechnology prefer:
Biotechnology

In Medical/Health prefer:
Medical/Health

In Industrial/Energy prefer:
Energy
Materials

In Other prefer:
Environment Responsible

Additional Information
Year Founded: 2001
Capital Under Management: $100,700,000
Current Activity Level : Actively seeking new investments

BASIS SET VENTURES LLC

325 Sharon Park Drive, Suite 603
Menlo Park, CA USA 94025

Type of Firm
Private Equity Firm

Project Preferences

Type of Financing Preferred:
Early Stage

Industry Preferences

In Computer Software prefer:
Artificial Intelligence

Additional Information
Year Founded: 2017
Current Activity Level : Actively seeking new investments

BASQUE, AUTONOMOUS COMMUNITY OF

Gran Via 85
Bilbao, Spain 48011
Phone: 0034945018000
Website: www.euskadi.net

Type of Firm
Government Affiliated Program

Project Preferences

Type of Financing Preferred:
Balanced

Additional Information
Year Founded: 1982
Capital Under Management: $3,305,000
Current Activity Level : Actively seeking new investments

BASSET INVESTMENT GROUP LLC

73 Spring Street
New York, NY USA 10012
Website: bassetinvestmentgroup.com

Management and Staff
Henry Guy, Managing Partner
Ryan Darnell, Principal

Type of Firm
Private Equity Firm

Project Preferences

Type of Financing Preferred:
Early Stage
Expansion
Balanced
Later Stage
Seed

Additional Information
Year Founded: 2010
Current Activity Level : Actively seeking new investments

BATANAI CAPITAL FINANCE PVT LTD

3 Lawson Avenue, Milton Park
P.O. Box A1480, Avondale
Harare, Zimbabwe

Management and Staff
Ndaba Mpofu, Managing Director
Nkosana Moyo, Founder

Type of Firm
Private Equity Firm

Additional Information
Year Founded: 1998
Current Activity Level : Actively seeking new investments

BATTELLE VENTURES LP

100 Princeton S. Corporate Ctr, Suite 150
Ewing, NJ USA 08628
Phone: 6099211456
Fax: 6099218703
E-mail: partners@battelleventures.com
Website: www.battelleventures.com

Management and Staff

Morton Colins, General Partner
Rakefet Kasdin, General Partner
Ralph Taylor-Smith, General Partner
Tammi Jantzen, Chief Financial Officer
Tracy Warren, General Partner

Type of Firm

Private Equity Firm

Project Preferences

Role in Financing:
Prefer role as deal originator but will also invest in deals created by others

Type of Financing Preferred:
Early Stage

Industry Preferences

In Medical/Health prefer:
Medical/Health

In Industrial/Energy prefer:
Energy
Environmental Related

Additional Information

Name of Most Recent Fund: Innovation Valley Partners
Most Recent Fund Was Raised: 08/19/2005
Year Founded: 2003
Capital Under Management: $255,000,000
Current Activity Level : Actively seeking new investments
Method of Compensation: Return on investment is of primary concern, do not charge fees

BATTERSON VENTURE CAPITAL

303 West Madison Street
Suite 1625
Chicago, IL USA 60606
Phone: 3122690300
Fax: 3122690021
Website: www.battersonvc.com

Management and Staff

AnnMarie Piotrowski, Vice President
Leonard Batterson, Chairman & CEO

Type of Firm

Private Equity Firm

Project Preferences

Role in Financing:
Will function either as deal originator or investor in deals created by others

Type of Financing Preferred:
Early Stage
Balanced
Seed
Startup

Geographical Preferences

United States Preferences:
Midwest

Industry Focus

(% based on actual investment)

Computer Software and Services	32.5%
Medical/Health	19.4%
Internet Specific	16.8%
Communications and Media	8.6%
Biotechnology	7.9%
Computer Hardware	4.5%
Industrial/Energy	4.0%
Other Products	3.2%
Semiconductors/Other Elect.	2.3%
Consumer Related	0.7%

Additional Information

Year Founded: 1988
Capital Under Management: $400,000,000
Current Activity Level : Actively seeking new investments
Method of Compensation: Return on invest. most important, but chg. closing fees, service fees, etc.

BATTERY VENTURES LP

One Marina Park Drive
Suite 1100
Boston, MA USA 02210
Phone: 6179483600
Fax: 6179483601
Website: www.battery.com

Other Offices

6 HaChoshlim Street
6th Floor
Herzliya, Israel 46724
Phone: 972-9-972-4300
Fax: 972-9-950-9484

260 Townsend Street
Seventh Floor
SAN FRANCISCO, CA USA 94107
Phone: 4154265900
Fax: 4154265901

Management and Staff

Abel Osorio, Vice President
Abhi Arunachalam, Vice President
Alexander Benik, Principal
Alexander Benik, Partner
Ben Johnston, Vice President
Blake Bartlett, Vice President
Brian O Malley, General Partner
Brian Lieber, Partner
Brian Lieber, Principal
Chelsea Stoner, Partner
Chelsea Stoner, General Partner
Chris Hanson, Chief Operating Officer
Chris Schiavo, Chief Financial Officer
Cornel Faucher, Partner
David Tabors, General Partner
David Sokolic, Vice President
Dharmesh Thakker, General Partner
Duncan Gills, Vice President
Eyal Shinar, Vice President
Itzik Parnafes, General Partner
Itzik Parnafes, General Partner
Jeffrey Lu, Vice President
Jesse Feldman, General Partner
Jesse Feldman, General Partner
Joe Porten, Vice President
Karen Bommart, Vice President
Kenneth Lawler, General Partner
Malvina Goldfeld, Vice President
Matthew Jacobson, Vice President
Matthew Garratt, Vice President
Michael Brown, General Partner
Michael Brown, General Partner
Mike Dauber, Principal
Mike Katz, Vice President
Morad Elhafed, Partner
Morad Elhafed, Vice President
Nakul Mandan, Vice President
Neeraj Agrawal, General Partner
Neeraj Agrawal, General Partner
Rebecca Buckman, Chief Financial Officer
Roger Lee, General Partner
Roger Lee, General Partner
Roland Anderson, Vice President
Russell Fleischer, General Partner
Sabrina Chiasson, Vice President
Satoshi Harris-Koizumi, Vice President
Scott Tobin, General Partner
Scott Tobin, General Partner
Shiran Shalev, Vice President
Sunil Dhaliwal, General Partner
Thomas Crotty, General Partner
Zack Smotherman, Principal
Zakary Ewen, Vice President

Type of Firm

Private Equity Firm

Association Membership

New England Venture Capital Association
Israel Venture Association
Western Association of Venture Capitalists (WAVC)
National Venture Capital Association - USA (NVCA)

Project Preferences

Role in Financing:
Prefer role as deal originator but will also invest in deals created by others

Type of Financing Preferred:
Leveraged Buyout
Early Stage
Expansion
Generalist PE
Balanced
Later Stage
Seed

Size of Investments Considered:
Min Size of Investment Considered (000s): $5,000
Max Size of Investment Considered (000s): $100,000

Geographical Preferences

United States Preferences:
North America

International Preferences:
Europe

Industry Focus

(% based on actual investment)
Computer Software and Services	39.4%
Internet Specific	26.6%
Communications and Media	13.1%
Semiconductors/Other Elect.	9.9%
Other Products	4.6%
Industrial/Energy	2.9%
Computer Hardware	2.5%
Medical/Health	0.8%
Biotechnology	0.2%

Additional Information

Name of Most Recent Fund: Battery Ventures X, L.P.
Most Recent Fund Was Raised: 02/21/2013
Year Founded: 1983
Capital Under Management: $4,700,000,000
Current Activity Level : Actively seeking new investments
Method of Compensation: Return on invest. most important, but chg. closing fees, service fees, etc.

BAY CAPITAL INVESTMENT PARTNERS LLC

One Turks Head Place
Suite 1492
Providence, RI USA 02903
Phone: 4012283833
Fax: 4012283835
Website: www.baycapllc.com

Management and Staff

Daniel Williams, Managing Director
Gregory Mulligan, Founder
Jacob Gaffey, Partner
Mary Halvey, Chief Financial Officer

Type of Firm

Investment Management Firm

Association Membership

Natl Assoc of Small Bus. Inv. Co (NASBIC)

Project Preferences

Type of Financing Preferred:
Leveraged Buyout
Expansion
Mezzanine
Management Buyouts
Acquisition
Recapitalizations

Geographical Preferences

United States Preferences:
Northeast

Industry Preferences

In Communications prefer:
Communications and Media

In Financial Services prefer:
Financial Services

In Business Serv. prefer:
Media

Additional Information

Name of Most Recent Fund: BCA Mezzanine Fund II, L.P.
Most Recent Fund Was Raised: 03/29/2012
Year Founded: 2006
Capital Under Management: $30,000,000
Current Activity Level : Actively seeking new investments

BAY CITY CAPITAL LLC

750 Battery Street
Suite 400
San Francisco, CA USA 94111
Phone: 4156763830
Fax: 4158370503
Website: baycitycapital.com

Management and Staff

Ashley Dombkowski, Managing Director
Carl Goldfischer, Managing Director
David Beier, Managing Director
David Milligan, Principal
Dayton Misfeldt, Partner
Douglass Given, Partner
Frederick Craves, Founder
Jeanne Cunicelli, Partner
Judy Koh, Chief Financial Officer
Lionel Carnot, Partner
Manuel Lopez-Figueroa, Vice President
Marge Josephson, Vice President
Min Cui, Principal
Rob Hopfner, Partner
Ross Bersot, Partner
William Gerber, Partner

Type of Firm

Private Equity Firm

Project Preferences

Role in Financing:
Prefer role as deal originator

Type of Financing Preferred:
Early Stage
Expansion
Balanced
Later Stage
Seed

Geographical Preferences

United States Preferences:

Industry Focus

(% based on actual investment)
Biotechnology	47.7%
Medical/Health	43.9%
Computer Software and Services	2.2%
Internet Specific	1.9%
Consumer Related	1.8%
Other Products	1.5%
Computer Hardware	1.0%

Additional Information

Name of Most Recent Fund: Bay City Capital Fund V, L.P.
Most Recent Fund Was Raised: 05/24/2007
Year Founded: 1997
Capital Under Management: $1,600,000,000
Current Activity Level : Actively seeking new investments

BAY GROVE CAPITAL LLC

423 Washington Street
Seventh floor
San Francisco, CA USA 94111
Phone: 4152297953
Fax: 4152297954
E-mail: info@baygrovecapital.com
Website: www.baygrovecapital.com

Management and Staff

Adam Forste, Managing Director
David Brandes, Managing Director
Kevin Marchetti, Managing Director

Type of Firm

Private Equity Firm

Project Preferences

Type of Financing Preferred:
Leveraged Buyout
Recapitalizations

Geographical Preferences

United States Preferences:
All U.S.

Industry Preferences

In Communications prefer:
Media and Entertainment

In Medical/Health prefer:
Medical/Health
Health Services

In Consumer Related prefer:
Consumer
Retail

In Industrial/Energy prefer:
Energy

In Financial Services prefer:
Financial Services

In Business Serv. prefer:
Distribution

In Manufact. prefer:
Manufacturing

Additional Information
Year Founded: 2009
Current Activity Level : Actively seeking new investments

BAY HILLS CAPITAL PARTNERS II LP

One Embarcadero Center
Suite 2839
San Francisco, CA USA 94111
Phone: 415-391-4240
Fax: 415-391-4210
Website: www.bayhillscapital.com

Management and Staff
Albert Chiang, Partner
David Smith, Partner
Joseph Zanone, Chief Financial Officer
Lance Mansbridge, Managing Partner

Type of Firm
Private Equity Advisor or Fund of Funds

Project Preferences

Type of Financing Preferred:
Fund of Funds
Leveraged Buyout
Fund of Funds of Second

Geographical Preferences

United States Preferences:
North America
All U.S.

Additional Information
Name of Most Recent Fund: Bay Hills Capital Partners III, L.P.
Most Recent Fund Was Raised: 03/26/2014
Year Founded: 2006
Capital Under Management: $127,055,000
Current Activity Level : Actively seeking new investments

BAY PARTNERS

2180 Sand Hill Road
Suite 345
Menlo Park, CA USA 94025
Phone: 6508541500
Fax: 6508541515
Website: www.baypartners.com

Management and Staff
Neal Dempsey, General Partner
Salil Deshpande, General Partner
Stuart Phillips, General Partner

Type of Firm
Private Equity Firm

Association Membership
Western Association of Venture Capitalists (WAVC)

Project Preferences

Role in Financing:
Will function either as deal originator or investor in deals created by others

Type of Financing Preferred:
Early Stage
Balanced
Later Stage
Seed
Startup

Geographical Preferences

United States Preferences:

Industry Focus
(% based on actual investment)

Computer Software and Services	45.4%
Communications and Media	18.2%
Internet Specific	15.9%
Semiconductors/Other Elect.	10.3%
Computer Hardware	3.3%
Industrial/Energy	3.0%
Other Products	1.6%
Biotechnology	1.2%
Consumer Related	0.9%
Medical/Health	0.2%

Additional Information
Year Founded: 1976
Capital Under Management: $980,000,000
Current Activity Level : Actively seeking new investments
Method of Compensation: Return on investment is of primary concern, do not charge fees

BAYBG BAYERISCHE BETEILIGUNGS-GESELLSCHAFT MBH

Koeniginstrasse 23
Munich, Germany 80539
Phone: 4989122280100
Fax: 4989122280101
E-mail: info@baybg.de
Website: www.baybg.de

Other Offices
Gewerbemuseumsplatz 2
Nuernberg, Germany 90403
Phone: 499112358605

Management and Staff
Guenther Henrich, Managing Director
Peter Pauli, Managing Director
Sonnfried Weber, Managing Director

Type of Firm
Private Equity Firm

Association Membership
German Venture Capital Association (BVK)

Project Preferences

Role in Financing:
Prefer role as deal originator

Type of Financing Preferred:
Leveraged Buyout
Early Stage
Turnaround
Later Stage
Seed
Management Buyouts
Startup
Recapitalizations

Size of Investments Considered:
Min Size of Investment Considered (000s): $26
Max Size of Investment Considered (000s): $1,962

Geographical Preferences

International Preferences:
Germany

Industry Preferences

In Communications prefer:
Telecommunications

In Computer Software prefer:
Software

In Semiconductor/Electr prefer:
Electronics
Electronic Components

In Consumer Related prefer:
Consumer

In Business Serv. prefer:
Services

Additional Information
Year Founded: 1972
Capital Under Management: $375,500,000
Current Activity Level : Actively seeking new investments

BAYBOSTON MANAGERS LLC

1280 Centre Street
Suite Two
Newton, MA USA 02459
E-mail: info@bayboston.com
Website: bayboston.com

Management and Staff
Carlos Garcia Espada, Chief Executive Officer
Liesl Sitton, Managing Partner
Richard Toomey, Principal
Richard Durkes, Partner

Type of Firm
Private Equity Firm

Project Preferences

Type of Financing Preferred:
Expansion
Later Stage
Special Situation

Size of Investments Considered:
Min Size of Investment Considered (000s): $5,000
Max Size of Investment Considered (000s): $10,000

Geographical Preferences

United States Preferences:

Industry Preferences

In Financial Services prefer:
Financial Services

Additional Information
Year Founded: 2015
Capital Under Management: $14,850,000
Current Activity Level : Actively seeking new investments

BAYERN KAPITAL GMBH

Laendgasse 135 A
Landshut, Germany 84028
Phone: 49871923250
Fax: 498719232555
E-mail: info@bayernkapital.de
Website: bayernkapital.de

Management and Staff
Georg Reid, Managing Director
Roman Huber, Managing Director

Type of Firm
Bank Affiliated

Association Membership
German Venture Capital Association (BVK)

Project Preferences

Type of Financing Preferred:
Early Stage
Seed
Startup

Size of Investments Considered:
Min Size of Investment Considered (000s): $1,000
Max Size of Investment Considered: No Limit

Geographical Preferences

International Preferences:
Germany

Industry Preferences

In Communications prefer:
Communications and Media

In Computer Software prefer:
Software

In Semiconductor/Electr prefer:
Electronics

In Biotechnology prefer:
Biotechnology

In Medical/Health prefer:
Medical/Health

In Industrial/Energy prefer:
Materials
Environmental Related

In Other prefer:
Environment Responsible

Additional Information
Name of Most Recent Fund: Clusterfonds Innovation GmbH
Most Recent Fund Was Raised: 03/27/2009
Year Founded: 1995
Capital Under Management: $95,000,000
Current Activity Level : Actively seeking new investments

BAYERNLB PRIVATE EQUITY MANAGEMENT GMBH

Ottostrasse 21
Munich, Germany 80333
Phone: 49895525630
Fax: 498955256390
E-mail: info@bayernlb-cp.de
Website: www.bayernlb-cp.de

Management and Staff
Karsten Buckenauer, Chief Financial Officer

Type of Firm
Private Equity Firm

Association Membership
German Venture Capital Association (BVK)

Project Preferences

Type of Financing Preferred:
Leveraged Buyout
Turnaround
Later Stage
Management Buyouts
Recapitalizations

Size of Investments Considered:
Min Size of Investment Considered (000s): $1,418
Max Size of Investment Considered (000s): $42,547

Geographical Preferences

International Preferences:
Germany

Industry Preferences

In Communications prefer:
Telecommunications

In Computer Software prefer:
Software

In Computer Other prefer:
Computer Related

In Medical/Health prefer:
Medical/Health

In Consumer Related prefer:
Consumer
Retail
Food/Beverage

In Industrial/Energy prefer:
Industrial Products

In Business Serv. prefer:
Services

Additional Information
Year Founded: 1969
Current Activity Level : Actively seeking new investments

BAYOU CITY ENERGY LP

1221 McKinney Street
Suite 2875
Houston, TX USA 77010
Phone: 4008210
E-mail: info@bayoucityenergy.com

Management and Staff
Kristin MacKelvey, Chief Financial Officer
Mark Stoner, Partner

Type of Firm
Private Equity Firm

Project Preferences

Type of Financing Preferred:
Generalist PE

Size of Investments Considered:
Min Size of Investment Considered (000s): $5,000
Max Size of Investment Considered (000s): $50,000

Geographical Preferences

United States Preferences:
North America

Industry Preferences

In Industrial/Energy prefer:
Energy

Additional Information

Year Founded: 2015
Capital Under Management: $468,870,000
Current Activity Level : Actively seeking new investments

BAYOU STEEL CORP

One Sound Shore Drive
Suite 200
Greenwich, CT USA 06830
Phone: 2035520888
E-mail: info@bdcm.com
Website: www.bayousteel.com

Other Offices

100 North Field Drive
Suite 170, One Conway Park
Lake Forest, IL USA 60045
Phone: 847-615-9000

68 Pall Mall
London, United Kingdom SW1Y 5ES
Phone: 442079683600

Management and Staff

James Zenni, President, Founder
Jean Fleischhacker, Senior Managing Director
Lanny Epperson, Managing Director
Mounir Nahas, Senior Managing Director
Philip Raygorodetsky, Managing Director
Stephen Deckoff, Founder

Type of Firm

Private Equity Firm

Project Preferences

Type of Financing Preferred:
Leveraged Buyout
Turnaround
Distressed Debt

Geographical Preferences

United States Preferences:

Additional Information

Name of Most Recent Fund: BDCM Opportunity Fund III, L.P.
Most Recent Fund Was Raised: 12/16/2009
Year Founded: 1995
Capital Under Management: $2,300,000,000
Current Activity Level : Actively seeking new investments

BAYSIDE CAPITAL INC

1450 Brickell Avenue
31st Floor
Miami, FL USA 33131
Phone: 3053798686
Fax: 3053793655
E-mail: bayside@bayside.com
Website: bayside.com

Other Offices

500 Boylston Street
Suite 1350
Boston, MA USA 02116
Phone: 6174255650
Fax: 6172621505

600 Fifth Avenue
24th Floor
New York, NY USA 10020
Phone: 2123141000
Fax: 2125060559

Management and Staff

Ahmed Hamdani, Managing Director
Appu Mundassery, Managing Director
David Robbins, Managing Director
Duncan Priston, Managing Director
Giuseppe Mirante, Managing Director
Jackson Craig, Managing Director
John Bolduc, Managing Director
Lionel Laurant, Managing Director
Sean Ozbolt, Managing Director

Type of Firm

Investment Management Firm

Project Preferences

Type of Financing Preferred:
Leveraged Buyout
Management Buyouts
Special Situation
Distressed Debt
Recapitalizations

Additional Information

Year Founded: 2004
Current Activity Level : Actively seeking new investments

BAYTECH VENTURE CAPITAL GMBH & CO KG

Theatinerstrasse 7
Munich, Germany 80333
Phone: 49892870090
Fax: 498928700911
E-mail: munich@baytechventure.com
Website: www.baytechventurecapital.de

Management and Staff

Jochen Walter, Partner
Michael Hochholzer, Partner
Rolf Schneider-Guenther, Managing Partner

Type of Firm

Bank Affiliated

Project Preferences

Type of Financing Preferred:
Early Stage
Mezzanine
Startup

Size of Investments Considered:
Min Size of Investment Considered (000s): $1,312
Max Size of Investment Considered (000s): $3,937

Geographical Preferences

International Preferences:
Western Europe
Germany
France

Industry Preferences

In Communications prefer:
Communications and Media
Telecommunications

In Computer Software prefer:
Software

In Internet Specific prefer:
Internet
Ecommerce

In Semiconductor/Electr prefer:
Semiconductor

In Medical/Health prefer:
Medical/Health

Additional Information

Year Founded: 2000
Capital Under Management: $89,100,000
Current Activity Level : Actively seeking new investments

BB CAPITAL BV

Tournooiveld 4
The Hague, Netherlands 2511 CX
Phone: 31703603066
Website: www.bbcapital.nl

Type of Firm
Private Equity Firm

Project Preferences

Type of Financing Preferred:
Leveraged Buyout
Early Stage
Expansion
Later Stage
Management Buyouts
Acquisition

Geographical Preferences

International Preferences:
Europe

Additional Information
Year Founded: 2014
Current Activity Level : Actively seeking new investments

BB&T CAPITAL PARTNERS LLC

101 North Cherry Street
Suite 700
Winston-Salem, NC USA 27101
Phone: 3367330350
Fax: 3367330349
Website: www.bbtcp.com

Management and Staff
Brad Clark, Chief Financial Officer
Christopher Jones, Partner
David Townsend, Managing Partner
Jonathan Blanco, Principal
Marshall White, Partner
Martin Gilmore, Partner
S. Whitfield Edwards, Principal
Scott Snow, Principal
Thomas Westbrook, Partner

Type of Firm
Bank Affiliated

Association Membership
Natl Assoc of Small Bus. Inv. Co (NASBIC)

Project Preferences

Role in Financing:
Prefer role as deal originator but will also invest in deals created by others

Type of Financing Preferred:
Fund of Funds
Leveraged Buyout
Mezzanine
Generalist PE
Management Buyouts
Acquisition
Recapitalizations

Geographical Preferences

United States Preferences:
Southeast

Industry Focus
(% based on actual investment)
Other Products	55.1%
Internet Specific	23.0%
Industrial/Energy	20.8%
Consumer Related	1.1%

Additional Information
Name of Most Recent Fund: Five Points Small Buyout Strategies II LLC
Most Recent Fund Was Raised: 06/26/2013
Year Founded: 1997
Capital Under Management: $725,000,000
Current Activity Level : Actively seeking new investments
Method of Compensation: Return on invest. most important, but chg. closing fees, service fees, etc.

BBVA VENTURES

55 Second Street, Suite 1900
San Francisco, CA USA 94105
Website: www.bbvaventures.com

Other Offices
55 Second Street
Suite 1900.
San Francisco, CA USA 94105

Type of Firm
Bank Affiliated

Association Membership
National Venture Capital Association - USA (NVCA)

Project Preferences

Type of Financing Preferred:
Leveraged Buyout
Early Stage
Expansion
Generalist PE

Geographical Preferences

United States Preferences:

International Preferences:
Latin America
Turkey
China
Mexico
Spain

Industry Preferences

In Financial Services prefer:
Financial Services

Additional Information
Year Founded: 2006
Current Activity Level : Actively seeking new investments

BC ADVANTAGE FUNDS LTD

221 West Esplanade
Suite 410
Vancouver, Canada V7M 3J3
Phone: 6046886877
Fax: 6046886166
E-mail: info@bcaf.ca
Website: www.bcadvantagefunds.com

Management and Staff
Ray Matthews, Vice President

Type of Firm
Private Equity Firm

Project Preferences

Type of Financing Preferred:
Early Stage
Expansion
Seed
Startup

Size of Investments Considered:
Min Size of Investment Considered (000s): $1,000
Max Size of Investment Considered (000s): $2,000

Geographical Preferences

Canadian Preferences:
All Canada
British Columbia

Industry Preferences

In Communications prefer:
Communications and Media

In Biotechnology prefer:
Biotechnology

In Medical/Health prefer:
Medical Products

In Industrial/Energy prefer:
Alternative Energy
Industrial Products

In Manufact. prefer:
Manufacturing

Additional Information
Year Founded: 2008
Capital Under Management: $94,000
Current Activity Level : Actively seeking new investments

BC BRANDENBURG CAPITAL GMBH

Steinstrasse 104-106
Potsdam, Germany 14480
Phone: 493316601698
Fax: 493316601699
E-mail: bc-capital@ilb.de
Website: www.bc-capital.de

Other Offices

Im Technologiepark 1
Frankfurt (Oder), Germany 15236
Phone: 49-335-5571690
Fax: 49-335-557-1699

Management and Staff

Michael Toenes, Managing Director
Olav Wilms, Managing Director

Type of Firm

Bank Affiliated

Association Membership

German Venture Capital Association (BVK)

Project Preferences

Type of Financing Preferred:
Early Stage
Expansion
Later Stage
Seed
Private Placement
Startup

Size of Investments Considered:
Min Size of Investment Considered (000s): $241
Max Size of Investment Considered (000s): $4,814

Geographical Preferences

International Preferences:
Germany

Industry Focus

(% based on actual investment)
Biotechnology	24.2%
Medical/Health	22.8%
Internet Specific	17.4%
Computer Software and Services	13.8%
Communications and Media	12.5%
Industrial/Energy	7.2%
Semiconductors/Other Elect.	2.1%

Additional Information

Year Founded: 1993
Capital Under Management: $33,000,000
Current Activity Level: Actively seeking new investments

BC GENERAL PARTNERS LLC

3841 Green Hills Village Drive
Suite 410
Nashville, TN USA 37215
Website: www.becknerclevypartners.com

Management and Staff

James Beckner, Partner
Tim Morris, Partner
W. Michael Clevy, Partner

Type of Firm

Private Equity Firm

Project Preferences

Type of Financing Preferred:
Leveraged Buyout
Acquisition

Geographical Preferences

United States Preferences:
North America

Additional Information

Year Founded: 2010
Capital Under Management: $250,000
Current Activity Level: Actively seeking new investments

BC PARTNERS LLP

40 Portman Square
London, United Kingdom W1H 6DA
Phone: 442070094800
Fax: 442070094899
E-mail: london@bcpartners.com
Website: www.bcpartners.com

Other Offices

667 Madison Avenue
NEW YORK, NY USA 10065
Phone: 212-891-2880
Fax: 212-891-2899

7 Quai du Mont Blanc
Geneva, Switzerland 1201
Phone: 41-22-757-8000
Fax: 41-22-757-8080

Via Brera 3
Milan, Italy 20121
Phone: 39-02-881-231
Fax: 39-02-8812-3290

Management and Staff

Amy Richards, Partner
Andreas Klab, Principal
Benjamin Hara, Partner
Benjamin Dupuy, Partner
Cedric Dubourdieu, Managing Partner
Charlie Bott, Managing Partner
Christian Mogge, Partner
Dale Ledbetter, Principal
Dimitrios Tzivelis, Principal
Ewald Walgenbach, Managing Partner
Fahim Ahmed, Partner
Fouad Jaidi, Principal
Idriss Soumare, Partner
Jacki Hamilton, Principal
Jamie Rivers, Partner
Jan Kengelbach, Partner
Jean-Baptiste Wautier, Managing Partner
Justin Bateman, Managing Partner
Laura Coquis, Partner
Maximilian Kastka, Partner
Moritz Elfers, Principal
Nikos Stathopoulos, Managing Partner
Raymond Svider, Managing Partner
Stefan Zuschke, Managing Partner
Stefano Quadrio-Curzio, Managing Partner
Xavier Lemonnier, Principal

Type of Firm

Private Equity Firm

Association Membership

Italian Venture Capital Association (AIFI)
British Venture Capital Association (BVCA)
French Venture Capital Association (AFIC)
German Venture Capital Association (BVK)
European Private Equity and Venture Capital Assoc.

Project Preferences

Role in Financing:
Prefer role as deal originator but will also invest in deals created by others

Type of Financing Preferred:
Leveraged Buyout
Acquisition

Geographical Preferences

International Preferences:
Europe

Industry Focus

(% based on actual investment)
Medical/Health	31.7%
Communications and Media	22.9%
Other Products	21.6%
Consumer Related	15.5%
Internet Specific	6.9%
Industrial/Energy	1.4%

Additional Information

Name of Most Recent Fund: BC European Capital IX
Most Recent Fund Was Raised: 12/31/2010
Year Founded: 1986
Capital Under Management: $15,484,000,000
Current Activity Level: Actively seeking new investments
Method of Compensation: Return on invest. most important, but chg. closing fees, service fees, etc.

BD VENTURE LTD

House 42 (2nd Floor)
Road 12, Block E, Banani
Dhaka, Bangladesh 1213
E-mail: info@bdventure.com

Type of Firm
Private Equity Firm

Project Preferences

Type of Financing Preferred:
Balanced

Additional Information
Year Founded: 2012
Current Activity Level : Actively seeking new investments

BDS CAPITAL MANAGEMENT LLC

500 N Broadway
Suite 241
Jericho, NY USA 11753
Phone: 5164662825
Website: www.bdscapital.net

Management and Staff
Brian Rubenstein, Founder

Type of Firm
Investment Management Firm

Project Preferences

Type of Financing Preferred:
Early Stage
Mezzanine
Generalist PE
Balanced
Opportunistic

Geographical Preferences

United States Preferences:
New York

Industry Preferences

In Computer Software prefer:
Applications Software

In Medical/Health prefer:
Medical Products

In Financial Services prefer:
Real Estate

Additional Information
Year Founded: 2009
Capital Under Management: $20,170,000
Current Activity Level : Actively seeking new investments

BDT CAPITAL PARTNERS LLC

401 North Michigan Avenue
Suite 3100
Chicago, IL USA 60611

Type of Firm
Private Equity Firm

Project Preferences

Type of Financing Preferred:
Leveraged Buyout

Additional Information
Name of Most Recent Fund: BDT Capital Partners Fund I, L.P.
Most Recent Fund Was Raised: 01/11/2011
Year Founded: 2011
Capital Under Management: $8,206,000,000
Current Activity Level : Actively seeking new investments

BE BETEILIGUNGEN GMBH & CO KG

Bismarckstrasse 30
Cologne, Germany 50672
Phone: 492215891890
Fax: 4922158918929
E-mail: info@be-beteiligungen.de
Website: www.be-beteiligungen.de

Management and Staff
Roland Eschmann, Co-Founder
Rolf Brodbeck, Co-Founder

Type of Firm
Private Equity Firm

Association Membership
German Venture Capital Association (BVK)

Project Preferences

Type of Financing Preferred:
Mezzanine
Acquisition

Geographical Preferences

International Preferences:
Switzerland
Austria
Germany

Additional Information
Year Founded: 2013
Current Activity Level : Actively seeking new investments

BE GREAT PARTNERS LLC

5900 Wilshire Boulevard
21st Floor, Suite 2100
Park La Brea, CA USA 90036
Phone: 8552478585
E-mail: incubate@begreatpartners.com
Website: www.begreatpartners.com

Type of Firm
Incubator/Development Program

Project Preferences

Type of Financing Preferred:
Startup

Size of Investments Considered:
Min Size of Investment Considered (000s): $25
Max Size of Investment Considered (000s): $50

Geographical Preferences

United States Preferences:
California

Additional Information
Year Founded: 2013
Capital Under Management: $100,000
Current Activity Level : Actively seeking new investments

BEACON NEW VENTURES

606 St. Kilda Road
Level 9
Melbourne, Australia 3004
Phone: 61395140688
Website: beaconnew.com.au

Other Offices
Three Pickering Street
Suite 02-17
Singapore, Singapore 048660

Type of Firm
Private Equity Firm

Project Preferences

Type of Financing Preferred:
Early Stage
Joint Ventures
Startup

Geographical Preferences

International Preferences:
Asia Pacific

Additional Information
Year Founded: 2012
Current Activity Level : Actively seeking new investments

BEACON PARTNERS INC

40 Powell Place
Stamford, CT USA 06902
Phone: 2033488858
Fax: 2033233188
E-mail: information@beaconpartnersinc.com
Website: www.beaconpartners.com

Management and Staff

Eric Vignola, Managing Director
John Nixon, Managing Director
Leonard Vignola, Partner

Type of Firm

Private Equity Firm

Project Preferences

Role in Financing:
Prefer role as deal originator

Type of Financing Preferred:
Second Stage Financing
Leveraged Buyout
Mezzanine
Turnaround
Recapitalizations

Size of Investments Considered:
Min Size of Investment Considered (000s): $300
Max Size of Investment Considered (000s): $1,000

Industry Focus

(% based on actual investment)
Consumer Related	39.8%
Industrial/Energy	19.2%
Other Products	17.3%
Internet Specific	8.6%
Computer Software and Services	5.1%
Medical/Health	4.9%
Communications and Media	3.5%
Semiconductors/Other Elect.	1.5%

Additional Information

Name of Most Recent Fund: Beacon Group Energy Investment Fund II
Most Recent Fund Was Raised: 03/17/1998
Year Founded: 1976
Capital Under Management: $1,000,000
Current Activity Level : Actively seeking new investments

BEAMONTE CAPITAL PARTNERS LLC

129 Newbury Street
Third Floor
Boston, MA USA 02116
Phone: 6172758960
E-mail: bcapital@beamonteinvestments.com
Website: www.beamontecapital.com

Management and Staff

Luis Trevino, Managing Director

Type of Firm

Investment Management Firm

Project Preferences

Type of Financing Preferred:
Leveraged Buyout
Expansion
Management Buyouts
Acquisition
Recapitalizations

Geographical Preferences

International Preferences:
Mexico
Colombia

Additional Information

Name of Most Recent Fund: Beamonte Capital Partners
Most Recent Fund Was Raised: 02/15/2012
Year Founded: 2012
Capital Under Management: $16,000,000
Current Activity Level : Actively seeking new investments

BEANSTALK VENTURES LP

53 Highridge Road
Hartsdale, NY USA 10530
Phone: 9172576643
Website: www.beanstalk.vc

Other Offices

Former HQ: 655 Magnolia Avenue
LARKSPUR, CA USA 94939
Phone: 9172576643

Type of Firm

Private Equity Firm

Project Preferences

Type of Financing Preferred:
Early Stage
Seed
Startup

Additional Information

Year Founded: 2013
Capital Under Management: $7,120,000
Current Activity Level : Actively seeking new investments

BEAUBRIDGE LTD

107 New Bond Street
London, United Kingdom W1S 1ED
Phone: 02075292543
Fax: 02075292549
E-mail: info@beaubridge.com
Website: www.beaubridge.com

Type of Firm

Private Equity Firm

Industry Preferences

In Medical/Health prefer:
Medical/Health

In Financial Services prefer:
Financial Services

Additional Information

Year Founded: 2017
Current Activity Level : Actively seeking new investments

BEAUFORT CAPITAL GMBH

Alsterarkaden 20
Hamburg, Germany 20354
Phone: 49403499996
Fax: 494034999977
E-mail: info@bo4.de
Website: www.bo4.de

Other Offices

Kurfuerstendamm 190-192
Berlin, Germany 10707

Management and Staff

Anja Moje, Co-Founder
Johann Herstatt, Co-Founder
Stefan Friese, Co-Founder

Type of Firm

Private Equity Firm

Association Membership

German Venture Capital Association (BVK)

Project Preferences

Type of Financing Preferred:
Leveraged Buyout
Early Stage
Later Stage
Acquisition

Size of Investments Considered:
Min Size of Investment Considered (000s): $2,659
Max Size of Investment Considered (000s): $15,951

Geographical Preferences

International Preferences:
Switzerland
Austria
Germany

Industry Preferences

In Communications prefer:
Communications and Media
Telecommunications
Wireless Communications

In Computer Software prefer:
Software
Systems Software
Applications Software

In Medical/Health prefer:
Medical/Health
Medical Products
Health Services

In Industrial/Energy prefer:
Environmental Related

In Financial Services prefer:
Financial Services

In Manufact. prefer:
Publishing

Additional Information
Year Founded: 2000
Current Activity Level : Actively seeking new investments

BECO CAPITAL INVESTMENT LLC

Grosvenor Business Tower
Dubai Internet City
Dubai, Utd. Arab Em. 333357
Phone: 97143687811
E-mail: info@becocapital.com
Website: becocapital.com

Type of Firm
Private Equity Firm

Project Preferences

Type of Financing Preferred:
Early Stage
Seed
Startup

Geographical Preferences

International Preferences:
Middle East
Africa

Industry Preferences

In Internet Specific prefer:
Internet
Ecommerce

In Financial Services prefer:
Financial Services

Additional Information
Year Founded: 1969
Current Activity Level : Actively seeking new investments

BEDFORD FUNDING CAPITAL MANAGEMENT LLC

Ten New King Street, Suite 104
White Plains, NY USA 10604
Phone: 9142874880
E-mail: info@bedfordfunding.com
Website: www.bedfordfunding.com

Management and Staff
Charles Jones, Managing Partner
Doug Ring, Principal
George Regnery, Principal

Type of Firm
Private Equity Firm

Project Preferences

Role in Financing:
Prefer role as deal originator

Type of Financing Preferred:
Leveraged Buyout
Later Stage
Acquisition

Geographical Preferences

United States Preferences:

Industry Preferences

In Medical/Health prefer:
Health Services

Additional Information
Name of Most Recent Fund: Bedford Funding II
Most Recent Fund Was Raised: 10/02/2012
Year Founded: 2006
Capital Under Management: $1,400,000,000
Current Activity Level : Actively seeking new investments

BEDMINSTER CAPITAL MANAGEMENT

350 Main Street
Suite 5
Bedminster, NJ USA 07921
Phone: 908-234-1063
Fax: 908-234-0664

Management and Staff
David Mathewson, Managing Director

Type of Firm
Other

Project Preferences

Type of Financing Preferred:
Generalist PE

Geographical Preferences

International Preferences:
Eastern Europe
Bulgaria
Romania

Additional Information
Year Founded: 2006
Current Activity Level : Actively seeking new investments

BEE PARTNERS, LLC

50 Osgood Place
Suite 220A
San Francisco, CA USA 94133
Phone: 4155194707
Website: beepartners.vc

Type of Firm
Incubator/Development Program

Association Membership
National Venture Capital Association - USA (NVCA)

Project Preferences

Type of Financing Preferred:
Seed
Startup

Size of Investments Considered:
Min Size of Investment Considered (000s): $200
Max Size of Investment Considered (000s): $400

Geographical Preferences

United States Preferences:

Industry Preferences

In Communications prefer:
Wireless Communications

In Computer Software prefer:
Data Processing
Applications Software

In Internet Specific prefer:
Ecommerce

In Consumer Related prefer:
Food/Beverage
Consumer Services

In Industrial/Energy prefer:
Materials

In Business Serv. prefer:
Services

Additional Information
Year Founded: 2009
Capital Under Management: $30,000,000
Current Activity Level : Actively seeking new investments

BEECHBROOK CAPITAL LLP

Nine Orange Street
First Floor
London, United Kingdom WC2H 7EA
Phone: 442035515965
Fax: 442078394736
E-mail: info@beechbrookcapital.com
Website: www.beechbrookcapital.com

Management and Staff

Jon Herbert, Managing Director
Mensah Lambie, Partner
Michiel Boorsma, Partner
Nick Fenn, Co-Founder
Paul Shea, Co-Founder
Sandeep Agarwal, Partner

Type of Firm

Private Equity Firm

Project Preferences

Type of Financing Preferred:
Leveraged Buyout
Expansion
Mezzanine
Generalist PE
Management Buyouts
Acquisition

Size of Investments Considered:
Min Size of Investment Considered (000s): $3,881
Max Size of Investment Considered (000s): $19,402

Geographical Preferences

International Preferences:
United Kingdom
Europe

Additional Information

Name of Most Recent Fund: Beechbrook Mezzanine II
Most Recent Fund Was Raised: 05/23/2013
Year Founded: 2008
Capital Under Management: $499,442,000
Current Activity Level : Actively seeking new investments

BEECHTREE CAPITAL LTD

34522 North Scottsdale Road
Suite 120-471
Scottsdale, AZ USA 85266
Phone: 9176561066
Fax: 4802689882
E-mail: info@beechtreecapital.com
Website: www.beechtreecapital.com

Other Offices

Former HQ: One Rockefeller Plaza
Suite 1600
New York, NY USA 10020
Phone: 212-541-6663
Fax: 212-541-8463

Management and Staff

John Oppenheimer, Managing Director
Romeo Laurel, Partner

Type of Firm

Investment Management Firm

Project Preferences

Type of Financing Preferred:
Leveraged Buyout
Early Stage
Expansion
Generalist PE
Balanced
Later Stage

Geographical Preferences

United States Preferences:
Arizona
California
New York

Industry Focus

(% based on actual investment)
Computer Software and Services 77.6%
Consumer Related 22.4%

Additional Information

Name of Most Recent Fund: Beechtree Capital Partners
Most Recent Fund Was Raised: 12/31/1992
Year Founded: 1992
Current Activity Level : Actively seeking new investments

BEECHWOOD CAPITAL

20 William Street
Suite 140
Wellesley, MA USA 02481
Phone: 7814499333
Fax: 7814499334
E-mail: info@beechwoodcap.com
Website: www.beechwoodcap.com

Type of Firm

Private Equity Firm

Project Preferences

Type of Financing Preferred:
Leveraged Buyout
Expansion
Generalist PE
Management Buyouts
Acquisition
Recapitalizations

Geographical Preferences

United States Preferences:
Northeast
All U.S.

Industry Preferences

In Consumer Related prefer:
Consumer

Additional Information

Year Founded: 1969
Current Activity Level : Actively seeking new investments

BEECKEN PETTY O'KEEFE & COMPANY LLC

131 South Dearborn Street
Suite 2800
Chicago, IL USA 60603
Phone: 3124350300
Fax: 3124350371
E-mail: partners@bpoc.com
Website: www.bpoc.com

Management and Staff

Adam Hentze, Vice President
David Beecken, Managing Director
David Cooney, Managing Director
Grant Patrick, Managing Director
Gregory Moerschel, President
John Kneen, Chief Financial Officer
Kenneth O Keefe, CEO & Managing Director
M. Troy Phillips, Managing Director
Mark Holmquist, Vice President
Peter Magas, Managing Director
Thomas Schlesinger, Managing Director
Timothy Sheehan, Managing Director
William Petty, Managing Director

Type of Firm

Private Equity Firm

Association Membership

Illinois Venture Capital Association
National Venture Capital Association - USA (NVCA)

Project Preferences

Role in Financing:
Will function either as deal originator or investor in deals created by others

Type of Financing Preferred:
Leveraged Buyout
Expansion
Later Stage
Management Buyouts
Acquisition
Recapitalizations

Geographical Preferences

United States Preferences:

Industry Focus

(% based on actual investment)
Medical/Health 71.3%
Computer Software and Services 24.7%
Internet Specific 2.3%
Biotechnology 1.2%
Communications and Media 0.6%

Additional Information

Name of Most Recent Fund: Beecken Petty O'Keefe Fund IV, L.P.
Most Recent Fund Was Raised: 12/05/2012
Year Founded: 1996
Capital Under Management: $1,185,000,000

Current Activity Level : Actively seeking new investments
Method of Compensation: Return on invest. most important, but chg. closing fees, service fees, etc.

BEEDIE CAPITAL PARTNERS

1580-1111 West Georgia Street
Vancouver, Canada V6E 4M3
Phone: 6046373321
E-mail: info@beediecapital.com
Website: beediecapital.com

Management and Staff

Dave Gormley, Vice President
Doug Nordan, Vice President
Eric Jensen, Vice President
Houtan Rafii, Vice President
Jim Bogusz, Chief Operating Officer
Maria Pacella, Vice President
Randy Garg, Managing Partner
Randy Strandt, Founder
Ryan Beedie, President
Todd Yuen, Vice President

Type of Firm

Private Equity Firm

Project Preferences

Type of Financing Preferred:
Expansion
Mezzanine
Generalist PE
Turnaround
Later Stage
Acquisition
Recapitalizations

Size of Investments Considered:
Min Size of Investment Considered (000s): $2,013
Max Size of Investment Considered (000s): $10,064

Geographical Preferences

United States Preferences:
Northwest

Canadian Preferences:
Western Canada

Additional Information

Year Founded: 2010
Capital Under Management: $130,000,000
Current Activity Level : Actively seeking new investments

BEEKMAN GROUP LLC

275 Madison Avenue, 37th Floor
New York, NY USA 10016
Phone: 6465023300
Fax: 6465023333
E-mail: info@thebeekmangroup.com
Website: www.thebeekmangroup.com

Management and Staff

Alexis Wolf, Vice President
Andrew Marolda, Managing Director
Andrew Brown, Managing Director
Christopher Artinian, Managing Director
Clement Dwyer, Managing Director
Michael Dobeck, Vice President

Type of Firm

Private Equity Firm

Project Preferences

Type of Financing Preferred:
Leveraged Buyout
Management Buyouts
Acquisition
Recapitalizations

Geographical Preferences

United States Preferences:

Canadian Preferences:
All Canada

Industry Preferences

In Medical/Health prefer:
Health Services

In Consumer Related prefer:
Consumer
Food/Beverage
Consumer Products
Consumer Services
Other Restaurants
Education Related

In Financial Services prefer:
Financial Services

In Business Serv. prefer:
Services
Distribution

Additional Information

Name of Most Recent Fund: Beekman Investment Partners II, L.P.
Most Recent Fund Was Raised: 01/15/2013
Year Founded: 2004
Capital Under Management: $100,000,000
Current Activity Level : Actively seeking new investments

BEENOS INC

4-7-35 Kitashinagawa Shinagawa
7F, Gotenyama Trust Tower
Tokyo, Japan 1400001
Phone: 81357393350
E-mail: pr@beenos.com
Website: beenos.com

Management and Staff

Hironori Maeda, Managing Partner
Koji Nakamura, Chief Financial Officer

Type of Firm

Private Equity Firm

Project Preferences

Type of Financing Preferred:
Early Stage
Seed
Startup

Additional Information

Year Founded: 2013
Current Activity Level : Actively seeking new investments

BEHRMAN CAPITAL

126 East 56th Street
27th Floor
New York, NY USA 10022
Phone: 2129806500
Fax: 2129807024
E-mail: contact.request@behrmancap.com
Website: www.behrmancap.com

Other Offices

One Maritime Plaza
Suite 1555
San Francisco, CA USA 94111
Phone: 415-434-7300
Fax: 415-434-7310

Management and Staff

Gary Dieber, Chief Financial Officer
Grant Behrman, Managing Partner
Jeffrey Wu, Partner
Michael Rapport, Vice President
Simon Lonergan, Partner
Tom Perlmutter, Partner
William Matthes, Managing Partner

Type of Firm

Private Equity Firm

Project Preferences

Role in Financing:
Prefer role as deal originator but will also invest in deals created by others

Type of Financing Preferred:
Leveraged Buyout
Management Buyouts
Acquisition
Recapitalizations

Geographical Preferences

United States Preferences:

Industry Focus

(% based on actual investment)

Industrial/Energy	65.8%
Other Products	11.9%
Internet Specific	8.2%
Medical/Health	7.2%
Computer Hardware	2.6%
Computer Software and Services	1.9%
Communications and Media	1.8%
Semiconductors/Other Elect.	0.5%

Additional Information

Name of Most Recent Fund: Behrman Capital PEP, L.P.
Most Recent Fund Was Raised: 09/10/2012
Year Founded: 1991
Capital Under Management: $3,100,000,000
Current Activity Level : Actively seeking new investments
Method of Compensation: Return on invest. most important, but chg. closing fees, service fees, etc.

BEIHANG INVESTMENT CO LTD

No. 7 Zhichun Road, Haidian Di
22F, Building A, Zhizhen Mansi
Beijing, China 100083
Phone: 861053859678
Website: www.beihangtou.com

Type of Firm
Private Equity Firm

Project Preferences

Type of Financing Preferred:
Balanced

Geographical Preferences

International Preferences:
China

Industry Preferences

In Internet Specific prefer:
Internet

In Industrial/Energy prefer:
Robotics

In Transportation prefer:
Aerospace

In Manufact. prefer:
Manufacturing

Additional Information
Year Founded: 2016
Capital Under Management: $1,000,000,000
Current Activity Level : Actively seeking new investments

BEIJIG DONGDONG INVESTMENT CO LTD

Dongda Street, Andingmen
A903, Yonghe Building
Beijing, China 100007
Fax: 861084031699
Website: 010dongdongtz.gotoip1.com

Type of Firm
Private Equity Firm

Project Preferences

Type of Financing Preferred:
Balanced

Geographical Preferences

International Preferences:
China

Industry Preferences

In Internet Specific prefer:
Internet

In Consumer Related prefer:
Education Related

In Industrial/Energy prefer:
Energy

Additional Information
Year Founded: 2013
Current Activity Level : Actively seeking new investments

BEIJING ANGEL AROUND INVESTMENT MANAGEMENT CO LTD

Zhongguancun Science and Techn
A District, Pinggu Park Hing V
Beijing, China
Website: aatouzi.com

Type of Firm
Private Equity Firm

Project Preferences

Type of Financing Preferred:
Seed
Startup

Size of Investments Considered:
Min Size of Investment Considered (000s): $152
Max Size of Investment Considered (000s): $1,518

Geographical Preferences

International Preferences:
China

Industry Preferences

In Communications prefer:
Telecommunications
Media and Entertainment

Additional Information
Year Founded: 2015
Current Activity Level : Actively seeking new investments

BEIJING ANGEL GROWTH TECHNOLOGY INCUBATOR CO LTD CO LTD

No.1 Zhongguancun Street
10F, Hailong Building
Beijing, China
Website: www.acjsq.com

Type of Firm
Incubator/Development Program

Project Preferences

Type of Financing Preferred:
Seed
Startup

Geographical Preferences

International Preferences:
China

Additional Information
Year Founded: 2015
Current Activity Level : Actively seeking new investments

BEIJING ANGELCRUNCH VENTURE FINANCIAL INFORMATION SERVICES

Jingyi Technology Building
R418-420, Block B
Beijing, China 100086
Phone: 861062670371
Fax: 861062670968
Website: www.angelcrunch.com

Type of Firm
Private Equity Firm

Project Preferences

Type of Financing Preferred:
Seed
Startup

Geographical Preferences

International Preferences:
China

Industry Preferences

In Communications prefer:
Entertainment

In Internet Specific prefer:
Internet

In Biotechnology prefer:
Biotech Related Research

In Consumer Related prefer:
Education Related

Additional Information
Year Founded: 2014
Current Activity Level : Actively seeking new investments

BEIJING APPLE FUNDS INVESTMENT LP

Huilongguan, Changping Distric
4F, Tower A, Tencent Maker Spa
Beijing, China
Phone: 861062751011
Fax: 861062759106
Website: www.applefunds.cn

Type of Firm
Private Equity Firm

Project Preferences

Type of Financing Preferred:
Balanced

Geographical Preferences

International Preferences:
China

Industry Preferences

In Internet Specific prefer:
Internet

Additional Information
Year Founded: 2015
Current Activity Level : Actively seeking new investments

BEIJING BEIDA MEDICAL INDUSTRIAL FUND MANAGEMENT CO LTD

Life Science Park Road
212,8/F, No.8 Yard
Beijing, China 102206
Phone: 861082524269

Type of Firm
Private Equity Firm

Project Preferences

Type of Financing Preferred:
Leveraged Buyout

Geographical Preferences

International Preferences:
China

Industry Preferences

In Medical/Health prefer:
Medical/Health

Additional Information
Year Founded: 2013
Current Activity Level : Actively seeking new investments

BEIJING BIGGER VENTURE TECHNOLOGY INCUBATOR CO LTD

1st Xiangheyuan Rd.,Dongzhimen
Bldg. B , Modern MOMA Art Dist
Beijing, China
Phone: 861084408427
Website: www.e-bigger.com

Type of Firm
Incubator/Development Program

Project Preferences

Type of Financing Preferred:
Start-up Financing
Recapitalizations

Geographical Preferences

International Preferences:
China

Industry Preferences

In Financial Services prefer:
Real Estate

Additional Information
Year Founded: 2015
Current Activity Level : Actively seeking new investments

BEIJING BO LE ZONG HENG INVESTMENT MANAGEMENT CENTER LP

Olympic Forest Park, Chaoyang
Chuiyitai, South Garden
Beijing, China 100101
Phone: 861064529179

Type of Firm
Private Equity Firm

Project Preferences

Type of Financing Preferred:
Balanced

Geographical Preferences

International Preferences:
China

Additional Information
Year Founded: 2014
Current Activity Level : Actively seeking new investments

BEIJING BO WEI ZHI HONG INVESTMENT CO LTD

No. A23 Huangsi Street, Deshen
1501-01, 15F, Building 1
Beijing, China
Phone: 861082090086
Website: www.bwinvest.cn

Type of Firm
Private Equity Firm

Project Preferences

Type of Financing Preferred:
Balanced

Geographical Preferences

International Preferences:
China

Industry Preferences

In Medical/Health prefer:
Medical/Health

Additional Information
Year Founded: 2008
Current Activity Level : Actively seeking new investments

BEIJING BOPAI QINGTIAN MANAGEMENT CONSULTING CO LTD

Chaoyang District
Beijing, China

Type of Firm
Private Equity Firm

Project Preferences

Type of Financing Preferred:
Early Stage
Seed
Startup

Geographical Preferences

International Preferences:
China

Industry Preferences

In Communications prefer:
Entertainment

In Internet Specific prefer:
Internet

Additional Information

Year Founded: 2014
Current Activity Level : Actively seeking new investments

BEIJING BOSI CHENGUANG ASSET MANAGEMENT CO LTD

No. 46, Fucheng Road
Haiyu Trade Building
Beijing, China

Type of Firm
Private Equity Firm

Project Preferences

Type of Financing Preferred:
Leveraged Buyout
Balanced
Later Stage

Geographical Preferences

International Preferences:
China

Industry Preferences

In Communications prefer:
Telecommunications

In Business Serv. prefer:
Services

Additional Information

Year Founded: 2010
Current Activity Level : Actively seeking new investments

BEIJING CAPITAL DYNAMICS INVESTMENT MANAGEMENT CO LTD

Beijing Oriental Plaza
Room 806, Tower E3
Beijing, China 100738
Phone: 36108518 5701
Fax: 861085185701
Website: www.capdyn.com.cn

Type of Firm
Private Equity Firm

Association Membership
China Venture Capital Association

Project Preferences

Type of Financing Preferred:
Fund of Funds
Leveraged Buyout
Generalist PE
Balanced

Geographical Preferences

International Preferences:
China

Additional Information

Year Founded: 2009
Current Activity Level : Actively seeking new investments

BEIJING CAPITAL EQUITY INVESTMENT FUND MANAGEMENT CO LTD

Financial Street
Beijing, China

Management and Staff
Gang Ke, Partner

Type of Firm
Investment Management Firm

Project Preferences

Type of Financing Preferred:
Leveraged Buyout

Geographical Preferences

International Preferences:
China

Industry Preferences

In Industrial/Energy prefer:
Energy
Energy Conservation Relat
Environmental Related

Additional Information

Year Founded: 2011
Current Activity Level : Actively seeking new investments

BEIJING CAPITAL INVESTMENT CO LTD

No.69 Zi Zhu Yuan, Haidian Dt.
Room 1808, China Arsenal Tower
Beijing, China 100089
Phone: 86-10-6896-4800
Fax: 86-10-6896-4810
E-mail: bcvc@capitalvc.com
Website: www.capitalvc.com

Management and Staff
Shaojun Wang, President
Wenyi Lu, Vice President

Type of Firm
Private Equity Firm

Project Preferences

Type of Financing Preferred:
Balanced
Startup

Geographical Preferences

International Preferences:
China

Additional Information

Year Founded: 1998
Current Activity Level : Actively seeking new investments

BEIJING CAPITAL SCIENCE AND TECHNOLOGY GROUP CO LTD

No.13 Gaoliangqiao Xiejie
R302
Beijing, China 100037
Phone: 1068338940

Management and Staff
Jian Li, Vice President

Type of Firm
Government Affiliated Program

Project Preferences

Type of Financing Preferred:
Leveraged Buyout

Geographical Preferences

International Preferences:
China

Additional Information

Year Founded: 1983
Current Activity Level : Actively seeking new investments

BEIJING CENTURY WANTONG SCIENCE & TECHNOLOGY INVESTMENT CO.

Hepingli North Street
6th Floor, Building 2
Beijing, China 100 013
Phone: 86-10-84290666

Fax: 86-10-8429104
Website: www.yhjcgroup.com.cn

Type of Firm
Investment Management Firm

Project Preferences

Type of Financing Preferred:
Balanced

Geographical Preferences

International Preferences:
China

Additional Information
Year Founded: 2000
Current Activity Level : Actively seeking new investments

BEIJING CHINA BRIDGE INVESTMENT MANAGEMENT CO LTD

No.50, Liangmaqiao Road
Yansha Center Office Building
Beijing, China 100125
Phone: 861064646066
Fax: 861064624966
Website: chinabridgecapital.com

Type of Firm
Bank Affiliated

Project Preferences

Type of Financing Preferred:
Leveraged Buyout

Geographical Preferences

International Preferences:
China

Industry Preferences

In Internet Specific prefer:
Internet

Additional Information
Year Founded: 2004
Current Activity Level : Actively seeking new investments

BEIJING CHUANGKEBANG TECHNOLOGY INCUBATOR CO LTD

No. 18, Zhongguanchun Street
ZhongguancunInternet eduCenter
Beijing, China
Phone: 86108289-8007
Website: www.91maker.com

Type of Firm
Incubator/Development Program

Project Preferences

Type of Financing Preferred:
Balanced
Start-up Financing
Seed

Geographical Preferences

International Preferences:
China

Industry Preferences

In Communications prefer:
Entertainment

In Computer Software prefer:
Software

In Internet Specific prefer:
Internet
Ecommerce

In Consumer Related prefer:
Education Related

In Financial Services prefer:
Financial Services

Additional Information
Year Founded: 2013
Current Activity Level : Actively seeking new investments

BEIJING CHUN XIN CAPITAL MANAGEMENT CORP LTD

No. 14, South Liangmahe Road
Tayuanwaijiaobangong Bldg.
Beijing, China 100060
Phone: 861085322299
Fax: 861085322676
Website: www.ecitic.com

Management and Staff
Xiang Liu, Vice President

Type of Firm
Investment Management Firm

Project Preferences

Type of Financing Preferred:
Balanced

Geographical Preferences

International Preferences:
China

Industry Preferences

In Manufact. prefer:
Manufacturing

Additional Information
Year Founded: 2009
Capital Under Management: $48,300,000
Current Activity Level : Actively seeking new investments

BEIJING CHUNFENG SHILI INVESTMENT CENTER LP

Xueyuan Road, Haidian Dist.
Rm, 1-002, Changfang dongqu
Beijing, China

Type of Firm
Private Equity Firm

Project Preferences

Type of Financing Preferred:
Seed
Startup

Geographical Preferences

International Preferences:
China

Industry Preferences

In Medical/Health prefer:
Medical/Health

Additional Information
Year Founded: 2015
Capital Under Management: $18,202,000
Current Activity Level : Actively seeking new investments

BEIJING CHUXIN YUANJING INVESTMENT MANAGEMENT CO LTD

Zhonguancun Avenue Haidian
8F No.18
Beijing, China
Phone: 861085996899
Website: www.initialvc.com

Type of Firm
Private Equity Firm

Project Preferences

Type of Financing Preferred:
Early Stage

Geographical Preferences

International Preferences:
China

Industry Preferences

In Communications prefer:
Entertainment

In Internet Specific prefer:
Internet

In Medical/Health prefer:
Medical/Health

In Consumer Related prefer:
Consumer
Retail

In Financial Services prefer:
Financial Services

Additional Information
Year Founded: 2014
Current Activity Level : Actively seeking new investments

BEIJING CLUTURAL CENTER CONSTRUCTION DVLPMT FUND MGMT CO LTD

jiangtai Rd, Chaoyang
20F, Nuojin Center, No. A2
Beijing, China
Phone: 861056826999
Fax: 861056826998
Website: www.bccf.com.cn

Type of Firm
Government Affiliated Program

Project Preferences

Type of Financing Preferred:
Balanced

Geographical Preferences

International Preferences:
China

Industry Preferences

In Consumer Related prefer:
Entertainment and Leisure

Additional Information
Year Founded: 2015
Capital Under Management: $2,965,640,000
Current Activity Level : Actively seeking new investments

BEIJING COLLEGE VENTURE CAPITAL COMPANY, LTD.

Industry Exploit Miyun County
Beijing, China
Phone: 86-10-8909-9027
Fax: 86-10-8909-9523

Type of Firm
University Program

Association Membership
Venture Capital Association of Beijing (VCAB)

Project Preferences

Type of Financing Preferred:
Startup

Geographical Preferences

International Preferences:
China

Industry Preferences

In Industrial/Energy prefer:
Materials

In Other prefer:
Environment Responsible

Additional Information
Year Founded: 2000
Current Activity Level : Actively seeking new investments

BEIJING COMPREHENSIVE INVESTMENT INC

2 Dewaixinfeng Ave, ,Xicheng
12/F, Tiancheng Tech Bldg.
Beijing, China 100088
Phone: 86-10-82271
Fax: 86-10-82271

Type of Firm
Government Affiliated Program

Additional Information
Year Founded: 1999
Current Activity Level : Actively seeking new investments

BEIJING CORNERSTONE CAPITAL MANAGEMENT CO LTD

No. 10, Caihefang Road
Zhongguancun
Haidian, Beijing, China 100080
Website: www.bjjsfund.com.cn

Type of Firm
Private Equity Firm

Project Preferences

Type of Financing Preferred:
Expansion

Size of Investments Considered:
Min Size of Investment Considered (000s): $3,207
Max Size of Investment Considered (000s): $16,036

Geographical Preferences

International Preferences:
China

Industry Preferences

In Industrial/Energy prefer:
Environmental Related

In Transportation prefer:
Transportation

In Manufact. prefer:
Manufacturing

Additional Information
Year Founded: 2011
Capital Under Management: $4,800,000
Current Activity Level : Actively seeking new investments

BEIJING DINGXIN CAPITAL CO LTD

No. 33 Jinrong Street, Xicheng
C917, Tongtai Plaza
Beijing, China 100033
Phone: 861088087251
Fax: 861088088849
E-mail: postmaster@dxcapital.com.cn
Website: www.dxcapital.com.cn

Type of Firm
Private Equity Firm

Project Preferences

Type of Financing Preferred:
Early Stage
Expansion
Balanced

Geographical Preferences

International Preferences:
China

Industry Preferences

In Medical/Health prefer:
Medical/Health

In Consumer Related prefer:
Sports
Consumer Products

In Industrial/Energy prefer:
Energy
Materials

In Manufact. prefer:
Manufacturing

In Agr/Forestr/Fish prefer:
Agriculture related

Additional Information
Year Founded: 2008
Current Activity Level : Actively seeking new investments

BEIJING DONGFANG HONGDAO ASSET MANAGEMENT CO LTD

No.7 Dongsihuan North Road
205, No.1 Building
Beijing, China

Type of Firm
Investment Management Firm

Project Preferences

Type of Financing Preferred:
Early Stage

Geographical Preferences

International Preferences:
China

Industry Preferences

In Internet Specific prefer:
Internet

Additional Information
Year Founded: 2009
Current Activity Level : Actively seeking new investments

BEIJING DONGFANG YOULIAN INVESTMENT CONSULTING CO LTD

15 Jian Guo Rd., Chaoyang Dist
Room 7-907, No A1 BeiAn 1292
Beijing, China

Type of Firm
Private Equity Firm

Project Preferences

Type of Financing Preferred:
Leveraged Buyout
Early Stage

Geographical Preferences

International Preferences:
China

Industry Preferences

In Communications prefer:
Telecommunications

In Business Serv. prefer:
Media

Additional Information
Year Founded: 2013
Current Activity Level : Actively seeking new investments

BEIJING DREAM LINK TECHNOLOGY CO LTD

No.39 E. 3rd Ring, Middle Rd.
27/F,Bldg.9,Jianwai SOHO
Beijing, China
Phone: 861059003909
Website: www.dreamlinker.cn

Type of Firm
Incubator/Development Program

Project Preferences

Type of Financing Preferred:
Seed
Startup

Geographical Preferences

International Preferences:
China

Additional Information
Year Founded: 2015
Current Activity Level : Actively seeking new investments

BEIJING E-TOWN INTERNATIONAL INVESTMENT & DEVELOPMENT CO LTD

2 Jingyuan N. St., ETDZ
Blk.61,BDA Intl Enterprise Ave
Beijing, China
Phone: 864008325066
Website: www.etowncapital.com

Type of Firm
Government Affiliated Program

Project Preferences

Type of Financing Preferred:
Fund of Funds
Leveraged Buyout
Balanced

Geographical Preferences

International Preferences:
China

Additional Information
Year Founded: 2009
Capital Under Management: $79,440,000
Current Activity Level : Actively seeking new investments

BEIJING ELECTRICITY INVESTMENT COMPANY, LTD.

No.2A Tianyin Mansion
FuXinMeng South Street
Beijing, China
Phone: 86-10-6641-1571
Fax: 86-10-6641-1104

Type of Firm
Private Equity Firm

Association Membership
Venture Capital Association of Beijing (VCAB)

Project Preferences

Type of Financing Preferred:
Balanced

Geographical Preferences

International Preferences:
China

Additional Information
Year Founded: 1993
Current Activity Level : Actively seeking new investments

BEIJING EXTENSIVE AND PROFOUND INFORMATION TECHNOLOGY CO LTD

Jiasheng Center
A-19, Dongsanhuan North Road
Beijing, China 100125
Phone: 86-10-58413138
E-mail: service@rootscap.com

Management and Staff
Lizhi Ran, Founder

Type of Firm
Private Equity Firm

Project Preferences

Type of Financing Preferred:
Seed
Startup

Size of Investments Considered:
Min Size of Investment Considered (000s): $152
Max Size of Investment Considered (000s): $3,048

Geographical Preferences

International Preferences:
China

Industry Preferences

In Medical/Health prefer:
Medical/Health

In Consumer Related prefer:
Consumer

Additional Information
Year Founded: 2013
Current Activity Level : Actively seeking new investments

BEIJING FAITH CAPITAL CO LTD

No.5 Guanghua Road
2202,Centry Caifu Center West
Beijing, China 100020
Phone: 861065847688
Fax: 861085875517
E-mail: info@faith-capital.com
Website: www.faith-capital.com

Type of Firm
Private Equity Firm

Project Preferences

Type of Financing Preferred:
Balanced

Geographical Preferences

International Preferences:
China

Industry Preferences

In Industrial/Energy prefer:
Energy

In Financial Services prefer:
Financial Services
Real Estate

Additional Information
Year Founded: 2014
Capital Under Management: $33,038,000
Current Activity Level : Actively seeking new investments

BEIJING FELLOW PARTNERS INVESTMENT MANAGEMENT LTD

Jianguomenwai Street, Chaoyang
2108B, Twin Tower Mansion
Beijing, China
Phone: 861051208266
Website: www.fellowcap.com

Type of Firm
Private Equity Firm

Project Preferences

Type of Financing Preferred:
Balanced

Geographical Preferences

International Preferences:
China

Industry Preferences

In Internet Specific prefer:
Internet

In Medical/Health prefer:
Medical/Health

In Financial Services prefer:
Financial Services

Additional Information
Year Founded: 2015
Capital Under Management: $3,000,000,000
Current Activity Level : Actively seeking new investments

BEIJING FENGBO HUIFU INVESTMENT MANAGEMENT CO LTD

Haidian District
Beijing, China 100080
Phone: 861082604563
Fax: 861082604563
Website: www.fengbocapital.com

Type of Firm
Investment Management Firm

Project Preferences

Type of Financing Preferred:
Balanced

Geographical Preferences

International Preferences:
China

Industry Preferences

In Communications prefer:
Telecommunications

In Computer Hardware prefer:
Integrated Turnkey System

In Biotechnology prefer:
Biotechnology

In Industrial/Energy prefer:
Energy

In Business Serv. prefer:
Media

Additional Information
Year Founded: 2014
Current Activity Level : Actively seeking new investments

BEIJING FLOURISH LIBRA VENTURE CAPITAL CO LTD

237, Chaoyang N Road, Chaoyang
Rm 2208, Fuxing International
Beijing, China 100020
Phone: 861059770939
Fax: 861059770929
Website: www.libravc.com

Other Offices
No. 122, Shuguang Road
Rm 803, Tower C, Shimao Center Plaza
Hangzhou, China
Phone: 8657187882122
Fax: 8657187882122

Management and Staff
Tinghe Chen, Managing Partner
Yang Xu, President

Type of Firm
Private Equity Firm

Project Preferences

Type of Financing Preferred:
Fund of Funds
Early Stage

Geographical Preferences

International Preferences:
China

Additional Information
Year Founded: 2010
Capital Under Management: $30,349,000
Current Activity Level : Actively seeking new investments

BEIJING FORISE ASSETS MANAGEMENT CO LTD

Jian Guo Men Wai Ave.
F38, Blk.A, IFC Building
Beijing, China 100022
Phone: 861059262266
Fax: 861059262277
E-mail: fh@foriseassets.com
Website: www.foriseassets.com

Type of Firm
Investment Management Firm

Project Preferences

Type of Financing Preferred:
Expansion

Industry Preferences

In Communications prefer:
Telecommunications

In Business Serv. prefer:
Media

Additional Information
Year Founded: 2010
Current Activity Level : Actively seeking new investments

BEIJING FUNDTURN INVESTMENT CO LTD

No.19, Zhongguancun Street
The Gate City Mall
Beijing, China
Phone: 861082607546
Website: www.fundturn.com

Type of Firm
Private Equity Firm

Project Preferences

Type of Financing Preferred:
Leveraged Buyout

Geographical Preferences

International Preferences:
China

Industry Preferences

In Communications prefer:
Telecommunications

In Medical/Health prefer:
Medical/Health
Drug/Equipmt Delivery

In Consumer Related prefer:
Consumer

In Industrial/Energy prefer:
Energy

In Business Serv. prefer:
Media

Additional Information
Year Founded: 2007
Current Activity Level : Actively seeking new investments

BEIJING GOLD FOUNT VENTURE CAPITAL CO LTD

17 Financial Str.,Xicheng Dist
6F, Bank of Beijing Building
Beijing, China 100140
Phone: 861066273888
Fax: 861066273706
E-mail: bj@gfvc.cn
Website: www.gfvc.cn

Type of Firm
Private Equity Firm

Association Membership
Venture Capital Association of Beijing (VCAB)

Project Preferences

Type of Financing Preferred:
Leveraged Buyout
Expansion
Later Stage
Acquisition

Geographical Preferences

International Preferences:
China

Industry Preferences

In Biotechnology prefer:
Genetic Engineering

In Medical/Health prefer:
Pharmaceuticals

In Industrial/Energy prefer:
Energy
Oil and Gas Exploration

In Financial Services prefer:
Financial Services
Insurance

Additional Information
Year Founded: 2006
Current Activity Level : Actively seeking new investments

BEIJING GOLDEN GROWTH INVESTMENT & MANAGEMENT CO LTD

No. 1 Zhongguancun East Road
Room 303, Chuangye Building
Beijing, China 100084
Phone: 861058727622
Fax: 861088223062

Other Offices
257 Des Voeux Road, Central
3/F, Kam Sang Building
Hong Kong, Hong Kong
Phone: 85225202727
Fax: 85225202336

Management and Staff
Winnie Li, Partner

Type of Firm
Private Equity Firm

Project Preferences

Type of Financing Preferred:
Balanced

Geographical Preferences

International Preferences:
China

Additional Information
Year Founded: 2007
Current Activity Level : Actively seeking new investments

BEIJING GRIT INVESTMENT MANAGEMENT CO LTD

798 Art District,Chaoyang Dist
F03-6-3, Qixing Middle St.,
Beijing, China
Website: www.gritvc.com

Other Offices
Qianwan Road 1
Room 201, Building A, No.1
Shenzhen, China

Type of Firm
Private Equity Firm

Project Preferences

Type of Financing Preferred:
Expansion
Seed
Startup

Geographical Preferences

United States Preferences:
All U.S.

International Preferences:
China

Industry Preferences

In Communications prefer:
Telecommunications

In Consumer Related prefer:
Consumer

In Business Serv. prefer:
Services
Media

Additional Information
Year Founded: 2015
Current Activity Level : Actively seeking new investments

BEIJING GUAN HUI CENTURY EQUITY INVESTMENT FUND CO LTD

No.11 Dongzhimen South Road
25F, A, Zhonghui Plaza
Beijing, China 100007
Phone: 861050928999
Fax: 861053502188
Website: ghsjfund.com

Type of Firm
Private Equity Firm

Project Preferences

Type of Financing Preferred:
Balanced

Geographical Preferences

International Preferences:
China

Additional Information
Year Founded: 2015
Current Activity Level : Actively seeking new investments

BEIJING GUANGNENG INVESTMENT FUND MANAGEMENT CO LTD

27 North 4th Ring Middle Road
2712, Pangudaguan A tower
Beijing, China
Phone: 861059393818
Fax: 86105939860
Website: www.gnfund.cn

Type of Firm
Private Equity Firm

Project Preferences

Type of Financing Preferred:
Leveraged Buyout

Geographical Preferences

International Preferences:
China

Industry Preferences

In Industrial/Energy prefer:
Coal Related

In Financial Services prefer:
Real Estate

In Agr/Forestr/Fish prefer:
Agriculture related

Additional Information
Year Founded: 2013
Current Activity Level : Actively seeking new investments

BEIJING GUIGE ANGEL INVESTMENT MANAGEMENT CO LTD

Yuanyang Guanghua Intl, Chaoya
1209, Blcok C
Beijing, China
Website: www.prestigeangel.com

Type of Firm
Private Equity Firm

Project Preferences

Type of Financing Preferred:
Early Stage
Seed
Startup

Geographical Preferences

International Preferences:
China

Industry Preferences

In Communications prefer:
Telecommunications
Media and Entertainment

In Computer Software prefer:
Artificial Intelligence

In Medical/Health prefer:
Medical/Health

Additional Information
Year Founded: 2015
Current Activity Level : Actively seeking new investments

BEIJING GUOHENG TECHNOLOGY GROUP CO LTD

Room 40419 Comity Hotel
Beijing, China
Phone: 86-10-8841-7748
Fax: 86-10-6871-1242

Type of Firm
Private Equity Firm

Association Membership
Venture Capital Association of Beijing (VCAB)

Project Preferences

Type of Financing Preferred:
Expansion
Startup

Geographical Preferences

International Preferences:
China

Industry Preferences

In Communications prefer:
Telecommunications

In Computer Software prefer:
Software

In Biotechnology prefer:
Biotechnology

In Medical/Health prefer:
Medical/Health

Additional Information
Year Founded: 1994
Current Activity Level : Actively seeking new investments

BEIJING GUOJU VENTURE CAPITAL CO LTD

#3 Jia, Yongan East Li
22/F, Tongyong Guiji Building
Beijing, China 100022
Phone: 861058795511
Fax: 861058793899
Website: www.guojuvc.com

Type of Firm
Private Equity Firm

Project Preferences

Type of Financing Preferred:
Leveraged Buyout
Balanced
Later Stage

Geographical Preferences

International Preferences:
China

Industry Preferences

In Biotechnology prefer:
Biotechnology

Additional Information
Year Founded: 2011
Current Activity Level : Actively seeking new investments

BEIJING GUOTAI VENTURE CAPITAL FUND MANAGEMENT CO LTD

No. 9 Financial Street A
905 Financial Street Center
Beijing, China 100033

Phone: 86-10-8885-4918
Fax: 86-10-8885-6409

Type of Firm
Private Equity Firm

Project Preferences

Type of Financing Preferred:
Balanced

Geographical Preferences

International Preferences:
China

Additional Information
Year Founded: 2009
Current Activity Level : Actively seeking new investments

BEIJING HAOXIANG CAPITAL MANAGEMENT CO LTD

Jianguomenwai Avenue
10F, Baogang Building
Beijing, China 100022
Phone: 861057610686
Fax: 861057610686
Website: www.dreamflyc.com

Type of Firm
Private Equity Firm

Project Preferences

Type of Financing Preferred:
Balanced

Geographical Preferences

International Preferences:
China

Additional Information
Year Founded: 2015
Current Activity Level : Actively seeking new investments

BEIJING HEPU YUNZHOU INVESTMENT MANAGEMENT CO LTD

No. A28, Xinxi Road, Haidian D
No. 155, Room 06C, 6F,, Buildi
Beijing, China 100088

Type of Firm
Investment Management Firm

Project Preferences

Type of Financing Preferred:
Balanced

Geographical Preferences

International Preferences:
China

Additional Information
Year Founded: 2015
Current Activity Level : Actively seeking new investments

BEIJING HEXIN DONGLI INVESTMENT MANAGEMENT CO LTD

No. 50, North of 3rd Ring Road
Beijing, China 100044
Phone: 861088418291
Fax: 861068317742
Website: www.hxvc.com.cn

Management and Staff
Hanliang Hu, Managing Partner
Wei Zhu, Vice President
Zhenglin Jiang, Vice President

Type of Firm
Private Equity Firm

Association Membership
Venture Capital Association of Beijing (VCAB)

Project Preferences

Type of Financing Preferred:
Balanced

Geographical Preferences

International Preferences:
China

Industry Preferences

In Communications prefer:
Telecommunications

In Biotechnology prefer:
Biotechnology

In Medical/Health prefer:
Pharmaceuticals

In Consumer Related prefer:
Consumer Products

In Industrial/Energy prefer:
Alternative Energy
Advanced Materials
Machinery

In Agr/Forestr/Fish prefer:
Agriculture related

Additional Information
Year Founded: 2010
Current Activity Level : Actively seeking new investments

BEIJING HOLCH INVESTMENT MANAGEMENT, LTD.

Beijing Wangjing Street
Chaoyang District, No. 10
Beijing, China
Phone: 01084770877
E-mail: hcc@holchcapital.com
Website: www.holchcapital.com

Management and Staff
Jiang Su, Co-Founder
Jianhua Zhu, Co-Founder
Jiaxing Li, Vice President
Liangyi Jia, Vice President
Yu Tong, Vice President

Type of Firm
Private Equity Firm

Project Preferences

Type of Financing Preferred:
Generalist PE
Balanced

Geographical Preferences

International Preferences:
China

Industry Preferences

In Internet Specific prefer:
Internet

In Financial Services prefer:
Real Estate

Additional Information
Year Founded: 2012
Capital Under Management: $10,000,000,000
Current Activity Level : Actively seeking new investments

BEIJING HONDEN CAPITAL CO LTD

Jianguomen Outer St., Chaoyang
28F, Block D, Central Internat
Beijing, China
Phone: 861080440886
Website: www.hdcap.com.cn

Type of Firm
Private Equity Firm

Project Preferences

Type of Financing Preferred:
Generalist PE

Geographical Preferences

International Preferences:
China

Industry Preferences

In Communications prefer:
Telecommunications

In Internet Specific prefer:
Internet

In Medical/Health prefer:
Medical/Health

In Industrial/Energy prefer:
Energy Conservation Relat

In Business Serv. prefer:
Media

Additional Information
Year Founded: 2010
Capital Under Management: $3,000,000,000
Current Activity Level : Actively seeking new investments

BEIJING HOSEN CAPITAL MANAGEMENT CENTER LP

Jianguomenwai Avenue
Suite 2508, Twin Towers W
Beijing, China 100022
Phone: 861058287188
Fax: 861065676087
Website: www.hosencapital.com

Other Offices
Pudongnan Road
Suite 1708, Huaxia Bank Tower
Shanghai, China 200120
Phone: 862151695033
Fax: 862151697259

Fuhua 1st Road
Suite 620, Tower A Guoji Shanghui Bldg.
Shenzhen, China 518048
Phone: 8675523832878
Fax: 8675523832848

Management and Staff
Hang Wang, Partner
Tianli Zhang, Partner

Type of Firm
Private Equity Firm

Project Preferences

Type of Financing Preferred:
Balanced

Geographical Preferences

International Preferences:
China

Industry Preferences

In Biotechnology prefer:
Biotechnology

In Consumer Related prefer:
Consumer
Food/Beverage

In Industrial/Energy prefer:
Alternative Energy
Advanced Materials

In Financial Services prefer:
Financial Services

In Business Serv. prefer:
Distribution

In Agr/Forestr/Fish prefer:
Agribusiness
Agriculture related

Additional Information
Year Founded: 2010
Capital Under Management: $791,132,000
Current Activity Level : Actively seeking new investments

BEIJING HUACHUANG PROPERTY INVESTMENT CO LTD

North 4th Ring, Haidian Dist.
7/F,Yingu Mansion, No.9 W. Rd.
Beijing, China 100080
Phone: 861082525299
Fax: 861082525299
Website: www.hczycapital.com

Type of Firm
Investment Management Firm

Project Preferences

Type of Financing Preferred:
Expansion
Seed
Startup

Geographical Preferences

International Preferences:
China

Industry Preferences

In Internet Specific prefer:
Internet

In Medical/Health prefer:
Health Services

In Consumer Related prefer:
Consumer

Additional Information
Year Founded: 2010
Capital Under Management: $1,000,000,000
Current Activity Level : Actively seeking new investments

BEIJING HUALIN HECHUANG INVESTMENT MANAGEMENT CO LTD

No.8 North of 2nd Haidian Road
Rm 506 Zhongguancun soho bldg
Beijing, China 100080
Phone: 861059718322
Fax: 861059718367
Website: www.hlvc.com.cn

Management and Staff
Min Zhou, Partner

Type of Firm
Investment Management Firm

Project Preferences

Type of Financing Preferred:
Expansion

Geographical Preferences

International Preferences:
China

Industry Preferences

In Internet Specific prefer:
Ecommerce

In Medical/Health prefer:
Medical/Health
Health Services

In Consumer Related prefer:
Consumer Products
Consumer Services

In Industrial/Energy prefer:
Energy
Energy Conservation Relat
Advanced Materials

In Business Serv. prefer:
Media

In Manufact. prefer:
Manufacturing

In Other prefer:
Environment Responsible

Additional Information
Year Founded: 2008
Current Activity Level : Actively seeking new investments

BEIJING HUINONG CAPITAL MANAGEMENT CO LTD

No. 105 Yaojiayuan Road
Wanqi Holdings Building
Beijing, China 100025
Phone: 86-10-5962-3322

Fax: 86-10-5962-3071
E-mail: hn@huinongfund.com
Website: www.huinongfund.com

Management and Staff

Guixin Dong, Vice President
Lidong Wei, President
Luping Zhao, Vice President
Sheng Cao, Vice President
Zhigang Xie, Vice President
Zhongqiu Zhao, Vice President

Type of Firm

Private Equity Firm

Project Preferences

Type of Financing Preferred:
Leveraged Buyout
Expansion
Mezzanine
Later Stage

Geographical Preferences

International Preferences:
China

Industry Preferences

In Biotechnology prefer:
Biotechnology

In Medical/Health prefer:
Medical/Health

In Consumer Related prefer:
Consumer
Food/Beverage

In Industrial/Energy prefer:
Energy
Materials

In Financial Services prefer:
Financial Services
Real Estate

In Agr/Forestr/Fish prefer:
Agribusiness
Agriculture related

Additional Information

Year Founded: 2009
Capital Under Management: $407,088,000
Current Activity Level : Actively seeking new investments

BEIJING INDUSTRIAL DEVELOPMENT INVESTMENT MANAGEMENT CO LTD

Building 19, Fukai, BlockB 9th
Beijing Financial Street
Beijing, Xicheng District, China 100027
Fax: 86-10-85235

Type of Firm

Private Equity Firm

Project Preferences

Type of Financing Preferred:
Balanced

Geographical Preferences

International Preferences:
China

Additional Information

Year Founded: 2010
Current Activity Level : Actively seeking new investments

BEIJING JIANGUANG ASSET MANAGEMENT CO LTD

No 21, Jianguomen Wai Ave
Rm 302, BJ Intl Club Office
Beijing, China 100020
Phone: 861085326007
Fax: 861085325935

Type of Firm

Government Affiliated Program

Project Preferences

Type of Financing Preferred:
Leveraged Buyout
Acquisition

Additional Information

Year Founded: 2014
Current Activity Level : Actively seeking new investments

BEIJING JIKE MENGGONGCHANG VENTURE CAPITAL CENTER (L.P.)

No.3, Xijing Road, Badachu
6833,3/F, Bdg3, High Tech Zone
Beijing, China

Management and Staff

Feng Wang, Founder
Jin Shang, Partner
Tao Jiang, Partner
Xin Feng, Partner

Type of Firm

Private Equity Firm

Project Preferences

Type of Financing Preferred:
Early Stage

Geographical Preferences

International Preferences:
China

Industry Preferences

In Communications prefer:
Entertainment

In Internet Specific prefer:
Internet

Additional Information

Year Founded: 2011
Capital Under Management: $2,276,000
Current Activity Level : Actively seeking new investments

BEIJING JILEI VENTURE CAPITAL INVESTMENT CO LTD

No.1 Dong 3rd Ring Middle Road
World Financial Center
Beijing, China 100020
Phone: 861059309966
Fax: 861056767790
Website: www.jileivc.com

Type of Firm

Private Equity Firm

Project Preferences

Type of Financing Preferred:
Leveraged Buyout
Early Stage
Expansion

Geographical Preferences

International Preferences:
China

Industry Preferences

In Medical/Health prefer:
Medical/Health
Pharmaceuticals

Additional Information

Year Founded: 2009
Current Activity Level : Actively seeking new investments

BEIJING JIN GUAN INVESTMENT CO LTD

No.801 Unit 3 Meihui Mansion
58 Dongzhong Street
Beijing, China
Phone: 86-10-6554-2710
Fax: 86-10-6554-2711

Type of Firm
Private Equity Firm

Association Membership
Venture Capital Association of Beijing (VCAB)

Project Preferences

Type of Financing Preferred:
Expansion

Geographical Preferences

International Preferences:
China

Industry Preferences

In Communications prefer:
Telecommunications

In Computer Software prefer:
Software

In Semiconductor/Electr prefer:
Electronics

In Biotechnology prefer:
Biotechnology

In Medical/Health prefer:
Medical/Health

Additional Information
Year Founded: 2000
Current Activity Level : Actively seeking new investments

BEIJING JINCHANG INVESTMENT & CONSULTATION CO LTD

17 Fuhua Mansion
8 Chaoyangmeng North Street
Beijing, China
Phone: 86-10-6554-1306
Fax: 85-10-6554-1678

Type of Firm
Private Equity Firm

Association Membership
Venture Capital Association of Beijing (VCAB)

Project Preferences

Type of Financing Preferred:
Startup

Geographical Preferences

International Preferences:
China

Industry Preferences

In Communications prefer:
Telecommunications

In Computer Software prefer:
Software

In Medical/Health prefer:
Medical/Health

Additional Information
Year Founded: 1999
Current Activity Level : Actively seeking new investments

BEIJING JINGANG VENTURE CAPITAL ADVISER CO LTD

Room 204 Taihua Commerce
13 Huayuan Street
Beijing, China
Phone: 86-10-6207-3380
Fax: 86-10-6207-3381

Type of Firm
Private Equity Firm

Association Membership
Venture Capital Association of Beijing (VCAB)

Project Preferences

Type of Financing Preferred:
Expansion
Startup

Geographical Preferences

International Preferences:
China

Industry Preferences

In Medical/Health prefer:
Medical/Health

In Industrial/Energy prefer:
Materials

Additional Information
Year Founded: 2000
Current Activity Level : Actively seeking new investments

BEIJING JINHUIFENG INVESTMENT MANAGEMENT CO LTD

Wangjing East Park, Chaoyang
RongkeWangjing Center
Beijing, China
Website: www.jhfinv.com

Type of Firm
Private Equity Firm

Project Preferences

Type of Financing Preferred:
Generalist PE

Geographical Preferences

International Preferences:
China

Additional Information
Year Founded: 2010
Current Activity Level : Actively seeking new investments

BEIJING JINKE HIGHTECH & INNOVATION VENTURES CO LTD

Chaoyang District
Beijing, China

Type of Firm
Private Equity Firm

Project Preferences

Type of Financing Preferred:
Expansion
Balanced

Geographical Preferences

International Preferences:
China

Industry Preferences

In Communications prefer:
Telecommunications

In Medical/Health prefer:
Medical/Health

In Business Serv. prefer:
Media

In Other prefer:
Environment Responsible

Additional Information
Year Founded: 2014
Capital Under Management: $19,160,000
Current Activity Level : Actively seeking new investments

BEIJING JUNHUI VENTURE CAPITAL CENTER

No. 2 Kexueyuan South Road
10th Floor, Rongkezixun Center
Beijing, China 100190
Phone: 861062509116
Fax: 861062509100

Type of Firm
Private Equity Firm

Project Preferences

Type of Financing Preferred:
Leveraged Buyout

Geographical Preferences

International Preferences:
China

Additional Information
Year Founded: 2008
Capital Under Management: $16,300,000
Current Activity Level : Actively seeking new investments

BEIJING JUXIN TAIHE ENERGY INVESTMENT FUND MANAGEMENT CO

C/o, CITIC Trust
6, Xinyuannan Road
Beijing, China 100004
Phone: 861084861324
Fax: 861084861385
E-mail: citict@citic.com
Website: qyxy.baic.gov.cn

Type of Firm
Service Provider

Project Preferences

Type of Financing Preferred:
Balanced

Geographical Preferences

International Preferences:
China

Industry Preferences

In Industrial/Energy prefer:
Coal Related

Additional Information
Year Founded: 2011
Current Activity Level : Actively seeking new investments

BEIJING KAIFU SHENGSHI INVESTMENT MANAGEMENT CO LTD

West Dawang Rd, Chaoyang
Room 2010, Lanbao Intl Center
Beijing, China
Phone: 861065820595
Fax: 861065820595
Website: www.keysfund.com

Type of Firm
Private Equity Advisor or Fund of Funds

Project Preferences

Type of Financing Preferred:
Fund of Funds

Geographical Preferences

International Preferences:
China

Industry Preferences

In Communications prefer:
Communications and Media
Telecommunications
Media and Entertainment

In Internet Specific prefer:
Internet
Ecommerce

In Medical/Health prefer:
Medical/Health

In Consumer Related prefer:
Retail
Consumer Services

In Industrial/Energy prefer:
Materials

Additional Information
Year Founded: 2011
Current Activity Level : Actively seeking new investments

BEIJING KAIXING CAPITAL MANAGEMENT CO LTD

No. 1, East Chang'an Avenue
Tower C1, Oriental Plaza
Beijing, China

Type of Firm
Private Equity Firm

Industry Preferences

In Business Serv. prefer:
Services
Media

Additional Information
Year Founded: 2013
Current Activity Level : Actively seeking new investments

BEIJING LAN XUE TECHNOLOGY VENTURE CAPITAL CO LTD

No. 66 South Litu Road
Room 506 Jianwei Building
Beijing, China
Phone: 86-10-6801-2922

Type of Firm
Private Equity Firm

Project Preferences

Type of Financing Preferred:
Balanced

Geographical Preferences

International Preferences:
China

Industry Preferences

In Biotechnology prefer:
Biotechnology

In Industrial/Energy prefer:
Materials
Environmental Related

In Agr/Forestr/Fish prefer:
Agriculture related

Additional Information
Year Founded: 1999
Current Activity Level : Actively seeking new investments

BEIJING LANGMAFENG VENTURE CAPITAL MANAGEMENT CO LTD

No.8, North 2nd Street
Room 1507
Beijing, China 100080
Phone: 861052486519
Fax: 861062680700
Website: www.lmfvc.com

Management and Staff
Xianhong Liang, President

Type of Firm
Private Equity Firm

Association Membership
Venture Capital Association of Beijing (VCAB)

Project Preferences

Type of Financing Preferred:
Balanced

Geographical Preferences

International Preferences:
China

Industry Preferences

In Communications prefer:
Wireless Communications

In Consumer Related prefer:
Retail
Consumer Services

In Industrial/Energy prefer:
Energy
Machinery

In Financial Services prefer:
Financial Services

In Business Serv. prefer:
Media

Additional Information
Year Founded: 2008
Current Activity Level : Actively seeking new investments

BEIJING LAPAMCAPITAL MANAGEMENT CONSULTING CENTER

No.27, Financial Street
Tower B, Investment Square
Beijing, China

Type of Firm
Private Equity Firm

Project Preferences

Type of Financing Preferred:
Balanced

Geographical Preferences

International Preferences:
China

Industry Preferences

In Biotechnology prefer:
Biotechnology

In Medical/Health prefer:
Medical/Health
Medical Therapeutics

Additional Information
Year Founded: 2010
Current Activity Level : Actively seeking new investments

BEIJING LEBANG LECHENG VENTURE INVESTMENT MANAGEMET CO LTD

No.16, Huilongguan West Ave.
R601, Longguan Business Center
Beijing, China 102208
Phone: 861053311901
E-mail: lebanglecheng@126.com
Website: www.leventure.cn

Management and Staff
Jichang Qiao, Chief Executive Officer

Type of Firm
Private Equity Firm

Project Preferences

Type of Financing Preferred:
Early Stage
Seed
Startup

Geographical Preferences

International Preferences:
China

Industry Preferences

In Computer Software prefer:
Software

In Internet Specific prefer:
Internet

In Biotechnology prefer:
Biotechnology

In Medical/Health prefer:
Medical Therapeutics
Pharmaceuticals

Additional Information
Year Founded: 2013
Current Activity Level : Actively seeking new investments

BEIJING LEYO CAPITAL MANAGEMENT CO LTD

Shangdi
Beijing, China
Website: www.leyocapital.com

Type of Firm
Private Equity Firm

Project Preferences

Type of Financing Preferred:
Early Stage
Start-up Financing
Seed

Geographical Preferences

International Preferences:
China

Industry Preferences

In Communications prefer:
Entertainment

In Internet Specific prefer:
Internet

Additional Information
Year Founded: 2015
Current Activity Level : Actively seeking new investments

BEIJING LF CAPITAL MANAGEMENT LTD

1, East Chang'an Street
1103, 11F , Tower W1
Beijing, China 100738
Phone: 86 10 8518 0809
Fax: 86 10 8518 0809
Website: www.lfcapital.com.cn

Type of Firm
Private Equity Firm

Project Preferences

Type of Financing Preferred:
Balanced

Geographical Preferences

International Preferences:
China

Industry Preferences

In Internet Specific prefer:
Internet

In Medical/Health prefer:
Medical/Health

In Consumer Related prefer:
Education Related

In Industrial/Energy prefer:
Energy Conservation Relat

In Other prefer:
Environment Responsible

Additional Information
Year Founded: 2014
Current Activity Level : Actively seeking new investments

BEIJING LIANDO INVESTMENT GROUP CO LTD

38 Longshan Road
5 Guli Garden
Xiaolan, China
Phone: 86-760-2102
Website: www.liando.cn

Type of Firm
Investment Management Firm

Additional Information
Year Founded: 2001
Current Activity Level : Actively seeking new investments

BEIJING MACRO VISION VENTURE CAPITAL MANAGEMENT CONSULTANCY

No.8 Haidian North 2nd Road
Rm 607, Haidan
Beijing, China 100080
Phone: 861059733359
Fax: 861059733359
Website: www.boguancapital.com

Management and Staff
Helen Zhao, Partner
Ivy Huang, Partner
Kai Zhang, Partner
Linda Lee, Partner
Shengyuan Shan, Partner

Type of Firm
Private Equity Firm

Project Preferences

Type of Financing Preferred:
Early Stage
Expansion
Balanced
Later Stage
Startup

Geographical Preferences

International Preferences:
China

Industry Preferences

In Communications prefer:
Communications and Media
Telecommunications

In Consumer Related prefer:
Retail
Consumer Products

In Industrial/Energy prefer:
Alternative Energy
Industrial Products
Advanced Materials

Additional Information
Year Founded: 2010
Capital Under Management: $6,540,000
Current Activity Level : Actively seeking new investments

BEIJING MAOXIN INVESTMENT MANAGEMENT CO LTD

Tongzhou District
157, Rixin East Road
Beijing, China

Type of Firm
Private Equity Firm

Project Preferences

Type of Financing Preferred:
Balanced

Geographical Preferences

International Preferences:
China

Industry Preferences

In Communications prefer:
Telecommunications
Media and Entertainment

In Medical/Health prefer:
Medical/Health

In Manufact. prefer:
Manufacturing

In Agr/Forestr/Fish prefer:
Agriculture related

Additional Information
Year Founded: 2013
Current Activity Level : Actively seeking new investments

BEIJING MILLENNIUM CAPITAL SERVICES CO LTD

6-01/E CITIC Building 19
JianGuomen Wai Street
Beijing, China 100004
Phone: 86-10-8526-2728
Fax: 86-10-6500-7699
E-mail: services@mschina.com
Website: www.mcschina.com

Other Offices
13th Floor, Room 8
150 Fu Hsin North Road
Taipei, Taiwan
Phone: 886-2-2713-4321
Fax: 886-2-2716-3731

No. 79 An Qing Road
He Fei
An Hui, China 230001
Phone: 86-551-267-5222
Fax: 86-551-267-7793

Unit 1106-7, Lippo Sun Plaza
28 Canton Road, Tsimshatsui
Kowloon, Hong Kong
Phone: 852-2375-0085
Fax: 852-2375-1601

20th Floor, Shartex Plaza
88 Zun Yi Road South
Shanghai, China 200336
Phone: 86-21-6219-6908
Fax: 86-21-6208-9555

Type of Firm
Bank Affiliated

Association Membership
Venture Capital Association of Beijing (VCAB)

Project Preferences

Type of Financing Preferred:
Balanced

Geographical Preferences

International Preferences:
China

Industry Preferences

In Communications prefer:
Telecommunications

In Medical/Health prefer:
Medical/Health

Additional Information
Year Founded: 2000
Current Activity Level : Actively seeking new investments

BEIJING MINGJIA INVESTMENT MANAGEMENT CO LTD

Chaoyang District
1/F, Block B, Tonghui Mansion
Beijing, China 100025

Type of Firm
Private Equity Firm

Project Preferences

Type of Financing Preferred:
Early Stage
Seed
Startup

Geographical Preferences

International Preferences:
China

Industry Preferences

In Communications prefer:
Media and Entertainment

In Consumer Related prefer:
Consumer

In Business Serv. prefer:
Services

Additional Information

Year Founded: 2015
Current Activity Level: Actively seeking new investments

BEIJING N5 CAPITAL CONSULTING CO LTD

DongCheng District
No.16 Jia, BeiXinCang Hutong
Beijing, China
Phone: 861064457337
Fax: 861064457397
E-mail: info@n5capital.com
Website: www.n5capital.com

Other Offices

PO Box 309
Ugland House
Grand Cayman, Cayman Islands KY1-1104

Management and Staff

Weiguo Zhao, Founder

Type of Firm

Private Equity Firm

Project Preferences

Type of Financing Preferred:
Early Stage

Geographical Preferences

International Preferences:
China

Industry Preferences

In Internet Specific prefer:
Internet

In Medical/Health prefer:
Medical/Health

In Consumer Related prefer:
Consumer Products

In Business Serv. prefer:
Media

Additional Information

Year Founded: 2012
Current Activity Level: Actively seeking new investments

BEIJING ORIENTAL-FOCUS INVESTMENT MANAGEMENT CO LTD

No. 19 Financial Street
1005, Fukai Building B
Beijing, China 100033
Phone: 86-10-6657-4898
Fax: 86-10-6657-4889

Management and Staff

Qingyun Peng, Partner
Zhiyuan Peng, President

Type of Firm

Private Equity Firm

Project Preferences

Type of Financing Preferred:
Early Stage
Balanced
Later Stage
Seed

Geographical Preferences

International Preferences:
China

Industry Preferences

In Communications prefer:
Communications and Media

In Biotechnology prefer:
Biotechnology

In Medical/Health prefer:
Medical/Health

In Consumer Related prefer:
Consumer

In Industrial/Energy prefer:
Energy
Environmental Related

Additional Information

Year Founded: 2010
Current Activity Level: Actively seeking new investments

BEIJING PACIFIC UNION TECHNOLOGY VENTURE FUND CO LTD

Fuwai Street, Xicheng District
25/F, Sichuan Building
Beijing, China
Phone: 86-10-88382295
Fax: 86-10-68365354
Website: www.bptv.com.cn

Type of Firm

Private Equity Firm

Project Preferences

Type of Financing Preferred:
Balanced

Geographical Preferences

International Preferences:
China

Industry Preferences

In Communications prefer:
Telecommunications

In Computer Software prefer:
Software

In Industrial/Energy prefer:
Energy

Additional Information

Year Founded: 1993
Current Activity Level: Actively seeking new investments

BEIJING PANGU VENTURE CAPITAL LTD

Nongda South Rd., Haidian Dist
Room 605, Building 4
Bejing, China
Phone: 861085910318
Website: www.grainsvalley.com

Type of Firm

Private Equity Firm

Project Preferences

Type of Financing Preferred:
Early Stage
Expansion

Geographical Preferences

International Preferences:
China

Industry Preferences

In Communications prefer:
Telecommunications
Entertainment

In Consumer Related prefer:
Consumer Products

In Industrial/Energy prefer:
Energy

Additional Information
Year Founded: 2007
Current Activity Level : Actively seeking new investments

BEIJING PEAKVALLEY CAPITAL MANAGEMENT CO LTD

Shunyi District, Beijing
No. 7 Green Jinxiu Ecological
Beijing, China
Phone: 861053313987
Website: peakvalleycap.com

Type of Firm
Private Equity Firm

Project Preferences

Type of Financing Preferred:
Balanced

Geographical Preferences

International Preferences:
China

Additional Information
Year Founded: 2014
Current Activity Level : Actively seeking new investments

BEIJING PHOENIX CAPITAL INVESTMENT MANAGEMENT CO LTD

Chaoyang District
No. 5, West St. Sanlitun
Beijing, China 100027
Phone: 861084682298
Fax: 861084682298
Website: www.phoenixfortune.com

Type of Firm
Private Equity Firm

Project Preferences

Type of Financing Preferred:
Balanced

Geographical Preferences

International Preferences:
China

Industry Preferences

In Communications prefer:
Media and Entertainment

In Internet Specific prefer:
Internet

In Medical/Health prefer:
Medical/Health

In Consumer Related prefer:
Consumer

In Financial Services prefer:
Financial Services

In Business Serv. prefer:
Services

In Manufact. prefer:
Manufacturing

Additional Information
Year Founded: 2011
Capital Under Management: $60,700,000
Current Activity Level : Actively seeking new investments

BEIJING PROPHET CAPITAL INVESTMENT MANAGEMENT CO LTD

Dongfang Plaza, No. 1
613, East No.1 Building
Beijing, China
Phone: 8610-85183380
Fax: info@prophetcap
Website: prophetcapital.com.cn

Type of Firm
Private Equity Firm

Project Preferences

Type of Financing Preferred:
Balanced

Geographical Preferences

International Preferences:
China

Industry Preferences

In Communications prefer:
Entertainment

In Computer Software prefer:
Artificial Intelligence

In Financial Services prefer:
Financial Services

Additional Information
Year Founded: 2014
Current Activity Level : Actively seeking new investments

BEIJING QIANSHAN CAPITAL MANAGEMENT CO LTD

No.18 Chaoyangmenwai Street
Fenglian Plaza A
Beijing, China
Phone: 861065889989
Website: www.qianshancapital.com

Type of Firm
Private Equity Firm

Project Preferences

Type of Financing Preferred:
Early Stage
Later Stage
Seed
Startup

Geographical Preferences

International Preferences:
China

Industry Preferences

In Communications prefer:
Telecommunications
Data Communications
Media and Entertainment

In Computer Software prefer:
Artificial Intelligence

In Medical/Health prefer:
Medical/Health

In Financial Services prefer:
Financial Services

Additional Information
Year Founded: 2016
Current Activity Level : Actively seeking new investments

BEIJING QINGSHAN TONGCHUANG INVESTMENT CO LTD

Shuguang Xili A, Chaoyang Dist
U201, Bldg.21, Yard 5
Beijing, China
Website: www.hwazing.com

Type of Firm
Private Equity Firm

Project Preferences

Type of Financing Preferred:
Start-up Financing
Seed

Geographical Preferences

International Preferences:
China

Industry Preferences

In Communications prefer:
Entertainment

Additional Information

Year Founded: 2011
Current Activity Level : Actively seeking new investments

BEIJING RICH LAND CAPITAL MANAGEMENT CENTER LP

1, East Chang An Avenue
08, 10/F,Oriental Plaza West
Beijing, China
Phone: 861085184365
Fax: 861085187626
Website: www.richlandcap.com

Type of Firm

Private Equity Firm

Project Preferences

Type of Financing Preferred:
Balanced

Geographical Preferences

International Preferences:
China

Industry Preferences

In Medical/Health prefer:
Medical/Health

In Consumer Related prefer:
Consumer Products
Education Related

In Industrial/Energy prefer:
Energy
Environmental Related

In Manufact. prefer:
Manufacturing

In Agr/Forestr/Fish prefer:
Agriculture related

Additional Information

Year Founded: 2011
Capital Under Management: $76,631,000
Current Activity Level : Actively seeking new investments

BEIJING RIVER INVESTMENT LTD

Zhongguancun, Haidian District
409BeijingRaycom InfoTech Park
Beijing, China
Phone: 861062509325
Fax: 861062509768
E-mail: bp@rivervc.com
Website: www.rivervc.com

Type of Firm

Private Equity Firm

Project Preferences

Type of Financing Preferred:
Early Stage
Seed

Geographical Preferences

International Preferences:
China

Industry Preferences

In Communications prefer:
Entertainment

In Computer Software prefer:
Software

In Internet Specific prefer:
Internet

In Medical/Health prefer:
Medical/Health

In Consumer Related prefer:
Consumer Services

Additional Information

Year Founded: 2014
Current Activity Level : Actively seeking new investments

BEIJING ROCK CAPITAL MANAGEMENT CO LTD

No.46 Haidian Road, Haidian
West Building, Beidaziyuan
Beijing, China
Phone: 861087157999
Website: www.tscapital.com.cn

Type of Firm

Investment Management Firm

Project Preferences

Type of Financing Preferred:
Leveraged Buyout
Balanced

Geographical Preferences

International Preferences:
China

Additional Information

Year Founded: 2001
Current Activity Level : Actively seeking new investments

BEIJING RUIFU TIMES INVESTMENT CO LTD

Rm.1505 Jingyu Mansion
100 Xisanhuan North Street
Beijing, China
Phone: 86-10-6842-9358
Fax: 86-10-6872-8868

Type of Firm

Private Equity Firm

Association Membership

Venture Capital Association of Beijing (VCAB)

Project Preferences

Type of Financing Preferred:
Expansion

Geographical Preferences

International Preferences:
China

Industry Preferences

In Communications prefer:
Telecommunications

In Semiconductor/Electr prefer:
Electronics

In Industrial/Energy prefer:
Energy

Additional Information

Year Founded: 2000
Current Activity Level : Actively seeking new investments

BEIJING SAID WISE FUND CO LTD

No.9 West of N. 4th Ring Road
12B02 Yingu Buildinng
Beijing, China 100190
Phone: 861082525202
Fax: 861082525077
Website: www.saidwise.com

Management and Staff
Xing Zhou, Partner

Type of Firm
Private Equity Firm

Project Preferences

Type of Financing Preferred:
Leveraged Buyout

Geographical Preferences

International Preferences:
China

Additional Information
Year Founded: 2010
Capital Under Management: $80,100,000
Current Activity Level : Actively seeking new investments

BEIJING SANXING CAPITAL MANAGEMENT CO LTD

C No 12, Guanghua Rd, Chaoyang
Rm 1607, Digital 01 Mansion
Beijing, China 100020
Phone: 861065068290
Website: www.triniticapital.com

Type of Firm
Private Equity Firm

Project Preferences

Type of Financing Preferred:
Early Stage
Seed
Startup

Geographical Preferences

International Preferences:
China

Industry Preferences

In Communications prefer:
Telecommunications
Media and Entertainment

In Internet Specific prefer:
Internet

In Medical/Health prefer:
Medical/Health

In Consumer Related prefer:
Consumer

In Financial Services prefer:
Financial Services

Additional Information
Year Founded: 2015
Capital Under Management: $45,250,000
Current Activity Level : Actively seeking new investments

BEIJING SEEC INVESTMENT MANAGEMENT CO LTD

11 Fanli Plaza
22 Chaowai Street
Beijing, China 100020
Phone: 86-10-65888
Fax: 86-10-65885

Type of Firm
Private Equity Firm

Additional Information
Year Founded: 2010
Current Activity Level : Actively seeking new investments

BEIJING SHANGSHI INVESTMENT MANAGEMENT CO LTD

No.18, Zhongguancun Street
Room 01-47, Floor 8
Beijing, China 100086

Type of Firm
Private Equity Firm

Project Preferences

Type of Financing Preferred:
Balanced

Geographical Preferences

International Preferences:
China

Industry Preferences

In Internet Specific prefer:
Internet

In Medical/Health prefer:
Medical/Health

Additional Information
Year Founded: 2014
Current Activity Level : Actively seeking new investments

BEIJING SHENGJING WANGLIAN TECHNOLOGY CO LTD

Tsinghua Science Park Bldg.
Block B
Beijing, China 100084
Phone: 861062602800
Website: www.shengjing360.com

Type of Firm
Corporate PE/Venture

Project Preferences

Type of Financing Preferred:
Fund of Funds
Expansion

Geographical Preferences

International Preferences:
China

Industry Preferences

In Industrial/Energy prefer:
Energy
Materials

In Business Serv. prefer:
Services

In Agr/Forestr/Fish prefer:
Agriculture related

Additional Information
Year Founded: 2007
Capital Under Management: $369,592,000
Current Activity Level : Actively seeking new investments

BEIJING SHENGSHI HONGMING INVESTMENT FUND MANAGEMENT CO LTD

No. 8 Guanghua Dongli
Zhonghai Square
Beijing, China
Phone: 861065018268
Fax: 861065016378
E-mail: info@cgpinvestment.com
Website: www.cgpinvestment.com

Other Offices
Rili Zhonglu 757
R 1503, Aux Central Building
Ningbo, China
Phone: 8657428830033
Fax: 8657428871856

Type of Firm
Private Equity Advisor or Fund of Funds

Project Preferences

Type of Financing Preferred:
Fund of Funds

Additional Information
Year Founded: 2010
Capital Under Management: $3,105,438,000
Current Activity Level : Actively seeking new investments

BEIJING SHENGSHIJING INVESTMENT CO LTD

Shouti South Rd., Haidian Dist
Room 1602, Block 4
Beijing, China 100048
Phone: 861088580505
Fax: 861088580910
Website: www.sensegain.com

Type of Firm
Private Equity Firm

Project Preferences

Type of Financing Preferred:
Leveraged Buyout
Balanced

Geographical Preferences

International Preferences:
China

Industry Preferences

In Communications prefer:
Telecommunications

In Medical/Health prefer:
Medical/Health

In Industrial/Energy prefer:
Energy

In Business Serv. prefer:
Media

Additional Information
Year Founded: 2006
Current Activity Level : Actively seeking new investments

BEIJING SHITELA VENTURE CAPITAL MANAGEMENT CO LTD

Dongbeiwang West Road
230, No.4 Building, No.8 Yuan
Beijing, China

Type of Firm
Private Equity Firm

Project Preferences

Type of Financing Preferred:
Early Stage

Geographical Preferences

International Preferences:
China

Industry Preferences

In Computer Software prefer:
Data Processing
Software
Systems Software

In Internet Specific prefer:
Internet

Additional Information
Year Founded: 2014
Capital Under Management: $4,956,000
Current Activity Level : Actively seeking new investments

BEIJING SHIXIN RONGZE INVESTMENT MANAGEMENT CO LTD

Yanqi Economic Dvpt. Zone
No.88, Yangyan Road
Beijing, China

Type of Firm
Private Equity Firm

Industry Preferences

In Industrial/Energy prefer:
Energy
Energy Conservation Relat
Materials

In Financial Services prefer:
Real Estate

Additional Information
Year Founded: 2012
Capital Under Management: $79,442,000
Current Activity Level : Actively seeking new investments

BEIJING SHOUYEN JUNLI INVESTMENT MANAGEMENT CO LTD

No.1 ChangAn Street East
910, Dongfang Plaza Wesr, Offb
Beijing, China
Phone: 861085186693
Fax: 861085186692
Website: www.leadingcap.net

Type of Firm
Private Equity Firm

Project Preferences

Type of Financing Preferred:
Generalist PE

Geographical Preferences

International Preferences:
China

Industry Preferences

In Communications prefer:
Telecommunications

In Medical/Health prefer:
Medical/Health

In Consumer Related prefer:
Consumer

In Business Serv. prefer:
Media

Additional Information
Year Founded: 2012
Current Activity Level : Actively seeking new investments

BEIJING SHULIAN CAPITAL INVESTMENT MANAGEMENT CO LTD

No.2 Landianchang Road
Jinyuanshidai Business Center
Beijing, China
Phone: 861088861269
Fax: 861088861268
Website: www.d2capital.cn

Type of Firm
Private Equity Firm

Project Preferences

Type of Financing Preferred:
Balanced

Geographical Preferences

International Preferences:
China

Industry Preferences

In Computer Software prefer:
Data Processing

In Semiconductor/Electr prefer:
Analytic/Scientific

Additional Information
Year Founded: 2014
Current Activity Level : Actively seeking new investments

BEIJING SILICON INDUSTRY INVESTMENT CO LTD

Room 109 Xueyan Mansion A
Tsinghua University
Beijing, China
Phone: 86-10-6277-0583
Fax: 86-10-6279-9779

Type of Firm
Private Equity Firm

Association Membership
Venture Capital Association of Beijing (VCAB)

Project Preferences

Type of Financing Preferred:
Startup

Geographical Preferences

International Preferences:
China

Industry Preferences

In Computer Software prefer:
Software

In Semiconductor/Electr prefer:
Electronics

In Medical/Health prefer:
Medical/Health

In Industrial/Energy prefer:
Materials

In Other prefer:
Environment Responsible

Additional Information
Year Founded: 2000
Current Activity Level : Actively seeking new investments

BEIJING STAR ANGEL EQUITY INVESTMENT FUND LP

Courtyard No.1, Baosheng
Building No.7
Beijing, China
Phone: 861084372755
Website: www.fengyun.vc

Type of Firm
Private Equity Firm

Project Preferences

Type of Financing Preferred:
Early Stage
Seed
Startup

Geographical Preferences

International Preferences:
China

Industry Preferences

In Internet Specific prefer:
Internet

In Consumer Related prefer:
Consumer

In Financial Services prefer:
Financial Services

Additional Information
Year Founded: 2015
Capital Under Management: $161,170,000
Current Activity Level : Actively seeking new investments

BEIJING SUCCESS GREAT CAPITAL MANAGEMENT CO LTD

No.3, Dawang Rd. W., Chaoyang
12/F, Blk1,Lanbao Intl' Center
Beijing, China 100022
Phone: 861085997287
Fax: 861085997288
Website: www.barbara53199.com

Type of Firm
Private Equity Firm

Project Preferences

Type of Financing Preferred:
Leveraged Buyout
Early Stage
Seed
Startup

Geographical Preferences

International Preferences:
China

Industry Preferences

In Communications prefer:
Telecommunications

In Medical/Health prefer:
Medical/Health

In Consumer Related prefer:
Consumer

In Business Serv. prefer:
Media

Additional Information
Year Founded: 2015
Current Activity Level : Actively seeking new investments

BEIJING TAIKANG INVESTMENT MANAGEMENT CO LTD

No. 156 Fuxingmen Inbound St.
10F Block B, Beijing Internati
Beijing, China 100031
Phone: 861057691835

Type of Firm
Insurance Firm Affiliate

Project Preferences

Type of Financing Preferred:
Balanced

Geographical Preferences

International Preferences:
China

Industry Preferences

In Medical/Health prefer:
Health Services
Hospital/Other Instit.

In Financial Services prefer:
Insurance

Additional Information
Year Founded: 2016
Capital Under Management: $734,700,000
Current Activity Level : Actively seeking new investments

BEIJING TAIYOU INVESTMENT MANAGEMENT CO LTD

No.1 Zhongguancun East Road
THU Tech park
Beijing, China
Website: www.taiyoufund.com

Type of Firm
Investment Management Firm

Project Preferences

Type of Financing Preferred:
Seed
Startup

Geographical Preferences

International Preferences:
China

Industry Preferences

In Internet Specific prefer:
Internet

In Biotechnology prefer:
Biotechnology

In Medical/Health prefer:
Medical/Health

In Industrial/Energy prefer:
Energy Conservation Relat
Materials

In Other prefer:
Environment Responsible

Additional Information

Year Founded: 2014
Current Activity Level : Actively seeking new investments

BEIJING TECHNOLOGY YUAN PORTFOLIO VALUATION CO., LTD.

No.9 Sanyimao
Haidian District
Beijing, China
Phone: 86-10-8269-0424
Fax: 86-10-8269-0506

Type of Firm

Government Affiliated Program

Association Membership

Venture Capital Association of Beijing (VCAB)

Project Preferences

Type of Financing Preferred:
Expansion
Seed

Geographical Preferences

International Preferences:
China

Industry Preferences

In Communications prefer:
Telecommunications

In Semiconductor/Electr prefer:
Electronics
Semiconductor

In Biotechnology prefer:
Biotechnology

In Medical/Health prefer:
Medical/Health

In Industrial/Energy prefer:
Energy
Materials

In Other prefer:
Environment Responsible

Additional Information

Year Founded: 1999
Current Activity Level : Actively seeking new investments

BEIJING TENGYE VENTURE CAPITAL MANAGEMENT CO LTD

No.28,Andingmen East Street
917,Tower F,Yonghe Mansion
Beijing, China
Phone: 861084080919
Fax: 861066290149
Website: www.tengye-vc.com

Type of Firm

Private Equity Advisor or Fund of Funds

Project Preferences

Type of Financing Preferred:
Fund of Funds

Geographical Preferences

International Preferences:
China

Additional Information

Year Founded: 2010
Capital Under Management: $5,000,000,000
Current Activity Level : Actively seeking new investments

BEIJING THE CAPITAL MANAGEMENT CO LTD

B 12 Chaoyangmenwai Street
2601 Kuntai Int'l Building
Beijing, China 100020
Phone: 861059051092
Fax: 861059051090
Website: www.the-capital.com.cn

Management and Staff

Dan Liu, President
Danping Liu, President

Type of Firm

Private Equity Firm

Project Preferences

Type of Financing Preferred:
Early Stage
Expansion
Mezzanine
Balanced
Later Stage

Geographical Preferences

International Preferences:
China

Additional Information

Year Founded: 2009
Capital Under Management: $133,898,000
Current Activity Level : Actively seeking new investments

BEIJING TIANXING CHUANGLIAN INVESTMENT MANAGEMENT CO., LTD.

No.8 North Second Street
810, SOHO Building
Beijing, China 100080
Phone: 861065660986
Fax: 861062682972
E-mail: office@bjtxcap.com
Website: www.bjtxcap.com

Other Offices

No.171, Zhongyuan Zhong Rd
0742, Wanda Plaza A
Zhengzhou, China 450007
Phone: 8637155057515
Fax: 8637155057515

Management and Staff

Bin Fei, Managing Partner
Changgao Li, Managing Partner
Chengxian Huang, Partner
Hui Zhang, Managing Partner
Jun Wang, President
Lei Wen, Managing Partner
Liguo Bai, Partner
Ling Yang, Partner
Liyu Zhu, Managing Partner
Peizhao He, Managing Partner
Tongyi Meng, Managing Partner
Wei Lei, Managing Partner
Xiaohu Huo, Managing Partner
Xiaopeng Zhou, Managing Partner
Xiaoqin Liu, Managing Partner
Xin Liu, Partner
Yi Gao, Managing Partner
Yi Wang, Managing Partner
Yong Yan, Managing Partner
Zhengjun Tan, Managing Partner
Zhiping Wang, Partner

Type of Firm

Private Equity Firm

Project Preferences

Type of Financing Preferred:
Later Stage

Geographical Preferences

International Preferences:
China

Industry Preferences

In Communications prefer:
Telecommunications

In Biotechnology prefer:
Biotech Related Research

In Industrial/Energy prefer:
Environmental Related

In Business Serv. prefer:
Media

In Manufact. prefer:
Manufacturing

Additional Information
Year Founded: 2012
Capital Under Management: $479,600,000
Current Activity Level : Actively seeking new investments

BEIJING TONGCHUANG JINDING INVESTMENT MANAGEMENT CO LTD

A22 Dongsishitiao, Dongcheng
Rma1007a, Xincang Intl' Masion
Beijing, China
Phone: 861051690907
Fax: 861051690907

Type of Firm
Private Equity Firm

Project Preferences

Type of Financing Preferred:
Generalist PE

Geographical Preferences

International Preferences:
China

Industry Preferences

In Industrial/Energy prefer:
Energy

In Financial Services prefer:
Financial Services

In Manufact. prefer:
Manufacturing

In Agr/Forestr/Fish prefer:
Agriculture related

Additional Information
Year Founded: 2013
Capital Under Management: $3,500,000,000
Current Activity Level : Actively seeking new investments

BEIJING TORCH CHENGXIN INVESTMENT & CONSULTATION CO LTD

Beijing Changchun Bridge 5
New Beginnings Bldgs. 4 2003
Beijing, China 100-089
Phone: 86-10-8256-2615
Fax: 86-10-8256-2616
E-mail: vci@vci.com.cn
Website: www.vci.com.cn

Type of Firm
Private Equity Firm

Association Membership
Venture Capital Association of Beijing (VCAB)

Project Preferences

Type of Financing Preferred:
Expansion
Seed
Startup

Geographical Preferences

International Preferences:
China

Industry Preferences

In Communications prefer:
Telecommunications

In Computer Software prefer:
Software

In Biotechnology prefer:
Biotechnology

In Medical/Health prefer:
Medical/Health

In Industrial/Energy prefer:
Materials

Additional Information
Year Founded: 1997
Current Activity Level : Actively seeking new investments

BEIJING UNION FORTUNE INVESTMENT MANAGEMENT CO LTD

7, Zhichun Rd, Haidian Dist
701, Tower 1, Zhizhen Mansion
Beijing, China
Phone: 861082263257
Fax: 861082263268
Website: www.yilianvc.com

Type of Firm
Private Equity Firm

Project Preferences

Type of Financing Preferred:
Early Stage
Seed
Startup

Geographical Preferences

International Preferences:
China

Industry Preferences

In Computer Software prefer:
Artificial Intelligence

In Internet Specific prefer:
Internet

In Medical/Health prefer:
Medical/Health

In Consumer Related prefer:
Consumer
Education Related

In Financial Services prefer:
Financial Services

Additional Information
Year Founded: 2011
Current Activity Level : Actively seeking new investments

BEIJING WANRONG TIMES CAPITAL MANAGEMENT CO LTD

GuanghuaRoad,ChaoYang District
7F,Building1,Century Wealth
Beijing, China
Website: www.wr-capital.com

Type of Firm
Private Equity Firm

Project Preferences

Type of Financing Preferred:
Leveraged Buyout
Balanced

Geographical Preferences

International Preferences:
China

Industry Preferences

In Internet Specific prefer:
Internet

In Medical/Health prefer:
Medical/Health

In Consumer Related prefer:
Consumer
Sports

In Financial Services prefer:
Financial Services

Additional Information
Year Founded: 2013
Current Activity Level : Actively seeking new investments

BEIJING WANZE INVESTMENT MANAGEMENT CO LTD

Xinyuanli North Road
Ping An Int'l Finance Center
Beijing, China 100027
Phone: 861064378886
Fax: 861064378886
E-mail: wanze@wz8886.com
Website: www.wz8886.com

Management and Staff
Anjie Li, President
Gang Kai, Managing Director

Type of Firm
Investment Management Firm

Project Preferences

Type of Financing Preferred:
Balanced

Geographical Preferences

International Preferences:
China

Industry Preferences

In Communications prefer:
Wireless Communications

In Internet Specific prefer:
Internet

In Medical/Health prefer:
Medical/Health

In Industrial/Energy prefer:
Energy
Alternative Energy
Energy Conservation Relat
Machinery

In Financial Services prefer:
Real Estate

In Business Serv. prefer:
Services
Media

In Manufact. prefer:
Manufacturing

In Agr/Forestr/Fish prefer:
Agriculture related

In Other prefer:
Environment Responsible

Additional Information
Year Founded: 2010
Capital Under Management: $5,600,000
Current Activity Level : Actively seeking new investments

BEIJING WU INVESTMENT MANAGEMENT CO LTD

No. 16 Middle Sun Palace Rd, B
Room 1902, Guanjie Building
Beijing, China
Phone: 861084899211
Website: wu-capital.com

Type of Firm
Private Equity Advisor or Fund of Funds

Project Preferences

Type of Financing Preferred:
Fund of Funds
Generalist PE

Geographical Preferences

International Preferences:
China

Industry Preferences

In Communications prefer:
Telecommunications
Media and Entertainment

In Medical/Health prefer:
Medical/Health

In Financial Services prefer:
Financial Services

Additional Information
Year Founded: 2013
Current Activity Level : Actively seeking new investments

BEIJING XIAOMAFENG INVESTMENT CONSULTING CO LTD

Floor 3, No. 55, Suzhou Street
Beijing, China

Type of Firm
Private Equity Firm

Project Preferences

Type of Financing Preferred:
Early Stage

Seed

Geographical Preferences

International Preferences:
China

Industry Preferences

In Internet Specific prefer:
Internet

In Consumer Related prefer:
Consumer

Additional Information
Year Founded: 2014
Current Activity Level : Actively seeking new investments

BEIJING XINDING RONGHUI CAPITAL MANAGEMENT CO LTD

No.15, Emerging East Lane
2/F, Building 10
Beijing, China
Phone: 861068332113
Website: www.xindingcapital.com

Type of Firm
Private Equity Firm

Project Preferences

Type of Financing Preferred:
Balanced

Geographical Preferences

International Preferences:
China

Industry Preferences

In Medical/Health prefer:
Medical/Health
Pharmaceuticals

In Consumer Related prefer:
Consumer

In Manufact. prefer:
Manufacturing

Additional Information
Year Founded: 2012
Current Activity Level : Actively seeking new investments

BEIJING XINGHAN LEGEND CAPITAL MANAGEMENT CO LTD

No.8 Yard Gongti North Road
Sanlitun SOHO, 8
Beijing, China
Phone: 861085270159
Website: www.skysaga.com.cn

Type of Firm
Private Equity Firm

Project Preferences

Type of Financing Preferred:
Early Stage
Expansion
Seed
Startup

Size of Investments Considered:
Min Size of Investment Considered (000s): $150
Max Size of Investment Considered (000s): $2,995

Geographical Preferences

International Preferences:
China

Industry Preferences

In Communications prefer:
Telecommunications
Media and Entertainment

In Internet Specific prefer:
Internet

In Biotechnology prefer:
Biotechnology

In Consumer Related prefer:
Sports
Consumer Services

In Industrial/Energy prefer:
Energy Conservation Relat
Industrial Products
Materials

Additional Information
Year Founded: 2015
Current Activity Level : Actively seeking new investments

BEIJING XINHE TAIDAO INVESTMENT MANAGEMENT CO LTD

Wanda Square, Tongzhou
Room 908, Tower C
Beijing, China
Phone: 8610-58682791
Fax: 8610-58682792

Type of Firm
Investment Management Firm

Project Preferences

Type of Financing Preferred:
Expansion
Later Stage
Seed

Geographical Preferences

International Preferences:
China

Industry Preferences

In Internet Specific prefer:
Internet

In Medical/Health prefer:
Medical/Health

In Consumer Related prefer:
Consumer

Additional Information
Year Founded: 2011
Current Activity Level : Actively seeking new investments

BEIJING YINGFEI HAILIN VENTURE CAPITAL CO LTD

North 2nd Zhongguancun Str.
15F, PE Building, Haidian Dist
Beijing, China 100080

Type of Firm
Private Equity Firm

Project Preferences

Type of Financing Preferred:
Balanced

Geographical Preferences

International Preferences:
China

Industry Preferences

In Semiconductor/Electr prefer:
Optoelectronics

In Biotechnology prefer:
Biotechnology

In Industrial/Energy prefer:
Energy
Materials
Environmental Related

In Financial Services prefer:
Financial Services

In Utilities prefer:
Utilities

Additional Information
Year Founded: 2011
Capital Under Management: $157,818,000
Current Activity Level : Actively seeking new investments

BEIJING YINGSHAN INVESTMENT CO LTD

Mantingfangyuan Neighborhood,
17F, Qingyun Contemporary Bldg
Beijing, China 10086
Phone: 861062111176

Type of Firm
Investment Management Firm

Project Preferences

Type of Financing Preferred:
Balanced

Geographical Preferences

International Preferences:
China

Industry Preferences

In Internet Specific prefer:
Internet

In Medical/Health prefer:
Medical/Health

In Consumer Related prefer:
Food/Beverage

Additional Information
Year Founded: 2014
Capital Under Management: $200,000,000
Current Activity Level : Actively seeking new investments

BEIJING YIRUN VENTURE CAPITAL CO LTD

No. 58, Liangguan St, Fangshan
C02
Beijing, China
Website: www.yiruntz.com

Type of Firm
Private Equity Firm

Project Preferences

Type of Financing Preferred:
Balanced

Geographical Preferences

International Preferences:
China

Pratt's Guide to Private Equity & Venture Capital Sources

Additional Information
Year Founded: 2007
Current Activity Level : Actively seeking new investments

BEIJING YUANXINGTU VENTURE CAPITAL INVESTMENT CO LTD

Chaoyang District, Beijing
Room 1552, Unit 01-06, 15F, Bl
Beijing, China
Phone: 861057306119

Type of Firm
Private Equity Firm

Project Preferences

Type of Financing Preferred:
Balanced

Geographical Preferences

International Preferences:
China

Additional Information
Year Founded: 2015
Current Activity Level : Actively seeking new investments

BEIJING ZENITH TAIFU INVESTMENT MANAGEMENT CO LTD

No. Jia 12 Jianguomenwai Str.
Rm1605 New China Insurance Twr
Beijing, China 100022
Phone: 861084464688
Fax: 861084417837
E-mail: contact@zenithcp.com
Website: www.zenithcp.com

Management and Staff
Shiguo Ding, President

Type of Firm
Investment Management Firm

Project Preferences

Type of Financing Preferred:
Generalist PE
Balanced

Geographical Preferences

International Preferences:
China

Industry Preferences

In Industrial/Energy prefer:
Energy
Materials

Additional Information
Year Founded: 2013
Capital Under Management: $1,582,544,000
Current Activity Level : Actively seeking new investments

BEIJING ZHENGYUAN STRATEGIC INVESTMENT CO LTD

#11, Chongwenmenwai Street
701, A Block
Beijing, China 100000
Phone: 861067080022

Type of Firm
Private Equity Firm

Project Preferences

Type of Financing Preferred:
Balanced

Geographical Preferences

International Preferences:
China

Industry Preferences

In Internet Specific prefer:
Internet

In Consumer Related prefer:
Consumer

In Business Serv. prefer:
Services

Additional Information
Year Founded: 2007
Current Activity Level : Actively seeking new investments

BEIJING ZHENRU INVESTMENT MANAGEMENT CO LTD

No. 1 Jianguomen Outer St., Ch
No. 12-19 45F, Block A, Guomao
Beijing, China 100020
Phone: 861084519901
Website: www.zrinvestment.com

Type of Firm
Investment Management Firm

Project Preferences

Type of Financing Preferred:
Balanced

Geographical Preferences

International Preferences:
China

Industry Preferences

In Communications prefer:
Telecommunications

In Medical/Health prefer:
Medical/Health

In Business Serv. prefer:
Media

Additional Information
Year Founded: 2011
Current Activity Level : Actively seeking new investments

BEIJING ZHONGCHENG YONGDAO INVESTMENT MANAGEMENT CENTER LP

No.11 Changchunqiao Rd., HD
Rm.606, Building 4
Beijing, China 100089
Phone: 861058818851

Type of Firm
Private Equity Firm

Project Preferences

Type of Financing Preferred:
Balanced

Geographical Preferences

International Preferences:
China

Additional Information
Year Founded: 2012
Current Activity Level : Actively seeking new investments

BEIJING ZHONGGUANCUN GAZELLA FUND MANAGEMENT CO LTD CO LTD

No.34 Zhongguancun S Road
Zhongguancun Tech Building
Beijing, China 100081
Phone: 861062113620

Type of Firm
Investment Management Firm

Project Preferences

Type of Financing Preferred:
Balanced

Geographical Preferences

International Preferences:
China

Industry Preferences

In Medical/Health prefer:
Medical/Health

In Agr/Forestr/Fish prefer:
Agriculture related

In Other prefer:
Environment Responsible

Additional Information
Year Founded: 2011
Capital Under Management: $48,100,000
Current Activity Level : Actively seeking new investments

BEIJING ZHONGJIN HUICAI INVESTMENT MANAGEMENT CO LTD

No.9, Gongyuan W St.,Dongcheng
Room 205, Floor 2
Beijing, China

Type of Firm
Private Equity Firm

Project Preferences

Type of Financing Preferred:
Early Stage

Geographical Preferences

International Preferences:
China

Industry Preferences

In Medical/Health prefer:
Medical/Health
Drug/Equipmt Delivery

Additional Information
Year Founded: 2012
Current Activity Level : Actively seeking new investments

BEIJING ZHONGLIAN GUOXIN INVESTMENT FUND MANAGEMENT CO., LTD

Liangmaqiao
F6, Diplomatic Office Building
Beijing, China

Type of Firm
Investment Management Firm

Project Preferences

Type of Financing Preferred:
Balanced

Geographical Preferences

International Preferences:
China

Additional Information
Year Founded: 2013
Current Activity Level : Actively seeking new investments

BEIJING ZHONGRONG DINGXIN INVESTMENT MANAGEMENT CO LTD

No. 8, Guanghua East, Chaoyang
Zhonghai Palace Mid Tower
Beijing, China
Phone: 861059772260
Fax: 861059772650
Website: www.zricapital.com

Type of Firm
Investment Management Firm

Project Preferences

Type of Financing Preferred:
Balanced

Geographical Preferences

International Preferences:
China

Additional Information
Year Founded: 2011
Current Activity Level : Actively seeking new investments

BEIJING ZHONGSHI RONGCHUAN EQUITY INVESTMENT MGMT CO LTD

Xiaoying Road, Chaoyang Dist.
Rm. 1001B, 9/F, Bldg.25
Beijing, China 100101

Type of Firm
Private Equity Firm

Project Preferences

Type of Financing Preferred:
Leveraged Buyout

Geographical Preferences

International Preferences:
China

Additional Information
Year Founded: 2012
Current Activity Level : Actively seeking new investments

BEIJING ZUOYU INVESTMENT MANAGEMENT CO LTD

No.3 A,West Dawanglu, Chaoyang
Rm.1802,Blk.1,Lanbao Intl' Cen
Beijing, China 100026
Phone: 86108599901
Website: www.zuoyucapital.com

Type of Firm
Bank Affiliated

Project Preferences

Type of Financing Preferred:
Leveraged Buyout
Early Stage
Expansion

Geographical Preferences

International Preferences:
China

Industry Preferences

In Communications prefer:
Entertainment

In Consumer Related prefer:
Sports

Additional Information
Year Founded: 2014
Current Activity Level : Actively seeking new investments

BELFIUS PRIVATE EQUITY

Boulevard Pacheco 44
Brussels, Belgium 1000
Phone: 3222221111
Fax: 3222221122
Website: www.belfius.be

Type of Firm
Bank Affiliated

Association Membership
Belgium Venturing Association

Project Preferences

Type of Financing Preferred:
Fund of Funds
Leveraged Buyout
Generalist PE
Later Stage
Acquisition

Pratt's Guide to Private Equity & Venture Capital Sources

Size of Investments Considered:
Min Size of Investment Considered (000s): $647
Max Size of Investment Considered (000s): $19,407

Geographical Preferences

International Preferences:
Luxembourg
Europe
Netherlands
Belgium

Industry Preferences

In Industrial/Energy prefer:
Environmental Related

In Other prefer:
Environment Responsible

Additional Information
Year Founded: 1996
Current Activity Level: Actively seeking new investments

BELGIAN INVEST NV

Avenue De Tervuren 188A b4
Brussels, Belgium 1150
Phone: 3227789999
Fax: 3227789990

Management and Staff
Hugo Bosmans, Chief Executive Officer

Type of Firm
Government Affiliated Program

Project Preferences

Type of Financing Preferred:
Fund of Funds
Early Stage
Mezzanine
Generalist PE
Later Stage
Acquisition

Size of Investments Considered:
Min Size of Investment Considered (000s): $350
Max Size of Investment Considered (000s): $7,000

Geographical Preferences

International Preferences:
Armenia
Vietnam
Angola
Bangladesh
Mongolia
Mauritania
Latin America
India
Rwanda
Tunisia
Ecuador
Kazakhstan
Luxembourg
Malawi
Nigeria
Europe
Gabon
Netherlands
Senegal
Uganda
Zambia
Bolivia
Paraguay
Tanzania
Burkina Faso
Egypt
Mali
Peru
Algeria
Ghana
Gambia
Ivory Coast
Kenya
Mexico
Middle East
El Salvador
Tajikistan
Afghanistan
Azerbaijan
Cambodia
Cameroon
Costa Rica
Nicaragua
Philippines
Togo
Belgium
Madagascar
Morocco
Sri Lanka
Asia
Colombia
Mozambique
Germany
Africa
Honduras

Additional Information
Year Founded: 2001
Current Activity Level: Actively seeking new investments

BELHEALTH INVESTMENT PARTNERS LLC

126 East 56th Street
23rd Floor
New York, NY USA 10022
Phone: 3473087011
E-mail: info@belhealth.com
Website: belhealth.com

Other Offices
26 Harbor Park Drive
PORT WASHINGTON, NY USA 11050
Phone: 516-626-5678

4100 Newport Place
Suite 255
NEWPORT BEACH, CA USA 92660
Phone: 949-200-6547

Management and Staff
Bert Brodsky, Managing Partner
David Sturek, Managing Director
Dennis Drislane, Co-Founder
Harold Blue, Co-Founder
Inder Tallur, Managing Director
Joseph Wynne, Chief Financial Officer
Joseph Wynne, Chief Financial Officer
Nathan Kronforst, Managing Director
Paul Barrett, Vice President
Scott Lee, Managing Director

Type of Firm
Private Equity Firm

Industry Preferences

In Medical/Health prefer:
Medical/Health
Health Services
Pharmaceuticals

Additional Information
Name of Most Recent Fund: BeLHealth Investment Fund, L.P.
Most Recent Fund Was Raised: 05/27/2011
Year Founded: 2011
Capital Under Management: $500,000,000
Current Activity Level: Actively seeking new investments

BELLE MICHIGAN FUND LP

217 Lakeshore Road
Grosse Pointe, MI USA 48236
Website: www.michbelles.com

Management and Staff
Carolyn Cassin, Co-Founder
Leslie Murphy, Partner
Marianne Udow-Phillips, Partner
Marie Klopf, Partner
Mary Brevard, Partner
Nancy Philippart, Co-Founder
Terese Hunwick, Co-Founder

Type of Firm
Private Equity Firm

Project Preferences

Type of Financing Preferred:
Early Stage

Geographical Preferences

United States Preferences:
Midwest
Michigan

Industry Preferences

In Internet Specific prefer:
Internet

In Medical/Health prefer:
Medical Products

In Manufact. prefer:
Manufacturing

In Other prefer:
Environment Responsible
Women/Minority-Owned Bus.

Additional Information
Year Founded: 2012
Capital Under Management: $1,130,000
Current Activity Level : Actively seeking new investments

BELLEVUE ASSET MANAGEMENT AG

Seestrasse 16
Kuesnacht, Switzerland 8700
Phone: 41442676700
Fax: 41442676701
E-mail: info@bellevue.ch
Website: www.bellevue.ch

Management and Staff
Daniel Jazbec, Chief Operating Officer
Jan Bootsma, Managing Director
Markus Peter, Vice President
Michael Hutter, Chief Financial Officer

Type of Firm
Investment Management Firm

Project Preferences

Type of Financing Preferred:
Early Stage
Expansion
Balanced
Later Stage
Seed
Startup

Geographical Preferences

United States Preferences:

Canadian Preferences:
All Canada

International Preferences:
Europe
Korea, South
All International

Industry Preferences

In Communications prefer:
Communications and Media
Telecommunications
Wireless Communications

In Computer Software prefer:
Software

In Semiconductor/Electr prefer:
Semiconductor

In Biotechnology prefer:
Biotechnology

In Medical/Health prefer:
Medical/Health
Medical Therapeutics
Medical Products
Health Services
Pharmaceuticals

Additional Information
Name of Most Recent Fund: BB Entrepreneur Europe Fund
Most Recent Fund Was Raised: 06/03/2013
Year Founded: 1993
Current Activity Level : Actively seeking new investments

BELMERT CAPITAL SA

Calle Azalea 1, Yuca 3
Parque empresarial Miniparc I
Alcobendas, Madrid, Spain 28109
Phone: 34916505488
Fax: 34916505488
Website: www.belmert.es

Management and Staff
Jesus Mendez, President
Miguel Valenzuela, Partner
Philippe Milliet, Partner

Type of Firm
Private Equity Firm

Project Preferences

Type of Financing Preferred:
Leveraged Buyout
Acquisition

Geographical Preferences

International Preferences:
Portugal
Spain

Industry Preferences

In Industrial/Energy prefer:
Advanced Materials

Additional Information
Year Founded: 2011
Current Activity Level : Actively seeking new investments

BELTRAE PARTNERS LTD

1 Corry Place
Belfast , Ireland BT3 9AH
Phone: 2890921282
Website: www.beltrae.com

Management and Staff
Conor McCullough, Co-Founder
Ian Kerr, Co-Founder

Type of Firm
Private Equity Firm

Project Preferences

Type of Financing Preferred:
Generalist PE
Balanced
Management Buyouts
Acquisition

Geographical Preferences

International Preferences:
Ireland

Additional Information
Year Founded: 2003
Current Activity Level : Actively seeking new investments

BEN FRANKLIN TECHNOLOGY PARTNERS OF CENTRAL AND NORTHERN PA

115 Technology Center
University Park, PA USA 16802
Phone: 8148634558
E-mail: info@cnp.benfranklin.org
Website: www.cnp.benfranklin.org

Other Offices
1010 North Seventh Street
Suite 397
WEST END, PA USA 17102
Phone: 7179486339

5340 Fryling Road
Suite 202, Knowledge Park
WESLEYVILLE, PA USA 16510
Phone: 8148986650

3900 Industrial Park Drive
Suite 6
ALTOONA, PA USA 16602
Phone: 8145691116

Type of Firm
Government Affiliated Program

Association Membership
National Venture Capital Association - USA (NVCA)

Project Preferences

Type of Financing Preferred:
Early Stage
Seed

Additional Information

Year Founded: 1983
Current Activity Level : Actively seeking new investments

BEN FRANKLIN TECHNOLOGY PARTNERS OF NORTHEASTERN PA

116 Research Drive
Bethlehem, PA USA 18015
Phone: 6107585200
E-mail: info@nep.benfranklin.org
Website: www.nep.benfranklin.org

Other Offices

Berks County Chamber of Commerce
Suite 101, 601 Penn Street
READING, PA USA 19601
Phone: 610-376-6766
Fax: 610-376-4135

Phoenix Plaza, Suite 200
22 E. Union Street
WILKES-BARRE, PA USA 18701
Phone: 570-819-4002
Fax: 570-819-8931

115 Research Drive
BETHLEHEM, PA USA 18015
Phone: 610-758-5261
Fax: 610-861-8247

115 Farley Circle
Suite 106
LEWISBURG, PA USA 17837
Phone: 570-522-9222
Fax: 570-522-9225

Management and Staff

Joseph Lane, Vice President
Kathy Ann Minnich, Chief Financial Officer

Type of Firm

Government Affiliated Program

Association Membership

National Venture Capital Association - USA (NVCA)

Project Preferences

Type of Financing Preferred:
Early Stage
Seed

Geographical Preferences

United States Preferences:
Pennsylvania

Industry Preferences

In Manufact. prefer:
Manufacturing

Additional Information

Year Founded: 1983
Current Activity Level : Actively seeking new investments

BEN FRANKLIN TECHNOLOGY PARTNERS SOUTHEASTERN PA

4801 S. Broad Street-Suite 200
Building 100 Innovation Center
Philadelphia, PA USA 19112
Phone: 2159726700
Fax: 2159725588
E-mail: info@sep.benfranklin.org
Website: www.sep.benfranklin.org

Other Offices

125 Goodman Drive
BETHLEHEM, PA USA 18015
Phone: 610-758-5200

200 North Third Street
Suite 400
HARRISBURG, PA USA 17101
Phone: 717-234-1748

115 Technology Center
PENN STATE UNIVERSITY, PA USA 16802
Phone: 814-863-4558

2000 Technology Drive
Suite 250
PITTSBURGH, PA USA 15219
Phone: 412-681-1520

Management and Staff

Anthony Green, Vice President
James Gambino, Vice President
Terrence Hicks, Vice President

Type of Firm

Government Affiliated Program

Association Membership

National Venture Capital Association - USA (NVCA)

Project Preferences

Role in Financing:
Will function either as deal originator or investor in deals created by others

Type of Financing Preferred:
Early Stage
Seed

Geographical Preferences

United States Preferences:
Pennsylvania

Industry Focus

(% based on actual investment)
Medical/Health	28.7%
Computer Software and Services	28.1%
Biotechnology	10.4%
Internet Specific	10.1%
Industrial/Energy	6.3%
Computer Hardware	5.3%
Consumer Related	4.4%
Other Products	2.7%
Communications and Media	2.4%
Semiconductors/Other Elect.	1.6%

Additional Information

Year Founded: 1983
Capital Under Management: $57,000,000
Current Activity Level : Actively seeking new investments

BENAROYA CAPITAL COMPANY

3600 136th Place Southeast
Suite 250
Bellevue, WA USA 98006
Phone: 4254406700
Fax: 4254406730
E-mail: general@benaroya.com
Website: www.benaroya.com

Type of Firm

Private Equity Firm

Project Preferences

Role in Financing:
Will function either as deal originator or investor in deals created by others

Type of Financing Preferred:
Balanced

Geographical Preferences

United States Preferences:
Northwest

Additional Information

Year Founded: 1995
Capital Under Management: $35,000,000
Current Activity Level : Actively seeking new investments
Method of Compensation: Return on investment is of primary concern, do not charge fees

BENCHMARK CAPITAL MANAGEMENT GESELLSCHAFT MBH IN LIQU

2965 Woodside Road
Redwood City, CA USA 94062
Phone: 6508548180
Fax: 6508548183
Website: www.benchmark.com

Other Offices

9 Hamanofim Street
Herzliya Pituach, Israel 46725
Phone: 972-9-961-7600
Fax: 972-9-961-7601

Market Street
San Francisco, CA USA 94107

988 Market Street
San Francisco, CA USA 94103

2480 Sand Hill Road
Suite 200
Menlo Park, CA USA 94025
Phone: 6508548180
Fax: 6508548183

Management and Staff

Alex Balkanski, General Partner
Bill Gurley, General Partner
Bruce Dunlevie, General Partner
Kevin Harvey, General Partner
Matthew Cohler, General Partner
Mitch Lasky, General Partner
Peter Fenton, General Partner
Richard Barton, Venture Partner
Robert Bearden, Venture Partner
Robert Kagle, General Partner

Type of Firm

Private Equity Firm

Association Membership

Western Association of Venture Capitalists (WAVC)
National Venture Capital Association - USA (NVCA)

Project Preferences

Role in Financing:
Prefer role as deal originator but will also invest in deals created by others

Type of Financing Preferred:
Early Stage
Balanced

Geographical Preferences

United States Preferences:

International Preferences:
Europe

Industry Focus
(% based on actual investment)

Internet Specific	36.8%
Computer Software and Services	29.7%
Semiconductors/Other Elect.	13.5%
Communications and Media	6.0%
Other Products	4.1%
Consumer Related	4.0%
Computer Hardware	3.7%
Industrial/Energy	1.4%
Medical/Health	0.8%

Additional Information

Name of Most Recent Fund: Benchmark Founders' Fund VIII, L.P.
Most Recent Fund Was Raised: 03/05/2014
Year Founded: 1995
Capital Under Management: $2,730,400,000
Current Activity Level : Actively seeking new investments
Method of Compensation: Return on invest. most important, but chg. closing fees, service fees, etc.

BENCIS CAPITAL PARTNERS BV

Zuidplein 76
WTC Amsterdam Tower H 9th Flr
Amsterdam, Netherlands 1077 XV
Phone: 31205400940
Fax: 31205400941
E-mail: info@bencis.nl
Website: www.bencis.com

Other Offices

Parklane
Culliganlaan 2C
Diegem, Belgium 1831
Phone: 32-2-610-0300
Fax: 32-2-610-0301

Management and Staff

Benoit Graulich, Partner
Eric-Joost Ernst, Partner
Jeroen Pit, Founder
Lesley van Zutphen, Partner
Zoran van Gessel, Founder

Type of Firm

Private Equity Firm

Association Membership

European Private Equity and Venture Capital Assoc.

Project Preferences

Type of Financing Preferred:
Leveraged Buyout

Geographical Preferences

International Preferences:
Luxembourg
Netherlands
Western Europe
Belgium

Industry Preferences

In Consumer Related prefer:
Consumer

In Industrial/Energy prefer:
Industrial Products

In Transportation prefer:
Transportation

In Financial Services prefer:
Financial Services

In Manufact. prefer:
Manufacturing

Additional Information

Name of Most Recent Fund: Bencis Buyout Fund IV
Most Recent Fund Was Raised: 11/11/2011
Year Founded: 1999
Capital Under Management: $560,902,000
Current Activity Level : Actively seeking new investments

BENDIGO PARTNERS LLC

Eleven East 44th Street
Suite 1602
New York, NY USA 10017
Phone: 2128674490
E-mail: info@bendigopartners.com
Website: www.bendigopartners.com

Type of Firm

Private Equity Firm

Project Preferences

Type of Financing Preferred:
Leveraged Buyout
Turnaround
Later Stage
Management Buyouts
Special Situation

Geographical Preferences

United States Preferences:

International Preferences:
United Kingdom
Hong Kong
Japan

Industry Preferences

In Financial Services prefer:
Financial Services

Additional Information

Year Founded: 2008
Current Activity Level : Actively seeking new investments

BENEFIT STREET PARTNERS LLC

Nine West 57th Street
Suite 4700
New York, NY USA 10019
E-mail: info@provequity.com
Website: www.provequity.com

Type of Firm
Private Equity Firm

Project Preferences

Type of Financing Preferred:
Mezzanine

Additional Information
Year Founded: 2008
Capital Under Management: $2,550,000,000
Current Activity Level : Actively seeking new investments

BENFORD CAPITAL PARTNERS LLC

One North Franklin
Suite 3310
Chicago, IL USA 60606
Phone: 3129320200
Fax: 3129320220
Website: www.benfordcapital.com

Management and Staff
Benjamin Riefe, Managing Director
Edward Benford, Managing Director

Type of Firm
Private Equity Firm

Project Preferences

Role in Financing:
Prefer role as deal originator

Type of Financing Preferred:
Leveraged Buyout
Management Buyouts
Acquisition
Recapitalizations

Geographical Preferences

United States Preferences:

Canadian Preferences:
All Canada

Industry Preferences

In Consumer Related prefer:
Consumer Products

In Industrial/Energy prefer:
Industrial Products

In Business Serv. prefer:
Distribution

In Manufact. prefer:
Manufacturing

Additional Information
Year Founded: 2004
Current Activity Level : Actively seeking new investments

BENHAMOU GLOBAL VENTURES LLC

540 Cowper Street
Suite 200
Palo Alto, CA USA 94301
Phone: 6503243680
Fax: 6504731347
Website: benhamouglobalventures.com

Other Offices
11 HaMenofim Street
Building B
Herzliya, Israel 46725

Management and Staff
Amir Nayyerhabibi, Partner
Anik Bose, General Partner
Barak Ben-Avinoam, Partner
Eric Buatois, General Partner
Janice Roberts, Partner
Marina Levinson, Partner
Yashwanth Hemaraj, Principal

Type of Firm
Private Equity Firm

Project Preferences

Type of Financing Preferred:
Seed

Geographical Preferences

United States Preferences:
All U.S.

International Preferences:
India
Israel
All International
France

Industry Preferences

In Communications prefer:
Wireless Communications

In Computer Software prefer:
Software
Artificial Intelligence

In Internet Specific prefer:
Internet

Additional Information
Year Founded: 2003
Capital Under Management: $152,000,000
Current Activity Level : Actively seeking new investments

BENNETT JONES VERCHERE

855 Second Street SW
4500 Bankers Hall East
Calgary, Canada T2P 4K7
Phone: 4032983100
Fax: 4032657219
Website: www.bj.com

Management and Staff
Darryl Barber, Partner
David Silver, Partner
Edward Goldenberg, Partner
Enzo Barichello, Managing Partner
Harinder Basra, Partner
J. Paul Barbeau, Partner
J. Scott Bodie, Partner
James McDermott, Managing Partner
John Batzel, Partner
Kimberly Henry, Chief Financial Officer
Melanie Aitken, Principal
Peter Banks, Partner
Philip Backman, Partner
Robert Booth, Partner
Ronald Barron, Partner
Scott Bower, Partner
Stephen Bowman, Managing Partner
Timothy Ross, Managing Partner

Type of Firm
Investment Management Firm

Project Preferences

Type of Financing Preferred:
Leveraged Buyout

Additional Information
Year Founded: 1922
Current Activity Level : Actively seeking new investments

BENSON OAK CAPITAL LTD

Spalena 14
Prague, Czech Republic 101 00
Phone: 420224056056
Fax: 420224056332
E-mail: boc@bensonoak.com
Website: www.bensonoak.com

Management and Staff
Gabriel Eichler, Founder
Jaroslav Sopuch, Vice President
Justin Fancher, Vice President
Robert Cohen, Managing Partner
Stanislav Spurny, Managing Director

Type of Firm
Private Equity Firm

Project Preferences

Type of Financing Preferred:
Leveraged Buyout
Early Stage
Expansion
Generalist PE
Later Stage
Acquisition

Geographical Preferences

International Preferences:
Slovak Repub.
Czech Republic

Industry Preferences

In Computer Software prefer:
Systems Software
Applications Software

In Consumer Related prefer:
Retail
Consumer Products

In Industrial/Energy prefer:
Industrial Products

In Manufact. prefer:
Manufacturing

Additional Information
Year Founded: 1991
Current Activity Level : Actively seeking new investments

BERENBERG-BALKAN-BALTIKUM-UNIVERSAL-FONDS

Am Hauptbahnhof 18
Frankfurt/Main, Germany 60079
Phone: 4969710430
Fax: 496971043700
E-mail: info@universal-investment.de
Website: www.universal-investment.de

Management and Staff
Markus Neubauer, Managing Director
Oliver Harth, Managing Director

Type of Firm
Bank Affiliated

Project Preferences

Type of Financing Preferred:
Generalist PE
Balanced

Geographical Preferences

International Preferences:
Europe

Additional Information
Year Founded: 1968
Current Activity Level : Actively seeking new investments

BERENSON & COMPANY LLC

667 Madison Avenue
New York, NY USA 10065
Website: www.berensonco.com

Type of Firm
Investment Management Firm

Project Preferences

Type of Financing Preferred:
Leveraged Buyout
Acquisition
Recapitalizations

Industry Preferences

In Communications prefer:
Telecommunications

Additional Information
Year Founded: 1990
Capital Under Management: $11,500,000
Current Activity Level : Actively seeking new investments

BERGEN ASSET MANAGEMENT LLC

1450 Broadway
36th Floor
New York, NY USA 10018
Phone: 12124882560
E-mail: contactus@bergenasset.com
Website: www.bergenasset.com

Management and Staff
Eugene Tablis, Chief Executive Officer
Petre Norton, Vice President
Robert Clisdell, Vice President

Type of Firm
Private Equity Firm

Project Preferences

Type of Financing Preferred:
Generalist PE

Additional Information
Year Founded: 2011
Current Activity Level : Actively seeking new investments

BERGGRUEN HOLDINGS INC

1114 Avenue of the Americas
41st Floor
New York, NY USA 10036
Phone: 2123802230
Fax: 2123820120
Website: www.berggruenholdings.com

Other Offices
8 Nachalat Benyamin Street
Tel Aviv, Israel 65161
Phone: 97236005620
Fax: 97236179059

Tesvikiye Caddesi no 97/8
Istanbul, Turkey
Phone: 902122363499
Fax: 902122272794

Wilhelmstrasse 138
Berlin, Germany 10963
Phone: 493025939960
Fax: 4930259399659

Markt 6
Beusichem, Netherlands 4112 JS
Phone: 31345509090
Fax: 31345501054

Management and Staff
Eric Hanson, Managing Director
Jared Bluestein, Chief Operating Officer
Kabir Kewalramani, Managing Director
Mary Klein, Chief Financial Officer
Mehmet Kosematoglu, Managing Director
Samuel Czarny, Managing Director
Thomas Crawford, Chief Financial Officer
Ton Trentelman, Managing Director
Yigal Zemah, Managing Director

Type of Firm
Investment Management Firm

Project Preferences

Type of Financing Preferred:
Value-Add
Turnaround
Startup
Recapitalizations

Geographical Preferences

United States Preferences:
North America
All U.S.

International Preferences:
Europe
Middle East
Asia

Industry Preferences

In Financial Services prefer:
Real Estate

Additional Information

Year Founded: 1984
Current Activity Level : Actively seeking new investments

BERINGEA LLC

32330 West 12 Mile Road
Farmington Hills, MI USA 48334
Phone: 2484899000
Fax: 2484898819
E-mail: info@beringea.com
Website: www.beringea.com

Management and Staff

Charles Rothstein, Co-Founder
Malcolm Moss, Partner
Mark Taylor, Partner
Michael Gross, Managing Director
Shane Elliott, Partner
Steven Tuckley, Chief Financial Officer
Stuart Veale, Managing Partner

Type of Firm

Private Equity Firm

Association Membership

British Venture Capital Association (BVCA)
National Venture Capital Association - USA (NVCA)
Natl Assoc of Small Bus. Inv. Co (NASBIC)

Project Preferences

Role in Financing:
Will function either as deal originator or investor in deals created by others

Type of Financing Preferred:
Leveraged Buyout
Early Stage
Balanced
Later Stage
Acquisition
Recapitalizations

Size of Investments Considered:
Min Size of Investment Considered (000s): $2,000
Max Size of Investment Considered (000s): $15,000

Geographical Preferences

United States Preferences:

International Preferences:
United Kingdom

Industry Preferences

In Medical/Health prefer:
Medical/Health

In Industrial/Energy prefer:
Environmental Related

In Business Serv. prefer:
Media

Additional Information

Name of Most Recent Fund: Michigan Growth Capital Partners II, L.P.
Most Recent Fund Was Raised: 02/11/2013
Year Founded: 1988
Capital Under Management: $617,000,000
Current Activity Level : Actively seeking new investments
Method of Compensation: Return on invest. most important, but chg. closing fees, service fees, etc.

BERINGER CAPITAL INC

141 Adelaide Street West
Suite 750
Toronto, Canada M5H 3L5
Phone: 4169282166
Fax: 4169281480
Website: www.beringercapital.com

Management and Staff

Andrea Nickel, Partner
Bill Kostenko, Managing Partner
Joe Prosperi, Managing Partner
Mike Sifton, Managing Partner

Type of Firm

Investment Management Firm

Project Preferences

Type of Financing Preferred:
Expansion
Acquisition

Industry Preferences

In Communications prefer:
Communications and Media

In Financial Services prefer:
Financial Services

In Business Serv. prefer:
Media

Additional Information

Name of Most Recent Fund: Beringer Capital Fund II (US), L.P.
Most Recent Fund Was Raised: 12/02/2011
Year Founded: 2011
Capital Under Management: $13,566,000
Current Activity Level : Actively seeking new investments

BERKSHIRE PARTNERS LLC

200 Clarendon Street
35th Floor
Boston, MA USA 02116
Phone: 6172270050
Fax: 6172276105
Website: www.berkshirepartners.com

Management and Staff

Alan Ghelberg, Principal
Benjamin Levy, Vice President
Blake Gottesman, Principal
Bradley Bloom, Co-Founder
Chris Hadley, Managing Director
D. Randolph Peeler, Managing Director
David Bordeau, Principal
Edward Whelan, Managing Director
Elizabeth Hoffman, Managing Director
Gary Giordano, Vice President
Greg Pappas, Managing Director
Jane Brock-Wilson, Managing Director
Jay Makadia, Principal
Jon Nuger, Vice President
Joshua Johnson, Vice President
Joshua Lutzker, Managing Director
Kevin Callaghan, Managing Director
Lawrence Hamelsky, Managing Director
Marni Payne, Principal
Matthew Janchar, Managing Director
Michael Ascione, Managing Director
Nii Amaah Ofosu-Amaah, Principal
Raleigh Shoemaker, Principal
Richard Lubin, Co-Founder
Robert Small, Managing Director
Ross Jones, Managing Director
Samantha Adams, Managing Director
Samuel Spirn, Principal
Tom Kuo, Managing Director

Type of Firm

Private Equity Firm

Project Preferences

Role in Financing:
Prefer role as deal originator but will also invest in deals created by others

Type of Financing Preferred:
Leveraged Buyout
Expansion
Management Buyouts
Acquisition
Recapitalizations

Geographical Preferences

United States Preferences:
North America

Industry Focus
(% based on actual investment)

Consumer Related	70.4%
Other Products	13.9%
Internet Specific	6.0%
Computer Software and Services	2.9%
Industrial/Energy	2.2%
Communications and Media	1.9%
Medical/Health	1.4%
Semiconductors/Other Elect.	1.3%

Additional Information
Name of Most Recent Fund: Berkshire Fund VIII, L.P.
Most Recent Fund Was Raised: 07/20/2011
Year Founded: 1984
Capital Under Management: $11,000,000,000
Current Activity Level : Actively seeking new investments
Method of Compensation: Return on invest. most important, but chg. closing fees, service fees, etc.

BERLIN VENTURES BG GMBH

Brunnenstrasse 181
Berlin, Germany 10119
Phone: 493063373135
Fax: 493063373136
E-mail: info@berlinventures.com
Website: www.berlinventures.com

Type of Firm
Private Equity Firm

Project Preferences

Type of Financing Preferred:
Early Stage
Seed
Startup

Geographical Preferences

United States Preferences:

International Preferences:
Turkey
Germany

Industry Preferences

In Communications prefer:
Communications and Media

In Computer Software prefer:
Software

In Internet Specific prefer:
E-Commerce Technology

Additional Information
Year Founded: 2007
Current Activity Level : Actively seeking new investments

BERTRAM CAPITAL MANAGEMENT LLC

800 Concar Drive
Suite 100
San Mateo, CA USA 94402
Phone: 6503585000
Fax: 6503585001
Website: www.bertramcapital.com

Management and Staff
Brian Wheeler, Partner
David Hellier, Partner
Ingrid Swenson, Chief Financial Officer
Jared Ruger, Partner
Jeff Giles, Vice President
Jeffrey Drazan, Managing Partner
Kenneth Drazan, Co-Founder
Kevin Yamashita, Partner
Ryan Craig, Partner
Tim Heston, Principal
Tom Beerle, Principal
Vimal Patel, Vice President

Type of Firm
Private Equity Firm

Association Membership
Australian Venture Capital Association (AVCAL)

Project Preferences

Role in Financing:
Prefer role as deal originator but will also invest in deals created by others

Type of Financing Preferred:
Leveraged Buyout
Expansion
Management Buyouts
Acquisition

Industry Preferences

In Communications prefer:
Communications and Media

In Medical/Health prefer:
Medical/Health
Health Services

In Consumer Related prefer:
Consumer

In Industrial/Energy prefer:
Industrial Products

In Financial Services prefer:
Financial Services

In Business Serv. prefer:
Services
Consulting Services

In Manufact. prefer:
Manufacturing

Additional Information
Year Founded: 2006
Capital Under Management: $884,000,000
Current Activity Level : Actively seeking new investments

BERWIND CORP

1500 Market Street
3000 Centre Square West
Philadelphia, PA USA 19102
Phone: 2155632800
Fax: 2155752314
E-mail: information@berwind.com
Website: www.berwind.com

Management and Staff
Charlie Lewis, Vice President

Type of Firm
Investment Management Firm

Project Preferences

Type of Financing Preferred:
Leveraged Buyout
Management Buyouts
Acquisition

Industry Preferences

In Medical/Health prefer:
Pharmaceuticals

In Industrial/Energy prefer:
Environmental Related

Additional Information
Name of Most Recent Fund: Berwind Leveraged Acquisitions
Most Recent Fund Was Raised: 03/01/1999
Year Founded: 1886
Current Activity Level : Actively seeking new investments

BERWIND PRIVATE EQUITY

Six Lancaster County Road
Harvard, MA USA 01451
Phone: 9783911244
Fax: 9783911255
E-mail: info@berwindprivateequity.com
Website: www.berwindprivateequity.com

Management and Staff
Larry Norton, Managing Director
Russell Shappy, Chief Financial Officer

Type of Firm
Private Equity Firm

Project Preferences

Type of Financing Preferred:
Leveraged Buyout
Early Stage
Expansion
Generalist PE
Balanced
Later Stage
Seed
Management Buyouts
Acquisition
Startup

Geographical Preferences

United States Preferences:
Northeast

Industry Preferences

In Industrial/Energy prefer:
Industrial Products
Materials

In Financial Services prefer:
Real Estate

In Manufact. prefer:
Manufacturing

Additional Information
Year Founded: 2011
Current Activity Level : Actively seeking new investments

BERYTECH SCAL

11-7503 Riad El Solh,
Mar Roukoz, Mkalles
Beirut, Lebanon 1107 2240
Phone: 9614533040
Fax: 9614533070
E-mail: info@berytech.org
Website: www.berytech.org

Type of Firm
Incubator/Development Program

Project Preferences

Type of Financing Preferred:
Early Stage
Expansion
Later Stage
Startup

Geographical Preferences

International Preferences:
Lebanon
Asia

Industry Preferences

In Medical/Health prefer:
Medical/Health

In Business Serv. prefer:
Media

Additional Information
Name of Most Recent Fund: Berytech Fund
Most Recent Fund Was Raised: 03/31/2008
Year Founded: 2002
Capital Under Management: $51,500,000
Current Activity Level : Actively seeking new investments

BESPOKE CAPITAL PARTNERS LLC

525 Okeechobee Boulevard
Suite 1650
West Palm Beach, FL USA 33401
Phone: 5612285381
Fax: 5616539942
Website: www.bespokecp.com

Type of Firm
Private Equity Firm

Project Preferences

Type of Financing Preferred:
Leveraged Buyout
Mezzanine

Geographical Preferences

United States Preferences:
All U.S.

International Preferences:
Europe

Industry Preferences

In Consumer Related prefer:
Consumer
Entertainment and Leisure

Additional Information
Year Founded: 2014
Current Activity Level : Actively seeking new investments

BESSEMER TRUST CO

630 Fifth Avenue
New York, NY USA 10111
Phone: 2127089100
Fax: 2122655826

Type of Firm
Private Equity Advisor or Fund of Funds

Project Preferences

Type of Financing Preferred:
Fund of Funds
Expansion

Geographical Preferences

International Preferences:
All International

Additional Information
Name of Most Recent Fund: Old Westbury Private Equity Fund XII LLC
Most Recent Fund Was Raised: 04/23/2013
Year Founded: 1998
Capital Under Management: $642,820,000
Current Activity Level : Actively seeking new investments

BESSEMER VENTURE PARTNERS

1865 Palmer Avenue
Suite 104
Larchmont, NY USA 10538
Phone: 9148339100
Fax: 9148339200
E-mail: press@bvp.com
Website: www.bvp.com

Other Offices

215 Nariman Point, Free Press Journal Rd
71 Free Press House, 7th Floor
Mumbai, India 400021
Phone: 91-22-6616-2000
Fax: 91-22-6616-2001

10 Abba Eban Boulevard
Ackerstein Tower C, Fourth Floor
Herzliya Piitauch, Israel 46725
Phone: 972-9-972-1200
Fax: 972-9-972-1220

40 Vittal Mallya Road
Second Floor
Bangalore, India 560 001
Phone: 918030829000
Fax: 918030829001

196 Broadway
Second Floor
CAMBRIDGE, MA USA 02139
Phone: 617-588-1700
Fax: 617-588-1701

Leopoldo Couto de Magalhaes Jr Str.758
New Century Building, 11th floor
Sao Paulo, Brazil
Phone: 5511981683901

Management and Staff
Aakash Goel, Vice President
Abhijeet Muzumdar, Vice President
Adam Fisher, Partner
Alex Ferrara, Partner
Ambar Bhattacharyya, Vice President
Aviad Ariel, Vice President
Bob Goodman, Partner
Brian Feinstein, Partner
Byron Deeter, Partner
Christopher Gabrieli, Partner
David Cowan, Partner
Ethan Kurzweil, Partner
G. Felda Hardymon, Partner

J. Edmund Colloton, Partner
Jeremy Levine, Partner
Kent Bennett, Partner
Nancy Straface, Vice President
Peter Lee, Vice President
Robert Stavis, Partner
Stephen Kraus, Partner
Subramanya S.V., Managing Director
Sunil Nagaraj, Vice President
Tiffany Spencer, Vice President
Trevor Oelschig, Partner
Umesh Padval, Partner
Vishal Gupta, Managing Director

Type of Firm
Private Equity Firm

Association Membership
New England Venture Capital Association
Israel Venture Association
National Venture Capital Association - USA (NVCA)

Project Preferences

Role in Financing:
Will function either as deal originator or investor in deals created by others

Type of Financing Preferred:
Early Stage
Expansion
Balanced
Seed
Startup

Geographical Preferences

United States Preferences:

International Preferences:
Israel
Russia

Industry Focus
(% based on actual investment)

Computer Software and Services	29.7%
Internet Specific	28.9%
Communications and Media	8.8%
Industrial/Energy	7.0%
Semiconductors/Other Elect.	6.7%
Other Products	5.5%
Medical/Health	4.1%
Computer Hardware	3.7%
Biotechnology	3.1%
Consumer Related	2.5%

Additional Information
Name of Most Recent Fund: Bessemer Venture Partners VIII
Most Recent Fund Was Raised: 03/31/2011
Year Founded: 1911
Capital Under Management: $2,000,000,000
Current Activity Level : Actively seeking new investments
Method of Compensation: Return on investment is of primary concern, do not charge fees

BEST PATTERSON CROTHERS & YEOHAM LTD

2200 Ross Avenue
Suite 3838
Dallas, TX USA 75201
Phone: 214-978-3800
Fax: 214-978-3899
Website: www.bpcy.com

Type of Firm
Private Equity Firm

Project Preferences

Type of Financing Preferred:
Recapitalizations

Additional Information
Year Founded: 1990
Current Activity Level : Actively seeking new investments

BESTIGE HOLDINGS LLC

2750 Rasmussen Road
Suite 100
Park City, UT USA 84098
Website: www.bestigeholdings.com

Management and Staff
Nathan Richey, President
Shawn Hassel, Co-Founder

Type of Firm
Investment Management Firm

Project Preferences

Type of Financing Preferred:
Leveraged Buyout
Acquisition

Additional Information
Year Founded: 2016
Current Activity Level : Actively seeking new investments

BETA BRIDGE CAPITAL

252 Nassau Street
Second Floor
Princeton, NJ USA 08542
Website: b2cap.com

Type of Firm
Private Equity Firm

Project Preferences

Type of Financing Preferred:
Early Stage
Seed

Geographical Preferences

United States Preferences:
Mid Atlantic
Midwest
Southern California

Industry Preferences

In Computer Software prefer:
Software

In Medical/Health prefer:
Health Services

Additional Information
Year Founded: 2015
Current Activity Level Actively seeking new investments

BETAWORKS STUDIO LLC

29 Little West
12th Street
New York, NY USA 10014
Website: betaworks.com

Management and Staff
Janet Balis, Partner
Josh Auerbach, Chief Financial Officer
Neil Wehrle, Vice President

Type of Firm
Private Equity Firm

Project Preferences

Type of Financing Preferred:
Seed

Additional Information
Year Founded: 2008
Current Activity Level : Actively seeking new investments

BETEILIGUNGSFONDS WIRTSCHAFTSFOERDERUNG MANNHEIM GMBH

Rathaus E 5
Mannheim, Germany 68159
Phone: 4962142561227
Website: https://www.mannheim.de/wirtschaft-entwickeln/bete

Management and Staff
Verena Eisenlohr, Managing Director

Type of Firm
Government Affiliated Program

Project Preferences

Type of Financing Preferred:
Early Stage
Seed
Startup

Geographical Preferences

International Preferences:
Germany

Industry Preferences

In Computer Software prefer:
Software

Additional Information

Year Founded: 2011
Current Activity Level : Actively seeking new investments

BETTER CAPITAL LLP

39-41 Charing Cross Road
Third Floor
London, United Kingdom WC2H 0AR
Phone: 442074400840
Fax: 442074400841
E-mail: info@bettercapital.co.uk
Website: www.bettercapital.co.uk

Other Offices

Heritage Hall, PO Box 225
Le Marchant Street, St Peter Port
Guernsey, United Kingdom GY1 4HY
Phone: 44-1481-716-000

Type of Firm

Private Equity Firm

Project Preferences

Type of Financing Preferred:
Leveraged Buyout
Turnaround
Management Buyouts
Acquisition
Distressed Debt

Geographical Preferences

International Preferences:
Ireland
United Kingdom
Europe

Additional Information

Name of Most Recent Fund: SME Turnaround Fund, The
Most Recent Fund Was Raised: 01/09/2013
Year Founded: 2009
Capital Under Management: $375,450,000
Current Activity Level : Actively seeking new investments

BETTER VENTURES LLC

2323 Broadway
Oakland, CA USA 94612
Phone: 5107259255
E-mail: hello@better.vc
Website: www.better.vc

Management and Staff

Rick Moss, Co-Founder
Wesley Selke, Co-Founder

Type of Firm

Incubator/Development Program

Project Preferences

Type of Financing Preferred:
Early Stage
Seed
Startup

Industry Preferences

In Communications prefer:
Wireless Communications

In Computer Software prefer:
Software

Additional Information

Year Founded: 2015
Capital Under Management: $20,910,000
Current Activity Level : Actively seeking new investments

BEV CAPITAL

764 Westover Drive
Stamford, CT USA 06902
Phone: 2037241100
Website: www.bevcapital.com

Management and Staff

Christopher Kirchen, Managing Partner
David Yarnell, Managing Partner
Marc Singer, General Partner
William Meurer, General Partner

Type of Firm

Private Equity Firm

Project Preferences

Role in Financing:
Will function either as deal originator or investor in deals created by others

Type of Financing Preferred:
Second Stage Financing
Early Stage
Expansion
Balanced
Later Stage
Private Placement

Size of Investments Considered:
Min Size of Investment Considered (000s): $1,000
Max Size of Investment Considered (000s): $10,000

Geographical Preferences

United States Preferences:
Mid Atlantic
Northeast

Industry Focus

(% based on actual investment)
Internet Specific	55.3%
Consumer Related	20.7%
Semiconductors/Other Elect.	11.1%
Industrial/Energy	5.3%
Computer Software and Services	4.0%
Other Products	3.5%

Additional Information

Name of Most Recent Fund: Brand Equity Ventures II, L.P.
Most Recent Fund Was Raised: 03/31/2000
Year Founded: 1997
Capital Under Management: $212,700,000
Current Activity Level : Actively seeking new investments
Method of Compensation: Return on investment is of primary concern, do not charge fees

---

BEVERLY CAPITAL LLC

630 Davis Street
Suite 201
Evanston, IL USA 60201
Phone: 8479619210
E-mail: info@beverlycap.com
Website: beverly-capital.com

Management and Staff

Barrett Willich, Vice President
Joseph Nolan, Founder

Type of Firm

Private Equity Firm

Project Preferences

Type of Financing Preferred:
Leveraged Buyout
Acquisition
Recapitalizations

Geographical Preferences

United States Preferences:

Industry Preferences

In Medical/Health prefer:
Health Services

In Business Serv. prefer:
Services

Additional Information
Year Founded: 2011
Current Activity Level : Actively seeking new investments

BEX CAPITAL SAS

6, rue Poussin
Paris, France 75016
Phone: 33145208922
Fax: 331981402640
Website: www.bexcapital.com

Management and Staff
Alexandre Covello, Managing Partner
Benjamin Revillon, Managing Director

Type of Firm
Private Equity Advisor or Fund of Funds

Project Preferences

Type of Financing Preferred:
Fund of Funds
Leveraged Buyout
Mezzanine
Fund of Funds of Second

Geographical Preferences

International Preferences:
Europe

Additional Information
Year Founded: 2009
Capital Under Management: $143,970,000
Current Activity Level : Actively seeking new investments

BEYOND CAPITAL PARTNERS GMBH

Mendelssohnstr. 75-77
Frankfurt am Main, Germany 60325
Phone: 496997583154
E-mail: info@beyondcapital-partners.com
Website: www.beyondcapital-partners.com

Type of Firm
Private Equity Firm

Project Preferences

Type of Financing Preferred:
Leveraged Buyout
Management Buyouts
Acquisition

Geographical Preferences

International Preferences:
Switzerland
Austria
Azerbaijan
Germany

Industry Preferences

In Industrial/Energy prefer:
Machinery

Additional Information
Year Founded: 2014
Current Activity Level : Actively seeking new investments

BEYOND NEXT VENTURES KK

2-4-11, Kudan-Minami, chiyoda
2F, Pacific Square Kudanminami
Tokyo, Japan
Website: beyondnextventures.com

Type of Firm
Private Equity Firm

Project Preferences

Type of Financing Preferred:
Early Stage
Seed

Additional Information
Year Founded: 2015
Current Activity Level : Actively seeking new investments

BEZOS EXPEDITIONS

505 5th Avenue South
Seattle, WA USA 98104
Phone: 2068128773
Fax: 2068128767
E-mail: info@bezosexpeditions.com
Website: www.bezosexpeditions.com

Type of Firm
Private Equity Firm

Project Preferences

Type of Financing Preferred:
Balanced

Geographical Preferences

United States Preferences:
All U.S.

Additional Information
Year Founded: 2003
Current Activity Level : Actively seeking new investments

BG CAPITAL GROUP LTD

A.P. 59223
Slot 2000
Nassau, Bahamas
Phone: 5613677979
Website: www.bgcapitalgroup.com

Type of Firm
Private Equity Firm

Additional Information
Year Founded: 2004

BHMS INVESTMENTS, L.P.

152 West 56th Street
19th Floor
New York, NY USA 10019
Phone: 6464816214
E-mail: contact@bhmsinvestments.com
Website: www.bhmsinvestments.com

Management and Staff
Kevin Angelis, Co-Founder
Robert Salamon, Co-Founder

Type of Firm
Private Equity Firm

Project Preferences

Type of Financing Preferred:
Leveraged Buyout
Acquisition
Special Situation
Distressed Debt

Geographical Preferences

United States Preferences:
North America

Additional Information
Name of Most Recent Fund: OCSPV, LP
Most Recent Fund Was Raised: 09/13/2010
Year Founded: 2010
Capital Under Management: $62,850,000
Current Activity Level : Actively seeking new investments

BID EQUITY ADVISORY GMBH

Neuer Wall 63
Hamburg, Germany 20354
Phone: 4940808093282
E-mail: contact@bidequity.de
Website: www.bidequity.de

Management and Staff
Axel Jansen, Managing Partner
Helge Hofmeister, Managing Partner
Lars Kloppsteck, Managing Partner

Type of Firm
Private Equity Firm

Project Preferences

Type of Financing Preferred:
Leveraged Buyout
Acquisition

Geographical Preferences

International Preferences:
Austria
Germany

Additional Information

Year Founded: 2015
Current Activity Level : Actively seeking new investments

BIG BANG VENTURES CVA

Rijnkaai 98
Hangar 26/27
Antwerpen, Belgium 2000
Phone: 3232923710
Fax: 3233035291
E-mail: info@hummingbird-ventures.com
Website: www.bbv.be

Other Offices

Esentepe Mah. Atom Sokak
King Plaza 18 6th Floor
Levent Istanbul, Turkey

2nd Floor, White Bear Yard
144a Clerkenwell Road
London, United Kingdom EC1R 5DF
Phone: 447944384251

Management and Staff

Barend Van den Brande, Managing Partner
Frank Maene, Managing Partner
Pamir Gelenbe, Partner

Type of Firm

Private Equity Firm

Project Preferences

Role in Financing:
Will function either as deal originator or investor in deals created by others

Type of Financing Preferred:
Early Stage
Seed
Startup

Size of Investments Considered:
Min Size of Investment Considered (000s): $679
Max Size of Investment Considered (000s): $2,039

Geographical Preferences

International Preferences:
Luxembourg
Turkey
Europe
Netherlands
Middle East
Belgium
Germany
Africa
France

Industry Preferences

In Communications prefer:
Communications and Media
Wireless Communications

In Computer Software prefer:
Computer Services
Software
Systems Software

In Internet Specific prefer:
E-Commerce Technology
Internet
Ecommerce

In Business Serv. prefer:
Services
Media

Additional Information

Name of Most Recent Fund: Hummingbird Ventures
Most Recent Fund Was Raised: 07/25/2011
Year Founded: 2000
Capital Under Management: $64,600,000
Current Activity Level : Actively seeking new investments

BIG BASIN PARTNERS LP

16541 Redmond Way, 287C
Redmond, WA USA 98052
Website: www.timark.net

Management and Staff

Frank Marshall, General Partner

Type of Firm

Private Equity Firm

Project Preferences

Type of Financing Preferred:
Early Stage

Industry Preferences

In Computer Software prefer:
Software

In Other prefer:
Environment Responsible

Additional Information

Year Founded: 1969
Current Activity Level : Actively seeking new investments

BIG CAPITAL LLC

1825 Main Street
Weston
Fort Lauderdale, FL USA 33326
Phone: 8007648584
Fax: 9543572350
E-mail: info@bigcapllc.com
Website: bigcapllc.com

Type of Firm

Private Equity Firm

Project Preferences

Type of Financing Preferred:
Leveraged Buyout
Management Buyouts
Acquisition

Industry Preferences

In Computer Software prefer:
Software

In Industrial/Energy prefer:
Energy

Additional Information

Year Founded: 2010
Current Activity Level : Actively seeking new investments

BIG SKY PARTNERS

One Gate Six Road, Suite 203, Building B
Sausalito, CA USA 94965
Phone: 4152891141
Fax: 4152891149

Management and Staff

Michael Schwab, Managing Director

Type of Firm

Private Equity Firm

Project Preferences

Role in Financing:
Will function either as deal originator or investor in deals created by others

Type of Financing Preferred:
Early Stage
Later Stage
Seed

Geographical Preferences

United States Preferences:
All U.S.

Industry Preferences

In Computer Software prefer:
Software

In Industrial/Energy prefer:
Alternative Energy
Energy Conservation Relat
Advanced Materials

Additional Information

Year Founded: 1999
Capital Under Management: $27,000,000
Current Activity Level : Actively seeking new investments
Method of Compensation: Return on investment is of primary concern, do not charge fees

BIG SUR VENTURES
Fdez. de la Hoz, 33, 5 cto-dc
Madrid, Spain 28010
Phone: 34916237731
Website: www.bigsurventures.es

Management and Staff
Jose Miguel Herrero, Founder

Type of Firm
Private Equity Firm

Project Preferences

Type of Financing Preferred:
Early Stage
Seed

Industry Preferences

In Internet Specific prefer:
Internet

In Industrial/Energy prefer:
Environmental Related

In Business Serv. prefer:
Services
Media

In Other prefer:
Environment Responsible

Additional Information
Year Founded: 2012
Current Activity Level : Actively seeking new investments

BIGCOLORS
144 Des Voeux Road
Level Nine
Central, Hong Kong
Website: www.bigcolors.com

Type of Firm
Incubator/Development Program

Project Preferences

Type of Financing Preferred:
Leveraged Buyout
Early Stage
Seed
Startup

Geographical Preferences

International Preferences:
Asia Pacific

Industry Preferences

In Computer Software prefer:
Software
Applications Software

In Internet Specific prefer:
Internet
Web Aggregration/Portals

Additional Information
Year Founded: 2013
Current Activity Level : Actively seeking new investments

BIHOOP VENTURES SL
C/ Almogavers 165
Barcelona, Spain 08018
Phone: 902789076
E-mail: info@bihoop.com
Website: www.bihoop.com

Type of Firm
Incubator/Development Program

Project Preferences

Type of Financing Preferred:
Seed
Startup

Additional Information
Year Founded: 2011
Current Activity Level : Actively seeking new investments

BILGOLA CAPITAL LLC
9408 Firethorn Court
Potomac, MD USA 20854
Website: www.bilgolacapital.com

Management and Staff
George Ferris, Founder

Type of Firm
Private Equity Firm

Project Preferences

Type of Financing Preferred:
Generalist PE
Acquisition

Industry Preferences

In Medical/Health prefer:
Health Services

In Financial Services prefer:
Financial Services

In Business Serv. prefer:
Services

Additional Information
Year Founded: 2008
Current Activity Level : Actively seeking new investments

BINARY CAPITAL
1550 Bryant Street
Suite 700
San Francisco, CA USA 94103
E-mail: info@binarycap.com
Website: www.binarycap.com

Type of Firm
Private Equity Firm

Project Preferences

Type of Financing Preferred:
Early Stage

Additional Information
Year Founded: 2016
Current Activity Level : Actively seeking new investments

BINARY CAPITAL MANAGEMENT LLC
1550 Bryant Street
Suite 700
San Francisco, CA USA 94103
E-mail: info@bcm-vidas.com
Website: www.binarycap.com

Type of Firm
Private Equity Firm

Project Preferences

Type of Financing Preferred:
Early Stage

Industry Preferences

In Consumer Related prefer:
Consumer

Additional Information
Year Founded: 2014
Capital Under Management: $300,000,000
Current Activity Level : Actively seeking new investments

BINOMIAL VENTURES
Presnenskaya nab 12
Moscow, Russia 123100
Website: www.binomial.vc

Type of Firm
Private Equity Firm

Project Preferences

Type of Financing Preferred:
Early Stage

Geographical Preferences

United States Preferences:
North America

International Preferences:
Europe

Industry Preferences

In Computer Software prefer:
Artificial Intelligence

In Financial Services prefer:
Financial Services

Additional Information
Year Founded: 2017
Current Activity Level : Actively seeking new investments

BIO EQUITY RISK MANAGEMENT LLC

75 Arlington Street
Suite 500
Boston, MA USA 02116
Phone: 857-241-3681
E-mail: admin@bioequityrisk.com
Website: www.bioequityrisk.com

Management and Staff
Joseph Siletto, Managing Partner

Type of Firm
Private Equity Firm

Project Preferences

Type of Financing Preferred:
Special Situation

Industry Preferences

In Medical/Health prefer:
Medical/Health

Additional Information
Year Founded: 2009
Current Activity Level : Actively seeking new investments

BIO WORLD VENTURE CAPITAL CORP

Min-Sheng East Road, Sec 2
Suite 143, Fifth Floor
Taipei, Taiwan 104
Phone: 25072960
Fax: 25006908

Type of Firm
Private Equity Firm

Association Membership
Taiwan Venture Capital Association(TVCA)

Project Preferences

Type of Financing Preferred:
Later Stage

Additional Information
Year Founded: 2000
Current Activity Level : Actively seeking new investments

BIO*ONE CAPITAL PTE LTD

20 Biopolis Way
#09-01 Centros
Singapore, Singapore 138668
Phone: 6563957700
Fax: 6563957796
E-mail: infohq@bio1capital.com

Management and Staff
Boon Ping Chua, Vice President
Sarah Ho, Founder
Serena Cho, Vice President
Swee-Yeok Chu, Chief Executive Officer

Type of Firm
Government Affiliated Program

Project Preferences

Type of Financing Preferred:
Early Stage
Expansion
Balanced
Seed
Startup

Geographical Preferences

United States Preferences:
All U.S.

International Preferences:
Singapore
All International

Industry Preferences

In Communications prefer:
Media and Entertainment

In Biotechnology prefer:
Biotechnology

In Medical/Health prefer:
Medical/Health
Medical Therapeutics
Health Services
Pharmaceuticals

In Business Serv. prefer:
Media

In Other prefer:
Environment Responsible

Additional Information
Year Founded: 1990
Capital Under Management: $790,000,000
Current Activity Level : Actively seeking new investments

BIO-INVESTIGATIONS LTD

32 Country Way
Madison, CT USA 06443
Phone: 2034213697
Website: www.bioinvestigationsltd.com

Management and Staff
Jonathan Rosenberg, Vice President
William Rosenberg, Vice President

Type of Firm
Private Equity Firm

Project Preferences

Role in Financing:
Prefer role as deal originator but will also invest in deals created by others

Type of Financing Preferred:
Balanced

Industry Preferences

In Communications prefer:
Communications and Media

In Computer Other prefer:
Computer Related

In Semiconductor/Electr prefer:
Electronic Components
Semiconductor
Controllers and Sensors
Component Testing Equipmt
Laser Related
Fiber Optics
Analytic/Scientific

In Biotechnology prefer:
Biotechnology

In Medical/Health prefer:
Medical/Health

In Consumer Related prefer:
Consumer
Education Related

In Industrial/Energy prefer:
Energy
Industrial Products

In Transportation prefer:
Transportation
Aerospace

In Business Serv. prefer:
Distribution

In Agr/Forestr/Fish prefer:
Agriculture related

Additional Information
Year Founded: 1987
Capital Under Management: $5,000,000
Current Activity Level : Actively seeking new investments
Method of Compensation: Return on invest. most important, but chg. closing fees, service fees, etc.

BIOADVANCE

3711 Market Street
Eighth Floor
Philadelphia, PA USA 19104
Phone: 6102300544
Fax: 2159666215
E-mail: info@bioadvance.com
Website: www.bioadvance.com

Other Offices
259 Radnor-Chester Road
Suite 220
SAINT DAVIDS, PA USA 19087
Phone: 610-230-0544
Fax: 610-230-0646

Management and Staff
Barbara Schilberg, CEO & Managing Director
Gregory Harriman, Venture Partner
Shahram Hejazi, Venture Partner

Type of Firm
Government Affiliated Program

Association Membership
National Venture Capital Association - USA (NVCA)

Project Preferences

Role in Financing:
Prefer role as deal originator

Type of Financing Preferred:
Seed
Startup

Geographical Preferences

United States Preferences:
Mid Atlantic

Industry Preferences

In Biotechnology prefer:
Human Biotechnology

In Medical/Health prefer:
Medical Diagnostics
Medical Therapeutics
Pharmaceuticals

Additional Information
Year Founded: 2002
Capital Under Management: $20,300,000
Current Activity Level : Actively seeking new investments
Method of Compensation: Return on investment is of primary concern, do not charge fees

BIOCROSSROADS

300 North Meridian Street
Suite 950
Indianapolis, IN USA 46204
Phone: 3172382450
Fax: 3172382451
Website: www.biocrossroads.com

Management and Staff
Matthew Hall, Founder

Type of Firm
Private Equity Firm

Project Preferences

Type of Financing Preferred:
Fund of Funds
Early Stage
Seed

Size of Investments Considered:
Min Size of Investment Considered (000s): $50,000
Max Size of Investment Considered (000s): $500,000

Geographical Preferences

United States Preferences:
Indiana

Industry Preferences

In Biotechnology prefer:
Biotechnology

In Medical/Health prefer:
Medical Diagnostics
Medical Products
Pharmaceuticals

Additional Information
Name of Most Recent Fund: Indiana Seed Fund II LLC
Most Recent Fund Was Raised: 12/23/2010
Year Founded: 2002
Capital Under Management: $13,250,000
Current Activity Level : Actively seeking new investments

BIOECONOMY CAPITAL GP LLC

3417 Evanston Avenue North
Suite 329
Seattle, WA USA 98103
Website: www.bioeconomycapital.com

Type of Firm
Private Equity Firm

Project Preferences

Type of Financing Preferred:
Early Stage

Industry Preferences

In Biotechnology prefer:
Biotechnology

Additional Information
Year Founded: 2015
Capital Under Management: $5,000,000
Current Activity Level : Actively seeking new investments

BIOENTERPRISE CORP

The Jaral Corporate Centre
120 Research Lane Suite 200
Guelph, Canada N1G 0B4
Phone: 5198212960
Fax: 5198217361
E-mail: info@bioenterprise.ca
Website: www.bioenterprise.ca

Other Offices
130 King Street West, The Exchange Tower
18th Floor
Toronto, Canada M5X 1E3

Type of Firm
Corporate PE/Venture

Association Membership
Canadian Venture Capital Association

Additional Information
Year Founded: 2003
Current Activity Level : Actively seeking new investments

BIOGENERATION VENTURES BV

Gooimeer 2-35
Naarden, Netherlands 1411 DC
Phone: 31356993000
Fax: 31356993001
E-mail: info@biogenerationventures.com
Website: www.biogenerationventures.com

Management and Staff
Edward van Wezel, Managing Partner
Joost Holthuis, Venture Partner
Wil Hazenberg, Partner

Type of Firm
Private Equity Firm

Project Preferences

Type of Financing Preferred:
Early Stage
Seed
Startup

Geographical Preferences

International Preferences:
Netherlands

Industry Preferences

In Biotechnology prefer:
Agricultural/Animal Bio.
Industrial Biotechnology

In Medical/Health prefer:
Pharmaceuticals

In Consumer Related prefer:
Food/Beverage

Additional Information
Year Founded: 2006
Capital Under Management: $95,500,000
Current Activity Level : Actively seeking new investments

BIOGENERATOR

4041 Forest Park Avenue
Suite 120
Saint Louis, MO USA 63108
Phone: 314-615-6355
Fax: 314-615-6351
E-mail: startup@biogenerator.org
Website: biogenerator.org

Management and Staff
Charlie Bolten, Vice President
Dan Broderick, Vice President
Eric Gulve, President

Type of Firm
Incubator/Development Program

Association Membership
Norwegian Venture Capital Association
National Venture Capital Association - USA (NVCA)

Project Preferences

Type of Financing Preferred:
Early Stage
Seed
Startup

Size of Investments Considered:
Min Size of Investment Considered (000s): $50
Max Size of Investment Considered (000s): $250

Geographical Preferences

United States Preferences:
Missouri

Industry Preferences

In Computer Other prefer:
Computer Related

In Biotechnology prefer:
Biotechnology

In Medical/Health prefer:
Medical Diagnostics
Medical Therapeutics
Medical Products
Health Services

In Industrial/Energy prefer:
Energy

Additional Information
Year Founded: 2003
Capital Under Management: $17,600,000
Current Activity Level : Actively seeking new investments

BIOM AG

Am Klopferspitz 19a
Martinsried, Germany 82152
Phone: 49898996790
Fax: 498989967979
E-mail: info@bio-m.org
Website: www.bio-m.org

Management and Staff
Horst Domdey, Managing Director

Type of Firm
Private Equity Firm

Project Preferences

Type of Financing Preferred:
Early Stage
Later Stage
Seed
Startup

Geographical Preferences

International Preferences:
Germany

Industry Preferences

In Biotechnology prefer:
Biotechnology

In Medical/Health prefer:
Medical/Health
Medical Diagnostics
Medical Therapeutics
Pharmaceuticals

Additional Information
Year Founded: 1997
Current Activity Level : Actively seeking new investments

BIOMARK CAPITAL

537 Steamboat Road
Greenwich, CT USA 06830
Phone: 2037692345
Fax: 2014021086
Website: www.biomarkcapital.com

Management and Staff
Bryant Fong, Managing Director
Craig Goos, Managing Partner
David Wetherell, Managing Partner
Douglas Lind, Managing Director

Type of Firm
Private Equity Firm

Project Preferences

Role in Financing:
Prefer role as deal originator but will also invest in deals created by others

Type of Financing Preferred:
Early Stage
Balanced

Size of Investments Considered:
Min Size of Investment Considered (000s): $5,000
Max Size of Investment Considered (000s): $10,000

Industry Preferences

In Medical/Health prefer:
Medical/Health
Medical Diagnostics
Diagnostic Test Products
Medical Therapeutics
Medical Products

Additional Information
Name of Most Recent Fund: Burrill Capital Fund IV, L.P.
Most Recent Fund Was Raised: 12/01/2011
Year Founded: 2013
Capital Under Management: $191,000,000
Current Activity Level : Actively seeking new investments

BIOMATICS CAPITAL PARTNERS LP

719 Second Avenue
Suite 1402
Seattle, WA USA 98104
Phone: 2064381822

Type of Firm
Private Equity Firm

Project Preferences

Type of Financing Preferred:
Balanced

Industry Preferences

In Medical/Health prefer:
Medical/Health

Additional Information
Year Founded: 2016
Capital Under Management: $200,000,000
Current Activity Level : Actively seeking new investments

BIOMEDPARTNERS AG

Elisabethenstrasse 23
Basel, Switzerland 4051
Phone: 41612703535
Fax: 41612703500
E-mail: info@biomedvc.com
Website: biomedvc.com

Management and Staff

Gerhard Ries, General Partner
Helmut Fenner, Venture Partner
Josef Bissig, Venture Partner
Karl Deres, Venture Partner
Markus Hosang, General Partner
Patrick Burgermeister, Venture Partner
Stefan Faes, Chief Financial Officer
Thomas Moeller, General Partner

Type of Firm

Private Equity Firm

Association Membership

Swiss Venture Capital Association (SECA)

Project Preferences

Role in Financing:
Will function either as deal originator or investor in deals created by others

Type of Financing Preferred:
Early Stage
Mezzanine
Later Stage
Seed
Startup

Size of Investments Considered:
Min Size of Investment Considered (000s): $360
Max Size of Investment Considered (000s): $3,600

Geographical Preferences

International Preferences:
Central Europe
Europe
Switzerland
Western Europe
Germany

Industry Preferences

In Biotechnology prefer:
Biotechnology
Biotech Related Research
Biotech Related Research

In Medical/Health prefer:
Medical/Health
Medical Diagnostics
Medical Therapeutics
Drug/Equipmt Delivery
Medical Products
Health Services
Pharmaceuticals

Additional Information

Name of Most Recent Fund: BioMedCredit AG
Most Recent Fund Was Raised: 09/01/2006
Year Founded: 2002
Capital Under Management: $75,250,000
Current Activity Level: Actively seeking new investments

BIOS PARTNERS

1401 Foch Street
Suite 140
Fort Worth, TX USA 76107
Phone: 817985964
E-mail: jfucci@biospartners.com
Website: biospartners.com

Type of Firm

Private Equity Firm

Project Preferences

Type of Financing Preferred:
Early Stage
Later Stage
Seed

Geographical Preferences

United States Preferences:

Industry Preferences

In Biotechnology prefer:
Biotechnology

In Medical/Health prefer:
Medical Products

Additional Information

Year Founded: 2017
Current Activity Level: Actively seeking new investments

BIOSCIENCE MANAGERS PTY LTD

530 Collins Street
Level 37
Melbourne, Australia 3000
Phone: 61396188216
Fax: 61396298882
Website: www.biosciencemanagers.com

Other Offices

Two Balfern Grove
London, United Kingdom W4 2JX
Phone: 44-20-7811-4034

Management and Staff

Jeremy Curnock Cook, Managing Director

Type of Firm

Investment Management Firm

Association Membership

Australian Venture Capital Association (AVCAL)

Project Preferences

Type of Financing Preferred:
Early Stage
Later Stage
Seed

Size of Investments Considered:
Min Size of Investment Considered (000s): $1,549
Max Size of Investment Considered (000s): $9,292

Geographical Preferences

International Preferences:
Asia Pacific
Australia
New Zealand

Additional Information

Year Founded: 2003
Capital Under Management: $75,200,000
Current Activity Level: Actively seeking new investments

BIOSTAR VENTURES II LLC

560 West Mitchell Street
Suite 480
Petoskey, MI USA 49770
Phone: 2134879186
Fax: 2134879183
E-mail: info@biostarventures.com

Management and Staff

Jeffrey O Donnell, Managing Director
Louis Cannon, Founder
Paul Scott, Chief Financial Officer
Renee Masi, Managing Director
Steven Almany, Managing Director

Type of Firm

Private Equity Firm

Project Preferences

Role in Financing:
Prefer role as deal originator but will also invest in deals created by others

Type of Financing Preferred:
Early Stage
Later Stage
Seed

Size of Investments Considered:
Min Size of Investment Considered (000s): $250
Max Size of Investment Considered (000s): $6,000

Industry Preferences

In Medical/Health prefer:
Medical/Health
Medical Products

Additional Information
Name of Most Recent Fund: BioStar Ventures II, L.P.
Most Recent Fund Was Raised: 03/11/2008
Year Founded: 2003
Capital Under Management: $10,100,000
Current Activity Level : Actively seeking new investments

BIOTECHONOMY VENTURES LLC

800 Boylston Street, Suite 1585
Boston, MA USA 02199
Phone: 6174215208
Fax: 6174509749
E-mail: info@biotechonomy.com
Website: www.biotechonomy.com

Management and Staff
Caleb Winder, Principal

Type of Firm
Private Equity Firm

Project Preferences

Role in Financing:
Will function either as deal originator or investor in deals created by others

Type of Financing Preferred:
Early Stage
Seed

Geographical Preferences

United States Preferences:

Industry Preferences

In Biotechnology prefer:
Biotechnology

In Medical/Health prefer:
Pharmaceuticals

In Industrial/Energy prefer:
Energy
Alternative Energy
Industrial Products
Advanced Materials

In Agr/Forestr/Fish prefer:
Agriculture related

Additional Information
Year Founded: 2005
Capital Under Management: $5,900,000
Current Activity Level : Actively seeking new investments

BIOTECHVEST LP

570 Seventh Avenue
New York, NY USA 10018
Phone: 2122624646
Fax: 2124624360

Management and Staff
Michael Ehrenreich, President

Type of Firm
Private Equity Firm

Project Preferences

Type of Financing Preferred:
Later Stage

Additional Information
Year Founded: 2009
Current Activity Level : Actively seeking new investments

BIOVEDA CAPITAL PTE LTD

50 Cuscaden Road
#07-02 HPL House
Singapore, Singapore 249724
Phone: 6562389200
Fax: 656733383
E-mail: info@biovedacapital.com
Website: www.biovedavc.com

Other Offices
Three Lagoon Drive
Suite 190
REDWOOD CITY, CA USA 94065
Phone: 650-508-1388
Fax: 650-508-1188

Management and Staff
Damien Lim, General Partner
Fredrik Nyberg, Venture Partner
Juanita Fu, General Partner
Kho Choon Joo, General Partner

Type of Firm
Private Equity Firm

Project Preferences

Type of Financing Preferred:
Early Stage
Expansion
Mezzanine
Balanced
Public Companies
Startup

Geographical Preferences

United States Preferences:

International Preferences:
China
Asia
Singapore

Industry Preferences

In Biotechnology prefer:
Biotechnology

In Medical/Health prefer:
Health Services

Additional Information
Year Founded: 2000
Capital Under Management: $32,000,000
Current Activity Level : Actively seeking new investments

BIOVEDA CHINA FUND

No.841, Mid Yan'an Road
Suit 1201, OOCL Plaza, Jing An
Shanghai, China 200040
Phone: 862151501800

Management and Staff
Bing Zhuo, Principal
Feng Lu, Partner
John Amos, Venture Partner
Xin Zhang, Partner
Yachao Zhao, Principal
Yi Li, Partner

Type of Firm
Private Equity Firm

Project Preferences

Type of Financing Preferred:
Early Stage
Expansion
Balanced
Later Stage

Geographical Preferences

International Preferences:
China

Industry Preferences

In Biotechnology prefer:
Biotechnology
Agricultural/Animal Bio.
Industrial Biotechnology

In Medical/Health prefer:
Medical/Health
Medical Diagnostics
Drug/Equipmt Delivery
Medical Products
Health Services
Pharmaceuticals

In Industrial/Energy prefer:
Environmental Related

Additional Information
Year Founded: 2005
Capital Under Management: $173,000,000
Current Activity Level : Actively seeking new investments

BIOVENTURES INVESTORS

70 Walnut Street
Suite 302
Wellesley, MA USA 02481
Phone: 6172523443
Fax: 6176217993
E-mail: info@bioventuresinvestors.com
Website: www.bioventuresinvestors.com

Management and Staff

Jeffrey Barnes, General Partner
Marc Goldberg, General Partner
Peter Feinstein, General Partner
Walter Gilbert, General Partner

Type of Firm

Private Equity Firm

Project Preferences

Role in Financing:
Will function either as deal originator or investor in deals created by others

Type of Financing Preferred:
Early Stage
Balanced
Seed

Size of Investments Considered:
Min Size of Investment Considered (000s): $3,000
Max Size of Investment Considered (000s): $10,000

Industry Preferences

In Biotechnology prefer:
Human Biotechnology

In Medical/Health prefer:
Medical/Health
Medical Therapeutics
Drug/Equipmt Delivery
Medical Products
Health Services
Pharmaceuticals

Additional Information

Name of Most Recent Fund: BioVentures Investors III, L.P.
Most Recent Fund Was Raised: 12/31/2005
Year Founded: 1997
Capital Under Management: $129,000,000
Current Activity Level : Actively seeking new investments
Method of Compensation: Return on investment is of primary concern, do not charge fees

BIP CAPITAL

3575 Piedmont Road
Building 15 7/F Suite 730
Atlanta, GA USA 30305
Phone: 4044955230
Website: www.bip-capital.com

Type of Firm

Private Equity Firm

Project Preferences

Type of Financing Preferred:
Early Stage
Seed
Startup

Geographical Preferences

United States Preferences:

Additional Information

Year Founded: 2007
Current Activity Level : Actively seeking new investments

BIP INVESTMENT PARTNERS SA

Rue des Coquelicots 1
Luxembourg, Luxembourg L-1356
Phone: 3522600261
Fax: 35226002650
E-mail: info@bip.lu
Website: www.bip.lu

Management and Staff

Viviane Graffe, Chief Financial Officer

Type of Firm

Investment Management Firm

Association Membership

European Private Equity and Venture Capital Assoc.

Project Preferences

Type of Financing Preferred:
Fund of Funds
Leveraged Buyout
Later Stage
Management Buyouts
Acquisition

Size of Investments Considered:
Min Size of Investment Considered (000s): $1,823
Max Size of Investment Considered (000s): $4,558

Geographical Preferences

International Preferences:
Luxembourg
Europe
Belgium
Germany
France

Industry Focus

(% based on actual investment)
Computer Software and Services 29.4%
Semiconductors/Other Elect. 27.9%
Biotechnology 15.1%
Internet Specific 12.3%
Computer Hardware 9.7%
Communications and Media 5.5%

Additional Information

Year Founded: 2000
Current Activity Level : Actively seeking new investments

BIRCH EQUITY PARTNERS LLC

3060 Peachtree Road NorthWest
Suite 1065,One Buckhead Plaza
Atlanta, GA USA 30305
Phone: 4046650200
Fax: 4046650300
E-mail: info@birchequity.com
Website: www.birchequity.com

Management and Staff

Holcombe Green, Co-Founder
R Godsey, Co-Founder
Vincent Oddo, Co-Founder

Type of Firm

Private Equity Firm

Project Preferences

Type of Financing Preferred:
Leveraged Buyout
Expansion
Later Stage
Management Buyouts
Acquisition
Recapitalizations

Industry Preferences

In Communications prefer:
Telecommunications
Entertainment

In Internet Specific prefer:
Internet

In Medical/Health prefer:
Medical/Health

In Consumer Related prefer:
Consumer Services
Education Related

In Financial Services prefer:
Financial Services

In Business Serv. prefer:
Services
Media

Additional Information
Year Founded: 2014
Current Activity Level: Actively seeking new investments

BIRCH HILL EQUITY PARTNERS MANAGEMENT INC

100 Wellington Street West
Suite 2300
Toronto, Canada M5K 1A1
Phone: 4167753800
Fax: 4163601688
E-mail: info@birchhillequity.com
Website: www.birchhillequity.com

Management and Staff
Andrew Fortier, Partner
David Samuel, Partner
Felix-Etienne Lebel, Vice President
Igor Gimelshtein, Vice President
John Loh, Partner
John MacIntyre, Co-Founder
Matthew Kunica, Partner
Michael Salamon, Partner
Michael Mazan, Partner
Neil McCarron, Vice President
Patrick Duncan, Vice President
Paul Henry, Partner
Peter Zissis, Chief Financial Officer
Stephen Dent, Co-Founder
Thecla Sweeney, Partner

Type of Firm
Private Equity Firm

Association Membership
Canadian Venture Capital Association

Project Preferences

Type of Financing Preferred:
Leveraged Buyout
Acquisition

Geographical Preferences

Canadian Preferences:
All Canada

Additional Information
Name of Most Recent Fund: Birch Hill Equity Partners IV, L.P.
Most Recent Fund Was Raised: 11/25/2009
Year Founded: 1995
Capital Under Management: $1,843,300,000
Current Activity Level: Actively seeking new investments

BIRCH VENTURE CAPITAL INC

Sec. 2 No.135 Jianguo North Rd
3rd Floor
Taipei, Taiwan 10484
Phone: 886225031190
Fax: 886225031506
Website: www.birchvc.com

Management and Staff
Terry Huang, Vice President

Type of Firm
Private Equity Firm

Project Preferences

Type of Financing Preferred:
Balanced

Geographical Preferences

United States Preferences:
California

International Preferences:
Taiwan
China

Industry Preferences

In Communications prefer:
Communications and Media
Wireless Communications

In Computer Software prefer:
Software

In Internet Specific prefer:
Internet

In Computer Other prefer:
Computer Related

In Semiconductor/Electr prefer:
Electronics
Semiconductor

In Industrial/Energy prefer:
Environmental Related

Additional Information
Year Founded: 2007
Current Activity Level: Actively seeking new investments

BIRCHMERE VENTURES

424 South 27th Street
Suite 203
Pittsburgh, PA USA 15203
Phone: 4123223300
Fax: 4123223226
E-mail: info@birchmerevc.com
Website: www.birchmerevc.com

Other Offices
530 Lytton Avenue
Second Floor
Palo Alto, CA USA 94301
Phone: 6507336286

Management and Staff
Mark Platshon, Partner
Ned Renzi, Partner
Sean Ammirati, Partner
Sean Sebastian, Founder

Type of Firm
Private Equity Firm

Project Preferences

Role in Financing:
Prefer role as deal originator but will also invest in deals created by others

Type of Financing Preferred:
Early Stage
Balanced
Seed
Startup

Geographical Preferences

United States Preferences:
Mid Atlantic
Pennsylvania

Industry Focus

(% based on actual investment)
Medical/Health	36.7%
Internet Specific	16.5%
Computer Software and Services	15.2%
Biotechnology	13.0%
Semiconductors/Other Elect.	7.4%
Communications and Media	3.3%
Industrial/Energy	2.9%
Other Products	2.5%
Computer Hardware	2.5%

Additional Information
Year Founded: 1996
Capital Under Management: $200,000,000
Current Activity Level: Actively seeking new investments
Method of Compensation: Return on investment is of primary concern, do not charge fees

BIRK VENTURE AS

Karenslyst Alle 8b
Oslo, Norway 0278
Phone: 4790871483
E-mail: post@birkventure.no
Website: www.birkventure.no

Management and Staff
Per-Oluf Olsen, Partner

Type of Firm
Private Equity Firm

Project Preferences

Type of Financing Preferred:
Seed
Startup

Geographical Preferences

International Preferences:
Scandanavia/Nordic Region

Additional Information

Year Founded: 2010
Current Activity Level : Actively seeking new investments

BISA

Rua Joao Suassuna
51 Boa Vista
Recife, Argentina
Phone: 8134237374
Fax: 8134234573
E-mail: bisa@bisa.com.br
Website: www.bisa.com.br

Management and Staff

Peter Davenport, Chief Executive Officer

Type of Firm

Private Equity Firm

Project Preferences

Type of Financing Preferred:
Balanced

Geographical Preferences

International Preferences:
Argentina

Additional Information

Year Founded: 1993
Current Activity Level : Actively seeking new investments

BISK VENTURES INC

585 Broadway Street
Redwood City, CA USA 94063
Phone: 8133724041
E-mail: info@biskventures.com
Website: www.biskventures.com

Type of Firm

Private Equity Firm

Project Preferences

Type of Financing Preferred:
Early Stage

Industry Preferences

In Consumer Related prefer:
Education Related

Additional Information

Year Founded: 1969
Current Activity Level : Actively seeking new investments

BISON CAPITAL ASSET MANAGEMENT LLC

233 Wilshire Boulevard, Suite 425
Santa Monica, CA USA 90401
Phone: 3102606570
Fax: 3102606576
Website: www.bisoncapital.com

Other Offices

401 North Tryon Street
Tenth Floor
Charlotte, NC USA 28202
Phone: 704-333-4899
Fax: 704-998-5770

780 Third Avenue
30th Floor
New York, NY USA 10017

Management and Staff

Andreas Hildebrand, Partner
Douglas Trussler, Founder
Kurt Pilecki, Vice President
Lou Caballero, Partner
Peter Macdonald, Partner
Richard Herdegen, Chief Financial Officer
Yee-Ping Chu, Partner

Type of Firm

Private Equity Firm

Project Preferences

Type of Financing Preferred:
Leveraged Buyout
Turnaround
Management Buyouts
Acquisition
Private Placement
Recapitalizations

Industry Preferences

In Medical/Health prefer:
Medical/Health

In Industrial/Energy prefer:
Energy
Industrial Products
Environmental Related

In Transportation prefer:
Transportation

In Financial Services prefer:
Financial Services

In Business Serv. prefer:
Services
Distribution

Additional Information

Year Founded: 2001
Capital Under Management: $110,000,000
Current Activity Level : Actively seeking new investments

BITKEMY VENTURES

Rajapraasadamu, Level 5
Wing 2B
Hyderabad, Telangana, India
Website: bitkemy.com

Type of Firm

Private Equity Firm

Project Preferences

Type of Financing Preferred:
Seed

Additional Information

Year Founded: 2012
Current Activity Level : Actively seeking new investments

BITKRAFT ESPORTS VENTURES GMBH & CO I GR KG

Axel Springer Strasse 54b
Berlin, Germany 10117
E-mail: info@bitkraft.net
Website: www.bitkraft.net

Type of Firm

Private Equity Firm

Industry Preferences

In Computer Software prefer:
Software

In Consumer Related prefer:
Sports

Additional Information

Year Founded: 2017
Capital Under Management: $19,580,000
Current Activity Level : Actively seeking new investments

BITTERFONTEIN BV

Laan van Meerdervoort 1224
The Hague, Netherlands 2555 CD
Phone: 31703639950
Website: bitterfontein.com

Type of Firm

Private Equity Firm

Project Preferences

Type of Financing Preferred:
Leveraged Buyout
Later Stage
Management Buyouts

Geographical Preferences

International Preferences:
Europe

Industry Preferences

In Medical/Health prefer:
Pharmaceuticals

In Consumer Related prefer:
Entertainment and Leisure

In Industrial/Energy prefer:
Alternative Energy
Industrial Products
Machinery

In Financial Services prefer:
Real Estate

In Business Serv. prefer:
Services

Additional Information

Year Founded: 2003
Capital Under Management: $60,600,000
Current Activity Level : Actively seeking new investments

BIZMEDTECH SASU

5, Avenue du Grand Sablon
La Tronche, France 38700
Phone: 33476549543
Website: bizmedtech.com

Type of Firm

Incubator/Development Program

Project Preferences

Type of Financing Preferred:
Early Stage
Expansion
Later Stage
Seed

Geographical Preferences

International Preferences:
France

Industry Preferences

In Computer Hardware prefer:
Computers

In Medical/Health prefer:
Medical/Health

Additional Information

Year Founded: 2012
Current Activity Level : Actively seeking new investments

BIZOVO CAPITAL (BEIJING) CO LTD

No. 29 Suzhou Street
607 Weiya Building
Beijing, China 100080
Phone: 861059732606
Fax: 861059732609
Website: www.bizovo.com

Other Offices

No. 169 Fuxi Street
B7A Huayu International
Taiyuan, China 030013
Phone: 86-351-5601-257
Fax: 86-351-5601-259

No. 610 Nathan Road, Mongkok
Room 1318 Hollywood Plaza
Kowloon, Hong Kong

4-13-13 Nakayoshida
Kokuraminami-ku
Kitakyushu, Japan 802-0001

Type of Firm

Bank Affiliated

Project Preferences

Type of Financing Preferred:
Early Stage
Balanced
Later Stage

Geographical Preferences

International Preferences:
China

Industry Preferences

In Internet Specific prefer:
Internet

In Medical/Health prefer:
Medical/Health

In Consumer Related prefer:
Consumer Products

In Industrial/Energy prefer:
Energy
Materials
Machinery
Environmental Related

In Transportation prefer:
Transportation

In Financial Services prefer:
Financial Services

In Business Serv. prefer:
Services
Media

In Agr/Forestr/Fish prefer:
Agriculture related
Mining and Minerals

Additional Information

Year Founded: 2009
Capital Under Management: $44,454,000
Current Activity Level : Actively seeking new investments

BJERT INVEST A/S

Kolding park 2
Kolding, Denmark 6000
Phone: 4576312590
E-mail: info@bjertinvest.dk
Website: www.bjertinvest.dk

Type of Firm

Investment Management Firm

Project Preferences

Type of Financing Preferred:
Leveraged Buyout
Management Buyouts
Acquisition

Geographical Preferences

International Preferences:
Denmark

Additional Information

Year Founded: 1980
Current Activity Level : Actively seeking new investments

BK INVESTMENT CO LTD

1817, Jungang Daero
Geumjeong-gu
Busan-si, South Korea
Phone: 82517448088
Fax: 82517448089
E-mail: ssyim@bkinvestment.co.kr
Website: www.bkinvestment.co.kr

Other Offices

41 Senteomdong-Ro, Haeundae-Gu
307 Senteom Tower
Busan, South Korea
Phone: 82517448088
Fax: 82517448089

Management and Staff

Su Hyeon Cho, Chief Executive Officer

Type of Firm

Private Equity Firm

Association Membership

Korean Venture Capital Association (KVCA)

Project Preferences

Type of Financing Preferred:
Early Stage
Startup

Geographical Preferences

International Preferences:
Korea, South

Industry Preferences

In Industrial/Energy prefer:
Industrial Products

In Manufact. prefer:
Manufacturing

Additional Information

Year Founded: 2009
Capital Under Management: $18,297,000
Current Activity Level : Actively seeking new investments

BKK INVESTITIONSFONDS GMBH

Teltowkanalstrasse 1
Berlin, Germany 12247
Phone: 49-30-7690-3206

Type of Firm
Private Equity Firm

Project Preferences

Type of Financing Preferred:
Expansion
Later Stage
Management Buyouts
Recapitalizations

Size of Investments Considered:
Min Size of Investment Considered (000s): $2,400
Max Size of Investment Considered: No Limit

Geographical Preferences

International Preferences:
Germany

Additional Information

Year Founded: 1990
Current Activity Level : Actively seeking new investments

BLACK CORAL CAPITAL LLC

60 East 42nd Street
Suite 2514
New York, NY USA 10165
Phone: 6464682646
E-mail: info@blackcoralcapital.com
Website: www.blackcoralcapital.com

Other Offices

55 Union Street
Third Floor
Boston, MA USA 02108

2000 McGill College
Suite 500
Montreal, Canada H3A 3H3

Management and Staff

Christian Zabbal, Managing Director
Nikhil Garg, Vice President
Robert Day, Partner

Type of Firm
Private Equity Firm

Project Preferences

Type of Financing Preferred:
Balanced

Industry Preferences

In Industrial/Energy prefer:
Alternative Energy
Environmental Related

Additional Information

Year Founded: 2008
Current Activity Level : Actively seeking new investments

BLACK DIAMOND FINANCIAL GROUP LLC

1610 Wynkoop Street
Suite 400
Denver, CO USA 80202
Phone: 3038932334
E-mail: info@bdfin.com
Website: bdfin.com

Management and Staff

Patrick Imeson, Managing Director

Type of Firm
Private Equity Firm

Project Preferences

Type of Financing Preferred:
Leveraged Buyout

Geographical Preferences

United States Preferences:
All U.S.

Industry Preferences

In Industrial/Energy prefer:
Coal Related

In Agr/Forestr/Fish prefer:
Mining and Minerals

Additional Information

Year Founded: 2014
Current Activity Level : Actively seeking new investments

BLACK DIAMOND VENTURES INC

400 North Brand Boulevard
Suite 950
Glendale, CA USA 91203
Phone: 8182456250
Fax: 8182456255
E-mail: info@bdventures.com
Website: www.bdventures.com

Management and Staff

Christopher Lucas, Managing Director
John Kispert, Managing Partner
Rob Ukropina, Managing Partner

Type of Firm
Private Equity Firm

Project Preferences

Type of Financing Preferred:
Balanced

Size of Investments Considered:
Min Size of Investment Considered (000s): $500
Max Size of Investment Considered (000s): $5,000

Industry Preferences

In Communications prefer:
Telecommunications
Wireless Communications

In Semiconductor/Electr prefer:
Semiconductor

In Biotechnology prefer:
Biotechnology

In Medical/Health prefer:
Medical/Health
Diagnostic Test Products

Additional Information

Year Founded: 1998
Current Activity Level : Actively seeking new investments

BLACK GRANITE CAPITAL

369 Lexington Avenue
26th Floor
Manhattan, NY USA 10017
Phone: 6467226110
E-mail: info@blackgranitecap.com
Website: www.blackgranitecap.com

Type of Firm
Private Equity Firm

Geographical Preferences

United States Preferences:

Industry Preferences

In Medical/Health prefer:
Health Services

Additional Information
Year Founded: 2017
Current Activity Level : Actively seeking new investments

BLACK OPAL EQUITY LLC

2500 Plaza 5
Harborside Financial Center
Jersey City, NJ USA 07311
Phone: 201-633-3655
Fax: 201-633-3656
E-mail: info@blackopalequity.com
Website: www.blackopalequity.com

Management and Staff
Matthew Day, Managing Partner

Type of Firm
Private Equity Firm

Project Preferences

Type of Financing Preferred:
Leveraged Buyout
Acquisition

Geographical Preferences

United States Preferences:
All U.S.

Industry Preferences

In Medical/Health prefer:
Medical/Health
Health Services

In Consumer Related prefer:
Retail

In Industrial/Energy prefer:
Energy
Alternative Energy
Environmental Related

In Transportation prefer:
Transportation

In Utilities prefer:
Utilities

Additional Information
Year Founded: 2009
Current Activity Level : Actively seeking new investments

BLACK PEARLS VC SA

al. Grunwaldzka 472
Olivia Four building, 1st floo
Gdansk, Poland 80-309
Phone: 48533643209
E-mail: office@blackpearls.vc
Website: blackpearls.vc

Management and Staff
Alexander Lubanski, Managing Partner
Ewa Treitz, Venture Partner
Hubert Szczolek, Chief Financial Officer
Marcin Kowalik, Managing Partner
Marcin Zagorski, Partner
Piotr Pagowski, Venture Partner
Tomasz Wozniak, Principal

Type of Firm
Private Equity Firm

Project Preferences

Type of Financing Preferred:
Early Stage
Seed

Geographical Preferences

International Preferences:
Poland
Eastern Europe

Industry Preferences

In Computer Software prefer:
Software
Systems Software
Applications Software

Additional Information
Year Founded: 2013
Capital Under Management: $3,790,000
Current Activity Level : Actively seeking new investments

BLACK RIVER ASSET MANAGEMENT LLC

9320 Excelsior Boulevard
Hopkins, MN USA 55343
Phone: 9529843863
Fax: 9529843992

Other Offices

Av Morumbi, 8234- Brooklin
Sao Paulo, Brazil 04703-002

Plot D4, Saket District Center
Unit 111, Rectangle One
New Delhi, India 110017

12700 Whitewater Drive
Minnetonka, MN USA 55343

623 Fifth Avenue
27th Floor
New York, NY USA 10022

1200 Park Place
Suite 300
San Mateo, CA USA 94403

Fairmile Lane, Cobham, Surrey
Knowle Hill Park
London, United Kingdom KT11 2PD

Chemin De-Normandie 14
Geneva, Switzerland 1206

Leningradsky Prospekt 37A
Building 14
Moscow, Russia 125167

999 Huai Hai Middle Road
10/F Shanghai International Commerce Ctr
Shanghai, China 200031

Carrera 7, Nr 72-13
Piso 3
Bogota, Colombia

300 Beach Road
#23-01, The Concourse
Singapore, Singapore 199555

No. 4 A Blok Bolum 8-9-10-11
Baglarbasi, Kisikli Cad
Istanbul, Turkey 34662

\
1 Piso
Buenos Aires, Argentina 1001

Management and Staff
Eric Larson, Principal
Gary Jarrett, Chief Executive Officer
Guilherme Schmidt, Principal
Jeffrey Drobny, Principal
Jeremy Llewelyn, Principal

Type of Firm
Investment Management Firm

Association Membership
Emerging Markets Private Equity Association

Project Preferences

Type of Financing Preferred:
Leveraged Buyout

Geographical Preferences

International Preferences:
China
Asia
Africa

Industry Preferences

In Consumer Related prefer:
Food/Beverage

In Industrial/Energy prefer:
Materials

In Agr/Forestr/Fish prefer:
Agriculture related
Mining and Minerals

Additional Information
Name of Most Recent Fund: Black River Agriculture Fund 2, L.P.
Most Recent Fund Was Raised: 07/11/2013
Year Founded: 2003
Capital Under Management: $585,311,000
Current Activity Level : Actively seeking new investments

BLACK SHEEP CAPITAL

102 Commercial Road
Level One
Brisbane, Australia QLD 4005
Website: www.blacksheepcapital.com.au

Type of Firm
Private Equity Firm

Project Preferences

Type of Financing Preferred:
Value-Add
Early Stage
Seed
Startup

Geographical Preferences

International Preferences:
Australia

Industry Preferences

In Financial Services prefer:
Real Estate

Additional Information
Year Founded: 2014
Current Activity Level : Actively seeking new investments

BLACK TORO CAPITAL LLP

AVENIDA DIAGONAL 640

BARCELONA, Spain 08017
Phone: 34932520889
Fax: 34934675389
E-mail: info@blacktorocapital.com
Website: www.blacktorocapital.com

Other Offices
Former HQ: 5-6 Carlos Place
London, United Kingdom W1K 3AP
Phone: 442079079748

Type of Firm
Private Equity Firm

Project Preferences

Type of Financing Preferred:
Turnaround
Distressed Debt

Geographical Preferences

United States Preferences:
Southeast
Southwest

International Preferences:
Europe

Additional Information
Year Founded: 2011
Capital Under Management: $219,620,000
Current Activity Level : Actively seeking new investments

BLACK WALL STREET INVESTMENTS LLC

One World Trade Center
85th Floor
Durham, NC USA 27709
E-mail: info@blackwallstreetinvestments.com
Website: www.blackwallstreetinvestments.com

Management and Staff
Clarissa Goodlett, Chief Operating Officer

Type of Firm
Private Equity Firm

Project Preferences

Type of Financing Preferred:
Start-up Financing
Startup

Additional Information
Year Founded: 2015
Current Activity Level : Actively seeking new investments

BLACKBERN PARTNERS LLC

295 Madison Avenue
24th Floor
New York, NY USA 10017
Phone: 6462142843
E-mail: info@blackbernpartners.com
Website: blackbernpartners.com

Management and Staff
Ian Black, Principal
Jon Bernstein, Principal

Type of Firm
Private Equity Firm

Additional Information
Year Founded: 2010
Current Activity Level : Actively seeking new investments

BLACKBIRD VENTURES

240 Riley Street
Surry Hills, Australia NSW 2010
Website: www.blackbird.vc

Type of Firm
Private Equity Firm

Project Preferences

Type of Financing Preferred:
Later Stage
Startup

Geographical Preferences

International Preferences:
Australia

Industry Preferences

In Computer Software prefer:
Software

In Internet Specific prefer:
Ecommerce

Additional Information
Year Founded: 2012
Capital Under Management: $29,400,000
Current Activity Level : Actively seeking new investments

BLACKEAGLE PARTNERS FUND L P

6905 Telegraph Road
Suite 205
Bloomfield Hills, MI USA 48301
Phone: 3136475340
Website: www.blackeaglepartners.com

Other Offices
750 Lexington Avenue
Suite 1501
New York, NY USA 10022
Phone: 9175916010

Management and Staff
Bryan Tolles, Vice President
Garrett Kanehann, Co-Founder
Harry Watson, Co-Founder
Jason Runco, Co-Founder
Michael Madden, Co-Founder
Michael Wheatley, Vice President
Mike Monroe, Vice President

Type of Firm
Private Equity Firm

Project Preferences

Type of Financing Preferred:
Leveraged Buyout
Turnaround
Distressed Debt

Size of Investments Considered:
Min Size of Investment Considered (000s): $5,000
Max Size of Investment Considered (000s): $40,000

Geographical Preferences

United States Preferences:
All U.S.

Industry Preferences

In Medical/Health prefer:
Medical/Health

In Consumer Related prefer:
Consumer Products
Consumer Services

In Industrial/Energy prefer:
Energy

In Transportation prefer:
Transportation
Aerospace

In Business Serv. prefer:
Services

In Manufact. prefer:
Manufacturing

Additional Information
Year Founded: 2005
Current Activity Level : Actively seeking new investments

BLACKFIN CAPITAL PARTNERS SAS

127 Avenue des Champs Elysees
Paris, France 75008
Phone: 33175000230
Fax: 33175000239
Website: www.blackfincp.com

Type of Firm
Private Equity Firm

Association Membership
French Venture Capital Association (AFIC)

Project Preferences

Type of Financing Preferred:
Leveraged Buyout
Generalist PE
Later Stage
Management Buyouts
Acquisition

Geographical Preferences

International Preferences:
Europe
France

Industry Preferences

In Financial Services prefer:
Financial Services

In Business Serv. prefer:
Distribution

Additional Information
Name of Most Recent Fund: BlackFin Financial Services Fund FCPR
Most Recent Fund Was Raised: 01/18/2010
Year Founded: 2008
Capital Under Management: $549,880,000
Current Activity Level : Actively seeking new investments

BLACKFORD CAPITAL LLC

190 Monroe Avenue
Suite 600
Grand Rapids, MI USA 49503
Phone: 6162333161
Fax: 6168285042
E-mail: info@blackfordcapital.com
Website: www.blackfordcapital.com

Other Offices
Former: 15 Ionia Southwest
Suite 320
GRAND RAPIDS, MI USA 49503

1112 Motana Avenue
Suite 131
SANTA MONICA, CA USA 90403
Phone: 6174707803
Fax: 6168285042

Management and Staff
Jeffrey Johnson, Managing Director
Martin Stein, Managing Director
Tony Kiehn, Managing Director

Type of Firm
Private Equity Firm

Project Preferences

Type of Financing Preferred:
Leveraged Buyout
Management Buyouts
Acquisition

Geographical Preferences

United States Preferences:
Michigan

Canadian Preferences:
All Canada

Industry Preferences

In Industrial/Energy prefer:
Industrial Products

In Financial Services prefer:
Financial Services

In Business Serv. prefer:
Services
Distribution

In Manufact. prefer:
Manufacturing

Additional Information
Year Founded: 2000
Current Activity Level : Actively seeking new investments

BLACKHORN VENTURES CAPITAL MANAGEMENT LLC

1023 Walnut Street
Suite 100
Boulder, CO USA 80302
Website: www.blackhornvc.com

Management and Staff
Philip Oconnor, Managing Partner
Raymond Levitt, Venture Partner
Trevor Zimmerman, Managing Partner

Type of Firm
Private Equity Firm

Project Preferences

Type of Financing Preferred:
Early Stage

Industry Preferences

In Biotechnology prefer:
Industrial Biotechnology

Additional Information
Year Founded: 2017
Capital Under Management: $13,580,000
Current Activity Level : Actively seeking new investments

BLACKPOYNT BRAND VENTURES

35A Hazleton Avenue
Toronto, Canada M5R 2E3
Phone: 4166555000

Type of Firm
Private Equity Firm

Project Preferences

Type of Financing Preferred:
Early Stage
Seed

Geographical Preferences

United States Preferences:
North America

Industry Preferences

In Internet Specific prefer:
Internet

In Consumer Related prefer:
Consumer Products
Consumer Services

Additional Information
Name of Most Recent Fund: BrandProject, L.P.
Most Recent Fund Was Raised: 08/02/2013
Year Founded: 2013
Capital Under Management: $14,373,000
Current Activity Level : Actively seeking new investments

BLACKROCK INC

55 East 52nd Street
Park Avenue Plaza
New York, NY USA 10055
Phone: 6092826970
Fax: 6092820761
Website: www.blackrock.com

Other Offices
One University Square Drive
Third Floor
PRINCETON TOWNSHIP, NJ USA 08540
Phone: 6092823642
Fax: 6092820761

2200 West Main Street
Suite 500
DURHAM, NC USA 27705

Management and Staff
Amy Schioldager, Senior Managing Director
David Blumerw, Managing Director
Derek Stein, Senior Managing Director
J Richard Kushel, Senior Managing Director
Jeffrey Smith, Senior Managing Director
Joe Sutka, Managing Partner
Ken Kroner, Senior Managing Director
Mark McCombe, Senior Managing Director
N.J. Charrington, Senior Managing Director
Patrick Olson, Senior Managing Director
Peter Fisher, Senior Managing Director
Quintin Price, Senior Managing Director
Robert Fairbairn, Senior Managing Director
Robert Kapito, President
Robert Goldstein, Chief Operating Officer
Russ Steenberg, Managing Director
Ryan Stork, Senior Managing Director

Type of Firm
Private Equity Firm

Association Membership
British Venture Capital Association (BVCA)
National Venture Capital Association - USA (NVCA)
European Private Equity and Venture Capital Assoc.

Project Preferences

Role in Financing:
Prefer role in deals created by others

Type of Financing Preferred:
Fund of Funds
Leveraged Buyout
Value-Add
Mezzanine
Generalist PE
Balanced
Opportunistic
Other
Special Situation
Distressed Debt
Fund of Funds of Second

Geographical Preferences

United States Preferences:

International Preferences:
United Kingdom
Europe
Rest of World
Australia
Japan

Industry Focus
(% based on actual investment)
Internet Specific	21.4%
Computer Software and Services	20.0%
Communications and Media	18.8%
Industrial/Energy	18.0%
Other Products	15.0%
Computer Hardware	4.4%
Biotechnology	1.5%
Medical/Health	0.8%

Additional Information
Name of Most Recent Fund: Blackrock Private Equity Partners VI US, L.P.
Most Recent Fund Was Raised: 07/22/2013
Year Founded: 1999
Capital Under Management: $17,200,000,000
Current Activity Level : Actively seeking new investments
Method of Compensation: Return on invest. most important, but chg. closing fees, service fees, etc.

BLACKROCK PRIVATE EQUITY PARTNERS AG

Mythenquai 50/60
PO Box
Zurich, Switzerland 8022
Phone: 41432852121
Fax: 41432852999

Other Offices
55 East 52nd Street
New York, NY USA 10055
Phone: 1-917-368-4002
Fax: 1-917-368-4386

Management and Staff
George Quinn, Chief Financial Officer
Stefan Lippe, Chief Executive Officer
Thomas Wellauer, Chief Operating Officer

Type of Firm
Private Equity Advisor or Fund of Funds

Association Membership
Swiss Venture Capital Association (SECA)
European Private Equity and Venture Capital Assoc.

Project Preferences

Type of Financing Preferred:
Fund of Funds

Geographical Preferences

United States Preferences:
All U.S.

International Preferences:
Europe
All International

Additional Information
Name of Most Recent Fund: Swiss Re Private Equity Partners III
Most Recent Fund Was Raised: 01/01/2005
Year Founded: 1863
Capital Under Management: $2,000,000,000
Current Activity Level : Actively seeking new investments

BLACKSTAR GROUP PLC

Saint Julian's Road
4th Floor, Avantech Building
San Gwann, Malta 2805
Phone: 35621446377
Fax: 35621446330
E-mail: info@blackstar.lu

Pratt's Guide to Private Equity & Venture Capital Sources

Other Offices
11 Crescent Drive
2nd floor
Melrose, South Africa 2076
Phone: 27112148500
Fax: 27112148511

Type of Firm
Investment Management Firm

Project Preferences

Type of Financing Preferred:
Leveraged Buyout
Mezzanine
Management Buyouts
Acquisition

Geographical Preferences

International Preferences:
Africa

Additional Information
Year Founded: 2009
Current Activity Level : Actively seeking new investments

BLACKSTONE GROUP LP

345 Park Avenue
31st Floor
New York, NY USA 10154
Phone: 2125835000
Fax: 2125835749
E-mail: BlackstoneInvestorRelations@blackstone.com
Website: m

Other Offices
Midtown Tower, 9-7-1 Akasaka, Minato-ku
22nd Floor
Tokyo, Japan 107-6222
Phone: 81-3-4577-8400
Fax: 81-3-4577-8401

No. 7, Finance Street
Unit F817-18, Winland Int'l Finance Ctr.
Beijing, China
Phone: 86-10-6649-7300
Fax: 86-10-6649-7301

Marina Bay Financial Tower 2
Ste 13-01/02, 10 Marina Blvd.
Singapore, Singapore 018983
Phone: 6568507500
Fax: 6568507501

8 Finance Street, Suite 901, 9th Floor
Two International Finance Center
Central, Hong Kong
Phone: 852-3656-8600
Fax: 852-3656-8601

1318 Lujiazui Ring Road
Unit 1101, DBS Bank Tower
Shanghai, China 200120
Phone: 86-21-6169-8188
Fax: 86-21-6169-8189

One Macquarie Place
Suite 3901
Sydney, Australia 2000
Phone: 61-2-8016-7200
Fax: 61-2-8016-7201

Express Towers
Nariman Point
Mumbai, India 400-021
Phone: 91-22-6752-8500
Fax: 91-22-6752-8531

3 rue Paul Cezanne
Paris, France 75008
Phone: 33-1-5669-1630
Fax: 33-1-5669-1631

Benrather Strasse 12
Dusseldorf, Germany 40213
Phone: 49-21-1862-8400
Fax: 49-21-1862-8401

1299 Ocean Avenue
Suite 320
SANTA MONICA, CA USA 90401
Phone: 310-310-6949
Fax: 310-310-6998

53 State Street
Exchange Place
BOSTON, MA USA 02109
Phone: 617-646-2900
Fax: 617-646-2905

4401 Northside Parkway
Suite 375
ATLANTA, GA USA 30327
Phone: 404-460-2321
Fax: 404-460-2337

2494 Sand Hill Road
Suite 200
MENLO PARK, CA USA 94025
Phone: 650-798-3800
Fax: 650-798-3801

280 Park Avenue
Eleventh Floor
New York, NY USA 10017
Phone: 2125032100
Fax: 2125036930

Management and Staff
A.J. Agarwal, Senior Managing Director
Abhimanyu Prakash, Principal
Adrian Millan, Principal
Akhilesh Gupta, Senior Managing Director
Akira Kosugi, Managing Director
Akshay Shah, Managing Director

Alan Milstein, Principal
Alan Yang, Principal
Alan Miyasaki, Senior Managing Director
Alberto Santulin, Managing Director
Alessandro Fiascaris, Principal
Alex Moomjy, Senior Managing Director
Alex Leonard, Principal
Alexander Zarzhevsky, Principal
Alexandra Hill, Managing Director
Alicia Corbin, Principal
Allen Otto, Vice President
Amit Dixit, Senior Managing Director
Amy Lee, Vice President
Andrea Valeri, Managing Director
Andrew Lax, Managing Director
Andrew Cheng, Vice President
Andrew Kuo, Senior Managing Director
Andy O Brien, Managing Director
Angelina Perkovic, Vice President
Angelo Acconcia, Managing Director
Anil Khera, Principal
Anjan Mukherjee, Senior Managing Director
Anna-Marie Horgan, Principal
Anne Simon, Vice President
Anthony Myers, Managing Director
Anthony Steains, Senior Managing Director
Anthony Leung, Senior Managing Director
Anthony Beovich, Managing Director
Araceli Corsini, Vice President
Arthur Liao, Managing Director
Asheesh Mohta, Principal
Axel Herberg, Senior Managing Director
Barry Gallagher, Vice President
Ben Hakim, Senior Managing Director
Beth Chartoff, Senior Managing Director
Brad Marshall, Managing Director
Brendan Boyle, Senior Managing Director
Brett Newman, Vice President
Brett Condron, Managing Director
Brian Kriebel, Principal
Brian Schwartz, Managing Director
Brian Levine, Senior Managing Director
Brian Shelby, Vice President
Brian Gavin, Senior Managing Director
Brian Kim, Managing Director
Bruce McEvoy, Principal
Byron Blount, Managing Director
C.J. Brown, Managing Director
Carol Kim, Managing Director
Cecilia Ott, Vice President
Chad Pike, Senior Managing Director
Charles Purse, Senior Managing Director
Chinh Chu, Senior Managing Director
Chisato Konda, Vice President
Chris Pasko, Senior Managing Director
Chris Sullivan, Managing Director
Christiana Voskarides, Managing Director
Christine Veschi, Principal
Christopher Nicolaou, Vice President
Christopher Heady, Senior Managing Director
Christopher Chung, Vice President
Christopher James, Managing Director
Colleen Longobardi, Principal
Cynthia Carter, Principal
Daigo Hirai, Principal

Daisuke Kitta, Principal
Daniel Hook, Vice President
Daniel Chang, Vice President
Daniel Fujii, Managing Director
Daniel McMullen, Managing Director
Daniel Prendergast, Senior Managing Director
Daniel Smith, Senior Managing Director
Darren Richman, Senior Managing Director
David Figur, Chief Financial Officer
David Mehenny, Vice President
David Tanzer, Vice President
David Krejci, Vice President
David Cunningham, Principal
David Barry, Principal
David Yoon, Principal
David Kim, Managing Director
David Hirsh, Managing Director
David Roth, Managing Director
David Foley, Senior Managing Director
David Riddell, Senior Managing Director
David Blitzer, Senior Managing Director
David Posnick, Senior Managing Director
Debra Anderson, Senior Managing Director
Denis Fabre, Senior Managing Director
Dennis Walsh, Managing Director
Dennis McDonagh, Senior Managing Director
Dermot Caden, Vice President
Diego San Jose, Principal
Dominik Brambring, Managing Director
Donald Scott, Senior Managing Director
Douglas Ostrover, Senior Managing Director
Douglas Logigian, Managing Director
Douglas Paolilo, Managing Director
Doyle Queally, Managing Director
Dustin Goodwin, Vice President
E. Blair Ritchie, Principal
Edward Huang, Managing Director
Edward Meyer, Managing Director
Edward Slapansky, Vice President
Elizabeth Coleman-Chen, Vice President
Elliot Eisenberger, Managing Director
Emily Sharko, Principal
Emily Reycroft, Managing Director
Eric McAlpine, Managing Director
Eric Storch, Managing Director
Eric Perlyn, Vice President
Eric Rosenberg, Managing Director
Erik Lisher, Managing Director
Erin Carney, Managing Director
Fabian Godbersen, Managing Director
Farhad Karim, Managing Director
Faris Saah, Managing Director
Florian Schaefer, Principal
Frank Cohen, Senior Managing Director
Frank Schmitz, Senior Managing Director
Gabriel Petersen, Managing Director
Garrett Moran, Senior Managing Director
Garrett Goldberg, Managing Director
Gary Sumers, Senior Managing Director
Geoffrey Strong, Principal
Geoffrey Stockwell, Principal
George Fan, Senior Managing Director
George Samoladas, Vice President
Gerry Murphy, Senior Managing Director
Gideon Berger, Senior Managing Director

Gilles Lengaigne, Principal
Glenn Alba, Managing Director
Go Yamashita, Vice President
Graham Martin, Principal
Greg Geiling, Senior Managing Director
Greg Blank, Principal
Greg Hewett, Senior Managing Director
Gregorio Bravo Garcia, Vice President
Gregory Hall, Senior Managing Director
Gregory Leong, Managing Director
Halbert Lindguist, Senior Managing Director
Harold Baron, Managing Director
Hayley Stein, Vice President
Helen Smither, Principal
Henry Hsu, Managing Director
Hwachie Lee, Principal
Ian Morris, Managing Director
Iliana Sobczak, Vice President
Ivan Brockman, Senior Managing Director
Jaime Hildreth, Vice President
Jake Cabala, Principal
James Lock, Managing Director
James Quella, Senior Managing Director
James Roche, Principal
James Christopher, Managing Director
James Westcott, Principal
James Lee, Managing Director
James Kiggen, Senior Managing Director
James Seppala, Managing Director
James Didden, Senior Managing Director
Jamie Baird, Vice President
Jamie O Connell, Managing Director
Jan Weidner, Senior Managing Director
Jane Lee, Managing Director
Jason New, Senior Managing Director
Jason Gregory, Vice President
Jason Giordano, Principal
Jason Wallace, Managing Director
Jay Liebowitz, Principal
Jay Parekh, Vice President
Jean-Manuel Richier, Senior Managing Director
Jean-Michel Steg, Senior Managing Director
Jeffrey Pribyl, Vice President
Jennifer Kaminsky, Vice President
Jennifer Tai Chang, Vice President
Jeppe Brondum, Vice President
Jerome Herschman, Managing Director
Jerry DeVito, Managing Director
Jessica Rosen, Principal
Jitesh Gadhia, Senior Managing Director
Joan Solotar, Senior Managing Director
John Cashwell, Managing Director
John Magliano, Managing Director
John Dionne, Senior Managing Director
John Estes, Vice President
John Studzinski, Senior Managing Director
John McCormick, Senior Managing Director
John Shields, Vice President
John-Paul Miller, Vice President
Jonas Agesand, Managing Director
Jonathan Lurvey, Managing Director
Jonathan Koplovitz, Senior Managing Director
Jonathan Kaufman, Principal
Jordan Steinberg, Vice President
Jordan Peer, Principal

Jose Mestres, Managing Director
Joseph Lohrer, Managing Director
Joseph Russell, Managing Director
Joseph Pedlow, Managing Director
Joseph DeFalco, Managing Director
Joseph Soares, Principal
Joseph Malangoni, Vice President
Joseph Herman, Senior Managing Director
Joshua Baumgarten, Managing Director
Joshua Peel, Principal
Joshua Krapf, Vice President
Joshua Rovine, Managing Director
Juan Sierra, Vice President
Judy Turchin, Managing Director
Juergen Pinker, Principal
Julia Kahr, Managing Director
Kallan Resnick, Principal
Karen Beyer, Managing Director
Karen Sprogis, Managing Director
Kashif Aslam, Vice President
Kathleen Hogan, Managing Director
Kathleen Skero, Managing Director
Kathleen McCarthy, Managing Director
Kearnon O Molony, Managing Director
Keigo Kuroda, Principal
Kemal Kaya, Senior Managing Director
Ken Duca, Vice President
Ken Nguyen, Vice President
Kenneth Caplan, Senior Managing Director
Kenneth Whitney, Senior Managing Director
Keri Gammill, Managing Director
Kevin Dinnie, Managing Director
Killian Maher, Vice President
Kristen Eshak, Managing Director
Lama Kanazeh, Principal
Larry Nath, Senior Managing Director
Laura Waitz, Managing Director
Lawrence Thuet, Senior Managing Director
Lawrence Guffey, Senior Managing Director
Lee Shaiman, Managing Director
Leif Lindback, Managing Director
Les Baquiran, Principal
Louis Salvatore, Senior Managing Director
Louis-Simon Ferland, Principal
Louise Somers, Vice President
Luv Parikh, Principal
Marc Baliotti, Managing Director
Marc-Antonio Bouyer, Principal
Maria Singer, Managing Director
Marion-Sophie Buten, Principal
Marisa Beeney, Managing Director
Mark Brown, Principal
Mark Moffat, Managing Director
Mark Miller, Vice President
Mark Buschmann, Managing Director
Martin Kandrac, Managing Director
Martin Brand, Managing Director
Martin Donnelly, Managing Director
Martin Gudgeon, Senior Managing Director
Martin Alderson Smith, Senior Managing Director
Mary Citrino, Senior Managing Director
Mary Lynn Eubanks, Managing Director
Matt Pedley, Principal
Matthew Tambellini, Vice President
Matthew Weidemoyer, Managing Director

Pratt's Guide to Private Equity & Venture Capital Sources

Matthew Skurbe, Managing Director
Matthew Quigley, Senior Managing Director
Matthew Tooth, Managing Director
Matthew Cyriac, Senior Managing Director
Mattia McDonough, Managing Director
Mayank Rawat, Principal
Menes Chee, Managing Director
Meng Gao, Managing Director
Michael Purvis, Managing Director
Michael Fronte, Managing Director
Michael Flanagan, Managing Director
Michael O Hara, Managing Director
Michael Fabiano, Principal
Michael Zawadzki, Principal
Michael Henningsen, Principal
Michael Pegler, Principal
Michael Chae, Chief Financial Officer
Michael Garrow, Vice President
Michael Nash, Senior Managing Director
Michael Genereux, Senior Managing Director
Michael Stark, Senior Managing Director
Michael Whitman, Senior Managing Director
Miguel Ramos-Fuentenebro, Managing Director
Mike Wilcox, Vice President
Mike Casey, Senior Managing Director
Mike Ramirez, Principal
Min-Yong Kim, Principal
Mustafa Siddiqui, Principal
Nadeem Meghji, Principal
Nacim El Gabbani, Principal
Natalie Hwang, Vice President
Nathaniel Bayko, Principal
Neal Denning, Managing Director
Neil Simpkins, Senior Managing Director
Nentcho Nentchev, Managing Director
Nicholas Leone, Senior Managing Director
Nicolas Hubert, Managing Director
Nicole Degnan, Managing Director
Nitin Karnani, Senior Managing Director
Nobuhito Nieda, Principal
Olivier Meyohas, Managing Director
Owen Boger, Principal
Patricia Lynett, Managing Director
Patrick Schumacher, Managing Director
Patrick Daly, Senior Managing Director
Patrick Gilligan, Principal
Patrick McKeon, Managing Director
Paul Hudson, Principal
Paul Braude, Vice President
Paul Heller, Principal
Paulo Eapen, Principal
Peter Mayer, Senior Managing Director
Peter Rose, Senior Managing Director
Peter Koffler, Senior Managing Director
Peter Stoll, Senior Managing Director
Peter Cohen, Senior Managing Director
Peter Wallace, Senior Managing Director
Peter Laurinaitis, Managing Director
Peter Rand, Managing Director
Peter Sotoloff, Managing Director
Philippe Chmelar, Vice President
Philippe Benaroya, Managing Director
Pierre Bourderye, Managing Director
Pilar Junco, Managing Director
Pinda Eng, Managing Director
Pithambar Gona, Vice President
Poh Heng Tan, Principal
Prakash Melwani, Senior Managing Director
Prashant Kanodia, Principal
Raffiq Nathoo, Senior Managing Director
Rafic Said, Senior Managing Director
Randall Rothschild, Managing Director
Randall Kessler, Principal
Rashmi Madan, Managing Director
Richard Dziurzynski, Managing Director
Richard Gannalo, Vice President
Richard Scarinci, Vice President
Robert Jordan, Managing Director
Robert Horn, Managing Director
Robert Harper, Managing Director
Robert Ramsauer, Principal
Robert Zable, Principal
Robert Kulperger, Principal
Robert Yang, Principal
Robert Kalik, Vice President
Robert Petrini, Senior Managing Director
Robert Cohen, Vice President
Robert McMullan, Senior Managing Director
Robert Reid, Senior Managing Director
Roger Coyle, Principal
Ronald Lintag, Vice President
Ruaraidh Campbell, Vice President
Saif Assam, Principal
Salvatore Paxia, Managing Director
Sarah McCormick, Vice President
Scott Soussa, Senior Managing Director
Scott Eisenberg, Principal
Scott Simon, Managing Director
Sean Keene, Senior Managing Director
Sean Klimczak, Managing Director
Sean Madnani, Managing Director
Sebastian Arango, Vice President
Shan Fu, Senior Managing Director
Shannon Gallagher, Principal
Sharon Burley, Managing Director
Shirish Joshi, Vice President
Shuk Fan Shek, Vice President
Siddhartha Gupta, Principal
Stephane Aubry, Vice President
Stephen Buehler, Vice President
Stephen Skrenta, Senior Managing Director
Stephens Sullens, Senior Managing Director
Steve Zelin, Senior Managing Director
Stuart Grant, Senior Managing Director
Susannah Lindenfield, Managing Director
Tania Daguere, Principal
Thomas Laroque, Vice President
Thomas Stoddard, Senior Managing Director
Thomas Roberts, Senior Managing Director
Thomas Morrison, Senior Managing Director
Thomas Middleton, Senior Managing Director
Thomas Kelly, Managing Director
Tia Breakley, Managing Director
Tim Wang, Managing Director
Tim Murray, Managing Director
Timothy White, Senior Managing Director
Timothy Johnson, Principal
Timothy Coleman, Senior Managing Director
Tom Campbell, Managing Director
Tuhin Parikh, Managing Director
Tyler Henritze, Managing Director
Valerie Kritsberg, Principal
Vijay Bharadia, Managing Director
Vikrant Sawhney, Senior Managing Director
Vincent Lu, Managing Director
Viral Patel, Managing Director
William Burt, Vice President
William Hobbs, Vice President
William Mulrow, Senior Managing Director
William Stein, Senior Managing Director
William Oglesby, Senior Managing Director
Wouter Mak, Principal
Xinyu Liu, Managing Director
Yanyan Gao, Managing Director
Yusuke Sasaki, Vice President
Zachary Stassi, Principal

Type of Firm
Investment Management Firm

Association Membership
Australian Venture Capital Association (AVCAL)
China Venture Capital Association
German Venture Capital Association (BVK)
Private Equity Council (PEC)
European Private Equity and Venture Capital Assoc.
Indian Venture Capital Association (IVCA)

Project Preferences

Type of Financing Preferred:
Leveraged Buyout
Value-Add
Mezzanine
Balanced
Opportunistic
Recapitalizations

Geographical Preferences

United States Preferences:
North America
All U.S.

International Preferences:
Asia Pacific
Australia
Asia
Korea, South
All International

Industry Focus
(% based on actual investment)

Other Products	55.8%
Consumer Related	13.1%
Industrial/Energy	8.5%
Computer Hardware	6.0%
Computer Software and Services	5.9%
Communications and Media	4.0%
Medical/Health	2.9%
Semiconductors/Other Elect.	2.7%
Internet Specific	1.0%
Biotechnology	0.2%

Additional Information
Year Founded: 1985
Capital Under Management: $84,300,000,000
Current Activity Level : Actively seeking new investments

BLACKSTREET CAPITAL MANAGEMENT LLC

5425 Wisconsin Avenue
Suite 701
Chevy Chase, MD USA 20815
Phone: 2402231330
Fax: 2402231331
E-mail: info@blackstreetcapital.com
Website: blackstreetcapital.com

Management and Staff
Aldus Chapin II, Managing Director
Angel Donchev, Vice President
Caroline Miller, Chief Financial Officer
Charlie Manry, Vice President
David Hartman, Vice President
Lawrence Berger, Managing Director
Murry Gunty, Managing Partner

Type of Firm
Bank Affiliated

Project Preferences

Type of Financing Preferred:
Leveraged Buyout
Turnaround

Geographical Preferences

United States Preferences:
Mid Atlantic
Midwest
Southeast
East Coast

Industry Preferences

In Communications prefer:
Commercial Communications

In Internet Specific prefer:
Internet

In Medical/Health prefer:
Medical/Health

In Consumer Related prefer:
Consumer
Retail
Other Restaurants
Education Related

In Industrial/Energy prefer:
Industrial Products

In Business Serv. prefer:
Distribution
Media

In Manufact. prefer:
Manufacturing

Additional Information
Name of Most Recent Fund: Black Street Capital Partners I, L.P. (AKA: BRP, FKA: MMP I)
Most Recent Fund Was Raised: 03/03/2003
Year Founded: 1996
Capital Under Management: $88,000,000
Current Activity Level : Actively seeking new investments

BLACKTHORNE PARTNERS, LTD.

375 Bishops Way, Suite 222
Brookfield, WI USA 53005
Phone: 2627865100
E-mail: info@blackthornepartners.com
Website: www.blackthornepartners.com

Management and Staff
John Syburg, President, Founder
Steve Balistreri, Managing Director

Type of Firm
Private Equity Firm

Project Preferences

Type of Financing Preferred:
Fund of Funds
Generalist PE
Acquisition

Geographical Preferences

United States Preferences:
Southeast
Wisconsin

Industry Preferences

In Business Serv. prefer:
Services
Distribution

In Manufact. prefer:
Manufacturing

Additional Information
Name of Most Recent Fund: Blackthorne Venture Fund LLC
Most Recent Fund Was Raised: 08/26/2010
Year Founded: 2007
Capital Under Management: $300,000
Current Activity Level : Actively seeking new investments

BLADE LLC

250 Consumer Street
Boston, MA USA 02210
Phone: 6174313910
E-mail: hello@blade.net
Website: www.blade.net

Management and Staff
Dennis Doughty, Vice President
Paul Schwenk, Co-Founder

Type of Firm
Incubator/Development Program

Project Preferences

Type of Financing Preferred:
Seed
Startup

Geographical Preferences

United States Preferences:
Massachusetts

Industry Preferences

In Computer Software prefer:
Software
Systems Software
Applications Software

In Computer Other prefer:
Computer Related

Additional Information
Year Founded: 2014
Current Activity Level : Actively seeking new investments

BLADE PARTNERS

27762 Antonio Parkway
Suite L1-426
Mission Viejo, CA USA 92694
Phone: 9492984595
Fax: 9495540181
Website: www.bladeventures.com

Management and Staff
Brian Flucht, Principal
Craig Gunther, Managing Director
Rajeev Varshneya, Venture Partner

Type of Firm
Private Equity Firm

Project Preferences

Role in Financing:
Prefer role as deal originator but will also invest in deals created by others

Type of Financing Preferred:
Early Stage
Balanced
Seed
Startup

Size of Investments Considered:
Min Size of Investment Considered (000s): $200
Max Size of Investment Considered (000s): $2,000

Geographical Preferences

United States Preferences:
All U.S.

Industry Preferences

In Semiconductor/Electr prefer:
Controllers and Sensors

In Medical/Health prefer:
Medical/Health
Medical Diagnostics

In Business Serv. prefer:
Media

Additional Information

Year Founded: 2005
Current Activity Level : Actively seeking new investments
Method of Compensation: Return on investment is of primary concern, do not charge fees

BLAZAR VENTURES LLC

211 North Union Street
Suite 100
Alexandria, VA USA 22314
Phone: 17035191214
E-mail: info@blazarventures.com
Website: www.blazarventures.com

Type of Firm
Private Equity Firm

Project Preferences

Type of Financing Preferred:
Leveraged Buyout
Generalist PE
Seed

Industry Preferences

In Computer Software prefer:
Artificial Intelligence

In Internet Specific prefer:
E-Commerce Technology
Internet

Additional Information

Year Founded: 2017
Current Activity Level : Actively seeking new investments

BLC INVEST SAL

Royal Tower Building
Nicolas Turk Street-Medawar
Beirut, Lebanon 2064-5809
Phone: 9611566207
Fax: 9611565311
E-mail: info@blcinvest.com

Type of Firm
Private Equity Firm

Project Preferences

Type of Financing Preferred:
Leveraged Buyout
Early Stage
Expansion
Later Stage
Management Buyouts

Geographical Preferences

International Preferences:
Lebanon

Industry Preferences

In Consumer Related prefer:
Food/Beverage

In Business Serv. prefer:
Services

In Manufact. prefer:
Manufacturing

In Utilities prefer:
Utilities

Additional Information

Year Founded: 1950
Current Activity Level : Actively seeking new investments

BLEU CAPITAL LLC

41 E 11th Street
11th Floor
New York, NY USA 10003
E-mail: hello@bleucap.com

Type of Firm
Private Equity Firm

Project Preferences

Type of Financing Preferred:
Early Stage

Additional Information

Year Founded: 2015
Current Activity Level : Actively seeking new investments

BLH VENTURE PARTNERS LLC

75 Fifth Street Northwest
Suite 422
Atlanta, GA USA 30308
Phone: 4049418780
Website: www.blhventures.com

Type of Firm
Private Equity Firm

Project Preferences

Type of Financing Preferred:
Early Stage

Industry Preferences

In Internet Specific prefer:
Internet
Ecommerce

In Consumer Related prefer:
Consumer

In Business Serv. prefer:
Media

Additional Information

Year Founded: 2010
Current Activity Level : Actively seeking new investments

BLOC VENTURES LTD

200 St Johns Street
London, United Kingdom EC1V 4RN
Phone: 442081233650
E-mail: info@blocventures.com
Website: www.blocventures.com

Management and Staff

Bruce Beckloff, Managing Partner
David Leftley, Managing Partner

Type of Firm
Private Equity Firm

Project Preferences

Type of Financing Preferred:
Early Stage

Geographical Preferences

International Preferences:
United Kingdom

Additional Information

Year Founded: 2017
Current Activity Level : Actively seeking new investments

BLOCK 26 LLC

3055 Overland Avenue
Suite 200
Los Angeles, CA USA 90034
Phone: 3104337066
E-mail: info@block26.com
Website: www.block26.com

Type of Firm
Incubator/Development Program

Project Preferences

Type of Financing Preferred:
Balanced
Startup

Industry Preferences

In Financial Services prefer:
Financial Services

Additional Information
Year Founded: 2015
Current Activity Level : Actively seeking new investments

BLOCK ONE CAPITAL INC

925 West Georgia Street
Suite 1000
Vancouver, Canada V6C 3L2
Website: www.blockonecap.com

Type of Firm
Private Equity Firm

Project Preferences

Type of Financing Preferred:
Early Stage

Additional Information
Year Founded: 2017
Current Activity Level : Actively seeking new investments

BLOCKCHAIN CAPITAL

One Ferry Building
Suite 255
San Francisco, CA USA 94111
Phone: 4156775440
E-mail: contact@ccp-lp.com
Website: www.blockchain.capital

Management and Staff
P. Bart Stephens, Co-Founder
W. Bradford Stephens, Co-Founder

Type of Firm
Private Equity Firm

Project Preferences

Type of Financing Preferred:
Seed
Startup

Additional Information
Year Founded: 2014
Capital Under Management: $73,820,000
Current Activity Level : Actively seeking new investments

BLOSSOM STREET VENTURES

5307 E Mockingbird Lane
Suite 802
Dallas, TX USA 75206
Website: www.blossomstreetventures.com

Type of Firm
Private Equity Firm

Project Preferences

Type of Financing Preferred:
Early Stage
Balanced
Seed

Geographical Preferences

United States Preferences:

Canadian Preferences:
All Canada

Industry Preferences

In Computer Software prefer:
Software

Additional Information
Year Founded: 2014
Capital Under Management: $6,600,000
Current Activity Level : Actively seeking new investments

BLS VENTURE CAPITAL GMBH

Darser Strasse 26
Berlin, Germany 14167
Phone: 493023271587
Fax: 491803551854427
E-mail: info@bls-venture.de
Website: www.bls-venture.de

Type of Firm
Private Equity Firm

Project Preferences

Type of Financing Preferred:
Early Stage
Seed
Startup

Geographical Preferences

International Preferences:
Germany

Industry Preferences

In Computer Software prefer:
Software

In Semiconductor/Electr prefer:
Semiconductor
Micro-Processing
Sensors

Additional Information
Year Founded: 1999
Current Activity Level : Actively seeking new investments

BLSW MANAGEMENT GMBH & CO KG

Obergruenewalder Strasse 8a
Wuppertal, Germany 42103
Phone: 4920287005170
Fax: 4920287005172
E-mail: info@blsw.de
Website: www.blsw.de

Type of Firm
Private Equity Firm

Project Preferences

Type of Financing Preferred:
Early Stage
Seed

Geographical Preferences

International Preferences:
Europe

Industry Preferences

In Computer Software prefer:
Software

Additional Information
Year Founded: 2015
Capital Under Management: $13,581,000
Current Activity Level : Actively seeking new investments

BLU VENTURE INVESTORS LLC

1577 Spring Hill Road
Suite 405
Vienna, VA USA 22182
Website: www.bluventureinvestors.com

Management and Staff

David Krauskopf, Principal
Dendy Young, Principal
Denis Seynhaeve, Principal
Eric Adler, Principal
G.L. Kohlenberger, Principal
Hal Shelton, Principal
J.S. Gamble, Principal
Jack Hangen, Principal
James Hunt, Co-Founder
Joe Callanan, Principal
Keith Bozeman, Principal
Kevin Hollins, Principal
Kim Nguyen, Principal
Lance Ullom, Principal
Matt Hanson, Principal
Mike Kostoff, Principal
Paul Silber, Principal
Peter Hayes, Principal
Pradeep Wahi, Principal
Pradeep Kaul, Principal
Robert Proctor, Co-Founder
Robert Struble, Principal
Steven Chen, Principal
T. Richard Stroupe, Principal
Tarun Upadhyay, Principal

Type of Firm
Angel Group

Project Preferences

Type of Financing Preferred:
Early Stage

Size of Investments Considered:
Min Size of Investment Considered (000s): $500
Max Size of Investment Considered (000s): $1,000

Geographical Preferences

United States Preferences:
Mid Atlantic
North Carolina
Maryland
Virginia
Washington
D. of Columbia

Industry Preferences

In Computer Software prefer:
Software

Additional Information
Year Founded: 2011
Capital Under Management: $10,600,000
Current Activity Level : Actively seeking new investments

BLUE BEAR CAPITAL LLC

1101 Fifth Avenue, Suite 100
San Rafael, CA USA 94901
E-mail: info@bluebearcap.com
Website: www.bluebearcap.com

Management and Staff

Brian Iversen, Venture Partner
Ernst Sack, Partner
Mark Leggett, Venture Partner
Martin Rajcan, Venture Partner
Oliver Richards, Venture Partner
Robert Macinnis, Partner
Timothy Kopra, Partner

Type of Firm
Private Equity Firm

Project Preferences

Type of Financing Preferred:
Balanced

Industry Preferences

In Industrial/Energy prefer:
Energy

Additional Information
Year Founded: 2016
Current Activity Level : Actively seeking new investments

BLUE CHIP VENTURE CO

312 Walnut Street
Suite 1120
Cincinnati, OH USA 45202
Phone: 5137232300
Fax: 513723306
E-mail: info@bcvc.com
Website: www.bcvc.com

Other Offices

11611 North Meridian Street
Suite 310
Carmel, IN USA 46032
Phone: 317-275-6800
Fax: 317-275-1100

Management and Staff

Susan Schieman, Chief Financial Officer

Type of Firm
Private Equity Firm

Project Preferences

Role in Financing:
Prefer role as deal originator

Type of Financing Preferred:
Early Stage
Balanced
Later Stage

Size of Investments Considered:
Min Size of Investment Considered (000s): $4,000
Max Size of Investment Considered (000s): $6,000

Geographical Preferences

United States Preferences:
Midwest
Northeast

Canadian Preferences:
All Canada

Industry Focus

(% based on actual investment)

Internet Specific	40.3%
Computer Software and Services	23.2%
Medical/Health	15.2%
Communications and Media	5.7%
Consumer Related	4.0%
Semiconductors/Other Elect.	3.4%
Other Products	2.9%
Biotechnology	2.4%
Industrial/Energy	1.8%
Computer Hardware	0.9%

Additional Information
Name of Most Recent Fund: Blue Chip VI LLC
Most Recent Fund Was Raised: 06/28/2013
Year Founded: 1990
Capital Under Management: $600,000,000
Current Activity Level : Actively seeking new investments
Method of Compensation: Return on investment is of primary concern, do not charge fees

---

BLUE CLOUD VENTURES

183 Madison Avenue
Suite 806
New York, NY USA 10016
Website: www.bluecloudventures.com

Management and Staff

Scott Chasin, Partner

Type of Firm
Private Equity Firm

Project Preferences

Type of Financing Preferred:
Expansion
Later Stage

Size of Investments Considered:
Min Size of Investment Considered (000s): $1,000
Max Size of Investment Considered (000s): $3,000

Industry Preferences

In Communications prefer:
Communications and Media
Media and Entertainment

In Computer Software prefer:
Software
Systems Software
Applications Software

In Internet Specific prefer:
E-Commerce Technology

Additional Information
Year Founded: 2012
Capital Under Management: $52,580,000
Current Activity Level : Actively seeking new investments

BLUE COAST SECURITIES INC

U.S. Bank Tower
633 West Fifth Street
Los Angeles, CA USA 90071
Phone: 3106017667
E-mail: info@BlueCoastPrivateClient.com
Website: www.bluecoastprivateclient.com

Type of Firm
Bank Affiliated

Project Preferences

Type of Financing Preferred:
Generalist PE
Balanced
Other

Geographical Preferences

United States Preferences:
North America

International Preferences:
Latin America
Europe
Asia

Industry Preferences

In Biotechnology prefer:
Biotechnology

In Medical/Health prefer:
Medical/Health

In Industrial/Energy prefer:
Energy
Oil and Gas Exploration
Oil & Gas Drilling,Explor

In Agr/Forestr/Fish prefer:
Mining and Minerals

Additional Information
Year Founded: 2008
Current Activity Level : Actively seeking new investments

BLUE CONSUMER CAPITAL

3419 Via Lido
Suite 516
Newport Beach, CA USA 92663
Website: blueconsumercapital.com

Type of Firm
Investment Management Firm

Project Preferences

Type of Financing Preferred:
Early Stage
Balanced

Industry Preferences

In Medical/Health prefer:
Health Services

In Consumer Related prefer:
Consumer
Food/Beverage

Additional Information
Year Founded: 2017
Current Activity Level : Actively seeking new investments

BLUE DELTA CAPITAL PARTNERS LLC

8280 Greensboro Drive
McLean, VA USA 22102
Website: bluedeltacapitalpartners.com

Management and Staff
Kevin Robbins, Co-Founder
Mark Frantz, Co-Founder

Type of Firm
Private Equity Firm

Project Preferences

Type of Financing Preferred:
Balanced

Size of Investments Considered:
Min Size of Investment Considered (000s): $2,000
Max Size of Investment Considered (000s): $5,000

Geographical Preferences

United States Preferences:
Mid Atlantic

Additional Information
Year Founded: 2014
Capital Under Management: $39,200,000
Current Activity Level : Actively seeking new investments

BLUE EQUITY LLC

333 East Main Street
Suite 200
Louisville, KY USA 40202
Phone: 5025898181
Fax: 5025887150
E-mail: info@blueequity.com
Website: www.blueequity.com

Management and Staff
Steven Whittingham, Managing Director
Terry Stapp, Chief Financial Officer
William Herrera, Vice President

Type of Firm
Private Equity Firm

Project Preferences

Type of Financing Preferred:
Leveraged Buyout

Geographical Preferences

United States Preferences:
All U.S.

Industry Preferences

In Medical/Health prefer:
Medical/Health

In Consumer Related prefer:
Entertainment and Leisure
Sports

In Financial Services prefer:
Financial Services
Real Estate

In Business Serv. prefer:
Media

In Manufact. prefer:
Manufacturing
Publishing

Additional Information
Year Founded: 2004
Current Activity Level : Actively seeking new investments

BLUE HERON CAPITAL LLC

8730 Stony Point Parkway
Suite 280
Richmond, VA USA 23235
Phone: 8042123400
Fax: 8042123400
E-mail: info@blueheroncap.com

Management and Staff
Andrew Tichenor, Partner
Sam Sezak, Partner
Tom Benedetti, Partner

Type of Firm
Private Equity Firm

Project Preferences

Type of Financing Preferred:
Early Stage
Balanced
Later Stage
Acquisition

Size of Investments Considered:
Min Size of Investment Considered (000s): $2,000
Max Size of Investment Considered (000s): $10,000

Geographical Preferences

United States Preferences:
Mid Atlantic

International Preferences:
All International

Additional Information
Name of Most Recent Fund: Blue Heron Capital Fund I, L.P.
Most Recent Fund Was Raised: 12/24/2013
Year Founded: 2012
Capital Under Management: $25,351,000
Current Activity Level : Actively seeking new investments

BLUE HILL PARTNERS LLC

40 West Evergreen Avenue
Philadelphia, PA USA 19118
Phone: 2152472400
Fax: 2152482381
Website: bluehillpartners.com

Management and Staff
Walter King, Partner

Type of Firm
Private Equity Firm

Project Preferences

Type of Financing Preferred:
Early Stage
Expansion
Mezzanine

Geographical Preferences

United States Preferences:
Pennsylvania

Industry Preferences

In Computer Software prefer:
Software

In Semiconductor/Electr prefer:
Sensors

In Industrial/Energy prefer:
Energy
Energy Conservation Relat
Process Control
Environmental Related

In Business Serv. prefer:
Services

In Agr/Forestr/Fish prefer:
Agribusiness

Additional Information
Year Founded: 2002
Capital Under Management: $5,000,000
Current Activity Level : Actively seeking new investments

BLUE HORIZON EQUITY LLC

615 Battery Street, Fourth Floor
San Francisco, CA USA 94111
Phone: 415-493-5190
Fax: 415-352-4060
Website: www.bluehorizonequity.com

Management and Staff
Alan Nichols, Managing Director
John Hommeyer, Managing Director
Scott Wu, Managing Director

Type of Firm
Private Equity Firm

Project Preferences

Type of Financing Preferred:
Leveraged Buyout
Public Companies
Later Stage
Management Buyouts
Acquisition
Industry Rollups
Distressed Debt

Industry Preferences

In Medical/Health prefer:
Medical/Health
Health Services

In Consumer Related prefer:
Consumer Products

In Industrial/Energy prefer:
Environmental Related

In Business Serv. prefer:
Services

Additional Information
Year Founded: 2008
Current Activity Level : Actively seeking new investments

BLUE LOOP CAPITAL LLC

7300 Central Parke Boulevard
Mason, OH USA 45040
Phone: 5132041739
Website: blueloopcapital.com

Management and Staff
Bill Jarvis, President & COO

Type of Firm
Private Equity Firm

Project Preferences

Type of Financing Preferred:
Leveraged Buyout
Turnaround
Acquisition
Distressed Debt

Industry Preferences

In Communications prefer:
Wireless Communications

In Computer Software prefer:
Software

In Semiconductor/Electr prefer:
Sensors

In Business Serv. prefer:
Distribution

In Manufact. prefer:
Manufacturing

Additional Information
Year Founded: 2011
Current Activity Level : Actively seeking new investments

BLUE NOTE VENTURES

831 EParl Street
Boulder, CO USA 80302
Website: bluenotevc.com

Type of Firm
Private Equity Firm

Project Preferences

Type of Financing Preferred:
Early Stage

Additional Information
Year Founded: 1969
Current Activity Level : Actively seeking new investments

BLUE OCEAN VENTURES

Seven Dharmaraja Mawatha
Colombo, Sri Lanka
Phone: 94112580852
E-mail: info@bov.lk
Website: www.bov.lk

Type of Firm
Private Equity Firm

Project Preferences

Type of Financing Preferred:
Early Stage
Seed
Startup

Geographical Preferences

United States Preferences:

International Preferences:
Australia
Asia

Additional Information
Year Founded: 1969
Capital Under Management: $13,720,000
Current Activity Level : Actively seeking new investments

BLUE POINT CAPITAL PARTNERS LP

127 Public Square
Suite 5100
Cleveland, OH USA 44114
Phone: 2165354700
Fax: 2165354701
Website: www.bluepointcapital.com

Other Offices
1201 Third Avenue
Suite 3090
Seattle, WA USA 98101
Phone: 2063329200
Fax: 2063329209

201 South Tryon Street
Suite 850
Charlotte, NC USA 28202
Phone: 7043471111
Fax: 7043471107

1233 Lujiazui Ring Road
Suite 1507, Azia Center
Shanghai, China 200120
Phone: 862150474700

Management and Staff
Ben Newman, Vice President
Brian Castleberry, Principal
Charley Geiger, Vice President
Chip Chaikin, Partner
David Given, Partner
Jack Guo, Vice President
Jeff Robich, Vice President
John Kirby, Partner
John LeMay, Partner
Julianne Marley, Partner
Lisa Root, Chief Financial Officer
Mark Morris, Partner
Sean Ward, Partner

Type of Firm
Private Equity Firm

Project Preferences

Type of Financing Preferred:
Leveraged Buyout
Expansion
Management Buyouts
Acquisition
Recapitalizations

Geographical Preferences

United States Preferences:
Midwest
Southeast
West Coast

International Preferences:
China

Industry Focus
(% based on actual investment)
    Other Products   100.0%

Additional Information
Year Founded: 1990
Capital Under Management: $800,000,000
Current Activity Level : Actively seeking new investments

BLUE RIDGE CAPITAL LLC

3715 Northside Parkway
Building 200, Suite 450
Atlanta, GA USA 30327
Phone: 4043649094
Fax: 4043649095
Website: www.blueridgecapital.com

Management and Staff
Kellie Snipes, Vice President
Steve Patrick, Vice President

Type of Firm
Private Equity Firm

Project Preferences

Type of Financing Preferred:
Value-Add
Generalist PE
Balanced
Opportunistic
Later Stage

Geographical Preferences

United States Preferences:
Southeast

Industry Preferences

In Financial Services prefer:
Real Estate

Additional Information
Name of Most Recent Fund: Blue Ridge China Partners II, L.P.
Most Recent Fund Was Raised: 02/05/2008
Year Founded: 1999

Capital Under Management: $440,900,000
Current Activity Level : Actively seeking new investments

BLUE ROAD CAPITAL

570 Lexington Avenue
32nd Floor
New York, NY USA 10022
Phone: 2128229710
Fax: 2128229711
E-mail: info@blueroad.com
Website: www.blueroad.com

Type of Firm
Private Equity Firm

Project Preferences

Type of Financing Preferred:
Leveraged Buyout
Acquisition

Industry Preferences

In Consumer Related prefer:
Consumer Products

In Agr/Forestr/Fish prefer:
Agribusiness
Agriculture related

Additional Information
Year Founded: 2014
Capital Under Management: $182,220,000
Current Activity Level : Actively seeking new investments

BLUE SAGE CAPITAL LP

114 West Seventh Street
Suite 820
Austin, TX USA 78701
Phone: 5125361900
Fax: 5122369215
E-mail: contact@bluesage.com
Website: www.bluesage.com

Management and Staff
Jim McBride, Co-Founder
Jonathan Pearce, Principal
Peter Huff, Co-Founder

Type of Firm
Private Equity Firm

Association Membership
Natl Assoc of Small Bus. Inv. Co (NASBIC)

Project Preferences

Role in Financing:
Prefer role as deal originator but will also invest in deals created by others

Type of Financing Preferred:
Leveraged Buyout
Later Stage
Acquisition
Recapitalizations

Geographical Preferences

United States Preferences:
Southwest
Texas

Industry Preferences

In Medical/Health prefer:
Medical/Health

In Industrial/Energy prefer:
Energy

In Business Serv. prefer:
Services
Distribution
Media

In Manufact. prefer:
Manufacturing

Additional Information

Name of Most Recent Fund: Blue Sage Capital II, L.P.
Most Recent Fund Was Raised: 08/17/2011
Year Founded: 2002
Capital Under Management: $250,000,000
Current Activity Level : Actively seeking new investments

BLUE SCORPION INVESTMENTS LP

402 West Broadway
3rd Floor
New York, NY USA 10012
Phone: 16464768728
Website: bluescorpioninv.com

Management and Staff

Gautam Ahuja, General Partner
Jamison Ernest, General Partner

Type of Firm

Private Equity Firm

Project Preferences

Type of Financing Preferred:
Early Stage
Expansion

Geographical Preferences

United States Preferences:

Industry Preferences

In Internet Specific prefer:
Ecommerce

In Semiconductor/Electr prefer:
Electronics

In Consumer Related prefer:
Consumer
Retail
Food/Beverage

Additional Information

Year Founded: 2016
Current Activity Level : Actively seeking new investments

BLUE SEA CAPITAL LLC

240 Royal Palm Way
Second Floor
Palm Beach, FL USA 33480
Phone: 5616558400
Fax: 5619228844
E-mail: info@blueseacapital.com
Website: www.blueseacapital.com

Type of Firm

Private Equity Firm

Project Preferences

Type of Financing Preferred:
Leveraged Buyout
Expansion
Acquisition

Geographical Preferences

United States Preferences:

Industry Preferences

In Medical/Health prefer:
Medical/Health

In Industrial/Energy prefer:
Materials
Machinery

In Transportation prefer:
Aerospace

In Business Serv. prefer:
Distribution

In Manufact. prefer:
Manufacturing

In Utilities prefer:
Utilities

Additional Information

Name of Most Recent Fund: Blue Sea Capital Fund I, L.P.
Most Recent Fund Was Raised: 10/29/2013
Year Founded: 2011
Capital Under Management: $327,000,000
Current Activity Level : Actively seeking new investments

BLUE SEED CAPITAL LLC

210 Avenue B
Apartment 2-S
New York, NY USA 10009
Phone: 9176561118

Type of Firm

Private Equity Firm

Project Preferences

Type of Financing Preferred:
Early Stage

Additional Information

Year Founded: 2014
Current Activity Level : Actively seeking new investments

BLUE SKY CAPITAL CORP

199 Bay Street, PO Box 459
Commerce Court West, Ste 2900
Toronto, Canada M5L 1G4
Website: www.blueskycapital.ca

Type of Firm

Private Equity Firm

Project Preferences

Type of Financing Preferred:
Early Stage

Industry Preferences

In Internet Specific prefer:
Internet

In Financial Services prefer:
Financial Services

Additional Information

Year Founded: 1969
Current Activity Level : Actively seeking new investments

BLUE SKY PRIVATE EQUITY

111 Eagle Street
Level 46
Brisbane, Australia 4000
Phone: 732707500
E-mail: investorservices@blueskyfunds.com.au
Website: www.blueskyfunds.com.au

Other Offices

501 Madison Ave, 5th Floor
Suite 501
MANHATTAN, NY USA 10022
Phone: 2129354494

111 Gawler Place, Level 10
Adelaide, Australia 5000
Phone: 882102371

Australia Square, 264-278 George Street
Suite 22.02, Level 22
Sydney, Australia 2000
Phone: 282820400

120 Collins Street
Level 34
Melbourne , Australia 3000
Phone: 392456200

315 Wakefield Street
Level One
, Australia

Management and Staff
Timothy Wilson, Managing Director

Type of Firm
Private Equity Firm

Association Membership
Australian Venture Capital Association (AVCAL)

Project Preferences

Type of Financing Preferred:
Leveraged Buyout
Generalist PE

Geographical Preferences

International Preferences:
Australia

Industry Preferences

In Industrial/Energy prefer:
Industrial Products

In Financial Services prefer:
Real Estate

In Agr/Forestr/Fish prefer:
Mining and Minerals

Additional Information
Name of Most Recent Fund: Blue Sky Private Equity EC2010 Fund
Most Recent Fund Was Raised: 11/30/2010
Year Founded: 2006
Capital Under Management: $41,500,000
Current Activity Level : Actively seeking new investments

BLUE SWELL CAPITAL

300 Clay Street
One Maritime Plaza, Suite 2250
San Francisco, CA USA 94111
Phone: 4157418922
Website: www.blueswellcapital.com

Management and Staff
Enrique Braquehais, General Partner

Type of Firm
Private Equity Firm

Project Preferences

Type of Financing Preferred:
Early Stage

Geographical Preferences

United States Preferences:
California

Industry Preferences

In Communications prefer:
Wireless Communications

In Internet Specific prefer:
E-Commerce Technology
Internet

Additional Information
Year Founded: 2014
Current Activity Level : Actively seeking new investments

BLUE WATER CAPITAL LLC

8400 Martingale Drive
McLean, VA USA 22102
Phone: 7038623296
Fax: 7035521322
Website: www.bluewatercapital.com

Management and Staff
Henry Barratt, Managing Director
James Loving, Chief Financial Officer
Kim Cooke, Managing Director
Michael Acheson, Managing Director
Wilbur Priester, Managing Director

Type of Firm
Private Equity Firm

Project Preferences

Role in Financing:
Prefer role as deal originator but will also invest in deals created by others

Type of Financing Preferred:
Expansion
Later Stage

Size of Investments Considered:
Min Size of Investment Considered (000s): $3,000
Max Size of Investment Considered (000s): $20,000

Geographical Preferences

United States Preferences:
Mid Atlantic

Canadian Preferences:
All Canada

Industry Focus
(% based on actual investment)
    Internet Specific   62.1%
    Computer Software and Services 16.4%
    Communications and Media   12.0%
    Other Products   9.4%
    Semiconductors/Other Elect.   0.2%

Additional Information
Name of Most Recent Fund: Blue Water Venture Fund III LLC
Most Recent Fund Was Raised: 04/30/2002
Year Founded: 1995
Capital Under Management: $98,700,000
Current Activity Level : Reducing investment activity
Method of Compensation: Return on investment is of primary concern, do not charge fees

BLUE WIRE CAPITAL LTD

200 Union Street
London, United Kingdom se1 0lx
E-mail: info@bluewirecapital.com
Website: www.bluewirecapital.com

Type of Firm
Private Equity Firm

Project Preferences

Type of Financing Preferred:
Early Stage
Seed

Size of Investments Considered:
Min Size of Investment Considered (000s): $150
Max Size of Investment Considered (000s): $2,000

Geographical Preferences

United States Preferences:
All U.S.

International Preferences:
Greece
Ireland
United Kingdom
Europe

Industry Preferences

In Biotechnology prefer:
Agricultural/Animal Bio.

In Consumer Related prefer:
Consumer
Food/Beverage
Consumer Services

Additional Information
Year Founded: 2015
Current Activity Level : Actively seeking new investments

353

BLUE WOLF CAPITAL PARTNERS LLC

One Liberty Plaza
52nd Floor, 165 Broadway
New York, NY USA 10006
Phone: 2124881340
Fax: 9176778233
E-mail: info@blue-wolf.com
Website: www.blue-wolf.com

Management and Staff

Aakash Patel, Principal
Adam Blumenthal, Managing Partner
Andrew Schwartz, Vice President
Charles Miller, Partner
Jeremy Kogler, Principal
Joshua Cherry-Seto, Chief Financial Officer
Michael Ranson, Partner
Mike Musuraca, Managing Director
Victor Caruso, Managing Director

Type of Firm

Private Equity Firm

Project Preferences

Type of Financing Preferred:
Leveraged Buyout
Turnaround
Acquisition
Special Situation
Distressed Debt

Geographical Preferences

United States Preferences:
All U.S.

Canadian Preferences:
All Canada

Additional Information

Name of Most Recent Fund: Blue Wolf Capital Fund III, L.P.
Most Recent Fund Was Raised: 07/18/2013
Year Founded: 2005
Capital Under Management: $840,000,000
Current Activity Level : Actively seeking new investments

BLUEBERRY VENTURES

25 Mara Vista Court
Belvedere Tiburon, CA USA 94920
Phone: 6508435000
Website: www.blueberryventures.vc

Type of Firm

Private Equity Firm

Project Preferences

Type of Financing Preferred:
Early Stage

Industry Preferences

In Consumer Related prefer:
Food/Beverage

Additional Information

Year Founded: 2015
Capital Under Management: $20,000,000
Current Activity Level : Actively seeking new investments

BLUEFIRE PARTNERS CAPITAL MARKETS GROUP

1300 Fifth Street Towers
150 South Fifth Street
Minneapolis, MN USA 55402
Phone: 612-344-1000
Fax: 612-344-1001

Other Offices

1300 Fifth Street Towers
150 South Fifth Street
Minneapolis, MN USA 55402
Phone: 612-344-1000
Fax: 612-344-1001

Management and Staff

Joanne Henry, Managing Director
Lee Schafer, Managing Director
William Bartkowsk, Chief Executive Officer

Type of Firm

Investment Management Firm

Project Preferences

Type of Financing Preferred:
Later Stage

Additional Information

Year Founded: 2009
Current Activity Level : Actively seeking new investments

BLUEGEM CAPITAL PARTNERS LLP

16 Berkeley Street
London, United Kingdom W1J 8DZ
Phone: 442076479710
Fax: 442076811304
E-mail: enquiries@bluegemcp.com
Website: www.bluegemcp.com

Management and Staff

Emilio Di Spiezio Sardo, Partner
Marco Capello, Co-Founder
Marco Anatriello, Co-Founder
Vishesh Srivastava, Partner

Type of Firm

Private Equity Firm

Project Preferences

Type of Financing Preferred:
Leveraged Buyout
Expansion
Management Buyouts
Acquisition
Recapitalizations

Geographical Preferences

International Preferences:
Italy
United Kingdom
Europe
Western Europe

Industry Preferences

In Consumer Related prefer:
Retail
Consumer Products

In Business Serv. prefer:
Services
Distribution

Additional Information

Name of Most Recent Fund: BlueGem II, L.P.
Most Recent Fund Was Raised: 01/07/2014
Year Founded: 2006
Capital Under Management: $285,300,000
Current Activity Level : Actively seeking new investments

BLUEGRASS ANGELS

330 East Main Street
Suite 210
Lexington, KY USA 40507
Phone: 8592571930
E-mail: admin@bluegrassangels.com
Website: www.bluegrassangels.com

Type of Firm

University Program

Project Preferences

Type of Financing Preferred:
Seed
Startup

Size of Investments Considered:
Min Size of Investment Considered (000s): $100
Max Size of Investment Considered (000s): $500

Geographical Preferences

United States Preferences:
Kentucky

Additional Information

Year Founded: 2004
Current Activity Level : Actively seeking new investments

BLUELINE BIOSCIENCE

101 College Street
Suite 401, South Tower
Toronto, Canada M5G 1L7
Phone: 4166738124
E-mail: info@bluelinebio.com
Website: www.bluelinebio.com

Type of Firm
Incubator/Development Program

Project Preferences

Type of Financing Preferred:
Early Stage

Geographical Preferences

Canadian Preferences:
All Canada

Industry Preferences

In Biotechnology prefer:
Biotechnology

Additional Information
Year Founded: 2013
Current Activity Level : Actively seeking new investments

BLUEOCEAN VENTURES SA

3 hemin du Pr-Fleuri
Geneva, Switzerland 1228
Phone: 41225523006
Fax: 41227793292
E-mail: info@blueocean-ventures.com
Website: www.blueocean-ventures.com

Management and Staff
Emmanuel De Watteville, Partner
Faris Sabeti, Partner
Maurice Olivier, Co-Founder
Sacha Haymoz, Partner

Type of Firm
Private Equity Firm

Project Preferences

Type of Financing Preferred:
Early Stage
Startup

Geographical Preferences

International Preferences:
Europe
Switzerland

Industry Preferences

In Medical/Health prefer:
Medical/Health

In Industrial/Energy prefer:
Industrial Products
Environmental Related

Additional Information
Year Founded: 2007
Capital Under Management: $25,877,000
Current Activity Level : Actively seeking new investments

BLUEPOINTE VENTURES LLC

999 Baker Way, Suite 150
San Mateo, CA USA 94404
Phone: 6502934545
E-mail: info@bluepointeventures.com
Website: www.bluepointeventures.com

Type of Firm
Private Equity Firm

Project Preferences

Type of Financing Preferred:
Fund of Funds
Start-up Financing

Industry Preferences

In Communications prefer:
Data Communications

In Computer Software prefer:
Software

Additional Information
Year Founded: 2014
Capital Under Management: $5,250,000
Current Activity Level : Actively seeking new investments

BLUERUN VENTURES LP

545 Middlefield Road, Suite 250
Menlo Park, CA USA 94025
Phone: 6504627250
Fax: 6504627252
Website: www.brv.com

Other Offices
1010 Huaihai Zhong Road
Room 2737-38, K. Wah Center
Shanghai, China 200031
Phone: 862161031386

No. 81 Jianguo Road
Unit 802, China Central Place
Beijing, China 100025
Phone: 861059695680
Fax: 861059695681

Management and Staff
Andrew Chen, Partner
Antti Kokkinen, Partner
David Young, Venture Partner
Jay Jamison, Partner
Jeff Tannenbaum, Principal
John Malloy, General Partner
Jonathan Ebinger, Partner
Jui Tan, Partner
Karen Eliadis, Chief Financial Officer
Kari-Pekka Wilska, Venture Partner
Kwan Yoon, Partner
W. Peter Buhl, Partner

Type of Firm
Private Equity Firm

Association Membership
Korean Venture Capital Association (KVCA)
Western Association of Venture Capitalists (WAVC)
National Venture Capital Association - USA (NVCA)

Project Preferences

Role in Financing:
Prefer role as deal originator but will also invest in deals created by others

Type of Financing Preferred:
Early Stage
Startup

Size of Investments Considered:
Min Size of Investment Considered (000s): $1,000
Max Size of Investment Considered (000s): $6,000

Geographical Preferences

United States Preferences:
West Coast

International Preferences:
Europe
China
Israel
Asia
Korea, South
All International

Industry Focus
(% based on actual investment)

Internet Specific	43.3%
Computer Software and Services	22.0%
Semiconductors/Other Elect.	12.0%
Communications and Media	10.9%
Computer Hardware	6.7%
Industrial/Energy	2.6%
Other Products	1.5%
Consumer Related	1.0%

Additional Information
Name of Most Recent Fund: BlueRun Ventures IV, L.P.
Most Recent Fund Was Raised: 02/12/2008
Year Founded: 1998
Capital Under Management: $2,000,000,000
Current Activity Level : Actively seeking new investments
Method of Compensation: Return on investment is of primary concern, do not charge fees

BLUESKY EQUITIES LTD

521 Third Avenue South West
Calgary, Canada T2P 3T3
Phone: 4032634337
Fax: 4032662214
E-mail: info@blueskyequities.com
Website: www.blueskyequities.com

Type of Firm
Private Equity Firm

Project Preferences

Type of Financing Preferred:
Value-Add
Generalist PE
Balanced
Acquisition
Startup
Recapitalizations

Geographical Preferences

United States Preferences:

Canadian Preferences:
All Canada

Industry Preferences

In Industrial/Energy prefer:
Energy

In Financial Services prefer:
Real Estate

Additional Information
Year Founded: 2008
Current Activity Level : Actively seeking new investments

BLUESTEM CAPITAL PARTNERS

122 South Phillips Avenue
Suite 300
Sioux Falls, SD USA 57104
Phone: 6053310091
E-mail: info@bluestemcapital.com
Website: www.bluestemcapital.com

Management and Staff
Nikole Mulder, Partner
Steve Kirby, Founding Partner
Tyler Stowater, Partner

Type of Firm
Private Equity Firm

Project Preferences

Role in Financing:
Will function either as deal originator or investor in deals created by others

Type of Financing Preferred:
Early Stage
Expansion
Balanced
Later Stage

Size of Investments Considered:
Min Size of Investment Considered (000s): $500
Max Size of Investment Considered (000s): $3,000

Geographical Preferences

United States Preferences:
Midwest
All U.S.

Industry Focus
(% based on actual investment)

Industrial/Energy	39.5%
Computer Software and Services	19.8%
Internet Specific	16.3%
Consumer Related	12.7%
Medical/Health	7.0%
Communications and Media	4.0%
Computer Hardware	0.3%
Other Products	0.3%

Additional Information
Name of Most Recent Fund: Bluestem Core Strategies Fund LLC
Most Recent Fund Was Raised: 10/29/2010
Year Founded: 1991
Capital Under Management: $76,000,000
Current Activity Level : Actively seeking new investments
Method of Compensation: Return on invest. most important, but chg. closing fees, service fees, etc.

BLUFF POINT ASSOCIATES CORP

274 Riverside Avenue
Second Floor
Westport, CT USA 06880
Phone: 2035579450
Website: www.bluffpt.com

Other Offices
285 Riverside Avenue
Suite 350
Westport, CT USA 06880
Phone: 2036423630
Fax: 2032278626

Management and Staff
J Jones, Partner
John McInerney, Managing Director
John Gilliam, Managing Director
Kevin Fahey, Managing Director
Neil Gabriele, Managing Director
Paula McInerney, President

Type of Firm
Private Equity Firm

Project Preferences

Type of Financing Preferred:
Leveraged Buyout

Geographical Preferences

United States Preferences:
All U.S.

Industry Preferences

In Medical/Health prefer:
Medical/Health

In Financial Services prefer:
Financial Services

Additional Information
Year Founded: 2005
Current Activity Level : Actively seeking new investments

BLUM CAPITAL PARTNERS LP

909 Montgomery Street
Suite 400
San Francisco, CA USA 94133
Phone: 4154341111
Fax: 4154343130
E-mail: info@blumcapital.com
Website: www.blumcapital.com

Other Offices
712 Fifth Avenue
39th Floor
New York, NY USA 10019
Phone: 212-397-1300
Fax: 212-397-1301

Management and Staff
Arthur Young, Partner
David Chung, Partner
Douglas Dossey, Partner
Gregory Hitchan, Chief Operating Officer
Gwen Reinke, Vice President
Jane Su, Partner
Jeff Green, Vice President
John Park, Partner
John Eidinger, Vice President
Judith Van Es, Vice President
Lee Fishman, Vice President
N. Colin Lind, Managing Partner
Paige Reeve Uher, Vice President
Peter Westley, Partner

Type of Firm
Private Equity Firm

Project Preferences

Type of Financing Preferred:
Leveraged Buyout
Turnaround
Acquisition

Geographical Preferences

United States Preferences:

Canadian Preferences:
All Canada

Industry Focus

(% based on actual investment)
Semiconductors/Other Elect.	37.8%
Other Products	23.2%
Computer Software and Services	12.9%
Medical/Health	12.9%
Consumer Related	10.2%
Internet Specific	1.1%
Industrial/Energy	1.1%
Biotechnology	0.8%

Additional Information

Name of Most Recent Fund: Blum Strategic Partners III, L.P.
Most Recent Fund Was Raised: 05/26/2005
Year Founded: 1975
Current Activity Level : Actively seeking new investments

BLUMBERG INTERNATIONAL PARTNERS LLC

No. 580, Howard Street
Suite 101
San Francisco, CA USA 94105
Phone: 4159055000
E-mail: info@blumbergcapital.com
Website: www.blumbergcapital.com

Management and Staff

Alon Lifshitz, Venture Partner
Ankur Jain, Vice President
Bruce Taragin, Managing Director
Chris Gottschalk, Vice President
Jon Soberg, Managing Director
Margot Giusti, Chief Financial Officer

Type of Firm

Private Equity Firm

Project Preferences

Role in Financing:
Will function either as deal originator or investor in deals created by others

Type of Financing Preferred:
Early Stage
Seed
Startup

Size of Investments Considered:
Min Size of Investment Considered (000s): $500
Max Size of Investment Considered (000s): $3,000

Geographical Preferences

United States Preferences:
All U.S.

International Preferences:
Israel

Industry Preferences

In Communications prefer:
Wireless Communications
Media and Entertainment

In Computer Software prefer:
Computer Services
Software
Systems Software
Applications Software

In Internet Specific prefer:
E-Commerce Technology
Internet

Additional Information

Name of Most Recent Fund: Blumberg Capital IV, L.P.
Most Recent Fund Was Raised: 02/04/2016
Year Founded: 2000
Capital Under Management: $356,600,000
Current Activity Level : Actively seeking new investments
Method of Compensation: Return on investment is of primary concern, do not charge fees

BLUME VENTURE ADVISORS

Santacruz West
Mumbai, India
Website: www.blumeventures.com

Management and Staff

Karthik Reddy, Managing Partner
Sanjay Nath, Managing Partner

Type of Firm

Private Equity Firm

Project Preferences

Type of Financing Preferred:
Early Stage
Seed
Special Situation

Geographical Preferences

International Preferences:
Asia

Additional Information

Year Founded: 2011
Capital Under Management: $82,371,000
Current Activity Level : Actively seeking new investments.

BM H BETEILIGUNGS MANAGEMENTGESELLSCHAFT HESSEN MBH

Schumannstrasse 4-6
Frankfurt am Main, Germany 60325
Phone: 49691338507840
Fax: 49691338507860
E-mail: info@bmh-hessen.de
Website: www.bmh-hessen.de

Management and Staff

Juergen Zabel, Managing Director
Pamela Roehrs-Guenther, Managing Director

Type of Firm

Government Affiliated Program

Project Preferences

Type of Financing Preferred:
Leveraged Buyout
Early Stage
Mezzanine
Generalist PE
Balanced
Later Stage
Seed
Startup

Size of Investments Considered:
Min Size of Investment Considered (000s): $164
Max Size of Investment Considered (000s): $1,894

Geographical Preferences

International Preferences:
Germany

Industry Preferences

In Computer Software prefer:
Software

In Semiconductor/Electr prefer:
Electronics

In Biotechnology prefer:
Biotechnology

In Medical/Health prefer:
Medical/Health
Pharmaceuticals

In Consumer Related prefer:
Retail

In Industrial/Energy prefer:
Industrial Products
Materials
Machinery

In Business Serv. prefer:
Media

Additional Information
Year Founded: 2004
Capital Under Management: $2,900,000
Current Activity Level : Actively seeking new investments

BM T BETEILIGUNGSMAN-AGEMENT

Gorkistrasse 9
Erfurt, Germany 99084
Phone: 493617447601
Fax: 493617447635
E-mail: info@bm-t.com

Management and Staff
Christian Damjakob, Managing Director

Type of Firm
Private Equity Firm

Association Membership
German Venture Capital Association (BVK)

Project Preferences

Type of Financing Preferred:
Early Stage
Later Stage
Seed
Management Buyouts
Startup

Size of Investments Considered:
Min Size of Investment Considered (000s): $141
Max Size of Investment Considered (000s): $7,056

Geographical Preferences

International Preferences:
Germany

Industry Preferences

In Communications prefer:
Telecommunications

In Semiconductor/Electr prefer:
Electronics
Micro-Processing
Optoelectronics

In Industrial/Energy prefer:
Process Control
Machinery

Additional Information
Year Founded: 2003
Capital Under Management: $268,100,000
Current Activity Level : Actively seeking new investments

BMO CAPITAL CORP

100 King Street West
11th Flr, First Canadian Place
Toronto, Canada M5X 1A1
Phone: 4168677341
Fax: 4168674108

Other Offices
100 King Street West
First Canadian Place, 11th Flo
Toronto, Canada M5X 1A1
Phone: 416-867-7341
Fax: 416-867-4108

Three Times Square
29th Floor
New York, NY USA 10036
Phone: 212-605-1512

111 West Monroe Streeet
Chicago, IL USA 60603
Phone: 312-461-3668

Management and Staff
Charlie Piermarini, Managing Director
Eric Tripp, President
Jamie Thorsen, Managing Director
Thomas Milroy, Chief Executive Officer

Type of Firm
Investment Management Firm

Association Membership
Canadian Venture Capital Association

Project Preferences

Type of Financing Preferred:
Leveraged Buyout
Mezzanine
Balanced

Geographical Preferences

Canadian Preferences:
Western Canada

International Preferences:
Western Europe

Additional Information
Year Founded: 1996
Current Activity Level : Actively seeking new investments

BNP PARIBAS CAPITAL PARTNERS SAS

1 Boulevard Haussmann
Paris, France 75009
Phone: 33158977575
Website: www.bnppe.com

Other Offices
Limmatquai 4
Zurich, Switzerland 8024
Phone: 4112679367
Fax: 4112679370

Management and Staff
Patrick Perez, Chief Operating Officer

Type of Firm
Bank Affiliated

Association Membership
European Private Equity and Venture Capital Assoc.

Project Preferences

Role in Financing:
Prefer role as deal originator but will also invest in deals created by others

Type of Financing Preferred:
Fund of Funds
Core
Leveraged Buyout
Early Stage
Mezzanine
Generalist PE
Balanced
Later Stage
Management Buyouts
Acquisition
Recapitalizations

Geographical Preferences

United States Preferences:

International Preferences:
Europe
Middle East
Germany
France

Industry Focus
(% based on actual investment)

Medical/Health	23.9%
Internet Specific	23.0%
Consumer Related	14.6%
Other Products	12.3%
Communications and Media	8.3%
Computer Software and Services	6.6%
Biotechnology	4.8%
Semiconductors/Other Elect.	4.7%
Industrial/Energy	1.1%
Computer Hardware	0.7%

Additional Information
Year Founded: 1998
Capital Under Management: $649,800,000
Current Activity Level : Actively seeking new investments
Method of Compensation: Return on investment is of primary concern, do not charge fees

BNP PARIBAS DEVELOPPEMENT SA

20 rue Chauchat
Paris, France 75009
Phone: 33140145578
Fax: 33140142968
Website: www.bnpparibasdeveloppement.com

Other Offices

5, boulevard de Dunkerque
Marseille, France 13002
Phone: 33491134399
Fax: 33491134346

7, rue Chanzy
Nancy, France 54004
Phone: 33383855399
Fax: 33383855368

4, allee de Turenne
Nantes, France 44001
Phone: 33251251261
Fax: 33251251289

140, Tour Lilleurope
11 Parvis de Rotterdam
Euralille, France 59777
Phone: 33320133499
Fax: 33320133243

10, allee de Tourny
Bordeaux, France 33024

41, rue Grenette
Lyon, France 69289
Phone: 33472565399
Fax: 33472562832

Type of Firm
Bank Affiliated

Association Membership
French Venture Capital Association (AFIC)

Project Preferences

Type of Financing Preferred:
Leveraged Buyout
Early Stage
Mezzanine
Generalist PE
Later Stage
Acquisition
Recapitalizations

Size of Investments Considered:
Min Size of Investment Considered (000s): $837
Max Size of Investment Considered (000s): $16,748

Geographical Preferences

International Preferences:
Europe
France

Industry Preferences

In Communications prefer:
Telecommunications

In Internet Specific prefer:
E-Commerce Technology

In Biotechnology prefer:
Biotechnology

In Consumer Related prefer:
Retail

In Business Serv. prefer:
Services
Distribution

In Manufact. prefer:
Manufacturing

Additional Information
Year Founded: 1988
Capital Under Management: $350,000,000
Current Activity Level : Actively seeking new investments

BNP PARIBAS FORTIS PRIVATE EQUITY GROWTH NV

Warandeberg 3
Brussels, Belgium 1000
Phone: 3225651111
Fax: 322564222
E-mail: info@fortisprivateequity.com

Other Offices

Archimedeslaan 6
Utrecht, Netherlands 3584 BA
Phone: 31-30-226-6222
Fax: 31-30-226-9835

6 rue de Ponthieu
Paris, France 75008
Phone: 33-1-5836-4460
Fax: 33-1-5836-4461

25 Allee de la Robertsau
Strasbourg, France 67000
Phone: 33-3-9022-1100
Fax: 33-3-9022-1101

Fortuny 37
3 Dcha.
Madrid, Spain 28010
Phone: 34-91-700-0501
Fax: 34-91-700-0514

Management and Staff
Brigitte Boone, Managing Director
Eric Spliet, Partner
Filip Dierckx, Chief Executive Officer
Frank Claeys, Managing Director
Georges Noel, Partner
Jean-Paul Votron, Chief Executive Officer
Julien Smets, Managing Director
Pieter Demuynck, Partner
Raf Moons, Partner

Type of Firm
Bank Affiliated

Association Membership
Belgium Venturing Association
European Private Equity and Venture Capital Assoc.

Project Preferences

Role in Financing:
Prefer role as deal originator but will also invest in deals created by others

Type of Financing Preferred:
Fund of Funds
Leveraged Buyout
Early Stage
Balanced
Later Stage
Seed
Acquisition
Startup
Recapitalizations

Size of Investments Considered:
Min Size of Investment Considered (000s): $471
Max Size of Investment Considered (000s): $7,533

Geographical Preferences

International Preferences:
Luxembourg
Netherlands
Belgium
Germany
France

Industry Focus
(% based on actual investment)
Biotechnology	25.5%
Other Products	22.4%
Consumer Related	21.2%
Medical/Health	9.8%
Semiconductors/Other Elect.	7.4%
Computer Software and Services	6.8%
Internet Specific	2.9%
Communications and Media	2.2%
Industrial/Energy	1.6%

Additional Information
Year Founded: 1987
Capital Under Management: $372,300,000
Current Activity Level : Actively seeking new investments
Method of Compensation: Return on invest. most important, but chg. closing fees, service fees, etc.

BOATHOUSE CAPITAL

200 West Lancaster Avenue
Suite 206
Wayne, PA USA 19087
Website: www.boathousecapital.com

Management and Staff
Chong Moua, Partner
Kenneth Jones, Managing Partner
Steven Gord, Partner
William Dyer, Partner

Type of Firm
Private Equity Firm

Association Membership
Nat'l Assoc of Small Bus. Inv. Co (NASBIC)

Project Preferences

Type of Financing Preferred:
Leveraged Buyout
Expansion
Mezzanine
Acquisition
Recapitalizations

Geographical Preferences

United States Preferences:
All U.S.

Industry Preferences

In Consumer Related prefer:
Consumer

Additional Information
Year Founded: 2008
Capital Under Management: $230,000,000
Current Activity Level : Actively seeking new investments

BOBCOCK & BROWN

680 George Street
Level 12
Sydney, Australia NSW2000
Phone: 612-8280-7452
E-mail: bobcockbrown@linkmarketservices.com.au
Website: www.bobcockbrown.com.au

Type of Firm
Private Equity Firm

Geographical Preferences

Canadian Preferences:
British Columbia

Additional Information
Year Founded: 2006
Current Activity Level : Actively seeking new investments

BOC INTERNATIONAL HOLDINGS LTD

1 Garden Road
26/F, Bank of China Tower
Hong Kong, Hong Kong
Phone: 85239886000
Fax: 85221479065
E-mail: info@bocigroup.com
Website: www.bocigroup.com

Other Offices
200 Yincheng Road Central, Pudong
39-40/F., Bank of China Tower
Shanghai, China 200120
Phone: 862168604866
Fax: 862158883554

Four Battery Road #04-00
Bank of China Building
Singapore, Singapore 049908
Phone: 6564128899
Fax: 6565343996

28 Finance Street, Xicheng District
15F,Tower2,Yingtai Business Center
Beijing, China 100032
Phone: 861066229000
Fax: 861066578950

90 Cannon Street
London, United Kingdom EC4N 6HA
Phone: 442070228888
Fax: 442070228877

1270 Avenue of the Americas
New York, NY USA 10020
Phone: 2122590888
Fax: 2122590889

One Garden Road
20/F, Bank of China Tower
Hong Kong, Hong Kong
Phone: 85228676333
Fax: 85225247327

Management and Staff
Jianzhong Gong, Chief Executive Officer
Simon Ting, Managing Director
Yan Wang, Chief Executive Officer

Type of Firm
Bank Affiliated

Association Membership
China Venture Capital Association

Project Preferences

Type of Financing Preferred:
Mezzanine
Balanced

Geographical Preferences

International Preferences:
Hong Kong
China

Industry Focus
(% based on actual investment)
Internet Specific	76.1%
Computer Hardware	11.5%
Industrial/Energy	4.9%
Consumer Related	4.0%
Other Products	3.5%

Additional Information
Year Founded: 1984
Capital Under Management: $806,000,000
Current Activity Level : Actively seeking new investments

BOCGI ZHESHANG INVESTMENT FUND MANAGEMENT ZHEJIANG CO LTD

No. 178-1 Nanshan Road
Hangzhou, Zhejiang, China 310002
Phone: 8657187929500
Fax: 8657187929555
E-mail: zs@bocgi-zs.com
Website: www.bocgi-zs.com

Management and Staff
Guoliang Jiang, Vice President
Zheng Qiu, President

Type of Firm
Bank Affiliated

Project Preferences

Type of Financing Preferred:
Balanced

Geographical Preferences

International Preferences:
China

Industry Preferences

In Medical/Health prefer:
Medical/Health

In Consumer Related prefer:
Consumer Products

In Industrial/Energy prefer:
Alternative Energy
Advanced Materials

In Financial Services prefer:
Real Estate

In Manufact. prefer:
Manufacturing

In Agr/Forestr/Fish prefer:
Agribusiness

Additional Information
Year Founded: 2009
Current Activity Level : Actively seeking new investments

BOCOM INT L (SHANGHAI) EQUITY INVEST MANAGEMENT CO., LTD.

c/o BOCOM Bank
No. 188 Yincheng Road
Shanghai, China 200120

Type of Firm
Bank Affiliated

Project Preferences

Type of Financing Preferred:
Balanced

Geographical Preferences

International Preferences:
China

Additional Information
Year Founded: 2011
Capital Under Management: $100,000,000
Current Activity Level : Actively seeking new investments

BOCOM INTERNATIONAL HOLDINGS CO LTD

68 Des Voeux Road
9/F, Man Yee Building
Central, Hong Kong
Phone: 852-3710-3328
Fax: 852-3798-0133
E-mail: enquiry@bocomgroup.com
Website: www.bocomgroup.com

Other Offices

No. 1 East Chang An Avenue
Suit 312, The Towers, Oriental Plaza
Beijing, China 100738
Phone: 86-10-8518-4068
Fax: 86-10-8518-0328

121 Des Voeux Road
3/F, Far East Consortium Building
Central, Hong Kong
Phone: 852-2297-9888
Fax: 852-3426-9702

22-28 Mody Road
1/F, CFC Tower
Kowloon, Hong Kong
Phone: 852-3189-7800
Fax: 852-3580-8087

Management and Staff
Chuange Cheng, Chief Executive Officer
Xuanhua Xi, Chief Executive Officer
Ying Li, President

Type of Firm
Bank Affiliated

Project Preferences

Type of Financing Preferred:
Later Stage
Recapitalizations

Geographical Preferences

International Preferences:
China
Asia

Industry Preferences

In Medical/Health prefer:
Medical/Health

In Consumer Related prefer:
Consumer

In Industrial/Energy prefer:
Environmental Related

In Transportation prefer:
Transportation

Additional Information
Year Founded: 1998
Capital Under Management: $53,500,000
Current Activity Level : Actively seeking new investments

BOE BANK LTD

196 Mandela Drive
1st Floor, PHG Building
Brandhof, South Africa 9301
Phone: 27-31-364-1567
Fax: 27-31-364-2936

Other Offices

21B Cascades Crescent, Cascades
Suite 2
Pietermaritzburg, South Africa 3201
Phone: 27-33-347-6940

28 Waterfront Drive
Ground Floor
Knysna, South Africa 6570
Phone: 27-44-302-2700

Umgazi Road, Menlo Park
Landmark Office Park, East Block
Pretoria, South Africa 0081
Phone: 27-12-470-6400
Fax: 27-12-470-6455

19 Hurst Grove
4th Floor Clifton Place
Musgrave, South Africa 4000
Phone: 27-31-203-9550

270 Cape Road, Newton Park
Port Elizabeth, P.O. Box 27528
Greenacres, South Africa 6045
Phone: 27-41-398-8080

135 Rivonia Road
Nedbank Sandton
Johannesburg, South Africa 2196
Phone: 27-11-294-8493

62 Cathedral Street
P.O. Box 1757
George, South Africa 6530
Phone: 27-44-802-7200

BoE Clocktower, Clocktower Precint
V&A Waterfront
Cape Town, South Africa 8001
Phone: 27-21-416-6000

Type of Firm
Bank Affiliated

Project Preferences

Type of Financing Preferred:
Leveraged Buyout
Early Stage
Expansion
Seed
Acquisition
Startup

Geographical Preferences

International Preferences:
South Africa

Additional Information
Year Founded: 1999
Current Activity Level : Actively seeking new investments

BOFORSSTIFTELSEN

Kopmangatan 23-25
Orebro, Sweden 702 23
Phone: 4619174804
E-mail: info@boforsstiftelsen.se
Website: www.boforsstiftelsen.se

Management and Staff
Ingemar Jonsson, Chief Executive Officer

Type of Firm
Private Equity Firm

Project Preferences

Type of Financing Preferred:
Balanced

Size of Investments Considered:
Min Size of Investment Considered (000s): $15
Max Size of Investment Considered (000s): $150

Geographical Preferences

International Preferences:
Sweden

Additional Information
Year Founded: 2006
Capital Under Management: $2,000,000
Current Activity Level : Actively seeking new investments

BOHAI HARVEST RST (SHANGHAI) EQUITY INVESTMENT FUND MGMT

No.188 Yesheng Road
Room 868H, A Building
Shanghai, China
Website: www.bhrpe.com

Type of Firm
Private Equity Firm

Project Preferences

Type of Financing Preferred:
Leveraged Buyout

Geographical Preferences

United States Preferences:
All U.S.

International Preferences:
Europe

Industry Preferences

In Consumer Related prefer:
Consumer

In Industrial/Energy prefer:
Energy

In Financial Services prefer:
Financial Services

In Manufact. prefer:
Manufacturing

Additional Information
Year Founded: 2013
Current Activity Level: Actively seeking new investments

BOHAI SEA REGION VENTURE CAPITAL MANAGEMENT CO LTD

7/F, No. 13 Bldg, Tibei
Weijin South Rd., Hexi Dist.
Tianjin, China 300060
Phone: 86-22-2334-1562
Fax: 86-22-2334-1533
E-mail: cvcm@cvcm.com.cn
Website: www.cvcm.com.cn

Management and Staff
Li Mingyan, Chief Financial Officer
Zhang Renliang, President

Type of Firm
Private Equity Firm

Project Preferences

Type of Financing Preferred:
Balanced

Geographical Preferences

International Preferences:
China

Additional Information
Year Founded: 2000
Current Activity Level : Actively seeking new investments

BOKWANG INVESTMENT CORP

946-1 Daechi-done
8F Glass Tower
Seoul, South Korea 135-280
Phone: 822-558-2092
Fax: 822-567-1673
Website: www.bokwang.co.kr

Management and Staff
Hong Seok-kyu, Chief Executive Officer
Kwang Lyul Oh, President
Moon Soo Park, Chief Executive Officer

Type of Firm
Private Equity Firm

Association Membership
Korean Venture Capital Association (KVCA)

Project Preferences

Type of Financing Preferred:
Balanced

Geographical Preferences

International Preferences:
Asia
Korea, South

Additional Information
Year Founded: 1989
Capital Under Management: $52,300,000
Current Activity Level : Actively seeking new investments

BOLD CAPITAL PARTNERS LP

225 Santa Monica Boulevard
Suite 500
Santa Monica, CA USA 90401
Website: www.boldcapitalpartners.com

Type of Firm
Private Equity Firm

Project Preferences

Type of Financing Preferred:
Balanced

Additional Information
Year Founded: 1969
Current Activity Level : Actively seeking new investments

BOLDER CAPITAL LLC

875 North Michigan Avenue
Suite 4020
Chicago, IL USA 60611
Phone: 3125736420
E-mail: info@boldercapital.com
Website: www.boldercapital.com

Management and Staff
Todd Hamilton, Senior Managing Director

Type of Firm
Private Equity Firm

Project Preferences

Type of Financing Preferred:
Leveraged Buyout
Expansion
Acquisition
Recapitalizations

Geographical Preferences

United States Preferences:
All U.S.

Canadian Preferences:
All Canada

Industry Preferences

In Business Serv. prefer:
Services

In Manufact. prefer:
Manufacturing

Additional Information
Year Founded: 2004
Current Activity Level : Actively seeking new investments

BOLDSTART VENTURES II LP

30 Irving Place
Sixth Floor
New York, NY USA 10003
Phone: 6464501941

Other Offices
56 West, 22nd Street
Ninth Floor
NEW YORK, NY USA 10010

Management and Staff
Justin Wohlstadter, Partner

Type of Firm
Private Equity Firm

Project Preferences

Type of Financing Preferred:
Seed
Startup

Size of Investments Considered:
Min Size of Investment Considered (000s): $100
Max Size of Investment Considered (000s): $300

Geographical Preferences

United States Preferences:
New York

Industry Preferences

In Computer Software prefer:
Data Processing
Software

Additional Information
Name of Most Recent Fund: BOLDstart Ventures II, L.P.
Most Recent Fund Was Raised: 02/28/2013
Year Founded: 2010
Capital Under Management: $63,910,000
Current Activity Level : Actively seeking new investments

BOLSHOI MANAGEMENT

Bolshoy Afanasievsky Perlevlok
Building 8/3, 3rd Floor
Moscow, Russia 121019
Phone: 7952343095
Fax: 7952343099

Other Offices
Rockefeller Center
630 5th Avenue, 16th Floor
New York, NY USA
Phone: 12123325100
Fax: 12123325120

Management and Staff
Evgeney Gorkov, Managing Director

Type of Firm
Government Affiliated Program

Association Membership
Russian Venture Capital Association (RVCA)

Project Preferences

Type of Financing Preferred:
Balanced

Size of Investments Considered:
Min Size of Investment Considered (000s): $300
Max Size of Investment Considered (000s): $3,000

Geographical Preferences

International Preferences:
Russia

Additional Information
Year Founded: 2000
Capital Under Management: $40,000,000
Current Activity Level : Actively seeking new investments

BOLT INNOVATION GROUP LLC

110 Chauncy Street
Boston, MA USA 02111
Phone: 6096582587
E-mail: info@bolt.io
Website: www.bolt.io

Management and Staff
Axel Bichara, Founder
Ben Einstein, Founder
Scott Miller, Founder

Type of Firm
Private Equity Firm

Project Preferences

Type of Financing Preferred:
Seed
Startup

Geographical Preferences

United States Preferences:

Industry Preferences

In Computer Software prefer:
Software
Systems Software
Applications Software

In Computer Other prefer:
Computer Related

Additional Information
Name of Most Recent Fund: Bolt Fund I, L.P.
Most Recent Fund Was Raised: 02/14/2013
Year Founded: 2013
Capital Under Management: $109,430,000
Current Activity Level : Actively seeking new investments

BONANZA INVESTMENT CO LTD

10th Bonade Building
Ahn Jung Xili, Chaoyang Dist.
Beijing, China 100029
Phone: 86-10-51961
Fax: 86-10-51961
Website: www.bonanza.com.cn

Type of Firm
Investment Management Firm

Project Preferences

Type of Financing Preferred:
Balanced

Geographical Preferences

International Preferences:
China

Additional Information
Year Founded: 1999
Current Activity Level : Actively seeking new investments

BONAVENTURE CAPITAL LLC

3104 Blue Lake Drive
Suite 120
Birmingham, AL USA 35243
Fax: 2058708050
E-mail: info@bonaventurecapital.net
Website: www.bonaventurecapital.net

Management and Staff
Misha Gordon, Partner
Steven Dauphin, Partner
William Reiser, Principal

Type of Firm
Private Equity Firm

Project Preferences

Type of Financing Preferred:
Early Stage

Size of Investments Considered:
Min Size of Investment Considered (000s): $500
Max Size of Investment Considered (000s): $1,500

Geographical Preferences

United States Preferences:
Southeast

Industry Preferences

In Computer Software prefer:
Software
Systems Software
Applications Software

In Industrial/Energy prefer:
Energy

In Financial Services prefer:
Financial Services

In Utilities prefer:
Utilities

Additional Information
Year Founded: 1998
Capital Under Management: $25,000,000
Current Activity Level : Actively seeking new investments

BOND CAPITAL PARTNERS, LTD.

1040 West Georgia Street
Suite 940
Vancouver, Canada V6E 4H1
Phone: 604-687-2663
Fax: 604-688-6527
E-mail: info@bondcapital.ca
Website: www.bondcapital.ca

Other Offices
1040 West Georgia Street
Suite 940
Vancouver, Canada
Phone: 604-687-2663
Fax: 604-688-6527

Type of Firm
Private Equity Firm

Association Membership
Canadian Venture Capital Association

Project Preferences

Type of Financing Preferred:
Mezzanine
Generalist PE
Later Stage
Management Buyouts

Geographical Preferences

United States Preferences:
Northwest

Canadian Preferences:
Western Canada

Industry Preferences

In Medical/Health prefer:
Health Services

In Consumer Related prefer:
Consumer
Education Related

In Financial Services prefer:
Financial Services

In Business Serv. prefer:
Distribution

In Manufact. prefer:
Manufacturing

Additional Information
Year Founded: 2003
Capital Under Management: $80,000,000
Current Activity Level : Actively seeking new investments

BONIFACIO CAPITAL

2E03-2E05 Building 5
Bonifacio High Street
Taguig City, Philippines
Phone: 6328561440
Fax: 6328563237
Website: bonifaciocapital.com

Management and Staff
Harvey Dychiao, Managing Director

Type of Firm
Private Equity Firm

Additional Information
Year Founded: 2012
Current Activity Level : Actively seeking new investments

BONSAI VENTURE CAPITAL SCR DE REGIMEN COMUN SA

Avda. Valdelaparra, 27
Alcobendas
Madrid, Spain 28108
Phone: 34-91-661-7987
Fax: 34-91-661-6658
E-mail: atencion.cliente@bonsaitech.com
Website: www.bonsaitech.com

Management and Staff
Javier Cebrian Sagarriga, President

Type of Firm
Private Equity Firm

Project Preferences

Type of Financing Preferred:
Balanced

Geographical Preferences

International Preferences:
Spain

Industry Preferences

In Internet Specific prefer:
Internet

In Biotechnology prefer:
Biotechnology

Additional Information
Year Founded: 2007
Current Activity Level : Actively seeking new investments

BOOKEND CAPITAL LLC

551 Fifth Avenue
Suite 1125
New York, NY USA 10176
Phone: 6463744477
E-mail: info@bookendcapital.com
Website: bookendcapital.com

Type of Firm
Private Equity Firm

Project Preferences

Type of Financing Preferred:
Leveraged Buyout
Management Buyouts

Geographical Preferences

United States Preferences:
All U.S.

Industry Preferences

In Consumer Related prefer:
Retail
Food/Beverage
Consumer Products

Additional Information
Year Founded: 2015
Current Activity Level : Actively seeking new investments

BOOMERANG CATAPULT LLC

236 2 East Front Street
Suite Six
Traverse City, MI USA 49686
Website: boomerangcatapult.com

Type of Firm
Private Equity Firm

Project Preferences

Type of Financing Preferred:
Early Stage

Geographical Preferences

United States Preferences:
Michigan

Additional Information
Year Founded: 2014
Current Activity Level : Actively seeking new investments

BOOOTUP WORLD

68 Willow Road
Menlo Park, CA USA 94025
Website: www.bootupworld.com/#!space/w0lu4

Type of Firm
Private Equity Firm

Project Preferences

Type of Financing Preferred:
Seed
Startup

Industry Preferences

In Medical/Health prefer:
Health Services

In Transportation prefer:
Transportation

In Financial Services prefer:
Financial Services

Additional Information
Year Founded: 2016
Current Activity Level : Actively seeking new investments

BOOST VC

55 East Third Avenue
San Mateo, CA USA 94401
E-mail: info@boost.vc
Website: www.boost.vc

Type of Firm
Incubator/Development Program

Project Preferences

Type of Financing Preferred:
Seed
Startup

Size of Investments Considered:
Min Size of Investment Considered (000s): $10
Max Size of Investment Considered (000s): $15

Industry Preferences

In Communications prefer:
Wireless Communications

In Computer Software prefer:
Software

In Internet Specific prefer:
Internet
Ecommerce

In Consumer Related prefer:
Consumer

In Financial Services prefer:
Financial Services

Additional Information
Year Founded: 2012
Capital Under Management: $29,030,000
Current Activity Level : Actively seeking new investments

BOOST&CO SAS

14 bis rue Daru
Paris, France 75008
Phone: 33619392423
E-mail: Info@boostandco.com
Website: www.boostandco.com

Management and Staff
Andrea Kowalski, Principal
Andrew Webster, Partner
Damien Bezancon, Principal
Lance Mysyrowicz, Partner
Nick Richardson, Chief Financial Officer
Sonia Powar, Partner

Type of Firm
Private Equity Firm

Project Preferences

Type of Financing Preferred:
Early Stage
Mezzanine
Startup
Distressed Debt

Size of Investments Considered:
Min Size of Investment Considered (000s): $2,527
Max Size of Investment Considered (000s): $10,106

Geographical Preferences

International Preferences:
United Kingdom
Germany

Additional Information
Year Founded: 2004
Current Activity Level : Actively seeking new investments

BOOTSTRAP INCUBATION LLC

10251 Vista Sorrento Parkway
Suite 100
San Diego, CA USA 92121
E-mail: contact@bootstrapincubation.com
Website: www.bootstrapincubation.com

Type of Firm
Private Equity Firm

Project Preferences

Type of Financing Preferred:
Startup

Industry Preferences

In Computer Software prefer:
Data Processing
Software

In Business Serv. prefer:
Consulting Services

Additional Information
Year Founded: 2012
Current Activity Level : Actively seeking new investments

BOOTSTRAPLABS LLC

541 Jefferson Avenue
Suite 100
Redwood City, CA USA 94063
Website: bootstraplabs.com

Other Offices
Lot 2-2 Technology Park MA
Lebuhraya Puchong-Sg.
Kuala Lumpur, Malaysia 57000
Phone: 60389941750
Fax: 60322975390

Type of Firm
Incubator/Development Program

Project Preferences

Type of Financing Preferred:
Early Stage
Seed
Startup

Geographical Preferences

United States Preferences:
Southeast
California

International Preferences:
Asia
Malaysia

Industry Preferences

In Computer Software prefer:
Software

Additional Information
Year Founded: 2009
Current Activity Level : Actively seeking new investments

BOPA MORUO

Suite 1, 1st Floor
3, Exchange Square
Sandton, South Africa 2196
Website: www.bopamoruo.co.za

Management and Staff
Boitumelo Thlabanelo, Co-Founder
Nthime Khoele, Co-Founder

Type of Firm
Private Equity Firm

Project Preferences

Type of Financing Preferred:
Leveraged Buyout
Management Buyouts
Acquisition

Geographical Preferences

International Preferences:
South Africa
Africa

Additional Information

Year Founded: 2006
Current Activity Level : Actively seeking new investments

BOQUAN INVESTMENT CONSULTATION SHANGHAI CO LTD

Hami Rd, Changning Dist
Rm 716, No 1947-1749
Shanghai, China 200000

Type of Firm
Investment Management Firm

Project Preferences

Type of Financing Preferred:
Early Stage
Expansion
Later Stage

Geographical Preferences

International Preferences:
China

Industry Preferences

In Communications prefer:
Telecommunications
Media and Entertainment

In Internet Specific prefer:
Internet

Additional Information

Year Founded: 2012
Current Activity Level : Actively seeking new investments

BOREALIS VENTURES

10 Allen Street
Upper Level
Hanover, NH USA 03755
Phone: 6036431500
Fax: 6036437600
E-mail: info@borealisventures.com
Website: www.borealisventures.com

Other Offices
26 Market Square
Portsmouth, NH USA 03801

Management and Staff
Jesse Devitte, Managing Director
Matt Harris, Managing General Partner
Matt Rightmire, Managing Director
Phil Ferneau, Managing Director

Type of Firm
Private Equity Firm

Association Membership
National Venture Capital Association - USA (NVCA)

Project Preferences

Role in Financing:
Prefer role as deal originator

Type of Financing Preferred:
Early Stage
Balanced
Seed
First Stage Financing
Startup

Size of Investments Considered:
Min Size of Investment Considered (000s): $100
Max Size of Investment Considered (000s): $2,500

Geographical Preferences

United States Preferences:
New Hampshire
Northeast
All U.S.

Industry Preferences

In Computer Software prefer:
Applications Software

In Internet Specific prefer:
Internet

In Biotechnology prefer:
Biotechnology

In Medical/Health prefer:
Medical/Health

Additional Information
Name of Most Recent Fund: Borealis Granite Fund, L.P.
Most Recent Fund Was Raised: 12/05/2012
Year Founded: 2002
Capital Under Management: $50,000,000
Current Activity Level : Actively seeking new investments
Method of Compensation: Return on investment is of primary concern, do not charge fees

---

BOREAN INNOVATION

Birk Centerpark 40
Herning, Denmark 7400
Phone: 4596270100
Fax: 4596270109
E-mail: info@borean.dk
Website: www.borean.dk

Other Offices
Bautavej 1 A
Arhus V, Denmark 8210

Havnegade 30
2nd floor
Vejle, Denmark 7100

Type of Firm
Incubator/Development Program

Association Membership
Danish Venture Capital Association (DVCA)

Project Preferences

Type of Financing Preferred:
Early Stage
Seed
Startup

Geographical Preferences

International Preferences:
Denmark

Industry Preferences

In Communications prefer:
Media and Entertainment

In Semiconductor/Electr prefer:
Electronics

In Consumer Related prefer:
Education Related

In Industrial/Energy prefer:
Energy
Energy Conservation Relat
Environmental Related

In Other prefer:
Environment Responsible

Additional Information
Year Founded: 1998
Current Activity Level : Actively seeking new investments

BORN2GROW & GMBH CO KG

Edisonstrasse 19
Heilbronn, Germany 74076
Phone: 4971313828474
Fax: 4971313829488
E-mail: info@born2grow.de
Website: www.born2grow.de

Type of Firm
Private Equity Firm

Project Preferences

Type of Financing Preferred:
Early Stage
Seed
Startup

Geographical Preferences

International Preferences:
Europe
Switzerland
Western Europe
Austria
Germany

Industry Preferences

In Semiconductor/Electr prefer:
Electronics

In Medical/Health prefer:
Medical Diagnostics

In Industrial/Energy prefer:
Energy
Environmental Related

Additional Information

Year Founded: 2013
Capital Under Management: $6,609,000
Current Activity Level : Actively seeking new investments

BOSPHERA ADVISORY, LTD.

Suleyman Seba Street No 48
BJK Plaza A Block D 115
Istanbul, Turkey 34357
Phone: 902122367751
Fax: 902122365370
E-mail: info@bosphera.com
Website: www.bosphera.com

Type of Firm
Private Equity Firm

Project Preferences

Type of Financing Preferred:
Leveraged Buyout
Early Stage
Expansion
Generalist PE
Later Stage
Management Buyouts
Acquisition

Geographical Preferences

International Preferences:
Turkey
Europe

Additional Information

Year Founded: 2012
Current Activity Level : Actively seeking new investments

BOSTON CAPITAL VENTURES LP

84 State Street
Suite 320
Boston, MA USA 02109
Phone: 6172276550
Fax: 6172273847

Other Offices

2250 Southwest Third Avenue
Suite 301
Miami, FL USA 33129

Management and Staff

Alex von der Goltz, Partner
Johan von der Goltz, General Partner
John Shields, General Partner

Type of Firm
Private Equity Firm

Project Preferences

Role in Financing:
Prefer role as deal originator but will also invest in deals created by others

Type of Financing Preferred:
Early Stage
Balanced
Startup

Size of Investments Considered:
Min Size of Investment Considered (000s): $1,000
Max Size of Investment Considered (000s): $10,000

Geographical Preferences

United States Preferences:
Northeast

Industry Focus

(% based on actual investment)
Computer Software and Services	29.5%
Internet Specific	27.7%
Communications and Media	16.2%
Other Products	11.9%
Medical/Health	8.9%
Consumer Related	1.6%
Industrial/Energy	1.2%
Semiconductors/Other Elect.	1.2%
Biotechnology	1.2%
Computer Hardware	0.6%

Additional Information

Name of Most Recent Fund: Boston Capital Ventures V, L.P.
Most Recent Fund Was Raised: 09/01/2000
Year Founded: 1982
Capital Under Management: $111,000,000
Current Activity Level : Actively seeking new investments
Method of Compensation: Return on investment is of primary concern, do not charge fees

---

BOSTON COMMUNITY CAPITAL INC

56 Warren Street
Suite 300
Boston, MA USA 02119
Phone: 6174278600
Fax: 6174279300
Website: www.bostoncommunitycapital.org

Management and Staff

Sharon Shepard, Managing Director

Type of Firm
Private Equity Firm

Association Membership

Community Development Venture Capital Alliance
New England Venture Capital Association

Project Preferences

Type of Financing Preferred:
Early Stage
Expansion
Later Stage
Seed

Size of Investments Considered:
Min Size of Investment Considered (000s): $250
Max Size of Investment Considered (000s): $1,500

Geographical Preferences

United States Preferences:
Northeast

Industry Preferences

In Other prefer:
Environment Responsible
Women/Minority-Owned Bus.

Additional Information

Year Founded: 2001
Current Activity Level : Actively seeking new investments

BOSTON GLOBAL VENTURES LLC

One Broadway
14th Floor
Cambridge, MA USA 02142
E-mail: info@bgv13.com
Website: bostonglobalventures.com

Type of Firm
Private Equity Firm

Project Preferences

Type of Financing Preferred:
Early Stage

Geographical Preferences

United States Preferences:
Massachusetts
New York

Canadian Preferences:
Alberta

International Preferences:
United Kingdom
China
Germany

Additional Information

Year Founded: 2013
Current Activity Level : Actively seeking new investments

BOSTON HARBOR CAPITAL PARTNERS LLC

400 Crown Colony Drive, Suite 104
Quincy, MA USA 02169
Phone: 617-513-3643
Website: www.bostonharborcapital.com

Management and Staff

Jeffrey Laughlin, Principal

Type of Firm

Private Equity Firm

Project Preferences

Type of Financing Preferred:
Leveraged Buyout
Management Buyouts
Acquisition
Recapitalizations

Industry Preferences

In Computer Software prefer:
Software

In Internet Specific prefer:
Internet

In Computer Other prefer:
Computer Related

In Medical/Health prefer:
Health Services

In Consumer Related prefer:
Consumer Products
Consumer Services

In Business Serv. prefer:
Services
Distribution

In Manufact. prefer:
Manufacturing

Additional Information

Year Founded: 1969
Current Activity Level : Actively seeking new investments

BOSTON MILLENNIA PARTNERS LP

30 Rowes Wharf, Suite 400
Boston, MA USA 02110
Phone: 6174285150
Fax: 6174285160
E-mail: info@millenniapartners.com
Website: www.bostonmillenniapartners.com

Management and Staff

A. Dana Callow, Managing Partner
Bradford Callow, Principal
Laurence Hagerty, Venture Partner
Martin Hernon, General Partner
Patrick Fortune, Partner
Robert Jevon, Partner
Robert Sherman, General Partner
Will DeGroot, Principal

Type of Firm

Private Equity Firm

Association Membership

New England Venture Capital Association
National Venture Capital Association - USA (NVCA)

Project Preferences

Role in Financing:
Prefer role as deal originator but will also invest in deals created by others

Type of Financing Preferred:
Early Stage
Expansion
Balanced
Later Stage

Size of Investments Considered:
Min Size of Investment Considered (000s): $3,000
Max Size of Investment Considered (000s): $15,000

Geographical Preferences

United States Preferences:
East Coast

Canadian Preferences:
All Canada

Industry Focus

(% based on actual investment)

Computer Software and Services	27.5%
Medical/Health	19.5%
Internet Specific	18.0%
Communications and Media	13.2%
Biotechnology	7.4%
Other Products	7.3%
Computer Hardware	3.9%
Semiconductors/Other Elect.	3.0%
Consumer Related	0.3%

Additional Information

Name of Most Recent Fund: Boston Millennia Partners III, L.P.
Most Recent Fund Was Raised: 07/15/2009
Year Founded: 1997
Capital Under Management: $700,000,000
Current Activity Level : Actively seeking new investments
Method of Compensation: Return on investment is of primary concern, do not charge fees

---

BOSTON SEED CAPITAL LLC

2310 Washington Street
Suite 420
Newton, MA USA 02462
Fax: 6176585649
E-mail: info@maddenasset.com
Website: www.bostonseed.com

Management and Staff

Peter Blacklow, Venture Partner

Type of Firm

Private Equity Firm

Project Preferences

Type of Financing Preferred:
Early Stage
Seed

Geographical Preferences

United States Preferences:
All U.S.

Industry Preferences

In Internet Specific prefer:
Internet

In Consumer Related prefer:
Consumer

Additional Information

Year Founded: 2010
Current Activity Level : Actively seeking new investments

BOSTON VENTURES

125 High Street
17th Floor
Boston, MA USA 02110
Phone: 6173501500
Fax: 6173501509
E-mail: info@bvlp.com
Website: www.bvlp.com

Other Offices

919 Third Avenue, Suite 620
New York, NY USA 10021
Phone: 212-593-0095
Fax: 212-593-0094

Management and Staff
Andrew Davis, Managing Director
Anthony Bolland, Co-Founder
Catherine Bird, Chief Financial Officer
Elizabeth Granville-Smith, Managing Director
Justin Harrison, Managing Director
Louis Bertocci, Managing Director
Matthew Kinsey, Managing Director
Michael Ricciardelli, Managing Partner
Roberto Ramirez, Chief Financial Officer
Roy Coppedge, Co-Founder
Vikrant Raina, Managing Director

Type of Firm
Private Equity Firm

Project Preferences

Role in Financing:
Prefer role as deal originator

Type of Financing Preferred:
Leveraged Buyout
Expansion
Management Buyouts
Acquisition
Recapitalizations

Industry Focus
(% based on actual investment)

Communications and Media	40.3%
Other Products	23.7%
Consumer Related	15.5%
Computer Software and Services	10.4%
Semiconductors/Other Elect.	4.0%
Internet Specific	3.5%
Biotechnology	1.5%
Computer Hardware	0.7%
Medical/Health	0.4%

Additional Information
Name of Most Recent Fund: BVIP Fund VIII, L.P.
Most Recent Fund Was Raised: 10/05/2012
Year Founded: 1983
Capital Under Management: $2,600,000,000
Current Activity Level : Actively seeking new investments
Method of Compensation: Return on investment is of primary concern, do not charge fees

---

BOTENYA ADVISORS (PTY) LTD

55 Regency Drive
Route 21 Corporate Park
Irene, South Africa 0046
Phone: 27123457571
Fax: 27123457603
Website: www.botenya.co.za

Type of Firm
Private Equity Firm

Project Preferences

Type of Financing Preferred:
Leveraged Buyout
Mezzanine
Generalist PE
Turnaround
Management Buyouts
Acquisition

Geographical Preferences

International Preferences:
South Africa

Industry Preferences

In Communications prefer:
Communications and Media

In Industrial/Energy prefer:
Energy

In Financial Services prefer:
Real Estate

In Agr/Forestr/Fish prefer:
Agriculture related

Additional Information
Year Founded: 2006
Current Activity Level : Actively seeking new investments

BOUBYAN BANK KSCP

Po Box 25507
Safat, Kuwait 13116
Phone: 96522325000
Fax: 96522454263
E-mail: info@bankboubyan.com
Website: boubyan.bankboubyan.com

Management and Staff
Abdul-Salam Al-Saleh, Chief Executive Officer
Abdulla Al-Tuwaijri, Chief Executive Officer
Adel Al-Majed, Chief Executive Officer
Mohamed Ismail, Chief Financial Officer

Type of Firm
Private Equity Firm

Project Preferences

Type of Financing Preferred:
Unknown

Geographical Preferences

International Preferences:
Middle East
Kuwait

Industry Preferences

In Financial Services prefer:
Real Estate

Additional Information
Year Founded: 2004
Current Activity Level : Actively seeking new investments

BOULDER BROOK PARTNERS LLC

24 Grasshopper Lane
Acton, MA USA 01720
Phone: 9787644227
Website: www.boulder-brook.com

Other Offices
22 Stanford Road
Wellesley, MA USA 02481
Phone: 7814430123

Management and Staff
Kevin Melia, Managing Director
Rob Rosen, Managing Director

Type of Firm
Private Equity Firm

Project Preferences

Type of Financing Preferred:
Leveraged Buyout
Management Buyouts
Recapitalizations

Geographical Preferences

United States Preferences:
Northern California
Northeast

Industry Preferences

In Business Serv. prefer:
Services
Distribution

In Manufact. prefer:
Manufacturing

Additional Information
Year Founded: 2012
Current Activity Level : Actively seeking new investments

BOULDER FOOD GROUP LLC

929 Pearl Street
Suite 300
Boulder, CO USA 80302
Phone: 3039544413
Website: bfgpartners.com

Management and Staff
Benjamin Fenton, Vice President
Dayton Miller, Partner

Type of Firm
Private Equity Firm

Industry Preferences

In Consumer Related prefer:
Consumer
Food/Beverage

Additional Information
Year Founded: 2014
Capital Under Management: $35,305,000
Current Activity Level : Actively seeking new investments

BOULDER INVESTMENT GROUP REPRISE

1871 Folsom Street
Suite 102
Boulder, CO USA 80301
Website: bigrventures.com

Type of Firm
Private Equity Firm

Project Preferences

Type of Financing Preferred:
Early Stage

Industry Preferences

In Consumer Related prefer:
Food/Beverage

Additional Information
Year Founded: 2015
Capital Under Management: $55,000,000
Current Activity Level : Actively seeking new investments

BOULDER VENTURES LTD

1941 Pearl Street
Suite 300
Boulder, CO USA 80302
Phone: 3034446950
Fax: 3034440267
Website: www.boulderventures.com

Management and Staff
Jonathan Perl, General Partner
Peter Roshko, General Partner

Type of Firm
Private Equity Firm

Association Membership
Mid-Atlantic Venture Association

Project Preferences

Role in Financing:
Will function either as deal originator or investor in deals created by others

Type of Financing Preferred:
Early Stage
Seed
Startup

Size of Investments Considered:
Min Size of Investment Considered (000s): $1,000
Max Size of Investment Considered (000s): $10,000

Geographical Preferences

United States Preferences:
Mid Atlantic
Colorado

Industry Focus
(% based on actual investment)

Computer Software and Services	50.7%
Internet Specific	12.7%
Biotechnology	11.1%
Communications and Media	10.7%
Other Products	5.6%
Semiconductors/Other Elect.	4.3%
Consumer Related	2.3%
Computer Hardware	1.4%
Industrial/Energy	0.7%
Medical/Health	0.5%

Additional Information
Name of Most Recent Fund: Boulder Ventures V
Most Recent Fund Was Raised: 05/03/2007
Year Founded: 1995
Capital Under Management: $344,000,000
Current Activity Level : Actively seeking new investments
Method of Compensation: Return on investment is of primary concern, do not charge fees

---

BOUNDS EQUITY PARTNERS, LLC

595 Elm Place
Suite 202
Highland Park, IL USA 60035
Phone: 847-266-6300
Fax: 847-433-1069
Website: www.boundsequity.com

Management and Staff
Mark Bounds, Founder
Stuart Skinner, Chief Financial Officer

Type of Firm
Private Equity Firm

Project Preferences

Type of Financing Preferred:
Leveraged Buyout
Later Stage
Management Buyouts
Acquisition

Geographical Preferences

United States Preferences:
Rocky Mountain

Industry Preferences

In Medical/Health prefer:
Medical/Health
Health Services

In Business Serv. prefer:
Services
Distribution

In Manufact. prefer:
Manufacturing

Additional Information
Year Founded: 1988
Current Activity Level : Actively seeking new investments

BOUNTY EQUITY FUND LLC

2 West 2nd Street
Suite # 210
Tulsa, OK USA 74103
Phone: 866-885-0264
Fax: 212-898-0397

Management and Staff
Elizabeth Kopple, Managing Partner

Type of Firm
Private Equity Advisor or Fund of Funds

Project Preferences

Type of Financing Preferred:
Early Stage
Public Companies
Seed

Geographical Preferences

United States Preferences:
All U.S.

Additional Information
Year Founded: 2007
Current Activity Level : Actively seeking new investments

BOW CAPITAL MANAGEMENT LLC

3307 Hillview Avenue
Palo Alto, CA USA 94304
Phone: 6508465001

Management and Staff
Grady Burnett, General Partner
Vivek Ranadive, Founder

Type of Firm
Private Equity Firm

Project Preferences

Type of Financing Preferred:
Balanced

Additional Information
Year Founded: 2016
Capital Under Management: $100,000,000
Current Activity Level : Actively seeking new investments

BOW RIVER CAPITAL PARTNERS LLC

1490 Lafayette Street
Suite 400
Denver, CO USA 80218
Phone: 303-861-8466
Fax: 303-861-8557
E-mail: noble@bowrivercapital.com
Website: www.bowrivercapital.com

Management and Staff
Ben Sykora, Vice President
Blair Richardson, Managing Partner
Bruno Darre, Co-Founder
Eric Wolf, Co-Founder
Jill Smith, Chief Financial Officer

Type of Firm
Private Equity Firm

Project Preferences

Role in Financing:
Prefer role as deal originator but will also invest in deals created by others

Type of Financing Preferred:
Leveraged Buyout
Expansion
Mezzanine
Turnaround
Later Stage
Management Buyouts
Acquisition
Recapitalizations

Size of Investments Considered:
Min Size of Investment Considered (000s): $1,000
Max Size of Investment Considered (000s): $5,000

Geographical Preferences

United States Preferences:
Northwest
Rocky Mountain
Colorado
West Coast
All U.S.

Canadian Preferences:
All Canada

Industry Preferences

In Consumer Related prefer:
Consumer Services

In Industrial/Energy prefer:
Energy
Oil & Gas Drilling,Explor

In Financial Services prefer:
Financial Services

In Business Serv. prefer:
Services
Distribution

Additional Information
Name of Most Recent Fund: Bow River Capital 2011 Fund, L.P.
Most Recent Fund Was Raised: 03/30/2012
Year Founded: 2004
Capital Under Management: $324,000,000
Current Activity Level : Actively seeking new investments

BOW VENTURES L.P.

3307 Hillview Avenue
Palo Alto, CA USA 94304

Type of Firm
Private Equity Firm

Project Preferences

Type of Financing Preferred:
Early Stage

Additional Information
Year Founded: 2016
Capital Under Management: $100,000,000
Current Activity Level : Actively seeking new investments

BOWERY CAPITAL

37 West 20th Street
Suite 901
New York, NY USA 10011
Phone: 4157353369
Website: www.bowerycap.com

Management and Staff
Mike Brown, Managing Partner

Type of Firm
Private Equity Firm

Association Membership
National Venture Capital Association - USA (NVCA)

Project Preferences

Type of Financing Preferred:
Early Stage
Seed
Startup

Additional Information
Name of Most Recent Fund: Bowery Capital I, L.P.
Most Recent Fund Was Raised: 05/01/2013
Year Founded: 2013
Capital Under Management: $93,000,000
Current Activity Level : Actively seeking new investments

BOWMARK CAPITAL LLP

Three Saint James's Square
London, United Kingdom SW1Y 4JU
Phone: 442071899000
Fax: 442071899044
E-mail: info@bowmark.com
Website: www.bowmark.com

Management and Staff
Charles Ind, Managing Partner
Kevin Grassby, Managing Partner

Type of Firm
Private Equity Firm

Association Membership
British Venture Capital Association (BVCA)

Project Preferences

Type of Financing Preferred:
Leveraged Buyout
Later Stage
Management Buyouts
Acquisition

Geographical Preferences

International Preferences:
United Kingdom

Industry Preferences

In Medical/Health prefer:
Medical/Health
Health Services

In Consumer Related prefer:
Entertainment and Leisure

In Business Serv. prefer:
Services
Media

Additional Information
Name of Most Recent Fund: Bowmark Capital Partners V, L.P.
Most Recent Fund Was Raised: 12/19/2013
Year Founded: 1997
Capital Under Management: $1,380,800,000
Current Activity Level : Actively seeking new investments

BOWSIDE CAPITAL LLC

954 Lexington Avenue
Suite 301
New York, NY USA 10021
Phone: 9173865564
Fax: 2122140744
Website: www.bowsidecapital.com

Other Offices

211 King Street
Suite 204
CHARLESTON, SC USA 29401
Phone: 8437257500

Management and Staff

Christian Albert, Managing Partner
Dru Rushing, Vice President

Type of Firm

Private Equity Advisor or Fund of Funds

Association Membership

Natl Assoc of Small Bus. Inv. Co (NASBIC)

Project Preferences

Type of Financing Preferred:
Fund of Funds
Leveraged Buyout
Fund of Funds of Second

Geographical Preferences

United States Preferences:
All U.S.

Additional Information

Name of Most Recent Fund: Bowside Capital Fund III, L.P.
Most Recent Fund Was Raised: 12/18/2013
Year Founded: 2009
Capital Under Management: $36,900,000
Current Activity Level: Actively seeking new investments

BOXIN CAPITAL

No. 3 Xinyuan South Road
10/F PingAn Int'l Finance Ctr
Beijing, China 100027
Phone: 861056300888
Fax: 861056300990
Website: www.boxincapital.com

Other Offices

No. 388, Fushan Road, Pudong New Area
Room 1206, Hongjia Plaza
Shanghai, China 200122
Phone: 862160453032
Fax: 36216045303

No. 26, Harbour Drive, Wanchai
Rm 2906, China Resources Building
Hong Kong, Hong Kong

Phone: 85231270600
Fax: 85231270666

Management and Staff

Bing Sun, Partner
Guohua Yao, Vice President
Lei Wang, Vice President
Linxuan Fu, Vice President
Weiming Lu, Partner
Xifeng Zhao, Vice President
Xin An, Partner
Yaofeng Xia, Vice President
Yue Peng, Partner

Type of Firm

Private Equity Firm

Association Membership

China Venture Capital Association

Project Preferences

Type of Financing Preferred:
Leveraged Buyout
Generalist PE
Balanced

Geographical Preferences

International Preferences:
China

Industry Preferences

In Communications prefer:
Commercial Communications

In Biotechnology prefer:
Biotechnology

In Medical/Health prefer:
Medical/Health
Pharmaceuticals

In Consumer Related prefer:
Consumer Services

In Industrial/Energy prefer:
Alternative Energy

In Business Serv. prefer:
Media

In Manufact. prefer:
Manufacturing

In Agr/Forestr/Fish prefer:
Agribusiness
Agriculture related
Mining and Minerals

Additional Information

Year Founded: 2008
Capital Under Management: $552,015,000
Current Activity Level: Actively seeking new investments

BOXWOOD CAPITAL PARTNERS LLC

Eleven South 12th Street
Fourth Floor
Richmond, VA USA 23219
Phone: 8043433300
Fax: 8043433440
Website: www.boxwoodpartnersllc.com

Management and Staff

Bobby Morris, Partner
Chris Deel, Partner
Patrick Galleher, Partner

Type of Firm

Bank Affiliated

Project Preferences

Role in Financing:
Prefer role as deal originator

Type of Financing Preferred:
Leveraged Buyout
Early Stage
Expansion
Management Buyouts
Acquisition

Size of Investments Considered:
Min Size of Investment Considered (000s): $2,000
Max Size of Investment Considered (000s): $20,000

Geographical Preferences

United States Preferences:
All U.S.

Industry Preferences

In Computer Software prefer:
Software
Systems Software
Applications Software

In Internet Specific prefer:
E-Commerce Technology
Internet
Ecommerce
Web Aggregation/Portals

In Medical/Health prefer:
Diagnostic Services
Medical Products
Health Services

In Consumer Related prefer:
Consumer
Entertainment and Leisure
Sports
Retail
Franchises(NEC)
Food/Beverage
Education Related

In Financial Services prefer:
Financial Services

In Business Serv. prefer:
Services
Distribution
Media

In Manufact. prefer:
Manufacturing

Additional Information
Year Founded: 2008
Current Activity Level : Actively seeking new investments

BOYER ALLAN INVESTMENT MANAGEMENT, LLP.

3 Garden Road, Citibank Plaza
Suite 1208,12th Floor
Central, Hong Kong
Phone: 852-3713-5888
Fax: 852-3713-5877
E-mail: enquiries@boyerallan.com
Website: www.boyerallan.com

Type of Firm
Private Equity Firm

Project Preferences

Type of Financing Preferred:
Early Stage
Balanced

Geographical Preferences

International Preferences:
Taiwan
Hong Kong
China
Asia
Japan

Additional Information
Year Founded: 1998
Current Activity Level : Actively seeking new investments

BOYNE CAPITAL PARTNERS LLC

2601 South Bayshore Drive
Suite 1475
Miami, FL USA 33133
Phone: 3058569500
E-mail: info@boynecapital.com
Website: www.boynecapital.com

Management and Staff
Derek McDowell, Founding Partner
James Malone, Founding Partner

Type of Firm
Private Equity Firm

Project Preferences

Type of Financing Preferred:
Leveraged Buyout
Management Buyouts
Acquisition
Recapitalizations

Geographical Preferences

United States Preferences:

Canadian Preferences:
All Canada

Industry Preferences

In Medical/Health prefer:
Medical/Health

In Consumer Related prefer:
Other Restaurants

In Industrial/Energy prefer:
Energy

In Financial Services prefer:
Financial Services

In Manufact. prefer:
Manufacturing

Additional Information
Year Founded: 2006
Capital Under Management: $70,000,000
Current Activity Level : Actively seeking new investments

BOZANO AGENTE AUTONOMO DE INVESTIMENTOS LTDA

Av Afranio de Melo Franco 29
Sl 503-Leblon
Rio de Janeiro, Brazil 22430-060
Phone: 552136871500
Fax: 552136871520
E-mail: contato@bozanoinvest.com
Website: www.bozanoinvestimentos.com.br

Other Offices
Nucleo Cidade de Deus S/N
4th Floor, Predio Novissimo
Osasco, Brazil 06029900

Management and Staff
Nelson Moreira Assad, President
Paulo Roberto Da Veiga Cardozo Monteiro, Partner

Type of Firm
Private Equity Firm

Association Membership
Brazilian Venture Capital Association (ABCR)

Project Preferences

Type of Financing Preferred:
Leveraged Buyout
Early Stage
Generalist PE
Later Stage
Management Buyouts
Acquisition

Geographical Preferences

International Preferences:
Brazil

Industry Preferences

In Computer Software prefer:
Software

In Medical/Health prefer:
Medical/Health

In Consumer Related prefer:
Food/Beverage

In Industrial/Energy prefer:
Advanced Materials

In Agr/Forestr/Fish prefer:
Agriculture related

Additional Information
Year Founded: 1998
Capital Under Management: $391,932,000
Current Activity Level : Actively seeking new investments

BPCE IMMOBILIER EXPLOITATION SAS

50 Avenue Pierre Mendes France
Paris, France 75013
Phone: 33153648770
Fax: 33153648773

Other Offices
5, Rue de Monttessuy
Paris, France 75007

Management and Staff
Alain Lemaire, President
Jean-Claude Crequit, Vice President

Type of Firm
Bank Affiliated

Association Membership
French Venture Capital Association (AFIC)

Project Preferences

Type of Financing Preferred:
Fund of Funds
Leveraged Buyout
Early Stage
Expansion
Generalist PE
Later Stage
Seed
Startup

Geographical Preferences

International Preferences:
Europe
France

Additional Information
Year Founded: 1995
Capital Under Management: $137,552,000
Current Activity Level : Actively seeking new investments

BPE INVESTIMENTOS

Avenida Paulista 949
16th Floor
Sao Paulo, Brazil 01311100
Phone: 551132695200
Fax: 551132856582
Website: www.bpei.com.br

Management and Staff
Claudio Pecanha, Partner
Luis Fernando Salem, Partner
Paulo Chueri, Partner
Robert Duncan Littlejohn, Partner

Type of Firm
Private Equity Firm

Project Preferences

Type of Financing Preferred:
Early Stage
Balanced
Later Stage

Geographical Preferences

International Preferences:
Brazil

Additional Information
Year Founded: 2006
Current Activity Level : Actively seeking new investments

BPE PARTNERS

Nile City Towers, South Tower
7th Floor, Corniche El Nil
Cairo, Egypt 2005A
Phone: 20224610300
Fax: 20224619851
E-mail: info.privateequity@beltonefinancial.com
Website: bpepartners.com

Management and Staff
Ahmed Madbouly, Chief Financial Officer
Aladdin Saba, Co-Founder

Type of Firm
Private Equity Firm

Association Membership
Emerging Markets Private Equity Association

Project Preferences

Role in Financing:
Will function either as deal originator or investor in deals created by others

Type of Financing Preferred:
Leveraged Buyout
Early Stage
Expansion
Unknown
Balanced
Acquisition
Recapitalizations

Size of Investments Considered:
Min Size of Investment Considered (000s): $4,443
Max Size of Investment Considered (000s): $177,718

Geographical Preferences

International Preferences:
Abu Dhabi
Qatar
Egypt
Middle East
Saudi Arabia
Libya
Africa
Sudan

Industry Preferences

In Communications prefer:
Telecommunications

In Biotechnology prefer:
Agricultural/Animal Bio.

In Transportation prefer:
Transportation

In Financial Services prefer:
Financial Services
Real Estate

In Manufact. prefer:
Manufacturing

In Agr/Forestr/Fish prefer:
Agribusiness

Additional Information
Year Founded: 2006
Capital Under Management: $1,884,000,000
Current Activity Level : Actively seeking new investments

BPE UNTERNEHMENS-BETEILIGUNGEN GMBH

Schleusenbruecke 1
Hamburg, Germany 20354
Phone: 49-403615700
Fax: 49-4036157070
E-mail: info@bpe.de
Website: www.bpe.de

Management and Staff
Aman Miran Khan, Partner
Andreas M. Odefey, Partner
Stephan Gummert, Partner

Type of Firm
Bank Affiliated

Association Membership
German Venture Capital Association (BVK)

Project Preferences

Type of Financing Preferred:
Leveraged Buyout
Mezzanine
Management Buyouts
Acquisition

Geographical Preferences

International Preferences:
Austria
Germany

Industry Focus
(% based on actual investment)
    Internet Specific   42.3%
    Semiconductors/Other Elect.   32.4%
    Other Products   25.3%

Additional Information
Name of Most Recent Fund: BPE2 Private Equity GmbH & Co. KG
Most Recent Fund Was Raised: 10/31/2005
Year Founded: 1998
Capital Under Management: $55,200,000
Current Activity Level : Actively seeking new investments

BPIFRANCE EPIC

27-31 Ave du General Leclerc
Maisons-Alfort, France 94710
Phone: 33141798000

Management and Staff
Francois Drouin, Chief Executive Officer

Type of Firm
Government Affiliated Program

Project Preferences

Type of Financing Preferred:
Leveraged Buyout
Early Stage
Mezzanine
Later Stage
Acquisition
Startup

Geographical Preferences

International Preferences:
Europe
France

Additional Information

Year Founded: 2005
Current Activity Level : Actively seeking new investments

BPIFRANCE INVESTISSEMENT REGIONS SAS

27-31 avenue du General Lecler
Maisons-Alfort, France 94710
Phone: 33
Fax: 33

Other Offices

22-28 Rue Joubert
Paris, France 75009
Phone: 33-1-5389-7701
Fax: 33-1-5389-7746

14 rue Peletier
Paris, France 75009
Phone: 33153895527

Immeuble Le 6eme Sens
186, avenue Thiers
Lyon cedex 06, France 69465
Phone: 33-4-7260-5759
Fax: 33-4-7260-5490

63 quai Magellan
BP 42304
Nantes, France 44023
Phone: 33-2-5172-9951
Fax: 33-2-4035-1899

Technopole de Nancy Brabois
10, route de l'Aviation
Villers les Nancy cedex, France 54602
Phone: 33-3-8367-2013
Fax: 33-3-8367-2015

Arche Jacques Coeur
222, place Ernest Granier
Montpellier cedex 2, France 34967
Phone: 33-4-6769-7611
Fax: 33-4-6769-7632

Immeuble Axe Europe
213 bd de Turin
Lille, France 59777
Phone: 33-3-2081-9448
Fax: 33-3-2081-9456

Type of Firm

Private Equity Firm

Association Membership

French Venture Capital Association (AFIC)

Project Preferences

Type of Financing Preferred:
Leveraged Buyout
Early Stage
Mezzanine
Generalist PE
Turnaround
Later Stage
Seed
Acquisition

Geographical Preferences

International Preferences:
Europe
France

Industry Preferences

In Biotechnology prefer:
Agricultural/Animal Bio.

In Medical/Health prefer:
Medical/Health
Health Services

In Consumer Related prefer:
Entertainment and Leisure
Hotels and Resorts

In Industrial/Energy prefer:
Industrial Products
Materials

In Business Serv. prefer:
Services

In Agr/Forestr/Fish prefer:
Agriculture related

In Utilities prefer:
Utilities

Additional Information

Year Founded: 1984
Capital Under Management: $65,600,000
Current Activity Level : Actively seeking new investments

BPIFRANCE INVESTISSEMENT SASU

137, rue de l'Universite
Paris, France 75007
Phone: 33158507171

E-mail: contact-cdcentreprises@cdcentreprises.fr
Website: www.bpifrance.fr

Other Offices

14, rue Le Peletier
Paris, France 75009
Phone: 330153897914

6-8, Boulevard Haussmann
Paris, France 75009

Management and Staff

Luc Heinrich, Chief Operating Officer
Pascal Lagarde, Chief Executive Officer

Type of Firm

Bank Affiliated

Association Membership

French Venture Capital Association (AFIC)

Project Preferences

Type of Financing Preferred:
Early Stage
Expansion
Later Stage
Seed
Startup

Size of Investments Considered:
Min Size of Investment Considered (000s): $648
Max Size of Investment Considered (000s): $12,978

Geographical Preferences

International Preferences:
France

Industry Preferences

In Computer Other prefer:
Computer Related

In Medical/Health prefer:
Medical Diagnostics
Pharmaceuticals

In Consumer Related prefer:
Entertainment and Leisure
Sports
Consumer Services
Other Restaurants
Hotels and Resorts

In Industrial/Energy prefer:
Energy Conservation Relat
Industrial Products
Environmental Related

In Transportation prefer:
Transportation

In Business Serv. prefer:
Media

In Manufact. prefer:
Manufacturing

Additional Information
Year Founded: 1994
Capital Under Management: $221,000,000
Current Activity Level : Actively seeking new investments

BPM CAPITAL OU

Roosikrantsi 11
Tallinn, Estonia 10119
Phone: 3726050073
Website: www.bpmcapital.eu

Management and Staff
Kalmer Kikas, Managing Partner
Kulli Kalamea, Chief Financial Officer
Martin Reinson, Partner
Pawel Zabrzycki, Partner
Pritt Veering, Partner

Type of Firm
Private Equity Firm

Project Preferences

Type of Financing Preferred:
Leveraged Buyout
Expansion
Mezzanine
Later Stage
Management Buyouts
Recapitalizations

Geographical Preferences

International Preferences:
Poland
Estonia
Latvia
Lithuania

Additional Information
Year Founded: 2015
Capital Under Management: $81,000,000
Current Activity Level : Actively seeking new investments

BR VENTURES

304 Sage Hall
Cornell University
Ithaca, NY USA 14850
Phone: 6072556599
Website: www.brventurefund.com

Management and Staff
Vinay Badami, Chief Operating Officer

Type of Firm
University Program

Project Preferences

Type of Financing Preferred:
Early Stage
Balanced
Seed
Startup

Size of Investments Considered:
Min Size of Investment Considered (000s): $50
Max Size of Investment Considered (000s): $200

Geographical Preferences

United States Preferences:

Additional Information
Year Founded: 2003
Current Activity Level : Actively seeking new investments

BRABANTSE ONTWIKKELINGS MAATSCHAPPIJ NV

Goirleseweg 15
Tilburg, Netherlands 5026 PB
Phone: 31888311120
Fax: 31888311121
E-mail: info@bom.nl
Website: www.bom.nl

Type of Firm
Corporate PE/Venture

Association Membership
Dutch Venture Capital Associaton (NVP)

Project Preferences

Type of Financing Preferred:
Early Stage
Later Stage

Size of Investments Considered:
Min Size of Investment Considered (000s): $100
Max Size of Investment Considered (000s): $2,500

Geographical Preferences

International Preferences:
Europe
Netherlands

Additional Information
Year Founded: 1983
Capital Under Management: $19,500,000
Current Activity Level : Actively seeking new investments

BRADFORD EQUITIES MANAGEMENT LLC

360 Hamilton Avenue
Suite 425
White Plains, NY USA 10601
Phone: 9149227171
Fax: 9149227172
Website: www.bradfordequities.com

Management and Staff
Richard Rudolph, Managing Director
Robert Simon, Senior Managing Director

Type of Firm
Private Equity Firm

Project Preferences

Role in Financing:
Prefer role as deal originator

Type of Financing Preferred:
Leveraged Buyout
Management Buyouts
Acquisition

Geographical Preferences

United States Preferences:

Industry Preferences

In Business Serv. prefer:
Distribution

In Manufact. prefer:
Manufacturing

Additional Information
Name of Most Recent Fund: Bradford Equities Fund III, L.P.
Most Recent Fund Was Raised: 08/15/2000
Year Founded: 1974
Capital Under Management: $120,000,000
Current Activity Level : Actively seeking new investments
Method of Compensation: Return on invest. most important, but chg. closing fees, service fees, etc.

BRAEMAR ENERGY VENTURES LP

350 Madison Avenue
23rd Floor
New York, NY USA 10017
Phone: 2126970900
Fax: 2122105788
Website: www.braemarenergy.com

Other Offices

470 Atlantic Avenue
Independence Wharf, Tenth Floor
BOSTON, MA USA 02210
Phone: 6177616550
Fax: 6177616552

166 Piccadilly
5th Floor, Foxglove House
London, United Kingdom W1J 9EF
Phone: 224075187007

Management and Staff
Dennis Costello, Managing Partner
Eric Schultz, Chief Financial Officer
Jiong Ma, Partner
Neil Suslak, Co-Founder
Scott DePasquale, Partner
William Lese, Co-Founder

Type of Firm
Private Equity Firm

Association Membership
New England Venture Capital Association
Norwegian Venture Capital Association
National Venture Capital Association - USA (NVCA)

Project Preferences
Type of Financing Preferred:
Early Stage
Expansion
Later Stage

Size of Investments Considered:
Min Size of Investment Considered (000s): $1,000
Max Size of Investment Considered (000s): $10,000

Industry Preferences
In Communications prefer:
Communications and Media

In Semiconductor/Electr prefer:
Semiconductor

In Industrial/Energy prefer:
Energy
Oil and Gas Exploration
Alternative Energy

Additional Information
Name of Most Recent Fund: Braemar Energy Ventures III, L.P.
Most Recent Fund Was Raised: 06/19/2012
Year Founded: 2002
Capital Under Management: $310,000,000
Current Activity Level : Actively seeking new investments

BRAHMAN MANAGEMENT LLC
350 Main Avenue
22nd Floor
New York, NY USA 10017
Phone: 212-681-9797

Management and Staff
Mitchell Kuflik, General Partner
Peter Hochfelder, General Partner
Robert Sobel, General Partner

Type of Firm
Private Equity Firm

Additional Information
Year Founded: 2002
Capital Under Management: $13,000,000
Current Activity Level : Actively seeking new investments

BRAIN ROBOTICS CAPITAL LLC
53 State Street
Suite 500
Boston, MA USA 02109
E-mail: contact@brainrobotcap.com
Website: www.brainrobotcap.com

Management and Staff
Feco Fong, Partner
Pei Qi, Managing Partner

Type of Firm
Private Equity Firm

Project Preferences
Type of Financing Preferred:
Balanced

Additional Information
Year Founded: 2014
Current Activity Level : Actively seeking new investments

BRAIN TRUST ACCELERATOR FUND LP
800 Airport Boulevard
Suite 508
Burlingame, CA USA 94010
Phone: 6503750200
Fax: 6503750230
Website: www.braintrustvc.com

Management and Staff
John Reher, Partner

Type of Firm
Private Equity Firm

Additional Information
Year Founded: 2016
Capital Under Management: $7,230,000
Current Activity Level : Actively seeking new investments

BRAINTIME SAS
21, Avenue des Hirondelles
Annecy, France 74000
Phone: 33458000388
Website: www.story-starter.fr

Type of Firm
Incubator/Development Program

Project Preferences
Type of Financing Preferred:
Early Stage
Seed

Geographical Preferences
International Preferences:
France

Industry Preferences
In Computer Software prefer:
Software

In Internet Specific prefer:
E-Commerce Technology
Internet
Ecommerce

Additional Information
Year Founded: 2013
Current Activity Level : Actively seeking new investments

BRAIT CAPITAL PARTNERS
177 Oxford Raod
2nd Floor, The Zone II
Johannesburg, South Africa
Phone: 27115071000
Fax: 27115071001
Website: www.brait.com

Other Offices
42, rue de la Valle'e
Luxembourg, Luxembourg L-2661
Phone: 3522692553297
Fax: 3522692553642

25 Protea Road
The Terraces Second Floor
Claremont, South Africa 7708
Phone: 27216737800
Fax: 27216737801

Le Caudan Waterfront
Suite 520 5th Floor, Barkly Wharf
Port Louis, Mauritius
Phone: 2302136909
Fax: 2302136913

Management and Staff
Antony Charles Ball, Chief Executive Officer

Type of Firm
Private Equity Firm

Association Membership
South African Venture Capital Association (SAVCA)

Project Preferences

Type of Financing Preferred:
Leveraged Buyout
Expansion
Balanced
Public Companies
Later Stage
Acquisition

Size of Investments Considered:
Min Size of Investment Considered (000s): $13,525
Max Size of Investment Considered (000s): $114,958

Geographical Preferences

International Preferences:
South Africa
Africa

Industry Preferences

In Communications prefer:
Communications and Media

In Medical/Health prefer:
Medical/Health

In Consumer Related prefer:
Consumer Products
Consumer Services

In Business Serv. prefer:
Mecia

In Manufact. prefer:
Manufacturing

Additional Information

Year Founded: 1991
Capital Under Management: $84,300,000
Current Activity Level : Actively seeking new investments

BRAMDEAN ASSET MANAGEMENT LLP

6 Derby Street
London, United Kingdom W1J 7AD
Phone: 44-20-7052-9272
Fax: 44-20-7052-9273
Website: www.bramdean.com

Management and Staff

Nicola Horlick, Chief Executive Officer
Richard Stewart, Chief Financial Officer

Type of Firm

Private Equity Advisor or Fund of Funds

Project Preferences

Type of Financing Preferred:
Fund of Funds

Additional Information

Year Founded: 2005
Current Activity Level : Actively seeking new investments

BRAND FOUNDRY VENTURES

250 Greenwich Street
Suite 4660
New York, NY USA 10007
Website: www.brandfoundryvc.com

Type of Firm

Private Equity Firm

Project Preferences

Type of Financing Preferred:
Early Stage

Geographical Preferences

United States Preferences:

Industry Preferences

In Computer Software prefer:
Applications Software

In Internet Specific prefer:
Ecommerce

In Consumer Related prefer:
Consumer
Consumer Products
Consumer Services

Additional Information

Year Founded: 2014
Current Activity Level : Actively seeking new investments

BRANDENBURG VENTURES GMBH

Platz der Luftbruecke 4 - 6
Berlin, Germany 12101
Phone: 4930609889060
Fax: 4930609889069
E-mail: info@brandenburg-ventures.com
Website: www.brandenburg-ventures.com

Type of Firm

Private Equity Firm

Project Preferences

Type of Financing Preferred:
Early Stage
Seed
Startup

Geographical Preferences

International Preferences:
Western Europe
Germany

Industry Preferences

In Communications prefer:
Media and Entertainment

In Internet Specific prefer:
E-Commerce Technology

Additional Information

Year Founded: 2011
Current Activity Level : Actively seeking new investments

BRANDON CAPITAL PARTNERS PTY LTD

210 George Street
Level Seven
Sydney, Australia 2000
Phone: 61292472577
Fax: 61292477344
E-mail: info@brandoncapital.com.au
Website: www.brandoncapital.com.au

Other Offices

459 Hamilton Ave
Suite 205
PALO ALTO, CA USA 94301

278 Collins Street
Level 9
, Australia
Phone: 61-3-9657-0700
Fax: 61-3-9657-0777

Management and Staff

Andrea Tobias, Venture Partner
Christopher Nave, Partner
David Fisher, Venture Partner
Kerensa Argyriou, Chief Financial Officer
Michael Ball, Chief Financial Officer
Stephen Thompson, Partner

Type of Firm

Private Equity Firm

Association Membership

Australian Venture Capital Association (AVCAL)

Project Preferences

Type of Financing Preferred:
Balanced
Seed

Size of Investments Considered:
Min Size of Investment Considered (000s): $521
Max Size of Investment Considered (000s): $20,842

Additional Information

Name of Most Recent Fund: MRCF IIF, L.P.
Most Recent Fund Was Raised: 05/17/2011
Year Founded: 2007
Capital Under Management: $105,300,000
Current Activity Level : Actively seeking new investments

BRANFORD CASTLE PARTNERS

150 East 58th Street
37th Floor
New York, NY USA 10155
Phone: 2123172004
Fax: 2123172153
Website: www.branfordcastle.com

Management and Staff
Eric Korsten, Vice President

Type of Firm
Private Equity Firm

Association Membership
Natl Assoc of Small Bus. Inv. Co (NASBIC)

Project Preferences

Role in Financing:
Prefer role as deal originator but will also invest in deals created by others

Type of Financing Preferred:
Leveraged Buyout
Expansion
Balanced

Geographical Preferences

United States Preferences:

Canadian Preferences:
All Canada

Industry Focus
(% based on actual investment)
Internet Specific   100.0%

Additional Information
Year Founded: 1986
Capital Under Management: $116,910,000
Current Activity Level : Actively seeking new investments
Method of Compensation: Return on investment is of primary concern, do not charge fees

---

BRANT POINT PARTNERS LLC

1150 First Avenue
Suite 150
King of Prussia, PA USA 19406
Phone: 6102917080
Website: www.brantpointpartners.net

Management and Staff
Robert Auritt, President

Type of Firm
Private Equity Firm

Project Preferences

Type of Financing Preferred:
Leveraged Buyout
Acquisition

Geographical Preferences

United States Preferences:
Mississippi

Industry Preferences

In Computer Software prefer:
Software

In Medical/Health prefer:
Health Services

In Business Serv. prefer:
Services

In Manufact. prefer:
Manufacturing

Additional Information
Year Founded: 1969
Current Activity Level : Actively seeking new investments

BRANTLEY VENTURE PARTNERS L P

3550 Lander Road
Suite 300
Pepper Pike, OH USA 44124
Phone: 2164648400
Fax: 2164648405
Website: www.brantleypartners.com

Management and Staff
Curtis Witchey, Chief Financial Officer
Robert Pinkas, Partner

Type of Firm
Private Equity Firm

Project Preferences

Role in Financing:
Prefer role as deal originator

Type of Financing Preferred:
Leveraged Buyout
Later Stage
Management Buyouts
Recapitalizations

Size of Investments Considered:
Min Size of Investment Considered (000s): $2,000
Max Size of Investment Considered (000s): $20,000

Geographical Preferences

United States Preferences:

Industry Focus
(% based on actual investment)
Other Products   57.5%
Industrial/Energy   15.0%
Computer Software and Services   7.5%
Consumer Related   7.3%
Medical/Health   5.0%
Biotechnology   4.4%
Semiconductors/Other Elect.   1.6%
Communications and Media   1.3%
Internet Specific   0.5%

Additional Information
Name of Most Recent Fund: Brantley Equity Partners
Most Recent Fund Was Raised: 06/30/2007
Year Founded: 1987
Capital Under Management: $310,000,000
Current Activity Level : Actively seeking new investments
Method of Compensation: Return on investment is of primary concern, do not charge fees

---

BRASIL PLURAL GESTAO DE RECURSOS LTDA

Rua Surubim 373
1st Floor
Sao Paulo, Brazil 04571050
Phone: 551132068000
Fax: 551132068001
Website: www.brasilplural.com.br

Other Offices
Rua Lauro Mller, 116
Salas 3304 / 3305
Rio de Janeiro, Brazil 22290-160
Phone: 552139233000
Fax: 552139233001

Management and Staff
Andre Schwartz, Chief Executive Officer
Rodolfo Riechert, Chief Executive Officer

Type of Firm
Investment Management Firm

Project Preferences

Type of Financing Preferred:
Early Stage
Balanced
Later Stage

Industry Preferences

In Consumer Related prefer:
Consumer Products

In Industrial/Energy prefer:
Oil and Gas Exploration
Oil & Gas Drilling,Explor

In Financial Services prefer:
Financial Services
Real Estate

Additional Information
Year Founded: 2009
Capital Under Management: $24,000,000
Current Activity Level : Actively seeking new investments

BRATENAHL CAPITAL PARTNERS LTD

700 West Street Clair Avenue
Suite 414
Cleveland, OH USA 44113
Phone: 2168204640
Website: www.bratenahlcapital.com

Management and Staff
Michael Howley, Managing Partner

Type of Firm
Private Equity Firm

Project Preferences

Type of Financing Preferred:
Fund of Funds
Mezzanine
Generalist PE

Additional Information
Year Founded: 2015
Current Activity Level : Actively seeking new investments

BRAVE VENTURES

1460 Broadway
New York, NY USA 10036
Website: www.braveventures.com

Type of Firm
Investment Management Firm

Project Preferences

Type of Financing Preferred:
Early Stage
Expansion
Later Stage

Industry Preferences

In Communications prefer:
Entertainment

In Business Serv. prefer:
Media

Additional Information
Year Founded: 2014
Current Activity Level : Actively seeking new investments

BRAVIA CAPITAL INVESTIMENTOS LTDA

Av Pres. Juscelino Kubitschek
1726, 7th floor
Sao Paulo, Brazil 04543-000
Phone: 551130741540
E-mail: contato@bravia.com.br
Website: www.bravia.com.br

Type of Firm
Private Equity Firm

Association Membership
Brazilian Venture Capital Association (ABCR)

Project Preferences

Type of Financing Preferred:
Leveraged Buyout
Mezzanine
Generalist PE
Balanced
Public Companies
Later Stage
Acquisition
Recapitalizations

Geographical Preferences

International Preferences:
Latin America
Brazil

Additional Information
Year Founded: 2009
Current Activity Level : Actively seeking new investments

BRAVIA CAPITAL PARTNERS INC

99 Queens Road
6511-13, The Center
Hong Kong, Hong Kong
Phone: 85226772104
E-mail: info@braviacapital.com
Website: www.braviacapital.com

Other Offices
11 The Executive center
Second Floor
Mumbai, India

312 Case del Sol Business Centre
Miramar, Panaji
, India
Phone: 8322465634
Fax: 8322452024

245 Park Avenue
39th Floor
New York, NY USA 10167
Phone: 2126721844

Orjin Building, Level Five
15 Boston Street Tesvikiye
Istanbul, Turkey
Phone: 2123739430
Fax: 2123739650

Management and Staff
Bharat Bhise, Chief Executive Officer
Hal Hayward, Managing Director
Ozgur Gen, Vice President

Type of Firm
Investment Management Firm

Association Membership
Hong Kong Venture Capital Association (HKVCA)

Project Preferences

Type of Financing Preferred:
Leveraged Buyout
Acquisition
Special Situation
Recapitalizations

Geographical Preferences

International Preferences:
India
China
Eastern Europe
Middle East
Asia
Africa

Industry Preferences

In Consumer Related prefer:
Entertainment and Leisure

In Transportation prefer:
Transportation
Aerospace

In Financial Services prefer:
Financial Services
Real Estate

Additional Information
Year Founded: 2000
Current Activity Level : Actively seeking new investments

BRAZOS PRIVATE EQUITY PARTNERS LLC

100 Crescent Court
Suite 1777
Dallas, TX USA 75201
Phone: 2147566500
Fax: 2147566505
Website: www.brazospartners.com

Management and Staff
Douglas Kennealey, Vice President
F. Russell Beard, Managing Director
Glenn Askew, Managing Director
Jason Sutherland, Vice President
Lucas Cutler, Managing Director
Michael Salim, Chief Operating Officer
Patrick McGee, Co-Founder
Patrick O Hara, Managing Director

Type of Firm
Private Equity Firm

Project Preferences

Role in Financing:
Will function either as deal originator or investor in deals created by others

Type of Financing Preferred:
Leveraged Buyout
Management Buyouts
Acquisition
Recapitalizations

Geographical Preferences

United States Preferences:

Industry Focus
(% based on actual investment)
Industrial/Energy	38.0%
Medical/Health	23.8%
Other Products	20.3%
Consumer Related	12.3%
Internet Specific	5.7%

Additional Information
Name of Most Recent Fund: Brazos Equity Fund, L.P.
Most Recent Fund Was Raised: 04/01/2000
Year Founded: 1999
Capital Under Management: $1,400,000,000
Current Activity Level : Actively seeking new investments
Method of Compensation: Return on invest. most important, but chg. closing fees, service fees, etc.

BREAKAWAY

399 Boylston Street
Fifth Floor
Boston, MA USA 02116
Phone: 6173990635
Fax: 6176710557
E-mail: huge@breakaway.com
Website: breakaway.com

Management and Staff
Marcus Wilson, Managing Director

Type of Firm
Private Equity Firm

Association Membership
New England Venture Capital Association

Project Preferences

Role in Financing:
Will function either as deal originator or investor in deals created by others

Type of Financing Preferred:
Early Stage
Balanced
Later Stage

Size of Investments Considered:
Min Size of Investment Considered (000s): $500
Max Size of Investment Considered (000s): $10,000

Geographical Preferences

United States Preferences:

International Preferences:
United Kingdom

Industry Preferences

In Communications prefer:
Media and Entertainment

In Internet Specific prefer:
Internet
Ecommerce

In Consumer Related prefer:
Consumer
Entertainment and Leisure
Retail
Food/Beverage
Consumer Products

Additional Information
Year Founded: 2006
Capital Under Management: $25,000,000
Current Activity Level : Actively seeking new investments
Method of Compensation: Return on investment is of primary concern, do not charge fees

BREAKAWAY CAPITAL PARTNERS LLC

2000 Avenue of the Stars
Suite 1100
Los Angeles, CA USA 90067
E-mail: info@breakawaycap.com
Website: www.breakawaycap.com

Type of Firm
Private Equity Firm

Project Preferences

Type of Financing Preferred:
Leveraged Buyout
Mezzanine
Acquisition
Recapitalizations

Size of Investments Considered:
Min Size of Investment Considered (000s): $3,000
Max Size of Investment Considered (000s): $7,000

Additional Information
Year Founded: 2014
Capital Under Management: $147,270,000
Current Activity Level : Actively seeking new investments

BREAKOUT CAPITAL LLC

954 West Washington Boulevard
Suite 730
Chicago, IL USA 60607
Website: www.breakoutcap.com

Management and Staff
Darwin Olympia, Chief Financial Officer
Jay Bhatt, Vice President
Keysha Washington, Vice President

Type of Firm
Private Equity Firm

Project Preferences

Type of Financing Preferred:
Balanced

Additional Information
Year Founded: 2014
Current Activity Level : Actively seeking new investments

BREAKOUT VENTURES INC

One Letterman Drive
Building C, Suite 400
San Francisco, CA USA 94129
Website: www.breakoutvc.com

Type of Firm
Private Equity Firm

Project Preferences

Type of Financing Preferred:
Early Stage

Additional Information
Year Founded: 2016
Capital Under Management: $60,100,000
Current Activity Level : Actively seeking new investments

BREAKTHROUGH ENERGY VENTURES LLC

4110 Carillon Point
Kirkland, WA USA 98033
Phone: 4254974303
Website: www.b-t.energy

Type of Firm
Endowment, Foundation or Pension Fund

Project Preferences

Type of Financing Preferred:
Balanced

Industry Preferences

In Other prefer:
Environment Responsible

Additional Information

Year Founded: 2016
Capital Under Management: $1,080,000,000
Current Activity Level : Actively seeking new investments

BREAKWATER INVESTMENT MANAGEMENT LLC

1999 Avenue of the Stars
Suite 3430
Los Angeles, CA USA 90067
Phone: 4247774000
Fax: 4247774001
E-mail: info@breakwaterfund.com
Website: www.breakwaterfund.com

Type of Firm
Private Equity Firm

Project Preferences

Type of Financing Preferred:
Early Stage
Expansion
Mezzanine
Acquisition
Recapitalizations

Industry Preferences

In Communications prefer:
Telecommunications

In Medical/Health prefer:
Medical/Health
Medical Products

In Consumer Related prefer:
Retail
Consumer Products

In Industrial/Energy prefer:
Energy
Alternative Energy

In Financial Services prefer:
Financial Services

In Manufact. prefer:
Manufacturing

Additional Information
Year Founded: 2008
Current Activity Level : Actively seeking new investments

BREED REPLY LTD

38, Grosvenor Gardens
London, United Kingdom SW1W 0EB
Phone: 442077306000
E-mail: info@breedreply.com
Website: www.reply.eu

Type of Firm
Incubator/Development Program

Project Preferences

Type of Financing Preferred:
Early Stage
Seed

Geographical Preferences

United States Preferences:

International Preferences:
Europe

Industry Preferences

In Computer Software prefer:
Software

In Internet Specific prefer:
Internet

In Medical/Health prefer:
Health Services

In Consumer Related prefer:
Sports

In Industrial/Energy prefer:
Energy

In Transportation prefer:
Transportation

In Manufact. prefer:
Manufacturing

Additional Information
Year Founded: 2014
Current Activity Level : Actively seeking new investments

BREEDINVEST BV

Naarderstraat 50
Laren, Netherlands 1250 AA
Phone: 31355393328
Fax: 31355393327

Type of Firm
Private Equity Firm

Association Membership
Dutch Venture Capital Associaton (NVP)

Project Preferences

Type of Financing Preferred:
Later Stage
Management Buyouts
Recapitalizations

Geographical Preferences

International Preferences:
Luxembourg
Netherlands
Belgium

Additional Information
Year Founded: 1969
Current Activity Level : Actively seeking new investments

BREEGA CAPITAL SARL

42 avenue Montaigne
Paris, France 75008
Phone: 33172741001
Fax: 33172741002
E-mail: contact@breega.com
Website: www.breega.com

Management and Staff
Benoit Marrel, Co-Founder
Francois Paulus, Co-Founder
Laurent Grimaldi, Venture Partner
Marc Deschamps, Venture Partner
Maximilien Bacot, Co-Founder

Type of Firm
Private Equity Firm

Project Preferences

Type of Financing Preferred:
Early Stage
Seed
Startup

Geographical Preferences

International Preferences:
France

Industry Preferences

In Communications prefer:
Communications and Media
Commercial Communications

In Computer Software prefer:
Applications Software

Additional Information
Year Founded: 2012
Capital Under Management: $139,857,000
Current Activity Level : Actively seeking new investments

BREGAL CAPITAL LLP

81 Fulham Road
Michelin House
London, United Kingdom SW3 6RD
Phone: 442075914200
Fax: 442075914222
E-mail: bregal@bregalcapital.com
Website: www.bregalcapital.com

Management and Staff

Adam Barron, Managing Partner
Edmund Lazarus, Managing Partner
Florian Schick, Partner
Olivier Morali, Partner
Patrik Johnson, Partner

Type of Firm

Private Equity Firm

Association Membership

British Venture Capital Association (BVCA)

Project Preferences

Type of Financing Preferred:
Leveraged Buyout
Management Buyouts
Acquisition

Additional Information

Year Founded: 2001
Capital Under Management: $1,432,870,000
Current Activity Level : Actively seeking new investments

BREGAL INVESTMENTS LLP

81 Fulham Road, Third Floor
London, United Kingdom SW3 6RD
Phone: 442074081663
Fax: 442074919228
E-mail: management@bregal.com
Website: www.bregal.com

Other Offices

La Route de la Liberation
Windward House, 2nd Floor, St Helier
Jersey, United Kingdom JE2 3BQ

277 Park Avenue
29th Floor
New York, NY USA 10172
Phone: 212-573-6235
Fax: 212-573-6234

Management and Staff

Adam Barron, Managing Partner
Adam Fuller, Vice President
Chuck Flynn, Managing Director
Daniel Kim, Partner
Daryl Yap, Vice President
Edmund Lazarus, Managing Partner
Edwin Niers, Chief Financial Officer
Florian Schick, Partner
Gene Yoon, Managing Partner
Jan Faber, Managing Director
Matthew Ford, Principal
Michael Anderson, Principal
Michael Kosty, Vice President
Olivier Morali, Partner
Patrik Johnson, Partner
Paul McGill, Principal
Pereklis Scott, Managing Partner
Philip Yates, Partner
Robert Bergmann, Managing Partner
Wolter Brenninkmeijer, Managing Director

Type of Firm

Private Equity Firm

Project Preferences

Type of Financing Preferred:
Fund of Funds
Leveraged Buyout
Generalist PE
Later Stage
Other
Management Buyouts
Acquisition
Special Situation
Fund of Funds of Second
Recapitalizations

Geographical Preferences

United States Preferences:
North America

Canadian Preferences:
All Canada

International Preferences:
Europe
Asia

Industry Preferences

In Industrial/Energy prefer:
Energy
Oil and Gas Exploration
Oil & Gas Drilling,Explor

Additional Information

Name of Most Recent Fund: Bregal Sagemount I, L.P.
Most Recent Fund Was Raised: 06/06/2012
Year Founded: 2002
Capital Under Management: $3,048,400,000
Current Activity Level : Actively seeking new investments

BREGAL UNTERNEHMER-KAPITAL GMBH

Marstallstrass 11
Munich, Germany 80539
Phone: 49894357150
E-mail: info@bregal.de
Website: www.bregal.de

Type of Firm

Private Equity Firm

Geographical Preferences

International Preferences:
Switzerland
Austria
Germany

Additional Information

Year Founded: 2014
Capital Under Management: $756,530,000
Current Activity Level : Actively seeking new investments

BREIZH UP SASU

283, Avenue General Patton
Rennes, France 35700
Website: breizhup.bretagne.bzh

Type of Firm

Government Affiliated Program

Project Preferences

Type of Financing Preferred:
Early Stage
Seed

Size of Investments Considered:
Min Size of Investment Considered (000s): $215
Max Size of Investment Considered (000s): $804

Geographical Preferences

International Preferences:
France

Industry Preferences

In Computer Software prefer:
Software

In Medical/Health prefer:
Medical/Health

In Consumer Related prefer:
Food/Beverage

In Industrial/Energy prefer:
Environmental Related

Additional Information

Year Founded: 2015
Current Activity Level : Actively seeking new investments

BRENTWOOD ASSOCIATES, L.P.

11150 Santa Monica Boulevard, Suite 1200
Los Angeles, CA USA 90025
Phone: 3104776611
Fax: 3104771011
E-mail: info@brentwood.com
Website: www.brentwood.com

Management and Staff

Anthony Choe, Partner
Craig Milius, Managing Director
Edward McCall, Partner
Eric Reiter, Partner
Jonathan Ang, Vice President
Matthew Whelan, Managing Director
Rahul Aggarwal, Managing Director
Randolph Brown, Principal
Roger Goddu, Partner
Steven Moore, Partner
Toros Yeremyan, Vice President
William Barnum, Partner

Type of Firm
Private Equity Firm

Project Preferences

Role in Financing:
Will function either as deal originator or investor in deals created by others

Type of Financing Preferred:
Leveraged Buyout
Early Stage
Expansion
Generalist PE
Management Buyouts
Recapitalizations

Size of Investments Considered:
Min Size of Investment Considered (000s): $20,000
Max Size of Investment Considered (000s): $200,000

Geographical Preferences

United States Preferences:

Industry Focus

(% based on actual investment)
Consumer Related	50.8%
Computer Hardware	10.4%
Internet Specific	9.6%
Other Products	7.3%
Communications and Media	5.4%
Semiconductors/Other Elect.	5.1%
Medical/Health	4.0%
Computer Software and Services	3.5%
Industrial/Energy	2.1%
Biotechnology	1.7%

Additional Information

Year Founded: 1972
Capital Under Management: $750,000,000
Current Activity Level: Actively seeking new investments
Method of Compensation: Return on invest. most important, but chg. closing fees, service fees, etc.

BRENTWOOD CAPITAL ADVISORS LLC

5000 Meridian Boulevard
Suite 350
Franklin, TN USA 37067
Phone: 6152243830
Fax: 6152243831
E-mail: info@brentwoodcapital.com
Website: www.brentwoodcap.com

Management and Staff

Jack Harrington, Partner
Kevin Murphy, Managing Partner
L.A. Galyon, Vice President
Nick Carteaux, Partner

Type of Firm
Bank Affiliated

Project Preferences

Type of Financing Preferred:
Leveraged Buyout
Mezzanine
Later Stage
Acquisition
Recapitalizations

Geographical Preferences

United States Preferences:
Southeast

Industry Preferences

In Medical/Health prefer:
Health Services

In Financial Services prefer:
Financial Services

In Business Serv. prefer:
Services

Additional Information

Year Founded: 1999
Capital Under Management: $15,200,000
Current Activity Level: Actively seeking new investments

BRENTWOOD VENTURE CAPITAL

11150 Santa Monica Blvd.
Suite 1200
West Los Angeles, CA USA 90025
Phone: 3104776611
Fax: 3104771011

Other Offices

450 Newport Center Drive
Suite 600
Newport Beach, CA USA 92660
Phone: 949-729-4500
Fax: 949-729-4501

3000 Sand Hill Road
Building Four, Suite 210
Menlo Park, CA USA 94025
Phone: 650-233-7877
Fax: 650-854-9513

Management and Staff

Anthony Choe, Partner
Eric Reiter, Partner
Jonathan Ang, Vice President
Matthew Whelan, Managing Director
Rahul Aggarwal, Managing Director
Randolph Brown, Principal
Steven Moore, Partner
Toros Yeremyan, Vice President
William Barnum, Partner

Type of Firm
Private Equity Firm

Project Preferences

Role in Financing:
Prefer role as deal originator but will also invest in deals created by others

Type of Financing Preferred:
Early Stage
Balanced
Seed
Startup

Geographical Preferences

United States Preferences:
West Coast

Industry Preferences

In Communications prefer:
Communications and Media

In Computer Software prefer:
Software

In Internet Specific prefer:
Internet

In Biotechnology prefer:
Biotechnology

In Medical/Health prefer:
Medical/Health
Health Services

In Consumer Related prefer:
Consumer
Retail
Food/Beverage
Other Restaurants
Education Related

In Business Serv. prefer:
Services
Distribution
Media

Additional Information
Year Founded: 1972
Capital Under Management: $675,000,000
Current Activity Level : Actively seeking new investments

BRETAGNE DE NESTADIO CAPITAL

Presqu'ile de Nestadio
Plouhinec, France 56680
Phone: 33297366674
Fax: 33297858849
E-mail: contact@nestadio-capital.com
Website: www.nestadio-capital.com

Management and Staff
Florent De Kersauson, President, Founder

Type of Firm
Private Equity Firm

Project Preferences

Type of Financing Preferred:
Early Stage
Balanced
Later Stage
Seed
Startup

Geographical Preferences

International Preferences:
Europe
France

Industry Preferences

In Computer Software prefer:
Systems Software

In Internet Specific prefer:
Internet

In Computer Other prefer:
Computer Related

In Consumer Related prefer:
Consumer
Food/Beverage
Consumer Products

In Industrial/Energy prefer:
Alternative Energy
Energy Conservation Relat
Environmental Related

In Transportation prefer:
Transportation
Aerospace

In Other prefer:
Socially Responsible

Additional Information
Year Founded: 2004
Current Activity Level : Actively seeking new investments

BRETAGNE PARTICIPATIONS SA

20 quai Duguay Trouin
Rennes, France 35000
Phone: 33299679769
Fax: 33299674600
E-mail: bretagne.participations@bretpart.com
Website: www.soderogestion.com

Type of Firm
Private Equity Firm

Project Preferences

Type of Financing Preferred:
Early Stage
Later Stage

Size of Investments Considered:
Min Size of Investment Considered (000s): $130
Max Size of Investment Considered (000s): $3,894

Geographical Preferences

International Preferences:
Europe
France

Additional Information
Year Founded: 1999
Capital Under Management: $13,700,000
Current Activity Level : Actively seeking new investments

BREYER CAPITAL

314 Lytton Avenue
Suite 200
Palo Alto, CA USA 94301
Phone: 4153106790
Fax: 4155209664
Website: www.breyercapital.com

Type of Firm
Private Equity Firm

Project Preferences

Type of Financing Preferred:
Leveraged Buyout
Early Stage
Mezzanine
Generalist PE
Acquisition
Recapitalizations

Industry Preferences

In Consumer Related prefer:
Retail
Education Related

In Business Serv. prefer:
Media

Additional Information
Year Founded: 1969
Current Activity Level : Actively seeking new investments

BRICK & MORTAR VENTURES

92 South Park
San Francisco, CA USA 94107
Phone: 4154837353
E-mail: info@brickmortar.vc
Website: www.brickmortar.vc

Other Offices
901 Hancock Avenue
West Hollywood, CA USA 90069
Phone: 2035361748

Type of Firm
Private Equity Firm

Project Preferences

Type of Financing Preferred:
Early Stage

Industry Preferences

In Communications prefer:
Communications and Media

In Computer Software prefer:
Software

Additional Information
Year Founded: 2015
Current Activity Level : Actively seeking new investments

BRIDGE CITY MANAGEMENT LLC

805 Southwest Broadway
Suite 2440
Portland, OR USA 97205
Phone: 5034193007
E-mail: info@portlandseedfund.com
Website: www.portlandseedfund.com

Management and Staff
Alexander Woodward, President
Angela Jackson, Partner
David Kiser, Vice President
Jim Huston, Partner
Stephen Brink, Co-Founder

Pratt's Guide to Private Equity & Venture Capital Sources

Type of Firm
Private Equity Firm

Project Preferences

Type of Financing Preferred:
Early Stage
Expansion
Balanced
Later Stage
Seed
Startup

Geographical Preferences

United States Preferences:
Oregon

Additional Information
Name of Most Recent Fund: Portland Seed Fund II, L.P.
Most Recent Fund Was Raised: 11/09/2012
Year Founded: 2011
Capital Under Management: $10,800,000
Current Activity Level : Actively seeking new investments

BRIDGE GROWTH PARTNERS LLC

787 Seventh Avenue
Floor 34, Suite 3408
New York, NY USA 10019
Phone: 2127288454
E-mail: info@bridgegrowthpartners.com
Website: bridgegrowthpartners.com

Type of Firm
Private Equity Firm

Project Preferences

Type of Financing Preferred:
Leveraged Buyout
Expansion
Acquisition

Industry Preferences

In Financial Services prefer:
Financial Services

Additional Information
Year Founded: 2013
Capital Under Management: $410,000,000
Current Activity Level : Actively seeking new investments

BRIDGE INVESTMENT FUND LP

11000 Cedar Avenue, Suite 100
Cleveland, OH USA 44106
Phone: 2166585470
Fax: 2166583998

Other Offices
11 Tuval Street
Ramat Gan, Israel 52522
Phone: 972-3-7529590

Management and Staff
Michael Goldberg, Founder

Type of Firm
Private Equity Firm

Project Preferences

Type of Financing Preferred:
Early Stage
Balanced

Size of Investments Considered:
Min Size of Investment Considered (000s): $250
Max Size of Investment Considered (000s): $1,000

Geographical Preferences

United States Preferences:
Ohio

International Preferences:
Israel

Industry Preferences

In Biotechnology prefer:
Biotechnology

In Medical/Health prefer:
Medical/Health
Medical Products

Additional Information
Name of Most Recent Fund: Bridge Investment Fund, L.P.
Most Recent Fund Was Raised: 12/20/2005
Year Founded: 2005
Capital Under Management: $5,400,000
Current Activity Level : Actively seeking new investments

BRIDGE INVESTMENTS LLC

600 Central Avenue,
Suite 310
Highland Park, IL USA 60035
Phone: 8476818881
Website: www.bridgeinvestments.com

Management and Staff
Robert Goldberg, Principal

Type of Firm
Private Equity Firm

Project Preferences

Type of Financing Preferred:
Leveraged Buyout
Mezzanine
Generalist PE
Balanced
Acquisition
Recapitalizations

Size of Investments Considered:
Min Size of Investment Considered (000s): $50
Max Size of Investment Considered (000s): $500

Industry Preferences

In Internet Specific prefer:
E-Commerce Technology

In Medical/Health prefer:
Medical/Health

In Financial Services prefer:
Real Estate

Additional Information
Year Founded: 1969
Capital Under Management: $3,000,000
Current Activity Level : Actively seeking new investments

BRIDGE STREET CAPITAL PARTNERS LLC

171 Monroe Avenue NW
Suite 410
Grand Rapids, MI USA 49503
Phone: 6167321050
Fax: 6167321055
Website: www.bridgestreetcapital.com

Other Offices
52 Village Place
Hinsdale, IL USA 60521
Phone: 630-323-9222
Fax: 630-323-9224

Management and Staff
John Meilner, Managing Director
William Kaczynski, Managing Director

Type of Firm
Private Equity Firm

Project Preferences

Role in Financing:
Prefer role as deal originator but will also invest in deals created by others

Type of Financing Preferred:
Early Stage
Expansion
Later Stage

Size of Investments Considered:
Min Size of Investment Considered (000s): $2,500
Max Size of Investment Considered (000s): $7,500

Geographical Preferences

United States Preferences:
Midwest

Industry Preferences

In Medical/Health prefer:
Medical/Health

In Consumer Related prefer:
Consumer Products

In Industrial/Energy prefer:
Industrial Products

In Business Serv. prefer:
Services
Distribution

In Manufact. prefer:
Manufacturing

Additional Information

Year Founded: 2004
Capital Under Management: $41,000,000
Current Activity Level : Actively seeking new investments
Method of Compensation: Return on investment is of primary concern, do not charge fees

---

BRIDGEPOINT ADVISERS II LTD

30 Warwick Street
London, United Kingdom W1B 5AL
Phone: 442074323500
Fax: 442074323600
E-mail: info@bridgepoint.eu
Website: www.bridgepoint.eu

Other Offices

Bridgepoint Oy
2 Etelaranta
Helsinki, Finland 00130
Phone: 358-9-5840-0044

2, avenue Charles de Gaulle
Luxembourg, Luxembourg L-1653
Phone: 352-26-4756

ul. Rondo ONZ 1
Warsaw, Poland 00-124
Phone: 48-22-544-8282

Via F.lli Gabba 1/a
Milan, Italy 20121
Phone: 39-02-806-951

999 Huahau Road
21F Unit 2110-2111, Shanghai One ICC
Shanghai, China 200031
Phone: 862161937688

Master Samuelsgatan 1
Stockholm, Sweden 111 44
Phone: 46-8-5451-6820

Calle de Rafael Calvo
39A-4
Madrid, Spain 28010
Phone: 34-91-702-2490

28 Neue Mainzer Strae
Frankfurt, Germany 60311
Phone: 49-69-210-8770

BJK Plaza no. 48 A blok 9.kat
Suleyman Seba Caddesi
Istanbul, Turkey D:93-94
Phone: 90-212-310-8252

37-39 rue de la
Bienfaisance
Paris, France 75008
Phone: 33-1-4429-2100

Management and Staff

Adrian Willetts, Partner
Alan Payne, Partner
Johan Dahlfors, Partner
Kevin Reynolds, Managing Partner
Pierre Colasson, Partner
Rod Selkirk, Managing Partner
Tim Thomas, Partner

Type of Firm

Private Equity Firm

Association Membership

British Venture Capital Association (BVCA)

Project Preferences

Type of Financing Preferred:
Leveraged Buyout
Expansion
Management Buyouts
Acquisition

Geographical Preferences

International Preferences:
United Kingdom
Europe
Scandanavia/Nordic Region
France

Industry Preferences

In Communications prefer:
Radio & TV Broadcasting

In Computer Software prefer:
Software

In Medical/Health prefer:
Medical Products
Health Services
Pharmaceuticals

In Consumer Related prefer:
Consumer
Entertainment and Leisure
Sports
Retail

In Industrial/Energy prefer:
Industrial Products
Environmental Related

In Transportation prefer:
Aerospace

In Financial Services prefer:
Financial Services
Insurance

In Business Serv. prefer:
Services
Media

In Manufact. prefer:
Manufacturing
Publishing

Additional Information

Name of Most Recent Fund: Hermes Private Equity Partners II
Most Recent Fund Was Raised: 09/12/2005
Year Founded: 2009
Current Activity Level : Actively seeking new investments

BRIDGEPOINT ADVISERS LTD

95 Wigmore Street
London, United Kingdom W1U 1FB
Phone: 442074323500
E-mail: info@bridgepoint.eu
Website: www.bridgepoint.eu

Other Offices

BJK Plaza No. 48, Suleyman Seba Caddesi
A Blok 9.kat, Visnezade Mahallesi
Istanbul, Turkey 93-94
Phone: 90-212-258-3437

Neue Mainzer Strasse 28
Frankfurt, Germany 60311
Phone: 49-69-210-8770

82 rue de Courcelles
Paris, France 75008
Phone: 33170225300

ul. Rondo ONZ 1
Warsaw, Poland 00-124
Phone: 48-22-544-8282

2, avenue Charles de
Gaulle, Luxembourg L-1653
Phone: 352-26-47-56

Calle de Rafael Calvo 39A-4
Madrid, Spain 28010
Phone: 34-91-702-2490

Via F.Ili Gabba 1/a
Milan, Italy 20121
Phone: 39-02-806-951

Master Samuelsgatan 1
Stockholm, Sweden 111 44
Phone: 46-8-5451-6820

999 Huaihai Road
21F Unit 2110-2111, Shanghai One ICC
Shanghai, China 200031
Phone: 86-21-6193-7688

Management and Staff
Adrian Willetts, Partner
Alan Payne, Partner
Alastair Gibbons, Partner
Benoit Bassi, Partner
Christopher Busby, Partner
Frederic Pescatori, Partner
Graham Oldroyd, Partner
Guy Weldon, Partner
Hakan Johansson, Partner
Hamish Grant, Partner
Ian Dugan, Managing Director
James Murray, Partner
Jamie Wyatt, Partner
Jason McGibbon, Partner
Johan Dahlfors, Partner
John Barber, Partner
Jose Maria Maldonado, Partner
Kevin Reynolds, Partner
Khai Tan, Partner
Martin Dunn, Partner
Michael Black, Partner
Michael Davy, Partner
Mikael Lovgren, Partner
Patrick Fox, Partner
Paul Gunner, Founder
Pierre Colasson, Partner
Robert Moores, Partner
Rod Selkirk, Partner
Timothy Thomas, Partner
Uwe Kolb, Partner
Vincent Gwilliam, Partner
William Paul, Partner
William Jackson, Managing Partner
Xavier Robert, Partner

Type of Firm
Private Equity Firm

Association Membership
Italian Venture Capital Association (AIFI)
British Venture Capital Association (BVCA)
French Venture Capital Association (AFIC)
German Venture Capital Association (BVK)
Swedish Venture Capital Association (SVCA)
Polish Venture Capital Association (PSIC/PPEA)
European Private Equity and Venture Capital Assoc.
Dutch Venture Capital Associaton (NVP)
Spanish Venture Capital Association (ASCRI)

Project Preferences

Type of Financing Preferred:
Leveraged Buyout
Turnaround
Management Buyouts
Acquisition
Recapitalizations

Geographical Preferences

International Preferences:
Europe

Industry Focus
(% based on actual investment)

Consumer Related	44.7%
Other Products	24.5%
Industrial/Energy	9.8%
Medical/Health	8.6%
Computer Hardware	4.1%
Communications and Media	2.6%
Internet Specific	1.9%
Computer Software and Services	1.6%
Biotechnology	1.2%
Semiconductors/Other Elect.	1.1%

Additional Information
Name of Most Recent Fund: Bridgepoint Europe IV
Most Recent Fund Was Raised: 10/28/2008
Year Founded: 1983
Capital Under Management: $8,000,000,000
Current Activity Level : Actively seeking new investments

BRIDGEPOINT INVESTMENT PARTNERS I LLLP

700 Locust Street
Suite 203
Des Moines, IA USA 50309
Website: www.bridgepointmb.com

Management and Staff
Dusty Friedman, Vice President
Joe Liss, Principal
Matt Plooster, Co-Founder

Type of Firm
Private Equity Firm

Additional Information
Year Founded: 1969
Current Activity Level : Actively seeking new investments

BRIDGEPOINT PORTFOLIO SERVICES SAS

47 Rue du
Faubourg Saint Honore
Paris, France 75008
Phone: 0033140172169
Fax: 0033140172391
Website: www.edmond-de-rothschild.fr

Other Offices
55, avenue Foch
Lyon, France 69006
Phone: 33-4-7282-3525
Fax: 33-4-7893-5956

Hotel de Saige
23, cours du Chapeau Rouge
Bordeaux, France 33000
Phone: 33-05-56-44-2066
Fax: 33-5-5651-6603

22, rue Croix Baragnon
Toulouse, France 31000
Phone: 33-5-6720-4900
Fax: 33-5-6173-4904

116 rue de Jemmapes
Lille, France 59800
Phone: 33-3-6253-7500
Fax: 33-3-2804-9620

10-12, R du President Herriot
Nantes, France 44000
Phone: 33-2-5359-1000
Fax: 33-2-5359-1009

5/7 rue Montalivet
Paris, France 75008

165, avenue du Prado
Marseille, France 13272
Phone: 33-4-9129-9080
Fax: 33-4-1290-9085

6, avenue de la Marseillaise
Strasbourg, France 67000
Phone: 33-3-6833-9000
Fax: 33-3-8835-6486

Management and Staff
Eric De Montgolfier, Managing Partner
Erick Fouque, Managing Partner
Francois Paillier, Partner
Herve Fonta, Partner

Type of Firm
Bank Affiliated

Association Membership
French Venture Capital Association (AFIC)

Project Preferences

Type of Financing Preferred:
Fund of Funds
Leveraged Buyout
Management Buyouts

Geographical Preferences

International Preferences:
Europe
France

Industry Preferences

In Communications prefer:
Media and Entertainment

In Medical/Health prefer:
Medical/Health

In Industrial/Energy prefer:
Industrial Products

In Business Serv. prefer:
Services
Distribution

Additional Information

Name of Most Recent Fund: Edmond de Rothschild LBO Fund
Most Recent Fund Was Raised: 07/11/2003
Year Founded: 2003
Current Activity Level : Actively seeking new investments

BRIDGES FUND MANAGEMENT LTD

38 Seymour Street
London, United Kingdom W1H 7BP
Phone: 4402037808000
Fax: 442072626389
E-mail: Info@bridgesventures.com
Website: www.bridgesfundmanagement.com

Management and Staff

Alistair Tillen, Partner
Anne-Marie Harris, Partner
Antony Ross, Partner
Brian Trelstad, Partner
Garret Turley, Partner
John Rogers, Partner
Michele Giddens, Co-Founder
Oliver Wyncoll, Partner
Paul Richings, Chief Financial Officer
Philip Newborough, Co-Founder
Simon Ringer, Partner

Type of Firm

Incubator/Development Program

Association Membership

Community Development Venture Capital Alliance
British Venture Capital Association (BVCA)

Project Preferences

Type of Financing Preferred:
Early Stage
Expansion
Generalist PE
Balanced
Management Buyouts
Startup

Geographical Preferences

International Preferences:
United Kingdom
Europe

Industry Preferences

In Medical/Health prefer:
Medical/Health
Health Services

In Consumer Related prefer:
Food/Beverage
Education Related

In Industrial/Energy prefer:
Environmental Related

Additional Information

Year Founded: 2002
Capital Under Management: $233,000,000
Current Activity Level : Actively seeking new investments

BRIDGESCALE PARTNERS LP

2200 Sand Hill Road
Suite 240
Menlo Park, CA USA 94025
Phone: 6508546100
Fax: 6506188745
Website: http://www.bridgescale.com

Other Offices

1259 El Camino Real
Suite 417
Menlo Park, CA USA 94025
Phone: 6508546100

Management and Staff

David Walrod, Venture Partner
Kevin Mello, Chief Financial Officer
Matthew Cowan, Co-Founder
Robert Chaplinsky, Co-Founder

Type of Firm

Private Equity Firm

Project Preferences

Type of Financing Preferred:
Leveraged Buyout
Early Stage
Expansion
Generalist PE
Balanced
Later Stage
Management Buyouts
Acquisition
Startup
Recapitalizations

Geographical Preferences

United States Preferences:
North America

Canadian Preferences:
All Canada

Industry Preferences

In Communications prefer:
Telecommunications
Wireless Communications

In Computer Hardware prefer:
Computer Graphics and D·g

In Computer Software prefer:
Software

In Internet Specific prefer:
Internet

In Computer Other prefer:
Computer Related

In Semiconductor/Electr prefer:
Semiconductor

In Consumer Related prefer:
Consumer

In Financial Services prefer:
Financial Services

In Business Serv. prefer:
Services
Consulting Services
Media

Additional Information

Name of Most Recent Fund: Bridgescale Partners, L.P.
Most Recent Fund Was Raised: 12/01/2005
Year Founded: 2005
Capital Under Management: $4,100,000
Current Activity Level : Actively seeking new investments

BRIGHT CAPITAL OOO

Bersenevskaya Emb. 6/3
Moscow, Russia 119072
Phone: 74959898540
Website: bright-capital.com

Management and Staff
Andrey Sergeev, Chief Financial Officer
Boris Ryabov, Managing Partner
Mikhail Chuchkevich, Managing Partner
Vadim Kulikov, Partner

Type of Firm
Private Equity Firm

Association Membership
European Private Equity and Venture Capital Assoc.

Project Preferences

Type of Financing Preferred:
Balanced

Geographical Preferences

International Preferences:
Europe
Russia

Industry Preferences

In Communications prefer:
Telecommunications

In Semiconductor/Electr prefer:
Electronics
Semiconductor

In Industrial/Energy prefer:
Environmental Related

Additional Information
Year Founded: 2010
Capital Under Management: $150,000,000
Current Activity Level : Actively seeking new investments

BRIGHT STONE INVESTMENT MANAGEMENT (HONG KONG) LTD

No. 213, Queen's Road East
Room 2209, 22F, Huzhong Plaza
Hong Kong, China BJ001740
Phone: 85239737725
Fax: 85230136410
E-mail: admin@chinabrightstone.com
Website: www.chinabrightstone.com

Other Offices
213 Queen's Road East, Wanchai
Unit 2209, 22/F, Wu Chung House
Hong Kong, Hong Kong 001740
Phone: 85239737725
Fax: 85230136410

Management and Staff
Jing Ni, Vice President
Peng Gao, Vice President
Qiangyun Zhang, Partner
Shaodong Wang, Chief Executive Officer
Tao Wang, President
Yu Miao, Partner
Yunhe Zhang, Managing Director
Zuqiang Lu, Partner

Type of Firm
Private Equity Firm

Project Preferences

Type of Financing Preferred:
Expansion
Balanced
Later Stage

Geographical Preferences

International Preferences:
China

Industry Preferences

In Communications prefer:
Communications and Media

In Biotechnology prefer:
Biotechnology

In Industrial/Energy prefer:
Energy
Energy Conservation Relat
Materials
Environmental Related

In Business Serv. prefer:
Media

In Agr/Forestr/Fish prefer:
Agriculture related

In Other prefer:
Environment Responsible

Additional Information
Year Founded: 2008
Capital Under Management: $2,007,400,000
Current Activity Level : Actively seeking new investments

BRIGHTBRIDGE VENTURES

One Hammersmith Broadway
London, United Kingdom W6 9DL
E-mail: info@brightbridgeventures.com
Website: www.brightbridgeventures.com

Type of Firm
Incubator/Development Program

Project Preferences

Type of Financing Preferred:
Seed
Startup

Additional Information
Year Founded: 1969
Current Activity Level : Actively seeking new investments

BRIGHTEYE ADVISORS SAS

23 Rue de Berri
Paris, France 75008
Phone: 330143591460
E-mail: info@brighteyevc.com
Website: www.brighteyevc.com

Type of Firm
Private Equity Firm

Project Preferences

Type of Financing Preferred:
Balanced
Seed

Geographical Preferences

United States Preferences:

International Preferences:
Europe
Israel

Additional Information
Year Founded: 2017
Capital Under Management: $52,630,000
Current Activity Level : Actively seeking new investments

BRIGHTON PARTNERS LLC

1201 Peachtree Street
400 Colony Square, Suite 530
Atlanta, GA USA 30361
Fax: 4049263497
Website: www.bpequity.com

Type of Firm
Private Equity Firm

Project Preferences

Type of Financing Preferred:
Leveraged Buyout
Acquisition
Recapitalizations

Geographical Preferences

United States Preferences:
Midwest
Southeast

Additional Information
Year Founded: 2007
Current Activity Level : Actively seeking new investments

BRIGHTPATH CAPITAL PARTNERS LP

One Kaiser Plaza
Suite 650
Oakland, CA USA 94612

Phone: 5104884140
Fax: 5102771949
E-mail: info@bcplp.com
Website: www.brightpathcapitalpartners.com

Management and Staff
Robert Davenport, Managing Partner
William Lewis, Vice President

Type of Firm
Private Equity Firm

Project Preferences

Type of Financing Preferred:
Later Stage

Size of Investments Considered:
Min Size of Investment Considered (000s): $1,000
Max Size of Investment Considered (000s): $5,000

Geographical Preferences

United States Preferences:
California
West Coast

Industry Preferences

In Medical/Health prefer:
Health Services

In Consumer Related prefer:
Food/Beverage
Education Related

In Industrial/Energy prefer:
Environmental Related

In Business Serv. prefer:
Services

In Manufact. prefer:
Manufacturing

Additional Information
Name of Most Recent Fund: Brightpath Capital Partners, L.P.
Most Recent Fund Was Raised: 12/20/2010
Year Founded: 2010
Capital Under Management: $34,500,000
Current Activity Level : Actively seeking new investments

BRIGHTSPARK VENTURES

101 College Street
Suite 140
Toronto, Canada M5G 1L7
Phone: 4164881999
Fax: 4164881988
E-mail: info@brightspark.com
Website: www.brightspark.com

Other Offices
481 Viger Street West
Suite 300
Montreal, Canada H2Z 1G6
Phone: 5147896421
Fax: 5143964354

Management and Staff
Mark Skapinker, Co-Founder
Sophie Forest, Managing Partner
Tony Davis, Partner

Type of Firm
Private Equity Firm

Project Preferences

Role in Financing:
Prefer role as deal originator but will also invest in deals created by others

Type of Financing Preferred:
Early Stage
Seed

Size of Investments Considered:
Min Size of Investment Considered (000s): $500
Max Size of Investment Considered (000s): $5,000

Geographical Preferences

United States Preferences:
Northwest
Northern California
Northeast

Canadian Preferences:
All Canada

Industry Preferences

In Communications prefer:
Commercial Communications
Telecommunications
Wireless Communications

In Computer Software prefer:
Computer Services
Software
Systems Software
Applications Software

In Internet Specific prefer:
E-Commerce Technology
Internet
Ecommerce

Additional Information
Name of Most Recent Fund: Brightspark Ventures II
Most Recent Fund Was Raised: 06/29/2005
Year Founded: 1999
Capital Under Management: $54,300,000
Current Activity Level : Actively seeking new investments
Method of Compensation: Return on investment is of primary concern, do not charge fees

BRIGHTSTAR CAPITAL PARTNERS GRS LP

450 Park Avenue
14th Floor
New York, NY USA 10022
Phone: 2124199850
E-mail: info@brightstarcapitalpartners.com

Type of Firm
Private Equity Firm

Project Preferences

Type of Financing Preferred:
Generalist PE

Additional Information
Year Founded: 2016
Capital Under Management: $218,630,000
Current Activity Level : Actively seeking new investments

BRIGHTSTONE VENTURE CAPITAL

510 First Ave North
Suite 200
Minneapolis, MN USA 55403
Phone: 6123457912
Website: www.brightstonevc.com

Management and Staff
David Dalvey, Principal
James Bernards, Principal

Type of Firm
Private Equity Firm

Project Preferences

Role in Financing:
Will function either as deal originator or investor in deals created by others

Type of Financing Preferred:
Early Stage
Expansion
Balanced
Later Stage

Size of Investments Considered:
Min Size of Investment Considered (000s): $250
Max Size of Investment Considered (000s): $5,000

Industry Preferences

In Communications prefer:
Communications and Media
Wireless Communications

In Computer Software prefer:
Software

In Internet Specific prefer:
Ecommerce

In Biotechnology prefer:
Biotechnology

In Medical/Health prefer:
Medical/Health

In Industrial/Energy prefer:
Energy

In Transportation prefer:
Transportation
Aerospace

In Business Serv. prefer:
Services

Additional Information
Year Founded: 1985
Capital Under Management: $125,000,000
Current Activity Level : Actively seeking new investments
Method of Compensation: Return on investment is of primary concern, do not charge fees

BRIGHTVENTURES

Willemsparkweg 58-3
Amsterdam, Netherlands 1071H)
E-mail: info@brightventures.com
Website: www.brightventures.nl

Management and Staff
Paul Montagne, Founder

Type of Firm
Private Equity Firm

Project Preferences

Type of Financing Preferred:
Early Stage

Additional Information
Year Founded: 2012
Current Activity Level : Actively seeking new investments

BRIGHTWOOD CAPITAL ADVISORS LLC

1540 Broadway
23rd Floor
New York, NY USA 10036
Phone: 6469579525
Fax: 6469579265
E-mail: info@brightwoodlp.com
Website: www.brightwoodlp.com

Management and Staff
Damien Dwin, Co-Founder
Russell Zomback, Chief Financial Officer
Sengal Selassie, Co-Founder

Type of Firm
Investment Management Firm

Association Membership
Natl Assoc of Small Bus. Inv. Co (NASBIC)

Project Preferences

Type of Financing Preferred:
Leveraged Buyout
Expansion
Acquisition
Recapitalizations

Additional Information
Year Founded: 2010
Capital Under Management: $15,480,000
Current Activity Level : Actively seeking new investments

BRINC

35. Aberdeen Street
7/f, Unit 701
Hong Kong Central, Hong Kong
Phone: 85251353620
Website: brinc.io

Type of Firm
Incubator/Development Program

Project Preferences

Type of Financing Preferred:
Seed

Industry Preferences

In Computer Software prefer:
Software

In Internet Specific prefer:
Internet

Additional Information
Year Founded: 2016
Current Activity Level : Actively seeking new investments

BRINKMERE CAPITAL PARTNERS LLC

One Independent Drive
Suite 2208
Jacksonville, FL USA 32202
Website: www.brinkmere.com

Type of Firm
Private Equity Firm

Project Preferences

Type of Financing Preferred:
Leveraged Buyout
Acquisition

Additional Information
Year Founded: 2014
Current Activity Level : Actively seeking new investments

BRITISH COLUMBIA IN-VESTMENT MANAGEMENT CORP

2940 Jutland Road
Suite 301
Victoria, Canada V8T 5K6
Phone: 2503560263
Fax: 2503877874
Website: www.bcimc.com

Other Offices
Sawmill Point, 2940 Jutland Rd
Victoria, Canada V8T 5K6
Phone: 250-356-0263
Fax: 250-387-7874

Management and Staff
Bryan Thomson, Vice President
Carol Iverson, Vice President
Daryl Jones, Vice President
Dean Atkins, Vice President
Douglas Pearce, Chief Executive Officer
Gina Pala, Vice President
Lincoln Webb, Vice President
Lynn Hannah, Vice President
Mary Garden, Vice President
Paul Flanagan, Vice President
Shauna Lukaitis, Vice President

Type of Firm
Endowment, Foundation or Pension Fund

Additional Information
Year Founded: 1999
Current Activity Level : Actively seeking new investments

BRITISH COLUMBIA MINISTRY OF ECONOMIC DEVELOPMENT

P.O. Box 9804
Victoria, Canada V8W 9W1
Phone: 2503876121
Fax: 2503875633
E-mail: EnquiryBC@gov.bc.ca
Website: www.bcbudget.gov.bc.ca/2007/sp/ed/default.a

Type of Firm
Government Affiliated Program

Association Membership
Canadian Venture Capital Association

Additional Information
Year Founded: 2008
Current Activity Level : Actively seeking new investments

BRITT PRIVATE CAPITAL LLC

24 Corporate Plaza
Suite 100
Newport Center, CA USA 92660
Phone: 9498613639
E-mail: info@brittprivatecapital.com
Website: www.brittprivatecapital.com

Management and Staff
Chris Britt, Principal

Type of Firm
Private Equity Firm

Project Preferences

Type of Financing Preferred:
Leveraged Buyout
Acquisition

Geographical Preferences

United States Preferences:
All U.S.

Industry Preferences

In Medical/Health prefer:
Health Services

In Consumer Related prefer:
Retail
Food/Beverage

In Business Serv. prefer:
Services
Distribution

In Manufact. prefer:
Manufacturing

Additional Information
Year Founded: 2016
Current Activity Level : Actively seeking new investments

BRIXEY & MEYER CAPITAL LLC

2991 Newmark Dr.
Miamisburg, OH USA 45342

Management and Staff
David Brixey, Co-Founder
Patrick Odell, Principal

Type of Firm
Private Equity Firm

Project Preferences

Type of Financing Preferred:
Generalist PE

Industry Preferences

In Medical/Health prefer:
Health Services

In Business Serv. prefer:
Distribution

In Manufact. prefer:
Manufacturing

Additional Information
Year Founded: 2015
Capital Under Management: $18,000,000
Current Activity Level : Actively seeking new investments

BRM CAPITAL LLC

825 Thirrd Avenue
32nd Floor
New York, NY USA 10022
Phone: 2129180551
Fax: 2129180674

Other Offices
One Bareket Building
Airport City
, Israel
Phone: 972.3.971.5100
Fax: 972.3.971.5101

10 Nissim Aloni Street
Tzameret Park
Tel Aviv, Israel 6291924
Phone: 97239715100
Fax: 97239715101

Akerstein Building B
11 Hamenofim Street
Herzliya Pituach , Israel 46725
Phone: 972-9-954-9555
Fax: 972-9-954-9557

Management and Staff
Alon Maor, Venture Partner
Eran Barkat, Partner
Yuval Rakavy, Co-Founder

Type of Firm
Private Equity Firm

Association Membership
Israel Venture Association

Project Preferences

Role in Financing:
Prefer role as deal originator but will also invest in deals created by others

Type of Financing Preferred:
Early Stage
Expansion
Balanced
Later Stage
Seed

Size of Investments Considered:
Min Size of Investment Considered (000s): $1,000
Max Size of Investment Considered (000s): $5,000

Geographical Preferences

International Preferences:
Israel

Industry Preferences

In Communications prefer:
Commercial Communications
Wireless Communications
Data Communications

In Computer Software prefer:
Software
Applications Software

In Internet Specific prefer:
Internet

In Semiconductor/Electr prefer:
Semiconductor

Additional Information
Year Founded: 2000
Capital Under Management: $150,000,000
Current Activity Level : Actively seeking new investments

BROAD SKY PARTNERS LLC

909 Third Avenue
27th Floor
New York, NY USA 10022
Phone: 2127358820
E-mail: info@BroadSkyPartners.com
Website: www.broadskypartners.com

Management and Staff
David Basto, Co-Founder
Heidi Vanhamme, Vice President
James Shillito, Principal
John Overbay, Principal
Tyler Zachem, Chief Executive Officer

Type of Firm
Private Equity Firm

Project Preferences

Type of Financing Preferred:
Leveraged Buyout
Acquisition
Recapitalizations

Geographical Preferences

United States Preferences:
All U.S.

Industry Preferences

In Communications prefer:
Communications and Media

In Consumer Related prefer:
Consumer Products

In Financial Services prefer:
Financial Services

In Business Serv. prefer:
Media

Additional Information
Year Founded: 2013
Current Activity Level : Actively seeking new investments

BROADHAVEN CAPITAL PARTNERS LLC

201 Broad Street
Fourth Floor
Stamford, CT USA 06901
Phone: 2033481200
Fax: 2033481207
E-mail: info@broadhaven.com
Website: www.broadhaven.com

Other Offices
5215 Old Orchard Road
Suite 630
Skokie, IL USA 60077
Phone: 8475814242
Fax: 8475814250

Gee Chang Hong Centre
65 Wong Chuk Hang
, Hong Kong
Phone: 85291302762

18 Floor Bund Centre
222 Yan An Road (East)
Shanghai, China 200002
Phone: 862161323808
Fax: 862163320643

Management and Staff
Christopher Spofford, Partner
Esther Tian, Principal
Gerard von Dohlen, Co-Founder
Greg Phillips, Co-Founder
James Denton, Partner
John Simpson, Partner
Joseph Zabik, Partner
Michael Deleray, Partner
Todd Owens, Partner

Type of Firm
Bank Affiliated

Project Preferences

Type of Financing Preferred:
Leveraged Buyout
Early Stage
Generalist PE
Management Buyouts
Acquisition

Industry Preferences

In Financial Services prefer:
Financial Services

Additional Information
Year Founded: 2009
Capital Under Management: $100,000,000
Current Activity Level : Actively seeking new investments

BROADLAKE CAPITAL LTD

Ardee Road
Hilton House, Rathmines
Dublin, Ireland 4
E-mail: info@broadlakecapital.com
Website: www.broadlakecapital.com

Other Offices
51 The Green, South Bar
, United Kingdom OX16 9AB

7, Manor Park
Banbury, Oxfordshire, United Kingdom OX16 3TB

Management and Staff
Peter Smyth, Chief Executive Officer

Type of Firm
Private Equity Firm

Project Preferences

Type of Financing Preferred:
Leveraged Buyout
Expansion
Balanced
Management Buyouts
Acquisition
Special Situation

Geographical Preferences

International Preferences:
Ireland
United Kingdom

Industry Preferences

In Consumer Related prefer:
Food/Beverage
Consumer Products
Education Related

In Business Serv. prefer:
Services
Media

In Manufact. prefer:
Manufacturing
Publishing

Additional Information
Year Founded: 2009
Capital Under Management: $132,600,000
Current Activity Level : Actively seeking new investments

BROADLINE CAPITAL LLC

110 Wall Street
Eleventh Floor
New York, NY USA 10005
E-mail: Info@BroadlineCapital.com
Website: www.broadlinecapital.com

Other Offices
Harbour View Street
1 IFC, 15th Floor
Hong Kong, Hong Kong

1 Corporate Avenue
15th Floor, Xintiandi
Shanghai, China 200021

Management and Staff
Christopher Thorne, Managing Partner
Kelly Chow, Managing Partner
Lin Lin Zhou, Managing Partner
Qi Pan, Partner

Type of Firm
Private Equity Firm

Project Preferences

Type of Financing Preferred:
Early Stage

Geographical Preferences

International Preferences:
China

Additional Information
Year Founded: 2008
Current Activity Level : Actively seeking new investments

BROADOAK CAPITAL PARTNERS LLC

7272 Wisconsin Avenue
Suite 320
Bethesda, MD USA 20814
Phone: 3013582692
Website: broadoak.com

Management and Staff
Bill Snider, Co-Founder
D. Kyle Wilson, Partner
Lars Hanan, Co-Founder
Matt McFarland, Vice President
Tara St. Amand, Vice President

Type of Firm
Bank Affiliated

Project Preferences

Type of Financing Preferred:
Leveraged Buyout
Expansion
Mezzanine
Acquisition
Distressed Debt
Recapitalizations

Industry Preferences

In Biotechnology prefer:
Biotechnology
Biotech Related Research

In Medical/Health prefer:
Medical/Health
Medical Diagnostics
Medical Therapeutics
Medical Products
Health Services
Pharmaceuticals

Additional Information
Name of Most Recent Fund: BroadOak Fund II LLC
Most Recent Fund Was Raised: 11/14/2012
Year Founded: 2006
Capital Under Management: $13,110,000
Current Activity Level : Actively seeking new investments

BROADSTREAM CAPITAL PARTNERS, LLC

4427 Gainsborough Avenue
Los Angeles, CA USA 90027
Website: broadstreamcapital.com

Type of Firm
Bank Affiliated

Project Preferences

Type of Financing Preferred:
Leveraged Buyout

Geographical Preferences

United States Preferences:
California

Additional Information
Year Founded: 2001
Current Activity Level : Actively seeking new investments

BROADVIEW VENTURES INC

125 High Street
Ninth floor
Boston, MA USA 02110
Phone: 6174575944
E-mail: info@broadviewventures.org
Website: www.broadviewventures.org

Type of Firm
Private Equity Firm

Association Membership
New England Venture Capital Association

Project Preferences

Type of Financing Preferred:
Early Stage

Industry Preferences

In Medical/Health prefer:
Medical/Health
Health Services

Additional Information
Year Founded: 2008
Current Activity Level : Actively seeking new investments

BROCKHAUS PRIVATE EQUITY GMBH

Myliusstrasse 30
Frankfurt Am Main, Germany 60323
Phone: 496971916170
Fax: 496971916171
Website: brockhaus-pe.de

Management and Staff
Jan-Daniel Neumann, Managing Director
Marcel Wilhelm, Managing Director
Marco Brockhaus, Founder

Type of Firm
Private Equity Firm

Association Membership
German Venture Capital Association (BVK)
European Private Equity and Venture Capital Assoc.

Project Preferences

Type of Financing Preferred:
Leveraged Buyout
Expansion
Generalist PE
Later Stage
Management Buyouts
Acquisition

Size of Investments Considered:
Min Size of Investment Considered (000s): $7,126
Max Size of Investment Considered (000s): $35,628

Geographical Preferences

International Preferences:
Europe
Germany

Industry Preferences

In Communications prefer:
Communications and Media
Telecommunications
Media and Entertainment
Entertainment

In Internet Specific prefer:
Internet

In Computer Other prefer:
Computer Related

In Semiconductor/Electr prefer:
Electronics

In Business Serv. prefer:
Services

Additional Information
Name of Most Recent Fund: Brockhaus Private Equity III GmbH & Co. KG
Most Recent Fund Was Raised: 01/17/2014
Year Founded: 2000
Capital Under Management: $224,600,000
Current Activity Level : Actively seeking new investments

BROCKWAY MORAN & PARTNERS INC

225 Northeast Mizner Boulevard
Suite 700
Boca Raton, FL USA 33432
Phone: 5617502000
Fax: 5617502001
E-mail: info@brockwaymoran.com
Website: www.brockwaymoran.com

Management and Staff
Ari Zur, Partner
H. Randall Litten, Partner
Lawrence Shagrin, Partner
Michael Moran, Managing Partner
Peter Brockway, Managing Partner

Type of Firm
Private Equity Firm

Association Membership
Private Equity Council (PEC)

Project Preferences

Role in Financing:
Prefer role as deal originator but will also invest in deals created by others

Type of Financing Preferred:
Leveraged Buyout
Expansion
Acquisition

Geographical Preferences

United States Preferences:

Industry Focus
(% based on actual investment)
Consumer Related	57.4%
Other Products	37.0%
Semiconductors/Other Elect.	5.3%
Industrial/Energy	0.4%

Additional Information
Name of Most Recent Fund: Brockway Moran & Partners Fund III, L.P.
Most Recent Fund Was Raised: 03/31/2006
Year Founded: 1998
Capital Under Management: $1,300,000,000
Current Activity Level : Actively seeking new investments
Method of Compensation: Return on invest. most important, but chg. closing fees, service fees, etc.

BROOK VENTURE PARTNERS LLC

301 Edgewater Place
Fourth Floor
Wakefield, MA USA 01880
Phone: 7812954000
Fax: 7812954007

Management and Staff
Brennan Mulcahey, Partner
Edward Williams, Partner
Frederic Morris, Partner
Jonathan Green, Partner
Kyle Stanbro, Partner
Peter DiCarlo, Chief Financial Officer
Walter Beinecke, Partner

Type of Firm
Private Equity Firm

Association Membership
New England Venture Capital Association
Natl Assoc of Small Bus. Inv. Co (NASBIC)

Project Preferences

Role in Financing:
Prefer role as deal originator but will also invest in deals created by others

Type of Financing Preferred:
Expansion
Generalist PE
Acquisition

Geographical Preferences

United States Preferences:
Mid Atlantic
Northeast

Industry Preferences

In Medical/Health prefer:
Medical/Health

Additional Information
Year Founded: 1995
Capital Under Management: $100,000,000
Current Activity Level : Actively seeking new investments
Method of Compensation: Return on investment is of primary concern, do not charge fees

BROOKE PRIVATE EQUITY ASSOCIATES MANAGEMENT LLC

84 State Street
Suite 320
Boston, MA USA 02109
Phone: 6172273160
Fax: 6172274128
E-mail: info@brookepea.com
Website: www.brookepea.com

Other Offices
114 State Street
Sixth Floor
Boston, MA USA 02109
Phone: 6172273160

Management and Staff
Christopher Austen, Managing Director
Daniel LeMoine, Principal
Johan von der Goltz, General Partner
John Brooke, Founder

Type of Firm
Private Equity Advisor or Fund of Funds

Project Preferences

Type of Financing Preferred:
Fund of Funds
Leveraged Buyout
Later Stage

Geographical Preferences

United States Preferences:

Industry Preferences

In Medical/Health prefer:
Medical/Health

Additional Information
Name of Most Recent Fund: BPEA Small Buyout & Growth Fund I, L.P.
Most Recent Fund Was Raised: 03/10/2011
Year Founded: 2002
Capital Under Management: $133,000,000
Current Activity Level : Actively seeking new investments

BROOKFIELD ASSET MANAGEMENT INC

181 Bay Street
Suite 300, Brookfield Place
Toronto, Canada M5J 2T3
Phone: 4163639491
Fax: 4163659642
Website: www.brookfield.com

Other Offices
Three World Financial Center
Eleventh Floor
New York, NY USA 10281
Phone: 212-417-7000
Fax: 212-417-7196

150 - 6 Avenue SW
Suite 3370
Calgary, Canada T2P 3Y7
Phone: 403-663-3335
Fax: 403-663-3340

181 Bay Street
Suite 330
Toronto, Ontario, Canada M5J 2T3
Phone: 416-369-2300
Fax: 416-369-2301

73 Front Street
5th Floor
Hamilton, Bermuda HM 12

Management and Staff
A. Silber, Vice President
Brett Fox, Managing Partner
Brian Lawson, Chief Financial Officer
Luiz Ildefonso Simones Lopes, Managing Partner

Type of Firm
Investment Management Firm

Association Membership
Brazilian Venture Capital Association (ABCR)
Emerging Markets Private Equity Association
Canadian Venture Capital Association
European Private Equity and Venture Capital Assoc.

Project Preferences

Type of Financing Preferred:
Core
Leveraged Buyout
Value-Add
Mezzanine
Generalist PE
Turnaround
Opportunistic
Later Stage
Other
Acquisition
Private Placement
Distressed Debt
Recapitalizations

Geographical Preferences

United States Preferences:
North America
All U.S.

Canadian Preferences:
All Canada

International Preferences:
Uruguay
Latin America
Europe
Brazil
Chile
Australia
New Zealand
Asia

Industry Preferences

In Industrial/Energy prefer:
Energy
Oil & Gas Drilling,Explor
Energy Conservation Relat
Industrial Products
Materials

In Transportation prefer:
Transportation

In Financial Services prefer:
Financial Services
Real Estate

In Business Serv. prefer:
Services

In Manufact. prefer:
Manufacturing

In Agr/Forestr/Fish prefer:
Agriculture related
Mining and Minerals

In Utilities prefer:
Utilities

Additional Information

Name of Most Recent Fund: Brookfield Infrastructure Fund II, L.P.
Most Recent Fund Was Raised: 07/09/2013
Year Founded: 2005
Capital Under Management: $3,918,500,000
Current Activity Level : Actively seeking new investments

BROOKLINE VENTURE PARTNERS

Four Cambridge Center, Second Floor
Cambridge, MA USA 02142
Phone: 6172526900

Management and Staff

Ken Levine, Founder
Mark Goodman, Founder

Type of Firm
Private Equity Firm

Project Preferences

Type of Financing Preferred:
Early Stage
Balanced

Size of Investments Considered:
Min Size of Investment Considered (000s): $250
Max Size of Investment Considered (000s): $10,000

Geographical Preferences

United States Preferences:
All U.S.

Additional Information

Year Founded: 2004
Current Activity Level : Actively seeking new investments

BROOKLYN BRIDGE VENTURES

55-C 9th Street
Brooklyn, NY USA 11215
Website: www.brooklynbridgeventures.com

Other Offices

456 Carroll Street
BROOKLYN, NY USA 11215
Phone: 3476617481

Management and Staff

Charles O Donnell, Founder

Type of Firm
Private Equity Firm

Project Preferences

Type of Financing Preferred:
Early Stage
Seed
Startup

Geographical Preferences

United States Preferences:
New York

Industry Preferences

In Internet Specific prefer:
E-Commerce Technology

Additional Information

Year Founded: 2012
Capital Under Management: $23,751,000
Current Activity Level : Actively seeking new investments

BROOKLYN EQUITY

80 State Street
Brooklyn, NY USA 11201
Phone: 6179359149
E-mail: brian@brooklyn-equity.com
Website: brooklyn-equity.com

Management and Staff

Brian Colton, Managing Partner

Type of Firm
Private Equity Firm

Project Preferences

Type of Financing Preferred:
Acquisition
Recapitalizations

Additional Information

Year Founded: 2015
Current Activity Level : Actively seeking new investments

BROOKLYN VENTURES BV

Straatweg 25
Breukelen, Netherlands 3621 BG
E-mail: info@brooklyn-ventures.com
Website: www.brooklyn-ventures.com

Management and Staff

Arg Jol, Partner
Hans Osnabrugge, Partner
Patrick Van der Tuin, Partner
Rutger Schouten, Partner
Wouter Van der Berg, Partner

Type of Firm
Private Equity Firm

Project Preferences

Type of Financing Preferred:
Early Stage
Balanced
Seed
Startup

Industry Preferences

In Communications prefer:
Communications and Media
Commercial Communications
Telecommunications

In Internet Specific prefer:
Internet

In Industrial/Energy prefer:
Energy
Oil and Gas Exploration
Alternative Energy
Energy Conservation Relat

In Other prefer:
Environment Responsible

Additional Information
Year Founded: 2011
Current Activity Level : Actively seeking new investments

BROOKSIDE INTERNATIONAL

201 Tresser Boulevard
Third Floor
Stamford, CT USA 06901
Phone: 2035954500
E-mail: info@brooksidegrp.com
Website: www.brooksidecapitalpartners.com

Management and Staff
Alex Troy, Managing Director
Donald Hawks, Managing Director
John Irwin, Managing Director
Philip Fitting, Managing Director
Raymond Weldon, Managing Director

Type of Firm
Private Equity Firm

Association Membership
Natl Assoc of Small Bus. Inv. Co (NASBIC)

Project Preferences

Type of Financing Preferred:
Leveraged Buyout
Mezzanine
Later Stage
Management Buyouts
Acquisition
Industry Rollups
Recapitalizations

Geographical Preferences

United States Preferences:

International Preferences:
Italy
United Kingdom
China
Eastern Europe
Spain
Asia
Germany
All International
France

Industry Focus
(% based on actual investment)
Biotechnology	42.1%
Internet Specific	25.9%
Computer Software and Services	19.8%
Medical/Health	5.2%
Computer Hardware	4.2%
Industrial/Energy	2.5%
Consumer Related	0.3%

Additional Information
Name of Most Recent Fund: Brookside Mezzanine Fund III, L.P.
Most Recent Fund Was Raised: 01/24/2013
Year Founded: 1977
Capital Under Management: $250,000,000
Current Activity Level : Actively seeking new investments
Method of Compensation: Return on investment is of primary concern, do not charge fees

BROOKSTONE PARTNERS LLP

317 Madison Avenue, Suite 405
New York, NY USA 10017
Phone: 2123020066
Fax: 2123025888

Other Offices
Boulevard Mohamed VI
Souissi
Rabat, Morocco

Management and Staff
Bardia Mesbah, Managing Director
Matthew Lipman, Principal
Michael Toporek, Managing Partner
Michael Toporek, Managing Partner
Perry Jacobson, Managing Director

Type of Firm
Private Equity Firm

Project Preferences

Type of Financing Preferred:
Leveraged Buyout
Expansion
Balanced
Acquisition

Size of Investments Considered:
Min Size of Investment Considered (000s): $3,000
Max Size of Investment Considered (000s): $30,000

Geographical Preferences

United States Preferences:
Mid Atlantic
Midwest
North America
Northeast
Southwest

International Preferences:
Morocco

Industry Preferences

In Semiconductor/Electr prefer:
Analytic/Scientific

In Industrial/Energy prefer:
Alternative Energy
Environmental Related

In Business Serv. prefer:
Services
Distribution

In Manufact. prefer:
Manufacturing

Additional Information
Year Founded: 2003
Current Activity Level : Actively seeking new investments

BROWN BROTHERS HARRIMAN & CO

140 Broadway
New York, NY USA 10005
Phone: 2124831818
E-mail: contactus@bbh.com
Website: www.bbh.com

Other Offices
40 Water Street
Boston, MA USA 02109-3661
Phone: 6177421818
Fax: 6177421148

Butterfield House, Fort Street
P.O. Box 2330, George Town
Grand Cayman, Cayman Islands
Phone: 3459452719

227 West Trade Street
Suite 2100 Carillion Building
Charlotte, NC USA 28202-1675
Phone: 7043700500

240 Royal Palm Way
Palm Beach, FL USA 33480
Phone: 5618324262

6801 South Tucson Way
Suite 100
Englewood, CO USA 80112
Phone: 3035666600

125 Finsbury Pavement
Veritas House
London, United Kingdom EC2A 1PN
Phone: 442075886166

70 Franklin Street
Boston, MA USA 02110
Phone: 6177421818

Park House
16-18 Finsbury Circus
London, England, United Kingdom EC2M 7EB
Phone: 442075886166

Styne House
Upper Hatch Street
Dublin, Ireland
Phone: 35316036200
Fax: 35316036300

Unit 1507, Level 15, Int'l Commerce Ctr.
1 Austin Road West
Kowloon, Hong Kong
Phone: 85237561600
Fax: 85237561799

1531 Walnut Street
Philadelphia, PA USA 19102-3098
Phone: 2158641818

1-2-8 Toranomon, Minato-ku
Toranomon Kotohira Tower 15F
Tokyo, Japan 105-0001
Phone: 81363616500

2-8 Avenue Charles De Gaulle
B.P. 403
Luxembourg, Luxembourg L-2014
Phone: 352474066
Fax: 352474058

Barengasse 25
Zurich, Switzerland CH-8001
Phone: 41442271818

50 Milk Street
Boston, MA USA 02109-3661
Phone: 6177421818

Room 1251, China Resources Bldg.
8, Jian Guo Men North Ave., Dongcheng
Beijing, China 100005
Phone: 861058111919

919 North Market Street
Suite 420
Wilmington, DE USA 19801
Phone: 3025524040

2001 Ross Avenue
Suite 2500
Dallas, TX USA 75201
Phone: 2143035600

150 South Wacker Drive
Suite 3250
Chicago, IL USA 60606
Phone: 3127817111
Fax: 8003251818

525 Washington Boulevard
Newport Tower
Jersey City, NJ USA 07310
Phone: 2014185600

Management and Staff

Alison Kelly, Vice President
Andrew Tucker, Partner
Andrew Hofer, Managing Director
Ben Neumann, Vice President
Bradley Langer, Managing Director
Charles Izard, Partner
Christian Romaglino, Vice President
Christopher Ling, Vice President
David Gorski, Vice President
Douglas Mark, Vice President
Douglas Maine, Partner
Francisco Vidal, Partner
Gregory Steier, Managing Director
J. Clark O Donoghue, Managing Director
Jared Keyes, Partner
Jason Johnson, Vice President
Jean-Pierre Paquin, Managing Director
Jeffrey Meskin, Partner
Jeffrey Schoenfeld, Partner
Jeffrey Scott, Managing Director
Jeffrey Adams, Vice President
John Santos, Managing Director
John Nelson, Managing Director
John Molner, Partner
Jonathan Wetreich, Vice President
Jorge Aseff, Vice President
Joseph Donlan, Managing Director
Kate Fuller, Vice President
Mark McCormick, Vice President
Marla Sims, Vice President
Maroa Velez, Partner
Matthew Hyman, Vice President
Matthew Salsbury, Vice President
Michael Townson, Vice President
Michael Keller, Managing Director
Michael Kim, Managing Director
Neel Panchal, Vice President
Nichol MacManus, Managing Director
Radford Klotz, Partner
Regina Lombardi, Managing Director
Richard Yeh, Vice President
Richard Witmer, Partner
Robert Paige, Principal
Robert Leverich, Vice President
Robert Davies, Vice President
S Hill, Managing Director
Scott Schultz, Managing Director
Susan O Donnell, Managing Director
Tatiana Vasilyev, Vice President
Timothy Urekew, Vice President
Timothy Hartch, Partner
Tripp Blum, Vice President
William Tyree, Partner
William Brennan, Vice President
Wyatt Courtney, Vice President

Type of Firm
Bank Affiliated

Project Preferences

Type of Financing Preferred:
Fund of Funds
Leveraged Buyout
Expansion
Mezzanine
Balanced
Turnaround
Opportunistic
Management Buyouts
Acquisition
Recapitalizations

Geographical Preferences

United States Preferences:

Industry Focus

(% based on actual investment)
Other Products	26.4%
Communications and Media	24.2%
Internet Specific	11.7%
Industrial/Energy	11.1%
Medical/Health	9.7%
Computer Software and Services	8.7%
Consumer Related	6.0%
Computer Hardware	2.0%
Semiconductors/Other Elect.	0.2%

Additional Information

Name of Most Recent Fund: BBH Capital Partners IV, L.P.
Most Recent Fund Was Raised: 01/18/2012
Year Founded: 1931
Capital Under Management: $2,000,000,000
Current Activity Level: Actively seeking new investments

BROWN GIBBONS LANG & COMPANY LLC

1111 Superior Avenue, Suite 900
Cleveland, OH USA 44114
Phone: 2162412800
Fax: 2162417417
Website: www.bglco.com

Other Offices

1809 Seventh Avenue
Suite 1209, Tower Building
Seattle, WA USA 98101
Phone: 2066234000

980 North Michigan Avenue
Suite 1880
Chicago, IL USA 60611
Phone: 3126581600

9980 South 300 West
Suite 200
Sandy, UT USA 84070
Phone: 8019533675
Fax: 8012857401

Management and Staff

Andrew Petryk, Managing Director
Clifford Sladnick, Managing Director
Effram Kaplan, Managing Director
John Riddle, Managing Director
John Tilson, Managing Director
Joseph Boleski, Vice President
Manfred Steiner, Managing Director
Michael Goettemoeller, Vice President
Michael Vinciquerra, Partner
Michael Gibbons, Managing Director
Robert Flanigan, Vice President
Scott Berlin, Managing Director
Thomas West, Chief Financial Officer

Type of Firm
Bank Affiliated

Project Preferences

Type of Financing Preferred:
Leveraged Buyout
Acquisition

Geographical Preferences

United States Preferences:
All U.S.

Industry Preferences

In Consumer Related prefer:
Consumer

In Industrial/Energy prefer:
Industrial Products

In Transportation prefer:
Transportation

Additional Information
Year Founded: 1989
Current Activity Level : Actively seeking new investments

BRUCKMANN ROSSER SHERRILL & CO LP

126 East 56th Street
29th Floor
New York, NY USA 10022
Phone: 2125213700
Fax: 2125213799
E-mail: info@brs.com

Management and Staff
Bruce Bruckmann, Managing Director
Nicholas Sheppard, Managing Director
Rashad Rahman, Principal
Stephen Sherrill, Managing Director
Thomas Baldwin, Managing Director
Tory Rooney, Principal

Type of Firm
Private Equity Firm

Project Preferences

Role in Financing:
Will function either as deal originator or investor in deals created by others

Type of Financing Preferred:
Expansion
Management Buyouts
Acquisition

Geographical Preferences

United States Preferences:

Industry Focus
(% based on actual investment)
Consumer Related	57.5%
Other Products	30.7%
Industrial/Energy	6.9%
Communications and Media	2.6%
Internet Specific	1.3%
Medical/Health	1.0%

Additional Information
Name of Most Recent Fund: Bruckmann, Rosser, Sherill & Co. II, L.P.
Most Recent Fund Was Raised: 05/21/1999
Year Founded: 1995
Capital Under Management: $1,400,000,000
Current Activity Level : Actively seeking new investments

BRUERE &ASSOCIES SARL

21, Rue de Lubeck
Paris, France 75116
Website: www.referenciaint.com

Type of Firm
Private Equity Firm

Project Preferences

Type of Financing Preferred:
Leveraged Buyout
Expansion
Turnaround
Later Stage
Management Buyouts
Acquisition

Geographical Preferences

International Preferences:
Italy
France

Industry Preferences

In Consumer Related prefer:
Consumer Products
Consumer Services

Additional Information
Year Founded: 2001
Current Activity Level : Actively seeking new investments

BRUIN SPORTS CAPITAL LLC

P.O. Box 8284
9149212762
White Plains, NY USA 10602
E-mail: info@bruinsc.com
Website: www.bruinsportscapital.com

Management and Staff
George Pyne, Founder

Type of Firm
Private Equity Firm

Project Preferences

Type of Financing Preferred:
Leveraged Buyout

Industry Preferences

In Consumer Related prefer:
Sports

Additional Information
Year Founded: 2015
Capital Under Management: $250,000,000
Current Activity Level : Actively seeking new investments

BRYANT STIBEL & COMPANY LLC

22761 Pacific Coast Highway
Garden Level
Malibu, CA USA 90265

Type of Firm
Private Equity Firm

Project Preferences

Type of Financing Preferred:
Balanced

Industry Preferences

In Business Serv. prefer:
Media

Additional Information
Year Founded: 2013
Capital Under Management: $100,000,000
Current Activity Level : Actively seeking new investments

BRYNWOOD PARTNERS L.P.

Eight Sound Shore Drive
Suite 265
Greenwich, CT USA 06830
Phone: 2036221790
Fax: 2036220559
E-mail: info@brynwoodpartners.com
Website: www.brynwoodpartners.com

Management and Staff
Dario Margve, Managing Partner
Guy Einav, Vice President
Hendrik Hartong, Managing Director
Ian MacTaggart, Managing Partner
Joan McCabe, Managing Partner
Kevin Hartnett, Managing Partner
Vipul Soni, Vice President

Type of Firm
Private Equity Firm

Project Preferences

Type of Financing Preferred:
Leveraged Buyout
Recapitalizations

Industry Focus
(% based on actual investment)
Consumer Related 66.0%
Other Products 32.3%
Computer Software and Services 1.3%
Industrial/Energy 0.4%

Additional Information
Name of Most Recent Fund: Brynwood Partners VII, L.P.
Most Recent Fund Was Raised: 09/25/2013
Year Founded: 1984
Capital Under Management: $500,000,000
Current Activity Level : Actively seeking new investments

BSCOPE PARTNERS INC

Changle Road 758
Shanghai, China 200040
Phone: 86-21-54048388
Fax: 86-21-54032921
Website: www.bscope.com

Management and Staff
Fitz De Smet, Venture Partner
Viktor Meng, Managing Partner

Type of Firm
Private Equity Firm

Project Preferences

Type of Financing Preferred:
Early Stage

Geographical Preferences

International Preferences:
China

Additional Information
Year Founded: 2004
Current Activity Level : Actively seeking new investments

BSD VENTURE CAPITAL LLC

2221 Camino del Rio South
Suite 308
San Diego, CA USA 92108
Phone: 619-682-3834
Website: www.bsdventurecapital.com

Management and Staff
Bruce Dolle, Managing Partner

Type of Firm
Private Equity Firm

Project Preferences

Type of Financing Preferred:
Balanced

Industry Preferences

In Medical/Health prefer:
Medical/Health
Medical Therapeutics
Health Services

Additional Information
Name of Most Recent Fund: BSD Venture Capital Fund I, L.P.
Most Recent Fund Was Raised: 02/09/2009
Year Founded: 2009
Capital Under Management: $250,000,000
Current Activity Level : Actively seeking new investments

BSEED INVESTMENTS LLC

40 Wall Street
New York, NY USA 10005
Phone: 2126039808
Website: bseedventure.com

Type of Firm
Private Equity Firm

Additional Information
Year Founded: 1969
Current Activity Level : Actively seeking new investments

BT VENTURE FUND MANAGEMENT LLC

175 Federal Street
Suite 1350
Boston, MA USA 02210
Phone: 617-439-0770

Management and Staff
Bagus Tjahjono, General Partner

Type of Firm
Private Equity Firm

Project Preferences

Type of Financing Preferred:
Balanced

Geographical Preferences

United States Preferences:

Additional Information
Name of Most Recent Fund: BT Venture Fund I, L.P.
Most Recent Fund Was Raised: 03/23/2004
Year Founded: 2004

Capital Under Management: $1,500,000
Current Activity Level : Actively seeking new investments

BT&T ASSET MANAGEMENT AG

Hardturmstrasse 11 / Puls 5
Zurich, Switzerland 8005
Phone: 41447358100
Fax: 41447358169
E-mail: info@btt.com
Website: www.btt.com

Other Offices
Dufourpark/Roetelistrasse 16
St. Gallen, Switzerland 9000
Phone: 41-71-274-2474
Fax: 41-71-274-2479

Management and Staff
Andreas Duesterhoeft, Chief Operating Officer

Type of Firm
Bank Affiliated

Project Preferences

Type of Financing Preferred:
Fund of Funds
Early Stage
Later Stage
Seed
Startup

Geographical Preferences

Canadian Preferences:
All Canada

International Preferences:
Europe
Switzerland
France

Industry Preferences

In Communications prefer:
Telecommunications
Media and Entertainment

In Biotechnology prefer:
Biotechnology

In Medical/Health prefer:
Medical/Health

In Consumer Related prefer:
Food/Beverage

In Industrial/Energy prefer:
Energy
Alternative Energy
Energy Conservation Relat
Environmental Related

In Financial Services prefer:
Financial Services

Pratt's Guide to Private Equity & Venture Capital Sources

Additional Information
Year Founded: 2003
Current Activity Level : Actively seeking new investments

BTG PACTUAL GESTORA DE INVESTIMENTOS ALTERNATIVOS LTDA

Praia de Botafogo 501
Torre Corcovado
Rio de Janeiro, Brazil 22250040

Type of Firm
Private Equity Firm

Project Preferences

Type of Financing Preferred:
Early Stage
Balanced
Seed

Geographical Preferences

International Preferences:
Brazil

Additional Information
Year Founded: 2007
Current Activity Level : Actively seeking new investments

BTH BERLIN TECHNOLOGIE HOLDING GMBH

Unter den Linden 16
Berlin, Germany 10117
Phone: 49 30408173214
Fax: 49 23273018210
E-mail: info@berlinholding.com
Website: berlinholding.com

Management and Staff
Hans Kompernass, Co-Founder
Hans Even, Venture Partner
Jan Webering, Venture Partner
Joern-Carlos Kuntze, Co-Founder

Type of Firm
Private Equity Firm

Project Preferences

Type of Financing Preferred:
Leveraged Buyout
Early Stage
Balanced
Seed
Management Buyouts
Acquisition
Startup

Geographical Preferences

International Preferences:
Germany

Industry Preferences

In Communications prefer:
Communications and Media

In Computer Software prefer:
Software

In Computer Other prefer:
Computer Related

In Industrial/Energy prefer:
Industrial Products

In Other prefer:
Environment Responsible

Additional Information
Year Founded: 2013
Current Activity Level : Actively seeking new investments

BTP CAPITAL INVESTISSEMENT SA

41, rue des Trois Fontanot
Parc de la Defense
Nanterre, France 92002
Phone: 33147248108
Fax: 33147248437
E-mail: btp@btp-banque.fr
Website: www.btpki.fr

Type of Firm
Bank Affiliated

Association Membership
French Venture Capital Association (AFIC)

Project Preferences

Type of Financing Preferred:
Leveraged Buyout
Early Stage
Generalist PE
Later Stage
Management Buyouts
Acquisition

Size of Investments Considered:
Min Size of Investment Considered (000s): $100
Max Size of Investment Considered (000s): $2,005

Geographical Preferences

International Preferences:
Europe
France

Industry Preferences

In Business Serv. prefer:
Services

Additional Information
Year Founded: 1974
Current Activity Level : Actively seeking new investments

BTV BETEILIGUNGSVERWALTUNG GMBH & CO. KG

Pettenkoferstrasse 37
Munich, Germany 80336
Phone: 49895446060
Fax: 498954460620
E-mail: btvbeteiligung@btv-holding.de

Management and Staff
Horst Goss, Managing Director

Type of Firm
Private Equity Firm

Project Preferences

Type of Financing Preferred:
Turnaround
Later Stage
Seed
Management Buyouts
Startup
Recapitalizations

Size of Investments Considered:
Min Size of Investment Considered (000s): $328
Max Size of Investment Considered (000s): $3,279

Geographical Preferences

United States Preferences:
All U.S.

International Preferences:
Europe
Germany

Industry Preferences

In Communications prefer:
Communications and Media

In Internet Specific prefer:
Internet

In Biotechnology prefer:
Biotechnology

In Consumer Related prefer:
Retail

In Financial Services prefer:
Financial Services

In Other prefer:
Environment Responsible

Additional Information
Year Founded: 1996
Current Activity Level : Actively seeking new investments

BTWINZ SAS

62, Rue de Caumartin
Paris, France 75009
Website: www.btwinz.com

Type of Firm
Private Equity Firm

Project Preferences

Type of Financing Preferred:
Early Stage
Seed

Size of Investments Considered:
Min Size of Investment Considered (000s): $55
Max Size of Investment Considered (000s): $1,095

Geographical Preferences

International Preferences:
Europe
France

Industry Preferences

In Computer Software prefer:
Data Processing
Software

In Internet Specific prefer:
E-Commerce Technology
Internet

Additional Information
Year Founded: 2013
Current Activity Level : Actively seeking new investments

BUCKHEAD INVESTMENT PARTNERS LLC

3575 Piedmont Road, Building 15, Suite 730
Atlanta, GA USA 30305
Phone: 4044955230
Fax: 4044955239
Website: www.buckheadinvestments.com

Management and Staff
Bill Harris, Co-Founder
Mark Buffington, Co-Founder

Type of Firm
Private Equity Firm

Project Preferences

Type of Financing Preferred:
Early Stage
Expansion
Generalist PE
Balanced
Later Stage
Seed
Startup

Size of Investments Considered:
Min Size of Investment Considered (000s): $500
Max Size of Investment Considered (000s): $4,000

Geographical Preferences

United States Preferences:
Georgia
All U.S.

International Preferences:
Gabon

Industry Preferences

In Communications prefer:
Media and Entertainment

In Computer Software prefer:
Software

In Internet Specific prefer:
Internet

In Medical/Health prefer:
Health Services

In Consumer Related prefer:
Franchises(NEC)

In Industrial/Energy prefer:
Alternative Energy
Energy Conservation Relat

In Financial Services prefer:
Financial Services

In Business Serv. prefer:
Services
Media

Additional Information
Name of Most Recent Fund: BIP Early Stage Fund I LP
Most Recent Fund Was Raised: 10/25/2013
Year Founded: 2007
Capital Under Management: $31,901,000
Current Activity Level : Actively seeking new investments

BUEPOINT PARTNERS

385-29 Doryong-dong, Usung-gu
Daejeon-city, South Korea 305-340
Phone: 82429363588
Fax: 82429363533
E-mail: contact@bluepoint.vc
Website: bluepoint-partners.com

Type of Firm
Private Equity Firm

Project Preferences

Type of Financing Preferred:
Start-up Financing

Additional Information
Year Founded: 2017
Current Activity Level : Actively seeking new investments

BUGIN CAPITAL CO LTD

1-10-8 Sakuragi-cho
Omiya shi
Saitama, Japan 331-0852
Phone: 81-48-657-0931
Fax: 81-48-657-0932

Type of Firm
Bank Affiliated

Additional Information
Year Founded: 1997
Current Activity Level : Actively seeking new investments

BUILDERS FUND L.P, THE

4319 21st Street
San Francisco, CA USA 94114
Website: www.thebuildersfund.com

Type of Firm
Private Equity Firm

Project Preferences

Type of Financing Preferred:
Leveraged Buyout
Acquisition

Industry Preferences

In Business Serv. prefer:
Services

Additional Information
Year Founded: 2014
Capital Under Management: $45,000,000
Current Activity Level : Actively seeking new investments

BUILDERS VC FUND I LP

370 Brannan Street
San Francisco, CA USA 94107

Type of Firm
Private Equity Firm

Project Preferences

Type of Financing Preferred:
Early Stage
Seed

Additional Information
Year Founded: 2016
Current Activity Level : Actively seeking new investments

BUILDGROUP MANAGEMENT LLC

3500 Jefferson Street, Suite 303
Austin, TX USA 78731
Phone: 5122206490
Website: www.buildgroup.com

Management and Staff
Klee Kleber, Partner
Pete Freeland, Co-Founder

Type of Firm
Private Equity Firm

Project Preferences

Type of Financing Preferred:
Balanced

Additional Information
Year Founded: 2016
Current Activity Level : Actively seeking new investments

BUILDING INDUSTRY PARTNERS LLC

10 Ware Street
Cambridge, MA USA 02138
Phone: 6174318333
Website: www.building-ip.com

Other Offices
301 Commerce Street
Suite 3025
FORT WORTH, TX USA 76102
Phone: 2145500405
Fax: 2145809595

Management and Staff
Matt Ogden, Managing Partner
Zach Coopersmith, Managing Partner

Type of Firm
Investment Management Firm

Project Preferences

Type of Financing Preferred:
Leveraged Buyout
Expansion
Management Buyouts
Recapitalizations

Geographical Preferences

United States Preferences:
All U.S.

Industry Preferences

In Industrial/Energy prefer:
Industrial Products
Machinery

In Manufact. prefer:
Manufacturing

In Agr/Forestr/Fish prefer:
Agribusiness

In Utilities prefer:
Utilities

Additional Information
Year Founded: 2005
Current Activity Level : Actively seeking new investments

BULGARIAN-AMERICAN ENTERPRISE FUND

333 West Wacker Drive
Suite 460
Chicago, IL USA 60606
Phone: 3126292500
Fax: 3126292929
Website: www.baefinvest.com

Other Offices
3 Shipka Street
Sofia, Bulgaria 1504
Phone: 35929460119
Fax: 35929460118

Management and Staff
Dennis Fiehler, Chief Financial Officer
Nancy Schiller, Managing Director
Tzvetomir Todorov, Managing Director

Type of Firm
Private Equity Firm

Project Preferences

Type of Financing Preferred:
Balanced

Size of Investments Considered:
Min Size of Investment Considered (000s): $100
Max Size of Investment Considered (000s): $5,000

Geographical Preferences

International Preferences:
No Preference
Bulgaria

Industry Preferences

In Internet Specific prefer:
Internet

In Medical/Health prefer:
Medical/Health

In Business Serv. prefer:
Distribution

In Manufact. prefer:
Manufacturing

In Agr/Forestr/Fish prefer:
Agribusiness

Additional Information
Year Founded: 1991
Current Activity Level : Actively seeking new investments

BULL CAPITAL PARTNERS LTD

Ugland House
Grand Cayman, Cayman Islands KYI-1104
E-mail: contact@bullcp.com
Website: www.bullcp.com

Other Offices
Room 905 Wheelock House
20 Pedder Street, Central
Hong kong, Hong Kong
Phone: 852-2899-7988
Fax: 852-2868-2897

Room 502-503, Kerry Centre
1515 Nanjing Road West
Shanghai, China 200040
Phone: 86-21-5298-6989
Fax: 86-21-5298-6979

Management and Staff
Friedrich Lung, Partner
Gilbert Wong, Managing Partner
Roy Li, Partner

Type of Firm
Private Equity Firm

Project Preferences

Type of Financing Preferred:
Early Stage
Expansion
Seed

Geographical Preferences

International Preferences:
Asia

Additional Information
Year Founded: 2008
Current Activity Level : Actively seeking new investments

BULL CITY VENTURE PARTNERS LLC

7780 Brier Creek Parkway, Suite 410
Raleigh, NC USA 27617
Phone: 9194428651
Website: www.bcvp.com

Management and Staff
David Jones, General Partner
Jason Caplain, Managing Director

Type of Firm
Private Equity Firm

Project Preferences

Type of Financing Preferred:
Early Stage
Balanced
Seed

Industry Preferences

In Communications prefer:
Communications and Media
Telecommunications
Data Communications

In Computer Software prefer:
Software

In Internet Specific prefer:
Ecommerce

In Medical/Health prefer:
Medical Diagnostics

Additional Information
Year Founded: 2013
Capital Under Management: $26,000,000
Current Activity Level : Actively seeking new investments

BULLDOG INNOVATION GROUP LLC

24 Dixwell Avenue
Suite 274
Hamden, CT USA 06518

Type of Firm
Private Equity Firm

Additional Information
Year Founded: 2015
Capital Under Management: $1,560,000
Current Activity Level : Actively seeking new investments

BULLNET CAPITAL SC R SA

Paseo del Club Deportivo,1
Edif. 3, Pozuelo de Alarcon
Madrid, Spain 28223
Phone: 34917997206
Fax: 34917995372
Website: www.grupobullnet.com

Management and Staff
Bruno Entrecanales, Co-Founder
Javier Ulecia, Partner
Miguel del Canizo, Partner

Type of Firm
Private Equity Firm

Association Membership
Spanish Venture Capital Association (ASCRI)

Project Preferences

Type of Financing Preferred:
Early Stage

Size of Investments Considered:
Min Size of Investment Considered (000s): $2,541
Max Size of Investment Considered (000s): $5,082

Geographical Preferences

International Preferences:
Spain

Industry Preferences

In Communications prefer:
Telecommunications

In Computer Software prefer:
Software

In Computer Other prefer:
Computer Related

In Medical/Health prefer:
Medical/Health

In Industrial/Energy prefer:
Industrial Products

In Business Serv. prefer:
Services
Media

Additional Information
Year Founded: 2001
Current Activity Level : Actively seeking new investments

BULLPEN CAPITAL LP

2108 Sand Hill Road
Menlo Park, CA USA 94025

Other Offices
2108 Sand Hill Road
Menlo Park, CA USA 94025

Management and Staff
Duncan Davidson, Managing Director
Eric Wiesen, General Partner
James Conlon, Principal
Paul Martino, Managing Director
Richard Melmon, Managing Director

Type of Firm
Private Equity Firm

Project Preferences

Type of Financing Preferred:
Early Stage
Seed

Geographical Preferences

United States Preferences:
All U.S.

Industry Preferences

In Internet Specific prefer:
Internet

Additional Information
Year Founded: 2010
Capital Under Management: $83,640,000
Current Activity Level : Actively seeking new investments

BUNKER HILL CAPITAL LP

260 Franklin Street, Suite 1860
Boston, MA USA 02110
Phone: 6177204030
Fax: 6177204037
Website: www.bunkerhillcapital.com

Management and Staff
Brian Kinsman, Co-Founder
Jared Paquette, Vice President
Jason Hurd, Co-Founder
Mark DeBlois, Co-Founder
Max McEwen, Vice President
Robert Dreier, Principal
Robert Clark, Co-Founder

Type of Firm
Private Equity Firm

Project Preferences

Type of Financing Preferred:
Leveraged Buyout
Acquisition

Industry Preferences

In Consumer Related prefer:
Retail
Consumer Products

In Industrial/Energy prefer:
Industrial Products

In Business Serv. prefer:
Services

Additional Information
Year Founded: 2003
Capital Under Management: $79,700,000
Current Activity Level : Actively seeking new investments

BURAN VENTURE CAPITAL

Khlebny Lane 8
Moscow, Russia 121069
Phone: 74955404842
E-mail: info@buranvc.com
Website: www.buranvc.com

Type of Firm
Private Equity Firm

Project Preferences

Type of Financing Preferred:
Early Stage
Expansion
Balanced
Later Stage
Seed

Geographical Preferences

International Preferences:
Armenia
Belarus
Kazakhstan
Kyrgyzstan
Tajikistan
Azerbaijan
Moldova
Israel
Uzbekistan
Russia

Industry Preferences

In Communications prefer:
Communications and Media
Media and Entertainment

In Computer Software prefer:
Software
Applications Software

In Internet Specific prefer:
E-Commerce Technology

Additional Information
Year Founded: 2010
Capital Under Management: $16,000,000
Current Activity Level : Actively seeking new investments

BURCH CREATIVE CAPITAL LLC

1115 Broadway, Fifth Floor
New York, NY USA 10010
Phone: 6465322000
E-mail: info@burchcreativecapital.com
Website: www.burchcreativecapital.com

Type of Firm
Incubator/Development Program

Project Preferences

Type of Financing Preferred:
Seed
Startup

Industry Preferences

In Communications prefer:
Wireless Communications

In Consumer Related prefer:
Retail
Consumer Products

Additional Information
Year Founded: 1969
Current Activity Level : Actively seeking new investments

BURDA DIGITAL VENTURES GMBH

Hauptstrasse 130
Offenburg, Germany 77652
Phone: 498992500
Fax: 498992502745
E-mail: info@actoncapital.de

Management and Staff
Christoph Braun, Managing Partner
Frank Seehaus, Managing Partner

Type of Firm
Corporate PE/Venture

Project Preferences

Type of Financing Preferred:
Early Stage
Later Stage
Startup

Geographical Preferences

International Preferences:
Europe
Germany

Industry Preferences

In Communications prefer:
Communications and Media
Commercial Communications
Media and Entertainment

In Internet Specific prefer:
Ecommerce

In Business Serv. prefer:
Media

Additional Information
Year Founded: 1999
Current Activity Level : Actively seeking new investments

BURE EQUITY AB

Nybrogatan Six
Stockholm, Sweden 114 34
Phone: 4686140020
Fax: 4686140038
E-mail: info@bure.se
Website: www.bure.se

Management and Staff
Max Jonson, Chief Financial Officer

Type of Firm
Private Equity Firm

Project Preferences

Type of Financing Preferred:
Leveraged Buyout
Expansion
Turnaround
Acquisition

Geographical Preferences

International Preferences:
Sweden
Scandanavia/Nordic Region

Industry Preferences

In Communications prefer:
Telecommunications

In Internet Specific prefer:
Internet

In Semiconductor/Electr prefer:
Electronics

In Medical/Health prefer:
Medical/Health

In Consumer Related prefer:
Entertainment and Leisure
Education Related

In Business Serv. prefer:
Media

Additional Information
Year Founded: 1993
Current Activity Level : Actively seeking new investments

BURRILL & COMPANY

One Embarcadero Center
Suite 2700
San Francisco, CA USA 94111
Phone: 4155915400
Fax: 4155915401
E-mail: burrill@b-c.com
Website: www.burrillandco.com

Management and Staff
Ann Hanham, Managing Director
Anton Gueth, Managing Director
Bryant Fong, Managing Director
Dag Dvergsten, Venture Partner
Daniel Levine, Managing Director
David Wetherell, President & COO
David Parke, Managing Director
Dirk Lammerts, Managing Director
Douglas Lind, Managing Director
Elemer Piros, Managing Director
Eric Laub, Managing Director
Greg Young, Managing Director
Hui Wu, Managing Director

Irena Melnikova, Managing Director
Joao Paulo Poiares Baptista, Managing Director
Kira Sheinerman, Managing Director
Konstantin Skryabin, Venture Partner
Martin Godbout, Managing Director
Michael Keyoung, Managing Director
Mike Carpenter, Managing Director
Paul Freiman, Venture Partner
Peter Fry, Managing Director
Reni Benjamin, Managing Director
Roger Wyse, President & COO
Stephen Sammut, Venture Partner
Sven Rohmann, Managing Director
Tee Wee Lee, Venture Partner
Wenyong Wang, Managing Director

Type of Firm
Bank Affiliated

Association Membership
Brazilian Venture Capital Association (ABCR)

Project Preferences

Role in Financing:
Will function either as deal originator or investor in deals created by others

Type of Financing Preferred:
Early Stage
Expansion
Mezzanine
Balanced
Later Stage
Seed
Startup

Size of Investments Considered:
Min Size of Investment Considered (000s): $5,000
Max Size of Investment Considered (000s): $15,000

Geographical Preferences

United States Preferences:
North America

International Preferences:
Europe
Brazil

Industry Focus
(% based on actual investment)
Biotechnology	54.8%
Medical/Health	37.0%
Consumer Related	3.6%
Computer Software and Services	2.7%
Internet Specific	2.0%

Additional Information
Year Founded: 1994
Capital Under Management: $695,000,000
Current Activity Level : Actively seeking new investments
Method of Compensation: Return on investment is of primary concern, do not charge fees

BUSINESS ANGELS NETWERK VLAANDEREN VZW

150, Hendrik Van Veldekesingel
Hasselt, Belgium 3500
Phone: 3211870910
Website: www.ban.be

Type of Firm
Bank Affiliated

Project Preferences

Type of Financing Preferred:
Early Stage
Expansion
Later Stage
Management Buyouts
Acquisition

Size of Investments Considered:
Min Size of Investment Considered (000s): $282
Max Size of Investment Considered (000s): $1,129

Geographical Preferences

International Preferences:
Belgium

Additional Information
Year Founded: 2007
Current Activity Level : Actively seeking new investments

BUSINESS ARTS, LTD.

90 Burnhhamthrope Road West
Suite 1504
Mississauga, Canada L5B 3C3
Phone: 905-281-0766
Fax: 905-281-2496

Other Offices
90 Burnhhamthrope Road West
Suite 1504
Mississauga, Canada L5B 3C3
Phone: 905-281-0766
Fax: 905-281-2496

Management and Staff
W. David Breukelman, President

Type of Firm
Private Equity Firm

Project Preferences

Type of Financing Preferred:
Later Stage

Additional Information
Year Founded: 2009
Current Activity Level : Actively seeking new investments

BUSINESS CREATION INVESTMENTS AG

c/o KPMG AG
Bogenstrasse 7
St. Gallen, Switzerland 9000

Management and Staff
Gerry Van der Sluys, Chief Executive Officer

Type of Firm
Private Equity Firm

Additional Information
Year Founded: 1998
Current Activity Level : Actively seeking new investments

BUSINESS DEVELOPMENT BANK OF CANADA

Five Place Ville Marie
Suite 400
Montreal, Canada H3B 5E7
Phone: 8772322269
Fax: 8773299232
Website: www.bdc.ca

Other Offices
505 Burrard Street
Suite 200, One Bentall Center
Vancouver, Canada V7X 1M3
Fax: 6046667650

444 - 7th Avenue South West
Suite 110, Barclay Center
Calgary, Canada T2P 0X8
Fax: 4032926951

Management and Staff
Charles Cazabon, Managing Partner
Danielle Landry, Vice President
Frank Pho, Vice President
Glenn Egan, Vice President
Matt Price, Managing Director
Michael Denham, President
Michelle Scarborough, Managing Director
Neal Hill, Vice President
Paula Cruickshank, Vice President
Robert Simon, Managing Partner
Senia Rapisarda, Vice President
Susan Rohac, Vice President
Timothy April, Managing Director

Type of Firm
Government Affiliated Program

Association Membership
Canadian Venture Capital Association

Project Preferences

Type of Financing Preferred:
Fund of Funds
Early Stage
Expansion
Mezzanine
Generalist PE
Balanced
Later Stage
Seed
Management Buyouts
Acquisition
Startup

Size of Investments Considered:
Min Size of Investment Considered (000s): $500
Max Size of Investment Considered (000s): $3,000

Geographical Preferences

Canadian Preferences:
All Canada

Industry Preferences

In Communications prefer:
Communications and Media
Telecommunications
Wireless Communications

In Computer Software prefer:
Software
Applications Software

In Internet Specific prefer:
Internet

In Computer Other prefer:
Computer Related

In Semiconductor/Electr prefer:
Electronics

In Biotechnology prefer:
Biotechnology

In Medical/Health prefer:
Medical/Health
Medical Diagnostics
Medical Therapeutics
Medical Products

In Industrial/Energy prefer:
Energy
Advanced Materials
Environmental Related

In Financial Services prefer:
Financial Services

In Manufact. prefer:
Manufacturing

Additional Information
Name of Most Recent Fund: BDC Venture Capital Healthcare Fund
Most Recent Fund Was Raised: 09/17/2013
Year Founded: 1970
Capital Under Management: $283,000,000
Current Activity Level : Actively seeking new investments

BUSINESS GROWTH FUND PLC

21 Palmer Street
London, United Kingdom SW1H 0AD
Phone: 448452668860
E-mail: enquiries@bgf.co.uk
Website: www.businessgrowthfund.co.uk

Management and Staff
Matthew Reed, Founder
Stephen Welton, Chief Executive Officer

Type of Firm
Government Affiliated Program

Project Preferences

Type of Financing Preferred:
Expansion
Generalist PE
Balanced
Later Stage
Acquisition

Size of Investments Considered:
Min Size of Investment Considered (000s): $3,245
Max Size of Investment Considered (000s): $16,226

Geographical Preferences

International Preferences:
United Kingdom

Industry Preferences

In Semiconductor/Electr prefer:
Electronics

In Medical/Health prefer:
Health Services

In Consumer Related prefer:
Consumer Services

In Industrial/Energy prefer:
Industrial Products
Environmental Related

In Manufact. prefer:
Manufacturing

In Other prefer:
Environment Responsible

Additional Information
Year Founded: 2011
Capital Under Management: $311,660,000
Current Activity Level : Actively seeking new investments

BUSINESS INSTINCTS GROUP

L120, 2303 4 Street South West
Calgary, Canada T2S 2S7
Phone: 4037816671
E-mail: hello@businessinstincts.ca
Website: businessinstincts.com

Management and Staff
Arden Styles, Chief Operating Officer
Cameron Chell, Chief Executive Officer
Erika Racicot, President
Robert Kennedy, Partner

Type of Firm
Private Equity Firm

Project Preferences

Type of Financing Preferred:
Balanced

Additional Information
Year Founded: 2014
Current Activity Level : Actively seeking new investments

BUSINESS PARTNERS LTD

Business Partners Centre
Parktown
Johannesburg, South Africa 2193
Phone: 27-11-480-8700
Fax: 27-11-642-2791
E-mail: enquiries@businesspartners.co.za
Website: www.businesspartners.co.za

Other Offices

3 Caxton Road
Industria
Johannesburg, South Africa 2000
Phone: 27-11-470-3111
Fax: 27 -11-470-3123

Business Partners Centre
266 Govan Mbeki Avenue
Port Elizabeth, South Africa 6000
Phone: 27-41-582-1601
Fax: 27-41-585-2297

Business Partners Centre
60 Sir Lowry Road
Cape Town, South Africa 8000
Phone: 27-21-464-3600
Fax: 27-21-461-8720

Business Partners Centre
23 Jan Hofmeyr Road
Westville, South Africa 3630
Phone: 27-31-240-7700
Fax: 27-31-266-3600

Management and Staff
Ben Bierman, Chief Financial Officer
J. Schwenke, Managing Director
Kerry Hodgkinson, Partner
Paul Malherbe, Chief Operating Officer
Willem Bosch, Chief Operating Officer

Type of Firm
Private Equity Firm

Association Membership
South African Venture Capital Association (SAVCA)

Project Preferences

Type of Financing Preferred:
Leveraged Buyout
Early Stage
Expansion
Turnaround
Seed
Startup

Geographical Preferences

International Preferences:
South Africa

Additional Information
Year Founded: 1981
Current Activity Level : Actively seeking new investments

BUSINESS VENTURE PARTNERS

Unit 23, Cubes 2
Beacon South Qtr, Sandyford
Dublin, Ireland 18
Phone: 35316572900
Fax: 35316572930
E-mail: eii@bvp.ie
Website: www.bvp.ie

Management and Staff
David Gavagan, Founder
Elliott Griffin, Founder

Type of Firm
Investment Management Firm

Project Preferences

Type of Financing Preferred:
Seed
Startup

Geographical Preferences

International Preferences:
Ireland
Europe

Industry Preferences

In Computer Software prefer:
Software

In Industrial/Energy prefer:
Energy
Energy Conservation Relat

Additional Information
Year Founded: 2004
Current Activity Level : Actively seeking new investments

BUTLER CAPITAL PARTNERS SA

30 Cours Albert 1er
Paris, France 75008
Phone: 0033145615580
Fax: 0033145619794
E-mail: contact@butlercapitalpartners.com
Website: www.butlercapitalpartners.com

Management and Staff
Laurent Parquet, Partner
Lise Nobre, Partner
Marc-Eric Flory, Founder
Michel Vedrines, Partner
Pierre Costes, Partner

Type of Firm
Private Equity Firm

Association Membership
French Venture Capital Association (AFIC)

Project Preferences

Role in Financing:
Prefer role as deal originator

Type of Financing Preferred:
Leveraged Buyout
Turnaround
Special Situation
Distressed Debt

Size of Investments Considered:
Min Size of Investment Considered (000s): $13,243
Max Size of Investment Considered (000s): $66,216

Geographical Preferences

International Preferences:
Europe
Switzerland
Belgium
France

Industry Preferences

In Communications prefer:
Other Communication Prod.

In Computer Other prefer:
Computer Related

In Semiconductor/Electr prefer:
Electronics

In Medical/Health prefer:
Medical/Health

In Consumer Related prefer:
Consumer

In Business Serv. prefer:
Services

Additional Information
Name of Most Recent Fund: France Private Equity III
Most Recent Fund Was Raised: 07/01/2005
Year Founded: 1991
Capital Under Management: $662,200,000
Current Activity Level : Actively seeking new investments
Method of Compensation: Return on invest. most important, but chg. closing fees, service fees, etc.

BUTTERFLY VENTURES OY

WTC, Aleksanterinkatu 17
Helsinki, Finland 00100

Type of Firm
Private Equity Firm

Association Membership
Finnish Venture Capital Association (FVCA)

Project Preferences

Type of Financing Preferred:
Early Stage
Seed
Startup

Geographical Preferences

International Preferences:
Europe
Finland

Industry Preferences

In Communications prefer:
Media and Entertainment
Entertainment

In Computer Software prefer:
Applications Software

In Consumer Related prefer:
Consumer Products

In Industrial/Energy prefer:
Energy

Additional Information
Year Founded: 2014
Current Activity Level : Actively seeking new investments

BUYSSE & PARTNERS BVBA

3, Esmoreitlaan
Antwerp, Belgium 2050
Phone: 3235689391
Fax: 3234017185
Website: www.buysse-partners.com

Type of Firm
Private Equity Firm

Project Preferences

Type of Financing Preferred:
Leveraged Buyout
Management Buyouts
Acquisition

Additional Information

Year Founded: 2008
Current Activity Level : Actively seeking new investments

BV CAPITAL PARTNERS LUXEMBURG SA

9A Boulevard du Prince Henri
Luxembourg, Luxembourg L-1724
Phone: 32473578890
Fax: 352691201057

Type of Firm
Private Equity Firm

Project Preferences

Type of Financing Preferred:
Leveraged Buyout
Management Buyouts
Acquisition
Recapitalizations

Geographical Preferences

International Preferences:
Luxembourg
Netherlands
Belgium

Industry Preferences

In Biotechnology prefer:
Industrial Biotechnology

In Medical/Health prefer:
Health Services
Pharmaceuticals

In Consumer Related prefer:
Consumer Products

In Industrial/Energy prefer:
Industrial Products
Environmental Related

In Financial Services prefer:
Financial Services

Additional Information

Year Founded: 2003
Current Activity Level : Actively seeking new investments

BV HOLDING AG

Hofgut
Vordere Dorfgasse 12
Guemligen, Switzerland 3073
Phone: 0313801850
Fax: 0313801859
Website: www.bvgroup.ch

Type of Firm
Private Equity Firm

Association Membership
Swiss Venture Capital Association (SECA)

Project Preferences

Type of Financing Preferred:
Leveraged Buyout
Early Stage
Turnaround
Later Stage
Management Buyouts
Acquisition
Recapitalizations

Geographical Preferences

International Preferences:
Italy
Liechtenstein
Switzerland
Germany
France

Industry Preferences

In Communications prefer:
Telecommunications

In Computer Software prefer:
Data Processing

In Internet Specific prefer:
Internet

In Biotechnology prefer:
Biotechnology

In Medical/Health prefer:
Medical/Health
Pharmaceuticals

In Industrial/Energy prefer:
Industrial Products

In Business Serv. prefer:
Media

Additional Information

Year Founded: 2001
Capital Under Management: $31,700,000
Current Activity Level : Actively seeking new investments

BVM CAPITAL LLC

820 Garrett Drive
Bossier City, LA USA 71111
Phone: 3187468430
Fax: 3187463771
Website: www.bvmcap.com

Other Offices

29 Constitution Court
Tuxedo Park, NY USA 10987
Phone: 914-588-7200
Fax: 318-746-3771

201 St. Charles Avenue
Suite 3700
New Orleans, LA USA 70170
Phone: 504-569-7904
Fax: 504-569-7910

Management and Staff
Ross Barrett, Managing Partner

Type of Firm
Private Equity Firm

Project Preferences

Role in Financing:
Will function either as deal originator or investor in deals created by others

Type of Financing Preferred:
Early Stage
Expansion
Balanced

Size of Investments Considered:
Min Size of Investment Considered (000s): $250
Max Size of Investment Considered (000s): $3,000

Geographical Preferences

United States Preferences:
Southeast
Northeast
Louisiana
New York

Industry Preferences

In Biotechnology prefer:
Biotech Related Research

In Medical/Health prefer:
Health Services
Hospitals/Clinics/Primary

In Industrial/Energy prefer:
Energy

Additional Information

Name of Most Recent Fund: TVP, L.P.
Most Recent Fund Was Raised: 03/01/2006
Year Founded: 2004
Capital Under Management: $36,000,000
Current Activity Level : Actively seeking new investments
Method of Compensation: Return on investment is of primary concern, do not charge fees

BVP BERLIN VENTURE PARTNERS GMBH

An der Kieler Bruecke 21
Berlin, Germany 10115
E-mail: info@berlin-venture-partners.com
Website: www.berlin-venture-partners.com

Management and Staff
Arend Iven, Managing Director
Ron Hillmann, Managing Director

Type of Firm
Private Equity Firm

Project Preferences

Type of Financing Preferred:
Early Stage
Seed
Startup

Geographical Preferences

International Preferences:
Germany

Industry Preferences

In Internet Specific prefer:
Ecommerce

Additional Information
Year Founded: 2007
Current Activity Level : Actively seeking new investments

BVT HOLDING GMBH & CO KG

Leopoldstrasse Seven
Munich, Germany 80802
Phone: 4989381650
Fax: 498938165100
E-mail: info@bvt.de
Website: www.bvt.de

Management and Staff
Christian Duerr, Managing Director
Claus Gaertner, Managing Director
Harald Von Scharfenberg, Managing Director
Robert List, Managing Director
Tibor Von Wiedebach-Nostitz, Managing Director

Type of Firm
Private Equity Firm

Project Preferences

Type of Financing Preferred:
Fund of Funds
Fund of Funds of Second

Geographical Preferences

United States Preferences:
All U.S.

International Preferences:
Europe
All International

Additional Information
Year Founded: 1976
Capital Under Management: $7,200,000
Current Activity Level : Actively seeking new investments

BWK GMBH UNTERNEH-MENSBETEILIGUNGS-GESELLSCHAFT

Thouretstrasse 2
Stuttgart, Germany 70173
Phone: 497112255760
Fax: 4971122557610
E-mail: stuttgart@bwku.de
Website: www.bw-kap.de

Management and Staff
Armin Schuler, Managing Director
Jochen Wolf, Managing Director
Matthias Heining, Managing Director

Type of Firm
Private Equity Firm

Association Membership
German Venture Capital Association (BVK)

Project Preferences

Type of Financing Preferred:
Leveraged Buyout
Later Stage
Management Buyouts

Geographical Preferences

International Preferences:
Switzerland
Austria
Germany

Industry Preferences

In Semiconductor/Electr prefer:
Electronics

In Medical/Health prefer:
Medical/Health
Pharmaceuticals

In Industrial/Energy prefer:
Factory Automation
Machinery

In Transportation prefer:
Transportation

In Business Serv. prefer:
Services

Additional Information
Year Founded: 1990
Current Activity Level : Actively seeking new investments

BXR GROUP BV

Jachthavenweg 109h
1081 KM
Amsterdam, Netherlands
E-mail: amsterdam@bxrgroup.com
Website: www.bxrgroup.com

Type of Firm
Private Equity Firm

Project Preferences

Type of Financing Preferred:
Leveraged Buyout
Acquisition

Geographical Preferences

United States Preferences:
All U.S.

International Preferences:
Europe
Pacific
Asia
Africa

Industry Preferences

In Communications prefer:
Telecommunications

In Computer Other prefer:
Computer Related

In Medical/Health prefer:
Medical/Health

In Consumer Related prefer:
Retail
Publishing-Retail

In Industrial/Energy prefer:
Oil and Gas Exploration
Industrial Products
Environmental Related

In Transportation prefer:
Transportation
Aerospace

In Financial Services prefer:
Financial Services
Real Estate

In Business Serv. prefer:
Services
Media

In Manufact. prefer:
Manufacturing

In Agr/Forestr/Fish prefer:
Agriculture related
Mining and Minerals

Additional Information

Year Founded: 1969
Current Activity Level : Actively seeking new investments

BY CAPITAL MANAGEMENT GMBH

Zehdenicker Strasse 1
Berlin, Germany 10119
E-mail: team@blueyard.com

Type of Firm
Private Equity Firm

Project Preferences

Type of Financing Preferred:
Early Stage

Geographical Preferences

International Preferences:
Europe

Additional Information

Year Founded: 2016
Capital Under Management: $111,000,000
Current Activity Level : Actively seeking new investments

- C -

C & M CAPITAL AB OY

Vattuniemenkuja 4
Helsinki, Finland 00210
Phone: 35896822966
Fax: 35896822988
E-mail: info@cmcapital.fi
Website: www.cmcapital.fi

Management and Staff
Christian Kolster, Managing Director

Type of Firm
Private Equity Firm

Project Preferences

Type of Financing Preferred:
Early Stage
Seed
Startup

Geographical Preferences

United States Preferences:

Canadian Preferences:
All Canada

International Preferences:
Central Europe
Finland

Industry Preferences

In Communications prefer:
Commercial Communications

Additional Information

Year Founded: 1999
Current Activity Level : Actively seeking new investments

C3 CAPITAL LLC

1511 Baltimore Avenue, Suite 500
Kansas City, MO USA 64108
Phone: 8167562225
Fax: 8167565552
Website: www.c3cap.com

Other Offices

14646 Kierland Boulevard
Suite 145
Scottsdale, AZ USA 85254
Phone: 4803896955
Fax: 8167565552

2828 North Harwood Street
Suite 1700
Dallas, TX USA 75201
Phone: 2142922000
Fax: 2142922007

Management and Staff
A. Baron Cass, Co-Founder
Bradley Harrop, Vice President
Christopher Roden, Managing Director
D. Patrick Curran, Co-Founder
Jared Poland, Managing Director
Mikala January, Chief Financial Officer
Patrick Healy, Co-Founder
Robert Smith, Co-Founder
Steven Swartzman, Co-Founder

Type of Firm
SBIC

Association Membership
Natl Assoc of Small Bus. Inv. Co (NASBIC)

Project Preferences

Role in Financing:
Prefer role as deal originator

Type of Financing Preferred:
Leveraged Buyout
Expansion
Mezzanine
Acquisition
Recapitalizations

Geographical Preferences

United States Preferences:
Midwest
Southwest

Industry Preferences

In Industrial/Energy prefer:
Energy
Materials

In Business Serv. prefer:
Services
Distribution

In Manufact. prefer:
Manufacturing

Additional Information

Year Founded: 1994
Capital Under Management: $260,000,000
Current Activity Level : Actively seeking new investments
Method of Compensation: Return on invest. most important, but chg. closing fees, service fees, etc.

C4 VENTURES

9 Queens Gate Place Mews
London, United Kingdom SW7 5BG
Website: www.c4v.com

Type of Firm
Private Equity Firm

Project Preferences

Type of Financing Preferred:
Early Stage
Later Stage
Seed

Geographical Preferences

International Preferences:
Europe

Additional Information
Year Founded: 2015
Current Activity Level : Actively seeking new investments

CABOT SQUARE CAPITAL ADVISORS LTD

One Connaught Place
London, United Kingdom W2 2ET
Phone: 442075799320
Fax: 442075799330
E-mail: contact@cabotsquare.com
Website: www.cabotsquare.com

Management and Staff
Billie Chasty, Chief Financial Officer
Chris Sales, Partner
James Clark, Partner
John Van Deventer, Founder
Keith Maddin, Partner

Type of Firm
Private Equity Firm

Association Membership
British Venture Capital Association (BVCA)

Project Preferences

Type of Financing Preferred:
Leveraged Buyout
Early Stage
Expansion
Generalist PE
Turnaround
Seed
Acquisition
Startup
Distressed Debt

Geographical Preferences

International Preferences:
United Kingdom
Europe
Western Europe

Industry Preferences

In Financial Services prefer:
Financial Services
Financial Services

Additional Information
Year Founded: 1996
Capital Under Management: $300,000,000
Current Activity Level : Actively seeking new investments

CAC CAPITAL MANAGEMENT CO LTD

No.8, Kefa Road
4C, Block 1, Financial Base
Shenzhen, China
Phone: 867558622776
Fax: 8675586627769
E-mail: contact@cac-capital.com
Website: www.cac-capital.com

Management and Staff
Chuan Zhan, Partner
Jiping Sun, Partner
Ran Yang, Partner
Yantao Wang, Partner
Yongbing Chang, Partner
Yu Liu, Partner

Type of Firm
Private Equity Firm

Project Preferences

Type of Financing Preferred:
Early Stage
Expansion
Seed

Size of Investments Considered:
Min Size of Investment Considered (000s): $158
Max Size of Investment Considered (000s): $4,751

Geographical Preferences

International Preferences:
China

Industry Preferences

In Internet Specific prefer:
Internet

In Medical/Health prefer:
Medical Products
Pharmaceuticals

In Consumer Related prefer:
Consumer Products

In Industrial/Energy prefer:
Materials
Advanced Materials
Environmental Related

In Transportation prefer:
Transportation

In Business Serv. prefer:
Services
Media

In Manufact. prefer:
Manufacturing

Additional Information
Year Founded: 2004
Capital Under Management: $158,400,000
Current Activity Level : Actively seeking new investments

CADMUS ORGANISATION LTD

Suite G, Kings Business Centre
Reeds Lane, Sayers Common
Hassocks, W Sussex, United Kingdom BN6 9LS
Phone: 441732363341
Fax: 441273835466
E-mail: enquiries@cadmus.uk.com
Website: www.cadmus.uk.com

Type of Firm
Bank Affiliated

Association Membership
British Venture Capital Association (BVCA)

Project Preferences

Type of Financing Preferred:
Expansion
Mezzanine
Balanced
Management Buyouts
Acquisition
Startup

Geographical Preferences

International Preferences:
United Kingdom

Additional Information
Year Founded: 1989
Capital Under Management: $6,300,000
Current Activity Level : Actively seeking new investments

CADRON CREEK CAPITAL LLC

P.O. Box 15
Conway, AR USA 72033
E-mail: Info@CadronCreekCapital.com
Website: cadroncreekcapital.com

Type of Firm
Private Equity Firm

Project Preferences

Type of Financing Preferred:
Early Stage
Seed

Geographical Preferences

United States Preferences:
Arkansas

Additional Information
Year Founded: 2015
Capital Under Management: $1,520,000
Current Activity Level : Actively seeking new investments

CAERUS VENTURES LLC

1601 Forum Place
Suite 1010
West Palm Beach, FL USA 33401
Phone: 5618551595
Fax: 561684765
Website: www.caerusventures.com

Management and Staff
Brodi Jackson, Managing Director
Gregory Borchardt, Managing Director
James Holmes, Co-Founder
Zachary Cherry, Co-Founder

Type of Firm
Private Equity Firm

Project Preferences

Type of Financing Preferred:
Early Stage
Balanced
Later Stage
Seed

Size of Investments Considered:
Min Size of Investment Considered (000s): $100
Max Size of Investment Considered (000s): $2,000

Industry Preferences

In Communications prefer:
Media and Entertainment

In Computer Software prefer:
Software

In Medical/Health prefer:
Medical/Health

In Consumer Related prefer:
Consumer

In Industrial/Energy prefer:
Energy

In Manufact. prefer:
Manufacturing

Additional Information
Year Founded: 2014
Capital Under Management: $4,500,000
Current Activity Level : Actively seeking new investments

CAFFEINATED CAPITAL LLC

2969 Jackson Street
San Francisco, CA USA 94115
Website: www.caffcap.com

Type of Firm
Private Equity Firm

Additional Information
Year Founded: 2016
Current Activity Level : Actively seeking new investments

CAI CAPITAL MANAGEMENT CO

595 Burrard Street
Suite 2833, Bentall Three
Vancouver, Canada V7X 1K8
Phone: 6046373411
Fax: 6046942524
E-mail: info@caifunds.com
Website: www.caifunds.com

Other Offices
767 Fifth Avenue
Fifth Floor
NEW YORK, NY USA 10153
Phone: 212-319-2525
Fax: 212-319-0232

3450 rue Drummond
Suite 140
Montreal, Canada H3G 1Y2
Phone: 5148491642
Fax: 5148491788

1508A - 999 West Hastings Street
PO Box 46
Vancouver, Canada V6C 2W2
Phone: 604-694-2525
Fax: 604-694-2524

70 East 55th Street
19th Floor
MANHATTAN, NY USA 10022
Phone: 212-319-2525
Fax: 212-319-0232

Management and Staff
Curtis Johansson, Partner
Tracey McVicar, Managing Partner

Type of Firm
Private Equity Firm

Association Membership
Canadian Venture Capital Association

Project Preferences

Type of Financing Preferred:
Leveraged Buyout
Expansion
Management Buyouts
Acquisition
Recapitalizations

Geographical Preferences

United States Preferences:
North America

Canadian Preferences:
All Canada

Additional Information
Year Founded: 1989
Capital Under Management: $277,000,000
Current Activity Level : Actively seeking new investments
Method of Compensation: Return on invest. most important, but chg. closing fees, service fees, etc.

CAIRN MERCHANT PARTNERS LP

101 College Street
MaRS Centre for Innovation
Toronto, Canada M5G 1L7
Website: cairnmp.com

Type of Firm
Private Equity Firm

Project Preferences

Type of Financing Preferred:
Leveraged Buyout

Additional Information
Year Founded: 2015
Current Activity Level : Actively seeking new investments

CAIRNGORM CAPITAL LTD

22 Cross Keys Close
Third Floor
London, United Kingdom W1H 6HNW1U
Phone: 2079691408
Website: www.cairngormcapital.com

Type of Firm
Private Equity Firm

Project Preferences

Type of Financing Preferred:
Leveraged Buyout
Management Buyouts
Acquisition
Recapitalizations

Industry Preferences

In Consumer Related prefer:
Consumer

Additional Information
Year Founded: 2015
Capital Under Management: $210,750,000
Current Activity Level : Actively seeking new investments

CAISSE D'EPARGNE NORD FRANCE INVESTISSEMENT SAS

135, Pont des Flandres
Lille, France 59350

Type of Firm
Bank Affiliated

Project Preferences

Type of Financing Preferred:
Early Stage
Expansion
Later Stage
Seed

Geographical Preferences

International Preferences:
France

Additional Information
Year Founded: 2014
Current Activity Level : Actively seeking new investments

CAISSE REGIONALE DE CREDIT AGRICOLE MUTUEL SUD RHONE ALPES

15, rue Paul Claudel
Grenoble, France 38100
Phone: 33476867070
Fax: 33476867099
Website: www.ca-sudrhonealpes.fr

Management and Staff
Christian Rouchon, Chief Executive Officer
Emmanuel Barras, Chief Executive Officer
Eric Campos, Chief Executive Officer

Type of Firm
Bank Affiliated

Project Preferences

Type of Financing Preferred:
Early Stage
Startup

Geographical Preferences

International Preferences:
France

Additional Information
Year Founded: 1995
Current Activity Level : Actively seeking new investments

CAIXA CAPITAL BV

Rua Barata Salgueiro, n 33
Lisbon, Portugal 1269-057
Phone: 351213137300
Fax: 351213526327
E-mail: caixabi@caixabi.pt

Other Offices
Paseo de la Castellana, n.21 - 1izq
Madrid, Spain 28046
Phone: 34-91-745-0504
Fax: 34-91-563-9559

Type of Firm
Bank Affiliated

Association Membership
Portuguese Venture Capital Association (APCRI)
European Private Equity and Venture Capital Assoc.

Project Preferences

Type of Financing Preferred:
Leveraged Buyout
Early Stage
Generalist PE
Balanced
Later Stage
Acquisition

Size of Investments Considered:
Min Size of Investment Considered (000s): $200
Max Size of Investment Considered (000s): $200,000

Geographical Preferences

International Preferences:
Europe

Industry Preferences

In Medical/Health prefer:
Medical/Health

In Consumer Related prefer:
Consumer

In Industrial/Energy prefer:
Energy
Industrial Products

In Manufact. prefer:
Manufacturing

Additional Information
Year Founded: 1990
Capital Under Management: $316,700,000
Current Activity Level : Actively seeking new investments

CAIXA CAPITAL DESARROLLO SCR

Avenida Diagonal 621-629
Barcelona, Spain 08028
Phone: 34-934-046-000
Fax: 34-933-395-703

Type of Firm
Bank Affiliated

Project Preferences

Type of Financing Preferred:
Leveraged Buyout
Early Stage
Expansion
Acquisition

Geographical Preferences

International Preferences:
Europe
Spain

Additional Information
Year Founded: 1844
Current Activity Level : Actively seeking new investments

CAIXA CAPITAL RISC SGEIC SA

Avinguda Diagonal, 613
3a Planta - B
Barcelona, Spain 08028
Phone: 34934094060
Fax: 34933309727
E-mail: info@caixacapitalrisc.es
Website: www.caixacapitalrisc.es

Management and Staff
Marcelino Armenter, Chief Executive Officer

Type of Firm
Bank Affiliated

Association Membership
Spanish Venture Capital Association (ASCRI)

Project Preferences

Type of Financing Preferred:
Early Stage
Seed
Startup

Geographical Preferences

International Preferences:
Europe
Spain

Industry Preferences

In Communications prefer:
Wireless Communications

In Computer Hardware prefer:
Computer Graphics and Dig

In Computer Software prefer:
Software

In Internet Specific prefer:
Internet

In Semiconductor/Electr prefer:
Electronic Components

In Biotechnology prefer:
Biotechnology

In Medical/Health prefer:
Medical/Health
Medical Therapeutics

In Industrial/Energy prefer:
Oil and Gas Exploration
Oil & Gas Drilling,Explor
Materials
Environmental Related

Additional Information

Year Founded: 2004
Capital Under Management: $206,416,000
Current Activity Level : Actively seeking new investments

CAJA DE SEGUROS REUNIDOS COMPANIA DE SEGUROS Y REASEGUROS SA

109 Avenida de Burgos
Madrid, Spain 28050
Phone: 34-90-201-1111
Fax: 34-91-595-5496
E-mail: informacion@caser.es
Website: www.caser.es

Management and Staff
Antonio Garcia Ortiz, Chief Financial Officer

Type of Firm
Insurance Firm Affiliate

Project Preferences

Type of Financing Preferred:
Balanced
Management Buyouts

Geographical Preferences

International Preferences:
Spain

Additional Information
Year Founded: 2010
Capital Under Management: $57,315,000
Current Activity Level : Actively seeking new investments

CAJASTUR CAPITAL SCR DE REGIMEN SIMPLIFICADO SA

Calle San Francisco 14
Oviedo, Spain 33003

Type of Firm
Private Equity Firm

Project Preferences

Type of Financing Preferred:
Balanced

Geographical Preferences

International Preferences:
Spain

Additional Information
Year Founded: 2006
Current Activity Level : Actively seeking new investments

CALAO FINANCE SAS

10, rue de Copenhague
Paris, France 75008
Phone: 33144907070
Fax: 33144907071
E-mail: info@calaofinance.com
Website: www.calaofinance.com

Type of Firm
Private Equity Firm

Association Membership
French Venture Capital Association (AFIC)

Project Preferences

Type of Financing Preferred:
Leveraged Buyout
Early Stage
Expansion
Generalist PE
Later Stage
Seed
Acquisition

Geographical Preferences

International Preferences:
Europe
France

Industry Preferences

In Communications prefer:
Communications and Media
Commercial Communications
Telecommunications
Wireless Communications
Media and Entertainment
Other Communication Prod.

In Internet Specific prefer:
E-Commerce Technology

In Consumer Related prefer:
Consumer
Entertainment and Leisure
Sports
Consumer Products
Consumer Services

In Industrial/Energy prefer:
Energy

In Transportation prefer:
Aerospace

In Business Serv. prefer:
Services

Additional Information
Year Founded: 2011
Current Activity Level : Actively seeking new investments

CALCIUM CAPITAL PARTNERS SAS

125 avenue des Champs-Elysees
Paris, France 75008
Website: www.calciumcapital.com

Management and Staff
Jean-Luc Biamonti, Co-Founder

Type of Firm
Private Equity Firm

Project Preferences

Type of Financing Preferred:
Leveraged Buyout
Early Stage
Generalist PE
Later Stage
Acquisition

Geographical Preferences

International Preferences:
France

Additional Information
Year Founded: 2012
Current Activity Level : Actively seeking new investments

CALDERA VENTURE PARTNERS LLC

500 North Michigan Avenue
Suite 2030
Chicago, IL USA 60611
Phone: 3124108400
Fax: 3124107228
E-mail: info@calderainvestmentgroup.com
Website: www.calderainvestmentgroup.com

Management and Staff

Christopher Ziobehr, Managing Partner
Neal Goyal, Chief Executive Officer

Type of Firm

Private Equity Firm

Project Preferences

Type of Financing Preferred:
Seed
Startup

Industry Preferences

In Industrial/Energy prefer:
Alternative Energy

Additional Information

Year Founded: 2013
Current Activity Level : Actively seeking new investments

CALERA CAPITAL MANAGEMENT INC

580 California Street
Suite 2200
San Francisco, CA USA 94104
Phone: 4156325200
Fax: 4156325201
E-mail: inquiry@caleracapital.com
Website: www.caleracapital.com

Other Offices

800 Boylston Street
Suite 1460
Boston, MA USA 02199
Phone: 6175780790
Fax: 6175780077

Management and Staff

Andrew Holmes, Vice President
Benjamin Abadi, Principal
Brian Fearnow, Principal
Ethan Thurow, Principal
James Farrell, Co-Founder
James Halow, Managing Director
Mark Williamson, Managing Partner
Michael Moon, Managing Director
Paul Walsh, Senior Managing Director
Robert Jaunich, Co-Founder

Type of Firm

Private Equity Firm

Project Preferences

Role in Financing:
Prefer role as deal originator

Type of Financing Preferred:
Leveraged Buyout
Acquisition
Recapitalizations

Industry Focus

(% based on actual investment)
Other Products	33.6%
Medical/Health	20.3%
Internet Specific	18.7%
Semiconductors/Other Elect.	16.6%
Communications and Media	6.0%
Computer Software and Services	3.5%
Computer Hardware	1.3%

Additional Information

Year Founded: 1991
Capital Under Management: $2,800,000,000
Current Activity Level : Actively seeking new investments
Method of Compensation: Return on invest. most important, but chg. closing fees, service fees, etc.

CALGARY ENTERPRISES INC

Four Park Avenue
Suite 12G
New York, NY USA 10016
Phone: 2126830119
Fax: 2126833119
Website: www.calgaryenterprises.com

Management and Staff

Steven Insalaco, President

Type of Firm

Investment Management Firm

Project Preferences

Role in Financing:
Prefer role as deal originator

Type of Financing Preferred:
Leveraged Buyout
Management Buyouts
Recapitalizations

Size of Investments Considered:
Min Size of Investment Considered (000s): $5,000
Max Size of Investment Considered: No Limit

Geographical Preferences

United States Preferences:
All U.S.

Industry Preferences

In Business Serv. prefer:
Consulting Services

In Manufact. prefer:
Manufacturing

In Agr/Forestr/Fish prefer:
Mining and Minerals

Additional Information

Year Founded: 1988
Current Activity Level : Actively seeking new investments
Method of Compensation: Professional fee required whether or not deal closes

CALIBRATE MANAGEMENT LTD

60 Gresham Street
London, United Kingdom EC2V 7BB
Phone: 44 (0)20 3440 9
E-mail: info@calibrate-partners.com
Website: www.calibrate-partners.com

Management and Staff

John White, Partner
John Pryor, Partner
Natasha Freedman, Partner
Remy Kesrouani, Partner
Zaid Al-Qaimi, Partner

Type of Firm

Private Equity Firm

Project Preferences

Type of Financing Preferred:
Early Stage
Seed

Geographical Preferences

International Preferences:
United Kingdom

Additional Information

Year Founded: 2017
Current Activity Level : Actively seeking new investments

CALIBRATE VENTURES LP

130 West Union Street
Pasadena, CA USA 91103

Type of Firm

Private Equity Firm

Project Preferences

Type of Financing Preferred:
Early Stage

Industry Preferences

In Computer Software prefer:
Software

Additional Information

Year Founded: 2017
Current Activity Level : Actively seeking new investments

CALIBRIUM LTD

Churerstrasse 70
Pfaeffikon, Switzerland 8808
Phone: 41555111222
Website: www.clbrm.com

Management and Staff

Frank Muehlenbeck, Partner
George Rehm, Managing Partner
Uwe Feuersenger, Managing Director

Type of Firm

Private Equity Firm

Association Membership

Swiss Venture Capital Association (SECA)
European Private Equity and Venture Capital Assoc.

Project Preferences

Type of Financing Preferred:
Leveraged Buyout
Early Stage
Mezzanine
Turnaround
Later Stage
Seed
Startup

Size of Investments Considered:
Min Size of Investment Considered (000s): $1,323
Max Size of Investment Considered (000s): $66,129

Geographical Preferences

United States Preferences:
All U.S.

International Preferences:
Europe
Switzerland
Austria
Germany

Industry Preferences

In Computer Software prefer:
Software

In Internet Specific prefer:
Internet

In Computer Other prefer:
Computer Related

In Biotechnology prefer:
Biotechnology

In Medical/Health prefer:
Medical/Health

Additional Information

Year Founded: 2006
Capital Under Management: $9,000,000
Current Activity Level : Actively seeking new investments

CALIDANT CAPITAL LLC

1901 North Akard Street
Old Cumberland Hill School
Dallas, TX USA 75201
Phone: 2149971170
Website: www.calidantcapital.com

Management and Staff

David Lai, Managing Partner
Drew Bagot, Managing Partner

Type of Firm

Private Equity Firm

Project Preferences

Type of Financing Preferred:
Generalist PE

Industry Preferences

In Communications prefer:
Telecommunications

In Consumer Related prefer:
Consumer Products

In Industrial/Energy prefer:
Energy

In Business Serv. prefer:
Services
Media

Additional Information

Year Founded: 2009
Current Activity Level : Actively seeking new investments

CALIFORNIA TECHNOLOGY VENTURES LLC

670 North Rosemead Boulevard
Suite 201
Pasadena, CA USA 91107
Phone: 6263513700
Fax: 6263513702
E-mail: info@ctventures.com
Website: ctventures.com

Management and Staff

Alexander Suh, Founder
Dorothy Pavloff, Managing Director
William Hanna, Managing Director

Type of Firm

Private Equity Firm

Project Preferences

Role in Financing:
Will function either as deal originator or investor in deals created by others

Type of Financing Preferred:
Early Stage
Later Stage
Seed
Startup

Size of Investments Considered:
Min Size of Investment Considered (000s): $250
Max Size of Investment Considered (000s): $5,000

Industry Preferences

In Communications prefer:
Communications and Media
Telecommunications

In Computer Software prefer:
Software

In Internet Specific prefer:
Internet

In Computer Other prefer:
Computer Related

In Semiconductor/Electr prefer:
Electronics
Semiconductor

Additional Information

Year Founded: 2000
Capital Under Management: $150,000,000
Current Activity Level : Actively seeking new investments
Method of Compensation: Return on investment is of primary concern, do not charge fees

CALIFORNIA UNIVERSITY OF LAW & BUSINESS

1111 Franklin Street
Oakland, CA USA 94607
Phone: 510-642-6000
Website: www.universityofcalifornia.edu

Management and Staff

Marie Berggren, Managing Director

Type of Firm

Endowment, Foundation or Pension Fund

Project Preferences

Type of Financing Preferred:
Fund of Funds

Geographical Preferences

United States Preferences:

International Preferences:
All International

Additional Information
Year Founded: 2002
Current Activity Level : Actively seeking new investments

CALLISTA HOLDINGS GMBH & CO KG

Konrad-Zuse-Platz 8
Munich, Germany 81829
Phone: 4989207042430
Fax: 4989207042431
E-mail: info@callista-pe.de
Website: www.callista-pe.de

Management and Staff
Marc Zube, Chief Operating Officer
Olaf Meier, Chief Executive Officer

Type of Firm
Private Equity Firm

Project Preferences

Type of Financing Preferred:
Leveraged Buyout
Turnaround
Acquisition

Additional Information
Year Founded: 2013
Current Activity Level : Actively seeking new investments

CALTIUS EQUITY PARTNERS

11766 Wilshire Boulevard, Suite 850
Los Angeles, CA USA 90025
Phone: 3109969585
Fax: 3109969577
E-mail: info@caltius.com
Website: www.caltius.com

Management and Staff
Garrick Ahn, Managing Director
Gregory Brackett, Chief Financial Officer
Jeffrey Kendig, Vice President
Jeffrey Holdsberg, Managing Director
Michael Morgan, Managing Director

Type of Firm
Private Equity Firm

Project Preferences

Role in Financing:
Prefer role as deal originator but will also invest in deals created by others

Type of Financing Preferred:
Leveraged Buyout
Expansion
Balanced
Management Buyouts
Acquisition
Recapitalizations

Size of Investments Considered:
Min Size of Investment Considered (000s): $1,000
Max Size of Investment Considered (000s): $20,000

Geographical Preferences

United States Preferences:
All U.S.

Industry Focus
(% based on actual investment)
Medical/Health	29.1%
Industrial/Energy	28.1%
Other Products	15.0%
Semiconductors/Other Elect.	14.2%
Consumer Related	13.5%

Additional Information
Year Founded: 1998
Capital Under Management: $133,000,000
Current Activity Level : Actively seeking new investments

CALTIUS MEZZANINE

11766 Wilshire Boulevard
Suite 850
Los Angeles, CA USA 90025
Phone: 3109969585
Fax: 3109969577
E-mail: info@caltius.com
Website: www.caltius.com

Management and Staff
Alisa Frederick, Managing Director
Don Jamieson, Vice President
Gavin Bates, Principal
Greg Howorth, Managing Director
Gregory Brackett, Chief Financial Officer
Michael Kane, Managing Director
Rick Shuart, Principal

Type of Firm
Private Equity Firm

Project Preferences

Role in Financing:
Will function either as deal originator or investor in deals created by others

Type of Financing Preferred:
Leveraged Buyout
Mezzanine
Turnaround
Management Buyouts
Acquisition
Recapitalizations

Geographical Preferences

United States Preferences:
West Coast

Industry Focus
(% based on actual investment)
Other Products	54.4%
Consumer Related	20.3%
Medical/Health	7.6%
Industrial/Energy	6.4%
Internet Specific	6.2%
Semiconductors/Other Elect.	4.6%
Biotechnology	0.5%

Additional Information
Name of Most Recent Fund: Caltius Partners IV, L.P.
Most Recent Fund Was Raised: 05/12/2008
Year Founded: 1997
Capital Under Management: $1,000,000,000
Current Activity Level : Actively seeking new investments
Method of Compensation: Return on invest. most important, but chg. closing fees, service fees, etc.

CALUMET VENTURE FUND

1245 East Washington Avenue, Suite 210
Madison, WI USA 53703
Phone: 6083103242
Fax: 8883103989
Website: www.calumetvc.com

Management and Staff
Judy Owen, General Partner
Tim Williams, General Partner
Toni Sikes, General Partner

Type of Firm
Private Equity Firm

Project Preferences

Type of Financing Preferred:
Early Stage
Startup

Size of Investments Considered:
Min Size of Investment Considered (000s): $200
Max Size of Investment Considered (000s): $3,000

Geographical Preferences

United States Preferences:
Midwest
Illinois
Michigan
Wisconsin
Minnesota

Industry Preferences

In Communications prefer:
Wireless Communications

In Computer Software prefer:
Software
Applications Software

In Internet Specific prefer:
Internet
Ecommerce

Additional Information
Year Founded: 2008
Current Activity Level : Actively seeking new investments

CALVERT FUND

4550 Montgomery Avenue
Suite 1125 N
Bethesda, MD USA 20814
Phone: 3019614788
Fax: 3016571982
Website: www.calvert.com

Management and Staff
Kathy Torrence, Vice President
Ronald Wolfsheimer, Chief Financial Officer
Stan Young, Vice President

Type of Firm
Bank Affiliated

Project Preferences

Role in Financing:
Prefer role in deals created by others

Type of Financing Preferred:
Fund of Funds
Early Stage
Other
Fund of Funds of Second

Size of Investments Considered:
Min Size of Investment Considered (000s): $100
Max Size of Investment Considered (000s): $2,500

Geographical Preferences

United States Preferences:
Mid Atlantic

Industry Preferences

In Biotechnology prefer:
Human Biotechnology

In Medical/Health prefer:
Medical Diagnostics
Diagnostic Services
Diagnostic Test Products
Medical Therapeutics
Drug/Equipmt Delivery
Medical Products
Health Services
Pharmaceuticals

In Consumer Related prefer:
Education Related

In Industrial/Energy prefer:
Energy
Process Control

In Other prefer:
Socially Responsible
Environment Responsible
Women/Minority-Owned Bus.

Additional Information
Year Founded: 1976
Capital Under Management: $30,000,000
Current Activity Level : Actively seeking new investments
Method of Compensation: Return on investment is of primary concern, do not charge fees

CALVERT SOCIAL VENTURE PARTNERS, L.P.

402 Maple Avenue West
Vienna, VA USA 22180
Phone: 7032554930
Fax: 7032554931
Website: www.calvertventures.com

Management and Staff
John May, Managing Partner
Steve Moody, Principal

Type of Firm
Private Equity Firm

Project Preferences

Role in Financing:
Will function either as deal originator or investor in deals created by others

Type of Financing Preferred:
Early Stage

Size of Investments Considered:
Min Size of Investment Considered (000s): $250
Max Size of Investment Considered (000s): $1,000

Geographical Preferences

United States Preferences:

Industry Preferences

In Other prefer:
Socially Responsible
Environment Responsible

Additional Information
Name of Most Recent Fund: Calvert Social Venture Partners
Most Recent Fund Was Raised: 12/31/1989
Year Founded: 1989
Capital Under Management: $10,000,000
Current Activity Level : Making few, if any, new investments
Method of Compensation: Return on investment is of primary concern, do not charge fees

CALVERT STREET CAPITAL PARTNERS INC

111 South Calvert Street, Suite 1800
Baltimore, MD USA 21202
Phone: 4435733700
Fax: 4435733702
E-mail: cscp@cscp.com
Website: www.cscp.com

Management and Staff
Aidan Riordan, Partner
Brian Guerin, Principal
Brian Mahoney, Co-Founder
Joseph Hasse, Partner
Joshua Hall, Co-Founder
Michael Booth, Partner
Steven Axel, Managing Director

Type of Firm
Private Equity Firm

Association Membership
Natl Assoc of Small Bus. Inv. Co (NASBIC)

Project Preferences

Role in Financing:
Prefer role as deal originator

Type of Financing Preferred:
Leveraged Buyout
Mezzanine
Acquisition

Geographical Preferences

United States Preferences:

Canadian Preferences:
All Canada

Industry Focus
(% based on actual investment)
Industrial/Energy	26.2%
Computer Hardware	20.5%
Internet Specific	19.5%
Consumer Related	14.7%
Computer Software and Services	11.5%
Biotechnology	6.2%
Other Products	1.5%

Additional Information
Name of Most Recent Fund: Calvert Street Capital Partners III, L.P.
Most Recent Fund Was Raised: 05/24/2005
Year Founded: 1995
Capital Under Management: $500,000,000
Current Activity Level : Actively seeking new investments
Method of Compensation: Return on invest. most important, but chg. closing fees, service fees, etc.

CAMBRIAN VENTURE CAPITAL

Huaihai Middle Road 98
Building 5
Shanghai, China 200021
Website: www.cambrianvc.com

Type of Firm
Private Equity Firm

Project Preferences

Type of Financing Preferred:
Seed
Startup

Geographical Preferences

International Preferences:
China

Industry Preferences

In Communications prefer:
Media and Entertainment

In Consumer Related prefer:
Consumer
Education Related

Additional Information
Year Founded: 2016
Current Activity Level : Actively seeking new investments

CAMBRIAN VENTURES INC

1686 Second Street
Suite 217
Livermore, CA USA 94550
Phone: 6509385900
Fax: 6509385959
E-mail: info@cambrianventures.com
Website: www.cambrianventures.com

Management and Staff
Anand Rajaraman, Partner
Henry Huff, Chief Financial Officer
Venky Harinarayan, Partner

Type of Firm
Private Equity Firm

Project Preferences

Role in Financing:
Will function either as deal originator or investor in deals created by others

Type of Financing Preferred:
Early Stage
Seed

Geographical Preferences

United States Preferences:

Industry Preferences

In Communications prefer:
Wireless Communications

In Computer Software prefer:
Software

In Internet Specific prefer:
Internet

Additional Information
Year Founded: 2000
Current Activity Level : Actively seeking new investments

CAMBRIDGE CAPITAL LLC

525 South Flagler Drive
Suite 200
West Palm Beach, FL USA 33401
Phone: 5619321601
Fax: 5616556232
E-mail: info@CambridgeCapital.com
Website: www.cambridgecapital.com

Management and Staff
Benjamin Gordon, Managing Partner

Type of Firm
Private Equity Firm

Project Preferences

Type of Financing Preferred:
Leveraged Buyout
Expansion
Balanced
Management Buyouts
Acquisition

Industry Preferences

In Industrial/Energy prefer:
Energy

In Business Serv. prefer:
Services
Distribution

Additional Information
Year Founded: 2009
Current Activity Level : Actively seeking new investments

CAMBRIDGE CAPITAL PARTNERS L L C

321 North Clark Street, Suite 1425
Chicago, IL USA 60654
Phone: 312-245-8920
Fax: 312-245-8930
E-mail: info@caldercapital.com
Website: www.caldercapital.com

Other Offices
520 Madison Avenue
27th Floor
New York, NY USA 10022
Phone: 212-822-7832
Fax: 212-822-7801

Fifth Floor, Star Tower
Yeoksam-Dong 737 Gangnam-Gu
Seoul, South Korea 150-010
Phone: 82-2-2112-1777
Fax: 82-2-2112-1778

Management and Staff
Bradley Morrow, Partner
Douglas Kitani, Partner
Joon Tae Yoo, Vice President
Michael Chorpash, Chief Financial Officer

Type of Firm
Private Equity Advisor or Fund of Funds

Project Preferences

Role in Financing:
Prefer role as deal originator but will also invest in deals created by others

Type of Financing Preferred:
Fund of Funds

Size of Investments Considered:
Min Size of Investment Considered (000s): $3,000
Max Size of Investment Considered (000s): $20,000

Geographical Preferences

United States Preferences:

International Preferences:
Europe
Asia
Korea, South

Industry Focus
(% based on actual investment)
   Other Products   100.0%

Additional Information
Year Founded: 2001
Capital Under Management: $100,000,000
Current Activity Level : Actively seeking new investments
Method of Compensation: Return on invest. most important, but chg. closing fees, service fees, etc.

CAMBRIDGE COMPANIES SPG LLC

660 Newport Center Drive
Suite 710
Newport Beach, CA USA 92660
Phone: 8886156166
E-mail: info@cambridgecompanies.us
Website: www.cambridgespg.com

Management and Staff
David Bartholomew, Managing Partner
David Patton, Managing Partner
Polina Chebotareva, Partner

Type of Firm
Private Equity Firm

Project Preferences

Type of Financing Preferred:
Value-Add
Early Stage
Later Stage
Seed
Acquisition

Geographical Preferences

United States Preferences:
All U.S.

Industry Preferences

In Financial Services prefer:
Real Estate

Additional Information
Year Founded: 2016
Current Activity Level : Actively seeking new investments

CAMBRIDGE INNOVATION CAPITAL

Three Charles Babbage Road
Hauser Forum
Cambridge, United Kingdom CB3 0GT
Phone: 4401223764875
Website: www.cambridgeinnovationcapital.com

Type of Firm
University Program

Project Preferences

Type of Financing Preferred:
Balanced
Later Stage
Seed

Geographical Preferences

International Preferences:
United Kingdom

Industry Preferences

In Computer Other prefer:
Computer Related

Additional Information
Year Founded: 2013
Capital Under Management: $98,540,000
Current Activity Level : Actively seeking new investments

CAMCO PRIVATE EQUITY GROUP

Four Farm Street
Rosebery House
London, United Kingdom W1J 5RD
E-mail: ah@camco.ch
Website: www.camco.ch

Management and Staff
Kevin Gould, Chief Operating Officer

Type of Firm
Private Equity Firm

Project Preferences

Type of Financing Preferred:
Leveraged Buyout
Acquisition

Industry Preferences

In Communications prefer:
Communications and Media

In Internet Specific prefer:
Internet
Ecommerce

In Consumer Related prefer:
Consumer Products

In Industrial/Energy prefer:
Oil and Gas Exploration
Alternative Energy

In Transportation prefer:
Transportation
Aerospace

In Financial Services prefer:
Financial Services
Real Estate

In Business Serv. prefer:
Services

In Manufact. prefer:
Manufacturing

Additional Information
Year Founded: 1969
Current Activity Level : Actively seeking new investments

CAMDEN PARTNERS HOLDINGS LLC

500 East Pratt Street
Suite 1200
Baltimore, MD USA 21202
Phone: 4108786800
Fax: 4108786850
E-mail: info@camdenpartners.com
Website: www.camdenpartners.com

Management and Staff
Christopher Kersey, Partner
Donald Hughes, Chief Operating Officer
J. Todd Sherman, Chief Financial Officer
Meghan McGuire, Principal
Patricia Woodward, Vice President
Richard Berkeley, Venture Partner

Type of Firm
Private Equity Firm

Project Preferences

Role in Financing:
Will function either as deal originator or investor in deals created by others

Type of Financing Preferred:
Fund of Funds
Leveraged Buyout
Early Stage
Expansion
Balanced
Later Stage
Acquisition
Recapitalizations

Geographical Preferences

United States Preferences:
All U.S.

International Preferences:
Europe

Industry Focus
(% based on actual investment)

Medical/Health	29.8%
Computer Software and Services	28.9%
Consumer Related	12.3%
Internet Specific	10.3%
Computer Hardware	9.1%
Other Products	8.4%
Biotechnology	1.2%
Communications and Media	0.1%

Additional Information
Name of Most Recent Fund: Camden Partners Strategic Fund V, L.P.
Most Recent Fund Was Raised: 09/19/2013
Year Founded: 1995
Capital Under Management: $525,000,000
Current Activity Level : Actively seeking new investments
Method of Compensation: Return on investment is of primary concern, do not charge fees

---

CAMELOT CAPITAL CORP

84 Winchester Street
Ontario, Canada M4X 1B2
Phone: 416-922-9172
Fax: 416-922-3189

Type of Firm
Private Equity Firm

Additional Information
Year Founded: 2009
Current Activity Level : Actively seeking new investments

CAMINO REAL CAPITAL PARTNERS LLC

128 Grant Avenue Suite 104
Santa Fe, NM USA 87501
Phone: 14326837200
E-mail: info@caminorealcap.com
Website: www.caminorealcap.com

Type of Firm
Private Equity Firm

Association Membership
Natl Assoc of Investment Cos. (NAIC)
Natl Assoc of Small Bus. Inv. Co (NASBIC)

Project Preferences

Type of Financing Preferred:
Startup

Geographical Preferences

United States Preferences:

Industry Preferences

In Medical/Health prefer:
Medical/Health

In Industrial/Energy prefer:
Energy

Additional Information
Year Founded: 1969
Current Activity Level : Actively seeking new investments

CAMP ONE VENTURES LLC

2501 20th Place South
Suite 275
Birmingham, AL USA 35223
Phone: 2052632332
Website: www.camponeventures.com

Management and Staff
J. Rainer Twiford, Principal
Madding King, Principal
Robert Claassen, Principal

Type of Firm
Private Equity Firm

Project Preferences

Type of Financing Preferred:
Early Stage

Geographical Preferences

United States Preferences:
Alabama
California

Industry Preferences

In Computer Software prefer:
Software

In Financial Services prefer:
Financial Services

In Business Serv. prefer:
Media

Additional Information
Name of Most Recent Fund: Camp One Ventures LLC
Most Recent Fund Was Raised: 05/31/2012
Year Founded: 2012
Capital Under Management: $1,150,000
Current Activity Level : Actively seeking new investments

CAMPBELL RESOURCES INC

1155, University
Suite 1405
Montreal, Canada H3B 3A7
Phone: 514-875-9033
Fax: 514-875-9764

Other Offices
1155, University
Suite 1405
Montreal, Canada
Phone: 514-875-9033
Fax: 514-875-9764

Management and Staff
Alain Blais, Vice President

Type of Firm
Private Equity Firm

Additional Information
Year Founded: 1950
Current Activity Level : Actively seeking new investments

CAMPFIRE CAPITAL

2580 Vine Street
Vancouver, Canada V6K 3L1
E-mail: contact@campfire-capital.com
Website: www.campfire-capital.com

Type of Firm
Private Equity Firm

Project Preferences

Type of Financing Preferred:
Startup

Geographical Preferences

United States Preferences:
North America

Industry Preferences

In Consumer Related prefer:
Consumer
Retail

Additional Information
Year Founded: 2014
Capital Under Management: $31,290,000
Current Activity Level : Actively seeking new investments

CAMPUS EVOLUTION INCUBATOR LLC

520 Eigth Avenue
New York, NY USA 10018
Website: www.company-x.com

Type of Firm
Incubator/Development Program

Project Preferences

Type of Financing Preferred:
Early Stage

Additional Information
Year Founded: 2013
Current Activity Level : Actively seeking new investments

CAMPVENTURES

280 Second Street, Suite 280
Los Altos, CA USA 94022
Phone: 6509490804
Fax: 6506181719

Management and Staff
Jerome Camp, General Partner
Kevin Negus, Venture Partner

Type of Firm
Private Equity Firm

Project Preferences

Type of Financing Preferred:
Seed

Size of Investments Considered:
Min Size of Investment Considered (000s): $500
Max Size of Investment Considered (000s): $1,500

Geographical Preferences

United States Preferences:

Additional Information
Name of Most Recent Fund: CampVentures III (Q), L.P.
Most Recent Fund Was Raised: 03/11/2009
Year Founded: 1997
Capital Under Management: $8,500,000
Current Activity Level : Actively seeking new investments

CAMWOOD CAPITAL GROUP LLC

2600 Via Fortuna Drive, Suite 420
Austin, TX USA 78746
E-mail: businesssolutions@camwoodcapitalgroup.com

Type of Firm
Private Equity Firm

Project Preferences

Type of Financing Preferred:
Leveraged Buyout
Acquisition

Geographical Preferences

United States Preferences:
North America

Additional Information
Year Founded: 2013
Current Activity Level : Actively seeking new investments

CANAAN PARTNERS

2765 Sand Hill Road, Suite 115
Menlo Park, CA USA 94025
Phone: 6508548092
Fax: 6508548127
Website: www.canaan.com

Other Offices
11 HaMenofim Street, Ackerstein Towers
Building B, Floor 10
Hertzliya Pituach, Israel 46120
Phone: 972-9-972-6858
Fax: 972-9-972-6859

508 Time
Mehrauli Gurgaon Road
Gurgaon, India 122001
Phone: 911244301841
Fax: 91-124-430-1850

95 Fifth Avenue, Fifth Floor
MANHATTAN, NY USA 10003
Phone: 6465967216

Management and Staff
Brendan Dickinson, Partner
Brenton Ahrens, General Partner
Colleen Feriod, Principal
Daniel Ciporin, General Partner
Deepak Kamra, General Partner
Eric Young, Co-Founder
Guy Russo, Chief Financial Officer
Hrach Simonian, General Partner
Izhar Shay, General Partner
John Balen, General Partner
Joydeep Bhattacharyya, Partner
Julie Papanek, Partner
Maha Ibrahim, General Partner
Michael Gilroy, Principal
Nina Kjellson, General Partner
Richard Boyle, Partner
Stephen Bloch, General Partner
Timothy Shannon, General Partner
Warren Lee, General Partner
Wende Hutton, General Partner

Type of Firm
Private Equity Firm

Association Membership
Israel Venture Association
Western Association of Venture Capitalists (WAVC)
National Venture Capital Association - USA (NVCA)
Indian Venture Capital Association (IVCA)

Project Preferences

Role in Financing:
Prefer role as deal originator but will also invest in deals created by others

Type of Financing Preferred:
Early Stage
Mezzanine
Balanced
Later Stage
Seed
Startup
Distressed Debt

Size of Investments Considered:
Min Size of Investment Considered (000s): $5,000
Max Size of Investment Considered (000s): $20,000

Geographical Preferences

United States Preferences:
Northeast
West Coast

International Preferences:
India
Israel
Asia

Industry Focus
(% based on actual investment)

Internet Specific	27.1%
Computer Software and Services	23.7%
Medical/Health	15.2%
Biotechnology	14.3%
Communications and Media	7.3%
Other Products	3.6%
Semiconductors/Other Elect.	3.5%
Computer Hardware	2.9%
Consumer Related	1.5%
Industrial/Energy	0.9%

Additional Information
Name of Most Recent Fund: Canaan IX, L.P.
Most Recent Fund Was Raised: 01/06/2012
Year Founded: 1987
Capital Under Management: $3,500,000,000
Current Activity Level : Actively seeking new investments

Method of Compensation: Return on investment is of primary concern, do not charge fees

CANACCORD GENUITY GROUP INC

609 Granville Street
Suite 2200, Pacific Centre
Vancouver, Canada V7Y 1H2
Phone: 6046437300
E-mail: contact@canaccordgenuity.com
Website: www.canaccordgenuity.com

Other Offices
350 Madison Avenue
New York, NY USA 10017
Phone: 212893000

161 Bay Street
Suite 3000, Brookfield Place
Toronto, Canada M5J 2S1
Phone: 416-869-7368
Fax: 416-869-7356

99 High Street
Suite 1200
Boston, MA USA 02110
Phone: 617-371-3900

535 Madison Avenue
Second Floor
New York, NY USA 10022
Phone: 2128493900

45, Seventh Street South
Suite 2640
Minneapolis, MN USA 55402
Phone: 6133322208

450, First Street Southwest
Suite 2200, TransCanada Tower
Calgary, Canada T2P 5P8
Phone: 4035083800

1880 Oak Avenue
Suite 135
Evanston, IL USA 60201
Phone: 8478641137

1250 Rene Levesque Blvd West
Suite 2000
Montreal, Canada H3B 4W8
Phone: 514-844-5443
Fax: 514-844-5216

1000 Louisiana Street
71st Floor, Wells Fargo Plaza
Houston, TX USA 77002
Phone: 7133319901

101 Montgomery Street
Suite 2000
San Francisco, CA USA 94104
Phone: 415-229-7171

Management and Staff
Arthur Gordon, Managing Director
David Morrison, Managing Director
John Esteireiro, Managing Director
Marcus Freeman, Managing Director
Mark Young, Managing Director
Rupert Woolfenden, Managing Director

Type of Firm
Private Equity Firm

Additional Information
Year Founded: 1992
Current Activity Level: Actively seeking new investments

CANADA PENSION PLAN INVESTMENT BOARD

One Queen Street East
Suite 2500, P.O. Box 101
Toronto, Canada M5C 2W5
Phone: 4168684075
Fax: 4168688689
E-mail: pac@cppib.ca
Website: www.cppib.com

Other Offices
33 Cavendish Square
7th Floor
London, United Kingdom W1G 0PW
Phone: 442032053500
Fax: 442032053420

15 Queen's Road Central
11/F York House, The Landmark
Central, Hong Kong
Phone: 85239738788
Fax: 85239738710

Three North Avenue, Maker Maxity
Fifth Floor
Mumbai, India 400051
Phone: 912261514400

Management and Staff
Alain Carrier, Senior Managing Director
Alain Bergeron, Vice President
Barry Rowland, Vice President
Cheryl Swan, Vice President
Chris Roper, Vice President
Chris Hawman, Vice President
Deborah Orida, Managing Director
Edwin Cass, Vice President
Geoffrey Rubin, Vice President
Graeme Eadie, Senior Managing Director
Jim Fasano, Vice President
Jimmy Phua, Vice President
Kevin Cunningham, Vice President
Martin Healey, Vice President
Patrice Walch-Watson, Senior Managing Director
Paul Mullins, Vice President
Pierre Lavallee, Senior Managing Director
Poul Winslow, Vice President
Rob Spindler, Vice President
Ryan Selwood, Managing Director
Scott Lawrence, Vice President
Shane Feeney, Senior Managing Director
Susan Bellingham, Vice President
Suyi Kim, Managing Director
Wenzel Hoberg, Managing Director

Type of Firm
Endowment, Foundation or Pension Fund

Association Membership
China Venture Capital Association
Canadian Venture Capital Association
European Private Equity and Venture Capital Assoc.

Project Preferences

Type of Financing Preferred:
Fund of Funds
Leveraged Buyout
Generalist PE
Later Stage
Management Buyouts
Acquisition
Fund of Funds of Second
Recapitalizations

Geographical Preferences

United States Preferences:
North America

Canadian Preferences:
All Canada

Industry Preferences

In Industrial/Energy prefer:
Oil and Gas Exploration
Alternative Energy

Additional Information
Year Founded: 1996
Current Activity Level: Actively seeking new investments

CANAL HOLDINGS LLC

1737 Georgetown Road
Suite A
Hudson, OH USA 44236
Phone: 3306506684
E-mail: info@canalholdings.us
Website: canalmezz.com

Management and Staff
Kevin Coyne, Founder

Type of Firm
Private Equity Firm

Project Preferences

Type of Financing Preferred:
Leveraged Buyout
Expansion
Mezzanine
Acquisition
Recapitalizations

Geographical Preferences

United States Preferences:
Midwest

Industry Preferences

In Medical/Health prefer:
Health Services

In Consumer Related prefer:
Consumer Products

In Financial Services prefer:
Financial Services

Additional Information
Name of Most Recent Fund: Canal Mezzanine Partners II, L.P.
Most Recent Fund Was Raised: 11/17/2011
Year Founded: 2005
Capital Under Management: $25,250,000
Current Activity Level: Actively seeking new investments

CANAL PARTNERS LLC

7114 East Stetson
Drive 360
Scottsdale, AZ USA 85251
Phone: 4802640238
Website: canalpartners.com

Management and Staff
Jim Armstrong, Managing Partner
Todd Belfer, Managing Partner

Type of Firm
Private Equity Firm

Project Preferences

Type of Financing Preferred:
Leveraged Buyout

Industry Preferences

In Computer Software prefer:
Software

In Internet Specific prefer:
Internet

Additional Information
Year Founded: 2008
Current Activity Level: Actively seeking new investments

CANBANK VENTURE CAPITAL FUND LTD

No. 14, M.G. Road
Sixth Floor Naveen Complex
Bangalore, India 560 001
Phone: 918025586506
Fax: 918025583909
E-mail: info@canbankventure.com
Website: www.canbankventure.com

Other Offices
P.O. Box 174, Longbow House
14/20 Chiswell St.
London, United Kingdom EC1Y4TW
Phone: 0171-628-2187
Fax: 0171-374-2468

Management and Staff
R Rajee, Vice President
S. Thiruvadi, Managing Director

Type of Firm
Bank Affiliated

Association Membership
Indian Venture Capital Association (IVCA)

Project Preferences

Role in Financing:
Prefer role as deal originator but will also invest in deals created by others

Type of Financing Preferred:
Early Stage
Expansion
Mezzanine
Balanced
Later Stage
Startup

Size of Investments Considered:
Min Size of Investment Considered (000s): $21
Max Size of Investment Considered (000s): $42

Geographical Preferences

International Preferences:
India

Industry Preferences

In Communications prefer:
Communications and Media
Telecommunications
Satellite Microwave Comm.

In Computer Software prefer:
Software

In Computer Other prefer:
Computer Related

In Semiconductor/Electr prefer:
Electronics
Semiconductor

In Biotechnology prefer:
Biotechnology
Industrial Biotechnology

In Medical/Health prefer:
Medical Diagnostics
Medical Therapeutics
Health Services
Pharmaceuticals

In Consumer Related prefer:
Consumer

In Industrial/Energy prefer:
Energy
Alternative Energy
Industrial Products
Materials
Factory Automation
Environmental Related

In Business Serv. prefer:
Distribution

In Manufact. prefer:
Manufacturing

Additional Information
Year Founded: 1989
Capital Under Management: $100,000
Current Activity Level : Actively seeking new investments
Method of Compensation: Return on invest. most important, but chg. closing fees, service fees, etc.

CANDESCENT PARTNERS LLC

Two Oliver Street
Tenth Floor
Boston, MA USA 02109
Website: www.candescentpartners.com

Management and Staff
Alexander McGrath, Managing Partner
Stephen Sahlman, Principal
Stephen Jenks, Managing Partner

Type of Firm
Private Equity Firm

Project Preferences

Type of Financing Preferred:
Leveraged Buyout
Expansion
Mezzanine
Recapitalizations

Industry Preferences

In Communications prefer:
Communications and Media

In Computer Software prefer:
Software

In Medical/Health prefer:
Medical/Health

In Consumer Related prefer:
Consumer Products
Consumer Services

In Financial Services prefer:
Financial Services

Additional Information
Year Founded: 2009
Current Activity Level : Actively seeking new investments

CANDOVER INVESTMENTS PLC

34 Lime Street
London, United Kingdom EC3M 7AT
Phone: 442074899848
E-mail: info@candover.com
Website: www.candoverinvestments.com

Other Offices
Via Boito 8
Milan, Italy 20121
Phone: 39-02-854-650
Fax: 39-02-7209-5679

Ste 1701, 17F, One Ex. Square
8 Connaught Place
Hong Kong, Hong Kong
Phone: 852-3665-1300
Fax: 852-2537-3990

Jorge Juan 15-1 Izq
Madrid, Spain 28001
Phone: 34-91-432-2497
Fax: 34-91-435-7043

4 Rond Point Des Champs-Elyses
Paris, France 75008
Phone: 33-1-5836-4350
Fax: 33-1-5836-4361

Rm 209, Taj Mahal Palace And Towers
Apollo Bunder
Mumbai, India 400 001
Phone: 91-22-6606-5555

Management and Staff
Charlie Green, Managing Director
Ian Gray, Managing Director
Javier Abad, Partner
Johnathan Arney, Managing Partner
Malcolm Fallen, Chief Executive Officer
Mark Dickinson, Partner
Nils Stoesser, Partner
Oliver Stratton, Managing Director
Simon Leefe, Partner

Type of Firm
Private Equity Firm

Association Membership
British Venture Capital Association (BVCA)

Project Preferences

Role in Financing:
Prefer role as deal originator

Type of Financing Preferred:
Leveraged Buyout
Management Buyouts
Acquisition

Geographical Preferences

International Preferences:
Europe

Industry Focus

(% based on actual investment)
Other Products	46.1%
Consumer Related	26.8%
Industrial/Energy	11.8%
Biotechnology	8.0%
Communications and Media	4.0%
Internet Specific	1.2%
Semiconductors/Other Elect.	1.1%
Computer Software and Services	0.6%
Medical/Health	0.3%
Computer Hardware	0.1%

Additional Information
Name of Most Recent Fund: Candover 1997 Fund
Most Recent Fund Was Raised: 01/22/1998
Year Founded: 1980
Capital Under Management: $13,017,400,000
Current Activity Level : Reducing investment activity
Method of Compensation: Return on invest. most important, but chg. closing fees, service fees, etc.

CANE INVESTMENT PARTNERS LLC

30 North LaSalle Street
17th Floor
Chicago, IL USA 60602
Phone: 8477457200
E-mail: info@caneip.com
Website: caneip.com

Management and Staff
Eli Davis, Managing Partner
Yaakov Spinrad, Venture Partner

Type of Firm
Private Equity Firm

Project Preferences

Type of Financing Preferred:
Early Stage

Industry Preferences

In Medical/Health prefer:
Health Services

In Industrial/Energy prefer:
Energy

In Financial Services prefer:
Financial Services
Real Estate

In Business Serv. prefer:
Services

Additional Information
Year Founded: 2014
Current Activity Level : Actively seeking new investments

CANNABIS GROWTH FUND I LP

2345 Bay Street
Unit 900
Toronto, Canada M3S 1B3
Phone: 9054445555
E-mail: info@thekushfund.com
Website: thekushfund.com

Type of Firm
Private Equity Firm

Additional Information
Year Founded: 2017
Current Activity Level : Actively seeking new investments

CANNON CAPITAL GP INC

161 Worcester Road
Suite 606
Framingham, MA USA 01701
Phone: 7747775276
E-mail: admin@cannon.pe
Website: www.cannon.pe

Type of Firm
Private Equity Firm

Project Preferences

Type of Financing Preferred:
Leveraged Buyout

Geographical Preferences

United States Preferences:
North America

Additional Information
Year Founded: 2016
Current Activity Level : Actively seeking new investments

CANOPYCENTRAL LLC

3269 28th Street
Suite 200
Boulder, CO USA 80301
Phone: 3035864745
Website: www.canopyboulder.com

Type of Firm
Incubator/Development Program

Project Preferences

Type of Financing Preferred:
Seed

Industry Preferences

In Medical/Health prefer:
Medical/Health

Additional Information
Year Founded: 2015
Capital Under Management: $1,200,000
Current Activity Level : Actively seeking new investments

CANSBRIDGE CAPITAL CORP

725-625 Howe Street
Vancouver, Canada V6C 2T6
Phone: 604-684-8368
Fax: 604-684-9369
Website: www.cansbridge.com

Other Offices
725-625 Howe Street
Vancouver, Canada V6C 2T6
Phone: 604-684-8368
Fax: 604-684-9369

Management and Staff
Diana Liu, Partner
William Yu, Partner

Type of Firm
Private Equity Firm

Additional Information
Year Founded: 1999
Current Activity Level : Actively seeking new investments

CANTER CAPITAL MANAGEMENT LLC

655 West Broadway
Suite 1650
San Diego, CA USA 92101
Phone: 6195460973
Fax: 6197956638
E-mail: info@cantercapital.com
Website: cantercapital.com

Pratt's Guide to Private Equity & Venture Capital Sources

Type of Firm
Private Equity Firm

Project Preferences

Type of Financing Preferred:
Balanced
Seed
Startup

Geographical Preferences

United States Preferences:

Industry Preferences

In Communications prefer:
Wireless Communications

In Industrial/Energy prefer:
Alternative Energy

In Business Serv. prefer:
Media

Additional Information
Year Founded: 1969
Current Activity Level : Actively seeking new investments

CANTON VENTURE CAPITAL CO LTD

11/F Metro Plaza
183 North Tianhe Road
Guangzhou, China 510075
Phone: 86-20-8755-6020
Fax: 86-20-8755-6023
E-mail: cvcc@c-vcc.com
Website: www.c-vcc.com

Management and Staff
HongHong Zheng, Chief Financial Officer

Type of Firm
Private Equity Firm

Project Preferences

Type of Financing Preferred:
Balanced
Later Stage
Seed
Startup

Geographical Preferences

International Preferences:
China

Industry Preferences

In Communications prefer:
Telecommunications

In Computer Software prefer:
Systems Software

In Internet Specific prefer:
Internet

In Biotechnology prefer:
Biotechnology

In Agr/Forestr/Fish prefer:
Agriculture related
Mining and Minerals

Additional Information
Year Founded: 1999
Capital Under Management: $75,000,000
Current Activity Level : Actively seeking new investments

CANTOR VENTURES

499 Park Avenue
New York, NY USA 10022
Phone: 2129385000

Other Offices
110 East, 59th Street
NEW YORK, NY USA 10022

Management and Staff
Douglas Barnard, Chief Financial Officer
Douglas Barnard, Chief Financial Officer
Laurence Rose, Senior Managing Director
Lori Pennay, Senior Managing Director
Michael Lehrman, Managing Director
Noel Kimmel, Senior Managing Director
Stephen Merkel, Managing Director
Steven Kantor, Managing Director
Thomas Anzalone, Senior Managing Director

Type of Firm
Private Equity Firm

Project Preferences

Type of Financing Preferred:
Opportunistic
Later Stage

Geographical Preferences

International Preferences:
Ireland

Industry Preferences

In Internet Specific prefer:
Ecommerce

In Financial Services prefer:
Real Estate

In Business Serv. prefer:
Services

Additional Information
Year Founded: 1945
Current Activity Level : Actively seeking new investments

CANVAS VENTURE FUND

2710 Sand Hill Road
Suite 100
Portola Valley, CA USA 94028
Phone: 6503887600
Fax: 6503887601
Website: www.canvas.vc

Other Offices
3200 Alpine Road
LADERA, CA USA 94028
Phone: 650887600

Management and Staff
Ben Narasin, Partner
Ching Wu, Partner
Gary Little, Partner
Paul Hsiao, Partner
Rebecca Lynn, Partner

Type of Firm
Private Equity Firm

Association Membership
National Venture Capital Association - USA (NVCA)

Project Preferences

Type of Financing Preferred:
Early Stage

Size of Investments Considered:
Min Size of Investment Considered (000s): $5,000
Max Size of Investment Considered (000s): $15,000

Geographical Preferences

United States Preferences:

Industry Preferences

In Computer Software prefer:
Software

Additional Information
Name of Most Recent Fund: Canvas Venture Fund, L.P.
Most Recent Fund Was Raised: 08/31/2013
Year Founded: 2013
Capital Under Management: $475,000,000
Current Activity Level : Actively seeking new investments

CANYON BRIDGE CAPITAL PARTNERS INC

228 Hamilton Avenue
Third Floor
Palo Alto, CA USA 94301
Phone: 4084561999
Website: canyonbridge.com

Type of Firm
Private Equity Firm

Project Preferences

Type of Financing Preferred:
Leveraged Buyout

Additional Information

Year Founded: 2016
Current Activity Level : Actively seeking new investments

CANYON CAPITAL ADVISORS LLC

2000 Avenue of the Stars
11th Floor
Los Angeles, CA USA 90067
Phone: 3102721000
Fax: 3102721997
E-mail: rcbe@canyonpartners.com
Website: www.canyonpartners.com

Other Offices

152 West 57th Street
25th Floor
New York, NY USA 10019
Phone: 212-314-1600
Fax: 212-314-1601

139 Piccadilly
First Floor
London, United Kingdom W1J 7NU
Phone: 44-20-7659-6800
Fax: 44-20-7629-2250

Management and Staff

Allen Ba, Partner
Chris Heine, Partner
Desmond Lynch, Partner
Dominique Mielle, Partner
George Jikovski, Partner
John Simpson, Chief Operating Officer
John Plaga, Chief Financial Officer
Joshua Friedman, Founding Partner
Mitchell Julis, Founding Partner
Patrick Dooley, Managing Director
Soon Pho, Partner
Todd Lemkin, Partner

Type of Firm

Private Equity Firm

Project Preferences

Type of Financing Preferred:
Mezzanine
Balanced
Distressed Debt

Additional Information

Year Founded: 1990
Capital Under Management: $3,500,000,000
Current Activity Level : Actively seeking new investments

CANYON HEALTHCARE PARTNERS LLC

4 Canyon Road
Ross, CA USA 94957
Phone: 4152658673
Website: www.canyonhcpartners.com

Type of Firm

Private Equity Firm

Project Preferences

Type of Financing Preferred:
Balanced

Industry Preferences

In Medical/Health prefer:
Health Services

Additional Information

Year Founded: 2017
Current Activity Level : Actively seeking new investments

CAP CREATION SARL

25 Chemin Des 3 Cypres
Aix-en-Provence, France
Phone: 33442527809
Fax: 33442527775
Website: www.ca-alpesprovence.fr

Type of Firm

Bank Affiliated

Project Preferences

Type of Financing Preferred:
Early Stage
Later Stage

Geographical Preferences

International Preferences:
Europe
France

Additional Information

Year Founded: 2005
Current Activity Level : Actively seeking new investments

CAP DECISIF MANAGEMENT SAS

45, rue Boissiere
Paris, France 75016
Phone: 33175000100
Fax: 33175000115
Website: www.cap-decisif.com

Management and Staff

Olivier Dubuisson, General Partner
Patrice Mesnier, Chief Operating Officer

Type of Firm

Private Equity Firm

Association Membership

French Venture Capital Association (AFIC)

Project Preferences

Type of Financing Preferred:
Early Stage
Later Stage
Startup

Size of Investments Considered:
Min Size of Investment Considered (000s): $120
Max Size of Investment Considered (000s): $6,510

Geographical Preferences

International Preferences:
Europe
Eastern Europe
France

Industry Preferences

In Communications prefer:
Commercial Communications

In Semiconductor/Electr prefer:
Electronics
Electronic Components

In Biotechnology prefer:
Biotechnology

In Industrial/Energy prefer:
Energy
Environmental Related

In Other prefer:
Environment Responsible

Additional Information

Name of Most Recent Fund: CapDecisif 3 FPCI
Most Recent Fund Was Raised: 01/28/2013
Year Founded: 2001
Capital Under Management: $121,000,000
Current Activity Level : Actively seeking new investments

CAPAGRO SAS

11 rue de Monceau
Paris, France 75008
Website: capagro.fr

Type of Firm

Private Equity Firm

Project Preferences

Type of Financing Preferred:
Early Stage
Later Stage

Geographical Preferences

International Preferences:
Europe
France

Industry Preferences

In Industrial/Energy prefer:
Alternative Energy
Industrial Products
Environmental Related

In Business Serv. prefer:
Services

In Agr/Forestr/Fish prefer:
Agribusiness
Agriculture related

In Other prefer:
Environment Responsible

Additional Information
Year Founded: 2014
Capital Under Management: $146,920,000
Current Activity Level : Actively seeking new investments

CAPALEPH ADVISORS INDIA PVT LTD

206, Prestige Omega,Whitefield
104 EPIP Zone, 2nd Floor
Bangalore, India 560066
Phone: 918032559698
E-mail: response@capaleph.com
Website: www.capaleph.com

Management and Staff
George Thomas, Managing Director

Type of Firm
Private Equity Firm

Project Preferences

Type of Financing Preferred:
Early Stage
Expansion
Balanced
Later Stage

Geographical Preferences

International Preferences:
Asia Pacific
India

Industry Preferences

In Medical/Health prefer:
Health Services

In Consumer Related prefer:
Consumer
Food/Beverage
Education Related

In Agr/Forestr/Fish prefer:
Agribusiness
Agriculture related

Additional Information
Year Founded: 2011
Current Activity Level : Actively seeking new investments

CAPATRIA SASU

Five-Seven, Rue De Monttessuy
Paris, France 75007
Phone: 33158194581
Fax: 33158192641
E-mail: atria@atria-partenaires.com
Website: www.atria-partenaires.com

Management and Staff
Dominique Oger, Partner
Patrick Bertiaux, Partner

Type of Firm
Private Equity Firm

Association Membership
French Venture Capital Association (AFIC)

Project Preferences

Type of Financing Preferred:
Leveraged Buyout
Early Stage
Later Stage
Management Buyouts
Startup

Geographical Preferences

International Preferences:
Europe
France

Additional Information
Year Founded: 1998
Capital Under Management: $783,400,000
Current Activity Level : Actively seeking new investments

CAPCELLENCE MITTELSTANDSPARTNER GMBH

Caffamacherreihe 7
Hamburg, Germany 20355
Phone: 494030700700
Fax: 494030700777
E-mail: info@CAPCELLENCE.com
Website: www.capcellence.com

Management and Staff
Holger Schragmann, Managing Partner
Jens Biermann, Partner
Matthias Feistel, Partner
Peter Karnitschnig, Partner
Spyros Chaveles, Managing Partner
Sven Goik, Partner
Thomas Meissner, Partner

Type of Firm
Private Equity Firm

Project Preferences

Type of Financing Preferred:
Leveraged Buyout
Later Stage
Management Buyouts
Acquisition

Geographical Preferences

International Preferences:
Switzerland
Austria
Germany

Industry Preferences

In Industrial/Energy prefer:
Energy
Industrial Products
Machinery

In Business Serv. prefer:
Services

Additional Information
Year Founded: 1971
Capital Under Management: $22,500,000
Current Activity Level : Actively seeking new investments

CAPE KAURI PARTNERS LLC

2711 Centerville Road
Suite 400
Wilmington, DE USA 19808

Type of Firm
Private Equity Firm

Additional Information
Year Founded: 2015
Current Activity Level : Actively seeking new investments

CAPELIA SAS

1, Rue des Rivieres
Lyon, France 69009
Phone: 33489851034
Website: www.capelia.net

Type of Firm
Private Equity Firm

Project Preferences

Type of Financing Preferred:
Leveraged Buyout
Early Stage
Expansion
Later Stage
Management Buyouts
Acquisition

Size of Investments Considered:
Min Size of Investment Considered (000s): $1,173
Max Size of Investment Considered (000s): $5,867

Additional Information
Year Founded: 2008
Current Activity Level: Actively seeking new investments

CAPGEN FINANCIAL GROUP LP

1185 Avenue of the Americas
Suite 2000
New York, NY USA 10036
Phone: 2125426868
Fax: 2125426879
Website: www.capgen.com

Management and Staff
Eugene Ludwig, Founder
John Sullivan, Managing Director
John Rose, Principal
Robert Merlino, Vice President
Robert Goldstein, Principal

Type of Firm
Private Equity Firm

Project Preferences

Type of Financing Preferred:
Leveraged Buyout
Expansion
Management Buyouts
Recapitalizations

Industry Preferences

In Financial Services prefer:
Financial Services

Additional Information
Year Founded: 2009
Current Activity Level: Actively seeking new investments

CAPHORN INVEST SAS

32 Avenue de l'Opera
Paris, France 75002
Website: www.caphorninvest.fr

Type of Firm
Private Equity Firm

Association Membership
French Venture Capital Association (AFIC)

Project Preferences

Type of Financing Preferred:
Early Stage
Expansion
Later Stage

Size of Investments Considered:
Min Size of Investment Considered (000s): $559
Max Size of Investment Considered (000s): $4,473

Geographical Preferences

International Preferences:
Europe
Eastern Europe
France

Industry Preferences

In Communications prefer:
Wireless Communications

In Computer Software prefer:
Software

In Internet Specific prefer:
Internet

In Other prefer:
Environment Responsible

Additional Information
Year Founded: 2010
Capital Under Management: $141,870,000
Current Activity Level: Actively seeking new investments

CAPI VENTURE

No.7 Hou Yuan En Si Lane
Jiaodaokou
Beijing, China
Phone: 86-10-8401-6277

Type of Firm
Private Equity Firm

Association Membership
Venture Capital Association of Beijing (VCAB)

Project Preferences

Type of Financing Preferred:
Balanced

Geographical Preferences

International Preferences:
China

Additional Information
Year Founded: 1998
Current Activity Level: Actively seeking new investments

CAPIDEA MANAGEMENT APS

Store Kongensgade 118 1 th
Copenhagen K, Denmark 1264
Phone: 4533386800
Fax: 4533386819
E-mail: info@capidea.dk
Website: www.capidea.dk

Management and Staff
Erik Balleby Jensen, Chief Executive Officer
Jens Thoger Hansen, Partner
Nicolai Jungersen, Partner

Type of Firm
Private Equity Firm

Association Membership
Danish Venture Capital Association (DVCA)

Project Preferences

Type of Financing Preferred:
Research and Development
Acquisition

Geographical Preferences

International Preferences:
Sweden
Denmark

Industry Preferences

In Consumer Related prefer:
Consumer Products

In Manufact. prefer:
Manufacturing

Additional Information
Name of Most Recent Fund: Capidea Kapital II
Most Recent Fund Was Raised: 03/05/2012
Year Founded: 2006
Capital Under Management: $270,900,000
Current Activity Level: Actively seeking new investments

CAPITAL BENOIT INC

1155 Metcalfe
Suite 1115
Montreal, Canada H3B2V6
Phone: 514-398-0960
Fax: 514-398-0962

Management and Staff
Bernard Deschamps, Vice President

Type of Firm
Private Equity Firm

Project Preferences

Type of Financing Preferred:
Leveraged Buyout
Expansion
Acquisition

Additional Information
Year Founded: 1970
Current Activity Level : Actively seeking new investments

CAPITAL BIDCO INC

6512 Centurion Drive
Suite 300
Lansing, MI USA 48917
Phone: 5173237772
Fax: 5173231999

Type of Firm
Private Equity Firm

Additional Information
Year Founded: 1993
Current Activity Level : Actively seeking new investments

CAPITAL CONNECT VENTURE PARTNERS AKES

Six Pontou Street
Kifisia, Greece 14563
Phone: 302106254063
Fax: 302106254763
E-mail: info@capitalconnect.gr
Website: www.capitalconnect.gr

Management and Staff
Mathios Rigas, Managing Director

Type of Firm
Private Equity Firm

Project Preferences

Type of Financing Preferred:
Early Stage
Startup

Size of Investments Considered:
Min Size of Investment Considered (000s): $1,322
Max Size of Investment Considered (000s): $3,967

Geographical Preferences

International Preferences:
Greece

Industry Preferences

In Communications prefer:
Communications and Media

In Computer Software prefer:
Software

In Computer Other prefer:
Computer Related

In Semiconductor/Electr prefer:
Electronics

In Biotechnology prefer:
Biotechnology

In Medical/Health prefer:
Medical/Health

In Industrial/Energy prefer:
Industrial Products

Additional Information
Name of Most Recent Fund: Capital Connect Venture Partners
Most Recent Fund Was Raised: 05/29/2003
Year Founded: 2003
Capital Under Management: $30,400,000
Current Activity Level : Actively seeking new investments

CAPITAL CRIATIVO SCR SA

Rua Alexandre Herculano 23
3rd, Frente
Lisbon, Portugal 1250008
Phone: 351213569800
Fax: 351213569809
E-mail: geral@capitalcriativo.com

Management and Staff
Alfredo Duarte Casimiro, Partner
Pedro Esteves de Carvalho, Partner
Tiago Vieira, Partner

Type of Firm
Private Equity Firm

Association Membership
Portuguese Venture Capital Association (APCRI)

Project Preferences

Type of Financing Preferred:
Expansion
Generalist PE
Management Buyouts

Geographical Preferences

International Preferences:
Portugal

Industry Preferences

In Communications prefer:
Communications and Media

In Computer Software prefer:
Software

In Internet Specific prefer:
Internet

In Business Serv. prefer:
Services

Additional Information
Year Founded: 2009
Capital Under Management: $104,583,000
Current Activity Level : Actively seeking new investments

CAPITAL CROISSANCE SAS

114, rue La Boetie
Paris, France 75008
Phone: 33180400410
Website: capitalcroissance.fr

Management and Staff
Eric Neuplanche, President, Founder
Regis Lamarche, Managing Partner

Type of Firm
Private Equity Firm

Association Membership
French Venture Capital Association (AFIC)

Project Preferences

Type of Financing Preferred:
Leveraged Buyout
Generalist PE
Later Stage
Management Buyouts
Acquisition

Size of Investments Considered:
Min Size of Investment Considered (000s): $1,112
Max Size of Investment Considered (000s): $11,120

Geographical Preferences

International Preferences:
Europe
France

Industry Preferences

In Internet Specific prefer:
E-Commerce Technology

In Consumer Related prefer:
Entertainment and Leisure

In Business Serv. prefer:
Services
Distribution

Additional Information
Name of Most Recent Fund: Cairn Capital I FCPR
Most Recent Fund Was Raised: 12/07/2012
Year Founded: 2010
Capital Under Management: $40,239,000
Current Activity Level : Actively seeking new investments

CAPITAL DYNAMICS SCA

2 Boulevard Konrad Adenauer
Luxembourg, Luxembourg L 1115
Phone: 2127983400

Type of Firm
Private Equity Firm

Project Preferences

Type of Financing Preferred:
Generalist PE

Geographical Preferences

International Preferences:
Europe
Eastern Europe

Additional Information
Year Founded: 2009
Capital Under Management: $77,000,000
Current Activity Level : Actively seeking new investments

CAPITAL DYNAMICS SDN BHD

Bahnhofstrasse 22
Zug, Switzerland 6301
Phone: 41417488444
Fax: 41417488440
E-mail: info@capdyn.com
Website: www.capitaldynamics.biz

Other Offices

2550 Sand Hill Road
Suite 150
Menlo Park, CA USA 94025
Phone: 650-388-7000
Fax: 650-388-7099

Av. Niemeyer 2,
Sala 102
Rio de Janeiro, Brazil 22450-220
Phone: 55-21-352-15010

Selnaustrasse 32
Zurich, Switzerland 8001
Phone: 41-41-748-8444
Fax: 41-41-748-8440

Possartstrasse 13
Munich, Germany 81679
Phone: 49-89-2000-4180
Fax: 49-89-200-041-899

21 Sackville Street
First Floor
London, United Kingdom W1S 3DN
Phone: 44-20-7297-0200
Fax: 44-20-7297-0299

1-5-1 Otemachi, Chiyoda-ku
East Tower, 4F, Otemachi First Square
Tokyo, Japan 100-0004
Phone: 81-3-5219-1358

645 Madison Avenue
19th Floor
New York, NY USA 10022
Phone: 212-798-3400
Fax: 212-798-3499

Spear Tower
One Market Street, 36th Floor
San Francisco, CA USA 94105
Phone: 415-243-4100
Fax: 415-293-8417

9 Colmore Row
Birmingham, United Kingdom B3 2BJ
Phone: 44-121-200-8800
Fax: 44-121-200-8899

16/F Nexxus Building
41 Connaught Road, Central
Hong Kong, Hong Kong
Phone: 852-3757-9818
Fax: 852-37579401

Management and Staff
Andrew Beaton, Managing Director
Anna Gredenhoff, Vice President
Anne Pearce, Vice President
Cynthia Duda, Managing Director
David Scaysbrook, Managing Director
David Reed, Vice President
David Smith, Managing Director
Elena Baly, Vice President
Emma Anderson, Chief Financial Officer
Ivan Herger, Managing Director
Janusz Heath, Managing Director
Joanne Southall, Vice President
John Gripton, Managing Director
Joseph Marks, Managing Director
Karl Olsoni, Managing Director
Kazushige Kobayashi, Managing Director
Manjia Guan, Vice President
Mark Drugan, Managing Director
Markus Ableitinger, Managing Director
Oliver Schumann, Managing Director
Richard Lyons, Vice President
Richard Grauel, Vice President
Rinat Yogev, Vice President
Rory Quinlan, Managing Director
Stefan Ammann, CEO & Managing Director
Timothy Chow, Vice President
Traci Pham, Vice President
Urs Rieder, Managing Director
Vanessa Buesser, Vice President
Warwick McDonald, Vice President

Type of Firm
Private Equity Firm

Association Membership
British Venture Capital Association (BVCA)
Emerging Markets Private Equity Association
Swiss Venture Capital Association (SECA)
European Private Equity and Venture Capital Assoc.

Project Preferences

Type of Financing Preferred:
Fund of Funds
Core
Leveraged Buyout
Early Stage
Expansion
Later Stage
Other
Seed
Management Buyouts
Fund of Funds of Second

Geographical Preferences

United States Preferences:
All U.S.

International Preferences:
Europe
Taiwan
Hong Kong
Western Europe
Australia
New Zealand
Asia
Singapore
Japan

Industry Preferences

In Industrial/Energy prefer:
Energy
Alternative Energy
Energy Conservation Relat
Environmental Related

In Financial Services prefer:
Real Estate

In Other prefer:
Environment Responsible

Additional Information
Name of Most Recent Fund: Capital Dynamics Clean Energy & Infrastructure, L.P.
Most Recent Fund Was Raised: 11/26/2013
Year Founded: 1988
Capital Under Management: $20,000,000,000
Current Activity Level : Actively seeking new investments

CAPITAL E GROUP

598 Madison Avenue
Ninth Floor
New York, NY USA 10022
Phone: 2127523566
Fax: 2123196551
Website: www.capitalegroup.com

Management and Staff
Anna Miller, Vice President
Charles Bastin, Managing Director
Patrick Hoogendijk, Chief Financial Officer

Type of Firm
Private Equity Advisor or Fund of Funds

Additional Information
Year Founded: 2003
Current Activity Level : Actively seeking new investments

CAPITAL ET DIRIGEANTS PARTENAIRES SARL

20, rue de Caumartin NGE
Paris, France 75009
Website: www.capital-dirigeants.com

Type of Firm
Private Equity Firm

Project Preferences

Type of Financing Preferred:
Leveraged Buyout
Early Stage
Expansion
Later Stage
Seed
Management Buyouts
Acquisition

Size of Investments Considered:
Min Size of Investment Considered (000s): $340
Max Size of Investment Considered (000s): $3,404

Geographical Preferences

International Preferences:
Europe
France

Additional Information
Year Founded: 2005
Current Activity Level : Actively seeking new investments

CAPITAL EXPORT SAS

28, Rue De Londres
Paris, France 75009
Phone: 33178423578
Website: www.capital-export.fr

Management and Staff
Jean de Puybaudet, Partner
Jean-Mathieu Sahy, Chief Executive Officer
Marc Hoffmeister, Partner

Type of Firm
Private Equity Firm

Association Membership
French Venture Capital Association (AFIC)

Project Preferences

Type of Financing Preferred:
Leveraged Buyout
Acquisition
Recapitalizations

Geographical Preferences

United States Preferences:
All U.S.

International Preferences:
Latin America
Europe
China
Middle East
Asia
Africa
France

Industry Preferences

In Medical/Health prefer:
Medical/Health

In Consumer Related prefer:
Food/Beverage
Consumer Products
Consumer Services

In Industrial/Energy prefer:
Industrial Products

In Business Serv. prefer:
Services

Additional Information
Year Founded: 2011
Current Activity Level : Actively seeking new investments

CAPITAL FACTORY PROPERTIES LLC

701 Brazos Street
Suite 500
Austin, TX USA 78701
Phone: 5126921881
Website: capitalfactory.com

Management and Staff
Georgia Thomsen, Managing Director

Type of Firm
Incubator/Development Program

Project Preferences

Type of Financing Preferred:
Seed
Startup

Additional Information
Year Founded: 2012
Capital Under Management: $2,700,000
Current Activity Level : Actively seeking new investments

CAPITAL FOR BUSINESS INC

Eleven South Meramec Street
Suite 1430
Clayton, MO USA 63105
Phone: 3147467427
E-mail: info@capitalforbusiness.com

Other Offices
1000 Walnut Street
18th Floor
Kansas City, MO USA 64106
Phone: 816-234-2375
Fax: 816-234-2952

Management and Staff
Paul Novak, Vice President
Stephen Broun, Managing Partner

Type of Firm
Investment Management Firm

Association Membership
Natl Assoc of Small Bus. Inv. Co (NASBIC)

Project Preferences

Role in Financing:
Will function either as deal originator or investor in deals created by others

Type of Financing Preferred:
Leveraged Buyout
Expansion
Generalist PE
Later Stage
Management Buyouts
Recapitalizations

Geographical Preferences

United States Preferences:
North America

Industry Focus

(% based on actual investment)

Industry	%
Industrial/Energy	34.0%
Other Products	25.6%
Medical/Health	12.8%
Internet Specific	7.5%
Communications and Media	5.7%
Consumer Related	4.6%
Semiconductors/Other Elect.	4.3%
Computer Hardware	3.2%
Biotechnology	2.3%

Additional Information
Name of Most Recent Fund: CFB Venture Fund III
Most Recent Fund Was Raised: 08/01/2001
Year Founded: 1959
Capital Under Management: $100,000,000
Current Activity Level : Actively seeking new investments
Method of Compensation: Return on investment is of primary concern, do not charge fees

CAPITAL FOR ENTERPRISE LTD

One Broadfield Close
Broadfield Business Park
Sheffield, South Yorkshire, United Kingdom S8 0XN
Phone: 441142062131
Fax: 441142062146
E-mail: info@capitalforenterprise.gov.uk
Website: www.capitalforenterprise.gov.uk

Management and Staff

David Campbell, Chief Financial Officer
Judith Ozcan, Managing Director
Ken Cooper, Managing Director
Richard Hepper, Chief Executive Officer
Rory Earley, Chief Executive Officer

Type of Firm

Private Equity Advisor or Fund of Funds

Association Membership

British Venture Capital Association (BVCA)

Project Preferences

Type of Financing Preferred:
Fund of Funds
Expansion

Size of Investments Considered:
Min Size of Investment Considered (000s): $131
Max Size of Investment Considered (000s): $2,637

Geographical Preferences

International Preferences:
Europe

Additional Information

Year Founded: 2008
Capital Under Management: $109,700,000
Current Activity Level : Actively seeking new investments

CAPITAL FOR FOUNDERS LLC

4845 Pearl East Circle
Suite 101
Boulder, CO USA 80301
Phone: 3039916170
E-mail: info@capitalforfounders.com
Website: capitalforfounders.com

Type of Firm

Private Equity Firm

Geographical Preferences

United States Preferences:

Industry Preferences

In Communications prefer:
Wireless Communications

In Computer Software prefer:
Software

In Transportation prefer:
Aerospace

In Manufact. prefer:
Manufacturing

Additional Information

Year Founded: 2013
Current Activity Level : Actively seeking new investments

CAPITAL GRAND EST SAS

9, Blvd Gonthier d'Andernach
Parc D'Innovation
Illkirch-Graffenstaden, France 67400
Phone: 33367106102
Fax: 33388431138
Website: alsacecapital.eu

Management and Staff

Jean-Lin Berge, President

Type of Firm

Private Equity Firm

Association Membership

French Venture Capital Association (AFIC)

Project Preferences

Type of Financing Preferred:
Leveraged Buyout
Early Stage
Generalist PE
Later Stage
Acquisition
Recapitalizations

Size of Investments Considered:
Min Size of Investment Considered (000s): $1,360
Max Size of Investment Considered (000s): $4,081

Geographical Preferences

International Preferences:
Europe
Switzerland
Germany
France

Industry Preferences

In Medical/Health prefer:
Medical/Health

In Industrial/Energy prefer:
Energy

Additional Information

Year Founded: 2011
Capital Under Management: $116,480,000
Current Activity Level : Actively seeking new investments

CAPITAL INDIGO

Guillermo Gonzalez Camarena
1450 Piso 2 Oficina D1
Santa Fe, Mexico 01210
Phone: 525511050861
E-mail: info@capitalindigo.mx
Website: www.capitalindigo.mx

Type of Firm

Private Equity Firm

Project Preferences

Type of Financing Preferred:
Mezzanine

Geographical Preferences

International Preferences:
Mexico

Additional Information

Year Founded: 1969
Current Activity Level : Actively seeking new investments

CAPITAL INNOVATORS LLC

611 Olive Street
Suite 1206
Saint Louis, MO USA 63101
Website: capitalinnovators.com

Management and Staff

Hal Gentry, Managing Partner
Judy Sindecuse, Chief Executive Officer

Type of Firm

Incubator/Development Program

Project Preferences

Type of Financing Preferred:
Seed
Startup

Geographical Preferences

United States Preferences:
Missouri

Additional Information

Year Founded: 2011
Current Activity Level : Actively seeking new investments

CAPITAL INTERNATIONAL INC

333 South Hope Street
53rd Floor
Los Angeles, CA USA 90071
Phone: 2134869200
Fax: 2134869035
Website: www.thecapitalgroup.com

Other Offices

181 Bay Street
Suite 3730, Brookfield Place
Toronto, Canada M5J 2T3

1230 Peachtree Street N.E.
Suite 3800, Promenade II
ATLANTA, GA USA 30309

Steuart Tower, 1 Market Street
Suite 2000
SAN FRANCISCO, CA USA 94105

630 Fifth Avenue,
36th Floor
NEW YORK, NY USA 10111

3500 Wiseman Boulevard
SAN ANTONIO, TX USA 78251

10 South Dearborn Street
25th floor
CHICAGO, IL USA 60603

5300 Robin Hood Road
NORFOLK, VA USA 23513

50 W. Liberty Street
Suite 650
RENO, NV USA 89501

2-1-1, Marunouchi, Chiyoda-ku
Meiji Yasuda Life Building, 14th floor
Tokyo, Japan 100-0005

3000 K Street N.W.
Suite 230, Washington Harbour
WASHINGTON, DC USA 20007

One Harbour View Street
2601 One International Finance Center
Hong Kong, Hong Kong
Phone: 852-2842-1000
Fax: 852-2810-6788

12811 N. Meridian Street
CARMEL, IN USA 46032

3rd floor, Unit 2 Vibgyor Tower
Block G, Plot C62
Mumbai, India 400051

40 Grosvenor Place
London, United Kingdom SW1X 7GG
Phone: 44-20-7864-5000
Fax: 44-20-7864-5773

440 Royal Palm Way
Suite 202
PALM BEACH, FL USA 33480

14636 N. Scottsdale Road
SCOTTSDALE, AZ USA 85254

No. 1 Jianguomenwai Avenue
Suite 3601, 36F, China World Tower
Beijing, China 100004

6455 Irvine Center Drive
IRVINE, CA USA 92618

Spring Street
Level 01, Suite 07/08
Sydney, Australia 2000

Three Place des Bergues
Geneva, Sweden 1201
Phone: 41-22-807-4000
Fax: 41-22-807-4001

Management and Staff

Anuj Girotra, Principal
Ashley Dunster, Managing Partner
Christian Skaanild, Partner
Guilherme Lins, Partner
Ian Cameron, Founder
Irina Grigorenko, Principal
James Ho, Partner
James McGuigan, Managing Partner
Koenraad Foulon, Managing Partner
Leandro Cuccioli, Principal
Leonard Kim, Managing Partner
Martin Diaz Plata, Partner
Nick Chen, Partner
Paul-Jeroen Van de Grampel, Principal
Umur Hursever, Principal
William Bannister-Parker, Managing Partner

Type of Firm
Private Equity Firm

Project Preferences

Type of Financing Preferred:
Generalist PE

Geographical Preferences

International Preferences:
All International

Industry Focus
(% based on actual investment)

Computer Software and Services	22.5%
Other Products	21.8%
Consumer Related	20.2%
Communications and Media	17.2%
Industrial/Energy	12.9%
Biotechnology	3.0%
Internet Specific	2.3%

Additional Information

Name of Most Recent Fund: Capital International Private Equity Fund VI, L.P.
Most Recent Fund Was Raised: 09/14/2011
Year Founded: 1992
Capital Under Management: $26,000,000,000
Current Activity Level: Actively seeking new investments

CAPITAL INVEST

30, Boulevard Moulay Youssef
Casablanca, Morocco 20000
Phone: 21222429120
Fax: 21222434684

Type of Firm
Private Equity Firm

Project Preferences

Type of Financing Preferred:
Balanced
Later Stage
Seed
Management Buyouts
Acquisition
Startup
Special Situation

Size of Investments Considered:
Min Size of Investment Considered (000s): $1,000
Max Size of Investment Considered (000s): $2,500

Geographical Preferences

International Preferences:
Morocco
Africa

Industry Preferences

In Semiconductor/Electr prefer:
Electronics

In Medical/Health prefer:
Health Services

In Consumer Related prefer:
Food/Beverage
Education Related

In Transportation prefer:
Transportation

In Business Serv. prefer:
Services
Distribution

In Manufact. prefer:
Manufacturing

In Agr/Forestr/Fish prefer:
Agriculture related

Additional Information
Name of Most Recent Fund: Capital North Africa Venture Fund II
Most Recent Fund Was Raised: 06/10/2013
Year Founded: 1999
Capital Under Management: $99,417,000
Current Activity Level : Actively seeking new investments

CAPITAL INVESTMENT LLC

P.O. Box 35666
Abu Dhabi, Utd. Arab Em.
Phone: 97126523999
Fax: 97126354606
E-mail: info@capitalinvestment.ae
Website: www.capitalinvestment.ae

Management and Staff
Ali Al Mansoori, Managing Director

Type of Firm
Private Equity Firm

Project Preferences

Type of Financing Preferred:
Leveraged Buyout
Early Stage
Expansion
Generalist PE
Later Stage

Industry Preferences

In Medical/Health prefer:
Medical/Health

In Consumer Related prefer:
Education Related

In Industrial/Energy prefer:
Oil and Gas Exploration

Additional Information
Year Founded: 1999
Current Activity Level : Actively seeking new investments

CAPITAL MIDWEST FUND LP

2675 North Mayfair Road
Suite 410
Milwaukee, WI USA 53226
Phone: 4144534488
Fax: 4144534831

Management and Staff
Alvin Vitangcol, Principal
Daniel Einhorn, Principal
Stephen Einhorn, Principal

Type of Firm
Private Equity Firm

Project Preferences

Type of Financing Preferred:
Early Stage

Geographical Preferences

United States Preferences:
Midwest
Wisconsin

Additional Information
Name of Most Recent Fund: Capital Midwest Fund II
Most Recent Fund Was Raised: 12/17/2010
Year Founded: 2008
Capital Under Management: $29,620,000
Current Activity Level : Actively seeking new investments

CAPITAL MILLS INVEST BV

Haarstraat 25
Gorinchem, Netherlands 4201 JA
Website: www.capitalmills.nl

Management and Staff
Erwin Van der Veen, Partner
Gijs Den Hartog, Partner

Type of Firm
Private Equity Firm

Project Preferences

Type of Financing Preferred:
Early Stage

Geographical Preferences

International Preferences:
Europe
Netherlands
Switzerland
Austria
Germany

Industry Preferences

In Communications prefer:
Telecommunications
Data Communications

In Computer Software prefer:
Software

In Internet Specific prefer:
Internet

In Medical/Health prefer:
Medical/Health
Health Services

In Consumer Related prefer:
Entertainment and Leisure
Sports
Education Related

Additional Information
Year Founded: 2014
Current Activity Level : Actively seeking new investments

CAPITAL NUTS

Chuangxin Mansion
Room 102B, Block A
Xiamen, China
E-mail: value@capitalnut.com
Website: www.capitalnuts.com

Type of Firm
Private Equity Firm

Project Preferences

Type of Financing Preferred:
Balanced

Geographical Preferences

International Preferences:
China

Industry Preferences

In Internet Specific prefer:
Internet

Additional Information
Year Founded: 2013
Current Activity Level : Actively seeking new investments

CAPITAL ONE CO LTD

1706-3 Seocho-Dong, Seocho-Gu
504, Beobjo Building
Seoul, South Korea 137070
Phone: 8225957450
Fax: 8225957577

Type of Firm
Private Equity Firm

Association Membership
Korean Venture Capital Association (KVCA)

Project Preferences

Type of Financing Preferred:
Balanced

Industry Preferences

In Communications prefer:
Media and Entertainment
Entertainment

Additional Information
Year Founded: 2009
Capital Under Management: $14,999,000
Current Activity Level : Actively seeking new investments

CAPITAL PARTNERS SA

ul. Krolewska 16
First Floor, Saski Crescent Bu
Warsaw, Poland 00 103
Phone: 48223306880
Fax: 48223306881
E-mail: biuro@c-p.pl
Website: www.c-p.pl

Type of Firm
Private Equity Firm

Association Membership
Polish Venture Capital Association (PSIC/PPEA)

Industry Preferences

In Computer Software prefer:
Software

In Semiconductor/Electr prefer:
Electronics

In Medical/Health prefer:
Medical/Health

In Consumer Related prefer:
Food/Beverage

In Manufact. prefer:
Manufacturing

Additional Information
Year Founded: 2002
Current Activity Level : Actively seeking new investments

CAPITAL PARTNERS, INC.

Eight Greenwich Office Park
Greenwich, CT USA 06831
Phone: 2036250770
Fax: 2036250423
E-mail: info@capitalpartners.com
Website: www.capitalpartners.com

Management and Staff
Brian Fitzgerald, Managing Director
Edwin Tan, Vice President
James Sidwa, Chief Financial Officer
John Willert, Principal
Mark Allsteadt, Managing Director
Robert Tucker, Managing Director

Type of Firm
Private Equity Firm

Project Preferences

Role in Financing:
Prefer role as deal originator

Type of Financing Preferred:
Core
Leveraged Buyout
Acquisition
Recapitalizations

Geographical Preferences

United States Preferences:
Northwest
North America
Northeast

Industry Focus
(% based on actual investment)

Consumer Related	48.7%
Other Products	27.8%
Industrial/Energy	9.4%
Computer Software and Services	5.9%
Internet Specific	5.0%
Communications and Media	2.6%
Semiconductors/Other Elect.	0.6%

Additional Information
Year Founded: 1982
Capital Under Management: $264,300,000
Current Activity Level : Actively seeking new investments

CAPITAL POINT LTD

132 Menachem Begin Rd.
Azrieli Ctr., Round Tower 22F
Tel Aviv, Israel 67021
Phone: 97236070320
Fax: 97236070323
E-mail: info@capitalpoint.co.il
Website: www.capitalpoint.co.il

Management and Staff
Boaz Kam, Chief Financial Officer
Limor Sela, Vice President

Type of Firm
Incubator/Development Program

Project Preferences

Type of Financing Preferred:
Early Stage
Seed
Startup

Geographical Preferences

International Preferences:
Israel

Industry Preferences

In Internet Specific prefer:
Internet

In Semiconductor/Electr prefer:
Electronics

In Biotechnology prefer:
Biotechnology

In Medical/Health prefer:
Medical Products

In Industrial/Energy prefer:
Environmental Related

Additional Information
Year Founded: 2000
Current Activity Level : Actively seeking new investments

CAPITAL POINT PARTNERS LLC

One Riveway, Suite 2020
Houston, TX USA 77056
Phone: 7135951420
Fax: 7135951421
E-mail: info@cappoint.com
Website: www.cappoint.com

Management and Staff
Keith Smith, Managing Director
Todd Stern, Managing Director

Type of Firm
Private Equity Firm

Project Preferences

Type of Financing Preferred:
Leveraged Buyout
Expansion
Mezzanine
Acquisition
Recapitalizations

Size of Investments Considered:
Min Size of Investment Considered (000s): $5,000
Max Size of Investment Considered (000s): $20,000

Geographical Preferences

United States Preferences:

Additional Information
Year Founded: 2006
Capital Under Management: $28,000,000
Current Activity Level : Actively seeking new investments

CAPITAL PROVENCE BUSINESS ANGELS SAS

Technopole de Chateau Gombert
45 Rue Joliot Curie Hotel
Marseille, France 13382
Phone: 33491118897
Fax: 33491118801
Website: www.provenceangels.com

Type of Firm
Private Equity Firm

Project Preferences

Type of Financing Preferred:
Early Stage
Seed
Startup

Geographical Preferences

International Preferences:
Europe
France

Additional Information
Year Founded: 2008
Current Activity Level : Actively seeking new investments

CAPITAL RESOURCE COMPANY OF CONNECTICUT

2558 Albany Avenue
West Hartford, CT USA 06117
Phone: 203-236-4336
Fax: 203-232-8161

Management and Staff
Morris Morgenstein, General Partner

Type of Firm
SBIC

Project Preferences

Type of Financing Preferred:
Expansion
Balanced

Geographical Preferences

United States Preferences:
Northeast

Additional Information
Year Founded: 1977
Capital Under Management: $5,500,000
Current Activity Level : Actively seeking new investments

CAPITAL RESOURCE PARTNERS

31 State Street
Sixth Floor
Boston, MA USA 02109
Phone: 6174789600
Fax: 6174789605
Website: www.crp.com

Management and Staff
Andrew Silverman, Principal
Peter Kagunye, Chief Financial Officer
Robert Ammerman, Managing Partner

Type of Firm
Private Equity Firm

Project Preferences

Role in Financing:
Prefer role as deal originator

Type of Financing Preferred:
Leveraged Buyout
Expansion
Management Buyouts
Acquisition
Recapitalizations

Geographical Preferences

United States Preferences:

Industry Focus
(% based on actual investment)
Computer Software and Services	20.4%
Medical/Health	18.4%
Other Products	15.9%
Consumer Related	14.8%
Communications and Media	10.5%
Industrial/Energy	9.6%
Internet Specific	7.3%
Semiconductors/Other Elect.	1.8%
Biotechnology	1.2%

Additional Information
Name of Most Recent Fund: Capital Resource Partners V, L.P.
Most Recent Fund Was Raised: 07/03/2003
Year Founded: 1987
Capital Under Management: $1,100,000,000
Current Activity Level : Actively seeking new investments
Method of Compensation: Return on invest. most important, but chg. closing fees, service fees, etc.

CAPITAL ROYALTY LP

1000 Main Street
Suite 2500
Houston, TX USA 77002
Phone: 7132097350
Fax: 7135593008
Website: www.capitalroyalty.com

Management and Staff
David Carter, Managing Director
Garth Monroe, Chief Financial Officer
Luke Duster, Managing Director
Mike Weinmann, Managing Director
Mike Cannon, Managing Director
Niles Chura, Managing Director
Scott Li, Principal

Type of Firm
Private Equity Firm

Project Preferences

Type of Financing Preferred:
Mezzanine

Industry Preferences

In Medical/Health prefer:
Health Services

Additional Information
Year Founded: 2003
Capital Under Management: $1,250,000,000
Current Activity Level : Actively seeking new investments

CAPITAL SERVICES & RESOURCES INC

5159 Wheelis Drive
Suite 106
Memphis, TN USA 38117
Phone: 9017612156
Fax: 9017670060

Management and Staff
Charles Bancroft, Principal

Type of Firm
Service Provider

Project Preferences

Role in Financing:
Prefer role as deal originator

Type of Financing Preferred:
Second Stage Financing
Leveraged Buyout
Expansion
Research and Development
Public Companies
Strategic Alliances
Special Situation
Recapitalizations

Size of Investments Considered:
Min Size of Investment Considered (000s): $10
Max Size of Investment Considered (000s): $15,000

Geographical Preferences

United States Preferences:
All U.S.

Canadian Preferences:
All Canada

Additional Information
Year Founded: 1976
Current Activity Level : Actively seeking new investments
Method of Compensation: Return on investment is of primary concern, do not charge fees

CAPITAL SOUTHWEST CORP

5400 Lyndon B. Johnson Freeway
Suite 1300
Dallas, TX USA 75240
Phone: 9722338242
Fax: 9722337362
E-mail: cscinfo@capitalsouthwest.com
Website: www.capitalsouthwest.com

Management and Staff
Kelly Tacke, Chief Financial Officer

Type of Firm
Private Equity Firm

Association Membership
Natl Assoc of Small Bus. Inv. Co (NASBIC)

Project Preferences

Role in Financing:
Will function either as deal originator or investor in deals created by others

Type of Financing Preferred:
Leveraged Buyout
Generalist PE
Later Stage
Management Buyouts
Acquisition
Recapitalizations

Geographical Preferences

United States Preferences:
Midwest
Southeast
Rocky Mountain
Southwest

Industry Focus

(% based on actual investment)
Other Products	21.1%
Industrial/Energy	18.1%
Consumer Related	18.0%
Internet Specific	9.5%
Computer Software and Services	9.2%
Communications and Media	7.8%
Medical/Health	7.7%
Computer Hardware	4.0%
Biotechnology	3.4%
Semiconductors/Other Elect.	1.1%

Additional Information
Name of Most Recent Fund: CSC Capital Corporation
Most Recent Fund Was Raised: 12/21/1998
Year Founded: 1961
Capital Under Management: $600,000,000
Current Activity Level : Actively seeking new investments
Method of Compensation: Return on investment is of primary concern, do not charge fees

CAPITAL SQUARE PARTNERS PTE LTD

One Raffles Place
20th Floor, Tower Two
Singapore, Singapore 048616
E-mail: info@capitalsquarepartners.com
Website: www.capitalsquarepartners.com

Management and Staff
Bharat Rao, Managing Partner
Mukesh Sharda, Managing Partner
Sanjay Chakrabarty, Managing Director

Type of Firm
Private Equity Firm

Geographical Preferences

International Preferences:
India
Asia

Industry Preferences

In Communications prefer:
Telecommunications

In Consumer Related prefer:
Consumer

In Business Serv. prefer:
Services
Media

Additional Information
Year Founded: 1969
Current Activity Level : Actively seeking new investments

CAPITAL STAGE AG

Grosse Elbstrasse 59
Hamburg, Germany 22767
Phone: 49403785620
Fax: 4940378562129
E-mail: info@capitalstage.com
Website: www.capitalstage.com

Management and Staff
Christoph Husmann, Chief Financial Officer
Holger Goetze, Chief Operating Officer

Type of Firm
Private Equity Firm

Project Preferences

Type of Financing Preferred:
Leveraged Buyout
Early Stage
Turnaround
Later Stage
Management Buyouts
Startup

Size of Investments Considered:
Min Size of Investment Considered (000s): $2,632
Max Size of Investment Considered (000s): $10,526

Geographical Preferences

International Preferences:
Europe
Switzerland
Austria
Germany

Industry Preferences

In Industrial/Energy prefer:
Alternative Energy
Energy Conservation Relat
Environmental Related

Additional Information
Year Founded: 1996
Capital Under Management: $80,800,000
Current Activity Level : Actively seeking new investments

CAPITAL STOCK SCR SA

Fortuny 45 Bjo Dcha.
Madrid, Spain 28010
Phone: 34-91-319-3301
Fax: 34-91-319-1839
E-mail: mpl@inversiones-europeas.com

Type of Firm
Private Equity Firm

Project Preferences

Type of Financing Preferred:
Leveraged Buyout
Expansion
Seed
Startup

Geographical Preferences

International Preferences:
Spain

Additional Information
Year Founded: 2001
Current Activity Level : Actively seeking new investments

CAPITAL STRATEGY MANAGEMENT CO

233 South Wacker Drive
Chicago, IL USA 60606
Phone: 312444170
Website: www.capitalstrategymanagement.com

Management and Staff
Eric von Bauer, President

Type of Firm
Private Equity Firm

Project Preferences

Role in Financing:
Prefer role as deal originator but will also invest in deals created by others

Type of Financing Preferred:
Early Stage
Expansion
Later Stage

Size of Investments Considered:
Min Size of Investment Considered (000s): $200
Max Size of Investment Considered (000s): $30,000

Geographical Preferences

United States Preferences:
Midwest

Industry Preferences

In Financial Services prefer:
Financial Services

In Business Serv. prefer:
Services

Additional Information

Year Founded: 1982
Current Activity Level : Actively seeking new investments
Method of Compensation: Return on invest. most important, but chg. closing fees, service fees, etc.

CAPITAL TECHNOLOGIES PTY LTD

Level 18
152-158 St. George's Terrace
Perth, Australia 6000
Phone: 618-9225-5034
Fax: 618-9221-0450

Type of Firm
Private Equity Firm

Project Preferences

Role in Financing:
Prefer role as deal originator

Type of Financing Preferred:
Research and Development
Seed
Startup

Size of Investments Considered:
Min Size of Investment Considered (000s): $51
Max Size of Investment Considered (000s): $255

Geographical Preferences

International Preferences:
Australia

Industry Preferences

In Communications prefer:
Commercial Communications
CATV & Pay TV Systems
Radio & TV Broadcasting
Telecommunications
Data Communications
Satellite Microwave Comm.

In Computer Hardware prefer:
Mini and Personal/Desktop
Computer Graphics and Dig

In Semiconductor/Electr prefer:
Electronics
Electronic Components
Semiconductor
Controllers and Sensors
Sensors
Laser Related
Fiber Optics
Analytic/Scientific

In Medical/Health prefer:
Other Therapeutic
Disposable Med. Products

In Industrial/Energy prefer:
Alternative Energy
Energy Conservation Relat
Robotics

In Business Serv. prefer:
Media

In Manufact. prefer:
Manufacturing

Additional Information

Year Founded: 1986
Capital Under Management: $3,800,000
Current Activity Level : Actively seeking new investments
Method of Compensation: Return on invest. most important, but chg. closing fees, service fees, etc.

CAPITAL TODAY CHINA GROWTH HK LTD

No. 88, Shiji Avenue
Rm. 3808, Jinmao Building
Shanghai, China 200121
Phone: 862150988886
Fax: 862150988050
E-mail: info@capitaltoday.com
Website: www.capitaltoday.com

Other Offices

Eight Finance Street, Central
Level 19, Two International Finance
Hong Kong, Hong Kong
Phone: 852-2868-5526
Fax: 852-3101-7913

Management and Staff

Baoma Wen, Partner
Xin Xu, President, Founder

Type of Firm
Private Equity Firm

Association Membership
China Venture Capital Association

Project Preferences

Type of Financing Preferred:
Expansion
Later Stage

Geographical Preferences

International Preferences:
China

Industry Preferences

In Internet Specific prefer:
Internet

In Medical/Health prefer:
Pharmaceuticals

In Consumer Related prefer:
Consumer
Retail
Consumer Products

Additional Information

Year Founded: 2005
Capital Under Management: $680,000,000
Current Activity Level : Actively seeking new investments

CAPITAL TRANSMISSION SA

4, rue de la Tour de Ille
Geneva, Switzerland 2251
Website: www.capitaltransmission.ch

Type of Firm
Private Equity Firm

Project Preferences

Type of Financing Preferred:
Generalist PE

Geographical Preferences

International Preferences:
Switzerland
France

Additional Information

Year Founded: 2008
Current Activity Level : Actively seeking new investments

CAPITAL TRUST LTD

49 Mount Street
London, United Kingdom W1K 2SD
Phone: 442074914230
Fax: 442074990524
Website: www.capitaltrustltd.com

Other Offices

Starco Center
Block C, Eight Floor
Beirut, Lebanon
Phone: 961-1-368-968
Fax: 961-1-368-324

655 Madison Avenue
17th Floor
LENOX HILL, NY USA 10021
Phone: 212-277-1010
Fax: 212-277-1011

8000 Towers Crescent Drive
Suite 1115
VIENNA, VA USA 22182
Phone: 571-730-4910
Fax: 571-730-4990

Management and Staff

Emad Odeh, Managing Partner
Romen Mathieu, Managing Director

Type of Firm

Bank Affiliated

Association Membership

Gulf Venture Capital Association

Project Preferences

Type of Financing Preferred:
Mezzanine
Generalist PE
Balanced

Geographical Preferences

United States Preferences:
All U.S.

International Preferences:
Tunisia
Jordan
Europe
Lebanon
Egypt
Algeria
Middle East
Morocco
Syria
South Africa
Africa

Industry Preferences

In Financial Services prefer:
Financial Services

Additional Information

Year Founded: 1985
Capital Under Management: $300,000,000
Current Activity Level : Actively seeking new investments

CAPITAL VC LTD

16-18 Queens Road
New World Tower, Room 602
Hong Kong, Hong Kong
Phone: 852-3421-0188
Fax: 852-3421-0198
E-mail: info@capital-vc.com
Website: www.capital-vc.com

Type of Firm

Private Equity Firm

Project Preferences

Type of Financing Preferred:
Leveraged Buyout

Geographical Preferences

International Preferences:
Hong Kong
China

Additional Information

Year Founded: 2002
Current Activity Level : Actively seeking new investments

CAPITAL Z PARTNERS LTD

142 West 57th Street
Third Floor
New York, NY USA 10019
Phone: 2129652400
Fax: 2129652301

Management and Staff

Bharath Subramanian, Principal
Chris Wolfe, Principal
Jonathan Kelly, Partner
Roland Bernardon, Chief Financial Officer

Type of Firm

Private Equity Firm

Project Preferences

Type of Financing Preferred:
Fund of Funds
Leveraged Buyout

Geographical Preferences

United States Preferences:

International Preferences:
Bermuda

Industry Focus

(% based on actual investment)
Other Products	88.8%
Internet Specific	7.7%
Medical/Health	2.2%
Computer Software and Services	1.4%

Additional Information

Year Founded: 1990
Capital Under Management: $4,840,000,000
Current Activity Level : Actively seeking new investments

CAPITAL-E NV

Karel Oomsstraat 4
Antwerpen, Belgium 2018
Phone: 3233033730
Fax: 3233033739
E-mail: contact@capital-e.be
Website: www.capital-e.eu

Management and Staff

Marc Wachsmuth, Partner
Pascal Vanluchene, Partner
Robert Jelski, Venture Partner
Ruud Van der Linden, Venture Partner
Sofie Baeten, Managing Partner

Type of Firm

Private Equity Firm

Project Preferences

Type of Financing Preferred:
Early Stage
Seed
Startup

Size of Investments Considered:
Min Size of Investment Considered (000s): $328
Max Size of Investment Considered (000s): $1,312

Geographical Preferences

International Preferences:
Ireland
United Kingdom
Western Europe
Belgium
Germany
France

Industry Preferences

In Communications prefer:
Communications and Media
Commercial Communications
CATV & Pay TV Systems
Radio & TV Broadcasting
Telecommunications

In Semiconductor/Electr prefer:
Electronics

In Medical/Health prefer:
Medical/Health
Medical Diagnostics

In Industrial/Energy prefer:
Energy
Alternative Energy

In Business Serv. prefer:
Media

In Other prefer:
Environment Responsible

Additional Information
Year Founded: 2006
Capital Under Management: $60,784,000
Current Activity Level : Actively seeking new investments

CAPITALA INVESTMENT ADVISORS LLC

4201 Congress Street
Suite 360
Charlotte, NC USA 28209
Phone: 7043765502
Fax: 7043765877

Type of Firm
Private Equity Firm

Project Preferences

Type of Financing Preferred:
Acquisition

Geographical Preferences

United States Preferences:
North America

Additional Information
Year Founded: 1998
Current Activity Level : Actively seeking new investments

CAPITALASIA GROUP

2077 Gold Street
Suite 281
Alviso, CA USA 95002
Website: www.capitalasia.com

Other Offices
2077 Gold Street
Suite #281 Alviso
Alviso, CA USA 95002

8 Finance Street, Central
19/F, Two Int Finance Centre
Hong Kong, Hong Kong

No.33 HuaYuanShiQiao Road
Rm. 2306, Citigroup Tower
Shanghai, China 200120

1066 West Hastings
2008, Oceanic Plaza,
Vancouver, Canada

No.1 Jianguomenwai Ave.
Suite 06, 15/ F, Tower 3, CWTC
Beijing, China 100004

Type of Firm
Private Equity Firm

Project Preferences

Type of Financing Preferred:
Leveraged Buyout
Early Stage
Expansion
Generalist PE
Seed

Geographical Preferences

United States Preferences:
North America

Canadian Preferences:
All Canada

International Preferences:
Hong Kong
China

Industry Preferences

In Communications prefer:
Telecommunications

In Consumer Related prefer:
Consumer

In Industrial/Energy prefer:
Energy
Oil and Gas Exploration
Oil & Gas Drilling,Explor
Environmental Related

In Financial Services prefer:
Real Estate

In Business Serv. prefer:
Media

In Agr/Forestr/Fish prefer:
Agriculture related
Mining and Minerals

Additional Information
Year Founded: 2006
Current Activity Level : Actively seeking new investments

CAPITALSOUTH PARTNERS LLC

4201 Congress Street, Suite 360
Charlotte, NC USA 28209
Phone: 7043765502
Fax: 7043765877

E-mail: info@capitalsouthpartners.com
Website: www.capitalsouthpartners.com

Other Offices
20 North Orange Avenue
Suite 804
Orlando, FL USA 32801
Phone: 4076485097
Fax: 4076419286

75 14th Street NorthWest
Suite 2700
Atlanta, GA USA 30309

100 Highland Park Village
Suite 200
Dallas, TX USA 75205
Phone: 2142953022
Fax: 2142953019

2530 Meridian Parkway
Suite 200 Research Triangle Park
Durham, NC USA 27713
Phone: 7043765502
Fax: 7043765877

333 East Main Street
Suite 310
Louisville, KY USA 40202
Phone: 5023878767
Fax: 5025859050

Management and Staff
Elyn Dortch, Managing Director
Hunt Broyhill, Partner
Jack McGlinn, Chief Operating Officer
Keith Carlson, Vice President
Richard Wheelahan, Vice President
Seth Ellis, Partner

Type of Firm
Private Equity Firm

Association Membership
Natl Assoc of Small Bus. Inv. Co (NASBIC)

Project Preferences

Role in Financing:
Will function either as deal originator or investor in deals created by others

Type of Financing Preferred:
Leveraged Buyout
Expansion
Mezzanine
Generalist PE
Management Buyouts
Acquisition
Recapitalizations

Size of Investments Considered:
Min Size of Investment Considered (000s): $5,000
Max Size of Investment Considered (000s): $25,000

Geographical Preferences

United States Preferences:
Southeast
All U.S.

Industry Preferences

In Medical/Health prefer:
Medical/Health

In Consumer Related prefer:
Consumer
Retail

In Industrial/Energy prefer:
Energy
Industrial Products

In Business Serv. prefer:
Services

Additional Information

Name of Most Recent Fund: CapitalSouth SBIC Fund IV, L.P.
Most Recent Fund Was Raised: 03/21/2013
Year Founded: 1998
Capital Under Management: $75,000,000
Current Activity Level : Actively seeking new investments
Method of Compensation: Return on investment is of primary concern, do not charge fees

CAPITALWORKS INVESTMENT PARTNERS (PTY) LTD

24 Central Bldg, 3rd Floor
cnr Gwen Lane & Fredman Dr.
Sandown, Sandton, South Africa 2196
Phone: 27113013000
Fax: 27118835560
E-mail: info@capitalworksip.com
Website: www.capitalworksip.com

Management and Staff

Chad Smart, Partner

Type of Firm

Private Equity Firm

Association Membership

South African Venture Capital Association (SAVCA)
Emerging Markets Private Equity Association

Project Preferences

Type of Financing Preferred:
Leveraged Buyout
Early Stage
Expansion
Generalist PE
Balanced
Later Stage
Management Buyouts
Acquisition

Geographical Preferences

International Preferences:
South Africa
Africa

Industry Preferences

In Communications prefer:
Wireless Communications

In Medical/Health prefer:
Health Services

In Consumer Related prefer:
Consumer
Education Related

In Financial Services prefer:
Financial Services

In Manufact. prefer:
Manufacturing

Additional Information

Name of Most Recent Fund: Capitalworks Private Equity Fund II, L.P.
Most Recent Fund Was Raised: 06/27/2013
Year Founded: 2006
Capital Under Management: $270,000,000
Current Activity Level : Actively seeking new investments

CAPITALWORKS LLC

1100 Superior Avenue
17th floor, Suite 1725
Cleveland, OH USA 44114
Phone: 2167813233
Fax: 2167816670
E-mail: info@capitalworks.net
Website: www.capitalworks.net

Management and Staff

John Mueller, Chief Executive Officer
Mikel Harding, Chief Financial Officer
Richard Hollington, President
W. Todd Martin, Principal

Type of Firm

Private Equity Firm

Association Membership

South African Venture Capital Association (SAVCA)

Project Preferences

Role in Financing:
Prefer role as deal originator but will also invest in deals created by others

Type of Financing Preferred:
Leveraged Buyout
Other
Acquisition
Special Situation

Geographical Preferences

United States Preferences:
Midwest
Rocky Mountain

Industry Preferences

In Transportation prefer:
Aerospace

In Financial Services prefer:
Financial Services

In Business Serv. prefer:
Services
Distribution

In Manufact. prefer:
Manufacturing

Additional Information

Name of Most Recent Fund: Short Vincent Partners III, L.P.
Most Recent Fund Was Raised: 10/15/2012
Year Founded: 1999
Capital Under Management: $100,000,000
Current Activity Level : Actively seeking new investments

CAPITAU ADVISORY LTD

Five Viscount Road
Capitau House
Bedfordview, South Africa 2007
Phone: 27116214900
Fax: 27116214901
Website: www.capitau.co.za

Management and Staff

Paul Sykes, Chief Financial Officer

Type of Firm

Private Equity Firm

Project Preferences

Type of Financing Preferred:
Leveraged Buyout
Management Buyouts
Acquisition

Geographical Preferences

International Preferences:
South Africa
Africa

Additional Information

Year Founded: 2005
Current Activity Level : Actively seeking new investments

CAPITECH VENTURE CAPITAL CO LTD

No.12 Gaoxin 2nd Road
Xi'an, China 710075
Phone: 862988356520
E-mail: capitech@mail.capitech.com.cn
Website: www.capitech.com.cn

Type of Firm
Private Equity Firm

Project Preferences

Type of Financing Preferred:
Early Stage
Balanced
Later Stage

Geographical Preferences

International Preferences:
China

Industry Preferences

In Communications prefer:
Telecommunications

In Computer Software prefer:
Software

In Semiconductor/Electr prefer:
Semiconductor

In Biotechnology prefer:
Biotechnology

In Medical/Health prefer:
Medical/Health

In Industrial/Energy prefer:
Alternative Energy

Additional Information
Year Founded: 1996
Capital Under Management: $15,753,000
Current Activity Level : Actively seeking new investments

CAPITEM PARTENAIRES SAS

3, Rue de Mailly
Caluire, France 69300
Phone: 33800401065
E-mail: contact@capitem.fr
Website: www.capitem.fr

Management and Staff
Frederic Fiore, Co-Founder
Herve Letoublon, Co-Founder
Stephane Gres, Co-Founder

Type of Firm
Private Equity Firm

Association Membership
French Venture Capital Association (AFIC)

Project Preferences

Type of Financing Preferred:
Leveraged Buyout
Generalist PE
Later Stage
Management Buyouts
Acquisition

Geographical Preferences

International Preferences:
Europe
France

Additional Information
Name of Most Recent Fund: Capitem I FCPR
Most Recent Fund Was Raised: 09/05/2013
Year Founded: 1996
Capital Under Management: $37,383,000
Current Activity Level : Actively seeking new investments

CAPITON AG

Bleibtreustrasse 33
Berlin, Germany 10707
Phone: 49303159450
Fax: 493031594557
E-mail: info@capiton.de
Website: www.capiton.de

Management and Staff
Andreas Denkmann, Partner
Christoph Karbenk, Partner
Christoph Spors, Partner
Frank-Markus Winkler, Partner
Gerwin Theiler, Founder
Manuel Hertweck, Partner

Type of Firm
Private Equity Firm

Association Membership
Swiss Venture Capital Association (SECA)
German Venture Capital Association (BVK)
European Private Equity and Venture Capital Assoc.

Project Preferences

Role in Financing:
Prefer role as deal originator

Type of Financing Preferred:
Leveraged Buyout
Generalist PE
Later Stage
Management Buyouts
Acquisition

Size of Investments Considered:
Min Size of Investment Considered (000s): $6,985
Max Size of Investment Considered (000s): $139,703

Geographical Preferences

International Preferences:
Switzerland
Austria
Germany

Industry Focus
(% based on actual investment)
Other Products	26.6%
Industrial/Energy	24.9%
Semiconductors/Other Elect.	20.9%
Computer Software and Services	14.1%
Consumer Related	9.4%
Communications and Media	2.4%
Internet Specific	1.7%

Additional Information
Year Founded: 1986
Capital Under Management: $1,227,300,000
Current Activity Level : Actively seeking new investments

CAPMAN OYJ

Korkeavuorenkatu 32
Helsinki, Finland 00130
Phone: 358207207500
Fax: 358207207510
Website: www.capman.fi

Other Offices

Grev Turegatan 30, Fifth Floor
P.O. Box 5745
Stockholm, Sweden 114 87
Phone: 46-8-5458-5470
Fax: 46-8-5458-5489

5, rue Guillaume Kroll
P.O. Box 2501
Luxembourg, Luxembourg L-1012
Phone: 352-48-18-281
Fax: 352-48-1828-3461

Dronning Mauds gate 3, Fourth floor
P.O. Box 1235
Oslo, Norway 0110
Phone: 47-2323-7575
Fax: 47-2323-7579

Hambro Hs, St. Julian's Avenue
P.O. Box 86, St. Peter Port
Guernsey, United Kingdom GY1 3AE
Phone: 44-1481-726-521
Fax: 44-1481-710-742

10, Arbat Street
Moscow, Russia 119002
Phone: 7-495-7813-730
Fax: 7-495-7813-729

Management and Staff
Joakim Frimodig, Chief Executive Officer
Johan Palsson, Managing Partner
Niko Haavisto, Chief Financial Officer
Pia Kall, Managing Partner

Type of Firm
Private Equity Firm

Association Membership
Finnish Venture Capital Association (FVCA)
Danish Venture Capital Association (DVCA)
Norwegian Venture Capital Association
Swedish Venture Capital Association (SVCA)
European Private Equity and Venture Capital Assoc.

Project Preferences

Type of Financing Preferred:
Second Stage Financing
Core
Leveraged Buyout
Value-Add
Early Stage
Mezzanine
Generalist PE
Balanced
Later Stage
Seed
Management Buyouts
Acquisition
Startup

Geographical Preferences

International Preferences:
Sweden
Europe
Rest of World
Iceland
Scandanavia/Nordic Region
Estonia
Finland
Norway
Denmark

Industry Focus
(% based on actual investment)

Medical/Health	22.9%
Other Products	15.4%
Computer Software and Services	12.2%
Consumer Related	11.9%
Communications and Media	11.8%
Internet Specific	9.2%
Industrial/Energy	9.2%
Semiconductors/Other Elect.	4.0%
Biotechnology	2.1%
Computer Hardware	1.3%

Additional Information
Name of Most Recent Fund: CapMan Nordic Real Estate
Most Recent Fund Was Raised: 03/06/2013
Year Founded: 1989
Capital Under Management: $4,747,300,000
Current Activity Level : Actively seeking new investments

CAPPELLO CAPITAL CORP

100 Wilshire Boulevard
Suite 1200
Santa Monica, CA USA 90401
Phone: 3103936632
Fax: 3103934838
Website: www.cappellocorp.com

Other Offices
Jewon Accounting Corp. Geonseol Bldg.
9th Floor #1-2, Nonhyeon-dong, Kangnam
South Korea, South Korea 135-010
Phone: 82-02-3442-3060
Fax: 82-02-3442-3010

Suite 812, South Tower, New World Center
3 Chongwenmenwai Street
Beijing, China 100062
Phone: 861067082350
Fax: 1067082292

401 Congress Avenure
Suite 1540
Austin, TX USA 78701
Phone: 5128524333
Fax: 5128524313

556 Eiercito Nacional, Suite 202A
Colonia Pilanco, Del Miguel Hidalgo
Rockville Centre, NY USA 11570
Phone: 2135939742
Fax: 3103934838

16th Floor, No. 456 Hsin Yi Road
Section 4, Taipei 106 - Ta An District
Taipei, Taiwan
Phone: 886287801536
Fax: 886227296579

Management and Staff
Alexander Cappello, Managing Director
David Losito, Managing Director
Gerard Cappello, Co-Founder
J. Randall Waterfield, Managing Director
Kay Booth, Managing Director
Richard Waterfield, Managing Director
Robert Deutsch, Managing Director
Rolando Pozos-Villarreal, Managing Director
Sean Kelly, Managing Director

Type of Firm
Private Equity Firm

Project Preferences

Type of Financing Preferred:
Acquisition
Recapitalizations

Geographical Preferences

United States Preferences:
All U.S.

International Preferences:
Europe
Middle East
Australia
Africa

Additional Information
Year Founded: 2007
Current Activity Level : Actively seeking new investments

CAPRIA VENTURES LLC

220 Second Avenue South
Seattle, WA USA 98104
Phone: 2069263700
Fax: 8884153030
Website: www.capria.vc

Other Offices
9/3 Kaiser-E-Hind
First Floor, Richmond Road
Bangalore, India 560 025
Phone: 918041120008
Fax: 918041120009

Management and Staff
Dave Richards, Managing Director

Type of Firm
Private Equity Firm

Project Preferences

Type of Financing Preferred:
Early Stage
Expansion
Seed
Strategic Alliances
Startup

Size of Investments Considered:
Min Size of Investment Considered (000s): $50
Max Size of Investment Considered (000s): $100

Geographical Preferences

International Preferences:
India

Industry Preferences

In Medical/Health prefer:
Health Services

In Consumer Related prefer:
Consumer
Education Related

In Business Serv. prefer:
Services

In Agr/Forestr/Fish prefer:
Agriculture related

In Other prefer:
Environment Responsible

Additional Information
Year Founded: 2012
Capital Under Management: $25,951,000
Current Activity Level : Actively seeking new investments

CAPRICORN CAPITAL PARTNERS

Capricorn House
32 Impala Road, Chislehurston
Johannesburg, South Africa 2196
Phone: 27-11-666-0700
Fax: 27-11-666-0702
E-mail: info@capricorncapital.co.uk
Website: www.capricornsa.com

Other Offices
22 Manchester Square
Third Floor
London, United Kingdom W1U 3PT
Phone: 44-207-725-1271

Management and Staff
Gavin Chadwick, Co-Founder

Type of Firm
Investment Management Firm

Project Preferences

Type of Financing Preferred:
Balanced

Geographical Preferences

International Preferences:
South Africa

Additional Information
Year Founded: 2004
Current Activity Level : Actively seeking new investments

CAPRICORN HOLDINGS LLC

30 East Elm Street
Greenwich, CT USA 06830
Phone: 2038616600
Fax: 2038616671
E-mail: info@capricornholdings.com
Website: www.capricornholdings.com

Management and Staff
Don Rice, General Partner
Herbert Winokur, Managing Partner
James Better, General Partner

Type of Firm
Private Equity Firm

Project Preferences

Role in Financing:
Prefer role as deal originator but will also invest in deals created by others

Type of Financing Preferred:
Leveraged Buyout
Acquisition
Recapitalizations

Size of Investments Considered:
Min Size of Investment Considered (000s): $3,000
Max Size of Investment Considered (000s): $35,000

Geographical Preferences

United States Preferences:
All U.S.

Canadian Preferences:
All Canada

Additional Information
Year Founded: 1987
Current Activity Level : Actively seeking new investments
Method of Compensation: Return on investment is of primary concern, do not charge fees

CAPRICORN INVESTMENT GROUP LLC

250 University Avenue
Suite 300
Palo Alto, CA USA 94301
Phone: 6503318800
E-mail: contact@capricornllc.com
Website: www.capricornllc.com

Management and Staff
Alan Chang, Principal
Andrew Hoffmann, Principal
John Jonson, Chief Operating Officer

Type of Firm
Private Equity Firm

Project Preferences

Type of Financing Preferred:
Generalist PE
Balanced
Public Companies
Recapitalizations

Geographical Preferences

United States Preferences:
All U.S.

Additional Information
Name of Most Recent Fund: Capricorn AIP - Venture Capital I, L.P.
Most Recent Fund Was Raised: 02/08/2008
Year Founded: 2006
Current Activity Level : Actively seeking new investments

CAPRICORN VENTURE PARTNERS NV

Lei 19/1
De Jonge St. Jacob
Leuven, Belgium 3000
Phone: 3216284100
Fax: 3216284108
E-mail: capricorn@capricorn.be
Website: www.capricorn.be

Management and Staff
Jos Peeters, Managing Partner
Tom Vanhoutte, Chief Financial Officer

Type of Firm
Private Equity Firm

Association Membership
Belgium Venturing Association
European Private Equity and Venture Capital Assoc.

Project Preferences

Role in Financing:
Prefer role as deal originator but will also invest in deals created by others

Type of Financing Preferred:
Early Stage
Balanced
Later Stage
Seed
Startup

Size of Investments Considered:
Min Size of Investment Considered (000s): $631
Max Size of Investment Considered (000s): $6,312

Geographical Preferences

United States Preferences:
All U.S.

International Preferences:
Latin America
Europe
Netherlands
Western Europe
Belgium
Asia
Germany
France

Industry Preferences

In Communications prefer:
Telecommunications

In Internet Specific prefer:
Internet

In Computer Other prefer:
Computer Related

In Biotechnology prefer:
Biotechnology
Biotech Related Research

In Medical/Health prefer:
Medical/Health
Medical Diagnostics
Pharmaceuticals

In Industrial/Energy prefer:
Alternative Energy
Energy Conservation Relat
Industrial Products
Materials
Advanced Materials

In Other prefer:
Environment Responsible

Additional Information
Name of Most Recent Fund: Capricorn ICT Arkiv NV
Most Recent Fund Was Raised: 12/18/2012
Year Founded: 1993
Capital Under Management: $189,400,000
Current Activity Level : Actively seeking new investments
Method of Compensation: Return on investment is of primary concern, do not charge fees

CAPSTAR PARTNERS LLC

1703 West Fifth Street
Austin, TX USA 78703
Phone: 5123407800
Website: www.capstarpartners.com

Management and Staff
R Hicks, President

Type of Firm
Private Equity Firm

Project Preferences

Type of Financing Preferred:
Leveraged Buyout
Value-Add
Generalist PE

Industry Preferences

In Internet Specific prefer:
Ecommerce

In Medical/Health prefer:
Health Services

In Financial Services prefer:
Financial Services
Real Estate

In Business Serv. prefer:
Media

Additional Information
Year Founded: 2000
Current Activity Level : Actively seeking new investments

CAPSTONE FINANCIAL GROUP

Eleven Palmetto Parkway
Suite 104
Hilton Head Island, SC USA 29926
Phone: 8436896450
Fax: 8436815938
Website: www.capfg.com

Management and Staff
Graham Payne, Managing Director
Kimberly Elkins, Vice President
M. Daniel Smith, President

Type of Firm
Bank Affiliated

Project Preferences

Type of Financing Preferred:
Leveraged Buyout
Turnaround
Management Buyouts
Recapitalizations

Geographical Preferences

United States Preferences:

Additional Information
Year Founded: 1988
Current Activity Level : Actively seeking new investments

CAPSTONE FINANCIAL PARTNERS LLC

3475 Lenox Road
Suite 400
Atlanta, GA USA 30326
Phone: 404-238-0550
Website: www.capstonefinancialpartners.com

Other Offices
423 Commonwealth Avenue
Newton Center, MA USA 02459

Management and Staff
James Eland, Principal
Jeff Walters, Managing Director
Michael Keaveney, Managing Director
Teo Forcht Dagi, General Partner

Type of Firm
Private Equity Firm

Project Preferences

Type of Financing Preferred:
Mezzanine

Geographical Preferences

United States Preferences:
All U.S.

Additional Information
Year Founded: 2005
Capital Under Management: $800,000
Current Activity Level : Actively seeking new investments

CAPSTONE PARTNERS LLC

1376-1bunji, Seocho Two-dong
1104, 11/F Seocho-Gu
Seoul, South Korea 137863
Phone: 8225751210
Fax: 8225753134
E-mail: hjkim@cspartners.co.kr
Website: www.cspartners.co.kr

Other Offices
77 Water Street,
8th Floor
New York, NY USA 10005

Management and Staff
Hwa Jin Choi, Partner
Tae Cheol Whang, Partner

Type of Firm
Private Equity Firm

Association Membership
Korean Venture Capital Association (KVCA)

Project Preferences

Type of Financing Preferred:
Early Stage
Balanced

Geographical Preferences

International Preferences:
Korea, South

Industry Preferences

In Internet Specific prefer:
Internet

Additional Information
Year Founded: 2008
Capital Under Management: $74,018,000
Current Activity Level : Actively seeking new investments

CAPSTREET GROUP LLC

600 Travis
Suite 6110
Houston, TX USA 77002
Phone: 7133322700
Fax: 7133322701
E-mail: info@capstreet.com
Website: capstreet.com

Management and Staff
Adrian Guerra, Vice President
M. Neil Kallmeyer, Managing Partner
Paul De Lisi, Principal
T. Michael Young, Managing Partner

Type of Firm
Private Equity Firm

Project Preferences

Role in Financing:
Prefer role as deal originator

Type of Financing Preferred:
Leveraged Buyout
Generalist PE
Management Buyouts
Acquisition
Recapitalizations

Geographical Preferences

United States Preferences:
Southeast
Southwest
Texas

Industry Focus
(% based on actual investment)

Industry	%
Computer Software and Services	26.7%
Industrial/Energy	19.9%
Internet Specific	14.1%
Other Products	13.4%
Consumer Related	11.9%
Communications and Media	5.0%
Biotechnology	5.0%
Semiconductors/Other Elect.	4.0%

Additional Information
Name of Most Recent Fund: CapStreet IV, L.P.
Most Recent Fund Was Raised: 12/20/2013
Year Founded: 1990
Capital Under Management: $570,000,000
Current Activity Level : Actively seeking new investments
Method of Compensation: Return on invest. most important, but chg. closing fees, service fees, etc.

CAPVENT AG

Dufourstrasse 24
Zurich, Switzerland 8008
Phone: 41435005070
Fax: 41435005079
E-mail: ch@capvent.com
Website: capvent.com

Other Offices
A 503, Leo Apts
24th Road, Off Linking Road
Mumbai, India 400052
Phone: 91-22-2648-9552
Fax: 91-22-2648-9551

7/2 Edward Road
Bangalore, India 560052
Phone: 91-80-4112-8900
Fax: 91-80-4112-7700

Room 1606, 16F, 258 Weihai Road
Merchant Plaza, South Wing
Shanghai, China 200041
Phone: 86-216-193-5742

321 North Clark Street
5th floor
Chicago, IL USA 60654
Phone: 212-984-0794

212, Gera Imperium
Patto Plaza
Panaji, Goa, India 403001
Phone: 91-832-664-7332
Fax: 91-832-664-7331

Management and Staff
Eric Oberfield, Vice President
Rohan Ajila, Managing Partner
Varun Sood, Managing Partner

Type of Firm
Private Equity Firm

Association Membership
Swiss Venture Capital Association (SECA)

Project Preferences

Type of Financing Preferred:
Fund of Funds
Leveraged Buyout
Early Stage
Mezzanine
Turnaround
Later Stage
Seed
Startup

Geographical Preferences

United States Preferences:

International Preferences:
Vietnam
Indonesia
Latin America
India
Europe
China
Thailand
Australia
Asia
Malaysia

Industry Preferences

In Internet Specific prefer:
Ecommerce

In Medical/Health prefer:
Medical/Health

In Consumer Related prefer:
Consumer
Food/Beverage
Consumer Services

In Industrial/Energy prefer:
Environmental Related

Additional Information
Name of Most Recent Fund: Capvent Asia Consumption Co-investment Fund
Most Recent Fund Was Raised: 11/22/2011
Year Founded: 2000
Capital Under Management: $425,000,000
Current Activity Level : Actively seeking new investments

CAPVEST LTD

100 Pall Mall
London, United Kingdom SW1Y 5NQ
Phone: 442073897900
Fax: 442073897901
E-mail: info@capvest.co.uk
Website: www.capvest.co.uk

Management and Staff
Christopher Campbell, Partner
Penelope Briant, Partner

Type of Firm
Private Equity Firm

Project Preferences

Type of Financing Preferred:
Expansion
Mezzanine
Acquisition

Geographical Preferences

International Preferences:
Ireland
United Kingdom
Western Europe
Scandanavia/Nordic Region

Additional Information
Name of Most Recent Fund: CapVest Equity Partners III, L.P.
Most Recent Fund Was Raised: 01/28/2013
Year Founded: 1999
Capital Under Management: $4,689,000,000
Current Activity Level : Actively seeking new investments

CAPVIS EQUITY PARTNERS AG

Grabenstrasse 17
Baar, Switzerland 6340
Phone: 41433005858
Fax: 4143005859
E-mail: info@capvis.com
Website: www.capvis.ch

Other Offices

21] Huadu Mansion
838 Zhangyang Road
Shanghai, China 200122
Phone: 86-21-5830-1200
Fax: 86-21-5830-1201

Bleichstrasse 64-66
4969247558715
Frankfurt am Main, Germany 60313
Phone: 4969247558715
Fax: 4969247558744

Florianstrasse 8
, Germany
Phone: 49-89-903-4390
Fax: 49-89-9048-0750

28 New Street
Saint Helier, United Kingdom JE23TE
Phone: 1534780789

Management and Staff

Andreas Simon, Partner
Daniel Flaig, Partner
Eric Trueb, Partner
Marc Battenfeld, Partner
Rolf Friedli, Partner
Stephan Lauer, Partner
Tobias Ursprung, Partner
Ueli Eckhardt, Partner

Type of Firm

Private Equity Firm

Association Membership

Swiss Venture Capital Association (SECA)
European Private Equity and Venture Capital Assoc.

Project Preferences

Role in Financing:
Prefer role as deal originator

Type of Financing Preferred:
Leveraged Buyout
Management Buyouts
Acquisition

Geographical Preferences

International Preferences:
United Kingdom
Switzerland
Western Europe
Austria
Spain
Belgium
Germany

Industry Preferences

In Medical/Health prefer:
Medical/Health
Pharmaceuticals

In Consumer Related prefer:
Consumer
Food/Beverage

In Industrial/Energy prefer:
Energy
Industrial Products

Additional Information

Name of Most Recent Fund: Capvis Equity IV L.P.
Most Recent Fund Was Raised: 01/09/2014
Year Founded: 1990
Capital Under Management: $1,822,900,000
Current Activity Level : Actively seeking new investments
Method of Compensation: Return on invest. most important, but chg. closing fees, service fees, etc.

CAPX PARTNERS III L L C

115 North Wacker Drive
#1760
Chicago, IL USA 60606
Phone: 3128937400
Fax: 3126292874
E-mail: info@capxpartners.com
Website: www.capxpartners.com

Other Offices

5 Penn Plazza
14th Floor
New York, NY USA 10001
Phone: 2123801706
Fax: 3023801708

60 Walnut Street
3rd Floor
Wellesley, MA USA 02481
Phone: 7812095049
Fax: 3126292874

4370 La Jolla Village Drive
#400
San Diego, CA USA 92122
Phone: 8587404156
Fax: 8582253495

Type of Firm

SBIC

Association Membership

Illinois Venture Capital Association

Project Preferences

Type of Financing Preferred:
Leveraged Buyout
Mezzanine
Later Stage
Acquisition
Recapitalizations

Size of Investments Considered:
Min Size of Investment Considered (000s): $2,000
Max Size of Investment Considered (000s): $20,000

Geographical Preferences

United States Preferences:

Industry Preferences

In Industrial/Energy prefer:
Industrial Products

In Business Serv. prefer:
Services
Distribution

In Manufact. prefer:
Manufacturing

Additional Information

Year Founded: 1999
Capital Under Management: $225,000,000
Current Activity Level : Actively seeking new investments

CARAVEL MANAGEMENT LLC

888 Seventh Avenue
16th Floor
New York, NY USA 10106
Phone: 2129949800
Website: caravelfund.com

Type of Firm

Investment Management Firm

Project Preferences

Type of Financing Preferred:
Leveraged Buyout
Later Stage
Acquisition

Geographical Preferences

United States Preferences:

Additional Information

Year Founded: 2004
Current Activity Level : Actively seeking new investments

CARDINAL EQUITY PARTNERS LLC

280 East 96th Street
Suite 350
Indianapolis, IN USA 46240
Phone: 3176630205
Fax: 3176630215
E-mail: info@cardinalep.com
Website: www.cardvent.com

Management and Staff

James Smeltzer, Co-Founder
John Ackerman, Co-Founder
Peter Munson, Co-Founder

Type of Firm
Private Equity Firm

Project Preferences

Type of Financing Preferred:
Leveraged Buyout
Balanced
Management Buyouts
Recapitalizations

Geographical Preferences

United States Preferences:
Midwest

Industry Preferences

In Business Serv. prefer:
Services
Distribution

In Manufact. prefer:
Manufacturing

Additional Information
Year Founded: 1993
Current Activity Level : Actively seeking new investments

CARDINAL VENTURE CAPITAL

325 Sharon Park Drive
Suite 107
Menlo Park, CA USA 94025
Phone: 6502894700
Fax: 6506144865
E-mail: info@cardinalvc.com
Website: www.cardinalvc.com

Management and Staff
Christian Borcher, Managing Director
Derek Blazensky, Founder

Type of Firm
Private Equity Firm

Project Preferences

Role in Financing:
Will function either as deal originator or investor in deals created by others

Type of Financing Preferred:
Early Stage

Industry Preferences

In Communications prefer:
Communications and Media
Data Communications

In Computer Software prefer:
Software

In Internet Specific prefer:
Internet

In Financial Services prefer:
Financial Services
Financial Services

Additional Information
Name of Most Recent Fund: Cardinal Venture Partners II, L.P.
Most Recent Fund Was Raised: 12/30/2009
Year Founded: 2000
Capital Under Management: $126,000,000
Current Activity Level : Actively seeking new investments
Method of Compensation: Return on investment is of primary concern, do not charge fees

CARDO PARTNERS AS

Bryggegata 7
P.O.Box 1979 Vika
Oslo, Norway 0125
Phone: 4722937370
Fax: 4722937371
Website: www.cardopartners.com

Management and Staff
Morten E. Luersen, Co-Founder

Type of Firm
Private Equity Firm

Project Preferences

Type of Financing Preferred:
Balanced

Geographical Preferences

International Preferences:
Scandanavia/Nordic Region

Additional Information
Year Founded: 2002
Current Activity Level : Actively seeking new investments

CARDUSO CAPITAL BV

2, L.J. Zielstraweg
Groningen, Netherlands 9713 GX
Phone: 31653751211
Website: www.cardusocapital.com

Management and Staff
Frits Kok, Partner
Koos Koops, Partner
Robert Polano, Partner

Type of Firm
Private Equity Firm

Project Preferences

Type of Financing Preferred:
Early Stage
Seed

Size of Investments Considered:
Min Size of Investment Considered (000s): $114
Max Size of Investment Considered (000s): $5,703

Geographical Preferences

International Preferences:
Netherlands

Industry Preferences

In Industrial/Energy prefer:
Energy

Additional Information
Year Founded: 2015
Current Activity Level : Actively seeking new investments

CARE CAPITAL LLC

47 Hulfish Street
Suite 310
Princeton, NJ USA 08542
Phone: 6096838300
Fax: 6096835787
E-mail: info@carecapital.com
Website: www.carecapital.com

Management and Staff
Argeris Karabelas, Partner
Daniel Cabo, Chief Financial Officer
David Ramsay, Co-Founder
Lorenzo Pellegrini, Partner
Richard Markham, Partner
Robert Seltzer, Partner

Type of Firm
Private Equity Firm

Project Preferences

Role in Financing:
Prefer role as deal originator but will also invest in deals created by others

Type of Financing Preferred:
Early Stage
Balanced
Later Stage

Size of Investments Considered:
Min Size of Investment Considered (000s): $5,000
Max Size of Investment Considered (000s): $20,000

Geographical Preferences

United States Preferences:

International Preferences:
Europe

Industry Preferences

In Medical/Health prefer:
Medical Therapeutics
Pharmaceuticals

Additional Information
Name of Most Recent Fund: Care Capital Investments III, LP
Most Recent Fund Was Raised: 01/06/2006
Year Founded: 2000
Capital Under Management: $100,000,000
Current Activity Level : Actively seeking new investments
Method of Compensation: Return on investment is of primary concern, do not charge fees

CARETTA PARTNERS LLC

220 N Green
Chicago, IL USA 60607
E-mail: partner@caretta.co
Website: caretta.co

Management and Staff
Eric Becker, Founder

Type of Firm
Private Equity Firm

Project Preferences

Type of Financing Preferred:
Generalist PE

Additional Information
Year Founded: 2015
Current Activity Level : Actively seeking new investments

CAREVENTURES SA

55 Val Fleuri
Luxembourg, Luxembourg 1526

Type of Firm
Private Equity Firm

Project Preferences

Type of Financing Preferred:
Early Stage
Expansion
Seed

Geographical Preferences

International Preferences:
Europe

Industry Preferences

In Medical/Health prefer:
Health Services
Hospitals/Clinics/Primary
Hospital/Other Instit.

Additional Information
Year Founded: 2017
Current Activity Level : Actively seeking new investments

CARIBBEAN DEVELOPMENT CAPITAL LTD

Ten Cipriani Boulevard
Port-of-Spain, Trinidad/Tob.
Phone: 868-623-4665
Fax: 868-623-3563
Website: www.devcapital.net

Management and Staff
Gerard Pemberton, CEO & Managing Director

Type of Firm
Private Equity Firm

Project Preferences

Type of Financing Preferred:
Balanced

Geographical Preferences

International Preferences:
Aruba
St Lucia
Grenada
Trinidad/Tob.
Guyana
Surinam

Industry Preferences

In Medical/Health prefer:
Health Services

In Consumer Related prefer:
Education Related

In Manufact. prefer:
Manufacturing

In Agr/Forestr/Fish prefer:
Agribusiness

Additional Information
Year Founded: 1988
Current Activity Level : Actively seeking new investments

CARIBBEAN EQUITY PARTNERS LTD

2nd Floor Kingston 5
Eight Dominica Drive
Kingston, Jamaica
Phone: 876-906-3372
Fax: 876-754-5875
E-mail: info@caribequity.com
Website: www.caribequity.com

Management and Staff
David Panton, Managing Director
Jeffrey Hall, Managing Director
Nigel Clarke, Managing Director

Type of Firm
Private Equity Firm

Project Preferences

Type of Financing Preferred:
Generalist PE
Balanced

Geographical Preferences

International Preferences:
Latin America

Additional Information
Year Founded: 2004
Current Activity Level : Actively seeking new investments

CARLSON INVEST AB

Acusticum 3
Pitea, Sweden 941 63
Website: www.cinvest.se

Management and Staff
Goran Carlson, Chief Executive Officer

Type of Firm
Private Equity Firm

Project Preferences

Type of Financing Preferred:
Expansion
Start-up Financing

Geographical Preferences

International Preferences:
Sweden

Industry Preferences

In Communications prefer:
Media and Entertainment

In Industrial/Energy prefer:
Alternative Energy
Energy Conservation Relat

In Business Serv. prefer:
Services

In Other prefer:
Environment Responsible

Additional Information
Year Founded: 2005
Current Activity Level : Actively seeking new investments

CARLYLE GROUP LP

1001 Pennsylvania Avenue, NW
Washington, DC USA 20004
Phone: 2027295626
Fax: 2023471818
Website: www.carlyle.com

Other Offices

Piazza Cavour 2
Milan, Italy 20121
Phone: 39-2-620-0461
Fax: 39-2-2901-3559

112, Avenue Kleber
Paris, France 75116
Phone: 331-5370-3520
Fax: 331-5370-3530

Shin-Marunouchi Building
1-5-1 Marunouchi, Chiyoda-ku
Tokyo, Japan 100-6535
Phone: 813-5208-4350
Fax: 813-5208-4351

Senckenberganlage 16
Frankfurt, Germany 60325
Phone: 49-69-5050-6570
Fax: 49-69-5050-65765

Cornish El Nil – Boulaq
Nile City Towers, South Tower
Cairo, Egypt 11221
Phone: 202-2461-8100
Fax: 202-2461-8110

Av Santo Toribio 115
Tempus Bldg 4&5
Lima, Peru 27
Phone: 5117128371
Fax: 5117128301

520 Madison Avenue
MANHATTAN, NY USA 10022
Phone: 212-381-4900
Fax: 212-381-4901

11100 Santa Monica Boulevard
SAWTELLE, CA USA 90025
Phone: 310-575-1700
Fax: 310-575-1740

Gagnam Finance Center
Yeoksam I-dong, Gangnam-gu
Seoul, South Korea 135-984
Phone: 822-2112-1900
Fax: 822-2112-1899

Intl. Financial Centre, Precinct Bldg. 3
Level 7 East, P.O. Box 506564
Dubai, Utd. Arab Em.
Phone: 971-4-427-5600
Fax: 971-4-427-5610

264 George Street
Sydney, Australia 2000
Phone: 61-2-9270-3500
Fax: 61-2-9270-3520

Alfred Rewane Road
39 Mulliner Towers
Lagos, Nigeria
Phone: 234144892678
Fax: 2341 4489210

2, Avenue Charles de Gaulle
Luxembourg, Luxembourg L-1653
Phone: 352-2686-2200
Fax: 352-2686-2110

1050 17th Street
Suite 1875
DENVER, CO USA 80265
Phone: 303-405-8300
Fax: 303-405-8310

Buyukdere Cad.
Yapi Kredi Plaza, B Blok
Istanbul, Turkey 34330
Phone: 90-212-385-9800
Fax: 90-212-385-9898

Pau Casals, 13
Barcelona, Spain 08021
Phone: 34-93-200-0906
Fax: 34-93-209-3510

1 Temasek Avenue
Millenia Tower
Singapore, Singapore 039192
Phone: 65-6212-9600
Fax: 65-6212-9620

Montes Urales, Suite 720
Colonia Lomas de Chapultepec
Mexico, Mexico 11000
Phone: 52-55-524-98020
Fax: 52-55-524-98030

No. 1 Guang Hua Road
2518-2521 Beijing Kerry Centre
Beijing, China 100020
Phone: 86-10-8529-8823
Fax: 86-10-8529-9877

Kungsgatan 30
Stockholm, Sweden 11135
Phone: 46-8-510-69600
Fax: 46-8-510-69610

128 South Tryon Street
CHARLOTTE, NC USA 28202
Phone: 704-632-0200
Fax: 704-632-0299

Promenadeplatz 8
Munich, Germany D-80333
Phone: 49-89-2444-600
Fax: 49-89-2444-604

Alexandra House
Sweepstakes, Ballbridge
Dublin, Ireland
Phone: 35316319730
Fax: 35316675170

12 Yoido-dong Youngdeungpo-gu
CCMM Building
Seoul, South Korea 150-869
Phone: 822-2004-8400
Fax: 822-2004-8440

Plaza 66 1266 Nan Jing Xi Road
Nanjing District
Shanghai, China
Phone: 86-21-6103-3200
Fax: 86-21-6103-3210

Quadrant A The IL&FS Financial Centre
Bandra-Kurla Complex
Mumbai, India 400 051
Phone: 91-22-6647-0800
Fax: 91-22-6647-0803

57 Berkeley Square
Lansdowne House
London, United Kingdom W1J 6ER
Phone: 44-20-7894-1200
Fax: 44-20-7894-1600

Calle Alcala 73
Madrid, Spain 28001
Phone: 34-91-432-9555
Fax: 34-91-432-9570

Avenue Brigadeiro
Faria Lima, 3900
Sao Paolo, Brazil 04538
Phone: 55-11-3568-7700
Fax: 55-11-3568-7750

Al Moutran Street
Building 142 Marfaa
Beirut, Lebanon 20127106
Phone: 961-197-2701
Fax: 961-197-2760

Third Melrose Boulevard
Unit 6a, First Floor
Melrose, North Johannesburg, South Africa 2196
Phone: 27110342004
Fax: 27110342020

Management and Staff

Aaron Gold, Principal
Adam Moss, Principal
Adam Palmer, Managing Director
Adam Glucksman, Managing Director
Adam Buchwald, Vice President
Alan Su, Managing Director
Alex Ying, Managing Director
Alex Wagenberg, Managing Director
Alexander Pietruska, Managing Director
Allan Holt, Managing Director
Alok Gaur, Managing Director

Pratt's Guide to Private Equity & Venture Capital Sources

Alp Guler, Vice President
Andre Domingos, Vice President
Andrea Pekala, Principal
Andres Obregon, Vice President
Andrew Chung, Managing Director
Andrew Burgess, Managing Director
Andrew Curry, Principal
Andrew Marino, Managing Director
Andrew Nimmer, Vice President
Anita Balaji, Vice President
Ann Siebecker, Vice President
Anna Tye, Vice President
Anne-Sophie Aude Pawlowski, Vice President
Artis Lin, Vice President
Barbara Murphy, Managing Director
Benoit Colas, Managing Director
Brandon Taylor, Vice President
Brett Wyard, Managing Director
Brian Nelsen, Principal
Brian McCarthy, Principal
Brian Hayhurst, Managing Director
Brian Bernasek, Managing Director
Brooke Coburn, Managing Director
Bruce Rosenblum, Managing Director
Bryan Lin, Principal
Bryan Corbett, Principal
Campbell Dyer, Managing Director
Can Deldag, Managing Director
Candice Szu, Vice President
Carey Davidson, Vice President
Carolyn Weimer, Managing Director
Catherine Simoni, Managing Director
Cedric Bobo, Principal
Charles Wu, Vice President
Charles Zyngier, Principal
Christopher Ullman, Managing Director
Christopher Lippman, Managing Director
Christopher Freeze, Managing Director
Christopher Cox, Principal
Christopher Finn, Managing Director
Claudius Watts, Managing Director
Colin Atkins, Managing Director
Curtis Buser, Chief Financial Officer
D. Scott Jenkins, Principal
Daniel Flaningan, Vice President
Daniel East, Vice President
Daniel Harris, Managing Director
Daniel Jordaan, Managing Director
Daniel Sterenberg, Principal
David Mew, Vice President
David Wen, Vice President
David Bluff, Vice President
David Gibson, Vice President
David Stonehill, Managing Director
David Daniel, Managing Director
David Albert, Managing Director
David Simmons, Vice President
David Johnson, Principal
David Tung, Managing Director
David Kingery, Principal
David Heilbrunn, Managing Director
David Pearson, Managing Director
Dayne Baird, Vice President
Debra Pedersen, Managing Director
Dennis Schulze, Managing Director

Derek Whang, Vice President
Devinjit Singh, Managing Director
Divya Misra, Vice President
Durant Schwimmer, Managing Director
Edward Samek, Managing Director
Eliot Merrill, Managing Director
Elliot Wagner, Managing Director
Eren Saricoglu, Vice President
Eric Brotman, Principal
Eric Herr, Principal
Eric Kump, Managing Director
Eric Zhang, Managing Director
Eric Sasson, Managing Director
Erica Herberg, Principal
Feng Xiao, Managing Director
Fernando Borges, Managing Director
Fernando Pinto, Principal
Firas Nasir, Managing Director
Francis Lolli, Managing Director
Francis Finelli, Managing Director
Franck Falezan, Managing Director
Gavin Lu, Vice President
Genevieve Sangudi, Managing Director
Genta Saito, Vice President
George Ruhlen, Managing Director
George Kurteson, Managing Director
Glenn Youngkin, President
Glori Holzman Graziano, Managing Director
Gregor Bohm, Managing Director
Gregory Ledford, Managing Director
Gregory Zeluck, Managing Director
Gregory Kares, Managing Director
Gregory MacDonald, Vice President
Gregory Summe, Managing Director
Gregory Nikodem, Vice President
Grishma Parekh, Principal
Han Chen, Managing Director
Harry Alverson, Managing Director
Heather Mitchell, Managing Director
Herman Chang, Managing Director
Hiroshi Kawahara, Managing Director
Hiroyuki Otsuka, Managing Director
Hisao Iijima, Vice President
Hugh Wilder, Managing Director
Hyun-Sup Byun, Vice President
Ian Fujiyama, Managing Director
Ian Sandler, Managing Director
J. Kevin Kenny, Managing Director
James Williams, Principal
James Attwood, Managing Director
James Kim, Vice President
James Sloan, Principal
James Burr, Managing Director
James Grippi, Vice President
Janie Chu, Vice President
Janine Feng, Managing Director
Jason Hart, Principal
Jason Kirschner, Managing Director
Jason Lee, Managing Director
Jason Thomas, Principal
Jay Sammons, Principal
Jean-Pierre Millet, Managing Director
Jennifer Haaz, Principal
Jeremy Anderson, Principal
Jesse Huff, Principal

Jessica Lee, Principal
Jessica Hoffman Brennan, Managing Director
Jim Larocque, Vice President
Jing Dong Lai, Vice President
Jiyuan Sun, Managing Director
John Flaherty, Principal
John Beczak, Principal
John Redett, Managing Director
Jonathan Bard, Vice President
Jonathan Colby, Managing Director
Jonathan Bylin, Managing Director
Joseph Cha, Vice President
Josh Dienstag, Managing Director
Juan Carlos Felix, Managing Director
Jumpei Ogura, Vice President
Justin Teltschik, Vice President
Justin Plouffe, Principal
Karen Vejseli, Principal
Karen Bechtel, Managing Director
Karthic Jayaraman, Principal
Katherine Elmore-Jones, Managing Director
Kazuhiro Yamada, Managing Director
Ken Tidwell, Managing Director
Kenneth Kencel, Managing Director
Kenneth Fahrman, Managing Director
Kevin Sweeney, Vice President
Kristen Ankerbrandt, Vice President
Lauren Dillard, Managing Director
Lee Carson, Managing Director
Leigh Oliver, Vice President
Leo Helmers, Managing Director
Leonard Tsomik, Managing Director
Linda Pace, Managing Director
Ling Yang, Vice President
Lori Sabet, Managing Director
Maki Mitsui, Managing Director
Manish Gaur, Vice President
Marco De Benedetti, Managing Director
Marius Jungerhans, Vice President
Mark Christopher, Managing Director
Mark Johnson, Managing Director
Mark Shottes, Vice President
Mark Harris, Managing Director
Mark Schoenfeld, Managing Director
Marlon Chigwende, Managing Director
Martin Sumner, Principal
Matthew LoRusso, Principal
Matthew Hunter, Managing Director
Matthew Stanczuk, Principal
Matthew Humbaugh, Principal
Mete Tuncel, Managing Director
Michael Gershenson, Principal
Michael Hadley, Principal
Michael Gozycki, Vice President
Michael Rasmussen, Vice President
Michael Stewart, Managing Director
Michael Wand, Managing Director
Michelle Dea, Managing Director
Miguel Valenzuela, Managing Director
Mitch Petrick, Managing Director
Nahar Houthan, Vice President
Nancy Palleschi, Principal
Natasha Nankivell, Managing Director
Nicholas Shao, Managing Director
Nikhil Mohta, Vice President

Nina Gong, Vice President
Norma Kuntz, Principal
Orit Mizrachi, Principal
Oussama Daher, Managing Director
P. Olivier Sarkozy, Managing Director
Parker Hayden, Vice President
Patrick Siewert, Managing Director
Patrick McCarter, Principal
Paul Ferraro, Principal
Paul Brady, Managing Director
Pedro De Esteban, Managing Director
Peter Rooney, Vice President
Polai Chan-Lee, Principal
Prabu Davamanirajan, Principal
R. Keith Taylor, Principal
Rahul Culas, Managing Director
Ram Jagannath, Vice President
Randal Quarles, Managing Director
Randall Whitestone, Principal
Raymond Whiteman, Managing Director
Richard Chang, Principal
Richard Casey, Principal
Robert Easton, Managing Director
Robert Kelly, Vice President
Robert Stuckey, Managing Director
Robert Konigsberg, Managing Director
Robert Dove, Managing Director
Robert Hodges, Managing Director
Rodney Cohen, Managing Director
Rodrigo Fonseca, Managing Director
Ronnie Jaber, Principal
Rory Macmillan, Principal
Russell Farscht, Principal
Sam Wu, Vice President
Sameer Bhargava, Principal
Samuel Kwon, Principal
Sandra Horbach, Managing Director
Sandra Lee, Managing Director
Sanghyun Lee, Managing Director
Satoru Hayashi, Managing Director
Sean Lu, Managing Director
Seok-Don Chu, Managing Director
Shalin Patel, Vice President
Shankar Narayanan, Managing Director
Shary Moalemzadeh, Managing Director
Shelley Guiley, Principal
Shirlene Song, Vice President
Siddartha Ahluwalia, Vice President
Simon Moore, Managing Director
Sinan Xin, Vice President
Skardon Baker, Managing Director
Stephen Bailey, Managing Director
Stephen Wise, Managing Director
Stephen Guillette, Principal
Sung Yong Choi, Vice President
Sunil Kaul, Managing Director
Susan Kasser, Principal
Takaomi Tomioka, Managing Director
Tamotsu Adachi, Managing Director
Tek Kaminski, Vice President
Thaddeus Paul, Managing Director
Theodore Gleser, Principal
Thomas Mayrhofer, Managing Director
Thomas Dwan, Principal
Thomas Lindstrom, Managing Director

Thomas Fousse, Managing Director
Thomas Wickwire, Managing Director
Thomas Hennigan, Vice President
Timothy Bruning, Vice President
Tom Levy, Principal
Tomas Peshkatari, Vice President
Tony Jiang, Vice President
Valeria Falcone, Managing Director
Vipul Amin, Principal
Vladimir Lasocki, Managing Director
Wael Bayazid, Managing Director
Wayne Wen-Tsui Tsou, Managing Director
Wesley Bieligk, Vice President
William Lee, Principal
William Allen, Vice President
William McMullan, Vice President
William Darman, Vice President
Willian Shiang, Vice President
Wulf Meinel, Managing Director
Xiang-dong Yang, Managing Director
Xiao-Bing Bai, Vice President
Yiru Liu, Vice President
Yong Li, Vice President
Youlee Nishimura, Vice President
Yuichi Tokumo, Vice President
Yusuke Watanabe, Vice President
Zade Zalatimo, Managing Director
Zubier Alim, Managing Director

Type of Firm
Private Equity Firm

Association Membership
South African Venture Capital Association (SAVCA)
Italian Venture Capital Association (AIFI)
Brazilian Venture Capital Association (ABCR)
Mid-Atlantic Venture Association
China Venture Capital Association
Emerging Markets Private Equity Association
French Venture Capital Association (AFIC)
Canadian Venture Capital Association
European Private Equity and Venture Capital Assoc.
Private Equity Council (PEC)
Singapore Venture Capital Association (SVCA)
Indian Venture Capital Association (IVCA)
African Venture Capital Association (AVCA)

Project Preferences

Role in Financing:
Prefer role as deal originator but will also invest in deals created by others

Type of Financing Preferred:
Leveraged Buyout
Value-Add
Early Stage
Expansion
Mezzanine
Generalist PE
Balanced
Opportunistic
Later Stage
Seed
Management Buyouts
Acquisition

Geographical Preferences

United States Preferences:
Southern California
North America
Northern California
West Coast
Washington
D. of Columbia
Indiana
New York
All U.S.

Canadian Preferences:
All Canada

International Preferences:
Italy
India
Tunisia
United Kingdom
Jordan
Europe
Qatar
Taiwan
Argentina
Hong Kong
Lebanon
Western Europe
China
Egypt
Utd. Arab Em.
Algeria
Mexico
Middle East
Saudi Arabia
Scandanavia/Nordic Region
Chile
Spain
Morocco
Asia
Colombia
South Africa
Korea, South
Germany
Japan
Kuwait
Libya
All International
France

Industry Focus
(% based on actual investment)

Other Products	34.8%
Medical/Health	18.5%
Communications and Media	13.1%
Computer Software and Services	10.7%
Consumer Related	8.3%
Industrial/Energy	6.3%
Semiconductors/Other Elect.	4.1%
Internet Specific	3.7%
Computer Hardware	0.4%
Biotechnology	0.1%

Additional Information
Year Founded: 1987
Capital Under Management: $97,700,000,000
Current Activity Level : Actively seeking new investments
Method of Compensation: Return on invest. most important, but chg. closing fees, service fees, etc.

CARMEL VENTURES IV PRINCIPALS FUND LP

12 Abba Eban Avenue
Ackerstein Towers Building D
Herzeliya, Israel 46725
Phone: 97299720400
Fax: 97199720401
E-mail: info@carmelventures.com
Website: www.carmelventures.com

Management and Staff
Assaf Ben-Ami, Founder
Avi Zeevi, General Partner
Dana Gross, Venture Partner
Debbie Levi, Principal
Doron Inbar, Venture Partner
Ohad Shperling, Principal
Ori Bendori, General Partner
Rina Shainski, General Partner
Ronen Nir, Partner
Ronit Amiaz, Vice President
Shlomo Dovrat, General Partner
Tomer Michaeli, Principal

Type of Firm
Private Equity Firm

Association Membership
Israel Venture Association

Project Preferences

Type of Financing Preferred:
Early Stage
Balanced
Seed
Startup

Geographical Preferences

United States Preferences:

International Preferences:
Europe
Israel

Industry Preferences

In Communications prefer:
Communications and Media
Telecommunications
Wireless Communications
Data Communications

In Computer Software prefer:
Software
Systems Software
Applications Software

In Internet Specific prefer:
Internet
Web Aggregation/Portals

In Semiconductor/Electr prefer:
Semiconductor

In Consumer Related prefer:
Retail
Consumer Products
Consumer Services

In Business Serv. prefer:
Media

In Agr/Forestr/Fish prefer:
Agribusiness

Additional Information
Name of Most Recent Fund: Carmel Ventures II
Most Recent Fund Was Raised: 05/03/2005
Year Founded: 2000
Capital Under Management: $600,000,000
Current Activity Level : Actively seeking new investments

CARMICHAEL PARTNERS LLC

4725 Piedmont Row Drive
Suite 210
Charlotte, NC USA 28210
Phone: 7043252255
E-mail: info@carmichaelpartners.com

Other Offices
2300 M Street, Northwest
Suite 800
Washington, DC USA 20037
Phone: 2029736442

Management and Staff
Brian Bailey, Managing Partner
Kevin Martin, Managing Partner

Type of Firm
Private Equity Firm

Project Preferences

Type of Financing Preferred:
Leveraged Buyout
Later Stage
Acquisition

Industry Preferences

In Communications prefer:
Communications and Media

In Business Serv. prefer:
Media

Additional Information
Year Founded: 2011
Current Activity Level : Actively seeking new investments

CAROUSEL CAPITAL PARTNERS

201 North Tryon Street
Suite 2450
Charlotte, NC USA 28202
Phone: 7043722040
Fax: 7043721040
Website: www.carouselcapital.com

Management and Staff
Alan Welch, Vice President
Charles Grigg, Managing Partner
Eric Heintschel, Chief Financial Officer
Erskine Bowles, Co-Founder
Jason Schmidly, Managing Partner
Nelson Schwab, Co-Founder
Peter Clark, Principal
Robert Kreidler, Chief Financial Officer
William Hobbs, Managing Partner

Type of Firm
Private Equity Firm

Project Preferences

Role in Financing:
Will function either as deal originator or investor in deals created by others

Type of Financing Preferred:
Leveraged Buyout
Acquisition
Recapitalizations

Geographical Preferences

United States Preferences:
Tennessee
Mississippi
Southeast
Alabama
North Carolina
South Carolina
Maryland
Virginia
Florida
Louisiana
Georgia
Arkansas
Kentucky

Industry Focus

(% based on actual investment)

Communications and Media	51.6%
Medical/Health	19.4%
Industrial/Energy	9.7%
Internet Specific	8.8%
Other Products	5.3%
Computer Software and Services	4.7%
Consumer Related	0.5%

Additional Information

Name of Most Recent Fund: Carousel Capital Partners IV, L.P.
Most Recent Fund Was Raised: 08/31/2011
Year Founded: 1996
Capital Under Management: $500,000,000
Current Activity Level : Actively seeking new investments
Method of Compensation: Return on invest. most important, but chg. closing fees, service fees, etc.

CARPEDIA CAPITAL LTD

123 Front Street West
Suite 902
Toronto, Canada M5J 2M2
Phone: 4163648842
Fax: 4163645999
E-mail: capital@carpediacapital.com
Website: www.carpediacapital.com

Other Offices

36 King Street East
Suite 820
, Canada M5C 1E5

Management and Staff

Glen Ampleford, Vice President

Type of Firm

Private Equity Firm

Association Membership

Canadian Venture Capital Association

Project Preferences

Type of Financing Preferred:
Management Buyouts

Industry Preferences

In Medical/Health prefer:
Medical/Health

In Consumer Related prefer:
Retail
Food/Beverage
Consumer Services
Hotels and Resorts

In Business Serv. prefer:
Distribution

In Manufact. prefer:
Manufacturing

Additional Information

Year Founded: 2010
Capital Under Management: $9,852,000
Current Activity Level : Actively seeking new investments

CARPENTER AND CO INC

Five Park Plaza
Suite 950
Irvine, CA USA 92614
Phone: 9492618888
Website: carpenterandcompanyinc.com

Management and Staff

Brett Lawrence, Vice President
John Flemming, President & COO

Type of Firm

Bank Affiliated

Project Preferences

Type of Financing Preferred:
Leveraged Buyout
Expansion
Acquisition
Recapitalizations

Geographical Preferences

United States Preferences:
All U.S.

Industry Preferences

In Financial Services prefer:
Financial Services

Additional Information

Name of Most Recent Fund: Carpenter Community BancFund, L.P.
Most Recent Fund Was Raised: 01/28/2008
Year Founded: 1974
Current Activity Level : Actively seeking new investments

CARRICK CAPITAL MANAGEMENT COMPANY LLC

160 Spear Street
Suite 1620
San Francisco, CA USA 94105
Phone: 4154324100

Management and Staff

Alexander Mason, Managing Director
James Madden, Co-Founder
Marc McMorris, Co-Founder
Paul Zolfaghari, Managing Director
Steve Unterberger, Managing Director

Type of Firm

Private Equity Firm

Project Preferences

Type of Financing Preferred:
Balanced
Strategic Alliances

Industry Preferences

In Communications prefer:
Data Communications

In Computer Software prefer:
Software
Systems Software
Applications Software

In Internet Specific prefer:
E-Commerce Technology

In Business Serv. prefer:
Services

Additional Information

Name of Most Recent Fund: Carrick Capital Partners, L.P.
Most Recent Fund Was Raised: 11/27/2012
Year Founded: 2012
Capital Under Management: $470,000,000
Current Activity Level : Actively seeking new investments

CARTESIAN CAPITAL GROUP LLC

505 Fifth Avenue
15th Floor
New York, NY USA 10017
Phone: 2124616363
Fax: 2124616366
Website: cartesiangroup.com

Other Offices

300 Huanhai Zhong Road
47th Floor
, China 200021

Av. Brigadeiro Faria Lima
3729, Fifth Floor
Sao Paolo, Brazil 04538-905

Management and Staff

Geoffrey Hamlin, Partner
Paul Pizzani, Partner
Peter Yu, Managing Partner
Thomas Armstrong, Partner
William Jarosz, Partner

Type of Firm

Private Equity Firm

Project Preferences

Type of Financing Preferred:
Leveraged Buyout
Acquisition

Geographical Preferences

United States Preferences:

International Preferences:
All International

Additional Information
Name of Most Recent Fund: Pangaea Two, L.P.
Most Recent Fund Was Raised: 04/28/2011
Year Founded: 2006
Capital Under Management: $2,000,000,000
Current Activity Level : Actively seeking new investments

CARTHONA CAPITAL FS PTY LTD

1 Alfred Street
Suite 1 Level 15
Sydney, Australia NSW 2000
Phone: 61280720621
Fax: 61280720622
E-mail: info@carthonacapital.com
Website: www.carthonacapital.com

Type of Firm
Private Equity Firm

Project Preferences

Type of Financing Preferred:
Balanced

Additional Information
Year Founded: 1969
Current Activity Level : Actively seeking new investments

CARUTH CAPITAL PARTNERS LLC

1528 Slocum Street
Dallas, TX USA 75207

Type of Firm
Private Equity Firm

Additional Information
Year Founded: 1969
Current Activity Level : Actively seeking new investments

CARVAL INVESTORS LLC

9320 Excelsior Boulevard
Seventh Floor
Hopkins, MN USA 55343
Phone: 9529843774
Fax: 9529843905
Website: www.carvalinvestors.com

Other Offices
25 Great Pulteney Street
Third Floor
London, United Kingdom W1F 9LT
Phone: 442072927700
Fax: 442072927777

1095 Avenue of the Americas
New York, NY USA 10036
Phone: 2124570147

11-13 Boulevard de la Foire
Luxembourg, Luxembourg L 1528
Phone: 35226975740
Fax: 35226202826

999 Huai Hai Road
10F, One ICC, Shanghai Intl Commerce Ctr
Shanghai, China 200031
Phone: 862123060888
Fax: 862123060606

3-1-1 Marunouchi Chiyoda-ku
Kokusai Building, Fourth floor
Tokyo, Japan 100 0005
Phone: 81332170768
Fax: 81332170760

Eleven Avenue Myron Herrick
Seventh Floor
Paris, France 75008
Phone: 33144823160
Fax: 33130618726

300 Beach Road #23-01
The Concourse
Singapore, Singapore 199555
Phone: 6562951112
Fax: 6563938898

Management and Staff
John Brice, President
Peter Alan Vorbrich, Chief Financial Officer

Type of Firm
Investment Management Firm

Project Preferences

Type of Financing Preferred:
Turnaround
Opportunistic

Industry Preferences

In Financial Services prefer:
Real Estate

Additional Information
Year Founded: 1987
Capital Under Management: $473,800,000
Current Activity Level : Actively seeking new investments

CARVEST CREDIT AGRICOLE REGIONS INVERTIS SAS

1, rue Pierre Truchis de Lays
Champagne au mont d'or, France 69410
E-mail: contact@carvest.fr
Website: www.carvest.fr

Other Offices
26, rue de la Godde
Saint Jean de Braye, France 45800

25, rue Libergier
Reims, France 51100
Phone: 33-3-2683-3050
Fax: 33-3-2683-3554

500, Rue Saint-Fuscien
Amiens, France 80095

Type of Firm
Bank Affiliated

Association Membership
French Venture Capital Association (AFIC)

Project Preferences

Type of Financing Preferred:
Leveraged Buyout
Generalist PE
Later Stage
Acquisition

Geographical Preferences

International Preferences:
Europe
France

Additional Information
Year Founded: 2004
Current Activity Level : Actively seeking new investments

CAS CAPITAL INC

2 Ichibancho, Chiyoda-Ku
5F Parkside House
Tokyo, Japan 102-0082
Phone: 81335565990
Fax: 81335565731
E-mail: cc@cascapital.com
Website: www.cascapital.com

Other Offices
NM Plaza Midosuji
3-6-3 Awajimachi, Chuo-ku
Osaka-shi, Japan 541-0047
Phone: 81-6-4706-5026

Unit 1505, Azia Center,
1233 Lujiazui Ring Road,
Shanghai, China 200120
Phone: 86-21-6160-8200

12F
No.100,Minsheng E. Road
Taipei City, Taiwan 105
Phone: 886-2-8712-3200

15F-4
No.101,Sec.1, Zihyou Rd.,
Taichung, Taiwan 403
Phone: 886-7-241-1800

17F Philam Life Tower,
8767 Paseo de Roxas,
Makati City, Manila, Philippines 1226
Phone: 63-2-856-0888

Management and Staff
Haruo Kawamura, Partner
Kazuyoshi Komiya, Partner
Yasuji Kibayashi, Partner

Type of Firm
Private Equity Firm

Project Preferences

Type of Financing Preferred:
Leveraged Buyout

Geographical Preferences

International Preferences:
Japan

Industry Preferences

In Consumer Related prefer:
Food/Beverage

Additional Information
Year Founded: 2003
Current Activity Level : Actively seeking new investments

CAS INVESTMENT MANAGEMENT CO LTD

1606 Ideal International Plaza
53 North, 4th Ring West
Beijing, China 100080
Phone: 861082607629
Fax: 861062137930
E-mail: casim@casim.cn
Website: www.casim.cn

Management and Staff
Jun Shao, Chief Financial Officer

Type of Firm
Private Equity Firm

Project Preferences

Type of Financing Preferred:
Early Stage
Expansion
Balanced
Later Stage

Geographical Preferences

International Preferences:
China

Industry Preferences

In Internet Specific prefer:
Internet

Additional Information
Year Founded: 1987
Current Activity Level : Actively seeking new investments

CAS JIAHE FUND MANAGEMENT CO

c/o CAS Holdings
No. 9 West 4th Ring Road
Beijing, China 100190
Phone: 86-10-6280-0115
Fax: 86-10-6280-0120

Type of Firm
Government Affiliated Program

Project Preferences

Type of Financing Preferred:
Early Stage
Expansion
Balanced
Later Stage

Geographical Preferences

International Preferences:
China

Industry Preferences

In Communications prefer:
Telecommunications

In Industrial/Energy prefer:
Energy
Environmental Related

In Business Serv. prefer:
Media

Additional Information
Year Founded: 2011
Capital Under Management: $208,579,000
Current Activity Level : Actively seeking new investments

CASA VERDE CAPITAL LLC

12530 Beatrice St
Los Angeles, CA USA 90066
E-mail: info@casaverdecapital.com
Website: www.casaverdecapital.com

Type of Firm
Private Equity Firm

Project Preferences

Type of Financing Preferred:
Early Stage
Seed
Startup

Geographical Preferences

United States Preferences:

Industry Preferences

In Medical/Health prefer:
Medical Therapeutics
Medical Products

Additional Information
Year Founded: 2014
Capital Under Management: $33,230,000
Current Activity Level : Actively seeking new investments

CASAFORTE INVESTIMENTOS SA

Av Eng Antonio de Goes, 60
Third Floor, Room 304
Recife, Brazil 51010-000
Phone: 558130393965
Fax: 558130393965
E-mail: contato@casaforteinvest.com.br
Website: www.casaforteinvestimentos.com.br

Management and Staff
Fernando Buarque, Founder
Kristopher Dowlin, Partner
Marcelo Reboucas, Founder
Pedro Magalhaes, Founder
Roberto Melo, Founder

Type of Firm
Private Equity Firm

Association Membership
Brazilian Venture Capital Association (ABCR)

Project Preferences

Type of Financing Preferred:
Leveraged Buyout

Geographical Preferences

International Preferences:
Brazil

Industry Preferences

In Consumer Related prefer:
Food/Beverage

In Industrial/Energy prefer:
Energy

In Agr/Forestr/Fish prefer:
Mining and Minerals

Additional Information
Year Founded: 2008
Current Activity Level : Actively seeking new investments

CASDIN CAPITAL LLC

1350 Avenue of the Americas
Suite 1140
New York, NY USA 10019
Phone: 2128975430
E-mail: info@casdincapital.com
Website: www.casdincapital.com

Management and Staff
Matt Ehrhart, Chief Financial Officer

Type of Firm
Private Equity Firm

Project Preferences

Type of Financing Preferred:
Balanced

Geographical Preferences

United States Preferences:

Industry Preferences

In Biotechnology prefer:
Biotechnology
Human Biotechnology

In Medical/Health prefer:
Medical/Health
Health Services

Additional Information
Year Founded: 2011
Current Activity Level : Actively seeking new investments

CASH CAPITAL

No.11 Dong Zhimen South Street
Rm 1803, Tower B
Beijing, China 100007
Phone: 861057636588
Fax: 861057636599
Website: en.cashcapital.cn

Type of Firm
Private Equity Firm

Project Preferences

Type of Financing Preferred:
Early Stage
Expansion
Later Stage
Startup

Industry Preferences

In Communications prefer:
Commercial Communications

In Computer Software prefer:
Software

In Internet Specific prefer:
Internet

In Semiconductor/Electr prefer:
Micro-Processing

In Medical/Health prefer:
Diagnostic Services
Medical Products
Health Services

Additional Information
Year Founded: 2011
Current Activity Level : Actively seeking new investments

CASPIAN ADVISORS PVT LTD

Road No. Ten, Banjara Hills
3rd Floor, 8-2-596/5/B/1
Hyderabad, India 500034
Phone: 914066297100
Fax: 914066465884
E-mail: info@caspian.in
Website: www.caspian.in

Other Offices
Sector 53, Golf Course Road
Level Four, Augusta Point
Gurgaon, India 122002
Phone: 91-124-435-4021
Fax: 91-124-435-4001

Management and Staff
S.Vishwanatha Prasad, Managing Director

Type of Firm
Private Equity Firm

Geographical Preferences

International Preferences:
India

Industry Preferences

In Consumer Related prefer:
Food/Beverage

In Financial Services prefer:
Financial Services

In Agr/Forestr/Fish prefer:
Agriculture related

Additional Information
Year Founded: 2004
Capital Under Management: $10,000,000
Current Activity Level : Actively seeking new investments

CASSELS BROCK & BLACKWELL LLP

2100 Scotia Plaza
40 King Street West
Toronto, Canada M5H3C2
Phone: 416-869-5300
Fax: 416-360-8877
E-mail: postmaster@casselsbrock.com
Website: www.casselsbrock.com

Other Offices
885 West Georgia Street
Suite 2200, HSBC Building
Vancouver, Canada V6C 3E8
Phone: 6046916100
Fax: 6046916120

Management and Staff
Lori Prokopich, Partner

Type of Firm
Private Equity Firm

Additional Information
Year Founded: 2009
Current Activity Level : Actively seeking new investments

CASSIA INVESTMENTS LTD

Yu Yuet Lai Building
43-55 Wyndham Street
Central Hong Kong, Hong Kong
Phone: 852 2796 356
E-mail: info@cassiainvest.com
Website: www.cassiainvest.com

Management and Staff
Faris Ayoub, Managing Director
Jake Astor, Principal
Yeung Kw, Chief Operating Officer

Type of Firm
Private Equity Firm

Project Preferences

Type of Financing Preferred:
Balanced

Geographical Preferences

International Preferences:
Asia Pacific

Additional Information

Year Founded: 2011
Current Activity Level : Actively seeking new investments

CASSIUS FAMILY MANAGEMENT LLC

2841 North Hills Drive
Atlanta, GA USA 30305

Type of Firm

Private Equity Firm

Project Preferences

Type of Financing Preferred:
Early Stage

Additional Information

Year Founded: 2017
Current Activity Level : Actively seeking new investments

CASTANEA PARTNERS INC

Three Newton Executive Park, Suite 304
Newton, MA USA 02462
Phone: 6176302400
Fax: 6176302424
E-mail: info@castaneapartners.com
Website: www.castaneapartners.com

Management and Staff

Adam Eveloff, Principal
Benjamin Tuttman, Principal
Brian Knez, Managing Partner
Colleen Love, Chief Financial Officer
Juan Hill, Partner
Lindsay Ting, Vice President
Michael Banu, Vice President
Paul Gibbons, Partner
Robert Smith, Managing Partner
Steven Berg, Managing Partner
Timothy Burke, Partner

Type of Firm

Private Equity Firm

Project Preferences

Role in Financing:
Prefer role as deal originator but will also invest in deals created by others

Type of Financing Preferred:
Leveraged Buyout
Management Buyouts
Acquisition
Industry Rollups
Special Situation

Industry Preferences

In Consumer Related prefer:
Sports
Retail
Food/Beverage
Consumer Products
Consumer Services
Education Related

In Manufact. prefer:
Publishing

Additional Information

Name of Most Recent Fund: Castanea Partners Fund IV, L.P.
Most Recent Fund Was Raised: 01/14/2014
Year Founded: 2001
Capital Under Management: $1,000,000,000
Current Activity Level : Actively seeking new investments
Method of Compensation: Return on investment is of primary concern, do not charge fees

CASTIK CAPITAL SARL

1 Boulevard de la Foire
Luxembourg, Luxembourg
Phone: 35228669097
E-mail: info@castik.lu
Website: www.castik.lu

Other Offices

Moehlstrasse 28
Munich, Germany 81675
Phone: 49899446640

Type of Firm

Bank Affiliated

Project Preferences

Type of Financing Preferred:
Leveraged Buyout
Mezzanine
Management Buyouts
Acquisition

Geographical Preferences

International Preferences:
Italy
Luxembourg
Czech Republic
Netherlands
Switzerland
Austria
Belgium
Germany
France

Additional Information

Year Founded: 2014
Capital Under Management: $1,266,754,000
Current Activity Level : Actively seeking new investments

CASTILE VENTURES

65 William Street, Suite 205
Wellesley, MA USA 02481
Phone: 7818900060
Fax: 7818900065
Website: www.castileventures.com

Management and Staff

Carl Stjernfeldt, General Partner
David Duval, Partner
Nina Saberi, Managing Partner
Roger Walton, General Partner
Skip Besthoff, General Partner

Type of Firm

Private Equity Firm

Association Membership

New England Venture Capital Association

Project Preferences

Role in Financing:
Prefer role as deal originator but will also invest in deals created by others

Type of Financing Preferred:
Early Stage

Geographical Preferences

United States Preferences:
Northeast

Industry Preferences

In Communications prefer:
Communications and Media
Telecommunications
Data Communications

In Computer Software prefer:
Software

In Internet Specific prefer:
Internet

Additional Information

Name of Most Recent Fund: Castile Ventures III, L.P.
Most Recent Fund Was Raised: 01/10/2006
Year Founded: 1998
Capital Under Management: $200,000,000
Current Activity Level : Actively seeking new investments
Method of Compensation: Return on investment is of primary concern, do not charge fees

CASTLE CREEK CAPITAL LLC

6051 El Tordo
Rancho Santa Fe, CA USA 92067
Phone: 8587568300
Fax: 8587568301
E-mail: accountinfo@castlecreek.com
Website: www.castlecreek.com

Management and Staff
J. Mikesell Thomas, Principal
John Pietrzak, Principal
John Eggemeyer, Co-Founder
Mark Merlo, Principal
William Ruh, Co-Founder

Type of Firm
Private Equity Firm

Project Preferences

Type of Financing Preferred:
Leveraged Buyout
Expansion
Turnaround
Later Stage
Acquisition
Distressed Debt
Recapitalizations

Geographical Preferences

United States Preferences:

Industry Preferences

In Financial Services prefer:
Financial Services

Additional Information
Name of Most Recent Fund: Castle Creek Capital Partners V, L.P.
Most Recent Fund Was Raised: 07/10/2013
Year Founded: 1992
Capital Under Management: $402,500,000
Current Activity Level : Actively seeking new investments

CASTLE HARLAN AUS MEZZANINE

31 Alfred Street
Level Four, Customs House
Sydney, Australia 2000
Phone: 61282488888
Fax: 61282488877
E-mail: champ@champequity.com.au
Website: www.champmbo.com

Other Offices
6 Battery Road
#12-08
Singapore, Singapore 049909
Phone: 65-6576-9179
Fax: 65-6576-9170

71 Eagle Street
Level 36 Riparian Plaza
Brisbane, Australia QLD 4000
Phone: 61731213122
Fax: 61731213030

150 East 58th Street
NEW YORK, NY USA 10155

Phone: 2126448600
Fax: 2122078042

Management and Staff
Benjamin Sebel, Managing Director
Cameron Buchanan, Managing Director
John Haddock, CEO & Managing Director
Joseph Skrzynski, Founder
Nathaniel Childres, Managing Director

Type of Firm
Bank Affiliated

Project Preferences

Role in Financing:
Prefer role as deal originator but will also invest in deals created by others

Type of Financing Preferred:
Leveraged Buyout
Management Buyouts
Acquisition

Size of Investments Considered:
Min Size of Investment Considered (000s): $50,000
Max Size of Investment Considered (000s): $150,000

Geographical Preferences

International Preferences:
Middle East

Industry Focus
(% based on actual investment)
Industrial/Energy	48.5%
Consumer Related	24.9%
Other Products	19.4%
Internet Specific	5.6%
Medical/Health	0.7%
Biotechnology	0.4%
Computer Hardware	0.3%
Semiconductors/Other Elect.	0.2%
Computer Software and Services	0.1%

Additional Information
Name of Most Recent Fund: CHAMP Buyout II Trust
Most Recent Fund Was Raised: 06/17/2005
Year Founded: 1987
Capital Under Management: $3,000,000,000
Current Activity Level : Actively seeking new investments
Method of Compensation: Return on invest. most important, but chg. closing fees, service fees, etc.

CASTLE HARLAN INC

150 East 58th Street
New York, NY USA 10155
Phone: 2126448600
Fax: 2122078042
E-mail: info@castleharlan.com
Website: castleharlan.com

Management and Staff
Anand Philip, Vice President
David Pittaway, Senior Managing Director
Heather Faust, Vice President
Joyce Demonteverde, Vice President
Lewis Raibley, Senior Managing Director
Marcel Fournier, Senior Managing Director
Murat Konuk, Vice President
Patrick Zyla, Vice President
Tariq Osman, Vice President

Type of Firm
Private Equity Firm

Project Preferences

Type of Financing Preferred:
Leveraged Buyout
Management Buyouts
Acquisition

Geographical Preferences

United States Preferences:
North America

International Preferences:
Europe
Australia

Industry Focus
(% based on actual investment)
Industrial/Energy	37.3%
Consumer Related	29.9%
Other Products	26.2%
Communications and Media	6.6%

Additional Information
Name of Most Recent Fund: Castle Harlan Partners V, L.P.
Most Recent Fund Was Raised: 03/18/2008
Year Founded: 1987
Capital Under Management: $3,200,000,000
Current Activity Level : Actively seeking new investments

CASTLE ISLAND PARTNERS LLC

470 Atlantic Avenue
Fourth Floor
Boston, MA USA 02210
Phone: 6176506236
Fax: 6176076045

Management and Staff
David Sullivan, Partner
Michael Barry, Partner
Ryan Kim, Managing Partner

Type of Firm
Investment Management Firm

Project Preferences

Type of Financing Preferred:
Leveraged Buyout
Turnaround
Acquisition
Recapitalizations

Industry Preferences

In Consumer Related prefer:
Food/Beverage
Consumer Products

In Business Serv. prefer:
Services
Distribution

In Manufact. prefer:
Manufacturing

Additional Information
Year Founded: 2005
Current Activity Level : Actively seeking new investments

CASTLE VENTURE GROUP LLC

1804 Williamson Court
Brentwood, TN USA 37027
Phone: 8449227853
Fax: 8003433467
Website: castleventure.com

Type of Firm
Private Equity Firm

Project Preferences

Type of Financing Preferred:
Leveraged Buyout
Acquisition

Additional Information
Year Founded: 2015
Current Activity Level : Actively seeking new investments

CASTLELAKE LP

4600 Wells Fargo Center
Minneapolis, MN USA 55402
Website: www.castlelake.com

Management and Staff
Brent Jong, Partner
Chris Buckley, Vice President
Chris Pelly, Vice President
Evan Carruthers, Managing Partner
Jeff Rangitsch, Vice President
Jim Davenport, Vice President
Joe McConnell, Managing Director
Jonathan Fragodt, Partner
Julian Rees, Vice President
Kevin Hiniker, Partner
Kevin Hackler, Partner
Luke Beltnick, Partner
Neil McCrossan, Vice President
Otto Verhoeff, Managing Director
Peter Glerum, Partner
Richard Dudley-Cave, Vice President
Rob Addison, Vice President
Rory O Neill, CEO & Managing Director
Sigfus Olafsson, Vice President

Type of Firm
Private Equity Firm

Project Preferences

Type of Financing Preferred:
Turnaround
Acquisition
Special Situation
Distressed Debt

Additional Information
Name of Most Recent Fund: Castlelake III, L.P.
Most Recent Fund Was Raised: 12/20/2013
Year Founded: 2005
Capital Under Management: $13,400,000,000
Current Activity Level : Actively seeking new investments

CASTLERAY LLC

900 North Franklin Street
Suite 610
Chicago, IL USA 60610
Phone: 3127894660
Fax: 3127894663
Website: www.castleray.com

Other Offices
6750 Hillcrest Plaza Drive
Suite 300
Dallas, TX USA 75230
Phone: 2143477760
Fax: 2143477711

1430 N. LaSalle Drive, G2
Chicago, IL USA 60610
Phone: 646-249-1364
Fax: 646-417-5262

Type of Firm
Private Equity Firm

Project Preferences

Type of Financing Preferred:
Leveraged Buyout
Special Situation
Recapitalizations

Geographical Preferences

United States Preferences:
North America

Canadian Preferences:
All Canada

Industry Preferences

In Consumer Related prefer:
Consumer Products

In Industrial/Energy prefer:
Industrial Products

In Business Serv. prefer:
Distribution

In Manufact. prefer:
Manufacturing

Additional Information
Name of Most Recent Fund: Castleray Fund IV LLC
Most Recent Fund Was Raised: 08/13/2010
Year Founded: 2005
Capital Under Management: $1,400,000
Current Activity Level : Actively seeking new investments

CASTLETOP CAPITAL

3600 N. Capital of Texas Hwy, Building B, Suite 320
Austin, TX USA 78746
Phone: 5123296600
E-mail: info@castletopcapital.com
Website: www.castletopcapital.com

Management and Staff
Alan Topfer, Managing Director
Morton Topfer, Managing Director
Richard Topfer, Managing Director

Type of Firm
Private Equity Firm

Project Preferences

Role in Financing:
Will function either as deal originator or investor in deals created by others

Type of Financing Preferred:
Value-Add
Balanced

Size of Investments Considered:
Min Size of Investment Considered (000s): $1,000
Max Size of Investment Considered (000s): $5,000

Geographical Preferences

United States Preferences:
Texas

Industry Preferences

In Financial Services prefer:
Real Estate

Additional Information
Year Founded: 2000
Capital Under Management: $63,000,000
Current Activity Level : Actively seeking new investments
Method of Compensation: Return on investment is of primary concern, do not charge fees

CASTROL INNOVENTURES

Castrol Technology Centre
Whitchurch Hill, Pangbourne
Berkshire, United Kingdom RG8 7QR
Phone: 4411898433
Website: castrolinnoventures.com

Type of Firm
Private Equity Firm

Project Preferences

Type of Financing Preferred:
Early Stage
Expansion
Later Stage
Seed

Industry Preferences

In Other prefer:
Environment Responsible

Additional Information
Year Founded: 1969
Current Activity Level : Actively seeking new investments

CATACAP MANAGEMENT A/S

Mollevej 9
4th floor
Niva, Denmark 2990
Phone: 4571991900
E-mail: info@catacap.dk
Website: catacap.dk

Management and Staff
Jens Hahn-Petersen, Partner
Peter Ryttergaard, Partner
Vilhelm Hahn-Petersen, Partner

Type of Firm
Private Equity Firm

Association Membership
Danish Venture Capital Association (DVCA)

Project Preferences

Type of Financing Preferred:
Leveraged Buyout

Geographical Preferences

International Preferences:
Denmark

Additional Information
Name of Most Recent Fund: CataCap 1 K/S
Most Recent Fund Was Raised: 12/21/2012
Year Founded: 2011
Capital Under Management: $192,942,000
Current Activity Level : Actively seeking new investments

CATAGONIA CAPITAL GMBH

Rosenthaler Strasse 42
Berlin, Germany 10178
Phone: 4930398213030
Fax: 4930398213031
E-mail: info@catagonia.com
Website: www.catagonia.com

Management and Staff
Christian Petersen, Venture Partner
Juha Christensen, Venture Partner
Sylvius Bardt, Venture Partner

Type of Firm
Private Equity Firm

Association Membership
German Venture Capital Association (BVK)

Project Preferences

Type of Financing Preferred:
Early Stage
Seed
Startup

Geographical Preferences

International Preferences:
Switzerland
Austria
Germany

Industry Preferences

In Communications prefer:
Wireless Communications

In Computer Software prefer:
Software

In Internet Specific prefer:
Internet
Ecommerce

Additional Information
Year Founded: 2009
Current Activity Level : Actively seeking new investments

CATALYST CAPITAL GROUP INC

181 Bay Street
Suite 4700
Toronto, Canada M5J 2T3
Phone: 4169453000
Fax: 4169453060
E-mail: info@catcapital.com
Website: www.catcapital.com

Other Offices
77 King Street West
Suite 4320, Royal Trust Tower
Toronto, Canada M5K 1J3

Type of Firm
Private Equity Firm

Project Preferences

Type of Financing Preferred:
Leveraged Buyout
Turnaround
Distressed Debt

Geographical Preferences

Canadian Preferences:
All Canada

Additional Information
Name of Most Recent Fund: Catalyst Fund Limited Partnership IV
Most Recent Fund Was Raised: 10/07/2013
Year Founded: 2002
Capital Under Management: $2,312,000,000
Current Activity Level : Actively seeking new investments

CATALYST EQUITY GROUP LLC

Three Compound Drive
Hutchinson, KS USA 67502
Phone: 6208993050
Fax: 8773496902
Website: www.catalystmanagementgroup.com

Type of Firm
Private Equity Firm

Project Preferences

Type of Financing Preferred:
Leveraged Buyout
Acquisition

Geographical Preferences

United States Preferences:

Additional Information
Year Founded: 2000
Current Activity Level : Actively seeking new investments

CATALYST FUND MANAGEMENT AND RESEARCH LTD

20 Old Street
4th Floor
London, United Kingdom EC1V 9AB
Phone: 442074909520

Management and Staff
Jussi Laurimaa, Co-Founder
Luca Bosatta, Partner
Robin Black, Managing Partner
Rodney Schwartz, Founding Partner

Type of Firm
Private Equity Firm

Project Preferences

Type of Financing Preferred:
Early Stage
Expansion
Later Stage
Seed
Startup

Size of Investments Considered:
Min Size of Investment Considered (000s): $1,600
Max Size of Investment Considered: No Limit

Geographical Preferences

International Preferences:
United Kingdom
Europe

Industry Preferences

In Internet Specific prefer:
E-Commerce Technology

In Medical/Health prefer:
Medical/Health
Health Services

In Consumer Related prefer:
Education Related

In Industrial/Energy prefer:
Alternative Energy
Energy Conservation Relat

In Business Serv. prefer:
Services

Additional Information
Year Founded: 1997
Capital Under Management: $64,700,000
Current Activity Level : Actively seeking new investments

CATALYST HEALTH AND TECHNOLOGY PARTNERS LLC

50 Braintree Hill Office Park
Suite 304
Braintree, MA USA 02184
Phone: 7812285228
Fax: 7812285150
E-mail: info@catalystpartners.com

Management and Staff
Darshana Zaveri, Partner
Joshua Phillips, Managing Partner
Kevin McCafferty, Partner
Robert Vigoda, Partner

Type of Firm
Private Equity Firm

Project Preferences

Role in Financing:
Prefer role as deal originator but will also invest in deals created by others

Type of Financing Preferred:
Early Stage

Size of Investments Considered:
Min Size of Investment Considered (000s): $7,000
Max Size of Investment Considered (000s): $12,000

Geographical Preferences

United States Preferences:
Northeast
Massachusetts
All U.S.

Industry Preferences

In Medical/Health prefer:
Medical/Health
Medical Diagnostics
Drug/Equipmt Delivery
Medical Products

Additional Information
Name of Most Recent Fund: Catalyst Health Ventures, L.P.
Most Recent Fund Was Raised: 02/15/2008
Year Founded: 1998
Capital Under Management: $35,000,000
Current Activity Level : Actively seeking new investments
Method of Compensation: Return on investment is of primary concern, do not charge fees

---

CATALYST INVESTMENT MANAGERS PTY, LTD.

151 Macquarie Street
Level 9
Sydney, Australia 2000
Phone: 61292701200
Fax: 61292701222
E-mail: enquiries@catalystinvest.com.au
Website: www.catalystinvest.com.au

Other Offices

91-93 Flinders Lane
Level Four
Melbourne, Australia 3000
Phone: 61396591800
Fax: 61396591899

2 The Esplanade
Level 17, Exchange Plaza
Perth, Australia 6000
Phone: 61892684200
Fax: 61892684299

Management and Staff
John Story, Managing Director
Simon Dighton, Managing Director
Tony Yap, Chief Financial Officer
Trent Peterson, Managing Director

Type of Firm
Private Equity Firm

Association Membership
Australian Venture Capital Association (AVCAL)

Project Preferences

Role in Financing:
Prefer role as deal originator but will also invest in deals created by others

Type of Financing Preferred:
Acquisition

Geographical Preferences

International Preferences:
Australia
New Zealand

Industry Focus
(% based on actual investment)

Consumer Related	52.3%
Other Products	22.7%
Internet Specific	11.5%
Industrial/Energy	10.3%
Semiconductors/Other Elect.	2.0%
Computer Software and Services	1.2%

Additional Information
Name of Most Recent Fund: Catalyst Buyout Fund 2
Most Recent Fund Was Raised: 03/16/2009
Year Founded: 1989
Capital Under Management: $145,700,000
Current Activity Level : Actively seeking new investments
Method of Compensation: Return on invest. most important, but chg. closing fees, service fees, etc.

CATALYST INVESTMENTS LP

3, Daniel Frish Street
Tel Aviv, Israel 64731
Phone: 972-3-695-0666
Fax: 972-3-695-0222
E-mail: info@catalyst-fund.com
Website: www.catalyst-fund.com

Management and Staff
Boaz Harel, Managing Partner
Edouard Cukierman, Chief Executive Officer
Joseph Sabet, Partner

Type of Firm
Bank Affiliated

Association Membership
Israel Venture Association

Project Preferences

Type of Financing Preferred:
Expansion
Later Stage

Geographical Preferences

International Preferences:
Switzerland
Israel

Industry Preferences

In Communications prefer:
Telecommunications

In Computer Software prefer:
Software

In Biotechnology prefer:
Biotechnology

Additional Information
Year Founded: 1999
Capital Under Management: $300,000,000
Current Activity Level : Actively seeking new investments

CATALYST INVESTORS LLC

711 Fifth Avenue, Suite 600
New York, NY USA 10022
Phone: 2128634848
Fax: 2123195771
E-mail: info@catalystinvestors.com
Website: www.catalystinvestors.com

Management and Staff
Brian Rich, Co-Founder
Christopher Shipman, Co-Founder
David Gordon, Vice President
Gene Wolfson, Partner
Mia Hegazy, Vice President
Ryan McNally, Co-Founder
Susan Bihler, Partner
Todd Clapp, Partner
Tyler Newton, Partner

Type of Firm
Private Equity Firm

Association Membership
National Venture Capital Association - USA (NVCA)

Project Preferences

Role in Financing:
Prefer role as deal originator but will also invest in deals created by others

Type of Financing Preferred:
Leveraged Buyout
Expansion
Generalist PE
Management Buyouts
Industry Rollups

Size of Investments Considered:
Min Size of Investment Considered (000s): $10,000
Max Size of Investment Considered (000s): $40,000

Geographical Preferences

United States Preferences:
North America

Canadian Preferences:
All Canada

International Preferences:
Europe

Industry Preferences

In Communications prefer:
Communications and Media
Telecommunications
Wireless Communications
Data Communications

In Computer Hardware prefer:
Computer Graphics and Dig

In Computer Software prefer:
Data Processing
Software

In Internet Specific prefer:
E-Commerce Technology
Internet
Ecommerce
Web Aggregation/Portals

In Medical/Health prefer:
Medical/Health
Health Services

In Consumer Related prefer:
Consumer Services
Education Related

In Financial Services prefer:
Financial Services

In Business Serv. prefer:
Services
Consulting Services

Additional Information
Name of Most Recent Fund: Catalyst Investors III, L.P.
Most Recent Fund Was Raised: 01/13/2012
Year Founded: 2000
Capital Under Management: $858,800,000
Current Activity Level : Actively seeking new investments
Method of Compensation: Return on investment is of primary concern, do not charge fees

CATALYST MICROFINANCE INVESTORS

ASA Tower, 23/3 Khilji Road
Shyamoli Mohammadpur
Dhaka, Bangladesh 1207
Phone: 880-2-911-6375
Fax: 880-2-912-1861
E-mail: dhaka@catalyst-microfinance.com
Website: www.catalyst-microfinance.com

Other Offices
Nieuwegracht 29
Utrecht, Netherlands 3512 LD
Phone: 31-30-234-3430
Fax: 31-30-233-1849

Type of Firm
Private Equity Firm

Project Preferences

Type of Financing Preferred:
Expansion

Geographical Preferences

International Preferences:
Pakistan
India
Ghana
Asia
Africa

Industry Preferences

In Financial Services prefer:
Financial Services

Additional Information
Year Founded: 2005
Current Activity Level : Actively seeking new investments

CATALYST PRINCIPAL PARTNERS LLC

Delta Riverside Office Park
3rd Floor Block 2
Nairobi, Kenya
Phone: 254204296000
Fax: 254204296100
E-mail: invest@catalystprincipal.com
Website: www.catalystprincipal.com

Management and Staff
Biniam Yohannes, Managing Director
Marlene Ngoyi, Principal
Paul Kavuma, Chief Executive Officer
Rajal Upadhyaya, Managing Director

Type of Firm
Private Equity Firm

Association Membership
Emerging Markets Private Equity Association
African Venture Capital Association (AVCA)

Project Preferences

Type of Financing Preferred:
Leveraged Buyout
Expansion
Management Buyouts
Acquisition
Recapitalizations

Geographical Preferences

International Preferences:
Ethiopia
Rwanda
Uganda
Zambia
Tanzania
Kenya
Congo, Dem Rep
Africa

Industry Preferences

In Communications prefer:
Telecommunications

In Consumer Related prefer:
Retail
Consumer Products

In Industrial/Energy prefer:
Industrial Products

In Financial Services prefer:
Financial Services

In Business Serv. prefer:
Services

In Manufact. prefer:
Manufacturing

Additional Information

Year Founded: 2009
Capital Under Management: $248,900,000
Current Activity Level : Actively seeking new investments

CATAMOUNT VENTURES LP

400 Pacific Avenue
Third Floor
San Francisco, CA USA 94133
Phone: 4152770300
Fax: 4152770301
E-mail: info@catamountventures.com
Website: www.catamountventures.com

Other Offices

3000 Sand Hill Road 1-100
Menlo Park, CA USA 94025

Management and Staff

James Joaquin, Partner
Jed Smith, Partner
Kate Chhabra, Partner
Mark Silverman, Partner
Patrick Fitzgerald, Principal
Tory Patterson, Partner

Type of Firm
Private Equity Firm

Association Membership
National Venture Capital Association - USA (NVCA)

Project Preferences

Type of Financing Preferred:
Early Stage

Industry Preferences

In Computer Software prefer:
Software

In Consumer Related prefer:
Consumer Products
Education Related

Additional Information
Name of Most Recent Fund: Catamount Ventures IV, L.P.
Most Recent Fund Was Raised: 12/10/2008
Year Founded: 2000
Capital Under Management: $206,000,000
Current Activity Level : Actively seeking new investments

CATAPULT PARTNERS PTY LTD

10 Eagle Street
Level 18
Brisbane, Australia QLD 4000
Phone: 61732201312
E-mail: catapult@catapultpartners.com.au
Website: catapultpartners.com.au

Type of Firm
Investment Management Firm

Project Preferences

Type of Financing Preferred:
Leveraged Buyout
Management Buyouts
Acquisition
Special Situation

Geographical Preferences

International Preferences:
Australia
New Zealand

Additional Information
Year Founded: 2015
Current Activity Level : Actively seeking new investments

CATAPULT VENTURE MANAGERS LTD

Melton Mowbray
11 Burrough Court Burrough on
Leicester, United Kingdom LE14 2QS
Phone: 441162388200
E-mail: mail@catapult-vm.co.uk
Website: www.catapult-vm.co.uk

Other Offices

One Victoria Square, Birmingham
West Midlands, United Kingdom B1 1BD
Phone: 441216160180
Fax: 441216160181

Management and Staff

Duncan Cameron, Chief Financial Officer
Mike Piper, Founder
Nick Wright, Chief Executive Officer
Rob Carroll, Managing Director

Type of Firm
Private Equity Firm

Association Membership
British Venture Capital Association (BVCA)

Project Preferences

Type of Financing Preferred:
Leveraged Buyout
Early Stage
Expansion
Generalist PE
Balanced
Later Stage
Management Buyouts
Acquisition

Size of Investments Considered:
Min Size of Investment Considered (000s): $314
Max Size of Investment Considered (000s): $3,139

Geographical Preferences

United States Preferences:
Midwest

International Preferences:
United Kingdom

Industry Preferences

In Communications prefer:
Communications and Media

In Computer Software prefer:
Software

In Medical/Health prefer:
Medical/Health

In Consumer Related prefer:
Consumer

In Industrial/Energy prefer:
Energy
Industrial Products
Environmental Related

In Business Serv. prefer:
Services

In Manufact. prefer:
Manufacturing

Additional Information
Year Founded: 1999
Capital Under Management: $125,600,000
Current Activity Level : Actively seeking new investments

CATCHA GROUP PTE LTD

45-7 The Boulevard
Lingkaran Syed Putra
Kuala Lumpur, Malaysia 59200
Phone: 6022970999
Fax: 6022970888
E-mail: enquiries@catchagroup.com
Website: www.catchagroup.com

Other Offices

Red Dot Traffic Building
28 Maxwell Road
, Singapore 069120

18/F, Tai Yip Building
141 Thomson Road
Wan Chai,, Hong Kong

Jl. Warung Jati Raya
36 Ragunan
Jakarta Selatan, Indonesia 12550

Type of Firm
Private Equity Firm

Project Preferences

Type of Financing Preferred:
Generalist PE
Seed
Acquisition
Startup

Geographical Preferences

International Preferences:
Indonesia
India
Taiwan
Hong Kong
China
Thailand
Philippines
Australia
Singapore
Malaysia

Industry Preferences

In Communications prefer:
Telecommunications
Media and Entertainment

In Internet Specific prefer:
E-Commerce Technology
Ecommerce

Additional Information
Year Founded: 1999
Current Activity Level : Actively seeking new investments

CATELLA AB

Birger Jarlsgatan Six
Stockholm, Sweden 102 40
Phone: 4684633310
Fax: 4684633395
E-mail: info@catella.se
Website: www.catella.com

Other Offices

Kongens Nytorv 26 1.
Copenhagen, Denmark 1050
Phone: 45-33-937-593
Fax: 45-33-938-593

15/25 boulevard de l'Amiral Bruix
Paris, France 75116
Phone: 33-1-5679-7979
Fax: 33-358-10522-0218

Aleksanterinkatu 15 B
Helsingfors, Finland 00100
Phone: 358-10-5220-100
Fax: 358-10-5220-218

Boulevard de la Woluwe 2 box 1
Brussels, Belgium 1150
Phone: 32-2-2307-000
Fax: 32-2-2307-700

Gertrudes 10/12
Riga, Latvia 1010
Phone: 370-5242-1101
Fax: 370-5278-4952

Management and Staff
Johan Nordenfalk, Chief Operating Officer
Marcus Holmstrand, Chief Financial Officer

Type of Firm
Investment Management Firm

Project Preferences

Type of Financing Preferred:
Leveraged Buyout
Early Stage
Generalist PE
Turnaround

Geographical Preferences

International Preferences:
Sweden
Europe

Industry Preferences

In Communications prefer:
Communications and Media
Publishing

In Internet Specific prefer:
Internet

Additional Information
Year Founded: 1987
Capital Under Management: $30,000,000
Current Activity Level : Actively seeking new investments

CATHAY CAPITAL PRIVATE EQUITY SAS

45 Avenue George V
Paris, France 75008
Phone: 33142252800
Fax: 33158285225
Website: www.cathay.fr

Other Offices

28, rue des Jardins
LILLE, France 59000

1901, Park Center
1088 Fangdian Road, Pudong
Shanghai, China 200120
Phone: 86-21-6888-8069

25, rue Marbeuf
Paris, France 75008
Phone: 33-1-4225-2800

Management and Staff
Edouard Moinet, Managing Partner
Mingpo Cai, President

Type of Firm
Private Equity Firm

Association Membership
French Venture Capital Association (AFIC)

Project Preferences

Type of Financing Preferred:
Leveraged Buyout
Early Stage
Expansion
Mezzanine
Generalist PE
Balanced
Acquisition
Startup

Size of Investments Considered:
Min Size of Investment Considered (000s): $2,505
Max Size of Investment Considered (000s): $18,789

Geographical Preferences

United States Preferences:

International Preferences:
Europe
China
Asia
Germany
France

Industry Preferences

In Communications prefer:
Wireless Communications
Media and Entertainment

In Computer Software prefer:
Data Processing
Software

In Internet Specific prefer:
E-Commerce Technology
Internet

In Medical/Health prefer:
Medical/Health
Pharmaceuticals

In Consumer Related prefer:
Consumer
Entertainment and Leisure
Retail
Franchises(NEC)
Food/Beverage
Consumer Products
Consumer Services

In Industrial/Energy prefer:
Industrial Products
Materials

In Business Serv. prefer:
Services

Additional Information
Year Founded: 2007
Capital Under Management: $1,176,838,000
Current Activity Level : Actively seeking new investments

CATHAY FINANCIAL HOLDING CO LTD

16th Floor, 296, Sec. 4
Ren Ai Road
Taipei, Taiwan 106
Phone: 886-2-2708-7698
Fax: 886-2-2325-2488
E-mail: service@cathayholdings.com.tw
Website: www.cathayholdings.com

Management and Staff
Cheng-Cheng Tung, President
Grace Chen, Chief Financial Officer

Type of Firm
Bank Affiliated

Association Membership
Taiwan Venture Capital Association(TVCA)

Project Preferences

Type of Financing Preferred:
Balanced

Geographical Preferences

International Preferences:
Taiwan

Additional Information
Year Founded: 2001
Current Activity Level : Actively seeking new investments

CATHAY FORTUNE CORP

Jinmao Tower, Suite 4403
Shanghai, China 200085
Website: www.cfc-group.cn

Type of Firm
Investment Management Firm

Additional Information
Year Founded: 2003
Current Activity Level : Actively seeking new investments

CATTERTON PARTNERS CORP

599 West Putnam Avenue
Greenwich, CT USA 06830
Phone: 2036294901
Fax: 2036294903
E-mail: info@cpequity.com
Website: www.cpequity.com

Management and Staff
Andrew Taub, Managing Partner
Christopher Casgar, Managing Director
David Gester, Partner
David Heidecorn, Partner
Dennis Ever, Partner
Farah Khan, Partner
Frankie Chan, Managing Director
Howard Steyn, Partner
James Hexter, Managing Partner
John Scerbo, Chief Financial Officer
Jonathan Owsley, Managing Partner
Marc Magliacano, Partner
Michael Farello, Managing Partner
Neda Daneshzadeh, Partner
Nikhil Thukral, Managing Partner
Sandra Kim-Suk, Chief Financial Officer

Type of Firm
Private Equity Firm

Project Preferences

Role in Financing:
Prefer role as deal originator but will also invest in deals created by others

Type of Financing Preferred:
Leveraged Buyout
Early Stage
Expansion
Turnaround
Acquisition
Recapitalizations

Geographical Preferences

United States Preferences:
North America

International Preferences:
Latin America

Industry Focus
(% based on actual investment)
Consumer Related	45.1%
Internet Specific	28.0%
Medical/Health	17.8%
Computer Software and Services	3.9%
Semiconductors/Other Elect.	2.2%
Computer Hardware	1.9%
Biotechnology	0.8%
Other Products	0.4%

Additional Information
Name of Most Recent Fund: Catterton Growth Partners II, L.P.
Most Recent Fund Was Raised: 09/18/2013
Year Founded: 1989
Capital Under Management: $2,500,000,000
Current Activity Level : Actively seeking new investments
Method of Compensation: Return on invest. most important, but chg. closing fees, service fees, etc.

CAURIS MANAGEMENT

68 av de la Liberation
BP 1172
Lome, Togo BP 1172
Phone: 228-222-5957
Fax: 228-222-5964
E-mail: cauris@caurismanagement.com
Website: www.caurismanagement.com

Other Offices
Terrasson de Fougeres and street Gourgas
4th Floor, BOA,
Abidjan, Ivory Coast 110690101
Phone: 225-2022-6463
Fax: 225-2022-6465

Management and Staff
Noel Eklo, Managing Director

Type of Firm
Private Equity Firm

Association Membership
Emerging Markets Private Equity Association
African Venture Capital Association (AVCA)

Project Preferences

Type of Financing Preferred:
Balanced
Later Stage
Acquisition

Size of Investments Considered:
Min Size of Investment Considered (000s): $180
Max Size of Investment Considered (000s): $3,866

Geographical Preferences

International Preferences:
Togo
Morocco
Africa

Industry Preferences

In Communications prefer:
Communications and Media

In Biotechnology prefer:
Agricultural/Animal Bio.

In Financial Services prefer:
Financial Services

Additional Information
Name of Most Recent Fund: Cauris Croissance
Most Recent Fund Was Raised: 07/20/2005
Year Founded: 1997
Capital Under Management: $17,300,000
Current Activity Level : Actively seeking new investments

CAUSEWAY CAPITAL PARTNERS I LP

4 Lower Hatch Street
Dublin, Ireland
Website: www.causewaycapital.eu

Management and Staff
Ben Merrifield, Partner
David Raethorne, Partner
Matthew Scaife, Partner

Type of Firm
Private Equity Firm

Project Preferences

Type of Financing Preferred:
Leveraged Buyout

Geographical Preferences

International Preferences:
Ireland
United Kingdom

Additional Information
Year Founded: 2016
Current Activity Level : Actively seeking new investments

CAUSEWAY MEDIA PARTNERS LP

226 Causeway Street
Fourth Floor
Boston, MA USA 02114
Phone: 6178548001
E-mail: info@causewaymp.com
Website: www.causewaymp.com

Type of Firm
Private Equity Firm

Project Preferences

Type of Financing Preferred:
Balanced

Industry Preferences

In Consumer Related prefer:
Sports

In Business Serv. prefer:
Media

Additional Information
Name of Most Recent Fund: Causeway Media Partners, L.P.
Most Recent Fund Was Raised: 06/06/2013
Year Founded: 2013
Capital Under Management: $332,836,000
Current Activity Level : Actively seeking new investments

CAVA CAPITAL

18 South Main Street
Third Floor
Norwalk, CT USA 06854
Phone: 2035293064
E-mail: info@cavacapital.com
Website: www.cavacapital.com

Other Offices
110 East 25th Street
NEW YORK, NY USA 10010

Management and Staff
Geoff Schneider, Founder
Geoff Schneider, Managing Partner
Kevin Lynch, Chief Financial Officer
Kevin Lynch, Chief Financial Officer
Mike Shim, Managing Partner
Peg Jackson, Venture Partner

Type of Firm
Private Equity Firm

Project Preferences

Type of Financing Preferred:
Early Stage

Size of Investments Considered:
Min Size of Investment Considered (000s): $1,000
Max Size of Investment Considered (000s): $5,000

Geographical Preferences

United States Preferences:
All U.S.

Industry Preferences

In Communications prefer:
Wireless Communications
Data Communications

In Computer Software prefer:
Software
Applications Software

In Internet Specific prefer:
E-Commerce Technology
Ecommerce

In Semiconductor/Electr prefer:
Analytic/Scientific

In Business Serv. prefer:
Services
Media

Additional Information
Year Founded: 2010
Capital Under Management: $14,000,000
Current Activity Level : Actively seeking new investments

CAVALRY INVESTMENTS LLC

Seven Skyline Drive
Hawthorne, NY USA 10532
Phone: 9143473440
Fax: 9143471973
Website: www.cavalryportfolioservices.com

Management and Staff
Andrew Zaro, Founder
Michael Godner, Chief Financial Officer

Type of Firm
Bank Affiliated

Project Preferences

Type of Financing Preferred:
Leveraged Buyout
Acquisition

Geographical Preferences

United States Preferences:

Industry Preferences

In Financial Services prefer:
Financial Services

Additional Information
Year Founded: 1991
Current Activity Level : Actively seeking new investments

CAVALRY MANAGEMENT GROUP LLC

Two Embarcadero Center
Suite 600
San Francisco, CA USA 94111
Phone: 4154397000

Type of Firm
Private Equity Firm

Additional Information
Year Founded: 2003
Capital Under Management: $129,100,000
Current Activity Level : Actively seeking new investments

CAVALRY VENTURES MANAGEMENT GMBH

Fehrbelliner Strasse 47e
c/o Rouven Dresselhaus
Berlin, Germany 10119
E-mail: deals@voltage.vc
Website: www.cavalry.vc

Type of Firm
Private Equity Firm

Project Preferences

Type of Financing Preferred:
Early Stage

Geographical Preferences

United States Preferences:
All U.S.

International Preferences:
Europe
Germany

Additional Information
Year Founded: 2011
Current Activity Level : Actively seeking new investments

CAVE CREEK CAPITAL MANAGEMENT

2355 East Camelback Road
Suite 510
Phoenix, AZ USA 85016
Phone: 4804786960
Fax: 4804786961
Website: www.cavecreekcapital.com

Management and Staff
G. Kevin Fechtmeyer, Managing Partner

Type of Firm
Private Equity Firm

Project Preferences

Type of Financing Preferred:
Leveraged Buyout
Mezzanine
Management Buyouts

Size of Investments Considered:
Min Size of Investment Considered (000s): $2,000
Max Size of Investment Considered (000s): $10,000

Industry Preferences

In Medical/Health prefer:
Health Services

In Consumer Related prefer:
Retail
Consumer Products
Consumer Services

In Financial Services prefer:
Financial Services

In Business Serv. prefer:
Services
Distribution

Additional Information
Year Founded: 2004
Current Activity Level : Actively seeking new investments

CAVENDISH IMPACT CAPITAL

6098 West Lake Road
Cooperstown, NY USA 13326

Type of Firm
Private Equity Firm

Project Preferences

Type of Financing Preferred:
Balanced

Industry Preferences

In Medical/Health prefer:
Health Services

In Consumer Related prefer:
Education Related

In Other prefer:
Environment Responsible

Additional Information
Year Founded: 2017
Current Activity Level : Actively seeking new investments

CAVIPAR SASU

68 rue du Faubourg
Saint-Honore
Paris, France 75008
Phone: 33139499703
Fax: 33134292297
E-mail: info@cavipar.com

Management and Staff
Charles-Henri Rossignol, Managing Partner
Richard Schreiber, Managing Partner

Type of Firm
Private Equity Firm

Association Membership
French Venture Capital Association (AFIC)

Project Preferences

Type of Financing Preferred:
Leveraged Buyout
Early Stage
Generalist PE
Turnaround
Later Stage

Size of Investments Considered:
Min Size of Investment Considered (000s): $6,489
Max Size of Investment Considered (000s): $38,935

Geographical Preferences

International Preferences:
Europe
France

Additional Information
Year Founded: 1999
Current Activity Level : Actively seeking new investments

CAVU VENTURE PARTNERS, LLC

515 West 20th Street
Suite 4W
New York, NY USA 10011
Phone: 2127162670
Website: www.cavuventures.com

Other Offices
Former HQ:350 Madison Avenue
Eight Floor
NEW YORK, NY USA 10001
Phone: 6468430578

Management and Staff
Bella Filer, Chief Financial Officer
Brett Thomas, Co-Founder
Clayton Christopher, Partner
Jacqueline Loken, Vice President
Rohan Oza, Partner

Type of Firm
Private Equity Firm

Project Preferences

Type of Financing Preferred:
Balanced

Industry Preferences

In Consumer Related prefer:
Food/Beverage

Additional Information
Year Founded: 2016
Capital Under Management: $155,980,000
Current Activity Level : Actively seeking new investments

CAYMUS EQUITY PARTNERS

3490 Piedmont Road North East
Suite 1040
Atlanta, GA USA 30305
Phone: 4049958300
Fax: 4049958340
Website: www.caymuspartners.com

Other Offices
641 Lexington Avenue
17th Floor
New York, NY USA 10022
Phone: 2127553600

Management and Staff
Geoffrey Faux, Managing Partner
John Maggard, Managing Partner

Type of Firm
Bank Affiliated

Project Preferences

Type of Financing Preferred:
Leveraged Buyout
Acquisition

Industry Preferences

In Communications prefer:
Wireless Communications

In Medical/Health prefer:
Medical Products
Health Services

In Consumer Related prefer:
Consumer
Retail
Consumer Products
Consumer Services

In Business Serv. prefer:
Services
Media

In Manufact. prefer:
Manufacturing

Additional Information
Year Founded: 2001
Current Activity Level : Actively seeking new investments

CAYUGA VENTURE FUND

15 Thornwood Drive
Cornell Business & Technology
Ithaca, NY USA 14850
Phone: 6072669266
Fax: 6072669267
Website: www.cayugaventures.com

Management and Staff
Cliff Lardin, Venture Partner
Jennifer Tegan, Partner
Jennifer Tegan, Partner
Ken Rother, Venture Partner
Philip Proujansky, Managing Partner
Ryoko Nozawa, Principal
Zachary Shulman, Managing Partner

Type of Firm
Private Equity Firm

Association Membership
National Venture Capital Association - USA (NVCA)

Project Preferences

Role in Financing:
Prefer role as deal originator but will also invest in deals created by others

Type of Financing Preferred:
Second Stage Financing
Early Stage
Expansion
Balanced
Seed

Size of Investments Considered:
Min Size of Investment Considered (000s): $200
Max Size of Investment Considered (000s): $3,000

Geographical Preferences

United States Preferences:
New York

Industry Preferences

In Computer Hardware prefer:
Computers

In Computer Other prefer:
Computer Related

In Semiconductor/Electr prefer:
Semiconductor
Laser Related

In Medical/Health prefer:
Medical/Health
Medical Diagnostics
Medical Products

In Consumer Related prefer:
Consumer

Additional Information
Name of Most Recent Fund: Cayuga Venture Fund IV, L.P.
Most Recent Fund Was Raised: 05/31/2011
Year Founded: 1994
Capital Under Management: $55,100,000
Current Activity Level : Actively seeking new investments
Method of Compensation: Return on investment is of primary concern, do not charge fees

CB ALLIANCE INC

350 Fifth Avenue
Empire State Bldg, Suite 7610
New York, NY USA 10118
Phone: 2124650600
Fax: 6463493532
Website: cballiancehq.com

Type of Firm
Investment Management Firm

Project Preferences

Type of Financing Preferred:
Early Stage
Startup

Industry Preferences

In Internet Specific prefer:
Internet

In Semiconductor/Electr prefer:
Analytic/Scientific

In Industrial/Energy prefer:
Alternative Energy

In Financial Services prefer:
Real Estate

Additional Information
Year Founded: 2011
Current Activity Level : Actively seeking new investments

CBC CAPITAL

Ju Fu Dian, Ritan Park
Beijing, China 100020
Phone: 861085635888
Fax: 861085635678
Website: www.cbc-capital.com

Other Offices

222 Yan An Road East
4104 Bund Center
Shanghai, China 200002
Phone: 86-21-6335-1177
Fax: 86-21-6335-0318

100 Cyberport Road
Unit 906, Level 9, Cyberport 2
Central, Hong Kong
Phone: 85221228400
Fax: 85221228410

Management and Staff

Jian Jiang, Partner
Wei Liu, Partner
Xingcha Fan, Partner
Ying Zhang, Founder
Yun Zhou, Partner
Zhiming Xu, Partner

Type of Firm
Private Equity Firm

Association Membership
China Venture Capital Association

Project Preferences

Type of Financing Preferred:
Balanced

Geographical Preferences

International Preferences:
China

Industry Preferences

In Communications prefer:
Communications and Media
Telecommunications
Wireless Communications

In Internet Specific prefer:
Internet

In Computer Other prefer:
Computer Related

In Industrial/Energy prefer:
Alternative Energy

Additional Information
Name of Most Recent Fund: China Broadband Capital Partners, L.P.
Most Recent Fund Was Raised: 05/16/2006
Year Founded: 2006
Current Activity Level : Actively seeking new investments

CBG COMMERZ BETEILI-GUNGSKAPITAL GMBH & CO KG

Kaiserstrasse 16
Frankfurt am Main, Germany 60311
Phone: 496913644494
Fax: 496913629336
E-mail: cbg@commerzbank.com
Website: www.cbg.commerzbank.com

Management and Staff

Klaus Sachse, Managing Director
Stephan Klier, Managing Director

Type of Firm
Bank Affiliated

Association Membership
German Venture Capital Association (BVK)

Project Preferences

Role in Financing:
Prefer role as deal originator

Type of Financing Preferred:
Leveraged Buyout
Mezzanine
Management Buyouts

Geographical Preferences

International Preferences:
Switzerland
Austria
Germany

Industry Preferences

In Communications prefer:
Communications and Media

In Semiconductor/Electr prefer:
Analytic/Scientific

In Medical/Health prefer:
Medical Diagnostics

In Consumer Related prefer:
Retail
Food/Beverage

In Industrial/Energy prefer:
Industrial Products
Materials

In Business Serv. prefer:
Services

In Agr/Forestr/Fish prefer:
Agriculture related

Additional Information
Year Founded: 1987
Capital Under Management: $160,500,000
Current Activity Level : Reducing investment activity
Method of Compensation: Return on investment is of primary concern, do not charge fees

CBPE CAPITAL LLP

Two George Yard
London, United Kingdom EC3V 9DH
Phone: 442070651100
Fax: 442075886815
E-mail: enquiries@cbpel.com
Website: www.cbpecapital.com

Management and Staff

Anne Hoffmann, Partner
Iain Slater, Partner
Mathew Hutchinson, Partner
Nick Macnay, Partner
Peter Gissel, Partner
Sean Dinnen, Partner

Type of Firm
Private Equity Firm

Association Membership
British Venture Capital Association (BVCA)

Project Preferences

Type of Financing Preferred:
Leveraged Buyout
Management Buyouts

Geographical Preferences

International Preferences:
United Kingdom

Industry Preferences

In Semiconductor/Electr prefer:
Electronics

In Medical/Health prefer:
Medical Diagnostics
Medical Products
Health Services
Pharmaceuticals

In Consumer Related prefer:
Consumer
Entertainment and Leisure
Retail
Food/Beverage
Consumer Products
Other Restaurants
Education Related

In Industrial/Energy prefer:
Oil & Gas Drilling,Explor
Industrial Products
Materials
Environmental Related

In Transportation prefer:
Transportation
Aerospace

In Business Serv. prefer:
Services
Distribution
Media

In Utilities prefer:
Utilities

Additional Information
Year Founded: 1984
Capital Under Management: $1,262,500,000
Current Activity Level : Actively seeking new investments

CBR MANAGEMENT GMBH

Theatinerstrasse 7
Munich, Germany 80333
Phone: 49892113777
Fax: 498921137788
E-mail: info@cbr-gmbh.de
Website: www.cbr-gmbh.de

Management and Staff
Eberhard Crain, Co-Founder
Michael Hessing, Partner
Michael Welzel, Co-Founder
Wolfgang Behrens-Ramberg, Co-Founder

Type of Firm
Private Equity Firm

Project Preferences

Type of Financing Preferred:
Leveraged Buyout
Turnaround
Later Stage
Management Buyouts
Recapitalizations

Geographical Preferences

International Preferences:
Switzerland
Austria
Germany

Additional Information
Year Founded: 1991
Capital Under Management: $140,000,000
Current Activity Level : Actively seeking new investments

CCB INTERNATIONAL GROUP HOLDINGS LTD

88 Queensway, Admiralty
34F Two Pacific Place
Central, Hong Kong
Phone: 85225326100
Fax: 85225301496

Management and Staff
Alvin Li, Managing Director
Hu Zhanghong, Chief Executive Officer

Type of Firm
Bank Affiliated

Project Preferences

Type of Financing Preferred:
Early Stage
Expansion
Balanced
Later Stage

Geographical Preferences

International Preferences:
Hong Kong
China

Industry Preferences

In Communications prefer:
Radio & TV Broadcasting
Publishing

In Internet Specific prefer:
Internet

In Medical/Health prefer:
Medical/Health
Other Therapeutic
Medical Products
Health Services
Pharmaceuticals

In Consumer Related prefer:
Entertainment and Leisure

In Industrial/Energy prefer:
Energy
Alternative Energy
Energy Conservation Relat
Materials
Environmental Related

In Financial Services prefer:
Financial Services

In Business Serv. prefer:
Services
Media

In Manufact. prefer:
Manufacturing

In Other prefer:
Environment Responsible

Additional Information
Year Founded: 2004
Capital Under Management: $417,376,000
Current Activity Level : Actively seeking new investments

CCBT PRIVATE EQUITY FUND

No.4, Naoshikou Avenue
4F, F Zone, 4th Road
Beijing, China 100031
Phone: 861067594352
Fax: 861067596590
Website: www.ccbtpe.com

Management and Staff
Xinghua Wu, Managing Director

Type of Firm
Bank Affiliated

Project Preferences

Type of Financing Preferred:
Later Stage

Geographical Preferences

International Preferences:
China

Industry Preferences

In Medical/Health prefer:
Medical/Health

In Industrial/Energy prefer:
Energy Conservation Relat
Environmental Related

In Business Serv. prefer:
Services
Media

In Manufact. prefer:
Manufacturing

In Agr/Forestr/Fish prefer:
Agriculture related

Additional Information
Year Founded: 2011
Capital Under Management: $455,235,000
Current Activity Level : Actively seeking new investments

CCM INVESTMENT ADVISERS LLC

1201 Main Street, Suite 1910
Columbia, SC USA 29201
Phone: 8032549500
Fax: 8032529530

E-mail: information@companioncm.com
Website: www.ccminc.com

Other Offices
Former: 4101 Percival Road
AX-200
Columbia, SC USA 29223
Phone: 803-264-5591
Fax: 803-264-8077

Management and Staff
Mike Mizeur, President

Type of Firm
Corporate PE/Venture

Project Preferences

Role in Financing:
Prefer role as deal originator

Type of Financing Preferred:
Second Stage Financing
Expansion
Balanced
Seed
First Stage Financing
Strategic Alliances
Startup

Size of Investments Considered:
Min Size of Investment Considered (000s): $5,000
Max Size of Investment Considered (000s): $100,000

Geographical Preferences

United States Preferences:
Southeast
All U.S.

Industry Preferences

In Computer Software prefer:
Software
Applications Software

In Medical/Health prefer:
Health Services

In Financial Services prefer:
Insurance
Financial Services

Additional Information
Year Founded: 2005
Capital Under Management: $5,600,000
Current Activity Level : Actively seeking new investments
Method of Compensation: Return on investment is of primary concern, do not charge fees

CCMP CAPITAL ADVISORS LP

245 Park Avenue, 16th Floor
New York, NY USA 10167
Phone: 2126009600
Fax: 2125993481
Website: www.ccmpcapital.com

Other Offices
28 King Street
Almack House
London, United Kingdom SW1Y6XA
Phone: 442073899100
Fax: 442078392192

24 Waterway Avenue
Suite 750
The Woodlands, TX USA 77380
Phone: 281-363-2013
Fax: 281-363-2097

Management and Staff
Alberto Joe Delgado, Managing Director
Allison Cole, Vice President
Allison Bernbach, Managing Director
Christopher Behrens, Managing Director
Christy Carter, Principal
Dina Colombo, Managing Director
Elizabeth Smith, Vice President
Esana Blank, Vice President
Greg Feig, Vice President
John Warner, Managing Director
Jonathan Lynch, Managing Director
Joseph Scharfenberger, Managing Director
Julie Casella-Esposito, Managing Director
Karl Kurz, Managing Director
Kevin O Brien, Managing Director
Leslie Brun, Managing Director
Mark McFadden, Principal
Mit Mehta, Principal
Nikki-Ann Trezza, Vice President
Richard Zannino, Managing Director
Richard Jansen, Managing Director
Robert Toth, Managing Director
Robert Stabile, Vice President
Ryan Anderson, Principal
Timothy Walsh, Managing Director
Trudy Capaldo, Vice President

Type of Firm
Private Equity Firm

Association Membership
Private Equity Council (PEC)

Project Preferences

Type of Financing Preferred:
Leveraged Buyout
Expansion

Geographical Preferences

United States Preferences:

International Preferences:
Europe
Asia

Industry Preferences

In Medical/Health prefer:
Medical/Health
Medical Products
Health Services
Pharmaceuticals

In Consumer Related prefer:
Consumer
Retail
Consumer Services

In Industrial/Energy prefer:
Energy
Industrial Products

In Business Serv. prefer:
Media

In Manufact. prefer:
Manufacturing

Additional Information
Name of Most Recent Fund: CCMP Capital Investors III, L.P.
Most Recent Fund Was Raised: 07/12/2013
Year Founded: 2006
Capital Under Management: $3,600,000,000
Current Activity Level : Actively seeking new investments

CD VENTURE GMBH

Bergheimer Strasse 45
Heidelberg, Germany 69115
Phone: 496221187870
E-mail: info@cd-venture.com
Website: www.cd-venture.com

Management and Staff
Christoph Boehringer, Managing Director
Dirk Wilken, Managing Director

Type of Firm
Private Equity Firm

Project Preferences

Type of Financing Preferred:
Balanced

Geographical Preferences

International Preferences:
Germany

Additional Information
Year Founded: 2003
Current Activity Level : Actively seeking new investments

CDBI PARTNERS

No. 1108, Nanjing West Road
Room 1108, Zhongxintaifu Plaza
Shanghai, China 200041
Phone: 862162609156
Fax: 862162609156
Website: www.cd-pe.com

Type of Firm
Private Equity Firm

Project Preferences

Type of Financing Preferred:
Fund of Funds
Balanced

Geographical Preferences

International Preferences:
China

Industry Preferences

In Medical/Health prefer:
Medical/Health
Pharmaceuticals

Additional Information
Year Founded: 2013
Capital Under Management: $2,000,000,000
Current Activity Level : Actively seeking new investments

CDC CLIMAT SA

47 Rue de la Victoire
Paris, France 75009
Phone: 33158508710
Website: www.cdcclimat.com

Management and Staff
Benoit Leguet, Managing Director
Herve Allegre, Managing Director
Jean-Pierre Sicard, Chief Executive Officer
Michel Laffitte, Managing Director

Type of Firm
Bank Affiliated

Project Preferences

Type of Financing Preferred:
Early Stage
Later Stage

Geographical Preferences

United States Preferences:
East Coast

International Preferences:
Europe
France

Industry Preferences

In Industrial/Energy prefer:
Energy Conservation Relat
Environmental Related

In Other prefer:
Environment Responsible

Additional Information
Year Founded: 2010
Current Activity Level : Actively seeking new investments

CDC GESTION SA

Rue du Lac Michigan
Residence LAKEO
Tunis, Tunisia 1053
Phone: 21671862660
Fax: 21671862730
Website: www.cdcgestion.tn

Type of Firm
Bank Affiliated

Project Preferences

Type of Financing Preferred:
Early Stage
Expansion
Later Stage
Recapitalizations

Geographical Preferences

International Preferences:
Tunisia

Additional Information
Year Founded: 2013
Current Activity Level : Actively seeking new investments

CDC GROUP PLC

123 Victoria Street
London, United Kingdom SW1E 6DE
Phone: 442079634700
Fax: 442079634750
E-mail: enquiries@cdcgroup.com
Website: www.cdcgroup.com

Other Offices
Room 2401, China World Tower 2
No. 1 Jian Guo Men Wai Street
Beijing, China 100004
Phone: 86-10-6505-6655
Fax: 86-10-6505-8111

16 Raffles Quay
#19-02 Hong Leong Building
Singapore, Singapore 048581
Phone: 65-6227-8632
Fax: 65-6227-1004

Management and Staff
Alagappan Murugappan, Managing Director
Colin Buckley, Chief Operating Officer
Colin Buckley, Chief Operating Officer
Diana Noble, Chief Executive Officer
Godfrey Davies, Chief Financial Officer
Godfrey Davies, Chief Financial Officer
Holger Rothenbusch, Managing Director
Mark Pay, Managing Director
Roderick Evison, Managing Director

Type of Firm
Government Affiliated Program

Association Membership
Emerging Markets Private Equity Association
European Private Equity and Venture Capital Assoc.
African Venture Capital Association (AVCA)

Project Preferences

Type of Financing Preferred:
Fund of Funds
Expansion
Mezzanine

Geographical Preferences

International Preferences:
Asia
Africa

Industry Preferences

In Communications prefer:
Communications and Media

In Medical/Health prefer:
Medical/Health

In Consumer Related prefer:
Education Related

In Financial Services prefer:
Financial Services
Real Estate

In Business Serv. prefer:
Services

In Manufact. prefer:
Manufacturing

In Agr/Forestr/Fish prefer:
Agribusiness
Mining and Minerals

Additional Information
Year Founded: 1948
Capital Under Management: $2,800,000,000
Current Activity Level : Actively seeking new investments

CDC INFRA MANAGEMENT SAS

56, rue de Lille
Paris, France 75007
Phone: 33158502090
E-mail: contact@cdcinfra.com
Website: www.cdcinfrastructure.com

Management and Staff
Eric Hayoun, Chief Financial Officer
Patrick Vandervoorde, Chief Executive Officer

Type of Firm
Bank Affiliated

Association Membership
French Venture Capital Association (AFIC)

Project Preferences

Type of Financing Preferred:
Early Stage
Later Stage

Geographical Preferences

International Preferences:
Europe
France

Industry Preferences

In Communications prefer:
Telecommunications

In Industrial/Energy prefer:
Energy

In Transportation prefer:
Transportation

Additional Information
Year Founded: 2010
Current Activity Level: Actively seeking new investments

CDC INTERNATIONAL CAPITAL SA

67, Rue de Lille
Paris, France 75007
E-mail: contact@cdcicapital.fr
Website: cdcicapital.fr

Type of Firm
Bank Affiliated

Project Preferences

Type of Financing Preferred:
Leveraged Buyout
Early Stage
Expansion
Later Stage
Management Buyouts
Acquisition

Size of Investments Considered:
Min Size of Investment Considered (000s): $15,924
Max Size of Investment Considered (000s): $84,926

Geographical Preferences

International Preferences:
France

Additional Information
Year Founded: 2008
Capital Under Management: $322,700,000
Current Activity Level: Actively seeking new investments

CDH CHINA MANAGEMENT CO., LTD.

No.5, East 3rd Ring Road
25F, Fortune Financial Center
Beijing, China 100020
Phone: 861085076998
Fax: 861085076999
E-mail: cdhir@cdhfund.com
Website: www.cdhfund.com

Other Offices
1503 International Commerce Center
1 Austin Road West
Kowloon, Hong Kong
Phone: 85235188000
Fax: 85228107083

Maples Corporate Services, Ltd
Ugland House
Grand Cayman, Cayman Islands KY1-1104
Phone: 85228107003

Management and Staff
Jason Zhang, Managing Director
Li Guo, Chief Financial Officer
Lin Wang, Founder
Meilan Gan, Managing Director
Ning Hu, Managing Director
Stuart Schonberger, Founder
Wei Ying, Managing Director
Xiaoling Hu, Founder
Xiaoming Song, Managing Director
Yan Huang, General Partner
Zhen Jiao, President
Zhenyu Wang, Founder

Type of Firm
Private Equity Firm

Association Membership
Venture Capital Association of Beijing (VCAB)
China Venture Capital Association
Hong Kong Venture Capital Association (HKVCA)

Project Preferences

Type of Financing Preferred:
Generalist PE
Balanced
Later Stage

Geographical Preferences

United States Preferences:

International Preferences:
Europe
China

Industry Preferences

In Medical/Health prefer:
Medical/Health
Health Services

In Consumer Related prefer:
Consumer
Consumer Products
Consumer Services
Education Related

In Industrial/Energy prefer:
Energy Conservation Relat

In Financial Services prefer:
Financial Services

In Business Serv. prefer:
Services
Media

Additional Information
Name of Most Recent Fund: CDH Special Opportunity Fund, L.P.
Most Recent Fund Was Raised: 04/26/2013
Year Founded: 2002
Capital Under Management: $600,000,000
Current Activity Level: Actively seeking new investments

CDI INVESTISSEMENT SASU

102C rue Amelot
Paris, France 75011
Phone: 33155280163
Fax: 33155287190
E-mail: cdi@groupe-sos.org

Type of Firm
Private Equity Firm

Project Preferences

Type of Financing Preferred:
Early Stage
Later Stage

Geographical Preferences

International Preferences:
Europe
Eastern Europe
France

Additional Information

Year Founded: 2012
Capital Under Management: $13,690,000
Current Activity Level : Actively seeking new investments

CDIB & MBS VENTURE CAPITAL CO LTD

ASEM Tower 35/F, 159-1
Samsung-dong, Kangnam-gu
Seoul, South Korea 135-798
Phone: 822-6001-5200
Fax: 822-6001-5240

Type of Firm

Private Equity Firm

Association Membership

Hong Kong Venture Capital Association (HKVCA)

Project Preferences

Type of Financing Preferred:
Balanced

Geographical Preferences

International Preferences:
Korea, South

Industry Preferences

In Semiconductor/Electr prefer:
Semiconductor

Additional Information

Year Founded: 1997
Capital Under Management: $17,000,000
Current Activity Level : Actively seeking new investments

CDIB BIOSCIENCE VENTURE MANAGEMENT

9191 Towne Centre Drive
Suite 575
San Diego, CA USA 92122
Phone: 8585526808
Fax: 8585526811
Website: www.cdibbiosciencevc.com

Other Offices

Peihsin Road
Ninth Floor-One, Suite 205, Section 3
Taipei, Taiwan
Phone: 886-2-8913-1956
Fax: 886-2-8913-1955

Management and Staff

Polong Chou, Vice President
Tai-Sen Soong, President

Type of Firm

Private Equity Firm

Association Membership

Taiwan Venture Capital Association(TVCA)

Project Preferences

Role in Financing:
Will function either as deal originator or investor in deals created by others

Type of Financing Preferred:
Early Stage
Balanced
Later Stage

Size of Investments Considered:
Min Size of Investment Considered (000s): $2,000
Max Size of Investment Considered (000s): $5,000

Geographical Preferences

United States Preferences:
North America

International Preferences:
Taiwan

Industry Preferences

In Medical/Health prefer:
Medical/Health

Additional Information

Year Founded: 2001
Capital Under Management: $75,000,000
Current Activity Level : Actively seeking new investments
Method of Compensation: Return on investment is of primary concern, do not charge fees

CDIB CAPITAL GROUP

No. 125 Nanking East Road
Section 5
Taipei, Taiwan 105-04
Phone: 886227638800
Website: www.cdibank.com

Other Offices

Kunshan
Jiangsu, China 215300

Management and Staff

Chia-Juch Chang, Managing Director
Ching-Yen Tsay, Managing Director
Paul Yang, Managing Director

Type of Firm

Bank Affiliated

Project Preferences

Role in Financing:
Prefer role as deal originator but will also invest in deals created by others

Type of Financing Preferred:
Fund of Funds
Early Stage
Expansion
Balanced

Geographical Preferences

United States Preferences:

International Preferences:
India
Taiwan
Hong Kong
Western Europe
China
Australia
Asia
Korea, South
Japan

Industry Preferences

In Communications prefer:
Telecommunications

In Medical/Health prefer:
Medical/Health

In Consumer Related prefer:
Consumer
Retail

In Industrial/Energy prefer:
Energy
Energy Conservation Relat
Industrial Products
Materials

In Transportation prefer:
Transportation

In Financial Services prefer:
Financial Services

In Business Serv. prefer:
Services
Media

Additional Information

Year Founded: 1959
Capital Under Management: $156,568,000
Current Activity Level : Actively seeking new investments

CDIB CAPITAL INTERNATIONAL CORP

ICBC Tower, Citibank Plaza
Suites 701-703
Hongkong, Hong Kong
Phone: 85222318600
Fax: 85222318601
Website: www.cdibcapital.com

Management and Staff
Gary Fung, Vice President
Hamilton Tang, Managing Director
Thomas Hu, Vice President
Xie Yinghai, Managing Director

Type of Firm
Bank Affiliated

Association Membership
China Venture Capital Association
Hong Kong Venture Capital Association (HKVCA)

Project Preferences

Type of Financing Preferred:
Leveraged Buyout
Expansion
Generalist PE
Later Stage
Recapitalizations

Size of Investments Considered:
Min Size of Investment Considered (000s): $20,000
Max Size of Investment Considered (000s): $75,000

Geographical Preferences

International Preferences:
Asia Pacific

Additional Information
Year Founded: 2006
Capital Under Management: $405,000,000
Current Activity Level : Actively seeking new investments

CDIB VENTURE CAPITAL CORP

11 Floor, 125, Section 5
Nanjing East Road
Taipei, Taiwan 10504
Phone: 886227638800
Website: www.cdibh.com

Type of Firm
Bank Affiliated

Geographical Preferences

International Preferences:
Taiwan

Industry Preferences

In Communications prefer:
Communications and Media

In Internet Specific prefer:
Internet

In Semiconductor/Electr prefer:
Electronic Components
Semiconductor

In Medical/Health prefer:
Medical/Health

In Consumer Related prefer:
Consumer Products

Additional Information
Year Founded: 2002
Current Activity Level : Actively seeking new investments

CDK VENTURES LLC

412 Olive Ave
Suite 619
Huntington Beach, CA USA 92648
E-mail: info@cdkventures.com
Website: www.cdkventures.com

Type of Firm
Private Equity Firm

Project Preferences

Type of Financing Preferred:
Balanced
Management Buyouts
Recapitalizations

Industry Preferences

In Computer Software prefer:
Software

Additional Information
Year Founded: 2016
Current Activity Level : Actively seeking new investments

CDP CAPITAL INC

2001 McGill College Avenue
Seventh Floor
Montreal, Canada H3A1G1
Phone: 514-847-2611
Fax: 514-847-5978
Website: www.cdpcapital.com

Management and Staff
Michel Lefebvre, Vice President

Type of Firm
Endowment, Foundation or Pension Fund

Project Preferences

Type of Financing Preferred:
Expansion
Balanced
Turnaround
Other
Acquisition

Geographical Preferences

Canadian Preferences:
All Canada
Quebec

Industry Preferences

In Computer Software prefer:
Software

In Manufact. prefer:
Manufacturing

Additional Information
Year Founded: 1994
Current Activity Level : Actively seeking new investments

CDP CAPITAL PRIVATE EQUITY

1000, place Jean-Paul-Riopelle
Montreal, Canada H2Z 2B3
Phone: 5148423261
Fax: 5148424833
Website: www.lacaisse.com

Type of Firm
Endowment, Foundation or Pension Fund

Project Preferences

Type of Financing Preferred:
Leveraged Buyout
Early Stage
Expansion
Mezzanine
Turnaround
Later Stage
Management Buyouts

Geographical Preferences

United States Preferences:
North America

Additional Information
Year Founded: 1982
Capital Under Management: $665,930,000
Current Activity Level : Actively seeking new investments

CDP EQUITY SPA

C.so Magenta, 71
Milan, Italy 20123
Phone: 39642214440
E-mail: segreteria@fondostrategico.it
Website: www.cdpequity.it

Management and Staff

Alessandro Mulas, Chief Operating Officer
Maurizio Tamagnini, Managing Director

Type of Firm

Private Equity Firm

Project Preferences

Type of Financing Preferred:
Acquisition

Geographical Preferences

International Preferences:
Italy

Industry Preferences

In Semiconductor/Electr prefer:
Fiber Optics

In Medical/Health prefer:
Pharmaceuticals

Additional Information

Year Founded: 2012
Current Activity Level : Actively seeking new investments

CE TECH INVEST BV

Haarstraat 25
Gorinchem, Netherlands 4201 JA
Website: www.cetechinvest.nl

Type of Firm

Private Equity Firm

Project Preferences

Type of Financing Preferred:
Early Stage

Geographical Preferences

United States Preferences:
All U.S.

International Preferences:
Europe
Asia

Additional Information

Year Founded: 2015
Current Activity Level : Actively seeking new investments

CEA INVESTISSEMENT SA

Immeuble Le Ponant D
25 Rue Leblanc
Paris, France 75015
Phone: 33438789400
Fax: 33438785674
E-mail: cea-investissement@cea.fr
Website: www.cea-investissement.com

Other Offices

Batiment 482
point courrier 62
Gif-sur-Yvette, France
Phone: 33438789400
Fax: 33438785674

Type of Firm

Government Affiliated Program

Association Membership

French Venture Capital Association (AFIC)

Project Preferences

Type of Financing Preferred:
Early Stage
Research and Development
Seed
Startup

Geographical Preferences

International Preferences:
Europe
France

Industry Preferences

In Communications prefer:
Telecommunications

In Biotechnology prefer:
Biotechnology

In Medical/Health prefer:
Medical/Health
Medical Diagnostics
Medical Therapeutics
Medical Products
Health Services

In Industrial/Energy prefer:
Energy
Advanced Materials

In Other prefer:
Environment Responsible

Additional Information

Year Founded: 1999
Current Activity Level : Actively seeking new investments

CEC CAPITAL GROUP

China Resources Building, 19 F
No.8 Jian Guo Men Bei Avenue
Beijing, China
Website: www.china-ecapital.com

Type of Firm

Bank Affiliated

Project Preferences

Type of Financing Preferred:
Leveraged Buyout
Balanced

Geographical Preferences

International Preferences:
China

Industry Preferences

In Communications prefer:
Telecommunications

In Medical/Health prefer:
Medical/Health

In Consumer Related prefer:
Consumer

In Business Serv. prefer:
Media

Additional Information

Year Founded: 2014
Current Activity Level : Actively seeking new investments

CEDAR CREEK PARTNERS

10936 West Port Washington Rd.
Number 180
Mequon, WI USA 53092
Phone: 414-272-5500
Fax: 414-272-1029
Website: www.cedarllc.com

Management and Staff

Daniel Jagla, Managing Director
Robert Cook, Managing Director

Type of Firm

Private Equity Firm

Project Preferences

Role in Financing:
Prefer role as deal originator but will also invest in deals created by others

Type of Financing Preferred:
Leveraged Buyout
Management Buyouts
Acquisition
Recapitalizations

Geographical Preferences

United States Preferences:

Industry Focus
(% based on actual investment)
Internet Specific	27.9%
Consumer Related	27.0%
Other Products	26.0%
Computer Software and Services	9.5%
Industrial/Energy	7.6%
Semiconductors/Other Elect.	2.0%

Additional Information
Year Founded: 1997
Capital Under Management: $100,000,000
Current Activity Level : Actively seeking new investments
Method of Compensation: Return on invest. most important, but chg. closing fees, service fees, etc.

CEDAR HILL ASSOCIATES LLC

120 South LaSalle Street
Suite 1750
Chicago, IL USA 60603
Phone: 3124452900
Fax: 3124452901
Website: www.cedhill.com

Management and Staff
Alan Cole, President
Asha Goldstein, Principal
Christopher Engelman, Managing Director
Daniel Kriser, Principal
Daniel Jones, Principal
Dawn Keach, Principal
Debbiann Frenzel, Principal
Robin Patinkin, Principal

Type of Firm
Investment Management Firm

Project Preferences

Type of Financing Preferred:
Core
Leveraged Buyout
Value-Add
Generalist PE
Balanced
Opportunistic

Additional Information
Name of Most Recent Fund: Cedar Hill Partners II LLC
Most Recent Fund Was Raised: 03/19/2012
Year Founded: 1984
Capital Under Management: $32,700,000
Current Activity Level : Actively seeking new investments

CEDAR SPRINGS CAPITAL LLC

3899 Maple Avenue
Old Parkland Campus Suite 150
Dallas, TX USA 75219
Phone: 4699303000
Website: www.cedarspringscapital.com

Management and Staff
Colin McGrady, Managing Partner
Mark Dunn, Venture Partner
Neset Pirkul, Principal

Type of Firm
Private Equity Firm

Project Preferences

Type of Financing Preferred:
Early Stage
Generalist PE
Acquisition
Recapitalizations

Geographical Preferences

United States Preferences:

Additional Information
Year Founded: 2015
Current Activity Level : Actively seeking new investments

CEDARPOINT INVESTMENTS INC

30 Saint Clair Avenue West
Suite 900
Toronto, Canada M4V3A1
Phone: 416-927-200
Fax: 416-927-2013

Management and Staff
Sydney Loftus, Managing Director

Type of Firm
Private Equity Firm

Additional Information
Year Founded: 1996
Current Activity Level : Actively seeking new investments

CEDRES PARTICIPATIONS SARL

268, Boulevard Saint Denis
Courbevoie, France 92400
Website: www.cedre-participations.com

Type of Firm
Private Equity Firm

Project Preferences

Type of Financing Preferred:
Early Stage
Seed

Size of Investments Considered:
Min Size of Investment Considered (000s): $22
Max Size of Investment Considered (000s): $544

Geographical Preferences

International Preferences:
Europe
France

Industry Preferences

In Computer Software prefer:
Software

In Internet Specific prefer:
Internet
Ecommerce

Additional Information
Year Founded: 2009
Current Activity Level : Actively seeking new investments

CEE EQUITY PARTNERS LTD

2 Prodromou & Dematrakopoulou
5th Floor
Nicosia, Cyprus CY-1090
Website: www.cee-equity.com

Other Offices
68-70, Blvd. de la Petrusse
Luxembourg, Luxembourg L-2320

Type of Firm
Bank Affiliated

Project Preferences

Type of Financing Preferred:
Leveraged Buyout
Expansion
Mezzanine
Later Stage
Management Buyouts
Acquisition

Size of Investments Considered:
Min Size of Investment Considered (000s): $20,000
Max Size of Investment Considered (000s): $65,000

Geographical Preferences

International Preferences:
Slovenia
Hungary
Slovak Repub.
Albania
Europe
Czech Republic
Macedonia
Poland
Croatia
Bulgaria
Estonia
Bosnia
Romania
Latvia
Lithuania

Industry Preferences

In Communications prefer:
Telecommunications

In Industrial/Energy prefer:
Energy
Industrial Products

In Manufact. prefer:
Manufacturing

Additional Information
Year Founded: 2012
Current Activity Level : Actively seeking new investments

CEE MANAGEMENT GMBH

Speersort 10
Hamburg, Germany 20095
Phone: 494068887880
Fax: 494068878870
Website: www.cee-holding.de

Management and Staff
Detlef Schreiber, Managing Director
Jan Kiel, Managing Director
Olaf Luedemann, Managing Director

Type of Firm
Private Equity Firm

Association Membership
German Venture Capital Association (BVK)

Project Preferences

Type of Financing Preferred:
Leveraged Buyout
Early Stage
Mezzanine
Later Stage
Acquisition
Startup

Size of Investments Considered:
Min Size of Investment Considered (000s): $1,443
Max Size of Investment Considered (000s): $7,216

Geographical Preferences

International Preferences:
Europe
Switzerland
Germany

Industry Preferences

In Industrial/Energy prefer:
Alternative Energy
Energy Conservation Relat
Environmental Related

In Other prefer:
Environment Responsible

Additional Information
Year Founded: 2006
Capital Under Management: $107,138,000
Current Activity Level : Actively seeking new investments

CEI COMMUNITY VENTURES INC

Two Portland Fish Pier
Suite 201
Portland, ME USA 04101
Phone: 2077725356
Fax: 2077725503
E-mail: info@ceicommunityventures.com

Management and Staff
Michael Gurau, President

Type of Firm
Private Equity Firm

Association Membership
Community Development Venture Capital Alliance

Project Preferences

Role in Financing:
Will function either as deal originator or investor in deals created by others

Type of Financing Preferred:
Early Stage
Expansion
Balanced
Later Stage

Size of Investments Considered:
Min Size of Investment Considered (000s): $250
Max Size of Investment Considered (000s): $750

Geographical Preferences

United States Preferences:
New Hampshire
Vermont
Maine

Additional Information
Year Founded: 2001
Capital Under Management: $10,000,000
Current Activity Level : Actively seeking new investments
Method of Compensation: Return on invest. most important, but chg. closing fees, service fees, etc.

CEI VENTURES INC

Two Portland Fish Pier, Suite 206
Cumberland Center, ME USA 04021
Phone: 2077725356
Fax: 2077725503
Website: www.ceiventures.com

Management and Staff
Nathaniel Henshaw, Managing Director

Type of Firm
Private Equity Firm

Association Membership
Community Development Venture Capital Alliance

Project Preferences

Role in Financing:
Will function either as deal originator or investor in deals created by others

Type of Financing Preferred:
Early Stage
Balanced
Later Stage

Size of Investments Considered:
Min Size of Investment Considered (000s): $250
Max Size of Investment Considered (000s): $1,000

Geographical Preferences

United States Preferences:
Maine

Additional Information
Name of Most Recent Fund: Coastal Ventures III, L.P.
Most Recent Fund Was Raised: 03/30/2011
Year Founded: 1994
Capital Under Management: $25,500,000
Current Activity Level : Actively seeking new investments

CEL VENTURE CAPITAL (SHENZHEN) LTD

No.4013, Shennan Road
8F Ind Bank Bldg, Futian Dist
Shenzhen, China
Phone: 8675583024017

Type of Firm
Investment Management Firm

Project Preferences

Type of Financing Preferred:
Expansion
Later Stage

Geographical Preferences

International Preferences:
China

Industry Preferences

In Communications prefer:
Telecommunications

In Computer Software prefer:
Software

In Semiconductor/Electr prefer:
Electronics
Semiconductor

In Biotechnology prefer:
Biotechnology

In Medical/Health prefer:
Medical/Health

In Industrial/Energy prefer:
Alternative Energy
Energy Conservation Relat

In Agr/Forestr/Fish prefer:
Agriculture related

In Other prefer:
Environment Responsible

Additional Information

Year Founded: 2001
Current Activity Level : Actively seeking new investments

CELERITY PARTNERS LP

1901 Avenue of the Stars
Suite 400
Los Angeles, CA USA 90067
Phone: 3102681710
Fax: 3107281756
E-mail: info@celeritypartners.com
Website: www.celeritypartners.com

Other Offices

3000 Sand Hill Road
Building Three, Suite 100
Menlo Park, CA USA 94025
Phone: 6506463624
Fax: 6502338230

635 Bryant Street
Third Floor
Palo Alto, CA USA 94301
Phone: 6503271325
Fax: 6502338230

Management and Staff

Mark Benham, Managing Partner
Matthew Kraus, Partner

Type of Firm

Private Equity Firm

Project Preferences

Role in Financing:
Will function either as deal originator or investor in deals created by others

Type of Financing Preferred:
Leveraged Buyout
Later Stage
Management Buyouts
Acquisition
Recapitalizations

Geographical Preferences

United States Preferences:

Industry Focus

(% based on actual investment)
Computer Hardware	37.3%
Semiconductors/Other Elect.	31.0%
Consumer Related	11.9%
Internet Specific	7.7%
Medical/Health	7.7%
Biotechnology	2.7%
Other Products	1.7%

Additional Information

Name of Most Recent Fund: Celerity Partners SBIC, L.P.
Most Recent Fund Was Raised: 09/30/2002
Year Founded: 1994
Capital Under Management: $191,000,000
Current Activity Level : Actively seeking new investments

CELGENE CORP

86 Morris Avenue
Summit, NJ USA 07901
Phone: 9086739000
Website: www.celgene.com

Management and Staff

Scott Smith, President & COO

Type of Firm

Corporate PE/Venture

Additional Information

Year Founded: 1986
Current Activity Level : Actively seeking new investments

CELTIC HOUSE VENTURE PARTNERS INC

101 College Street, Suite 155
MaRS Center, Heritage Building
Toronto, Canada M5G 1L7
Phone: 4169247000
Fax: 4169247090
E-mail: info@celtic-house.com
Website: www.celtic-house.com

Other Offices

MaRS Centre, Heritage Building
101 College Street, Suite 155
Toronto, Canada M5G 1L7
Phone: 416-924-7000
Fax: 416-924-7090

53 Davies Street
Suite 19
London, United Kingdom
Phone: 44-1453-836-370
Fax: 44-1453-835-203

Management and Staff

Brian Antonen, Partner
David Adderley, Partner
Julie Fallon, Chief Financial Officer
Pierre-Andre Meunier, Partner
Roger Maggs, Partner
Tomas Valis, Partner

Type of Firm

Private Equity Firm

Association Membership

Canadian Venture Capital Association

Project Preferences

Type of Financing Preferred:
Early Stage
Expansion
Balanced
Seed
Startup

Geographical Preferences

United States Preferences:

Canadian Preferences:
All Canada
New Brunswick
Quebec
Ontario
British Columbia

Industry Focus

(% based on actual investment)
Semiconductors/Other Elect.	46.7%
Computer Software and Services	25.0%
Communications and Media	13.9%
Internet Specific	7.7%
Medical/Health	3.7%
Computer Hardware	1.9%
Consumer Related	1.1%

Additional Information

Name of Most Recent Fund: Celtic House Venture Partners Fund IV, L.P.
Most Recent Fund Was Raised: 05/22/2012
Year Founded: 1994
Capital Under Management: $102,810,000
Current Activity Level : Actively seeking new investments
Method of Compensation: Return on invest. most important, but chg. closing fees, service fees, etc.

CENDANA CAPITAL GP LLC

Two Embarcadero Center
22nd Floor
San Francisco, CA USA 94111
Phone: 6503462914
E-mail: info@cendanacapital.com
Website: www.cendanacapital.com

Management and Staff
Michael Kim, Founder

Type of Firm
Private Equity Advisor or Fund of Funds

Project Preferences

Type of Financing Preferred:
Fund of Funds
Expansion
Later Stage

Additional Information
Name of Most Recent Fund: Cendana Capital, L.P.
Most Recent Fund Was Raised: 03/29/2013
Year Founded: 2009
Capital Under Management: $297,156,000
Current Activity Level : Actively seeking new investments

CENTANA GROWTH PARTNERS

54 West 40th Street
New York, NY USA 10018
E-mail: info@centanagrowth.com
Website: www.centanagrowth.com

Management and Staff
Ben Cukier, Managing Partner
Bonnie Kearns, Managing Partner

Type of Firm
Private Equity Firm

Association Membership
National Venture Capital Association - USA (NVCA)

Project Preferences

Type of Financing Preferred:
Early Stage

Geographical Preferences

United States Preferences:

Industry Preferences

In Computer Software prefer:
Software

In Internet Specific prefer:
Internet

In Financial Services prefer:
Financial Services

Additional Information
Year Founded: 2014
Capital Under Management: $250,000,000
Current Activity Level : Actively seeking new investments

CENTENIUM-PINETREE CHINA PRIVATE EQUITY

56 Boyun Road
Zhangjiang Hi-tech Park
Shanghai, China
Phone: 86-21-5855-9818

Other Offices
300 Park Avenue
17th Floor
New York, NY USA 10022
Phone: 212-572-4896

89 West Third Ring North Road
China Foreign Building B, Suite 1106
Beijing, China
Phone: 86-21-5855-8859

Management and Staff
Andy Yu, Vice President
Angela Luo, Vice President
Hong Ke, Vice President
Junbin Li, Vice President
Lynn Wang, Vice President
Tony Wang, Vice President

Type of Firm
Private Equity Advisor or Fund of Funds

Project Preferences

Type of Financing Preferred:
Leveraged Buyout
Acquisition

Geographical Preferences

International Preferences:
China

Industry Preferences

In Medical/Health prefer:
Health Services

In Industrial/Energy prefer:
Energy
Alternative Energy

In Business Serv. prefer:
Services

In Manufact. prefer:
Manufacturing

Additional Information
Year Founded: 2009
Capital Under Management: $6,000,000
Current Activity Level : Actively seeking new investments

CENTENNIAL VENTURES VII L P

1125 17th Street
Suite 740
Denver, CO USA 80202
Phone: 3034057500
Fax: 3034057575
Website: www.centennial.com

Other Offices
600 Congress Avenue
Suite 200
Austin, TX USA 78701
Phone: 5125054500
Fax: 5125054550

4605 Post Oak Place
Suite 202
Houston, TX USA 77027
Phone: 7136279200
Fax: 7136279292

Management and Staff
David Hull, Managing Director
Duncan Butler, Managing Director
Jeffrey Schutz, Managing Director
Neel Sarkar, Managing Director
Rand Lewis, Managing Director
Steven Halstedt, Managing Director

Type of Firm
Private Equity Firm

Project Preferences

Role in Financing:
Prefer role as deal originator but will also invest in deals created by others

Type of Financing Preferred:
Early Stage
Balanced
Later Stage

Industry Focus
(% based on actual investment)

Communications and Media	54.6%
Internet Specific	17.3%
Computer Hardware	9.7%
Semiconductors/Other Elect.	5.1%
Computer Software and Services	4.9%
Other Products	4.1%
Medical/Health	1.8%
Biotechnology	1.7%
Consumer Related	0.6%
Industrial/Energy	0.3%

Additional Information

Name of Most Recent Fund: Centennial Ventures VII, L.P.
Most Recent Fund Was Raised: 12/28/2000
Year Founded: 1982
Capital Under Management: $100,000,000
Current Activity Level : Actively seeking new investments
Method of Compensation: Return on investment is of primary concern, do not charge fees

CENTER FOR INNOVATION AND ENTREPRENEURSHIP

803 South College Road
Wilmington, NC USA 28403
Phone: 9109623000
E-mail: our@uncw.edu
Website: www.uncw.edu

Type of Firm

University Program

Project Preferences

Type of Financing Preferred:
Seed
Startup

Geographical Preferences

United States Preferences:
North Carolina

Additional Information

Year Founded: 2013
Current Activity Level : Actively seeking new investments

CENTER FOR INNOVATIVE TECHNOLOGY

2214 Rock Hill Road
Suite 600
Herndon, VA USA 20170
Phone: 7036893000
Fax: 7036893041
E-mail: gap@cit.org
Website: www.cit.org

Management and Staff

Nancy Vorona, Vice President
Paul McGowan, Vice President
Sandie Terry, Vice President
Susan Aitcheson, Chief Financial Officer
Tom Weithman, Vice President

Type of Firm

Government Affiliated Program

Association Membership

Mid-Atlantic Venture Association
National Venture Capital Association - USA (NVCA)

Project Preferences

Role in Financing:
Prefer role as deal originator but will also invest in deals created by others

Type of Financing Preferred:
Early Stage
Balanced
Seed

Geographical Preferences

United States Preferences:
Virginia

Industry Preferences

In Industrial/Energy prefer:
Energy

Additional Information

Year Founded: 2004
Capital Under Management: $6,500,000,000
Current Activity Level : Actively seeking new investments
Method of Compensation: Return on investment is of primary concern, do not charge fees

CENTERBRIDGE PARTNERS LP

375 Park Avenue
12th Floor
New York, NY USA 10019
Phone: 2126725000
Fax: 2126725001
Website: www.centerbridge.com

Other Offices

63 Brook Street
London, United Kingdom W1K 4HS
Phone: 44-20-3214-1100

Management and Staff

Jason Mozingo, Senior Managing Director
Jeffrey Gelfand, Managing Director
Jeffrey Aronson, Founder
Mark Gallogly, Co-Founder
Steven Price, Managing Partner

Type of Firm

Private Equity Firm

Project Preferences

Type of Financing Preferred:
Leveraged Buyout
Turnaround
Acquisition
Special Situation
Distressed Debt

Additional Information

Name of Most Recent Fund: Centerbridge Special Credit Partners II, L.P.
Most Recent Fund Was Raised: 03/15/2012
Year Founded: 2006
Capital Under Management: $6,627,950,000
Current Activity Level : Actively seeking new investments

CENTERFIELD CAPITAL PARTNERS LP

Ten West Market Street
3000 Market Tower
Indianapolis, IN USA 46204
Phone: 3172372323
Fax: 3172372325
Website: www.centerfieldcapital.com

Management and Staff

Faraz Abbasi, Partner
Jackie Byers, Chief Financial Officer
Jill Margetts, Principal
Mark Hollis, Partner
Matthew Hook, Partner
Michael Miller, Partner
Scott Lutzke, Partner
Thomas Hiatt, Partner

Type of Firm

Private Equity Firm

Association Membership

Natl Assoc of Small Bus. Inv. Co (NASBIC)

Project Preferences

Role in Financing:
Will function either as deal originator or investor in deals created by others

Type of Financing Preferred:
Mezzanine
Management Buyouts
Acquisition
Recapitalizations

Geographical Preferences

United States Preferences:
Midwest

Canadian Preferences:
All Canada

Industry Preferences

In Medical/Health prefer:
Health Services

In Consumer Related prefer:
Food/Beverage
Consumer Products
Consumer Services
Education Related

In Industrial/Energy prefer:
Materials

In Business Serv. prefer:
Services
Distribution

In Manufact. prefer:
Manufacturing

Additional Information
Name of Most Recent Fund: Centerfield Capital Partners III, L.P.
Most Recent Fund Was Raised: 05/31/2011
Year Founded: 1998
Capital Under Management: $260,000,000
Current Activity Level : Actively seeking new investments
Method of Compensation: Return on invest. most important, but chg. closing fees, service fees, etc.

CENTERGATE CAPITAL LP

2700 Via Fortuna
Suite 145
Austin, TX USA 78746
Phone: 5127177100
E-mail: info@centergatecapital.com
Website: centergatecapital.com

Management and Staff
Lewis Schoenwetter, Managing Director
Paul Langley, Vice President
Stenning Schueppert, Co-Founder
Tiffany Kosch, Managing Director
Timothy Liu, Principal

Type of Firm
Private Equity Firm

Project Preferences

Type of Financing Preferred:
Leveraged Buyout
Expansion
Generalist PE
Balanced
Later Stage
Management Buyouts
Acquisition

Geographical Preferences

United States Preferences:
Midwest

Industry Preferences

In Consumer Related prefer:
Consumer Products

In Industrial/Energy prefer:
Industrial Products

In Financial Services prefer:
Financial Services

In Manufact. prefer:
Manufacturing

Additional Information
Year Founded: 1969
Capital Under Management: $350,000,000
Current Activity Level : Actively seeking new investments

CENTERMAN CAPITAL

50 Dedham Avenue
Suite R2
Needham, MA USA 02492
Website: www.centermancapital.com

Type of Firm
Private Equity Firm

Project Preferences

Type of Financing Preferred:
Early Stage

Additional Information
Year Founded: 2012
Current Activity Level : Actively seeking new investments

CENTEROAK PARTNERS LLC

100 Crescent Court
Suite 1700
Dallas, TX USA 75201
Phone: 2143014201
Fax: 2148535090
E-mail: info@centeroakpartners.com
Website: www.centeroakpartners.com

Management and Staff
Ben Adams, Vice President
Jeffrey Moredock, Vice President
Lucas Cutler, Partner
Randall Fojtasek, Managing Partner
Tully Wyatt, Vice President

Type of Firm
Private Equity Firm

Project Preferences

Type of Financing Preferred:
Leveraged Buyout
Recapitalizations

Geographical Preferences

United States Preferences:
Southwest

International Preferences:
Latin America

Industry Preferences

In Communications prefer:
Communications and Media
Wireless Communications

In Internet Specific prefer:
E-Commerce Technology

In Medical/Health prefer:
Health Services

In Consumer Related prefer:
Consumer
Retail
Food/Beverage
Consumer Products
Consumer Services
Other Restaurants

In Industrial/Energy prefer:
Industrial Products

In Business Serv. prefer:
Services
Distribution

Additional Information
Year Founded: 2014
Capital Under Management: $420,000,000
Current Activity Level : Actively seeking new investments

CENTERPOINT VENTURE PARTNERS LP

13455 Noel Road
Two Galleria Tower, 16th Floor
Dallas, TX USA 75240
Phone: 9727021101
Fax: 9727021103
Website: www.cpventures.com

Other Offices
6300 Bridge Point Parkway
Building One, Suite 500
Austin, TX USA 78730
Phone: 512-795-5800
Fax: 512-795-5849

Management and Staff
Robert Paluck, Managing Director
Terence Rock, Managing Director

Type of Firm
Private Equity Firm

Project Preferences

Role in Financing:
Prefer role as deal originator but will also invest in deals created by others

Type of Financing Preferred:
Early Stage

Size of Investments Considered:
Min Size of Investment Considered (000s): $5,000
Max Size of Investment Considered (000s): $15,000

Geographical Preferences

United States Preferences:
Southwest
Texas

Industry Focus

(% based on actual investment)
Communications and Media	31.0%
Computer Software and Services	22.1%
Internet Specific	12.8%
Semiconductors/Other Elect.	12.0%
Computer Hardware	8.5%
Medical/Health	6.0%
Industrial/Energy	3.2%
Other Products	2.9%
Consumer Related	1.6%

Additional Information

Name of Most Recent Fund: CenterPoint Venture Fund III, L.P.
Most Recent Fund Was Raised: 02/01/2001
Year Founded: 1996
Capital Under Management: $425,000,000
Current Activity Level : Actively seeking new investments

CENTERVIEW PARTNERS LLC

31 West 52nd Street, 22nd Floor
New York, NY USA 10019
Phone: 2123802650
Fax: 2123802651
Website: www.centerviewpartners.com

Other Offices

555 California Street
Suite 3305
San Francisco, CA USA 94104
Phone: 4154000900
Fax: 4154000901

10250 Constellation Boulevard
Suite 2815
Los Angeles, CA USA 90067
Phone: 4242305950
Fax: 4242305951

45 Old Bond Street
3rd Floor
London, United Kingdom W1S 4QT
Phone: 442074099700
Fax: 442074099704

Management and Staff

Adam Chinn, Co-Founder
Alexander Glantz, Partner
Anthony Kim, Partner
Blair Effron, Co-Founder
Buno Pati, Partner
David St. Jean, Partner
David Cohen, Partner
David Handler, Partner
Mark Robinson, Partner
Nicholas Reid, Partner
Robert Pruzan, Co-Founder
Robin Budenberg, Partner
Todd Davison, Partner

Type of Firm

Private Equity Firm

Project Preferences

Type of Financing Preferred:
Leveraged Buyout
Acquisition

Geographical Preferences

United States Preferences:

Industry Preferences

In Consumer Related prefer:
Consumer
Food/Beverage
Consumer Products
Consumer Services

Additional Information

Year Founded: 2006
Capital Under Management: $500,000,000
Current Activity Level : Actively seeking new investments

CENTINELA CAPITAL PARTNERS LLC

152 West 57th Street
34th Floor
New York, NY USA 10019
Phone: 212-823-0280
E-mail: admin@centinelacapital.com
Website: www.centinelacapital.com

Other Offices

777 South Figueroa Street
Suite 390
Los Angeles, CA USA 90017
Phone: 213-542-1800

Management and Staff

Cesar Baez, Managing Partner
Christopher Farrington, Partner
Fidel Vargas, Partner
Jan Le Chang, Vice President
Mark Perry, Vice President
Robert Taylor, Partner
Sophie Liang, Vice President

Type of Firm

Private Equity Advisor or Fund of Funds

Project Preferences

Type of Financing Preferred:
Fund of Funds
Expansion
Mezzanine
Balanced
Fund of Funds of Second

Additional Information

Year Founded: 2006
Capital Under Management: $400,000,000
Current Activity Level : Actively seeking new investments

CENTRAL INVESTMENT GROUP

Economic & Tech Dev'l Zone
4/F Haiheng Building
Hefei, Anhui, China
Phone: 86-551-3876-028
Fax: 86-551-3876-010
Website: www.chinachg.com

Type of Firm

Investment Management Firm

Project Preferences

Type of Financing Preferred:
Balanced

Geographical Preferences

International Preferences:
China

Industry Preferences

In Financial Services prefer:
Real Estate

Additional Information

Year Founded: 2004
Current Activity Level : Actively seeking new investments

CENTRAL PARK GROUP LLC

805 Third Avenue 18th floor
New York, NY USA 10022
Phone: 2123179200
Fax: 2128131543
E-mail: info@centralparkgroup.com
Website: www.centralparkgroup.com

Type of Firm

Investment Management Firm

Project Preferences

Type of Financing Preferred:
Generalist PE

Industry Preferences

In Medical/Health prefer:
Medical/Health

In Financial Services prefer:
Real Estate

In Business Serv. prefer:
Media

Additional Information
Year Founded: 2006
Current Activity Level : Actively seeking new investments

CENTRAS CAPITAL PARTNERS

32-A Manas Street
SAT Business Center
Almaty, Kazakhstan 050008
Phone: 77273111111
Fax: 77272378478
E-mail: mail@centrascapital.com
Website: www.centrascapital.com

Management and Staff
Dauren Alipbayev, Managing Director
Eldar Abdrazakov, Managing Director
Igor Churbanov, Founding Partner

Type of Firm
Investment Management Firm

Association Membership
Emerging Markets Private Equity Association
European Private Equity and Venture Capital Assoc.

Project Preferences

Type of Financing Preferred:
Leveraged Buyout
Early Stage
Turnaround
Seed
Startup

Size of Investments Considered:
Min Size of Investment Considered (000s): $4,500
Max Size of Investment Considered (000s): $7,500

Geographical Preferences

International Preferences:
Kazakhstan
Asia
Russia

Industry Preferences

In Communications prefer:
Telecommunications

In Consumer Related prefer:
Consumer

In Industrial/Energy prefer:
Energy
Alternative Energy
Energy Conservation Relat
Materials
Advanced Materials
Environmental Related

In Financial Services prefer:
Financial Services
Insurance

In Other prefer:
Environment Responsible

Additional Information
Year Founded: 2004
Current Activity Level : Actively seeking new investments

CENTRE CAPITAL DEVELOPPEMENT

38 Rue de la Marine de Loire
Le Verlaine
Orleans, France 45100
Phone: 33238223060
Fax: 33238566225
E-mail: ccd@sofimacpartners.com
Website: www.centrecapitaldeveloppement.com

Type of Firm
Private Equity Firm

Association Membership
French Venture Capital Association (AFIC)

Project Preferences

Type of Financing Preferred:
Early Stage
Generalist PE
Later Stage
Acquisition

Geographical Preferences

International Preferences:
Europe
France

Industry Preferences

In Consumer Related prefer:
Consumer

In Industrial/Energy prefer:
Industrial Products

In Business Serv. prefer:
Services
Distribution

Additional Information
Year Founded: 1987
Current Activity Level : Actively seeking new investments

CENTRE LANE PARTNERS LLC

60 East 42nd Street
Suite 1400, One Grand Central
New York, NY USA 10165
Phone: 6468430710
E-mail: info@centrelanepartners.com
Website: centrelanepartners.com

Management and Staff
Nathan Richey, Managing Director
William Tomai, Chief Financial Officer

Type of Firm
Private Equity Firm

Project Preferences

Type of Financing Preferred:
Leveraged Buyout
Acquisition

Geographical Preferences

United States Preferences:
North America

Additional Information
Name of Most Recent Fund: Centre Lane Partners III, L.P.
Most Recent Fund Was Raised: 12/15/2011
Year Founded: 2010
Capital Under Management: $404,500,000
Current Activity Level : Actively seeking new investments

CENTRE PARTNERS MANAGEMENT LLC

825 Third Avenue
40th floor
New York, NY USA 10022
Phone: 2123325800
Fax: 2127581830
E-mail: info@CentrePartners.com
Website: www.centrepartners.com

Other Offices
11726 San Vicente Boulevard
Suite 450
Los Angeles, CA USA 90049
Phone: 310-207-9170
Fax: 310-207-9180

Management and Staff
Andrew Vandekerckhove, Principal
Bruce Pollack, Managing Partner
Christopher Sand, Principal
Daniel Brinkenhoff, Principal
David Jaffe, Managing Partner
Jeffrey Bartoli, Managing Director
Lester Pollack, Founder
Michael Schnabel, Managing Director

Type of Firm
Private Equity Firm

Project Preferences

Role in Financing:
Prefer role as deal originator but will also invest in deals created by others

Type of Financing Preferred:
Leveraged Buyout
Management Buyouts
Recapitalizations

Geographical Preferences

United States Preferences:
North America

Industry Focus
(% based on actual investment)
Other Products	66.8%
Consumer Related	25.3%
Computer Software and Services	2.8%
Industrial/Energy	2.4%
Semiconductors/Other Elect.	1.4%
Internet Specific	0.8%
Communications and Media	0.4%

Additional Information
Name of Most Recent Fund: Centre Capital Investors VI, L.P.
Most Recent Fund Was Raised: 12/06/2013
Year Founded: 1986
Capital Under Management: $2,600,000,000
Current Activity Level : Actively seeking new investments
Method of Compensation: Return on invest. most important, but chg. closing fees, service fees, etc.

CENTRICA INNOVATIONS UK LTD

Maidenhead Road
Millstream
Berkshire, United Kingdom SL4 5GD
Phone: 441753494000
Fax: 441753494001

Type of Firm
Incubator/Development Program

Project Preferences

Type of Financing Preferred:
Early Stage

Industry Preferences

In Industrial/Energy prefer:
Energy

Additional Information
Year Founded: 2017
Current Activity Level : Actively seeking new investments

CENTRIPETAL CAPITAL PARTNERS LLC

One Landmark Square
Suite 620
Stamford, CT USA 06901
Phone: 2033267600
Fax: 2035691924
E-mail: info@centricap.com
Website: www.centricap.com

Other Offices
57 Danbury Road
Suite 103
WILTON, CT USA 06897
Phone: 2038346222
Fax: 2038342473

Management and Staff
E. Bulkeley Griswold, Managing Director
Jeffrey Brodlieb, Principal
Stephen Rossetter, Principal
Steven Chrust, Managing Director

Type of Firm
Private Equity Firm

Project Preferences

Type of Financing Preferred:
Leveraged Buyout
Early Stage
Mezzanine
Management Buyouts
Acquisition

Size of Investments Considered:
Min Size of Investment Considered (000s): $5,000
Max Size of Investment Considered (000s): $100,000

Geographical Preferences

United States Preferences:
All U.S.

Additional Information
Year Founded: 2004
Current Activity Level : Actively seeking new investments

CENTRO PARA EL DESARROLLO TECNOLOGICO INDUSTRIAL

C/ Cid, Four
Madrid, Spain 28001
Phone: 34-91-581-5500
Fax: 34-91-581-5594
E-mail: info@cdti.es
Website: www.cdti.es

Type of Firm
Private Equity Firm

Association Membership
Spanish Venture Capital Association (ASCRI)

Project Preferences

Type of Financing Preferred:
Early Stage
Expansion

Size of Investments Considered:
Min Size of Investment Considered (000s): $211
Max Size of Investment Considered (000s): $4,226

Geographical Preferences

International Preferences:
Spain

Additional Information
Year Founded: 2004
Capital Under Management: $735,357,000
Current Activity Level : Actively seeking new investments

CENTRUM CAPITAL LTD

Centrum House, CST Road
Vidyanagari Marg
Kalina Mumbai, India 400098
Website: www.centrum.co.in

Management and Staff
Shailendra Apte, Chief Financial Officer

Type of Firm
Investment Management Firm

Project Preferences

Type of Financing Preferred:
Generalist PE

Industry Preferences

In Medical/Health prefer:
Medical/Health

In Consumer Related prefer:
Consumer
Education Related

In Financial Services prefer:
Financial Services

Additional Information
Year Founded: 1977
Current Activity Level : Actively seeking new investments

CENTUM INVESTMENT COMPANY PLC

International Life House
Mama Ngina Street
Nairobi, Kenya
Phone: 254202286000
Fax: 254202286120
E-mail: pe@centum.co.ke
Website: www.centum.co.ke

Management and Staff
James Mworia, Chief Executive Officer

Type of Firm
Private Equity Firm

Association Membership
African Venture Capital Association (AVCA)

Project Preferences

Type of Financing Preferred:
Leveraged Buyout
Balanced
Later Stage
Acquisition

Geographical Preferences

International Preferences:
Kenya
Africa

Additional Information
Year Founded: 1967
Current Activity Level : Actively seeking new investments

CENTURION INVESTMENT MANAGEMENT PTE LTD

47 Scotts Road
18-01 Goldbell Towers
Singapore, Singapore 228233
Phone: 6563383190
Fax: 6567362330
Website: www.centurion-investment.com

Other Offices
183 Queen's Road Central
Unit 2506, 25th Floor, COSCO Tower
Hong Kong, Hong Kong
Phone: 852-2169-0966
Fax: 852-2907-7669

No.222 Hubin Road, One Corporate Avenue
Suit 1567, 15th Floor
Shanghai, China
Phone: 86-21-6340-4081
Fax: 86-21-6340-4187

Management and Staff
Kay Hua Tang, Chief Executive Officer

Type of Firm
Private Equity Firm

Project Preferences

Type of Financing Preferred:
Expansion
Generalist PE
Management Buyouts

Geographical Preferences

International Preferences:
China
Asia

Industry Preferences

In Consumer Related prefer:
Consumer
Food/Beverage

In Manufact. prefer:
Manufacturing

In Other prefer:
Environment Responsible

Additional Information
Year Founded: 2004
Capital Under Management: $90,000,000
Current Activity Level : Actively seeking new investments

CENTURION TECHNOLOGY INVESTMENT CORP

168-28, Samsung-Dong
Gangnam-Gu
Seoul, South Korea 135-090
Phone: 822-556-2563
Fax: 822-556-2514

Management and Staff
Dae Young Huh, President
Euiyong Lee, Managing Director

Type of Firm
Corporate PE/Venture

Project Preferences

Type of Financing Preferred:
Fund of Funds
Generalist PE
Balanced

Geographical Preferences

International Preferences:
Korea, South

Industry Preferences

In Communications prefer:
Media and Entertainment

In Biotechnology prefer:
Biotechnology

Additional Information
Year Founded: 2000
Capital Under Management: $36,400,000
Current Activity Level : Actively seeking new investments

CENTURY CAPITAL MANAGEMENT / MASSACHUSETTS INC

100 Federal Street
29th Floor
Boston, MA USA 02110
Phone: 8003211928
Fax: 6175429398

Management and Staff
Charles Kline, Managing Director
Chris Lalonde, Principal
David Borah, Partner
David Sherwood, Managing Director
Davis Fulkerson, Managing Director
Donald Bisson, Partner
Frank Bazos, Managing Director
Gerard Vecchio, Managing Director
Gregory DiMarzio, Partner
Jared Hobson, Partner
Kevin Maclaughlan, Chief Financial Officer
Kevin Callahan, Partner
Lanny Thorndike, Managing Partner
Peter Whitlock, Partner
Stephen Marquardt, Principal

Type of Firm
Private Equity Firm

Project Preferences

Type of Financing Preferred:
Leveraged Buyout
Early Stage
Generalist PE
Balanced
Later Stage
Acquisition

Size of Investments Considered:
Min Size of Investment Considered (000s): $10,000
Max Size of Investment Considered (000s): $30,000

Geographical Preferences

United States Preferences:

Canadian Preferences:
All Canada

International Preferences:
United Kingdom
Bermuda

Industry Focus

(% based on actual investment)
Other Products	58.1%
Internet Specific	25.5%
Computer Software and Services	6.1%
Computer Hardware	5.5%
Medical/Health	4.7%
Communications and Media	0.1%

Additional Information

Name of Most Recent Fund: Century Focused Fund III, L.P.
Most Recent Fund Was Raised: 09/27/2010
Year Founded: 1928
Capital Under Management: $224,000,000
Current Activity Level : Actively seeking new investments

CENTURY PARK CAPITAL PARTNERS LLC

2101 Rosecrans Avenue
Suite 4275
El Segundo, CA USA 90245
Phone: 3108672210
Fax: 3108672212
E-mail: info@cpclp.com
Website: www.centuryparkcapital.com

Other Offices

750 Menlo Avenue
Suite 200
MENLO PARK, CA USA 94025
Phone: 650-324-1956
Fax: 650-322-1550

Management and Staff

Guy Zaczepinski, Managing Partner
Kurt Gula, Vice President

Type of Firm

Private Equity Firm

Project Preferences

Type of Financing Preferred:
Leveraged Buyout
Expansion
Management Buyouts
Recapitalizations

Industry Focus

(% based on actual investment)
Other Products	50.8%
Consumer Related	49.2%

Additional Information

Year Founded: 1999
Capital Under Management: $107,000,000
Current Activity Level : Actively seeking new investments

CENTURYLINK INC

100 CenturyLink Drive
Monroe, LA USA 71203
Phone: 3183889000
Website: www.centurylink.com

Management and Staff

Jeffrey Storey, President & COO
R. Stewart Ewing, Chief Financial Officer

Type of Firm

Private Equity Firm

Project Preferences

Type of Financing Preferred:
Balanced

Geographical Preferences

International Preferences:
All International

Additional Information

Year Founded: 1968
Current Activity Level : Actively seeking new investments

CEO VENTURES

1200 Abernathy Road
17th Flr., 600 Northpark Bldg.
Atlanta, GA USA 30328
Phone: 770-998-9999
E-mail: info@ceoventures.com
Website: www.ceoventures.com

Management and Staff

Michael Price, General Partner

Type of Firm

Private Equity Firm

Project Preferences

Type of Financing Preferred:
Seed
Startup

Industry Preferences

In Computer Software prefer:
Software
Systems Software

Additional Information

Year Founded: 2010
Capital Under Management: $8,000,000
Current Activity Level : Actively seeking new investments

CERBERUS CAPITAL MANAGEMENT LP

875 Third Avenue, Eleventh Floor
New York, NY USA 10022
Phone: 2128912100
Fax: 2128911545
E-mail: info@cerberuscapital.com
Website: www.cerberuscapital.com

Other Offices

155 North Wacker Drive
Suite 4250
CHICAGO, IL USA 60606
Phone: 3127558137

Management and Staff

Andrew Kandel, Managing Director
Andrew Frank, Managing Director
Daniel Wolf, Senior Managing Director
David Abrams, Senior Managing Director
David Teitelbaum, Managing Director
Eric Miller, Senior Managing Director
Frank Bruno, Senior Managing Director
Josh Weintraub, Managing Director
Kevin Genda, Senior Managing Director
Lee Millstein, Senior Managing Director
Lenard Tessler, Senior Managing Director
Lou Forster, Senior Managing Director
Lynn Topham, Vice President
Mark Neporent, Chief Operating Officer
Robert Davenport, Senior Managing Director
Ronald Kravit, Senior Managing Director
Ronald Rawald, Managing Director
Steven Mayer, Senior Managing Director
W. Brett Ingersoll, Senior Managing Director
William Richter, Senior Managing Director

Type of Firm

Private Equity Firm

Association Membership

China Venture Capital Association
European Private Equity and Venture Capital Assoc.

Project Preferences

Type of Financing Preferred:
Leveraged Buyout
Turnaround
Acquisition
Recapitalizations

Geographical Preferences

United States Preferences:

Canadian Preferences:
All Canada

International Preferences:
Thailand
Asia
Japan
All International

Industry Focus
(% based on actual investment)

Other Products	84.0%
Internet Specific	5.8%
Consumer Related	5.4%
Computer Software and Services	1.7%
Biotechnology	1.2%
Communications and Media	1.0%
Industrial/Energy	0.8%

Additional Information
Name of Most Recent Fund: Cerberus Institutional Partners, L.P., Series Five
Most Recent Fund Was Raised: 04/19/2012
Year Founded: 1993
Capital Under Management: $7,000,000,000
Current Activity Level : Actively seeking new investments

CEREA PARTENAIRE SAS

23 Avenue de Neuilly
Paris, France 75116
Phone: 33175777800
Fax: 33144311650
E-mail: contact@cereagestion.com
Website: www.cerea.com

Management and Staff
Fabrice Vidal, Managing Director
Gilles Sicard, Managing Director
Jean-Francois Laurain, President
Michel Chabanel, Chief Executive Officer

Type of Firm
Private Equity Firm

Association Membership
French Venture Capital Association (AFIC)

Project Preferences

Role in Financing:
Prefer role as deal originator

Type of Financing Preferred:
Leveraged Buyout
Mezzanine

Geographical Preferences

International Preferences:
Europe
France

Industry Preferences

In Biotechnology prefer:
Agricultural/Animal Bio.

In Consumer Related prefer:
Food/Beverage

In Agr/Forestr/Fish prefer:
Agriculture related

Additional Information
Year Founded: 2004
Capital Under Management: $423,460,000
Current Activity Level : Actively seeking new investments
Method of Compensation: Return on invest. most important, but chg. closing fees, service fees, etc.

CERIUM TECHNOLOGY LLC

2101 Rosecrans Avenue, Suite 5282
El Segundo, CA USA 90245
Phone: 3103599211
Website: cerium-technology.com

Other Offices
1717 Mckinney Avenue
Suite 700
Dallas, TX USA 75202
Phone: 2144326323

Management and Staff
Eldon Klaassen, Founder

Type of Firm
Private Equity Firm

Project Preferences

Type of Financing Preferred:
Early Stage

Industry Preferences

In Industrial/Energy prefer:
Energy
Oil & Gas Drilling,Explor
Alternative Energy
Energy Conservation Relat

In Other prefer:
Environment Responsible

Additional Information
Year Founded: 2014
Current Activity Level : Actively seeking new investments

CERRACAP VENTURES LLC

650 Town Center Drive
Costa Mesa, CA USA 92626
E-mail: info@cerracap.com
Website: www.cerracap.com

Type of Firm
Private Equity Firm

Project Preferences

Type of Financing Preferred:
Early Stage

Additional Information
Year Founded: 2015
Capital Under Management: $7,500,000
Current Activity Level : Actively seeking new investments

CERTUS CAPITAL PARTNERS

935 South Main Street
Suite 300
Greenville, SC USA 29601
Phone: 8647041803
Website: www.certuscapitalpartners.com

Other Offices
1170 Peachtree Street NE
Suite 2350
Atlanta, GA USA 30309
Phone: 6782931899

Type of Firm
Private Equity Firm

Project Preferences

Type of Financing Preferred:
Mezzanine

Size of Investments Considered:
Min Size of Investment Considered (000s): $4,000
Max Size of Investment Considered (000s): $15,000

Geographical Preferences

United States Preferences:
Southeast

Industry Preferences

In Communications prefer:
Telecommunications

In Medical/Health prefer:
Medical/Health

In Business Serv. prefer:
Services
Distribution
Media

In Manufact. prefer:
Manufacturing

Additional Information
Year Founded: 2013
Capital Under Management: $225,000,000
Current Activity Level : Actively seeking new investments

CERVIN VENTURES

2882 Sand Hill Road
Suite 210
Fremont, CA USA 94539
Phone: 8232764726
E-mail: info@cervinventures.com
Website: cervinventures.com

Other Offices
2882 Sand Hill Road, Suite 210
MENLO PARK, CA USA 94025

Management and Staff
Neeraj Gupta, Managing Director
Preetish Nijhawan, Managing Director

Type of Firm
Private Equity Firm

Project Preferences

Type of Financing Preferred:
Early Stage
Startup

Industry Preferences

In Communications prefer:
Wireless Communications
Media and Entertainment

In Computer Software prefer:
Software

In Computer Other prefer:
Computer Related

Additional Information
Name of Most Recent Fund: Cervin Ventures Fund II, L.P.
Most Recent Fund Was Raised: 01/11/2012
Year Founded: 2011
Capital Under Management: $33,700,000
Current Activity Level : Actively seeking new investments

CEVIAN CAPITAL AB

Engelbrektsgatan Five
Stockholm, Sweden 114 32
Phone: 46854567550
Fax: 46854567560
E-mail: info@ceviancapital.com
Website: www.ceviancapital.com

Other Offices
Seedammstrasse 3
Pfaffikon, Switzerland 8808
Phone: 41-55-417-4620
Fax: 41-55-417-4621

17 Cavendish Square
London, United Kingdom W1G 0PH
Phone: 44-20-3178-4953
Fax: 44-20-3178-4954

Management and Staff
Christer Gardell, Managing Partner
Goran Casserlov, Chief Financial Officer
Ilias Laber, Partner
Jens Tischendorf, Partner
Jonas Synnergren, Partner
Lars Forberg, Managing Partner
Marcus Alexanderson, Partner
Martin Oliw, Partner

Type of Firm
Private Equity Firm

Project Preferences

Type of Financing Preferred:
Generalist PE
Public Companies

Geographical Preferences

International Preferences:
Europe
Greenland
Iceland
Scandanavia/Nordic Region

Additional Information
Year Founded: 2002
Capital Under Management: $4,682,900,000
Current Activity Level : Actively seeking new investments

CEYUAN VENTURES MANAGEMENT LLC

No. 35, Qinlao Hutong Road
Dongcheng District
Beijing, China 100009
Phone: 861084028800
Fax: 861084020999
E-mail: info@ceyuanvc.com
Website: www.ceyuan.com

Other Offices
18 Harcourt Road, Tower II
Room 605, Admiralty Centre
Hong Kong, Hong Kong
Phone: 85225271010
Fax: 85225201680

Management and Staff
Bo Feng, Founder
Chris Wadsworth, Partner
Darren Wong, Partner
Silin Huang, Partner
Tao Feng, Co-Founder
Ye Yuan, Partner
Yi Wang, Chief Financial Officer
Zhao Weiguo, Partner

Type of Firm
Private Equity Firm

Project Preferences

Role in Financing:
Prefer role as deal originator but will also invest in deals created by others

Type of Financing Preferred:
Early Stage
Expansion
Balanced
Seed

Geographical Preferences

International Preferences:
China

Industry Preferences

In Communications prefer:
Wireless Communications

In Computer Software prefer:
Software

In Internet Specific prefer:
Internet

In Semiconductor/Electr prefer:
Semiconductor

Additional Information
Year Founded: 2005
Capital Under Management: $282,241,000
Current Activity Level : Actively seeking new investments

CF INVESTMENT, CO.

104 South Main Street
Poinsett Plaza
Greenville, SC USA 29601
Phone: 864-255-4919
Fax: 864-239-6423

Type of Firm
Bank Affiliated

Project Preferences

Type of Financing Preferred:
Balanced

Size of Investments Considered:
Min Size of Investment Considered (000s): $100
Max Size of Investment Considered (000s): $1,000

Additional Information
Year Founded: 1997
Capital Under Management: $3,000,000
Current Activity Level : Actively seeking new investments

CFH BETEILIGUNGSGESELLSCHAFT MBH

Loehrstrasse 16
Leipzig, Germany 04105
Phone: 4934122038802
Fax: 4934122038809
E-mail: cfh@cfh.de
Website: www.cfh.de

Management and Staff
Christian Vogel, Chief Executive Officer

Type of Firm
Bank Affiliated

Pratt's Guide to Private Equity & Venture Capital Sources

Association Membership
German Venture Capital Association (BVK)

Project Preferences

Type of Financing Preferred:
Fund of Funds
Early Stage
Mezzanine
Balanced
Later Stage
Seed
Management Buyouts
Startup
Fund of Funds of Second
Recapitalizations

Geographical Preferences

International Preferences:
Europe
Germany

Industry Preferences

In Communications prefer:
Communications and Media
Wireless Communications
Media and Entertainment

In Internet Specific prefer:
E-Commerce Technology

In Semiconductor/Electr prefer:
Electronics
Semiconductor
Sensors

In Medical/Health prefer:
Medical/Health
Medical Diagnostics

In Industrial/Energy prefer:
Energy
Industrial Products
Materials
Machinery
Environmental Related

In Transportation prefer:
Transportation

In Business Serv. prefer:
Services
Media

Additional Information
Name of Most Recent Fund: CHF Growth Fund
Most Recent Fund Was Raised: 02/03/2012
Year Founded: 1995
Capital Under Management: $130,100,000
Current Activity Level : Actively seeking new investments

CFI CAPITAL

229 Niagara Street
Toronto, Canada M6J 2L5
Phone: 416-364-6191
Fax: 416-364-1012
E-mail: info@corpfinance.ca

Management and Staff
Andre Nadon, Vice President
David Bell, Managing Director
Eric Skillins, Vice President
Gerry Hway, Vice President
Jacques Huot, Vice President
Michael Breen, Vice President
Peter Heffernan, Vice President

Type of Firm
Investment Management Firm

Additional Information
Year Founded: 1984
Current Activity Level : Actively seeking new investments

CGW SOUTHEAST PARTNERS

2970 Peachtree Road, NorthWest
Suite 510, One Buckhead Plaza
Atlanta, GA USA 30305
Phone: 4048413325
Fax: 6787059940
Website: www.cgwlp.com

Other Offices
Former HQ: 3060 Peachtree Road
Suite 895
Atlanta, GA USA 30305
Phone: 4048413325
Fax: 6787059940

Management and Staff
Bart McLean, Partner
Edwin Wahlen, Managing Partner
Michael Long, Partner
Richard Cravey, Managing Partner

Type of Firm
Private Equity Firm

Project Preferences

Role in Financing:
Prefer role as deal originator but will also invest in deals created by others

Type of Financing Preferred:
Leveraged Buyout
Acquisition
Recapitalizations

Geographical Preferences

United States Preferences:
Southeast

Industry Focus
(% based on actual investment)

Other Products	37.9%
Industrial/Energy	26.5%
Consumer Related	22.5%
Medical/Health	6.6%
Communications and Media	6.1%
Internet Specific	0.3%

Additional Information
Name of Most Recent Fund: CGW Southeast Partners IV, L.P.
Most Recent Fund Was Raised: 05/01/1999
Year Founded: 1984
Capital Under Management: $750,000,000
Current Activity Level : Reducing investment activity
Method of Compensation: Return on invest. most important, but chg. closing fees, service fees, etc.

CHAAC VENTURES

c/o Princeton University
Princeton, NJ USA 08544
E-mail: info@ChaacVentures.com

Type of Firm
University Program

Project Preferences

Type of Financing Preferred:
Seed
Startup

Geographical Preferences

United States Preferences:

Industry Preferences

In Computer Software prefer:
Software

In Internet Specific prefer:
Internet

In Computer Other prefer:
Computer Related

Additional Information
Year Founded: 2015
Current Activity Level : Actively seeking new investments

CHALLENGE JAPAN INVEST CO LTD

2-5-1 Kita-Aoyama
Minato-ku
Tokyo, Japan 107-0061
Phone: 81-3-3497-8633

Fax: 81-3-3408-5781

Other Offices
Chuo-ku, 4-1-3
Taro Hisashi-cho
Osaka, Japan 541-0056
Phone: 83-6-6241-3383
Fax: 83-6-6241-3387

Management and Staff
Tadashi Nakamura, President

Type of Firm
Corporate PE/Venture

Additional Information
Year Founded: 2003
Current Activity Level : Actively seeking new investments

CHALMERS INNOVATION

Stena Center 1D
Gothenburg, Sweden 412 92
Phone: 46317728100
Fax: 46317728091
Website: www.chalmersinnovation.com

Other Offices
Lindholmspiren 5
Gothenburg, Sweden 402 78
Phone: 46317728100
Fax: 4631221932

Management and Staff
Olle Stenberg, Chief Executive Officer

Type of Firm
Incubator/Development Program

Association Membership
Swedish Venture Capital Association (SVCA)

Project Preferences

Type of Financing Preferred:
Early Stage
Seed
Startup

Geographical Preferences

International Preferences:
Sweden
Europe

Industry Preferences

In Communications prefer:
Telecommunications
Wireless Communications

In Computer Software prefer:
Software

In Biotechnology prefer:
Biotechnology

In Medical/Health prefer:
Medical/Health

In Business Serv. prefer:
Services

Additional Information
Year Founded: 1999
Capital Under Management: $1,700,000
Current Activity Level : Actively seeking new investments

CHAMELEON INVEST SCA

66, Rue X Octobre
Bereldange, Luxembourg 7243
Phone: 35227849482
E-mail: info@chameleoninvest.com
Website: www.chameleoninvest.com

Management and Staff
Serge Rollinger, Chief Executive Officer

Type of Firm
Private Equity Firm

Project Preferences

Type of Financing Preferred:
Early Stage
Seed
Startup

Geographical Preferences

International Preferences:
Europe

Industry Preferences

In Internet Specific prefer:
Internet

Additional Information
Year Founded: 2011
Current Activity Level : Actively seeking new investments

CHAMP VENTURES PTY LTD

31 Alfred Street
Level Four Customs House
Sydney, Australia 2000
Phone: 61282488822
Fax: 61292517655
E-mail: info@CHAMPVentures.com
Website: www.champventures.com

Other Offices
71 Eagle Street
Level 36 Riparian Plaza
Brisbane, Australia 4000
Phone: 617-3121-3098
Fax: 617-3121-3030

Type of Firm
Private Equity Firm

Association Membership
Australian Venture Capital Association (AVCAL)

Project Preferences

Geographical Preferences

International Preferences:
Pacific
Australia
New Zealand

Industry Preferences

In Internet Specific prefer:
Internet

In Medical/Health prefer:
Medical/Health
Health Services

In Consumer Related prefer:
Retail
Food/Beverage
Consumer Products

In Industrial/Energy prefer:
Energy

In Transportation prefer:
Transportation

In Financial Services prefer:
Financial Services

In Business Serv. prefer:
Services
Distribution

In Manufact. prefer:
Manufacturing

In Agr/Forestr/Fish prefer:
Agriculture related
Mining and Minerals

In Utilities prefer:
Utilities

Additional Information
Name of Most Recent Fund: CHAMP Ventures Investments Trust No. 7
Most Recent Fund Was Raised: 06/30/2011
Year Founded: 1987
Capital Under Management: $629,200,000
Current Activity Level : Actively seeking new investments

CHAMPLAIN CAPITAL PARTNERS LP

44 Montgomery Street, Suite 1920
San Francisco, CA USA 94104
Phone: 4152814181
Fax: 4153623211
Website: www.champlaincapital.com

Other Offices
20 Park Plaza
Suite 472
Boston, MA USA 02116
Phone: 6179482578
Fax: 9784055063

Management and Staff
Claire Porter, Founding Partner
Dennis Leary, Partner
Pierre Simard, Partner
Warren Feldberg, Partner

Type of Firm
Private Equity Firm

Association Membership
Natl Assoc of Small Bus. Inv. Co (NASBIC)

Project Preferences

Type of Financing Preferred:
Leveraged Buyout
Recapitalizations

Size of Investments Considered:
Min Size of Investment Considered (000s): $20,000
Max Size of Investment Considered (000s): $100,000

Geographical Preferences

United States Preferences:

Canadian Preferences:
All Canada

Industry Preferences

In Business Serv. prefer:
Services
Distribution

In Manufact. prefer:
Manufacturing

Additional Information
Year Founded: 2002
Current Activity Level : Actively seeking new investments

CHANCENKAPITALFONDS DER KREISSPARKASSE BIBERACH GMBH
Zeppelinring 27-29
Biberach, Germany 88400
Phone: 4973515702020
Fax: 4973515702340
E-mail: info@ksk-bc.de
Website: www.ksk-bc.de

Type of Firm
Bank Affiliated

Project Preferences

Type of Financing Preferred:
Early Stage
Later Stage
Startup

Geographical Preferences

International Preferences:
Germany

Industry Preferences

In Semiconductor/Electr prefer:
Electronics

In Biotechnology prefer:
Biotechnology

In Medical/Health prefer:
Medical/Health

In Consumer Related prefer:
Consumer

In Industrial/Energy prefer:
Energy
Industrial Products
Machinery

In Business Serv. prefer:
Services

Additional Information
Year Founded: 1998
Capital Under Management: $7,000,000
Current Activity Level : Actively seeking new investments

CHANGAN BLUE OAK VENTURE CAPITAL CO LTD
No. 7 Jianguomenwai Avenue
Rm 307 Guanghua Chang'an Bldg.
Beijing, China 100005
Phone: 86-10-59111086
Fax: 86-10-59111089
Website: www.blueoakcapital.com.cn

Other Offices
Dorland House 20
Regent Street
London, United Kingdom SW1Y 4PH
Phone: 44-20-7024-4645
Fax: 44-20-7024-4699

Management and Staff
Huaizhong Yuan, Chief Executive Officer

Type of Firm
Investment Management Firm

Project Preferences

Type of Financing Preferred:
Generalist PE
Later Stage

Geographical Preferences

International Preferences:
China

Industry Preferences

In Consumer Related prefer:
Consumer
Retail
Consumer Products
Consumer Services

In Industrial/Energy prefer:
Energy
Alternative Energy
Materials
Environmental Related

In Transportation prefer:
Transportation

In Manufact. prefer:
Manufacturing

Additional Information
Year Founded: 2003
Capital Under Management: $100,002,000
Current Activity Level : Actively seeking new investments

CHANGAN CAPITAL
No.23 Xihaibeiyan
Xicheng District
Beijing, China 100035
Phone: 861084002728
Fax: 861084002716
Website: www.changancap.com

Management and Staff
Li Xie, Founder
Tao Wu, Vice President
Xiang Jun Qu, Founder

Type of Firm
Private Equity Firm

Project Preferences

Type of Financing Preferred:
Balanced

Geographical Preferences

International Preferences:
China

Industry Preferences

In Consumer Related prefer:
Consumer

In Industrial/Energy prefer:
Environmental Related

In Agr/Forestr/Fish prefer:
Agribusiness

Additional Information
Year Founded: 1998
Current Activity Level : Actively seeking new investments

CHANGCHUN S&T VENTURE CAPITAL CO LTD

Rm 501, Tower A, High-Tech Bldg
3003 Qianjin Ave
Changchun, China 130012
Phone: 86-43-1518-6638
Fax: 86-43-1518-8007
E-mail: master@chinacvc.com

Type of Firm
Private Equity Firm

Project Preferences

Type of Financing Preferred:
Early Stage
Start-up Financing
Later Stage
Seed

Geographical Preferences

International Preferences:
China

Industry Preferences

In Biotechnology prefer:
Biotechnology

In Business Serv. prefer:
Services

Additional Information
Year Founded: 2000
Current Activity Level : Actively seeking new investments

CHANGE CAPITAL PARTNERS LLP

272 Kings Road
Second Floor, College House
London, United Kingdom SW3 5AW
Phone: 442078089110
Fax: 442078089111
E-mail: info@changecapitalpartners.com
Website: www.changecapitalpartners.com

Management and Staff
Andrew Wood, Chief Financial Officer
Roger Holmes, Partner
Stephan Lobmeyr, Partner
Steven Petrow, Partner

Type of Firm
Private Equity Firm

Project Preferences

Type of Financing Preferred:
Leveraged Buyout
Turnaround
Management Buyouts
Private Placement

Geographical Preferences

International Preferences:
Italy
United Kingdom
Europe
Germany
France

Industry Preferences

In Consumer Related prefer:
Consumer
Retail
Consumer Products
Consumer Services

Additional Information
Year Founded: 2003
Capital Under Management: $683,500,000
Current Activity Level : Actively seeking new investments

CHANGE PARTNERS

Av. da Boavista, 3769, L-25
Porto, Portugal 4100-139
Phone: 351226075700
Fax: 351226075709
E-mail: cppe@changepartners.pt
Website: www.changepartners.pt

Management and Staff
Hugo Ramos, Partner
Mario Pereira Pinto, Founder
Patricia Costa, Partner

Type of Firm
Private Equity Firm

Association Membership
European Private Equity and Venture Capital Assoc.

Project Preferences

Type of Financing Preferred:
Leveraged Buyout
Early Stage
Expansion
Balanced
Later Stage
Seed
Management Buyouts
Startup

Geographical Preferences

International Preferences:
Portugal
Spain

Industry Preferences

In Communications prefer:
Communications and Media
Telecommunications

In Computer Hardware prefer:
Computers
Terminals
Disk Relat. Memory Device

In Computer Software prefer:
Computer Services
Software

In Computer Other prefer:
Computer Related

In Semiconductor/Electr prefer:
Electronics

In Biotechnology prefer:
Biotechnology

In Medical/Health prefer:
Medical/Health

In Consumer Related prefer:
Consumer
Consumer Products

In Industrial/Energy prefer:
Energy
Industrial Products

In Business Serv. prefer:
Media

Additional Information
Year Founded: 2000
Capital Under Management: $32,000,000
Current Activity Level : Actively seeking new investments

CHANGSHA SCIENCE & TECHNOLOGY VENTURE CAPITAL CO LTD

No.101 Xiangjiang Road
5F Huiyuan Building
Changsha, China 410205
Phone: 867318286892
Fax: 867318286892
Website: www.csvvc.cn

Management and Staff
Ce Jiang, President

Type of Firm
Government Affiliated Program

Project Preferences

Type of Financing Preferred:
Early Stage
Expansion
Balanced
Later Stage
Startup

Size of Investments Considered:
Min Size of Investment Considered (000s): $293
Max Size of Investment Considered (000s): $2,933

Geographical Preferences

International Preferences:
China

Industry Preferences

In Semiconductor/Electr prefer:
Electronics

In Biotechnology prefer:
Biotechnology

In Medical/Health prefer:
Medical/Health

In Industrial/Energy prefer:
Energy
Materials
Environmental Related

In Agr/Forestr/Fish prefer:
Agriculture related

Additional Information

Year Founded: 2000
Current Activity Level : Actively seeking new investments

CHANGZHOU AOYANG VENTURE CAPITAL CO LTD

Wujin Economic Dev'l Zone
Changzhou, China

Type of Firm

Private Equity Firm

Project Preferences

Type of Financing Preferred:
Balanced

Geographical Preferences

International Preferences:
China

Additional Information

Year Founded: 2009
Current Activity Level : Actively seeking new investments

CHANGZHOU HEJIA CAPITAL MANAGEMENT CO LTD

Xinbei District
Room 502, Block E, Hi-tech Sci
Changzhou, China
Phone: 8651985176186

Type of Firm

Investment Management Firm

Project Preferences

Type of Financing Preferred:
Balanced

Geographical Preferences

International Preferences:
China

Additional Information

Year Founded: 2016
Current Activity Level : Actively seeking new investments

CHANGZHOU HENUO CAPITAL MANAGEMENT CO LTD

Xinbei District
Room 503, Block E, Hi-tech Sci
Changzhou, China
Phone: 8651985176186

Type of Firm

Investment Management Firm

Project Preferences

Type of Financing Preferred:
Balanced

Geographical Preferences

International Preferences:
China

Additional Information

Year Founded: 2016
Capital Under Management: $30,810,000
Current Activity Level : Actively seeking new investments

CHANGZHOU HIGH-TECH VENTURE CAPITAL CO LTD

Hanjiang Rd., Xinbei District
Hi-tech Park
Changzhou, China 213000

Type of Firm

Government Affiliated Program

Project Preferences

Type of Financing Preferred:
Early Stage
Seed
Startup

Geographical Preferences

International Preferences:
China

Additional Information

Year Founded: 2012
Current Activity Level : Actively seeking new investments

CHANNEL GROUP LLC, THE

1133 Broadway
Suite 706
New York, NY USA 10010
Phone: 2123308076
Fax: 2126278877
E-mail: info@thechannelgroup.com
Website: www.thechannelgroup.com

Management and Staff

Allan Goldberg, Co-Founder
Philip Sussman, Managing Partner
Shmuel Einav, Partner
Vijay Aggarwal, Managing Partner
Walter Flamenbaum, Managing Partner

Type of Firm

Incubator/Development Program

Project Preferences

Type of Financing Preferred:
Leveraged Buyout
Mezzanine
Management Buyouts
Acquisition
Recapitalizations

Industry Preferences

In Medical/Health prefer:
Medical/Health
Pharmaceuticals

Additional Information

Year Founded: 2001
Current Activity Level : Actively seeking new investments

CHANNEL MARK VENTURES

50 Tice Boulevard
Suite 340
Woodcliff Lake, NJ USA 07677
Phone: 2016905105
E-mail: funding@channelmark.com
Website: www.channelmark.com

Type of Firm
Private Equity Firm

Project Preferences

Type of Financing Preferred:
Early Stage
Expansion
Balanced
Later Stage
Seed
Private Placement
Startup

Geographical Preferences

United States Preferences:
California
New Jersey
New York

Industry Preferences

In Communications prefer:
Communications and Media
Wireless Communications
Entertainment

In Computer Software prefer:
Software
Applications Software
Artificial Intelligence

In Internet Specific prefer:
Internet
Ecommerce

In Consumer Related prefer:
Entertainment and Leisure
Consumer Products
Consumer Services

In Business Serv. prefer:
Media

Additional Information
Year Founded: 2013
Current Activity Level: Actively seeking new investments

CHARENTE PERIGORD EXPANSION SASU

Rue dEpagnac
Soyaux, France 16800
Phone: 33545204700
Website: http://www.ca-charente-perigord.fr/

Type of Firm
Bank Affiliated

Project Preferences

Type of Financing Preferred:
Leveraged Buyout
Early Stage
Expansion
Later Stage
Management Buyouts
Acquisition

Geographical Preferences

International Preferences:
France

Additional Information
Year Founded: 2009
Current Activity Level: Actively seeking new investments

CHARLES RIVER VENTURES LLC

One Broadway
15th Floor
Cambridge, MA USA 02142
Phone: 7817686000
Fax: 7817686100
Website: www.crv.com

Management and Staff
Adam Amero, Chief Financial Officer
Annie Kadavy, General Partner
Bruce Sachs, General Partner
Devdutt Yellurkar, General Partner
Dylan Morris, General Partner
George Zachary, General Partner
Izhar Armony, General Partner
Jon Auerbach, General Partner
Max Gazor, General Partner
Michael Zak, Partner
Murat Bicer, General Partner
Rafael Corrales, General Partner
Saar Gur, General Partner
William Tai, Partner

Type of Firm
Private Equity Firm

Association Membership
New England Venture Capital Association
National Venture Capital Association - USA (NVCA)

Project Preferences

Role in Financing:
Will function either as deal originator or investor in deals created by others

Type of Financing Preferred:
Early Stage
Balanced
Seed
Startup

Industry Focus
(% based on actual investment)

Internet Specific	33.8%
Computer Software and Services	28.5%
Communications and Media	15.2%
Semiconductors/Other Elect.	4.7%
Computer Hardware	4.4%
Other Products	3.8%
Industrial/Energy	3.6%
Medical/Health	2.7%
Consumer Related	2.3%
Biotechnology	1.0%

Additional Information
Name of Most Recent Fund: Charles River Partnership XV
Most Recent Fund Was Raised: 02/28/2012
Year Founded: 1970
Capital Under Management: $2,000,000,000
Current Activity Level: Actively seeking new investments
Method of Compensation: Return on investment is of primary concern, do not charge fees

---

CHARLESBANK CAPITAL PARTNERS LLC

200 Clarendon Street
54th Floor, John Hancock Tower
Boston, MA USA 02116
Phone: 6176195400
Fax: 6176195402
Website: www.charlesbank.com

Other Offices
70 East 55th Street
20th Floor, Heron Tower
New York, NY USA 10022
Phone: 212-903-1880
Fax: 212-903-1890

Management and Staff
Andrew Janower, Managing Director
Brandon White, Managing Director
David Kwan, Vice President
J. Ryan Carroll, Managing Director
Jason Pike, Managing Director
John Fiyod, Chief Financial Officer
John Vander Vort, Chief Operating Officer
Jon Biotti, Managing Director
Joshua Beer, Managing Director
Joshua Klevens, Managing Director
Kim Davis, Co-Founder
Mark Rosen, Co-Founder
Matthew Jacobson, Principal
Maura Turner, Vice President
Michael Choe, Chief Executive Officer
Michael Thonis, Co-Founder
Richard Owens, Vice President
Samuel Bartlett, Managing Director
Sandor Hau, Managing Director
Tim Palmer, Co-Founder

Type of Firm
Private Equity Firm

Project Preferences

Role in Financing:
Prefer role as deal originator but will also invest in deals created by others

Type of Financing Preferred:
Leveraged Buyout
Expansion
Mezzanine
Opportunistic
Management Buyouts
Acquisition
Private Placement
Recapitalizations

Geographical Preferences

United States Preferences:
North America

Canadian Preferences:
All Canada

Industry Focus
(% based on actual investment)

Consumer Related	40.2%
Other Products	23.0%
Communications and Media	15.4%
Medical/Health	11.0%
Biotechnology	5.3%
Computer Software and Services	2.8%
Semiconductors/Other Elect.	2.1%

Additional Information
Name of Most Recent Fund: CB Offshore Equity Fund VI, L.P.
Most Recent Fund Was Raised: 06/08/2005
Year Founded: 1991
Capital Under Management: $1,500,000,000
Current Activity Level : Actively seeking new investments
Method of Compensation: Return on invest. most important, but chg. closing fees, service fees, etc.

CHARLOTTE ANGEL PARTNERS

5615 Laurium Road
Charlotte, NC USA 28266
Phone: 7043624659
Fax: 7043624659

Type of Firm
Angel Group

Project Preferences

Role in Financing:
Prefer role in deals created by others

Type of Financing Preferred:
Early Stage
Expansion

Size of Investments Considered:
Min Size of Investment Considered (000s): $1,000
Max Size of Investment Considered (000s): $26,000

Geographical Preferences

United States Preferences:
North Carolina
South Carolina
Virginia

Additional Information
Year Founded: 2000
Capital Under Management: $8,000,000
Current Activity Level : Actively seeking new investments
Method of Compensation: Return on investment is of primary concern, do not charge fees

CHARME CAPITAL PARTNERS SGR SPA

Via Mangili Giuseppe 38/A
Roma, Italy 00197
Website: www.charmecapitalpartners.com

Management and Staff
Matteo Di Montezemolo, Chief Executive Officer

Type of Firm
Investment Management Firm

Project Preferences

Role in Financing:
Will function either as deal originator or investor in deals created by others

Type of Financing Preferred:
Leveraged Buyout

Geographical Preferences

International Preferences:
Italy
Europe

Additional Information
Year Founded: 2009
Capital Under Management: $451,110,000
Current Activity Level : Actively seeking new investments
Method of Compensation: Function primarily in service area, receive contingent fee in cash or equity

CHARMEX VENTURES LTD

The Oast House
5 Mead Lane
Farnham, United Kingdom GU9 7DY
Phone: 44-12-5273-4411
Fax: 44-12-5273-4536

Type of Firm
Private Equity Firm

Project Preferences

Type of Financing Preferred:
Early Stage
Expansion
Turnaround
Seed
Startup

Geographical Preferences

International Preferences:
Europe

Industry Preferences

In Communications prefer:
Communications and Media

In Internet Specific prefer:
Internet

In Biotechnology prefer:
Biotechnology

In Medical/Health prefer:
Medical/Health

Additional Information
Year Founded: 1998
Capital Under Management: $1,500,000
Current Activity Level : Actively seeking new investments

CHARMIDES CAPITAL

501 Congressional Boulevard
Suite 220
Carmel, IN USA 46032
Phone: 3177105416
Website: www.charmidescapital.com

Type of Firm
Private Equity Firm

Project Preferences

Type of Financing Preferred:
Early Stage

Geographical Preferences

United States Preferences:
Indiana

Additional Information
Year Founded: 2015
Current Activity Level : Actively seeking new investments

CHART VENTURE PARTNERS LP

75 Rockefeller Plaza
14th Floor
New York, NY USA 10019
Phone: 2123508224
Website: www.chartventure.com

Other Offices
3305 Main Road
Suite 104
Picatinny Arsenal, NJ USA 07806

Management and Staff
Christopher Brady, Managing Partner
Cole Nice, Partner
Matthew McCooe, Managing Partner
Ted Hobart, Partner
Timothy Teen, Managing Partner

Type of Firm
Private Equity Firm

Project Preferences

Role in Financing:
Will function either as deal originator or investor in deals created by others

Type of Financing Preferred:
Early Stage

Geographical Preferences

United States Preferences:

Additional Information
Year Founded: 2006
Capital Under Management: $83,000,000
Current Activity Level : Actively seeking new investments
Method of Compensation: Return on investment is of primary concern, do not charge fees

CHARTER LIFE SCIENCES II L P

2041 Mission College Boulevard
Suite 210
Santa Clara, CA USA 95054
Phone: 4087584700
Fax: 4087584848

Other Offices
2120 East Galbraith Road
Building A, Room 161
CINCINNATI, OH USA 45237
Phone: 5135586324
Fax: 5135586364

Management and Staff
Gino Di Sciullo, Partner
Nelson Teng, Managing Partner

Type of Firm
Private Equity Firm

Association Membership
Western Association of Venture Capitalists (WAVC)

Project Preferences

Role in Financing:
Prefer role as deal originator but will also invest in deals created by others

Type of Financing Preferred:
Early Stage

Size of Investments Considered:
Min Size of Investment Considered (000s): $1,000
Max Size of Investment Considered (000s): $5,000

Geographical Preferences

United States Preferences:

Additional Information
Name of Most Recent Fund: Charter Life Sciences II, L.P.
Most Recent Fund Was Raised: 05/05/2008
Year Founded: 2003
Capital Under Management: $66,300,000
Current Activity Level : Actively seeking new investments
Method of Compensation: Return on investment is of primary concern, do not charge fees

CHARTER OAK EQUITY, L.P.

Ten Wright Street
Suite 220
Westport, CT USA 06880
Phone: 2032214752
Fax: 2032222720
Website: www.charteroak-equity.com

Other Offices
10 Wright Street
Suite 230
Westport, CT USA
Phone: 2032214752

Management and Staff
Mark Ullman, General Partner
Stephen Noe, Principal
Zubin Avari, General Partner

Type of Firm
Private Equity Firm

Project Preferences

Type of Financing Preferred:
Leveraged Buyout
Generalist PE
Acquisition

Size of Investments Considered:
Min Size of Investment Considered (000s): $15,000
Max Size of Investment Considered (000s): $50,000

Geographical Preferences

United States Preferences:

Canadian Preferences:
All Canada

Industry Preferences

In Medical/Health prefer:
Medical Products
Health Services
Pharmaceuticals

In Consumer Related prefer:
Consumer Products

In Industrial/Energy prefer:
Advanced Materials

In Financial Services prefer:
Financial Services

In Manufact. prefer:
Manufacturing

Additional Information
Year Founded: 2006
Capital Under Management: $400,000,000
Current Activity Level : Actively seeking new investments

CHARTERHOUSE CAPITAL PARTNERS LLP

Paternoster Square
7th Floor, Warwick Court
London, United Kingdom EC4M 7DX
Phone: 442073345300
Fax: 442073345344
Website: www.charterhouse.co.uk

Other Offices
1, rue Paul Cezanne
Paris, France 75008
Phone: 33-1-7039-7500
Fax: 33-1-7039-7549

Management and Staff
Duncan Aldred, Partner
Giuseppe Prestia, Partner
Lionel Giacomotto, Managing Partner

Type of Firm
Private Equity Firm

Association Membership
British Venture Capital Association (BVCA)
French Venture Capital Association (AFIC)

Project Preferences

Role in Financing:
Prefer role as deal originator but will also invest in deals created by others

Type of Financing Preferred:
Leveraged Buyout
Acquisition

Geographical Preferences

International Preferences:
Western Europe

Industry Focus

(% based on actual investment)
Other Products	40.9%
Consumer Related	34.8%
Internet Specific	22.9%
Semiconductors/Other Elect.	1.0%
Industrial/Energy	0.2%
Medical/Health	0.1%
Computer Hardware	0.1%
Computer Software and Services	0.0%

Additional Information

Name of Most Recent Fund: Charterhouse Capital Partners IX
Most Recent Fund Was Raised: 12/22/2008
Year Founded: 1934
Capital Under Management: $16,870,500,000
Current Activity Level : Actively seeking new investments
Method of Compensation: Return on invest. most important, but chg. closing fees, service fees, etc.

CHARTERHOUSE GROUP INC

92 River Road
Summit, NJ USA 07901
Phone: 12125843200
Fax: 12125843233

Management and Staff

C. Taylor Cole, Managing Director
Cheri Lieberman, Chief Financial Officer
Cheri Lieberman, Chief Financial Officer
David Hoffman, Managing Director
Jay Gates, Managing Director
Robert Haisch, Principal
Thomas Dircks, Managing Partner
Todd Neustat, Vice President
William Landuyt, Managing Director

Type of Firm

Private Equity Firm

Project Preferences

Type of Financing Preferred:
Leveraged Buyout
Mezzanine
Acquisition

Geographical Preferences

United States Preferences:
North America

Industry Focus

(% based on actual investment)
Communications and Media	29.0%
Other Products	20.9%
Consumer Related	13.4%
Medical/Health	12.0%
Industrial/Energy	11.9%
Computer Software and Services	6.1%
Semiconductors/Other Elect.	5.4%
Computer Hardware	0.9%
Internet Specific	0.4%

Additional Information

Year Founded: 1973
Current Activity Level : Actively seeking new investments

CHARTLINE CAPITAL PARTNERS

1105 Market Street
18th Floor, Suite 1800
Wilmington, DE USA 19801
Phone: 3026541597
Fax: 3603612275
Website: www.chartline.com

Other Offices

3-15-5, Kanda Nishiki-cho, Chiyoda-ku
2nd Floor Kawasaki Park Bldg. I
Tokyo, Japan
Phone: 81-3-5217-0217
Fax: 81-3-5217-0218

Management and Staff

Benjamin du Pont, President, Founder
Emma Hughes, Vice President
Eugene Buff, Vice President
Hideyuki Fujii, Vice President

Type of Firm

Private Equity Firm

Association Membership

National Venture Capital Association - USA (NVCA)

Project Preferences

Type of Financing Preferred:
Balanced

Industry Preferences

In Computer Software prefer:
Software

In Semiconductor/Electr prefer:
Electronics
Electronic Components

In Medical/Health prefer:
Medical/Health
Medical Products

In Consumer Related prefer:
Consumer

In Industrial/Energy prefer:
Alternative Energy
Environmental Related

Additional Information

Name of Most Recent Fund: Yet2Ventures
Most Recent Fund Was Raised: 06/20/2011
Year Founded: 2009
Capital Under Management: $15,000,000
Current Activity Level : Actively seeking new investments

CHARTWELL INVESTMENTS, INC.

500 Fifth Avenue
50th Floor
New York, NY USA 10110
Phone: 2125215500
Fax: 2125215533
Website: www.chartwellinvestments.com

Management and Staff

C. Larry Davis, Partner
Mark Woods, Principal
Michael Shein, Co-Founder
Michael Rolland, Partner

Type of Firm

Private Equity Firm

Project Preferences

Role in Financing:
Prefer role as deal originator but will also invest in deals created by others

Type of Financing Preferred:
Leveraged Buyout
Expansion
Management Buyouts
Recapitalizations

Geographical Preferences

United States Preferences:

International Preferences:
Europe

Industry Focus

(% based on actual investment)
Consumer Related	61.0%
Other Products	39.0%

Additional Information

Year Founded: 1992
Capital Under Management: $750,000,000
Current Activity Level : Actively seeking new investments
Method of Compensation: Return on invest. most important, but chg. closing fees, service fees, etc.

CHATHAM CAPITAL

400 Galleria Parkway
Suite 1950
Atlanta, GA USA 30339
Phone: 7706182100
Fax: 7706182101
Website: www.chathamcapital.com

Other Offices

100 Crescent Court
Seventh Floor
Dallas, TX USA 75201
Phone: 2144593311

220 West Exchange Street
Providence, RI USA 02903
Phone: 4013306716

Management and Staff

Brian Reynolds, Managing Partner
Frank Caprio, Managing Director
Lin Wang, Senior Managing Director
Nick Anacreonte, Partner
Patty Totaro, Chief Financial Officer
Scott Kray, Managing Director

Type of Firm

Private Equity Firm

Association Membership

Natl Assoc of Small Bus. Inv. Co (NASBIC)

Project Preferences

Role in Financing:
Will function either as deal originator or investor in deals created by others

Type of Financing Preferred:
Leveraged Buyout
Expansion
Mezzanine
Turnaround
Later Stage
Management Buyouts
Acquisition
Private Placement

Size of Investments Considered:
Min Size of Investment Considered (000s): $2,000
Max Size of Investment Considered (000s): $60,000

Geographical Preferences

United States Preferences:
Mid Atlantic
Midwest
Southeast

Industry Preferences

In Medical/Health prefer:
Medical/Health
Medical Diagnostics
Medical Products
Health Services
Hospitals/Clinics/Primary

In Financial Services prefer:
Financial Services

In Business Serv. prefer:
Services
Distribution

In Manufact. prefer:
Manufacturing

Additional Information

Name of Most Recent Fund: Chatham Investment Fund IV LLC
Most Recent Fund Was Raised: 06/08/2012
Year Founded: 2001
Capital Under Management: $150,000,000
Current Activity Level : Actively seeking new investments
Method of Compensation: Return on invest. most important, but chg. closing fees, service fees, etc.

CHATHAM VENTURE PARTNERS

20 East 91st Street
Suite 200
Indianapolis, IN USA 46240
E-mail: info@chathamvp.com
Website: www.chathamvp.com

Type of Firm

Private Equity Firm

Project Preferences

Type of Financing Preferred:
Early Stage
Seed

Geographical Preferences

United States Preferences:
Midwest

Additional Information

Year Founded: 1969
Current Activity Level : Actively seeking new investments

CHAZEN CAPITAL PARTNERS

150 East 58th Street
27th Floor
New York, NY USA 10155
Phone: 2128887800
Fax: 21288814580
E-mail: info@chazen.com
Website: www.chazen.com

Type of Firm

Private Equity Firm

Industry Preferences

In Consumer Related prefer:
Consumer Products

In Manufact. prefer:
Manufacturing

Additional Information

Year Founded: 1997
Current Activity Level : Actively seeking new investments

CHECKETTS PARTNERS INVESTMENT GP LLC

200 Park Avenue
16th Floor
New York, NY USA 10166
Phone: 2124901414

Type of Firm

Investment Management Firm

Project Preferences

Type of Financing Preferred:
Generalist PE

Additional Information

Name of Most Recent Fund: Checketts Partners Investment Fund, L.P.
Most Recent Fund Was Raised: 06/22/2011
Year Founded: 2011
Capital Under Management: $50,000,000
Current Activity Level : Actively seeking new investments

CHEERS CAPITAL PARTNERS CO., LTD.

918 Huaihai Millde Rd.
Blk.17E, Jiushifuxingg Bldg.
Shanghai, China
Phone: 862165568993
Website: cheerscapital.com

Type of Firm

Private Equity Firm

Project Preferences

Type of Financing Preferred:
Expansion
Start-up Financing
Seed

Geographical Preferences

International Preferences:
China

Pratt's Guide to Private Equity & Venture Capital Sources

Industry Preferences

In Communications prefer:
Entertainment

In Internet Specific prefer:
Internet

In Consumer Related prefer:
Retail
Consumer Products
Education Related

In Business Serv. prefer:
Media

Additional Information
Year Founded: 2015
Current Activity Level : Actively seeking new investments

CHEEVER CAPITAL MANAGEMENT LLC

2360 14th Avenue SouthEast
Albany, OR USA 97322
Fax: 5419673627
Website: www.cheevercapitalmgmt.com

Management and Staff
Edward Cheever, Co-Founder
Milton Cheever, Co-Founder

Type of Firm
Private Equity Firm

Project Preferences

Type of Financing Preferred:
Seed
Startup

Industry Preferences

In Medical/Health prefer:
Medical Products

In Utilities prefer:
Utilities

Additional Information
Year Founded: 2010
Capital Under Management: $4,212,000
Current Activity Level : Actively seeking new investments

CHEMELOT VENTURES MANAGEMENT BV

Urmonderbaan 22
Geleen, Netherlands 6167 RD
Website: chemelotventures.com

Type of Firm
Private Equity Firm

Project Preferences

Type of Financing Preferred:
Early Stage
Expansion
Later Stage
Seed

Geographical Preferences

International Preferences:
Netherlands

Industry Preferences

In Semiconductor/Electr prefer:
Analytic/Scientific

In Biotechnology prefer:
Biotechnology
Agricultural/Animal Bio.

In Medical/Health prefer:
Medical/Health
Diagnostic Services
Diagnostic Test Products

In Industrial/Energy prefer:
Materials

Additional Information
Year Founded: 2014
Current Activity Level : Actively seeking new investments

CHENGDAO TIANHUA INVESTMENT MANAGEMENT CO LTD

Number 6008, Shennan Avenue
21A, Baoye Plaza
Shenzhen, China 518009
Phone: 8675533065618
Fax: 8675533065618
E-mail: cdzb@chengdaocapital.com
Website: www.chengdaocapital.com

Type of Firm
Investment Management Firm

Association Membership
Venture Capital Association of Beijing (VCAB)

Project Preferences

Type of Financing Preferred:
Generalist PE

Geographical Preferences

International Preferences:
China

Industry Preferences

In Semiconductor/Electr prefer:
Electronics

In Medical/Health prefer:
Medical Products
Pharmaceuticals

In Consumer Related prefer:
Consumer

In Industrial/Energy prefer:
Energy
Energy Conservation Relat
Materials

In Manufact. prefer:
Manufacturing

Additional Information
Year Founded: 2012
Current Activity Level : Actively seeking new investments

CHENGDU CHINA RAILWAY HIDEA EQUITY INVESTMENT FUND MANAGEMEN

Ladefangsi Building
Number 311, 3rd Floor
Chengdu, China

Type of Firm
Private Equity Firm

Project Preferences

Type of Financing Preferred:
Balanced

Geographical Preferences

International Preferences:
China

Industry Preferences

In Transportation prefer:
Transportation

In Manufact. prefer:
Manufacturing

Additional Information
Year Founded: 2012
Capital Under Management: $48,795,000
Current Activity Level : Actively seeking new investments

CHENGDU DINXING INVESTMENT MANAGEMENT CO LTD

Dong chenggenshang Street
10F, Chengzheng Mansion, 95
Chengdu, China
Phone: 8628-61503040

Type of Firm
Bank Affiliated

Project Preferences

Type of Financing Preferred:
Balanced

Geographical Preferences

International Preferences:
China

Additional Information

Year Founded: 2013
Current Activity Level : Actively seeking new investments

CHENGDU GAOTOU VENTURE CAPITAL CO LTD

No. 966,Tianfu Dadao
2F, 2,Tianfu Int'l Finance Ctr
Chengdu, China

Type of Firm

Private Equity Firm

Project Preferences

Type of Financing Preferred:
Balanced

Geographical Preferences

International Preferences:
China

Industry Preferences

In Biotechnology prefer:
Biotechnology

In Medical/Health prefer:
Pharmaceuticals

In Industrial/Energy prefer:
Materials
Machinery

Additional Information

Year Founded: 2004
Capital Under Management: $47,600,000
Current Activity Level : Actively seeking new investments

CHENGDU HI-TECH INNOVATION INVESTMENT CO LTD

No.18 N. Tianfu Avenue
6/F Tower A Hi-Tech Int'l Plaz
Chengdu, China
Phone: 862885327999
Fax: 862885327888
E-mail: info@cdhtgroup.com

Type of Firm

Government Affiliated Program

Project Preferences

Type of Financing Preferred:
Early Stage
Expansion
Later Stage
Seed

Geographical Preferences

International Preferences:
China

Industry Preferences

In Communications prefer:
Wireless Communications

In Internet Specific prefer:
Internet

In Biotechnology prefer:
Biotechnology

In Medical/Health prefer:
Pharmaceuticals

In Manufact. prefer:
Manufacturing

Additional Information

Year Founded: 2012
Capital Under Management: $12,711,000
Current Activity Level : Actively seeking new investments

CHENGDU MERCHANTS YINKE VENTURE CAPITAL MANAGEMENT CO LTD

No.539 Jincheng Avenue
Yingchuang Dongli Mansion
Chengdu, China
Phone: 862885336380
Website: www.ykvc.cn

Type of Firm

Private Equity Firm

Project Preferences

Type of Financing Preferred:
Balanced

Geographical Preferences

International Preferences:
China

Industry Preferences

In Biotechnology prefer:
Agricultural/Animal Bio.

In Industrial/Energy prefer:
Energy
Materials

In Business Serv. prefer:
Services

In Manufact. prefer:
Manufacturing

In Other prefer:
Environment Responsible

Additional Information

Year Founded: 2010
Capital Under Management: $77,500,000
Current Activity Level : Actively seeking new investments

CHENGDU QIDIAN CHUANGKE ENTERPRISE MANAGEMENT CONSULTING CO

No. 1480 Tianfu Avenue, Chengd
Room 1501, Block A, Deshang In
Chengdu, China
Website: www.desunfund.com

Type of Firm

Private Equity Firm

Project Preferences

Type of Financing Preferred:
Balanced

Geographical Preferences

International Preferences:
China

Industry Preferences

In Communications prefer:
Entertainment

In Internet Specific prefer:
Internet

In Medical/Health prefer:
Health Services

In Consumer Related prefer:
Sports

In Business Serv. prefer:
Services

Additional Information

Year Founded: 2015
Current Activity Level : Actively seeking new investments

CHENGDU TIANZHUAN JIA-WA TECHNOLOGY CO LTD

Hi Tech Zone, Chengdu
B8-201 Block B Tianfu Software
Sichuang, China
Phone: 862883119005
Website: www.evervc.com

Type of Firm
Private Equity Firm

Project Preferences

Type of Financing Preferred:
Seed

Geographical Preferences

International Preferences:
China

Industry Preferences

In Internet Specific prefer:
Internet

In Consumer Related prefer:
Entertainment and Leisure

In Financial Services prefer:
Financial Services

Additional Information
Year Founded: 2015
Current Activity Level: Actively seeking new investments

CHENGDU YINGCHUANG XINGKE EQUITY INVEST. FUND MGMT CO., LTD.

No. 539, Jincheng Avenue
Room 503, 5F, Unit 1
Chengdu, China

Type of Firm
Private Equity Firm

Project Preferences

Type of Financing Preferred:
Seed
Startup

Geographical Preferences

International Preferences:
China

Additional Information
Year Founded: 2014
Capital Under Management: $16,519,000
Current Activity Level: Actively seeking new investments

CHENGWEI VENTURES

No. 33, Lane 672, Changle Road
Suite C
Shanghai, China 200040
Phone: 862154048566
Fax: 862154048766
Website: www.chengwei.com

Other Offices
58 West Portal Avenue #146
San Francisco, CA USA 94127

60 Wyndham Street
Suite 3206
Central, Hong Kong
Phone: 85225378133
Fax: 85225260533

Management and Staff
Griffith Baker, Venture Partner
Pei Kang, Managing Director
Ping Ping, Managing Director
Ye Sha, Managing Director

Type of Firm
Private Equity Firm

Association Membership
China Venture Capital Association

Project Preferences

Type of Financing Preferred:
Early Stage
Expansion
Balanced

Geographical Preferences

International Preferences:
China

Industry Preferences

In Communications prefer:
Communications and Media

In Computer Software prefer:
Software

In Internet Specific prefer:
E-Commerce Technology

In Semiconductor/Electr prefer:
Electronic Components

In Medical/Health prefer:
Medical/Health

In Financial Services prefer:
Financial Services

In Business Serv. prefer:
Media

In Manufact. prefer:
Manufacturing

Additional Information
Year Founded: 1999
Capital Under Management: $100,000,000
Current Activity Level: Actively seeking new investments

CHENJUN BEIJING ASSET MANAGEMENT CO LTD

No. 3 Guangqu Road, Chaoyang D
26B, Jingyuan Art Center
Beijing, China
Phone: 861087529506
Fax: 861087529554
Website: www.chenjunamc.com

Type of Firm
Private Equity Firm

Project Preferences

Type of Financing Preferred:
Balanced

Geographical Preferences

International Preferences:
China

Additional Information
Year Founded: 2014
Current Activity Level: Actively seeking new investments

CHEQUERS CAPITAL PARTNERS SA

48 Bis, Avenue Montaigne
Paris, France 75008
Phone: 33153576100
Fax: 33153576111
E-mail: mail@chequerscapital.com
Website: www.chequerscapital.com

Other Offices
Schackstrasse 3
Munchen, Germany 80539
Phone: 498945206950

Via Gaetano Negri 8
Milano, Italy 20123
Phone: 33153576100

Management and Staff
Denis Metzger, President
Dominique Du Peloux, Managing Director

Type of Firm
Private Equity Firm

Association Membership
French Venture Capital Association (AFIC)

Project Preferences

Type of Financing Preferred:
Leveraged Buyout
Management Buyouts
Acquisition
Recapitalizations

Geographical Preferences

International Preferences:
Italy
United Kingdom
Europe
Spain
Belgium
Germany
France

Industry Preferences

In Consumer Related prefer:
Consumer Services

In Industrial/Energy prefer:
Industrial Products

In Business Serv. prefer:
Services
Distribution

Additional Information

Name of Most Recent Fund: Chequers Capital XVI FCPR
Most Recent Fund Was Raised: 07/04/2011
Year Founded: 1972
Capital Under Management: $2,464,593,000
Current Activity Level : Actively seeking new investments

CHERRY VENTURES GMBH

Rosenstrasse 2
Berlin, Germany 10785
E-mail: team@cherry-vc.com
Website: www.cherry-vc.com

Type of Firm
Private Equity Firm

Project Preferences

Type of Financing Preferred:
Early Stage
Seed
Startup

Additional Information
Year Founded: 2012
Capital Under Management: $171,430,000
Current Activity Level : Actively seeking new investments

CHESTNUT HILL VENTURES LLC

60 Wiliam Street
Suite 230
Wellesley, MA USA 02481
Phone: 7814891200

Type of Firm
Private Equity Firm

Project Preferences

Role in Financing:
Prefer role as deal originator but will also invest in deals created by others

Type of Financing Preferred:
Balanced

Additional Information
Year Founded: 2002
Capital Under Management: $350,000,000
Current Activity Level : Actively seeking new investments
Method of Compensation: Return on investment is of primary concern, do not charge fees

---

CHESTNUT STREET PARTNERS INC

75 State Street
Suite 2500
Boston, MA USA 02109
Phone: 617-345-7220
Fax: 617-345-7201

Management and Staff
David Croll, Vice President

Type of Firm
Private Equity Firm

Project Preferences

Role in Financing:
Prefer role as deal originator but will also invest in deals created by others

Type of Financing Preferred:
Balanced

Industry Preferences

In Communications prefer:
Communications and Media
Telecommunications
Wireless Communications

In Computer Software prefer:
Software

In Internet Specific prefer:
Internet

Additional Information
Year Founded: 1995
Capital Under Management: $10,000,000
Current Activity Level : Actively seeking new investments

CHEVRON TECHNOLOGY VENTURES L L C

1200 Smith Street, Ste. 30.023
Houston, TX USA 77002
Phone: 7136544802
E-mail: techventures@chevron.com

Other Offices
3901 Briarpark
HOUSTON, TX USA 77042
Phone: 713-954-6360
Fax: 925-807-0385

Management and Staff
Matt McElhattan, Principal
Richard Pardoe, Principal
Trond Unneland, Vice President

Type of Firm
Corporate PE/Venture

Association Membership
National Venture Capital Association - USA (NVCA)

Project Preferences

Role in Financing:
Prefer role in deals created by others

Type of Financing Preferred:
Early Stage
Expansion
Balanced
Later Stage
Seed
Startup

Industry Preferences

In Communications prefer:
Commercial Communications
Wireless Communications

In Computer Software prefer:
Software

In Semiconductor/Electr prefer:
Analytic/Scientific

In Biotechnology prefer:
Industrial Biotechnology

In Industrial/Energy prefer:
Energy
Oil and Gas Exploration
Oil & Gas Drilling,Explor
Alternative Energy
Industrial Products
Materials
Advanced Materials

Additional Information
Year Founded: 1999
Capital Under Management: $320,000,000
Current Activity Level: Actively seeking new investments
Method of Compensation: Return on investment is of primary concern, do not charge fees

CHIBAGIN CAPITAL CO LTD

Nihon Kowa Bldg.
8-4 Chibakou, Chuo-ku
Chiba-shi, Japan 260-0026
Phone: 81-43-248-8822
Fax: 81-43-248-8821

Type of Firm
Private Equity Firm

Project Preferences

Type of Financing Preferred:
Balanced

Geographical Preferences

International Preferences:
Japan

Additional Information
Year Founded: 1984
Capital Under Management: $9,800,000
Current Activity Level: Actively seeking new investments

CHICAGO GROWTH PARTNERS LLC

222 West Merchandise
Mart Plaza, Suite 1212
Chicago, IL USA 60606
Phone: 3126986300
Website: cgp.com

Other Offices
1200 Prospect Street
Suite 425
LA JOLLA, CA USA 92037
Phone: 312-698-6300

Management and Staff
Arda Minocherhomjee, Managing Partner
Corey Dossett, Chief Financial Officer
David Chandler, Managing Partner
Devin Mathews, Managing Partner
Jeffery Farrero, Principal
Kristina Heinze, Principal
Robert Healy, Managing Partner
Robert Blank, Partner
Ron Davies, Partner
Ron Huberman, Chief Operating Officer
Ryan Milligan, Vice President
Sean Barrette, Vice President
Timothy Murray, Partner

Type of Firm
Private Equity Firm

Project Preferences

Role in Financing:
Prefer role as deal originator but will also invest in deals created by others

Type of Financing Preferred:
Leveraged Buyout
Expansion
Management Buyouts
Recapitalizations

Geographical Preferences

United States Preferences:

Industry Focus
(% based on actual investment)
Medical/Health	20.4%
Other Products	18.7%
Consumer Related	17.8%
Industrial/Energy	14.4%
Computer Software and Services	10.9%
Internet Specific	6.2%
Biotechnology	5.6%
Communications and Media	2.4%
Computer Hardware	2.2%
Semiconductors/Other Elect.	1.4%

Additional Information
Year Founded: 1982
Capital Under Management: $1,200,000,000
Current Activity Level: Actively seeking new investments
Method of Compensation: Return on investment is of primary concern, do not charge fees

CHICAGO INNOVATION EXCHANGE

1452 East 53rd Street
Chicago, IL USA 60615
Website: cie.uchicago.edu

Type of Firm
University Program

Project Preferences

Type of Financing Preferred:
Early Stage
Startup

Additional Information
Year Founded: 1969
Current Activity Level: Actively seeking new investments

CHICAGO PACIFIC FOUNDERS FUND LP

400 North Michigan Avenue
Suite 560
Chicago, IL USA 60611
Phone: 3122734750

Management and Staff
Krista Hatcher, Partner
Lawrence Leisure, Managing Partner

Type of Firm
Private Equity Firm

Project Preferences

Type of Financing Preferred:
Generalist PE

Industry Preferences

In Medical/Health prefer:
Medical/Health
Medical Diagnostics
Medical Therapeutics
Health Services

Additional Information
Year Founded: 2014
Capital Under Management: $325,000,000
Current Activity Level: Actively seeking new investments

CHICAGO VENTURES

222 West Merchandise Mart Plaz
Suite 212
Chicago, IL USA 60654
Phone: 3122828211
E-mail: info@I2Afund.com
Website: chicagoventures.com

Other Offices
222 W Merchandise Mart Plaza
Suite 1212
CHICAGO, IL USA 60654

Management and Staff
Jason Felger, Venture Partner
Kapil Chaudhary, Managing Director
Kevin Willer, Partner
Stuart Larkins, Partner

Type of Firm
Private Equity Firm

Association Membership
Illinois Venture Capital Association

Project Preferences

Type of Financing Preferred:
Early Stage
Seed

Size of Investments Considered:
Min Size of Investment Considered (000s): $250
Max Size of Investment Considered (000s): $1,000

Geographical Preferences

United States Preferences:
Midwest
Illinois

Industry Preferences

In Communications prefer:
Communications and Media

In Consumer Related prefer:
Consumer
Retail
Consumer Products
Consumer Services
Education Related

Additional Information
Name of Most Recent Fund: Chicago Ventures Fund, L.P.
Most Recent Fund Was Raised: 03/23/2012
Year Founded: 2007
Capital Under Management: $106,000,000
Current Activity Level : Actively seeking new investments

CHIESI VENTURES

75 Arlington Street, Unit 500
Boston, MA USA 02116
Website: www.chiesiventures.com

Type of Firm
Private Equity Firm

Project Preferences

Type of Financing Preferred:
Early Stage

Industry Preferences

In Biotechnology prefer:
Biotechnology

In Medical/Health prefer:
Medical/Health
Pharmaceuticals

Additional Information
Year Founded: 2014
Current Activity Level : Actively seeking new investments

CHIFUFUND INVESTMENT CONSULTING SHANGHAI CO LTD

Century Avenue 1528
Lujiazui Fund Building
Shanghai, China 200333
Phone: 862151215988
Website: www.chifufund.com

Type of Firm
Investment Management Firm

Project Preferences

Type of Financing Preferred:
Balanced

Geographical Preferences

International Preferences:
China

Additional Information
Year Founded: 2011
Current Activity Level : Actively seeking new investments

CHILANGO VENTURES LLC

201 Spear Street 1100
San Francisco, CA USA 94105
Phone: 4159699007
E-mail: hello@chilangoventures.com
Website: www.chilangoventures.com

Management and Staff
Carlos Ochoa, CEO & Managing Director
Juan Yrigoyen, Partner
Neha Jain, Partner
Yamandu Rodriguez, Partner

Type of Firm
Private Equity Firm

Project Preferences

Type of Financing Preferred:
Early Stage
Seed

Geographical Preferences

United States Preferences:

International Preferences:
Mexico

Additional Information
Year Founded: 2014
Current Activity Level : Actively seeking new investments

CHILTERN CAPITAL LLP

31 Southampton Row
London, United Kingdom WC1B 5HJ
Phone: 02036375620
E-mail: enquiry@chilterncapital.co.uk
Website: chilterncapital.co.uk

Type of Firm
Private Equity Firm

Project Preferences

Type of Financing Preferred:
Leveraged Buyout
Start-up Financing
Management Buyouts
Acquisition

Size of Investments Considered:
Min Size of Investment Considered (000s): $1,462
Max Size of Investment Considered (000s): $14,621

Geographical Preferences

International Preferences:
United Kingdom

Industry Preferences

In Internet Specific prefer:
Ecommerce

Additional Information
Year Founded: 1969
Current Activity Level : Actively seeking new investments

CHIMERA PARTNERS LTD

3 More London Riverside
First Floor
London, United Kingdom
Phone: 4402032834403
Website: chimerapartners.com

Type of Firm
Private Equity Firm

Project Preferences

Type of Financing Preferred:
Balanced

Additional Information
Year Founded: 2014
Current Activity Level : Actively seeking new investments

CHINA CANADA ANGELS ALLIANCE LTD

156 Front Street West
Toronto, Canada M5J 2L6
Phone: 6472800652
E-mail: info@cc-angels.com
Website: www.cc-angels.com

Management and Staff
Alan Yang, Vice President
Qiao Qian, Co-Founder
Yingna Liu, Co-Founder
Zhishuo Liu, President

Type of Firm
Incubator/Development Program

509

Project Preferences

Type of Financing Preferred:
Startup

Geographical Preferences

Canadian Preferences:
All Canada

International Preferences:
China

Additional Information

Year Founded: 1969
Current Activity Level : Actively seeking new investments

CHINA CAPITAL MANAGEMENT LTD

415, Tower B, Tongtai Mansion
33 Finance St., Xicheng Dist.
Beijing, China 100032
Phone: 86-10-8808-7300
Fax: 86-10-8808-7216
E-mail: invest@ccmcllc.com

Other Offices

2206, Bank of America Tower
12 Harcourt Road
Central, Hong Kong
Phone: 852-2810-8155
Fax: 852-2522-9976

5784 Post Road, Suite 5
East Greenwich, RI USA 02818
Phone: 401-398-0260
Fax: 401-885-4686

Management and Staff

Cui Ming, Managing Director
Penny Fang, Chief Financial Officer
Samuel Lou, Managing Director

Type of Firm

Private Equity Firm

Project Preferences

Type of Financing Preferred:
Leveraged Buyout
Balanced
Turnaround
Later Stage
Acquisition

Geographical Preferences

International Preferences:
China

Additional Information

Year Founded: 2004
Current Activity Level : Actively seeking new investments

CHINA CENTURY VENTURE CAPITAL

No.68 Xinzhong Street
Dongcheng District
Beijing, China
Phone: 86-10-6708-3157
Website: www.ccvc.com.cn

Type of Firm

Private Equity Firm

Association Membership

Venture Capital Association of Beijing (VCAB)

Project Preferences

Type of Financing Preferred:
Expansion
Startup

Geographical Preferences

International Preferences:
No Preference
China

Industry Preferences

In Communications prefer:
Telecommunications

In Computer Software prefer:
Software

In Semiconductor/Electr prefer:
Electronics

In Biotechnology prefer:
Biotechnology

In Industrial/Energy prefer:
Energy
Materials

In Other prefer:
Environment Responsible

Additional Information

Year Founded: 2000
Current Activity Level : Actively seeking new investments

CHINA CULTURE INDUSTRIAL INVESTMENT FUND MANAGEMENT CO LTD

5001 Shennan East Road
Rm. 502, China Resources Bldg.
Shenzhen, China
Phone: 010-57503518
Fax: 010-57503528
E-mail: info@chinacf.com
Website: www.chinacf.com

Other Offices

28th Pacific Insurance
Room 1206, Building B
Beijing, China

Type of Firm

Government Affiliated Program

Project Preferences

Type of Financing Preferred:
Generalist PE

Geographical Preferences

International Preferences:
China

Industry Preferences

In Communications prefer:
Radio & TV Broadcasting
Wireless Communications

In Internet Specific prefer:
Internet

In Consumer Related prefer:
Entertainment and Leisure

In Business Serv. prefer:
Distribution
Media

In Manufact. prefer:
Publishing

Additional Information

Year Founded: 2011
Capital Under Management: $943,249,000
Current Activity Level : Actively seeking new investments

CHINA DEVELOPMENT BANK

No.7, Finance Street
1111-1117, Yinglan Int Fin Ctr
Beijing, China 100034
Website: www.cdb.com.cn

Type of Firm

Bank Affiliated

Project Preferences

Type of Financing Preferred:
Balanced

Geographical Preferences

International Preferences:
China

Additional Information

Year Founded: 2009
Capital Under Management: $4,000,000,000
Current Activity Level : Actively seeking new investments

CHINA DEVELOPMENT FINANCE CO., LTD.

c/o China Development Bank
No. 29 Fucheng Menwai Street
Beijing, China 100037
Phone: 86-10-6830-6688
Fax: 86-10-6830-6699

Type of Firm
Bank Affiliated

Project Preferences

Type of Financing Preferred:
Generalist PE

Geographical Preferences

International Preferences:
China

Additional Information
Year Founded: 2009
Capital Under Management: $988,878,000
Current Activity Level : Actively seeking new investments

CHINA ECAPITAL CORP

Vanton Plaza
Room 803, Building C
Beijing, China 100020
Phone: 861059070682
Website: www.dragonwings-cap.com

Type of Firm
Bank Affiliated

Project Preferences

Type of Financing Preferred:
Generalist PE

Geographical Preferences

International Preferences:
China

Additional Information
Year Founded: 2014
Current Activity Level : Actively seeking new investments

CHINA EVERBRIGHT LTD

16 Harcourt Road
46/F, Far East Finance Centre
Hong Kong, Hong Kong
Phone: 852-25289882
Fax: 852-225290177
Website: www.everbright.com

Other Offices
No. 28 Ping An Li West Street
Room 1600 Everbright
Beijing, China 100081
Phone: 86-10-6894-7857
Fax: 86-10-6894-0009

4013 Shennan Road
8/F Industrial Bank Building
Shenzhen, China
Phone: 86-755-8302-4017

Management and Staff
Chi Chun Tang, Chief Financial Officer
Shuang Chen, Chief Executive Officer

Type of Firm
Investment Management Firm

Project Preferences

Type of Financing Preferred:
Core
Early Stage
Expansion
Mezzanine
Balanced
Opportunistic
Later Stage

Size of Investments Considered:
Min Size of Investment Considered (000s): $5,000
Max Size of Investment Considered (000s): $30,000

Geographical Preferences

International Preferences:
Asia Pacific
Hong Kong
China

Industry Preferences

In Biotechnology prefer:
Biotechnology

In Medical/Health prefer:
Medical/Health
Health Services
Pharmaceuticals

In Consumer Related prefer:
Consumer
Retail
Consumer Products

In Industrial/Energy prefer:
Energy
Alternative Energy
Materials
Environmental Related

In Financial Services prefer:
Financial Services
Real Estate

In Business Serv. prefer:
Services

In Manufact. prefer:
Manufacturing

In Agr/Forestr/Fish prefer:
Agriculture related

Additional Information
Year Founded: 1972
Capital Under Management: $3,007,570,000
Current Activity Level : Actively seeking new investments

CHINA EXPORT & CREDIT INSURANCE CORP

88 Shiji Dadao, Century Blvd.
Jin Mao Tower Suite 1705
Pudong New Area, Shanghai, China 200120
Phone: 866222398855
Fax: 886222392977
E-mail: inquiry@maximavc.com
Website: www.sinosure.com.cn

Other Offices
10F-3, No. 89, Song Ren Rd.
Taipei 110, Taiwan
Phone: 886-2-27200011
Fax: 886-2-27202106

Management and Staff
David Tai, Partner

Type of Firm
Private Equity Firm

Association Membership
Taiwan Venture Capital Association(TVCA)

Project Preferences

Type of Financing Preferred:
Early Stage

Geographical Preferences

United States Preferences:

International Preferences:
Taiwan
China

Industry Preferences

In Communications prefer:
Wireless Communications

In Computer Software prefer:
Software

In Semiconductor/Electr prefer:
Electronic Components
Semiconductor

Additional Information
Year Founded: 2002
Current Activity Level : Actively seeking new investments

CHINA FINANCIAL INTERNATIONAL INVESTMENTS LTD

18 Harbour Road
Central Plaza, 58th Floor
Hong Kong, Hong Kong 5802
Phone: 85235425373
Fax: 85235425370
E-mail: info@cfii.com.hk

Other Offices
Futian District
3301-3302 Excellence Times Pl.
Shenzhen, China
Phone: 8675582560385
Fax: 8675582560382

Type of Firm
Investment Management Firm

Project Preferences

Type of Financing Preferred:
Balanced

Geographical Preferences

International Preferences:
Hong Kong
China

Industry Preferences

In Internet Specific prefer:
Internet

In Industrial/Energy prefer:
Alternative Energy
Advanced Materials

In Financial Services prefer:
Financial Services
Real Estate

In Agr/Forestr/Fish prefer:
Mining and Minerals

In Utilities prefer:
Utilities

In Other prefer:
Environment Responsible

Additional Information
Year Founded: 2006
Capital Under Management: $158,629,000
Current Activity Level: Actively seeking new investments

CHINA GALAXY INVESTMENT MANAGEMENT CO LTD

No.35, Finance Avenue, Xicheng
16F, Int'l Enterprise Bldg C
Beijing, China 100140
Phone: 861066568168
Fax: 861066568253
Website: china-galaxy-inv.com

Type of Firm
Investment Management Firm

Project Preferences

Type of Financing Preferred:
Early Stage
Balanced
Seed
Startup

Geographical Preferences

International Preferences:
China

Industry Preferences

In Communications prefer:
Telecommunications

In Biotechnology prefer:
Biotechnology

In Medical/Health prefer:
Medical/Health

In Consumer Related prefer:
Entertainment and Leisure
Food/Beverage
Education Related

In Industrial/Energy prefer:
Alternative Energy
Energy Conservation Relat
Advanced Materials

In Transportation prefer:
Transportation

In Financial Services prefer:
Financial Services
Real Estate

In Business Serv. prefer:
Services

In Agr/Forestr/Fish prefer:
Agriculture related

In Other prefer:
Environment Responsible

Additional Information
Year Founded: 2000
Current Activity Level: Actively seeking new investments

CHINA HIGHRUN CAPITAL LTD

No.2012 Shennan Street Futian
39F Shenzhen Stock Exchange Sq
Shenzhen, China 518038
Website: www.chrcapital.cn

Type of Firm
Investment Management Firm

Project Preferences

Type of Financing Preferred:
Leveraged Buyout
Mezzanine
Generalist PE

Geographical Preferences

International Preferences:
China

Additional Information
Year Founded: 2014
Current Activity Level: Actively seeking new investments

CHINA INTERNATIONAL CAPITAL CORP LTD

No. 1, Jianguomenwai Avenue
28F, China World Office 2
Beijing, China 100004
Phone: 861065051166
Fax: 861065051156
E-mail: info@cicc.com.cn
Website: www.cicc.com.cn

Other Offices
Six Battery Road
Suite 39-04
, Singapore 049909
Phone: 6565721999
Fax: 6563271278

1233 Lujiazui Ring Road
32F Azia Center
Shanghai, China 200120
Phone: 862158796226
Fax: 862158888976

7088 Shennan Road
25/F, Room 2503
Shenzhen, China 518040
Phone: 8675583195000
Fax: 8675583199229

350 Park Avenue
28th Floor
New York, NY USA 10022
Phone: 6467948800
Fax: 6467948801

125 Old Broad Street
Level 25
London, United Kingdom ECN2N 1AR
Phone: 442073675718
Fax: 442073675719

One Harbour View Street
29th Floor
, Hong Kong
Phone: 85228722000
Fax: 85228722100

Management and Staff
Gang Chu, Chief Operating Officer
Jie Xin, Chief Financial Officer
Mingjian Bi, Chief Executive Officer

Type of Firm
Bank Affiliated

Project Preferences

Type of Financing Preferred:
Leveraged Buyout
Expansion
Generalist PE
Balanced
Public Companies
Later Stage
Acquisition

Geographical Preferences

International Preferences:
China

Industry Preferences

In Medical/Health prefer:
Medical/Health
Pharmaceuticals

In Consumer Related prefer:
Consumer
Education Related

In Industrial/Energy prefer:
Energy
Alternative Energy

In Transportation prefer:
Transportation

In Financial Services prefer:
Financial Services
Insurance
Financial Services

Additional Information
Year Founded: 1998
Capital Under Management: $826,629,000
Current Activity Level : Actively seeking new investments

CHINA INTERNET INVESTMENT FUND MNAGEMENT CO LTD

Xicheng District
Beijing, China 100120

Type of Firm
Government Affiliated Program

Project Preferences

Type of Financing Preferred:
Balanced

Geographical Preferences

International Preferences:
China

Industry Preferences

In Internet Specific prefer:
Internet

Additional Information
Year Founded: 2016
Capital Under Management: $4,364,970,000
Current Activity Level : Actively seeking new investments

CHINA INVESTMENT CORP

No.1 Chaoyangmen Beidajie
New Poly Plaza, Dongcheng
Beijing, China 100010
Phone: 861084096277
Fax: 861064086908
E-mail: pr@china-inv.cn
Website: www.china-inv.cn

Management and Staff
Xiqing Gao, President

Type of Firm
Investment Management Firm

Project Preferences

Type of Financing Preferred:
Generalist PE

Geographical Preferences

International Preferences:
China

Additional Information
Year Founded: 2007
Current Activity Level : Actively seeking new investments

CHINA INVESTMENT FORTUNE CAPITAL MANAGEMENT (TIANJIN) CO LTD

126 Middle District B1
Floor 201-118, Eco-City Bldg.
Tianjin, China

Type of Firm
Investment Management Firm

Project Preferences

Type of Financing Preferred:
Early Stage
Expansion
Balanced
Later Stage

Geographical Preferences

International Preferences:
China

Additional Information
Year Founded: 2011
Current Activity Level : Actively seeking new investments

CHINA KING LINK CORP

No 1, Dongzhimen South Ave
7F, Raffles City Office Bldg
Beijing, China 100007
Phone: 861064028852
Fax: 861064025652
E-mail: info@chinasoftcapital.com
Website: www.chinakinglink.com

Other Offices
No.89 Queenway, Hong Kong
2310 Room, 2 Block, Lippo Centre
Hong Kong, Hong Kong
Phone: 85225229906
Fax: 8525378930

No.1600 West Zhongshan Road
2106-2107 Tower A
Shanghai, China
Phone: 862161289556
Fax: 862161289558

Taihu East Road, Xinbei Dist
Room 1306-1, No. 9-1
Changzhou, China

No. 3850 Jiangnan Avenue
1812 Chuangxin Building
Hangzhou, China 310053
Phone: 8657128290599
Fax: 8657128290600

Management and Staff
Guangyu Wang, President, Founder
Pengcheng Jiang, Chief Financial Officer
Shijian Pan, Vice President
Yong Zhang, Vice President
Yulin Pan, Vice President

Type of Firm
Private Equity Firm

Association Membership
Beijing Private Equity Association (BPEA)
Hong Kong Venture Capital Association (HKVCA)
Czech Venture Capital Association (CVCA)

Project Preferences

Type of Financing Preferred:
Leveraged Buyout
Balanced
Acquisition

Geographical Preferences

International Preferences:
China

Industry Preferences

In Communications prefer:
Entertainment
Publishing

In Computer Software prefer:
Software

In Medical/Health prefer:
Medical/Health
Medical Products
Health Services

In Consumer Related prefer:
Consumer

In Industrial/Energy prefer:
Energy

In Business Serv. prefer:
Services

In Manufact. prefer:
Manufacturing

In Other prefer:
Environment Responsible

Additional Information
Year Founded: 2010
Capital Under Management: $369,389,000
Current Activity Level : Actively seeking new investments

CHINA LIFE INVESTMENT HOLDING CO LTD

12th Floor, China Life Center
Xicheng District
Beijing, China 100033
Phone: 861066581000
Website: www.chinalifeinvest.com

Type of Firm
Insurance Firm Affiliate

Project Preferences

Type of Financing Preferred:
Generalist PE

Geographical Preferences

International Preferences:
China

Industry Preferences

In Medical/Health prefer:
Medical/Health

In Financial Services prefer:
Real Estate

Additional Information
Year Founded: 2007
Capital Under Management: $100,000,000,000
Current Activity Level : Actively seeking new investments

CHINA MATERIALIA LLC

No. 248, University Road, Yang
15th Floor
Shanghai, China 200433
Phone: 862135322611
E-mail: info@chinamaterialia.com
Website: www.chinamaterialia.com

Management and Staff
Charles Kwon, Venture Partner
Ed Hotard, Venture Partner
Jean-Claude Pierre, Venture Partner
Min Zhou, Founder
Patrick Berbon, Founder
Xiaoxia Gai, Venture Partner

Type of Firm
Private Equity Firm

Project Preferences

Type of Financing Preferred:
Early Stage

Geographical Preferences

International Preferences:
China

Industry Preferences

In Medical/Health prefer:
Medical/Health

Additional Information
Year Founded: 2010
Current Activity Level : Actively seeking new investments

CHINA MEDIA CAPITAL CO LTD

No. 989, Changle Road
Unit 3607B-08, The Center
Shanghai, China 200031
Phone: 862154668282
Fax: 862154661250
Website: www.chinamediacapital.com

Other Offices
No. 1 Guanghua Road
30/F, South Tower, Beijing Kerry Centre
Beijing, China 100020
Phone: 86-10-6561-1860
Fax: 86-10-6561-1002

Management and Staff
Shoujing Li, Chief Operating Officer
Xiaowan Zhang, Principal
Youchuan Liang, Vice President

Type of Firm
Private Equity Firm

Project Preferences

Type of Financing Preferred:
Leveraged Buyout
Management Buyouts
Acquisition

Geographical Preferences

International Preferences:
China
All International

Industry Preferences

In Communications prefer:
Media and Entertainment

In Consumer Related prefer:
Entertainment and Leisure
Consumer Services

In Business Serv. prefer:
Media

Additional Information
Year Founded: 2009
Capital Under Management: $303,700,000
Current Activity Level : Actively seeking new investments

CHINA MERCHANTS CAPITAL CO LTD

No7888 Shennan Road, Futian
Dongnan Intl Center
Shenzhen, China
Website: www.cmcapital.com.cn

Type of Firm
Corporate PE/Venture

Project Preferences

Type of Financing Preferred:
Generalist PE

Additional Information
Year Founded: 2012
Capital Under Management: $805,860,000
Current Activity Level : Actively seeking new investments

CHINA MERCHANTS CHINA DIRECT INVESTMENTS LTD

1803 China Merchants Tower
168-200 Connaught Road
Central, Hong Kong
Phone: 85228589089
Fax: 85228588455
E-mail: info@cmcdi.com.hk
Website: www.cmcdi.com.hk

Type of Firm
Bank Affiliated

Project Preferences

Type of Financing Preferred:
Leveraged Buyout
Generalist PE
Balanced

Geographical Preferences

International Preferences:
China

Industry Preferences

In Industrial/Energy prefer:
Energy

In Financial Services prefer:
Financial Services

In Business Serv. prefer:
Media

In Manufact. prefer:
Manufacturing

Additional Information
Year Founded: 1993
Current Activity Level : Actively seeking new investments

CHINA MERCHANTS KUN-LUN EQUITY INVEST MANAGEMENT CO LTD

Guomao Office Building, No.1
901, Block 2,
Beijing, China

Phone: 861059611919
Fax: 861059611090
E-mail: info@cmkcapital.com
Website: www.cmkcapital.com

Management and Staff
Duanyi Mao, Vice President
Guang Yang, Managing Director
Hongtao Feng, Managing Director
Jian Guo, Chief Executive Officer
Ju Zhang, Managing Director

Type of Firm
Bank Affiliated

Project Preferences

Type of Financing Preferred:
Fund of Funds
Leveraged Buyout
Expansion
Mezzanine
Later Stage

Geographical Preferences

International Preferences:
China

Industry Preferences

In Medical/Health prefer:
Medical/Health

In Consumer Related prefer:
Consumer
Retail

In Industrial/Energy prefer:
Energy

In Transportation prefer:
Transportation

In Financial Services prefer:
Financial Services

In Business Serv. prefer:
Services

In Agr/Forestr/Fish prefer:
Agriculture related

In Utilities prefer:
Utilities

Additional Information
Year Founded: 2011
Capital Under Management: $1,222,000,000
Current Activity Level : Actively seeking new investments

CHINA MERCHANTS SECURITIES CO LTD

38/F, Block A, Jiangsu Bldg
Yitian Road
Shenzhen, China 518026

Website: www.newone.com.cn

Other Offices
Central Trade Plaza
48/F, Phase 1
Hong Kong, Hong Kong
Phone: 852-2530-0698
Fax: 852-2810-0162

Management and Staff
Jiantao Xiong, Vice President
Yizheng Sun, Vice President
Zongjun Li, Vice President

Type of Firm
Bank Affiliated

Project Preferences

Type of Financing Preferred:
Balanced
Later Stage

Geographical Preferences

International Preferences:
China

Industry Preferences

In Communications prefer:
Communications and Media
Media and Entertainment

In Biotechnology prefer:
Agricultural/Animal Bio.

In Medical/Health prefer:
Health Services

In Industrial/Energy prefer:
Alternative Energy
Industrial Products
Environmental Related

In Agr/Forestr/Fish prefer:
Agriculture related

Additional Information
Year Founded: 2009
Capital Under Management: $446,560,000
Current Activity Level : Actively seeking new investments

CHINA OPERVESTORS INC

28 Xiang Jun Bei Li
Suite 807-9, Hanhai Culture
Beijing, China 100020
Phone: 86-10-6508-5686
Fax: 86-10-6508-5986
E-mail: info@chinaopervestors.com
Website: www.covgroup.cn

Pratt's Guide to Private Equity & Venture Capital Sources

Other Offices
1221 Xie Tu Road
RM105 Zhi Jun Building
Shanghai, China
Phone: 862151712216
Fax: 862151712215

Two Ice House Street
Room 303, St. George Building
Central, Hong Kong
Phone: 85228400683
Fax: 85228015618

Management and Staff
Warren Law, Managing Director

Type of Firm
Investment Management Firm

Additional Information
Year Founded: 2005
Current Activity Level : Actively seeking new investments

CHINA ORIENT ASSET MANAGEMENT INTERNATIONAL HOLDING LTD

No. 28, Jianguomennei Street
Minsheng Financial
Beijing, China
Website: www.coamc.com.cn

Other Offices
Yangshupu Road
Fengui International Building
Shenzhen, China 200082
Phone: 862165686591

Type of Firm
Investment Management Firm

Project Preferences

Type of Financing Preferred:
Value-Add
Balanced

Additional Information
Year Founded: 2011
Capital Under Management: $573,652,000
Current Activity Level : Actively seeking new investments

CHINA PEACE(BEIJING) INVEST CO

East Chang'an Street
Building.3, No. 6
Beijing, China 100006
Phone: 86-10-85115
Fax: 86-10-85115

Type of Firm
Government Affiliated Program

Industry Preferences

In Industrial/Energy prefer:
Energy

In Agr/Forestr/Fish prefer:
Agriculture related

In Other prefer:
Environment Responsible

Additional Information
Year Founded: 1999
Current Activity Level : Actively seeking new investments

CHINA PROSPER INVESTMENT & MANAGEMENT TIANJIN CO LTD

No. 166 West 3rd Avenue
Airport Logistic Process Zone
Tianjin, China
Phone: 86-22-8319-5158

Type of Firm
Private Equity Firm

Project Preferences

Type of Financing Preferred:
Balanced

Geographical Preferences

International Preferences:
Taiwan
China

Additional Information
Year Founded: 2008
Current Activity Level : Actively seeking new investments

CHINA REFORM FUND MANAGEMENT CO LTD

Haidian District, Beijing
6F, Block A, Yuhui Building, N
Beijing, China 100036
Phone: 861088656901
Website: www.chinareformfund.com

Type of Firm
Government Affiliated Program

Project Preferences

Type of Financing Preferred:
Balanced

Geographical Preferences

International Preferences:
China

Industry Preferences

In Biotechnology prefer:
Biotechnology

In Medical/Health prefer:
Medical Products

In Manufact. prefer:
Manufacturing

Additional Information
Year Founded: 2014
Capital Under Management: $15,909,540,000
Current Activity Level : Actively seeking new investments

CHINA RENAISSANCE CAPITAL INVESTMENT LTD

Two Ice House Street
Suite 305, St. George's Bldg.
Central, Hong Kong
Phone: 85225218013
Fax: 85225218023

Other Offices
One East Chang An Avenue
Suite 805, Tower E1
Beijing, China 100738
Phone: 861085185686
Fax: 861085151898

999 Huai Hai Road
Suite 1504, Shanghai Int'l Center
Shanghai, China 200031
Phone: 862163351018
Fax: 862163351919

Management and Staff
Frances Wang, Vice President

Type of Firm
Investment Management Firm

Project Preferences

Type of Financing Preferred:
Early Stage
Expansion
Balanced

Geographical Preferences

International Preferences:
Macau
Taiwan
Hong Kong
China

Additional Information
Year Founded: 2005
Capital Under Management: $180,000,000
Current Activity Level : Actively seeking new investments

CHINA RESOURCES INVESTMENT MANAGEMENT CO LTD

Room 712, Tower 1
Bright China Chang An Building
Beijing, China 100005
Phone: 86-10-65102
Fax: 86-10-65180
Website: www.vc-china.com

Other Offices
1311 Mason Street
San Francisco, CA USA 94133
Phone: 9252080012
Fax: 9258305173

Type of Firm
Private Equity Firm

Project Preferences

Type of Financing Preferred:
Generalist PE
Balanced
Opportunistic

Geographical Preferences

International Preferences:
China

Industry Preferences

In Transportation prefer:
Transportation

Additional Information
Year Founded: 1998
Capital Under Management: $265,000,000
Current Activity Level : Actively seeking new investments

CHINA SCIENCE & MERCHANTS INVESTMENT MANAGEMENT GROUP CO LTD

No. 12 Yumin Rd. Madianqiao
Inte'l Sci&Tech Convention Ctr
Beijing, China 100029
Phone: 861051658558
Fax: 861082250616
Website: www.leadvc.com

Management and Staff
Jerry Song, General Partner
John Wang, General Partner
Shuangxiang Shan, President & Chairman

Type of Firm
Private Equity Firm

Project Preferences

Type of Financing Preferred:
Fund of Funds
Leveraged Buyout
Early Stage
Expansion
Mezzanine
Balanced
Later Stage
Seed
Startup

Geographical Preferences

International Preferences:
China

Industry Preferences

In Communications prefer:
CATV & Pay TV Systems
Entertainment

In Internet Specific prefer:
Internet

In Medical/Health prefer:
Drug/Equipmt Delivery
Pharmaceuticals

In Consumer Related prefer:
Franchises(NEC)
Consumer Products

In Industrial/Energy prefer:
Energy
Alternative Energy
Advanced Materials

In Financial Services prefer:
Financial Services

In Business Serv. prefer:
Media

In Manufact. prefer:
Manufacturing

In Agr/Forestr/Fish prefer:
Agriculture related
Mining and Minerals

Additional Information
Year Founded: 2000
Capital Under Management: $5,211,619,000
Current Activity Level : Actively seeking new investments

CHINA SDIC HI-TECH INDUSTRIAL INVESTMENT CO

No. 1, South Binhe Road
Gaoxin Bldg. Xicheng District
Beijing, China 100055
Phone: 861063288613
Fax: 861063288606
Website: www.gaoxin-china.com.cn

Other Offices
No. 1, South Binhe Road
Gaoxin Bldg. Xicheng District
Beijing, China
Phone: 861063588613
Fax: 861063288606

Type of Firm
Government Affiliated Program

Project Preferences

Type of Financing Preferred:
Balanced

Geographical Preferences

International Preferences:
China

Industry Preferences

In Biotechnology prefer:
Biotechnology

In Medical/Health prefer:
Medical/Health
Pharmaceuticals

In Industrial/Energy prefer:
Energy
Energy Conservation Relat
Materials
Environmental Related

Additional Information
Year Founded: 1987
Current Activity Level : Actively seeking new investments

CHINA UNITED FORTUNE INTL. INVEST. FUND MGMT (BEIJING)

SK Building
R3008, Block B
Beijing, China 100022
Phone: 861085670048
Fax: 861085670059
Website: www.zhonglianfund.com

Type of Firm
Private Equity Firm

Pratt's Guide to Private Equity & Venture Capital Sources

Association Membership
China Venture Capital Association

Project Preferences

Type of Financing Preferred:
Leveraged Buyout
Generalist PE
Later Stage

Geographical Preferences

International Preferences:
China

Industry Preferences

In Industrial/Energy prefer:
Energy

In Financial Services prefer:
Real Estate

In Business Serv. prefer:
Media

Additional Information
Year Founded: 2011
Current Activity Level : Actively seeking new investments

CHINA US STRATEGY CAPITAL GROUP, LTD.

1330 Avenue of the Americas
20/F, The Financial Times Bldg
New York, NY USA 10019
Phone: 646-200-6353
Fax: 646-200-6354
E-mail: CUSC@chinausgroup.com
Website: www.chinausgroup.com

Other Offices
No. 33 Huayuan Shiqiao Road
21/F, Citi Group Tower
Shanghai, China
Phone: 86-21-6105-0200
Fax: 86-21-6105-0201

Type of Firm
Investment Management Firm

Project Preferences

Type of Financing Preferred:
Early Stage
Balanced
Later Stage

Geographical Preferences

International Preferences:
China

Industry Preferences

In Semiconductor/Electr prefer:
Semiconductor

In Consumer Related prefer:
Consumer

In Industrial/Energy prefer:
Energy
Materials

In Business Serv. prefer:
Services

In Agr/Forestr/Fish prefer:
Agriculture related

Additional Information
Year Founded: 2011
Capital Under Management: $75,873,000
Current Activity Level : Actively seeking new investments

CHINA VENTURE CAPITAL CO LTD

No. 208, Chaowai Street
Chaoyang District
Beijing, China 100020
Phone: 861085698024
Fax: 861085698023
E-mail: cvc@c-vc.com.cn
Website: www.c-vc.com.cn

Management and Staff
Aimin Li, Partner
Chunsheng Huang, Partner
Jiping Sun, Partner
Xiaobing Liu, Partner
Yijun Wang, President

Type of Firm
Private Equity Firm

Association Membership
Venture Capital Association of Beijing (VCAB)

Project Preferences

Type of Financing Preferred:
Early Stage
Expansion
Balanced
Later Stage
Seed

Geographical Preferences

International Preferences:
China

Industry Preferences

In Semiconductor/Electr prefer:
Electronics

In Biotechnology prefer:
Biotechnology

In Medical/Health prefer:
Medical/Health
Pharmaceuticals

In Industrial/Energy prefer:
Energy
Energy Conservation Relat
Materials
Advanced Materials
Machinery
Environmental Related

In Manufact. prefer:
Manufacturing

In Other prefer:
Environment Responsible

Additional Information
Year Founded: 2000
Capital Under Management: $31,092,000
Current Activity Level : Actively seeking new investments

CHINA VENTURE CAPITAL RESEARCH INSTITUTE LTD

No.9 Science Museum Road
New East Ocean Centre
Tsim Sha Tsui, Kowloon, Hong Kong
Phone: 852-2722 0989
Fax: 852 2723 0060
E-mail: cvcri@cvcri.com
Website: www.cvcri.com

Other Offices
6019 Shennan Boulevard
17/F, Jinrun Building
Shenzhen, China 518040
Phone: 755-8280-0020
Fax: 755-8280-0039

Management and Staff
Gongmen Chen, President

Type of Firm
Private Equity Advisor or Fund of Funds

Project Preferences

Type of Financing Preferred:
Fund of Funds

Geographical Preferences

International Preferences:
China

Additional Information
Year Founded: 2010
Current Activity Level : Actively seeking new investments

CHINA VENTURE LABS LTD

3rd Floor, Tower B, Gemdale Pl
No. 91 Jianguo Road, Chaoyang
Beijing, China 100022
Phone: 86-10-8571-2688
Fax: 86-10-822-1201
E-mail: info@chinaventurelabs.com
Website: www.chinaventurelabs.com

Type of Firm
Private Equity Firm

Project Preferences

Type of Financing Preferred:
Early Stage
Seed
Startup

Geographical Preferences

International Preferences:
China

Industry Preferences

In Communications prefer:
Media and Entertainment

In Internet Specific prefer:
Internet

Additional Information
Year Founded: 2010
Current Activity Level: Actively seeking new investments

CHINA WESTERN ECONOMIC DEVELOPMENT CO LTD

No.8 North 4th Ring Middle Rd.
2/F, Athletes Restaurant
Beijing, China

Type of Firm
Private Equity Firm

Project Preferences

Type of Financing Preferred:
Leveraged Buyout

Geographical Preferences

International Preferences:
China

Industry Preferences

In Communications prefer:
Entertainment

In Biotechnology prefer:
Biotechnology

In Consumer Related prefer:
Retail
Hotels and Resorts

In Financial Services prefer:
Real Estate

Additional Information
Year Founded: 2006
Current Activity Level: Actively seeking new investments

CHINA ZHESHANG BANK LONGWAN BRANCH

No. 2988, Yongqiang Avenue
Longwan District
Wenzhou, China
Phone: 8657785989779

Type of Firm
Bank Affiliated

Project Preferences

Type of Financing Preferred:
Balanced

Geographical Preferences

International Preferences:
China

Additional Information
Current Activity Level: Actively seeking new investments

CHINA-AFRICA DEVELOPMENT FUND

No.28 Fuxinmennei Street
F10/F11, Tower C, Chemsunny
Beijing, China 100031
Phone: 861059566800
Fax: 861059566969
Website: www.cadfund.com

Other Offices

Plot No.6953, Birdcage Walk, Longacres
Villa No .42, Millennium Village
Lusaka, Zambia
Phone: 00260-211 258121
Fax: 00260-211 258121

House No.420, Kebele 03/05
P.O.Box 3052
Addis Ababa, Ethiopia
Phone: 00251-116-626821
Fax: 00251-116-626822

No.95, Grasyton Drive, Santon
F1,China,Construction Bank
Johannesburg, South Africa 2196
Phone: 0027-11-7833919
Fax: 0027-11-7833763

Management and Staff
Jianxin Chi, Chief Executive Officer

Type of Firm
Government Affiliated Program

Project Preferences

Type of Financing Preferred:
Fund of Funds
Generalist PE

Geographical Preferences

International Preferences:
Africa

Industry Preferences

In Communications prefer:
Telecommunications

In Industrial/Energy prefer:
Energy
Oil and Gas Exploration

In Transportation prefer:
Transportation

In Manufact. prefer:
Manufacturing

In Agr/Forestr/Fish prefer:
Agribusiness
Agriculture related

Additional Information
Year Founded: 2007
Current Activity Level: Actively seeking new investments

CHINAEQUITY GROUP INC

No.10, Jingtong West Road
10F, Block A, Office Park
Beijing, China 100020
Phone: 861085906800
Fax: 861085906900
E-mail: admin@chinaequity.net
Website: www.chinaequity.net

Management and Staff
Jing Zhang, Partner
Zhaochen Liu, Partner

Type of Firm
Bank Affiliated

Association Membership
China Venture Capital Association

Project Preferences

Type of Financing Preferred:
Early Stage
Expansion
Balanced

Geographical Preferences

International Preferences:
China
Australia
New Zealand
All International

Industry Preferences

In Communications prefer:
Telecommunications
Wireless Communications
Media and Entertainment

In Internet Specific prefer:
Internet

In Semiconductor/Electr prefer:
Optoelectronics

In Biotechnology prefer:
Biotechnology

In Medical/Health prefer:
Medical/Health
Pharmaceuticals

In Consumer Related prefer:
Consumer
Retail
Consumer Products

In Industrial/Energy prefer:
Energy
Alternative Energy
Energy Conservation Relat
Materials
Advanced Materials
Machinery
Environmental Related

In Transportation prefer:
Transportation

In Business Serv. prefer:
Services
Media

In Manufact. prefer:
Manufacturing

In Agr/Forestr/Fish prefer:
Agriculture related

In Other prefer:
Environment Responsible

Additional Information
Year Founded: 1999
Capital Under Management: $986,343,000
Current Activity Level : Actively seeking new investments

CHINALLIANCE VENTURE PARTNERS LTD

No. 5 Chaoyangmen North Street
506A Fifth Square B, Dongcheng
Beijing, China 100010
Phone: 861052188784
Fax: 861052188757
E-mail: eric@chinalliancevc.com
Website: www.chinalliancevc.com

Type of Firm
Private Equity Firm

Project Preferences

Type of Financing Preferred:
Early Stage
Expansion
Balanced

Geographical Preferences

International Preferences:
China

Industry Preferences

In Semiconductor/Electr prefer:
Electronics

In Medical/Health prefer:
Medical Products
Pharmaceuticals

In Consumer Related prefer:
Retail
Consumer Products

In Industrial/Energy prefer:
Energy
Industrial Products
Machinery
Environmental Related

In Transportation prefer:
Transportation

In Business Serv. prefer:
Services

Additional Information
Year Founded: 2008
Capital Under Management: $13,710,000
Current Activity Level : Actively seeking new investments

CHINAROCK CAPITAL MANAGEMENT, LTD.

One Maritime Plaza
Suite 1107
San Francisco, CA USA 94111
Phone: 4155785700
E-mail: info@chinarockcapital.com
Website: www.chinarockcapital.com

Other Offices
30 Queen's Road Central
Unit B, 26th Floor, Entertainment Bldg.
Central, Hong Kong
Phone: 85231967888

68 Yincheng Road (C)
22nd Floor
Shanghai, China 200120
Phone: 862161946600

Type of Firm
Investment Management Firm

Project Preferences

Type of Financing Preferred:
Generalist PE

Geographical Preferences

International Preferences:
China

Additional Information
Name of Most Recent Fund: CRCM Opportunity Fund, L.P.
Most Recent Fund Was Raised: 03/16/2012
Year Founded: 2012
Capital Under Management: $82,600,000
Current Activity Level : Actively seeking new investments

CHINARUN CAPITAL PARTNERS CHONGQING LTD

No.1, Jianxin S.Road, Jiangbei
8-9-2, CITIC Plaza
Chongqing, China 400020
Phone: 862363807808
Fax: 862363318955
E-mail: Service@chinarunvc.com
Website: www.chinarunvc.com

Other Offices
No.105, Dunhua South Road
Room B, 26F
Taipei, Taiwan
Phone: 88622706
Fax: 886227062800

Management and Staff
David Tai, Partner
Roland Chen, Founder

Type of Firm
Private Equity Firm

Project Preferences

Type of Financing Preferred:
Balanced

Geographical Preferences

International Preferences:
Taiwan
China

Industry Preferences

In Biotechnology prefer:
Biotechnology

In Medical/Health prefer:
Medical/Health

In Industrial/Energy prefer:
Energy

Additional Information
Year Founded: 2000
Capital Under Management: $73,386,000
Current Activity Level : Actively seeking new investments

CHL MEDICAL PARTNERS LP

1055 Washington Boulevard
Sixth Floor
Stamford, CT USA 06901
Phone: 2033247700
Fax: 2033243636
E-mail: info@chlmedical.com
Website: www.chlmedical.com

Management and Staff
David Steffy, Venture Partner
Gregory Weinhoff, Partner
Jeffrey Collinson, Co-Founder
Myles Greenberg, Partner
Timothy Howe, Partner

Type of Firm
Private Equity Firm

Project Preferences

Role in Financing:
Will function either as deal originator or investor in deals created by others

Type of Financing Preferred:
Early Stage
Seed
Startup

Size of Investments Considered:
Min Size of Investment Considered (000s): $100
Max Size of Investment Considered (000s): $15,000

Geographical Preferences

United States Preferences:

Industry Focus
(% based on actual investment)
Medical/Health	67.4%
Biotechnology	24.7%
Computer Software and Services	5.1%
Other Products	1.7%
Internet Specific	1.0%

Additional Information
Year Founded: 1990
Capital Under Management: $220,000,000
Current Activity Level : Actively seeking new investments
Method of Compensation: Return on investment is of primary concern, do not charge fees

CHOBANI FOOD INCUBATOR

147 State Highway 320
Norwich, NY USA 13815
Website: www.chobanifoodincubator.com

Type of Firm
Incubator/Development Program

Project Preferences

Type of Financing Preferred:
Early Stage

Industry Preferences

In Consumer Related prefer:
Food/Beverage

Additional Information
Year Founded: 2014
Current Activity Level : Actively seeking new investments

CHONGQING CHUNGSHUI EQUITY INVESTMENT CO LTD

No.39 Beichengtian Street
Tongchang International Commer
Chongqing, China 400020
Phone: 862367721278

Type of Firm
Private Equity Firm

Project Preferences

Type of Financing Preferred:
Leveraged Buyout

Geographical Preferences

International Preferences:
China

Additional Information
Year Founded: 2011
Current Activity Level : Actively seeking new investments

CHONGQING GAOTEJIA EQUITY INVESTMENT FUND MANAGEMENT CO LTD

Xingai Avenue, Longxi Neighbor
Chuanyu Xiangnai Residence
Chongqing, China 401120

Type of Firm
Investment Management Firm

Project Preferences

Type of Financing Preferred:
Balanced

Geographical Preferences

International Preferences:
China

Industry Preferences

In Medical/Health prefer:
Medical Therapeutics
Medical Products
Pharmaceuticals

Additional Information
Year Founded: 2016
Current Activity Level : Actively seeking new investments

CHONGQING HI-TECH VENTURE CAPIAL RED HORSE MANAGEMENT CO LTD

12F, Kangtian Kaixuan
Xinpaifang, Yubei District
Chongqing, China 400023
Phone: 86236799099
Fax: 86236799097
Website: www.cqrhcapital.com

Type of Firm
Investment Management Firm

Project Preferences

Type of Financing Preferred:
Balanced

Geographical Preferences

International Preferences:
China

Additional Information
Year Founded: 2014
Capital Under Management: $198,230,000
Current Activity Level : Actively seeking new investments

CHONGQING HI-TECH VENTURE CAPITAL CO LTD

No. 5, Keyuan 1 Road
Chongqing High-tech Zone
Chongqing, China
Phone: 862368605101
Fax: 862368694994

Type of Firm
Government Affiliated Program

Project Preferences

Type of Financing Preferred:
Balanced

Geographical Preferences

International Preferences:
China

Additional Information
Year Founded: 2011
Current Activity Level : Actively seeking new investments

CHONGQING LIANGZI COAL FUND PARTNER ENTERPRISE

No.127, Zhongshan 3rd Road
5F, Xinshancheng business bldg
Chongqing, China 400010
Phone: 862367862537
Fax: 862363628188
Website: www.liangzijijin.com

Type of Firm
Private Equity Firm

Project Preferences

Type of Financing Preferred:
Balanced

Geographical Preferences

International Preferences:
China

Industry Preferences

In Industrial/Energy prefer:
Alternative Energy
Coal Related

Additional Information
Year Founded: 2007
Capital Under Management: $157,575,000
Current Activity Level : Actively seeking new investments

CHONGQING WARP VENTURE CAPITAL MANAGEMENT CO LTD

No.24, Honghu West Road Yubei
20F B Block Software Park
Chongqing, China
Phone: 862388922560
Website: www.warpcapital.com

Type of Firm
Private Equity Firm

Project Preferences

Type of Financing Preferred:
Balanced

Geographical Preferences

International Preferences:
China

Industry Preferences

In Communications prefer:
Entertainment

In Internet Specific prefer:
Internet

Additional Information
Year Founded: 2015
Capital Under Management: $161,170,000
Current Activity Level : Actively seeking new investments

CHONGQING ZHENGYIN GUANGHUI EQUITY INVESTMENT MGMT CO., LTD.

No. 38, Qingnian Road, Yuzhong
22-3, Guomao Center Bldg
Chongqing, China 400010
Phone: 862363107199
Fax: 862363107299
E-mail: cqzygh@cqzygh.com
Website: www.cqzygh.com

Management and Staff
Jun Zhang, Chief Executive Officer

Type of Firm
Private Equity Firm

Project Preferences

Type of Financing Preferred:
Balanced

Geographical Preferences

International Preferences:
China

Industry Preferences

In Biotechnology prefer:
Biotechnology

In Medical/Health prefer:
Pharmaceuticals

In Industrial/Energy prefer:
Energy
Materials

In Business Serv. prefer:
Services

In Manufact. prefer:
Manufacturing

In Agr/Forestr/Fish prefer:
Agriculture related

Additional Information
Year Founded: 2011
Capital Under Management: $44,153,000
Current Activity Level : Actively seeking new investments

CHOONGNAM VENTURE CAPITAL

409 Mutimedia Center
511 Sameun-ri, Jiksan-eup
Chungcheongnam-do, South Korea 330-816
Phone: 8241-589-0820
Fax: 8241-589-0822

Other Offices
2nd Floor, Room 7, Haseong Building
548-1 Kumhodong 4 Ga
Seoul, South Korea 133-809

Type of Firm
Bank Affiliated

Project Preferences

Type of Financing Preferred:
Balanced

Geographical Preferences

International Preferences:
Korea, South

Additional Information
Year Founded: 2007
Current Activity Level : Actively seeking new investments

CHP MANAGEMENT INC

230 Nassau Street
Princeton, NJ USA 08542
Phone: 6099246452
Fax: 6096830174
E-mail: info@cardinalpartners.com
Website: www.cardinalpartners.com

Other Offices

Two Embarcadero Center
Suite 1670
SAN FRANCISCO, CA USA 94111
Phone: 415-438-3300

1200 Liberty Ridge Drive
Suite 300
WAYNE, PA USA 19087
Phone: 610-254-4212
Fax: 610-964-8136

Management and Staff

Brandon Hull, Co-Founder
Charles Hadley, Partner
John Clarke, Managing Partner
Thomas McKinley, Partner

Type of Firm

Private Equity Firm

Association Membership

National Venture Capital Association - USA (NVCA)

Project Preferences

Role in Financing:
Will function either as deal originator or investor in deals created by others

Type of Financing Preferred:
Early Stage

Size of Investments Considered:
Min Size of Investment Considered (000s): $6,000
Max Size of Investment Considered (000s): $12,000

Industry Focus

(% based on actual investment)
Medical/Health	38.7%
Biotechnology	19.5%
Internet Specific	12.5%
Computer Software and Services	10.6%
Computer Hardware	8.2%
Semiconductors/Other Elect.	3.2%
Communications and Media	3.0%
Industrial/Energy	1.8%
Other Products	1.4%
Consumer Related	1.2%

Additional Information

Name of Most Recent Fund: CHP III, L.P.
Most Recent Fund Was Raised: 12/05/2006
Year Founded: 1996
Capital Under Management: $400,000,000
Current Activity Level : Actively seeking new investments
Method of Compensation: Return on investment is of primary concern, do not charge fees

---

CHRYSALIS CAPITAL ADVISORS INC

438-11th Avenue Southeast, Suite 600
Calgary, Canada T2G 0Y4
Phone: 4032522911
Website: www.chrysaliscapital.ca

Type of Firm

Private Equity Firm

Project Preferences

Type of Financing Preferred:
Leveraged Buyout
Management Buyouts
Acquisition

Geographical Preferences

Canadian Preferences:
All Canada

Additional Information

Year Founded: 2015
Current Activity Level : Actively seeking new investments

CHRYSALIS VENTURES INC

101 South Fifth Street
Suite 1650
Louisville, KY USA 40202
Phone: 5025837644
Fax: 5025837648
E-mail: info@chrysalisventures.com
Website: www.chrysalisventures.com

Other Offices

6701 Carnegie Avenue
CLEVELAND, OH USA 44103
Phone: 2164531299
Fax: 2162740244

2000 Technology Drive
Suite 250
PITTSBURGH, PA USA 15219
Phone: 412-235-0302

115 West Huron Street
Third Floor
ANN ARBOR, MI USA 48104
Phone: 734-864-0237

Management and Staff

David Jones, Partner
Douglas Cobb, Co-Founder
Irving Bailey, Partner
John Willmoth, Venture Partner
Wright Steenrod, Partner

Type of Firm

Private Equity Firm

Association Membership

Illinois Venture Capital Association

Project Preferences

Role in Financing:
Will function either as deal originator or investor in deals created by others

Type of Financing Preferred:
Early Stage
Expansion
Balanced
Later Stage

Size of Investments Considered:
Min Size of Investment Considered (000s): $2,000
Max Size of Investment Considered (000s): $15,000

Geographical Preferences

United States Preferences:
Midwest
Southeast
Southwest

Industry Focus

(% based on actual investment)
Computer Software and Services	30.8%
Internet Specific	30.0%
Medical/Health	22.6%
Other Products	4.1%
Industrial/Energy	4.0%
Consumer Related	3.3%
Computer Hardware	2.2%
Biotechnology	1.4%
Communications and Media	1.1%
Semiconductors/Other Elect.	0.6%

Additional Information

Year Founded: 1993
Capital Under Management: $400,000,000
Current Activity Level : Actively seeking new investments
Method of Compensation: Return on invest. most important, but chg. closing fees, service fees, etc.

CHRYSALIX ENERGY

1055 West Georgia Street
Suite 2480, Box 11102
Vancouver, Canada V6E 3P3
Phone: 6046595499
Fax: 6046595479
E-mail: info@chrysalix.com
Website: www.chrysalix.com

Management and Staff

Alfred Lam, Vice President
Fred Van Beuningen, Managing Partner
Joe Blair, Vice President
Michael Sherman, Managing Partner
Richard MacKellar, Managing Partner
Wendy Leong, Vice President

Type of Firm

Private Equity Firm

Project Preferences

Role in Financing:
Will function either as deal originator or investor in deals created by others

Type of Financing Preferred:
Early Stage
Start-up Financing
Seed
First Stage Financing
Startup

Geographical Preferences

United States Preferences:

Canadian Preferences:
All Canada

International Preferences:
United Kingdom
Europe
Western Europe
China
Eastern Europe
Israel
Germany
France

Industry Preferences

In Industrial/Energy prefer:
Energy
Alternative Energy
Energy Conservation Relat
Industrial Products
Environmental Related

In Other prefer:
Environment Responsible

Additional Information
Name of Most Recent Fund: Chrysalix Energy, L.P. III
Most Recent Fund Was Raised: 05/11/2010
Year Founded: 2001
Capital Under Management: $216,000,000
Current Activity Level : Actively seeking new investments

CHRYSCAPITAL MANAGEMENT CO

Suit 504 St James Court
Port Louis, Mauritius
Phone: 2302115410
Fax: 2302086413
Website: www.chryscapital.com

Other Offices
Suite 111, Maker Chambers IV
11th Floor, Nariman Point
Mumbai, India 400021
Phone: 91-22-4066-8000
Fax: 91-22-4066-8080

Suite 101, The Oberoi
Dr. Zakir Hussain Marg
New Delhi, India 110003
Phone: 91-11-4129-1000
Fax: 91-11-4129-1010

285, Hamilton Ave.
Suite 300
Palo Alto, CA USA 94301
Phone: 650-752-0890
Fax: 650-752-0891

Management and Staff
Ashish Dhawan, Senior Managing Director

Type of Firm
Private Equity Firm

Association Membership
Emerging Markets Private Equity Association
Indian Venture Capital Association (IVCA)

Project Preferences

Type of Financing Preferred:
Leveraged Buyout
Early Stage
Expansion
Mezzanine
Generalist PE
Balanced
Later Stage
Management Buyouts
Acquisition

Size of Investments Considered:
Min Size of Investment Considered (000s): $10,000
Max Size of Investment Considered (000s): $30,000

Geographical Preferences

International Preferences:
India
Asia
All International

Industry Focus
(% based on actual investment)
Other Products	52.4%
Computer Software and Services	24.0%
Medical/Health	10.6%
Communications and Media	6.6%
Internet Specific	4.6%
Industrial/Energy	1.9%

Additional Information
Name of Most Recent Fund: ChrysCapital VI LLC
Most Recent Fund Was Raised: 11/11/2011
Year Founded: 1999
Capital Under Management: $2,250,000,000
Current Activity Level : Actively seeking new investments

CHS CAPITAL LLC

Ten South Wacker Drive
Suite 3175
Chicago, IL USA 60606
Phone: 3128761840
Fax: 3128763854
Website: www.chsonline.com

Management and Staff
Brian Simmons, Managing Partner
Cameron Smith, Vice President
Daniel Hennessy, Partner
David Hawkins, Partner
Doug Knoch, Principal
Edward Lhee, Partner
Jocelyn Stanley, Vice President
Laura Lester, Vice President
Marcus George, Partner
Michael Keesey, Chief Financial Officer
Richard Lobo, Partner
Robert Hogan, Principal
Ronelle DeShazer, Vice President
Thomas Formolo, Partner
Todd Schneider, Chief Financial Officer

Type of Firm
Private Equity Firm

Association Membership
Illinois Venture Capital Association

Project Preferences

Role in Financing:
Prefer role as deal originator

Type of Financing Preferred:
Leveraged Buyout
Expansion
Acquisition

Industry Focus
(% based on actual investment)
Other Products	45.6%
Consumer Related	14.6%
Medical/Health	14.4%
Industrial/Energy	12.5%
Computer Hardware	11.5%
Semiconductors/Other Elect.	0.8%
Communications and Media	0.7%

Additional Information
Name of Most Recent Fund: CHS Private Equity V LP
Most Recent Fund Was Raised: 02/18/2005
Year Founded: 1988
Capital Under Management: $2,300,000,000
Current Activity Level : Actively seeking new investments
Method of Compensation: Return on invest. most important, but chg. closing fees, service fees, etc.

CHUGIN LEASE CO LTD

1-14-17 Marunouchi
Okayama-shi, Japan 700-0823
Phone: 81-86-232-7060
Website: www.chugin.co.jp

Type of Firm
Private Equity Firm

Additional Information
Year Founded: 1982
Current Activity Level : Actively seeking new investments

CHUNSHAN PUJIANG SHANGHAI INVESTMENT MANAGEMENT CO LTD

No. 333, Huanhu West 1 Road
Room 303-40
Shanghai, China

Type of Firm
Private Equity Firm

Project Preferences

Type of Financing Preferred:
Fund of Funds
Balanced

Geographical Preferences

International Preferences:
China

Industry Preferences

In Financial Services prefer:
Financial Services

Additional Information
Year Founded: 2014
Current Activity Level : Actively seeking new investments

CHURCHILL EQUITY INC

333 South Seventh Street
Suite 3100
Minneapolis, MN USA 55402
Phone: 6126736680
Fax: 6126736732
Website: www.churchillequity.com

Management and Staff
Michael Bender, Vice President
Sameer Vijayakar, Partner

Type of Firm
Private Equity Firm

Project Preferences

Role in Financing:
Prefer role as deal originator but will also invest in deals created by others

Type of Financing Preferred:
Leveraged Buyout
Mezzanine
Later Stage
Management Buyouts
Acquisition
Recapitalizations

Geographical Preferences

United States Preferences:

Canadian Preferences:
All Canada

Industry Focus
(% based on actual investment)
Industrial/Energy	43.1%
Other Products	26.7%
Consumer Related	13.4%
Medical/Health	11.3%
Semiconductors/Other Elect.	4.7%
Computer Software and Services	0.8%

Additional Information
Year Founded: 1987
Capital Under Management: $558,000,000
Current Activity Level : Actively seeking new investments
Method of Compensation: Return on invest. most important, but chg. closing fees, service fees, etc.

CHV CAPITAL INC

340 West Tenth Street, Suite 2100
Indianapolis, IN USA 46202
Phone: 3179637800
Fax: 3179637801
E-mail: submitaplan@chvcapital.com
Website: www.chvcapital.com

Management and Staff
Kyle Salyers, Managing Director

Type of Firm
Corporate PE/Venture

Project Preferences

Type of Financing Preferred:
Early Stage

Size of Investments Considered:
Min Size of Investment Considered (000s): $500
Max Size of Investment Considered (000s): $3,000

Geographical Preferences

United States Preferences:
Indiana

Industry Preferences

In Biotechnology prefer:
Biotechnology

In Medical/Health prefer:
Medical/Health
Medical Products
Pharmaceuticals

Additional Information
Year Founded: 2008
Capital Under Management: $35,000,000
Current Activity Level : Actively seeking new investments

CI CAPITAL PARTNERS LLC

500 Park Avenue
Eighth Floor
New York, NY USA 10022
Phone: 2127521850
Fax: 2128329450
E-mail: info@cicapllc.com
Website: www.cicapllc.com

Management and Staff
Evan Weinstein, Vice President
Joost Thesseling, Managing Director
Robert Kopera, Vice President
Steven Lefkowitz, President
Thomas Ritchie, Managing Director
Timothy Hall, Managing Director

Type of Firm
Private Equity Firm

Project Preferences

Role in Financing:
Prefer role in deals created by others

Type of Financing Preferred:
Leveraged Buyout
Acquisition

Geographical Preferences

United States Preferences:
North America

Industry Focus
(% based on actual investment)
Consumer Related	74.3%
Other Products	18.7%
Computer Software and Services	5.8%
Biotechnology	1.1%

Additional Information
Name of Most Recent Fund: CI Capital Investors II, L.P.
Most Recent Fund Was Raised: 03/31/2011
Year Founded: 1993
Capital Under Management: $2,000,000,000
Current Activity Level : Actively seeking new investments

CIA ESPANOLA DE FINAN-CIACION DEL DESARROL-LO COFIDES SA SME

C/. Gran Va de les Corts Cat.
630 - 4 planta
Catalonia, Barcelona, Spain 08007
Phone: 3493270262
Fax: 34902095568
E-mail: cofides@cofides.es
Website: www.cofides.es

Other Offices

Avenida Presidente Mazaryk, 473
Mexico D.F., Spain 11510
Phone: 52-55-5280-9577
Fax: 52-55-9138-6045

Pau Claris n 172
Planta 5 Puerta 2A
Barcelona, Spain 08037
Phone: 34-93-215-1303
Fax: 34-93-467-5346

Type of Firm
Government Affiliated Program

Association Membership
Spanish Venture Capital Association (ASCRI)

Project Preferences

Type of Financing Preferred:
Second Stage Financing
Expansion
Balanced
Seed

Geographical Preferences

International Preferences:
Hungary
Latin America
China
Morocco
All International

Industry Preferences

In Consumer Related prefer:
Consumer Products
Consumer Services

In Industrial/Energy prefer:
Industrial Products

In Business Serv. prefer:
Services

In Other prefer:
Environment Responsible

Additional Information
Year Founded: 1988
Current Activity Level: Actively seeking new investments

CIC PARTNERS, L.P.

500 Crescent Court
Suite 250
Dallas, TX USA 75201
Phone: 2148716263
Fax: 2148804491
E-mail: info@cicpartners.com
Website: www.cicpartners.com

Management and Staff
Amir Yoffe, Principal
Drew Johnson, Co-Founder
Fouad Bashour, Co-Founder
Jay Bradford, Chief Financial Officer

Type of Firm
Private Equity Firm

Project Preferences

Type of Financing Preferred:
Leveraged Buyout
Later Stage
Management Buyouts
Recapitalizations

Industry Preferences

In Medical/Health prefer:
Health Services

In Consumer Related prefer:
Retail
Food/Beverage
Other Restaurants

In Industrial/Energy prefer:
Energy

Additional Information
Name of Most Recent Fund: CIC III, L.P.
Most Recent Fund Was Raised: 01/13/2012
Year Founded: 1973
Capital Under Management: $500,000,000
Current Activity Level: Actively seeking new investments

CIC VIZILLE CAPITAL INNOVATION

28 avenue de l'Opera
Paris, France 75002
E-mail: contact@vci-bdv.com
Website: www.banquedevizille.fr

Management and Staff
Olivier Levy, Partner

Type of Firm
Bank Affiliated

Association Membership
French Venture Capital Association (AFIC)

Project Preferences

Type of Financing Preferred:
Early Stage
Later Stage
Seed
Startup

Size of Investments Considered:
Min Size of Investment Considered (000s): $656
Max Size of Investment Considered (000s): $3,938

Geographical Preferences

International Preferences:
Europe
France

Industry Preferences

In Communications prefer:
Telecommunications

In Computer Software prefer:
Software

In Semiconductor/Electr prefer:
Electronics

In Biotechnology prefer:
Biotech Related Research

In Industrial/Energy prefer:
Energy
Materials
Environmental Related

In Other prefer:
Environment Responsible

Additional Information
Year Founded: 2003
Capital Under Management: $11,280,000
Current Activity Level: Actively seeking new investments

CICLAD PARTICIPATIONS SAS

22, av Franklin-Roosevelt
Paris, France 75008
Phone: 33156597733
Fax: 33153762210
E-mail: info@ciclad.com
Website: www.ciclad.com

Management and Staff
Jean-Francois Vaury, Partner
Lionel Lambert, Partner
Thierry Thomann, Partner

Type of Firm
Private Equity Firm

Association Membership
French Venture Capital Association (AFIC)

Project Preferences

Role in Financing:
Prefer role as deal originator but will also invest in deals created by others

Type of Financing Preferred:
Leveraged Buyout
Management Buyouts
Acquisition
Special Situation

Size of Investments Considered:
Min Size of Investment Considered (000s): $2,674
Max Size of Investment Considered (000s): $20,061

Geographical Preferences

International Preferences:
Europe
France

Additional Information
Name of Most Recent Fund: CICLAD 5 FCPR
Most Recent Fund Was Raised: 03/31/2011
Year Founded: 1998
Capital Under Management: $401,200,000
Current Activity Level : Actively seeking new investments
Method of Compensation: Return on invest. most important, but chg. closing fees, service fees, etc.

CID CAPITAL INC

201 West 103rd Street
Suite 200
Indianapolis, IN USA 46290
Phone: 3174183067
Fax: 3176442914
E-mail: info@cidcap.com
Website: www.cidcap.com

Other Offices

200 West Madison Street
Suite 3500
Chicago, IL USA 60606
Phone: 312-578-5350
Fax: 312-578-5358

180 East Broad Street
Suite 810
Columbus, OH USA 43215
Phone: 614-222-8185
Fax: 614-222-8190

4181 East 96th Street
Suite 200
Indianapolis, IN USA 46240
Phone: 3178439704
Fax: 3178449815

400 West Wilson Bridge Road
Suite 130
Worthington, OH USA 43085
Phone: 6144294236

Management and Staff
Eric Bruun, Managing Director
John Aplin, Managing Director
Peter Kleinhenz, Managing Director
Robert O Brien, Managing Director
Scot Swenberg, Managing Director

Type of Firm
Private Equity Firm

Project Preferences

Role in Financing:
Prefer role as deal originator but will also invest in deals created by others

Type of Financing Preferred:
Leveraged Buyout
Early Stage
Expansion
Mezzanine
Generalist PE
Balanced
Later Stage
Seed
Acquisition
Recapitalizations

Size of Investments Considered:
Min Size of Investment Considered (000s): $500
Max Size of Investment Considered (000s): $3,000

Geographical Preferences

United States Preferences:
Midwest

Canadian Preferences:
All Canada

Industry Focus
(% based on actual investment)

Computer Software and Services	34.6%
Medical/Health	17.6%
Other Products	13.9%
Biotechnology	7.0%
Communications and Media	6.3%
Consumer Related	5.7%
Semiconductors/Other Elect.	5.0%
Industrial/Energy	4.2%
Computer Hardware	3.8%
Internet Specific	2.0%

Additional Information
Name of Most Recent Fund: CID Capital Opportunity Fund II, L.P.
Most Recent Fund Was Raised: 09/18/2013
Year Founded: 1981
Capital Under Management: $45,100,000
Current Activity Level : Actively seeking new investments
Method of Compensation: Return on investment is of primary concern, do not charge fees

CID GROUP

97 Tun Hwa South Road Section2
25th Floor
Taipei, Taiwan 106
Phone: 886223257998
Fax: 886223257933
E-mail: inquiries@cidgroup.com
Website: www.cidgroup.com

Other Offices

No. 1 Jianguomenwai Avenue
Suite 710, China World Trade Ctr Tower 2
Beijing, China 100004
Phone: 86-10-6505-7734
Fax: 86-10-6505-7934

9F-2, JiaNianHua Building
9 Guan YinQiao Pedestrian
Chongqing, China 400020
Phone: 862367005461
Fax: 862367005484

No. 150 Hubin Road
1701-02, 17/F, Five Corporate Avenue
Shanghai, China 200021
Phone: 862153835566
Fax: 862163335621

Management and Staff
Alex Zhu, Vice President
Charles Chang, Co-Founder
Chris Pan, Vice President
Cory Chen, Vice President
David Yang, Partner
David Yang, Partner
Eric Tan, Vice President
Han-Fei Lin, Partner
Howard Lee, Partner
Jack Tsai, Partner
James Liang, Partner
Jason Hsieh, Partner
Lisa Lo, Partner
Po-Yen Lu, Partner
Rachel Sang, Vice President
Steve Yang, Partner
Tony Huang, Partner
Vincent Hou, Partner
Zach Chen, Vice President

Type of Firm
Private Equity Firm

Association Membership
Taiwan Venture Capital Association(TVCA)

Geographical Preferences

United States Preferences:

International Preferences:
Taiwan
China

Industry Preferences

In Communications prefer:
Telecommunications
Wireless Communications
Data Communications

In Medical/Health prefer:
Medical/Health

In Consumer Related prefer:
Retail
Education Related

In Agr/Forestr/Fish prefer:
Agriculture related

In Other prefer:
Environment Responsible

Additional Information
Year Founded: 1998
Capital Under Management: $1,000,000,000
Current Activity Level : Actively seeking new investments

CIELO MANAGEMENT LLC

500 North Capital of Texas Hwy
Building Three, Second Floor
Austin, TX USA 78746
Phone: 5126376989
E-mail: info@cielopef.com
Website: www.cielopef.com

Management and Staff
Daniel Urbina, Chief Financial Officer
Mehron Azarmehr, Venture Partner
Philip Pompa, Venture Partner
Teofilo Tijerina, Venture Partner
Thomas Rini, Venture Partner

Type of Firm
Private Equity Firm

Project Preferences

Type of Financing Preferred:
Early Stage
Expansion
Mezzanine
Generalist PE
Other
Seed
Acquisition
Recapitalizations

Industry Preferences

In Industrial/Energy prefer:
Energy
Oil and Gas Exploration

In Financial Services prefer:
Real Estate

Additional Information
Name of Most Recent Fund: Cielo Private Equity Fund, L.P.
Most Recent Fund Was Raised: 04/19/2011
Year Founded: 2011
Capital Under Management: $200,000
Current Activity Level : Actively seeking new investments

CIG SECURITIES INC

1000 Town Center
Suite 2500
Southfield, MI USA 48075
Phone: 2488271010
Fax: 2488277167
E-mail: info@cigcorporation.com
Website: www.cigcorporation.com

Management and Staff
David Martin, Vice President
Paul Schapira, Vice President
Richard Gonzales, Chief Operating Officer
Yusuf Hai, Vice President

Type of Firm
Investment Management Firm

Project Preferences

Type of Financing Preferred:
Early Stage
Expansion
Balanced

Industry Preferences

In Medical/Health prefer:
Medical/Health
Medical Products
Health Services

Additional Information
Name of Most Recent Fund: CIG Capital Partners, L.P.
Most Recent Fund Was Raised: 09/19/2011
Year Founded: 1997
Capital Under Management: $9,670,000
Current Activity Level : Actively seeking new investments

CIMARRON HEALTHCARE CAPITAL

50 Monument Road
Suite 201
Cynwyd, PA USA 19004
Phone: 4844341910
E-mail: info@cimarronhc.com
Website: cimarronhc.com

Type of Firm
Private Equity Firm

Project Preferences

Type of Financing Preferred:
Leveraged Buyout
Management Buyouts
Acquisition
Recapitalizations

Industry Preferences

In Medical/Health prefer:
Health Services

Additional Information
Year Founded: 2014
Current Activity Level : Actively seeking new investments

CIMB PRIVATE EQUITY SDN BHD

Eight Jalan Damanlela
Lot 3-03 Level 3 Annexe Block
Kuala Lumpur, Malaysia 50490
Phone: 60327238648
Fax: 60320922316
E-mail: ir@cimb.com
Website: www.cimb.com

Other Offices
The Jakarta Stock Exchange Bldg. II
20/F Jl Jend, Sudirman Kav 52-53
Jakarta, India 12190
Phone: 62-21-515-1330
Fax: 62-21-515-1335

Unit 3502 35/F, Q. House Lumpini Bldg.
1 South Sathorn Road
Bangkok, Thailand 10120
Phone: 662-687-0888
Fax: 662-677-7538

50 Raffles Place
#19-00 Singapore Land Tower
Singapore, Singapore 048623
Phone: 65-6225-1228
Fax: 65-6225-1522

540 Madison Avenue
Eleventh Floor
New York, NY USA 10022
Phone: 212-616-8600
Fax: 212-828-9633

Almoayyed Tower, Suite 304
Road 283, Al Seef 428
Manama, Bahrain

25th Floor Central Tower
28 Queen's Road Central
Hong Kong, Hong Kong
Phone: 852-2868-0380
Fax: 852-2537-1928

27 Knightbridge
London, United Kingdom SW1X 7YB
Phone: 44-207-201-2199
Fax: 44-207-201-2191

14th Floor PGGMB Building
Jalan Kianggeh
Bandar Seri Begawan, Brunei BS8811
Phone: 673-224-1888
Fax: 673-224-0999

35 (D) Pyay Road
7th Miles Mayangone Tsp
Yangon, Burma
Phone: 951-660-919
Fax: 951-650-838

Management and Staff
Kenny Kim, Chief Financial Officer
Mohamed Nazir bin Abdul Razak, CEO & Managing Director

Type of Firm
Bank Affiliated

Association Membership
Malaysian Venture Capital Association

Project Preferences

Type of Financing Preferred:
Leveraged Buyout
Early Stage
Expansion
Mezzanine
Balanced
Management Buyouts
Startup

Geographical Preferences

United States Preferences:

International Preferences:
Vietnam
Indonesia
Bahrain
India
United Kingdom
Hong Kong
Brunei
China
Thailand
Cambodia
Sri Lanka
Asia
Singapore
Malaysia

Additional Information
Year Founded: 2004
Capital Under Management: $130,000,000
Current Activity Level : Actively seeking new investments

CIMBRIA CAPITAL

1155 Dairy Ashford
Houston, TX USA 77079
Phone: 2177205865
E-mail: info@cimbriacapital.com
Website: www.cimbriacapital.com

Type of Firm
Private Equity Firm

Project Preferences

Type of Financing Preferred:
Leveraged Buyout
Acquisition

Industry Preferences

In Agr/Forestr/Fish prefer:
Agriculture related

Additional Information
Year Founded: 2014
Current Activity Level : Actively seeking new investments

CINCYTECH

1311 Vine Street
Suite 300
Cincinnati, OH USA 45202
Phone: 5132632720
Fax: 5133815093
E-mail: contactus@cincytechusa.com
Website: www.cincytechusa.com

Management and Staff
Mike Venerable, Managing Director
Robert Coy, President

Type of Firm
Private Equity Firm

Association Membership
National Venture Capital Association - USA (NVCA)

Project Preferences

Type of Financing Preferred:
Early Stage
Seed
Startup

Geographical Preferences

United States Preferences:
Ohio

Industry Preferences

In Communications prefer:
Media and Entertainment

In Computer Hardware prefer:
Computer Graphics and Dig

In Computer Software prefer:
Applications Software

In Internet Specific prefer:
Internet

In Biotechnology prefer:
Biotechnology

In Medical/Health prefer:
Health Services

In Consumer Related prefer:
Consumer Services

In Industrial/Energy prefer:
Advanced Materials

In Manufact. prefer:
Manufacturing

Additional Information
Name of Most Recent Fund: CincyTech Fund III LLC
Most Recent Fund Was Raised: 12/14/2012
Year Founded: 2007
Capital Under Management: $62,700,000
Current Activity Level : Actively seeking new investments

CINDA CAPITAL MANAGEMENT CO LTD

Binhai District
Tianjin, China

Management and Staff
Lingjia Zhang, President

Type of Firm
Investment Management Firm

Project Preferences

Type of Financing Preferred:
Leveraged Buyout
Balanced

Geographical Preferences

International Preferences:
China

Industry Preferences

In Agr/Forestr/Fish prefer:
Agriculture related

Additional Information
Year Founded: 2008
Capital Under Management: $641,436,000
Current Activity Level : Actively seeking new investments

CINTRIFUSE

299 East Sixth Street
Cincinnati, OH USA 45202
Phone: 5132462700
E-mail: info@cintrifuse.com
Website: cintrifuse.com

Type of Firm
Private Equity Advisor or Fund of Funds

Project Preferences

Type of Financing Preferred:
Fund of Funds

Geographical Preferences

United States Preferences:
Ohio

Industry Preferences

In Consumer Related prefer:
Consumer Products
Consumer Services

In Industrial/Energy prefer:
Energy

Additional Information

Name of Most Recent Fund: Cintrifuse Early Stage Capital Fund I LLC
Most Recent Fund Was Raised: 01/02/2013
Year Founded: 2012
Capital Under Management: $57,000,000
Current Activity Level : Actively seeking new investments

CINVEN GROUP LTD

Warwick Court
Paternoster Square
London, United Kingdom EC4M 7AG
Phone: 442076613333
Fax: 442076613888
E-mail: info@cinven.com
Website: www.cinven.com

Other Offices

Via Manzoni, 30
Milan, Italy 20121
Phone: 39-02-3211-1700
Fax: 39-02-3211-1800

4, rue Albert Borschette
Ballade B2 Building
, Luxembourg L-1246
Phone: 352-2609-5200
Fax: 352-2609-5230

Neue Mainzer Str 52
Main Tower
Frankfurt am Main, Germany 60311
Phone: 49-69-900-270
Fax: 49-69-9002-7100

P.O. Box 656, Third Floor
Tudor House Le Bordage
St. Peter Port, United Kingdom
Phone: 44 (0)1481 749 705

8 Finance Street
Suite 5812-14
Hong Kong, Hong Kong
Phone: 852-3665-2880
Fax: 852-3665-2980

Management and Staff

Alexandra Hess, Partner
Andrea Bertolini, Principal
Anthony Cardona, Principal
Anthony Santospirito, Principal
Bruno Schick, Partner
Caspar Berendsen, Partner
Chris Good, Partner
David Barker, Partner
Eugenio Preve, Principal
Guy Davison, Partner
Immo Rupf, Partner
Ivan Kwok, Partner
Jonas Nilsson, Partner
Jorge Quemada, Partner
Joseph Wan, Partner
Julien Lammoglia, Principal
Matthew Sabben-Clare, Partner
Matthew Norton, Principal
Maxim Crewe, Partner
Nicolas Paulmier, Partner
Peter Catterall, Partner
Pontus Pettersson, Partner
Soeren Christensen, Partner
Stuart Anderson McAlpine, Managing Partner
Supraj Rajagopalan, Partner
Thilo Sautter, Partner
Thomas Railhac, Partner
Xavier Geismar, Partner
Yalin Karadogan, Partner

Type of Firm

Private Equity Firm

Association Membership

British Venture Capital Association (BVCA)
German Venture Capital Association (BVK)
European Private Equity and Venture Capital Assoc.
Dutch Venture Capital Associaton (NVP)
Spanish Venture Capital Association (ASCRI)

Project Preferences

Role in Financing:
Prefer role as deal originator but will also invest in deals created by others

Type of Financing Preferred:
Leveraged Buyout
Management Buyouts
Acquisition

Geographical Preferences

International Preferences:
Europe

Industry Focus

(% based on actual investment)
Other Products	32.7%
Medical/Health	24.6%
Consumer Related	17.5%
Industrial/Energy	13.5%
Communications and Media	11.2%
Computer Hardware	0.5%
Computer Software and Services	0.1%
Internet Specific	0.0%
Biotechnology	0.0%

Additional Information

Name of Most Recent Fund: Fifth Cinven Fund, The
Most Recent Fund Was Raised: 03/13/2012
Year Founded: 1977
Capital Under Management: $16,679,500,000
Current Activity Level : Actively seeking new investments
Method of Compensation: Return on invest. most important, but chg. closing fees, service fees, etc.

CIP CAPITAL

400 Madison Avenue
Suite 3A
New York, NY USA 10017
Phone: 2122575000
Fax: 2127029587
E-mail: info@cip-capital.com
Website: www.cip-capital.com

Management and Staff

Bobby Kelly, Managing Director
Justin Lipton, Managing Director
Scott Marden, Managing Partner

Type of Firm

Bank Affiliated

Project Preferences

Type of Financing Preferred:
Leveraged Buyout
Later Stage
Acquisition

Geographical Preferences

United States Preferences:
North America

Industry Preferences

In Communications prefer:
Radio & TV Broadcasting
Media and Entertainment
Entertainment

In Internet Specific prefer:
Ecommerce

In Medical/Health prefer:
Medical/Health
Health Services

In Consumer Related prefer:
Consumer
Education Related

In Industrial/Energy prefer:
Energy

In Financial Services prefer:
Financial Services

In Business Serv. prefer:
Services
Consulting Services
Media

Additional Information
Name of Most Recent Fund: CIP Capital Fund, L.P.
Most Recent Fund Was Raised: 11/09/2011
Year Founded: 2010
Capital Under Management: $537,500,000
Current Activity Level : Actively seeking new investments

CIPIO PARTNERS GMBH

Ottostrasse 8
Palais Am Lenbachplatz
Munich, Germany 80333
Phone: 49895506960
Fax: 498955069699
E-mail: info@cipiopartners.com
Website: www.cipiopartners.com

Other Offices
560 South Winchester Boulevard
Suite 500
San Jose, CA USA 95128
Phone: 408-236-7654
Fax: 408-236-7651

Management and Staff
Achim Lederle, Venture Partner
Maximilian Schroeck, Managing Partner
Roland Dennert, Managing Partner

Type of Firm
Private Equity Firm

Association Membership
German Venture Capital Association (BVK)
European Private Equity and Venture Capital Assoc.

Project Preferences

Type of Financing Preferred:
Leveraged Buyout
Early Stage
Mezzanine
Later Stage
Acquisition

Geographical Preferences

United States Preferences:
All U.S.

Canadian Preferences:
All Canada

International Preferences:
Europe
Israel
Singapore
Germany
All International

Industry Preferences

In Communications prefer:
Communications and Media
Telecommunications

In Computer Software prefer:
Software

In Computer Other prefer:
Computer Related

In Semiconductor/Electr prefer:
Electronics
Semiconductor
Optoelectronics

In Medical/Health prefer:
Medical/Health

In Industrial/Energy prefer:
Energy

In Financial Services prefer:
Financial Services

Additional Information
Name of Most Recent Fund: Cipio Partners Fund VI
Most Recent Fund Was Raised: 06/17/2009
Year Founded: 2003
Capital Under Management: $174,000,000
Current Activity Level : Actively seeking new investments

CIRCLE PEAK CAPITAL LLC

270 Lafayette Street, Suite 1400
New York, NY USA 10012
Phone: 6462308812
Fax: 6463492743
E-mail: info@circlepeakcapital.com
Website: www.circlepeakcapital.com

Management and Staff
R. Adam Smith, President

Type of Firm
Private Equity Firm

Project Preferences

Role in Financing:
Prefer role as deal originator but will also invest in deals created by others

Size of Investments Considered:
Min Size of Investment Considered (000s): $50,000
Max Size of Investment Considered (000s): $500,000

Industry Preferences

In Medical/Health prefer:
Health Services

In Consumer Related prefer:
Retail
Food/Beverage
Consumer Products

In Business Serv. prefer:
Services
Distribution

In Manufact. prefer:
Manufacturing

Additional Information
Year Founded: 2002
Current Activity Level : Actively seeking new investments

CIRCLEUP NETWORK INC

30 Maiden Lane
Sixth Floor
San Francisco, CA USA 94108
Phone: 4155297408
Website: circleup.com

Management and Staff
Rory Eakin, Co-Founder
Ross Davisson, Vice President
Yael Gavish, Vice President

Type of Firm
Private Equity Firm

Industry Preferences

In Consumer Related prefer:
Retail
Food/Beverage
Consumer Products

Additional Information
Year Founded: 2006
Capital Under Management: $165,480,000
Current Activity Level : Actively seeking new investments

CIRCULARITY CAPITAL LLP

Eight Albany Street
Edinburgh, United Kingdom EH1 3QB
Phone: 44135640370
E-mail: info@circularitycapital.com
Website: circularitycapital.com

Type of Firm
Private Equity Firm

Project Preferences

Type of Financing Preferred:
Generalist PE

Additional Information
Year Founded: 1969
Current Activity Level : Actively seeking new investments

CIRRUS INVESTMENT PARTNERS LLC

1560 Broadway
Suite 2200
Denver, CO USA 80202
Phone: 303-863-3015
Fax: 303-863-3006

Management and Staff
Fred Hamilton, Managing Partner
Thomas Hamilton, Managing Partner

Type of Firm
Private Equity Firm

Project Preferences

Type of Financing Preferred:
Other

Additional Information
Year Founded: 2002
Capital Under Management: $3,200,000
Current Activity Level : Actively seeking new investments

CIRTECH FUND

89E Medinat HaYehudim
11th Floor
Herzliya, Israel
E-mail: israel@cirtechfund.com
Website: www.cirtechfund.com

Type of Firm
Private Equity Firm

Project Preferences

Type of Financing Preferred:
Balanced

Geographical Preferences

United States Preferences:

International Preferences:
Hong Kong
China
Israel
Germany

Industry Preferences

In Communications prefer:
Data Communications

In Computer Software prefer:
Software

In Medical/Health prefer:
Medical/Health

In Industrial/Energy prefer:
Energy

Additional Information
Year Founded: 2015
Current Activity Level : Actively seeking new investments

CISCO INVESTMENTS INC

170 West Tasman Drive
SJC10-5
San Jose, CA USA 95134
Website: www.ciscoinvestments.com

Management and Staff
Derek Idemoto, Vice President
Janey Hoe, Vice President
Rob Salvagno, Vice President

Type of Firm
Private Equity Firm

Association Membership
National Venture Capital Association - USA (NVCA)

Project Preferences

Type of Financing Preferred:
Balanced

Geographical Preferences

Canadian Preferences:
All Canada

International Preferences:
India
China
Israel

Industry Preferences

In Computer Software prefer:
Software

In Internet Specific prefer:
Internet

In Semiconductor/Electr prefer:
Semiconductor
Analytic/Scientific

Additional Information
Year Founded: 2014
Current Activity Level : Actively seeking new investments

CISCO SYSTEMS INC

170 West Tasman Drive
SJC10-5
San Jose, CA USA 95134
Phone: 4085264000
Website: www.cisco.com

Other Offices
181 Bay Street
Suite 3400, Bay Wellington
Toronto, Canada M5J 2T3
Phone: 4163067000
Fax: 4163067099

Type of Firm
Corporate PE/Venture

Project Preferences

Type of Financing Preferred:
Early Stage
Expansion
Startup

Size of Investments Considered:
Min Size of Investment Considered (000s): $2,000
Max Size of Investment Considered (000s): $60,000

Geographical Preferences

United States Preferences:

International Preferences:
India
Europe
China
Israel

Industry Preferences

In Communications prefer:
Communications and Media
Telecommunications

In Internet Specific prefer:
Internet

In Semiconductor/Electr prefer:
Electronics

Additional Information
Year Founded: 1984
Capital Under Management: $390,911,000
Current Activity Level : Actively seeking new investments

CIT GROUP INC

11 West 42 Street
New York, NY USA 10036
Phone: 2124615200
E-mail: info@cit.com
Website: www.cit.com

Other Offices
1211 Avenue of the Americas
New York, NY USA 10036
Phone: 212-536-1211

One CIT Drive
Livingston, NJ USA 07039
Phone: 973-740-5000

Management and Staff

Adrian Pang, Managing Director
Claude Mattesich, Managing Director
Fernando Fiore, Managing Director
Jason Meek, Managing Director
Jay Beckman, Managing Director
Meggan Walsh, Managing Director
Mike Lorusso, Managing Director
Mike Kahmann, Managing Director
Neil Wessan, Managing Director
Nick Small, Managing Director
Robert Bielinski, Managing Director
Steve Reedy, Managing Director
Todd Harrington, Managing Director
Tom Westdyk, Managing Director
Vincent Belcastro, Managing Director
W. Taylor Kamp, Managing Director
Wade Layton, Managing Director
Wesley Smith, Managing Director

Type of Firm

Corporate PE/Venture

Project Preferences

Role in Financing:
Prefer role as deal originator but will also invest in deals created by others

Type of Financing Preferred:
Second Stage Financing
Leveraged Buyout
Mezzanine
Balanced
First Stage Financing

Size of Investments Considered:
Min Size of Investment Considered (000s): $3,000
Max Size of Investment Considered: No Limit

Geographical Preferences

United States Preferences:
All U.S.

International Preferences:
All International

Industry Focus

(% based on actual investment)

Consumer Related	39.1%
Internet Specific	13.0%
Communications and Media	10.6%
Computer Software and Services	9.5%
Other Products	8.7%
Medical/Health	6.6%
Semiconductors/Other Elect.	5.7%
Computer Hardware	3.6%
Biotechnology	1.6%
Industrial/Energy	1.4%

Additional Information

Year Founded: 1908
Capital Under Management: $15,000,000
Current Activity Level : Actively seeking new investments

Method of Compensation: Return on invest. most important, but chg. closing fees, service fees, etc.

CITA GESTION SA

11 Bis Rue Balzac
Paris, France 75008
Phone: 33142257676
Fax: 33142257685
E-mail: info@cita.fr
Website: www.cita.fr

Management and Staff

Philippe Queveau, Managing Director

Type of Firm

Bank Affiliated

Association Membership

French Venture Capital Association (AFIC)

Project Preferences

Type of Financing Preferred:
Leveraged Buyout
Early Stage
Generalist PE
Later Stage
Acquisition

Size of Investments Considered:
Min Size of Investment Considered (000s): $1,293
Max Size of Investment Considered (000s): $15,517

Geographical Preferences

International Preferences:
Europe
France

Industry Preferences

In Communications prefer:
Communications and Media

In Biotechnology prefer:
Biotechnology

In Business Serv. prefer:
Services

Additional Information

Year Founded: 1985
Capital Under Management: $133,700,000
Current Activity Level : Actively seeking new investments

CITIC ASSET MANAGEMENT CORP LTD

Xinyuan South Road Chaoyang
Jingcheng Bldg No.6
Beijing, China 100004
Phone: 861064660088
Fax: 861064661186
Website: amc.ecitic.com

Type of Firm

Investment Management Firm

Project Preferences

Type of Financing Preferred:
Balanced

Geographical Preferences

International Preferences:
China

Additional Information

Year Founded: 2002
Current Activity Level : Actively seeking new investments

CITIC CAPITAL PARTNERS LTD

1 Tim Mei Avenue, Central
28/F, CITIC Tower
Hong Kong, Hong Kong
Phone: 85237106888
Fax: 85225238312
E-mail: info@citiccapital.com
Website: www.citiccapital.com

Other Offices

1168 West Nan Jing Road
Unit 4101, CITIC Square
Shanghai, China 200040
Phone: 86-21-6170-5555
Fax: 86-21-3218-0303

No.1 Dongzhimen South St.
22/F Raffles City Beijing Office Tower
Beijing, China 100007
Phone: 86-10-5802-3999
Fax: 86-10-5802-3600

9F BUREX Kojimachi
3-5-2 Kojimachi, Chiyoda-ku
Tokyo, Japan 102-0083
Phone: 81-3-5211-3830
Fax: 81-3-5211-3824

Maples Corporate Services, Ltd
Ugland House
Grand Cayman, Cayman Islands KY1-1104
Phone: 3459457099

1120 Avenue of the Americas
Suite 1501
New York, NY USA 10036
Phone: 212-395-9767
Fax: 212-395-9787

Management and Staff

Annie Fung, Managing Director
Ching Ju Yeh, Managing Director
Emil Cheung, Managing Director
Eric Chan, Chief Financial Officer
Eric Xin, Managing Director
Fanglu Wang, Senior Managing Director
Hironobu Nakano, Senior Managing Director
Jerry Zhang, Senior Managing Director
Jian Li, Managing Director
Karen Li, Managing Director
Rikizo Matsukawa, Managing Director
Robert Lie, Managing Director
Stanley Ching, Managing Director
Xiaopin Liu, Senior Managing Director
Yichen Zhang, Chief Executive Officer
Zhijie Zeng, Senior Managing Director

Type of Firm

Investment Management Firm

Association Membership

China Venture Capital Association
Emerging Markets Private Equity Association

Project Preferences

Type of Financing Preferred:
Core
Leveraged Buyout
Early Stage
Expansion
Later Stage
Management Buyouts
Acquisition

Geographical Preferences

International Preferences:
Asia Pacific
China
Japan
All International

Industry Preferences

In Communications prefer:
Telecommunications

In Consumer Related prefer:
Franchises(NEC)
Consumer Products

In Industrial/Energy prefer:
Environmental Related

In Business Serv. prefer:
Distribution
Media

In Manufact. prefer:
Manufacturing

Additional Information

Name of Most Recent Fund: CITIC Capital Flying High Investment Fund, L.P.
Most Recent Fund Was Raised: 08/06/2012
Year Founded: 2002
Capital Under Management: $2,600,000,000
Current Activity Level : Actively seeking new investments

CITIC PRIVATE EQUITY FUNDS MANAGEMENT CO LTD

89 Jinbao St, Dongcheng Dist
11/F, Jinbao Tower
Beijing, China 100005
Phone: 861085079000
Fax: 861085221872
E-mail: BusinessContact@citicpe.com
Website: www.citicpe.com

Management and Staff

Lefei Liu, Chief Executive Officer
Tao Zhuang, Managing Director
Yibing Wu, President

Type of Firm

Bank Affiliated

Association Membership

China Venture Capital Association

Project Preferences

Type of Financing Preferred:
Leveraged Buyout
Expansion
Mezzanine
Generalist PE
Balanced
Later Stage
Acquisition

Geographical Preferences

International Preferences:
China

Industry Preferences

In Medical/Health prefer:
Medical/Health

In Consumer Related prefer:
Consumer
Retail

In Industrial/Energy prefer:
Energy
Industrial Products

In Financial Services prefer:
Financial Services

In Business Serv. prefer:
Services

In Manufact. prefer:
Manufacturing

Additional Information

Year Founded: 2008
Capital Under Management: $2,654,793,000
Current Activity Level : Actively seeking new investments

CITIC SECURITIES INTERNATIONAL PRTNS LTD

26/F, CITIC Tower
1 Tim Mei Avenue
Central, Hong Kong
Phone: 852-2237-6899
Fax: 852-2104-6862
E-mail: info@citics.com.hk
Website: www.citics.com.hk

Management and Staff

Rui Zhang, Managing Director

Type of Firm

Bank Affiliated

Project Preferences

Type of Financing Preferred:
Leveraged Buyout
Expansion
Management Buyouts

Geographical Preferences

International Preferences:
China

Industry Preferences

In Medical/Health prefer:
Medical/Health
Health Services

In Consumer Related prefer:
Consumer
Food/Beverage

In Industrial/Energy prefer:
Energy
Environmental Related

In Agr/Forestr/Fish prefer:
Agriculture related

Additional Information

Year Founded: 2009
Current Activity Level : Actively seeking new investments

CITICS PROPERTY FUND MANAGEMENT CO LTD

Science and Technology Innovat
Room 312, Rongying Building
Beijing, China 4000001
Phone: 861084865655
Website: www.chinaxy-fund.com

Type of Firm
Corporate PE/Venture

Project Preferences

Type of Financing Preferred:
Value-Add
Expansion
Mezzanine

Geographical Preferences

International Preferences:
China

Industry Preferences

In Consumer Related prefer:
Consumer

In Financial Services prefer:
Real Estate

In Business Serv. prefer:
Services

In Agr/Forestr/Fish prefer:
Agriculture related

Additional Information
Year Founded: 2011
Current Activity Level : Actively seeking new investments

CITIGROUP PRIVATE EQUITY LP

731 Lexington Avenue, 27th Floor
New York, NY USA 10022
Phone: 2127831088

Other Offices
33 Cavendish Square
8th Floor
London, United Kingdom W1A 2SY

Parliament Street
New Delhi, India 110001
Phone: 91-11-2371-4211
Fax: 91-11-2374-7450

Management and Staff
Cali Cole, Managing Director
Craig Farnsworth, Partner
Darren Friedman, Partner
Hunter Reisner, Managing Partner
Michael Whitman, Partner
Robert Womsley, Partner

Type of Firm
Bank Affiliated

Project Preferences

Role in Financing:
Will function either as deal originator or investor in deals created by others

Type of Financing Preferred:
Fund of Funds
Leveraged Buyout
Mezzanine
Generalist PE

Geographical Preferences

United States Preferences:
All U.S.

International Preferences:
All International

Industry Preferences

In Medical/Health prefer:
Pharmaceuticals

In Consumer Related prefer:
Retail

In Industrial/Energy prefer:
Energy

Additional Information
Year Founded: 1998
Capital Under Management: $8,300,000,000
Current Activity Level : Actively seeking new investments

Method of Compensation: Return on investment is of primary concern, do not charge fees

---

CITIZEN CAPITAL PARTENAIRES SAS

16, rue Martel
Paris, France 75010
Phone: 33176747720
Fax: 33176747729
E-mail: contact@citizencapital.fr
Website: www.citizencapital.fr

Management and Staff
Laurence Mehaignerie, President
Pierre-Olivier Barennes, Chief Executive Officer

Type of Firm
Private Equity Firm

Association Membership
French Venture Capital Association (AFIC)

Project Preferences

Type of Financing Preferred:
Leveraged Buyout
Early Stage
Generalist PE
Later Stage
Acquisition

Size of Investments Considered:
Min Size of Investment Considered (000s): $381
Max Size of Investment Considered (000s): $2,794

Geographical Preferences

International Preferences:
Europe
France

Additional Information
Year Founded: 2008
Capital Under Management: $40,248,000
Current Activity Level : Actively seeking new investments

CITY CAPITAL VENTURES LLC

444 North Michigan
Suite 3250
Chicago, IL USA 60611
Phone: 3125467999
Website: citycapitalventures.com

Management and Staff
Allen Tibshrany, Managing Director
Michael Humenansky, Vice President

Type of Firm
Private Equity Firm

Project Preferences

Type of Financing Preferred:
Generalist PE

Additional Information
Year Founded: 2015
Current Activity Level : Actively seeking new investments

CITY HILL VENTURES LLC

11575 Sorrento Valley Road
Suite 200
San Diego, CA USA 92121
E-mail: info@cityhillventures.com
Website: www.cityhillventures.com

Type of Firm
Private Equity Firm

Project Preferences

Type of Financing Preferred:
Early Stage
Seed

Size of Investments Considered:
Min Size of Investment Considered (000s): $2,000
Max Size of Investment Considered (000s): $200,000

Geographical Preferences

United States Preferences:
California
All U.S.

Industry Preferences

In Communications prefer:
Wireless Communications

In Medical/Health prefer:
Medical/Health
Medical Diagnostics
Diagnostic Services
Medical Therapeutics

Additional Information

Name of Most Recent Fund: City Hill Venture Partners I, LLC
Most Recent Fund Was Raised: 08/17/2011
Year Founded: 2010
Capital Under Management: $8,000,000
Current Activity Level : Actively seeking new investments

CITY LIGHT CAPITAL

370 Lexington Avenue, Suite 1704
New York, NY USA 10017
Phone: 2124039575
E-mail: info@citylightcap.com
Website: www.citylightcap.com

Management and Staff

Bill Lyons, Venture Partner
Josh Cohen, Managing Partner
Matt Cohen, Principal
Tom Groos, Partner

Type of Firm

Private Equity Firm

Project Preferences

Type of Financing Preferred:
Early Stage
Balanced
Later Stage

Geographical Preferences

United States Preferences:

Industry Preferences

In Consumer Related prefer:
Education Related

In Industrial/Energy prefer:
Energy
Energy Conservation Relat
Environmental Related

In Business Serv. prefer:
Media

Additional Information

Name of Most Recent Fund: Impact Ventures II, L.P.
Most Recent Fund Was Raised: 07/17/2009
Year Founded: 2004
Capital Under Management: $75,000,000
Current Activity Level : Actively seeking new investments

CITY STAR PRIVATE EQUITY SAS

11, rue des Pyramides
Paris, France 75001
Phone: 33153642200
Fax: 33145001716
E-mail: la@clavel-invest.fr
Website: www.citystarcapital.com

Other Offices

55 street 78
No Problem Villa House
Phnom Penh , Cambodia 12207
Phone: 855-23-223-695
Fax: 855-23-223-690

80 Rafles Place
Level 35 UOB Plaza 1
Singapore, Singapore
Phone: 65-9817-9909
Fax: 65-6735-1131

Management and Staff

Davis Chong, Founder
Frederic Jugi, Founder
Jean-Louis Charon, President

Type of Firm

Private Equity Firm

Association Membership

French Venture Capital Association (AFIC)

Project Preferences

Type of Financing Preferred:
Leveraged Buyout
Turnaround
Later Stage
Management Buyouts

Geographical Preferences

International Preferences:
Europe
Asia
France

Additional Information

Year Founded: 2004
Current Activity Level : Actively seeking new investments

CIVC PARTNERS LP

191 North Wacker Drive
Suite 1100
Chicago, IL USA 60606
Phone: 3128737300
Fax: 3128737301
E-mail: civc_partners@civc.com
Website: www.civc.com

Management and Staff

Christopher Perry, Partner
Christopher Geneser, Chief Financial Officer
Christopher McLaughlin, Principal
Daniel Helle, Partner
David Miller, Principal
Doug Potters, Vice President
J.D. Wright, Vice President
John Compall, Partner
Keith Yamada, Partner
Marc McManus, Principal
Marcus Wedner, Partner
Scott Schwartz, Partner

Type of Firm

Private Equity Firm

Project Preferences

Role in Financing:
Prefer role as deal originator but will also invest in deals created by others

Type of Financing Preferred:
Leveraged Buyout
Expansion
Management Buyouts
Recapitalizations

Geographical Preferences

United States Preferences:

Industry Preferences

In Financial Services prefer:
Financial Services

In Business Serv. prefer:
Services

Additional Information

Name of Most Recent Fund: CIVC Partners Fund II
Most Recent Fund Was Raised: 01/01/1999
Year Founded: 1970
Capital Under Management: $1,300,000,000
Current Activity Level : Actively seeking new investments
Method of Compensation: Return on invest. most important, but chg. closing fees, service fees, etc.

CIVETA INVESTMENT SA

Francisco Silvela 47
Madrid, Spain
E-mail: contacto@civeta.es
Website: www.civeta.es

Type of Firm

Private Equity Firm

Project Preferences

Type of Financing Preferred:
Early Stage
Seed

CIVILIZATION VENTURES

500 Sansome Street
San Francisco, CA USA 94111
Website: www.civilizationventures.com

Type of Firm
Private Equity Firm

Industry Preferences

In Biotechnology prefer:
Biotechnology

In Medical/Health prefer:
Health Services

Additional Information
Year Founded: 2017
Current Activity Level : Actively seeking new investments

Geographical Preferences

International Preferences:
Europe

Additional Information
Year Founded: 2013
Current Activity Level : Actively seeking new investments

CLAIRVEST GROUP INC

22 St Clair Avenue East
Suite 1700
Toronto, Canada M4T 2S3
Phone: 4169259270
Fax: 4169255753
Website: www.clairvest.com

Management and Staff
Aly Champsi, Vice President
Daniel Cheng, Chief Financial Officer
Jeffrey Parr, Managing Director
Kenneth Rotman, CEO & Managing Director
Sebastien Dhonte, Vice President
Steve Frenkiel, Vice President

Type of Firm
Private Equity Firm

Association Membership
Canadian Venture Capital Association

Project Preferences

Role in Financing:
Prefer role as deal originator

Type of Financing Preferred:
Leveraged Buyout
Management Buyouts
Acquisition

Geographical Preferences

United States Preferences:
North America

Industry Focus
(% based on actual investment)
Other Products 31.6%
Industrial/Energy 23.8%
Consumer Related 19.9%
Computer Software and Services 10.2%
Internet Specific 7.7%
Medical/Health 5.2%
Communications and Media 1.5%

Additional Information
Year Founded: 1987
Capital Under Management: $1,537,000,000
Current Activity Level : Actively seeking new investments
Method of Compensation: Return on invest. most important, but chg. closing fees, service fees, etc.

CLAL VENTURE CAPITAL FUND MANAGEMENT, LTD.

3 Azrieli Center
45 floor
Tel Aviv, Israel 67023
Phone: 97236075777
Fax: 97236075778
E-mail: cii@cii.co.il
Website: www.cii.co.il

Type of Firm
Corporate PE/Venture

Project Preferences

Type of Financing Preferred:
Early Stage
Expansion
Startup

Geographical Preferences

International Preferences:
Middle East
Israel

Industry Preferences

In Computer Software prefer:
Software

In Biotechnology prefer:
Biotechnology

In Medical/Health prefer:
Medical/Health

In Consumer Related prefer:
Consumer Products

In Industrial/Energy prefer:
Alternative Energy

In Manufact. prefer:
Manufacturing

Additional Information
Year Founded: 1995
Capital Under Management: $36,000,000
Current Activity Level : Actively seeking new investments

CLAREMONT CREEK VENTURES LP

300 Frank H. Ogawa Plaza
Suite 350
Oakland, CA USA 94612
Phone: 5107405001

Management and Staff
Brad Webb, Venture Partner
Nat Goldhaber, Co-Founder
Randy Hawks, Co-Founder

Type of Firm
Private Equity Firm

Association Membership
Western Association of Venture Capitalists (WAVC)

Project Preferences

Role in Financing:
Prefer role as deal originator

Type of Financing Preferred:
Early Stage
Seed

Industry Preferences

In Communications prefer:
Wireless Communications

In Internet Specific prefer:
Ecommerce

In Medical/Health prefer:
Medical/Health

In Industrial/Energy prefer:
Energy

Additional Information
Name of Most Recent Fund: Claremont Creek Ventures II, L.P.
Most Recent Fund Was Raised: 09/30/2008
Year Founded: 2005
Capital Under Management: $305,000,000
Current Activity Level : Actively seeking new investments

CLARENDON FUND MANAGERS LTD

11-13 Gloucester Street
8th Floor, City Exchange
Belfast, United Kingdom BT1 4LS
Phone: 442890326465
Fax: 442890326473
E-mail: info@clarendon-fm.co.uk
Website: www.clarendon-fm.co.uk

Other Offices
12 Cromac Place
Belfast, United Kingdom BT7 2JB

Type of Firm
Private Equity Firm

Project Preferences

Type of Financing Preferred:
Early Stage
Startup

Geographical Preferences

International Preferences:
Ireland

Industry Preferences

In Business Serv. prefer:
Services

In Manufact. prefer:
Manufacturing

Additional Information
Year Founded: 2001
Capital Under Management: $52,630,000
Current Activity Level : Actively seeking new investments

CLARICA LIFE INSURANCE CO

227 King Street South
Waterloo, Canada N2J4C5
Phone: 888-864-5463

Type of Firm
Endowment, Foundation or Pension Fund

Additional Information
Year Founded: 2009
Current Activity Level : Actively seeking new investments

CLARIDGE INC

1170 Peel, Suite 800
Montreal, Canada H3B 4P2
Phone: 5148785200
E-mail: info@claridgeinc.com
Website: www.claridgeinc.com

Type of Firm
Endowment, Foundation or Pension Fund

Project Preferences

Type of Financing Preferred:
Leveraged Buyout
Later Stage
Management Buyouts
Acquisition

Geographical Preferences

International Preferences:
Israel

Additional Information
Year Founded: 1987
Current Activity Level : Actively seeking new investments

CLARION CAPITAL PARTNERS LLC

527 Madison Avenue
Suite 1000
New York, NY USA 10022
Phone: 2128210170
Fax: 2123717597
Website: www.clarion-capital.com

Management and Staff
Brandon Katz, Vice President
David Ragins, Managing Director
Douglas Mellinger, Managing Director
Edward Martin, Vice President
Eric Kogan, Partner
Janice Chan, Chief Financial Officer
Jonathan Haas, Managing Director
Marc Utay, Managing Partner
Matthew Feldman, Principal
Thomas Goundrey, Managing Director

Type of Firm
Private Equity Firm

Project Preferences

Type of Financing Preferred:
Leveraged Buyout
Acquisition
Distressed Debt
Recapitalizations

Industry Preferences

In Communications prefer:
Media and Entertainment

In Medical/Health prefer:
Health Services

In Consumer Related prefer:
Retail
Consumer Products

In Financial Services prefer:
Financial Services

In Business Serv. prefer:
Services

Additional Information
Year Founded: 1999
Capital Under Management: $399,600,000
Current Activity Level : Actively seeking new investments

CLARION OFFSHORE PARTNERS LLC

2700 Post Oak Boulevard
Suite 300
Houston, TX USA 77056
Phone: 2819144783
E-mail: www.clarionoffshore.com
Website: www.clarionoffshore.com

Type of Firm
Investment Management Firm

Industry Preferences

In Industrial/Energy prefer:
Oil and Gas Exploration

Additional Information
Year Founded: 2015
Current Activity Level : Actively seeking new investments

CLARITAS CAPITAL LLC

Thirty Burton Hills Boulevard
Suite 100
Nashville, TN USA 37215
Phone: 6156658550
Website: claritascapital.com

Other Offices
2211 Michelson Drive
Suite 300
IRVINE, CA USA 92612
Phone: 9495028277

Management and Staff
J. Donald McLemore, Managing Director
John Chadwick, Managing Director
Lee Ballew, Vice President
Mark McManigal, Managing Director
R. Burton Harvey, Managing Director
Robert Fisher, Managing Director
Theresa Sexton, Managing Director

Type of Firm
Private Equity Firm

Association Membership
Natl Assoc of Small Bus. Inv. Co (NASBIC)
National Venture Capital Association - USA (NVCA)

Project Preferences

Role in Financing:
Prefer role as deal originator

Type of Financing Preferred:
Core
Early Stage
Expansion
Mezzanine
Balanced
Later Stage
Startup

Size of Investments Considered:
Min Size of Investment Considered (000s): $500
Max Size of Investment Considered: No Limit

Geographical Preferences

United States Preferences:
Southeast
North America
West Coast
Texas

Industry Preferences

In Medical/Health prefer:
Medical/Health
Health Services

In Consumer Related prefer:
Retail

In Financial Services prefer:
Financial Services
Real Estate

In Business Serv. prefer:
Services
Distribution

In Manufact. prefer:
Manufacturing

Additional Information
Name of Most Recent Fund: CCSD II, L.P.
Most Recent Fund Was Raised: 07/27/2012
Year Founded: 2002
Capital Under Management: $70,000,000
Current Activity Level : Actively seeking new investments
Method of Compensation: Return on investment is of primary concern, do not charge fees

CLARKE INC

6009 Quinpool Road
Ninth Floor
Halifax, Canada B3K 5J7
Phone: 9024423000
Fax: 9024420187

Management and Staff
Dennis Amirault, Vice President
Dustin Haw, Vice President
Kim Langille, Chief Financial Officer

Type of Firm
Private Equity Firm

Additional Information
Year Founded: 1997
Current Activity Level : Actively seeking new investments

CLARUS VENTURES LLC

101 Main Street
Suite 1210
Cambridge, MA USA 02142
Phone: 6179492200
Fax: 6179492201
Website: www.clarusventures.com

Management and Staff
Ari Brettman, Principal
Barry Gertz, Venture Partner
Dennis Henner, Managing Director
Emmett Cunningham, Managing Director
Kiran Reddy, Venture Partner
Kurt Wheeler, Managing Director
Markus Orchowski, Vice President
Michele Park, Partner
Nicholas Simon, Managing Director
Nicholas Galakatos, Managing Director
Robert DeBenedetto, Venture Partner
Robert Liptak, Managing Director
Scott Requadt, Managing Director
William Young, Venture Partner

Type of Firm
Private Equity Firm

Association Membership
New England Venture Capital Association
National Venture Capital Association - USA (NVCA)

Project Preferences

Type of Financing Preferred:
Expansion
Later Stage

Industry Preferences

In Biotechnology prefer:
Biotechnology

In Medical/Health prefer:
Medical Diagnostics
Medical Products
Pharmaceuticals

Additional Information
Name of Most Recent Fund: Clarus Lifesciences II, L.P.
Most Recent Fund Was Raised: 02/15/2008
Year Founded: 2005
Capital Under Management: $2,000,000,000
Current Activity Level : Actively seeking new investments

CLAVE MAYOR SA SGECR

C/Emilio Arrieta
11 bis-2
Pamplona, Spain 31002
Phone: 34948203960
Fax: 948228902
E-mail: info@clavemayor.com
Website: www.clavemayor.com

Other Offices
C/ Duque de la Victoria, 13-2
Edif. Duvicentro
Valladolid, Spain 47001
Phone: 983363359
Fax: 983339795

C/ La Paz
44-1-2
Valencia, Spain 46003
Phone: 963516556
Fax: 963516568

Type of Firm
Private Equity Firm

Association Membership
Spanish Venture Capital Association (ASCRI)

Project Preferences

Type of Financing Preferred:
Early Stage
Expansion
Balanced
Startup

Geographical Preferences

International Preferences:
Europe
Spain

Industry Preferences

In Communications prefer:
Communications and Media

In Semiconductor/Electr prefer:
Electronics

In Biotechnology prefer:
Biotechnology

In Medical/Health prefer:
Medical Diagnostics
Medical Therapeutics
Medical Products
Health Services

In Industrial/Energy prefer:
Industrial Products
Environmental Related

In Transportation prefer:
Transportation

In Business Serv. prefer:
Services

Additional Information
Year Founded: 2002
Capital Under Management: $3,595,000
Current Activity Level : Actively seeking new investments

CLAVIS CAPITAL PARTNERS LLC

10440 North Central Expressway
Suite 1150
Dallas, TX USA 75225
Phone: 2149897050
Website: www.claviscp.com

Management and Staff
Todd Dauphinais, Managing Partner

Type of Firm
Investment Management Firm

Project Preferences

Type of Financing Preferred:
Early Stage
Expansion
Later Stage

Industry Preferences

In Industrial/Energy prefer:
Energy

In Transportation prefer:
Transportation
Aerospace

In Agr/Forestr/Fish prefer:
Mining and Minerals

Additional Information
Year Founded: 2014
Current Activity Level : Actively seeking new investments

CLAYTON ASSOCIATES LLC

5121 Maryland Way
Suite 100
Brentwood, TN USA 37027
Phone: 6153203070
Fax: 6159633847
E-mail: info@claytonassociates.com
Website: www.claytonassociates.com

Management and Staff
John Burch, Partner
Matthew King, Managing Partner
Nancy Allen, Chief Financial Officer

Type of Firm
Investment Management Firm

Project Preferences

Role in Financing:
Will function either as deal originator or investor in deals created by others

Type of Financing Preferred:
Early Stage
Expansion

Geographical Preferences

United States Preferences:
Southeast

Industry Preferences

In Computer Software prefer:
Software

In Medical/Health prefer:
Medical Therapeutics
Medical Products

In Business Serv. prefer:
Media

Additional Information
Name of Most Recent Fund: Rolling Hills Ventures I, L.P.
Most Recent Fund Was Raised: 03/20/2014
Year Founded: 1996
Capital Under Management: $140,000,000
Current Activity Level : Actively seeking new investments
Method of Compensation: Return on invest. most important, but chg. closing fees, service fees, etc.

CLAYTON DUBILIER & RICE LLC

375 Park Avenue
18th Floor
New York, NY USA 10152
Phone: 2124075200
Fax: 2124075252
E-mail: info@cdr-ltd.com
Website: www.cdr-inc.com

Management and Staff
Christian Storch, Principal
Christian Rochat, Partner
David Wasserman, Partner
David Novak, Partner
Derek Strum, Principal
Donald Gogel, Chairman & CEO
Edward Liddy, Partner
Eric Rahe, Managing Director
Eric Rouzier, Principal
Fred Kindle, Partner
George Tamke, Partner
George Jaquette, Partner
Gregory Lai, Principal
J. L. Zrebiec, Principal
James Berges, Partner
James Ahn, Managing Director
John Malfettone, Senior Managing Director
Joseph Rice, Founder
Kenneth Giuriceo, Partner
Kevin Conway, Managing Partner
Kevin Smith, Principal
Manvinder Singh Banga, Partner
Marco Herbst, Managing Director
Michael Babiarz, Partner
Nathan Sleeper, Partner
Paul Pressler, Partner
Richard Schnall, Partner
Roberto Quarta, Partner
Sarah Kim, Principal
Sonja Terraneo, Partner
Stephen Shapiro, Principal
Theresa Gore, Principal
Thomas Franco, Partner

Type of Firm
Private Equity Firm

Association Membership
British Venture Capital Association (BVCA)
Emerging Markets Private Equity Association

Project Preferences

Type of Financing Preferred:
Leveraged Buyout
Management Buyouts
Acquisition

Industry Focus
(% based on actual investment)

Other Products	45.0%
Consumer Related	21.0%
Industrial/Energy	21.0%
Communications and Media	9.0%
Computer Hardware	2.1%
Internet Specific	1.7%
Medical/Health	0.3%
Computer Software and Services	0.1%
Semiconductors/Other Elect.	0.0%

Additional Information
Name of Most Recent Fund: Clayton, Dubilier & Rice Fund IX, L.P.
Most Recent Fund Was Raised: 08/23/2013
Year Founded: 1978
Capital Under Management: $21,000,000,000
Current Activity Level : Actively seeking new investments

CLB PARTNERS LLC

1160 East Jericho Turnpike
Suite 207
Huntington, NY USA 11743
Phone: 631-425-0710
Fax: 631-824-9118
Website: www.clb-partners.com

Management and Staff
Alex Abreu, Managing Director

Type of Firm
Bank Affiliated

Project Preferences

Type of Financing Preferred:
Leveraged Buyout

Additional Information
Year Founded: 2004
Capital Under Management: $40,000,000
Current Activity Level : Actively seeking new investments

CLEAN ENERGY INVEST CVBA

22, Meiboom
Halle, Belgium 1500
Website: cleanenergyinvest.be

Type of Firm
Private Equity Firm

Project Preferences

Type of Financing Preferred:
Leveraged Buyout
Early Stage
Expansion
Later Stage
Management Buyouts
Acquisition

Industry Preferences

In Industrial/Energy prefer:
Energy
Energy Conservation Relat
Environmental Related

In Other prefer:
Environment Responsible

Additional Information
Year Founded: 2009
Current Activity Level : Actively seeking new investments

CLEAN ENERGY VENTURE GROUP

101 Stedman Street
Brookline, MA USA 02446
Phone: 8775319017
E-mail: info@cleanenergyvg.com

Management and Staff
Carl Nelson, Partner
Daniel Goldman, Co-Founder
Ralph Earle, Co-Founder

Type of Firm
Private Equity Firm

Project Preferences

Type of Financing Preferred:
Early Stage
Seed

Geographical Preferences

United States Preferences:
Northeast

Industry Preferences

In Industrial/Energy prefer:
Energy

In Other prefer:
Environment Responsible

Additional Information
Year Founded: 2009
Capital Under Management: $36,540,000
Current Activity Level : Actively seeking new investments

CLEAN PACIFIC VENTURES MANAGEMENT LLC

505 Sansome Street, Suite 1200
Two Transamerica Center
San Francisco, CA USA 94111
Phone: 4154330123
Fax: 4154330161
Website: www.cleanpacific.com

Management and Staff
Dave Herron, General Partner
Dewey Chambers, Chief Financial Officer
Jeff Barnes, General Partner
Sean Schickedanz, General Partner

Type of Firm
Private Equity Firm

Project Preferences

Role in Financing:
Will function either as deal originator or investor in deals created by others

Type of Financing Preferred:
Early Stage
Seed

Size of Investments Considered:
Min Size of Investment Considered (000s): $2,000
Max Size of Investment Considered (000s): $4,000

Industry Preferences

In Consumer Related prefer:
Food/Beverage

In Industrial/Energy prefer:
Energy Conservation Relat
Materials
Environmental Related

In Other prefer:
Environment Responsible

Additional Information
Year Founded: 2007
Capital Under Management: $15,000,000
Current Activity Level : Actively seeking new investments

CLEAR VENTURE MANAGEMENT LLC

3340 Hillview Ave
Palo Alto, CA USA 94304
Phone: 8662532714
E-mail: inbox@clear.ventures
Website: clear.ventures

Management and Staff
Christopher Rust, Co-Founder
Rajeev Madhavan, Co-Founder

Type of Firm
Private Equity Firm

Project Preferences

Type of Financing Preferred:
Early Stage

Geographical Preferences

United States Preferences:

International Preferences:
India
Europe
Israel

Industry Preferences

In Internet Specific prefer:
Internet

Additional Information
Year Founded: 2016
Capital Under Management: $121,200,000
Current Activity Level : Actively seeking new investments

CLEAR VENTURE PARTNERS INC

Nine Norton Farm Road
Freeport, ME USA 04032
Phone: 8888028778
Fax: 2072211184
E-mail: info@clearvcs.com
Website: www.clearvcs.com

Management and Staff
Michael Gurau, Managing Partner

Type of Firm
Private Equity Firm

Project Preferences

Type of Financing Preferred:
Early Stage

Geographical Preferences

United States Preferences:
New Hampshire
Rhode Island
Vermont
Northeast
Massachusetts
Connecticut
Maine

Industry Preferences

In Communications prefer:
Wireless Communications

In Computer Software prefer:
Software
Systems Software
Applications Software

In Medical/Health prefer:
Medical/Health
Medical Products
Health Services

In Consumer Related prefer:
Consumer
Food/Beverage
Consumer Products

In Industrial/Energy prefer:
Energy
Industrial Products
Advanced Materials
Environmental Related

In Transportation prefer:
Transportation

In Manufact. prefer:
Manufacturing

In Agr/Forestr/Fish prefer:
Agriculture related

In Other prefer:
Environment Responsible

Additional Information

Year Founded: 2007
Current Activity Level : Actively seeking new investments

CLEARBRIDGE PARTNERS LTD

61 Hoi Yuen Road
Suite 1803, Kwun Tong
Kowloon, Hong Kong
E-mail: contactus@clearbridgepartners.com
Website: www.clearbridgepartners.com

Other Offices

20 Ayer Rajah Crescent
#08-03 Technopreneur Centre
Singapore, Singapore 139964

40/41 Great Castle Street
Fourth Floor, Windsor House
London, United Kingdom W1W 8LU

Type of Firm
Private Equity Firm

Association Membership
Hong Kong Venture Capital Association (HKVCA)

Project Preferences

Type of Financing Preferred:
Early Stage
Expansion
Balanced
Seed
Startup

Geographical Preferences

International Preferences:
United Kingdom
Europe
Asia

Additional Information

Year Founded: 2002
Current Activity Level : Actively seeking new investments

CLEARBROOK CAPITAL PARTNERS LLP

25 Grosvenor Street
London, United Kingdom W1K 4QN
Phone: 44-20-7907-9650
Fax: 44-20-7907-9651
E-mail: info@clearbrook.com
Website: www.clearbrook.com

Management and Staff
Robin Saunders, Managing Partner

Type of Firm
Private Equity Firm

Project Preferences

Type of Financing Preferred:
Generalist PE
Management Buyouts

Geographical Preferences

International Preferences:
Europe

Additional Information

Year Founded: 2004
Current Activity Level : Actively seeking new investments

CLEARLAKE CAPITAL GROUP LP

233 Wilshire Boulevard
Suite 800
Santa Monica, CA USA 90401
Phone: 3104008800
E-mail: info@clearlakecapital.com
Website: www.clearlakecapital.com

Other Offices

650 Madison Avenue
23rd Floor
New York, NY USA 10022

Management and Staff
Behdad Eghbali, Co-Founder
Colin Leonard, Partner
James Pade, Principal
Jose Feliciano, Co-Founder
Nate Mejias, Vice President
Patrick Gilligan, Managing Director
Paul Huber, Vice President
Steven Chang, Co-Founder
Xavier Gutierrez, Managing Director

Type of Firm
Private Equity Firm

Association Membership
Natl Assoc of Investment Cos. (NAIC)
Australian Venture Capital Association (AVCAL)

Project Preferences

Type of Financing Preferred:
Expansion
Special Situation

Industry Preferences

In Communications prefer:
Communications and Media

In Medical/Health prefer:
Medical/Health

In Consumer Related prefer:
Retail

In Industrial/Energy prefer:
Energy
Industrial Products

In Business Serv. prefer:
Services
Media

Additional Information

Name of Most Recent Fund: Clearlake Capital Partners III, L.P.
Most Recent Fund Was Raised: 12/31/2012
Year Founded: 2006
Capital Under Management: $2,191,738,000
Current Activity Level : Actively seeking new investments

CLEARLIGHT PARTNERS LLC

100 Bayview Circle
Suite 5000
Newport Beach, CA USA 92660
Phone: 9497256610
Fax: 9497256611
Website: www.clearlightpartners.com

Management and Staff
David Reed, Principal
Doug Scherrer, Principal
Huy DangVu, Chief Financial Officer
Jay Shepherd, Partner
Joshua Mack, Partner
Mark Gartner, Vice President
Peter Kim, Principal

Type of Firm
Private Equity Firm

Project Preferences

Type of Financing Preferred:
Leveraged Buyout
Mezzanine
Management Buyouts

Geographical Preferences

United States Preferences:

Canadian Preferences:
All Canada

Industry Preferences

In Medical/Health prefer:
Health Services

In Consumer Related prefer:
Consumer Products
Consumer Services
Education Related

In Industrial/Energy prefer:
Industrial Products

In Financial Services prefer:
Financial Services

In Business Serv. prefer:
Services
Distribution

In Manufact. prefer:
Manufacturing

Additional Information
Name of Most Recent Fund: ClearLight Partners III LLC
Most Recent Fund Was Raised: 11/27/2012
Year Founded: 2000
Capital Under Management: $900,000,000
Current Activity Level : Actively seeking new investments

CLEARPOINT INVESTMENT PARTNERS LLC

400 South El Camino Real
Suite 260
San Mateo, CA USA 94402
Phone: 4158905828
Fax: 4153248302
E-mail: info@clearpointinvest.com
Website: clearpointinvest.com

Management and Staff
Carty Chock, Co-Founder
Ingrid Mazul, Co-Founder
Taimur Shaikh, Principal

Type of Firm
Private Equity Firm

Project Preferences

Type of Financing Preferred:
Leveraged Buyout
Acquisition
Recapitalizations

Industry Preferences

In Financial Services prefer:
Financial Services

Additional Information
Year Founded: 2017
Current Activity Level : Actively seeking new investments

CLEARSIGHT INVESTMENTS AG

Churerstrasse 23
Pfaeffikon, Switzerland 8808
Phone: 41442514087
E-mail: info@clearsight-invest.com
Website: www.clearsight-invest.com

Management and Staff
Jakub Crhonek, Managing Director

Type of Firm
Private Equity Advisor or Fund of Funds

Geographical Preferences

International Preferences:
Europe

Additional Information
Year Founded: 2008
Current Activity Level : Actively seeking new investments

CLEARSKY POWER & TECHNOLOGY FUND I LLC

700 Universe Boulevard
North Palm Beach, FL USA 33408
Phone: 5616917770
Website: www.clear-sky.com

Management and Staff
James Huff, Managing Director

Type of Firm
Private Equity Firm

Project Preferences

Type of Financing Preferred:
Expansion
Later Stage

Industry Preferences

In Industrial/Energy prefer:
Energy

Additional Information
Name of Most Recent Fund: ClearSky Power & Technology Fund I LLC
Most Recent Fund Was Raised: 03/29/2012
Year Founded: 2012
Capital Under Management: $422,515,000
Current Activity Level : Actively seeking new investments

CLEARSPRING CAPITAL PARTNERS

Brookfield Place, 161 Bay St.
Suite 4540, P.O. Box 709
Toronto, Canada M5J 2S1
Phone: 4168684900
Fax: 4168684910
E-mail: info@callistocapital.ca
Website: www.cscap.ca

Management and Staff
Aly Hadibhai, Vice President
James Walker, Managing Director
Joseph Shlesinger, Managing Director
Lawrence Stevenson, Managing Director

Type of Firm
Private Equity Firm

Association Membership
Canadian Venture Capital Association

Project Preferences

Type of Financing Preferred:
Leveraged Buyout
Acquisition

Geographical Preferences

Canadian Preferences:
All Canada

Industry Preferences

In Medical/Health prefer:
Medical/Health
Pharmaceuticals

In Consumer Related prefer:
Retail
Food/Beverage

In Business Serv. prefer:
Services

Additional Information

Name of Most Recent Fund: Callisto Capital III LP
Most Recent Fund Was Raised: 12/31/2007
Year Founded: 2002
Capital Under Management: $371,510,000
Current Activity Level : Actively seeking new investments

CLEARSTONE VENTURE MANAGEMENT SERVICES LLC

1351 Fourth Street
Fourth Floor
Santa Monica, CA USA 90401
Phone: 3104607900
Fax: 3104607901
E-mail: info@clearstone.com
Website: www.clearstone.com

Other Offices

720 University Avenue
Suite 200
PALO ALTO, CA USA 94301
Phone: 6502340400
Fax: 6502340401

Management and Staff

Anilkumar Patel, Venture Partner
Dana Moraly, Chief Financial Officer
David Stern, Venture Partner
James Armstrong, Managing Director
Rajan Mehra, Venture Partner
Sumant Mandal, Managing Director
T.M. Ravi, Venture Partner
William Quigley, Managing Director

Type of Firm

Private Equity Firm

Project Preferences

Role in Financing:
Prefer role as deal originator but will also invest in deals created by others

Type of Financing Preferred:
Early Stage
Seed
Startup

Geographical Preferences

United States Preferences:
Southern California
California

International Preferences:
India

Industry Focus

(% based on actual investment)
Internet Specific	46.4%
Computer Software and Services	29.7%
Communications and Media	12.2%
Other Products	4.3%
Semiconductors/Other Elect.	3.2%
Computer Hardware	2.1%
Industrial/Energy	1.7%
Consumer Related	0.5%

Additional Information

Year Founded: 1997
Capital Under Management: $651,000,000
Current Activity Level : Actively seeking new investments
Method of Compensation: Return on investment is of primary concern, do not charge fees

CLEARVIEW CAPITAL LLC

1010 Washington Boulevard
11th Floor
Stamford, CT USA 06901
Phone: 2036982777
Fax: 2036989194
Website: www.clearviewcap.com

Other Offices

180 North Stetson Avenue
Suite 1300, Two Prudential Plaza
CHICAGO, IL USA 60601
Phone: 3122880123
Fax: 3125831700

12100 Wilshire Boulevard
Suite 800
LOS ANGELES, CA USA 90025
Phone: 3108069555
Fax: 3108069556

Management and Staff

Anthony Veith, Principal
Harold Doolittle, Founder
James Tucker, Principal
John Cerra, Chief Financial Officer
Jon Van Tuin, Principal
Lawrence Simon, Principal
Matt Rumilly, Principal
Matthew Blevins, Principal
Paul Caliento, Partner
William Case, Partner

Type of Firm

Private Equity Firm

Project Preferences

Role in Financing:
Prefer role as deal originator

Type of Financing Preferred:
Leveraged Buyout
Management Buyouts
Acquisition
Recapitalizations

Geographical Preferences

United States Preferences:
North America

Industry Focus

(% based on actual investment)
Industrial/Energy	44.4%
Other Products	26.7%
Consumer Related	26.3%
Biotechnology	1.4%
Medical/Health	1.3%

Additional Information

Name of Most Recent Fund: Clearview Capital Fund III, L.P.
Most Recent Fund Was Raised: 06/24/2013
Year Founded: 1999
Capital Under Management: $360,000,000
Current Activity Level : Actively seeking new investments
Method of Compensation: Return on invest. most important, but chg. closing fees, service fees, etc.

CLEARVISION EQUITY PARTNERS LLC

4320 La Jolla Village Drive
Suite 200
San Diego, CA USA 92122
Phone: 8582993950
Fax: 8582993960
E-mail: info@cvequity.com
Website: clearvisionequity.com

Management and Staff

Jim Burdick, Founder

Type of Firm

Private Equity Firm

Project Preferences

Type of Financing Preferred:
Leveraged Buyout
Balanced
Startup

Geographical Preferences

United States Preferences:
Southern California

Additional Information
Year Founded: 2017
Current Activity Level: Actively seeking new investments

CLEARVUE PARTNERS, L.P.

428, South Yanggao Rd, Pudong
10D Bldg2 Youyou Century Plaza
Shanghai, China 200127
Phone: 862150318996

Management and Staff
Irene Cai, Managing Director

Type of Firm
Private Equity Firm

Project Preferences

Type of Financing Preferred:
Balanced

Geographical Preferences

International Preferences:
China

Industry Preferences

In Communications prefer:
Wireless Communications

In Consumer Related prefer:
Consumer
Food/Beverage
Consumer Products

Additional Information
Year Founded: 2012
Capital Under Management: $624,000,000
Current Activity Level: Actively seeking new investments

CLEARWATER CAPITAL MANAGEMENT

614 Academy Avenue
Sewickley, PA USA 15143
Phone: 4127490396
Fax: 4127491220
E-mail: info@clearwatercapital.com
Website: www.clearwatercapital.com

Type of Firm
Private Equity Firm

Project Preferences

Type of Financing Preferred:
Early Stage
Other

Additional Information
Year Founded: 2003
Current Activity Level: Actively seeking new investments

CLEARWATER CAPITAL PARTNERS CYPRUS LTD

One Grand Central Place
Suite 4600
New York, NY USA 10165
Phone: 2122018544
E-mail: information@clearwatercp.com
Website: www.clearwatercapitalpartners.com

Other Offices
4 Battery Road #34-01
Bank of China Building
Singapore, Singapore 049908

No. 9 Queens Road
Suite 3205
Central, Hong Kong

149, Seorin Dong, Jongro Gu
8F, Chunggye 11 Bldg.
Seoul, South Korea 110-726

201, 2nd Floor, Central Plaza
166 CST Road Kalina
Mumbai, India 400 098

Management and Staff
Amit Gupta, Co-Founder
Jaewoo Shim, Managing Director
Michael Capasso, Managing Director
Robert Petty, Co-Founder
Subhashree Dutta, Managing Director
Yao-Chye Chiang, Chief Operating Officer

Type of Firm
Private Equity Firm

Association Membership
Emerging Markets Private Equity Association
Indian Venture Capital Association (IVCA)

Project Preferences

Type of Financing Preferred:
Leveraged Buyout
Turnaround

Geographical Preferences

United States Preferences:

International Preferences:
India
Hong Kong
China
Asia
Singapore

Additional Information
Year Founded: 2001
Capital Under Management: $818,300,000
Current Activity Level: Actively seeking new investments

CLERMONT GROUP

80 Raffles Place
Level 46, UOB Plaza 1
Singapore, Singapore 048624
Phone: 6562105555
Fax: 6562105556
E-mail: info@clermont.com
Website: www.clermont.com

Type of Firm
Private Equity Firm

Project Preferences

Type of Financing Preferred:
Generalist PE

Industry Preferences

In Medical/Health prefer:
Health Services

In Consumer Related prefer:
Consumer

In Industrial/Energy prefer:
Energy

In Financial Services prefer:
Financial Services

Additional Information
Year Founded: 1986
Current Activity Level: Actively seeking new investments

CLESSIDRA SOCIETA DI GESTIONE DEL RISPARMIO SPA

Via del Lauro 7
Milan, Italy 20121
Phone: 3928695221
Fax: 392869522522
E-mail: info@clessidrasgr.it
Website: www.clessidrasgr.it

Management and Staff
Alessandro Papetti, Partner
Manuel Catalano, Partner
Matteo Ricatti, Partner
Maurizio Bottinelli, Partner

Type of Firm
Private Equity Firm

Association Membership
Italian Venture Capital Association (AIFI)
European Private Equity and Venture Capital Assoc.

Project Preferences

Type of Financing Preferred:
Leveraged Buyout
Management Buyouts

Geographical Preferences

International Preferences:
Italy
Europe

Additional Information
Name of Most Recent Fund: Clessidra Capital Partners II
Most Recent Fund Was Raised: 03/11/2009
Year Founded: 2003
Capital Under Management: $1,340,100,000
Current Activity Level : Actively seeking new investments

CLEVELAND AVENUE LLC

222 North Canal Street
Chicago, IL USA 60606
Phone: 3123836700
E-mail: info@clevelandave.com
Website: www.clevelandavenue.com

Management and Staff
Diana Ferguson, Chief Financial Officer

Type of Firm
Incubator/Development Program

Project Preferences

Type of Financing Preferred:
Early Stage

Industry Preferences

In Consumer Related prefer:
Food/Beverage

Additional Information
Year Founded: 1969
Current Activity Level : Actively seeking new investments

CLEVELAND HEALTH-TECH CORRIDOR, THE

5C00 Euclid
Suite 100
Cleveland, OH USA 44103
Phone: 2163915080
E-mail: jepstein@healthtechcorridor.com
Website: www.healthtechcorridor.com

Type of Firm
Private Equity Firm

Project Preferences

Type of Financing Preferred:
Generalist PE

Industry Preferences

In Medical/Health prefer:
Medical/Health
Health Services

In Financial Services prefer:
Real Estate

Additional Information
Year Founded: 2010
Current Activity Level : Actively seeking new investments

CLI VENTURES

1069 E Meadow Cir
Palo Alto, CA USA 94303
Phone: 5132766735
Website: www.cli.ventures

Type of Firm
Private Equity Firm

Project Preferences

Type of Financing Preferred:
Early Stage

Geographical Preferences

United States Preferences:

International Preferences:
China

Additional Information
Year Founded: 2014
Current Activity Level : Actively seeking new investments

CLIMATE CHANGE CAPITAL LTD

Three More London Riverside
London, United Kingdom SE1 2AQ
Phone: 442079395000
Fax: 442079395030

Other Offices
One Guanghua Road
405-406 North Tower, Beijing Kerry Ctr
Beijing, China 100020
Phone: 86-10-6589-0888
Fax: 86-10-8525-3197

Management and Staff
Bruno Derungs, Managing Director
Ian Temperton, Managing Director
John Betts, Managing Director
Simon Drury, Managing Director

Type of Firm
Investment Management Firm

Association Membership
China Venture Capital Association

Project Preferences

Role in Financing:
Will function either as deal originator or investor in deals created by others

Type of Financing Preferred:
Leveraged Buyout
Generalist PE
Balanced
Later Stage
Management Buyouts
Acquisition

Size of Investments Considered:
Min Size of Investment Considered (000s): $15,637
Max Size of Investment Considered (000s): $31,274

Geographical Preferences

United States Preferences:

International Preferences:
India
Soviet Union
United Kingdom
Europe
China

Industry Preferences

In Industrial/Energy prefer:
Energy
Energy Conservation Relat
Environmental Related

In Business Serv. prefer:
Services

In Other prefer:
Environment Responsible

Additional Information
Year Founded: 2004
Capital Under Management: $1,600,000,000
Current Activity Level : Actively seeking new investments

CLOCKTOWER TECHNOLOGY VENTURES LLC

225 Santa Monica Blvd
Tenth Floor
Santa Monica, CA USA 90401
Phone: 3104582003
Website: www.clocktowerventures.com

Type of Firm
Private Equity Firm

Project Preferences

Type of Financing Preferred:
Early Stage
Expansion
Balanced
Start-up Financing
Later Stage
Seed

Industry Preferences

In Financial Services prefer:
Financial Services

Additional Information
Year Founded: 2015
Capital Under Management: $5,000,000
Current Activity Level : Actively seeking new investments

CLOSED LOOP CAPITAL

259 North Radnor-Chester Road
Wayne, PA USA 19087
E-mail: info@closedloopcapital.com
Website: closedloopcapital.com

Management and Staff
James Macon, Co-Founder
Jason Ingle, Co-Founder

Type of Firm
Private Equity Firm

Project Preferences

Type of Financing Preferred:
Early Stage

Geographical Preferences

United States Preferences:

Canadian Preferences:
All Canada

Industry Preferences

In Agr/Forestr/Fish prefer:
Agriculture related

Additional Information
Year Founded: 2015
Current Activity Level : Actively seeking new investments

CLOSED LOOP PARTNERS LLC

817 BROADWAY
5TH FLOOR
New York, NY USA 10003
Phone: 9178226476
Website: www.closedlooppartners.com

Type of Firm
Private Equity Firm

Project Preferences

Type of Financing Preferred:
Early Stage

Additional Information
Year Founded: 2016
Capital Under Management: $3,500,000
Current Activity Level : Actively seeking new investments

CLOUD APPS MANAGEMENT LLC

One Sutter Street
Suite 900
San Francisco, CA USA 94104
Phone: 6503865103
Website: www.cloudappscapital.com

Management and Staff
Judy Loehr, Venture Partner
Matt Holleran, General Partner

Type of Firm
Private Equity Firm

Industry Preferences

In Computer Software prefer:
Software

In Internet Specific prefer:
Internet

Additional Information
Year Founded: 2013
Capital Under Management: $53,700,000
Current Activity Level : Actively seeking new investments

CLOUD EQUITY GROUP LLC

14 Wall Street
20th Floor
New York, NY USA 10005
Phone: 2126181298
Fax: 2126181298
E-mail: info@cloudequitygroup.com
Website: www.cloudequitygroup.com

Management and Staff
Kevin Wilson, Managing Partner
Sean Frank, Managing Partner

Type of Firm
Private Equity Firm

Project Preferences

Type of Financing Preferred:
Leveraged Buyout
Mezzanine
Acquisition

Industry Preferences

In Internet Specific prefer:
Internet

Additional Information
Year Founded: 2013
Current Activity Level : Actively seeking new investments

CLOUDBREAK CAPITAL LLC

6255 La Pintura Drive
San Diego, CA USA 92137
Phone: 8584562590
Fax: 8662125104
Website: www.cloudbreakcap.com

Type of Firm
Private Equity Firm

Project Preferences

Type of Financing Preferred:
Leveraged Buyout

Industry Preferences

In Business Serv. prefer:
Services

In Manufact. prefer:
Manufacturing

Additional Information
Year Founded: 2011
Current Activity Level : Actively seeking new investments

CLOVE CAPITAL PARTNERS LTD

194-204 Johnston Road
501 Wanchai Commercial Center
Hong Kong, Hong Kong
Phone: 85225292866
Fax: 85225291991

Management and Staff
Andy Law, Chief Financial Officer
Bharat Parashar, Managing Partner
Chung Min Pang, Partner

Type of Firm
Private Equity Firm

Project Preferences

Type of Financing Preferred:
Expansion
Balanced
Turnaround
Later Stage

Geographical Preferences

International Preferences:
Indonesia
India
China
Thailand
Philippines
Asia
Malaysia

Industry Preferences

In Communications prefer:
Telecommunications

In Industrial/Energy prefer:
Energy
Oil and Gas Exploration
Oil & Gas Drilling,Explor
Industrial Products

In Transportation prefer:
Transportation

In Business Serv. prefer:
Services

In Manufact. prefer:
Manufacturing

In Agr/Forestr/Fish prefer:
Agribusiness
Agriculture related
Mining and Minerals

Additional Information

Year Founded: 2010
Current Activity Level : Actively seeking new investments

CLOVER VENTURE GMBH

Ottostrasse 1
Starnberg, Germany 82319
Phone: 49 81514443795
Website: cloverventure.squarespace.com

Management and Staff

Michael Munz, Managing Director

Type of Firm

Private Equity Firm

Project Preferences

Type of Financing Preferred:
Early Stage
Seed
Startup

Geographical Preferences

International Preferences:
Western Europe
Germany

Industry Preferences

In Internet Specific prefer:
Ecommerce

Additional Information

Year Founded: 2009
Current Activity Level : Actively seeking new investments

CLOVERLAY

101 West Elm Street
Suite 425
Conshohocken, PA USA 19428
Phone: 14842625020
E-mail: info@cloverlay.com
Website: www.cloverlay.com

Type of Firm

Investment Management Firm

Project Preferences

Type of Financing Preferred:
Leveraged Buyout
Generalist PE
Balanced
Other

Industry Preferences

In Financial Services prefer:
Financial Services
Financial Services

Additional Information

Year Founded: 2015
Capital Under Management: $80,830,000
Current Activity Level : Actively seeking new investments

CLOVERLEAF GROUP

1115 Broadway
12th Floor
New York, NY USA 10010
E-mail: info@cloverleafgroup.eu
Website: www.cloverleafgroup.eu

Other Offices

6 avenue des Citronniers
Les Acanthes
Monte Carlo, Monaco 98000

Type of Firm

Private Equity Firm

Project Preferences

Type of Financing Preferred:
Leveraged Buyout
Early Stage
Expansion
Generalist PE
Balanced
Turnaround
Later Stage
Management Buyouts
Acquisition
Distressed Debt

Size of Investments Considered:
Min Size of Investment Considered (000s): $2,000
Max Size of Investment Considered (000s): $10,000

Industry Preferences

In Medical/Health prefer:
Medical/Health
Health Services

Additional Information

Year Founded: 2011
Current Activity Level : Actively seeking new investments

CLS CAPITAL LTD

10-11 Park Place
London, United Kingdom SW1A 1LP
Phone: 442071484499
Fax: 442074998087
E-mail: nfo@clscapital.com

Other Offices

24th Flr
1040, Avenue of the Americas
New York, NY USA 10018
Phone: 12127649200

Management and Staff

Andrey Kozlov, Managing Director
Nikolay Danilov, Founder
Sergei Petukhov, Managing Director

Type of Firm

Private Equity Firm

Project Preferences

Type of Financing Preferred:
Early Stage
Expansion
Balanced
Later Stage

Geographical Preferences

United States Preferences:
All U.S.

International Preferences:
United Kingdom
Europe
Russia

Industry Preferences

In Biotechnology prefer:
Biotechnology

In Medical/Health prefer:
Medical Diagnostics
Medical Products

Additional Information

Year Founded: 2010
Current Activity Level : Actively seeking new investments

CLSA CAPITAL PARTNERS HK LTD

89, Queensway
19F, Tower II, Lippo Centre
Hong Kong, Hong Kong
Phone: 85226008888
Fax: 85228680189
E-mail: capital.partners@clsa.com

Other Offices

Room 910, 9/F
100 Century Avenue, Pudong New Area
Shanghai, China 200120
Phone: 86-21-2020-5888
Fax: 86-21-2020-5666

8/F Dalamal House
Nariman Point
Mumbai, India 400 021
Phone: 91-22-5650-5050
Fax: 91-22-2284-0271

20 Hunter Street
Level 15, CLSA House
Sydney, Australia NSW 2000
Phone: 612-8571-4200
Fax: 612-9221-1188

Unit 10-12, Level 25, China World Twr 2
1 Jian Guo Men Wai Ave.
Beijing, China 100004
Phone: 86-10-6505-0248
Fax: 86-10-6505-2209

Shiodome Sumitomo Building 14F
1-9-2, Higashi-Shimbashi, Minato-ku
Tokyo, Japan 105-0021
Phone: 81-3-4580-5050
Fax: 81-3-4580-5251

Management and Staff

Byron Zhao, Managing Director
Chris Boyle, Managing Director
Christopher Seaver, Chief Executive Officer
David Cheung, Chief Financial Officer
Hirotaka Uchiyama, Managing Director
Jit Meng Ng, Managing Director
John Pattar, Managing Director
Megumi Kiyozuka, Managing Director
Miranda Tang, Managing Director
Naotsugu Saito, Managing Director
Peter Min, Managing Director
Peter Kennedy, Managing Director
Randy Wilbert, Chief Operating Officer
Stephane Delatte, Managing Director
Thomas Tan, Managing Director

Type of Firm

Investment Management Firm

Association Membership

Hong Kong Venture Capital Association (HKVCA)
Singapore Venture Capital Association (SVCA)

Project Preferences

Type of Financing Preferred:
Expansion
Mezzanine
Balanced

Size of Investments Considered:
Min Size of Investment Considered (000s): $25,000
Max Size of Investment Considered (000s): $75,000

Geographical Preferences

International Preferences:
Asia Pacific
Taiwan
Australia
Asia
Japan

Industry Preferences

In Medical/Health prefer:
Medical/Health

In Consumer Related prefer:
Consumer
Retail
Food/Beverage
Consumer Products
Education Related

In Industrial/Energy prefer:
Energy

In Financial Services prefer:
Real Estate

In Manufact. prefer:
Manufacturing

In Utilities prefer:
Utilities

Additional Information

Name of Most Recent Fund: Fudo Capital III, L.P.
Most Recent Fund Was Raised: 03/10/2014
Year Founded: 1995
Capital Under Management: $2,700,000,000
Current Activity Level : Actively seeking new investments

CLUB AUTO SPORT SILICON VALLEY L L C

521 Charcot Avenue
San Jose, CA USA 95131
Phone: 4087701200
Website: www.clubautosport.net

Management and Staff

John Davis, Founder
Ralph Borelli, Founder

Type of Firm

Incubator/Development Program

Project Preferences

Type of Financing Preferred:
Seed

Geographical Preferences

United States Preferences:
All U.S.

Industry Preferences

In Industrial/Energy prefer:
Energy Conservation Relat

In Transportation prefer:
Transportation

Additional Information

Year Founded: 2010
Current Activity Level : Actively seeking new investments

CLUB DIGITALE SRL

Via Timavo, 34
Milano, Italy 20124
Website: clubdigitale.it

Type of Firm

Private Equity Firm

Project Preferences

Type of Financing Preferred:
Start-up Financing
Seed
Startup

Geographical Preferences

International Preferences:
Italy

Industry Preferences

In Computer Software prefer:
Software

In Internet Specific prefer:
E-Commerce Technology
Internet

Additional Information
Year Founded: 2015
Current Activity Level : Actively seeking new investments

CLYDESDALE BANK PLC
30 St. Vincent Place
Glasgow, United Kingdom G1 2HL
Phone: 441419517320
Website: www.cbonline.co.uk

Management and Staff
David Thorburn, Chief Executive Officer
Scott Butterworth, Chief Financial Officer

Type of Firm
Bank Affiliated

Project Preferences
Type of Financing Preferred:
Balanced

Geographical Preferences
International Preferences:
Europe

Additional Information
Year Founded: 1838
Current Activity Level : Actively seeking new investments

CM CIC INVESTISSEMENT SA
4 Rue Gaillon
Paris, France 75002
Phone: 33142667663
Website: www.cmcic-investissement.com

Other Offices
28 avenue de l'Opera
Paris, France 75002
Phone: 33-1-4266-7959

2 bis rue Duguay Trouin
Rouen, France 76000
Phone: 33-2-3508-6406

33 avenue Le Corbusier
Lille, France 59000
Phone: 33-3-2012-6729

4 Place Andre Maginot
Nancy, France 84000
Phone: 33-3-8334-5192

31 rue Jean Wenger-Valentin
Strasbourg, France 67000
Phone: 33-3-8837-7485

Management and Staff
Antoine Jarmak, Chief Executive Officer
Sydney Cabessa, Chief Executive Officer

Type of Firm
Private Equity Firm

Association Membership
French Venture Capital Association (AFIC)

Project Preferences
Type of Financing Preferred:
Leveraged Buyout
Early Stage
Generalist PE
Later Stage
Acquisition

Size of Investments Considered:
Min Size of Investment Considered (000s): $635
Max Size of Investment Considered (000s): $127,032

Geographical Preferences
United States Preferences:
All U.S.

International Preferences:
Europe
Asia
France

Industry Preferences
In Communications prefer:
Communications and Media

In Computer Software prefer:
Software

In Medical/Health prefer:
Health Services
Hospitals/Clinics/Primary

In Consumer Related prefer:
Retail

In Industrial/Energy prefer:
Industrial Products

In Financial Services prefer:
Real Estate

In Business Serv. prefer:
Services

Additional Information
Year Founded: 1956
Current Activity Level : Actively seeking new investments

CM CIC MEZZANINE SAS
60, rue de la Victoire
Paris, France 75009
Phone: 33153483512
Fax: 3342668082
E-mail: cicmezzanine@cic.fr

Management and Staff
Francois Petit, President

Type of Firm
Bank Affiliated

Association Membership
French Venture Capital Association (AFIC)

Project Preferences
Type of Financing Preferred:
Leveraged Buyout
Mezzanine
Management Buyouts
Recapitalizations

Size of Investments Considered:
Min Size of Investment Considered (000s): $3,741
Max Size of Investment Considered (000s): $24,943

Geographical Preferences
International Preferences:
Europe
France

Additional Information
Year Founded: 2003
Capital Under Management: $319,490,000
Current Activity Level : Actively seeking new investments

CM EQUITY PARTNERS LP
900 Third Avenue, 33rd Floor
New York, NY USA 10022
Phone: 2129098400
Fax: 2123717254
Website: www.cmequity.com

Management and Staff
Daniel Colon, Partner
Joel Jacks, Managing Partner
Peter Schulte, Managing Partner
Robert Hopkins, Managing Partner
Robert Speer, Chief Financial Officer
Wesley Gaus, Partner

Type of Firm
Bank Affiliated

Project Preferences
Type of Financing Preferred:
Leveraged Buyout
Acquisition

Geographical Preferences
United States Preferences:

Canadian Preferences:
All Canada

Industry Focus
(% based on actual investment)
Other Products	97.8%
Communications and Media	1.4%
Internet Specific	0.8%

CM-CIC CAPITAL PRIVE SA

28, Avenue De L'Opera
Paris, France 75002
Phone: 33142667959
Fax: 33142667086
E-mail: info@cic.fr
Website: www.cmciccapitalprive.com

Management and Staff
Helen Mareschal, Chief Executive Officer

Type of Firm
Bank Affiliated

Association Membership
French Venture Capital Association (AFIC)

Project Preferences

Type of Financing Preferred:
Leveraged Buyout
Early Stage
Generalist PE
Later Stage
Management Buyouts
Acquisition
Startup

Geographical Preferences

International Preferences:
Europe
France

Industry Preferences

In Communications prefer:
Telecommunications
Media and Entertainment
Publishing

In Computer Hardware prefer:
Integrated Turnkey System

In Computer Software prefer:
Software

In Internet Specific prefer:
Internet

In Biotechnology prefer:
Biotechnology

In Medical/Health prefer:
Medical/Health
Health Services

In Industrial/Energy prefer:
Energy
Industrial Products
Environmental Related

In Business Serv. prefer:
Services
Distribution
Consulting Services
Media

In Agr/Forestr/Fish prefer:
Agriculture related

In Other prefer:
Environment Responsible

Additional Information
Year Founded: 1990
Capital Under Management: $22,100,000
Current Activity Level : Actively seeking new investments

CMA VENTURES INC

2600 Grand Avenue
Suite 410
Des Moines, IA USA 50312
Phone: 5153093018
E-mail: info@cmaventures.net
Website: www.cmaventures.net

Type of Firm
Private Equity Firm

Project Preferences

Type of Financing Preferred:
Balanced

Geographical Preferences

United States Preferences:
Midwest
Iowa

Industry Preferences

In Computer Software prefer:
Software

Additional Information
Year Founded: 1969
Current Activity Level : Actively seeking new investments

CMB ADVISORY PTY LTD

PO Box K421
Haymarket Post Shop
Sydney, Australia 2000
Phone: 61280781600
E-mail: info@cmbcapital.com.au
Website: www.cmbcapital.com.au

Management and Staff
Jamie Olsen, Founder

Type of Firm
Investment Management Firm

Project Preferences

Type of Financing Preferred:
Balanced

Industry Preferences

In Internet Specific prefer:
Internet

Additional Information
Year Founded: 2010

CMBIGROUP

10655 Northeast Fourth Street
Suite 706
Bellevue, WA USA 98004
Phone: 2067934063
Fax: 2066225161
Website: www.cmbigroup.net

Management and Staff
Aaron Stolpman, Partner
Mike Cadigan, Partner
Shane Cadigan, Partner

Type of Firm
Private Equity Firm

Project Preferences

Type of Financing Preferred:
Leveraged Buyout

Geographical Preferences

United States Preferences:
Oregon
West Coast
Idaho
Washington

Canadian Preferences:
All Canada

Industry Preferences

In Consumer Related prefer:
Retail

In Business Serv. prefer:
Services
Distribution

In Manufact. prefer:
Manufacturing

Additional Information
Year Founded: 1994
Current Activity Level : Actively seeking new investments

Additional Information
Name of Most Recent Fund: CM Equity Partners, L.P.
Most Recent Fund Was Raised: 04/16/1997
Year Founded: 1992
Current Activity Level : Actively seeking new investments

CMEA DEVELOPMENT COMPANY LLC

One Letterman Drive
Building C, Suite CM500
San Francisco, CA USA 94129
Phone: 4153521520
Fax: 4153521524
Website: www.cmea.com

Management and Staff

Andy Perlman, Venture Partner
David Tuckerman, Venture Partner
David Collier, Managing Director
Erick Sebusch, Partner
Faysal Sohail, General Partner
James Watson, Managing Partner
Jim Larrick, Venture Partner
Jim Hornthal, Venture Partner
John Haag, Chief Operating Officer
Karl Handelsman, Managing Director
Maurice Gunderson, Venture Partner
Michael Melnick, Venture Partner
Rachel Sheinbein, Partner
Saad Khan, Partner
Thomas Baruch, Partner

Type of Firm

Private Equity Firm

Project Preferences

Role in Financing:
Will function either as deal originator or investor in deals created by others

Industry Focus

(% based on actual investment)

Biotechnology	22.9%
Medical/Health	18.4%
Semiconductors/Other Elect.	13.3%
Computer Software and Services	12.1%
Industrial/Energy	12.1%
Other Products	10.4%
Internet Specific	4.9%
Communications and Media	4.0%
Computer Hardware	1.8%

Additional Information

Name of Most Recent Fund: Presidio Partners 2007
Most Recent Fund Was Raised: 06/29/2007
Year Founded: 1989
Capital Under Management: $1,044,700,000
Current Activity Level : Actively seeking new investments
Method of Compensation: Return on investment is of primary concern, do not charge fees

CMIA CAPITAL PARTNERS PTE LTD

1 Kim Seng Promenade
#13-08 Great World City West
Singapore, Singapore 237994
Phone: 6562361288
Fax: 6565366316
E-mail: contactus@cmia.com
Website: www.cmia.com

Other Offices

8 Connaught Road Central
Suite 1606, Chater House
Central, Hong Kong
Phone: 852-2251-1968
Fax: 852-2849-4185

No. 233 Taicang Road
Platinum, 20/F Unit 4, Luwan
Shanghai, China
Phone: 86-21-6141-5788
Fax: 86-21-6141-5700

Management and Staff

Chong Min Lee, Managing Partner
Esther Laska, Partner
Jimmy Wang, Partner
Kian Woon Yap, Partner
Lee Li Meng, Principal
Yong Ho Hsiang, Chief Financial Officer

Type of Firm

Private Equity Firm

Association Membership

Emerging Markets Private Equity Association
Singapore Venture Capital Association (SVCA)

Project Preferences

Type of Financing Preferred:
Leveraged Buyout
Expansion

Geographical Preferences

International Preferences:
Asia
Singapore

Industry Preferences

In Biotechnology prefer:
Biotechnology
Agricultural/Animal Bio.

In Medical/Health prefer:
Medical/Health
Pharmaceuticals

In Consumer Related prefer:
Consumer

In Industrial/Energy prefer:
Industrial Products
Environmental Related

In Transportation prefer:
Transportation

In Manufact. prefer:
Manufacturing

In Agr/Forestr/Fish prefer:
Agribusiness
Mining and Minerals

Additional Information

Year Founded: 2003
Capital Under Management: $200,000
Current Activity Level : Actively seeking new investments

CMP CAPITAL MANAGEMENT PARTNERS GMBH

Leipziger Platz 15
Mosse Palais
Berlin, Germany 10117
Phone: 49303940690
Fax: 493039406925
E-mail: kontakt@cm-p.de
Website: www.cm-p.de

Management and Staff

Kai Brandes, Managing Partner
Ludger Vonnahme, Managing Partner

Type of Firm

Private Equity Firm

Project Preferences

Type of Financing Preferred:
Leveraged Buyout
Turnaround
Special Situation

Geographical Preferences

International Preferences:
Switzerland
Austria
Germany

Industry Preferences

In Medical/Health prefer:
Medical/Health

In Consumer Related prefer:
Consumer
Food/Beverage

In Industrial/Energy prefer:
Industrial Products
Machinery

Additional Information

Name of Most Recent Fund: CMP German Opportunity Fund II
Most Recent Fund Was Raised: 03/31/2011
Year Founded: 2000
Capital Under Management: $531,006,000
Current Activity Level : Actively seeking new investments

CMS MEZZANINE FUND

308 East Lancaster Avenue
Suite 300
Wynnewood, PA USA 19096
Phone: 6108962080
Fax: 6108963339
Website: www.cmsmezz.com

Management and Staff

David Clapper, Chief Financial Officer
Morey Goldberg, Managing Director
Paul Silberberg, President
William Landman, Chief Executive Officer

Type of Firm

Investment Management Firm

Project Preferences

Type of Financing Preferred:
Leveraged Buyout
Mezzanine
Generalist PE
Later Stage

Additional Information

Year Founded: 1969
Capital Under Management: $1,000,000,000
Current Activity Level : Actively seeking new investments

CMS OPUS PRIVATE EQUITY SDN BHD

Level 33 Suite A Menara Maxis
Kuala Lumpur City Centre
Kuala Lumpur, Malaysia 50088
Phone: 603-2031-9008
Fax: 603-2031-4008

Type of Firm

Private Equity Firm

Association Membership

Malaysian Venture Capital Association

Additional Information

Year Founded: 2009
Current Activity Level : Actively seeking new investments

CN PRIVATE EQUITY PARTNERS

900 Third Avenue
19th Floor
New York, NY USA 10022
Phone: 212-418-9600
Fax: 212-308-6623
E-mail: info@columbusnova.com
Website: www.columbusnova.com

Other Offices

Former HQ: 153 East 53rd Street
58th Floor
New York, NY USA 10022
Phone: 212-418-9600
Fax: 212-308-6623

Management and Staff

Jason Epstein, Partner
Jay Haft, Partner
Ji Ham, Vice President
Paul Lipari, Partner

Type of Firm

Investment Management Firm

Project Preferences

Type of Financing Preferred:
Leveraged Buyout
Expansion
Recapitalizations

Geographical Preferences

United States Preferences:

Canadian Preferences:
All Canada

Industry Preferences

In Consumer Related prefer:
Entertainment and Leisure
Consumer Products
Consumer Services
Education Related

In Industrial/Energy prefer:
Energy

In Business Serv. prefer:
Media

In Manufact. prefer:
Manufacturing

In Utilities prefer:
Utilities

Additional Information

Year Founded: 2005
Current Activity Level : Actively seeking new investments

CNF INVESTMENTS LLC

c/o Clark Enterprises, Inc
7500 Old Georgetown Road, 15/F
Bethesda, MD USA 20814
Phone: 3016577100
Fax: 3016577263
E-mail: cnfinvestments@clarkus.com
Website: www.clarkenterprisesinc.com

Management and Staff

Jennifer Hsin, Chief Financial Officer
Joe Del Guercio, Managing Director
Robert Flanagan, Managing Director

Type of Firm

Private Equity Firm

Association Membership

Mid-Atlantic Venture Association

Project Preferences

Type of Financing Preferred:
Early Stage
Expansion
Balanced
Later Stage

Geographical Preferences

United States Preferences:

Industry Preferences

In Communications prefer:
Communications and Media
Telecommunications

In Computer Software prefer:
Software

In Medical/Health prefer:
Medical Products

In Consumer Related prefer:
Consumer Products

In Industrial/Energy prefer:
Energy
Oil and Gas Exploration
Alternative Energy

In Financial Services prefer:
Financial Services

Additional Information

Year Founded: 1997
Capital Under Management: $225,000,000
Current Activity Level : Actively seeking new investments

CNSTAR CAPITAL PTE LTD

No. 375 Sung-Chiang Road
Room 3F-1
Taipei, Taiwan 104
Phone: 886-2-2506-6227
E-mail: Client.First@cnstar.com.tw
Website: www.cnstar.com.tw

Other Offices

63 Market Street
#09-02
Singapore, Singapore 048942
Phone: 65-6837-0568
Fax: 65-6837-2660

88 Zhangyang Road, Pudong
Room 604, Binjiang Mansion
Shanghai, China 200122
Phone: 86-21-5840-3619
Fax: 86-21-5840-7161

Management and Staff
Frank Shen, Managing Partner
Gary Ting, Managing Partner

Type of Firm
Bank Affiliated

Project Preferences
Type of Financing Preferred:
Early Stage
Later Stage

Size of Investments Considered:
Min Size of Investment Considered (000s): $1,000
Max Size of Investment Considered (000s): $10,000

Geographical Preferences
International Preferences:
China

Industry Preferences
In Communications prefer:
Communications and Media
Commercial Communications

In Computer Software prefer:
Software

In Internet Specific prefer:
Ecommerce
Web Aggregation/Portals

In Biotechnology prefer:
Biotechnology

In Medical/Health prefer:
Medical/Health

In Consumer Related prefer:
Consumer

In Industrial/Energy prefer:
Environmental Related

Additional Information
Year Founded: 2005
Current Activity Level : Actively seeking new investments

CNSTONE

No. 555 West Nanjing Road
Room 605, Jingan District
Shanghai, China 200041
Phone: 86-21-6253-5602
Fax: 86-21-6253-5361
Website: www.cnstone-pb.com

Type of Firm
Private Equity Advisor or Fund of Funds

Project Preferences
Type of Financing Preferred:
Fund of Funds
Balanced

Geographical Preferences
International Preferences:
China

Industry Preferences
In Consumer Related prefer:
Consumer
Retail

Additional Information
Year Founded: 2009
Capital Under Management: $439,500,000
Current Activity Level : Actively seeking new investments

CO INVESTOR AG

Kreuzstrasse 26
Zuerich, Switzerland 8008
Phone: 41435216111
Fax: 41435216110
E-mail: office@co-investor.com
Website: www.co-investor.com

Management and Staff
Farsin Yadergardjam, Partner
Nicolai von Engelhardt, Managing Partner
Thomas Hoch, Partner

Type of Firm
Private Equity Firm

Association Membership
Swiss Venture Capital Association (SECA)

Project Preferences
Type of Financing Preferred:
Early Stage
Mezzanine
Later Stage
Management Buyouts

Size of Investments Considered:
Min Size of Investment Considered (000s): $1,859
Max Size of Investment Considered (000s): $27,882

Geographical Preferences
International Preferences:
Switzerland
Austria
Germany

Industry Preferences
In Computer Software prefer:
Software

In Semiconductor/Electr prefer:
Electronics

In Medical/Health prefer:
Medical/Health

In Consumer Related prefer:
Food/Beverage
Consumer Products

In Industrial/Energy prefer:
Energy
Industrial Products
Environmental Related

In Manufact. prefer:
Manufacturing

Additional Information
Year Founded: 2000
Capital Under Management: $167,700,000
Current Activity Level : Actively seeking new investments

COACH & CAPITAL NORDIC 1 AB

Birger Jarlsgatan 37
Stockholm, Sweden 111 45
Phone: 46707296404
Website: www.coachandcapital.se

Management and Staff
Anders Ingestrom, Managing Partner

Type of Firm
Private Equity Firm

Project Preferences
Type of Financing Preferred:
Early Stage
Seed
Startup

Size of Investments Considered:
Min Size of Investment Considered (000s): $150
Max Size of Investment Considered (000s): $1,500

Geographical Preferences
International Preferences:
Sweden

Industry Preferences
In Communications prefer:
Communications and Media
Commercial Communications
Telecommunications

In Internet Specific prefer:
Internet

In Computer Other prefer:
Computer Related

In Semiconductor/Electr prefer:
Electronics

In Biotechnology prefer:
Biotechnology

In Medical/Health prefer:
Medical/Health
Pharmaceuticals

In Industrial/Energy prefer:
Energy
Industrial Products

Additional Information
Year Founded: 2007
Capital Under Management: $11,000,000
Current Activity Level : Actively seeking new investments

COAST INVESTMENT AND DEVELOPMENT CO KSCP

Shuhada Street
Coast Bldg., Al Sharq Area
Safat, Kuwait 13128
Phone: 96522230510
Fax: 96522415364
E-mail: cidco@coast.com.kw
Website: www.coast.com.kw

Management and Staff
Khalid Al Usaimi, Chief Executive Officer

Type of Firm
Private Equity Firm

Project Preferences

Type of Financing Preferred:
Early Stage
Generalist PE
Later Stage
Acquisition

Industry Preferences

In Financial Services prefer:
Real Estate

Additional Information
Year Founded: 1975
Current Activity Level : Actively seeking new investments

COAST2COAST INVESTMENTS PTY LTD

Unit C7 & C8, Westlake Square
Westlake
Cape Town, South Africa 7945
Phone: 27-21-701-2232
Fax: 27-86-510-8865
E-mail: info@coast2coast.co.za
Website: coast2coast.co.za

Management and Staff
Cris Dillon, Chief Operating Officer
Gary Shayne, Chief Executive Officer

Type of Firm
Private Equity Firm

Association Membership
South African Venture Capital Association (SAVCA)

Project Preferences

Type of Financing Preferred:
Leveraged Buyout
Acquisition

Geographical Preferences

International Preferences:
South Africa
Africa

Industry Preferences

In Consumer Related prefer:
Consumer
Food/Beverage
Consumer Products

In Financial Services prefer:
Real Estate

In Business Serv. prefer:
Distribution

In Manufact. prefer:
Manufacturing

Additional Information
Year Founded: 2006
Current Activity Level : Actively seeking new investments

COASTLINE CAPITAL LLC

244 Fifth Avenue
Suite C-225
New York, NY USA 10001
Phone: 5164962256
E-mail: cstein@coastlinecapital.com
Website: www.coastlinecapital.com

Type of Firm
Private Equity Firm

Project Preferences

Type of Financing Preferred:
Leveraged Buyout
Special Situation
Recapitalizations

Geographical Preferences

United States Preferences:

Canadian Preferences:
All Canada

Industry Preferences

In Consumer Related prefer:
Retail
Consumer Services

In Industrial/Energy prefer:
Industrial Products

In Business Serv. prefer:
Distribution

In Manufact. prefer:
Manufacturing

Additional Information
Year Founded: 1999
Current Activity Level : Actively seeking new investments

COATUE MANAGEMENT LLC

9 West 57th Street
25th Floor
New York, NY USA 10019
Website: www.coatue.com

Management and Staff
Philippe Laffont, Founder

Type of Firm
Investment Management Firm

Project Preferences

Type of Financing Preferred:
Early Stage
Expansion
Balanced
Later Stage

Industry Preferences

In Communications prefer:
Telecommunications

In Transportation prefer:
Aerospace

Additional Information
Year Founded: 1999
Current Activity Level : Actively seeking new investments

COBE EQUITIES LLC

708 Third Avenue, 31st Floor
New York, NY USA 10017
Phone: 2123380235
E-mail: info@CoBeCapital.com
Website: www.cobecapital.com

Other Offices
Gieberallee 19, Willich
, Germany 47877
Phone: 49-70-0476-30000

Management and Staff
Darren McKenzie Chaffee, Managing Director
Neal Cohen, Founder
Thomas Kermorgant, Managing Director

Type of Firm
Private Equity Firm

Industry Preferences

In Consumer Related prefer:
Education Related

In Transportation prefer:
Transportation

In Financial Services prefer:
Real Estate

Additional Information
Year Founded: 1994
Current Activity Level : Actively seeking new investments

COBURN VENTURES LLC

Ten Chestnut Street
Pleasantville, NY USA 10570
E-mail: info@coburnventures.com
Website: coburnventures.com

Management and Staff
Adam Emrich, Partner
Dave Bujnowski, Partner
David Harvey, Chief Operating Officer
Faye Hou, Partner
Fazia Merhai, Founder
Pip Coburn, Founder

Type of Firm
Private Equity Firm

Project Preferences

Type of Financing Preferred:
Balanced

Geographical Preferences

United States Preferences:

Additional Information
Year Founded: 2005
Current Activity Level : Actively seeking new investments

COCO SPACE INVESTMENT (SHANGHAI) CO LTD

No.600, No.615, Ningqiao Road
Jinqiao Export Process Zone
Shanghai, China
Fax: 862150301286
Website: www.cocospace.com.cn

Type of Firm
Private Equity Firm

Project Preferences

Type of Financing Preferred:
Early Stage

Geographical Preferences

International Preferences:
China

Industry Preferences

In Other prefer:
Environment Responsible

Additional Information
Year Founded: 2013
Current Activity Level : Actively seeking new investments

COCOON CAPITAL PTE LTD

20 Upper Circular Road
#02-10/12
The Riverwalk, Singapore

Type of Firm
Private Equity Firm

Project Preferences

Type of Financing Preferred:
Early Stage

Geographical Preferences

United States Preferences:
Southeast

International Preferences:
India

Additional Information
Year Founded: 2016
Capital Under Management: $7,030,000
Current Activity Level : Actively seeking new investments

COELI PRIVATE EQUITY MANAGEMENT AB

Vasagatan 11
Stockholm, Sweden 11120
Phone: 46854591640
Fax: 46854591641
E-mail: info@coelipe.se

Management and Staff
Karl-Anders Falk, Chief Executive Officer

Type of Firm
Private Equity Advisor or Fund of Funds

Association Membership
Swedish Venture Capital Association (SVCA)
European Private Equity and Venture Capital Assoc.

Project Preferences

Type of Financing Preferred:
Fund of Funds

Geographical Preferences

International Preferences:
Scandanavia/Nordic Region

Additional Information
Year Founded: 2006
Current Activity Level : Actively seeking new investments

COENT VENTURE PARTNERS PTE. LTD.

79 Emerald Hill Road
Singapore, Singapore 29355
Website: www.coent.sg

Other Offices
10 Anson Road
#13-13Am Int'l Plaza
, Singapore

Type of Firm
Private Equity Firm

Project Preferences

Type of Financing Preferred:
Balanced
Seed

Geographical Preferences

International Preferences:
Asia

Additional Information
Year Founded: 1969
Current Activity Level : Actively seeking new investments

COFIRI SPA

26 Via Compagni
Rome, Italy 00187
Phone: 39-06-47-331
Fax: 39-0-6853-31410
E-mail: e.arduini@cofiri.it

Management and Staff
Alfredo De Marzio, President

Type of Firm
Bank Affiliated

Project Preferences

Type of Financing Preferred:
Early Stage
Startup

Geographical Preferences

International Preferences:
Italy

Industry Preferences

In Communications prefer:
Telecommunications

In Biotechnology prefer:
Biotechnology

In Industrial/Energy prefer:
Energy
Materials

In Transportation prefer:
Transportation

Additional Information

Year Founded: 1999
Capital Under Management: $13,500,000
Current Activity Level : Actively seeking new investments

COFOUNDERS CAPITAL MANAGEMENT LLC

122 East Chatham Street
Suite 301
Cary, NC USA 27511
Website: cofounderscapital.com

Other Offices

102 Anna Lake Lane
Cary, NC USA 27513
Phone: 919-244-3048

Type of Firm

Incubator/Development Program

Project Preferences

Type of Financing Preferred:
Seed
Startup

Geographical Preferences

International Preferences:
Western Europe

Additional Information

Year Founded: 2015
Capital Under Management: $10,700,000
Current Activity Level : Actively seeking new investments

COGNITE VENTURES LLC

210 Mission Street
Santa Cruz, CA USA 95060
Phone: +1 408 334 036
E-mail: info@cogniteventures.com
Website: www.cogniteventures.com

Type of Firm

Corporate PE/Venture

Project Preferences

Type of Financing Preferred:
Startup

Additional Information

Year Founded: 2018
Current Activity Level : Actively seeking new investments

COGNITIVE CAPITAL PARTNERS LLC

250 North Michigan Avenue
Suite 2000
Chicago, IL USA 60601
Phone: 3122686012
Fax: 3122768678
Website: www.cognitivecap.com

Type of Firm

Private Equity Firm

Project Preferences

Type of Financing Preferred:
Leveraged Buyout
Management Buyouts
Recapitalizations

Industry Preferences

In Communications prefer:
Telecommunications

In Medical/Health prefer:
Health Services

In Consumer Related prefer:
Consumer
Retail

In Industrial/Energy prefer:
Energy
Environmental Related

In Financial Services prefer:
Insurance
Financial Services

In Business Serv. prefer:
Services
Consulting Services

In Manufact. prefer:
Manufacturing

In Utilities prefer:
Utilities

Additional Information

Year Founded: 2006
Current Activity Level : Actively seeking new investments

COGR INC

200 Park Avenue
20th Floor
New York, NY USA 10166
Phone: 2123705600
Fax: 2126824195
Website: www.cortecgroup.com

Management and Staff

David Schnadig, Managing Partner
Eugene Nesbeda, Partner
Jack Miner, Vice President
James Tucker, Vice President
Jeffrey Shannon, Managing Director
Jeffrey Lipsitz, Managing Partner
Jeremy Lack, Managing Director
Jonathan Stein, Partner
Michael Najjar, Partner
R. Scott Schafler, Managing Partner
Robert Whipple, Managing Director

Type of Firm

Private Equity Firm

Project Preferences

Type of Financing Preferred:
Acquisition
Recapitalizations

Geographical Preferences

United States Preferences:

Industry Focus

(% based on actual investment)
Industrial/Energy	69.9%
Consumer Related	21.0%
Biotechnology	4.0%
Semiconductors/Other Elect.	4.0%
Other Products	1.1%

Additional Information

Name of Most Recent Fund: Cortec Group Fund V, L.P.
Most Recent Fund Was Raised: 12/17/2010
Year Founded: 1984
Capital Under Management: $560,000,000
Current Activity Level : Actively seeking new investments

COHEN & COMPANY FINANCIAL LTD

23, College Hill
6th Floor
London, United Kingdom EC4R 2RP
Phone: 442035406000
Fax: 442035406001
Website: www.cohenandcompany.com

Other Offices
40, Avenue Monterey
Luxembourg, Luxembourg L2163
Phone: 3524967671

Management and Staff
Edward Cahill, Managing Director
Gareth Noonan, Managing Director
Henrik Woergaard, Managing Director
Jason Wolfe, Managing Director
Linda Koster, Managing Director
Paul Vernhes, Managing Director
Sherjeel Khan, Managing Director

Type of Firm
Bank Affiliated

Project Preferences

Type of Financing Preferred:
Leveraged Buyout
Early Stage
Expansion
Mezzanine
Later Stage
Management Buyouts
Acquisition

Additional Information
Year Founded: 2006
Capital Under Management: $55,050,000
Current Activity Level : Actively seeking new investments

COHEN PRIVATE VENTURES LLC

72 Cummings Point Road
Stamford, CT USA 06902

Type of Firm
Private Equity Firm

Project Preferences

Type of Financing Preferred:
Generalist PE

Additional Information
Year Founded: 2017
Current Activity Level : Actively seeking new investments

COHESIVE CAPITAL PARTNERS

650 Fifth Avenue
31st Floor
New York, NY USA 10019
Phone: 2126169678
Fax: 2126169676
Website: www.cohesivecapital.com

Management and Staff
Anthony Bienstock, Partner
Gregory Angrist, Partner
John Barber, Managing Partner

Type of Firm
Private Equity Firm

Project Preferences

Type of Financing Preferred:
Leveraged Buyout
Management Buyouts
Acquisition
Recapitalizations

Additional Information
Name of Most Recent Fund: Cohesive Capital Partners, L.P.
Most Recent Fund Was Raised: 11/23/2010
Year Founded: 2011
Capital Under Management: $476,653,000
Current Activity Level : Actively seeking new investments

COLLABORATIVE CAPITAL L L C

535 Park Avenue
New York, NY USA 10065
Phone: 212-421-5007
Fax: 212-599-2287
Website: www.elvey.com

Other Offices
1819 Polk Street
Suite 133
San Francisco, CA USA 94109
Fax: 2675432801

Management and Staff
Gavin Beekman, Partner
Gene Spence, Partner
Malcolm Elvey, Principal
Matthew Elvey, Partner

Type of Firm
Service Provider

Project Preferences

Role in Financing:
Prefer role in deals created by others

Type of Financing Preferred:
Early Stage

Size of Investments Considered:
Min Size of Investment Considered (000s): $50
Max Size of Investment Considered (000s): $250

Geographical Preferences

United States Preferences:

Industry Preferences

In Internet Specific prefer:
Internet

In Medical/Health prefer:
Health Services

In Consumer Related prefer:
Retail

In Transportation prefer:
Transportation

In Financial Services prefer:
Financial Services

Additional Information
Year Founded: 1999
Capital Under Management: $2,200,000
Current Activity Level : Actively seeking new investments
Method of Compensation: Return on invest. most important, but chg. closing fees, service fees, etc.

COLLABORATIVE FUND

400 Park Avenue
21st Floor
New York, NY USA 10022
Phone: 4154138360
E-mail: info@collabfund.com
Website: www.collaborativefund.com

Management and Staff
Douglas Smith, Venture Partner
Rachel Botsman, Venture Partner

Type of Firm
Private Equity Firm

Project Preferences

Type of Financing Preferred:
Startup

Industry Preferences

In Communications prefer:
Wireless Communications

In Internet Specific prefer:
Internet

Additional Information
Name of Most Recent Fund: Collaborative II, L.P.
Most Recent Fund Was Raised: 03/01/2013
Year Founded: 2010

Capital Under Management: $98,125,000
Current Activity Level : Actively seeking new investments

COLLABORATIVE SEED AND GROWTH PARTNERS LLC

1340 Centre Street
Suite 207
Newton, MA USA 02459
Phone: 6179693066

Management and Staff
Walter Winshall, Managing Director

Type of Firm
Private Equity Firm

Project Preferences

Type of Financing Preferred:
Early Stage
Expansion

Geographical Preferences

United States Preferences:
All U.S.

Additional Information
Name of Most Recent Fund: Alpha Technology Fund, LP
Most Recent Fund Was Raised: 01/10/2005
Year Founded: 2001
Capital Under Management: $1,300,000
Current Activity Level : Actively seeking new investments

COLLE CAPITAL

606 W 28th Street
Level 7
New York, NY USA 10001
E-mail: info@collecapital.com
Website: www.collecapital.com

Type of Firm
Private Equity Firm

Project Preferences

Type of Financing Preferred:
Early Stage

Industry Preferences

In Communications prefer:
Telecommunications

In Financial Services prefer:
Financial Services

Additional Information
Year Founded: 2015
Current Activity Level : Actively seeking new investments

COLLER CAPITAL LTD

33 Cavendish Square
London, United Kingdom W1G 0TT
Phone: 442076318500
Fax: 442076318555
Website: www.collercapital.com

Other Offices
950 Third Avenue
MANHATTAN, NY USA 10022
Phone: 212-644-8500
Fax: 212-644-9133

Eight Finance Street
Two International Finance Centre
Central, Hong Kong
Phone: 85222511594

Management and Staff
Amyn Hassanally, Partner
Ashley Johansen, Partner
Axel Hansing, Partner
Christopher McDermott, Partner
David Jolly, Partner
Edward Goldstein, Partner
Frank Ochsenfeld, Partner
Frank Morgan, Partner
Gerald Carton, Principal
Giovanni Orsi, Principal
Hiromichi Mizuno, Partner
Jonathan Freeman, Partner
Joseph Mahon, Partner
Krys Grudniewicz, Partner
Luca Salvato, Partner
Michael Alfano, Principal
Paige Brotherton, Partner
Paul Koffel, Partner
Paul Lanna, Partner
Peter Hutton, Partner
Peter Kim, Partner
Philipp Patschkowski, Principal
Remco Haaxman, Principal
Rune Munk, Partner
Sebastien Burdel, Partner
Stephen Ziff, Partner
Stephen Marquardt, Partner
Susan Flynn, Partner
Taro Morimoto, Principal
Timothy Jones, Chief Executive Officer

Type of Firm
Private Equity Advisor or Fund of Funds

Association Membership
Brazilian Venture Capital Association (ABCR)
Australian Venture Capital Association (AVCAL)
British Venture Capital Association (BVCA)
China Venture Capital Association
French Venture Capital Association (AFIC)
German Venture Capital Association (BVK)
Canadian Venture Capital Association
European Private Equity and Venture Capital Assoc.

Project Preferences

Type of Financing Preferred:
Fund of Funds
Fund of Funds of Second

Size of Investments Considered:
Min Size of Investment Considered (000s): $1,000
Max Size of Investment Considered: No Limit

Industry Focus

(% based on actual investment)
Other Products	49.1%
Biotechnology	10.9%
Medical/Health	9.5%
Computer Software and Services	9.0%
Communications and Media	7.1%
Internet Specific	5.2%
Semiconductors/Other Elect.	4.6%
Industrial/Energy	2.5%
Computer Hardware	1.8%
Consumer Related	0.2%

Additional Information
Name of Most Recent Fund: Coller International Partners VI, L.P.
Most Recent Fund Was Raised: 04/27/2011
Year Founded: 1990
Capital Under Management: $17,000,000,000
Current Activity Level : Actively seeking new investments

COLLINA VENTURES LLC

3548 Club Estates Drive
Carmel, IN USA 46033
Website: collinaventures.com

Management and Staff
Karen A. Hill, Managing Partner
Mark E. Hill, Managing Partner

Type of Firm
Private Equity Firm

Project Preferences

Type of Financing Preferred:
Early Stage

Geographical Preferences

United States Preferences:
Indiana

Additional Information
Year Founded: 1969
Current Activity Level : Actively seeking new investments

COLLINS PRIVATE EQUITY HOLDINGS PTY LTD

164 Springfield Road
Morningside
Durban, South Africa 4000
Phone: 27312086266
Fax: 27312086014

Type of Firm
Private Equity Firm

Association Membership
South African Venture Capital Association (SAVCA)

Project Preferences

Type of Financing Preferred:
Leveraged Buyout
Early Stage
Generalist PE
Balanced
Later Stage
Management Buyouts
Acquisition

Geographical Preferences

International Preferences:
South Africa
Africa

Additional Information
Year Founded: 2011
Capital Under Management: $22,710,000
Current Activity Level : Actively seeking new investments

COLONIAL FIRST STATE PRIVATE EQUITY PTY, LTD.

52 Martin Place
Level Six
Sydney, Australia 2000
Phone: 61293033000
Fax: 61293033200
E-mail: investments@colonialfirststate.com.au
Website: www.colonialfirststate.com.au

Management and Staff
Linda Elkins, Chief Executive Officer

Type of Firm
Private Equity Firm

Project Preferences

Role in Financing:
Prefer role as deal originator but will also invest in deals created by others

Type of Financing Preferred:
Expansion
Balanced
Later Stage

Geographical Preferences

International Preferences:
Pacific
Australia

Industry Focus
(% based on actual investment)
Other Products	41.9%
Computer Software and Services	24.6%
Medical/Health	13.2%
Consumer Related	8.3%
Communications and Media	4.5%
Internet Specific	2.5%
Computer Hardware	2.3%
Semiconductors/Other Elect.	1.5%
Biotechnology	1.0%
Industrial/Energy	0.3%

Additional Information
Name of Most Recent Fund: Diversified Private Equity Fund
Most Recent Fund Was Raised: 07/31/2001
Year Founded: 1984
Capital Under Management: $234,200,000
Current Activity Level : Actively seeking new investments
Method of Compensation: Return on investment is of primary concern, do not charge fees

COLONY CAPITAL LLC

2450 Broadway
Sixth Floor
Santa Monica, CA USA 90404
Phone: 3102828820

Other Offices

7 Savile Row
Second Floor
London, United Kingdom W1S 3PE
Phone: 44-20-7440-0500

3 Piazza Ara Coeli
Palazzo Pecci Blunt
Rome, Italy 00186
Phone: 390669941890

Foch Street
Second Floor, Building 230
Beirut, Lebanon
Phone: 9611985123

Two International Place
Suite 2500
BOSTON, MA USA 02110
Phone: 617-235-6300

No. 460 Hsin Yi Road, Section 4
16th Floor
Taipei, Taiwan 110
Phone: 886-227-2278-68

660 Madison Avenue
Suite 1600
NEW YORK, NY USA 10065
Phone: 212-230-3300

737 Yeoksam-dong, Gangnam-gu
16/F Gangnam Finance Center Building
Seoul, South Korea 135-984
Phone: 822-3468-2700

6, rue Christophe Colomb
Paris, France 75008
Phone: 33-1-5357-4600

No. 1 East Chang An Avenue, Dong Cheng
Unit 1901, 19/F, Tower E2 Oriental Plaza
Beijing , China 100738
Phone: 86-10-852-00596

11 Fernando el Santo
Madrid, Spain 28010
Phone: 34-91-308-2653

Management and Staff
Aleksandra Dubrova, Vice President
Allen Lau, Managing Director
Andrea Nicholas, Vice President
Andrew Goodman, Vice President
Andrew Witt, Vice President
Brian Lee, Vice President
Christian Fuqua, Vice President
Christophe De Taurines, Managing Director
Darren Tangen, Principal
David Belford, Vice President
David Monahan, Principal
Ed Dailey, Principal
Jinho Seo, Managing Director
Justin Chang, Principal
Kevin Traenkle, Principal
Paul Fuhrman, Principal
Richard Welch, Principal
Richard Nanula, Principal
Richard Saltzman, President
Ronald Sanders, Principal
Ryan McManus, Vice President
Sebastien Bazin, Principal
Sylvio Tabet, Managing Director
Thomas Harrison, Principal
Todd Sammann, Principal

Type of Firm
Private Equity Firm

Association Membership
French Venture Capital Association (AFIC)

Project Preferences

Type of Financing Preferred:
Opportunistic

Geographical Preferences

United States Preferences:
North America

International Preferences:
Europe
Middle East
Asia

Industry Preferences

In Financial Services prefer:
Real Estate

Additional Information
Year Founded: 1991
Current Activity Level : Actively seeking new investments

COLT VENTURES

2101 Cedar Springs Road
Suite 1230
Dallas, TX USA 75201
Phone: 2143970176
Website: www.coltventures.com

Type of Firm
Private Equity Firm

Industry Preferences

In Biotechnology prefer:
Biotechnology

In Industrial/Energy prefer:
Oil and Gas Exploration

In Financial Services prefer:
Real Estate

Additional Information
Year Founded: 2017
Current Activity Level : Actively seeking new investments

COLUMBIA CAPITAL GROUP, INC.

3924 Forest Drive
Suite 9
Columbia, SC USA 29204
Phone: 8037825666
Fax: 8037820056
E-mail: info@columbiacapitalgroup.com
Website: www.columbiacapitalgroup.com

Management and Staff
Lloyd Arrington, President
Richard Williams, Jr., Vice President

Type of Firm
Government Affiliated Program

Project Preferences

Role in Financing:
Prefer role as deal originator but will also invest in deals created by others

Type of Financing Preferred:
Second Stage Financing
Mezzanine
First Stage Financing

Geographical Preferences

United States Preferences:
D. of Columbia

Industry Focus
(% based on actual investment)
Communications and Media   53.8%
Semiconductors/Other Elect.   26.7%
Computer Software and Services 15.9%
Computer Hardware   3.5%

Additional Information
Year Founded: 1988
Capital Under Management: $10,000,000
Current Activity Level : Actively seeking new investments
Method of Compensation: Return on invest. most important, but chg. closing fees, service fees, etc.

COLUMBIA CAPITAL LP

204 South Union Street
Alexandria, VA USA 22314
Phone: 7035192000
Fax: 7035195870
Website: www.colcap.com

Other Offices
1601 Trapelo Road
Suite 154
Waltham, MA USA 02451
Phone: 781-290-2240
Fax: 781-290-2241

Management and Staff
Arun Gupta, Partner
Donald Gips, Venture Partner
Evan DeCorte, Vice President
Jason Booma, Partner
Jeffrey Patterson, Partner
Jim Fleming, Partner
John Siegel, Partner
Monish Kundra, Partner
Patrick Hendy, Partner

Type of Firm
Private Equity Firm

Association Membership
Mid-Atlantic Venture Association
National Venture Capital Association - USA (NVCA)

Project Preferences

Role in Financing:
Prefer role as deal originator but will also invest in deals created by others

Type of Financing Preferred:
Early Stage
Balanced
Later Stage
Seed

Size of Investments Considered:
Min Size of Investment Considered (000s): $15,000
Max Size of Investment Considered (000s): $40,000

Industry Preferences

In Communications prefer:
Wireless Communications

In Computer Software prefer:
Software

In Internet Specific prefer:
Internet

In Business Serv. prefer:
Media

Additional Information
Year Founded: 1989
Capital Under Management: $2,482,000,000
Current Activity Level : Actively seeking new investments

COLUMBIA LAKE PARTNERS GROWTH LENDING (HOLDINGS SUB) LTD

41 Lothbury
London, United Kingdom EC2R 7HF
Phone: 7919324970

Type of Firm
Private Equity Firm

Project Preferences

Type of Financing Preferred:
Balanced

Additional Information
Year Founded: 2014
Capital Under Management: $25,000,000
Current Activity Level : Actively seeking new investments

COLUMBIA PACIFIC ADVISORS LLC

1910 Fairview Avenue East
Suite 200
Seattle, WA USA 98102
Phone: 2067289063
E-mail: info@col-pac.com

Management and Staff
Alan Spragins, Chief Operating Officer
Alexander Washburn, Co-Founder
Daniel Baty, Founder
Jack Ferry, Chief Financial Officer
Jeff Schrock, Managing Director
Joe Kelly, Managing Director
Kevin Barber, Managing Director
Stanley Baty, Founder
Todd Seneker, Managing Director

Type of Firm
Private Equity Firm

Project Preferences

Type of Financing Preferred:
Generalist PE
Opportunistic

Geographical Preferences

United States Preferences:

International Preferences:
United Kingdom

Industry Preferences

In Financial Services prefer:
Real Estate

Additional Information
Year Founded: 2006
Capital Under Management: $193,750,000
Current Activity Level: Actively seeking new investments

COLUMBIA PARTNERS PRIVATE CAPITAL

5425 Wisconsin Avenue
Suite 700
Chevy Chase, MD USA 20815
Phone: 2404820400
Fax: 2404820401
Website: www.columbiaptrs.com

Management and Staff
Christopher Lane, Principal
Christopher Doherty, Managing Director
Jason Crist, Managing Director
K. Dunlop Scott, President
Rhys Williams, Principal
Terence Collins, Principal
Thomas Bain, Vice President
Timothy Talley, Principal

Type of Firm
Investment Management Firm

Project Preferences

Type of Financing Preferred:
Fund of Funds
Expansion
Generalist PE
Later Stage

Industry Preferences

In Communications prefer:
Communications and Media
Telecommunications

In Industrial/Energy prefer:
Energy

In Business Serv. prefer:
Services
Media

Additional Information
Year Founded: 1995
Capital Under Management: $250,000,000
Current Activity Level: Actively seeking new investments

COLUMBUS NOVA TECHNOLOGY PARTNER

900 Third Avenue
19th Floor
New York, NY USA 10022
Phone: 2124189600
Fax: 2123086623
E-mail: info@cntp.com
Website: www.cntp.com

Other Offices
3000 Sand Hill Road
Building 3 Suite 190
Menlo Park, CA USA 94025
Phone: 4082346519

Type of Firm
Private Equity Firm

Project Preferences

Type of Financing Preferred:
Balanced
Startup

Additional Information
Year Founded: 2013
Current Activity Level: Actively seeking new investments

COLUMN GROUP

1700 Owens Street
Suite 500
San Francisco, CA USA 94158
Phone: 4158652050
Fax: 4152552048
E-mail: info@thecolumngroup.net
Website: www.thecolumngroup.net

Management and Staff
David Baltimore, Partner
David Goeddel, Managing Partner
Joseph Goldstein, Partner
Michael Brown, Partner
Richard Klausner, Partner
Roger Perlmutter, Partner
Tim Kutzkey, Partner
Tom Maniatis, Partner

Type of Firm
Private Equity Firm

Project Preferences

Type of Financing Preferred:
Early Stage
Seed

Size of Investments Considered:
Min Size of Investment Considered (000s): $15,000
Max Size of Investment Considered (000s): $30,000

Industry Preferences

In Biotechnology prefer:
Biotechnology

In Medical/Health prefer:
Pharmaceuticals

Additional Information
Name of Most Recent Fund: Column Group II, L.P.
Most Recent Fund Was Raised: 03/10/2010
Year Founded: 2005
Capital Under Management: $239,540,000
Current Activity Level: Actively seeking new investments

COLUMNA CAPITAL LLP

108 New Bond Street
Floor
London, United Kingdom
Phone: 442033225301
Fax: 442033225249
E-mail: info@columnacapital.com
Website: www.columnacapital.com

Type of Firm
Private Equity Firm

Project Preferences

Type of Financing Preferred:
Leveraged Buyout
Later Stage
Management Buyouts
Acquisition

Geographical Preferences

International Preferences:
Europe

Additional Information
Year Founded: 2009

Capital Under Management: $101,210,000
Current Activity Level : Actively seeking new investments

COLVILLE CAPITAL LLC

201 South College Street, Suite 2770
Charlotte, NC USA 28244
Phone: 7043234400
Fax: 7043234420
Website: www.colvillecapital.com

Management and Staff
Daniel Sanderson, Principal
Mark Mealy, Managing Partner

Type of Firm
Private Equity Firm

Project Preferences

Type of Financing Preferred:
Leveraged Buyout
Management Buyouts
Acquisition
Recapitalizations

Industry Preferences

In Manufact. prefer:
Manufacturing

Additional Information
Year Founded: 2006
Current Activity Level : Actively seeking new investments

COMBINE VC

52 Zoe Street
San Francisco, CA USA 94107
Phone: 6283335337
Website: combine.vc

Type of Firm
Private Equity Firm

Project Preferences

Type of Financing Preferred:
Early Stage
Seed

Additional Information
Year Founded: 2017
Capital Under Management: $10,920,000
Current Activity Level : Actively seeking new investments

COMCAST VENTURES

1701 John F. Kennedy Boulevard
55th Floor, One Comcast Center
Philadelphia, PA USA 19103
Phone: 4159265540
E-mail: info@comcastventures.com
Website: www.comcastventures.com

Other Offices
588 Broadway
Suite 202
NEW YORK, NY USA 10012

480 Cowper Street
Suite 200
PALO ALTO, CA USA 94301

5 Times Square
Tenth Floor
NEW YORK, NY USA 10036

Management and Staff
Amy Banse, Managing Director
Andrew Cleland, Managing Director
Callum King, Principal
Daniel Gulati, Partner
David Zilberman, Managing Director
Dinesh Moorjani, Managing Director
Frances Schwiep, Principal
Gil Beyda, Managing Director
Louis Toth, Managing Director
Michael Yang, Managing Director
Rick Prostko, Managing Director
Sam Landman, Managing Director

Type of Firm
Corporate PE/Venture

Association Membership
Mid-Atlantic Venture Association

Project Preferences

Type of Financing Preferred:
Early Stage
Expansion
Later Stage
Seed

Size of Investments Considered:
Min Size of Investment Considered (000s): $2,000
Max Size of Investment Considered (000s): $15,000

Geographical Preferences

United States Preferences:

Industry Preferences

In Communications prefer:
Communications and Media
Commercial Communications

In Computer Software prefer:
Software

In Internet Specific prefer:
Internet
Ecommerce

In Consumer Related prefer:
Consumer
Entertainment and Leisure

In Business Serv. prefer:
Services

Additional Information
Year Founded: 1999
Capital Under Management: $500,000,000
Current Activity Level : Actively seeking new investments

COME UP CAPITAL

Fourth Street South East
29 University Park Plaza
Minneapolis, MN USA 55414
E-mail: info@comeup.capital
Website: www.comeup.capital

Type of Firm
Private Equity Firm

Project Preferences

Type of Financing Preferred:
Early Stage
Startup

Geographical Preferences

United States Preferences:

Additional Information
Year Founded: 2016
Current Activity Level : Actively seeking new investments

COMERICA INC

1717 Main Street, Comerica Bank Tower
Dallas, TX USA 75201
Phone: 8002921300
Website: www.comerica.com

Management and Staff
Karen Parkhill, Chief Financial Officer

Type of Firm
Bank Affiliated

Association Membership
Canadian Venture Capital Association

Project Preferences

Type of Financing Preferred:
Leveraged Buyout
Acquisition

Geographical Preferences

United States Preferences:

Canadian Preferences:
All Canada

Additional Information
Year Founded: 2001
Current Activity Level : Actively seeking new investments

COMERICA VENTURE CAPITAL GROUP

1717 Main Street
Comerica Bank Tower
Dallas, TX USA 75201
Phone: 2149696476
Fax: 3139654648
E-mail: info@comerica.com
Website: campaign.comerica.com/business/technology/v

Other Offices

211 North Union Street #100
Alexandria, VA USA 22314
Phone: 703-684-4829
Fax: 703-838-5579

11512 El Camino Real
Suite 350
San Diego, CA USA 92103
Phone: 858-509-2370
Fax: 858-509-2365

1100 Glendon Avenue
Suite 2020
Westwood, CA USA 90024
Phone: 310-481-1001
Fax: 310-481-1099

Management and Staff

J. Michael Fulton, President
J. Patrick Faubion, President
Mark Horn, Vice President
Thomas Ogden, President

Type of Firm

Corporate PE/Venture

Association Membership

Western Association of Venture Capitalists (WAVC)

Project Preferences

Role in Financing:
Prefer role as deal originator but will also invest in deals created by others

Type of Financing Preferred:
Balanced

Size of Investments Considered:
Min Size of Investment Considered (000s): $500
Max Size of Investment Considered (000s): $2,000

Geographical Preferences

United States Preferences:
California

Industry Preferences

In Semiconductor/Electr prefer:
Electronics

In Medical/Health prefer:
Medical/Health

Additional Information

Year Founded: 1849
Capital Under Management: $18,000,000
Current Activity Level : Actively seeking new investments
Method of Compensation: Other

COMET LABS INC

818 Mission Street
San Francisco, CA USA 94103
E-mail: hi@cometlabs.io

Type of Firm

Incubator/Development Program

Project Preferences

Type of Financing Preferred:
Startup

Industry Preferences

In Industrial/Energy prefer:
Robotics

Additional Information

Year Founded: 2015
Current Activity Level : Actively seeking new investments

COMMERCE VENTURES MANAGEMENT LLC

680 Mission Street, Unit 11E
San Francisco, CA USA 94105
Phone: 4155005352
E-mail: info@commercevc.com
Website: www.commercevc.com

Management and Staff

Daniel Rosen, Founder

Type of Firm

Private Equity Firm

Project Preferences

Type of Financing Preferred:
Early Stage
Seed
Startup

Industry Preferences

In Internet Specific prefer:
Ecommerce

Additional Information

Name of Most Recent Fund: Commerce Ventures, L.P.
Most Recent Fund Was Raised: 02/14/2014
Year Founded: 2013
Capital Under Management: $45,600,000
Current Activity Level : Actively seeking new investments

COMMERCIAL DRONE FUND

4000 Westerly Place
Newport Beach, CA USA 92660
Website: www.commercialdronefund.com

Type of Firm

Private Equity Firm

Project Preferences

Type of Financing Preferred:
Early Stage
Seed

Size of Investments Considered:
Min Size of Investment Considered (000s): $250
Max Size of Investment Considered (000s): $1,000

Geographical Preferences

United States Preferences:
All U.S.

Canadian Preferences:
All Canada

International Preferences:
United Kingdom
Europe
Austria

Industry Preferences

In Computer Software prefer:
Software
Applications Software

In Semiconductor/Electr prefer:
Analytic/Scientific

Additional Information

Year Founded: 2015
Current Activity Level : Actively seeking new investments

COMMERZBANK AG

Kaiserplatz
Frankfurt, Germany 60311
Phone: 496913620
Fax: 4969285389
E-mail: info@commerzbank.com
Website: www.commerzbank.de

Management and Staff

Frank Annuscheit, Chief Operating Officer
Stephen Engels, Chief Financial Officer

Type of Firm

Bank Affiliated

Project Preferences

Type of Financing Preferred:
Generalist PE

Geographical Preferences

International Preferences:
Europe

Additional Information
Year Founded: 1870
Current Activity Level : Actively seeking new investments

COMMISSION FOR TECHNOLOGY AND INNOVATION CTI

Einsteinstrasse 2
Bern, Switzerland 3003
Phone: 41584622440
E-mail: regula.leuenberger@kti.admin.ch
Website: www.kti.admin.ch

Management and Staff
Beda Stadler, Vice President
Lutz Nolte, Vice President
Martin Riediker, Vice President
Matthias Kaiserswerth, Vice President
Myriam Meyer Stutz, Vice President
Walter Steinlin, President

Type of Firm
Government Affiliated Program

Project Preferences

Type of Financing Preferred:
Early Stage
Seed

Geographical Preferences

International Preferences:
Europe

Additional Information
Year Founded: 2009
Current Activity Level : Actively seeking new investments

COMMITTED ADVISORS SAS

9 rue Daru
Paris, France 75008
Phone: 33172283530
Fax: 33142274619
E-mail: contact@committedadvisors.info
Website: www.committedadvisors.com

Other Offices
Level 21, Darling Park Tower 2
201 Sussex Street
Sydney, Australia NSW 2000

Type of Firm
Private Equity Advisor or Fund of Funds

Association Membership
French Venture Capital Association (AFIC)

Project Preferences

Type of Financing Preferred:
Fund of Funds
Leveraged Buyout
Turnaround
Later Stage
Fund of Funds of Second

Geographical Preferences

United States Preferences:
All U.S.

International Preferences:
Europe
Australia
Asia

Additional Information
Name of Most Recent Fund: Committed Advisors Secondary Fund I
Most Recent Fund Was Raised: 07/11/2011
Year Founded: 2010
Capital Under Management: $2,156,852,000
Current Activity Level : Actively seeking new investments

COMMITTED CAPITAL, LTD.

107 New Bond Street
London, United Kingdom W1S 1ED
Phone: 44-20-7529-1350
Fax: 44-20-3004-1183
E-mail: info@committedcapital.co.uk
Website: www.committedcapital.co.uk

Management and Staff
Steven Harris, Chief Executive Officer

Type of Firm
Investment Management Firm

Project Preferences

Type of Financing Preferred:
Expansion
Balanced
Management Buyouts

Geographical Preferences

International Preferences:
United Kingdom

Industry Preferences

In Consumer Related prefer:
Entertainment and Leisure
Retail

In Manufact. prefer:
Manufacturing

Additional Information
Year Founded: 2011
Current Activity Level : Actively seeking new investments

COMMONFUND CAPITAL INC

15 Old Danbury Road
Wilton, CT USA 06897
Phone: 2035635000
Website: www.commonfund.org

Other Offices
1801 Century Park East
Suite 2220
Los Angeles, CA USA 90067
Phone: 310-286-6500

Berkeley Square
Berkeley Square House, Second Floor
London, United Kingdom W1J 6BD
Phone: 44-20-7887-1540
Fax: 44-20-7887-1541

Management and Staff
Alec Rapaport, Managing Director
Brijesh Jeevarathnam, Managing Director
E. Lyndon Tefft, Chief Operating Officer
Ellen Blix, Managing Director
Jeffrey Long, Managing Director
Keith Luke, Managing Director
Leenong Li, Managing Director
Mark Hoeing, Managing Director
Sarah Clark, Managing Director
Susan Carter, Chief Executive Officer
Tim Yates, Managing Director

Type of Firm
Private Equity Advisor or Fund of Funds

Project Preferences

Role in Financing:
Prefer role in deals created by others

Type of Financing Preferred:
Fund of Funds

Geographical Preferences

United States Preferences:
Southeast

International Preferences:
Utd. Arab Em.

Industry Focus
(% based on actual investment)
Other Products	86.6%
Medical/Health	5.9%
Internet Specific	4.5%
Computer Software and Services	3.1%

Additional Information

Name of Most Recent Fund: Commonfund Capital Emerging Markets 2013, L.P.
Most Recent Fund Was Raised: 02/11/2013
Year Founded: 1971
Capital Under Management: $12,700,000,000
Current Activity Level : Actively seeking new investments
Method of Compensation: Return on invest. most important, but chg. closing fees, service fees, etc.

COMMONFUND REALTY

15 Old Danbury Road
Wilton, CT USA 06897
Phone: 203-563-5000
Fax: 203-762-0921

Management and Staff

Hugh Scott, Managing Director
Timothy Shine, Managing Director

Type of Firm

Private Equity Advisor or Fund of Funds

Project Preferences

Type of Financing Preferred:
Fund of Funds
Value-Add

Geographical Preferences

United States Preferences:

Industry Preferences

In Financial Services prefer:
Real Estate

Additional Information

Year Founded: 1987
Current Activity Level : Actively seeking new investments

COMMONVIEW CAPITAL LLC

61 Brundige Drive
Goldens Bridge, NY USA 10526
Website: www.commonviewcapital.com

Type of Firm

Private Equity Firm

Project Preferences

Type of Financing Preferred:
Leveraged Buyout
Acquisition

Geographical Preferences

United States Preferences:
North America

Industry Preferences

In Medical/Health prefer:
Medical Products
Health Services

In Consumer Related prefer:
Food/Beverage

In Transportation prefer:
Transportation

In Business Serv. prefer:
Distribution

In Manufact. prefer:
Manufacturing

Additional Information

Year Founded: 2017
Capital Under Management: $32,000,000
Current Activity Level : Actively seeking new investments

COMMONWEALTH CAPITAL VENTURES

400 West Cumkings Park
Suite 1725-134
Woburn, MA USA 01801
Phone: 7818905554
Fax: 7818903414
Website: www.commonwealthvc.com

Management and Staff

Brian Annese, Partner
Elliot Katzman, General Partner
Jeffrey Hurst, Co-Founder
Justin Perreault, General Partner
Michael Fitzgerald, Co-Founder
R. Stephen McCormack, Co-Founder

Type of Firm

Private Equity Firm

Association Membership

New England Venture Capital Association

Project Preferences

Role in Financing:
Will function either as deal originator or investor in deals created by others

Type of Financing Preferred:
Early Stage
Balanced
Later Stage

Size of Investments Considered:
Min Size of Investment Considered (000s): $2,000
Max Size of Investment Considered (000s): $8,000

Geographical Preferences

United States Preferences:
Northeast

Industry Focus

(% based on actual investment)

Computer Software and Services	40.6%
Internet Specific	14.9%
Computer Hardware	13.0%
Semiconductors/Other Elect.	7.3%
Industrial/Energy	6.8%
Medical/Health	6.8%
Communications and Media	4.7%
Biotechnology	2.2%
Other Products	2.2%
Consumer Related	1.3%

Additional Information

Name of Most Recent Fund: Commonwealth Capital Ventures IV, L.P.
Most Recent Fund Was Raised: 02/09/2007
Year Founded: 1995
Capital Under Management: $580,000,000
Current Activity Level : Actively seeking new investments
Method of Compensation: Return on investment is of primary concern, do not charge fees

COMMONWEALTH SEED CAPITAL LLC

300 West Vine Street
Suite 600
Lexington, KY USA 40507

Type of Firm

Government Affiliated Program

Project Preferences

Type of Financing Preferred:
Early Stage

Geographical Preferences

United States Preferences:
Kentucky

Industry Preferences

In Communications prefer:
Communications and Media

In Medical/Health prefer:
Health Services

In Industrial/Energy prefer:
Energy
Environmental Related

In Manufact. prefer:
Manufacturing

Additional Information

Year Founded: 1969
Current Activity Level : Actively seeking new investments

COMMUNITAS CAPITAL PARTNERS LLC

1177 Avenue of the Americas
Fifth Floor
New York, NY USA 10036
Phone: 6499656699
E-mail: info@communitascapital.com

Type of Firm
Private Equity Firm

Project Preferences

Type of Financing Preferred:
Balanced

Industry Preferences

In Financial Services prefer:
Financial Services

Additional Information
Year Founded: 2018
Capital Under Management: $14,960,000
Current Activity Level : Actively seeking new investments

COMMUNITECH LTD

295 Hagey Boulevard
Suite 16, Accelerator Centre
Waterloo, Canada N2L 6R5
Phone: 5198889944
Fax: 5198887007

Management and Staff
Kevin Tuer, Vice President
Lynn Forgeron, Chief Financial Officer
Steve Currie, Vice President

Type of Firm
Incubator/Development Program

Project Preferences

Type of Financing Preferred:
Early Stage
Balanced
Seed
Startup

Geographical Preferences

Canadian Preferences:
Ontario

Additional Information
Year Founded: 1997
Capital Under Management: $30,990,000
Current Activity Level : Actively seeking new investments

COMMUNITY INVESTMENT MANAGEMENT LLC

755 Sansome Street
Suite #450
San Francisco, CA USA 94111
Phone: 4158573233
E-mail: info@cim-llc.com
Website: cim-llc.com

Management and Staff
Jacob Haar, Managing Partner
Michael Hokenson, Managing Partner
Olympia De Castro, Partner

Type of Firm
Incubator/Development Program

Project Preferences

Type of Financing Preferred:
Early Stage

Additional Information
Year Founded: 2015
Current Activity Level : Actively seeking new investments

COMO VENTURE SRL

Via per Cernobbio, 11
Como, Italy 22100
Phone: 390312287624
E-mail: segreteria@comoventure.it
Website: www.comoventure.it

Management and Staff
Filippo Arcioni, Managing Director
Lino Moscatelli, Managing Director

Type of Firm
Private Equity Firm

Association Membership
Italian Venture Capital Association (AIFI)

Additional Information
Year Founded: 2014
Current Activity Level : Actively seeking new investments

COMPAGNIE BENELUX PARTICIPATIONS SA

Rue de la Chancellerie 2 box 1
Brussels, Belgium 1000
Phone: 3222133210
Fax: 3225131702
E-mail: info@cobepa.be
Website: www.cobepa.com

Management and Staff
Jean-Marie Laurent Josi, Managing Director
Xavier de Walque, Chief Financial Officer

Type of Firm
Private Equity Firm

Project Preferences

Type of Financing Preferred:
Leveraged Buyout
Generalist PE
Later Stage
Management Buyouts
Acquisition

Geographical Preferences

United States Preferences:
All U.S.

International Preferences:
Italy
Latin America
Luxembourg
Europe
Netherlands
Switzerland
Belgium
Asia
France

Industry Preferences

In Medical/Health prefer:
Medical/Health

In Industrial/Energy prefer:
Industrial Products

In Transportation prefer:
Transportation

In Business Serv. prefer:
Services

In Other prefer:
Environment Responsible

Additional Information
Year Founded: 1957
Current Activity Level : Actively seeking new investments

COMPAS PRIVATE EQUITY

Av. Diagonal 442 Bis Principal
Barcelona, Spain 08037
Phone: 34933685640
Website: www.compaspe.es

Type of Firm
Private Equity Firm

Project Preferences

Type of Financing Preferred:
Balanced

Geographical Preferences

International Preferences:
Spain
All International

Additional Information
Year Founded: 2008
Current Activity Level : Actively seeking new investments

COMPASS CAPITAL FOR FINANCIAL INVESTMENTS

2 Wadi El Nile Street
Mohandeseen
Giza, Egypt
Phone: 20233050700
Fax: 20233050711
E-mail: info@compass-cap.com
Website: www.ramedapharma.com

Type of Firm
Private Equity Firm

Project Preferences

Type of Financing Preferred:
Generalist PE
Opportunistic

Geographical Preferences

International Preferences:
Egypt
Middle East

Industry Preferences

In Medical/Health prefer:
Health Services

In Consumer Related prefer:
Consumer

In Industrial/Energy prefer:
Oil and Gas Exploration

Additional Information
Year Founded: 2010
Current Activity Level : Actively seeking new investments

COMPASS CAPITAL SERVICES INC

7525 Southeast 24th Street
Suite 650
Mercer Island, WA USA 98040
Phone: 2062362100
Fax: 2069262300
E-mail: info@compasscapital.com

Management and Staff
Bradley Hallock, Managing Partner
Carrie Rorem, Chief Operating Officer
Chris Nicholson, Managing Partner
James Ellison, Managing Partner
Robert Hild, Managing Partner
Todd Barton, Managing Director

Type of Firm
Private Equity Firm

Project Preferences

Role in Financing:
Prefer role as deal originator but will also invest in deals created by others

Type of Financing Preferred:
Early Stage
Later Stage
Industry Rollups

Size of Investments Considered:
Min Size of Investment Considered (000s): $500
Max Size of Investment Considered (000s): $5,000

Geographical Preferences

United States Preferences:

Canadian Preferences:
All Canada

Industry Preferences

In Communications prefer:
Wireless Communications

In Computer Software prefer:
Software
Systems Software
Applications Software

In Semiconductor/Electr prefer:
Semiconductor
Controllers and Sensors
Sensors
Laser Related
Fiber Optics

In Biotechnology prefer:
Human Biotechnology
Industrial Biotechnology
Biosensors
Biotech Related Research

In Medical/Health prefer:
Medical Diagnostics
Diagnostic Services
Drug/Equipmt Delivery
Medical Products

Additional Information
Year Founded: 1994
Current Activity Level : Actively seeking new investments
Method of Compensation: Return on investment is of primary concern, do not charge fees

COMPASS INVESTMENT MANAGEMENT LTD

33 Cork Street
London, United Kingdom W1X 1HB
Phone: 44-20-74343488
Fax: 44-20-74343155
E-mail: info@compass.uk.com

Management and Staff
Dennis Hallahane, Partner
Peter Dale, Partner

Type of Firm
Bank Affiliated

Association Membership
British Venture Capital Association (BVCA)

Project Preferences

Role in Financing:
Prefer role as deal originator but will also invest in deals created by others

Type of Financing Preferred:
Second Stage Financing
Leveraged Buyout
Early Stage
Expansion
Special Situation
Recapitalizations

Geographical Preferences

United States Preferences:

Canadian Preferences:
All Canada

International Preferences:
United Kingdom
Western Europe

Industry Preferences

In Communications prefer:
Telecommunications
Data Communications

In Semiconductor/Electr prefer:
Electronic Components
Sensors
Component Testing Equipmt

In Medical/Health prefer:
Drug/Equipmt Delivery
Other Therapeutic
Medical Products
Disposable Med. Products
Pharmaceuticals

In Consumer Related prefer:
Entertainment and Leisure
Food/Beverage
Consumer Products
Other Restaurants

In Industrial/Energy prefer:
Industrial Products
Materials
Factory Automation
Machinery
Environmental Related

Additional Information
Year Founded: 1986
Capital Under Management: $5,900,000
Current Activity Level : Actively seeking new investments
Method of Compensation: Return on invest. most important, but chg. closing fees, service fees, etc.

COMPASS PARTNERS INTERNATIONAL LLC

825 Third Avenue
32nd Floor
New York, NY USA 10001
Phone: 2127029800
E-mail: info@compasspartners.com
Website: compasspartners.com

Other Offices
Ordnance House, 31 Pier Road
Jersey, United Kingdom JE4 8PW
Phone: 441534825274

Management and Staff
Allan Chapin, Partner
Antoine Pupin, Partner
Eugene Co, Managing Director
Frank Rudd, Partner
James Waters, Vice President
Thomas Tullo, Managing Director
Ze ev Goldberg, Partner

Type of Firm
Investment Management Firm

Project Preferences

Type of Financing Preferred:
Generalist PE

Additional Information
Year Founded: 2007
Capital Under Management: $401,490,000
Current Activity Level : Actively seeking new investments

COMPASS PARTNERS INTERNATIONAL LLP

33 Lowndes Street
London, United Kingdom SW1X 9HX
Phone: 44-20-7761-2000
Fax: 44-20-7761-2020
E-mail: info@cpil.co.uk

Management and Staff
Anthony Marraccino, Chief Financial Officer
Eugene Kim, Managing Director
Franklin J. Rudd, Partner
Steve Waters, Founding Partner
Tim Wright, Partner
Trevor Peterson, Managing Director

Type of Firm
Private Equity Firm

Project Preferences

Type of Financing Preferred:
Leveraged Buyout
Turnaround
Acquisition
Joint Ventures

Geographical Preferences

United States Preferences:

International Preferences:
Europe

Industry Focus
(% based on actual investment)
Other Products 72.0%
Consumer Related 28.0%

Additional Information
Name of Most Recent Fund: Compass Partners European Equity Fund, L.P.
Most Recent Fund Was Raised: 07/31/1999
Year Founded: 1997
Current Activity Level : Actively seeking new investments

COMPOUND SEMICONDUCTOR TECHNOLOGIES GLOBAL LTD

Four Stanley Boulevard
Hamilton Technology Park
Scotland, United Kingdom G72 0BN
Phone: 44-16-9872-2072
Fax: 44-16-9882-1101
Website: www.compoundsemi.co.uk

Management and Staff
Neil Martin, Chief Executive Officer

Type of Firm
Incubator/Development Program

Project Preferences

Type of Financing Preferred:
Early Stage
Seed
Startup

Geographical Preferences

International Preferences:
United Kingdom

Industry Preferences

In Communications prefer:
Telecommunications

In Semiconductor/Electr prefer:
Electronics
Semiconductor
Fiber Optics

Additional Information
Year Founded: 1999
Capital Under Management: $10,900,000
Current Activity Level : Actively seeking new investments

COMPOUND VENTURES

257 Park Avenue South
Floor 5
New York, NY USA 10010
Phone: 2122093366
E-mail: info@metamorphic.vc
Website: www.compound.vc

Management and Staff
David Hirsch, Managing Partner
Lewis Gersh, Managing Partner
Marc Michel, Managing Partner
Michael Dempsey, Principal

Type of Firm
Private Equity Firm

Project Preferences

Role in Financing:
Will function either as deal originator or investor in deals created by others

Type of Financing Preferred:
Early Stage
Seed
Startup

Geographical Preferences

United States Preferences:
New York

Industry Preferences

In Computer Software prefer:
Software

In Internet Specific prefer:
E-Commerce Technology
Internet

In Business Serv. prefer:
Media

Additional Information
Name of Most Recent Fund: Metamorphic Ventures II, L.P.
Most Recent Fund Was Raised: 07/02/2013
Year Founded: 2006
Capital Under Management: $7,000,000
Current Activity Level : Actively seeking new investments
Method of Compensation: Return on investment is of primary concern, do not charge fees

COMSPACE DEVELOPMENT LLC

12521 Manderlay Way
Oak Hill, VA USA 20171
Phone: 7037160675
Website: www.comspacedev.com

Management and Staff
Michael Miller, Managing Director

Type of Firm
Investment Management Firm

Project Preferences

Type of Financing Preferred:
Early Stage
Expansion

Industry Preferences

In Communications prefer:
Wireless Communications

In Transportation prefer:
Aerospace

Additional Information
Year Founded: 1997
Capital Under Management: $10,000,000
Current Activity Level : Actively seeking new investments

COMVEST HOLDING GMBH

Joachimsthaler Strasse 34
Berlin, Germany 10719
Phone: 4930531449916
Fax: 4930531449915
E-mail: info@comvest-holding.de
Website: www.comvest-holding.de

Type of Firm
Private Equity Firm

Additional Information
Year Founded: 2014
Current Activity Level : Actively seeking new investments

COMVEST PARTNERS

525 Okeechobee Boulevard
Suite 1050
West Palm Beach, FL USA 33401
Phone: 5617272000
Website: www.comvest.com

Other Offices
830 Third Avenue
Eighth Floor
NEW YORK, NY USA 10022
Phone: 2128295825

295 Madison Avenue
17th Floor
NEW YORK, NY USA 10017
Phone: 2128295825

Management and Staff
Adam Bentkover, Vice President
Al Wood, Partner
Brad Nii, Managing Director
Bryce Peterson, Vice President
Carlo Porreca, Vice President
Cecilio Rodriguez, Chief Financial Officer
Cecilio Rodriguez, Chief Financial Officer
Daniel Lee, Managing Director
Greg Reynolds, Managing Director
Jared Grigg, Principal
Jared Grigg, Principal
Jason Gelberd, Partner
John Caple, Managing Director
Jon Huitink, Principal
Joseph Pallota, Vice President
Justin Chen, Vice President
Kevin LaHatte, Vice President
Lee Bryan, Partner
Lee Bryan, Vice President
Louis Colosimo, Managing Director
Mark Hughes, Managing Director
Marshall Griffin, Vice President
Marshall Griffin, Principal
Matt Gullen, Partner
Michael Falk, Managing Partner
Palmer Rosemond, Vice President
Peter Kight, Managing Partner
Peter Nortrup, Vice President
Robert O Sullivan, Partner
Robert Priddy, Managing Partner
Roger Marrero, Managing Partner
Roger Marrero, Managing Director
Tom Goila, Managing Director
Tom Clark, Managing Director
Tom Clark, Partner

Type of Firm
Private Equity Firm

Project Preferences

Role in Financing:
Prefer role as deal originator

Type of Financing Preferred:
Leveraged Buyout
Mezzanine
Turnaround
Management Buyouts
Industry Rollups
Recapitalizations

Geographical Preferences

United States Preferences:

Industry Preferences

In Communications prefer:
Telecommunications

In Computer Software prefer:
Software

In Medical/Health prefer:
Medical/Health
Health Services

In Industrial/Energy prefer:
Industrial Products
Materials

In Transportation prefer:
Transportation

In Financial Services prefer:
Financial Services

In Business Serv. prefer:
Services

In Manufact. prefer:
Manufacturing

Additional Information
Name of Most Recent Fund: Comvest Investment Partners IV, L.P.
Most Recent Fund Was Raised: 07/16/2010
Year Founded: 1988
Capital Under Management: $1,300,000,000
Current Activity Level : Actively seeking new investments
Method of Compensation: Return on invest. most important, but chg. closing fees, service fees, etc.

CONCENTRIC EQUITY PARTNERS, L.P.

50 East Washington Street
Suite 400
Chicago, IL USA 60602
Phone: 3124944513
Fax: 3124941494
Website: www.fic-cep.com

Management and Staff
David Gervase, Chief Financial Officer
Ian Ross, Principal
Jennifer Steans, Chief Executive Officer
Kenneth Hooten, Co-Founder
Nicholas Sayers, Vice President

Type of Firm
Private Equity Firm

Association Membership
Illinois Venture Capital Association

Project Preferences

Role in Financing:
Will function either as deal originator or investor in deals created by others

Type of Financing Preferred:
Leveraged Buyout
Expansion
Generalist PE
Later Stage
Management Buyouts
Acquisition

Size of Investments Considered:
Min Size of Investment Considered (000s): $10,000
Max Size of Investment Considered (000s): $30,000

Industry Preferences

In Consumer Related prefer:
Consumer Services

In Financial Services prefer:
Financial Services

In Business Serv. prefer:
Services

Additional Information
Name of Most Recent Fund: Concentric Equity Partners, L.P.
Most Recent Fund Was Raised: 08/21/2003
Year Founded: 2003
Capital Under Management: $650,000,000
Current Activity Level : Actively seeking new investments
Method of Compensation: Return on invest. most important, but chg. closing fees, service fees, etc.

CONCORDE CAPITAL TOV

Mechnikova, 2
Parus Business Center, Floor 16
Kiev, Ukraine 01601
Phone: 380443915577
Fax: 380443915571
Website: concorde.ua

Type of Firm
Investment Management Firm

Project Preferences

Type of Financing Preferred:
Early Stage
Turnaround
Seed
Distressed Debt
Recapitalizations

Geographical Preferences

International Preferences:
Ukraine

Additional Information
Year Founded: 2004
Capital Under Management: $310,000,000
Current Activity Level : Actively seeking new investments

CONDOR CAPITAL MANAGEMENT CORP

1973 Washington Valley road
Martinsville, NJ USA 08836
Phone: 732-356-7323
Fax: 732-356-5875
Website: www.condorcapital.com

Management and Staff
Andrew Novick, Vice President
Kenneth Schapiro, President, Founder
Stephen Tipping, Vice President

Type of Firm
Private Equity Firm

Additional Information
Year Founded: 1988
Current Activity Level : Actively seeking new investments
Method of Compensation: Return on invest. most important, but chg. closing fees, service fees, etc.

CONDUIT VENTURES LTD

59-61 Hatton Garden
Unit B, 2/F, Colonial Bldgs.
London, United Kingdom EC1N 8LS
Phone: 442078313131
Fax: 442078415808

Other Offices
Room 504 Shanghai
1634 Huai Hai Zhong Road
Shanghai, China 200 031
Phone: 86-21-6433-3028
Fax: 86-21-6433-7796

Management and Staff
Linda Zheng, Principal
Yuenong Tong, Principal

Type of Firm
Private Equity Firm

Project Preferences

Type of Financing Preferred:
Early Stage
Expansion
Balanced
Later Stage
Startup

Geographical Preferences

United States Preferences:

Canadian Preferences:
All Canada

International Preferences:
Europe

Industry Preferences

In Industrial/Energy prefer:
Energy
Advanced Materials

In Other prefer:
Environment Responsible

Additional Information
Year Founded: 2001
Current Activity Level : Actively seeking new investments

CONECTOR SL

Calabria 169
7th floor
Barcelona, Spain 08015
Phone: 93 2269950
E-mail: conector@conector.com
Website: www.conector.com

Type of Firm
Incubator/Development Program

Project Preferences

Type of Financing Preferred:
Seed
Startup

Geographical Preferences

International Preferences:
Spain

Additional Information
Year Founded: 2013
Current Activity Level : Actively seeking new investments

CONEXUS CAPITAL MANAGEMENT, INC.

Post Office Box 835
Somerville, NJ USA 08876
Phone: 908-231-9101
Fax: 908-231-9103
E-mail: info@conexuscapital.com
Website: www.conexuscapital.com

Management and Staff
Dietmar Hirt, Managing Director
G. Robert Marcus, Managing Director
Graham May, Managing Director

Type of Firm
Private Equity Firm

Project Preferences

Role in Financing:
Prefer role as deal originator but will also invest in deals created by others

Type of Financing Preferred:
Early Stage

Size of Investments Considered:
Min Size of Investment Considered (000s): $1,000
Max Size of Investment Considered (000s): $2,000

Geographical Preferences

United States Preferences:
Mid Atlantic
Northeast

Additional Information
Name of Most Recent Fund: Conexus Financial Partners, L.P.
Most Recent Fund Was Raised: 05/01/2001
Year Founded: 2000
Capital Under Management: $45,000,000
Current Activity Level : Actively seeking new investments
Method of Compensation: Return on investment is of primary concern, do not charge fees

CONFRAPAR ADMINISTRACAO E GESTAO DE RECURSOS SA

Avenida do Contorno 6594
17th floor, Santo Antonio
Belo Horizonte, Brazil 30110044
Phone: 553135553566
Website: confrapar.com.br

Other Offices
RB1 Av. Rio Branco
12th Floor Centro
Rio de Janeiro, Brazil 20.090-003
Phone: 552125888068

12995 Edificio Plaza Centenario
Tenth Floor Av. das Nacoes Unidas
Sao Paulo, Brazil 04578-000
Phone: 551155036621

Management and Staff
Carlos Eduardo Guillaume, Chief Executive Officer
Rodrigo Esteves, Chief Financial Officer

Type of Firm
Private Equity Firm

Association Membership
Brazilian Venture Capital Association (ABCR)

Project Preferences

Type of Financing Preferred:
Early Stage
Balanced
Later Stage

Geographical Preferences

United States Preferences:

International Preferences:
Brazil

Industry Preferences

In Communications prefer:
Communications and Media
Telecommunications
Entertainment

In Medical/Health prefer:
Medical/Health

In Consumer Related prefer:
Education Related

In Industrial/Energy prefer:
Energy
Oil and Gas Exploration

In Business Serv. prefer:
Media

Additional Information
Year Founded: 2005
Capital Under Management: $21,093,000
Current Activity Level : Actively seeking new investments

CONGRUENT INVESTMENT PARTNERS LLC

3131 McKinney Avenue
Suite 850
Dallas, TX USA 75204
Website: www.congruentinv.com

Management and Staff
Preston Massey, Co-Founder
Travis Baldwin, Co-Founder

Type of Firm
Investment Management Firm

Project Preferences

Type of Financing Preferred:
Leveraged Buyout
Expansion
Acquisition
Recapitalizations

Geographical Preferences

United States Preferences:
North America

Industry Preferences

In Computer Software prefer:
Software

In Medical/Health prefer:
Medical/Health

In Consumer Related prefer:
Consumer Products

In Industrial/Energy prefer:
Energy

In Transportation prefer:
Transportation

In Financial Services prefer:
Financial Services
Real Estate

In Business Serv. prefer:
Services
Distribution
Media

In Manufact. prefer:
Manufacturing

Additional Information
Name of Most Recent Fund: Congruent Credit Opportunities Fund III, L.P.
Most Recent Fund Was Raised: 06/10/2013
Year Founded: 2009
Capital Under Management: $312,893,000
Current Activity Level : Actively seeking new investments

CONGRUENT VENTURES LLC

6114 La Salle Avenue, Suite 443
Oakland, CA USA 94611
Website: www.congruentvc.com

Type of Firm
Private Equity Firm

Project Preferences

Type of Financing Preferred:
Balanced

Industry Preferences

In Other prefer:
Environment Responsible

Additional Information
Year Founded: 2017
Current Activity Level : Actively seeking new investments

CONISTON CAPITAL CORP

10 Town Square
Suite 200
Chatham, NJ USA 07928

Phone: 9737017712
Website: www.coniston-capital.com

Type of Firm
Private Equity Firm

Project Preferences

Type of Financing Preferred:
Startup

Industry Preferences

In Communications prefer:
Entertainment

In Business Serv. prefer:
Services
Media

Additional Information
Year Founded: 1969
Current Activity Level : Actively seeking new investments

CONNECT VENTURES LLP

89 Great Eastern Street
4th Floor
London, United Kingdom EC2A 3HX
E-mail: info@connectventures.co.uk
Website: connectventures.co.uk

Management and Staff
Bill Earner, Managing Partner
Pietro Bezza, Managing Partner
Sitar Teli, Managing Director

Type of Firm
Private Equity Firm

Project Preferences

Type of Financing Preferred:
Early Stage
Seed

Size of Investments Considered:
Min Size of Investment Considered (000s): $376
Max Size of Investment Considered (000s): $1,252

Geographical Preferences

International Preferences:
United Kingdom
Europe

Industry Preferences

In Communications prefer:
Wireless Communications

In Internet Specific prefer:
Internet
Web Aggregation/Portals

Additional Information
Year Founded: 2011

Capital Under Management: $21,056,000
Current Activity Level : Actively seeking new investments

CONNECTEDVC

22 West 21st Street
New York, NY USA 10001
E-mail: team@connectedvc.com
Website: connectedvc.com

Type of Firm
Private Equity Firm

Project Preferences

Type of Financing Preferred:
Early Stage

Additional Information
Year Founded: 1969
Current Activity Level : Actively seeking new investments

CONNECTICUT INNOVATIONS INC

865 Brook Street
Rocky Hill, CT USA 06067
Phone: 8605635851
Fax: 8605634877
E-mail: info@ctinnovations.com
Website: www.ctinnovations.com

Management and Staff
Antonio Roberto, Managing Director
Colin Tedeschi, Vice President
Matthew McCooe, Chief Executive Officer

Type of Firm
Government Affiliated Program

Association Membership
New England Venture Capital Association
National Venture Capital Association - USA (NVCA)

Project Preferences

Role in Financing:
Will function either as deal originator or investor in deals created by others

Type of Financing Preferred:
Early Stage
Mezzanine
Balanced
Later Stage
Seed
Startup

Geographical Preferences

United States Preferences:
Connecticut

Industry Focus
(% based on actual investment)

Computer Software and Services	24.5%
Biotechnology	22.1%
Industrial/Energy	19.7%
Internet Specific	15.3%
Medical/Health	9.9%
Semiconductors/Other Elect.	2.5%
Computer Hardware	2.1%
Communications and Media	1.9%
Other Products	1.3%
Consumer Related	0.7%

Additional Information
Year Founded: 1989
Capital Under Management: $147,000,000
Current Activity Level : Actively seeking new investments
Method of Compensation: Return on investment is of primary concern, do not charge fees

CONNECTING CAPITAL SWEDEN AB

Wallingatan Two
Stockholm, Sweden 111 60
Phone: 4686796610
E-mail: contact@connectingcapital.se
Website: www.connectingcapital.se

Management and Staff
Jeanine Bergstrom, Partner
Lina Nilsson, Partner
Nils Bergstrom, Chief Executive Officer

Type of Firm
Private Equity Firm

Association Membership
Swedish Venture Capital Association (SVCA)

Project Preferences

Type of Financing Preferred:
Generalist PE

Geographical Preferences

International Preferences:
Scandanavia/Nordic Region

Industry Preferences

In Industrial/Energy prefer:
Industrial Products

Additional Information
Year Founded: 1896
Current Activity Level : Actively seeking new investments

CONNECTION CAPITAL LLP

Four Park Place
London, United Kingdom SW1A 1LP
Phone: 442031782453
E-mail: enquiries@connectioncapital.co.uk
Website: www.connectioncapital.co.uk

Management and Staff

Bernard Dale, Partner
Claire Madden, Partner
Steve Wilson, Partner
Sue Heard, Partner

Type of Firm

Corporate PE/Venture

Project Preferences

Type of Financing Preferred:
Leveraged Buyout
Value-Add
Mezzanine
Later Stage
Acquisition

Geographical Preferences

International Preferences:
United Kingdom

Industry Preferences

In Financial Services prefer:
Real Estate

Additional Information

Year Founded: 2010
Current Activity Level : Actively seeking new investments

CONNEXUS EQUITY MANAGEMENT PARTNERS LLC

P. O. Box 10522
Newport Beach, CA USA 92658
Phone: 9496399710
E-mail: info@connexuspartners.com
Website: www.connexuspartners.com

Type of Firm

Private Equity Firm

Project Preferences

Type of Financing Preferred:
Early Stage
Expansion
Later Stage
Startup

Industry Preferences

In Internet Specific prefer:
Ecommerce

In Consumer Related prefer:
Sports
Retail
Food/Beverage
Consumer Products
Hotels and Resorts

In Manufact. prefer:
Manufacturing

Additional Information

Year Founded: 2013
Current Activity Level : Actively seeking new investments

CONOR VENTURE PARTNERS OY

Tekniikantie 14
Innopoli 2
Espoo, Finland 02150
Phone: 358925177370
Fax: 35898127305
Website: www.conor.vc

Management and Staff

Jari Mieskonen, Managing Partner
Jarkko Penttila, Partner
Manu Makela, Co-Founder
Sami Ahvenniemi, Co-Founder

Type of Firm

Private Equity Firm

Association Membership

Finnish Venture Capital Association (FVCA)
Swedish Venture Capital Association (SVCA)
European Private Equity and Venture Capital Assoc.

Project Preferences

Type of Financing Preferred:
Early Stage
Seed
Startup

Size of Investments Considered:
Min Size of Investment Considered (000s): $710
Max Size of Investment Considered (000s): $2,131

Geographical Preferences

International Preferences:
Sweden
Estonia
Finland
Latvia
Lithuania

Industry Preferences

In Communications prefer:
Communications and Media
Wireless Communications

In Computer Software prefer:
Software

In Semiconductor/Electr prefer:
Electronics
Semiconductor
Fiber Optics

In Medical/Health prefer:
Pharmaceuticals

In Industrial/Energy prefer:
Alternative Energy

Additional Information

Name of Most Recent Fund: Conor Technology Fund II
Most Recent Fund Was Raised: 05/05/2010
Year Founded: 2005
Capital Under Management: $21,800,000
Current Activity Level : Actively seeking new investments

CONSECO GLOBAL INVESTMENTS

18/F, Room 18
China World Tower 1
Beijing, China
Phone: 86-10-6505-0636
Fax: 86-10-6505-5635
E-mail: conseco@public.bta.net.cn

Type of Firm

Insurance Firm Affiliate

Association Membership

Venture Capital Association of Beijing (VCAB)

Project Preferences

Type of Financing Preferred:
Balanced

Geographical Preferences

International Preferences:
China

Additional Information

Year Founded: 1997
Current Activity Level : Actively seeking new investments

CONSEIL PLUS GESTION SAS

5, rue Charles Duchesne
Aix-en-Provence, France 13290
Website: www.cpgfinance.com

Type of Firm

Private Equity Firm

Project Preferences

Type of Financing Preferred:
Leveraged Buyout
Early Stage
Expansion
Later Stage
Seed
Management Buyouts
Acquisition

Geographical Preferences

International Preferences:
Europe
France

Additional Information

Year Founded: 1999
Current Activity Level : Actively seeking new investments

CONSENSUS CAPITAL PRIVATE EQUITY LTD

45, Charlotte Square
Edinburgh, United Kingdom EH24HQ
Phone: 441315100289
Fax: 441315100302
E-mail: info@ccpe.net
Website: ccpe.net

Management and Staff

Charlie Clements, Chief Executive Officer

Type of Firm

Private Equity Firm

Project Preferences

Type of Financing Preferred:
Leveraged Buyout
Early Stage
Expansion
Generalist PE
Balanced
Later Stage
Management Buyouts
Acquisition

Geographical Preferences

United States Preferences:
All U.S.

International Preferences:
United Kingdom
Europe
Middle East

Additional Information

Year Founded: 2011
Current Activity Level : Actively seeking new investments

CONSIGLIERE BRAND CAPITAL LLC

111 Eigth Avenue
15th Floor
New York, NY USA 10011
Phone: 2126345857
E-mail: hey@theconsig.com
Website: www.theconsig.com

Management and Staff

Mike Duda, Founder
Steve Nash, Founder

Type of Firm

Investment Management Firm

Project Preferences

Type of Financing Preferred:
Seed
Startup

Geographical Preferences

United States Preferences:
New York

Industry Preferences

In Consumer Related prefer:
Consumer
Consumer Products
Consumer Services

Additional Information

Year Founded: 2010
Current Activity Level : Actively seeking new investments

CONSILIUM SGR PA

Via Sacchi 7
Milan, Italy 20121
Phone: 39027260191
Fax: 390272095768
E-mail: info@consiliumsgr.it
Website: www.consiliumsgr.it

Management and Staff

Antonio Glorioso, Partner
Roberto De Rossi, Partner
Stefano Iamoni, Partner

Type of Firm

Private Equity Firm

Association Membership

Italian Venture Capital Association (AIFI)

Project Preferences

Type of Financing Preferred:
Leveraged Buyout
Recapitalizations

Size of Investments Considered:
Min Size of Investment Considered (000s): $3,811
Max Size of Investment Considered (000s): $7,621

Geographical Preferences

International Preferences:
Italy

Additional Information

Year Founded: 2005
Capital Under Management: $56,900,000
Current Activity Level : Actively seeking new investments

CONSILLA PARTNERS LTD

Three Hardman Street
Tenth Floor
Manchester, United Kingdom M3 3HF
Phone: 441619321485
E-mail: info@consiliapartners.com
Website: www.consiliapartners.com

Type of Firm

Private Equity Firm

Project Preferences

Type of Financing Preferred:
Leveraged Buyout
Acquisition

Geographical Preferences

International Preferences:
United Kingdom
Europe

Industry Preferences

In Business Serv. prefer:
Services
Distribution

In Manufact. prefer:
Manufacturing

Additional Information

Year Founded: 2015
Current Activity Level : Actively seeking new investments

CONSOLIDATED INVESTMENT GROUP INC

18 Inverness Place East
Englewood, CO USA 80112
Phone: 3037892664
Fax: 3037892696
E-mail: info@ciginvest.com
Website: www.ciginvest.com

Management and Staff

Juanita Belle, Vice President
Tim Bertoch, Vice President

Type of Firm
Investment Management Firm

Project Preferences

Type of Financing Preferred:
Leveraged Buyout
Early Stage
Expansion
Generalist PE
Balanced
Later Stage
Acquisition
Recapitalizations

Size of Investments Considered:
Min Size of Investment Considered (000s): $5,000
Max Size of Investment Considered (000s): $20,000

Geographical Preferences

United States Preferences:
All U.S.

International Preferences:
All International

Industry Preferences

In Consumer Related prefer:
Food/Beverage

Additional Information
Year Founded: 2001
Current Activity Level : Actively seeking new investments

CONSONANCE CAPITAL PARTNERS LP

1370 Avenue of the Americas
33rd Floor
New York, NY USA 10019
Phone: 2126608060
Fax: 2126608098
Website: consonancecapital.com

Management and Staff
Benjamin Edmands, Co-Founder
Javier Starkand, Principal
Mitchell Blutt, Co-Founder
Nancy-Ann DeParle, Co-Founder
Sapna Jethwa, Vice President
Sean Breen, Principal
Stephen McKenna, Co-Founder
Wencell Fowler, Chief Financial Officer

Type of Firm
Private Equity Firm

Project Preferences

Type of Financing Preferred:
Leveraged Buyout
Expansion
Acquisition
Recapitalizations

Geographical Preferences

United States Preferences:

Industry Preferences

In Medical/Health prefer:
Medical/Health

Additional Information
Name of Most Recent Fund: Consonance Private Equity, L.P.
Most Recent Fund Was Raised: 01/31/2013
Year Founded: 2011
Capital Under Management: $1,000,000,000
Current Activity Level : Actively seeking new investments

CONSTELLATION CAPITAL AG

Kantonsstrasse 77
Freienbach, Switzerland 8807
Phone: 41444826666
Fax: 41444826663
E-mail: info@constellation.ch
Website: www.constellation.ch

Other Offices
400 Embassy Row Northeast
Suite 100
Atlanta, GA USA 30328
Phone: 4157263676
Fax: 4158990219

Industriestrasse 47
Zug, Switzerland 6300
Phone: 41417110801
Fax: 41417110170

12 rue des Minimes
Paris, France 75003
Phone: 33141802500
Fax: 33141802523

Management and Staff
Rainer Froehlich, Managing Partner
Ralf Flore, Managing Partner

Type of Firm
Private Equity Firm

Association Membership
Swiss Venture Capital Association (SECA)
European Private Equity and Venture Capital Assoc.

Project Preferences

Type of Financing Preferred:
Leveraged Buyout
Turnaround
Later Stage
Management Buyouts
Acquisition
Recapitalizations

Geographical Preferences

International Preferences:
Switzerland
Austria
Germany

Industry Preferences

In Medical/Health prefer:
Medical/Health
Health Services

In Consumer Related prefer:
Education Related

In Financial Services prefer:
Financial Services
Financial Services

In Business Serv. prefer:
Services

Additional Information
Year Founded: 1992
Capital Under Management: $149,421,000
Current Activity Level : Actively seeking new investments

CONSTITUTION CAPITAL PARTNERS LLC

300 Brickstone Square
Tenth Floor
Andover, MA USA 01810
Phone: 9787499600
Fax: 9787499669
E-mail: info@concp.com
Website: www.concp.com

Management and Staff
Alexander Tatum, Principal
Dan Cahill, Managing Partner
Daniel Clare, Partner
John Guinee, Managing Partner
Peter Melanson, Partner
Robert Hatch, Partner
Vicente Miguel Ramos, Partner
William Richardson, Partner

Type of Firm
Private Equity Advisor or Fund of Funds

Geographical Preferences

United States Preferences:
North America

Additional Information
Name of Most Recent Fund: Ironsides Partnership Fund III, L.P.
Most Recent Fund Was Raised: 06/19/2013
Year Founded: 2008
Capital Under Management: $1,728,100,000
Current Activity Level : Actively seeking new investments

CONSUS ASSET MANAGEMENT CO LTD

23Yeouido-Dong,Yeongdeungpo Gu
F9,Shinhan Inv Tower
Seoul, South Korea
Phone: 82220775000
Fax: 82220775019
Website: www.consus.co.kr

Type of Firm
Investment Management Firm

Project Preferences

Type of Financing Preferred:
Leveraged Buyout
Later Stage

Geographical Preferences

International Preferences:
Korea, South

Industry Preferences

In Medical/Health prefer:
Medical/Health

In Financial Services prefer:
Financial Services

Additional Information
Year Founded: 2004
Current Activity Level : Actively seeking new investments

CONTINENTAL CAPITAL MARKETS LTD

Eight Wilfred Street
CCP House
London, United Kingdom SW1E 6PL
Phone: 44-20-7630-2010
Fax: 44-20-7630-2011
E-mail: info@dealmaker.co.uk
Website: www.ccpltd.net

Management and Staff
Roger C. Luscombe, Founder

Type of Firm
Private Equity Firm

Project Preferences

Type of Financing Preferred:
Fund of Funds
Leveraged Buyout
Mezzanine
Generalist PE
Management Buyouts
Acquisition
Private Placement
Recapitalizations

Geographical Preferences

International Preferences:
United Kingdom
Europe

Additional Information
Year Founded: 1997
Current Activity Level : Actively seeking new investments

CONTINENTAL INVESTORS LIFE INC

227 West Monroe Street
Suite 5045
Chicago, IL USA 60606
Phone: 3126282451

Type of Firm
Private Equity Firm

Project Preferences

Type of Financing Preferred:
Generalist PE
Balanced

Size of Investments Considered:
Min Size of Investment Considered (000s): $3,000
Max Size of Investment Considered (000s): $12,000

Industry Preferences

In Consumer Related prefer:
Consumer

In Financial Services prefer:
Financial Services

Additional Information
Year Founded: 2006
Current Activity Level : Actively seeking new investments

CONTINUITY CAPITAL

12 Moore Street
Level 8
Canberra, Australia ACT 2601
Phone: 61262454100
Fax: 61262628746
Website: www.continuitycp.com

Other Offices
2 Queen's Road, Cheung Kong Center
Level 19
Central, Hong Kong
Phone: 85234695588
Fax: 85234695000

Type of Firm
Private Equity Firm

Project Preferences

Type of Financing Preferred:
Fund of Funds
Expansion

Additional Information
Year Founded: 2010
Current Activity Level : Actively seeking new investments

CONTINUUM CAPITAL LLC

One Montgomery Street
25th Floor
San Francisco, CA USA 94104
Website: www.continuumcapital.com

Management and Staff
Tyson Carter, Vice President
Vladimir Jacimovic, Managing Director

Type of Firm
Private Equity Firm

Project Preferences

Type of Financing Preferred:
Leveraged Buyout
Expansion
Acquisition

Industry Preferences

In Computer Software prefer:
Software

In Business Serv. prefer:
Services

Additional Information
Year Founded: 2007
Current Activity Level : Actively seeking new investments

CONTOUR VENTURE PARTNERS

475 Park Avenue South
6th Floor
New York, NY USA 10016
Website: www.contourventures.com

Management and Staff
I. Robert Greene, Co-Founder
Matthew Gorin, Co-Founder

Type of Firm
Private Equity Firm

Project Preferences

Role in Financing:
Prefer role as deal originator but will also invest in deals created by others

Type of Financing Preferred:
Early Stage
Seed
First Stage Financing
Startup

Size of Investments Considered:
Min Size of Investment Considered (000s): $250
Max Size of Investment Considered (000s): $1,500

Geographical Preferences

United States Preferences:
Northeast

Industry Preferences

In Computer Software prefer:
Software

In Internet Specific prefer:
Internet

In Financial Services prefer:
Financial Services

In Business Serv. prefer:
Services
Media

Additional Information
Name of Most Recent Fund: Contour Venture Partners II, L.P.
Most Recent Fund Was Raised: 10/09/2009
Year Founded: 2006
Capital Under Management: $23,500,000
Current Activity Level : Actively seeking new investments

CONTRARIAN CAPITAL INDIA PARTNERS PVT LTD

Dr. E. Moses Road
Turf Estate, 215, 2nd Floor
Mumbai, India 400011
Phone: 02266170902
E-mail: team@contrariancapindia.com
Website: www.contrariancapindia.com

Type of Firm
Private Equity Firm

Project Preferences

Type of Financing Preferred:
Early Stage
Expansion
Balanced

Geographical Preferences

International Preferences:
India
Asia

Industry Preferences

In Medical/Health prefer:
Health Services

In Consumer Related prefer:
Food/Beverage
Education Related

In Industrial/Energy prefer:
Energy

In Agr/Forestr/Fish prefer:
Agribusiness

Additional Information
Year Founded: 2013
Current Activity Level : Actively seeking new investments

CONVALUE INVESTMENT GMBH

Rooseveltplatz 10
Vienna, Austria A-1090
E-mail: office@convalue.at
Website: www.convalue.at

Management and Staff
Daniel Gaertner, Chief Operating Officer

Type of Firm
Private Equity Firm

Association Membership
Austrian PE and Venture Capital Association (AVCO)

Project Preferences

Type of Financing Preferred:
Leveraged Buyout
Expansion
Turnaround
Acquisition
Recapitalizations

Geographical Preferences

International Preferences:
Switzerland
Austria
Germany

Industry Preferences

In Consumer Related prefer:
Retail

In Business Serv. prefer:
Services
Distribution

In Manufact. prefer:
Manufacturing

Additional Information
Year Founded: 2009
Current Activity Level : Actively seeking new investments

CONVENTIONAL WISDOM CAPITAL LTD

No. 4009 Shennan Avenue
2101, Investment Building
Shenzhen, China 518048
Phone: 86-755-33368756
Fax: 86-755-33368755
E-mail: master@szcwcl.com
Website: www.szcwcl.com

Type of Firm
Private Equity Firm

Project Preferences

Role in Financing:
Prefer role in deals created by others

Type of Financing Preferred:
Later Stage

Geographical Preferences

International Preferences:
China

Additional Information
Year Founded: 2008
Current Activity Level : Actively seeking new investments

CONVERGE

101 Main Street
Cambridge, MA USA 02142
Website: converge.vc

Other Offices
1000 Winter Street
Suite 4000
WALTHAM, MA USA 02451
Phone: 7812749124

Management and Staff
Ash Egan, Principal
Maia Heymann, General Partner
Roberto Ramirez, Chief Financial Officer

Type of Firm
Private Equity Firm

Association Membership
New England Venture Capital Association

Project Preferences

Role in Financing:
Prefer role as deal originator

Type of Financing Preferred:
Early Stage
Seed

Size of Investments Considered:
Min Size of Investment Considered (000s): $250
Max Size of Investment Considered (000s): $1,000

Geographical Preferences

United States Preferences:
Northeast
Massachusetts
New York

Canadian Preferences:
All Canada

Additional Information
Name of Most Recent Fund: CommonAngels Ventures Fund IV, L.P.
Most Recent Fund Was Raised: 12/11/2013
Year Founded: 1998
Capital Under Management: $50,000,000
Current Activity Level : Actively seeking new investments

CONVERGENCE ACCEL

Jl H.R. Rasuna Said Kav 20
H-Tower 18/F
Jakarta, Indonesia 12940
Phone: 622129718644
Fax: 622129718601
E-mail: info@convergenceaccel.com
Website: convergenceaccel.com

Type of Firm
Private Equity Firm

Project Preferences

Type of Financing Preferred:
Early Stage

Geographical Preferences

International Preferences:
Indonesia

Industry Preferences

In Internet Specific prefer:
E-Commerce Technology
Ecommerce

Additional Information
Year Founded: 2014
Capital Under Management: $25,000,000
Current Activity Level : Actively seeking new investments

CONVERGENCE PARTNERS INVESTMENTS (PTY) LTD

33 Fricker Road, Illovo
Johannesburg, South Africa 2196
Phone: 27115505320
Fax: 27115505321
E-mail: info@convergencepartners.co.za
Website: www.convergencepartners.co.za

Other Offices
Postnet 232
Pvt Bag X11
Craighall, South Africa 2024

Type of Firm
Private Equity Firm

Project Preferences

Type of Financing Preferred:
Leveraged Buyout
Early Stage
Expansion
Balanced
Later Stage
Acquisition

Geographical Preferences

International Preferences:
Middle East
Asia
South Africa
Africa

Industry Preferences

In Communications prefer:
Communications and Media
Commercial Communications

Additional Information
Year Founded: 2006
Capital Under Management: $200,000,000
Current Activity Level : Actively seeking new investments

CONVERGENCE VENTURES

Jl. KH. Mas Mansyur Kav. 121
Citylofts Sudirman, 26th Floor
Jakarta, Indonesia 10220
Phone: 622129264177
Fax: 62212971860
E-mail: info@convergencevc.com
Website: www.convergencevc.com

Other Offices
Jl. KH. Mas Mansyur Kav. 121
Citylofts Sudirman 26th Floor
Jakarta, Indonesia 10220
Phone: 622129264177
Fax: 62212971860

Type of Firm
Private Equity Firm

Project Preferences

Type of Financing Preferred:
Early Stage

Geographical Preferences

International Preferences:
Indonesia

Additional Information
Year Founded: 2016
Capital Under Management: $30,000,000
Current Activity Level : Actively seeking new investments

CONVERGENT CAPITAL PARTNERS

505 North Highway 169
Suite 245
Minneapolis, MN USA 55441
Phone: 7634324080
Fax: 7634324085
Website: www.cvcap.com

Type of Firm
Private Equity Firm

Association Membership
Natl Assoc of Small Bus. Inv. Co (NASBIC)

Project Preferences

Type of Financing Preferred:
Expansion
Management Buyouts
Acquisition
Recapitalizations

Geographical Preferences

United States Preferences:

Additional Information
Year Founded: 1998
Current Activity Level : Actively seeking new investments

CONVERSION CAPITAL LLC

902 Broadway
Suite 1611
New York, NY USA 10011
Phone: 9176279539
E-mail: Info@ConversionCapital.com
Website: www.conversioncapital.com

Type of Firm
Private Equity Firm

Project Preferences

Type of Financing Preferred:
Balanced

Industry Preferences

In Business Serv. prefer:
Services

Additional Information

Year Founded: 2012
Capital Under Management: $8,350,000
Current Activity Level : Actively seeking new investments

CONVERSION VENTURE CAPITAL LLC

216 East 45th Street
Sixth Floor
New York, NY USA 10017
Phone: 2128121417
Website: www.cvc2.com

Type of Firm

Private Equity Firm

Project Preferences

Type of Financing Preferred:
Leveraged Buyout
Expansion
Generalist PE
Acquisition

Additional Information

Year Founded: 2012
Current Activity Level : Actively seeking new investments

COOL JAPAN FUND INC

6-10-1, Roppongi, Minato-ku
17F Roppongi Hills Mori Tower
Tokyo, Japan 106-6117
Phone: 81364067500
Fax: 81364067501
Website: www.cj-fund.co.jp

Type of Firm

Government Affiliated Program

Project Preferences

Type of Financing Preferred:
Balanced

Geographical Preferences

International Preferences:
Japan

Industry Preferences

In Communications prefer:
Media and Entertainment

In Consumer Related prefer:
Retail
Food/Beverage

In Business Serv. prefer:
Services

Additional Information

Year Founded: 2013
Current Activity Level : Actively seeking new investments

COOLEY LLP

101 California Street
Fifth Floor
San Francisco, CA USA 94111
Phone: 4156932000
Website: www.cooley.com

Other Offices

3000 El Camino Real
Five Palo Alto Square
Palo Alto, CA USA 94306
Phone: 6508435000

3175 Hanover Street
Palo Alto, CA USA 94304
Phone: 6508435000

1114 Avenue of the Americas
The Grace Building
New York, NY USA 10036
Phone: 2124796000

1299 Pennsylvania Avenue Northwest
Suite 700
Washington, DC USA 20004
Phone: 2028427800

500 Boylston Street
Boston, MA USA 02116
Phone: 6179372300

1700 Seventh Avenue
Suite 1900
Seattle, WA USA 98101
Phone: 2064528700

380 Interlocken Crescent
Suite 900
Broomfield, CO USA 80021
Phone: 7205664000

4401 Eastgate Mall
San Diego, CA USA 92121
Phone: 8585506000

11951 Freedom Drive
One Freedom Square, Reston Town Center
Herndon, VA USA 20190
Phone: 7034568000

Eight Century Avenue
International Finance Center, Tower 2
Shanghai, China 200120
Phone: 862160627238

Management and Staff

Alan Levine, Partner
Alfred Browne, Partner
Barbara Kosacz, Partner
C. Christopher Shoff, Partner
Craig Dauchy, Partner
David Hernand, Partner
David Young, Partner
Eric Schwartzman, Partner
Frank Pietrantonio, Partner
Frederick Muto, Partner
Ian Smith, Partner
James Strawbridge, Partner
James Linfield, Partner
Jamie Leigh, Partner
Jennifer Massey, Partner
Joe Conroy, Chief Executive Officer
John Dwyer, Partner
John Robertson, Partner
Kathleen Goodhart, Partner
Kevin Rooney, Partner
Louis Lehot, Partner
Mark Pitchford, Partner
Michael Rhodes, Partner
Michael Attanasio, Partner
Patrick Gunn, Partner
R. Ronald Hopkinson, Partner
Ryan Naftulin, Partner
Shira Nadich Levin, Partner
Stephen Rosen, Partner
Steve Tonsfeldt, Partner
Thomas Hopkins, Partner
Warren Martin, Chief Operating Officer
Wendy Goldstein, Partner

Type of Firm

Service Provider

Association Membership

Mid-Atlantic Venture Association

Project Preferences

Type of Financing Preferred:
Balanced

Industry Preferences

In Medical/Health prefer:
Medical/Health
Health Services

In Consumer Related prefer:
Retail

In Industrial/Energy prefer:
Energy
Environmental Related

In Financial Services prefer:
Real Estate

Additional Information
Year Founded: 1920
Current Activity Level : Actively seeking new investments

COOLHOUSE LABS LLC

277 East Main Street
Harbor Springs, MI USA 49740
Phone: 4356591294
E-mail: info@coolhouselabs.com
Website: coolhouselabs.com

Type of Firm
Incubator/Development Program

Project Preferences

Type of Financing Preferred:
Early Stage
Seed
Startup

Size of Investments Considered:
Min Size of Investment Considered (000s): $25
Max Size of Investment Considered (000s): $100

Additional Information
Year Founded: 2013
Capital Under Management: $1,000,000
Current Activity Level : Actively seeking new investments

COOLIDGE CORNER INVESTMENT

707-24 Yeoksamdong, Gangnamgu
911-913, Hanshin Intervalley24
Seoul, South Korea
Phone: 82221832740
Fax: 82221832750
E-mail: ccvc1@ccvc.co.kr
Website: www.ccvc.co.kr

Type of Firm
Private Equity Firm

Association Membership
Korean Venture Capital Association (KVCA)

Project Preferences

Type of Financing Preferred:
Early Stage
Seed

Geographical Preferences

International Preferences:
Korea, South

Industry Preferences

In Communications prefer:
Communications and Media
Radio & TV Broadcasting
Media and Entertainment
Entertainment
Publishing

In Internet Specific prefer:
E-Commerce Technology
Internet
Ecommerce

In Consumer Related prefer:
Entertainment and Leisure
Retail

Additional Information
Year Founded: 2010
Capital Under Management: $15,091,000
Current Activity Level : Actively seeking new investments

COOPER INVESTMENT PARTNERS

1633 BROADWAY
18TH FLOOR
New York, NY USA 10019
Phone: 2122752800
Website: www.cooperinvest.net

Type of Firm
Private Equity Firm

Project Preferences

Type of Financing Preferred:
Recapitalizations

Geographical Preferences

United States Preferences:
All U.S.

Additional Information
Year Founded: 2010
Current Activity Level : Actively seeking new investments

COOPFOND SPA

Via Guattani, 9
Rome, Italy 00161
Phone: 39064424935
Fax: 390644249659
Website: www.coopfond.it

Other Offices
Via Cairoli, 11
Bologna, Italy 40121
Phone: 39-051-5282-811
Fax: 39-051-5282-888

Type of Firm
Private Equity Firm

Additional Information
Year Founded: 1992
Current Activity Level : Actively seeking new investments

COPACABANA HOUSE VENTURES

22, Rua Xavier Silveira
Rio De Janeiro, Brazil
Phone: 552199497767
Website: www.copacabanahouse.com.br

Type of Firm
Private Equity Firm

Project Preferences

Type of Financing Preferred:
Early Stage
Recapitalizations

Geographical Preferences

International Preferences:
Brazil

Industry Preferences

In Communications prefer:
Data Communications

In Computer Software prefer:
Software

In Consumer Related prefer:
Education Related

Additional Information
Year Founded: 2015
Current Activity Level : Actively seeking new investments

COPARION GMBH & CO KG

Charles-de-Gaulle-Platz 1d
Cologne, Germany 50679
Phone: 493058584400
E-mail: info@coparion.de
Website: www.coparion.de

Type of Firm
Private Equity Firm

Additional Information
Year Founded: 2016
Capital Under Management: $254,550,000
Current Activity Level : Actively seeking new investments

COPELEY CAPITAL PARTNERS I LP

129 West Trade Street, Suite 1225
Charlotte, NC USA 28202
Phone: 7044093070
Fax: 7044093075

Management and Staff
Lane Faison, Managing Partner
Richard Jones, Principal

Type of Firm
Private Equity Firm

Project Preferences

Type of Financing Preferred:
Leveraged Buyout
Expansion
Management Buyouts
Acquisition

Geographical Preferences

United States Preferences:
Mid Atlantic
Southeast

Industry Preferences

In Medical/Health prefer:
Medical/Health

In Industrial/Energy prefer:
Materials

In Business Serv. prefer:
Services

In Manufact. prefer:
Manufacturing

Additional Information
Year Founded: 2003
Capital Under Management: $20,000,000
Current Activity Level : Actively seeking new investments

COPIA AGRO AND FOOD LTD

32 Neve Reim Street
Ramat Hasharon, Israel
Phone: 97235353043
Fax: 97237618001
E-mail: info@copia-agro.com
Website: copia-agro.com

Other Offices
32 Neve Reim Street
Ramat Hasharon, Israel
Phone: 97235353043
Fax: 97237618001

Type of Firm
Private Equity Firm

Project Preferences

Type of Financing Preferred:
Early Stage
Seed

Geographical Preferences

International Preferences:
Israel

Industry Preferences

In Semiconductor/Electr prefer:
Analytic/Scientific

In Biotechnology prefer:
Biotechnology
Agricultural/Animal Bio.
Biotech Related Research

In Consumer Related prefer:
Food/Beverage

In Agr/Forestr/Fish prefer:
Agriculture related

Additional Information
Year Founded: 2014
Current Activity Level : Actively seeking new investments

COPLEX VENTURES FUND I LP

515 East Grant Street
Phoenix, AZ USA 85004
Phone: 4802488261
Website: www.coplexventures.com

Type of Firm
Corporate PE/Venture

Project Preferences

Type of Financing Preferred:
Balanced

Industry Preferences

In Computer Software prefer:
Software

In Internet Specific prefer:
E-Commerce Technology

In Business Serv. prefer:
Media

Additional Information
Year Founded: 2017
Capital Under Management: $5,000,000
Current Activity Level : Actively seeking new investments

COPLEY EQUITY PARTNERS LLC

101 Huntington Avenue
Fifth Floor
Boston, MA USA 02199
Phone: 6178804305
E-mail: info@copleyequity.com
Website: copleyequity.com

Management and Staff
Andrew Miller, Co-Founder
Matthew Bryson, Vice President
Peter Trovato, Co-Founder
Robert Hale, Co-Founder

Type of Firm
Private Equity Firm

Project Preferences

Type of Financing Preferred:
Leveraged Buyout
Balanced
Management Buyouts
Acquisition

Industry Preferences

In Communications prefer:
Communications and Media
Media and Entertainment

In Computer Software prefer:
Applications Software

In Internet Specific prefer:
E-Commerce Technology

In Other prefer:
Environment Responsible

Additional Information
Year Founded: 1969
Capital Under Management: $500,000,000
Current Activity Level : Actively seeking new investments

CORADIN INC

675, Saint Charles
Marieville, Canada J3M1B3
Phone: 514-658-0661
Fax: 514-658-9158

Management and Staff
Pierre Lizotte, Vice President

Type of Firm
Private Equity Firm

Additional Information
Year Founded: 1976
Current Activity Level : Actively seeking new investments

CORAL VENTURES INC

60 South Sixth Street, Suite 2410
Minneapolis, MN USA 55402
Phone: 6123358666
Website: www.coralventures.com

Management and Staff
Christopher Smith, Managing Director
Mark Headrick, Managing Director
Miki Granski, Managing Director
Richard Siber, Managing Director

Type of Firm
Private Equity Firm

Project Preferences

Role in Financing:
Will function either as deal originator or investor in deals created by others

Type of Financing Preferred:
Early Stage
Expansion
Balanced
Later Stage

Size of Investments Considered:
Min Size of Investment Considered (000s): $3,000
Max Size of Investment Considered (000s): $15,000

Geographical Preferences

United States Preferences:

International Preferences:
Europe
Israel

Industry Focus

(% based on actual investment)

Industry	%
Internet Specific	25.7%
Communications and Media	23.8%
Medical/Health	19.4%
Computer Software and Services	15.9%
Semiconductors/Other Elect.	5.6%
Biotechnology	4.4%
Computer Hardware	2.6%
Industrial/Energy	2.0%
Other Products	0.5%

Additional Information
Year Founded: 1990
Capital Under Management: $350,000,000
Current Activity Level : Actively seeking new investments
Method of Compensation: Return on investment is of primary concern, do not charge fees

CORAZON CAPITAL LLC

222 W. Merchandise Mart Plaza
Chicago, IL USA 60654
Phone: 6128170589
Website: www.corazoncap.com

Management and Staff
Chris Coyne, Co-Founder
Christian Rudder, Co-Founder
Max Krohn, Co-Founder
Sam Yagan, Co-Founder
Steven Farsht, Co-Founder
Zach Kaplan, Co-Founder

Type of Firm
Private Equity Firm

Project Preferences

Type of Financing Preferred:
Balanced

Additional Information
Name of Most Recent Fund: Corazon Capital LLC
Most Recent Fund Was Raised: 01/10/2014
Year Founded: 2014
Capital Under Management: $43,615,000
Current Activity Level : Actively seeking new investments

CORBEL STRUCTURED EQUITY PARTNERS

12400 Wilshire Boulevard
Suite 645
West Los Angeles, CA USA 90025
Phone: 3104427011
Website: www.corbelsep.com

Type of Firm
Private Equity Firm

Project Preferences

Type of Financing Preferred:
Leveraged Buyout
Expansion
Acquisition
Recapitalizations

Industry Preferences

In Consumer Related prefer:
Retail
Consumer Products
Consumer Services

In Business Serv. prefer:
Services

In Manufact. prefer:
Manufacturing

Additional Information
Name of Most Recent Fund: Corbel Structured Equity Partners, L.P.
Most Recent Fund Was Raised: 12/24/2013
Year Founded: 2013
Capital Under Management: $21,425,000
Current Activity Level : Actively seeking new investments

CORDIANT CAPITAL INC

1002 Sherbrooke St. West
Suite 2800
Montreal, Canada H3A 3L6
Phone: 5142861142
E-mail: info@cordiantcap.com
Website: cordiantcap.com

Other Offices
1010 Sherbrooke Street West
Suite 2400
Montreal, Canada H3A 2R7

Type of Firm
Private Equity Firm

Association Membership
Emerging Markets Private Equity Association

Project Preferences

Type of Financing Preferred:
Leveraged Buyout
Expansion
Mezzanine
Generalist PE
Later Stage
Management Buyouts

Geographical Preferences

International Preferences:
Asia Pacific
Latin America
Central Europe
China
Mexico
Eastern Europe
Middle East
Brazil
Asia
Russia
Africa

Additional Information
Name of Most Recent Fund: Canada Investment Fund for Africa (CIFA)
Most Recent Fund Was Raised: 05/31/2004
Year Founded: 1999
Capital Under Management: $930,000,000
Current Activity Level : Actively seeking new investments

CORDISH PRIVATE VENTURES LLC

601 East Pratt Street
6th Floor
Baltimore, MD USA 21202
Phone: 4107525444
Website: www.cordish.com

Type of Firm
Corporate PE/Venture

Project Preferences

Type of Financing Preferred:
Fund of Funds
Leveraged Buyout
Mezzanine
Generalist PE
Balanced
Acquisition
Distressed Debt

Additional Information

Year Founded: 1998
Current Activity Level : Actively seeking new investments

CORE CAPITAL MANAGEMENT CO LTD

No. 87, West 3rd Ring Road
Room 702-703, Tower C
Beijing, China
Phone: 861088820200
Fax: 861088820975
Website: www.yszbgroup.com

Management and Staff

Chunfang Liu, Managing Partner

Type of Firm

Private Equity Firm

Project Preferences

Type of Financing Preferred:
Leveraged Buyout

Geographical Preferences

International Preferences:
China

Additional Information

Year Founded: 2014
Current Activity Level : Actively seeking new investments

CORE CAPITAL PARTNERS II L P

1717 K Street North West
Suite 920
Washington, DC USA 20006
Phone: 2025890090
Fax: 2025890091
E-mail: info@core-capital.com
Website: www.core-capital.com

Management and Staff

Mark Levine, Managing Director
Pascal Luck, Managing Director
Randy Klueger, Chief Financial Officer
Thomas Wheeler, Managing Director
William Dunbar, Managing Director

Type of Firm

Private Equity Firm

Association Membership

Mid-Atlantic Venture Association
Natl Assoc of Small Bus. Inv. Co (NASBIC)

Project Preferences

Role in Financing:
Prefer role as deal originator but will also invest in deals created by others

Type of Financing Preferred:
Early Stage
Expansion
Balanced
Later Stage

Size of Investments Considered:
Min Size of Investment Considered (000s): $2,000
Max Size of Investment Considered (000s): $5,000

Geographical Preferences

United States Preferences:
East Coast

Industry Preferences

In Communications prefer:
Communications and Media
Wireless Communications

In Business Serv. prefer:
Services

Additional Information

Year Founded: 1999
Capital Under Management: $370,000,000
Current Activity Level : Actively seeking new investments
Method of Compensation: Return on investment is of primary concern, do not charge fees

CORE CAPITAL PARTNERS LLP

9, South Street
London, United Kingdom W1K 2XA
Phone: 02031790925
Fax: 02031790902
E-mail: info@core-cap.com
Website: www.core-cap.com

Management and Staff

David Steel, Partner
James Smallridge, Partner
Stephen Edwards, Managing Partner
Walid Fakhry, Managing Partner

Type of Firm

Private Equity Firm

Association Membership

British Venture Capital Association (BVCA)

Project Preferences

Type of Financing Preferred:
Leveraged Buyout
Mezzanine
Turnaround
Management Buyouts
Acquisition
Distressed Debt

Geographical Preferences

International Preferences:
United Kingdom

Additional Information

Year Founded: 2004
Capital Under Management: $85,000,000
Current Activity Level : Actively seeking new investments

CORE INDUSTRIAL PARTNERS

200 North LaSalle Street
Suite 2360
Chicago, IL USA 60601
Phone: 3125664880
Website: coreipfund.com

Type of Firm

Private Equity Firm

Project Preferences

Type of Financing Preferred:
Leveraged Buyout
Management Buyouts

Geographical Preferences

United States Preferences:
North America

Industry Preferences

In Industrial/Energy prefer:
Industrial Products

In Manufact. prefer:
Manufacturing

Additional Information

Year Founded: 2017
Current Activity Level : Actively seeking new investments

CORE INNOVATION CAPITAL I LP

1680 Vine Street
Suite 606
Los Angeles, CA USA 90028
Phone: 6465800046
E-mail: info@corevc.com
Website: www.corevc.com

Other Offices
Former HQ: 611 Broadway Avenue
Suite 510
New York, NY USA 10012
Phone: 2127800193

Management and Staff
Arjan Schutte, Managing Partner
Michael Harris, Managing Partner

Type of Firm
Private Equity Firm

Project Preferences

Role in Financing:
Prefer role as deal originator but will also invest in deals created by others

Type of Financing Preferred:
Expansion
Balanced
Seed

Size of Investments Considered:
Min Size of Investment Considered (000s): $500
Max Size of Investment Considered (000s): $3,000

Industry Preferences

In Financial Services prefer:
Financial Services

Additional Information
Year Founded: 2010
Capital Under Management: $30,000,000
Current Activity Level : Actively seeking new investments

CORE PARTNERS LLC

120-Tenth Street North West
Suite 200
Calgary, Canada T2N1V3
Phone: 403-270-9772
Fax: 403-270-4594

Management and Staff
Don Short, Partner
Jim Gibson, Partner
Ken MacLean, Partner
Kevin Weatherston, Partner
Martin Bunting, Partner
Neil Bowker, Partner
Rick Shannon, Partner

Type of Firm
Private Equity Firm

Project Preferences

Type of Financing Preferred:
Early Stage

Geographical Preferences

United States Preferences:
East Coast

Additional Information
Year Founded: 2005
Current Activity Level : Actively seeking new investments

CORECO HOLDINGS LLC

200 Mts Norte Escuela Espana
San Antonio de Belen
Heredia, Costa Rica
Phone: 50622390391
Fax: 3057043334
Website: www.corecoholding.com

Other Offices
2121 Southwest Third Avenue
Suite 200
Miami, FL USA 33129
Phone: 3057043344
Fax: 3057043334

14 Calle 3-51, Zona 10
Edificio Murano Center, Oficina 504
Guatemala City, Guatemala
Phone: 50222291324

Management and Staff
Alex von der Goltz, Managing Partner
Roberto Ponce Romay, Managing Partner
Will Muecke, Managing Partner

Type of Firm
Private Equity Firm

Association Membership
Emerging Markets Private Equity Association

Project Preferences

Type of Financing Preferred:
Expansion
Later Stage

Geographical Preferences

International Preferences:
Latin America
Dominican Rep.
Belize
El Salvador
Panama
Costa Rica
Nicaragua
Guatemala
Honduras

Industry Preferences

In Communications prefer:
Telecommunications
Wireless Communications

In Computer Software prefer:
Software
Systems Software
Applications Software

In Internet Specific prefer:
Internet

In Medical/Health prefer:
Medical/Health

In Consumer Related prefer:
Retail
Consumer Products

In Transportation prefer:
Transportation

In Financial Services prefer:
Financial Services

Additional Information
Year Founded: 2009
Capital Under Management: $54,000,000
Current Activity Level : Actively seeking new investments

COREST GMBH CORPORATE RESTRUCTURING

Inselstrasse 24
Duesseldorf, Germany 40479
Phone: 4902115136472
Fax: 4902115136449
E-mail: info@COREST.de
Website: www.microventure.de

Management and Staff
Andre Peto, Managing Director
Dietmar Klein, Managing Director

Type of Firm
Private Equity Firm

Project Preferences

Type of Financing Preferred:
Leveraged Buyout
Early Stage
Mezzanine
Turnaround
Later Stage
Management Buyouts
Startup

Geographical Preferences

International Preferences:
Germany

Industry Preferences

In Semiconductor/Electr prefer:
Micro-Processing
Sensors

Additional Information
Year Founded: 2000
Current Activity Level : Actively seeking new investments

CORIGIN PRIVATE EQUITY GROUP

505 Fifth Avenue
New York, NY USA 10017
Phone: 212-775-1111
E-mail: contact@corigin.com
Website: www.corigin.com

Management and Staff
Gregory Gleason, Founder
Thomas Landherr, Chief Financial Officer
Will Olivares, Vice President

Type of Firm
Private Equity Firm

Project Preferences

Type of Financing Preferred:
Core
Value-Add
Generalist PE

Geographical Preferences

United States Preferences:
New York

Industry Preferences

In Consumer Related prefer:
Food/Beverage

In Transportation prefer:
Transportation

In Financial Services prefer:
Financial Services
Real Estate

Additional Information
Year Founded: 2010
Current Activity Level : Actively seeking new investments

CORIGIN VENTURES

505 Fifth Avenue
New York, NY USA 10017
Website: coriginventures.com

Type of Firm
Private Equity Firm

Project Preferences

Type of Financing Preferred:
Early Stage

Industry Preferences

In Internet Specific prefer:
Internet
Ecommerce

In Medical/Health prefer:
Health Services

In Consumer Related prefer:
Retail

In Financial Services prefer:
Real Estate

Additional Information
Year Founded: 1969
Current Activity Level : Actively seeking new investments

CORINTHIAN CAPITAL GROUP LLC

601 Lexington Avenue
59th Floor
New York, NY USA 10022
Phone: 2129202300
Fax: 2129202399
E-mail: contact@corinthiancap.com
Website: www.corinthiancap.com

Other Offices
60 Station Street
Hingham, MA USA 02043
Phone: 6175909090
Fax: 7817494467

70 West Madison Street
Suite 1400
Chicago, IL USA 60602
Phone: 3128999988
Fax: 3128999099

Management and Staff
Abhaya Shrestha, Vice President
Adam Fitzner, Vice President
C. Kenneth Clay, Founder
James McNair, Senior Managing Director
Jason Caporrino, Vice President
Luis Mercader, Vice President
Nora de la Serna, Chief Financial Officer

Type of Firm
Private Equity Firm

Project Preferences

Role in Financing:
Prefer role as deal originator

Type of Financing Preferred:
Leveraged Buyout
Acquisition
Recapitalizations

Geographical Preferences

United States Preferences:
North America

Industry Preferences

In Consumer Related prefer:
Consumer Products

In Business Serv. prefer:
Services
Distribution

In Manufact. prefer:
Manufacturing

Additional Information
Name of Most Recent Fund: Corinthian Equity Fund II, L.P.
Most Recent Fund Was Raised: 01/07/2014
Year Founded: 2005
Capital Under Management: $315,000,000
Current Activity Level : Actively seeking new investments
Method of Compensation: Return on invest. most important, but chg. closing fees, service fees, etc.

CORNERSTONE ADVISORS INC

7272 East Indian School Road
Suite 400
Scottsdale, AZ USA 85251
Phone: 4804232030
Fax: 4804816076
Website: www.crnrstone.com

Management and Staff
Bill McFarland, Managing Director
Bob Roth, Managing Director
Carl Faulkner, Principal
Eric Weikart, Managing Director
Steve Williams, Co-Founder
Terence Roche, Co-Founder

Type of Firm
Investment Management Firm

Project Preferences

Type of Financing Preferred:
Balanced

Industry Preferences

In Financial Services prefer:
Financial Services

Additional Information
Year Founded: 1983
Capital Under Management: $1,700,000,000
Current Activity Level : Actively seeking new investments

CORNERSTONE CAPITAL HOLDINGS LLC

12400 Wilshire Boulevard
Suite 1180
West Los Angeles, CA USA 90025
Phone: 3104995670
Fax: 3122757855
Website: www.cstonecapital.com

Management and Staff
Andrew Bushell, Founder
Jonathan Alt, Founder
Lili Zhou, Chief Financial Officer

Type of Firm
Private Equity Firm

Project Preferences

Type of Financing Preferred:
Leveraged Buyout

Geographical Preferences

United States Preferences:

Industry Preferences

In Semiconductor/Electr prefer:
Electronic Components

In Transportation prefer:
Aerospace

In Business Serv. prefer:
Distribution

In Manufact. prefer:
Manufacturing

Additional Information
Year Founded: 2000
Current Activity Level : Actively seeking new investments

CORNERSTONE EQUITY PARTNERS

Yeoildo-Dong, Yeungdeungpo-Gu
18/ Korea Investment Securitie
Seoul, South Korea
Phone: 82232765109
Fax: 82232765099

Type of Firm
Private Equity Firm

Project Preferences

Type of Financing Preferred:
Leveraged Buyout
Management Buyouts

Geographical Preferences

International Preferences:
Asia
Korea, South

Additional Information
Year Founded: 2006
Current Activity Level : Actively seeking new investments

CORNERSTONE PARTNERS SP. Z O.O.

Aleja Szucha 6
Warsaw, Poland 00582
Phone: 48222121900
Fax: 48222121999
Website: www.cornerstone.pl

Type of Firm
Private Equity Firm

Project Preferences

Type of Financing Preferred:
Generalist PE

Geographical Preferences

International Preferences:
Central Europe
Poland
Eastern Europe

Additional Information
Year Founded: 2013
Current Activity Level : Actively seeking new investments

CORNERSTONECAPITAL VERWALTUNGS AG

Ziegelhaeuser Landstrasse 1
Heidelberg, Germany 69120
Phone: 4962216492470
Fax: 4962216492476
E-mail: equity@cornerstonecapital.de

Other Offices
Westendstrasse 41
Frankfurt am Main, Germany 60325
Phone: 49-69-7890-470
Fax: 49-69-7890-4710

Management and Staff
Stephan Helmstaedter, Managing Partner

Type of Firm
Private Equity Firm

Association Membership
German Venture Capital Association (BVK)
European Private Equity and Venture Capital Assoc.

Project Preferences

Type of Financing Preferred:
Leveraged Buyout
Public Companies
Later Stage
Management Buyouts

Size of Investments Considered:
Min Size of Investment Considered (000s): $2,633
Max Size of Investment Considered (000s): $9,213

Geographical Preferences

International Preferences:
Switzerland
Austria
Germany

Industry Preferences

In Computer Software prefer:
Software

In Semiconductor/Electr prefer:
Electronics

In Medical/Health prefer:
Medical/Health

In Industrial/Energy prefer:
Industrial Products

In Business Serv. prefer:
Services

Additional Information
Name of Most Recent Fund: CornerstoneCapital II AG & Co. KG
Most Recent Fund Was Raised: 11/12/2007
Year Founded: 2001
Capital Under Management: $41,300,000
Current Activity Level : Actively seeking new investments

CORPACQ LTD

20 Market Street, Suite 1.3
Cheshire, United Kingdom
Phone: 0161 927 3113
Fax: 0161 927 3101
E-mail: enquiries@corpacqplc.com
Website: www.corpacqplc.com

Management and Staff
David Martin, Managing Director
Simon Orange, Founder

Type of Firm
Private Equity Firm

Project Preferences

Type of Financing Preferred:
Leveraged Buyout
Expansion
Management Buyouts
Acquisition

Geographical Preferences

International Preferences:
United Kingdom
Europe

Additional Information
Year Founded: 2006
Current Activity Level: Actively seeking new investments

CORPFIN CAPITAL ASESORES SA SGEIC

Serrano 57, 5th floor
Madrid, Spain 28006
Phone: 34917812800
Fax: 34915778583
E-mail: contacto@corpfincapital.com
Website: www.corpfincapital.com

Other Offices
Serrano 57
Madrid, Spain 28006
Phone: 34917812800

Management and Staff
Carlos Lavilla, Partner
Patrick Gandarias, Partner

Type of Firm
Private Equity Firm

Association Membership
European Private Equity and Venture Capital Assoc.
Spanish Venture Capital Association (ASCRI)

Project Preferences

Role in Financing:
Prefer role as deal originator but will also invest in deals created by others

Type of Financing Preferred:
Management Buyouts
Acquisition

Size of Investments Considered:
Min Size of Investment Considered (000s): $13,702
Max Size of Investment Considered (000s): $52,412

Geographical Preferences

International Preferences:
Spain

Industry Focus

(% based on actual investment)
Consumer Related	37.5%
Other Products	20.9%
Industrial/Energy	20.6%
Medical/Health	12.2%
Semiconductors/Other Elect.	8.9%

Additional Information
Name of Most Recent Fund: Corpfin Capital Fund III
Most Recent Fund Was Raised: 09/30/2006
Year Founded: 1990
Capital Under Management: $622,700,000
Current Activity Level: Actively seeking new investments
Method of Compensation: Return on invest. most important, but chg. closing fees, service fees, etc.

CORPORACION INVERSIONES ABONO SUPER SA

Cra. 7 No. 71-21 Torre B
Piso 12
Bogota, Colombia
Phone: 5713139800
Website: www.inversor.org.co

Type of Firm
Private Equity Firm

Project Preferences

Type of Financing Preferred:
Balanced

Geographical Preferences

United States Preferences:

International Preferences:
Colombia

Industry Preferences

In Medical/Health prefer:
Medical/Health

In Industrial/Energy prefer:
Alternative Energy

In Business Serv. prefer:
Services

In Agr/Forestr/Fish prefer:
Agribusiness
Agriculture related

In Other prefer:
Environment Responsible

Additional Information
Year Founded: 2010
Capital Under Management: $3,000,000
Current Activity Level: Actively seeking new investments

CORPORACION SANTIAGO INNOVA

Manuel Rodriguez Sur 749
Santiago, Chile
Phone: 5627704200
Fax: 5627704299
Website: www.innova.cl

Type of Firm
Incubator/Development Program

Project Preferences

Type of Financing Preferred:
Seed
Startup

Additional Information
Year Founded: 1969
Current Activity Level: Actively seeking new investments

CORPORATE FINANCE ASSOCIATES WORLDWIDE INC

24461 Ridge Route Drive
Suite 200
Laguna Hills, CA USA 92653
Phone: 949-305-6710
Fax: 949-305-6713
E-mail: info@cfaw.com
Website: www.cfaw.com

Other Offices
671 Camden Yard Court
Columbus, OH USA 43235
Phone: 614-457-9219
Fax: 614-457-9211

3333 Founders Road
Indianapolis, IN USA 46268
Phone: 317-872-5155
Fax: 317-872-8501

6065 Lake Forrest Drive
Suite 250
Atlanta, GA USA 30328
Phone: 404-459-0130
Fax: 636-444-1969

3906 Quail Ridge Road
Lafayette, CA USA 94549
Phone: 925-299-0386
Fax: 925-299-0387

268 North 115th Street
Suite Six
Omaha, NE USA 68154
Phone: 402-330-2160
Fax: 402-330-2461

6240 West 135th Street
Suite 200
Shawnee Mission, KS USA 66223
Phone: 913-648-0185
Fax: 913-273-0080

75 Market Street, Suite 305
Portland, ME USA 04101
Phone: 207-772-2221
Fax: 207-772-2227

23046 Avenida de la Carlota
Suite 600
Laguna Hills, CA USA 92653
Phone: 949-457-8990
Fax: 949-587-9688

2431 East 51st Street
Suite 600
Tulsa, OK USA 74105
Phone: 918-743-1130
Fax: 918-743-1131

770 Beacon Street
Suite A
Dundee, IL USA 60118
Phone: 847-836-7035
Fax: 847-836-7254

950 West Bannock Street
Eleventh Floor
Boise, ID USA 83701
Phone: 208-386-9000
Fax: 208-386-9900

5970 Fairview Road
Suite 720
Charlotte, NC USA 28210
Phone: 704-716-8572
Fax: 704-556-7260

6336 Shady Grove East
Memphis, TN USA 38120
Phone: 901-751-8880
Fax: 901-471-3800

725 Cool Springs Boulevard
Suite 600
Franklin, TN USA 37067
Phone: 615-732-6141
Fax: 866-283-3418

10802 Golden Maple Place
Louisville, KY USA 40223
Phone: 502-493-7990
Fax: 502-805-0653

5100 Westheimer
Suite 105
Houston, TX USA 77056
Phone: 713-465-4055
Fax: 713-465-0102

102 Brooke Avenue
Toronto
Ontario, Canada M5M 2K4
Phone: 416-485-9547
Fax: 416-485-8970

13750 San Pedro Avenue
Suite 600
San Antonio, TX USA 78232
Phone: 210-804-0716
Fax: 210-568-2520

223 West Wall
Suite 825
Midland, TX USA 79701
Phone: 432-687-4916
Fax: 432-684-8963

106 Fulton Street
Boston, MA USA 02109
Phone: 617-742-7440
Fax: 617-742-7358

160 East State Street
Suite 202
Traverse City, MI USA 49684
Phone: 231-932-1280
Fax: 231-935-3895

303 South Cascade Avenue
Suite 200
Colorado Springs, CO USA 80903
Phone: 719-635-4667
Fax: 719-635-4988

551 Valley Road
PMB 105
Montclair, NJ USA 07043
Phone: 888-452-3269
Fax: 973-860-0757

1540 Cornwall
Suite 211, Oakville
Ontario, Canada L6J 7W3
Phone: 905-845-4340
Fax: 905-845-4358

Management and Staff
Gary Parker, Vice President

Type of Firm
Service Provider

Project Preferences

Role in Financing:
Prefer role as deal originator

Type of Financing Preferred:
Second Stage Financing
Leveraged Buyout
Early Stage
Expansion
Mezzanine
First Stage Financing
Acquisition
Recapitalizations

Geographical Preferences

United States Preferences:
Southeast

Industry Focus
(% based on actual investment)
Internet Specific   100.0%

Additional Information
Year Founded: 1997
Current Activity Level : Actively seeking new investments

CORPORATE FINANCE PARTNERS CFP BERA-TUNGS GMBH

Palais 22
Kennedyallee 70a
Frankfurt am Main, Germany D-60596
E-mail: contact@venturecapital.de
Website: www.cfpartners.com

Other Offices
1054 Szechenyi u. 1/D
Budapest, Hungary 1054
Phone: 36-1-301-0218
Fax: 36-1-302-7616

286 Madison Avenue
Suite 2001
New York, NY USA 10017
Phone: 6466883552
Fax: 6469243530

Akasaka Park Building 3 F
5-2-20 Akasaka, Minato-ku
Tokyo, Japan 107-6130
Phone: 91-3-3587-9574

Herrengasse 6 - 8/7/1
Vienna, Austria 1010
Phone: 43-1-5352-9370
Fax: 43-1-535293710

Niedenau 36
Frankfurt am Main, Germany 60325
Phone: 49-69-907-4660
Fax: 49-69-9074-6620

600 Montgomery Street
43rd floor
San Francisco, CA USA 94111
Phone: 650-641-0833

1111 Brickell Avenue
Floor 11
Miami, FL USA 33131
Phone: 305-395-4049
Fax: 305-675-3175

Grosse Praesidentenstrasse 10
Berlin, Germany 10178
Phone: 49-30-814564166
Fax: 49-30-814564135

Grosse Elbstrasse 86
Hamburg, Germany 22767
Phone: 49-40-211076660
Fax: 49-40-211076669

Management and Staff
Andreas Thuemmler, Founder
Malte von der Ropp, Managing Director

Type of Firm
Investment Management Firm

Association Membership
German Venture Capital Association (BVK)

Project Preferences

Type of Financing Preferred:
Balanced

Geographical Preferences

United States Preferences:
All U.S.

International Preferences:
Europe
Germany

Industry Preferences

In Communications prefer:
Telecommunications
Wireless Communications

In Computer Software prefer:
Software

In Internet Specific prefer:
Internet
Ecommerce

In Business Serv. prefer:
Services

Additional Information
Year Founded: 1998
Current Activity Level : Actively seeking new investments

CORPORATE GROWTH ASSISTANCE LTD

One Benvenuto Place
Suite 420
Toronto, Canada M4V 2L1
Phone: 416-222-7772
Fax: 416-222-6091
Website: www.corporategrowthassistance.com

Management and Staff
Millard Roth, President

Type of Firm
Investment Management Firm

Project Preferences

Role in Financing:
Prefer role as deal originator but will also invest in deals created by others

Type of Financing Preferred:
Second Stage Financing
Leveraged Buyout
Mezzanine
Generalist PE
Recapitalizations

Size of Investments Considered:
Min Size of Investment Considered (000s): $1,000
Max Size of Investment Considered: No Limit

Geographical Preferences

United States Preferences:
Midwest
Northwest

Canadian Preferences:
Ontario
Western Canada

Industry Preferences

In Communications prefer:
CATV & Pay TV Systems
Data Communications
Other Communication Prod.

In Computer Software prefer:
Computer Services
Applications Software

In Semiconductor/Electr prefer:
Component Testing Equipmt

In Medical/Health prefer:
Disposable Med. Products
Hospital/Other Instit.
Pharmaceuticals

In Consumer Related prefer:
Food/Beverage
Consumer Products
Consumer Services

In Industrial/Energy prefer:
Energy Conservation Relat
Industrial Products
Materials
Machinery

In Manufact. prefer:
Publishing

Additional Information
Year Founded: 1967
Current Activity Level : Actively seeking new investments
Method of Compensation: Return on invest. most important, but chg. closing fees, service fees, etc.

CORPORATE STRATEGIES LLC

123 N Post Oak Lane
Suite 440
Houston, TX USA 77024
Website: www.corporatestrategies.net

Type of Firm
Bank Affiliated

Project Preferences

Type of Financing Preferred:
Leveraged Buyout

Additional Information
Year Founded: 2005
Current Activity Level : Actively seeking new investments

CORPORATION FINANCIERE CHAMPLAIN CANADA INC

1010 Sherbrooke Street West, Suite 1606
Montreal, Canada H3A 2R7
Phone: 5142823585

Management and Staff
Pierre Simard, Managing Partner
Robert Zeidel, Vice President

Type of Firm
Private Equity Firm

Project Preferences

Type of Financing Preferred:
Leveraged Buyout
Acquisition

Geographical Preferences

United States Preferences:
All U.S.

Canadian Preferences:
All Canada

Industry Preferences

In Medical/Health prefer:
Medical/Health
Health Services

In Consumer Related prefer:
Consumer
Retail

In Manufact. prefer:
Manufacturing

Additional Information
Year Founded: 2006
Current Activity Level : Actively seeking new investments

CORPOSANA CAPITAL INC

1000, rue du Haut-Bois, First Floor
Sherbrooke, Canada J1N 3V4
Phone: 8198291469
Website: www.corposanacapital.com

Type of Firm
Private Equity Firm

Project Preferences

Type of Financing Preferred:
Balanced
Later Stage

Industry Preferences

In Biotechnology prefer:
Agricultural/Animal Bio.

In Industrial/Energy prefer:
Alternative Energy
Energy Conservation Relat
Environmental Related

In Business Serv. prefer:
Services
Distribution

In Manufact. prefer:
Manufacturing

Additional Information
Year Founded: 2005
Current Activity Level : Actively seeking new investments

CORRELATION VENTURES LP

9255 Towne Cente Drive
Suite 350
San Diego, CA USA 92121
Phone: 8584128500
Website: correlationvc.com

Other Offices
600 Hansen Way
Suite 200
PALO ALTO, CA USA 94304
Phone: 6508433210

Management and Staff
Anu Pathria, Partner
Collin West, Principal
David Coats, Founder
Grace Chui-Miller, Chief Financial Officer
Moiz Saifee, Principal
Trevor Kienzle, Founder

Type of Firm
Private Equity Firm

Project Preferences

Type of Financing Preferred:
Early Stage
Expansion
Balanced
Later Stage
Seed

Size of Investments Considered:
Min Size of Investment Considered (000s): $250
Max Size of Investment Considered (000s): $4,000

Geographical Preferences

United States Preferences:
All U.S.

Additional Information
Name of Most Recent Fund: Correlation Ventures Executives Fund, L.P.
Most Recent Fund Was Raised: 06/23/2011
Year Founded: 2006
Capital Under Management: $365,000,000
Current Activity Level : Actively seeking new investments

CORRIDOR CAPITAL LLC

12400 Wilshire Boulevard
Suite 645
West Los Angeles, CA USA 90025
Phone: 3104427000
Website: www.corridorcapital.com

Management and Staff
Cameron Reilly, Principal
Edward Monnier, Managing Director
Jessamyn Davis, Chief Financial Officer
Rohit Bassi, Managing Director

Type of Firm
Private Equity Firm

Project Preferences

Type of Financing Preferred:
Leveraged Buyout
Later Stage
Special Situation

Geographical Preferences

United States Preferences:
All U.S.

Industry Preferences

In Consumer Related prefer:
Entertainment and Leisure

In Business Serv. prefer:
Services
Media

In Manufact. prefer:
Manufacturing

In Other prefer:
Environment Responsible

Additional Information
Name of Most Recent Fund: Corridor Capital II, L.P.
Most Recent Fund Was Raised: 09/30/2011
Year Founded: 2005
Capital Under Management: $100,000
Current Activity Level : Actively seeking new investments

CORSA VENTURES

103 East Fifth Street, Suite 208
Austin, TX USA 78701
Phone: 5127710550
E-mail: info@corsaventures.com
Website: www.corsaventures.com

Management and Staff
Alexander Gruzen, General Partner
Brian Grigsby, General Partner

Type of Firm
Private Equity Firm

Project Preferences

Type of Financing Preferred:
Early Stage
Balanced
Startup

Geographical Preferences

United States Preferences:
Southwest
Texas

Industry Preferences

In Communications prefer:
Wireless Communications
Data Communications

In Computer Software prefer:
Data Processing

In Business Serv. prefer:
Media

Additional Information
Name of Most Recent Fund: Corsa Fund 2012, L.P.
Most Recent Fund Was Raised: 03/14/2012
Year Founded: 2012
Capital Under Management: $5,000,000
Current Activity Level : Actively seeking new investments

CORSAIR CAPITAL LLC

717 Fifth Avenue, 24th Floor
New York, NY USA 10022
Phone: 2122249400
Fax: 2122249445
E-mail: corsair@corsair-capital.com
Website: www.corsair-capital.com

Management and Staff
Clifford Brokaw, Managing Director
D.T. Jayanti, President
Derrick Estes, Vice President
Hari Rajan, Principal
James Kirk, Managing Director
Jeremy Schein, Principal
Marwan El-Asmar, Vice President
Raja Haji-Touma, Principal

Type of Firm
Private Equity Firm

Project Preferences

Type of Financing Preferred:
Leveraged Buyout
Expansion
Acquisition
Distressed Debt

Geographical Preferences

International Preferences:
All International

Industry Preferences

In Financial Services prefer:
Financial Services
Insurance
Investment Groups

Additional Information
Year Founded: 1992
Capital Under Management: $773,829,000
Current Activity Level : Actively seeking new investments

CORSTONE CORP

6707 Democracy Boulevard, Suite 300
Bethesda, MD USA 20817
Phone: 8663672100
Fax: 2402385012
E-mail: info@corstone.com
Website: www.corstone.com

Other Offices
2 London Wall Building
2nd Floor
, United Kingdom EC2 M5PP
Phone: 442070489400
Fax: 442070489409

357 Bayi Road
Room 2401, Tower A, Fortune Plaza
Nanchang City, China 330004
Phone: 8607916278039
Fax: 8607916278639

39-1, Seosomoon Dong, Jung Gu
2nd Floor 203 Shin-A B/D
Jung Gu, South Korea 100-813
Phone: 8223191206
Fax: 8223190070

6 Eu Tong Sen Street
Suite 11-08, The Central
Singapore, Singapore 059817
Phone: 6562389600
Fax: 6562389601

Management and Staff
Charles Ehrig, Managing Director
Choi Sunho, General Partner
Jin Park, Vice President
John Herring, Partner
Thomas Cho, General Partner
Zhao Haiching, Managing Director

Type of Firm
Bank Affiliated

Project Preferences

Type of Financing Preferred:
Early Stage
Balanced
Later Stage

Geographical Preferences

United States Preferences:
North America

International Preferences:
Europe
Australia
Asia

Industry Preferences

In Consumer Related prefer:
Education Related

In Industrial/Energy prefer:
Energy

In Financial Services prefer:
Financial Services

In Business Serv. prefer:
Services

In Manufact. prefer:
Manufacturing

Additional Information
Year Founded: 1991
Capital Under Management: $100,000,000
Current Activity Level : Actively seeking new investments

CORTLANDT PRIVATE CAPITAL LLC

28 William Puckey Drive
Cortlandt Manor, NY USA 10567
Phone: 9147394892
Fax: 9144204708
Website: www.cortlandtprivatecapital.com

Management and Staff
Howard Goldstein, Managing Partner

Type of Firm
Private Equity Firm

Project Preferences

Type of Financing Preferred:
Balanced

Geographical Preferences

United States Preferences:

Industry Preferences

In Communications prefer:
Communications and Media

In Computer Software prefer:
Software

In Internet Specific prefer:
Internet

In Biotechnology prefer:
Biotechnology

In Medical/Health prefer:
Medical/Health

In Consumer Related prefer:
Consumer
Retail
Food/Beverage

Additional Information
Year Founded: 2013
Current Activity Level : Actively seeking new investments

CORVM CAPITAL PARTNERS SAS

19 bis, rue Pierre Fontaine
Paris, France 75009
Phone: 33954479000
Fax: 33959479000
E-mail: eu.contact@corvmcapital.com
Website: www.corvmcapital.com

Other Offices
73 Spring Street, Suite 309
New York, NY USA 10012
Phone: 26465393977
Fax: 16466523127

Management and Staff
Arthur Dessenante, Chief Executive Officer

Type of Firm
Private Equity Firm

Project Preferences

Type of Financing Preferred:
Leveraged Buyout
Generalist PE
Later Stage
Management Buyouts
Acquisition
Recapitalizations

Geographical Preferences

United States Preferences:

International Preferences:
Europe

Additional Information
Year Founded: 2014
Current Activity Level : Actively seeking new investments

CORVUS CAPITAL GMBH

Alte Berg 15
Malsch, Germany 69254
Phone: 497253278713
Fax: 497253278712
E-mail: info@corvus-capital.de
Website: www.corvus-capital.de

Management and Staff
Joachim Rabe, Managing Director

Type of Firm
Private Equity Firm

Project Preferences

Type of Financing Preferred:
Early Stage
Seed
Management Buyouts
Acquisition
Startup

Geographical Preferences

International Preferences:
Germany

Additional Information
Year Founded: 2002
Current Activity Level : Actively seeking new investments

COSIMO VENTURES

535 Boylston Street
Sixth Stree
Boston, MA USA 02116
Phone: 6179100406
E-mail: info@cosimoventures.com
Website: cosimoventures.com

Type of Firm
Private Equity Firm

Project Preferences

Type of Financing Preferred:
Early Stage

Additional Information
Year Founded: 2014
Current Activity Level : Actively seeking new investments

COSTANOA VENTURE CAPITAL, L.P.

755 Page Mill Road
Suite A-200
Palo Alto, CA USA 94304
Phone: 16504166009
E-mail: info@costanoavc.com
Website: costanoavc.com

Type of Firm
Private Equity Firm

Project Preferences

Type of Financing Preferred:
Early Stage

Size of Investments Considered:
Min Size of Investment Considered (000s): $500
Max Size of Investment Considered (000s): $3,000

Industry Preferences

In Communications prefer:
Data Communications

In Computer Software prefer:
Systems Software
Applications Software

In Consumer Related prefer:
Consumer Services

Additional Information
Name of Most Recent Fund: Costanoa Venture Capital I, L.P.
Most Recent Fund Was Raised: 12/13/2012
Year Founded: 2012
Capital Under Management: $421,532,000
Current Activity Level : Actively seeking new investments

COTA CAPITAL INC

455 Market Street
Suite 1850
San Francisco, CA USA 94105
Website: cotacapital.com

Management and Staff
Babak Poushanchi, Co-Founder
Bobby Yazdani, Co-Founder
Nina Achadjian, Principal
Victoria Liang, Principal

Type of Firm
Private Equity Firm

Project Preferences

Type of Financing Preferred:
Balanced

Industry Preferences

In Computer Software prefer:
Applications Software

In Internet Specific prefer:
Internet

Additional Information
Year Founded: 2015
Current Activity Level : Actively seeking new investments

COTTON CREEK CAPITAL MANAGEMENT LLC

500 North Akard Street
2820 Lincoln Plaza
Dallas, TX USA 75201
Phone: 2142420700
Fax: 2142194654
Website: www.cottoncreekcapital.com

Other Offices
6300 Bee Cave Road
Palisades West II, Suite 445
Austin, TX USA 78746
Phone: 512412330
Fax: 5124123322

301 Commerce Street
Suite 3655
Fort Worth, TX USA 76102
Phone: 8173482751
Fax: 8173398998

Management and Staff
Antonio DiGesualdo, Managing Director
James Braden, Managing Director
Smith Brownlie, Managing Director
Steven Lankenau, Chief Financial Officer

Type of Firm
Private Equity Firm

Project Preferences

Type of Financing Preferred:
Leveraged Buyout
Acquisition
Recapitalizations

Geographical Preferences

United States Preferences:
Southwest

Industry Preferences

In Medical/Health prefer:
Health Services

In Consumer Related prefer:
Consumer Products

In Industrial/Energy prefer:
Energy
Industrial Products
Materials
Advanced Materials
Environmental Related

In Transportation prefer:
Aerospace

In Business Serv. prefer:
Services
Distribution

In Manufact. prefer:
Manufacturing

Additional Information
Name of Most Recent Fund: Cotton Creek Capital Partners II, L.P.
Most Recent Fund Was Raised: 06/13/2012
Year Founded: 2006
Capital Under Management: $311,793,000
Current Activity Level : Actively seeking new investments

COTTONWOOD CAPITAL PARTNERS LLC

406 West Overland Drive, Suite 110
El Paso, TX USA 79901
Phone: 5054128537

Other Offices
228 Griffin Street
SANTA FE, NM USA 87505
Phone: 505-412-8537

4200 West Jemez Road
Suite 301
LOS ALAMOS, NM USA 87544

Hengelosestraat 500
7521
Enschede, Netherlands

Management and Staff
Jeffrey Gochnour, President
John West, Chief Financial Officer
John West, Chief Executive Officer

Type of Firm
Private Equity Firm

Association Membership
National Venture Capital Association - USA (NVCA)

Project Preferences

Role in Financing:
Prefer role as deal originator but will also invest in deals created by others

Type of Financing Preferred:
Early Stage
Seed

Size of Investments Considered:
Min Size of Investment Considered (000s): $500
Max Size of Investment Considered (000s): $1,500

Geographical Preferences

United States Preferences:
New Mexico
Arizona
Southwest

International Preferences:
Europe

Industry Preferences

In Semiconductor/Electr prefer:
Electronics

In Medical/Health prefer:
Health Services

In Industrial/Energy prefer:
Energy
Factory Automation
Environmental Related

In Transportation prefer:
Aerospace

In Manufact. prefer:
Manufacturing

Additional Information
Name of Most Recent Fund: Cottonwood Technology Fund II
Most Recent Fund Was Raised: 06/30/2013
Year Founded: 2009
Capital Under Management: $13,000,000
Current Activity Level : Actively seeking new investments

COTTONWOOD VENTURE PARTNERS LLC

4306 Yoakum Boulevard
Suite 302
Houston, TX USA 77006
E-mail: contact@cottonwoodvp.com
Website: www.cottonwoodvp.com

Management and Staff
Jeremy Arendt, Managing Partner
Ryan Gurney, Managing Partner

Type of Firm
Private Equity Firm

Project Preferences

Type of Financing Preferred:
Early Stage

Industry Preferences

In Industrial/Energy prefer:
Oil and Gas Exploration

Additional Information
Year Founded: 2016
Capital Under Management: $6,100,000
Current Activity Level : Actively seeking new investments

COUGAR CAPITAL LLC

1261 South 1000 East
Orem, UT USA 84097
Website: byucougarcapital.org

Type of Firm
Private Equity Firm

Project Preferences

Type of Financing Preferred:
Early Stage

Additional Information
Year Founded: 2005
Current Activity Level : Actively seeking new investments

COUGHLIN CAPITAL LLC

1010 B Street
Suite 319
San Rafael, CA USA 94901
Website: www.coughlincapital.com

Management and Staff
Carl Coughlin, Partner
Francis Coughlin, Partner
Kevin Coughlin, Partner

Type of Firm
Private Equity Firm

Project Preferences

Type of Financing Preferred:
Leveraged Buyout
Later Stage
Management Buyouts
Acquisition
Recapitalizations

Industry Preferences

In Consumer Related prefer:
Sports

In Transportation prefer:
Transportation

In Financial Services prefer:
Real Estate

In Business Serv. prefer:
Services

In Manufact. prefer:
Manufacturing

COULTON CREEK CAPITAL LLC

5613 DTC Parkway
Suite 830
Englewood, CO USA 80111
Phone: 7205021149
Website: ccrcapital.com

Management and Staff
Christopher Hanks, Managing Director

Type of Firm
Private Equity Firm

Project Preferences

Type of Financing Preferred:
Mezzanine

Size of Investments Considered:
Min Size of Investment Considered (000s): $500
Max Size of Investment Considered (000s): $3,000

Additional Information
Year Founded: 2013
Current Activity Level : Actively seeking new investments

COUNCIL CAPITAL

30 Burton Hills Boulevard, Suite 576
Nashville, TN USA 37215
Phone: 6152553707
Fax: 6152553709
E-mail: info@councilcapital.com
Website: www.councilcapital.com

Management and Staff
Dennis Bottorff, Co-Founder
Eric Keen, General Partner
Grant Jackson, Managing Partner
John Davis, Vice President
Katie Gambill, Co-Founder

Type of Firm
Private Equity Firm

Project Preferences

Role in Financing:
Will function either as deal originator or investor in deals created by others

Type of Financing Preferred:
Leveraged Buyout
Early Stage
Expansion
Balanced
Later Stage
Acquisition
Recapitalizations

Industry Preferences

In Medical/Health prefer:
Medical/Health
Medical Products
Health Services
Pharmaceuticals

Additional Information
Name of Most Recent Fund: Council & Enhanced Tennessee Fund LLC
Most Recent Fund Was Raised: 11/05/2009
Year Founded: 2000
Capital Under Management: $200,000,000
Current Activity Level : Actively seeking new investments
Method of Compensation: Return on investment is of primary concern, do not charge fees

COUNTERPOINT CAPITAL PARTNERS LLC

1605 Hope Street
Suite 320
South Pasadena, CA USA 91030
Phone: 4242592228
E-mail: info@counterpointcp.com
Website: www.counterpointcp.com

Management and Staff
Christopher Iorillo, Managing Partner
Eric Willis, Managing Partner
Stephen Rossi, Managing Partner

Type of Firm
Private Equity Firm

Project Preferences

Type of Financing Preferred:
Leveraged Buyout
Later Stage
Management Buyouts
Acquisition
Private Placement
Recapitalizations

Geographical Preferences

United States Preferences:
North America

Canadian Preferences:
All Canada

Industry Preferences

In Communications prefer:
Telecommunications

In Computer Software prefer:
Software

In Industrial/Energy prefer:
Industrial Products

In Financial Services prefer:
Financial Services

In Business Serv. prefer:
Services
Distribution
Consulting Services

In Manufact. prefer:
Manufacturing

Additional Information
Year Founded: 2011
Current Activity Level : Actively seeking new investments

COURT SQUARE CAPITAL PARTNERS LP

55 East 52nd Street
34th Floor, Park Avenue Plaza
New York, NY USA 10055
Phone: 2127526110
Fax: 2127526184
Website: www.courtsquare.com

Management and Staff
Anthony Mirra, Chief Financial Officer
Christopher Bloise, Partner
David Nguyen, Vice President
David Thomas, Managing Partner
Doron Grosman, Partner
Ian Highet, Managing Partner
Jeffrey Vogel, Principal
John Civantos, Partner
John Weber, Managing Partner
John Overbay, Vice President
Joseph Silvestri, Managing Partner
Kevin White, Vice President
Kevin Brown, Principal
Kurt Hilzinger, Partner
Michael Delaney, Managing Partner
Michael Finley, Partner
Sendil Rajendran, Vice President
Thomas McWilliams, Managing Partner
William Comfort, Managing Partner

Type of Firm
Private Equity Firm

Project Preferences

Type of Financing Preferred:
Leveraged Buyout

Industry Preferences

In Communications prefer:
Telecommunications

In Medical/Health prefer:
Medical/Health

In Industrial/Energy prefer:
Industrial Products

In Business Serv. prefer:
Services
Media

In Manufact. prefer:
Publishing

Additional Information
Name of Most Recent Fund: Court Square Capital Partners III, L.P.
Most Recent Fund Was Raised: 09/14/2012
Year Founded: 2002
Capital Under Management: $2,534,036,000
Current Activity Level : Actively seeking new investments

COURT SQUARE VENTURES LLC

455 Second Street Southeast
Suite 401
Charlottesville, VA USA 22902
Phone: 4348173300
Fax: 4348173299

Management and Staff
Brian Kannry, Principal
Christopher Holden, General Partner
James Murray, General Partner
Randy Castleman, General Partner

Type of Firm
Private Equity Firm

Project Preferences

Role in Financing:
Prefer role as deal originator but will also invest in deals created by others

Type of Financing Preferred:
Early Stage

Geographical Preferences

United States Preferences:

Industry Preferences

In Communications prefer:
Communications and Media
Telecommunications

In Business Serv. prefer:
Media

Additional Information
Year Founded: 2001
Capital Under Management: $118,000,000
Current Activity Level : Actively seeking new investments
Method of Compensation: Return on investment is of primary concern, do not charge fees

COURTIN INVESTMENT SAS

91, rue du Faubourg
Paris, France 75008
E-mail: contact@courtin-investment.com
Website: courtin-investment.com

Type of Firm
Private Equity Firm

Project Preferences

Type of Financing Preferred:
Early Stage
Expansion
Later Stage
Seed

Size of Investments Considered:
Min Size of Investment Considered (000s): $55
Max Size of Investment Considered (000s): $1,106

Geographical Preferences

United States Preferences:

Canadian Preferences:
All Canada

International Preferences:
Europe

Additional Information
Year Founded: 2015
Current Activity Level : Actively seeking new investments

COURTNEY GROUP INC

500 Newport Center Drive
Suite 580
Newport Beach, CA USA 92660
Phone: 9497063600
Fax: 9496257900
E-mail: info@thecourtneygroup.com

Type of Firm
Bank Affiliated

Project Preferences

Type of Financing Preferred:
Leveraged Buyout
Later Stage
Management Buyouts
Recapitalizations

Geographical Preferences

United States Preferences:

Industry Preferences

In Computer Software prefer:
Software

In Computer Other prefer:
Computer Related

In Medical/Health prefer:
Medical Products
Health Services

In Industrial/Energy prefer:
Alternative Energy
Industrial Products
Environmental Related

In Financial Services prefer:
Financial Services

In Business Serv. prefer:
Services

In Manufact. prefer:
Manufacturing

Additional Information
Year Founded: 1995
Current Activity Level : Actively seeking new investments

COURTSIDE VENTURE PARTNERS RG LLC

1555 Broadway Street
New York, NY USA 10011
E-mail: hello@courtsidevc.com
Website: www.courtsidevc.com

Type of Firm
Private Equity Firm

Project Preferences

Type of Financing Preferred:
Early Stage

Geographical Preferences

United States Preferences:

International Preferences:
All International

Industry Preferences

In Consumer Related prefer:
Sports

In Business Serv. prefer:
Media

Additional Information
Year Founded: 2014
Capital Under Management: $3,750,000
Current Activity Level : Actively seeking new investments

COVE HILL PARTNERS LLC

888 Boylston Street
Boston, MA USA 02199
Phone: 8572456060

E-mail: info@coverhillpartners.com

Management and Staff
Andrew Balson, Managing Partner
Justin Roberts, Managing Director
Keith Power, Chief Financial Officer
Lara Moskowitz, Chief Operating Officer

Type of Firm
Private Equity Firm

Project Preferences

Type of Financing Preferred:
Leveraged Buyout

Geographical Preferences

United States Preferences:
North America

Additional Information
Year Founded: 2017
Capital Under Management: $1,000,000,000
Current Activity Level : Actively seeking new investments

COVENT TOKE BEFEKTETO ZARTKORUEN MUKODO RT

Maros u 27
Budapest, Hungary 1122
Phone: 3613552493
Fax: 3612022381
Website: www.covent.hu

Management and Staff
Janos Bolyky, Chief Executive Officer
Margit Szasz, Founder

Type of Firm
Private Equity Firm

Project Preferences

Role in Financing:
Prefer role as deal originator but will also invest in deals created by others

Type of Financing Preferred:
Leveraged Buyout
Acquisition

Geographical Preferences

International Preferences:
Hungary
Sweden
Europe
Scandanavia/Nordic Region

Industry Preferences

In Financial Services prefer:
Real Estate

In Business Serv. prefer:
Consulting Services

Additional Information
Year Founded: 1993
Capital Under Management: $7,900,000
Current Activity Level : Actively seeking new investments

COVENTURE LLC

60 East 42nd Street
Third Floor
New York, NY USA 10165
Phone: 8183077964
Website: www.coventure.vc

Management and Staff
Ali Hamed, Managing Partner

Type of Firm
Private Equity Firm

Project Preferences

Type of Financing Preferred:
Seed
Startup

Geographical Preferences

United States Preferences:

Industry Preferences

In Computer Software prefer:
Software

Additional Information
Year Founded: 2014
Capital Under Management: $10,100,000
Current Activity Level : Actively seeking new investments

COVERA VENTURES LP

6836 Bee Caves Road, Suite 275
Austin, TX USA 78746
Phone: 5127955870
Website: www.coveraventures.com

Other Offices
13455 Noel Road
Suite 1670, Two Galleria Tower
Dallas, TX USA 75240
Phone: 9727761575

Management and Staff
Jeff Williams, Managing Director
Steve Coffey, Managing Director
Thomas Huseby, Venture Partner

Type of Firm
Private Equity Firm

Project Preferences

Role in Financing:
Will function either as deal originator or investor in deals created by others

Type of Financing Preferred:
Early Stage

Size of Investments Considered:
Min Size of Investment Considered (000s): $1,000
Max Size of Investment Considered (000s): $5,000

Geographical Preferences

United States Preferences:

Canadian Preferences:
All Canada

Industry Preferences

In Communications prefer:
Telecommunications
Wireless Communications

In Computer Software prefer:
Software

In Business Serv. prefer:
Services
Media

Additional Information
Name of Most Recent Fund: Hunt Ventures Fund I, L.P.
Most Recent Fund Was Raised: 04/22/2004
Year Founded: 1998
Capital Under Management: $100,000,000
Current Activity Level : Actively seeking new investments
Method of Compensation: Return on investment is of primary concern, do not charge fees

COVESTIA CAPITAL PARTNERS

60 South Sixth Street
Suite 3720
Minneapolis, MN USA 55402
Phone: 612-333-0130
Fax: 612-333-0122
Website: www.covestia.com

Other Offices
280 Park Avenue
22nd Floor
New York, NY USA 10017
Phone: 212-883-0130

11111 Santa Monica Boulevard
Suite 1620
West Los Angeles, CA USA 90025
Phone: 310-444-0130
Fax: 310-444-6393

Management and Staff
Jim D Aquila, Managing Director
Randy Bort, Managing Director

Type of Firm
Bank Affiliated

Project Preferences

Type of Financing Preferred:
Leveraged Buyout
Expansion
Recapitalizations

Industry Preferences

In Medical/Health prefer:
Medical/Health
Health Services

In Consumer Related prefer:
Consumer
Retail

In Business Serv. prefer:
Services

In Manufact. prefer:
Manufacturing

Additional Information
Year Founded: 2008
Capital Under Management: $30,000,000
Current Activity Level : Actively seeking new investments

COVEVIEW CAPITAL PARTNERS LLC

177 Broad Street
Tenth Floor
White Plains, NY USA 10601
Phone: 2033271200
Website: www.coveviewcapital.com

Management and Staff
Daniel Tredwell, Managing Partner
Matthew Faust, Vice President
Steve Lamb, Managing Director

Type of Firm
Private Equity Firm

Project Preferences

Type of Financing Preferred:
Leveraged Buyout
Turnaround
Management Buyouts
Recapitalizations

Industry Preferences

In Industrial/Energy prefer:
Industrial Products
Factory Automation

In Transportation prefer:
Aerospace

In Manufact. prefer:
Manufacturing
Office Automation Equipmt

Additional Information
Year Founded: 1969
Current Activity Level : Actively seeking new investments

COVINGTON CAPITAL CORP

87 Front Street East
Suite 400
Toronto, Canada M5E 1B8
Phone: 4163655227
E-mail: info@covingtonfunds.com
Website: www.covingtonfunds.com

Management and Staff
Derrick Ho, Vice President
Grant Brown, Managing Partner
Lily Lam, Vice President
Lisa Low, Chief Financial Officer
Philip Reddon, Managing Partner
Scott Clark, Managing Partner

Type of Firm
Investment Management Firm

Association Membership
Canadian Venture Capital Association

Project Preferences

Type of Financing Preferred:
Early Stage
Expansion
Balanced
Later Stage

Size of Investments Considered:
Min Size of Investment Considered (000s): $1,000
Max Size of Investment Considered (000s): $15,000

Geographical Preferences

United States Preferences:

Canadian Preferences:
All Canada
Ontario

Industry Preferences

In Communications prefer:
Wireless Communications

In Internet Specific prefer:
Internet

In Consumer Related prefer:
Consumer

Additional Information
Year Founded: 1994
Current Activity Level : Actively seeking new investments

COWBOY CAPITAL

2750 Sand Hill Road
Menlo Park, CA USA 94025
Phone: 6502333320
Website: www.cowboy.vc

Management and Staff
Aileen Lee, Founding Partner

Type of Firm
Private Equity Firm

Association Membership
National Venture Capital Association - USA (NVCA)

Project Preferences

Type of Financing Preferred:
Seed

Geographical Preferences

United States Preferences:

Additional Information
Name of Most Recent Fund: Cowboy Capital Fund I LLC
Most Recent Fund Was Raised: 07/27/2012
Year Founded: 2012
Capital Under Management: $36,005,000
Current Activity Level : Actively seeking new investments

COWBOY TECHNOLOGIES LLC

505 South Main Street
Stillwater, OK USA 74074
Phone: 4057442325
Fax: 4057442329
E-mail: info@cowboytechllc.com
Website: www.cowboytechllc.com

Management and Staff
Steve Wood, Chief Executive Officer

Type of Firm
Private Equity Firm

Project Preferences

Type of Financing Preferred:
Early Stage
Seed
Startup

Geographical Preferences

United States Preferences:
Oklahoma

Additional Information
Year Founded: 2011
Current Activity Level : Actively seeking new investments

COWEN CAPITAL PARTNERS LLC

1221 Avenue of the Americas
14th Floor
New York, NY USA 10020
Phone: 6465621189
Website: www.cowencapitalpartners.com

Other Offices

181 West Madison Street
Chicago, IL USA 60602
Phone: 312-578-5000
Fax: 312-578-5099

3200 Cherry Creek South Drive
Suite 280
Denver, CO USA 80209
Phone: 303-282-3100
Fax: 303-778-7340

118, Rue du Rhone
Geneva, Switzerland 1204
Phone: 41-22-707-6900
Fax: 41-22-707-6999

Tour Societe Generale
17 Cours Valmy
Paris la Defense, France
Phone: 331-4213-5500
Fax: 331-4244-1745

100 Yonge Street
Suite 1002
Toronto, Canada M5C 2W1
Phone: 416-362-2229
Fax: 416-362-5373

Talstrasse 20
Zurich, Switzerland 8001
Phone: 411-225-2040
Fax: 411-225-2040

Exchange House
Primrose Street
London, United Kingdom EC2A 2DD
Phone: 44-207-762-4444
Fax: 44-207-762-5578

Four Embarcadero Center
Suite 1200
San Francisco, CA USA 94111
Phone: 415-646-7200
Fax: 415-646-7455

Trammel Crow Center
2001 Ross Avenue, 49th Floor
Dallas, TX USA 75201
Phone: 214-979-2735
Fax: 214-979-2795

Two International Place
Boston, MA USA 02110
Phone: 617-946-3700
Fax: 617-946-3758

20006 Detroit Road
Suite 100
Cleveland, OH USA 44116
Phone: 440-331-3631
Fax: 440-331-7237

Management and Staff

Andrew Stein, Managing Director
David Seaburg, Managing Director
Stephen Lasota, Chief Financial Officer

Type of Firm

Bank Affiliated

Project Preferences

Role in Financing:
Prefer role in deals created by others

Type of Financing Preferred:
Leveraged Buyout
Generalist PE
Balanced
Turnaround
Management Buyouts
Distressed Debt

Geographical Preferences

United States Preferences:

Industry Focus

(% based on actual investment)

Medical/Health	27.7%
Biotechnology	19.3%
Internet Specific	16.2%
Semiconductors/Other Elect.	14.7%
Computer Software and Services	12.2%
Communications and Media	5.4%
Computer Hardware	2.4%
Other Products	2.1%

Additional Information

Year Founded: 1996
Capital Under Management: $500,000,000
Current Activity Level: Actively seeking new investments
Method of Compensation: Return on investment is of primary concern, do not charge fees

CPS CAPITAL

63 Keefer Place
Suite 2508
Vancouver, Canada V6B 6N6
E-mail: info@cpscapital.com
Website: www.cpscapital.com

Type of Firm

Private Equity Firm

Geographical Preferences

United States Preferences:

Canadian Preferences:
All Canada

International Preferences:
Hong Kong

Additional Information

Year Founded: 2017
Current Activity Level: Actively seeking new investments

CRAFTSMAN CAPITAL PARTNERS

8117 Preston Road
Suite 300
Dallas, TX USA 75225
Website: www.craftsmancapitalpartners.com

Type of Firm

Private Equity Firm

Project Preferences

Type of Financing Preferred:
Leveraged Buyout
Management Buyouts

Industry Preferences

In Medical/Health prefer:
Health Services

In Consumer Related prefer:
Consumer Products
Education Related

In Industrial/Energy prefer:
Energy

In Business Serv. prefer:
Services

In Manufact. prefer:
Manufacturing

Additional Information

Year Founded: 2014
Current Activity Level: Actively seeking new investments

CRAIC BV

Wilhelminalaan 3
Baarn, Netherlands 3743DB
Phone: 31352400230
E-mail: info@craic.nl
Website: www.craic.nl

Type of Firm

Private Equity Firm

Project Preferences

Type of Financing Preferred:
Leveraged Buyout
Later Stage
Management Buyouts

Geographical Preferences

International Preferences:
Europe
Netherlands

Additional Information

Year Founded: 2008
Current Activity Level : Actively seeking new investments

CRAIG CAPITAL CORP

127 Pecksland Road
Greenwich, CT USA 06831
Phone: 2038697700
Fax: 2038698594
Website: www.craigcapitalcorp.com

Other Offices

100 Royal Palm Way
Palm Beach, FL USA 33480
Phone: (561) 832-1558

4076 Shelburne Road
Suite Six
Shelburne, VT USA 05482
Phone: (802) 658-7747

Management and Staff

Daniel Bryan, Managing Director
Miroslav Boublik, Managing Director

Type of Firm

Private Equity Firm

Project Preferences

Type of Financing Preferred:
Leveraged Buyout
Management Buyouts
Recapitalizations

Geographical Preferences

United States Preferences:

Additional Information

Year Founded: 1985
Current Activity Level : Actively seeking new investments
Method of Compensation: Return on invest. most important, but chg. closing fees, service fees, etc.

CRANBERRY CAPITAL LLC

300 Trolley Boulevard
Rochester, NY USA 14606
Website: crancap.com

Management and Staff

Algimantas Chesonis, Partner
Arunas Chesonis, Partner
Keith Wilson, Co-Founder

Type of Firm

Private Equity Firm

Project Preferences

Type of Financing Preferred:
Early Stage

Additional Information

Year Founded: 1969
Current Activity Level : Actively seeking new investments

CRANE STREET CAPITAL LLC

2989 Woodside Road
Woodside
Redwood City, CA USA 94062
Phone: 6503289100
E-mail: info@cranestreetcapital.com
Website: www.cranestreetcapital.com

Type of Firm

Private Equity Firm

Project Preferences

Type of Financing Preferred:
Leveraged Buyout
Expansion
Acquisition

Geographical Preferences

United States Preferences:
Midwest
Northwest
California
Southwest

Industry Preferences

In Internet Specific prefer:
Internet

In Consumer Related prefer:
Education Related

In Business Serv. prefer:
Services

In Manufact. prefer:
Manufacturing

Additional Information

Year Founded: 2009
Current Activity Level : Actively seeking new investments

CRANE VENTURE PARTNERS LLP

24 Florian Road
London, United Kingdom SW15 2NL
Website: www.crane.vc

Type of Firm

Private Equity Firm

Project Preferences

Type of Financing Preferred:
Early Stage

Geographical Preferences

United States Preferences:

Industry Preferences

In Computer Software prefer:
Software

Additional Information

Year Founded: 2015
Current Activity Level : Actively seeking new investments

CRANRIDGE CAPITAL LP

216 East 45th Street
6th Floor
New York, NY USA 10017
Phone: 2128121421
E-mail: nmarks@cranridge.com
Website: www.cranridge.com

Management and Staff

Edward Koch, Co-Founder
Neil Marks, Co-Founder
Norm Lieu, Managing Director

Type of Firm

Private Equity Firm

Project Preferences

Type of Financing Preferred:
Generalist PE

Geographical Preferences

United States Preferences:

Industry Preferences

In Financial Services prefer:
Financial Services

Additional Information

Year Founded: 2014
Capital Under Management: $35,050,000
Current Activity Level : Actively seeking new investments

CRATON EQUITY PARTNERS LLC

315 South Beverly Drive
Suite 250
Beverly Hills, CA USA 90212
Phone: 3109542220
Fax: 3109542255
E-mail: info@cratonep.com
Website: www.cratonep.com

Management and Staff
Bob Baxter, Chief Financial Officer
Daniel Furey, Principal
David Asarnow, Principal
Kevin Wall, Managing Partner
Luke Hayes, Principal
Robert MacDonald, Managing Partner
Tom Soto, Co-Founder

Type of Firm
Private Equity Firm

Project Preferences

Type of Financing Preferred:
Balanced

Industry Preferences

In Industrial/Energy prefer:
Energy
Alternative Energy

In Manufact. prefer:
Manufacturing

Additional Information
Name of Most Recent Fund: Craton Equity Investors I, L.P.
Most Recent Fund Was Raised: 05/21/2008
Year Founded: 2005
Capital Under Management: $82,500,000
Current Activity Level : Actively seeking new investments

CRAWFORD CAPITAL CORP

125 Main Street, South East
Suite 270
Minneapolis, MN USA 55414
Phone: 6126761436
Fax: 6126761438
Website: www.crawcap.com

Type of Firm
Private Equity Firm

Project Preferences

Type of Financing Preferred:
Startup

Industry Preferences

In Medical/Health prefer:
Medical/Health

Additional Information
Year Founded: 1990
Current Activity Level : Actively seeking new investments

CRCM VENTURE CAPITAL

1 Maritime Plaza
Suite 1107
San Francisco, CA USA 94111
Phone: 4155785700
E-mail: vc@crcm.com
Website: www.crcmvc.com

Type of Firm
Private Equity Firm

Project Preferences

Type of Financing Preferred:
Early Stage
Seed

Geographical Preferences

United States Preferences:

International Preferences:
China

Industry Preferences

In Computer Software prefer:
Software

In Consumer Related prefer:
Consumer Services

Additional Information
Year Founded: 2014
Current Activity Level : Actively seeking new investments

CREADEV SAS

64, bd de Cambrai
Roubaix, France 59100
Phone: 33158652013
E-mail: contact@creadev.fr
Website: www.creadev.fr

Other Offices
26, bd Malesherbes
Paris, France 75008
Phone: 33-1-5865-2013
Fax: 33-1-4482-0015

Management and Staff
Jerome Mulliez, President

Type of Firm
Private Equity Firm

Association Membership
French Venture Capital Association (AFIC)

Project Preferences

Type of Financing Preferred:
Leveraged Buyout
Early Stage
Generalist PE
Later Stage
Management Buyouts
Acquisition

Size of Investments Considered:
Min Size of Investment Considered (000s): $1,247
Max Size of Investment Considered (000s): $99,775

Geographical Preferences

International Preferences:
Europe
France

Industry Preferences

In Medical/Health prefer:
Medical/Health
Health Services

In Industrial/Energy prefer:
Energy
Environmental Related

In Business Serv. prefer:
Services

In Other prefer:
Environment Responsible

Additional Information
Year Founded: 2002
Current Activity Level : Actively seeking new investments

CREADOR CAPITAL GROUP

285, Jalan Ma'arof
8th Floor, Menara BRDB
Kuala Lumpur, Malaysia 59000
Phone: 60321826888
Fax: 60321826889
Website: www.creador.com

Other Offices
651, Regus Citi Centre
Level 6, Chennai Citi Centre
Chennai, India 600004
Phone: 914442218532

IFS Court TwentyEight Cybercity
Ebene, Mauritius
Phone: 2304673000
Fax: 2304674000

PT Creador
15th Floor, One Pacific Place
Jakarta, Indonesia
Phone: 622125502529
Fax: 622125502555

Type of Firm
Private Equity Firm

Project Preferences

Type of Financing Preferred:
Leveraged Buyout
Early Stage
Expansion
Generalist PE
Balanced
Later Stage
Management Buyouts
Acquisition

Geographical Preferences

United States Preferences:
Southeast

International Preferences:
Indonesia
India
Asia
Singapore
Malaysia

Additional Information
Year Founded: 2011
Capital Under Management: $847,000,000
Current Activity Level: Actively seeking new investments

CREAFUND MANAGEMENT NV
Kapitein Maenhoutstraat 77B
Sint-Martens-Latem, Belgium 9830
Phone: 3292726200
Fax: 3292726209
E-mail: info@creafund.be
Website: www.creafund.be

Type of Firm
Private Equity Firm

Association Membership
Belgium Venturing Association

Project Preferences

Type of Financing Preferred:
Early Stage
Later Stage
Management Buyouts
Acquisition

Geographical Preferences

International Preferences:
Europe
Belgium

Industry Preferences

In Communications prefer:
Telecommunications

In Computer Software prefer:
Software

In Biotechnology prefer:
Biotechnology

In Transportation prefer:
Transportation

In Business Serv. prefer:
Media

In Manufact. prefer:
Manufacturing

Additional Information
Year Founded: 1997
Capital Under Management: $34,400,000
Current Activity Level: Actively seeking new investments

CREANDUM AB
Jakobsbergsgatan 18
Stockholm, Sweden 111 44
Phone: 46852463630
Fax: 468221175
E-mail: info@creandum.com
Website: www.creandum.com

Management and Staff
Asa Lindencrona, Chief Financial Officer
Daniel Blomquist, Principal
Fredrik Cassel, General Partner
Hjalmar Winbladh, Venture Partner
Johan Brenner, General Partner
Martin Hauge, General Partner
Staffan Helgesson, General Partner

Type of Firm
Private Equity Firm

Association Membership
Swedish Venture Capital Association (SVCA)
European Private Equity and Venture Capital Assoc.

Project Preferences

Type of Financing Preferred:
Early Stage
Balanced
Later Stage
Seed
Startup

Size of Investments Considered:
Min Size of Investment Considered (000s): $147
Max Size of Investment Considered (000s): $11,032

Geographical Preferences

International Preferences:
Scandanavia/Nordic Region

Industry Preferences

In Communications prefer:
Communications and Media
Wireless Communications
Entertainment

In Computer Software prefer:
Software

In Internet Specific prefer:
Internet

In Computer Other prefer:
Computer Related

In Semiconductor/Electr prefer:
Electronics
Electronic Components
Semiconductor

In Consumer Related prefer:
Entertainment and Leisure

Additional Information
Name of Most Recent Fund: Creandum III
Most Recent Fund Was Raised: 05/15/2012
Year Founded: 2002
Capital Under Management: $163,800,000
Current Activity Level: Actively seeking new investments

CREATHOR VENTURE MANAGEMENT GMBH
Marienbader Platz 1
Bad Homburg, Germany 61348
Phone: 496172139720
Fax: 4961721397229
E-mail: creathor@creathor.de
Website: www.creathor.de

Other Offices
Technoparkstr. 1
Zurich, Switzerland 8005
Phone: 41-44-271-1358

Management and Staff
Cedric Koehler, Partner
Gert Koehler, Chief Executive Officer
Ingo Franz, Partner
Karlheinz Schmelig, Partner
Martin Neumann, Chief Financial Officer

Type of Firm
Private Equity Firm

Association Membership
Swiss Venture Capital Association (SECA)
Swedish Venture Capital Association (SVCA)
European Private Equity and Venture Capital Assoc.

Project Preferences

Type of Financing Preferred:
Early Stage
Seed
Startup

Geographical Preferences

United States Preferences:
All U.S.

International Preferences:
Europe
Switzerland
Austria
Asia
Germany
All International
France

Industry Preferences

In Communications prefer:
Communications and Media
Telecommunications
Wireless Communications
Media and Entertainment

In Internet Specific prefer:
Internet

In Computer Other prefer:
Computer Related

In Semiconductor/Electr prefer:
Electronics

In Biotechnology prefer:
Biotechnology

In Medical/Health prefer:
Medical/Health

In Industrial/Energy prefer:
Energy
Alternative Energy
Industrial Products
Materials
Environmental Related

Additional Information

Name of Most Recent Fund: Creathor Venture Fonds III
Most Recent Fund Was Raised: 09/05/2011
Year Founded: 1984
Capital Under Management: $103,053,000
Current Activity Level : Actively seeking new investments

CREATION CAPITAL L L C

485 Underhill Boulevard
Suite 301
Syosset, NY USA 11791
Phone: 5166724333
Fax: 5166822220
Website: www.creationcapital.com

Management and Staff

Michael Morris, President

Type of Firm

Bank Affiliated

Project Preferences

Type of Financing Preferred:
Early Stage
Expansion
Later Stage

Geographical Preferences

United States Preferences:
All U.S.

Industry Preferences

In Biotechnology prefer:
Biotechnology

Additional Information

Year Founded: 2001
Current Activity Level : Actively seeking new investments

CREATION INVESTMENTS CAPITAL MANAGEMENT LLC

30 South Wacker Drive, Suite 1600
Chicago, IL USA 60606
Phone: 3127843988
Fax: 13127843991
E-mail: information@creationinvestments.com
Website: www.creationinvestments.com

Management and Staff

Adam Code, Vice President
Bryan Wagner, Partner
Ken Vander Weele, Co-Founder
Patrick Fisher, Co-Founder
Tyler Day, Vice President

Type of Firm

Private Equity Firm

Project Preferences

Role in Financing:
Prefer role as deal originator but will also invest in deals created by others

Type of Financing Preferred:
Leveraged Buyout
Balanced
Acquisition

Geographical Preferences

International Preferences:
Latin America
Eastern Europe
Asia

Industry Preferences

In Medical/Health prefer:
Medical/Health

In Industrial/Energy prefer:
Alternative Energy

In Financial Services prefer:
Insurance
Financial Services

In Agr/Forestr/Fish prefer:
Agriculture related

In Other prefer:
Socially Responsible
Environment Responsible

Additional Information

Name of Most Recent Fund: Creation Investments Social Ventures Fund II, L.P.
Most Recent Fund Was Raised: 05/31/2012
Year Founded: 2007
Capital Under Management: $337,000,000
Current Activity Level : Actively seeking new investments

CREDENCE PARTNERS PTE LTD

3A Tank Road
Singapore, Singapore 238060
Phone: 6563232440
E-mail: hello@credencepartners.com
Website: www.credence-investment.com

Management and Staff

Chow Boon Tan, Managing Partner

Type of Firm

Private Equity Firm

Association Membership

Singapore Venture Capital Association (SVCA)

Project Preferences

Type of Financing Preferred:
Leveraged Buyout
Early Stage
Expansion
Generalist PE
Balanced
Later Stage
Acquisition

Geographical Preferences

International Preferences:
Indonesia
Thailand
Asia
Singapore
Malaysia

Industry Preferences

In Internet Specific prefer:
E-Commerce Technology

In Consumer Related prefer:
Consumer

In Transportation prefer:
Transportation

In Business Serv. prefer:
Services

In Manufact. prefer:
Manufacturing

Additional Information

Year Founded: 2012
Capital Under Management: $160,947,000
Current Activity Level : Actively seeking new investments

CREDIT AGRICOLE ALPES DEVELOPPEMENT SNC

15- 17, Rue Paul Claudel
Grenoble, France 38100

Type of Firm
Bank Affiliated

Project Preferences

Type of Financing Preferred:
Leveraged Buyout
Early Stage
Expansion
Later Stage
Seed
Acquisition

Geographical Preferences

International Preferences:
France

Additional Information

Year Founded: 2009
Current Activity Level : Actively seeking new investments

CREDIT AGRICOLE AQUITAINE EXPANSION SAS

304 Boulevard du Pdt Wilson
Bordeaux, France 33076
Phone: 33556904040
E-mail: credit.agricole.en.ligne@ca-aquitaine.fr
Website: www.ca-aquitaine.fr

Management and Staff
Jean-Pierre Pargade, President

Type of Firm
Bank Affiliated

Project Preferences

Type of Financing Preferred:
Leveraged Buyout
Early Stage
Mezzanine
Generalist PE
Later Stage
Startup

Geographical Preferences

International Preferences:
Europe
France

Industry Preferences

In Internet Specific prefer:
Internet

In Consumer Related prefer:
Consumer

In Industrial/Energy prefer:
Energy
Alternative Energy

In Financial Services prefer:
Financial Services

In Agr/Forestr/Fish prefer:
Agriculture related

Additional Information

Year Founded: 2001
Current Activity Level : Actively seeking new investments

CREDIT AGRICOLE CORPORATE AND INVESTMENT BANK SA

9 Quai President Paul Doumer
Paris-la-Defense-Cedex, France 92820
Phone: 33141890000
E-mail: externalcommunications@ca-cib.com
Website: www.ca-cib.fr

Other Offices

Ruben Dario 281
Piso 21
Mexico D. F., Mexico 11580
Phone: 52-55-9138-1380
Fax: 52-55-5280-9720

227 W Monroe Street
Suite 3800
CHICAGO, IL USA 60606
Phone: 1-312-641-0500
Fax: 1-312-641-0527

Savoie, 11, avenue d'Albigny
Annecy Cedex, France 74000
Phone: 33-4-5066-2063
Fax: 33-4-5027-8833

Succursale Aquitaine, 31
Allees de Chartres
Bordeaux Cedex, France 33025
Phone: 33-5-5600-2550
Fax: 33-5-5648-2869

30, rue Thiers
Lille Cedex, France 59005
Phone: 33-3-20-63-6300
Fax: 33-3-20-57-6374

39 Allee Scheffer
Luxembourg, Luxembourg 2520
Phone: 352-4767-2659
Fax: 352-4767-3659

Alameda ITU, 852
16 Andar, Cerqueira Cesar
Sao Paulo, Brazil 01421-001
Phone: 55-11-3896-6300
Fax: 55-11-3896-6363

Circunvalacion Durango 1378
Plaza Zabala
Montevideo, Uruguay 1100
Phone: 11-598-2916-3514
Fax: 11-598-2916-3520

Succursale de Dijon, 3 Place Grangier
Dijon, France 21024
Phone: 33-3-80-54-1770
Fax: 33-3-80-49-9752

1301 Travis Street
Suite 2100
DALLAS, TX USA 75201
Phone: 1-713-890-8600
Fax: 1-713-890-8668

A.M.G. Building, Rue du lac Windermere
Les Berges du lac
Tunis, Tunisia 1053
Phone: 21-67-196-0008
Fax: 21-67-196-0029

Aleksanterinkatu 15 B, P.O. Box 688
Helsinki, Finland FI-00101
Phone: 35-89-69-6991
Fax: 35-89-6969-9200

2000 McGill College Ave
Suite 1900
Montreal, Canada H3A 3H3
Phone: 1-51-4982-6200
Fax: 1-51-4982-6298

Algeria Building, , Business Center Moha
Les Pins Maritimes
Alger, Algeria 16000
Phone: 213-2189-1300
Fax: 213-2189-1199

7, Route du Loc'h
Quimper, France 29000
Phone: 33298760529

2200 Ross Avenue
Suite 4400W
DALLAS, TX USA 75201
Phone: 1-214-220-2300
Fax: 1-214-220-2323

Torre Mene Grande, Piso 9, Ofic. 9-4
Avenida Francisco de Miranda, Los Paolos
Caracas, Venezuela 1060
Phone: 58-21-2285-1942
Fax: 58-21-2285-3254

Succursale Dauphine, 5, rue Felix Poulat
Grenoble Cedex, France 38010
Phone: 33-4-76-86-6400
Fax: 33-4-76-86-0325

4 quai General Guisan
Geneva, Switzerland 1204
Phone: 41-58-321-9000
Fax: 41-58-321-9100

23 Melrose Boulevard, Melrose North
Johannesburg, South Africa 2076
Phone: 27-11-448-3300
Fax: 27-11-448-3370

Succursale de Bruxelles
Chaussee de la Hulpe 166
Brussels, Belgium B1170
Phone: 32-2661-3350
Fax: 32-2661-3360

44/F One Exchange Square
8 Connaught Place
Central, Hong Kong
Phone: 852-2820-7373
Fax: 852-2868-1524

Torre Alem Plaza
Avda. Leonardo N. Alem 855 - piso 24
Buenos Aires, Argentina 1001
Phone: 54-11-4317-7900
Fax: 54-11-4317-7950

122 Leadenhall Street
London, United Kingdom EC3V 4QH
Phone: 44-20-7971-4454
Fax: 44-20-7971-4362

Management and Staff
Frederic Coudreau, Chief Operating Officer
Frederic Meron, Chief Financial Officer
Jacques Prost, Chief Executive Officer
Jean-Yves Hocher, Chief Executive Officer
Paul de Leusse, Chief Executive Officer
Regis Monfront, Chief Executive Officer

Type of Firm
Bank Affiliated

Association Membership
Australian Venture Capital Association (AVCAL)
British Venture Capital Association (BVCA)
Hong Kong Venture Capital Association (HKVCA)

Project Preferences

Type of Financing Preferred:
Leveraged Buyout
Mezzanine
Generalist PE
Later Stage
Management Buyouts
Recapitalizations

Geographical Preferences

International Preferences:
Europe

Additional Information
Year Founded: 1996
Capital Under Management: $56,600,000
Current Activity Level : Actively seeking new investments

CREDIT AGRICOLE CREATION SAS

1, rue Truchis de Lays
Champagne au Mont d'Or, France 69410
Phone: 33472528000
Fax: 33472526999
Website: www.credit-agricole.com

Type of Firm
Bank Affiliated

Project Preferences

Type of Financing Preferred:
Startup

Geographical Preferences

International Preferences:
France

Industry Preferences

In Internet Specific prefer:
Internet

In Consumer Related prefer:
Consumer

In Industrial/Energy prefer:
Energy
Alternative Energy

In Financial Services prefer:
Financial Services

In Agr/Forestr/Fish prefer:
Agriculture related

Additional Information
Year Founded: 1998
Current Activity Level : Actively seeking new investments

CREDIT AGRICOLE DES SAVOIE CAPITAL SAS

Passage des Glaisins
Annecy-le-Vieux, France 74940
Phone: 33825826816

Type of Firm
Bank Affiliated

Project Preferences

Type of Financing Preferred:
Leveraged Buyout
Early Stage
Expansion
Later Stage
Management Buyouts
Acquisition

Geographical Preferences

International Preferences:
France

Additional Information
Year Founded: 1983
Current Activity Level : Actively seeking new investments

CREDIT INDUSTRIEL ET COMMERCIAL SA

6, avenue de Provence
Paris, France 75452
Phone: 33145969696
Website: www.cic.fr

Management and Staff
Alain Fradin, Chief Executive Officer
Daniel Baal, Chief Executive Officer
Philippe Vidal, Chief Executive Officer

Type of Firm
Bank Affiliated

Project Preferences

Type of Financing Preferred:
Leveraged Buyout
Generalist PE
Later Stage
Acquisition

Geographical Preferences

International Preferences:
France

Additional Information
Year Founded: 1990
Current Activity Level : Actively seeking new investments

CREDIT SUISSE ASSET MANAGEMENT LLC

Eleven Madison Avenue
New York, NY USA 10010
Phone: 2123252000
Fax: 2123256665
Website: www.credit-suisse.com

Other Offices
Giesshuebelstrasse 40
PO Box 800
Zurich, Switzerland 8070
Phone: 41-1-333-42-45
Fax: 41-1-333-41-98

Management and Staff
Robert Shafir, Chief Executive Officer

Type of Firm
Bank Affiliated

Association Membership
Hong Kong Venture Capital Association (HKVCA)
Natl Assoc of Small Bus. Inv. Co (NASBIC)

Additional Information
Year Founded: 1999
Current Activity Level : Actively seeking new investments

CREDITEASE VENTURE

88 Jianguo Rd., Chaoyang Dist.
16/F, Block C,SOHO New Town
Beijing, China 100022
Phone: 864008106699
Fax: 861057382188
Website: www.creditease.cn

Type of Firm
Private Equity Firm

Additional Information
Year Founded: 2012
Capital Under Management: $65,000,000
Current Activity Level : Actively seeking new investments

CREDO VENTURES AS

Krizova 2598/4
TechSquare
Prague, Czech Republic 150 00
Phone: 420211153210
E-mail: info@credoventures.com
Website: www.credoventures.com

Management and Staff
Jan Habermann, Partner
Karel Obluk, Venture Partner
Ondrej Bartos, Founder
Tomas Orlik, Venture Partner
Vladislav Jez, Partner

Type of Firm
Private Equity Firm

Association Membership
Czech Venture Capital Association (CVCA)

Project Preferences

Type of Financing Preferred:
Early Stage
Expansion
Seed
Startup

Geographical Preferences

International Preferences:
Slovak Repub.
Central Europe

Industry Preferences

In Communications prefer:
Wireless Communications

In Medical/Health prefer:
Health Services

Additional Information
Name of Most Recent Fund: Credo Stage 1
Most Recent Fund Was Raised: 10/28/2010
Year Founded: 2009
Capital Under Management: $18,100,000
Current Activity Level : Actively seeking new investments

CREINVEST CHAMPAGNE BOURGOGNE SAS

18, Rue d'Avout
Dijon, France 21000

Type of Firm
Bank Affiliated

Project Preferences

Type of Financing Preferred:
Early Stage
Seed

Size of Investments Considered:
Min Size of Investment Considered (000s): $56
Max Size of Investment Considered (000s): $111

Geographical Preferences

International Preferences:
France

Additional Information
Year Founded: 2013
Current Activity Level : Actively seeking new investments

CRESCENDO CAPITAL PARTNERS LLC

10833 Wilshire Boulevard, Suite 331
Westwood, CA USA 90024
Website: www.crescendocap.com

Management and Staff
Mark Hopkins, Managing Partner

Type of Firm
Private Equity Firm

Project Preferences

Type of Financing Preferred:
Leveraged Buyout
Acquisition
Recapitalizations

Industry Preferences

In Communications prefer:
Telecommunications

In Medical/Health prefer:
Health Services

In Consumer Related prefer:
Retail
Food/Beverage

In Business Serv. prefer:
Distribution

In Manufact. prefer:
Manufacturing

Additional Information
Year Founded: 2005
Current Activity Level : Actively seeking new investments

CRESCENDO PARTNERS CAPITAL PTY LTD

71 Macquarie Street, Level Four
Sydney, Australia 2000
Phone: 61293347600
Fax: 61293347660
E-mail: info@crescendopartners.com.au
Website: www.crescendopartners.com.au

Management and Staff
Joseph Crepaldi, Managing Director

Type of Firm
Service Provider

Project Preferences

Type of Financing Preferred:
Leveraged Buyout
Later Stage
Management Buyouts
Acquisition
Private Placement

Geographical Preferences

International Preferences:
Australia
New Zealand

Additional Information
Year Founded: 2011
Current Activity Level : Actively seeking new investments

CRESCENDO VENTURE MANAGEMENT LLC

600 Hansen Way
Palo Alto, CA USA 94304
Phone: 6504701200
Fax: 6504701201
E-mail: investorservices@crescendoventures.com
Website: www.crescendoventures.com

Management and Staff
David Spreng, Managing Partner
John Borchers, General Partner
Peter van Cuylenberg, General Partner
Wayne Cantwell, General Partner

Type of Firm
Private Equity Firm

Project Preferences

Role in Financing:
Prefer role as deal originator but will also invest in deals created by others

Type of Financing Preferred:
Early Stage
Seed
Startup

Geographical Preferences

United States Preferences:
Midwest

International Preferences:
Europe
Western Europe
Israel
Asia

Industry Focus
(% based on actual investment)

Communications and Media	25.5%
Internet Specific	24.5%
Computer Software and Services	17.7%
Semiconductors/Other Elect.	17.6%
Medical/Health	4.5%
Other Products	3.3%
Computer Hardware	3.2%
Biotechnology	1.8%
Industrial/Energy	1.2%
Consumer Related	0.8%

Additional Information
Year Founded: 1993
Capital Under Management: $1,000,000,000
Current Activity Level : Actively seeking new investments
Method of Compensation: Return on investment is of primary concern, do not charge fees

---

CRESCENT CAPITAL GROUP LP

11100 Santa Monica Boulevard
Suite 2000
West Los Angeles, CA USA 90025
Phone: 3102355900
E-mail: info@crescentcap.com
Website: www.crescentcap.com

Management and Staff
Adam Stern, Managing Director
Amir Rao, Vice President
Christine Vanden Beukel, Managing Director
Christopher Wright, Managing Director
Daniel Honeker, Managing Director
Elizabeth Ko, Vice President
Jean-Marc Chapus, Managing Partner
John Fekete, Managing Director
John Hwang, Vice President
Jonathan Insull, Managing Director
Joseph Keenan, Chief Financial Officer
Joshua Grumer, Vice President
Kimberly Frazier, Vice President
Kimberly Grant, Vice President
Louis Lavoie, Managing Director
M. Mark Albert, Managing Director
Mark Attanasio, Managing Partner
Matthew Miller, Managing Director
Melissa Weiler, Managing Director
Meric Topbas, Vice President
Michael Parks, Managing Director
Patrick Turner, Managing Director
Philip Kenney, Vice President
Raymond Barrios, Vice President
Seth Healy, Vice President
Steven Novick, Managing Director
Yev Kuznetsov, Vice President

Type of Firm
Investment Management Firm

Association Membership
Natl Assoc of Small Bus. Inv. Co (NASBIC)

Project Preferences

Type of Financing Preferred:
Leveraged Buyout
Mezzanine
Acquisition
Recapitalizations

Geographical Preferences

International Preferences:
Europe

Additional Information
Name of Most Recent Fund: Crescent Mezzanine Partners VI, L.P.
Most Recent Fund Was Raised: 04/16/2012
Year Founded: 2012
Capital Under Management: $8,000,000,000
Current Activity Level : Actively seeking new investments

CRESCENT CAPITAL NI LTD

7 Upper Crescent
Belfast, United Kingdom BT7 1NT
Phone: 442890233633
Fax: 442890329525
E-mail: mail@crescentcapital.co.uk
Website: www.crescentcapital.co.uk

Management and Staff
Colin Walsh, Managing Director
Ed Finnegan, Chief Financial Officer

Type of Firm
Private Equity Firm

Association Membership
Australian Venture Capital Association (AVCAL)
Emerging Markets Private Equity Association

Project Preferences

Type of Financing Preferred:
Early Stage
Expansion
Management Buyouts

Size of Investments Considered:
Min Size of Investment Considered (000s): $391
Max Size of Investment Considered (000s): $2,348

Geographical Preferences

International Preferences:
Ireland

Industry Preferences

In Manufact. prefer:
Manufacturing

Additional Information
Name of Most Recent Fund: Crescent Capital III, L.P.
Most Recent Fund Was Raised: 12/20/2013
Year Founded: 1995
Capital Under Management: $20,500,000
Current Activity Level: Actively seeking new investments

CRESCENT CAPITAL PARTNERS LTD
One Farrer Place
Gov. Phillip Tower, Level 29
Sydney, Australia 2000
Phone: 61292208100
Fax: 61292208199
E-mail: mail@crescentcap.com.au
Website: www.crescentcap.com.au

Management and Staff
Peter Lyon-Mercado, Chief Financial Officer

Type of Firm
Private Equity Firm

Association Membership
New Zealand Venture Capital Association

Project Preferences

Role in Financing:
Prefer role as deal originator

Type of Financing Preferred:
Leveraged Buyout
Expansion
Generalist PE
Acquisition

Geographical Preferences

International Preferences:
Pacific
Australia
New Zealand

Industry Preferences

In Communications prefer:
Telecommunications

In Computer Other prefer:
Computer Related

In Medical/Health prefer:
Medical Diagnostics

In Consumer Related prefer:
Food/Beverage

In Financial Services prefer:
Insurance
Financial Services

In Business Serv. prefer:
Services

In Manufact. prefer:
Manufacturing

Additional Information
Name of Most Recent Fund: Crescent Capital Fund IV
Most Recent Fund Was Raised: 01/14/2011
Year Founded: 2000
Capital Under Management: $1,000,000,000
Current Activity Level: Actively seeking new investments
Method of Compensation: Return on invest. most important, but chg. closing fees, service fees, etc.

CRESCENT ENTERPRISES
P.O. Box 211
Sharjah, Utd. Arab Em.
Phone: 97165727000
Fax: 97165726000
E-mail: mail@crescententerprises.ae
Website: www.crescententerprises.ae

Management and Staff
Badr Jafar, Chief Executive Officer

Type of Firm
Private Equity Firm

Project Preferences

Type of Financing Preferred:
Leveraged Buyout
Early Stage
Expansion
Generalist PE
Later Stage

Industry Preferences

In Communications prefer:
Media and Entertainment

Additional Information
Year Founded: 1969
Current Activity Level: Actively seeking new investments

CRESCENT HYDEPARK INVESTMENT CONSULTING SHANGHAI CO LTD
Wukang Road, Xuhui District
Room 601-603, No.378 Wukang Rd
Shanghai, China

Type of Firm
Private Equity Firm

Project Preferences

Type of Financing Preferred:
Early Stage
Expansion

Geographical Preferences

International Preferences:
China

Industry Preferences

In Consumer Related prefer:
Retail
Consumer Products

Additional Information
Year Founded: 2007
Current Activity Level: Actively seeking new investments

CRESCENT POINT ENERGY CORP
111 - 5th Avenue Southwest
Suite 2800
Calgary, Canada T2P 3Y6
Phone: 4036930020
Fax: 4036930070
Website: www.crescentpointenergy.com

Other Offices
555, 17th Street
Suite 750
DENVER, CO USA 80202
Phone: 7208803610
Fax: 303292562

Management and Staff
Bradley Borggard, Vice President
C. Neil Smith, Chief Operating Officer
Kenneth Lamont, Chief Financial Officer
Mark Eade, Vice President
Ryan Gritzfeldt, Vice President
Steven Toews, Vice President

Type of Firm
Private Equity Firm

Additional Information
Year Founded: 2001
Current Activity Level: Actively seeking new investments

CRESCENT POINT GROUP
One Temasek Avenue
Suite 20-01 Millenia Tower
Singapore, Singapore 039192
Phone: 6565113088
Fax: 6562235992
E-mail: info@cgcm.com
Website: www.cgcm.com

Other Offices
378 Wukang Road
Sixth Floor
Shanghai, China 200031
Phone: 862164185599
Fax: 862164185569

Bin Homran Commercial Centre
Aziz St. (Tahlia St.), 603A & 604A
Jeddah, Saudi Arabia
Phone: 992-2-660-8776
Fax: 992-2-682-8801

62 Kehua Bei Road
Unit 1301, Lippo Tower
Chengdu, China 610041
Phone: 862162519292
Fax: 862162519293

Management and Staff
Thomas Pompidou, Managing Director

Type of Firm
Private Equity Firm

Project Preferences

Type of Financing Preferred:
Balanced
Acquisition
Special Situation

Geographical Preferences

International Preferences:
Middle East
Pacific
Asia

Industry Preferences

In Medical/Health prefer:
Medical/Health

In Consumer Related prefer:
Consumer
Retail
Education Related

In Industrial/Energy prefer:
Environmental Related

In Financial Services prefer:
Financial Services

In Agr/Forestr/Fish prefer:
Agriculture related

Additional Information
Year Founded: 2003
Current Activity Level : Actively seeking new investments

CRESCENT RIDGE PARTNERS INC

400 Continental Boulevard
Suite 160
El Segundo, CA USA 90245
Website: www.cpartnersinc.com

Type of Firm
Private Equity Firm

Project Preferences

Type of Financing Preferred:
Early Stage
Seed
Startup

Additional Information
Year Founded: 2013
Current Activity Level : Actively seeking new investments

CRESSEY AND COMPANY LP

155 North Wacker Drive
Suite 4500
Chicago, IL USA 60606
Phone: 3129455700
Fax: 3129455701
E-mail: chicago@cresseyco.com
Website: www.cresseyco.com

Other Offices
2525 West End Avenue
Suite 1250
Nashville, TN USA 37203
Phone: 6153698400
Fax: 6153698444

Management and Staff
Bryan Cressey, Partner
David Schuppan, Partner
David Rogero, Partner
Merrick Axel, Partner
Peter Ehrich, Partner
Ralph Davis, Partner
Scott Maskalunas, Chief Financial Officer
William Frist, Partner

Type of Firm
Private Equity Firm

Association Membership
Illinois Venture Capital Association

Project Preferences

Type of Financing Preferred:
Leveraged Buyout
Later Stage
Acquisition

Geographical Preferences

United States Preferences:
North America

Industry Preferences

In Medical/Health prefer:
Medical/Health
Health Services

Additional Information
Name of Most Recent Fund: Cressey & Co Fund V, L.P.
Most Recent Fund Was Raised: 12/08/2014
Year Founded: 2008
Capital Under Management: $385,000,000
Current Activity Level : Actively seeking new investments

CREST CAPITAL PARTNERS

50 Raffles Place #34-03
Singapore Land Tower
Singapore, Singapore 048623
Phone: 65-6533-2002
Fax: 65-6532-2002
E-mail: contact@crestcapitalasia.com
Website: www.crestcapitalasia.com

Other Offices
Plaza ABDA 23rd floor
Jalan Jend. Sudirman Kav 59
Jakarta, Indonesia 12190
Phone: 62-21-5140-1133
Fax: 62-21-5140-1599

Suite 8-1, Level 8, Faber Imperial Court
Jaltan Sultan Ismail
Kuala Lumpur, Malaysia 50250
Phone: 603-2693-8008
Fax: 603-2698-2088

16th FL, FKI B/D,
28-1, Yoido-dong
Seoul, South Korea
Phone: 821-6231-7601

Room 1212A No. 689 Guang Dong Road
Haitong Securities Tower
Shanghai, China 200001
Phone: 86-21-6341-0319
Fax: 86-21-6341-0329

Management and Staff
Angela Tan, Principal
David Tan, Principal
Glendon Tan, Principal
Peter Chan, Managing Partner

Type of Firm
Private Equity Firm

Project Preferences

Type of Financing Preferred:
Expansion
Public Companies
Later Stage
Management Buyouts
Acquisition

Geographical Preferences

International Preferences:
Asia

Industry Preferences

In Communications prefer:
Communications and Media
Telecommunications

In Computer Software prefer:
Software

In Internet Specific prefer:
E-Commerce Technology
Internet

In Consumer Related prefer:
Consumer
Food/Beverage

In Industrial/Energy prefer:
Industrial Products

In Business Serv. prefer:
Services

In Manufact. prefer:
Manufacturing

Additional Information
Year Founded: 1987
Capital Under Management: $21,790,000
Current Activity Level : Actively seeking new investments

CREST GROUP LLC

38 Kings Highway
Hauppauge, NY USA 11788
E-mail: info@thecrestgroupllc.com
Website: www.thecrestgroupllc.com

Type of Firm
Private Equity Firm

Project Preferences

Type of Financing Preferred:
Value-Add
Management Buyouts
Acquisition
Recapitalizations

Industry Preferences

In Financial Services prefer:
Real Estate

Additional Information
Year Founded: 2009
Current Activity Level : Actively seeking new investments

CRESTLIGHT VENTURE PRODUCTIONS LLC

3633 Vireo Avenue
Santa Clara, CA USA 95051
Phone: 4082439702
E-mail: info@crestlight.com
Website: www.crestlight.com

Management and Staff
David Borlo, Managing Partner
Jay Sethuram, Managing Partner
Jens Horstmann, Managing Partner

Type of Firm
Private Equity Firm

Project Preferences

Type of Financing Preferred:
Early Stage
Seed
Startup

Size of Investments Considered:
Min Size of Investment Considered (000s): $200
Max Size of Investment Considered (000s): $750

Geographical Preferences

United States Preferences:
West Coast

Industry Preferences

In Computer Software prefer:
Software

In Internet Specific prefer:
Internet

Additional Information
Name of Most Recent Fund: Crestlight Venture Partners Fund I, L.P.
Most Recent Fund Was Raised: 03/29/2013
Year Founded: 2012
Capital Under Management: $1,290,000
Current Activity Level : Actively seeking new investments

CRESTONE CAPITAL LLC

1050 Walnut Street
Suite 500
Boulder, CO USA 80302
Phone: 3034424587
Fax: 303424587
Website: www.crestonecapital.com

Management and Staff
Eric Kramer, Chief Executive Officer
Jack Swift, President
Jeremy Shevlin, Partner
Randi Grassgreen, Partner

Type of Firm
Private Equity Advisor or Fund of Funds

Additional Information
Year Founded: 2001
Capital Under Management: $101,580,000
Current Activity Level : Actively seeking new investments

CRESTVIEW ADVISORS, LLC

667 Madison Avenue, 10th Floor
New York, NY USA 10065
Phone: 2129060700
E-mail: information@crestview.com
Website: www.crestview.com

Management and Staff
Adam Klein, Partner
Alex Binderow, Principal
Alex Rose, Partner
Bob Hurst, Partner
Bradford Williams, Vice President
Brian Cassidy, Partner
Caroline Bliss, Principal
Cindy Cheung, Principal
Daniel Wellman, Vice President
Daniel Kilpatrick, Principal
Evelyn Pellicone, Chief Financial Officer
Jeffrey Marcus, Partner
Katherine Chung, Principal
Quentin Chu, Partner
Richard DeMartini, Partner
Thomas Murphy, Co-Founder

Type of Firm
Private Equity Firm

Association Membership
Private Equity Council (PEC)

Project Preferences

Type of Financing Preferred:
Leveraged Buyout
Turnaround
Special Situation
Distressed Debt

Size of Investments Considered:
Min Size of Investment Considered (000s): $100,000
Max Size of Investment Considered (000s): $250,000

Industry Preferences

In Medical/Health prefer:
Medical/Health

In Industrial/Energy prefer:
Energy
Industrial Products

In Financial Services prefer:
Financial Services

In Business Serv. prefer:
Media

Additional Information
Name of Most Recent Fund: Crestview Partners II, L.P.
Most Recent Fund Was Raised: 12/18/2007
Year Founded: 2004
Capital Under Management: $6,000,000,000
Current Activity Level : Actively seeking new investments

CRIMSON CAPITAL CHINA

Unit 1025, Tower 1
China World Trade Center
Beijing, China 100004
Phone: 86-10-6505-8668
Fax: 86-10-6505-8667
E-mail: info@crimcap.com
Website: www.crimcap.com

Other Offices

Unit 4808, Tower 2
Plaza 66, #1366, West Nanjing Road
Shanghai, China 200040
Phone: 86-21-6113-0177
Fax: 86-21-6113-0176

Management and Staff

Eileen Yang, Managing Director
Real Lin, Vice President
Zack Ren, Managing Director

Type of Firm
Private Equity Firm

Project Preferences

Type of Financing Preferred:
Expansion
Generalist PE
Opportunistic

Geographical Preferences

International Preferences:
China

Additional Information

Year Founded: 1991
Current Activity Level : Actively seeking new investments

CRIMSON INVESTMENTS LTD

260 Sheridan Avenue
Suite 300
Palo Alto, CA USA 94306
Phone: 650-233-6900
Fax: 650-233-6919

Other Offices

2F, North Wing
35 SiNan Road
Shanghai, China 200020
Phone: 86-21-5306-2299
Fax: 86-21-6386-0166

13F, 109, Sec. 3
Min Sheng E. Road
Taipei 105, Taiwan
Phone: 886-22717-9900
Fax: 886-22546-2302

Type of Firm
Private Equity Firm

Additional Information
Year Founded: 1993
Current Activity Level : Actively seeking new investments

CRIMSON VENTURES LLC

6957 West Highway 10
Suite 206
Anoka, MN USA 55303
Website: www.crimsonventuresllc.com

Type of Firm
Investment Management Firm

Project Preferences

Type of Financing Preferred:
Early Stage
Expansion
Later Stage

Additional Information
Year Founded: 1969
Current Activity Level : Actively seeking new investments

CRITICAL CAPITAL GROWTH FUND L P

90 Park Avenue
New York, NY USA 10016
Phone: 212-697-5200
Fax: 212-697-1096

Management and Staff
Charlie Robinson, Managing Director
Jeff Krentz, Vice President

Type of Firm
Private Equity Firm

Project Preferences

Type of Financing Preferred:
Expansion
Mezzanine
Management Buyouts

Size of Investments Considered:
Min Size of Investment Considered (000s): $1,000
Max Size of Investment Considered (000s): $2,000

Geographical Preferences

United States Preferences:
All U.S.

Industry Preferences

In Communications prefer:
Communications and Media

In Semiconductor/Electr prefer:
Electronics

In Consumer Related prefer:
Consumer

In Industrial/Energy prefer:
Machinery

In Business Serv. prefer:
Services

In Manufact. prefer:
Manufacturing

Additional Information
Year Founded: 1999
Capital Under Management: $10,000,000
Current Activity Level : Actively seeking new investments

CROCKER CAPITAL, INC.

One Post Street
Suite 2515
San Francisco, CA USA 94104
Phone: 4159565250
Fax: 4159565710

Management and Staff
Asad Madni, Managing Director

Type of Firm
Private Equity Firm

Project Preferences

Role in Financing:
Prefer role as deal originator

Type of Financing Preferred:
Early Stage
Generalist PE
Acquisition

Geographical Preferences

United States Preferences:

Industry Preferences

In Communications prefer:
Telecommunications

In Computer Software prefer:
Software

In Semiconductor/Electr prefer:
Electronic Components
Controllers and Sensors
Sensors

In Biotechnology prefer:
Biotechnology

In Medical/Health prefer:
Medical Products

In Industrial/Energy prefer:
Industrial Products

In Transportation prefer:
Aerospace

Additional Information
Year Founded: 1969
Capital Under Management: $50,000,000
Current Activity Level : Actively seeking new investments
Method of Compensation: Return on investment is of primary concern, do not charge fees

CROFT & BENDER LLC

4200 Northside Parkway, NW
Building One, Suite 100
Atlanta, GA USA 30327
Phone: 4048413131
Fax: 4048413135
E-mail: info@croft-bender.com
Website: www.croft-bender.com

Management and Staff
Edward Croft, Managing Director
Erik Zalenski, Vice President
Frank Briggs, Managing Director
Nathan Barbour, Vice President
R. Neale Fisher, Vice President
Ronald Goldman, Managing Director
Steve Tye, Managing Director
Theodore Bender, Managing Director

Type of Firm
Bank Affiliated

Project Preferences

Role in Financing:
Prefer role as deal originator but will also invest in deals created by others

Type of Financing Preferred:
Leveraged Buyout
Early Stage
Expansion
Generalist PE
Later Stage
Acquisition
Recapitalizations

Geographical Preferences

United States Preferences:
Southeast

Industry Focus
(% based on actual investment)

Other Products	50.5%
Computer Software and Services	24.2%
Internet Specific	12.4%
Medical/Health	8.7%
Communications and Media	2.3%
Biotechnology	1.2%
Semiconductors/Other Elect.	0.7%

Additional Information
Name of Most Recent Fund: C&B Capital II, L.P.
Most Recent Fund Was Raised: 03/27/2006
Year Founded: 1986
Capital Under Management: $122,800,000
Current Activity Level : Actively seeking new investments
Method of Compensation: Return on investment is of primary concern, do not charge fees

CROFTON CAPITAL LLC

2227 Washington Street
2 Newton Exec. Park, Suite 202
Newton, MA USA 02462
Phone: 7815913070
Website: www.croftoncap.com

Management and Staff
Phil Ivey, Managing Director

Type of Firm
Private Equity Firm

Project Preferences

Type of Financing Preferred:
Leveraged Buyout
Management Buyouts
Acquisition

Geographical Preferences

United States Preferences:
Northeast

Industry Preferences

In Computer Software prefer:
Software

In Consumer Related prefer:
Consumer Products
Consumer Services

In Business Serv. prefer:
Services
Distribution

In Manufact. prefer:
Manufacturing

Additional Information
Year Founded: 2009
Current Activity Level : Actively seeking new investments

CROISSANCE NORD PAS DE CALAIS SAS

2 avenue de Kaarst
BP 52004
Euralille, France 59777
Phone: 33359302004
Fax: 33359302059
E-mail: contact@groupeird.fr

Website: www.groupeird.fr

Other Offices
Euroalliance Port A
2 avenue de Kaarst BP52004
Euralille, France 59777
Phone: 33-3-5930-2004
Fax: 33-3-5930-2059

Type of Firm
Private Equity Firm

Association Membership
French Venture Capital Association (AFIC)

Project Preferences

Type of Financing Preferred:
Leveraged Buyout
Early Stage
Generalist PE
Later Stage
Acquisition

Size of Investments Considered:
Min Size of Investment Considered (000s): $68
Max Size of Investment Considered (000s): $2,030

Geographical Preferences

International Preferences:
France

Industry Preferences

In Semiconductor/Electr prefer:
Electronics

In Biotechnology prefer:
Biotechnology

In Medical/Health prefer:
Medical/Health

In Consumer Related prefer:
Retail
Other Restaurants

In Industrial/Energy prefer:
Industrial Products

In Business Serv. prefer:
Services

In Agr/Forestr/Fish prefer:
Agribusiness

Additional Information
Year Founded: 1991
Capital Under Management: $35,200,000
Current Activity Level : Actively seeking new investments

CRONOS GROUP INC

76 Stafford Street, Suite 302
Toronto, Canada M6J 2S1
Phone: 4165040004
E-mail: info@pharmacancapital.com

Website: thecronosgroup.com

Management and Staff
Michael Gorenstein, President
William Hilson, Chief Financial Officer

Type of Firm
Investment Management Firm

Project Preferences

Type of Financing Preferred:
Generalist PE

Geographical Preferences

Canadian Preferences:
All Canada

Industry Preferences

In Biotechnology prefer:
Biotech Related Research

In Medical/Health prefer:
Other Therapeutic
Health Services

Additional Information
Year Founded: 2013
Current Activity Level : Actively seeking new investments

CRONUS VENTURES

6517, 151st PL Southeast
Bellevue, WA USA 98006
Phone: 425-641-4497
Fax: 419-793-1451
E-mail: info@cronusventures.com
Website: www.cronusventures.com

Management and Staff
Rao Remala, Partner

Type of Firm
Private Equity Firm

Additional Information
Year Founded: 2000
Current Activity Level : Actively seeking new investments

CROSBIE & CO INC

150 King Street West
15th Floor, P.O. Box 95
Toronto, Canada M5H 1J9
Phone: 4163627726
Fax: 4163623447
E-mail: info@crosbieco.com

Management and Staff
Asim Siddiqui, Vice President
Colin Walker, Managing Director
Ed Giacomelli, Managing Director
Ian Maconell, Managing Director
Jeffrey Ng, Vice President
Mel Margolese, Managing Director

Type of Firm
Investment Management Firm

Additional Information
Year Founded: 1995
Current Activity Level : Actively seeking new investments

CROSS ATLANTIC CAPITAL PARTNERS LLC

100 Matsonford Road
Suite 555, 5 Radnor Corp. Ctr.
Radnor, PA USA 19087
Phone: 6109952650
Fax: 6109712062
E-mail: info@xacp.com
Website: www.xacp.com

Other Offices
Alexandra House
The Sweepstakes
Dublin, Ireland
Phone: 353-1-664-1721
Fax: 353-1-664-1806

Management and Staff
Frederick Tecce, Managing Partner
Rahul Singh, Principal
Richard Fox, Managing Director

Type of Firm
Private Equity Firm

Project Preferences

Role in Financing:
Will function either as deal originator or investor in deals created by others

Type of Financing Preferred:
Early Stage
Expansion
Balanced

Geographical Preferences

United States Preferences:

International Preferences:
Ireland
United Kingdom

Industry Focus
(% based on actual investment)
Computer Software and Services	35.7%
Internet Specific	22.4%
Semiconductors/Other Elect.	10.2%
Communications and Media	9.7%
Other Products	8.6%
Biotechnology	6.5%
Computer Hardware	5.9%
Industrial/Energy	0.9%

Additional Information
Name of Most Recent Fund: Co-Investment Fund II, The
Most Recent Fund Was Raised: 11/17/2005
Year Founded: 1998
Capital Under Management: $523,000,000
Current Activity Level : Actively seeking new investments
Method of Compensation: Return on investment is of primary concern, do not charge fees

---

CROSS ATLANTIC PARTNERS

445 Park Avenue
3rd Floor
New York, NY USA 10022
Phone: 6465217500
Fax: 6464970061
E-mail: info@crossatlanticpartners.com
Website: www.crossatlanticpartners.com

Management and Staff
James Dougherty, Venture Partner
John Cassis, Managing Partner
Paula Allamby, Partner
Sandra Panem, Managing Partner
Steven Soignet, Venture Partner

Type of Firm
Private Equity Firm

Project Preferences

Role in Financing:
Will function either as deal originator or investor in deals created by others

Type of Financing Preferred:
Later Stage

Size of Investments Considered:
Min Size of Investment Considered (000s): $1,000
Max Size of Investment Considered (000s): $3,000

Geographical Preferences

United States Preferences:

Industry Preferences

In Medical/Health prefer:
Medical/Health
Medical Products
Health Services

Additional Information
Name of Most Recent Fund: Cross Atlantic Partners V, K/S
Most Recent Fund Was Raised: 03/31/2004
Year Founded: 1994
Capital Under Management: $155,000,000
Current Activity Level : Actively seeking new investments
Method of Compensation: Return on investment is of primary concern, do not charge fees

CROSS CREEK CAPITAL LP

150 Social Hall Avenue
Fourth Floor
Salt Lake City, UT USA 84111
Phone: 8015330777
Fax: 8015339828
E-mail: info@crosscreekadvisors.com
Website: www.crosscreekadvisors.com

Management and Staff
Dan Fellars, Venture Partner
Karey Barker, Managing Director

Type of Firm
Investment Management Firm

Association Membership
Norwegian Venture Capital Association
National Venture Capital Association - USA (NVCA)

Project Preferences

Type of Financing Preferred:
Fund of Funds
Generalist PE
Later Stage

Industry Preferences

In Computer Other prefer:
Computer Related

In Consumer Related prefer:
Consumer

Additional Information
Name of Most Recent Fund: Cross Creek Capital Partners II, L.P.
Most Recent Fund Was Raised: 08/02/2011
Year Founded: 2006
Capital Under Management: $111,000,000
Current Activity Level : Actively seeking new investments

CROSS CULTURE VENTURES

10351 Washington Boulevard
Culver City, CA USA 90232
Phone: 2129603948
Website: www.cultturevc.com

Type of Firm
Private Equity Firm

Project Preferences

Type of Financing Preferred:
Early Stage

Additional Information
Year Founded: 2015
Capital Under Management: $10,500,000
Current Activity Level : Actively seeking new investments

CROSS EQUITY PARTNERS AG

Bahnhofstrasse 1
Pfaeffikon, Switzerland 8808
Phone: 41442699393
Fax: 41442699394
E-mail: info@crossequitypartners.ch
Website: www.crossequity.ch

Other Offices
29/31 ESPLANADE
South tower, 3rd Floor
Jersey, Channel Islands JE4 5SJ

Management and Staff
Markus Reich, Managing Partner
Michael Petersen, Managing Partner

Type of Firm
Private Equity Firm

Association Membership
Swiss Venture Capital Association (SECA)

Project Preferences

Type of Financing Preferred:
Early Stage
Seed
Management Buyouts
Startup

Geographical Preferences

International Preferences:
Germany

Industry Preferences

In Consumer Related prefer:
Consumer

In Industrial/Energy prefer:
Industrial Products

In Business Serv. prefer:
Services

Additional Information
Year Founded: 2008
Capital Under Management: $165,141,000
Current Activity Level : Actively seeking new investments

CROSS ROAD BIOTECH SCR DE REGIMEN COMUN SA

Calle De Almagro One, Derecha
Madrid, Spain 28010
Phone: 34914467897
Fax: 34917021018
E-mail: info@crbinverbio.com

Management and Staff
Enrique Castellon, President

Type of Firm
Private Equity Firm

Association Membership
Spanish Venture Capital Association (ASCRI)

Project Preferences

Type of Financing Preferred:
Early Stage
Seed
Startup

Geographical Preferences

International Preferences:
Spain

Industry Preferences

In Biotechnology prefer:
Biotechnology
Biotech Related Research

In Medical/Health prefer:
Medical/Health
Medical Diagnostics
Medical Therapeutics
Health Services

Additional Information
Name of Most Recent Fund: CRB Bio II FCR
Most Recent Fund Was Raised: 04/26/2012
Year Founded: 2001
Capital Under Management: $44,532,000
Current Activity Level : Actively seeking new investments

CROSS VALLEY CAPITAL

1680 Michigan Avenue
Suite 815
Miami Beach, FL USA 33139
E-mail: info@crossvalley.vc
Website: crossvalley.vc

Management and Staff
David Kabakoff, Partner
Garheng Kong, Managing Partner
Randy Scott, Partner
Richard Lin, Partner
Thomas Callaway, Venture Partner

Type of Firm
Private Equity Firm

Project Preferences

Type of Financing Preferred:
Early Stage
Later Stage
Seed

Additional Information
Year Founded: 2015
Current Activity Level : Actively seeking new investments

CROSSCUT VENTURES MANAGEMENT LLC

373 Rose Avenue
Venice, CA USA 90291
Phone: 3106504777
E-mail: info@crosscutventures.com
Website: www.crosscut.vc

Management and Staff
Adam Goldenberg, Venture Partner
Brett Brewer, Co-Founder
Brian Garrett, Co-Founder
Rick Smith, Co-Founder
Zaw Thet, Venture Partner

Type of Firm
Private Equity Firm

Project Preferences

Size of Investments Considered:
Min Size of Investment Considered (000s): $250
Max Size of Investment Considered (000s): $750

Geographical Preferences

United States Preferences:
Southern California

Industry Preferences

In Communications prefer:
Telecommunications

In Computer Software prefer:
Software

In Internet Specific prefer:
Internet

In Consumer Related prefer:
Consumer Services

Additional Information
Name of Most Recent Fund: Crosscut Ventures 2, L.P.
Most Recent Fund Was Raised: 03/15/2012
Year Founded: 2008
Capital Under Management: $100,000,000
Current Activity Level : Actively seeking new investments

CROSHARBOR CAPITAL PARTNERS

One Boston Place
Suite 2300
Boston, MA USA 02108
Phone: 6176248300
Fax: 6176248399
E-mail: info@crossharborcapital.com
Website: www.crossharborcapital.com

Management and Staff
Daniel Jacobson, Vice President
David Jones, Vice President
Gregory Dewitt, Managing Director
Jay Hart, Chief Operating Officer
Stephen Steinour, Managing Partner
William Kremer, Managing Partner

Type of Firm
Private Equity Firm

Project Preferences

Role in Financing:
Prefer role as deal originator

Type of Financing Preferred:
Leveraged Buyout
Acquisition
Distressed Debt

Geographical Preferences

United States Preferences:

International Preferences:
Rest of World

Industry Preferences

In Financial Services prefer:
Financial Services
Real Estate

In Business Serv. prefer:
Services

Additional Information
Name of Most Recent Fund: CrossHarbor Institutional Partners II, L.P.
Most Recent Fund Was Raised: 01/05/2011
Year Founded: 1993
Capital Under Management: $906,400,000
Current Activity Level : Actively seeking new investments

CROSSLINK CAPITAL INC

Two Embarcadero Center
Suite 2200
San Francisco, CA USA 94111
Phone: 4156171800
Fax: 4156171801
E-mail: info@crosslinkcapital.com
Website: www.crosslinkcapital.com

Management and Staff
Bill Dauphinais, Partner
Carl Rydbeck, Vice President
Daniel Myers, Partner
David Silverman, Partner
Eric Gonsenheim, Vice President
Eric Chin, Partner
Gary Hromadko, Partner
Grant Cleghorn, Partner
James Feuille, Partner
Joel Hausman, Partner
John Perkins, Partner
Marcelo Desio, Partner
Matt Bigge, Partner
Michael Stark, Founder
Mihaly Szigeti, Chief Financial Officer
Omar El-Ayat, Partner
Sy Kaufman, Founder
Thomas Bliska, Partner

Type of Firm
Private Equity Firm

Association Membership
National Venture Capital Association - USA (NVCA)

Project Preferences

Role in Financing:
Prefer role as deal originator but will also invest in deals created by others

Type of Financing Preferred:
Early Stage
Expansion
Balanced
Later Stage
Seed

Geographical Preferences

United States Preferences:
California

Industry Focus
(% based on actual investment)

Internet Specific	37.8%
Computer Software and Services	27.7%
Semiconductors/Other Elect.	19.3%
Communications and Media	5.6%
Computer Hardware	5.1%
Industrial/Energy	2.4%
Other Products	0.8%
Consumer Related	0.6%
Medical/Health	0.5%
Biotechnology	0.2%

Additional Information
Name of Most Recent Fund: Crosslink Crossover Fund VI, L.P.
Most Recent Fund Was Raised: 04/30/2011
Year Founded: 1989
Capital Under Management: $1,700,000,000
Current Activity Level : Actively seeking new investments

CROSSOVER ADVISORS PVT LTD

318, Maker Chambers V,
Nariman Point,
Mumbai, India 400 021
Phone: 91-22-6610-7030
Fax: 91-22-6610-7033
E-mail: info@crossoveradvisors.com
Website: www.crossoveradvisors.com

Other Offices
A1, Deepak Complex
6, National Games Road, Yerawada
Pune, India 411006

Bharat Mekani, 1 , Amber Road
#17-03 Amber point
Singapore, Singapore 439845

Management and Staff
S Chandrasekaran, Chief Operating Officer
Vinnie Vyas, Chief Executive Officer

Type of Firm
Private Equity Firm

Project Preferences

Type of Financing Preferred:
Balanced
Later Stage

Size of Investments Considered:
Min Size of Investment Considered (000s): $2,000
Max Size of Investment Considered (000s): $20,000

Geographical Preferences

International Preferences:
India
China

Industry Preferences

In Financial Services prefer:
Financial Services

In Manufact. prefer:
Manufacturing

Additional Information
Year Founded: 2007
Current Activity Level : Actively seeking new investments

CROSSPACIFIC CAPITAL PARTNERS

428 220 Cambie Street
Vancouver, Canada V6B 2M9
Phone: 7787270286
Fax: 7787280167
E-mail: info@xpcp.ca
Website: xpcp.ca

Management and Staff
Frank Christiaens, Partner
Marc Van der Chijs, Managing Director

Type of Firm
Private Equity Firm

Association Membership
Canadian Venture Capital Association

Project Preferences

Type of Financing Preferred:
Later Stage

Geographical Preferences

United States Preferences:
North America

Canadian Preferences:
All Canada

International Preferences:
Asia

Industry Preferences

In Communications prefer:
Communications and Media
Wireless Communications

In Computer Software prefer:
Software

In Internet Specific prefer:
Internet

In Consumer Related prefer:
Entertainment and Leisure

In Industrial/Energy prefer:
Alternative Energy
Environmental Related

Additional Information
Year Founded: 1969
Current Activity Level : Actively seeking new investments

CROSSPOINT VENTURE PARTNERS 2001 LP

670 Woodside Road
Redwood City, CA USA 94061
Phone: 6508517600
Fax: 6508517661

Other Offices
2925 Woodside Road
The Pioneer Hotel Building
Woodside, CA USA 94062

Management and Staff
Bob Hoff, General Partner
Don Milder, General Partner
James Dorrian, General Partner
John Mumford, Partner
Rich Shapero, Managing Partner
Seth Neiman, Managing Partner

Type of Firm
Private Equity Firm

Project Preferences

Role in Financing:
Prefer role as deal originator

Type of Financing Preferred:
Early Stage

Industry Preferences

In Communications prefer:
Telecommunications
Wireless Communications
Data Communications

In Internet Specific prefer:
Ecommerce

In Business Serv. prefer:
Services

Additional Information
Name of Most Recent Fund: Crosspoint Ventures 2000 Late Stage Fund, L.P.
Most Recent Fund Was Raised: 06/01/2000
Year Founded: 1972
Capital Under Management: $2,000,000,000
Current Activity Level : Making few, if any, new investments
Method of Compensation: Return on investment is of primary concern, do not charge fees

CROSSROADS LIQUIDATING TRUST

5251 DTC Parkway
Suite 1100
Greenwood Village, CO USA 80111
Phone: 7208890139
E-mail: info@keatinginvestments.com
Website: www.xroadscap.com

Management and Staff
Daniel Morris, Vice President
David Hadani, Chief Financial Officer
Frederic Schweiger, President
Rexford Darko, Managing Director

Type of Firm
Private Equity Firm

Project Preferences

Type of Financing Preferred:
Balanced
Later Stage

Geographical Preferences

United States Preferences:

Additional Information

Year Founded: 1997
Current Activity Level : Actively seeking new investments

CROSSWINDS HOLDINGS INC

225a Macpherson Avenue
Suite 201
Toronto, Canada M4V 1A1
Phone: 4162145985
Fax: 4168618166
E-mail: info@cabancorp.com
Website: www.crosswindsinc.com

Other Offices

130 King St West, Suite 2810
The Exchange Tower
Toronto, Canada M5X 1A4
Phone: 416-214-5985
Fax: 416-861-8166

Management and Staff

Helen Martin, Chief Operating Officer
Susan McCormick, Chief Financial Officer

Type of Firm

Investment Management Firm

Project Preferences

Type of Financing Preferred:
Leveraged Buyout
Mezzanine
Acquisition

Geographical Preferences

Canadian Preferences:
All Canada
Ontario

Industry Preferences

In Financial Services prefer:
Real Estate
Investment Groups
Financial Services

Additional Information

Year Founded: 2005
Current Activity Level : Actively seeking new investments

CROWDCUBE LTD

Rennes Dr,University of Exeter
The Innovation Centre
Exeter, United Kingdom EX4 4RN
Phone: 441392241319
Website: www.crowdcube.com

Management and Staff

Jerry Davison, Chief Financial Officer

Type of Firm

Private Equity Firm

Project Preferences

Type of Financing Preferred:
Early Stage
Expansion
Startup
Special Situation

Geographical Preferences

International Preferences:
United Kingdom

Industry Preferences

In Communications prefer:
Media and Entertainment

In Internet Specific prefer:
Internet

In Consumer Related prefer:
Retail
Consumer Products

In Industrial/Energy prefer:
Environmental Related

In Business Serv. prefer:
Services

Additional Information

Year Founded: 2010
Current Activity Level : Actively seeking new investments

CROWDFUNDER INC

3435 Ocean Park Boulevard
Suite 202
Santa Monica, CA USA 90405
E-mail: info@crowdfunder.com
Website: www.crowdfunder.com

Type of Firm

Private Equity Firm

Project Preferences

Type of Financing Preferred:
Seed

Additional Information

Year Founded: 2016
Capital Under Management: $150,000
Current Activity Level : Actively seeking new investments

CROWN CAPITAL PARTNERS INC

77 King Street West
Suite 3730
Toronto, Canada M5K 1H6
Phone: 4166406715
Fax: 4166406722
Website: www.crowncapital.ca

Other Offices

175 Bloor Street East
Suite 1316
Toronto, Canada M4W 3R8
Phone: 4169271851
Fax: 4169270863

175, 601-10 Avenue SW
Calgary, Canada T2R 0B2
Phone: 4035399569
Fax: 4035086120

Management and Staff

Michael Overvelde, Chief Financial Officer

Type of Firm

Private Equity Firm

Project Preferences

Type of Financing Preferred:
Mezzanine
Special Situation
Distressed Debt

Size of Investments Considered:
Min Size of Investment Considered (000s): $5,000
Max Size of Investment Considered (000s): $25,000

Geographical Preferences

United States Preferences:

Additional Information

Year Founded: 2000
Capital Under Management: $150,000,000
Current Activity Level : Actively seeking new investments

CRP COMPANHIA DE PARTICIPACOES

Avenida Soledade, 550
Cojunto 1001
Porto Alegre, Brazil 90470340
Phone: 555132110777
Fax: 555132110777
E-mail: crp@crp.com.br
Website: www.crp.com.br

Other Offices
AV. Rio Branco 404/sala 901
Florianopolis, SC, Brazil 88015-201
Phone: 5551-3211-0777
Fax: 5551-3211-0777

Management and Staff
Andre Lenz, Partner
Dalton Schmitt, Chief Operating Officer
Joao Marcelo Franca e Leite Eboli, Partner

Type of Firm
Private Equity Firm

Association Membership
Brazilian Venture Capital Association (ABCR)
Emerging Markets Private Equity Association

Project Preferences

Type of Financing Preferred:
Early Stage
Expansion
Mezzanine
Generalist PE
Balanced
Public Companies
Later Stage
Seed
Acquisition
Startup

Geographical Preferences

International Preferences:
Brazil

Industry Preferences

In Communications prefer:
Communications and Media
Telecommunications
Wireless Communications
Data Communications

In Computer Hardware prefer:
Mainframes / Scientific

In Computer Software prefer:
Software

In Semiconductor/Electr prefer:
Electronic Components

In Biotechnology prefer:
Biotechnology

In Medical/Health prefer:
Medical/Health

In Industrial/Energy prefer:
Energy

In Business Serv. prefer:
Services
Consulting Services
Media

Additional Information
Year Founded: 1981
Capital Under Management: $12,000,000
Current Activity Level : Actively seeking new investments

CRP-FANYA INVESTMENT CONSULTANTS BEIJING CO LTD

No.6 Jianguomenwai Avenue
21F Tower C
Beijing, China 100022
Phone: 861085679988
Fax: 861085679989
Website: www.chinarenaissance.com

Management and Staff
Guoyu Qu, Managing Director
Jiachang Lin, Managing Director
Shijun Liu, Chief Operating Officer
Xinwei Wang, Chief Financial Officer
Yang Diao, Managing Director
Yaozhou Xin, Managing Director
Yi Lu, Managing Director
Yijing Xie, Managing Director
Yongbo Du, Managing Director

Type of Firm
Bank Affiliated

Project Preferences

Type of Financing Preferred:
Leveraged Buyout
Expansion
Seed
Startup

Geographical Preferences

International Preferences:
China

Industry Preferences

In Communications prefer:
Telecommunications

In Biotechnology prefer:
Biotechnology

In Medical/Health prefer:
Medical Therapeutics
Health Services

In Consumer Related prefer:
Consumer

In Business Serv. prefer:
Media

Additional Information
Year Founded: 2005
Capital Under Management: $161,170,000
Current Activity Level : Actively seeking new investments

CRUNCHFUND

801 California Street
Mountain View, CA USA 94041
Phone: 6503945901

Management and Staff
Michael Arrington, General Partner
Patrick Gallagher, General Partner

Type of Firm
Private Equity Firm

Project Preferences

Type of Financing Preferred:
Early Stage
Seed

Additional Information
Name of Most Recent Fund: Crunch Fund I, L.P.
Most Recent Fund Was Raised: 09/14/2011
Year Founded: 2011
Capital Under Management: $20,000,000
Current Activity Level : Actively seeking new investments

CRYSTAL PARTNERS & COMPANY LLP

Chancery Lane
1 Quality Court
London, United Kingdom WC2A 1HR
Phone: 44-20-7061-6250
Fax: 44-20-7061-6251
E-mail: info@crystalpartners-llp.com
Website: www.crystalpartners-llp.com

Type of Firm
Private Equity Advisor or Fund of Funds

Project Preferences

Type of Financing Preferred:
Fund of Funds

Geographical Preferences

United States Preferences:
All U.S.

International Preferences:
Western Europe
Asia

Additional Information
Year Founded: 2005
Current Activity Level : Actively seeking new investments

CSA PARTNERS LLC

555 East Wells Street, Suite 1630
Milwaukee, WI USA 53202
Website: www.csapartnersllc.com

Management and Staff
Pat Farley, Managing Director

Type of Firm
Private Equity Firm

Project Preferences

Type of Financing Preferred:
Early Stage
Expansion
Later Stage
Seed

Geographical Preferences

United States Preferences:
Midwest

Additional Information
Year Founded: 2013
Capital Under Management: $10,000,000
Current Activity Level : Actively seeking new investments

CSFB PRIVATE EQUITY ADVISERS

Eleven Madison Avenue
New York, NY USA 10010
Phone: 2123252000
Fax: 2123256665
E-mail: private.equity@credit-suisse.com

Other Offices

One Raffles Link
Number 05-02
Singapore, Singapore 039393
Phone: 65-6212-6000
Fax: 65-6212-6200

Campos Eliseos # 345
Piso 9
Chapultepec Polanco, Mexico 11560
Phone: 52-5-5283-8900
Fax: 52-5-5283-8930

1250 Rene Levesque Boulevard West
Suite 3935
Montreal , Canada H3B 4W8
Phone: 514-933-8774
Fax: 514-933-7699

2400 Hanover Street
Palo Alto, CA USA 94304
Phone: 650-614-5000
Fax: 650-614-5030

34 Chervonoarmiyska Street
Kiev, Ukraine 252004
Phone: 380-44-247-1900
Fax: 380-44-247-5790

Izumi Garden Tower
6-1, Roppongi 1-Chome, Minato-ku
Tokyo, Japan 106-6024
Phone: 81-3-4550-9000
Fax: 81-3-4550-9800

Paradeplatz 8
Zurich, Switzerland 8070
Phone: 41-44-212-1616
Fax: 41-44-333-2587

21 Boulevard de la Madeleine
Cedex 01
Paris, France 75001
Phone: 33-1-40-76-8888
Fax: 33-1-42-56-1082

5/39 Free Press House, 3rd Floor
215 Free Press Journal Marg, Nariman Pt.
Mumbai, India 400 021
Phone: 91-22-230-6333
Fax: 91-22-285-1949

Karntner Ring 11-13
Wien, Austria A-1010
Phone: 43-1-512-3023
Fax: 43-1-512-3023-23

Mina Road, ADPC Admin Bldg.
Second Floor
Abu Dhabi, Utd. Arab Em. 45005
Phone: 971-2-698-8000
Fax: 971-2-698-8001

5 Nikitsky Pereulok
Moscow, Russia 103 009
Phone: 7-501-967-8200
Fax: 7-501-967-8210

6th Floor, Union Enterprise Plaza
No. 109, Section 3, Min Sheng East Road
Taipei, Taiwan
Phone: 886-2-2715-6388
Fax: 886-2-2718-8934

Rua Leopoldo Couto de Magalhaes Jr.
700/10 andar
Sao Paulo, Brazil 04542 000
Phone: 55-11-3701-6000
Fax: 55-11-3701-6900

Via Principe Amedeo 2
Milano, Italy 20121
Phone: 39-02-7702-1
Fax: 39-02-7702-2216

101 Collins Street
27th Floor
Melbourne, Victoria , Australia 3000
Phone: 61-3-9280-1666
Fax: 61-3-9280-1890

Eight Connaught Place
Three Exchange Square
Central, Hong Kong
Phone: 852-2101-6000
Fax: 852-2101-7990

Bahamas Financial Centre, 4th Floor
Shirley & Charlotte St., P.O. Box N4928
Nassau, Bahamas
Phone: 242-356-8100
Fax: 242-326-6589

One Cabot Square
London, United Kingdom E14 4QJ
Phone: 44-20-7888-8888
Fax: 44-20-7888-1600

BritCay House
P.O. Box 10344 APO
Grand Cayman, Cayman Islands
Phone: 345-946-9920
Fax: 345-946-9921

Ortega y Gasset
22 24 Floor 6th
Madrid, Spain 28006
Phone: 34-91-423-1600
Fax: 34-91-423-1638

Management and Staff
Brady Dougan, Chief Executive Officer
David Mathers, Chief Financial Officer
Eddy Sze, Managing Director

Type of Firm
Bank Affiliated

Association Membership
Natl Assoc of Investment Cos. (NAIC)
Australian Venture Capital Association (AVCAL)

Project Preferences

Type of Financing Preferred:
Early Stage
Later Stage
Other
Acquisition
Fund of Funds of Second

Geographical Preferences

International Preferences:
Turkey
China

Industry Focus
(% based on actual investment)
Other Products	38.9%
Industrial/Energy	11.9%
Internet Specific	11.8%
Consumer Related	10.6%
Computer Software and Services	10.0%
Medical/Health	5.7%
Biotechnology	5.5%
Communications and Media	3.4%
Semiconductors/Other Elect.	1.2%
Computer Hardware	1.0%

Additional Information
Year Founded: 1985
Capital Under Management: $28,000,000,000
Current Activity Level : Actively seeking new investments

CSFC MANAGEMENT CO, LLC

575 Lexington Avenue
28th Floor
New York, NY USA 10022
Phone: 2129810140
Website: www.capitalspring.com

Other Offices
488 Madison Avenue
24th Floor
MANHATTAN, NY USA 10022
Phone: 2129810148
Fax: 2129810159

950 Third Avenue
24th Floor
MANHATTAN, NY USA 10022

Management and Staff
Jim Ellis, Vice President
Lara Adin, Vice President

Type of Firm
Private Equity Firm

Project Preferences

Type of Financing Preferred:
Leveraged Buyout
Mezzanine

Geographical Preferences

United States Preferences:

Industry Preferences

In Consumer Related prefer:
Franchises(NEC)

Additional Information
Year Founded: 2005
Capital Under Management: $980,935,000
Current Activity Level : Actively seeking new investments

CSI

2317 Westwood Avenue, Suite 204
Richmond, VA USA 23230
Phone: 804-340-1988
Fax: 804-340-2836
Website: www.vcdlf.org

Other Offices
The Mason Enterprise Center
4031 University Drive, Suite 200
Fairfax, VA USA 22030
Phone: 703-277-7706

Management and Staff
Kirsten Sachwitz, Managing Director

Type of Firm
Incubator/Development Program

Project Preferences

Type of Financing Preferred:
Early Stage

Size of Investments Considered:
Min Size of Investment Considered (000s): $50
Max Size of Investment Considered (000s): $500

Geographical Preferences

United States Preferences:
Maryland
Virginia
D. of Columbia

Industry Preferences

In Business Serv. prefer:
Services

Additional Information
Year Founded: 1995
Capital Under Management: $3,000,000
Current Activity Level : Actively seeking new investments

CT INVESTMENT MANAGEMENT CO LLC

410 Park Avenue, 14th Floor
New York, NY USA 10022
Phone: 212-655-0220
Fax: 212-655-0044
E-mail: investorrelations@capitaltrust.com
Website: www.capitaltrust.com

Management and Staff
John Klopp, Chief Executive Officer
Stephen Plavin, Chief Operating Officer

Type of Firm
Investment Management Firm

Project Preferences

Type of Financing Preferred:
Value-Add
Mezzanine

Geographical Preferences

United States Preferences:

Additional Information
Year Founded: 2000
Current Activity Level : Actively seeking new investments

CT INVESTMENT PARTNERS LLP

27-45 Stamford Street
Dorset House, Fourth Floor
London, United Kingdom SE1 9NT
Phone: 442078324601
E-mail: invest@350ip.co.uk
Website: www.350ip.co.uk

Other Offices
The Innovation Centre
Queen's Road, Queen's Island
Belfast, United Kingdom BT3 9DT
Phone: 44-2890-737-912

Albion House
Oxford Street, Nantgarw
Cardiff, United Kingdom CF15 7TR
Phone: 44-1443-845-944

The Technology Centre
Scottish Enterprise Technology Park
East Kilbride, United Kingdom G75 0QF
Phone: 44-1355-581-810

Management and Staff
Adam Workman, Co-Founder
Jonathan Bryers, Co-Founder
Peter Linthwaite, Managing Partner

Type of Firm
Corporate PE/Venture

Association Membership
European Private Equity and Venture Capital Assoc.

Project Preferences

Type of Financing Preferred:
Early Stage
Expansion
Balanced

Geographical Preferences

International Preferences:
United Kingdom
Europe
No Preference
Qatar
Middle East

Industry Preferences

In Industrial/Energy prefer:
Energy
Alternative Energy
Energy Conservation Relat
Environmental Related

In Other prefer:
Environment Responsible

Additional Information
Year Founded: 2006
Current Activity Level : Actively seeking new investments

CTECHBA PTY LTD

299 Sussex Street
Suite 101
Sydney, Australia NSW 2000
Phone: 292646655
Website: www.ctechba.com

Management and Staff
Adam Townley, Principal
Bruce Cottrill, Principal
Karl Sussebach, Principal
Paul Anthony Young, Principal
Song Duan, Principal

Type of Firm
Incubator/Development Program

Association Membership
Australian Venture Capital Association (AVCAL)

Project Preferences

Type of Financing Preferred:
Early Stage
Balanced
Turnaround
Later Stage
Seed
Startup

Industry Preferences

In Biotechnology prefer:
Biotechnology
Biotech Related Research

In Medical/Health prefer:
Health Services

In Consumer Related prefer:
Food/Beverage

In Industrial/Energy prefer:
Energy
Energy Conservation Relat
Environmental Related

In Transportation prefer:
Transportation

In Manufact. prefer:
Manufacturing

In Utilities prefer:
Utilities

Additional Information
Year Founded: 1969
Current Activity Level : Actively seeking new investments

CTI CAPITAL SECURITIES INC

One Place Ville Marie
Suite 1635
Montreal, Canada H3B 2B6
Phone: 5148613500
Fax: 5148613230
Website: www.cticap.com

Management and Staff
Mark Chadakhtzian, Chief Financial Officer
Robert LaCroix, Vice President

Type of Firm
Private Equity Firm

Association Membership
Canadian Venture Capital Association

Project Preferences

Type of Financing Preferred:
Expansion
Balanced
Start-up Financing

Geographical Preferences

Canadian Preferences:
All Canada

Industry Preferences

In Biotechnology prefer:
Biotechnology

In Medical/Health prefer:
Medical Products

Additional Information
Name of Most Recent Fund: CTI Life Sciences Fund II
Most Recent Fund Was Raised: 03/31/2014
Year Founded: 2006
Capital Under Management: $244,500,000
Current Activity Level : Actively seeking new investments

CUDOS ADVISORS GMBH

Spiegelgasse 2/26
Wien, Austria 1010
Phone: 431360730
Fax: 4313607350
E-mail: office@cudos-group.com
Website: www.cudos-group.com

Management and Staff
Andreas Frech, Founder

Type of Firm
Private Equity Firm

Project Preferences

Type of Financing Preferred:
Leveraged Buyout
Turnaround
Later Stage
Management Buyouts
Special Situation
Distressed Debt

Geographical Preferences

International Preferences:
Central Europe
Switzerland
Austria
Eastern Europe
Germany

Industry Preferences

In Industrial/Energy prefer:
Industrial Products

Additional Information
Year Founded: 2011
Current Activity Level : Actively seeking new investments

CUE BALL GROUP LLC

One Faneuil Hall Square
Seventh Floor
Boston, MA USA 02109
Phone: 6175420100
Fax: 6175420033
E-mail: ping@cueball.com
Website: www.cueball.com

Management and Staff
Anthony Tjan, CEO & Managing Director
John Hamel, Partner
Mats Lederhausen, General Partner

Type of Firm
Private Equity Firm

Association Membership
New England Venture Capital Association
National Venture Capital Association - USA (NVCA)

Project Preferences

Type of Financing Preferred:
Early Stage
Expansion
Seed

Geographical Preferences

United States Preferences:

Industry Preferences

In Consumer Related prefer:
Consumer

In Business Serv. prefer:
Services
Media

Additional Information

Name of Most Recent Fund: Cue Ball Capital, L.P.
Most Recent Fund Was Raised: 06/20/2008
Year Founded: 2008
Capital Under Management: $50,000,000
Current Activity Level : Actively seeking new investments

CULBRO LLC

880 Third Avenue
18th Floor
New York, NY USA 10022
Phone: 646-461-9270
E-mail: info@culbro.com
Website: www.culbro.com

Management and Staff

Jack LoParco, Vice President

Type of Firm

Private Equity Firm

Project Preferences

Type of Financing Preferred:
Balanced

Size of Investments Considered:
Min Size of Investment Considered (000s): $10,000
Max Size of Investment Considered (000s): $20,000

Geographical Preferences

United States Preferences:
All U.S.

Industry Preferences

In Internet Specific prefer:
Ecommerce

In Consumer Related prefer:
Consumer
Food/Beverage
Education Related

In Business Serv. prefer:
Services

Additional Information

Year Founded: 2005
Current Activity Level : Actively seeking new investments

CULTIVATE VENTURES LLC

1425 Euclid Street
NW #12
Washington, DC USA 20009
Phone: 2025509710
Website: www.cultivateventures.co

Type of Firm

Private Equity Firm

Project Preferences

Type of Financing Preferred:
Balanced

Industry Preferences

In Medical/Health prefer:
Health Services

In Consumer Related prefer:
Food/Beverage

In Agr/Forestr/Fish prefer:
Agriculture related

Additional Information

Year Founded: 2016
Current Activity Level : Actively seeking new investments

CULTIVATION CAPITAL

911 Washington Avenue
Suite 801
Saint Louis, MO USA 63101
Phone: 3142162051
Website: www.cultivationcapital.com

Management and Staff

Brian Matthews, Co-Founder
Cliff Holekamp, General Partner
Jim McKelvey, General Partner
Kyle Welborn, Co-Founder
Peter Esparrago, Co-Founder
Rick Holton, General Partner

Type of Firm

Private Equity Firm

Project Preferences

Type of Financing Preferred:
Early Stage
Seed
Startup

Geographical Preferences

United States Preferences:
Missouri

Additional Information

Name of Most Recent Fund: Cultivation Capital Life Sciences Fund LLC
Most Recent Fund Was Raised: 06/17/2013
Year Founded: 2012
Capital Under Management: $65,000,000
Current Activity Level : Actively seeking new investments

CULTIVIAN SANDBOX VENTURE PARTNERS LLC

1000 West Fulton Market
Suite 213
Chicago, IL USA 60607
E-mail: contactus@cultiviansbx.com
Website: cultiviansbx.com

Management and Staff

Ron Meeusen, Managing Director

Type of Firm

Private Equity Firm

Association Membership

National Venture Capital Association - USA (NVCA)

Project Preferences

Type of Financing Preferred:
Early Stage
Balanced
Later Stage

Size of Investments Considered:
Min Size of Investment Considered (000s): $5,000
Max Size of Investment Considered (000s): $15,000

Industry Preferences

In Biotechnology prefer:
Agricultural/Animal Bio.

In Consumer Related prefer:
Food/Beverage

In Agr/Forestr/Fish prefer:
Agriculture related

Additional Information

Year Founded: 1969
Current Activity Level : Actively seeking new investments

CULTIVIAN VENTURES LLC

11550 North Meridian Street
Suite 310
Carmel, IN USA 46032
Phone: 3172083333
Website: www.midpointvc.com

Management and Staff
Andrew Ziolkowski, Partner
Ronald Meeusen, Partner

Type of Firm
Private Equity Firm

Project Preferences

Role in Financing:
Will function either as deal originator or investor in deals created by others

Type of Financing Preferred:
Early Stage
Expansion
Balanced

Size of Investments Considered:
Min Size of Investment Considered (000s): $1,000
Max Size of Investment Considered (000s) $3,000

Geographical Preferences

United States Preferences:
Midwest
North America

Industry Preferences

In Medical/Health prefer:
Other Therapeutic

In Consumer Related prefer:
Food/Beverage
Consumer Products

In Industrial/Energy prefer:
Energy
Environmental Related

In Agr/Forestr/Fish prefer:
Agriculture related

In Other prefer:
Environment Responsible

Additional Information
Name of Most Recent Fund: Cultivian Ventures, L.P.
Most Recent Fund Was Raised: 12/16/2003
Year Founded: 2008
Capital Under Management: $30,000,000
Current Activity Level : Actively seeking new investments

CUPOLA GROUP

Dubai Outsource Zone (DOZ)
P.O.Box 500220
Dubai, Utd. Arab Em.
Phone: 97143662000
Fax: 97143662002
Website: www.cupolagroup.com

Management and Staff
Arif Naqvi, Founder
Shabbir Jivanji, Chief Financial Officer

Type of Firm
Private Equity Firm

Association Membership
Gulf Venture Capital Association

Project Preferences

Type of Financing Preferred:
Early Stage
Balanced
Later Stage

Geographical Preferences

United States Preferences:

International Preferences:
Europe
Middle East
Asia

Industry Preferences

In Consumer Related prefer:
Retail
Franchises(NEC)

In Business Serv. prefer:
Distribution

In Manufact. prefer:
Manufacturing

Additional Information
Year Founded: 1998
Current Activity Level : Actively seeking new investments

CURACAO GROWTH FUND CV

Kaya Richard J. Beaujon
Willemstad, Curacao, Neth. Antilles
Website: www.curacaogrowthfund.com

Type of Firm
Private Equity Firm

Project Preferences

Type of Financing Preferred:
Leveraged Buyout
Early Stage
Expansion
Turnaround
Later Stage
Acquisition
Distressed Debt

Geographical Preferences

International Preferences:
Neth. Antilles

Industry Preferences

In Communications prefer:
Telecommunications

In Semiconductor/Electr prefer:
Laser Related

In Medical/Health prefer:
Health Services

In Consumer Related prefer:
Entertainment and Leisure
Food/Beverage

In Industrial/Energy prefer:
Energy

In Financial Services prefer:
Financial Services
Insurance

In Manufact. prefer:
Manufacturing

Additional Information
Year Founded: 2015
Current Activity Level : Actively seeking new investments

CURIOUS CAPITAL

111 S Jackson St
Seattle, WA USA 98104
E-mail: a@curiouscap.com
Website: curiouscap.com

Type of Firm
Private Equity Firm

Project Preferences

Type of Financing Preferred:
Seed

Geographical Preferences

United States Preferences:

Additional Information
Year Founded: 2017
Capital Under Management: $50,000
Current Activity Level : Actively seeking new investments

CURIOUS MINDS

8560 West Sunset Boulevard
Tenth Floor
West Hollywood, CA USA 90069
Phone: 3102765900
E-mail: info@curiousminds.com
Website: www.curiousminds.com

Management and Staff
David Gonen, Co-Founder

Type of Firm
Private Equity Firm

Project Preferences

Type of Financing Preferred:
Seed
Startup

Additional Information
Year Founded: 2004
Current Activity Level : Actively seeking new investments

CURRAN COMPANIES

1511 Baltimore Avenue
#500
Kansas City, MO USA 64108
Phone: 8167562225
Fax: 8167565552
Website: http://www.currancos.com/

Type of Firm
Private Equity Firm

Project Preferences

Type of Financing Preferred:
Leveraged Buyout

Additional Information
Year Founded: 1969
Current Activity Level : Actively seeking new investments

CURRENT CAPITAL LLC

555 Madison Avenue
19th Floor
New York, NY USA 10022
E-mail: info@currentcap.com
Website: www.currentcap.com

Management and Staff
Jonathan Foster, Founder
Stephen Cortinovis, Managing Director
Steven Martin, Managing Director

Type of Firm
Private Equity Firm

Project Preferences

Type of Financing Preferred:
Leveraged Buyout
Acquisition

Industry Preferences

In Industrial/Energy prefer:
Industrial Products

In Business Serv. prefer:
Services

Additional Information
Year Founded: 2008
Current Activity Level : Actively seeking new investments

CURZON PARK CAPITAL LTD

14 Cornhill
London, United Kingdom EC3V 3ND
Phone: 442072809700
Fax: 442072809719

Management and Staff
Cedriane Marie De Boucaud, Partner
Jeffrey Belkin, Partner
Olivia Bloomfield, Partner

Type of Firm
Private Equity Firm

Project Preferences

Type of Financing Preferred:
Balanced

Size of Investments Considered:
Min Size of Investment Considered (000s): $7,696
Max Size of Investment Considered (000s): $76,960

Geographical Preferences

International Preferences:
United Kingdom

Industry Preferences

In Industrial/Energy prefer:
Alternative Energy

In Other prefer:
Environment Responsible

Additional Information
Year Founded: 2007
Current Activity Level : Actively seeking new investments

CVC ASIA PACIFIC LTD

Citibank Plaza, 3 Garden Road
Suite 901-3, ICBC Tower
Hong Kong, Hong Kong
Phone: 85235186360
Fax: 85235186380

Other Offices
Jianguomenwai Dajie No.1, Chaoyang Dist.
Lvl 16, Units 25-29, China World Tower 1
Beijing, China
Phone: 86-10-6535-1800
Fax: 86-10-6535-1811

2-5-1 Atago, Minato-ku
Atago Green Hills MORI Tower 38F
Tokyo, Japan 105-6238
Phone: 813-5402-5300
Fax: 813-5402-5301

One Temasek Avenue
#24-01A Millenia Tower
Singapore, Singapore 039192
Phone: 65-6500-7328
Fax: 65-6500-7323

5 Place du Theatrec
Luxembourg, Luxembourg L-2613
Phone: 352-2647-8368
Fax: 352-2647-8367

Jose Ortega y Gasset 25 - 1
Madrid, Spain 28006
Phone: 34-91-436-4280
Fax: 34-91-436-4282

Via Senato 12
Milan, Italy 20121
Phone: 39-02-760-7571
Fax: 39-02-7607-5799

Hamngatan 13
Stockholm, Sweden 11147
Phone: 46-8-407-8790
Fax: 46-8-611-0565

Bahnhofstrasse 94
Zurich, Switzerland 8001
Phone: 41-1-217-7000
Fax: 41-1-217-7001

Taepyeongro 1-ga, Jung-gu
21/F Seoul Finance Center
Seoul, South Korea 100-768
Phone: 82-2-2075-8500
Fax: 82-2-2075-8511

Chaussee de la Hulpe 166
Brussels, Belgium 1170
Phone: 32-2-663-8090
Fax: 32-2-663-8099

Bredgade 31
3rd Floor
Copenhagen, Denmark 1260 K
Phone: 45-33-120-010
Fax: 45-33-120-015

40 rue La Perouse
Paris, France 75116
Phone: 33-1-4502-2300
Fax: 33-1-4502-2301

111 Strand
London, United Kingdom WC2R 0AG
Phone: 44-20-7420-4200
Fax: 44-20-7420-4231

712 Fifth Avenue
43rd Floor
New York, NY USA 10019
Phone: 212-265-6222
Fax: 212-265-6375

Schiphol Boulevard 285, Luchthaven
Schiphol Airport, Tower B, 6F
Amsterdam, Netherlands 1118BH
Phone: 31-20-354-8051
Fax: 31-20-354-8052

Bockenheimer Landsstrasse 24
WestendDuo
Frankfurt, Germany D-60323
Phone: 49-69-975-8350
Fax: 49-69-9758-3511

18-22 Grenville Street
St. Heller, United Kingdom JE4 8PX
Phone: 44-15-3460-9000
Fax: 44-15-3460-9333

Two Park Street
Level 45, Citigroup Center
Sydney, Australia 2000
Phone: 61-2-9260-9800
Fax: 61-2-9260-9820

Management and Staff
Allen Han, Senior Managing Director
Alvin Lam, Managing Director
Brian Hong, Senior Managing Director
Graham Brooke, Managing Director
Hans Wang, Senior Managing Director
Hemal Mirani, Senior Managing Director
John Kim, Managing Director
Kei Mizukami, Senior Managing Director
Maarten Ruijs, Managing Partner
Norimitsu Niwa, Managing Director
Roy Kuan, Managing Director
Sigit Prasetya, Managing Partner
William Ho, Partner

Type of Firm
Private Equity Firm

Association Membership
China Venture Capital Association
Singapore Venture Capital Association (SVCA)

Project Preferences

Type of Financing Preferred:
Leveraged Buyout
Management Buyouts
Acquisition

Geographical Preferences

United States Preferences:
North America

International Preferences:
Indonesia
Europe
China
Thailand
Philippines
Asia
Singapore
Korea, South
Japan
Malaysia

Industry Preferences

In Medical/Health prefer:
Medical/Health

In Consumer Related prefer:
Retail
Consumer Services

In Financial Services prefer:
Financial Services

Additional Information
Year Founded: 1999
Capital Under Management: $6,845,000,000
Current Activity Level : Actively seeking new investments

CVC CAPITAL PARTNERS LTD

20 Avenue Monterey
L-2163
Luxembourg, Luxembourg L 2163
Phone: 35226478368
Fax: 35226478367
Website: www.cvc.com

Other Offices

1 Temasek Avenue
24-01A Millenia Tower
Singapore, Singapore 039192
Phone: 65-6500-7328
Fax: 65-6500-7323

1266 Najing West Road
Suite 3918, 39/F, Plaza 66
Shanghai, China 200040
Phone: 86-21-6103-8115
Fax: 86-32-6103-8111

Bockenheimer Landsstrasse 24
WestendDuo
Frankfurt am Main, Germany D-60323
Phone: 49-69-975-8350
Fax: 49-69-9758-3511

One Maritime Plaza
Suite 1610
SAN FRANCISCO, CA USA 94111
Phone: 4158723900

63 Avenue des Champs Elysees
Paris, France 75008
Phone: 33-1-4502-2300
Fax: 33-1-4502-2301

World Trade Center, Schiphol Airport
Tower B, 6/F Schiphol Boulevard 285
Amsterdam, Netherlands 1118BH
Phone: 31-20-354-8051
Fax: 31-20-354-8052

Hamngatan 13
Stockholm, Sweden 11147
Phone: 46-8-407-8790
Fax: 46-8-611-0565

Level 29, The Offices at Centralworld
Suite 2921
Bangkik, Thailand 10330
Phone: 66-2207-2328
Fax: 66-2207-8633

Three Garden Road
Suite 901-3, ICBC Tower, Citibank Plaza
Central Hong Kong, Hong Kong
Phone: 852-3518-6360
Fax: 852-3518-6380

Chaussee de la Hulpe 166
Brussels, Belgium 1170
Phone: 32-2-663-8090
Fax: 32-2-663-8099

20 Avenue Monterey
Luxembourg, Luxembourg L-2163
Phone: 352-26-47-8368
Fax: 352-26-47-8367

Bahnhofstrasse 94
Zurich, Switzerland 8001
Phone: 41-44-217-7000
Fax: 41-44-217-7001

Taepyeongro 1-ga, Jung-gu
21/F Seoul Finance Center
Seoul, South Korea 100-768
Phone: 822-2075-8500
Fax: 822-2075-8511

2-5-1 Atago, Minato-ku, Green Hills MORI
Tower 38F, Kabushiki Kaisha Atago
Tokyo, Japan 105-6238
Phone: 813-5402-5300
Fax: 813-5402-5301

18-22 Grenville Street
St. Helier, United Kingdom JE4 8PX
Phone: 44-15-3460-9000
Fax: 44-15-3460-9333

Jianguomenwai Dajie No. 1
16th Flr, Units 25-29, China World Tower
Beijing, China 100004
Phone: 86-10-6535-1800
Fax: 86-10-6535-1811

Pratt's Guide to Private Equity & Venture Capital Sources

Bredgade 31
Third Floor
Copenhagen, Denmark 1260 K
Phone: 45-33-12-0010
Fax: 45-33-12-0015

Via Senato 12
Milan, Italy 20121
Phone: 39-2-760-7571
Fax: 39-2-7607-5799

712 Fifth Avenue
43rd Floor
NEW YORK, NY USA 10019
Phone: 212-265-6222
Fax: 212-265-6375

Two Park Street
Level 45, Citigroup Center
Sydney, Australia 2000
Phone: 61-2-9260-9800
Fax: 61-2-9260-9820

Management and Staff

Alexander Fotakidis, Senior Managing Director
Alexis Martineau, Managing Director
Alfredo Zamarriego, Managing Director
Allen Han, Partner
Alvin Lam, Senior Managing Director
Andrew Davies, Managing Director
Andy Nugroho Purwohardono, Managing Director
Bas Becks, Managing Director
Benjamin Edgar, Founder
Bertrand Meunier, Managing Partner
Bo Liu, Senior Managing Director
Brandon Bradkin, Partner
Brian Hong, Senior Managing Director
Cameron Breitner, Senior Managing Director
Carl Hansen, Senior Managing Director
Caroline Benton, Managing Director
Cathrin Petty, Partner
Christoph Rottele, Partner
Christopher Hojlo, Managing Director
Christopher Allen, Partner
Christopher Colpitts, Senior Managing Director
Daniel Pindur, Managing Director
Dirk Muhl, Managing Director
Emanuela Brero, Managing Director
Fazle Husain, Partner
Fred Watt, Managing Partner
Geert Duyck, Managing Partner
Giampiero Mazza, Senior Managing Director
Giorgio De Palma, Managing Director
Graham Brooke, Managing Director
Gregor Hilverkus, Managing Director
Gretchen Bergstresser, Partner
Iain Parham, Co-Founder
Inaki Cobo Bachiller, Senior Managing Director
Istvan Szoke, Partner
James Mahoney, Senior Managing Director
Janish Patel, Managing Director
Jay Bryant, Senior Managing Director
Jean-Christophe Germani, Senior Managing Director
Jennifer Patrickakos, Vice President
John Kim, Managing Director
John Clark, Managing Partner
Jonathan Feuer, Managing Partner
Jonathan Bowers, Partner
Kei Mizukami, Senior Managing Director
Ken Young, Senior Managing Director
Kevin O Meara, Managing Director
Lars Haegg, Managing Director
Lisa Lee, Managing Director
Lorne Somerville, Partner
Marc Rachman, Managing Director
Marc St John, Partner
Marc Boughton, Managing Partner
Mark Grizzelle, Partner
Mark Ku, Managing Director
Mark Denatale, Partner
Michael Lavrysen, Managing Director
Neale Broadhead, Managing Director
Nicholas Clarry, Partner
Nick Archer, Partner
Norimitsu Niwa, Managing Director
Pablo Costi Ruiz, Managing Director
Peter Rutland, Managing Director
Pev Hooper, Partner
Philip Raciti, Managing Director
Ran Landmann, Managing Director
Richard Perris, Managing Director
Robert Lucas, Managing Partner
Rolly Van Rappard, Managing Partner
Roy Kuan, Managing Partner
Scott Bynum, Managing Director
Siddharth Patel, Managing Director
Sigit Prasetya, Managing Partner
Soren Vestergaard-Poulsen, Partner
Stephen Vineburg, Partner
Steven Buyse, Senior Managing Director
Stuart Levett, Managing Director
Tim Cundy, Partner
Tom Newberry, Partner
Victor Blanchard, Managing Director
Wai Hoong Fock, Managing Director
William Ho, Partner

Type of Firm
Private Equity Firm

Association Membership
Italian Venture Capital Association (AIFI)
Hong Kong Venture Capital Association (HKVCA)
British Venture Capital Association (BVCA)
French Venture Capital Association (AFIC)
Danish Venture Capital Association (DVCA)
German Venture Capital Association (BVK)
Swedish Venture Capital Association (SVCA)
European Private Equity and Venture Capital Assoc.
Dutch Venture Capital Associaton (NVP)
Spanish Venture Capital Association (ASCRI)

Project Preferences

Role in Financing:
Prefer role as deal originator but will also invest in deals created by others

Type of Financing Preferred:
Leveraged Buyout
Management Buyouts
Acquisition

Geographical Preferences

United States Preferences:
North America

International Preferences:
Europe
Asia

Industry Focus

(% based on actual investment)
Consumer Related	30.7%
Other Products	29.8%
Industrial/Energy	29.2%
Communications and Media	6.6%
Internet Specific	1.7%
Medical/Health	1.1%
Computer Software and Services	0.8%
Semiconductors/Other Elect.	0.1%
Biotechnology	0.0%

Additional Information

Name of Most Recent Fund: CVC European Equity Partners VI, L.P.
Most Recent Fund Was Raised: 07/19/2013
Year Founded: 1981
Capital Under Management: $41,941,000,000
Current Activity Level : Actively seeking new investments
Method of Compensation: Return on investment is of primary concern, do not charge fees

CVC MANAGERS PTY LTD

259 George Street
Level 42, Suncorp Place
Sydney, Australia 2000
Phone: 61290878000
Fax: 61290878088
E-mail: cvc@cvcltd.com.au
Website: www.cvc.com.au

Other Offices
24 Marcus Clarke Street
Level 3
Canberra, Australia 2601
Phone: 61262570000
Fax: 61262570003

Type of Firm
Private Equity Firm

Project Preferences

Role in Financing:
Will function either as deal originator or investor in deals created by others

Type of Financing Preferred:
Leveraged Buyout
Early Stage
Expansion
Mezzanine
Generalist PE
Balanced
Later Stage
Seed
Management Buyouts
Acquisition
Joint Ventures
Startup
Recapitalizations

Size of Investments Considered:
Min Size of Investment Considered (000s): $1,000
Max Size of Investment Considered (000s): $15,000

Geographical Preferences

International Preferences:
Pacific
Australia

Industry Focus

(% based on actual investment)
Other Products	49.5%
Industrial/Energy	20.3%
Medical/Health	11.0%
Consumer Related	6.6%
Semiconductors/Other Elect.	6.2%
Biotechnology	3.2%
Computer Software and Services	1.5%
Communications and Media	0.9%
Internet Specific	0.8%

Additional Information

Name of Most Recent Fund: CVC Sustainable Investments, Ltd.
Most Recent Fund Was Raised: 06/30/2002
Year Founded: 1985
Capital Under Management: $73,300,000
Current Activity Level : Actively seeking new investments
Method of Compensation: Return on invest. most important, but chg. closing fees, service fees, etc.

CVENTURES PARTICI-PACOES S.A.

Rodovia SC 401
ParqTec Alfa 600
Florianopolis, Brazil 88030901
Phone: 554832392150
Fax: 554832392009
E-mail: contato@cventures.com.br
Website: www.cventures.com.br

Type of Firm

Private Equity Firm

Association Membership

Brazilian Venture Capital Association (ABZR)

Project Preferences

Type of Financing Preferred:
Early Stage
Seed
Startup

Geographical Preferences

International Preferences:
Brazil

Additional Information

Year Founded: 2008
Capital Under Management: $42,948,000
Current Activity Level : Actively seeking new investments

CVF CAPITAL PARTNERS LLC

1590 Drew Avenue
Suite 110
Davis, CA USA 95618
Phone: 5307577004
Fax: 5307571316
Website: www.centralvalleyfund.com

Other Offices

5010 Woodrow Avenue, Lyles Center
Suite WC 142
Fresno, CA USA 93740
Phone: 559-294-6668
Fax: 559-294-6655

Management and Staff

Brad Triebsch, Principal
Daniel Jessee, Principal
Edward McNulty, Principal
Jose Blanco, Principal

Type of Firm

Private Equity Firm

Association Membership

Natl Assoc of Small Bus. Inv. Co (NASBIC)

Project Preferences

Role in Financing:
Will function either as deal originator or investor in deals created by others

Type of Financing Preferred:
Expansion
Mezzanine
Generalist PE
Later Stage
Management Buyouts
Acquisition
Recapitalizations

Size of Investments Considered:
Min Size of Investment Considered (000s): $2,000
Max Size of Investment Considered (000s): $10,000

Geographical Preferences

United States Preferences:
Southern California
Northern California
California

Industry Preferences

In Medical/Health prefer:
Medical/Health
Health Services

In Consumer Related prefer:
Consumer Services
Education Related

In Industrial/Energy prefer:
Energy
Industrial Products

In Business Serv. prefer:
Services
Distribution

In Manufact. prefer:
Manufacturing

Additional Information

Name of Most Recent Fund: Central Valley Fund II, L.P.
Most Recent Fund Was Raised: 04/17/2012
Year Founded: 2005
Capital Under Management: $55,000,000
Current Activity Level : Actively seeking new investments
Method of Compensation: Return on invest. most important, but chg. closing fees, service fees, etc.

CVF TECHNOLOGIES CORP

8604 Main Street
Suite One
Williamsville, NY USA 14221
Phone: 716-565-4711
Fax: 716-565-4717
E-mail: cvf@cvftechnologies.com
Website: www.cvfcorp.com

Management and Staff

Robert Nally, Chief Operating Officer

Type of Firm

Private Equity Firm

Project Preferences

Role in Financing:
Prefer role as deal originator but will also invest in deals created by others

Type of Financing Preferred:
Early Stage
Balanced

Geographical Preferences

United States Preferences:
All U.S.

Canadian Preferences:
Central Canada

Industry Preferences

In Internet Specific prefer:
E-Commerce Technology

In Biotechnology prefer:
Industrial Biotechnology

In Other prefer:
Environment Responsible

Additional Information
Year Founded: 1989
Capital Under Management: $30,000,000
Current Activity Level : Actively seeking new investments

CX PARTNERS

D-15, 1st Floor
Defence Colony
New Delhi, India 110024
Phone: 911147640000
Website: www.cxpartners.in

Management and Staff
Amit Bhatiani, Founder
Jayanta Basu, Founder
Tarun Khanna, Principal
Vivek Chhachhi, Partner

Type of Firm
Private Equity Firm

Association Membership
Indian Venture Capital Association (IVCA)

Project Preferences

Type of Financing Preferred:
Leveraged Buyout
Expansion
Mezzanine
Generalist PE
Balanced
Later Stage
Acquisition
Recapitalizations

Geographical Preferences

International Preferences:
India

Industry Preferences

In Manufact. prefer:
Manufacturing

Additional Information
Year Founded: 2008
Capital Under Management: $70,000,000
Current Activity Level : Actively seeking new investments

CXO COLLECTIVE INTERNATIONAL LLC

4300 South US Highway 1
Suite 2013-117
Jupiter, FL USA 33477
Website: www.cxocollective.com

Type of Firm
Private Equity Firm

Project Preferences

Type of Financing Preferred:
Leveraged Buyout
Acquisition

Additional Information
Year Founded: 2013
Current Activity Level : Actively seeking new investments

CYBERNAUT (CHINA) VENTURE CAPITAL MANAGEMENT CO LTD

176 Tianmu Shan Road
No.11 Bldg, WestLake Soyea
Hangzhou, China 310012
Phone: 8657189939898
Fax: 8657189939834
E-mail: contact@cybernaut.com.cn
Website: www.cybernaut.com.cn

Other Offices

20/F China Everbright Bank Building
Zhu Zi Lin, Futian District
Shenzhen, China 518040

No.777, Zhongguan West Road
Ningbo, China

No. 11 Chang Chun Bridge Road
Room 1502 Wan Liu Yi Cheng Center
, China
Phone: 86-158819698
Fax: 86158819566

No. 200 Yincheng Middle Road
Room 2705 Bank of China Tower
Shanghai, China 200120
Phone: 862150372257

Management and Staff
Daryl Magana, Partner
David Ren, General Partner
Jason Zhao, General Partner
Lan Shi, Partner
Nick Archibald, Partner
Sha Wang, Principal
Thomas Chen, General Partner
Wei Lu, Partner
Wilson Wu, Principal
Xuanyu Shang, General Partner
Yan Gu, Partner
Yingqi Su, Partner

Type of Firm
Private Equity Firm

Project Preferences

Type of Financing Preferred:
Early Stage
Expansion
Balanced

Geographical Preferences

International Preferences:
China

Industry Preferences

In Consumer Related prefer:
Consumer
Consumer Services
Education Related

In Industrial/Energy prefer:
Energy

In Financial Services prefer:
Financial Services

In Business Serv. prefer:
Services

In Manufact. prefer:
Manufacturing

Additional Information
Year Founded: 2006
Capital Under Management: $55,324,000
Current Activity Level : Actively seeking new investments

CYBERSEC 3 LLC

5540 N Harbor Vlg Dr
Vero Beach, FL USA 32967

Type of Firm
Private Equity Firm

Project Preferences

Type of Financing Preferred:
Early Stage

Additional Information
Year Founded: 2017
Current Activity Level : Actively seeking new investments

CYCAD GROUP LLC

1270 Coast Village Circle
Suite 100
Santa Barbara, CA USA 93108
Phone: 8056846515
Fax: 8056846511
Website: www.cycadvc.com

Management and Staff

K. Leonard Judson, President
Robert Balch, Vice President

Type of Firm

Private Equity Firm

Project Preferences

Type of Financing Preferred:
Early Stage

Geographical Preferences

United States Preferences:
All U.S.

Industry Preferences

In Semiconductor/Electr prefer:
Electronics

In Biotechnology prefer:
Biotechnology

In Medical/Health prefer:
Medical/Health
Medical Products
Pharmaceuticals

In Industrial/Energy prefer:
Energy
Advanced Materials

Additional Information

Year Founded: 2000
Current Activity Level : Actively seeking new nvestments

CYCLE CAPITAL MANAGEMENT (CCM) INC

1000 Sherbrooke Ouest
Bureau 1610
Montreal, Canada H3A 3G4
Phone: 5144951022
Fax: 5144958034
Website: www.cyclecapital.com

Management and Staff

Andree-Lise Methot, Founder
Claude Vachet, Managing Partner
Colin Ryan, Partner
Jean-Francois Giroux, Partner
Michel Lambert, Partner
Pascal Drouin, Partner
Richard Legault, Venture Partner

Type of Firm

Private Equity Firm

Association Membership

Canadian Venture Capital Association

Project Preferences

Type of Financing Preferred:
Early Stage
Expansion
Seed
Startup

Geographical Preferences

United States Preferences:
Northeast

Canadian Preferences:
Quebec

Industry Preferences

In Industrial/Energy prefer:
Environmental Related

Additional Information

Name of Most Recent Fund: Cycle Capital Fund III
Most Recent Fund Was Raised: 03/20/2012
Year Founded: 2003
Capital Under Management: $231,000,000
Current Activity Level : Actively seeking new investments

CYHAWK VENTURES LTD

6 Hanechoshet Street
First Floor
Tel Aviv, Israel 69710
Phone: 97236247117
Fax: 97236247116
E-mail: website@cyhawk.com
Website: www.cyhawkventures.com

Type of Firm

Private Equity Firm

Project Preferences

Type of Financing Preferred:
Early Stage
Seed

Geographical Preferences

International Preferences:
Israel

Industry Preferences

In Communications prefer:
Media and Entertainment

In Computer Software prefer:
Applications Software

In Internet Specific prefer:
E-Commerce Technology

In Business Serv. prefer:
Media

Additional Information

Year Founded: 2001
Current Activity Level : Actively seeking new investments

CYNOSURE GROUP, THE

79 South Man Street
First Security Building
Salt Lake City, UT USA 84184

Type of Firm

Private Equity Firm

Project Preferences

Type of Financing Preferred:
Balanced

Additional Information

Year Founded: 2014
Current Activity Level : Actively seeking new investments

CYPRESS & KINGWIN CAPITAL GROUP LTD

Shenzhen Int'l Chamber Bldg.
Room 1803, Block A
Futian, China 518000
Phone: 867582048351
Fax: 8675582934053
E-mail: jiangy@cypresscapital.com.cn
Website: cypresscapital.com.cn

Type of Firm

Investment Management Firm

Project Preferences

Type of Financing Preferred:
Balanced

Geographical Preferences

International Preferences:
China

Industry Preferences

In Communications prefer:
Media and Entertainment

In Medical/Health prefer:
Medical/Health

In Consumer Related prefer:
Retail

In Industrial/Energy prefer:
Energy

Additional Information
Year Founded: 2007
Current Activity Level : Actively seeking new investments

CYPRESS ADVISORS, L.P.
437 Madison Avenue
33rd Floor
New York, NY USA 10022
Phone: 2127050150
Fax: 2127050199
E-mail: contact@cypressgp.com
Website: www.cypressgp.com

Management and Staff
Christopher Harned, Managing Director
Jonathan Saltzman, Principal
Joseph Parzick, Managing Director

Type of Firm
Bank Affiliated

Project Preferences
Type of Financing Preferred:
Leveraged Buyout
Management Buyouts

Industry Focus
(% based on actual investment)
Other Products	39.4%
Consumer Related	23.5%
Medical/Health	10.4%
Communications and Media	10.2%
Semiconductors/Other Elect.	6.8%
Computer Hardware	6.6%
Internet Specific	3.2%

Additional Information
Year Founded: 1989
Capital Under Management: $3,426,000,000
Current Activity Level : Actively seeking new investments

CYPRESS CAPITAL CORP
188 The Embarcadero
Suite 420
San Francisco, CA USA 94105
Phone: 4152813020
Fax: 4152813021
Website: www.cypressleasing.com

Type of Firm
Private Equity Firm

Project Preferences
Type of Financing Preferred:
Balanced
Acquisition

Geographical Preferences
Canadian Preferences:
Ontario

Industry Preferences
In Medical/Health prefer:
Diagnostic Test Products
Medical Therapeutics
Medical Products

Additional Information
Year Founded: 1985
Current Activity Level : Actively seeking new investments

CYPRESS GROWTH CAPITAL LLC
100 Crescent Court
Suite 700
Dallas, TX USA 75201
Phone: 2144598118
E-mail: inquiries@cypressgrowthcapital.com
Website: www.cypressgrowthcapital.com

Other Offices
297 Kingsbury Grade
Suite 228
Stateline, NV USA 89449
Phone: 7755892126

Type of Firm
Private Equity Firm

Project Preferences
Type of Financing Preferred:
Expansion
Later Stage
Other

Size of Investments Considered:
Min Size of Investment Considered (000s): $1,000
Max Size of Investment Considered (000s): $8,000

Geographical Preferences
United States Preferences:
Southwest

Industry Preferences
In Computer Software prefer:
Software

In Business Serv. prefer:
Services

Additional Information
Year Founded: 2010
Capital Under Management: $92,000,000
Current Activity Level : Actively seeking new investments

CYPRESS HILLS PARTNERS INC
409 - 1080 Mainland Street
Vancouver, Canada V6B 2T4
Phone: 6047325840
E-mail: info@cypresshillspartners.com
Website: www.cypresshillspartners.com

Management and Staff
Dean Linden, Managing Partner
Kelly Klatik, Managing Partner

Type of Firm
Private Equity Firm

Additional Information
Year Founded: 2015
Current Activity Level : Actively seeking new investments

CYPRESSTREE INVESTMENT MANAGEMENT COMPANY INC
One Washington Mall
6th Floor
Boston, MA USA 02108
Phone: 617-371-9300
Fax: 617-371-9362

Management and Staff
Paul Foley, Chief Financial Officer

Type of Firm
Bank Affiliated

Additional Information
Year Founded: 1998
Current Activity Level : Actively seeking new investments

CYPRIUM INVESTMENT PARTNERS LLC
200 Public Square, Suite 2020
Cleveland, OH USA 44114
Phone: 2164534500
Fax: 2164534520
Website: www.cyprium.com

Other Offices
461 Fifth Avenue
26th Floor
New York, NY USA 10017
Phone: 646571620
Fax: 6465711619

Management and Staff
Beth Laschinger, Partner
Cindy Babitt, Managing Partner
Daniel Kessler, Partner
Dennis Wagner, Chief Financial Officer

Leland Lewis, Managing Partner
Michael Conaton, Managing Partner
Nicholas Stone, Principal
Patrick Rond, Principal
Wes Owen, Managing Director

Type of Firm
Private Equity Firm

Project Preferences

Type of Financing Preferred:
Leveraged Buyout
Mezzanine
Generalist PE
Later Stage
Management Buyouts
Acquisition
Private Placement

Geographical Preferences

United States Preferences:

Canadian Preferences:
All Canada

Industry Preferences

In Business Serv. prefer:
Services
Distribution

In Manufact. prefer:
Manufacturing

Additional Information
Name of Most Recent Fund: Cyprium Investors IV, L.P.
Most Recent Fund Was Raised: 10/30/2012
Year Founded: 2011
Capital Under Management: $813,000,000
Current Activity Level : Actively seeking new investments

CYRUS CAPITAL PARTNERS LLC
399 Park Avenue
39th Floor
New York, NY USA 10022
Phone: 2123805800
Fax: 2123805801
Website: www.cyruscapital.com

Management and Staff
Brennan McCaw, Chief Financial Officer
James Tucker, Chief Operating Officer
Stephen Freidheim, Founder

Type of Firm
Investment Management Firm

Project Preferences

Type of Financing Preferred:
Leveraged Buyout
Special Situation
Distressed Debt

Geographical Preferences

United States Preferences:
North America

International Preferences:
Europe

Additional Information
Year Founded: 1969
Current Activity Level : Actively seeking new investments

CZR CAPITAL LLC
230 Park Avenue South
11th Floor
New York, NY USA 10003
Phone: 852-2230-98
Website: www.czrcapital.com

Type of Firm
Private Equity Advisor or Fund of Funds

Project Preferences

Type of Financing Preferred:
Fund of Funds

Additional Information
Year Founded: 2007
Current Activity Level : Actively seeking new investments

- D -

D E SHAW & CO LP
1166 Avenue of the Americas
Ninth Floor
New York, NY USA 10036
Phone: 2124780000
Fax: 2124780100
E-mail: inquiries@deshaw.com
Website: www.deshaw.com

Other Offices
44 Church Street West
Hamilton, Bermuda HM 12
Phone: 1-441-294-6650
Fax: 1-441-294-6670

7300 College Boulevard
Suite 620
Overland Park, KS USA 66210
Phone: 212-478-0050
Fax: 212-478-0060

166 Lujiazui Ring Road, Pudong
Suite 20, 20/F Mirae Asset Tower
Shanghai, China 200120
Phone: 86-21-5174-8830
Fax: 86-21-5174-8715

55 Baker Street
Seventh Floor
London, United Kingdom W1U 8EW
Phone: 44-20-7409-4300
Fax: 44-20-7409-4350

20400 Stevens Creek Boulevard
Suite 850
Cupertino, CA USA 95014
Phone: 408-352-9600
Fax: 408-352-9650

8-2-120/113, Road No. 2
Banjara Hills
Hyderabad, India 500 034
Phone: 91-40-40164284

180 Linden Street
2nd Floor
Wellesley, MA USA 02482

Dr. Annie Besant Road, Shiv Sagar Estate
305, Ceejay House, Third Floor
Mumbai, India 400 018
Phone: 91-22-4341-2000
Fax: 91-22-6747-0990

10-1 Roppongi 6-chome, Minato-ku
Roppongi Hills Mori Tower 37th Floor
Tokyo, Japan 106-6137
Phone: 81-3-5414-5400
Fax: 81-3-5414-5302

15 Queen's Road Central
19th Floor, York House, The Landmark
Hong Kong, Hong Kong
Phone: 852-3521-2500
Fax: 852-3521-2600

Management and Staff
Alexander Wong, Managing Director
Anne Dinning, Managing Director
David Shaw, Founder
Eric Wepsic, Managing Director
Julius Gaudio, Managing Director
Louis Salkind, Managing Director
Max Stone, Managing Director
Zoltan Berty, Vice President

Type of Firm
Corporate PE/Venture

Project Preferences

Role in Financing:
Will function either as deal originator or investor in deals created by others

Type of Financing Preferred:
Leveraged Buyout
Early Stage
Generalist PE
Balanced
Later Stage

Additional Information
Name of Most Recent Fund: D E Shaw & Co VI, L.P.
Most Recent Fund Was Raised: 01/07/2015
Year Founded: 1988
Capital Under Management: $32,000,000,000
Current Activity Level : Actively seeking new investments

D&F EQUITY INVESTMENT FUND MANAGEMENT CO LTD

907, A block, Fortune Center.
No.7,Dongsanhuanzhong Road.
Beijing, China 100020
Phone: 86-10-65330211
Fax: 86-10-65330212
Website: www.df-capital.com

Type of Firm
Investment Management Firm

Project Preferences

Type of Financing Preferred:
Leveraged Buyout
Expansion
Later Stage
Acquisition

Geographical Preferences

International Preferences:
China

Industry Preferences

In Consumer Related prefer:
Sports

Additional Information
Year Founded: 2010
Capital Under Management: $30,802,000
Current Activity Level : Actively seeking new investments

D5 CAPITAL (UK) LTD

53 Chandos Place
London, United Kingdom WC2N 4HS
Phone: 442078126567
Website: www.d5capital.com

Type of Firm
Private Equity Firm

Project Preferences

Type of Financing Preferred:
Early Stage
Expansion
Later Stage
Private Placement
Startup

Industry Preferences

In Communications prefer:
Wireless Communications
Media and Entertainment
Entertainment

In Computer Software prefer:
Software
Applications Software

In Internet Specific prefer:
Ecommerce

In Consumer Related prefer:
Food/Beverage

In Business Serv. prefer:
Media

Additional Information
Year Founded: 2010
Current Activity Level : Actively seeking new investments

DA VINCI CAPITAL MANAGEMENT LTD

Martello Court
Admiral Park, St Peter Port
Guernsey, United Kingdom GY1 3HB
Phone: 441481812080
E-mail: info@dvcap.com
Website: www.dvcap.com

Other Offices
136 Dostyk Avenue
RFCA Business Center 11 floor
Almaty, Kazakhstan
Phone: 77273302323

Northern Tower Business Center
19th Floor, Testovskaya 10
Moscow, Russia 123317
Phone: 74957756222

7 Old Park Lane, Level 7
Mayfair
London, United Kingdom W1K 1QR
Phone: 442075296647

Gazetny lane 17/9
4th floor, building 2
Moscow, Russia 123317
Phone: 7-495-785-3331

Management and Staff
Eric Maillebiau, Managing Director
Evgeny Fetisov, Managing Director
Oleg Konev, Managing Partner
Oleg Jelezko, Managing Partner

Type of Firm
Private Equity Firm

Project Preferences

Type of Financing Preferred:
Leveraged Buyout
Early Stage
Acquisition

Size of Investments Considered:
Min Size of Investment Considered (000s): $10,000
Max Size of Investment Considered (000s): $25,000

Geographical Preferences

International Preferences:
Armenia
Belarus
Kazakhstan
Europe
Kyrgyzstan
Tajikistan
Azerbaijan
Moldova
Ukraine
Uzbekistan

Industry Preferences

In Financial Services prefer:
Financial Services

In Business Serv. prefer:
Services

Additional Information
Year Founded: 2007
Capital Under Management: $400,000,000
Current Activity Level : Actively seeking new investments

DACE VENTURES

230 Third Avenue
Third Floor
North Waltham, MA USA 02451
Phone: 7812500600
Fax: 7812500611
E-mail: info@daceventures.com
Website: www.daceventures.com

Management and Staff

David Andonian, Managing Partner
Doug Chertok, Venture Partner
Jonathan Chait, Partner

Type of Firm

Private Equity Firm

Association Membership

New England Venture Capital Association
National Venture Capital Association - USA (NVCA)

Project Preferences

Type of Financing Preferred:
Early Stage

Size of Investments Considered:
Min Size of Investment Considered (000s): $250
Max Size of Investment Considered (000s): $3,000

Industry Preferences

In Communications prefer:
Wireless Communications

In Internet Specific prefer:
Internet

In Consumer Related prefer:
Consumer

In Business Serv. prefer:
Services
Media

Additional Information

Year Founded: 2007
Capital Under Management: $74,000,000
Current Activity Level : Actively seeking new investments

DAEDEOK INVESTMENT

764, Gwanpyeongdong, Yuseonggu
Daejeon, South Korea
Phone: 827077703210
Fax: 82429362300

Type of Firm

Private Equity Firm

Association Membership

Korean Venture Capital Association (KVCA)

Project Preferences

Type of Financing Preferred:
Balanced

Geographical Preferences

International Preferences:
Korea, South

Additional Information

Year Founded: 2011
Capital Under Management: $25,459,000
Current Activity Level : Actively seeking new investments

DAEKYO CO LTD

158-9, Samseongdong, Gangnamgu
4F, Dongsung Blgd
Seoul, South Korea
Phone: 82234521236
Fax: 82234521525
Website: www.daekyoinvest.com

Type of Firm

Private Equity Firm

Association Membership

Korean Venture Capital Association (KVCA)

Project Preferences

Type of Financing Preferred:
Early Stage
Expansion
Balanced

Geographical Preferences

International Preferences:
Korea, South

Additional Information

Year Founded: 2011
Capital Under Management: $26,470,000
Current Activity Level : Actively seeking new investments

DAESUNG PRIVATE EQUITY INC

400 World Cup North Road
9-10F,Culture Contents Center
Seoul, South Korea 121270
Phone: 82231532960
Fax: 82231532965
Website: www.daesungpe.com

Other Offices

548-8, Oseon-dong
Gwwangsan-gu
Gwangju, South Korea
Phone: 82-62-952-2971
Fax: 82-62-952-2974

1893, Sindang-dong
Dalseo-gu
Daegu, South Korea
Phone: 82-53-587-7624
Fax: 82-53-587-7626

Type of Firm

Corporate PE/Venture

Association Membership

Korean Venture Capital Association (KVCA)

Project Preferences

Type of Financing Preferred:
Expansion
Balanced
Seed
Startup

Geographical Preferences

International Preferences:
Korea, South

Industry Preferences

In Communications prefer:
Communications and Media
Telecommunications
Media and Entertainment
Entertainment

In Computer Software prefer:
Software

In Semiconductor/Electr prefer:
Semiconductor

In Biotechnology prefer:
Biotechnology

In Medical/Health prefer:
Medical/Health

In Consumer Related prefer:
Entertainment and Leisure
Food/Beverage

In Industrial/Energy prefer:
Energy
Industrial Products
Machinery
Environmental Related

In Business Serv. prefer:
Distribution
Media

Additional Information

Year Founded: 1987
Capital Under Management: $81,300,000
Current Activity Level : Actively seeking new investments

DAHER CAPITAL

Riad el Solh Street
Arab Bank Bldg. 2nd Fl.
Beirut Central District, Lebanon
E-mail: info@dahercapital.com

Type of Firm
Private Equity Firm

Project Preferences

Type of Financing Preferred:
Core
Leveraged Buyout
Value-Add
Generalist PE
Balanced
Opportunistic
Acquisition

Industry Preferences

In Financial Services prefer:
Financial Services

In Business Serv. prefer:
Distribution

In Manufact. prefer:
Manufacturing

In Agr/Forestr/Fish prefer:
Agriculture related

Additional Information
Year Founded: 1969
Current Activity Level: Actively seeking new investments

DAIWA CORPORATE INVESTMENT CO LTD

Marunouchi
GranTokyo North Tower 1-9-1
Chiyodaku, Tokyo, Japan 100-6756
Phone: 81-3-55556300
Fax: 81355550877
E-mail: info@daiwa-inv.co.jp
Website: www.daiwa-inv.co.jp

Other Offices

88 Queensway
Suites 2506-08, 25F, Two Pacific Place
Hong Kong, Hong Kong
Phone: 85229184111
Fax: 85229184666

2 Ngo Duc Ke Street, District 1
Room 616, Me Linh Point Tower
Ho Chi Minh City, Vietnam
Phone: 8485203045
Fax: 8485202800

2-8-13, Chuo, Aoba-ku
Daiwashouken Sendai Building
Sendai, China 980-0021
Phone: 81227167261
Fax: 81222215132

No.1000 Lujiazui Ring Road
Room 131, 45/F, HSBC Tower, Pudong
Shanghai, China
Phone: 862158794255
Fax: 862168410038

1-13-20, Sonezakishinchi, Kita-ku
Daiwashouken Osakashiten Building
Osaka, Japan 530-0001
Phone: 81663460955
Fax: 81663460965

Management and Staff
Akihiko Ogino, Senior Managing Director
Kazuhiko Suruta, Senior Managing Director
Kenichi Atogami, Managing Director
Koshiro Taniguchi, Senior Managing Director
Sumiyuki Akaiwa, Senior Managing Director
Teruaki Ueda, President
Tsuneo Hasegawa, Senior Managing Director
Yoshihide Shimamura, Senior Managing Director
Yoshio Narukage, Senior Managing Director

Type of Firm
Private Equity Firm

Association Membership
Japan Venture Capital Association

Project Preferences

Type of Financing Preferred:
Leveraged Buyout
Early Stage
Expansion
Generalist PE
Balanced
Public Companies
Later Stage
Seed
Management Buyouts

Geographical Preferences

United States Preferences:

International Preferences:
Europe
Asia
Japan

Industry Preferences

In Consumer Related prefer:
Other Restaurants

In Financial Services prefer:
Financial Services

In Business Serv. prefer:
Services
Distribution
Media

Additional Information
Year Founded: 1983
Capital Under Management: $735,300,000
Current Activity Level: Actively seeking new investments

DAIWA SECURITIES SMBC PRINCIPAL INVESTMENTS CO., LTD.

1-9-1, Marunouchi
Gran Tokyo North Tower
Chiyoda-Ku, Tokyo, Japan 1006754
Phone: 81355556111
Fax: 81332861815
Website: www.daiwasmbcpi.co.jp

Other Offices

1-14-5 Eidai
Koto-ku
Tokyo, Japan 135-0034
Phone: 81-3-5620-7111

3-15-30, Nishiki
Naka-ku
Nagoya, Japan 460-8691
Phone: 81-52-963-7200

1-13-20, Sonezakishinchi
Kita-ku
Osaka, Japan 530-8231
Phone: 81-6-6454-7000

Management and Staff
Geokyeow Ong, Managing Director
Hideki Araki, President
Kenichi Kawasaki, Vice President

Type of Firm
Bank Affiliated

Association Membership
China Venture Capital Association

Project Preferences

Type of Financing Preferred:
Balanced

Geographical Preferences

International Preferences:
Taiwan
Japan

Additional Information
Year Founded: 2010
Capital Under Management: $18,300,000
Current Activity Level: Actively seeking new investments

DAKOTA VENTURE GROUP INC

4200 James Ray Drive
Grand Forks, ND USA 58203
E-mail: information@dakotaventuregroup.com
Website: www.dakotaventuregroup.com

Management and Staff

Andrew Allen, Managing Director
Austin Emineth, Managing Director
Jacob Oleksik, Managing Director
Luke Schields, Managing Director

Type of Firm

University Program

Project Preferences

Type of Financing Preferred:
Balanced

Geographical Preferences

United States Preferences:
All U.S.

Additional Information

Year Founded: 2006
Current Activity Level : Actively seeking new investments

DALIAN CHENGDA TECH INVEST

71 Renmin Road, Zhongshan Dist
Room 906, Bldg 71
Dalian, China 116001
Phone: 86-411-2657060
Fax: 86-411-2632037

Type of Firm

Private Equity Firm

Project Preferences

Type of Financing Preferred:
Later Stage

Additional Information

Year Founded: 2010
Current Activity Level : Actively seeking new investments

DALIAN INNOVATION INVESTMENT MANAGEMENT CO LTD

No. 82, Yongping Street
Shahekou District
Dalian, Liaoning, China

Type of Firm

Private Equity Firm

Project Preferences

Type of Financing Preferred:
Later Stage

Geographical Preferences

International Preferences:
China

Additional Information

Year Founded: 2012
Capital Under Management: $63,673,000
Current Activity Level : Actively seeking new investments

DALIAN KAIDA VENTURE CAPITAL CO LTD

Rm. 2201, Xiwang Bldg.
Dalian, China 116001
Phone: 8641139856899
Fax: 8641139805933
E-mail: vc@dlkdvc.com
Website: www.dlkdvc.com

Management and Staff

Yefei Liu, Chief Financial Officer

Type of Firm

Private Equity Firm

Project Preferences

Type of Financing Preferred:
Expansion
Later Stage

Geographical Preferences

United States Preferences:

International Preferences:
China

Industry Preferences

In Biotechnology prefer:
Biotechnology

In Medical/Health prefer:
Medical/Health
Health Services

In Industrial/Energy prefer:
Energy

In Financial Services prefer:
Financial Services

Additional Information

Year Founded: 2008
Current Activity Level : Actively seeking new investments

DALIT INDIAN CHAMBER OF COMMERCE & INDUSTRY

Pune Station Road
114, Parmar Chambers
Pune, India 411001
Phone: 912026068800
E-mail: info@dicci.org
Website: www.dicci.org

Type of Firm

Government Affiliated Program

Project Preferences

Type of Financing Preferred:
Early Stage
Expansion
Balanced

Geographical Preferences

International Preferences:
India
Asia

Additional Information

Year Founded: 2011
Capital Under Management: $97,000
Current Activity Level : Actively seeking new investments

DALLAS VENTURE PARTNERS LP

5950 Berkshire Lane
Suite 800
Dallas, TX USA 75225
E-mail: info@dallasventurepartners.com
Website: dallasventurepartners.com

Management and Staff

Jim Duda, Managing Partner
Matt Himelfarb, Managing Partner
Michael Coppola, Managing Partner

Type of Firm

Private Equity Firm

Project Preferences

Type of Financing Preferred:
Early Stage
Balanced

Geographical Preferences

United States Preferences:
Midwest
Texas

Industry Preferences

In Communications prefer:
Wireless Communications
Media and Entertainment

In Computer Software prefer:
Software

In Internet Specific prefer:
Web Aggregation/Portals

In Other prefer:
Environment Responsible

Additional Information

Year Founded: 2012
Current Activity Level : Actively seeking new investments

DANA NAYE VENTURES

409 Black Street
Whitehorse, Canada
Phone: 867-668-6925
Fax: 867-668-3127
Website: www.dananaye.yk.net

Type of Firm
Other

Project Preferences

Type of Financing Preferred:
Early Stage
Expansion
Balanced

Geographical Preferences

Canadian Preferences:
All Canada
Yukon

Industry Preferences

In Financial Services prefer:
Financial Services
Investment Groups

Additional Information

Year Founded: 1985
Current Activity Level : Actively seeking new investments

DANE CREEK CAPITAL CORP

6541 Mississauga Road
Suite A
Mississauga, Canada L5N 1A6
Phone: 9052910103
Fax: 9052961165
Website: danecreekcap.com

Management and Staff

Glen Tennison, President

Type of Firm
Private Equity Firm

Project Preferences

Type of Financing Preferred:
Leveraged Buyout
Acquisition

Additional Information

Year Founded: 2015
Current Activity Level : Actively seeking new investments

DANEVEST TECH FUND ADVISORS

8215 Greenway Boulevard
Suite 560
Middleton, WI USA 53562
Phone: 6088302990
E-mail: dvc@danevestcapital.com
Website: www.danevestcapital.com

Management and Staff

Joseph Hildebrandt, Managing Director
Leon Wilkosz, President

Type of Firm
Private Equity Firm

Project Preferences

Type of Financing Preferred:
Early Stage

Geographical Preferences

United States Preferences:
Midwest
Wisconsin

Industry Preferences

In Consumer Related prefer:
Consumer

In Business Serv. prefer:
Services

Additional Information

Name of Most Recent Fund: DaneVest Tech Fund I, L.P.
Most Recent Fund Was Raised: 12/11/2007
Year Founded: 2007
Capital Under Management: $2,800,000
Current Activity Level : Actively seeking new investments

DANHUA CAPITAL LP

435 Tasso Street
Suite 305
Palo Alto, CA USA 94301
Phone: 6502892301

Type of Firm
Private Equity Firm

Project Preferences

Type of Financing Preferred:
Early Stage
Expansion

Industry Preferences

In Internet Specific prefer:
Internet

Additional Information

Year Founded: 2014
Capital Under Management: $341,250,000
Current Activity Level : Actively seeking new investments

DANONE MANIFESTO VENTURES INC

111 Eighth Avenue
New York, NY USA 10011
Website: www.danoneventures.com

Type of Firm
Private Equity Firm

Project Preferences

Type of Financing Preferred:
Early Stage

Industry Preferences

In Consumer Related prefer:
Food/Beverage

Additional Information

Year Founded: 2016
Current Activity Level : Actively seeking new investments

DANSK GENERATIONSSKIFTE

Filippavej 57
Flintholm
Vester Skerninge, Denmark 5762
Phone: 4562241741
Fax: 5 6224 1743
Website: www.danskgenerationsskifte.dk

Type of Firm
Private Equity Firm

Project Preferences

Type of Financing Preferred:
Leveraged Buyout
Management Buyouts

Geographical Preferences

International Preferences:
Denmark

Additional Information

Year Founded: 1997
Current Activity Level : Actively seeking new investments

DANSKE PRIVATE EQUITY A/S

Ny Kongensgade 10
Copenhagen, Denmark 1472
Phone: 4533446300
Fax: 4533446301
E-mail: info@danskeprivateequity.com
Website: www-2.danskebank.com

Management and Staff

Carsten Ronfeldt, Chief Financial Officer
Dan Kjerulf, Partner
John Danielsen, Managing Partner
Klaus Friis, Partner
Michael Maigaard, Partner

Type of Firm

Private Equity Advisor or Fund of Funds

Association Membership

European Private Equity and Venture Capital Assoc.

Project Preferences

Role in Financing:
Other

Geographical Preferences

United States Preferences:
North America

International Preferences:
Europe
Western Europe
Scandanavia/Nordic Region
Denmark

Industry Preferences

In Medical/Health prefer:
Medical/Health

In Consumer Related prefer:
Consumer Products

In Industrial/Energy prefer:
Industrial Products
Materials

In Financial Services prefer:
Financial Services

Additional Information

Name of Most Recent Fund: Danske Private Equity Partners V
Most Recent Fund Was Raised: 02/07/2012
Year Founded: 1999
Capital Under Management: $3,282,400,000
Current Activity Level : Actively seeking new investments
Method of Compensation: Other

DAOSHENG FUJIAN INVESTMENT CO LTD

Shiji Ave., Meiling Community
2407,Blk.A,Wanda Center
Quanzhou, China
Phone: 8659528889999

Type of Firm

Private Equity Firm

Project Preferences

Type of Financing Preferred:
Balanced
Later Stage

Geographical Preferences

International Preferences:
China

Industry Preferences

In Internet Specific prefer:
Internet

Additional Information

Year Founded: 2010
Capital Under Management: $30,000,000
Current Activity Level : Actively seeking new investments

DAOYUAN CAPITAL MANAGEMENT BEIJING CO LTD

No.2 Easr Ring North Road
2703, Nanyin Building
Beijing, China
Phone: 861056293025
Fax: 861064108001
Website: www.taocapital.cn

Type of Firm

Private Equity Firm

Project Preferences

Type of Financing Preferred:
Generalist PE

Geographical Preferences

International Preferences:
China

Industry Preferences

In Biotechnology prefer:
Biotech Related Research

In Medical/Health prefer:
Medical/Health
Medical Diagnostics
Pharmaceuticals

Additional Information

Year Founded: 2013
Current Activity Level : Actively seeking new investments

DAPHNI SAS

67 rue d'Aboukir
Paris, France 75002
Website: daphni.com

Type of Firm

Private Equity Firm

Project Preferences

Type of Financing Preferred:
Startup

Additional Information

Year Founded: 2015
Capital Under Management: $162,940,000
Current Activity Level : Actively seeking new investments

DARBY OVERSEAS INVESTMENTS, LTD.

1133 Connecticut Avenue, NW
Suite 400
Washington, DC USA 20036
Phone: 2028720500
Fax: 2028721816
Website: www.darbyoverseas.com

Other Offices

Montes Urales 770
Oficina 401
Col. Lomas de Chapultepec, Mexico DF 11000
Phone: 525550020660
Fax: 525526232643

Bank Centre, Citibank Tower, First Floor
Szabadsag ter 7
Budapest, Hungary H-1054
Phone: 3613543700
Fax: 3613543710

Carrera Seven #24-89
Piso 33
Bogota, Colombia
Phone: 5712827877
Fax: 5712827879

8 Connaught Road
17th floor Chater House
Central, Hong Kong
Phone: 85229109200
Fax: 85225219815

Templeton Research Poland
Rondo 1, 29th floor
Warsaw, Poland 00-124
Phone: 48223371380
Fax: 48223371373

12 Youido-dong, Youngdungpo-gu
10th Floor, CCMM Building
Seoul, South Korea 150-968
Phone: 82237740605
Fax: 82237740667

Dr. Karl Lueger-Ring 10
Vienna, Austria A-1010
Phone: 431532265500
Fax: 431532265550

Wockhardt Tower (East), 4F
Bandra Kurla Complex
Mumbai, India 400051
Phone: 9102267519100
Fax: 9102266391277

Sun Plaza 15th Floor
Maslak
Istanbul, Turkey 34367
Phone: 902123679205
Fax: 902123679202

Avenida Brigadeiro Faria Lima
5 andar, 3311
Sao Paulo, Brazil 04538-133
Phone: 551132060080
Fax: 551130713775

200 South Biscayne Boulevard
Suite 3050
MIAMI, FL USA 33131
Phone: 3053721260
Fax: 3059821593

15, Rue Edward Steichen
Luxembourg, Luxembourg 2540

Management and Staff
David Hudson, Senior Managing Director
Jon Potokin, Managing Director

Type of Firm
Private Equity Firm

Association Membership
Brazilian Venture Capital Association (ABCR)
Emerging Markets Private Equity Association
Polish Venture Capital Association (PSIC/PPEA)

Project Preferences

Role in Financing:
Prefer role as deal originator but will also invest in deals created by others

Type of Financing Preferred:
Leveraged Buyout
Early Stage
Expansion
Generalist PE
Balanced
Turnaround
Later Stage
Other
Management Buyouts
Acquisition
Recapitalizations

Geographical Preferences

International Preferences:
Latin America
Central Europe
Eastern Europe
Asia
Korea, South

Industry Focus
(% based on actual investment)

Industrial/Energy	42.7%
Other Products	23.8%
Consumer Related	11.5%
Communications and Media	9.1%
Medical/Health	4.2%
Internet Specific	3.2%
Computer Hardware	3.0%
Computer Software and Services	2.0%
Biotechnology	0.4%

Additional Information
Name of Most Recent Fund: Fondo de Infraestructura en Transporte
Most Recent Fund Was Raised: 08/31/2010
Year Founded: 1994
Capital Under Management: $1,800,000,000
Current Activity Level: Actively seeking new investments
Method of Compensation: Return on invest. most important, but chg. closing fees, service fees, etc.

DARIEN BUSINESS DEVELOPMENT CORP

2073 Avenida Paulista
Sao Paulo, Brazil

Other Offices
Ehad Ha'Am 72
Tel Aviv, Israel

Management and Staff
Daniel Carneiro Da Cunha, Partner
Harpreet Nijjar, Chief Financial Officer
Roi Carthy, Managing Partner

Type of Firm
Private Equity Firm

Project Preferences

Type of Financing Preferred:
Early Stage
Seed
Startup

Size of Investments Considered:
Min Size of Investment Considered (000s): $100
Max Size of Investment Considered (000s): $300

Geographical Preferences

International Preferences:
Brazil
Israel

Industry Preferences

In Internet Specific prefer:
E-Commerce Technology
Web Aggregation/Portals

Additional Information
Year Founded: 2011
Current Activity Level: Actively seeking new investments

DARLING VENTURES LLC

32 Heron St
San Francisco, CA USA 94103

Type of Firm
Private Equity Firm

Project Preferences

Type of Financing Preferred:
Leveraged Buyout
Acquisition

Additional Information
Year Founded: 2013
Current Activity Level: Actively seeking new investments

DARR GLOBAL HOLDINGS INC

779 Allison Court
Moorestown, NJ USA 08057
Phone: 856-840-0800
Fax: 856-840-0885
Website: www.darrglobal.com

Management and Staff
Dinesh Desai, President
Eric Bulock, Partner
Stephen Donnelly, Chief Financial Officer

Type of Firm
Private Equity Firm

Project Preferences

Type of Financing Preferred:
Leveraged Buyout
Turnaround
Management Buyouts
Recapitalizations

Geographical Preferences

United States Preferences:

International Preferences:
India
United Kingdom

Additional Information
Year Founded: 1986
Current Activity Level : Actively seeking new investments

DARUAN VENTURE CAPITAL SCR DE REGIMEN SIMPLIFICADO SA

Calle Rafael Boti 2
Aravaca
Madrid, Spain 20023
Phone: 34917991330
Website: www.daruanvc.com

Type of Firm
Private Equity Firm

Project Preferences

Type of Financing Preferred:
Seed

Geographical Preferences

International Preferences:
Spain

Additional Information
Year Founded: 2013
Capital Under Management: $3,966,000
Current Activity Level : Actively seeking new investments

DARWIN PRIVATE EQUITY LLP

21-22 New Row
London, United Kingdom WC2N 4LE
Phone: 442074200750
Fax: 442074200799
E-mail: contact@darwinpe.com
Website: www.darwinpe.com

Management and Staff
Alan Maynard, Partner
Derek Elliott, Partner
Katie Beck, Principal
Kevin Street, Partner

Type of Firm
Private Equity Firm

Association Membership
British Venture Capital Association (BVCA)

Project Preferences

Type of Financing Preferred:
Leveraged Buyout
Expansion
Turnaround
Management Buyouts
Acquisition

Geographical Preferences

International Preferences:
United Kingdom

Industry Preferences

In Consumer Related prefer:
Consumer

In Industrial/Energy prefer:
Industrial Products

In Financial Services prefer:
Financial Services

In Business Serv. prefer:
Services
Media

Additional Information
Year Founded: 2007
Capital Under Management: $96,000,000
Current Activity Level : Actively seeking new investments

DARWIN VENTURE CAPITAL CO LTD

No. 1407 SK Leader's View
168 Dogok-dong, Gangam-gu
Seoul, South Korea 135-270
Phone: 822-575-5200
Fax: 822-575-3223

Management and Staff
Yongdong Yeo, Chief Executive Officer

Type of Firm
Private Equity Firm

Project Preferences

Type of Financing Preferred:
Balanced

Additional Information
Year Founded: 2008
Current Activity Level : Actively seeking new investments

DASH VENTURES LTD

Jabal Weibdeh
Amman, Jordan
E-mail: info@dashventures.com
Website: www.dashventures.com

Type of Firm
Private Equity Firm

Project Preferences

Type of Financing Preferred:
Early Stage
Seed

Geographical Preferences

International Preferences:
Jordan
Middle East
Africa

Industry Preferences

In Communications prefer:
Entertainment

In Computer Software prefer:
Software

In Internet Specific prefer:
Internet
Web Aggregation/Portals

In Medical/Health prefer:
Health Services

In Industrial/Energy prefer:
Alternative Energy

In Financial Services prefer:
Financial Services

In Business Serv. prefer:
Media

In Other prefer:
Environment Responsible

Additional Information
Year Founded: 2011
Current Activity Level : Actively seeking new investments

DASOS CAPITAL OY

Tekniikantie 12
Espoo, Finland 02150
Phone: 358985606100
Fax: 358985606101
E-mail: info@dasos.fi
Website: www.dasos.fi

Management and Staff
Johanna Lindroos, Partner
Kaisa Anttila, Partner
Olli Haltia, Chief Executive Officer
Petteri Seppanen, Partner
Sami Veijalainen, Partner

Type of Firm
Private Equity Firm

Association Membership
Finnish Venture Capital Association (FVCA)

Project Preferences

Type of Financing Preferred:
Generalist PE

Geographical Preferences

International Preferences:
All International

Industry Preferences

In Industrial/Energy prefer:
Alternative Energy
Energy Conservation Relat

In Other prefer:
Environment Responsible

Additional Information
Name of Most Recent Fund: Dasos Timberland Fund II
Most Recent Fund Was Raised: 03/01/2013
Year Founded: 2005
Capital Under Management: $254,919,000
Current Activity Level: Actively seeking new investments

DASYM INVESTMENT STRATEGIES BV
Flevolaan 41a
Naarden, Netherlands 1411 KC
Phone: 31356959090
Fax: 31356959044
E-mail: info@cyrte.com
Website: www.dasym.com

Management and Staff
Frank Botman, Founder

Type of Firm
Private Equity Firm

Project Preferences

Type of Financing Preferred:
Generalist PE

Geographical Preferences

United States Preferences:
All U.S.

International Preferences:
United Kingdom
Western Europe

Industry Preferences

In Communications prefer:
Telecommunications
Media and Entertainment

In Computer Other prefer:
Computer Related

In Business Serv. prefer:
Media

Additional Information
Year Founded: 2000
Capital Under Management: $2,927,000,000
Current Activity Level: Actively seeking new investments

DATA COLLECTIVE LLC
665 3rd Street
Suite 150
San Francisco, CA USA 94107
Website: www.dcvc.com

Other Offices
317 University Avenue
Suite 200
Palo Alto, CA USA 94301

537 Hamilton Avenue
PALO ALTO, CA USA 94301

Management and Staff
Matt Ocko, Co-Founder
Zachary Bogue, Co-Founder

Type of Firm
Private Equity Firm

Project Preferences

Type of Financing Preferred:
Early Stage

Industry Preferences

In Computer Software prefer:
Software

In Internet Specific prefer:
Internet

In Semiconductor/Electr prefer:
Analytic/Scientific

Additional Information
Year Founded: 2012
Capital Under Management: $596,390,000
Current Activity Level: Actively seeking new investments

DATA POINT CAPITAL I LP
280 Congress Street
Suite 1360
Boston, MA USA 02210
E-mail: info@datapointcapital.com
Website: datapointcapital.com

Management and Staff
Michael Majors, Managing Partner
Scott Savitz, Founder

Type of Firm
Private Equity Firm

Association Membership
New England Venture Capital Association

Project Preferences

Type of Financing Preferred:
Early Stage
Seed

Industry Preferences

In Internet Specific prefer:
Ecommerce
Web Aggregation/Portals

In Consumer Related prefer:
Consumer

Additional Information
Name of Most Recent Fund: Data Point Capital I, L.P.
Most Recent Fund Was Raised: 07/12/2012
Year Founded: 2012
Capital Under Management: $14,490,000
Current Activity Level: Actively seeking new investments

DATABANK PRIVATE EQUITY LTD
61 Barnes Road Adabraka
Accra, Ghana
Phone: 233302610610
Fax: 233302681443
E-mail: info@databankgroup.com
Website: www.databankgroup.com

Type of Firm
Investment Management Firm

Project Preferences

Type of Financing Preferred:
Early Stage
Generalist PE
Turnaround
Later Stage
Management Buyouts
Recapitalizations

Size of Investments Considered:
Min Size of Investment Considered (000s): $50
Max Size of Investment Considered (000s): $500

Geographical Preferences

International Preferences:
Latin America
Ghana
Middle East
Africa

Industry Preferences

In Consumer Related prefer:
Food/Beverage

In Financial Services prefer:
Financial Services

In Agr/Forestr/Fish prefer:
Agribusiness

Additional Information
Year Founded: 1990
Capital Under Management: $7,000,000
Current Activity Level : Actively seeking new investments

DATATRIBE

8115 Maple Lawn Boulevard
Fulton, MD USA 20759
Website: www.datatribe.com

Type of Firm
Incubator/Development Program

Project Preferences

Type of Financing Preferred:
Early Stage

Additional Information
Year Founded: 2017
Current Activity Level : Actively seeking new investments

DAVIES WARD PHILLIPS & VINEBER

100 King Street West 44th/F
First Canadian Place
Toronto, Canada M5X1B1
Phone: 416-367-6972
Fax: 416-863-0871
E-mail: mduncan@dwpv.com
Website: www.dwpv.com

Other Offices

900 Third Avenue
24th Floor
New York, NY USA 10022
Phone: 2125885500
Fax: 2123080132

1501 McGill College Avenue
26th Floor
Montreal, Canada H3A 3N9
Phone: 5148416400
Fax: 5148416499

Management and Staff
Carol Pennycook, Partner

Type of Firm
Private Equity Firm

Additional Information
Year Founded: 2009
Current Activity Level : Actively seeking new investments

DAWN CAPITAL LLP

21-22 Warwick Street
London, United Kingdom W1B 5NE
Website: www.dawncapital.co.uk

Management and Staff
Haakon Overli, General Partner
Josh Bell, General Partner
Norman Fiore, Co-Founder

Type of Firm
Private Equity Firm

Association Membership
British Venture Capital Association (BVCA)

Project Preferences

Type of Financing Preferred:
Early Stage
Expansion
Balanced
Later Stage

Geographical Preferences

International Preferences:
United Kingdom
Europe

Industry Preferences

In Communications prefer:
Communications and Media
Telecommunications

In Computer Software prefer:
Software

In Internet Specific prefer:
Internet

In Medical/Health prefer:
Medical/Health
Health Services

In Consumer Related prefer:
Consumer

In Financial Services prefer:
Financial Services

Additional Information
Year Founded: 2008
Capital Under Management: $93,656,000
Current Activity Level : Actively seeking new investments

DAWNAY DAY GROUP

74-82 Queen Victoria Street
York House
London, United Kingdom EC4N 4SJ
Phone: 442079797575
Fax: 442079797585
E-mail: info@D2L.com
Website: www.dawnayday.com

Management and Staff
Jonathan Lander, Chief Executive Officer

Type of Firm
Private Equity Firm

Project Preferences

Type of Financing Preferred:
Early Stage
Balanced
Later Stage
Seed
Startup

Geographical Preferences

International Preferences:
United Kingdom
Europe
Middle East

Industry Preferences

In Communications prefer:
Telecommunications

In Computer Software prefer:
Software

In Internet Specific prefer:
Internet

In Computer Other prefer:
Computer Related

In Semiconductor/Electr prefer:
Electronics
Semiconductor

In Biotechnology prefer:
Biotechnology

In Medical/Health prefer:
Medical/Health

Additional Information
Year Founded: 1998
Current Activity Level : Actively seeking new investments

DAY ONE CAPITAL KOCK-AZATI TOKEALAP KEZELO ZRT

Alkotas utca 53
MOM Park Building B 5th floor
Budapest, Hungary H-1123
E-mail: info@dayonecapital.com
Website: www.dayonecapital.com

Management and Staff
Gyorgy Simo, Managing Partner

Type of Firm
Private Equity Firm

Project Preferences

Type of Financing Preferred:
Early Stage
Seed
Startup

Geographical Preferences

International Preferences:
Central Europe
Eastern Europe

Industry Preferences

In Computer Software prefer:
Software

In Internet Specific prefer:
Internet

In Biotechnology prefer:
Biotechnology

In Medical/Health prefer:
Health Services

Additional Information
Year Founded: 2010
Capital Under Management: $5,600,000
Current Activity Level: Actively seeking new investments

DB CAPITAL PARTNERS LTD

17 - 19 Wellington Street
701 Hong Kong House
Central, Hong Kong
Website: www.dbcapital-partners.com

Type of Firm
Private Equity Firm

Association Membership
Hong Kong Venture Capital Association (HKVCA)

Project Preferences

Type of Financing Preferred:
Leveraged Buyout

Geographical Preferences

International Preferences:
Indonesia
Taiwan
Hong Kong
China
Singapore
Malaysia

Industry Preferences

In Communications prefer:
Communications and Media

In Medical/Health prefer:
Health Services

In Consumer Related prefer:
Consumer

In Industrial/Energy prefer:
Industrial Products

In Transportation prefer:
Transportation

In Financial Services prefer:
Financial Services
Financial Services

Additional Information
Year Founded: 1969
Current Activity Level: Actively seeking new investments

DB PRIVATE EQUITY GMBH

Elsa-Braendstroem-Str. 10-12
Cologne, Germany 50668
Phone: 492219370850
Fax: 4922193708519
E-mail: dbpe-info@db.com
Website: www.dbpe.com

Other Offices
One Appold Street
London, United Kingdom EC2A 2UU

One Raffles Quay
#15-00, South Tower
Singapore, Singapore

345 Park Avenue
New York, NY USA

Type of Firm
Private Equity Advisor or Fund of Funds

Association Membership
German Venture Capital Association (BVK)
European Private Equity and Venture Capital Assoc.

Project Preferences

Type of Financing Preferred:
Fund of Funds
Leveraged Buyout
Mezzanine
Turnaround
Fund of Funds of Second

Geographical Preferences

United States Preferences:
All U.S.

International Preferences:
United Kingdom
Middle East
Germany

Additional Information
Name of Most Recent Fund: Deutsche Bank Private Equity Global Select Fund VI
Most Recent Fund Was Raised: 04/08/2013
Year Founded: 2008
Capital Under Management: $8,400,000,000
Current Activity Level: Actively seeking new investments

DB1 VENTURES GMBH

Mergenthalerallee 61
Eschborn, Germany 65760
Website: deutsche-boerse.com

Type of Firm
Bank Affiliated

Project Preferences

Type of Financing Preferred:
Early Stage

Additional Information
Year Founded: 2016
Current Activity Level: Actively seeking new investments

DBH INVESTMENT ZRT

Gabor Denes u.2. Infopark D
Budapest, Hungary H1117
Phone: 36-1-464-9500
Fax: 36-1-464-9540
E-mail: info@dbh-group.com
Website: www.dbh-group.com

Other Offices
Arany Janos u. 55.
Debrecen, Hungary H4025
Phone: 36-52-453-101
Fax: 36-52-502-461

Str. Buzesti Nr. 50-52, Sector 1
Bukarest, Romania 011015
Phone: 40-21-30-21-111
Fax: 40-21-401-1025

Kriva 21, 04001
Kosice, Slovakia
Phone: 42-1-55-622-0678

Beursplein 37, 3011 AA
World Trade Center
Rotterdam, Neth. Antilles 30077
Phone: 31-10-205-3350
Fax: 31-10-205-3355

Management and Staff
Sandor Erdei, Chief Executive Officer

Type of Firm
Investment Management Firm

Project Preferences

Type of Financing Preferred:
Early Stage
Expansion
Balanced
Later Stage
Seed
Startup

Geographical Preferences

International Preferences:
Hungary
Europe
Eastern Europe

Additional Information
Year Founded: 1994
Capital Under Management: $26,890,000
Current Activity Level : Actively seeking new investments

DBJ CAPITAL CO., LTD

No.2-1 Otemachi 2-Chome
12F, Nippon Bldg.
Tokyo, Japan 100-0004
Phone: 81332312381
Fax: 81332312380
Website: www.dbj-cap.jp

Management and Staff
Ryoma Tsuchida, Managing Director
Shigeyuki Soeda, Managing Director
Yasuhisa Yamaguchi, Managing Director

Type of Firm
Bank Affiliated

Association Membership
Japan Venture Capital Association

Project Preferences

Type of Financing Preferred:
Balanced

Geographical Preferences

International Preferences:
Japan

Industry Preferences

In Semiconductor/Electr prefer:
Electronics

In Biotechnology prefer:
Biotechnology

In Medical/Health prefer:
Medical/Health

In Industrial/Energy prefer:
Environmental Related

In Business Serv. prefer:
Services

In Manufact. prefer:
Manufacturing

Additional Information
Year Founded: 1990
Capital Under Management: $739,400,000
Current Activity Level : Actively seeking new investments

DBL INVESTORS

One Montgomery Street
Suite 2375
San Francisco, CA USA 94104
Phone: 4155682901
Fax: 4159562561
Website: www.dblpartners.vc

Management and Staff
Cynthia Ringo, Managing Partner
Mark Perutz, Partner

Type of Firm
Private Equity Firm

Association Membership
National Venture Capital Association - USA (NVCA)

Project Preferences

Type of Financing Preferred:
Later Stage

Geographical Preferences

United States Preferences:

Industry Preferences

In Medical/Health prefer:
Medical/Health

In Industrial/Energy prefer:
Environmental Related

In Other prefer:
Environment Responsible

Additional Information
Name of Most Recent Fund: DBL Equity Fund - BAEF II, L.P.
Most Recent Fund Was Raised: 12/23/2008
Year Founded: 2008
Capital Under Management: $140,000,000
Current Activity Level : Actively seeking new investments

DBW FM LTD

14-16 Park Place
Oakleigh House
Cardiff, United Kingdom CF10 3DQ
Phone: 448005874140
Fax: 442920338139
E-mail: info@financewales.co.uk

Type of Firm
Investment Management Firm

Project Preferences

Type of Financing Preferred:
Early Stage
Mezzanine
Seed

Size of Investments Considered:
Min Size of Investment Considered (000s): $80
Max Size of Investment Considered (000s): $1,590

Geographical Preferences

International Preferences:
United Kingdom

Industry Preferences

In Semiconductor/Electr prefer:
Electronics

In Industrial/Energy prefer:
Energy
Environmental Related

Additional Information
Year Founded: 1984
Current Activity Level : Actively seeking new investments

DC CAPITAL PARTNERS LLC

11 Canal Center Plaza, Suite 350
Alexandria, VA USA 22314
Phone: 2027375220
Fax: 2027375225
E-mail: info@dccapitalpartners.com
Website: www.dccapitalpartners.com

Management and Staff
Andrew Campbell, Partner
Douglas Lake, Partner
Jeffrey Weber, Partner
Jerry Chernock, Vice President
T. Gail Dady, Partner

Type of Firm
Private Equity Firm

Project Preferences

Type of Financing Preferred:
Leveraged Buyout

Geographical Preferences

United States Preferences:
All U.S.

Additional Information
Year Founded: 1988
Current Activity Level : Actively seeking new investments

DCA CAPITAL PARTNERS LP

3721 Douglas Boulevard
Suite 350
Roseville, CA USA 95661
Phone: 9169605350
Fax: 9169605360
E-mail: info@dcapartners.com
Website: dcapartners.com

Management and Staff
Casey Layton, Chief Financial Officer
Curtis Rocca, Managing Partner
Ronald Crane, Managing Director
Steven Mills, General Partner

Type of Firm
Private Equity Firm

Project Preferences

Type of Financing Preferred:
Leveraged Buyout
Later Stage
Acquisition
Recapitalizations

Size of Investments Considered:
Min Size of Investment Considered (000s): $2,000
Max Size of Investment Considered (000s): $6,000

Geographical Preferences

United States Preferences:
California
Southwest

Industry Preferences

In Medical/Health prefer:
Health Services

In Consumer Related prefer:
Retail
Food/Beverage
Consumer Products

In Industrial/Energy prefer:
Alternative Energy

In Business Serv. prefer:
Services
Distribution
Media

In Manufact. prefer:
Manufacturing
Publishing

In Agr/Forestr/Fish prefer:
Agribusiness

Additional Information
Year Founded: 2005
Capital Under Management: $12,475,000
Current Activity Level : Actively seeking new investments

DCM PRIVATE EQUITY

One Righter Parkway
Suite 3200
Wilmington, DE USA 19803
Website: dupontcapital.com

Type of Firm
Private Equity Advisor or Fund of Funds

Project Preferences

Type of Financing Preferred:
Fund of Funds

Additional Information
Year Founded: 2005
Capital Under Management: $155,360,000
Current Activity Level : Actively seeking new investments

DE NOVO VENTURES LLC

14612 Big Basin Way
Suite B
Saratoga, CA USA 95070
Phone: 6503291999
Fax: 6503291315
Website: www.denovovc.com

Management and Staff
Frederick Dotzler, Co-Founder
Joseph Mandato, Managing Director
Richard Ferrari, Co-Founder

Type of Firm
Private Equity Firm

Association Membership
Western Association of Venture Capitalists (WAVC)

Project Preferences

Role in Financing:
Will function either as deal originator or investor in deals created by others

Type of Financing Preferred:
Early Stage
Expansion
Balanced
Later Stage

Industry Preferences

In Biotechnology prefer:
Biotechnology
Biotech Related Research

In Medical/Health prefer:
Medical/Health
Medical Therapeutics
Medical Products
Pharmaceuticals

Additional Information
Name of Most Recent Fund: De Novo Ventures III, L.P.
Most Recent Fund Was Raised: 08/01/2006
Year Founded: 2000
Capital Under Management: $650,000,000
Current Activity Level : Actively seeking new investments
Method of Compensation: Return on investment is of primary concern, do not charge fees

DECATHLON CAPITAL PARTNERS LLC

1389 Center Drive
Suite 200
Park City, UT USA 84098
Phone: 6504701200
Website: www.decathloncapital.com

Type of Firm
Private Equity Firm

Project Preferences

Type of Financing Preferred:
Leveraged Buyout
Management Buyouts
Acquisition

Additional Information
Year Founded: 2011
Capital Under Management: $29,650,000
Current Activity Level : Actively seeking new investments

DECHENG CAPITAL LLC

35 Si Nan Road
Fourth Floor South
Shanghai, China 200020
Phone: 862153831999
Fax: 862153831997
Website: www.decheng.com

Management and Staff
Fay Xing, Principal
Min Cui, Managing Director
Nick Pliam, Venture Partner
Qiang Xu, Principal
Victor Tong, Principal

Type of Firm
Private Equity Firm

Project Preferences

Type of Financing Preferred:
Balanced
Public Companies
Turnaround

Geographical Preferences

International Preferences:
China

Industry Preferences

In Biotechnology prefer:
Agricultural/Animal Bio.
Industrial Biotechnology

In Medical/Health prefer:
Diagnostic Services
Medical Therapeutics
Health Services
Pharmaceuticals

In Manufact. prefer:
Manufacturing

Additional Information
Year Founded: 2011
Capital Under Management: $123,002,000
Current Activity Level : Actively seeking new investments

DECORUM CAPITAL PARTNERS PTY LTD

37 Peter Place
Bryanston
Johannesburg, South Africa
Phone: 27117061442
E-mail: enquiries@namf.co.za
Website: www.namf.co.za

Type of Firm
Private Equity Firm

Project Preferences

Type of Financing Preferred:
Early Stage
Expansion
Later Stage

Geographical Preferences

International Preferences:
South Africa
Africa

Industry Preferences

In Agr/Forestr/Fish prefer:
Mining and Minerals

Additional Information
Name of Most Recent Fund: New Africa Mining Fund II
Most Recent Fund Was Raised: 01/31/2011
Year Founded: 2000
Capital Under Management: $50,000,000
Current Activity Level : Actively seeking new investments

DEEP FORK CAPITAL

3000 Sand Hill Road
Building Two, Suite 130
Menlo Park, CA USA 94025
Phone: 6509269850
Fax: 6509269882
E-mail: info@deepforkcapital.com

Management and Staff
Andre De Baubigny, Managing Partner
Tim Komada, Managing Partner

Type of Firm
Private Equity Firm

Project Preferences

Type of Financing Preferred:
Balanced

Industry Preferences

In Communications prefer:
Media and Entertainment

In Industrial/Energy prefer:
Alternative Energy

Additional Information
Year Founded: 2008
Current Activity Level : Actively seeking new investments

DEEPBLUE VENTURES LLC

1900 McCathy Blvd
Suite 105
Milpitas, CA USA 95035
E-mail: bp@deepbluevc.com
Website: www.deepbluevc.com

Type of Firm
Private Equity Firm

Project Preferences

Type of Financing Preferred:
Early Stage

Industry Preferences

In Computer Software prefer:
Artificial Intelligence

In Internet Specific prefer:
Internet

Additional Information
Year Founded: 1969
Current Activity Level : Actively seeking new investments

DEEPBRIDGE CAPITAL LLP

Honeycomb East
Deepbridge House
Chester, United Kingdom CH4 9QN
Phone: 1244746000
Website: www.deepbridgecapital.com

Management and Staff
Andrew Aldridge, Partner
Andrew Hughes, Partner
Ian Warwick, Managing Partner
Kieran O Gorman, Partner
Louise Farley, Partner
Ray Eugeni, Partner
Rick Parry, Partner
Savvas Neophytou, Partner

Type of Firm
Private Equity Firm

Project Preferences

Type of Financing Preferred:
Balanced

Industry Preferences

In Industrial/Energy prefer:
Energy

Additional Information
Year Founded: 2010
Current Activity Level : Actively seeking new investments

DEERFIELD MANAGEMENT COMPANY LP

780 Third Avenue
37th Floor
New York, NY USA 10017
Phone: 2125511600
Fax: 2125993075
Website: www.deerfield.com

Management and Staff
Adam Greene, Partner
Alex Karnal, Partner
Avi Kometz, Partner
Brian Bizoza, Partner
CAMERON WHEELER, Principal
ELISE WANG, Principal
ELLIOT PRESS, Partner
Howie Furest, Partner
JAMES FLYNN, Managing Partner
JEAN KIM, Partner
JEFF KAPLAN, Partner
Jonathan Leff, Partner
Kevin Berg, Partner
LAWRENCE ATINSKY, Partner
LESLIE HENSHAW, Partner
PETER STEELMAN, Partner
Robert Jackson, Partner
Robert Olan, Partner
Sumner Anderson, Partner
VINCE MELLET, Partner

Type of Firm
Investment Management Firm

Association Membership
National Venture Capital Association - USA (NVCA)

Project Preferences

Type of Financing Preferred:
Leveraged Buyout
Mezzanine
Generalist PE
Balanced
Joint Ventures

Industry Preferences

In Biotechnology prefer:
Human Biotechnology
Industrial Biotechnology

In Medical/Health prefer:
Medical/Health
Health Services
Pharmaceuticals

Additional Information
Year Founded: 1994
Capital Under Management: $2,941,750,000
Current Activity Level : Actively seeking new investments

DEERPATH CAPITAL MANAGEMENT LP

405 Lexington Avenue
71st Floor
New York, NY USA 10174
E-mail: info@deerpathcapital.com
Website: www.deerpathcapital.com

Management and Staff
Anish Bahl, Chief Financial Officer
David Vavrichek, Vice President
James Kirby, President
Steve Brune, Vice President
Tas Hasan, Vice President

Type of Firm
Private Equity Firm

Association Membership
Natl Assoc of Small Bus. Inv. Co (NASBIC)

Project Preferences

Type of Financing Preferred:
Leveraged Buyout
Expansion
Mezzanine
Acquisition
Recapitalizations

Industry Preferences

In Communications prefer:
Communications and Media

In Medical/Health prefer:
Medical/Health

In Industrial/Energy prefer:
Energy

In Financial Services prefer:
Financial Services

In Business Serv. prefer:
Services
Distribution

In Manufact. prefer:
Manufacturing

Additional Information
Name of Most Recent Fund: Deerpath Capital II, L.P.
Most Recent Fund Was Raised: 10/07/2011
Year Founded: 2008
Capital Under Management: $62,094,000
Current Activity Level : Actively seeking new investments

DEFI GESTION SA

Boulevard de Grancy 1
Lausanne, Switzerland 1006
Phone: 41216143444
Fax: 41216143445
E-mail: defi@defigestion.ch
Website: www.defigestion.com

Management and Staff
Gabriel Gomez, Principal
Mohammed Diab, Managing Director

Type of Firm
Private Equity Firm

Association Membership
French Venture Capital Association (AFIC)

Project Preferences

Type of Financing Preferred:
Leveraged Buyout
Early Stage
Later Stage
Seed
Management Buyouts
Acquisition
Startup

Geographical Preferences

International Preferences:
Europe
Netherlands
Switzerland
Belgium

Industry Focus
(% based on actual investment)
Biotechnology	38.1%
Medical/Health	35.9%
Other Products	16.4%
Consumer Related	6.6%
Semiconductors/Other Elect.	3.1%

Additional Information
Year Founded: 1990
Capital Under Management: $141,300,000
Current Activity Level : Actively seeking new investments

DEFOE PARTNERS & CO

48 Wall Street
11th Floor
New York, NY USA 10005
Phone: 2127960495
Website: www.defoepartners.com

Other Offices
16 Hanover Square
Mayfair
London, United Kingdom W1S 1HT
Phone: 442033724334

Type of Firm
Bank Affiliated

Project Preferences

Type of Financing Preferred:
Leveraged Buyout
Acquisition
Distressed Debt

Additional Information
Year Founded: 2011
Current Activity Level : Actively seeking new investments

DEFTA PARTNERS

111 Pine Street
Suite 1410
San Francisco, CA USA 94111
Phone: 4154332262
Fax: 4154332264
E-mail: information@deftapartners.com
Website: www.deftapartners.com

Other Offices

Nihonbashi Hongoku-cho 4-4-20
Mitsui 2nd Annex 7th Floor
Chuo-ku Tokyo, Japan 103-0021
Phone: 81362252790
Fax: 81362252791

6 Alon Street
Rosh Ha'ain, Israel 48560
Phone: 972-3-938-4940
Fax: 972-3-938-8965

Marpol House 6 The Green
Richmond, Surrey, United Kingdom TW9 1PL
Phone: 44-208-940-1001
Fax: 44-208-940-6792

Management and Staff

Kyoko Watanabe, Founder
Masa Isono, Principal
Stan Sakai, Partner
Stuart Gannes, Venture Partner

Type of Firm

Private Equity Firm

Association Membership

National Venture Capital Association - USA (NVCA)

Project Preferences

Role in Financing:
Prefer role in deals created by others

Type of Financing Preferred:
Early Stage
Seed
Startup

Size of Investments Considered:
Min Size of Investment Considered (000s): $500
Max Size of Investment Considered (000s): $3,000

Industry Focus

(% based on actual investment)

Computer Software and Services	45.6%
Internet Specific	28.7%
Semiconductors/Other Elect.	18.2%
Medical/Health	3.7%
Communications and Media	1.4%
Computer Hardware	1.2%
Biotechnology	1.2%

Additional Information

Year Founded: 1984
Capital Under Management: $20,000,000
Current Activity Level : Actively seeking new investments
Method of Compensation: Professional fee required whether or not deal closes

DEFU FUND MANAGEMENT CO LTD

Futian District
2701, Tower A, Union Square
Shenzhen, China
Phone: 86755-66603728
Fax: 86755-83872291
E-mail: admin@defufm.com
Website: www.defufm.com

Type of Firm

Investment Management Firm

Project Preferences

Type of Financing Preferred:
Leveraged Buyout
Value-Add
Balanced

Geographical Preferences

International Preferences:
China

Industry Preferences

In Internet Specific prefer:
Internet

Additional Information

Year Founded: 2013
Capital Under Management: $16,006,000

DEFY PARTNERS MANAGEMENT LLC

3340 Hillview Avenue
Palo Alto, CA USA 94304
Website: defy.vc

Type of Firm

Private Equity Firm

Project Preferences

Type of Financing Preferred:
Balanced

Additional Information

Year Founded: 2017
Capital Under Management: $151,000,000
Current Activity Level : Actively seeking new investments

DEG DEUTSCHE INVESTITIONS- UND ENTWICKLUNGSGESELLSCHAFT MBH

Kaemmergasse 22
Cologne, Germany 50676
Phone: 4922149860
Fax: 4922149861290
E-mail: info@deginvest.de
Website: www.deginvest.de

Management and Staff

Bruno Wenn, Managing Director
Michael Bornmann, Managing Director
Philipp Kreutz, Managing Director

Type of Firm

Private Equity Firm

Association Membership

Emerging Markets Private Equity Association

Project Preferences

Type of Financing Preferred:
Leveraged Buyout
Mezzanine
Generalist PE
Balanced

Geographical Preferences

International Preferences:
Latin America
Eastern Europe
Asia
Africa

Industry Preferences

In Industrial/Energy prefer:
Industrial Products

In Financial Services prefer:
Financial Services

In Business Serv. prefer:
Services

In Manufact. prefer:
Manufacturing

In Agr/Forestr/Fish prefer:
Agriculture related

In Other prefer:
Socially Responsible

Additional Information

Year Founded: 1962
Capital Under Management: $1,480,000,000
Current Activity Level : Actively seeking new investments

DELANY CAPITAL MANAGEMENT CORP

6972 Southeast Harbor Circle
Stuart, FL USA 34996
Phone: 7723342451
Fax: 6035164865
Website: www.dcmcorp.com

Management and Staff
Jim Elsner, Principal
Joel Motley, Principal
Logan Delany, President

Type of Firm
Private Equity Firm

Project Preferences

Type of Financing Preferred:
Leveraged Buyout

Industry Preferences

In Semiconductor/Electr prefer:
Electronic Components

In Business Serv. prefer:
Services

Additional Information
Year Founded: 2005
Current Activity Level : Actively seeking new investments

DELAVACO HOLDINGS INC

2300 East Las Olas Boulevard
Fifth Floor
Fort Lauderdale, FL USA 33301
Phone: 9547791930
Fax: 9547791933
Website: www.delavaco.com

Other Offices
Avenue Carrera Nine No. 113-52
Of. 1203
Bogota, Colombia
Phone: 5716373200
Fax: 5716373200

1 Richmond Street West
Suite 500
Toronto, Canada M5H 3W4
Phone: 4163624441
Fax: 4163622528

Management and Staff
John Martin, Chief Financial Officer
Michael Galloro, Chief Financial Officer

Type of Firm
Private Equity Firm

Project Preferences

Type of Financing Preferred:
Leveraged Buyout
Early Stage
Seed
Management Buyouts
Acquisition

Geographical Preferences

International Preferences:
Latin America
Eastern Europe
Africa

Industry Preferences

In Consumer Related prefer:
Retail
Other Restaurants

In Industrial/Energy prefer:
Energy

In Financial Services prefer:
Real Estate

In Agr/Forestr/Fish prefer:
Agriculture related
Mining and Minerals

Additional Information
Year Founded: 2007
Capital Under Management: $525,900,000
Current Activity Level : Actively seeking new investments

DELIN CAPITAL UK LTD

35 Portman Square
London, United Kingdom W1H 6LR
Phone: 4402074871244

Type of Firm
Private Equity Firm

Project Preferences

Type of Financing Preferred:
Early Stage

Additional Information
Year Founded: 2016
Current Activity Level : Actively seeking new investments

DELPHI VENTURES

160 Bovet Road
Suite 408
San Mateo, CA USA 94402
Phone: 6508549650
Website: www.delphiventures.com

Management and Staff
David Douglass, Partner
Deepika Pakianathan, Managing Partner
Douglas Roeder, Managing Partner
James Bochnowski, Founder

Type of Firm
Private Equity Firm

Association Membership
Western Association of Venture Capitalists (WAVC)
National Venture Capital Association - USA (NVCA)

Project Preferences

Role in Financing:
Will function either as deal originator or investor in deals created by others

Type of Financing Preferred:
Early Stage

Size of Investments Considered:
Min Size of Investment Considered (000s): $500
Max Size of Investment Considered (000s): $12,000

Geographical Preferences

United States Preferences:

Industry Focus
(% based on actual investment)
Medical/Health	66.5%
Biotechnology	21.0%
Internet Specific	4.8%
Computer Software and Services	2.9%
Computer Hardware	2.0%
Other Products	1.4%
Industrial/Energy	1.2%
Communications and Media	0.1%

Additional Information
Name of Most Recent Fund: Delphi Ventures VIII, L.P.
Most Recent Fund Was Raised: 06/10/2008
Year Founded: 1988
Capital Under Management: $1,100,000,000
Current Activity Level : Actively seeking new investments
Method of Compensation: Return on investment is of primary concern, do not charge fees

DELTA CAPITAL MANAGEMENT LLC

420 Lexington Avenue
Suite 1633
New York, NY USA 10170
Phone: 2129864040
E-mail: info@delta-capital.com

Management and Staff
Don Mundie, Managing Partner
William Coughlin, Managing Partner

Type of Firm
Private Equity Firm

Project Preferences

Role in Financing:
Will function either as deal originator or investor in deals created by others

Type of Financing Preferred:
Early Stage
Balanced
Later Stage

Size of Investments Considered:
Min Size of Investment Considered (000s): $500
Max Size of Investment Considered (000s): $1,500

Geographical Preferences

United States Preferences:
Tennessee
Mississippi
Southeast
Alabama
Arkansas

Industry Preferences

In Communications prefer:
Telecommunications
Wireless Communications

In Computer Software prefer:
Software
Applications Software

In Internet Specific prefer:
Internet
Ecommerce

In Medical/Health prefer:
Medical/Health
Medical Diagnostics
Diagnostic Services
Diagnostic Test Products
Medical Therapeutics
Drug/Equipmt Delivery
Medical Products
Disposable Med. Products
Health Services

In Transportation prefer:
Transportation

In Business Serv. prefer:
Distribution

Additional Information
Year Founded: 1992
Capital Under Management: $90,000,000
Current Activity Level : Actively seeking new investments
Method of Compensation: Return on investment is of primary concern, do not charge fees

DELTA CAPITAL MYANMAR

Bogyoke Aung San Street
380, FMI Centre, Office 701
Yangon, Burma
Phone: 951240363
E-mail: info@deltacapital.com
Website: www.deltacapital.com

Type of Firm
Private Equity Firm

Project Preferences

Type of Financing Preferred:
Balanced

Geographical Preferences

International Preferences:
Burma

Industry Preferences

In Communications prefer:
Telecommunications

In Medical/Health prefer:
Health Services

In Consumer Related prefer:
Consumer

In Financial Services prefer:
Financial Services

Additional Information
Year Founded: 2013
Capital Under Management: $80,000,000
Current Activity Level : Actively seeking new investments

DELTA PARTNERS FZ LLC

Media One, Dubai Media City
Level 29, P.O. Box 502428
Dubai, Utd. Arab Em.
Phone: 971-43692999
Fax: 971-43688408
E-mail: info@deltapartnersgroup.com
Website: www.deltapartnersgroup.com

Other Offices
P.O. Box 783719
Santon
Johannesburg, South Africa 2146
Phone: 27-11-881-5957
Fax: 27-11-881-5611

Management and Staff
Alberto Pamias, Managing Partner
Josep Maria Moya, Partner
Kristoff Puelinckx, Managing Director
Victor Font, Managing Director

Type of Firm
Investment Management Firm

Association Membership
Emerging Markets Private Equity Association

Project Preferences

Type of Financing Preferred:
Leveraged Buyout
Early Stage
Expansion
Generalist PE
Balanced
Later Stage
Acquisition

Geographical Preferences

International Preferences:
Central Europe
Eastern Europe
Middle East
Asia
Africa

Industry Preferences

In Communications prefer:
Communications and Media
Radio & TV Broadcasting
Telecommunications
Media and Entertainment

In Business Serv. prefer:
Media

Additional Information
Year Founded: 2006
Capital Under Management: $200,000,000
Current Activity Level : Actively seeking new investments

DELTA PARTNERS LTD

South County Business Park
Leopardstown
Dublin, Ireland 18
Phone: 35312940870
Fax: 35312940877
Website: www.delta.ie

Other Offices
55 Newman Street
London, United Kingdom W1T 3EB
Phone: 442036429329

Management and Staff
Dermot Berkery, General Partner
Frank Kenny, Founder
John O Sullivan, Chief Financial Officer
Maurice Roche, General Partner
Rob Johnson, Venture Partner

Type of Firm
Private Equity Firm

Association Membership
Irish Venture Capital Association
European Private Equity and Venture Capital Assoc.

Project Preferences

Role in Financing:
Prefer role as deal originator but will also invest in deals created by others

Type of Financing Preferred:
Early Stage
Balanced

Size of Investments Considered:
Min Size of Investment Considered (000s): $655
Max Size of Investment Considered (000s): $3,929

Geographical Preferences

International Preferences:
Ireland
United Kingdom
Europe

Industry Focus
(% based on actual investment)

Computer Software and Services	30.3%
Internet Specific	20.3%
Other Products	20.1%
Medical/Health	15.1%
Communications and Media	6.1%
Biotechnology	4.4%
Semiconductors/Other Elect.	3.7%

Additional Information
Name of Most Recent Fund: Bank of Ireland Start-up & Emerging Sectors Equity Fund 2010
Most Recent Fund Was Raised: 12/21/2010
Year Founded: 1994
Capital Under Management: $360,500,000
Current Activity Level : Actively seeking new investments
Method of Compensation: Return on investment is of primary concern, do not charge fees

DELTA PROJET SICAR

2 Avenue de France
Tunis, Tunisia 1000
Phone: 216 71762516
Fax: 21671762824

Type of Firm
Private Equity Firm

Project Preferences

Type of Financing Preferred:
Early Stage
Later Stage
Startup

Geographical Preferences

International Preferences:
Tunisia
Africa

Additional Information
Year Founded: 2004
Current Activity Level : Actively seeking new investments

DELTA-V CAPITAL LLC

4514 Cole Avenue
Suite 1225
Boulder, CO USA 80302
Website: www.deltavcapital.com

Type of Firm
Private Equity Firm

Project Preferences

Type of Financing Preferred:
Later Stage

Size of Investments Considered:
Min Size of Investment Considered (000s): $2,000
Max Size of Investment Considered (000s): $20,000

Additional Information
Year Founded: 2009
Capital Under Management: $232,000,000
Current Activity Level : Actively seeking new investments

DELTAPOINT CAPITAL MANAGEMENT LLC

45 East Avenue, Sixth Floor
Rochester, NY USA 14604
Phone: 5854546990
Fax: 5854543204
E-mail: info@deltapointcapital.com
Website: www.deltapointcapital.com

Management and Staff
David Waterman, Managing Director
Jason Hall, Vice President
John Cordes, Managing Director
Kevin Halpin, Managing Director
Thomas Cimino, Co-Founder
Thomas Cimino, Managing Director

Type of Firm
Private Equity Firm

Project Preferences

Role in Financing:
Prefer role as deal originator but will also invest in deals created by others

Type of Financing Preferred:
Leveraged Buyout
Management Buyouts
Acquisition
Recapitalizations

Geographical Preferences

United States Preferences:
Northeast

Industry Preferences

In Business Serv. prefer:
Services
Distribution

In Manufact. prefer:
Manufacturing

Additional Information
Year Founded: 1997
Capital Under Management: $100,000,000
Current Activity Level : Actively seeking new investments
Method of Compensation: Return on investment is of primary concern, do not charge fees

DEMETER SAS

7-9 rue de la Boetie
Paris, France 75008
Phone: 33143125333
Fax: 33143125330
E-mail: contact@demeter-partners.com

Other Offices
c/ Jose Abascal 52 2izda
Madrid, Spain 28003
Phone: 34-915-639-704
Fax: 34-915-619-506

Kurfurstendamm 119
Berlin, Germany 10711
Phone: 49-30-8906-82968
Fax: 49-30-8906-82961

Management and Staff
Lionel Cormier, Partner
Marcos Semmler, Venture Partner
Michel Ronc, Partner
Sophie Paturle Guesnerot, Partner
Stephane Villecroze, Partner

Type of Firm
Private Equity Firm

Association Membership
French Venture Capital Association (AFIC)
German Venture Capital Association (BVK)
Spanish Venture Capital Association (ASCRI)

Project Preferences

Type of Financing Preferred:
Leveraged Buyout
Early Stage
Generalist PE
Later Stage
Seed
Acquisition
Startup

Size of Investments Considered:
Min Size of Investment Considered (000s): $2,736
Max Size of Investment Considered (000s): $20,522

Geographical Preferences

International Preferences:
Europe
Spain
Germany
France

Industry Preferences

In Industrial/Energy prefer:
Energy
Alternative Energy
Energy Conservation Relat
Environmental Related

In Other prefer:
Environment Responsible

Additional Information

Name of Most Recent Fund: Demeter 3 Amorcage FCPR
Most Recent Fund Was Raised: 09/20/2012
Year Founded: 2005
Capital Under Management: $321,500,000
Current Activity Level : Actively seeking new investments

DEMPSEY VENTURES INC

217 Grandville Avenue SW
Suite 402
Grand Rapids, MI USA 49503
Phone: 6166089693
E-mail: info@dempseyventures.com
Website: dempseyventures.com

Type of Firm
Private Equity Firm

Project Preferences

Type of Financing Preferred:
Leveraged Buyout
Later Stage
Acquisition
Recapitalizations

Geographical Preferences

United States Preferences:

Industry Preferences

In Medical/Health prefer:
Medical/Health
Medical Products

In Business Serv. prefer:
Distribution

In Manufact. prefer:
Manufacturing

Additional Information
Year Founded: 2006
Current Activity Level : Actively seeking new investments

DENOVO HEALTH PARTNERS LLC

11111 Santa Monica Boulevard, Suite 1125
West Los Angeles, CA USA 90025
Phone: 3104556355
Fax: 3104925012
E-mail: Info@DenovoHealthPartners.com
Website: denovohealthpartners.com

Management and Staff
Glenn Golenberg, Co-Founder
Jonathan Doctor, Co-Founder
Sherwin Voss, Co-Founder

Type of Firm
Private Equity Firm

Project Preferences

Type of Financing Preferred:
Leveraged Buyout
Management Buyouts
Acquisition

Geographical Preferences

United States Preferences:

Industry Preferences

In Computer Software prefer:
Software

In Medical/Health prefer:
Medical/Health
Medical Products
Health Services

In Industrial/Energy prefer:
Process Control

In Business Serv. prefer:
Services

In Manufact. prefer:
Manufacturing

Additional Information
Year Founded: 1969
Current Activity Level : Actively seeking new investments

DENTSUCOM

1-8-1 Higashi-Shinkyo
Minato-Ku
Tokyo, Japan 1057001
Phone: 81362521703
Fax: 81362521705
E-mail: info@dentsu-digital.co.jp
Website: www.dentsu-digital.co.jp

Type of Firm
Corporate PE/Venture

Project Preferences

Type of Financing Preferred:
Early Stage
Balanced
Public Companies
Later Stage
Joint Ventures

Geographical Preferences

United States Preferences:
All U.S.

International Preferences:
Europe
China
Asia
Japan

Industry Preferences

In Communications prefer:
Communications and Media
Wireless Communications

In Computer Hardware prefer:
Computer Graphics and Dig

Additional Information
Year Founded: 2000
Capital Under Management: $107,530,000
Current Activity Level : Actively seeking new investments

DEPARTMENT OF VENTURES

Kommendorsgatan 5
Stockholm, Sweden 114 48
Phone: 46841045555
E-mail: info@departmentofventures.com
Website: departmentofventures.se

Type of Firm
Private Equity Firm

Project Preferences

Type of Financing Preferred:
Early Stage
Seed
Startup

Size of Investments Considered:
Min Size of Investment Considered (000s): $145
Max Size of Investment Considered (000s): $1,448

Geographical Preferences

International Preferences:
Scandanavia/Nordic Region

651

Additional Information
Year Founded: 2009
Current Activity Level : Actively seeking new investments

DERWENT LONDON PLC
25 Savile Row
London, United Kingdom W1S 2ER
Phone: 442076593000
Fax: 442076593100
E-mail: mail@derwentlondon.com
Website: www.derwentlondon.com

Management and Staff
Glenn Payne, Chief Executive Officer
John Burns, Chief Executive Officer
Tony Sweet, Chief Financial Officer

Type of Firm
Private Equity Firm

Project Preferences

Role in Financing:
Prefer role in deals created by others

Type of Financing Preferred:
Early Stage
Expansion
Balanced

Geographical Preferences

United States Preferences:

International Preferences:
United Kingdom
No Preference
All International

Industry Preferences

In Communications prefer:
Communications and Media

In Computer Software prefer:
Software

In Internet Specific prefer:
Internet

Additional Information
Name of Most Recent Fund: Westpool Investment Trust PLC
Most Recent Fund Was Raised: 08/01/1983
Year Founded: 1984
Capital Under Management: $200,000,000
Current Activity Level : Actively seeking new investments
Method of Compensation: Return on investment is of primary concern, do not charge fees

DESERT CEDARS LLC
5346 Calle Del Norte
Phoenix, AZ USA 85018
Phone: 602-840-8611

Management and Staff
Michael Koslow, Managing Partner
Patricia Koslow, Managing Partner

Type of Firm
Private Equity Firm

Project Preferences

Type of Financing Preferred:
Core

Industry Preferences

In Financial Services prefer:
Real Estate

Additional Information
Year Founded: 2002
Capital Under Management: $1,900,000
Current Activity Level : Actively seeking new investments

DESHI ZHONGYUAN INVESTMENT MANAGEMENT CO LTD
C/o, Orica Capital.
Shanghai, China

Type of Firm
Private Equity Firm

Project Preferences

Type of Financing Preferred:
Balanced

Geographical Preferences

International Preferences:
China

Industry Preferences

In Medical/Health prefer:
Medical Diagnostics

In Consumer Related prefer:
Education Related

In Industrial/Energy prefer:
Energy Conservation Relat
Advanced Materials
Machinery

In Business Serv. prefer:
Services

In Manufact. prefer:
Manufacturing

In Agr/Forestr/Fish prefer:
Agriculture related

In Other prefer:
Environment Responsible

Additional Information
Year Founded: 2011
Current Activity Level : Actively seeking new investments

DESIGNER FUND
164 Townsend
Unit 3
San Francisco, CA USA 94107
Website: designerfund.com

Type of Firm
Private Equity Firm

Project Preferences

Type of Financing Preferred:
Startup

Industry Preferences

In Medical/Health prefer:
Health Services

In Consumer Related prefer:
Education Related

In Industrial/Energy prefer:
Energy

Additional Information
Year Founded: 1969
Capital Under Management: $20,000,000
Current Activity Level : Actively seeking new investments

DESIMONE GROUP INVESTMENTS LLC
Six Esterbrook Lane
Cherry Hill, NJ USA 08003
Phone: 8567610740
Fax: 8567610749
E-mail: info@desimonegroup.com
Website: www.desimonegroup.com

Management and Staff
John Goodwin, Managing Partner
Kendra Brill, Managing Partner

Type of Firm
Private Equity Firm

Project Preferences

Type of Financing Preferred:
Early Stage
Expansion
Balanced
Later Stage
Seed

Geographical Preferences

United States Preferences:
Pennsylvania

Industry Preferences

In Industrial/Energy prefer:
Energy

In Manufact. prefer:
Manufacturing

Additional Information

Year Founded: 1969
Current Activity Level : Actively seeking new investments

DESJARDINS CAPITAL

2. Complexe Desjardins
bureau 1717, Case postale 760
Montreal, Canada H5B 1B8
Phone: 5142817131
Fax: 5142817808
Website: www.dcrdesjardins.com

Management and Staff

Luc Menard, Chief Operating Officer
Sylvain Dupuis, Vice President

Type of Firm

Bank Affiliated

Project Preferences

Role in Financing:
Prefer role as deal originator but will also invest in deals created by others

Type of Financing Preferred:
Leveraged Buyout
Early Stage
Expansion
Mezzanine
Generalist PE
Later Stage
Seed
Acquisition
Startup

Geographical Preferences

Canadian Preferences:
Quebec

Industry Focus

(% based on actual investment)
Other Products	35.5%
Consumer Related	16.3%
Computer Software and Services	11.3%
Industrial/Energy	8.1%
Communications and Media	8.1%
Medical/Health	5.4%
Semiconductors/Other Elect.	5.3%
Biotechnology	4.9%
Internet Specific	4.2%
Computer Hardware	0.9%

Additional Information

Name of Most Recent Fund: Capital croissance PME II
Most Recent Fund Was Raised: 01/01/2014
Year Founded: 1974
Capital Under Management: $150,000,000
Current Activity Level : Actively seeking new investments
Method of Compensation: Return on invest. most important, but chg. closing fees, service fees, etc.

DETROIT RENAISSANCE

600 Renaissance Center
Suite 1760
Detroit, MI USA 48243
Phone: 3132595400
E-mail: info@businessleadersformichigan.com
Website: www.businessleadersformichigan.com

Management and Staff

Kelly Chesney, Vice President
Sabrina Keeley, Chief Operating Officer
Tim Sowton, Vice President

Type of Firm

Private Equity Advisor or Fund of Funds

Project Preferences

Type of Financing Preferred:
Fund of Funds

Geographical Preferences

United States Preferences:
Michigan

Additional Information

Name of Most Recent Fund: Renaissance Venture Capital Fund II, L.P.
Most Recent Fund Was Raised: 05/22/2012
Year Founded: 2007
Capital Under Management: $131,000,000
Current Activity Level : Actively seeking new investments

DETROIT VENTURE PARTNERS LLC

1555 Broadway Street, Third Floor
Detroit, MI USA 48226
E-mail: Info@DetroitVenturePartners.com
Website: detroitventurepartners.com

Management and Staff

Dan Gilbert, General Partner
Jared Stasik, Vice President

Type of Firm

Private Equity Firm

Association Membership

National Venture Capital Association - USA (NVCA)

Project Preferences

Type of Financing Preferred:
Early Stage
Seed

Geographical Preferences

United States Preferences:
Michigan

Industry Preferences

In Computer Software prefer:
Software
Applications Software

Additional Information

Name of Most Recent Fund: Detroit Venture Partners, L.P.
Most Recent Fund Was Raised: 08/13/2013
Year Founded: 2010
Capital Under Management: $55,000,000
Current Activity Level : Actively seeking new investments

DEUTSCHE BETEILIGUNGS AG

Boersenstrasse 1
Frankfurt, Germany 60313
Phone: 49699578701
Fax: 496995787199
E-mail: welcome@deutsche-beteiligung.de
Website: www.dbag.com

Management and Staff

Andreas Paulke, Chief Financial Officer
Susanne Zeidler, Chief Financial Officer

Type of Firm

Private Equity Firm

Association Membership

German Venture Capital Association (BVK)

Project Preferences

Role in Financing:
Prefer role as deal originator but will also invest in deals created by others

Type of Financing Preferred:
Leveraged Buyout
Later Stage
Management Buyouts

Geographical Preferences

International Preferences:
Europe
Switzerland
Austria
Germany

Industry Focus

(% based on actual investment)
Other Products	50.7%
Industrial/Energy	30.9%
Internet Specific	14.2%
Consumer Related	4.3%

Additional Information
Name of Most Recent Fund: DBAG Fund VI
Most Recent Fund Was Raised: 06/29/2012
Year Founded: 2004
Capital Under Management: $1,780,300,000
Current Activity Level : Actively seeking new investments

DEUTSCHE EFFECTEN UND WECHSEL BETEILIGUNGS-GESELLSCHAFT AG

Fraunhoferstrasse 1
Jena, Germany 07743
Phone: 4936413100030
Fax: 4936413100040
E-mail: info@dewb-vc.com

Management and Staff
Bertram Kohler, Chief Executive Officer

Type of Firm
Private Equity Firm

Association Membership
German Venture Capital Association (BVK)

Project Preferences

Type of Financing Preferred:
Leveraged Buyout
Early Stage
Later Stage
Seed
Management Buyouts
Acquisition
Startup

Size of Investments Considered:
Min Size of Investment Considered (000s): $1,438
Max Size of Investment Considered (000s): $10,066

Geographical Preferences

International Preferences:
Switzerland
Austria
Germany

Industry Preferences

In Communications prefer:
Telecommunications

In Semiconductor/Electr prefer:
Controllers and Sensors
Sensors
Fiber Optics
Optoelectronics

In Biotechnology prefer:
Biotechnology

Additional Information
Year Founded: 1997
Capital Under Management: $110,900,000
Current Activity Level : Actively seeking new investments

DEUTSCHE MITTELSTAND-SHOLDING GMBH

Guiollettstrasse 19
Frankfurt am Main, Germany 60325
Phone: 496994597814
Fax: 496958607904
Website: deutschemittelstandsholding.de

Type of Firm
Private Equity Firm

Project Preferences

Type of Financing Preferred:
Leveraged Buyout
Turnaround
Acquisition
Special Situation

Geographical Preferences

International Preferences:
Europe
Western Europe
Germany

Industry Preferences

In Consumer Related prefer:
Sports

In Industrial/Energy prefer:
Machinery

Additional Information
Year Founded: 2012
Current Activity Level : Actively seeking new investments

DEUTSCHE TELEKOM AG

Winterfeldtstr 21
Berlin, Germany 10781
Phone: 492281810
E-mail: contact@hubraum.com
Website: www.telekom.com

Management and Staff
Thomas Dannenfeldt, Chief Financial Officer

Type of Firm
Incubator/Development Program

Project Preferences

Type of Financing Preferred:
Early Stage
Seed
Startup

Geographical Preferences

International Preferences:
Europe
Germany

Additional Information
Year Founded: 2012
Current Activity Level : Actively seeking new investments

DEUTSCHE TELEKOM STRATEGIC INVESTMENTS

Graurheindorfer
Str 153-159
Bonn, Germany 53117
Phone: 49228308480
Fax: 4922830848819
E-mail: t-venture@telekom.de
Website: www.telekom.com

Other Offices
950 Tower Lane
Suite 1600
SAN MATEO, CA USA 94404
Phone: 650-358-2011
Fax: 650-292-8353

Management and Staff
Georg Schwegler, CEO & Managing Director
Patrick Meisberger, Managing Director

Type of Firm
Corporate PE/Venture

Association Membership
German Venture Capital Association (BVK)
European Private Equity and Venture Capital Assoc.

Project Preferences

Type of Financing Preferred:
Early Stage
Expansion
Balanced
Later Stage
Seed
Startup

Size of Investments Considered:
Min Size of Investment Considered (000s): $670
Max Size of Investment Considered (000s): $6,700

Geographical Preferences

United States Preferences:
All U.S.

Canadian Preferences:
All Canada

International Preferences:
Ireland
United Kingdom
Europe
Netherlands
Switzerland
China
Austria
Israel
Asia
Germany
France

Industry Preferences

In Communications prefer:
Communications and Media
Telecommunications
Wireless Communications
Other Communication Prod.

In Computer Software prefer:
Applications Software

In Internet Specific prefer:
Internet

In Business Serv. prefer:
Services

Additional Information

Year Founded: 1997
Capital Under Management: $440,400,000
Current Activity Level : Actively seeking new investments

DEV EQUITY LLC

877 South Alvernon Way
Suite 200A
Tucson, AZ USA 85711
Phone: 5203183810
E-mail: contact@devequity.com
Website: devequity.com

Management and Staff
Carl Reinhardt, General Partner
Farzad Alvi, General Partner
Forrest Metz, Founder
Jim Kolbe, General Partner
Jonathan Lewis, General Partner

Type of Firm
Private Equity Firm

Project Preferences

Type of Financing Preferred:
Leveraged Buyout
Acquisition

Geographical Preferences

International Preferences:
Latin America

Industry Preferences

In Industrial/Energy prefer:
Environmental Related

In Other prefer:
Socially Responsible
Environment Responsible

Additional Information
Name of Most Recent Fund: Dev Equity, L.P.
Most Recent Fund Was Raised: 07/13/2011
Year Founded: 2011
Capital Under Management: $5,005,000
Current Activity Level : Actively seeking new investments

DEVELOPING WORLD MARKETS INC

750 Washington Boulevard
Suite 500
Stamford, CT USA 06901
Phone: 2036555453
Fax: 2036569528
E-mail: info@dwmarkets.com
Website: www.dwmarkets.com

Management and Staff
Aleem Remtula, Vice President
Bogdan Tatarchevskiy, Vice President
Brad Swanson, Partner
Courtland Walker, Vice President
Gretell Merlo, Vice President
James Kaddaras, Partner
Kathryn Barrios, Managing Director
Patrick Ball, Vice President
Peter Johnson, Partner

Type of Firm
Investment Management Firm

Project Preferences

Type of Financing Preferred:
Leveraged Buyout
Acquisition

Geographical Preferences

United States Preferences:

International Preferences:
Eastern Europe
Middle East
Asia
Russia
Africa

Additional Information
Year Founded: 1994
Current Activity Level : Actively seeking new investments

DEVELOPMENT BANK OF WALES PUBLIC LTD CO

Oakleigh House
Park Place
Cardiff, United Kingdom CF10 3DQ
Phone: 442920338100
Fax: 442920338101
E-mail: info@financewales.co.uk
Website: www.financewales.co.uk

Other Offices
St. David's House
New Road
Newtown, United Kingdom SY16 1RB
Phone: 44-1686-613-352

Llys Llewelyn, St Asaph Business Park
Ffordd Richard Davies
St Asaph, United Kingdom LL17 0LJ
Phone: 44-1745-582-501

Axis 3, Axis Court, Mallard Way
Riverside Business Park
Swansea, United Kingdom SA7 0AJ
Phone: 44-1792-762-350

Type of Firm
Incubator/Development Program

Association Membership
British Venture Capital Association (BVCA)

Project Preferences

Type of Financing Preferred:
Leveraged Buyout
Early Stage
Expansion
Mezzanine
Balanced
Seed
Startup

Geographical Preferences

International Preferences:
United Kingdom

Industry Preferences

In Computer Software prefer:
Software

In Semiconductor/Electr prefer:
Electronics

In Medical/Health prefer:
Medical/Health
Medical Products

In Industrial/Energy prefer:
Energy
Environmental Related

Additional Information

Name of Most Recent Fund: Finance Wales IV
Most Recent Fund Was Raised: 04/24/2009
Year Founded: 1999
Capital Under Management: $38,000,000
Current Activity Level : Actively seeking new investments

DEVELOPMENT PARTNERS INTERNATIONAL LLP

28 Chelsea Wharf, Lots Road
London, United Kingdom SW10 0QJ
Phone: 442073495030
Fax: 442073495038
E-mail: info@dpi-llp.com
Website: www.dpi-llp.com

Management and Staff

Eduardo Gutierrez, Partner
Idris Mohammed, Partner
Miles Morland, Partner
Sarah Shackleton, Partner
Sofiane Lahmar, Partner

Type of Firm

Private Equity Firm

Association Membership

South African Venture Capital Association (SAVCA)
Emerging Markets Private Equity Association
African Venture Capital Association (AVCA)

Project Preferences

Type of Financing Preferred:
Leveraged Buyout
Expansion

Geographical Preferences

International Preferences:
Guernsey
Africa

Industry Preferences

In Medical/Health prefer:
Health Services

In Consumer Related prefer:
Consumer
Consumer Services

In Industrial/Energy prefer:
Oil and Gas Exploration

In Transportation prefer:
Transportation

In Financial Services prefer:
Real Estate
Financial Services

Additional Information

Name of Most Recent Fund: African Development Partners II, L.P.
Most Recent Fund Was Raised: 07/23/2013
Year Founded: 2007
Capital Under Management: $725,000,000
Current Activity Level : Actively seeking new investments

DEVELOPPEMENT ET PARTENARIAT PME SAS

152 avenue de Malakoff
Paris, France 75116
Phone: 33156797900
Fax: 33156797910
E-mail: contact@developart.com
Website: www.dp-finance.fr

Management and Staff

Didier Calmels, President
Thierry Jullien, Vice President

Type of Firm

Private Equity Firm

Association Membership

French Venture Capital Association (AFIC)

Project Preferences

Type of Financing Preferred:
Leveraged Buyout
Early Stage
Generalist PE
Turnaround
Later Stage
Management Buyouts
Acquisition
Recapitalizations

Geographical Preferences

International Preferences:
Europe
France

Industry Preferences

In Industrial/Energy prefer:
Industrial Products

In Business Serv. prefer:
Services

Additional Information

Name of Most Recent Fund: Developpement et Partenariats V FCPR
Most Recent Fund Was Raised: 12/22/2010
Year Founded: 2003
Capital Under Management: $83,500,000
Current Activity Level : Actively seeking new investments

DEVON PARK BIOVENTURES LP

1400 Liberty Ridge Drive
Suite 103
Wayne, PA USA 19087
Phone: 4843204900
Fax: 4843204920
Website: www.dpbioventures.com

Management and Staff

Christopher Moller, General Partner
Devang Kantesaria, General Partner
John Leaman, Principal
Marc Ostro, General Partner

Type of Firm

Private Equity Firm

Project Preferences

Role in Financing:
Prefer role as deal originator but will also invest in deals created by others

Type of Financing Preferred:
Later Stage

Industry Preferences

In Biotechnology prefer:
Biotechnology

In Medical/Health prefer:
Medical/Health
Medical Therapeutics
Drug/Equipmt Delivery
Medical Products

Additional Information

Name of Most Recent Fund: Devon Park Bioventures, L.P.
Most Recent Fund Was Raised: 02/17/2006
Year Founded: 2006
Capital Under Management: $100,000,000
Current Activity Level : Actively seeking new investments
Method of Compensation: Return on investment is of primary concern, do not charge fees

DFJ ATHENA

55 East Third Avenue
San Mateo, CA USA 94401
E-mail: info@dfjathena.com
Website: www.dfjathena.com

Other Offices

#712 Seocho-gu Heolleung-no 7
7th Floor
Seoul, South Korea 137-749

Management and Staff

Charles Rim, Venture Partner
Daniel Chang, Venture Partner
Henry Chung, Managing Director
John Rockwell, Venture Partner
Perry Ha, Founder
Steven Lee, Venture Partner
Warren Packard, Venture Partner

Type of Firm

Private Equity Firm

Project Preferences

Role in Financing:
Will function either as deal originator or investor in deals created by others

Type of Financing Preferred:
Early Stage
Expansion
Seed
Startup

Geographical Preferences

United States Preferences:

International Preferences:
Korea, South

Industry Focus

(% based on actual investment)

Internet Specific	33.8%
Computer Software and Services	21.6%
Computer Hardware	17.0%
Semiconductors/Other Elect.	9.3%
Industrial/Energy	8.6%
Communications and Media	4.4%
Other Products	3.8%
Consumer Related	1.5%

Additional Information

Name of Most Recent Fund: DFJ Athena, L.P.
Most Recent Fund Was Raised: 12/28/2007
Year Founded: 2007
Capital Under Management: $150,000,000
Current Activity Level : Actively seeking new investments

DFW CAPITAL PARTNERS LP

300 Frank West Burr Boulevard
Glenpointe Centre East, 5th Fl
Teaneck, NJ USA 07666
Phone: 2018366000
Fax: 2018365666
Website: www.dfwcapital.com

Other Offices

1050 Connecticut Avenue Northwest
Connecticut Ave. NorthWest Suite 1019
Washington, DC USA 20036
Phone: 2027721068

Management and Staff

Brett Prager, Managing Partner
Brian Tilley, General Partner
Cheri Lieberman, Chief Financial Officer
Donald DeMuth, General Partner
Douglas Gilbert, General Partner
Keith Pennell, Managing Partner

Type of Firm

Private Equity Firm

Project Preferences

Role in Financing:
Prefer role as deal originator but will also invest in deals created by others

Type of Financing Preferred:
Leveraged Buyout
Expansion
Generalist PE
Management Buyouts
Acquisition
Recapitalizations

Size of Investments Considered:
Min Size of Investment Considered (000s): $5,000
Max Size of Investment Considered (000s): $10,000

Geographical Preferences

United States Preferences:
All U.S.

Industry Focus

(% based on actual investment)

Medical/Health	47.8%
Consumer Related	10.3%
Internet Specific	8.9%
Communications and Media	8.8%
Semiconductors/Other Elect.	6.3%
Computer Hardware	6.3%
Computer Software and Services	3.6%
Other Products	3.3%
Biotechnology	3.0%
Industrial/Energy	1.6%

Additional Information

Name of Most Recent Fund: DFW Capital Partners IV, L.P.
Most Recent Fund Was Raised: 11/29/2012
Year Founded: 1983
Capital Under Management: $40,000,000
Current Activity Level : Actively seeking new investments
Method of Compensation: Return on investment is of primary concern, do not charge fees

DGC CAPITAL INC

999 de Maisonneuve Boulevard W
Suite 1000
Montreal, Canada H3A 3L4

Type of Firm

Private Equity Firm

Additional Information

Year Founded: 2017
Current Activity Level : Actively seeking new investments

DGF INVESTIMENTOS GESTAO DE FUNDOS LTDA

Av Paulista 1337
Andar 2, Conj 21, Bela Vista
Sao Paulo, Brazil 01311200
Phone: 551133723300
Website: www.dgf.com.br

Management and Staff

Antonio J.L. Duarte, Principal
Celso Nunes, Principal
Dario Boralli, Partner
Frederico Greve, Managing Partner
Humberto Casagrande, Managing Partner
Patrick Arippol, Principal
Sidney Chameh, Partner

Type of Firm

Private Equity Firm

Association Membership

Brazilian Venture Capital Association (ABCR)

Project Preferences

Type of Financing Preferred:
Early Stage
Balanced
Startup

Geographical Preferences

International Preferences:
Latin America
Brazil

Industry Preferences

In Computer Software prefer:
Software

In Medical/Health prefer:
Medical/Health

In Consumer Related prefer:
Consumer
Consumer Products
Consumer Services

In Industrial/Energy prefer:
Energy

In Transportation prefer:
Transportation

In Financial Services prefer:
Financial Services
Insurance

In Business Serv. prefer:
Services

Additional Information
Name of Most Recent Fund: DGF Capital III
Most Recent Fund Was Raised: 06/22/2012
Year Founded: 2001
Capital Under Management: $171,938,000
Current Activity Level : Actively seeking new investments

DGNL VENTURES LP

915 Broadwat, 20th Floor
New York, NY USA 10010
Phone: 2126270001
Website: www.dgnl.vc

Management and Staff
Desiree Gruber, Co-Founder
Nir Liberboim, Co-Founder

Type of Firm
Private Equity Firm

Industry Preferences

In Communications prefer:
Entertainment

In Internet Specific prefer:
Ecommerce

In Medical/Health prefer:
Health Services

In Consumer Related prefer:
Food/Beverage
Consumer Services

Additional Information
Year Founded: 2016
Current Activity Level : Actively seeking new investments

DHV MANAGEMENT GMBH

Exerzierstrasse 17
Berlin, Germany 13357
Phone: 493072024994

Website: dhventures.de

Type of Firm
Private Equity Firm

Project Preferences

Type of Financing Preferred:
Early Stage

Industry Preferences

In Medical/Health prefer:
Health Services

Additional Information
Year Founded: 2014
Current Activity Level : Actively seeking new investments

DIAMOND CAPITAL MANAGEMENT LLC

5311 N Plaza Drive
Menomonee Falls, WI USA 53051
Phone: 262-790-9175
Fax: 262-790-9175
Website: www.diamondcapitalmgmt.com

Type of Firm
Private Equity Firm

Additional Information
Year Founded: 2009
Current Activity Level : Actively seeking new investments

DIAMOND CASTLE HOLDINGS LLC

280 Park Avenue
25th Floor, East Tower
New York, NY USA 10017
Phone: 2123001900
Fax: 2129831234
Website: www.dchold.com

Management and Staff
Andrew Rush, Co-Founder
Ari Benacerraf, Co-Founder
David Wittels, Co-Founder
Eric Nadan, Principal
Lee Wright, Senior Managing Director
Linda Grogan, Chief Financial Officer
Michael Langer, Principal
Michael Ranger, Co-Founder
Simon Roberts, Senior Managing Director
Stephen Bassford, Senior Managing Director

Type of Firm
Private Equity Firm

Project Preferences

Type of Financing Preferred:
Leveraged Buyout
Expansion
Acquisition
Special Situation
Recapitalizations

Geographical Preferences

United States Preferences:

Canadian Preferences:
All Canada

Industry Preferences

In Communications prefer:
Communications and Media

In Medical/Health prefer:
Medical/Health

In Consumer Related prefer:
Retail

In Industrial/Energy prefer:
Energy

In Financial Services prefer:
Financial Services

In Business Serv. prefer:
Services

Additional Information
Name of Most Recent Fund: Diamond Castle Partners IV, L.P.
Most Recent Fund Was Raised: 10/27/2005
Year Founded: 2004
Capital Under Management: $1,850,000,000
Current Activity Level : Actively seeking new investments

DIAMOND STATE VENTURES LP

445 Hamilton Avenue
Suite 1102
White Plains, NY USA 10601
Phone: 9142208337
Fax: 9144284001
Website: www.diamondstateventures.com

Other Offices
445 Hamilton Avenue
Suite 1102
White Plains, NY USA 10601
Phone: 914-220-8337
Fax: 914-428-4001

Type of Firm
Private Equity Firm

Project Preferences

Type of Financing Preferred:
Management Buyouts

Size of Investments Considered:
Min Size of Investment Considered (000s): $10,000
Max Size of Investment Considered (000s): $100,000

Geographical Preferences

United States Preferences:
All U.S.

Industry Preferences

In Consumer Related prefer:
Retail
Consumer Products

Additional Information

Year Founded: 2005
Current Activity Level : Actively seeking new investments

DIAMOND STATE VENTURES, L.P.

200 River Market Avenue
Suite 400
Little Rock, AR USA 72201
Phone: 5013749247
Fax: 5013749425
Website: www.diamondstateventures.com

Other Offices

2905 King Street
Jonesboro, AR USA 72403
Phone: 870-932-8002
Fax: 870-932-0135

The Chamber Building
West 3rd
Fordyce, AR USA 71742
Phone: 870-352-2853
Fax: 870-352-5126

700 Research Centre Boulevard
Suite 1608
Fayetteville, AR USA 72701
Phone: 479-444-8881
Fax: 479-444-8882

Management and Staff

Joe Hays, Founder
Larry Carter, Managing Director

Type of Firm

Private Equity Firm

Association Membership

Natl Assoc of Small Bus. Inv. Co (NASBIC)

Project Preferences

Role in Financing:
Will function either as deal originator or investor in deals created by others

Type of Financing Preferred:
Leveraged Buyout
Turnaround
Later Stage
Management Buyouts
Acquisition
Recapitalizations

Size of Investments Considered:
Min Size of Investment Considered (000s): $1,000
Max Size of Investment Considered (000s): $6,000

Geographical Preferences

United States Preferences:
Midwest
Southeast
Southwest
Arkansas

Industry Preferences

In Medical/Health prefer:
Health Services

In Consumer Related prefer:
Consumer Products
Education Related

In Business Serv. prefer:
Services
Media

In Manufact. prefer:
Manufacturing

Additional Information

Name of Most Recent Fund: Diamond State Ventures III, L.P.
Most Recent Fund Was Raised: 02/03/2014
Year Founded: 1999
Capital Under Management: $56,000,000
Current Activity Level : Actively seeking new investments
Method of Compensation: Return on invest. most important, but chg. closing fees, service fees, etc.

DIAMOND TECHVENTURES

360 Bryant Street
Suite 100
Palo Alto, CA USA 94301
Phone: 6508380813
Fax: 4134032106
E-mail: info@diamondtechventures.com
Website: www.diamondtechventures.com

Other Offices

No.1, Summer Palace Road
Peking Univ. Resource Hotel, Suite 1412
Beijing, China 100080
Phone: 86-139-11715700

Management and Staff

Henry Wong, Founder

Type of Firm

Private Equity Firm

Project Preferences

Type of Financing Preferred:
Balanced

Geographical Preferences

International Preferences:
China

Industry Preferences

In Communications prefer:
Wireless Communications

Additional Information

Year Founded: 2010
Current Activity Level : Actively seeking new investments

DIANA CAPITAL SGECR SA

Torre Europa Building
Paseo Castellana 95
Madrid, Spain 28046
Phone: 34914262329
Fax: 34914262330
E-mail: diana@dianacapital.com
Website: www.dianacapital.com

Other Offices

Ninth Street
Suite 99 - 45
Bogota, Colombia
Phone: 5715209770
Fax: 5715205872

Paseo de la Castellana, 95
29th Floor
, Spain 28046

Management and Staff

Daniel Sandoval, Principal
David Polo, Principal
Elena Pajarin, Principal
Francisco Gomez-Zubeldia, Managing Director

Type of Firm

Private Equity Firm

Association Membership

European Private Equity and Venture Capital Assoc.
Spanish Venture Capital Association (ASCRI)

Project Preferences

Role in Financing:
Prefer role as deal originator

Type of Financing Preferred:
Leveraged Buyout
Acquisition

Geographical Preferences

International Preferences:
Portugal
Bolivia
Peru
Spain
Colombia

Industry Focus

(% based on actual investment)
Other Products	63.8%
Consumer Related	18.9%
Industrial/Energy	17.4%

Additional Information

Year Founded: 2000
Capital Under Management: $227,200,000
Current Activity Level : Actively seeking new investments

DIANKO HOLDINGS SA

Sina 36
Athens, Greece 10672
Phone: 30-210-360-3255
Website: www.dianko.eu

Type of Firm
Private Equity Firm

Association Membership
Hellenic Venture Capital Association

Project Preferences

Type of Financing Preferred:
Early Stage

Geographical Preferences

International Preferences:
Greece
Europe

Industry Preferences

In Financial Services prefer:
Real Estate

Additional Information

Year Founded: 2004
Current Activity Level : Actively seeking new investments

DIANLIAN VENTURE CAPITAL CO LTD

Jiargneng Bldg
8 Fengqi E Rd
Hangzhou, China
Phone: 86-571-8604

Type of Firm
Private Equity Firm

Project Preferences

Type of Financing Preferred:
Balanced

Additional Information

Year Founded: 2010
Current Activity Level : Actively seeking new investments

DIANLIANG INVESTMENT MANAGEMENT SHANGHAI CO LTD

No.77,Jiangning Rd,Jingan dist
7th Floor
Shanghai, China 200041
Phone: 862161310612
E-mail: contact@dlcapitals.com
Website: www.dlcapitals.com

Type of Firm
Private Equity Firm

Project Preferences

Type of Financing Preferred:
Early Stage
Start-up Financing
Seed

Geographical Preferences

International Preferences:
China

Industry Preferences

In Communications prefer:
Telecommunications

In Internet Specific prefer:
Internet

In Medical/Health prefer:
Medical/Health

In Business Serv. prefer:
Media

Additional Information

Year Founded: 2013
Current Activity Level : Actively seeking new investments

DIATEM NETWORKS INC

350 Terry Fox Drive
Suite 320
Ottawa, Canada K2K2W5
Phone: 613-592-3525
Fax: 613-592-4570
E-mail: info@diatem.com

Type of Firm
Private Equity Firm

Additional Information

Year Founded: 2009
Current Activity Level : Actively seeking new investments

DICK ISRAEL & PARTNERS

8929 Wilshire Boulevard
Suite 214
Beverly Hills, CA USA 90211
Phone: 310-208-1234
Fax: 310-657-4486

Type of Firm
Private Equity Firm

Project Preferences

Role in Financing:
Prefer role as deal originator

Type of Financing Preferred:
Generalist PE

Size of Investments Considered:
Min Size of Investment Considered (000s): $10,000
Max Size of Investment Considered: No Limit

Geographical Preferences

United States Preferences:
All U.S.

Industry Preferences

In Communications prefer:
Commercial Communications
Radio & TV Broadcasting

In Internet Specific prefer:
Internet

In Medical/Health prefer:
Diagnostic Services
Disposable Med. Products

In Consumer Related prefer:
Entertainment and Leisure
Retail
Computer Stores
Franchises(NEC)
Food/Beverage
Consumer Products
Consumer Services
Education Related

In Industrial/Energy prefer:
Factory Automation
Machinery

In Financial Services prefer:
Financial Services
Real Estate

In Business Serv. prefer:
Distribution
Consulting Services

In Manufact. prefer:
Publishing

In Agr/Forestr/Fish prefer:
Agriculture related

Additional Information
Year Founded: 1974
Current Activity Level : Actively seeking new investments
Method of Compensation: Function primarily in service area, receive contingent fee in cash or equity

DIEVINI HOPP BIOTECH HOLDING GMBH & CO KG

Johann-Jakob-Astor-Str. 57
Walldorf, Germany 69190
Phone: 4962278608462
Fax: 4962278608470
E-mail: contact@devini.com
Website: www.dievini.com

Management and Staff
Christof Hettich, Co-Founder
Friedrich von Bohlen, Co-Founder
Mathias Hothum, Managing Director

Type of Firm
Private Equity Firm

Project Preferences

Type of Financing Preferred:
Leveraged Buyout
Early Stage
Balanced
Later Stage
Seed
Acquisition
Startup

Geographical Preferences

International Preferences:
Europe
Germany

Industry Preferences

In Medical/Health prefer:
Health Services

Additional Information
Year Founded: 2005
Current Activity Level : Actively seeking new investments

DIFFERENCE CAPITAL FINANCIAL INC

130 Adelaide Street West, Suite 1010
Toronto, Canada M5H 3P5
Phone: 4166495085
E-mail: info@differencecapital.com
Website: differencecapital.com

Management and Staff
Henry Kneis, Chief Executive Officer
Jamie Brown, Managing Partner
Victor Duong, Chief Financial Officer

Type of Firm
Private Equity Firm

Association Membership
Canadian Venture Capital Association

Industry Preferences

In Medical/Health prefer:
Medical/Health

In Industrial/Energy prefer:
Environmental Related

In Business Serv. prefer:
Media

Additional Information
Year Founded: 2012
Capital Under Management: $107,700,000
Current Activity Level : Actively seeking new investments

DIGITAL ASSETS DEPLOYMENT SL

c/ Doctor Castelo 10
Local 1
Madrid, Spain 28009
Phone: 34915747190
E-mail: info@dad.es
Website: www.dad.es

Type of Firm
Incubator/Development Program

Project Preferences

Type of Financing Preferred:
Seed
Startup

Geographical Preferences

United States Preferences:

International Preferences:
Latin America
Europe
China
Spain

Industry Preferences

In Internet Specific prefer:
Internet

Additional Information
Year Founded: 2006
Current Activity Level : Actively seeking new investments

DIGITAL CAPITAL AG

Hofstrasse 1
Zug, Switzerland ACH-6300
Phone: +41445087111
Website: www.digitalcapital.ch

Management and Staff
Stewart Kosoy, Co-Founder
W. Todd Tribell, Co-Founder

Type of Firm
Private Equity Firm

Project Preferences

Type of Financing Preferred:
Early Stage
Seed
Startup

Industry Preferences

In Computer Software prefer:
Software

In Internet Specific prefer:
E-Commerce Technology

Additional Information
Year Founded: 2011
Current Activity Level : Actively seeking new investments

DIGITAL ENTERTAINMENT VENTURES LLC

1501 Broadway
New York, NY USA 10036
E-mail: info@devny.vc
Website: devny.vc

Management and Staff
Alan McGlade, Managing Director
Damian Manning, Venture Partner
Michael Yang, Managing Director

Type of Firm
Private Equity Firm

Project Preferences

Type of Financing Preferred:
Early Stage
Seed
Startup

Geographical Preferences

United States Preferences:
New York

Industry Preferences

In Communications prefer:
Media and Entertainment

In Manufact. prefer:
Publishing

Additional Information
Year Founded: 2012
Current Activity Level : Actively seeking new investments

DIGITAL FUEL CAPITAL LLC

339 Auburn Street
Suite 12
Auburndale, MA USA 02466
Phone: 6172748400
Website: www.digitalfuelcapital.com

Type of Firm
Private Equity Firm

Project Preferences

Type of Financing Preferred:
Leveraged Buyout
Acquisition

Geographical Preferences

United States Preferences:

Industry Preferences

In Internet Specific prefer:
Ecommerce
Web Aggregation/Portals

In Consumer Related prefer:
Consumer Products

Additional Information
Year Founded: 2015
Current Activity Level : Actively seeking new investments

DIGITAL FUTURE

Kostyantynivska str. 34
Kyiv, Ukraine 04071
Phone: 380638979342
Website: digital-future.org

Management and Staff
Alex Kharchyshyn, Chief Operating Officer

Type of Firm
Private Equity Firm

Project Preferences

Type of Financing Preferred:
Early Stage
Expansion
Later Stage
Seed
Startup

Size of Investments Considered:
Min Size of Investment Considered (000s): $20
Max Size of Investment Considered (000s): $1,000

Geographical Preferences

International Preferences:
Armenia
Belarus
Kazakhstan
Kyrgyzstan
Tajikistan
Turkmenistan
Azerbaijan
Moldova
Ukraine
Uzbekistan
Russia
Georgia

Industry Preferences

In Internet Specific prefer:
E-Commerce Technology

Additional Information
Year Founded: 2014
Current Activity Level : Actively seeking new investments

DIGITAL GARAGE INC

3-5-7 Ebisu Minami, Shibuya-ku
DG Bldg.
Tokyo, Japan 150-0022
Phone: 81363671111
Fax: 81363671119
Website: www.garage.co.jp

Type of Firm
Incubator/Development Program

Additional Information
Year Founded: 1995
Current Activity Level : Actively seeking new investments

DIGITAL MAGICS SPA

Via B Quaranta, 40
Milano, Italy 20139
Phone: 3902525051
Fax: 390236598402
E-mail: investorrelations@digitalmagics.com
Website: digitalmagics.com

Type of Firm
Private Equity Firm

Project Preferences

Type of Financing Preferred:
Early Stage
Seed
Startup

Geographical Preferences

International Preferences:
Italy
All International

Additional Information
Year Founded: 2004
Current Activity Level : Actively seeking new investments

DIGITAL MEDIA PARTNERS PTE LTD

56B Pagoda Street
Singapore, Singapore 059215
Phone: 6562241449
Website: digitalmedia.vc

Other Offices
12 Eu Tong Sen Street
Soho Two
, Singapore 059819

Management and Staff
Chieh Suang Khor, Principal
Dmitry Levit, General Partner
Lee Buckerfield, Chief Financial Officer
Maria Shevtsova, General Partner
Mark Suckling, Principal

Type of Firm
Private Equity Firm

Project Preferences

Type of Financing Preferred:
Early Stage

Size of Investments Considered:
Min Size of Investment Considered (000s): $500
Max Size of Investment Considered (000s): $1,000

Geographical Preferences

International Preferences:
China
Brazil
Asia
Singapore
Russia

Industry Preferences

In Communications prefer:
Telecommunications
Media and Entertainment

In Computer Software prefer:
Software

In Internet Specific prefer:
Internet

In Financial Services prefer:
Financial Services

Additional Information
Year Founded: 2011
Current Activity Level : Actively seeking new investments

DIGITAL SPACE VENTURES SCSP

7, Rue Robert Stuemper
Luxembourg, Luxembourg 2557
Website: www.digital.space

Type of Firm
Private Equity Firm

Project Preferences

Type of Financing Preferred:
Early Stage

Additional Information
Year Founded: 2016
Capital Under Management: $50,000,000
Current Activity Level : Actively seeking new investments

DIGITALIS VENTURES LLC

11 Times Square, Suite 1500a
New York, NY USA 10036
Phone: 16464917988
Website: www.digitalisventures.com

Management and Staff
Amit Bansal, Principal
Drew Taylor, Partner
Steve Allen, Partner

Type of Firm
Private Equity Firm

Project Preferences

Type of Financing Preferred:
Early Stage

Industry Preferences

In Biotechnology prefer:
Biotechnology

In Medical/Health prefer:
Medical/Health
Medical Diagnostics
Medical Therapeutics

Additional Information
Year Founded: 2016
Current Activity Level : Actively seeking new investments

DIGITALPLUS GMBH

Ohmstr. 22
Munich, Germany 80802
Phone: 4989125012800
Fax: 4989125012899
Website: dplus.partners

Type of Firm
Private Equity Firm

Additional Information
Year Founded: 2015
Capital Under Management: $138,030,000
Current Activity Level : Actively seeking new investments

DIGITECH VENTURE CAPITAL FUND INC

11757 Katy Freeway
Suite 1300
Houston, TX USA 77079
Website: digitechvcfund.com

Management and Staff
James Vogel, Co-Founder
Paul Watson, CEO & Managing Director
Samuel Whitley, Co-Founder

Type of Firm
Private Equity Firm

Project Preferences

Type of Financing Preferred:
Early Stage
Seed

Additional Information
Year Founded: 2015
Capital Under Management: $110,000
Current Activity Level : Actively seeking new investments

DIGITX PARTNERS LLC

601 Gateway Boulevard
Suite 350
South San Francisco, CA USA 94080
E-mail: info@digitx.vc
Website: www.digitxpartners.com

Type of Firm
Private Equity Firm

Project Preferences

Type of Financing Preferred:
Early Stage

Industry Preferences

In Medical/Health prefer:
Health Services

Additional Information
Year Founded: 2016
Capital Under Management: $10,500,000
Current Activity Level : Actively seeking new investments

DILA CAPITAL

Bosques de Cidros 54 - 404
Bosques de las Lomas
Mexico DF, Mexico 11910
Phone: 5255259182
E-mail: info@dilacapital.com
Website: www.dilacapital.com

Type of Firm
Private Equity Firm

Project Preferences

Type of Financing Preferred:
Balanced

Geographical Preferences

International Preferences:
Mexico

Additional Information
Year Founded: 1969
Current Activity Level : Actively seeking new investments

DIOGENES BUSINESS INCUBATOR UNIVERSITY OF CYPRUS

2 Limassol Avenue Wights
Building
Nicosia, Cyprus 1678
Phone: 35722895110
Fax: 35722895055
E-mail: info@diogenes.com.cy
Website: www.diogenes-incubator.com

Management and Staff
George Kassinis, Vice President

Type of Firm
Incubator/Development Program

Project Preferences

Type of Financing Preferred:
Early Stage
Startup

Geographical Preferences

International Preferences:
Cyprus

Industry Preferences

In Other prefer:
Socially Responsible

Additional Information
Year Founded: 2003
Current Activity Level : Actively seeking new investments

DIOKO HEALTH VENTURES GP LLC

525 Vine Street
Suite 130
Winston-Salem, NC USA 27101

Type of Firm
Private Equity Firm

Project Preferences

Type of Financing Preferred:
Early Stage
Seed

Additional Information
Year Founded: 2015
Capital Under Management: $7,000,000
Current Activity Level : Actively seeking new investments

DIPL.-KFM. WUNDERLICH & PARTNER

Braeuhausstrasse 4b
Plannegg, Germany 82152
Phone: 498989948860
Fax: 4989899488899
E-mail: info@wunderlich-partner.de
Website: www.wunderlich-partner.de

Management and Staff
Hans-Dieter Wunderlich, Managing Partner
Marc Diekmann, Managing Director

Type of Firm
Private Equity Firm

Project Preferences

Type of Financing Preferred:
Early Stage
Later Stage

Geographical Preferences

International Preferences:
Germany

Additional Information
Year Founded: 1986
Current Activity Level : Actively seeking new investments

DIRECT CAPITAL PRIVATE EQUITY

Two Kitchener Street
Level Six
Auckland, New Zealand 1141
Phone: 6493072562
Fax: 6493072349
Website: www.directcapital.co.nz

Management and Staff
Ross George, Managing Director

Type of Firm
Private Equity Firm

Association Membership
New Zealand Venture Capital Association

Project Preferences

Role in Financing:
Prefer role as deal originator but will also invest in deals created by others

Type of Financing Preferred:
Expansion
Generalist PE
Management Buyouts
Acquisition
Recapitalizations

Size of Investments Considered:
Min Size of Investment Considered (000s): $15,000
Max Size of Investment Considered (000s): $60,000

Geographical Preferences

International Preferences:
Australia
New Zealand

Additional Information
Name of Most Recent Fund: Direct Capital Partners III
Most Recent Fund Was Raised: 04/01/2005
Year Founded: 1994
Capital Under Management: $699,800,000
Current Activity Level : Actively seeking new investments
Method of Compensation: Return on invest. most important, but chg. closing fees, service fees, etc.

DIRECTIONAL AVIATION CAPITAL

355 Richmond Road
Richmond Heights, OH USA 44143
Phone: 2162613000
Website: www.directionalaviation.com

Management and Staff
Kenneth Ricci, Principal
Michael Rossi, Principal

Type of Firm
Private Equity Firm

Project Preferences

Type of Financing Preferred:
Leveraged Buyout
Acquisition

Industry Preferences

In Transportation prefer:
Aerospace

Additional Information
Year Founded: 2005
Current Activity Level : Actively seeking new investments

DISCOVERY ANGEL INVESTMENT MANAGEMENT BEIJING CO LTD

No. 2 Jianguomen Outer Street,
Building A, Yintai Center
Beijing, China 100022
Website: www.faxianvc.com

Type of Firm
Private Equity Firm

Project Preferences

Type of Financing Preferred:
Seed
Startup

Geographical Preferences

International Preferences:
China

Industry Preferences

In Consumer Related prefer:
Consumer

Additional Information
Year Founded: 2015
Current Activity Level : Actively seeking new investments

DISCOVERY CAPITAL CORP

1285 West Pender Street
Suite 570
Vancouver, Canada V6E 4B1
Phone: 6046833000
Fax: 6046623457
E-mail: info@discoverycapital.com
Website: www.discoverycapital.com

Type of Firm
Private Equity Firm

Association Membership
Canadian Venture Capital Association

Project Preferences

Role in Financing:
Prefer role as deal originator

Type of Financing Preferred:
Early Stage
Balanced
Startup

Geographical Preferences

United States Preferences:
All U.S.

Canadian Preferences:
All Canada
Ontario
British Columbia

Industry Preferences

In Communications prefer:
Communications and Media

In Internet Specific prefer:
Internet

Additional Information
Year Founded: 1986
Current Activity Level : Actively seeking new investments

DISCOVERY VENTURES GMBH & CO KG

Kollwitzstrasse 51
Berlin, Germany 10405

Type of Firm
Private Equity Firm

Additional Information
Year Founded: 2016
Current Activity Level : Actively seeking new investments

DISRUPTION CORPORATION

2231 Crystal Drive
Suite 1000
Arlington, VA USA 22202
E-mail: nfo@disruption.vc
Website: disruption.vc

Management and Staff
Paul Singh, General Partner

Type of Firm
Investment Management Firm

Project Preferences

Type of Financing Preferred:
Early Stage
Startup

Industry Preferences

In Internet Specific prefer:
Internet

Additional Information
Year Founded: 2014
Current Activity Level : Actively seeking new investments

DISRUPTIVE CAPITAL PTY LTD

74 Castlereagh Street
Level 14
Sydney, Australia NSW 2000
Phone: 61292486988
Fax: 61292486989
E-mail: contact@disruptivecapital.com.au
Website: www.disruptivecapital.com.au

Other Offices
Nine Battery Road
11/F & 12/F Straits Trading Building
Singapore, Singapore 049910
Phone: 6596818368

230 Balaclava Road
Level Two
Melbourne, Australia VIC 3161

Management and Staff
Adir Shiffman, Partner
Calvin Ng, Partner
Eric Chan, Partner

Type of Firm
Investment Management Firm

Project Preferences

Type of Financing Preferred:
Early Stage
Expansion
Seed

Additional Information
Year Founded: 2012
Current Activity Level : Actively seeking new investments

DISRUPTIVE TECHNOLOGIES LP

11 Hamanofim street
Kerstein Buildings, Building B
Herzeliya, Israel
Website: www.disrupt-ive.com

Type of Firm
Private Equity Firm

Project Preferences

Type of Financing Preferred:
Early Stage
Seed

Additional Information
Year Founded: 2014
Current Activity Level : Actively seeking new investments

DISRUPTOR INC

315A Cameron Street
Alexandria, VA USA 22314
E-mail: info@disruptor.com
Website: disruptor.com

Type of Firm
Private Equity Firm

Project Preferences

Type of Financing Preferred:
Seed
Startup

Additional Information
Year Founded: 2012
Current Activity Level : Actively seeking new investments

DISTRICT 5 INVESTMENTS LP

100 East Royal Ln
Irving, TX USA 75039
Phone: 4697262946
Website: www.d5inv.com

Type of Firm
Private Equity Firm

Project Preferences

Type of Financing Preferred:
Leveraged Buyout
Mezzanine
Management Buyouts
Acquisition

Geographical Preferences

United States Preferences:
North America

Industry Preferences

In Industrial/Energy prefer:
Energy
Oil and Gas Exploration

Additional Information
Year Founded: 2016
Current Activity Level : Actively seeking new investments

DISTRICT VENTURES

2540 Kensington Road Northwest
Calgary, Canada T2N 3S3
Website: www.districtventures.ca

665

Type of Firm
Incubator/Development Program

Project Preferences

Type of Financing Preferred:
Early Stage

Industry Preferences

In Medical/Health prefer:
Health Services

In Consumer Related prefer:
Food/Beverage

Additional Information
Year Founded: 2015
Current Activity Level : Actively seeking new investments

DIVERGENT VENTURE PARTNERS AFFILIATES I LP

1652 20th Avenue
Seattle, WA USA 98122
Phone: 4259545704
Fax: 2067093008
E-mail: info@divergent.com

Management and Staff
Kevin Ober, Managing Director
Robert Shurtleff, Managing Director
Tocd Warren, Managing Partner

Type of Firm
Private Equity Firm

Association Membership
National Venture Capital Association - USA (NVCA)

Project Preferences

Role in Financing:
Prefer role as deal originator but will also invest in deals created by others

Type of Financing Preferred:
Early Stage

Size of Investments Considered:
Min Size of Investment Considered (000s): $200
Max Size of Investment Considered (000s): $1,000

Geographical Preferences

United States Preferences:
Northwest
West Coast

Industry Preferences

In Communications prefer:
Data Communications

In Computer Software prefer:
Software

In Internet Specific prefer:
Internet

Additional Information
Name of Most Recent Fund: Divergent Venture Partners III, L.P.
Most Recent Fund Was Raised: 06/19/2012
Year Founded: 2003
Capital Under Management: $100,000,000
Current Activity Level : Actively seeking new investments
Method of Compensation: Return on investment is of primary concern, do not charge fees

DIVERSIFIED TRUST COMPANY INC

6075 Poplar Avenue, Suite 900
Memphis, TN USA 38119
Phone: 9017617979
Website: www.diversifiedtrust.com

Management and Staff
Brook Lester, Principal
Carol Womack, Principal
Carolyn Hicks, Vice President
F. Kneeland Gammill, Principal
J. Hal Daughdrill, Co-Founder
Jason Lioon, Principal
Jason Wheat, Vice President
Jay Davis, Vice President
Kevin Jamison, Vice President
Larry Bryan, Co-Founder
Max Rowland, Vice President
Selden Frisbee, Principal
William Spitz, Co-Founder

Type of Firm
Investment Management Firm

Project Preferences

Type of Financing Preferred:
Fund of Funds

Additional Information
Year Founded: 1994
Capital Under Management: $25,000,000
Current Activity Level : Actively seeking new investments

DIVERSIS CAPITAL LLC

3110 Main Street, Suite 200
Santa Monica, CA USA 90405
Phone: 3103964200
Fax: 3108297151
E-mail: info@diversiscapital.com
Website: diversiscapital.com

Management and Staff
Joseph Lok, Vice President
Kevin Ma, Co-Founder
Ron Nayot, Co-Founder
Ryan Tanaka, Vice President

Type of Firm
Private Equity Firm

Project Preferences

Type of Financing Preferred:
Leveraged Buyout
Expansion
Turnaround
Acquisition
Special Situation
Recapitalizations

Geographical Preferences

United States Preferences:
North America

Industry Preferences

In Communications prefer:
Telecommunications

In Computer Software prefer:
Software

In Internet Specific prefer:
Ecommerce

In Medical/Health prefer:
Health Services

In Consumer Related prefer:
Consumer
Food/Beverage
Education Related

In Industrial/Energy prefer:
Machinery

In Transportation prefer:
Aerospace

In Business Serv. prefer:
Services
Distribution
Media

Additional Information
Year Founded: 2013
Current Activity Level : Actively seeking new investments

DJAKNE SS II AB

Djaknegatan 9
Malmo, Sweden 21135
Website: www.djakne.co

Type of Firm
Private Equity Firm

Project Preferences

Type of Financing Preferred:
Early Stage

Additional Information
Year Founded: 2017
Current Activity Level : Actively seeking new investments

DLD VENTURES GMBH

Arabellastrasse 23
Munich, Germany 81925
Phone: 498992504135

Type of Firm
Private Equity Firm

Project Preferences

Type of Financing Preferred:
Early Stage
Expansion
Balanced
Later Stage

Industry Preferences

In Consumer Related prefer:
Consumer

Additional Information
Year Founded: 1969
Current Activity Level : Actively seeking new investments

DLJ MERCHANT BANKING PARTNERS

Eleven Madison Avenue
New York, NY USA 10010
Phone: 2125380644

Other Offices
One Cabot Square
London, United Kingdom E14 4QJ
Phone: 44-207-888-8888
Fax: 44-207-888-1600

#05-02, One Raffles Link
Singapore, Singapore 039393
Phone: 65-6212-6000
Fax: 65-6212-6200

Av. Brig. Faria Lima
3064 - 13 andar, Jardim Paulistano
Sao Paulo, Brazil 01451 000

Paradeplatz 8
Zurich, Switzerland 8070
Phone: 41-44-333-1111
Fax: 41-44-332-5555

Three Exchange Square
8 Connaught Place
Central, Hong Kong
Phone: 852-2101-6000
Fax: 852-2101-7990

Roppongi 1-Chome, Minato-ku
Izumi Garden Tower, 6-1
Tokyo, Japan 106-6024
Phone: 81-3-4550-9000
Fax: 81-3-4550-9800

Management and Staff
Colin Taylor, Managing Director
Edward Johnson, Managing Director

Type of Firm
Bank Affiliated

Project Preferences

Type of Financing Preferred:
Fund of Funds
Leveraged Buyout
Mezzanine
Generalist PE
Later Stage
Seed
Startup
Fund of Funds of Second

Size of Investments Considered:
Min Size of Investment Considered (000s): $20,000
Max Size of Investment Considered (000s): $200,000

Geographical Preferences

United States Preferences:

International Preferences:
United Kingdom
Europe

Industry Focus
(% based on actual investment)
Industrial/Energy	30.1%
Other Products	22.2%
Medical/Health	14.7%
Consumer Related	11.1%
Communications and Media	10.3%
Computer Software and Services	5.1%
Internet Specific	3.8%
Semiconductors/Other Elect.	2.3%
Computer Hardware	0.3%
Biotechnology	0.2%

Additional Information
Year Founded: 1972
Current Activity Level : Actively seeking new investments

DLM INVISTA GESTAO DE RECURSOS LTDA

Rua Felipe dos Santos 901
11th Floor, Lourdes
Belo Horizonte, Brazil 30180160
Phone: 553133478009
Fax: 553133478012
E-mail: relacionamento@dlminvista.com.br
Website: www.dlminvista.com.br

Other Offices
Rua Haddock Lobo 746
6th Floor, Jardins
Sao Paulo, Brazil 01414000
Phone: 551130630059
Fax: 551123610530

Avenida Paulista 1111
2nd Floor, Bela Vista
Sao Paulo, Brazil 01311920

Management and Staff
Jorge Steffens, Partner
Paulo Sergio Caputo, Partner

Type of Firm
Private Equity Firm

Association Membership
Brazilian Venture Capital Association (ABCR)

Project Preferences

Type of Financing Preferred:
Early Stage
Balanced
Later Stage
Seed
Startup

Size of Investments Considered:
Min Size of Investment Considered (000s): $4,929
Max Size of Investment Considered (000s): $19,714

Geographical Preferences

International Preferences:
Brazil

Industry Preferences

In Computer Software prefer:
Software

Additional Information
Year Founded: 2012
Capital Under Management: $88,543,000
Current Activity Level : Actively seeking new investments

DMB DEUTSCHE MITTEL-STANDSBETEILIGUNGS GMBH

Colonnaden 25
Hamburg, Germany 20354
Phone: 49403748340
Fax: 494037483410
E-mail: info@dmb-beteiligungen.de
Website: www.dmb-beteiligungen.de

Other Offices
Colonnaden 25
Hamburg, Germany

Management and Staff
Christian Kuehn, Partner
Dirk Tetzlaff, Chief Executive Officer
Jens Roehr, Partner
Peter Welge, Chief Executive Officer

Type of Firm
Private Equity Firm

Association Membership
German Venture Capital Association (BVK)

Project Preferences

Type of Financing Preferred:
Leveraged Buyout

Geographical Preferences

International Preferences:
Europe
Switzerland
Austria
Germany

Additional Information
Year Founded: 2011
Current Activity Level : Actively seeking new investments

DMG :: INFORMATION
3 Stamford Landing
Suite 400
Stamford, CT USA 06902
Phone: 2039732940
Website: www.dmginfo.com

Type of Firm
Private Equity Firm

Project Preferences

Type of Financing Preferred:
Early Stage
Balanced
Later Stage

Geographical Preferences

United States Preferences:

International Preferences:
United Kingdom
Europe
Australia
Singapore

Additional Information
Year Founded: 1990
Current Activity Level : Actively seeking new investments

DN CAPITAL GLOBAL VENTURE CAPITAL II LP
Dartmouth Street
Two Queen Anne's Gate Bldg.
London, United Kingdom SW1H 9BP
Phone: 442073401600
Fax: 442073401601
E-mail: info@dncapital.com
Website: www.dncapital.com

Other Offices
228 Hamilton Avenue, Third Floor
PALO ALTO, CA USA 94301
Phone: 650-798-5424

Management and Staff
Imran Akram, Principal
John Helm, Venture Partner
Simon Greenman, Venture Partner
Steven Schlenker, Managing Partner
Tom Bradley, Partner

Type of Firm
Private Equity Firm

Association Membership
European Private Equity and Venture Capital Assoc.

Project Preferences

Role in Financing:
Will function either as deal originator or investor in deals created by others

Type of Financing Preferred:
Early Stage
Expansion
Balanced
Later Stage
Seed

Size of Investments Considered:
Min Size of Investment Considered (000s): $100
Max Size of Investment Considered (000s): $100,000

Geographical Preferences

United States Preferences:

International Preferences:
Sweden
United Kingdom
Central Europe
Europe
Western Europe
Eastern Europe
Iceland
Scandanavia/Nordic Region
Israel
Finland
Norway
Germany
Denmark
France

Industry Preferences

In Communications prefer:
Communications and Media
Wireless Communications

In Computer Software prefer:
Software
Applications Software

In Internet Specific prefer:
E-Commerce Technology
Internet
Ecommerce

In Computer Other prefer:
Computer Related

In Semiconductor/Electr prefer:
Electronics

In Business Serv. prefer:
Media

Additional Information
Year Founded: 2000
Capital Under Management: $309,700,000
Current Activity Level : Actively seeking new investments

DN PARTNERS LLC
180 North LaSalle Street, Suite 2630
Chicago, IL USA 60601
Phone: 3123320856

Management and Staff
John Dancewicz, Managing Partner
Maury Bell, Managing Partner

Type of Firm
Private Equity Firm

Project Preferences

Role in Financing:
Prefer role as deal originator but will also invest in deals created by others

Type of Financing Preferred:
Leveraged Buyout
Management Buyouts
Acquisition
Recapitalizations

Geographical Preferences

United States Preferences:
Midwest
Illinois
Ohio
Minnesota

Industry Preferences

In Consumer Related prefer:
Consumer Products
Consumer Services

In Industrial/Energy prefer:
Industrial Products

In Business Serv. prefer:
Services
Distribution

In Manufact. prefer:
Manufacturing

Additional Information
Name of Most Recent Fund: DN Partners
Most Recent Fund Was Raised: 11/30/1999
Year Founded: 1995
Capital Under Management: $250,000,000
Current Activity Level : Actively seeking new investments

DNS CAPITAL LLC

400 N. Michigan Avenue
Suite 1310
Chicago, IL USA 60611
Phone: 3129820047

Type of Firm
Private Equity Firm

Project Preferences

Type of Financing Preferred:
Leveraged Buyout
Acquisition

Geographical Preferences

United States Preferences:

Industry Preferences

In Consumer Related prefer:
Consumer

In Industrial/Energy prefer:
Industrial Products

In Financial Services prefer:
Real Estate

Additional Information
Year Founded: 1969
Current Activity Level : Actively seeking new investments

DOCOMO INNOVATIONS INC

3240 Hillview Avenue
Palo Alto, CA USA 94304

Management and Staff
Byron Haigh, Principal
Jay Onda, Principal
Neil Sadaranganey, Managing Director

Type of Firm
Corporate PE/Venture

Project Preferences

Type of Financing Preferred:
Expansion
Later Stage

Geographical Preferences

United States Preferences:
Northern California

Industry Preferences

In Communications prefer:
Wireless Communications

Additional Information
Year Founded: 2005
Current Activity Level : Actively seeking new investments

DOCOR INTERNATIONAL BV

65 Yigal Alon Street
Toyota Tower, 14th Floor
Tel Aviv, Israel 67443
Phone: 97235620311
Fax: 97235620312
E-mail: info@docor.com
Website: www.docor.com

Management and Staff
Adi Goldin, Vice President
Alon Dumanis, Chief Executive Officer
Tsachy Shasha, Vice President

Type of Firm
Endowment, Foundation or Pension Fund

Project Preferences

Type of Financing Preferred:
Balanced
Startup

Geographical Preferences

International Preferences:
No Preference
Israel

Industry Preferences

In Computer Software prefer:
Software

In Biotechnology prefer:
Biotechnology

In Medical/Health prefer:
Medical Products

In Industrial/Energy prefer:
Industrial Products
Materials

Additional Information
Year Founded: 2003
Current Activity Level : Actively seeking new investments

DOEN PARTICIPATIES BV

Van Eeghenstraat 70
Amsterdam, Netherlands 1071 GK
Phone: 31205737333
Fax: 31205737370
E-mail: doen@doen.nl
Website: www.doen.nl

Management and Staff
Jasper Snoek, Chief Financial Officer
Nina Tellegen, Chief Executive Officer

Type of Firm
Private Equity Firm

Association Membership
Dutch Venture Capital Associaton (NVP)

Project Preferences

Type of Financing Preferred:
Fund of Funds
Early Stage
Seed

Geographical Preferences

International Preferences:
Europe
Netherlands

Industry Preferences

In Other prefer:
Socially Responsible
Environment Responsible

Additional Information
Year Founded: 1991
Capital Under Management: $29,300,000
Current Activity Level : Actively seeking new investments

DOJANE CAPITAL

1155, Fangdian Road, Pudong
Room 3701, Kerry Parkside
Shanghai, China 201204
Phone: 862161049522
Fax: 862161049527
E-mail: info@dojane.com.cn
Website: www.dojane.com.cn

Management and Staff
Tiecheng Yu, Managing Partner

Type of Firm
Bank Affiliated

Project Preferences

Type of Financing Preferred:
Early Stage
Later Stage

Size of Investments Considered:
Min Size of Investment Considered (000s): $10,000
Max Size of Investment Considered (000s): $100,000

Geographical Preferences

International Preferences:
China
Asia

Industry Preferences

In Biotechnology prefer:
Agricultural/Animal Bio.

In Medical/Health prefer:
Health Services

In Consumer Related prefer:
Consumer

In Industrial/Energy prefer:
Alternative Energy
Environmental Related

In Business Serv. prefer:
Services

Additional Information
Year Founded: 2004
Current Activity Level : Actively seeking new investments

DOLBY FAMILY VENTURES LP

999 Brannan Street
Suite 114
San Francisco, CA USA 94103
Phone: 4154491005
E-mail: info@dolbyventures.com
Website: www.dolbyventures.com

Type of Firm
Private Equity Firm

Project Preferences

Type of Financing Preferred:
Balanced
Later Stage
Seed

Geographical Preferences

United States Preferences:

International Preferences:
All International

Industry Preferences

In Medical/Health prefer:
Medical/Health

In Business Serv. prefer:
Media

Additional Information
Year Founded: 2014
Current Activity Level : Actively seeking new investments

DOLIK VENTURES LLC

142 E 16th Street
New York, NY USA 10003
Website: www.dolikventures.com

Type of Firm
Private Equity Firm

Project Preferences

Type of Financing Preferred:
Early Stage
Seed

Additional Information
Year Founded: 2017
Current Activity Level : Actively seeking new investments

DOLL CAPITAL MANAGEMENT INC

2420 Sand Hill Road, Suite 200
Menlo Park, CA USA 94025
Phone: 6502331400
Fax: 6508549159
Website: www.dcm.com

Other Offices

Unit 1, Level 10, Tower W2
Oriental No. 1 East Chang An
Beijing, China 100738
Phone: 8610-8515-1180
Fax: 8610-8515-1179

NBF Hibiya Building 5F
1-1-7 Uchisaiwaicho, Chiyoda-ku
Tokyo, Japan 100-0011
Phone: 11-813-3580-1451
Fax: 11-813-3580-5840

Management and Staff
Andre Levi, Chief Financial Officer
David Chao, Co-Founder
Dixon Doll, Co-Founder
Hurst Lin, Co-Founder
Jason Krikorian, General Partner
Osuke Honda, General Partner
Peter Moran, General Partner
Ramon Zeng, General Partner
Rudolph Rehm, Co-Founder
Thomas Blaisdell, General Partner

Type of Firm
Private Equity Firm

Association Membership
Western Association of Venture Capitalists (WAVC)
National Venture Capital Association - USA (NVCA)

Project Preferences

Role in Financing:
Will function either as deal originator or investor in deals created by others

Type of Financing Preferred:
Early Stage
Expansion
Balanced
Later Stage

Size of Investments Considered:
Min Size of Investment Considered (000s): $3,000
Max Size of Investment Considered (000s): $7,000

Geographical Preferences

United States Preferences:
All U.S.

International Preferences:
China
Japan

Industry Focus
(% based on actual investment)

Internet Specific	40.4%
Computer Software and Services	33.5%
Semiconductors/Other Elect.	7.9%
Communications and Media	5.8%
Other Products	4.4%
Computer Hardware	2.9%
Consumer Related	2.4%
Industrial/Energy	1.4%
Medical/Health	1.2%

Additional Information
Name of Most Recent Fund: A-Fund, L.P.
Most Recent Fund Was Raised: 04/21/2011
Year Founded: 1996
Capital Under Management: $3,000,000,000
Current Activity Level : Actively seeking new investments
Method of Compensation: Return on investment is of primary concern, do not charge fees

---

DOLPHIN CAPITAL GROUP LLC

136 Heber Avenue
Suite 101
Park City, UT USA 84060
Phone: 4356496482
E-mail: info@dolphincapitalgroup.com
Website: www.dolphincapitalgroup.com

Other Offices

Three Devon Road
Westport, CT USA 06880
Phone: 917-860-7440

Management and Staff

Chris Infurchia, Partner
Daniel Schley, Co-Founder
Jill Krishnamurthy, Partner
Ken Jacquin, Partner
Mike Dutton, Partner

Type of Firm

Private Equity Firm

Project Preferences

Type of Financing Preferred:
Leveraged Buyout
Expansion
Acquisition

Geographical Preferences

United States Preferences:
Rocky Mountain

Additional Information

Name of Most Recent Fund: Dolphin Capital Partners II, L.P.
Most Recent Fund Was Raised: 01/14/2013
Year Founded: 2005
Capital Under Management: $17,000,000
Current Activity Level : Actively seeking new investments

DOMAIN ASSOCIATES LLC

One Palmer Square
Suite 515
Princeton, NJ USA 08542
Phone: 6096835656
Fax: 6096839789
Website: domainvc.com

Other Offices

12481 High Bluff Drive
Suite 150
FAIRBANKS COUNTRY CLUB, CA USA 92130

Management and Staff

Brian Dovey, Partner
Brian Halak, Partner
Debra Liebert, Managing Director
Dennis Podlesak, Partner
Eckard Weber, Partner
James Blair, Partner
Jesse Treu, Partner
Kim Kamdar, Partner
Lisa Kraeutler, Managing Director
Nicole Vitullo, Partner

Type of Firm

Private Equity Firm

Association Membership

National Venture Capital Association - USA (NVCA)

Project Preferences

Role in Financing:
Will function either as deal originator or investor in deals created by others

Type of Financing Preferred:
Early Stage
Later Stage
Seed
Startup

Industry Focus
(% based on actual investment)
Biotechnology	53.5%
Medical/Health	41.1%
Internet Specific	1.5%
Consumer Related	1.4%
Other Products	0.9%
Computer Software and Services	0.9%
Industrial/Energy	0.6%
Semiconductors/Other Elect.	0.1%

Additional Information

Year Founded: 1985
Capital Under Management: $2,600,400,000
Current Activity Level : Actively seeking new investments
Method of Compensation: Return on investment is of primary concern, do not charge fees

DOMINET DIGITAL CORPORATION PTY LTD

44 Gwynne Street
Cremorne, Australia
Website: www.dominet.com.au

Type of Firm

Private Equity Firm

Project Preferences

Type of Financing Preferred:
Early Stage
Seed

Additional Information

Year Founded: 2017
Current Activity Level : Actively seeking new investments

DOMINION INVESTMENT GROUP

4301 Commuter Drive
Virginia Beach, VA USA 23462
Phone: 7572269440
Website: www.dominioninvestmentgroup.com

Other Offices

13 Culpeper Street
Warrenton, VA USA 20186
Phone: 5403472125

Type of Firm

Insurance Firm Affiliate

Project Preferences

Type of Financing Preferred:
Balanced

Industry Preferences

In Computer Software prefer:
Data Processing

In Computer Other prefer:
Computer Related

In Consumer Related prefer:
Consumer Services

Additional Information

Year Founded: 2003
Current Activity Level : Actively seeking new investments

DOMINUS CAPITAL LP

135 West 50th Street
19th Floor
New York, NY USA 10020
Phone: 212-784-5440
Fax: 212-784-5441
E-mail: Dominus@dominuscap.com
Website: www.dominuscap.com

Management and Staff

Ashish Rughwani, Partner
Gary Binning, Managing Partner
Robert Haswell, Partner

Type of Firm

Private Equity Firm

Project Preferences

Type of Financing Preferred:
Leveraged Buyout
Management Buyouts
Acquisition

Geographical Preferences

United States Preferences:

Industry Preferences

In Consumer Related prefer:
Food/Beverage
Consumer Services
Other Restaurants

In Industrial/Energy prefer:
Industrial Products
Materials

In Business Serv. prefer:
Distribution

In Manufact. prefer:
Manufacturing

Additional Information
Year Founded: 2008
Capital Under Management: $400,000,000
Current Activity Level: Actively seeking new investments

DONGGUAN HUICHUANG ZHICHENG VENTURE CAPITAL ENTERPRISE LP

Xiaqiao Qiaoyuan Villa
Floor 2, Tower C
Gongguan, China

Type of Firm
Private Equity Firm

Project Preferences

Type of Financing Preferred:
Balanced

Geographical Preferences

International Preferences:
China

Additional Information
Year Founded: 2011
Current Activity Level: Actively seeking new investments

DONGGUAN LAKE VENTURE CAPITAL MANAGEMENT INC

Songshan Lake High Tech Park
3F, Administration Bldg.
Dongguan, China
Phone: 86-769-22892023
Fax: 86-769-22892022
E-mail: sqwu@lakevc.com
Website: www.lakevc.com

Type of Firm
Investment Management Firm

Project Preferences

Type of Financing Preferred:
Early Stage
Balanced
Later Stage

Geographical Preferences

International Preferences:
China

Industry Preferences

In Semiconductor/Electr prefer:
Electronics

In Biotechnology prefer:
Biotechnology

In Consumer Related prefer:
Consumer Products

In Industrial/Energy prefer:
Alternative Energy
Environmental Related

In Manufact. prefer:
Manufacturing

Additional Information
Year Founded: 2008
Current Activity Level: Actively seeking new investments

DONGGUAN RONGKE INVESTMENT CONSULTING CO LTD

Dongcheng Street, Dongguan
Room 204, 2F, Dongshun Buildin
Dongguan, China

Type of Firm
Private Equity Firm

Project Preferences

Type of Financing Preferred:
Balanced

Geographical Preferences

International Preferences:
China

Additional Information
Year Founded: 2013
Current Activity Level: Actively seeking new investments

DONGGUAN RONGYI INNOVATION INVESTMENT CO., LTD.

D220, Chuangyi Shenghuo Cheng
Songshanhu District
Dongguan, Guangdong, China 523000
Phone: 8676923076212
Fax: 8676923075508
E-mail: rongyidg@gmail.com
Website: www.ry168.cn

Type of Firm
Private Equity Firm

Project Preferences

Type of Financing Preferred:
Expansion
Balanced
Later Stage

Geographical Preferences

International Preferences:
China

Industry Preferences

In Biotechnology prefer:
Biotechnology

In Medical/Health prefer:
Medical/Health

In Industrial/Energy prefer:
Energy
Energy Conservation Relat
Advanced Materials
Environmental Related

Additional Information
Year Founded: 2011
Capital Under Management: $49,720,000
Current Activity Level: Actively seeking new investments

DONNELLY PENMAN & PARTNERS INC

1760 Kercheval Avenue
Grasse Pointe
Grosse Pointe Park, MI USA 48230
Phone: 3134469900
Fax: 3134469955
Website: www.donnellypenman.com

Management and Staff
Andrew Christians, Vice President
James Penman, Managing Director
John Lewis, Managing Director
John Donnelly, Managing Director
Mark Cleland, Chief Financial Officer

Type of Firm
Bank Affiliated

Project Preferences

Type of Financing Preferred:
Early Stage

Geographical Preferences

United States Preferences:

Industry Preferences

In Medical/Health prefer:
Health Services

In Consumer Related prefer:
Retail

In Financial Services prefer:
Financial Services

In Business Serv. prefer:
Services
Distribution

In Manufact. prefer:
Manufacturing

Additional Information
Year Founded: 2006
Current Activity Level : Actively seeking new investments

DORADO CAPITAL PTY LTD

Level 9
190 Street George's Terrace
Perth, Australia 6000
Phone: 418924811
Website: doradocapital.com.au

Type of Firm
Private Equity Firm

Industry Preferences

In Computer Software prefer:
Software

In Semiconductor/Electr prefer:
Electronic Components

In Industrial/Energy prefer:
Oil and Gas Exploration

In Agr/Forestr/Fish prefer:
Mining and Minerals

Additional Information
Year Founded: 1969
Current Activity Level : Actively seeking new investments

DORAZIO CAPITAL PARTNERS, LLC

190 South LaSalle
Suite 3025
Chicago, IL USA 60603
Phone: 3123575670
Website: www.doracm.com

Type of Firm
Private Equity Firm

Project Preferences

Type of Financing Preferred:
Early Stage

Additional Information
Year Founded: 2015
Current Activity Level : Actively seeking new investments

DOS RIOS PARTNERS LP

205 Wild Basin Road South
Building Three, Suite 100
Austin, TX USA 78746
Website: www.dosriospartners.com

Management and Staff
Bo Baskin, Partner

Type of Firm
Private Equity Firm

Association Membership
Natl Assoc of Small Bus. Inv. Co (NASBIC)

Project Preferences

Type of Financing Preferred:
Leveraged Buyout
Mezzanine
Management Buyouts
Acquisition
Recapitalizations

Geographical Preferences

United States Preferences:
New Mexico
Oklahoma
Colorado
Louisiana
Arkansas
Texas

Additional Information
Name of Most Recent Fund: Dos Rios Partners, L.P.
Most Recent Fund Was Raised: 05/14/2013
Year Founded: 2013
Capital Under Management: $225,000,000
Current Activity Level : Actively seeking new investments

DOUBLE C CAPITAL

485 Underhill Boulevard
Suite 200
Syosset, NY USA 11791
Website: www.doubleccapital.com

Management and Staff
Cody Cohen, Co-Founder

Type of Firm
Private Equity Firm

Project Preferences

Type of Financing Preferred:
Early Stage
Balanced
Later Stage

Geographical Preferences

United States Preferences:
New York

Additional Information
Year Founded: 2013
Current Activity Level : Actively seeking new investments

DOUBLE M PARTNERS LP

11812 San Vicente Blvd
Suite 510
Brentwood, CA USA 90049
Website: www.doublempartners.com

Management and Staff
Mark Mullen, Managing Partner

Type of Firm
Private Equity Firm

Project Preferences

Type of Financing Preferred:
Early Stage
Balanced

Industry Preferences

In Communications prefer:
Communications and Media

In Computer Software prefer:
Software

In Internet Specific prefer:
Internet

Additional Information
Name of Most Recent Fund: Double M Partners, L.P.
Most Recent Fund Was Raised: 08/10/2012
Year Founded: 2012
Capital Under Management: $9,200,000
Current Activity Level : Actively seeking new investments

DOUBLEROCK LLC

2200 Sand Hill Road
Suite 160
Menlo Park, CA USA 94025
Phone: 6503914797
Fax: 6506144880
Website: www.doublerock.com

Management and Staff
Morgan Moncada, Venture Partner
Nick Dani, General Partner
Suraj Rajwani, Co-Founder

Type of Firm
Private Equity Firm

Project Preferences

Type of Financing Preferred:
Early Stage
Expansion

Size of Investments Considered:
Min Size of Investment Considered (000s): $2,000
Max Size of Investment Considered (000s): $15,000

Geographical Preferences

United States Preferences:
All U.S.

International Preferences:
India
China
Brazil

Industry Preferences

In Communications prefer:
Communications and Media
Commercial Communications
Telecommunications

In Computer Software prefer:
Data Processing
Software
Systems Software
Applications Software

In Internet Specific prefer:
E-Commerce Technology
Internet
Ecommerce

Additional Information

Year Founded: 2011
Current Activity Level : Actively seeking new investments

DOUGHTY HANSON AND CO.

45 Pall Mall
London, United Kingdom SW1Y 5JG
Phone: 442076639300
Fax: 442076639352
E-mail: info@doughtyhanson.com
Website: www.doughtyhanson.com

Other Offices

Lenbachplatz 3
Munich, Germany 80333
Phone: 49-89-552-793-450
Fax: 49-89-2444-0688

C/Serrano 26
Madrid, Spain 28001
Phone: 34-9-1436-4420
Fax: 34-91-745-6626

Platz der Einheit 2
Frankfurt, Germany 60327
Phone: 49-69-971-2020
Fax: 49-69-9712-0299

Via Dei Bossi 4
Milan, Italy 20121
Phone: 39-02-806-0681
Fax: 39-02-8060-6820

28 Boulevard Royal
Luxembourg, Luxembourg 2449
Phone: 352-26-27-561
Fax: 352-26-275-620

60 Avenue Hoche
Paris, France 75008
Phone: 33-1-5668-5515
Fax: 33-1-5668-5524

Management and Staff

Adam Black, Principal
Alessandro Baroni, Principal
Alex Moss, Principal
Christopher Fielding, Principal
David Torralba, Principal
John Gemmell, Principal
Jon Higginson, Principal
Karl Eidem, Principal
Matt Appleton, Principal
Mike Youlden, Principal
Richard Lund, Chief Financial Officer
Stephen Marquardt, Chief Executive Officer
Thomas Neumann, Principal
Tim Robson, Principal

Type of Firm

Private Equity Firm

Association Membership

British Venture Capital Association (BVCA)
French Venture Capital Association (AFIC)

Project Preferences

Type of Financing Preferred:
Leveraged Buyout
Value-Add
Early Stage
Generalist PE
Opportunistic

Geographical Preferences

International Preferences:
Europe

Industry Focus

(% based on actual investment)
Other Products	29.9%
Consumer Related	23.8%
Communications and Media	17.0%
Semiconductors/Other Elect.	11.1%
Medical/Health	6.1%
Computer Software and Services	5.3%
Industrial/Energy	3.3%
Internet Specific	2.8%
Computer Hardware	0.6%
Biotechnology	0.2%

Additional Information

Name of Most Recent Fund: Doughty Hanson & Co European Real Estate III LP
Most Recent Fund Was Raised: 09/25/2012
Year Founded: 1985
Capital Under Management: $7,362,000,000
Current Activity Level : Actively seeking new investments

DOVE CAPITAL PARTNERS LLC

219 Borders Road
P.O. Box 4357
Beaver Creek, CO USA 81620
Phone: 9707488594
Fax: 9709496029
Website: www.dovecapitalpartners.com

Management and Staff

David Dove, Managing Partner
Matt Harris, Managing Partner

Type of Firm

Investment Management Firm

Project Preferences

Type of Financing Preferred:
Early Stage
Expansion
Seed
Startup

Industry Preferences

In Financial Services prefer:
Financial Services

Additional Information

Year Founded: 2010
Capital Under Management: $75,000,000
Current Activity Level : Actively seeking new investments

DOWLING CAPITAL PARTNERS I LP

190 Farmington Avenue
Farmington, CT USA 06032
Phone: 8606767300
E-mail: info@dowlingcapitalpartners.com
Website: www.dowlingcapitalpartners.com

Management and Staff
Jeffery Cappel, Partner
Vincent Dowling, Partner

Type of Firm
Private Equity Firm

Project Preferences

Type of Financing Preferred:
Leveraged Buyout
Acquisition

Industry Preferences

In Financial Services prefer:
Insurance

In Business Serv. prefer:
Services
Distribution

Additional Information
Name of Most Recent Fund: Dowling Capital Partners I, L.P.
Most Recent Fund Was Raised: 05/11/2011
Year Founded: 2011
Capital Under Management: $288,358,000
Current Activity Level : Actively seeking new investments

DOWN2EARTH CAPITAL NV

Hessenstraatje 20
Antwerp, Belgium 2000
Phone: 3236894501
Website: d2e.be

Type of Firm
Private Equity Firm

Project Preferences

Type of Financing Preferred:
Leveraged Buyout

Geographical Preferences

International Preferences:
Belgium

Additional Information
Name of Most Recent Fund: Down2Earth Capital
Most Recent Fund Was Raised: 08/12/2013
Year Founded: 2013
Capital Under Management: $70,820,000
Current Activity Level : Actively seeking new investments

DOWNING PARTNERS LLC

590 Madison Avenue, 21st Floor
New York, NY USA 10022
Phone: 2125214368
E-mail: infor@downingpartners.com
Website: www.downingpartners.com

Type of Firm
Private Equity Firm

Project Preferences

Type of Financing Preferred:
Early Stage

Additional Information
Year Founded: 2014
Capital Under Management: $1,950,000
Current Activity Level : Actively seeking new investments

DP WORLD LTD

JAFZA Building 17, 5th Floor
Jebel Ali Free Zone
Dubai, Utd. Arab Em.
Phone: 0097148811110
Fax: 0097148811344
E-mail: info@dpworld.com
Website: www.dpworld.com

Management and Staff
Simon Pitout, Vice President

Type of Firm
Private Equity Firm

Project Preferences

Type of Financing Preferred:
Fund of Funds
Leveraged Buyout

Geographical Preferences

International Preferences:
All International

Industry Preferences

In Communications prefer:
Telecommunications

In Medical/Health prefer:
Health Services

In Industrial/Energy prefer:
Energy

In Financial Services prefer:
Real Estate
Financial Services

Additional Information
Year Founded: 2007
Current Activity Level : Actively seeking new investments

DPE DEUTSCHE PRIVATE EQUITY GMBH

Ludwigstrasse 7
Munich, Germany 80539
Phone: 49892000380
Fax: 4989200038111
E-mail: info@pdpe.de
Website: www.dpe.de

Management and Staff
Frank Mueller, Partner
Guido Prehn, Partner
Lars Becker, Partner
Marc Thiery, Co-Founder
Richard Lancaster, Chief Financial Officer
Volker Hichert, Co-Founder

Type of Firm
Private Equity Firm

Project Preferences

Type of Financing Preferred:
Leveraged Buyout
Acquisition

Geographical Preferences

International Preferences:
Switzerland
Austria

Industry Preferences

In Industrial/Energy prefer:
Alternative Energy
Industrial Products
Environmental Related

In Financial Services prefer:
Financial Services
Insurance
Investment Groups

In Business Serv. prefer:
Services

Additional Information
Name of Most Recent Fund: Deutsche Private Equity II
Most Recent Fund Was Raised: 03/21/2013
Year Founded: 2007
Capital Under Management: $660,400,000
Current Activity Level : Actively seeking new investments

DR ENGELHARDT KAUPP KIEFER BETEILIGUNGS-BERATUNG GMBH

Marienstrasse 39
Stuttgart, Germany 70178
Phone: 4971151876400
Fax: 4971151876401
E-mail: info@ekkub.de
Website: www.ekkub.de

Other Offices
Leipziger Platz 7
Berlin, Germany 10117

Management and Staff
Betina Fecker, Partner
Georg Kiefer, Managing Director
Karl-Friedrich Kaupp, Managing Director
Thomas Heiden, Partner
Tobias Engelhardt, Managing Director
Volker Horst, Partner

Type of Firm
Private Equity Firm

Association Membership
German Venture Capital Association (BVK)

Project Preferences

Type of Financing Preferred:
Early Stage
Turnaround
Later Stage
Special Situation

Size of Investments Considered:
Min Size of Investment Considered (000s): $132
Max Size of Investment Considered (000s): $791

Geographical Preferences

International Preferences:
Germany

Industry Preferences

In Industrial/Energy prefer:
Environmental Related

In Business Serv. prefer:
Services

Additional Information
Year Founded: 2001
Current Activity Level : Actively seeking new investments

DRAGONBRIDGE CAPITAL LLC

1000 Bishop Street
Suite 902
Honolulu, HI USA 96813
Phone: 808-546-2288
Fax: 808-546-2211
E-mail: info@dragonbridgecapital.com

Type of Firm
Bank Affiliated

Project Preferences

Type of Financing Preferred:
Early Stage

Geographical Preferences

International Preferences:
Asia

Industry Preferences

In Industrial/Energy prefer:
Energy

In Other prefer:
Environment Responsible

Additional Information
Year Founded: 2010
Capital Under Management: $30,000,000
Current Activity Level : Actively seeking new investments

DRAGONVENTURE, INC.

2882 Sand Hill Road
Suite 150
Menlo Park, CA USA 94025
Phone: 6502339000
Fax: 6502348533
E-mail: info@dragonventure.com
Website: www.dragonventure.com

Other Offices
133 Amoy Street
#02-01
Singapore, Singapore 049962

801 Haidian Science Plaza
3 Zhong Guan Cun Rd. South, Haidian Dist
Beijing, China

Suite 301, Tower A, 560 Songtao Road
Zhangjiang High-tech Park
Shanghai, China

Management and Staff
Gang Mai, Venture Partner
Henry Ines, Venture Partner
Jie Tian, General Partner
K. Bobby Chao, Co-Founder
Tony Luh, Co-Founder

Type of Firm
Investment Management Firm

Project Preferences

Type of Financing Preferred:
Early Stage
Expansion
Balanced
Seed

Geographical Preferences

United States Preferences:

International Preferences:
Asia Pacific
China
Pacific
Asia

Industry Preferences

In Communications prefer:
Telecommunications

In Computer Software prefer:
Software

In Internet Specific prefer:
Internet

In Computer Other prefer:
Computer Related

In Semiconductor/Electr prefer:
Semiconductor

Additional Information
Name of Most Recent Fund: DFJ DragonFund China II, L.P.
Most Recent Fund Was Raised: 11/12/2008
Year Founded: 2000
Current Activity Level : Actively seeking new investments

DRAPER ASSOCIATES INC

55 East Third Avenue
San Mateo, CA USA 94401
Phone: 6502339000
Website: www.draper.vc

Other Offices
2882 Sand Hill Road
Suite 150
MENLO PARK, CA USA 94025
Phone: 6502339000

Management and Staff
Joel Yarmon, Venture Partner

Type of Firm
Private Equity Firm

Project Preferences

Type of Financing Preferred:
Early Stage
Seed

Industry Preferences

In Internet Specific prefer:
E-Commerce Technology
Ecommerce

In Medical/Health prefer:
Medical/Health

In Consumer Related prefer:
Consumer

In Financial Services prefer:
Financial Services

Additional Information
Year Founded: 1985
Capital Under Management: $190,000,000
Current Activity Level : Actively seeking new investments

DRAPER ESPRIT PLC

20 Garrick Street
London, United Kingdom WC2E 9BT
Phone: 442079318800
Fax: 442079318866
Website: www.dfjesprit.com

Other Offices
Building 1010
Cambourne Business Park
Cambridge, United Kingdom CB23 6DP
Phone: 44-1223-307-770
Fax: 44-1223-307-771

Management and Staff
Alan Duncan, Co-Founder
Benjamin Wilkinson, Chief Financial Officer
Brian Caulfield, Partner
David Cummings, Venture Partner
Jonathan Freuchet-Sibilia, Partner
Mikko Suonenlahti, Venture Partner
Philip O Reilly, Principal
Richard Marsh, Partner
Simon Cook, Chief Executive Officer
Stuart Chapman, Partner
Vinoth Jayakumar, Principal
Vishal Gulati, Venture Partner

Type of Firm
Private Equity Firm

Association Membership
Irish Venture Capital Association
British Venture Capital Association (BVCA)
European Private Equity and Venture Capital Assoc.

Project Preferences

Type of Financing Preferred:
Early Stage
Expansion
Seed
Startup

Geographical Preferences

International Preferences:
United Kingdom
Europe
Western Europe

Industry Preferences

In Communications prefer:
Telecommunications

In Computer Software prefer:
Software

In Internet Specific prefer:
Internet

In Semiconductor/Electr prefer:
Electronics

In Medical/Health prefer:
Medical/Health

In Industrial/Energy prefer:
Environmental Related

Additional Information
Name of Most Recent Fund: DFJ Esprit II
Most Recent Fund Was Raised: 06/19/2008
Year Founded: 2006
Capital Under Management: $500,000,000
Current Activity Level : Actively seeking new investments

DRAPER ESPRIT SECONDARIES LLP

52 Jermyn Street
London, United Kingdom SW1Y 6LX
Phone: 442072557500
Fax: 442072557501
Website: www.tempo-cap.com

Management and Staff
Annabelle De St. Quentin, Chief Financial Officer
David Tate, Co-Founder
Hansjorg Ruof, Venture Partner
Olav Ostin, Co-Founder
Stefan Elsser, Venture Partner

Type of Firm
Private Equity Advisor or Fund of Funds

Association Membership
European Private Equity and Venture Capital Assoc.

Project Preferences

Type of Financing Preferred:
Fund of Funds
Fund of Funds of Second

Geographical Preferences

International Preferences:
Europe

Additional Information
Name of Most Recent Fund: TempoPark II (FKA) Viventures I
Most Recent Fund Was Raised: 10/01/1998
Year Founded: 2006
Current Activity Level : Actively seeking new investments

DRAPER FISHER JURVETSON

2882 Sand Hill Road
Suite 150
Menlo Park, CA USA 94025
Phone: 6502339000
E-mail: pitch@dfj.com
Website: www.dfj.com

Other Offices
1366 West Nanjing Road
Plaza 6611, Suite 4709
Shanghai, China 200040
Phone: 86-21-6288-4000

16 Infantry Road
Bangalore, India 560001
Phone: 91-80-6644-5100
Fax: 91-80-6644-5200

Management and Staff
Andreas Stavropoulos, Partner
Barry Schuler, Partner
Carol Wentworth, Partner
Donald Wood, Venture Partner
Emily Melton, Partner
John Fisher, Co-Founder
Josh Stein, Partner
Mark Bailey, Partner
Randall Glein, Partner
Sam Fort, Partner
Steve Jurvetson, Co-Founder
Timothy Draper, Co-Founder
William Bryant, Partner

Type of Firm
Private Equity Firm

Association Membership
Western Association of Venture Capitalists (WAVC)
National Venture Capital Association - USA (NVCA)

Project Preferences

Role in Financing:
Prefer role as deal originator but will also invest in deals created by others

Type of Financing Preferred:
Early Stage
Expansion
Balanced
Later Stage
Seed

Geographical Preferences

United States Preferences:
North America

International Preferences:
China

Industry Focus

(% based on actual investment)
Computer Software and Services	31.0%
Internet Specific	28.0%
Semiconductors/Other Elect.	12.0%
Industrial/Energy	8.1%
Biotechnology	6.0%
Communications and Media	5.1%
Other Products	4.9%
Computer Hardware	3.0%
Medical/Health	1.2%
Consumer Related	0.8%

Additional Information

Name of Most Recent Fund: DFJ Venture XI, L.P.
Most Recent Fund Was Raised: 02/04/2014
Year Founded: 1985
Capital Under Management: $5,000,000,000
Current Activity Level : Actively seeking new investments
Method of Compensation: Function primarily in service area, receive contingent fee in cash or equity

DRAPER NEXUS VENTURE PARTNERS LLC

55 East 3rd Avenue, Suite 210
San Mateo, CA USA 94401
Phone: 8584494173

Management and Staff

Akira Kurabayashi, Managing Director
Dave Pearce, Venture Partner
Hironobu Maeda, Managing Director
Masaru Tange, Venture Partner
Mitch Kitamura, Managing Director
Quaeed Motiwala, Managing Director
Tetsujiro Nakagaki, Managing Director

Type of Firm

Private Equity Firm

Association Membership

National Venture Capital Association - USA (NVCA)

Project Preferences

Type of Financing Preferred:
Seed

Industry Preferences

In Communications prefer:
Wireless Communications

In Computer Software prefer:
Data Processing
Applications Software

In Semiconductor/Electr prefer:
Electronics
Sensors

In Consumer Related prefer:
Consumer

In Industrial/Energy prefer:
Energy
Industrial Products
Advanced Materials
Environmental Related

In Financial Services prefer:
Financial Services

In Business Serv. prefer:
Services
Media

Additional Information

Year Founded: 2011
Capital Under Management: $175,000,000
Current Activity Level : Actively seeking new investments

DRAPER RICHARDS KAPLAN FOUNDATION

1600 El Camino Real
Suite 155
Menlo Park, CA USA 94025
Phone: 6503197808
Fax: 6503234060
Website: www.drkfoundation.org

Type of Firm

Endowment, Foundation or Pension Fund

Association Membership

National Venture Capital Association - USA (NVCA)

Additional Information

Year Founded: 2001
Current Activity Level : Actively seeking new investments

DRAPER TRIANGLE VENTURES LP

Two Gateway Center
Suite 2000
Pittsburgh, PA USA 15222
Phone: 4122889800
Fax: 4122889799

Other Offices

30 West Third Street
Sixth Floor
CINCINNATI, OH USA 45202
Phone: 5132632732
Fax: 5133815093

10816 Millington Ct
CINCINNATI, OH USA 45242
Phone: 513 984-7980

6701 Carnegie Avenue
Suite 100
CLEVELAND, OH USA 44103
Phone: 2163635300

737 Bolivar Road
Suite 1500
CLEVELAND, OH USA 44115
Phone: 2163635300
Fax: 2163635440

Management and Staff

D. Thompson Jones, Co-Founder
Jay Katarincic, Co-Founder
Jonathan Murray, Managing Director
Michael Stubler, Co-Founder
Will Indest, Managing Director

Type of Firm

Private Equity Firm

Project Preferences

Role in Financing:
Will function either as deal originator or investor in deals created by others

Type of Financing Preferred:
Early Stage
Balanced
Seed
Startup

Size of Investments Considered:
Min Size of Investment Considered (000s): $250
Max Size of Investment Considered (000s): $2,000

Geographical Preferences

United States Preferences:
Midwest

Industry Preferences

In Internet Specific prefer:
Internet

In Semiconductor/Electr prefer:
Electronic Components

In Medical/Health prefer:
Medical Products

Additional Information

Name of Most Recent Fund: Draper Triangle Ventures III, L.P.
Most Recent Fund Was Raised: 02/20/2013
Year Founded: 1999
Capital Under Management: $204,000,000
Current Activity Level : Actively seeking new investments
Method of Compensation: Return on investment is of primary concern, do not charge fees

DRAYTON PARK CAPITAL LP

259 North Radnor-Chester Road
Suite 210
Wayne, PA USA 19087
Phone: 4842532259
E-mail: info@draytonparkcapital.com
Website: www.draytonparkcapital.com

Management and Staff
Charles Bodie, Partner

Type of Firm
Private Equity Firm

Project Preferences

Type of Financing Preferred:
Leveraged Buyout
Management Buyouts
Acquisition

Size of Investments Considered:
Min Size of Investment Considered (000s): $500
Max Size of Investment Considered (000s): $10,000

Geographical Preferences

United States Preferences:

Additional Information
Year Founded: 1969
Current Activity Level : Actively seeking new investments

DREAM INCUBATOR INC

3-2-6 Kasumigaseki, Chiyoda-Ku
Tokyo Club Building, 4th Floor
Tokyo, Japan 100-0013
Phone: 81355323200
Fax: 81355323201
E-mail: info@dreamincubator.co.jp
Website: www.dreamincubator.co.jp

Management and Staff
Takayoshi Yamakawa, President

Type of Firm
Service Provider

Project Preferences

Type of Financing Preferred:
Balanced

Geographical Preferences

International Preferences:
Vietnam
Japan

Industry Preferences

In Consumer Related prefer:
Retail
Consumer Products

Additional Information
Year Founded: 2000
Capital Under Management: $54,625,000
Current Activity Level : Actively seeking new investments

DREAM VENTURE INVESTMENT CO LTD

316, G-Five Central Plaza
1685-8, Seocho-dong
Seoul, South Korea 137-070
Phone: 82-2-539-7220
Fax: 82-2-539-8995
Website: www.dreamvi.co.kr

Management and Staff
Chung Hae Lim, President

Type of Firm
Corporate PE/Venture

Project Preferences

Type of Financing Preferred:
Mezzanine

Geographical Preferences

International Preferences:
Korea, South

Additional Information
Year Founded: 2000
Current Activity Level : Actively seeking new investments

DREAMIT VENTURES

3401 Market Street
Suite 201
Philadelphia, PA USA 19104
E-mail: info@dreamitventures.com
Website: www.dreamit.com

Other Offices
417 North Eighth Street
PHILADELPHIA, PA USA 19123
Phone: 2159956889

Management and Staff
Andrew Ackerman, Managing Director
Avi Savar, Managing Partner
Ben Rubin, Co-Founder
Bharani Rajakumar, Co-Founder
Khushboo Shah, Co-Founder
Mark Wachen, Managing Director
Phil Christian, Managing Director
Russ D Souza, Co-Founder
Seth Berk, Partner

Type of Firm
Private Equity Firm

Association Membership
National Venture Capital Association - USA (NVCA)

Project Preferences

Type of Financing Preferred:
Startup

Geographical Preferences

United States Preferences:
Pennsylvania

Industry Preferences

In Medical/Health prefer:
Medical Products
Health Services

Additional Information
Name of Most Recent Fund: DreamIt Fund II, L.P.
Most Recent Fund Was Raised: 12/31/2012
Year Founded: 2007
Capital Under Management: $22,000,000
Current Activity Level : Actively seeking new investments

DREAMLAB FINANCE LTD

1 North Shore Road
Suite 102, Saint James Court
Hamilton, Bermuda FL04
Website: dreamlabfinance.com

Type of Firm
Private Equity Firm

Additional Information
Year Founded: 1969
Current Activity Level : Actively seeking new investments

DRESNER CAPITAL RESOURCES INC

20 North Clark Street
Suite 3550
Chicago, IL USA 60602
Phone: 3127263600
Fax: 3127267448
E-mail: info@dresnerco.com
Website: www.dresnerco.biz

Management and Staff
Alan Mustacchi, Managing Director
Jamie Lisac, Managing Director
Joseph Kacergis, Vice President
Kevin McMurchy, Senior Managing Director
M. Mark Sarchet, Managing Director
Michelle Moreno, Managing Director
Mitchell Stern, Managing Director
Omar Diaz, Managing Director
Steven Dresner, President

Type of Firm
Bank Affiliated

Project Preferences

Role in Financing:
Prefer role as deal originator

Type of Financing Preferred:
Second Stage Financing
Leveraged Buyout
Mezzanine

Size of Investments Considered:
Min Size of Investment Considered (000s): $500
Max Size of Investment Considered (000s): $1,000

Geographical Preferences

International Preferences:
No Preference

Industry Preferences

In Communications prefer:
Commercial Communications
Telecommunications
Data Communications
Satellite Microwave Comm.

In Computer Hardware prefer:
Computers
Mini and Personal/Desktop
Computer Graphics and Dig
Disk Relat. Memory Device

In Computer Software prefer:
Computer Services
Systems Software
Applications Software

In Internet Specific prefer:
Internet

In Semiconductor/Electr prefer:
Semiconductor
Sensors
Circuit Boards
Component Testing Equipmt
Laser Related
Fiber Optics
Analytic/Scientific

In Medical/Health prefer:
Medical/Health
Medical Products

In Consumer Related prefer:
Entertainment and Leisure
Retail
Computer Stores
Franchises(NEC)
Food/Beverage
Consumer Products
Consumer Services
Other Restaurants

In Industrial/Energy prefer:
Industrial Products
Materials
Factory Automation
Robotics
Machinery

In Financial Services prefer:
Financial Services

In Business Serv. prefer:
Consulting Services

In Manufact. prefer:
Office Automation Equipmt
Publishing

Additional Information
Year Founded: 1991
Current Activity Level : Actively seeking new investments
Method of Compensation: Return on investment is of primary concern, do not charge fees

---

DRIEHAUS PRIVATE EQUITY LLC

17 East Erie Street
Chicago, IL USA 60611
Phone: 3129323605
E-mail: info@driehauspe.com
Website: www.driehauspe.com

Management and Staff
Eli Boufis, Managing Director
Richard Driehaus, Founder

Type of Firm
Private Equity Firm

Project Preferences

Type of Financing Preferred:
Leveraged Buyout
Expansion
Management Buyouts
Acquisition
Recapitalizations

Geographical Preferences

United States Preferences:
All U.S.

Additional Information
Name of Most Recent Fund: Driehaus Private Equity Growth Fund I LLC
Most Recent Fund Was Raised: 07/15/2011
Year Founded: 2011
Capital Under Management: $42,205,000
Current Activity Level : Actively seeking new investments

DRIVE CAPITAL LLC

629 North High Street
Sixth Street
Columbus, OH USA 43215
Phone: 6142578243
E-mail: info@drivecapital.com
Website: drivecapital.com

Management and Staff
Chris Olsen, Co-Founder
Mark Kvamme, Co-Founder

Type of Firm
Private Equity Firm

Project Preferences

Type of Financing Preferred:
Early Stage
Expansion
Balanced

Size of Investments Considered:
Min Size of Investment Considered (000s): $100
Max Size of Investment Considered (000s): $10,000

Geographical Preferences

United States Preferences:
Midwest

Industry Preferences

In Medical/Health prefer:
Medical/Health

In Consumer Related prefer:
Consumer

In Business Serv. prefer:
Services

Additional Information
Name of Most Recent Fund: Drive Capital Fund I, L.P.
Most Recent Fund Was Raised: 08/06/2013
Year Founded: 2013
Capital Under Management: $550,000,000
Current Activity Level : Actively seeking new investments

DROIA NV

Brusselsesteenweg 11
Meise, Belgium 1860
Phone: 3228806730
E-mail: contact@droiagroup.com
Website: droia.be

Type of Firm
Private Equity Firm

Industry Preferences

In Biotechnology prefer:
Biotechnology

In Medical/Health prefer:
Health Services

Additional Information
Year Founded: 2012
Current Activity Level : Actively seeking new investments

DRUMMOND ROAD CAPITAL INC

1801 East 9th Street
Cleveland, OH USA 44114
Website: www.drummondroad.com

Type of Firm
Private Equity Firm

Project Preferences

Type of Financing Preferred:
Early Stage
Seed

Industry Preferences

In Computer Software prefer:
Software

In Business Serv. prefer:
Media

Additional Information
Year Founded: 1969
Current Activity Level : Actively seeking new investments

DRYDOCK VENTURES LP

300 Pond Street
Randolph, MA USA 02368
Phone: 7819641405
Website: www.drydockventures.com

Management and Staff
Jed Swan, Managing Partner
Ted Acworth, Managing Partner

Type of Firm
Private Equity Firm

Project Preferences

Type of Financing Preferred:
Early Stage

Size of Investments Considered:
Min Size of Investment Considered (000s): $500
Max Size of Investment Considered (000s): $2,500

Geographical Preferences

United States Preferences:
Northeast

Industry Preferences

In Computer Software prefer:
Applications Software

In Internet Specific prefer:
Internet

In Financial Services prefer:
Financial Services

In Business Serv. prefer:
Services
Distribution

In Manufact. prefer:
Manufacturing

Additional Information
Year Founded: 2009
Current Activity Level : Actively seeking new investments

DSC INVESTMENT INC

678-10, Yeoksamdong, Gangnamgu
6F, BMY-Tower
Seoul, South Korea
Phone: 82234533190
Fax: 82234533189
Website: www.dscinvestment.com

Management and Staff
Tae Hun Ha, Managing Director

Type of Firm
Private Equity Firm

Association Membership
Korean Venture Capital Association (KVCA)

Project Preferences

Type of Financing Preferred:
Early Stage
Balanced

Geographical Preferences

International Preferences:
Asia
South Africa

Industry Preferences

In Industrial/Energy prefer:
Environmental Related

Additional Information
Year Founded: 2012
Capital Under Management: $8,630,000
Current Activity Level : Actively seeking new investments

DSE INVESTMENT SERVICES LTD

38/F Dah Sing Financial Centre
108 Gloucester Road
Wanchai, Hong Kong
Phone: 85225078122
Fax: 85228459926
E-mail: ops@dahsing.com.hk

Management and Staff
Nicholas Mayhew, Managing Director

Type of Firm
Bank Affiliated

Association Membership
Hong Kong Venture Capital Association (HKVCA)

Project Preferences

Role in Financing:
Prefer role as deal originator but will also invest in deals created by others

Type of Financing Preferred:
Early Stage
Expansion
Mezzanine
Balanced
Turnaround
Later Stage

Size of Investments Considered:
Min Size of Investment Considered (000s): $1,281
Max Size of Investment Considered (000s): $12,814

Geographical Preferences

International Preferences:
Hong Kong
China

Industry Preferences

In Communications prefer:
Telecommunications

In Semiconductor/Electr prefer:
Electronic Components

In Medical/Health prefer:
Pharmaceuticals

In Consumer Related prefer:
Entertainment and Leisure
Food/Beverage
Consumer Products
Consumer Services

In Industrial/Energy prefer:
Machinery

In Financial Services prefer:
Financial Services

In Business Serv. prefer:
Distribution

Additional Information
Year Founded: 1995
Capital Under Management: $60,000,000
Current Activity Level: Actively seeking new investments
Method of Compensation: Return on invest. most important, but chg. closing fees, service fees, etc.

DSM VENTURING BV

Mauritslaan 49
Urmond, Netherlands 6129 EL
Phone: 31464763684
Fax: 31455719753
E-mail: info.venturing@dsm.com
Website: www.dsm-venturing.com

Management and Staff
Marcel Lubben, Managing Director

Type of Firm
Corporate PE/Venture

Association Membership
National Venture Capital Association - USA (NVCA)

Project Preferences

Type of Financing Preferred:
Early Stage
Later Stage
Seed
Startup

Geographical Preferences

United States Preferences:
All U.S.

International Preferences:
Europe
Netherlands
China

Industry Preferences

In Biotechnology prefer:
Biotechnology

In Medical/Health prefer:
Health Services

In Industrial/Energy prefer:
Energy
Industrial Products
Materials

Additional Information
Year Founded: 1902
Current Activity Level: Actively seeking new investments

DT CAPITAL PARTNERS

No.1 Gao Lan Road
Shanghai, China 200020
Phone: 862153835999
Fax: 862153835998
E-mail: info@dtcap.com
Website: www.dtcap.com

Other Offices
19 Des Voeux Road, Central
Suite 1505 World Wide Hous
Hong Kong, Hong Kong
Phone: 852-3107-0682
Fax: 852-3107-0683

62 Xingguang Road
C-2-2 Neptune Building
Chongqing, China 401121
Phone: 862367889909
Fax: 862367889908

100 Jingxi Road, Binhu District
Suite 204, Block 7, Area B
Wuxi, China 214125
Phone: 8651085187018
Fax: 8651085187018

No. 235 Science Road
Suite 901-902, 9F, Block A3
Guangzhou, China 510663
Phone: 862032290780
Fax: 862032290780

No.13 The Fourth Gaoxin Road
Room 12403, Langchen Mansion
Xi'an, China 710075
Phone: 862988894811
Fax: 862988894811810

No.1480 Northern Section of Tianfu Ave
1406, West Bldg, La Defense
Chengdu, China 610042
Phone: 862885231260
Fax: 862885231897

Enping Street, OCT, Nanshan Dist
Building 2
Shenzhen, China 518053
Phone: 8675588311638
Fax: 8675588312178

3000 Sand Hill Road
Building 1, Suite 150
Menlo Park, CA USA 94025
Phone: 650-854-8301
Fax: 650-233-9352

3850 Jiangnan Avenue
Suite 1811, Renovation Building
Hangzhou, China 310053
Phone: 8657186690980
Fax: 8657186690981

No.8 Jianguomenbei Avenue
Rm 1005A, China Resources Building
Beijing, China 100005
Phone: 86-10-8519-2121
Fax: 86-10-8519-2100

8 Haidian Beier Street, Haidian
Suite 707, PE Building
Beijing, China 100080
Phone: 861059733367
Fax: 86105973 3367-805

Management and Staff
Charles Zhang, Partner
Daming Zhu, Partner
Greg Penner, General Partner
Guoxiang Sun, Venture Partner
Joe Tian, Managing Partner
Jun Zhao, Managing Partner
Kevin Li, Partner
Roman Shaw, Partner

Type of Firm
Private Equity Firm

Association Membership
China Venture Capital Association

Project Preferences

Type of Financing Preferred:
Early Stage
Expansion
Balanced

Geographical Preferences

International Preferences:
Asia Pacific
China
Asia

Industry Preferences

In Medical/Health prefer:
Medical/Health

In Consumer Related prefer:
Consumer

In Industrial/Energy prefer:
Energy
Alternative Energy
Machinery
Environmental Related

In Transportation prefer:
Transportation

In Business Serv. prefer:
Media

In Manufact. prefer:
Manufacturing

Additional Information
Year Founded: 2006
Capital Under Management: $135,500,000
Current Activity Level : Actively seeking new investments

DTI CAPITAL LLC

590 Madison Avenue
New York, NY USA 10022
Phone: 2125214400
E-mail: info@dticapital.com
Website: www.dticapital.com

Other Offices
851 North Spoede Road
Saint Louis, MO USA 63141

Management and Staff
George Creel, Managing Director
John Wehrle, Managing Partner
Matthew Pennycard, Managing Director

Type of Firm
Private Equity Firm

Project Preferences

Type of Financing Preferred:
Leveraged Buyout
Turnaround
Management Buyouts
Acquisition
Recapitalizations

Geographical Preferences

United States Preferences:
All U.S.

International Preferences:
Europe

Industry Preferences

In Industrial/Energy prefer:
Energy

In Financial Services prefer:
Financial Services

In Business Serv. prefer:
Services

Additional Information
Year Founded: 2011
Current Activity Level : Actively seeking new investments

DUBAG DEUTSCHE UNTERNEHMENSBETEILIGUNGEN AG

Maximilianstrasse 58
Munich, Germany 80538
Phone: 498945209450
Fax: 4989452094545
E-mail: info@dubag.eu
Website: www.dubag.eu

Type of Firm
Private Equity Firm

Project Preferences

Type of Financing Preferred:
Leveraged Buyout
Special Situation

Geographical Preferences

International Preferences:
Europe
Western Europe

Additional Information
Year Founded: 2009
Current Activity Level : Actively seeking new investments

DUBAI INTERNATIONAL CAPITAL LLC

The Gate, East Wing
13th Floor, DIFC
Dubai, Utd. Arab Em.
Phone: 97143621888
Fax: 97143620888
E-mail: info@dubaiic.com
Website: www.dubaiic.com

Other Offices
9th Floor
21 Palmer Street
London, United Kingdom SW1H 0AD
Phone: 44-207-808-1700

Management and Staff
Anand Krishnan, Chief Executive Officer
Thomas Pereira, Chief Financial Officer

Type of Firm
Private Equity Firm

Association Membership
British Venture Capital Association (BVCA)

Project Preferences

Type of Financing Preferred:
Leveraged Buyout
Other
Acquisition

Geographical Preferences

International Preferences:
India
United Kingdom
Jordan
Netherlands
Western Europe
China
Utd. Arab Em.
Middle East
Japan
Africa

Industry Preferences

In Communications prefer:
Communications and Media

In Consumer Related prefer:
Consumer Services
Education Related

In Industrial/Energy prefer:
Oil and Gas Exploration

In Transportation prefer:
Transportation

In Manufact. prefer:
Manufacturing

In Utilities prefer:
Utilities

Additional Information
Year Founded: 2004
Current Activity Level : Actively seeking new investments

DUBAI INVESTMENT GROUP

Emirates Towers, Level 30
Sheikh Zayed Road
Dubai, Utd. Arab Em.
Phone: 97143300707
Fax: 97143303260
E-mail: info@dubaigroup.com
Website: dubaiinvestmentsgroup.org

Other Offices
4th Floor, DIFC, 5th Precinct
Sheikh Zayed Road
Dubai, Utd. Arab Em.
Phone: 971-4-363-7070
Fax: 971-4-363-7066

1 Rockefeller Plaza
30th Floor, Suite 3001
New York, NY USA 10020
Phone: 212-218-7400
Fax: 212-218-7401

3107 - 3109 AIG Tower
1 Connaught Road
Central, Hong Kong
Phone: 852-2-219-2111
Fax: 852-2-219-2112

58th Floor, Petronas Twin Towers
Kuala Lumpur City Centre
Kuala Lumpur, Malaysia 50088
Phone: 60-3-216-85288
Fax: 60-3-2168-5388

5th Floor, Berkeley Square House
Berkeley Square
London, United Kingdom W1J 6BR
Phone: 44-20-7907-2992
Fax: 44-20-7907-2990

Management and Staff
Fadhel Al Ali, Chief Executive Officer

Type of Firm
Private Equity Firm

Project Preferences

Type of Financing Preferred:
Leveraged Buyout
Expansion
Mezzanine
Balanced
Public Companies
Later Stage
Acquisition

Geographical Preferences

United States Preferences:
All U.S.

International Preferences:
India
Europe
Middle East
Asia

Industry Preferences

In Communications prefer:
Telecommunications

In Consumer Related prefer:
Hotels and Resorts

In Industrial/Energy prefer:
Energy
Industrial Products

In Transportation prefer:
Transportation

In Financial Services prefer:
Financial Services
Insurance

Additional Information
Year Founded: 2007
Current Activity Level : Actively seeking new investments

DUBLIN BUSINESS INNOVATION CENTRE

1st Flr, The Tower, Pearse St.
Trinity Tech. & Enterprise Ctr
Dublin 2, Ireland
Phone: 35316713111
E-mail: info@dublinbic.ie
Website: dublinbic.ie

Type of Firm
Incubator/Development Program

Association Membership
Irish Venture Capital Association
European Private Equity and Venture Capital Assoc.

Project Preferences

Type of Financing Preferred:
Early Stage
Start-up Financing
Seed
Startup

Geographical Preferences

International Preferences:
Ireland

Industry Preferences

In Communications prefer:
Telecommunications
Wireless Communications

In Computer Software prefer:
Software

In Internet Specific prefer:
Internet

In Computer Other prefer:
Computer Related

In Biotechnology prefer:
Biotechnology
Biotech Related Research

In Medical/Health prefer:
Medical Products
Health Services

In Consumer Related prefer:
Consumer Products

In Industrial/Energy prefer:
Alternative Energy
Industrial Products

In Financial Services prefer:
Financial Services

In Manufact. prefer:
Manufacturing

Additional Information
Year Founded: 1987
Capital Under Management: $3,000,000
Current Activity Level : Actively seeking new investments

DUBLIN CAPITAL PARTNERS LP

500 North Gulph Road
Suite 401
Norristown, PA USA 19406
Phone: 6102561740
Fax: 6107194646
Website: www.dublincapitalpartners.com

Management and Staff
Christopher Noe, General Partner

Type of Firm
Private Equity Firm

Project Preferences

Type of Financing Preferred:
Early Stage
Balanced
Later Stage

Industry Preferences

In Computer Software prefer:
Software

In Business Serv. prefer:
Media

Additional Information
Year Founded: 1969
Current Activity Level : Actively seeking new investments

DUCHOSSOIS TECHNOLOGY PARTNERS LLC

845 Larch Avenue
Elmhurst, IL USA 60126
Phone: 6302793600
Fax: 6309938644
Website: www.dcmllc.com

Other Offices
5001 Plaza on Lake Boulevard
Building 1, Suite 500
Austin, TX USA 78730
Phone: 5127955814
Fax: 5127955849

Management and Staff
Robert Fealy, Managing Director
Rohit Seth, General Partner

Type of Firm
Private Equity Firm

Association Membership
National Venture Capital Association - USA (NVCA)
Illinois Venture Capital Association

Project Preferences

Role in Financing:
Will function either as deal originator or investor in deals created by others

Type of Financing Preferred:
Early Stage
Expansion
Balanced
Later Stage

Size of Investments Considered:
Min Size of Investment Considered (000s): $2,000
Max Size of Investment Considered (000s): $7,000

Geographical Preferences

United States Preferences:

Industry Preferences

In Communications prefer:
Commercial Communications
Wireless Communications

In Computer Software prefer:
Software

In Semiconductor/Electr prefer:
Semiconductor
Sensors

In Medical/Health prefer:
Medical/Health

In Consumer Related prefer:
Consumer
Education Related

In Industrial/Energy prefer:
Energy
Process Control

In Transportation prefer:
Transportation

Additional Information
Year Founded: 1998
Capital Under Management: $85,000,000
Current Activity Level : Actively seeking new investments
Method of Compensation: Return on investment is of primary concern, do not charge fees

DUET CAPITAL LTD

27 Hill Street
London, United Kingdom W1J 5LP
Phone: 442072909800
E-mail: info@duetgroup.net
Website: www.duetgroup.net

Management and Staff
Alain Schibl, Co-Founder
Alina Gorbacheva, Vice President
Carlos Stelin, Vice President
Clive Smalley, Chief Financial Officer
Henry Gabay, Chief Executive Officer
Jun Muto, Managing Director
Nemer Bechara, Vice President
Tayfun Ozturk, Chief Operating Officer

Type of Firm
Private Equity Firm

Project Preferences

Type of Financing Preferred:
Core
Early Stage
Generalist PE
Turnaround
Opportunistic
Later Stage
Acquisition
Startup

Geographical Preferences

International Preferences:
United Kingdom
Europe
Western Europe
Israel

Industry Preferences

In Communications prefer:
Communications and Media

In Computer Software prefer:
Software

In Internet Specific prefer:
Ecommerce

In Medical/Health prefer:
Medical/Health

In Consumer Related prefer:
Sports

Additional Information
Name of Most Recent Fund: European Real Estate Debt Fund II L.P.
Most Recent Fund Was Raised: 11/13/2013
Year Founded: 2002
Capital Under Management: $1,608,072,000
Current Activity Level : Actively seeking new investments

DUFF ACKERMAN & GOODRICH LLC

251 Lytton Avenue, Suite 200
Palo Alto, CA USA 94301
Phone: 4157882755
Fax: 4157887311
E-mail: dag@dagllc.com
Website: www.dagllc.com

Other Offices
Former HQ: Two Embarcadero Center
Suite 1670
SAN FRANCISCO, CA USA 94111

Management and Staff
Arnold Ackerman, Co-Founder
Greg Williams, Managing Director
Greg Paulson, Venture Partner
Jim McBride, Partner
John Cadeddu, Managing Director
John Duff, Managing Director
Joseph Zanone, Chief Financial Officer
Nicholas Pianim, Managing Director
R. Thomas Goodrich, Managing Director
Young Chung, Managing Director

Type of Firm
Private Equity Firm

Association Membership
National Venture Capital Association - USA (NVCA)

Project Preferences

Type of Financing Preferred:
Leveraged Buyout
Early Stage
Generalist PE
Balanced
Acquisition

Industry Focus
(% based on actual investment)

Internet Specific	26.5%
Computer Software and Services	23.1%
Semiconductors/Other Elect.	10.1%
Communications and Media	10.0%
Biotechnology	9.3%
Industrial/Energy	8.7%
Medical/Health	5.2%
Other Products	4.4%
Computer Hardware	2.5%
Consumer Related	0.0%

Additional Information
Year Founded: 1991
Capital Under Management: $1,343,300,000
Current Activity Level : Actively seeking new investments

DUKE EQUITY PARTNERS INC

6255 Sunset Boulevard
Suite 800
Los Angeles, CA USA 90028
Phone: 3238712223
Fax: 3238711258
E-mail: info@duke-industries.com
Website: www.dukeequity.com

Other Offices
IndiaCo Innovation Center
2/4 Navi Peth, L.B.S. Marg
Pune, India 411 030
Phone: 91-20-2433-5710
Fax: 91-20-2433-4978

Management and Staff
Gopal Patwardhan, CEO & Managing Director
Patwardhan Gopal, Managing Partner

Type of Firm
Private Equity Firm

Project Preferences

Type of Financing Preferred:
Public Companies
Private Placement

Size of Investments Considered:
Min Size of Investment Considered (000s): $2,000
Max Size of Investment Considered (000s): $6,000

Geographical Preferences

United States Preferences:
All U.S.

International Preferences:
India

Industry Preferences

In Communications prefer:
Telecommunications
Wireless Communications
Data Communications

In Computer Software prefer:
Applications Software

In Semiconductor/Electr prefer:
Semiconductor
Controllers and Sensors

In Biotechnology prefer:
Biotechnology

In Medical/Health prefer:
Medical Diagnostics
Medical Therapeutics
Medical Products

In Industrial/Energy prefer:
Alternative Energy

In Financial Services prefer:
Financial Services

In Manufact. prefer:
Manufacturing

Additional Information
Year Founded: 2011
Current Activity Level: Actively seeking new investments

DUKE STREET CAPITAL LTD
103 Wigmore Street
Nations House
London, United Kingdom W1U 1QS
Phone: 442076638500
Fax: 442076638501
E-mail: mail@dukestreet.com
Website: www.dukestcapital.com

Other Offices
29 rue de Bassano
Paris, France 75009
Phone: 33-1-5343-5444
Fax: 33-1-5343-5440

Management and Staff
Ben Long, Partner
Buchan Scott, Partner
Charlie Troup, Managing Partner
Didier Bismuth, Partner
Iain Kennedy, Partner
James Almond, Partner
Jason Lawford, Partner
Jean-Marc Dayan, Partner
John Harper, Partner
Nikola Sutherland, Partner
Peter Taylor, Managing Partner
Stuart McMinnies, Managing Partner

Type of Firm
Private Equity Firm

Association Membership
British Venture Capital Association (BVCA)
French Venture Capital Association (AFIC)

Project Preferences

Role in Financing:
Prefer role as deal originator but will also invest in deals created by others

Type of Financing Preferred:
Leveraged Buyout
Management Buyouts
Acquisition

Geographical Preferences

International Preferences:
United Kingdom
France

Industry Focus
(% based on actual investment)

Consumer Related	55.1%
Medical/Health	22.1%
Industrial/Energy	13.6%
Communications and Media	7.3%
Other Products	1.9%
Internet Specific	0.1%

Additional Information
Name of Most Recent Fund: Duke Street Capital VI, L.P.
Most Recent Fund Was Raised: 06/15/2008
Year Founded: 1988
Capital Under Management: $1,522,700,000
Current Activity Level: Actively seeking new investments
Method of Compensation: Return on invest. most important, but chg. closing fees, service fees, etc.

DUNAMIS VENTURES
Office F-39, Block 2A
Dubai Knowledge Village
Dubai, Utd. Arab Em.
Website: www.dunamisventures.com

Management and Staff
Tanzil Sayed, Managing Partner

Type of Firm
Private Equity Firm

Project Preferences

Type of Financing Preferred:
Early Stage
Startup

Geographical Preferences

International Preferences:
United Kingdom
Utd. Arab Em.

Industry Preferences

In Biotechnology prefer:
Biotechnology

In Consumer Related prefer:
Food/Beverage
Consumer Products
Consumer Services
Education Related

Additional Information
Year Founded: 2016
Current Activity Level: Actively seeking new investments

DUNDEE SAREA LP
1250 Guy Street
Suite 710
Montreal, Canada H3H 2T4
Phone: 15144229279
E-mail: info@dundeesarea.com
Website: www.dundeesarea.com

Management and Staff
Barry Downing, Managing Partner
Sam Ramadori, Managing Partner

Type of Firm
Private Equity Firm

Project Preferences

Type of Financing Preferred:
Leveraged Buyout
Special Situation

Geographical Preferences

United States Preferences:
North America

International Preferences:
Europe

Industry Preferences

In Industrial/Energy prefer:
Energy
Industrial Products

In Agr/Forestr/Fish prefer:
Agriculture related

Additional Information
Year Founded: 2015
Capital Under Management: $86,430,000
Current Activity Level : Actively seeking new investments

DUNDEE VENTURE CAPITAL

1111 North 13th Street
Studio 119
Omaha, NE USA 68102
Phone: 4028501802

Management and Staff
Mark Hasebroock, Founder

Type of Firm
Private Equity Firm

Association Membership
National Venture Capital Association - USA (NVCA)

Project Preferences

Type of Financing Preferred:
Seed
Startup

Size of Investments Considered:
Min Size of Investment Considered (000s): $10
Max Size of Investment Considered (000s): $500

Geographical Preferences

United States Preferences:

Industry Preferences

In Computer Software prefer:
Software

In Internet Specific prefer:
Ecommerce
Web Aggregation/Portals

Additional Information
Year Founded: 2010
Capital Under Management: $36,214,000
Current Activity Level : Actively seeking new investments

DUNEDIN CAPITAL PARTNERS LTD

20 Castle Terrace
Saltire Court
Edinburgh, United Kingdom EH1 2EN
Phone: 441312256699
Fax: 441317182300
E-mail: info@dunedin.com
Website: www.dunedin.com

Other Offices
32 Duke Street St James's
Dukes Court
London, United Kingdom W1S 2EU
Phone: 2072922110
Fax: 2072922111

Management and Staff
David Williams, Partner
Dougal Bennett, Partner
Giles Derry, Partner
Mark Ligertwood, Partner
Nicol Fraser, Partner
Oliver Bevan, Partner
Shaun Middleton, Managing Partner

Type of Firm
Bank Affiliated

Association Membership
British Venture Capital Association (BVCA)
European Private Equity and Venture Capital Assoc.

Project Preferences

Role in Financing:
Prefer role as deal originator but will also invest in deals created by others

Type of Financing Preferred:
Leveraged Buyout
Later Stage
Management Buyouts
Acquisition

Geographical Preferences

International Preferences:
United Kingdom
Europe

Industry Preferences

In Medical/Health prefer:
Medical/Health

In Consumer Related prefer:
Consumer

In Industrial/Energy prefer:
Energy
Industrial Products

In Financial Services prefer:
Financial Services
Financial Services

In Business Serv. prefer:
Services

Additional Information
Year Founded: 1969
Capital Under Management: $320,800,000
Current Activity Level : Actively seeking new investments
Method of Compensation: Return on invest. most important, but chg. closing fees, service fees, etc.

DUNES POINT CAPITAL

411 Theodore Fremd Avenue
Suite 125
Rye, NY USA 10580
Phone: 9142692020
E-mail: info@dunespointcapital.com
Website: www.dunespointcapital.com

Type of Firm
Private Equity Firm

Project Preferences

Type of Financing Preferred:
Leveraged Buyout
Acquisition

Industry Preferences

In Industrial/Energy prefer:
Energy
Industrial Products

Additional Information
Year Founded: 2013
Current Activity Level : Actively seeking new investments

DUNROBIN VENTURES LLC

590 Territorial Drive
Unit H
Chicago, IL USA 60290
Website: dunrobinventures.com

Management and Staff
Jonathan Lee, Co-Founder

Type of Firm
Private Equity Firm

Project Preferences

Type of Financing Preferred:
Start-up Financing

Additional Information
Year Founded: 2015
Capital Under Management: $50,000
Current Activity Level : Actively seeking new investments

DUPONT VENTURES

Chestnut Run Plaza
P.O. Box 80708
Wilmington, DE USA 19880
Phone: 3029992927
Fax: 3029994083
Website: www2.dupont.com/Ventures/en_US/index.html

Management and Staff
Michael Blaustein, Managing Director

Type of Firm
Corporate PE/Venture

Association Membership
National Venture Capital Association - USA (NVCA)

Project Preferences

Type of Financing Preferred:
Balanced
Later Stage

Additional Information
Year Founded: 1985
Current Activity Level : Actively seeking new investments

DVR CAPITAL SPA

Largo Augusto, Seven
Milan, Italy 20122
Phone: 3927623261
Fax: 392762326210
E-mail: info@dvrcapital.it
Website: www.dvrcapital.it

Management and Staff
Fabrizio De Simone, Partner
Martin Miszerak, Managing Director
Nicola Gualmini, Partner
Stefano Baiardo, Partner

Type of Firm
Bank Affiliated

Project Preferences

Geographical Preferences

International Preferences:
Italy

Additional Information
Year Founded: 2007
Capital Under Management: $40,000,000
Current Activity Level : Actively seeking new investments

DW HEALTHCARE PARTNERS

66 Wellington Street West
TD Bank Tower, Suite 4030
Toronto, Canada M5K 1J5
Phone: 4165832420
Website: www.dwhp.com

Other Offices
66 Wellington Street West
TD Bank Tower, Suite 4030
Toronto, Canada M5K 1J5
Phone: 4165832420
Fax: 4165832425

1413 Center Drive
Suite 220
PARK CITY, UT USA 84098
Phone: 4356454050
Fax: 4356454065

Management and Staff
Aly Champsi, Managing Director
Doug Schillinger, Managing Director
Gabriel Becher, Principal
Jay Benear, Founder
Justin Pettit, Vice President
Lisa Downey, Vice President
Liz Null, Vice President
Rod Boone, Managing Director

Type of Firm
Private Equity Firm

Project Preferences

Type of Financing Preferred:
Leveraged Buyout
Acquisition

Geographical Preferences

United States Preferences:
North America

Industry Preferences

In Medical/Health prefer:
Medical/Health
Medical Diagnostics
Diagnostic Services
Diagnostic Test Products
Medical Products
Health Services

Additional Information
Name of Most Recent Fund: DW Healthcare Partners III, L.P.
Most Recent Fund Was Raised: 01/05/2012

Year Founded: 2002
Capital Under Management: $800,000,000
Current Activity Level : Actively seeking new investments

DWP INVESTMENTS LLC

7114 East Stetson Drive
Suite 350
Scottsdale, AZ USA 85251
Website: www.dwpinvestments.com

Management and Staff
David Paul, Managing Director

Type of Firm
Private Equity Firm

Project Preferences

Type of Financing Preferred:
Early Stage

Geographical Preferences

United States Preferences:
Arizona
Southern California
Colorado

Industry Preferences

In Computer Software prefer:
Software

Additional Information
Year Founded: 2016
Current Activity Level : Actively seeking new investments

DYMON ASIA EQUITY PTE LTD

One Temasek Avenue
Suite 11-01
Singapore, Singapore 039192
E-mail: enquiries@dymonasia.com
Website: www.dymonasia.com

Management and Staff
Keith Tan, Managing Partner

Type of Firm
Private Equity Firm

Project Preferences

Type of Financing Preferred:
Leveraged Buyout
Acquisition

Geographical Preferences

United States Preferences:
Southeast

DYNAMIC VENTURE OPPORTUNITIES FUND LTD

1 Adelaide Street East
29th Floor
Toronto, Canada M5C 2V9
Phone: 5149083212
Fax: 4163634179
Website: www.dynamic.ca

Other Offices

350 Seventh Avenue South West
Suite 3250
Calgary, Canada T2B 3N9

1055 Dunsmuir Street
Suite 3434, Four Bentall Centre
Vancouver, Canada V7X 1K8

1200 McGill College Avenue
Suite 2300
Montreal, Canada H3B 4G7

Type of Firm
Private Equity Firm

Additional Information
Name of Most Recent Fund: Dynamic Ventures Opportunities Fund
Most Recent Fund Was Raised: 03/31/2002
Year Founded: 1993
Current Activity Level : Actively seeking new investments
Year Founded: 2012
Capital Under Management: $166,216,000
Current Activity Level : Actively seeking new investments

DYNAMIS ADVISORS LLC

310 Fourth Street
Suite 101
Charlottesville, VA USA 22902
Phone: 434-220-0234
E-mail: info@dynamis.com
Website: www.dynamisfunds.com

Management and Staff
George McVey, Chief Financial Officer

Type of Firm
Private Equity Firm

Project Preferences

Type of Financing Preferred:
Balanced

Geographical Preferences

United States Preferences:
All U.S.

Additional Information
Name of Most Recent Fund: Dynamis Venture Partners, LP
Most Recent Fund Was Raised: 10/02/2007
Year Founded: 2007
Capital Under Management: $9,000,000
Current Activity Level : Making few, if any, new investments

DYNAMK CAPITAL LLC

473 Sylvan Avenue
Englewood, NJ USA 07632
Website: www.dynamkcapital.com

Management and Staff
Daniella Kranjac, Co-Founder
Mario Kranjac, Co-Founder

Type of Firm
Private Equity Firm

Project Preferences

Type of Financing Preferred:
Startup

Additional Information
Year Founded: 2016
Current Activity Level : Actively seeking new investments

DYNAMO ACCELERATOR

800 Market Street
Suite 200
Chattanooga, TN USA 37402
Website: dynamo.vc

Type of Firm
Incubator/Development Program

Project Preferences

Type of Financing Preferred:
Early Stage
Seed
Startup

Additional Information
Year Founded: 2016
Capital Under Management: $18,000,000
Current Activity Level : Actively seeking new investments

DZETA CONSEIL SAS

48, rue Saint Anne
Paris, France 75002
Phone: 33143167120
Fax: 33142605180
Website: www.dzetaconseil.com

Type of Firm
Private Equity Firm

Project Preferences

Type of Financing Preferred:
Leveraged Buyout
Management Buyouts

Geographical Preferences

International Preferences:
France

Industry Preferences

In Medical/Health prefer:
Medical/Health

In Consumer Related prefer:
Entertainment and Leisure

In Financial Services prefer:
Real Estate
Financial Services

In Business Serv. prefer:
Distribution

Additional Information
Year Founded: 2009
Current Activity Level : Actively seeking new investments

- E -

8 MILES LLP

55 Strand
Fifth Floor
London, United Kingdom WC2N 5LR
Phone: 442070689999
Website: www.8miles.com

Other Offices

7-10 Adam Street
The Strand
London, United Kingdom WC2N 6AA
Phone: 442075209446
Fax: 442075209410

Management and Staff

Doug Agble, Partner
Hemen Shah, Partner
Nathan Mintah, Partner

Type of Firm

Private Equity Firm

Project Preferences

Type of Financing Preferred:
Leveraged Buyout
Management Buyouts
Acquisition
Recapitalizations

Geographical Preferences

International Preferences:
Africa

Industry Preferences

In Communications prefer:
Telecommunications

In Medical/Health prefer:
Medical/Health
Pharmaceuticals

In Consumer Related prefer:
Consumer
Retail
Consumer Products
Consumer Services

In Industrial/Energy prefer:
Energy

In Transportation prefer:
Transportation

In Financial Services prefer:
Financial Services
Real Estate

In Business Serv. prefer:
Services
Media

In Agr/Forestr/Fish prefer:
Agribusiness

In Utilities prefer:
Utilities

Additional Information

Name of Most Recent Fund: 8 Miles Fund, L.P.
Most Recent Fund Was Raised: 02/19/2012
Year Founded: 2009
Current Activity Level : Actively seeking new investments

819 CAPITAL LLC

Pier 1, Bay 2
The Embarcadero
San Francisco, CA USA 94111
Website: www.819capital.com

Management and Staff

John Bickford, Co-Founder
Joseph Lerner, Co-Founder

Type of Firm

Private Equity Firm

Project Preferences

Type of Financing Preferred:
Early Stage
Generalist PE
Balanced
Later Stage
Other
Seed

Industry Preferences

In Consumer Related prefer:
Consumer Products

In Financial Services prefer:
Real Estate

Additional Information

Year Founded: 1969
Current Activity Level : Actively seeking new investments

88 GREEN VENTURES

88 Collins Street
Level 1
Melbourne, Australia 3000
Phone: 61396633207
E-mail: info@88greenventures.com
Website: www.88greenventures.com

Type of Firm

Private Equity Firm

Project Preferences

Type of Financing Preferred:
Early Stage

Additional Information

Year Founded: 2016
Current Activity Level : Actively seeking new investments

88MPH GARAGE

66 Albert Road, Woodstock
Block A, Fourth Floor
Cape Town, South Africa 7925
Website: www.88mph.ac

Other Offices

Fourth Floor Piedmont Plaza
671 Ngong Road
, Kenya

Type of Firm

Incubator/Development Program

Project Preferences

Type of Financing Preferred:
Early Stage
Seed
Startup

Geographical Preferences

International Preferences:
Nigeria
South Africa
Africa

Industry Preferences

In Communications prefer:
Telecommunications
Wireless Communications

In Internet Specific prefer:
Internet
Web Aggregation/Portals

Additional Information

Year Founded: 2011
Current Activity Level : Actively seeking new investments

8VC

501 2nd Street
Suite 300
San Francisco, CA USA 94107
E-mail: media@eight.vc
Website: eight.vc

Type of Firm

Private Equity Firm

Project Preferences

Type of Financing Preferred:
Early Stage

Additional Information
Year Founded: 1969
Capital Under Management: $425,000,000
Current Activity Level : Actively seeking new investments

E & I VENTURES LLC

55 North Arizona Place
Suite 203
Chandler, AZ USA 85225
Phone: 4803202520
E-mail: info@eandiventuresllc.com
Website: eandiventuresllc.com

Type of Firm
Private Equity Firm

Project Preferences

Type of Financing Preferred:
Early Stage
Seed

Geographical Preferences

United States Preferences:
West Coast
Southwest

Additional Information
Year Founded: 2016
Current Activity Level : Actively seeking new investments

E CAPITAL MANAGEMENT SCRL

273, avenue de Tervueren
Brussels, Belgium 1150
Phone: 3226422000
Fax: 3226422009
E-mail: info@e-capital.be

Management and Staff
Eric Van Zujilen, Partner
Jerome Lamfalussy, Partner
Yvan Jansen, Partner
Yves Trouveroy, Partner

Type of Firm
Private Equity Firm

Association Membership
Belgium Venturing Association

Project Preferences

Type of Financing Preferred:
Leveraged Buyout
Management Buyouts

Size of Investments Considered:
Min Size of Investment Considered (000s): $5,112
Max Size of Investment Considered (000s): $15,337

Geographical Preferences

International Preferences:
Luxembourg
Europe
Netherlands
Belgium
France

Industry Preferences

In Computer Other prefer:
Computer Related

In Semiconductor/Electr prefer:
Electronics
Component Testing Equipmt

In Biotechnology prefer:
Biotechnology

In Medical/Health prefer:
Medical/Health

In Industrial/Energy prefer:
Industrial Products
Materials

In Business Serv. prefer:
Services

Additional Information
Name of Most Recent Fund: E-Capital III
Most Recent Fund Was Raised: 06/17/2011
Year Founded: 1999
Capital Under Management: $31,300,000
Current Activity Level : Actively seeking new investments

E I CAPITAL LLP

41-42 Berners Street
London, United Kingdom W1T 3NB
Phone: 442071837592
E-mail: info@encorecapital.co.uk
Website: www.encorecapital.co.uk

Management and Staff
Dimitri Tzililis, Partner
Ed Shah, Partner
Khilan Dodhia, Partner
Rajesh Shah, Partner
Shirin Gandhi, Partner

Type of Firm
Private Equity Firm

Project Preferences

Type of Financing Preferred:
Leveraged Buyout
Expansion
Management Buyouts

Geographical Preferences

International Preferences:
United Kingdom
Uganda

Industry Preferences

In Computer Software prefer:
Software

In Medical/Health prefer:
Health Services

Additional Information
Year Founded: 2009
Current Activity Level : Actively seeking new investments

E MERGE SA

480, av. Louiselaan
IT Tower - 15th Floor
Brussels, Belgium 1082
Fax: 3224668776
E-mail: info@emerge.be
Website: www.emerge.be

Type of Firm
Private Equity Firm

Project Preferences

Type of Financing Preferred:
Early Stage
Startup

Size of Investments Considered:
Min Size of Investment Considered (000s): $196
Max Size of Investment Considered (000s): $1,308

Geographical Preferences

International Preferences:
Europe
Belgium

Industry Focus
(% based on actual investment)
  Computer Software and Services   100.0%

Additional Information
Year Founded: 1998
Current Activity Level : Actively seeking new investments

E TRUST VENTURE CAPITAL

1480-3, YeonHyangdong, Sunchon
Seoul, South Korea
Phone: 822-3424-1988
Fax: 822-3424-1983

Type of Firm
Private Equity Firm

Association Membership
Korean Venture Capital Association (KVCA)

Project Preferences

Type of Financing Preferred:
Balanced

Geographical Preferences

International Preferences:
Korea, South

Industry Preferences

In Semiconductor/Electr prefer:
Electronics

Additional Information

Year Founded: 1999
Capital Under Management: $13,100,000
Current Activity Level : Actively seeking new investments

E-TRUST INVESTMENT GROUP

Regus business center
3, Smolenskaya sq.
Moscow, Russia 119099
Phone: 70959338944
Fax: 70959378290
E-mail: info@e-trustgroup.com
Website: www.e-trustgroup.com

Management and Staff

Maxim Karimov, Managing Director

Type of Firm

Private Equity Firm

Project Preferences

Type of Financing Preferred:
Startup

Geographical Preferences

International Preferences:
Russia

Additional Information

Year Founded: 2003
Current Activity Level : Actively seeking new investments

E.VENTURES

600 Montgomery Street, 43rd Floor
San Francisco, CA USA 94111
Phone: 4158695200
Fax: 4158695201
E-mail: info@eventures.vc
Website: www.eventures.vc

Other Offices

4 34 23 Yoha Setagaya-ku
Tokyo, Japan 1580097
Phone: 819014672730

Rua Joaquim Floriano, 1120 A
cj. 92, Itaim Bibi
Sao Paolo, Brazil 04534
Phone: 551140636061

Am Kupfergraben 6a
Berlin, Germany 10117
Phone: 4930467249770

Dongsi Bei St. Dongcheng District
Tianhai Busines Building B, Suite 107
Beijing, China

Management and Staff

Akio Tanaka, Partner
Anderson Thees, Partner
Andreas Haug, General Partner
Christian Leybold, General Partner
Damian Doberstein, Partner
Hirofumi Ono, Partner
Jan Buettner, Partner
Maren Eckloff-Boehme, Chief Financial Officer
Masashi Kobayashi, Partner
Mathias Schilling, General Partner
Thomas Gieselman, Founder
Yann De Vries, Partner

Type of Firm

Private Equity Firm

Project Preferences

Role in Financing:
Will function either as deal originator or investor in deals created by others

Type of Financing Preferred:
Early Stage
Balanced

Geographical Preferences

United States Preferences:
All U.S.

International Preferences:
Europe
Brazil
Asia
Russia

Industry Focus

(% based on actual investment)
Internet Specific	60.8%
Computer Software and Services	29.2%
Communications and Media	5.0%
Consumer Related	2.4%
Computer Hardware	1.0%
Other Products	0.9%
Medical/Health	0.7%

Additional Information

Name of Most Recent Fund: Bertelsmann Ventures
Most Recent Fund Was Raised: 09/01/1999
Year Founded: 1997
Capital Under Management: $750,000,000

Current Activity Level : Actively seeking new investments
Method of Compensation: Return on investment is of primary concern, do not charge fees

E14 GP LLC

15 Walnut Street
Suite 150
Wellesley, MA USA 02481

Type of Firm

Private Equity Firm

Project Preferences

Type of Financing Preferred:
Early Stage
Seed

Industry Preferences

In Biotechnology prefer:
Biotechnology

In Consumer Related prefer:
Consumer Products

In Manufact. prefer:
Manufacturing

Additional Information

Year Founded: 2017
Capital Under Management: $9,500,000
Current Activity Level : Actively seeking new investments

E3 MEDIA LTD

Unit 2.1-2.3, Paintworks
Bath Road
Bristol, United Kingdom BS4 3EH
Phone: 44-117-902-1333
Fax: 44-117-902-1334
E-mail: info@e3media.co.uk
Website: www.e3.co.uk

Management and Staff

Dougal Templeton, Co-Founder
Mike Bennett, Co-Founder
Scott Davidson, Co-Founder
Stuart Avery, Co-Founder

Type of Firm

Incubator/Development Program

Project Preferences

Type of Financing Preferred:
Early Stage
Seed
Startup

Geographical Preferences

International Preferences:
No Preference

Industry Preferences

In Communications prefer:
Media and Entertainment

In Internet Specific prefer:
Internet

Additional Information

Year Founded: 2000
Current Activity Level : Actively seeking new investments

EAGLE MERCHANT PARTNERS

3060 Peachtree Road, NorthWest
One Buckhead Plaza, Suite 360
Atlanta, GA USA 30305
Phone: 4049742480
Website: www.eaglemerchantpartners.com

Management and Staff

Andrew Hirsekorn, Principal
Bill Lundstrom, Partner
E. Stockton Croft, Partner
Ransom James, Partner

Type of Firm

Private Equity Firm

Project Preferences

Type of Financing Preferred:
Leveraged Buyout

Geographical Preferences

United States Preferences:
Southeast

Industry Preferences

In Consumer Related prefer:
Consumer
Retail
Other Restaurants

In Industrial/Energy prefer:
Industrial Products

In Business Serv. prefer:
Services
Distribution

In Manufact. prefer:
Manufacturing

Additional Information

Year Founded: 2013
Current Activity Level : Actively seeking new investments

EAGLE PRIVATE CAPITAL LLC

One North Brentwood
Suite 1550
Saint Louis, MO USA 63105
Phone: 3147541400
Fax: 3147541430
Website: www.eagleprivatecapital.com

Management and Staff

James O Donnell, President
John Brown, Managing Director

Type of Firm

Investment Management Firm

Association Membership

Natl Assoc of Small Bus. Inv. Co (NASBIC)

Project Preferences

Type of Financing Preferred:
Leveraged Buyout
Expansion
Mezzanine
Later Stage
Management Buyouts
Recapitalizations

Geographical Preferences

United States Preferences:
Midwest

Industry Preferences

In Consumer Related prefer:
Consumer
Retail
Consumer Products

In Business Serv. prefer:
Services
Distribution
Consulting Services

In Manufact. prefer:
Manufacturing

Additional Information

Name of Most Recent Fund: Eagle Fund III, L.P.
Most Recent Fund Was Raised: 08/02/2012
Year Founded: 1986
Capital Under Management: $250,000,000
Current Activity Level : Actively seeking new investments

EAGLE TRADING SYSTEMS INC

47 Hulfish Street, Suite 410
Princeton, NJ USA 08542
Phone: 609-688-2060
Fax: 609-688-2099
E-mail: eagleinfo@eaglets.com
Website: www.eaglets.com

Management and Staff

Menachem Sternberg, Chief Executive Officer

Type of Firm

Private Equity Firm

Additional Information

Year Founded: 2002
Capital Under Management: $16,300,000
Current Activity Level : Actively seeking new investments

EAGLEHILL ADVISORS LLC

150 East 52nd Street
Suite 5004
New York, NY USA 10022
Phone: 2124051200
E-mail: info@eaglehillcapital.com
Website: www.eaglehillcapital.com

Management and Staff

Jason Cunningham, Co-Founder
Marcos Garcia, Vice President
Marcus Villanueva, Principal
Michael Zicari, Co-Founder

Type of Firm

Investment Management Firm

Project Preferences

Type of Financing Preferred:
Mezzanine
Acquisition
Recapitalizations

Geographical Preferences

United States Preferences:

Additional Information

Year Founded: 2016
Capital Under Management: $100,000,000
Current Activity Level : Actively seeking new investments

EAGLETREE CAPITAL, LP

1301 Avenue of the Americas
41st Floor
New York, NY USA 10019
Phone: 2127025600
Fax: 2127025635
Website: www.eagletree.com

Other Offices

1705 El Camino Real
PALO ALTO, CA USA 94306
Phone: 650-473-2300
Fax: 650-473-2332

1999 Avenue of the Stars
Suite 2840
CENTURY CITY, CA USA 90067
Phone: 3102863315
Fax: 3102863325

Management and Staff

George Majoros, President & COO
Nitin Singhal, Vice President
Rengarajan Ramesh, Managing Director
Robert Mersten, Chief Financial Officer
Robert Fogelson, Managing Director
Rohan Rai, Vice President
Stuart Martin, Vice President
Thomas Huang, Managing Director

Type of Firm

Private Equity Firm

Project Preferences

Role in Financing:
Prefer role as deal originator but will also invest in deals created by others

Type of Financing Preferred:
Leveraged Buyout
Balanced
Acquisition

Geographical Preferences

United States Preferences:

Industry Focus

(% based on actual investment)

Communications and Media	60.4%
Internet Specific	14.5%
Consumer Related	6.9%
Medical/Health	4.3%
Semiconductors/Other Elect.	4.0%
Other Products	3.6%
Computer Hardware	2.2%
Computer Software and Services	2.2%
Industrial/Energy	1.8%

Additional Information

Year Founded: 2001
Capital Under Management: $300,000,000
Current Activity Level : Actively seeking new investments
Method of Compensation: Return on investment is of primary concern, do not charge fees

EARLSFIELD CAPITAL

253 Earlsfield Road
London, United Kingdom
E-mail: info@earlsfieldcapital.com
Website: earlsfield.com

Type of Firm

Private Equity Firm

Project Preferences

Type of Financing Preferred:
Early Stage

Geographical Preferences

International Preferences:
India

Industry Preferences

In Medical/Health prefer:
Medical/Health

In Consumer Related prefer:
Food/Beverage
Education Related

In Financial Services prefer:
Financial Services

Additional Information

Year Founded: 2008
Current Activity Level : Actively seeking new investments

EARLY STAGE PARTNERS LP

1801 East Ninth Street
Suite 1700
Cleveland, OH USA 44114
Phone: 2167814600
E-mail: inbox@esplp.com
Website: www.esplp.com

Other Offices

201 South Main Street
Suite 900
Ann Arbor, MI USA 48103
Phone: 7342143007

Management and Staff

Charles MacMillan, Chief Financial Officer
Ethan Cohen, Managing Director
Jim Petras, General Partner
Jonathan Murray, Co-Founder
Mike Bunker, Managing Director

Type of Firm

Private Equity Firm

Project Preferences

Role in Financing:
Will function either as deal originator or investor in deals created by others

Type of Financing Preferred:
Early Stage

Geographical Preferences

United States Preferences:
Midwest

Industry Preferences

In Medical/Health prefer:
Medical/Health

In Industrial/Energy prefer:
Industrial Products

In Manufact. prefer:
Manufacturing

Additional Information

Name of Most Recent Fund: Early Stage Partners II, L.P.
Most Recent Fund Was Raised: 03/10/2008
Year Founded: 2001
Capital Under Management: $100,000,000
Current Activity Level : Actively seeking new investments
Method of Compensation: Return on investment is of primary concern, do not charge fees

EARLYBIRD VENTURE CAPITAL GMBH & CO KG

Maximilianstrasse 14
Munich, Germany 80539
Phone: 49892907020
E-mail: info@earlybird.com
Website: www.earlybird.de

Management and Staff

Andrea Baldini, Principal
Barbara Poggiali, Partner
Cem Sertoglu, Partner
Christian Nagel, Managing Partner
Ciaran O Leary, Partner
Dan Lupu, Partner
Evren Ucok, Partner
Jason Whitmire, General Partner
John Yianni, Venture Partner
Konstantin Guericke, Venture Partner
Lionel Carnot, Partner
Maximilian Claussen, Principal
Michele Novelli, Partner
Roland Manger, Founder
Rolf Mathies, Partner
Thom Rasche, Partner
Wolfgang Seibold, Partner

Type of Firm

Private Equity Firm

Association Membership

German Venture Capital Association (BVK)
European Private Equity and Venture Capital Assoc.

Project Preferences

Role in Financing:
Will function either as deal originator or investor in deals created by others

Type of Financing Preferred:
Early Stage
Later Stage
Seed
Startup

Size of Investments Considered:
Min Size of Investment Considered (000s): $1,323
Max Size of Investment Considered (000s): $19,844

Geographical Preferences

United States Preferences:

International Preferences:
Turkey
Central Europe
Europe
Eastern Europe
Germany

Industry Focus

(% based on actual investment)
Internet Specific	40.5%
Computer Software and Services	27.6%
Medical/Health	10.5%
Biotechnology	6.3%
Semiconductors/Other Elect.	5.3%
Industrial/Energy	4.1%
Computer Hardware	2.1%
Communications and Media	2.1%
Other Products	1.5%

Additional Information
Name of Most Recent Fund: Earlybird Digital East Fund
Most Recent Fund Was Raised: 01/21/2014
Year Founded: 1997
Capital Under Management: $800,000,000
Current Activity Level : Actively seeking new investments
Method of Compensation: Return on investment is of primary concern, do not charge fees

EARLYMARKET LLP

Six A Addison Avenue
London, United Kingdom W11 4QR
Phone: 442076022334
Website: www.earlymarket.com

Type of Firm
Incubator/Development Program

Project Preferences

Type of Financing Preferred:
Seed
Startup

Industry Preferences

In Medical/Health prefer:
Hospitals/Clinics/Primary
Hospital/Other Instit.

In Transportation prefer:
Aerospace

In Financial Services prefer:
Financial Services
Financial Services

Additional Information
Year Founded: 2013
Current Activity Level : Actively seeking new investments

EARLYSTAGE.NYC

1430 Broadway
Suite 503
New York, NY USA 10018
Phone: 9177633500
Website: www.earlystage.nyc

Type of Firm
Incubator/Development Program

Project Preferences

Type of Financing Preferred:
Early Stage
Seed
Startup

Geographical Preferences

United States Preferences:

Additional Information
Year Founded: 2015
Capital Under Management: $800,000
Current Activity Level : Actively seeking new investments

EARTH CAPITAL PARTNERS LLP

34 St James's Street
Third Floor
London, United Kingdom SW1A 1HD
Phone: 02078114500
E-mail: info@earthcp.com
Website: www.earthcp.com

Type of Firm
Investment Management Firm

Project Preferences

Type of Financing Preferred:
Generalist PE

Industry Preferences

In Industrial/Energy prefer:
Energy

In Other prefer:
Environment Responsible

Additional Information
Year Founded: 2017
Current Activity Level : Actively seeking new investments

EAST AFRICA CAPITAL PARTNERS

Off Langata Road
Wilson Business Park
Nairobi, Kenya
Phone: 254206006521
Fax: 254206006526
E-mail: info@eacp.co.ke

Other Offices
Berkley Square House
1st Floor, Berkley Square
London, United Kingdom W1J 6BD

Management and Staff
Ali Mufuruki, Partner
James Gachui, Partner
Jimnah Mbaru, Partner
Mandhir Grewal, Chief Financial Officer
Richard Bell, Chief Executive Officer

Type of Firm
Private Equity Firm

Association Membership
Emerging Markets Private Equity Association

Project Preferences

Type of Financing Preferred:
Leveraged Buyout
Expansion
Balanced

Size of Investments Considered:
Min Size of Investment Considered (000s): $500
Max Size of Investment Considered (000s): $5,000

Geographical Preferences

International Preferences:
Rwanda
Malawi
Uganda
Tanzania
Kenya
Africa

Industry Preferences

In Communications prefer:
Communications and Media
Telecommunications

In Financial Services prefer:
Real Estate

In Business Serv. prefer:
Media

Additional Information
Year Founded: 2005
Current Activity Level : Actively seeking new investments

EAST BRIDGE PARTNERS

6th Floor, Ukyeong Building
239-1 Nonhyeon 2-dong
Seoul, South Korea
Phone: 82262175100
Fax: 82262175110
Website: www.eastbridge.asia

Type of Firm
Private Equity Firm

Project Preferences

Type of Financing Preferred:
Generalist PE

Geographical Preferences

International Preferences:
China
Korea, South
Japan

Additional Information
Year Founded: 2011
Current Activity Level : Actively seeking new investments

EAST CAPITAL PRIVATE EQUITY AB

Kungsgatan 33
Stockholm, Sweden 111 93
Phone: 46850588500
Fax: 46850588590
E-mail: info@eastcapital.com

Other Offices
13/F Wyndham Place
40-44 Wyndham Street
Hong Kong, China
Phone: 85236550550
Fax: 85236550554

Leonardo Business Center
17/52 B/ Khmelnitskogo St.
Kyiv, Ukraine 01030

Joe street 2B
Tallinn, Estonia
Phone: 3726406650
Fax: 3726406660

Kronprinsesse Marthas Plass 1
P.O. Box 1811
Oslo, Norway
Phone: 4722396690
Fax: 4794772395

Romanov Dvor Business Centre
4, Romanov Lane
Moscow, Russia 125009
Phone: 74953801500
Fax: 74953801501

39 Avenue d'Iena
Duncanville, France 75116
Phone: 33140730080
Fax: 33140730081

11F Aurora Plaza
No.99 Fu Cheng Road
Shanghai, China 200120
Phone: 862160589143

Management and Staff
Aivaras Abromavicius, Partner
Albin Rosengren, Partner
Jacob Grapengiesser, Partner
Karine Hirn, Partner
Kestutis Sasnauskas, Chief Executive Officer

Type of Firm
Investment Management Firm

Project Preferences

Type of Financing Preferred:
Core
Leveraged Buyout
Value-Add
Generalist PE
Balanced
Later Stage
Special Situation
Distressed Debt

Geographical Preferences

International Preferences:
Armenia
Hungary
Slovak Repub.
Belarus
Kazakhstan
Central Europe
Europe
Czech Republic
Rest of World
Poland
Kyrgyzstan
Eastern Europe
Tajikistan
Azerbaijan
Moldova
Ukraine
Estonia
Uzbekistan
Latvia
Lithuania
Russia
Georgia

Industry Preferences

In Consumer Related prefer:
Consumer

In Industrial/Energy prefer:
Energy

In Financial Services prefer:
Financial Services
Real Estate

In Business Serv. prefer:
Services
Distribution

Additional Information
Year Founded: 2003
Capital Under Management: $647,900,000
Current Activity Level : Actively seeking new investments

EAST GATE PARTNERS LLC

300-6 Yeomgok-dong, Seocho-gu
No.816 IKP Bldg
Seoul, South Korea
Phone: 82222650503
Fax: 82222612509
Website: www.egpartners.co.kr

Type of Firm
Private Equity Firm

Association Membership
Korean Venture Capital Association (KVCA)

Project Preferences

Type of Financing Preferred:
Balanced

Geographical Preferences

International Preferences:
Korea, South

Industry Preferences

In Communications prefer:
Communications and Media
Media and Entertainment

Additional Information
Year Founded: 2010
Capital Under Management: $29,206,000
Current Activity Level : Actively seeking new investments

EAST HILL MANAGEMENT CO LLC

Ten Memorial Boulevard
Suite 902
Providence, RI USA 02903
Phone: 4014900700
Website: www.easthillmgt.com

Other Offices
Oxford University Begbroke Science Park
Sandy Lane, Yarnton
Oxford, United Kingdom OX5 1PF
Phone: 44-1865-283-792

Type of Firm
Private Equity Firm

Project Preferences

Type of Financing Preferred:
Early Stage
Balanced

Geographical Preferences

United States Preferences:
All U.S.

International Preferences:
United Kingdom

Industry Preferences

In Biotechnology prefer:
Biotechnology

Additional Information
Year Founded: 2000
Capital Under Management: $16,800,000
Current Activity Level : Actively seeking new investments

EAST VALLEY VENTURES INC

12 Smythe Street
Suite 214
Saint John, Canada E2L 5G5
Phone: 5066429384
Website: www.eastvalleyventures.com

Type of Firm
Private Equity Firm

Project Preferences

Type of Financing Preferred:
Early Stage

Geographical Preferences

Canadian Preferences:
Nova Scotia
Prince Edward Island
New Brunswick
Newfoundland

Additional Information
Year Founded: 2012
Current Activity Level : Actively seeking new investments

EAST WEST CAPITAL PARTNERS PTE LTD

14 Robinson Road
06-01 Far East Finanace Bldg.
Singapore, Singapore 048545
Phone: 65-9675-6436
Fax: 65-6325-2789
Website: www.eastwestcap.com

Management and Staff
Duncan Moore, Partner
Hans Brenner, Partner
Ram Radhakrishnan, Partner
Sanjay Sehgal, CEO & Managing Director

Type of Firm
Private Equity Firm

Project Preferences

Role in Financing:
Prefer role as deal originator

Type of Financing Preferred:
Second Stage Financing
Early Stage
Research and Development
Public Companies
Turnaround
Later Stage
Management Buyouts
First Stage Financing
Private Placement
Special Situation
Recapitalizations

Geographical Preferences

International Preferences:
India
China
Asia

Industry Preferences

In Biotechnology prefer:
Biotechnology
Human Biotechnology

In Medical/Health prefer:
Medical Products
Health Services
Hospitals/Clinics/Primary
Pharmaceuticals

Additional Information
Year Founded: 2005
Current Activity Level : Actively seeking new investments

EASTERLY CAPITAL LLC

138 Conant Street
Beverly, MA USA 01915
Phone: 6172314300
E-mail: info@easterlycapital.com
Website: easterlycapital.com

Type of Firm
Investment Management Firm

Project Preferences

Type of Financing Preferred:
Core
Value-Add
Generalist PE
Later Stage

Industry Preferences

In Financial Services prefer:
Real Estate

Additional Information
Year Founded: 2013
Capital Under Management: $114,300,000
Current Activity Level : Actively seeking new investments

EASTERN BELL VENTURE CAPITAL CO LTD

1777 Century Ave
Block C, Bldg 7, East Hope
Shanghai, China 200120
Phone: 862161652668
Fax: 862161652668
E-mail: info@easternbellvc.com
Website: www.ebvc.com.cn

Other Offices
Yuetan North Ave.
2116, No.25 Yard
Suzhou, China 100834
Phone: 8668392116
Fax: 8668392116

Management and Staff
Chris Evdemon, Venture Partner
Tang Tao, Managing Partner
Yan Li, Managing Partner

Type of Firm
Private Equity Firm

Geographical Preferences

International Preferences:
China

Industry Preferences

In Consumer Related prefer:
Consumer Services

In Industrial/Energy prefer:
Environmental Related

In Transportation prefer:
Transportation

In Business Serv. prefer:
Distribution

Additional Information
Year Founded: 2009
Capital Under Management: $114,383,000
Current Activity Level: Actively seeking new investments

EASTLINK CAPITAL

63 Willow Road, Suite 168
Menlo Park, CA USA 94025
Phone: 6506483188
Fax: 6508544303
E-mail: info@eastlinkcap.com
Website: www.eastlinkcap.com

Type of Firm
Private Equity Firm

Project Preferences

Type of Financing Preferred:
Early Stage

Geographical Preferences

United States Preferences:
California

Industry Preferences

In Computer Software prefer:
Data Processing
Software

In Consumer Related prefer:
Consumer

Additional Information
Year Founded: 2013
Current Activity Level: Actively seeking new investments

EASTON HUNT CAPITAL PARTNERS LP

767 Third Avenue, Seventh Floor
New York, NY USA 10017
Phone: 2127020950
Fax: 2127020950
Website: www.eastoncapital.com

Other Offices
520 Alhambra Circle
Coral Gables
Miami, FL USA 33134

Management and Staff
Charles Hughes, Managing Director
Francisco Garcia, Managing Director
Kresimir Letinic, Managing Director
Lisa Rhoads, Managing Director
Richard Schneider, Managing Director
Thomas Jackson, Venture Partner

Type of Firm
Private Equity Firm

Project Preferences

Role in Financing:
Prefer role as deal originator but will also invest in deals created by others

Type of Financing Preferred:
Early Stage
Balanced
Later Stage

Size of Investments Considered:
Min Size of Investment Considered (000s): $10,000
Max Size of Investment Considered (000s): $20,000

Geographical Preferences

United States Preferences:

Industry Preferences

In Medical/Health prefer:
Medical/Health
Drug/Equipmt Delivery
Health Services

Additional Information
Year Founded: 1999
Capital Under Management: $140,000,000
Current Activity Level: Actively seeking new investments
Method of Compensation: Return on invest. most important, but chg. closing fees, service fees, etc.

EASTSIDE PARTNERS

207 East Side Square
Second Floor
Huntsville, AL USA 35801
Phone: 2563278777
Fax: 2568838558
E-mail: info@eastsidepartners.com

Management and Staff
Emerson Fann, Managing Partner
Paul Reaves, Venture Partner

Type of Firm
Private Equity Firm

Project Preferences

Type of Financing Preferred:
Early Stage
Expansion

Size of Investments Considered:
Min Size of Investment Considered (000s): $1,000
Max Size of Investment Considered (000s): $5,000

Geographical Preferences

United States Preferences:
Southeast

Industry Preferences

In Medical/Health prefer:
Health Services

In Financial Services prefer:
Financial Services

Additional Information
Year Founded: 1998
Capital Under Management: $60,000,000
Current Activity Level: Actively seeking new investments

EASTWARD CAPITAL PARTNERS LLC

432 Cherry Street
West Newton, MA USA 02465
Phone: 6179696700
Fax: 6179697900
E-mail: contacts@eastwardcp.com
Website: www.eastwardcp.com

Management and Staff
Dennis Cameron, Co-Founder
Edward Dresner, Managing Director
Nancy Malone, Principal

Type of Firm
Private Equity Firm

Project Preferences

Type of Financing Preferred:
Mezzanine

Industry Preferences

In Communications prefer:
Communications and Media
Commercial Communications

In Medical/Health prefer:
Medical/Health

In Industrial/Energy prefer:
Alternative Energy
Environmental Related

Additional Information
Name of Most Recent Fund: Eastward Capital Partners VI, L.P.
Most Recent Fund Was Raised: 09/26/2013
Year Founded: 1994
Capital Under Management: $300,000,000
Current Activity Level: Actively seeking new investments

EBERHART CAPITAL LLC

10632 North Scottsdale Road
Suite B187
Scottsdale, AZ USA 85254
E-mail: info@eberhartcapital.com

Type of Firm
Private Equity Firm

Project Preferences

Type of Financing Preferred:
Leveraged Buyout
Early Stage
Acquisition

Geographical Preferences

United States Preferences:
All U.S.

Industry Preferences

In Industrial/Energy prefer:
Oil and Gas Exploration
Industrial Products

In Transportation prefer:
Transportation
Aerospace

In Manufact. prefer:
Manufacturing

Additional Information
Year Founded: 2014
Current Activity Level : Actively seeking new investments

EBRICKS DIGITAL

Avenida Republica do Libano
8 andar
Sao Paulo, Brazil 04501-000
Phone: 3050-0750
E-mail: contato@ebricksdigital.com.br
Website: www.ebricksdigital.com.br

Management and Staff
Fabio Bruggioni, Chief Executive Officer
Ricardo Hudson, Chief Financial Officer

Type of Firm
Private Equity Firm

Project Preferences

Type of Financing Preferred:
Early Stage
Balanced
Later Stage

Geographical Preferences

United States Preferences:

International Preferences:
Brazil

Industry Preferences

In Communications prefer:
Communications and Media
Commercial Communications
Telecommunications
Wireless Communications
Media and Entertainment

In Internet Specific prefer:
E-Commerce Technology
Ecommerce

Additional Information
Year Founded: 2012
Capital Under Management: $100,000,000
Current Activity Level : Actively seeking new investments

EBT VENTURE FUND LTD

38-42 Hill Street
Belfast, Ireland BT1 2LB
Phone: 44-28-9031-1770
Fax: 44-28-9031-1880
E-mail: info@emergingbusinesstrust.com
Website: www.emergingbusinesstrust.com

Type of Firm
Private Equity Firm

Additional Information
Current Activity Level : Actively seeking new investments

EC1 CAPITAL LTD

86-90 Paul Street
Third Floor
London, United Kingdom EC2A 4NE
E-mail: info@ec1capital.com
Website: www.ec1capital.com

Management and Staff
Julian Carter, Co-Founder

Type of Firm
Private Equity Firm

Project Preferences

Type of Financing Preferred:
Early Stage
Seed

Size of Investments Considered:
Min Size of Investment Considered (000s): $40
Max Size of Investment Considered (000s): $317

Geographical Preferences

International Preferences:
United Kingdom
Europe

Industry Preferences

In Computer Software prefer:
Software

In Internet Specific prefer:
Internet

Additional Information
Year Founded: 2011
Current Activity Level : Actively seeking new investments

ECAPITAL ENTREPRE-NEURIAL PARTNERS AG

Hafenweg 24
Muenster, Germany 48155
Phone: 492517037670
Fax: 4925170376722
E-mail: info@ecapital.de
Website: ecapital.de

Management and Staff
Michael Luebbenhusen, Managing Partner
Paul Grunow, Venture Partner
V. Desai, Venture Partner

Type of Firm
Private Equity Firm

Association Membership
German Venture Capital Association (BVK)
European Private Equity and Venture Capital Assoc.

Project Preferences

Type of Financing Preferred:
Early Stage
Later Stage
Seed
Startup

Geographical Preferences

International Preferences:
Europe
Switzerland
Austria
Germany

Industry Preferences

In Communications prefer:
Communications and Media
Wireless Communications

In Computer Software prefer:
Software

In Internet Specific prefer:
Internet

In Semiconductor/Electr prefer:
Optoelectronics

In Biotechnology prefer:
Biotechnology

In Medical/Health prefer:
Medical/Health

In Industrial/Energy prefer:
Alternative Energy
Industrial Products
Materials
Advanced Materials
Machinery
Environmental Related

Additional Information
Year Founded: 1999
Current Activity Level : Actively seeking new investments

ECART INVEST 1 BV

Javastraat 78
Den Haag, Netherlands 2585 AS
Phone: 31703554788
Fax: 31703500523
E-mail: info@ecart.nl
Website: www.ecart.nl

Type of Firm
Private Equity Firm

Association Membership
Dutch Venture Capital Associaton (NVP)

Project Preferences

Type of Financing Preferred:
Early Stage
Balanced
Later Stage

Size of Investments Considered:
Min Size of Investment Considered (000s): $88
Max Size of Investment Considered (000s): $1,104

Geographical Preferences

International Preferences:
Europe
Netherlands

Industry Preferences

In Consumer Related prefer:
Retail

In Business Serv. prefer:
Services

In Manufact. prefer:
Manufacturing

Additional Information
Year Founded: 1993
Capital Under Management: $37,800,000
Current Activity Level : Actively seeking new investments

ECHELON CAPITAL LLC

121 West Wacker Drive
Suite 2156
Chicago, IL USA 60601
Phone: 3122630263
Fax: 3122630262
Website: www.echeloncapital.com

Type of Firm
Private Equity Firm

Project Preferences

Type of Financing Preferred:
Leveraged Buyout
Turnaround
Acquisition

Geographical Preferences

United States Preferences:

International Preferences:
Nauru

Industry Preferences

In Semiconductor/Electr prefer:
Electronic Components

In Industrial/Energy prefer:
Industrial Products
Materials
Machinery

In Manufact. prefer:
Manufacturing

Additional Information
Year Founded: 2002
Current Activity Level : Actively seeking new investments

ECHELON VENTURES LLC

303 Wyman Street
Suite 300
Waltham, MA USA 02451
Phone: 7814199850
Fax: 7814199851
E-mail: info@echelonventures.com
Website: www.echelonventures.com

Management and Staff
Alfred Woodworth, Managing Director

Type of Firm
Private Equity Firm

Project Preferences

Role in Financing:
Prefer role as deal originator but will also invest in deals created by others

Type of Financing Preferred:
Early Stage

Size of Investments Considered:
Min Size of Investment Considered (000s): $1,000
Max Size of Investment Considered (000s): $5,000

Geographical Preferences

United States Preferences:
Northeast

Industry Preferences

In Computer Software prefer:
Software

In Semiconductor/Electr prefer:
Semiconductor

In Biotechnology prefer:
Human Biotechnology

In Medical/Health prefer:
Medical Diagnostics

In Industrial/Energy prefer:
Alternative Energy

Additional Information
Name of Most Recent Fund: Echelon Ventures II, L.P.
Most Recent Fund Was Raised: 08/04/2004
Year Founded: 2000
Capital Under Management: $15,700,000
Current Activity Level : Actively seeking new investments
Method of Compensation: Return on invest. most important, but chg. closing fees, service fees, etc.

ECHO CAPITAL

1001, boul. de Maisonneuve O.
Bureau 205
Montreal, Canada H3A 3C8
Phone: 5149071440
Fax: 5149071444
Website: www.echocapital.ca

Other Offices
25 Laurier Street
Seventh Floor
, Canada J8X 4C8
Phone: 8195558888

Type of Firm
Government Affiliated Program

Additional Information
Year Founded: 2007
Current Activity Level : Actively seeking new investments

ECHO HEALTH VENTURES LLC

1800 Ninth Avenue, Suite 250
Seattle, WA USA 98101
E-mail: general@echohealthventures.com
Website: www.echohealthventures.com

Management and Staff
Michael Mankowski, Chief Operating Officer
Rob Coppedge, Chief Executive Officer

Type of Firm
Private Equity Firm

Project Preferences

Type of Financing Preferred:
Early Stage

Industry Preferences

In Medical/Health prefer:
Health Services

Additional Information
Year Founded: 2016
Current Activity Level : Actively seeking new investments

ECHO STREET CAPITAL ADVISORS LLC

850 Third Avenue
New York, NY USA 10022

Type of Firm
Private Equity Firm

Project Preferences

Type of Financing Preferred:
Other

Additional Information
Year Founded: 2002
Capital Under Management: $3,600,000
Current Activity Level : Actively seeking new investments

ECHOVC PARTNERS LLC

806 Lose Robles Avenue
Palo Alto, CA USA 94306
Phone: 4088960695
Website: www.echovc.com

Management and Staff
Amber Fowler, Partner
Shadi Mehraein, Partner

Type of Firm
Private Equity Firm

Project Preferences

Type of Financing Preferred:
Balanced

Geographical Preferences

International Preferences:
Africa

Industry Preferences

In Communications prefer:
Wireless Communications
Media and Entertainment

In Computer Software prefer:
Software
Applications Software

In Internet Specific prefer:
Internet
Ecommerce

In Consumer Related prefer:
Consumer
Entertainment and Leisure

In Other prefer:
Environment Responsible

Additional Information
Year Founded: 2011
Capital Under Management: $16,180,000
Current Activity Level : Actively seeking new investments

ECI PARTNERS LLP

Lancaster Place (South)
Brettenham House
London, United Kingdom WC2E 7EN
Phone: 442076061000
Fax: 442072405050
E-mail: enquiries@ecipartners.com
Website: www.ecipartners.com

Management and Staff
Chris Watt, Partner
Chris Warren, Partner
Ken Landsberg, Managing Director
Ken Lindsay, Partner
Lewis Bantin, Partner
Philip Shuttleworth, Partner
Richard Chapman, Partner
Sean Whelan, Managing Director
Steven Tudge, Managing Partner
Tim Raffle, Managing Director
Tom Wrenn, Partner

Type of Firm
Private Equity Firm

Association Membership
British Venture Capital Association (BVCA)
European Private Equity and Venture Capital Assoc.

Project Preferences

Role in Financing:
Prefer role as deal originator but will also invest in deals created by others

Type of Financing Preferred:
Leveraged Buyout
Balanced
Management Buyouts

Industry Focus
(% based on actual investment)
Consumer Related 23.9%
Industrial/Energy 18.1%
Computer Software and Services 14.9%
Communications and Media 14.6%
Computer Hardware 10.8%
Other Products 9.9%
Internet Specific 6.0%
Biotechnology 1.2%
Medical/Health 0.6%

Additional Information
Name of Most Recent Fund: ECI 9
Most Recent Fund Was Raised: 08/12/2008
Year Founded: 1976
Capital Under Management: $1,001,400,000
Current Activity Level : Actively seeking new investments
Method of Compensation: Return on invest. most important, but chg. closing fees, service fees, etc.

ECKERT WAGNISKAPITAL UND FRUEHPHASENFINAN- ZIERUNG GMBH

Friedenstrasse 2
Panketal, Germany 16341
Phone: 493094414129

Type of Firm
Private Equity Firm

Project Preferences

Type of Financing Preferred:
Early Stage
Seed
Startup

Geographical Preferences

International Preferences:
Germany

Industry Preferences

In Biotechnology prefer:
Biotechnology

In Medical/Health prefer:
Medical Diagnostics
Pharmaceuticals

Additional Information
Year Founded: 1990
Current Activity Level : Actively seeking new investments

ECLIPSE RT

Alkotas ut 50.
Budapest, Hungary 1123
Phone: 3614892286
Fax: 3614892290

Type of Firm
Private Equity Firm

Project Preferences

Type of Financing Preferred:
Early Stage
Balanced
Seed
Startup

Geographical Preferences

International Preferences:
Europe

Additional Information
Year Founded: 2011
Current Activity Level : Actively seeking new investments

ECLIPSE VENTURES

514 High Street
Suite 4
Palo Alto, CA USA 94301
Website: eclipse.vc

Type of Firm
Private Equity Firm

Project Preferences

Type of Financing Preferred:
Early Stage
Balanced

Geographical Preferences

United States Preferences:
All U.S.

Industry Preferences

In Semiconductor/Electr prefer:
Electronic Components

Additional Information
Year Founded: 2015
Capital Under Management: $308,780,000
Current Activity Level : Actively seeking new investments

ECLOSION2 SA

Chemin des Aulx 14
Plan les Ouates, Switzerland 1228
Phone: 41228801010
Fax: 41228801013
Website: www.eclosion2.com

Type of Firm
Private Equity Firm

Project Preferences

Type of Financing Preferred:
Early Stage
Seed
Startup

Industry Preferences

In Biotechnology prefer:
Human Biotechnology
Biotech Related Research

In Medical/Health prefer:
Medical/Health
Medical Diagnostics
Diagnostic Services
Diagnostic Test Products
Medical Therapeutics

Additional Information
Year Founded: 2011
Current Activity Level : Actively seeking new investments

ECM EQUITY CAPITAL MANAGEMENT GMBH

Taunusanlage 18
Main Building Taunusanlage
Frankfurt am Main, Germany 60325
Phone: 4969971020
Fax: 49699710224
E-mail: info@ecm-pe.de
Website: www.ecm-pe.de

Management and Staff
Axel Eichmeyer, Managing Partner
Harald Sipple, Partner
Melanie Buesing, Founder
Richard Gritsch, Partner

Type of Firm
Private Equity Firm

Association Membership
Swiss Venture Capital Association (SECA)
German Venture Capital Association (BVK)
European Private Equity and Venture Capital Assoc.

Project Preferences

Type of Financing Preferred:
Management Buyouts

Geographical Preferences

International Preferences:
Switzerland
Austria
Germany

Industry Preferences

In Medical/Health prefer:
Medical/Health

In Consumer Related prefer:
Food/Beverage
Consumer Products
Consumer Services

In Industrial/Energy prefer:
Energy

In Transportation prefer:
Transportation

In Business Serv. prefer:
Services

In Manufact. prefer:
Manufacturing

Additional Information
Name of Most Recent Fund: German Equity Partners IV
Most Recent Fund Was Raised: 06/29/2012
Year Founded: 1994
Capital Under Management: $753,900,000
Current Activity Level : Actively seeking new investments

ECM-BULGARIAN POST-PRIVATISATION FUND

Svoboda Square 1, Fourth Floor
Sofia, Bulgaria 1421
Phone: 35929600200
Fax: 35929815812

Management and Staff
Antonio Perez-Montes, Managing Director

Type of Firm
Private Equity Firm

Project Preferences

Type of Financing Preferred:
Balanced

Geographical Preferences

International Preferences:
Europe
Bulgaria

Additional Information
Year Founded: 2005
Current Activity Level : Actively seeking new investments

ECO

Private Bag x9, Suite 352
Benmore, South Africa 2010
Phone: 27-11-269-4069
Fax: 27-11-269-4090
E-mail: info@iveri.com
Website: www.iveri.co.za

Management and Staff
Sheldon Cohen, Chief Executive Officer

Type of Firm
Incubator/Development Program

Project Preferences

Type of Financing Preferred:
Seed
Startup

Geographical Preferences

International Preferences:
Africa

Industry Preferences

In Internet Specific prefer:
Internet

In Computer Other prefer:
Computer Related

In Financial Services prefer:
Financial Services

Additional Information
Year Founded: 1999
Current Activity Level : Actively seeking new investments

ECOENTERPRISES FUND

200E and 100S of Plaza Mayor
Centro Corporativo Nunziatura
San Jose, Costa Rica
Phone: 50622961501
Fax: 50622961451
E-mail: ecoe@ecoenterprisesfund.com
Website: ecoenterprisesfund.com

Other Offices
Apdo. Postal 230-1225
Plaza Mayor
San Jose, Costa Rica
Phone: 506-296-5000
Fax: 506-220-2551

Management and Staff
Eugenia Villalobos Baldioceda, Vice President
Tammy Newmark, President

Type of Firm
Private Equity Firm

Project Preferences

Type of Financing Preferred:
Expansion
Mezzanine
Balanced
Later Stage

Size of Investments Considered:
Min Size of Investment Considered (000s): $50
Max Size of Investment Considered (000s): $800

Geographical Preferences

International Preferences:
Latin America
Ecuador
Bolivia
Peru
Mexico
Brazil
Costa Rica
Colombia
Guatemala

Industry Preferences

In Industrial/Energy prefer:
Environmental Related

In Business Serv. prefer:
Services

In Agr/Forestr/Fish prefer:
Agriculture related

In Other prefer:
Socially Responsible
Environment Responsible

Additional Information
Name of Most Recent Fund: EcoEnterprises Partners II, L.P.
Most Recent Fund Was Raised: 12/28/2011
Year Founded: 1998
Capital Under Management: $5,000,000
Current Activity Level : Actively seeking new investments

ECOFOREST

Gonzalo Crance Street
Suite 176 Ciudad del Saber
Panama City, Panama
Phone: 5073173400
Fax: 5073173422
E-mail: info@grupoecos.com
Website: www.grupoecos.com

Management and Staff
Andreas Eggenberg, Chief Executive Officer
Jose Guardiola, Chief Financial Officer

Type of Firm
Private Equity Firm

Project Preferences

Type of Financing Preferred:
Leveraged Buyout
Expansion
Turnaround

Geographical Preferences

International Preferences:
Latin America

Industry Preferences

In Industrial/Energy prefer:
Energy
Alternative Energy
Environmental Related

In Agr/Forestr/Fish prefer:
Agriculture related

Additional Information
Year Founded: 2009
Current Activity Level : Actively seeking new investments

ECOLUTIONS MANAGEMENT GMBH

Grueneburgweg 18
Frankfurt am Main, Germany 60322
Phone: 49-69-9150-1080
Fax: 49-69-915010811
E-mail: info@ecolutions.de

Other Offices
1505, Block 15; China Central Place
89 Jianguo Road
Beijing, China 100025
Phone: 86-10-5203-6828
Fax: 86-10-5203-6827

Unit #15,Ground Floor,Mahinder Chambers,
619/28,W.T.Patil Marg,Opp. Dukes Factory
Mumbai, India 400 071
Phone: 91-22-2520-0500
Fax: 91-22-2520-1743

Management and Staff
David Zimmer, Managing Director
Petra Leue-Bahns, Managing Director

Type of Firm
Private Equity Firm

Project Preferences

Type of Financing Preferred:
Early Stage
Seed

Geographical Preferences

Canadian Preferences:
All Canada

International Preferences:
Italy
India
Germany
France

Industry Preferences

In Industrial/Energy prefer:
Energy
Alternative Energy
Energy Conservation Relat
Materials
Advanced Materials
Environmental Related

In Other prefer:
Environment Responsible

Additional Information
Year Founded: 2007
Current Activity Level : Actively seeking new investments

ECOMACHINES VENTURES LTD

One Canada Square
Canary Wharf
London, United Kingdom E145AB
Phone: 442037616
Website: www.ecomachinesventures.com

Management and Staff
Ian Cooke, Venture Partner
Igor Turevsky, Venture Partner
Ilian Iliev, Co-Founder

Type of Firm
Private Equity Firm

Project Preferences

Type of Financing Preferred:
Early Stage
Expansion
Later Stage
Seed

Size of Investments Considered:
Min Size of Investment Considered (000s): $744
Max Size of Investment Considered (000s): $2,976

Geographical Preferences

International Preferences:
United Kingdom
Europe
Israel

Industry Preferences

In Communications prefer:
Data Communications

In Computer Software prefer:
Software

In Industrial/Energy prefer:
Energy

In Transportation prefer:
Transportation

Additional Information
Year Founded: 2013
Current Activity Level : Actively seeking new investments

ECOMOBILITY VENTURES

117, av des Champs Elysees
Paris, France 75008
Phone: 33185761907
E-mail: contact@em-v.com
Website: ecomobility-ventures.com

Type of Firm
Private Equity Firm

Project Preferences

Type of Financing Preferred:
Early Stage
Later Stage
Startup

Geographical Preferences

International Preferences:
Europe

Industry Preferences

In Transportation prefer:
Transportation

Additional Information
Year Founded: 2011
Current Activity Level : Actively seeking new investments

ECONA AG

Chausseestr. 8E
Berlin, Germany 10115
Phone: 493020089966
Fax: 493020089967
E-mail: info@econa.com
Website: www.econa.com

Management and Staff
Bernd Hardes, Managing Director

Type of Firm
Private Equity Firm

Project Preferences

Type of Financing Preferred:
Leveraged Buyout
Generalist PE
Balanced

Geographical Preferences

International Preferences:
Europe
Germany

Industry Preferences

In Communications prefer:
Media and Entertainment
Publishing

In Internet Specific prefer:
Internet
Ecommerce
Web Aggregation/Portals

Additional Information
Year Founded: 1999
Capital Under Management: $105,600,000
Current Activity Level : Making few, if any, new investments

ECONERGY INTERNATIONAL CORP

1881 Ninth Street
Suite 300
Boulder, CO USA 80302
Phone: 303-473-9007
Fax: 303-473-9060
Website: www.econergy.net

Other Offices
Plaza Roble, Escazu
Edificio El Portico, Piso 1
San Jose, Costa Rica
Phone: 506-201-1543

1925 K Street North West
Washington, DC USA 20006
Phone: 202-822-4980
Fax: 202-822-4986

Avenida Angelica 2530
Conjunto 111
Sao Paulo, Brazil 01228-200
Phone: 55-11-3555-5700
Fax: 55-11-3555-5735

22 Billiter Street
London, United Kingdom EC3M 2RY
Phone: 44-203-102-3403
Fax: 44-203-102-3401

Management and Staff
Lee Atkins, Chief Financial Officer
Rick Renner, Chief Operating Officer
Thomas Stoner, General Partner

Type of Firm
Corporate PE/Venture

Project Preferences

Type of Financing Preferred:
Early Stage

Geographical Preferences

International Preferences:
Latin America

Industry Preferences

In Industrial/Energy prefer:
Energy
Alternative Energy
Energy Conservation Relat

Additional Information

Year Founded: 1994
Capital Under Management: $16,300,000
Current Activity Level : Actively seeking new investments

ECOR1 CAPITAL LLC

409 Illinois Street
San Francisco, CA USA 94158
Phone: 4157543517
E-mail: info@ecor1cap.com
Website: ecor1cap.com

Type of Firm
Investment Management Firm

Project Preferences

Type of Financing Preferred:
Balanced

Industry Preferences

In Biotechnology prefer:
Human Biotechnology
Biotech Related Research

Additional Information

Year Founded: 2012
Current Activity Level : Actively seeking new investments

ECOSYSTEM VENTURES LLC

P.O. Box 3347
Saratoga, CA USA 95070
Phone: 4084268040
Fax: 4088671441
E-mail: info@ecosystemventures.com
Website: www.ecosystemventures.com

Other Offices

60 Weingartenstrasse
Mannedorf
Zurich, Switzerland 8708
Phone: 41-44-586-7108
Fax: 41-44-790-2187

Management and Staff

Alexander Fries, President, Founder

Type of Firm
Private Equity Firm

Project Preferences

Type of Financing Preferred:
Early Stage
Seed

Geographical Preferences

International Preferences:
Europe

Additional Information

Year Founded: 2005
Current Activity Level : Actively seeking new investments

ECS CAPITAL SA

Rua Castilho 20, Sixth Floor
Lisbon, Portugal 1250069
Phone: 351213802500
Fax: 351213802499
E-mail: info@ecscapital.com
Website: www.ecs.pt

Management and Staff

Diogo Chalbert Santos, Principal
Fernando Esmeraldo, Chief Executive Officer
Goncalo Batalha, Partner
Goncalo Lucas Mendes, Principal
Gracinda Raposo, Partner
Manuel Noronha Andrade, Partner
Renato Arie, Partner
Tomas Figueira, Founder

Type of Firm
Private Equity Firm

Association Membership

Portuguese Venture Capital Association (APCRI)
European Private Equity and Venture Capital Assoc.

Project Preferences

Type of Financing Preferred:
Leveraged Buyout
Recapitalizations

Size of Investments Considered:
Min Size of Investment Considered (000s): $6,344
Max Size of Investment Considered (000s): $21,183

Geographical Preferences

International Preferences:
Portugal
Spain

Additional Information

Name of Most Recent Fund: Fundo Recuperacao, FCR
Most Recent Fund Was Raised: 07/31/2009
Year Founded: 2006
Capital Under Management: $634,400,000
Current Activity Level : Actively seeking new investments

ECT MERCHANT INVESTMENTS CORP

Four Houston Center
1331 Lamar, Suite 1600
Houston, TX USA 77010
Phone: 713-853-6161
Website: www.enron.com

Type of Firm
Private Equity Firm

Additional Information

Year Founded: 2009
Current Activity Level : Actively seeking new investments

ECUS ADMINISTRADORA GENERAL DE FONDOS SA

Magdalena 140
Fifth Floor
Las Condes, Chile 7550104
Phone: 5625772200
Fax: 5625772222
E-mail: desk@ecuscapital.com
Website: www.ecuscapital.com

Management and Staff

Francois Edant, Co-Founder
Gustavo Rivera, Managing Partner
Jose Canete, Chief Financial Officer

Type of Firm
Private Equity Firm

Project Preferences

Type of Financing Preferred:
Leveraged Buyout
Early Stage
Generalist PE
Acquisition

Geographical Preferences

International Preferences:
Chile
France

Industry Preferences

In Consumer Related prefer:
Food/Beverage

In Industrial/Energy prefer:
Energy
Energy Conservation Relat

In Agr/Forestr/Fish prefer:
Agribusiness
Agriculture related

EDB INVESTMENTS PTE LTD

250 North Bridge Road
Suite 28-00 Raffles City Tower
Singapore, Singapore 179101
Phone: 6568326832
Fax: 6568326838
E-mail: infoHQ@edbi.com
Website: www.edbi.com

Other Offices
One International Place
Eight Floor
Boston, MA USA 022110
Phone: 617-261-9981
Fax: 617-261-9983

250A, Twin Dolphin Drive
Redwood City, CA USA 94065
Phone: 650-591-9102
Fax: 650-591-1328

Management and Staff
Jeremy Loh, Vice President
Keat Chuan Yeo, Managing Director

Type of Firm
Government Affiliated Program

Project Preferences

Type of Financing Preferred:
Early Stage
Expansion
Balanced
Later Stage
Seed

Geographical Preferences

International Preferences:
Asia

Industry Preferences

In Internet Specific prefer:
Internet

In Biotechnology prefer:
Biotechnology

In Medical/Health prefer:
Medical Therapeutics
Medical Products
Health Services

In Industrial/Energy prefer:
Alternative Energy

In Business Serv. prefer:
Media

In Other prefer:
Environment Responsible

Additional Information
Year Founded: 1991
Capital Under Management: $400,000,000
Current Activity Level : Actively seeking new investments
Method of Compensation: Return on investment is of primary concern, do not charge fees

EDCO VENTURES

1107 South Eighth Street
Austin, TX USA 78704
Phone: 9155395552
Fax: 5123547443
Website: edcoventures.org

Management and Staff
Teofilo Tijerina, Co-Founder

Type of Firm
Private Equity Firm

Association Membership
Community Development Venture Capital Alliance

Project Preferences

Type of Financing Preferred:
Early Stage
Expansion
Seed
Startup

Size of Investments Considered:
Min Size of Investment Considered (000s): $1,000
Max Size of Investment Considered (000s): $100,000

Geographical Preferences

United States Preferences:
Texas

Industry Preferences

In Computer Software prefer:
Software

In Biotechnology prefer:
Biotechnology

In Industrial/Energy prefer:
Environmental Related

In Other prefer:
Environment Responsible

Additional Information
Year Founded: 2008
Current Activity Level : Actively seeking new investments

Additional Information
Year Founded: 2001
Capital Under Management: $130,000,000
Current Activity Level : Actively seeking new investments

EDELWEISS & BERGE UG HAFTUNGSBESCHRAENKT & CO KG

Maximiliansplatz 17
Munich, Germany 80333
Phone: 49700333593477
Website: www.the-foo.de

Management and Staff
Werner Roth, Managing Director

Type of Firm
Private Equity Firm

Project Preferences

Type of Financing Preferred:
Balanced

Geographical Preferences

International Preferences:
Europe

Industry Preferences

In Other prefer:
Environment Responsible

Additional Information
Year Founded: 2009
Current Activity Level : Actively seeking new investments

EDELWEISS FINANCIAL SERVICES LTD

Edelweiss House, Off. C.S.T Rd
Kalina
Mumbai, India 400 098
Phone: 912222864400
Fax: 912222882119
E-mail: info@edelcap.com
Website: www.edelweissfin.com

Other Offices
Empire State Building
350 Fifth Avenue, Suite 5013
New York, NY USA 10118
Phone: 212 564 1634
Fax: 212 563 4534

Management and Staff
Himanshu Kaji, Chief Operating Officer
S. Ranganathan, Chief Financial Officer

Type of Firm
Bank Affiliated

Project Preferences

Type of Financing Preferred:
Early Stage
Mezzanine

Balanced
Later Stage

Geographical Preferences

International Preferences:
India
Asia

Additional Information

Year Founded: 1995
Current Activity Level : Actively seeking new investments

EDEN VENTURES LTD

14 Golden Square
London, United Kingdom W1F 9JF
Phone: 442077583440

Other Offices

Fourteen London Square
London, United Kingdom W1F 9JF
Phone: 44-207-758-3440

Management and Staff

Ben Tompkins, Partner
Charles Grimsdale, Co-Founder
David Embleton, Co-Founder
Mark Caroe, Partner
Mark Farmer, Co-Founder
Peter Jones, Partner

Type of Firm

Private Equity Firm

Association Membership

European Private Equity and Venture Capital Assoc.

Project Preferences

Type of Financing Preferred:
Early Stage
Seed

Geographical Preferences

International Preferences:
Ireland
United Kingdom
Europe

Industry Preferences

In Communications prefer:
Telecommunications
Media and Entertainment

In Computer Software prefer:
Software

Additional Information

Year Founded: 2002
Capital Under Management: $58,700,000
Current Activity Level : Actively seeking new investments

EDF VENTURES

425 North Main Street
Ann Arbor, MI USA 48104
Phone: 7346633213
Fax: 7346637358
Website: www.edfventures.com

Other Offices

4670 Fulton Street East
Suite 202
Ada, MI USA 49301
Phone: 616-956-8025
Fax: 616-956-8026

Management and Staff

Mary Campbell, Managing Director
Michael DeVries, Managing Director

Type of Firm

Private Equity Firm

Project Preferences

Role in Financing:
Will function either as deal originator or investor in deals created by others

Type of Financing Preferred:
Early Stage
Seed
Startup

Size of Investments Considered:
Min Size of Investment Considered (000s): $1,500
Max Size of Investment Considered (000s): $6,000

Industry Focus

(% based on actual investment)
Medical/Health	30.2%
Other Products	18.1%
Computer Software and Services	16.8%
Internet Specific	12.7%
Communications and Media	9.7%
Biotechnology	6.8%
Semiconductors/Other Elect.	3.0%
Computer Hardware	1.5%
Consumer Related	1.1%
Industrial/Energy	0.0%

Additional Information

Year Founded: 1987
Capital Under Management: $140,000,000
Current Activity Level : Actively seeking new investments
Method of Compensation: Return on investment is of primary concern, do not charge fees

EDG PARTNERS LLC

5445 Triangle Parkway, Suite 260
Atlanta, GA USA 30092
Phone: 7704538000
Fax: 7704538001
Website: www.edgpartners.com

Other Offices

2760 Eisenhower Avenue
Suite 406
Alexandria, VA USA 22314
Phone: 7032489510
Fax: 7704538025

Management and Staff

Alan Dahl, Co-Founder
Harrison Perry, Vice President
J. Stephen Eaton, Co-Founder
Justin Stark, Vice President
Michael Gaffney, Co-Founder
Robert Carlin, Vice President

Type of Firm

Private Equity Firm

Project Preferences

Type of Financing Preferred:
Leveraged Buyout
Later Stage

Geographical Preferences

United States Preferences:
Mid Atlantic
Southeast
Georgia
Southwest

Industry Preferences

In Medical/Health prefer:
Medical/Health
Hospitals/Clinics/Primary

In Business Serv. prefer:
Services
Distribution

In Manufact. prefer:
Manufacturing

Additional Information

Name of Most Recent Fund: EDG Partners Fund II, L.P.
Most Recent Fund Was Raised: 01/15/2010
Year Founded: 2004
Current Activity Level : Actively seeking new investments

EDGE INVESTMENTS LTD

1, Marylebone High Street
London, United Kingdom W1U 4LZ
Phone: 442073171300
Fax: 442073171313
E-mail: info@edge.uk.com
Website: www.edge.uk.com

Management and Staff

Alison McCarthy, Chief Financial Officer

Type of Firm

Private Equity Firm

Project Preferences

Type of Financing Preferred:
Early Stage
Expansion
Seed

Geographical Preferences

International Preferences:
United Kingdom
Europe

Industry Preferences

In Consumer Related prefer:
Entertainment and Leisure

In Business Serv. prefer:
Media

Additional Information

Year Founded: 2006
Current Activity Level : Actively seeking new investments

EDGE PTY LTD

82 Grayston
Grayston Drive, Third Floor
Sandton, South Africa
Phone: 27112927974
Fax: 27112927911
Website: www.edgegrowth.com

Type of Firm

Private Equity Firm

Association Membership

South African Venture Capital Association (SAVCA)

Project Preferences

Type of Financing Preferred:
Early Stage
Expansion
Balanced
Later Stage
Seed

Geographical Preferences

International Preferences:
South Africa
Africa

Additional Information

Year Founded: 2008
Current Activity Level : Actively seeking new investments

EDGEWATER CAPITAL GROUP, INC.

28601 Chagrin Boulevard, Suite 205
Cleveland, OH USA 44122
Phone: 2162923838
Fax: 2162923879
E-mail: info@edgewatercapital.com
Website: www.edgewatercapital.com

Management and Staff

Chris Childres, Managing Partner
Ryan Meany, Partner

Type of Firm

Private Equity Firm

Project Preferences

Type of Financing Preferred:
Leveraged Buyout
Management Buyouts

Geographical Preferences

United States Preferences:
All U.S.

Industry Focus

(% based on actual investment)
Other Products   100.0%

Additional Information

Name of Most Recent Fund: Edgewater Capital Partners III, L.P.
Most Recent Fund Was Raised: 02/12/2014
Year Founded: 1982
Capital Under Management: $85,000,000
Current Activity Level : Actively seeking new investments

EDGEWATER FUNDS

900 North Michigan Avenue
Suite 1800
Chicago, IL USA 60611
Phone: 3126495666
Fax: 3126648649
Website: www.edgewaterfunds.com

Management and Staff

Brian Peiser, Vice President
David Tolmie, Partner
Gerald Saltarelli, Vice President
Gregory Jones, Partner
James Gordon, Managing Partner
Jeffrey Frient, Partner
John Malloy, Vice President
Matt Norris, Chief Financial Officer
Phillip Lorenzini, Partner
Robert Growney, Partner
Scott Meadow, Partner
Stephen Natali, Vice President
Trish Gilbert, Vice President

Type of Firm

Private Equity Firm

Association Membership

Illinois Venture Capital Association
Private Equity Council (PEC)

Project Preferences

Role in Financing:
Prefer role as deal originator but will also invest in deals created by others

Type of Financing Preferred:
Leveraged Buyout
Early Stage
Generalist PE
Later Stage
Acquisition

Geographical Preferences

United States Preferences:
North America

Industry Preferences

In Computer Software prefer:
Software

In Medical/Health prefer:
Medical/Health

In Consumer Related prefer:
Consumer Products
Consumer Services

In Financial Services prefer:
Financial Services

In Business Serv. prefer:
Services

Additional Information

Name of Most Recent Fund: Edgewater Growth Capital Partners III, L.P.
Most Recent Fund Was Raised: 06/05/2009
Year Founded: 1991
Capital Under Management: $2,000,000,000
Current Activity Level : Actively seeking new investments
Method of Compensation: Return on investment is of primary concern, do not charge fees

EDISON PARTNERS

281 Witherspoon Street
Princeton, NJ USA 08540
Phone: 6098961900
Fax: 6098960066
Website: www.edisonpartners.com

Other Offices

11000 Cedar Avenue
Suite 100
CLEVELAND, OH USA 44106

Management and Staff

Chris Sugden, Managing Partner
Chris Sklarin, Vice President
Christopher Sugden, Managing Partner
David Nevas, Partner
David Nevas, Principal
Gary Golding, General Partner

Joe Allegra, General Partner
John Martinson, Founder
Joseph Allegra, General Partner
Kelly Buckley, Partner
Kelly Ford, Partner
Lenard Marcus, Partner
Michael Kopelman, General Partner
Ryan Ziegler, General Partner
Sever Totia, Partner
Tom Vander Schaaff, Partner
Tom Schaaff, General Partner

Type of Firm
Private Equity Firm

Association Membership
Mid-Atlantic Venture Association
New England Venture Capital Association

Project Preferences

Role in Financing:
Prefer role as deal originator but will also invest in deals created by others

Type of Financing Preferred:
Expansion

Size of Investments Considered:
Min Size of Investment Considered (000s): $5,000
Max Size of Investment Considered (000s): $8,000

Geographical Preferences

United States Preferences:

Industry Focus

(% based on actual investment)
Computer Software and Services	53.0%
Internet Specific	19.6%
Computer Hardware	7.7%
Other Products	7.4%
Communications and Media	3.9%
Medical/Health	3.2%
Industrial/Energy	3.1%
Consumer Related	1.1%
Semiconductors/Other Elect.	0.9%

Additional Information
Name of Most Recent Fund: Edison Venture Fund VII, L.P.
Most Recent Fund Was Raised: 09/30/2010
Year Founded: 1986
Capital Under Management: $924,000,000
Current Activity Level : Actively seeking new investments
Method of Compensation: Return on investment is of primary concern, do not charge fees

EDISON.VC

15 Rochdelskaya Street 16a
Moscow, Russia 123022
Website: www.edison.vc

Type of Firm
Private Equity Firm

Project Preferences

Type of Financing Preferred:
Expansion
Later Stage

Geographical Preferences

United States Preferences:
All U.S.

International Preferences:
Asia Pacific
Europe
Israel

Industry Preferences

In Internet Specific prefer:
E-Commerce Technology

Additional Information
Year Founded: 2014
Current Activity Level : Actively seeking new investments

EDMOND DE ROTHSCHILD INVESTMENT PARTNERS SAS

47, Rue du Faubourg
Saint-Honore
Paris, France 75401
Phone: 33140172525
Fax: 33140172402
Website: www.edmond-de-rothschild.com

Other Offices
No.166 East Lujiazui Road
28F China Insurance Building
Shanghai, China 200120
Phone: 862160862503
Fax: 862160862550

45, Av. de la Belle Gabrielle
Jardin Tropical
Nogent-sur-Marne, France 94737

Management and Staff
Jerome Bevierre, Chief Financial Officer

Type of Firm
Bank Affiliated

Association Membership
French Venture Capital Association (AFIC)

Project Preferences

Type of Financing Preferred:
Leveraged Buyout
Early Stage
Expansion
Balanced
Public Companies
Later Stage
Open Market
Seed
Startup

Size of Investments Considered:
Min Size of Investment Considered (000s): $446
Max Size of Investment Considered (000s): $13,371

Geographical Preferences

United States Preferences:
All U.S.

International Preferences:
United Kingdom
Europe
Switzerland
Israel
Asia
Germany
France

Industry Preferences

In Communications prefer:
Communications and Media
Telecommunications
Wireless Communications

In Internet Specific prefer:
Internet

In Computer Other prefer:
Computer Related

In Biotechnology prefer:
Biotechnology

In Medical/Health prefer:
Medical/Health
Medical Diagnostics
Health Services
Pharmaceuticals

In Consumer Related prefer:
Consumer
Food/Beverage
Consumer Products

In Industrial/Energy prefer:
Energy
Industrial Products
Machinery
Environmental Related

In Financial Services prefer:
Financial Services

In Business Serv. prefer:
Services
Distribution
Media

Pratt's Guide to Private Equity & Venture Capital Sources

In Agr/Forestr/Fish prefer:
Agriculture related

Additional Information
Name of Most Recent Fund: BioDiscovery 4 FCPR
Most Recent Fund Was Raised: 07/10/2012
Year Founded: 2002
Capital Under Management: $693,500,000
Current Activity Level : Actively seeking new investments

EDUCATION GROWTH PARTNERS LLC

One Landmark Square
21st Floor
Stamford, CT USA 06901
Phone: 2036588100
E-mail: administrator@edgrowthllc.com
Website: edgrowthpartners.com

Management and Staff
Brian Nairn, Managing Partner

Type of Firm
Private Equity Firm

Project Preferences

Type of Financing Preferred:
Leveraged Buyout
Acquisition
Recapitalizations

Industry Preferences

In Consumer Related prefer:
Education Related

In Manufact. prefer:
Publishing

Additional Information
Year Founded: 2011
Current Activity Level : Actively seeking new investments

EDWARDS CAPITAL LLC

676 North Michigan Avenue, Suite 3300
Chicago, IL USA 60611
Phone: 3123274520
Fax: 3123274525
Website: flexpointford.com

Other Offices
650 Madison Avenue, Suite 1902
New York, NY USA 10022
Phone: 646-217-7555
Fax: 646-217-7855

Management and Staff
Alex Saporito, Managing Director
Christopher Ackerman, Principal
Daniel Edelman, Principal
Jonathan Oka, Vice President

Kara O Brien, Vice President
Michael Vostrizansky, Principal
Michael Tyree, Vice President
Michael Fazekas, Principal
Perry Ballard, Principal
Steven Michienzi, Principal

Type of Firm
Private Equity Firm

Project Preferences

Role in Financing:
Prefer role as deal originator

Type of Financing Preferred:
Leveraged Buyout
Turnaround
Acquisition
Distressed Debt

Industry Preferences

In Medical/Health prefer:
Medical/Health

In Financial Services prefer:
Financial Services

Additional Information
Year Founded: 2004
Capital Under Management: $1,000,000,000
Current Activity Level : Actively seeking new investments

EEQUITY AB

Kungsgatan 24
5th Floor
Stockholm, Sweden 111 35
Phone: 46853482300
Website: www.eequity.se

Type of Firm
Private Equity Firm

Association Membership
Swedish Venture Capital Association (SVCA)

Project Preferences

Type of Financing Preferred:
Balanced

Geographical Preferences

International Preferences:
Sweden

Industry Preferences

In Internet Specific prefer:
E-Commerce Technology

In Consumer Related prefer:
Consumer
Entertainment and Leisure

Additional Information
Year Founded: 2014
Current Activity Level : Actively seeking new investments

EES VENTURES

616 FM 1960 West
Suite 605
Houston, TX USA 77090
Website: eesventures.com

Type of Firm
Private Equity Firm

Project Preferences

Type of Financing Preferred:
Early Stage
Seed

Industry Preferences

In Industrial/Energy prefer:
Energy

Additional Information
Year Founded: 2016
Capital Under Management: $4,170,000
Current Activity Level : Actively seeking new investments

EESTI ARENGUFOND

Tornimae 5
Talinn, Estonia 10145
Phone: 3726161100
Fax: 3726161101
E-mail: info@arengufond.ee
Website: www.arengufond.ee

Type of Firm
Government Affiliated Program

Association Membership
Estonian Private Equity and Venture Capital Assoc
European Private Equity and Venture Capital Assoc.

Project Preferences

Type of Financing Preferred:
Early Stage
Later Stage
Seed

Geographical Preferences

International Preferences:
Europe

Industry Preferences

In Communications prefer:
Commercial Communications

In Internet Specific prefer:
Internet

Additional Information
Year Founded: 2007
Current Activity Level : Actively seeking new investments

EFESO CONSULTING GROUP SA

14 Rue de Bassano
Paris, France 75116
Website: www.efeso.com

Management and Staff
Gilles Lorang, Vice President

Type of Firm
Private Equity Firm

Project Preferences

Type of Financing Preferred:
Leveraged Buyout

Geographical Preferences

International Preferences:
France

Additional Information
Year Founded: 2010
Current Activity Level : Actively seeking new investments

EFG HERMES HOLDINGS SAE

Km 28 Cairo Alexandria Road
Building No. B129
6 October, Egypt 12577
Phone: 20235356499
Fax: 20235370942
E-mail: pegroup@efg-hermes.com
Website: efghermes.com

Other Offices
Mohamed Darwish El-Dib (Ismailiya)
39 Roshdy
Alexandria, Egypt
Phone: 20-3-544-2100
Fax: 20-3-544-2101

5 Gomhoreya we Assaf Street
Dakahleya
Mansoura, Egypt
Phone: 20-050-229-5300
Fax: 20-050-229-5301

Emirates Towers, 11th Floor
Sheikh Zayed Road
Dubai, Utd. Arab Em.
Phone: 971-4-306-9471
Fax: 971-4-330-0046

Management and Staff
Karim Awad, Chief Executive Officer
Mohamed Abdel Khabir, Chief Financial Officer
Mohamed El Wakeel, Chief Operating Officer
Yasser El Mallawany, Chief Executive Officer

Type of Firm
Bank Affiliated

Association Membership
Gulf Venture Capital Association

Project Preferences

Type of Financing Preferred:
Leveraged Buyout
Early Stage
Expansion
Generalist PE
Balanced
Turnaround
Later Stage
Seed
Management Buyouts

Size of Investments Considered:
Min Size of Investment Considered (000s): $500
Max Size of Investment Considered (000s): $7,000

Geographical Preferences

International Preferences:
Albania
Ecuador
Jordan
Egypt
Utd. Arab Em.
Middle East
Saudi Arabia
Syria
Africa

Industry Preferences

In Communications prefer:
Communications and Media
Telecommunications

In Biotechnology prefer:
Agricultural/Animal Bio.

In Consumer Related prefer:
Food/Beverage

In Industrial/Energy prefer:
Energy
Oil and Gas Exploration
Oil & Gas Drilling,Explor
Materials

In Financial Services prefer:
Financial Services
Real Estate
Financial Services

In Manufact. prefer:
Manufacturing

In Utilities prefer:
Utilities

Additional Information
Year Founded: 1984
Capital Under Management: $1,000,000,000
Current Activity Level : Actively seeking new investments

EFG WEALTH MANAGEMENT INDIA PVT LTD

1st Floor, Marshall Building
Shoorji Vallabhdhas Marg
Mumbai, India 400 038
Phone: 91-22-6634-9946
Fax: 91-22-2264-2393
E-mail: info@strategicindia.net

Other Offices
Marshall Building, 1st Floor
Shoorji Vallabhdhas Marg, Ballard Estate
Mumbai , India 400 038

Management and Staff
Atul Sud, Managing Director

Type of Firm
Bank Affiliated

Project Preferences

Type of Financing Preferred:
Balanced

Geographical Preferences

International Preferences:
India

Industry Preferences

In Financial Services prefer:
Insurance
Real Estate
Investment Groups

In Business Serv. prefer:
Services

Additional Information
Year Founded: 1995
Current Activity Level : Actively seeking new investments

EFROMOVICH/SILVA CAPITAL PARTNERS

Calle 75 #8-77 Of, 102
Bogota, Colombia
Phone: 571313921
E-mail: info@efromovichsilva.com
Website: efromovichsilva.info

Other Offices

Rcdrguez Marn 88
Madrid, Spain 28016
Phone: 34917823660

1250 Connecticut Avenue, NW
Suite 200
Washington, DC USA 20036
Phone: 2022613564

Management and Staff

Felipe Daza, Chief Financial Officer
Maria Claudia Correa, Chief Operating Officer

Type of Firm

Private Equity Firm

Project Preferences

Type of Financing Preferred:
Early Stage
Balanced

Geographical Preferences

International Preferences:
Latin America
Portugal
Peru
Brazil
Spain
Colombia

Additional Information

Year Founded: 2013
Current Activity Level : Actively seeking new investments

EG CAPITAL GROUP LLC

39 West 54th Street
New York, NY USA 10019
Phone: 2129562600
Fax: 2129562699
Website: www.egcapitalgroup.com

Type of Firm

Private Equity Firm

Project Preferences

Type of Financing Preferred:
Leveraged Buyout
Early Stage
Expansion

Geographical Preferences

United States Preferences:
All U.S.

Canadian Preferences:
All Canada

Industry Preferences

In Consumer Related prefer:
Retail
Food/Beverage
Other Restaurants

Additional Information

Year Founded: 2003
Current Activity Level : Actively seeking new investments

EGAN MANAGED CAPITAL LP

30 Federal Street
Boston, MA USA 02110
Phone: 6176952600
Fax: 6176952699
Website: www.egancapital.com

Management and Staff

Frank Andrasco, Partner
John Egan, Co-Founder
Michael Shanahan, Co-Founder
Travis Connors, Partner

Type of Firm

Private Equity Firm

Association Membership

New England Venture Capital Association

Project Preferences

Role in Financing:
Will function either as deal originator or investor in deals created by others

Type of Financing Preferred:
Early Stage

Geographical Preferences

United States Preferences:
New Hampshire
Rhode Island
Vermont
Northeast
Massachusetts
Connecticut
Maine

Industry Focus

(% based on actual investment)
Computer Software and Services 45.8%
Internet Specific 43.8%
Semiconductors/Other Elect. 7.4%
Communications and Media 1.7%
Computer Hardware 1.2%

Additional Information

Name of Most Recent Fund: Egan-Managed Capital III
Most Recent Fund Was Raised: 10/01/2003
Year Founded: 1997
Capital Under Management: $233,000,000

Current Activity Level : Reducing investment activity
Method of Compensation: Return on investment is of primary concern, do not charge fees

EGARDEN VENTURES HONG KONG LTD

Bank of America Tower
12 Harcourt Road
Central, Hong Kong 0000
Phone: 85223117996
Fax: 85223121909
Website: www.egardenvc.com

Type of Firm

Private Equity Firm

Project Preferences

Type of Financing Preferred:
Balanced

Geographical Preferences

International Preferences:
China
Asia

Industry Preferences

In Communications prefer:
Telecommunications
Wireless Communications
Media and Entertainment

In Internet Specific prefer:
Internet

In Medical/Health prefer:
Health Services

In Consumer Related prefer:
Consumer Products

Additional Information

Year Founded: 2000
Capital Under Management: $1,000,000
Current Activity Level : Actively seeking new investments

EGELI & CO TARIM GIRISIM SERMAYESI YATIRIM ORTAKLIGI AS

Abdi Ipekci Caddesi
No 40/10 Nisantasi
Istanbul, Turkey 34367
Phone: 902123430626
Fax: 902123430627
E-mail: info@egcyo.com
Website: www.egcyo.com

Type of Firm

Private Equity Firm

Project Preferences

Type of Financing Preferred:
Leveraged Buyout
Early Stage
Expansion
Generalist PE
Later Stage
Management Buyouts
Acquisition

Geographical Preferences

International Preferences:
Turkey
Europe

Industry Preferences

In Agr/Forestr/Fish prefer:
Agriculture related

Additional Information
Year Founded: 1994
Current Activity Level : Actively seeking new investments

EGERIA BV

Sarphatikade 12
Amsterdam, Netherlands 1017 WV
Phone: 31205306868
Fax: 31205306869
E-mail: egeria@egeria.nl
Website: www.egeria.nl

Management and Staff
Floris Muijser, Partner
Frank van Trigt, Chief Financial Officer
Geert Glimmerveen, Partner
Mark Wetzels, Partner
Peter Visser, Managing Partner

Type of Firm
Private Equity Firm

Association Membership
European Private Equity and Venture Capital Assoc.
Dutch Venture Capital Associaton (NVP)

Project Preferences

Type of Financing Preferred:
Leveraged Buyout
Mezzanine
Later Stage
Management Buyouts
Recapitalizations

Size of Investments Considered:
Min Size of Investment Considered (000s): $20,970
Max Size of Investment Considered (000s): $69,901

Geographical Preferences

International Preferences:
Europe
Netherlands
Germany

Industry Preferences

In Communications prefer:
Communications and Media

In Medical/Health prefer:
Medical/Health

In Consumer Related prefer:
Consumer

In Industrial/Energy prefer:
Energy
Industrial Products

Additional Information
Name of Most Recent Fund: Egeria Private Equity Fund IV
Most Recent Fund Was Raised: 12/12/2012
Year Founded: 1997
Capital Under Management: $1,537,800,000
Current Activity Level : Actively seeking new investments

EGIS CAPITAL PARTNERS

19 West 44th Street
Suite 812
New York, NY USA 10036
Phone: 9739940606
Fax: 2127680977

Management and Staff
John Mack, Partner
Robert Chefitz, Partner

Type of Firm
Private Equity Firm

Project Preferences

Type of Financing Preferred:
Leveraged Buyout
Management Buyouts

Size of Investments Considered:
Min Size of Investment Considered (000s): $5,000
Max Size of Investment Considered (000s): $40,000

Geographical Preferences

United States Preferences:
Virginia
California

Industry Preferences

In Medical/Health prefer:
Medical Diagnostics

Additional Information
Year Founded: 1997
Current Activity Level : Actively seeking new investments

EGYPTIAN-AMERICAN ENTERPRISE FUND

888 Seventh Avenue, 16th floor
New York, NY USA 10106
Phone: 2129949819
Fax: 2129949811
E-mail: aenan@eaefund.org

Type of Firm
Private Equity Firm

Project Preferences

Type of Financing Preferred:
Leveraged Buyout
Early Stage
Expansion
Acquisition

Geographical Preferences

International Preferences:
Egypt

Additional Information
Year Founded: 2013
Capital Under Management: $300,000,000
Current Activity Level : Actively seeking new investments

EHEALTH TECHNOLOGY BUSINESS INCUBATOR

A-Block PIXEL Park
1 KM Before Electronics City
Bangalore, India 560 100
Phone: 080-25743600
Fax: 080-25743700
E-mail: ehealthtbi@mail2business.com
Website: www.ehealthtbi.com

Type of Firm
Incubator/Development Program

Project Preferences

Type of Financing Preferred:
Early Stage

Geographical Preferences

International Preferences:
India

Industry Preferences

In Medical/Health prefer:
Medical/Health
Health Services

In Consumer Related prefer:
Education Related

Additional Information
Year Founded: 2013
Capital Under Management: $5,467,000
Current Activity Level : Actively seeking new investments

EHEALTH VENTURES ISRAEL LTD

2 Koifman Street
Tel Aviv, Israel 6158101
Phone: 97236588809
Website: www.ehealthventures.com

Type of Firm
Incubator/Development Program

Geographical Preferences

International Preferences:
Israel

Industry Preferences

In Computer Software prefer:
Software

In Internet Specific prefer:
Internet
Ecommerce

In Medical/Health prefer:
Medical/Health
Medical Therapeutics
Medical Products

Additional Information
Year Founded: 2016
Current Activity Level : Actively seeking new investments

EIG VENTURE CAPITAL LTD

Floragatan 19
Stockholm, Sweden 114 31
Phone: 46734232255
E-mail: evc@eigcapital.com

Type of Firm
Private Equity Firm

Project Preferences

Type of Financing Preferred:
Later Stage

Geographical Preferences

International Preferences:
Sweden

Industry Preferences

In Industrial/Energy prefer:
Alternative Energy
Energy Conservation Relat

In Other prefer:
Environment Responsible

Additional Information
Year Founded: 2001
Current Activity Level : Actively seeking new investments

EIGHT ROADS VENTURES EUROPE

25 Cannon Street
London, United Kingdom EC4M 5TA
Phone: 442070745400
Website: www.eightroads.com

Management and Staff
Davor Hebel, Partner
Gaurav Tuli, Principal
Joe Chang, Partner
John Moorhead, Chief Operating Officer
Kevin Kimber, Venture Partner
Michael Treskow, Partner
Rohit Krishnan, Vice President
Simon Clark, Managing Partner
Vytautas Balsys, Vice President

Type of Firm
Private Equity Firm

Project Preferences

Type of Financing Preferred:
Expansion
Balanced

Geographical Preferences

International Preferences:
Europe

Industry Preferences

In Computer Software prefer:
Data Processing
Software

In Internet Specific prefer:
E-Commerce Technology

In Financial Services prefer:
Financial Services

Additional Information
Year Founded: 2010
Capital Under Management: $250,000,000
Current Activity Level : Actively seeking new investments

EILESES CAPITAL LLC

595 Market Street
Suite 2430
San Francisco, CA USA 94105
Phone: 6288882500
E-mail: info@eileses.com
Website: eileses.com

Type of Firm
Private Equity Firm

Additional Information
Year Founded: 1969
Current Activity Level : Actively seeking new investments

EIV CAPITAL MANAGEMENT COMPANY LLC

1616 South Voss Road
Suite 940
Houston, TX USA 77057
Phone: 2817604907
Fax: 7133532793
Website: www.eivcapital.com

Management and Staff
A. Anthony Annunziato, President, Founder
Jennifer Gottschalk, Principal
Patricia Melcher, Chief Executive Officer

Type of Firm
Private Equity Firm

Project Preferences

Type of Financing Preferred:
Other

Size of Investments Considered:
Min Size of Investment Considered (000s): $5,000
Max Size of Investment Considered (000s): $20,000

Industry Preferences

In Industrial/Energy prefer:
Oil and Gas Exploration
Oil & Gas Drilling,Explor
Alternative Energy

Additional Information
Name of Most Recent Fund: EIV Capital Fund II, L.P.
Most Recent Fund Was Raised: 08/29/2013
Year Founded: 2007
Capital Under Management: $717,000,000
Current Activity Level : Actively seeking new investments

EKKOFUND SA

28, Boulevard Initialis
Mons, Belgium 7000
Phone: 32231889
Website: www.ekkofund.com

Type of Firm
Private Equity Firm

Project Preferences

Type of Financing Preferred:
Management Buyouts
Acquisition

Geographical Preferences

International Preferences:
Belgium

Additional Information

Year Founded: 2015
Current Activity Level : Actively seeking new investments

EKUITI NASIONAL BHD

No. 1 Jalan PJU 7/3
Level 13, Surian Tower
Petaling Jaya, Selangor, Malaysia 47810
Phone: 60377107171
Fax: 60377107173
Website: www.ekuinas.com.my

Type of Firm

Government Affiliated Program

Project Preferences

Type of Financing Preferred:
Generalist PE
Joint Ventures

Geographical Preferences

International Preferences:
Malaysia

Additional Information

Year Founded: 2009
Capital Under Management: $41,901,000
Current Activity Level : Actively seeking new investments

EL DORADO VENTURES

850 Oak Grove Avenue
Menlo Park, CA USA 94025
Phone: 6508541200
Fax: 6508541202
E-mail: info@eldorado.com
Website: www.eldorado.com

Other Offices

601 Carlson Parkway
Suite 1160
Minnetonka, MN USA 55305
Phone: 952-995-7450
Fax: 952-995-7493

Management and Staff

Charles Beeler, General Partner
Jeff Hinck, General Partner
Jim Kunse, Chief Financial Officer
Michael Irwin, General Partner
Thomas Peterson, General Partner

Type of Firm

Private Equity Firm

Association Membership

Western Association of Venture Capitalists (WAVC)

Project Preferences

Role in Financing:
Prefer role as deal originator but will also invest in deals created by others

Type of Financing Preferred:
Early Stage
Balanced
Seed
Startup

Geographical Preferences

United States Preferences:
California
West Coast

Industry Focus

(% based on actual investment)
Internet Specific	30.1%
Computer Software and Services	29.9%
Semiconductors/Other Elect.	17.4%
Communications and Media	14.5%
Computer Hardware	4.5%
Medical/Health	1.0%
Other Products	1.0%
Consumer Related	0.7%
Industrial/Energy	0.5%
Biotechnology	0.3%

Additional Information

Name of Most Recent Fund: El Dorado Technology '05, L.P.
Most Recent Fund Was Raised: 11/15/2005
Year Founded: 1986
Capital Under Management: $750,000,000
Current Activity Level : Actively seeking new investments
Method of Compensation: Return on investment is of primary concern, do not charge fees

ELAB VENTURES

505 E. Liberty Street
Suite LL500
Ann Arbor, MI USA 48104
Website: elabvc.com

Type of Firm

Private Equity Firm

Project Preferences

Type of Financing Preferred:
Early Stage
Startup

Additional Information

Year Founded: 1969
Current Activity Level : Actively seeking new investments

ELAGHMORE PARTNERS LLP

Cale Cross House, Pilgrim St
Newcastle Upon Tyne
Tyne And Wear, United Kingdom NE1 6SU

Type of Firm

Private Equity Firm

Project Preferences

Type of Financing Preferred:
Generalist PE

Geographical Preferences

International Preferences:
United Kingdom

Additional Information

Year Founded: 2016
Capital Under Management: $76,070,000
Current Activity Level : Actively seeking new investments

ELAH FUND I LP

11 Menachem Begin Road
C/O Raveh Haber & Co
Ramat Gan, Israel 5268104
Phone: 6464701291
Website: www.elahfund.com

Type of Firm

Private Equity Firm

Geographical Preferences

International Preferences:
Israel

Additional Information

Year Founded: 2016
Current Activity Level : Actively seeking new investments

ELAIA PARTNERS SAS

54, Rue De Ponthieu
Paris, France 75008
Phone: 33176749250
Fax: 33176749260
E-mail: contact@elaia.com
Website: www.elaia.com

Management and Staff

Marie Ekeland, Partner
Philippe Gire, Partner
Xavier Lazarus, Partner

Type of Firm

Private Equity Firm

Association Membership
French Venture Capital Association (AFIC)

Project Preferences

Type of Financing Preferred:
Early Stage
Later Stage
Seed
Startup

Size of Investments Considered:
Min Size of Investment Considered (000s): $1,247
Max Size of Investment Considered (000s): $2,494

Geographical Preferences

International Preferences:
United Kingdom
Europe
Spain
France

Industry Preferences

In Computer Software prefer:
Data Processing
Software

In Internet Specific prefer:
Internet

In Computer Other prefer:
Computer Related

In Medical/Health prefer:
Medical/Health

In Industrial/Energy prefer:
Industrial Products

In Business Serv. prefer:
Services

Additional Information
Name of Most Recent Fund: Elaia Alpha
Most Recent Fund Was Raised: 10/29/2012
Year Founded: 2002
Capital Under Management: $59,600,000
Current Activity Level : Actively seeking new investments

ELAIS CAPITAL SAS

17, avenue Georges V
Paris, France 75008
Phone: 33184851290
Fax: 33184851299
E-mail: contact@elais.eu
Website: www.elais.eu

Type of Firm
Private Equity Firm

Project Preferences

Type of Financing Preferred:
Leveraged Buyout
Early Stage
Expansion
Management Buyouts
Acquisition

Size of Investments Considered:
Min Size of Investment Considered (000s): $11,277
Max Size of Investment Considered (000s): $56,383

Geographical Preferences

International Preferences:
Europe
France

Additional Information
Year Founded: 2014
Current Activity Level : Actively seeking new investments

ELBRUS KAPITAL OOO

10 Presnenskaya Nab.
52/F, Naberezhnaya Twr, Blk. C
Moscow, Russia 123317
Phone: 74956637400
Fax: 74956637407
E-mail: info@elbcp.com
Website: elbcp.ru

Management and Staff
Alexander Savin, Partner
Andrey Aksenov, Vice President
Dmitri Krukov, Partner
Maria Lashina, Chief Financial Officer
Rob Thielen, Partner

Type of Firm
Private Equity Firm

Association Membership
Emerging Markets Private Equity Association
Russian Venture Capital Association (RVCA)

Project Preferences

Type of Financing Preferred:
Leveraged Buyout
Acquisition

Geographical Preferences

International Preferences:
Armenia
Belarus
Kazakhstan
Western Europe
Kyrgyzstan
Tajikistan
Turkmenistan
Azerbaijan
Moldova
Ukraine
Uzbekistan
Russia

Industry Preferences

In Communications prefer:
Communications and Media
CATV & Pay TV Systems
Media and Entertainment

In Medical/Health prefer:
Health Services

In Consumer Related prefer:
Retail
Consumer Services

Additional Information
Name of Most Recent Fund: Elbrus Capital Fund II LP
Most Recent Fund Was Raised: 11/21/2012
Year Founded: 2007
Capital Under Management: $550,000,000
Current Activity Level : Actively seeking new investments

ELCANO CAPITAL LP

PO Box 6001
Fairfield Gardens, Australia 4301
E-mail: info@elcanocapital.com
Website: www.elcanocapital.com

Management and Staff
Andrew Rettie, Managing Partner
Darren Lelliott, Partner
Kevin Mumford, Partner
Shonna Lelliott, Partner

Type of Firm
Private Equity Firm

Project Preferences

Type of Financing Preferred:
Early Stage
Expansion
Seed

Geographical Preferences

International Preferences:
Australia

Industry Preferences

In Industrial/Energy prefer:
Energy

In Transportation prefer:
Transportation

In Other prefer:
Socially Responsible
Environment Responsible

Additional Information
Year Founded: 2009
Current Activity Level : Actively seeking new investments

ELDERSTREET INVESTMENTS LTD

10-11 Charterhouse Square
London, United Kingdom WC1R 4HE
Phone: 442078315088
Fax: 448436593491
E-mail: info@elderstreet.com
Website: www.elderstreet.com

Management and Staff
Barnaby Terry, Partner
Paul Frew, Managing Partner
Vinodka Murria, Partner

Type of Firm
Private Equity Firm

Association Membership
British Venture Capital Association (BVCA)

Project Preferences

Type of Financing Preferred:
Early Stage
Expansion
Balanced
Later Stage
Seed
Management Buyouts

Size of Investments Considered:
Min Size of Investment Considered (000s): $763
Max Size of Investment Considered (000s): $7,630

Geographical Preferences

International Preferences:
United Kingdom
Western Europe

Industry Focus
(% based on actual investment)
Computer Software and Services	45.7%
Internet Specific	43.5%
Communications and Media	5.3%
Consumer Related	2.9%
Semiconductors/Other Elect.	1.8%
Other Products	0.8%

Additional Information
Year Founded: 1990
Capital Under Management: $169,800,000
Current Activity Level : Actively seeking new investments

ELECTRA PRIVATE EQUITY PLC

50, Grosvenor Hill, 1st floor
London, United Kingdom W1K 3QT
Phone: 442038748300
E-mail: info@electrapartners.com
Website: www.electrapartners.com

Management and Staff
Alexander Cooper-Evans, Partner
Alexander Fortescue, Partner
Charles Elkington, Partner
Christopher Hanna, Partner
David Symondson, Managing Partner
Hugh Mumford, Managing Partner
Stephen Ozin, Partner

Type of Firm
Private Equity Firm

Association Membership
British Venture Capital Association (BVCA)

Project Preferences

Type of Financing Preferred:
Leveraged Buyout
Expansion
Mezzanine
Public Companies
Later Stage
Acquisition

Geographical Preferences

International Preferences:
United Kingdom
Western Europe

Additional Information
Name of Most Recent Fund: Acuity VCT 2 (FKA: Electra Kingsway VCT 2)
Most Recent Fund Was Raised: 12/31/2004
Year Founded: 1976
Capital Under Management: $2,725,000,000
Current Activity Level : Actively seeking new investments

ELEMENTS CAPITAL PARTNERS LTD

8, Kennedy Avenue
Office 205
Nicosia, Cyprus 1087
Phone: 35722764030
Fax: 35722763190
Website: www.elements-capital.com

Type of Firm
Private Equity Firm

Project Preferences

Type of Financing Preferred:
Generalist PE

Geographical Preferences

International Preferences:
Europe

Industry Preferences

In Industrial/Energy prefer:
Alternative Energy

In Financial Services prefer:
Financial Services
Real Estate

Additional Information
Year Founded: 2013
Current Activity Level : Actively seeking new investments

ELEPHANT PARTNERS LP

ONE MARINA PARK DRIVE
SUITE 900
Boston, MA USA 02210
Phone: 6176489100
Website: elephantvc.com

Type of Firm
Private Equity Firm

Project Preferences

Type of Financing Preferred:
Early Stage

Industry Preferences

In Computer Software prefer:
Software

In Internet Specific prefer:
Internet

Additional Information
Year Founded: 2015
Capital Under Management: $156,360,000
Current Activity Level : Actively seeking new investments

ELEPHANT VENTURES LLC

259 West 30th Street
Suite 403
New York, NY USA 10001
Phone: 2127306710
Fax: 9175912809
E-mail: info@elephantventures.com
Website: www.elephantventures.com

Management and Staff
Art Shectman, President, Founder
Miles Kafka, Principal

Type of Firm
Private Equity Firm

Project Preferences

Type of Financing Preferred:
Early Stage

Industry Preferences

In Computer Software prefer:
Software

In Internet Specific prefer:
Internet

Additional Information

Year Founded: 2015
Current Activity Level : Actively seeking new investments

ELEVAR EQUITY ADVISORS PVT LTD

Off M.G. Road
No. 21/8, Craig Park Layout
Bangalore, India 560 001
Phone: 918043356666
Fax: 918041120009
E-mail: info@elevarequity.com
Website: elevarequity.com

Management and Staff

Akshay Chandrasekhar, Vice President
Ayesha Gopal, Vice President
Chris Brookfield, Co-Founder
Danielle Wainer, Vice President
Johanna Posada, Co-Founder
Jyotsna Krishnan, Managing Director
Maya Chorengel, Co-Founder
Nethra Bhat, Vice President
Paula Arango, Vice President
Rana Muminoglu, Vice President
Sandeep Farias, Co-Founder

Type of Firm

Private Equity Firm

Project Preferences

Type of Financing Preferred:
Early Stage
Expansion
Start-up Financing
First Stage Financing

Geographical Preferences

International Preferences:
Indonesia
India
Peru
Mexico
Brazil
Philippines

Industry Preferences

In Other prefer:
Socially Responsible

Additional Information

Name of Most Recent Fund: Elevar Equity III, L.P.
Most Recent Fund Was Raised: 12/30/2013

Year Founded: 2008
Capital Under Management: $144,000,000
Current Activity Level : Actively seeking new investments

ELEVATE INNOVATION PARTNERS LLC

148 Lincoln Street
Garden City, NY USA 11530
Website: www.eipfund.com

Management and Staff

Greg Brown, Chief Financial Officer
Pranav Pai, General Partner
Shreyas Chityala, Co-Founder
Thomas Rudy, Co-Founder

Type of Firm

Private Equity Firm

Project Preferences

Type of Financing Preferred:
Early Stage
Expansion
Balanced
Seed

Size of Investments Considered:
Min Size of Investment Considered (000s): $100
Max Size of Investment Considered (000s): $400

Geographical Preferences

United States Preferences:
North Carolina
California
Florida
New York

Industry Preferences

In Communications prefer:
Entertainment

In Computer Software prefer:
Data Processing
Software

In Industrial/Energy prefer:
Energy

In Financial Services prefer:
Financial Services

Additional Information

Year Founded: 2016
Capital Under Management: $15,000,000
Current Activity Level : Actively seeking new investments

ELEVATE VENTURES INC

50 East 91st Street, Suite 213
Indianapolis, IN USA 46240
Phone: 3172520258

Fax: 3172520255

Other Offices

Former HQ: One North Capital Avenue
Suite 900
Indianapolis, IN USA 46204
Phone: 3172345671
Fax: 3174541367

Management and Staff

David Clark, Venture Partner
John Bodman, Venture Partner
Linda O Keefe, Chief Financial Officer
Stephen Hourigan, Chief Executive Officer
Ting Gootee, Vice President

Type of Firm

Incubator/Development Program

Project Preferences

Type of Financing Preferred:
Early Stage
Seed
Startup

Geographical Preferences

United States Preferences:
Indiana

Industry Preferences

In Communications prefer:
Wireless Communications
Other Communication Prod.

In Computer Hardware prefer:
Computers

In Computer Software prefer:
Software

In Internet Specific prefer:
Internet

In Semiconductor/Electr prefer:
Electronics
Electronic Components
Semiconductor

In Biotechnology prefer:
Biotechnology

In Medical/Health prefer:
Health Services

In Consumer Related prefer:
Consumer Products
Consumer Services
Education Related

In Industrial/Energy prefer:
Environmental Related

In Manufact. prefer:
Manufacturing

In Other prefer:
Environment Responsible
Women/Minority-Owned Bus.

Additional Information
Name of Most Recent Fund: Indiana Diversity Investment Fund
Most Recent Fund Was Raised: 06/04/2013
Year Founded: 2011
Capital Under Management: $100,000,000
Current Activity Level : Actively seeking new investments

ELEVATION CHINA CAPITAL

B118, Jianguo Road, Chaoyang
Rm.1106, Jinghui Building
Beijing, China 100022
Phone: 861065678505
Fax: 861065678515
E-mail: info@ecc-capital.com
Website: www.ecc-capital.com

Management and Staff
Bo Lin, Partner
Kainan Tang, Partner
Man Li, Founder
Ruizhong Wu, Partner
Xiaofeng Ma, Partner
Zhixian Xu, Partner
Zhongqing Liu, Partner

Type of Firm
Private Equity Firm

Project Preferences

Type of Financing Preferred:
Balanced

Geographical Preferences

International Preferences:
China

Industry Preferences

In Communications prefer:
Telecommunications

In Medical/Health prefer:
Medical/Health

In Industrial/Energy prefer:
Alternative Energy
Advanced Materials

In Business Serv. prefer:
Media

In Manufact. prefer:
Manufacturing

In Agr/Forestr/Fish prefer:
Agriculture related

Additional Information
Year Founded: 2006
Current Activity Level : Actively seeking new investments

ELEVATION PARTNERS LP

70 East 55th Street
12th Floor
New York, NY USA 10022
Phone: 2123176555
Fax: 2123176556
E-mail: info@elevation.com
Website: www.elevation.com

Other Offices
2800 Sand Hill Road
Suite 160
Menlo Park, CA USA 94025
Phone: 6506876700
Fax: 6506876710

Management and Staff
Adam Hopkins, Principal
Avadis Tevanian, Managing Director
Bret Pearlman, Co-Founder
Frederick Anderson, Co-Founder
Paul Hewson, Co-Founder
Roger McNamee, Co-Founder
Sherwin Chen, Principal
Tracy Hogan, Chief Financial Officer

Type of Firm
Private Equity Firm

Project Preferences

Type of Financing Preferred:
Leveraged Buyout
Management Buyouts
Acquisition

Geographical Preferences

United States Preferences:

Industry Preferences

In Communications prefer:
Media and Entertainment

In Consumer Related prefer:
Consumer

In Business Serv. prefer:
Media

Additional Information
Name of Most Recent Fund: Elevation Partners, L.P.
Most Recent Fund Was Raised: 09/03/2004
Year Founded: 2004
Capital Under Management: $1,900,000,000
Current Activity Level : Actively seeking new investments

ELEVEN ACCELERATOR VENTURE FUND

Gurko 4
Sofia, Bulgaria 1000
Phone: 359886852881
E-mail: eleven@eleven.bg
Website: www.blog.eleven.bg/about/

Type of Firm
Private Equity Firm

Project Preferences

Type of Financing Preferred:
Early Stage
Seed

Size of Investments Considered:
Min Size of Investment Considered (000s): $33
Max Size of Investment Considered (000s): $267

Geographical Preferences

International Preferences:
Central Europe
Eastern Europe
Bulgaria

Additional Information
Year Founded: 2012
Capital Under Management: $15,732,000
Current Activity Level : Actively seeking new investments

ELGNER GROUP INVESTMENTS LTD

3300 Bloor Street West
Suite 3100
Toronto, Canada M8X 2X3
Phone: 6474260380
Fax: 6474260376
Website: www.elgnergroup.com

Type of Firm
Corporate PE/Venture

Additional Information
Year Founded: 1993
Current Activity Level : Actively seeking new investments

ELI LILLY AND CO

Lilly Corporate Center
Indianapolis, IN USA 46285
Phone: 3172762000
Fax: 3172764878
Website: www.lilly.com

Other Offices

Sannomiya Plaza Building
7-1-5 Isogami-dori, Chuo-ku
Kobe, Japan 651-0086
Phone: 81-78-242-9000
Fax: 87-78-242-9502

3650 Danforth Avenue
Toronto, Canada M1N 2E8
Phone: 800-268-5123
Fax: 416-693-3604

Erl Wood Manor
Sunninghill Road
Windlesham, United Kingdom GU20 6PH
Phone: 44-1276-483-000
Fax: 44-1276-484-921

Koelblgasse 8-10
Vienna, Austria A-1030
Phone: 43-1-711-780
Fax: 43-1-711-783-12

112 Wharf Road
West Ryde, Australia 2114
Phone: 612-9325-4440
Fax: 612-9325-4400

Management and Staff
Erik Fyrwarld, President

Type of Firm
Corporate PE/Venture

Project Preferences

Type of Financing Preferred:
Early Stage
Balanced

Geographical Preferences

United States Preferences:

International Preferences:
Australia

Industry Preferences

In Biotechnology prefer:
Biotechnology

In Medical/Health prefer:
Pharmaceuticals

Additional Information
Year Founded: 1901
Current Activity Level: Actively seeking new investments

ELITE CAPITAL

#1239 Century Avenue, Pudong
01-A Bld 13-Bld 2
Shanghai, China
Website: www.oncocapital.com

Type of Firm
Private Equity Firm

Project Preferences

Type of Financing Preferred:
Balanced

Industry Preferences

In Medical/Health prefer:
Health Services

Additional Information
Year Founded: 1969
Current Activity Level: Actively seeking new investments

ELITE CAPITAL

#1 Zuojiazhuang, Chaoyang Dist
2U, Blk A Guomen Bldg
Beijing, China 100028
Phone: 861084517085
Website: elite-capital.com

Type of Firm
Private Equity Firm

Project Preferences

Type of Financing Preferred:
Balanced

Additional Information
Year Founded: 2010
Current Activity Level: Actively seeking new investments

ELLERSTON CAPITAL LTD

Level 11, 179 Elizabeth Street
Sydney, Australia 2000
Phone: 61290217797
Fax: 61292610528
E-mail: info@ellerstoncapital.com
Website: www.ellerstoncapital.com

Type of Firm
Investment Management Firm

Project Preferences

Type of Financing Preferred:
Early Stage

Additional Information
Year Founded: 2016
Capital Under Management: $50,000,000
Current Activity Level: Actively seeking new investments

ELLIPSE CAPITAL LLC

One North Franklin Street, Suite 1500
Chicago, IL USA 60606
Phone: 3122678750
Fax: 3122676025
Website: www.ellipsecapital.com

Management and Staff
David Schumacher, Vice President
Jennifer Levinson, Principal
Peter Gotsch, Managing Partner

Type of Firm
Private Equity Firm

Project Preferences

Type of Financing Preferred:
Leveraged Buyout

Size of Investments Considered:
Min Size of Investment Considered (000s): $15,000
Max Size of Investment Considered (000s): $75,000

Industry Preferences

In Business Serv. prefer:
Distribution

Additional Information
Name of Most Recent Fund: Ellipse Capital Fund I
Most Recent Fund Was Raised: 11/20/2009
Year Founded: 2008
Capital Under Management: $6,000,000
Current Activity Level: Actively seeking new investments

ELLIS CAPITAL

888 3rd Street NW
Atlanta, GA USA 30318
Website: www.elliscapital.net

Type of Firm
Private Equity Firm

Project Preferences

Type of Financing Preferred:
Early Stage
Expansion
Later Stage

Industry Preferences

In Communications prefer:
Telecommunications

In Internet Specific prefer:
Internet

In Medical/Health prefer:
Health Services

In Financial Services prefer:
Financial Services
Real Estate

In Business Serv. prefer:
Media

ELM CREEK PARTNERS

5949 Sherry Lane
Suite 1070
Dallas, TX USA 75225
Phone: 2148715650
Fax: 2149755650
Website: www.elmcreekpartners.com

Management and Staff
Aaron Handler, Co-Founder
Zach Wooldridge, Co-Founder

Type of Firm
Private Equity Firm

Association Membership
Natl Assoc of Small Bus. Inv. Co (NASBIC)

Project Preferences

Type of Financing Preferred:
Leveraged Buyout
Acquisition

Size of Investments Considered:
Min Size of Investment Considered (000s): $3,000
Max Size of Investment Considered (000s): $6,000

Geographical Preferences

United States Preferences:
Texas

Industry Preferences

In Financial Services prefer:
Financial Services

In Business Serv. prefer:
Distribution

In Manufact. prefer:
Manufacturing

Additional Information
Year Founded: 2008
Current Activity Level : Actively seeking new investments

ELM EQUITY PARTNERS LLC

222 Broadway, 19th Floor
New York, NY USA 10011
E-mail: contact@elmeqp.com
Website: www.elmeqp.com

Management and Staff
Elliot Luchansky, Managing Partner
Michael Mazzeo, Partner
Percy Rueda, Vice President

Type of Firm
Private Equity Firm

Project Preferences

Type of Financing Preferred:
Leveraged Buyout
Acquisition

Geographical Preferences

United States Preferences:

Canadian Preferences:
All Canada

Industry Preferences

In Medical/Health prefer:
Medical/Health

In Consumer Related prefer:
Education Related

In Business Serv. prefer:
Services

Additional Information
Year Founded: 2014
Current Activity Level : Actively seeking new investments

ELM STREET VENTURES LP

33 Whitney Avenue
New Haven, CT USA 06510
Phone: 2034014201
Fax: 2034014235
E-mail: venture@elmvc.com
Website: www.elmvc.com

Management and Staff
Barry Schweitzer, Venture Partner
Brian Dixon, Venture Partner
Christopher McLeod, Venture Partner
Richard Stahl, Venture Partner

Type of Firm
Private Equity Firm

Association Membership
New England Venture Capital Association
National Venture Capital Association - USA (NVCA)

Project Preferences

Role in Financing:
Will function either as deal originator or investor in deals created by others

Type of Financing Preferred:
Early Stage
Seed

Geographical Preferences

United States Preferences:
Connecticut
New York

Industry Preferences

In Communications prefer:
Wireless Communications

In Medical/Health prefer:
Medical Diagnostics
Diagnostic Services
Diagnostic Test Products
Medical Therapeutics
Medical Products
Health Services

In Industrial/Energy prefer:
Alternative Energy

Additional Information
Name of Most Recent Fund: Elm Street Ventures, L.P.
Most Recent Fund Was Raised: 02/21/2006
Year Founded: 2004
Capital Under Management: $22,000,000
Current Activity Level : Actively seeking new investments

ELMCORE GROUP INC

3900 Paradise Road
Suite 101
Las Vegas, NV USA 89169
Phone: 7026379600
Fax: 7029405462
E-mail: info@elmcore.com
Website: www.elmcore.com

Management and Staff
Kim Schmidt, Chief Operating Officer

Type of Firm
Investment Management Firm

Project Preferences

Type of Financing Preferred:
Leveraged Buyout

Industry Preferences

In Communications prefer:
Media and Entertainment

In Computer Software prefer:
Software

In Internet Specific prefer:
Internet

In Semiconductor/Electr prefer:
Semiconductor

In Medical/Health prefer:
Drug/Equipmt Delivery

In Consumer Related prefer:
Consumer Products

Additional Information
Year Founded: 1996
Current Activity Level : Actively seeking new investments

In Transportation prefer:
Transportation
Aerospace

In Financial Services prefer:
Financial Services
Real Estate

In Manufact. prefer:
Manufacturing

In Agr/Forestr/Fish prefer:
Mining and Minerals

Additional Information
Year Founded: 2011
Current Activity Level : Actively seeking new investments

ELRON ELECTRONIC INDUSTRIES LTD

3 Azrieli Center
The Triangle Tower, 42nd Floor
Tel Aviv, Israel 6702301
Phone: 97236075555
Fax: 97236075556
E-mail: info@elron.com
Website: www.elron.com

Management and Staff
Ari Bronshtein, Chief Executive Officer

Type of Firm
Corporate PE/Venture

Project Preferences

Type of Financing Preferred:
Early Stage
Balanced
Seed
Startup

Geographical Preferences

International Preferences:
Israel
Asia

Additional Information
Year Founded: 1962
Current Activity Level : Actively seeking new investments

ELSEWHERE PARTNERS

300 West Sixth Street
Austin, TX USA 78701
Website: elsewhere.partners

Type of Firm
Private Equity Firm

Project Preferences

Type of Financing Preferred:
Later Stage

Geographical Preferences

United States Preferences:
All U.S.

Industry Preferences

In Computer Software prefer:
Software

Additional Information
Year Founded: 2017
Current Activity Level : Actively seeking new investments

ELVASTON CAPITAL MANAGEMENT GMBH

Kurfuerstendamm 214
Berlin, Germany 10719
Phone: 49308871427
Fax: 49308871427
E-mail: info@elvaston.com
Website: www.elvaston.com

Management and Staff
Oliver Thum, Partner
Thomas Keul, Partner

Type of Firm
Private Equity Firm

Project Preferences

Type of Financing Preferred:
Leveraged Buyout
Management Buyouts
Acquisition
Special Situation

Geographical Preferences

International Preferences:
Switzerland
Austria
Germany

Additional Information
Year Founded: 2013
Capital Under Management: $200,000,000
Current Activity Level : Actively seeking new investments

ELYSIAN CAPITAL LLP

15 John Adam Street
Ingram House
London, United Kingdom WC2N 6LU
Phone: 442079258050
Fax: 442079258069
Website: www.elysiancapital.com

Management and Staff
Edward Brett, Partner
Kenneth Terry, Chief Executive Officer
Philip Greves, Partner
Richard Ramsey, Partner

Type of Firm
Private Equity Firm

Project Preferences

Type of Financing Preferred:
Leveraged Buyout
Mezzanine
Management Buyouts
Acquisition

Size of Investments Considered:
Min Size of Investment Considered (000s): $19,680
Max Size of Investment Considered (000s): $137,760

Geographical Preferences

International Preferences:
United Kingdom

Additional Information
Year Founded: 2008
Capital Under Management: $381,330,000
Current Activity Level : Actively seeking new investments

EMALTERNATIVES LLC

2020 Pennsylvania Avenue
Suite 283
Washington, DC USA 20006
Phone: 2026595959
Fax: 2026595960
E-mail: info@emalternatives.com
Website: www.emalternatives.com

Other Offices

6th Floor, Building Kennemerhaghe
Leidsevaartweg 99
Heemstede, Netherlands 2106 AS
Phone: 31-23-510-0560
Fax: 31-23-510-0569

Level 5, North Block
159 Madang Road
Shanghai, China 200021
Phone: 86-21-6135-7208
Fax: 86-21-6135-7207

Management and Staff
Alexandra Gardiner, Chief Financial Officer
John Stephens, Managing Partner
Nicholas Morriss, Managing Partner

Type of Firm
Private Equity Advisor or Fund of Funds

Project Preferences

Type of Financing Preferred:
Fund of Funds

Geographical Preferences

United States Preferences:

International Preferences:
Latin America
India
Soviet Union
Central Europe
China
Eastern Europe
Middle East
Australia
Asia
Korea, South
Japan
Africa

Additional Information
Year Founded: 2007
Current Activity Level : Actively seeking new investments

EMBARK VENTURES LP

610 Santa Monica Boulevard
Suite 226
Los Angeles, CA USA 90036
Phone: 4157460615
Website: www.embark.vc

Type of Firm
Private Equity Firm

Project Preferences

Type of Financing Preferred:
Seed

Industry Preferences

In Internet Specific prefer:
Internet

Additional Information
Year Founded: 2016
Capital Under Management: $45,000,000
Current Activity Level : Actively seeking new investments

EMBED CAPITAL SRL

Via Giacomo Leopardi 12
Milan, Italy 20123
Phone: 390289682020
E-mail: info@embedcapital.it
Website: www.embedcapital.com

Management and Staff
Edoardo Bosio, Chief Executive Officer
Emanuele Bosio, President

Type of Firm
Private Equity Firm

Additional Information
Year Founded: 2014
Current Activity Level : Actively seeking new investments

EMBL VENTURES GMBH

Boxbergring 107
Heidelberg, Germany 69126
Phone: 496221389330
Fax: 4962213893311
E-mail: info@embl-ventures.com
Website: www.embl-ventures.com

Management and Staff
Jan Adams, Managing Director
Stefan Herr, Managing Director

Type of Firm
Corporate PE/Venture

Project Preferences

Type of Financing Preferred:
Early Stage
Expansion
Seed
Startup

Geographical Preferences

International Preferences:
Europe
Switzerland
Austria
Australia
Germany

Industry Preferences

In Biotechnology prefer:
Biotechnology

In Medical/Health prefer:
Medical/Health
Medical Diagnostics
Medical Therapeutics

In Industrial/Energy prefer:
Advanced Materials

Additional Information
Name of Most Recent Fund: EMBL Technology Fund II GmbH & Co. KG
Most Recent Fund Was Raised: 12/07/2011
Year Founded: 2001
Capital Under Management: $82,900,000
Current Activity Level : Actively seeking new investments

EME CAPITAL LLP

32 Street James Street
London, United Kingdom SW1A 1HD
E-mail: info@eme-capital.com
Website: www.eme-capital.com

Other Offices
51, Rue Francois Ier
Paris, France 75008

23, Level 3
Gate Village 10, DIFC
Dubai, Utd. Arab Em. 125115

Type of Firm
Private Equity Firm

Project Preferences

Type of Financing Preferred:
Leveraged Buyout
Management Buyouts
Acquisition

Geographical Preferences

International Preferences:
United Kingdom
Europe
Utd. Arab Em.
France

Additional Information
Year Founded: 2010
Current Activity Level : Actively seeking new investments

EMEDICI CAPITAL INC

427 Eleventh Avenue North East
Calgary, Canada T2E0Z4
Phone: 403-701-2700
Fax: 403-221-0909
Website: www.emedici.net/accolade_capital.shtml

Management and Staff
Grant Howard, President
Stace Wills, Managing Partner

Type of Firm
Private Equity Firm

Project Preferences

Type of Financing Preferred:
Seed

Geographical Preferences

Canadian Preferences:
All Canada

Additional Information
Year Founded: 2009
Current Activity Level : Actively seeking new investments

EMERALD DEVELOPMENT MANAGERS LP

9C9 Third Avenue
Floor 15
New York, NY USA 10022
Phone: 2123172250
Fax: 2123172255
Website: www.emeraldmanagers.com

Management and Staff
Charles Collins, Managing Director
Mark Mitchell, Vice President
Stephen Case, Managing Director
Thomas Gallo, Principal

Type of Firm
Private Equity Firm

Project Preferences

Type of Financing Preferred:
Early Stage

Additional Information
Year Founded: 2016
Current Activity Level : Actively seeking new investments

EMERALD HILL CAPITAL PARTNERS LTD

16 Ice House Street
19th Floor
Central, Hong Kong
Phone: 852-2248-8000
Fax: 852-2248-8001
E-mail: admin@ehcp.com
Website: www.ehcp.com

Other Offices
355 South Teller Street
Suite 200
Lakewood, CO USA 80226
Phone: 303-825-3550
Fax: 303-825-1874

Management and Staff
David Spencer, Managing Director
S. Eugene Choung, Managing Director
Tommy Y. Yip, Principal

Type of Firm
Private Equity Advisor or Fund of Funds

Project Preferences

Type of Financing Preferred:
Fund of Funds

Geographical Preferences

United States Preferences:
Southeast

International Preferences:
India
China
Asia

Additional Information
Year Founded: 2005
Capital Under Management: $999,900,000
Current Activity Level : Actively seeking new investments

EMERALD STAGE2 CAPITAL VENTURES LP

4801 S. Broad St.,
Suite 400
Philadelphia, PA USA 19112
Phone: 2159721502

Other Offices
1835 Market-Frankford Line
Suite 1100
PHILADELPHIA, PA USA 19103
Phone: 2159721502

Management and Staff
Bruce Luehrs, Partner

Type of Firm
Private Equity Firm

Association Membership
National Venture Capital Association - USA (NVCA)

Project Preferences

Role in Financing:
Prefer role as deal originator but will also invest in deals created by others

Type of Financing Preferred:
Early Stage

Size of Investments Considered:
Min Size of Investment Considered (000s): $1,000
Max Size of Investment Considered (000s): $3,000

Geographical Preferences

United States Preferences:
Mid Atlantic
Pennsylvania

Industry Preferences

In Medical/Health prefer:
Medical/Health
Pharmaceuticals

In Financial Services prefer:
Financial Services

Additional Information
Name of Most Recent Fund: Emerald Stage2 Ventures, L.P.
Most Recent Fund Was Raised: 03/05/2008
Year Founded: 2006
Capital Under Management: $15,000,000
Current Activity Level : Actively seeking new investments
Method of Compensation: Return on investment is of primary concern, do not charge fees

EMERALD TECHNOLOGY VENTURES AG

Seefeldstrasse 215
Zurich, Switzerland 8008
Phone: 41442696100
Fax: 41442696101
E-mail: info@emerald-ventures.com
Website: www.emerald-ventures.com

Other Offices
Trafalgar Court, Les Banques
St Peter Port, Channel Islands GY1 3QL

495 King Street West
2nd floor
, Canada
Phone: 416-900-3453
Fax: 416-900-3457

Management and Staff
Charles Vaslet, Partner
Gina Domanig, Managing Partner
Hans Dellenbach, Chief Financial Officer
Markus Moor, Partner

Type of Firm
Private Equity Firm

Association Membership
Swiss Venture Capital Association (SECA)
Canadian Venture Capital Association
European Private Equity and Venture Capital Assoc.

Project Preferences

Role in Financing:
Will function either as deal originator or investor in deals created by others

Type of Financing Preferred:
Early Stage
Later Stage
Startup

Geographical Preferences

United States Preferences:
All U.S.

Canadian Preferences:
All Canada

International Preferences:
Europe

Industry Preferences

In Semiconductor/Electr prefer:
Semiconductor

In Industrial/Energy prefer:
Energy
Alternative Energy
Coal Related
Materials
Advanced Materials
Environmental Related

Additional Information
Name of Most Recent Fund: Emerald Cleantech Fund III
Most Recent Fund Was Raised: 12/31/2012
Year Founded: 2000
Capital Under Management: $473,600,000
Current Activity Level : Actively seeking new investments

EMERAM CAPITAL PARTNERS GMBH

Muehlbaurstrasse 1
Munich, Germany 81677
Phone: 498941999670
Fax: 4989419996710
E-mail: info@emeram.com
Website: www.emeram.com

Management and Staff
Christian Naether, Co-Founder
Eckhard Cordes, Co-Founder
Kai Koppen, Co-Founder
Kai Obring, Co-Founder
Korbinian Knoblach, Co-Founder
Volker Schmidt, Co-Founder

Type of Firm
Private Equity Firm

Geographical Preferences

International Preferences:
Europe
Switzerland
Germany

Industry Preferences

In Medical/Health prefer:
Health Services

In Business Serv. prefer:
Services

Additional Information
Year Founded: 2012
Current Activity Level : Actively seeking new investments

EMERGE VENTURE CAPITAL

70 Danbury Road, Second Floor
Wilton, CT USA 06897
Phone: 203-210-7477
E-mail: info@emergevc.com
Website: www.emergevc.com

Management and Staff
Geoff Schneider, Managing Partner

Type of Firm
Private Equity Firm

Project Preferences

Type of Financing Preferred:
Early Stage
Seed

Additional Information
Year Founded: 2008
Current Activity Level : Actively seeking new investments

EMERGE VENTURES CAPITAL LTD

10 Totseret Haarets St
2nd Floor
Tel Aviv, Israel
E-mail: hi@emerge.co.il
Website: www.emerge.co.il

Type of Firm
Private Equity Firm

Project Preferences

Type of Financing Preferred:
Early Stage

Geographical Preferences

International Preferences:
Israel
Asia

Industry Preferences

In Computer Software prefer:
Data Processing
Software
Artificial Intelligence

Additional Information
Year Founded: 2015
Current Activity Level : Actively seeking new investments

EMERGENCE CAPITAL PARTNERS

160 Bovet Road
Suite 300
San Mateo, CA USA 94402
Phone: 6505733100
Fax: 6505733119
E-mail: hello@emcap.com
Website: www.emcap.com

Management and Staff
Alison Wagonfeld, Partner
Brian Jacobs, Co-Founder
Cathy Minshall, Chief Financial Officer
Everett Cox, Venture Partner
Gordon Ritter, Co-Founder
Jake Saper, Principal
Jason Green, Co-Founder
Joe Floyd, Partner
Kevin Spain, General Partner
Santiago Subotousky, General Partner

Type of Firm
Private Equity Firm

Association Membership
National Venture Capital Association - USA (NVCA)

Project Preferences

Role in Financing:
Prefer role as deal originator but will also invest in deals created by others

Type of Financing Preferred:
Early Stage
Expansion
Seed

Geographical Preferences

United States Preferences:

Industry Preferences

In Communications prefer:
Communications and Media
Wireless Communications
Media and Entertainment

In Computer Software prefer:
Computer Services
Software

In Internet Specific prefer:
Internet

In Semiconductor/Electr prefer:
Electronics

In Consumer Related prefer:
Consumer Services

In Business Serv. prefer:
Services

Additional Information
Name of Most Recent Fund: Emergence Capital Partners III, L.P.
Most Recent Fund Was Raised: 02/29/2012
Year Founded: 2003
Capital Under Management: $915,000,000
Current Activity Level : Actively seeking new investments
Method of Compensation: Return on investment is of primary concern, do not charge fees

EMERGENCE VENTURE PARTNERS LLC

813 Heinz Avenue
Berkeley, CA USA 94710
Phone: 5108092535
Fax: 5108092510
Website: www.emergence-llc.com

Management and Staff
George Pitarra, Managing Director

Type of Firm
Private Equity Firm

Project Preferences

Type of Financing Preferred:
Early Stage
Seed

Size of Investments Considered:
Min Size of Investment Considered (000s): $250
Max Size of Investment Considered (000s): $3,000

Industry Preferences

In Biotechnology prefer:
Biotechnology

In Industrial/Energy prefer:
Advanced Materials

Additional Information
Name of Most Recent Fund: Emergence Venture Fund II, L.P.
Most Recent Fund Was Raised: 08/06/2009
Year Founded: 2007
Capital Under Management: $3,100,000
Current Activity Level : Actively seeking new investments

EMERGENCES SARL

12 cours Xavier Arnozan
Bordeaux, France 33000
Phone: 33556440407
Fax: 33556793311
Website: www.emergences.com

Type of Firm
Service Provider

Project Preferences

Type of Financing Preferred:
Leveraged Buyout
Early Stage
Expansion
Seed
Startup

Geographical Preferences

International Preferences:
France

Additional Information
Year Founded: 2001
Current Activity Level : Actively seeking new investments

EMERGENT MEDICAL PARTNERS LP

3282 Alpine Road
Portola Valley, CA USA 94028
Phone: 6508510091
Fax: 6508510095
E-mail: eassist@emvllp.com
Website: www.emvllp.com

Management and Staff
Allan May, Managing Director
Chris Adams, Chief Financial Officer
Robert Brownell, Managing Director
Thomas Fogarty, Managing Director

Type of Firm
Private Equity Firm

Project Preferences

Role in Financing:
Will function either as deal originator or investor in deals created by others

Type of Financing Preferred:
Early Stage

Industry Preferences

In Medical/Health prefer:
Medical/Health
Medical Products

Additional Information
Name of Most Recent Fund: Emergent Medical Partners II, L.P.
Most Recent Fund Was Raised: 09/11/2013
Year Founded: 2007
Capital Under Management: $70,000,000
Current Activity Level : Actively seeking new investments
Method of Compensation: Return on investment is of primary concern, do not charge fees

EMERGEVEST LTD

190 Elgin Avenue
George Town, Cayman Islands KY1-9005
E-mail: info@emergevest.com
Website: www.emergevest.com

Type of Firm
Private Equity Firm

Project Preferences

Type of Financing Preferred:
Leveraged Buyout
Acquisition

Additional Information
Year Founded: 2014
Capital Under Management: $236,000,000
Current Activity Level : Actively seeking new investments

EMERGING CAPITAL PARTNERS

1602 L Street North West
Sixth Floor
Washington, DC USA 20036
Phone: 2022806200
Fax: 2023318255
Website: www.ecpinvestments.com

Other Offices

8th Floor, The Forum Building
Corner 5th and Maude
Johannesburg, South Africa 2196
Phone: 27-11-685-0830
Fax: 27-11-784-9112

219, Boulevard Zerktouni
Casablanca, Morocco 20100
Phone: 212-522-94-41-95
Fax: 212-522-94-41-96

316 Victoria Street
4th Floor, Victoria Building
Douala, Cameroon 753
Phone: 237-33-424-861
Fax: 237-33-424-851

9 West, Ring Road
9th Floor
Parklands, Kenya 2568-00621

29 Avenue Hoche
3rd Floor
Paris, France
Phone: 33-1-44-01-16-84
Fax: 33-1-44-01-02-81

Immeuble N'Zarama
Boulevard Lagunaire - Plateau
Abidjan, Ivory Coast
Phone: 225-20-310-731
Fax: 225-203-338-651

Immeuble Miniar Bloc B 2eme Etage
Les Berges du Lac
Tunis, Tunisia 1053
Phone: 216-71-962-590
Fax: 216-71-962-608

Management and Staff
Alex-Handrah Aime, Managing Director
Aurore Bahounoui, Vice President
Bryce Fort, Partner
Carolyn Campbell, Partner
Ferdinand Ngon, Managing Director
Ghislaine El Alami, Vice President
Manil Nedjar, Managing Director

Mariam Tchibanda, Vice President
Marie-France Mathes, Managing Director
Michael Jansa, Managing Director
Namita Shah, Vice President
Zain Laher, Vice President

Type of Firm
Private Equity Firm

Association Membership
South African Venture Capital Association (SAVCA)
Emerging Markets Private Equity Association
African Venture Capital Association (AVCA)

Project Preferences

Type of Financing Preferred:
Leveraged Buyout
Expansion
Generalist PE
Acquisition
Startup
Distressed Debt
Recapitalizations

Geographical Preferences

International Preferences:
Mauritania
Turkey
Djibouti
Africa

Industry Preferences

In Communications prefer:
Telecommunications

In Consumer Related prefer:
Food/Beverage

In Industrial/Energy prefer:
Environmental Related

In Transportation prefer:
Transportation

In Financial Services prefer:
Financial Services
Financial Services

In Manufact. prefer:
Manufacturing

In Agr/Forestr/Fish prefer:
Agribusiness
Agriculture related

In Utilities prefer:
Utilities

In Other prefer:
Environment Responsible

Additional Information
Year Founded: 2000
Capital Under Management: $100,000,000
Current Activity Level : Actively seeking new investments

EMERGING ENERGY & ENVIRONMENT LLC

Six Landmark Square
Suite 400
Stamford, CT USA 06901
Phone: 2033595670
Fax: 2033595870
Website: www.emergingenergy.com

Management and Staff
Anadi Jauhari, Senior Managing Director
Ernesto Hanhausen, Principal
John Paul Moscarella, Senior Managing Director
Jorge Barrigh, Managing Director
Raul Ortega, Vice President

Type of Firm
Private Equity Firm

Project Preferences

Type of Financing Preferred:
Balanced

Geographical Preferences

International Preferences:
Latin America
Peru
Mexico
Brazil
Chile
Colombia

Industry Preferences

In Medical/Health prefer:
Medical/Health

In Industrial/Energy prefer:
Energy
Alternative Energy
Energy Conservation Relat
Environmental Related

Additional Information
Year Founded: 2009
Capital Under Management: $10,000,000
Current Activity Level : Actively seeking new investments

EMERGING INVESTMENT PARTNERS CO

Abdul Razzak Building, 2nd floor, Abdul Hamid Karami St.
Beirut, Lebanon
Phone: 96101998598
E-mail: info@eip-capital.com
Website: www.eip-capital.com

Other Offices
Abdul Razzak Building, 2nd floor, Abdul Hamid Karami St.
Beirut, Lebanon
Phone: 96101998598

Type of Firm
Private Equity Firm

Project Preferences

Type of Financing Preferred:
Leveraged Buyout
Acquisition

Geographical Preferences

International Preferences:
Middle East
Africa

Industry Preferences

In Medical/Health prefer:
Health Services

In Consumer Related prefer:
Food/Beverage
Education Related

In Financial Services prefer:
Financial Services

Additional Information
Year Founded: 2014
Capital Under Management: $50,000,000
Current Activity Level : Actively seeking new investments

EMERGO VENTURES

Prodromou & Demetrakopoulou 2
Nicosia, Cyprus 1090
Phone: 35722449122
E-mail: info@emergoventures.net
Website: www.emergoventures.net

Type of Firm
Investment Management Firm

Project Preferences

Type of Financing Preferred:
Early Stage
Expansion
Balanced
Later Stage
Startup

Geographical Preferences

International Preferences:
Europe

Additional Information
Year Founded: 2011
Current Activity Level : Actively seeking new investments

EMERILLON CAPITAL, INC.

2, Complexe Desjardins E. Towe
Suite 1717
Montreal, Canada
E-mail: contact@emerilloncapital.com
Website: www.emerilloncapital.com

Type of Firm
Private Equity Firm

Project Preferences

Type of Financing Preferred:
Early Stage
Seed
Startup

Geographical Preferences

United States Preferences:
Northeast

Canadian Preferences:
All Canada

Industry Preferences

In Communications prefer:
Communications and Media

In Medical/Health prefer:
Medical/Health

In Industrial/Energy prefer:
Environmental Related

Additional Information
Name of Most Recent Fund: Emerillon Capital
Most Recent Fund Was Raised: 06/26/2013
Year Founded: 2013
Capital Under Management: $95,493,000
Current Activity Level : Actively seeking new investments

EMERISQUE BRANDS UK LTD

53 Davies Street
London, United Kingdom
Phone: 4402071526347
E-mail: contact@emerisque.com
Website: www.emerisque.com

Type of Firm
Private Equity Firm

Project Preferences

Type of Financing Preferred:
Leveraged Buyout
Generalist PE
Later Stage
Acquisition

Geographical Preferences

United States Preferences:
All U.S.

International Preferences:
Italy
India
Switzerland
China
Middle East
Germany
Russia
Africa
France

Industry Preferences

In Consumer Related prefer:
Consumer
Entertainment and Leisure
Consumer Products
Consumer Services

Additional Information
Year Founded: 2004
Current Activity Level : Actively seeking new investments

EMERTEC

17 Rue De La Frise
Grenoble, France 38000
Phone: 33438123895
Fax: 33438123464
E-mail: info@emertec.fr

Other Offices

44 bis rue Pasquier
Paris, France 75008
Phone: 33-1-8018-1124
Fax: 33-1-8018-1124

3, rue Marconi
Metz, France 57070

Type of Firm
Private Equity Firm

Association Membership
French Venture Capital Association (AFIC)

Project Preferences

Type of Financing Preferred:
Early Stage
Expansion
Later Stage
Seed
Startup

Geographical Preferences

International Preferences:
Luxembourg
Europe
Netherlands
Switzerland
Belgium
Germany
France

Industry Preferences

In Computer Other prefer:
Computer Related

In Semiconductor/Electr prefer:
Semiconductor

In Biotechnology prefer:
Biotech Related Research

In Industrial/Energy prefer:
Energy
Alternative Energy
Industrial Products
Materials
Advanced Materials
Robotics
Environmental Related

In Agr/Forestr/Fish prefer:
Agriculture related

Additional Information
Name of Most Recent Fund: Emertec 5 FCPR
Most Recent Fund Was Raised: 03/06/2014
Year Founded: 1999
Capital Under Management: $17,100,000
Current Activity Level : Actively seeking new investments

EMF CAPITAL PARTNERS LTD

43 London Wall
London, United Kingdom EC2M 5TF
Phone: 442074483540
E-mail: info@emfcp.com
Website: www.emfcp.com

Type of Firm
Private Equity Firm

Project Preferences

Type of Financing Preferred:
Expansion

Geographical Preferences

International Preferences:
Armenia
Belarus
United Kingdom
Turkey
Macedonia
Moldova
Ukraine
Russia
Georgia

Industry Preferences

In Financial Services prefer:
Insurance

Additional Information
Year Founded: 2012
Current Activity Level : Actively seeking new investments

EMIGRANT CAPITAL

Six East 43rd Street, Eight Floor
New York, NY USA 10017
Phone: 9172625245
Website: www.emigrantcapital.com

Type of Firm
Bank Affiliated

Project Preferences

Role in Financing:
Will function either as deal originator or investor in deals created by others

Type of Financing Preferred:
Leveraged Buyout
Mezzanine
Generalist PE
Later Stage
Recapitalizations

Size of Investments Considered:
Min Size of Investment Considered (000s): $5,000
Max Size of Investment Considered (000s): $15,000

Geographical Preferences

United States Preferences:

Industry Focus
(% based on actual investment)
Biotechnology	40.4%
Computer Software and Services	32.1%
Other Products	17.8%
Industrial/Energy	5.0%
Consumer Related	4.7%

Additional Information
Year Founded: 1999
Capital Under Management: $150,000,000
Current Activity Level : Actively seeking new investments

EMINENT VENTURE CAPITAL CORP

No.19-11 San Choung Road
11 Floor, Nan Kang
Taipei, Taiwan
Phone: 88626553010
Fax: 88626553209

Type of Firm
Private Equity Firm

Association Membership
Taiwan Venture Capital Association(TVCA)

Project Preferences

Type of Financing Preferred:
Balanced

Geographical Preferences

International Preferences:
No Preference

Additional Information
Year Founded: 2005
Current Activity Level : Actively seeking new investments

EMIRATES INVESTMENT AND DEVELOPMENT PSC

PO Box 62220
Dubai, Utd. Arab Em.
Phone: 97144298200
Fax: 97144298221

Type of Firm
Private Equity Firm

Project Preferences

Type of Financing Preferred:
Early Stage
Seed

Industry Preferences

In Consumer Related prefer:
Education Related

In Financial Services prefer:
Financial Services
Real Estate

In Manufact. prefer:
Manufacturing

Additional Information
Year Founded: 1997
Current Activity Level : Actively seeking new investments

EMK CAPITAL PARTNERS LP

17 Connaught Place
Lex House
London, United Kingdom W2 2ES
Phone: 442075914200

Other Offices
17 Connaught Place
Lex House
London, United Kingdom W2 2ES
Phone: 442075914200

Type of Firm
Private Equity Firm

Project Preferences

Type of Financing Preferred:
Leveraged Buyout

Additional Information
Year Founded: 2016
Current Activity Level : Actively seeking new investments

EMPEIRIA CAPITAL PARTNERS LLC

142 West 57th Street, 12th Floor
New York, NY USA 10019
Website: www.empeiria.com

Management and Staff
Joseph Fong, Partner
Keith Oster, Partner

Type of Firm
Private Equity Firm

Project Preferences

Type of Financing Preferred:
Leveraged Buyout
Acquisition

Geographical Preferences

United States Preferences:
All U.S.

Industry Preferences

In Consumer Related prefer:
Food/Beverage
Consumer Products

In Industrial/Energy prefer:
Energy
Industrial Products

Additional Information
Year Founded: 2013
Current Activity Level : Actively seeking new investments

EMPIRE INVESTMENT HOLDINGS LLC

1000 Northwest 57th Court, Ninth Floor
Miami, FL USA 33126
Phone: 3054031111
Fax: 3054031112
E-mail: info@empireih.com
Website: www.empireih.com

Management and Staff
Dennis Mahoney, Managing Director
Michael Greif, Managing Director
Paul Miller, Managing Director
Thomas Dalfonso, Vice President

Type of Firm
Private Equity Firm

Project Preferences

Type of Financing Preferred:
Leveraged Buyout

Size of Investments Considered:
Min Size of Investment Considered (000s): $10,000
Max Size of Investment Considered (000s): $100,000

Geographical Preferences

United States Preferences:
All U.S.

Industry Preferences

In Business Serv. prefer:
Services
Distribution

In Manufact. prefer:
Manufacturing

Additional Information
Year Founded: 2004
Capital Under Management: $28,000,000
Current Activity Level : Actively seeking new investments

EMPOWER INVESTMENT
Pudong New District, Shanghai
Room 3069, Block 24, No. 2 Xin
Shanghai, China
Phone: 2161671921
Website: www.empowerinvestment.com

Type of Firm
Private Equity Firm

Project Preferences

Type of Financing Preferred:
Early Stage

Geographical Preferences

International Preferences:
Asia Pacific

Industry Preferences

In Communications prefer:
Telecommunications

In Internet Specific prefer:
Internet

In Consumer Related prefer:
Consumer

In Business Serv. prefer:
Media

Additional Information
Year Founded: 1969
Current Activity Level : Actively seeking new investments

EMPRESA NACIONAL DE INNOVACION SA
Paseo de la Castellana, 141
Madrid, Spain C 28046
Phone: 34-91-570-8200
Fax: 34-91-570-4199
Website: www.enisa.es

Management and Staff
Begona Cristeto, Chief Operating Officer

Type of Firm
Government Affiliated Program

Association Membership
Spanish Venture Capital Association (ASCRI)

Project Preferences

Type of Financing Preferred:
Early Stage
Seed
Startup

Geographical Preferences

International Preferences:
Europe
Spain

Industry Preferences

In Biotechnology prefer:
Biotechnology

Additional Information
Year Founded: 2003
Capital Under Management: $51,787,000
Current Activity Level : Actively seeking new investments

EMPRESARIA GROUP PLC
Old Church House, Sandy Lane
Crawley Down, Crawley
West Sussex, United Kingdom RH10 4HS
Phone: 44-1342-711-430
Fax: 44-1342-711-449
E-mail: info@empresaria.com
Website: www.empresaria.com

Management and Staff
Joost Kreulen, Chief Executive Officer

Type of Firm
Private Equity Firm

Project Preferences

Type of Financing Preferred:
Startup

Geographical Preferences

International Preferences:
United Kingdom

Industry Preferences

In Communications prefer:
Telecommunications

In Medical/Health prefer:
Health Services

In Transportation prefer:
Transportation

In Financial Services prefer:
Financial Services

In Business Serv. prefer:
Services
Media

Additional Information
Year Founded: 1996
Current Activity Level : Actively seeking new investments

EMPRESARIO DIGITAL
Av. Duque de Avila, no. 23
Lisboa, Portugal 1000 138
Phone: 351213100164
Fax: 351213526314
E-mail: info@empresariodigital.pt
Website: www.empresariodigital.pt

Management and Staff
Patrician Goncalves, Partner

Type of Firm
Incubator/Development Program

Project Preferences

Type of Financing Preferred:
Startup

Geographical Preferences

International Preferences:
Europe
Portugal

Additional Information
Year Founded: 2000
Current Activity Level : Actively seeking new investments

EMR CAPITAL GROUP

89 Nexus Way
Camana Bay
Grand Cayman, Cayman Islands KY1-9007
E-mail: admin@emrcapital.com
Website: www.emrcapital.com

Other Offices

333 Collins Street
Level Seven
Melbourne, Austria 3000
Phone: 61386441353

151 Macquarie Street
Level 11
Sydney, Australia 2000
Phone: 61283982037

Type of Firm

Private Equity Firm

Project Preferences

Type of Financing Preferred:
Leveraged Buyout

Size of Investments Considered:
Min Size of Investment Considered (000s): $774
Max Size of Investment Considered (000s): $38,715

Industry Preferences

In Agr/Forestr/Fish prefer:
Mining and Minerals

Additional Information

Name of Most Recent Fund: EMR Capital Resources Fund 1, L.P.
Most Recent Fund Was Raised: 12/26/2013
Year Founded: 2011
Capital Under Management: $77,400,000
Current Activity Level : Actively seeking new investments

EMX CAPITAL PARTNERS LP

Montes Urales 720
5th Floor-Lomas de Chapultepec
Mexico City, Mexico 11000
Phone: 525552498020
E-mail: contact@emxcapital.com
Website: emxcapital.com

Management and Staff

Joaquin Avila, Co-Founder

Type of Firm

Private Equity Firm

Association Membership

Emerging Markets Private Equity Association

Project Preferences

Type of Financing Preferred:
Leveraged Buyout
Expansion
Later Stage

Geographical Preferences

International Preferences:
Mexico

Additional Information

Name of Most Recent Fund: EMX Capital Partners, L.P.
Most Recent Fund Was Raised: 03/03/2011
Year Founded: 2005
Capital Under Management: $205,300,000
Current Activity Level : Actively seeking new investments

ENABLIS FINANCIAL CORPORATION SA (PTY) LTD

217 Nupen Cresent
Palms Office Park, Midrand
Johannesburg, South Africa
Phone: 27112342526
Fax: 27112342527
Website: www.enablis.org

Other Offices

26, Murray Street
Nelspruit, South Africa 1200
Phone: 27137525816

116, Florida Road
Suite 4, Morningside
Durban, South Africa 4001
Phone: 27313124233
Fax: 27313124232

46, Schroder Street
Upington, South Africa 8800
Phone: 27543383397

302, Manhattan Place
130, Bree Street
Cape Town, South Africa 8001
Phone: 27214220690
Fax: 27214220744

7 Mellis Road
2nd Floor, North Tower
Rivonia, South Africa 2192
Phone: 27112342526
Fax: 27112342527

Type of Firm

Private Equity Firm

Association Membership

South African Venture Capital Association (SAVCA)

Project Preferences

Type of Financing Preferred:
Early Stage
Expansion
Balanced
Later Stage

Geographical Preferences

International Preferences:
Kenya
South Africa
Africa

Additional Information

Year Founded: 2002
Current Activity Level : Actively seeking new investments

ENBW NEW VENTURES GMBH

Durlacher Allee 93
Karlsruhe, Germany 76131
Phone: 497216313490
E-mail: New.Ventures@enbw.com
Website: www.enbw.com

Type of Firm

Private Equity Firm

Additional Information

Year Founded: 2016
Current Activity Level : Actively seeking new investments

ENCORE CONSUMER CAPITAL FUND L P

111 Pine Street
Suite 1825
San Francisco, CA USA 94111
Phone: 4152969850
Fax: 4152969075
E-mail: info@encoreconsumercapital.com
Website: www.encoreconsumercapital.com

Other Offices

100 California Street
Suite 670
San Francisco, CA USA 94111
Phone: 415-296-9850
Fax: 415-296-9075

Management and Staff

Bill Shen, Managing Director
Gary Smith, Co-Founder
Kevin Murphy, Managing Director
Megan Pirsch, Vice President
Robert Brown, Co-Founder
Scott Sellers, Co-Founder
Tom DeMott, Managing Partner

Type of Firm
Private Equity Firm

Project Preferences

Role in Financing:
Prefer role as deal originator

Type of Financing Preferred:
Leveraged Buyout
Expansion
Management Buyouts
Acquisition
Recapitalizations

Geographical Preferences

United States Preferences:

Industry Preferences

In Consumer Related prefer:
Consumer
Food/Beverage
Consumer Products

Additional Information
Name of Most Recent Fund: Encore Consumer Capital Fund II, L.P.
Most Recent Fund Was Raised: 01/04/2012
Year Founded: 2005
Capital Under Management: $175,000,000
Current Activity Level : Actively seeking new investments

ENDEAVOUR CAPITAL INC

920 Southwest Sixth Avenue
Suite 1400
Portland, OR USA 97204
Phone: 5032232721
Fax: 5032231384
Website: www.endeavourcapital.com

Other Offices

44 Cook Street
Suite 100
Denver, CO USA 80206
Phone: 3033553553
Fax: 5032231384

601 West Fifth Street
Suite 700
Los Angeles, CA USA 90071
Phone: 2138910115
Fax: 2133476399

1001 Fourth Avenue
Suite 4301
Seattle, WA USA 98154
Phone: 2066217060
Fax: 2066211075

Management and Staff
Aaron Richmond, Managing Director
Bradaigh Wagner, Managing Director
Chad Heath, Managing Director
D. Mark Dorman, Managing Director
David Goldberg, Vice President
Derek Eve, Vice President
Dietz Fry, Managing Director
John Schlegell, Co-Founder
Leland Jones, Managing Director
Rachel Foltz, Vice President
Randy Miller, Chief Financial Officer
Rocky Dixon, Managing Director
Stephen Babson, Managing Director

Type of Firm
Private Equity Firm

Project Preferences

Type of Financing Preferred:
Leveraged Buyout
Early Stage
Mezzanine
Management Buyouts
Acquisition
Recapitalizations

Geographical Preferences

United States Preferences:
Midwest
West Coast
All U.S.

Industry Focus
(% based on actual investment)
Other Products	75.3%
Internet Specific	10.1%
Consumer Related	6.9%
Medical/Health	4.1%
Communications and Media	3.5%
Industrial/Energy	0.1%

Additional Information
Name of Most Recent Fund: Endeavour Capital Fund VI, L.P.
Most Recent Fund Was Raised: 10/13/2011
Year Founded: 1991
Capital Under Management: $400,000,000
Current Activity Level : Actively seeking new investments

ENDEAVOUR VENTURES LTD

41 Devonshire Street
London, United Kingdom W1G 7AJ
Phone: 442076374102
E-mail: enquiries@endven.com
Website: www.endven.com

Other Offices

15635 Alton Parkway, Suite 100
Irvine, CA USA 92618

Management and Staff
Richard Hargreaves, Co-Founder

Type of Firm
Private Equity Firm

Project Preferences

Type of Financing Preferred:
Early Stage
Expansion
Startup

Size of Investments Considered:
Min Size of Investment Considered (000s): $817
Max Size of Investment Considered (000s): $12,257

Geographical Preferences

International Preferences:
United Kingdom

Industry Preferences

In Computer Other prefer:
Computer Related

In Semiconductor/Electr prefer:
Fiber Optics

In Financial Services prefer:
Financial Services

In Business Serv. prefer:
Media

Additional Information
Year Founded: 2005
Current Activity Level : Actively seeking new investments

ENDEAVOUR VISION SA

Six Rue De La Croix D'Or
Geneva, Switzerland 1204
Phone: 41225446000
Fax: 41225446006
E-mail: info@endeavourvision.com
Website: www.endeavourvision.com

Management and Staff
Bernard Vogel, Managing Partner
Dominik Ellenrieder, Venture Partner
Dominique Pitteloud, Partner
Eric Milledge, Venture Partner
Olivier Valdenaire, Venture Partner
Sven Lingjaerde, Managing Partner

Type of Firm
Private Equity Firm

Association Membership
European Private Equity and Venture Capital Assoc.

Project Preferences

Type of Financing Preferred:
Early Stage
Later Stage
Seed
Startup

Size of Investments Considered:
Min Size of Investment Considered (000s): $3,948
Max Size of Investment Considered (000s): $10,529

Geographical Preferences

United States Preferences:

International Preferences:
Europe
Switzerland
Israel

Industry Preferences

In Communications prefer:
Commercial Communications
Wireless Communications
Data Communications

In Computer Hardware prefer:
Computer Graphics and Dig
Integrated Turnkey System

In Internet Specific prefer:
Internet

In Semiconductor/Electr prefer:
Semiconductor

In Biotechnology prefer:
Biotechnology
Human Biotechnology
Industrial Biotechnology
Biosensors
Biotech Related Research

In Medical/Health prefer:
Medical Diagnostics
Medical Products

Additional Information
Name of Most Recent Fund: Endeavour LP
Most Recent Fund Was Raised: 06/08/2000
Year Founded: 1989
Capital Under Management: $142,800,000
Current Activity Level : Actively seeking new investments

ENDIYA PARTNERS

Level 1, am@10, MB Towers
Road No.:10, Banjara Hills
Hyderabad, India 500034
E-mail: info@endiya.com

Management and Staff
Ramesh Byrapaneni, Managing Director
Sateesh Andra, Managing Director
Sruti Komarappagari, Vice President

Type of Firm
Private Equity Firm

Project Preferences

Type of Financing Preferred:
Early Stage

Industry Preferences

In Consumer Related prefer:
Consumer Services

In Industrial/Energy prefer:
Advanced Materials

Additional Information
Year Founded: 2016
Capital Under Management: $14,960,000
Current Activity Level : Actively seeking new investments

ENDLESS LLP

Three Whitehall Quay
Leeds, United Kingdom LS1 4BF
Phone: 441132104000
Fax: 448452802411
Website: www.endlessllp.com

Other Offices

Waterloo House
Waterloo Street
Birmingham, United Kingdom B2 5TB
Phone: 441216335600

102 Park Street
Mayfair
London, United Kingdom W1K 6NE
Phone: 442075144000

13 Police Street
Fourth Floor, The Chambers
Manchester, United Kingdom M2 7LQ
Phone: 441618376030

Management and Staff
Christopher Clegg, Managing Director
Darren Forshaw, Partner
Garry Wilson, Partner

Type of Firm
Private Equity Firm

Project Preferences

Type of Financing Preferred:
Leveraged Buyout
Turnaround
Management Buyouts
Acquisition
Special Situation
Recapitalizations

Geographical Preferences

International Preferences:
United Kingdom

Additional Information
Name of Most Recent Fund: Endless Fund III
Most Recent Fund Was Raised: 07/25/2011
Year Founded: 2005
Capital Under Management: $648,900,000
Current Activity Level : Actively seeking new investments

ENDURANCE CAPITAL HOLDINGS LLC

1661 Worcester Road
Suite 303
Framingham, MA USA 01701
Phone: 5086654800
Fax: 5086654801
Website: www.endurancecap.net

Other Offices

Five Milk Street
Suite 301
Portland, ME USA 04101
Phone: 2077721332
Fax: 2078740868

Management and Staff
Diane McDonald, Chief Financial Officer
Jeffrey Diggins, Managing Director
John McDonough, Managing Director
Michael Hullinger, President

Type of Firm
Private Equity Firm

Project Preferences

Type of Financing Preferred:
Mezzanine
Turnaround

Geographical Preferences

United States Preferences:

Industry Preferences

In Manufact. prefer:
Manufacturing

Additional Information
Year Founded: 2005
Current Activity Level : Actively seeking new investments

ENDURE CAPITAL

228 Hamiltion Ave, 3rd Floor
Palo Alto, CA USA 94301
Phone: 16507985267
E-mail: tf@endurecap.com
Website: www.endurecap.com

Other Offices
228 Hamiltion Ave
3rd Floor
PALO ALTO, CA USA 94301
Phone: 16507985267

Type of Firm
Private Equity Firm

Project Preferences

Type of Financing Preferred:
Early Stage
Seed

Geographical Preferences

United States Preferences:

Canadian Preferences:
All Canada

International Preferences:
Middle East
Germany

Industry Preferences

In Computer Software prefer:
Software

In Internet Specific prefer:
Internet

Additional Information
Year Founded: 2015
Current Activity Level : Actively seeking new investments

ENEAS ALTERNATIVE INVESTMENTS SL

Paseo de la Castellana, 149
2 Planta
Madrid, Spain 28046

Type of Firm
Investment Management Firm

Project Preferences

Type of Financing Preferred:
Leveraged Buyout
Generalist PE

Additional Information
Year Founded: 2015
Current Activity Level : Actively seeking new investments

ENEAS CAPITAL SL

Paseo de la Castellana
172 6 izq
Madrid, Spain 28046
Phone: 34913430710
Fax: 34913508456

E-mail: eneas@eneascf.com

Management and Staff
German Rovira, Partner
Juan Carlos Smith, Partner
Michael Page, Partner
Miguel Marin, Partner
Miguel Arrese, Partner

Type of Firm
Investment Management Firm

Project Preferences

Type of Financing Preferred:
Fund of Funds
Leveraged Buyout
Expansion
Later Stage
Seed
Startup

Size of Investments Considered:
Min Size of Investment Considered (000s): $4,158
Max Size of Investment Considered (000s): $13,860

Geographical Preferences

International Preferences:
Spain

Additional Information
Year Founded: 2003
Current Activity Level : Actively seeking new investments

ENERCAP CAPITAL PARTNERS

Burzovni palac
Rybna 14
Prague, Czech Republic 110 00
Phone: 420-227-316-222
Fax: 420-227-316-444
Website: www.enercap.com

Management and Staff
Alastair Hammond, Chief Operating Officer
Ewan Gibb, Partner
George Formandl, Partner
Jim Campion, Partner
Michael White, Partner
Shane Woodroffe, Partner

Type of Firm
Private Equity Firm

Project Preferences

Type of Financing Preferred:
Leveraged Buyout
Acquisition

Geographical Preferences

International Preferences:
Central Europe
Europe
Eastern Europe

Industry Preferences

In Industrial/Energy prefer:
Energy
Alternative Energy
Energy Conservation Relat

Additional Information
Year Founded: 2007
Capital Under Management: $108,800,000
Current Activity Level : Actively seeking new investments

ENERDIGM VENTURES LLC

825 San Antonio Road
Palo Alto, CA USA 94303
Phone: 4152373478
Fax: 6503835523
E-mail: idea@enerdigm.com
Website: www.enerdigm.com

Other Offices
Former: 2660 Waiwai Loop
Suite 200
Honolulu, HI USA 96819
Phone: 808-833-4747

Management and Staff
Michael Shimoko, Partner

Type of Firm
Private Equity Firm

Project Preferences

Type of Financing Preferred:
Early Stage

Size of Investments Considered:
Min Size of Investment Considered (000s): $500
Max Size of Investment Considered (000s): $1,000

Geographical Preferences

United States Preferences:
Hawaii
Northern California

Industry Preferences

In Computer Software prefer:
Software

In Industrial/Energy prefer:
Environmental Related

In Business Serv. prefer:
Services

Additional Information
Year Founded: 2007
Current Activity Level : Actively seeking new investments

ENERGI INVEST FYN A/S

Forskeparken 10
Odense, Denmark 5230
Phone: 4563157034
Website: www.energiinvestfyn.dk

Management and Staff
Jens Damsgaard, Chief Executive Officer

Type of Firm
Private Equity Firm

Association Membership
European Private Equity and Venture Capital Assoc.

Project Preferences

Type of Financing Preferred:
Early Stage

Geographical Preferences

International Preferences:
Denmark

Industry Preferences

In Communications prefer:
Telecommunications

In Semiconductor/Electr prefer:
Electronic Components

In Industrial/Energy prefer:
Energy

Additional Information
Year Founded: 2010
Current Activity Level : Actively seeking new investments

ENERGY & ENVIRONMENT INVESTMENT INC

5-20-7, Gohanda
Shinakawa, Tokyo, Japan 1410022
E-mail: info@ee-investment.jp
Website: www.ee-investment.jp

Type of Firm
Private Equity Firm

Project Preferences

Type of Financing Preferred:
Balanced
Startup

Geographical Preferences

United States Preferences:
All U.S.

International Preferences:
Japan

Industry Preferences

In Industrial/Energy prefer:
Energy
Energy Conservation Relat
Environmental Related

Additional Information
Year Founded: 2006
Capital Under Management: $25,960,000
Current Activity Level : Actively seeking new investments

ENERGY ACCESS VENTURES SAS

7 Boulevard Malesherbes
Paris, France 75008
Website: www.eavafrica.com

Management and Staff
Emmanuel Beau, Co-Founder
Michael Gera, Co-Founder

Type of Firm
Private Equity Firm

Project Preferences

Type of Financing Preferred:
Early Stage

Geographical Preferences

International Preferences:
Africa

Industry Preferences

In Industrial/Energy prefer:
Energy

In Other prefer:
Environment Responsible

Additional Information
Year Founded: 2014
Current Activity Level : Actively seeking new investments

ENERGY CAPITAL MANAGEMENT AS

Stortingsgaten 22
Third floor
Oslo, Norway 0161
Website: innovate.statoil.com

Type of Firm
Corporate PE/Venture

Project Preferences

Type of Financing Preferred:
Early Stage
Seed

Size of Investments Considered:
Min Size of Investment Considered (000s): $1,493
Max Size of Investment Considered (000s): $14,931

Geographical Preferences

United States Preferences:
North America

Canadian Preferences:
All Canada

International Preferences:
Europe

Industry Preferences

In Industrial/Energy prefer:
Energy
Oil and Gas Exploration
Oil & Gas Drilling,Explor
Alternative Energy

Additional Information
Year Founded: 2001
Capital Under Management: $25,000,000
Current Activity Level : Actively seeking new investments

ENERGY FUTURE INVEST AS

Stortingsgata 28
Oslo, Norway 0161
Phone: 4721631700
Website: www.energyfutureinvest.com

Type of Firm
Private Equity Firm

Project Preferences

Type of Financing Preferred:
Balanced

Size of Investments Considered:
Min Size of Investment Considered (000s): $1,500
Max Size of Investment Considered (000s): $3,000

Geographical Preferences

International Preferences:
Scandinavia/Nordic Region

Industry Preferences

In Industrial/Energy prefer:
Alternative Energy
Energy Conservation Relat

In Other prefer:
Environment Responsible

Additional Information
Year Founded: 2001
Capital Under Management: $71,100,000
Current Activity Level : Actively seeking new investments

ENERGY IMPACT PARTNERS LLC

622 3rd Avenue
37th Floor
New York, NY USA 10017
Phone: 2128999700
E-mail: contact@energyimpactpartners.com
Website: energyimpactpartners.com

Type of Firm
Private Equity Firm

Project Preferences

Type of Financing Preferred:
Early Stage
Balanced

Industry Preferences

In Industrial/Energy prefer:
Energy

Additional Information
Year Founded: 2015
Capital Under Management: $150,000,000
Current Activity Level : Actively seeking new investments

ENERGY INNOVATION CAPITAL

3720 Carillon Point
Kirkland, WA USA 98033
Website: energyinnovationcapital.com

Type of Firm
Private Equity Firm

Project Preferences

Type of Financing Preferred:
Balanced

Industry Preferences

In Industrial/Energy prefer:
Energy
Oil and Gas Exploration
Oil & Gas Drilling,Explor

Additional Information
Year Founded: 2016
Capital Under Management: $42,800,000
Current Activity Level : Actively seeking new investments

ENERGY TECHNOLOGY VENTURES

3135 Easton Turnpike
Fairfield, CT USA 06828
E-mail: EnergyTechnologyVentures@ge.com

Type of Firm
Private Equity Firm

Project Preferences

Type of Financing Preferred:
Balanced

Geographical Preferences

United States Preferences:
North America

International Preferences:
Europe
Israel

Industry Preferences

In Industrial/Energy prefer:
Energy
Oil and Gas Exploration
Alternative Energy
Coal Related
Environmental Related

Additional Information
Year Founded: 2011
Capital Under Management: $300,000,000
Current Activity Level : Actively seeking new investments

ENERGY VENTURES AS

Kongsgaardbakken One
Stavanger, Norway 4005
Phone: 4751841295
E-mail: mail@energyventures.no
Website: www.energyventures.no

Other Offices
15 Albert Street
Aberdeen, United Kingdom AB25 1XX
Phone: 44-1224-628-280
Fax: 44-1224-628-290

10375 Richmond Avenue
Suit 295
HOUSTON, TX USA 77042
Phone: 281-768-6725
Fax: 281-768-6726

Management and Staff
Anoop Poddar, Partner
Einar Gamman, Partner
Greg Herrera, Partner
Helge Tveit, Partner
Jim Sledzik, President
Kjell Jacobsen, Partner
Leif Andre Skare, Partner
Ole Melberg, Managing Partner
Pelle Bildtsen, Chief Financial Officer

Type of Firm
Private Equity Firm

Association Membership
Brazilian Venture Capital Association (ABCR)
Norwegian Venture Capital Association

Project Preferences

Type of Financing Preferred:
Other

Size of Investments Considered:
Min Size of Investment Considered (000s): $5,000
Max Size of Investment Considered (000s): $20,000

Geographical Preferences

United States Preferences:

Canadian Preferences:
All Canada

International Preferences:
Scandanavia/Nordic Region

Industry Preferences

In Industrial/Energy prefer:
Energy
Oil and Gas Exploration
Oil & Gas Drilling,Explor
Alternative Energy

Additional Information
Year Founded: 2002
Capital Under Management: $750,000,000
Current Activity Level : Actively seeking new investments

ENERGY VENTURES GROUP LLC

3050 K Street, Northwest
Suite 205
Washington, DC USA 20007
Phone: 2029444141
Fax: 2029444145
Website: www.energyvg.com

Type of Firm
Private Equity Firm

Project Preferences

Type of Financing Preferred:
Early Stage
Later Stage
Startup

Industry Preferences

In Industrial/Energy prefer:
Energy

Additional Information
Year Founded: 2001
Current Activity Level : Actively seeking new investments

ENERTECH CAPITAL

1235 Bay Street
Suite 801
Toronto, Canada M5R 3K4
Phone: 4165152759
Website: www.enertechcapital.com

Other Offices

1235 Bay Street
Suite 801
Toronto, Canada M5R 3K4

One Tower Bridge 100 Front St
Suite 1225
CONSHOHOCKEN, PA USA 19428
Phone: 4845391872
Fax: 4845391870

Management and Staff

Anne-Marie Bourgeois, Vice President
Chris Buckman, Vice President
Dean Sciorillo, Managing Director
Jarett Carson, Managing Director
Scott Ungerer, Founder
Wally Hunter, Managing Director
William Kingsley, Managing Director

Type of Firm
Private Equity Firm

Association Membership
National Venture Capital Association - USA (NVCA)
Canadian Venture Capital Association

Project Preferences

Role in Financing:
Prefer role as deal originator

Type of Financing Preferred:
Early Stage
Expansion
Later Stage

Geographical Preferences

United States Preferences:

Canadian Preferences:
All Canada

Industry Focus
(% based on actual investment)

Industrial/Energy	30.8%
Internet Specific	25.0%
Computer Software and Services	14.5%
Other Products	11.2%
Semiconductors/Other Elect.	9.6%
Communications and Media	4.1%
Computer Hardware	3.8%
Biotechnology	0.8%
Consumer Related	0.4%

Additional Information
Name of Most Recent Fund: EnerTech Capital Partners IV, L.P.
Most Recent Fund Was Raised: 02/14/2012
Year Founded: 1996
Capital Under Management: $450,000,000
Current Activity Level : Actively seeking new investments
Method of Compensation: Return on investment is of primary concern, do not charge fees

ENGIE NEW VENTURES SA

1 Place Samuel De Champlain
Courbevoie, France 92400

Type of Firm
Private Equity Firm

Project Preferences

Type of Financing Preferred:
Early Stage
Seed
Startup

Geographical Preferences

United States Preferences:
All U.S.

International Preferences:
Europe
Israel
Asia

Industry Preferences

In Industrial/Energy prefer:
Energy

Additional Information
Year Founded: 2014
Current Activity Level : Actively seeking new investments

ENGINE, THE

501 Massachusetts Ave.
Cambridge, MA USA 02139
E-mail: info@engine.xyz
Website: www.engine.xyz

Type of Firm
Incubator/Development Program

Project Preferences

Type of Financing Preferred:
Balanced

Additional Information
Year Founded: 2016
Capital Under Management: $200,000,000
Current Activity Level : Actively seeking new investments

ENGINEERING CAPITAL LLC

1175 Stanley Way
Palo Alto, CA USA 94303
Phone: 6509615914
Website: www.engineeringcapital.com

Type of Firm
Private Equity Firm

Project Preferences

Type of Financing Preferred:
Early Stage

Geographical Preferences

United States Preferences:

Industry Preferences

In Industrial/Energy prefer:
Process Control

Additional Information
Year Founded: 2015
Capital Under Management: $78,880,000
Current Activity Level : Actively seeking new investments

ENGLAND CAPITAL PARTNERS LLC

Two Wisconsin Circle
Suite 700
Chevy Chase, MD USA 20815
Phone: 301-880-7350
Fax: 877-430-6964
Website: www.englandco.com

Management and Staff

Bruce Craig, Managing Director
Craig England, Managing Director
Glenn Tofil, Managing Director
Timothy Brown, Vice President
Timothy Johnson, Managing Director

Type of Firm
Investment Management Firm

Project Preferences

Type of Financing Preferred:
Leveraged Buyout
Balanced
Acquisition

Industry Preferences

In Medical/Health prefer:
Medical/Health

In Industrial/Energy prefer:
Energy

In Financial Services prefer:
Financial Services
Financial Services

In Business Serv. prefer:
Media

Additional Information
Year Founded: 2007
Capital Under Management: $500,000
Current Activity Level : Actively seeking new investments

ENHANCED CAPITAL PARTNERS LLC

60 Lexington Avenue
Suite 1401
New York, NY USA 10022
Phone: 2122073385
Fax: 2122079031
E-mail: info@enhancedcap.com
Website: enhancedcapital.com

Other Offices

8310 South Valley Highway
Third Floor
ENGLEWOOD, CO USA 80112
Phone: 303-524-1213
Fax: 303-524-1278

201 St. Charles Avenue
Suite 3700
NEW ORLEANS, LA USA 70170
Phone: 5045697900
Fax: 5045697910

150 2nd Avenue, North
Suite 415
NASHVILLE, TN USA 37201
Phone: 6152553707
Fax: 6152553709

170 East Broadway
Suite 100A
JACKSON, WY USA 83001
Phone: 3072011440
Fax: 3072011441

1055 Washington Boulevard
Eighth Floor
STAMFORD, CT USA 06901
Phone: 2036148770

2802 Flintrock Trace
Suite 220
AUSTIN, TX USA 78738
Phone: 5126105555
Fax: 5126105550

444 North Capitol Street NW
Suite 715
WASHINGTON, DC USA 20001
Phone: 2024574825
Fax: 2024574825

201 E. Kennedy Boulevard
Suite 325
TAMPA, FL USA 33602
Phone: 8137121073

Management and Staff

ALAN LANGE, Managing Partner
BRITTANY MAJOR, Vice President
CARLING DINKLER, Vice President
CATHERINE BLUME, Vice President
Elizabeth Karter, Managing Director
Gingee Prince, Managing Director
Hitesh Shah, Vice President
Mark Slusar, Managing Director
Paul Kasper, Managing Director
Philip Hodges, Managing Director
Richard Montgomery, Managing Director
Roddy Clark, Managing Partner
SUNIL KHANNA, Managing Director
Shane McCarthy, Chief Financial Officer

Type of Firm
SBIC

Association Membership
Community Development Venture Capital Alliance
Natl Assoc of Small Bus. Inv. Co (NASBIC)

Project Preferences

Type of Financing Preferred:
Early Stage
Expansion
Mezzanine
Balanced

Size of Investments Considered:
Min Size of Investment Considered (000s): $500
Max Size of Investment Considered (000s): $3,000

Geographical Preferences

United States Preferences:
Tennessee
Wyoming
Alabama
Colorado
Connecticut
Florida
Louisiana
Washington
New York
Texas
All U.S.

Industry Preferences

In Communications prefer:
Communications and Media

In Biotechnology prefer:
Biotechnology

In Medical/Health prefer:
Health Services

In Business Serv. prefer:
Services

In Manufact. prefer:
Manufacturing

Additional Information
Name of Most Recent Fund: Enhanced Small Business Investment Company, L.P.
Most Recent Fund Was Raised: 03/13/2012
Year Founded: 1999
Capital Under Management: $33,074,000
Current Activity Level : Actively seeking new investments

ENHANCED EQUITY FUND, L.P.

601 Lexington Avenue
55th Floor
New York, NY USA 10022
Phone: 2122073386
Fax: 2122079031
E-mail: eef@enhancedequity.com
Website: www.enhancedequity.com

Management and Staff

Andrew Paul, Co-Founder
Brett Fliegler, Partner
Christopher Garcia, Managing Partner
David Pegg, Principal
Kenton Rosenberry, Partner
Malcolm Kostuchenko, Co-Founder
Mark Tricolli, Partner
Matthew Thompson, Vice President
Samarth Chandra, Principal
Victoria Konfong, Chief Financial Officer

Type of Firm
Private Equity Firm

Project Preferences

Type of Financing Preferred:
Leveraged Buyout
Later Stage
Acquisition
Recapitalizations

Industry Preferences

In Medical/Health prefer:
Medical/Health
Health Services

Additional Information
Year Founded: 2005
Capital Under Management: $600,000,000
Current Activity Level : Actively seeking new investments

ENHANCED PERFORMANCE INDEXED CREDIT TR

179 Waldoncroft Crescent
Burlington, Canada

Type of Firm
Private Equity Firm

Additional Information
Year Founded: 1996
Current Activity Level : Actively seeking new investments

ENIAC VENTURES LP

240 West 23rd Street
New York, NY USA 10017
Phone: 4154208798
Website: www.eniac.vc

Management and Staff
Nihal Mehta, Founder
Tim Young, Founder
Vic Singh, Founder

Type of Firm
Private Equity Firm

Project Preferences

Type of Financing Preferred:
Early Stage
Seed
Startup

Size of Investments Considered:
Min Size of Investment Considered (000s): $100
Max Size of Investment Considered (000s): $300

Geographical Preferences

United States Preferences:
Northern California

Industry Preferences

In Communications prefer:
Telecommunications
Wireless Communications
Entertainment
Other Communication Prod.

In Computer Software prefer:
Software

In Internet Specific prefer:
Internet
Web Aggregration/Portals

Additional Information
Name of Most Recent Fund: ENIAC Ventures II, L.P.
Most Recent Fund Was Raised: 09/26/2013
Year Founded: 2009
Capital Under Management: $167,900,000
Current Activity Level : Actively seeking new investments

ENJOYVENTURE MANAGEMENT GMBH

Elberfelder Strasse 2
Duesseldorf, Germany 40213
Phone: 4921123955170
Fax: 4921123955177
E-mail: office@enjoyventure.de
Website: www.enjoyventure.de

Other Offices
Ueckendorfer Strasse 237e
Gelsenkirchen, Germany 45886
Phone: 49-209-95718500
Fax: 49-209-95718507

Vahrenwalder Strasse 7
Hannover, Germany 30165
Phone: 49-511-30033322
Fax: 49-511-30033399

Management and Staff
Bert Brinkhaus, Managing Director
Peter Wolff, Managing Director
Wolfgang Lubert, Managing Director

Type of Firm
Private Equity Firm

Project Preferences

Role in Financing:
Will function either as deal originator or investor in deals created by others

Type of Financing Preferred:
Early Stage
Seed
Startup

Geographical Preferences

International Preferences:
Germany

Industry Preferences

In Communications prefer:
Communications and Media
Telecommunications

In Computer Software prefer:
Software

In Semiconductor/Electr prefer:
Electronics
Micro-Processing
Laser Related

In Medical/Health prefer:
Medical/Health

In Industrial/Energy prefer:
Energy
Industrial Products
Factory Automation

In Business Serv. prefer:
Services

In Manufact. prefer:
Manufacturing

Additional Information
Year Founded: 2000
Capital Under Management: $24,800,000
Current Activity Level : Actively seeking new investments

ENKO CAPITAL MANAGEMENT LLP

56 Sloane Square
London, United Kingdom SW1W 8AX
Phone: 442078810030
Fax: 442078810039
E-mail: info@enkocapital.com
Website: www.enkocapital.com

Other Offices
85-89 Protea Road
Kingsley Park, 1F Block B
Chislehurston, South Africa 2196
Phone: 27117840232
Fax: 27117840238

Management and Staff
Alain Nkontchou, Managing Partner
Cyrille Nkontchou, Managing Partner
Ralph Gilchrist, Partner

Type of Firm
Private Equity Firm

Project Preferences

Type of Financing Preferred:
Later Stage

Geographical Preferences

International Preferences:
Africa

Industry Preferences

In Medical/Health prefer:
Medical/Health

In Consumer Related prefer:
Retail
Education Related

In Agr/Forestr/Fish prefer:
Agribusiness

Additional Information
Year Founded: 2013
Capital Under Management: $48,250,000
Current Activity Level : Actively seeking new investments

ENLIGHTENED HOSPITALITY INVESTMENTS LP

24 Union Square East
New York, NY USA 10003

Type of Firm
Private Equity Firm

Project Preferences

Type of Financing Preferred:
Balanced

Additional Information
Year Founded: 2017
Capital Under Management: $207,220,000
Current Activity Level : Actively seeking new investments

ENLIGHTENMENT CAPITAL

4445 Willard Avenue
11th Floor
Chevy Chase, MD USA 20815
E-mail: info@enlightencap.com
Website: www.enlightencap.com

Other Offices
1300 Wilson Boulevard
Suite 500
Arlington, VA USA 22209

Management and Staff
Devin Talbott, Co-Founder
Jeffrey Guffey, Chief Financial Officer
Pierre Chao, Co-Founder

Type of Firm
Private Equity Firm

Project Preferences

Type of Financing Preferred:
Mezzanine
Acquisition

Industry Preferences

In Transportation prefer:
Aerospace

Additional Information
Name of Most Recent Fund: Enlightenment Capital Solutions Fund I, L.P.
Most Recent Fund Was Raised: 11/22/2013
Year Founded: 2012
Capital Under Management: $227,000,000
Current Activity Level : Actively seeking new investments

ENLIGHTENMENT CAPITAL

No.10 Wangjing Street
Room 811, 8F, C, WanggjingSOHO
Beijing, China
Website: mingzhaocap.com

Type of Firm
Private Equity Firm

Project Preferences

Type of Financing Preferred:
Early Stage
Seed
Startup

Geographical Preferences

International Preferences:
China

Industry Preferences

In Semiconductor/Electr prefer:
Sensors

In Industrial/Energy prefer:
Industrial Products
Advanced Materials

Additional Information
Year Founded: 2015
Current Activity Level : Actively seeking new investments

ENNISMORE CAPITAL

53 - 54, Grosvenor Street
London, United Kingdom W1K 3HU
Phone: 442077545577
Fax: 442077545580
E-mail: info@ennismorecapital.com
Website: ennismorecapital.com

Type of Firm
Private Equity Firm

Project Preferences

Type of Financing Preferred:
Leveraged Buyout
Balanced
Management Buyouts
Acquisition

Geographical Preferences

International Preferences:
United Kingdom
Europe

Industry Preferences

In Consumer Related prefer:
Hotels and Resorts

In Financial Services prefer:
Real Estate

Additional Information
Year Founded: 2010
Current Activity Level : Actively seeking new investments

ENR RUSSIA INVEST SA

Place du Molard 2-4
Geneva, Switzerland 1211
Phone: 41227161000
Fax: 41227161001
E-mail: contact@enr.ch
Website: www.enr.ch

Management and Staff
Ben de Bruyn, Chief Executive Officer

Type of Firm
Investment Management Firm

Project Preferences

Type of Financing Preferred:
Leveraged Buyout
Early Stage
Balanced
Later Stage
Acquisition

Geographical Preferences

International Preferences:
Armenia
Belarus
Kazakhstan
Kyrgyzstan
Tajikistan
Turkmenistan
Azerbaijan
Moldova
Ukraine
Uzbekistan
Russia
Georgia

Industry Preferences

In Industrial/Energy prefer:
Energy
Oil and Gas Exploration

In Financial Services prefer:
Real Estate

Additional Information
Year Founded: 2007
Current Activity Level : Actively seeking new investments

ENSO VENTURES LTD

10-11 Park Place
London, United Kingdom SW1A 1LP
Phone: 442071486499
E-mail: info@ensoventures.com
Website: www.ensoventures.com

Other Offices
747 Third Avenue, 2nd floor
New York, NY USA 10017
Phone: 6466960056

Management and Staff
Andrey Kozlov, Partner
Kim Berknov, Partner
Nikolay Danilov, Managing Director
Sergei Petukhov, Partner

Type of Firm
Private Equity Firm

Association Membership
European Private Equity and Venture Capital Assoc.

Project Preferences

Type of Financing Preferred:
Early Stage

Geographical Preferences

United States Preferences:

International Preferences:
Europe
Russia

Industry Preferences

In Biotechnology prefer:
Biotechnology

Additional Information
Year Founded: 2013
Current Activity Level : Actively seeking new investments

ENSPIRE CAPITAL PTE LTD

317 Outram Road
#B1-07 Holiday Inn Atrium
Singapore, Singapore 169075
Phone: 65-63490836
Fax: 65-62340532
E-mail: admin@enspire-capital.com
Website: www.enspire-capital.com

Other Offices
30 Marsiling Industrial
Estate Road 8
Singapore, Singapore 739193

Management and Staff
Lung Yeh, Managing Director

Type of Firm
Private Equity Firm

Project Preferences

Type of Financing Preferred:
Early Stage

Geographical Preferences

International Preferences:
Taiwan
Hong Kong
China
Pacific
Singapore

Industry Preferences

In Communications prefer:
Telecommunications

In Biotechnology prefer:
Human Biotechnology

In Industrial/Energy prefer:
Alternative Energy

In Business Serv. prefer:
Media

Additional Information
Year Founded: 2004
Current Activity Level : Actively seeking new investments

ENTANGLED VENTURES LLC

C/O Galvanize 543 Howard St
5th floor
San Francisco, CA USA 94105
Phone: 4155709321
Website: www.entangled.ventures

Management and Staff
Daniel Kuo, Vice President
Jason Sanders, Chief Operating Officer

Type of Firm
Private Equity Firm

Project Preferences

Type of Financing Preferred:
Balanced

Geographical Preferences

United States Preferences:

Industry Preferences

In Consumer Related prefer:
Education Related

Additional Information
Year Founded: 2014
Capital Under Management: $2,255,000
Current Activity Level : Actively seeking new investments

ENTERPRISE EQUITY VENTURE CAPITAL GROUP

Dublin Road
Teagasc Building
Dundalk, Ireland
Phone: 353429333167
Fax: 353429334857
E-mail: info@enterpriseequity.ie
Website: www.enterpriseequity.ie

Other Offices
Ballybrit Business Park
Galway, Ireland
Phone: 353-91-764-614
Fax: 353-91-764-615

NSC Campus
Mahon
Cork, Ireland
Phone: 353-21-230-7127
Fax: 353-21-230-7070

Arena Rd, Sandyford 18
Dublin, Ireland
Phone: 353-01-213-0720
Fax: 353-01-213-0866

Management and Staff
Conor O Connor, Managing Partner
Eric Reed, Partner
Frank Walsh, Partner
Rory Hynes, Partner
Tom Shinkwin, Partner

Type of Firm
Private Equity Firm

Association Membership
Irish Venture Capital Association
British Venture Capital Association (BVCA)
European Private Equity and Venture Capital Assoc.

Project Preferences

Role in Financing:
Prefer role as deal originator but will also invest in deals created by others

Type of Financing Preferred:
Early Stage
Balanced
Later Stage
Seed
Startup

Size of Investments Considered:
Min Size of Investment Considered (000s): $100
Max Size of Investment Considered (000s): $1,960

Geographical Preferences

International Preferences:
Ireland
United Kingdom
Europe

Industry Preferences

In Communications prefer:
Data Communications

In Computer Software prefer:
Computer Services
Applications Software

In Internet Specific prefer:
Internet

In Semiconductor/Electr prefer:
Semiconductor
Sensors
Component Testing Equipmt
Analytic/Scientific

In Biotechnology prefer:
Industrial Biotechnology
Biosensors

In Medical/Health prefer:
Medical Diagnostics
Diagnostic Services
Diagnostic Test Products
Drug/Equipmt Delivery
Medical Products

In Consumer Related prefer:
Entertainment and Leisure
Food/Beverage
Consumer Products

In Industrial/Energy prefer:
Alternative Energy
Industrial Products
Factory Automation
Environmental Related

In Manufact. prefer:
Publishing

In Agr/Forestr/Fish prefer:
Agriculture related

Additional Information

Year Founded: 1987
Capital Under Management: $20,000,000
Current Activity Level : Actively seeking new investments
Method of Compensation: Return on invest. most important, but chg. closing fees, service fees, etc.

ENTERPRISE INVESTORS SP Z O O

Emilii Plater, 53, Floor 31
Warsaw, Poland 00-113
Phone: 48224588500
Fax: 48224588555
E-mail: info@ei.com.pl
Website: www.ei.com.pl

Other Offices

Domus Center, Str. Stirbei Voda
Nr. 36, Etaj 5
Bucharest, Romania
Phone: 40213146685
Fax: 40213148191

Management and Staff

Dariusz Pronczuk, Managing Partner
Jacek Wozniak, Partner
Michal Kedzia, Partner
Michal Rusiecki, Managing Partner
Rafal Bator, Partner
Robert Manz, Managing Partner
Sebastian Krol, Partner
Tomasz Ciborowski, Partner

Type of Firm

Private Equity Firm

Association Membership

Czech Venture Capital Association (CVCA)
Polish Venture Capital Association (PSIC/PPEA)
South Eastern Europes Private Equity Association
European Private Equity and Venture Capital Assoc.

Project Preferences

Role in Financing:
Prefer role as deal originator but will also invest in deals created by others

Type of Financing Preferred:
Leveraged Buyout
Expansion
Later Stage
Management Buyouts

Size of Investments Considered:
Min Size of Investment Considered (000s): $3,000
Max Size of Investment Considered (000s): $30,000

Geographical Preferences

International Preferences:
Slovenia
Hungary
Slovak Repub.
Central Europe
Czech Republic
Poland
Eastern Europe
Croatia
Ukraine
Bulgaria
Estonia
Romania
Latvia
Lithuania

Industry Preferences

In Communications prefer:
Communications and Media
Telecommunications
Media and Entertainment

In Computer Hardware prefer:
Integrated Turnkey System

In Computer Software prefer:
Computer Services
Systems Software
Applications Software

In Internet Specific prefer:
Internet

In Computer Other prefer:
Computer Related

In Semiconductor/Electr prefer:
Electronic Components
Sensors
Component Testing Equipmt
Analytic/Scientific

In Biotechnology prefer:
Industrial Biotechnology

In Medical/Health prefer:
Medical/Health
Medical Diagnostics
Medical Therapeutics
Health Services
Pharmaceuticals

In Consumer Related prefer:
Consumer
Entertainment and Leisure
Retail
Computer Stores
Franchises(NEC)
Food/Beverage
Consumer Products
Consumer Services
Education Related

In Industrial/Energy prefer:
Energy Conservation Relat
Materials
Factory Automation
Machinery
Environmental Related

In Transportation prefer:
Transportation

In Financial Services prefer:
Financial Services

In Business Serv. prefer:
Distribution
Media

In Manufact. prefer:
Manufacturing
Office Automation Equipmt
Publishing

In Agr/Forestr/Fish prefer:
Agriculture related
Mining and Minerals

Additional Information

Name of Most Recent Fund: Polish Enterprise Fund VII LP
Most Recent Fund Was Raised: 05/25/2012
Year Founded: 1990
Capital Under Management: $1,354,200,000
Current Activity Level : Actively seeking new investments
Method of Compensation: Return on investment is of primary concern, do not charge fees

ENTERPRISE IRELAND

The Plaza
East Point Business Park
Dublin 3, Ireland
Phone: 35317272000
Fax: 35318082020
E-mail: client.service@enterprise-ireland.com
Website: www.enterprise-ireland.com

Other Offices

4500 Atlantic Avenue
Westpark, Shannon
County Clare, Ireland
Phone: 35361777000
Fax: 35361777001

Type of Firm

Government Affiliated Program

Project Preferences

Type of Financing Preferred:
Early Stage
Expansion
Balanced
Seed
Startup

Geographical Preferences

International Preferences:
Ireland

Industry Preferences

In Communications prefer:
Telecommunications
Media and Entertainment

In Computer Software prefer:
Software
Applications Software

In Internet Specific prefer:
Internet

In Medical/Health prefer:
Medical Products
Pharmaceuticals

In Consumer Related prefer:
Food/Beverage
Consumer Products

In Industrial/Energy prefer:
Alternative Energy
Industrial Products
Environmental Related

In Financial Services prefer:
Financial Services

In Business Serv. prefer:
Services

In Manufact. prefer:
Manufacturing

In Other prefer:
Environment Responsible

Additional Information

Name of Most Recent Fund: Competitive Start Fund
Most Recent Fund Was Raised: 01/23/2013
Year Founded: 1998
Capital Under Management: $999,000
Current Activity Level : Actively seeking new investments

ENTERPRISE PARTNERS MANAGEMENT LLC

2223 Avenida De La Playa
Suite 300
La Jolla, CA USA 92037
Phone: 8587310300
Website: www.epvc.com

Management and Staff

Andrew Senyei, Managing Director
Carl Eibl, Managing Director
James Berglund, Founder

Type of Firm

Private Equity Firm

Project Preferences

Role in Financing:
Will function either as deal originator or investor in deals created by others

Type of Financing Preferred:
Leveraged Buyout
Early Stage
Later Stage
Seed
Acquisition

Size of Investments Considered:
Min Size of Investment Considered (000s): $3,000
Max Size of Investment Considered (000s): $10,000

Geographical Preferences

United States Preferences:
Southern California
California
New York

Canadian Preferences:
All Canada

Industry Focus

(% based on actual investment)
Computer Software and Services	25.7%
Communications and Media	18.1%
Biotechnology	14.6%
Medical/Health	11.3%
Semiconductors/Other Elect.	10.5%
Internet Specific	9.4%
Consumer Related	4.6%
Industrial/Energy	2.4%
Computer Hardware	1.9%
Other Products	1.5%

Additional Information

Year Founded: 1985
Capital Under Management: $1,100,000,000
Current Activity Level : Actively seeking new investments
Method of Compensation: Return on invest. most important, but chg. closing fees, service fees, etc.

ENTERPRISE PRIVATE EQUITY LTD

176 Upper Richmond Road
Apsley House
London, United Kingdom SW15 2SH
Phone: 442087800883
Fax: 442087891711
Website: www.enterprisepe.com

Type of Firm

Private Equity Firm

Project Preferences

Type of Financing Preferred:
Balanced

Size of Investments Considered:
Min Size of Investment Considered (000s): $31,478
Max Size of Investment Considered (000s): $786,950

Geographical Preferences

International Preferences:
United Kingdom
Europe

Additional Information

Year Founded: 1992
Current Activity Level : Actively seeking new investments

ENTREPRENEUR CAPITAL INC

600 De Maisonneuve West
Suite 1700
Montreal, Canada H3A 3J2
Phone: 8884548884
E-mail: info@entrepreneurcapital.ca
Website: www.entrepreneurcapital.ca

Management and Staff
Andre La Forge, Partner
Eric Doyon, Partner
Guy Bessette, Partner

Type of Firm
Private Equity Firm

Project Preferences

Type of Financing Preferred:
Leveraged Buyout
Management Buyouts

Additional Information
Year Founded: 2013
Current Activity Level: Actively seeking new investments

ENTREPRENEUR FIRST INVESTMENT MANAGER LLP

Clements Road
Block M, The Biscuit Factory
London, United Kingdom SE16 4DG
E-mail: info@joinef.com
Website: www.joinef.com

Management and Staff
Alice Bentinck, Co-Founder
Chris Mairs, Venture Partner
Tim Davey, Venture Partner

Type of Firm
Incubator/Development Program

Project Preferences

Type of Financing Preferred:
Seed
Startup

Geographical Preferences

International Preferences:
Europe

Additional Information
Year Founded: 2011
Capital Under Management: $18,306,000
Current Activity Level: Actively seeking new investments

ENTREPRENEUR PARTNERS LP

2000 Market Street
Suite 720
Philadelphia, PA USA 19103
Phone: 2673227000
Fax: 2673227001
E-mail: info@epfunds.com
Website: www.entrepreneurpartners.com

Management and Staff
Bruce Newman, Partner
Salem Shuchman, Managing Partner

Type of Firm
Private Equity Firm

Project Preferences

Type of Financing Preferred:
Leveraged Buyout
Management Buyouts
Acquisition

Geographical Preferences

United States Preferences:

Industry Preferences

In Consumer Related prefer:
Consumer
Retail

In Business Serv. prefer:
Services

In Manufact. prefer:
Publishing

Additional Information
Year Founded: 2005
Capital Under Management: $15,000,000
Current Activity Level: Actively seeking new investments

ENTREPRENEUR VENTURE GESTION SA

39, Av. Pierre 1er de Serbie
Paris, France 75008
Phone: 33158186180
Fax: 33158186189
E-mail: entrepreneur@entrepreneurventure.com
Website: www.entrepreneurventure.com

Other Offices
128 Lockhart Road
Wanchai
Hong Kong, Hong Kong
Phone: 852-9131-8099
Fax: 852-2520-1213

Type of Firm
Private Equity Firm

Association Membership
French Venture Capital Association (AFIC)

Project Preferences

Type of Financing Preferred:
Early Stage
Later Stage
Seed
Startup

Size of Investments Considered:
Min Size of Investment Considered (000s): $472
Max Size of Investment Considered (000s): $3,777

Geographical Preferences

International Preferences:
Europe
France

Industry Preferences

In Communications prefer:
Commercial Communications

In Computer Software prefer:
Software

In Internet Specific prefer:
Ecommerce

In Industrial/Energy prefer:
Energy
Alternative Energy

In Business Serv. prefer:
Services
Distribution
Media

Additional Information
Year Founded: 2000
Current Activity Level: Actively seeking new investments

ENTREPRENEURS FACTORY SAS

154, Boulevard Hausmann
Paris, France 75008

Type of Firm
Private Equity Firm

Project Preferences

Type of Financing Preferred:
Early Stage
Expansion
Later Stage
Seed

Geographical Preferences

International Preferences:
Europe
France

Additional Information
Year Founded: 2014
Current Activity Level: Actively seeking new investments

ENTREPRENEURS FUND LP

1900 South Norfolk Street, Suite 219
San Mateo, CA USA 94403
E-mail: info@tef3.com
Website: www.tefunds.com

Management and Staff

David Sifry, Venture Partner
Jeffrey Webber, Managing Director
Kenneth Gardner, Venture Partner
Manoj Saxena, Managing Director
Stephen Turner, Venture Partner
Stephen Plume, Managing Director
Tal Broda, Venture Partner
Tom Chavez, Venture Partner
Umair Khan, Venture Partner

Type of Firm

Private Equity Firm

Project Preferences

Type of Financing Preferred:
Early Stage
Seed
Startup

Industry Preferences

In Communications prefer:
Data Communications

In Computer Software prefer:
Computer Services
Data Processing
Software

Additional Information

Year Founded: 2013
Capital Under Management: $27,450,000
Current Activity Level : Actively seeking new investments

ENTREPRENEURS FUND MANAGEMENT LLP

3rd Floor, Standbrook House
2-5 Old Bond Street
London, United Kingdom W1S 4PD
Phone: 442073551011
Fax: 442073556199
E-mail: info@entrepreneursfund.com

Other Offices

2nd Floor, Windward House
La Route de la Liberation
Channel Islands, France JE2 3BQ

Management and Staff

Dennis Brenninkmeijer, Partner
Klaas de Boer, Managing Partner

Type of Firm

Private Equity Firm

Project Preferences

Type of Financing Preferred:
Early Stage
Expansion

Industry Preferences

In Communications prefer:
Communications and Media

In Medical/Health prefer:
Medical/Health

In Consumer Related prefer:
Retail

In Industrial/Energy prefer:
Energy
Materials

In Other prefer:
Environment Responsible

Additional Information

Year Founded: 2002
Current Activity Level : Actively seeking new investments

ENTREPRISES INTERACTION SEC

5333 Casgrain
Suite 701
Montreal, Canada H2T 1X3
Website: www.interaction.vc

Type of Firm

Private Equity Firm

Project Preferences

Type of Financing Preferred:
Early Stage
Seed

Geographical Preferences

United States Preferences:
North America

Industry Preferences

In Computer Software prefer:
Software

In Internet Specific prefer:
Ecommerce

Additional Information

Year Founded: 2014
Current Activity Level : Actively seeking new investments

ENTWICKLUNGSUND BETEILIGUNGS-GESELLSCHAFT OSTBELGIENS AG

Hutte 79
Box 20
Eupen, Belgium 4700
Phone: 3287568205
Fax: 3287743350
E-mail: info@obi.be
Website: www.obi.be

Management and Staff

Robert Nelles, Vice President
Yves Noel, President

Type of Firm

Private Equity Firm

Association Membership

Belgium Venturing Association

Project Preferences

Type of Financing Preferred:
Early Stage
Later Stage

Size of Investments Considered:
Min Size of Investment Considered (000s): $67
Max Size of Investment Considered (000s): $1,697

Geographical Preferences

International Preferences:
Europe
Belgium

Additional Information

Year Founded: 1989
Current Activity Level : Actively seeking new investments

ENVEST VENTURES

2101 Parks Avenue
Suite 401
Virginia Beach, VA USA 23451
Phone: 7574373000
Fax: 7574373884
Website: www.envestventures.com

Management and Staff

David Kaufman, Co-Founder
David Wolfe, Co-Founder
John Garel, Co-Founder
Lisa Parks, Vice President
Paul Hirschbiel, Co-Founder

Type of Firm

Private Equity Firm

Project Preferences

Role in Financing:
Prefer role as deal originator but will also invest in deals created by others

Type of Financing Preferred:
Generalist PE

Size of Investments Considered:
Min Size of Investment Considered (000s): $2,500
Max Size of Investment Considered (000s): $7,500

Geographical Preferences

United States Preferences:
East Coast

Industry Preferences

In Computer Software prefer:
Software

In Medical/Health prefer:
Medical/Health

In Consumer Related prefer:
Retail
Franchises(NEC)

In Financial Services prefer:
Financial Services

In Business Serv. prefer:
Services

In Manufact. prefer:
Manufacturing

Additional Information

Year Founded: 2000
Capital Under Management: $162,000,000
Current Activity Level : Actively seeking new investments
Method of Compensation: Return on investment is of primary concern, do not charge fees

ENVESTORS LTD

One Lancaster Place
London, United Kingdom WC2E 7ED
Phone: 442072400202
Website: www.envestorslondon.co.uk

Other Offices

PO Box 74327
Dubai, Utd. Arab Em.
Phone: 9714311 6618

1st Floor, Liberation Place
St Helier
Jersey, United Kingdom JE1 1BB
Phone: 441534 448805

The Boardwalk, Third Floor
21 Little Peter Street
Manchester, United Kingdom M15 4PS
Phone: 441616350001
Fax: 441612281569

Type of Firm

Private Equity Firm

Project Preferences

Type of Financing Preferred:
Early Stage
Expansion
Seed

Size of Investments Considered:
Min Size of Investment Considered (000s): $45
Max Size of Investment Considered (000s): $1,784

Geographical Preferences

International Preferences:
United Kingdom
Europe

Additional Information

Year Founded: 2004
Current Activity Level : Actively seeking new investments

ENVISAGE EQUITY

610 Newport Center Drive
Suite 800
Newport Beach, CA USA 92660
Website: www.envisageequity.com

Type of Firm

Private Equity Firm

Project Preferences

Type of Financing Preferred:
Leveraged Buyout
Acquisition

Additional Information

Year Founded: 1969
Current Activity Level : Actively seeking new investments

ENVISION CAPITAL

1512 Larimer Street
Sutie 710
Denver, CO USA 80202
Phone: 720-399-5060
E-mail: inquiries@envision-bc.com
Website: www.envision-bc.com

Type of Firm

Investment Management Firm

Project Preferences

Type of Financing Preferred:
Early Stage
Expansion

Additional Information

Year Founded: 2012
Current Activity Level : Actively seeking new investments

ENVISION CAPITAL

66 Hua Yuan Shi Qiao Road
1303/F, BEA Finance Tower
Shanghai, China 200120
Phone: 862133830038
Fax: 862133830040
Website: www.evcap.com.cn

Type of Firm

Private Equity Firm

Project Preferences

Type of Financing Preferred:
Balanced

Geographical Preferences

International Preferences:
China
Asia

Industry Preferences

In Consumer Related prefer:
Consumer

In Industrial/Energy prefer:
Alternative Energy
Energy Conservation Relat
Environmental Related

In Manufact. prefer:
Manufacturing

In Agr/Forestr/Fish prefer:
Agriculture related

In Other prefer:
Environment Responsible

Additional Information

Year Founded: 2009
Capital Under Management: $223,881,000
Current Activity Level : Actively seeking new investments

ENVOY CAPITAL MANAGEMENT LLC

216 East 45th Street
6th Floor
New York, NY USA 10017

Type of Firm
Private Equity Firm

Project Preferences

Type of Financing Preferred:
Leveraged Buyout
Mezzanine
Management Buyouts
Acquisition
Recapitalizations

Additional Information
Year Founded: 2013
Current Activity Level : Actively seeking new investments

EONCAPITAL, LLC

7430 East Caley Avenue
Suite 200
Centennial, CO USA 80111
Phone: 3038509300
E-mail: inquiry@eonbusiness.com
Website: www.eoncapital.com

Management and Staff
Dave Carlson, Founder
Rob Hooke, Managing Director

Type of Firm
Private Equity Firm

Project Preferences

Type of Financing Preferred:
Early Stage
Seed

Industry Preferences

In Communications prefer:
Wireless Communications

In Computer Software prefer:
Software

In Business Serv. prefer:
Services

Additional Information
Year Founded: 1997
Current Activity Level : Actively seeking new investments

EOS PARTNERS LP

320 Park Avenue
9th Floor
New York, NY USA 10022
Phone: 2128325800
Fax: 2128325815
E-mail: mfirst@eospartners.com
Website: www.eospartners.com

Management and Staff
Aakash Patel, Vice President
Adam Gruber, Principal
Beth Bernstein, Chief Financial Officer
Brendan Moore, Principal
Brian Young, Managing Partner
David Steenkiste, Principal
Mark First, Managing Director
Samuel Levine, Managing Director
Simon Bachleda, Principal
Steven Friedman, Managing Partner

Type of Firm
Private Equity Firm

Project Preferences

Role in Financing:
Prefer role as deal originator but will also invest in deals created by others

Type of Financing Preferred:
Leveraged Buyout
Later Stage
Management Buyouts
Acquisition
Recapitalizations

Size of Investments Considered:
Min Size of Investment Considered (000s): $3,000
Max Size of Investment Considered: No Limit

Geographical Preferences

United States Preferences:
All U.S.

Canadian Preferences:
All Canada

International Preferences:
South Africa

Industry Focus
(% based on actual investment)

Other Products	39.5%
Industrial/Energy	34.7%
Communications and Media	8.2%
Medical/Health	5.7%
Consumer Related	4.3%
Semiconductors/Other Elect.	3.5%
Computer Software and Services	3.1%
Internet Specific	1.1%

Additional Information
Year Founded: 1994
Capital Under Management: $300,000,000
Current Activity Level : Making few, if any, new investments
Method of Compensation: Return on investment is of primary concern, do not charge fees

---

EPI-V LLP

19-20 Piccadilly
Denman House, third floor
London, United Kingdom W1J 0DG
Phone: 4402077343689
Fax: 4402077343689
E-mail: info@epi-v.com
Website: www.epi-v.com

Management and Staff
Glynn Williams, Co-Founder
Robert Preston, Co-Founder

Type of Firm
Private Equity Firm

Association Membership
British Venture Capital Association (BVCA)

Project Preferences

Type of Financing Preferred:
Early Stage
Expansion
Generalist PE
Start-up Financing
Acquisition
Startup

Size of Investments Considered:
Min Size of Investment Considered (000s): $3,917
Max Size of Investment Considered (000s): $19,587

Geographical Preferences

United States Preferences:
All U.S.

Canadian Preferences:
All Canada

International Preferences:
United Kingdom
Europe
Western Europe

Industry Preferences

In Industrial/Energy prefer:
Energy
Oil and Gas Exploration
Oil & Gas Drilling,Explor

Additional Information
Year Founded: 2007
Current Activity Level : Actively seeking new investments

EPIC CAPITAL MANAGEMENT INC

Two Toronto Street
Toronto, Canada M5C 2B6
Phone: 4167034441
Website: www.epiccapitalmanagement.ca

Type of Firm
Private Equity Firm

Project Preferences

Type of Financing Preferred:
Balanced

Geographical Preferences

Canadian Preferences:
All Canada

Industry Preferences

In Medical/Health prefer:
Medical/Health

Additional Information
Year Founded: 2014
Current Activity Level : Actively seeking new investments

EPIC VENTURES INC

15 West South Temple
Suite 500
Salt Lake City, UT USA 84101
Phone: 8015248939
Fax: 8015248941
E-mail: info@epicvc.com
Website: www.epicvc.com

Other Offices
317 Commercial Street NorthEast
ALBUQUERQUE, NM USA 87102
Phone: 5059803392

310 North Second East
Suite 113
REXBURG, ID USA 83440
Phone: 2083565009

Management and Staff
Geoffrey Woolley, Venture Partner
Kent Madsen, Managing Director
Nicholaus Efstratis, Managing Director
Robert Pothier, Venture Partner
Ryan Davis, Chief Financial Officer

Type of Firm
Private Equity Firm

Project Preferences

Role in Financing:
Prefer role as deal originator but will also invest in deals created by others

Type of Financing Preferred:
Early Stage
Seed

Geographical Preferences

United States Preferences:
New Mexico
Northwest
Northeast
Rocky Mountain
Massachusetts
California
West Coast
Southwest

Industry Focus

(% based on actual investment)
Computer Software and Services	34.9%
Internet Specific	33.5%
Semiconductors/Other Elect.	6.5%
Industrial/Energy	5.4%
Computer Hardware	4.9%
Communications and Media	3.2%
Consumer Related	3.0%
Biotechnology	3.0%
Medical/Health	2.9%
Other Products	2.6%

Additional Information
Name of Most Recent Fund: Epic Venture Fund IV
Most Recent Fund Was Raised: 03/24/2008
Year Founded: 1994
Capital Under Management: $220,000,000
Current Activity Level : Actively seeking new investments
Method of Compensation: Return on invest. most important, but chg. closing fees, service fees, etc.

EPIDAREX CAPITAL

7910 Woodmont Avenue
Suite 1210
Bethesda, MD USA 20814
Phone: 3012985455
Fax: 3013578517
E-mail: info@rockspringventures.com
Website: www.rockspringventures.com

Other Offices
157-27 Samsung-dong, Kangnam-gu
18th Floor Kyungam Building
Seoul, South Korea 135-090
Phone: 8225017727

125 Princes Street
Fifth Floor
Scotland, United Kingdom EH2 4AD
Phone: 442034630810

5-22-3 Shimbashi, Minato-ku
4F Le Gratte-Ciel Bldg. 3
Tokyo, Japan 105-0004
Phone: 81364590258

Management and Staff
Isao Kikuchi, Managing Director
Kyparissia Sirinakis, Managing Partner
Samuel Lee, Managing Director
Sinclair Dunlop, Managing Partner

Type of Firm
Private Equity Firm

Association Membership
Mid-Atlantic Venture Association

Project Preferences

Type of Financing Preferred:
Early Stage
Seed
Startup

Geographical Preferences

United States Preferences:
Mid Atlantic

International Preferences:
United Kingdom
Europe

Industry Preferences

In Biotechnology prefer:
Biotechnology

In Medical/Health prefer:
Medical/Health
Diagnostic Services
Medical Products
Health Services
Pharmaceuticals

Additional Information
Name of Most Recent Fund: Epidarex Capital II, L.P.
Most Recent Fund Was Raised: 02/04/2013
Year Founded: 2011
Capital Under Management: $79,830,000
Current Activity Level : Actively seeking new investments

EPIRIS LLP

65, Saint Paul's Churchyard
Paternoster House
London, United Kingdom EC4M 8AB
Phone: 442072144200
Fax: 442072144201
Website: www.epiris.co.uk

Type of Firm
Private Equity Firm

Project Preferences

Type of Financing Preferred:
Leveraged Buyout
Management Buyouts
Acquisition

Geographical Preferences

International Preferences:
United Kingdom
Europe

Additional Information
Year Founded: 2017
Current Activity Level : Actively seeking new investments

EPISODE 1 VENTURES LLP

229-231 High Holborn
Kingsbourne House
London, United Kingdom WC1 V7DA
Phone: 442074864841
Fax: 442072241567
E-mail: info@episode1.com
Website: www.episode1.com

Management and Staff
Adrian Lloyd, Partner
Damien Lane, Founder
Perry Blacher, Founding Partner
Richard Tahta, Founding Partner
Simon Murdoch, Founding Partner

Type of Firm
Private Equity Firm

Project Preferences

Type of Financing Preferred:
Early Stage

Size of Investments Considered:
Min Size of Investment Considered (000s): $654
Max Size of Investment Considered (000s): $1,961

Geographical Preferences

International Preferences:
United Kingdom

Industry Preferences

In Communications prefer:
Telecommunications

In Computer Software prefer:
Software

In Internet Specific prefer:
Internet

Additional Information
Name of Most Recent Fund: Episode 1 Fund, The.
Most Recent Fund Was Raised: 10/08/2013
Year Founded: 1999
Capital Under Management: $100,000,000
Current Activity Level : Actively seeking new investments

EPLANET CAPITAL

5300 Stevens Creek Boulevard
Suite 430
San Jose, CA USA 95129
Phone: 4082366500
Fax: 4085546600
E-mail: siliconvalley@eplanetcapital.com
Website: www.eplanetcapital.com

Other Offices
30th Floor ASEM Tower
159-1 Samsung-dong, Kangnam-ku
Seoul, South Korea 135-798
Phone: 822-6001-2920
Fax: 822-6001-2922

66/F, The Centre
99 Queens Road
Central, Hong Kong
Phone: 85239606545
Fax: 85239653222

1168 Nanjing Xi Road
Suite 4105, CITIC Square
Shanghai, China 200041
Phone: 86-21-5292-9911
Fax: 86-21-5292-5026

Level 11 Park West Building
6-2-1 Nishi-Shinjuku
Shinjuku-ku, Tokyo, Japan
Phone: 81-3-5325-3212
Fax: 81-3-3816-5689

Room 2113-2114, Tower I
No. 1 Jianguomen Wai Da Jie
Beijing, China 100004
Phone: 86-10-6505-9398
Fax: 86-10-6505-9395

W-2 First Floor
Greater Kailash Part I
New Delhi, India 110 048
Phone: 91-11-4141-4107

30 Cecil Street
Prudential Tower 27th Floor
Singapore, Singapore 049712
Phone: 65-6538-3353
Fax: 65-6538-5755

202 B Rear, II Floor
Sobha Alexander Plaza, Commissariat Road
Bangalore, India 560 001
Phone: 91-80-4154-0240
Fax: 91-80-4154-0250

29 Farm Street
London, United Kingdom W1J 5RL
Phone: 442030087155
Fax: 442031708101

Management and Staff
Dennis Atkinson, Managing Partner
Fang Liu, Vice President
Hemant Khatwani, Vice President
Ilhyun Cho, Managing Partner
Nisreen Malik, Vice President

Type of Firm
Bank Affiliated

Project Preferences

Type of Financing Preferred:
Balanced

Geographical Preferences

United States Preferences:

International Preferences:
Indonesia
Latin America
India
Turkey
Europe
China
Brazil
Chile
Asia
Korea, South

Industry Preferences

In Communications prefer:
Telecommunications

In Internet Specific prefer:
Internet
Ecommerce

In Consumer Related prefer:
Consumer

In Business Serv. prefer:
Media

Additional Information
Name of Most Recent Fund: ePlanet Ventures III
Most Recent Fund Was Raised: 06/25/2010
Year Founded: 1999
Capital Under Management: $4,500,000,000
Current Activity Level : Actively seeking new investments

EQ INDIA ADVISORS

63, Free Press House
Nariman Point
Mumbai, India 400021
Phone: 912266156300
Website: www.eqindiaadvisors.com

Management and Staff
Hetal Jain, Vice President
K Srinivas, Managing Partner
Shaji Varghese, Partner
Subhash Baliga, Partner
Sudershan Tirumala, Vice President

Type of Firm
Private Equity Firm

Association Membership
Indian Venture Capital Association (IVCA)

Project Preferences

Type of Financing Preferred:
Leveraged Buyout
Early Stage
Expansion
Generalist PE
Balanced
Later Stage
Management Buyouts
Acquisition

Geographical Preferences

International Preferences:
India

Industry Preferences

In Biotechnology prefer:
Biotechnology
Industrial Biotechnology

In Medical/Health prefer:
Pharmaceuticals

In Transportation prefer:
Transportation

In Business Serv. prefer:
Services

In Manufact. prefer:
Manufacturing

In Agr/Forestr/Fish prefer:
Agribusiness

Additional Information
Year Founded: 1997
Current Activity Level : Actively seeking new investments

EQ OYJ

Mikonkatu 9
Helsinki, Finland 00100
Phone: 358-968178777
Website: www.eq.fi

Management and Staff
Antti Lyytikainen, Chief Financial Officer
Janne Larma, Chief Executive Officer

Type of Firm
Private Equity Advisor or Fund of Funds

Association Membership
Finnish Venture Capital Association (FVCA)

Project Preferences

Type of Financing Preferred:
Fund of Funds
Fund of Funds of Second

Geographical Preferences

United States Preferences:

Canadian Preferences:
All Canada

International Preferences:
Western Europe
Eastern Europe
Scandanavia/Nordic Region
Russia

Additional Information
Name of Most Recent Fund: Amanda V East, L.P.
Most Recent Fund Was Raised: 06/30/2011
Year Founded: 2000
Capital Under Management: $3,684,800,000
Current Activity Level : Actively seeking new investments

EQT FUNDS MANAGEMENT LTD

St Julian's Court
Level Four (North)
Guernsey, United Kingdom GY1 1WA
Phone: 441481722278
Website: www.eqt.se

Other Offices
Taunusanlage 16
mainBuilding
Frankfurt, Germany 60325
Phone: 49-69-247-0450
Fax: 49-69-247-045-122

Grzybowska 5a Street
Grzybowska Park, 7th floor
Warsaw, Poland 00-132
Phone: 48-22-324-5828
Fax: 48-22-324-5838

80 Raffles Place, Suite 44-02
UOB Plaza 1
Singapore, Singapore 048624
Phone: 65-6595-1830
Fax: 65-6595-0062

Postboks 1241 Vika
Oslo, Norway 0110
Phone: 47-2323-7550
Fax: 47-2323-7560

Leopoldstrasse 8
Munich, Germany D-80802
Phone: 49-89-2554-9990
Fax: 49-89-2554-9999

50 Lothian Road
Festival Square
Edinburgh, United Kingdom EH3 9WJ
Phone: 31 20 577 66 70

Pohjoisesplanadi 25A
Helsinki, Finland 00100
Phone: 358-9-696-2470
Fax: 358-9-6962-4710

One North Lexington Avenue
11th Floor
WHITE PLAINS, NY USA 10601
Phone: 914-220-0900
Fax: 914-428-0649

Bahnhofstrasse 61
Zurich, Switzerland CH-8001
Phone: 41-44-266-6800
Fax: 41-44-266-6810

15 Golden Square
London, United Kingdom W1F 9JG
Phone: 442074305510

P.O. Box 16409
Stockholm, Sweden 10327
Phone: 46-8-5065-5300
Fax: 46-8-5065-5319

1366 Nanjing West Rd
16/F, Unit 1606, Tower II
Shanghai, China 200040
Phone: 86-21-6113-5868
Fax: 86-21-6113-5866

10 Harcourt Road
1701 Hutchison House
Central, Hong Kong
Phone: 85-2-2801-6823
Fax: 85-2-2810-4188

1114 Avenue of the Americas
45th Floor
New York, NY USA 10036
Phone: 9172810850

Management and Staff
Andreas Huber, Partner
Asa Hallert, Partner
Carina Chai, Chief Financial Officer
Caspar Callerstrom, Partner
Chris Puscasiu, Partner
Glen Matsumoto, Partner
Hans Ragnesjo, Chief Financial Officer
Jens Moritz, Partner
Lennart Blecher, Managing Partner
Martin Mok, Partner
Morten Hummelmose, Partner
Patrick Weber, Founder
Piotr Czapski, Partner
Samir Kamal, Partner
Stefan Gleven, Partner
Sumeet Gulati, Partner
Tomas Aubell, Partner

Type of Firm
Private Equity Firm

Association Membership
Finnish Venture Capital Association (FVCA)
Hong Kong Venture Capital Association (HKVCA)
Danish Venture Capital Association (DVCA)
Norwegian Venture Capital Association
German Venture Capital Association (BVK)
Polish Venture Capital Association (PSIC/PPEA)
Swedish Venture Capital Association (SVCA)
European Private Equity and Venture Capital Assoc.
Dutch Venture Capital Associaton (NVP)

Project Preferences

Type of Financing Preferred:
Leveraged Buyout
Mezzanine
Other
Acquisition

Geographical Preferences

United States Preferences:
Southeast
North America

International Preferences:
Sweden
Central Europe
Europe
Switzerland
China
Austria
Iceland
Asia
Finland
Norway
Germany
Denmark

Industry Focus
(% based on actual investment)

Industrial/Energy	25.0%
Consumer Related	16.4%
Medical/Health	15.0%
Communications and Media	14.7%
Computer Hardware	10.9%
Other Products	10.8%
Computer Software and Services	3.7%
Semiconductors/Other Elect.	2.0%
Internet Specific	1.5%

Additional Information
Name of Most Recent Fund: EQT Mid Market
Most Recent Fund Was Raised: 01/21/2014
Year Founded: 1994
Capital Under Management: $13,522,200,000
Current Activity Level : Actively seeking new investments

EQUATOR CAPITAL PARTNERS LLC

135 South LaSalle Street, Suite 2125
Chicago, IL USA 60603
Phone: 3126379430
Website: www.equatorcap.net

Type of Firm
SBIC

Project Preferences

Type of Financing Preferred:
Balanced

Additional Information
Year Founded: 2017
Capital Under Management: $48,950,000
Current Activity Level : Actively seeking new investments

EQUI SICAV SIF SCA

2, Boulevard de la Foire
Luxembourg, Luxembourg L-1528
Phone: 3522484681

Type of Firm
Investment Management Firm

Project Preferences

Type of Financing Preferred:
Leveraged Buyout
Early Stage
Expansion
Mezzanine
Later Stage
Management Buyouts
Acquisition
Recapitalizations

Geographical Preferences

International Preferences:
Luxembourg
Europe

Additional Information
Year Founded: 2010
Current Activity Level : Actively seeking new investments

EQUICAPITA INCOME LP

5920 Macleod Trail South West
Suite 803
Calgary, Canada T2K 0H2
Phone: 5878871541
Website: www.equicapita.com

Type of Firm
Private Equity Firm

Project Preferences

Type of Financing Preferred:
Leveraged Buyout
Acquisition

Geographical Preferences

Canadian Preferences:
All Canada

Additional Information
Year Founded: 2013
Current Activity Level : Actively seeking new investments

EQUIFIN CAPITAL PARTNERS

Seven Times Square
Suite 2106
New York, NY USA 10036
Phone: 212-382-6000
Website: www.equifincapital.com

Management and Staff
Daniel Ury, Principal
Douglas Goodman, Partner
Joseph Tomei, Managing Partner
Mani Sadeghi, Managing Partner
Stephane Chevrier, Managing Partner

Type of Firm
Private Equity Firm

Project Preferences

Type of Financing Preferred:
Generalist PE

Geographical Preferences

United States Preferences:
All U.S.

Additional Information
Year Founded: 2005
Current Activity Level : Actively seeking new investments

EQUINOX SECURITIES LTD

29 Harley Street
61-65 Conduit Street
London, United Kingdom WIG9QR
Phone: 44-20-7509-9500
Fax: 44-20-7509-9602
E-mail: information@equinoxonline.com
Website: www.equinoxonline.com

Type of Firm
Private Equity Firm

Additional Information
Year Founded: 2010
Current Activity Level : Actively seeking new investments

EQUIP VENTURES LLC

60 East 42nd Street
Suite 501
New York, NY USA 10165
Phone: 646-291-6310
Fax: 646-205-9136
E-mail: info@equipventures.com

Other Offices
2626 Hidden Valley Road
La Jolla, CA USA 92037
Phone: 858-551-1280
Fax: 858-551-1708

Management and Staff
David Waxman, Managing Partner
Mark Goros, Managing Partner

Type of Firm
Private Equity Firm

Project Preferences

Type of Financing Preferred:
Early Stage
Seed
Startup

Geographical Preferences

United States Preferences:
Southern California

International Preferences:
Israel

Industry Preferences

In Communications prefer:
Communications and Media

In Computer Software prefer:
Software

Additional Information
Year Founded: 2002
Current Activity Level : Actively seeking new investments

EQUISTONE PARTNERS EUROPE LTD

Saint Paul's Churchyard
Condor House
London, United Kingdom EC4M 8AL
Phone: 442076535300
Fax: 442076535301
Website: www.equistonepe.com

Other Offices
Foro Bounaparte 51
Milan, Italy 20121
Phone: 39249533000
Fax: 39249533005

1st Floor, Bank House
8 Cherry Street
Birmingham, United Kingdom B2 5AL
Phone: 44-121-631-4220
Fax: 44-121-631-1071

6th Floor
55 King Street
Manchester, United Kingdom M2 4LQ
Phone: 44-161-214-0800
Fax: 44-161-214-0805

General Guisan Quai 34
Zurich, Switzerland CH-8002
Phone: 41-44-289-8090
Fax: 41-44-289-8091

Platzl 4
80331 Munchen
Munich, Germany 80331
Phone: 49-89-242-0640
Fax: 49-89-242-06433

Management and Staff
Christiian Marriott, Partner
Guillaume Jacqueau, Managing Partner
Michael Bork, Managing Director
Peter Hammermann, Managing Director
Robert Myers, Managing Director
Simon Brown, Chief Financial Officer
Steven Whitaker, Chief Operating Officer

Type of Firm
Private Equity Firm

Association Membership
British Venture Capital Association (BVCA)
French Venture Capital Association (AFIC)
Swiss Venture Capital Association (SECA)
European Private Equity and Venture Capital Assoc.

Project Preferences

Type of Financing Preferred:
Leveraged Buyout
Mezzanine
Balanced
Turnaround
Management Buyouts
Acquisition
Recapitalizations

Geographical Preferences

International Preferences:
Switzerland
Germany
France

Industry Focus
(% based on actual investment)
Other Products	38.3%
Consumer Related	21.7%
Internet Specific	9.7%
Semiconductors/Other Elect.	9.2%
Industrial/Energy	7.7%
Medical/Health	5.3%
Communications and Media	3.9%
Computer Software and Services	2.6%
Biotechnology	1.7%

Additional Information
Name of Most Recent Fund: Equistone Partners Europe Fund IV
Most Recent Fund Was Raised: 12/31/2011
Year Founded: 1979
Capital Under Management: $8,779,600,000
Current Activity Level : Actively seeking new investments

EQUITIS GESTION SAS

6 Place De La Rep. Dominicaine
Paris, France 75017
Phone: 33156881616
Fax: 33156881618
E-mail: contact@equitis.fr
Website: www.equitis.fr

Management and Staff
Denis Henrion, Partner
Gilles Astruc, Venture Partner
Philippe Bertin, Partner
Raffy Kazandjian, Venture Partner
Stephan Catoire, Partner

Type of Firm
Private Equity Firm

Association Membership
French Venture Capital Association (AFIC)

Project Preferences

Type of Financing Preferred:
Early Stage
Balanced
Later Stage

Geographical Preferences

International Preferences:
Europe
France

Additional Information
Year Founded: 2000
Current Activity Level : Actively seeking new investments

EQUITRUST AG

Hohe Bleichen 12
Hamburg, Germany 20354
Phone: 494030081431
Fax: 494030081431
E-mail: info@equitrust.de
Website: www.equitrust.de

Type of Firm
Private Equity Advisor or Fund of Funds

Project Preferences

Type of Financing Preferred:
Fund of Funds

Geographical Preferences

United States Preferences:
All U.S.

International Preferences:
Europe
Switzerland
Austria
Asia
Germany
All International

Industry Preferences

In Consumer Related prefer:
Retail

In Industrial/Energy prefer:
Industrial Products

In Business Serv. prefer:
Services

Additional Information
Year Founded: 1999
Capital Under Management: $305,100,000
Current Activity Level : Actively seeking new investments

EQUITY GROUP INVESTMENTS

Two North Riverside Plaza
Suite 600
Chicago, IL USA 60606
Website: www.egizell.com

Type of Firm
Private Equity Firm

Project Preferences

Type of Financing Preferred:
Generalist PE

Industry Preferences

In Medical/Health prefer:
Health Services

In Industrial/Energy prefer:
Energy

In Transportation prefer:
Transportation

In Manufact. prefer:
Manufacturing

Additional Information
Year Founded: 2017
Current Activity Level : Actively seeking new investments

EQUITY PARTNERS

201 Kent Street
Level 12
Sydney, Australia 2000
Phone: 61282985100
Fax: 61282985150
E-mail: enquiries@equitypartners.com.au
Website: www.equitypartners.com.au

Management and Staff
Quentin Jones, Partner
Rajeev Dhawan, Partner
Sue Rosen, Chief Financial Officer

Type of Firm
Private Equity Firm

Association Membership
Australian Venture Capital Association (AVCAL)

Project Preferences

Role in Financing:
Will function either as deal originator or investor in deals created by others

Type of Financing Preferred:
Leveraged Buyout
Expansion
Management Buyouts
Acquisition
Private Placement
Recapitalizations

Geographical Preferences

International Preferences:
Pacific
Australia
New Zealand

Industry Focus
(% based on actual investment)
Consumer Related	29.4%
Other Products	28.7%
Internet Specific	15.2%
Computer Software and Services	11.6%
Medical/Health	11.6%
Industrial/Energy	3.3%

Additional Information
Year Founded: 1995
Capital Under Management: $144,600,000
Current Activity Level : Actively seeking new investments
Method of Compensation: Return on invest. most important, but chg. closing fees, service fees, etc.

EQUITY VENTURE PARTNERS PTY LTD

Suite 606A
3 Waverley Street
Bondi Junction, Australia 2022
Website: www.equityventures.com.au

Management and Staff
Howard Leibman, Co-Founder
Les Szekely, Co-Founder
Matthew Tribe, Chief Financial Officer

Type of Firm
Investment Management Firm

Project Preferences

Type of Financing Preferred:
Early Stage

Additional Information
Year Founded: 1995
Capital Under Management: $76,000,000
Current Activity Level : Actively seeking new investments

EQVENTURE GMBH

Karmeliterplatz 4
Graz, Austria 8010
Phone: 433162321260
E-mail: office@eqventure.com
Website: www.eqventure.com

Type of Firm
Private Equity Firm

Additional Information
Year Founded: 2016
Current Activity Level : Actively seeking new investments

ERGO MEDIA CAPITAL LLC

853 Broadway
Suite 1406
New York, NY USA 10010
Phone: 6469981060
Fax: 6462740846
Website: www.ergomediacapital.com

Type of Firm
Private Equity Firm

Project Preferences

Type of Financing Preferred:
Expansion
Generalist PE
Later Stage
Startup

Industry Preferences

In Communications prefer:
Radio & TV Broadcasting
Media and Entertainment

In Consumer Related prefer:
Entertainment and Leisure

In Business Serv. prefer:
Media

Additional Information

Year Founded: 2010
Current Activity Level : Actively seeking new investments

ERHVERVSINVEST MANAGEMENT A/S

Nybrogade 12
2nd Floor
Copenhagen K, Denmark 1203
Phone: 4570203295
Fax: 4533910445
E-mail: info@erhvervsinvest.dk
Website: erhvervsinvest.dk

Management and Staff

Thomas Marstrand, Managing Partner

Type of Firm

Private Equity Firm

Project Preferences

Type of Financing Preferred:
Leveraged Buyout
Management Buyouts

Geographical Preferences

International Preferences:
Denmark

Industry Preferences

In Consumer Related prefer:
Casino/Gambling
Retail
Other Restaurants

In Industrial/Energy prefer:
Energy
Coal Related
Industrial Products
Materials
Machinery

In Transportation prefer:
Transportation

In Manufact. prefer:
Manufacturing

Additional Information

Name of Most Recent Fund: Erhvervsinvest III K/S
Most Recent Fund Was Raised: 06/26/2013
Year Founded: 2004
Capital Under Management: $28,300,000
Current Activity Level : Actively seeking new investments

ERNE VENTURES SA

Aleja Jana Pawa II 27
Warszawa, Poland 00-867
Phone: 4822208 78 48
Fax: 4822203 53 93
Website: erne.pl

Type of Firm

Private Equity Firm

Project Preferences

Type of Financing Preferred:
Early Stage
Startup

Geographical Preferences

International Preferences:
Poland

Industry Preferences

In Biotechnology prefer:
Biotechnology

In Consumer Related prefer:
Entertainment and Leisure

In Industrial/Energy prefer:
Environmental Related

In Transportation prefer:
Transportation

Additional Information

Year Founded: 2007
Current Activity Level : Actively seeking new investments

ERNST & YOUNG LLP

Five Times Square
New York, NY USA 10036
Phone: 2127733000
Fax: 2127736350
Website: www.ey.com

Management and Staff

Carmine DiSibio, Managing Partner
David Holtze, Chief Financial Officer
Ibi Krukrubo, Managing Partner
Joe Muscat, Managing Partner
Lou Pagnutti, Managing Partner
Stephen Howe, Managing Partner
Tim Tasker, Managing Partner

Type of Firm

Corporate PE/Venture

Association Membership

Mid-Atlantic Venture Association
New Zealand Venture Capital Association
Emerging Markets Private Equity Association
Israel Venture Association
Canadian Venture Capital Association
Indian Venture Capital Association (IVCA)

Additional Information

Year Founded: 1989
Current Activity Level : Actively seeking new investments

ESANG TECHNOLOGY INVESTMENT

No. 239-4, Gasan-dong
3/F, ES Bldg, Geumcheon-gu
Seoul, South Korea
Phone: 82233970060
Fax: 82233970065
E-mail: esangvc@e-sang.net
Website: www.esangvc.com

Management and Staff

Jong Pil Kim, Chief Executive Officer
Yeong Chan Kim, Vice President

Type of Firm

Private Equity Firm

Association Membership

Korean Venture Capital Association (KVCA)

Project Preferences

Type of Financing Preferred:
Balanced

Geographical Preferences

International Preferences:
Asia
Korea, South

Industry Preferences

In Computer Software prefer:
Software

Additional Information

Year Founded: 2009
Capital Under Management: $11,880,000
Current Activity Level : Actively seeking new investments

ESAS HOLDING AS

Esas Plaza Ruzgarlibahce
Mahallesi Kavak Sokak No:3
Istanbul, Turkey 34398
Phone: 902166818500
Fax: 902166818560
E-mail: esas@esas.com.tr
Website: www.esas.com.tr

Other Offices
12 Stanhope Gate
London, United Kingdom W1K 1AW
Phone: 442074080240
Fax: 442074914331

Management and Staff
Benan Cetin, Founder
Huseyin Ozdogru, Chief Executive Officer
Inan Tanriover, Chief Financial Officer

Type of Firm
Investment Management Firm

Project Preferences

Type of Financing Preferred:
Leveraged Buyout
Early Stage
Expansion
Generalist PE
Balanced
Later Stage
Management Buyouts
Acquisition

Geographical Preferences

International Preferences:
Turkey
Europe

Industry Preferences

In Computer Hardware prefer:
Integrated Turnkey System

In Medical/Health prefer:
Medical Products
Health Services

In Consumer Related prefer:
Food/Beverage

In Transportation prefer:
Transportation

In Financial Services prefer:
Financial Services
Insurance
Real Estate
Financial Services

Additional Information
Year Founded: 2000
Current Activity Level : Actively seeking new investments

ESCALATE CAPITAL I L P

300 W. Sixth Street
Suite 2300
Austin, TX USA 78701
Phone: 5126512100
E-mail: info@escalatecapital.com
Website: www.escalatecapital.com

Other Offices
300 West Sixth Street
Suite 2250
Austin, TX USA 78701
Phone: 512-651-2100
Fax: 408-200-0099

Management and Staff
Chris Julich, Principal
Larry Bradshaw, Principal
Ross Cockrell, Managing Director
Tony Schell, Managing Director

Type of Firm
Private Equity Firm

Association Membership
Natl Assoc of Small Bus. Inv. Co (NASBIC)

Project Preferences

Type of Financing Preferred:
Mezzanine
Later Stage
Acquisition
Recapitalizations

Size of Investments Considered:
Min Size of Investment Considered (000s): $5,000
Max Size of Investment Considered (000s): $15,000

Geographical Preferences

United States Preferences:
All U.S.

Industry Preferences

In Communications prefer:
Wireless Communications

In Computer Software prefer:
Software

Additional Information
Name of Most Recent Fund: Escalate Capital I, L.P.
Most Recent Fund Was Raised: 05/15/2005
Year Founded: 2005
Capital Under Management: $235,000,000
Current Activity Level : Actively seeking new investments

ESFIN GESTION SA

2 place des Vosges
Immeuble La Fayette
Courbevoie, France 92400
Phone: 33155230710
Fax: 33149001982
E-mail: esfin-gestion@esfingestion.fr
Website: www.esfingestion.fr

Type of Firm
Private Equity Firm

Association Membership
French Venture Capital Association (AFIC)

Project Preferences

Type of Financing Preferred:
Leveraged Buyout
Early Stage
Expansion
Generalist PE
Later Stage

Size of Investments Considered:
Min Size of Investment Considered (000s): $131
Max Size of Investment Considered (000s): $1,315

Geographical Preferences

International Preferences:
Europe
France

Industry Preferences

In Industrial/Energy prefer:
Industrial Products
Environmental Related

In Business Serv. prefer:
Services
Distribution

In Other prefer:
Socially Responsible

Additional Information
Year Founded: 1983
Capital Under Management: $83,484,000
Current Activity Level : Actively seeking new investments

ESHBOL INVESTMENT IN VITAL LP

Hazait 13
Kfar Malal, Israel
Phone: 97299660527
Website: www.eshbol.com

Type of Firm
Private Equity Firm

Project Preferences

Type of Financing Preferred:
Early Stage
Seed
Startup

Geographical Preferences

International Preferences:
Israel

Industry Preferences

In Computer Software prefer:
Software

In Internet Specific prefer:
Ecommerce

In Financial Services prefer:
Financial Services

Additional Information

Year Founded: 2013
Current Activity Level : Actively seeking new investments

ESPERANTE BV

Siriusdreef 22
Hoofddorp, Netherlands 2132 WT
Phone: 31235560466
Fax: 31235560461
Website: www.esperanteventures.com

Other Offices

216 Boulevard Saint Germain
Paris, France 75007
Phone: 33153635087
Fax: 33153635090

Management and Staff

Dean Slagel, Managing Director

Type of Firm

Private Equity Firm

Project Preferences

Type of Financing Preferred:
Early Stage
Balanced
Seed
Startup

Size of Investments Considered:
Min Size of Investment Considered (000s): $264
Max Size of Investment Considered (000s): $1,318

Geographical Preferences

United States Preferences:
All U.S.

International Preferences:
Europe

Industry Preferences

In Medical/Health prefer:
Medical/Health
Medical Therapeutics
Other Therapeutic

Additional Information

Year Founded: 2004
Current Activity Level : Actively seeking new investments

ESPIGA CAPITAL GESTION SGCR SA

4 izquierda
Alfonso XII, 22
Madrid, Spain 28014
Phone: 34915317277
Fax: 34915312552
E-mail: contact@espiga.com
Website: www.espiga.com

Management and Staff

Carlos Prado, Co-Founder
Carlos Prado Perez-Seoane, Managing Partner
Juan Carvajal, Managing Partner
Juan Carvajal Arguelles, Co-Founder

Type of Firm

Private Equity Firm

Association Membership

European Private Equity and Venture Capital Assoc.
Spanish Venture Capital Association (ASCRI)

Project Preferences

Role in Financing:
Will function either as deal originator or investor in deals created by others

Type of Financing Preferred:
Leveraged Buyout
Management Buyouts
Acquisition

Geographical Preferences

International Preferences:
Portugal
Spain

Industry Focus

(% based on actual investment)
Consumer Related	43.1%
Semiconductors/Other Elect.	24.0%
Other Products	23.0%
Industrial/Energy	5.6%
Computer Software and Services	3.0%
Communications and Media	1.3%

Additional Information

Year Founded: 1998
Capital Under Management: $198,100,000
Current Activity Level : Actively seeking new investments

ESPRESSO CAPITAL PARTNERS

999 West Hastings Street
Suite 400
Vancouver, Canada V6C 2W2
Phone: 6047733
Website: www.espressocapital.com

Type of Firm

Corporate PE/Venture

Association Membership

Canadian Venture Capital Association

Additional Information

Year Founded: 2009
Current Activity Level : Actively seeking new investments

ESSDOCS VENTURES

171 Old Bakery Street
Valletta, Malta VLT 1455
E-mail: malta@essdocs.com
Website: www.essdocs.com

Type of Firm

Private Equity Firm

Geographical Preferences

United States Preferences:

International Preferences:
Europe
Asia

Additional Information

Year Founded: 2005
Current Activity Level : Actively seeking new investments

ESSEC VENTURES 1 SAS

3, Avenue Bernard Hirsch
Cergy, France 95000
Website: http://www.essec.fr/lessec/essec-ventures

Type of Firm

University Program

Project Preferences

Type of Financing Preferred:
Early Stage
Seed

Geographical Preferences

International Preferences:
France

Additional Information

Year Founded: 2006
Current Activity Level : Actively seeking new investments

ESSEDEL OY

Aleksanterinkatu 46 C
Helsinki, Finland 00100
Phone: 358 9 454 0300
Fax: 358 9 454 0302
E-mail: info@essedel.com
Website: www.essedel.com

Management and Staff
Andrei Novitsky, Partner
Mihail Malkov, Managing Partner

Type of Firm
Private Equity Firm

Project Preferences

Type of Financing Preferred:
Leveraged Buyout
Management Buyouts
Acquisition

Geographical Preferences

International Preferences:
Russia

Additional Information
Year Founded: 1997
Current Activity Level : Actively seeking new investments

ESTANCIA CAPITAL MANAGEMENT LLC

20865 North 90th Place
Suite 200
Scottsdale, AZ USA 85255
Phone: 4809987000
Website: www.estanciapartners.com

Management and Staff
Daniel Kang, Partner
Michael Mendez, Partner
Takashi Moriuchi, Partner

Type of Firm
Private Equity Firm

Project Preferences

Type of Financing Preferred:
Leveraged Buyout
Expansion
Management Buyouts

Industry Preferences

In Financial Services prefer:
Financial Services

In Business Serv. prefer:
Services

Additional Information
Name of Most Recent Fund: Estancia Capital Partners, L.P.
Most Recent Fund Was Raised: 01/04/2012
Year Founded: 2009
Capital Under Management: $180,667,000
Current Activity Level : Actively seeking new investments

ESTERAD INVESTMENT CO BSC

Almoayyed Tower, 5th Floor
Suite 503, Seef District
Manama, Bahrain
Phone: 97317585400
Fax: 97317585444
E-mail: mail@esterad.net
Website: www.esterad.net

Management and Staff
Abdul Samad Zaman, Chief Operating Officer
Abdulrahman Jamsheer, Managing Director
Faisal Janahi, Chief Executive Officer
Jamshir Nasimi, Chief Financial Officer

Type of Firm
Private Equity Firm

Project Preferences

Type of Financing Preferred:
Leveraged Buyout
Early Stage
Generalist PE
Balanced
Later Stage
Acquisition

Geographical Preferences

International Preferences:
Middle East
Asia
Africa

Industry Preferences

In Financial Services prefer:
Real Estate
Investment Groups
Financial Services

Additional Information
Year Founded: 1973
Current Activity Level : Actively seeking new investments

ESW CAPITAL LLC

401 Congress Avenue
Suite 2650
Austin, TX USA 78701
Website: www.eswcapital.com

Type of Firm
Private Equity Firm

Project Preferences

Type of Financing Preferred:
Leveraged Buyout

Industry Preferences

In Computer Software prefer:
Software

Additional Information
Year Founded: 2008
Current Activity Level : Actively seeking new investments

ESW MANAGE PTE LTD

Harbourfront Centre
1 Maritime Square, Ste 09-50/54
Singapore, Singapore 099253
Phone: 6562740321
Fax: 6563760248
E-mail: enquiry@eswmanage.com
Website: esw-manage.com

Management and Staff
Choon Tong Seah, Co-Founder

Type of Firm
Private Equity Firm

Project Preferences

Type of Financing Preferred:
Leveraged Buyout
Early Stage
Expansion
Generalist PE
Balanced
Later Stage
Management Buyouts
Acquisition

Geographical Preferences

International Preferences:
Vietnam
China
Asia
Singapore
Korea, South
Japan

Additional Information
Year Founded: 2011
Current Activity Level : Actively seeking new investments

ETERNITY CAPITAL ADVISORS LTD

80 Park Lane
London, United Kingdom W1K 7TR
Phone: 442034402785
Fax: 442034402786
E-mail: info@eternitycapital.co.uk

Type of Firm
Private Equity Firm

Association Membership
British Venture Capital Association (BVCA)

Project Preferences

Type of Financing Preferred:
Early Stage
Expansion
Balanced
Later Stage

Geographical Preferences

International Preferences:
United Kingdom
Europe

Industry Preferences

In Industrial/Energy prefer:
Energy Conservation Relat
Environmental Related

Additional Information
Year Founded: 2010
Current Activity Level : Actively seeking new investments

ETF PARTNERS LLP

20 Berkeley Square
London, United Kingdom W1J 6EQ
Phone: 442073180700
Fax: 442076293338
E-mail: info@etf.eu.com
Website: www.etf.eu.com

Management and Staff
Ame Morteani, Principal
Fabrice Bienfait, Principal
Henrik Olsen, Managing Partner
Jorg Uberla, Venture Partner
Klas Hillstrom, Venture Partner
Patrick Sheehan, Partner
Per Ericsson, Venture Partner
Peter Horsburgh, Partner
Robert Genieser, Partner

Type of Firm
Private Equity Firm

Association Membership
European Private Equity and Venture Capital Assoc.

Project Preferences

Role in Financing:
Prefer role as deal originator but will also invest in deals created by others

Type of Financing Preferred:
Early Stage
Expansion
Later Stage

Size of Investments Considered:
Min Size of Investment Considered (000s): $7,483
Max Size of Investment Considered (000s): $17,959

Geographical Preferences

International Preferences:
Europe

Industry Preferences

In Semiconductor/Electr prefer:
Electronic Components
Semiconductor

In Industrial/Energy prefer:
Energy
Alternative Energy
Energy Conservation Relat
Environmental Related

In Transportation prefer:
Transportation

In Manufact. prefer:
Manufacturing

In Agr/Forestr/Fish prefer:
Agriculture related

In Utilities prefer:
Utilities

Additional Information
Name of Most Recent Fund: Environmental Technologies Fund II
Most Recent Fund Was Raised: 09/30/2013
Year Founded: 2006
Capital Under Management: $258,200,000
Current Activity Level : Actively seeking new investments

ETHOS CAPITAL PARTNERS

3475 Lenox Road
Suite 970
Atlanta, GA USA 30326
Website: www.ethospartners.com

Type of Firm
Private Equity Firm

Project Preferences

Type of Financing Preferred:
Leveraged Buyout
Early Stage
Mezzanine
Generalist PE
Balanced
Turnaround
Later Stage
Special Situation
Recapitalizations

Geographical Preferences

United States Preferences:
Southeast
Georgia

Industry Preferences

In Computer Software prefer:
Applications Software

In Medical/Health prefer:
Medical/Health

In Financial Services prefer:
Financial Services
Real Estate

Additional Information
Year Founded: 2014
Capital Under Management: $16,700,000
Current Activity Level : Actively seeking new investments

ETHOS PRIVATE EQUITY (PROPRIETARY) LTD

35 Fricker Road
Illovo, South Africa 2196
Phone: 27113287400
Fax: 27113287410
Website: www.ethos.co.za

Management and Staff
Anthonie De Beer, Partner
Bill Ashmore, Partner
Christo Roos, Partner
Garry Boyd, Partner
Ngalaah Chuphi, Partner
Shaun Zagnoev, Partner
Stuart Mackenzie, Partner

Type of Firm
Private Equity Firm

Association Membership
South African Venture Capital Association (SAVCA)
Emerging Markets Private Equity Association

Project Preferences

Type of Financing Preferred:
Leveraged Buyout
Later Stage
Management Buyouts
Acquisition
Recapitalizations

Size of Investments Considered:
Min Size of Investment Considered (000s): $107,293
Max Size of Investment Considered (000s): $429,171

Geographical Preferences

International Preferences:
Nigeria
Uganda
Tanzania
Ghana
Kenya
South Africa
Africa

Industry Focus

(% based on actual investment)
Other Products 41.1%
Consumer Related 39.7%
Communications and Media 18.8%
Computer Hardware 0.3%

Additional Information

Name of Most Recent Fund: Ethos Private Equity VI, L.P.
Most Recent Fund Was Raised: 01/23/2013
Year Founded: 1984
Capital Under Management: $800,000,000
Current Activity Level : Actively seeking new investments

ETOILE D AQUITAINE

59 Boulevard Haussman
Paris, France 75008
Phone: 33140224022
Fax: 33142471234
Website: www.mercedesbordeaux.com

Type of Firm
Private Equity Firm

Association Membership
French Venture Capital Association (AFIC)

Project Preferences

Type of Financing Preferred:
Leveraged Buyout
Generalist PE
Balanced

Size of Investments Considered:
Min Size of Investment Considered (000s): $619
Max Size of Investment Considered (000s): $2,474

Geographical Preferences

International Preferences:
France

Additional Information
Year Founded: 1985
Current Activity Level : Actively seeking new investments

EUCLID OPPORTUNITIES LTD

Two Broadgate
London, United Kingdom EC2M 7UR
E-mail: ideas@euclidopportunities.com
Website: www.euclidopportunities.com

Type of Firm
Private Equity Firm

Project Preferences

Type of Financing Preferred:
Early Stage
Startup

Additional Information
Year Founded: 2010
Current Activity Level : Actively seeking new investments

EUGLENA SMBC NIKKO LEAVE-A-NEST CAPITAL LLC

Shiba 5-chome
Morinaga Plaza Building 22F
Tokyo, Japan 108-0014
Website: www.realtech.fund

Type of Firm
Private Equity Firm

Project Preferences

Type of Financing Preferred:
Early Stage
Seed

Additional Information
Year Founded: 2014
Current Activity Level : Actively seeking new investments

EURATECHNOLOGIES

165, Avenue De Bretagne
Lille, France 59000
Phone: 33359083230
Website: www.euratechnologies.com

Type of Firm
Incubator/Development Program

Project Preferences

Type of Financing Preferred:
Early Stage
Seed

Geographical Preferences

International Preferences:
Europe
France

Industry Preferences

In Communications prefer:
Data Communications

In Computer Software prefer:
Data Processing
Software

In Internet Specific prefer:
Internet

Additional Information
Year Founded: 2012
Current Activity Level : Actively seeking new investments

EURAZEO PME CAPITAL SAS

32 rue de Monceau
Paris, France 75008
Phone: 33153838160
Fax: 33153838174
E-mail: contact@eurazeo-pme.com
Website: www.eurazeo-pme.com

Management and Staff
Elisabeth Auclair, Chief Financial Officer
Erwann Le Ligne, Managing Director
Pierre Meignen, Managing Director

Type of Firm
Private Equity Firm

Association Membership
French Venture Capital Association (AFIC)
European Private Equity and Venture Capital Assoc.

Project Preferences

Size of Investments Considered:
Min Size of Investment Considered (000s): $20,973
Max Size of Investment Considered (000s): $104,866

Industry Preferences

In Semiconductor/Electr prefer:
Semiconductor

In Consumer Related prefer:
Consumer

In Industrial/Energy prefer:
Energy

In Transportation prefer:
Transportation

In Financial Services prefer:
Financial Services

In Manufact. prefer:
Manufacturing

Additional Information
Year Founded: 2007
Capital Under Management: $554,076,000
Current Activity Level : Actively seeking new investments

EURAZEO SA

1, rue Georges Berger
Paris, France 75017
Phone: 33144150111
Fax: 33147668441
Website: www.eurazeo.com

Management and Staff
Philippe Audouin, Chief Financial Officer
Virginie Morgan, Chief Executive Officer

Type of Firm
Private Equity Firm

Association Membership
French Venture Capital Association (AFIC)
European Private Equity and Venture Capital Assoc.

Project Preferences

Type of Financing Preferred:
Leveraged Buyout
Early Stage
Generalist PE
Later Stage
Acquisition

Geographical Preferences

United States Preferences:
All U.S.

International Preferences:
Europe
Asia
France

Industry Preferences

In Communications prefer:
Communications and Media

In Internet Specific prefer:
Internet

In Semiconductor/Electr prefer:
Electronics

In Consumer Related prefer:
Consumer

In Industrial/Energy prefer:
Industrial Products

In Business Serv. prefer:
Media

Additional Information
Year Founded: 2001
Capital Under Management: $3,387,300,000
Current Activity Level : Actively seeking new investments

EUREFI SA

Maison de la Formation
Centre Jean Monnet
Longwy, France 54414
Phone: 333523072891
Fax: 3335230728944
E-mail: info@eurefi.org
Website: www.eurefi.eu

Other Offices
24, rue Robert Krieps
Europe et Croissance
Petange, Luxembourg L-4702
Phone: 3523072891
Fax: 3523072894

Management and Staff
Bernard Moreau, Vice President
Georges Schmit, President
Rene Delcomminette, Vice President

Type of Firm
Private Equity Firm

Association Membership
French Venture Capital Association (AFIC)

Project Preferences

Type of Financing Preferred:
Leveraged Buyout
Early Stage
Generalist PE
Later Stage
Acquisition

Geographical Preferences

International Preferences:
Luxembourg
Europe
Belgium
Germany
France

Additional Information
Year Founded: 1995
Current Activity Level : Actively seeking new investments

EUREKA GROWTH CAPITAL

1717 Arch Street
34/F, 3420 Bell Atlantic Tower
Philadelphia, PA USA 19103
Phone: 2672384200
Fax: 2672384201
Website: www.eurekagrowth.com

Management and Staff
Alexandra Oswald, Principal
Christian Miller, Partner
Christopher Hanssens, Co-Founder
Jonathan Chou, Partner
Jonathan Zimbalist, Co-Founder
Lisa Millhauser, Vice President
Michael Foran, Chief Financial Officer

Type of Firm
Private Equity Firm

Project Preferences

Role in Financing:
Prefer role as deal originator but will also invest in deals created by others

Type of Financing Preferred:
Leveraged Buyout
Expansion
Management Buyouts
Acquisition
Recapitalizations

Geographical Preferences

United States Preferences:
Mid Atlantic
Southeast
Northeast

Industry Focus
(% based on actual investment)
Other Products	49.1%
Computer Hardware	19.0%
Medical/Health	17.2%
Consumer Related	5.1%
Computer Software and Services	4.8%
Internet Specific	3.5%
Industrial/Energy	1.2%

Additional Information
Name of Most Recent Fund: Eureka III, L.P.
Most Recent Fund Was Raised: 12/21/2012
Year Founded: 1999
Capital Under Management: $305,000,000
Current Activity Level : Actively seeking new investments
Method of Compensation: Return on invest. most important, but chg. closing fees, service fees, etc.

EUREKAP SAS

28 Cours De Verdun
Lyon, France 69002
Website: www.eurekap.eu

Management and Staff
Bruno Rousset, Co-Founder
Christian Lameloise, Co-Founder
Jacques Dancer, Co-Founder
Jacques Moyrand, Co-Founder

Type of Firm
Private Equity Firm

Project Preferences

Type of Financing Preferred:
Early Stage
Seed
Startup
Distressed Debt

Geographical Preferences

International Preferences:
Europe
France

Industry Preferences

In Computer Other prefer:
Computer Related

Additional Information

Year Founded: 2011
Current Activity Level : Actively seeking new investments

EURO CAPITAL SAS

3 rue Francois de Curel
Metz, France 57021
Phone: 33387377065
Fax: 33387377196
E-mail: contact@euro-capital.fr
Website: www.euro-capital.fr

Management and Staff

Lionel Werner, Founder

Type of Firm

Bank Affiliated

Project Preferences

Type of Financing Preferred:
Leveraged Buyout
Early Stage
Generalist PE
Later Stage
Acquisition

Size of Investments Considered:
Min Size of Investment Considered (000s): $612
Max Size of Investment Considered (000s): $2,446

Geographical Preferences

International Preferences:
Europe
France

Additional Information

Year Founded: 2000
Current Activity Level : Actively seeking new investments

EURO PRIVATE EQUITY SA

chemin du Pavillon 5
Le Grand-Saconnex, Switzerland 1218
Phone: 41227885371
Website: www.private-equity-geneve.com

Type of Firm

Private Equity Firm

Additional Information

Year Founded: 2005
Capital Under Management: $234,880,000
Current Activity Level : Actively seeking new investments

EUROMEZZANINE GESTION SAS

11, Rue Scribe
Paris, France 75009
Phone: 33153302330
Fax: 33153302340

Management and Staff

Ajit Jayaratnam, Partner
Bruno Froideval, Managing Partner
Charles Mercier, Partner
Francois Carre, Managing Partner
Marie-Cecile Matar, Partner

Type of Firm

Investment Management Firm

Association Membership

French Venture Capital Association (AFIC)
European Private Equity and Venture Capital Assoc.

Project Preferences

Role in Financing:
Will function either as deal originator or investor in deals created by others

Type of Financing Preferred:
Leveraged Buyout
Mezzanine
Turnaround
Management Buyouts
Acquisition
Recapitalizations

Geographical Preferences

International Preferences:
Europe
France

Industry Focus

(% based on actual investment)
Semiconductors/Other Elect.	49.4%
Industrial/Energy	22.6%
Other Products	16.8%
Biotechnology	5.0%
Computer Software and Services	3.9%
Consumer Related	2.3%

Additional Information

Year Founded: 1990
Capital Under Management: $1,939,200,000
Current Activity Level : Actively seeking new investments

EUROPEAN BANK FOR RECONSTRUCTION AND DEVELOPMENT

One Exchange Square
London, United Kingdom EC2A 2JN
Phone: 442073386000
Fax: 442073386100
E-mail: generalenquiries@ebrd.com
Website: www.ebrd.com

Other Offices

Buyukdere Caddesi, 185
Kanyon Ofis Binasi Kat 2
Istanbul, Turkey 34394
Phone: 9021-2386-1100
Fax: 9021-2386-1199

27/23 Sofiyvska Street
Kiev, United Kingdom 01001
Phone: 380-44270-6132
Fax: 380-44270-6813

Europeum Business Centre
Suche Myto 1
Bratislava, Slovakia 81103
Phone: 421-2591-01700
Fax: 421-2591-01750

26 Geologichesk Pereoulok
Bishkek, Kyrgyzstan 720005
Phone: 996-321-530-012
Fax: 996-312-666-284

3rd Floor, MCS Plaza
Seoul Street - 4A
Ulaanbaatar, Mongolia 210644
Phone: 976-1131-7974
Fax: 976-1131-5844

53 Emili Plater Street
Warsaw Financial Center, Suite 1300
Warsaw, Poland 00113
Phone: 4822-520-5700
Fax: 4822-520-5800

Pratt's Guide to Private Equity & Venture Capital Sources

6 Marjanishvili street
Tbilisi, Georgia 0105
Phone: 995-3244-74100
Fax: 995-3292-0512

Makosped building, 3rd Floor
Makedonija Street, 19
Skopje, Macedonia 1000
Phone: 389-2329-7800
Fax: 389-2323-1238

International and Banking Financial Ctr
1 Turab Tula Street, 4th Floor
Tashkent, Uzbekistan 700066
Phone: 998-7123-94014
Fax: 998-7112-06121

Landmark I, 4th Floor
96 Nizami Street
Baku, Azerbaijan 370010
Phone: 994-12-497-1014
Fax: 994-12-497-1019

Seimyniskiu 1A
4th Floor
Vilnius, Lithuania 2600
Phone: 370-5263-8480
Fax: 370-5263-8481

Metropolis Center
56-60, Iancu de Hunedoara Bd, 3rd floor
Bucharest, Romania
Phone: 4021-202-7100
Fax: 4021-202-7110

17 Moskovska Street
Sofia, Bulgaria 1000
Phone: 359-2932-1414
Fax: 359-2932-1441

Miramarska 23
3rd Floor
Zagreb, Croatia 10000
Phone: 385-1600-0310
Fax: 385-1619-7218

Rokoczi ut 42
Budapest, Hungary 1072
Phone: 361-486-3020
Fax: 361-486-3030

Kalku Street
Riga, Latvia 1050
Phone: 371-7-830-300
Fax: 371-7-830-301

Ducat Place III, Second floor
6 Gasheka Street
Moscow, Russia 125047
Phone: 495-787-1111
Fax: 495-787-1122

85/22 Internatsionalnaya Street
Dushanbe, Tajikistan 734001
Phone: 999-372-231-543
Fax: 992-372-219-832

Yimpas Business Center, 2nd Floor
Suite 201, 54, Turkmenbashi Ave
Ashgabat, Turkmenistan 744000
Phone: 993-1245-5118
Fax: 993-1245-3922

Torre Drin Building, 4th Floor
Abdi Toptani Street
Tirana, Algeria
Phone: 355-4223-2898
Fax: 355-4223-0580

Almaty office, 41 Kazybek bi Street
Entrance 3, 3rd Floor
Almaty, Kazakhstan 480100
Phone: 727-2581-42176
Fax: 727-2581-422

34A Engelsa Street, Building 2
Minsk, Belarus 220030
Phone: 375-17-210-4787
Fax: 375-17-328-3522

15th Floor, Tower B, Unitic Towers
Fra Andela Zvizdovica1
Sarajevo, Bosnia/Herz. 71000
Phone: 387-33-667-945
Fax: 387-33-667-950

12, Samal microdistrict
Astana Tower Business Centre
Astana, Kazakhstan 010000
Phone: 7172-580-204
Fax: 7172-580-201

10th floor, 63 Vlaicu Pircalab Street
Sky Tower building
Chisinau, Moldova 2012
Phone: 373-210-000
Fax: 373-210-011

Citadel Business Centre, 105/1 Teryan St
4th Floor, Suite 407
Yerevan, Armenia 0009
Phone: 374-1051-4805
Fax: 374-1051-4810

Management and Staff

Alain Pilloux, Managing Director
Alan Rousso, Managing Director
Alistair Clark, Managing Director
Betsey Nelson, Vice President
Chris Holyoak, Managing Director
David Klingensmith, Managing Director
Hans Peter Lankes, Vice President
Hildegard Gacek, Managing Director
Horst Reichenbach, Vice President
Jean-Marc Peterschmitt, Managing Director
Josue Tanaka, Managing Director
Kanako Sekine, Managing Director

Natasha Khanjenkova, Managing Director
Nick Tesseyman, Managing Director
Olivier Descamps, Managing Director
Paulo Sousa, Managing Director
Riccardo Puliti, Managing Director
Suma Chakrabarti, President
Thomas Maier, Managing Director
Varel Freeman, Vice President

Type of Firm
Government Affiliated Program

Association Membership
Emerging Markets Private Equity Association
Russian Venture Capital Association (RVCA)
European Private Equity and Venture Capital Assoc.

Project Preferences

Type of Financing Preferred:
Fund of Funds
Generalist PE

Industry Preferences

In Communications prefer:
Telecommunications

In Industrial/Energy prefer:
Energy

In Transportation prefer:
Transportation

In Financial Services prefer:
Financial Services

In Business Serv. prefer:
Services

In Manufact. prefer:
Manufacturing

In Agr/Forestr/Fish prefer:
Agribusiness

In Other prefer:
Environment Responsible

Additional Information
Year Founded: 1991
Capital Under Management: $130,340,000
Current Activity Level : Actively seeking new investments

EUROPEAN CAPITAL

25 Bedford Street
London, United Kingdom WC2E 9ES
Phone: 442075397000
Fax: 442075397001
E-mail: info@europeancapital.com
Website: www.europeancapital.com/

Other Offices

37 Avenue Pierre 1er de Serbie
Paris, France 75008
Phone: 33-1-4068-0666
Fax: 33-1-4068-0688

Management and Staff

Didier Lefevre, Managing Director
Ira Wagner, President
Nathalie Beaulieu, Managing Director
Roland Cline, Partner
Tristan Parisot, Managing Director

Type of Firm

Private Equity Firm

Association Membership

French Venture Capital Association (AFIC)

Project Preferences

Type of Financing Preferred:
Leveraged Buyout
Mezzanine
Management Buyouts
Acquisition
Recapitalizations

Geographical Preferences

International Preferences:
United Kingdom
Europe

Additional Information

Name of Most Recent Fund: European Capital Ltd.
Most Recent Fund Was Raised: 08/18/2005
Year Founded: 2005
Capital Under Management: $1,306,800,000
Current Activity Level : Actively seeking new investments

EUROPEAN CAPITAL FINANCIAL SERVICES LTD

25 Bedford Street
London, United Kingdom WC2E 9ES
Phone: 442075397000
Fax: 442075397001
E-mail: Info@EuropeanCapital.com
Website: www.europeancapital.com

Other Offices

37 Avenue Pierre 1er de Serbie
Paris, France 75008
Phone: 33140680666
Fax: 3314068688

Management and Staff

Clare Copeland, Vice President
Didier Lefevre, Managing Director
Etienne Haubold, Managing Director
Giles Cheek, Managing Director
Ira Wagner, President
Jerry Tebbutt, Managing Director
Julien Darsy, Vice President
Matthew Clark, Managing Director
Nathalie Faure Beaulieu, Managing Director
Richard Smith, Vice President
Stephane Legrand, Managing Director
Tristan Parisot, Managing Director

Type of Firm

Private Equity Firm

Project Preferences

Type of Financing Preferred:
Leveraged Buyout
Expansion
Mezzanine
Turnaround
Management Buyouts
Acquisition
Recapitalizations

Geographical Preferences

International Preferences:
Europe

Industry Preferences

In Business Serv. prefer:
Services
Distribution

In Manufact. prefer:
Manufacturing

Additional Information

Year Founded: 2005
Current Activity Level : Actively seeking new investments

EUROPEAN FINANCE ASSOCIATES SA

7 Stratigi Street
Neo Psichiko, Greece 15451
Phone: 302106728610
Fax: 302106728624
E-mail: t-potsis@efagroup.gr
Website: www.efagroup.gr

Type of Firm

Bank Affiliated

Project Preferences

Type of Financing Preferred:
Early Stage
Balanced
Later Stage
Startup

Geographical Preferences

International Preferences:
All International

Additional Information

Year Founded: 1989
Current Activity Level : Actively seeking new investments

EUROPEAN HOTEL CAPITAL BV

Herengracht 469
Amsterdam, Netherlands 1017 BS
Phone: 31205226330
Fax: 31205226333
Website: www.europeanhotelcapital.nl

Type of Firm

Private Equity Firm

Project Preferences

Type of Financing Preferred:
Leveraged Buyout

Geographical Preferences

International Preferences:
Italy
Netherlands
Portugal
Western Europe
Spain
Belgium
Germany
France

Industry Preferences

In Consumer Related prefer:
Hotels and Resorts

In Financial Services prefer:
Real Estate

Additional Information

Year Founded: 2003
Current Activity Level : Actively seeking new investments

EUROPEAN INVESTMENT BANK

98-100, boulevard Konrad Adenauer
Luxembourg, Luxembourg 2950
Phone: 35243791
Fax: 352437704
E-mail: info@eib.org
Website: www.eib.org

Management and Staff

Dario Scannapieco, Vice President
Jonathan Taylor, Vice President
Pim van Ballekom, Vice President
Roman Escolano Olivares, Vice President

Type of Firm
Bank Affiliated

Association Membership
African Venture Capital Association (AVCA)

Project Preferences

Type of Financing Preferred:
Fund of Funds
Generalist PE
Balanced
Later Stage

Size of Investments Considered:
Min Size of Investment Considered (000s): $2,368
Max Size of Investment Considered (000s): $11,841

Geographical Preferences

International Preferences:
Tunisia
Jordan
Europe
Lebanon
Egypt
Algeria
Pacific Rim
Israel
Morocco
Syria
Africa

Industry Preferences

In Communications prefer:
Communications and Media

In Internet Specific prefer:
Internet

In Computer Other prefer:
Computer Related

In Semiconductor/Electr prefer:
Electronics
Semiconductor

In Biotechnology prefer:
Biotechnology

In Medical/Health prefer:
Medical/Health

In Consumer Related prefer:
Consumer
Education Related

In Industrial/Energy prefer:
Energy

In Transportation prefer:
Transportation
Aerospace

In Financial Services prefer:
Real Estate
Financial Services

In Manufact. prefer:
Manufacturing

In Utilities prefer:
Utilities

Additional Information
Year Founded: 1968
Capital Under Management: $462,900,000
Current Activity Level : Actively seeking new investments

EUROPEAN INVESTMENT FUND

96, Avenue J.F. Kennedy
Luxembourg, Luxembourg 2968
Phone: 35124851
Fax: 352248581301
E-mail: info@eif.org
Website: www.eif.org

Other Offices
29 Calle Jose Ortega y Gaset
Madrid, Spain 28006

227 Rue de la Loi
Brussels, Belgium 1040

Management and Staff
Jean-Marie Magnette, Chief Executive Officer
Richard Pelly, Chief Executive Officer

Type of Firm
Government Affiliated Program

Association Membership
European Private Equity and Venture Capital Assoc.
Spanish Venture Capital Association (ASCRI)

Project Preferences

Type of Financing Preferred:
Fund of Funds

Size of Investments Considered:
Min Size of Investment Considered (000s): $1,000
Max Size of Investment Considered: No Limit

Geographical Preferences

International Preferences:
Italy
Luxembourg
Europe
Spain
Belgium

Industry Preferences

In Computer Software prefer:
Software

In Biotechnology prefer:
Industrial Biotechnology

Additional Information
Name of Most Recent Fund: Baltic Innovation Fund
Most Recent Fund Was Raised: 09/26/2012
Year Founded: 1994
Capital Under Management: $3,619,800,000
Current Activity Level : Actively seeking new investments

EUROPLAY CAPITAL ADVISORS LLC

15260 Ventura Boulevard
20th Floor Sherman Oaks
Sherman Oaks, CA USA 91403
Phone: 8184444400
Website: europlaycapital.com

Management and Staff
Joseph Miller, Managing Director

Type of Firm
Private Equity Firm

Project Preferences

Type of Financing Preferred:
Early Stage
Seed
Startup

Industry Preferences

In Communications prefer:
Communications and Media
Entertainment

In Internet Specific prefer:
Internet

Additional Information
Year Founded: 2013
Current Activity Level : Actively seeking new investments

EUROVENTURES CAPITAL TANACSADO KFT

Martonhegyi Ut 61/A
Budapest, Hungary 1124
Phone: 3613097900
Fax: 3613194762
E-mail: office@euroventures.hu
Website: www.euroventures.hu

Management and Staff
Andras Geszti, Founder
Peter Tanczos, Partner
Thomas Howells, Partner

Type of Firm
Private Equity Firm

Association Membership
Hungarian Venture Capital Association (HVCA)

Project Preferences

Type of Financing Preferred:
Early Stage

Size of Investments Considered:
Min Size of Investment Considered (000s): $2,761
Max Size of Investment Considered (000s): $11,042

Geographical Preferences

International Preferences:
Hungary
Central Europe

Industry Preferences

In Consumer Related prefer:
Consumer

In Industrial/Energy prefer:
Industrial Products

In Transportation prefer:
Transportation
Aerospace

In Business Serv. prefer:
Services

Additional Information
Name of Most Recent Fund: Euroventures Hungary III
Most Recent Fund Was Raised: 06/30/2005
Year Founded: 1989
Capital Under Management: $99,400,000
Current Activity Level : Actively seeking new investments

EUROVESTECH PLC

29 Curzon Street
London, United Kingdom W1J 7TL
Phone: 442074910770
Fax: 442074919595
E-mail: enquiries@eurovestech.com
Website: eurovestech.com

Management and Staff
Richard Bernstein, Chief Executive Officer

Type of Firm
Private Equity Firm

Project Preferences

Type of Financing Preferred:
Early Stage

Geographical Preferences

International Preferences:
United Kingdom
Europe
Israel

Additional Information
Year Founded: 2000
Capital Under Management: $14,000,000
Current Activity Level : Actively seeking new investments

EVA BASEL LIFE SCIENCES AGENCY

Hochbergerstrasse 60c
Basel, Switzerland 4057
Phone: 41612838485
Fax: 41612838486
E-mail: info@eva-basel.ch
Website: www.eva-basel.ch

Management and Staff
Peter Burckhardt, Managing Director

Type of Firm
Private Equity Firm

Project Preferences

Type of Financing Preferred:
Early Stage
Seed
Startup

Geographical Preferences

International Preferences:
Switzerland

Industry Preferences

In Semiconductor/Electr prefer:
Analytic/Scientific

In Biotechnology prefer:
Biotechnology
Biotech Related Research

In Medical/Health prefer:
Medical/Health
Pharmaceuticals

Additional Information
Year Founded: 1996
Current Activity Level : Actively seeking new investments

EVALUE VENTURES AG

Kennedydamm 1
Duesseldorf, Germany 40476
Phone: 492115209940
Fax: 4921152099411
E-mail: service@evalueeurope.com
Website: www.evalueventures.de

Other Offices
36 W 25th Street
7th floor
New York, NY USA 10010

Rosental 4
Munich, Germany 80331
Phone: 4989383980320
Fax: 498938398099

Type of Firm
Private Equity Firm

Project Preferences

Type of Financing Preferred:
Leveraged Buyout
Early Stage
Later Stage
Acquisition
Startup

Geographical Preferences

International Preferences:
Germany

Industry Preferences

In Communications prefer:
Communications and Media
Wireless Communications
Media and Entertainment

In Internet Specific prefer:
Internet
Ecommerce

Additional Information
Year Founded: 1962
Capital Under Management: $2,000,000
Current Activity Level : Actively seeking new investments

EVC VENTURES

1111 Superior Avenue
Suite 310
Cleveland, OH USA 44114
E-mail: info@edutechvc.com
Website: evc.ventures

Type of Firm
Incubator/Development Program

Project Preferences

Type of Financing Preferred:
Early Stage

Industry Preferences

In Computer Software prefer:
Software

In Internet Specific prefer:
Internet

Additional Information
Year Founded: 2016
Current Activity Level : Actively seeking new investments

EVENTI CAPITAL PARTNERS INC

5000 Yonge Street
Suite 1503
Toronto, Canada M2N 7E9
Phone: 4169278887
Fax: 18888691045
Website: www.eventi.ca

Other Offices
2200 Yonge Street
14th Floor
Toronto, Canada M4S 2C6

Type of Firm
Corporate PE/Venture

Association Membership
Canadian Venture Capital Association

Additional Information
Year Founded: 2002
Current Activity Level : Actively seeking new investments

EVENTURE CAPITAL PARTNERS GMBH

Hohe Bleichen 21
Hamburg, Germany 20354
Phone: 494082225550
Fax: 49408222555999
E-mail: info@eventures.vc
Website: www.evcpartners.com

Other Offices
600 Montgomery Street
43rd Floor
San Francisco, CA USA 94111
Phone: 001-315-347-3320
Fax: 001-415-347-3321

7V Baseina
3nd floor, office. 303
Kiev, Ukraine 01004
Phone: 38-50-8477-122

Management and Staff
Akio Tanaka, Partner
Anderson Thees, Partner
Andreas Haug, General Partner
Charles Yim, Venture Partner
Christian Leybold, General Partner
Damian Doberstein, Partner
Hirofumi Ono, Partner
Jan Henric Buettner, Partner
Maren Eckloff-Boehme, Chief Financial Officer
Masashi Kobayashi, Partner
Mathias Schilling, General Partner
Thomas Gieselmann, General Partner
Yann De Vries, Partner

Type of Firm
Corporate PE/Venture

Project Preferences

Type of Financing Preferred:
Early Stage
Seed

Geographical Preferences

United States Preferences:

International Preferences:
Central Europe
Eastern Europe

Industry Preferences

In Communications prefer:
Media and Entertainment

In Internet Specific prefer:
E-Commerce Technology
Internet
Ecommerce

Additional Information
Year Founded: 1998
Current Activity Level : Actively seeking new investments

EVENTURES EUROPE BV

Oud Blaricumerweg 40
PO BOX 301
Bussum, Netherlands 1400 AH
Phone: 31356470682
Fax: 31356470683
E-mail: info@eva-fund.com
Website: www.eventures.nl

Management and Staff
Brian Hirman, Managing Director
Vincent Kouwenhoven, President, Founder

Type of Firm
Private Equity Firm

Project Preferences

Type of Financing Preferred:
Early Stage
Later Stage

Geographical Preferences

International Preferences:
Europe
Netherlands
Ghana
Kenya
Africa

Industry Preferences

In Internet Specific prefer:
E-Commerce Technology
Internet
Ecommerce

Additional Information
Year Founded: 2000
Current Activity Level : Actively seeking new investments

EVERBRIGHT JINKONG SHANGHAI INVESTMENT MANAGEMENT CO LTD

791 Nong Xiangyin Road
1402,1st Floor,13 Building
Shanghai, China

Management and Staff
Guijun Yan, President

Type of Firm
Private Equity Firm

Project Preferences

Type of Financing Preferred:
Leveraged Buyout

Geographical Preferences

International Preferences:
China

Additional Information
Year Founded: 2011
Capital Under Management: $62,000,000
Current Activity Level : Actively seeking new investments

EVERCORE INC

55 East 52nd Street
43rd Floor
New York, NY USA 10055
Phone: 2128573100
Fax: 2128573101
Website: www.evercore.com

Other Offices
1099 New York Avenue, North West
Suite 650
Washington, DC USA 20001
Phone: 202-471-3500
Fax: 202-471-3510

321 North Clark Street
Fifth Floor
Chicago, IL USA 60654
Phone: 3124456440
Fax: 3124456501

Avenida Lazaro Cardenas 2400 Pte
Torre D, 3er piso, Oficina D33
Garza Garcia, Nuevo Leon, Mexico 66267
Phone: 528181335550
Fax: 528181335526

601 South Figueroa Street
44th Floor
Los Angeles, CA USA 90017
Phone: 213-443-2620
Fax: 212-443-2630

Paseo de la Castellana 259-C
Pl. 18 Torre de Cristal
Madrid, Spain 28046
Phone: 34911190584

1000 Winter Street
Suite 4400
Waltham, MA USA 02451
Phone: 7813704700
Fax: 7813704747

50 Carden Place
Bishop House
Aberdeen, United Kingdom AB10 1UP
Phone: 441224218504
Fax: 441224218510

Avenida Borges de Medeiros
633 Sala 206
Rio de Janeiro, Brazil 22430 042
Phone: 552132059180
Fax: 552132059181

15 Stanhope Gate
London, United Kingdom WIK ILN
Phone: 442076536000
Fax: 442076536001

Avenida Brigadeiro Faria Lima 3311
Tenth Floor
Sao Paulo, Brazil 04538 133
Phone: 551130146868
Fax: 551130146869

Two Exchange Square
Suite 1405-1407
Central, Hong Kong
Phone: 85239832600
Fax: 85228690319

150 South fifth Street
Suite 1330
Minneapolis, MN USA 55402
Phone: 6126562820
Fax: 6126562830

Three Embarcadero Center
Suite 560
San Francisco, CA USA 94111
Phone: 415-989-8900
Fax: 415-989-8929

Blvd. Manuel Avila Camacho 36
piso 22 Torre Esmeralda II
Mexico City, Distrito Federal, Mexico 11000

909 Fannin
2 Houston Center
Houston, TX USA 77010
Phone: 713-403-2440
Fax: 713-403-2444

Management and Staff

A. Mark Finkelstein, Managing Director
Alan Gould, Managing Director
Alexander Russ, Managing Director
Alkesh Shah, Managing Director
Andrew Donovan, Managing Director
Andrew Marquardt, Managing Director
Angela Dalton, Managing Director
Angus Winther, Senior Managing Director
Anthony Scali, Managing Director
Antonio Souza, Senior Managing Director
Ben Catt, Managing Director
Bradley Ball, Managing Director
Brendan Panda, Managing Director
Brett Pickett, Senior Managing Director
Charles Myers, Senior Managing Director
Christopher Brand, Managing Director
Christopher Allen, Managing Director
Christopher Juban, Managing Director
Christopher Lynch, Managing Director
Christopher Solmssen, Managing Director
Christopher Nicholson, Managing Director
Ciara Burnham, Senior Managing Director
Corrado Varoli, Senior Managing Director
Daniel Celentano, Senior Managing Director
Daniel Mendelow, Senior Managing Director
Dato Sandroshvili, Managing Director
David Togut, Managing Director
David Ying, Senior Managing Director
David Waring, Senior Managing Director
Dominic Freely, Senior Managing Director
Douglas DePietro, Managing Director
Douglas Arthur, Managing Director
Edward Banks, Senior Managing Director
Edwin Roseberry, Managing Director
Egan Antill, Managing Director
Elaine Sun, Managing Director
Eric Mandl, Senior Managing Director
F.Perkins Hixon, Senior Managing Director
Fernando Aportela, Senior Managing Director
Francois Maisonrouge, Senior Managing Director
George Estey, Senior Managing Director
Gideon Asher, Managing Director
Greg Brooks, Managing Director
Gustavus Christensen, Managing Director
Hichem Zebidi, Managing Director
Hugh Baker, Managing Director
Hugo Garza, Managing Director
James Byrnes, Managing Director
James Oliver, Managing Director
James Swindell, Managing Director
Jamie Easton, Managing Director
Jane Gladstone, Senior Managing Director
Jason Colavita, Managing Director
Jason Sobol, Senior Managing Director

Jeff Easter, Managing Director
Jeffrey Reisenberg, Managing Director
Jim Birle, Senior Managing Director
Joe Chambers, Managing Director
John Kimm, Managing Director
John Venezia, Managing Director
John Honts, Senior Managing Director
John Pancari, Managing Director
Jonathan Schildkraut, Managing Director
Jonathan Chappell, Managing Director
Jonathan Apter, Vice President
Jonathan Knee, Senior Managing Director
Jorge Marcos, Senior Managing Director
Jose Miguel Smith, Managing Director
Julian Oakley, Senior Managing Director
Justin Steil, Managing Director
Kathleen Reiland, Senior Managing Director
Ken Sena, Managing Director
Lance Dardis, Managing Director
Leslie Fabuss, Senior Managing Director
Lincoln Singleton, Managing Director
Liz Lynch, Senior Managing Director
Lloyd Sprung, Senior Managing Director
Lowell Strug, Senior Managing Director
Marcelo Andre Lajchter, Senior Managing Director
Marcus Thompson, Managing Director
Mark Hennessy, Managing Director
Mark Williamson, Managing Director
Mark Whatley, Managing Director
Mark Connell, Senior Managing Director
Mark Friedman, Senior Managing Director
Martin Copeland, Managing Director
Marty Cicco, Senior Managing Director
Matthew Page, Managing Director
Matthew Lindsey-Clark, Senior Managing Director
Michael Price, Senior Managing Director
Nancy Valiente, Managing Director
Nancy Bryson, Managing Director
Naveen Nataraj, Senior Managing Director
Neeraj Mital, Senior Managing Director
Nick Chapman, Managing Director
Nico Master, Managing Director
Ollie Clayton, Managing Director
Patrick Wang, Managing Director
Paul Billyard, Managing Director
Peter Seibold, Managing Director
Philip Kassin, Senior Managing Director
Pierre Oustinow, Managing Director
Qazi Fazal, Senior Managing Director
Rafael Polanco, Managing Director
Raymond Strong, Senior Managing Director
Read Gomm, Senior Managing Director
Renato Klarnet, Senior Managing Director
Richard Anthony, Senior Managing Director
Rob Cihra, Managing Director
Robert Walsh, Chief Financial Officer
Robert Pacha, Senior Managing Director
Saul Goodman, Senior Managing Director
Scott Seymour, Managing Director
Scott Barishaw, Managing Director
Scott Patrick, Managing Director
Sergio Sanchez, Senior Managing Director
Sesh Raghavan, Managing Director
Shaun Finnie, Senior Managing Director
Slava Brin, Managing Director

767

Stephen Worth, Senior Managing Director
Stephen CuUnjieng, Senior Managing Director
Stephen Schaible, Senior Managing Director
Stephen Hannan, Senior Managing Director
Stephen Goldstein, Senior Managing Director
Stewart Kirk Materne, Managing Director
Stuart Britton, Managing Director
Tiarnan O Rourke, Managing Director
Tim Main, Senior Managing Director
Tim Carlson, Senior Managing Director
Timothy LaLonde, Senior Managing Director
Tony Magro, Senior Managing Director
Tony D Souza, Managing Director
William Shutzer, Senior Managing Director

Type of Firm
Investment Management Firm

Project Preferences

Type of Financing Preferred:
Leveraged Buyout
Early Stage
Acquisition

Geographical Preferences

United States Preferences:

International Preferences:
Mexico

Industry Focus
(% based on actual investment)
Other Products	50.1%
Medical/Health	20.7%
Computer Software and Services	20.2%
Communications and Media	4.6%
Internet Specific	3.4%
Computer Hardware	0.8%
Biotechnology	0.2%

Additional Information
Name of Most Recent Fund: Evercore Mexico Capital Partners III, L.P.
Most Recent Fund Was Raised: 06/18/2013
Year Founded: 1996
Capital Under Management: $1,500,000,000
Current Activity Level : Actively seeking new investments

EVEREST INVESTMENT MANAGEMENT LLC

P.O. Box 27395
Omaha, NE USA 68127
Phone: 4025485600
Fax: 4025057592
Website: www.everestcpi.com

Management and Staff
Vinod Gupta, Managing Partner

Type of Firm
Private Equity Firm

Association Membership
National Venture Capital Association - USA (NVCA)

Project Preferences

Type of Financing Preferred:
Leveraged Buyout
Early Stage
Generalist PE
Seed
Acquisition
Startup

Geographical Preferences

United States Preferences:

Industry Preferences

In Computer Software prefer:
Software

In Business Serv. prefer:
Services

Additional Information
Year Founded: 1987
Capital Under Management: $10,000,000
Current Activity Level : Actively seeking new investments

EVERGREEN GROUP VENTURES LLC

Rosecrans Avenue
Media Center, 4th Floor, 1600
Manhattan Beach, CA USA 90266
Website: www.the-evergreen-group.com

Management and Staff
Jim Wagner, Managing Director

Type of Firm
Private Equity Firm

Project Preferences

Type of Financing Preferred:
Leveraged Buyout
Early Stage
Generalist PE
Acquisition

Industry Preferences

In Communications prefer:
Media and Entertainment

Additional Information
Year Founded: 1969
Current Activity Level : Actively seeking new investments

EVERGREEN INDUSTRIES LLC

2501 Panama Street
Philadelphia, PA USA 19103
Phone: 2155455863
Fax: 2155458961
Website: www.evergreenind.com

Type of Firm
Private Equity Firm

Project Preferences

Type of Financing Preferred:
Leveraged Buyout
Management Buyouts
Acquisition
Recapitalizations

Geographical Preferences

United States Preferences:
Mid Atlantic

Industry Preferences

In Medical/Health prefer:
Health Services

In Industrial/Energy prefer:
Industrial Products

In Manufact. prefer:
Manufacturing

Additional Information
Year Founded: 1969
Current Activity Level : Actively seeking new investments

EVERGREEN PACIFIC PARTNERS GP LLC

1700 Seventh Avenue
Suite 2300
Seattle, WA USA 98101
Phone: 2062624709
Fax: 2062624715
E-mail: general@eppcapital.com
Website: www.eppcapital.com

Other Offices
10940 Wilshire Boulevard
Suite 600
Los Angeles, CA USA 90024
Phone: 3104742515
Fax: 3104742816

Management and Staff
Chris Brenes, Vice President
Michael Nibarger, Co-Founder
Thomas McGill, Co-Founder
Timothy Brillon, Chief Financial Officer
Timothy Bernardez, Co-Founder

Type of Firm
Private Equity Firm

Project Preferences

Type of Financing Preferred:
Leveraged Buyout
Expansion
Management Buyouts
Acquisition

Geographical Preferences

United States Preferences:
North America
West Coast

Canadian Preferences:
All Canada

Industry Preferences

In Communications prefer:
CATV & Pay TV Systems
Radio & TV Broadcasting

In Consumer Related prefer:
Consumer Products

In Business Serv. prefer:
Distribution
Media

In Manufact. prefer:
Manufacturing

Additional Information
Name of Most Recent Fund: Evergreen Pacific Partners II, L.P.
Most Recent Fund Was Raised: 08/01/2008
Year Founded: 2003
Capital Under Management: $700,000,000
Current Activity Level : Actively seeking new investments

EVERGREEN VENTURE PARTNERS

25 Habarzel Street
Tel Aviv, Israel 69710
Phone: 97237108282
Fax: 97237108210
E-mail: info@evergreen.co.il
Website: www.evergreen.co.il

Other Offices
Former HQ: 96 Rothschild Boulevard
P.O. Box 14111
Tel Aviv, Israel 65224
Phone: 97237108282
Fax: 97237108210

Management and Staff
Adi Gan, General Partner
Boaz Dinte, General Partner
Erez Shachar, General Partner
Jacob Burak, Founder
Ofer Neeman, Founder
Ronit Bendori, General Partner

Type of Firm
Private Equity Firm

Project Preferences

Role in Financing:
Prefer role as deal originator but will also invest in deals created by others

Type of Financing Preferred:
Early Stage
Expansion
Balanced
Startup

Geographical Preferences

International Preferences:
Israel
Asia

Industry Preferences

In Communications prefer:
Communications and Media

In Computer Software prefer:
Software

In Internet Specific prefer:
Internet

In Medical/Health prefer:
Medical/Health

In Business Serv. prefer:
Media

Additional Information
Name of Most Recent Fund: Evergreen Partners Fund IV, L.P.
Most Recent Fund Was Raised: 09/16/2003
Year Founded: 1987
Capital Under Management: $650,000,000
Current Activity Level : Actively seeking new investments
Method of Compensation: Return on investment is of primary concern, do not charge fees

EVERPINE CAPITAL LTD

No. 93 Huangpu District
Shanghai, China
Phone: 862163235207
Fax: 862163235207
Website: www.everpinecapital.com

Type of Firm
Private Equity Firm

Project Preferences

Type of Financing Preferred:
Leveraged Buyout
Early Stage
Expansion
Later Stage
Management Buyouts
Acquisition

Geographical Preferences

International Preferences:
China
All International

Additional Information
Year Founded: 2014
Current Activity Level : Actively seeking new investments

EVERSTONE CAPITAL MANAGEMENT, LTD.

One Indiabulls Center
16/F,Twr 2A,Jupiter Mills Comp
Mumbai, India 400013
Phone: 912240436000
Website: www.everstonecapital.com

Other Offices
19 Cybercity
Third Floor, Raffles Tower
Ebene, Mauritius
Phone: 2304677986
Fax: 2304648308

Ugland House
George Town, Cayman Islands KY1-1104

250 North Bridge Road
13-01A Raffles City Tower
Singapore, Singapore 179101
Phone: 6565116883
Fax: 6565116899

Management and Staff
Abhijit Malkani, Managing Director
Aloke Bhuniya, Managing Director
Arun Patkie, Managing Director
Ashutosh Lavakare, Chief Financial Officer
Brian Oravec, Partner
Deep Mishra, Managing Director
Jason Breeman, Managing Director
Jaspal Sabarwal, Partner
Joanna Desouza, Managing Director
Kazi Arif Uz Zaman, Managing Director
Pankaj Thapar, Managing Director
Rahul Nair, Managing Director
Roopa Purushothaman, Managing Director
Sanjoy Chatterjee, Chief Operating Officer
Shishir Baijal, Partner

Type of Firm
Investment Management Firm

Association Membership
Singapore Venture Capital Association (SVCA)
Indian Venture Capital Association (IVCA)

Project Preferences

Type of Financing Preferred:
Leveraged Buyout
Early Stage
Expansion
Generalist PE
Balanced
Opportunistic
Later Stage
Management Buyouts
Acquisition

Geographical Preferences

International Preferences:
Asia Pacific
India
Asia

Industry Preferences

In Medical/Health prefer:
Medical/Health
Health Services

In Consumer Related prefer:
Consumer
Entertainment and Leisure
Retail
Consumer Products
Consumer Services
Education Related

In Industrial/Energy prefer:
Energy

In Financial Services prefer:
Real Estate
Financial Services

In Business Serv. prefer:
Media

Additional Information
Name of Most Recent Fund: IndoSpace Logistics Parks II (Cayman), Ltd.
Most Recent Fund Was Raised: 05/21/2013
Year Founded: 2005
Capital Under Management: $1,640,000,000
Current Activity Level: Actively seeking new investments

EVERYOUNG CAPITAL MANAGEMENT CO LTD

#6D08 Shennan Street
10/F, Newspaper Bldg. B
Shenzhen, China 518009
Phone: 86-755-82960701
Fax: 86-755-82960703
E-mail: everyoungw@163.com

Website: www.everyoungcapital.com

Type of Firm
Private Equity Firm

Additional Information
Year Founded: 2001
Current Activity Level: Actively seeking new investments

EVI CAPITAL PARTNERS LLP

Nelson Mandela Square
4th Floor, West Tower
Johannesburg, South Africa 2196
Phone: 27-86-100-0659
E-mail: enquiries@evicap.com
Website: www.evicap.com

Other Offices
Medius House
2 Sheraton Street
London, United Kingdom W1F 8BH
Phone: 44-870-366-9949
Fax: 44-845-862-2198

Management and Staff
Zola Fihlani, CEO & Managing Director

Type of Firm
Private Equity Firm

Project Preferences

Type of Financing Preferred:
Leveraged Buyout
Expansion
Mezzanine
Management Buyouts
Acquisition
Recapitalizations

Size of Investments Considered:
Min Size of Investment Considered (000s): $25,000
Max Size of Investment Considered (000s): $250,000

Geographical Preferences

International Preferences:
Middle East
Africa

Industry Preferences

In Communications prefer:
Telecommunications

In Industrial/Energy prefer:
Energy
Oil and Gas Exploration

In Financial Services prefer:
Financial Services
Real Estate

Additional Information
Year Founded: 2009
Capital Under Management: $100,000,000
Current Activity Level: Actively seeking new investments

EVIA CAPITAL PARTNERS PTE LTD

Eight Eu Tong Sen Street
Suite 20-92 The Central
Singapore, Singapore 059818
Phone: 6565383345
Fax: 6565368129
Website: www.eviacp.com

Management and Staff
Kiam Cheow Low, Partner
Tee Khiang Ng, Partner

Type of Firm
Private Equity Firm

Project Preferences

Type of Financing Preferred:
Early Stage
Expansion
Later Stage

Size of Investments Considered:
Min Size of Investment Considered (000s): $817
Max Size of Investment Considered (000s): $8,169

Geographical Preferences

International Preferences:
Asia
Singapore

Industry Preferences

In Communications prefer:
Communications and Media

In Consumer Related prefer:
Consumer Products
Consumer Services

In Industrial/Energy prefer:
Environmental Related

In Manufact. prefer:
Manufacturing

In Other prefer:
Environment Responsible

Additional Information
Year Founded: 2012
Current Activity Level: Actively seeking new investments

EVO VENTURE PARTNERS

Kabelweg 21
Amsterdam, Netherlands 1014 BA
Website: www.evoventurepartners.com

Management and Staff
Dave Dirks, Managing Partner
Dennis Bruin, Managing Partner
Jaap Goch, Chief Financial Officer
Willem Harmsel, Partner

Type of Firm
Private Equity Firm

Project Preferences

Type of Financing Preferred:
Early Stage
Start-up Financing
Seed

Industry Preferences

In Computer Software prefer:
Data Processing
Software

Additional Information
Year Founded: 2014
Current Activity Level : Actively seeking new investments

EVOK INNOVATIONS

200 - 560 Beatty Street
Vancouver, Canada V6B 2L3
E-mail: info@evokinnovations.com
Website: www.evokinnovations.com

Type of Firm
Incubator/Development Program

Project Preferences

Type of Financing Preferred:
Early Stage

Geographical Preferences

Canadian Preferences:
All Canada

Industry Preferences

In Other prefer:
Environment Responsible

Additional Information
Year Founded: 2016
Capital Under Management: $69,650,000
Current Activity Level : Actively seeking new investments

EVOLEM 2 SAS

6, quai Saint Antoine
CS 60026
Lyon, France 69289
Phone: 33472689800
Fax: 33472689809
E-mail: contact@evolem.fr
Website: www.evolem.fr

Other Offices
11, rue de la Rpublique
Lyon, France 69281
Phone: 33472689800
Fax: 33472689809

Type of Firm
Private Equity Firm

Association Membership
French Venture Capital Association (AFIC)

Project Preferences

Type of Financing Preferred:
Leveraged Buyout
Later Stage
Management Buyouts

Size of Investments Considered:
Min Size of Investment Considered (000s): $1,307
Max Size of Investment Considered (000s): $19,618

Geographical Preferences

International Preferences:
Europe
France

Industry Preferences

In Communications prefer:
Communications and Media
Commercial Communications

In Medical/Health prefer:
Medical/Health
Medical Therapeutics

In Business Serv. prefer:
Services

Additional Information
Year Founded: 2002
Current Activity Level : Actively seeking new investments

EVOLUTION CAPITAL PARTNERS LLC

3333 Richmond Road
Suite 480
Cleveland, OH USA 44122
Phone: 2165930402
Fax: 2165930403
Website: www.evolutioncp.com

Other Offices
Former HQ: 29325 Chagrin Boulevard
Suite 302
WARRENSVILLE HEIGHTS, OH USA 44122
Phone: 2165930402
Fax: 2165930403

105 West Adams Street
Suite 2125
CHICAGO, IL USA 60603
Phone: 3122635080

Management and Staff
Brendan Anderson, Co-Founder
Gary Kunkle, Partner
Gene Marino, Partner
Jeffrey Kadlic, Co-Founder
Marlene Tehi, Chief Financial Officer

Type of Firm
Private Equity Firm

Association Membership
Natl Assoc of Small Bus. Inv. Co (NASBIC)

Project Preferences

Type of Financing Preferred:
Leveraged Buyout
Turnaround
Management Buyouts
Acquisition
Recapitalizations

Geographical Preferences

United States Preferences:
Midwest
Ohio
All U.S.

Additional Information
Name of Most Recent Fund: Evolution Investments II LLC
Most Recent Fund Was Raised: 01/21/2011
Year Founded: 2005
Capital Under Management: $240,400,000
Current Activity Level : Actively seeking new investments

EVOLUTION CORPORATE ADVISORS LLC

515 Madison Avenue
Suite 1500
New York, NY USA 10022
Phone: 2128885826
Fax: 6465367136
E-mail: info@evolutionadvisorsllc.com
Website: www.evolutionadvisorsllc.com

Management and Staff
Gregg Smith, Founder

Type of Firm
Incubator/Development Program

Project Preferences

Type of Financing Preferred:
Early Stage

Industry Preferences

In Communications prefer:
Telecommunications

In Medical/Health prefer:
Health Services

In Consumer Related prefer:
Consumer
Retail

In Industrial/Energy prefer:
Energy

Additional Information
Year Founded: 2007
Current Activity Level : Actively seeking new investments

EVOLUTION EQUITY PARTNERS GMBH

Genferstrasse 23
Zurich, Switzerland 8002
E-mail: info@evolutionequity.com
Website: www.evolutionequity.com

Type of Firm
Private Equity Firm

Project Preferences

Type of Financing Preferred:
Balanced

Geographical Preferences

United States Preferences:

International Preferences:
Switzerland

Additional Information
Year Founded: 2008
Capital Under Management: $70,000,000
Current Activity Level : Actively seeking new investments

EVOLUTION MEDIA PARTNERS

2000 Avenue of the Stars
Los Angeles, CA USA 90067
E-mail: info@evolutionmediacapital.com
Website: www.evolutionmediacapital.com

Type of Firm
Investment Management Firm

Project Preferences

Type of Financing Preferred:
Balanced

Industry Preferences

In Communications prefer:
Entertainment

In Internet Specific prefer:
E-Commerce Technology

In Business Serv. prefer:
Distribution
Media

Additional Information
Year Founded: 2008
Current Activity Level : Actively seeking new investments

EVOLUTION PARTNERS PARTICIPACOES SA

R Florida 1670
Conj 52, Cidade Moncoes
Sao Paulo, Brazil 04565001
Phone: 551138114562

Type of Firm
Private Equity Firm

Association Membership
Brazilian Venture Capital Association (ABCR)

Project Preferences

Type of Financing Preferred:
Early Stage
Balanced
Seed
Startup

Geographical Preferences

International Preferences:
Brazil

Additional Information
Year Founded: 2011
Current Activity Level : Actively seeking new investments

EVOLUTION VENTURE CAPITAL FUND I ISRAEL LP

32A Habarzel Street
Tel Aviv, Israel 69710
Phone: 97237686776
Fax: 97236484104
E-mail: info@evolutionvc.com
Website: www.evolutionvc.com

Management and Staff
Zohar Alon, Venture Partner

Type of Firm
Private Equity Firm

Project Preferences

Type of Financing Preferred:
Expansion
Later Stage

Geographical Preferences

International Preferences:
Israel
Asia

Additional Information
Year Founded: 2006
Current Activity Level : Actively seeking new investments

EVOLVE CAPITAL LTD

2200 Ross Avenue
Suite 4050
Dallas, TX USA 75201
Phone: 2142204800
E-mail: evolve@evolvecapital.com
Website: www.evolvecapital.com

Management and Staff
Mike Crothers, Founder

Type of Firm
Private Equity Firm

Project Preferences

Type of Financing Preferred:
Leveraged Buyout
Expansion
Balanced
Acquisition
Recapitalizations

Industry Preferences

In Communications prefer:
Wireless Communications

In Semiconductor/Electr prefer:
Electronics

In Biotechnology prefer:
Biotechnology

In Medical/Health prefer:
Medical/Health

In Transportation prefer:
Transportation

In Business Serv. prefer:
Services

Additional Information
Year Founded: 2005
Current Activity Level : Actively seeking new investments

EVOLVENCE CAPITAL LTD

Sheik Zayed Road, Level 15
Park Place Tower
Dubai, Utd. Arab Em.
Phone: 97143158100
Fax: 97143296500
E-mail: info@evolvence.com
Website: www.evolvence.com

Other Offices

150 East 58th Street, 14th Floor
New York, NY USA 10155

8th Floor, Narain Manzil
Barakhamba Road
New Delhi, India 110 001
Phone: 91-11-4151-9292
Fax: 91-11-4151-9393

Management and Staff

Ajit Kumar, Managing Director
Benjamin Lee, Managing Director
Ezaldeen El-Araj, Chief Financial Officer
Nitin Kripalani, Vice President
Paresh Thakker, Managing Director
Robert Pardi, Chief Operating Officer
Rohit Batra, Vice President

Type of Firm

Private Equity Firm

Project Preferences

Type of Financing Preferred:
Fund of Funds
Leveraged Buyout
Early Stage
Expansion
Unknown
Generalist PE
Balanced
Later Stage
Other
Seed
Management Buyouts
Acquisition

Geographical Preferences

International Preferences:
India
Middle East
Asia

Industry Preferences

In Biotechnology prefer:
Biotechnology

In Medical/Health prefer:
Medical/Health
Medical Products
Health Services
Hospital/Other Instit.
Pharmaceuticals

In Consumer Related prefer:
Education Related

In Financial Services prefer:
Real Estate

In Utilities prefer:
Utilities

Additional Information

Year Founded: 2000
Capital Under Management: $144,095,000
Current Activity Level : Actively seeking new investments

EVOLVER INVESTMENT GROUP LTD

Torggatan 5
4th floor
Mariehamn, Finland 22100
Phone: 358405491518
Fax: 3581822107
Website: evolver.ax

Management and Staff

Erik Flodin, Partner
Lars Porko, Co-Founder
Lasse Aspback, Co-Founder
Pentti Kulmala, Co-Founder
Peter Lindstrom, Co-Founder

Type of Firm

Private Equity Firm

Project Preferences

Type of Financing Preferred:
Leveraged Buyout

Geographical Preferences

International Preferences:
Sweden
Finland

Industry Preferences

In Consumer Related prefer:
Consumer Products

In Industrial/Energy prefer:
Industrial Products

In Manufact. prefer:
Manufacturing

Additional Information

Year Founded: 2009
Current Activity Level : Actively seeking new investments

EVOLVERE CAPITAL SAS

Calle 79B No. 8-21floor 3
Bogota D.C., Colombia 110221
Phone: 34627451993

E-mail: info@evolverecapital.com
Website: www.evolverecapital.com

Type of Firm

Private Equity Firm

Project Preferences

Type of Financing Preferred:
Leveraged Buyout
Acquisition

Geographical Preferences

International Preferences:
Peru
Colombia

Additional Information

Year Founded: 2012
Current Activity Level : Actively seeking new investments

EW HEALTHCARE PARTNERS

335 Bryant Street
Third Floor
Palo Alto, CA USA 94301
Phone: 6505431555
Fax: 6503279755
E-mail: paloalto@ewhv.com
Website: www.essexwoodlands.com

Other Offices

Suite 522, Shanghai Centre
1376 Nanjing Road West
Shanghai, China 200040
Phone: 862162898770
Fax: 862162898779

21 Waterway Avenue
Suite 225
SHENANDOAH, TX USA 77380
Phone: 2813641555
Fax: 2813649755

280 Park Avenue
27th Floor East
MANHATTAN, NY USA 10017
Phone: 6464291251
Fax: 2129220551

Berkeley Square House
Berkeley Square
London, United Kingdom W1J 6BR
Phone: 44-20-7529-2500
Fax: 44-20-7529-2501

Management and Staff

Brooks Andrews, Vice President
C. Thomas Caskey, Partner
Evis Hursever, Principal
Frank Young, Partner
Immanuel Thangaraj, Managing Director
James Currie, Co-Founder
Jeffrey Himawan, Managing Director
Martin Sutter, Managing Director
Peter Lafer, Vice President
Petri Vainio, Managing Director
Richard Kolodziejcyk, Chief Financial Officer
Ronald Eastman, Managing Director
Scott Barry, Managing Director
Shaunak Parikh, Vice President
Steve Wiggins, Managing Director
Toby Sykes, Managing Director

Type of Firm
Private Equity Firm

Project Preferences

Role in Financing:
Prefer role as deal originator but will also invest in deals created by others

Type of Financing Preferred:
Leveraged Buyout
Early Stage
Expansion
Balanced
Later Stage
Seed
Acquisition

Size of Investments Considered:
Min Size of Investment Considered (000s): $20,000
Max Size of Investment Considered (000s): $60,000

Geographical Preferences

United States Preferences:

International Preferences:
Latin America
Europe
Asia

Industry Focus

(% based on actual investment)

Industry	%
Medical/Health	49.7%
Biotechnology	40.7%
Computer Software and Services	5.2%
Internet Specific	2.1%
Consumer Related	1.4%
Communications and Media	0.7%
Other Products	0.3%
Industrial/Energy	0.1%

Additional Information

Name of Most Recent Fund: Essex Woodlands Health Ventures Fund VIII, L.P.
Most Recent Fund Was Raised: 02/11/2008
Year Founded: 1985
Capital Under Management: $2,500,000,000
Current Activity Level: Actively seeking new investments
Method of Compensation: Return on investment is of primary concern, do not charge fees

EXCEL VENTURE MANAGEMENT

800 Boylston Street
Suite 2825
Boston, MA USA 02199
Phone: 6174509800
Fax: 6174509749
E-mail: info@excelvm.com
Website: www.excelvm.com

Management and Staff

Enrico Petrillo, Managing Director
Frederick Blume, Managing Director
Gaye Bok, Venture Partner
Jeanne Henry, Chief Financial Officer
Juan Enriquez, Managing Director
Steven Gullans, Managing Director

Type of Firm
Private Equity Firm

Association Membership
New England Venture Capital Association
National Venture Capital Association - USA (NVCA)

Project Preferences

Role in Financing:
Will function either as deal originator or investor in deals created by others

Type of Financing Preferred:
Early Stage
Balanced
Later Stage

Size of Investments Considered:
Min Size of Investment Considered (000s): $1,000
Max Size of Investment Considered (000s): $5,000

Industry Preferences

In Medical/Health prefer:
Medical/Health
Medical Diagnostics
Medical Products
Health Services

Additional Information

Name of Most Recent Fund: Excel Medical Fund
Most Recent Fund Was Raised: 02/15/2008
Year Founded: 2007
Capital Under Management: $100,000,000
Current Activity Level: Actively seeking new investments

EXCELERATE HEALTH VENTURES LLC

Two Davis Drive
Suite 105
Durham, NC USA 27709
Phone: 9199601540
E-mail: info@exceleratehealth.com
Website: www.exceleratehealth.com

Management and Staff

Bobby Bahram, Managing Partner
Cam Patterson, Venture Partner
Gary Abrahams, Managing Partner

Type of Firm
Private Equity Firm

Project Preferences

Type of Financing Preferred:
Early Stage
Seed
Startup

Geographical Preferences

United States Preferences:
Southeast
North Carolina

Industry Preferences

In Computer Software prefer:
Software

In Medical/Health prefer:
Medical/Health
Medical Products

In Business Serv. prefer:
Services

Additional Information

Name of Most Recent Fund: Physician Fund, L.P.
Most Recent Fund Was Raised: 07/01/2013
Year Founded: 2013
Capital Under Management: $6,900,000
Current Activity Level: Actively seeking new investments

EXCELESTAR VENTURES

One Elm Square
Andover, MA USA 01810
Phone: 9782965270
Fax: 9782965259
Website: www.excelestarventures.com

Management and Staff

Tasneem Dohadwala, General Partner

Type of Firm
Private Equity Firm

Project Preferences

Type of Financing Preferred:
Expansion
Later Stage

Additional Information

Year Founded: 2011
Current Activity Level : Actively seeking new investments

EXCELL PARTNERS INC

343 State Street
Second Floor
Rochester, NY USA 14650
Phone: 5854587333
Fax: 58545873333
E-mail: info@excellny.com
Website: www.excellny.com

Management and Staff

Rami Katz, Chief Operating Officer

Type of Firm

Private Equity Firm

Project Preferences

Type of Financing Preferred:
Seed
Startup

Size of Investments Considered:
Min Size of Investment Considered (000s): $50
Max Size of Investment Considered (000s): $350

Geographical Preferences

United States Preferences:
New York

Additional Information

Name of Most Recent Fund: Excell Innovate NY Fund, L.P.
Most Recent Fund Was Raised: 12/31/2012
Year Founded: 2005
Capital Under Management: $10,000,000
Current Activity Level : Actively seeking new investments

EXCELLERE CAPITAL MANAGEMENT LLC

3033 East First Avenue
Suite 700
Denver, CO USA 80206
Phone: 3037652400
Fax: 3037652411
Website: www.excellerepartners.com

Other Offices

100 Fillmore Street, Suite 300
Denver, CO USA 80206
Phone: 3037652400
Fax: 3037652411

Management and Staff

Brad Cornell, Partner
David Kessenich, Managing Partner
Eric Mattson, Principal
John Lanier, Partner
Justin Unertl, Vice President
Matthew Hicks, Partner
Michael Geldart, Partner
Nate Raulin, Vice President
Patrick O Keefe, Principal
Robert Martin, Managing Partner
Ryan Glaws, Partner
Scott Friar, Vice President

Type of Firm

Private Equity Firm

Project Preferences

Type of Financing Preferred:
Leveraged Buyout
Management Buyouts
Acquisition
Recapitalizations

Geographical Preferences

United States Preferences:

Industry Preferences

In Computer Software prefer:
Data Processing
Software

In Medical/Health prefer:
Medical/Health
Diagnostic Services
Health Services
Hospitals/Clinics/Primary
Pharmaceuticals

In Consumer Related prefer:
Food/Beverage

In Industrial/Energy prefer:
Energy
Oil and Gas Exploration
Industrial Products

In Business Serv. prefer:
Services
Distribution

In Utilities prefer:
Utilities

Additional Information

Name of Most Recent Fund: Excellere Capital Fund II, L.P.
Most Recent Fund Was Raised: 12/22/2010
Year Founded: 2006
Capital Under Management: $730,000,000
Current Activity Level : Actively seeking new investments

EXEO CAPITAL

Barinors Vineyard South
Bellville, South Africa 7530
Phone: 219138950
E-mail: office@exeocapital.com
Website: www.exeocapital.com

Type of Firm

Private Equity Firm

Geographical Preferences

International Preferences:
South Africa

Additional Information

Year Founded: 2013
Current Activity Level : Actively seeking new investments

EXFINITY VENTURE PARTNERS LLP

Sukh Sagar, 5th A Block
Pragati Mansion, 12, 3rd Floor
Bangalore, India 560095
Phone: 918043420700
Fax: 918043420719
E-mail: info@reservoir.co.in
Website: exfinityventures.com

Other Offices

Millers Road, Grace Towers
No. 70, 2nd and 3rd Floor
Bangalore, India 560052

Type of Firm

Private Equity Firm

Project Preferences

Type of Financing Preferred:
Early Stage
Startup

Industry Preferences

In Communications prefer:
Telecommunications

In Internet Specific prefer:
Ecommerce

In Medical/Health prefer:
Medical/Health

In Consumer Related prefer:
Retail
Education Related

In Manufact. prefer:
Manufacturing

Additional Information
Year Founded: 2013
Capital Under Management: $81,554,000
Current Activity Level : Actively seeking new investments

EXHILWAY GLOBAL

Two Allen Center
1200 Smith Street, 16th floor
Houston, TX USA 77002
Phone: 01204804938
E-mail: investor@exhilway.com
Website: www.exhilway.com

Other Offices
SB Tower, 5th floor, Sector 16A
New Okhla, Industrial Development Area
Uttar Pradesh, India 201301
Phone: 0120 480 4938

Type of Firm
Private Equity Firm

Project Preferences

Type of Financing Preferred:
Leveraged Buyout
Acquisition

Geographical Preferences

United States Preferences:

International Preferences:
Indonesia
Kazakhstan
Turkey
Peru
Ukraine
Asia
Africa

Industry Preferences

In Consumer Related prefer:
Retail

In Business Serv. prefer:
Services
Media

In Agr/Forestr/Fish prefer:
Mining and Minerals

Additional Information
Name of Most Recent Fund: Exhilway Global Opportunities Fund, L.P.
Most Recent Fund Was Raised: 11/20/2013
Year Founded: 1974
Capital Under Management: $200,000,000
Current Activity Level : Actively seeking new investments

EXIGENT CAPITAL MANAGEMENT LLC

250 Park Avenue
New York, NY USA 10177
Phone: 6465069450
E-mail: info@exigentcap.com
Website: www.exigent.capital

Other Offices
5 Wyndham Deedes
Jerusalem, Israel 93106

Type of Firm
Private Equity Firm

Project Preferences

Type of Financing Preferred:
Generalist PE

Additional Information
Year Founded: 2009
Current Activity Level : Actively seeking new investments

EXIGENT VENTURES INC

2202 Timberloch Place
Suite 118
Spring, TX USA 77380
Phone: 2813630363
Fax: 2813639079
Website: www.exigentventures.com

Type of Firm
Private Equity Firm

Project Preferences

Type of Financing Preferred:
Balanced

Industry Preferences

In Financial Services prefer:
Financial Services

Additional Information
Year Founded: 2012
Current Activity Level : Actively seeking new investments

EXIUM PARTNERS LLC

144 Village Landing
Suite 276
Fairport, NY USA 14450
Phone: 8889839486
E-mail: info@exiumpartners.com
Website: www.exiumpartners.com

Type of Firm
Private Equity Firm

Project Preferences

Type of Financing Preferred:
Leveraged Buyout
Recapitalizations

Geographical Preferences

United States Preferences:

Canadian Preferences:
All Canada

Industry Preferences

In Communications prefer:
Telecommunications

In Computer Software prefer:
Software

In Financial Services prefer:
Financial Services

In Business Serv. prefer:
Services
Media

In Manufact. prefer:
Manufacturing

Additional Information
Year Founded: 2013
Current Activity Level : Actively seeking new investments

EXMARQ CAPITAL PARTNERS INC

5850 Opus Parkway
Suite 240
Hopkins, MN USA 55343
Phone: 9527674000
Website: www.exmarqcapital.com

Management and Staff
Dale Olsen, Principal
Ryan McKinney, President
Steve Morgan, Principal
Wes Olsen, Principal

Type of Firm
Private Equity Firm

Project Preferences

Type of Financing Preferred:
Expansion
Management Buyouts
Recapitalizations

Geographical Preferences

United States Preferences:
Midwest

Industry Preferences

In Business Serv. prefer:
Services
Distribution

In Manufact. prefer:
Manufacturing

Additional Information

Year Founded: 2011
Current Activity Level : Actively seeking new investments

EXPA CAPITAL LLC

555 Mission Street
Suite 1850
San Francisco, CA USA 94105
Phone: 4155006680
Website: www.expa.com

Type of Firm
Private Equity Firm

Project Preferences

Type of Financing Preferred:
Seed
Startup

Industry Preferences

In Communications prefer:
Wireless Communications

In Computer Software prefer:
Applications Software

Additional Information
Name of Most Recent Fund: Expa Capital LLC
Most Recent Fund Was Raised: 03/14/2014
Year Founded: 2014
Capital Under Management: $150,000,000
Current Activity Level : Actively seeking new investments

EXPANSINVEST SASU

2, Avenue Du Gresivaudan
Corenc, France 38700
Phone: 33405072638
Website: www.expansinvest.fr

Type of Firm
Bank Affiliated

Project Preferences

Type of Financing Preferred:
Leveraged Buyout
Early Stage
Generalist PE
Later Stage
Acquisition
Startup

Size of Investments Considered:
Min Size of Investment Considered (000s): $127
Max Size of Investment Considered (000s): $381

Geographical Preferences

International Preferences:
France

Industry Preferences

In Medical/Health prefer:
Medical/Health
Health Services

In Business Serv. prefer:
Services

Additional Information
Year Founded: 2003
Current Activity Level : Actively seeking new investments

EXPANSION CAPITAL PARTNERS LLC

30 Old Kings Highway South
Darien, CT USA 06820
E-mail: info@expansioncapital.com
Website: www.expansioncapital.com

Other Offices

140 Rowayton Avenue
Second floor
Norwalk, CT USA 06853

1350 Avenue of the Americas
29th floor
New York, NY USA 10019
Phone: 212-786-7408
Fax: 646-514-8492

Two Summer Street
Suite Two
Natick, MA USA 01760
Phone: 508-651-2277

Management and Staff
Bernardo Llovera, General Partner

Type of Firm
Private Equity Firm

Project Preferences

Role in Financing:
Prefer role as deal originator

Type of Financing Preferred:
Expansion
Later Stage

Geographical Preferences

United States Preferences:
North America

Canadian Preferences:
All Canada

Industry Preferences

In Industrial/Energy prefer:
Alternative Energy
Advanced Materials
Environmental Related

In Transportation prefer:
Transportation

In Manufact. prefer:
Manufacturing

Additional Information
Name of Most Recent Fund: Clean Technology Fund II, L.P.
Most Recent Fund Was Raised: 09/30/2005
Year Founded: 2002
Capital Under Management: $103,100,000
Current Activity Level : Actively seeking new investments
Method of Compensation: Return on investment is of primary concern, do not charge fees

EXPANSO CAPITAL SAS

25, cours du Marechal Foch
Bordeaux, France 33076
Phone: 33556008610
Fax: 33556815715
E-mail: contact@expanso.com
Website: www.expanso.com

Type of Firm
Private Equity Firm

Project Preferences

Type of Financing Preferred:
Early Stage
Later Stage
Startup

Size of Investments Considered:
Min Size of Investment Considered (000s): $65
Max Size of Investment Considered (000s): $392

Geographical Preferences

International Preferences:
France

Industry Preferences

In Industrial/Energy prefer:
Industrial Products

In Financial Services prefer:
Real Estate

In Business Serv. prefer:
Services

Additional Information
Year Founded: 1957
Capital Under Management: $13,100,000
Current Activity Level : Actively seeking new investments

EXPARA PTE LTD

Blk 71 Ayer Rajah Crescent
Suite 02-10/11
Singapore, Singapore 139951
Phone: 6563233084
Fax: 6568733120
E-mail: inquiries@expara.com
Website: expara.com

Type of Firm
Incubator/Development Program

Project Preferences

Type of Financing Preferred:
Seed
Startup

Geographical Preferences

United States Preferences:
Southeast

International Preferences:
Thailand
Malaysia

Industry Preferences

In Business Serv. prefer:
Media

Additional Information
Year Founded: 2015
Current Activity Level : Actively seeking new investments

EXPEDITION CAPITAL PARTNERS LLC

2918 North Sheffield Avenue
Suite 1S
Chicago, IL USA 60657
Phone: 7738570210
Website: www.expedition-partners.com

Management and Staff
Busn Helzberg, Managing Partner

Type of Firm
Private Equity Firm

Project Preferences

Type of Financing Preferred:
Leveraged Buyout
Acquisition
Recapitalizations

Geographical Preferences

United States Preferences:

Canadian Preferences:
All Canada

Industry Preferences

In Medical/Health prefer:
Health Services

In Consumer Related prefer:
Consumer Products
Consumer Services
Education Related

In Business Serv. prefer:
Services
Distribution

In Manufact. prefer:
Manufacturing

Additional Information
Year Founded: 2010
Current Activity Level : Actively seeking new investments

EXPERIENCED CAPITAL MANAGEMENT SAS

174, Rue de Rivoli
Paris, France 75001
Phone: 33140137213
Website: www.excp.com

Type of Firm
Private Equity Firm

Project Preferences

Type of Financing Preferred:
Leveraged Buyout
Early Stage
Expansion
Later Stage
Management Buyouts
Acquisition

Size of Investments Considered:
Min Size of Investment Considered (000s): $2,244
Max Size of Investment Considered (000s): $22,437

Industry Preferences

In Consumer Related prefer:
Entertainment and Leisure
Food/Beverage
Consumer Products
Consumer Services

Additional Information
Year Founded: 2016
Capital Under Management: $45,120,000
Current Activity Level : Actively seeking new investments

EXPLORER GROUP, THE

1327 North Carolan Avenue
Burlingame, CA USA 94010
Website: www.theexplorergroup.com

Type of Firm
Private Equity Firm

Project Preferences

Type of Financing Preferred:
Early Stage

Additional Information
Year Founded: 2015
Current Activity Level : Actively seeking new investments

EXPLORER INVESTMENTS SOCIEDADE DE CAPITAL DE RISCO SA

Avenida Eng. Duarte Pacheco
26, 8th Floor
Lisbon, Portugal 1070110
Phone: 351213241820
Fax: 351213241829
E-mail: explorer@explorerinvestments.com
Website: www.explorerinvestments.com

Management and Staff
Elizabeth Rothfield, Partner
Marco Lebre, Partner
Rodrigo Guimaraes, Partner

Type of Firm
Private Equity Firm

Association Membership
Portuguese Venture Capital Association (APCRI)
European Private Equity and Venture Capital Assoc.

Project Preferences

Type of Financing Preferred:
Leveraged Buyout
Expansion
Acquisition

Geographical Preferences

International Preferences:
Europe
Portugal
Spain

Additional Information
Name of Most Recent Fund: Explorer III
Most Recent Fund Was Raised: 12/31/2011
Year Founded: 2003
Capital Under Management: $720,500,000
Current Activity Level : Actively seeking new investments

EXPON CAPITAL SARL

13-15, Parc dActivites Capelle
Capellen, Luxembourg 8308
Website: www.exponcapital.com

Type of Firm
Private Equity Firm

Project Preferences

Type of Financing Preferred:
Early Stage
Seed

Geographical Preferences

International Preferences:
Europe

Industry Preferences

In Communications prefer:
Telecommunications

In Computer Software prefer:
Software

In Internet Specific prefer:
E-Commerce Technology
Internet
Ecommerce

In Business Serv. prefer:
Media

Additional Information
Year Founded: 2015
Capital Under Management: $22,560,000
Current Activity Level : Actively seeking new investments

EXPONENT PRIVATE EQUITY LLP

12 Henrietta Street
London, United Kingdom WC2E 8LH
Phone: 442078458520
Fax: 442078458521
E-mail: info@exponentpe.com
Website: www.exponentpe.com

Management and Staff
Chris Graham, Co-Founder
Hugh Richards, Co-Founder
Richard Campin, Co-Founder
Simon Davidson, Partner
Tom Sweet-Escott, Co-Founder

Type of Firm
Private Equity Firm

Association Membership
British Venture Capital Association (BVCA)

Project Preferences

Type of Financing Preferred:
Leveraged Buyout
Management Buyouts
Acquisition

Size of Investments Considered:
Min Size of Investment Considered (000s): $29,586
Max Size of Investment Considered (000s): $147,930

Geographical Preferences

International Preferences:
United Kingdom
Europe

Industry Preferences

In Communications prefer:
Media and Entertainment

In Medical/Health prefer:
Medical/Health
Health Services

In Financial Services prefer:
Financial Services

In Business Serv. prefer:
Services
Media

Additional Information
Name of Most Recent Fund: Exponent Private Equity Partners
Most Recent Fund Was Raised: 08/13/2004
Year Founded: 2004
Capital Under Management: $1,467,000,000
Current Activity Level : Actively seeking new investments

EXPONENTIA CAPITAL PARTNERS LLP

407, Trade Center
Bandra Kurla Complex
Mumbai, India 400 098
Phone: 912261945555
Fax: 912261955599
E-mail: contact@exponentia.in
Website: www.exponentiacap.com

Management and Staff
P.R. Srinivasan, CEO & Managing Director

Type of Firm
Private Equity Firm

Association Membership
Indian Venture Capital Association (IVCA)

Project Preferences

Type of Financing Preferred:
Balanced

Size of Investments Considered:
Min Size of Investment Considered (000s): $9,479
Max Size of Investment Considered (000s): $28,436

Geographical Preferences

International Preferences:
India

Additional Information
Year Founded: 2010
Current Activity Level : Actively seeking new investments

EXPORT DEVELOPMENT CANADA

150 Slater Street
Ottawa, Canada K1A 1K3
Phone: 6135982500
Website: www.edc.ca

Type of Firm
Government Affiliated Program

Association Membership
Emerging Markets Private Equity Association
Canadian Venture Capital Association

Project Preferences

Type of Financing Preferred:
Early Stage
Expansion

Geographical Preferences

United States Preferences:
All U.S.

Canadian Preferences:
All Canada

Additional Information
Year Founded: 1994
Capital Under Management: $1,896,000,000
Current Activity Level : Actively seeking new investments

EXPORT VENTURE CAPITAL CORPORATION (PTY) LTD

5 Roodehek Street,
10 Het Atelier
Cape Town, South Africa 8001
Phone: 27-21-462-7862
Fax: 27-21-462-7863
E-mail: info@exportcapital.co.za
Website: www.exportcapital.co.za

Other Offices
Mill Street
PO Box 12842
, South Africa 8010

Management and Staff
Pieter Wesselink, Managing Director

Type of Firm
Private Equity Firm

Project Preferences

Type of Financing Preferred:
Leveraged Buyout
Early Stage
Later Stage
Seed
Management Buyouts
First Stage Financing
Startup

Geographical Preferences

International Preferences:
South Africa

Industry Preferences

In Business Serv. prefer:
Services

Additional Information
Year Founded: 2003
Current Activity Level : Actively seeking new investments

EXTENDAM SA
79, rue La Boetie
Paris, France 75008
Website: www.extendam.com

Management and Staff
Matthieu Dracs, Chief Executive Officer

Type of Firm
Private Equity Firm

Project Preferences

Type of Financing Preferred:
Core
Leveraged Buyout
Value-Add
Early Stage
Expansion
Opportunistic
Later Stage
Acquisition

Geographical Preferences

International Preferences:
France

Industry Preferences

In Consumer Related prefer:
Hotels and Resorts

In Financial Services prefer:
Real Estate

Additional Information
Year Founded: 2012
Current Activity Level : Actively seeking new investments

EXTENS SASU
14, Avenue de l'Opera
Paris, France 75001
Website: www.extens.eu

Type of Firm
Private Equity Firm

Project Preferences

Type of Financing Preferred:
Early Stage
Expansion
Later Stage

Geographical Preferences

International Preferences:
United Kingdom
Germany
France

Industry Preferences

In Computer Software prefer:
Software

In Internet Specific prefer:
Internet

In Medical/Health prefer:
Medical Diagnostics
Medical Therapeutics
Medical Products

Additional Information
Year Founded: 2013
Current Activity Level : Actively seeking new investments

EXTO PARTNERS PTY LTD
19A Boundary Street
Suite 302
Rushcutters Bay, Sydney, Australia 2011
Phone: 61293320600
Fax: 61293322862
E-mail: info@extopartners.com
Website: www.extopartners.com

Management and Staff
H. William Deane, Co-Founder
Peter Hammond, Managing Director

Type of Firm
Private Equity Firm

Project Preferences

Type of Financing Preferred:
Expansion
Balanced
Later Stage

Size of Investments Considered:
Min Size of Investment Considered (000s): $386
Max Size of Investment Considered (000s): $7,711

Industry Preferences

In Biotechnology prefer:
Biotechnology

In Medical/Health prefer:
Health Services

In Consumer Related prefer:
Consumer Services
Education Related

In Industrial/Energy prefer:
Energy
Industrial Products

Additional Information
Year Founded: 2003
Capital Under Management: $34,700,000
Current Activity Level : Actively seeking new investments

EXTOL CAPITAL
190 N. Canon Drive
Beverly Hills, CA USA 90210
E-mail: kenan@extolcap.com
Website: www.extolcap.com

Type of Firm
Private Equity Firm

Project Preferences

Type of Financing Preferred:
Generalist PE

Geographical Preferences

United States Preferences:

International Preferences:
China

Industry Preferences

In Communications prefer:
Entertainment

In Business Serv. prefer:
Media

Additional Information
Year Founded: 2016
Current Activity Level : Actively seeking new investments

EXTOREL GMBH

Nussbaumstrasse 12
Munich, Germany 80336
Phone: 4989207030
Fax: 492890703398
E-mail: info@extorel.de
Website: www.extorel.de

Management and Staff
Falk F. Strascheg, Founding Partner
Mathias Lindermeir, Chief Executive Officer

Type of Firm
Private Equity Advisor or Fund of Funds

Association Membership
European Private Equity and Venture Capital Assoc.

Project Preferences

Type of Financing Preferred:
Fund of Funds
Early Stage
Later Stage
Seed
Startup

Size of Investments Considered:
Min Size of Investment Considered (000s): $342,091
Max Size of Investment Considered: No Limit

Geographical Preferences

United States Preferences:
All U.S.

International Preferences:
Europe
Switzerland
Austria
Israel
Germany

Industry Preferences

In Communications prefer:
Communications and Media

In Internet Specific prefer:
Internet

In Computer Other prefer:
Computer Related

In Semiconductor/Electr prefer:
Electronics

In Medical/Health prefer:
Medical/Health

Additional Information
Year Founded: 1997
Capital Under Management: $470,800,000
Current Activity Level : Actively seeking new investments

EXTREMADURA AVANTE SL

Avda. Jose Fernandez Lopez, 4
Merida, Spain 06800
Phone: 34924319159
Fax: 34924319212
E-mail: informacion@sofiex.es
Website: www.sofiex.es

Type of Firm
Government Affiliated Program

Association Membership
Spanish Venture Capital Association (ASCRI)

Project Preferences

Type of Financing Preferred:
Expansion
Balanced
Startup

Geographical Preferences

International Preferences:
Europe
Spain

Industry Preferences

In Computer Software prefer:
Computer Services

In Biotechnology prefer:
Agricultural/Animal Bio.

In Consumer Related prefer:
Food/Beverage

In Industrial/Energy prefer:
Industrial Products
Machinery

In Business Serv. prefer:
Services

In Agr/Forestr/Fish prefer:
Agriculture related

Additional Information
Year Founded: 1987
Current Activity Level : Actively seeking new investments

EXTREME STARTUPS

69 Yonge Street
Suite 600
Toronto, Canada M5E 1K3
E-mail: info@extremestartups.com
Website: www.extremestartups.com

Type of Firm
Incubator/Development Program

Project Preferences

Type of Financing Preferred:
Seed
Startup

Geographical Preferences

United States Preferences:
All U.S.

Canadian Preferences:
All Canada

Additional Information
Name of Most Recent Fund: Extreme Startups
Most Recent Fund Was Raised: 01/31/2012
Year Founded: 2012
Capital Under Management: $7,000,000
Current Activity Level : Actively seeking new investments

EXTREME VENTURE PARTNERS INC

69 Yonge Street
Suite 600
Toronto, Canada M5E 1K3
Website: www.extremevp.com

Other Offices
170A University Avenue
Palo Alto, CA USA 94301

Management and Staff
Amar Varma, Managing Partner
Imran Bashir, Partner
Ken Teslia, Partner
Ray Sharma, Partner
Sundeep Madra, Managing Partner

Type of Firm
Private Equity Firm

Project Preferences

Type of Financing Preferred:
Early Stage
Seed

Geographical Preferences

Canadian Preferences:
All Canada

Industry Preferences

In Communications prefer:
Wireless Communications

In Computer Software prefer:
Software

In Internet Specific prefer:
Internet

In Semiconductor/Electr prefer:
Analytic/Scientific

Additional Information
Year Founded: 2008
Current Activity Level : Actively seeking new investments

EZDEHAR MANAGEMENT

Km 22 Cairo Alex Desert Road
Giza, Egypt
Phone: 20235362915
E-mail: Info@ezdehar.com
Website: www.ezdehar.com

Type of Firm
Private Equity Firm

Project Preferences

Type of Financing Preferred:
Early Stage
Seed

Geographical Preferences

International Preferences:
Egypt

Industry Preferences

In Consumer Related prefer:
Consumer

Additional Information
Year Founded: 2015
Capital Under Management: $15,000,000
Current Activity Level : Actively seeking new investments

4.0 PARTNERS

3009 Webster Street
San Francisco, CA USA 94123
Phone: 4152548868

Type of Firm
Private Equity Firm

Project Preferences

Type of Financing Preferred:
Balanced

Industry Preferences

In Computer Software prefer:
Software
Artificial Intelligence

In Semiconductor/Electr prefer:
Electronics

In Consumer Related prefer:
Education Related

In Financial Services prefer:
Financial Services

Additional Information
Year Founded: 2017
Current Activity Level : Actively seeking new investments

404 GROUP

Krasnogo Kursanta, 25
Saint Petersburg, Russia 197110
Phone: 78126778975
E-mail: info@404-group.com
Website: 404-group.com

Type of Firm
Incubator/Development Program

Project Preferences

Type of Financing Preferred:
Early Stage
Seed
Startup

Industry Preferences

In Communications prefer:
Media and Entertainment

In Internet Specific prefer:
Internet

Additional Information
Year Founded: 2015
Current Activity Level : Actively seeking new investments

406 VENTURES LLC

470 Atlantic Avenue
12th Floor
Boston, MA USA 02210
Phone: 6174063300
Fax: 6174063301
E-mail: contact@406ventures.com
Website: www.406ventures.com

Management and Staff
Graham Brooks, Principal
Greg Dracon, Principal
Lawrence Begley, Co-Founder
Liam Donohue, Co-Founder
Maria Cirino, Co-Founder
So-June Min, Chief Financial Officer

Type of Firm
Private Equity Firm

Association Membership
New England Venture Capital Association
National Venture Capital Association - USA (NVCA)

Project Preferences

Role in Financing:
Prefer role as deal originator

Type of Financing Preferred:
Early Stage

Size of Investments Considered:
Min Size of Investment Considered (000s): $1,000
Max Size of Investment Considered (000s): $4,000

Geographical Preferences

United States Preferences:
Northeast

Industry Preferences

In Internet Specific prefer:
Web Aggregation/Portals

In Medical/Health prefer:
Medical/Health

In Industrial/Energy prefer:
Energy

In Financial Services prefer:
Financial Services

In Business Serv. prefer:
Services
Media

Additional Information
Name of Most Recent Fund: Point 406 Ventures II, L.P.
Most Recent Fund Was Raised: 11/23/2011
Year Founded: 2006
Capital Under Management: $633,000,000
Current Activity Level : Actively seeking new investments
Method of Compensation: Return on invest. most important, but chg. closing fees, service fees, etc.

4BIO VENTURES MANAGEMENT LTD

78 Pall Mall
London, United Kingdom SW1Y 5ES
Phone: 442038655365
E-mail: info@4biocapital.com
Website: www.4biocapital.com

Management and Staff
Andrey Kozlov, Partner
Dmitry Kuzmin, Partner
Kieran Mudryy, Partner
Vasily Fedorin, Principal
Vladimir Guber, Partner
Yury Kukushkin, Principal

Type of Firm
Private Equity Firm

Project Preferences

Type of Financing Preferred:
Generalist PE

Additional Information
Year Founded: 1969
Current Activity Level: Actively seeking new investments

4C CAPITAL LLC

1401 Shadwell Circle
Lake Mary
Lake Mary, FL USA 32746
Website: www.4ccapitalllc.com

Type of Firm
Private Equity Firm

Project Preferences

Type of Financing Preferred:
Leveraged Buyout

Geographical Preferences

United States Preferences:

Industry Preferences

In Medical/Health prefer:
Medical/Health

Additional Information
Year Founded: 2013
Current Activity Level: Actively seeking new investments

4D GLOBAL ENERGY ADVISORS SAS

15 Rue de la Baume
Paris, France 75008
Phone: 33156433860
Fax: 33142255459
E-mail: contact@4dgea.com
Website: www.4dgea.com

Management and Staff
David Kabile, Vice President
Jerome Halbout, Partner
Simon Eyers, Partner
Tighe Noonan, Partner

Type of Firm
Private Equity Firm

Association Membership
French Venture Capital Association (AFIC)

Project Preferences

Type of Financing Preferred:
Other

Geographical Preferences

International Preferences:
Europe
France

Industry Preferences

In Industrial/Energy prefer:
Energy

Additional Information
Year Founded: 2002
Capital Under Management: $216,001,000
Current Activity Level: Actively seeking new investments

4G VENTURES LLC

8871 Research Drive
Irvine, CA USA 92618
Phone: 9497486100

Type of Firm
Private Equity Firm

Project Preferences

Type of Financing Preferred:
Core
Balanced

Industry Preferences

In Communications prefer:
Wireless Communications

In Consumer Related prefer:
Retail
Other Restaurants

In Financial Services prefer:
Real Estate
Investment Groups

Additional Information
Year Founded: 2016
Current Activity Level: Actively seeking new investments

4K INVEST INTERNATIONAL LTD

Sendlinger Strasse 10
Munich, Germany 80331
Phone: 49891894260
Fax: 4989189426499
E-mail: info@4k.ag
Website: www.4k.ag

Other Offices
Rue Gabriel Lippmann 1 C
Munsbach, Luxembourg 5365

Sendlinger Strasse 10
Munich, Germany 80331
Phone: 49891894260
Fax: 4989189426499

Type of Firm
Private Equity Firm

Project Preferences

Type of Financing Preferred:
Leveraged Buyout
Acquisition

Geographical Preferences

International Preferences:
Europe

Additional Information
Year Founded: 2013
Current Activity Level: Actively seeking new investments

4TH LEVEL VENTURES

75 Saint Stephen's Green
Dublin, Ireland
Phone: 35316333603
Fax: 35316333889
E-mail: info@4thlevelventures.ie
Website: www.4thlevelventures.ie

Management and Staff
Dennis Jennings, Co-Founder
Ray Naughton, Co-Founder
Ronan Reid, Managing Director

Type of Firm
Private Equity Firm

Project Preferences

Type of Financing Preferred:
Early Stage
Balanced
Later Stage
Seed
Startup

Geographical Preferences

International Preferences:
Ireland
Europe

Industry Preferences

In Communications prefer:
Communications and Media

Additional Information
Name of Most Recent Fund: 4th Level Ventures University Seed Fund
Most Recent Fund Was Raised: 12/31/2002
Year Founded: 2002
Current Activity Level: Actively seeking new investments

783

5 M VENTURES SAS

28 place de la Bourse
Paris, France 75002
Phone: 33184164515
Website: www.5m-ventures.com

Type of Firm
Private Equity Firm

Project Preferences

Type of Financing Preferred:
Early Stage
Seed
Startup

Geographical Preferences

International Preferences:
France

Industry Preferences

In Communications prefer:
Communications and Media
Commercial Communications
Media and Entertainment

Additional Information
Year Founded: 2013
Current Activity Level : Actively seeking new investments

50 PARTNERS SAS

62, Rue Jean-Jacques Rousseau
Paris, France 75001
Website: www.50partners.fr

Type of Firm
Incubator/Development Program

Project Preferences

Type of Financing Preferred:
Early Stage
Seed

Geographical Preferences

International Preferences:
Europe
France

Industry Preferences

In Computer Software prefer:
Software

In Internet Specific prefer:
Internet
Ecommerce

In Consumer Related prefer:
Consumer Products
Consumer Services

Additional Information
Year Founded: 2012
Current Activity Level : Actively seeking new investments

50 SOUTH CAPITAL ADVISORS LLC

50 South LaSalle Street
Chicago, IL USA 60603
Phone: 13126306000
Website: www.50southcapital.com

Management and Staff
Adam Freda, Vice President
Anthony Chiaverini, Vice President
Christopher McCrory, Vice President
James Hart, Vice President
Kevin Kresnicka, Vice President
Mike Marderosian, Vice President

Type of Firm
Bank Affiliated

Project Preferences

Type of Financing Preferred:
Fund of Funds
Fund of Funds of Second

Additional Information
Year Founded: 2015
Capital Under Management: $546,612,000
Current Activity Level : Actively seeking new investments

500 MEXICO CITY

Chihuahua 230
Colonia Roma
Mexico, Mexico 06700
Website: 500mexicocity.com

Other Offices
444 Castro Street
Suite 1200
Mountain View, CA USA 94041

Type of Firm
Incubator/Development Program

Project Preferences

Type of Financing Preferred:
Seed
Startup

Size of Investments Considered:
Min Size of Investment Considered (000s): $25
Max Size of Investment Considered (000s): $350

Geographical Preferences

International Preferences:
Mexico

Additional Information
Year Founded: 2013
Current Activity Level : Actively seeking new investments

500 STARTUPS, L.P.

444 Castro Street
Suite 1200
Mountain View, CA USA 94041
Phone: 6507434738
Website: www.500startups.com

Other Offices
Chihuahua 230
Colonia Roma
Mexico, Mexico 06700

Global Business Hub Tokyo
Third Floor
Chiyoda-ku, Japan 100-0004

Management and Staff
Andrea Barrica, Venture Partner
Arjun Arora, Partner
Bedy Yang, Managing Partner
Christine Tsai, Partner
David McClure, Partner
Diana Moldavsky, Partner
Edith Yeung, Partner
Elizabeth Yin, Partner
Emily Chiu, Partner
James Riney, Partner
Jon Liao, Partner
Khailee Ng, Managing Partner
Krating Poonpol, Venture Partner
Marvin Liao, Partner
Max Fram-Schwartz, Venture Partner
Mojan Movassate, Partner
Pankaj Jain, Partner
Paul Yoo, Chief Financial Officer
Rui Ma, Partner
Santiago Zavala, Partner
Sean Percival, Partner
Shalini Prakash, Principal
Sheel Mohnot, Partner
Tanya Soman, Principal
Tim Chae, Partner
Tristan Pollock, Venture Partner
Zafer Younis, Partner

Type of Firm
Private Equity Firm

Association Membership
National Venture Capital Association - USA (NVCA)

Project Preferences

Type of Financing Preferred:
Seed

Size of Investments Considered:
Min Size of Investment Considered (000s): $10
Max Size of Investment Considered (000s): $250

Pratt's Guide to Private Equity & Venture Capital Sources

Geographical Preferences

United States Preferences:

International Preferences:
Thailand
Japan
All International

Industry Preferences

In Communications prefer:
Communications and Media
Wireless Communications

In Computer Software prefer:
Software

In Internet Specific prefer:
Internet
Ecommerce

In Medical/Health prefer:
Medical/Health

In Consumer Related prefer:
Entertainment and Leisure

In Transportation prefer:
Transportation

In Financial Services prefer:
Financial Services
Real Estate

In Business Serv. prefer:
Media

Additional Information
Name of Most Recent Fund: 500 Luchadores, L.P.
Most Recent Fund Was Raised: 01/27/2014
Year Founded: 2010
Capital Under Management: $307,600,000
Current Activity Level : Actively seeking new investments

54 CAPITAL LTD

38 Park Street
London, United Kingdom W1K 2JF
Phone: 4402070168355
E-mail: info@54capital.com
Website: www.54capital.com

Management and Staff
Saad Aouad, Founder
Yassine Benjelloun, Partner

Type of Firm
Investment Management Firm

Geographical Preferences

International Preferences:
Morocco
Mozambique
Africa

Industry Preferences

In Communications prefer:
Telecommunications

In Medical/Health prefer:
Health Services
Pharmaceuticals

In Consumer Related prefer:
Retail
Education Related

In Financial Services prefer:
Financial Services

Additional Information
Year Founded: 2015
Current Activity Level : Actively seeking new investments

57 STARS LLC

616 H Street Northwest
Suite 450
Washington, DC USA 20001
Phone: 2028241600
Fax: 2028244300
E-mail: info@57stars.net
Website: www.57stars.net

Other Offices
Maximilianstrasse 13
Muenchen, Germany 80539
Phone: 498928890177
Fax: 49892889045

12707 High Bluff Drive
Suite 200
San Diego, CA USA 92130
Phone: 8587941452
Fax: 8587941450

One Fullerton
1 Fullerton Road #02-01
Singapore, Singapore 049213
Phone: 6564083895
Fax: 6564083801

Av. Brigadeiro Faria Lima
3729 - 5 andar
Sao Paulo, Brazil 04538-905

Management and Staff
Amit Chandra, Vice President
Charles Toy, Managing Director
Gene Pohren, Managing Director
John Engel, Vice President
Stephen O Neill, Managing Director
Steven Cowan, Managing Director

Type of Firm
Private Equity Advisor or Fund of Funds

Project Preferences

Type of Financing Preferred:
Fund of Funds

Additional Information
Name of Most Recent Fund: 57 Stars Global Opportunity Fund 3, L.P.
Most Recent Fund Was Raised: 04/23/2012
Year Founded: 2011
Capital Under Management: $337,821,000
Current Activity Level : Actively seeking new investments

5AM VENTURES LLC

2200 Sand Hill Road
Suite 110
Menlo Park, CA USA 94025
Phone: 6502338600
Fax: 6502338923
Website: www.5amventures.com

Other Offices
890 Winter Street, Suite 140
Waltham Woods Corporate Center
WALTHAM, MA USA 02451
Phone: 7818904480
Fax: 7818903565

Management and Staff
Brian Daniels, Venture Partner
David Allison, Principal
James Young, Venture Partner
Joseph Victor, Venture Partner
Kush Parmar, Managing Partner
Mason Freeman, Venture Partner
Paul Stone, Partner
Peter Kim, Venture Partner
Rebecca Lucia, Chief Financial Officer
Richard Ulevitch, Venture Partner
Scott Rocklage, Managing Partner

Type of Firm
Private Equity Firm

Association Membership
Norwegian Venture Capital Association
National Venture Capital Association - USA (NVCA)

Project Preferences

Role in Financing:
Prefer role as deal originator but will also invest in deals created by others

Type of Financing Preferred:
Early Stage
Seed

Geographical Preferences

United States Preferences:

Industry Preferences

In Biotechnology prefer:
Biotechnology

In Medical/Health prefer:
Medical Therapeutics
Drug/Equipmt Delivery
Medical Products

Additional Information

Name of Most Recent Fund: 5AM Ventures IV, L.P.
Most Recent Fund Was Raised: 11/08/2013
Year Founded: 2002
Capital Under Management: $969,600,000
Current Activity Level : Actively seeking new investments

5SQUARE BV

Torenlaan 19A
Laren, Netherlands 1251 HE
Phone: 31880086405
Website: www.5square.nl

Management and Staff

Ewout Wegman, Partner
Mark Gitsels, Co-Founder
Remco Van den Heuvel, Co-Founder
Sean Wever, Partner

Type of Firm

Private Equity Firm

Association Membership

Dutch Venture Capital Associaton (NVP)

Project Preferences

Type of Financing Preferred:
Leveraged Buyout
Early Stage
Generalist PE
Balanced
Later Stage
Seed
Recapitalizations

Size of Investments Considered:

Min Size of Investment Considered (000s): $1,337
Max Size of Investment Considered (000s): $6,683

Geographical Preferences

International Preferences:
Luxembourg
Europe
Netherlands
Belgium

Industry Preferences

In Consumer Related prefer:
Retail
Consumer Services

In Manufact. prefer:
Manufacturing

Additional Information

Year Founded: 2004
Current Activity Level : Actively seeking new investments

F & H FUND MANAGEMENT PTE LTD

238A Thomson Rd, Novena Square
Suite 18-10 Tower A
Singapore, Singapore 307684
Phone: 65-62218805
Fax: 65-62218815
E-mail: inquiry@fnh.com.sg
Website: fnh.com.sg

Other Offices

No. 9 Qingchun Road
Hangzhou, China 310005

No. 99 Jinyu Avenue
26/F Qibo Building
Chongqing, China

No. 333 Huaihai Zhong Road
Room 1823 Ruian Plaza
Shanghai, China

Chaowai Street, Chaoyang District
Room 1010 Youtang Office
Beijing, China

No. 9 Fuxi Street
Taiyuan, China

Management and Staff

Matt Hu, Chief Executive Officer

Type of Firm

Private Equity Firm

Project Preferences

Type of Financing Preferred:
Leveraged Buyout
Early Stage
Balanced
Later Stage
Joint Ventures

Geographical Preferences

United States Preferences:
Southeast

International Preferences:
China
Singapore

Industry Preferences

In Internet Specific prefer:
Internet

In Consumer Related prefer:
Consumer

Additional Information

Year Founded: 2009
Capital Under Management: $24,300,000
Current Activity Level : Actively seeking new investments

F HOFFMANN LA ROCHE AG

Grenzacherstrasse 124
Basel, Switzerland 4070
Phone: 41616881111
Fax: 41616919391
E-mail: roche.venturefund@roche.com
Website: www.roche.com

Management and Staff

Alan Hippe, Chief Financial Officer

Type of Firm

Corporate PE/Venture

Project Preferences

Type of Financing Preferred:
Early Stage
Startup

Size of Investments Considered:

Min Size of Investment Considered (000s): $1,112
Max Size of Investment Considered (000s): $5,558

Geographical Preferences

United States Preferences:
All U.S.

International Preferences:
Europe
Pacific

Industry Preferences

In Biotechnology prefer:
Biotechnology

In Medical/Health prefer:
Medical/Health
Medical Diagnostics
Pharmaceuticals

Additional Information

Year Founded: 1989
Current Activity Level : Actively seeking new investments

F&C ASSET MANAGEMENT PLC

80 George Street
Edinburgh, United Kingdom EH2 3BU
Phone: 442076288000
Fax: 441317181283
E-mail: privateequityfunds@fandc.com
Website: www.bmo.com

Other Offices

265 Franklin Street
16th Floor
Boston, MA USA 02110
Phone: 6174269050

Exchange House
Primrose Street
London, United Kingdom EC2A 2NY
Phone: 442070114444

Block Five, Harcourt Centre
Dublin 2
Dublin, Ireland
Phone: 35314364000

Niederlassung Deutschland
Oeder Weg 113
Frankfurt a.M., Germany 60318
Phone: 49695979908

99 Queen's Road
66th Floor, Suite 01, The Center
Central, Hong Kong

Rua de Campolide, 372 - 1
Gestao de Patrimonios, S.A.
Lisboa, Portugal 1070 - 040

Management and Staff

David Logan, Chief Financial Officer
Richard Wilson, Chief Executive Officer

Type of Firm

Private Equity Advisor or Fund of Funds

Association Membership

European Private Equity and Venture Capital Assoc.

Project Preferences

Type of Financing Preferred:
Fund of Funds
Leveraged Buyout

Geographical Preferences

International Preferences:
Europe

Industry Preferences

In Industrial/Energy prefer:
Environmental Related

In Other prefer:
Environment Responsible

Additional Information

Year Founded: 1980
Capital Under Management: $158,729,000
Current Activity Level : Actively seeking new investments

F&C EQUITY PARTNERS PLC

100 Wood Street
Second Floor
London, United Kingdom EC2V 7AN
Phone: 442075065600
Fax: 442075065665
Website: www.livingbridge.com

Other Offices

Three New York Street
Second Floor, The Exchange
Manchester, United Kingdom M1 4HN
Phone: 441619126500
Fax: 441612532313

8 Cherry Street
Bank House
Birmingham, United Kingdom B2 5AN
Phone: 441212531600
Fax: 441212531616

Management and Staff

Adam Holloway, Partner
Andrew Garside, Partner
Daniel Smith, Partner
Liz Jones, Partner
Mark Advani, Partner
Mark Turner, Partner
Paul Morris, Partner
Pete Clarke, Partner
Shani Zindel, Partner
Wol Kolade, Managing Partner

Type of Firm

Private Equity Firm

Project Preferences

Role in Financing:
Prefer role as deal originator but will also invest in deals created by others

Type of Financing Preferred:
Leveraged Buyout
Early Stage
Expansion
Generalist PE
Balanced
Management Buyouts
Acquisition

Size of Investments Considered:
Min Size of Investment Considered (000s): $3,159
Max Size of Investment Considered (000s): $63,184

Geographical Preferences

International Preferences:
United Kingdom
Europe

Industry Focus

(% based on actual investment)
Consumer Related	29.4%
Other Products	21.2%
Internet Specific	14.4%
Medical/Health	11.0%
Communications and Media	11.0%
Computer Software and Services	7.6%
Biotechnology	2.6%
Computer Hardware	1.9%
Industrial/Energy	0.9%

Additional Information

Year Founded: 1983
Capital Under Management: $1,737,600,000
Current Activity Level : Actively seeking new investments

F-PRIME CAPITAL PARTNERS

One Main Street
13th Floor
Cambridge, MA USA 02142
Phone: 6172312400
Fax: 6172312425
E-mail: FidelityBiosciences@fmr.com
Website: fprimecapital.com

Other Offices

82 Devonshire Street
EPC13A
BOSTON, MA USA 02109

Management and Staff

Alexander Pasteur, Partner
Ben Malka, Partner
Ben Auspitz, Partner
David Jegen, Partner
Gaurav Tuli, Principal
Jenny Rooke, Venture Partner
Jon Lim, Partner
Ketan Patel, Partner
Mary Pendergast, Chief Financial Officer
Robert Weisskoff, Partner
Sanjay Aggarwal, Venture Partner

Type of Firm

Corporate PE/Venture

Association Membership

New England Venture Capital Association
National Venture Capital Association - USA (NVCA)

Project Preferences

Role in Financing:
Will function either as deal originator or investor in deals created by others

Type of Financing Preferred:
Early Stage
Expansion
Balanced

Geographical Preferences

United States Preferences:

International Preferences:
All International

Industry Preferences

In Biotechnology prefer:
Biotechnology

In Medical/Health prefer:
Medical/Health
Medical Therapeutics
Medical Products
Health Services
Pharmaceuticals

Additional Information
Name of Most Recent Fund: Beacon Bioventures Fund III
Most Recent Fund Was Raised: 01/06/2012
Year Founded: 2002
Capital Under Management: $1,500,000,000
Current Activity Level : Actively seeking new investments
Method of Compensation: Return on investment is of primary concern, do not charge fees

F.J. STORK HOLDINGS, LTD.

541 Mill Street
Suite One
Kitchener, Canada N2G 2Y5
Phone: 519-744-8765

Type of Firm
Private Equity Firm

Project Preferences

Type of Financing Preferred:
Expansion
Seed

Additional Information
Year Founded: 2006
Current Activity Level : Actively seeking new investments

F1 BIOVENTURES LLC

505 S Flagler Dr
Suite 900
West Palm Beach, FL USA 33401
E-mail: info@f1bioventures.com
Website: www.f1bioventures.com

Type of Firm
Private Equity Firm

Additional Information
Year Founded: 1969
Current Activity Level : Actively seeking new investments

FA DIESE 2 SAS

59 boulevard Exelmans
Paris, France 75016
Phone: 33147435097
Fax: 33147439663
Website: www.fadiese.fr

Type of Firm
Private Equity Firm

Association Membership
French Venture Capital Association (AFIC)

Project Preferences

Type of Financing Preferred:
Early Stage
Seed
Startup

Size of Investments Considered:
Min Size of Investment Considered (000s): $263
Max Size of Investment Considered (000s): $1,969

Geographical Preferences

International Preferences:
Europe
France

Additional Information
Year Founded: 2001
Current Activity Level : Actively seeking new investments

FA TECHNOLOGY VENTURES CORP

1000 High Street, Suite 1105
Boston, MA USA 02110
Phone: 6177573883
Fax: 6177573881
E-mail: info@fatechventures.com
Website: www.fatechventures.com

Management and Staff
Claire Wadlington, Partner
George McNamee, Managing Partner
Gregory Hulecki, Co-Founder
Kenneth Mabbs, Co-Founder
Laura Rippy, General Partner

Type of Firm
Bank Affiliated

Project Preferences

Role in Financing:
Will function either as deal originator or investor in deals created by others

Type of Financing Preferred:
Early Stage
Expansion

Size of Investments Considered:
Min Size of Investment Considered (000s): $3,000
Max Size of Investment Considered (000s): $15,000

Geographical Preferences

United States Preferences:
Northeast

Industry Preferences

In Industrial/Energy prefer:
Energy
Materials
Environmental Related

Additional Information
Name of Most Recent Fund: FA Technology Ventures I
Most Recent Fund Was Raised: 10/20/2000
Year Founded: 2000
Capital Under Management: $175,000,000
Current Activity Level : Actively seeking new investments
Method of Compensation: Return on investment is of primary concern, do not charge fees

FAIR VALUE CAPITAL

No. 107, Zunyi Road
Rm. 402-409, Antai Bldg.
Shanghai, China 200100
Phone: 862162375485
E-mail: anyi@fvinvest.com
Website: www.anyitz.com

Management and Staff
Dongbing Ma, Founder
Li Yu, Partner
Longquan Du, Partner
Peifeng Zhu, Partner
Yongzhi Mao, Partner

Type of Firm
Private Equity Firm

Project Preferences

Type of Financing Preferred:
Balanced

Geographical Preferences

International Preferences:
China

Industry Preferences

In Semiconductor/Electr prefer:
Electronics

In Industrial/Energy prefer:
Industrial Products

In Other prefer:
Socially Responsible

Additional Information
Year Founded: 1997
Capital Under Management: $78,756,000
Current Activity Level : Actively seeking new investments

FAIRBRIDGE VENTURE PARTNERS

1105 North Market Street
Sutie 1800
Wilmington, DE USA 19801
Website: www.fairbridgepartners.com

Management and Staff
Benjamin DuPont, Managing Director
Phil Stern, Managing Director
Scott Lockledge, Venture Partner
Tim Bernstein, Managing Director

Type of Firm
Private Equity Firm

Project Preferences

Type of Financing Preferred:
Early Stage

Geographical Preferences

United States Preferences:

Additional Information
Year Founded: 1969
Current Activity Level : Actively seeking new investments

FAIRFAX AFRICA FUND LLC

95 Wellington Street West
Suite 800
Toronto, Canada M5J 2N7
Phone: 4163674941
Fax: 4163674946
E-mail: info@fairfaxafrica.com
Website: www.fairfaxafrica.com

Other Offices
8200 Greensboro Drive
Suite 900
MCLEAN, VA USA 22101
Phone: 7036773455
Fax: 7034625437

Type of Firm
Private Equity Firm

Project Preferences

Type of Financing Preferred:
Leveraged Buyout
Acquisition
Startup

Geographical Preferences

International Preferences:
Africa

Additional Information
Year Founded: 2017
Current Activity Level : Actively seeking new investments

FAIRFAX FINANCIAL HOLDINGS LTD

95 Wellington Street West
Suite 800
Toronto, Canada M5J 2N7
Phone: 4163674941
Fax: 4163674946
Website: www.fairfax.ca

Management and Staff
Bradley Martin, Vice President
Eric Salsberg, Vice President
Jean Cloutier, Vice President
John Varnell, Vice President
Paul Rivett, President
Ronald Schokking, Vice President

Type of Firm
Investment Management Firm

Project Preferences

Type of Financing Preferred:
Leveraged Buyout
Mezzanine
Acquisition

Additional Information
Year Founded: 1985
Current Activity Level : Actively seeking new investments

FAIRFAX INDIA HOLDINGS CORP

95 Wellington Street West
Suite 800
Toronto, Canada M5J 2N7
Website: www.fairfaxindia.ca

Type of Firm
Investment Management Firm

Project Preferences

Type of Financing Preferred:
Leveraged Buyout
Acquisition

Geographical Preferences

International Preferences:
India

Additional Information
Year Founded: 2014
Capital Under Management: $500,000,000
Current Activity Level : Actively seeking new investments

FAIRHAVEN CAPITAL PARTNERS, L.P.

One Hampshire Street
Suite 7R
Cambridge, MA USA 02139
Phone: 6174520800
Fax: 6174520801
E-mail: info@fairhavencapial.com
Website: www.fairhavencapital.com

Management and Staff
Daniel Keshian, Co-Founder
James Goldinger, Partner
Mark Hatfield, Partner
Paul Ciriello, Partner
Richard Grinnell, Managing Director
Rick Grinnell, Partner
Rudina Seseri, Partner
Wan Li Zhu, Principal

Type of Firm
Private Equity Firm

Association Membership
New England Venture Capital Association
National Venture Capital Association - USA (NVCA)

Project Preferences

Type of Financing Preferred:
Early Stage

Industry Preferences

In Communications prefer:
Wireless Communications

In Computer Software prefer:
Software

In Internet Specific prefer:
Internet

In Consumer Related prefer:
Consumer

In Industrial/Energy prefer:
Materials

In Financial Services prefer:
Financial Services

In Business Serv. prefer:
Media

Additional Information
Name of Most Recent Fund: Fairhaven Capital Partners, L.P.
Most Recent Fund Was Raised: 03/31/2008
Year Founded: 2007

Capital Under Management: $400,000,000
Current Activity Level: Actively seeking new investments

FAIRVENTURES

105 Adelaide St W
Suite 1010
Toronto, Canada M5H 1P9
Website: www.fairventures.ca

Type of Firm
Incubator/Development Program

Project Preferences

Type of Financing Preferred:
Early Stage

Additional Information
Year Founded: 2016
Current Activity Level: Actively seeking new investments

FAIRWATER GROWTH RESOURCES, INC.

130 Adelaide Street West
Suite 1010
Toronto, Canada M5H3P5
Phone: 416-369-1499
Fax: 416-369-0280
E-mail: info@fairwater.ca

Management and Staff
Terry Mactaggart, President

Type of Firm
Private Equity Firm

Project Preferences

Type of Financing Preferred:
Later Stage

Additional Information
Year Founded: 2001
Current Activity Level: Actively seeking new investments

FAITH CAPITAL HOLDING KSCC

Floor 65 Al Hamra Tower
Al-Shuhada St
Sharq, Kuwait
Phone: 96522270355

Other Offices
Floor 65 Al Hamra Tower
Al-Shuhada St
Sharq, Kuwait
Phone: 96522270355

Type of Firm
Private Equity Firm

Project Preferences

Type of Financing Preferred:
Early Stage
Expansion
Later Stage
Seed
Acquisition

Geographical Preferences

International Preferences:
Oman
Qatar
Utd. Arab Em.
Saudi Arabia
Kuwait

Additional Information
Year Founded: 2016
Current Activity Level: Actively seeking new investments

FAJR CAPITAL LTD

Gate Village 5, Level 3, DIFC,
P.O. Box 506738
Dubai, Utd. Arab Em.
Phone: 97143735900
Fax: 97143278874
Website: www.fajrcapital.com

Other Offices
4, Royal Mint Court
London, United Kingdom EC3N 4HJ
Phone: 4420-7073-7960
Fax: 4420-7073-7951

Management and Staff
Aamir Rehman, Managing Director
Asad Zafar, Managing Director
Javed Ahmad, Managing Director
Noor Azman Aziz, Managing Director

Type of Firm
Private Equity Firm

Project Preferences

Type of Financing Preferred:
Leveraged Buyout

Geographical Preferences

International Preferences:
Middle East

Industry Preferences

In Financial Services prefer:
Financial Services

Additional Information
Year Founded: 2009
Capital Under Management: $2,203,600,000
Current Activity Level: Actively seeking new investments

FALCON INVESTMENT ADVISORS LLC

21 Custom House Street
10th Floor
Boston, MA USA 02110
Phone: 6174122700
Website: www.falconinvestments.com

Other Offices
600 Lexington Avenue
35rh Floor
New York, NY USA 10022
Phone: 2123000200

Management and Staff
Christopher Thorsheim, Vice President
Eric Rogoff, Partner
Irene Wang, Vice President
John Schnabel, Partner
Matthew White, Vice President
Matthew Prout, Vice President
Rafael Fogel, Partner
Sandeep Alva, Managing Partner
Sven Grasshoff, Principal
Wesley Fuller, Principal
William Kennedy, Managing Partner

Type of Firm
Private Equity Firm

Association Membership
Emerging Markets Private Equity Association

Project Preferences

Role in Financing:
Will function either as deal originator or investor in deals created by others

Type of Financing Preferred:
Leveraged Buyout
Expansion
Mezzanine
Management Buyouts
Acquisition
Recapitalizations

Geographical Preferences

United States Preferences:
North America

Additional Information
Year Founded: 2000
Capital Under Management: $1,000,000,000
Current Activity Level: Actively seeking new investments

FALCONER BELLOMO & CO LTD

Sargood House, Suite 404
73 Flinders Lane
Melbourne, Australia 3000
Phone: 613-9650-8911
Fax: 613-9650-4911
E-mail: falconerbellomo@bigpond.com

Type of Firm
Private Equity Firm

Project Preferences

Role in Financing:
Prefer role as deal originator

Type of Financing Preferred:
Early Stage
Expansion
Mezzanine
Later Stage
First Stage Financing
Acquisition
Private Placement

Geographical Preferences

International Preferences:
China
Australia

Industry Preferences

In Communications prefer:
Telecommunications
Wireless Communications
Satellite Microwave Comm.

In Biotechnology prefer:
Agricultural/Animal Bio.

In Consumer Related prefer:
Entertainment and Leisure
Sports
Food/Beverage
Hotels and Resorts

In Industrial/Energy prefer:
Energy

In Financial Services prefer:
Financial Services

In Business Serv. prefer:
Media

In Agr/Forestr/Fish prefer:
Agribusiness
Agriculture related
Mining and Minerals

Additional Information
Year Founded: 1997
Current Activity Level : Actively seeking new investments
Method of Compensation: Function primarily in service area, receive contingent fee in cash or equity

FALCONHEAD CAPITAL LLC

450 Park Avenue
3rd Floor
New York, NY USA 10022
Phone: 2126343304
Fax: 2126343305
E-mail: info@falconheadcapital.com
Website: www.falconheadcapital.com

Management and Staff
Brian Crosby, Partner
David Gubbay, General Partner
Glen Bushery, Chief Financial Officer
Jason Turowsky, General Partner
Robert Fioretti, Managing Director
Zuher Ladak, General Partner

Type of Firm
Private Equity Firm

Project Preferences

Role in Financing:
Prefer role as deal originator but will also invest in deals created by others

Type of Financing Preferred:
Leveraged Buyout
Acquisition

Geographical Preferences

United States Preferences:

Industry Preferences

In Consumer Related prefer:
Consumer
Entertainment and Leisure
Sports
Food/Beverage
Consumer Products
Consumer Services

In Business Serv. prefer:
Media

Additional Information
Name of Most Recent Fund: Falconhead Capital Partners II, L.P.
Most Recent Fund Was Raised: 01/05/2006
Year Founded: 1998
Capital Under Management: $500,000,000
Current Activity Level : Actively seeking new investments
Method of Compensation: Return on invest. most important, but chg. closing fees, service fees, etc.

FALFURRIAS CAPITAL PARTNERS LP

100 North Tryon Street
Suite 4100
Charlotte, NC USA 28202
Phone: 7043713220
Fax: 7043330185
Website: www.falfurriascapital.com

Management and Staff
Joseph Schonberg, Chief Financial Officer
Marc Oken, Co-Founder
Todd Taylor, Partner
W. Edwin McMahan, Partner

Type of Firm
Private Equity Firm

Project Preferences

Type of Financing Preferred:
Leveraged Buyout
Expansion
Recapitalizations

Geographical Preferences

United States Preferences:
All U.S.

Industry Preferences

In Medical/Health prefer:
Medical/Health

In Consumer Related prefer:
Consumer Products
Education Related

In Industrial/Energy prefer:
Industrial Products

In Financial Services prefer:
Financial Services

In Business Serv. prefer:
Services

In Manufact. prefer:
Manufacturing

Additional Information
Name of Most Recent Fund: Falfurrias Capital Partners II, L.P.
Most Recent Fund Was Raised: 11/18/2011
Year Founded: 2006
Capital Under Management: $401,300,000
Current Activity Level : Actively seeking new investments

FALL LINE CAPITAL GP LLC

119 South B Street
San Mateo, CA USA 94401
Phone: 6502354032
E-mail: info@fall-line-cap.com
Website: www.fall-line-capital.com

Management and Staff

Clay Mitchell, Managing Director
Eric O Brien, Managing Director

Type of Firm

Private Equity Firm

Project Preferences

Type of Financing Preferred:
Value-Add
Early Stage
Startup

Industry Preferences

In Financial Services prefer:
Real Estate

In Agr/Forestr/Fish prefer:
Agribusiness
Agriculture related

Additional Information

Name of Most Recent Fund: Fall Line Farms Fund I, L.P.
Most Recent Fund Was Raised: 02/27/2012
Year Founded: 1969
Capital Under Management: $127,000,000
Current Activity Level : Actively seeking new investments

FAMA PRIVATE EQUITY

R. Samuel Morse
Brooklin
Sao Paulo, Brazil 04576-060
Phone: 551155081188
E-mail: contato@famape.com.br
Website: www.famape.com.br

Management and Staff

Fabio Alperwitch, Founder

Type of Firm

Private Equity Firm

Project Preferences

Type of Financing Preferred:
Leveraged Buyout
Management Buyouts
Acquisition

Geographical Preferences

International Preferences:
Brazil

Additional Information

Year Founded: 2008
Current Activity Level : Actively seeking new investments

FAMILIE GRAEF HOLDING GMBH

Dietrich-Bonhoeffer-Strasse 5
Huerth, Germany 50354
Website: www.fg-holding.com

Type of Firm

Incubator/Development Program

Project Preferences

Type of Financing Preferred:
Early Stage
Seed
Startup

Geographical Preferences

International Preferences:
Germany

Industry Preferences

In Internet Specific prefer:
Internet
Ecommerce

In Consumer Related prefer:
Consumer

Additional Information

Year Founded: 2008
Current Activity Level : Actively seeking new investments

FANG GROUP CO LTD

No. 19A, East 3rd Ring Rd. N
Suite 3901, Nexus Center
Beijing, China 100020
Phone: 861065025588
Fax: 861065035588
E-mail: info@fanggroup.com
Website: www.fanggroup.com

Management and Staff

Cynthia Qiu, Managing Partner
Rong Guo, Partner

Type of Firm

Investment Management Firm

Project Preferences

Type of Financing Preferred:
Early Stage
Expansion
Balanced

Geographical Preferences

International Preferences:
China

Industry Preferences

In Consumer Related prefer:
Consumer Products
Consumer Services

In Industrial/Energy prefer:
Energy

In Business Serv. prefer:
Media

Additional Information

Year Founded: 2010
Capital Under Management: $75,873,000
Current Activity Level : Actively seeking new investments

FANISI CAPITAL, LTD.

14 Riverside Drive
4th Floor Arlington Block
Nairobi, Kenya 00800
Phone: 254204207000
Fax: 254204207222
E-mail: info@fanisi.com
Website: www.fanisi.com

Other Offices

Two, boulevard Konrad Adenauer
Luxembourg, Luxembourg 1115

Type of Firm

Private Equity Firm

Association Membership

Emerging Markets Private Equity Association

Project Preferences

Type of Financing Preferred:
Early Stage
Expansion
Startup

Size of Investments Considered:
Min Size of Investment Considered (000s): $500
Max Size of Investment Considered (000s): $3,000

Geographical Preferences

International Preferences:
Rwanda
Uganda
Tanzania
Africa

Industry Preferences

In Medical/Health prefer:
Hospitals/Clinics/Primary

In Consumer Related prefer:
Retail
Consumer Products
Consumer Services
Education Related

In Industrial/Energy prefer:
Energy

Additional Information
Year Founded: 2009
Capital Under Management: $40,057,000
Current Activity Level : Actively seeking new investments

FAR PACIFIC CAPITAL LTD

6th Floor Change House
150 Featherstone Street
Wellington, New Zealand
Phone: 644-473-3877
Fax: 644-473-3836
E-mail: info@far.co.nz
Website: www.farpacific.co.nz

Type of Firm
Private Equity Firm

Project Preferences

Type of Financing Preferred:
Early Stage
Expansion
Turnaround
Seed
Startup

Geographical Preferences

International Preferences:
New Zealand

Additional Information
Year Founded: 2001
Current Activity Level : Actively seeking new investments

FARALLON CAPITAL MANAGEMENT LLC

One Maritime Plaza
Suite 2100
San Francisco, CA USA 94111
Phone: 4154212132
Website: www.faralloncapital.com

Other Offices
87 Mary Street, George Town
Walker House
Grand Cayman, Cayman Islands KY1-9005

Management and Staff
Colby Clark, Managing Director
Daniel Meade, Managing Director
David Kim, Managing Director
Eric Gorham, Managing Director
Gregory Swart, Chief Financial Officer
Jacquelyn Suen, Managing Director
Joshua Dapice, Managing Director
Kirstin Lynch, Managing Director
Lee Hicks, Managing Director
Matthew Trentini, Managing Director
Richard Bollini, Managing Director
Stephen Heath, Managing Director
William Seybold, Managing Director

Type of Firm
Investment Management Firm

Project Preferences

Type of Financing Preferred:
Leveraged Buyout
Value-Add
Opportunistic
Acquisition
Recapitalizations

Geographical Preferences

International Preferences:
Cayman Islands
Asia

Industry Preferences

In Medical/Health prefer:
Medical/Health

In Industrial/Energy prefer:
Energy

In Financial Services prefer:
Real Estate

Additional Information
Name of Most Recent Fund: Farallon Real Estate Partners, L.P.
Most Recent Fund Was Raised: 08/12/2013
Year Founded: 1986
Capital Under Management: $2,595,719,000
Current Activity Level : Actively seeking new investments

FAROL ASSET MANAGEMENT LP

48 Wall Street
11th Floor
New York, NY USA 10005
Phone: 2129184533
Fax: 2129184800
Website: www.farol-group.com

Management and Staff
Charles Barringer, Chief Financial Officer
Robert Azeke, Founder

Type of Firm
Private Equity Firm

Project Preferences

Type of Financing Preferred:
Leveraged Buyout
Expansion
Distressed Debt
Recapitalizations

Industry Preferences

In Communications prefer:
Telecommunications

In Medical/Health prefer:
Medical/Health

In Consumer Related prefer:
Retail
Franchises(NEC)
Consumer Products
Education Related

In Industrial/Energy prefer:
Energy
Industrial Products
Materials
Advanced Materials

In Transportation prefer:
Transportation
Aerospace

In Financial Services prefer:
Financial Services
Insurance

In Business Serv. prefer:
Services
Distribution
Media

Additional Information
Year Founded: 1969
Current Activity Level : Actively seeking new investments

FARRAGUT CAPITAL PARTNERS

5425 Wisconsin Avenue
Suite 401
Chevy Chase, MD USA 20815
Phone: 3019135296
Website: www.farragutcapitalpartners.com

Management and Staff
Javier Aguirre, Partner
Philip McNeill, Managing Partner

Type of Firm
Private Equity Firm

Association Membership
Natl Assoc of Small Bus. Inv. Co (NASBIC)

Project Preferences

Type of Financing Preferred:
Leveraged Buyout
Mezzanine
Later Stage
Management Buyouts
Acquisition
Recapitalizations

Geographical Preferences

United States Preferences:

Additional Information

Name of Most Recent Fund: Farragut Mezzanine Partners III, L.P.
Most Recent Fund Was Raised: 09/23/2011
Year Founded: 2012
Capital Under Management: $100,000,000
Current Activity Level : Actively seeking new investments

FASHION CAPITAL PARTNERS SAS

88, Rue de Courcelles
Paris, France 75008
Website: fashioncapitalpartners.com

Type of Firm

Private Equity Firm

Project Preferences

Type of Financing Preferred:
Early Stage
Seed

Geographical Preferences

United States Preferences:

International Preferences:
Europe

Industry Preferences

In Communications prefer:
Data Communications

In Computer Software prefer:
Software

In Internet Specific prefer:
E-Commerce Technology
Internet

In Consumer Related prefer:
Consumer Products

In Business Serv. prefer:
Consulting Services

Additional Information

Year Founded: 2014
Current Activity Level : Actively seeking new investments

FASHION ZONE AT RYERSON UNIVERSITY

Ten Dundas Street East
Toronto, Canada ON M5B
E-mail: info@fashionzone.ca
Website: www.fashionzone.ca

Type of Firm

Incubator/Development Program

Project Preferences

Type of Financing Preferred:
Early Stage

Geographical Preferences

Canadian Preferences:
All Canada

Industry Preferences

In Consumer Related prefer:
Entertainment and Leisure
Retail

Additional Information

Year Founded: 2015
Current Activity Level : Actively seeking new investments

FAST LANE VENTURES OOO

12, Dvintsev Street
Building 1, 9th Floor
Moscow, Russia 127018
Phone: 74952213351
Fax: 74952213352
E-mail: info@fastlaneventures.ru
Website: www.fastlaneventures.ru

Type of Firm

Private Equity Firm

Project Preferences

Type of Financing Preferred:
Early Stage
Seed
Startup

Geographical Preferences

International Preferences:
Russia

Industry Preferences

In Internet Specific prefer:
Internet
Ecommerce

Additional Information

Year Founded: 2010
Current Activity Level : Actively seeking new investments

FASTLANE VENTURES GMBH

Jungfernstieg 30
Hamburg, Germany 20354
Phone: 4940808011120
Fax: 4940808011121
E-mail: office@shortcut.vc
Website: www.shortcut.vc

Type of Firm

Private Equity Firm

Project Preferences

Type of Financing Preferred:
Early Stage
Seed
Startup

Size of Investments Considered:
Min Size of Investment Considered (000s): $659
Max Size of Investment Considered (000s): $2,637

Geographical Preferences

International Preferences:
Germany

Industry Preferences

In Communications prefer:
Wireless Communications
Media and Entertainment

In Internet Specific prefer:
Internet

Additional Information

Year Founded: 2011
Current Activity Level : Actively seeking new investments

FATFISH MEDIALAB PTE LTD

71 Ayer Rajah Cresent #02-15
Fusionopolis, Singapore 139951
E-mail: media@fatfishlab.com
Website: www.fatfishgroup.com

Other Offices

Cityloft-Citywalk Sudirman 12 floor
unit 1219J.L.K.H Mas Mansyur no.121
Jakarta Pusat, Indonesia 10220

A-3-3-5 Solaris Dutamas
Jalan Dutamas 1
Kuala Lumpur, Malaysia 50480

Management and Staff

Kin Wai Lau, Partner

Type of Firm

Incubator/Development Program

Project Preferences

Type of Financing Preferred:
Early Stage
Expansion
Later Stage
Seed
Startup

Geographical Preferences

International Preferences:
Singapore

Industry Preferences

In Communications prefer:
Telecommunications
Media and Entertainment
Entertainment

In Computer Software prefer:
Applications Software

In Internet Specific prefer:
Internet
Ecommerce

In Biotechnology prefer:
Biotechnology
Agricultural/Animal Bio.

In Business Serv. prefer:
Media

Additional Information

Year Founded: 2013
Current Activity Level : Actively seeking new investments

FDC CAPITAL PARTNERS INC

611 Alexander Street
Suite 308
Vancouver, Canada V6A 1E1
Phone: 6042554255
Fax: 6042553800
Website: www.fdccapital.com

Type of Firm
Private Equity Firm

Project Preferences

Type of Financing Preferred:
Generalist PE

Size of Investments Considered:
Min Size of Investment Considered (000s): $1,974
Max Size of Investment Considered (000s): $9,871

Additional Information

Year Founded: 2010
Current Activity Level : Actively seeking new investments

FE CLEAN ENERGY GROUP INC

22 Thorndal Circle South
Darien, CT USA 06820
Phone: 2036629293
Fax: 2036629297
E-mail: ekmiecik@fecleanenergy.com
Website: www.fecleanenergy.com

Type of Firm
Private Equity Firm

Project Preferences

Type of Financing Preferred:
Expansion
Generalist PE
Later Stage

Geographical Preferences

International Preferences:
Latin America
Europe
Asia

Industry Preferences

In Industrial/Energy prefer:
Energy

Additional Information

Year Founded: 1997
Current Activity Level : Actively seeking new investments

FEDERAL ECONOMIC DEVELOPMENT AGENCY FOR SOUTHERN ONTARIO

101 Frederick Street
Fourth floor
Kitchener, Canada N2H 6R2
Phone: 866-593-5505
Fax: 519-571-5750
Website: www.feddevontario.gc.ca

Other Offices

61 Lorne Avenue East Three
Stratford, Canada N5A 6S4
Phone: 866-593-5505
Fax: 519-271-5274

143 Simcoe Street
Peterborough, Canada K9H 0A3
Phone: 8665935505

151 Yonge Street
Toronto, Canada M5C 2W7
Phone: 866-593-5505

185 King Street
Peterborough, Canada K9J 2R8
Phone: 866-593-5505
Fax: 705-750-4827

155 Queen Street
14th floor
Ottawa, Canada K1P 6L1
Phone: 613-960-7012
Fax: 866-593-5505

Management and Staff
Bruce Archibald, President
Jeff Moore, Vice President

Type of Firm
Private Equity Firm

Project Preferences

Type of Financing Preferred:
Balanced

Geographical Preferences

United States Preferences:
All U.S.

Canadian Preferences:
All Canada

Additional Information

Year Founded: 2009
Current Activity Level : Actively seeking new investments

FEDERAL FINANCE GESTION SA

One, Allee Louis Lichou
Le Relecq-Kerhuon, France 29480
Phone: 33969320032
E-mail: contact@federal-finance.fr
Website: www.federal-finance.fr

Type of Firm
Bank Affiliated

Project Preferences

Type of Financing Preferred:
Fund of Funds
Leveraged Buyout
Early Stage
Generalist PE
Turnaround
Later Stage
Management Buyouts
Acquisition

Geographical Preferences

International Preferences:
France

Additional Information
Year Founded: 2008
Current Activity Level : Actively seeking new investments

FEIMA FUND

3131, Jinshajiang Road
5-103, Innovation Park
Shanghai, China
E-mail: feima@feimalv.com
Website: www.feimalv.com

Management and Staff
Boquan He, Partner
Chengjian Zhou, Partner
Huajin Deng, Partner
Min Fan, Partner
Minhong Yu, Partner
Nanchun Jiang, Partner
Qinan Ji, Partner
Qinghua Hong, Partner
Qinqi Zhu, Partner
Zhenyu Yang, Partner
Zhonghua Chen, Partner

Type of Firm
Private Equity Firm

Project Preferences

Type of Financing Preferred:
Early Stage
Expansion
Balanced

Geographical Preferences

International Preferences:
China

Industry Preferences

In Communications prefer:
Entertainment

In Internet Specific prefer:
Ecommerce

In Transportation prefer:
Transportation

Additional Information
Year Founded: 2011
Current Activity Level : Actively seeking new investments

FELICIS VENTURES

530 Lytton Avenue
Suite 305
Palo Alto, CA USA 94301
Phone: 6502514031
Fax: 6505491976
Website: www.felicis.com

Management and Staff
Anthony Matusich, Chief Financial Officer
Aydin Senkut, Founder
Guergana Tomova, Chief Financial Officer
Niki Pezeshki, Vice President
Renata Streit Quintini, Partner
Sundeep Peechu, Managing Director
Wesley Chan, Managing Director

Type of Firm
Private Equity Firm

Association Membership
National Venture Capital Association - USA (NVCA)

Project Preferences

Role in Financing:
Will function either as deal originator or investor in deals created by others

Type of Financing Preferred:
Early Stage
Seed

Geographical Preferences

United States Preferences:

Canadian Preferences:
All Canada

International Preferences:
Australia
Israel
Finland

Industry Preferences

In Communications prefer:
Wireless Communications

In Computer Software prefer:
Systems Software
Applications Software

In Internet Specific prefer:
E-Commerce Technology

In Medical/Health prefer:
Medical/Health

In Consumer Related prefer:
Education Related

Additional Information
Name of Most Recent Fund: Felicis Ventures III, L.P.
Most Recent Fund Was Raised: 06/29/2012
Year Founded: 2006
Capital Under Management: $445,000,000
Current Activity Level : Actively seeking new investments
Method of Compensation: Other

FELIX CAPITAL PARTNERS LLP

21A Kingly Street
London, United Kingdom W1B 5QA
Website: www.felixcap.com

Management and Staff
Antoine Nussenbaum, Co-Founder
Frederic Court, Co-Founder
Les Gabb, Co-Founder

Type of Firm
Private Equity Firm

Project Preferences

Type of Financing Preferred:
Balanced

Geographical Preferences

International Preferences:
United Kingdom
Europe

Industry Preferences

In Internet Specific prefer:
Internet
Ecommerce

Additional Information
Year Founded: 2015
Capital Under Management: $270,000,000
Current Activity Level : Actively seeking new investments

FEMTO STARTUP LLP

Higashi-ikebukuro 3-1-1
37/F Sunshine60, Toshima-ku
Tokyo, Japan 170-6037
Website: www.femto.st

Management and Staff
Tadashi Yokoyama, Partner

Type of Firm
Private Equity Firm

Project Preferences

Type of Financing Preferred:
Seed
Startup

Size of Investments Considered:
Min Size of Investment Considered (000s): $26
Max Size of Investment Considered (000s): $39

Geographical Preferences

International Preferences:
Japan

FEMUI QUI SA SA

Maison du Parc Technologique
ZI Erbajolo
Bastia, France 20601
Phone: 33495315946
Fax: 33955777075
E-mail: femuqui@mic.fr
Website: www.femu-qui.com

Type of Firm
Private Equity Firm

Project Preferences

Type of Financing Preferred:
Early Stage
Later Stage

Size of Investments Considered:
Min Size of Investment Considered (000s): $69
Max Size of Investment Considered (000s): $837

Geographical Preferences

International Preferences:
France

Additional Information
Year Founded: 1992
Capital Under Management: $500,000
Current Activity Level : Actively seeking new investments

FENBUSHI CAPITAL

Lujiazui Road 99
Pudong
Shanghai, China
E-mail: contact@fenbushi.vc
Website: fenbushi.vc

Type of Firm
Private Equity Firm

Project Preferences

Type of Financing Preferred:
Balanced

Additional Information
Year Founded: 2015
Current Activity Level : Actively seeking new investments

FENGHOU CAPITAL

East City District
R 309, Liangdian Design Center
Beijing, China
Phone: 861089508968
Website: www.fhcapital.cn

Type of Firm
Private Equity Firm

Project Preferences

Type of Financing Preferred:
Early Stage
Seed
Startup

Geographical Preferences

International Preferences:
China

Industry Preferences

In Communications prefer:
Entertainment

In Internet Specific prefer:
Internet

In Consumer Related prefer:
Consumer

In Financial Services prefer:
Financial Services

Additional Information
Year Founded: 2012
Current Activity Level : Actively seeking new investments

FENGLI FORTUNE (BEIJING) INTERNATIONAL CAPITAL MANAGEMENT CO

No.18 Xizhimenwai Street
506 C2 Bldg Jinmao Tower
Beijing, China 100044
Phone: 861088332627
Fax: 861066217131
Website: www.flfortune.com

Type of Firm
Private Equity Firm

Project Preferences

Type of Financing Preferred:
Leveraged Buyout

Additional Information
Year Founded: 2008
Current Activity Level : Actively seeking new investments

Industry Preferences

In Internet Specific prefer:
Internet

Additional Information
Year Founded: 2012
Current Activity Level : Actively seeking new investments

FENGYANG CAPITAL

Yangpu District, Shanghai
3F, Block A, No. 32 Qinhuangda
Shanghai, China 200000
Phone: 862131009068

Type of Firm
Private Equity Firm

Project Preferences

Type of Financing Preferred:
Balanced

Geographical Preferences

International Preferences:
China

Industry Preferences

In Semiconductor/Electr prefer:
Electronics

In Industrial/Energy prefer:
Advanced Materials
Robotics

Additional Information
Year Founded: 2015
Current Activity Level : Actively seeking new investments

FENNO MANAGEMENT OY

Toppelundintie 5 B 10
Espoo, Finland 02170
Phone: 358400706072
Fax: 358925172202
Website: www.fennomanagement.com

Management and Staff
Aaro Cantell, Managing Partner

Type of Firm
Private Equity Firm

Project Preferences

Type of Financing Preferred:
Leveraged Buyout
Acquisition

Size of Investments Considered:
Min Size of Investment Considered (000s): $1,000
Max Size of Investment Considered (000s): $35,000

Geographical Preferences

International Preferences:
Finland

Additional Information
Year Founded: 1997
Capital Under Management: $100,600,000
Current Activity Level : Actively seeking new investments

FENOX VENTURE CAPITAL INC

1641 North First Street
Suite 110
San Jose, CA USA 95112
Phone: 4086455532
E-mail: contact@fenoxvc.com
Website: www.fenoxvc.com

Management and Staff

Anis Uzzaman, General Partner
Evgeny Zhilinsky, Vice President
Shameem Ahsan, General Partner
TOSHITADA NAGUMO, Chief Executive Officer
Vitaliy Arbuzov, General Partner

Type of Firm

Private Equity Firm

Project Preferences

Type of Financing Preferred:
Early Stage
Expansion
Balanced
Later Stage
Seed
Startup

Geographical Preferences

United States Preferences:
Northwest
North America

International Preferences:
Bangladesh
Europe
Middle East
Asia

Industry Preferences

In Communications prefer:
Wireless Communications

In Computer Hardware prefer:
Computers

In Computer Software prefer:
Software
Applications Software

In Internet Specific prefer:
Internet

In Medical/Health prefer:
Medical/Health
Health Services

In Consumer Related prefer:
Retail
Consumer Products
Consumer Services

In Business Serv. prefer:
Media

In Other prefer:
Environment Responsible

Additional Information

Year Founded: 1989
Capital Under Management: $65,202,000
Current Activity Level : Actively seeking new investments

FENWAY PARTNERS LLC

152 West 57th Street
27th Floor
New York, NY USA 10019
Phone: 2126989400
Fax: 2125811205
E-mail: info@fenwaypartners.com
Website: www.fenwaypartners.com

Management and Staff

Gregg Smart, Managing Director
Peter Lamm, Co-Founder
Richard Dresdale, Co-Founder
Ross Lipson, Principal
Walter Wiacek, Chief Financial Officer

Type of Firm

Private Equity Firm

Project Preferences

Role in Financing:
Prefer role as deal originator but will also invest in deals created by others

Type of Financing Preferred:
Leveraged Buyout
Management Buyouts
Acquisition
Recapitalizations

Geographical Preferences

United States Preferences:

Industry Focus

(% based on actual investment)
Consumer Related	50.5%
Other Products	28.7%
Internet Specific	16.1%
Computer Software and Services	2.2%
Communications and Media	1.6%
Industrial/Energy	0.7%
Semiconductors/Other Elect.	0.1%

Additional Information

Name of Most Recent Fund: Fenway Partners Capital Fund III, L.P.
Most Recent Fund Was Raised: 02/24/2006
Year Founded: 1994
Capital Under Management: $2,100,000,000
Current Activity Level : Actively seeking new investments
Method of Compensation: Return on investment is of primary concern, do not charge fees

FENWAY SUMMER VENTURES LP

7315 Wisconsin Avenue
Suite 400 West
Bethesda, MD USA 20814
Phone: 3018875990
E-mail: info@fsv.vc
Website: fenwaysummer.com

Management and Staff

Anna Roth, Principal
Javier Saade, Managing Director
Mark Lefanowicz, Managing Director
Matthew Perlman, Principal
Rajeev Date, Managing Director

Type of Firm

Private Equity Firm

Project Preferences

Type of Financing Preferred:
Balanced

Industry Preferences

In Financial Services prefer:
Financial Services

Additional Information

Year Founded: 2015
Current Activity Level : Actively seeking new investments

FENWICK BRANDS INC

110 Office Park Drive
Suite 300
Birmingham, AL USA 35223
Phone: 2053134815
E-mail: info@fenwickbrands.com
Website: www.fenwickbrands.com

Type of Firm

Private Equity Firm

Project Preferences

Type of Financing Preferred:
Turnaround
Management Buyouts
Acquisition
Recapitalizations

Industry Preferences

In Consumer Related prefer:
Food/Beverage
Consumer Products

Additional Information

Year Founded: 2005
Capital Under Management: $33,550,000
Current Activity Level : Actively seeking new investments

FEO VENTURES PTE LTD

14 Scotts Road
#06-00 Far East Plaza
Singapore, Singapore 228213
Phone: 65-6235-2411
Fax: 65-6235-3316
E-mail: feoca@fareast.com.sg
Website: www.fareast.com.sg

Other Offices

1 Tanglin Road
#04-18 Orchard Parade Hotel
Singapore, Singapore 247905
Phone: 65-833-6666
Fax: 75-736-2043

Management and Staff

Philip Ng, Chief Executive Officer

Type of Firm

Corporate PE/Venture

Project Preferences

Role in Financing:
Will function either as deal originator or investor in deals created by others

Type of Financing Preferred:
Expansion
Start-up Financing

Geographical Preferences

International Preferences:
Asia

Industry Preferences

In Internet Specific prefer:
Internet

Additional Information

Year Founded: 2000
Capital Under Management: $1,700,000
Current Activity Level : Actively seeking new investments
Method of Compensation: Return on investment is of primary concern, do not charge fees

FEP CAPITAL

10 Rostom Street
Office 702 & 802, Garden City
Cairo, Egypt
Phone: 20227933308
Fax: 20227962596
E-mail: info@fep-capital.com
Website: fep-capital.com

Management and Staff

Mahmoud Khalifa, Vice President

Type of Firm

Bank Affiliated

Project Preferences

Type of Financing Preferred:
Leveraged Buyout
Expansion
Distressed Debt
Recapitalizations

Geographical Preferences

International Preferences:
Egypt
Africa

Industry Preferences

In Consumer Related prefer:
Food/Beverage

In Manufact. prefer:
Manufacturing

Additional Information

Year Founded: 1995
Capital Under Management: $140,000,000
Current Activity Level : Actively seeking new investments

FERD CAPITAL PARTNERS AS

Strandveien 50
P.O.Box 34
Lysaker, Norway 1324
Phone: 4767108000
Fax: 4767108001
E-mail: post@ferd.no
Website: www.ferd.no

Management and Staff

Bjorn Reinseth, Partner
Erik Olsen, Managing Partner
Peter Sunde, Partner

Type of Firm

Private Equity Firm

Association Membership

Norwegian Venture Capital Association

Project Preferences

Type of Financing Preferred:
Generalist PE

Size of Investments Considered:
Min Size of Investment Considered (000s): $711
Max Size of Investment Considered (000s): $1,777

Geographical Preferences

International Preferences:
Scandanavia/Nordic Region

Industry Preferences

In Communications prefer:
Commercial Communications
Wireless Communications

In Computer Software prefer:
Software

In Biotechnology prefer:
Biotechnology

In Consumer Related prefer:
Consumer Products

In Industrial/Energy prefer:
Oil and Gas Exploration

In Business Serv. prefer:
Services

Additional Information

Year Founded: 2007
Capital Under Management: $900,500,000
Current Activity Level : Actively seeking new investments

FERRER FREEMAN & CO LLC

10 Glenville Street
Greenwich, CT USA 06831
Phone: 2035328011
Fax: 2035328016
Website: www.ffandco.com

Management and Staff

Carlos Ferrer, Co-Founder
Justin Yang, Principal
Nicole Sansone, Chief Financial Officer
Theodore Lundberg, Partner
 Freeman, Co-Founder

Type of Firm

Private Equity Firm

Project Preferences

Role in Financing:
Prefer role as deal originator but will also invest in deals created by others

Type of Financing Preferred:
Leveraged Buyout
Expansion
Generalist PE
Later Stage
Management Buyouts
Acquisition

Size of Investments Considered:
Min Size of Investment Considered (000s): $10,000
Max Size of Investment Considered (000s): $40,000

Geographical Preferences

United States Preferences:

International Preferences:
Europe

Industry Preferences

In Medical/Health prefer:
Medical/Health
Medical Diagnostics
Medical Therapeutics
Medical Products
Health Services
Pharmaceuticals

Additional Information
Name of Most Recent Fund: FFC Partners III, L.P.
Most Recent Fund Was Raised: 07/15/2004
Year Founded: 1995
Capital Under Management: $900,000,000
Current Activity Level : Actively seeking new investments
Method of Compensation: Return on investment is of primary concern, do not charge fees

FERRO MANAGEMENT GROUP INC

185 Wind Chime Court
Suite 201
Raleigh, NC USA 27615
Phone: 9196762533
Fax: 9196760630
Website: www.ferromg.com

Management and Staff
Markus Isenrich, Founder

Type of Firm
Private Equity Firm

Project Preferences

Role in Financing:
Prefer role as deal originator but will also invest in deals created by others

Type of Financing Preferred:
Leveraged Buyout
Expansion
Management Buyouts
Acquisition
Recapitalizations

Geographical Preferences

United States Preferences:
Mid Atlantic
Southeast

Additional Information
Year Founded: 1995
Capital Under Management: $120,000,000
Current Activity Level : Actively seeking new investments
Method of Compensation: Return on invest. most important, but chg. closing fees, service fees, etc.

FERST CAPITAL PARTNERS INC

642 Rue de Courcelle #403
Montreal, Canada H4C 3C5
Website: www.ferstcapital.com

Type of Firm
Private Equity Firm

Project Preferences

Type of Financing Preferred:
Early Stage

Geographical Preferences

Canadian Preferences:
All Canada

Industry Preferences

In Financial Services prefer:
Financial Services

Additional Information
Year Founded: 2012
Current Activity Level : Actively seeking new investments

FERTITTA CAPITAL INC

9220 West Sunset Boulevard
Suite 210
Los Angeles, CA USA 90069
Phone: 2133283130
Website: www.fertittacapital.com

Management and Staff
David Hirschfeld, Vice President
Sam Bakhshandehpour, Managing Director

Type of Firm
Private Equity Firm

Project Preferences

Type of Financing Preferred:
Generalist PE

Industry Preferences

In Communications prefer:
Entertainment

In Consumer Related prefer:
Consumer

In Business Serv. prefer:
Media

Additional Information
Year Founded: 2017
Current Activity Level : Actively seeking new investments

FF VENTURE CAPITAL

989 Avenue of the Americas
Third Floor
New York, NY USA 10018
Phone: 9734887110
Website: www.ffvc.com

Other Offices
101 Eisenhower Parkway
Suite 300
ROSELAND, NJ USA 07068

Management and Staff
Adam Plotkin, Partner
David Teten, Partner
John Frankel, Partner
Kathryn Hume, Venture Partner
Michael Faber, Partner
Michael Yavonditte, Founder
Ryan Armburst, Managing Director

Type of Firm
Private Equity Firm

Association Membership
Canadian Venture Capital Association
National Venture Capital Association - USA (NVCA)

Project Preferences

Type of Financing Preferred:
Early Stage

Size of Investments Considered:
Min Size of Investment Considered (000s): $75
Max Size of Investment Considered (000s): $1,000

Industry Preferences

In Internet Specific prefer:
Internet

Additional Information
Name of Most Recent Fund: ff Rose (III) Venture Capital Fund, L.P.
Most Recent Fund Was Raised: 11/22/2013
Year Founded: 1999
Capital Under Management: $86,400,000
Current Activity Level : Actively seeking new investments

FFP SA

75, Avenue de la Grande Armee
Paris, France 75116
Phone: 33140664211
Fax: 33140665992
Website: www.groupe-ffp.fr

Management and Staff
Alain Chagnon, Chief Executive Officer

Type of Firm
Bank Affiliated

Project Preferences

Type of Financing Preferred:
Leveraged Buyout
Later Stage
Acquisition

Geographical Preferences

International Preferences:
Italy
India
Europe
China
Spain
Asia
France

Additional Information
Year Founded: 1929
Current Activity Level : Actively seeking new investments

FFR CAPITAL PARTNERS

141 Avondale Road
Ridgewood, NJ USA 07450
Website: www.frrcapital.com

Management and Staff
Robert Rosenberg, Partner
Thomas Ferguson, Partner

Type of Firm
Private Equity Advisor or Fund of Funds

Project Preferences

Type of Financing Preferred:
Leveraged Buyout

Geographical Preferences

United States Preferences:
Midwest
Northeast

Additional Information
Year Founded: 2006
Current Activity Level : Actively seeking new investments

FGF MANAGEMENT LTD

57-59 St James's Street
London, United Kingdom SW1A 1LD
Phone: 442076471400
Fax: 442076471440
E-mail: mail@greenparkcapital.com
Website: www.greenparkcapital.com

Other Offices
Level 10, Central Building
1-3 Pedder Street
Central Hong Kong, Hong Kong
Phone: 852-3975-2909
Fax: 852-3975-2800

Management and Staff
Andrew French, Founder

Type of Firm
Private Equity Advisor or Fund of Funds

Association Membership
German Venture Capital Association (BVK)

Project Preferences

Type of Financing Preferred:
Fund of Funds
Fund of Funds of Second

Additional Information
Year Founded: 2000
Capital Under Management: $1,800,000,000
Current Activity Level : Actively seeking new investments

FGI CAPITAL PARTNERS INC

2-7-16 Toranomon, Minato-ku
Toranomon Towers Office 304
Tokyo, Japan 205-0001
Website: www.fgicp.com

Management and Staff
Hajime Yoda, Managing Director
Yasuhito Doi, Managing Director

Type of Firm
Bank Affiliated

Project Preferences

Type of Financing Preferred:
Early Stage
Balanced
Seed

Geographical Preferences

United States Preferences:
All U.S.

International Preferences:
Europe
China
Japan

Industry Preferences

In Communications prefer:
Communications and Media

In Industrial/Energy prefer:
Advanced Materials

Additional Information
Year Founded: 2007
Current Activity Level : Actively seeking new investments

FIANCHETTO CAPITAL AB

Telegrafgatan 8A
Epsilon bld. fl.2
Stockholm, Sweden 169 72
Phone: 46-8-558-01433
Fax: 46-8-558-01434
E-mail: info@fianchettocapital.com
Website: www.fianchettocapital.com

Management and Staff
Gustav Kamperman, Managing Director

Type of Firm
Private Equity Firm

Project Preferences

Type of Financing Preferred:
Leveraged Buyout

Size of Investments Considered:
Min Size of Investment Considered (000s): $4,419
Max Size of Investment Considered (000s): $43,751

Geographical Preferences

International Preferences:
Europe
Scandanavia/Nordic Region

Industry Preferences

In Medical/Health prefer:
Medical/Health

Additional Information
Year Founded: 2005
Current Activity Level : Actively seeking new investments

FIBA KAPITAL HOLDING AS

First Levent Plaza No 173/A
Floor 9
Istanbul, Turkey
Phone: 902123391900
Fax: 902123391872
E-mail: info@fibacapital.com
Website: www.fibaholding.com.tr

Management and Staff
Burak Emin Sahin, Principal
Karani Gulec, Managing Director
Turan Sert, Managing Director

Type of Firm
Private Equity Firm

Project Preferences

Type of Financing Preferred:
Early Stage
Expansion
Balanced
Later Stage

Geographical Preferences

International Preferences:
Turkey
Europe

Industry Preferences

In Consumer Related prefer:
Retail

In Industrial/Energy prefer:
Energy

In Transportation prefer:
Transportation
Aerospace

In Financial Services prefer:
Real Estate
Financial Services

Additional Information

Year Founded: 2005
Current Activity Level : Actively seeking new investments

FIDEA VENTURE CAPITAL LTD

2F Shogin Yamagata Bldg.
1-4-21 Honcho
Yamagata-shi, Japan 990-0043
Phone: 81236355030
Fax: 81236252626
Website: www.fidea-venture.co.jp

Type of Firm
Bank Affiliated

Project Preferences

Type of Financing Preferred:
Balanced

Geographical Preferences

International Preferences:
Japan

Additional Information

Year Founded: 1995
Current Activity Level : Actively seeking new investments

FIDELIS CAPITAL LLC

820 Shades Creek Parkway, Suite 1200
Birmingham, AL USA 35209
Phone: 2055886022
E-mail: info@fideliscapital.net
Website: www.fideliscapital.net

Management and Staff

John Stein, Co-Founder
Steven Dauphin, Co-Founder
William Reiser, Co-Founder

Type of Firm
Private Equity Firm

Project Preferences

Type of Financing Preferred:
Leveraged Buyout
Generalist PE
Balanced
Acquisition

Geographical Preferences

United States Preferences:
Southeast

Additional Information

Year Founded: 2012
Current Activity Level : Actively seeking new investments

FIDELITY GROWTH PARTNERS ASIA

88 Queensway, Admiralty
Suite 2201 Level 22, 2 Pacific
Hong Kong, Hong Kong
Phone: 85226292800
Fax: 85225090371
E-mail: FGPA@fil.com
Website: www.fidelitygrowthpartners.asia

Other Offices

Eight Century Avenue
Unit 3313-14, Two IFC, Shanghai IFC
Shanghai, China 200120
Phone: 862163406555
Fax: 862163406618

No. 79 Jianguo Road, Chaoyang District
Unit 2908, 29th Floor, Tower 2
Beijing, China 100025
Phone: 861065989336
Fax: 861065989335

Management and Staff

Albert Cheng, Partner
Bing Chung Tam, Partner
Daniel Auerbach, Managing Partner
Dianna Qian, Principal
Leon Chen, Partner
Norman Chen, Partner
Qian Yu, Principal
Rebecca Lin, Principal
Ted Chua, Partner

Type of Firm
Investment Management Firm

Association Membership
Hong Kong Venture Capital Association (HKVCA)
China Venture Capital Association

Project Preferences

Type of Financing Preferred:
Early Stage
Expansion
Mezzanine
Later Stage
Seed
Startup

Geographical Preferences

International Preferences:
China
Asia

Industry Preferences

In Communications prefer:
Telecommunications
Other Communication Prod.

In Computer Hardware prefer:
Computers

In Computer Other prefer:
Computer Related

In Medical/Health prefer:
Medical/Health

In Consumer Related prefer:
Consumer
Education Related

In Financial Services prefer:
Financial Services

In Business Serv. prefer:
Distribution
Media

Additional Information

Year Founded: 1994
Capital Under Management: $250,000,000
Current Activity Level : Actively seeking new investments

FIDELITY INVESTMENT FUNDS II

82 Devonshire Street
Boston, MA USA 02109
Phone: 6175637000
Fax: 6175636150

Management and Staff

Abigail Johnson, Chief Executive Officer

Type of Firm
Investment Management Firm

Project Preferences

Type of Financing Preferred:
Balanced

Geographical Preferences

United States Preferences:
All U.S.

Additional Information
Name of Most Recent Fund: Fidelity Investors VI Limited Partnership
Most Recent Fund Was Raised: 07/13/2004
Year Founded: 1946
Current Activity Level : Actively seeking new investments

FIDELIUM FINANCE

North Urban Center
Block B, 1st Floor, No. B 1-1
Tunis, Tunisia 1083
Phone: 21671948135
Fax: 21671948168
Website: www.fidelium-finance.com.tn

Type of Firm
Investment Management Firm

Association Membership
Tunisian Venture Capital Association
French Venture Capital Association (AFIC)

Project Preferences

Type of Financing Preferred:
Leveraged Buyout
Early Stage
Unknown
Generalist PE
Later Stage
Acquisition
Recapitalizations

Geographical Preferences

International Preferences:
Tunisia
Africa
All International

Additional Information
Year Founded: 2007
Capital Under Management: $46,927,000
Current Activity Level : Actively seeking new investments

FIDES BUSINESS PARTNER AG

Hirschengraben 28
Zurich, Switzerland 8001
Phone: 41 44 241 30 00
E-mail: info@fidesbusinesspartner.ch
Website: www.fidesbusinesspartner.ch

Management and Staff
Johannes Gugl, Co-Founder
Manfred Handle, Co-Founder
Martin Risch, Co-Founder
Rene Steiner, Co-Founder

Type of Firm
Investment Management Firm

Association Membership
Swiss Venture Capital Association (SECA)

Project Preferences

Type of Financing Preferred:
Leveraged Buyout
Turnaround

Geographical Preferences

International Preferences:
Italy
Switzerland
Austria
Germany

Additional Information
Year Founded: 2011
Current Activity Level : Actively seeking new investments

FIDES CAPITAL SL

Paseo de la castellana, n 100
escalera derecha 2 B
Madrid, Spain 28046
Phone: 34-91-781-1638
Fax: 34-91-564-4514
E-mail: fmb@fidescapital.es
Website: www.fidescapital.es

Management and Staff
Julia De la Calle Negro, Chief Executive Officer

Type of Firm
Private Equity Firm

Project Preferences

Type of Financing Preferred:
Second Stage Financing
Expansion

Size of Investments Considered:
Min Size of Investment Considered (000s): $1,924
Max Size of Investment Considered (000s): $7,697

Geographical Preferences

International Preferences:
Europe
Spain

Industry Preferences

In Internet Specific prefer:
Internet

Additional Information
Year Founded: 1999
Capital Under Management: $20,900,000
Current Activity Level : Actively seeking new investments

FIDI TOSCANA SPA

Piazza della Repubblica 6
Florence, Italy 50123
Phone: 39-55-238-41
Fax: 39-55-212-805
E-mail: mail@fiditoscana.it
Website: www.fiditoscana.it

Management and Staff
Duilio Mannaioni, Vice President
Paolo Rafanelli, President

Type of Firm
Private Equity Firm

Project Preferences

Type of Financing Preferred:
Expansion
Mezzanine

Geographical Preferences

International Preferences:
Italy

Industry Preferences

In Industrial/Energy prefer:
Energy
Alternative Energy

Additional Information
Year Founded: 1975
Current Activity Level : Actively seeking new investments

FIDURA CAPITAL CONSULT GMBH

Bavariaring 44
Munich, Germany 80336
Phone: 4923889810
Fax: 4923889819
E-mail: info@fidura-fonds.de
Website: www.fidura.net

Type of Firm
Private Equity Firm

Association Membership
German Venture Capital Association (BVK)

Project Preferences

Type of Financing Preferred:
Early Stage
Balanced
Later Stage
Seed
Startup

Geographical Preferences

International Preferences:
Switzerland
Western Europe
Austria
Germany

Additional Information

Year Founded: 2001
Current Activity Level : Actively seeking new investments

FIDUS CAPITAL LLC

227 West Trade Street
Suite 1910
Charlotte, NC USA 28202
Phone: 7043342222
Fax: 7043342202
Website: www.fiduspartners.com

Other Offices

190 South LaSalle Street
Suite 2140
Chicago, IL USA 60603
Phone: 312-284-5200
Fax: 312-284-5212

70 East 55th Street
Tenth Floor
New York, NY USA 10022
Phone: 212-750-6400
Fax: 212-750-6411

Management and Staff

B. Bragg Comer, Managing Partner
Cary Schaefer, Vice President
Christopher Haza, Vice President
Edward Ross, Managing Director
Edward Imbrogno, Managing Partner
J. Stephen Dockery, Managing Partner
John Grigg, Managing Partner
John Ross, Managing Partner
John Cheek, Vice President
Robert Kreidler, Chief Operating Officer
Ted Swimmer, Managing Partner
W. Andrew Worth, Principal

Type of Firm

Bank Affiliated

Association Membership

Natl Assoc of Small Bus. Inv. Co (NASBIC)

Project Preferences

Type of Financing Preferred:
Leveraged Buyout
Expansion
Mezzanine
Later Stage
Management Buyouts
Acquisition
Recapitalizations

Geographical Preferences

United States Preferences:

Industry Preferences

In Computer Software prefer:
Software

In Medical/Health prefer:
Health Services

In Consumer Related prefer:
Consumer
Retail
Franchises(NEC)
Food/Beverage
Consumer Products

In Industrial/Energy prefer:
Industrial Products

In Transportation prefer:
Aerospace

In Business Serv. prefer:
Services
Distribution

In Manufact. prefer:
Manufacturing

Additional Information

Year Founded: 2005
Capital Under Management: $200,000,000
Current Activity Level : Actively seeking new investments

FIEDLER CAPITAL GMBH

Donau-City-Strasse 6
Vienna, Austria A-1220
E-mail: info@fiedlercapital.com
Website: www.fiedlercapital.com

Management and Staff

David Douglas, Venture Partner
Jordan Bocskov, Managing Partner
Robert Hegedus, Managing Partner

Type of Firm

Private Equity Firm

Project Preferences

Type of Financing Preferred:
Early Stage
Seed

Additional Information

Year Founded: 2017
Current Activity Level : Actively seeking new investments

FIELDS GROUP BV

Claude Debussylaan 10
Amsterdam, Netherlands 1082 MD
Phone: 31202623532
Website: fields.nl

Type of Firm

Private Equity Firm

Project Preferences

Type of Financing Preferred:
Leveraged Buyout
Turnaround
Recapitalizations

Geographical Preferences

International Preferences:
Europe
Netherlands

Industry Preferences

In Industrial/Energy prefer:
Industrial Products
Materials
Machinery

In Manufact. prefer:
Manufacturing

Additional Information

Year Founded: 2012
Current Activity Level : Actively seeking new investments

FIER PARTNERS LP

413, rue Saint-Jacques
Suite 500
Montreal, Canada H2Y 1N9
Phone: 5148739287
Fax: 5148731494
Website: www.fierpartenaires.com

Type of Firm

Private Equity Advisor or Fund of Funds

Additional Information

Year Founded: 2005
Current Activity Level : Actively seeking new investments

FIER SUCCES

350 Rue Franquet
Porte 20, Sainte-Foy
Quebec, Canada G1P 4N3
Phone: 4186830011
Fax: 4186502359
Website: www.fiersucces.com

Type of Firm
Government Affiliated Program

Additional Information
Year Founded: 2005
Current Activity Level : Actively seeking new investments

FIERA CAPITAL (UK) LTD

39 St James's Street
London, United Kingdom SW1A 1JD
Phone: 44-207-518-2100
Fax: 44-207-518-2199
E-mail: marketing@charlemagnecapital.com
Website: www.charlemagnecapital.com

Other Offices

Tsum Business Centre
2 Kniagina Maria Louisa
Sofia, Bulgaria 1550
Phone: 359-2-926-0600
Fax: 359-2-926-0692

16-18 Ridgeway Street
Douglas
Isle of Man, United Kingdom IM1 1EN
Phone: 44-1624-640-200
Fax: 44-1624-614-474

Management and Staff
Hans Van Griethuysen, Chief Executive Officer

Type of Firm
Investment Management Firm

Project Preferences

Type of Financing Preferred:
Leveraged Buyout
Expansion
Balanced
Turnaround
Other
Management Buyouts
Acquisition

Geographical Preferences

International Preferences:
Abu Dhabi
Slovenia
Turkey
Central Europe
Qatar
Argentina
Eastern Europe
Middle East
Croatia
Saudi Arabia
Bulgaria
Romania

Additional Information
Year Founded: 1997
Current Activity Level : Actively seeking new investments

FIFTH FORCE GMBH

Cuvrystrasse 4
Berlin, Germany 10997
Phone: 491703507819
E-mail: hello@neufund.org
Website: www.neufund.org

Type of Firm
Private Equity Firm

Additional Information
Year Founded: 2016
Current Activity Level : Actively seeking new investments

FIFTH STREET CAPITAL LLC

777 West Putnam Avenue
Third Floor
Greenwich, CT USA 06830
Phone: 2036813600
Fax: 2036813879
Website: www.fifthstreetfinance.com

Other Offices

311 South Wacker Drive
Suite 3380
Chicago, IL USA 60606
Phone: 3123487205
Fax: 3123487613

Two Greenwich Office Park
Second Floor, 51 Weaver Street
Greenwich, CT USA 06831
Phone: 2039924533
Fax: 2039924549

5023 North Parkway Calabasas
Suite 14
Calabasas, CA USA 91302
Phone: 8188769665

Management and Staff
Alexander Frank, Chief Financial Officer
Brian Finkelstein, Managing Director
Casey Zmijeski, Partner
Gregory Browne, Managing Director
Ivelin Dimitrov, Partner
Jennifer Blank Tremblay, Vice President
John Trentos, Managing Director
Juan Alva, Partner
Sunny Khorana, Partner

Type of Firm
Private Equity Firm

Association Membership
Natl Assoc of Small Bus. Inv. Co (NASBIC)

Project Preferences

Type of Financing Preferred:
Leveraged Buyout
Expansion
Mezzanine
Later Stage
Management Buyouts
Acquisition
Recapitalizations

Industry Preferences

In Computer Software prefer:
Software

In Internet Specific prefer:
Internet

In Medical/Health prefer:
Medical/Health

In Consumer Related prefer:
Food/Beverage
Consumer Products
Other Restaurants
Education Related

In Industrial/Energy prefer:
Energy

In Transportation prefer:
Aerospace

In Business Serv. prefer:
Services

In Manufact. prefer:
Manufacturing

Additional Information
Year Founded: 1998
Capital Under Management: $500,000,000
Current Activity Level : Actively seeking new investments

FIFTH WALL VENTURES

3115 Ocean Front Walk
Suite 202
Marina del Rey, CA USA 90292
Phone: 4242651112
Website: fifthwall.vc

Type of Firm
Private Equity Firm

Project Preferences

Type of Financing Preferred:
Early Stage

Additional Information
Year Founded: 2016
Capital Under Management: $210,000,000
Current Activity Level: Actively seeking new investments

FIGHT AGAINST CANCER INNOVATION TRUST

661 University Avenue
Suite 510
Toronto, Canada M5G 0A3
Website: facit.ca

Management and Staff
Jeff Courtney, President

Type of Firm
Government Affiliated Program

Project Preferences

Type of Financing Preferred:
Early Stage

Industry Preferences

In Medical/Health prefer:
Medical/Health

Additional Information
Year Founded: 2014
Current Activity Level: Actively seeking new investments

FII CAPITAL PARTNERS LLC

500 North Michigan Avenue
Suite 300
Chicago, IL USA 60611
Phone: 3123964165
E-mail: info@fiicp.com
Website: www.fiicp.com

Other Offices
Former HQ 191 Peachtree Street Northeast
Suite 3300
Atlanta, GA USA 30303
Phone: 4044627548
Fax: 4044202810

Management and Staff
Milo Hall, Chief Financial Officer
Redell Vincent Napper II, Managing Partner

Type of Firm
Private Equity Firm

Project Preferences

Type of Financing Preferred:
Balanced

Additional Information
Year Founded: 2011
Current Activity Level: Actively seeking new investments

FIKA VENTURES LP

3222 Selby Avenue
Los Angeles, CA USA 90034
Phone: 6505564776

Type of Firm
Private Equity Firm

Project Preferences

Type of Financing Preferred:
Early Stage

Geographical Preferences

United States Preferences:
California

Additional Information
Year Founded: 2016
Capital Under Management: $40,000,000
Current Activity Level: Actively seeking new investments

FIL CAPITAL ADVISORS (INDIA) PVT LTD

5 President John Kennedy St.
Rogers House
Mauritius, India 400 021
Phone: 912266554200
Fax: 912266554220
E-mail: info@fidelityindiacapital.com
Website: www.fidelitygrowthpartners.in

Other Offices
Nariman Point
6th Floor, Mafatlal Centre
Mumbai, India 400 021
Phone: 912266554400

Management and Staff
Raj Dugar, Senior Managing Director
Raul Rai, Managing Director

Type of Firm
Private Equity Firm

Project Preferences

Type of Financing Preferred:
Early Stage
Expansion

Size of Investments Considered:
Min Size of Investment Considered (000s): $10,000
Max Size of Investment Considered (000s): $50,000

Geographical Preferences

International Preferences:
India

Industry Preferences

In Communications prefer:
Telecommunications

In Medical/Health prefer:
Medical/Health

In Consumer Related prefer:
Retail
Education Related

In Industrial/Energy prefer:
Energy

In Financial Services prefer:
Financial Services

In Business Serv. prefer:
Media

Additional Information
Year Founded: 2009
Current Activity Level: Actively seeking new investments

FILLMORE CAPITAL PARTNERS LLC

Four Embarcadero Center
Suite 710
San Francisco, CA USA 94111
Phone: 4159341477
Website: www.fillmorecap.com

Other Offices
250 West Old Wilson Bridge Road
Suite 122
Worthington, OH USA 43085
Phone: 6147811420

Management and Staff
Brandon Ribar, Vice President
Nicholas Finn, Vice President

Type of Firm
Private Equity Firm

Project Preferences

Type of Financing Preferred:
Value-Add
Generalist PE
Opportunistic
Special Situation

Industry Preferences

In Medical/Health prefer:
Medical/Health

In Consumer Related prefer:
Hotels and Resorts

In Financial Services prefer:
Real Estate

Additional Information
Year Founded: 2003
Current Activity Level : Actively seeking new investments

FILSA BV

Wilhelminaplein 2
Wassenaar, Netherlands 2243HE
Phone: 31622522276
E-mail: info@filsa.nl
Website: www.filsa.com

Type of Firm
Private Equity Firm

Project Preferences

Type of Financing Preferred:
Early Stage
Seed

Geographical Preferences

International Preferences:
Netherlands

Industry Preferences

In Communications prefer:
Telecommunications

In Internet Specific prefer:
Internet

Additional Information
Year Founded: 2012
Current Activity Level : Actively seeking new investments

FINADVANCE SA

570 avenue du Club Hippique
Le Derby
Aix en Provence, France 13090
Phone: 33442529130
Fax: 33442529139
E-mail: contact@finadvance.fr
Website: www.finadvance.fr

Other Offices
82 rue Saint-Lazare
Paris, France 75009
Phone: 33148747770
Fax: 33148742169

Management and Staff
Herve Legoupil, Founder
Olivier Gillot, Founder

Type of Firm
Private Equity Firm

Association Membership
French Venture Capital Association (AFIC)

Project Preferences

Role in Financing:
Prefer role as deal originator but will also invest in deals created by others

Type of Financing Preferred:
Leveraged Buyout
Later Stage
Management Buyouts
Acquisition

Size of Investments Considered:
Min Size of Investment Considered (000s): $2,665
Max Size of Investment Considered (000s): $15,995

Geographical Preferences

International Preferences:
Europe
France

Industry Preferences

In Industrial/Energy prefer:
Industrial Products

In Business Serv. prefer:
Services

Additional Information
Year Founded: 1988
Capital Under Management: $41,000,000
Current Activity Level : Actively seeking new investments
Method of Compensation: Return on invest. most important, but chg. closing fees, service fees, etc.

FINAM GLOBAL

Nastasinskiy Pereulok, 7
Building 2
Moscow, Russia 127006
Phone: 74957969388
E-mail: invest@finamglobal.com

Management and Staff
Victor Remsha, Founder

Type of Firm
Private Equity Firm

Project Preferences

Type of Financing Preferred:
Generalist PE

Geographical Preferences

International Preferences:
Russia

Industry Preferences

In Communications prefer:
Communications and Media
Telecommunications
Media and Entertainment

In Computer Software prefer:
Software

In Internet Specific prefer:
Internet

In Computer Other prefer:
Computer Related

In Business Serv. prefer:
Media

Additional Information
Year Founded: 1994
Capital Under Management: $143,000,000
Current Activity Level : Actively seeking new investments

FINANCE YORKSHIRE LTD

One Capitol Court, Dodworth
Capitol Business Park
Barnsley, United Kingdom S75 3TZ
Phone: 448456490000
E-mail: info@finance-yorkshire.com
Website: www.finance-yorkshire.com

Management and Staff
Alex McWhirter, Chief Executive Officer

Type of Firm
Private Equity Firm

Project Preferences

Type of Financing Preferred:
Leveraged Buyout
Early Stage
Expansion
Generalist PE
Acquisition
Startup

Geographical Preferences

International Preferences:
United Kingdom

Additional Information
Year Founded: 1969
Current Activity Level : Actively seeking new investments

FINANCE ZEALAND MANAGEMENT APS

Marienbergvej 132
Vordingborg, Denmark 4760
Phone: 4531377331
Website: financezealand.dk

Management and Staff
Joachim Vanggaard, Managing Partner

Type of Firm
Private Equity Firm

Project Preferences

Type of Financing Preferred:
Acquisition

Geographical Preferences

International Preferences:
Denmark

Additional Information

Year Founded: 2017
Capital Under Management: $4,230,000
Current Activity Level : Actively seeking new investments

FINANCIADORA DE ESTUDOS E PROJETOS FINEP

SCN Q 2 Bloco D Torre A
Sala 1102, Liberty Mall
Brasilia, Brazil 70712904
Phone: 556130357150
E-mail: seac@finep.gov.br
Website: www.finep.gov.br

Management and Staff

Mauro Marcondes Rodrigues, President

Type of Firm

Government Affiliated Program

Association Membership

Emerging Markets Private Equity Association

Project Preferences

Type of Financing Preferred:
Expansion
Seed
Startup

Geographical Preferences

International Preferences:
Brazil

Industry Preferences

In Communications prefer:
Communications and Media

In Computer Software prefer:
Software

In Biotechnology prefer:
Biotechnology

In Medical/Health prefer:
Medical/Health

In Financial Services prefer:
Financial Services

In Business Serv. prefer:
Services

Additional Information

Year Founded: 1967
Current Activity Level : Actively seeking new investments

FINANCIAL CORPORATION CO SAOG

Near Bank Melli Iran
P.O. Box 782
Muscat, Oman 131
Phone: 96824822300
Fax: 96824822390
E-mail: fincorp@fincorp.org
Website: www.fincorp.org

Management and Staff

AJV Jayachander, Chief Operating Officer
Nasr Al Hosni, Chief Executive Officer

Type of Firm

Investment Management Firm

Project Preferences

Type of Financing Preferred:
Early Stage
Balanced
Later Stage
Startup

Geographical Preferences

International Preferences:
India
Oman
Middle East

Industry Preferences

In Industrial/Energy prefer:
Industrial Products

In Financial Services prefer:
Investment Groups
Financial Services

In Manufact. prefer:
Manufacturing

Additional Information

Year Founded: 2003
Capital Under Management: $51,989,000
Current Activity Level : Actively seeking new investments

FINANCIAL TECHNOLOGY VENTURES

555 California Street
Suite 2900
San Francisco, CA USA 94104
Phone: 4152293000
Fax: 4152293005
Website: www.ftvcapital.com

Other Offices

540 Madison Avenue
Suite 2800
MANHATTAN, NY USA 10022
Phone: 212-682-4800
Fax: 212-682-4480

Management and Staff

Aly Lovett, Vice President
Ben Cukier, Partner
Brad Bernstein, Partner
Christopher Winship, Partner
Christopher Tan, Principal
Eric Byunn, Partner
James Hale, Managing Partner
Karen Gilbert, Partner
Kyle Griswold, Principal
Liron Gitig, Partner
Richard Garman, Managing Partner
Robert Huret, Managing Partner
Robert Anderson, Vice President
Robert Kaufman, Vice President

Type of Firm

Private Equity Firm

Association Membership

Western Association of Venture Capitalists (WAVC)

Project Preferences

Role in Financing:
Prefer role as deal originator but will also invest in deals created by others

Type of Financing Preferred:
Leveraged Buyout
Expansion
Generalist PE
Later Stage
Management Buyouts
Acquisition
Recapitalizations

Geographical Preferences

United States Preferences:

International Preferences:
All International

Industry Focus

(% based on actual investment)
Computer Software and Services   41.6%
Internet Specific   22.8%
Other Products   21.2%
Computer Hardware   14.4%

Additional Information

Name of Most Recent Fund: FTV IV, L.P.
Most Recent Fund Was Raised: 11/26/2013
Year Founded: 1998
Capital Under Management: $935,000,000
Current Activity Level : Actively seeking new investments
Method of Compensation: Other

FINANCIERE FONDS PRIVES SAS

136, Rue du Faubourg
Paris, France 75008
Website: www.financiere-fondsprives.com

Type of Firm
Private Equity Firm

Project Preferences

Type of Financing Preferred:
Early Stage
Expansion
Later Stage
Seed

Geographical Preferences

International Preferences:
Europe
France

Additional Information
Year Founded: 2008
Current Activity Level : Actively seeking new investments

FINANCIERE MEESCHAERT SA

12 Rond-Point Des Champs-
-Elysees
Paris, France 75008
Phone: 33 1 53 40 2020
E-mail: contact@meeschaert.com
Website: meeschaert.com

Type of Firm
Bank Affiliated

Project Preferences

Type of Financing Preferred:
Leveraged Buyout
Early Stage
Mezzanine
Balanced
Turnaround
Later Stage
Seed
Acquisition
Recapitalizations

Geographical Preferences

International Preferences:
Europe
France

Additional Information
Year Founded: 1987
Current Activity Level : Actively seeking new investments

FINANZIARIA REGIONALE FRIULI VENEZIA GIULIA SPA

Via Locchi, 19
Trieste, Italy 34123
Phone: 3904031971
Fax: 390403197400
E-mail: mail@friulia.it
Website: www.friulia.it

Other Offices
Via Liruti, 18
Udine, Italy 33100
Phone: 39-0432-275-911
Fax: 39-0432-501-290

Piazzetta del Portello n. 2
Pordenone, Italy 33170
Phone: 39-0434-247-666
Fax: 39-0434-246-304

Management and Staff
Marco Signori, Founder
Stefano Milanese, Vice President

Type of Firm
Government Affiliated Program

Project Preferences

Role in Financing:
Prefer role as deal originator but will also invest in deals created by others

Type of Financing Preferred:
Leveraged Buyout
Early Stage
Mezzanine
Turnaround
Later Stage
Seed
Startup

Geographical Preferences

International Preferences:
Italy

Industry Focus
(% based on actual investment)

Consumer Related	54.1%
Industrial/Energy	30.6%
Other Products	7.4%
Computer Software and Services	6.9%
Medical/Health	1.0%

Additional Information
Year Founded: 1967
Capital Under Management: $234,500,000
Current Activity Level : Actively seeking new investments
Method of Compensation: Professional fee required whether or not deal closes

FINAPERE CAPITAL SAS

22-24 Rue de Belfort
Courbevoie, France 92400
Phone: 33147682007
Fax: 33607442980
E-mail: contact@finapere.com
Website: www.finapere.com

Management and Staff
Jean-Pierre Miege, President

Type of Firm
Private Equity Firm

Project Preferences

Type of Financing Preferred:
Leveraged Buyout
Early Stage
Generalist PE
Later Stage
Management Buyouts
Acquisition

Geographical Preferences

International Preferences:
France

Additional Information
Year Founded: 2011
Current Activity Level : Actively seeking new investments

FINATEM FONDS MANAGEMENT VERWALTUNGS GMBH

Feldbergstrasse 35
Frankfurt am Main, Germany 60323
Phone: 49695095640
Fax: 496950956430
E-mail: info@finatem.de
Website: www.finatem.de

Management and Staff
Christophe Hemmerle, Managing Partner
Daniel Kartje, Partner
Eric Jungblut, Partner
Irmgard Schade, Partner

Type of Firm
Private Equity Firm

Association Membership
Austrian PE and Venture Capital Association (AVCO)
German Venture Capital Association (BVK)

Project Preferences

Type of Financing Preferred:
Leveraged Buyout
Turnaround
Management Buyouts
Acquisition
Recapitalizations

Geographical Preferences

International Preferences:
Switzerland
Austria
Germany

Industry Preferences

In Industrial/Energy prefer:
Industrial Products

Additional Information

Name of Most Recent Fund: Finatem III
Most Recent Fund Was Raised: 01/14/2010
Year Founded: 2000
Capital Under Management: $195,653,000
Current Activity Level : Actively seeking new investments

FINAVENTURES

3000 Ocean Park Boulevard
Suite 1022
Santa Monica, CA USA 90405
Phone: 3103995011
Fax: 3104525492
E-mail: contact@finaventures.com

Management and Staff

David Espitallier, Principal
Rachid Sefrioui, Managing Director
Sam Lee, Managing Director

Type of Firm

Private Equity Firm

Project Preferences

Role in Financing:
Will function either as deal originator or investor in deals created by others

Type of Financing Preferred:
Early Stage
Balanced
Later Stage

Geographical Preferences

United States Preferences:
Southern California
Northern California

Additional Information

Name of Most Recent Fund: Fina Fund I, L.P.
Most Recent Fund Was Raised: 10/24/2000
Year Founded: 1999
Capital Under Management: $21,000,000
Current Activity Level : Actively seeking new investments

Method of Compensation: Return on investment is of primary concern, do not charge fees

FINAVES I SA

Avenida Pearson, 21
Barcelona, Spain 08034
Phone: 34932534200
Fax: 34932534343
E-mail: finaves@iese.edu

Other Offices

Pacellistr. 4
Munich, Germany 80333
Phone: 49 89 24 20 97 90
Fax: 49 89 24 20 97 99

Camino del Cerro del guila, 3
Madrid, Spain 28023
Phone: 34 91 211 30 00
Fax: 34 91 357 29 13

165 West 57th Street
New York, NY USA 10019
Phone: 1 646 346 8850
Fax: 1 646 346 8852

Rua Martiniano de Carvalho, 573
Sao Paulo, Brazil 01321001
Phone: 55 11 3177 8200

Management and Staff

Adelaide Cracco, Chief Executive Officer
Pedro Nueno, President, Founder

Type of Firm

University Program

Project Preferences

Type of Financing Preferred:
Early Stage
Mezzanine
Seed
Startup

Geographical Preferences

United States Preferences:

International Preferences:
Europe
Spain
Germany
All International

Additional Information

Name of Most Recent Fund: Finaves IV
Most Recent Fund Was Raised: 03/30/2011
Year Founded: 2000
Capital Under Management: $2,600,000
Current Activity Level : Actively seeking new investments

FINCALABRA SPA

Via Pugliese, 30
Catanzaro, Italy 88100
Phone: 39-09-6177-0775
Fax: 39-09-6177-0226
E-mail: info@fincalabra.it
Website: www.fincalabra.it

Management and Staff

Domenico Lecce, President
Giuseppe Speziali, President
Umberto De Rose, President

Type of Firm

Incubator/Development Program

Project Preferences

Type of Financing Preferred:
Balanced

Geographical Preferences

International Preferences:
Italy

Industry Preferences

In Industrial/Energy prefer:
Industrial Products
Materials

In Manufact. prefer:
Manufacturing

Additional Information

Year Founded: 1999
Current Activity Level : Actively seeking new investments

FINCH CAPITAL PARTNERS BV

Concertgebouwplein 9
Amsterdam, Netherlands 1071 LL
Phone: 31207607800
E-mail: info@ogc-partners.com
Website: www.ogc-partners.com

Management and Staff

Aman Ghei, Principal
Hans De Back, Partner
Radboud Vlaar, Partner
Reinier Musters, Partner

Type of Firm

Private Equity Firm

Project Preferences

Type of Financing Preferred:
Early Stage
Expansion
Later Stage

Size of Investments Considered:
Min Size of Investment Considered (000s): $317
Max Size of Investment Considered (000s): $12,670

Geographical Preferences

International Preferences:
Europe

Industry Preferences

In Computer Software prefer:
Applications Software

In Internet Specific prefer:
E-Commerce Technology
Ecommerce
Web Aggregation/Portals

In Financial Services prefer:
Financial Services
Insurance

Additional Information

Year Founded: 2013
Current Activity Level : Actively seeking new investments

FIND INVEST GROW LTD

B51.1, 56 Wood Lane
London, United Kingdom W12 7SB
Phone: 448700349633
E-mail: info@findinvestgrow.com
Website: www.fig.vc

Management and Staff

James Herbert, Co-Founder
James King, Co-Founder
Marco Geninazza, Co-Founder
Mark Hanington, Co-Founder
Simon Hill, Managing Director

Type of Firm

Private Equity Firm

Project Preferences

Type of Financing Preferred:
Early Stage
Expansion
Seed

Geographical Preferences

International Preferences:
United Kingdom
Europe

Additional Information

Year Founded: 2009
Current Activity Level : Actively seeking new investments

FINDOS INVESTOR GMBH

Frauenstrasse 30
Munich, Germany 80469
Phone: 498920000950
Fax: 4989200009595
E-mail: findos@findos.eu
Website: www.findos.eu

Management and Staff

Hans Freudenberg, Partner
Olaf Kensy, Partner
Olaf Rogowski, Partner
Oliver Nell, Partner
Verena Mohaupt, Partner
Wolfgang Ziegler, Partner

Type of Firm

Private Equity Firm

Project Preferences

Type of Financing Preferred:
Leveraged Buyout

Geographical Preferences

International Preferences:
Germany

Additional Information

Year Founded: 2006
Current Activity Level : Actively seeking new investments

FINEMATIKA OOO

Glinishchevskiy pereulok 3
Moscow, Russia 125009
Phone: 74955425858
E-mail: info@finematika.ru
Website: www.finematika.ru

Type of Firm

Investment Management Firm

Association Membership

Russian Venture Capital Association (RVCA)

Project Preferences

Type of Financing Preferred:
Leveraged Buyout
Expansion
Acquisition

Geographical Preferences

International Preferences:
Russia

Additional Information

Year Founded: 2015
Current Activity Level : Actively seeking new investments

FINERGY CAPITAL

One East Chang An Avenue
12/F, Tower W2, Oriental Plaza
Dong Cheng District, Beijing, China 100738
Phone: 861057387888
E-mail: finergy@ryfund.com
Website: www.finergyfund.com

Type of Firm

Private Equity Firm

Project Preferences

Type of Financing Preferred:
Expansion
Later Stage

Geographical Preferences

International Preferences:
China

Industry Preferences

In Industrial/Energy prefer:
Energy
Machinery

In Financial Services prefer:
Financial Services

In Manufact. prefer:
Manufacturing

Additional Information

Year Founded: 2011
Current Activity Level : Actively seeking new investments

FINEXT STARTUP KOCKA-ZATI TOKEALAP-KEZELO ZRT

47-53 Runner Street
6th Floor
Budapest, Hungary 1082
Phone: 3617833749
Fax: 3617833849
E-mail: finextstartup@finextstartup.hu
Website: finext.hu

Type of Firm

Private Equity Firm

Project Preferences

Role in Financing:
Will function either as deal originator or investor in deals created by others

Type of Financing Preferred:
Early Stage
Expansion
Later Stage

Geographical Preferences

International Preferences:
Hungary
Europe

Industry Preferences

In Communications prefer:
Commercial Communications
Telecommunications

In Biotechnology prefer:
Biotechnology

In Medical/Health prefer:
Health Services

In Consumer Related prefer:
Food/Beverage

In Industrial/Energy prefer:
Energy
Environmental Related

In Agr/Forestr/Fish prefer:
Agriculture related

Additional Information
Year Founded: 2011
Current Activity Level : Actively seeking new investments

FININT PARTNERS SRL

Via Vittorio Alfieri 1
Conegliano, Italy 31015
Phone: 39-04-3836-0900
Fax: 39-04-3841-1901
E-mail: finint@finint.it
Website: www.finintprivatequity.it

Management and Staff
Domenico Tonussi, Managing Director
Piergiorgio Fantin, Partner

Type of Firm
Bank Affiliated

Association Membership
Italian Venture Capital Association (AIFI)

Project Preferences

Type of Financing Preferred:
Expansion
Generalist PE

Geographical Preferences

International Preferences:
Italy

Industry Preferences

In Industrial/Energy prefer:
Industrial Products

In Utilities prefer:
Utilities

Additional Information
Year Founded: 1980
Current Activity Level : Actively seeking new investments

FINISTERE VENTURES L L C

4365 Executive Drive
Suite 1500
San Diego, CA USA 92121
Phone: 8589263009
Fax: 8587937120
E-mail: info@finistere.com
Website: www.finistereventures.com

Management and Staff
Arama Kukutai, Managing Director
Bruce Brumfield, Managing Director
David Duncan, Venture Partner
Eyal Rosenthal, Venture Partner
Gil Meron, Venture Partner
Jerry Caulder, Managing Director
Kenneth Selzer, Venture Partner
Paul Zorner, Venture Partner

Type of Firm
Private Equity Firm

Project Preferences

Type of Financing Preferred:
Balanced
Later Stage
Seed
Startup

Geographical Preferences

United States Preferences:

International Preferences:
Australia
New Zealand

Industry Preferences

In Biotechnology prefer:
Agricultural/Animal Bio.
Industrial Biotechnology

In Medical/Health prefer:
Medical/Health
Medical Diagnostics
Medical Products
Disposable Med. Products
Pharmaceuticals

In Consumer Related prefer:
Food/Beverage

In Industrial/Energy prefer:
Energy Conservation Relat

In Agr/Forestr/Fish prefer:
Agriculture related

In Other prefer:
Environment Responsible

Additional Information
Name of Most Recent Fund: Finistere-AgResearch Strategic Fund I, L.P.
Most Recent Fund Was Raised: 09/05/2005
Year Founded: 2002
Capital Under Management: $32,000,000
Current Activity Level : Actively seeking new investments

FINLAB AG

Grueneburgweg 18
Frankfurt am Main, Germany 60322
Phone: 4969719128000
Fax: 49697191280999
E-mail: info@altira-group.de
Website: www.finlab.de

Type of Firm
Private Equity Firm

Project Preferences

Type of Financing Preferred:
Fund of Funds
Early Stage
Mezzanine
Later Stage
Seed
Startup

Size of Investments Considered:
Min Size of Investment Considered (000s): $471
Max Size of Investment Considered (000s): $2,825

Geographical Preferences

International Preferences:
Europe
Germany
Africa

Industry Preferences

In Communications prefer:
Communications and Media
Telecommunications

In Computer Software prefer:
Software

In Internet Specific prefer:
E-Commerce Technology
Internet

In Computer Other prefer:
Computer Related

In Semiconductor/Electr prefer:
Electronics
Semiconductor
Laser Related
Fiber Optics

In Biotechnology prefer:
Biotechnology

In Medical/Health prefer:
Medical/Health
Pharmaceuticals

In Industrial/Energy prefer:
Energy
Oil and Gas Exploration
Alternative Energy
Environmental Related

In Financial Services prefer:
Financial Services

In Business Serv. prefer:
Media

Additional Information
Year Founded: 2003
Capital Under Management: $35,700,000
Current Activity Level : Actively seeking new investments

FINLEAP GMBH

Rosa-Luxemburg-Strasse 2
Berlin, Germany 10178
Phone: 4930577025820
E-mail: info@finleap.com
Website: www.finleap.com

Management and Staff
Hendrik Krawinkel, Co-Founder
Jan Beckers, Founder
Ramin Niroumand, Co-Founder

Type of Firm
Private Equity Firm

Additional Information
Year Founded: 2014
Current Activity Level : Actively seeking new investments

FINLES NV

Euclideslaan 151
Utrecht, Netherlands 3584
Phone: 310302974975
Fax: 310302974959
E-mail: info@finles.nl
Website: www.finlescapitalmanagement.nl

Management and Staff
Jan van Oudvorst, Chief Financial Officer
Rob van Kuijk, Chief Executive Officer

Type of Firm
Investment Management Firm

Additional Information
Year Founded: 1977
Current Activity Level : Actively seeking new investments

FINORIS AG

Gotthardstrasse 56
Zurich, Switzerland 8027
Phone: 41445153800
Fax: 41445153810
E-mail: info@finoris.com
Website: www.finoris.com

Type of Firm
Private Equity Firm

Project Preferences

Type of Financing Preferred:
Expansion
Later Stage

Industry Preferences

In Medical/Health prefer:
Medical/Health

In Industrial/Energy prefer:
Energy

Additional Information
Year Founded: 2010
Current Activity Level : Actively seeking new investments

FINORPA PP SAS

23 Rue du 11 Novembre
BP 351
Lens, France 62300
Phone: 33321136060
Fax: 33321136069
E-mail: finorpa@finorpa.fr
Website: www.finorpa.fr

Other Offices
50 Boulevard Jacquard
Calais, France 62100
Phone: 33321855460
Fax: 33321850758

17 rue Capron
Valenciennes, France 59300
Phone: 33327474707
Fax: 33327335177

21 avenue Le Corbusier
Lille, France 59800
Phone: 33320315954
Fax: 33320312265

Management and Staff
Antoine Harleaux, Chief Executive Officer

Type of Firm
Incubator/Development Program

Project Preferences

Type of Financing Preferred:
Leveraged Buyout
Early Stage
Mezzanine
Later Stage
Startup
Special Situation

Size of Investments Considered:
Min Size of Investment Considered (000s): $69
Max Size of Investment Considered (000s): $3,475

Geographical Preferences

International Preferences:
Europe
France

Industry Preferences

In Semiconductor/Electr prefer:
Electronics

In Consumer Related prefer:
Food/Beverage

In Industrial/Energy prefer:
Industrial Products
Materials

In Manufact. prefer:
Manufacturing
Publishing

Additional Information
Year Founded: 2005
Current Activity Level : Actively seeking new investments

FINOVAM SAS

323, Boulevard du Hoover
Lille, France 59000

Type of Firm
Private Equity Firm

Project Preferences

Type of Financing Preferred:
Early Stage
Seed

Size of Investments Considered:
Min Size of Investment Considered (000s): $55
Max Size of Investment Considered (000s): $1,660

Geographical Preferences

International Preferences:
France

Industry Preferences

In Communications prefer:
Communications and Media

In Biotechnology prefer:
Biotechnology

In Medical/Health prefer:
Medical/Health

In Industrial/Energy prefer:
Energy
Materials
Factory Automation

In Transportation prefer:
Transportation

Additional Information
Year Founded: 2014
Capital Under Management: $34,616,000
Current Activity Level : Actively seeking new investments

FINPIEMONTE PARTECI-PAZIONI SPA

Galleria San Federico 54
Turin, Italy 10121
Phone: 390115717711
Fax: 39011545759
E-mail: finanziamenti@finpiemonte.it
Website: www.finpiemonte-partecipazioni.it

Management and Staff
Fina Laura, President
Maria Rovero, President
Mario Calderini, President
Valerio Cattaneo, Vice President

Type of Firm
Private Equity Firm

Project Preferences

Type of Financing Preferred:
Expansion

Geographical Preferences

International Preferences:
Europe

Additional Information
Year Founded: 1976
Current Activity Level : Actively seeking new investments

FINSTAR FINANCIAL GROUP

8 Presnenskaya Nab
bld.1, off. 12B
Moscow, Russia 123317
Website: www.finstar.com

Type of Firm
Private Equity Firm

Project Preferences

Type of Financing Preferred:
Leveraged Buyout
Management Buyouts

Geographical Preferences

United States Preferences:

Canadian Preferences:
All Canada

International Preferences:
Europe
Poland
Ukraine
Scandanavia/Nordic Region
Spain
Asia
South Africa
Germany
Russia

Industry Preferences

In Communications prefer:
Telecommunications

In Consumer Related prefer:
Retail

In Financial Services prefer:
Financial Services
Real Estate

Additional Information
Year Founded: 1996
Current Activity Level : Actively seeking new investments

FINTECH COLLECTIVE INC

419 Park Avenue South
Second Floor
New York, NY USA 10016
Website: www.fintech.io

Management and Staff
Brooks Gibbins, Co-Founder
Gareth Jones, Co-Founder

Type of Firm
Private Equity Firm

Project Preferences

Type of Financing Preferred:
Early Stage
Balanced
Seed

Industry Preferences

In Internet Specific prefer:
E-Commerce Technology

In Financial Services prefer:
Financial Services

Additional Information
Year Founded: 2012
Capital Under Management: $93,830,000
Current Activity Level : Actively seeking new investments

FINTOP CAPITAL LLC

7101 Executive Center Drive
Suite 197
Brentwood, TN USA 37027
Website: www.fintopcapital.com

Type of Firm
Private Equity Firm

Industry Preferences

In Computer Software prefer:
Software

In Financial Services prefer:
Financial Services

Additional Information
Year Founded: 2017
Current Activity Level : Actively seeking new investments

FIR CAPITAL PARTNERS GESTAO DE INVESTIMENTOS SA

Praca Carlos Chagas 49, 7th Floor
Belo Horizonte, Brazil 30170020
Phone: 553130740020
Fax: 553130740015
E-mail: info@fircapital.com
Website: www.fircapital.com

Management and Staff
David Travesso Neto, Chief Executive Officer
Marcus Regueira, Partner

Type of Firm
Private Equity Firm

Association Membership
Brazilian Venture Capital Association (ABCR)
Emerging Markets Private Equity Association

Project Preferences

Type of Financing Preferred:
Early Stage
Balanced
Later Stage
Seed
Startup

Size of Investments Considered:
Min Size of Investment Considered (000s): $100
Max Size of Investment Considered (000s): $2,000

Geographical Preferences

International Preferences:
Brazil

Industry Preferences

In Computer Software prefer:
Software

In Biotechnology prefer:
Biotechnology
Human Biotechnology
Industrial Biotechnology

In Medical/Health prefer:
Medical/Health

In Business Serv. prefer:
Services

Additional Information

Year Founded: 1999
Capital Under Management: $65,000,000
Current Activity Level : Actively seeking new investments

FIRA FINANZIARIA REGIONALE ABRUZZESE SPA

Via Ferrari, 155
Pescara, Italy 65124
Phone: 390854213832
Fax: 390854213834
Website: www.fira.it

Type of Firm
Private Equity Firm

Project Preferences

Type of Financing Preferred:
Early Stage
Acquisition
Startup

Geographical Preferences

International Preferences:
Italy

Additional Information

Year Founded: 2016
Current Activity Level : Actively seeking new investments

FIRE CAPITAL FUND MAURITIUS PRIVATE LTD

Caudan,
4th Floor, IBL House,
Port Louis, Mauritius
Phone: 2302032020
E-mail: contactus@firecapital.com
Website: www.firecapital.com

Management and Staff
Om Chaudhry, Managing Director

Type of Firm
Private Equity Firm

Project Preferences

Type of Financing Preferred:
Early Stage
Expansion
Balanced
Later Stage

Geographical Preferences

International Preferences:
India
Asia

Industry Preferences

In Consumer Related prefer:
Hotels and Resorts

In Financial Services prefer:
Real Estate

Additional Information

Year Founded: 2004
Current Activity Level : Actively seeking new investments

FIREBRAND MANAGEMENT LLC

8510 West 127th Place
Overland Park, KS USA 66213
Website: www.firebrandvc.com

Management and Staff
John Fein, Founder

Type of Firm
Private Equity Firm

Project Preferences

Type of Financing Preferred:
Early Stage

Geographical Preferences

United States Preferences:
Midwest

Industry Preferences

In Computer Software prefer:
Software

Additional Information

Year Founded: 2016
Capital Under Management: $8,440,000
Current Activity Level : Actively seeking new investments

FIRELAKE CAPITAL MANAGEMENT LLC

575 High Street
Suite 330
Palo Alto, CA USA 94301
Phone: 6503210880
Fax: 6503210882
E-mail: bp@firelakecapital.com

Management and Staff
Candice Eggerss, Managing Director
Fred Kittler, Managing Director
Lisa Lee, Chief Financial Officer
Martin Lagod, Managing Director
Peter Shannon, Managing Director

Type of Firm
Private Equity Firm

Project Preferences

Type of Financing Preferred:
Early Stage

Industry Preferences

In Communications prefer:
Communications and Media

In Industrial/Energy prefer:
Environmental Related

Additional Information

Name of Most Recent Fund: Firelake Strategic Technology Fund II, L.P.
Most Recent Fund Was Raised: 02/13/2008
Year Founded: 2002
Current Activity Level : Actively seeking new investments

FIREMAN CAPITAL PARTNERS LLC

800 Boylston Street, 24th Floor
Boston, MA USA 02199
Phone: 6176710555
E-mail: info@firemancapital.com
Website: www.firemancapital.com

Other Offices

3801 PGA Boulevard
Suite 910
Palm Beach Gardens, FL USA 33410

Management and Staff
Andrew Spellman, Founder
Bryan Doherty, Vice President
Chris Akelman, Principal
Clara Maddox, Vice President
Daniel Fireman, Managing Partner
Ekta Sharma, Vice President
Liam Patrick, Partner
Marla Sabo, Partner

Type of Firm
Private Equity Firm

Project Preferences

Type of Financing Preferred:
Leveraged Buyout
Generalist PE
Later Stage

Geographical Preferences

United States Preferences:

Industry Preferences

In Consumer Related prefer:
Consumer
Retail
Food/Beverage
Consumer Products
Consumer Services

In Business Serv. prefer:
Services

Additional Information
Name of Most Recent Fund: Fireman Capital CPF NR, L.P.
Most Recent Fund Was Raised: 08/25/2011
Year Founded: 2008
Capital Under Management: $216,500,000
Current Activity Level : Actively seeking new investments

FIREPOWER CAPITAL CORP

Three Church Street
Suite 601
Toronto, Canada M5E 1M2
Phone: 6472602069
Fax: 6477235108
Website: www.firepowercapital.com

Type of Firm
Private Equity Firm

Project Preferences

Type of Financing Preferred:
Mezzanine

Geographical Preferences

Canadian Preferences:
All Canada

Additional Information
Year Founded: 2012
Capital Under Management: $75,640,000
Current Activity Level : Actively seeking new investments

FIRESTARTER FUND LLC

222 West Hubbard, Suite 310
Chicago, IL USA 60610

Type of Firm
Private Equity Firm

Project Preferences

Type of Financing Preferred:
Early Stage
Balanced
Seed
Startup

Size of Investments Considered:
Min Size of Investment Considered (000s): $25
Max Size of Investment Considered (000s): $350

Geographical Preferences

United States Preferences:
Illinois

Industry Preferences

In Communications prefer:
Wireless Communications

In Computer Software prefer:
Software

In Internet Specific prefer:
Ecommerce

In Business Serv. prefer:
Media

Additional Information
Name of Most Recent Fund: FireStarter Fund LLC
Most Recent Fund Was Raised: 12/14/2011
Year Founded: 2011
Capital Under Management: $5,700,000
Current Activity Level : Actively seeking new investments

FIRESTARTER PARTNERS LLC

1055 Minnesota Avenue
Suite 3
San Jose, CA USA 95125
Phone: 408-288-5100
Fax: 408-873-0550
Website: www.firestarter-llc.com

Management and Staff
Peter Verbica, Managing Partner

Type of Firm
Private Equity Advisor or Fund of Funds

Project Preferences

Type of Financing Preferred:
Fund of Funds
Early Stage
Expansion
Mezzanine
Seed

Geographical Preferences

United States Preferences:

Additional Information
Year Founded: 1999
Current Activity Level : Making few, if any, new investments

FIRM FACTORY NETWORK AB

Karlavagen 50
Stockholm, Sweden 114 49
Phone: 46709102580
E-mail: info@firmfactory.com
Website: www.firmfactory.com

Management and Staff
Alexander Murad, Partner
Arwind Malhotra, Founder
Daniel Kaplan, Managing Partner
David Ekenvi, Partner
Lars Procheus, Partner
Maria Groschopp, Founder
Oskar Bjursten, Founder
Peter Ahlgren, Founder
Peter Settman, Partner
Samuel Asarnoj, Partner

Type of Firm
Private Equity Firm

Association Membership
Swedish Venture Capital Association (SVCA)

Project Preferences

Type of Financing Preferred:
Seed
Startup

Geographical Preferences

International Preferences:
Sweden

Industry Preferences

In Communications prefer:
Communications and Media
Wireless Communications

In Internet Specific prefer:
Internet

In Industrial/Energy prefer:
Alternative Energy
Energy Conservation Relat

In Other prefer:
Environment Responsible

Additional Information
Year Founded: 2005
Capital Under Management: $9,300,000
Current Activity Level : Actively seeking new investments

FIRST ABU DHABI BANK PJSC

One Nbad Tower, Sheikh
Khalifa St, PO Box 4
Abu Dhabi, Utd. Arab Em. 2993
Phone: 97126111111
Fax: 97126275738
Website: www.bankfortheuae.com

Management and Staff

Abdulla AbdulRaheem, Chief Executive Officer
Abdullah Abdul Rahim, Chief Executive Officer
Abhijit Choudhury, Chief Executive Officer
Akram Yassin, Senior Managing Director
Andy Cairns, Managing Director
Ashraf Mazahreh, Managing Director
Claude-Henri Chavanon, Managing Director
Frank Beckers, Managing Director
Hein Van Der Wielen, Managing Director
James Burdett, Chief Financial Officer
Jamil ElHalabi, Chief Financial Officer
Jonathan Macdonald, Managing Director
Mahmood Al Aradi, Senior Managing Director
Nilanjan Ray, Managing Director
Omar Mehanna, Managing Director
Rola Abu Manneh, Senior Managing Director
Saeed Al Khouri, Managing Director
Saif Al Shehhi, Senior Managing Director
Suvrat Saigal, Managing Director
Vivek Mohra, Managing Director

Type of Firm
Bank Affiliated

Association Membership
Gulf Venture Capital Association

Project Preferences

Type of Financing Preferred:
Expansion
Mezzanine
Generalist PE
Startup

Geographical Preferences

International Preferences:
Bahrain
Oman
Qatar
Utd. Arab Em.
Saudi Arabia
Kuwait

Industry Preferences

In Financial Services prefer:
Financial Services

Additional Information
Year Founded: 1968
Capital Under Management: $21,782,000
Current Activity Level : Actively seeking new investments

FIRST ALVERSTONE PARTNERS PTE LTD

80 Raffles Place
36th Floor UOB Plaza One
Singapore, Singapore 048624
Website: www.firstalverstone.com

Management and Staff
Ron Tan, Partner
Selena Cheng, Managing Director

Type of Firm
Private Equity Firm

Association Membership
Singapore Venture Capital Association (SVCA)

Project Preferences

Type of Financing Preferred:
Leveraged Buyout
Acquisition

Geographical Preferences

International Preferences:
Asia

Additional Information
Year Founded: 2005
Current Activity Level : Actively seeking new investments

FIRST ANALYSIS CORP

One South Wacker Drive
Suite 3900
Chicago, IL USA 60606
Phone: 3122581400
Website: www.firstanalysis.com

Management and Staff
Anita McFarlane, Principal
Brian Friedman, Managing Director
Charles Zent, Managing Director
Clement Erbmann, Managing Director
Corey- Greendale, Vice President
Craig Nankervis, Vice President
Daniel Smereczynski, Vice President
Dave Leshuk, Managing Director
David Hess, Vice President
Frank Sparacino, Vice President
Howard Smith, Managing Director
James MacDonald, Managing Director
Joshua Moses, Vice President
Kenneth Patsey, Vice President
Lawrence Berlin, Vice President
Matthew Nicklin, Managing Director
Michael Siemplenski, Managing Director
Michael Harrison, Vice President
Oliver Nicklin, President, Founder
Richard Conklin, Managing Director
Thomas Ianiro, Managing Director
Thomas Swann, Vice President
Todd Van Fleet, Vice President
Tracy Marshbanks, Managing Director

Type of Firm
Private Equity Firm

Association Membership
Illinois Venture Capital Association

Project Preferences

Role in Financing:
Prefer role as deal originator but will also invest in deals created by others

Type of Financing Preferred:
Early Stage
Expansion
Balanced
Later Stage

Size of Investments Considered:
Min Size of Investment Considered (000s): $3,000
Max Size of Investment Considered (000s): $10,000

Geographical Preferences

United States Preferences:

Industry Focus

(% based on actual investment)
Computer Software and Services	26.2%
Internet Specific	20.4%
Other Products	14.3%
Industrial/Energy	12.3%
Medical/Health	7.8%
Communications and Media	7.3%
Computer Hardware	4.3%
Semiconductors/Other Elect.	3.0%
Biotechnology	2.7%
Consumer Related	1.7%

Additional Information
Name of Most Recent Fund: First Analysis Private Equity Fund V, L.P.
Most Recent Fund Was Raised: 06/28/2012
Year Founded: 1981
Capital Under Management: $280,000,000
Current Activity Level : Actively seeking new investments
Method of Compensation: Return on investment is of primary concern, do not charge fees

FIRST ASIA VENTURE CAPITAL INC

Herrera Corner Alfaro Street
6/F, PDPC Bank Center
Makati City, Philippines
Phone: 6328925462
Fax: 6328926464
E-mail: first.asia@gmail.com
Website: www.firstasia.com.ph

Management and Staff
Saturnino Belen, President

Type of Firm
Private Equity Firm

Project Preferences

Type of Financing Preferred:
Balanced
Seed

Geographical Preferences

International Preferences:
Philippines

Industry Preferences

In Semiconductor/Electr prefer:
Electronics

In Consumer Related prefer:
Hotels and Resorts
Education Related

In Industrial/Energy prefer:
Industrial Products

In Transportation prefer:
Transportation
Aerospace

In Financial Services prefer:
Real Estate

In Manufact. prefer:
Publishing

In Other prefer:
Environment Responsible

Additional Information
Year Founded: 1983
Capital Under Management: $12,400,000
Current Activity Level : Actively seeking new investments

FIRST ATLANTIC CAPITAL, LTD.

477 Madison Avenue
Suite 330
New York, NY USA 10022
Phone: 2122070300
Fax: 2122078842
E-mail: info@first-atlantic.com
Website: www.firstatlanticcapital.com

Management and Staff
Brinda Cherian, Vice President
Emilio Pedroni, Managing Director
Peter Patricola, Chief Financial Officer
Thomas Berglund, Managing Director

Type of Firm
Private Equity Firm

Project Preferences

Type of Financing Preferred:
Leveraged Buyout
Management Buyouts
Acquisition

Geographical Preferences

United States Preferences:

Industry Preferences

In Consumer Related prefer:
Food/Beverage
Consumer Products

In Industrial/Energy prefer:
Industrial Products
Materials

In Business Serv. prefer:
Services

Additional Information
Name of Most Recent Fund: Atlantic Equity Partners IV, L.P.
Most Recent Fund Was Raised: 07/17/2006
Year Founded: 1989
Capital Under Management: $490,000,000
Current Activity Level : Actively seeking new investments

FIRST AVENUE PARTNERS, L.P.

30 Burton Hills Boulevard
Suite 550
Nashville, TN USA 37215
Phone: 6153700056
Fax: 6153766310
Website: www.1stpartners.com

Management and Staff
David Wilds, Managing Partner
Mark Isaacs, Partner
Patricia Chalian, Principal
Patrick Shuttleworth, Vice President

Type of Firm
Private Equity Firm

Association Membership
Emerging Markets Private Equity Association

Project Preferences

Type of Financing Preferred:
Later Stage

Size of Investments Considered:
Min Size of Investment Considered (000s): $3,000
Max Size of Investment Considered (000s): $4,000

Geographical Preferences

United States Preferences:

Industry Preferences

In Medical/Health prefer:
Health Services

Additional Information
Name of Most Recent Fund: First Avenue Partners II
Most Recent Fund Was Raised: 08/01/2005
Year Founded: 1998
Current Activity Level : Actively seeking new investments

FIRST CANADIAN TITLE COMPANY LTD

1290 Central Parkway West
Suite 900
Mississauga, Canada L5C 4R3
Phone: 905-566-0425
Fax: 905-566-8613
Website: www.fct.ca

Type of Firm
Investment Management Firm

Additional Information
Year Founded: 1996
Current Activity Level : Actively seeking new investments

FIRST CAPITAL GROUP MANAGEMENT COMPANY LLC

12400 Coit Road
Suite 910
Dallas, TX USA 75251
Phone: 2143821916
Fax: 2143821915
E-mail: info@firstcapitalgroup.com
Website: www.firstcapitalgroup.com

Other Offices
12400 Coit Road
Suite 910
Dallas, TX USA 75251
Phone: 214-382-1916
Fax: 214-382-1915

Management and Staff
Jeffrey Blanchard, Founder
Paul Williams, Principal

Type of Firm
Private Equity Firm

Association Membership
Natl Assoc of Small Bus. Inv. Co (NASBIC)

Project Preferences

Role in Financing:
Will function either as deal originator or investor in deals created by others

Type of Financing Preferred:
Leveraged Buyout
Early Stage
Generalist PE
Later Stage
Management Buyouts
Acquisition

Size of Investments Considered:
Min Size of Investment Considered (000s): $1,000
Max Size of Investment Considered (000s): $6,000

Geographical Preferences

United States Preferences:
Southwest
Texas

Industry Focus

(% based on actual investment)
Semiconductors/Other Elect.	27.0%
Communications and Media	24.9%
Computer Software and Services	14.7%
Internet Specific	14.4%
Other Products	5.2%
Medical/Health	4.1%
Industrial/Energy	3.9%
Consumer Related	3.8%
Computer Hardware	1.9%
Biotechnology	0.2%

Additional Information

Name of Most Recent Fund: First Capital Group of Texas Fund III, L.P.
Most Recent Fund Was Raised: 01/01/2001
Year Founded: 1984
Capital Under Management: $150,000,000
Current Activity Level : Actively seeking new investments
Method of Compensation: Return on investment is of primary concern, do not charge fees

---

FIRST CAPITAL PARTNERS LLC

1620 Dodge Street
Suite 800
Omaha, NE USA 68102
Phone: 4027188850
Fax: 4027188860
E-mail: info@fcpcapital.com
Website: www.firstcapitalpartners.com

Management and Staff

Andrew Kemp, Principal
David McLeese, Managing Partner
Wes Hampp, Managing Director
Young Park, Managing Director

Type of Firm

Private Equity Firm

Project Preferences

Type of Financing Preferred:
Leveraged Buyout
Mezzanine
Management Buyouts
Recapitalizations

Size of Investments Considered:
Min Size of Investment Considered (000s): $2,000
Max Size of Investment Considered (000s): $8,000

Industry Preferences

In Manufact. prefer:
Manufacturing

Additional Information

Name of Most Recent Fund: FCP Fund II, L.P.
Most Recent Fund Was Raised: 04/21/2011
Year Founded: 2006
Capital Under Management: $91,000,000
Current Activity Level : Actively seeking new investments

FIRST CAPITAL VENTURES LLC

50 South Steele Street
Suite 500
Denver, CO USA 80209
Website: www.firstcapitalventures.com

Management and Staff

Scott Morris, Chief Financial Officer

Type of Firm

Private Equity Firm

Project Preferences

Type of Financing Preferred:
Balanced

Additional Information

Year Founded: 2005
Current Activity Level : Actively seeking new investments

FIRST EASTERN INVESTMENT GROUP

No. 8 Finance Street
Central, Hong Kong
Phone: 85229563838
Fax: 85229561132

Management and Staff

Chunqi Yam, Vice President
Elizabeth Kan, Managing Director

Type of Firm

Private Equity Firm

Association Membership

Hong Kong Venture Capital Association (HKVCA)

Project Preferences

Type of Financing Preferred:
Leveraged Buyout
Expansion
Generalist PE
Later Stage
Management Buyouts
Acquisition

Size of Investments Considered:
Min Size of Investment Considered (000s): $1,000
Max Size of Investment Considered (000s): $10,000

Geographical Preferences

Canadian Preferences:
Nova Scotia

International Preferences:
Indonesia
Taiwan
Hong Kong
China
Thailand
Philippines
Asia
Singapore
Korea, South
Malaysia

Industry Preferences

In Medical/Health prefer:
Medical/Health
Health Services
Hospitals/Clinics/Primary

In Consumer Related prefer:
Food/Beverage

In Financial Services prefer:
Real Estate
Financial Services

In Manufact. prefer:
Manufacturing

Additional Information

Year Founded: 1988
Capital Under Management: $500,000,000
Current Activity Level : Actively seeking new investments

FIRST EASTERN SHANGHAI EQUITY INVESTMENT MANAGEMENT LTD

No. 68 Yincheng East Road
33/F Shidai Finance Building
Shanghai, China

Type of Firm
Private Equity Firm

Project Preferences

Type of Financing Preferred:
Balanced

Geographical Preferences

International Preferences:
China

Industry Preferences

In Industrial/Energy prefer:
Environmental Related

Additional Information
Year Founded: 2009
Capital Under Management: $5,000,000
Current Activity Level : Actively seeking new investments

FIRST EQUITY PARTNERS WLL

P.O.Box 60260
Manama, Bahrain
Phone: 97317588788
Fax: 97317581212
E-mail: info@firstequity-partners.com
Website: www.firstequity-partners.com

Type of Firm
Private Equity Firm

Project Preferences

Type of Financing Preferred:
Leveraged Buyout
Acquisition

Geographical Preferences

International Preferences:
Middle East
Asia
Africa

Industry Preferences

In Medical/Health prefer:
Health Services

In Consumer Related prefer:
Food/Beverage

In Industrial/Energy prefer:
Energy
Materials

In Transportation prefer:
Transportation

In Financial Services prefer:
Real Estate
Financial Services

In Manufact. prefer:
Manufacturing

In Agr/Forestr/Fish prefer:
Mining and Minerals

Additional Information
Year Founded: 2011
Current Activity Level : Actively seeking new investments

FIRST FUNDS LTD

90 Awolowo Road
Ikoyi
Lagos, Nigeria 1001
Phone: 234-1-279-3910
Fax: 234-1-279-3919
E-mail: info@firstfunds.com.ng
Website: www.firstfundsltd.com

Management and Staff
Yemisi Tayo-Aboaba, CEO & Managing Director

Type of Firm
Private Equity Firm

Project Preferences

Type of Financing Preferred:
Early Stage
Generalist PE
Balanced
Startup

Size of Investments Considered:
Min Size of Investment Considered (000s): $77
Max Size of Investment Considered (000s): $1,536

Geographical Preferences

International Preferences:
Nigeria

Industry Preferences

In Communications prefer:
Other Communication Prod.

In Biotechnology prefer:
Agricultural/Animal Bio.

In Medical/Health prefer:
Medical/Health

In Industrial/Energy prefer:
Energy

In Manufact. prefer:
Manufacturing

Additional Information
Year Founded: 2003
Capital Under Management: $42,500,000
Current Activity Level : Actively seeking new investments

FIRST ISRAEL MEZZANINE INVESTORS LTD

98 Yigal Alon Street
Electra Tower
Tel Aviv, Israel 67891
Phone: 97235652244
Fax: 97235652245
E-mail: fimi@fimi.co.il
Website: www.fimi.co.il

Other Offices
Former HQ: 37 Menachem Begin Road
FIMI Rubinstein House
Tel Aviv, Israel 67137

Management and Staff
Ami Boehm, Partner
Chelly Pardo, Partner
Ron Ben-Haim, Partner

Type of Firm
Private Equity Firm

Project Preferences

Type of Financing Preferred:
Leveraged Buyout
Management Buyouts
Acquisition

Geographical Preferences

International Preferences:
Israel

Industry Focus
(% based on actual investment)

Other Products	46.0%
Industrial/Energy	20.1%
Computer Software and Services	16.8%
Internet Specific	10.6%
Consumer Related	6.5%

Additional Information
Year Founded: 1996
Capital Under Management: $600,000,000
Current Activity Level : Actively seeking new investments

FIRST NATIONS EQUITY INC

746 Avenue Road
Toronto, Canada M5P 2K2
Phone: 4164833475
Fax: 4164835117
E-mail: info@firstnationsequity.com
Website: www.firstnationsequity.com

Management and Staff
Andrew Szonyi, Managing Partner
Brian Davey, Founder

Type of Firm
Private Equity Firm

Project Preferences

Type of Financing Preferred:
Expansion
Start-up Financing

Geographical Preferences

United States Preferences:
Northwest

Canadian Preferences:
Yukon

Additional Information

Year Founded: 2000
Current Activity Level : Actively seeking new investments

FIRST QUAY CAPITAL PTY LTD

71 Macquarie Street
Circular Quay
Sydney, Australia 2000
E-mail: info@quaycapital.com.au

Type of Firm

Private Equity Firm

Project Preferences

Type of Financing Preferred:
Early Stage

Industry Preferences

In Medical/Health prefer:
Medical/Health

In Consumer Related prefer:
Education Related

In Financial Services prefer:
Financial Services

Additional Information

Year Founded: 2016
Current Activity Level : Actively seeking new investments

FIRST RESERVE CORP

One Lafayette Place
Greenwich, CT USA 06830
Phone: 2036616601
Fax: 2036616729
E-mail: info@firstreserve.com

Other Offices

25 Victoria Street
Seventh Floor
London, United Kingdom SW1H OEX
Phone: 442079302120
Fax: 442079302130

600 Travis
Suite 6000
Houston, TX USA 77002
Phone: 7132277890
Fax: 7132240771

8 Connaught Place
Level 8, Two Exchange Square
Central, Hong Kong
Phone: 85221680625

Management and Staff

Alan Schwartz, Managing Director
Alex Rogers, Vice President
Alexander Williams, Managing Director
Barrett Schick, Vice President
Cathleen Ellsworth, Managing Director
Christopher Pietersen, Vice President
David Posner, Managing Director
Eduard Fidler, Vice President
Francesco Giuliani, Managing Director
George DeMontrond, Vice President
Irene Mavroyannis, Managing Director
James Brooks, Vice President
Jamie Paton, Managing Director
Jeffrey Quake, Managing Director
Joel Lambert, Vice President
John Mogford, Managing Director
John Barry, Managing Director
Joshua Weiner, Managing Director
Kenneth Moore, Managing Director
Lauren De Paola, Vice President
Mark Florian, Managing Director
Michael France, Managing Director
Neil Hartley, Managing Director
Neil Wizel, Managing Director
Rosario Corcione, Vice President
Will Honeybourne, Managing Director
William Brown, Vice President

Type of Firm

Private Equity Firm

Association Membership

Hong Kong Venture Capital Association (HKVCA)

Project Preferences

Role in Financing:
Prefer role as deal originator but will also invest in deals created by others

Type of Financing Preferred:
Other

Industry Focus

(% based on actual investment)
Industrial/Energy	62.7%
Other Products	37.2%
Computer Software and Services	0.1%

Additional Information

Name of Most Recent Fund: First Reserve Energy Infrastructure Fund, L.P.
Most Recent Fund Was Raised: 05/04/2011
Year Founded: 1983
Capital Under Management: $4,700,000,000
Current Activity Level : Actively seeking new investments
Method of Compensation: Return on investment is of primary concern, do not charge fees

---

FIRST ROUND CAPITAL

4040 Locust Street
Philadelphia, PA USA 19104
Phone: 6108341461

Other Offices

60 Madison Avenue
Suite 1001
NEW YORK, NY USA 10010

217 Second Street
Fifth Floor
SAN FRANCISCO, CA USA 94105
Phone: 415-646-0072
Fax: 415-646-0074

Management and Staff

Bill Trenchard, Partner
Brett Berson, Vice President
Christopher Fralic, Partner
Hayley Barna, General Partner
Howard Morgan, Partner
Jeffrey Donnon, Chief Financial Officer
Josh Kopelman, Partner
Phin Barnes, Partner
Robert Hayes, Partner

Type of Firm

Private Equity Firm

Association Membership

National Venture Capital Association - USA (NVCA)

Project Preferences

Type of Financing Preferred:
Seed

Geographical Preferences

United States Preferences:
California

Industry Preferences

In Computer Software prefer:
Software

Additional Information

Name of Most Recent Fund: StartupPHL Seed Fund I, L.P.
Most Recent Fund Was Raised: 07/25/2013
Year Founded: 2004
Capital Under Management: $852,000,000
Current Activity Level : Actively seeking new investments

FIRST SOUTH INVESTMENT MANAGERS (PTY) LTD

181 Jan Smuts Avenue
Macquarie First S. Office Park
Rosebank, South Africa 2121
Phone: 27-11-343-2200
Fax: 27-11-880-3648
E-mail: info@firstsouth.co.za
Website: www.firstsouth.co.za

Management and Staff

Duarte Da Silva, Co-Founder
Fawzia Suliman, Chief Financial Officer
Jayendra Naidoo, Chief Executive Officer

Type of Firm
Investment Management Firm

Project Preferences

Type of Financing Preferred:
Balanced

Size of Investments Considered:
Min Size of Investment Considered (000s): $1,517
Max Size of Investment Considered (000s): $7,586

Geographical Preferences

International Preferences:
South Africa

Industry Preferences

In Industrial/Energy prefer:
Industrial Products

In Financial Services prefer:
Financial Services

Additional Information
Year Founded: 2003
Capital Under Management: $34,900,000
Current Activity Level : Actively seeking new investments

FIRST STEP LTD

Jefferson House, Eglinton Road
Donnybrook
Dublin, Ireland 4
Phone: 353-1-260-0988
Fax: 353-1-260-0989
E-mail: firststep@eircom.net
Website: www.first-step.ie

Management and Staff
Pauline Irwin O Toole, Chief Operating Officer

Type of Firm
Private Equity Firm

Project Preferences

Type of Financing Preferred:
Early Stage
Balanced
Later Stage
Startup

Geographical Preferences

International Preferences:
Ireland
United Kingdom
Europe

Additional Information
Year Founded: 1991
Current Activity Level : Actively seeking new investments

FIRST STONE VENTURE PARTNERS INC

35 Bridge Street
Picton, Canada K0K 2T0
Phone: 6139025464
E-mail: info@fsvp.ca
Website: fsvp.ca

Management and Staff
Don Wilford, Co-Founder
Geoff Salter, Co-Founder
Margo Langford, Co-Founder
Matthew Davis, Co-Founder
Mauro Lollo, Co-Founder
Pierre Rainville, Co-Founder

Type of Firm
Private Equity Firm

Project Preferences

Type of Financing Preferred:
Startup

Geographical Preferences

Canadian Preferences:
Ontario

Additional Information
Year Founded: 2012
Current Activity Level : Actively seeking new investments

FIRST UNITED VENTURE CAPITAL CORP

1400 West Main Street
Durant, OK USA 74701
Phone: 580-924-2256
Fax: 580-924-2228
Website: www.firstunitedbank.com

Type of Firm
Bank Affiliated

Project Preferences

Type of Financing Preferred:
Early Stage
Expansion
Balanced

Size of Investments Considered:
Min Size of Investment Considered (000s): $500
Max Size of Investment Considered (000s): $1,000

Geographical Preferences

United States Preferences:
Oklahoma
Texas

Additional Information
Year Founded: 1998
Capital Under Management: $3,000,000
Current Activity Level : Actively seeking new investments

FIRST WEST CAPITAL

6470 201 Street
Langley, Canada V2Y 2X4
Phone: 5014260
Website: firstwestcapital.ca

Type of Firm
Investment Management Firm

Association Membership
Canadian Venture Capital Association

Project Preferences

Type of Financing Preferred:
Leveraged Buyout
Early Stage
Expansion
Mezzanine
Management Buyouts
Acquisition

Geographical Preferences

United States Preferences:
Northwest

Canadian Preferences:
All Canada

Additional Information
Year Founded: 2013
Capital Under Management: $100,786,000
Current Activity Level : Actively seeking new investments

FIRSTENERGY CAPITAL CORP

1100, 311-6th Avenue SouthWest
Calgary, Canada T2P 3H2
Phone: 403-262-0600
Fax: 403-262-0666
Website: gmpsecurities.com

Type of Firm
Investment Management Firm

Additional Information
Year Founded: 2002
Current Activity Level : Actively seeking new investments

FIRSTFLOOR CAPITAL SDN BHD

Level 7, PNB Damansara
19 Lorong Dungun, Damansara
Kuala Lumpur, Malaysia 50490
Phone: 60320934043
Fax: 60320938244
Website: www.firstfloorcapital.com

Management and Staff
Mohd Fahmi Tengku Hamzah, Partner
Mohd Nizar Ali, Managing Director
Muhammad Zauqi, Partner

Type of Firm
Private Equity Firm

Association Membership
Malaysian Venture Capital Association

Project Preferences

Type of Financing Preferred:
Early Stage
Expansion
Balanced
Later Stage
Seed

Geographical Preferences

United States Preferences:
Southeast

International Preferences:
Malaysia

Industry Preferences

In Communications prefer:
Telecommunications

In Computer Software prefer:
Artificial Intelligence

In Computer Other prefer:
Computer Related

In Biotechnology prefer:
Human Biotechnology

In Industrial/Energy prefer:
Energy

In Business Serv. prefer:
Services

In Manufact. prefer:
Manufacturing

Additional Information
Year Founded: 2000
Capital Under Management: $20,300,000
Current Activity Level : Actively seeking new investments

FIRSTHAND CAPITAL MANAGEMENT INC

P.O. Box 9836
Providence, RI USA 02940
Phone: 8888842675
E-mail: info@firsthandfunds.com
Website: www.firsthandfunds.com

Type of Firm
Private Equity Firm

Project Preferences

Type of Financing Preferred:
Balanced

Additional Information
Year Founded: 1994
Current Activity Level : Actively seeking new investments

FIRSTHAND TECHNOLOGY VALUE FUND INC

150 Almaden Boulevard
Suite 1250
San Jose, CA USA 95113
Phone: 4088867096
E-mail: vc@firsthandtvf.com
Website: www.firsthandtvf.com

Management and Staff
Omar Billawala, Chief Financial Officer

Type of Firm
Private Equity Firm

Project Preferences

Type of Financing Preferred:
Expansion
Balanced
Later Stage

Geographical Preferences

United States Preferences:

Industry Preferences

In Computer Software prefer:
Applications Software

In Industrial/Energy prefer:
Alternative Energy
Energy Conservation Relat
Superconductivity

Additional Information
Year Founded: 2010
Current Activity Level : Actively seeking new investments

FIRSTMARK CAPITAL LLC

100, Fifth Avenue
Third Floor
New York, NY USA 10011
Phone: 2127922200
Fax: 2123915700
E-mail: info@firstmarkcap.com
Website: www.firstmarkcap.com

Other Offices
500 Nyala Farm Road
WESTPORT, CT USA 06880
Phone: 2034292200

Management and Staff
Amish Jani, Co-Founder
Beth Ferreira, Managing Director
Brian Kempner, Chief Operating Officer
Catherine Ulrich, Managing Director
Chris Ahearn, Venture Partner
Gerald Poch, Co-Founder
Gus Warren, Venture Partner
Joseph Essas, Venture Partner
Josh Abramson, Venture Partner
Larry Wilson, Venture Partner
Lawrence Lenihan, Co-Founder
Martin Nisenholtz, Venture Partner
Matt Turck, Managing Director
Neil Vogel, Venture Partner
Nick Marsh, Venture Partner
Paul Cianciolo, Vice President
Richard Nucci, Venture Partner
Rick Heitzmann, Co-Founder
Tasso Argyros, Venture Partner

Type of Firm
Private Equity Firm

Project Preferences

Role in Financing:
Prefer role as deal originator but will also invest in deals created by others

Type of Financing Preferred:
Early Stage
Balanced
Later Stage

Size of Investments Considered:
Min Size of Investment Considered (000s): $250
Max Size of Investment Considered (000s): $10,000

Geographical Preferences

United States Preferences:
New York

Industry Preferences

In Communications prefer:
Communications and Media

In Computer Software prefer:
Software

In Internet Specific prefer:
Internet
Ecommerce

In Computer Other prefer:
Computer Related

In Medical/Health prefer:
Medical/Health

In Consumer Related prefer:
Entertainment and Leisure
Education Related

Additional Information
Name of Most Recent Fund: FirstMark Capital III
Most Recent Fund Was Raised: 11/12/2013
Year Founded: 1997
Capital Under Management: $2,000,000,000
Current Activity Level : Actively seeking new investments
Method of Compensation: Return on investment is of primary concern, do not charge fees

FIRSTMINUTE CAPITAL I LP

Young Street
Northcliffe House
London, United Kingdom W8 5EH
Phone: 4402039055854

Type of Firm
Private Equity Firm

Project Preferences

Type of Financing Preferred:
Early Stage
Seed

Geographical Preferences

International Preferences:
United Kingdom
Europe

Additional Information
Year Founded: 2017
Capital Under Management: $60,000,000
Current Activity Level : Actively seeking new investments

FIRSTTRACKS VENTURES LLC

3033 East First Avenue
Suite 415
Denver, CO USA 80206

Type of Firm
Private Equity Firm

Project Preferences

Type of Financing Preferred:
Early Stage
Balanced
Seed
Startup

Geographical Preferences

United States Preferences:
Colorado

Industry Preferences

In Internet Specific prefer:
E-Commerce Technology

Additional Information
Year Founded: 2017
Current Activity Level : Actively seeking new investments

FISCHER BUCHSCHACHER GRUPPE AG

Susenbergstrasse 31
Zurich, Switzerland 8044
Phone: 41442661060
Fax: 41442661069
E-mail: office@fischer-buchschacher.ch
Website: www.fischerinvestment.ch

Other Offices
Zirkusweg 1
Hamburg, Germany 20359

Management and Staff
Hakan Solak, Chief Executive Officer

Type of Firm
Private Equity Firm

Project Preferences

Type of Financing Preferred:
Leveraged Buyout
Turnaround
Later Stage
Management Buyouts

Geographical Preferences

International Preferences:
Switzerland
Western Europe
Austria
Israel
Germany

Industry Preferences

In Financial Services prefer:
Real Estate

Additional Information
Year Founded: 1969
Current Activity Level : Actively seeking new investments

FISHER CAPITAL PARTNERS LTD

7887 East Belleview Avenue
Suite 810
Englewood, CO USA 80111
Phone: 3034149900
Fax: 3034149905
E-mail: info@fisher-capital.com
Website: www.fisher-capital.com

Management and Staff
Don Fisher, Co-Founder
William Fisher, Co-Founder

Type of Firm
Private Equity Firm

Project Preferences

Type of Financing Preferred:
Balanced

Industry Preferences

In Financial Services prefer:
Real Estate

Additional Information
Year Founded: 1991
Current Activity Level : Actively seeking new investments

FISHHAWK ADVISORS LLC

6363 Woodway, Suite 960
Houston, TX USA 77057
Phone: 7139745000
Website: www.fishhawkllc.com

Type of Firm
Private Equity Firm

Project Preferences

Type of Financing Preferred:
Leveraged Buyout
Expansion

Geographical Preferences

United States Preferences:
Southeast
Southwest
Texas

Industry Preferences

In Business Serv. prefer:
Services
Distribution

In Manufact. prefer:
Manufacturing

Additional Information
Year Founded: 2013
Capital Under Management: $30,000,000
Current Activity Level : Actively seeking new investments

FISK VENTURES INC

555 North Main Street
Suite 500
Racine, WI USA 53403

Management and Staff
H. Johnson, President, Founder

Type of Firm
Private Equity Firm

Additional Information
Year Founded: 2003
Current Activity Level : Actively seeking new investments

FITCH CROWN VENTURE CAPITAL MANAGEMENT (SHENZHEN) CO LTD

Rm 2202, CEC Info Tower
1 Xinwen Road, Futian
Shenzhen, China
Phone: 86-755-83733704
Fax: 86-755-83733664
E-mail: info@itechvc.com
Website: www.itechvc.com

Management and Staff
Boyd R. Jones, Partner
Eric Liu, Partner
Yongzhong Du, Partner

Type of Firm
Private Equity Firm

Project Preferences

Type of Financing Preferred:
Early Stage
Balanced
Later Stage
Seed

Geographical Preferences

International Preferences:
China

Industry Preferences

In Internet Specific prefer:
Internet

In Transportation prefer:
Transportation

Additional Information
Year Founded: 2010
Current Activity Level : Actively seeking new investments

FITZRANDOLPH GATEWAY MANAGEMENT LLC

3100 Edloe Street
Suite 270
Houston, TX USA 77027

Type of Firm
Private Equity Firm

Project Preferences

Type of Financing Preferred:
Early Stage

Geographical Preferences

United States Preferences:
All U.S.

Additional Information
Year Founded: 2016
Capital Under Management: $10,000,000
Current Activity Level : Actively seeking new investments

FIVE CROWNS CAPITAL INC

2721 Pacific Coast Highway
Suite B Newport Beach
Newport Beach, CA USA 92663
E-mail: Inquiries@fivecrownscapital.com
Website: www.fivecrownscapital.com

Management and Staff
David McReynolds, Managing Partner
John Stroh, Managing Director
Timothy O Brien, Chief Financial Officer

Type of Firm
Private Equity Firm

Project Preferences

Type of Financing Preferred:
Leveraged Buyout
Management Buyouts
Acquisition
Recapitalizations

Geographical Preferences

United States Preferences:

Canadian Preferences:
All Canada

Additional Information
Year Founded: 2003
Current Activity Level : Actively seeking new investments

FIVE ELMS CAPITAL LLC

3500 West 75th Street
Suite 350
Prairie Village, KS USA 66208
Phone: 8162000402
Website: www.fiveelms.com

Management and Staff
Fred Coulson, Managing Director
Saran Ferraro, Chief Financial Officer

Type of Firm
Private Equity Firm

Project Preferences

Type of Financing Preferred:
Later Stage

Size of Investments Considered:
Min Size of Investment Considered (000s): $1,000
Max Size of Investment Considered (000s): $10,000

Geographical Preferences

United States Preferences:

Industry Preferences

In Computer Software prefer:
Applications Software

In Internet Specific prefer:
Internet

In Medical/Health prefer:
Medical Diagnostics
Health Services

In Consumer Related prefer:
Consumer
Entertainment and Leisure

In Financial Services prefer:
Financial Services

In Business Serv. prefer:
Services

Additional Information
Name of Most Recent Fund: Five Elms Equity Fund II, L.P.
Most Recent Fund Was Raised: 05/29/2013
Year Founded: 2007
Capital Under Management: $22,000,000
Current Activity Level : Actively seeking new investments

FIVE PEAKS CAPITAL MANAGEMENT

105 Rowayton Avenue
First Floor
Norwalk, CT USA 06853
E-mail: info@fivepeakscapital.com
Website: www.fivepeakscapital.com

Management and Staff
John Almeida, Managing Partner
Mark Edwards, Partner

Type of Firm
Private Equity Firm

Project Preferences

Type of Financing Preferred:
Leveraged Buyout
Management Buyouts
Acquisition
Recapitalizations

Size of Investments Considered:
Min Size of Investment Considered (000s): $5,000
Max Size of Investment Considered (000s): $40,000

Geographical Preferences

United States Preferences:
All U.S.

Canadian Preferences:
All Canada

Industry Preferences

In Communications prefer:
Communications and Media
Data Communications
Publishing

In Computer Software prefer:
Software

In Consumer Related prefer:
Education Related

In Financial Services prefer:
Financial Services

In Business Serv. prefer:
Services
Consulting Services

Additional Information
Year Founded: 2012
Current Activity Level : Actively seeking new investments

FJ LABS
19 West 24th Street
10th Floor
New York, NY USA 10010
Website: www.fjlabs.com

Type of Firm
Private Equity Firm

Project Preferences

Type of Financing Preferred:
Seed

Geographical Preferences

United States Preferences:
All U.S.

International Preferences:
United Kingdom
Turkey
Brazil
Germany
Russia

Additional Information
Year Founded: 1969
Current Activity Level : Actively seeking new investments

FJORD VENTURES LLC
26051 Merit Circle
Suite 102
Laguna Hills, CA USA 92653
Phone: 9493481188
Fax: 9493481866
E-mail: info@fjordventures.com
Website: fjordventures.com

Management and Staff
Hugh Neuharth, Chief Financial Officer
Olav Bergheim, Managing Director
Roy Cosan, Managing Director

Type of Firm
Private Equity Firm

Project Preferences

Type of Financing Preferred:
Early Stage
Startup

Additional Information
Name of Most Recent Fund: Fjord Capital Partners I, L.P.
Most Recent Fund Was Raised: 02/18/2010
Year Founded: 2005
Capital Under Management: $11,800,000
Current Activity Level : Actively seeking new investments

FLAG CAPITAL MANAGEMENT LLC
1266 East Main Street
Fifth Floor
Stamford, CT USA 06902
Phone: 2033520440
Fax: 2033520441
E-mail: flag@flagcapital.com
Website: www.squadroncapital.com

Other Offices
Level 8, Two Exchange Square
8, Connaught Place
Central, Hong Kong
Phone: 85221680842

3 Garden Road
21/F ICBC Tower, Citibank Plaza
Central, Hong Kong
Phone: 852-2273-5445

One Beacon Street, 23rd Floor
Boston, MA USA 02108
Phone: 617-557-0028
Fax: 617-557-0029

Management and Staff
Aliza Samuels, Vice President
Daniel Iamiceli, Chief Financial Officer
Diana Frazier, Managing Partner
Jim Gasperoni, Partner
John Dickie, Principal
Kirsten Morin, Vice President
Louis Sciarretta, Partner
Peter Denious, Partner
Peter Lawrence, Managing Partner
Scott Reed, Partner
Timothy Fritzinger, Principal
Tina Wei, Principal

Type of Firm
Private Equity Advisor or Fund of Funds

Project Preferences

Type of Financing Preferred:
Fund of Funds

Geographical Preferences

United States Preferences:
North America

International Preferences:
Asia Pacific
Europe

Industry Preferences

In Medical/Health prefer:
Medical/Health

In Industrial/Energy prefer:
Energy

In Agr/Forestr/Fish prefer:
Agriculture related
Mining and Minerals

Additional Information
Year Founded: 1994
Capital Under Management: $4,200,000,000
Current Activity Level : Actively seeking new investments

FLAGSHIP PIONEERING
55 Cambridge Parkway
Suite 800E
Cambridge, MA USA 02142
Phone: 6178681888
Fax: 6178681115
Website: flagshippioneering.com

Other Offices
122 South Main Street
Suite 230
ANN ARBOR, MI USA 48104
Phone: 7349269783

Management and Staff
Avak Kahvejian, Partner
Brian Baynes, Partner
Chuck Carelli, Chief Financial Officer
Daniel McIntyre, Partner
David Berry, General Partner
Douglas Cole, Managing Partner
Ed Kania, Co-Founder
Ignacio Martinez, Partner
Miguel Ilzarbe, Vice President
Noubar Afeyan, Chief Executive Officer
Robert Berendes, Venture Partner
Robert Connelly, Venture Partner
Stacie Rader, Partner

Type of Firm
Private Equity Firm

Association Membership
New England Venture Capital Association
National Venture Capital Association - USA (NVCA)

Project Preferences

Role in Financing:
Prefer role as deal originator but will also invest in deals created by others

Type of Financing Preferred:
Early Stage
Balanced
Later Stage
Seed
Startup

Size of Investments Considered:
Min Size of Investment Considered (000s): $500
Max Size of Investment Considered (000s): $15,000

Geographical Preferences

United States Preferences:
Northeast
West Coast

Industry Focus
(% based on actual investment)

Biotechnology	55.1%
Computer Software and Services	11.3%
Medical/Health	8.4%
Communications and Media	8.0%
Industrial/Energy	4.7%
Semiconductors/Other Elect.	4.3%
Internet Specific	4.0%
Computer Hardware	2.7%
Other Products	1.1%
Consumer Related	0.4%

Additional Information
Name of Most Recent Fund: Flagship Ventures Fund V, L.P.
Most Recent Fund Was Raised: 03/26/2015
Year Founded: 2000
Capital Under Management: $929,000,000
Current Activity Level : Actively seeking new investments
Method of Compensation: Return on investment is of primary concern, do not charge fees

FLARE CAPITAL PARTNERS
200 Newbury Street
Boston, MA USA 02116
Phone: 6176075060
Website: www.flarecapital.com

Type of Firm
Private Equity Firm

Project Preferences

Type of Financing Preferred:
Early Stage

Industry Preferences

In Medical/Health prefer:
Health Services

Additional Information
Year Founded: 2015
Capital Under Management: $200,000,000
Current Activity Level : Actively seeking new investments

FLASHSTARTS INC
1621 Euclid Avenue, Suite 2150
Penthouse at the Palace
Cleveland, OH USA 44115
Phone: 2162200200
E-mail: info@flashstarts.com
Website: www.flashstarts.com

Type of Firm
Incubator/Development Program

Project Preferences

Type of Financing Preferred:
Seed
Startup

Industry Preferences

In Communications prefer:
Wireless Communications

In Medical/Health prefer:
Medical/Health

Additional Information
Name of Most Recent Fund: FlashStarts Partners Fund I, L.P.
Most Recent Fund Was Raised: 07/12/2013
Year Founded: 2012
Capital Under Management: $6,545,000
Current Activity Level : Actively seeking new investments

FLAT6LABS
1 Dr Mohamed Soubhi Street,
Second Floor, Flat 6, Giza
Cairo, Egypt 12511
Phone: 20235685856
E-mail: info@flat6labs.com
Website: www.flat6labs.com

Other Offices
15, Rue de Carthage
Tunis, Tunisia

Al Fakhr, Al Khalidiyah
First floor, office number 106
Jeddah, Saudi Arabia
Phone: 96623237927

1 Dr Mohamed Soubhi Street,
Second Floor, Flat 6
Cairo, Egypt

Park Rotana Complex
5th floor
Abu Dhabi, Utd. Arab Em.
Phone: 97126220365

Type of Firm
Incubator/Development Program

Project Preferences

Type of Financing Preferred:
Seed
Startup

Geographical Preferences

International Preferences:
Middle East
Africa

Industry Preferences

In Computer Software prefer:
Software

In Internet Specific prefer:
Ecommerce
Web Aggregation/Portals

Additional Information
Year Founded: 2011
Capital Under Management: $1,500,000
Current Activity Level : Actively seeking new investments

FLATWORLD CAPITAL LLC

220 East, 42nd Street
The News Building, 29th Floor
New York, NY USA 10118
Phone: 2127964001
Fax: 2127964002
E-mail: info@flatworldcapital.com
Website: www.flatworldcapital.com

Other Offices
Usha Kiran 1-8-165
S.D. Road
Secunderabad, India 500-033
Phone: 91-40-2781-0633

Management and Staff
Gilbert Lamphere, Partner
Jeffrey Valenty, Partner
Raj Gupta, Partner
Vivek Selot, Vice President

Type of Firm
Private Equity Firm

Project Preferences

Type of Financing Preferred:
Leveraged Buyout
Expansion
Acquisition
Recapitalizations

Geographical Preferences

United States Preferences:
North America

International Preferences:
India
China

Industry Preferences

In Business Serv. prefer:
Services

Additional Information
Year Founded: 2008
Current Activity Level : Actively seeking new investments

FLEDGE LLC

220 Second Avenue South
Seattle, WA USA 98104
Phone: 2065507109
Website: www.fledge.co

Management and Staff
Michael Libes, Founder

Type of Firm
Incubator/Development Program

Project Preferences

Type of Financing Preferred:
Seed
Startup

Industry Preferences

In Biotechnology prefer:
Biotechnology

In Medical/Health prefer:
Medical/Health

Additional Information
Name of Most Recent Fund: Fledge LLC
Most Recent Fund Was Raised: 01/31/2015
Year Founded: 2011
Capital Under Management: $865,000
Current Activity Level : Actively seeking new investments

FLETCHER SPAGHT VENTURES LP

222 Berkeley Street
20th Floor
Boston, MA USA 02116
Phone: 6172476700
Fax: 6172477757

Management and Staff
Bob Schmidt, Venture Partner
Guy Fish, Vice President
Linda Tufts, Vice President
Lisa Granick, Vice President
Pearson Spaght, President
Peter Kleinhenz, Venture Partner

Type of Firm
Private Equity Firm

Association Membership
New England Venture Capital Association

Project Preferences

Role in Financing:
Will function either as deal originator or investor in deals created by others

Type of Financing Preferred:
Early Stage
Balanced

Geographical Preferences

United States Preferences:
All U.S.

Industry Preferences

In Communications prefer:
Telecommunications
Wireless Communications
Data Communications
Satellite Microwave Comm.

In Computer Hardware prefer:
Mainframes / Scientific
Computer Graphics and Dig
Integrated Turnkey System

In Computer Software prefer:
Computer Services
Data Processing
Software
Systems Software
Applications Software
Artificial Intelligence

In Internet Specific prefer:
E-Commerce Technology
Web Aggregation/Portals

In Semiconductor/Electr prefer:
Electronic Components
Semiconductor
Micro-Processing
Controllers and Sensors
Sensors
Circuit Boards
Component Testing Equipmt
Laser Related
Fiber Optics
Analytic/Scientific
Optoelectronics

In Biotechnology prefer:
Human Biotechnology
Genetic Engineering
Agricultural/Animal Bio.
Industrial Biotechnology
Biotech Related Research

In Medical/Health prefer:
Medical/Health
Medical Diagnostics
Drug/Equipmt Delivery
Pharmaceuticals

In Industrial/Energy prefer:
Factory Automation
Robotics

In Transportation prefer:
Aerospace

In Financial Services prefer:
Financial Services

Additional Information
Year Founded: 2001
Capital Under Management: $100,600,000
Current Activity Level : Actively seeking new investments

FLEXIS CAPITAL LLC

509 Madison Avenue, 6th Floor
New York, NY USA 10022
Phone: 2123784000
Fax: 2123784178
E-mail: info@flexiscapital.com
Website: www.flexiscapital.com

Management and Staff
Andrea Hagan, Managing Director
Jonathan Dobres, Managing Director
Robert Wu, Principal

Type of Firm
Private Equity Firm

Project Preferences

Type of Financing Preferred:
Leveraged Buyout

Industry Preferences

In Communications prefer:
Communications and Media

In Consumer Related prefer:
Consumer

Additional Information
Year Founded: 2009
Current Activity Level : Actively seeking new investments

FLINT CAPITAL OOO
75 Passeig de Garcia Faria
Barcelona, Spain
E-mail: info@flintcap.com

Type of Firm
Private Equity Firm

Project Preferences

Type of Financing Preferred:
Distressed Debt

Size of Investments Considered:
Min Size of Investment Considered (000s): $500
Max Size of Investment Considered (000s): $2,000

Geographical Preferences

International Preferences:
Europe
Tajikistan
Turkmenistan
Azerbaijan
Moldova
Ukraine
Uzbekistan
Russia
Georgia

Industry Preferences

In Communications prefer:
Communications and Media
Media and Entertainment

In Computer Hardware prefer:
Computers

Additional Information
Year Founded: 2013
Capital Under Management: $30,000,000
Current Activity Level : Actively seeking new investments

FLOODGATE FUND, L.P.
820 Ramona Street
Suite 200
Palo Alto, CA USA 94301
Phone: 6502047990
Website: www.floodgate.com

Management and Staff
Ann Miura-Ko, Partner
Michael Maples, Managing Partner

Type of Firm
Private Equity Firm

Association Membership
National Venture Capital Association - USA (NVCA)

Project Preferences

Type of Financing Preferred:
Balanced

Size of Investments Considered:
Min Size of Investment Considered (000s): $150
Max Size of Investment Considered (000s): $1,000

Geographical Preferences

United States Preferences:

Industry Preferences

In Communications prefer:
Data Communications

In Computer Software prefer:
Software

In Internet Specific prefer:
Internet

In Consumer Related prefer:
Consumer

Additional Information
Year Founded: 2006
Capital Under Management: $279,500,000
Current Activity Level : Actively seeking new investments

FLOOR 13 GMBH
Seestrasse 9
Utting am Ammersee, Germany 86919
Phone: 4988069576430
Fax: 4981439576432
E-mail: info@floor13.de
Website: www.floor13.de

Management and Staff
Stefan Schneider, Managing Partner
Thomas Nagano, Partner

Type of Firm
Private Equity Firm

Project Preferences

Type of Financing Preferred:
Early Stage
Balanced
Later Stage
Seed

Geographical Preferences

International Preferences:
Europe
Austria
Germany

Industry Preferences

In Medical/Health prefer:
Medical/Health

Additional Information
Year Founded: 2012
Current Activity Level : Actively seeking new investments

FLORAC SAS
16, Avenue Robert Schuman
Paris, France 75007
Phone: 33156603051
Website: www.florac.eu

Management and Staff
Leopold Meyer, Chief Executive Officer
Marie-Jeanne Meyer, President

Type of Firm
Private Equity Firm

Association Membership
French Venture Capital Association (AFIC)

Project Preferences

Type of Financing Preferred:
Leveraged Buyout
Generalist PE
Later Stage
Management Buyouts
Acquisition

Geographical Preferences

International Preferences:
Europe
France

Additional Information
Year Founded: 2009
Current Activity Level : Actively seeking new investments

FLORENCE VENTURE PARTNERS

401 Florence Street
Palo Alto, CA USA 94301
Phone: 8883418243
Fax: 6506181863
Website: florencevp.com

Type of Firm
Private Equity Firm

Project Preferences

Type of Financing Preferred:
Early Stage

Industry Preferences

In Computer Software prefer:
Software
Applications Software

In Business Serv. prefer:
Media

Additional Information
Year Founded: 2012
Current Activity Level : Actively seeking new investments

FLORESCENCE CAPITAL CO LTD

1266 Nan Jing West Road
Shanghai Plaza 66, 2nd Tower
Shanghai, China 200002
E-mail: info@florescencecapital.com
Website: www.florescencecapital.com

Other Offices

805 Third Avenue
New York, NY USA 10022
Phone: 2128385000

2255 Glades Road
Boca Raton, FL USA 33431
Phone: 5612138606

Management and Staff
Andrew Stein, Partner
Christopher Schneider, Managing Partner

Type of Firm
Investment Management Firm

Project Preferences

Type of Financing Preferred:
Leveraged Buyout
Balanced
Public Companies
Later Stage
Acquisition

Size of Investments Considered:
Min Size of Investment Considered (000s): $770
Max Size of Investment Considered (000s): $7,704

Geographical Preferences

International Preferences:
China
Asia

Industry Preferences

In Medical/Health prefer:
Medical/Health
Pharmaceuticals

In Consumer Related prefer:
Consumer
Entertainment and Leisure
Retail
Education Related

In Industrial/Energy prefer:
Energy
Advanced Materials
Environmental Related

In Business Serv. prefer:
Services
Media

In Manufact. prefer:
Manufacturing

In Agr/Forestr/Fish prefer:
Agriculture related

Additional Information
Year Founded: 1999
Capital Under Management: $100,000,000
Current Activity Level : Actively seeking new investments

FLORESCENCE HUAMAO EQUITY CAPITAL MANAGEMENT CO LTD

1266 Nan Jing West Road
2nd Tower, Suite 4709
Shanghai, China 200002
E-mail: info@florescencecapital.com
Website: www.florescencecapital.com

Management and Staff
Andrew Stein, Partner
Christopher Schneider, Managing Partner

Type of Firm
Private Equity Firm

Project Preferences

Type of Financing Preferred:
Balanced

Geographical Preferences

International Preferences:
China

Industry Preferences

In Computer Software prefer:
Software

In Internet Specific prefer:
Internet

In Biotechnology prefer:
Biotechnology

In Medical/Health prefer:
Medical/Health

In Consumer Related prefer:
Consumer

In Industrial/Energy prefer:
Alternative Energy
Energy Conservation Relat
Materials
Environmental Related

In Agr/Forestr/Fish prefer:
Agriculture related

Additional Information
Year Founded: 1999
Capital Under Management: $45,524,000
Current Activity Level : Actively seeking new investments

FLORIDA CAPITAL PARTNERS INC

500 North Westshore Boulevard
Suite 605
Tampa, FL USA 33609
Phone: 8132228000
Fax: 8132228001
Website: www.fcpinvestors.com

Management and Staff
Felix Wong, Managing Director
Peter Franz, Managing Director

Type of Firm
Private Equity Firm

Project Preferences

Role in Financing:
Prefer role as deal originator but will also invest in deals created by others

Type of Financing Preferred:
Leveraged Buyout
Management Buyouts
Recapitalizations

Geographical Preferences

United States Preferences:

Industry Focus

(% based on actual investment)
Consumer Related	46.1%
Other Products	28.8%
Industrial/Energy	19.3%
Medical/Health	5.8%

Additional Information

Name of Most Recent Fund: FCP Investors VI
Most Recent Fund Was Raised: 10/01/2000
Year Founded: 1988
Capital Under Management: $350,000,000
Current Activity Level : Actively seeking new investments
Method of Compensation: Return on invest. most important, but chg. closing fees, service fees, etc.

FLORIDA FIRST PARTNERS

250 Park Avenue South
Suite 360
Winter Park, FL USA 32789

Other Offices

Eleven Madison Avenue
16th Floor
New York, NY USA 10010

Type of Firm

Private Equity Advisor or Fund of Funds

Project Preferences

Type of Financing Preferred:
Fund of Funds

Geographical Preferences

United States Preferences:
Florida

Industry Preferences

In Industrial/Energy prefer:
Alternative Energy

In Transportation prefer:
Aerospace

In Manufact. prefer:
Manufacturing

Additional Information

Year Founded: 2008
Current Activity Level : Actively seeking new investments

FLORIDA INSTITUTE FOR COMMERCIALIZATION OF PUBLIC RESEARCH

3651 FAU Boulevard
Suite 400
Boca Raton, FL USA 33431
Website: www.florida-institute.com

Management and Staff

Jackson Streeter, Chief Executive Officer
Jane Teague, Chief Operating Officer

Type of Firm

Government Affiliated Program

Project Preferences

Type of Financing Preferred:
Seed

Additional Information

Year Founded: 2014
Current Activity Level : Actively seeking new investments

FLUKE VENTURE PARTNERS II LP

520 Kirkland Way
Suite 300
Kirkland, WA USA 98033
Phone: 4258964322
Fax: 4258274683

Management and Staff

Denny Weston, Senior Managing Director
Kevin Gabelein, Managing Director

Type of Firm

Private Equity Firm

Project Preferences

Role in Financing:
Will function either as deal originator or investor in deals created by others

Type of Financing Preferred:
Expansion
Later Stage

Geographical Preferences

United States Preferences:
Northwest

Industry Focus

(% based on actual investment)
Computer Software and Services	28.8%
Medical/Health	16.2%
Internet Specific	16.0%
Communications and Media	10.1%
Other Products	9.2%
Computer Hardware	6.1%
Semiconductors/Other Elect.	5.2%
Consumer Related	5.0%
Industrial/Energy	2.1%
Biotechnology	1.5%

Additional Information

Name of Most Recent Fund: Fluke Venture Partners II
Most Recent Fund Was Raised: 04/13/2004
Year Founded: 1982
Capital Under Management: $100,000,000
Current Activity Level : Actively seeking new investments
Method of Compensation: Return on investment is of primary concern, do not charge fees

FLUXUS VENTURES LLP

530 Lytton Avenue
Palo Alto, CA USA 94301
Website: fluxusventures.com

Management and Staff

John van Oost, Managing Partner
Jonathan Bartelt, Partner
Mark Sasongko, Partner

Type of Firm

Private Equity Firm

Project Preferences

Type of Financing Preferred:
Early Stage

Industry Preferences

In Industrial/Energy prefer:
Energy
Industrial Products

Additional Information

Year Founded: 2015
Current Activity Level : Actively seeking new investments

FLY VENTURES MANAGEMENT GMBH

Ackerstrasse 6
Berlin, Germany 10115
Website: www.fly.vc

Type of Firm

Private Equity Firm

Project Preferences

Type of Financing Preferred:
Early Stage
Seed

Additional Information

Year Founded: 2016
Capital Under Management: $41,000,000
Current Activity Level : Actively seeking new investments

FLYBRIDGE CAPITAL PARTNERS

500 Boylston Street
18th Floor
Boston, MA USA 02116
Phone: 6173079292
Fax: 6173079293
Website: www.flybridge.com

Other Offices

31 St. James Avenue
Sixth Floor
BOSTON, MA USA 02108

578 Broadway
Seventh Floor
NEW YORK, NY USA 10012
Phone: 9175220065

Management and Staff

Bruce Revzin, Chief Financial Officer
Charles Hazard, General Partner
David Aronoff, General Partner
Jeffrey Bussgang, General Partner
John Karlen, General Partner
Matthew Witheiler, Principal
Michael Greeley, General Partner

Type of Firm

Private Equity Firm

Association Membership

New England Venture Capital Association
National Venture Capital Association - USA (NVCA)

Project Preferences

Role in Financing:
Prefer role as deal originator but will also invest in deals created by others

Type of Financing Preferred:
Early Stage
Balanced
Seed
Startup

Geographical Preferences

United States Preferences:

Industry Focus

(% based on actual investment)
Computer Software and Services	32.6%
Internet Specific	25.8%
Semiconductors/Other Elect.	13.5%
Computer Hardware	6.0%
Biotechnology	5.8%
Other Products	4.9%
Communications and Media	4.5%
Medical/Health	3.1%
Consumer Related	2.5%
Industrial/Energy	1.1%

Additional Information

Name of Most Recent Fund: Flybridge Capital Partners III, L.P.
Most Recent Fund Was Raised: 03/21/2008
Year Founded: 2001
Capital Under Management: $625,000,000
Current Activity Level : Actively seeking new investments
Method of Compensation: Other

FLYCAP AIFP SIA

15A Matrozu Str.
Riga, Latvia LV-1010
Website: www.flycap.lv

Management and Staff

Girts Milgravis, Partner
Janis Skutelis, Founder
Janis Liepins, Partner

Type of Firm

Private Equity Firm

Project Preferences

Type of Financing Preferred:
Early Stage
Expansion

Industry Preferences

In Medical/Health prefer:
Health Services

In Business Serv. prefer:
Distribution

Additional Information

Year Founded: 2013
Capital Under Management: $1,500,000
Current Activity Level : Actively seeking new investments

FLYING FISH MANAGEMENT LLC

801 Blanchard Street
Suite 200
Seattle, WA USA 98121
E-mail: info@flyingfish.vc
Website: www.flyingfish.vc

Type of Firm

Private Equity Firm

Project Preferences

Type of Financing Preferred:
Early Stage
Seed

Geographical Preferences

United States Preferences:
Northwest

International Preferences:
Pacific

Industry Preferences

In Computer Software prefer:
Artificial Intelligence

Additional Information

Year Founded: 2016
Capital Under Management: $5,040,000
Current Activity Level : Actively seeking new investments

FLYWHEEL VENTURES

341 East Alameda Street
Santa Fe, NM USA 87501
Phone: 5052251618
Fax: 5056727053
Website: www.flywheelventures.com

Other Offices

9204 San Mateo Boulevard North East
ALBUQUERQUE, NM USA 87113

Management and Staff

Chris Traylor, Venture Partner
David Jargiello, Venture Partner
Lawrence Chavez, Venture Partner

Type of Firm

Private Equity Firm

Association Membership

National Venture Capital Association - USA (NVCA)

Project Preferences

Role in Financing:
Prefer role as deal originator but will also invest in deals created by others

Type of Financing Preferred:
Early Stage
Seed

Size of Investments Considered:
Min Size of Investment Considered (000s): $50
Max Size of Investment Considered (000s): $1,000

Geographical Preferences

United States Preferences:

Industry Preferences

In Industrial/Energy prefer:
Energy

In Business Serv. prefer:
Services

In Utilities prefer:
Utilities

Additional Information

Year Founded: 1999
Capital Under Management: $50,000,000
Current Activity Level : Actively seeking new investments
Method of Compensation: Return on investment is of primary concern, do not charge fees

FOCAL POINT VENTURES LLC

4N701 School Road
Saint Charles, IL USA 60175
Phone: 2245237838
Fax: 2245237839
E-mail: info@focalpointventures.com
Website: www.focalpointventures.com

Management and Staff

Charles Muscarello, Partner
Darren Niemann, Partner

Type of Firm

Private Equity Firm

Project Preferences

Type of Financing Preferred:
Early Stage
Balanced

Geographical Preferences

United States Preferences:
All U.S.

International Preferences:
Europe
Middle East
Asia

Industry Preferences

In Industrial/Energy prefer:
Energy
Environmental Related

Additional Information

Name of Most Recent Fund: Focal Point Ventures Investment IV, L.P.
Most Recent Fund Was Raised: 08/31/2011
Year Founded: 2011

Capital Under Management: $600,000
Current Activity Level : Actively seeking new investments

FOCUS ACQUISITION PARTNERS

23 South Main Street
Suite 3B
Hanover, NH USA 03755
Phone: 6032779491
E-mail: infor@focusacquisition.com
Website: www.focusacquisition.com

Management and Staff

Chris Nesbitt, Partner
Craig Allsopp, Partner
David Parsons, Partner
Hilton Schwartz, Managing Director
Jack Miller, Managing Director
Paul Pappageorge, Managing Director

Type of Firm

Investment Management Firm

Project Preferences

Type of Financing Preferred:
Leveraged Buyout
Later Stage
Acquisition
Recapitalizations

Geographical Preferences

United States Preferences:
North America

Industry Preferences

In Medical/Health prefer:
Medical/Health
Diagnostic Test Products

In Consumer Related prefer:
Food/Beverage

In Business Serv. prefer:
Services
Distribution

In Manufact. prefer:
Manufacturing

Additional Information

Year Founded: 2009
Capital Under Management: $25,000,000
Current Activity Level : Actively seeking new investments

FOCUS HEALTHCARE PARTNERS LLC

200 West Madison Street
Suite 2650
Chicago, IL USA 60606

Phone: 3125332728
E-mail: info@focushp.com
Website: www.focushealthcarepartners.com

Management and Staff

Curt Schaller, Co-Founder
Paul Froning, Co-Founder

Type of Firm

Private Equity Firm

Project Preferences

Type of Financing Preferred:
Value-Add
Mezzanine
Special Situation
Distressed Debt

Industry Preferences

In Medical/Health prefer:
Health Services

In Financial Services prefer:
Real Estate

Additional Information

Year Founded: 2009
Capital Under Management: $312,000,000
Current Activity Level : Actively seeking new investments

FOCUS VENTURES LTD

525 University Avenue
Suite 225
Palo Alto, CA USA 94301
Phone: 6503257400
Fax: 6503258400
Website: www.focusventuresltd.com

Management and Staff

Chris Adams, Chief Financial Officer
James Boettcher, General Partner
Kevin McQuillan, General Partner
Kevin Bales, Chief Financial Officer
Steve Bird, General Partner

Type of Firm

Private Equity Firm

Association Membership

Western Association of Venture Capitalists (WAVC)

Project Preferences

Role in Financing:
Will function either as deal originator or investor in deals created by others

Type of Financing Preferred:
Expansion
Later Stage

Size of Investments Considered:
Min Size of Investment Considered (000s): $3,000
Max Size of Investment Considered (000s): $8,000

Geographical Preferences

United States Preferences:

International Preferences:
Latin America
Asia

Industry Focus

(% based on actual investment)
Internet Specific	38.2%
Computer Software and Services	30.7%
Communications and Media	14.7%
Semiconductors/Other Elect.	7.4%
Computer Hardware	5.0%
Consumer Related	2.0%
Other Products	0.9%
Medical/Health	0.6%
Biotechnology	0.3%
Industrial/Energy	0.2%

Additional Information

Year Founded: 1997
Capital Under Management: $830,000,000
Current Activity Level : Actively seeking new investments
Method of Compensation: Return on investment is of primary concern, do not charge fees

FOLLOW SEED AUSTRALIA PTY LTD

152/177 Bellevue Road
Bellevue Hill
Sydney, Australia 2023
Website: followtheseed.vc

Management and Staff

Ajoy Mallik, Co-Founder
Curt Shi, Partner
Eliav Alaluf, Partner

Type of Firm

Private Equity Firm

Project Preferences

Type of Financing Preferred:
Early Stage
Seed

Industry Preferences

In Computer Software prefer:
Software

Additional Information

Year Founded: 2015
Current Activity Level : Actively seeking new investments

FOND RAZVITIYA INTERNET-INITSIATIV

Serebryanicheskaya nab. 29
Serebryanyi Gorod
Moscow, Russia
E-mail: info@iidf.ru
Website: www.iidf.ru

Type of Firm

Government Affiliated Program

Project Preferences

Type of Financing Preferred:
Early Stage
Seed
Startup

Geographical Preferences

International Preferences:
Russia

Additional Information

Year Founded: 2013
Current Activity Level : Actively seeking new investments

FOND SODEYSTVIYA RAZVITIYU MFP V NAUCH-TEKH SFERE

1 3-y Obedinskiy Pereulok
Moscow, Romania 119034
Phone: 74952311901
Fax: 74952311902
Website: www.fasie.ru

Type of Firm

Government Affiliated Program

Association Membership

Russian Venture Capital Association (RVCA)

Project Preferences

Type of Financing Preferred:
Balanced

Geographical Preferences

International Preferences:
Europe
Russia

Additional Information

Year Founded: 1994
Current Activity Level : Actively seeking new investments

FONDACTION CSN

2175, bd De Maisonneuve Est
Bureau 103
Montreal, Canada
Phone: 5145255505
E-mail: investissement@fondaction.com
Website: www.fondaction.com

Other Offices

125, boul. Charest Est
Bureau 602
, Canada G1K 3G5
Phone: 4185228650

Management and Staff

Genevieve Morin, Chief Financial Officer

Type of Firm

Private Equity Firm

Association Membership

Canadian Venture Capital Association

Project Preferences

Type of Financing Preferred:
Early Stage
Expansion
Generalist PE
Balanced
Startup

Geographical Preferences

Canadian Preferences:
Quebec

Industry Preferences

In Communications prefer:
Commercial Communications

In Computer Hardware prefer:
Computers

In Internet Specific prefer:
Internet

In Semiconductor/Electr prefer:
Electronics

In Manufact. prefer:
Manufacturing

Additional Information

Year Founded: 1996
Current Activity Level : Actively seeking new investments

FONDATIONS CAPITAL FRANCE SAS

29-31 Rue Saint-Augustin
Paris, France 75002
Phone: 33156758500
Fax: 33153458748
E-mail: info@ciclbopartners.fr
Website: www.fondationscapital.com

Type of Firm
Private Equity Firm

Association Membership
French Venture Capital Association (AFIC)

Project Preferences

Type of Financing Preferred:
Leveraged Buyout
Management Buyouts

Size of Investments Considered:
Min Size of Investment Considered (000s): $6,440
Max Size of Investment Considered (000s): $51,526

Geographical Preferences

International Preferences:
Europe
France

Industry Preferences

In Communications prefer:
Communications and Media
Commercial Communications
Telecommunications
Wireless Communications

In Medical/Health prefer:
Health Services

In Industrial/Energy prefer:
Environmental Related

In Business Serv. prefer:
Services
Distribution

In Other prefer:
Environment Responsible

Additional Information
Year Founded: 2004
Current Activity Level : Actively seeking new investments

FONDATIONS CAPITAL SA

5 rue Guillaume Kroll
Luxembourg, Luxembourg L-1182
Phone: 3524818281
Fax: 352481863
E-mail: contact@fondcap.com
Website: www.fondationscapital.com

Other Offices
3 rue Paul Cezanne
Paris, France 75008
Phone: 33-1-5535-5500
Fax: 33-1-5535-5529

Management and Staff
Philippe Renaud, Partner

Type of Firm
Private Equity Firm

Association Membership
French Venture Capital Association (AFIC)

Project Preferences

Role in Financing:
Prefer role as deal originator but will also invest in deals created by others

Type of Financing Preferred:
Generalist PE
Later Stage
Acquisition

Geographical Preferences

International Preferences:
Europe
France

Industry Preferences

In Other prefer:
Socially Responsible
Environment Responsible

Additional Information
Year Founded: 2007
Current Activity Level : Actively seeking new investments
Method of Compensation: Return on invest. most important, but chg. closing fees, service fees, etc.

FONDO DE FONDOS

Av. Insurgentes Sur 863
11-1st Floor
Colonia Napoles, Mexico 03810
Phone: 525544334500
Fax: 525544334530
E-mail: info@fondodefondos.com.mx
Website: www.fondodefondos.com.mx

Management and Staff
Felipe Vila Gonzalez, Chief Executive Officer

Type of Firm
Private Equity Advisor or Fund of Funds

Project Preferences

Type of Financing Preferred:
Fund of Funds

Geographical Preferences

International Preferences:
Mexico

Additional Information
Year Founded: 2006
Capital Under Management: $40,000,000
Current Activity Level : Actively seeking new investments

FONDO ITALIANO D'INVESTIMENTO SGR SPA

Via Turati 16/18
Milan, Italy 20121
Phone: 3902635321
Fax: 390263532222
Website: www.fondoitaliano.it

Management and Staff
Marco Vitale, President

Type of Firm
Government Affiliated Program

Association Membership
Italian Venture Capital Association (AIFI)

Project Preferences

Type of Financing Preferred:
Leveraged Buyout
Early Stage
Balanced
Later Stage
Acquisition

Geographical Preferences

International Preferences:
Italy

Additional Information
Year Founded: 2010
Capital Under Management: $1,432,870,000
Current Activity Level : Actively seeking new investments

FONDS DE RESERVE POUR LES RETRAITES

56, Rue de Lille
Paris, France 75007
Phone: 33158509912
Website: www.fondsdereserve.fr

Type of Firm
Endowment, Foundation or Pension Fund

Project Preferences

Type of Financing Preferred:
Core
Leveraged Buyout
Value-Add
Early Stage
Expansion
Opportunistic
Later Stage
Management Buyouts
Acquisition

Geographical Preferences

International Preferences:
Europe
France

Additional Information
Year Founded: 2002
Current Activity Level : Actively seeking new investments

FONDS INNOVEXPORT

125 Boulevard, Charest Est.
Second Floor
Quebec, Canada G1K 3G5
Phone: 4183805514
E-mail: info@fondsinnovexport.com
Website: www.fondsinnovexport.com

Type of Firm
Private Equity Firm

Project Preferences

Type of Financing Preferred:
Early Stage
Seed

Additional Information
Year Founded: 2017
Current Activity Level : Actively seeking new investments

FONDS MANUFACTURIER QUEBECOIS SEC

100 rue Landsowne
Bureau 209
Saint-Bruno, Canada J3V 0B3
Phone: 6531414
Fax: 6530533
E-mail: info@fondsmanufacturier.com
Website: fondsmanufacturier.com

Type of Firm
Corporate PE/Venture

Project Preferences

Type of Financing Preferred:
Generalist PE
Later Stage

Geographical Preferences

Canadian Preferences:
All Canada

Industry Preferences

In Manufact. prefer:
Manufacturing

Additional Information
Year Founded: 2006
Current Activity Level : Actively seeking new investments

FONDUL ROMAN PENTRU EFICIENTA ENERGIEI

Str. Johann Strauss nr. 2A
Sector 2
Bucharest, Romania 020312
Phone: 40212338801
Fax: 40212338802
E-mail: office@free.org.ro
Website: www.free.org.ro

Type of Firm
Private Equity Firm

Project Preferences

Type of Financing Preferred:
Leveraged Buyout
Early Stage
Balanced
Later Stage
Seed
Management Buyouts
Acquisition
Startup

Geographical Preferences

International Preferences:
Europe
Romania

Industry Preferences

In Industrial/Energy prefer:
Energy

Additional Information
Year Founded: 2003
Current Activity Level : Actively seeking new investments

FONGIT SEED INVEST SA

Three Chemin Du Pre-Fleuri
Plan-les-Ouates, Switzerland 1228
Phone: 41228848300
Fax: 41227946665
E-mail: info@fongit.ch
Website: www.fongitseedinvest.ch

Type of Firm
Incubator/Development Program

Project Preferences

Type of Financing Preferred:
Early Stage
Seed
Startup

Size of Investments Considered:
Min Size of Investment Considered (000s): $103
Max Size of Investment Considered (000s): $516

Geographical Preferences

International Preferences:
Switzerland
France

Industry Preferences

In Communications prefer:
Telecommunications

In Biotechnology prefer:
Biotechnology

In Medical/Health prefer:
Medical/Health
Medical Products
Pharmaceuticals

In Industrial/Energy prefer:
Energy
Industrial Products

Additional Information
Year Founded: 1997
Current Activity Level : Actively seeking new investments

FONTERELLI GMBH & CO KGAA

Widenmayerstrasse 27
Munich, Germany 80538
Phone: 49-89-211-2120
Fax: 49-89-2112-1212
E-mail: info@fonterelli.de
Website: www.fonterelli.de

Management and Staff
Andreas Beyer, Managing Director

Type of Firm
Bank Affiliated

Project Preferences

Type of Financing Preferred:
Leveraged Buyout
Management Buyouts

Geographical Preferences

International Preferences:
Europe
Germany

Additional Information

Year Founded: 2007
Current Activity Level : Actively seeking new investments

FONTINALIS PARTNERS LLC

One Woodward Avenue
Suite 1600
Detroit, MI USA 48226
Phone: 3134320321
Fax: 3134327847
E-mail: info@fontinalis.com
Website: www.fontinalispartners.com

Other Offices

800 Boylston Street
Prudential Tower, Suite 3310
Boston, MA USA 02199

645 Griswold Street
Penobscot Building, Suite 4321
Detroit, MI USA 48226

Management and Staff

Chris Thomas, Principal
Chris Cheever, Principal
Laura Petterle, Chief Financial Officer
Mark Schulz, Partner
Ralph Booth, Partner
William Ford, Partner

Type of Firm

Private Equity Firm

Project Preferences

Type of Financing Preferred:
Balanced
Later Stage
Seed

Size of Investments Considered:

Min Size of Investment Considered (000s): $100
Max Size of Investment Considered (000s): $10,000

Industry Preferences

In Computer Software prefer:
Software

In Semiconductor/Electr prefer:
Analytic/Scientific

In Transportation prefer:
Transportation

In Manufact. prefer:
Manufacturing

Additional Information

Year Founded: 2009
Capital Under Management: $100,000,000
Current Activity Level : Actively seeking new investments

FOOD AND BEVERAGE PRIVATE EQUITY SASU

39, avenue d'Ina
Paris, France 75116
Website: fnb.pe

Type of Firm

Private Equity Firm

Project Preferences

Type of Financing Preferred:
Leveraged Buyout
Early Stage
Expansion
Later Stage
Management Buyouts
Acquisition

Geographical Preferences

International Preferences:
Italy
United Kingdom
Luxembourg
Netherlands
Portugal
Spain
Belgium
France

Industry Preferences

In Consumer Related prefer:
Food/Beverage

Additional Information

Year Founded: 2017
Current Activity Level : Actively seeking new investments

FOOD CAPITALS PCL

999/9 Rama I Road Pathumwan
Centralworld,1912
Bangkok, Thailand 10330
Phone: 6622072900
Fax: 6622072929
Website: foodcapitals.com

Management and Staff

Na Chanok Ratanadaros, Chief Operating Officer
Naravadee Waravanitcha, Chief Executive Officer
Pattama Joednapa, Chief Financial Officer
Sayarm Tongkrabin, Chief Operating Officer

Type of Firm

Investment Management Firm

Association Membership

Thai Venture Capital Association

Project Preferences

Type of Financing Preferred:
Balanced

Geographical Preferences

International Preferences:
Asia

Industry Preferences

In Communications prefer:
Media and Entertainment

In Internet Specific prefer:
Ecommerce

In Consumer Related prefer:
Hotels and Resorts

In Financial Services prefer:
Financial Services
Real Estate

Additional Information

Year Founded: 1999
Current Activity Level : Actively seeking new investments

FOODLAB CAPITAL LTD

13 Hamesila Road
Rishpon, Israel 4691500
Phone: 197298850512
E-mail: info@foodlabcapital.com
Website: foodlabcapital.com

Type of Firm

Private Equity Firm

Project Preferences

Type of Financing Preferred:
Early Stage

Geographical Preferences

International Preferences:
Israel

Industry Preferences

In Consumer Related prefer:
Food/Beverage

Additional Information

Year Founded: 2015
Current Activity Level : Actively seeking new investments

FOOTPRINT VENTURES

Plot 16, 1st Block,
2F, 7th Main, Koramangala
Bangalore, India 560 034
Phone: 918041101910
Fax: 918041101913
E-mail: info@footprintventures.com
Website: www.footprintventures.com

Management and Staff
Josh Bornstein, Partner
Linda Brownstein, Co-Founder
Neill Brownstein, General Partner

Type of Firm
Private Equity Firm

Project Preferences

Type of Financing Preferred:
Early Stage
Balanced

Geographical Preferences

United States Preferences:

International Preferences:
India
Israel

Industry Preferences

In Communications prefer:
Telecommunications
Wireless Communications

In Computer Software prefer:
Software

In Biotechnology prefer:
Biotechnology

In Medical/Health prefer:
Health Services

In Consumer Related prefer:
Consumer Services

In Industrial/Energy prefer:
Alternative Energy

Additional Information
Year Founded: 2007
Current Activity Level : Actively seeking new investments

FORAGEN TECHNOLOGIES MANAGEMENT INC

111 Research Drive
Suite 105
Saskatoon, Canada S7N 3R2
Phone: 3066511066
Fax: 3066511067
Website: www.foragen.com

Other Offices
7333 rue Berri
Montreal, Canada H2R 2G6
Phone: 514 217-6775
Fax: 514 217-1754

105-111 Research Drive
, Canada S7N 3R2
Phone: 306-651-1066
Fax: 306-651-1067

Management and Staff
Armand Lavoie, Managing Director
David Gauthier, Vice President

Type of Firm
Private Equity Firm

Project Preferences

Type of Financing Preferred:
Early Stage
Seed

Geographical Preferences

Canadian Preferences:
All Canada

Industry Preferences

In Agr/Forestr/Fish prefer:
Agriculture related

Additional Information
Year Founded: 2000
Current Activity Level : Actively seeking new investments

FORBES ALLIANCE PARTNERS INC

4880, Sherbrooke St. West, Suite 170
Montreal, Canada H3Z 1H1
Phone: 514-282-1500
Fax: 514-369-9223
E-mail: info@forbesalliance.com
Website: www.forbesalliance.com

Management and Staff
Eric Melka, President

Type of Firm
Incubator/Development Program

Project Preferences

Role in Financing:
Prefer role as deal originator

Type of Financing Preferred:
Early Stage
Expansion

Size of Investments Considered:
Min Size of Investment Considered (000s): $1,000
Max Size of Investment Considered (000s): $5,000

Geographical Preferences

United States Preferences:

Canadian Preferences:
All Canada

Industry Preferences

In Internet Specific prefer:
Internet

Additional Information
Year Founded: 2000
Current Activity Level : Actively seeking new investments

FORBION CAPITAL PARTNERS

Gooimeer 2-35
Naarden, Netherlands 1411 DC
Phone: 31356993000
Fax: 31356993001
E-mail: info@forbion.com
Website: www.forbion.com

Other Offices
Maximilanstrasse 36
Munchen, Germany 80539
Phone: 4989416161950
Fax: 4989416161959

Management and Staff
Avi Molcho, Venture Partner
Christina Takke, Partner
Geert-Jan Mulder, General Partner
Holger Reithinger, General Partner
Marco Boorsma, Principal
Philip Astley-Sparke, Venture Partner
Sander Slootweg, Managing Partner
Sander van Deventer, General Partner

Type of Firm
Private Equity Firm

Association Membership
European Private Equity and Venture Capital Assoc.

Project Preferences

Role in Financing:
Prefer role as deal originator but will also invest in deals created by others

Type of Financing Preferred:
Later Stage

Size of Investments Considered:
Min Size of Investment Considered (000s): $4,080
Max Size of Investment Considered (000s): $9,520

Geographical Preferences

International Preferences:
Netherlands

Industry Preferences

In Biotechnology prefer:
Biotechnology

In Medical/Health prefer:
Medical/Health

Additional Information

Year Founded: 2000
Capital Under Management: $272,000,000
Current Activity Level : Actively seeking new investments

FORDAHL CAPITAL SA

Passeig Gaudi, 7 4-1
Banyoles, Spain 17820
Phone: 34972580025
Fax: 34972576744
Website: www.fordahlcapital.com

Management and Staff

John Pinnell, Managing Partner
Tom Bouman, Managing Partner

Type of Firm

Investment Management Firm

Project Preferences

Type of Financing Preferred:
Leveraged Buyout
Acquisition

Geographical Preferences

International Preferences:
United Kingdom
Luxembourg
Europe
Netherlands
Spain
Belgium
Germany
France

Industry Preferences

In Consumer Related prefer:
Retail
Franchises(NEC)

In Business Serv. prefer:
Services

In Manufact. prefer:
Manufacturing

Additional Information

Year Founded: 1969
Current Activity Level : Actively seeking new investments

FORE C INVESTMENT AB

Nasets Backavag 60
Vastra Frolunda, Sweden 421 66
Phone: 46704331320
Fax: 4631681320
E-mail: info@4c.se
Website: www.4c.se

Type of Firm

Private Equity Firm

Project Preferences

Type of Financing Preferred:
Balanced

Geographical Preferences

International Preferences:
Sweden

Additional Information

Year Founded: 2003
Current Activity Level : Actively seeking new investments

FORENTIS PARTNERS LLC

26442 Beckman Court
Murrieta, CA USA 92562
Phone: 9517046792

Management and Staff

Jay Goth, Managing Partner

Type of Firm

Private Equity Firm

Industry Preferences

In Biotechnology prefer:
Biotech Related Research

In Medical/Health prefer:
Diagnostic Services
Pharmaceuticals

Additional Information

Year Founded: 2016
Capital Under Management: $5,000,000
Current Activity Level : Actively seeking new investments

FORERUNNER VENTURES LLC

1161 Mission Street
Suite 300
San Francisco, CA USA 94103
Phone: 4156771441
E-mail: info@forerunnerventures.com
Website: www.forerunnerventures.com

Management and Staff

Kirsten Green, Managing Partner

Type of Firm

Private Equity Firm

Project Preferences

Type of Financing Preferred:
Early Stage
Seed
Startup

Geographical Preferences

United States Preferences:

Industry Preferences

In Internet Specific prefer:
E-Commerce Technology
Internet
Ecommerce

In Consumer Related prefer:
Consumer
Retail
Consumer Services

Additional Information

Name of Most Recent Fund: Forerunner Partners II, L.P.
Most Recent Fund Was Raised: 12/24/2013
Year Founded: 2007
Capital Under Management: $239,430,000
Current Activity Level : Actively seeking new investments

FORESIGHT GROUP LLP

The Shard
32 London Bridge Street
London, United Kingdom SE1 9SG
Phone: 441732471800
Fax: 441732471810
E-mail: info@foresightgroup.eu
Website: www.foresightgroup.eu

Other Offices

Torre Europa
Paseo de la Castellana 95 - 15
Madrid, Spain
Phone: 34-914-185-006
Fax: 44-1732-471-810

Via Marche 23
Rome, Italy 00187
Phone: 39-0645-506-734
Fax: 44-1732-471-810

Management and Staff
Andrew Page, Partner
David Hughes, Partner
Donald Maclennan, Partner
Federico Giannandrea, Partner
Gary Fraser, Founder
Humberto Santillana, Partner
Jamie Richards, Partner
Matt Smith, Partner
Michael Currie, Partner
Minal Patel, Partner
Nigel Aitchison, Partner
Peter English, Partner
Pietro Zerauschek, Managing Partner
Ricardo Pineiro, Partner
Russell Healey, Partner

Type of Firm
Private Equity Firm

Project Preferences

Type of Financing Preferred:
Second Stage Financing
Leveraged Buyout
Early Stage
Generalist PE
Balanced
Later Stage
Seed
Management Buyouts
Acquisition

Size of Investments Considered:
Min Size of Investment Considered (000s): $1,562
Max Size of Investment Considered (000s): $7,809

Geographical Preferences

United States Preferences:

International Preferences:
Italy
Greece
United Kingdom
Europe

Industry Preferences

In Communications prefer:
Communications and Media
Commercial Communications
Telecommunications

In Computer Software prefer:
Software

In Internet Specific prefer:
Internet

In Computer Other prefer:
Computer Related

In Semiconductor/Electr prefer:
Electronics

In Industrial/Energy prefer:
Energy Conservation Relat
Environmental Related

In Manufact. prefer:
Manufacturing

In Other prefer:
Environment Responsible

Additional Information
Year Founded: 1984
Capital Under Management: $83,400,000
Current Activity Level : Actively seeking new investments

FORESITE CAPITAL MANAGEMENT LLC

101 California Street
Suite 4100
San Francisco, CA USA 94111
Phone: 4158774887
Fax: 4155670091
Website: foresitecapital.com

Other Offices
Former: 120 Kearny Street
Suite 2500
San Francisco, CA USA 94104

1345 Avenue of the Americas
Third Floor
New York, NY USA 10105

Management and Staff
Dennis Ryan, Chief Financial Officer
Molly He, Venture Partner

Type of Firm
Private Equity Firm

Project Preferences

Type of Financing Preferred:
Expansion
Later Stage

Size of Investments Considered:
Min Size of Investment Considered (000s): $10,000
Max Size of Investment Considered (000s): $50,000

Industry Preferences

In Biotechnology prefer:
Biotechnology

In Medical/Health prefer:
Medical/Health
Medical Diagnostics
Diagnostic Services
Diagnostic Test Products
Medical Therapeutics
Medical Products
Health Services

Additional Information
Name of Most Recent Fund: Foresite Capital Fund II, L.P.
Most Recent Fund Was Raised: 03/03/2014
Year Founded: 2011
Capital Under Management: $866,184,000
Current Activity Level : Actively seeking new investments

FOREST HILL PARTNERS LLC

422 N. Northwest Highway
Suite 140
Park Ridge, IL USA 60068
Phone: 847-692-2426
Fax: 847-939-1700
E-mail: info@foresthillpartners.com
Website: www.foresthillpartners.com

Other Offices
1115 Aldine Avenue
Park Ridge, IL USA 60068
Phone: 773-909-1239
Fax: 847-939-1700

1001 West 13 Mile Road
Madison Heights, MI USA 48071
Phone: 248-798-6915
Fax: 734-264-6127

Management and Staff
John Carretta, Partner
Michael Sullivan, Partner

Type of Firm
Private Equity Firm

Project Preferences

Type of Financing Preferred:
Leveraged Buyout
Expansion
Management Buyouts
Acquisition
Recapitalizations

Geographical Preferences

United States Preferences:
Midwest
North America

Industry Preferences

In Industrial/Energy prefer:
Industrial Products

In Transportation prefer:
Transportation
Aerospace

In Business Serv. prefer:
Services
Distribution

In Manufact. prefer:
Manufacturing

Additional Information
Year Founded: 2002
Current Activity Level : Actively seeking new investments

FORESTEFFECT FUND

Zuid Hollandlaan 7
Den Haag, Netherlands 2596AL
Phone: 3170361734
E-mail: info@foresteffectfund.com
Website: www.foresteffectfund.com

Type of Firm
SBIC

Project Preferences

Type of Financing Preferred:
Expansion

Geographical Preferences

International Preferences:
Netherlands

Industry Preferences

In Biotechnology prefer:
Agricultural/Animal Bio.

In Agr/Forestr/Fish prefer:
Agribusiness
Agriculture related

Additional Information
Year Founded: 2016
Current Activity Level : Actively seeking new investments

FORMATION 8 PARTNERS LP

501 Second Street
Suite 300
San Francisco, CA USA 94107
Phone: 5108250367
E-mail: info@formation8.com

Other Offices
306 Bongeunsa-ro
NK Building, 12th Floor
Seoul, South Korea

300 Beach Road
#25-07, The Concourse Singapore
Singapore, Singapore 199555

#906 Broadtec
Building 221, Wangjingxiyuan
Beijing, China

525 University Avenue
Suite 100
Palo Alto, CA USA 94301
Phone: 5108250367

Great Wall Building
32nd Floor, No. 3000, North Zhongshan Rd
Shanghai, China

Management and Staff
Jim Kim, Partner
Joel Sng, Partner
Lior Susan, Partner

Type of Firm
Private Equity Firm

Project Preferences

Type of Financing Preferred:
Early Stage
Expansion
Balanced
Later Stage

Geographical Preferences

United States Preferences:

International Preferences:
Asia Pacific
Israel
Asia

Industry Preferences

In Semiconductor/Electr prefer:
Electronic Components

In Industrial/Energy prefer:
Energy

Additional Information
Name of Most Recent Fund: Formation8 Partners Fund I, L.P.
Most Recent Fund Was Raised: 04/01/2013
Year Founded: 2011
Capital Under Management: $948,000,000
Current Activity Level : Actively seeking new investments

FORMATION GROUP INC

435 Tasso Street
Suite 315
Palo Alto, CA USA 94301
E-mail: info@formationgroup.com
Website: formationgroup.com

Management and Staff
Jin Lee, Partner
Lae Jang, Partner
Sungjoon Cho, Partner

Type of Firm
Private Equity Firm

Additional Information
Year Founded: 1969
Capital Under Management: $357,000,000
Current Activity Level : Actively seeking new investments

FORMATIVE VENTURES

2905 Stender Way
Number Two
Santa Clara, CA USA 95054
E-mail: info@formative.com
Website: www.formative.com

Management and Staff
Bernard Xavier, Venture Partner
Bill Burger, Venture Partner
Brian Connors, Co-Founder
Brooke Seawell, Venture Partner
Clint Chao, Co-Founder
Dino Vendetti, Managing Director
Douglas Laird, Venture Partner
Ian Crayford, Venture Partner
James Burke, Venture Partner
John Hagedorn, Venture Partner
Joseph Hutt, Venture Partner
Michael Ricks, Venture Partner
Mike Ingster, Venture Partner
Mike Boich, Venture Partner
Peter Zaballos, Venture Partner
Ziya Boyacigiller, Venture Partner

Type of Firm
Private Equity Firm

Project Preferences

Role in Financing:
Will function either as deal originator or investor in deals created by others

Type of Financing Preferred:
Early Stage

Size of Investments Considered:
Min Size of Investment Considered (000s): $2,000
Max Size of Investment Considered (000s): $5,000

Industry Preferences

In Communications prefer:
Communications and Media
Wireless Communications

In Internet Specific prefer:
Internet

Additional Information
Year Founded: 2000
Capital Under Management: $90,200,000
Current Activity Level : Actively seeking new investments
Method of Compensation: Return on investment is of primary concern, do not charge fees

FORMER CHARTER COMMUNICATIONS PARENT INC

12405 Powerscout Drive
Saint Louis, MO USA 63131
Phone: 8884382427
Website: www.charter.com

Management and Staff
John Bickham, Chief Operating Officer

Type of Firm
Private Equity Firm

Additional Information
Year Founded: 2000
Current Activity Level: Actively seeking new investments

FORSTMANN LITTLE & CO

767 Fifth Avenue
44th Floor
New York, NY USA 10153
Phone: 2123555656
Fax: 2127597059

Other Offices
2 N. Riverside Plaza
Suite 600
Chicago, IL USA 60606
Phone: 312-454-1800
Fax: 312-454-0610

Management and Staff
Chris Davis, General Partner
Daniel Akerson, General Partner
J. Anthony Forstmann, Partner
Michael Miles, Partner

Type of Firm
Private Equity Firm

Project Preferences

Type of Financing Preferred:
Leveraged Buyout
Mezzanine
Management Buyouts
Acquisition
Recapitalizations

Industry Focus
(% based on actual investment)

Internet Specific	68.7%
Communications and Media	18.3%
Other Products	8.6%
Industrial/Energy	2.9%
Consumer Related	1.4%
Medical/Health	0.1%

Additional Information
Name of Most Recent Fund: Forstmann Little Sub. Debt & Equity MBO Fund VIII
Most Recent Fund Was Raised: 06/30/2000
Year Founded: 1978
Current Activity Level: Making few, if any, new investments

FORSYTH CAPITAL INVESTORS LLC

8040 Forsyth Boulevard
Saint Louis, MO USA 63105
Phone: 3147262152
Fax: 3147262132
Website: www.forsythcapital.com

Management and Staff
Chet Walker, Senior Managing Director
Kyle Chapman, Managing Director
Ryan Gable, Managing Director

Type of Firm
Private Equity Firm

Project Preferences

Type of Financing Preferred:
Leveraged Buyout
Expansion
Management Buyouts
Special Situation
Recapitalizations

Size of Investments Considered:
Min Size of Investment Considered (000s): $10,000
Max Size of Investment Considered (000s): $30,000

Industry Preferences

In Communications prefer:
Telecommunications

In Medical/Health prefer:
Health Services

In Consumer Related prefer:
Consumer Products

In Financial Services prefer:
Financial Services
Insurance

In Business Serv. prefer:
Services
Distribution
Media

In Manufact. prefer:
Manufacturing

Additional Information
Year Founded: 2009
Current Activity Level: Actively seeking new investments

FORT ROCK CAPITAL LTD

32 Sackville Street
London, United Kingdom W1S 3EA
Phone: 442033724919
E-mail: enquiries@fortrockcapital.com
Website: www.fortrockcapital.com

Type of Firm
Private Equity Firm

Project Preferences

Type of Financing Preferred:
Early Stage
Expansion
Later Stage

Geographical Preferences

International Preferences:
Europe

Additional Information
Year Founded: 2014
Current Activity Level: Actively seeking new investments

FORT WASHINGTON CAPITAL

303 Broadway
Suite 1200
Cincinnati, OH USA 45202
Phone: 5133617600
Fax: 5133617605
Website: www.fortwashington.com

Other Offices
The Huntington Center, Suite 2495
41 South High Street
Columbus, OH USA 43215
Phone: 614-222-6500
Fax: 614-222-6535

299 South Main Street
Suite 1301
Salt Lake City, UT USA 84111
Phone: 801-535-4350
Fax: 801-535-4351

263 Staab Street
Santa Fe, NM USA 87501
Phone: 505-986-1552
Fax: 505-986-1592

Management and Staff
Jeffrey Meek, Chief Financial Officer
John O Connor, Managing Director
Joseph Woods, Managing Director
Joseph Michael, Managing Director
Mark Frietch, Managing Director
Michele Hawkins, Managing Director
Paul Cohn, Managing Director

Type of Firm
Private Equity Advisor or Fund of Funds

Project Preferences

Type of Financing Preferred:
Fund of Funds
Fund of Funds of Second

Additional Information
Name of Most Recent Fund: Fort Washington Private Equity Investors VIII, L.P.
Most Recent Fund Was Raised: 01/03/2014
Year Founded: 1999
Capital Under Management: $1,866,200,000
Current Activity Level : Actively seeking new investments
Method of Compensation: Return on investment is of primary concern, do not charge fees

FORTE CAPITAL ADVISORS LLC

c/o Forte Management LLC
170 Varick St 2nd Flr
New York, NY USA 10013
Website: fortecapitaladvisory.com

Management and Staff
Greg DeYonker, Chief Operating Officer

Type of Firm
Investment Management Firm

Project Preferences

Type of Financing Preferred:
Generalist PE

Additional Information
Year Founded: 2003
Current Activity Level : Actively seeking new investments

FORTE VENTURES

3423 Piedmont Road, NE
Second Floor
Atlanta, GA USA 30305
Phone: 7027034295
Fax: 4048552840
Website: www.forteventures.com

Other Offices
4501 Dudley Lane, NW
Atlanta, GA USA 30327
Phone: 7027034295

3000 Sand Hill Road
Building One, Suite 205
Menlo Park, CA USA 94025

Management and Staff
Tom Hawkins, Managing Partner

Type of Firm
Private Equity Firm

Association Membership
National Venture Capital Association – USA (NVCA)

Project Preferences

Role in Financing:
Will function either as deal originator or investor in deals created by others

Size of Investments Considered:
Min Size of Investment Considered (000s): $100
Max Size of Investment Considered (000s): $3,000

Industry Preferences

In Communications prefer:
Wireless Communications

In Industrial/Energy prefer:
Industrial Products

In Financial Services prefer:
Financial Services

In Business Serv. prefer:
Media

Additional Information
Name of Most Recent Fund: Forte Ventures, L.P.
Most Recent Fund Was Raised: 05/15/2013
Year Founded: 2012
Capital Under Management: $30,000,000
Current Activity Level : Actively seeking new investments

FORTEX CAPITAL INC

800 West El Camino Real
Suite 180
Mountain View, CA USA 94040
Phone: 6463744336
Fax: 6506144880
Website: www.fortexcapital.com

Other Offices
26-27 Mahatma Gandhi Road
Level 9, Raheja Towers
Bangalore, India 560 001
Phone: 918041800800
Fax: 918041800900

1168 Nanjing Xi Lu
3501 Citic Square
Shanghai, China 200041
Phone: 862152524618
Fax: 862152524616

405 Lexington Avenue
25th & 26th Floor, Chrysler Building
New York, NY USA 10174
Phone: 2129076400
Fax: 9173688005

1 Northumberland Avenue
Trafalgar Square
London, United Kingdom WC2N 5BW
Phone: 442078725500
Fax: 442078725611

2 Jianguomenwai Avenue
15/F, Yintai Office Tower C, Chaoyang
Beijing, China
Phone: 861065637888
Fax: 861065637999

Nehru place
15th Floor
New Delhi, India 110 019
Phone: 911142235223
Fax: 911142235222

12 Abba Hillel Street
16th Floor, Ayalon House
Ramat-Gan, Israel 52136
Phone: 97237541111
Fax: 97237541100

Management and Staff
Kevin Dane, General Partner
Suraj Luke, General Partner

Type of Firm
Private Equity Firm

Project Preferences

Type of Financing Preferred:
Leveraged Buyout
Mezzanine
Balanced
Seed
Acquisition
Startup
Special Situation
Recapitalizations

Size of Investments Considered:
Min Size of Investment Considered (000s): $5,000
Max Size of Investment Considered (000s): $20,000

Industry Preferences

In Communications prefer:
Communications and Media

In Computer Software prefer:
Software

In Internet Specific prefer:
Internet

In Semiconductor/Electr prefer:
Electronics
Semiconductor

In Medical/Health prefer:
Medical/Health

In Consumer Related prefer:
Consumer

In Industrial/Energy prefer:
Alternative Energy

In Financial Services prefer:
Financial Services

In Business Serv. prefer:
Services
Media

Additional Information
Year Founded: 2011
Current Activity Level : Actively seeking new investments

FORTIFY VENTURES LLC

1627 K Street Northwest
Washington, DC USA 20006
E-mail: bringit@fortify.vc

Management and Staff
Adam Fazackerley, General Partner
Jonathon Perrelli, Partner

Type of Firm
Private Equity Firm

Project Preferences

Type of Financing Preferred:
Early Stage
Seed
Startup

Geographical Preferences

United States Preferences:
Washington

Additional Information
Year Founded: 2011
Current Activity Level : Actively seeking new investments

FORTINO CAPITAL ARKIV COMM.VA

3, Belgicastraat
ZaZaventem, Belgium 1930
Phone: 3226691050
Website: fortino.be

Other Offices
3, Belgicastraat
Zaventem, Belgium 1930
Phone: 3226691050

Type of Firm
Private Equity Firm

Project Preferences

Type of Financing Preferred:
Early Stage
Expansion
Later Stage
Seed
Acquisition

Industry Preferences

In Internet Specific prefer:
E-Commerce Technology

In Computer Other prefer:
Computer Related

Additional Information
Year Founded: 2016
Capital Under Management: $148,090,000
Current Activity Level : Actively seeking new investments

FORTISSIMO CAPTIAL FUND ISRAEL LP

14 Hamelacha Street
Park Afek, POB 11704
Rosh Haayin, Israel 48091
Phone: 97239157400
Fax: 97239157411
E-mail: info@ffcapital.com
Website: www.ffcapital.com

Management and Staff
Eli Blatt, Partner
Marc Lesnick, Partner
Shmoulik Barashi, Partner
Yoav Hineman, Partner
Yochai Hacohen, Partner

Type of Firm
Private Equity Firm

Project Preferences

Type of Financing Preferred:
Leveraged Buyout
Expansion
Turnaround
Later Stage
Management Buyouts

Geographical Preferences

International Preferences:
Europe
Israel
All International

Industry Preferences

In Communications prefer:
Telecommunications

In Industrial/Energy prefer:
Industrial Products

Additional Information
Year Founded: 2004
Capital Under Management: $665,000,000
Current Activity Level : Actively seeking new investments

FORTRESS INVESTMENT GROUP LLC

1345 Avenue of the Americas
46th Floor
New York, NY USA 10105
Phone: 2127986100
Fax: 2127986092
Website: www.fortress.com

Other Offices
200 South Wacker Drive
31st Floor
CHICAGO, IL USA 60606
Phone: 312-674-4954

6-10-1 Roppongi, Minato-ku
29F Roppongi Hills Mori Tower
Tokyo, Japan 106-6129
Phone: 81-3-6438-4400

220 Elm Street
Suite 201
NEW CANAAN, CT USA 06840
Phone: 203-442-2450

Drawbridge (Suisse) SARL
Place Longemalle 6-8
Geneva, Switzerland 1204
Phone: 41-22-310-5790

5221 North O'Connor Boulevard
Suite 700
IRVING, TX USA 75039
Phone: 972-532-4300

One Market Street
Spear Tower, 35th Floor
SAN FRANCISCO, CA USA 94105
Phone: 415-293-7965

1717 Arch Street
15th Floor
MIDDLE CITY WEST, PA USA 19103
Phone: 267-330-0000

1 Raffles Place
Level 24
Singapore, Singapore 048616
Phone: 65-6408-0566

No. 1717, Nanjing West Road
Suite 2580, Wheelock Square, Jing An Dst
Shanghai, China
Phone: 862161575322

Via Mario Carucci, 131
Rome, Italy 00143
Phone: 39-06-47971

5 Savile Row
London, United Kingdom W1S 3PD
Phone: 44-207-290-5600

10250 Constellation Boulevard
23rd Floor
CENTURY CITY, CA USA 90067
Phone: 310-228-3030

Level 43, AMP Centre
50 Bridge Street
Sydney, Australia 2000
Phone: 612-8239-1900

Junghofstrasse 22
Frankfurt, Germany 60311
Phone: 49-69-2549-670

Cheung Kong Centre, Suite 4701
2 Queen's Road
Central, Hong Kong
Phone: 852-2251-1881

750 B Street
Suite 2700
SAN DIEGO, CA USA 92101
Phone: 619-881-6910

Feringastr. 6
Munich, Germany 85774
Phone: 49-89-9921-6265

Bay Wellington Tower, Suite 3210
181 Bay Street, BCE Place
Toronto, Canada M5J 2T3
Phone: 416-862-8720

Management and Staff
A. Todd Ladda, Managing Director
Adam Levinson, Managing Director
Alexander Cook, Managing Director
Allison Thrush, Managing Director
Andrew McKnight, Managing Director
Andrew Dempsey, Managing Director
Anthony Tufariello, Managing Director
Constantine Dakolias, Managing Director
Daniel Bass, Chief Financial Officer
David Brooks, Vice President
Jonathan Ashley, Managing Director
Joseph Adams, Managing Director
Jude Driscoll, Managing Director
Kenneth Gershenfeld, Managing Director
Lilly Donohue, Managing Director
Marc Furstein, Managing Director
Peter McTeague, Managing Director
Peter Smith, Managing Director
Randal Nardone, Chief Executive Officer
Stuart Bohart, Senior Managing Director
Thomas Pulley, Managing Director
Thomas Chan-Soo Kang, Managing Director
William Callanan, Managing Director

Type of Firm
Investment Management Firm

Project Preferences

Type of Financing Preferred:
Leveraged Buyout
Generalist PE
Balanced
Opportunistic
Distressed Debt

Geographical Preferences

United States Preferences:
North America

International Preferences:
Western Europe
Japan
All International

Industry Preferences

In Industrial/Energy prefer:
Energy
Machinery

In Transportation prefer:
Transportation

In Financial Services prefer:
Real Estate

In Utilities prefer:
Utilities

Additional Information
Name of Most Recent Fund: Fortress Japan Opportunity Fund II
Most Recent Fund Was Raised: 12/27/2011
Year Founded: 1998
Capital Under Management: $22,000,000,000
Current Activity Level : Actively seeking new investments

FORTUNE VENTURE CAPITAL CO LTD

Special Zone Press Building
23rd Floor
Shenzhen, China 518009
Phone: 8675583515108
Fax: 8675583515115
E-mail: Fortune@fortunevc.com
Website: www.fortunevc.com

Other Offices
No. 1088 Pudong S Rd, Pudong New Dist
Room 1301, Zhongrong International Plaza
Shanghai, China 200120
Phone: 862168880068
Fax: 862168886698

No. 159, North Shaoshan Road
Rm 1910-1916, 19/F, Dolton Hotel
Changsha, China 410011
Phone: 8673189821028
Fax: 8673189821838

No. 7, Financial St, Xicheng District
F201, Level 2, Windland Int'l Fiance Ctr
Beijing, China 100026
Phone: 861066553328
Fax: 861066555321

No. 28, Huaxiang Road, Zhujiang New City
Room 1608, Fuli Yingxin Plaza
Guangzhou, China 510623
Phone: 862085608312
Fax: 862085608313

No.46 Long She Road
Room 909, Diamond Office Building
Hangzhou, China 310000
Phone: 8657187078792
Fax: 8657187078962

Management and Staff
Dehua Hu, Partner
Guozhi Liang, Partner
Hongxia Shao, Partner
Renjie Xiong, Partner
Shen Qi, Partner
Xufeng Liu, Partner
Zhihong Yu, Partner
Zhonghong Fu, Partner

Type of Firm
Private Equity Firm

Project Preferences

Type of Financing Preferred:
Early Stage
Expansion
Balanced
Later Stage

Size of Investments Considered:
Min Size of Investment Considered (000s): $734
Max Size of Investment Considered (000s): $14,685

Geographical Preferences

International Preferences:
China

Industry Preferences

In Communications prefer:
Telecommunications
Wireless Communications

In Computer Software prefer:
Software

In Internet Specific prefer:
Internet

In Semiconductor/Electr prefer:
Semiconductor

In Biotechnology prefer:
Biotechnology

In Medical/Health prefer:
Medical/Health

In Consumer Related prefer:
Consumer Products
Consumer Services

In Industrial/Energy prefer:
Energy
Energy Conservation Relat
Materials
Advanced Materials
Machinery
Environmental Related

In Business Serv. prefer:
Media

In Manufact. prefer:
Manufacturing

In Agr/Forestr/Fish prefer:
Agriculture related

In Other prefer:
Environment Responsible

Additional Information
Year Founded: 2000
Capital Under Management: $10,500,000,000
Current Activity Level : Actively seeking new investments

FORTUNE VENTURE CAPITAL CORP

No. 333, Tun-Hwa South Road, 18 F
Taipei, Taiwan
Phone: 886227006999
Fax: 886227026208

Management and Staff
Bing Xiao, Managing Partner
Dehua Hu, Partner
Guozhi Liang, Partner
Margaret Shao, Partner
Renjie Xiong, Partner
Robert Tsao, President & Chairman
Shen Qi, Partner
Xufeng Liu, Partner
Zhihong Yu, Partner
Zhonghong Fu, Partner
Zhou Liu, Founder

Type of Firm
Private Equity Firm

Association Membership
Taiwan Venture Capital Association(TVCA)

Project Preferences

Type of Financing Preferred:
Early Stage
Expansion
Start-up Financing
Turnaround
Later Stage
Seed

Geographical Preferences

International Preferences:
Taiwan
China

Industry Preferences

In Communications prefer:
Telecommunications

In Computer Software prefer:
Software

In Semiconductor/Electr prefer:
Semiconductor
Circuit Boards

Additional Information
Year Founded: 1993
Capital Under Management: $62,100,000
Current Activity Level : Actively seeking new investments

FORUM CAPITAL PARTNER

140 East 45th Street, 40th Floor
New York, NY USA 10017
Phone: 2122901787
Fax: 2122901763
E-mail: info@forumcp.com

Management and Staff
Andrew Harris, Vice President
Jeffrey Stern, Managing Director
Robert Schwabe, Managing Partner

Type of Firm
Private Equity Firm

Additional Information
Year Founded: 2001
Current Activity Level : Actively seeking new investments

FORUM SYNERGIES INDIA PE FUND MANAGERS P LTD

Yemlur Main Road
Suite No VI, A1- Epsilon
Bangalore, India 560 037
Phone: 91-80-4000-6400
Fax: 91-80-4117-9500

Management and Staff
Hemchandra Javeri, Co-Founder
Prashant Goyal, Chief Operating Officer
Samir Inamdar, Co-Founder

Type of Firm
Private Equity Firm

Association Membership
Indian Venture Capital Association (IVCA)

Project Preferences

Type of Financing Preferred:
Balanced
Later Stage

Size of Investments Considered:
Min Size of Investment Considered (000s): $3,000
Max Size of Investment Considered (000s): $15,000

Geographical Preferences

International Preferences:
India

Industry Preferences

In Communications prefer:
Commercial Communications
Telecommunications

In Semiconductor/Electr prefer:
Electronics
Electronic Components

In Biotechnology prefer:
Biotechnology

In Medical/Health prefer:
Medical/Health
Pharmaceuticals

In Consumer Related prefer:
Retail
Consumer Products
Consumer Services

In Transportation prefer:
Transportation

In Financial Services prefer:
Real Estate

In Other prefer:
Environment Responsible

Additional Information
Year Founded: 2008
Current Activity Level : Actively seeking new investments

FORWARD INVESTMENT PARTNERS

Centre Point
103, New Oxford Street
London, United Kingdom WC1A1DD
Website: www.forwardinvestmentpartners.com

Management and Staff
Carl Gaywood, Partner
Nicholas Brisbourne, Managing Partner

Type of Firm
Private Equity Firm

Project Preferences

Type of Financing Preferred:
Early Stage
Expansion
Balanced
Later Stage
Seed

Geographical Preferences

International Preferences:
United Kingdom
Europe

Industry Preferences

In Computer Software prefer:
Software

In Internet Specific prefer:
E-Commerce Technology
Internet
Web Aggregation/Portals

In Business Serv. prefer:
Media

In Manufact. prefer:
Publishing

Additional Information
Year Founded: 2013
Current Activity Level : Actively seeking new investments

FORWARD PARTNERS LTD

124 East Road
Unit 2, Aurora Building
London, United Kingdom N1 6FD
Phone: 4402030210684
Website: www.forwardpartners.com

Management and Staff
David Norris, Partner
Nicholas Brisbourne, Managing Partner

Type of Firm
Private Equity Firm

Project Preferences

Type of Financing Preferred:
Early Stage
Startup

Industry Preferences

In Internet Specific prefer:
Ecommerce

Additional Information
Year Founded: 2014
Capital Under Management: $74,660,000
Current Activity Level : Actively seeking new investments

FORWARD VENTURES

4747 Executive Drive
Suite 700
San Diego, CA USA 92121
Phone: 8586776077
Fax: 8584528799
E-mail: info@forwardventures.com
Website: www.forwardventures.com

Management and Staff
Ivor Royston, Co-Founder
Standish Fleming, Co-Founder
Stuart Collinson, Partner

Type of Firm
Private Equity Firm

Project Preferences

Role in Financing:
Prefer role as deal originator but will also invest in deals created by others

Type of Financing Preferred:
Early Stage
Balanced
Seed
Startup

Size of Investments Considered:
Min Size of Investment Considered (000s): $1,000
Max Size of Investment Considered (000s): $15,000

Geographical Preferences

United States Preferences:
North America

International Preferences:
Europe

Industry Focus
(% based on actual investment)

Biotechnology	69.5%
Medical/Health	30.0%
Internet Specific	0.5%

Additional Information
Name of Most Recent Fund: Forward Ventures V, L.P.
Most Recent Fund Was Raised: 04/28/2003
Year Founded: 1993
Capital Under Management: $500,000,000
Current Activity Level : Actively seeking new investments
Method of Compensation: Return on investment is of primary concern, do not charge fees

FOS CAPITAL PARTNERS LLC

535 Fifth Avenue, 4th Floor
New York, NY USA 10017
E-mail: info@fos-advisors.com

Type of Firm
Investment Management Firm

Project Preferences

Type of Financing Preferred:
Balanced

Geographical Preferences

United States Preferences:
North America

Canadian Preferences:
All Canada

Industry Preferences

In Medical/Health prefer:
Medical/Health
Health Services

Additional Information
Year Founded: 2016
Capital Under Management: $25,000,000
Current Activity Level : Actively seeking new investments

FOSHAN JI CHENG VENTURE CAPITAL CO., LTD.

No. 61 Nanhai Avenue
4/F Minsheng Building
Foshan, China 528200
Phone: 86-757-83216333
Fax: 86-757-83206999
Website: www.gdjcvc.com

Type of Firm
Private Equity Firm

Project Preferences

Type of Financing Preferred:
Early Stage
Balanced
Later Stage
Seed

Geographical Preferences

International Preferences:
China

Industry Preferences

In Internet Specific prefer:
Internet

In Medical/Health prefer:
Medical/Health

In Consumer Related prefer:
Retail
Consumer Products
Education Related

In Industrial/Energy prefer:
Energy
Environmental Related

In Financial Services prefer:
Financial Services

In Business Serv. prefer:
Media

In Manufact. prefer:
Manufacturing

In Agr/Forestr/Fish prefer:
Agriculture related

Additional Information
Year Founded: 2008
Capital Under Management: $45,423,000
Current Activity Level : Actively seeking new investments

FOSHAN KEHAI VENTURE CAPITAL CO LTD

Innovation Centere B306
Shishan Town, Nanhai
Foshan City, China 528222
Phone: 86-757-86683131
Fax: 86-757-86683130

Type of Firm
Private Equity Firm

Project Preferences

Type of Financing Preferred:
Balanced

Geographical Preferences

International Preferences:
Taiwan
All International

Additional Information
Year Founded: 2002
Current Activity Level : Actively seeking new investments

FOSHAN SHUNDE DEXIN VENTURE CAPITAL CO LTD

Demin Road District, Shunde
6/F Gov't Building
Foshan, China

Type of Firm
Private Equity Firm

Project Preferences

Type of Financing Preferred:
Balanced

Geographical Preferences

International Preferences:
China

Industry Preferences

In Biotechnology prefer:
Biotechnology

In Industrial/Energy prefer:
Energy
Industrial Products
Materials
Environmental Related

Additional Information
Year Founded: 2010
Current Activity Level : Actively seeking new investments

FOUNDATION CAPITAL LLC

250 Middlefield Road
Menlo Park, CA USA 94025
Phone: 6506140500
E-mail: info@foundationcapital.com
Website: www.foundationcapital.com

Management and Staff
Ashu Garg, General Partner
Charles Moldow, General Partner
David Singer, Chief Financial Officer
Joanne Chen, Partner
Jonathan Ehrlich, Partner
Meg Sloan, Partner
Michael Schuh, General Partner
Paul Koontz, General Partner
Paul Holland, General Partner
Rodolfo Gonzalez, Partner
Steven Vassallo, General Partner
Warren Weiss, General Partner
William Elmore, General Partner
Zach Noorani, Partner

Type of Firm
Private Equity Firm

Association Membership
Western Association of Venture Capitalists (WAVC)
National Venture Capital Association - USA (NVCA)

Project Preferences

Role in Financing:
Prefer role as deal originator but will also invest in deals created by others

Type of Financing Preferred:
Early Stage
Balanced
Startup

Size of Investments Considered:
Min Size of Investment Considered (000s): $1,000
Max Size of Investment Considered (000s): $10,000

Industry Focus
(% based on actual investment)

Computer Software and Services	48.0%
Internet Specific	18.5%
Communications and Media	10.0%
Industrial/Energy	6.5%
Semiconductors/Other Elect.	5.4%
Computer Hardware	4.9%
Other Products	3.8%
Consumer Related	2.1%
Medical/Health	0.5%
Biotechnology	0.2%

Additional Information
Name of Most Recent Fund: Foundation Capital VII, L.P.
Most Recent Fund Was Raised: 04/09/2013
Year Founded: 1995
Capital Under Management: $2,400,000,000
Current Activity Level : Actively seeking new investments
Method of Compensation: Return on investment is of primary concern, do not charge fees

FOUNDATION MEDICAL PARTNERS LP

200 Newbury Street
Boston, MA USA 02116
Phone: 6176075060
Website: www.foundmed.com

Other Offices
105 Rowayton Avenue
NORWALK, CT USA 06853
Phone: 2038513900

Management and Staff
A. Marc Gillinov, Partner
Amit Shah, Partner
Andrew Firlik, Managing Partner
Harry Rein, Partner
John Sullivan, Partner
Kevin Sharer, Partner
Lawrence Calcano, Venture Partner
Lee Wrubel, Managing Partner

Type of Firm
Private Equity Firm

Association Membership
New England Venture Capital Association
National Venture Capital Association - USA (NVCA)

Project Preferences

Role in Financing:
Will function either as deal originator or investor in deals created by others

Type of Financing Preferred:
Startup

Industry Preferences

In Computer Software prefer:
Software

In Medical/Health prefer:
Medical Products
Health Services
Pharmaceuticals

Additional Information

Year Founded: 2001
Capital Under Management: $216,000,000
Current Activity Level : Actively seeking new investments
Method of Compensation: Return on investment is of primary concern, do not charge fees

FOUNDATION SPECIALTY FINANCING FUND LLC

7244 South Perth Way
Aurora, CO USA 80016
Phone: 3032567604
E-mail: info@fsff.biz
Website: www.fsff.biz

Type of Firm
Private Equity Firm

Project Preferences

Type of Financing Preferred:
Mezzanine
Management Buyouts
Recapitalizations

Size of Investments Considered:
Min Size of Investment Considered (000s): $1,000
Max Size of Investment Considered (000s): $5,000

Industry Preferences

In Financial Services prefer:
Financial Services

Additional Information

Year Founded: 2012
Capital Under Management: $15,590,000
Current Activity Level : Actively seeking new investments

FOUNDATION VENTURE CAPITAL GROUP LLC

120 Albany Street
Tower II, Eighth Floor
New Brunswick, NJ USA 08901
Phone: 7322355400
Website: www.foundationventure.com

Management and Staff

Dale Heffler, Vice President
George Heinrich, Chief Executive Officer
James Golubieski, President

Type of Firm
Private Equity Firm

Project Preferences

Type of Financing Preferred:
Startup

Geographical Preferences

United States Preferences:
New Jersey

Industry Preferences

In Biotechnology prefer:
Biotech Related Research

In Medical/Health prefer:
Diagnostic Test Products
Medical Products

Additional Information

Year Founded: 2006
Current Activity Level : Actively seeking new investments

FOUNDCENTER INVESTMENT GMBH

Schoenhauser Allee 59B
Berlin, Germany 10437
Phone: 493099006195
Website: www.foundcenter.com

Type of Firm
Private Equity Firm

Project Preferences

Type of Financing Preferred:
Early Stage
Seed

Additional Information

Year Founded: 2016
Current Activity Level : Actively seeking new investments

FOUNDER COLLECTIVE LP

One Mifflin Place
Suite 300
Cambridge, MA USA 02138
Phone: 6174532250
E-mail: contact@foundercollective.com
Website: www.foundercollective.com

Other Offices

580 Broadway
Suite 303
NEW YORK, NY USA 10012

Management and Staff

Caterina Fake, Partner
David Frankel, Managing Partner
Eric Paley, Managing Partner
Gaurav Jain, Principal
Micah Rosenbloom, Managing Partner
Raj De Datta, Partner
Zach Klein, Partner

Type of Firm
Private Equity Firm

Association Membership
New England Venture Capital Association

Project Preferences

Type of Financing Preferred:
Seed
Startup

Geographical Preferences

United States Preferences:
East Coast

Additional Information

Name of Most Recent Fund: Founder Collective II, L.P.
Most Recent Fund Was Raised: 09/11/2012
Year Founded: 2009
Capital Under Management: $200,000,000
Current Activity Level : Actively seeking new investments

FOUNDER EQUITY LLC

118 North Peoria
Suite 3S
Chicago, IL USA 60607
Phone: 3122266468
E-mail: investors@founderequity.com
Website: founderequity.com

Type of Firm
Incubator/Development Program

Project Preferences

Type of Financing Preferred:
Seed
Strategic Alliances
Startup

Size of Investments Considered:
Min Size of Investment Considered (000s): $2,000
Max Size of Investment Considered (000s): $2,500

Industry Preferences

In Internet Specific prefer:
E-Commerce Technology

Additional Information

Year Founded: 2013
Capital Under Management: $7,690,000
Current Activity Level : Actively seeking new investments

Pratt's Guide to Private Equity & Venture Capital Sources

FOUNDERFUEL
51 Sherbrooke West
Montreal, Canada H2X 1X2
Website: founderfuel.com

Other Offices
51 Sherbrooke West
Montreal, Canada H2X 1X2

Type of Firm
Incubator/Development Program

Project Preferences

Type of Financing Preferred:
Early Stage
Seed
Startup

Size of Investments Considered:
Min Size of Investment Considered (000s): $10
Max Size of Investment Considered (000s): $153

Geographical Preferences

Canadian Preferences:
Quebec

Industry Preferences

In Communications prefer:
Wireless Communications

In Internet Specific prefer:
Internet

Additional Information
Year Founded: 2011
Current Activity Level : Actively seeking new investments

FOUNDERS A/S
Skelbaekgade 2, 5.
Copenhagen , Denmark 1717
Website: www.founders.as

Type of Firm
Private Equity Firm

Project Preferences

Type of Financing Preferred:
Early Stage
Seed
Startup

Additional Information
Year Founded: 2012
Current Activity Level : Actively seeking new investments

FOUNDERS CAPITAL PARTNERS
1615 Lasuen Road
Santa Barbara, CA USA 93103
Phone: 8059634600
Fax: 8059634704
Website: www.founderscapitalpartners.com

Management and Staff
L. Robert Johnson, Managing Partner
Robert Johnson, Managing Partner

Type of Firm
Angel Group

Project Preferences

Type of Financing Preferred:
Early Stage
Balanced

Size of Investments Considered:
Min Size of Investment Considered (000s): $100
Max Size of Investment Considered (000s): $5,000

Geographical Preferences

United States Preferences:
California

Industry Preferences

In Computer Software prefer:
Software

In Internet Specific prefer:
Internet

In Semiconductor/Electr prefer:
Electronics
Sensors

In Biotechnology prefer:
Industrial Biotechnology

In Industrial/Energy prefer:
Industrial Products

Additional Information
Year Founded: 1988
Capital Under Management: $54,500,000
Current Activity Level : Actively seeking new investments

FOUNDERS CIRCLE CAPITAL
27 South Park Street
Suite 101
San Francisco, CA USA 94107
E-mail: info@fcc.vc
Website: www.founderscirclecapital.com

Type of Firm
Private Equity Firm

Project Preferences

Type of Financing Preferred:
Balanced

Additional Information
Name of Most Recent Fund: Founders Circle Capital I, L.P.
Most Recent Fund Was Raised: 11/13/2013
Year Founded: 2013
Capital Under Management: $38,900,000
Current Activity Level : Actively seeking new investments

FOUNDERS CLUB LP
123-125 Ladbroke Road
11 Mead House
London, United Kingdom W11 3PU
Phone: 447815901066
E-mail: info@Founders-Club.com
Website: www.founders-club.com

Other Offices
5050 El Camino Real
Suite 104
Los Altos, CA USA 94022
Phone: 6504756877

Management and Staff
Andrew Romans, General Partner
BC Brant, General Partner
Christopher Burke, Venture Partner

Type of Firm
Private Equity Firm

Project Preferences

Type of Financing Preferred:
Early Stage
Expansion
Later Stage
Seed

Industry Preferences

In Communications prefer:
Communications and Media

In Biotechnology prefer:
Biotechnology

In Medical/Health prefer:
Medical Products
Health Services
Pharmaceuticals

In Industrial/Energy prefer:
Environmental Related

Additional Information
Year Founded: 2010
Current Activity Level : Actively seeking new investments

FOUNDERS CO OP

1100 Northeast Campus Parkway
Second Floor
Seattle, WA USA 98105
Website: www.founderscoop.com

Management and Staff
Andy Sack, Partner
Chris DeVore, Partner
Rudy Gadre, Partner

Type of Firm
Private Equity Firm

Project Preferences

Type of Financing Preferred:
Early Stage
Seed
Startup

Size of Investments Considered:
Min Size of Investment Considered (000s): $50
Max Size of Investment Considered (000s): $250

Geographical Preferences

United States Preferences:
Northwest
Oregon
Washington

Canadian Preferences:
All Canada

Industry Preferences

In Communications prefer:
Wireless Communications

Additional Information
Name of Most Recent Fund: Founder's Co-Op II LLC
Most Recent Fund Was Raised: 01/06/2012
Year Founded: 2008
Capital Under Management: $17,950,000
Current Activity Level : Actively seeking new investments

FOUNDERS EQUITY, INC.

711 Fifth Avenue
Fifth Floor
New York, NY USA 10022
Phone: 2128290900
Fax: 2128290901
E-mail: info@fequity.com
Website: www.fequity.com

Management and Staff
J. Ryan Kelly, Partner
John White, Partner
John Teeger, Partner
Thomas Ghegan, Principal
Warren Haber, Partner

Type of Firm
Private Equity Firm

Association Membership
Natl Assoc of Small Bus. Inv. Co (NASBIC)

Project Preferences

Role in Financing:
Prefer role as deal originator but will also invest in deals created by others

Type of Financing Preferred:
Leveraged Buyout
Expansion
Turnaround
Later Stage
Management Buyouts
Special Situation
Recapitalizations

Size of Investments Considered:
Min Size of Investment Considered (000s): $3,000
Max Size of Investment Considered (000s): $15,000

Geographical Preferences

United States Preferences:
North America

Industry Preferences

In Medical/Health prefer:
Medical/Health

In Consumer Related prefer:
Consumer Products

In Industrial/Energy prefer:
Environmental Related

In Financial Services prefer:
Financial Services

In Business Serv. prefer:
Services
Distribution

In Manufact. prefer:
Manufacturing

Additional Information
Year Founded: 1969
Capital Under Management: $160,000,000
Current Activity Level : Actively seeking new investments
Method of Compensation: Return on invest. most important, but chg. closing fees, service fees, etc.

FOUNDERS FACTORY LTD

17 Old Court Place
London, United Kingdom W8 4PL
Website: www.foundersfactory.com

Management and Staff
Louis Warner, Chief Operating Officer

Type of Firm
Incubator/Development Program

Project Preferences

Type of Financing Preferred:
Early Stage

Additional Information
Year Founded: 2015
Current Activity Level : Actively seeking new investments

FOUNDERS FUND, THE

One Letterman Drive
Building D, Suite 500
San Francisco, CA USA 94129
Phone: 4152305800
E-mail: info@thefoundersfund.com
Website: www.thefoundersfund.com

Management and Staff
Brian Singerman, Partner
Geoff Lewis, Principal
Ken Howery, Partner
Lauren Gross, Principal
Luke Nosek, Partner
Peter Thiel, Partner
Scott Nolan, Principal

Type of Firm
Private Equity Firm

Project Preferences

Type of Financing Preferred:
Early Stage
Seed
Startup

Size of Investments Considered:
Min Size of Investment Considered (000s): $500
Max Size of Investment Considered (000s): $1,000

Geographical Preferences

United States Preferences:

Industry Preferences

In Computer Software prefer:
Software
Artificial Intelligence

In Internet Specific prefer:
Internet

In Biotechnology prefer:
Biotechnology

In Medical/Health prefer:
Medical/Health

In Consumer Related prefer:
Consumer

In Industrial/Energy prefer:
Energy
Machinery

In Transportation prefer:
Transportation
Aerospace

In Business Serv. prefer:
Media

Additional Information
Name of Most Recent Fund: Founders Fund V, L.P.
Most Recent Fund Was Raised: 03/05/2014
Year Founded: 2005
Capital Under Management: $50,000,000
Current Activity Level : Actively seeking new investments

FOUNDRY GROUP LLC

1050 Walnut Street
Suite 210
Boulder, CO USA 80302

Management and Staff
Bradley Feld, Co-Founder
Chris Moody, Partner
Jason Mendelson, Managing Director
Ryan McIntyre, Managing Director
Seth Levine, Managing Director

Type of Firm
Private Equity Firm

Association Membership
National Venture Capital Association - USA (NVCA)

Project Preferences

Type of Financing Preferred:
Early Stage
Balanced
Later Stage
Seed
Startup

Size of Investments Considered:
Min Size of Investment Considered (000s): $250
Max Size of Investment Considered (000s): $500

Geographical Preferences

United States Preferences:
North America
All U.S.

Industry Preferences

In Computer Software prefer:
Software

In Internet Specific prefer:
Internet

Additional Information
Name of Most Recent Fund: Foundry Group Select Fund, L.P.
Most Recent Fund Was Raised: 08/05/2013
Year Founded: 1996
Capital Under Management: $695,900,000
Current Activity Level : Actively seeking new investments

FOUNTAINVEST PARTNERS ASIA LTD

No. 1539, Nanjing West Road
Building 2, 22F
Shanghai, China
Phone: 862124190800
Fax: 862124190888
E-mail: enquiry@fountainvest.com
Website: www.fountainvest.com

Other Offices
3 Garden Road
Suite 705-8 ICBC Tower
Central, Hong Kong
Phone: 85239723900
Fax: 85231072490

No.1 Jianguomenwai Avenue
Suite 3410, China World Office 1
Beijing, China
Phone: 861057766288
Fax: 861057766299

Management and Staff
Chenning Zhao, Managing Director
George Chuang, Managing Director
Terry Yongmin Hu, Managing Director

Type of Firm
Private Equity Firm

Association Membership
China Venture Capital Association

Project Preferences

Type of Financing Preferred:
Leveraged Buyout
Acquisition

Geographical Preferences

International Preferences:
China

Additional Information
Year Founded: 2007
Capital Under Management: $950,000,000
Current Activity Level : Actively seeking new investments

FOUR RIVERS PARTNERS LP

156 Second Street
San Francisco, CA USA 94105
Phone: 4152504643
Website: www.fourriversgroup.com

Management and Staff
Farouk Ladha, Managing Partner
Joe Greenstein, Partner
Kevin Mello, Chief Financial Officer
Lew Cirne, Partner
Rick Thompson, Partner
Russell Fradin, Partner

Type of Firm
Private Equity Firm

Project Preferences

Type of Financing Preferred:
Expansion
Balanced

Additional Information
Name of Most Recent Fund: Four Rivers Partners III, L.P.
Most Recent Fund Was Raised: 12/10/2013
Year Founded: 2006
Capital Under Management: $154,000,000
Current Activity Level : Actively seeking new investments

FOURIERTRANSFORM AB

Sveavagen 17
10th Floor
Stockholm, Sweden 111 57
Phone: 46841040600
Fax: 46841040640
Website: www.fouriertransform.se

Management and Staff
Per Nordberg, Chief Executive Officer
Ulf Jarvenas, Chief Financial Officer

Type of Firm
Government Affiliated Program

Association Membership
Swedish Venture Capital Association (SVCA)

Project Preferences

Type of Financing Preferred:
Balanced

Geographical Preferences

International Preferences:
Scandanavia/Nordic Region

Industry Preferences

In Transportation prefer:
Transportation

Additional Information

Year Founded: 2009
Capital Under Management: $427,600,000
Current Activity Level : Actively seeking new investments

FOURSAN GROUP

PO Box 143154
Amman, Jordan 11814
Phone: 962-6-562-4562
Fax: 962-6-552-6489
E-mail: mail@4san.com
Website: www.4san.com

Other Offices

P.O. Box 143154
Amman, Jordan 11814
Phone: 9626562452
Fax: 96265526489

186 Sloane Street
London, United Kingdom
Phone: 44-20-7235-0277
Fax: 44-20-7235-0467

Management and Staff

Nashat Masri, Founder

Type of Firm

Private Equity Firm

Association Membership

Emerging Markets Private Equity Association

Project Preferences

Type of Financing Preferred:
Leveraged Buyout
Early Stage
Generalist PE
Balanced
Seed
Acquisition
Startup

Geographical Preferences

International Preferences:
United Kingdom
Jordan
Middle East
Jamaica
Africa

Industry Preferences

In Communications prefer:
Wireless Communications

In Computer Software prefer:
Software

In Internet Specific prefer:
Internet

In Medical/Health prefer:
Pharmaceuticals

In Consumer Related prefer:
Food/Beverage
Education Related

In Financial Services prefer:
Financial Services

Additional Information

Year Founded: 2000
Current Activity Level : Actively seeking new investments

FOX THREE PARTNERS LLC

1072 Laskin Road
Suite 201
Virginia Beach, VA USA 23451
Phone: 7572963454
Website: www.fox3partners.com

Type of Firm

Private Equity Firm

Project Preferences

Type of Financing Preferred:
Leveraged Buyout
Acquisition

Geographical Preferences

United States Preferences:
East Coast

Industry Preferences

In Medical/Health prefer:
Health Services

In Industrial/Energy prefer:
Industrial Products

In Transportation prefer:
Aerospace

In Business Serv. prefer:
Services
Distribution

In Manufact. prefer:
Manufacturing

Additional Information

Year Founded: 2014
Current Activity Level : Actively seeking new investments

FOXHAVEN ASSET MANAGEMENT LP

410 E. Water Street, Suite 888
Charlottesville, VA USA 22902
Phone: 4343265300
E-mail: info@foxhavencap.com

Type of Firm

Investment Management Firm

Project Preferences

Type of Financing Preferred:
Later Stage

Additional Information

Year Founded: 2013
Current Activity Level : Actively seeking new investments

FPE CAPITAL LLP

15 Suffolk Street
London, United Kingdom
Website: www.fpecapital.com

Management and Staff

Dan Walker, Partner
David Barbour, Managing Partner
Henry Sallitt, Managing Partner
Llewellyn John, Partner

Type of Firm

Private Equity Firm

Project Preferences

Type of Financing Preferred:
Leveraged Buyout
Acquisition

Geographical Preferences

International Preferences:
United Kingdom

Additional Information

Year Founded: 2017
Capital Under Management: $131,500,000
Current Activity Level : Actively seeking new investments

FRAMESTORE VENTURES

Nine Noel Street
London , United Kingdom W1F 8GH
Website: www.framestore.com

Management and Staff

Lucy Killick, Managing Director
Mel Sullivan, Chief Operating Officer
William Sargent, Chief Executive Officer

Type of Firm

Private Equity Firm

Additional Information

Year Founded: 2016
Current Activity Level : Actively seeking new investments

FRAMEWORK CAPITAL PARTNERS LLC

1700 Post Oak Blvd
2BLVD Place, Suite 600
Houston, TX USA 77056
Phone: 7138269351
E-mail: info@frameworkcapitalpartners.com
Website: www.frameworkcapitalpartners.com

Type of Firm
Private Equity Firm

Project Preferences

Type of Financing Preferred:
Leveraged Buyout
Acquisition

Industry Preferences

In Industrial/Energy prefer:
Oil and Gas Exploration

In Transportation prefer:
Transportation

In Manufact. prefer:
Manufacturing

In Other prefer:
Environment Responsible

Additional Information
Year Founded: 1969
Current Activity Level: Actively seeking new investments

FRANCISCO PARTNERS LP

One Letterman Drive
Building C, Suite 410
San Francisco, CA USA 94129
Phone: 4154182900
Fax: 4154182999
E-mail: info@franciscopartners.com
Website: www.franciscopartners.com

Other Offices

201 Sloane Street
Second Floor
London, United Kingdom SW1Y 9QX
Phone: 44-207-907-8600
Fax: 44-207-907-8650

Management and Staff
Andrew Kowal, Partner
Billy Deitch, Vice President
Brian Decker, Principal
Chris Adams, Partner
Dipanjan Deb, Chief Executive Officer
Evan Daar, Vice President
Jason Brein, Principal
Jonh Herr, Chief Financial Officer
Jonathan Murphy, Vice President

Keith Geeslin, Partner
Leonid Rozkin, Vice President
Mario Razzini, Vice President
Matt Spetzler, Partner
Peter Christodoulo, Partner
Petri Oksanen, Partner
Robert Maclean, Principal
Thomas Ludwig, Chief Operating Officer

Type of Firm
Private Equity Firm

Project Preferences

Role in Financing:
Prefer role as deal originator

Type of Financing Preferred:
Leveraged Buyout
Management Buyouts
Acquisition

Industry Focus
(% based on actual investment)
Computer Software and Services	45.0%
Internet Specific	29.6%
Semiconductors/Other Elect.	14.8%
Computer Hardware	5.8%
Other Products	4.7%
Medical/Health	0.0%

Additional Information
Year Founded: 1999
Capital Under Management: $4,831,900,000
Current Activity Level: Actively seeking new investments

FRANGER INVESTMENT KGAA

Dahlienweg 15
Ketsch, Germany 68775
Phone: 4962323126018
Fax: 4962323127026
Website: www.frangerinvestment.com

Management and Staff
Bernhard Franger, Partner
Helmut Franger, Founder
Stefan Franger, Managing Partner

Type of Firm
Private Equity Firm

Project Preferences

Type of Financing Preferred:
Core
Leveraged Buyout
Early Stage
Balanced
Later Stage
Acquisition
Startup

Geographical Preferences

International Preferences:
Western Europe
Germany

Industry Preferences

In Financial Services prefer:
Real Estate

Additional Information
Year Founded: 2011
Current Activity Level: Actively seeking new investments

FRANK RUSSELL CAPITAL CO

1301 Second Avenue
18th Floor
Seattle, WA USA 98101
Phone: 12065057877
Website: www.russell.com

Other Offices

1 First Canadian Place
100 King St. W, Ste 5900, PO Box 476
Toronto, Canada M5X 1E4
Phone: 416-362-8411

100 East Wisconsin Avenue
Suite 1550
Milwaukee, WI USA 53202
Phone: 414-203-5800

1511 North Westshore Boulevard
1511 N. Westshore Boulevard
Tampa, FL USA 33607
Phone: 813-472-8200

1095 Avenue of the Americas
14th Floor
New York, NY USA 10036
Phone: 212-702-7900
Fax: 212-702-7944

6 Shenton Way #25-11 A
DBS Building Tower Two
Singapore, Singapore 068809
Phone: 65-325-4336

PO Box 105-191
Auckland, New Zealand
Phone: 649-357-6633

4330 La Jolla Village Drive
Suite 300
San Diego, CA USA 92122
Phone: 858-458-1125

6 Rue Christophe Colomb
Paris, France 75008
Phone: 331-5357-4020
Fax: 331-5357-4021

Level 24, Maritime Centre
207 Kent Street
Sydney, Australia NSW 2000
Phone: 612-9770-8000

71 Wacker Drive
Suite 2040
Chicago, IL USA 60606
Phone: 312-780-7100

One Maritime Plaza
Suite 1900
San Francisco, CA USA 94111
Phone: 415-403-6900

Place Canada
7-3-37, Akasaka
Minato-ku, Tokyo, Japan 107-0052
Phone: 81-3-5411-3500

Rex House
10 Regent Street
London, United Kingdom SW1Y 4PE
Phone: 44-20-7024-6000

Management and Staff
Helen Steers, Managing Director
Jeff Watts, Managing Director
Karl Smith, Managing Director
Michael Phillips, Chairman & CEO

Type of Firm
Private Equity Advisor or Fund of Funds

Project Preferences

Type of Financing Preferred:
Fund of Funds

Additional Information
Year Founded: 1936
Capital Under Management: $3,127,000,000
Current Activity Level : Actively seeking new investments

FRANKLIN TEMPLETON INVESTIMENTOS BRASIL LTDA

Avenida Paulista 1450
Sixth Floor, Bela Vista
Sao Paulo, Brazil 01310917
Phone: 551121786600
E-mail: bram@bram.bradesco.com.br
Website: www.franklintempleton.com.br

Type of Firm
Bank Affiliated

Project Preferences

Type of Financing Preferred:
Balanced

Geographical Preferences

International Preferences:
Brazil

Industry Preferences

In Communications prefer:
Communications and Media

In Semiconductor/Electr prefer:
Electronic Components

In Biotechnology prefer:
Agricultural/Animal Bio.

In Consumer Related prefer:
Retail

In Industrial/Energy prefer:
Energy
Oil and Gas Exploration
Oil & Gas Drilling,Explor

In Financial Services prefer:
Financial Services

In Agr/Forestr/Fish prefer:
Agribusiness
Agriculture related

Additional Information
Year Founded: 1998
Capital Under Management: $1,200,000,000
Current Activity Level : Actively seeking new investments

FRANSABANK SAL

PO Box 11-0393
Hamra Street
Riad El Solh Beirut, Lebanon 11072803
Phone: 9611734000
Website: www.fransabank.com

Type of Firm
Bank Affiliated

Project Preferences

Type of Financing Preferred:
Unknown

Geographical Preferences

International Preferences:
Qatar
Middle East

Additional Information
Year Founded: 2007
Current Activity Level : Actively seeking new investments

FRASER MCCOMBS CAPITAL

1035 Pearl Street, Suite 403
Boulder, CO USA 80302
Phone: 2104476150
E-mail: info@FMCap.com
Website: www.fmcap.com

Other Offices
220 North Green Street
CHICAGO, IL USA 60607

Management and Staff
Chase Fraser, Managing Partner
Tony Rimas, Managing Partner

Type of Firm
Private Equity Firm

Project Preferences

Type of Financing Preferred:
Early Stage

Industry Preferences

In Transportation prefer:
Transportation

Additional Information
Name of Most Recent Fund: Fraser McCombs Ventures, L.P.
Most Recent Fund Was Raised: 03/16/2012
Year Founded: 2012
Capital Under Management: $104,686,000
Current Activity Level : Actively seeking new investments

FRAZIER MANAGEMENT LLC

601 Union, Two Union Square, Suite 3200
Seattle, WA USA 98101
Phone: 2066217200
Fax: 2066211848
Website: www.frazierhealthcare.com

Other Offices
70 Willow Road
Suite 200
MENLO PARK, CA USA 94025
Phone: 6503255156
Fax: 6503255157

Management and Staff
Alan Levy, Venture Partner
Alan Frazier, Managing Partner
Ben Magnano, Principal
Brian Morfitt, Partner
Bridget Rauvola, Partner
Dan Estes, Partner
David Socks, Venture Partner
James Topper, General Partner
Kent Berkley, Vice President
Nader Naini, General Partner
Nathan Every, General Partner
Patrick Heron, General Partner
Remy Durand, Vice President
Steve Bailey, Chief Financial Officer
W.Michael Gallatin, Venture Partner

Type of Firm
Private Equity Firm

Association Membership
National Venture Capital Association - USA (NVCA)

Project Preferences

Role in Financing:
Prefer role as deal originator but will also invest in deals created by others

Type of Financing Preferred:
Leveraged Buyout
Early Stage
Generalist PE
Balanced
Later Stage
Seed
Recapitalizations

Geographical Preferences

United States Preferences:
All U.S.

Industry Focus

(% based on actual investment)
Medical/Health	47.3%
Biotechnology	34.6%
Other Products	5.7%
Internet Specific	5.3%
Computer Software and Services	3.2%
Consumer Related	1.7%
Computer Hardware	0.9%
Communications and Media	0.8%
Industrial/Energy	0.2%
Semiconductors/Other Elect.	0.2%

Additional Information
Name of Most Recent Fund: Frazier Healthcare VII, L.P.
Most Recent Fund Was Raised: 05/03/2013
Year Founded: 1991
Capital Under Management: $2,900,000,000
Current Activity Level : Actively seeking new investments
Method of Compensation: Return on investment is of primary concern, do not charge fees

FRDCM SICAR

Place Fasteur
Gafsa, Tunisia 2100
Phone: 21676228788
Fax: 21676224036
E-mail: frdcmgafsa@tunet.tn
Website: www.frdcmgafsa.com.tn

Type of Firm
Private Equity Firm

Association Membership
Tunisian Venture Capital Association

Project Preferences

Type of Financing Preferred:
Early Stage
Later Stage

Geographical Preferences

International Preferences:
Tunisia
Africa

Industry Preferences

In Consumer Related prefer:
Consumer
Consumer Services
Hotels and Resorts

In Industrial/Energy prefer:
Industrial Products

In Business Serv. prefer:
Services

In Agr/Forestr/Fish prefer:
Agriculture related

Additional Information
Year Founded: 1991
Current Activity Level : Actively seeking new investments

FREDRICK D SCOTT LLC

1120 Avenue of the Americas
Fourth Floor
New York, NY USA 10036
Phone: 2126266901
Fax: 2126266999
E-mail: info@fredrickdscott.com
Website: www.fredrickdscott.com

Management and Staff
Fredrick Scott, Founder

Type of Firm
Private Equity Firm

Project Preferences

Type of Financing Preferred:
Generalist PE
Balanced
Acquisition
Startup

Geographical Preferences

United States Preferences:

Industry Preferences

In Medical/Health prefer:
Medical/Health
Health Services

In Industrial/Energy prefer:
Oil and Gas Exploration

In Financial Services prefer:
Financial Services
Insurance

In Other prefer:
Women/Minority-Owned Bus.

Additional Information
Year Founded: 1969
Current Activity Level : Actively seeking new investments

FREEDOM 3 CAPITAL

1185 Avenue of the Americas
30th Floor
New York, NY USA 10036
Phone: 2122352160
Website: www.freedom3capital.com

Type of Firm
Private Equity Firm

Project Preferences

Type of Financing Preferred:
Mezzanine

Size of Investments Considered:
Min Size of Investment Considered (000s): $10,000
Max Size of Investment Considered (000s): $100,000

Additional Information
Year Founded: 1969
Current Activity Level : Actively seeking new investments

FREELANDS VENTURES LLP

34 Park Street
London, United Kingdom W1K 2JD
E-mail: hello@freelandsventures.com
Website: freelandsventures.com

Type of Firm
Private Equity Firm

Project Preferences

Type of Financing Preferred:
Early Stage

Additional Information
Year Founded: 2014
Current Activity Level : Actively seeking new investments

FREEMAN GROUP LLC

100 Crescent Court, Suite 1450
Dallas, TX USA 75201
Phone: 2145501220
Fax: 2145501221

E-mail: info@freemangp.com
Website: thefreemangroupllc.com

Management and Staff
Brandon Freeman, President, Founder
Crystal Moore, Chief Financial Officer

Type of Firm
Investment Management Firm

Project Preferences

Type of Financing Preferred:
Generalist PE

Additional Information
Year Founded: 2004
Current Activity Level : Actively seeking new investments

FREEMAN SPOGLI & CO LLC

11100 Santa Monica Boulevard
Suite 1900
Los Angeles, CA USA 90025
Phone: 3104441822
Fax: 3104441870
E-mail: IR@freemanspogli.com
Website: www.freemanspogli.com

Other Offices
299 Park Avenue
20th Floor
New York, NY USA 10171
Phone: 212-758-2555
Fax: 212-758-7499

Management and Staff
Brad Brutocao, General Partner
Bradford Freeman, Founder
Lou Losorelli, Chief Financial Officer
Richard Riordan, Founder
William Wardlaw, General Partner

Type of Firm
Private Equity Firm

Project Preferences

Type of Financing Preferred:
Leveraged Buyout
Management Buyouts
Acquisition
Recapitalizations

Geographical Preferences

United States Preferences:
North America

Industry Focus
(% based on actual investment)
Consumer Related	45.1%
Other Products	33.3%
Industrial/Energy	7.3%
Communications and Media	4.2%
Internet Specific	3.9%
Medical/Health	3.4%
Semiconductors/Other Elect.	2.8%

Additional Information
Year Founded: 1983
Capital Under Management: $1,250,000,000
Current Activity Level : Actively seeking new investments
Method of Compensation: Return on investment is of primary concern, do not charge fees

FREEPORT FINANCIAL PARTNERS LLC

300 North LaSalle
Suite 5300
Chicago, IL USA 60654
Phone: 3122814600
E-mail: freeportfinancial@moelis.com
Website: www.moelis.com

Management and Staff
Dave Allen, Co-Founder
Joe Walker, Co-Founder
Joseph Gambino, Vice President
Josh Howie, Co-Founder
Matt Gerdes, Managing Director
Steve Papalas, Co-Founder

Type of Firm
Private Equity Firm

Association Membership
Natl Assoc of Small Bus. Inv. Co (NASBIC)

Project Preferences

Type of Financing Preferred:
Mezzanine
Generalist PE

Industry Preferences

In Medical/Health prefer:
Medical/Health

In Consumer Related prefer:
Retail
Consumer Products
Education Related

In Industrial/Energy prefer:
Oil and Gas Exploration
Industrial Products

In Transportation prefer:
Transportation

In Financial Services prefer:
Financial Services

In Business Serv. prefer:
Services
Distribution

Additional Information
Name of Most Recent Fund: Freeport Financial SBIC Fund, L.P.
Most Recent Fund Was Raised: 11/20/2012
Year Founded: 2005
Capital Under Management: $230,000,000
Current Activity Level : Actively seeking new investments

FREESTONE PARTNERS LLC

808 Travis Street
Suite 540
Houston, TX USA 77002
Phone: 7135331888
Fax: 7135331811
E-mail: freestone@freestonepartners.com
Website: www.freestonepartners.com

Management and Staff
George Clark, Managing Director
Jim Briggs, Managing Director
Mark Leyerle, Managing Director

Type of Firm
Private Equity Firm

Project Preferences

Type of Financing Preferred:
Leveraged Buyout
Early Stage
Generalist PE
Management Buyouts
Acquisition

Geographical Preferences

United States Preferences:
Southeast
Southwest

Industry Preferences

In Consumer Related prefer:
Food/Beverage

In Business Serv. prefer:
Services
Distribution

In Manufact. prefer:
Manufacturing

Additional Information
Year Founded: 2001
Current Activity Level : Actively seeking new investments

FREESTYLE CAPITAL

One Lovell Avenue
Mill Valley, CA USA 94941
Phone: 4152508651
Website: freestyle.vc

Management and Staff

Dave Samuel, Co-Founder
Jennifer Lefcourt, Partner
Josh Felser, Co-Founder

Type of Firm

Private Equity Firm

Industry Preferences

In Computer Software prefer:
Software

In Internet Specific prefer:
Internet

In Consumer Related prefer:
Consumer

Additional Information

Name of Most Recent Fund: Freestyle Capital Fund II, L.P.
Most Recent Fund Was Raised: 02/14/2013
Year Founded: 2009
Capital Under Management: $230,995,000
Current Activity Level : Actively seeking new investments

FREETEL CAPITAL (PTY) LTD

82 Grayston Drive, Sandton
Ground Floor
Johannesburg, South Africa 2196
Phone: 27112637900
Fax: 27112637904
Website: www.freetelcapital.com

Type of Firm

Private Equity Firm

Project Preferences

Type of Financing Preferred:
Expansion
Acquisition

Size of Investments Considered:
Min Size of Investment Considered (000s): $1,216
Max Size of Investment Considered (000s): $12,157

Geographical Preferences

International Preferences:
South Africa
Africa

Industry Preferences

In Communications prefer:
Communications and Media

In Agr/Forestr/Fish prefer:
Agriculture related

Additional Information

Year Founded: 2011
Current Activity Level : Actively seeking new investments

FREMONT GROUP LLC

199 Fremont Street
Suite 2400
San Francisco, CA USA 94105
Phone: 415-284-8500
Fax: 415-284-8187
E-mail: info@fremontgroup.com
Website: www.fremontgroup.com

Type of Firm

Private Equity Firm

Project Preferences

Type of Financing Preferred:
Balanced

Additional Information

Year Founded: 2000
Current Activity Level : Actively seeking new investments

FRENCHFOOD CAPITAL SAS

2, avenue de Messine
Paris, France 75008
Website: frenchfoodcapital.com

Type of Firm

Private Equity Firm

Project Preferences

Type of Financing Preferred:
Early Stage
Expansion
Later Stage

Industry Preferences

In Consumer Related prefer:
Food/Beverage
Consumer Products
Consumer Services

In Business Serv. prefer:
Distribution

Additional Information

Year Founded: 2017
Current Activity Level : Actively seeking new investments

FRESH SOURCE CAPITAL LLC

250 Main Street
P.O. Box #425908
Cambridge, MA USA 02142
Phone: 6174352291
E-mail: info@freshsourcecapital.com
Website: www.freshsourcecapital.com

Type of Firm

Private Equity Firm

Project Preferences

Type of Financing Preferred:
Mezzanine

Geographical Preferences

United States Preferences:
Northeast

Industry Preferences

In Agr/Forestr/Fish prefer:
Agriculture related

Additional Information

Year Founded: 2015
Current Activity Level : Actively seeking new investments

FRESHTRACKS CAPITAL LP

29 Harbor Road
Suite 200
Shelburne, VT USA 05482
Phone: 8029231500
Fax: 8029231506
E-mail: info1@freshtrackscap.com
Website: www.freshtrackscap.com

Management and Staff

Cairn Cross, Co-Founder
Charles Kireker, Co-Founder
Lee Bouyea, Managing Director
Timothy Davis, Managing Director

Type of Firm

Private Equity Firm

Project Preferences

Role in Financing:
Prefer role as deal originator but will also invest in deals created by others

Type of Financing Preferred:
Early Stage
Seed
First Stage Financing

Geographical Preferences

United States Preferences:
New Hampshire
Vermont
New York

Industry Preferences

In Communications prefer:
Communications and Media
Telecommunications

In Computer Software prefer:
Software
Applications Software

In Semiconductor/Electr prefer:
Electronics
Semiconductor

In Biotechnology prefer:
Biotechnology

In Medical/Health prefer:
Medical Products
Health Services

In Consumer Related prefer:
Consumer

In Industrial/Energy prefer:
Energy
Factory Automation

In Business Serv. prefer:
Media

Additional Information

Name of Most Recent Fund: FreshTracks Capital III, L.P.
Most Recent Fund Was Raised: 09/26/2013
Year Founded: 2000
Capital Under Management: $40,000,000
Current Activity Level : Actively seeking new investments
Method of Compensation: Return on investment is of primary concern, do not charge fees

---

FREUDENBERG VENTURE CAPITAL GMBH

Hoehnerweg 2-4
Weinheim, Germany 69469
Phone: 496201807107
Fax: 496201883094
E-mail: info@freudenberg-Venture.de
Website: www.fnt-kg.de

Management and Staff

Hans-Juergen Wendelken, Chief Operating Officer
Joerg Boecking, Managing Director
Wolfgang Scheffler, Managing Director

Type of Firm

Corporate PE/Venture

Association Membership

German Venture Capital Association (BVK)

Project Preferences

Type of Financing Preferred:
Early Stage
Later Stage
Seed
Startup

Geographical Preferences

International Preferences:
Europe
Germany

Industry Preferences

In Computer Software prefer:
Software

In Semiconductor/Electr prefer:
Sensors

In Industrial/Energy prefer:
Materials
Advanced Materials
Machinery

In Manufact. prefer:
Manufacturing

In Other prefer:
Environment Responsible

Additional Information

Year Founded: 2001
Current Activity Level : Actively seeking new investments

FRIEDMAN CAPITAL

2120 L Street NW
Suite 215
Washington, DC USA 20037
Website: www.friedmancap.com

Type of Firm

Investment Management Firm

Project Preferences

Type of Financing Preferred:
Leveraged Buyout
Acquisition

Geographical Preferences

United States Preferences:
North America

Industry Preferences

In Medical/Health prefer:
Health Services

In Financial Services prefer:
Real Estate

In Business Serv. prefer:
Distribution

Additional Information

Year Founded: 2010
Current Activity Level : Actively seeking new investments

FRIEDMAN FLEISCHER & LOWE CAP PTNRS L P

One Maritime Plaza
22nd Floor
San Francisco, CA USA 94111
Phone: 4154022100
Fax: 4154022111
E-mail: contact@fflpartners.com
Website: www.fflpartners.com

Management and Staff

Aaron Money, Managing Director
Alex Albert, Vice President
Cas Schneller, Managing Director
Christopher Masto, Senior Managing Director
Geoff Evans, Vice President
Gregory Ruiz, Vice President
Jason Lee, Vice President
John Tudor, Managing Director
Nancy Graham Ford, Managing Director
Patricia Nykodym, Chief Financial Officer
Rajat Duggal, Managing Director
Spencer Fleischer, President

Type of Firm

Private Equity Firm

Project Preferences

Type of Financing Preferred:
Leveraged Buyout

Industry Focus

(% based on actual investment)
Other Products	85.6%
Consumer Related	11.5%
Computer Software and Services	1.9%
Computer Hardware	1.0%

Additional Information

Year Founded: 1997
Capital Under Management: $2,000,000,000
Current Activity Level : Actively seeking new investments

FRIEND SKOLER & CO. LLC

160 Pehle Avenue
Suite 303
Saddle Brook, NJ USA 07663
Phone: 2017120075
Fax: 2017121525
E-mail: mail@friendskoler.com
Website: www.friendskoler.com

Management and Staff
Alexander Friend, Managing Director
Gregory Sullivan, Chief Financial Officer
Steven Skoler, Managing Director

Type of Firm
Private Equity Firm

Project Preferences

Type of Financing Preferred:
Leveraged Buyout
Acquisition

Industry Preferences

In Internet Specific prefer:
E-Commerce Technology

In Consumer Related prefer:
Retail
Consumer Products

In Business Serv. prefer:
Services
Distribution

In Manufact. prefer:
Manufacturing

Additional Information
Name of Most Recent Fund: Friend Skoler Equity Investors
Most Recent Fund Was Raised: 11/17/2003
Year Founded: 1998
Current Activity Level : Actively seeking new investments

FRIULIA VENETO SVILUPPO SGR SPA

Via Locchi, 19
Trieste, Italy 34143
Phone: 3940306590
Fax: 3940307364
E-mail: mail@friuliasgr.it
Website: www.friuliasgr.it

Type of Firm
Private Equity Firm

Association Membership
Italian Venture Capital Association (AIFI)

Industry Preferences

In Biotechnology prefer:
Biotechnology

In Medical/Health prefer:
Medical Products

Additional Information
Year Founded: 2009
Capital Under Management: $64,238,000
Current Activity Level : Actively seeking new investments

FROG CAPITAL LTD

1A Birkenhead Street
The Mews
London, United Kingdom WC1H 8BA
Phone: 442078330555
Fax: 442078338322
E-mail: info@foursome.net
Website: www.frogcapital.com

Management and Staff
Iyad Omari, Partner
Jens Duing, Principal
Joseph Krancki, Partner
Mike Reid, Managing Partner
Rob Shaw, Chief Financial Officer
Stephen Lowery, Partner
Sue Hunter, Partner

Type of Firm
Private Equity Firm

Association Membership
British Venture Capital Association (BVCA)
European Private Equity and Venture Capital Assoc.

Project Preferences

Type of Financing Preferred:
Expansion
Later Stage

Geographical Preferences

International Preferences:
Europe

Industry Preferences

In Computer Software prefer:
Software

In Internet Specific prefer:
Internet

In Industrial/Energy prefer:
Energy Conservation Relat
Environmental Related

Additional Information
Year Founded: 1998
Capital Under Management: $166,200,000
Current Activity Level : Actively seeking new investments

FRONT STREET CAPITAL

33 Yonge Street
Suite 600
Toronto, Canada M5E 1G4
Phone: 4165979595
Fax: 4163648893
Website: www.frontstreetcapital.com

Management and Staff
David Conway, Chief Operating Officer
Normand Lamarche, Partner
Susan Johnson, Chief Financial Officer

Type of Firm
Private Equity Firm

Additional Information
Year Founded: 2002
Current Activity Level : Actively seeking new investments

FRONTENAC COMPANY LLC

135 South LaSalle Street
38th Floor
Chicago, IL USA 60603
Phone: 3123680044
Fax: 3123689520
E-mail: info@frontenac.com
Website: www.frontenac.com

Management and Staff
Brian Rowe, Founder
Elizabeth Williamson, Vice President
James Cowie, Managing Director
Jeremy Silverman, Managing Director
Martin Koldyke, Founder
Michael Langdon, Principal
Parker Davis, Vice President
Paul Carbery, Managing Director
Ronald Kuehl, Principal
Walter Florence, Managing Director

Type of Firm
Private Equity Firm

Association Membership
Illinois Venture Capital Association

Project Preferences

Role in Financing:
Prefer role as deal originator

Type of Financing Preferred:
Leveraged Buyout
Early Stage
Mezzanine
Balanced
Later Stage
Acquisition

Geographical Preferences

United States Preferences:

Industry Focus
(% based on actual investment)

Other Products	23.8%
Consumer Related	21.2%
Computer Software and Services	14.7%
Internet Specific	13.2%
Medical/Health	12.1%
Industrial/Energy	7.9%
Communications and Media	5.1%
Computer Hardware	1.1%
Semiconductors/Other Elect.	0.5%
Biotechnology	0.3%

Additional Information
Year Founded: 1971
Capital Under Management: $1,500,000,000
Current Activity Level : Actively seeking new investments
Method of Compensation: Return on investment is of primary concern, do not charge fees

FRONTERIS CONSULTING AG

Ziegetsdorfer Strasse 109
Regensburg, Germany 93051
Phone: 4994199208860
Fax: 4994199208839
E-mail: info@fronteris.de
Website: www.fronteris.de

Management and Staff
Max Rauch, Partner
Michael Schoernig, Partner
Raimund Stummer, Chief Executive Officer

Type of Firm
Private Equity Firm

Project Preferences

Type of Financing Preferred:
Leveraged Buyout
Early Stage
Mezzanine
Turnaround
Later Stage
Acquisition
Startup

Geographical Preferences

International Preferences:
Switzerland
Austria
Germany

Industry Preferences

In Industrial/Energy prefer:
Energy
Alternative Energy

In Financial Services prefer:
Financial Services

Additional Information
Year Founded: 2006
Capital Under Management: $19,646,000
Current Activity Level : Actively seeking new investments

FRONTIER CAPITAL LLC

525 North Tryon Street
Suite 1900
Charlotte, NC USA 28202
Phone: 7044142880
Fax: 7044142881
Website: www.frontiercapital.com

Management and Staff
Andrew Lindner, Co-Founder
David Pandullo, Vice President
J. Michael Ramich, Partner
Joel Lanik, Partner
Lori Shell, Chief Financial Officer
Michael Ramich, Partner
Richard Maclean, Co-Founder
Scott Hoch, Principal
Scott Hoch, Partner
Seth Harward, Partner
Seth Harward, Principal
Steven Harris, Vice President

Type of Firm
Private Equity Firm

Project Preferences

Role in Financing:
Will function either as deal originator or investor in deals created by others

Type of Financing Preferred:
Leveraged Buyout
Generalist PE
Later Stage
Management Buyouts
Acquisition

Geographical Preferences

United States Preferences:
Mid Atlantic
Southeast
North America

Industry Preferences

In Communications prefer:
Communications and Media

In Computer Software prefer:
Software

In Internet Specific prefer:
E-Commerce Technology
Internet

In Medical/Health prefer:
Medical/Health
Health Services

In Business Serv. prefer:
Services

Additional Information
Name of Most Recent Fund: Frontier Fund III, L.P.
Most Recent Fund Was Raised: 11/01/2010
Year Founded: 1999
Capital Under Management: $755,000,000
Current Activity Level : Actively seeking new investments
Method of Compensation: Return on investment is of primary concern, do not charge fees

FRONTIER CAPITAL PARTNERS

444 St. Mary Avenue
Suite 1445
Winnipeg, Canada R3C 3T1
Phone: 204-925-8402
Fax: 204-949-0602
E-mail: frontier.capital@shawlink.ca

Type of Firm
Private Equity Firm

Additional Information
Year Founded: 2002
Current Activity Level : Actively seeking new investments

FRONTIER EQUITIES VC LLC

45 West 60th Street
Suite 5A
New York, NY USA 10023
E-mail: mmolin@frontierequitiesvc.com
Website: www.frontierequitiesvc.com

Management and Staff
Marit Molin, Founder

Type of Firm
Private Equity Firm

Project Preferences

Type of Financing Preferred:
Early Stage
Balanced
Later Stage

Size of Investments Considered:
Min Size of Investment Considered (000s): $100
Max Size of Investment Considered (000s): $5,000

Additional Information
Year Founded: 2014
Current Activity Level : Actively seeking new investments

FRONTIER INVESTMENT & CAPITAL ADVISORS PTE LTD

5 Shenton Way
#26-01 UIC Building
Singapore, Singapore 068808
Phone: 65-8121-0031
Fax: 65-6333-6487
Website: www.ficadvisors.com

Other Offices
166 Norodom Boulevard
7th Floor, B-ray Tower
Phnom Penh, Cambodia 12301
Phone: 85523993903
Fax: 85523993903

Management and Staff
Kim Song Tan, Partner
Marvin Yeo, Partner

Type of Firm
Private Equity Firm

Project Preferences

Type of Financing Preferred:
Balanced

Geographical Preferences

International Preferences:
Laos
Vietnam
Mongolia
Cambodia

Industry Preferences

In Consumer Related prefer:
Consumer
Consumer Services

In Industrial/Energy prefer:
Energy
Oil and Gas Exploration

In Financial Services prefer:
Real Estate
Financial Services

In Business Serv. prefer:
Services

In Manufact. prefer:
Manufacturing

In Agr/Forestr/Fish prefer:
Agribusiness
Agriculture related

Additional Information
Year Founded: 2008
Capital Under Management: $50,000,000
Current Activity Level : Actively seeking new investments

FRONTIER INVESTMENT CORP

169, Samsung-Dong, Gangnam
6/F Daehwa Venture Plaza
Seoul, South Korea 135100
Phone: 8225523611
Fax: 8225523613

Type of Firm
Bank Affiliated

Project Preferences

Type of Financing Preferred:
Early Stage

Geographical Preferences

International Preferences:
Korea, South
All International

Industry Preferences

In Computer Software prefer:
Software

In Internet Specific prefer:
Internet

In Consumer Related prefer:
Entertainment and Leisure

In Business Serv. prefer:
Media

In Manufact. prefer:
Manufacturing

Additional Information
Year Founded: 2000
Capital Under Management: $27,000,000
Current Activity Level : Actively seeking new investments

FRONTIER TECH VENTURES

1062 Folsom Street
Suite 200
San Francisco, CA USA 94103
Website: www.rothenbergventures.com

Type of Firm
Private Equity Firm

Project Preferences

Type of Financing Preferred:
Startup

Size of Investments Considered:
Min Size of Investment Considered (000s): $10
Max Size of Investment Considered (000s): $100

Industry Preferences

In Internet Specific prefer:
Internet

Additional Information
Year Founded: 2012
Capital Under Management: $47,247,000
Current Activity Level : Actively seeking new investments

FRONTIER VENTURE CAPITAL

100 Wilshire Boulevard
Suite 1270
Santa Monica, CA USA 90401
Phone: 4243542244
Website: www.frontiervc.com

Other Offices
1120 North West Couch Street
Seventh Floor
OLDTOWN-CHINATOWN, OR USA 97209
Phone: 503-943-0846

800 Anacapa Street
Suite A
SANTA BARBARA, CA USA 93101

Management and Staff
David Cremin, Co-Founder
Eric Rosenfeld, Venture Partner
Frank Foster, Managing Director
Jim Schraith, Venture Partner
Robert Perille, Venture Partner
Scott Lenet, Co-Founder

Type of Firm
Private Equity Firm

Project Preferences

Role in Financing:
Prefer role as deal originator but will also invest in deals created by others

Type of Financing Preferred:
Early Stage
Seed

Size of Investments Considered:
Min Size of Investment Considered (000s): $50
Max Size of Investment Considered (000s): $500

Geographical Preferences

United States Preferences:
West Coast

Industry Preferences

In Computer Software prefer:
Software

In Internet Specific prefer:
Internet

Additional Information
Name of Most Recent Fund: DFJ Frontier Fund II, L.P.
Most Recent Fund Was Raised: 06/25/2007
Year Founded: 2002
Capital Under Management: $91,200,000
Current Activity Level : Actively seeking new investments
Method of Compensation: Return on investment is of primary concern, do not charge fees

---

FRONTIER VENTURES

1st Magistralny Tupik, Five
Magistral Plaza, 1st Floor
Moscow, Russia 123290
Phone: 74955404255
E-mail: ir@frontier.ru
Website: www.frontier.ru

Management and Staff
Dmitry Alimov, Managing Partner
Oleg Tumanov, Venture Partner

Type of Firm
Private Equity Firm

Project Preferences

Type of Financing Preferred:
Early Stage

Size of Investments Considered:
Min Size of Investment Considered (000s): $100
Max Size of Investment Considered (000s): $10,000

Geographical Preferences

International Preferences:
Eastern Europe
Russia

Industry Preferences

In Internet Specific prefer:
Internet
Ecommerce

In Consumer Related prefer:
Consumer Services

In Business Serv. prefer:
Media

Additional Information
Year Founded: 2011
Capital Under Management: $50,000,000
Current Activity Level : Actively seeking new investments

FRONTLINE BIOVENTURE CO LTD

Zhangheng Road 1000, Building 33
Shanghai, China 201203
Phone: 862120287698
Fax: 862120287996
Website: www.frontlinebioventures.com

Type of Firm
Private Equity Firm

Project Preferences

Type of Financing Preferred:
Balanced

Geographical Preferences

International Preferences:
China

Industry Preferences

In Communications prefer:
Media and Entertainment

In Internet Specific prefer:
Internet

In Biotechnology prefer:
Biotechnology

In Medical/Health prefer:
Medical/Health

Additional Information
Year Founded: 2012
Current Activity Level : Actively seeking new investments

FRONTLINE VENTURES (GP) LTD

26-28 Lombard Street East
First Floor
Dublin, Ireland 2
Phone: 353014498717
Website: www.frontline.vc

Other Offices
Central Working
6-8 Bonhill Street
London, United Kingdom EC2A 4BX
Phone: 44077 4822 2112

Management and Staff
Stephen McIntyre, Venture Partner
William McQuillan, Partner

Type of Firm
Private Equity Firm

Association Membership
Irish Venture Capital Association

Project Preferences

Type of Financing Preferred:
Early Stage
Seed

Size of Investments Considered:
Min Size of Investment Considered (000s): $215
Max Size of Investment Considered (000s): $3,226

Geographical Preferences

International Preferences:
Europe

Industry Preferences

In Communications prefer:
Telecommunications

In Computer Software prefer:
Data Processing
Software

In Internet Specific prefer:
Internet

Additional Information
Year Founded: 2013
Capital Under Management: $117,370,000
Current Activity Level : Actively seeking new investments

FRONTRANGE CAPITAL PARTNERS LLC

5251 DTC Parkway
Suite 1150
Englewood, CO USA 80111
Phone: 7209615490
E-mail: info@FrontRangeCap.com
Website: www.frontrangecap.com

Management and Staff
David Robertson, Chief Executive Officer

Type of Firm
Private Equity Firm

Project Preferences

Type of Financing Preferred:
Value-Add
Generalist PE
Balanced
Acquisition

Additional Information
Name of Most Recent Fund: FrontRange Property Fund II, L.P.
Most Recent Fund Was Raised: 03/20/2014
Year Founded: 2010
Capital Under Management: $64,850,000
Current Activity Level : Actively seeking new investments

FROST DATA CAPITAL

31910 Del Obispo, Suite 100
San Juan Capistrano, CA USA 92675
E-mail: info@frostvp.com
Website: www.frostdatacapital.com

Management and Staff
Anthony Howcroft, General Partner
Holly Self, Vice President

Type of Firm
Incubator/Development Program

Project Preferences

Type of Financing Preferred:
Early Stage
Seed
Startup

Industry Preferences

In Computer Software prefer:
Data Processing

In Internet Specific prefer:
Internet

In Medical/Health prefer:
Health Services

In Industrial/Energy prefer:
Machinery

Additional Information
Year Founded: 2012
Capital Under Management: $73,000,000
Current Activity Level : Actively seeking new investments

FRUMKVODULL EHF

Sigtur 42
Reykjavik, Iceland 105
Phone: 3545787800
Fax: 3545787819

Type of Firm
Corporate PE/Venture

Project Preferences

Type of Financing Preferred:
Early Stage
Later Stage

Size of Investments Considered:
Min Size of Investment Considered (000s): $300
Max Size of Investment Considered (000s): $3,000

Geographical Preferences

United States Preferences:

International Preferences:
Europe
Iceland
Scandanavia/Nordic Region

Industry Preferences

In Communications prefer:
Communications and Media
Telecommunications

In Computer Software **prefer:**
Software

In Internet Specific prefer:
Internet

In Computer Other prefer:
Computer Related

In Biotechnology prefer:
Biotechnology

In Consumer Related prefer:
Consumer

Additional Information
Year Founded: 2000
Capital Under Management: $12,800,000
Current Activity Level : Actively seeking new investments

FRYE-LOUIS CAPITAL ADVISORS LLC

225 West Wacker Drive, Suite 1000
Chicago, IL USA 60606
Phone: 312-541-4650
Fax: 312-541-9140
Website: www.fryelouis.com

Type of Firm
Private Equity Advisor or Fund of Funds

Project Preferences

Type of Financing Preferred:
Fund of Funds

Geographical Preferences

United States Preferences:

Additional Information
Year Founded: 1992
Capital Under Management: $70,000,000
Current Activity Level : Actively seeking new investments

FS VENCUBE GMBH

Sommermannstrasse 9-11
Frankfurt am Main, Germany 60314
Phone: 4969154008629
Fax: 4969154008698
E-mail: startup@fsvencube.de
Website: www.frankfurt-school.de/content/de/vencube

Management and Staff
Christoph Kauter, Managing Director
Omid Dogmeh Saz, Managing Director

Type of Firm
University Program

Project Preferences

Type of Financing Preferred:
Seed
Startup

Geographical Preferences

International Preferences:
Germany

Additional Information
Year Founded: 2012
Capital Under Management: $1,300,000
Current Activity Level : Actively seeking new investments

FSE CIC

4 Meadows Business Park
Riverside House, Blackwater
Camberley, United Kingdom GU17 9AB
Phone: 441276608510
Fax: 441276608539
E-mail: mail@financesoutheast.com
Website: www.thefsegroup.com

Management and Staff
Sally Goodsell, Chief Executive Officer

Type of Firm
Incubator/Development Program

Association Membership
British Venture Capital Association (BVCA)

Project Preferences

Type of Financing Preferred:
Early Stage
Seed
Startup

Geographical Preferences

International Preferences:
United Kingdom
Europe

Additional Information
Year Founded: 2002
Current Activity Level : Actively seeking new investments

FSN CAPITAL PARTNERS AS

Karl Johansgate 27
Oslo, Norway 0159
Phone: 4724147300
Fax: 4724147301
E-mail: admin@fsncapital.no
Website: www.fsncapital.com

Other Offices
Master Samuelsgatan 4
Stockholm, Sweden 111 44
Phone: 46-8-5450-3930
Fax: 46-8-611-3305

Ostergade 22
4th floor
Copenhagen, Denmark 1100
Phone: 45-3313-4800

Management and Staff
Cato Holmsen, Founder
Frode Strand-Nielsen, Managing Partner
Henrik Lisaeth, Partner
Morten Welo, Chief Operating Officer
Peter Moller, Partner
Thomas Broe-Andersen, Partner

Type of Firm
Private Equity Firm

Association Membership
Danish Venture Capital Association (DVCA)
Norwegian Venture Capital Association
Swedish Venture Capital Association (SVCA)
European Private Equity and Venture Capital Assoc.

Project Preferences

Type of Financing Preferred:
Leveraged Buyout

Size of Investments Considered:
Min Size of Investment Considered (000s): $4,513
Max Size of Investment Considered (000s): $25,270

Geographical Preferences

International Preferences:
Sweden
Scandanavia/Nordic Region
Finland
Denmark

Industry Preferences

In Communications prefer:
Communications and Media

In Medical/Health prefer:
Health Services

In Consumer Related prefer:
Consumer Products
Consumer Services
Education Related

In Industrial/Energy prefer:
Industrial Products
Materials

In Business Serv. prefer:
Services
Consulting Services

In Manufact. prefer:
Manufacturing

Additional Information
Name of Most Recent Fund: FSN Capital IV L.P.
Most Recent Fund Was Raised: 07/26/2013
Year Founded: 2000
Capital Under Management: $1,517,200,000

Current Activity Level : Actively seeking new investments

FTFD FUND DISTRIBUTOR INC

3175 Oregon Pike
P.O. Box 10666
Leola, PA USA 17540
Phone: 7173961116
Fax: 6103379230
E-mail: info@teamemerald.com
Website: www.teamemerald.com

Other Offices
500 North Gulph Road
Suite 101
Norristown, PA USA 19406
Phone: 6103379230

100 Kingston Drive
Wilkins Township
Pittsburgh, PA USA 15235
Phone: 4128161776

500 N. Gulph Road
Suite 401
Norristown, PA USA 19406

429 Forbes Avenue
Suite 809
Pittsburgh, PA USA 15219

Management and Staff
Joseph Witthohn, Vice President
Richard Juliano, Chief Operating Officer

Type of Firm
Private Equity Firm

Project Preferences

Type of Financing Preferred:
Balanced

Size of Investments Considered:
Min Size of Investment Considered (000s): $2,000
Max Size of Investment Considered (000s): $6,000

Geographical Preferences

United States Preferences:

Industry Preferences

In Communications prefer:
Communications and Media
Telecommunications

Additional Information
Year Founded: 2000
Current Activity Level : Actively seeking new investments

FTL CAPITAL LLC

120 South Central Avenue
Suite 1000
Saint Louis, MO USA 63105
Phone: 3143925257
Fax: 3145842058
E-mail: information@ftlcapital.com
Website: www.ftlcapital.com

Management and Staff
Todd Spener, Managing Director

Type of Firm
Private Equity Firm

Project Preferences

Type of Financing Preferred:
Leveraged Buyout
Turnaround
Distressed Debt

Additional Information
Year Founded: 2001
Current Activity Level : Actively seeking new investments

FUBON FINANCIAL HOLDING VENTURE CO LTD

237 Chien Kuo South Road
Section One
Taipei, Taiwan
Phone: 886266366636
Fax: 886266360111
E-mail: ir@fubon.com
Website: www.fubon.com

Type of Firm
Investment Management Firm

Association Membership
Taiwan Venture Capital Association(TVCA)

Project Preferences

Type of Financing Preferred:
Balanced

Geographical Preferences

International Preferences:
Taiwan

Industry Preferences

In Communications prefer:
Media and Entertainment

In Biotechnology prefer:
Biotechnology

In Medical/Health prefer:
Medical/Health

In Transportation prefer:
Transportation

Additional Information
Year Founded: 2004
Current Activity Level : Actively seeking new investments

FUDAN QUANTUM VENTURE CAPITAL MANAGEMENT CO LTD

No. 234 Songhu Road
2/F KIC Plaza
Shanghai, China 200433
Phone: 86-21-6563-2555
Fax: 86-21-6514-8999
E-mail: master@fudan-venture.com
Website: www.fudan-venture.com

Management and Staff
Allen Lu, Chief Executive Officer

Type of Firm
University Program

Project Preferences

Type of Financing Preferred:
Early Stage
Balanced
Later Stage
Seed

Geographical Preferences

International Preferences:
China

Industry Preferences

In Computer Software prefer:
Software
Applications Software

In Biotechnology prefer:
Biotechnology

In Consumer Related prefer:
Education Related

In Industrial/Energy prefer:
Alternative Energy
Environmental Related

In Business Serv. prefer:
Media

Additional Information
Year Founded: 2000
Current Activity Level : Actively seeking new investments

FUJIAN INVESTMENT AND DEVELOPMENT COMPANY LTD

No. 169 Hudong Road
14/F Zhongmin Tianao Building
Fuzhou, Fujian, China 350001

Type of Firm
Government Affiliated Program

Project Preferences

Type of Financing Preferred:
Early Stage
Expansion
Balanced
Later Stage
Seed

Geographical Preferences

International Preferences:
China

Additional Information
Year Founded: 1988
Capital Under Management: $87,900,000
Current Activity Level : Actively seeking new investments

FUJIAN RED BRIDGE CAPITAL MANAGEMENT CO LTD

17/F, Zengjing CCB Building
Jinjiang, China
Phone: 8659582032099
Website: www.hqcapital.com.cn

Management and Staff
Zhenmu Wang, Vice President

Type of Firm
Private Equity Firm

Project Preferences

Type of Financing Preferred:
Expansion
Balanced
Later Stage

Geographical Preferences

International Preferences:
China

Industry Preferences

In Internet Specific prefer:
Internet

In Biotechnology prefer:
Biotechnology

In Medical/Health prefer:
Medical/Health

In Consumer Related prefer:
Consumer
Entertainment and Leisure
Food/Beverage

In Industrial/Energy prefer:
Energy
Machinery
Environmental Related

In Business Serv. prefer:
Media

In Manufact. prefer:
Manufacturing

In Agr/Forestr/Fish prefer:
Agriculture related

Additional Information
Year Founded: 2008
Capital Under Management: $144,644,000
Current Activity Level : Actively seeking new investments

FUJIAN VENTURE CAPITAL CO LTD

Software Park B11
Room 510-511
Fuzhou, Fujian, China 350001
Phone: 86-591-87303311
Fax: 86-591-87303322
Website: www.fjvc.com.cn

Other Offices

No. 820 Xiahe Road
Room 1308 Dihao Building
Xiamen, Fujian, China 361004
Phone: 86-592-2966-650
Fax: 86-592-2966-656

No. 1000 Maanshan South Road
Room 3101 Xinduhui Huanqiu
Hafei, Anhui, China 230001
Phone: 86-551-4682-777
Fax: 86-551-4681-877

No. 13 Wenhua West Road
Room 808 Haichen Building B
Jinan, Shandong, China 250014
Phone: 86-531-82660679
Fax: 86-531-82660679

Management and Staff
Shaobing Huang, President

Type of Firm
Private Equity Firm

Project Preferences

Type of Financing Preferred:
Early Stage
Balanced
Later Stage
Startup

Geographical Preferences

International Preferences:
China

Industry Preferences

In Communications prefer:
Telecommunications

In Internet Specific prefer:
Internet

In Consumer Related prefer:
Sports
Consumer Products

In Business Serv. prefer:
Media

Additional Information
Year Founded: 2000
Current Activity Level : Actively seeking new investments

FULCRUM CAPITAL PARTNERS INC

79 Wellington Street West
Suite 3510
Toronto, Canada M5K 1K7
Phone: 4168642761
Website: www.fulcrumcapital.ca

Other Offices

70 York Street
7th Floor
Toronto, Canada M5J 1S9
Phone: 4168642761
Fax: 4168680067

885 West Georgia Street
Suite 1020
Vancouver, Canada V6C 3E8
Phone: 6046318088
Fax: 6044088892

Management and Staff
Graham Flater, Principal
Gregory Collings, Partner
Johan Lemmer, Chief Financial Officer
John Philp, Managing Partner
Klemens Wilhelm, Principal
Lindsay Wilson, Partner
Michael Berkson, Partner
Neil Johansen, Managing Partner
Paul Eldridge, Partner
Paul Rowe, Partner

Type of Firm
Private Equity Firm

Association Membership
Canadian Venture Capital Association

Project Preferences

Type of Financing Preferred:
Fund of Funds
Leveraged Buyout
Expansion
Mezzanine
Later Stage
Management Buyouts
Acquisition
Recapitalizations

Geographical Preferences

Canadian Preferences:
All Canada

Industry Focus
(% based on actual investment)
Other Products	35.9%
Consumer Related	28.2%
Industrial/Energy	22.7%
Internet Specific	6.9%
Communications and Media	5.3%
Computer Hardware	0.9%

Additional Information
Name of Most Recent Fund: Fulcrum Capital Partners Fund IV
Most Recent Fund Was Raised: 03/31/2010
Year Founded: 1993
Capital Under Management: $782,000,000
Current Activity Level : Actively seeking new investments

FULCRUM EQUITY PARTNERS

5555 Glenridge Connector
Glenridge Highlands One # 930
Atlanta, GA USA 30342
Phone: 7705516300
Fax: 7705516330
Website: fulcrumep.com

Management and Staff
Alston Gardner, Founder
Frank Dalton, Founder
James Douglass, Partner
Jeffrey Muir, Founder
Philip Lewis, Principal
Thomas Greer, Founder

Type of Firm
Private Equity Firm

Association Membership
National Venture Capital Association - USA (NVCA)

Project Preferences

Type of Financing Preferred:
Leveraged Buyout
Mezzanine
Generalist PE
Later Stage
Management Buyouts
Recapitalizations

Geographical Preferences

United States Preferences:
Southeast

Industry Preferences

In Medical/Health prefer:
Medical/Health
Health Services

In Business Serv. prefer:
Services

Additional Information
Name of Most Recent Fund: Fulcrum Growth Fund II LLC
Most Recent Fund Was Raised: 05/31/2011
Year Founded: 2006
Capital Under Management: $140,000,000
Current Activity Level : Actively seeking new investments

FULCRUM MANAGEMENT INC

245 Park Avenue
24th Floor
New York, NY USA 10167
Phone: 212-439-1512
Fax: 212-208-6810
Website: www.fulcrummgt.com

Management and Staff
Robert Crary, Managing Director

Type of Firm
Private Equity Firm

Project Preferences

Role in Financing:
Prefer role as deal originator but will also invest in deals created by others

Type of Financing Preferred:
Leveraged Buyout
Expansion
Management Buyouts
Acquisition
Recapitalizations

Size of Investments Considered:
Min Size of Investment Considered (000s): $10,000
Max Size of Investment Considered (000s): $75,000

FULCRUM VENTURE CAPITAL CORP

10940 Wilshire Boulevard
Suite 1626
Los Angeles, CA USA 90024
Phone: 3104434281
Fax: 3104434282
E-mail: info@fulcrumventures.com

Management and Staff
Josh Drake, Vice President
Roy Doumani, Venture Partner

Type of Firm
Investment Management Firm

Project Preferences

Type of Financing Preferred:
Leveraged Buyout
Expansion
Acquisition
Recapitalizations

Geographical Preferences

United States Preferences:
Southern California

Industry Preferences

In Communications prefer:
Commercial Communications

In Consumer Related prefer:
Consumer Services

In Manufact. prefer:
Manufacturing

In Other prefer:
Women/Minority-Owned Bus.

Additional Information
Year Founded: 1977
Current Activity Level: Actively seeking new investments

FULCRUM VENTURE INDIA

Dr. Radhakrishna Nagar Road
Shristi Apartments, 43/22
Chennai, India 600041
Phone: 914443511620

Management and Staff
Ethan Khatri, Principal
Krishna Ramanathan, Partner

Type of Firm
Private Equity Firm

Association Membership
Indian Venture Capital Association (IVCA)

Project Preferences

Type of Financing Preferred:
Expansion
Seed

Industry Preferences

In Medical/Health prefer:
Health Services
Hospitals/Clinics/Primary
Pharmaceuticals

In Consumer Related prefer:
Retail
Consumer Products
Consumer Services

In Financial Services prefer:
Financial Services

Additional Information
Year Founded: 2000
Capital Under Management: $16,040,000
Current Activity Level: Actively seeking new investments

FULHAM & CO INC

593 Washington Street
Wellesley, MA USA 02482
Phone: 7812352266
Fax: 7812352009
Website: www.fulhamco.com

Management and Staff
John Fulham, Managing Partner
Susan Sullivan, Chief Financial Officer
Timothy Fulham, Managing Partner

Type of Firm
Private Equity Firm

Association Membership
Natl Assoc of Small Bus. Inv. Co (NASBIC)

Project Preferences

Type of Financing Preferred:
Leveraged Buyout
Management Buyouts
Acquisition

Industry Preferences

In Manufact. prefer:
Manufacturing

Geographical Preferences

United States Preferences:

Additional Information
Year Founded: 1994
Current Activity Level: Actively seeking new investments
Method of Compensation: Return on invest. most important, but chg. closing fees, service fees, etc.

Additional Information
Name of Most Recent Fund: Fulham Investors II, L.P.
Most Recent Fund Was Raised: 08/05/2005
Year Founded: 1984
Capital Under Management: $280,000,000
Current Activity Level: Actively seeking new investments

FULL STACK FOUNDRY GP

55 East Cordova
Unit 604
Vancouver, Canada V6A 0A5
Website: fullstack.ca

Type of Firm
Private Equity Firm

Project Preferences

Type of Financing Preferred:
Early Stage
Balanced
Later Stage
Seed
Startup

Industry Preferences

In Computer Software prefer:
Applications Software

Additional Information
Year Founded: 2012
Current Activity Level: Actively seeking new investments

FULTON CAPITAL LLC

601 Skokie Boulevard
Suite 204
Northbrook, IL USA 60062
Website: www.fulton-capital.com

Management and Staff
David Schlossberg, Founder
Phillip Gerber, Founder

Type of Firm
Private Equity Firm

Project Preferences

Type of Financing Preferred:
Leveraged Buyout
Acquisition

Geographical Preferences

United States Preferences:

Industry Preferences

In Business Serv. prefer:
Services
Distribution

In Manufact. prefer:
Manufacturing

Additional Information
Year Founded: 2004
Current Activity Level : Actively seeking new investments

FUNAI CAPITAL CO LTD

5F Urban Square Yaesu
2-4-13 Yaesu, Chuo-ku
Tokyo, Japan 104-0028
Phone: 81-3-6225-5911
Fax: 81-3-6225-5912
E-mail: info@funaicapital.co.jp
Website: www.funaicapital.co.jp

Type of Firm
Private Equity Firm

Project Preferences

Type of Financing Preferred:
Expansion
Balanced

Geographical Preferences

International Preferences:
Japan

Additional Information
Year Founded: 1990
Current Activity Level : Actively seeking new investments

FUND + NV

60, Groot Begijnhof
Leuven, Belgium 3000
Phone: 3216905000
Fax: 3216795025
E-mail: info@fundplus.be
Website: fundplus.be

Type of Firm
Private Equity Firm

Project Preferences

Type of Financing Preferred:
Early Stage
Seed

Size of Investments Considered:
Min Size of Investment Considered (000s): $3,142
Max Size of Investment Considered (000s): $10,472

Geographical Preferences

International Preferences:
Belgium

Industry Preferences

In Medical/Health prefer:
Medical Diagnostics
Medical Therapeutics
Medical Products

Additional Information
Year Founded: 2015
Current Activity Level : Actively seeking new investments

FUND EVALUATION GROUP LLC

201 East Fifth Street
Suite 1600
Cincinnati, OH USA 45202
Phone: 5139774400
Fax: 5139774430
Website: www.feg.com

Management and Staff
Anthony Festa, Chief Operating Officer
Brian Gray, Vice President
Carolyn McClintock, Vice President
Douglas Harrell, Vice President
Douglas Walouke, Vice President
Emily Crail, Vice President
Jeffrey Weisker, Vice President
Jeffrey Davis, Vice President
Jeremiah Whiteley, Vice President
Kevin Kersting, Vice President
Maureen Kiefer-Goldenberg, Vice President
Ralph Doering, Vice President
Stephen Hodson, Vice President
W. Quincy Brown, Vice President

Type of Firm
Investment Management Firm

Geographical Preferences

International Preferences:
Asia

Additional Information
Name of Most Recent Fund: FEG Private Opportunities Fund, L.P.
Most Recent Fund Was Raised: 08/12/2011
Year Founded: 1988
Capital Under Management: $544,058,000
Current Activity Level : Actively seeking new investments

FUNDACI CATALANA PER A LA RECERCA I LA INNOVACI

Passeig Lluis Companys, 23
Barcelona, Spain 08010
Phone: 34932687700
Fax: 34933150140
E-mail: info@fundaciorecerca.cat
Website: www.fundaciorecerca.cat

Type of Firm
Government Affiliated Program

Project Preferences

Type of Financing Preferred:
Early Stage
Balanced
Later Stage

Geographical Preferences

International Preferences:
Spain

Additional Information
Year Founded: 2013
Current Activity Level : Actively seeking new investments

FUNDACION CREAS

C/Gobernador 26, bajo
Madrid, Spain 28014
Phone: 34-619-780-049
E-mail: info@creas.org.es
Website: www.creas.org.es

Other Offices
Refugio Ten, Local Left
Zaragoza, Spain 50001
Phone: 34-976-301-702

Santa Feliciana Five, Seven B
Madrid, Spain 28010
Phone: 34-619-780-049

Type of Firm
Endowment, Foundation or Pension Fund

Project Preferences

Type of Financing Preferred:
Early Stage
Expansion
Startup

Geographical Preferences

International Preferences:
Spain

Industry Preferences

In Other prefer:
Socially Responsible
Environment Responsible

Additional Information
Year Founded: 2008
Capital Under Management: $2,064,000
Current Activity Level : Actively seeking new investments

FUNDAMENTAL ADVISORS LP

745 Fifth Avenue
25th Floor
New York, NY USA 10151
E-mail: ir@fundamentaladvisorslp.com
Website: www.fundamentaladvisorslp.com

Management and Staff
Dana Fusaris, Co-Founder
Danford Peterson, Managing Director
Hector Negroni, Principal
Jason Black, Managing Director
Jonathan Stern, Managing Director
Justin Vinci, Chief Financial Officer
Nicholas Campany, Managing Director
Robert Jacobsen, Managing Director
Sandy Goldstein, Vice President
Sudar Purushothaman, Managing Director

Type of Firm
Private Equity Firm

Project Preferences
Type of Financing Preferred:
Special Situation
Distressed Debt

Industry Preferences
In Medical/Health prefer:
Health Services

In Industrial/Energy prefer:
Energy

In Financial Services prefer:
Real Estate

Additional Information
Year Founded: 2007
Capital Under Management: $1,442,200,000
Current Activity Level : Actively seeking new investments

FUNDAMENTAL CAPITAL MANAGEMENT LLC

201 Mission Street
Suite 1850
San Francisco, CA USA 94105
Phone: 4157820000
E-mail: info@fundamentalcapital.com
Website: fundamental2.hedgecowebsites.com

Management and Staff
Kevin Keenley, Founder
Rich McNally, President

Type of Firm
Private Equity Firm

Project Preferences
Type of Financing Preferred:
Leveraged Buyout
Expansion
Generalist PE
Other
Management Buyouts
Recapitalizations

Size of Investments Considered:
Min Size of Investment Considered (000s): $2,000
Max Size of Investment Considered (000s): $10,000

Geographical Preferences
United States Preferences:
All U.S.

Industry Preferences
In Consumer Related prefer:
Retail
Consumer Products

In Business Serv. prefer:
Services
Distribution

In Manufact. prefer:
Manufacturing

Additional Information
Year Founded: 2004
Current Activity Level : Actively seeking new investments

FUNDAMENTAL MANAGEMENT CORP

8567 Coral Way
Suite 138
Miami, FL USA 33165
Phone: 305-288-3020

Management and Staff
Carl Singer, Founder

Type of Firm
Private Equity Firm

Additional Information
Name of Most Recent Fund: Active Investors II
Most Recent Fund Was Raised: 12/31/1994
Year Founded: 1993
Current Activity Level : Actively seeking new investments

FUNDCORP INC

550 Bailey Avenue
Suite 650
Fort Worth, TX USA 76147
E-mail: info@FundCorpInc.com
Website: www.fundcorpinc.com

Type of Firm
Private Equity Firm

Industry Preferences
In Industrial/Energy prefer:
Energy

In Financial Services prefer:
Real Estate

In Business Serv. prefer:
Distribution

In Manufact. prefer:
Manufacturing

Additional Information
Year Founded: 2004
Current Activity Level : Actively seeking new investments

FUNDERSCLUB INC

One Bluxome Street, Suite 405
San Francisco, CA USA 94107
E-mail: contact@thefundersclub.com
Website: fundersclub.com

Management and Staff
Boris Silver, President

Type of Firm
Private Equity Firm

Association Membership
National Venture Capital Association - USA (NVCA)

Project Preferences
Type of Financing Preferred:
Seed
Startup

Additional Information
Name of Most Recent Fund: Accelerate FC Fund IV LLC
Most Recent Fund Was Raised: 01/16/2014
Year Founded: 2012
Capital Under Management: $8,494,000
Current Activity Level : Actively seeking new investments

FUNDERSGUILD

26 Broadway
New York, NY USA 10004
Website: fundersguild.com/

Type of Firm
Private Equity Firm

Project Preferences
Type of Financing Preferred:
Early Stage
Seed

Geographical Preferences

United States Preferences:
New York

International Preferences:
Israel

Additional Information
Year Founded: 1969
Current Activity Level : Actively seeking new investments

FUNDRX INC

43 West 23rd Street
Sixth Floor
New York, NY USA 10010
Phone: 1646751794
E-mail: team@fundrx.com
Website: fundrx.com

Management and Staff

Aran Ron, Partner
Darryl Finkton, Partner
Eric Golding, Partner
Gurdane Bhutani, Managing Partner
Jainal Bhuiyan, Partner
Zachary Frankel, Partner
Zeshan Muhammedi, Chief Executive Officer

Type of Firm
Private Equity Firm

Project Preferences

Type of Financing Preferred:
Balanced

Geographical Preferences

United States Preferences:

Industry Preferences

In Medical/Health prefer:
Hospitals/Clinics/Primary

Additional Information
Year Founded: 2015
Current Activity Level : Actively seeking new investments

FUSE CAPITAL

800 Menlo Avenue
Suite 220
Menlo Park, CA USA 94025
Phone: 6503259600
Fax: 6503259608
E-mail: info@fusecapital.com
Website: www.fusecapital.com

Management and Staff

David Britts, Managing Partner
Keyur Patel, Managing Partner
Roland Van der Meer, Managing Partner

Type of Firm
Private Equity Firm

Project Preferences

Role in Financing:
Prefer role as deal originator but will also invest in deals created by others

Type of Financing Preferred:
Early Stage
Expansion
Balanced
Seed

Geographical Preferences

United States Preferences:

International Preferences:
India
China

Industry Focus
(% based on actual investment)
Communications and Media	37.3%
Internet Specific	30.7%
Computer Software and Services	14.8%
Semiconductors/Other Elect.	11.7%
Industrial/Energy	2.7%
Computer Hardware	1.6%
Other Products	1.2%

Additional Information
Name of Most Recent Fund: ComVentures VI, L.P.
Most Recent Fund Was Raised: 09/29/2003
Year Founded: 1987
Capital Under Management: $1,500,000,000
Current Activity Level : Actively seeking new investments
Method of Compensation: Return on investment is of primary concern, do not charge fees

FUSION CAPITAL

1st Ngong Ave, Off Bishops Rd.
ACK Garden House,Blk.A G/F
Nairobi, Kenya 00100
Phone: 254202710149
Fax: 254202711396
E-mail: info@fusioncapital.co.ke
Website: www.fusioncapitalafrica.com

Management and Staff
David Webster, Founder

Type of Firm
Private Equity Firm

Project Preferences

Type of Financing Preferred:
Core
Balanced

Geographical Preferences

International Preferences:
Rwanda
Uganda
Tanzania
Kenya
Burundi

Industry Preferences

In Financial Services prefer:
Real Estate

Additional Information
Year Founded: 2006
Current Activity Level : Actively seeking new investments

FUSIONX VENTURES

15890 Bernardo Center Dr
San Diego, CA USA 92127
Website: www.fusionxventures.com

Type of Firm
Private Equity Firm

Project Preferences

Type of Financing Preferred:
Early Stage

Industry Preferences

In Internet Specific prefer:
Internet

Additional Information
Year Founded: 2016
Capital Under Management: $10,000,000
Current Activity Level : Actively seeking new investments

FUTURE CAPITAL PARTNERS LTD

10 Old Burlington Street
London, United Kingdom W1S 3AG
Phone: 442070096600
Fax: 442070096601
E-mail: info@capitalpartners.com
Website: www.futurecapitalpartners.com

Management and Staff
Gordon Deas, Founder
Graham Webber, Founder
Tim Levy, Founder

Type of Firm
Private Equity Firm

Project Preferences

Type of Financing Preferred:
Leveraged Buyout
Early Stage
Expansion
Balanced
Later Stage
Acquisition

Geographical Preferences

International Preferences:
United Kingdom
Europe

Industry Preferences

In Medical/Health prefer:
Health Services

In Consumer Related prefer:
Entertainment and Leisure

In Industrial/Energy prefer:
Energy

In Financial Services prefer:
Real Estate

In Business Serv. prefer:
Media

Additional Information
Year Founded: 2000
Current Activity Level : Actively seeking new investments

FUTURE FUND

215 South Main Street
Suite One
Zelienople, PA USA 16063
Phone: 724-453-6150
Fax: 724-453-6151
Website: www.future-fund.com

Management and Staff
Esther Dormer, Founder
Richard Madden, Founder

Type of Firm
Private Equity Firm

Project Preferences

Role in Financing:
Will function either as deal originator or investor in deals created by others

Type of Financing Preferred:
Seed
Startup

Size of Investments Considered:
Min Size of Investment Considered (000s): $100
Max Size of Investment Considered (000s): $1,500

Industry Preferences

In Communications prefer:
Data Communications

In Computer Software prefer:
Software
Systems Software

In Internet Specific prefer:
Internet

In Semiconductor/Electr prefer:
Electronic Components

In Biotechnology prefer:
Human Biotechnology
Biotech Related Research

In Medical/Health prefer:
Diagnostic Services
Diagnostic Test Products

In Business Serv. prefer:
Services

Additional Information
Name of Most Recent Fund: Future Fund, The
Most Recent Fund Was Raised: 07/01/1999
Year Founded: 1999
Capital Under Management: $10,000,000
Current Activity Level : Making few, if any, new investments
Method of Compensation: Return on investment is of primary concern, do not charge fees

FUTURE INTERNATIONAL LTD

4-6-21-301
Takanawa, Minato-ku
Tokyo, Japan
Phone: 81-3-5447-6581
Fax: 81-3-5447-6583

Type of Firm
Private Equity Firm

Association Membership
Japan Venture Capital Association

Additional Information
Year Founded: 1997
Current Activity Level : Actively seeking new investments

FUTURE PERFECT VENTURES LLC

77 Bleecker Street
Suite 916
New York, NY USA 10012
Website: www.futureperfectventures.com

Type of Firm
Private Equity Firm

Project Preferences

Type of Financing Preferred:
Early Stage

Industry Preferences

In Computer Software prefer:
Software
Artificial Intelligence

In Internet Specific prefer:
E-Commerce Technology

In Medical/Health prefer:
Medical/Health

In Consumer Related prefer:
Education Related

In Business Serv. prefer:
Media

Additional Information
Year Founded: 2014
Current Activity Level : Actively seeking new investments

FUTURE PLANET CAPITAL

18 St Swithin's Lane
London, United Kingdom EC4N 8AD
Website: futureplanetcapital.com

Type of Firm
Private Equity Firm

Project Preferences

Type of Financing Preferred:
Early Stage

Additional Information
Year Founded: 2016
Current Activity Level : Actively seeking new investments

FUTURE VALUE VENTURES INC

330 East Kibourn Avenue, Suite 711
Milwaukee, WI USA 53203
Phone: 414-278-0377
Fax: 414-278-7321
E-mail: fvvventures@aol.com

Management and Staff
William Beckett, President

Type of Firm
SBIC

Project Preferences

Role in Financing:
Prefer role as deal originator but will also invest in deals created by others

Type of Financing Preferred:
Second Stage Financing
Mezzanine
Start-up Financing
First Stage Financing

Size of Investments Considered:
Min Size of Investment Considered (000s): $100
Max Size of Investment Considered (000s): $300

Geographical Preferences

United States Preferences:
All U.S.

Additional Information
Year Founded: 1984
Capital Under Management: $3,500,000
Current Activity Level : Actively seeking new investments
Method of Compensation: Return on invest. most important, but chg. closing fees, service fees, etc.

FUTURE VENTURE CAPITAL CO LTD

659 Tearaimizu-cho, Nakagyo-ku
4F, Karasuma-Chuo Building
Kyoto, Japan 604-8152
Phone: 81752576656
Fax: 81752116965
E-mail: info@fvc.co.jp
Website: www.fvc.co.jp

Type of Firm
Private Equity Firm

Association Membership
Japan Venture Capital Association

Project Preferences

Type of Financing Preferred:
Early Stage
Balanced

Geographical Preferences

International Preferences:
Japan

Industry Focus

(% based on actual investment)
Other Products	21.6%
Consumer Related	17.0%
Medical/Health	15.2%
Internet Specific	12.4%
Industrial/Energy	11.9%
Communications and Media	7.8%
Computer Software and Services	6.2%
Semiconductors/Other Elect.	5.7%
Computer Hardware	2.3%

Additional Information
Year Founded: 1998
Capital Under Management: $7,000,000
Current Activity Level : Actively seeking new investments

FUZHOU INVESTMENT MANAGEMENT CO

No. 106 Guangda Road
Taijiang District
Fuzhou, Fujian, China 350005

Type of Firm
Government Affiliated Program

Project Preferences

Type of Financing Preferred:
Balanced

Geographical Preferences

International Preferences:
China

Additional Information
Year Founded: 2011
Capital Under Management: $19,727,000
Current Activity Level : Actively seeking new investments

FW ASSET MANAGEMENT LTD

IFS Court
28 Cybercity
Ebene, Mauritius
E-mail: communicate@fidelisworld.com
Website: www.fidelisworld.com

Type of Firm
Private Equity Firm

Project Preferences

Type of Financing Preferred:
Early Stage
Balanced
Later Stage

Geographical Preferences

United States Preferences:
Southeast

International Preferences:
India
Middle East
Asia

Industry Preferences

In Consumer Related prefer:
Sports

Additional Information
Year Founded: 2013
Capital Under Management: $100,000,000
Current Activity Level : Actively seeking new investments

FW CAPITAL LTD

100 Old Hall Street
The Plaza
Liverpool, United Kingdom L3 9QJ
Phone: 01516005336
E-mail: info@fwcapital.co.uk
Website: www.fwcapital.co.uk

Other Offices

Lowry House
17 Marble Street
Manchester, United Kingdom M2 3AW
Phone: 441616389208

Lockside Road
7 Lockside Office Park
Preston, United Kingdom PR2 2YS
Phone: 441772298435

Cuthbert House
City Road, All Saints
Newcastle Upon Tyne, United Kingdom NE1 2ET
Phone: 441913506310

Type of Firm
Private Equity Firm

Project Preferences

Type of Financing Preferred:
Early Stage
Expansion

Geographical Preferences

United States Preferences:
Northwest
Northeast

International Preferences:
United Kingdom

Additional Information
Year Founded: 2009
Capital Under Management: $540,000,000
Current Activity Level : Actively seeking new investments

FYRFLY VENTURE PARTNERS LLC

200 Middlefield Road
Suite 102
Menlo Park, CA USA 94025
Website: www.fyrfly.vc

Type of Firm
Private Equity Firm

873

- G -

G 51 CAPITAL MANAGEMENT LLC

900 South Capital of Texas Hwy
Suite 151, Las Cimas IV
Austin, TX USA 78746
Phone: 5129295151
Fax: 5127320886
E-mail: info@g51.com
Website: www.g51.com

Management and Staff
John Kinnaird, Venture Partner
Lauranne Jarrett, Managing General Partner
Pat Horner, Venture Partner
Rudy Garza, Managing General Partner
Theresa Garza, Venture Partner

Type of Firm
Private Equity Firm

Association Membership
National Venture Capital Association - USA (NVCA)

Project Preferences

Role in Financing:
Prefer role as deal originator but will also invest in deals created by others

Type of Financing Preferred:
Early Stage
Seed

Size of Investments Considered:
Min Size of Investment Considered (000s): $250
Max Size of Investment Considered (000s): $2,000

Geographical Preferences

United States Preferences:

Industry Focus
(% based on actual investment)
Computer Software and Services	48.5%
Internet Specific	28.6%
Computer Hardware	12.0%
Consumer Related	10.9%

Additional Information
Year Founded: 1996
Capital Under Management: $20,000,000
Current Activity Level : Actively seeking new investments
Method of Compensation: Return on investment is of primary concern, do not charge fees

G SQUARE HEALTHCARE PRIVATE EQUITY FUND LLP

17c, Curzon Street
London, United Kingdom W1J5HU

Project Preferences

Type of Financing Preferred:
Early Stage

Industry Preferences

In Computer Software prefer:
Software

Additional Information
Year Founded: 2015
Current Activity Level : Actively seeking new investments

Phone: 44203757
Fax: 33147030620
E-mail: contact@gsquarecapital.com
Website: www.gsquarecapital.com

Management and Staff
Edward de Nor, Partner
Joelle Preaux, Chief Operating Officer
Laurent Ganem, Chief Executive Officer
Renaud Dessertenne, Partner
Sebastian Shea, Principal

Type of Firm
Private Equity Firm

Association Membership
French Venture Capital Association (AFIC)
European Private Equity and Venture Capital Assoc.

Project Preferences

Type of Financing Preferred:
Leveraged Buyout
Early Stage
Generalist PE
Later Stage
Management Buyouts
Acquisition

Geographical Preferences

International Preferences:
Europe
Switzerland
Spain
Congo, Dem Rep
Germany
France

Industry Preferences

In Medical/Health prefer:
Medical/Health
Medical Diagnostics
Medical Therapeutics
Medical Products
Health Services
Hospitals/Clinics/Primary
Hospital/Other Instit.
Pharmaceuticals

Additional Information
Name of Most Recent Fund: G Square Capital I
Most Recent Fund Was Raised: 01/06/2011
Year Founded: 2007
Capital Under Management: $478,000,000
Current Activity Level : Actively seeking new investments

G20 ASSOCIATES LLC

500 Boylston Street
Suite 1380
Boston, MA USA 02116
Phone: 6178509777
E-mail: info@g20vc.com
Website: g20vc.com

Management and Staff
Michael Troiano, Partner
Robert Hower, Co-Founder
William Wiberg, Co-Founder

Type of Firm
Private Equity Firm

Association Membership
New England Venture Capital Association

Project Preferences

Type of Financing Preferred:
Early Stage

Geographical Preferences

United States Preferences:
North Carolina
Massachusetts
New York
East Coast

International Preferences:
Utd. Arab Em.

Industry Preferences

In Computer Software prefer:
Software
Systems Software
Applications Software

In Internet Specific prefer:
Internet

Additional Information
Year Founded: 2014
Capital Under Management: $61,575,000
Current Activity Level : Actively seeking new investments

G2T3V LLC

351 West Hubbard Street
Chicago, IL USA 60654
Website: www.g2t3v.com

Management and Staff
Howard Tullman, Managing Partner

Type of Firm
Private Equity Firm

Project Preferences

Type of Financing Preferred:
Early Stage

Geographical Preferences

United States Preferences:

Industry Preferences

In Communications prefer:
Communications and Media

In Computer Software prefer:
Data Processing

In Consumer Related prefer:
Education Related

In Transportation prefer:
Transportation

In Financial Services prefer:
Insurance

In Business Serv. prefer:
Media

Additional Information
Year Founded: 2013
Current Activity Level : Actively seeking new investments

G2VP LLC

2742 sand Hill Road
Menlo Park, CA USA 94025
E-mail: info@g2vp.com
Website: www.g2vp.com

Type of Firm
Private Equity Firm

Industry Preferences

In Industrial/Energy prefer:
Energy

In Transportation prefer:
Transportation

In Manufact. prefer:
Manufacturing

In Agr/Forestr/Fish prefer:
Agriculture related

Additional Information
Year Founded: 2017
Current Activity Level : Actively seeking new investments

G3W VENTURES LLC

333 South Grand Ave
28th Floor
Los Angeles, CA USA 90049
Phone: 2138306300
Fax: 2138306293
Website: www.gfienergy.com

Management and Staff
Andrew Osler, Managing Director
Ian Schapiro, Co-Founder
James Lee, Vice President
Mark Chesler, Managing Director
Michael Harmon, Managing Director
Steve Kaplan, Principal
Ulysses Fowler, Vice President

Type of Firm
Private Equity Firm

Project Preferences

Type of Financing Preferred:
Other

Industry Preferences

In Industrial/Energy prefer:
Energy
Oil and Gas Exploration
Alternative Energy
Environmental Related

In Business Serv. prefer:
Distribution

In Utilities prefer:
Utilities

Additional Information
Year Founded: 1995
Current Activity Level : Actively seeking new investments

G8 CAPITAL LLC

999 Corporate Drive
Suite 215
Ladera Ranch, CA USA 92694
Phone: 9495456996
Fax: 9495456999
Website: www.g8cap.com

Management and Staff
Aaron Murray, Vice President
Brett Gilliland, Vice President
Evan Gentry, Chief Executive Officer
Kurt Mullen, Chief Financial Officer

Type of Firm
Private Equity Firm

Project Preferences

Type of Financing Preferred:
Leveraged Buyout
Generalist PE
Balanced
Opportunistic

Geographical Preferences

United States Preferences:
North America
All U.S.

Industry Preferences

In Financial Services prefer:
Real Estate

Additional Information
Name of Most Recent Fund: G8 Opportunity Fund VIII LLC
Most Recent Fund Was Raised: 09/30/2011
Year Founded: 2007
Capital Under Management: $3,200,000
Current Activity Level : Actively seeking new investments

GABES INVEST SICAR PLC

Centre Dorra,Esc A Appt n 8
El Manar III
Tunis, Tunisia 2092
Phone: 21671886922
Fax: 21671887477
Website: www.gabesinvest-sicar.com

Type of Firm
Corporate PE/Venture

Association Membership
Tunisian Venture Capital Association

Project Preferences

Type of Financing Preferred:
Early Stage
Later Stage
Startup

Geographical Preferences

International Preferences:
Tunisia
Africa

Industry Preferences

In Industrial/Energy prefer:
Industrial Products
Materials

In Manufact. prefer:
Manufacturing

Additional Information
Year Founded: 2002
Current Activity Level : Actively seeking new investments

GAIN CAPITAL PARTICIPATIONS GMBH

Schwarzenbergplatz 5
Vienna, Austria 1030
Phone: 4315333298
Fax: 431533329839
E-mail: office@gain-capital.at
Website: www.gain-capital.at

Management and Staff
Gert Reinhard Jonke, Managing Director

Type of Firm
Private Equity Firm

Project Preferences

Type of Financing Preferred:
Fund of Funds
Core
Generalist PE

Geographical Preferences

International Preferences:
Central Europe
Europe
Switzerland
Western Europe
Austria
Eastern Europe
Germany

Industry Preferences

In Computer Other prefer:
Computer Related

In Consumer Related prefer:
Consumer

In Industrial/Energy prefer:
Energy
Industrial Products

In Transportation prefer:
Transportation

In Financial Services prefer:
Real Estate
Financial Services

Additional Information
Year Founded: 2007
Capital Under Management: $42,099,000
Current Activity Level : Actively seeking new investments

GAINLINE CAPITAL PARTNERS, L.P.

700 Canal Street
Fifth Floor
Stamford, CT USA 06902
Phone: 2123193023
Website: www.gainlinecapital.com

Other Offices
250 Park Avenue
Seventh Floor
NEW YORK, NY USA 10177
Phone: 2123193023

Management and Staff
Allan Weinstein, Managing Partner
Harry Clouston, Vice President
Kerri McNicholas, Principal
Rick Sullivan, Managing Director

Type of Firm
Private Equity Firm

Project Preferences

Type of Financing Preferred:
Leveraged Buyout
Management Buyouts
Acquisition
Recapitalizations

Geographical Preferences

United States Preferences:
North America

Additional Information
Year Founded: 2017
Capital Under Management: $66,320,000
Current Activity Level : Actively seeking new investments

GAJA CAPITAL PARTNERS

Kamala Mill Compound
Ground Flr, Publicis Zen House
Mumbai, India 400 013
Phone: 912224903047
Fax: 912224903057
E-mail: info@gajacapital.com
Website: www.gajacapital.com

Management and Staff
Avinash Luthria, Partner
Gopal Jain, Managing Partner
Imran Jafar, Partner
Ranjit Shah, Managing Partner
Sanjay Patel, Co-Founder
Sriranjan Seshadri, Principal

Type of Firm
Private Equity Firm

Association Membership
Indian Venture Capital Association (IVCA)

Project Preferences

Type of Financing Preferred:
Leveraged Buyout
Expansion
Balanced
Turnaround
Later Stage
Acquisition

Geographical Preferences

International Preferences:
India

Industry Preferences

In Consumer Related prefer:
Consumer
Education Related

In Financial Services prefer:
Financial Services

In Business Serv. prefer:
Services

In Manufact. prefer:
Manufacturing

Additional Information
Year Founded: 2004
Capital Under Management: $370,000,000
Current Activity Level : Actively seeking new investments

GALA CAPITAL PARTNERS SL

Calle Serrano 57
Madrid, Spain 28006
Website: www.galacapital.com

Management and Staff
Carlos Tejera, Co-Founder

Type of Firm
Private Equity Firm

Project Preferences

Type of Financing Preferred:
Leveraged Buyout
Balanced

Geographical Preferences

International Preferences:
Europe
No Preference
Spain

Additional Information
Year Founded: 2004
Current Activity Level : Actively seeking new investments

GALAXY INTERNET HOLDING BEIJING CO LTD

18, Information Rd., Haidian
Shangdi Innovation Building
Beijing, China 100085
Phone: 861059065002
Website: www.galaxyinternet.com

Type of Firm
Private Equity Firm

Project Preferences

Type of Financing Preferred:
Early Stage

Geographical Preferences

International Preferences:
China

Industry Preferences

In Communications prefer:
Entertainment

In Internet Specific prefer:
Internet

Additional Information
Year Founded: 2009
Current Activity Level : Actively seeking new investments

GALDANA VENTURES

Avenida Diagonal 409, 6B
Barcelona, Spain 08008
E-mail: info@galdanaventures.com
Website: www.galdanaventures.com

Type of Firm
Private Equity Firm

Project Preferences

Type of Financing Preferred:
Fund of Funds

Geographical Preferences

International Preferences:
Latin America
Spain

Industry Preferences

In Communications prefer:
Telecommunications

In Computer Software prefer:
Software

Additional Information
Year Founded: 2015
Current Activity Level : Actively seeking new investments

GALEN ASSOCIATES INC

680 Washington Boulevard, 11th Floor
Stamford, CT USA 06901
Phone: 2036536400
Fax: 2036536499
E-mail: info@galen.com
Website: www.galen.com

Management and Staff
Bill Williams, Venture Partner
Bruce Wesson, Partner
David Jahns, Managing Director
David Azad, Managing Director
Judith Starkey, Venture Partner
L. John Wilkerson, Founder
Michael Burcham, Venture Partner
Stacey Bauer, Chief Financial Officer
Steve Shapiro, Venture Partner
Terry Gregg, Venture Partner

Zubeen Shroff, Managing Partner

Type of Firm
Private Equity Firm

Project Preferences

Role in Financing:
Prefer role as deal originator but will also invest in deals created by others

Type of Financing Preferred:
Expansion
Balanced
Later Stage

Size of Investments Considered:
Min Size of Investment Considered (000s): $10,000
Max Size of Investment Considered (000s): $30,000

Industry Focus
(% based on actual investment)
Medical/Health	56.9%
Internet Specific	12.1%
Computer Software and Services	11.5%
Computer Hardware	5.3%
Consumer Related	5.2%
Communications and Media	3.3%
Biotechnology	3.0%
Other Products	2.8%

Additional Information
Name of Most Recent Fund: Galen Partners V, L.P.
Most Recent Fund Was Raised: 07/11/2007
Year Founded: 1990
Capital Under Management: $397,000,000
Current Activity Level : Actively seeking new investments
Method of Compensation: Return on investment is of primary concern, do not charge fees

GALENA ASSET MANAGEMENT LTD

Portman House
2, Portman Street
London, United Kingdom W1H 6DU
Phone: 442071732200
Fax: 442071707800

Other Offices

10, Collyer Quay
Ocean Financial Centre
Singapore, Singapore 049315
Phone: 6563192960
Fax: 6567349448

Amsterdam, Geneva Branch
5, Rue de Jargonnant
Geneva, Switzerland 1207
Phone: 41225946900
Fax: 41225946901

Management and Staff
Gerard Lynch, Chief Operating Officer
Jeremy Weir, Chief Executive Officer
Jesus Fernandez, Principal

Type of Firm
Investment Management Firm

Project Preferences

Type of Financing Preferred:
Leveraged Buyout
Early Stage
Expansion
Generalist PE
Balanced
Later Stage
Acquisition
Distressed Debt

Geographical Preferences

International Preferences:
United Kingdom
Europe

Industry Preferences

In Agr/Forestr/Fish prefer:
Mining and Minerals

Additional Information
Name of Most Recent Fund: Galena Private Equity Resources Fund
Most Recent Fund Was Raised: 01/10/2013
Year Founded: 2003
Capital Under Management: $400,000,000
Current Activity Level : Actively seeking new investments

GALIA GESTION SAS
2, rue des Piliers de Tutelle
Bordeaux, France 33025
Phone: 33557818810
Fax: 33556521734
E-mail: contact@galia-gestion.com
Website: www.galia-gestion.com

Management and Staff
Christian Joubert, President

Type of Firm
Private Equity Firm

Association Membership
French Venture Capital Association (AFIC)

Project Preferences

Type of Financing Preferred:
Leveraged Buyout
Early Stage
Generalist PE
Later Stage
Management Buyouts
Acquisition

Size of Investments Considered:
Min Size of Investment Considered (000s): $401
Max Size of Investment Considered (000s): $4,009

Geographical Preferences

International Preferences:
Europe
France

Industry Preferences

In Communications prefer:
Telecommunications

In Computer Software prefer:
Software

In Semiconductor/Electr prefer:
Electronics

In Biotechnology prefer:
Biotechnology
Biotech Related Research

In Medical/Health prefer:
Pharmaceuticals

In Consumer Related prefer:
Consumer Products
Consumer Services

In Industrial/Energy prefer:
Industrial Products

In Business Serv. prefer:
Services
Distribution

In Agr/Forestr/Fish prefer:
Agriculture related

Additional Information
Year Founded: 2002
Capital Under Management: $30,259,000
Current Activity Level : Actively seeking new investments

GALIENA CAPITAL SAS
39, Avenue d'Iena
Paris, France 75116
Phone: 3317141714
Website: www.galiena-capital.com

Type of Firm
Private Equity Firm

Project Preferences

Type of Financing Preferred:
Leveraged Buyout
Early Stage
Expansion
Later Stage
Management Buyouts
Acquisition

Geographical Preferences

International Preferences:
France

Additional Information
Year Founded: 2007
Current Activity Level : Actively seeking new investments

GALILEO PARTNERS
109, Boulevard Haussmann
Paris, France 75008
Phone: 33153594500
Fax: 33153599200
E-mail: email@galileo.fr
Website: www.galileo.fr

Management and Staff
Joel Flichy, Co-Founder
Louis-Michel Angue, Co-Founder
Tig Krekel, Partner

Type of Firm
Private Equity Firm

Association Membership
French Venture Capital Association (AFIC)

Project Preferences

Type of Financing Preferred:
Leveraged Buyout
Early Stage
Turnaround
Later Stage
Recapitalizations

Size of Investments Considered:
Min Size of Investment Considered (000s): $1,413
Max Size of Investment Considered (000s): $7,067

Geographical Preferences

International Preferences:
United Kingdom
Europe
France

Industry Preferences

In Communications prefer:
Communications and Media
Telecommunications

In Computer Software prefer:
Software

In Internet Specific prefer:
Internet

In Computer Other prefer:
Computer Related

In Semiconductor/Electr prefer:
Electronics
Semiconductor

In Medical/Health prefer:
Medical/Health

In Business Serv. prefer:
Services
Media

Additional Information
Name of Most Recent Fund: Galileo II B
Most Recent Fund Was Raised: 03/31/2002
Year Founded: 1989
Capital Under Management: $400,000
Current Activity Level : Actively seeking new investments

GALLATIN POINT CAPITAL LLC

660 Steamboat Road
First Floor
Greenwich, CT USA 06830
Phone: 2037420200
E-mail: info@gallatinpoint.com
Website: gallatinpoint.com

Management and Staff
Lewis Sachs, Co-Founder
Matthew Botein, Co-Founder

Type of Firm
Investment Management Firm

Additional Information
Year Founded: 1969
Current Activity Level : Actively seeking new investments

GALTERE LTD

597 Fifth Avenue
12th Floor
New York, NY USA 10017
Phone: 212-598-1837
E-mail: info@galtere.com
Website: www.galtere.com

Management and Staff
Kurt Spero, Chief Operating Officer

Type of Firm
Investment Management Firm

Project Preferences

Type of Financing Preferred:
Balanced

Geographical Preferences

International Preferences:
Uruguay
Brazil
Australia

Industry Preferences

In Agr/Forestr/Fish prefer:
Agribusiness

Additional Information
Year Founded: 1997
Current Activity Level : Actively seeking new investments

GALVANIZE VENTURES

1062 Delaware Street
Denver, CO USA 80204
Phone: 3038234170
E-mail: info@galvanize.it
Website: galvanize.it

Type of Firm
Private Equity Firm

Project Preferences

Type of Financing Preferred:
Early Stage

Geographical Preferences

United States Preferences:

Industry Preferences

In Computer Hardware prefer:
Computer Graphics and Dig

In Computer Software prefer:
Systems Software

Additional Information
Year Founded: 2014
Capital Under Management: $9,700,000
Current Activity Level : Actively seeking new investments

GAME BCN

Roc Boronat 117, 2 Planta
Barcelona Growth Centre
Barcelona, Spain 08018
E-mail: info@gamebcn.co
Website: www.gamebcn.co

Type of Firm
Incubator/Development Program

Project Preferences

Type of Financing Preferred:
Early Stage
Seed
Startup

Geographical Preferences

International Preferences:
Europe
Spain

Industry Preferences

In Computer Software prefer:
Software
Applications Software

In Internet Specific prefer:
Internet
Web Aggregation/Portals

In Consumer Related prefer:
Entertainment and Leisure

Additional Information
Year Founded: 2014
Current Activity Level : Actively seeking new investments

GAMUT CAPITAL MANAGEMENT LP

250 West 55th Street
25th Floor
New York, NY USA 10019
Website: www.gamutcapital.com

Type of Firm
Private Equity Firm

Project Preferences

Type of Financing Preferred:
Leveraged Buyout
Distressed Debt

Additional Information
Year Founded: 2015
Capital Under Management: $1,000,000,000
Current Activity Level : Actively seeking new investments

GANESH CAPITAL LLC

P.O. Box 991
Boulder, CO USA 80302
E-mail: info@ganeshcapital.com
Website: www.ganeshcapital.com

Type of Firm
Private Equity Firm

Project Preferences

Type of Financing Preferred:
Seed
Startup

Size of Investments Considered:
Min Size of Investment Considered (000s): $50
Max Size of Investment Considered (000s): $5,000

Additional Information
Year Founded: 2014
Current Activity Level : Actively seeking new investments

GANOT CAPITAL LLC

4000 Hollywood Boulevard
Suite 530N
Hollywood, FL USA 33021
Phone: 9549852400
Fax: 9549850396
Website: www.ganotcapital.com

Type of Firm
Private Equity Firm

Project Preferences

Type of Financing Preferred:
Leveraged Buyout
Early Stage
Generalist PE
Balanced
Later Stage
Acquisition

Geographical Preferences

United States Preferences:
All U.S.

International Preferences:
Israel

Industry Preferences

In Biotechnology prefer:
Biotechnology
Human Biotechnology

In Medical/Health prefer:
Medical/Health
Medical Diagnostics
Diagnostic Services

In Financial Services prefer:
Real Estate

Additional Information
Year Founded: 1964
Current Activity Level : Actively seeking new investments

GARAGE TECHNOLOGY VENTURES LLC

101 First Street,
Suite 210
Los Altos, CA USA 94022
Phone: 6503971359
E-mail: info@garage.com
Website: www.garage.com

Management and Staff
Bill Reichert, Managing Director
Guy Kawasaki, Founder
Henry Wong, Venture Partner
Joyce Chung, Managing Director

Type of Firm
Private Equity Firm

Association Membership
Hong Kong Venture Capital Association (HKVCA)

Project Preferences

Role in Financing:
Will function either as deal originator or investor in deals created by others

Type of Financing Preferred:
Early Stage
Seed

Size of Investments Considered:
Min Size of Investment Considered (000s): $500
Max Size of Investment Considered (000s): $3,000

Geographical Preferences

United States Preferences:
California
West Coast

Industry Preferences

In Communications prefer:
Telecommunications

In Computer Software prefer:
Software
Applications Software

In Industrial/Energy prefer:
Materials

In Business Serv. prefer:
Services

In Other prefer:
Environment Responsible

Additional Information
Year Founded: 1997
Capital Under Management: $10,000,000
Current Activity Level : Actively seeking new investments

GARANZIA PARTECIPAZIONI E FINANZIAMENTI SPA

Via Campo di Marte n.9
Perugia, Italy 06124
Phone: 39-075-500-9811
Fax: 39-075-500-5156
E-mail: gepafin@Krenet.it
Website: www.gepafin.it

Other Offices
Piazza Gabriotti
Ufficio Economico del Comune di Citta
Citta di Castello, Italy
Phone: 39-075-852-1501

Management and Staff
Marco Tili, Managing Director

Type of Firm
Private Equity Firm

Association Membership
Italian Venture Capital Association (AIFI)
European Private Equity and Venture Capital Assoc.

Project Preferences

Type of Financing Preferred:
Second Stage Financing
Leveraged Buyout
Expansion
Startup

Geographical Preferences

International Preferences:
Italy

Industry Preferences

In Industrial/Energy prefer:
Industrial Products

In Business Serv. prefer:
Services

Additional Information
Year Founded: 1987
Capital Under Management: $13,200,000
Current Activity Level : Actively seeking new investments

GARIBALDI MEZZO SAS

141, rue Garibaldi
Lyon, France 69003
Phone: 33478955412
Fax: 33478955739
Website: www.garibaldi-mezzo.com

Management and Staff
Olivier De Marignan, Chief Executive Officer

Type of Firm
Bank Affiliated

Project Preferences

Type of Financing Preferred:
Mezzanine

Size of Investments Considered:
Min Size of Investment Considered (000s): $412
Max Size of Investment Considered (000s): $2,062

Geographical Preferences

International Preferences:
Europe
France

Additional Information
Year Founded: 2009
Current Activity Level : Actively seeking new investments

GARIBALDI PARTICIPATIONS SAS
141, rue Garibaldi
Lyon, France 69003
Website: www.garibaldi-participations.com

Other Offices
1, place de l'Hotel de Ville
Saint-Etienne, France 42000

Type of Firm
Bank Affiliated

Association Membership
French Venture Capital Association (AFIC)

Project Preferences
Type of Financing Preferred:
Early Stage
Generalist PE
Later Stage
Acquisition

Size of Investments Considered:
Min Size of Investment Considered (000s): $390
Max Size of Investment Considered (000s): $2,605

Geographical Preferences
International Preferences:
Europe
France

Additional Information
Year Founded: 2004
Current Activity Level : Actively seeking new investments

GARNETT & HELFRICH CAPITAL LP
1200 Park Place
Suite 330
San Mateo, CA USA 94403
Phone: 6502344200
Fax: 6502344299
E-mail: info@garnetthelfrich.com
Website: www.garnetthelfrich.com

Management and Staff
David Helfrich, Co-Founder
Terence Garnett, Managing Director
Terry Garnett, Co-Founder

Type of Firm
Private Equity Firm

Project Preferences
Type of Financing Preferred:
Leveraged Buyout
Acquisition

Industry Preferences
In Communications prefer:
Communications and Media
Commercial Communications

In Computer Software prefer:
Software

In Internet Specific prefer:
Internet

In Semiconductor/Electr prefer:
Semiconductor

Additional Information
Year Founded: 2004
Capital Under Management: $350,400,000
Current Activity Level : Actively seeking new investments

GARNETT THEIS CAPITAL
1200 Park Place
Suite 330
San Mateo, CA USA 94403

Type of Firm
Private Equity Firm

Project Preferences
Type of Financing Preferred:
Leveraged Buyout
Acquisition

Geographical Preferences
United States Preferences:

Industry Preferences
In Computer Software prefer:
Software

In Internet Specific prefer:
Internet

Additional Information
Year Founded: 2014
Current Activity Level : Actively seeking new investments

GARON FINANCIAL GROUP
1220 Howard Avenue
Second Floor
Burlingame, CA USA 94011
Phone: 650-548-9511

Type of Firm
Service Provider

Project Preferences
Role in Financing:
Will function either as deal originator or investor in deals created by others

Type of Financing Preferred:
Second Stage Financing
Research and Development
Start-up Financing
Seed
First Stage Financing
Special Situation

Size of Investments Considered:
Min Size of Investment Considered (000s): $100
Max Size of Investment Considered (000s): $1,000

Geographical Preferences
International Preferences:
No Preference

Additional Information
Year Founded: 1994
Current Activity Level : Actively seeking new investments
Method of Compensation: Function primarily in service area, receive contingent fee in cash or equity

GARRISON INVESTMENT GROUP LP
1290 Avenue of the Americas
Suite 914
New York, NY USA 10104
Phone: 2123729500
Fax: 2123729525
Website: www.garrisoninv.com

Other Offices
1350 Avenue of the Americas
Suite 905
New York, NY USA 10019
Phone: 2123729500
Fax: 2123729525

Type of Firm
Private Equity Firm

Association Membership
Natl Assoc of Small Bus. Inv. Co (NASBIC)

Project Preferences
Type of Financing Preferred:
Leveraged Buyout
Generalist PE
Turnaround
Opportunistic
Distressed Debt

Geographical Preferences
United States Preferences:
North America

Industry Preferences

In Communications prefer:
Communications and Media
Radio & TV Broadcasting

In Consumer Related prefer:
Retail

In Transportation prefer:
Transportation

In Financial Services prefer:
Real Estate

In Business Serv. prefer:
Services
Distribution

In Manufact. prefer:
Manufacturing

Additional Information
Name of Most Recent Fund: Garrison Opportunity Fund LLC
Most Recent Fund Was Raised: 10/30/2009
Year Founded: 2007
Capital Under Management: $553,135,000
Current Activity Level : Actively seeking new investments

GARUDA CAPITAL PARTNERS

Plaza Bapindo- Citibank Tower
12/F, Jl Jendral Sudirman
Jakarta, Indonesia
Phone: 62-21-524-030
Fax: 62-21-526-7516

Management and Staff
Patrick Alexander, Managing Partner

Type of Firm
Private Equity Firm

Project Preferences

Type of Financing Preferred:
Leveraged Buyout
Management Buyouts

Geographical Preferences

International Preferences:
Indonesia

Industry Preferences

In Consumer Related prefer:
Consumer

In Industrial/Energy prefer:
Energy

In Agr/Forestr/Fish prefer:
Agriculture related

Additional Information
Year Founded: 2004
Current Activity Level : Actively seeking new investments

GARVIN HILL CAPITAL PARTNERS LLC

Three Buckingham Terrace
Wellesley, MA USA 02482
Phone: 617-640-4679

Management and Staff
Mark Hastings, Managing Partner

Type of Firm
Private Equity Firm

Project Preferences

Type of Financing Preferred:
Early Stage
Later Stage

Industry Preferences

In Computer Software prefer:
Software

In Internet Specific prefer:
Internet

Additional Information
Name of Most Recent Fund: Garvin Hill Capital Fund LLC
Most Recent Fund Was Raised: 07/22/2009
Year Founded: 2009
Capital Under Management: $186,300,000
Current Activity Level : Actively seeking new investments

GASPAR GLOBAL VENTURES LLC

437 Madison Avenue
Suite 33A
New York, NY USA 10022
Website: www.gasparglobal.com

Management and Staff
Andrew Gaspar, Principal

Type of Firm
Private Equity Firm

Project Preferences

Type of Financing Preferred:
Leveraged Buyout
Early Stage
Expansion
Seed
Startup

Industry Preferences

In Business Serv. prefer:
Services
Media

Additional Information
Year Founded: 1983
Current Activity Level : Actively seeking new investments

GASTON CAPITAL PARTNERS LP

PMB 510, 2212 Union Road
Suite 700
Gastonia, NC USA 28054
Phone: 7046162737
E-mail: gastoncapitalpartners@gmail.com
Website: gastoncapitalpartners.com

Type of Firm
Private Equity Firm

Project Preferences

Type of Financing Preferred:
Balanced

Industry Preferences

In Medical/Health prefer:
Medical/Health
Health Services
Pharmaceuticals

In Industrial/Energy prefer:
Industrial Products

Additional Information
Name of Most Recent Fund: William Gaston Fund LLC
Most Recent Fund Was Raised: 06/13/2013
Year Founded: 2006
Capital Under Management: $5,070,000
Current Activity Level : Actively seeking new investments

GATCOMBE PARK VENTURES LTD

10-11 Charterhouse Square
Welken House
London, United Kingdom EC1M 6EH
Fax: 448701254861
E-mail: contact@gpventures.co.uk

Type of Firm
Private Equity Firm

Project Preferences

Type of Financing Preferred:
Balanced

Geographical Preferences

International Preferences:
United Kingdom
Bulgaria
Germany

Industry Preferences

In Internet Specific prefer:
Ecommerce

In Financial Services prefer:
Financial Services
Financial Services

Additional Information

Year Founded: 2010
Current Activity Level : Actively seeking new investments

GATES GROUP CAPITAL PARTNERS LLC

6120 Parkland Boulevard
Suite 202
Mayfield Heights, OH USA 44124
Phone: 4406849900
Website: www.gatesgroupcp.com

Management and Staff

E. De Windt, Chief Executive Officer

Type of Firm

Private Equity Firm

Project Preferences

Type of Financing Preferred:
Leveraged Buyout
Acquisition
Recapitalizations

Geographical Preferences

United States Preferences:

Industry Preferences

In Consumer Related prefer:
Consumer Services

In Transportation prefer:
Transportation

Additional Information

Year Founded: 2002
Current Activity Level : Actively seeking new investments

GATEWAY GLOBAL (FKA NW BROWN CAPITAL PARTNERS)

Highfield Court, Church Lane
Madingley
Cambridgeshire, United Kingdom CB3 8AG
Phone: 441954211515
Fax: 441954211516

Type of Firm

Private Equity Firm

Project Preferences

Type of Financing Preferred:
Early Stage
Expansion
Balanced
Later Stage
Seed
Startup

Geographical Preferences

International Preferences:
United Kingdom
Europe

Industry Preferences

In Biotechnology prefer:
Biotechnology

In Industrial/Energy prefer:
Environmental Related

Additional Information

Year Founded: 1974
Capital Under Management: $46,500,000
Current Activity Level : Actively seeking new investments

GATEWAY INCUBATOR LLC

330 Second Street
Oakland, CA USA 94607
Phone: 5108336766
E-mail: info@gtwy.co
Website: www.gtwy.co

Type of Firm

Incubator/Development Program

Project Preferences

Type of Financing Preferred:
Early Stage
Startup

Additional Information

Year Founded: 2015
Current Activity Level : Actively seeking new investments

GATEWAY INTERNATIONAL INVESTMENT CO LTD

25 Qingchun Road
12th Floor, Yuanyang Plaza
Hangzhou, China 310004
Phone: 86-571-8724
Fax: 86-571-8724

Type of Firm

Private Equity Firm

Additional Information

Year Founded: 2010
Current Activity Level : Actively seeking new investments

GATEWOOD CAPITAL PARTNERS LLC

419 Park Avenue South
New York, NY USA 10016
Phone: 9949590
E-mail: info@gatewoodcapital.com
Website: www.gatewoodcapital.com

Management and Staff

Alan Weinfeld, Partner
Ami Samuels, Partner
Heidi Shiachy, Vice President
Oren Yahav, Managing Partner

Type of Firm

Private Equity Firm

Project Preferences

Type of Financing Preferred:
Mezzanine
Balanced
Distressed Debt

Geographical Preferences

United States Preferences:
North America

International Preferences:
Western Europe

Industry Preferences

In Financial Services prefer:
Real Estate

Additional Information

Year Founded: 2015
Capital Under Management: $220,000,000
Current Activity Level : Actively seeking new investments

GATX EUROPEAN TECHNOLOGY VENTURES

Tendernden Street
First Floor
London, United Kingdom W1S1TA
Phone: 44-20-7499-0163
Fax: 44-20-7491-1935
Website: www.gatxetv.com

Management and Staff
Humphrey Nokes, Managing Director

Type of Firm
Private Equity Firm

Additional Information
Year Founded: 2010
Current Activity Level : Actively seeking new investments

GAUGE CAPITAL LLC

1256 Main Street
Suite 256
Grapevine, TX USA 76092
Phone: 6823345800
Fax: 2145559876
Website: www.gaugecapital.com

Management and Staff
Drew Johnson, Co-Founder
Tom McKelvey, Co-Founder
Whitney Bowman, Partner

Type of Firm
Private Equity Firm

Project Preferences

Type of Financing Preferred:
Leveraged Buyout
Management Buyouts
Acquisition
Recapitalizations

Geographical Preferences

United States Preferences:

Canadian Preferences:
All Canada

Industry Preferences

In Medical/Health prefer:
Health Services

In Consumer Related prefer:
Food/Beverage

In Business Serv. prefer:
Services

Additional Information
Year Founded: 2014
Capital Under Management: $750,000,000
Current Activity Level : Actively seeking new investments

GAVEA INVESTIMENTOS LTDA

Av Ataulfo de Paiva 1100
7th Floor, Leblon
Rio De Janeiro, Brazil 22440035
Phone: 552135269150
Fax: 552135269180
E-mail: gavea@gaveainvest.com.br
Website: www.gavea.com.br

Management and Staff
Luiz Henrique Fraga, Partner

Type of Firm
Private Equity Firm

Association Membership
Brazilian Venture Capital Association (ABCR)
Emerging Markets Private Equity Association

Project Preferences

Type of Financing Preferred:
Leveraged Buyout
Early Stage
Generalist PE
Balanced
Later Stage
Seed
Management Buyouts
Acquisition
Startup

Geographical Preferences

United States Preferences:
All U.S.

International Preferences:
Brazil

Industry Preferences

In Consumer Related prefer:
Consumer Products

Additional Information
Year Founded: 2003
Capital Under Management: $3,000,000,000
Current Activity Level : Actively seeking new investments

GAXQ EMERGING INDUSTRY DEVELOPMENT FUND MANAGEMENT CO LTD

Room A124, 1F, 11 Bldg
Guian New District Temporary A
Guiyang, China
Phone: 8685184722453

Type of Firm
Private Equity Firm

Project Preferences

Type of Financing Preferred:
Balanced

Geographical Preferences

International Preferences:
China

Additional Information
Year Founded: 2016
Current Activity Level : Actively seeking new investments

GB CREDIT PARTNERS LLC

1350 Avenue of the Americas
Suite 2802
New York, NY USA 10020
Phone: 2122186800
Fax: 2122186802
E-mail: equityinfo@gbmerchantpartners.com
Website: www.gbcredit.com

Other Offices
101 Huntington Avenue
Tenth Floor
Boston, MA USA 02199
Phone: 888-424-1903
Fax: 617-210-7141

Management and Staff
Brian Cooper, Vice President
James Rhee, Principal
James Dworkin, Principal
Larry Klaff, Principal
Matthew Kahn, Principal
Michael Cassetta, Managing Director
Scott Strasser, Managing Director

Type of Firm
Bank Affiliated

Project Preferences

Type of Financing Preferred:
Turnaround
Management Buyouts
Recapitalizations

Industry Preferences

In Consumer Related prefer:
Retail
Consumer Products
Consumer Services

In Business Serv. prefer:
Distribution

In Manufact. prefer:
Manufacturing

Additional Information

Year Founded: 2003
Current Activity Level : Actively seeking new investments

GBS VENTURE PARTNERS

71 Collins Street
Harley House, Level Five
Melbourne, Australia 3000
Phone: 61386509900
Fax: 61386509901
E-mail: investment@gbsventures.com.au
Website: www.gbsventures.com.au

Management and Staff

Ben Gust, Partner
Brigitte Smith, Co-Founder
Geoffrey Brooke, Co-Founder

Type of Firm

Private Equity Firm

Association Membership

Australian Venture Capital Association (AVCAL)

Project Preferences

Role in Financing:
Prefer role as deal originator but will also invest in deals created by others

Type of Financing Preferred:
Early Stage
Later Stage
Seed
Startup

Size of Investments Considered:
Min Size of Investment Considered (000s): $50
Max Size of Investment Considered (000s): $12,000

Geographical Preferences

International Preferences:
Australia

Industry Preferences

In Biotechnology prefer:
Biotechnology

In Medical/Health prefer:
Medical/Health
Medical Diagnostics
Medical Therapeutics
Medical Products

Additional Information

Year Founded: 1998
Capital Under Management: $436,900,000
Current Activity Level : Actively seeking new investments
Method of Compensation: Return on investment is of primary concern, do not charge fees

GBT CAPITAL LLC

8521 E Princess Dr
Scottsdale, AZ USA 85255
E-mail: info@gbtcapital.com
Website: www.gbtcapital.com

Management and Staff

Anthony Wanger, Co-Founder
George Slessman, Co-Founder
William Slessman, Co-Founder

Type of Firm

Private Equity Firm

Project Preferences

Type of Financing Preferred:
Balanced

Additional Information

Year Founded: 2006
Current Activity Level : Actively seeking new investments

GC CAPITAL INC

150 Spear Street
Suite 950
San Francisco, CA USA 94105
Phone: 4155470033
Website: www.gc-cap.com

Management and Staff

Chip Linehan, Co-Founder
Greg Chiate, Co-Founder

Type of Firm

Private Equity Firm

Project Preferences

Type of Financing Preferred:
Leveraged Buyout
Expansion
Acquisition
Recapitalizations

Industry Preferences

In Business Serv. prefer:
Services
Distribution

In Manufact. prefer:
Manufacturing

Additional Information

Year Founded: 1969
Current Activity Level : Actively seeking new investments

GC&H PARTNERS

One Maritime Plaza
Room 2000
San Francisco, CA USA 94111
Phone: 4156932000

Other Offices

1200 17th Street
Denver, CO USA 80202
Phone: 303-606-4800

Type of Firm

Private Equity Firm

Project Preferences

Type of Financing Preferred:
Early Stage
Balanced

Additional Information

Year Founded: 1981
Capital Under Management: $2,200,000
Current Activity Level : Actively seeking new investments

GCC PRIVATE EQUITY

Suhad Complex
Fahad Al-Salem Street
Kuwait, Kuwait
Phone: 965-1-840-000
Fax: 965-2-243-1435
E-mail: info@bayaninvest.com
Website: www.bayaninvest.com

Type of Firm

Investment Management Firm

Project Preferences

Type of Financing Preferred:
Leveraged Buyout

Geographical Preferences

International Preferences:
Middle East
Kuwait

Additional Information

Year Founded: 2009
Current Activity Level : Actively seeking new investments

GCP CAPITAL PARTNERS HOLDINGS LLC

600 Lexington Avenue
New York, NY USA 10022
Website: www.gcpcapital.com

Type of Firm
Private Equity Firm

Project Preferences

Type of Financing Preferred:
Leveraged Buyout
Acquisition

Industry Preferences

In Industrial/Energy prefer:
Energy

In Financial Services prefer:
Financial Services

In Business Serv. prefer:
Services

Additional Information
Name of Most Recent Fund: Greenhill Capital Partners III, L.P.
Most Recent Fund Was Raised: 12/31/2010
Year Founded: 2009
Capital Under Management: $640,990,000
Current Activity Level : Actively seeking new investments

GCP GAMMA CAPITAL PARTNERS BERATUNGS & BETEILIGUNGS AG

Schoenbrunnerstrasse 218-220
Stiege A / Top 4.04
Vienna, Austria 1120
Phone: 4315131072
Fax: 4315131072200
E-mail: office@gamma-capital.com
Website: www.gamma-capital.com

Other Offices
Zamocka 22
Bratislava, Slovakia 81101
Phone: 421-2-5413-1378
Fax: 43-1-513-107-2200

Management and Staff
Burkhard Feurstein, Founder
Oliver Grabherr, Partner
Paul Weinberger, Venture Partner

Type of Firm
Private Equity Firm

Association Membership
Austrian PE and Venture Capital Association (AVCO)
Swiss Venture Capital Association (SECA)
German Venture Capital Association (BVK)
Czech Venture Capital Association (CVCA)
European Private Equity and Venture Capital Assoc.

Project Preferences

Role in Financing:
Prefer role as deal originator but will also invest in deals created by others

Type of Financing Preferred:
Leveraged Buyout
Early Stage
Mezzanine
Later Stage
Seed
Startup

Size of Investments Considered:
Min Size of Investment Considered (000s): $639
Max Size of Investment Considered (000s): $5,089

Geographical Preferences

International Preferences:
Slovenia
Hungary
Slovak Repub.
Central Europe
Europe
Czech Republic
Switzerland
Austria
Eastern Europe
Germany

Industry Preferences

In Communications prefer:
Communications and Media
Telecommunications

In Computer Software prefer:
Software

In Internet Specific prefer:
Internet

In Computer Other prefer:
Computer Related

In Semiconductor/Electr prefer:
Electronics

In Biotechnology prefer:
Biotechnology

In Medical/Health prefer:
Medical/Health
Medical Products
Pharmaceuticals

In Industrial/Energy prefer:
Alternative Energy
Materials
Advanced Materials

In Business Serv. prefer:
Services

Additional Information
Year Founded: 2000
Capital Under Management: $114,600,000
Current Activity Level : Actively seeking new investments

GCP MEMBER LTD

112 Jermyn Street
Second Floor
London, United Kingdom SW1Y 6LS
Phone: 442070249800
Fax: 442076917878
E-mail: gcp@growthcapital.co.uk

Management and Staff
Garrett Curran, Partner
James Blake, Partner
Simon Jobson, Partner
William Crossan, Managing Partner

Type of Firm
Private Equity Firm

Project Preferences

Type of Financing Preferred:
Leveraged Buyout
Early Stage
Expansion
Mezzanine
Management Buyouts
Acquisition

Size of Investments Considered:
Min Size of Investment Considered (000s): $8,729
Max Size of Investment Considered (000s): $43,645

Geographical Preferences

International Preferences:
United Kingdom
Western Europe
Eastern Europe

Industry Focus
(% based on actual investment)
Other Products	61.1%
Industrial/Energy	27.8%
Internet Specific	11.2%

Additional Information
Year Founded: 1999
Capital Under Management: $71,200,000
Current Activity Level : Actively seeking new investments

GE ENERGY FINANCIAL SERVICES INC

3135 Easton Turnpike
Fairfield, CT USA 06828
Phone: 2033732211
Website: www.geenergyfinancialservices.com

Type of Firm
Investment Management Firm

Project Preferences

Type of Financing Preferred:
Balanced
Public Companies
Later Stage
Acquisition
Recapitalizations

Industry Preferences

In Industrial/Energy prefer:
Energy

Additional Information
Year Founded: 1991
Current Activity Level : Actively seeking new investments

GEBRUDER HELLER DINKLAGE

Driebergseweg 17
Zeist, Netherlands 3708 JA
Phone: 31306971410
Fax: 31306971411
E-mail: ah@nimbus.com
Website: www.nimbus.com

Other Offices
Maximilianstrasse 32
Munich, Germany 80539
Phone: 498920500300
Fax: 498920500333

Management and Staff
Ed Van Dijk, Partner
Edwin Puijpe, Partner
Gert Jan Hubers, Partner
Kaj Grichnik, Partner
Marc Renne, Partner
Paul Frohn, Partner

Type of Firm
Private Equity Firm

Project Preferences

Type of Financing Preferred:
Leveraged Buyout
Turnaround
Later Stage
Management Buyouts

Geographical Preferences

International Preferences:
Sweden
United Kingdom
Luxembourg
Europe
Netherlands
Eastern Europe
Belgium
Norway
Germany
Denmark
France

Industry Preferences

In Consumer Related prefer:
Consumer

In Industrial/Energy prefer:
Industrial Products

In Business Serv. prefer:
Services

In Manufact. prefer:
Manufacturing

Additional Information
Year Founded: 1993
Current Activity Level : Actively seeking new investments

GED GROUP

Montalban 7
3a Planta
Madrid, Spain 28014
Phone: 34917020250
Fax: 34914021764
E-mail: madrid@gedcapital.com
Website: www.gedcapital.com

Other Offices
R. Viana de Lima 155
Porto, Portugal 4100
Phone: 35-917-270-040

14, Saborna Str.,
Second Floor
Sofia, Bulgaria 1000
Phone: 359-29-817-469
Fax: 359-29-817-467

Strada Frumoasa 42 A
Sector 1
Bucharest, Romania 010987
Phone: 40-213-175-884
Fax: 40-213-181-483

Almirante Lobo 2, 4 planta
Seville, Spain 41001
Phone: 34954490180
Fax: 34954560857

Management and Staff
Enrique Centelles Echeverria, President
Enrique Centelles Satrustegui, Managing Partner
Felix Guerrero Igea, Co-Founder
Javier Echarri Eraso, Managing Partner
Joaquim Hierro Lopes, Managing Partner
Juan Puertas, Chief Financial Officer
Robert Luke, Co-Founder

Type of Firm
Private Equity Firm

Association Membership
European Private Equity and Venture Capital Assoc.
Spanish Venture Capital Association (ASCRI)

Project Preferences

Type of Financing Preferred:
Second Stage Financing
Leveraged Buyout
Early Stage
Expansion
Balanced
Startup

Size of Investments Considered:
Min Size of Investment Considered (000s): $3,899
Max Size of Investment Considered (000s): $32,493

Geographical Preferences

International Preferences:
Portugal
Western Europe
Eastern Europe
Bulgaria
Spain
Romania

Industry Preferences

In Communications prefer:
Telecommunications

In Computer Software prefer:
Software

In Internet Specific prefer:
Internet

In Medical/Health prefer:
Pharmaceuticals

In Consumer Related prefer:
Food/Beverage
Hotels and Resorts

In Industrial/Energy prefer:
Industrial Products

In Other prefer:
Environment Responsible

Additional Information
Name of Most Recent Fund: GED Sur
Most Recent Fund Was Raised: 11/01/2005
Year Founded: 1996
Capital Under Management: $454,900,000
Current Activity Level : Actively seeking new investments

GEDIK GIRISIM SERMAYESI YATIRIM ORTAKLIGI AS

Cumhuriyet Mahallesi E-5 Yolu
Yanyol No:29 Kat:3
Istanbul, Turkey
Phone: 902164523624
Fax: 902163771136
E-mail: bilgi@gedikgirisim.com
Website: www.gedikgirisim.com

Type of Firm
Private Equity Firm

Project Preferences

Type of Financing Preferred:
Leveraged Buyout
Early Stage
Generalist PE
Later Stage
Seed
Management Buyouts
Acquisition
Recapitalizations

Geographical Preferences

International Preferences:
Turkey
Europe

Industry Preferences

In Internet Specific prefer:
Ecommerce

In Consumer Related prefer:
Food/Beverage
Consumer Products

Additional Information
Year Founded: 2006
Current Activity Level : Actively seeking new investments

GEEKDOM LC

110 East Houston
Seventh & Eight Floor
San Antonio, TX USA 78205
Phone: 2108653782
E-mail: info@geekdom.com
Website: www.geekdom.com

Management and Staff
David Garcia, Chief Operating Officer
Graham Weston, Co-Founder
Lorenzo Gomez, Chief Executive Officer
Nicholas Longo, Founder

Type of Firm
Private Equity Firm

Geographical Preferences

United States Preferences:
Texas

Additional Information
Name of Most Recent Fund: Geekdom Fund I, L.P.
Most Recent Fund Was Raised: 12/30/2014
Year Founded: 2014
Capital Under Management: $23,396,000
Current Activity Level : Actively seeking new investments

GEF MANAGEMENT CORP

5471 Wisconsin Avenue
Suite 300
Chevy Chase, MD USA 20815
Phone: 2404828900
Fax: 2404828908
Website: gefcapital.com

Management and Staff
Alipt Sharma, Principal
Anibal Wadih, Managing Director
Anneliese Mueller, Vice President
Ben Fritz, Principal
Benjamin Sessions, Managing Director
Brian Foist, Chief Financial Officer
Derek Beaty, Vice President
Elizabeth Lewis, Principal
George McPherson, Managing Director
George McPherson, Managing Director
Gloria Mamba, Managing Director
Gordon Carrihill, Managing Director
H. Jeffrey Leonard, Chief Executive Officer
James Castanino, Vice President
Jim Heyes, Principal
Joan Larrea, Managing Director
Justin Heyman, Vice President
Kevin Tidwell, Principal
Kumar Shah, Vice President
Lisa Schule, Managing Director
Mauricio Marcal, Principal
Mirtcho Spassov, Vice President
Nakul Zaveri, Vice President
Ole Sand, Managing Partner
Peter Tynan, Managing Director
Philo Tran, Principal
Raj Pai, Managing Director
Scott Vicary, Managing Director
Scott MacLeod, Managing Partner
Sridhar Narayan, Principal
Sulanji Siwale, Managing Director
Todd Cater, Managing Director
Yue Tian, Vice President

Type of Firm
Private Equity Firm

Association Membership
South African Venture Capital Association (SAVCA)
Emerging Markets Private Equity Association
African Venture Capital Association (AVCA)

Project Preferences

Role in Financing:
Prefer role as deal originator but will also invest in deals created by others

Type of Financing Preferred:
Generalist PE
Balanced
Later Stage
Other

Geographical Preferences

United States Preferences:
Southeast
Hawaii
Southwest
Alaska
New York

International Preferences:
Latin America
India
Turkey
China
Mexico
Eastern Europe
Brazil
Sri Lanka
Asia
South Africa
Africa

Industry Preferences

In Medical/Health prefer:
Medical/Health
Health Services

In Industrial/Energy prefer:
Energy
Alternative Energy
Energy Conservation Relat
Industrial Products
Environmental Related

In Transportation prefer:
Transportation

In Manufact. prefer:
Manufacturing

In Utilities prefer:
Utilities

In Other prefer:
Socially Responsible
Environment Responsible

GEFINOR VENTURES

375, Park Avenue
Suite 3607
New York, NY USA 10152
Phone: 2123081111
Fax: 2123081182
E-mail: kreesing@gefinor.com
Website: www.gefinorventures.com

Other Offices

375 Park Avenue
Suite 3607
New York, NY USA 10152
Phone: 212-308-1111
Fax: 212-308-1182

Management and Staff

Bobby Inman, Managing Director
Chris Davis, Principal
Greg Carlisle, Managing Director
Mimo Ousseimi, Managing Director
Robert Porell, Principal
Thomas Inman, Principal
William Beckett, Managing Director

Type of Firm

Private Equity Firm

Association Membership

Western Association of Venture Capitalists (WAVC)
National Venture Capital Association - USA (NVCA)
Natl Assoc of Small Bus. Inv. Co (NASBIC)

Project Preferences

Role in Financing:
Will function either as deal originator or investor in deals created by others

Type of Financing Preferred:
Early Stage
Later Stage

Size of Investments Considered:
Min Size of Investment Considered (000s): $1,000
Max Size of Investment Considered (000s): $2,000

Geographical Preferences

United States Preferences:
California
Colorado
D. of Columbia
New York
Texas

Industry Preferences

In Communications prefer:
Wireless Communications

In Computer Software prefer:
Software

In Internet Specific prefer:
Internet

In Semiconductor/Electr prefer:
Semiconductor

In Medical/Health prefer:
Medical/Health

In Consumer Related prefer:
Consumer Products

In Financial Services prefer:
Financial Services

In Manufact. prefer:
Manufacturing

Additional Information

Name of Most Recent Fund: GEFUS SBIC, L.P.
Most Recent Fund Was Raised: 03/01/2000
Year Founded: 1995
Capital Under Management: $43,500,000
Current Activity Level : Actively seeking new investments
Method of Compensation: Return on investment is of primary concern, do not charge fees

GEMCORP CAPITAL LLP

36 Queen Street
London, United Kingdom EC4R 1BN
Phone: 442038371120
E-mail: info@gemcorp.net
Website: www.gemcorp.net

Management and Staff

Anya Kopyleva, Principal
Atanas Bostandjiev, Managing Partner
Bojidar Savkov, Partner
Ines Cruz, Vice President
Parvoleta Shtereva, Managing Partner
Philip Hamilton, Managing Partner
Reginald Crawford, Principal
Sarah Walton, Principal
Selim Basak, Managing Partner
Tue Sando, Partner

Type of Firm

Private Equity Firm

Project Preferences

Type of Financing Preferred:
Expansion
Mezzanine

Geographical Preferences

International Preferences:
Latin America
Europe
Middle East
Asia
Africa

Industry Preferences

In Industrial/Energy prefer:
Industrial Products
Materials

In Financial Services prefer:
Financial Services

In Agr/Forestr/Fish prefer:
Mining and Minerals

In Utilities prefer:
Utilities

Additional Information

Year Founded: 2013
Current Activity Level : Actively seeking new investments

GEMINI CAPITAL FUND MGMT LTD

9 Hamenofim Street
Herzliya, Israel 46725
Phone: 97299719111
Fax: 97299584842
E-mail: info@gemini.co.il
Website: www.gemini.co.il

Management and Staff

Adi Pundak-Mintz, Venture Partner
Anat Shukhman, Vice President
Daniel Cohen, General Partner
David Cohen, General Partner
Ed Mlavsky, Partner
Einat Metzer, Principal
Eran Wagner, General Partner
Menashe Ezra, Managing Partner
Omer Regev, Chief Financial Officer
Yossi Sela, Managing Partner

Type of Firm

Private Equity Firm

Association Membership

Israel Venture Association

Project Preferences

Role in Financing:
Prefer role as deal originator but will also invest in deals created by others

Type of Financing Preferred:
Early Stage
Seed

Additional Information

Name of Most Recent Fund: GEF U.S. Growth Fund II, L.P.
Most Recent Fund Was Raised: 11/01/2010
Year Founded: 1990
Capital Under Management: $1,000,000,000
Current Activity Level : Actively seeking new investments

Pratt's Guide to Private Equity & Venture Capital Sources

Geographical Preferences

International Preferences:
Israel
All International

Industry Focus

(% based on actual investment)

Computer Software and Services	33.2%
Communications and Media	19.5%
Internet Specific	16.5%
Semiconductors/Other Elect.	15.5%
Medical/Health	8.4%
Computer Hardware	3.8%
Other Products	2.1%
Industrial/Energy	0.6%
Biotechnology	0.3%

Additional Information

Year Founded: 1993
Capital Under Management: $700,000,000
Current Activity Level : Actively seeking new investments
Method of Compensation: Return on investment is of primary concern, do not charge fees

GEMINI INVESTMENT CORP

10/F, Seoyeong Building, 158-1
Samseung-dong, Kangnam-gu
Seoul, South Korea 135-760
Phone: 82220519640
Fax: 82220519639
Website: www.geminivc.co.kr

Management and Staff

Takyoung Kang, President

Type of Firm

Private Equity Firm

Association Membership

Korean Venture Capital Association (KVCA)

Project Preferences

Type of Financing Preferred:
Early Stage
Expansion
Balanced
Seed
Startup

Geographical Preferences

United States Preferences:

International Preferences:
Korea, South

Industry Preferences

In Internet Specific prefer:
Internet

In Biotechnology prefer:
Biotechnology

In Consumer Related prefer:
Entertainment and Leisure

Additional Information

Year Founded: 1986
Capital Under Management: $17,700,000
Current Activity Level : Actively seeking new investments

GEMINI INVESTORS INC

20 William Street
Suite 250
Wellesley, MA USA 02481
Phone: 7812377001
Fax: 7812377233
Website: www.gemini-investors.com

Other Offices

225 South Sixth Street
Suite 4350
Minneapolis, MN USA 55402
Phone: 612-766-4074
Fax: 612-766-4040

111 West Olmos Drive
San Antonio, TX USA 78212
Phone: 210-601-1057
Fax: 210-824-1807

Management and Staff

David Millet, Managing Director
Dean Pernisie, Vice President
James Goodman, President
James Rich, Managing Director
Jeffrey Newton, Managing Director
Matthew Keis, Managing Director
Robert Menn, Vice President

Type of Firm

Private Equity Firm

Association Membership

Natl Assoc of Small Bus. Inv. Co (NASBIC)

Project Preferences

Role in Financing:
Will function either as deal originator or investor in deals created by others

Type of Financing Preferred:
Leveraged Buyout
Generalist PE
Balanced
Later Stage
Management Buyouts
Acquisition
Recapitalizations

Size of Investments Considered:
Min Size of Investment Considered (000s): $3,000
Max Size of Investment Considered (000s): $8,000

Geographical Preferences

United States Preferences:

Industry Focus

(% based on actual investment)

Consumer Related	31.8%
Other Products	15.7%
Computer Software and Services	15.5%
Internet Specific	11.5%
Medical/Health	9.6%
Communications and Media	6.7%
Semiconductors/Other Elect.	4.0%
Computer Hardware	2.7%
Industrial/Energy	2.6%

Additional Information

Name of Most Recent Fund: Gemini Investors IV, L.P.
Most Recent Fund Was Raised: 07/22/2005
Year Founded: 1993
Capital Under Management: $450,000,000
Current Activity Level : Actively seeking new investments
Method of Compensation: Return on invest. most important, but chg. closing fees, service fees, etc.

GEMINI NEW MEDIA VENTURES LLP

12th Road, Chembur East
Plot Number 514, Number Two
Mumbai, India 400071
Phone: 912225216065
E-mail: contact@imgemini.com
Website: www.imgemini.com

Management and Staff

Deep Malhotra, Managing Partner
Ramesh Malhotra, Partner

Type of Firm

Incubator/Development Program

Project Preferences

Type of Financing Preferred:
Early Stage
Balanced
Startup

Geographical Preferences

International Preferences:
India
Asia

Industry Preferences

In Communications prefer:
Communications and Media
Media and Entertainment

In Business Serv. prefer:
Services
Media

GEMINI PARTNERS, INC.

10900 Wilshire Boulevard
Suite 300
Los Angeles, CA USA 90024
Phone: 3106964001
Fax: 3105070263
Website: www.geminipartners.net

Management and Staff

Horace Usry, Managing Director
Jeff Kovick, Vice President
Matthew Johnson, Managing Partner
Nathan Johnson, Managing Partner

Type of Firm

Bank Affiliated

Project Preferences

Type of Financing Preferred:
Leveraged Buyout
Expansion
Mezzanine
Generalist PE
Public Companies
Private Placement
Distressed Debt

Size of Investments Considered:
Min Size of Investment Considered (000s): $1,000
Max Size of Investment Considered (000s): $5,000

Geographical Preferences

United States Preferences:

International Preferences:
Europe

Additional Information

Year Founded: 2003
Current Activity Level : Actively seeking new investments

GEMMA FRISIUS FONDS K.U.LEUVEN SA

Waaistraat 6
Leuven, Belgium 3000
Phone: 3216326500
Fax: 3216326515
E-mail: lrd@kuleuven.be
Website: www.lrd.kuleuven.be

Type of Firm

Private Equity Firm

Association Membership

Belgium Venturing Association

Project Preferences

Type of Financing Preferred:
Balanced
Seed
Startup

Geographical Preferences

International Preferences:
Belgium

Industry Preferences

In Communications prefer:
Data Communications

In Biotechnology prefer:
Biotechnology

Additional Information

Year Founded: 1997
Capital Under Management: $32,900,000
Current Activity Level : Actively seeking new investments

GEMMES VENTURE SA

13 Rue Paul Valery
Paris, France 75116
Website: www.gemmes-venture.com

Management and Staff

Philippe Monnot, Chief Executive Officer

Type of Firm

Private Equity Firm

Project Preferences

Type of Financing Preferred:
Leveraged Buyout
Generalist PE
Later Stage
Acquisition

Geographical Preferences

International Preferences:
France

Industry Preferences

In Communications prefer:
Communications and Media

In Internet Specific prefer:
Internet

In Medical/Health prefer:
Medical/Health

In Industrial/Energy prefer:
Alternative Energy

In Financial Services prefer:
Financial Services

Additional Information

Year Founded: 1999
Current Activity Level : Actively seeking new investments

GEMSPRING CAPITAL LLC

17 Bridge Square
Westport, CT USA 06880
E-mail: info@gemspring.com
Website: www.gemspring.com

Management and Staff

Alexander Shakibnia, Vice President
Aron Grossman, Principal
Bennet Grill, Vice President
Bret Wiener, Managing Partner
Geoff Broglio, Principal
Ravdeep Chanana, Vice President
Thomas Zanios, Managing Director

Type of Firm

Private Equity Firm

Project Preferences

Type of Financing Preferred:
Leveraged Buyout
Recapitalizations

Geographical Preferences

United States Preferences:

Canadian Preferences:
All Canada

Industry Preferences

In Medical/Health prefer:
Health Services

Additional Information

Year Founded: 2016
Capital Under Management: $350,000,000
Current Activity Level : Actively seeking new investments

GEN CAP AMERICA INC

40 Burton Hills Boulevard
Suite 420
Nashville, TN USA 37215
Phone: 6152560231
Fax: 6152562487
E-mail: info@gencapamerica.com
Website: www.gencapamerica.com

Management and Staff

Andrew Ginsberg, Vice President

Type of Firm

Private Equity Firm

Project Preferences

Role in Financing:
Prefer role as deal originator

Type of Financing Preferred:
Leveraged Buyout
Mezzanine
Management Buyouts
Acquisition
Recapitalizations

Industry Focus
(% based on actual investment)
Other Products 100.0%

Additional Information
Name of Most Recent Fund: Southvest Fund V, L.P.
Most Recent Fund Was Raised: 12/30/2004
Year Founded: 1985
Capital Under Management: $255,000,000
Current Activity Level : Actively seeking new investments

GEN3 PARTNERS, INC.

20 Winthrop Square
Second Floor
Boston, MA USA 02110
Phone: 6177287000
Fax: 6177287500
E-mail: info@gen3.com
Website: www.gen3partners.com

Management and Staff
Alex Lyubomirskiy, Principal
Andrey Prokofiev, Principal
Arthur Toscanini, Chief Financial Officer
Douglas Hoon, Managing Director
Howard Soriano, Managing Director
Igor Petiy, Principal
Irina Sigalovsky, Principal
Luba Mitnik-Gankin, Principal
Michael Treacy, Co-Founder
Oleg Feygenson, Principal
Patrick Casey, Principal
Pavel Yu Koblents, Principal
Prokofiev Andrey, Principal
Simon Litvin, Co-Founder

Type of Firm
Service Provider

Project Preferences

Type of Financing Preferred:
Early Stage
Balanced

Industry Preferences

In Medical/Health prefer:
Medical Products

In Consumer Related prefer:
Consumer Products

In Industrial/Energy prefer:
Industrial Products

Additional Information
Name of Most Recent Fund: GEN3 Capital I, L.P.
Most Recent Fund Was Raised: 07/31/2005
Year Founded: 1999
Current Activity Level : Actively seeking new investments

GEN7 INVESTMENT LLC

101 Fifth Street North
Fargo, ND USA 58102
E-mail: info@Gen7investments.com
Website: www.gen7investments.com

Management and Staff
John Hajostek, Chief Financial Officer
Paul Amundson, Vice President

Type of Firm
Private Equity Firm

Project Preferences

Type of Financing Preferred:
Generalist PE

Geographical Preferences

United States Preferences:
All U.S.

Additional Information
Year Founded: 2017
Current Activity Level : Actively seeking new investments

GENECHEM FINANCIAL CORP

One Westmount Square, Suite 800
Montreal, Canada H3Z 2P9
Phone: 5148497696
Fax: 5148495191
E-mail: info@genechem.com
Website: www.genechem.com

Management and Staff
Elizabeth Douville, General Partner
Ines Holzbaur, General Partner
John Clement, General Partner
Louis Lacasse, General Partner
Martial Lacroix, General Partner

Type of Firm
Private Equity Firm

Project Preferences

Type of Financing Preferred:
Early Stage
Balanced
Later Stage
Seed

Geographical Preferences

United States Preferences:

Canadian Preferences:
All Canada
Quebec

International Preferences:
Europe

Industry Preferences

In Medical/Health prefer:
Medical Therapeutics
Other Therapeutic

Additional Information
Name of Most Recent Fund: AmorChem, L.P.
Most Recent Fund Was Raised: 01/28/2011
Year Founded: 1997
Capital Under Management: $33,100,000
Current Activity Level : Actively seeking new investments

GENER8TOR

309 North Water Street
Milwaukee, WI USA 53202
Phone: 4145028880
Website: www.gener8tor.com

Other Offices
30 West Mifflin
Fifth Floor
Madison, WI USA 53703

One East Main Street
Plymouth, WI USA 53073

Management and Staff
Dan Armbrust, Co-Founder
Daniel Bader, Co-Founder
Joe Kirgues, Co-Founder
Joel Abraham, Co-Founder
Jon Eckhardt, Co-Founder
Troy Vosseller, Co-Founder

Type of Firm
Incubator/Development Program

Project Preferences

Type of Financing Preferred:
Early Stage
Seed
Startup

Geographical Preferences

United States Preferences:
Wisconsin

Industry Preferences

In Computer Software prefer:
Software

In Internet Specific prefer:
Internet

In Industrial/Energy prefer:
Industrial Products

In Business Serv. prefer:
Services

Additional Information

Year Founded: 1969
Capital Under Management: $3,679,000
Current Activity Level : Actively seeking new investments

GENERA CAPITAL LLC

167 Tellico Port Road
Vonore, TN USA 37885
Phone: 4238844110
Fax: 4238844129
E-mail: info@generaenergy.com
Website: www.generaenergy.net

Other Offices

Former HQ: 2450 E.J. Chapman Drive
Suite 216
Knoxville, TN USA 37996
Phone: 8659748258
Fax: 8659748301

Type of Firm

Private Equity Firm

Project Preferences

Type of Financing Preferred:
Startup

Geographical Preferences

United States Preferences:
Tennessee

Industry Preferences

In Industrial/Energy prefer:
Energy
Energy Conservation Relat

Additional Information

Year Founded: 2011
Current Activity Level : Actively seeking new investments

GENERAL ATLANTIC LLC

600 Steamboat Road
Suite 105
Greenwich, CT USA 06830
Phone: 2036298600
Fax: 2036228818
E-mail: generalatlantic@generalatlantic.com
Website: www.generalatlantic.com

Other Offices

Rua Dr. Renato Paes de Barros
1017, 15 Andar
Sao Paulo, Brazil 04538-133
Phone: 551132966100
Fax: 551132966144

Maximillianstrasse 35b
Munich, Germany 80359
Phone: 49-89-3803-8910

Express Towers
17th Floor, Nariman Point
Mumbai, India 400 021
Phone: 91-22-6656-1400
Fax: 91-22-6631-7893

Park Avenue Plaza
55 East 52nd Street
NEW YORK, NY USA 10055
Phone: 212-715-4000
Fax: 212-759-5708

One Jianguomenwai Avenue
Room 1708-12, China World Office One
Beijing, China 100022
Phone: 861059652500
Fax: 861058669533

Two IFC, Eight Finance Street
Suite 5815, 58th Floor
Hong Kong, Hong Kong
Phone: 852-3602-2600
Fax: 852-3602-2611

228 Hamilton Avenue
PALO ALTO, CA USA 94301
Phone: 650-251-7800
Fax: 650-251-9672

Asia Square Tower One
Eight Marina View, Suite 41-04
Singapore, Singapore 018960
Phone: 6566616700

1101 CM Amsterdam Zuidoost
Luna ArenA 5th floor
Herikerbergweg, Netherlands 152
Phone: 31-20-60-90-301

Management and Staff

Alan Ghelberg, Principal
Amit Soni, Principal
Andrew Crawford, Managing Director
Andrew Ferrer, Principal
Anna Golynskaya, Vice President
Anton Levy, Managing Director
Brett Rochkind, Managing Director
Bryant Christanto, Vice President
Chris Caulkin, Principal
Chris Lanning, Managing Director
Christian Figge, Vice President
Cory Eaves, Managing Director
Daniel Lessner, Vice President
David George, Vice President
David Caluori, Principal
David Hodgson, Managing Director
Drew Pearson, Managing Director
Eduardo Samara, Principal
Eloho Omame, Vice President
Eric Zhang, Managing Director
Erin Chang, Vice President
Frederico Ferreira, Vice President
Gabriel Caillaux, Managing Director
Graves Tompkins, Managing Director
Hans Reuter, Vice President
Joern Nikolay, Managing Director
John Bernstein, Managing Director
Jonathan Korngold, Managing Director
Ke Wei, Managing Director
Lucia Rigo, Vice President
Luis Cervantes, Vice President
Mark Dzialga, Managing Director
Martin Escobari, Managing Director
Melis Kahya, Vice President
Michelle Dipp, Managing Director
Montes Piard, Vice President
Nathalie Bruls, Vice President
Nick Hammerschlag, Vice President
Pamela Fang, Managing Director
Paul Stamas, Principal
Peter Munzig, Principal
Rajat Sood, Principal
Raphael Osnoss, Vice President
Rene Kern, Managing Director
Robbert Vorhoff, Managing Director
Rodrigo Catunda, Vice President
Roni Elchahal, Principal
Sandeep Naik, Managing Director
Sara Dillon, Vice President
Shantanu Rastogi, Principal
Shaw Joseph, Vice President
Tim Cook, Vice President
Timothy Cook, Vice President
Tom Davis, Vice President
William Ford, Chief Executive Officer
Zachary Kaplan, Vice President

Type of Firm

Private Equity Firm

Association Membership

Venture Capital Association of Beijing (VCAB)
Hong Kong Venture Capital Association (HKVCA)
Malaysian Venture Capital Association
Singapore Venture Capital Association (SVCA)
Indian Venture Capital Association (IVCA)

Project Preferences

Role in Financing:
Prefer role as deal originator but will also invest in deals created by others

Type of Financing Preferred:
Leveraged Buyout
Generalist PE
Balanced

Size of Investments Considered:
Min Size of Investment Considered (000s): $75,000
Max Size of Investment Considered (000s): $400,000

Geographical Preferences

United States Preferences:
North America

International Preferences:
Latin America
India
Europe
Asia

Industry Focus

(% based on actual investment)
Other Products	29.9%
Internet Specific	27.5%
Computer Software and Services	20.4%
Computer Hardware	13.0%
Industrial/Energy	3.5%
Medical/Health	1.7%
Consumer Related	1.6%
Communications and Media	1.5%
Biotechnology	0.7%
Semiconductors/Other Elect.	0.1%

Additional Information

Name of Most Recent Fund: General Atlantic Partners 93, L.P.
Most Recent Fund Was Raised: 07/10/2013
Year Founded: 1980
Capital Under Management: $17,000,000,000
Current Activity Level : Actively seeking new investments

GENERAL CATALYST PARTNERS LLC

20 University Road
Fourth Floor
Cambridge, MA USA 02138
Phone: 6172347000
Fax: 6172347040
Website: www.generalcatalyst.com

Other Offices

444 High Street
Suite 400
Palo Alto, CA USA 94301
Phone: 6506185900
Fax: 6506185950

Management and Staff

Adam Valkin, General Partner
Bilal Zuberi, Principal
Brian Shortsleeve, Managing Director
Chris Farmer, Venture Partner
David Orfao, Co-Founder
David Fialkow, Co-Founder
Deepak Kumar, Partner
Gabe Ling, Partner
George Bell, Managing Director
Hemant Taneja, Managing Director
Holly McConnell, Managing Director
Joel Cutler, Co-Founder
John Simon, Co-Founder
Jonathan Teo, Managing Director
Kevin Colleran, Venture Partner
Kyle Doherty, Managing Director
Lawrence Bohn, Managing Director
Matt Tara, Vice President
Michelle Daubar, Vice President
Neil Sequeira, Managing Director
Niko Bonatsos, Managing Director
Peter Freeland, Vice President
Phil Libin, Managing Director
Spencer Lazar, Partner
Stephen Herrod, Managing Director
Terrell Jones, Venture Partner
William Fitzgerald, Co-Founder

Type of Firm
Private Equity Firm

Association Membership
New England Venture Capital Association
National Venture Capital Association - USA (NVCA)

Project Preferences

Role in Financing:
Prefer role as deal originator but will also invest in deals created by others

Type of Financing Preferred:
Leveraged Buyout
Early Stage
Expansion
Generalist PE
Balanced
Seed
Management Buyouts
Acquisition
Recapitalizations

Size of Investments Considered:
Min Size of Investment Considered (000s): $50
Max Size of Investment Considered (000s): $250

Geographical Preferences

United States Preferences:
Northern California
Massachusetts
New York
All U.S.

Industry Focus

(% based on actual investment)
Internet Specific	48.2%
Computer Software and Services	29.2%
Other Products	5.1%
Medical/Health	3.9%
Computer Hardware	3.3%
Industrial/Energy	2.7%
Communications and Media	2.3%
Biotechnology	2.3%
Semiconductors/Other Elect.	1.8%
Consumer Related	1.3%

Additional Information

Name of Most Recent Fund: General Catalyst Group VII, L.P.
Most Recent Fund Was Raised: 12/23/2013
Year Founded: 2000
Capital Under Management: $3,000,000,000
Current Activity Level : Actively seeking new investments

GENERALI PRIVATE EQUITY INVESTMENTS GMBH

Unter Sachsenhausen 27
Cologne, Germany 50667
Phone: 491801163616
Fax: 4922142035444

Other Offices

5, Allee Scheffer
Luxembourg, Luxembourg 2520

Management and Staff

Britta Lindhorst, Managing Director
Klaus Wiener, Managing Director

Type of Firm
Insurance Firm Affiliate

Association Membership
German Venture Capital Association (BVK)

Project Preferences

Type of Financing Preferred:
Fund of Funds

Geographical Preferences

United States Preferences:

International Preferences:
Luxembourg
Europe
Eastern Europe

Additional Information

Year Founded: 2002
Capital Under Management: $208,800,000
Current Activity Level : Actively seeking new investments

GENERATION GROWTH CAPITAL INC

411 East Wisconsin Avenue, Suite 1710
Milwaukee, WI USA 53202
Phone: 4142918908
Fax: 4142918918
E-mail: info@generationgrowth.com
Website: www.generationgrowth.com

Other Offices

300 North LaSalle Street, Suite 4000
Chicago, IL USA 60654
Phone: 3126605992

Management and Staff
Cory Nettles, Managing Director

Type of Firm
Private Equity Firm

Project Preferences

Type of Financing Preferred:
Leveraged Buyout
Turnaround
Management Buyouts
Acquisition
Recapitalizations

Geographical Preferences

United States Preferences:
Midwest

Industry Preferences

In Business Serv. prefer:
Services
Distribution

In Manufact. prefer:
Manufacturing

Additional Information
Name of Most Recent Fund: Generation Growth Capital Fund II, L.P.
Most Recent Fund Was Raised: 01/19/2012
Year Founded: 2006
Capital Under Management: $63,600,000
Current Activity Level : Actively seeking new investments

GENERATION INVESTMENT MANAGEMENT LLP

20 Air Street
London, United Kingdom W1B 5AN
Phone: 442075344700
Fax: 442075344701
E-mail: info@generationim.com
Website: www.generationim.com

Other Offices

One Bryant Park
48th Floor
New York, NY USA 10036
Phone: 212-584-3650
Fax: 212-584-3652

Ugland House
P.O. Box 309
Grand Cayman, Cayman Islands KY1-1104
Phone: 44-207-534-4700

29 Chifley Tower
2 Chifley Square
Sydney, Australia 2000
Phone: 61-2-9375-2243
Fax: 61-2-9375-2121

Management and Staff
David Blood, Managing Partner
Peter Harris, Chief Operating Officer

Type of Firm
Private Equity Firm

Project Preferences

Type of Financing Preferred:
Early Stage
Expansion
Balanced

Geographical Preferences

International Preferences:
Cayman Islands
Africa

Industry Preferences

In Industrial/Energy prefer:
Energy
Alternative Energy
Energy Conservation Relat

In Other prefer:
Environment Responsible

Additional Information
Year Founded: 2004
Current Activity Level : Actively seeking new investments

GENERATION PARTNERS LP

Two Lafayette Court
Greenwich, CT USA 06830
Phone: 2034228215
Website: www.generation.com

Other Offices

9606 North Mopac Express Way
Austin, TX USA 78759
Phone: 2034228200
Fax: 2034228250

One Maritime Plaza
Suite 1555
San Francisco, CA USA 94111
Phone: 415-646-8620
Fax: 415-646-8625

Management and Staff
Andrew Hertzmark, Managing Partner
Andrew Hertzmark, Partner

Type of Firm
Private Equity Firm

Project Preferences

Role in Financing:
Prefer role as deal originator but will also invest in deals created by others

Type of Financing Preferred:
Leveraged Buyout
Expansion
Generalist PE
Balanced
Acquisition

Size of Investments Considered:
Min Size of Investment Considered (000s): $10,000
Max Size of Investment Considered (000s): $40,000

Industry Focus
(% based on actual investment)
Internet Specific	75.6%
Consumer Related	8.4%
Communications and Media	6.5%
Medical/Health	5.8%
Computer Software and Services	2.0%
Semiconductors/Other Elect.	1.4%
Other Products	0.3%

Additional Information
Name of Most Recent Fund: Generation Capital Partners Donuts, L.P.
Most Recent Fund Was Raised: 05/07/2012
Year Founded: 1995
Capital Under Management: $350,000,000
Current Activity Level : Actively seeking new investments
Method of Compensation: Return on invest. most important, but chg. closing fees, service fees, etc.

GENERIS CAPITAL PARTNERS SAS

8 Rue Montesquieu
Paris, France 75001
Phone: 33149260310
Fax: 33149263031
E-mail: generis@generiscapital.com
Website: www.generiscapital.com

Management and Staff
Philippe Charquet, Managing Partner
Thibaut De Roux, Managing Partner

Type of Firm
Private Equity Firm

Association Membership
French Venture Capital Association (AFIC)

Project Preferences

Type of Financing Preferred:
Early Stage
Public Companies
Later Stage
Seed

Geographical Preferences

United States Preferences:
All U.S.

International Preferences:
United Kingdom
Luxembourg
Europe
Netherlands
Scandanavia/Nordic Region
Belgium
Asia
Germany
France

Industry Preferences

In Communications prefer:
Communications and Media
Commercial Communications

In Internet Specific prefer:
Ecommerce

In Medical/Health prefer:
Medical/Health
Health Services
Hospitals/Clinics/Primary

In Industrial/Energy prefer:
Energy
Industrial Products
Environmental Related

In Business Serv. prefer:
Services

In Other prefer:
Environment Responsible

Additional Information

Year Founded: 2008
Capital Under Management: $56,760,000
Current Activity Level: Actively seeking new investments

GENERO CAPITAL LLC

8th Floor, Shangri-La Hotel
Sheikh Zayed Road
Dubai, Utd. Arab Em.
Phone: 97143546311
Fax: 97143546312
E-mail: Info@genero.ae
Website: genero.ae

Type of Firm
Private Equity Firm

Project Preferences

Type of Financing Preferred:
Early Stage
Seed
Acquisition

Geographical Preferences

International Preferences:
Egypt
Utd. Arab Em.
Middle East
Africa

Industry Preferences

In Computer Software prefer:
Software

In Consumer Related prefer:
Food/Beverage
Education Related

In Financial Services prefer:
Real Estate
Investment Groups

Additional Information

Year Founded: 2011
Current Activity Level: Actively seeking new investments

GENESIS ANGELS

45 Broadway Manhattan
New York, NY USA 10006
Website: genesisangels.com

Other Offices
One St. Peters Square
St Petersburg
Moscow, Russia

One Regents Street
London, United Kingdom

Hilazon Five
Third Floor
Ramat Gan, Israel

Management and Staff
Kenges Rakishev, Co-Founder
Moshe Hogeg, Co-Founder

Type of Firm
Private Equity Firm

Project Preferences

Type of Financing Preferred:
Early Stage
Seed
Startup

Size of Investments Considered:
Min Size of Investment Considered (000s): $200
Max Size of Investment Considered (000s): $2,000

Industry Preferences

In Industrial/Energy prefer:
Robotics

Additional Information
Year Founded: 2013
Current Activity Level: Actively seeking new investments

GENESIS CAPITAL ADVISORS LLC

3414 Peachtree Road NE
Suite 700
Atlanta, GA USA 30326
Phone: 4048167540
Fax: 4048167553
E-mail: info@genesis-capital.com
Website: www.gencappartners.com

Type of Firm
Private Equity Advisor or Fund of Funds

Project Preferences

Type of Financing Preferred:
Early Stage

Geographical Preferences

United States Preferences:

Additional Information
Year Founded: 2003
Current Activity Level: Actively seeking new investments

GENESIS CAPITAL CONSULTING & MANAGEMENT LTD

No. 1 East Chang An Ave,
Suite 1907/08, Tower E1
Beijing, China 100022
Phone: 861085188998
Fax: 861085189998
Website: www.genesis-cap.com

Other Offices
Former HQ: 20/F, Rouy Chai Int'l Bldg.
No. 8 Yong An Dongli
Beijing, China 100022
Phone: 861085288998
Fax: 861085288890

Suite 3008, 30/F One Int'l Finance Ctr.
1 Harbour View Street Central
Hong Kong, Hong Kong
Phone: 852-2295-1120
Fax: 852-2295-1121

Management and Staff
Pu Zhang, Managing Director
Stan Yue, Managing Director

Type of Firm
Private Equity Firm

Association Membership
Venture Capital Association of Beijing (VCAB)

Project Preferences

Type of Financing Preferred:
Early Stage
Balanced
Startup

Geographical Preferences

International Preferences:
China

Industry Preferences

In Communications prefer:
Telecommunications

In Consumer Related prefer:
Consumer Products

In Industrial/Energy prefer:
Alternative Energy

In Business Serv. prefer:
Services

In Manufact. prefer:
Manufacturing

Additional Information

Year Founded: 2000
Current Activity Level : Actively seeking new investments

GENESIS CAPITAL SRO

Na Safrance 22
Prague, Czech Republic 101 00
Phone: 420271740207
Fax: 420271740208
E-mail: genesis@genesis.cz
Website: www.genesis.cz

Management and Staff

Jan Tauber, Managing Partner
Marek Hoscalek, Partner
Ondrej Vicar, Partner
Radan Hanzl, Partner
Radim Jasek, Partner

Type of Firm

Private Equity Firm

Association Membership

Czech Venture Capital Association (CVCA)

Project Preferences

Role in Financing:
Prefer role as deal originator but will also invest in deals created by others

Type of Financing Preferred:
Leveraged Buyout
Early Stage
Expansion
Generalist PE
Balanced
Later Stage
Management Buyouts
Acquisition

Size of Investments Considered:
Min Size of Investment Considered (000s): $2,673
Max Size of Investment Considered (000s): $12,027

Geographical Preferences

International Preferences:
Slovak Repub.
Czech Republic
Eastern Europe

Industry Preferences

In Communications prefer:
Communications and Media

In Consumer Related prefer:
Consumer Products

In Industrial/Energy prefer:
Energy

In Manufact. prefer:
Manufacturing

Additional Information

Name of Most Recent Fund: Genesis Private Equity Fund
Most Recent Fund Was Raised: 02/07/2003
Year Founded: 1999
Capital Under Management: $133,600,000
Current Activity Level : Actively seeking new investments

GENESIS FINANCIAL SERVICES FUND LLC

7244 South Perth Way
Aurora, CO USA 80016
Phone: 3032567604
Website: genesisfinancialfund.com

Management and Staff

Edward Sondker, Co-Founder
Leon Parma, Co-Founder
Matthew Carpenter, Co-Founder

Type of Firm

Private Equity Firm

Project Preferences

Type of Financing Preferred:
Mezzanine
Management Buyouts
Recapitalizations

Size of Investments Considered:
Min Size of Investment Considered (000s): $1,000
Max Size of Investment Considered (000s): $3,000

Industry Preferences

In Financial Services prefer:
Financial Services

Additional Information

Year Founded: 2007
Capital Under Management: $5,970,000
Current Activity Level : Actively seeking new investments

GENESIS PARK, L.P.

2131 San Felipe
Houston, TX USA 77019
Phone: 7135211980
E-mail: info@genesis-park.com
Website: www.genesis-park.com

Management and Staff

Cathy Leeson, Chief Financial Officer
Neil Kelley, Founding Partner
Peter Shaper, Founding Partner
Steven Gibson, Founding Partner

Type of Firm

Private Equity Firm

Project Preferences

Role in Financing:
Prefer role as deal originator but will also invest in deals created by others

Type of Financing Preferred:
Leveraged Buyout
Early Stage
Generalist PE
Balanced
Later Stage
Acquisition

Geographical Preferences

United States Preferences:
Texas

Industry Preferences

In Communications prefer:
Telecommunications

In Computer Software prefer:
Software

In Industrial/Energy prefer:
Energy

In Business Serv. prefer:
Media

Additional Information

Name of Most Recent Fund: Genesis Park Ventures
Most Recent Fund Was Raised: 03/01/2000
Year Founded: 2000
Capital Under Management: $27,000,000
Current Activity Level : Actively seeking new investments
Method of Compensation: Return on investment is of primary concern, do not charge fees

GENESIS PARTNERS LTD

11 HaMenofim Street
Ackerstein, Bldg B, 4th Floor
Herzliya Pituach, Israel 46733
Phone: 97299729000
Fax: 97299729001
Website: www.genesispartners.com

Other Offices

Ackerstein Towers, Building B
11 Hamenofim Street, 4th Floor
Herzliya Pituach, Israel

Management and Staff

Eddy Shalev, Co-Founder
Eden Shochat, General Partner
Eyal Kishon, Co-Founder
Gary Gannot, General Partner
Jonathan Saacks, General Partner
Roi Bar-Kat, Principal

Type of Firm

Private Equity Firm

Association Membership

Israel Venture Association

Project Preferences

Type of Financing Preferred:
Early Stage
Balanced
Seed
Startup

Size of Investments Considered:
Min Size of Investment Considered (000s): $2,000
Max Size of Investment Considered (000s): $6,000

Geographical Preferences

International Preferences:
Middle East
Israel

Industry Focus

(% based on actual investment)
Computer Software and Services	39.5%
Semiconductors/Other Elect.	22.6%
Communications and Media	17.7%
Industrial/Energy	9.2%
Internet Specific	8.6%
Other Products	1.1%
Medical/Health	1.0%
Biotechnology	0.4%

Additional Information

Name of Most Recent Fund: Genesis Partners III, L.P.
Most Recent Fund Was Raised: 03/29/2005
Year Founded: 1996
Capital Under Management: $618,000,000
Current Activity Level : Actively seeking new investments

GENESYS CAPITAL PARTNERS INC

123 Front Street West
Suite 1503 PO Box 34
Toronto, Canada M5J 2M2
Phone: 4165984900
Fax: 4165983328
E-mail: info@genesyscapital.com
Website: www.genesyscapital.com

Management and Staff

Damian Lamb, Managing Director
Damian Lamb, Co-Founder
Jamie Stiff, Partner
Kelly Holman, Managing Director
Kelly Holman, Co-Founder
Kent Plumley, Partner

Type of Firm

Private Equity Firm

Association Membership

Canadian Venture Capital Association

Project Preferences

Type of Financing Preferred:
Early Stage
Expansion
Seed
Startup

Geographical Preferences

Canadian Preferences:
All Canada
Ontario

Industry Preferences

In Biotechnology prefer:
Biotech Related Research

In Medical/Health prefer:
Medical Products

Additional Information

Year Founded: 2001
Capital Under Management: $90,000,000
Current Activity Level : Actively seeking new investments

GENEVA VENTURE GROUP INC

50 California Street
Suite 1500
San Francisco, CA USA 94111
Phone: 4154334646
Fax: 4154336635
E-mail: info@genevagroup.com
Website: www.genevagroup.com

Management and Staff

Igor Sill, Managing Director
Robert Troy, General Partner

Type of Firm

Private Equity Firm

Project Preferences

Type of Financing Preferred:
Fund of Funds
Early Stage
Generalist PE
Seed
Startup

Geographical Preferences

United States Preferences:
California

Industry Focus

(% based on actual investment)
Computer Software and Services	35.0%
Communications and Media	22.3%
Biotechnology	19.3%
Internet Specific	14.1%
Other Products	6.2%
Industrial/Energy	3.1%

Additional Information

Year Founded: 1983
Current Activity Level : Actively seeking new investments

GENIUS VENTURE CAPITAL GMBH

Hagenower Strasse 73
Schwerin, Germany 19061
Phone: 493853993500
Fax: 493853993510
E-mail: info@genius-vc.de
Website: www.genius-vc.de

Management and Staff

Uwe Braeuer, Managing Director

Type of Firm

Private Equity Firm

Association Membership

German Venture Capital Association (BVK)

Project Preferences

Type of Financing Preferred:
Early Stage
Seed
Startup

Size of Investments Considered:
Min Size of Investment Considered (000s): $136
Max Size of Investment Considered (000s): $2,046

Geographical Preferences

International Preferences:
Germany

Industry Preferences

In Communications prefer:
Communications and Media

In Biotechnology prefer:
Biotechnology

In Medical/Health prefer:
Medical/Health

In Industrial/Energy prefer:
Advanced Materials

Additional Information

Year Founded: 1998
Current Activity Level : Actively seeking new investments

GENNEXT INNOVATION HUB

Reliance Corporate Park
Ghansoli
Mumbai, India 400701
E-mail: innovation.hub@gennextventures.com
Website: www.gennexthub.com

Type of Firm
Incubator/Development Program

Project Preferences

Type of Financing Preferred:
Seed
Startup

Industry Preferences

In Communications prefer:
Communications and Media
Telecommunications
Entertainment

In Computer Software prefer:
Software

In Internet Specific prefer:
Internet

In Medical/Health prefer:
Medical/Health

In Consumer Related prefer:
Education Related

In Other prefer:
Environment Responsible

Additional Information

Year Founded: 2014
Current Activity Level : Actively seeking new investments

GENNX360 CAPITAL PARTNERS LP

590 Madison Avenue
27th Floor
New York, NY USA 10022
Phone: 8882156992
Fax: 2125726472
E-mail: info@gennx360.com
Website: www.gennx360.com

Other Offices

701 Fifth Avenue
42nd Floor
Seattle, WA USA 98104

Prateek Park, Ring Road,
Bangalore, India 561229

245 First Street
Suite 1800
Cambridge, MA USA 02142

DLF City, PhaseV
Churchill, 2nd Floor, Sector 53, Gurgaon
Haryana, India 122002
Phone: 91-124-402-3047

Management and Staff

Charles Castine, Partner
Chris Allen, Vice President
James Shepard, Managing Partner
Lloyd Trotter, Managing Partner
Matthew Guenther, Partner
Monty Yort, Managing Partner
Mukesh Sawlani, Managing Director
Neil Schaefer, Vice President
Rahul Mahajan, Managing Director
Rena Clark, Partner
Rishi Verma, Managing Director
Ronald Blaylock, Managing Partner
Sumit Tony, Chief Financial Officer
W. Andrew Shea, Managing Partner

Type of Firm
Private Equity Firm

Association Membership
Natl Assoc of Investment Cos. (NAIC)

Project Preferences

Type of Financing Preferred:
Leveraged Buyout

Geographical Preferences

International Preferences:
All International

Industry Preferences

In Industrial/Energy prefer:
Industrial Products
Materials

In Transportation prefer:
Transportation
Aerospace

In Business Serv. prefer:
Services

In Manufact. prefer:
Manufacturing

In Agr/Forestr/Fish prefer:
Agriculture related

Additional Information

Name of Most Recent Fund: GenNx360 Capital Partners II, L.P.
Most Recent Fund Was Raised: 08/26/2013
Year Founded: 2006
Capital Under Management: $535,000,000
Current Activity Level : Actively seeking new investments

GENOME CANADA

150 Metcalfe Street
Suite 2100
Ottawa, Canada K2P 1P1
Phone: 6137514460
Fax: 6137514474
E-mail: info@genomecanada.ca
Website: www.genomecanada.ca

Management and Staff

Dale Patterson, Vice President
Jacques Guerette, Vice President
Karl Tibelius, Vice President

Type of Firm
Government Affiliated Program

Additional Information

Year Founded: 2013
Current Activity Level : Actively seeking new investments

GENSPRING HOLDINGS INC

3801 P.G.A. Boulevard
Suite 555
Palm Beach Gardens, FL USA 33410
Phone: 5617468444

Type of Firm
Private Equity Advisor or Fund of Funds

Project Preferences

Type of Financing Preferred:
Fund of Funds

Additional Information

Name of Most Recent Fund: AMA Eagle Private Equity Fund, L.P.
Most Recent Fund Was Raised: 08/09/2005
Year Founded: 1988
Current Activity Level : Actively seeking new investments

GENSTAR CAPITAL LLC

Four Embarcadero Center
Suite 1900
San Francisco, CA USA 94111
Phone: 4158342350
Fax: 4158342383
E-mail: info@gencap.com
Website: www.gencap.com

Management and Staff

Anthony Salewski, Principal
Benjamin Marshall, Principal
David Golde, Vice President
Eli Weiss, Principal
J. Ryan Clark, President
James Nadauld, Principal
Katie Solomon, Managing Director
Mark Hanson, Managing Director
Rob Rutledge, Principal
Robert Weltman, Managing Director
Roman Margolin, Vice President

Type of Firm

Private Equity Firm

Association Membership

Private Equity Council (PEC)

Project Preferences

Role in Financing:
Prefer role as deal originator but will also invest in deals created by others

Type of Financing Preferred:
Leveraged Buyout
Later Stage
Management Buyouts
Acquisition
Recapitalizations

Geographical Preferences

United States Preferences:
North America

Canadian Preferences:
All Canada

Industry Focus

(% based on actual investment)
Other Products 53.5%
Computer Software and Services 24.5%
Medical/Health 13.4%
Industrial/Energy 4.8%
Biotechnology 2.1%
Communications and Media 1.6%

Additional Information

Year Founded: 1988
Capital Under Management: $810,800,000
Current Activity Level : Actively seeking new investments
Method of Compensation: Return on invest. most important, but chg. closing fees, service fees, etc.

GENTRY VENTURE PARTNERS

205 North Michigan Avenue
Suite 3770
Chicago, IL USA 60601
Phone: 3125527160
Fax: 3125527161

Type of Firm

Private Equity Firm

Industry Preferences

In Industrial/Energy prefer:
Energy

In Other prefer:
Environment Responsible

Additional Information

Year Founded: 2006
Capital Under Management: $50,000,000
Current Activity Level : Actively seeking new investments

GENUI GMBH

Neuer Wall 80
Hamburg, Germany 20354
Phone: 494032086690
Fax: 4940320866980
E-mail: sg@genui.de
Website: www.genui.de

Type of Firm

Private Equity Firm

Project Preferences

Type of Financing Preferred:
Early Stage
Expansion
Balanced
Later Stage
Seed
Startup

Geographical Preferences

International Preferences:
Switzerland
Austria
Germany

Industry Preferences

In Consumer Related prefer:
Retail

Additional Information

Year Founded: 2014
Current Activity Level : Actively seeking new investments

GENUINE STARTUPS KK

2-10-7, Dogenzaka
1020, Shin Otsu Bldg. 2
Tokyo, Japan 150-0043
Website: genuine-startups.com

Management and Staff

Kanako Inoue, Vice President
Kengo Ito, Co-Founder
Makoto Takano, Co-Founder
Mamoru Taniya, Co-Founder
Masahisa Kido, Vice President

Type of Firm

Incubator/Development Program

Project Preferences

Type of Financing Preferred:
Early Stage

Additional Information

Year Founded: 2012
Current Activity Level : Actively seeking new investments

GEO INVESTMENT CO LTD

2nd Floor, Samsung Fire
1329-3, Seocho-dong, Seocho-ku
Seoul, South Korea
Phone: 82-2-523-0256
Fax: 82-2-523-0618

Type of Firm

Corporate PE/Venture

Project Preferences

Type of Financing Preferred:
Early Stage
Seed

Geographical Preferences

International Preferences:
Asia

Industry Preferences

In Semiconductor/Electr prefer:
Semiconductor

In Biotechnology prefer:
Biotechnology

Additional Information
Year Founded: 1996
Current Activity Level : Actively seeking new investments

GEODESIC CAPITAL

950 Tower Lane
Suite 1100
Palo Alto, CA USA 94304
Phone: 6507810400
Website: www.geodesiccap.com

Type of Firm
Private Equity Firm

Industry Preferences

In Consumer Related prefer:
Consumer

Additional Information
Year Founded: 2015
Capital Under Management: $335,000,000
Current Activity Level : Actively seeking new investments

GEORGETOWN VENTURE PARTNERS

123-125 Ladbroke Road
11 Mead House
London, United Kingdom W11 3PU
Phone: 44-20-7373-4823
Fax: 801-681-3604
E-mail: inquiries@georgetownventures.com
Website: www.georgetownventures.com

Management and Staff
Andrew Romans, Managing Partner
John Cusick, Managing Partner
Ronald Tetteroo, Managing Partner

Type of Firm
Private Equity Firm

Project Preferences

Type of Financing Preferred:
Expansion

Size of Investments Considered:
Min Size of Investment Considered (000s): $5,000
Max Size of Investment Considered (000s): $50,000

Geographical Preferences

United States Preferences:

Canadian Preferences:
All Canada

International Preferences:
United Kingdom
Europe

Industry Preferences

In Communications prefer:
Communications and Media

Additional Information
Year Founded: 2004
Current Activity Level : Actively seeking new investments

GEORGIA OAK PARTNERS LLC

3223 Paces Ferry Pl Northwest
Atlanta, GA USA 30305
Phone: 4049617201
E-mail: info@georgiaoakpartners.com
Website: www.georgiaoakpartners.com

Management and Staff
A. Frazier, President
A.D. Frazier, President
Michael Lonergan, Co-Founder

Type of Firm
Private Equity Firm

Project Preferences

Role in Financing:
Other

Type of Financing Preferred:
Leveraged Buyout
Expansion
Turnaround
Management Buyouts
Acquisition
Special Situation
Recapitalizations

Geographical Preferences

United States Preferences:
Southeast

Industry Preferences

In Consumer Related prefer:
Consumer Products
Consumer Services
Other Restaurants

In Industrial/Energy prefer:
Industrial Products
Materials
Environmental Related

In Transportation prefer:
Transportation

In Business Serv. prefer:
Services
Distribution

In Manufact. prefer:
Manufacturing

Additional Information
Year Founded: 2011
Current Activity Level : Actively seeking new investments

GEORGIAN PARTNERS GROWTH FUND FOUNDERS INTERNATIONAL I LP

Two St Clair Avenue West
Suite 1400
Toronto, Canada M4V 1L5
Phone: 4168689696
Fax: 4168681514
E-mail: info@georgianpartners.com

Other Offices
Eight Price Street
Third Floor
Toronto, Canada M4W 1Z4
Phone: 416-868-9696
Fax: 416-868-1514

Management and Staff
John Berton, Managing Partner
Justin LaFayette, Managing Partner
Simon Chong, Managing Partner
Steve Leightell, Principal
Tyson Baber, Principal

Type of Firm
Private Equity Firm

Association Membership
Canadian Venture Capital Association

Project Preferences

Type of Financing Preferred:
Expansion
Later Stage
Acquisition

Geographical Preferences

Canadian Preferences:
All Canada
Ontario

Industry Preferences

In Communications prefer:
Communications and Media
Media and Entertainment

In Computer Software prefer:
Software

In Internet Specific prefer:
Internet

Additional Information
Name of Most Recent Fund: Georgian Partners Growth Fund II, L.P.
Most Recent Fund Was Raised: 02/11/2014
Year Founded: 2008
Capital Under Management: $545,800,000
Current Activity Level : Actively seeking new investments

GERA VENTURE CAPITAL

Avenida Epitacio Pessoa 1674
Ipanema
Rio de Janeiro, Brazil 22411071
Phone: 552132028862
Fax: 552132028850
Website: www.geraventure.com.br

Type of Firm
Private Equity Firm

Project Preferences

Type of Financing Preferred:
Early Stage
Balanced

Geographical Preferences

International Preferences:
Brazil

Industry Preferences

In Consumer Related prefer:
Education Related

Additional Information
Year Founded: 2013
Current Activity Level : Actively seeking new investments

GERBERA CAPITAL ASESORES SC

Pasec de las Palmas 1715
Lomas de Chapultepec
Mexico Distrito Federal, Mexico 11000
Phone: 5552515332
E-mail: contacto@gerberacapital.com
Website: www.gerberacapital.com

Other Offices
Paseo Lomas Atlas 4520
Col. Lomas Atlas
Zapopan, Jalisco, Mexico 45128
Phone: 3312010154
Fax: 3312010154

Management and Staff
Alejandra Gaona Sanchez, Founder
Alonso B. Diaz Etienne, Managing Partner
Israel Zavala Resendiz, Vice President
Raul A. Uranga Lamadrid, Managing Partner

Type of Firm
Private Equity Firm

Project Preferences

Type of Financing Preferred:
Balanced

Size of Investments Considered:
Min Size of Investment Considered (000s): $3,000
Max Size of Investment Considered (000s): $10,000

Geographical Preferences

International Preferences:
Mexico

Additional Information
Year Founded: 2012
Current Activity Level : Actively seeking new investments

GERKEN CAPITAL ASSOCIATES

110 Tiburon Boulevard
Suite Five
Mill Valley, CA USA 94941
Phone: 4153831464
Fax: 4153831253
E-mail: info@gerkencapital.com
Website: www.gerkencapital.com

Type of Firm
Private Equity Firm

Project Preferences

Type of Financing Preferred:
Fund of Funds
Leveraged Buyout
Early Stage
Expansion
Mezzanine
Balanced
Later Stage
Acquisition
Distressed Debt

Geographical Preferences

United States Preferences:

International Preferences:
India
Europe
China
Middle East
Brazil
Asia
Russia
Africa

Additional Information
Year Founded: 1989
Current Activity Level : Actively seeking new investments

GERMAN STARTUPS GROUP BERLIN GMBH & CO KGAA

Platz der Luftbruecke 4-6
Berlin, Germany 12101
Phone: 4930609889080
Fax: 4930609889089
E-mail: info@german-startups.com
Website: www.german-startups.com

Management and Staff
Christoph Gerlinger, Chief Executive Officer
Nikolas Samios, Chief Operating Officer

Type of Firm
Private Equity Firm

Association Membership
German Venture Capital Association (BVK)
European Private Equity and Venture Capital Assoc.

Project Preferences

Type of Financing Preferred:
Early Stage
Expansion
Acquisition

Additional Information
Year Founded: 2011
Current Activity Level : Actively seeking new investments

GESTALT EQUITY PARTNERS

243 Queen Street West
Second Floor
Toronto, Canada M5V 1Z4
Website: www.gestaltequity.com

Type of Firm
Private Equity Firm

Project Preferences

Type of Financing Preferred:
Leveraged Buyout
Management Buyouts
Acquisition

Geographical Preferences

Canadian Preferences:
All Canada
Ontario

Additional Information

Year Founded: 2012
Current Activity Level : Actively seeking new investments

GESTION DE CAPITAL RIESGO DEL

Alameda de Urquijo, 36
Edif. Plaza Bizkaia, 2 planta
Bilbao, Spain 48011
Phone: 34944790192
Fax: 34944790050
E-mail: capitalriesgo@spri.es
Website: www.gestioncapitalriesgo.com

Management and Staff

Aitor Cobanera, Managing Director

Type of Firm

Private Equity Firm

Association Membership

Spanish Venture Capital Association (ASCRI)

Project Preferences

Type of Financing Preferred:
Leveraged Buyout
Early Stage
Expansion
Generalist PE
Balanced
Later Stage
Seed
Management Buyouts
Acquisition
Startup

Geographical Preferences

International Preferences:
Europe
Spain

Industry Preferences

In Communications prefer:
Communications and Media

In Computer Software prefer:
Software

In Internet Specific prefer:
Internet

In Semiconductor/Electr prefer:
Electronics
Fiber Optics

In Biotechnology prefer:
Biotechnology

In Medical/Health prefer:
Medical/Health

In Consumer Related prefer:
Entertainment and Leisure
Food/Beverage
Consumer Products
Consumer Services
Hotels and Resorts

In Industrial/Energy prefer:
Energy
Industrial Products
Materials
Environmental Related

In Transportation prefer:
Aerospace

In Financial Services prefer:
Financial Services

In Business Serv. prefer:
Media

In Manufact. prefer:
Manufacturing

In Agr/Forestr/Fish prefer:
Agriculture related

Additional Information

Year Founded: 1985
Capital Under Management: $885,200,000
Current Activity Level : Actively seeking new investments

GEVAERT SA

Septestraat 27
Mortsel, Belgium 2640
Phone: 3234442111
Fax: 3234447094
E-mail: directie@gevaert.be
Website: www.agfa.com

Management and Staff

Albert Follens, Vice President
Kris Hoornaert, Chief Financial Officer
Luc Delagaye, President
Stefaan Vanhooren, President

Type of Firm

Private Equity Firm

Project Preferences

Type of Financing Preferred:
Early Stage
Later Stage

Geographical Preferences

International Preferences:
Europe
Belgium

Additional Information

Year Founded: 2004
Current Activity Level : Actively seeking new investments

GF CAPITAL MANAGEMENT & ADVISORS LLC

767 Fifth Avenue
46th Floor
New York, NY USA 10153
Phone: 2124331234
Fax: 2124331239
E-mail: info@gfcap.com
Website: www.gfcap.com

Management and Staff

Erik Baker, Managing Director
James Taussig, Managing Director
Neil Shapiro, Managing Director
William Kahane, Managing Director

Type of Firm

Private Equity Firm

Project Preferences

Type of Financing Preferred:
Leveraged Buyout
Value-Add
Opportunistic
Acquisition
Recapitalizations

Industry Preferences

In Communications prefer:
Telecommunications
Media and Entertainment

In Computer Software prefer:
Software

In Consumer Related prefer:
Consumer Products

In Financial Services prefer:
Real Estate

Additional Information

Name of Most Recent Fund: GF Capital Real Estate I, LLC
Most Recent Fund Was Raised: 04/26/2004
Year Founded: 2001
Current Activity Level : Actively seeking new investments

GF XINDE INVESTMENT MANAGEMENT CO LTD

38/F, Da Du Hui Square
No.183, Tianhebei Road
Guangzhou, China 510075
Phone: 86-20-87555888
Fax: 86-20-87553579
Website: www.gfinvestment.cn

Type of Firm
Investment Management Firm

Project Preferences

Type of Financing Preferred:
Leveraged Buyout
Balanced
Later Stage

Geographical Preferences

International Preferences:
China

Industry Preferences

In Communications prefer:
Telecommunications

In Medical/Health prefer:
Medical/Health

In Consumer Related prefer:
Retail
Consumer Products

In Industrial/Energy prefer:
Energy
Materials

In Business Serv. prefer:
Media

In Manufact. prefer:
Manufacturing

Additional Information
Year Founded: 2008
Capital Under Management: $317,768,000
Current Activity Level: Actively seeking new investments

GFH CAPITAL LTD

402, Level 4
Precinct Building 3, The Gate
Dubai, Utd. Arab Em.
Phone: 97143651500
Fax: 97143637324
E-mail: info@injazatcapital.com
Website: www.gcap.ae

Management and Staff
Declan Duff, Vice President
Fawzi Zeine, Principal
Morten Kvammen, Chief Operating Officer
Rami Bazzi, Vice President

Type of Firm
Private Equity Firm

Project Preferences

Type of Financing Preferred:
Leveraged Buyout
Early Stage
Generalist PE
Balanced
Seed
Acquisition
Startup

Geographical Preferences

International Preferences:
Utd. Arab Em.
Middle East

Industry Preferences

In Communications prefer:
Telecommunications

In Computer Software prefer:
Software
Systems Software
Applications Software

In Medical/Health prefer:
Medical/Health
Medical Diagnostics
Medical Therapeutics

In Consumer Related prefer:
Consumer
Food/Beverage
Consumer Products
Consumer Services
Other Restaurants

In Industrial/Energy prefer:
Energy
Oil and Gas Exploration
Oil & Gas Drilling,Explor
Alternative Energy
Industrial Products

In Financial Services prefer:
Financial Services
Insurance
Real Estate
Financial Services

In Business Serv. prefer:
Consulting Services

In Agr/Forestr/Fish prefer:
Agribusiness

Additional Information
Year Founded: 2001
Current Activity Level: Actively seeking new investments

GFH FINANCIAL GROUP BSC

Bahrain Financial Harbour
Manama, Bahrain
Phone: 97317538538
Fax: 97317540006
Website: www.gfh.com

Management and Staff
Chandan Gupta, Chief Financial Officer
Hisham Al Rayes, Chief Executive Officer

Type of Firm
Bank Affiliated

Project Preferences

Type of Financing Preferred:
Leveraged Buyout
Early Stage
Expansion
Generalist PE
Acquisition

Industry Preferences

In Industrial/Energy prefer:
Industrial Products

In Financial Services prefer:
Financial Services

Additional Information
Year Founded: 1999
Current Activity Level: Actively seeking new investments

GGV CAPITAL

3000 Sand Hill Road
Suite 230
Menlo Park, CA USA 94025
Phone: 6504752150
Fax: 6504752151
E-mail: info@ggvc.com
Website: www.ggvc.com

Other Offices

8 Century Avenue, Pudong District
Unit 3501, Two IFC
China
Phone: 86-21-6161-1717
Fax: 86-21-5403-5580

Suite 19, 9th Floor, China Central Place
79 Jianguo Road, Chaoyang District
China
Phone: 86-10-5920-4491
Fax: 86-10-5920-4492

1-3 Xinyuan South Road
Unit 2308, Tower A, Pingan International
Beijing, China 100027
Phone: 861059897988

Management and Staff

Bruce Yu, Partner
Crystal Huang, Vice President
Eric Xu, Managing Partner
Erica Yu, Vice President
Fumin Zhuo, Partner
Glenn Solomon, Managing Partner
Hans Tung, Managing Partner
Hany Nada, Managing Partner
Haojun Li, Vice President
Hong Wei Lee, Managing Partner
Jeff Richards, Managing Partner
Jenny Lee, Managing Partner
Jessie Jin, Partner
Jixun Foo, Managing Partner
Joel Kellman, Co-Founder
Joshua Wu, Vice President
Kheng Nam Lee, Venture Partner
Lei Sheng, Vice President
Mark Pols, Principal
Scott Bonham, Managing Partner
Stephen Hyndman, Chief Financial Officer
Terry Tian, Vice President

Type of Firm

Private Equity Firm

Association Membership

China Venture Capital Association
National Venture Capital Association - USA (NVCA)

Project Preferences

Role in Financing:
Will function either as deal originator or investor in deals created by others

Type of Financing Preferred:
Early Stage
Expansion
Balanced
Seed
First Stage Financing

Size of Investments Considered:
Min Size of Investment Considered (000s): $500
Max Size of Investment Considered (000s): $25,000

Geographical Preferences

United States Preferences:

International Preferences:
China

Industry Preferences

In Communications prefer:
Communications and Media
Wireless Communications

In Computer Software prefer:
Software
Applications Software

In Internet Specific prefer:
E-Commerce Technology
Internet
Ecommerce

In Medical/Health prefer:
Medical/Health

In Consumer Related prefer:
Consumer
Entertainment and Leisure

In Business Serv. prefer:
Media

Additional Information

Name of Most Recent Fund: GGV Capital IV, L.P.
Most Recent Fund Was Raised: 05/17/2011
Year Founded: 2000
Capital Under Management: $3,800,000,000
Current Activity Level : Actively seeking new investments
Method of Compensation: Return on investment is of primary concern, do not charge fees

GHO CAPITAL PARTNERS LLP

44 Davies Street
London, United Kingdom W1K 5JA
Phone: 442037007440
E-mail: enquiries@ghocapital.com
Website: ghocapital.com

Management and Staff

Alan Mackay, Co-Founder
Andrea Ponti, Co-Founder
Irina Haivas, Principal
Janine Nicholls, Chief Operating Officer
Ken Eichmann, Principal
Michael Mortimer, Co-Founder

Type of Firm

Private Equity Firm

Project Preferences

Type of Financing Preferred:
Leveraged Buyout
Expansion
Generalist PE

Industry Preferences

In Medical/Health prefer:
Medical/Health

Additional Information

Year Founded: 2013
Capital Under Management: $202,860,000
Current Activity Level : Actively seeking new investments

GI PARTNERS

188 The Embarcadero, Suite 700
San Francisco, CA USA 94105
Phone: 4156884800
Fax: 4156884801
E-mail: info@gipartners.com
Website: www.gipartners.com

Other Offices

Karl-Scharnagel-Ring 5
Munich, Germany 80539
Phone: 49-89-21568830
Fax: 49-89-21568249

150 S. Wacker Dr., Suite 1315
Chicago, IL USA 60606
Phone: 3126467880

35 Portman Square, Fifth Floor
London, United Kingdom W1H 6LR
Phone: 44-20-7034-1120
Fax: 44-20-7034-1156

283 Greenwich Avenue, Suite 300
Greenwich, CT USA 06830
Phone: 2036612000
Fax: 2036612008

Management and Staff

Achi Yaffe, Principal
Alexander Fraser, Managing Director
Alfred Foglio, Managing Director
Amin Hariri, Vice President
Brad Altberger, Managing Director
David Kreter, Vice President
Hoon Cho, Managing Director
Howard Park, Managing Director
John Saer, Managing Director
Mark Tagliaferri, Managing Director
Michael Wong, Vice President
Philip Kaziewicz, Managing Director
Philip Yau, Managing Director
Richard Magnuson, Managing Director
Roman Braslavsky, Vice President
Roy Kelvin, Chief Financial Officer
Tony Lin, Vice President

Type of Firm

Private Equity Firm

Project Preferences

Role in Financing:
Prefer role as deal originator

Type of Financing Preferred:
Core
Leveraged Buyout
Expansion
Generalist PE
Turnaround
Management Buyouts
Acquisition
Recapitalizations

Geographical Preferences

United States Preferences:
North America

International Preferences:
Europe

Industry Focus
(% based on actual investment)

Other Products	67.5%
Consumer Related	12.8%
Computer Software and Services	9.1%
Industrial/Energy	6.0%
Internet Specific	2.3%
Semiconductors/Other Elect.	2.3%

Additional Information
Name of Most Recent Fund: GI Partners Fund IV, L.P.
Most Recent Fund Was Raised: 01/03/2014
Year Founded: 2001
Capital Under Management: $3,900,700,000
Current Activity Level : Actively seeking new investments

GIBRALTAR & COMPANY

77 King Street West, 21st Flr
Toronto-Dominion Centre
Toronto, Canada M5K 1G8
Website: gibraltarcompany.ca

Type of Firm
Private Equity Firm

Project Preferences

Type of Financing Preferred:
Early Stage

Geographical Preferences

Canadian Preferences:
All Canada

Industry Preferences

In Consumer Related prefer:
Consumer

Additional Information
Year Founded: 2013
Capital Under Management: $12,000,000
Current Activity Level : Actively seeking new investments

GIC SPECIAL INVESTMENTS PTE LTD

168 Robinson Road
#37-01 Capital Tower
Singapore, Singapore 068912
Phone: 6568898888
Fax: 6568898722
E-mail: contactsi@gic.com.sg
Website: www.gic.com.sg

Other Offices

No. 1 Jian Guo Men Wai Avenue
Level 19, Unit 1828, China World Tower 1
Beijing, China 100004
Phone: 861065351010
Fax: 861065351078

335 Madison Avenue
24th Floor
New York, NY USA 10017
Phone: 6466582200
Fax: 6466582122

45 Seymoure Street
First & Second Floor, York House
London, United Kingdom W1H 7LX
Phone: 442077253888
Fax: 442077253506

84 Taepyungro 1-ga Chung-gu
Tenth Floor, Seoul Finance Center
Seoul, South Korea 100-768
Phone: 8227263300
Fax: 8227263318

1-5-2 Higashi-shimabashi Minato-ku
Tenth Floor, Shiodome City Center
Tokyo, Japan 105-7110
Phone: 81335727188
Fax: 81355372208

One Bush Street
Suite 1100
San Francisco, CA USA 94104
Phone: 4152291800
Fax: 4152291812

1233 Lujiazui Ring Road
Room 805, The Azia Centre
Shanghai, China
Phone: 862161651919
Fax: 862161651900

Av. Cidade Jardim, 803-Cj.
71,7 andar
Sao Paulo, Brazil 01453-000
Phone: 551135141600
Fax: 551135141601

Three North Avenue, Maker Maxity
8th Floor, Unit 83, Banda Kurla Complex
Mumbai, India 400051
Phone: 912261502888
Fax: 912261502850

255 Shoreline Drive
Suite 600
Redwood City, CA USA 94065
Phone: 6508021200
Fax: 6508021213

Management and Staff
Siong Guan S. Lim, President
Tay Lim Hock, President

Type of Firm
Government Affiliated Program

Association Membership
China Venture Capital Association
Singapore Venture Capital Association (SVCA)

Project Preferences

Type of Financing Preferred:
Leveraged Buyout
Early Stage
Mezzanine
Generalist PE
Balanced
Later Stage
Special Situation
Distressed Debt

Additional Information
Year Founded: 1982
Current Activity Level : Actively seeking new investments

GIDEON HIXON FUND LP

800 Ancapa Street
Suite A
Santa Barbara, CA USA 93101
Phone: 8059632277
Fax: 8055650929
Website: www.gideonhixonfund.com

Other Offices

315 East Commerce Street
Suite 300
San Antonio, TX USA 78205
Phone: 210-225-3053
Fax: 210-225-5910

Management and Staff
Benson Whitney, Managing Partner
Bryan Simpson, General Partner
Debra Geiger, General Partner
Dylan Hixon, General Partner
Eric Hixon, General Partner
Frank Foster, General Partner

Type of Firm
Private Equity Firm

Project Preferences

Role in Financing:
Prefer role as deal originator but will also invest in deals created by others

Type of Financing Preferred:
Early Stage
Balanced
Later Stage

Size of Investments Considered:
Min Size of Investment Considered (000s): $100
Max Size of Investment Considered (000s): $1,500

Geographical Preferences

United States Preferences:

Industry Focus
(% based on actual investment)
Internet Specific	29.8%
Biotechnology	29.2%
Medical/Health	23.0%
Computer Software and Services	9.0%
Other Products	3.6%
Industrial/Energy	3.3%
Semiconductors/Other Elect.	2.0%

Additional Information
Year Founded: 1989
Capital Under Management: $30,000,000
Current Activity Level : Actively seeking new investments
Method of Compensation: Return on investment is of primary concern, do not charge fees

GIFUSHIN SOGO FINANCE KK

7-66 Shikishima-cho
Gifu-shi, Japan 500-8369
Phone: 81-58-252-3130

Type of Firm
Bank Affiliated

Additional Information
Year Founded: 2007
Current Activity Level : Actively seeking new investments

GIGAFUND

1200 Seaport Boulevard
Redwood City, CA USA 94063
Phone: 6508140643
E-mail: info@gigafund.com
Website: www.gigafund.com

Type of Firm
Private Equity Firm

Project Preferences

Type of Financing Preferred:
Balanced

Additional Information
Year Founded: 2017
Current Activity Level : Actively seeking new investments

GILBERT GLOBAL EQUITY CAPITAL LLC

277 Park Avenue
49th Floor
New York, NY USA 10172
Phone: 2125846200
Fax: 2125846211
Website: www.gilbertglobal.com

Other Offices
P.O. Box 984
New Canaan, CT USA 06840
Phone: 203-966-6022
Fax: 203-972-0250

Management and Staff
Richard Gaenzle, Partner

Type of Firm
Private Equity Firm

Project Preferences

Type of Financing Preferred:
Leveraged Buyout
Expansion
Generalist PE
Balanced
Turnaround
Later Stage
Management Buyouts
Acquisition
Distressed Debt

Geographical Preferences

United States Preferences:

International Preferences:
Asia Pacific
Latin America
Europe
All International

Industry Focus
(% based on actual investment)
Other Products	42.0%
Communications and Media	25.0%
Semiconductors/Other Elect.	20.3%
Internet Specific	7.1%
Computer Software and Services	3.2%
Computer Hardware	1.5%
Consumer Related	0.8%

Additional Information
Name of Most Recent Fund: Gilbert Global Equity Partners, L.P.
Most Recent Fund Was Raised: 05/01/1999
Year Founded: 1997
Capital Under Management: $1,158,600,000
Current Activity Level : Actively seeking new investments

GILDE BUY OUT PARTNERS BV

Herculesplein 104
Utrecht, Netherlands 3584 AA
Phone: 31882202600
Fax: 31882202601
Website: www.gilde.com

Other Offices
69, Boulevard Haussmann
Paris, France 75008
Phone: 33140980515
Fax: 33140980518

Rue de la Regence 58
Brussels, Belgium 1000
Phone: 3225030627
Fax: 3225027336

Neue Rothofstrasse 19
Frankfurt, Germany 60313
Phone: 4969209767500

Seefeldstrasse 40
Zurich, Switzerland 8008
Phone: 41432682030
Fax: 41432682035

Management and Staff
Alexander Friedrich, Partner
Boudewijn Molenaar, Partner
Hein Ploegmakers, Partner
Martijn Schreurs, Partner
Maurits Boomsma, Partner
Nicolas Linkens, Partner
Nikolai Pronk, Partner
Paul A. Bekx, Partner
Ralph Wyss, Partner
Rogier Engelsma, Partner
Tom Muizers, Partner
, Partner

Type of Firm
Private Equity Firm

Association Membership
Belgium Venturing Association
German Venture Capital Association (BVK)
Dutch Venture Capital Associaton (NVP)

Project Preferences

Role in Financing:
Prefer role as deal originator

Type of Financing Preferred:
Leveraged Buyout
Mezzanine
Management Buyouts

Geographical Preferences

International Preferences:
Luxembourg
Europe
Netherlands
Austria
Belgium
Germany
France

GILDE EQUITY MANAGEMENT GEM BENELUX PARTNERS BV

Newtonlaan 91
P.O. Box 85067
Utrecht, Netherlands 3508 AB
Phone: 31302192555
Fax: 31302192575
E-mail: GEM@gilde.nl
Website: gembenelux.com

Management and Staff
Gerhard Nordemann, Managing Partner
Remko Jager, Managing Partner

Type of Firm
Private Equity Firm

Association Membership
Belgium Venturing Association
Dutch Venture Capital Associaton (NVP)

Project Preferences

Type of Financing Preferred:
Leveraged Buyout
Management Buyouts

Size of Investments Considered:
Min Size of Investment Considered (000s): $19,402
Max Size of Investment Considered (000s): $194,024

Geographical Preferences

International Preferences:
Luxembourg
Netherlands
Belgium

Additional Information
Year Founded: 2006
Capital Under Management: $643,257,000
Current Activity Level: Actively seeking new investments

GILDE HEALTHCARE PARTNERS BV

Newtonlaan 91
Utrecht, Netherlands 3584 BP
Phone: 31302192565
Fax: 31302192596
E-mail: healthcare@gilde.nl
Website: gildehealthcare.com

Other Offices
222 Third Street, Suite 1321
Cambridge, MA USA 02142

Management and Staff
Arthur Franken, Partner
Dirk Kersten, Partner
Edwin de Graaf, Managing Partner
Geoff Pardo, Partner
Janke Dittmer, Partner
Marc Perret, Managing Partner
Pieter van der Meer, Managing Partner

Type of Firm
Private Equity Firm

Association Membership
Dutch Venture Capital Associaton (NVP)
European Private Equity and Venture Capital Assoc.

Project Preferences

Type of Financing Preferred:
Leveraged Buyout
Early Stage
Balanced
Later Stage

Geographical Preferences

United States Preferences:
All U.S.

International Preferences:
Europe

Industry Preferences

In Medical/Health prefer:
Medical/Health
Medical Diagnostics
Diagnostic Services
Diagnostic Test Products
Medical Therapeutics
Other Therapeutic
Medical Products

Additional Information
Name of Most Recent Fund: Gilde Healthcare III
Most Recent Fund Was Raised: 10/13/2011
Year Founded: 1999
Capital Under Management: $381,000,000
Current Activity Level: Actively seeking new investments

GILDE INVESTMENT MANAGEMENT BV

Newtonlaan 91
P.O. Box 85067
Utrecht, Netherlands 3508 AB
Phone: 31302192525
Fax: 31302192575
E-mail: info@gilde.nl
Website: www.gilde.nl

Other Offices
Holbeinstrasse 31
Zurich, Switzerland 8008
Phone: 41432682030
Fax: 41432682035

69 Boulevard Haussmann
Haussmann
Paris, France 75008
Phone: 33140980515
Fax: 33140980518

Management and Staff
Boudewijn Molenaar, Managing Director
Dirk Kersten, Partner
Paul A. Bekx, Managing Director
Ralph Wyss, Managing Director
Remko A. Jager, Managing Partner
Robert Thole, Managing Director

Type of Firm
Private Equity Firm

Association Membership
Swiss Venture Capital Association (SECA)
Dutch Venture Capital Associaton (NVP)
European Private Equity and Venture Capital Assoc.

Project Preferences

Role in Financing:
Prefer role as deal originator but will also invest in deals created by others

Type of Financing Preferred:
Fund of Funds
Second Stage Financing
Leveraged Buyout
Early Stage
Mezzanine
Generalist PE
Balanced
Later Stage
Management Buyouts
First Stage Financing
Startup

Size of Investments Considered:
Min Size of Investment Considered (000s): $4,708
Max Size of Investment Considered (000s): $9,416

Geographical Preferences

United States Preferences:
All U.S.

Canadian Preferences:
All Canada

Additional Information
Year Founded: 1982
Capital Under Management: $1,817,400,000
Current Activity Level: Actively seeking new investments

International Preferences:
Italy
United Kingdom
Luxembourg
Europe
Netherlands
Bermuda
Middle East
Scandanavia/Nordic Region
Spain
Australia
Belgium
Israel
Germany
France

Industry Focus
(% based on actual investment)
Biotechnology	23.7%
Computer Software and Services	21.7%
Communications and Media	15.2%
Internet Specific	14.2%
Industrial/Energy	9.6%
Medical/Health	7.6%
Semiconductors/Other Elect.	3.2%
Other Products	2.6%
Computer Hardware	2.1%

Additional Information
Year Founded: 1982
Capital Under Management: $1,979,900,000
Current Activity Level : Actively seeking new investments
Method of Compensation: Return on invest. most important, but chg. closing fees, service fees, etc.

GILFUS VENTURE PARTNERS LLC

1050 Connecticut Avenue
Tenth Floor
Washington, DC USA 20036
Phone: 2026036035
Fax: 2023184328
E-mail: info@gilfusventures.com
Website: www.gilfusventurepartners.com

Other Offices
13800 Coppermine Road
Third Floor
Herndon, VA USA 20191

Management and Staff
Frank Ganis, General Partner
Stephen Gilfus, General Partner

Type of Firm
Private Equity Firm

Project Preferences

Type of Financing Preferred:
Early Stage

Industry Preferences

In Internet Specific prefer:
E-Commerce Technology

In Consumer Related prefer:
Education Related

In Business Serv. prefer:
Services

Additional Information
Year Founded: 1969
Current Activity Level : Actively seeking new investments

GIMAR CAPITAL INVESTISSEMENT SCA

9, Avenue de l'Opera
Paris, France 75001
Phone: 33155047100
Fax: 33155047104
E-mail: contact@gimar-finance.com

Management and Staff
Pierre Dauvillaire, Managing Partner

Type of Firm
Private Equity Advisor or Fund of Funds

Association Membership
French Venture Capital Association (AFIC)

Project Preferences

Type of Financing Preferred:
Fund of Funds

Geographical Preferences

International Preferences:
Europe
France

Industry Preferences

In Industrial/Energy prefer:
Energy
Oil & Gas Drilling,Explor

In Financial Services prefer:
Financial Services
Insurance
Real Estate

In Business Serv. prefer:
Media

Additional Information
Year Founded: 2005
Current Activity Level : Actively seeking new investments

GIMPO IND INVEST FUND MGMT CO

No. 68 Yin Cheng Central
Rm 4901,49/F One Lujiazui
Shanghai, China 200120
Phone: 862120329333
Fax: 8622120329222
E-mail: contact@gpcapital.com.cn
Website: www.gpcapital.com.cn

Management and Staff
Houjun Lv, Chief Executive Officer

Type of Firm
Government Affiliated Program

Project Preferences

Type of Financing Preferred:
Generalist PE

Geographical Preferences

International Preferences:
China

Industry Preferences

In Consumer Related prefer:
Consumer Products

In Industrial/Energy prefer:
Alternative Energy

In Financial Services prefer:
Financial Services
Insurance
Financial Services

In Manufact. prefer:
Manufacturing

In Agr/Forestr/Fish prefer:
Agriculture related
Mining and Minerals

Additional Information
Year Founded: 2009
Current Activity Level : Actively seeking new investments

GIMV ASIA MANAGEMENT PTE LTD

298 Tiong Bahru Rd.
#08-04 Central Plaza
Singapore, Singapore 168730
Phone: 65-6278-3881
Fax: 65-6278-3991
E-mail: info@gimv.com
Website: www.gimv.com

Type of Firm
Bank Affiliated

Project Preferences

Type of Financing Preferred:
Fund of Funds
Leveraged Buyout
Expansion
Balanced
Startup
Recapitalizations

Geographical Preferences

International Preferences:
Indonesia
Taiwan
Hong Kong
China
Thailand
Philippines
Asia
Singapore
Malaysia

Industry Preferences

In Communications prefer:
Communications and Media
Telecommunications

In Computer Software prefer:
Software
Applications Software

In Internet Specific prefer:
Internet

In Semiconductor/Electr prefer:
Semiconductor

In Consumer Related prefer:
Entertainment and Leisure
Food/Beverage
Consumer Products

In Business Serv. prefer:
Distribution
Media

Additional Information

Year Founded: 1999
Capital Under Management: $60,000,000
Current Activity Level : Actively seeking new investments

GIMV INVESTERING-SMAATSCHAPPIJ VOOR VLANDEREN NV

Karel Oomsstraat 37
Antwerp, Belgium 2018
Phone: 3232902100
Fax: 3232902105
E-mail: info@gimv.com
Website: www.gimv.com

Other Offices

38, Avenue Hoche
Paris, France 75008
Phone: 33-1-5836-4560

Lange Voorhout 9
The Hague, Netherlands 2514 EA
Phone: 31-70-361-8618
Fax: 31-70-361-8616

Barckhausstrasse 12-16
Frankfurt am Main, Germany 60325
Phone: 49-69-242-5330
Fax: 49-69-236-866

Promenadeplatz 12
Munich, Germany 80333
Phone: 498944232750

60 Cannon Street
London, United Kingdom EC4N 6NP
Phone: 44-20-7618-6428
Fax: 44-20-7618-8498

Management and Staff

Alex Brabers, Chief Operating Officer
Elderd Land, Partner
Geoffroy Dubus, Partner
Jim Van Heusden, Partner
Karl Naegler, Partner
Koen Dejonckheere, Chief Executive Officer
Kristof Vande Capelle, Chief Financial Officer
Manu Vandenbulcke, Managing Director
Patrick Van Beneden, Partner
Robert Gallenberger, Principal
Steven Coppens, Partner

Type of Firm

Private Equity Firm

Association Membership

Belgium Venturing Association
French Venture Capital Association (AFIC)
German Venture Capital Association (BVK)
Czech Venture Capital Association (CVCA)
Dutch Venture Capital Associaton (NVP)
European Private Equity and Venture Capital Assoc.

Project Preferences

Role in Financing:
Prefer role as deal originator but will also invest in deals created by others

Type of Financing Preferred:
Leveraged Buyout
Early Stage
Expansion
Balanced
Start-up Financing
Turnaround
Later Stage
Seed
Management Buyouts
Recapitalizations

Size of Investments Considered:

Min Size of Investment Considered (000s): $1,883
Max Size of Investment Considered (000s): $28,248

Geographical Preferences

United States Preferences:
All U.S.

International Preferences:
Central Europe
Europe
Western Europe
Eastern Europe
Russia
France

Industry Focus

(% based on actual investment)

Biotechnology	21.9%
Consumer Related	16.4%
Other Products	13.4%
Medical/Health	10.4%
Computer Software and Services	10.0%
Industrial/Energy	7.7%
Internet Specific	7.0%
Communications and Media	7.0%
Semiconductors/Other Elect.	4.8%
Computer Hardware	1.2%

Additional Information

Name of Most Recent Fund: Health & Care Fund
Most Recent Fund Was Raised: 02/27/2013
Year Founded: 1980
Capital Under Management: $1,138,300,000
Current Activity Level : Actively seeking new investments

GINKGO GROUP CO LTD

Yinhu Road
D1 Jinhu Villa
Shenzhen, China 518000
Phone: 8675583664444
Fax: 8675583663588
Website: www.ginkgo.net.cn

Management and Staff

Feng Zhang, Partner

Type of Firm

Private Equity Firm

Project Preferences

Type of Financing Preferred:
Expansion

Geographical Preferences

International Preferences:
China

Additional Information

Year Founded: 2003
Current Activity Level : Actively seeking new investments

GINKGO VENTURE CAPITAL MANAGEMENT BEIJING CO LTD

Tsinghua Tech Park, Haidian
Room 1702, Tower C, Tech Bldg
Beijing, China
Phone: 861082159800
Website: www.th-vc.com

Type of Firm
Corporate PE/Venture

Project Preferences

Type of Financing Preferred:
Early Stage
Seed
Startup

Geographical Preferences

International Preferences:
China

Additional Information
Year Founded: 2015
Capital Under Management: $725,270,000
Current Activity Level : Actively seeking new investments

GINKO VENTURES SARL

Avenue de Secheron 15
Geneva, Switzerland 1202
Phone: 41229104248
Website: www.ginkopartners.com

Type of Firm
Private Equity Firm

Project Preferences

Type of Financing Preferred:
Early Stage
Expansion
Later Stage
Seed
Startup

Geographical Preferences

International Preferences:
Europe
Israel

Industry Preferences

In Semiconductor/Electr prefer:
Electronics

Additional Information
Year Founded: 2014
Current Activity Level : Actively seeking new investments

GIZA VENTURE CAPITAL

40 Einstein Street
12th Floor, Ramat Aviv Tower
Tel Aviv, Israel 61175
Phone: 97236402323
Fax: 97236402319
Website: www.gizavc.com

Other Offices
Trakt Lubelski 40a
Warsaw, Poland 04870
Phone: 48222086242

Management and Staff
Eyal Niv, Managing Director
Ezer Soref, Venture Partner
Haim Shechter, Co-Founder
Moshe Nazarathy, Venture Partner
Ori Kirshner, Managing Partner
Shmuel Chafets, Venture Partner
Shuki Ehrlich, Venture Partner
Yuval Avni, Partner

Type of Firm
Private Equity Firm

Project Preferences

Role in Financing:
Prefer role as deal originator

Type of Financing Preferred:
Early Stage
Balanced
Seed

Geographical Preferences

International Preferences:
Israel

Industry Focus
(% based on actual investment)
Computer Software and Services	28.2%
Medical/Health	20.6%
Semiconductors/Other Elect.	18.0%
Internet Specific	16.9%
Communications and Media	7.9%
Computer Hardware	5.0%
Biotechnology	3.4%

Additional Information
Year Founded: 1992
Capital Under Management: $316,000,000
Current Activity Level : Actively seeking new investments
Method of Compensation: Return on investment is of primary concern, do not charge fees

---

GKL GROWTH CAPITAL AB

Engelbrektsplan 2
Box 55643
Stockholm, Sweden 102 14
Phone: 46-8-679-4451
Fax: 46-8-679-4499
Website: www.gklcapital.se

Management and Staff
Karl-Magnus Karlsson, Partner
Lars Guldstrand, Partner
Peter Lindh, Partner

Type of Firm
Private Equity Firm

Project Preferences

Type of Financing Preferred:
Balanced

Geographical Preferences

International Preferences:
Scandanavia/Nordic Region

Industry Preferences

In Communications prefer:
Media and Entertainment

In Industrial/Energy prefer:
Industrial Products
Environmental Related

Additional Information
Year Founded: 2009
Current Activity Level : Actively seeking new investments

GKM NEWPORT GENERATION FUNDS

11150 Santa Monica Boulevard
Suite 825
Los Angeles, CA USA 90025
Phone: 310-268-2650
Fax: 310-268-0870
Website: www.gkmnewport.com

Management and Staff
Anthony Rust, Managing Director
Diane Peek, Managing Director
Erica Bushner, Managing Director
Jeff Scheinrock, Managing Director
Jonathan Bloch, Managing Director

Type of Firm
Private Equity Advisor or Fund of Funds

Project Preferences

Type of Financing Preferred:
Fund of Funds

Additional Information
Name of Most Recent Fund: GKM Newport/NY Venture Capital Fund, L.P.
Most Recent Fund Was Raised: 11/29/2004
Year Founded: 2002
Capital Under Management: $39,000,000
Current Activity Level : Actively seeking new investments

GLADE BROOK CAPITAL LLC

80 Field Point Road
Greenwich, CT USA 06830
Phone: 2038613000
Fax: 2038613050
Website: www.gladebrookcapital.com

Type of Firm
Investment Management Firm

Project Preferences

Type of Financing Preferred:
Generalist PE

Industry Preferences

In Communications prefer:
Telecommunications

In Consumer Related prefer:
Consumer

In Business Serv. prefer:
Media

Additional Information
Year Founded: 2016
Capital Under Management: $174,790,000
Current Activity Level : Actively seeking new investments

GLADSTONE INVESTMENT CORP

1521 Westbranch Drive
Suite 200
McLean, VA USA 22102
Phone: 7032875893
E-mail: info@gladstonecompanies.com
Website: ir.gladstoneinvestment.com

Management and Staff
Nicole Schaltenbrand, Chief Financial Officer

Type of Firm
Investment Management Firm

Association Membership
Natl Assoc of Small Bus. Inv. Co (NASBIC)

Project Preferences

Type of Financing Preferred:
Core
Leveraged Buyout
Expansion
Mezzanine
Generalist PE
Acquisition
Recapitalizations

Geographical Preferences

United States Preferences:

Industry Preferences

In Financial Services prefer:
Real Estate

In Agr/Forestr/Fish prefer:
Agriculture related

Additional Information
Year Founded: 2005
Current Activity Level : Actively seeking new investments

GLASSWING VENTURES LLC

33 Arch Street
20th Floor
Boston, MA USA 02110
Website: www.glasswing.vc

Type of Firm
Private Equity Firm

Project Preferences

Type of Financing Preferred:
Early Stage

Industry Preferences

In Computer Software prefer:
Artificial Intelligence

Additional Information
Year Founded: 2016
Current Activity Level : Actively seeking new investments

GLC MERCHANT BANKING

805 Third Avenue
20th Floor
New York, NY USA 10022
Phone: 2128359940
Fax: 6466194122
Website: www.glcllc.com

Other Offices
451 Jackson Street
Second Floor
San Francisco, CA USA 94111
Phone: 4159628500
Fax: 4159628501

Type of Firm
Bank Affiliated

Association Membership
Natl Assoc of Small Bus. Inv. Co (NASBIC)

Project Preferences

Type of Financing Preferred:
Leveraged Buyout
Expansion
Mezzanine
Management Buyouts
Acquisition
Distressed Debt
Recapitalizations

Industry Preferences

In Communications prefer:
Communications and Media

In Medical/Health prefer:
Medical/Health

In Consumer Related prefer:
Entertainment and Leisure
Consumer Products

In Manufact. prefer:
Manufacturing

Additional Information
Year Founded: 2005
Current Activity Level : Actively seeking new investments

GLD INVEST AB

Hovslagargatan 5B
Box 559 06
Stockholm, Sweden 102 16
E-mail: info@gldinvest.com
Website: www.gldinvest.com

Type of Firm
Private Equity Firm

Association Membership
Swedish Venture Capital Association (SVCA)

Project Preferences

Type of Financing Preferred:
Early Stage
Seed
Startup

Geographical Preferences

International Preferences:
Sweden

Industry Preferences

In Biotechnology prefer:
Biotechnology

In Industrial/Energy prefer:
Energy
Environmental Related

Additional Information
Year Founded: 2009
Current Activity Level : Actively seeking new investments

GLEDDEN VENTURES

19 Martin Place
Level 14, MLC Centre
Sydney, Australia 2000
Phone: 61418350737
Website: www.gledden.com

Type of Firm
Private Equity Firm

Project Preferences

Type of Financing Preferred:
Early Stage

Additional Information
Year Founded: 1969
Current Activity Level : Actively seeking new investments

GLENCOE CAPITAL LLC

227 West Monroe Street, Suite 38880
Chicago, IL USA 60606
Phone: 3127956300
Fax: 3127950455
Website: www.glencap.com

Other Offices
300 Park Street
Suite 380
Birmingham, MI USA 48009
Phone: 2485662580

Management and Staff
Christopher Yoo, Vice President
Douglas Kearney, Principal
G. Douglas Patterson, Managing Director
Jason Duzan, Managing Director
Julie Vuotto, Chief Financial Officer
Timothy Flannery, Vice President

Type of Firm
Private Equity Firm

Project Preferences

Role in Financing:
Prefer role as deal originator but will also invest in deals created by others

Type of Financing Preferred:
Leveraged Buyout
Generalist PE
Balanced
Later Stage
Acquisition

Geographical Preferences

United States Preferences:
Michigan
North America

Industry Focus
(% based on actual investment)

Communications and Media	81.1%
Consumer Related	9.3%
Industrial/Energy	4.4%
Other Products	3.1%
Internet Specific	1.1%
Medical/Health	0.9%
Semiconductors/Other Elect.	0.1%
Biotechnology	0.0%

Additional Information
Year Founded: 1994
Capital Under Management: $1,008,000,000
Current Activity Level : Actively seeking new investments
Method of Compensation: Return on invest. most important, but chg. closing fees, service fees, etc.

GLENDONTODD CAPITAL LLC

2101 Cedar Springs Road, Suite 1540
Dallas, TX USA 75201
Phone: 2143101094
E-mail: info@glendonTodd.com
Website: glendontodd.com

Management and Staff
Eric Wenick, Partner
Mary Hatcher, Chief Financial Officer
Wade Barker, Partner

Type of Firm
Private Equity Firm

Project Preferences

Type of Financing Preferred:
Leveraged Buyout
Value-Add

Geographical Preferences

United States Preferences:

Industry Preferences

In Medical/Health prefer:
Medical/Health

In Financial Services prefer:
Real Estate
Financial Services

In Business Serv. prefer:
Services

Additional Information
Year Founded: 2010
Current Activity Level : Actively seeking new investments

GLENGARY LLC

25200 Chagrin Blvd.
Suite 300
Beachwood, OH USA 44122
Phone: 2163789200
Website: www.glengaryventures.com

Management and Staff
Albert Ratner, Partner
David Brennan, Partner
David Kall, Partner
Gary Oatey, Partner
James Bennett, Partner
Maura Corrigan, Partner
Michael Merriman, Partner
Pat Roche, Partner
Peter Rea, Partner
Randall Myeroff, Partner
Stephen Haynes, Managing Partner
Thomas Sullivan, Partner
Thomas Tyrrell, Co-Founder
William Ryan, Partner
William Summers, Partner

Type of Firm
Private Equity Firm

Project Preferences

Type of Financing Preferred:
Early Stage

Size of Investments Considered:
Min Size of Investment Considered (000s): $100
Max Size of Investment Considered (000s): $1,500

Geographical Preferences

United States Preferences:
Ohio

Industry Preferences

In Computer Software prefer:
Software

In Medical/Health prefer:
Medical Products
Health Services

In Consumer Related prefer:
Consumer Products

In Business Serv. prefer:
Services

Additional Information
Year Founded: 2003
Current Activity Level : Actively seeking new investments

GLENHOVE FUND MANAGERS (PTY) LTD

151 Katherine St, Vunani House
Athol Ridge Office Park
Sandton, South Africa 2196
Phone: 27-11-263-9538
Fax: 27-11-784-3135
E-mail: info@wpef.co.za
Website: www.wpef.co.za

Management and Staff
Leonard Fine, Chief Executive Officer

Type of Firm
Private Equity Firm

Project Preferences

Type of Financing Preferred:
Balanced

Size of Investments Considered:
Min Size of Investment Considered (000s): $284
Max Size of Investment Considered (000s): $2,699

Geographical Preferences

International Preferences:
South Africa

Industry Preferences

In Other prefer:
Women/Minority-Owned Bus.

Additional Information
Year Founded: 2003
Capital Under Management: $12,700,000
Current Activity Level : Actively seeking new investments

GLENMONT PARTNERS, LLC

54 State Street
Suite 110
Albany, NY USA 12207
Phone: 518-431-1300
Fax: 518-431-1302

Management and Staff
Dara Shareef, Partner
Jeffrey Wetherbee, Partner
Laura Mann, Partner

Type of Firm
Private Equity Firm

Project Preferences

Type of Financing Preferred:
Early Stage

Geographical Preferences

United States Preferences:
Pennsylvania
Massachusetts
Connecticut
New Jersey
New York

Additional Information
Year Founded: 2007
Current Activity Level : Actively seeking new investments

GLENWOOD CAPITAL LLC

757 3rd Ave. 17th Floor
New York, NY USA 10017
Website: www.glenwoodcapital.net

Type of Firm
Private Equity Firm

Project Preferences

Type of Financing Preferred:
Generalist PE

Additional Information
Year Founded: 2016
Current Activity Level : Actively seeking new investments

GLG GREEN LIFESTYLE GMBH

Deichstrasse 47
Hamburg, Germany 20459
Phone: 494070383990
Website: www.greenlifestylegroup.de

Type of Firm
Private Equity Firm

Project Preferences

Type of Financing Preferred:
Early Stage
Expansion
Balanced
Later Stage
Seed
Startup

Industry Preferences

In Internet Specific prefer:
Ecommerce

Additional Information
Year Founded: 2013
Current Activity Level : Actively seeking new investments

GLILOT CAPITAL INVESTMENTS GP LTD

America House
35 Shaul Hamelech Ave
Tel Aviv, Israel 61181
Phone: 972737055755
Fax: 972377055750
E-mail: info@glilotcapital.com
Website: www.glilotcapital.com

Management and Staff
Kobi Sambourskiy, Co-Founder

Type of Firm
Private Equity Firm

Industry Preferences

In Computer Software prefer:
Software
Systems Software
Applications Software

In Internet Specific prefer:
Internet

Additional Information
Year Founded: 2011
Capital Under Management: $77,000,000
Current Activity Level : Actively seeking new investments

GLL INVESTORS (TWO) INC

3200 North Lake Shore Drive
Chicago, IL USA 60657
Phone: 773-525-3038
Fax: 773-525-3019
E-mail: info@gllinvestors.com

Type of Firm
Private Equity Firm

Project Preferences

Type of Financing Preferred:
Generalist PE

Additional Information
Year Founded: 1995
Capital Under Management: $31,400,000
Current Activity Level : Actively seeking new investments

GLOBAL & ASSOCIATES INC

Nonhyun-dong 25, Kangnam-gu
4/F, G&A Hakdong Park
Seoul, South Korea
Phone: 82262617700
Fax: 82262617719
Website: www.gnakorea.co.kr

Type of Firm
Investment Management Firm

Project Preferences

Type of Financing Preferred:
Leveraged Buyout
Early Stage
Start-up Financing
Startup

Additional Information
Year Founded: 2000
Current Activity Level : Actively seeking new investments

GLOBAL ASIA PARTNERS

699, Bonnie Drive
Stateline, NV USA 89449
Phone: 4153597998
Website: www.gapvc.com

Other Offices
Unit No. 114, 1st Floor
BPTP Park, Centra, NH-8
Sector 30, Gurgaon, India 122002
Phone: 01244720300
Fax: 911244720316

Management and Staff
John Cornell, Principal

Type of Firm
Private Equity Firm

Project Preferences

Type of Financing Preferred:
Early Stage

Geographical Preferences

United States Preferences:
All U.S.

International Preferences:
Europe
Asia

Industry Preferences

In Communications prefer:
Telecommunications
Wireless Communications

In Medical/Health prefer:
Health Services

In Business Serv. prefer:
Services
Distribution

In Manufact. prefer:
Manufacturing

Additional Information
Year Founded: 2002
Current Activity Level : Actively seeking new investments

GLOBAL BANKING CORPORATION BSCC

GBCORP Tower
Bahrain Financial Harbour
Manama, Bahrain
Phone: 97317200200
Fax: 97317200300
E-mail: info@gbcorponline.com
Website: www.gbcorponline.com

Management and Staff
Abdul Monaim Bastaki, Chief Operating Officer
Oscar Silva, Chief Executive Officer

Type of Firm
Private Equity Firm

Project Preferences

Type of Financing Preferred:
Leveraged Buyout
Early Stage
Generalist PE

Industry Preferences

In Communications prefer:
Telecommunications

In Biotechnology prefer:
Agricultural/Animal Bio.

In Medical/Health prefer:
Health Services

In Consumer Related prefer:
Food/Beverage
Education Related

In Financial Services prefer:
Financial Services
Real Estate

Additional Information
Year Founded: 2007
Current Activity Level : Actively seeking new investments

GLOBAL BRAIN CORP

Shibuya-ku
10-11, Sakuragaoka-cho
Tokyo, Japan 150-0031
Website: globalbrains.com

Management and Staff
Ayu Shinoyama, Chief Financial Officer
Daisuke Furukawa, Venture Partner
Hidetaka Aoki, Venture Partner
Isao Yasuda, Partner
Jiro Kumakura, Partner
Jung Yong Kim, Venture Partner
Kaori Akiba, Venture Partner
Kazuhiko Miyama, Partner
Keisuke Tatsuoka, Partner
Kenta Kitsuka, Venture Partner
Masaru Kaneshiro, Venture Partner
Naoki Kamimaeda, Venture Partner
Nobutake Suzuki, Partner
Taisuke Nakagawa, Partner
Takashi Sano, Venture Partner
Takashi Kato, Partner
Tomoaki Ishikure, Venture Partner
Yusuke Miyazawa, Venture Partner

Type of Firm
Private Equity Firm

Project Preferences

Role in Financing:
Prefer role as deal originator

Type of Financing Preferred:
Early Stage
Balanced
Seed
Startup

Geographical Preferences

United States Preferences:
All U.S.

International Preferences:
Pacific
Asia
Japan

Industry Preferences

In Communications prefer:
Media and Entertainment

In Computer Software prefer:
Software

In Internet Specific prefer:
E-Commerce Technology
Internet

In Biotechnology prefer:
Biotechnology

In Medical/Health prefer:
Medical/Health

In Consumer Related prefer:
Entertainment and Leisure

In Industrial/Energy prefer:
Environmental Related

In Business Serv. prefer:
Media

Additional Information
Year Founded: 1998
Capital Under Management: $100,000,000
Current Activity Level : Actively seeking new investments

GLOBAL CAPITAL FINANCE

4 Manhattanville Road
Suite 104
Purchase, NY USA 10577
Phone: 212-660-7600
Fax: 212-660-7660
E-mail: info@globalcapitalfinance.com
Website: www.globalcapitalfinance.com

Other Offices

45 Lime Street
Suite 403
Sydney, Australia NSW 2000
Phone: 61-2-9279-0443
Fax: 61-2-9279-0283

Bertalanffy u. 49
Szombathely, Hungary 9700
Phone: 36-94-344-745
Fax: 36-94-344-745

1 Ropemaker Street
London, United Kingdom EC2Y 9HD

10th Fl, 120, 2-ka Taepyungro
Chung-ku
Seoul, South Korea 110-724
Phone: 82-2-772-2872
Fax: 82-2-772-2835

Burgemeester Haspelslaan 67
Amstelveen, United Kingdom 1181 NB
Phone: 31-20-347-5015
Fax: 31-20-347-5011

Narodni 41/973
Prague, United Kingdom 110 00
Phone: 420-225-574-460
Fax: 420-574-999

Stadiongasse 5/2a
Vienna, Austria 1010
Phone: 43-1-990-7174
Fax: 43-1-990-2393

Mohrlistrasse 97
Zurich, United Kingdom CH-8006
Phone: 41-44-363-9436
Fax: 41-44-363-9436

Management and Staff
Christine Brockwell, Vice President
Juergen Moessner, President

Type of Firm
Bank Affiliated

Project Preferences

Type of Financing Preferred:
Expansion
Acquisition

Geographical Preferences

United States Preferences:
All U.S.

Canadian Preferences:
All Canada

International Preferences:
United Kingdom
Australia

Industry Preferences

In Industrial/Energy prefer:
Energy

In Transportation prefer:
Transportation
Aerospace

In Financial Services prefer:
Real Estate

In Utilities prefer:
Utilities

Additional Information
Current Activity Level : Actively seeking new investments

GLOBAL CAPITAL PARTNERS

155 University Avenue
Suite 1220
Toronto, Canada M5H 3B7
Phone: 416-867-9099
Fax: 416-867-9232
E-mail: info@globalcp.com
Website: www.globalcp.com

Type of Firm
Private Equity Firm

Project Preferences

Type of Financing Preferred:
Mezzanine

Geographical Preferences

Canadian Preferences:
Ontario

Industry Preferences

In Manufact. prefer:
Manufacturing

Additional Information
Year Founded: 2006
Current Activity Level : Actively seeking new investments

GLOBAL CAPITAL PRIVATE EQUITY

21 West Street
Houghton
Johannesburg, South Africa 2198
Phone: 27-11-728-0255
Fax: 27-11-728-8921
E-mail: info@glocapital.com
Website: www.glocapital.com

Management and Staff
Frank Boner, Chief Executive Officer

Type of Firm
Private Equity Firm

Association Membership
South African Venture Capital Association (SAVCA)

Project Preferences

Type of Financing Preferred:
Early Stage
Balanced
Later Stage

Geographical Preferences

United States Preferences:

International Preferences:
United Kingdom
Australia
South Africa
Africa

Additional Information
Year Founded: 1998
Current Activity Level : Actively seeking new investments

GLOBAL CATALYST PARTNERS

530 Lytton Avenue
Second Floor
Palo Alto, CA USA 94301
Phone: 6504862420
Fax: 6505930419
Website: www.gc-partners.com

Other Offices

4-3-20 Toranomon, Minato-ku
Kamiyacho MT Building 14th Floor
Tokyo, Japan 105-0001
Phone: 81354043835
Fax: 81354043401

Management and Staff
Arthur Schneiderman, Co-Founder
Koji Osawa, Co-Founder
Patty O Malley, Chief Financial Officer

Type of Firm
Private Equity Firm

Project Preferences

Role in Financing:
Will function either as deal originator or investor in deals created by others

Type of Financing Preferred:
Early Stage
Balanced
Later Stage

Geographical Preferences

United States Preferences:

International Preferences:
China
Israel
Japan

Additional Information
Name of Most Recent Fund: Global Catalyst Partners III, L.P.
Most Recent Fund Was Raised: 04/07/2005
Year Founded: 1999
Capital Under Management: $245,000,000
Current Activity Level : Actively seeking new investments
Method of Compensation: Return on investment is of primary concern, do not charge fees

GLOBAL CLEANTECH CAPITAL BV

Herengracht 338
Amsterdam, Netherlands 1016 CG
Phone: 31207766280
Fax: 31208907687
E-mail: Info@gccfund.net
Website: www.gccfund.com

Management and Staff
Paul Kloppenborg, Chief Executive Officer

Type of Firm
Private Equity Firm

Association Membership
European Private Equity and Venture Capital Assoc.

Project Preferences

Type of Financing Preferred:
Later Stage

Geographical Preferences

International Preferences:
Europe

Industry Preferences

In Industrial/Energy prefer:
Energy
Alternative Energy
Environmental Related

In Other prefer:
Environment Responsible

Additional Information
Year Founded: 2011
Capital Under Management: $66,961,000
Current Activity Level : Actively seeking new investments

GLOBAL DERAYAH

P.O. Box: 13111
Riyadh, Saudi Arabia 11493
Phone: 96612102424
Fax: 96612102277
E-mail: info@gdme.net
Website: gdme.net

Type of Firm
Private Equity Firm

Project Preferences

Type of Financing Preferred:
Leveraged Buyout
Early Stage
Generalist PE

Industry Preferences

In Consumer Related prefer:
Consumer

In Industrial/Energy prefer:
Industrial Products

In Financial Services prefer:
Financial Services
Real Estate

Additional Information
Year Founded: 1969
Current Activity Level : Actively seeking new investments

GLOBAL DIGITAL PRIMA PT

Jl. Letjen S. Parman 77, Slipi
Wisma 77 Tower 2, 8th Floor
Jakarta Barat, Indonesia 11410
E-mail: reach@gdpventure.com

Other Offices
Jl. Letjen S. Parman No. 77, Slipi
Wisma 77 Tower 2, 8th Floor
Jakarta Barat, Indonesia 11410

Type of Firm
Private Equity Firm

Project Preferences

Type of Financing Preferred:
Start-up Financing

Geographical Preferences

International Preferences:
Indonesia

Industry Preferences

In Communications prefer:
Media and Entertainment

In Internet Specific prefer:
E-Commerce Technology

Additional Information
Year Founded: 2010
Current Activity Level : Actively seeking new investments

GLOBAL EMERGING MARKETS

590 Madison Avenue
27th Floor
New York, NY USA 10022
Phone: 2125823400
Fax: 2122654035
E-mail: mlhom@gemny.com
Website: www.gemny.com

Other Offices
10 Hardcourt Road
1818 Suite, Hutchison House
Central, Hong Kong
Phone: 85229018222
Fax: 85228418891

54, Avenue Montaigne
Paris, France 75008
Phone: 33153532010
Fax: 33145637622

81 Fulham Road
Michelin House
London, United Kingdom SW3 6RD

Management and Staff
Cheikh Faye, Managing Director
Harpal Randhawa, Founder
Haykel Hajjaji, Managing Director
Javier Saade, Managing Director
Mansoor Ali, Managing Director

Type of Firm
Private Equity Firm

Project Preferences

Type of Financing Preferred:
Leveraged Buyout
Expansion
Later Stage
Management Buyouts
Acquisition
Recapitalizations

Geographical Preferences

International Preferences:
Rest of World
All International

Industry Preferences

In Business Serv. prefer:
Services

In Manufact. prefer:
Manufacturing

Additional Information

Year Founded: 1991
Current Activity Level : Actively seeking new investments

GLOBAL EQUITY ADMINISTRADORA DE RECURSOS SA

Rua Lauro Muller, 116 sl. 1802
Torre do Rio Sul
Rio de Janeiro, Brazil 22290-160
Phone: 552121258300
Fax: 552121258301
Website: www.globalequity.com.br

Type of Firm
Private Equity Firm

Association Membership
Brazilian Venture Capital Association (ABCR)

Project Preferences

Type of Financing Preferred:
Generalist PE

Industry Preferences

In Consumer Related prefer:
Food/Beverage

In Financial Services prefer:
Real Estate

In Agr/Forestr/Fish prefer:
Agribusiness
Agriculture related

Additional Information

Year Founded: 1994
Capital Under Management: $1,469,400,000
Current Activity Level : Actively seeking new investments

GLOBAL FOUNDERS CAPITAL MANAGEMENT GMBH

Luisenstrasse 14
Munich, Germany 80333
E-mail: info@europeanfounders.com
Website: www.globalfounders.vc

Management and Staff
Alexander Samwer, Managing Director
Marc Samwer, Managing Director
Oliver Samwer, Managing Director

Type of Firm
Private Equity Firm

Project Preferences

Type of Financing Preferred:
Early Stage
Later Stage

Size of Investments Considered:
Min Size of Investment Considered (000s): $500
Max Size of Investment Considered (000s): $2,000

Geographical Preferences

United States Preferences:

Canadian Preferences:
All Canada

International Preferences:
Europe
Poland
Germany

Industry Preferences

In Communications prefer:
Wireless Communications

In Computer Software prefer:
Software
Applications Software

In Internet Specific prefer:
E-Commerce Technology
Internet

In Business Serv. prefer:
Services

Additional Information

Year Founded: 2006
Capital Under Management: $198,282,000
Current Activity Level : Actively seeking new investments

GLOBAL IMPACT INVESTORS

c/o J.Barrymore
20 Berkeley Square
London, United Kingdom W1J 6LH
E-mail: contact@globalimpactinvestors.com
Website: www.globalimpactinvestors.com

Management and Staff
Varun Sahni, Founder

Type of Firm
Private Equity Firm

Project Preferences

Type of Financing Preferred:
Balanced

Size of Investments Considered:
Min Size of Investment Considered (000s): $5,000
Max Size of Investment Considered (000s): $15,000

Geographical Preferences

International Preferences:
India
Asia

Industry Preferences

In Medical/Health prefer:
Medical/Health
Health Services

In Consumer Related prefer:
Education Related

Additional Information

Year Founded: 2010
Current Activity Level : Actively seeking new investments

GLOBAL INFRASTRUCTURE HOLDINGS

12 East 49th Street
New York, NY USA 10017
Phone: 2123158100
Website: www.global-infra.com

Other Offices

Five Wilton Road
The Peak
, United Kingdom
Phone: 442077980400

225 High Ridge Road
Suite 260
STAMFORD, CT USA 06905
Phone: 2033553270

Management and Staff
Alan Bowman, Principal
Andrew Gillespie-Smith, Principal
Ari Droga, Principal
Brian Nailor, Principal
Bruce MacLennan, Principal
Colin Gilligan, Principal
Damien Flanagan, Principal
Deepak Agrawal, Principal
Erik Einset, Principal

Glenn Johnson, Principal
Gregg Myers, Founder
Harry Quarls, Managing Director
Howard Sykes, Principal
James Jenkins, Managing Director
John Cole, Principal
Jonathan Bram, Partner
Mark Levitt, Chief Operating Officer
Matthew Harris, Partner
Mehrdad Noorani, Partner
Michael McGhee, Partner
Raj Rao, Partner
Randy Robertson, Principal
Robert Callahan, Principal
Robert O Brien, Managing Director
Salim Samaha, Principal
Samad Momin, Principal
Scott Stanley, Principal
Susan Healy, Principal
William Woodburn, Partner
William Brilliant, Partner

Type of Firm
Private Equity Firm

Project Preferences

Type of Financing Preferred:
Leveraged Buyout
Other

Industry Preferences

In Industrial/Energy prefer:
Energy

In Transportation prefer:
Transportation

In Other prefer:
Environment Responsible

Additional Information
Year Founded: 2006
Capital Under Management: $5,640,000,000
Current Activity Level : Actively seeking new investments

GLOBAL INNOVATION FUND

68-80, Hanbury Street
Second Home
London, United Kingdom E1 5JL
Website: www.globalinnovation.fund

Type of Firm
Government Affiliated Program

Project Preferences

Type of Financing Preferred:
Early Stage
Expansion
Later Stage
Seed

Size of Investments Considered:
Min Size of Investment Considered (000s): $48
Max Size of Investment Considered (000s): $15,904

Additional Information
Year Founded: 2014
Current Activity Level : Actively seeking new investments

GLOBAL INVEST SICAR

3, R.Jenner
Tunis, Tunisia 1002
Phone: 21371848230
Fax: 213-71840557
Website: www.ubci.com.tn

Type of Firm
Private Equity Firm

Project Preferences

Type of Financing Preferred:
Early Stage
Balanced
Later Stage
Startup

Geographical Preferences

International Preferences:
Tunisia

Industry Preferences

In Communications prefer:
Radio & TV Broadcasting
Telecommunications
Wireless Communications

In Industrial/Energy prefer:
Industrial Products

In Business Serv. prefer:
Services

Additional Information
Year Founded: 2004
Current Activity Level : Making few, if any, new investments

GLOBAL INVESTMENT HOUSE KSCC

Global Tower, Sharq
Shuhada Street, P.O. Box 28807
Safat, Kuwait 13149
Phone: 96522951000
Fax: 96522951005
Website: www.globalinv.net

Other Offices

7 Abdel Hadi Salah Street
El-Nasr Tower
Giza, Egypt 12411
Phone: 20-2-3760-9398
Fax: 20-2-3760-9506

AL-Mather Street
PO. Box 66930
Riyadh, Saudi Arabia 11586
Phone: 966-1-219-9966
Fax: 966-1-217-8481

Abu Dhabi Commercial Bank Building
Intersection of Al Salam and Electra St.
Abu Dhabi, Utd. Arab Em.
Phone: 971-2-678-9808
Fax: 971-2-6790-0601

First Floor, Flat No. 2
Sagar Apartments, CBD Belapur
Navi Mumbai, India 400 614
Phone: 91-982-078-2884
Fax: 91-981-940-0280

Bldg. No. 131, Office No. 191
P.O.Box 855
Manama, Bahrain
Phone: 973-17-210-011
Fax: 973-17-210-222

Burj Dubai Square
Bldg 1- Office 402, Sheikh Zayed Road
Dubai, Utd. Arab Em.
Phone: 971-4-425-7977
Fax: 971-4-425-7960

Khartoum - Al Barakah Tower
1st Floor - Flat 407
Sudan, Sudan
Phone: 249-1-8376-7324
Fax: 249-1-8374-7260

Al-Jazaer St., Sana'a Trade Center
Northern Tower, 3rd Floor
Sana'a, Yemen
Phone: 967-1-448-3502
Fax: 967-1-448-353

Shmeisani - Al Sharef Abdelhameed
Sharaf Street
, Jordan 11180
Phone: 962-6-500-5060
Fax: 962-6-500-5066

QFC Tower, Office 1902
P.O.Box: 18126
Doha, Qatar
Phone: 974-496-7305
Fax: 974-496-7307

Management and Staff
Maha Al-Ghunaim, Chairman & Managing Director
Nawal Mulla-Hussein, Chief Operating Officer
Samer Abbouchi, Vice President
Sulaiman Al-Rubaie, Chief Executive Officer
Sunny Bhatia, Chief Financial Officer

Type of Firm
Investment Management Firm

Project Preferences

Type of Financing Preferred:
Fund of Funds
Leveraged Buyout
Value-Add
Mezzanine
Generalist PE
Balanced
Public Companies

Geographical Preferences

International Preferences:
Pakistan
Bahrain
India
Oman
Turkey
Qatar
China
Utd. Arab Em.
Middle East
Saudi Arabia
Asia
Kuwait
Africa
All International

Industry Preferences

In Medical/Health prefer:
Medical/Health
Disposable Med. Products

In Consumer Related prefer:
Retail

In Industrial/Energy prefer:
Industrial Products

In Transportation prefer:
Transportation

In Financial Services prefer:
Investment Groups
Financial Services

Additional Information
Year Founded: 1998
Capital Under Management: $766,000,000
Current Activity Level : Actively seeking new investments

GLOBAL LEISURE PARTNERS LLC

17/18 Old Bond Street
London, United Kingdom W1S4PT
Phone: 44- 2070168050
Fax: 44-2070168060
E-mail: info@glp.uk.com
Website: www.globalleisurepartners.com

Management and Staff
Mervyn Metcalf, Managing Partner
Robert Decker, Managing Director
Tina Palastanga, Vice President
W.B. Harms, CEO & Managing Director

Type of Firm
Bank Affiliated

Project Preferences

Type of Financing Preferred:
Balanced

Geographical Preferences

International Preferences:
United Kingdom

Industry Preferences

In Consumer Related prefer:
Entertainment and Leisure

Additional Information
Year Founded: 2004
Current Activity Level : Actively seeking new investments

GLOBAL LIFE SCIENCE VENTURES GMBH

Maximilianstrasse 35 C
Munich, Germany 80539
Phone: 49892881510
Fax: 498928815130
E-mail: mailbox@glsv-vc.com
Website: www.glsv-vc.com

Other Offices
Postplatz 1
Zug, Switzerland 6301
Phone: 41-41-727-1940
Fax: 41-41-727-1945

Management and Staff
Hanns-Peter Wiese, Partner
Hans Kuepper, Partner
Peter Reinisch, Partner

Type of Firm
Private Equity Firm

Project Preferences

Role in Financing:
Prefer role as deal originator but will also invest in deals created by others

Type of Financing Preferred:
Leveraged Buyout
Early Stage
Later Stage
Startup
Special Situation

Geographical Preferences

United States Preferences:

International Preferences:
United Kingdom
Europe
Switzerland
Austria
Germany

Industry Focus
(% based on actual investment)
    Biotechnology   59.8%
    Medical/Health   39.9%
    Computer Software and Services   0.3%

Additional Information
Year Founded: 1996
Capital Under Management: $84,500,000
Current Activity Level : Actively seeking new investments

GLOBAL MINING CAPITAL CORP

330 Bay Street
Toronto, Canada M5H 2S8
Phone: 4163620007
E-mail: info@globalmining.ca
Website: www.globalmining.ca

Other Offices
A22 Dongsi Shitiao, Dongcheng
Suite A 508
Beijing, China
Phone: 861064096455

Management and Staff
Keith Spence, President
Neil Morgan, Partner
Peng Mun Foo, Partner
Robert Khayrullin, Vice President

Type of Firm
Private Equity Firm

Project Preferences

Type of Financing Preferred:
Leveraged Buyout
Acquisition

Pratt's Guide to Private Equity & Venture Capital Sources

Geographical Preferences

Canadian Preferences:
All Canada

International Preferences:
Asia Pacific
Latin America
Argentina
China
Peru
Brazil
Australia

Industry Preferences

In Agr/Forestr/Fish prefer:
Mining and Minerals

Additional Information

Year Founded: 1969
Current Activity Level : Actively seeking new investments

GLOBAL PARTNERSHIPS

1932 First Avenue, Suite 400
Seattle, WA USA 98101
Website: www.globalpartnerships.org

Management and Staff

Aaron Nasurutia, Vice President
Jason Henning, Vice President
Jim Villanueva, Managing Director
Kusi Hornberger, Vice President
Mark Coffey, Chief Operating Officer
Nathalia Vega, Vice President
Ricardo Visbal, Vice President
Tara Forde, Vice President

Type of Firm

Endowment, Foundation or Pension Fund

Project Preferences

Type of Financing Preferred:
Early Stage

Geographical Preferences

International Preferences:
Africa

Industry Preferences

In Medical/Health prefer:
Medical/Health

In Consumer Related prefer:
Education Related

In Agr/Forestr/Fish prefer:
Agriculture related

Additional Information

Year Founded: 2016
Capital Under Management: $2,000,000
Current Activity Level : Actively seeking new investments

GLOBAL PRIVATE EQUITY PLC

4 Royal Mint Court
London, United Kingdom EC3N 4HJ
Phone: 44-20-7073-7888
Fax: 44-20-7073-7889
E-mail: mailto:info@global.cn
Website: www.globalprivateequity.plc.uk

Management and Staff

Adam Palin, Chief Executive Officer
Johnny Hon, Chairman & CEO
Rebecca Wong, Chief Financial Officer
Simmy Ho, Chief Operating Officer

Type of Firm

Private Equity Firm

Project Preferences

Type of Financing Preferred:
Leveraged Buyout
Early Stage
Seed
Acquisition

Geographical Preferences

International Preferences:
Vietnam
Indonesia
United Kingdom
China
Thailand
Philippines
Singapore
Korea, South
Malaysia

Industry Preferences

In Communications prefer:
Communications and Media

In Semiconductor/Electr prefer:
Electronic Components

In Consumer Related prefer:
Entertainment and Leisure

In Industrial/Energy prefer:
Alternative Energy

In Financial Services prefer:
Financial Services

Additional Information

Year Founded: 2008
Current Activity Level : Actively seeking new investments

GLOBAL TECHNOLOGY INVESTMENT

150 East 58th Street, 24th Floor
New York, NY USA 10155
Phone: 2123232600
Fax: 2123232601
E-mail: info@gticapitalgroup.com
Website: www.gticapitalgroup.com

Other Offices

11th Floor, Narain Manzil Building
23 Barakhamba Road
New Delhi, India 110001
Phone: 911143621200
Fax: 911141501333

Management and Staff

Gaurav Dalmia, Partner
Jonathan Schulhof, Managing Director
Madhav Dhar, Managing Director
Michael Schulhof, Managing Director
Rahul Agrawal, Vice President
Rahul Dhir, Venture Partner
Sanjay Aggarwal, Venture Partner
Tejpreet Singh Chopra, Venture Partner

Type of Firm

Private Equity Firm

Association Membership

Indian Venture Capital Association (IVCA)

Project Preferences

Type of Financing Preferred:
Balanced

Geographical Preferences

International Preferences:
All International

Additional Information

Year Founded: 2005
Current Activity Level : Actively seeking new investments

GLOBAL VENTURE CAPITAL INC

2-7-5 Toranomon Minato-Ku
3F BUREX Toranomon
Tokyo, Japan 1050001
Phone: 81335077707
Fax: 81335077706
Website: www.gvc.jp

Management and Staff

Hirokazu Hasegawa, Co-Founder
Kazukiyo Toyoshima, Partner
Michael Korver, Co-Founder
Tomohiko Hasegawa, Partner
Yoshitaka Matsubara, Partner

Type of Firm
Private Equity Firm

Project Preferences

Type of Financing Preferred:
Early Stage
Balanced

Geographical Preferences

International Preferences:
Japan
All International

Industry Preferences

In Communications prefer:
Telecommunications

In Medical/Health prefer:
Medical/Health
Health Services

In Consumer Related prefer:
Consumer Services

In Industrial/Energy prefer:
Alternative Energy

Additional Information
Year Founded: 1996
Current Activity Level : Actively seeking new investments

GLOBESPAN CAPITAL PARTNERS

One Boston Place
Suite 2810
Boston, MA USA 02108
Phone: 6173052300
Fax: 6173052301
E-mail: businessplan@globespancapital.com
Website: www.globespancapital.com

Management and Staff
Andrew Goldfarb, Co-Founder
David Fachetti, Managing Director

Type of Firm
Private Equity Firm

Association Membership
New England Venture Capital Association
Western Association of Venture Capitalists (WAVC)
National Venture Capital Association - USA (NVCA)

Project Preferences

Role in Financing:
Will function either as deal originator or investor in deals created by others

Type of Financing Preferred:
Early Stage
Balanced
Startup

Geographical Preferences

United States Preferences:

International Preferences:
All International

Industry Focus
(% based on actual investment)

Computer Software and Services	29.7%
Internet Specific	26.5%
Communications and Media	14.9%
Semiconductors/Other Elect.	11.1%
Industrial/Energy	5.0%
Consumer Related	4.4%
Computer Hardware	3.4%
Biotechnology	2.2%
Medical/Health	1.7%
Other Products	1.0%

Additional Information
Name of Most Recent Fund: Globespan Capital Partners V, L.P.
Most Recent Fund Was Raised: 06/28/2006
Year Founded: 1984
Capital Under Management: $1,100,000,000
Current Activity Level : Actively seeking new investments
Method of Compensation: Return on investment is of primary concern, do not charge fees

GLOBIS CAPITAL PARTNERS & CO

5-1 Nibancho, Chiyoda-ku
Sumitomo Fudosan Kojimachi Bld
Tokyo, Japan 1020084
Phone: 81352753939
Fax: 81352753825
E-mail: info-gcp@globis.co.jp
Website: www.globiscapital.co.jp

Other Offices
No.10, Cayman Center
118, Dorcy
Dr. George Town, Cayman Islands KY1-1007
Phone: 81352753644

Management and Staff
Akihiro Ideguchi, Principal
Keisuke Ide, Principal
Minoru Imano, Partner
Shinichi Takamiya, Partner
Shoichi Kariyazono, Managing Partner
Tetsushi Kawaguchi, Principal
Yoshito Hori, Managing Partner

Type of Firm
Private Equity Firm

Association Membership
Japan Venture Capital Association

Project Preferences

Type of Financing Preferred:
Early Stage
Expansion
Balanced
Later Stage

Geographical Preferences

International Preferences:
Asia
Japan

Industry Preferences

In Communications prefer:
Communications and Media
Telecommunications

In Internet Specific prefer:
Web Aggregation/Portals

In Medical/Health prefer:
Health Services

In Consumer Related prefer:
Education Related

In Business Serv. prefer:
Services
Media

Additional Information
Name of Most Recent Fund: Globis Fund IV, L.P.
Most Recent Fund Was Raised: 01/16/2013
Year Founded: 1999
Capital Under Management: $180,000,000
Current Activity Level : Actively seeking new investments

GLOBON CO LTD

20/F, Gangnam Finance Center
Yeoksam1-dong737,Gangnam-gu
Seoul, South Korea 135081
Phone: 82-2-21126200
Website: www.globon.co.kr

Type of Firm
Investment Management Firm

Association Membership
Venture Capital Association of Beijing (VCAB)

Project Preferences

Type of Financing Preferred:
Early Stage
Expansion
Balanced
Later Stage

Geographical Preferences

International Preferences:
No Preference
Asia
Korea, South

Industry Preferences

In Industrial/Energy prefer:
Industrial Products

In Business Serv. prefer:
Services

Additional Information

Year Founded: 1986
Capital Under Management: $10,100,000
Current Activity Level : Actively seeking new investments

GLORY VENTURES

No.721 Lingshi Road
Unite 822A, Le Square
Shanghai, China
Website: glory-ventures.com

Type of Firm

Private Equity Firm

Project Preferences

Type of Financing Preferred:
Early Stage

Geographical Preferences

International Preferences:
China

Industry Preferences

In Internet Specific prefer:
Internet

In Consumer Related prefer:
Consumer

Additional Information

Year Founded: 2015
Current Activity Level : Actively seeking new investments

GLOUSTON CAPITAL PARTNERS LLC

800 Boylston Street
Suite 1325, Prudential Tower
Boston, MA USA 02199
Phone: 6175875300
Fax: 6175875301
E-mail: info@permalcapital.com
Website: www.permalcapital.com

Management and Staff

Aaron Bright, Vice President
Adriaan Zur Muhlen, Managing Director
Benjamin Marino, Managing Director & CFO
David Navins, Vice President
Michael D Agostino, Principal
Robert Di Geronimo, Managing Director

Type of Firm

Private Equity Advisor or Fund of Funds

Project Preferences

Role in Financing:
Prefer role as deal originator but will also invest in deals created by others

Type of Financing Preferred:
Fund of Funds
Leveraged Buyout
Balanced
Fund of Funds of Second

Geographical Preferences

United States Preferences:

Additional Information

Name of Most Recent Fund: Permal Private Equity Holdings 2000, L.P
Most Recent Fund Was Raised: 09/27/2000
Year Founded: 1990
Capital Under Management: $800,000,000
Current Activity Level : Actively seeking new investments
Method of Compensation: Return on investment is of primary concern, do not charge fees

---

GLYNN CAPITAL MANAGEMENT LLC

3000 Sand Hill Road
Building 3, Suite 230
Menlo Park, CA USA 94025
Phone: 6508542215
Fax: 6508548083
Website: www.glynncapital.com

Management and Staff

Carl Anderson, Managing Director
David Glynn, Managing Director
Jacqueline Brandin, Managing Director
John Fogelsong, Principal
John Glynn, Founder
Scott Jordon, Managing Director
Sebastian Zahedi, Principal
Vivian Nahmias, Chief Financial Officer
Vivian Loh Nahmias, Chief Financial Officer

Type of Firm

Private Equity Firm

Association Membership

Western Association of Venture Capitalists (WAVC)
National Venture Capital Association - USA (NVCA)

Project Preferences

Role in Financing:
Prefer role as deal originator but will also invest in deals created by others

Type of Financing Preferred:
Early Stage
Expansion
Later Stage

Geographical Preferences

United States Preferences:

Industry Preferences

In Communications prefer:
Communications and Media
Wireless Communications

In Computer Software prefer:
Software

In Internet Specific prefer:
E-Commerce Technology
Internet
Ecommerce

In Semiconductor/Electr prefer:
Semiconductor

In Medical/Health prefer:
Medical/Health
Medical Products

In Business Serv. prefer:
Services
Media

Additional Information

Name of Most Recent Fund: Glynn Partners III, L.P.
Most Recent Fund Was Raised: 08/08/2012
Year Founded: 1970
Capital Under Management: $190,000,000
Current Activity Level : Actively seeking new investments
Method of Compensation: Return on investment is of primary concern, do not charge fees

---

GMF CAPITAL GMBH

Bellevue 19
Hamburg, Germany 22301
Phone: 496997544639
Fax: 4969505027301
E-mail: info@gmf-group.com
Website: http://www.gmf-group.de/

Type of Firm

Private Equity Firm

Project Preferences

Type of Financing Preferred:
Leveraged Buyout
Early Stage
Expansion
Generalist PE
Balanced
Later Stage
Acquisition

Industry Preferences

In Medical/Health prefer:
Medical/Health
Pharmaceuticals

Additional Information
Year Founded: 2012
Current Activity Level : Actively seeking new investments

GMG CAPITAL PARTNERS LP

575 Lexington Avenue
15th Floor
New York, NY USA 10022
Phone: 2128324013
Fax: 2129801695
Website: www.e-hoffman.net

Other Offices
9350 South 150 East
9th Floor
Salt Lake City, UT USA 84107
Phone: 801-208-8100
Fax: 801-937-8101

Management and Staff
Bill Kesselring, General Partner
David Mock, General Partner
Jeffrey Gilfix, Managing Director
Joachim Gfoeller, Managing Partner

Type of Firm
Private Equity Firm

Project Preferences

Type of Financing Preferred:
Early Stage

Geographical Preferences

United States Preferences:

Industry Preferences

In Communications prefer:
Telecommunications
Data Communications

In Internet Specific prefer:
Internet

Additional Information
Year Founded: 1997
Current Activity Level : Actively seeking new investments

GMH VENTURES

Ten Campus Boulevard
Newtown Square, PA USA 19073
Website: www.gmh-ventures.com

Management and Staff
Dennis O Leary, President

Type of Firm
Private Equity Firm

Project Preferences

Type of Financing Preferred:
Leveraged Buyout
Expansion
Recapitalizations

Geographical Preferences

United States Preferences:

Industry Preferences

In Business Serv. prefer:
Services
Distribution

In Manufact. prefer:
Manufacturing

Additional Information
Year Founded: 2008
Current Activity Level : Actively seeking new investments

GMO VENTUREPARTNERS INC

26-1, Sakuraoka-Cho, Shibuya-K
11F Cerulean Tower
Tokyo, Japan 150-8512
Phone: 81354588663
Website: www.gmo-vp.com

Type of Firm
Corporate PE/Venture

Project Preferences

Type of Financing Preferred:
Balanced
Startup

Geographical Preferences

International Preferences:
China
Asia
Japan

Industry Preferences

In Communications prefer:
Wireless Communications

In Internet Specific prefer:
E-Commerce Technology
Internet

Additional Information
Year Founded: 2005
Capital Under Management: $6,496,000
Current Activity Level : Actively seeking new investments

GMP SECURITIES LTD

145 King Street West
Suite 300
Toronto, Canada M5H 1J8
Phone: 4163678600
Fax: 4163678164

Other Offices
525, Eighth Avenue Southwest
Suite 4800
Calgary, Canada T2P 1G1
Phone: 4035433030
Fax: 4035433038

331 Madison Avenue
New York, NY USA 10017
Phone: 2126925100
Fax: 2126925174

5601 Granite Parkway
Suite 660
Plano, TX USA 75024
Phone: 2143870255
Fax: 2143873063

19495 Biscayne Boulevard
Suite 408
Miami, FL USA 33180
Phone: 3057924221
Fax: 3057924590

1250 Rene Levesque Boulevard
15th Floor
Montreal, Canada H3B 4W8
Phone: 5142887774
Fax: 5142881574

Management and Staff
Simon Catt, Partner

Type of Firm
Investment Management Firm

Project Preferences

Type of Financing Preferred:
Leveraged Buyout

Geographical Preferences

Canadian Preferences:
Ontario

Industry Preferences

In Communications prefer:
Communications and Media
Commercial Communications

Additional Information
Year Founded: 1995
Current Activity Level : Actively seeking new investments

GMPVC GERMAN MEDIA POOL GMBH

Meinekestrasse 5
Berlin, Germany 10719
Phone: 4930609847838
E-mail: info@gmpvc.com
Website: www.germanmediapool.com

Type of Firm
Private Equity Firm

Geographical Preferences

International Preferences:
Germany

Additional Information
Year Founded: 2011
Current Activity Level : Actively seeking new investments

GMT COMMUNICATIONS PARTNERS LLP

40 Piccadilly
Sackville House
London, United Kingdom W1J 0DR
Phone: 442072929333
Fax: 442072929390
Website: www.gmtpartners.com

Management and Staff
Ashley Long, Partner
Francois Stoessel, Principal
Jean-Sebastien Talbot, Principal
Timothy Green, Co-Founder
Vikram Krishna, Partner

Type of Firm
Private Equity Firm

Association Membership
British Venture Capital Association (BVCA)
European Private Equity and Venture Capital Assoc.

Project Preferences

Role in Financing:
Prefer role as deal originator but will also invest in deals created by others

Type of Financing Preferred:
Leveraged Buyout
Management Buyouts
Acquisition

Geographical Preferences

International Preferences:
Europe
Western Europe

Industry Focus
(% based on actual investment)

Communications and Media	68.8%
Computer Software and Services	14.3%
Internet Specific	12.5%
Consumer Related	2.7%
Other Products	1.6%

Additional Information
Name of Most Recent Fund: GMT Communications Partners III, L.P.
Most Recent Fund Was Raised: 05/11/2006
Year Founded: 1993
Capital Under Management: $1,117,400,000
Current Activity Level : Actively seeking new investments

GO CAPITAL ASSET MANAGEMENT BV

Johannes Vermeerstraat 14
Amsterdam, Netherlands 1071 DR
Phone: 31205703045
Fax: 31205703047
E-mail: info@go-capital.nl
Website: www.gocapital.nl

Management and Staff
Albert Jellema, Managing Partner
Corneille Couwenberg, Managing Partner
Mike Kranenburg, Managing Partner

Type of Firm
Private Equity Firm

Association Membership
French Venture Capital Association (AFIC)

Project Preferences

Type of Financing Preferred:
Early Stage
Startup

Geographical Preferences

International Preferences:
Europe

Industry Preferences

In Computer Software prefer:
Software

Additional Information
Year Founded: 2000
Capital Under Management: $17,100,000
Current Activity Level : Actively seeking new investments

GO CAPITAL LLC

45 Page Avenue
Staten Island, NY USA 10309
Website: www.gocapllc.com

Management and Staff
Chris Duggan, Managing Partner
Phillip Brennan, Managing Partner

Type of Firm
Private Equity Firm

Project Preferences

Type of Financing Preferred:
Leveraged Buyout
Management Buyouts

Geographical Preferences

United States Preferences:

Industry Preferences

In Internet Specific prefer:
Web Aggregation/Portals

In Consumer Related prefer:
Consumer

Additional Information
Year Founded: 2015
Current Activity Level : Actively seeking new investments

GO CAPITAL SAS

103A, Avenue Henri Freville
Rennes, France 35200
Phone: 33299350400
Fax: 33299350022
E-mail: contact@gocapital.fr
Website: www.gocapital.fr

Management and Staff
Marc Frouin, Venture Partner
Thao Lane, Venture Partner

Type of Firm
Private Equity Firm

Project Preferences

Type of Financing Preferred:
Early Stage
Balanced
Later Stage
Seed
Startup

Size of Investments Considered:
Min Size of Investment Considered (000s): $414
Max Size of Investment Considered (000s): $3,450

Geographical Preferences

International Preferences:
Europe
France

Industry Preferences

In Communications prefer:
Communications and Media
Telecommunications

In Computer Hardware prefer:
Mainframes / Scientific

In Computer Software prefer:
Software

In Semiconductor/Electr prefer:
Electronics

In Biotechnology prefer:
Biotechnology

In Medical/Health prefer:
Medical/Health
Medical Diagnostics
Diagnostic Services
Medical Therapeutics
Medical Products

In Consumer Related prefer:
Consumer Products

In Industrial/Energy prefer:
Environmental Related

In Business Serv. prefer:
Media

In Other prefer:
Environment Responsible

Additional Information
Name of Most Recent Fund: Go Capital Amorcage FCPR
Most Recent Fund Was Raised: 06/07/2012
Year Founded: 2003
Capital Under Management: $191,400,000
Current Activity Level : Actively seeking new investments

GO4IT ESPORTES E ENTRE-TENIMENTO SA

Av. Delfim Moreira, 120
3rd floor - Leblon
Rio de Janeiro, Brazil
Phone: 552136272505
E-mail: hello@go4.it
Website: go4.it

Type of Firm
Private Equity Firm

Industry Preferences

In Consumer Related prefer:
Sports

Additional Information
Year Founded: 2015
Current Activity Level : Actively seeking new investments

GOBI PARTNERS

No.2088, Room303
Xietu Road, Xuhui District
Shanghai, China 20032
Phone: 862151601618
Fax: 862152929730
E-mail: mail@gobivc.com
Website: www.gobivc.com

Other Offices
No. 399, Keyuan Road
7B, Zhangjiang Innovation Park
, China 201203

4th Floor, Sohu.com, Internet Plaza
1 East Zhongguan Road, Haidian District
, China
Phone: 86-10-8215-1502
Fax: 86-10-8215-1503

9/F, 33 Des Voeux Road Central
Hong Kong, Hong Kong

Management and Staff
Don Jiang, Partner
Filippo Huang, Chief Financial Officer
James Tong, Venture Partner
Ken Xu, Partner
Ku Kay Mok, Partner
Lawrence Tse, Co-Founder
May Wang, Vice President
Michael Zhu, Vice President
Soo Wei Shaw, Partner
Thomas Tsao, Founder
Wai Kit Lau, Co-Founder
William Tong, Managing Director

Type of Firm
Private Equity Firm

Association Membership
China Venture Capital Association
Singapore Venture Capital Association (SVCA)

Project Preferences

Type of Financing Preferred:
Early Stage
Expansion
Balanced
Seed
Startup

Size of Investments Considered:
Min Size of Investment Considered (000s): $1,000
Max Size of Investment Considered (000s): $3,000

Geographical Preferences

International Preferences:
China
Singapore

Industry Preferences

In Communications prefer:
Telecommunications
Wireless Communications

In Internet Specific prefer:
Internet

In Industrial/Energy prefer:
Energy

In Financial Services prefer:
Financial Services

In Business Serv. prefer:
Media

Additional Information
Year Founded: 2002
Capital Under Management: $51,800,000
Current Activity Level : Actively seeking new investments

GOEAST VENTURES LTD

Universal House
88-94 Wentworth Street
London, United Kingdom E1 7SA
Phone: 44-20-7456-0448
Fax: 44-20-7247-8729

Management and Staff
Eddie Yongo, Chief Executive Officer

Type of Firm
Private Equity Firm

Project Preferences

Type of Financing Preferred:
Balanced

Geographical Preferences

International Preferences:
No Preference

Additional Information
Year Founded: 2002
Current Activity Level : Actively seeking new investments

GOFF CAPITAL PARTNERS, L.P.

500 Commerce Street, Suite 700
Fort Worth, TX USA 76102

Phone: 8175093951
Fax: 8173340666
E-mail: info@goffcp.com
Website: www.goffcp.com

Other Offices

6465 South Greenwood Plaza
Suite 1075
Centennial, CO USA 80111
Phone: 303-395-1890
Fax: 866-929-4578

6312 South Fiddlers Green Circle
Suite 435N
Greenwood Village, CO USA 80111
Phone: 303-395-1890
Fax: 866-929-4578

1266 East Main Street
Eighth Floor
Stamford, CT USA 06902
Phone: 203-504-5062
Fax: 203-504-5068

Management and Staff

Darla Moore, Principal
Hugh Balloch, Principal
John Goff, Managing Director

Type of Firm

Private Equity Firm

Project Preferences

Type of Financing Preferred:
Value-Add
Early Stage

Industry Focus

(% based on actual investment)
Computer Software and Services	38.7%
Communications and Media	29.9%
Internet Specific	15.6%
Consumer Related	14.5%
Semiconductors/Other Elect.	1.3%

Additional Information

Year Founded: 1998
Capital Under Management: $2,000,000,000
Current Activity Level : Actively seeking new investments

GOGIN CAPITAL CO LTD

71 Shirakata Hon-machi
Matsue-shi, Japan 690-0061
Phone: 81-852-28-7170
Fax: 81-852-28-7177
E-mail: info@g-cp.jp
Website: www.g-cp.jp

Management and Staff

Hiroshi Watanabe, President
Shohei Ikebuchi, Managing Director

Type of Firm

Private Equity Firm

Association Membership

Japan Venture Capital Association

Project Preferences

Type of Financing Preferred:
Balanced

Geographical Preferences

International Preferences:
Japan

Additional Information

Year Founded: 1996
Current Activity Level : Actively seeking new investments

GOGREEN CAPITAL SA

Avenue de la Faisanderie 34
Brussels, Belgium 1150
Phone: 3227720674
Fax: 3228886793
Website: gogreencapital.be

Type of Firm

Private Equity Firm

Project Preferences

Type of Financing Preferred:
Early Stage
Later Stage

Geographical Preferences

United States Preferences:
All U.S.

International Preferences:
Europe

Industry Preferences

In Industrial/Energy prefer:
Alternative Energy
Environmental Related

In Agr/Forestr/Fish prefer:
Agriculture related

In Other prefer:
Environment Responsible

Additional Information

Year Founded: 2000
Current Activity Level : Actively seeking new investments

GOLD HILL CAPITAL MANAGEMENT LLC

One Almaden Boulevard
Suite 630
San Jose, CA USA 95113
Phone: 4082007840
Fax: 4082007841
E-mail: info@goldhillcapital.com
Website: www.goldhillcapital.com

Other Offices

35 Braintree Hill Office Park
Suite 301
BRAINTREE, MA USA 02184
Phone: 7817964200
Fax: 7817964210

Management and Staff

David Fischer, Founder
Frank Tower, Founder
Glenn Marasigan, Principal
Rob Helm, Co-Founder
Sean Lynden, Founder
Tim Waterson, Founder

Type of Firm

Private Equity Firm

Association Membership

Mid-Atlantic Venture Association
New England Venture Capital Association

Project Preferences

Type of Financing Preferred:
Mezzanine
Balanced
Later Stage

Size of Investments Considered:
Min Size of Investment Considered (000s): $1,000
Max Size of Investment Considered (000s): $15,000

Additional Information

Year Founded: 2003
Capital Under Management: $19,800,000
Current Activity Level : Actively seeking new investments

GOLD INNOVATION (BEIJING) INTERNATIONAL INVESTMENT MGMT.

No. 39 East 4th Ring Middle Rd
Huaye International Center
Beijing, China 100025
Phone: 861087888808
Fax: 861085711077
E-mail: zhongjinchuangxin@gmail.com
Website: www.cfiivc.com

Type of Firm

Private Equity Firm

Project Preferences

Type of Financing Preferred:
Leveraged Buyout
Balanced

Geographical Preferences

International Preferences:
China

Additional Information

Year Founded: 2011
Current Activity Level : Actively seeking new investments

GOLD RIDGE ASSET MANAGEMENT LLC

130 Gardeners Circle
Suite 139
Johns Island, SC USA 29455
Phone: 2038376079
E-mail: info@goldridgeasset.com
Website: goldridgeasset.com

Type of Firm
Private Equity Firm

Project Preferences

Type of Financing Preferred:
Early Stage
Expansion
Balanced
Seed
Startup

Geographical Preferences

United States Preferences:
East Coast

Additional Information

Year Founded: 2013
Current Activity Level : Actively seeking new investments

GOLD STONE INVESTMENT LTD

48, Liangmaqiao Rd, Chaoyang
17/F, CITIC Securities Tower
Beijing, China 100125
Phone: 861060837800
Fax: 861060837899

Type of Firm
Bank Affiliated

Association Membership
China Venture Capital Association

Project Preferences

Type of Financing Preferred:
Leveraged Buyout
Balanced
Later Stage

Geographical Preferences

International Preferences:
China
Asia

Industry Preferences

In Communications prefer:
Media and Entertainment

In Medical/Health prefer:
Medical/Health
Pharmaceuticals

In Consumer Related prefer:
Consumer

In Industrial/Energy prefer:
Energy
Materials
Machinery

In Financial Services prefer:
Financial Services
Financial Services

In Business Serv. prefer:
Services

In Manufact. prefer:
Manufacturing

In Agr/Forestr/Fish prefer:
Agriculture related
Mining and Minerals

Additional Information

Year Founded: 2007
Capital Under Management: $786,225,000
Current Activity Level : Actively seeking new investments

GOLDCREST INVESTMENTS LP

5956 Sherry LN, Suite 930
Dallas, TX USA 75225
E-mail: info@goldcrest.co

Type of Firm
Private Equity Firm

Project Preferences

Type of Financing Preferred:
Balanced

Additional Information

Year Founded: 2015
Current Activity Level : Actively seeking new investments

GOLDEN BRIDGE VENTURE CAPITAL, L.P.

Daxue West Road
Room 1212, Xuefukangdu A Bldg
Hohhot, Inner Mongolia, China
Phone: 864713382391
Fax: 864713382392
E-mail: gbvc@gbvc.com.cn
Website: www.gbvc.com.cn

Management and Staff
Hongjun Bai, Managing Partner
Jinxia Li, Managing Partner
Luanduo Zhang, Managing Partner

Type of Firm
Private Equity Firm

Project Preferences

Type of Financing Preferred:
Balanced

Geographical Preferences

International Preferences:
Mongolia
China

Industry Preferences

In Consumer Related prefer:
Retail
Consumer Services
Education Related

In Industrial/Energy prefer:
Energy Conservation Relat
Environmental Related

Additional Information

Year Founded: 2010
Capital Under Management: $8,810,000
Current Activity Level : Actively seeking new investments

GOLDEN EQUATOR CAPITAL PTE LTD

1 Marina Blvd
Singapore, Singapore 018989
Website: www.goldenequatorcapital.com

Management and Staff
Daren Tan, Managing Partner
Steven Tseng, Managing Partner

Type of Firm
Investment Management Firm

Project Preferences

Type of Financing Preferred:
Balanced

Additional Information
Year Founded: 2015
Capital Under Management: $40,000,000
Current Activity Level : Actively seeking new investments

GOLDEN GATE CAPITAL INC

One Embarcadero Center
39th Floor
San Francisco, CA USA 94111
Phone: 4159832700
Fax: 4159832701
E-mail: info@goldengatecap.com
Website: www.goldengatecap.com

Management and Staff
David Dominik, Managing Director
Felix Lo, Principal
Jake Mizrahi, Managing Director
Jim Rauh, Principal
John Knoll, Managing Director
Josh Cohen, Principal
Joshua Olshansky, Managing Director
Ken Diekroeger, Managing Director
Prescott Ashe, Managing Director
Rajeev Amara, Managing Director
Rishi Chandna, Principal
Rob Little, Chief Operating Officer

Type of Firm
Private Equity Firm

Project Preferences

Type of Financing Preferred:
Leveraged Buyout
Expansion
Generalist PE
Balanced
Management Buyouts
Recapitalizations

Industry Focus
(% based on actual investment)
Consumer Related	28.4%
Other Products	26.6%
Computer Software and Services	18.3%
Computer Hardware	9.8%
Communications and Media	8.1%
Semiconductors/Other Elect.	4.1%
Internet Specific	3.9%
Medical/Health	0.8%

Additional Information
Year Founded: 2000
Capital Under Management: $12,000,000,000
Current Activity Level : Actively seeking new investments

GOLDEN GATE VENTURES PTE LTD

73B Duxton Road
Singapore, Singapore 089532
E-mail: hello@goldengate.vc
Website: goldengate.vc

Other Offices
113, Somerset Road
, Singapore 238165

Management and Staff
Justin Hall, Principal
Michael Lints, Venture Partner

Type of Firm
Private Equity Firm

Project Preferences

Type of Financing Preferred:
Early Stage
Expansion
Seed
Startup

Geographical Preferences

International Preferences:
Vietnam
Indonesia
Thailand
Philippines
Asia
Singapore
Malaysia

Industry Preferences

In Computer Software prefer:
Software

In Internet Specific prefer:
Internet

Additional Information
Year Founded: 2012
Capital Under Management: $60,000,000
Current Activity Level : Actively seeking new investments

GOLDEN SUNFLOWER CAPITAL MANAGEMENT CO LTD

Haidian East Three Street
10F, Internet Financial Center
Beijing, China 100080
Phone: 861059608000
Fax: 861059608023
Website: www.gsfcap.com

Type of Firm
Investment Management Firm

Project Preferences

Type of Financing Preferred:
Leveraged Buyout

Geographical Preferences

International Preferences:
China

Industry Preferences

In Internet Specific prefer:
Internet

In Medical/Health prefer:
Medical/Health

In Agr/Forestr/Fish prefer:
Agriculture related

Additional Information
Year Founded: 2014
Current Activity Level : Actively seeking new investments

GOLDEN VENTURE PARTNERS INC

20 Maud Street
Suite 207
Toronto, Canada M5V 2M5
E-mail: info@goldenvp.com

Management and Staff
Bert Amato, Venture Partner
Matt Golden, Managing Partner

Type of Firm
Private Equity Firm

Association Membership
Canadian Venture Capital Association

Project Preferences

Type of Financing Preferred:
Early Stage
Seed
Startup

Geographical Preferences

Canadian Preferences:
All Canada

Industry Preferences

In Communications prefer:
Communications and Media
Telecommunications
Wireless Communications

Additional Information
Year Founded: 2011
Capital Under Management: $52,520,000
Current Activity Level : Actively seeking new investments

GOLDENMOUNT CAPITAL INTERNATIONAL INC

250 Consumer Road, Unit 1009
North York, Canada M2J 4R4
Phone: 14164989818
Fax: 14164989868
Website: www.goldenmountcapital.ca

Management and Staff
Bob Guo, President
Junaid Saleem, Managing Director

Type of Firm
Private Equity Firm

Project Preferences

Type of Financing Preferred:
Early Stage
Expansion
Generalist PE
Acquisition
Startup

Industry Preferences

In Industrial/Energy prefer:
Environmental Related

In Financial Services prefer:
Real Estate

In Agr/Forestr/Fish prefer:
Mining and Minerals

Additional Information
Year Founded: 2008
Current Activity Level : Actively seeking new investments

GOLDIN VENTURES CO

150 Locust Street
Macungie, PA USA 18062
Website: www.goldinventures.com

Management and Staff
Michael Doyle, President
Steven Markowitz, Chief Executive Officer

Type of Firm
Private Equity Firm

Project Preferences

Role in Financing:
Will function either as deal originator or investor in deals created by others

Type of Financing Preferred:
Leveraged Buyout
Early Stage
Expansion
Generalist PE
Acquisition

Geographical Preferences

United States Preferences:
Mid Atlantic

Industry Preferences

In Communications prefer:
Communications and Media
Telecommunications

Additional Information
Year Founded: 2007
Current Activity Level : Actively seeking new investments

GOLDING CAPITAL PARTNERS GMBH

Moehlstrasse 7
Munich, Germany 81675
Phone: 49894199970
Fax: 498941999750
E-mail: info@goldingcapital.com
Website: www.goldingcapital.com

Other Offices
Ave Marie-Therese 6
Luxembourg, Luxembourg 2132

One Embarcadero Center, Suite 500
SAN FRANCISCO, CA USA 94111
Phone: 1-415-623-2018
Fax: 1-415-433-5994

Management and Staff
Andreas Rizos, Principal
Edouard Georges, Managing Director
Hubertus Theile-Ochel, Partner
Jeremy Golding, Managing Partner
Linda Behnke, Partner
Silvan Trachsler, Managing Director

Type of Firm
Private Equity Advisor or Fund of Funds

Association Membership
German Venture Capital Association (BVK)
European Private Equity and Venture Capital Assoc.

Project Preferences

Type of Financing Preferred:
Fund of Funds
Fund of Funds of Second

Geographical Preferences

United States Preferences:
All U.S.

International Preferences:
United Kingdom
Europe
Scandanavia/Nordic Region
Asia
Germany
France

Additional Information
Name of Most Recent Fund: Golding Buyout Europe SICAV VI
Most Recent Fund Was Raised: 03/25/2014
Year Founded: 1999
Capital Under Management: $1,215,357,000
Current Activity Level : Actively seeking new investments

GOLDIS BHD

199 Jalan Tun Razak
Suite 28-03, Level 28, GTower
Kuala Lumpur, Malaysia 50400
Phone: 60321681888
Fax: 60321637020
Website: www.go.dis.com

Management and Staff
Tan Lei Cheng, Chairman & CEO

Type of Firm
Private Equity Firm

Project Preferences

Type of Financing Preferred:
Leveraged Buyout
Balanced

Geographical Preferences

International Preferences:
China
Malaysia

Industry Preferences

In Industrial/Energy prefer:
Environmental Related

In Financial Services prefer:
Real Estate

In Agr/Forestr/Fish prefer:
Agriculture related

Additional Information
Year Founded: 2000
Current Activity Level : Actively seeking new investments

GOLDMAN SACHS & CO LLC

200 West Street, 29th Floor
New York, NY USA 10282
Phone: 2129020300
E-mail: gs-investor-relations@gs.com
Website: www.goldmansachs.com

Other Offices

1735 Market Street
Mellon Bank Center, 26th Floor
Philadelphia, PA USA 19103
Phone: 215-656-7800

2121 Avenue of the Stars
Fox Plaza, Suite 2600
Los Angeles, CA USA 90067
Phone: 310-407-5700

Winland International Center, 17th Floor
7 Finance Street, Xicheng District
Beijing, China 100140
Phone: 86-10-6627-3333

14th Floor, Ducat III
6, Gasheka Street
Moscow, Russia 125047
Phone: 7-495-645-4000
Fax: 7-495-645-4050

63 Wireless Road, Athenee Tower
23/F, Suite 33
Bangkok, Thailand 10330
Phone: 6621268076

101 Constitution Avenue, Northwest
Suite 1000 East
Washington, DC USA 20001
Phone: 202-637-3700

777 South Flagler
Suite 1200 - East Tower
West Palm Beach, FL USA 33401
Phone: 561-650-1600

Gardenia Court, Suite 3307
45 Market Street
Camana Bay, Cayman Islands KY1-1103
Phone: 345-949-6770

555 California Street
45th Floor
San Francisco, CA USA 94104
Phone: 415-393-7500

QFC Branch, Qatar Financial Centre
West Bay
Doha, Qatar
Phone: 974-496-7560
Fax: 974-496-7570

Daniel House
133 Fleet Street
London, United Kingdom EC4A 2BB
Phone: 44-20-7774-1000

Avda. del Libertador, 498
19th Floor
Buenos Aires, Argentina 1001
Phone: 54-11-4323-0500

2, rue de Thann
Paris, France 75017
Phone: 33-1-4212-1000

MesseTurm
Friedrich-Ebert-Anlage 49
Frankfurt am Main, Germany 60308
Phone: 49-69-7532-1000

Taipei Metro Tower, 11th Floor
207 Tun Hua South Road, Sec. 2
Taipei, Taiwan 10675
Phone: 886-2-2730-4000

2502 Rocky Point Drive
Suite 500
Tampa, FL USA 33607
Phone: 813-288-7500

Petershill
1 Carter Lane
London, United Kingdom EC4V 5ER
Phone: 44-20-7774-1000

125 High Street
17th Floor
Boston, MA USA 02110
Phone: 617-204-2000

200 South Biscayne Boulevard
First Union Financial Center, Suite 3700
Miami, FL USA 33131
Phone: 305-755-1000

30 Hudson Street
Jersey City, NJ USA 07302
Phone: 212-902-1000

Av. Presidente Juscelino
Kubitscheck, 510-6th Floor
Sao Paulo, Brazil 04543-000
Phone: 55-11-3371-0700

1310, 311 - 6 Ave. SW
Calgary, Canada T2P 3H2
Phone: 403-269-1333

21/F, HungKuk Life Insurance Building
226 Shin Mun Ro 1Ga, Chong Ro-Gu
Seoul, South Korea 110-786
Phone: 82-2-3788-1000

Crystal Downs
Embassy Golf Links Business Park
Bangalore, India 560 071

Museum Tower
4 Berkowitz Street, 16th Floor
Tel Aviv, Israel 64238
Phone: 972-3-564-1600

Le George V
14 Avenue de Grande-Bretagne
Monte Carlo, Monaco 98000
Phone: 377-97-982-830
Fax: 377-97-982-831

Kingdom Tower
25th Floor
Riyadh, Saudi Arabia 11573
Phone: 966-1279-4800

440 South LaSalle Street
Suite 1600
Chicago, IL USA 60605

Level 5, Gate Precinct Building 1
Dubai International Financial Centre
Dubai, Utd. Arab Em.
Phone: 971-442-82444

100 Crescent Court
Suite 1000
Dallas, TX USA 75201
Phone: 214-855-1000

Christchurch Court
10-15 Newgate Street
London, United Kingdom EC1A 7HD
Phone: 44-20-7774-1000

River Court
120 Fleet Street
, United Kingdom EC4A BB
Phone: 44-20-7774-1000

719 Second Avenue
Suite 1300
Seattle, WA USA 98104
Phone: 206-613-5500

3835,855 2nd Street SW
Bankers Hall - East Tower
Calgary, Canada T2P 4J8
Phone: 403-233-9293

Royal Trust Tower
77 King Street West, Suite 3400
Toronto, Canada M5K 1B7
Phone: 416-343-8900

43/F, The Center
989 Chang Le Road
Shanghai, China 200031
Phone: 86-21-2401-8888

Birger Jarlsgatan, 12
Second Floor
Stockholm, Sweden 114 34
Phone: 46-8-407-0500

Munsterhof 4
Postfach
Zurich, Sweden 8022
Phone: 41-44-224-1000

Pratt's Guide to Private Equity & Venture Capital Sources

3414 Peachtree Road, Northeast
Suite 600
Atlanta, GA USA 30326
Phone: 404-846-7200

71 South Wacker Drive
Suite 500
Chicago, IL USA 60606
Phone: 312-655-4600

Peterborough Court
133 Fleet Street
London, United Kingdom EC4A 2BB
Phone: 44-20-7774-1000
Fax: 44-207-774-4123

701 Mt. Lucas Road
Princeton, NJ USA 08540
Phone: 609-497-5500

1 Raffles Link
07-01 South Lobby
Singapore, Singapore 039393
Phone: 65-6889-1000

13th Floor, The Forum
2 Maude Street, Sandton
Johannesburg, South Africa 2196
Phone: 27-11-303-2700

Maria de Molina, 6-5a
Madrid, Spain 28006
Phone: 34-91-700-6000

1 Rue des Moulins
Geneva, Sweden 1211
Phone: 41-228-166-000

295 Chipeta Way
Salt Lake City, UT USA 84108
Phone: 801-884-1000

Cheung Kong Center, 68th Floor
2 Queen's Road
Central, Hong Kong
Phone: 852-2978-1000
Fax: 852-2978-0440

Second Floor
Hardwicke House, Upper Hatch Street
Dublin, Ireland
Phone: 353-1-439-6000

Passaggio Centrale 2
Milan, Italy 20123
Phone: 39-2-8022-1000

Roppongi Hills Mori Tower, Level 43-48
10-1, Roppongi 6-chrome, Minato-ku
Tokyo, Japan 106-6147
Phone: 81-3-6437-1000

Torre Optima Bldg., Paseo de las Palmas
Col. Lomas de Chapultepec
Mexico, Mexico 11000
Phone: 52-55-5540-8100

6011 Connection Drive
Irving, TX USA 75039
Phone: 9723682200

951-A, Appasaheb Marathe Marg
Prabhadevi
Mumbai, India 400 025
Phone: 91-22-6616-9000
Fax: 91-22-6616-9001

1000 Louisiana Street
Suite 550
Houston, TX USA 77002
Phone: 713-654-8400

Management and Staff
Alice Jane Murphy, Partner
Alicia Glen, Managing Director
Gary Cohn, President & COO

Type of Firm
Bank Affiliated

Association Membership
China Venture Capital Association
Israel Venture Association
Natl Assoc of Small Bus. Inv. Co (NASBIC)
European Private Equity and Venture Capital Assoc.

Project Preferences

Type of Financing Preferred:
Fund of Funds
Leveraged Buyout
Value-Add
Early Stage
Expansion
Mezzanine
Generalist PE
Balanced
Turnaround
Opportunistic
Later Stage
Other
Acquisition
Distressed Debt
Fund of Funds of Second
Recapitalizations

Size of Investments Considered:
Min Size of Investment Considered (000s): $50,000
Max Size of Investment Considered (000s): $800,000

Geographical Preferences

United States Preferences:
All U.S.

International Preferences:
Europe
Asia
All International

Industry Focus
(% based on actual investment)
Other Products	35.6%
Computer Software and Services	16.8%
Internet Specific	13.8%
Consumer Related	9.2%
Industrial/Energy	8.1%
Communications and Media	7.8%
Medical/Health	5.1%
Semiconductors/Other Elect.	2.0%
Computer Hardware	1.1%
Biotechnology	0.4%

Additional Information
Name of Most Recent Fund: Goldman Sachs Vintage Fund VI, L.P.
Most Recent Fund Was Raised: 06/27/2012
Year Founded: 1991
Capital Under Management: $79,000,000,000
Current Activity Level : Actively seeking new investments

GOLDMAN SACHS SPECIALTY LENDING GROUP LP

200 West Street
New York, NY USA 10282
Phone: 2129021000

Type of Firm
Corporate PE/Venture

Project Preferences

Type of Financing Preferred:
Leveraged Buyout
Expansion
Turnaround
Management Buyouts

Geographical Preferences

United States Preferences:

Canadian Preferences:
All Canada

Industry Preferences

In Communications prefer:
Telecommunications
Wireless Communications

In Computer Software prefer:
Software

In Medical/Health prefer:
Health Services

In Consumer Related prefer:
Retail
Franchises(NEC)
Consumer Products

In Industrial/Energy prefer:
Oil and Gas Exploration

In Business Serv. prefer:
Media

Additional Information
Year Founded: 1969
Current Activity Level : Actively seeking new investments

GOLDNER HAWN JOHNSON & MORRISON INC

90 South Seventh Street
3700 Wells Fargo Center
Minneapolis, MN USA 55402
Phone: 6123385912
Fax: 6123382860
E-mail: reporting@ghjm.com
Website: www.ghjm.com

Management and Staff
Aaron Goldstein, Chief Financial Officer
Andrew Tomashek, Vice President
Chad Cornell, Managing Director
Jason Brass, Managing Director
John Morrison, Managing Director
Joseph Helms, Vice President
Joseph Heinen, Managing Director
Peter Settle, Managing Director
Timothy Johnson, Managing Partner
Van Hawn, Managing Director

Type of Firm
Private Equity Firm

Association Membership
Natl Assoc of Small Bus. Inv. Co (NASBIC)

Project Preferences

Role in Financing:
Prefer role as deal originator

Type of Financing Preferred:
Leveraged Buyout
Management Buyouts
Acquisition
Recapitalizations

Geographical Preferences

United States Preferences:
Midwest
Northwest

Industry Preferences

In Consumer Related prefer:
Consumer
Retail
Food/Beverage
Other Restaurants

In Industrial/Energy prefer:
Industrial Products

In Transportation prefer:
Transportation

In Business Serv. prefer:
Services
Distribution

In Manufact. prefer:
Manufacturing

In Agr/Forestr/Fish prefer:
Agribusiness

Additional Information
Name of Most Recent Fund: Trailhead Fund, L.P.
Most Recent Fund Was Raised: 03/28/2012
Year Founded: 1989
Capital Under Management: $325,000,000
Current Activity Level : Actively seeking new investments
Method of Compensation: Return on invest. most important, but chg. closing fees, service fees, etc.

GOLDPOINT PARTNERS LLC

51 Madison Avenue
Suite 1600
New York, NY USA 10010
Phone: 2125766500
E-mail: info@goldpointpartners.com
Website: www.goldpointpartners.com

Other Offices
1180 Avenue of the Americas
NEW YORK, NY USA 10036
Phone: 212-938-6500

Management and Staff
A. Vijay Palkar, Principal
Charles Cocuzza, Vice President
Matthew Cashion, Principal
Paul Roberts, Principal
Scott Iorio, Vice President
Sean Gelb, Chief Financial Officer
Thomas Haubenstricker, Chief Executive Officer

Type of Firm
Insurance Firm Affiliate

Project Preferences

Role in Financing:
Prefer role in deals created by others

Type of Financing Preferred:
Fund of Funds
Leveraged Buyout
Mezzanine
Generalist PE
Management Buyouts
Recapitalizations

Geographical Preferences

United States Preferences:
All U.S.

International Preferences:
Europe
Western Europe

Industry Focus
(% based on actual investment)

Other Products	55.5%
Biotechnology	9.9%
Internet Specific	7.7%
Computer Hardware	6.6%
Communications and Media	6.2%
Computer Software and Services	5.3%
Medical/Health	5.2%
Industrial/Energy	1.9%
Semiconductors/Other Elect.	1.0%
Consumer Related	0.7%

Additional Information
Name of Most Recent Fund: GoldPoint Partners Co-Investment V, L.P.
Most Recent Fund Was Raised: 11/14/2012
Year Founded: 1999
Capital Under Management: $10,047,000,000
Current Activity Level : Actively seeking new investments
Method of Compensation: Return on invest. most important, but chg. closing fees, service fees, etc.

GOLDROCK CAPITAL

16 Hata'asiyah St
A Industrial Zone
Har Tuv, Israel 99100
Phone: 972722221344
Fax: 972722221345
Website: www.goldrockcap.com

Type of Firm
Private Equity Firm

Project Preferences

Type of Financing Preferred:
Leveraged Buyout
Early Stage
Expansion
Generalist PE

Balanced
Later Stage
Management Buyouts
Acquisition

Size of Investments Considered:
Min Size of Investment Considered (000s): $1,000
Max Size of Investment Considered (000s): $5,000

Geographical Preferences

International Preferences:
Israel

Industry Preferences

In Communications prefer:
Communications and Media
Radio & TV Broadcasting
Telecommunications
Wireless Communications
Media and Entertainment

In Computer Software prefer:
Software
Systems Software
Applications Software

In Internet Specific prefer:
Internet

In Business Serv. prefer:
Mecia

Additional Information
Year Founded: 1988
Current Activity Level : Actively seeking new investments

GOLDTEL VENTURE CAPITAL FUND

GolcTel Park
West Hi-tech Zone, Sichuan
Chendu, China 611731
Phone: 862887827222
Fax: 862887827221
Website: www.guoteng.com.cn

Type of Firm
Incubator/Development Program

Project Preferences

Type of Financing Preferred:
Early Stage
Seec
Startup

Geographical Preferences

International Preferences:
China

Additional Information
Year Founded: 2011
Current Activity Level : Actively seeking new investments

GOLUB CAPITAL MASTER FUNDING LLC

150 South Wacker Drive
Suite 800
Chicago, IL USA 60606
Phone: 3122055050
Fax: 3122019167
E-mail: info@golubcapital.com
Website: www.golubcapital.com

Other Offices
666 Fifth Avenue
Suite 800
New York, NY USA 10103
Phone: 2127506060
Fax: 2127505505

3343 Peachtree Road, North East
East Tower, Suite 331
Atlanta, GA USA 30326
Phone: 404-495-4520
Fax: 404-495-4526

Management and Staff
Brian Davis, Managing Director
Charles Riceman, Managing Director
Chip Cushman, Managing Director
David Golub, President
Gregory Cashman, Senior Managing Director
Gregory Robbins, Managing Director
Hyun Chang, Managing Director
Jason Van Dussen, Managing Director
John Geisler, Chief Financial Officer
Jonathan Pearl, Vice President
Joseph Wilson, Managing Director
Joseph Longosz, Managing Director
Marc Robinson, Managing Director
Marcus Lindberg, Vice President
Michael Meagher, Managing Director
Michael Griffin, Vice President
Patrick Hayes, Principal
Paul Stern, Vice President
Pierre-Olivier Lamoureux, Vice President
Robert Tuchscherer, Managing Director
Sean Coleman, Managing Director
Spyro Alexopoulos, Managing Director
Stefano Robertson, Managing Director
Troy Oder, Managing Director

Type of Firm
Private Equity Firm

Association Membership
Natl Assoc of Small Bus. Inv. Co (NASBIC)

Project Preferences

Role in Financing:
Will function either as deal originator or investor in deals created by others

Type of Financing Preferred:
Mezzanine
Generalist PE
Balanced
Later Stage
Distressed Debt
Recapitalizations

Geographical Preferences

United States Preferences:

Industry Preferences

In Computer Software prefer:
Software

In Semiconductor/Electr prefer:
Semiconductor

In Medical/Health prefer:
Medical/Health
Diagnostic Services
Health Services

In Consumer Related prefer:
Consumer
Sports
Retail
Consumer Products
Other Restaurants
Hotels and Resorts
Education Related

In Industrial/Energy prefer:
Industrial Products
Factory Automation
Process Control

In Transportation prefer:
Transportation
Aerospace

In Business Serv. prefer:
Services
Distribution
Media

In Manufact. prefer:
Manufacturing

Additional Information
Name of Most Recent Fund: Golub Capital Partners IX, L.P.
Most Recent Fund Was Raised: 01/13/2014
Year Founded: 1994
Capital Under Management: $8,000,000,000
Current Activity Level : Actively seeking new investments
Method of Compensation: Return on invest. most important, but chg. closing fees, service fees, etc.

GOOD ENERGIES AG

Grafenauweg 10
Zug, Switzerland 6301
Phone: 41417296902
Website: www.goodenergies.org

Other Offices

277 Park Avenue
29th Floor
NEW YORK, NY USA 10172
Phone: 212-704-3000
Fax: 212-704-3001

2-5 Old Bond Street
Standbrook House
London, United Kingdom W1S 4PD
Phone: 44-20-7659-3300
Fax: 44-20-7569-3305

Management and Staff

Edwin Niers, Chief Financial Officer
Marcel Brenninkmeijer, Founder

Type of Firm

Private Equity Firm

Project Preferences

Type of Financing Preferred:
Generalist PE
Balanced

Geographical Preferences

United States Preferences:
All U.S.

Canadian Preferences:
All Canada

International Preferences:
United Kingdom
Europe
Germany
All International

Industry Preferences

In Industrial/Energy prefer:
Energy
Alternative Energy
Environmental Related

In Other prefer:
Environment Responsible

Additional Information

Year Founded: 2001
Current Activity Level : Actively seeking new investments

GOOD WORKS VENTURES LLC

72702 Heart View Lane
Arlee, MT USA 59821
Website: www.goodworksventures.com

Type of Firm

Private Equity Firm

Project Preferences

Type of Financing Preferred:
Early Stage

Geographical Preferences

United States Preferences:
Montana

Additional Information

Year Founded: 2012
Current Activity Level : Actively seeking new investments

GOODE PARTNERS LLC

767 Third Avenue, 22nd Floor
New York, NY USA 10017
Phone: 6467229450
Fax: 2123172827
E-mail: info@goodepartners.com
Website: www.goodepartners.com

Other Offices

767 Third Avenue, 22nd Floor
New York, NY USA 10017
Phone: 6467229450
Fax: 2123172827

150 North Santa Anita Avenue, Suite 300
Arcadia, CA USA 91006
Phone: 626-821-1877
Fax: 626-821-1876

Management and Staff

Daniel Bonoff, Partner
David Oddi, Founder
Jose Ferreira, Founder
Keith Miller, Partner
Michael Stanley, Vice President
Paula Semelmacher, Chief Financial Officer
Ron Beegle, Founder

Type of Firm

Private Equity Firm

Project Preferences

Type of Financing Preferred:
Leveraged Buyout
Expansion
Management Buyouts

Geographical Preferences

United States Preferences:

Industry Preferences

In Consumer Related prefer:
Consumer
Retail
Consumer Products
Consumer Services
Other Restaurants

Additional Information

Name of Most Recent Fund: Goode Partners Consumer Fund II, L.P.
Most Recent Fund Was Raised: 10/25/2012
Year Founded: 2005
Capital Under Management: $240,400,000
Current Activity Level : Actively seeking new investments

GOODVENT BETEILIGUNGSMANAGEMENT GMBH & CO KG

Kantstrasse 5
Magdeburg, Germany 39104
Phone: 493031519080
Fax: 493031519099
E-mail: info@goodvent.net
Website: www.goodvent.net

Other Offices

Kurfuerstendamm 57
Berlin, Germany 10707
Phone: 493031012300
Fax: 493031012441

Management and Staff

Dinnies von der Osten, Chief Executive Officer
Eric Bourgett, Partner
Guido Heine, Partner

Type of Firm

Private Equity Firm

Project Preferences

Type of Financing Preferred:
Early Stage
Later Stage
Seed
Startup

Geographical Preferences

International Preferences:
Germany

Industry Preferences

In Computer Software prefer:
Software

In Semiconductor/Electr prefer:
Electronics
Electronic Components
Semiconductor

In Medical/Health prefer:
Medical/Health
Pharmaceuticals

In Industrial/Energy prefer:
Energy
Industrial Products
Materials
Process Control
Environmental Related

Additional Information
Year Founded: 2007
Current Activity Level : Actively seeking new investments

GOODWELL INVESTMENTS BV

Herengracht 201
Amsterdam, Netherlands 1016BE
Phone: 31852737462
Website: goodwell.nl

Type of Firm
Private Equity Firm

Project Preferences

Type of Financing Preferred:
Early Stage

Geographical Preferences

International Preferences:
India
Nigeria
Ghana
Kenya
Africa

Industry Preferences

In Computer Software prefer:
Software

In Internet Specific prefer:
Internet

In Financial Services prefer:
Financial Services

Additional Information
Year Founded: 2006
Capital Under Management: $20,820,000
Current Activity Level : Actively seeking new investments

GOPHER ASSET MANAGEMENT CO LTD

c/o, Noah Private Wealth
No. 58, Yincheng Mid Road
Shanghai, China 200120
Phone: 862138602388
Fax: 862138602300
Website: www.gopherasset.com

Other Offices
No.25 Culture Road, Jinghu
Wuhu, China

Type of Firm
Private Equity Advisor or Fund of Funds

Project Preferences

Type of Financing Preferred:
Fund of Funds
Balanced

Geographical Preferences

International Preferences:
China

Industry Preferences

In Communications prefer:
Telecommunications

In Consumer Related prefer:
Consumer

In Financial Services prefer:
Real Estate

In Manufact. prefer:
Manufacturing

Additional Information
Name of Most Recent Fund: Gopher S Fund
Most Recent Fund Was Raised: 04/15/2013
Year Founded: 2010
Capital Under Management: $321,200,000
Current Activity Level : Actively seeking new investments

GORDON RIVER CAPITAL

2950 Golden Gate Parkway #101
Naples, FL USA 34105
Phone: 2396590288
Fax: 2392622212
Website: www.gulfshorecap.com

Management and Staff
Patrick George, Principal
Richard Molloy, Principal

Type of Firm
Private Equity Firm

Project Preferences

Type of Financing Preferred:
Early Stage
Expansion
Later Stage

Geographical Preferences

United States Preferences:
Southeast
Florida

Industry Preferences

In Internet Specific prefer:
Internet

In Medical/Health prefer:
Medical Products
Health Services

In Consumer Related prefer:
Consumer Products

In Industrial/Energy prefer:
Industrial Products

In Business Serv. prefer:
Services

Additional Information
Year Founded: 2005
Current Activity Level : Actively seeking new investments

GORE RANGE CAPITAL LLC

2121 N Frontage Rd West
#253
Vail, CO USA 81657
E-mail: info@gorerangecapital.com
Website: gorerangecapital.com

Type of Firm
Private Equity Firm

Project Preferences

Type of Financing Preferred:
Early Stage

Industry Preferences

In Medical/Health prefer:
Health Services

Additional Information
Year Founded: 2015
Capital Under Management: $460,000
Current Activity Level : Actively seeking new investments

GORES GROUP LLC

9800 Wilshire Boulevard
Beverly Hills, CA USA 90212
Phone: 3102093010
Fax: 3102093310
E-mail: investorrelations@gores.com
Website: www.gores.com

Other Offices
52 Conduit Street
4th Floor
London, United Kingdom W1S 2YX
Phone: 448700601190
Fax: 448700601191

6260 Lookout Road
Boulder, CO USA 80301
Phone: 3035313100
Fax: 3035313200

Bockenheimer Landstrasse 17/19
Frankfurt, Germany 60325F

Management and Staff
Andrew Freedman, Managing Director
Anthony Guagliano, Managing Director
Ashley Abdo, Managing Director
David Fredston, Principal
Desmond Nugent, Principal
Edward Johnson, Managing Director
Eric Harnish, Managing Director
Fernando Goni, Managing Director
Gina Pollack, Vice President
Igor Chacartegui, Principal
Jeffrey Schwartz, Managing Director
Jennifer Kwon, Principal
Jonathan Huberman, Managing Director
Jonathan Gimbel, Principal
Jordan Katz, Managing Director
Joseph Page, Chief Operating Officer
Lindsay Wynter, Managing Director
Mark Stone, Senior Managing Director
Michael Adkins, Principal
Michael Eblin, Managing Director
Mike Nutting, Managing Director
Ray LeClercq, Managing Director
Robbie Reynders, Managing Director
Ryan Wald, Managing Director
Saad Hammad, Managing Director
Steven Yager, Senior Managing Director
Tarek Kutrieh, Principal
Thomas Waldman, Managing Director
Timothy Meyer, Managing Director
Victor Otley, Managing Director

Type of Firm
Private Equity Firm

Project Preferences

Role in Financing:
Prefer role as deal originator

Type of Financing Preferred:
Leveraged Buyout
Turnaround
Acquisition
Special Situation

Geographical Preferences

United States Preferences:
North America

International Preferences:
Europe

Industry Preferences

In Communications prefer:
Telecommunications

In Medical/Health prefer:
Medical/Health
Health Services

In Consumer Related prefer:
Consumer
Retail
Food/Beverage
Consumer Products
Consumer Services

In Industrial/Energy prefer:
Industrial Products

In Financial Services prefer:
Financial Services

In Business Serv. prefer:
Services
Media

Additional Information
Name of Most Recent Fund: Gores Small Capitalization Partners, L.P.
Most Recent Fund Was Raised: 03/07/2012
Year Founded: 1987
Capital Under Management: $400,000,000
Current Activity Level : Actively seeking new investments

GORGE HOLDINGS LLC

317 SW Alder Street
Suite 510
Portland, OR USA 97204
E-mail: info@gorgeholdings.com
Website: www.gorgeholdings.com

Management and Staff
David Altman, Co-Founder
Richard Diforio, Co-Founder

Type of Firm
Private Equity Firm

Project Preferences

Type of Financing Preferred:
Leveraged Buyout

Geographical Preferences

United States Preferences:
West Coast

Industry Preferences

In Business Serv. prefer:
Services
Distribution

In Manufact. prefer:
Manufacturing

Additional Information
Year Founded: 2003
Current Activity Level : Actively seeking new investments

GOTHAM PRIVATE EQUITY PARTNERS LP

355 Lexington Avenue
Fourth Floor
New York, NY USA 10017
Phone: 212-818-1818
Fax: 212-818-1994
E-mail: info@gothamequity.com
Website: www.gothamequity.com

Management and Staff
Daniel Gaspar, Vice President
Gregory Prata, Vice President

Type of Firm
Private Equity Firm

Project Preferences

Type of Financing Preferred:
Leveraged Buyout
Expansion
Management Buyouts
Acquisition
Special Situation
Recapitalizations

Additional Information
Year Founded: 2009
Current Activity Level : Actively seeking new investments

GOTHAM VENTURES LLC

425 Madison Avenue
Suite 1801
Manhattan, NY USA 10017
Phone: 2122793980
Fax: 2122793835
Website: gothamvc.com

Management and Staff
Daniel Schultz, Co-Founder
Joy Marcus, Venture Partner
Lucas Nelson, Principal
Ross Goldstein, Co-Founder
Thatcher Bell, Venture Partner
Thatcher Bell, Managing Director
Timothy Draper, Co-Founder

Type of Firm
Private Equity Firm

Project Preferences

Type of Financing Preferred:
Early Stage
Seed

Size of Investments Considered:
Min Size of Investment Considered (000s): $100
Max Size of Investment Considered (000s): $500

Geographical Preferences

United States Preferences:
Northeast

International Preferences:
Israel

Industry Preferences

In Communications prefer:
Wireless Communications

In Internet Specific prefer:
Ecommerce

In Financial Services prefer:
Financial Services

In Business Serv. prefer:
Media

Additional Information

Year Founded: 2000
Capital Under Management: $180,000,000
Current Activity Level : Actively seeking new investments

GOVIN CAPITAL PTE LTD

21 Bukit, Batok Crescent
#05-74 WCEGA Tower
Singapore, Singapore 658065
Phone: 6566595946
E-mail: govincapital@yahoo.com

Type of Firm

Incubator/Development Program

Project Preferences

Type of Financing Preferred:
Startup

Additional Information

Year Founded: 2002
Current Activity Level : Actively seeking new investments

GOVTECH FUND

912 Cole Street
Suite 174
San Francisco, CA USA 94117
Website: http://govtechfund.com/

Type of Firm

Private Equity Firm

Project Preferences

Type of Financing Preferred:
Seed
Startup

Geographical Preferences

United States Preferences:

Additional Information

Year Founded: 2014
Capital Under Management: $23,000,000
Current Activity Level : Actively seeking new investments

GP INVESTIMENTOS LTDA

Ingham & Wilkinson Building
129, Front Street, Penthouse
Hamilton, Bermuda HM12
Fax: 4412790600
Website: www.gp.com.br

Other Offices

Avenida Brigadeiro Faria Lima
3900, 7th Floor
Sao Paulo, Brazil 04538-132
Fax: 551135565505

Management and Staff

Alvaro Lopes da Silva, Chief Financial Officer
Danilo Gamboa, Managing Director
Eduardo Alcalay, Managing Director
Mara Pedretti, Managing Director
Octavio Pereira Lopes, Managing Director
Thiago Rodrigues, Managing Director

Type of Firm

Private Equity Firm

Association Membership

Brazilian Venture Capital Association (ABCR)
Emerging Markets Private Equity Association

Project Preferences

Role in Financing:
Prefer role as deal originator

Type of Financing Preferred:
Leveraged Buyout
Management Buyouts
Acquisition

Size of Investments Considered:
Min Size of Investment Considered (000s): $50,000
Max Size of Investment Considered (000s): $200,000

Geographical Preferences

International Preferences:
Latin America
Argentina
Peru
Mexico
Brazil
Chile
Colombia

Additional Information

Name of Most Recent Fund: GP Capital Partners III, L.P.
Most Recent Fund Was Raised: 06/17/2005
Year Founded: 1993
Capital Under Management: $4,000,000,000
Current Activity Level : Actively seeking new investments
Method of Compensation: Function primarily in service area, receive contingent fee in cash or equity

GPF CAPITAL

Joaquin Costa 26
Madrid, Spain 28002
Phone: 34915902121
E-mail: info@gpf-capital.com
Website: gpf-capital.com

Type of Firm

Private Equity Firm

Project Preferences

Type of Financing Preferred:
Expansion
Later Stage

Geographical Preferences

International Preferences:
Spain

Additional Information

Year Founded: 2015
Capital Under Management: $177,240,000
Current Activity Level : Actively seeking new investments

GPI CAPITAL

437 Madison Avenue
28th Floor
Manhattan, NY USA 10022
Phone: 6463573144
E-mail: info@gpicap.com
Website: www.gpicap.com

Type of Firm

Private Equity Firm

Project Preferences

Type of Financing Preferred:
Generalist PE
Later Stage
Acquisition

Additional Information

Year Founded: 1969
Current Activity Level : Actively seeking new investments

GRA VENTURE FUND LLC

191 Peachtree Street Northeas
Suite 849
Atlanta, GA USA 30303
Phone: 4043329770
E-mail: info@gra.org
Website: www.graventurefund.org

Management and Staff
Michelle Jarrard, Managing Director

Type of Firm
Private Equity Firm

Project Preferences

Type of Financing Preferred:
Early Stage

Geographical Preferences

United States Preferences:
Georgia

Industry Preferences

In Biotechnology prefer:
Biotechnology

In Manufact. prefer:
Manufacturing

In Agr/Forestr/Fish prefer:
Agriculture related

Additional Information
Name of Most Recent Fund: GRA Venture Fund
Most Recent Fund Was Raised: 06/26/2009
Year Founded: 2008
Current Activity Level : Actively seeking new investments

GRACE ASSETS MANAGEMENT LLP

No. 1 East Chang-an Avenue
Rm1901, Block E2, Oriental Plz
Beijing, China 100738
Phone: 861085200381
Fax: 861085322933
E-mail: admin@graceam.com
Website: www.graceam.com

Other Offices
No.1 North Road of Worker's Stadium
Building 3-2-41
Beijing, China

8 Finance Street, Central
1909, Level 19, Two Int'l Finance Centre
Hong Kong, Hong Kong

Management and Staff
Fatima Xia, Vice President
Kevin Cruise, Venture Partner
Midas L.G. Nieh, Managing Partner
Shuhe Wang, Venture Partner
Taiou Kimura, Vice President
Vivian Washington, Chief Financial Officer
Wen Sin Tien-Hurter, Venture Partner
William Chai, Managing Partner

Type of Firm
Private Equity Firm

Project Preferences

Type of Financing Preferred:
Fund of Funds
Expansion
Later Stage

Geographical Preferences

International Preferences:
China

Industry Preferences

In Communications prefer:
Telecommunications

In Consumer Related prefer:
Consumer

In Industrial/Energy prefer:
Energy
Alternative Energy
Environmental Related

In Business Serv. prefer:
Media

In Agr/Forestr/Fish prefer:
Agriculture related

Additional Information
Year Founded: 2010
Capital Under Management: $88,561,000
Current Activity Level : Actively seeking new investments

GRADIENTE SGR SPA

Piazza Duomo, 14
Padova, Italy 35141
Phone: 39498234870
Fax: 39498234879
Website: www.gradientesgr.it

Management and Staff
Lara Farina, Chief Financial Officer

Type of Firm
Private Equity Firm

Association Membership
Italian Venture Capital Association (AIFI)

Project Preferences

Type of Financing Preferred:
Leveraged Buyout
Later Stage
Acquisition
Recapitalizations

Size of Investments Considered:
Min Size of Investment Considered (000s): $5,338
Max Size of Investment Considered (000s): $13,346

Geographical Preferences

International Preferences:
Italy

Additional Information
Year Founded: 2010
Capital Under Management: $100,100,000
Current Activity Level : Actively seeking new investments

GRAFTON CAPITAL LTD

81 Fulham Road
Michelin House
London, United Kingdom SW3 6RD
Phone: 442038260095
E-mail: info@graftoncapital.com
Website: graftoncapital.com

Management and Staff
Edward Brown, Co-Founder
Oliver Thomas, Co-Founder

Type of Firm
Private Equity Firm

Project Preferences

Type of Financing Preferred:
Expansion
Later Stage

Industry Preferences

In Computer Software prefer:
Data Processing
Software

In Internet Specific prefer:
Ecommerce

Additional Information
Year Founded: 2014
Current Activity Level : Actively seeking new investments

GRAHAM PARTNERS INC

3811 West Chester Pike
Building Two, Suite 200
Newtown Square, PA USA 19073
Phone: 6104080500
Fax: 6104080600
Website: www.grahampartners.net

Management and Staff
Anthony Folino, Chief Financial Officer
Joseph Heinmiller, Principal
Sara Boyd, Founder
William McKee, Chief Operating Officer
William Timmerman, Principal

Type of Firm
Corporate PE/Venture

Project Preferences

Type of Financing Preferred:
Leveraged Buyout
Management Buyouts
Acquisition

Geographical Preferences

United States Preferences:
North America

Industry Focus
(% based on actual investment)
Industrial/Energy	76.9%
Other Products	15.0%
Internet Specific	6.0%
Communications and Media	1.2%
Computer Software and Services	0.8%

Additional Information
Year Founded: 1988
Capital Under Management: $1,600,000,000
Current Activity Level : Actively seeking new investments

GRAMAX CAPITAL AG
Maximilianstr. 30
Munich, Germany 80539
E-mail: info@gramax-capital.com
Website: www.gramax-capital.com

Type of Firm
Private Equity Firm

Project Preferences

Type of Financing Preferred:
Leveraged Buyout
Management Buyouts

Geographical Preferences

International Preferences:
Slovenia
Luxembourg
Czech Republic
Netherlands
Switzerland
Poland
Austria
Belgium
Germany
Denmark
France

Industry Preferences

In Consumer Related prefer:
Consumer Products

In Business Serv. prefer:
Services

In Manufact. prefer:
Manufacturing

Additional Information
Year Founded: 2011
Current Activity Level : Actively seeking new investments

GRAMERCY INC
20 Dayton Avenue
Greenwich, CT USA 06830
Phone: 2035521900
Fax: 2035521901
E-mail: inquiries@gramecy.com
Website: www.gramecy.com

Other Offices
1 Knightsbridge Green
London, United Kingdom SW1X 7NE
Phone: 2033300545

One Raffles Quay, North Tower
Level 25
, Singapore 048583
Phone: 6566225602

Reforma 404
Piso Eight, Col. Juarez
, Mexico 06600
Phone: 525510843500

Eight Connaught Place
Suite 735, Two Exchange Square
Central, Hong Kong
Phone: 85237982687

Management and Staff
Ajay Jani, Managing Director
Andrew Williams, Managing Director
Artun Alparslan, Vice President
Belinda Hill, Managing Director
Bob Joannou, Managing Director
Brian Nunes, Vice President
David Britts, Managing Partner
David Herzberg, Managing Director
Dennis Wilson, Vice President
Franklin Mejia, Vice President
Gunter Heiland, Managing Director
Gustavo Ferraro, Managing Director
J. Robert Young, Managing Director
James Conroy, Vice President
James Taylor, Managing Director
Jason Cook, Managing Director
Jeffrey Grills, Managing Director
Jose Cerritelli, Managing Director
Kathleen Fennelly, Vice President
Kelly Griffin, Managing Director
Martin Dunn, Vice President
Matthew Christ, Vice President
Robert Rauch, Partner
Robert Lanava, Partner
Robert Koenigsberger, Founder
Rodd Kauffman, Partner
Scott Seaman, Partner
Stephen LaVersa, Managing Director
Tony Tessitore, Managing Director
Warren Harvey, Managing Director
William Shia, Managing Director

Type of Firm
Private Equity Firm

Association Membership
Emerging Markets Private Equity Association

Project Preferences

Type of Financing Preferred:
Generalist PE
Private Placement
Special Situation
Distressed Debt

Geographical Preferences

International Preferences:
Latin America
Argentina
Peru
Mexico
Brazil
Colombia

Industry Preferences

In Communications prefer:
Telecommunications

In Medical/Health prefer:
Medical/Health
Health Services

In Consumer Related prefer:
Consumer
Retail

In Industrial/Energy prefer:
Oil and Gas Exploration
Industrial Products

In Financial Services prefer:
Financial Services

In Business Serv. prefer:
Media

Additional Information
Year Founded: 1998
Capital Under Management: $670,990,000
Current Activity Level : Actively seeking new investments

GRAMERCY PRIVATE EQUITY LLC

548 Market Street, Suite 27695
San Francisco, CA USA 94104
Phone: 4152954650
Fax: 4153543487
E-mail: info@gramercype.com
Website: www.gramercype.com

Management and Staff
Elaine Harris, Partner
Michael Gale, Managing Partner

Type of Firm
Bank Affiliated

Project Preferences

Type of Financing Preferred:
Balanced

Geographical Preferences

United States Preferences:

International Preferences:
India
China
Asia
South Africa

Additional Information
Year Founded: 1969
Capital Under Management: $250,000,000
Current Activity Level : Actively seeking new investments

GRAN PRIVATE EQUITY ZRT

53 Alkotas Street
Budapest, Hungary
Phone: 3613740937
Fax: 3613740937
Website: www.granpe.hu

Type of Firm
Private Equity Firm

Project Preferences

Type of Financing Preferred:
Early Stage
Later Stage
Seed
Startup

Geographical Preferences

International Preferences:
Hungary
Europe

Additional Information
Year Founded: 2013
Current Activity Level : Actively seeking new investments

GRANATUS VENTURES CJSC

Melik Adamyan, 2/1
Yerevan, Armenia 0010
Phone: 37410546436
E-mail: info@granatusventures.com
Website: granatusventures.com

Management and Staff
Pierre Hennes, Partner
Yervand Sarkisyan, Partner

Type of Firm
Private Equity Firm

Industry Preferences

In Communications prefer:
Wireless Communications

In Semiconductor/Electr prefer:
Analytic/Scientific

Additional Information
Year Founded: 2013
Current Activity Level : Actively seeking new investments

GRAND CROSSING CAPITAL LLC

311 South Wacker Drive
Suite 2525
Chicago, IL USA 60606
Phone: 3129975900
E-mail: info@grandcrossing.com
Website: www.grandcrossing.com

Management and Staff
Brian Jacobsen, Managing Partner
Clay Naccarato, Managing Partner
Justin Demes, Principal
Patrick Collins, Managing Partner

Type of Firm
Private Equity Firm

Project Preferences

Type of Financing Preferred:
Expansion

Geographical Preferences

United States Preferences:
All U.S.

Additional Information
Year Founded: 2014
Current Activity Level : Actively seeking new investments

GRAND GROUP INVESTMENT PLC

Room 2023, South Building
Wuhu Road
Jiangsu, China
Website: www.grandgroupplc.com

Type of Firm
Private Equity Firm

Project Preferences

Type of Financing Preferred:
Later Stage

Geographical Preferences

International Preferences:
China

Additional Information
Year Founded: 2014
Current Activity Level : Actively seeking new investments

GRAND SUD OUEST CAPITAL SA

304 Bd du President Wilson
Bordeaux, France 33076
Phone: 33556904287
Fax: 33556904296
E-mail: gsocapital@gsocapital.com
Website: www.gsocapital.com

Other Offices
9 rue Ozenne
Toulouse, France 31000
Phone: 33561145004
Fax: 33561145032

Management and Staff
Didier Mathieu, Partner
Laurent Mazard, Partner

Type of Firm
Bank Affiliated

Association Membership
French Venture Capital Association (AFIC)

Project Preferences

Type of Financing Preferred:
Leveraged Buyout
Early Stage
Generalist PE
Later Stage
Management Buyouts
Acquisition

Size of Investments Considered:
Min Size of Investment Considered (000s): $260
Max Size of Investment Considered (000s): $1,951

Geographical Preferences

International Preferences:
Europe
Eastern Europe
France

Industry Preferences

In Communications prefer:
Communications and Media

In Computer Software prefer:
Software

In Semiconductor/Electr prefer:
Electronics

In Biotechnology prefer:
Biotechnology

In Medical/Health prefer:
Medical/Health

In Consumer Related prefer:
Sports
Hotels and Resorts

In Business Serv. prefer:
Services

In Manufact. prefer:
Manufacturing

In Agr/Forestr/Fish prefer:
Agriculture related

Additional Information

Year Founded: 2002
Current Activity Level : Actively seeking new investments

GRAND VENTURES

38 Fulton Street West
Suite 308
Grand Rapids, MI USA 49503
Website: www.grandvcp.com

Type of Firm
Private Equity Firm

Project Preferences

Type of Financing Preferred:
Seed

Geographical Preferences

United States Preferences:
Midwest
Michigan

Additional Information

Year Founded: 2017
Current Activity Level : Actively seeking new investments

GRANDBANKS CAPITAL

75 Second Avenue
Suite 360
Needham, MA USA 02494
Phone: 7819974300
Fax: 7819974301
E-mail: info@grandbankscapital.com
Website: www.grandbankscapital.com

Management and Staff

Alden Reid, Principal
Charles Lax, Co-Founder
JJ Healy, Venture Partner
Jeffrey Parker, Venture Partner
Tim Wright, General Partner

Type of Firm
Private Equity Firm

Association Membership
New England Venture Capital Association

Project Preferences

Role in Financing:
Prefer role as deal originator but will also invest in deals created by others

Type of Financing Preferred:
Early Stage

Geographical Preferences

United States Preferences:
East Coast

Industry Preferences

In Communications prefer:
Wireless Communications

In Computer Software prefer:
Data Processing
Software

In Internet Specific prefer:
Internet

In Financial Services prefer:
Financial Services

In Business Serv. prefer:
Services
Media

Additional Information

Year Founded: 2000
Capital Under Management: $250,000,000
Current Activity Level : Actively seeking new investments
Method of Compensation: Return on investment is of primary concern, do not charge fees

GRANITE CREEK PARTNERS LLC

222 West Adams Street
Suite 1980
Chicago, IL USA 60606
Phone: 3128954500
Fax: 3128954509
E-mail: info@granitecreek.com
Website: www.granitecreek.com

Other Offices

No. 121 YongHua Street
Shi Qiao Road, Xia Cheng Qu
Hangzhou, China 310022

Management and Staff

Brian Boorstein, Managing Partner
James Clark, Managing Partner
John He, Managing Partner
Mark Radzik, Managing Partner
Peter Lehman, Managing Partner

Type of Firm
Private Equity Firm

Project Preferences

Type of Financing Preferred:
Leveraged Buyout
Management Buyouts
Acquisition
Recapitalizations

Size of Investments Considered:
Min Size of Investment Considered (000s): $10,000
Max Size of Investment Considered (000s): $50,000

Geographical Preferences

United States Preferences:
All U.S.

Industry Preferences

In Computer Other prefer:
Computer Related

In Biotechnology prefer:
Biotechnology
Agricultural/Animal Bio.

In Medical/Health prefer:
Medical Products
Disposable Med. Products

In Consumer Related prefer:
Food/Beverage

In Transportation prefer:
Transportation

Additional Information

Year Founded: 2005
Current Activity Level : Actively seeking new investments

GRANITE EQUITY PARTNERS LLC

122 12th Avenue North
Suite 201
Saint Cloud, MN USA 56303
Phone: 3202511800
Fax: 3202511804
Website: www.graniteequity.com

Other Offices

158 Water Street North
Suite 4B
Northfield, MN USA 55057
Phone: 6126058017
Fax: 6123959295

Management and Staff

Arthur Monaghan, Co-Founder
Greg Schumacher, Partner
Patrick Edeburn, Co-Founder
Richard Bauerly, Managing Partner
Shelly Kopel, Partner

Type of Firm

Private Equity Firm

Project Preferences

Type of Financing Preferred:
Leveraged Buyout
Recapitalizations

Geographical Preferences

United States Preferences:
South Dakota
North Dakota
Wisconsin
Minnesota

Industry Preferences

In Communications prefer:
Media and Entertainment

In Business Serv. prefer:
Services
Distribution

In Manufact. prefer:
Manufacturing

In Agr/Forestr/Fish prefer:
Agriculture related

Additional Information

Year Founded: 2002
Current Activity Level : Actively seeking new investments

GRANITE HALL PARTNERS INC

190 South LaSalle Street
Suite 540
Chicago, IL USA 60603
Phone: 3124446360
Fax: 3124446369
E-mail: info@granitehall.com
Website: www.granitehall.com

Management and Staff

Bradley Leshnock, Founder
James Flanigan, Managing Director
John Wagner, Managing Director

Type of Firm

Private Equity Advisor or Fund of Funds

Project Preferences

Type of Financing Preferred:
Fund of Funds
Leveraged Buyout

Geographical Preferences

United States Preferences:

Additional Information

Year Founded: 2000
Capital Under Management: $10,000,000
Current Activity Level : Actively seeking new investments

GRANITE HILL CAPITAL PARTNERS LLC

1300 South El Camino
Suite 380
San Mateo, CA USA 94402
Phone: 6507872716
E-mail: info@granitehill.net
Website: www.granitehill.net

Management and Staff

Kamil Hasan, General Partner
Sameet Mehta, General Partner
Shailesh Mehta, Managing Partner
Shraddha Ghadiali, Partner
Talat Hasan, Venture Partner

Type of Firm

Private Equity Firm

Project Preferences

Type of Financing Preferred:
Expansion
Balanced
Later Stage

Geographical Preferences

International Preferences:
India

Industry Preferences

In Communications prefer:
Communications and Media

In Medical/Health prefer:
Medical/Health

In Consumer Related prefer:
Education Related

In Financial Services prefer:
Financial Services

Additional Information

Name of Most Recent Fund: Granite Hill India Opportunities Fund, L.P.
Most Recent Fund Was Raised: 07/02/2008
Year Founded: 1969
Current Activity Level : Actively seeking new investments

GRANITE PARTNERS

20 Eglinton Avenue
Suite 1501
Toronto, Canada M4R 1K8
Phone: 4163645311
Fax: 6477291548
Website: www.granitepartners.ca

Management and Staff

Doug Buchanan, President

Type of Firm

Private Equity Firm

Project Preferences

Type of Financing Preferred:
Leveraged Buyout
Management Buyouts

Geographical Preferences

Canadian Preferences:
All Canada

Industry Preferences

In Industrial/Energy prefer:
Industrial Products

In Business Serv. prefer:
Services

Additional Information

Year Founded: 1996
Current Activity Level : Actively seeking new investments

GRANITE VENTURES LLC

101 Second Street
Suite 570
San Francisco, CA USA 94104
Phone: 4155917700
Fax: 4155917720
E-mail: info@granitevc.com

Management and Staff

Brian Panoff, Principal
Chris Hollenbeck, Managing Director
Chris McKay, Managing Director
Christopher Hollenbeck, Managing Director
Eric Zimits, Managing Director
Samuel Kingsland, Managing Director
Standish O Grady, Managing Director
Tom Furlong, Managing Director

Type of Firm

Private Equity Firm

Project Preferences

Role in Financing:
Prefer role as deal originator but will also invest in deals created by others

Type of Financing Preferred:
Early Stage
Balanced
Seed
Startup

Size of Investments Considered:
Min Size of Investment Considered (000s): $500
Max Size of Investment Considered (000s): $10,000

Geographical Preferences

United States Preferences:

Industry Focus

(% based on actual investment)
Computer Software and Services	46.3%
Internet Specific	27.1%
Communications and Media	12.1%
Semiconductors/Other Elect.	9.5%
Computer Hardware	1.3%
Consumer Related	1.2%
Medical/Health	1.2%
Other Products	1.0%
Biotechnology	0.2%
Industrial/Energy	0.2%

Additional Information

Name of Most Recent Fund: Granite Ventures II, L.P.
Most Recent Fund Was Raised: 06/27/2005
Year Founded: 1992
Capital Under Management: $1,000,000,000
Current Activity Level : Actively seeking new investments
Method of Compensation: Return on investment is of primary concern, do not charge fees

GRANO RETAIL INVESTMENTS INC

89 Tycos
Toronto, Canada M6B 1W3
Phone: 4166427342
Website: www.granoretail.com

Management and Staff

Lawrence Pollack, Partner
Naomi Levinson, Partner
Stephen Granovsky, Partner

Type of Firm

Investment Management Firm

Project Preferences

Type of Financing Preferred:
Leveraged Buyout
Acquisition

Industry Preferences

In Consumer Related prefer:
Retail
Consumer Products

In Business Serv. prefer:
Distribution

In Manufact. prefer:
Manufacturing

Additional Information

Year Founded: 2007
Current Activity Level : Actively seeking new investments

GRAPH VENTURES LLC

120 Hawthorne Avenue
Palo Alto, CA USA 94301

Type of Firm

Private Equity Firm

Project Preferences

Type of Financing Preferred:
Balanced

Additional Information

Year Founded: 1969
Current Activity Level : Actively seeking new investments

GRAPHENE VENTURES

530 Lytton Avenue
Second Floor
Palo Alto, CA USA 94301
Website: www.graphene.vc

Type of Firm

Private Equity Firm

Project Preferences

Type of Financing Preferred:
Early Stage

Industry Preferences

In Computer Software prefer:
Software

Additional Information

Year Founded: 2015
Current Activity Level : Actively seeking new investments

GRAPHITE CAPITAL MANAGEMENT LLP

Berkeley Square House
Berkeley Square
London, United Kingdom W1J 6BQ
Phone: 442078255300
Fax: 442078255399
Website: www.graphitecapital.com

Management and Staff

James Markham, Partner
Jennifer Michelman, Partner
Jeremy Gough, Partner
John O Neill, Partner
Kane Bayliss, Partner
Mark Hall, Partner
Mudassir Khan, Partner
Rod Richards, Managing Partner
Tim Spence, Founder

Type of Firm

Private Equity Firm

Association Membership

British Venture Capital Association (BVCA)

Project Preferences

Role in Financing:
Prefer role as deal originator but will also invest in deals created by others

Type of Financing Preferred:
Leveraged Buyout
Expansion
Later Stage
Management Buyouts
Acquisition

Geographical Preferences

International Preferences:
United Kingdom
Europe

Industry Focus
(% based on actual investment)

Other Products	30.9%
Consumer Related	26.3%
Medical/Health	24.7%
Industrial/Energy	9.2%
Communications and Media	4.6%
Computer Hardware	1.7%
Computer Software and Services	1.4%
Semiconductors/Other Elect.	1.1%
Biotechnology	0.1%

Additional Information
Name of Most Recent Fund: Graphite Capital Partners VIII
Most Recent Fund Was Raised: 09/25/2013
Year Founded: 1981
Capital Under Management: $1,200,000,000
Current Activity Level : Actively seeking new investments
Method of Compensation: Return on invest. most important, but chg. closing fees, service fees, etc.

GRAUE MILL PARTNERS LLC

2215 York Road
Suite 308
Oak Brook, IL USA 60523
Phone: 6305751540
Fax: 6305751544
E-mail: info@grauemillpartners.com
Website: www.grauemillpartners.com

Management and Staff
Mark Rothschild, Partner
Robert Whitelaw, Founder

Type of Firm
Private Equity Firm

Project Preferences

Type of Financing Preferred:
Leveraged Buyout
Value-Add
Later Stage
Management Buyouts
Acquisition
Recapitalizations

Industry Preferences

In Financial Services prefer:
Financial Services

In Business Serv. prefer:
Services
Distribution

In Manufact. prefer:
Manufacturing

Additional Information
Year Founded: 2000
Current Activity Level : Actively seeking new investments

GRAY & CO

3333 Piedmont Road NE
Suite 1250
Atlanta, GA USA 30305
Phone: 4048832500
Fax: 4048832501
Website: www.egrayco.com

Management and Staff
Laurence Gray, President, Founder
Marc Hardy, Chief Financial Officer

Type of Firm
Investment Management Firm

Project Preferences

Type of Financing Preferred:
Core
Leveraged Buyout
Value-Add
Generalist PE
Balanced
Opportunistic
Special Situation

Industry Preferences

In Financial Services prefer:
Real Estate
Investment Groups

Additional Information
Name of Most Recent Fund: GrayCo Alternative Partners II, L.P.
Most Recent Fund Was Raised: 12/20/2012
Year Founded: 2012
Capital Under Management: $83,000,000
Current Activity Level : Actively seeking new investments

GRAY GHOST VENTURES

2200 Century Parkway
Suite 100
Atlanta, GA USA 30345
Phone: 6783654700
Fax: 6783654752
E-mail: info@grayghostventures.com
Website: www.grayghostventures.com

Other Offices
One, Sreyas Visalakshi
Cenotaph First Street
Chennai, India 600018

H. No 3-6-2/1
Third Floor
Hyderabad, India 500029

Management and Staff
Brian Cayce, Vice President

Type of Firm
Private Equity Firm

Association Membership
Emerging Markets Private Equity Association
National Venture Capital Association - USA (NVCA)

Project Preferences

Type of Financing Preferred:
Early Stage
Balanced
Startup

Geographical Preferences

United States Preferences:
Southeast

International Preferences:
India
Asia
Africa

Industry Preferences

In Communications prefer:
Wireless Communications

In Consumer Related prefer:
Education Related

In Financial Services prefer:
Financial Services

In Other prefer:
Socially Responsible

Additional Information
Year Founded: 2004
Capital Under Management: $25,000,000
Current Activity Level : Actively seeking new investments

GRAY MATTERS CAPITAL INC

2200 Century Pkwy
Atlanta, GA USA 30345

Type of Firm
Private Equity Firm

Project Preferences

Type of Financing Preferred:
Early Stage

Additional Information
Year Founded: 2006
Current Activity Level : Actively seeking new investments

GRAYCLIFF PARTNERS LP

452 Fifth Avenue
New York, NY USA 10018
Phone: 2123002900
Fax: 6464390871
Website: graycliffpartners.com

Other Offices
Rua Tabapua, 1123
24th floor
Sao Paulo, Brazil 04533-014
Phone: 551138475734

Management and Staff
Andrew Trigg, Managing Director
Carl Barcoma, Vice President
Cristiano Boccia, Managing Director
Dave Mullen, Managing Director
Duke Punhong, Principal
Guilherme Cunha, Principal
James Marley, Managing Director
Javier Ledesma-Arocena, Principal
Stephen Hindmarch, Managing Director
Steven Schaefer, Chief Financial Officer
Will Henderson, Principal

Type of Firm
Private Equity Firm

Association Membership
Brazilian Venture Capital Association (ABCR)
Natl Assoc of Small Bus. Inv. Co (NASBIC)

Project Preferences

Type of Financing Preferred:
Leveraged Buyout
Expansion
Generalist PE
Later Stage
Management Buyouts
Recapitalizations

Geographical Preferences

United States Preferences:

Additional Information
Name of Most Recent Fund: Graycliff Mezzanine II, L.P.
Most Recent Fund Was Raised: 11/08/2012
Year Founded: 2011
Capital Under Management: $78,720,000
Current Activity Level : Actively seeking new investments

GRAYHAWK CAPITAL

5050 North 40th Street
Suite 380
Phoenix, AZ USA 85018
Phone: 6029568700
Website: www.grayhawkcapital.us

Management and Staff
Brian Burns, Managing Partner
Sherman Chu, Managing Partner

Type of Firm
SBIC

Project Preferences

Role in Financing:
Will function either as deal originator or investor in deals created by others

Type of Financing Preferred:
Leveraged Buyout
Early Stage
Expansion
Generalist PE
Later Stage
Acquisition

Geographical Preferences

United States Preferences:
New Mexico
Nevada
Arizona
Southern California
Colorado
Utah
Southwest
Texas

Industry Focus
(% based on actual investment)

Computer Software and Services	56.7%
Internet Specific	20.6%
Other Products	8.1%
Computer Hardware	6.4%
Medical/Health	2.4%
Semiconductors/Other Elect.	2.4%
Communications and Media	1.8%
Biotechnology	1.5%

Additional Information
Name of Most Recent Fund: Grayhawk Venture Fund II, L.P.
Most Recent Fund Was Raised: 09/23/2011
Year Founded: 1995
Capital Under Management: $150,000,000
Current Activity Level : Actively seeking new investments
Method of Compensation: Return on investment is of primary concern, do not charge fees

GRAYSON & ASSOCIATES INC

10147 Bluffmont Lane
Lone Tree, CO USA 80124

Other Offices
5209 Ocean Front Walk, Suite 302
Marina del Rey, CA USA 90292
Phone: 310-306-0850
Fax: 303-484-7679

2638 Juniper Hills Road
Aspen, CO USA 81611
Phone: 970-925-4049
Fax: 303-484-7679

155 Riverside Drive
Suite 7B
New York, NY USA 10024
Phone: 212-580-8817
Fax: 212-580-8827

Management and Staff
F. Joseph Daugherty, Managing Director
Gerald Grayson, President

Type of Firm
Service Provider

Project Preferences

Role in Financing:
Prefer role as deal originator but will also invest in deals created by others

Type of Financing Preferred:
Later Stage

Size of Investments Considered:
Min Size of Investment Considered (000s): $1,000
Max Size of Investment Considered: No Limit

Geographical Preferences

United States Preferences:

Industry Preferences

In Biotechnology prefer:
Human Biotechnology

In Medical/Health prefer:
Medical Diagnostics
Diagnostic Services
Diagnostic Test Products
Medical Therapeutics
Drug/Equipmt Delivery
Medical Products
Disposable Med. Products

Additional Information
Year Founded: 1986
Current Activity Level : Actively seeking new investments
Method of Compensation: Function primarily in service area, receive contingent fee in cash or equity

GRAZIA EQUITY GMBH

Breitscheidstrasse 10
Stuttgart, Germany 70174
Phone: 497119071090
Fax: 4971190710988
E-mail: info@grazia.com
Website: www.grazia.com

Management and Staff
Erich Rauschenbusch, Partner
Jochen Klueppel, Partner
Torsten Kreindl, Partner

Type of Firm
Private Equity Firm

Association Membership
German Venture Capital Association (BVK)

Project Preferences

Type of Financing Preferred:
Early Stage
Later Stage
Startup

Geographical Preferences

United States Preferences:
All U.S.

International Preferences:
Europe
Germany

Industry Preferences

In Communications prefer:
Communications and Media

In Internet Specific prefer:
Internet

In Biotechnology prefer:
Biotechnology

In Industrial/Energy prefer:
Energy

In Other prefer:
Environment Responsible

Additional Information
Year Founded: 2000
Current Activity Level : Actively seeking new investments

GREAT HILL EQUITY PARTNERS LLC

One Liberty Square
Boston, MA USA 02109
Phone: 6177909400
Fax: 6177909401
Website: www.greathillpartners.com

Management and Staff
Anne Hawkins, Vice President
Charles Papazian, Vice President
Christopher Cavanagh, Vice President
Christopher Busby, Principal
Christopher Gaffney, Managing Partner
Craig Byrnes, Vice President
Drew Loucks, Vice President
John Hayes, Co-Founder
Laurie Gerber, Chief Financial Officer
Mark Taber, Managing Partner
Mark Taber, Managing Partner
Mary Kate Bertke, Vice President
Matthew Vettel, Managing Partner
Michael Kumin, Managing Partner
Nicholas Cayer, Principal
Peter Garran, Partner
Rafael Cofino, Partner
Sarah Pinto Peyronel, Vice President
Sarah Pinto, Vice President
Tanzeen Syed, Vice President

Type of Firm
Private Equity Firm

Project Preferences

Role in Financing:
Prefer role as deal originator but will also invest in deals created by others

Type of Financing Preferred:
Leveraged Buyout
Expansion
Later Stage
Acquisition
Recapitalizations

Size of Investments Considered:
Min Size of Investment Considered (000s): $30,000
Max Size of Investment Considered (000s): $150,000

Industry Focus
(% based on actual investment)

Internet Specific	47.8%
Computer Software and Services	17.2%
Other Products	12.5%
Computer Hardware	9.1%
Communications and Media	6.4%
Semiconductors/Other Elect.	4.0%
Consumer Related	2.9%
Medical/Health	0.1%

Additional Information
Name of Most Recent Fund: Great Hill Equity Partners V, L.P.
Most Recent Fund Was Raised: 12/20/2013
Year Founded: 1993
Capital Under Management: $2,671,000,000
Current Activity Level : Actively seeking new investments

GREAT OAKS VENTURE CAPITAL LLC

660 Madison Avenue
Suite 1405
New York, NY USA 10065
Phone: 2128211800
E-mail: info@greatoaksvc.com

Other Offices
122 West 26th Street
Fifth Floor
New York, NY USA 10001

Management and Staff
Andrew Boszhardt, Managing Partner
Ben Lin, Managing Partner
Celine Kwok, Chief Financial Officer
John Philosophos, Partner

Type of Firm
Private Equity Firm

Project Preferences

Type of Financing Preferred:
Early Stage

Size of Investments Considered:
Min Size of Investment Considered (000s): $50
Max Size of Investment Considered (000s): $500

Industry Preferences

In Computer Software prefer:
Software

In Internet Specific prefer:
Internet
Ecommerce

In Consumer Related prefer:
Consumer

In Business Serv. prefer:
Distribution

Additional Information
Name of Most Recent Fund: Great Oaks Venture Fund, L.P.
Most Recent Fund Was Raised: 09/12/2012
Year Founded: 2005
Capital Under Management: $40,220,000
Current Activity Level : Actively seeking new investments

GREAT POINT PARTNERS LLC

165 Mason Street
Third Floor
Greenwich, CT USA 06830
Phone: 2039713300
Fax: 2039713320
Website: www.gppfunds.com

Management and Staff
Adam Dolder, Managing Director
David Kroin, Co-Founder
Jeffrey Jay, Managing Director
Joseph Pesce, Managing Director
Rohan Saikia, Vice President
Ron Panzier, Chief Financial Officer
Scott Davidson, Managing Director

Type of Firm
Private Equity Firm

Pratt's Guide to Private Equity & Venture Capital Sources

Project Preferences

Type of Financing Preferred:
Leveraged Buyout
Expansion
Generalist PE
Balanced
Public Companies
Later Stage
Management Buyouts
Acquisition
Recapitalizations

Size of Investments Considered:
Min Size of Investment Considered (000s): $10,000
Max Size of Investment Considered (000s): $50,000

Industry Preferences

In Biotechnology prefer:
Biotechnology

In Medical/Health prefer:
Medical/Health
Medical Products
Health Services
Hospitals/Clinics/Primary
Hospital/Other Instit.
Pharmaceuticals

In Manufact. prefer:
Manufacturing

Additional Information

Name of Most Recent Fund: Great Point Partners II, L.P.
Most Recent Fund Was Raised: 10/02/2012
Year Founded: 2003
Capital Under Management: $215,000,000
Current Activity Level : Actively seeking new investments

GREAT RANGE CAPITAL

11250 Tomahawk Creek Parkway
Leawood
Shawnee Mission, KS USA 66211
Phone: 9133780855
Website: www.greatrangecapital.com

Management and Staff

Chris Freitag, Vice President
Paul Maxwell, Managing Partner
Ryan Sprott, Managing Partner

Type of Firm
Private Equity Firm

Project Preferences

Type of Financing Preferred:
Leveraged Buyout
Expansion
Later Stage
Management Buyouts
Acquisition
Recapitalizations

Geographical Preferences

United States Preferences:
Midwest

Industry Preferences

In Medical/Health prefer:
Medical/Health
Health Services

In Consumer Related prefer:
Consumer
Retail

In Financial Services prefer:
Financial Services

In Business Serv. prefer:
Services
Media

In Manufact. prefer:
Manufacturing

Additional Information

Name of Most Recent Fund: Great Range Capital Fund I, L.P.
Most Recent Fund Was Raised: 07/06/2012
Year Founded: 2010
Capital Under Management: $4,350,000
Current Activity Level : Actively seeking new investments

GREAT RIVER CAPITAL LLC

131 West Second Street
Suite 305
Davenport, IA USA 52801
Phone: 7817710074
E-mail: grc.info@greatrivercap.com
Website: www.greatriverllc.com

Management and Staff

Andrew Axel, Chief Operating Officer

Type of Firm
Private Equity Advisor or Fund of Funds

Project Preferences

Type of Financing Preferred:
Fund of Funds

Geographical Preferences

United States Preferences:
Iowa

Industry Preferences

In Biotechnology prefer:
Biotechnology

Additional Information

Year Founded: 2002
Current Activity Level : Actively seeking new investments

GREAT WALL SECURITIES CO LTD

Shenzhen Special Area
6008 Shennan Rd., Futian Dist.
Shenzhen, China
Phone: 86-755-82288968
Website: www.cgws.com

Type of Firm
Bank Affiliated

Project Preferences

Type of Financing Preferred:
Balanced

Additional Information

Year Founded: 1995
Current Activity Level : Actively seeking new investments

GREATPOINT VENTURES

One Broadway
14th Floor
Cambridge, MA USA 02142
Phone: 617-225-4391
Fax: 617-225-4475
E-mail: info@greatpointventures.com

Other Offices

1130 West Monroe
Suite 310
Chicago, IL USA 60607
Phone: 3123002328

Management and Staff

Aaron Mandell, Managing Partner
Andrew Perlman, Managing Partner
Avi Goldberg, Managing Partner
Brian Freeman, Venture Partner
Dan Goldman, Vice President
David Gerzof, Venture Partner

Type of Firm
Private Equity Firm

Project Preferences

Type of Financing Preferred:
Seed
Startup

Geographical Preferences

United States Preferences:

Industry Preferences

In Semiconductor/Electr prefer:
Semiconductor

In Industrial/Energy prefer:
Materials

In Other prefer:
Socially Responsible

Additional Information
Year Founded: 2004
Capital Under Management: $199,000,000
Current Activity Level : Actively seeking new investments

GREEN ACRE CAPITAL

Two Bloor St. West
Suite 1805
Toronto, Canada M4W 3E2
Website: greenacrecapital.ca

Type of Firm
Private Equity Firm

Project Preferences

Type of Financing Preferred:
Early Stage

Geographical Preferences

Canadian Preferences:
All Canada

Industry Preferences

In Medical/Health prefer:
Medical/Health

Additional Information
Year Founded: 2017
Capital Under Management: $20,120,000
Current Activity Level : Actively seeking new investments

GREEN BAY ADVISORS LLC

480 PACIFIC AVE
SUITE 200
San Francisco, CA USA 94133
Phone: 4157809980
Website: greenbayadvisors.com

Type of Firm
Private Equity Firm

Additional Information
Year Founded: 2015
Current Activity Level : Actively seeking new investments

GREEN CAMPUS INNOVATIONS OY

Ahventie 4
Espoo, Finland 02750
Phone: 358 40 5573232
Website: greencampusinnovations.fi

Type of Firm
University Program

Project Preferences

Type of Financing Preferred:
Early Stage
Seed
Startup

Industry Preferences

In Industrial/Energy prefer:
Energy
Alternative Energy
Energy Conservation Relat
Environmental Related

In Other prefer:
Environment Responsible

Additional Information
Year Founded: 2000
Current Activity Level : Actively seeking new investments

GREEN CENTURY INVESTMENT

4789 Yonge Street, Unit 706
Toronto, Canada M2N 0G3
Website: www.greencenturyinvestment.com

Type of Firm
Private Equity Firm

Project Preferences

Type of Financing Preferred:
Early Stage
Seed

Industry Preferences

In Communications prefer:
Entertainment

In Consumer Related prefer:
Consumer Products

In Industrial/Energy prefer:
Energy
Industrial Products

In Business Serv. prefer:
Media

Additional Information
Year Founded: 1969
Current Activity Level : Actively seeking new investments

GREEN HARBOR MANAGEMENT SHENZHEN CO LTD

Taiping Bridge, Xicheng Dis.
Fenghuishidai East
Shenzhen, China
Phone: 861058362240
Website: www.greenharbor-inv.com

Type of Firm
Private Equity Firm

Project Preferences

Type of Financing Preferred:
Early Stage
Expansion
Balanced

Geographical Preferences

International Preferences:
China

Industry Preferences

In Internet Specific prefer:
Internet

In Medical/Health prefer:
Medical/Health

In Consumer Related prefer:
Consumer

In Financial Services prefer:
Financial Services

Additional Information
Year Founded: 2016
Current Activity Level : Actively seeking new investments

GREEN LION PARTNERS LLC

1307 22nd Street
Denver, CO USA 80205
Website: www.greenlionpartners.com

Management and Staff
Jeffrey Zucker, President
Mike Bologna, Chief Executive Officer

Type of Firm
Private Equity Firm

Project Preferences

Type of Financing Preferred:
Early Stage

Additional Information
Year Founded: 2015
Current Activity Level : Actively seeking new investments

GREEN MANNING & BUNCH LTD

1515 Wynkoop Street
Suite 800
Denver, CO USA 80202
Phone: 3035924800
Website: www.gmbltd.com

Management and Staff
Aaron Bachik, Managing Director
Alan Mayer, Managing Director
Chris Hammond, Managing Director
Greg Anderson, Managing Director
Laurel Kenny, Chief Operating Officer
Seth Benson, Vice President
Thomas Fencl, Managing Director
Warren Henson, President

Type of Firm
Bank Affiliated

Project Preferences

Role in Financing:
Will function either as deal originator or investor in deals created by others

Type of Financing Preferred:
Leveraged Buyout
Mezzanine
Management Buyouts
Recapitalizations

Geographical Preferences

United States Preferences:
Rocky Mountain
West Coast

Additional Information
Year Founded: 1988
Current Activity Level : Actively seeking new investments
Method of Compensation: Return on invest. most important, but chg. closing fees, service fees, etc.

GREEN PARK & GOLF VENTURES LLC

5910 North Central Expressway
Suite 1480
Dallas, TX USA 75206
Phone: 2149165750
Website: gpgventures.com

Management and Staff
Carl Soderstrom, Partner
JR Garcia, Principal
Kevin Rowden, Vice President

Type of Firm
Private Equity Firm

Project Preferences

Type of Financing Preferred:
Early Stage
Startup

Size of Investments Considered:
Min Size of Investment Considered (000s): $16,250
Max Size of Investment Considered (000s): $24,375

Geographical Preferences

United States Preferences:
All U.S.

Industry Preferences

In Computer Software prefer:
Software

In Internet Specific prefer:
Internet

In Medical/Health prefer:
Medical/Health
Medical Diagnostics
Medical Therapeutics
Health Services

Additional Information
Year Founded: 2011
Current Activity Level : Actively seeking new investments

GREEN TREE CAPITAL

135 Camino Dorado
Suite Number Seven
Napa, CA USA 94558
Phone: 70725-0994
Fax: 7072510940
E-mail: info@greentreecapital.com
Website: www.greentreecapital.com

Type of Firm
Private Equity Firm

Project Preferences

Role in Financing:
Prefer role as deal originator

Type of Financing Preferred:
Leveraged Buyout
Management Buyouts
Acquisition
Recapitalizations

Geographical Preferences

United States Preferences:
West Coast

Additional Information
Year Founded: 1985
Current Activity Level : Actively seeking new investments

GREEN VISOR CAPITAL

101 California Street, Suite 4100
San Francisco, CA USA 94111
E-mail: info@greenvisorcapital.com
Website: www.greenvisorcapital.com

Type of Firm
Private Equity Firm

Project Preferences

Type of Financing Preferred:
Early Stage
Seed

Industry Preferences

In Financial Services prefer:
Financial Services

Additional Information
Year Founded: 2014
Capital Under Management: $51,280,000
Current Activity Level : Actively seeking new investments

GREENBANK CAPITAL INC

100 King Street West, Suite 5700
Toronto, Canada M5X 1C7
Phone: 6479319768
Website: www.greenbankcapitalinc.com

Type of Firm
Bank Affiliated

Project Preferences

Type of Financing Preferred:
Early Stage
Acquisition

Additional Information
Year Founded: 2013
Current Activity Level : Actively seeking new investments

GREENBRIAR EQUITY GROUP LLC

555 Theodore Fremd Avenue, Suite A-201
Rye, NY USA 10580
Phone: 9149259600
Fax: 9149259699
E-mail: info@greenbriarequity.com
Website: www.greenbriarequity.com

Management and Staff
Jill Raker, Managing Director
John Daileader, Managing Director
Jonathan Pressnell, Principal
Niall McComiskey, Managing Director
Nisha Kumar, Chief Financial Officer
Noah Roy, Managing Director
Raynard Benvenuti, Managing Director

Type of Firm
Private Equity Firm

Project Preferences

Role in Financing:
Prefer role as deal originator but will also invest in deals created by others

Type of Financing Preferred:
Leveraged Buyout
Expansion
Management Buyouts
Recapitalizations

Industry Focus
(% based on actual investment)
Other Products 92.6%
Industrial/Energy 7.4%

Additional Information
Name of Most Recent Fund: Greenbriar Equity Fund III, L.P.
Most Recent Fund Was Raised: 11/20/2013
Year Founded: 1999
Capital Under Management: $1,500,000,000
Current Activity Level : Actively seeking new investments
Method of Compensation: Return on invest. most important, but chg. closing fees, service fees, etc.

GREENCOAT CAPITAL LLP

Francis Street
Greencoat House
London, United Kingdom SW1P 1DH
Phone: 442078329400
Fax: 442078329499
Website: www.greencoat-capital.com

Other Offices

Maximilianstr. 35a
Munchen, Germany 80539
Phone: 498924218205

27 Lower Fitzwilliam Street
Dublin, Ireland
Phone: 353-1-702-7905
Fax: 353-1-669-2438

Management and Staff

Ann Markey, Partner
Bertrand Gautier, Partner
John McKiernan, Partner
Richard Nourse, Managing Partner
Robert Schrimpff, Partner

Type of Firm
Private Equity Firm

Association Membership
Irish Venture Capital Association

Project Preferences

Type of Financing Preferred:
Early Stage
Expansion
First Stage Financing
Startup

Geographical Preferences

International Preferences:
Europe

Industry Preferences

In Industrial/Energy prefer:
Energy
Alternative Energy
Energy Conservation Relat

In Other prefer:
Environment Responsible

Additional Information
Year Founded: 2009
Current Activity Level : Actively seeking new investments

GREENER CAPITAL PARTNERS LP

128 Alvarado Road
Berkeley, CA USA 94705
Phone: 8664318709
E-mail: sfoffice@greenercap.com
Website: www.greenercap.com

Other Offices

645 Buena Vista Way
Laguna Beach, CA USA 92651
Phone: 8664318709

Campeche
Suite 430
, Mexico 01640
Phone: 1525551050518

Management and Staff

Charles Finnie, Managing Partner
Charlie Lewis, Vice President
Michael Katz, Partner
Thomas Cain, Managing Partner

Type of Firm
Private Equity Firm

Project Preferences

Type of Financing Preferred:
Early Stage
Balanced
Later Stage

Industry Preferences

In Biotechnology prefer:
Biotechnology

In Industrial/Energy prefer:
Oil and Gas Exploration
Alternative Energy
Energy Conservation Relat
Environmental Related

In Transportation prefer:
Transportation

In Agr/Forestr/Fish prefer:
Agriculture related

In Other prefer:
Environment Responsible

Additional Information
Name of Most Recent Fund: Greener Capital Partners II, L.P.
Most Recent Fund Was Raised: 10/05/2011
Year Founded: 2009
Capital Under Management: $16,000,000
Current Activity Level : Actively seeking new investments

GREENFIELD CAPITAL GROUP, INC.

2166 Chisin Street
San Jose, CA USA 95121
Phone: 4088881576
Fax: 4085219666
E-mail: usa@gfcapital.net
Website: www.gfcapital.net

Other Offices

425 Zhenning Road
Shanghai, China
Phone: 862152397982
Fax: 862162253385

105-334 East Kent Avenue South
BC Southbridge Business Park
Vancouver, Canada V5X 4N6
Phone: 6043258111
Fax: 6043258116

Suite 7-7, B3 Xinghai Plaza
Shahekou District
Dalian, China
Phone: 8641182810033
Fax: 8641182640077

33 Huayuan Shiqiao Road
23F Citigroup Tower
Shanghai, China
Phone: 862161010101
Fax: 862161010102

1 East Changan Avenue
19F, Tower E2, Oriental Plaza
Beijing, China
Phone: 861085200264
Fax: 861085200220

Type of Firm
Investment Management Firm

Project Preferences

Type of Financing Preferred:
Value-Add
Generalist PE
Opportunistic
Later Stage

Geographical Preferences

United States Preferences:
North America

International Preferences:
Europe
China
Asia
Africa

Industry Preferences

In Communications prefer:
Telecommunications

In Medical/Health prefer:
Medical/Health

In Consumer Related prefer:
Consumer
Retail

In Industrial/Energy prefer:
Energy
Industrial Products

In Transportation prefer:
Transportation
Aerospace

In Financial Services prefer:
Financial Services
Real Estate

In Business Serv. prefer:
Services
Media

Additional Information
Year Founded: 2005
Current Activity Level : Actively seeking new investments

GREENFIELD CAPITAL PARTNERS BV

Huizerstraatweg 111
het Berghuis
Naarden, Netherlands 1411 GM
Phone: 31356993900
Fax: 31356950444
E-mail: info@greenfield.nl
Website: www.greenfield.nl

Other Offices

747 Third Avenue
Suite 34A
New York, NY USA 10017
Phone: 2123172662
Fax: 2126792940

Scharlooweg 81
Willemstad
Curacao, Neth. Antilles
Phone: 59994618866
Fax: 59994618130

Management and Staff
Bart Zandbergen, Partner
Evert Dorhout Mees, Partner
Paul Janssens, Partner
Stef van Doesburg, Managing Partner

Type of Firm
Private Equity Firm

Association Membership
Dutch Venture Capital Associaton (NVP)

Project Preferences

Type of Financing Preferred:
Fund of Funds
Leveraged Buyout
Early Stage
Mezzanine
Generalist PE
Turnaround
Later Stage
Management Buyouts
Acquisition

Size of Investments Considered:
Min Size of Investment Considered (000s): $942
Max Size of Investment Considered (000s): $4,708

Geographical Preferences

United States Preferences:
All U.S.

International Preferences:
Luxembourg
Europe
Netherlands
Western Europe
Belgium

Industry Focus
(% based on actual investment)
Other Products	67.2%
Communications and Media	17.7%
Computer Software and Services	7.0%
Internet Specific	4.8%
Consumer Related	3.1%
Industrial/Energy	0.1%

Additional Information
Name of Most Recent Fund: GCF III
Most Recent Fund Was Raised: 09/01/2010
Year Founded: 1995
Capital Under Management: $264,000,000
Current Activity Level : Actively seeking new investments

GREENFIELDS VENTURE CAPITAL (PTY) LTD

Main Road, Claremont
Suite 102, Stadium On Main
Cape Town, South Africa 7735
Phone: 27-21-671-2820
Fax: 27-21-683-3214
E-mail: info@gvc.co.za
Website: www.gvc.co.za

Type of Firm
Private Equity Advisor or Fund of Funds

Project Preferences

Type of Financing Preferred:
Early Stage
Expansion
Seed
Startup

Geographical Preferences

International Preferences:
South Africa

Additional Information
Year Founded: 1999
Current Activity Level : Actively seeking new investments

GREENHALL CAPITAL PARTNERS LLC

2400 M Street Northwest
Washington, DC USA 20036
Phone: 2022967566
E-mail: info@greenhallcapital.com
Website: www.greenhallcapital.com

Other Offices
140 E 56th Street
New York, NY USA 10014
Phone: 6463891185

Management and Staff
Curtis Ofori, Principal
Otis Ofori, Principal

Type of Firm
Investment Management Firm

Project Preferences

Type of Financing Preferred:
Core
Leveraged Buyout
Value-Add
Generalist PE
Balanced
Opportunistic
Management Buyouts
Recapitalizations

Industry Preferences

In Medical/Health prefer:
Medical/Health

In Consumer Related prefer:
Consumer
Education Related

In Industrial/Energy prefer:
Industrial Products

In Financial Services prefer:
Real Estate

In Business Serv. prefer:
Services
Media

Additional Information
Name of Most Recent Fund: Greenhall Capital Partners LLC
Most Recent Fund Was Raised: 05/01/2013
Year Founded: 2013
Capital Under Management: $2,000,000
Current Activity Level : Actively seeking new investments

GREENHILL CAPITAL PARTNERS LP

48 Dover Street
1st Floor
London, United Kingdom W1S 4FF
Phone: 442037475700
E-mail: contactus@kestercapital.com
Website: www.kestercapital.com

Management and Staff
Birger Berendes, Vice President
Boris Gutin, Managing Director
Cyrus Hormazdi, Principal
Ian Wood, Vice President
Robert Deutsch, Managing Director
V. Frank Pottow, Managing Director

Type of Firm
Private Equity Firm

Association Membership
British Venture Capital Association (BVCA)

Project Preferences

Type of Financing Preferred:
Leveraged Buyout
Acquisition

Geographical Preferences

United States Preferences:
North America

International Preferences:
United Kingdom
Europe

Industry Focus
(% based on actual investment)

Communications and Media	48.5%
Industrial/Energy	40.0%
Other Products	9.4%
Internet Specific	1.3%
Consumer Related	0.5%
Computer Software and Services	0.4%

Additional Information
Year Founded: 2007
Capital Under Management: $1,900,000,000
Current Activity Level : Actively seeking new investments

GREENHOUSE CAPITAL PARTNERS

One Gate Six Road
Suite 203, Building B
Sausalito, CA USA 94965
Website: www.greenhousecapital.net

Management and Staff
Charlene Schachter, Principal
Michael Schwab, General Partner

Type of Firm
Private Equity Firm

Association Membership
Community Development Venture Capital Alliance

Project Preferences

Type of Financing Preferred:
Seed
Startup

Industry Preferences

In Industrial/Energy prefer:
Alternative Energy

In Other prefer:
Environment Responsible

Additional Information
Name of Most Recent Fund: Greenhouse Capital Partners II, L.P.
Most Recent Fund Was Raised: 09/27/2016
Year Founded: 2006
Current Activity Level : Actively seeking new investments

GREENLAND VENTURE A/S

P.O. Box 1068
Nuuk, Greenland 3900
Phone: 299342880
Fax: 299342881
E-mail: greenland@venture.gl
Website: www.venture.gl

Type of Firm
Private Equity Firm

Project Preferences

Type of Financing Preferred:
Balanced

Geographical Preferences

International Preferences:
Greenland
Denmark

Industry Preferences

In Consumer Related prefer:
Consumer
Retail
Food/Beverage
Consumer Products
Consumer Services

In Financial Services prefer:
Real Estate

In Agr/Forestr/Fish prefer:
Agriculture related

Additional Information
Year Founded: 2000
Current Activity Level : Actively seeking new investments

GREENLINE VENTURES LLC

1324 15th Street
Denver, CO USA 80202
Phone: 3035868000
Fax: 3035868039
E-mail: info@greenlineventures.com
Website: www.greenlineventures.com

Management and Staff
Andy Walvoord, Vice President
Charles Jensen, Vice President
Fred Koch, Vice President
Kelly Morse, Vice President
Nathan Perry, Vice President
Patrick Vahey, President

Type of Firm
Incubator/Development Program

Project Preferences

Type of Financing Preferred:
Balanced

Geographical Preferences

United States Preferences:

Additional Information
Year Founded: 2011
Capital Under Management: $2,000,000
Current Activity Level : Actively seeking new investments

953

GREENMONT CAPITAL PARTNERS

1634 Walnut Street, Suite 301
Boulder, CO USA 80302
Phone: 3034440599
Fax: 3034440603
E-mail: contact@greenmontcapital.com
Website: www.greenmontcapital.com

Management and Staff

Barney Feinblum, Managing Director
Bryan Meehan, Venture Partner
David Haynes, Managing Director
Hass Hassan, Managing Director
John Shields, Venture Partner
Kim Bixel, Partner
Mark Retzloff, Venture Partner
Michelle Goolsby, Venture Partner
Pam Shepherd, Vice President
Steven Demos, Venture Partner
Todd Woloson, Managing Director

Type of Firm
Private Equity Firm

Project Preferences

Role in Financing:
Will function either as deal originator or investor in deals created by others

Type of Financing Preferred:
Early Stage
Balanced
Later Stage
Seed

Geographical Preferences

United States Preferences:
Colorado

Industry Preferences

In Consumer Related prefer:
Consumer Products

Additional Information

Name of Most Recent Fund: Greenmont Capital Partners II, L.P.
Most Recent Fund Was Raised: 06/20/2008
Year Founded: 2004
Capital Under Management: $20,000,000
Current Activity Level : Actively seeking new investments
Method of Compensation: Return on investment is of primary concern, do not charge fees

GREENOAKS CAPITAL PARTNERS LLC

535 Pacific Avenue, Fourth Floor
San Francisco, CA USA 94133
Website: www.greenoakscap.com

Type of Firm
Private Equity Firm

Project Preferences

Type of Financing Preferred:
Generalist PE

Additional Information
Year Founded: 1969
Current Activity Level : Actively seeking new investments

GREENPOINT INVESTMENT COUNSEL

1200 John Q Hammons Drive
Suite 501
Madison, WI USA 53717
Phone: 6082153875
Website: www.greenpointfunds.com

Type of Firm
Investment Management Firm

Project Preferences

Type of Financing Preferred:
Balanced

Geographical Preferences

United States Preferences:

Industry Preferences

In Manufact. prefer:
Manufacturing

Additional Information
Name of Most Recent Fund: Greenpoint Global Mittelstand Fund I LLC
Most Recent Fund Was Raised: 01/03/2014
Year Founded: 2014
Capital Under Management: $1,500,000
Current Activity Level : Actively seeking new investments

GREENRIDGE INVESTMENT PARTNERS

600 Congress Avenue
Suite 300
Austin, TX USA 73301
E-mail: info@greenridgeinv.com
Website: www.greenridgeinv.com

Management and Staff

Ben Moss, Co-Founder
Jack Cardwell, Co-Founder
Shelley McAfee, Chief Financial Officer

Type of Firm
Private Equity Firm

Project Preferences

Type of Financing Preferred:
Leveraged Buyout
Acquisition

Geographical Preferences

United States Preferences:
Texas

Industry Preferences

In Communications prefer:
Media and Entertainment

In Medical/Health prefer:
Medical/Health

In Industrial/Energy prefer:
Oil and Gas Exploration

Additional Information
Year Founded: 2014
Current Activity Level : Actively seeking new investments

GREENSKY CAPITAL INC

40 University Avenue
Suite 70
Toronto, Canada M5J 1T1
E-mail: info@greenskycapital.com
Website: www.greenskycapital.com

Type of Firm
Investment Management Firm

Project Preferences

Type of Financing Preferred:
Early Stage

Geographical Preferences

Canadian Preferences:
All Canada

Industry Preferences

In Medical/Health prefer:
Medical/Health

In Industrial/Energy prefer:
Environmental Related

Additional Information
Year Founded: 2007
Capital Under Management: $6,576,000
Current Activity Level : Actively seeking new investments

GREENSOIL INVESTMENTS MANAGEMENT LTD

Beit Bonei Binyan HaMelacha 2, Third Floor
Ra anana, Israel 43657
Phone: 97297887011
E-mail: info@greensoil-investments.com
Website: greensoil-investments.com

Other Offices

61 Yorkville Avenue
Toronto, Canada M5R 2B1

Stadhouderskade 140
Amsterdam, Netherlands 1074 BA

Type of Firm

Private Equity Firm

Additional Information

Year Founded: 2011
Capital Under Management: $40,460,000
Current Activity Level : Actively seeking new investments

GREENSPRING ASSOCIATES INC

100 Painters Mill Road
Suite 700
Owings Mills, MD USA 21117
Phone: 4103632725
Fax: 4103639075
E-mail: info@gspring.com
Website: greenspringassociates.com

Other Offices

228 Hamilton Avenue
Third Floor
PALO ALTO, CA USA 94301
Phone: 6507985392
Fax: 6507985001

Management and Staff

Adair Newhall, Principal
Ashton Newhall, Co-Founder
Brittany Hargest, Vice President
Eric Thompson, Chief Operating Officer
Hunter Somerville, Partner
James Lim, General Partner
John Wuestling, Vice President
John Avirett, Partner
Lindsay Redfield, Chief Financial Officer
R. Todd Ruppert, Venture Partner

Type of Firm

Private Equity Advisor or Fund of Funds

Association Membership

National Venture Capital Association - USA (NVCA)

Project Preferences

Role in Financing:
Prefer role in deals created by others

Type of Financing Preferred:
Fund of Funds
Later Stage
Fund of Funds of Second

Geographical Preferences

United States Preferences:
North America

International Preferences:
Europe
Australia
Asia

Industry Preferences

In Business Serv. prefer:
Services

Additional Information

Name of Most Recent Fund: Greenspring GE III, L.P.
Most Recent Fund Was Raised: 03/27/2014
Year Founded: 2000
Capital Under Management: $3,902,000,000
Current Activity Level : Actively seeking new investments
Method of Compensation: Return on invest. most important, but chg. closing fees, service fees, etc.

GREENVIEW ASSOCIATES LLC

1200 High Ridge Road
Suite Seven
Stamford, CT USA 06905
Phone: 2035045000
Fax: 2122024641
E-mail: info@greenviewassociates.com
Website: www.greenviewassociates.com

Management and Staff

A. Martin Cannon, Managing Partner
Stephen W.G. Yip, Partner

Type of Firm

Private Equity Firm

Project Preferences

Type of Financing Preferred:
Leveraged Buyout
Expansion
Mezzanine
Recapitalizations

Additional Information

Year Founded: 2005
Current Activity Level : Actively seeking new investments

GREENWOODS ASSET MANAGEMENT LTD

1518 Minsheng Road, Pudong
Jinying Tower B, Tenth Floor
Shanghai, China 200135
Phone: 862168548938
Fax: 862161049577
E-mail: info@greenwoodsasset.com

Other Offices

1 Connaught Place
Suite 805-08, 8/F, Jardine House
Hong Kong, Hong Kong
Phone: 85229076280
Fax: 85229076208

Management and Staff

Di Pan, Vice President
Hao Wang, Partner
Hong Shi, Partner
Shangjun Wang, Partner
Xiaodong Chen, Vice President
Xiaodong Wang, Vice President
Zhijun Wen, Managing Director
Zhongyuan Zhu, Managing Director

Type of Firm

Investment Management Firm

Project Preferences

Type of Financing Preferred:
Expansion

Size of Investments Considered:
Min Size of Investment Considered (000s): $772
Max Size of Investment Considered (000s): $4,630

Industry Preferences

In Communications prefer:
Telecommunications

In Semiconductor/Electr prefer:
Electronics

In Medical/Health prefer:
Medical/Health

In Industrial/Energy prefer:
Energy
Materials
Environmental Related

In Transportation prefer:
Transportation

In Business Serv. prefer:
Services
Media

In Manufact. prefer:
Manufacturing

GREENWOODS CAPITAL PARTNERS

24 Greenwoods Road West
P.O. Box 572
Norfolk, CT USA 06058
Phone: 8605423935
Fax: 8605423936
Website: www.greenwoodscapital.com

Management and Staff
Justin Vagliano, Principal

Type of Firm
Private Equity Firm

Project Preferences

Type of Financing Preferred:
Expansion
Management Buyouts
Acquisition

Size of Investments Considered:
Min Size of Investment Considered (000s): $1,000
Max Size of Investment Considered (000s): $3,000

Industry Preferences

In Consumer Related prefer:
Retail

In Business Serv. prefer:
Services

Additional Information
Year Founded: 2005
Current Activity Level : Actively seeking new investments

GREER CAPITAL ADVISORS LLC

2200 Woodcrest Place
Suite 309
Birmingham, AL USA 35209
Phone: 2054450800
Fax: 2054451013
E-mail: info@greercap.com

Management and Staff
Allan Dean, Managing Partner
Lawrence Greer, Founder

Type of Firm
Private Equity Firm

Project Preferences

Role in Financing:
Will function either as deal originator or investor in deals created by others

Type of Financing Preferred:
Early Stage
Expansion
Mezzanine
Balanced
Later Stage

Size of Investments Considered:
Min Size of Investment Considered (000s): $100
Max Size of Investment Considered (000s): $2,000

Geographical Preferences

United States Preferences:
Southeast
Alabama

Industry Preferences

In Biotechnology prefer:
Biotechnology

In Medical/Health prefer:
Medical/Health
Medical Diagnostics
Medical Products
Pharmaceuticals

Additional Information
Name of Most Recent Fund: Birmingham Technology Fund LLC
Most Recent Fund Was Raised: 06/27/2006
Year Founded: 2002
Capital Under Management: $18,000,000
Current Activity Level : Actively seeking new investments
Method of Compensation: Return on investment is of primary concern, do not charge fees

---

GRESHAM HOUSE STRATEGIC PLC

Five St John's Lane
London, United Kingdom EC1M 4BH
Phone: 442081230665
E-mail: enquiries@sparkventures.com
Website: www.ghsplc.com

Other Offices
33 Glasshouse Street
Fourth Floor
London, United Kingdom W1B 5DG
Phone: 442078517777
Fax: 442078517770

Type of Firm
Private Equity Firm

Association Membership
British Venture Capital Association (BVCA)

Project Preferences

Role in Financing:
Prefer role as deal originator but will also invest in deals created by others

Type of Financing Preferred:
Early Stage

Geographical Preferences

International Preferences:
United Kingdom

Industry Focus
(% based on actual investment)
Internet Specific	24.6%
Biotechnology	16.3%
Communications and Media	15.1%
Computer Software and Services	14.3%
Semiconductors/Other Elect.	9.3%
Other Products	8.0%
Medical/Health	5.6%
Computer Hardware	3.1%
Consumer Related	1.9%
Industrial/Energy	1.9%

Additional Information
Name of Most Recent Fund: Lachesis Fund
Most Recent Fund Was Raised: 01/07/2002
Year Founded: 1984
Capital Under Management: $292,400,000
Current Activity Level : Actively seeking new investments
Method of Compensation: Return on invest. most important, but chg. closing fees, service fees, etc.

GRESHAM LLP

Two London Bridge
Third Floor
London, United Kingdom SE1 9RA
Phone: 442073095000
Fax: 442073740707
E-mail: info@greshampe.com
Website: www.greshampe.com

Other Offices
King Street
Venturers House
Bristol, United Kingdom BS1 4PB
Phone: 441179154005

82 King Street
Manchester, United Kingdom M2 4WQ
Phone: 441618337500
Fax: 441618337575

2 Snow Hill, Snow Hill Queensway
Suite 231
Birmingham, United Kingdom B3 3GT
Phone: 441212000050
Fax: 441212000055

Additional Information (Greenwoods Capital Partners)
Year Founded: 2004
Capital Under Management: $88,425,000
Current Activity Level : Actively seeking new investments

Management and Staff
Andy Marsh, Partner
Iain Wolstenholme, Partner
James Slipper, Partner
Paul Franks, Partner
Paul Thomas, Partner
Pauline Abbie, Partner
Simon Hemley, Partner
Simon Inchley, Chief Executive Officer

Type of Firm
Private Equity Firm

Association Membership
British Venture Capital Association (BVCA)

Project Preferences

Type of Financing Preferred:
Leveraged Buyout
Management Buyouts
Acquisition

Geographical Preferences

International Preferences:
United Kingdom
Europe

Industry Focus
(% based on actual investment)

Other Products	46.2%
Consumer Related	33.9%
Communications and Media	6.7%
Medical/Health	4.4%
Computer Hardware	4.2%
Computer Software and Services	2.9%
Semiconductors/Other Elect.	1.6%

Additional Information
Name of Most Recent Fund: Gresham IV
Most Recent Fund Was Raised: 06/30/2006
Year Founded: 1982
Capital Under Management: $262,800,000
Current Activity Level : Actively seeking new investments

GREY MOUNTAIN PARTNERS LLC

1470 Walnut Street
Suite 400
Boulder, CO USA 80302
Phone: 3034495692
Fax: 3034493194
E-mail: info@greymountain.com
Website: www.greymountain.com

Other Offices
590 Madison Avenue
21st Floor
New York, NY USA 10022
Phone: 212-588-8845
Fax: 212-588-8853

Management and Staff
Alexandr Khizver, Chief Financial Officer
Ben Ault, Managing Director
Beth Lesniak, Vice President
Brad Starkweather, Vice President
Jeff Kuo, Co-Founder
Jeff Vincent, Managing Director
Rob Wright, Co-Founder

Type of Firm
Private Equity Firm

Association Membership
Natl Assoc of Investment Cos. (NAIC)

Project Preferences

Role in Financing:
Prefer role as deal originator

Type of Financing Preferred:
Leveraged Buyout
Turnaround
Management Buyouts
Acquisition
Recapitalizations

Geographical Preferences

United States Preferences:
North America

Industry Preferences

In Medical/Health prefer:
Health Services

In Consumer Related prefer:
Food/Beverage

In Industrial/Energy prefer:
Energy
Industrial Products
Advanced Materials

In Transportation prefer:
Transportation
Aerospace

In Financial Services prefer:
Financial Services

In Business Serv. prefer:
Services
Distribution

In Manufact. prefer:
Manufacturing

Additional Information
Name of Most Recent Fund: Grey Mountain Partners Fund III, L.P.
Most Recent Fund Was Raised: 06/28/2013
Year Founded: 2003
Capital Under Management: $424,045,000
Current Activity Level : Actively seeking new investments
Method of Compensation: Return on investment is of primary concern, do not charge fees

---

GREYBIRD VENTURES LLC

31 Pond View Lane Concord
Concord, MA USA 01742
Website: www.greybirdventures.com

Type of Firm
Private Equity Firm

Project Preferences

Type of Financing Preferred:
Early Stage

Industry Preferences

In Medical/Health prefer:
Medical/Health

Additional Information
Year Founded: 2013
Current Activity Level : Actively seeking new investments

GREYCROFT PARTNERS LLC

292 Madison Avenue
New York, NY USA 10017
Phone: 2127563508
Fax: 2128320117
Website: greycroft.com

Other Offices
100 Wilshire Boulevard
Suite 1830
SANTA MONICA, CA USA 90401
Phone: 3105665960

Management and Staff
Alan Patricof, Co-Founder
Bo Peabody, Venture Partner
Dana Settle, Co-Founder
Dylan Pearce, Principal
Ellie Wheeler, Partner
Ian Sigalow, Co-Founder
John Elton, Partner
Jon Goldman, Venture Partner
Kamran Ansari, Venture Partner
Mark Terbeek, Partner
Matt Parker, Chief Financial Officer
Paul Bricault, Venture Partner

Type of Firm
Private Equity Firm

Project Preferences

Type of Financing Preferred:
Balanced
Startup

Size of Investments Considered:
Min Size of Investment Considered (000s): $100
Max Size of Investment Considered (000s): $20,000

Geographical Preferences

United States Preferences:
California
West Coast
New York

Industry Preferences

In Communications prefer:
Wireless Communications
Media and Entertainment

In Computer Software prefer:
Software

In Internet Specific prefer:
Internet
Ecommerce

In Consumer Related prefer:
Consumer

In Business Serv. prefer:
Services
Media

Additional Information
Name of Most Recent Fund: Greycroft Partners III, L.P.
Most Recent Fund Was Raised: 11/26/2012
Year Founded: 2006
Capital Under Management: $1,000,000,000
Current Activity Level: Actively seeking new investments

GREYLOCK ISRAEL GLOBAL MANAGEMENT LTD

Sderot Abba Eban 10
Bldg. C, 9th Floor
Herzliya, Israel 4673303
Website: www.83north.com

Other Offices
Sderot Abba Eban 10
Bldg. C, 9th Floor
Herzliya, Israel

Management and Staff
Arnon Dinur, Partner
Asaf Horesh, Principal
Erez Ofer, Co-Founder
Laurel Bowden, Partner
Tilli Kalisky-Bannett, Venture Partner
Yoram Snir, Co-Founder

Type of Firm
Private Equity Firm

Project Preferences

Type of Financing Preferred:
Balanced

Geographical Preferences

International Preferences:
Ireland
Europe
Israel

Industry Preferences

In Communications prefer:
Data Communications
Media and Entertainment

In Computer Software prefer:
Data Processing
Software
Systems Software

In Internet Specific prefer:
E-Commerce Technology
Ecommerce

In Consumer Related prefer:
Consumer Services

In Industrial/Energy prefer:
Environmental Related

In Financial Services prefer:
Financial Services

In Business Serv. prefer:
Media

Additional Information
Year Founded: 2006
Capital Under Management: $800,000,000
Current Activity Level: Actively seeking new investments

GREYLOCK PARTNERS LLC

2550 Sand Hill Road
Suite 200
Menlo Park, CA USA 94025
Phone: 6504935525
Fax: 6504935575
Website: www.greylock.com

Other Offices
No. 79 Jianguo Road
3207A, Tower 2 China Central Place
Beijing, China 100025
Phone: 861057696500
Fax: 861059696185

Level 2, No 104 EPIP Zone
Prestige Omega Building, Whitefield
Bangalore, India 560066
Phone: 91-80-4060-0664
Fax: 91-80-4060-0700

10 Abba Eban Boulevard
Building C, Nineth Floor
Herzliya Pituach, Israel 46733
Phone: 972-9-958-0007
Fax: 972-9-958-0009

Management and Staff
Aneel Bhusri, Partner
Arvin Babu, Partner
Asheem Chandna, Partner
Chad Waite, Partner
Dan Portillo, Vice President
Daniel Gregory, Partner
David Strohm, Partner
David Thacker, Venture Partner
David Sze, Partner
Dev Ittycheria, Venture Partner
Donald Fischer, Principal
Donald Sullivan, Partner
Elisa Schreiber, Vice President
Howard Cox, Partner
James Slavet, Partner
Jeff Markowitz, Partner
Jerry Chen, Partner
John Lilly, Partner
Joseph Ansanelli, Partner
Josh McFarland, Partner
Josh Elman, Principal
Kristin Richards, Vice President
Michael Ahearn, Partner
Reid Hoffman, Partner
Robert Henderson, Partner
Roger Evans, Partner
Sarah Tavel, Partner
Thomas Bogan, Venture Partner
Tom Frangione, Chief Operating Officer
William Helman, Partner
William Elfers, Partner
William Kaiser, Partner

Type of Firm
Private Equity Firm

Association Membership
New England Venture Capital Association
Israel Venture Association

Project Preferences

Role in Financing:
Prefer role as deal originator but will also invest in deals created by others

Type of Financing Preferred:
Early Stage
Expansion
Balanced
Later Stage
Seed
Startup

Size of Investments Considered:
Min Size of Investment Considered (000s): $50
Max Size of Investment Considered (000s): $10,000

Geographical Preferences

United States Preferences:

International Preferences:
India
China
Israel

Industry Focus

(% based on actual investment)
Computer Software and Services	40.9%
Internet Specific	33.3%
Communications and Media	7.0%
Computer Hardware	6.0%
Semiconductors/Other Elect.	5.2%
Other Products	3.1%
Industrial/Energy	1.4%
Biotechnology	1.1%
Consumer Related	1.0%
Medical/Health	0.9%

Additional Information

Name of Most Recent Fund: Greylock XIV, L.P.
Most Recent Fund Was Raised: 09/10/2013
Year Founded: 1965
Capital Under Management: $2,200,000,000
Current Activity Level : Actively seeking new investments
Method of Compensation: Return on investment is of primary concern, do not charge fees

GREYROCK CAPITAL GROUP

10 Westport Road
Suite C204
Wilton, CT USA 06897
Fax: 2034292010

Other Offices

582 Market Street
Suite 1117
San Francisco, CA USA 94104
Fax: 4152880284

230 West Monroe Street
Suite 2000
Chicago, IL USA 60606
Fax: 3128490000

Management and Staff

Mark Shufro, Managing Partner
Mark French, Principal
Stephen Etter, Partner
Steve Dempsey, Partner
Todd Osburn, Partner
Tracy Perkins, Partner

Type of Firm

Private Equity Firm

Project Preferences

Type of Financing Preferred:
Leveraged Buyout
Mezzanine
Recapitalizations

Geographical Preferences

United States Preferences:

Industry Preferences

In Consumer Related prefer:
Consumer

In Industrial/Energy prefer:
Industrial Products
Materials

In Business Serv. prefer:
Services

In Manufact. prefer:
Manufacturing

Additional Information

Name of Most Recent Fund: GCG Investors III, L.P.
Most Recent Fund Was Raised: 03/15/2013
Year Founded: 2002
Capital Under Management: $370,900,000
Current Activity Level : Actively seeking new investments

GREYWOLF

10100 Santa Monica Boulevard
Suite 925
Los Angeles, CA USA 90067
E-mail: info@greywolf.vc
Website: greywolf.vc

Type of Firm

Private Equity Firm

Project Preferences

Type of Financing Preferred:
Early Stage
Expansion
Balanced

Industry Preferences

In Financial Services prefer:
Real Estate

Additional Information

Year Founded: 2015
Current Activity Level : Actively seeking new investments

GRIDIRON CAPITAL LLC

220 Elm Street
New Canaan, CT USA 06840
Phone: 2039721100
Fax: 2038010602
Website: www.gridironcapital.com

Management and Staff

Brian Rachal, Chief Financial Officer
Christopher King, Vice President
Douglas Rosenstein, Vice President
Eugene Conese, Co-Founder
Geoffrey Spillane, Managing Director
Joseph Saldutti, Managing Director
Josh Gault, Vice President
Kallie Hapgood, Managing Director
Kevin Jackson, Senior Managing Director
Owen Tharrington, Managing Director
Paul Sun, Managing Director
Sean Kelley, Principal
Thomas Burger, Co-Founder
Timothy Clark, Managing Director
William Hausberg, Managing Director

Type of Firm

Private Equity Firm

Project Preferences

Type of Financing Preferred:
Leveraged Buyout
Acquisition

Geographical Preferences

United States Preferences:

Canadian Preferences:
All Canada

Industry Preferences

In Consumer Related prefer:
Consumer Products
Consumer Services

In Business Serv. prefer:
Services

In Manufact. prefer:
Manufacturing

Additional Information

Name of Most Recent Fund: Gridiron Capital Fund II, L.P.
Most Recent Fund Was Raised: 06/01/2011
Year Founded: 2005
Capital Under Management: $1,275,000,000
Current Activity Level : Actively seeking new investments

GRIFFIN HOLDINGS LLC

2121 Avenue Of The Stars
Suite 2575
Los Angeles, CA USA 90067
Phone: 4242454423
Fax: 4242454623
E-mail: info@griffinhld.com
Website: griffinhld.com

Type of Firm

Private Equity Firm

Project Preferences

Type of Financing Preferred:
Leveraged Buyout
Expansion
Management Buyouts
Acquisition
Recapitalizations

Industry Preferences

In Consumer Related prefer:
Retail
Food/Beverage
Consumer Products
Consumer Services

In Industrial/Energy prefer:
Materials

In Business Serv. prefer:
Distribution

In Manufact. prefer:
Manufacturing

Additional Information

Year Founded: 2008
Current Activity Level : Actively seeking new investments

GRIFFON CAPITAL

38 Golfam Street Unit 101
Africa Boulevard
Tehran, Iran
Phone: 982126231278
Fax: 982126231275
E-mail: info@griffoncapital.com
Website: www.griffoncapital.com

Type of Firm
Private Equity Firm

Geographical Preferences

International Preferences:
Iran

Additional Information
Year Founded: 2014
Current Activity Level : Actively seeking new investments

GRIFFON VENTURE PARTNERS

6711 Forest Glen Road
Pittsburgh, PA USA 15217
Phone: 4129044743

Management and Staff
Gary Schwager, Managing Partner

Type of Firm
Private Equity Advisor or Fund of Funds

Project Preferences

Type of Financing Preferred:
Fund of Funds

Additional Information
Year Founded: 2008
Current Activity Level : Actively seeking new investments

GRISHIN ROBOTICS

112 West 34th Street
New York, NY USA 10120
Phone: 2125023093
E-mail: info@grishinrobotics.com
Website: grishinrobotics.com

Management and Staff
Dmitry Grishin, Founder

Type of Firm
Private Equity Firm

Project Preferences

Type of Financing Preferred:
Seed
Startup

Size of Investments Considered:
Min Size of Investment Considered (000s): $250
Max Size of Investment Considered (000s): $1,000

Additional Information
Year Founded: 2012
Capital Under Management: $25,000,000
Current Activity Level : Actively seeking new investments

GRO CAPITAL A/S

Gothersgade 103
Copenhagen, Denmark 1123
Phone: 4533157030
Fax: 4533369444
E-mail: dankap@dankap.dk
Website: www.grocapital.dk

Management and Staff
Jesper Johansen, Partner
Lars Dybkjaer, Managing Partner

Type of Firm
Private Equity Firm

Project Preferences

Type of Financing Preferred:
Fund of Funds
Leveraged Buyout
Turnaround
Recapitalizations

Size of Investments Considered:
Min Size of Investment Considered (000s): $6,906
Max Size of Investment Considered (000s): $18,588

Geographical Preferences

International Preferences:
Denmark

Industry Focus
(% based on actual investment)
Medical/Health	32.3%
Biotechnology	19.9%
Semiconductors/Other Elect.	14.4%
Internet Specific	13.8%
Other Products	8.9%
Industrial/Energy	8.6%
Computer Software and Services	2.1%

Additional Information
Year Founded: 1984
Capital Under Management: $275,000,000
Current Activity Level : Actively seeking new investments

GROEP BRUSSEL LAMBERT NV

24, Avenue Marnix
Brussels, Belgium 1000
Phone: 3222891717
Fax: 3222891737
Website: www.gbl.be

Management and Staff
Baron Albert Frere, CEO & Managing Director
William Blomme, Chief Financial Officer

Type of Firm
Private Equity Firm

Project Preferences

Type of Financing Preferred:
Fund of Funds
Leveraged Buyout
Early Stage
Generalist PE
Public Companies
Later Stage

Geographical Preferences

United States Preferences:
All U.S.

International Preferences:
Italy
Luxembourg
Europe
Netherlands
Switzerland
Spain
Belgium
France

Industry Preferences

In Biotechnology prefer:
Biotechnology

In Medical/Health prefer:
Medical/Health

In Industrial/Energy prefer:
Industrial Products

Additional Information

Year Founded: 1902
Current Activity Level : Actively seeking new investments

GROFIN CAPITAL (PTY) LTD

Building D, 224 Loristo Street
Pretorius Park
Pretoria, South Africa 0010
Phone: 27129988280
Fax: 27129988401
E-mail: info@grofin.com
Website: www.grofin.com

Other Offices

Amman Gate Building
7th Circle, Sweifieh
Amman, Jordan
Phone: 96265851811

9 Abimbola Awoniyi Close
Lagos, Nigeria
Phone: 234-1-279-8046
Fax: 234-1-279-8049

Jumeirah Business Centre 5
Jumeirah Lake Towers
Dubai, Utd. Arab Em. 487747
Phone: 97143752424

No 7 NME Lane
Airport Residential Area
Accra, Ghana
Phone: 233-21-774-777
Fax: 233-21-760-457

4th Floor Tele10 Building
Airport Boulevard, Nyarutarama, Remera
Kigali, Rwanda
Phone: 250-587-150
Fax: 250-587-152

Basrah International Hotel
Al Corneesh Street, Al Ashar
Basra, Iraq
Phone: 964775601111

DG35
Block D Ruisseau Creole La Mivoie
Black River, Mauritius
Phone: 230-483-6782
Fax: 230-483-8498

Suite 203
Standard Bank Building,1 Millenium Blvd.
Durban, South Africa
Phone: 27-31-584-6079
Fax: 27-31-566-3075

Ground Floor, CIC Plaza
Mara Road, Upper Hill
Nairobi, Kenya
Phone: 254-20-273-0280
Fax: 254-20-273-0279

224 Loristo Street
Building F, Pretorius Park
Pretoria, South Africa
Phone: 27-12-998-8280
Fax: 27-12-998-8401

Office 229A, 2nd Floor
Harbour View Towers Centre, Samora Ave.
Dar es Salaam, Tanzania
Phone: 255-22-212-0815
Fax: 255-22-212-0871

1st Floor, Global house
Plot 38B Winsor Crescent
Kampala, Uganda
Phone: 256-41-423-7482
Fax: 256-41-423-7481

House No 1305, Way No 3017
Shatti Al Qurum
Muscat, Oman
Phone: 968-24-697-949
Fax: 968-24-697-323

Management and Staff

Anton Wewege, Founder
Jurie Willemse, Managing Director
William Morkel, Chief Financial Officer

Type of Firm

Private Equity Firm

Project Preferences

Type of Financing Preferred:
Leveraged Buyout
Early Stage
Expansion
Balanced
Later Stage
Other
Management Buyouts
Startup

Size of Investments Considered:
Min Size of Investment Considered (000s): $50
Max Size of Investment Considered (000s): $1,500

Geographical Preferences

International Preferences:
Oman
Jordan
Zambia
Middle East
Africa
Iraq

Additional Information

Year Founded: 2004
Capital Under Management: $250,000,000
Current Activity Level : Actively seeking new investments

GROKVENTURES PTY LTD

251 Riley Street
Surry Hills, Australia NSW 2010
E-mail: hi@grok.ventures
Website: grok.ventures

Type of Firm

Private Equity Firm

Project Preferences

Type of Financing Preferred:
Early Stage
Later Stage

Additional Information

Year Founded: 1969
Current Activity Level : Actively seeking new investments

GROSVENOR CAPITAL MANAGEMENT LP

900 North Michigan Avenue
Suite 1100
Chicago, IL USA 60611
Phone: 3125066500
Website: www.grosvenorcapitalmanagement.com

Management and Staff

Aris Hatch, Managing Director
Dasha Dwin, Managing Director
Jeremy Katz, Managing Director
Jonathan Levin, Managing Director
Peter Braffman, Managing Director
Stephen Brewster, Managing Director

Type of Firm

Investment Management Firm

Project Preferences

Type of Financing Preferred:
Generalist PE

Additional Information

Year Founded: 2016
Capital Under Management: $22,280,000
Current Activity Level : Actively seeking new investments

GROTECH VENTURES

8000 Towers Crescent Drive, Suite 850
Hunt Valley, MD USA 21031
Phone: 7036379555
Fax: 7038279088
Website: www.grotech.com

Other Offices
100 Fillmore Street
Suite 500
DENVER, CO USA 80206
Phone: 7203994952
Fax: 3036485168

Management and Staff
Don Rainey, General Partner
Joseph Zell, General Partner
Julia Taxin, Vice President
Lawson DeVries, General Partner
Stephen Fredrick, General Partner

Type of Firm
Private Equity Firm

Association Membership
National Venture Capital Association - USA (NVCA)

Project Preferences

Role in Financing:
Prefer role as deal originator

Type of Financing Preferred:
Early Stage
Expansion
Balanced
Later Stage
Seed
Startup

Size of Investments Considered:
Min Size of Investment Considered (000s): $500
Max Size of Investment Considered (000s): $5,000

Geographical Preferences

United States Preferences:
Mid Atlantic
Southeast

Industry Focus
(% based on actual investment)
Internet Specific	36.5%
Computer Software and Services	23.0%
Consumer Related	11.2%
Medical/Health	8.9%
Communications and Media	7.6%
Semiconductors/Other Elect.	4.5%
Other Products	3.4%
Industrial/Energy	2.5%
Computer Hardware	1.4%
Biotechnology	0.8%

Additional Information
Name of Most Recent Fund: Grotech Ventures II, L.P.
Most Recent Fund Was Raised: 03/28/2013
Year Founded: 1984
Capital Under Management: $1,000,000,000
Current Activity Level : Actively seeking new investments
Method of Compensation: Return on invest. most important, but chg. closing fees, service fees, etc.

GROUNDWORK EQUITY LLC

826 Calle Plano
Camarillo, CA USA 93012
Phone: 8053836288
Fax: 8054132009
Website: www.groundworkequity.com

Management and Staff
Fredrick Ackourey, Partner
Michael Edell, Managing Partner
Ron Means, Partner

Type of Firm
Private Equity Firm

Project Preferences

Type of Financing Preferred:
Early Stage
Seed
Startup

Geographical Preferences

United States Preferences:
All U.S.

Additional Information
Year Founded: 1969
Current Activity Level : Actively seeking new investments

GROUP MC NV

467, Luikesteenweg
Hasselt, Belgium 3500
Phone: 3211283550
Website: www.groupmc.be

Type of Firm
Private Equity Firm

Project Preferences

Type of Financing Preferred:
Leveraged Buyout
Expansion
Later Stage
Management Buyouts
Acquisition

Additional Information
Year Founded: 1999
Current Activity Level : Actively seeking new investments

GROUPE ALISTON INC

400, Laurier Avenue West, Suite 600
Montreal, Canada H2V 2K7
Phone: 5142745777
Fax: 5142745701
Website: www.aliston.com

Type of Firm
Private Equity Firm

Additional Information
Year Founded: 2012
Current Activity Level : Actively seeking new investments

GROUPE ARNAULT SE

41, Avenue Montaigne
Paris, France 75008
Phone: 33120244000

Management and Staff
Denis Dalibot, Founder

Type of Firm
Corporate PE/Venture

Project Preferences

Type of Financing Preferred:
Leveraged Buyout
Early Stage
Generalist PE
Start-up Financing
Acquisition

Geographical Preferences

International Preferences:
Europe
France

Additional Information
Year Founded: 1978
Current Activity Level : Actively seeking new investments

GROUPE IRD SA

40, rue Eugene Jacquert
Marcq-en-Baroeul, France 59708
Phone: 330359302004
Fax: 330359302059
Website: www.groupeird.fr

Type of Firm
Private Equity Firm

Project Preferences

Type of Financing Preferred:
Core
Leveraged Buyout
Value-Add
Early Stage
Expansion
Opportunistic
Later Stage
Management Buyouts
Acquisition

Size of Investments Considered:
Min Size of Investment Considered (000s): $212
Max Size of Investment Considered (000s): $7,436

Geographical Preferences

International Preferences:
France

Additional Information
Year Founded: 1956
Current Activity Level : Actively seeking new investments

GROVEPOINT CAPITAL LLP

4 Bentinck Street
Heron House
London, United Kingdom W1U 2EF
Phone: 442074865954
E-mail: info@grovepoint.co.uk
Website: www.grovepoint.co.uk

Management and Staff
Bradley Fried, Co-Founder
Leon Blitz, Co-Founder

Type of Firm
Private Equity Firm

Project Preferences

Type of Financing Preferred:
Leveraged Buyout
Generalist PE
Later Stage

Additional Information
Year Founded: 2010
Current Activity Level : Actively seeking new investments

GROVEST VENTURE CAPITAL CO (PTY) LTD

164 Katherine Street
Pinmill Office Park Building 2
Strathavon-Johannesburg, South Africa 2196
Phone: 27112626433
Fax: 27112626308
E-mail: invest@grovest.co.za
Website: www.grovest.co.za

Type of Firm
Private Equity Firm

Association Membership
South African Venture Capital Association (SAVCA)

Project Preferences

Type of Financing Preferred:
Early Stage
Expansion
Later Stage
Seed
Startup

Geographical Preferences

International Preferences:
South Africa

Industry Preferences

In Communications prefer:
Telecommunications

Additional Information
Year Founded: 2013
Current Activity Level : Actively seeking new investments

GROW MICHIGAN LLC

801 W. Ann Arbor Trail
Suite 220
Plymouth, MI USA 48170
Phone: 8889639149
E-mail: info@growmicapital.com
Website: growmicapital.com

Other Offices
180 West Michigan Avenue
Suite 800
Jackson, MI USA 49201
Phone: 5175138923

Type of Firm
Private Equity Firm

Project Preferences

Type of Financing Preferred:
Expansion
Mezzanine
Management Buyouts
Acquisition
Recapitalizations

Geographical Preferences

United States Preferences:
Michigan

Industry Preferences

In Industrial/Energy prefer:
Machinery

In Transportation prefer:
Transportation

In Business Serv. prefer:
Distribution

In Manufact. prefer:
Manufacturing

Additional Information
Name of Most Recent Fund: Grow Michigan LLC
Most Recent Fund Was Raised: 01/09/2013
Year Founded: 2013
Capital Under Management: $67,200,000
Current Activity Level : Actively seeking new investments

GROWCORP GROUP LTD

3015 Lake Drive
National Digital Park
Dublin, Ireland
Phone: 35314661000
Fax: 35314661002
E-mail: grow@growcorp.net
Website: www.growcorp.net

Management and Staff
Fintan Maher, Managing Director

Type of Firm
Incubator/Development Program

Project Preferences

Type of Financing Preferred:
Seed
Startup

Geographical Preferences

International Preferences:
Ireland
United Kingdom
Europe

Industry Preferences

In Communications prefer:
Communications and Media

In Biotechnology prefer:
Biotechnology

In Medical/Health prefer:
Medical Diagnostics
Medical Products

Additional Information
Name of Most Recent Fund: European Bioscience Fund 1, The
Most Recent Fund Was Raised: 12/17/2002
Year Founded: 1999
Capital Under Management: $8,700,000
Current Activity Level : Reducing investment activity

GROWLAB VENTURES INC

116 West Hastings Street
2nd Floor
Vancouver, Canada V6B 1G8
Phone: 6046523230
E-mail: info@growlab.ca
Website: www.growlab.ca

Management and Staff
Boris Wertz, Co-Founder
Debbie Landa, Co-Founder
Jason Bailey, President
Leonard Brody, Co-Founder

Type of Firm
Corporate PE/Venture

Project Preferences

Type of Financing Preferred:
Early Stage

Additional Information
Year Founded: 2014
Capital Under Management: $2,179,000
Current Activity Level : Actively seeking new investments

GROWTH CATALYST PARTNERS LLC

318 West Adams Street
16th Floor
Chicago, IL USA 60606
Phone: 3123850850
Website: www.growthcatalystpartners.com

Type of Firm
Private Equity Firm

Project Preferences

Type of Financing Preferred:
Leveraged Buyout
Acquisition

Industry Preferences

In Business Serv. prefer:
Services
Media

Additional Information
Year Founded: 2017
Capital Under Management: $57,000,000
Current Activity Level : Actively seeking new investments

GROWTH ENTERPRISE MARKET

21/F, 3 Huaaozhongxin Apt.
31 Zhizhuyuan Haidian District
Beijing, China
Phone: 86-10-6872-8858
Fax: 86-10-6841-0981

Type of Firm
Private Equity Firm

Association Membership
Venture Capital Association of Beijing (VCAB)

Project Preferences

Type of Financing Preferred:
Balanced

Geographical Preferences

International Preferences:
China

Additional Information
Year Founded: 1999
Current Activity Level : Actively seeking new investments

GROWTH FUND, THE

Suite 2, Level 33 Chifley Tower
Two Chifley Square
Sydney, Australia
Website: thegrowthfund.com.au

Type of Firm
Private Equity Firm

Project Preferences

Type of Financing Preferred:
Leveraged Buyout
Management Buyouts
Acquisition

Geographical Preferences

International Preferences:
Australia
New Zealand

Additional Information
Year Founded: 2011
Capital Under Management: $450,000,000
Current Activity Level : Actively seeking new investments

GROWTH STREET MANAGEMENT LLC

130 Seale Avenue
San Francisco, CA USA 94101
E-mail: info@growthstreetpartners.com
Website: growthstreetpartners.com

Management and Staff
Nathan Grossman, Co-Founder
Stephen Wolfe, Co-Founder

Type of Firm
Private Equity Firm

Project Preferences

Type of Financing Preferred:
Early Stage

Geographical Preferences

United States Preferences:

Industry Preferences

In Computer Software prefer:
Software

In Business Serv. prefer:
Services

Additional Information
Year Founded: 2017
Capital Under Management: $70,000,000
Current Activity Level : Actively seeking new investments

GROWTH UP GROUP

L. Tolstogo, 3
Floor 4
Kiev, Ukraine
E-mail: pr@growthup.com
Website: www.growthup.com

Type of Firm
Incubator/Development Program

Project Preferences

Type of Financing Preferred:
Seed
Startup

Geographical Preferences

International Preferences:
Ukraine
Russia

Industry Preferences

In Computer Software prefer:
Systems Software
Applications Software

In Internet Specific prefer:
E-Commerce Technology

Additional Information
Year Founded: 2013
Current Activity Level : Actively seeking new investments

GROWTH WORKS CAPITAL LTD

2600-1055 West Georgia Street
Box 11170, Royal Centre
Vancouver, Canada V6E 3R5
Phone: 8002688244
Fax: 8666883431
E-mail: info@growthworks.ca
Website: www.growthworks.ca

Other Offices

77 Westmorland Street
Fredericton, Canada E3B 6Z3
Phone: 506-444-0091
Fax: 506-444-0816

1801 Hollis Street
Suite 310
Halifax, Canada B3J 3N4
Phone: 902-492-5164
Fax: 902-421-1808

200 Graham Avenue
Suite 1120
Winnipeg, Canada R3C 4L5
Phone: 204-949-3700
Fax: 204-949-0591

275 Slater Street
Suite 900
Ottawa, Canada K1P 5H9
Phone: 613-567-3225
Fax: 613-567-3979

130 King Street West, Suite 2200
Exchange Tower, PO Box 422
Toronto, Canada M5X 1E3
Phone: 416-934-7777
Fax: 416-929-0901

Management and Staff

Alex Irwin, Chief Operating Officer
Carol Crow, Vice President
Clint Matthews, Chief Financial Officer
David Wilson, Vice President
Joe Timlin, Vice President
John Proven, Vice President
Les Lyall, Chief Operating Officer
Pat Brady, Vice President
Peter Clark, Vice President
Richard Charlebois, Vice President
Rolf Dekleer, Vice President
Steven Stang, Vice President
Todd Farrell, Vice President

Type of Firm

Private Equity Firm

Association Membership

Canadian Venture Capital Association

Project Preferences

Role in Financing:
Will function either as deal originator or investor in deals created by others

Type of Financing Preferred:
Early Stage
Expansion
Mezzanine
Balanced
Later Stage
Acquisition
Startup

Geographical Preferences

Canadian Preferences:
All Canada

Industry Preferences

In Industrial/Energy prefer:
Environmental Related

In Manufact. prefer:
Manufacturing

Additional Information

Year Founded: 1992
Capital Under Management: $750,000,000
Current Activity Level : Actively seeking new investments
Method of Compensation: Return on invest. most important, but chg. closing fees, service fees, etc.

GROWTHFIRE LLC

4235 Foxberry Court
Hamel, MN USA 55340
Phone: 9522005438
Website: www.growthfire.com

Type of Firm

Private Equity Firm

Project Preferences

Type of Financing Preferred:
Leveraged Buyout
Acquisition

Geographical Preferences

United States Preferences:
North America

Industry Preferences

In Computer Software prefer:
Software

In Consumer Related prefer:
Consumer Services

In Business Serv. prefer:
Services

Additional Information

Name of Most Recent Fund: GrowthFire LLC
Most Recent Fund Was Raised: 06/05/2013
Year Founded: 2013
Capital Under Management: $16,955,000
Current Activity Level : Actively seeking new investments

GROWTHX

44 Tehama Street
San Francisco, CA USA 94105
Website: www.growthx.com

Type of Firm

Incubator/Development Program

Project Preferences

Type of Financing Preferred:
Seed

Additional Information

Year Founded: 2015
Current Activity Level : Actively seeking new investments

GRREN BUSAN INVESTMENT CO LTD

1470 Wudong, Haewundae-gu
808, 8/F, Ace hightech 21
Busan, South Korea 600-014
Phone: 82-51-465-1214
Fax: 82-51-465-1216
Website: www.greeninvestments.co.kr

Other Offices

705-19 Yeoksam-Dong, Gangam-Gu
7/F Green Non-Insurance Building
Seoul, South Korea 135-922

Type of Firm

Private Equity Firm

Association Membership

Korean Venture Capital Association (KVCA)

Project Preferences

Type of Financing Preferred:
Balanced

Geographical Preferences

International Preferences:
Korea, South

Industry Preferences

In Consumer Related prefer:
Consumer

Additional Information

Year Founded: 2008
Capital Under Management: $8,860,000
Current Activity Level : Actively seeking new investments

GRUENDERFONDS GMBH CO KEG

Walcherstrasse 11A
Vienna, Austria 1020
Phone: 431501750
Fax: 43150175709
E-mail: office@gruenderfonds.at

Management and Staff

Gero Parfuss, Managing Director

965

Type of Firm
Bank Affiliated

Association Membership
Swiss Venture Capital Association (SECA)

Project Preferences

Type of Financing Preferred:
Early Stage
Later Stage

Size of Investments Considered:
Min Size of Investment Considered (000s): $383
Max Size of Investment Considered (000s): $2,551

Geographical Preferences

International Preferences:
Austria

Industry Focus

(% based on actual investment)
Semiconductors/Other Elect.	33.5%
Biotechnology	23.4%
Medical/Health	17.6%
Industrial/Energy	9.4%
Computer Software and Services	8.0%
Internet Specific	7.5%
Other Products	0.6%

Additional Information
Year Founded: 2001
Current Activity Level : Actively seeking new investments

GRUENWALD EQUITY MANAGEMENT GMBH

Suedliche Muenchner Strasse 10
Gruenwald, Germany 82031
Phone: 498950080860
Fax: 49895008086160
Website: www.gruenwaldequity.de

Management and Staff
Constantin Liechtenstein, Managing Partner
Raimund Koenig, Managing Partner
Thomas Trauttmansdorff, Managing Partner

Type of Firm
Private Equity Firm

Project Preferences

Type of Financing Preferred:
Leveraged Buyout
Later Stage
Acquisition

Geographical Preferences

International Preferences:
Switzerland
Austria
Germany

Industry Preferences

In Semiconductor/Electr prefer:
Electronics
Circuit Boards

In Consumer Related prefer:
Retail
Education Related

In Industrial/Energy prefer:
Industrial Products
Environmental Related

In Transportation prefer:
Transportation

In Financial Services prefer:
Financial Services
Financial Services

In Business Serv. prefer:
Services

In Manufact. prefer:
Manufacturing
Office Automation Equipmt

Additional Information
Year Founded: 2001
Current Activity Level : Actively seeking new investments

GRUPARA, INC.

Gedung Medco Ampera I, 3F, JL.
Ampera Raya no.20
Jakarta Selatan, Indonesia 10160
Phone: 62217892163
Fax: 62217892164
E-mail: incubation@gruparainc.com
Website: gruparainc.com

Type of Firm
Private Equity Firm

Project Preferences

Type of Financing Preferred:
Early Stage
Expansion
Seed
Startup

Size of Investments Considered:
Min Size of Investment Considered (000s): $5
Max Size of Investment Considered (000s): $1,500

Geographical Preferences

International Preferences:
Indonesia
Asia

Additional Information
Year Founded: 2011
Current Activity Level : Actively seeking new investments

GRUPPA SPUTNIK OOO

11 Derbenevskaya naberezhnaya
10 floor
Moscow, Russia 115114
Phone: 74957255000
Fax: 74957255001
Website: www.spkgroup.com

Management and Staff
Dmitriy Bakatin, Managing Director
Sergei Riabtsov, Managing Director

Type of Firm
Private Equity Firm

Project Preferences

Type of Financing Preferred:
Balanced

Geographical Preferences

International Preferences:
Russia

Industry Preferences

In Communications prefer:
Communications and Media

In Computer Software prefer:
Software

In Internet Specific prefer:
Internet

In Medical/Health prefer:
Medical Therapeutics

In Financial Services prefer:
Financial Services
Insurance

In Business Serv. prefer:
Media

Additional Information
Year Founded: 1998
Capital Under Management: $50,000,000
Current Activity Level : Actively seeking new investments

GRUSS ASSET MANAGEMENT LP

667 Madison Avenue, Third Floor
New York, NY USA 10021
Phone: 212-688-1500
Fax: 212-688-2138
E-mail: ir@gruss.com
Website: www.gruss.com

Other Offices
103 Mount Street
London, United Kingdom W1K 2TJ

St. George's Building, 2 Ice House Stree
Central, Hong Kong

Type of Firm
Private Equity Firm

Project Preferences

Type of Financing Preferred:
Leveraged Buyout
Turnaround
Distressed Debt

Additional Information
Year Founded: 2001
Capital Under Management: $26,600,000
Current Activity Level : Actively seeking new investments

GRYFFINDOR CAPITAL PARTNERS LLC

150 North Wacker Drive
Suite 800
Chicago, IL USA 60606
Phone: 3128272280
Fax: 3128272281

Management and Staff
Shelby Pruett, Managing Partner
Stuart Fuchs, Managing Partner

Type of Firm
Private Equity Firm

Project Preferences

Role in Financing:
Will function either as deal originator or investor in deals created by others

Type of Financing Preferred:
Early Stage
Mezzanine
Generalist PE
Balanced
Later Stage
Acquisition

Size of Investments Considered:
Min Size of Investment Considered (000s): $500
Max Size of Investment Considered (000s): $2,000

Geographical Preferences

United States Preferences:

Industry Preferences

In Computer Software prefer:
Software

In Semiconductor/Electr prefer:
Electronic Components
Controllers and Sensors
Sensors
Analytic/Scientific

In Medical/Health prefer:
Medical Therapeutics
Drug/Equipmt Delivery
Medical Products
Health Services
Pharmaceuticals

In Consumer Related prefer:
Consumer
Entertainment and Leisure

In Industrial/Energy prefer:
Energy

In Business Serv. prefer:
Services
Distribution
Media

Additional Information
Year Founded: 1996
Capital Under Management: $2,000,000,000
Current Activity Level : Actively seeking new investments
Method of Compensation: Return on investment is of primary concern, do not charge fees

GRYPHON INVESTORS INC

One Maritime Plaza
Suite 2300
San Francisco, CA USA 94111
Phone: 14152177400
Fax: 14152177447
E-mail: info@gryphoninvestors.com
Website: www.gryphon-inv.com

Management and Staff
Alex Earls, Partner
Alexander Earls, Partner
Ankit Kumar, Vice President
Christine Bucklin, Managing Director
Darren Gold, Partner
Dell Larcen, Partner
Dennis O Brien, Partner
Dennis O Brien, Partner
Dorian Faust, Principal
Dorian Faust, Partner
Drew Meyers, Principal
Felix Park, Principal
Gabe Stephenson, Vice President
Janet Kluzik, Vice President
Jef Rogers, Principal
John Geisler, Partner
John Rogers, Partner
Justin Saks, Vice President
Keith Stimson, Partner
Luke Schroeder, Principal
Matt Farron, Principal
Michael Gillen, Partner
Nicholas Orum, President
Philip Petrocelli, Partner
R. David Andrews, Chief Executive Officer
Robert Grady, Partner
Ryan Fagan, Vice President
Tim Bradley, Principal

Vincent Carey, Principal
Wes Lucas, Partner
Williard Lynn, Partner

Type of Firm
Private Equity Firm

Project Preferences

Type of Financing Preferred:
Leveraged Buyout
Expansion
Management Buyouts
Acquisition

Geographical Preferences

United States Preferences:

Industry Focus
(% based on actual investment)
Other Products	27.0%
Medical/Health	26.6%
Consumer Related	19.2%
Industrial/Energy	18.2%
Semiconductors/Other Elect.	6.0%
Computer Software and Services	1.4%
Internet Specific	0.7%
Communications and Media	0.4%
Biotechnology	0.4%

Additional Information
Year Founded: 1995
Capital Under Management: $1,153,000,000
Current Activity Level : Actively seeking new investments

GSM INDUSTRIES GMBH

Hans-Stiessberger-Strasse 2b
Haar, Germany 85540
Phone: 498921669617
E-mail: gsm@gsm-industries.com

Type of Firm
Private Equity Firm

Geographical Preferences

International Preferences:
Europe

Additional Information
Year Founded: 1999
Current Activity Level : Actively seeking new investments

GSR VENTURES MANAGEMENT LLC

No. 1 Jianguomenwai Street
Room 5620
Beijing, China 100004
Phone: 861057069898
Fax: 861057069899
Website: www.gsrventures.com

Other Offices

101 University Avenue, Fourth Floor
Palo Alto, CA USA 94301
Phone: 6503317300
Fax: 6503317301

18 Harbour Road
Suite 4801, 48/F Central Plaza
Wanchai, Hong Kong
Phone: 85222016300
Fax: 85228779833

Management and Staff

Alex Pan, Managing Director
Hai Liu, Partner
Haichen Hu, Partner
Hua Jiang, Partner
James Ding, Managing Director
Kevin Yin, Partner
Richard Lim, Co-Founder
Simon Vieira-Ribeiro, Partner
Sonny Wu, Co-Founder
Xiaohu Zhu, Managing Director
Yinan Li, Partner
Zhiwei Yang, Partner

Type of Firm

Private Equity Firm

Association Membership

China Venture Capital Association

Project Preferences

Type of Financing Preferred:
Leveraged Buyout
Early Stage
Expansion
Balanced
Later Stage

Geographical Preferences

International Preferences:
Europe
China

Industry Preferences

In Communications prefer:
Communications and Media
Wireless Communications

In Internet Specific prefer:
Internet

In Semiconductor/Electr prefer:
Electronics
Electronic Components
Semiconductor

In Medical/Health prefer:
Pharmaceuticals

In Industrial/Energy prefer:
Energy
Environmental Related

In Financial Services prefer:
Financial Services

Additional Information

Year Founded: 2004
Capital Under Management: $1,000,000,000
Current Activity Level : Actively seeking new investments

GSTC HEALTH INNOVATIONS LTD

9 King s Head Yard
London, United Kingdom SE1 1NA
Website: www.gsttcharity.org.uk

Type of Firm

Endowment, Foundation or Pension Fund

Project Preferences

Type of Financing Preferred:
Seed
Startup

Geographical Preferences

International Preferences:
United Kingdom

Industry Preferences

In Medical/Health prefer:
Health Services

Additional Information

Year Founded: 1969
Current Activity Level : Actively seeking new investments

GSV ACCELERATION FUND I LP

425 Broadway Street
Redwood City, CA USA 94063

Type of Firm

Incubator/Development Program

Project Preferences

Type of Financing Preferred:
Startup

Additional Information

Year Founded: 2016
Capital Under Management: $95,890,000
Current Activity Level : Actively seeking new investments

GTCR GOLDER RAUNER LLC

300 North LaSalle Street, Suite 5600
Chicago, IL USA 60654
Phone: 3123822200
Fax: 3123822201
E-mail: info@gtcr.com
Website: www.gtcr.com

Management and Staff

Aaron Cohen, Principal
Anna May Trala, Chief Financial Officer
Barry Dunn, Principal
Benjamin Daverman, Managing Director
Collin Roche, Principal
Constantine Mihas, Principal
Craig Bondy, Principal
David Donnini, Principal
George Sperzel, Principal
James Cantu, Vice President
Jeffrey Heh, Principal
John Kos, Principal
Joseph Nolan, Principal
Joshua Earl, Vice President
Justin DuPere, Vice President
Lawrence Fey, Managing Director
Mark Anderson, Principal
Michael Hollander, Vice President
Philip Canfield, Principal
Sean Cunningham, Principal
Stephen Jeschke, Principal
Tannaz Chapman, Vice President
Travis Krueger, Vice President

Type of Firm

Private Equity Firm

Association Membership

Illinois Venture Capital Association
Private Equity Council (PEC)

Project Preferences

Role in Financing:
Prefer role as deal originator

Type of Financing Preferred:
Leveraged Buyout
Expansion
Management Buyouts
Acquisition
Recapitalizations

Industry Focus

(% based on actual investment)

Medical/Health	25.5%
Communications and Media	18.7%
Computer Software and Services	18.1%
Other Products	16.3%
Consumer Related	6.0%
Internet Specific	5.1%
Biotechnology	4.3%
Semiconductors/Other Elect.	4.0%
Industrial/Energy	1.5%
Computer Hardware	0.5%

Additional Information

Name of Most Recent Fund: GTCR Fund XI, L.P.
Most Recent Fund Was Raised: 11/26/2013
Year Founded: 1980
Capital Under Management: $8,000,000,000

Current Activity Level : Actively seeking new investments
Method of Compensation: Return on invest. most important, but chg. closing fees, service fees, etc.

GTI CAPITAL, INC.

255, Rue Saint-Jacques
2nd Floor
Montreal, Canada H2Y 1M6
Phone: 5148453800
Fax: 5148453810
E-mail: info@gticapital.com

Management and Staff
Francois Veilleux, Chief Financial Officer

Type of Firm
Private Equity Firm

Project Preferences

Type of Financing Preferred:
Early Stage
Expansion
Seed
Startup

Geographical Preferences

Canadian Preferences:
Quebec
Eastern Canada

Industry Preferences

In Communications prefer:
Telecommunications
Wireless Communications

In Computer Other prefer:
Computer Related

In Semiconductor/Electr prefer:
Electronics

Additional Information
Year Founded: 1993
Capital Under Management: $100,000,000
Current Activity Level : Actively seeking new investments

GTJA INNOVATION INVESTMENT CO LTD

c/o Guotai Junan Securities Co
29/F, Shanghai Bank Building
Shanghai, China 200120
Fax: 86-21-3867-0666
Website: www.gtjaiic.com

Type of Firm
Bank Affiliated

Project Preferences

Type of Financing Preferred:
Generalist PE

Geographical Preferences

International Preferences:
China
Asia

Industry Preferences

In Medical/Health prefer:
Medical/Health

In Consumer Related prefer:
Consumer Products

In Industrial/Energy prefer:
Environmental Related

In Financial Services prefer:
Real Estate

In Business Serv. prefer:
Services

In Manufact. prefer:
Manufacturing

Additional Information
Year Founded: 2009
Capital Under Management: $108,913,000
Current Activity Level : Actively seeking new investments

GUANGDONG 100 CAPITAL CO LTD

No. 512 Fenjiang Zhonlu
Room 603, Bdlg. 6
Foshan, China 528000
Phone: 8675782367768
Website: www.100capital.com.cn

Other Offices
Former HQ: Jihua 5 Road, Chancheng
9/F Jinhai Plaza
Foshan, Guangdong, China 528000
Phone: 8675782903122
Fax: 8675782903120

Management and Staff
Wensheng Huang, Vice President

Type of Firm
Corporate PE/Venture

Project Preferences

Type of Financing Preferred:
Early Stage
Expansion
Balanced
Later Stage

Geographical Preferences

International Preferences:
China

Industry Preferences

In Biotechnology prefer:
Biotechnology

In Medical/Health prefer:
Medical/Health

In Consumer Related prefer:
Consumer Products
Consumer Services

In Industrial/Energy prefer:
Energy
Materials

In Manufact. prefer:
Manufacturing

Additional Information
Year Founded: 2010
Capital Under Management: $14,650,000
Current Activity Level : Actively seeking new investments

GUANGDONG DEYI CAPITAL MANAGEMENT CO LTD

Siming District, Xiamen
Block V7, Haiyuan Villa, Haiyu
Foshan, China
Phone: 865922518818

Type of Firm
Private Equity Firm

Project Preferences

Type of Financing Preferred:
Balanced

Geographical Preferences

International Preferences:
China

Additional Information
Year Founded: 2016
Current Activity Level : Actively seeking new investments

GUANGDONG FINANCE INVESTMENT HOLDINGS CO LTD

No.481, Dongfeng Zhong Road
15/F, Yuecai Plaza
Guangzhou, China
Phone: 862083063888
Website: www.utrust.cn

Pratt's Guide to Private Equity & Venture Capital Sources

Type of Firm
Investment Management Firm

Project Preferences

Type of Financing Preferred:
Balanced

Geographical Preferences

International Preferences:
China

Additional Information
Year Founded: 1984
Capital Under Management: $7,940,000
Current Activity Level : Actively seeking new investments

GUANGDONG GUANGKEN HEJIN MODERN AGRICULTURE INVESTMENT MGMT

No.28 Huaxia Road
2510 Fuli Yingxin Bldg
Guangzhou, China 510623
Phone: 862038398051
Fax: 862038398623
Website: hejintz.com

Type of Firm
Private Equity Firm

Project Preferences

Type of Financing Preferred:
Later Stage

Geographical Preferences

International Preferences:
China

Industry Preferences

In Agr/Forestr/Fish prefer:
Agriculture related

Additional Information
Year Founded: 2012
Capital Under Management: $39,361,000
Current Activity Level : Actively seeking new investments

GUANGDONG HUIYU YIHAO INVESTMENT MANAGEMENT CO LTD

Tancun Road, Tianhe District
Guangzhou, China

Type of Firm
Private Equity Firm

Project Preferences

Type of Financing Preferred:
Leveraged Buyout

Geographical Preferences

International Preferences:
China

Additional Information
Year Founded: 2014
Capital Under Management: $16,519,000
Current Activity Level : Actively seeking new investments

GUANGDONG INFORE CAPITAL MANAGEMENT CO LTD

c/o iFirst Group
No. 6 North Jiaomeizhen Avenue
Foshan, China 528311
Phone: 8675726666669
Fax: 8675726663346
Website: www.ifirstcapital.com.cn

Management and Staff
Dan Lu, Partner
Jun Zhang, Partner
Yi Duan, Partner

Type of Firm
Investment Management Firm

Project Preferences

Type of Financing Preferred:
Early Stage
Expansion
Balanced
Later Stage

Size of Investments Considered:
Min Size of Investment Considered (000s): $3,050
Max Size of Investment Considered (000s): $6,099

Geographical Preferences

International Preferences:
China

Industry Preferences

In Communications prefer:
Telecommunications
Wireless Communications

In Internet Specific prefer:
Internet

In Semiconductor/Electr prefer:
Electronics

In Medical/Health prefer:
Medical/Health

In Consumer Related prefer:
Consumer
Retail
Food/Beverage
Consumer Services
Education Related

In Industrial/Energy prefer:
Energy
Materials
Machinery
Environmental Related

In Business Serv. prefer:
Services

In Manufact. prefer:
Manufacturing

In Agr/Forestr/Fish prefer:
Agriculture related

Additional Information
Year Founded: 2007
Capital Under Management: $114,477,000
Current Activity Level : Actively seeking new investments

GUANGDONG INVESTMENT LTD

28F & 29F Guandong Inv. Tower
148 Connaught Rd.
Central, Hong Kong
Phone: 852-2860-4368
Fax: 852-2528-4386
Website: www.gdi.com.hk

Management and Staff
Hon Nam Tsang, Chief Financial Officer
Wen Yinheng, Managing Director

Type of Firm
Private Equity Firm

Project Preferences

Type of Financing Preferred:
Expansion

Geographical Preferences

International Preferences:
China

Industry Preferences

In Semiconductor/Electr prefer:
Electronics

In Consumer Related prefer:
Food/Beverage
Consumer Products

In Industrial/Energy prefer:
Industrial Products
Materials

Additional Information
Year Founded: 1993
Current Activity Level : Actively seeking new investments

GUANGDONG JINHAI ASSET MANAGEMENT CO LTD

No. 142 Yuhe Rd., Foshan New C
Section 7, No. 2101 Jinhai Cul
Foshan, China
Phone: 8675728781111
Website: www.jinhaizc.com

Type of Firm
Investment Management Firm

Project Preferences

Type of Financing Preferred:
Balanced

Geographical Preferences

International Preferences:
China

Additional Information
Year Founded: 2015
Current Activity Level : Actively seeking new investments

GUANGDONG JINRI INVESTMENT LTD

183-187, Tianhe North Road
Room 3213-3215
Guangzhou, China 510000
Phone: 862087553248
Fax: 862087555221
E-mail: jinri@nowinvest.cn
Website: www.nowinvest.cn

Management and Staff
Minjian Shi, President

Type of Firm
Private Equity Firm

Project Preferences

Type of Financing Preferred:
Balanced
Seed
Startup

Geographical Preferences

International Preferences:
China

Industry Preferences

In Internet Specific prefer:
Ecommerce

In Medical/Health prefer:
Medical Products

In Consumer Related prefer:
Retail
Hotels and Resorts

In Financial Services prefer:
Financial Services

In Agr/Forestr/Fish prefer:
Agriculture related

Additional Information
Year Founded: 2003
Current Activity Level : Actively seeking new investments

GUANGDONG PACIFIC TECHNOLOGY VENTURE CO LTD

y
Guanzhou, China
Phone: 86-20-87377435
Fax: 86-20-87377597
E-mail: gdptv@sti.gd.cn

Management and Staff
Fei Yang, Vice President

Type of Firm
Private Equity Firm

Additional Information
Year Founded: 1994
Current Activity Level : Actively seeking new investments

GUANGDONG RC EQUITY INVESTMENT FUND MANAGEMENT CO LTD

MeiHua Road, Futian District
1Floor,1block Merlin Duoli
Shenzhen, China
Phone: 4009987522
E-mail: gdrcgq@163.com
Website: www.gdrcgq.com.cn

Type of Firm
Investment Management Firm

Project Preferences

Type of Financing Preferred:
Leveraged Buyout

Geographical Preferences

International Preferences:
China

Additional Information
Year Founded: 2013
Capital Under Management: $8,059,000
Current Activity Level : Actively seeking new investments

GUANGDONG TECHNOLOGY VENTURE INVESTMENT CO LTD

No.17, Zhujiang West Road
F43, Guangcheng Intl. Building
Guangzhou, China 510623
Phone: 862087680388
Fax: 862087682766
E-mail: gvcgc@gvcgc.com
Website: www.gvcgc.com

Type of Firm
Investment Management Firm

Project Preferences

Type of Financing Preferred:
Fund of Funds
Early Stage
Expansion
Balanced
Later Stage
Seed
Startup

Size of Investments Considered:
Min Size of Investment Considered (000s): $1,572
Max Size of Investment Considered (000s): $4,716

Geographical Preferences

International Preferences:
China

Industry Preferences

In Biotechnology prefer:
Biotechnology

In Medical/Health prefer:
Medical Products
Pharmaceuticals

In Industrial/Energy prefer:
Energy Conservation Relat
Materials

In Manufact. prefer:
Manufacturing

Additional Information
Year Founded: 2000
Capital Under Management: $413,711,000
Current Activity Level : Actively seeking new investments

GUANGDONG XIYU INVESTMENT MANAGEMENT CO LTD

No. 689, Hebei Road
C4, 30/F, Everbright Bank Blg
Guangzhou, Guangdong, China 510630
Phone: 862038732749
Fax: 862038730127
Website: www.xiyuinvestment.com

Management and Staff
Jianping Wang, Managing Director

Type of Firm
Investment Management Firm

Project Preferences

Type of Financing Preferred:
Balanced
Later Stage

Geographical Preferences

International Preferences:
China

Industry Preferences

In Biotechnology prefer:
Biotechnology

In Medical/Health prefer:
Medical/Health

In Manufact. prefer:
Manufacturing

In Agr/Forestr/Fish prefer:
Mining and Minerals

Additional Information
Year Founded: 2007
Capital Under Management: $32,230,000
Current Activity Level : Actively seeking new investments

GUANGHUA 898 CAPITAL MANAGEMENT CO LTD

No. 14 Jiangtai Road, Jiuxian
Builcing 6
Beijing, China 100016
Phone: 861067788898
Website: www.guanghua898cap.com

Type of Firm
Private Equity Firm

Project Preferences

Type of Financing Preferred:
Balanced

Geographical Preferences

International Preferences:
China

Industry Preferences

In Medical/Health prefer:
Medical/Health

In Consumer Related prefer:
Education Related

Additional Information
Year Founded: 2016
Current Activity Level : Actively seeking new investments

GUANGXI GUIDONG HAIDA INVESTMENT MANAGEMENT CO LTD

Xingguang Road, Babu District
Store No. 2001, 2F, Block C
Hezhou, China

Type of Firm
Private Equity Firm

Project Preferences

Type of Financing Preferred:
Early Stage
Expansion
Seed
Startup

Geographical Preferences

International Preferences:
China

Industry Preferences

In Industrial/Energy prefer:
Energy

In Manufact. prefer:
Manufacturing

Additional Information
Year Founded: 2014
Current Activity Level : Actively seeking new investments

GUANGXIN INVESTMENT MANAGEMENT BEIJING CO LTD

Guanghua Road No.1
South Bldg., Jiali Center
Beijing, China
Phone: 861085299890
Fax: 861085299892
E-mail: info@gxcapital.com.cn
Website: www.gxcapital.com.cn

Management and Staff
Rui Ding, Partner
Wei Lu, Partner
Yue Yang, Partner
Yuming Ye, Partner
Zhenni Hu, Partner

Type of Firm
Private Equity Firm

Project Preferences

Type of Financing Preferred:
Balanced

Geographical Preferences

International Preferences:
China

Industry Preferences

In Communications prefer:
Telecommunications

In Medical/Health prefer:
Medical/Health

In Business Serv. prefer:
Media

Additional Information
Year Founded: 2014
Current Activity Level : Actively seeking new investments

GUANGZHOU ANGEL INVESTMENT CO LTD

No.241, Science City
13F,Block A4,HQ Economic Zone
Guangzhou, China 510663
Phone: 862032210058
Fax: 862032210058
Website: www.gzangel.cn

Type of Firm
Private Equity Firm

Project Preferences

Type of Financing Preferred:
Start-up Financing
Seed

Geographical Preferences

International Preferences:
China

Industry Preferences

In Internet Specific prefer:
Internet

In Other prefer:
Environment Responsible

Additional Information
Year Founded: 2014
Current Activity Level : Actively seeking new investments

GUANGZHOU ANJIANXIN INVESTMENT MANAGEMENT CO LTD

No.19, Xiangshan Road
Room 103
Guangzhou, China

Management and Staff
Sheng Ying, Founder

Type of Firm
Private Equity Firm

Project Preferences

Type of Financing Preferred:
Leveraged Buyout
Generalist PE
Balanced

Geographical Preferences

International Preferences:
China

Industry Preferences

In Biotechnology prefer:
Biotechnology

In Medical/Health prefer:
Medical/Health

Additional Information
Year Founded: 2014
Current Activity Level : Actively seeking new investments

GUANGZHOU BLACK HOLE INVESTMENT CO LTD

Chaoyangmen,Dongcheng
50803, Block D, Galaxy Soho
Beijing, China
Website: www.blackholecap.com

Type of Firm
Private Equity Firm

Project Preferences

Type of Financing Preferred:
Early Stage
Expansion
Generalist PE
Seed
Startup

Size of Investments Considered:
Min Size of Investment Considered (000s): $150
Max Size of Investment Considered (000s): $29,982

Geographical Preferences

International Preferences:
Rest of World
China

Industry Preferences

In Computer Software prefer:
Software

In Internet Specific prefer:
Internet

In Medical/Health prefer:
Medical/Health

In Industrial/Energy prefer:
Energy

In Business Serv. prefer:
Services

Additional Information
Year Founded: 2014
Current Activity Level : Actively seeking new investments

GUANGZHOU GET CAPITAL CO LTD

237, Kexue Avenue Science City
9/F, A2, Economics Park
Guangzhou, China 510663
Phone: 862082116611
Fax: 862032211146

Type of Firm
Private Equity Firm

Project Preferences

Type of Financing Preferred:
Early Stage
Expansion
Balanced
Later Stage
Seed
Startup

Geographical Preferences

International Preferences:
China
Asia

Industry Preferences

In Biotechnology prefer:
Biotechnology

In Medical/Health prefer:
Pharmaceuticals

Additional Information
Year Founded: 2008
Capital Under Management: $48,132,000
Current Activity Level : Actively seeking new investments

GUANGZHOU HENGZHAOYUAN INVESTMENT MANAGEMENT CENTER LP

No. 9 Huaming Road, Zhujiang N
1902, West Tower, Huapu Plaza
Guangzhou, China 510623
Phone: 862022382191

Type of Firm
Investment Management Firm

Project Preferences

Type of Financing Preferred:
Balanced

Geographical Preferences

International Preferences:
China

Additional Information
Year Founded: 2014
Current Activity Level : Actively seeking new investments

GUANGZHOU HUIYIN AOFENG EQUITY INVESTMENT FUND MANAGEMENT

No.171, Haibin Road, Nansha
11F, Nansha Financial Bldg.
Guangzhou, China
Website: www.cgtz.com

Type of Firm
Investment Management Firm

Project Preferences

Type of Financing Preferred:
Balanced

Geographical Preferences

International Preferences:
China

Additional Information
Year Founded: 2014
Current Activity Level : Actively seeking new investments

GUANGZHOU INDUSTRIAL INVESTMENT FUND MANAGEMENT CO LTD

No.5 Zhujiang Rd. (west)
Guangzhou int'l Finance Centre
Guangzhou, China
Phone: 862023388666
Fax: 862023388789
Website: www.sfund.com

Type of Firm
Government Affiliated Program

Project Preferences

Type of Financing Preferred:
Leveraged Buyout
Balanced
Public Companies

Geographical Preferences

International Preferences:
China

Additional Information
Year Founded: 2013
Current Activity Level : Actively seeking new investments

GUANGZHOU INNOHUB ACCELERATION TECHNOLOGY CO LTD

106 North Keyun Road
Tianhe District
Guangzhou, China
Website: www.chuang.ba

Type of Firm
Incubator/Development Program

Project Preferences

Type of Financing Preferred:
Start-up Financing
Seed

Geographical Preferences

International Preferences:
China

Additional Information
Year Founded: 2014
Current Activity Level : Actively seeking new investments

GUANGZHOU INNOVATION VALLEY INCUBATOR ACCELERATOR

Nanshan District
No.9, Shekou Industrial Road 6
Shenzhen, China 518067
Website: www.innovalley.com.cn

Other Offices
No.315, Huangpu Road
Building1-14, Yangcheng Creative Park
Guangzhou, China 510000

Type of Firm
Incubator/Development Program

Project Preferences

Type of Financing Preferred:
Seed

Size of Investments Considered:
Min Size of Investment Considered (000s): $79
Max Size of Investment Considered (000s): $315

Geographical Preferences

International Preferences:
China

Industry Preferences

In Communications prefer:
Telecommunications

In Internet Specific prefer:
Internet

In Business Serv. prefer:
Media

Additional Information
Year Founded: 2012
Current Activity Level : Actively seeking new investments

GUANGZHOU SINVO SPRING INVESTMENT MANAGEMENT CO LTD

No.1 North Zhongguancun Avenue
Yiyuan, Youyi Hotel
Beijing, China 100873
Phone: 861068949996
Fax: 861068941717
E-mail: investment@sinvocapital.com
Website: www.sinvocapital.com

Management and Staff
Haixia Huang, Vice President
Lei Zhang, Vice President
Xiaobo Hu, Vice President

Type of Firm
Investment Management Firm

Project Preferences

Type of Financing Preferred:
Leveraged Buyout
Early Stage
Mezzanine
Balanced
Opportunistic
Later Stage
Other
Open Market

Geographical Preferences

International Preferences:
China

Industry Preferences

In Biotechnology prefer:
Biotechnology

In Medical/Health prefer:
Pharmaceuticals

In Industrial/Energy prefer:
Energy
Materials

In Financial Services prefer:
Real Estate

In Agr/Forestr/Fish prefer:
Agriculture related

Additional Information
Name of Most Recent Fund: Dalian Sinvo Hengtai Equity Investment Mgmt Center, L.P.
Most Recent Fund Was Raised: 09/15/2011
Year Founded: 2010
Capital Under Management: $32,100,000
Current Activity Level : Actively seeking new investments

GUANGZHOU SUIYONG ORIGINAL CAPITAL CO LTD

Zhujiang New City, Tianhe
59F, West Tower, No.5
Guangzhou, China 510630

Type of Firm
Private Equity Firm

Project Preferences

Type of Financing Preferred:
Balanced

Geographical Preferences

International Preferences:
China

Additional Information
Year Founded: 2016
Current Activity Level : Actively seeking new investments

GUANGZHOU VENTURE CAPITAL CO LTD
No. 191, Science Road
Rm. 1001-1002, Commerce Sq. A1
Guangzhou, China 510663
Phone: 862032210188
Fax: 862032219983

Type of Firm
Private Equity Firm

Project Preferences

Type of Financing Preferred:
Early Stage
Balanced
Later Stage
Seed

Geographical Preferences

International Preferences:
China

Industry Preferences

In Biotechnology prefer:
Biotechnology

In Medical/Health prefer:
Medical/Health
Pharmaceuticals

In Industrial/Energy prefer:
Energy
Alternative Energy
Materials
Advanced Materials
Environmental Related

In Manufact. prefer:
Manufacturing

In Agr/Forestr/Fish prefer:
Agriculture related

In Other prefer:
Environment Responsible

Additional Information
Year Founded: 2002
Current Activity Level : Actively seeking new investments

GUANGZHOU ZHISHANG EQUITY INVESTMENT CENTER LP
No. 191, Science Ave., Science
Room 503, Blcok A1, Business S
Guangzhou, China 510663
Phone: 862082118908

Type of Firm
Private Equity Firm

Project Preferences

Type of Financing Preferred:
Balanced

Geographical Preferences

International Preferences:
China

Additional Information
Year Founded: 2015
Current Activity Level : Actively seeking new investments

GUANGZHOU ZHONGDA VENTURE CAPITAL MANAGEMENT CO LTD
No. 135 West Xingang Road
Haizhu District
Guangzhou, China 510275
Phone: 862084112088
Fax: 862084115661
Website: www.zdvc.com.cn

Management and Staff
Haibo Hu, Vice President

Type of Firm
University Program

Project Preferences

Type of Financing Preferred:
Later Stage

Geographical Preferences

International Preferences:
China

Industry Preferences

In Industrial/Energy prefer:
Energy
Materials

In Business Serv. prefer:
Services

In Agr/Forestr/Fish prefer:
Agriculture related

Additional Information
Year Founded: 2010
Capital Under Management: $15,404,000
Current Activity Level : Actively seeking new investments

GUANGZHOU ZHUOSHI INVESTMENT MANAGEMENT CO LTD
No. 1 Pazhou Avenue, Haizhu
Room 2006, South Tower of Poly
Guangzhou, China
Website: www.midascapital.cn

Type of Firm
Private Equity Firm

Project Preferences

Type of Financing Preferred:
Generalist PE

Geographical Preferences

International Preferences:
China

Industry Preferences

In Communications prefer:
Entertainment

In Medical/Health prefer:
Medical/Health

In Consumer Related prefer:
Consumer

Additional Information
Year Founded: 2014
Current Activity Level : Actively seeking new investments

GUARDIAN CAPITAL PARTNERS
353 West Lancaster Avenue
Suite 130
Wayne, PA USA 19087
Phone: 6109641500
Fax: 6104658900
E-mail: gcp@guardiancp.com
Website: www.guardiancp.com

Management and Staff
Adrian Ironside, Principal
Hugh Kenworthy, Managing Partner
Peter Haabestad, Managing Partner
Scott Evans, Managing Partner

Type of Firm
Private Equity Firm

Association Membership
Emerging Markets Private Equity Association

Project Preferences

Type of Financing Preferred:
Leveraged Buyout
Management Buyouts
Acquisition

Geographical Preferences

United States Preferences:

Industry Preferences

In Medical/Health prefer:
Medical/Health
Medical Products
Health Services

In Consumer Related prefer:
Consumer Products

In Industrial/Energy prefer:
Industrial Products

In Financial Services prefer:
Financial Services

In Business Serv. prefer:
Services
Consulting Services

In Manufact. prefer:
Manufacturing

Additional Information
Year Founded: 2008
Capital Under Management: $153,500,000
Current Activity Level : Actively seeking new investments

GUB UNTERNEHMENS-BETEILIGUNGEN GMBH & CO KGAA

Wartburgstrasse 19
Plauen, Germany 08525
Phone: 32121192357
Fax: 32121192357
E-mail: gub@gub-ag.de
Website: www.gub.de

Other Offices
An den Treptowers 1
Berlin, Germany 12435
Phone: 49 30-536072-0
Fax: 49 30-536072-29

Glockegiesserwall 22
Hamburg, Germany 20095
Phone: 49 40-30382990
Fax: 49 40-30382980

Marktplatz 4
St. Gallen, Switzerland CH-9004

Technologiezentrum am Europaplatz
Aachen, Germany 52068
Phone: 49 241-9632870
Fax: 49 241-9632877

Friedrichstrasse 9a
Stuttgart, Germany 70174
Phone: 49 711-2245100
Fax: 49 711-22451033

Dreifaltigkeitsgasse 9
Salzburg, Austria A-5020

Type of Firm
Private Equity Firm

Project Preferences

Type of Financing Preferred:
Early Stage
Expansion
Mezzanine
Seed
Management Buyouts
Startup

Size of Investments Considered:
Min Size of Investment Considered (000s): $500
Max Size of Investment Considered (000s): $50,000

Geographical Preferences

United States Preferences:

International Preferences:
United Kingdom
Luxembourg
Netherlands
Switzerland
Austria
Scandinavia/Nordic Region
Belgium
Germany
France

Industry Preferences

In Communications prefer:
Communications and Media

In Internet Specific prefer:
Internet

In Medical/Health prefer:
Medical/Health

In Industrial/Energy prefer:
Materials

In Business Serv. prefer:
Media

Additional Information
Year Founded: 1994
Capital Under Management: $134,000,000
Current Activity Level : Actively seeking new investments

GUIDA INVEST OY

Televisiokatu 1-3
Helsinki, Finland 00240
Phone: 358290300200
Website: www.guida.fi

Management and Staff
Jari Vesanen, Partner

Type of Firm
Private Equity Firm

Association Membership
Finnish Venture Capital Association (FVCA)

Project Preferences

Type of Financing Preferred:
Seed
Startup

Geographical Preferences

International Preferences:
Finland

Additional Information
Year Founded: 2011
Current Activity Level : Actively seeking new investments

GUIDEPOST GROWTH EQUITY

950 Winter Street
North Entrance
Waltham, MA USA 02451
Phone: 7814667800
Fax: 6503570017
E-mail: info@northbridge.com
Website: guidepostgrowth.com

Other Offices
950 Winter Street
North Entrance
WALTHAM, MA USA 02451
Phone: 781-290-0004
Fax: 781-290-0999

Management and Staff
Jeffrey McCarthy, Partner
Paul Santinelli, Partner
Richard D Amore, Co-Founder

Type of Firm
Private Equity Firm

Association Membership
New England Venture Capital Association
National Venture Capital Association - USA (NVCA)

Project Preferences

Role in Financing:
Prefer role as deal originator

Type of Financing Preferred:
Early Stage
Balanced
Later Stage
Seed

Size of Investments Considered:
Min Size of Investment Considered (000s): $50
Max Size of Investment Considered (000s): $75,000

Geographical Preferences

United States Preferences:
North America

Industry Focus

(% based on actual investment)
Industry	%
Computer Software and Services	37.0%
Internet Specific	19.9%
Communications and Media	17.4%
Semiconductors/Other Elect.	8.7%
Industrial/Energy	6.7%
Other Products	2.9%
Biotechnology	2.9%
Computer Hardware	2.6%
Medical/Health	1.5%
Consumer Related	0.3%

Additional Information
Name of Most Recent Fund: North Bridge Growth Equity II, L.P.
Most Recent Fund Was Raised: 10/30/2013
Year Founded: 1994
Capital Under Management: $3,200,000,000
Current Activity Level : Actively seeking new investments
Method of Compensation: Return on investment is of primary concern, do not charge fees

GUIDON CAPITAL PARTNERS

2030 S Tryon Street
Suite 3G
Charlotte, NC USA 28203
Phone: 7043223525
Website: guidoncapitalpartners.com

Management and Staff
Kyle Caniglia, President
Mike Deely, Co-Founder
Phillips Dee, Co-Founder

Type of Firm
Private Equity Firm

Project Preferences

Type of Financing Preferred:
Leveraged Buyout
Acquisition

Industry Preferences

In Computer Software prefer:
Software

In Financial Services prefer:
Financial Services

In Manufact. prefer:
Manufacturing

Additional Information
Year Founded: 2015
Capital Under Management: $150,000
Current Activity Level : Actively seeking new investments

GUIGU TIANTANG VENTURE CAPITAL CO LTD

12, Zhongguancun South St A
Huantai Building
Beijing, China 100081
Website: www.ggttvc.com

Other Offices
Qintai Wenhua Yishu Center
No. 8 Gujianzhu A District
Wuhan, China 430050
Phone: 86-27-8484-2218
Fax: 86-27-8484-2228

No.188, Rixin Rd., Binhai Science Park
R503, F5
Tianjin, China

Jintian Road, Futian District
Rongchao Jingmao Center
Shenzhen, China 518035
Phone: 86-755-33226099
Fax: 86-755-33226069

No. 439 Chunxiao Road
Zhangjiang Gaokeji Yuan District
Shanghai, China 201203
Phone: 86-21-5027-4986
Fax: 86-21-5027-5016

No. 76 Yuhuang Shan Road
Building 2-3
Hangzhou, China 310002
Phone: 8657187083018
Fax: 8657187089718

Management and Staff
Xin Feng, Vice President
Yue Bao, Chief Executive Officer

Type of Firm
Private Equity Firm

Project Preferences

Type of Financing Preferred:
Early Stage
Expansion
Balanced
Public Companies
Later Stage
Special Situation

Geographical Preferences

International Preferences:
Aruba
Asia

Industry Preferences

In Communications prefer:
Wireless Communications
Entertainment

In Computer Other prefer:
Computer Related

In Consumer Related prefer:
Entertainment and Leisure

In Industrial/Energy prefer:
Environmental Related

In Financial Services prefer:
Real Estate

In Manufact. prefer:
Publishing

In Agr/Forestr/Fish prefer:
Agribusiness

Additional Information
Year Founded: 2001
Capital Under Management: $215,468,000
Current Activity Level : Actively seeking new investments

GUILD CAPITAL LLC

222 West Hubbard Street
Suite 200
Chicago, IL USA 60654
Website: guildcap.com

Type of Firm
Private Equity Firm

Project Preferences

Type of Financing Preferred:
Expansion
Balanced
Later Stage

Industry Preferences

In Communications prefer:
Communications and Media

Additional Information
Year Founded: 1969
Current Activity Level : Actively seeking new investments

GUIYIN ZHONGKE INDUSTRIAL INVESTMENT FUND MANAGEMENT LTD

GuiAn New District
2F, Government Affair Hall
GuiAn New District, China

Type of Firm
Bank Affiliated

Project Preferences

Type of Financing Preferred:
Leveraged Buyout

Geographical Preferences

International Preferences:
China

Industry Preferences

In Medical/Health prefer:
Pharmaceuticals

In Consumer Related prefer:
Food/Beverage

In Manufact. prefer:
Manufacturing

Additional Information
Year Founded: 2014
Capital Under Management: $162,880,000
Current Activity Level : Actively seeking new investments

GULF CAPITAL PVT JSC

Al Sila Tower, 25th Floor
Sowwah Sq., Al Maryah Island
Abu Dhabi, Utd. Arab Em.
Phone: 97126716060
Fax: 97126942703
E-mail: info@gulfcapital.com
Website: www.gulfcapital.com

Management and Staff
Kenneth Himmel, Managing Partner
Nasser Alsowaidi, Co-Founder

Type of Firm
Private Equity Firm

Association Membership
Gulf Venture Capital Association
Emerging Markets Private Equity Association

Project Preferences

Type of Financing Preferred:
Leveraged Buyout
Early Stage
Expansion
Mezzanine
Generalist PE
Later Stage
Management Buyouts
Acquisition

Geographical Preferences

International Preferences:
Jordan
Turkey
Utd. Arab Em.
Asia

Industry Preferences

In Communications prefer:
Telecommunications

In Industrial/Energy prefer:
Oil & Gas Drilling,Explor

In Manufact. prefer:
Manufacturing

Additional Information
Name of Most Recent Fund: Gulf Credit Opportunities Fund LP I
Most Recent Fund Was Raised: 04/01/2013
Year Founded: 2006
Capital Under Management: $1,140,000,000
Current Activity Level : Actively seeking new investments

GULF INVESTMENT CORPORATION SAG

PO Box 3402
Safat, Kuwait 13035
Phone: 96522225000
Fax: 96522225010
E-mail: info@gic.com.kw
Website: www.gic.com.kw

Management and Staff
Ibrahim Al Qadhi, Chief Executive Officer
Rashid Bin Rasheed, Chief Executive Officer
Russell Read, Chief Executive Officer
Shawki Khalaf, Chief Operating Officer

Type of Firm
Private Equity Firm

Project Preferences

Type of Financing Preferred:
Balanced

Geographical Preferences

International Preferences:
Middle East

Industry Preferences

In Industrial/Energy prefer:
Oil and Gas Exploration
Oil & Gas Drilling,Explor

In Financial Services prefer:
Financial Services

In Utilities prefer:
Utilities

Additional Information
Year Founded: 2008
Current Activity Level : Actively seeking new investments

GULF ISLAMIC INVESTMENTS LLC

PO Box 215931, Suite 1102
Boulevard Plaza II, Downtown
Dubai, Utd. Arab Em.
Phone: 97143253686
Fax: 97143253709
E-mail: info@gii.ae
Website: gii.ae

Type of Firm
Private Equity Firm

Industry Preferences

In Medical/Health prefer:
Health Services

In Consumer Related prefer:
Retail
Education Related

In Industrial/Energy prefer:
Energy
Industrial Products

In Transportation prefer:
Transportation

In Financial Services prefer:
Financial Services

In Manufact. prefer:
Manufacturing

Additional Information
Year Founded: 2015
Current Activity Level : Actively seeking new investments

GUOJIN DINGXING CO., LTD.

No.1088 Fangdian Road
Rm501 Zizhu Int'l Building
Shanghai, China 201204
Phone: 862168826827
Website: www.gjcc.com.cn

Type of Firm
Bank Affiliated

Project Preferences

Type of Financing Preferred:
Leveraged Buyout
Mezzanine
Balanced

Geographical Preferences

International Preferences:
China

Industry Preferences

In Medical/Health prefer:
Medical Therapeutics

In Consumer Related prefer:
Consumer

In Industrial/Energy prefer:
Energy
Environmental Related

In Business Serv. prefer:
Media

Additional Information
Year Founded: 2012
Capital Under Management: $247,782,000
Current Activity Level : Actively seeking new investments

GUOSEN BOLE EQUITY INVESTMENT MANAGEMENT CO LTD

6002, Shennan Middle Road
17, West Renmin Building
Shenzhen, Guangdong, China
Phone: 8675583065000
Fax: 8675583067481
E-mail: shiyl@hanxinchina.com
Website: www.guosenbole.com

Management and Staff
Peng Chen, Partner
Qiu Hu, Partner
Xiaoyong Liu, Partner

Type of Firm
Private Equity Firm

Project Preferences

Type of Financing Preferred:
Expansion
Later Stage

Geographical Preferences

International Preferences:
China

Industry Preferences

In Communications prefer:
Telecommunications

In Internet Specific prefer:
Internet

In Semiconductor/Electr prefer:
Electronics

In Medical/Health prefer:
Medical/Health

In Consumer Related prefer:
Consumer
Entertainment and Leisure
Retail
Education Related

In Industrial/Energy prefer:
Alternative Energy
Advanced Materials

In Financial Services prefer:
Financial Services

In Business Serv. prefer:
Services
Media

In Manufact. prefer:
Manufacturing

In Agr/Forestr/Fish prefer:
Agriculture related

Additional Information
Year Founded: 2011
Capital Under Management: $75,873,000
Current Activity Level : Actively seeking new investments

GUOSEN H&S INVESTMENT CO LTD

No. 1010 Hongling Zhong Road
11/F Int'l Trust Building
Shenzhen, China
Phone: 8675525472612
Website: hs.guosen.com.cn

Management and Staff
Hui Huang, Vice President

Type of Firm
Service Provider

Project Preferences

Type of Financing Preferred:
Balanced

Geographical Preferences

International Preferences:
China

Additional Information
Year Founded: 2008
Capital Under Management: $321,022,000
Current Activity Level : Actively seeking new investments

GUOSEN SECURITIES HK ASSET MANAGEMENT CO LTD

189 Des Voeux Road
8/F, Li Po Chun Chambers
Central, Hong Kong
Phone: 85228998300
Fax: 85228998346
E-mail: asm@guosen.com.hk
Website: www.guosen.com.hk

Type of Firm
Private Equity Firm

Project Preferences

Type of Financing Preferred:
Acquisition

Geographical Preferences

International Preferences:
China

Industry Preferences

In Agr/Forestr/Fish prefer:
Agriculture related

Additional Information
Year Founded: 2011
Current Activity Level : Actively seeking new investments

GURNET POINT CAPITAL LLC

55 Cambridge Parkway
Suite 401
Cambridge, MA USA 02142
Phone: 6175884900
E-mail: info@gurnetpointcapital.com
Website: www.gurnetpointcapital.com

Management and Staff
Fereydoun Firouz, Managing Partner

Type of Firm
Private Equity Firm

Project Preferences

Type of Financing Preferred:
Leveraged Buyout
Early Stage
Expansion
Generalist PE
Later Stage
Seed
Acquisition

Size of Investments Considered:
Min Size of Investment Considered (000s): $500
Max Size of Investment Considered (000s): $20,000

Industry Preferences

In Biotechnology prefer:
Biotechnology
Human Biotechnology

In Medical/Health prefer:
Medical/Health
Medical Diagnostics
Medical Therapeutics
Health Services

Additional Information
Year Founded: 1969
Current Activity Level : Actively seeking new investments

GUSM CAPITAL MANAGEMENT CO LTD

Dongfang East Road, Chaoyang
Rm 605, Block D1, Liangmaqiao
Beijing, China
Phone: 861085315116
Fax: 861085315299
Website: www.gsum.cn

Type of Firm
Private Equity Firm

Project Preferences

Type of Financing Preferred:
Early Stage
Balanced

Geographical Preferences

International Preferences:
China

Industry Preferences

In Medical/Health prefer:
Medical/Health

In Consumer Related prefer:
Entertainment and Leisure
Consumer Services

Additional Information
Year Founded: 2015
Current Activity Level : Actively seeking new investments

GUSTAFSON & CO INC

1866 Commerce Street
Yorktown Heights, NY USA 10598
Phone: 914-962-2200
Fax: 914-962-2204

Management and Staff
Mark Gustafson, President

Type of Firm
Private Equity Firm

Project Preferences

Type of Financing Preferred:
Leveraged Buyout
Turnaround
Management Buyouts
Recapitalizations

Geographical Preferences

United States Preferences:

International Preferences:
United Kingdom
France

Additional Information
Year Founded: 1989
Current Activity Level : Actively seeking new investments
Method of Compensation: Return on invest. most important, but chg. closing fees, service fees, etc.

GUYIN INTERNATIONAL INVESTMENT FUND MGMT BEIJING CO LTD

Gaoliangqiao Byway, Haidian
4F,Shanxi Security Center
Beijing, China
Phone: 861057272939
Website: www.guyinfund.com

Type of Firm
Private Equity Firm

Project Preferences

Type of Financing Preferred:
Balanced

Geographical Preferences

International Preferences:
China

Industry Preferences

In Computer Software prefer:
Artificial Intelligence

In Consumer Related prefer:
Consumer Services

In Manufact. prefer:
Manufacturing

Additional Information
Year Founded: 2014
Current Activity Level : Actively seeking new investments

GVA CAPITAL LLC

910 Broadway
San Francisco, CA USA 94133
Phone: 7347307812
E-mail: contact@gva.capital

Type of Firm
Private Equity Firm

Project Preferences

Type of Financing Preferred:
Startup

Geographical Preferences

United States Preferences:

International Preferences:
Europe

Industry Preferences

In Business Serv. prefer:
Media

Additional Information
Year Founded: 2011
Current Activity Level : Actively seeking new investments

GVA LAUNCHGURUS

Pereulok Kapranova 3
Moscow, Russia 123242Pere
Phone: 74996537890
E-mail: contact@gvalg.com
Website: www.gvalaunch.guru

Type of Firm
Private Equity Firm

Industry Preferences

In Computer Software prefer:
Software

In Business Serv. prefer:
Media

In Other prefer:
Environment Responsible

Additional Information
Year Founded: 2015
Capital Under Management: $11,000,000
Current Activity Level : Actively seeking new investments

GVC HOLDINGS INC

210 Summit Avenue
Montvale, NJ USA 07645
E-mail: info@gvcholdings.com
Website: gvcholdings.com

Type of Firm
Private Equity Firm

Project Preferences

Type of Financing Preferred:
Leveraged Buyout
Balanced
Management Buyouts
Acquisition

Industry Preferences

In Medical/Health prefer:
Medical/Health

In Industrial/Energy prefer:
Industrial Products
Advanced Materials

Additional Information
Year Founded: 1992
Current Activity Level : Actively seeking new investments

GVFL LTD

B/h Popular House, Ashram Road
1st Flr, Premchand House Annex
Ahmedabad, India 380 009
Phone: 917940213900
Fax: 917926585226
E-mail: info@gvfl.com
Website: www.gvfl.com

Management and Staff
Mihir Joshi, Chief Executive Officer

Type of Firm
Private Equity Firm

Association Membership
Indian Venture Capital Association (IVCA)

Project Preferences

Role in Financing:
Prefer role as deal originator but will also invest in deals created by others

Type of Financing Preferred:
Leveraged Buyout
Value-Add
Early Stage
Expansion
Balanced
Opportunistic
Seed
Management Buyouts
Startup

Size of Investments Considered:
Min Size of Investment Considered (000s): $55
Max Size of Investment Considered (000s): $2,200

Geographical Preferences

International Preferences:
India

Industry Focus
(% based on actual investment)
Industrial/Energy	20.2%
Other Products	16.7%
Communications and Media	16.2%
Internet Specific	15.4%
Computer Software and Services	9.6%
Semiconductors/Other Elect.	9.0%
Computer Hardware	5.1%
Consumer Related	3.8%
Medical/Health	2.7%
Biotechnology	1.3%

Additional Information
Name of Most Recent Fund: Golden Gujarat Growth Fund Series - 1
Most Recent Fund Was Raised: 03/24/2012
Year Founded: 1990
Capital Under Management: $34,600,000
Current Activity Level : Actively seeking new investments
Method of Compensation: Return on investment is of primary concern, do not charge fees

GXP GERMAN PROPERTIES AG

Schopenstehl 22
Hamburg, Germany 20095
Phone: 494067958022
Fax: 494067958052
E-mail: ir@kimon.de
Website: www.gxpag.com

Management and Staff
Johannes Meran, Chief Executive Officer

Type of Firm
Private Equity Firm

Project Preferences

Type of Financing Preferred:
Early Stage
Later Stage
Seed
Startup

Geographical Preferences

International Preferences:
Germany

Industry Preferences

In Internet Specific prefer:
Internet

In Biotechnology prefer:
Biotechnology

Additional Information
Year Founded: 2000
Current Activity Level : Actively seeking new investments

- H -

H BARTON ASSET MANAGEMENT LLC

2882 Sand Hill Road
Suite 241
Menlo Park, CA USA 94025
Phone: 6502090226
E-mail: info@bartonam.com
Website: bartonam.com

Type of Firm
Investment Management Firm

Project Preferences

Type of Financing Preferred:
Early Stage
Startup

Additional Information
Year Founded: 1969
Current Activity Level : Actively seeking new investments

H KATZ CAPITAL GROUP INC

928 Jaymor Road
Suite A-100
Southampton, PA USA 18966
Phone: 2153640400
Fax: 2153645025
Website: www.katzgroup.com

Other Offices
Former HQ: 238 Second Street Pike
Suite 150
Southampton, PA USA 18966

Management and Staff
Brian Siegel, Managing Director

Type of Firm
Private Equity Firm

Project Preferences

Type of Financing Preferred:
Leveraged Buyout
Mezzanine
Management Buyouts
Acquisition
Joint Ventures
Recapitalizations

Industry Preferences

In Medical/Health prefer:
Medical/Health

In Consumer Related prefer:
Consumer
Franchises(NEC)

In Financial Services prefer:
Insurance
Financial Services

In Business Serv. prefer:
Media

Additional Information
Year Founded: 1996
Current Activity Level : Actively seeking new investments

H SIEDENTOPF GMBH & CO KG

Lloydstr. 4-6
Bremen, Germany 28217
Phone: 49421800470
Fax: 494218004752
E-mail: info@siedentopf.de
Website: www.siedentopf.de

Type of Firm
Private Equity Firm

Project Preferences

Type of Financing Preferred:
Core
Leveraged Buyout
Value-Add
Early Stage
Balanced
Later Stage
Management Buyouts
Acquisition

Geographical Preferences

International Preferences:
No Preference
Germany

Industry Preferences

In Computer Software prefer:
Software

In Financial Services prefer:
Real Estate

Additional Information
Year Founded: 2006
Current Activity Level : Actively seeking new investments

H&Q ASIA PACIFIC, LTD.

228 Hamilton Avenue
3rd Floor
Palo Alto, CA USA 94301
Phone: 6508388025
Fax: 6508380801
E-mail: hqap@hqap.com
Website: www.hqap.com

Other Offices

3F Wonseo Bldg., 171 Wonseo-Dong
Jongno-Gu
Seoul, South Korea 110-280
Phone: 8227822288
Fax: 82237754589

MID Nihonbashi-Horidome-cho Bldg. 7F
1-7-7 Nihonbashi-Horidome-cho, Chuo-ku
Tokyo, Japan 103-0012
Phone: 81362062399
Fax: 81332495950

Suite 2011, 20/FL Citigroup Tower
33 HuaYuanShiQiao Road
Shanghai, China 200120
Phone: 862168878080
Fax: 862168878011

Suite 2018, Hutchison House
10 Harcourt Road, Central
Hong Kong, Hong Kong
Phone: 85228684800
Fax: 85228104883

32F-1, International Trade Bldg.
333 Keelung Road, Sec.1
Taipei, Taiwan 110
Phone: 886227209855
Fax: 886227222106

Management and Staff
Howard Shen, Managing Director
Jarlon Tsang, Managing Director
Jong Won Lee, Managing Director
Jung Jin Lee, Managing Director
Mark Hsu, Managing Director
Rick Chiang, Managing Director
Robert Shen, Managing Director
Steven Lee, Managing Director
Yuchul Rhim, Managing Director

Type of Firm
Private Equity Firm

Association Membership
Hong Kong Venture Capital Association (HKVCA)
Taiwan Venture Capital Association(TVCA)

Project Preferences

Role in Financing:
Prefer role as deal originator but will also invest in deals created by others

Type of Financing Preferred:
Leveraged Buyout
Early Stage
Generalist PE
Balanced
Later Stage

Geographical Preferences

United States Preferences:

International Preferences:
China
Asia
Korea, South
Japan

Industry Focus
(% based on actual investment)

Category	%
Other Products	25.7%
Internet Specific	22.5%
Computer Software and Services	10.8%
Semiconductors/Other Elect.	10.7%
Industrial/Energy	10.4%
Consumer Related	8.7%
Computer Hardware	7.0%
Biotechnology	1.9%
Medical/Health	1.2%
Communications and Media	1.1%

Additional Information
Year Founded: 1985
Capital Under Management: $2,691,000,000
Current Activity Level : Actively seeking new investments

H-FARM SPA

Via Sile, 41
Tenuta Ca'Tron
Roncade Treviso, Italy 31056
Phone: 390422789611
Fax: 390422789666
E-mail: info@h-farmventures.com
Website: www.h-farm.com

Other Offices

Harbour Yard
Unit 2.14
London, United Kingdom SW10 0XD

911 Western Ave Suite 420
Maritime Building
Seattle, WA USA 98104

101/102, Vyom Arcade
Off Subhash Road
Mumbai, India 400057

Management and Staff
Luca Valerio, Chief Financial Officer

Type of Firm
Incubator/Development Program

Project Preferences

Type of Financing Preferred:
Seed
Startup

Geographical Preferences

United States Preferences:
All U.S.

International Preferences:
Italy
India
United Kingdom

Industry Preferences

In Internet Specific prefer:
Internet

Additional Information
Year Founded: 2005
Current Activity Level : Actively seeking new investments

H2 EQUITY PARTNERS BV

Oosteinde 19
Amsterdam, Netherlands 1017 WT
Phone: 31206790822
Fax: 31206758359
E-mail: info@h2.nl
Website: www.h2.nl

Other Offices

Kranhaus 1
Im Zzollhafen 18
Koeln, Germany 50678
Phone: 4922165060580
Fax: 4922165060500

100 Wingmore Street
London, United Kingdom W1U 3RN
Phone: 442070090440

Management and Staff
Age Hollander, Co-Founder
Gert Jan Van der Hoeven, Managing Partner
Harmen Geerts, Partner
Oliver Thum, Partner
Patrick Kalverboer, Managing Partner
Peter Kroeze, Partner
Simon Gilbert, Principal
Tonn Van de Laar, Partner

Type of Firm
Private Equity Firm

Project Preferences

Type of Financing Preferred:
Leveraged Buyout
Turnaround
Later Stage
Recapitalizations

Geographical Preferences

International Preferences:
United Kingdom
Europe
Netherlands
Belgium
Germany

Industry Preferences

In Medical/Health prefer:
Medical/Health
Pharmaceuticals

In Consumer Related prefer:
Consumer
Food/Beverage
Hotels and Resorts
Education Related

In Industrial/Energy prefer:
Industrial Products

In Business Serv. prefer:
Services
Media

Additional Information
Year Founded: 1991
Capital Under Management: $688,900,000
Current Activity Level : Actively seeking new investments

H2 PROPERTIES GMBH

Drehbahn 47-48
Hamburg, Germany 20354
Phone: 494060943720
Fax: 4940609437290
Website: www.h2-investments.com

Management and Staff
Heiko Hubertz, Chief Executive Officer

Type of Firm
Private Equity Firm

Project Preferences

Type of Financing Preferred:
Early Stage
Balanced
Later Stage
Seed
Startup

Geographical Preferences

International Preferences:
Germany

Additional Information
Year Founded: 2011
Current Activity Level : Actively seeking new investments

H2 VENTURES PTY LTD

Level Two
50 Bridge Street
Sydney, Australia 2068
Phone: 61280909365
E-mail: contact@h2.vc
Website: www.h2.vc

Type of Firm
Incubator/Development Program

Project Preferences

Type of Financing Preferred:
Later Stage

Size of Investments Considered:
Min Size of Investment Considered (000s): $100
Max Size of Investment Considered (000s): $1,000

Geographical Preferences

International Preferences:
Australia

Industry Preferences

In Communications prefer:
Data Communications

In Computer Software prefer:
Software

In Financial Services prefer:
Insurance
Real Estate
Financial Services

Additional Information
Year Founded: 1969
Current Activity Level : Actively seeking new investments

H2O VENTURE PARTNERS PE LTD

33-35 George Street
Oxford, United Kingdom OX1 2AY
Phone: 44-1865-251-000
Fax: 44-1865-204-114
E-mail: Info@h2ovp.com
Website: www.h2ovp.com

Management and Staff
Andrew Baum, Venture Partner
Martin Hunt, Venture Partner
Paul Coleman, Co-Founder
William Pope, Venture Partner

Type of Firm
Private Equity Firm

Project Preferences

Type of Financing Preferred:
Early Stage
Balanced
Seed
Startup

Geographical Preferences

International Preferences:
United Kingdom
Europe
Western Europe

Additional Information
Year Founded: 2006
Current Activity Level : Actively seeking new investments

HAATCH LTD

Orion House, Barn Hill
Stamford
Lincolnshire, United Kingdom PE9 2AE
Phone: 01780408491
E-mail: hello@haatch.com
Website: www.haatch.com

Management and Staff
Elaine Weavers-Wright, Co-Founder
Fred Soneya, Co-Founder
Scott Weavers-Wright, Co-Founder
Sophie Weavers-Wright, Co-Founder

Type of Firm
Incubator/Development Program

Project Preferences

Type of Financing Preferred:
Seed
Startup

Geographical Preferences

International Preferences:
United Kingdom

Additional Information
Year Founded: 2013
Current Activity Level : Actively seeking new investments

HACHIJUNI CAPITAL CO LTD

6F Choei Dai-ichi Bldg. 282-11
MinamiSekidomachi,Oaza-Minami-
Nagano, Nagano-shi, Japan 380-0824
Phone: 026-227-6887
Fax: 026-227-6989
Website: www.hcc82.co.jp

Type of Firm
Private Equity Firm

Project Preferences

Type of Financing Preferred:
Balanced

Geographical Preferences

International Preferences:
Japan

Industry Preferences

In Computer Other prefer:
Computer Related

In Consumer Related prefer:
Consumer Services

Additional Information
Year Founded: 1984
Capital Under Management: $50,500,000
Current Activity Level : Actively seeking new investments

HACKFWD GMBH & CO KG

Gaensemarkt 43
Hamburg, Germany 20354
Phone: 494044191700
Fax: 4940209325429
Website: www.hackfwd.com

Management and Staff
Lars Hinrichs, Chief Executive Officer

Type of Firm
Private Equity Firm

Project Preferences

Type of Financing Preferred:
Seed

Geographical Preferences

International Preferences:
Europe
Switzerland
Austria
Belgium

Industry Preferences

In Communications prefer:
Wireless Communications
Media and Entertainment

In Computer Software prefer:
Software

In Internet Specific prefer:
Ecommerce

Additional Information
Year Founded: 2011
Current Activity Level : Actively seeking new investments

HACKING HEALTH ACCELERATOR INC

2100 Drummond
Montreal, Canada QC H3G
E-mail: hello@hhaccelerator.com
Website: www.hhaccelerator.com

Management and Staff
Etienne Lagace, Co-Founder
Luc Sirois, Co-Founder

Type of Firm
Incubator/Development Program

Additional Information
Year Founded: 2015
Current Activity Level : Actively seeking new investments

HADDINGTON VENTURES LLC

2603 Augusta
Suite 900
Houston, TX USA 77057
Phone: 7135327992
Fax: 7135329922
E-mail: sec@hvllc.com
Website: www.hvllc.com

Management and Staff
J. Chris Jones, Managing Director
Jim Wise, Managing Director
John Strom, Managing Director
M. Scott Jones, Managing Director
Samuel Pyne, Vice President

Type of Firm
Private Equity Firm

Project Preferences

Role in Financing:
Prefer role as deal originator but will also invest in deals created by others

Type of Financing Preferred:
Leveraged Buyout
Balanced
Other
Acquisition

Size of Investments Considered:
Min Size of Investment Considered (000s): $5,000
Max Size of Investment Considered (000s): $50,000

Geographical Preferences

United States Preferences:
North America
All U.S.

Canadian Preferences:
All Canada

Industry Preferences

In Industrial/Energy prefer:
Energy
Oil and Gas Exploration

In Utilities prefer:
Utilities

Additional Information

Name of Most Recent Fund: Haddington Energy Partners IV, L.P.
Most Recent Fund Was Raised: 10/12/2010
Year Founded: 1997
Capital Under Management: $150,000,000
Current Activity Level : Actively seeking new investments
Method of Compensation: Return on invest. most important, but chg. closing fees, service fees, etc.

HADLEY CAPITAL

1200 Central Avenue
Suite 300 Chase Bank Building
Wilmette, IL USA 60091
Phone: 8479065300
Fax: 8479065301
E-mail: info@hadleycapital.com
Website: www.hadleycapital.com

Management and Staff

Clay Brock, Partner
Marc Summe, Vice President
Paul Wormley, Partner
Scott Dickes, Partner

Type of Firm

Private Equity Firm

Project Preferences

Type of Financing Preferred:
Leveraged Buyout
Expansion
Management Buyouts
Acquisition
Recapitalizations

Industry Preferences

In Financial Services prefer:
Financial Services

In Business Serv. prefer:
Services
Distribution

In Manufact. prefer:
Manufacturing

Additional Information

Year Founded: 1998
Capital Under Management: $40,000,000
Current Activity Level : Actively seeking new investments

HAHN & COMPANY EYE HOLDINGS CO LTD

100-201, 21 Floor, Ferrumtower
66 Juong-gu, Suha-dong
Seoul, South Korea
Phone: 0263537900
Fax: 0263537990

Type of Firm

Private Equity Firm

Project Preferences

Type of Financing Preferred:
Leveraged Buyout

Geographical Preferences

International Preferences:
Asia
Korea, South

Additional Information

Year Founded: 2011
Capital Under Management: $1,950,000,000
Current Activity Level : Actively seeking new investments

HAISHI EQUITY INVESTMENT FUND MANAGEMENT CO., LTD.

New Hope, High-tech Zone
1521 Tower B
Chengdu, China
Phone: 862883154028
Website: www.aviorcapital.cn

Type of Firm

Private Equity Firm

Project Preferences

Type of Financing Preferred:
Balanced

Geographical Preferences

International Preferences:
China

Additional Information

Year Founded: 2012
Current Activity Level : Actively seeking new investments

HAITONG BUYOUT CAPITAL MANAGEMENT SHANGHAI CO LTD

No.99, Huanhu West Roard
R201-1, Building 16, Block A
Shanghai, China

Type of Firm

Private Equity Firm

Project Preferences

Type of Financing Preferred:
Leveraged Buyout

Geographical Preferences

International Preferences:
China

Additional Information

Year Founded: 2014
Current Activity Level : Actively seeking new investments

HAITONG CAPITAL CO LTD

No. 689, Guangdong Road
26F, Haitong Securities Plaza
Shanghai, China 200001
Phone: 86-21-63410311
Fax: 86-21-63410815
E-mail: admin@htcc.sh.cn

Type of Firm

Investment Management Firm

Project Preferences

Type of Financing Preferred:
Leveraged Buyout
Balanced

Geographical Preferences

International Preferences:
China

Pratt's Guide to Private Equity & Venture Capital Sources

Industry Preferences

In Communications prefer:
Communications and Media
Radio & TV Broadcasting
Media and Entertainment
Publishing

In Internet Specific prefer:
Internet

In Biotechnology prefer:
Biotechnology

In Medical/Health prefer:
Medical/Health
Pharmaceuticals

In Consumer Related prefer:
Entertainment and Leisure
Consumer Products

In Industrial/Energy prefer:
Energy
Materials
Machinery

In Business Serv. prefer:
Media

In Manufact. prefer:
Manufacturing

In Other prefer:
Environment Responsible

Additional Information
Year Founded: 2008
Capital Under Management: $474,993,000
Current Activity Level : Actively seeking new investments

HAITONG CAPITAL SCR SA

Rua Alexandre Herculano, 38
1st Floor
Lisbon, Portugal 1269161
Phone: 351213515840
Fax: 351213515846
E-mail: es-capital@ip.pt

Other Offices

Calle Serrano
88-4 Planta
Madrid, Spain 28006
Phone: 34-91-400-5464
Fax: 34-91-435-3593

Av. Brigadeiro Faria Lima
3729-6 Itaim Bibi
Sao Paulo, Brazil 04538-905
Phone: 55-11-3074-7445
Fax: 55-11-3074-7462

Management and Staff
Antonio Almeida, Vice President
Antonio Silva Ricciardi, Managing Director
Emilia Franco Frazao, Managing Director
Joao Arantes E Oliveira, Chief Executive Officer

Type of Firm
Bank Affiliated

Association Membership
Portuguese Venture Capital Association (APCRI)
European Private Equity and Venture Capital Assoc.

Project Preferences

Role in Financing:
Will function either as deal originator or investor in deals created by others

Type of Financing Preferred:
Generalist PE
Later Stage
Acquisition

Size of Investments Considered:
Min Size of Investment Considered (000s): $2,626
Max Size of Investment Considered (000s): $13,130

Geographical Preferences

International Preferences:
Liberia
Europe
Portugal
Switzerland
Brazil
Spain
Norway
France

Additional Information
Name of Most Recent Fund: Espirito Santo Infrastructure Fund I
Most Recent Fund Was Raised: 07/31/2007
Year Founded: 1988
Capital Under Management: $319,800,000
Current Activity Level : Actively seeking new investments

HAITONG JIHE PRIVATE EQUITY INVESTMENT FUND MANAGEMENT CO

No. 222, YanAn East Road
Unit 3303, Bund Center
Shanghai, China
Phone: 862163351166
Fax: 862163351219
E-mail: info@htjhpe.com.cn
Website: www.htjhpe.com.cn

Type of Firm
Private Equity Firm

Project Preferences

Type of Financing Preferred:
Leveraged Buyout
Generalist PE

Geographical Preferences

International Preferences:
China

Industry Preferences

In Biotechnology prefer:
Agricultural/Animal Bio.

In Manufact. prefer:
Manufacturing

Additional Information
Year Founded: 2014
Capital Under Management: $8,259,000
Current Activity Level : Actively seeking new investments

HAIXIANG TIANJIN VENTURE CAPITAL MANAGEMENT CO LTD

No. 482, Dongman Middle Road
Rm. 203-077, Chuangzhi Bldg
Tianjin, China

Type of Firm
Private Equity Firm

Project Preferences

Type of Financing Preferred:
Balanced

Geographical Preferences

International Preferences:
China

Additional Information
Year Founded: 2012
Current Activity Level : Actively seeking new investments

HAIYIN CAPITAL

310 Block B, Winterless Center
No.1 West Dawang road
Beijing, China 100026
Website: www.haiyindtfund.com

Type of Firm
Private Equity Firm

Project Preferences

Type of Financing Preferred:
Balanced

Geographical Preferences

United States Preferences:

Industry Preferences

In Medical/Health prefer:
Medical/Health

In Industrial/Energy prefer:
Alternative Energy

In Transportation prefer:
Aerospace

Additional Information
Year Founded: 2014
Current Activity Level : Actively seeking new investments

HAL INVESTMENTS BV

Weena 696
Millennium Tower
Rotterdam, Netherlands 3012 CN
Phone: 31102816500
Fax: 31102816528
E-mail: info@halinvestments.nl
Website: www.halinvestments.nl

Other Offices

Tower D, 4th Floor
Schiphol Boulevard 123
Schiphol Airport, Netherlands 1118 BG
Phone: 31204469555
Fax: 31204469550

Rua Dr. Rafael de Barros,
209 - 10 andar
, Brazil 04003-040
Phone: 551131712016

Type of Firm
Bank Affiliated

Project Preferences

Type of Financing Preferred:
Leveraged Buyout
Balanced
Acquisition
Recapitalizations

Geographical Preferences

United States Preferences:

International Preferences:
Europe
Western Europe

Industry Focus
(% based on actual investment)
Other Products	96.6%
Internet Specific	3.4%

Additional Information
Year Founded: 1989
Current Activity Level : Actively seeking new investments

HALE FUND MANAGEMENT, L.P.

570 Lexington Avenue
49th Floor
New York, NY USA 10022
Phone: 2127518228
Website: www.halefunds.com

Management and Staff
Jason Koenig, Vice President
Martin Hale, Chief Executive Officer
Nathaniel Klein, Vice President

Type of Firm
Private Equity Firm

Project Preferences

Type of Financing Preferred:
Leveraged Buyout
Acquisition
Recapitalizations

Additional Information
Year Founded: 2007
Current Activity Level : Actively seeking new investments

HALIFAX GROUP LLC

1133 Connecticut Avenue, NW
Suite 700
Washington, DC USA 20036
Phone: 2025308300
Fax: 2022967133
E-mail: inquiry@thehalifaxgroup.com
Website: www.thehalifaxgroup.com

Other Offices

3605 Glenwood Avenue
Suite 490
Raleigh, NC USA 27612
Phone: 919-786-4420
Fax: 919-786-4428

200 Crescent Court
Suite 1030
Dallas, TX USA 75201
Phone: 2148558700
Fax: 2148558712

Management and Staff
Allie Atwood, Vice President
Brent Williams, Managing Director
Chris Cathcart, Partner
David Dupree, Chief Executive Officer
David Calder, Vice President
David Bonderman, Co-Founder
Davis Hostetter, Vice President
Katherine Trainor, Vice President
Kenneth Doyle, Managing Director
Michael Marshall, Chief Financial Officer
Scott Van Duinen, Partner
Scott Plumridge, Partner
Thomas Barrack, Co-Founder
William Rogers, Co-Founder

Type of Firm
Private Equity Firm

Project Preferences

Type of Financing Preferred:
Leveraged Buyout
Later Stage
Management Buyouts
Recapitalizations

Geographical Preferences

United States Preferences:
North America

Canadian Preferences:
All Canada

Industry Focus
(% based on actual investment)
Medical/Health	43.9%
Internet Specific	27.5%
Other Products	25.7%
Communications and Media	3.0%

Additional Information
Name of Most Recent Fund: Halifax Capital Partners III, L.P.
Most Recent Fund Was Raised: 12/23/2011
Year Founded: 1999
Capital Under Management: $200,000,000
Current Activity Level : Actively seeking new investments

HALL CAPITAL LLC

9225 Lake Hefner Parkway
Suite 200
Oklahoma City, OK USA 73120
Phone: 4052312400
Fax: 4052312405
Website: www.hall-capital.com

Other Offices

2000 McKinney Avenue
Suite 1200
Dallas, TX USA 75201
Phone: 9726306303
Fax: 2149549995

One Westminster Place
Suite 108
Lake Forest, IL USA 60045
Phone: 8472954214
Fax: 8475745850

Management and Staff
David Holsted, Partner
John Kobza, Partner
Jonathan Adamson, Partner
Maya Lowder, Chief Financial Officer

Type of Firm
Private Equity Firm

Project Preferences

Type of Financing Preferred:
Leveraged Buyout
Value-Add
Management Buyouts
Acquisition
Recapitalizations

Size of Investments Considered:
Min Size of Investment Considered (000s): $2,000
Max Size of Investment Considered (000s): $25,000

Geographical Preferences

United States Preferences:
Midwest
All U.S.

Industry Preferences

In Financial Services prefer:
Real Estate

In Business Serv. prefer:
Services
Distribution

In Manufact. prefer:
Manufacturing

Additional Information
Year Founded: 2010
Capital Under Management: $59,330,000
Current Activity Level: Actively seeking new investments

HALL CAPITAL PARTNERS LLC

One Maritime Plaza
Fifth Floor
San Francisco, CA USA 94111
Phone: 4152880544
Website: www.hallcapital.com

Other Offices
850 Third Avenue
19th Floor
New York, NY USA 10022
Phone: 2124070700

Management and Staff
Ann Barber, Managing Director
Charles Kurz, Principal
Charlie Lamm, Vice President
Edward Patron, Principal
Eric Alt, Managing Director
Helane Morrison, Managing Director
Jack Crowley, Vice President
Jessica Reed Saouaf, Managing Director
Joanne Hagopian, Managing Director
John Buoymaster, President
Kurt Rieke, Managing Director
Laurie Deaton, Principal
Lou Fernandes, Vice President
Matthew Burns, Vice President
Pamela Blakey-Hart, Vice President
Paul Muller, Managing Director
Promit Bhattacharya, Vice President
Rachel Kort, Vice President
Sarah Whitelaw, Vice President
Sarah Stein, Managing Director
Simon Krinsky, Managing Director
Stephen Florance, Managing Director

Type of Firm
Private Equity Advisor or Fund of Funds

Project Preferences

Type of Financing Preferred:
Fund of Funds

Industry Preferences

In Industrial/Energy prefer:
Energy
Environmental Related

In Financial Services prefer:
Real Estate

Additional Information
Name of Most Recent Fund: HCP Private Equity Fund VI, L.P.
Most Recent Fund Was Raised: 01/25/2013
Year Founded: 1994
Capital Under Management: $2,000,000,000
Current Activity Level: Actively seeking new investments

HALLEY VENTURE PARTNERS LP

876 Revere Road
Lafayette, CA USA 94549
E-mail: info@halleyvp.com
Website: www.halleyvp.com

Type of Firm
Private Equity Firm

Project Preferences

Type of Financing Preferred:
Early Stage

Industry Preferences

In Agr/Forestr/Fish prefer:
Agribusiness

Additional Information
Year Founded: 2017
Current Activity Level: Actively seeking new investments

HALO FUND L P

2665 Marine Way
Suite 1150
Mountain View, CA USA 94043
Phone: 6508570700
Fax: 6508570773
Website: www.halofund.com

Management and Staff
Craig Sirnio, Partner
Ed Esber, Partner
Leif Langensand, Partner
Nagesh Mhatre, Partner
Phil Schlein, Partner

Type of Firm
Private Equity Firm

Project Preferences

Type of Financing Preferred:
Early Stage

Industry Preferences

In Consumer Related prefer:
Consumer Products

In Other prefer:
Environment Responsible

Additional Information
Year Founded: 1969
Current Activity Level: Actively seeking new investments

HALOGEN VENTURES PARTNERS LLC

212 26th Street
Suite 223
Santa Monica, CA USA 90402
Website: halogenvc.com

Type of Firm
Private Equity Firm

Project Preferences

Type of Financing Preferred:
Early Stage

Additional Information
Year Founded: 1969
Current Activity Level: Actively seeking new investments

HALYARD CAPITAL

600 Fifth Avenue
17th Floor
New York, NY USA 10020
Phone: 2125542121
Fax: 2125542120
E-mail: info@halyard.com
Website: www.halyard.com

Management and Staff

Brendyn Grimaldi, Principal
Bruce Eatroff, Founder
Jonathan Barnes, Partner
Robert Nolan, Managing Partner
Sarah Kim, Managing Director

Type of Firm

Private Equity Firm

Project Preferences

Type of Financing Preferred:
Leveraged Buyout
Expansion
Turnaround
Management Buyouts
Acquisition

Geographical Preferences

United States Preferences:
North America

International Preferences:
Europe

Industry Preferences

In Communications prefer:
Communications and Media
Radio & TV Broadcasting
Wireless Communications
Media and Entertainment

In Medical/Health prefer:
Health Services

In Consumer Related prefer:
Education Related

In Business Serv. prefer:
Services
Distribution

In Manufact. prefer:
Publishing

Additional Information

Year Founded: 2000
Capital Under Management: $600,000,000
Current Activity Level : Actively seeking new investments

HAMBRO PERKS LTD

Eight Greencoat Place
London, United Kingdom SW1P 1PL
Phone: 4402033274861
E-mail: info@hambroperks.com
Website: www.hambroperks.com

Management and Staff

Andrew Wyke, Partner
Dominic Perks, Co-Founder
George Davies, Partner
Kate Burns, Chief Executive Officer
Rupert Hambro, Co-Founder

Type of Firm

Incubator/Development Program

Project Preferences

Type of Financing Preferred:
Balanced

Additional Information

Year Founded: 2011
Current Activity Level : Actively seeking new investments

HAMILTON INVESTMENTS INC

515 Madison Avenue
Suite 27W
New York, NY USA 10022
Phone: 6462850341
Fax: 6462850347
Website: www.hamiltonrisk.com

Management and Staff

Brian Fenty, Vice President
Douglas Hamilton, Managing Partner
Veronica La Voun, Chief Operating Officer

Type of Firm

Private Equity Firm

Project Preferences

Type of Financing Preferred:
Early Stage

Size of Investments Considered:
Min Size of Investment Considered (000s): $4,000
Max Size of Investment Considered (000s): $8,000

Geographical Preferences

United States Preferences:
Mid Atlantic
Northeast

Industry Preferences

In Consumer Related prefer:
Consumer
Education Related

In Industrial/Energy prefer:
Energy

In Financial Services prefer:
Financial Services

In Business Serv. prefer:
Services
Distribution

In Manufact. prefer:
Manufacturing

Additional Information

Year Founded: 1969
Current Activity Level : Actively seeking new investments

HAMILTON LANE ADVISORS LLC

One Presidential Boulevard
Fourth Floor
Bala Cynwyd, PA USA 19004
Phone: 6109342222
Fax: 6106179853
E-mail: information@hamiltonlane.com
Website: www.hamiltonlane.com

Other Offices

1-1-1, Uchisaiwai-cho
17F, Imperial Tower
Tokyo, Japan 100-0011
Phone: 81335804000
Fax: 81335804600

7777 Fay Avenue
Suite 206
LA JOLLA, CA USA 92037
Phone: 8584109967
Fax: 8584109968

3753 Howard Hughes Parkway
Suite 200
LAS VEGAS, NV USA 89169
Phone: 702-784-7690

Two Ice House Building
St. George's Building, 10th Floor
Central, Hong Kong
Phone: 852-3987-7191
Fax: 852-3987-7198

825 Third Avenue
35th Floor
MANHATTAN, NY USA 10022
Phone: 2127527667
Fax: 2127527865

N 2 Room 102, Leblon
Avenida Niemeyer, Brazil
Phone: 552180333600

200 Southwest First Avenue
Suite 880
FORT LAUDERDALE, FL USA 33301
Phone: 9547452780
Fax: 9547452799

200 California Street
Suite 400
SAN FRANCISCO, CA USA 94111
Phone: 4153651056
Fax: 4153651057

14 Shenkar Street
Nolton House
Herzalia Pituach, Israel 46733
Phone: 97299586670
Fax: 97299568205

Management and Staff

Alice Lindenauer, Managing Director
Ana Lei Ortiz, Managing Director
Andrea Kramer, Managing Director
Andrew Schardt, Managing Director
Anthony Donofrio, Principal
Brian Gildea, Managing Director
Christian Kallen, Managing Director
Collwyn Tan, Principal
David Helgerson, Managing Director
Demetrius Sidberry, Principal
Dennis Scharf, Managing Director
Edward D Onofrio, Vice President
Emily Nomeir, Principal
Filipe Caldas, Vice President
Greg Baty, Principal
Ilene Levinson, Principal
Jacqueline Rantanen, Managing Director
James Noon, Principal
Janet Bauman, Managing Director
Jeffrey Meeker, Managing Director
Jerome Gates, Managing Director
Jim Strang, Managing Director
Jisoo Noh, Principal
John Brecker, Vice President
Josh Jacob, Managing Director
Joshua Kahn, Managing Director
Juan Delgado-Moreira, Managing Director
Katie Moore, Vice President
Keith Brittain, Managing Director
Kevin Lucey, Chief Operating Officer
Kristin Williamson, Principal
Lars Pace, Principal
Laura Warren, Vice President
Limor Beker, Managing Director
Mario Giannini, Chief Executive Officer
Matthew Silverio, Principal
Matthew Pellini, Principal
Mei Ni Yang, Vice President
Melissa Nigro, Vice President
Michael Kelly, Managing Director
Michael Ryan, Principal
Michael Koenig, Principal
Miguel Luina, Principal
Mingchen Xia, Managing Director
Mitesh Pabari, Principal
N. Grant Saul, Principal

Napoleon Stephenson, Managing Director
Olin Honore, Managing Director
Paul Yett, Managing Director
Paul Waller, Partner
Peter Larsen, Principal
Randy Stilman, Chief Financial Officer
Ricardo Fernandez, Managing Director
Richard Hope, Managing Director
Robert Flanigan, Principal
Sarah Mehra, Vice President
Sonia Lopez, Vice President
Stephen Brennan, Managing Director
Sungji An, Principal
Tammy Mahn, Vice President
Tara Blackburn, Managing Director
Tarang Katira, Principal
Thomas Kerr, Managing Director
Tomoko Kitao, Managing Director
Trevor Messerly, Principal
Vesna Sipp, Managing Director
Vesna Dukic, Vice President

Type of Firm
Private Equity Firm

Association Membership
Brazilian Venture Capital Association (ABCR)
Emerging Markets Private Equity Association
Israel Venture Association
Natl Assoc of Small Bus. Inv. Co (NASBIC)
European Private Equity and Venture Capital Assoc.

Project Preferences

Type of Financing Preferred:
Fund of Funds
Fund of Funds of Second

Geographical Preferences

International Preferences:
Brazil

Industry Focus
(% based on actual investment)

Other Products	77.7%
Communications and Media	8.5%
Medical/Health	6.9%
Computer Software and Services	3.0%
Internet Specific	1.8%
Consumer Related	1.0%
Computer Hardware	0.8%
Industrial/Energy	0.3%

Additional Information
Name of Most Recent Fund: HL Brazil FIQFIP
Most Recent Fund Was Raised: 03/12/2014
Year Founded: 1991
Capital Under Management: $15,000,000,000
Current Activity Level : Actively seeking new investments

HAMILTON PORTFOLIO LTD

20 Renfield Street
Sterling House
Glasgow, United Kingdom G2 5AP
Phone: 44-141-221-4400
Fax: 44-141-227-7519
E-mail: inbox@hamiltonportfolio.co.uk
Website: www.hamiltonportfolio.co.uk

Management and Staff
Andrew Lapping, Managing Director

Type of Firm
Private Equity Firm

Project Preferences

Type of Financing Preferred:
Later Stage

Size of Investments Considered:
Min Size of Investment Considered (000s): $400
Max Size of Investment Considered (000s): $400,000

Geographical Preferences

International Preferences:
United Kingdom
Europe

Additional Information
Year Founded: 1999
Current Activity Level : Actively seeking new investments

HAMILTON ROBINSON LLC

281 Tresser Boulevard
Suite 1000
Stamford, CT USA 06901
Phone: 2036020011
Fax: 2036022206
Website: www.hrco.com

Management and Staff

Christian Lund, Partner
Owen Crihfield, Partner
Phillip Cagnassola, Partner
Scott Oakford, Managing Partner

Type of Firm
Private Equity Firm

Association Membership
Natl Assoc of Small Bus. Inv. Co (NASBIC)

Project Preferences

Role in Financing:
Prefer role as deal originator

Type of Financing Preferred:
Leveraged Buyout
Acquisition
Recapitalizations

Industry Preferences

In Industrial/Energy prefer:
Industrial Products
Environmental Related

In Business Serv. prefer:
Services
Distribution

In Manufact. prefer:
Manufacturing

Additional Information

Name of Most Recent Fund: Cygnet Capital Partners, L.P.
Most Recent Fund Was Raised: 06/01/2001
Year Founded: 1984
Capital Under Management: $100,000,000
Current Activity Level : Actively seeking new investments
Method of Compensation: Return on invest. most important, but chg. closing fees, service fees, etc.

HAMILTON VENTURES LLC

75 Fifth Street
Suite 311
Atlanta, GA USA 30308
Phone: 4049813444
Website: www.hamilton-ventures.com

Type of Firm
Private Equity Firm

Project Preferences

Type of Financing Preferred:
Early Stage

Geographical Preferences

United States Preferences:
Georgia

Industry Preferences

In Communications prefer:
Communications and Media

In Internet Specific prefer:
Ecommerce

In Medical/Health prefer:
Medical/Health

Additional Information
Year Founded: 2012
Current Activity Level : Actively seeking new investments

HAMMERMAN CAPITAL LLC

3470 Mount Diablo Boulevard, Suite A130
Boston, MA USA 02110
Phone: 617-574-6150
Website: www.hammermancapital.com

Type of Firm
Private Equity Firm

Additional Information
Year Founded: 2001
Capital Under Management: $79,000,000
Current Activity Level : Actively seeking new investments

HAMMOND KENNEDY WHITNEY & COMPANY INC

8888 Keystone Crossing
Suite 600
Indianapolis, IN USA 46240
Phone: 3175746900
Fax: 3175747515
E-mail: hk@hkwinc.com
Website: www.hkwinc.com

Other Offices
420 Lexington Avenue
Suite 2633
New York, NY USA 10170
Phone: 2128671010

Management and Staff
Caroline Young, Partner
James Snyder, Partner
John Carsello, Principal
Luke Phenicie, Partner
Mark Becker, Partner
Michael Foisy, Partner
Ryan Grand, Vice President
Ted Kramer, Partner

Type of Firm
Private Equity Firm

Project Preferences

Role in Financing:
Prefer role as deal originator

Type of Financing Preferred:
Leveraged Buyout
Management Buyouts
Acquisition
Recapitalizations

Geographical Preferences

United States Preferences:
North America

Industry Focus

(% based on actual investment)
Other Products	50.1%
Industrial/Energy	37.6%
Computer Software and Services	6.7%
Internet Specific	5.7%

Additional Information
Name of Most Recent Fund: HKW Capital Partners IV, L.P.
Most Recent Fund Was Raised: 07/15/2013
Year Founded: 1903
Capital Under Management: $250,000,000
Current Activity Level : Actively seeking new investments
Method of Compensation: Return on invest. most important, but chg. closing fees, service fees, etc.

HANA DAETOO SECURITIES CO LTD

27-3, Yeoyuido-dong
Yeongdeungpo-gu
Seoul, South Korea 150705
Phone: 820237717114
Fax: 820237717080
Website: www.hanaw.com

Management and Staff
Byeong Wun Seo, Managing Director
C Lee, Managing Director
Chang Sup Rhim, Chairman & CEO
Hyeon Jun Cho, Managing Director
Jae Ho Lee, Managing Director
Jae Wuk Jung, Managing Director
Jeong Ho Choi, Managing Director
Ji-whan Kim, Managing Director
Seung Heon Baek, Managing Director
Yeong Bae Jeon, Managing Director
Yik Su Joo, Managing Director
Yong Choo, Managing Director
Yong Cheol Lee, Managing Director

Type of Firm
Bank Affiliated

Project Preferences

Type of Financing Preferred:
Balanced

Additional Information
Year Founded: 1977
Capital Under Management: $26,340,000
Current Activity Level : Actively seeking new investments

HANCOCK CAPITAL MANAGEMENT LLC

197 Clarendon Street
Second Floor
Boston, MA USA 02116
Phone: 6175721372
Fax: 6175726454
Website: www.hancockcapitalllc.com

Other Offices
1120 Avenue of the Americas
15th Floor, Suite 1502
New York, NY USA 10036

Management and Staff
Daniel Budde, Senior Managing Director
Lorn Davis, Managing Director
Paul Fishbin, Managing Director
Saverio Costa, Managing Director
Scott McFetridge, Senior Managing Director
Scott Garfield, Managing Director
Stephen Blewitt, Senior Managing Director

Type of Firm
Insurance Firm Affiliate

Project Preferences

Type of Financing Preferred:
Mezzanine

Industry Focus
(% based on actual investment)
Other Products	44.1%
Consumer Related	39.6%
Semiconductors/Other Elect.	12.9%
Computer Software and Services	3.4%

Additional Information
Name of Most Recent Fund: Hancock Capital Partners V, L.P.
Most Recent Fund Was Raised: 08/31/2012
Year Founded: 1998
Capital Under Management: $619,000,000
Current Activity Level : Actively seeking new investments

HANCOCK PARK ASSOCIATES A CALIFORNIA LP

1880 Century Park East
Suite 900
Los Angeles, CA USA 90067
Phone: 3102286900
Fax: 3102286939
E-mail: info@hpcap.com
Website: www.hpcap.com

Other Offices
1980 Post Oak
Suite 2150
Houston, TX USA 77056
Phone: 713-333-2580
Fax: 713-209-7451

Management and Staff
J. Webb Jennings, Vice President
Kenneth Watler, Partner
Kenton Van Harten, Partner
Kevin Listen, Partner
Martin Irani, Vice President
Michael Fourticq, Managing Partner
Michael Fourticq, Partner
Ted Fourticq, Principal

Type of Firm
Private Equity Firm

Project Preferences

Type of Financing Preferred:
Leveraged Buyout
Expansion
Acquisition

Size of Investments Considered:
Min Size of Investment Considered (000s): $5,000
Max Size of Investment Considered (000s): $10,000

Geographical Preferences

United States Preferences:
Northwest
West Coast
Southwest

Industry Focus
(% based on actual investment)
Consumer Related	74.9%
Other Products	25.1%

Additional Information
Name of Most Recent Fund: Hancock Park Capital II, L.P.
Most Recent Fund Was Raised: 11/22/2002
Year Founded: 1986
Capital Under Management: $158,000,000
Current Activity Level : Actively seeking new investments

HANDSON3 LLC

3003 Pennsylvania Avenue
Santa Monica, CA USA 90404
E-mail: info@handson3.com
Website: www.handson3.com

Management and Staff
Andrej Jonovic, Managing Director
Ashim Ahuja, Managing Director
David Levene, Principal
Jito Chadha, Partner
Kanwar Chadha, Principal
Matthew Brown, Vice President
Prakash Shukla, Partner
Rohit Jain, Partner
Ronald Cogburn, Principal
Sarah Jonovic, Partner
Shao-Shao Cheng, Principal
Sunil Rajadhyaksha, Partner
Surinder Rametra, Partner
Vik Negi, Principal
W. Tompie Hall, Partner
Xin Cheng, Partner

Type of Firm
Private Equity Firm

Project Preferences

Type of Financing Preferred:
Leveraged Buyout

Geographical Preferences

United States Preferences:

International Preferences:
India
United Kingdom
China
Brazil
Russia

Industry Preferences

In Computer Software prefer:
Data Processing
Systems Software

In Industrial/Energy prefer:
Alternative Energy
Environmental Related

In Business Serv. prefer:
Services

Additional Information
Year Founded: 2002
Current Activity Level : Actively seeking new investments

HANFOR (BEIJING) INVESTMENT CO LTD

No. 92, Jianguo Road, Chaoyang
20F, Block B, Shimao Tower
Beijing, China 100022
Phone: 861062136860
Fax: 861062138291
E-mail: hanfor@hanfor.cn
Website: www.hanfor.cn

Management and Staff
Hui Wang, Vice President
Pengcheng Feng, Partner

Type of Firm
Bank Affiliated

Project Preferences

Type of Financing Preferred:
Expansion
Later Stage

Geographical Preferences

International Preferences:
China

Additional Information
Year Founded: 2011
Current Activity Level : Actively seeking new investments

HANGAR VENTURES LLC

211 North Ervay
Dallas, TX USA 75201
E-mail: info@hangarventures.com
Website: www.hangarventures.com

Management and Staff
Jason Story, Partner
Jeff Williams, Partner

Type of Firm
Private Equity Firm

Project Preferences

Type of Financing Preferred:
Early Stage
Expansion
Later Stage
Seed

Industry Preferences

In Internet Specific prefer:
Internet

Additional Information
Year Founded: 2015
Capital Under Management: $50,000,000
Current Activity Level : Actively seeking new investments

HANGHAI SMALLVILLE FINANCIAL ADVISOR CO LTD

88 Century Avenue
Jin Mao edifice 24/F, 50/F
Shanghai, China
Phone: 862150496669
Fax: 862150496668
Website: sv-fa.com

Management and Staff
Zhen Wang, Partner

Type of Firm
Investment Management Firm

Project Preferences

Type of Financing Preferred:
Fund of Funds
Balanced

Geographical Preferences

International Preferences:
China

Industry Preferences

In Consumer Related prefer:
Consumer
Education Related

In Industrial/Energy prefer:
Energy Conservation Relat
Environmental Related

In Manufact. prefer:
Manufacturing

Additional Information
Year Founded: 2007
Capital Under Management: $17,727,000
Current Activity Level : Actively seeking new investments

HANGZHOU ALI VENTURE CAPITAL CO LTD

Room 301, 3F, Building 1, 699
Wangshang Road, Binjiang
Hangzhou, China 310012

Type of Firm
Private Equity Firm

Project Preferences

Type of Financing Preferred:
Balanced

Geographical Preferences

International Preferences:
China

Additional Information
Year Founded: 2006
Current Activity Level : Actively seeking new investments

HANGZHOU BANGSHI INVESTMENT MANAGEMENT CO LTD

No.550 Xixi Road Xihu Dist
3F B Block No.6 Xixi New Build
Hangzhou, China
Phone: 8657188311217
Website: www.vcchina.com

Type of Firm
Private Equity Firm

Project Preferences

Type of Financing Preferred:
Early Stage

Geographical Preferences

International Preferences:
China

Industry Preferences

In Communications prefer:
Telecommunications

In Medical/Health prefer:
Medical/Health

In Consumer Related prefer:
Consumer Products

In Business Serv. prefer:
Media

Additional Information
Year Founded: 2014
Current Activity Level : Actively seeking new investments

HANGZHOU BEIJIA INVESTMENT MANAGEMENT CO LTD

Donghu Subdistrict Economic
No.355 Xingzhong Road
Hangzhou, China 311100
Phone: 8657189263217

Type of Firm
Investment Management Firm

Project Preferences

Type of Financing Preferred:
Balanced

Geographical Preferences

International Preferences:
China

Industry Preferences

In Biotechnology prefer:
Biotechnology

In Medical/Health prefer:
Medical/Health
Medical Products

Additional Information
Year Founded: 2016
Current Activity Level : Actively seeking new investments

HANGZHOU CHONGDONG INVESTMENT MANAGEMENT CO LTD

Qianmo Road 459
C2-109, Juguang Center
Hangzhou, China
Website: www.warpspeedcap.com

Type of Firm
Private Equity Firm

Project Preferences

Type of Financing Preferred:
Early Stage
Seed
Startup

Geographical Preferences

International Preferences:
China

Industry Preferences

In Internet Specific prefer:
Internet

In Financial Services prefer:
Insurance
Financial Services

Additional Information

Year Founded: 2014
Current Activity Level : Actively seeking new investments

HANGZHOU DATOU INVESTMENT MANAGEMENT CO LTD

Beishan Subdistrict, Xihu Dis
Annex Building, Inside East Bl
Hangzhou, China 310000
Phone: 8657188370000

Type of Firm
Investment Management Firm

Project Preferences

Type of Financing Preferred:
Balanced

Geographical Preferences

International Preferences:
China

Additional Information

Year Founded: 2015
Current Activity Level : Actively seeking new investments

HANGZHOU DENENG EQUITY INVESTMENT PARTNERSHIP LP

Xiarghu Financial Village, Xia
Room 113, AF, Building 3, Sout
Hangzhou, China 311200
Phone: 8657183780880

Type of Firm
Private Equity Firm

Project Preferences

Type of Financing Preferred:
Balanced

Geographical Preferences

International Preferences:
China

Additional Information

Year Founded: 2016
Current Activity Level : Actively seeking new investments

HANGZHOU DINGJU INVESTMENT MANAGEMENT CO LTD

1785, Jianghan Road, Binjiang
22F, Block 4, Shuangcheng Intl
Hangzhou, China
Phone: 86-571-87082841
Website: www.djcapital.cn

Type of Firm
Private Equity Firm

Project Preferences

Type of Financing Preferred:
Balanced

Geographical Preferences

International Preferences:
China

Industry Preferences

In Communications prefer:
Telecommunications
Media and Entertainment

In Business Serv. prefer:
Services

Additional Information

Year Founded: 2011
Current Activity Level : Actively seeking new investments

HANGZHOU HAIBANG INVESTMENT MANAGEMENT CO LTD

No. 998, Wenyi West Road
Building 1, Haichuang Park
Hangzhou, China 310012
Phone: 8657188212200
Fax: 8657181022997
E-mail: office@hbvc.com.cn
Website: www.hbvc.com.cn

Management and Staff
Gang Liang, President
Li Xie, President

Type of Firm
Private Equity Firm

Project Preferences

Type of Financing Preferred:
Early Stage
Expansion

Geographical Preferences

International Preferences:
China

Industry Preferences

In Biotechnology prefer:
Biotechnology

In Medical/Health prefer:
Pharmaceuticals

In Industrial/Energy prefer:
Energy
Energy Conservation Relat
Materials

Additional Information

Year Founded: 2011
Capital Under Management: $45,524,000
Current Activity Level : Actively seeking new investments

HANGZHOU HI-TECH VENTURE CAPITAL CO LTD

Fifth Floor, Keji Building
Number Two, Huixing Road
Hangzhou, China 310001
Phone: 86-8706-2201
Fax: 86-8706-2201
E-mail: ed@hznet.com.cn

Type of Firm
Private Equity Firm

Project Preferences

Type of Financing Preferred:
Early Stage

Geographical Preferences

International Preferences:
China

Additional Information

Year Founded: 2010
Current Activity Level : Actively seeking new investments

HANGZHOU INCAPITAL MANAGEMENT CO., LTD.

No. 391 Wener Road, Xihu Dist
B1-1201 Xihu Int'l S&T Bldg
Hangzhou, China 310007
Phone: 8657187997755
Fax: 8657187960022
E-mail: admin@incapital.cn
Website: www.incapital.cn

Management and Staff
Jianbiao Xiang, Founder
Qiudong Chen, Vice President

Type of Firm
Private Equity Firm

Project Preferences
Type of Financing Preferred:
Early Stage
Expansion
Later Stage

Geographical Preferences
International Preferences:
China

Industry Preferences
In Industrial/Energy prefer:
Energy
Energy Conservation Relat
Materials
Machinery
Environmental Related

In Manufact. prefer:
Manufacturing

In Other prefer:
Environment Responsible

Additional Information
Year Founded: 2009
Current Activity Level : Actively seeking new investments

HANGZHOU JINYING INVESTMENT MANAGEMENT CO LTD

No. 111 Yisheng Road
Nongfu Product Logistics Park
Hangzhou, China 310007
Phone: 86-571-85117038
Fax: 86-571-89011158
E-mail: jytz@hzjytz.com
Website: www.hzjytz.com

Type of Firm
Investment Management Firm

Project Preferences
Type of Financing Preferred:
Balanced

Geographical Preferences
International Preferences:
China

Industry Preferences
In Industrial/Energy prefer:
Energy

In Financial Services prefer:
Real Estate

Additional Information
Year Founded: 2002
Current Activity Level : Actively seeking new investments

HANGZHOU JISU INVESTMENT PARTNERS ENTERPRISE LP

Beigan Street, Xiaoshan
Hangzhou, China

Type of Firm
Private Equity Firm

Project Preferences
Type of Financing Preferred:
Balanced

Geographical Preferences
International Preferences:
China

Additional Information
Year Founded: 2015
Current Activity Level : Actively seeking new investments

HANGZHOU JUNSHANG INVESTMENT MANAGEMENT CO LTD

No. 262, Wantang Road, Xihu Di
Room 6-9, Building 6
Hangzhou, China

Type of Firm
Investment Management Firm

Project Preferences
Type of Financing Preferred:
Balanced

Geographical Preferences
International Preferences:
China

Additional Information
Year Founded: 2012
Current Activity Level : Actively seeking new investments

HANGZHOU KEDI CAPITAL GROUP CO LTD

Shangtang Road 15
20F, Wulinshidai
Hangzhou, China 310014

Type of Firm
Private Equity Firm

Project Preferences
Type of Financing Preferred:
Balanced

Geographical Preferences
International Preferences:
China

Additional Information
Year Founded: 2007
Current Activity Level : Actively seeking new investments

HANGZHOU QIYI INVESTMENT MANAGEMENT CO LTD

Liuhe Road, Xihu District
C, Huifeng Intl Building
Hangzhou, China
Website: qiyicap.com

Type of Firm
Investment Management Firm

Project Preferences
Type of Financing Preferred:
Balanced

Geographical Preferences
International Preferences:
China

Industry Preferences
In Communications prefer:
Media and Entertainment

In Internet Specific prefer:
Internet

Additional Information
Year Founded: 2015
Current Activity Level : Actively seeking new investments

HANGZHOU RIVER HILL FUND CAPITAL MANAGEMENT CO LTD

699, Wangshang Rd., Binjiang
Hangzhou, China 310000
Phone: 8657185022088
Website: www.riverhillfund.com

Type of Firm
Private Equity Firm

Project Preferences

Type of Financing Preferred:
Early Stage
Expansion
Seed

Geographical Preferences

International Preferences:
China

Industry Preferences

In Communications prefer:
Wireless Communications

In Internet Specific prefer:
Internet

In Medical/Health prefer:
Medical/Health

In Consumer Related prefer:
Education Related

In Industrial/Energy prefer:
Energy

In Financial Services prefer:
Financial Services

In Business Serv. prefer:
Media

In Manufact. prefer:
Manufacturing

Additional Information
Year Founded: 2014
Current Activity Level : Actively seeking new investments

HANGZHOU TAIHENG INVESTMENT MANAGEMENT CO LTD

Sijiqing Street Community, Jia
30F, No. 2-6 Qingchun East Rd.
Hangzhou, China 310016

Type of Firm
Investment Management Firm

Project Preferences

Type of Financing Preferred:
Balanced

Geographical Preferences

International Preferences:
China

Additional Information
Year Founded: 2010
Current Activity Level : Actively seeking new investments

HANGZHOU TOBON VENTURE CAPITAL INVESTMENT CO LTD

155 Qingchun Road
16th F, Zhongcaifazhan Edifice
Hangzhou, China
Phone: 8657187247828
Fax: 8657187247828
Website: www.tobonvc.com

Type of Firm
Private Equity Firm

Project Preferences

Type of Financing Preferred:
Balanced

Geographical Preferences

International Preferences:
China

Additional Information
Year Founded: 2008
Current Activity Level : Actively seeking new investments

HANGZHOU TOUTOU SHIDAO INVESTMENT PARTNERSHIP ENTERPRISE LP

No. 138, Guyu Road
Huangzhou Yuquan Hotel
Hangzhou, China

Type of Firm
Investment Management Firm

Project Preferences

Type of Financing Preferred:
Balanced

Geographical Preferences

International Preferences:
China

Additional Information
Year Founded: 2015
Current Activity Level : Actively seeking new investments

HANGZHOU YUANZHI INVESTMENT MANAGEMENT CO LTD

Dream Town, Yuhang District
Building 3, Tianshi Village
Hangzhou, China
Phone: 8657188579775
Website: www.yuanzhivc.com

Type of Firm
Private Equity Firm

Project Preferences

Type of Financing Preferred:
Start-up Financing
Seed

Geographical Preferences

International Preferences:
China

Industry Preferences

In Internet Specific prefer:
Internet

Additional Information
Year Founded: 2013
Current Activity Level : Actively seeking new investments

HANGZHOU ZHEKE YOUYE INVESTMENT MANAGEMENT CO LTD

No. 207,Qigudeng, Gongshu
R113, 1F, Tower A
Hangzhou, China

Type of Firm
Investment Management Firm

Pratt's Guide to Private Equity & Venture Capital Sources

Project Preferences

Type of Financing Preferred:
Leveraged Buyout
Balanced

Geographical Preferences

International Preferences:
China

Industry Preferences

In Communications prefer:
Telecommunications

In Internet Specific prefer:
Ecommerce

In Medical/Health prefer:
Medical/Health

In Industrial/Energy prefer:
Energy Conservation Relat

In Business Serv. prefer:
Media

Additional Information

Year Founded: 2011
Current Activity Level : Actively seeking new investments

HANJU INVESTMENT CO LTD

14-15 Yoido-dong
Yongdungpo-gu
Seoul, South Korea
Phone: 822-783-7101
Fax: 822-783-7104

Management and Staff

Oh Jin Kim, President

Type of Firm

Private Equity Firm

Project Preferences

Type of Financing Preferred:
Balanced

Geographical Preferences

International Preferences:
Korea, South

Additional Information

Year Founded: 2000
Current Activity Level : Actively seeking new investments

HANKING INTERNATIONAL CO LTD

No.99 Huangpu Road
13F, Shanghaitan Intl Building
Shanghai, China
Website: www.hkfof.com

Type of Firm

Private Equity Advisor or Fund of Funds

Project Preferences

Type of Financing Preferred:
Fund of Funds

Industry Preferences

In Internet Specific prefer:
Internet

In Medical/Health prefer:
Medical/Health

In Consumer Related prefer:
Consumer
Education Related

In Industrial/Energy prefer:
Energy

In Financial Services prefer:
Financial Services

Additional Information

Year Founded: 2013
Current Activity Level : Actively seeking new investments

HANNOVER FINANZ GMBH

Guenther-Wagner-Allee 13
Hannover, Germany 30177
Phone: 49511280070
Fax: 495112800737
E-mail: mail@hannoverfinanz.de
Website: www.hannoverfinanz.de

Other Offices

Guenthergasse 3
Wien, Austria 1090
Phone: 43150580000
Fax: 431505800030

Management and Staff

Andreas Schober, Chief Executive Officer

Type of Firm

Private Equity Firm

Association Membership

German Venture Capital Association (BVK)
European Private Equity and Venture Capital Assoc.

Project Preferences

Type of Financing Preferred:
Leveraged Buyout
Later Stage
Management Buyouts

Size of Investments Considered:
Min Size of Investment Considered (000s): $3,847
Max Size of Investment Considered (000s): $64,119

Geographical Preferences

International Preferences:
Europe
Switzerland
Austria
Germany

Additional Information

Year Founded: 1979
Capital Under Management: $366,400,000
Current Activity Level : Actively seeking new investments

HANSE VENTURES BSJ GMBH

Am Sandtorkai 71-72
Hamburg, Germany 20457
Phone: 494030388660
E-mail: info@hanseventures.com
Website: www.hanseventures.com

Management and Staff

Bernd Kundrun, Co-Founder
Jochen Maass, Chief Executive Officer
Rolf Schmidt-Holtz, Co-Founder
Sarik Weber, Co-Founder

Type of Firm

Incubator/Development Program

Project Preferences

Type of Financing Preferred:
Seed
Startup

Geographical Preferences

International Preferences:
Germany

Industry Preferences

In Internet Specific prefer:
Internet
Ecommerce
Web Aggregration/Portals

Additional Information

Year Founded: 2010
Current Activity Level : Actively seeking new investments

HANSEATIC CAPITAL AS

Roosikrantsi 11
Tallinn, Estonia 10119
Phone: 3726676250
Fax: 3726676251
Website: www.hanseaticcapital.net

Other Offices
Marynarska Point
Postepu 15C
Warsaw, Poland 02676
Phone: 48223816072
Fax: 48223816073

Management and Staff
Kalmer Kikas, Managing Director

Type of Firm
Private Equity Firm

Association Membership
Estonian Private Equity and Venture Capital Assoc
Polish Venture Capital Association (PSIC/PPEA)
European Private Equity and Venture Capital Assoc.

Project Preferences

Type of Financing Preferred:
Leveraged Buyout
Mezzanine
Later Stage
Management Buyouts

Geographical Preferences

International Preferences:
Europe
Poland
Eastern Europe
Estonia
Latvia
Lithuania

Industry Preferences

In Transportation prefer:
Transportation

In Financial Services prefer:
Financial Services

In Business Serv. prefer:
Distribution

Additional Information
Year Founded: 2003
Current Activity Level : Actively seeking new investments

HANSEATISCHE VC GMBH

Am Brill 2-4
Bremen, Germany 28195
Phone: 491724203902
Fax: 49420379536
E-mail: info@hvc-bremen.de
Website: www.hvc-bremen.de

Management and Staff
Bernd Wilhelm, Chief Executive Officer

Type of Firm
Private Equity Firm

Project Preferences

Type of Financing Preferred:
Leveraged Buyout
Early Stage
Turnaround
Later Stage
Seed
Management Buyouts
Acquisition
Startup

Geographical Preferences

International Preferences:
Germany
All International

Industry Preferences

In Communications prefer:
Media and Entertainment

In Biotechnology prefer:
Biotechnology

Additional Information
Year Founded: 2002
Current Activity Level : Actively seeking new investments

HANWHA INVESTMENT CORP

60 Youido-dong, Yongdungpo-gu
150-763 Korea Life, 63 Bldg.
Seoul, South Korea 135846
Phone: 8225592699
Website: www.hwvc.co.kr

Management and Staff
Jun Tae Park, Chief Executive Officer

Type of Firm
Corporate PE/Venture

Association Membership
Korean Venture Capital Association (KVCA)

Project Preferences

Type of Financing Preferred:
Fund of Funds
Leveraged Buyout
Early Stage
Expansion
Generalist PE
Balanced
Turnaround
Later Stage
Seed
Management Buyouts
Acquisition
Joint Ventures
Startup
Distressed Debt
Fund of Funds of Second
Recapitalizations

Geographical Preferences

International Preferences:
Asia
Korea, South

Industry Preferences

In Communications prefer:
Wireless Communications
Entertainment

In Computer Hardware prefer:
Computer Graphics and Dig

In Internet Specific prefer:
Internet

In Computer Other prefer:
Computer Related

In Semiconductor/Electr prefer:
Electronics
Semiconductor

In Biotechnology prefer:
Biotechnology
Human Biotechnology
Agricultural/Animal Bio.

In Medical/Health prefer:
Medical/Health
Medical Diagnostics
Medical Products

In Consumer Related prefer:
Consumer
Education Related

In Industrial/Energy prefer:
Energy
Industrial Products
Robotics
Environmental Related

In Manufact. prefer:
Manufacturing

Additional Information
Year Founded: 2000
Capital Under Management: $118,700,000
Current Activity Level : Actively seeking new investments

HAO CAPITAL

No. 9 Dongdaqiao Road
Tower C, Parkview Green
Beijing, China 100020
Phone: 861064620909
Fax: 861064627001
E-mail: info@haocapital.net
Website: www.haocapital.net

Other Offices

20 Pedder Street
17th Floor, Wheelock House
Hong Kong, Hong Kong
Phone: 85236269214
Fax: 85236269213

Management and Staff

Anthony Hopson, Managing Director
Elaine Wong, Founder
Eric Zhang, Principal
Kenneth Yan, Principal
Sidney Tsang, Chief Financial Officer
Yang Sheng Liu, Founder
Zane Li, Partner

Type of Firm

Private Equity Firm

Association Membership

China Venture Capital Association
Hong Kong Venture Capital Association (HKVCA)

Project Preferences

Type of Financing Preferred:
Expansion
Later Stage

Size of Investments Considered:
Min Size of Investment Considered (000s): $12,691
Max Size of Investment Considered (000s): $47,592

Geographical Preferences

International Preferences:
China

Industry Preferences

In Medical/Health prefer:
Medical/Health

In Consumer Related prefer:
Consumer

In Industrial/Energy prefer:
Energy Conservation Relat
Industrial Products
Environmental Related

In Other prefer:
Environment Responsible

Additional Information

Year Founded: 2005
Capital Under Management: $499,500,000
Current Activity Level : Actively seeking new investments

HAPPY FARM LLP

ul. Lesi Ukrainky 14
Kyiv region
Schaslyve village, Ukraine
Phone: +38 044 379 34
Fax: +38 044 379 34
E-mail: info@happyfarm.com.ua
Website: www.happyfarm.com.ua

Type of Firm

Incubator/Development Program

Project Preferences

Type of Financing Preferred:
Startup

Geographical Preferences

International Preferences:
Italy
Belarus
China
Ukraine
Spain
Uzbekistan
Russia

Additional Information

Year Founded: 2009
Current Activity Level : Actively seeking new investments

HARBERT MANAGEMENT CORP

2100 Third Avenue North
Suite 600
Birmingham, AL USA 35203
Phone: 2059875500
Fax: 2059875568
Website: www.harbert.net

Other Offices

555 Madison Avenue
16th Floor
NEW YORK, NY USA 10022

44 Davies Street
Fifth Floor, Brookfield House
London, United Kingdom W1K 5JA
Phone: 44-207-408-4123
Fax: 44-207-408-4121

Suite 204, Second Floor
Pinar 5
Madrid, Spain 28006

29 rue de Bassano
Paris, France 75008

3715 Northside Parkway
Northcreek Building 300, Suite 150
ATLANTA, GA USA 30327

1210 East Cary Street
Suite 400
RICHMOND, VA USA 23219

Two Russell Street
Level 7
Melbourne, Australia 3000

618 Church Street
Suite 500
NASHVILLE, TN USA 37219

575 Market Street
Suite 2925
SAN FRANCISCO, CA USA 94105

Management and Staff

Brian Carney, Principal
Donald Beard, Vice President
Eric Desautel, Principal
G. Huw Davies, Vice President
Gregory Jordan, Senior Managing Director
Heather Barlow, Managing Director
J. Travis Pritchett, Vice President
James Flood, Vice President
Jeffrey Seidman, Vice President
Jeremy Steele, Vice President
Jerry Phillips, Vice President
John Harrison, Senior Managing Director
John Scott, Managing Director
Jon-Paul Momsen, Vice President
Kenneth Freeman, Managing Director
Lynette Horton, Managing Director
Melissa Babb, Senior Managing Director
Michael Luce, President & COO
Michael Larsen, Senior Managing Director
Michael White, Vice President
Neil Kennedy, Senior Managing Director
Peter Land, Principal
Richard Brereton, Managing Director
Robert Bourquin, Managing Director
Robert Crutchfield, Venture Partner
Roque Rotaeche, Principal
Scott O Donnell, Vice President
Thomas Roberts, Partner
Todd Jordan, Managing Director
Todd Nunnelley, Senior Managing Director
Tor Tveitane, Managing Director
Wayne Hunter, Managing Partner
William Brooke, Managing Partner
Winston Gillum, Vice President

Type of Firm

Private Equity Firm

Pratt's Guide to Private Equity & Venture Capital Sources

Association Membership
Australian Venture Capital Association (AVCAL)
Natl Assoc of Small Bus. Inv. Co (NASBIC)
National Venture Capital Association - USA (NVCA)

Project Preferences

Type of Financing Preferred:
Leveraged Buyout
Generalist PE
Turnaround
Opportunistic
Other
Special Situation
Distressed Debt

Geographical Preferences

United States Preferences:
Southeast
Alaska

International Preferences:
United Kingdom

Industry Preferences

In Biotechnology prefer:
Biotechnology

Additional Information
Name of Most Recent Fund: Harbert Power Fund V LLC
Most Recent Fund Was Raised: 02/07/2013
Year Founded: 1993
Capital Under Management: $110,000,000
Current Activity Level : Actively seeking new investments

HARBIN ISRAEL VENTURE CAPITAL MANAGEMENT CO LTD

c/o Harbin Venture Capital
6/F, Yangtze River Int'l Bldg.
Harbin, Heilongjiang, China
Phone: 86-451-82668766

Type of Firm
Private Equity Firm

Project Preferences

Type of Financing Preferred:
Balanced

Geographical Preferences

International Preferences:
China

Industry Preferences

In Biotechnology prefer:
Biotechnology

In Industrial/Energy prefer:
Machinery

In Manufact. prefer:
Manufacturing

In Agr/Forestr/Fish prefer:
Agriculture related

Additional Information
Year Founded: 2010
Capital Under Management: $73,243,000
Current Activity Level : Actively seeking new investments

HARBIN S&T VENTURE CAPITAL INVESTMENT CENTER

No. 86 Youyi Road
Daoli District
Harbin, China 150010
Phone: 8645184686551
Fax: 8645184686552

Type of Firm
Government Affiliated Program

Project Preferences

Type of Financing Preferred:
Early Stage
Seed

Geographical Preferences

International Preferences:
China

Industry Preferences

In Biotechnology prefer:
Biotechnology

In Medical/Health prefer:
Pharmaceuticals

In Industrial/Energy prefer:
Materials
Environmental Related

In Agr/Forestr/Fish prefer:
Agriculture related

Additional Information
Year Founded: 1998
Capital Under Management: $1,700,000
Current Activity Level : Actively seeking new investments

HARBIN VENTURE CAPITAL MANAGEMENT CO LTD

No.7 Shanghai Street, Daoli
22/F Block B Haishang Ginza
Shanghai, China

Phone: 8645182668766
E-mail: services@hrbvc.com.cn
Website: www.hrbvc.com.cn

Type of Firm
Government Affiliated Program

Project Preferences

Type of Financing Preferred:
Early Stage
Expansion
Balanced
Later Stage

Geographical Preferences

International Preferences:
Taiwan
China

Industry Preferences

In Biotechnology prefer:
Biotechnology

In Medical/Health prefer:
Pharmaceuticals

Additional Information
Year Founded: 2009
Capital Under Management: $62,804,000
Current Activity Level : Actively seeking new investments

HARBINGER CAPITAL PARTNERS

450 Park Avenue
30th Floor
New York, NY USA 10022
Phone: 2123395800
Website: www.harbingercapital.com

Type of Firm
Private Equity Firm

Project Preferences

Type of Financing Preferred:
Leveraged Buyout
Turnaround
Special Situation
Distressed Debt

Additional Information
Year Founded: 2001
Current Activity Level : Actively seeking new investments

HARBINGER VENTURE MANAGEMENT

Three Results Way
Cupertino, CA USA 95014
Phone: 4088613645

E-mail: USContact@harbingervc.com
Website: www.harbingervc.com

Other Offices
No. 187 Tiding Boulevard
7th Floor, Sec 2, Neihu
Taipei, Taiwan 114
Phone: 886-22657-9368

10th Floor, Tower D
No. 1068 Tian Shan West Road
Shanghai, China
Phone: 86-21-6120-9980

Management and Staff
Chih-Kai Cheng, Co-Founder
John Tzeng, Vice President
Moun-Rong Lin, Venture Partner
Ronald Han, Vice President
Ru Guang Bai, Vice President
T.C. Chou, President

Type of Firm
Private Equity Firm

Association Membership
Taiwan Venture Capital Association(TVCA)

Project Preferences

Role in Financing:
Will function either as deal originator or investor in deals created by others

Type of Financing Preferred:
Early Stage
Expansion
Balanced
Later Stage

Size of Investments Considered:
Min Size of Investment Considered (000s): $1,000
Max Size of Investment Considered (000s): $5,000

Geographical Preferences

United States Preferences:
North America

International Preferences:
Asia

Industry Preferences

In Communications prefer:
Communications and Media

In Computer Software prefer:
Software
Applications Software

In Internet Specific prefer:
Internet

In Computer Other prefer:
Computer Related

In Semiconductor/Electr prefer:
Semiconductor

In Consumer Related prefer:
Consumer

Additional Information
Year Founded: 2000
Capital Under Management: $150,000,000
Current Activity Level : Actively seeking new investments
Method of Compensation: Return on investment is of primary concern, do not charge fees

HARBINGER VENTURES LLC

2897 Mapleton Avenue
Suite 100
Boulder, CO USA 80304
Phone: 2035367323
Website: www.harbingerventuresllc.com

Type of Firm
Private Equity Firm

Project Preferences

Type of Financing Preferred:
Early Stage

Additional Information
Year Founded: 2016
Capital Under Management: $1,120,000
Current Activity Level : Actively seeking new investments

HARBOR BEACH CAPITAL LLC

401 East Las Olas Boulevard
Suite 1400
Fort Lauderdale, FL USA 33301
Phone: 9545948001
E-mail: info@harborbeachcapital.com

Type of Firm
Private Equity Firm

Project Preferences

Type of Financing Preferred:
Leveraged Buyout
Management Buyouts
Acquisition
Recapitalizations

Industry Preferences

In Medical/Health prefer:
Health Services

In Consumer Related prefer:
Consumer Products
Consumer Services

In Industrial/Energy prefer:
Energy
Environmental Related

In Business Serv. prefer:
Services

In Manufact. prefer:
Manufacturing

Additional Information
Year Founded: 2016
Current Activity Level : Actively seeking new investments

HARBOR LIGHT CAPITAL PARTNERS LLC

38 Central Square
Keene, NH USA 03431
Phone: 6033559954
Fax: 6033551158
E-mail: info@harborlightcp.com
Website: www.hlcp.com

Management and Staff
Darby Kopp, Principal
Richard Upton, General Partner
Todd Warden, Managing Partner

Type of Firm
Private Equity Firm

Project Preferences

Type of Financing Preferred:
Early Stage
Expansion

Size of Investments Considered:
Min Size of Investment Considered (000s): $1,000
Max Size of Investment Considered (000s): $5,000

Geographical Preferences

United States Preferences:
Northeast

Industry Preferences

In Medical/Health prefer:
Medical/Health
Health Services

Additional Information
Year Founded: 1911
Current Activity Level : Actively seeking new investments

HARBOR PACIFIC CAPITAL LLC

525 University Avenue
Suite 100
Palo Alto, CA USA 94301
Phone: 6503228088
Fax: 6503228092
E-mail: info@harborpac.com

Pratt's Guide to Private Equity & Venture Capital Sources

Management and Staff
Moon Kim, Venture Partner

Type of Firm
Private Equity Firm

Project Preferences

Type of Financing Preferred:
Early Stage
Expansion

Size of Investments Considered:
Min Size of Investment Considered (000s): $250
Max Size of Investment Considered (000s): $3,000

Geographical Preferences

United States Preferences:

International Preferences:
China
North Korea
Asia
Korea, South

Industry Preferences

In Communications prefer:
Wireless Communications
Media and Entertainment

In Computer Software prefer:
Software

In Internet Specific prefer:
E-Commerce Technology
Internet
Ecommerce

In Consumer Related prefer:
Consumer

In Industrial/Energy prefer:
Alternative Energy

In Business Serv. prefer:
Services

Additional Information
Name of Most Recent Fund: Harbor Pacific Capital Partners I, L.P.
Most Recent Fund Was Raised: 02/26/2010
Year Founded: 2010
Capital Under Management: $32,800,000
Current Activity Level : Actively seeking new investments

HARBOUR GROUP LTD

7701 Forsyth Boulevard
Suite 600
Saint Louis, MO USA 63105
Phone: 3147275550
Website: www.harbourgroup.com

Management and Staff
Gregory Fox, President
Jim Janning, President
Mike Santoni, Chief Financial Officer
Steven Fox, Managing Director

Type of Firm
Private Equity Firm

Project Preferences

Role in Financing:
Prefer role as deal originator but will also invest in deals created by others

Type of Financing Preferred:
Leveraged Buyout
Mezzanine
Acquisition

Geographical Preferences

United States Preferences:
North America

Industry Focus
(% based on actual investment)
Other Products   100.0%

Additional Information
Name of Most Recent Fund: Harbour Group Investments VI, L.P.
Most Recent Fund Was Raised: 07/03/2012
Year Founded: 1976
Capital Under Management: $706,500,000
Current Activity Level : Actively seeking new investments
Method of Compensation: Return on investment is of primary concern, do not charge fees

HARBOUR POINT CAPITAL

745 Fifth Avenue, Floor Seven
New York, NY USA 10151
E-mail: info@harbourpointcapital.com
Website: www.harbourpointcapital.com

Management and Staff
Bob Juneja, Co-Founder
Bret Bowerman, Co-Founder

Type of Firm
Private Equity Firm

Project Preferences

Type of Financing Preferred:
Leveraged Buyout
Management Buyouts
Acquisition

Industry Preferences

In Medical/Health prefer:
Medical/Health
Medical Diagnostics
Health Services

Additional Information
Year Founded: 2015
Current Activity Level : Actively seeking new investments

HARBOURVEST PARTNERS LLC

One Financial Center
44th Floor
Boston, MA USA 02111
Phone: 6173483707
Fax: 6173500305
E-mail: usinfo@harbourvest.com
Website: www.harbourvest.com

Other Offices

1 Jianguomenwai Avenue
5608,56/F China World Tower
Beijing, China
Phone: 861057068600
Fax: 861057068601

100 King West
Suite 5600 First Canadian Place
Toronto, Canada M5X 1C9
Phone: 4166428895
Fax: 4166448801

33 Jermyn Street
3rd Floor
London, United Kingdom SW1Y 6DN

Kyobo Building 15th Floor
1 Jongno
Seoul, South Korea 110-714
Phone: 82 2 2010 8916
Fax: 82 2 2010 8899

2-4-1 Marunouchi Building
26th Floor, Marunouchi
Tokyo, Japan 100-6326
Phone: 81-3-3284-4320
Fax: 81-3-3217 1077

Calle 113 No. 7 - 21
Torre A Oficina 1101
Bogot, Colombia
Phone: 57-1-658-5848

Anson Place Mill Court
La Charroterie St Peter Port
Guernsey, United Kingdom GY1 3JE
Phone: 44 1481 722 260

Management and Staff
Alexander Barker, Principal
Aris Hatch, Managing Director
Cory Cook, Vice President
David Atterbury, Managing Director
David Zug, Principal
Dustin Willard, Principal
Francisco Arboleda, Principal
George Anson, Managing Director

Gregory Ciesielski, Principal
James Kase, Managing Director
Jason Frigiani, Vice President
Kathleen Bacon, Managing Director
Kelli Finnegan, Vice President
Kelvin Yap, Managing Director
McComma Grayson, Principal
Nathan Bishop, Managing Director
Nhora Otalora, Principal
Ryan Jones, Principal
Ryan Gunther, Managing Director
Sandra Pasquale, Vice President
Senia Rapisarda, Managing Director
Shumin Gong, Principal
Simon Lund, Principal
Simon Jennings, Managing Director
W. Fran Peters, Principal

Type of Firm
Private Equity Firm

Association Membership
Hong Kong Venture Capital Association (HKVCA)
British Venture Capital Association (BVCA)
China Venture Capital Association
Emerging Markets Private Equity Association
German Venture Capital Association (BVK)
National Venture Capital Association – USA (NVCA)
Canadian Venture Capital Association
European Private Equity and Venture Capital Assoc.

Project Preferences

Role in Financing:
Prefer role as deal originator but will also invest in deals created by others

Type of Financing Preferred:
Fund of Funds
Leveraged Buyout
Expansion
Mezzanine
Generalist PE
Balanced
Turnaround
Acquisition
Special Situation
Distressed Debt
Fund of Funds of Second
Recapitalizations

Geographical Preferences

United States Preferences:

Canadian Preferences:
All Canada

International Preferences:
Latin America
Europe
Australia
Asia
Africa

Industry Focus
(% based on actual investment)

Other Products	24.4%
Computer Software and Services	19.2%
Internet Specific	15.7%
Communications and Media	12.3%
Consumer Related	7.5%
Medical/Health	7.0%
Industrial/Energy	6.1%
Computer Hardware	3.7%
Semiconductors/Other Elect.	2.7%
Biotechnology	1.3%

Additional Information
Name of Most Recent Fund: HarbourVest Partners 2013 Direct Fund, L.P.
Most Recent Fund Was Raised: 06/28/2012
Year Founded: 1982
Capital Under Management: $35,551,000,000
Current Activity Level : Actively seeking new investments
Method of Compensation: Return on invest. most important, but chg. closing fees, service fees, etc.

HARD 8 VENTURE CAPITAL

141 West Jackson Boulevard
Chicago, IL USA 60604
E-mail: seeding@hard8trading.com
Website: www.hard8trading.com/seeding.html

Type of Firm
Investment Management Firm

Project Preferences

Type of Financing Preferred:
Seed

Industry Preferences

In Financial Services prefer:
Financial Services
Investment Groups

Additional Information
Year Founded: 2013
Current Activity Level : Actively seeking new investments

HARDGAMMA VENTURES SP Z O O

c/o UBIK BC
Emilii Plater 53,Warsaw Fin Ct
Warsaw, Poland 00-113
E-mail: info@hardgamma.com

Management and Staff
Krzysztof Kowalczyk, Managing Partner
Piotr Sienkiewicz, Partner

Type of Firm
Private Equity Firm

Project Preferences

Type of Financing Preferred:
Early Stage
Seed
Startup

Geographical Preferences

International Preferences:
Central Europe
Poland
Eastern Europe

Industry Preferences

In Communications prefer:
Wireless Communications
Data Communications

In Computer Software prefer:
Data Processing
Software

In Internet Specific prefer:
E-Commerce Technology
Internet
Ecommerce
Web Aggregation/Portals

In Biotechnology prefer:
Biotechnology

Additional Information
Year Founded: 2009
Current Activity Level : Actively seeking new investments

HARDY CAPITAL PARTNERS

2390 1055 West Hastings
Penthouse
Vancouver, Canada V6E 2E9
Phone: 6042355550
Website: www.hardycapital.com

Type of Firm
Bank Affiliated

Project Preferences

Type of Financing Preferred:
Leveraged Buyout
Acquisition
Recapitalizations

Additional Information
Year Founded: 1969
Current Activity Level : Actively seeking new investments

HARGETT HUNTER CAPITAL PARTNERS

1122 Oberlin Road
Suite 200
Raleigh, NC USA 27605
Phone: 9196752204
Website: hargetthunter.com

Type of Firm
Investment Management Firm

Project Preferences

Type of Financing Preferred:
Leveraged Buyout
Acquisition
Recapitalizations

Industry Preferences

In Consumer Related prefer:
Food/Beverage

Additional Information
Year Founded: 2015
Current Activity Level : Actively seeking new investments

HARITH GENERAL PARTNERS (PTY) LTD

1 Chislehurston
34 Impala Road
Sandton, South Africa 2196
Phone: 27113844000
Website: www.harith.co.za

Type of Firm
Private Equity Firm

Project Preferences

Type of Financing Preferred:
Leveraged Buyout
Early Stage
Expansion
Later Stage
Seed
Acquisition
Startup

Geographical Preferences

International Preferences:
Africa

Industry Preferences

In Industrial/Energy prefer:
Energy

In Transportation prefer:
Transportation

Additional Information
Year Founded: 2009
Current Activity Level : Actively seeking new investments

HARKNESS CAPITAL PARTNERS LLC

444 Madison Avenue
23rd Floor
New York, NY USA 10022
Website: www.harknesscapital.com

Management and Staff
Ted Dardani, Partner

Type of Firm
Private Equity Firm

Project Preferences

Type of Financing Preferred:
Leveraged Buyout
Acquisition

Industry Preferences

In Business Serv. prefer:
Services

In Manufact. prefer:
Manufacturing

Additional Information
Year Founded: 2014
Current Activity Level : Actively seeking new investments

HARLYN CAPITAL

No.35, Dongzhimenwai Avenue
Dongcheng District
Beijing, China 100027
Phone: 861064240026
Fax: 861064240856
E-mail: gengxy@hlcapital.com.cn
Website: www.hlcapital.com.cn

Management and Staff
Yajun Ge, Managing Director

Type of Firm
Private Equity Firm

Project Preferences

Type of Financing Preferred:
Balanced

Geographical Preferences

International Preferences:
China

Industry Preferences

In Biotechnology prefer:
Biotechnology

In Medical/Health prefer:
Pharmaceuticals

In Consumer Related prefer:
Consumer Products

In Industrial/Energy prefer:
Energy

In Financial Services prefer:
Real Estate

In Agr/Forestr/Fish prefer:
Agriculture related

Additional Information
Year Founded: 2011
Current Activity Level : Actively seeking new investments

HARMONY PARTNERS

2200 Sand Hill Road, Suite 240
Menlo Park, CA USA 94025
Phone: 6506462835
E-mail: info@harmonyvp.com
Website: www.harmonyvp.com

Other Offices
655 Madison Avenue, 20th Floor
New York, NY USA 10065
Phone: 2129409670

Management and Staff
Daniel Lane, Principal
Gregory Eaton, General Partner
Mark Lotke, General Partner
Michael Chou, Partner

Type of Firm
Private Equity Firm

Project Preferences

Type of Financing Preferred:
Early Stage
Expansion
Balanced
Later Stage

Geographical Preferences

United States Preferences:

Industry Preferences

In Consumer Related prefer:
Consumer

Additional Information
Name of Most Recent Fund: Harmony Partners Fund I, L.P.
Most Recent Fund Was Raised: 03/14/2011

Year Founded: 2011
Capital Under Management: $210,500,000
Current Activity Level : Actively seeking new investments

HARPETH VENTURES LLC

3100 West End Avenue
Suite 710
Nashville, TN USA 37203
Phone: 6152969850
Fax: 6152162175

Type of Firm
Corporate PE/Venture

Project Preferences

Type of Financing Preferred:
Generalist PE

Additional Information
Year Founded: 1999
Current Activity Level : Actively seeking new investments

HARREN EQUITY PARTNERS

200 Garrett Street
The Gleason Building, Suite F
Charlottesville, VA USA 22902
Phone: 4342455800
Fax: 4342455802
Website: www.harrenequity.com

Other Offices
350 East Las Olas Boulevard
Suite 980
Fort Lauderdale, FL USA 33301
Phone: 9547459000
Fax: 9547459001

Management and Staff
Garrick Brown, Vice President
George Urban, Partner
Jonathan Earnhardt, Partner
Lee Monahan, Partner
Richard Grosshandler, Vice President

Type of Firm
Private Equity Firm

Project Preferences

Type of Financing Preferred:
Leveraged Buyout
Expansion
Turnaround
Management Buyouts
Acquisition
Distressed Debt
Recapitalizations

Geographical Preferences

United States Preferences:
North America

Industry Preferences

In Medical/Health prefer:
Medical Products
Health Services

In Consumer Related prefer:
Retail
Food/Beverage
Consumer Products
Other Restaurants

In Industrial/Energy prefer:
Energy
Industrial Products
Materials
Machinery
Environmental Related

In Transportation prefer:
Aerospace

In Business Serv. prefer:
Services
Distribution

In Manufact. prefer:
Manufacturing

In Utilities prefer:
Utilities

Additional Information
Name of Most Recent Fund: Harren Investors III, L.P.
Most Recent Fund Was Raised: 07/16/2013
Year Founded: 2000
Capital Under Management: $275,000,000
Current Activity Level : Actively seeking new investments

HARRISON METAL CAPITAL

291 Alma Street
Palo Alto, CA USA 94301

Type of Firm
Private Equity Firm

Project Preferences

Type of Financing Preferred:
Early Stage

Geographical Preferences

United States Preferences:
All U.S.

Industry Preferences

In Communications prefer:
Communications and Media

In Computer Software prefer:
Software

In Internet Specific prefer:
Internet

Additional Information
Year Founded: 2006
Capital Under Management: $68,000,000
Current Activity Level : Actively seeking new investments

HARTENBERG CAPITAL SRO

Na Prikope 22
Prague, Czech Republic 11000
Phone: 420245501180
Fax: 420221451751
Website: www.hartenbergcapital.com

Type of Firm
Private Equity Firm

Project Preferences

Type of Financing Preferred:
Leveraged Buyout
Acquisition

Geographical Preferences

International Preferences:
Central Europe

Industry Preferences

In Consumer Related prefer:
Retail
Food/Beverage
Consumer Services

In Utilities prefer:
Utilities

Additional Information
Year Founded: 2013
Capital Under Management: $264,375,000
Current Activity Level : Actively seeking new investments

HARVARD MANAGEMENT COMPANY INC

600 Atlantic Avenue
Boston, MA USA 02210
Phone: 6175234400
E-mail: general@hmc.harvard.edu
Website: www.hmc.harvard.edu

Management and Staff
Andrew Wiltshire, Managing Director
Jennifer Pline, Managing Director
Kathryn Murtagh, Managing Director
Neil Mason, Managing Director
Stephen Blyth, Managing Director

Type of Firm
Endowment, Foundation or Pension Fund

Additional Information
Year Founded: 1974
Current Activity Level : Actively seeking new investments

HARVARD SCHOOL OF ENGINEERING AND APPLIED SCIENCES

33 Oxford St, Maxwell-Dworkin
Cambridge, MA USA 02138
E-mail: hello@experimentfund.com
Website: www.experimentfund.com

Management and Staff
Harry Dumay, Chief Financial Officer

Type of Firm
University Program

Project Preferences

Type of Financing Preferred:
Seed
Startup

Geographical Preferences

United States Preferences:
Massachusetts

Additional Information
Year Founded: 2011
Capital Under Management: $100,000,000
Current Activity Level : Actively seeking new investments

HARVEST PARTNERS LP

280 Park Avenue
25th Floor
New York, NY USA 10017
Phone: 2125996300
Fax: 2128120100
Website: www.harvestpartners.com

Management and Staff
Andrew Schoenthal, Managing Director
Christopher Whalen, Managing Director
David Schwartz, Vice President
Debra Bricker, Chief Financial Officer
Harvey Mallement, Co-Founder
Harvey Wertheim, Co-Founder
Ira Kleinman, Senior Managing Director
Jay Wilkins, Senior Managing Director
Joseph Hegenbart, Managing Director
Michael DeFlorio, Senior Managing Director
Paige Daly, Principal
Simon Roberts, Managing Director
Stephen Eisenstein, Senior Managing Director
Stephen Carlson, Vice President
Thomas Arenz, Senior Managing Director

Type of Firm
Private Equity Firm

Project Preferences

Role in Financing:
Will function either as deal originator or investor in deals created by others

Type of Financing Preferred:
Leveraged Buyout
Expansion
Management Buyouts
Acquisition
Recapitalizations

Geographical Preferences

United States Preferences:
North America

Canadian Preferences:
All Canada

Industry Focus
(% based on actual investment)
Other Products	69.3%
Consumer Related	21.0%
Internet Specific	4.1%
Industrial/Energy	3.9%
Medical/Health	1.7%

Additional Information
Name of Most Recent Fund: Harvest Partners VI, L.P.
Most Recent Fund Was Raised: 06/01/2011
Year Founded: 1981
Capital Under Management: $1,400,000,000
Current Activity Level : Actively seeking new investments
Method of Compensation: Return on invest. most important, but chg. closing fees, service fees, etc.

HARWELL CAPITAL SPC

89 Nexus Way Camana Bay
Grand Cayman, Cayman Islands KY1-9007
E-mail: info@harwellcapital.com
Website: harwellcapital.com

Management and Staff
Rupert Gladitz, Chief Executive Officer

Type of Firm
Private Equity Firm

Project Preferences

Type of Financing Preferred:
Early Stage
Expansion
Balanced
Later Stage
Startup

Geographical Preferences

International Preferences:
United Kingdom

Additional Information
Year Founded: 2007
Current Activity Level : Actively seeking new investments

HARWOOD CAPITAL LLP

6, Stratton Street
Mayfair
London, United Kingdom W1J8LD
Phone: 442076403200
Fax: 442076403299
E-mail: privateequity@harwoodcapital.co.uk
Website: www.harwoodcapital.co.uk

Management and Staff
Faye Foster, Partner
James Agnew, Partner
Jeremy Brade, Partner
Keith Jelley, Partner
Timothy Sturm, Partner

Type of Firm
Investment Management Firm

Project Preferences

Type of Financing Preferred:
Leveraged Buyout
Management Buyouts
Acquisition

Geographical Preferences

International Preferences:
United Kingdom
Europe

Additional Information
Year Founded: 2004
Capital Under Management: $1,454,400,000
Current Activity Level : Actively seeking new investments

HASPA BETEILIGUNGS-GESELLSCHAFT FUER DEN MITTELSTAND MBH

Herrengraben 1
Hamburg, Germany 20459
Phone: 494082220950
Fax: 4940822209595
E-mail: info@haspa-bgm.de
Website: www.haspa-bgm.de

Type of Firm
Bank Affiliated

Association Membership
German Venture Capital Association (BVK)

Project Preferences

Type of Financing Preferred:
Leveraged Buyout
Early Stage
Mezzanine
Balanced
Turnaround
Later Stage
Management Buyouts
Acquisition
Startup

Geographical Preferences

International Preferences:
Germany

Industry Preferences

In Consumer Related prefer:
Consumer

In Industrial/Energy prefer:
Industrial Products

In Business Serv. prefer:
Media

Additional Information
Year Founded: 1998
Capital Under Management: $13,500,000
Current Activity Level : Actively seeking new investments

HASSO PLATTNER VENTURES MANAGEMENT GMBH

Rudolf-Breitscheid-Strasse 187
Potsdam, Germany 14482
Phone: 4933197992101
Fax: 4933197992130
E-mail: info@hp-ventures.com
Website: www.hp-ventures.com

Other Offices
2 Fir Street
Black River Park
Cape Town, South Africa
Phone: 27214861060

Management and Staff
Hasso Plattner, Founder
Rouven Westphal, Partner
Yaron Valler, Partner

Type of Firm
Private Equity Firm

Project Preferences

Type of Financing Preferred:
Early Stage
Later Stage

Size of Investments Considered:
Min Size of Investment Considered (000s): $695
Max Size of Investment Considered (000s): $13,897

Geographical Preferences

International Preferences:
Europe
Switzerland
Austria
Israel
South Africa
Germany

Industry Preferences

In Computer Software prefer:
Software

In Internet Specific prefer:
Internet
Web Aggregation/Portals

In Industrial/Energy prefer:
Alternative Energy

In Other prefer:
Environment Responsible

Additional Information
Name of Most Recent Fund: Hasso Plattner Ventures I
Most Recent Fund Was Raised: 06/13/2005
Year Founded: 2005
Current Activity Level : Actively seeking new investments

HASTINGS EQUITY PARTNERS LLC

250 First Avenue, Suite 100
Needham, MA USA 02494
Phone: 7812098801
Fax: 7812098802
Website: www.hastingsequity.com

Other Offices
4203 Montrose Boulevard
Suite 350
HOUSTON, TX USA 77006
Phone: 2814074845

179 Bear Hill Road
WALTHAM, MA USA 02451
Phone: 7812098801

600 Travis Street
2800 JPMorgan Chase Tower
HOUSTON, TX USA 77002
Phone: 7132261207

Management and Staff
Bruce MacRae, Managing Director
Grant Reckhow, Vice President
Katrina Starr-Frederick, Chief Financial Officer
Marco Rodriguez, Vice President
Ted Patton, Managing Director

Type of Firm
Private Equity Firm

Project Preferences

Type of Financing Preferred:
Leveraged Buyout
Other
Management Buyouts
Acquisition
Recapitalizations

Size of Investments Considered:
Min Size of Investment Considered (000s): $5,000
Max Size of Investment Considered (000s): $20,000

Geographical Preferences

United States Preferences:
North America

Industry Preferences

In Industrial/Energy prefer:
Energy
Oil and Gas Exploration
Oil & Gas Drilling,Explor

Additional Information
Year Founded: 2002
Capital Under Management: $172,000,000
Current Activity Level : Actively seeking new investments

HASTINGS PRIVATE EQUITY FUND IIA PTY LTD

35 Collins Street
Level 27
Melbourne, Australia 3000
Phone: 61386503600
Fax: 61386503701
E-mail: investor_relations@hfm.com.au
Website: www.hfm.com.au

Other Offices
575 Fifth Avenue
39th Floor
New York, NY USA 10017
Phone: 2126812524

23 Camomile Street
Camomile Court
London, United Kingdom EC3A 7LL
Phone: 442073376720
Fax: 442079292502

55 Market Street
Level 10
Sydney, Australia 2000
Phone: 61292878700
Fax: 61292878801

Management and Staff

Andrew Day, Chief Executive Officer

Type of Firm

Investment Management Firm

Project Preferences

Role in Financing:
Will function either as deal originator or investor in deals created by others

Type of Financing Preferred:
Leveraged Buyout
Expansion
Later Stage
Management Buyouts
Acquisition

Geographical Preferences

International Preferences:
Australia

Additional Information

Name of Most Recent Fund: Hastings Private Equity Fund 1
Most Recent Fund Was Raised: 02/09/2001
Year Founded: 1993
Capital Under Management: $200,600,000
Current Activity Level : Actively seeking new investments
Method of Compensation: Return on investment is of primary concern, do not charge fees

HAT HOLDING ALL TOGETHER SPA

Foro Buonaparte 12
Milan, Italy 20121
Phone: 390289286200
Fax: 39289286209
E-mail: info@hat-holding.it
Website: www.hat-holding.it

Other Offices

Via Crispi 26
Naples, Italy
Phone: 39-81-7613-235
Fax: 39-81-7612-227

Corso Garibaldi 4
Padova, Italy 35122
Phone: 39-49-876-6670
Fax: 39-49-876-6671

Management and Staff

Antonio Attanasio, President
Massimo Esposito, Managing Director

Type of Firm

Private Equity Firm

Association Membership

Italian Venture Capital Association (AIFI)

Project Preferences

Type of Financing Preferred:
Expansion
Seed
Startup

Geographical Preferences

International Preferences:
Italy

Industry Preferences

In Communications prefer:
Media and Entertainment

In Medical/Health prefer:
Medical Diagnostics

In Industrial/Energy prefer:
Energy
Industrial Products

In Transportation prefer:
Transportation
Aerospace

In Financial Services prefer:
Insurance
Real Estate

In Business Serv. prefer:
Consulting Services

In Manufact. prefer:
Publishing

Additional Information

Year Founded: 2008
Current Activity Level : Actively seeking new investments

HATCHD INC

191 Salcedo Street
Unit A-51,5/F Zeta II Building
Makati City, Philippines 1229
E-mail: info@hatchddigital.com
Website: www.hatchddigital.com

Type of Firm

Incubator/Development Program

Project Preferences

Type of Financing Preferred:
Seed

Geographical Preferences

International Preferences:
Philippines

Additional Information

Year Founded: 2010
Current Activity Level : Actively seeking new investments

HATCHER PTE LTD

Ayer Rajah Crescent
Block 71 Suite 01-12
Singapore, Singapore 139951
Website: hatcher.com

Type of Firm

Private Equity Firm

Project Preferences

Type of Financing Preferred:
Early Stage
Later Stage
Seed
Startup

Geographical Preferences

International Preferences:
Latin America
Asia

Industry Preferences

In Financial Services prefer:
Financial Services

Additional Information

Year Founded: 2015
Current Activity Level : Actively seeking new investments

HATTERAS VENTURE PARTNERS

280 South Mangum Street
Suite 350
Durham, NC USA 27701
Phone: 9194840730
Fax: 9194840364
Website: www.hatterasvp.com

Management and Staff

Christy Shaffer, Venture Partner
Clay Thorp, General Partner
Dana Fowlkes, Venture Partner
Douglas Reed, General Partner
Fred Goldwater, Venture Partner
John Crumpler, General Partner
Kenneth Lee, General Partner
Myla Lai-Goldman, Venture Partner
Robert Morff, Venture Partner
Robert Ingram, General Partner

Type of Firm

Private Equity Firm

Association Membership

Natl Assoc of Small Bus. Inv. Co (NASBIC)

Project Preferences

Role in Financing:
Will function either as deal originator or investor in deals created by others

Type of Financing Preferred:
Early Stage
Later Stage
Seed
Startup

Size of Investments Considered:
Min Size of Investment Considered (000s): $500
Max Size of Investment Considered (000s): $4,000

Geographical Preferences

United States Preferences:
Mid Atlantic
Southeast
North Carolina

Industry Preferences

In Biotechnology prefer:
Biotechnology
Human Biotechnology

In Medical/Health prefer:
Medical/Health
Medical Diagnostics
Medical Products
Pharmaceuticals

Additional Information

Name of Most Recent Fund: Hatteras Venture Partners IV, L.P.
Most Recent Fund Was Raised: 08/10/2011
Year Founded: 2000
Capital Under Management: $250,000,000
Current Activity Level : Actively seeking new investments

HATTERY

414 Brannan Street
San Francisco, CA USA 94107
Phone: 1415230018
E-mail: info@hattery.com
Website: hattery.com

Other Offices

Ten East 21st Street
Fourth Floor
New York, NY USA 10010

Type of Firm

Private Equity Firm

Project Preferences

Type of Financing Preferred:
Early Stage
Seed

Geographical Preferences

United States Preferences:
California

Industry Preferences

In Computer Software prefer:
Software
Applications Software

Additional Information

Year Founded: 1969
Current Activity Level : Actively seeking new investments

HATTINGTON INVESTMENT PARTNERS LLP

22-23 Old Burlington Street
Fourth Floor
London, United Kingdom W1S 2JJ
Phone: 442030068440
Website: www.hattington.com

Type of Firm

Private Equity Firm

Project Preferences

Type of Financing Preferred:
Leveraged Buyout
Management Buyouts
Acquisition
Recapitalizations

Geographical Preferences

International Preferences:
Ireland
United Kingdom
Europe

Industry Preferences

In Consumer Related prefer:
Consumer
Retail

In Industrial/Energy prefer:
Energy
Industrial Products

Additional Information

Year Founded: 2014
Current Activity Level : Actively seeking new investments

HAUSER PRIVATE EQUITY

8260 Northcreek Drive
Suite 200
Cincinnati, OH USA 45236
Phone: 5139367372
Website: www.hauserprivateequity.com

Other Offices

801 Pennsylvania Avenue NW
Suite 610
Washington, DC USA 20004
Phone: 2022361089

233 Wilshire Boulevard
Suite 900
Santa Monica, CA USA 90401
Phone: 3103939147

Management and Staff

Daniel Heidenreich, Principal
Janna Laudato, Managing Director

Type of Firm

Private Equity Firm

Project Preferences

Type of Financing Preferred:
Fund of Funds
Leveraged Buyout

Geographical Preferences

United States Preferences:
North America

Additional Information

Name of Most Recent Fund: Hauser Private Equity Core Fund II LLC
Most Recent Fund Was Raised: 10/04/2013
Year Founded: 1969
Capital Under Management: $212,550,000
Current Activity Level : Actively seeking new investments

HAVENVEST PRIVATE EQUITY MIDDLE EAST LTD

Office 4, Level 5
Gate Precinct 3, DIFC
Dubai, Utd. Arab Em.
Phone: 97144449300
Fax: 97144449333
E-mail: havenvest@hpeme.com
Website: www.havenvest.com

Other Offices

8 Canada Square
London, United Kingdom E14 5HQ

Management and Staff

Niall Booker, Chief Executive Officer

Type of Firm

Private Equity Firm

Project Preferences

Type of Financing Preferred:
Leveraged Buyout
Early Stage
Expansion
Unknown
Generalist PE
Later Stage
Management Buyouts
Acquisition

Geographical Preferences

International Preferences:
Middle East
Asia

Industry Preferences

In Consumer Related prefer:
Consumer
Retail

In Industrial/Energy prefer:
Energy
Industrial Products

In Financial Services prefer:
Financial Services

In Manufact. prefer:
Manufacturing

Additional Information
Year Founded: 2001
Current Activity Level : Actively seeking new investments

HAWK CAPITAL PARTNERS LP

111 Presidential Boulevard
Suite 201
Bala Cynwyd, PA USA 19004
Phone: 6106672600
Fax: 6106672604
Website: hawkcapital.com

Management and Staff
Jim Mirage, Co-Founder
Michael Hagan, Co-Founder

Type of Firm
Private Equity Firm

Project Preferences

Type of Financing Preferred:
Leveraged Buyout

Geographical Preferences

United States Preferences:
Mid Atlantic
Southeast

Industry Preferences

In Internet Specific prefer:
Internet

In Consumer Related prefer:
Food/Beverage
Consumer Products
Consumer Services

In Industrial/Energy prefer:
Energy

In Financial Services prefer:
Financial Services

In Business Serv. prefer:
Services
Distribution

In Manufact. prefer:
Manufacturing

Additional Information
Year Founded: 1969
Current Activity Level : Actively seeking new investments

HAWKESBRIDGE CAPITAL

23 Hunter Street
Level 14, Currency House
Sydney, Australia 2000
Phone: 61292337200
Fax: 61292337544
E-mail: contact@hawkesbridge.com.au
Website: www.hawkesbridge.com.au

Other Offices
10 Airlie Street
Claremont
Perth, Australia 6010
Phone: 618-9384-3963
Fax: 618-9284-4915

Management and Staff
David Plumridge, Managing Partner
Joshua Rowe, Managing Partner
Mark Darling, Partner
Mark Lewis, Partner

Type of Firm
Private Equity Firm

Association Membership
Australian Venture Capital Association (AVCAL)

Project Preferences

Role in Financing:
Will function either as deal originator or investor in deals created by others

Type of Financing Preferred:
Leveraged Buyout
Expansion
Generalist PE
Later Stage
Management Buyouts

Size of Investments Considered:
Min Size of Investment Considered (000s): $5,211
Max Size of Investment Considered (000s): $20,842

Geographical Preferences

International Preferences:
Australia
New Zealand

Industry Preferences

In Medical/Health prefer:
Health Services

In Consumer Related prefer:
Consumer

In Industrial/Energy prefer:
Industrial Products

Additional Information
Name of Most Recent Fund: Hawkesbridge Debt Fund 1
Most Recent Fund Was Raised: 03/31/2011
Year Founded: 2002
Capital Under Management: $238,600,000
Current Activity Level : Actively seeking new investments
Method of Compensation: Return on investment is of primary concern, do not charge fees

HAWTHORN EQUITY PARTNERS

40 King Street West
Suite 4900, Scotia Plaza
Toronto, Canada M5H 3Y2
Phone: 416-603-6000
Fax: 416-603-3099
E-mail: investor.relations@genuitycm.com
Website: www.hawthornep.com

Other Offices
Bentall Tower Five
1068-550 Burrard Street
Vancouver, Canada V6C 2B5
Phone: 604-331-1444
Fax: 604-331-1446

1800 McGill College Avenue
Suite 3000
Montreal, Canada H3A 3J6
Phone: 514-281-3250
Fax: 514-281-3022

717 Fifth Avenue
Suite 1403
NEW YORK, NY USA 10022
Phone: 212-644-0001
Fax: 212-644-1341

1700 Stock Exchange Tower
300 Fifth Avenue SouthWest
Calgary, Canada T2P 3C4
Phone: 403-266-3400
Fax: 403-266-1755

One Federal Street
25th Floor
BOSTON, MA USA 02110
Phone: 617-338-1008
Fax: 617-338-1016

Type of Firm
Private Equity Firm

Project Preferences

Type of Financing Preferred:
Leveraged Buyout
Expansion
Generalist PE
Strategic Alliances
Acquisition
Joint Ventures
Recapitalizations

Geographical Preferences

United States Preferences:
North America

Canadian Preferences:
All Canada

Industry Preferences

In Consumer Related prefer:
Consumer

In Business Serv. prefer:
Services
Media

Additional Information
Year Founded: 2005
Current Activity Level : Actively seeking new investments

HAWTHORNE GROUP

381 Mansfield Avenue
Pittsburgh, PA USA 15220
Phone: 4129287700

Management and Staff
Henry Posner, Co-Founder
Thomas Wright, Co-Founder

Type of Firm
Private Equity Firm

Project Preferences

Type of Financing Preferred:
Leveraged Buyout

Additional Information
Year Founded: 1987
Current Activity Level : Actively seeking new investments

HAYNES AND BOONE LLC

2505 North Plano Road
Suite 4000
Richardson, TX USA 75082
Phone: 9727396900
Fax: 9726807551
Website: www.haynesboone.com

Management and Staff
Aimee Minick Furness, Partner
Albert Tan, Partner
Alberto De la Pena, Partner
Amy Christine Moss, Partner
Andrew Ehmke, Partner
Ann Richardson Knox, Partner
Anne Johnson, Partner
Anthony Newton, Partner
Antonio Diez de Bonilla Martinez, Partner
Antonio Franck, Partner
Ariel Ramos, Partner
Arthur Carter, Partner
Arthur Cohen, Partner
Arthur Howard, Partner
Arthur Nathan, Partner
Barry McNeil, Partner
Bart Greenberg, Partner
Ben Mesches, Partner
Bernard Clark, Partner
Bill Kleinman, Partner
Bill Morrison, Partner
Brad Lowry, Partner
Bradley Olson, Partner
Bradley Richards, Partner
Brandon Jones, Partner
Brian Barnard, Partner
Bruce Newsome, Partner
Bruce Merwin, Partner
Bruce McNamara, Partner
C. Kyle Musgrove, Partner
Carrie Huff, Partner
Charles Beckham, Partner
Charles Plenge, Partner
Cheryl Rosenberg, Partner
Daniel Gold, Partner
Darrel Rice, Partner
David O Dell, Partner
David Taubenfeld, Partner
David Oden, Partner
David McCombs, Partner
David Fields, Partner
David Fleischer, Partner
David Bell, Partner
David Harper, Partner
Debbie McComas, Partner
Deborah Coldwell, Partner
Debra Gatison Hatter, Partner
Dennis Cassell, Partner
Diana Liebmann, Partner
Donald Jackson, Partner
Doug Edwards, Partner
Dustin Johnson, Partner
Edward Kwok, Partner
Ellen Gibson McGinnis, Partner
Eric Terry, Partner
Erika Bright Blomquist, Partner
Ernest Martin, Partner
Felicity Fowler, Partner
Garrett Devries, Partner
Gary Edwards, Partner
George Bramblett, Partner
Gilbert Porter, Partner
Greg Michelson, Partner
Gregg Miller, Partner
Greta Cowart, Partner
Henry Flores, Partner
Herbert Glaser, Partner
Ian Peck, Partner
J. Andrew Lowes, Partner
J. Kent Friedman, Partner
Jan Gilbert, Partner
Jeff Dorrill, Partner
Jeff Nichols, Partner
Jeff Dinerstein, Partner
Jeff Civins, Partner
Jeffrey Becker, Partner
Jennifer Lantz, Partner
Jeremy Kernodle, Partner
Jesse Gelsomini, Partner
John Penn, Partner
John Eldridge, Partner
John McGowan, Partner
John Hintz, Partner
John Collins, Partner
John Turner, Partner
Jonathan Hallman, Partner
Jorge Labastida, Partner
Joyce Mazero, Partner
Judith Elkin, Partner
Karen Denney, Partner
Karen Precella, Partner
Karen Nelson, Partner
Kathleen Beasley, Partner
Kathryn Garner, Partner
Kenneth Rogers, Partner
Kenneth Rubinstein, Partner
Kenneth Hurwitz, Partner
Kenneth Bezozo, Partner
Kenneth Parker, Partner
Kenneth Friedman, Partner
Kenneth Broughton, Partner
Kenneth Herz, Partner
Kenric Kattner, Partner
Kent Rutter, Partner
Kimberley Chen Nobles, Partner
Kit Addleman, Partner
Lamont Jefferson, Partner
Larry Pascal, Partner
Laura O Donnell, Partner
Laurie Grant Lang, Partner

Pratt's Guide to Private Equity & Venture Capital Sources

Lawrence Gaydos, Partner
Lawrence Mittman, Partner
Lenard Parkins, Partner
Luis Moreno Trevino, Partner
Lynne Liberato, Partner
Madelyn Calabrese, Partner
Mark Trachtenberg, Partner
Mark Tidwell, Partner
Mark Erickson, Partner
Mark Mullin, Partner
Marty Brimmage, Partner
Mary Simmons Mendoza, Partner
Matt Holley, Partner
Matthew Thomas Deffebach, Partner
Melissa Goodman, Partner
Michael Boone, Co-Founder
Michael Hood, Partner
Michael Powell, Partner
Michael Mazzone, Partner
Nicholas Even, Partner
Nina Cortell, Partner
Patrick Hughes, Partner
Patrick Keating, Partner
Paul Amiel, Partner
Paul Dickerson, Partner
Pavel Pogodin, Partner
Philip Hampton, Partner
Philip Philbin, Partner
Purvi Patel, Partner
Rafael Anchia, Partner
Ralph Arpajian, Partner
Randall Brown, Partner
Randall Colson, Partner
Ricardo Garcia-Moreno, Partner
Richard Anigian, Partner
Richard Martin, Partner
Richard Fijolek, Partner
Richard Rochford, Partner
Richard Ripley, Partner
Robert Lauer, Partner
Robert Albergotti, Partner
Robert Reetz, Partner
Robert Ladd, Partner
Robin Phelan, Partner
Ronald Breaux, Partner
Russell Emerson, Partner
Sarah Teachout, Partner
Sashe Dimitroff, Partner
Scott Night, Partner
Scott Everett, Partner
Scott Drablos, Partner
Sergei Lomako, Partner
Stacy Brainin, Partner
Stan Perry, Partner
Stephen Pezanosky, Partner
Steve Levitan, Partner
Steve Allison, Partner
Steven Jenkins, Partner
Steven Buxbaum, Partner
Steven Koch, Partner
Stuart Mass, Partner
Sue Murphy, Partner
Terry Conner, Managing Partner
Thad Behrens, Partner
Theresa Einhorn, Partner

Thomas Cordell, Partner
Thomas Kurth, Partner
Timothy Powers, Partner
Tom Chen, Partner
Tom Harris, Partner
Trace Ryan Blair, Partner
Trevor Hoffmann, Partner
Trey Monsour, Partner
Vicki Martin-Odette, Partner
Werner Powers, Partner
William Nash, Partner
William Buckley, Partner
William Ratliff, Partner
William Nelson, Partner
Yasser Madriz, Partner

Type of Firm
Service Provider

Project Preferences

Type of Financing Preferred:
Balanced

Industry Preferences

In Semiconductor/Electr prefer:
Electronics

In Consumer Related prefer:
Entertainment and Leisure
Food/Beverage

In Business Serv. prefer:
Distribution

In Manufact. prefer:
Manufacturing

Additional Information
Year Founded: 1970
Current Activity Level : Actively seeking new investments

HAYSTACK

737 Harvard Avenue
Menlo Park, CA USA 94025
Phone: 4158685024
Website: blog.semilshah.com/haystack

Type of Firm
Private Equity Firm

Project Preferences

Type of Financing Preferred:
Early Stage

Additional Information
Year Founded: 2013
Current Activity Level : Actively seeking new investments

HAYSTACK PARTNERS

515 Madison Avenue
Suite 1910
New York, NY USA 10022
Phone: 6468834777
E-mail: info@haystackpartners.com
Website: www.haystackpartners.com

Type of Firm
Private Equity Firm

Project Preferences

Type of Financing Preferred:
Early Stage
Seed

Additional Information
Year Founded: 2015
Capital Under Management: $38,000,000
Current Activity Level : Actively seeking new investments

HBC INVESTMENTS

3963 Maple Avenue
Suite 450, 3-963 Maple Ave.
Dallas, TX USA 75219
Phone: 2144514640
Website: www.hbcinvestments.com

Type of Firm
Private Equity Firm

Project Preferences

Type of Financing Preferred:
Leveraged Buyout
Expansion
Mezzanine
Generalist PE
Acquisition
Recapitalizations

Size of Investments Considered:
Min Size of Investment Considered (000s): $10,000
Max Size of Investment Considered (000s): $50,000

Geographical Preferences

United States Preferences:

Canadian Preferences:
All Canada

Industry Preferences

In Consumer Related prefer:
Retail
Consumer Products

In Industrial/Energy prefer:
Energy

In Business Serv. prefer:
Media

In Manufact. prefer:
Manufacturing

Additional Information
Year Founded: 2012
Current Activity Level : Actively seeking new investments

HBM HEALTHCARE INVESTMENTS AG

Bundesplatz 1
Zug, Switzerland 6300
Phone: 41438887171
Fax: 41438887172
E-mail: info@hbmbioventures.com
Website: www.hbmhealthcare.com

Other Offices
2454 West Bay Road
Centennial Towers, 3rd Floor
Grand Cayman, Cayman Islands
Phone: 345-946-8002
Fax: 345-946-8003

Management and Staff
Andreas Wicki, Chief Executive Officer
Erwin Troxler, Chief Financial Officer
Jean-Marc LeSieur, Chairman & Managing Director
John Arnold, Chairman & Managing Director

Type of Firm
Private Equity Firm

Association Membership
Swiss Venture Capital Association (SECA)
European Private Equity and Venture Capital Assoc.

Project Preferences

Type of Financing Preferred:
Early Stage
Later Stage

Geographical Preferences

United States Preferences:
All U.S.

International Preferences:
Europe
Asia

Industry Preferences

In Biotechnology prefer:
Biotechnology

In Medical/Health prefer:
Medical/Health
Medical Diagnostics
Medical Products
Pharmaceuticals

Additional Information
Name of Most Recent Fund: HBM BioCapital II
Most Recent Fund Was Raised: 02/13/2012
Year Founded: 2001
Capital Under Management: $1,100,000,000
Current Activity Level : Actively seeking new investments

HBM HOLDINGS CO

101 South Hanley Road
Suite 1050
Saint Louis, MO USA 63105
E-mail: info@hbmholdings.com
Website: hbmholdings.com

Management and Staff
Daniel Wright, Vice President
Michael Chill, Vice President
Michael DeCola, Chief Executive Officer

Type of Firm
Private Equity Firm

Project Preferences

Type of Financing Preferred:
Leveraged Buyout
Acquisition

Geographical Preferences

United States Preferences:
North America

Industry Preferences

In Industrial/Energy prefer:
Energy
Industrial Products

In Transportation prefer:
Transportation

Additional Information
Year Founded: 2014
Current Activity Level : Actively seeking new investments

HCI EQUITY LLC

1730 Pennsylvania Avenue, NW
Suite 525
Washington, DC USA 20006
Phone: 2023710150
Fax: 2023125300
E-mail: info@hciequity.com
Website: www.hciequity.com

Other Offices
80 South Eighth Street
IDS Center, Suite 4508
Minneapolis, MN USA 55402
Phone: 612-332-2335
Fax: 612-332-2012

1033 Skokie Boulevard, Suite 260
Northbrook, IL USA 60062
Phone: 8472919259
Fax: 8478976212

Management and Staff
Bonnie Price, Vice President
Brendon Biddle, Vice President
Carl Nelson, Managing Director
Dan Moorse, Managing Director
Daniel Dickinson, Managing Partner
Douglas McCormick, Managing Partner
James Forese, Chief Operating Officer
Judith Vijums, Managing Director
Scott Rued, Managing Partner
Scott Gibaratz, Managing Director
Tim Frend, Vice President

Type of Firm
Private Equity Firm

Project Preferences

Role in Financing:
Prefer role as deal originator but will also invest in deals created by others

Type of Financing Preferred:
Leveraged Buyout
Management Buyouts
Acquisition

Geographical Preferences

United States Preferences:
North America

Industry Focus
(% based on actual investment)
Semiconductors/Other Elect.	28.4%
Consumer Related	25.2%
Other Products	22.6%
Industrial/Energy	13.0%
Communications and Media	5.6%
Computer Software and Services	3.6%
Internet Specific	1.6%
Biotechnology	0.1%

Additional Information
Name of Most Recent Fund: HCI Equity Partners IV, L.P.
Most Recent Fund Was Raised: 09/30/2013
Year Founded: 1994
Capital Under Management: $775,000,000
Current Activity Level : Actively seeking new investments
Method of Compensation: Return on invest. most important, but chg. closing fees, service fees, etc.

HCI PRIVATE EQUITY GMBH

Moehlstrasse 7
Munich, Germany 81675
Phone: 498941073830
Fax: 498941073850

Management and Staff
Jeremy Golding, Managing Director

Type of Firm
Private Equity Firm

Project Preferences

Type of Financing Preferred:
Fund of Funds

Geographical Preferences

International Preferences:
Europe
Germany

Additional Information

Year Founded: 2000
Current Activity Level : Actively seeking new investments

HCM HANDWERK CONSULT MITTELSTANDSBERATUNG EK

Heideweg 29a
Quickborn, Germany 25451
Phone: 49410677420
Fax: 494106774220
E-mail: hcm@hcminfo.de
Website: www.hcminfo.de

Other Offices

Bahnhofstrasse 14
Scheessel, Germany 27383
Phone: 49-4263-302-880
Fax: 49-4263-302-8820

Management and Staff

Franco Ottavio Mathias, Chief Executive Officer

Type of Firm

Private Equity Firm

Association Membership

German Venture Capital Association (BVK)

Project Preferences

Type of Financing Preferred:
Early Stage
Later Stage

Geographical Preferences

International Preferences:
Germany

Industry Preferences

In Consumer Related prefer:
Retail
Consumer Services

In Industrial/Energy prefer:
Alternative Energy
Industrial Products

In Transportation prefer:
Transportation

In Business Serv. prefer:
Services

Additional Information

Year Founded: 1996
Current Activity Level : Actively seeking new investments

HCS BETEILIGUNGS-GESELLSCHAFT MBH

Bockenheimer Landstrasse 2-4
Frankfurt am Main, Germany 60306
Phone: 4969264846280
Fax: 4969264846281
E-mail: info@hcs-beteiligungen.de
Website: www.hcs-beteiligungen.de

Type of Firm

Private Equity Firm

Additional Information

Year Founded: 2003
Current Activity Level : Actively seeking new investments

HDFC VENTURE CAPITAL LTD

Ramon House, 169, Backbay
HT Parekh Marg, Churchgate
Mumbai, India 400 020
Phone: 912266316000
Fax: 912222048834
E-mail: info@hdfc.com

Management and Staff

K. G. Krishnamurthy, CEO & Managing Director

Type of Firm

Bank Affiliated

Project Preferences

Type of Financing Preferred:
Core
Value-Add
Opportunistic

Geographical Preferences

International Preferences:
India

Industry Preferences

In Financial Services prefer:
Real Estate

Additional Information

Year Founded: 2005
Capital Under Management: $250,000,000
Current Activity Level : Actively seeking new investments

HEADHAUL CAPITAL PARTNERS LLC

600 Mamaroneck Avenue
Suite 400
Harrison, NY USA 10528
Website: www.headhaulcapital.com

Management and Staff

James Cannaday, Principal
Jason Grant, Co-Founder
Mindy Luxenberg-Grant, Co-Founder
Seth Wilson, Co-Founder

Type of Firm

Private Equity Firm

Project Preferences

Type of Financing Preferred:
Leveraged Buyout
Acquisition
Recapitalizations

Industry Preferences

In Transportation prefer:
Transportation

In Business Serv. prefer:
Distribution

Additional Information

Year Founded: 2014
Current Activity Level : Actively seeking new investments

HEADLANDS CAPITAL MANAGEMENT LLC

One Ferry Building
Suite 255
San Francisco, CA USA 94111
Phone: 4152637310
Website: www.headlandscap.com

Management and Staff

David Park, Managing Partner
Francois Joly, Partner

Type of Firm

Private Equity Advisor or Fund of Funds

Geographical Preferences

United States Preferences:

International Preferences:
Europe

Additional Information

Name of Most Recent Fund: Headlands Capital Secondary Fund, L.P.
Most Recent Fund Was Raised: 09/15/2011
Year Founded: 2006

Capital Under Management: $308,975,000
Current Activity Level : Actively seeking new investments

HEADWATER EQUITY PARTNERS INC

1111 West Georgia Street
Suite 1890
Vancouver, Canada V6E 4M3
E-mail: info@headwaterequity.com
Website: www.headwaterequity.com

Type of Firm
Private Equity Firm

Association Membership
Canadian Venture Capital Association

Project Preferences

Type of Financing Preferred:
Leveraged Buyout
Expansion
Later Stage
Management Buyouts
Acquisition

Geographical Preferences

Canadian Preferences:
Western Canada

Additional Information
Year Founded: 2012
Current Activity Level : Actively seeking new investments

HEADWATERS BD LLC

One Tabor Center
1200 17th Street, Suite 900
Denver, CO USA 80202
Phone: 303-572-6000
Fax: 303-572-6001
Website: www.headwatersmb.com

Other Offices

50 Cocoanut Row
Suite 212
Palm Beach, FL USA 33480
Phone: 5619321600
Fax: 5616556232

One Main Street
Burlington, VT USA 05401
Phone: 802-658-7733

Two Sound View Drive
Suite 100
Greenwich, CT USA 06830
Phone: 2036221328
Fax: 2038699815

23 Corporate Plaza
Suite 135
Newport Beach, CA USA 92660
Phone: 9496798550
Fax: 9496799550

135 Main Street
Suite 800
San Francisco, CA USA 94105
Phone: 4157663860

1999 K Street, Northwest
Suite 700
Washington, DC USA 20006
Phone: 2029575155
Fax: 2024672074

950 Bannock Street
Suite 1100
Boise, ID USA 83702
Phone: 2128516103

400 Tradecenter 128
Suite 5900
Woburn, MA USA 01801
Phone: 7812736062

30 South Wacker Drive
22nd Floor
Chicago, IL USA 60606
Phone: 3124665700
Fax: 3126047850

One Van de Graaff Drive
Burlington, MA USA 01803
Phone: 781-273-6062
Fax: 781-240-6050

2211 Michelson Drive
Suite 530
Irvine, CA USA 92612
Phone: 714-800-1770
Fax: 949-679-9550

500 Fifth Avenue
Suite 2440
New York, NY USA 10110
Phone: 6464358989

Management and Staff
Aaron Osmundson, Principal
Anant Vashi, Managing Director
Andrew Paff, Managing Director
Bradley Rosborough, Managing Director
Brian Mulvaney, Managing Director
Dave Prieto, Principal
David Traylor, Managing Director
David Dodson, Managing Director
Diane O Connor, Principal
Don Warriner, Managing Director
Doug Usifer, Managing Director
Douglas Reynolds, Managing Director
Edward Shaoul, Principal
Grant Garbers, Managing Director
Gretchen Lium, Managing Director
Horacio Facca, Managing Director
James Von Kreuter, Managing Director
Jason Ficken, Managing Director
Jeffrey Schottler, Managing Director
Jerry Sturgill, Managing Director
John Ippolito, Managing Director
Joseph Radecki, Managing Director
Mark Guilford, Principal
Matt Huebner, Principal
Michael Thomsic, Principal
Patrick Seese, Managing Director
Paul Janson, Chief Operating Officer
Rob Heilbronner, Managing Director
Roberta Laraway, Founder
Scott Teagle, Principal
Sivaprakash Siva Shanmugam, Principal
Toby Nuber, Principal
Todd Hellman, Managing Director
Travis Rue, Principal
Tucker Morrison, Managing Director
W. Bradley Hall, Managing Director

Type of Firm
Bank Affiliated

Project Preferences

Type of Financing Preferred:
Leveraged Buyout
Expansion
Management Buyouts
Acquisition
Recapitalizations

Geographical Preferences

United States Preferences:
All U.S.

Canadian Preferences:
All Canada

Additional Information
Year Founded: 2002
Current Activity Level : Actively seeking new investments

HEADWAY CAPITAL PARTNERS LLP

25 Maddox Street
Second Floor
London, United Kingdom W1S 2QN
Phone: 442075188888
Fax: 442079003160
E-mail: info@headwaycap.com
Website: www.headwaycap.com

Management and Staff
Christiaan de Lint, Co-Founder
Laura Lefranc, Co-Founder
Sebastian Junoy, Co-Founder
Tushar Pabari, Chief Financial Officer
Ulrich Hardt, Vice President
Zoe Karkaletsos, Vice President

Type of Firm
Private Equity Firm

Association Membership
European Private Equity and Venture Capital Assoc.

Project Preferences

Type of Financing Preferred:
Leveraged Buyout
Acquisition

Geographical Preferences

United States Preferences:
North America

International Preferences:
Western Europe

Additional Information
Name of Most Recent Fund: Headway Investment Partners III, L.P.
Most Recent Fund Was Raised: 04/25/2013
Year Founded: 2004
Capital Under Management: $131,322,000
Current Activity Level : Actively seeking new investments

HEALTH CATALYST CAPITAL MANAGEMENT LLC

767 Fifth Avenue
18th Floor
New York, NY USA 10153
Phone: 2127522225
Website: www.healthcatalystcapital.com

Management and Staff
Charles Boorady, Managing Director

Type of Firm
Private Equity Firm

Project Preferences

Type of Financing Preferred:
Early Stage

Geographical Preferences

United States Preferences:

Industry Preferences

In Medical/Health prefer:
Health Services

Additional Information
Year Founded: 2015
Capital Under Management: $27,790,000
Current Activity Level : Actively seeking new investments

HEALTH ENTERPRISE PARTNERS LP

565 Fifth Avenue
26th Floor
New York, NY USA 10017
Phone: 2129816901
E-mail: info@hepfund.com
Website: www.hepfund.com

Management and Staff
Daniel Cain, General Partner
David Tamburi, General Partner
Richard Stowe, General Partner
Robert Schulz, General Partner

Type of Firm
Private Equity Firm

Project Preferences

Type of Financing Preferred:
Leveraged Buyout
Balanced
Acquisition

Geographical Preferences

United States Preferences:

Industry Preferences

In Biotechnology prefer:
Biotechnology

In Medical/Health prefer:
Medical/Health
Health Services

Additional Information
Name of Most Recent Fund: Health Enterprise Partners II, L.P.
Most Recent Fund Was Raised: 08/01/2012
Year Founded: 2005
Capital Under Management: $193,450,000
Current Activity Level : Actively seeking new investments

HEALTH INNOVATIONS BV

Computerweg 11
Utrecht, Netherlands 3542 DP
Phone: 31346752188
E-mail: healthpitch@healthinnovations.nl
Website: www.healthinnovations.nl

Type of Firm
Private Equity Firm

Association Membership
Dutch Venture Capital Associaton (NVP)

Project Preferences

Type of Financing Preferred:
Early Stage
Turnaround
Seed
Startup

Size of Investments Considered:
Min Size of Investment Considered (000s): $129
Max Size of Investment Considered (000s): $1,294

Geographical Preferences

International Preferences:
Europe
Netherlands

Industry Preferences

In Medical/Health prefer:
Medical/Health
Medical Diagnostics
Medical Therapeutics
Medical Products
Health Services

Additional Information
Year Founded: 2007
Current Activity Level : Actively seeking new investments

HEALTH VELOCITY CAPITAL

One Letterman Drive, Building D, Suite 3700
San Francisco, CA USA 94129
E-mail: bruce@healthvelocitycapital.com
Website: healthvelocitycap.com

Type of Firm
Private Equity Firm

Industry Preferences

In Computer Software prefer:
Software

In Medical/Health prefer:
Health Services

Additional Information
Year Founded: 2017
Capital Under Management: $76,140,000
Current Activity Level : Actively seeking new investments

HEALTH WILDCATTERS

2700 Fairmount Street
Dallas, TX USA 75201
Phone: 2147991450
E-mail: info@healthwildcatters.com
Website: www.healthwildcatters.com

Management and Staff
Carl Soderstrom, Co-Founder
Clay Heighten, Co-Founder
Gabriella Draney, Co-Founder
Hubert Zajicek, Co-Founder

Type of Firm
Incubator/Development Program

Project Preferences

Type of Financing Preferred:
Early Stage
Seed
Startup

Size of Investments Considered:
Min Size of Investment Considered (000s): $30
Max Size of Investment Considered (000s): $250

Geographical Preferences

United States Preferences:
Texas

Industry Preferences

In Computer Software prefer:
Software

In Medical/Health prefer:
Medical/Health
Medical Diagnostics
Medical Products
Pharmaceuticals

Additional Information
Year Founded: 2013
Current Activity Level : Actively seeking new investments

HEALTHBOX LLC

213 N Racine
Chicago, IL USA 60607
E-mail: info@healthbox.com
Website: www.healthbox.com

Other Offices

4-5 Bonhill Street
London, United Kingdom EC2A 4BX

Five West Forsyth Street
Jacksonville, FL USA 32202

41 Peabody Street
Nashville, TN USA 37210

213 North Racine
Chicago, IL USA 60607

Management and Staff
Celine Druilhe, Vice President
Neil Patel, President & COO

Type of Firm
Incubator/Development Program

Project Preferences

Type of Financing Preferred:
Early Stage
Seed
Startup

Geographical Preferences

United States Preferences:
Illinois
Tennessee
Massachusetts
Florida

International Preferences:
United Kingdom

Industry Preferences

In Medical/Health prefer:
Medical/Health

Additional Information
Year Founded: 2012
Capital Under Management: $37,900,000
Current Activity Level : Actively seeking new investments

HEALTHCAP PARTNERS LLC

5910 North Central Expressway
Suite 1000
Dallas, TX USA 75206
Phone: 2149531722
E-mail: info@healthcappartners.com
Website: healthcap.com

Management and Staff
Chrisman Jackson, Managing Partner
Jason Dodd, Partner
Matthew Nurkin, Managing Director
Stephanie Toliver, Chief Financial Officer
William Hutchison, Partner

Type of Firm
Private Equity Firm

Project Preferences

Type of Financing Preferred:
Leveraged Buyout
Management Buyouts
Acquisition
Recapitalizations

Industry Preferences

In Medical/Health prefer:
Medical/Health
Health Services

Additional Information
Year Founded: 2012
Current Activity Level : Actively seeking new investments

HEALTHCARE VENTURES LLC

47 Thorndike Street, Suite B1-1
Cambridge, MA USA 02141
Phone: 6172524343
Fax: 6172524342
E-mail: info@hcven.com

Management and Staff
Augustine Lawlor, Managing Director
Christopher Mirabelli, Managing Director
Harold Werner, Founder
James Cavanaugh, Managing Director
John Littlechild, Managing Director

Type of Firm
Private Equity Firm

Project Preferences

Role in Financing:
Will function either as deal originator or investor in deals created by others

Type of Financing Preferred:
Early Stage
Balanced
Seed
Startup

Industry Focus

(% based on actual investment)
Biotechnology	60.1%
Medical/Health	38.1%
Consumer Related	1.4%
Internet Specific	0.4%

Additional Information
Name of Most Recent Fund: HealthCare Ventures Strategic Fund, L.P.
Most Recent Fund Was Raised: 12/08/2009
Year Founded: 1985
Capital Under Management: $1,409,100,000
Current Activity Level : Actively seeking new investments
Method of Compensation: Return on investment is of primary concern, do not charge fees

---

HEALTHCOR PARTNERS MANAGEMENT LP

152 West 57th Street
Carnegie Hall Tower
New York, NY USA 10019
Website: www.healthcorpartners.com

Management and Staff
Arthur Cohen, Senior Managing Director
Jeffrey Lightcap, Senior Managing Director
John Sailer, Vice President
Joseph Healey, Senior Managing Director
Michael Mashaal, Managing Director
Steven Musumeci, Chief Operating Officer

Type of Firm
Private Equity Firm

Project Preferences

Type of Financing Preferred:
Later Stage

Industry Preferences

In Medical/Health prefer:
Medical/Health
Medical Diagnostics
Medical Therapeutics
Medical Products
Health Services

In Industrial/Energy prefer:
Energy

Additional Information
Name of Most Recent Fund: Healthcor Partners Fund II, L.P.
Most Recent Fund Was Raised: 01/05/2012
Year Founded: 2005
Capital Under Management: $100,842,000
Current Activity Level : Actively seeking new investments

HEALTHEDGE INVESTMENT PARTNERS LLC
5550 West Executive Drive
Suite 230
Tampa, FL USA 33609
Phone: 8134907100
Fax: 8134907111
E-mail: info@HealthEdgePartners.com
Website: www.healthedgepartners.com

Other Offices
Former HQ: 100 South Ashley Drive
Suite 650
Tampa, FL USA 33602
Phone: 8134907100
Fax: 8134907111

Management and Staff
A. Scott Lee, Principal
Brian Anderson, Managing Partner
Phillip Dingle, Managing Partner
Ralph Nelson, Chief Financial Officer

Type of Firm
Private Equity Firm

Project Preferences

Type of Financing Preferred:
Leveraged Buyout
Acquisition
Recapitalizations

Geographical Preferences
United States Preferences:

Industry Preferences

In Medical/Health prefer:
Medical/Health
Medical Products
Health Services
Pharmaceuticals

In Business Serv. prefer:
Distribution

Additional Information
Name of Most Recent Fund: HealthEdge Investment Fund II, L.P.
Most Recent Fund Was Raised: 12/30/2011
Year Founded: 2005
Capital Under Management: $86,525,000
Current Activity Level : Actively seeking new investments

HEALTHPOINTCAPITAL LLC
505 Park Avenue
12th Floor
New York, NY USA 10022
Phone: 2129357780
Fax: 2129356878
E-mail: info@healthpointcapital.com
Website: www.healthpointcapital.com

Management and Staff
Jacques Bizot, Founder
John Chopack, Managing Director
John McCormick, Managing Director
John Steffens, Managing Partner
Joseph Fitzpatrick, Chief Financial Officer
Laing Rikkers, Managing Director
Mortimer Berkowitz, President
Stephen O Neil, Founder

Type of Firm
Private Equity Firm

Project Preferences

Type of Financing Preferred:
Leveraged Buyout
Expansion
Later Stage
Acquisition

Industry Preferences

In Medical/Health prefer:
Medical/Health
Medical Therapeutics
Health Services

Additional Information
Year Founded: 2002
Capital Under Management: $800,000,000
Current Activity Level : Actively seeking new investments

HEALTHQUAD ADVISORS PVT LTD
Shaheed Jeet Singh Marg
D1, Qutab Hotel Complex
New Delhi, India 110 016
E-mail: contact@healthquad.in
Website: www.healthquad.in

Type of Firm
Private Equity Firm

Project Preferences

Type of Financing Preferred:
Early Stage
Seed

Geographical Preferences
International Preferences:
India

Industry Preferences

In Medical/Health prefer:
Medical/Health
Health Services

Additional Information
Year Founded: 2016
Current Activity Level : Actively seeking new investments

HEALTHQUEST CAPITAL
3000 Sand Hill Rd
Bldg 4, Ste. 250
Menlo Park, CA USA 94025
Website: www.healthquestcapital.com

Other Offices
1230 Peachtree Street NE
Suite 3875
ATLANTA, GA USA 30309
Phone: 14049202051

Management and Staff
David Kabakoff, Partner
Randy Scott, Partner
Thomas Callaway, Venture Partner

Type of Firm
Private Equity Firm

Project Preferences

Type of Financing Preferred:
Early Stage

Size of Investments Considered:
Min Size of Investment Considered (000s): $7,000
Max Size of Investment Considered (000s): $10,000

Industry Preferences

In Medical/Health prefer:
Medical Diagnostics
Medical Products

Additional Information

Name of Most Recent Fund: HealthQuest Capital Fund I
Most Recent Fund Was Raised: 07/16/2013
Year Founded: 2013
Capital Under Management: $338,400,000
Current Activity Level : Actively seeking new investments

HEALTHRIGHT PARTNERS

10939 N. Alpine Highway
Suite 505
American Fork, UT USA 84003
Phone: 801-772-0403
Website: www.healthright.org

Management and Staff

Alisa Lycheva, Chief Financial Officer
Rachel Madenyika, Chief Financial Officer
Shawn Smart, General Partner

Type of Firm

Private Equity Firm

Project Preferences

Type of Financing Preferred:
Balanced

Additional Information

Name of Most Recent Fund: HealthRight Partners, L.P.
Most Recent Fund Was Raised: 11/21/2005
Year Founded: 2005
Capital Under Management: $2,000,000
Current Activity Level : Actively seeking new investments

HEALTHSHARESTM INC

420 Lexington Avenue
Suite 2550
New York, NY USA 10170
Phone: 212-867-7400
Fax: 212-867-3857
Website: www.healthsharesinc.com

Management and Staff

Anthony Dudzinski, Vice President

Type of Firm

Private Equity Firm

Project Preferences

Type of Financing Preferred:
Early Stage
Balanced

Geographical Preferences

United States Preferences:
All U.S.

Industry Preferences

In Biotechnology prefer:
Biotechnology

In Medical/Health prefer:
Medical/Health

Additional Information

Name of Most Recent Fund: WellSpring BioCapital Partners, LLC
Most Recent Fund Was Raised: 05/11/2004
Year Founded: 2004
Capital Under Management: $1,100,000
Current Activity Level : Actively seeking new investments

HEALTHVIEW CAPITAL PARTNERS LLC

3124 Zebulon Road
Rocky Mount, NC USA 27804

Type of Firm

Private Equity Firm

Project Preferences

Type of Financing Preferred:
Early Stage
Generalist PE
Later Stage

Industry Preferences

In Medical/Health prefer:
Medical/Health
Health Services

Additional Information

Year Founded: 2014
Current Activity Level : Actively seeking new investments

HEALTHX MANAGEMENT LLC

111 North Fairchild Street, Suite 240
Madison, WI USA 53703
Phone: 6086183863
E-mail: contact@healthxventures.com
Website: www.healthxventures.com

Type of Firm

Private Equity Firm

Project Preferences

Type of Financing Preferred:
Early Stage
Seed

Geographical Preferences

United States Preferences:
Midwest
Wisconsin

Industry Preferences

In Medical/Health prefer:
Medical/Health
Medical Diagnostics
Medical Therapeutics
Medical Products
Health Services

Additional Information

Year Founded: 2015
Capital Under Management: $21,000,000
Current Activity Level : Actively seeking new investments

HEALTHY VENTURES MANAGEMENT LLC

One Letterman Drive
Building D, Suite 3700
San Francisco, CA USA 94129
Phone: 4159027864
Website: www.healthy.vc

Management and Staff

Anya Schiess, General Partner
Enmi Kendall, General Partner

Type of Firm

Private Equity Firm

Project Preferences

Type of Financing Preferred:
Early Stage

Industry Preferences

In Medical/Health prefer:
Medical/Health

Additional Information

Year Founded: 2015
Capital Under Management: $16,980,000
Current Activity Level : Actively seeking new investments

HEALY CIRCLE CAPITAL LLC

153 East 53rd Street
48th Floor
New York, NY USA 10022
Phone: 212-446-2440

Type of Firm

Private Equity Firm

Project Preferences

Type of Financing Preferred:
Other

Additional Information
Year Founded: 2002
Capital Under Management: $10,400,000
Current Activity Level : Actively seeking new investments

HEARTLAND VENTURES LLC

545 E. John Carpenter Freeway
Suite 300
Coppell, TX USA 75019
Phone: 9727392100
Website: heartland-ventures.com

Type of Firm
Private Equity Firm

Project Preferences

Role in Financing:
Prefer role as deal originator but will also invest in deals created by others

Type of Financing Preferred:
Early Stage
Startup

Size of Investments Considered:
Min Size of Investment Considered (000s): $1,000
Max Size of Investment Considered (000s): $2,500

Geographical Preferences

United States Preferences:
Texas

Industry Preferences

In Medical/Health prefer:
Medical Products

Additional Information
Year Founded: 2005
Current Activity Level : Actively seeking new investments

HEATHQUEST CAPITAL

3000 Sand Hill Road
Building Four Suite 250
Menlo Park, CA USA 94025
Phone: 6506818420
Website: www.healthquestcapital.com

Management and Staff
David Kabakoff, Partner
Garheng Kong, Managing Partner
Nathalie Auber, Chief Financial Officer
Randy Scott, Partner
Richard Lin, Partner
Thomas Callaway, Venture Partner

Type of Firm
Private Equity Firm

Project Preferences

Type of Financing Preferred:
Early Stage
Expansion

Geographical Preferences

United States Preferences:
North America

Industry Preferences

In Medical/Health prefer:
Medical/Health

Additional Information
Year Founded: 2013
Current Activity Level : Actively seeking new investments

HEAVEN-SENT CAPITAL MANAGEMENT GROUP CO LTD

No. 76, Yuhuang Road
Building 3
Hangzhou, China 310002
Phone: 8657187083018
Fax: 8657187089718
E-mail: ttgg@ttgg.com.cn
Website: www.ggttvc.com

Management and Staff
Weigang Yuan, President

Type of Firm
Private Equity Firm

Project Preferences

Type of Financing Preferred:
Leveraged Buyout
Expansion
Balanced
Later Stage
Seed
Acquisition
Startup

Geographical Preferences

International Preferences:
China

Industry Preferences

In Communications prefer:
Satellite Microwave Comm.

In Semiconductor/Electr prefer:
Controllers and Sensors

In Biotechnology prefer:
Biotechnology

In Medical/Health prefer:
Pharmaceuticals

In Industrial/Energy prefer:
Alternative Energy
Energy Conservation Relat

Additional Information
Year Founded: 2000
Capital Under Management: $76,995,000
Current Activity Level : Actively seeking new investments

HEAVYBIT

325 Ninth Street
San Francisco, CA USA 94101
Website: www.heavybit.com

Type of Firm
Incubator/Development Program

Project Preferences

Type of Financing Preferred:
Balanced

Additional Information
Year Founded: 2017
Current Activity Level : Actively seeking new investments

HEBEI TECHNOLOGY VENTURE CAPITAL CO LTD

No. 55 Kunlun Street
Gaoxin Technology Dev'l
Shijiazhuang, China 050035
Phone: 86-311-85961617
Fax: 86-311-85961613
E-mail: hebvc@hebvc.com
Website: www.hebvc.com

Type of Firm
Private Equity Firm

Project Preferences

Type of Financing Preferred:
Early Stage
Balanced
Seed

Geographical Preferences

International Preferences:
China

Industry Preferences

In Semiconductor/Electr prefer:
Electronics
Fiber Optics

In Biotechnology prefer:
Biotechnology

In Medical/Health prefer:
Medical/Health
Pharmaceuticals

In Industrial/Energy prefer:
Alternative Energy
Industrial Products
Materials
Advanced Materials
Machinery

In Manufact. prefer:
Manufacturing

Additional Information
Year Founded: 2001
Capital Under Management: $206,390,000
Current Activity Level : Actively seeking new investments

HEBEI XINGSHI VENTURE CAPITAL CO LTD

No. 55, Kunlun Avenue
203, Bldg. A, Gaoxin District
Shijiazhuang, China
Phone: 8631185961615

Type of Firm
Private Equity Firm

Project Preferences

Type of Financing Preferred:
Balanced

Geographical Preferences

International Preferences:
China

Industry Preferences

In Semiconductor/Electr prefer:
Electronics
Fiber Optics

In Biotechnology prefer:
Biotechnology

In Medical/Health prefer:
Pharmaceuticals

In Industrial/Energy prefer:
Alternative Energy
Advanced Materials
Machinery

In Manufact. prefer:
Manufacturing

Additional Information
Year Founded: 2009
Capital Under Management: $15,090,000
Current Activity Level : Actively seeking new investments

HEBEI XUANYUAN PRIVATE EQUITY INVESTMENT FUND MANAGEMENT CO.

No. 319 Xiangjiang Road
Building 10, Zhenhai Tower
Shijiazhuang, China 050000
Phone: 8631185831551
Fax: 8631185831559
Website: www.xytzjj.com

Type of Firm
Private Equity Firm

Project Preferences

Type of Financing Preferred:
Balanced

Geographical Preferences

International Preferences:
China

Industry Preferences

In Consumer Related prefer:
Entertainment and Leisure
Sports

Additional Information
Year Founded: 2011
Capital Under Management: $156,900,000
Current Activity Level : Actively seeking new investments

HEBEI YANHAI INDUSTRIAL INVESTMENT FUND MANAGEMENT CO LTD

Caofeidian industrial Zone
5F, Tower B, Jindao Mansion
Tangshan, China 063200
Phone: 863155072586
E-mail: cyfunds@hbcyjj.com
Website: www.hbcyjj.com

Management and Staff
Fengtao Gong, President

Type of Firm
Government Affiliated Program

Project Preferences

Type of Financing Preferred:
Leveraged Buyout

Geographical Preferences

International Preferences:
China

Additional Information
Year Founded: 2013
Capital Under Management: $825,940,000
Current Activity Level : Actively seeking new investments

HEDA VENTURES

19 Davis Drive
Suite 203
Belmont, CA USA 94002
E-mail: info@hedaventures.com
Website: www.hedaventures.com

Type of Firm
Private Equity Firm

Project Preferences

Type of Financing Preferred:
Early Stage
Seed

Geographical Preferences

United States Preferences:

International Preferences:
China

Industry Preferences

In Communications prefer:
Telecommunications

In Biotechnology prefer:
Biotechnology

In Industrial/Energy prefer:
Energy
Materials

In Business Serv. prefer:
Media

Additional Information
Year Founded: 2017
Current Activity Level : Actively seeking new investments

HEDGEHOG SP Z O O

Prosta 51
Warszawa, Poland 00-838
Website: www.hedgehogfund.pl

Type of Firm
Private Equity Firm

Geographical Preferences

International Preferences:
Poland

Additional Information
Year Founded: 2012
Current Activity Level : Actively seeking new investments

HEDGEWOOD INC

8 Brentcliffe Road
Suite 200
Toronto, Canada M4G 3Y2
Phone: 4164224828
Fax: 4164220051
Website: www.hedgewood.com

Management and Staff
Wayne Bigby, President

Type of Firm
Private Equity Firm

Project Preferences

Type of Financing Preferred:
Core
Leveraged Buyout
Value-Add
Mezzanine
Balanced
Opportunistic
Acquisition

Geographical Preferences

United States Preferences:

Canadian Preferences:
All Canada

International Preferences:
All International

Industry Preferences

In Internet Specific prefer:
Internet

In Medical/Health prefer:
Health Services

In Consumer Related prefer:
Food/Beverage

In Industrial/Energy prefer:
Alternative Energy

In Financial Services prefer:
Real Estate

Additional Information
Year Founded: 1969
Current Activity Level : Actively seeking new investments

HEFEI HI-TECH VENTURE CAPITAL CO LTD

436 Changjia Road
Suite 1108, Jincheng Bldg.
Hefei, China
Phone: 865512832321
Fax: 865512832320

Type of Firm
Private Equity Firm

Project Preferences

Type of Financing Preferred:
Generalist PE

Additional Information
Year Founded: 2012
Current Activity Level : Actively seeking new investments

HEFEI STATE-OWNED ASSETS HOLDING CO LTD

No.100, Qianshan Road
Hupo Wuhuan International
Hefei, China

Type of Firm
Government Affiliated Program

Project Preferences

Type of Financing Preferred:
Balanced

Geographical Preferences

International Preferences:
China

Additional Information
Year Founded: 1996
Current Activity Level : Actively seeking new investments

HEIDE PROBSTEL TRUST

1231 Calle Cerrito Alto
Santa Barbara, CA USA 93101
Phone: 8058987059
Fax: 8058982049
E-mail: info@probstel.com
Website: www.probstel.com

Type of Firm
Service Provider

Project Preferences

Role in Financing:
Prefer role as deal originator but will also invest in deals created by others

Type of Financing Preferred:
Early Stage

Geographical Preferences

United States Preferences:
California

International Preferences:
Germany
France

Industry Preferences

In Computer Software prefer:
Software

In Internet Specific prefer:
Internet

Additional Information
Year Founded: 1994
Current Activity Level : Actively seeking new investments
Method of Compensation: Function primarily in service area, receive contingent fee in cash or equity

HEIDELBERGCAPITAL ASSET MANAGEMENT GMBH

Alte Glockengiesserei 9
Der Turm
Heidelberg, Germany 69115
Phone: 496221867630
Fax: 4962218676310
E-mail: kontakt@hdcpe.de
Website: www.heidelbergcapital.de

Management and Staff
Clemens Doppler, Managing Partner
Martin Weiblen, Managing Partner

Type of Firm
Private Equity Firm

Project Preferences

Type of Financing Preferred:
Fund of Funds
Leveraged Buyout
Later Stage
Acquisition

Geographical Preferences

International Preferences:
Germany

Industry Preferences

In Computer Software prefer:
Software

In Semiconductor/Electr prefer:
Laser Related

In Biotechnology prefer:
Biotechnology

In Medical/Health prefer:
Medical/Health
Pharmaceuticals

In Consumer Related prefer:
Consumer

In Industrial/Energy prefer:
Industrial Products

Additional Information
Year Founded: 2007
Current Activity Level : Actively seeking new investments

HEIDRICK & STRUGGLES INTERNATIONAL INC

233 South Wacker Drive
Willis Tower, Suite 4200
Chicago, IL USA 60606
Phone: 3124961200
Fax: 3124961048
E-mail: InvestorRelations@heidrick.com
Website: www.heidrick.com

Other Offices
950 Tower Lane
Sixth Floor
Foster City, CA USA 94404
Phone: 650-234-1500
Fax: 650-350-1000

Management and Staff
Bradley Holden, Managing Partner
Guy Sava, Partner
Jean-Louis Alpeyrie, Partner
Jeff Markowitz, Managing Partner
Michael Hunter, Principal

Type of Firm
Corporate PE/Venture

Project Preferences

Type of Financing Preferred:
Early Stage

Geographical Preferences

International Preferences:
All International

Additional Information
Year Founded: 1968
Current Activity Level : Actively seeking new investments

HEIRS CAPITAL LTD

H.E.I.R. Place, 33A Bishop
Aboyade Cole, V/I
Lagos, Nigeria
Phone: 234-1-461-6466
Fax: 234-1-262-6799
Website: www.heirsalliance.com

Type of Firm
Private Equity Firm

Project Preferences

Type of Financing Preferred:
Balanced

Geographical Preferences

International Preferences:
Nigeria
No Preference

Additional Information
Year Founded: 2004
Current Activity Level : Actively seeking new investments

HEJUN CAPITAL CO LTD

Yard 86, Beiyuan Rd, Chaoyang
1-3/F, Block 213, District E
Beijing, China 100101
Phone: 861084108866
Fax: 861084108899
Website: www.hejun.com

Type of Firm
Private Equity Firm

Project Preferences

Type of Financing Preferred:
Leveraged Buyout
Early Stage
Generalist PE
Public Companies
Later Stage
Seed
Startup

Geographical Preferences

International Preferences:
China

Industry Preferences

In Communications prefer:
Telecommunications

In Biotechnology prefer:
Biotechnology

In Medical/Health prefer:
Pharmaceuticals

In Consumer Related prefer:
Education Related

In Industrial/Energy prefer:
Energy Conservation Relat
Environmental Related

In Business Serv. prefer:
Media

In Manufact. prefer:
Manufacturing

Additional Information
Year Founded: 2000
Capital Under Management: $137,064,000
Current Activity Level: Actively seeking new investments

HELIAD EQUITY PARTNERS GMBH & CO KGAA

Grueneburgweg 18
Frankfurt am Main, Germany 60322
Phone: 4969719159650
Fax: 496971915965603
E-mail: info@heliad.com
Website: www.heliad.com

Management and Staff
Thomas Hanke, Managing Director

Type of Firm
Private Equity Firm

Association Membership
German Venture Capital Association (BVK)
European Private Equity and Venture Capital Assoc.

Project Preferences

Type of Financing Preferred:
Leveraged Buyout
Public Companies
Turnaround
Private Placement

Geographical Preferences

International Preferences:
Germany

Industry Preferences

In Medical/Health prefer:
Medical/Health
Health Services

In Financial Services prefer:
Financial Services

In Business Serv. prefer:
Services

Additional Information
Year Founded: 2004
Current Activity Level : Actively seeking new investments

HELIANT INVESTMENT MANAGEMENT, LTD.

7/F, KinOn Commercial Building
49-51, Jervois Street
Sheung Wan, Hong Kong

Type of Firm
Private Equity Firm

Project Preferences

Type of Financing Preferred:
Early Stage
Expansion
Balanced
Later Stage

Geographical Preferences

International Preferences:
Hong Kong
Israel
Asia

Industry Preferences

In Computer Software prefer:
Software
Applications Software

Additional Information

Year Founded: 2012
Current Activity Level : Actively seeking new investments

HELICONIA CAPITAL MANAGEMENT PTE LTD

9 Temasek Boulevard #24-03
Suntec Tower Two
Singapore, Singapore 038989
E-mail: enquiries@heliconiacapital.com
Website: www.heliconiacapital.com

Type of Firm

Private Equity Firm

Project Preferences

Type of Financing Preferred:
Generalist PE

Geographical Preferences

International Preferences:
Singapore

Additional Information

Year Founded: 2010
Current Activity Level : Actively seeking new investments

HELION VENTURE PARTNERS LLC

Les Cascades Building
Edith Cavell Street
Port Louis, Mauritius
Phone: 2302129800
Fax: 2302129833
E-mail: contact@helionvc.com
Website: www.helionvc.com

Other Offices

Block B, 9th Floor
Vatika Towers, Sector 54
Gurgaon, India 122 002

Phone: 91-124-461-5333
Fax: 91-124-461-5345

First Floor, Pine Valley, Embassy
Golflinks Business Park, Koramangala
Bangalore , India 560 071
Phone: 91-80-4018-3333
Fax: 91-80-4018-3456

Management and Staff

Ashish Gupta, Senior Managing Director
Kanwaljit Singh, Senior Managing Director
Natarajan Ranganathan, Managing Director & CFO
Rahul Chandra, Managing Director
Sanjeev Aggarwal, Senior Managing Director

Type of Firm

Private Equity Firm

Association Membership

Indian Venture Capital Association (IVCA)

Project Preferences

Type of Financing Preferred:
Early Stage
Expansion
Balanced
Seed
Startup

Size of Investments Considered:
Min Size of Investment Considered (000s): $2,000
Max Size of Investment Considered (000s): $10,000

Geographical Preferences

International Preferences:
India
Asia

Industry Preferences

In Communications prefer:
Wireless Communications

In Internet Specific prefer:
Internet

In Medical/Health prefer:
Health Services

In Consumer Related prefer:
Consumer Services
Education Related

In Financial Services prefer:
Financial Services

In Business Serv. prefer:
Services
Media

Additional Information

Year Founded: 2006
Capital Under Management: $140,000,000
Current Activity Level : Actively seeking new investments

HELIOS INVESTMENT PARTNERS LLP

12 Charles II Street
2nd Floor, St. James's
London, United Kingdom SW1Y 4QU
Phone: 442074847700
Fax: 442074847750
E-mail: Info@HeliosLLP.com
Website: www.heliosinvestment.com

Other Offices

7b Olu Holloway Road
Ikoyi
Lagos, Niger
Phone: 23416310330

14 Riverside Drive
4B Grosvenor Suite
Nairobi, Kenya
Phone: 254708985818

12 Charles II Street, St. James's
London, United Kingdom SW1Y 4QU
Phone: 442074847700
Fax: 442074847750

Management and Staff

Babatunde Soyoye, Managing Director
Dabney Tonelli, Partner
Tope Lawani, Managing Director

Type of Firm

Private Equity Firm

Association Membership

Emerging Markets Private Equity Association
African Venture Capital Association (AVCA)

Project Preferences

Type of Financing Preferred:
Fund of Funds
Leveraged Buyout
Early Stage
Expansion
Generalist PE
Balanced
Public Companies
Seed
Acquisition
Startup
Recapitalizations

Size of Investments Considered:
Min Size of Investment Considered (000s): $15,000
Max Size of Investment Considered (000s): $200,000

Geographical Preferences

International Preferences:
Angola
India
Nigeria
Uganda
Tanzania
Ghana
Kenya
Brazil
South Africa
Africa

Industry Preferences

In Communications prefer:
Communications and Media
Telecommunications

In Biotechnology prefer:
Agricultural/Animal Bio.

In Medical/Health prefer:
Medical/Health

In Consumer Related prefer:
Entertainment and Leisure
Consumer Products

In Industrial/Energy prefer:
Energy

In Transportation prefer:
Transportation
Aerospace

In Financial Services prefer:
Financial Services

In Business Serv. prefer:
Distribution

In Agr/Forestr/Fish prefer:
Agribusiness

In Utilities prefer:
Utilities

Additional Information

Year Founded: 2004
Capital Under Management: $400,000
Current Activity Level : Actively seeking new investments

HELIX CENTER BIOTECH INCUBATOR

1100 Corporate Square Drive
Creve Coeur
Saint Louis, MO USA 63132
Phone: 3144322672
Website: www.helixcenter.com

Type of Firm

Incubator/Development Program

Project Preferences

Type of Financing Preferred:
Early Stage
Seed
Startup

Geographical Preferences

United States Preferences:
Missouri

Industry Preferences

In Biotechnology prefer:
Biotechnology

Additional Information

Year Founded: 2010
Current Activity Level : Actively seeking new investments

HELIX VENTURES

125 University Avenue
Suite 88
Palo Alto, CA USA 94301
Phone: 6503532523
E-mail: info@helixventure.com
Website: www.helixventure.com

Management and Staff

Evgeny Zaytsev, General Partner
Graham Crooke, General Partner
Philip Sawyer, General Partner

Type of Firm

Private Equity Firm

Project Preferences

Type of Financing Preferred:
Early Stage
Later Stage

Industry Preferences

In Medical/Health prefer:
Medical/Health
Health Services
Pharmaceuticals

Additional Information

Year Founded: 2008
Capital Under Management: $150,000,000
Current Activity Level : Actively seeking new investments

HELLMAN & FRIEDMAN LLC

One Maritime Plaza
Twelfth Floor
San Francisco, CA USA 94111
Phone: 4157885111
Fax: 4157880176
E-mail: info@hf.com
Website: hf.com

Other Offices

30th Floor Millbank Tower
21-24 Millbank
London, United Kingdom SW1P 4QP
Phone: 44-20-7839-5111
Fax: 44-20-7839-5711

390 Park Avenue
21st Floor
New York, NY USA 10022
Phone: 212-871-6680
Fax: 212-871-6688

Management and Staff

Adrien Motte, Principal
Allen Thorpe, Managing Director
Anupam Mishra, Managing Director
Blake Kleinman, Managing Director
Brian Powers, Managing Director
Brian Doyle, Managing Director
C. Andrew Ballard, Managing Director
David Tunnell, Managing Director
Deepak Advani, Managing Director
Emily Johnson, Principal
Erik Ragatz, Managing Director
F. Warren Hellman, Co-Founder
Jeffrey Goldstein, Managing Director
P. Hunter Philbrick, Managing Director
Patrick Healy, Chief Executive Officer
Philip Meicler, Principal
Philip Sternheimer, Principal
Philip Hammarskjold, Chief Executive Officer
Philip Hammarskjold, Chief Executive Officer
Robert Henske, Managing Director
Sameer Narang, Principal
Stefan Goetz, Managing Director
Stuart Banks, Managing Director
Tarim Wasim, Managing Director
Thomas Steyer, Managing Director
Trevor Watt, Managing Director
Zita Saurel, Managing Director

Type of Firm

Private Equity Firm

Association Membership

Private Equity Council (PEC)

Project Preferences

Role in Financing:
Prefer role as deal originator

Type of Financing Preferred:
Leveraged Buyout
Management Buyouts
Acquisition
Recapitalizations

Geographical Preferences

United States Preferences:

International Preferences:
Europe

1025

Industry Focus
(% based on actual investment)

Computer Software and Services	30.9%
Other Products	26.3%
Consumer Related	20.7%
Computer Hardware	13.9%
Communications and Media	3.2%
Internet Specific	2.8%
Medical/Health	1.2%
Semiconductors/Other Elect.	1.1%
Biotechnology	0.1%

Additional Information
Name of Most Recent Fund: Hellman & Friedman Capital Partners VII, L.P.
Most Recent Fund Was Raised: 10/01/2009
Year Founded: 1984
Capital Under Management: $8,000,000,000
Current Activity Level : Actively seeking new investments

HELMSMAN FUNDS MANAGEMENT, LTD.

23 Hunter Street
Suite 503, Level Five
Sydney, Australia 2000
Phone: 61292398100
Fax: 61292398199
E-mail: info@helmsman.com.au
Website: www.helmsman.com.au

Management and Staff
Douglas Potter, Managing Director
Ian Johnson, Managing Director
Kerensa Argyriou, Chief Financial Officer
Peter Watt, Managing Director

Type of Firm
Bank Affiliated

Association Membership
Australian Venture Capital Association (AVCAL)

Project Preferences

Role in Financing:
Prefer role as deal originator but will also invest in deals created by others

Type of Financing Preferred:
Turnaround
Special Situation

Geographical Preferences

International Preferences:
Australia
New Zealand

Industry Preferences

In Business Serv. prefer:
Distribution

Additional Information
Name of Most Recent Fund: Helmsman Capital Fund
Most Recent Fund Was Raised: 12/23/2002
Year Founded: 2002
Capital Under Management: $124,900,000
Current Activity Level : Actively seeking new investments
Method of Compensation: Return on invest. most important, but chg. closing fees, service fees, etc.

HELSINN INVESTMENT FUND SA

7-9 Avenue de Grande Bretagne
Monaco, Monaco MC-98000
Phone: 37797983080
E-mail: hif@helsinn.com
Website: helsinninvestmentfund.com

Type of Firm
Private Equity Firm

Project Preferences

Type of Financing Preferred:
Early Stage

Industry Preferences

In Biotechnology prefer:
Biotech Related Research

In Medical/Health prefer:
Medical/Health
Pharmaceuticals

Additional Information
Year Founded: 1969
Current Activity Level : Actively seeking new investments

HEMERA SAS

74, Avenue Thiers
Bordeaux, France 33100
Website: hemera.camp

Type of Firm
Incubator/Development Program

Project Preferences

Type of Financing Preferred:
Early Stage
Seed

Geographical Preferences

International Preferences:
France

Industry Preferences

In Computer Software prefer:
Software

In Internet Specific prefer:
Internet

In Consumer Related prefer:
Consumer Products
Consumer Services

Additional Information
Year Founded: 2015
Current Activity Level : Actively seeking new investments

HEMI VENTURES FUND I LP

228 Hamilton Avenue
Third Floor
Palo Alto, CA USA 94301
Website: www.hemi.vc

Type of Firm
Private Equity Firm

Project Preferences

Type of Financing Preferred:
Seed

Size of Investments Considered:
Min Size of Investment Considered (000s): $250
Max Size of Investment Considered (000s): $500

Additional Information
Year Founded: 2016
Capital Under Management: $18,000,000
Current Activity Level : Actively seeking new investments

HEMISPHERE CAPITAL LLC

84 Brook Street
London, United Kingdom W1K 5EY
Phone: 44-20-7866-6028
E-mail: info@hemispherecapital.com
Website: www.hemispherecapital.com

Management and Staff
Heather Killen, Managing Partner
Matt Rothman, Managing Partner

Type of Firm
Private Equity Firm

Project Preferences

Type of Financing Preferred:
Later Stage

Size of Investments Considered:
Min Size of Investment Considered (000s): $3,000
Max Size of Investment Considered (000s): $5,000

Geographical Preferences

International Preferences:
Sweden
United Kingdom
Iceland
Finland
Norway
Denmark

Industry Preferences

In Communications prefer:
Telecommunications

Additional Information

Year Founded: 2004
Current Activity Level : Actively seeking new investments

HEMP DEPOSIT AND DISTRIBUTION CORP

2665 Ariane Drive, Suite 207
San Diego, CA USA 92117
Phone: 8558522622
E-mail: Corporate@mycannabank.com
Website: www.cannabank.com

Type of Firm
Private Equity Firm

Project Preferences

Type of Financing Preferred:
Generalist PE

Industry Preferences

In Medical/Health prefer:
Medical/Health

In Industrial/Energy prefer:
Alternative Energy

In Financial Services prefer:
Real Estate
Financial Services

In Agr/Forestr/Fish prefer:
Agriculture related

Additional Information
Year Founded: 2012
Current Activity Level : Actively seeking new investments

HENAN AGRICULTURE INVESTMENT FUND MANAGEMENT CO LTD

A-22, Shangwu Waihuan Road
19/F, Italy Graham Building
Zhengzhou, Henan, China 450046
Phone: 8637169176396
Fax: 8637169176382
E-mail: haif@haifund.com
Website: www.haifund.com

Type of Firm
Government Affiliated Program

Project Preferences

Type of Financing Preferred:
Balanced

Geographical Preferences

International Preferences:
China

Industry Preferences

In Agr/Forestr/Fish prefer:
Agriculture related

Additional Information
Year Founded: 2010
Capital Under Management: $87,889,000
Current Activity Level : Actively seeking new investments

HENAN HUAXIA HAINA VENTURE CAPITAL CO LTD

Y06, No. 11,Changchun Road
Zhengzhou National HIDZ
Zhengzhou, Henan, China
Phone: 8637186068166
Fax: 8637186068126
Website: www.huaxiahn.com

Type of Firm
Private Equity Firm

Project Preferences

Type of Financing Preferred:
Early Stage
Expansion
Balanced

Geographical Preferences

International Preferences:
China

Industry Preferences

In Biotechnology prefer:
Biotechnology

In Medical/Health prefer:
Pharmaceuticals

In Consumer Related prefer:
Food/Beverage

In Industrial/Energy prefer:
Alternative Energy
Energy Conservation Relat
Industrial Products
Advanced Materials

In Agr/Forestr/Fish prefer:
Agriculture related

In Other prefer:
Environment Responsible

Additional Information
Year Founded: 2008
Current Activity Level : Actively seeking new investments

HENAN JIN EN INVESTMENT CO LTD

South of Jishui E. Road
No.01 12F, B Unit Suit1
Zhengzhou, China

Type of Firm
Private Equity Firm

Project Preferences

Type of Financing Preferred:
Balanced

Geographical Preferences

International Preferences:
China

Additional Information
Year Founded: 2011
Current Activity Level : Actively seeking new investments

HENAN ZHONGCAI VENTURE CAPITAL MANAGEMENT CO LTD

No.1, Inner Ring Road, CBD
16/F, CITIC Tower
Zhengzhou, Henan, China
Phone: 8637155623759
Website: www.ceptm.com

Type of Firm
Investment Management Firm

Project Preferences

Type of Financing Preferred:
Balanced

Geographical Preferences

International Preferences:
China

Additional Information
Year Founded: 2011
Capital Under Management: $15,600,000
Current Activity Level : Actively seeking new investments

HENDERSON GLOBAL INVESTORS LTD

201 Bishopgate
London, United Kingdom EC2M 3AE
Phone: 442078181818
Fax: 442078181819

Other Offices

Miguel Angel 21, Five
Madrid, Spain 28010

Falkestrasse One
Vienna, Austria A-1010
Phone: 43-1-319-3222-18
Fax: 43-1-319-3222-90

6-15-1 Roppongi Minato-ku
Fourth Keyakizaka Terrace
Tokyo, Japan 106-0032
Phone: 813-5413-2130
Fax: 813-5413-2131

Via Agnello Eight
Milan, Italy 20121
Phone: 39-02-7214-731
Fax: 39-02-7214-7350

Suites 4108 Jardine House
1 Connaught Place
Central, Hong Kong
Phone: 852-2905-5188
Fax: 852-2905-5138

737 North Michigan Avenue
Olympia Centre, Suite 1700
Chicago, IL USA 60611
Phone: 312-397-1122
Fax: 312-397-1494

WestEndDuo
Bockenheimer Landstrasse 24
Frankfurt, Germany 60323
Phone: 49-69-86003-0
Fax: 49-69-86003-355

Rennweg 28
Zurich, Switzerland 8001
Phone: 41-043-888-6262
Fax: 41-043-888-6263

1 Financial Plaza
19th Floor
Hartford, CT USA 06103
Phone: 860-723-8600
Fax: 860-723-8601

43-45 Roemer Visscherstraat
Amsterdam, Netherlands 1054EW
Phone: 31-20-675-0146
Fax: 31-20-675-7197

Seven, rue Scribe
Paris, France
Phone: 33-1-5305-4480
Fax: 33-1-4451-9422

4a rue Henri Schnadt
Gasperich, Luxembourg L-2530
Phone: 352-2619-2124
Fax: 352-2689-3535

6 Battery Road, #12-01
Singapore, Singapore 049909
Phone: 65-6836-3900
Fax: 65-6221-0039

Suite 705, Nexus Center
No.19A East 3rd Ring Road North
Beijing, China
Phone: 86-10-5967-0509
Fax: 86-10-5967-0125

C/-The Oberoi Hotel
Suite 110, Dr. Zakir Hussain Marg
New Delhi, India 110003
Phone: 91-11-2430-4029
Fax: 91-11-2430-4030

Management and Staff

Andrew Formica, Chief Executive Officer
Andy Boorman, Managing Director
Andy Andy, Managing Director
David Jacob, Managing Director
James Darkins, Managing Director
Roger Greville, Managing Director
Shirley Garrood, Chief Operating Officer
Toby Hiscock, Chief Financial Officer

Type of Firm

Investment Management Firm

Association Membership

Hong Kong Venture Capital Association (HKVCA)

Project Preferences

Type of Financing Preferred:
Fund of Funds
Core
Leveraged Buyout
Value-Add
Expansion
Generalist PE
Balanced
Opportunistic
Management Buyouts
Acquisition

Size of Investments Considered:
Min Size of Investment Considered (000s): $10,000
Max Size of Investment Considered (000s): $50,000

Geographical Preferences

United States Preferences:
North America

International Preferences:
India
Europe
Switzerland
Western Europe
China
Austria
Eastern Europe
Asia
Korea, South
Germany

Industry Preferences

In Communications prefer:
Telecommunications

In Medical/Health prefer:
Health Services

In Consumer Related prefer:
Entertainment and Leisure
Retail
Consumer Products

In Industrial/Energy prefer:
Alternative Energy

In Transportation prefer:
Transportation

In Financial Services prefer:
Financial Services
Real Estate

In Business Serv. prefer:
Distribution
Media

Additional Information

Name of Most Recent Fund: CASA Partners VI, L.P.
Most Recent Fund Was Raised: 09/23/2013
Year Founded: 1998
Capital Under Management: $2,400,000,000
Current Activity Level: Actively seeking new investments

HENGJI PUYE ASSET MANAGEMENT CO LTD

Xuhui District
No. 158, Fenyang Road
Shanghai, China
Website: www.hpasset.com

Type of Firm

Private Equity Firm

Project Preferences

Type of Financing Preferred:
Balanced

Geographical Preferences

International Preferences:
China

Additional Information
Year Founded: 2011
Current Activity Level : Actively seeking new investments

HENKEL AG & CO KGAA
Henkelstrasse 67
Duesseldorf, Germany 40191
Phone: 492117971331
Fax: 492117982342
E-mail: venture.capital@henkel.de
Website: www.henkel.de

Type of Firm
Corporate PE/Venture

Project Preferences

Type of Financing Preferred:
Early Stage
Seed
Startup

Geographical Preferences

United States Preferences:
All U.S.

International Preferences:
Europe

Industry Preferences

In Biotechnology prefer:
Biotechnology

In Consumer Related prefer:
Consumer Products

In Industrial/Energy prefer:
Materials
Factory Automation

Additional Information
Year Founded: 2001
Current Activity Level : Actively seeking new investments

HENQ INVEST BV
Herengracht 124-128
Amsterdam, Netherlands 1015 BT
Phone: 31104521346
Fax: 31104528846
E-mail: info@henq.nl
Website: www.henq.nl

Management and Staff
Herman Hintzen, Chief Financial Officer

Type of Firm
Private Equity Firm

Project Preferences

Type of Financing Preferred:
Early Stage
Seed
Startup

Geographical Preferences

International Preferences:
Netherlands

Industry Preferences

In Communications prefer:
Communications and Media
Commercial Communications
Wireless Communications
Media and Entertainment

In Computer Software prefer:
Software

In Internet Specific prefer:
Internet

Additional Information
Year Founded: 2006
Capital Under Management: $56,408,000
Current Activity Level : Actively seeking new investments

HENRY INVESTMENT TRUST LP
255 South 17th Street
Suite 2501
Philadelphia, PA USA 19103
Phone: 215-985-4484

Type of Firm
Private Equity Firm

Additional Information
Year Founded: 2001
Capital Under Management: $5,800,000
Current Activity Level : Actively seeking new investments

HERA CAPITAL PARTNERS PTE LTD
30A Kandahar Street
Singapore, Singapore 198890
E-mail: contact@hera-capital.com
Website: hera-capital.com

Management and Staff
Sebastien Guillaud, Co-Founder
Thierry de Panafieu, Co-Founder

Type of Firm
Private Equity Firm

Project Preferences

Type of Financing Preferred:
Balanced

Size of Investments Considered:
Min Size of Investment Considered (000s): $1,000
Max Size of Investment Considered (000s): $10,000

Geographical Preferences

United States Preferences:
Southeast

Industry Preferences

In Consumer Related prefer:
Consumer
Retail

In Business Serv. prefer:
Media

Additional Information
Year Founded: 2012
Current Activity Level : Actively seeking new investments

HERCULES CAPITAL INC
400 Hamilton Avenue
Suite 310
Palo Alto, CA USA 94301
Phone: 6502893060
Fax: 6504739194
E-mail: info@htgc.com
Website: www.htgc.com

Other Offices
777 Church Street
ELMHURST, IL USA 60126
Phone: 8475421858

10955 Westmoor Drive
Suite 400
BROOMFIELD, CO USA 80021
Phone: 3034104417
Fax: 8662121031

31 St. James Avenue
Suite 790
BOSTON, MA USA 02116
Phone: 6173149973
Fax: 6173149997

100 Park Avenue
34th Floor
NEW YORK, NY USA 10017
Phone: 2127743611

1600 Tysons Boulevard
Eighth Floor
MCLEAN, VA USA 22102
Phone: 7032453184
Fax: 7032453001

Management and Staff

Ancy Laszlo, Managing Director
Brad Pritchard, Managing Director
Bryan Jadot, Managing Director
Chad Norman, Managing Director
David Lund, Chief Financial Officer
Glen Mello, Managing Director
Janice Bourque, Managing Director
Kathy Conte, Managing Director
Kevin Grossman, Managing Director
Patrick White, Managing Director
Paul Enderle, Managing Director
Roy Liu, Managing Director
Steve Kuo, Managing Director
Tim McDonough, Principal

Type of Firm

Private Equity Firm

Association Membership

Beijing Private Equity Association (BPEA)
Mid-Atlantic Venture Association
National Venture Capital Association - USA (NVCA)
Natl Assoc of Small Bus. Inv. Co (NASBIC)

Project Preferences

Type of Financing Preferred:
Leveraged Buyout
Early Stage
Expansion
Mezzanine
Generalist PE
Balanced
Later Stage
Acquisition
Recapitalizations

Industry Preferences

In Communications prefer:
Communications and Media
Wireless Communications

In Computer Software prefer:
Data Processing
Software

In Internet Specific prefer:
Ecommerce

In Semiconductor/Electr prefer:
Electronics
Semiconductor

In Biotechnology prefer:
Biotechnology

In Medical/Health prefer:
Medical Diagnostics
Drug/Equipmt Delivery
Medical Products
Health Services
Pharmaceuticals

In Consumer Related prefer:
Consumer

In Industrial/Energy prefer:
Energy
Alternative Energy
Industrial Products
Materials
Advanced Materials
Environmental Related

In Transportation prefer:
Transportation

In Business Serv. prefer:
Services
Media

In Manufact. prefer:
Manufacturing

In Other prefer:
Environment Responsible

Additional Information

Name of Most Recent Fund: Hercules Technology II, L.P.
Most Recent Fund Was Raised: 10/06/2006
Year Founded: 2003
Capital Under Management: $906,300,000
Current Activity Level : Actively seeking new investments

HERCULIS PARTNERS SA

30, rue du 23 Juin
Porrentruy, Switzerland 2900
Phone: 41325520220
Fax: 41324465018
E-mail: info@herculispartners.ch
Website: www.herculispartners.ch

Type of Firm

Investment Management Firm

Project Preferences

Type of Financing Preferred:
Leveraged Buyout
Early Stage
Balanced
Later Stage
Acquisition

Additional Information

Year Founded: 2009
Current Activity Level : Actively seeking new investments

HERITAGE GROUP LLC

40 Burton Hills Boulevard
Suite 250
Nashville, TN USA 37215
Phone: 6156658220
Fax: 6152637800
E-mail: info@heritagegroupusa.com
Website: www.heritagegroupusa.com

Other Offices

2324 Crestmoor Road
Nashville, TN USA 37215
Phone: 6157770001
Fax: 6159865200

Management and Staff

David McClellan, Managing Director
Rock Morphis, Managing Director

Type of Firm

Investment Management Firm

Project Preferences

Type of Financing Preferred:
Balanced
Later Stage

Industry Preferences

In Medical/Health prefer:
Medical Diagnostics
Health Services
Hospitals/Clinics/Primary
Hospital/Other Instit.
Pharmaceuticals

Additional Information

Name of Most Recent Fund: Heritage Healthcare Innovation Fund, L.P.
Most Recent Fund Was Raised: 01/25/2011
Year Founded: 1986
Capital Under Management: $377,050,000
Current Activity Level : Actively seeking new investments

HERKULES CAPITAL AS

PO Box 1973
Vika
Oslo, Norway 0125
Phone: 4722048000
Fax: 4722048001
E-mail: post@herkules.no
Website: www.herkulescapital.no

Management and Staff

Gert Munthe, Managing Partner
Patrik Egeland, Partner
Rikke Reinemo, Partner
Sverre Flaskjer, Partner

Type of Firm

Private Equity Firm

Association Membership

Norwegian Venture Capital Association
European Private Equity and Venture Capital Assoc.

Project Preferences

Type of Financing Preferred:
Leveraged Buyout
Acquisition

Size of Investments Considered:
Min Size of Investment Considered (000s): $17,250
Max Size of Investment Considered (000s): $200,000

Geographical Preferences

International Preferences:
Sweden
Scandanavia/Nordic Region
Finland
Norway
Denmark

Industry Preferences

In Communications prefer:
Communications and Media
Telecommunications

In Medical/Health prefer:
Medical/Health
Health Services

In Consumer Related prefer:
Consumer
Consumer Products
Consumer Services

In Industrial/Energy prefer:
Energy
Oil and Gas Exploration
Industrial Products

In Business Serv. prefer:
Services

Additional Information

Name of Most Recent Fund: Herkules III
Most Recent Fund Was Raised: 11/05/2008
Year Founded: 2000
Capital Under Management: $2,275,500,000
Current Activity Level : Actively seeking new investments

HERMED CAPITAL CO LTD

Xuhui District
3F, A Tower, No.1289 Yishan Rd
Shanghai, China 200233
Phone: 862133987651
Fax: 862133987651
E-mail: info@hermedcapital.com
Website: hermedcapital.com

Type of Firm
Private Equity Firm

Project Preferences

Type of Financing Preferred:
Balanced

Geographical Preferences

International Preferences:
China

Industry Preferences

In Medical/Health prefer:
Health Services

Additional Information
Year Founded: 2016
Current Activity Level : Actively seeking new investments

HERMES GPE LLP

One Portsoken Street
Lloyds Chambers
London, United Kingdom E1 8HZ
Phone: 442076803880
E-mail: contact@hermesgpe.com
Website: www.hermesgpe.com

Other Offices

225 Franklin Street
26th Floor
Boston, MA USA 02110
Phone: 6178928990

One Raffles Place
Level 20-61, Tower 2
Singapore, Singapore 048616
Phone: 6568085855

Management and Staff
Alan MacKay, Chief Executive Officer
Hamish de Run, Principal
Janine Nicholls, Chief Operating Officer

Type of Firm
Private Equity Advisor or Fund of Funds

Association Membership
British Venture Capital Association (BVCA)
European Private Equity and Venture Capital Assoc.

Project Preferences

Type of Financing Preferred:
Fund of Funds
Core
Value-Add
Other
Fund of Funds of Second

Geographical Preferences

International Preferences:
United Kingdom

Industry Preferences

In Industrial/Energy prefer:
Alternative Energy
Energy Conservation Relat
Industrial Products

In Financial Services prefer:
Real Estate

In Other prefer:
Environment Responsible

Additional Information
Year Founded: 2009
Capital Under Management: $33,943,500,000
Current Activity Level : Actively seeking new investments

HERMES GROWTH PARTNERS LTD

96 Kensington High Street
Kensington Pavilion
London, United Kingdom W8 4SG
E-mail: info@hermesgp.com
Website: www.hermesgrowthpartners.com

Management and Staff
Bobby Yerramilli-Rao, Co-Founder
Juan Villalonga, Co-Founder

Type of Firm
Private Equity Firm

Project Preferences

Type of Financing Preferred:
Expansion
Later Stage
Acquisition

Size of Investments Considered:
Min Size of Investment Considered (000s): $10,000
Max Size of Investment Considered (000s): $20,000

Geographical Preferences

International Preferences:
United Kingdom

Industry Preferences

In Communications prefer:
Wireless Communications

In Computer Software prefer:
Data Processing
Software
Systems Software

Additional Information
Year Founded: 2011
Current Activity Level : Actively seeking new investments

HERMITAGE EQUITY PARTNERS

539 Armistead Place
Nashville, TN USA 37215
Phone: 6153003025
Fax: 6152926583
Website: /www.hermitageequity.com

Type of Firm
Private Equity Firm

Project Preferences

Type of Financing Preferred:
Leveraged Buyout
Acquisition

Additional Information
Year Founded: 2017
Current Activity Level : Actively seeking new investments

HERON CAPITAL EQUITY PARTNERS

11550 North Meridian Street
Suite 115, the SePRO Tower
Carmel, IN USA 46032
Phone: 317-686-1950
Fax: 317-686-1954
Website: www.heroncap.com

Management and Staff
Greg Maurer, Managing Director
Kevin Etzkorn, Managing Director

Type of Firm
Private Equity Firm

Project Preferences

Type of Financing Preferred:
Leveraged Buyout
Acquisition
Recapitalizations

Geographical Preferences

United States Preferences:
Midwest

Industry Preferences

In Medical/Health prefer:
Medical/Health

In Manufact. prefer:
Manufacturing

Additional Information
Year Founded: 2010
Current Activity Level : Actively seeking new investments

HERON CAPITAL LLC

11550 North Meridian Street
Suite 115, The SePRO Tower
Carmel, IN USA 46032
Phone: 3176861950
Fax: 3176861954

Management and Staff
Greg Maurer, Managing Director
Kevin Etzkorn, Managing Director
Michael Shepard, Principal

Type of Firm
Private Equity Firm

Project Preferences

Role in Financing:
Will function either as deal originator or investor in deals created by others

Type of Financing Preferred:
Early Stage
Expansion
Balanced
Later Stage

Geographical Preferences

United States Preferences:
All U.S.

Industry Preferences

In Medical/Health prefer:
Medical/Health
Medical Diagnostics
Medical Therapeutics
Medical Products
Health Services

Additional Information
Name of Most Recent Fund: Heron Capital Venture Fund I, L.P.
Most Recent Fund Was Raised: 02/01/2006
Year Founded: 2005
Capital Under Management: $24,000,000
Current Activity Level : Actively seeking new investments

HERRERA PARTNERS

1010 Lamar
Suite 600
Houston, TX USA 77002
Phone: 713-978-6590
Fax: 713-978-6599
Website: www.herrera.com

Management and Staff
Gilbert Herrera, Founder
J. Finley Biggerstaff, Managing Director

Type of Firm
Private Equity Firm

Project Preferences

Role in Financing:
Will function either as deal originator or investor in deals created by others

Type of Financing Preferred:
Leveraged Buyout
Value-Add
Mezzanine
Turnaround
Acquisition
Private Placement
Recapitalizations

Size of Investments Considered:
Min Size of Investment Considered (000s): $500
Max Size of Investment Considered (000s): $25,000

Geographical Preferences

United States Preferences:
Southwest
Texas

Additional Information
Year Founded: 1992
Current Activity Level : Actively seeking new investments
Method of Compensation: Professional fee required whether or not deal closes

HERRIKOA SCA

3, Rue du Pont de l'Aveugle
Anglet, France 64600
Phone: 33559253730
Fax: 559253734
Website: herrikoa.com

Type of Firm
Private Equity Firm

Project Preferences

Type of Financing Preferred:
Leveraged Buyout
Early Stage
Expansion
Later Stage
Seed
Management Buyouts
Acquisition

Size of Investments Considered:
Min Size of Investment Considered (000s): $17
Max Size of Investment Considered (000s): $169

Geographical Preferences

International Preferences:
France

Industry Preferences

In Communications prefer:
Telecommunications

In Industrial/Energy prefer:
Energy
Industrial Products
Environmental Related

In Business Serv. prefer:
Services

In Other prefer:
Environment Responsible

Additional Information
Year Founded: 1980
Current Activity Level : Actively seeking new investments

HEURISTIC CAPITAL PARTNERS MANAGEMENT CO LLC

5201 Great America Parkway
Suite 320
Santa Clara, CA USA 95054

Type of Firm
Private Equity Firm

Project Preferences

Type of Financing Preferred:
Balanced

Industry Preferences

In Financial Services prefer:
Financial Services

In Manufact. prefer:
Manufacturing

Additional Information
Year Founded: 2016
Capital Under Management: $17,000,000
Current Activity Level : Actively seeking new investments

HEXAGON INVESTMENTS LLC

730 17Th Street
Suite 800
Denver, CO USA 80202
Phone: 3035711010
Fax: 3035711221
E-mail: info@hexagoninc.com
Website: www.hexagoninc.com

Type of Firm
Private Equity Firm

Additional Information
Year Founded: 1999
Current Activity Level : Actively seeking new investments

HFPX HOLDING LTDA

Rua Doutor Placido Gomes 610, Sala 204
Joinville, Brazil
Phone: 554730290172
E-mail: contato@hfpx.com.br
Website: www.hfpx.com.br

Management and Staff
Hugo Fabiano Cordeiro, Chief Executive Officer
Priscila Lamb, Chief Financial Officer

Type of Firm
Private Equity Firm

Project Preferences

Type of Financing Preferred:
Seed
Startup

Industry Preferences

In Internet Specific prefer:
E-Commerce Technology

Additional Information
Year Founded: 2012
Current Activity Level : Actively seeking new investments

HGCAPITAL TRUST PLC

Two More London Riverside
London, United Kingdom SE1 2AP
Phone: 442070897888
Fax: 442070897999
E-mail: info@hgcapital.com
Website: www.hgcapitaltrust.com

Management and Staff
Nic Humphries, Chief Executive Officer

Type of Firm
Private Equity Firm

Association Membership
British Venture Capital Association (BVCA)
German Venture Capital Association (BVK)
European Private Equity and Venture Capital Assoc.

Project Preferences

Type of Financing Preferred:
Leveraged Buyout
Later Stage
Management Buyouts
Acquisition

Geographical Preferences

International Preferences:
Ireland
United Kingdom
East Germany
Western Europe
Germany

Industry Preferences

In Communications prefer:
Telecommunications

In Medical/Health prefer:
Health Services

In Industrial/Energy prefer:
Alternative Energy
Industrial Products

In Business Serv. prefer:
Services
Media

Additional Information
Name of Most Recent Fund: HgCapital 7, L.P.
Most Recent Fund Was Raised: 04/15/2013
Year Founded: 2000
Capital Under Management: $3,816,000,000
Current Activity Level : Actively seeking new investments

HGGC LLC

1950 University Avenue
Palo Alto, CA USA 94303
Phone: 6503214910
Fax: 6503214911
E-mail: ir@hggc.com
Website: www.hggc.com

Other Offices

26 Patriot Place
Foxboro, MA USA 02035
Phone: 5085498800
Fax: 5085467867

9815 South Monroe Street, Suite 500
Sandy, UT USA 84070
Phone: 8019842700
Fax: 8019842701

222 Lakeview Avenue
West Palm Beach, FL USA 33401
Phone: 5614916300
Fax: 5614916301

Management and Staff
David Topham, Principal
David Parkin, Partner
Donald Miller, Partner
Farouk Hussein, Principal
Gregory Benson, Co-Founder
Hudson Smith, Managing Director
J. Steven Young, Co-Founder
Jacob Hodgman, Principal
James Learner, Managing Partner
Jay Tabu, Vice President
Jonathon Gay, Vice President
Judy Frodigh, Partner
Kunal Agarwal, Vice President
Neil White, Managing Director
Patrick Dugoni, Vice President
Rhett Neuenschwander, Partner
Richard Lawson, Co-Founder
Robert Gay, Chief Executive Officer
Robert Connors, Vice President
Ryan Stratton, Principal
Steven Smith, Vice President
Steven Leistner, Principal

Pratt's Guide to Private Equity & Venture Capital Sources

Type of Firm
Private Equity Firm

Project Preferences

Type of Financing Preferred:
Leveraged Buyout
Acquisition

Size of Investments Considered:

Min Size of Investment Considered (000s): $25,000
Max Size of Investment Considered (000s): $100,000

Geographical Preferences

United States Preferences:
All U.S.

Industry Preferences

In Computer Software prefer:
Software

In Semiconductor/Electr prefer:
Electronics

In Medical/Health prefer:
Medical/Health
Health Services

In Consumer Related prefer:
Consumer
Retail
Consumer Products

In Industrial/Energy prefer:
Energy
Oil and Gas Exploration
Oil & Gas Drilling,Explor

In Transportation prefer:
Aerospace

In Financial Services prefer:
Financial Services

In Business Serv. prefer:
Media

In Manufact. prefer:
Manufacturing

Additional Information
Year Founded: 2007
Capital Under Management: $3,167,000,000
Current Activity Level : Actively seeking new investments

HGI FINAVES CHINA FUND

889 Yan'an Road
26/F, Pacific Center
Shanghai, China
Phone: 862152402800
Fax: 862152402988
E-mail: investor@hgifinaves.com
Website: www.hgifinaves.com

Other Offices
No. 12, Harcourt Road Central
Suite 1212, Bank of America Tower
Hong Kong, Hong Kong
Phone: 85235202959
Fax: 85235202950

Management and Staff
Bin Luo, Vice President
Lei Zhou, Partner
Yonghan Zhang, Managing Partner
Yongmin Hu, Partner

Type of Firm
University Program

Project Preferences

Type of Financing Preferred:
Early Stage
Seed

Geographical Preferences

International Preferences:
China

Industry Preferences

In Communications prefer:
Entertainment

In Internet Specific prefer:
Internet
Ecommerce

In Consumer Related prefer:
Retail

In Business Serv. prefer:
Services
Media

Additional Information
Year Founded: 2012
Capital Under Management: $47,665,000
Current Activity Level : Actively seeking new investments

HI INOV SAS

30 B Rue Sainte Helene
Lyon, France 69002
Website: www.hiinov.com

Type of Firm
Private Equity Firm

Association Membership
French Venture Capital Association (AFIC)

Project Preferences

Type of Financing Preferred:
Early Stage
Seed
Startup

Geographical Preferences

United States Preferences:

International Preferences:
Europe
Israel
France

Industry Preferences

In Communications prefer:
Communications and Media
Wireless Communications
Data Communications

In Computer Software prefer:
Software

In Internet Specific prefer:
Internet
Ecommerce

Additional Information
Year Founded: 2012
Capital Under Management: $82,424,000
Current Activity Level : Actively seeking new investments

HI INVESTMENT & SECURITIES CO LTD

25-15, Youido-dong
Youngdeungpo-gu
Seoul, South Korea 150-878
Phone: 8223189111
Fax: 82221229030
Website: www.hi-ib.com

Management and Staff
Byeong Chun Yoon, Managing Director

Type of Firm
Corporate PE/Venture

Project Preferences

Type of Financing Preferred:
Leveraged Buyout
Generalist PE
Balanced

Geographical Preferences

International Preferences:
Korea, South

Additional Information
Year Founded: 1989
Capital Under Management: $8,920,000
Current Activity Level : Actively seeking new investments

1034

HI-FORTUNE CAPITAL MANAGEMENT LTD

No.168, Xizhimenwai Street
609,Tengda Building
Beijing, China 100000

Type of Firm
Private Equity Firm

Project Preferences

Type of Financing Preferred:
Balanced

Geographical Preferences

International Preferences:
China

Additional Information
Year Founded: 2015
Current Activity Level : Actively seeking new investments

HICKS EQUITY PARTNERS LLC

c/o Hicks Holdings LLC
100 Crescent Court, Ste 1200
Dallas, TX USA 75201

Management and Staff
Robert Swartz, Managing Director

Type of Firm
Private Equity Firm

Project Preferences

Type of Financing Preferred:
Leveraged Buyout

Geographical Preferences

United States Preferences:
All U.S.

Canadian Preferences:
Alberta

Additional Information
Year Founded: 2004
Current Activity Level : Actively seeking new investments

HIDDEN HARBOR CAPITAL PARTNERS LLC

550 West Cypress Creek Road
Suite 420
Fort Lauderdale, FL USA 33309
Phone: 9549907934
Website: www.hh-cp.com

Management and Staff
Andrew Joy, Principal
Brett Craig, Principal
David Block, Co-Founder
John Caple, Co-Founder

Type of Firm
Private Equity Firm

Project Preferences

Type of Financing Preferred:
Leveraged Buyout
Acquisition

Geographical Preferences

United States Preferences:
North America

Industry Preferences

In Biotechnology prefer:
Industrial Biotechnology

In Consumer Related prefer:
Retail
Consumer Products

In Industrial/Energy prefer:
Industrial Products

In Transportation prefer:
Transportation

In Business Serv. prefer:
Services

Additional Information
Year Founded: 2016
Current Activity Level : Actively seeking new investments

HIG CAPITAL LLC

1450 Brickell Avenue
31st Floor
Miami, FL USA 33131
Phone: 3053792322
Fax: 3053792013
E-mail: info@higcapital.com
Website: higcapital.com

Other Offices

200 Crescent Court
Suite 1414
DALLAS, TX USA 75201
Phone: 214-855-2999
Fax: 214-855-2998

3438 Peachtree Road NE
Suite 1425
ATLANTA, GA USA 30326
Phone: 404-504-9333
Fax: 404-504-9370

One Market - Spear Tower
18th Floor
SAN FRANCISCO, CA USA 94105
Phone: 415-439-5500
Fax: 415-439-5525

Avenida Ataulfo de Pavia
N 1351 7 E 8 Andares - Leblon
Rio de Janeiro, Brazil 22431-050
Phone: 552139588392

Calle Alfonso XII 38, 5a Planta
Madrid, Spain 28014
Phone: 34917375050
Fax: 34917375049

155 N Wacker Drive
Suite 4180
CHICAGO, IL USA 60606
Phone: 312-214-1234

Warburgstrasse 50
Hamburg, Germany 20354
Phone: 49-40-4133-06100
Fax: 49-40-4133-06200

Via Santa Maria Segreta, 6
Milan, Italy 20123
Phone: 39 02 62 03 3115
Fax: 39 02 62 03 4000

25 St. George Street
First Floor, Mayfair
London, United Kingdom W1S 1FS
Phone: 44-207-318-5700
Fax: 44-207-318-5749

44, avenue George V
Paris, France 75008
Phone: 33-1-5357-5060
Fax: 33-1-5357-5089

600 Fifth Avenue
23rd Floor
NEW YORK, NY USA 10020
Phone: 212-506-0500
Fax: 212-506-0559

Management and Staff

Andrew Freeman, Managing Director
Brian Schwartz, Managing Director
Camilo Horvilleur, Managing Director
Carl Harring, Managing Director
Douglas Berman, Managing Director
Elliot Maluth, Managing Director
Fernando Oliveira, Managing Director
Fraser Preston, Managing Director
Jaime Bergel, Managing Director
Jeff Zanarini, Managing Director
Jeff Bohl, Managing Director
Kenneth Borton, Managing Director
Keval Patel, Managing Director
Marcelo Cecchetto, Managing Director
Richard Stokes, Managing Director
Rick Rosen, Managing Director
Rob Wolfson, Managing Director
Ruth Brophy, Chief Financial Officer
Sanjoy Chattopadhyay, Managing Director
Tenno Tsai, Managing Director
William Nolan, Managing Director
Wolfgang Biedermann, Managing Director

Type of Firm
Private Equity Firm

Association Membership
French Venture Capital Association (AFIC)
German Venture Capital Association (BVK)
Illinois Venture Capital Association
Spanish Venture Capital Association (ASCRI)

Project Preferences

Role in Financing:
Will function either as deal originator or investor in deals created by others

Type of Financing Preferred:
Leveraged Buyout
Early Stage
Expansion
Generalist PE
Balanced
Turnaround
Later Stage
Management Buyouts
Acquisition
Distressed Debt
Recapitalizations

Geographical Preferences

United States Preferences:

International Preferences:
United Kingdom
Europe

Industry Focus
(% based on actual investment)

Other Products	24.3%
Industrial/Energy	19.2%
Consumer Related	16.4%
Medical/Health	12.5%
Internet Specific	12.5%
Computer Software and Services	4.2%
Communications and Media	4.1%
Biotechnology	3.6%
Semiconductors/Other Elect.	2.7%
Computer Hardware	0.5%

Additional Information
Name of Most Recent Fund: H.I.G. Middle Market LBO Fund II, L.P.
Most Recent Fund Was Raised: 02/10/2014
Year Founded: 1998
Capital Under Management: $8,500,000,000
Current Activity Level : Actively seeking new investments
Method of Compensation: Return on invest. most important, but chg. closing fees, service fees, etc.

HIGH ALPHA CO-INVESTMENT LLC

55 Monument Circle
14th Floor
Indianapolis, IN USA 46204
E-mail: info@highalpha.com
Website: www.highalpha.com

Type of Firm
Private Equity Firm

Association Membership
National Venture Capital Association - USA (NVCA)

Project Preferences

Type of Financing Preferred:
Early Stage

Geographical Preferences

United States Preferences:

Industry Preferences

In Internet Specific prefer:
Internet

Additional Information
Year Founded: 2015
Capital Under Management: $15,400,000
Current Activity Level : Actively seeking new investments

HIGH COUNTRY VENTURE LLC

831 Pearl Street
Boulder, CO USA 80302
Phone: 3033812638
E-mail: info@highcountryventure.com
Website: www.highcountryventure.com

Type of Firm
Private Equity Firm

Project Preferences

Role in Financing:
Will function either as deal originator or investor in deals created by others

Type of Financing Preferred:
Early Stage
Seed

Geographical Preferences

United States Preferences:
Rocky Mountain
Colorado
All U.S.

Industry Preferences

In Internet Specific prefer:
Internet

In Biotechnology prefer:
Biotechnology

In Medical/Health prefer:
Medical Diagnostics
Medical Products

Additional Information
Year Founded: 2005
Capital Under Management: $25,000,000
Current Activity Level : Actively seeking new investments
Method of Compensation: Return on investment is of primary concern, do not charge fees

HIGH PARK CAPITAL PARTNERS

51 Wolseley Street
Suite 308
Toronto, Canada M5T 1A4

Type of Firm
Private Equity Firm

Project Preferences

Type of Financing Preferred:
Leveraged Buyout

Geographical Preferences

Canadian Preferences:
All Canada

Industry Preferences

In Computer Software prefer:
Software

In Medical/Health prefer:
Medical/Health

In Consumer Related prefer:
Education Related

In Industrial/Energy prefer:
Industrial Products

Additional Information
Year Founded: 2011
Current Activity Level : Actively seeking new investments

HIGH ROAD CAPITAL PARTNERS LLC

1251 Avenue of the Americas
Suite 825
New York, NY USA 10020
Phone: 2125543265
Fax: 2125543284
Website: www.highroadcap.com

Management and Staff
Ben Schnakenberg, Partner
Daniel Gaspar, Partner
Eojin Lee, Vice President
Jeffrey Goodrich, Co-Founder
Jerome Anderson, Partner
Kristin Newhall, Partner
Nicholas Martino, Partner
Richard Prestegaard, Partner
Robert Fitzsimmons, Co-Founder
Scott Rubino, Principal
Steven Siwinski, Partner
William Hobbs, Partner
William Connell, Co-Founder

Type of Firm
Private Equity Firm

Project Preferences

Role in Financing:
Prefer role as deal originator

Type of Financing Preferred:
Leveraged Buyout
Management Buyouts
Acquisition
Recapitalizations

Geographical Preferences

United States Preferences:
North America

Industry Preferences

In Medical/Health prefer:
Medical/Health

In Business Serv. prefer:
Services
Distribution
Media

In Manufact. prefer:
Manufacturing

Additional Information
Name of Most Recent Fund: High Road Capital Partners Fund II, L.P.
Most Recent Fund Was Raised: 04/10/2013
Year Founded: 2007
Capital Under Management: $472,900,000
Current Activity Level : Actively seeking new investments
Method of Compensation: Return on invest. most important, but chg. closing fees, service fees, etc.

HIGH STREET CAPITAL

150 North Wacker Drive
Suite 2420
Chicago, IL USA 60606
Phone: 3124232650
Fax: 3122672861
E-mail: Info@HighStreetCapital.com
Website: www.highstreetcapital.com

Management and Staff
Andrew Simmons, Principal
Charles Bossart, Vice President
Joseph Katcha, Principal
Kent Haeger, Co-Founder
Richard McClain, Principal
Robert France, Principal

Type of Firm
Private Equity Firm

Association Membership
Illinois Venture Capital Association
Natl Assoc of Small Bus. Inv. Co (NASBIC)

Project Preferences

Role in Financing:
Prefer role as deal originator but will also invest in deals created by others

Type of Financing Preferred:
Leveraged Buyout
Expansion
Management Buyouts
Acquisition
Recapitalizations

Geographical Preferences

United States Preferences:

Industry Preferences

In Medical/Health prefer:
Health Services

In Financial Services prefer:
Insurance

In Business Serv. prefer:
Services
Distribution

In Manufact. prefer:
Manufacturing

Additional Information
Year Founded: 1997
Capital Under Management: $120,000,000
Current Activity Level : Actively seeking new investments
Method of Compensation: Return on investment is of primary concern, do not charge fees

HIGH TECH GRUNDERFONDS MANAGEMENT GMBH UNSPECIFIED FUND

Schlegelstrasse 2
Bonn, Germany 53175
Phone: 4922882300100
Fax: 4922882300050
E-mail: info@high-tech-gruenderfonds.de

Management and Staff
Alexander Von Frankenberg, Managing Director
Guido Schlitzer, Chief Financial Officer
Michael Brandkamp, Managing Director

Type of Firm
Government Affiliated Program

Association Membership
German Venture Capital Association (BVK)
European Private Equity and Venture Capital Assoc.

Project Preferences

Type of Financing Preferred:
Seed
Startup

Geographical Preferences

International Preferences:
Germany
All International

Additional Information
Year Founded: 2005
Capital Under Management: $369,700,000
Current Activity Level : Actively seeking new investments

HIGHBAR VENTURES

3150 Porter Drive
Palo Alto, CA USA 94304
E-mail: info@highbarventures.com
Website: www.highbarventures.com

Management and Staff
John Kim, Managing Partner
Roy Thiele-Sardina, Managing Partner

Type of Firm
Private Equity Firm

Project Preferences

Type of Financing Preferred:
Early Stage

Industry Preferences

In Computer Software prefer:
Software
Systems Software

Additional Information
Name of Most Recent Fund: HighBAR Entrepreneur Partners II, L.P.
Most Recent Fund Was Raised: 02/14/2013
Year Founded: 1995
Capital Under Management: $339,000,000
Current Activity Level : Actively seeking new investments

HIGHCAPE PARTNERS LP

10751 Falls Road
SUITE 30
Timonium, MD USA 21093
Phone: 4103750050

Management and Staff
Kevin Rakin, Co-Founder
Matt Zuga, Co-Founder

Type of Firm
Private Equity Firm

Project Preferences

Type of Financing Preferred:
Balanced
Later Stage

Additional Information
Year Founded: 2014
Capital Under Management: $985,000
Current Activity Level : Actively seeking new investments

HIGHGATE VENTURE CAPITAL FUND

Eight King Street East
Suite 202
Toronto, Canada M5C 1B5
Phone: 416-362-7668
Fax: 416-863-5161

Type of Firm
Private Equity Firm

Additional Information
Year Founded: 1988
Current Activity Level : Actively seeking new investments

HIGHLAND CAPITAL MANAGEMENT LP

300 Crescent Court
Suite 700
Dallas, TX USA 75201
Phone: 9726284100
Fax: 9726284147
Website: highlandcapital.com

Other Offices
Av. Juscelino Kubitschek
12o Andar, Itaim Bibi
So Paulo, Brazil 04542-080
Phone: 551130788191

136, Sejong-daero, Jung-gu
21st Floor, Seoul Finance Center
Seoul, South Korea 100-768
Phone: 82 2 3782 4500
Fax: 82 2 3782 4555

130 Jermyn Street
Fourth Floor
London, United Kingdom SW1Y 4UR
Phone: 11-44-20-7747-8000
Fax: 11-44-20-7747-8001

Nine West 57th Street
38th Floor
New York, NY USA 10019
Phone: 212-792-6900
Fax: 212-792-6920

Six Battery Road
Level 31
Singapore, Singapore 049909
Phone: 65-6550-9608
Fax: 65-6225-9060

Management and Staff
Brian Rice, Managing Director
Clay Shumway, Managing Director
Frank Waterhouse, Chief Financial Officer
James Dondero, President
Jess Larsen, Managing Director
John Honis, Partner
Jonathan Lamensdorf, Managing Director
Josh Terry, Managing Director
Lane Britain, Partner
Mark Okada, Co-Founder
Michael Gregory, Managing Director
Patrick Boyce, Partner
Paul Adkins, Managing Director
Philip Braner, Managing Director
Ted Dameris, Managing Director

Type of Firm
Investment Management Firm

Project Preferences

Type of Financing Preferred:
Expansion
Turnaround
Special Situation
Distressed Debt

Geographical Preferences

United States Preferences:
All U.S.

International Preferences:
Europe

Additional Information
Year Founded: 1993
Capital Under Management: $147,000,000
Current Activity Level : Actively seeking new investments

HIGHLAND CAPITAL PARTNERS (UK), LLP

12 Golden Square
London, United Kingdom W1F 9JE
Website: www.highlandeurope.com

Type of Firm
Private Equity Firm

Geographical Preferences

United States Preferences:

International Preferences:
Ireland
Europe
Switzerland
Spain
Israel

Additional Information
Name of Most Recent Fund: Highland Europe Technology Growth, L.P.
Most Recent Fund Was Raised: 02/13/2014
Year Founded: 2012
Capital Under Management: $721,830,000
Current Activity Level : Actively seeking new investments

HIGHLAND CAPITAL PARTNERS LLC

One Broadway
16th Floor
Cambridge, MA USA 02142
Phone: 6174014500

Other Offices
8 Clifford Street
, United Kingdom W1S2LQ
Phone: 44-20-7851-6140

288 Nan Jin Road
Financial Center, Suite 2606
Shanghai, China 200003
Phone: 86-21-2890-9698
Fax: 86-21-2890-9999

18 rue du Marche
Geneva, Switzerland 1204
Phone: 41-22-817-7200
Fax: 41-22-817-7219

11 - 15 Seaton Place
St. Helier, United Kingdom JE4 0QH
Phone: 441534833000

Management and Staff

Alex Taussig, Principal
Andrew Miller, General Partner
Bijan Salehizadeh, General Partner
Bob Davis, Partner
Chris Protasewich, Principal
Chuan Thor, Managing Director
Chuan Thor, Managing Director
Corey Mulloy, General Partner
Corey Mulloy, Partner
Craig Driscoll, Partner
Daniel Nova, Partner
Daniel Rosen, Principal
Daniel Nova, General Partner
David Delmore, Chief Financial Officer
Fergal Mullen, General Partner
Gajan Rajanathan, Principal
Gaurav Tewari, Principal
Irena Goldenberg, Principal
Jean-Luc Abaziou, Venture Partner
Jeremiah Daly, Principal
Jessica Pelletier, Chief Financial Officer
Kuantai Yeh, Managing Director
Laurence Garrett, General Partner
Manish Patel, General Partner
Paul Maeder, General Partner
Peter Bell, Partner
Peter Bell, General Partner
Richard De Silva, Venture Partner
Rob Bemis, Vice President
Robert Davis, General Partner
Robert Higgins, General Partner
Sam Brooks, Principal
Sean Dalton, General Partner
Sean Dalton, Partner
Ted Philip, Managing Partner
Thomas Stemberg, Managing Partner
Thomas Guilfoile, General Partner
Yaping Yao, Principal

Type of Firm

Private Equity Firm

Association Membership

New England Venture Capital Association
Western Association of Venture Capitalists (WAVC)
National Venture Capital Association - USA (NVCA)

Project Preferences

Role in Financing:
Prefer role as deal originator but will also invest in deals created by others

Type of Financing Preferred:
Seed
Startup

Geographical Preferences

International Preferences:
Europe

Industry Focus

(% based on actual investment)
Internet Specific	33.9%
Computer Software and Services	23.1%
Communications and Media	12.4%
Consumer Related	7.8%
Medical/Health	5.1%
Biotechnology	4.9%
Other Products	4.3%
Semiconductors/Other Elect.	4.3%
Computer Hardware	2.4%
Industrial/Energy	1.8%

Additional Information

Name of Most Recent Fund: Leap Fund, The
Most Recent Fund Was Raised: 06/20/2013
Year Founded: 1988
Capital Under Management: $3,085,000,000
Current Activity Level : Actively seeking new investments
Method of Compensation: Return on invest. most important, but chg. closing fees, service fees, etc.

HIGHLAND VENTURE CAPITAL

Three Attadale Road
Inverness, United Kingdom IV3 5QH
Phone: 441463712588

Type of Firm

Government Affiliated Program

Project Preferences

Type of Financing Preferred:
Early Stage
Expansion
Start-up Financing

Size of Investments Considered:
Min Size of Investment Considered (000s): $117
Max Size of Investment Considered (000s): $1,553

Geographical Preferences

International Preferences:
United Kingdom
Europe

Industry Preferences

In Industrial/Energy prefer:
Alternative Energy
Energy Conservation Relat
Environmental Related

Additional Information

Year Founded: 2006
Current Activity Level : Actively seeking new investments

HIGHLAND VENTURES GROUP LLC

1630 30th Street
Suite A, #125
Boulder, CO USA 80301
E-mail: info@highlandvg.com

Management and Staff

Mark Loch, Founder

Type of Firm

Private Equity Firm

Project Preferences

Type of Financing Preferred:
Early Stage

Geographical Preferences

United States Preferences:

Industry Preferences

In Industrial/Energy prefer:
Energy

Additional Information

Year Founded: 2013
Current Activity Level : Actively seeking new investments

HIGHLAND WEST CAPITAL LTD

1508-999 West Hastings Street
Vancouver, Canada V6C 2W2
Phone: 6045584925
E-mail: info@hwcl.ca
Website: www.hwcl.ca

Management and Staff

David Schellenberg, Managing Director
David Rowntree, Founder
David Mullen, Managing Director

Type of Firm

Private Equity Firm

Association Membership

Canadian Venture Capital Association

Pratt's Guide to Private Equity & Venture Capital Sources

Geographical Preferences

United States Preferences:

Canadian Preferences:
All Canada
Western Canada

Industry Preferences

In Financial Services prefer:
Financial Services

In Business Serv. prefer:
Services

In Manufact. prefer:
Manufacturing

Additional Information
Year Founded: 2017
Current Activity Level : Actively seeking new investments

HIGHLANDER PARTNERS LP

3811 Turtle Creek Boulevard
Suite 250
Dallas, TX USA 75219
Phone: 2142455000
Fax: 2142455015
Website: www.highlander-partners.com

Other Offices
pl. Marszalka Josefa Pilsudskiego 3
Warszawa, Poland 00-078
Phone: 48224490012
Fax: 48224490001

Management and Staff
Alex Guiva, Partner
Ben Slater, Vice President
Dawid Walendowski, Managing Partner
Michael Nicolais, President
Robert Sussman, Partner
Stanley Bould, Partner

Type of Firm
Private Equity Firm

Association Membership
Polish Venture Capital Association (PSIC/PPEA)

Project Preferences

Type of Financing Preferred:
Leveraged Buyout
Expansion
Mezzanine
Management Buyouts
Recapitalizations

Geographical Preferences

United States Preferences:
North America

International Preferences:
Hungary
Slovak Repub.
Central Europe
Czech Republic
Poland
Romania

Industry Preferences

In Medical/Health prefer:
Medical/Health
Health Services

In Consumer Related prefer:
Retail
Food/Beverage
Consumer Products

In Industrial/Energy prefer:
Materials

In Business Serv. prefer:
Services

In Manufact. prefer:
Manufacturing

Additional Information
Year Founded: 2004
Current Activity Level : Actively seeking new investments

HIGHLIGHT CAPITAL

No. 1468, Nanjing West Road
2602-2603, Zhongxin Building
Shanghai, China 200040
Phone: 862162790750
Website: www.highlightcapital.com

Management and Staff
Bing Chen, Vice President
Gang Zhao, Founder
Hui Wang, Founder
Jingran Yan, Vice President
Li Hu, Chief Financial Officer
Zhongyuan Zhu, Founder

Type of Firm
Private Equity Firm

Project Preferences

Type of Financing Preferred:
Early Stage
Expansion
Balanced

Geographical Preferences

International Preferences:
China

Industry Preferences

In Medical/Health prefer:
Medical/Health
Medical Therapeutics
Health Services
Pharmaceuticals

Additional Information
Year Founded: 2014
Capital Under Management: $528,830,000
Current Activity Level : Actively seeking new investments

HIGHLINE EQUITY PARTNERS LLC

1620 Market Street
Suite 5E
Denver, CO USA 80202
Phone: 3035226687
Website: www.highlineequitypartners.com

Type of Firm
Private Equity Firm

Project Preferences

Type of Financing Preferred:
Leveraged Buyout
Management Buyouts
Acquisition
Recapitalizations

Geographical Preferences

United States Preferences:

Industry Preferences

In Business Serv. prefer:
Services
Distribution

In Manufact. prefer:
Manufacturing

Additional Information
Year Founded: 2008
Current Activity Level : Actively seeking new investments

HIGHSTAR CAPITAL LP

277 Park Avenue
45th Floor
New York, NY USA 10172
Phone: 6468578700
Fax: 6468578848
E-mail: info@highstarcapital.com
Website: www.highstarcapital.com

Other Offices
2929 Allen Parkway
Suite 2222
Houston, TX USA 77019
Phone: 7138313729
Fax: 7138312447

1040

Management and Staff
Christopher Lee, Founder

Type of Firm
Private Equity Firm

Project Preferences

Type of Financing Preferred:
Leveraged Buyout
Other

Industry Preferences

In Industrial/Energy prefer:
Energy

In Transportation prefer:
Transportation

In Other prefer:
Environment Responsible

Additional Information
Name of Most Recent Fund: Highstar Capital IV, L.P.
Most Recent Fund Was Raised: 10/27/2011
Year Founded: 1998
Capital Under Management: $1,128,105,000
Current Activity Level : Actively seeking new investments

HIGHVIEW CAPITAL LLC

1175 Wilshire Boulevard
Suite 1400
Los Angeles, CA USA 90025
Phone: 3108069780
Website: highviewcp.com

Management and Staff
David Cohen, Co-Founder
Ryan McCarthy, Co-Founder

Type of Firm
Private Equity Firm

Project Preferences

Type of Financing Preferred:
Leveraged Buyout
Management Buyouts
Recapitalizations

Industry Preferences

In Consumer Related prefer:
Retail

In Industrial/Energy prefer:
Energy

Additional Information
Year Founded: 2016
Current Activity Level : Actively seeking new investments

HIGHWAY 12 VENTURES

802 West Bannock
Seventh Floor, Hoff Building
Boise, ID USA 83702
Phone: 2083458383
Fax: 2083458484
E-mail: inform@highway12ventures.com

Management and Staff
Archie Clemins, Venture Partner
Derek Keller, Principal
Mark Solon, Managing Partner
Phil Reed, General Partner
Phillip Reed, General Partner

Type of Firm
Private Equity Firm

Project Preferences

Role in Financing:
Will function either as deal originator or investor in deals created by others

Type of Financing Preferred:
Early Stage
Expansion
Seed

Size of Investments Considered:
Min Size of Investment Considered (000s): $50
Max Size of Investment Considered (000s): $5,000

Geographical Preferences

United States Preferences:
West Coast

Additional Information
Year Founded: 2001
Capital Under Management: $100,000,000
Current Activity Level : Actively seeking new investments
Method of Compensation: Return on investment is of primary concern, do not charge fees

HILCO CONSUMER CAPITAL CORP

5 Revere Drive
Suite 206
Northbrook, IL USA 60062
Phone: 8475091100
E-mail: mail@hilcocc.com
Website: www.hilcocc.com

Management and Staff
Benjamin Nortman, Managing Director
Eric Kaup, Managing Director
Jheff Branman, Senior Managing Director

Type of Firm
Private Equity Firm

Project Preferences

Type of Financing Preferred:
Leveraged Buyout

Industry Preferences

In Business Serv. prefer:
Services
Distribution

In Manufact. prefer:
Manufacturing

Additional Information
Year Founded: 2006
Current Activity Level : Actively seeking new investments

HILCO EQUITY MANAGEMENT LLC

Five Revere Drive
Suite 300
Northbrook, IL USA 60062
Phone: 8475091100
Fax: 8477141580
E-mail: mail@hilcoequity.com
Website: www.hilcoequity.com

Other Offices
38/F One Exchange Square
8 Connaught Place
Central, Hong Kong
Phone: 852-3101-7385
Fax: 852-3101-7384

Management and Staff
John Tomes, Managing Director
Keith Freeman, Principal
Ryan Bohr, Principal

Type of Firm
Private Equity Firm

Project Preferences

Type of Financing Preferred:
Leveraged Buyout
Expansion
Management Buyouts
Acquisition
Recapitalizations

Geographical Preferences

United States Preferences:
North America

Canadian Preferences:
All Canada

Industry Preferences

In Consumer Related prefer:
Retail
Consumer Products

In Business Serv. prefer:
Services

In Manufact. prefer:
Manufacturing

Additional Information
Year Founded: 2002
Capital Under Management: $73,000,000
Current Activity Level : Actively seeking new investments

HILDRED CAPITAL PARTNERS LLC

745 Fifth Avenue, Suite 1702
New York, NY USA 10151
Phone: 6463625965
Fax: 6463625966
E-mail: office@hildredpartners.com
Website: www.hildredpartners.com

Type of Firm
Private Equity Firm

Additional Information
Year Founded: 2017
Current Activity Level : Actively seeking new investments

HILL CAPITAL PARTNERS LLP

22 Manchester Square
London, United Kingdom W1U 3PT
Phone: 442079474454
Website: www.hillcap.co.uk

Type of Firm
Private Equity Firm

Project Preferences

Type of Financing Preferred:
Balanced

Geographical Preferences

International Preferences:
United Kingdom

Industry Preferences

In Consumer Related prefer:
Consumer Services
Other Restaurants

Additional Information
Year Founded: 2010
Current Activity Level : Actively seeking new investments

HILL PATH CAPITAL LP

150 East 58th St, 32 Fl
New York, NY USA 10155
E-mail: info@hillpathcap.com

Type of Firm
Private Equity Firm

Project Preferences

Type of Financing Preferred:
Generalist PE

Additional Information
Year Founded: 2016
Capital Under Management: $303,790,000
Current Activity Level : Actively seeking new investments

HILLCREST CAPITAL PARTNERS LP

225 South Sixth Street, Suite 2660
Minneapolis, MN USA 55401
Phone: 6123339922
Fax: 6127672186

Management and Staff
Jeffrey Turner, Managing Partner

Type of Firm
Private Equity Firm

Project Preferences

Type of Financing Preferred:
Leveraged Buyout

Geographical Preferences

United States Preferences:
Midwest

Industry Preferences

In Consumer Related prefer:
Food/Beverage

In Industrial/Energy prefer:
Industrial Products

In Financial Services prefer:
Financial Services

In Manufact. prefer:
Manufacturing

Additional Information
Year Founded: 2002
Current Activity Level : Actively seeking new investments

HILLCREST VENTURE PARTNERS

950 North Isabel Street
Glendale, CA USA 91207
Phone: 8184929800
Website: www.hillcrestvp.com

Type of Firm
Private Equity Firm

Project Preferences

Type of Financing Preferred:
Early Stage

Industry Preferences

In Communications prefer:
Communications and Media

Additional Information
Year Founded: 2008
Current Activity Level : Actively seeking new investments

HILLTOP CAPITAL PARTNERS LLC

40 Cuttermill Road Suite 400
Great Neck, NY USA 11021
Website: www.hilltopcapital.com

Type of Firm
Private Equity Firm

Project Preferences

Type of Financing Preferred:
Early Stage
Expansion
Later Stage

Industry Preferences

In Computer Software prefer:
Software

In Consumer Related prefer:
Consumer Products

In Industrial/Energy prefer:
Energy

Additional Information
Year Founded: 2016
Current Activity Level : Actively seeking new investments

HILLTOP PRIVATE CAPITAL LLC

509 Madison Avenue, 14th Floor
New York, NY USA 10022
Phone: 9173010980
Fax: 9149673188
Website: www.hilltopprivatecapital.com

Management and Staff
Edwin Moss, Partner
Katherine Lehman, Managing Partner
W. Andrew Shea, Managing Partner

Type of Firm
Private Equity Firm

Project Preferences

Type of Financing Preferred:
Leveraged Buyout
Acquisition

Geographical Preferences

United States Preferences:
All U.S.

Industry Preferences

In Industrial/Energy prefer:
Industrial Products

In Business Serv. prefer:
Services

Additional Information
Year Founded: 1969
Current Activity Level : Actively seeking new investments

HIMALAYA CAPITAL PARTNERS L P

301 East Colorado Boulevard
Suite 501
Diamond Bar, CA USA 91765
Phone: 6266897539
Fax: 6265840182
Website: www.himalayacapital.com

Type of Firm
Private Equity Firm

Project Preferences

Role in Financing:
Prefer role as deal originator

Type of Financing Preferred:
Early Stage

Size of Investments Considered:
Min Size of Investment Considered (000s): $500
Max Size of Investment Considered (000s): $3,000

Geographical Preferences

United States Preferences:
Northeast
Connecticut
New Jersey
New York

Industry Preferences

In Computer Software prefer:
Software

In Biotechnology prefer:
Biotechnology

In Medical/Health prefer:
Medical/Health

In Business Serv. prefer:
Media

Additional Information
Name of Most Recent Fund: Himalaya Capital Ventures II, L.P.
Most Recent Fund Was Raised: 01/14/2003
Year Founded: 1998
Capital Under Management: $40,000,000
Current Activity Level : Actively seeking new investments

HIMEL CAPITAL

7083 Hollywood Boulevard
Los Angeles, CA USA 90004
E-mail: info@himelcapital.com
Website: himelcapital.com

Type of Firm
Investment Management Firm

Project Preferences

Type of Financing Preferred:
Early Stage
Generalist PE

Additional Information
Year Founded: 1969
Current Activity Level : Actively seeking new investments

HINA CAPITAL PARTNERS

No. 79, Jianguo Road
14F, T2, China Central Place
Beijing, China 100020
Phone: 861085889000
Fax: 861085889001
E-mail: info@hinagroup.com.cn
Website: www.hinagroup.com

Other Offices
Suite 2310, Two Embarcadero Center
San Francisco, CA USA 94111
Phone: 14158358880

1010 Huaihai Road
2760, 27/F, K Wah Center
Shanghai, China 200031
Phone: 862161031234
Fax: 862161031288

Management and Staff
Chun Li, Managing Director
Eric Clow, Chief Financial Officer
Jinyi Li, Chief Financial Officer
Yi Lu, Managing Partner
Zheng Dong, Managing Director
Zongzhi Li, Managing Director

Type of Firm
Private Equity Firm

Association Membership
National Venture Capital Association - USA (NVCA)

Project Preferences

Type of Financing Preferred:
Balanced

Geographical Preferences

United States Preferences:
All U.S.

International Preferences:
China

Industry Preferences

In Communications prefer:
Telecommunications
Wireless Communications

In Computer Software prefer:
Software
Applications Software

In Internet Specific prefer:
E-Commerce Technology
Internet

In Consumer Related prefer:
Consumer
Food/Beverage

In Industrial/Energy prefer:
Materials
Environmental Related

In Transportation prefer:
Transportation

In Business Serv. prefer:
Media

Additional Information
Year Founded: 2003
Capital Under Management: $93,166,000
Current Activity Level : Actively seeking new investments

HIPERION CAPITAL MANAGEMENT SGECR SA

Manuel Silvela, One, Four D
Madrid, Spain 28010
Phone: 915930884
Fax: 915933256
E-mail: hiperion@hiperioncapital.com
Website: www.hiperioncapital.com

Type of Firm
Private Equity Firm

Project Preferences

Type of Financing Preferred:
Special Situation
Distressed Debt

Geographical Preferences

International Preferences:
Spain

Additional Information

Year Founded: 2011
Current Activity Level : Actively seeking new investments

HIROGIN CAPITAL CO LTD

1-3-8 Kamiya machi
Naka-ku
Hiroshima City, Japan
Phone: 81-82-504-3979
Fax: 81-82-246-7002

Type of Firm
Private Equity Firm

Project Preferences

Type of Financing Preferred:
Balanced

Geographical Preferences

International Preferences:
Japan

Additional Information

Year Founded: 1995
Capital Under Management: $16,400,000
Current Activity Level : Actively seeking new investments

HIROSHIMA INNOVATION NETWORK INC

Three-17 Fukuromachi, Naka-ku
Shishinyo Building, 10th Floor
Hiroshima, Japan 730-0036
Phone: 81825452860
Fax: 81825452866
Website: www.hinet.co.jp

Type of Firm
Government Affiliated Program

Project Preferences

Type of Financing Preferred:
Generalist PE
Later Stage
Management Buyouts

Geographical Preferences

International Preferences:
Japan

Additional Information

Year Founded: 2011
Capital Under Management: $134,678,000
Current Activity Level : Actively seeking new investments

HIROSHIMA VENTURE CAPITAL CO LTD

3-1, Kayama-cho, Naka-Ku
6F, Hiroshima High Building21
Hiroshima-shi, Japan 730-0031
Phone: 81825043979
Fax: 81822467002
Website: www.h-vc.co.jp

Type of Firm
Private Equity Firm

Association Membership
Japan Venture Capital Association

Additional Information

Year Founded: 1995
Current Activity Level : Actively seeking new investments

HIRTLE CALLAGHAN & CO LLC

300 Barr Harbor Drive
Five Tower Bridge, Suite 500
West Conshohocken, PA USA 19428
Phone: 6108287200
Fax: 6108287425
E-mail: emails@hirtlecallaghan.com
Website: www.hirtlecallaghan.com

Type of Firm
Private Equity Advisor or Fund of Funds

Project Preferences

Type of Financing Preferred:
Fund of Funds

Additional Information

Name of Most Recent Fund: Hirtle Callaghan Private Equity Fund V, L.P.
Most Recent Fund Was Raised: 11/17/2005
Year Founded: 1988
Current Activity Level : Actively seeking new investments

HISPANIA CAPITAL PARTNERS LLC

200 West Madison Street
Suite 970
Chicago, IL USA 60606
Phone: 3126974611
Fax: 3126974598
Website: www.hcpcompany.com

Other Offices

2029 Century Park East, Suite 820
Los Angeles, CA USA 90067
Phone: 310-284-8008
Fax: 310-284-8130

2725 Southwest Third Avenue
Miami, FL USA 33129
Phone: 305-285-4160
Fax: 305-285-4115

Management and Staff
Carlos Signoret, Co-Founder
Victor Maruri, Co-Founder

Type of Firm
SBIC

Association Membership
Natl Assoc of Investment Cos. (NAIC)

Project Preferences

Type of Financing Preferred:
Leveraged Buyout
Expansion
Later Stage
Acquisition

Industry Preferences

In Medical/Health prefer:
Medical/Health
Health Services

In Consumer Related prefer:
Consumer Products
Education Related

In Financial Services prefer:
Financial Services

In Business Serv. prefer:
Services

Additional Information

Name of Most Recent Fund: Hispania Private Equity
Most Recent Fund Was Raised: 03/11/2003
Year Founded: 2003
Capital Under Management: $215,000,000
Current Activity Level : Actively seeking new investments

HITECVISION AS

Jattavagveien 7
Building A
Stavanger, Norway 4020
Phone: 4751202020
Fax: 4751202051
E-mail: contact@hitecvision.com
Website: www.hitecvision.com

Other Offices

Dronning Mauds gate 11
Oslo, Norway 0250
Phone: 4722014030

8909 Jackrabbit Road
Houston, TX USA 77095
Phone: 2818557643

Management and Staff
Andreas Oulie, Partner
Arne Rise, Partner
Cathrine Bjaarstad, Partner
Einar Gjelsvik, Partner
Endre Folge, Partner
Joachim Modahl, Partner
Liv Lundby, Chief Financial Officer
Mariann Baerheim, Chief Operating Officer
Ola Saetre, Partner
Ole Ertvaag, Chief Executive Officer
Pal Reed, Chief Executive Officer

Type of Firm
Private Equity Firm

Association Membership
Norwegian Venture Capital Association

Project Preferences

Type of Financing Preferred:
Leveraged Buyout
Later Stage
Acquisition

Size of Investments Considered:
Min Size of Investment Considered (000s): $30,000
Max Size of Investment Considered (000s): $150,000

Geographical Preferences

United States Preferences:
North America
All U.S.

International Preferences:
United Kingdom
Europe
Norway

Industry Preferences

In Computer Software prefer:
Software

In Semiconductor/Electr prefer:
Electronics

In Industrial/Energy prefer:
Energy
Oil and Gas Exploration
Oil & Gas Drilling,Explor
Industrial Products

In Business Serv. prefer:
Services
Consulting Services

Additional Information
Name of Most Recent Fund: HitecVision VII
Most Recent Fund Was Raised: 04/04/2014
Year Founded: 1985
Capital Under Management: $808,000,000
Current Activity Level : Actively seeking new investments

HIVE LLC
720 University Avenue
Suite 200
Palo Alto, CA USA 94301
E-mail: info@hivedata.com
Website: hivedata.com

Other Offices
1351 4th Street
Fourth Floor
Santa Monica, CA USA 90401

153 Townsend Street
San Francisco, CA USA 94107

Management and Staff
Sumant Mandal, Co-Founder
T. Ravi, Co-Founder

Type of Firm
Incubator/Development Program

Project Preferences

Type of Financing Preferred:
Seed
Startup

Size of Investments Considered:
Min Size of Investment Considered (000s): $1,000
Max Size of Investment Considered (000s): $1,500

Geographical Preferences

United States Preferences:

International Preferences:
India

Industry Preferences

In Communications prefer:
Data Communications

In Computer Software prefer:
Data Processing

Additional Information
Year Founded: 2012
Capital Under Management: $32,020,000
Current Activity Level : Actively seeking new investments

HIVENTURES KOCKAZATI TOKEALAP-KEZELO ZRT
1027 Budapest Kaps u. 6-12
Budapest, Hungary
Phone: 3614525780
Website: www.hiventures.hu

Type of Firm
Private Equity Firm

Project Preferences

Type of Financing Preferred:
Early Stage
Seed
Startup

Geographical Preferences

International Preferences:
Hungary
Europe

Additional Information
Year Founded: 2005
Current Activity Level : Actively seeking new investments

HIVEST CAPITAL PARTNERS SASU
121, Avenue des Champs-Elysees
Paris, France 75008
Phone: 33142890277
Website: www.hivestcapital.com

Type of Firm
Private Equity Firm

Project Preferences

Type of Financing Preferred:
Leveraged Buyout
Management Buyouts
Acquisition

Geographical Preferences

International Preferences:
France

Additional Information
Year Founded: 2016
Capital Under Management: $130,680,000
Current Activity Level : Actively seeking new investments

HLD SCA
41, Rue St Dominique
Paris, France 75007
Website: www.groupehld.com

Type of Firm
Private Equity Firm

Project Preferences

Type of Financing Preferred:
Leveraged Buyout
Early Stage
Expansion
Later Stage
Management Buyouts
Acquisition

Size of Investments Considered:
Min Size of Investment Considered (000s): $10,593
Max Size of Investment Considered (000s): $105,932

Geographical Preferences

International Preferences:
Europe
France

Additional Information
Year Founded: 2010
Current Activity Level : Actively seeking new investments

HLM MANAGEMENT CO LLC

222 Berkeley Street, 20th Floor
Boston, MA USA 02116
Phone: 6172660030
Fax: 6172663619
E-mail: submit@hlmvp.com
Website: www.hlmvp.com

Other Offices

116 Huntington Avenue
Ninth Floor
BOSTON, MA USA 02116
Phone: 6172660030

201 Mission Street
Suite 2240
SAN FRANCISCO, CA USA 94105
Phone: 4158146110
Fax: 4159863050

Management and Staff

Daniel Galles, Partner
Edward Cahill, Partner
Enrico Picozza, Venture Partner
Martin Felsenthal, Partner
Peter Grua, Partner
Russell Ray, Partner
Teo Forcht Dagi, Partner
Vincent Fabiani, Partner
Yumin Choi, Vice President
Yumin Choi, Partner

Type of Firm
Private Equity Firm

Association Membership
New England Venture Capital Association
National Venture Capital Association - USA (NVCA)

Project Preferences

Role in Financing:
Will function either as deal originator or investor in deals created by others

Type of Financing Preferred:
Expansion
Balanced
Later Stage

Geographical Preferences

United States Preferences:

Industry Preferences

In Medical/Health prefer:
Medical/Health
Medical Diagnostics
Medical Products
Health Services

Additional Information
Name of Most Recent Fund: HLM Venture Partners II, LP
Most Recent Fund Was Raised: 04/04/2006
Year Founded: 1983
Capital Under Management: $1,000,000,000
Current Activity Level : Actively seeking new investments
Method of Compensation: Other

HNA TOURISM GROUP CO LTD

East Third Ring North Road
Hainan Aviation Building
Beijing, China 100027
Phone: 861059156800
Fax: 861059156800

Type of Firm
Corporate PE/Venture

Project Preferences

Type of Financing Preferred:
Later Stage

Geographical Preferences

International Preferences:
China

Industry Preferences

In Communications prefer:
Entertainment

Additional Information
Year Founded: 2002
Capital Under Management: $88,640,000
Current Activity Level : Actively seeking new investments

HOF CAPITAL INC

100 11th Avenue
New York, NY USA 10011
Website: www.hof.capital

Management and Staff

Ben Fester, Venture Partner
David Teten, Managing Partner
Fady Yacoub, Co-Founder
Hisham El Haddad, Co-Founder
Neeraj Singhal, Venture Partner
Neha Manaktala, Venture Partner
Neil Devani, Venture Partner
Onsi Sawiris, Co-Founder
Philipp Petrescu, Venture Partner
Varun Kapur, Venture Partner
Victor Wang, Principal

Type of Firm
Private Equity Firm

Project Preferences

Type of Financing Preferred:
Early Stage
Seed

Additional Information
Year Founded: 1969
Current Activity Level : Actively seeking new investments

HOFAN VENTURE CAPITAL

Qian Wan Yi Road 1
Room 201, Building A
Shenzhen, China
Phone: 8675583661390
Website: www.hofan.cn

Type of Firm
Incubator/Development Program

Project Preferences

Type of Financing Preferred:
Seed
Startup

Geographical Preferences

International Preferences:
China

Industry Preferences

In Internet Specific prefer:
Internet
Ecommerce

Additional Information
Year Founded: 2006
Current Activity Level : Actively seeking new investments

HOKURIKU CAPITAL

1-8-10 Marunouchi
Toyama-shi, Japan 930-0085
Phone: 81-76-431-2440
Fax: 81-76-431-2401

Type of Firm
Private Equity Firm

Additional Information
Year Founded: 2007
Current Activity Level : Actively seeking new investments

HOLDING DI INIZIATIVA INDUSTRIALE SPA

Via Barberini 95
Roma, Italy 00187
Phone: 390642020712
Fax: 390642013508
E-mail: h2ispa@h2ispa.com
Website: www.h2ispa.com

Type of Firm
Private Equity Firm

Project Preferences

Type of Financing Preferred:
Early Stage
Expansion
Balanced
Later Stage
Seed

Geographical Preferences

International Preferences:
Europe

Industry Preferences

In Communications prefer:
Commercial Communications

In Consumer Related prefer:
Consumer Products

In Industrial/Energy prefer:
Factory Automation

In Agr/Forestr/Fish prefer:
Agribusiness

Additional Information
Year Founded: 2007
Current Activity Level : Actively seeking new investments

HOLLAND FOOD VENTURES BV

Agro Business Park 10
Wageningen, Netherlands 6708 PW
Phone: 31317466269
Website: www.hfv-bv.nl

Type of Firm
Private Equity Firm

Project Preferences

Type of Financing Preferred:
Early Stage
Expansion
Later Stage
Seed
Management Buyouts

Geographical Preferences

International Preferences:
Europe
Netherlands

Industry Preferences

In Consumer Related prefer:
Food/Beverage

Additional Information
Year Founded: 2008
Current Activity Level : Actively seeking new investments

HOLLAND PRIVATE EQUITY BV

Gustav Mahlerplein 3
Amsterdam, Netherlands 1082 MS
Phone: 31207143400
Fax: 31207143419
E-mail: info@hollandpe.com
Website: www.hpegrowthcapital.com

Other Offices
Koenigsallee 62
Dusseldorf, Germany 40212
Phone: 4921160258800
Fax: 4921160258819

Management and Staff
Corne Jansen, Vice President
Titus Schurink, Chief Financial Officer

Type of Firm
Private Equity Firm

Association Membership
European Private Equity and Venture Capital Assoc.
Dutch Venture Capital Associaton (NVP)

Project Preferences

Type of Financing Preferred:
Balanced
Public Companies
Later Stage

Size of Investments Considered:
Min Size of Investment Considered (000s): $13,175
Max Size of Investment Considered (000s): $26,351

Geographical Preferences

International Preferences:
Netherlands
Belgium
Germany

Industry Preferences

In Communications prefer:
Wireless Communications

In Computer Software prefer:
Software

In Semiconductor/Electr prefer:
Electronics

In Medical/Health prefer:
Medical/Health

In Industrial/Energy prefer:
Energy
Oil and Gas Exploration
Alternative Energy
Energy Conservation Relat
Industrial Products
Factory Automation
Environmental Related

In Financial Services prefer:
Financial Services

Additional Information
Name of Most Recent Fund: HPE PRO Institutional Fund BV
Most Recent Fund Was Raised: 01/01/2010
Year Founded: 2008
Capital Under Management: $97,400,000
Current Activity Level : Actively seeking new investments

HOLLAND STARTUP BV

Boothstraat 5
UTRECHT, Netherlands 3512 BT
Phone: 31303200222
Website: www.hollandstartup.com

Management and Staff
Maurice Bakker, Co-Founder

Type of Firm
Private Equity Firm

Project Preferences

Type of Financing Preferred:
Start-up Financing
Seed

Geographical Preferences

International Preferences:
Netherlands

Industry Preferences

In Computer Software prefer:
Applications Software

Pratt's Guide to Private Equity & Venture Capital Sources

Additional Information
Year Founded: 2014
Current Activity Level: Actively seeking new investments

HOLLAND VENTURE BV

Krijn Taconiskade 416
Amsterdam, Netherlands 1087 HW
Phone: 31203119411
Fax: 31203119412
E-mail: info@hollandventure.com

Management and Staff
Ewout Prins, Managing Partner
Hubert Verbeek, Managing Partner

Type of Firm
Private Equity Firm

Association Membership
Dutch Venture Capital Associaton (NVP)

Project Preferences

Type of Financing Preferred:
Leveraged Buyout
Early Stage
Later Stage
Seed
Management Buyouts
Acquisition

Size of Investments Considered:
Min Size of Investment Considered (000s): $125
Max Size of Investment Considered (000s): $6,250

Geographical Preferences

International Preferences:
Luxembourg
Europe
Netherlands
Scandanavia/Nordic Region
Belgium
Israel

Industry Focus
(% based on actual investment)

Computer Software and Services	35.5%
Internet Specific	26.3%
Communications and Media	25.9%
Computer Hardware	10.0%
Medical/Health	2.4%

Additional Information
Year Founded: 1981
Capital Under Management: $135,900,000
Current Activity Level: Actively seeking new investments

HOLLYHIGH INTL CAPITAL CO LTD

Nan'an District
2-2607, Wanda Plaza
Chongqing, China 400060
Phone: 862367003702
Fax: 862367003702
E-mail: hhic@hollyhigh.cn
Website: www.hollyhigh.cn

Other Offices
No. 59 Soth Maoming Road
1EF Grosvenor House
Shanghai, China 200020
Phone: 86-21-5466-7326
Fax: 86-21-5466-6120

Management and Staff
Jiangtao Qiao, Managing Director
Lin Gong, Managing Director
Sinian Qiu, Partner
Zhanbin Liu, Vice President
Zhengjin Hua, Partner

Type of Firm
Bank Affiliated

Project Preferences

Type of Financing Preferred:
Leveraged Buyout
Acquisition

Geographical Preferences

International Preferences:
China

Industry Preferences

In Biotechnology prefer:
Biotechnology

In Medical/Health prefer:
Pharmaceuticals

In Industrial/Energy prefer:
Energy
Materials
Environmental Related

Additional Information
Year Founded: 2010
Capital Under Management: $73,185,000
Current Activity Level: Actively seeking new investments

HOLLYPORT CAPITAL CAPITAL LLP

56 Conduit Street
London, United Kingdom W1S 2YZ
Phone: 442074783970
Fax: 442074398138
Website: www.hollyportcapital.com

Type of Firm
Private Equity Advisor or Fund of Funds

Project Preferences

Type of Financing Preferred:
Fund of Funds

Additional Information
Year Founded: 2006
Current Activity Level: Actively seeking new investments

HOLTZBRINCK VENTURES GMBH

Landsberger Strasse 187
Munich, Germany 80687
Phone: 4989452285100
Fax: 4989452285200
Website: www.holtzbrinck-ventures.com

Management and Staff
Markus Schunk, Managing Director

Type of Firm
Corporate PE/Venture

Project Preferences

Type of Financing Preferred:
Early Stage
Seed
Startup

Size of Investments Considered:
Min Size of Investment Considered (000s): $1,265
Max Size of Investment Considered (000s): $6,324

Geographical Preferences

International Preferences:
Europe
Switzerland
Austria
Germany

Industry Preferences

In Communications prefer:
Communications and Media
Media and Entertainment

In Internet Specific prefer:
Internet
Ecommerce

In Business Serv. prefer:
Media

Additional Information
Name of Most Recent Fund: HV Holtzbrinck Ventures Fund IV
Most Recent Fund Was Raised: 01/11/2011
Year Founded: 2000

Capital Under Management: $52,300,000
Current Activity Level : Actively seeking new investments

HOMEBREW LLC

300 Brannan Street
Suite 308
San Francisco, CA USA 94107
Phone: 9177444940
Website: www.homebrew.co

Management and Staff

Hunter Walk, Partner
Satya Patel, Partner

Type of Firm

Private Equity Firm

Project Preferences

Type of Financing Preferred:
Startup

Additional Information

Name of Most Recent Fund: Homebrew Ventures I, L.P.
Most Recent Fund Was Raised: 04/26/2013
Year Founded: 2013
Capital Under Management: $120,000,000
Current Activity Level : Actively seeking new investments

HOMELAND DEFENSE VENTURES

153 East 53rd Street
35th Floor
New York, NY USA 10022
Phone: 212-651-3545
Fax: 212-655-0174
Website: www.homelanddefenseventures.com

Management and Staff

Ken Jennings, Partner
Richard Barker, Partner
Valerie Ceva, Partner

Type of Firm

Private Equity Firm

Project Preferences

Type of Financing Preferred:
Balanced

Industry Preferences

In Computer Software prefer:
Artificial Intelligence

In Semiconductor/Electr prefer:
Sensors

In Biotechnology prefer:
Industrial Biotechnology

In Medical/Health prefer:
Pharmaceuticals

In Other prefer:
Socially Responsible

Additional Information

Year Founded: 2001
Current Activity Level : Actively seeking new investments

HONGHUA CAPITAL MANAGEMENT SHENZHEN CO LTD

Mintian Road, Futian Central A
1309-1310, Xinhua Insurance Ma
Shenzhen, China
Phone: 8675582766123
Fax: 8675582735839
Website: www.szhhzb.cn

Type of Firm

Investment Management Firm

Project Preferences

Type of Financing Preferred:
Balanced

Geographical Preferences

International Preferences:
China

Additional Information

Year Founded: 2013
Current Activity Level : Actively seeking new investments

HONGJIN JIYE (BEIJING) INVESTMENT MANAGEMENT CO LTD

Haidian N Road, Haidian Dist
1002, Zhongguancun SOHO
Beijing, China
Phone: 861062682028
Fax: 861062684522
Website: www.hj-invest.com

Type of Firm

Investment Management Firm

Project Preferences

Type of Financing Preferred:
Early Stage
Expansion
Balanced
Seed

Size of Investments Considered:

Min Size of Investment Considered (000s): $32
Max Size of Investment Considered (000s): $315

Geographical Preferences

International Preferences:
China

Industry Preferences

In Communications prefer:
Telecommunications

In Computer Software prefer:
Software

In Internet Specific prefer:
Internet

In Consumer Related prefer:
Consumer Products
Consumer Services

In Industrial/Energy prefer:
Energy
Energy Conservation Relat

In Business Serv. prefer:
Services
Media

In Other prefer:
Environment Responsible

Additional Information

Year Founded: 2011
Current Activity Level : Actively seeking new investments

HONGQIAO CAPITAL

Shanghai
Shanghai, China
Phone: 861084535220

Type of Firm

Private Equity Firm

Project Preferences

Type of Financing Preferred:
Balanced

Geographical Preferences

International Preferences:
China

Industry Preferences

In Communications prefer:
Telecommunications
Media and Entertainment

In Internet Specific prefer:
Internet
Ecommerce

In Consumer Related prefer:
Sports
Education Related

Additional Information
Year Founded: 2012
Current Activity Level : Actively seeking new investments

HONGTA HOTLAND ASSET MANAGEMENT CO LTD

4068 Qiaoxiang Rd Nanshan Dist
A801 Zhihui Square
Shenzhen, China 518052
Phone: 8675536855888
Fax: 8675533379033
Website: www.htamc.com.cn

Type of Firm
Investment Management Firm

Project Preferences

Type of Financing Preferred:
Balanced

Geographical Preferences

International Preferences:
China

Additional Information
Year Founded: 2012
Capital Under Management: $31,600,000
Current Activity Level : Actively seeking new investments

HONY CAPITAL BEIJING CO LTD

No. 2, South Kexueyuan Road
Raycom InfoTech Park
Beijing, China 100190
Phone: 861082655888
Fax: 861082658000
E-mail: honymaster@honycapital.com
Website: www.honycapital.com

Other Offices

No. 149, Yuanmingyuan Road, Huangpu Dist
Hami Plaza
Shanghai, China
Phone: 862160322888
Fax: 862160322800

One Exchange Square
Suite 2701, Central
Hong Kong, Hong Kong
Phone: 85239619700
Fax: 85239719799

Management and Staff

Bing Yuan, Managing Director
Bruce Wang, Managing Director
Gary Chaucer, Managing Director
Hong Song, Managing Director
Jun Ma, Managing Director
Linda Wang, Managing Director
Mason Xu, Managing Director
Minglei Guo, Managing Director
Owen Guo, Managing Director
Sheng Lin, Managing Director
Shuai Chen, Managing Director
Shunlong Wang, Managing Director
Tracy Cui, Managing Director
Wen Chen, Managing Director
Xiaobin Bao, Managing Director
Xihong Deng, Managing Director
Yonghong Sun, Managing Director
Zhongwei Qiu, Managing Director

Type of Firm
Private Equity Firm

Association Membership
China Venture Capital Association

Project Preferences

Type of Financing Preferred:
Leveraged Buyout
Expansion
Generalist PE

Geographical Preferences

International Preferences:
China
Asia

Industry Preferences

In Communications prefer:
Media and Entertainment

In Medical/Health prefer:
Medical/Health
Medical Products
Pharmaceuticals

In Consumer Related prefer:
Consumer
Retail
Consumer Products

In Industrial/Energy prefer:
Alternative Energy
Materials
Advanced Materials

In Financial Services prefer:
Financial Services
Financial Services

In Manufact. prefer:
Manufacturing

In Agr/Forestr/Fish prefer:
Mining and Minerals

In Utilities prefer:
Utilities

In Other prefer:
Environment Responsible

Additional Information
Year Founded: 2003
Capital Under Management: $125,000,000
Current Activity Level : Actively seeking new investments

HOPE INVESTMENTS MANAGEMENT CO LTD

Chaoyangmenwai Avenue
5F, Zhongguorenshou Bldg
Beijing, China 100020

Type of Firm
Private Equity Firm

Project Preferences

Type of Financing Preferred:
Leveraged Buyout

Geographical Preferences

International Preferences:
China
Asia

Additional Information
Year Founded: 2007
Capital Under Management: $2,000,000,000
Current Activity Level : Actively seeking new investments

HOPEN LIFE SCIENCE VENTURES

171 Monroe NW
Suite 410
Grand Rapids, MI USA 49503
Phone: 6163252110
Fax: 6163252111
E-mail: info@hopenls.com
Website: www.hopenls.com

Management and Staff

Jerry Callahan, Managing Director
Mark Olesnavage, Managing Director

Type of Firm
Private Equity Firm

Project Preferences

Type of Financing Preferred:
Early Stage
Expansion
Balanced

Size of Investments Considered:
Min Size of Investment Considered (000s): $150
Max Size of Investment Considered (000s): $5,000

Geographical Preferences

United States Preferences:
Midwest

Industry Preferences

In Medical/Health prefer:
Diagnostic Services
Diagnostic Test Products
Medical Therapeutics
Other Therapeutic
Medical Products
Pharmaceuticals

Additional Information
Name of Most Recent Fund: Hopen Life Science Ventures Fund II, L.P.
Most Recent Fund Was Raised: 08/04/2011
Year Founded: 2006
Capital Under Management: $65,000,000
Current Activity Level : Actively seeking new investments

HOPEWELL VENTURES

20 North Wacker Drive
Suite 2200
Chicago, IL USA 60606
Phone: 3123579600
Fax: 3123579620
E-mail: info@hopewellventures.com
Website: www.hopewellventures.com

Other Offices
801 Main Street
Peoria, IL USA 61606
Phone: 309-495-7251
Fax: 309-495-7255

Management and Staff
Brian Williams, Venture Partner
Craig Overmyer, Principal
Jeffrey Lampe, Principal
Matthew McCue, Vice President
Thomas Parkinson, Principal
William Sutter, Senior Managing Director

Type of Firm
Private Equity Firm

Project Preferences

Role in Financing:
Will function either as deal originator or investor in deals created by others

Type of Financing Preferred:
Early Stage
Expansion
Balanced
Later Stage

Size of Investments Considered:
Min Size of Investment Considered (000s): $2,000
Max Size of Investment Considered (000s): $7,000

Geographical Preferences

United States Preferences:
Midwest

Industry Preferences

In Medical/Health prefer:
Medical/Health
Medical Products

In Manufact. prefer:
Manufacturing

Additional Information
Name of Most Recent Fund: Hopewell Ventures, L.P.
Most Recent Fund Was Raised: 05/05/2004
Year Founded: 2003
Capital Under Management: $110,000,000
Current Activity Level : Actively seeking new investments
Method of Compensation: Return on investment is of primary concern, do not charge fees

HORIZON CAPITAL MANAGEMENT

Mykoly Raevskoho, 4
Kiev, Ukraine 01042
Phone: 380444905580
Fax: 380444905589
E-mail: info@horizoncapital.com.ua
Website: www.horizoncapital.com.ua

Other Offices
175 West Jackson Boulevard
Suite 2225
CHICAGO, IL USA 60604
Phone: 3129397003
Fax: 3129397004

Management and Staff
Denis Tafintsev, Principal
Iryna Starodubova, Partner
Jeffrey Neal, Partner
Konstantin Magaletskyi, Principal
Natalie Chaus, Founder
Natalie Jaresko, Chief Executive Officer
Oksana Strashna, Partner

Type of Firm
Private Equity Firm

Project Preferences

Type of Financing Preferred:
Leveraged Buyout
Early Stage
Expansion
Mezzanine
Balanced
Later Stage

Size of Investments Considered:
Min Size of Investment Considered (000s): $15,000
Max Size of Investment Considered (000s): $40,000

Geographical Preferences

International Preferences:
Belarus
Moldova
Ukraine

Industry Preferences

In Consumer Related prefer:
Retail
Consumer Products

In Industrial/Energy prefer:
Industrial Products

In Financial Services prefer:
Financial Services

In Manufact. prefer:
Manufacturing

Additional Information
Year Founded: 1995
Capital Under Management: $647,000,000
Current Activity Level : Actively seeking new investments

HORIZON EQUITY PARTNERS PTY LTD

Two Commerce Square
39 Rivonia Road, Sandhurst
Sandton, South Africa 2196
Phone: 27115026940
Fax: 27112682275
E-mail: info@horizonequity.co.za
Website: www.horizonequity.co.za

Management and Staff
Garth Jarvis, Managing Director
Richard Flett, Managing Director
Steven Lipchin, Managing Director

Type of Firm
Private Equity Firm

Association Membership
South African Venture Capital Association (SAVCA)
Emerging Markets Private Equity Association

Project Preferences

Type of Financing Preferred:
Leveraged Buyout
Early Stage
Expansion
Public Companies
Later Stage
Management Buyouts
Acquisition
Startup
Recapitalizations

Size of Investments Considered:
Min Size of Investment Considered (000s): $966
Max Size of Investment Considered (000s): $9,657

Geographical Preferences

International Preferences:
South Africa

Industry Preferences

In Communications prefer:
Telecommunications
Wireless Communications

In Computer Software prefer:
Software

In Internet Specific prefer:
E-Commerce Technology
Internet

In Semiconductor/Electr prefer:
Electronics

In Biotechnology prefer:
Biotechnology

In Medical/Health prefer:
Medical/Health
Pharmaceuticals

In Consumer Related prefer:
Food/Beverage

Additional Information

Year Founded: 1992
Capital Under Management: $47,700,000
Current Activity Level : Actively seeking new investments

HORIZON HOLDINGS LLC

Three Embarcadero Center
Suite 2360
San Francisco, CA USA 94111
Phone: 4157882000
Fax: 4157882030
E-mail: hh@horizonholdings.com
Website: www.horizonholdings.com

Management and Staff

James Shorin, Managing Partner
Philip Estes, Managing Partner

Type of Firm

Private Equity Firm

Project Preferences

Type of Financing Preferred:
Leveraged Buyout

Geographical Preferences

United States Preferences:

Additional Information

Year Founded: 1989
Current Activity Level : Actively seeking new investments

HORIZON PARTNERS, LTD.

3838 Tamiami Trail N
Suite 408
Naples, FL USA 34103
Phone: 2392610020
Fax: 2392610225
Website: www.horizonpartnersltd.com

Management and Staff

William Schaar, Chief Financial Officer

Type of Firm

Private Equity Firm

Association Membership

Western Association of Venture Capitalists (WAVC)

Project Preferences

Role in Financing:
Prefer role as deal originator but will also invest in deals created by others

Type of Financing Preferred:
Leveraged Buyout
Turnaround

Industry Focus

(% based on actual investment)
Consumer Related	69.4%
Computer Software and Services	17.0%
Other Products	11.9%
Internet Specific	1.7%

Additional Information

Name of Most Recent Fund: Horizon Capital Partners, L.P.
Most Recent Fund Was Raised: 12/31/1992
Year Founded: 1988
Capital Under Management: $100,000,000
Current Activity Level : Actively seeking new investments
Method of Compensation: Return on invest. most important, but chg. closing fees, service fees, etc.

HORIZON TECHNOLOGY FINANCE MANAGEMENT LLC

312 Farminton Avenue
Farmington, CT USA 06032
Phone: 8606768654
Fax: 8606768655
Website: www.horizontechfinance.com

Other Offices

1646 North California Boulevard, Suite 650
Walnut Creek, CA USA 94596
Phone: 9259352924
Fax: 9259779488

Management and Staff

Gary Moro, Vice President
Greg Clark, Managing Director
Jerry Michaud, President
Kevin Walsh, Vice President
Kevin May, Managing Director
Kristen Kosofsky, Managing Director
Mike Lederman, Managing Director
Paul Gibson, Managing Director
Todd McDonald, Managing Director

Type of Firm

Investment Management Firm

Association Membership

Mid-Atlantic Venture Association

Project Preferences

Type of Financing Preferred:
Balanced

Geographical Preferences

United States Preferences:

Industry Preferences

In Communications prefer:
Communications and Media
Commercial Communications
Wireless Communications

In Computer Software prefer:
Software

In Semiconductor/Electr prefer:
Semiconductor

In Biotechnology prefer:
Biotechnology

In Medical/Health prefer:
Medical/Health
Health Services
Pharmaceuticals

In Industrial/Energy prefer:
Alternative Energy
Environmental Related

Additional Information

Year Founded: 2004
Current Activity Level : Actively seeking new investments

HORIZON VENTURES

Four Main Street
Suite 50
Los Altos, CA USA 94022
Phone: 6509174100
Website: www.horizonvc.com

Management and Staff

Arthur Reidel, Managing Director
Ash Dhar, Venture Partner
Doug Tsui, Venture Partner
George Schneer, Venture Partner
Jack Carsten, Managing Director
John Hall, Managing Director

Type of Firm
Private Equity Firm

Association Membership
China Venture Capital Association

Project Preferences

Role in Financing:
Will function either as deal originator or investor in deals created by others

Type of Financing Preferred:
Early Stage
Seed
Startup

Geographical Preferences

United States Preferences:

Industry Focus
(% based on actual investment)
Computer Software and Services	38.9%
Internet Specific	33.0%
Semiconductors/Other Elect.	10.5%
Consumer Related	6.9%
Communications and Media	5.4%
Other Products	2.4%
Computer Hardware	2.3%
Industrial/Energy	0.6%

Additional Information
Name of Most Recent Fund: Horizon Ventures Fund II, L.P.
Most Recent Fund Was Raised: 11/19/2003
Year Founded: 1999
Capital Under Management: $176,800,000
Current Activity Level : Making few, if any, new investments
Method of Compensation: Return on investment is of primary concern, do not charge fees

HORIZON21 AG

Poststrasse 4
Pfaeffikon, Switzerland 8808
Phone: 41554152000
Fax: 41554152001
E-mail: info@horizon21.com
Website: www.horizon21.ch

Other Offices
20 Genesis Close
Grand Cayman, Cayman Islands KY1-1108
Phone: 13459436660
Fax: 13459436669

Type of Firm
Private Equity Advisor or Fund of Funds

Project Preferences

Type of Financing Preferred:
Fund of Funds
Leveraged Buyout

Geographical Preferences

United States Preferences:
All U.S.

International Preferences:
Europe
Asia

Additional Information
Year Founded: 2004
Current Activity Level : Actively seeking new investments

HORIZONONE ASSET MANAGEMENT INC

220 Bay Street
Suite 1500
Toronto, Canada M5J 2W4
Phone: 4168001784
Fax: 4169280421
E-mail: info@horizonone.com
Website: www.horizonone.com

Management and Staff
James Mahoney, President, Founder

Type of Firm
Investment Management Firm

Project Preferences

Type of Financing Preferred:
Leveraged Buyout
Expansion
Generalist PE
Other
Recapitalizations

Geographical Preferences

Canadian Preferences:
All Canada

Industry Preferences

In Communications prefer:
Communications and Media

In Biotechnology prefer:
Biotechnology

In Industrial/Energy prefer:
Energy
Oil & Gas Drilling,Explor
Alternative Energy

Additional Information
Year Founded: 2001
Current Activity Level : Actively seeking new investments

HORIZONS VENTURES LTD

Two Queen's Road
7/F Cheung Kong Center
Central, Hong Kong
Phone: 85221288888
E-mail: general@horizons.com.hk
Website: horizonsventures.com

Management and Staff
Gilad Novik, Vice President
Jason Wong, Chief Financial Officer
Mabel Chu, Managing Director
Solina Chau, Co-Founder

Type of Firm
Private Equity Firm

Project Preferences

Type of Financing Preferred:
Early Stage

Geographical Preferences

United States Preferences:

Canadian Preferences:
All Canada

International Preferences:
Sweden
United Kingdom
Luxembourg
Europe
China
Estonia
Spain
Israel
Asia
Germany

Industry Preferences

In Communications prefer:
Radio & TV Broadcasting
Telecommunications
Wireless Communications
Data Communications
Media and Entertainment

In Computer Software prefer:
Data Processing

In Semiconductor/Electr prefer:
Electronics

In Medical/Health prefer:
Health Services
Hospitals/Clinics/Primary

In Consumer Related prefer:
Education Related

In Financial Services prefer:
Financial Services

1053

In Other prefer:
Socially Responsible

Additional Information
Year Founded: 2006
Current Activity Level : Actively seeking new investments

HORSLEY BRIDGE PARTNERS LLC

505 Montgomery Street
21st Floor
San Francisco, CA USA 94111
Phone: 4159867733
E-mail: info@horsleybridge.com

Other Offices
8 Jianguomenbei Avenue
Beijing, China
Phone: 86165175988
Fax: 86165175788

Management and Staff
Alfred Giuffrida, Managing Director
Clara Vu, Chief Financial Officer
Du Chai, Managing Director
Elizabeth Obershaw, Managing Director
Josh Freeman, Managing Director
Kathryn Mayne, Managing Director
Lance Cottrill, Managing Director
Mark Moore, Principal
Yi Sun, Managing Director

Type of Firm
Private Equity Advisor or Fund of Funds

Project Preferences

Type of Financing Preferred:
Fund of Funds

Size of Investments Considered:
Min Size of Investment Considered (000s): $25,000
Max Size of Investment Considered (000s): $500,000

Geographical Preferences

United States Preferences:
All U.S.

International Preferences:
India
Europe
Australia
Israel
Asia
All International

Industry Focus
(% based on actual investment)

Other Products	49.9%
Computer Hardware	21.3%
Communications and Media	7.7%
Computer Software and Services	6.6%
Semiconductors/Other Elect.	3.6%
Industrial/Energy	2.7%
Biotechnology	2.7%
Consumer Related	2.5%
Medical/Health	1.9%
Internet Specific	1.2%

Additional Information
Name of Most Recent Fund: Horsley Bridge X Growth Buyout, L.P.
Most Recent Fund Was Raised: 01/09/2014
Year Founded: 1979
Capital Under Management: $11,452,000,000
Current Activity Level : Actively seeking new investments
Method of Compensation: Return on invest. most important, but chg. closing fees, service fees, etc.

HOSPITAL HOLDING SPA

Via Borgogna 7
Milan, Italy 20122
Website: www.hospitalholding.it

Type of Firm
Private Equity Firm

Project Preferences

Type of Financing Preferred:
Early Stage
Seed
Startup

Geographical Preferences

International Preferences:
Italy

Industry Preferences

In Medical/Health prefer:
Health Services
Hospitals/Clinics/Primary

Additional Information
Year Founded: 2016
Capital Under Management: $400,000
Current Activity Level : Actively seeking new investments

HOTSPUR CAPITAL DEVELOPMENT LTD

Bothal Castle
Bothal, Northumberland, United Kingdom NE61 6SL
Phone: 447973252644

Type of Firm
Private Equity Firm

Project Preferences

Type of Financing Preferred:
Early Stage
Expansion

Geographical Preferences

International Preferences:
United Kingdom
Western Europe

Industry Preferences

In Communications prefer:
Wireless Communications

In Computer Software prefer:
Software

In Internet Specific prefer:
Internet

Additional Information
Year Founded: 2007
Current Activity Level : Actively seeking new investments

HOTUNG INTERNATIONAL CO LTD

261 Sung Chiang Road
Nineth Floor
Taipei, Taiwan
Phone: 886225006700
Fax: 886225029716
Website: www.hotung.com.tw

Other Offices
5201 Great America Parkway, No. 356
Techmart
SANTA CLARA, CA USA 95054
Phone: 408-577-1380
Fax: 408-907-0147

Type of Firm
Private Equity Firm

Association Membership
Taiwan Venture Capital Association (TVCA)

Project Preferences

Role in Financing:
Prefer role as deal originator

Type of Financing Preferred:
Early Stage
Expansion
Balanced
Later Stage

Geographical Preferences

International Preferences:
Taiwan

Industry Preferences

In Communications prefer:
Communications and Media

In Internet Specific prefer:
Ecommerce

In Biotechnology prefer:
Biotechnology

In Industrial/Energy prefer:
Machinery

In Agr/Forestr/Fish prefer:
Agriculture related

Additional Information
Year Founded: 1997
Capital Under Management: $511,300,000
Current Activity Level : Actively seeking new investments
Method of Compensation: Return on investment is of primary concern, do not charge fees

---

HOULIHAN LOKEY INC

10250 Constellation Boulevard
Fifth Floor
Los Angeles, CA USA 90067
Phone: 3105538871
Fax: 3105532173
Website: www.hl.com

Other Offices

Citicorp Center - One Sansome Street
Suite 1700
San Francisco, CA USA 94104
Phone: 415-974-5888
Fax: 415-974-5969

11/F Hong Kong Club Building
3A Chater Road
Hong Kong, China
Phone: 852-3551-2300
Fax: 852-3551-2551

200 Crescent Court
Suite 1900
Dallas, TX USA 75201
Phone: 214-220-8470
Fax: 214-220-3808

225 South Sixth Street
Suite 4950
Minneapolis, MN USA 55402
Phone: 612-338-2910
Fax: 612-338-2938

123 North Wacker Drive
Fourth Floor
Chicago, IL USA 60606
Phone: 312-456-4700
Fax: 312-346-0951

3475 Piedmont Road
Suite 950
Atlanta, GA USA 30305
Phone: 404-495-7000
Fax: 404-495-9545

Taunusanlage 1 (Skyper)
60329 Frankfurt am Main
Frankfurt, Germany
Phone: 49-692-562-460
Fax: 49-692-5624-6136

1800 Tysons Boulevard
Suite 300
McLean, VA USA 22102
Phone: 703-847-5225
Fax: 703-848-9667

15/17 rue Auber
Paris, France 75009
Phone: 33-1-7500-1400
Fax: 33-1-7500-1499

83 Pall Mall
3rd Floor
London, United Kingdom SW1Y 5ES
Phone: 442078393355
Fax: 442078395566

245 Park Avenue
New York, NY USA 10167-0001
Phone: 212-497-4100
Fax: 212-661-3070

Management and Staff
J Alley, Chief Financial Officer

Type of Firm
Bank Affiliated

Project Preferences

Role in Financing:
Prefer role as deal originator but will also invest in deals created by others

Type of Financing Preferred:
Leveraged Buyout
Management Buyouts
Acquisition
Recapitalizations

Geographical Preferences

United States Preferences:

Industry Focus
(% based on actual investment)
Internet Specific   93.5%
Industrial/Energy   6.5%

Additional Information
Year Founded: 1970
Current Activity Level : Actively seeking new investments
Method of Compensation: Unknown

HOUSATONIC PARTNERS MANAGEMENT CO INC

One Post Street
Suite 2600
San Francisco, CA USA 94104
Phone: 4159559020
Fax: 4159559053
Website: www.housatonicpartners.com

Other Offices

800 Boylston Street
Suite 2220, Prudential Tower
Boston, MA USA 02199
Phone: 617-399-9200
Fax: 617-267-5565

Management and Staff
Barry Reynolds, Managing Director
Eliot Wadsworth, Partner
H. Irving Grousbeck, Partner
Jill Raimondi, Chief Financial Officer
Joseph Niehaus, Managing Director
Karen Liesching, Principal
Mark Hilderbrand, Managing Director
Michael Jackson, Partner
William Thorndike, Managing Director
William Kuntz, Vice President

Type of Firm
Private Equity Firm

Project Preferences

Type of Financing Preferred:
Leveraged Buyout
Generalist PE
Balanced
Later Stage
Management Buyouts
Acquisition
Recapitalizations

Geographical Preferences

United States Preferences:

Canadian Preferences:
All Canada

Industry Preferences

In Communications prefer:
Communications and Media
Radio & TV Broadcasting
Telecommunications

In Financial Services prefer:
Financial Services

In Business Serv. prefer:
Services
Media

Additional Information
Year Founded: 1994
Capital Under Management: $600,000,000
Current Activity Level : Actively seeking new investments

HOUSE FUND LP
1506 Hyde Street
San Francisco, CA USA 94109
Website: thehouse.fund

Type of Firm
University Program

Project Preferences
Type of Financing Preferred:
Start-up Financing
Seed
Startup

Industry Preferences
In Consumer Related prefer:
Education Related

Additional Information
Year Founded: 2016
Capital Under Management: $6,000,000
Current Activity Level : Actively seeking new investments

HOUSTON HEALTH VENTURES LLC
3733 Westheimer Road
Suite 1039
Houston, TX USA 77027
Phone: 2818150689
Website: www.houstonhealthventures.com

Management and Staff
David Franklin, Co-Founder
Huan Le, Co-Founder
James Tao, Co-Founder

Type of Firm
Incubator/Development Program

Project Preferences
Type of Financing Preferred:
Balanced

Industry Preferences
In Medical/Health prefer:
Medical/Health

Additional Information
Year Founded: 2014
Current Activity Level : Actively seeking new investments

HOUSTON VENTURES
600 Travis
Suite 3550
Houston, TX USA 77002
Phone: 8889087716
E-mail: info@houven.com
Website: www.houven.com

Management and Staff
Charles Davis, Managing Partner
Jim Newell, Managing Partner

Type of Firm
Private Equity Firm

Project Preferences
Type of Financing Preferred:
Early Stage
Expansion
Later Stage

Geographical Preferences
United States Preferences:
New Mexico
Oklahoma
Colorado
Louisiana
Texas

Industry Preferences
In Industrial/Energy prefer:
Energy
Oil and Gas Exploration
Oil & Gas Drilling,Explor

Additional Information
Year Founded: 1996
Capital Under Management: $5,660,000
Current Activity Level : Actively seeking new investments

HOVDE PRIVATE EQUITY ADVISORS LLC
1826 Jefferson Place Northwest
Washington, DC USA 20036
Phone: 2028228117
Fax: 2028228117
Website: www.hovdeprivateequity.com

Management and Staff
Allyson Savin, Vice President
Jeffrey Kashdin, Chief Financial Officer
Joseph Thomas, Managing Director
Shaun Murphy, Managing Director

Type of Firm
Bank Affiliated

Project Preferences
Type of Financing Preferred:
Leveraged Buyout
Turnaround

Industry Preferences
In Financial Services prefer:
Financial Services
Insurance
Investment Groups

Additional Information
Year Founded: 1994
Current Activity Level : Actively seeking new investments

HOYA CORP
2-7-5, Naka-Ochiai
Shinjuku-ku
Tokyo, Japan 161-8525
Phone: 81339521151
Fax: 81339521314
Website: www.hoya.co.jp

Management and Staff
Eiichiro Ikeda, Chief Operating Officer
Ryo Hirooka, Chief Financial Officer

Type of Firm
Corporate PE/Venture

Project Preferences
Type of Financing Preferred:
Balanced

Geographical Preferences
International Preferences:
Japan

Additional Information
Year Founded: 1944
Current Activity Level : Actively seeking new investments

HPEF CAPITAL PARTNERS LTD
1301, AIA Central
1 Connaught Road Central
Hong Kong, Hong Kong
Phone: 85237988388
Fax: 85237988389
E-mail: info@headlandcp.com

Other Offices
The Capital 701
C-70, G Block, 7th Floor
Mumbai, India 400 055
Phone: 91-22-3953-7447
Fax: 91-22-3953-7413

10 Collyer Quay
Ocean Financial Center
Singapore
Phone: 6568086288
Fax: 6568086299

Room 1503
1788 Nanjing Road West
Shanghai, China 200120
Phone: 86-21-6841-3396
Fax: 86-21-6841-3397

Management and Staff

Alok Gupta, Partner
Amy Kwok, Principal
Bernard Man, Principal
Christina Tsang, Principal
Christine Li, Principal
Clara Ho, Partner
Glory Gunawan, Principal
James Stewart, Chief Operating Officer
James Savage, Partner
Jerry Gu, Principal
Jessica Lau, Partner
Jimmy Wang, Partner
Jung Yup Lee, Principal
Junlee Hsu, Principal
Laetitia Yu, Principal
Lance Hong, Partner
Raymond Wong, Principal
Shane Yau, Chief Financial Officer
Sonny Chan, Partner

Type of Firm

Private Equity Firm

Association Membership

Hong Kong Venture Capital Association (HKVCA)
China Venture Capital Association
Emerging Markets Private Equity Association
Singapore Venture Capital Association (SVCA)
Indian Venture Capital Association (IVCA)

Project Preferences

Role in Financing:
Prefer role as deal originator but will also invest in deals created by others

Type of Financing Preferred:
Leveraged Buyout
Early Stage
Expansion
Generalist PE
Balanced
Later Stage
Acquisition

Geographical Preferences

United States Preferences:
Southeast

International Preferences:
India
Taiwan
China
Asia
Korea, South

Industry Focus

(% based on actual investment)
Other Products	39.7%
Consumer Related	22.3%
Semiconductors/Other Elect.	8.4%
Communications and Media	7.8%
Industrial/Energy	7.4%
Computer Software and Services	6.1%
Computer Hardware	3.0%
Internet Specific	2.7%
Medical/Health	2.5%

Additional Information

Year Founded: 1988
Capital Under Management: $2,400,000,000
Method of Compensation: Return on investment is of primary concern, do not charge fees

HPS INVESTMENT PARTNERS LLC

40 West 57th Street
33rd Floor
New York, NY USA 10019
Phone: 1 212 287 6767
E-mail: investor-relations@highbridge.com
Website: www.hpspartners.com

Management and Staff

Clifford Friedman, Founder
George Brokaw, Managing Director
Liza Boyd, Managing Director
Payne Brown, Managing Director
Thomas Wasserman, Managing Director

Type of Firm

Investment Management Firm

Project Preferences

Role in Financing:
Will function either as deal originator or investor in deals created by others

Type of Financing Preferred:
Early Stage
Mezzanine
Generalist PE
Balanced

Geographical Preferences

United States Preferences:
Northeast
West Coast
All U.S.

Canadian Preferences:
All Canada

International Preferences:
Western Europe

Industry Focus

(% based on actual investment)
Other Products	39.1%
Industrial/Energy	17.3%
Computer Software and Services	15.8%
Internet Specific	13.1%
Communications and Media	8.4%
Consumer Related	6.3%

Additional Information

Name of Most Recent Fund: HPS Mezzanine Partners Fund II
Most Recent Fund Was Raised: 03/18/2013
Year Founded: 1998
Capital Under Management: $650,000,000
Current Activity Level : Actively seeking new investments
Method of Compensation: Return on investment is of primary concern, do not charge fees

HQ EQUITA GMBH

Am Pilgerrain 15
Inge Quandt Haus
Bad Homburg vor der Hohe, Germany 61352
Phone: 49617294410
Fax: 4961729441299
E-mail: info@equita.de
Website: hqequita.com

Management and Staff

Hans Moock, Managing Director
Hansjorg Schnabel, Managing Partner
Michael Honig, Managing Partner

Type of Firm

Private Equity Firm

Project Preferences

Type of Financing Preferred:
Management Buyouts
Acquisition
Recapitalizations

Geographical Preferences

International Preferences:
Austria

Industry Preferences

In Communications prefer:
Communications and Media

In Computer Other prefer:
Computer Related

In Semiconductor/Electr prefer:
Electronics
Electronic Components

In Industrial/Energy prefer:
Materials
Machinery

Additional Information
Name of Most Recent Fund: Equita GmbH & Co. CoVest KGaA
Most Recent Fund Was Raised: 07/26/2012
Year Founded: 1992
Capital Under Management: $141,226,000
Current Activity Level : Actively seeking new investments

HSBC PRIVATE EQUITY INVESTMENTS (UK) LTD

8 Canada Square
Level four
London, United Kingdom E14 5HQ
Phone: 442073369955
Fax: 442073369961

Other Offices
Level 17, HSBC Main Building
1 Queen's Road Central
Hong Kong, Hong Kong
Phone: 852-2845-7688
Fax: 852-2845-9992

Type of Firm
Bank Affiliated

Association Membership
British Venture Capital Association (BVCA)

Project Preferences

Type of Financing Preferred:
Leveraged Buyout
Expansion
Management Buyouts
Recapitalizations

Size of Investments Considered:
Min Size of Investment Considered (000s): $32,880
Max Size of Investment Considered (000s): $16,440

Geographical Preferences

International Preferences:
United Kingdom
Europe

Additional Information
Year Founded: 1968
Current Activity Level : Actively seeking new investments

HT CAPITAL ADVISORS LLC

437 Madison Avenue
New York, NY USA 10022
Phone: 2127599080
Fax: 2127590199
E-mail: finance@htcapital.com
Website: www.htcapital.com

Management and Staff
C.A. Burkhardt, Senior Managing Director
Eric Lomas, President
Peter Offermann, Managing Director
Sharif Tanamli, Managing Director

Type of Firm
Bank Affiliated

Project Preferences

Role in Financing:
Will function either as deal originator or investor in deals created by others

Type of Financing Preferred:
Leveraged Buyout
Turnaround
Acquisition
Recapitalizations

Size of Investments Considered:
Min Size of Investment Considered (000s): $2,000
Max Size of Investment Considered (000s): $10,000

Geographical Preferences

United States Preferences:

International Preferences:
Europe

Additional Information
Year Founded: 1932
Current Activity Level : Actively seeking new investments
Method of Compensation: Return on invest. most important, but chg. closing fees, service fees, etc.

HTG VENTURES AG

Rothusstrasse 21
Huenenberg, Switzerland 6331
E-mail: investment@htgventures.com
Website: www.htgventures.com

Management and Staff
Jorn Sievers, Chief Executive Officer

Type of Firm
Private Equity Firm

Project Preferences

Type of Financing Preferred:
Early Stage
Seed
Startup

Additional Information
Year Founded: 1969
Current Activity Level : Actively seeking new investments

HU INVESTMENTS LLC

321 Upper Mountain Avenue
Montclair, NJ USA 07043
Phone: 9735092190
Fax: 9735099682
E-mail: info@huinvestments.com
Website: www.huinvestments.com

Type of Firm
Private Equity Firm

Project Preferences

Type of Financing Preferred:
Early Stage

Industry Preferences

In Manufact. prefer:
Manufacturing

Additional Information
Year Founded: 2011
Current Activity Level : Actively seeking new investments

HUA CAPITAL MANAGEMENT CO LTD

Haidian District
15F, Block A, Beihang Zhizhen
Beijing, China
Phone: 861059943900
Website: www.hua-capital.com

Type of Firm
Private Equity Firm

Project Preferences

Type of Financing Preferred:
Balanced

Geographical Preferences

International Preferences:
Asia

Industry Preferences

In Semiconductor/Electr prefer:
Semiconductor
Circuit Boards

Additional Information
Year Founded: 2014
Current Activity Level : Actively seeking new investments

HUA YU INVESTMENT MANAGEMENT LTD

Suite 51, 5F New Henry House
10 Ice House Street
Central, Hong Kong
Phone: 852-2804-6188
Fax: 852-2804-6197

Type of Firm
Investment Management Firm

Project Preferences

Type of Financing Preferred:
Balanced

Geographical Preferences

International Preferences:
Hong Kong

Additional Information
Year Founded: 2002
Current Activity Level : Actively seeking new investments

HUAMEI CAPITAL CO INC

48th Floor, One Exchange Square
Central, Hong Kong
Phone: 852-3189-6888
Fax: 86-755-8294
E-mail: enquiry@huameicapital.com

Type of Firm
Investment Management Firm

Project Preferences

Type of Financing Preferred:
Later Stage

Geographical Preferences

International Preferences:
China

Industry Preferences

In Communications prefer:
Communications and Media

In Medical/Health prefer:
Health Services

In Financial Services prefer:
Real Estate
Financial Services

Additional Information
Year Founded: 2006
Current Activity Level : Actively seeking new investments

HUANAN VENTURE CAPITAL CO LTD

38, Sec. 1
Chungching South Road
Taipei, Taiwan
Phone: 886-2-2371-3111
Fax: 886-2-2331-6741
E-mail: public@hnfhc.com.tw

Type of Firm
Bank Affiliated

Association Membership
Taiwan Venture Capital Association (TVCA)

Project Preferences

Type of Financing Preferred:
Balanced

Geographical Preferences

International Preferences:
Taiwan

Additional Information
Year Founded: 2001
Capital Under Management: $1,832,400,000
Current Activity Level : Actively seeking new investments

HUARONG RONGDE ASSET MANAGEMENT CO LTD

No. 6 Wudinghou Street, Xichen
Room 306
Beijing, China
Phone: 861059315310
Website: www.rongdeamc.com

Type of Firm
Private Equity Firm

Project Preferences

Type of Financing Preferred:
Balanced

Geographical Preferences

International Preferences:
Asia

Industry Preferences

In Industrial/Energy prefer:
Energy

In Financial Services prefer:
Real Estate

In Manufact. prefer:
Manufacturing

Additional Information
Year Founded: 2006
Current Activity Level : Actively seeking new investments

HUARONG TIANZE INVESTMENT CO LTD

Zhongshan East 2nd Road, Huang
No. 15
Shanghai, China 200002
Phone: 862163266082

Type of Firm
Private Equity Firm

Project Preferences

Type of Financing Preferred:
Balanced

Geographical Preferences

International Preferences:
China

Additional Information
Year Founded: 2012
Current Activity Level : Actively seeking new investments

HUATAI RUITONG INVESTMENT MANAGEMENT CO LTD

No.90, Zhongshan E. Road
Huatai Securities Building
Nanjing, China 210002

Type of Firm
Investment Management Firm

Project Preferences

Type of Financing Preferred:
Leveraged Buyout

Geographical Preferences

International Preferences:
China

Industry Preferences

In Biotechnology prefer:
Biotechnology

In Medical/Health prefer:
Pharmaceuticals

In Industrial/Energy prefer:
Energy
Advanced Materials
Machinery

In Business Serv. prefer:
Services

In Manufact. prefer:
Manufacturing

Additional Information
Year Founded: 2012
Capital Under Management: $8,000,000
Current Activity Level : Actively seeking new investments

HUAXIN INVESTMENT MANAGEMENT CO LTD

Golden Eagle Intl. Plaza, 19-A
Xin Jie Kou
Nanjing, China 210029
Phone: 862584711223
Fax: 862584711222

Type of Firm
Private Equity Firm

Project Preferences

Type of Financing Preferred:
Early Stage

Geographical Preferences

International Preferences:
China

Additional Information
Year Founded: 2011
Current Activity Level : Actively seeking new investments

HUAXING VENTURE

268 Lake Road
Securities Building 8
Fuzhou, China 350003
Phone: 87857096
Fax: 37858275
Website: www.fjhxvc.com

Type of Firm
Private Equity Firm

Project Preferences

Type of Financing Preferred:
Balanced

Additional Information
Year Founded: 2010
Current Activity Level : Actively seeking new investments

HUB VENTURES

901 Mission Street, Suite 105
San Francisco, CA USA 94103
Website: www.hub-ventures.com

Management and Staff
Rick Moss, Founder
Wesley Selke, Founder

Type of Firm
Incubator/Development Program

Project Preferences

Type of Financing Preferred:
Early Stage
Seed
Startup

Size of Investments Considered:
Min Size of Investment Considered (000s) $10
Max Size of Investment Considered (000s): $20

Industry Preferences

In Communications prefer:
Wireless Communications

In Computer Software prefer:
Software

In Medical/Health prefer:
Medical/Health

In Consumer Related prefer:
Food/Beverage
Education Related

In Industrial/Energy prefer:
Energy
Energy Conservation Relat
Environmental Related

Additional Information
Name of Most Recent Fund: Hub Ventures Fund
Most Recent Fund Was Raised: 12/31/2012
Year Founded: 2010
Capital Under Management: $400,000
Current Activity Level : Actively seeking new investments

HUBEI AOXIN VENTURE CAPITAL CO LTD

c/o Aoxin Investments Group
No. 31 Yunlin Street
Wuhan, Hubei, China
Phone: 86-27-8555-0880
Fax: 86-27-8555-0876
Website: www.aoxin-wh.com

Type of Firm
Bank Affiliated

Project Preferences

Type of Financing Preferred:
Leveraged Buyout
Expansion
Mezzanine
Balanced
Later Stage

Geographical Preferences

International Preferences:
China

Industry Preferences

In Industrial/Energy prefer:
Environmental Related

In Agr/Forestr/Fish prefer:
Agriculture related

In Other prefer:
Environment Responsible

Additional Information
Year Founded: 2008
Capital Under Management: $44,180,000
Current Activity Level : Actively seeking new investments

HUBEI JINDINGSHENG EQUITY INVESTMENT FUND CO LTD

No. 81, Hongshan Road,Wuchang
5/F, The Hongshan Hall
Wuhan, China 430071
Phone: 862787892606
Fax: 862787892608
Website: www.gpchn.com.cn

Type of Firm
Private Equity Firm

Project Preferences

Type of Financing Preferred:
Generalist PE

Geographical Preferences

International Preferences:
China

Additional Information
Year Founded: 2013
Current Activity Level : Actively seeking new investments

HUBEI PROVINCIAL HIGH TECHNOLOGY INDUSTRY INVESTMENT CO LTD

716 Luoyu Road
12/F, Huale Business Centre
Wuhan, China 430074
Phone: 862787440549
Fax: 862787440849
Website: www.cnhbgt.com

Type of Firm
Private Equity Firm

Project Preferences

Type of Financing Preferred:
Fund of Funds
Early Stage
Expansion
Balanced
Later Stage
Seed

Geographical Preferences

International Preferences:
China
Asia

Industry Preferences

In Communications prefer:
Communications and Media

In Medical/Health prefer:
Medical/Health

In Industrial/Energy prefer:
Energy
Energy Conservation Relat
Materials
Environmental Related

In Manufact. prefer:
Manufacturing

Additional Information

Year Founded: 2005
Capital Under Management: $140,215,000
Current Activity Level : Actively seeking new investments

HUDSON CLEAN ENERGY PARTNERS

400 Frank W. Burr Boulevard
Suite 37
Teaneck, NJ USA 07666
Phone: 2012874100
E-mail: ideas@hudsoncep.com
Website: www.hudsoncep.com

Other Offices

No. 1 Dong San Huan Zhong Road
10/F East Tower
Beijing, China

Three Sheldon Square
Paddington Central
London, United Kingdom W2 6HY
Phone: 44-20-7121-0530

Management and Staff

Bill Rogers, Managing Director
Craig Cornelius, Managing Director
Gene Kakaulin, Vice President
Geoff Broglio, Vice President
John Cavalier, Managing Partner
Joseph Slamm, Partner
Larry Henry, Partner
Natasha Furquharson, Vice President
Neil Auerbach, Managing Partner
Paul Ho, Managing Director
Sean Reilly, Chief Financial Officer
Shaun Kingsbury, Partner
Zhongmin Shen, Partner

Type of Firm

Private Equity Firm

Project Preferences

Type of Financing Preferred:
Early Stage
Other

Geographical Preferences

International Preferences:
China

Industry Preferences

In Industrial/Energy prefer:
Energy
Alternative Energy

Additional Information

Name of Most Recent Fund: Hudson Solar Infrastructure Program
Most Recent Fund Was Raised: 09/10/2013
Year Founded: 2008
Capital Under Management: $1,024,000,000
Current Activity Level : Actively seeking new investments

HUDSON FERRY CAPITAL LLC

275 Madison Avenue
36th Floor
New York, NY USA 10017
Phone: 2123083079
Fax: 2123083893
E-mail: info@hudsonferry.com
Website: www.hudsonferry.com

Management and Staff

Bruce Robertson, Co-Founder
Mark Deutsch, Co-Founder
Robert Athas, Vice President
Stephen Fisher, Co-Founder
Timothy Ross, Co-Founder

Type of Firm

Private Equity Firm

Association Membership

Natl Assoc of Small Bus. Inv. Co (NASBIC)

Project Preferences

Type of Financing Preferred:
Leveraged Buyout
Acquisition

Size of Investments Considered:
Min Size of Investment Considered (000s): $100,000
Max Size of Investment Considered (000s): $300,000

Geographical Preferences

United States Preferences:
All U.S.

Industry Preferences

In Business Serv. prefer:
Services

In Manufact. prefer:
Manufacturing

Additional Information

Name of Most Recent Fund: Hudson Ferry Capital II, L.P.
Most Recent Fund Was Raised: 06/21/2011
Year Founded: 2006
Capital Under Management: $165,000,000
Current Activity Level : Actively seeking new investments

HUDSON RIVER CAPITAL

645 Madison Avenue
New York, NY USA 10022
Phone: 2124469600
Fax: 2125936127
E-mail: info@hudsonrivercapital.com
Website: www.hudsonrivercapital.com

Type of Firm

Private Equity Firm

Project Preferences

Type of Financing Preferred:
Leveraged Buyout
Mezzanine
Management Buyouts
Acquisition

Geographical Preferences

United States Preferences:
All U.S.

Industry Focus

(% based on actual investment)
Other Products	30.6%
Computer Software and Services	24.3%
Internet Specific	24.2%
Semiconductors/Other Elect.	20.9%

Additional Information

Name of Most Recent Fund: Hudson River Co-Investment Fund
Most Recent Fund Was Raised: 02/15/2001
Year Founded: 1994
Current Activity Level : Actively seeking new investments

HUFF CAPITAL INC

61 Valecrest Drive
Toronto, Canada M9A 4P5
Phone: 4168813489
Website: huffcapitalinc.com

Type of Firm
Private Equity Firm

Project Preferences

Type of Financing Preferred:
Early Stage

Additional Information
Year Founded: 2015
Current Activity Level : Actively seeking new investments

HUIDING CAPITAL MANAGEMENT CO LTD

Zhujiang West Road, Tianhe Dis
Room 4301-4302, International
Guangzhou, China
Website: www.huidingcapital.com

Type of Firm
Private Equity Firm

Project Preferences

Type of Financing Preferred:
Balanced

Geographical Preferences

International Preferences:
China

Additional Information
Year Founded: 2015
Current Activity Level : Actively seeking new investments

HUILI BEIJNG INVESTMENT FUND MANAGEMENT CO LTD

5 Guanghua Road, Chaoyang
19F, Tower 1, Prosper Center
Beijing, China 100020
Phone: 861057611888
Fax: 861057611899
E-mail: info@huilifund.com
Website: www.huilifund.com

Type of Firm
Private Equity Firm

Project Preferences

Type of Financing Preferred:
Leveraged Buyout
Value-Add
Generalist PE

Geographical Preferences

International Preferences:
China

Industry Preferences

In Communications prefer:
Media and Entertainment

In Medical/Health prefer:
Medical/Health

In Industrial/Energy prefer:
Energy

In Financial Services prefer:
Real Estate

In Agr/Forestr/Fish prefer:
Mining and Minerals

Additional Information
Year Founded: 2009
Capital Under Management: $606,980,000
Current Activity Level : Actively seeking new investments

HUIZHOU ZHONGKAI HI-TECH ZONE TECHNOLOGY PARK CO LTD

No.16, Huifeng Donger Road
Zhongkai High Teck Zone
Huizhou, Guangdong, China

Type of Firm
Government Affiliated Program

Project Preferences

Type of Financing Preferred:
Early Stage
Seed

Geographical Preferences

International Preferences:
China

Additional Information
Year Founded: 2011
Current Activity Level : Actively seeking new investments

HULL CAPITAL MANAGEMENT LLC

78 Forest Avenue
Locust Valley, NY USA 11560
Phone: 516-609-2500
Fax: 516-977-3058
E-mail: mhull@hullcap.com
Website: www.hullcap.com

Management and Staff
George Holland, Managing Director
James Mitchell Hull, Managing Director

Type of Firm
Private Equity Firm

Project Preferences

Type of Financing Preferred:
Other

Additional Information
Year Founded: 2003
Current Activity Level : Actively seeking new investments
Method of Compensation: Unknown

HUMMER WINBLAD VENTURE PARTNER

Pier 33 South, The Embarcadero
Suites 200 & 300
San Francisco, CA USA 94111
Phone: 4159799600
Fax: 4159799601
Website: www.humwin.com

Management and Staff
Ann Winblad, Co-Founder
Ingrid Chiavacci, Chief Financial Officer
John Hummer, Co-Founder
Lars Leckie, Managing Director
Mitchell Kertzman, Managing Director
Steven Kishi, Managing Director

Type of Firm
Private Equity Firm

Association Membership
Western Association of Venture Capitalists (WAVC)

Project Preferences

Role in Financing:
Prefer role as deal originator but will also invest in deals created by others

Type of Financing Preferred:
Early Stage
Startup

Industry Focus
(% based on actual investment)

Computer Software and Services	59.2%
Internet Specific	33.6%
Communications and Media	2.2%
Consumer Related	2.2%
Other Products	1.8%
Computer Hardware	1.1%

Additional Information
Name of Most Recent Fund: Hummer Winblad Venture Partners VI, L.P.
Most Recent Fund Was Raised: 08/03/2007
Year Founded: 1989
Capital Under Management: $1,000,000,000
Current Activity Level : Actively seeking new investments
Method of Compensation: Return on investment is of primary concern, do not charge fees

HUNAN EVERASSION EQUITY INVESTMENT MANAGEMENT CO LTD

SINOCHEM Building A2
12/F, Fuxingmenwai St
Beijing, China
Phone: 861068567989
Fax: 861068567922
E-mail: fund@everassion.com
Website: www.everassion.cn

Management and Staff
Anyu Zhao, Chief Financial Officer

Type of Firm
Investment Management Firm

Project Preferences

Type of Financing Preferred:
Generalist PE
Balanced

Geographical Preferences

International Preferences:
China

Industry Preferences

In Financial Services prefer:
Real Estate

Additional Information
Year Founded: 2008
Capital Under Management: $79,442,000
Current Activity Level : Actively seeking new investments

HUNAN HAIJIE INVESTMENT CO LTD

No.389 Wuyi Road
1908-1909, Huameiou Building
Changsha, China 410005
Phone: 8673188780176
Fax: 8673188780198
Website: www.hiyield.cn

Type of Firm
Private Equity Firm

Project Preferences

Type of Financing Preferred:
Generalist PE

Geographical Preferences

International Preferences:
China

Industry Preferences

In Communications prefer:
Data Communications
Entertainment

In Medical/Health prefer:
Medical/Health

In Consumer Related prefer:
Sports
Education Related

In Industrial/Energy prefer:
Materials

Additional Information
Year Founded: 2015
Capital Under Management: $599,500,000
Current Activity Level : Actively seeking new investments

HUNAN HIGH-TECH VENTURE CAPITAL CO LTD

No. 1, West Southcity Road
Changsha, China 410015
Phone: 8673185165403
Fax: 8673185165400
E-mail: admin@hhtvc.com

Management and Staff
Shaojun Liu, President

Type of Firm
Government Affiliated Program

Project Preferences

Type of Financing Preferred:
Leveraged Buyout
Early Stage
Expansion
Balanced
Later Stage
Seed

Geographical Preferences

International Preferences:
China

Industry Preferences

In Biotechnology prefer:
Biotechnology

In Medical/Health prefer:
Pharmaceuticals

In Consumer Related prefer:
Entertainment and Leisure

In Industrial/Energy prefer:
Energy
Alternative Energy
Energy Conservation Relat
Materials
Advanced Materials

In Transportation prefer:
Transportation

In Manufact. prefer:
Manufacturing

In Agr/Forestr/Fish prefer:
Agriculture related
Mining and Minerals

In Other prefer:
Environment Responsible

Additional Information
Year Founded: 2007
Capital Under Management: $1,193,398,000
Current Activity Level : Actively seeking new investments

HUNAN HIGH-TECH VENTURE CAPITAL FORTUNE MANAGEMENT CO LTD

No. 508, Furong Middle Road
Floor 2, Junyi Kangnian Hotel
Changsha, China
Phone: 8673182671699
Fax: 8673182671699
Website: www.hhtvccf.com

Type of Firm
Government Affiliated Program

Geographical Preferences

International Preferences:
China

Additional Information
Year Founded: 2013
Current Activity Level : Actively seeking new investments

HUNAN XIANGTOU HIGH-TECH VENTURE CAPITAL CO LTD

No. 999, North Hanpu Road
Xiangtou Holding Group Bldg.
Changsha, China 410012
Phone: 8673185188640
Fax: 8673185188649
E-mail: hnhvc0731@hnhvc.com
Website: www.hnhvc.com

Type of Firm
Private Equity Firm

Project Preferences

Type of Financing Preferred:
Balanced

Geographical Preferences

International Preferences:
China

Industry Preferences

In Semiconductor/Electr prefer:
Electronics

In Biotechnology prefer:
Biotechnology

In Medical/Health prefer:
Medical/Health

In Industrial/Energy prefer:
Energy
Materials

Additional Information
Year Founded: 2000
Current Activity Level: Actively seeking new investments

HUNAN XIANGTOU HOLDINGS GROUP CO LTD

No.279, Furong Road
15th Floor, Goldsourcehotel
Changsha, China 410635
Phone: 867315558888
Fax: 867315161509
Website: www.hnxtkg.com

Management and Staff
Fangjun Ma, Vice President
Lina Luo, Vice President
Xin Cheng, President
Yunlin Wang, Vice President

Type of Firm
Government Affiliated Program

Project Preferences

Type of Financing Preferred:
Balanced

Geographical Preferences

International Preferences:
China

Industry Preferences

In Financial Services prefer:
Financial Services

In Manufact. prefer:
Manufacturing

In Agr/Forestr/Fish prefer:
Agriculture related
Mining and Minerals

Additional Information
Year Founded: 1992
Current Activity Level: Actively seeking new investments

HUNTINGTON CAPITAL I

3636 Nobel Drive
Suite 401
San Diego, CA USA 92122
Phone: 8582597654
Fax: 8582590074
E-mail: info@huntingtoncapital.com

Management and Staff
Barry Wilson, Managing Partner
Frank Mora, Partner
Hope Mago, Principal
Joel Gragg, Principal
Kurt Noyes, Chief Financial Officer
Morgan Miller, Managing Partner
Nicolas Lopez, Principal
Tim Bubnack, Managing Partner

Type of Firm
Private Equity Firm

Project Preferences

Type of Financing Preferred:
Mezzanine
Acquisition

Size of Investments Considered:
Min Size of Investment Considered (000s): $2,000
Max Size of Investment Considered (000s): $7,000

Geographical Preferences

United States Preferences:
California
Southwest

Industry Preferences

In Medical/Health prefer:
Medical/Health
Health Services

In Business Serv. prefer:
Services
Consulting Services

In Manufact. prefer:
Manufacturing

Additional Information
Name of Most Recent Fund: Huntington Capital Fund III, L.P.
Most Recent Fund Was Raised: 06/14/2013
Year Founded: 2000

Capital Under Management: $92,647,000
Current Activity Level: Actively seeking new investments

HUNTSMAN FAMILY INVESTMENTS LLC

500 Huntsman Way
Salt Lake City, UT USA 84108
Phone: 8015845921
Website: www.hfinvestments.com

Management and Staff
Benjamin Wu, Partner

Type of Firm
Investment Management Firm

Project Preferences

Type of Financing Preferred:
Core
Leveraged Buyout
Value-Add
Public Companies
Opportunistic
Acquisition

Geographical Preferences

United States Preferences:

International Preferences:
All International

Additional Information
Year Founded: 2014
Current Activity Level: Actively seeking new investments

HUNTSMAN-LION CAPITAL LLC

535 Madison Avenue
Fourth Floor
New York, NY USA 10022
Phone: 2123555500
Fax: 2123556283
E-mail: info@huntsmanlion.com
Website: huntsmanlion.com

Type of Firm
Private Equity Firm

Project Preferences

Type of Financing Preferred:
Balanced

Industry Preferences

In Industrial/Energy prefer:
Industrial Products
Materials

Additional Information

Year Founded: 2013
Current Activity Level : Actively seeking new investments

HUPOMONE CAPITAL PARTNERS PTE, LTD.

79 Robinson Road
1501 CPF Building
Singapore, Singapore 068897
Phone: 6565363733
Fax: 6564380802
Website: www.hupomone.com

Type of Firm
Private Equity Firm

Project Preferences

Type of Financing Preferred:
Balanced

Geographical Preferences

International Preferences:
China
Asia

Industry Preferences

In Medical/Health prefer:
Medical/Health

In Industrial/Energy prefer:
Energy
Environmental Related

Additional Information

Year Founded: 2004
Current Activity Level : Actively seeking new investments

HURON CAPITAL PARTNERS LLC

500 Griswold, Suite 2700
Detroit, MI USA 48226
Phone: 3139625800
Fax: 3139625820
Website: www.huroncapital.com

Other Offices

Four King Street West
Suite 1300
Toronto, Canada M5H 1B6
Phone: 416-234-0313
Fax: 416-234-1980

Management and Staff

Brian Schwartz, Vice President
Brian Demkowicz, Co-Founder
Charles Sheridan, Principal
Christopher Sheeren, Partner
David Reynolds, Partner
Douglas Sutton, Partner
Gretchen Perkins, Partner
James Mahoney, Partner
Mark Miller, Vice President
Matthew Hare, Vice President
Nicholas Barker, Partner
Sean Roberts, Vice President
William McKinley, Co-Founder

Type of Firm
Private Equity Firm

Project Preferences

Role in Financing:
Prefer role as deal originator but will also invest in deals created by others

Type of Financing Preferred:
Leveraged Buyout
Management Buyouts
Acquisition
Special Situation
Recapitalizations

Geographical Preferences

United States Preferences:

Canadian Preferences:
All Canada

Industry Focus
(% based on actual investment)
Other Products   79.7%
Consumer Related   18.0%
Medical/Health   2.4%

Additional Information

Name of Most Recent Fund: Huron Fund IV L.P., The
Most Recent Fund Was Raised: 01/15/2013
Year Founded: 1999
Capital Under Management: $1,100,000,000
Current Activity Level : Actively seeking new investments
Method of Compensation: Return on invest. most important, but chg. closing fees, service fees, etc.

HURON RIVER VENTURE PARTNERS LLC

320 North Main Street
Suite 400
Ann Arbor, MI USA 48104
Phone: 6464830809
E-mail: info@huronrivervc.com
Website: huronriverventures.com

Other Offices

38 Fulton Street West
Suite 308
Grand Rapids, MI USA 49503

Management and Staff

Ryan Waddington, Managing Director
Tim Streit, Managing Director

Type of Firm
Corporate PE/Venture

Project Preferences

Type of Financing Preferred:
Early Stage
Seed
Startup

Size of Investments Considered:
Min Size of Investment Considered (000s): $50
Max Size of Investment Considered (000s): $1,500

Geographical Preferences

United States Preferences:
Midwest
Michigan

Industry Preferences

In Computer Software prefer:
Software

In Consumer Related prefer:
Food/Beverage

In Industrial/Energy prefer:
Energy

In Transportation prefer:
Transportation

In Agr/Forestr/Fish prefer:
Agriculture related

Additional Information

Name of Most Recent Fund: Huron River Ventures I, L.P.
Most Recent Fund Was Raised: 04/12/2011
Year Founded: 2010
Capital Under Management: $11,000,000
Current Activity Level : Actively seeking new investments

HURRAY INC

1-12-1 Dogenzaka
18/F, Shibuya Mark City West
Tokyo, Japan 150-0043
Phone: 81354561232
Fax: 81354561177

Type of Firm
Private Equity Firm

Association Membership
Japan Venture Capital Association

Project Preferences

Type of Financing Preferred:
Balanced

Geographical Preferences

International Preferences:
Japan

Additional Information

Year Founded: 2004
Current Activity Level: Actively seeking new investments

HUSTLE FUND

751 Laurel Street
Suite 337
San Carlos, CA USA 94070
Website: www.hustlefund.vc

Type of Firm
Private Equity Firm

Project Preferences

Type of Financing Preferred:
Early Stage

Additional Information

Year Founded: 2017
Current Activity Level: Actively seeking new investments

HUTTON COLLINS PARTNERS LLP

50 Pall Mall
London, United Kingdom SW1Y 5JH
Phone: 442070047000
Fax: 442070047001
E-mail: enquiries@huttoncollins.com
Website: www.huttoncollins.com

Management and Staff
Dominic Barbour, Founder
Graham Hutton, Founder
Matthew Collins, Founder

Type of Firm
Private Equity Firm

Project Preferences

Type of Financing Preferred:
Leveraged Buyout
Expansion
Mezzanine
Management Buyouts
Acquisition

Geographical Preferences

International Preferences:
Italy
United Kingdom
Europe
Western Europe
Spain
France

Industry Preferences

In Medical/Health prefer:
Medical/Health

In Consumer Related prefer:
Entertainment and Leisure

In Financial Services prefer:
Financial Services

In Business Serv. prefer:
Services

Additional Information

Year Founded: 2002
Current Activity Level: Actively seeking new investments

HW CAPITAL GMBH

Pienzenauerstrasse 2
Munchen, Germany D-81679
Phone: 4989809912940
Fax: 4989809912950
E-mail: info@hwcapital.de
Website: www.hwcapital.de

Management and Staff
Marcus Wolsdorf, Managing Director
Robert Haselsteiner, Managing Director

Type of Firm
Private Equity Firm

Project Preferences

Type of Financing Preferred:
Early Stage
Seed
Startup

Geographical Preferences

International Preferences:
Germany

Industry Preferences

In Internet Specific prefer:
Ecommerce

In Financial Services prefer:
Financial Services

Additional Information

Year Founded: 2011
Current Activity Level: Actively seeking new investments

HYDE PARK HOLDINGS INC

701 North Franklin Street
Tampa, FL USA 33602
Phone: 8133830202
Fax: 8133830209
Website: www.hydeparkcapital.com

Management and Staff
Jeffrey Bridge, Vice President
John Hill, Senior Managing Director
John McDonald, Senior Managing Director

Type of Firm
Bank Affiliated

Project Preferences

Type of Financing Preferred:
Leveraged Buyout
Management Buyouts
Acquisition
Recapitalizations

Geographical Preferences

United States Preferences:
Southeast
Florida

Industry Focus
(% based on actual investment)
    Consumer Related   97.5%
    Internet Specific   2.5%

Additional Information

Year Founded: 1989
Current Activity Level: Actively seeking new investments

HYDE PARK VENTURE PARTNERS

225 West Washington Street
Suite 1500
Chicago, IL USA 60606
Phone: 2039046930
Website: www.hydeparkvp.com

Management and Staff
Greg Barnes, Principal
Guy Turner, Partner
Ira Weiss, Founder
James Gagnard, Venture Partner
Nancy Corrie, Chief Financial Officer
Nancy Corrie, Chief Financial Officer
Sam Yagan, Venture Partner
Timothy Kopp, Partner

Type of Firm
Private Equity Firm

Association Membership
Illinois Venture Capital Association

Project Preferences

Type of Financing Preferred:
Early Stage

Size of Investments Considered:
Min Size of Investment Considered (000s): $750,000
Max Size of Investment Considered: No Limit

Geographical Preferences

United States Preferences:
Midwest
Illinois

Industry Preferences

In Medical/Health prefer:
Medical/Health

In Consumer Related prefer:
Consumer Services

In Business Serv. prefer:
Services

Additional Information
Name of Most Recent Fund: Hyde Park Venture Partners Fund, L.P.
Most Recent Fund Was Raised: 12/15/2011
Year Founded: 2011
Capital Under Management: $90,000,000
Current Activity Level : Actively seeking new investments

HYDERABAD INFORMATION TECHNOLOGY VENTURE ENTERPRISES LTD

Fateh Maidan Road
First Floor Fateh
Hyderabad, India 500044
Phone: 914023237995
Fax: 914023235516
E-mail: info@hitvel.co.in

Management and Staff
C. Balagopal, Chief Executive Officer

Type of Firm
Government Affiliated Program

Project Preferences

Role in Financing:
Prefer role as deal originator but will also invest in deals created by others

Type of Financing Preferred:
Early Stage
Expansion
Seed
Startup

Size of Investments Considered:
Min Size of Investment Considered (000s): $250
Max Size of Investment Considered (000s): $750

Geographical Preferences

International Preferences:
India

Industry Preferences

In Computer Hardware prefer:
Computers

In Computer Software prefer:
Software

In Computer Other prefer:
Computer Related

Additional Information
Year Founded: 1998
Capital Under Management: $3,300,000
Current Activity Level : Actively seeking new investments

HYDRA VENTURES BV

Hoogoorddreef 9a
Amsterdam, Netherlands 1101 BA
Website: www.hydra-ventures.com

Type of Firm
Private Equity Firm

Project Preferences

Type of Financing Preferred:
Early Stage
Later Stage
Seed
Startup

Geographical Preferences

United States Preferences:
All U.S.

International Preferences:
Europe

Industry Preferences

In Consumer Related prefer:
Consumer
Sports
Consumer Products

Additional Information
Year Founded: 2011
Current Activity Level : Actively seeking new investments

HYIELD CONSULTING GROUP

Section 1, 380 Fu Hsing S Rd
5F
Taipei, Taiwan
Phone: 886227081915
Fax: 886227081932

Management and Staff
Hong-Jen Chung, President

Type of Firm
Private Equity Firm

Association Membership
Taiwan Venture Capital Association(TVCA)

Project Preferences

Type of Financing Preferred:
Expansion
Mezzanine
Balanced
Seed

Geographical Preferences

International Preferences:
Taiwan

Industry Preferences

In Communications prefer:
Telecommunications

In Computer Software prefer:
Software

In Semiconductor/Electr prefer:
Electronic Components
Semiconductor

Additional Information
Year Founded: 1995
Capital Under Management: $58,800,000
Current Activity Level : Actively seeking new investments

HYPATIA CAPITAL GROUP LLC

750 Lexington Avenue
Sixth Floor
New York, NY USA 10022
Phone: 2124727500
Fax: 2124727501
E-mail: info@hypatiacapital.com
Website: www.hypatiacapital.com

Management and Staff
Irina Anguelova, Managing Director
Mercedes Tech, Managing Director
Patricia Lizarraga, Managing Partner

Type of Firm
Private Equity Firm

Project Preferences

Type of Financing Preferred:
Leveraged Buyout
Generalist PE
Later Stage
Management Buyouts
Acquisition

Industry Preferences

In Communications prefer:
Communications and Media

In Consumer Related prefer:
Retail
Food/Beverage
Consumer Products
Other Restaurants
Education Related

In Financial Services prefer:
Financial Services

In Business Serv. prefer:
Services

Additional Information
Year Founded: 2007
Current Activity Level : Actively seeking new investments

HYPERPLANE VENTURE CAPITAL

75 Park Plaza
Boston, MA USA 02116
Website: www.hyperplane.vc

Type of Firm
Private Equity Firm

Project Preferences

Type of Financing Preferred:
Balanced

Geographical Preferences

United States Preferences:

Industry Preferences

In Financial Services prefer:
Financial Services

In Business Serv. prefer:
Services

Additional Information
Year Founded: 2016
Current Activity Level : Actively seeking new investments

HYPOID PARTNERS

2359 Lakeshore Road West
Suite 100
Oakville, Canada L6L 1H4
Website: www.hypoidpartners.com

Management and Staff
Les Barsony, Managing Director
Matthew Kay, Principal
Nick Bobrow, Managing Director
Robert Mohri, Managing Director

Type of Firm
Private Equity Firm

Project Preferences

Type of Financing Preferred:
Leveraged Buyout
Turnaround
Later Stage
Management Buyouts
Acquisition
Recapitalizations

Industry Preferences

In Communications prefer:
Commercial Communications

In Consumer Related prefer:
Retail

In Industrial/Energy prefer:
Oil and Gas Exploration
Industrial Products
Robotics

In Manufact. prefer:
Manufacturing

In Agr/Forestr/Fish prefer:
Mining and Minerals

Additional Information
Year Founded: 2010
Current Activity Level : Actively seeking new investments

HYUNDAI VENTURE INVESTMENT CORP

Mookyo-dong, Chung-ku
4F, Nat'l Info Soc Agency Bldg
Seoul, South Korea 100-170
Phone: 8227288990
Fax: 8227288999
Website: www.hvic.co.kr

Type of Firm
Corporate PE/Venture

Association Membership
Korean Venture Capital Association (KVCA)

Project Preferences

Type of Financing Preferred:
Early Stage
Expansion
Balanced
Startup

Geographical Preferences

International Preferences:
No Preference
Korea, South

Industry Preferences

In Computer Hardware prefer:
Computers

In Computer Software prefer:
Software

In Internet Specific prefer:
Internet

In Semiconductor/Electr prefer:
Electronics
Electronic Components

In Biotechnology prefer:
Biotechnology
Agricultural/Animal Bio.

In Industrial/Energy prefer:
Materials

Additional Information
Year Founded: 1997
Capital Under Management: $24,200,000
Current Activity Level : Actively seeking new investments

- I -

I SQUARED CAPITAL ADVISORS (US) LLC

410 Park Avenue
Suite 830
New York, NY USA 10022
E-mail: info@isquaredcapital.com
Website: www.isquaredcapital.com

Type of Firm
Private Equity Firm

Project Preferences

Type of Financing Preferred:
Leveraged Buyout

Industry Preferences

In Industrial/Energy prefer:
Energy

In Transportation prefer:
Transportation

In Utilities prefer:
Utilities

Additional Information
Year Founded: 2012
Capital Under Management: $3,000,000,000
Current Activity Level : Actively seeking new investments

I&P SARL

9, Notre-Dame des Victoires
Paris, France 75002
Phone: 33158185710
Fax: 33158185719
Website: www.ietp.com

Type of Firm
Private Equity Firm

Project Preferences

Type of Financing Preferred:
Expansion
Later Stage

Geographical Preferences

International Preferences:
Mauritania
Gabon
Senegal
Burkina Faso
Ghana
Ivory Coast
Kenya
Niger
Benin
Cameroon
Namibia
Madagascar
Congo, Dem Rep

Additional Information
Year Founded: 2002
Capital Under Management: $71,770,000
Current Activity Level : Actively seeking new investments

I-4 CAPITAL PARTNERS LLC

150 North Orange Avenue
Suite 410
Orlando, FL USA 32801
Phone: 3212362921
Website: www.i4fund.com

Type of Firm
Private Equity Firm

Project Preferences

Type of Financing Preferred:
Early Stage

Industry Preferences

In Medical/Health prefer:
Medical/Health

In Consumer Related prefer:
Education Related

In Industrial/Energy prefer:
Alternative Energy

In Other prefer:
Socially Responsible
Environment Responsible

Additional Information
Year Founded: 2013
Current Activity Level : Actively seeking new investments

I/O VENTURES

780 Valencia Street
San Francisco, CA USA 94107
E-mail: info@ventures.io
Website: www.ventures.io

Management and Staff
Aber Whitcomb, Partner
Ashwin Navin, Partner
Dan Bragiel, Partner
Paul Bragiel, Partner

Type of Firm
Incubator/Development Program

Project Preferences

Type of Financing Preferred:
Early Stage
Startup

Industry Preferences

In Computer Software prefer:
Software

In Internet Specific prefer:
Web Aggregration/Portals

In Consumer Related prefer:
Entertainment and Leisure

In Business Serv. prefer:
Media

Additional Information
Year Founded: 2010
Current Activity Level : Actively seeking new investments

I2BF GLOBAL VENTURES

Bolshaia Polianka 2/10
Building 1
Moscow, Russia 119180
Phone: 74957800111
Fax: 74957833049
E-mail: info@i2bf.com
Website: www.i2bf.com

Other Offices
Suite 600, 110 Greene Str
New York, NY USA 10012
Phone: 12122267320

The Dubai International Financial Centre
Building 3, Level 5
Dubai, Utd. Arab Em.
Phone: 971043588220
Fax: 971043588188

3 Queen Str
Mayfair
London, United Kingdom W1J 5PR
Phone: 442034051974
Fax: 442074913613

Management and Staff
Ahmad Soubra, Chief Financial Officer
Alexey Belyakov, Partner
Andrei Lisyansky, Partner
David Waserstein, Partner
Ilya Golubovich, Managing Partner
Nizar El Hachem, Partner
Timothy Lewin, Partner

Type of Firm
Private Equity Firm

Association Membership
European Private Equity and Venture Capital Assoc.

Project Preferences

Type of Financing Preferred:
Early Stage
Mezzanine
Balanced
Public Companies
Later Stage
Seed
Startup

Size of Investments Considered:
Min Size of Investment Considered (000s): $17
Max Size of Investment Considered (000s): $341

Geographical Preferences

International Preferences:
Latin America
Kazakhstan
Asia
Russia

Industry Preferences

In Internet Specific prefer:
E-Commerce Technology

In Semiconductor/Electr prefer:
Electronics

In Biotechnology prefer:
Industrial Biotechnology

Additional Information
Year Founded: 2005
Capital Under Management: $1,576,000
Current Activity Level : Actively seeking new investments

I2E, INC
840 Research Parkway
Suite 250
Oklahoma City, OK USA 73104
Phone: 4052352305
Fax: 4052352252
Website: www.i2e.org

Other Offices
618 East Third Street, Suite 1
Tulsa, OK USA 74120

Phone: 9185825592
Fax: 8003376822

Management and Staff
David Thomison, Vice President
David Daviee, Founder
Sarah Seagraves, Vice President
Wayne Embree, Vice President

Type of Firm
Corporate PE/Venture

Project Preferences

Type of Financing Preferred:
Early Stage
Expansion
Balanced
Seed
Startup

Size of Investments Considered:
Min Size of Investment Considered (000s): $50
Max Size of Investment Considered (000s): $200

Geographical Preferences

United States Preferences:
Oklahoma

Industry Preferences

In Consumer Related prefer:
Consumer Products
Consumer Services

In Business Serv. prefer:
Services
Distribution

In Manufact. prefer:
Manufacturing

Additional Information
Year Founded: 1997
Capital Under Management: $12,000,000
Current Activity Level : Actively seeking new investments

I5 EMPRESAS CONSULTORIA E PARTICIPACOES LTDA
Av. Paisagista Jose Silva de
Azevedo Neto 200
Rio de Janeiro, Brazil 22640102
Phone: 552136139000
Fax: 552136139001
E-mail: i5@i5empresas.com.br
Website: www.i5participacoes.com.br

Management and Staff
Alexandre Icaza, Partner
Gabriella Icaza, Partner
Leonidas Moura, Founder

Type of Firm
Private Equity Firm

Project Preferences

Type of Financing Preferred:
Balanced

Geographical Preferences

International Preferences:
Brazil

Additional Information
Year Founded: 2002
Current Activity Level : Actively seeking new investments

I5INVEST BERATUNGS GMBH
Spengergasse 37-39
Vienna, Austria
Website: www.i5invest.com

Management and Staff
Bernhard Lehner, Managing Director
Markus Wagner, Managing Director
Paul Weinberger, Managing Director
Stefan Kalteis, Managing Director

Type of Firm
Incubator/Development Program

Project Preferences

Type of Financing Preferred:
Seed
Startup

Geographical Preferences

International Preferences:
Austria

Industry Preferences

In Communications prefer:
Wireless Communications

In Internet Specific prefer:
Internet

Additional Information
Year Founded: 2011
Current Activity Level : Actively seeking new investments

IA CAPITAL GROUP INC
419 Park Avenue South, Suite 807
New York, NY USA 10016
Phone: 2125812000
Website: www.iacapgroup.com

Management and Staff
Alex Maffeo, Vice President
Andrew Lerner, Managing Partner
Brett Baris, Partner
Richard Viton, Partner

Type of Firm
Private Equity Firm

Project Preferences

Type of Financing Preferred:
Early Stage
Expansion
Balanced
Later Stage

Geographical Preferences

United States Preferences:

Industry Preferences

In Consumer Related prefer:
Consumer Services

In Financial Services prefer:
Financial Services

In Business Serv. prefer:
Services

Additional Information
Name of Most Recent Fund: Inter-Atlantic Fund II, L.P.
Most Recent Fund Was Raised: 12/30/2005
Year Founded: 1992
Capital Under Management: $76,000,000
Current Activity Level : Actively seeking new investments

IA VENTURES

156 Fifth Avenue, Suite 1119
New York, NY USA 10010
Phone: 2122423310
E-mail: info@iaventurepartners.com
Website: www.iaventures.com

Management and Staff
Ben Siscovick, General Partner
Brad Gillespie, General Partner
Roger Ehrenberg, Managing Partner

Type of Firm
Private Equity Firm

Project Preferences

Role in Financing:
Will function either as deal originator or investor in deals created by others

Type of Financing Preferred:
Early Stage
Seed

Geographical Preferences

United States Preferences:
California
Washington
New York

International Preferences:
United Kingdom
Israel

Industry Preferences

In Computer Software prefer:
Computer Services
Software

In Computer Other prefer:
Computer Related

Additional Information
Name of Most Recent Fund: IA Venture Strategies Fund II, L.P.
Most Recent Fund Was Raised: 09/19/2011
Year Founded: 2010
Capital Under Management: $315,000,000
Current Activity Level : Actively seeking new investments

IBB BETEILIGUNGS GMBH

Bundesallee 171
Berlin, Germany 10715
Phone: 493021253201
Fax: 493021253202
E-mail: venture@ibb-bet.de
Website: www.ibb-bet.de

Management and Staff
Marco Zeller, Managing Director
Roger Bendisch, Managing Director

Type of Firm
Bank Affiliated

Association Membership
German Venture Capital Association (BVK)

Project Preferences

Type of Financing Preferred:
Early Stage
Mezzanine
Start-up Financing
Later Stage
Seed
Startup

Geographical Preferences

International Preferences:
Germany

Industry Preferences

In Communications prefer:
Communications and Media
Radio & TV Broadcasting
Media and Entertainment

In Computer Hardware prefer:
Computers

In Computer Software prefer:
Software

In Internet Specific prefer:
Internet

In Semiconductor/Electr prefer:
Electronics

In Biotechnology prefer:
Biotechnology

In Medical/Health prefer:
Medical/Health

In Industrial/Energy prefer:
Energy
Materials
Environmental Related

In Transportation prefer:
Transportation

In Manufact. prefer:
Publishing

Additional Information
Name of Most Recent Fund: IBB Beteilgungs-gesellschaft
Most Recent Fund Was Raised: 10/01/1997
Year Founded: 2010
Capital Under Management: $25,500,000
Current Activity Level : Actively seeking new investments

IBERIAN CAPITAL III SICAR

20, rue de la Poste
Luxembourg, Luxembourg L-2346

Type of Firm
Private Equity Firm

Geographical Preferences

International Preferences:
Spain

Additional Information
Year Founded: 2008
Capital Under Management: $69,300,000
Current Activity Level : Actively seeking new investments

IBERO AMERICAN INVESTORS CORP

104 Scio Street
Rochester, NY USA 14604
Phone: 5852623440
Fax: 5852623441
E-mail: iberoinv@rochester.rr.com
Website: www.iberoinvestors.com

Management and Staff
George Dickinson, Chief Financial Officer

Type of Firm
SBIC

Project Preferences

Type of Financing Preferred:
Early Stage
Expansion
Start-up Financing
Management Buyouts

Size of Investments Considered:
Min Size of Investment Considered (000s): $50
Max Size of Investment Considered (000s): $500

Geographical Preferences

United States Preferences:
All U.S.

Industry Preferences

In Consumer Related prefer:
Entertainment and Leisure
Retail

In Business Serv. prefer:
Services
Distribution

In Manufact. prefer:
Manufacturing

Additional Information
Year Founded: 1979
Capital Under Management: $8,000,000
Current Activity Level : Actively seeking new investments

IBG BETEILIGUNGS-GESELLSCHAFT

Kantstrasse 5
c/o bmp Beteiligungsmanagement
Magdeburg, Germany 39104

Type of Firm
Incubator/Development Program

Project Preferences

Type of Financing Preferred:
Early Stage
Expansion
Seed
Startup

Geographical Preferences

International Preferences:
Germany

Industry Preferences

In Semiconductor/Electr prefer:
Micro-Processing

In Industrial/Energy prefer:
Machinery
Environmental Related

Additional Information
Year Founded: 2000
Capital Under Management: $53,660,000
Current Activity Level : Actively seeking new investments

IBID HOLDINGS LTD

Covent Garden
22 Long Acre
London, United Kingdom WC2E 9LY
Website: ibidgroup.com

Other Offices
99 Queen's Road Central
Suite 6601, 66/F The Center
Hong Kng, Hong Kong

Type of Firm
Private Equity Firm

Project Preferences

Type of Financing Preferred:
Generalist PE

Industry Preferences

In Internet Specific prefer:
Internet

Additional Information
Year Founded: 2016
Current Activity Level : Actively seeking new investments

IBIONEXT SASU

74,R.du Faubourg Saint-Antoine
Paris, France 75012
Phone: 33176214750
Website: ibionext.com

Type of Firm
Private Equity Firm

Project Preferences

Type of Financing Preferred:
Early Stage
Seed

Industry Preferences

In Communications prefer:
Data Communications

In Biotechnology prefer:
Biotechnology

In Medical/Health prefer:
Medical/Health
Medical Diagnostics
Medical Products

Additional Information
Year Founded: 2012

Capital Under Management: $51,700,000
Current Activity Level : Actively seeking new investments

IBK CAPITAL CORP

414 Teheran-ro,
14-21F L&B Tower Kangnam-gu
Seoul, South Korea 135-080
Phone: 82215771885
Fax: 8225319789
Website: www.ibkcapital.co.kr

Management and Staff
Yun Hui Lee, Chief Executive Officer

Type of Firm
Bank Affiliated

Association Membership
Korean Venture Capital Association (KVCA)

Project Preferences

Role in Financing:
Prefer role as deal originator but will also invest in deals created by others

Type of Financing Preferred:
Second Stage Financing
Leveraged Buyout
Mezzanine
Research and Development
Balanced

Size of Investments Considered:
Min Size of Investment Considered (000s): $5,000
Max Size of Investment Considered: No Limit

Geographical Preferences

United States Preferences:
West Coast
All U.S.

Canadian Preferences:
All Canada

International Preferences:
United Kingdom
No Preference
Korea, South
Germany
Japan
France

Industry Preferences

In Communications prefer:
Telecommunications
Data Communications
Satellite Microwave Comm.
Other Communication Prod.

In Computer Hardware prefer:
Integrated Turnkey System
Disk Relat. Memory Device

In Computer Software prefer:
Systems Software
Applications Software

In Internet Specific prefer:
Internet

In Semiconductor/Electr prefer:
Electronics
Electronic Components
Semiconductor
Fiber Optics

In Biotechnology prefer:
Industrial Biotechnology
Biotech Related Research

In Medical/Health prefer:
Medical Diagnostics
Diagnostic Test Products
Medical Products

In Consumer Related prefer:
Franchises(NEC)
Hotels and Resorts

In Industrial/Energy prefer:
Alternative Energy
Industrial Products
Materials
Machinery
Environmental Related

In Agr/Forestr/Fish prefer:
Mining and Minerals

Additional Information
Year Founded: 1986
Capital Under Management: $166,000,000
Current Activity Level : Actively seeking new investments
Method of Compensation: Return on investment is of primary concern, do not charge fees

IBRC CAPITAL PARTNERS LTD

18/21 St. Stephens Green
Stephen Court
Dublin, Ireland
Phone: 353-1-616-2000
Fax: 353-1-616-2488
E-mail: enquiries@angloirishbank.ie
Website: www.angloirishbank.ie

Other Offices
1 Burlington Road
Dublin, Ireland 4
Phone: 353-631-0000
Fax: 353-631-0098

Type of Firm
Bank Affiliated

Project Preferences

Type of Financing Preferred:
Leveraged Buyout
Expansion

Geographical Preferences

International Preferences:
Ireland
United Kingdom
Europe

Additional Information
Year Founded: 2004
Current Activity Level : Actively seeking new investments

IC AFRICA PRIVATE EQUITY LTD

TMF Place
Road Town
Tortola, Br. Virgin I.
E-mail: info@icafrica-pe.com
Website: www.icafrica-pe.com

Type of Firm
Private Equity Firm

Project Preferences

Type of Financing Preferred:
Expansion
Management Buyouts
Acquisition

Geographical Preferences

International Preferences:
Liberia
Senegal
Ghana
Gambia
Sierra Leone
Africa

Industry Preferences

In Communications prefer:
Communications and Media
Telecommunications

In Biotechnology prefer:
Agricultural/Animal Bio.

In Financial Services prefer:
Financial Services
Real Estate

In Business Serv. prefer:
Media

In Agr/Forestr/Fish prefer:
Agriculture related

Additional Information
Year Founded: 2008
Capital Under Management: $75,000,000
Current Activity Level : Actively seeking new investments

IC2 CAPITAL

Three Bunhill Row
London, United Kingdom EC1Y 8YZ
Phone: 44-20-7847-4020
Fax: 44-20-7847-4005
E-mail: info@ic2capital.co.uk
Website: ic2capital.co.uk

Other Offices
A-67 Mount Kailash
New Delhi, India 110065
Phone: 91-99-103-35485

Management and Staff
Anmol Nayyar, Managing Director
Kuldip Clair, Chief Operating Officer

Type of Firm
Private Equity Firm

Project Preferences

Type of Financing Preferred:
Leveraged Buyout
Expansion
Acquisition

Size of Investments Considered:
Min Size of Investment Considered (000s): $5,000
Max Size of Investment Considered (000s): $30,000

Geographical Preferences

United States Preferences:

International Preferences:
India
Europe
Middle East

Industry Preferences

In Medical/Health prefer:
Medical/Health
Health Services
Hospitals/Clinics/Primary

In Transportation prefer:
Transportation
Aerospace

In Business Serv. prefer:
Services
Media

In Manufact. prefer:
Manufacturing

In Agr/Forestr/Fish prefer:
Agriculture related

In Other prefer:
Socially Responsible

Additional Information
Year Founded: 2008
Current Activity Level : Actively seeking new investments

ICA GRUPPEN AB

Svetsarvagen 16
P.O. Box 1508
Solna, Sweden 171 29
Phone: 46855339900
Fax: 46855339933
Website: www.icagruppen.se

Management and Staff
Anders Svensson, Chief Executive Officer
Per Stromberg, Chief Executive Officer
Sven Lindskog, Chief Financial Officer

Type of Firm
Private Equity Firm

Project Preferences

Type of Financing Preferred:
Leveraged Buyout
Acquisition

Geographical Preferences

International Preferences:
Scandanavia/Nordic Region
Estonia
Latvia
Lithuania

Industry Preferences

In Consumer Related prefer:
Retail

Additional Information
Year Founded: 2000
Current Activity Level : Actively seeking new investments

ICAPITAL M SDN BHD

11th Floor, Block C
Kelana Centrepoint Petaling Ja
Selangor, Malaysia
Phone: 603-7491-9100
Fax: 603-7491-9101

Management and Staff
Christine Lim, Partner
Nethan Pillai, Partner

Type of Firm
Private Equity Firm

Project Preferences

Type of Financing Preferred:
Seed

Geographical Preferences

International Preferences:
Hong Kong
Philippines
Singapore
Malaysia

Industry Preferences

In Internet Specific prefer:
Internet

Additional Information
Year Founded: 2000
Current Activity Level : Actively seeking new investments

ICC VENTURE CAPITAL

Bank of Scotland House
124 -127 St Stephens Green
Dublin, Ireland
Phone: 353-1-267-4000
Fax: 353-1-267-4010
E-mail: ventcap@icc.ie
Website: www.iccvc.ie

Management and Staff
Anne Bannon, Partner
Brendan Spierin, Founder
David Fassbender, Managing Director
Martin O Brian, Partner
Maurice McHenry, Partner
Prisca Grady, Partner
Tom Kirwan, Partner

Type of Firm
Bank Affiliated

Project Preferences

Role in Financing:
Prefer role as deal originator

Type of Financing Preferred:
Expansion
Balanced
Later Stage

Size of Investments Considered:
Min Size of Investment Considered (000s): $700
Max Size of Investment Considered: No Limit

Geographical Preferences

International Preferences:
Ireland
Europe
Western Europe

Industry Focus
(% based on actual investment)
Computer Software and Services	36.6%
Consumer Related	18.6%
Communications and Media	13.0%
Other Products	8.8%
Industrial/Energy	6.3%
Semiconductors/Other Elect.	5.3%
Internet Specific	4.8%
Biotechnology	4.1%
Medical/Health	2.4%

Additional Information
Year Founded: 1987
Capital Under Management: $245,000,000
Current Activity Level : Reducing investment activity
Method of Compensation: Return on invest. most important, but chg. closing fees, service fees, etc.

ICCP VENTURE PARTNERS INC

6783 Ayala Avenue
17F Robinsons Summit Center
Makati City, Philippines 1226
Phone: 6328114656
Fax: 6328190941
E-mail: info@iccventureparnters.com
Website: www.iccpventurepartners.com

Management and Staff
Edwin Lau, Managing Director
William Valtos, Senior Managing Director

Type of Firm
Bank Affiliated

Project Preferences

Role in Financing:
Will function either as deal originator or investor in deals created by others

Type of Financing Preferred:
Leveraged Buyout
Early Stage
Expansion
Mezzanine
Turnaround
Startup

Size of Investments Considered:
Min Size of Investment Considered (000s): $500
Max Size of Investment Considered (000s): $500,000

Geographical Preferences

United States Preferences:

International Preferences:
Europe
Hong Kong
Philippines
Singapore

Industry Preferences

In Communications prefer:
Telecommunications

In Computer Other prefer:
Computer Related

In Semiconductor/Electr prefer:
Electronics

In Consumer Related prefer:
Consumer Products
Consumer Services

In Business Serv. prefer:
Services

Additional Information
Year Founded: 1998
Current Activity Level : Actively seeking new investments

ICENTIS CAPITAL SP Z O O

Postepu 15C
Warszawa, Poland 02-676
Phone: 48 22 325 34 80
Fax: 48 22 325 34 81
E-mail: office@icentiscapital.com
Website: www.icentiscapital.pl

Management and Staff
Adam Pietruszkiewicz, Partner
Igor Chalupec, Co-Founder
Pawel Szymanski, Co-Founder

Type of Firm
Private Equity Firm

Project Preferences

Type of Financing Preferred:
Leveraged Buyout
Turnaround
Acquisition
Recapitalizations

Geographical Preferences

International Preferences:
Poland

Industry Preferences

In Communications prefer:
Telecommunications

In Consumer Related prefer:
Consumer
Retail

In Business Serv. prefer:
Media

In Manufact. prefer:
Manufacturing

Additional Information
Year Founded: 2008
Current Activity Level : Actively seeking new investments

ICF CAPITAL SGEIC SAU

Gran Via de les Corts Catalane
635 6a planta
Barcelona, Spain 08010
Phone: 902227237
Website: www.icf.cat

Other Offices
Gran Via de les Corts Catalanes
680, 5a planta
Barcelona, Spain
Phone: 34-93-318-8686

Management and Staff
Josep Ramon Sanroma, Chief Executive Officer

Type of Firm
Investment Management Firm

Association Membership
Spanish Venture Capital Association (ASCRI)

Project Preferences

Type of Financing Preferred:
Expansion
Balanced
Later Stage

Geographical Preferences

International Preferences:
Europe
Spain

Industry Preferences

In Communications prefer:
Telecommunications

In Biotechnology prefer:
Biotechnology

In Industrial/Energy prefer:
Energy Conservation Relat

In Business Serv. prefer:
Media

Additional Information
Name of Most Recent Fund: Capital Expansio
Most Recent Fund Was Raised: 06/26/2013
Year Founded: 2007
Capital Under Management: $400,000
Current Activity Level : Actively seeking new investments

ICHIGO INC

No. 1-chome Chiyoda-ku
Imperial Tower No. 1
Tokyo, Japan 100-0011
Phone: 81-3-3502-4800
Website: www.ichigo.gr.jp

Other Offices
Room 1108-09, Bank of America Tower
12 Harcourt Road
Central, Hong Kong
Phone: 85225218222
Fax: 85225219100

Management and Staff
Eric Yip, Chief Executive Officer
Minoru Ishihara, Chief Operating Officer
Savio Cheung, Vice President

Type of Firm
Investment Management Firm

Project Preferences

Role in Financing:
Prefer role as deal originator but will also invest in deals created by others

Type of Financing Preferred:
Fund of Funds

Geographical Preferences

International Preferences:
Asia
Japan

Industry Preferences

In Financial Services prefer:
Real Estate

Additional Information
Year Founded: 2000
Capital Under Management: $160,300,000
Current Activity Level : Actively seeking new investments

ICICI VENTURE FUNDS MANAGEMENT COMPANY LTD

Appasaheb Marathe Marg
ICICI Venture House, Ground Fl.
Mumbai, Maharashtra, India 400025
Phone: 912266555050
Fax: 912266555055
E-mail: info@iciciventure.com
Website: www.iciciventure.com

Other Offices
Ground Floor, Scindia House
N.M.Marg, Ballard Estate
Mumbai, India 400 038
Phone: 9122-266-4767

Fax: 9122-266-4769

ICICI Towers
Bandra Kurla Complex
Mumbai, India 400051
Phone: 9122-653-8818

10th Floor, Prestige Obelisk
Kasturba Road
Bangalore, India 560 001
Phone: 91-80-4149-7021
Fax: 91-80-4149-7027

501, 5th Floor, World Trade Tower,
Barakhamba Road, Connaught Place
New Delhi, India 110001
Phone: 91-11-6618-4440
Fax: 91-11-6618-4450

Management and Staff
Abdul Suriya, Vice President
Awadh Agrawal, Vice President
Beena Chotai, Chief Financial Officer
Birit Saraf, Vice President
Chhina Gagandeep, Vice President
Krishnan Ganesan, Vice President
Kunal Patil, Vice President
Manikkan Sangameswaran, President
Naresh Patwari, Vice President
Parth Gandhi, President
Partha Dey, President
Prashant Purker, Chief Executive Officer
Sanjeev Dasgupta, President
Shrinivas Chellapa, Vice President
Suketu Kumar, Vice President

Type of Firm
Bank Affiliated

Association Membership
Indian Venture Capital Association (IVCA)

Project Preferences
Role in Financing:
Prefer role as deal originator but will also invest in deals created by others

Type of Financing Preferred:
Leveraged Buyout
Early Stage
Expansion
Mezzanine
Generalist PE
Balanced
Turnaround
Opportunistic
Later Stage
Other
Acquisition
Special Situation

Geographical Preferences
International Preferences:
India

Industry Focus
(% based on actual investment)
Other Products	29.9%
Consumer Related	27.6%
Internet Specific	15.4%
Medical/Health	15.1%
Computer Software and Services	3.1%
Communications and Media	2.8%
Industrial/Energy	2.1%
Biotechnology	1.9%
Computer Hardware	1.3%
Semiconductors/Other Elect.	0.6%

Additional Information
Year Founded: 1988
Capital Under Management: $2,000,000,000
Current Activity Level : Actively seeking new investments

ICOS CAPITAL MANAGEMENT BV

Schipholweg 275
Skyline Plaza
Badhoevedorp, Netherlands 1171 PK
Phone: 31204530777
Fax: 31204529286
E-mail: info@icoscapital.com
Website: www.icoscapital.com

Management and Staff
Bart Bouwmeester, Partner
Daan Den Ouden, Partner
Fred Van Efferink, Partner
Ger Spruijtenburg, Partner
John Gardner, Partner
Marco De Rooij, Partner
Nityen Lal, Chief Executive Officer
Rop Zoetemeijer, Partner
Willem Trommels, Partner

Type of Firm
Private Equity Firm

Association Membership
European Private Equity and Venture Capital Assoc.

Project Preferences
Type of Financing Preferred:
Early Stage
Later Stage
Startup

Size of Investments Considered:
Min Size of Investment Considered (000s): $143
Max Size of Investment Considered (000s): $3,581

Geographical Preferences
International Preferences:
Europe
Netherlands

Industry Preferences
In Consumer Related prefer:
Food/Beverage

In Industrial/Energy prefer:
Alternative Energy
Energy Conservation Relat
Environmental Related

In Other prefer:
Socially Responsible

Additional Information
Year Founded: 2006
Capital Under Management: $26,500,000
Current Activity Level : Actively seeking new investments

ICP INC

2-5-8, Nishi-Kanda, Chiyoda-ku
8F, Kyowa No.15
Tokyo, Japan 101-0065
Phone: 81332213505
Fax: 8132213506
Website: www.icp5.co.jp

Type of Firm
Private Equity Firm

Project Preferences
Type of Financing Preferred:
Early Stage
Seed

Industry Preferences
In Communications prefer:
Communications and Media

Additional Information
Year Founded: 1998
Current Activity Level : Actively seeking new investments

ICS PARTNERS GMBH

Baarerstrasse 78
Zug, Switzerland 6301
E-mail: info@icspartners.net
Website: www.icspartners.net

Other Offices
Westhafenplatz 1
Frankfurt a.M., Germany 60327
Phone: 496996866011
Fax: 496996866012

Management and Staff
Ingo Zemke, Managing Director

Type of Firm
Private Equity Firm

Association Membership
German Venture Capital Association (BVK)

Project Preferences

Type of Financing Preferred:
Leveraged Buyout
Mezzanine
Acquisition

Geographical Preferences

International Preferences:
Switzerland
Western Europe
Austria
Germany

Additional Information
Year Founded: 2005
Current Activity Level : Actively seeking new investments

ICV PARTNERS LLC

810 Seventh Avenue
35th Floor
New York, NY USA 10019
Phone: 2124559600
Fax: 2124559603
Website: icvcapital.com

Management and Staff
Cory Mims, Managing Director
Ira Moreland, Managing Director
Jermaine Warren, Vice President
Lloyd Metz, Managing Director
Qian Elmore, Principal
Sheldon Howell, Vice President
Willie Woods, President
Zeena Rao, Managing Director

Type of Firm
Private Equity Firm

Association Membership
Natl Assoc of Investment Cos. (NAIC)

Project Preferences

Type of Financing Preferred:
Leveraged Buyout
Expansion
Management Buyouts
Recapitalizations

Geographical Preferences

United States Preferences:
All U.S.

Industry Focus
(% based on actual investment)
Consumer Related	65.0%
Medical/Health	18.6%
Computer Software and Services	11.6%
Semiconductors/Other Elect.	4.9%

Additional Information
Name of Most Recent Fund: ICV Partners III, L.P.
Most Recent Fund Was Raised: 12/03/2012
Year Founded: 1998
Capital Under Management: $400,000,000
Current Activity Level : Actively seeking new investments

ID CAPITAL

1250 Rene-Levesque Blvd. West
38th Floor
Montreal, Canada H3B 4W8
Phone: 5143978477
Fax: 5146738477
E-mail: info@idcapital.ca
Website: www.idcapital.ca

Management and Staff
Daniel Cyr, Managing Partner
David Bernardi, Managing Partner
Denis Sirois, Managing Partner
Francois-Charles Sirois, President
Jean Paul Tardif, Managing Partner
Thomas Birch, Managing Partner

Type of Firm
Private Equity Firm

Project Preferences

Type of Financing Preferred:
Early Stage
Seed
Startup

Geographical Preferences

Canadian Preferences:
Quebec

Industry Preferences

In Communications prefer:
Communications and Media

Additional Information
Year Founded: 2006
Capital Under Management: $75,000,000
Current Activity Level : Actively seeking new investments

IDA CAPITAL KK

8F New Kudan Building
3-7-1 Kandajimbo-cho,Chiyodaku
Tokyo, Japan 101-0051
Phone: 813-3288-2786
Fax: 813-3288-2787
E-mail: info@idacapital.co.jp

Type of Firm
Private Equity Firm

Project Preferences

Type of Financing Preferred:
Mezzanine
Balanced
Management Buyouts

Geographical Preferences

International Preferences:
Asia

Additional Information
Year Founded: 2002
Current Activity Level : Actively seeking new investments

IDEA

Calle Torneo 26
Seville, Spain 41002
Phone: 34-95-503-0700
Fax: 34-95-503-0780
E-mail: informacion@central.ifa.es
Website: www.ifa.es

Other Offices
C/ Cister, 5
Malaga, Spain
Phone: 34-951-042-902

C/angel, 3
Granada, Spain
Phone: 34-958-002-500

Carrera De Jesus, 9, bajo
Jaen, Spain
Phone: 34-951-042-902

Plaza Cardenal Toldeo, 6
Bajo
Cordoba, Spain
Phone: 34-957-005-000

Avda. Alemania, 3
Huelva, Spain
Phone: 34-959-011-200

C/Adriano del Valle, 7
Local 1
Sevilla, Spain
Phone: 34-95-503-0900

Avda. Pablo Iglesias, 24
Almeria, Spain
Phone: 34-950-006-808

Alameda Apodaca, 20
Cadiz, Spain
Phone: 34-956-009-510

Type of Firm
Private Equity Firm

Project Preferences

Type of Financing Preferred:
Expansion
Balanced

Geographical Preferences

International Preferences:
Europe
Spain

Industry Preferences

In Financial Services prefer:
Financial Services

Additional Information

Year Founded: 1987
Current Activity Level : Actively seeking new investments

IDEA CAPITAL FUNDS SOCIETA DI GESTIONE DEL RISPARMIO SPA

Via Brera 21
Milan, Italy 20121
Phone: 3922906631
Fax: 39229066320
E-mail: info@ideasgr.com
Website: www.ideasgr.com

Management and Staff

Danilo Beltramino, Chief Financial Officer
Franco Mosca, Managing Director
Mario Barozzi, Chief Executive Officer
Sergio Buonanno, Managing Director

Type of Firm

Investment Management Firm

Association Membership

European Private Equity and Venture Capital Assoc.

Project Preferences

Type of Financing Preferred:
Fund of Funds
Acquisition

Geographical Preferences

International Preferences:
Italy

Industry Preferences

In Agr/Forestr/Fish prefer:
Agriculture related

Additional Information

Year Founded: 2006
Capital Under Management: $422,777,000
Current Activity Level : Actively seeking new investments

IDEA FUND PARTNERS LLC

104 City Hall Plaza
Suite 201
Durham, NC USA 27701
Phone: 9198084000
E-mail: info@ideafundpartners.com
Website: www.ideafundpartners.com

Management and Staff

Lister Delgado, Managing Partner
Richard Fox, Venture Partner

Type of Firm

Private Equity Firm

Project Preferences

Role in Financing:
Will function either as deal originator or investor in deals created by others

Type of Financing Preferred:
Early Stage
Seed

Size of Investments Considered:
Min Size of Investment Considered (000s): $100
Max Size of Investment Considered (000s): $1,500

Geographical Preferences

United States Preferences:
Southeast
North Carolina
Florida
All U.S.

Industry Preferences

In Computer Software prefer:
Software

In Medical/Health prefer:
Medical/Health
Medical Diagnostics

Additional Information

Name of Most Recent Fund: IDEA Fund II, L.P.
Most Recent Fund Was Raised: 08/02/2013
Year Founded: 2003
Capital Under Management: $54,900,000
Current Activity Level : Actively seeking new investments
Method of Compensation: Return on investment is of primary concern, do not charge fees

IDEABOX VENTURES

Jl. Letjen S. Parman Kav.62-63
Wisma Barito Pacific Tower A
Jakarta, Indonesia 11410
Website: www.ideabox.co.id

Other Offices
Jl. Letjen S. Parman Kav. 62-63
Wisma Barito Pacific Tower A, Level 6
Jakarta, Indonesia 11410

Type of Firm

Incubator/Development Program

Project Preferences

Type of Financing Preferred:
Early Stage
Seed

Industry Preferences

In Communications prefer:
Telecommunications

Additional Information

Year Founded: 2016
Current Activity Level : Actively seeking new investments

IDEALAB

130 West Union Street
Pasadena, CA USA 91103
Phone: 6265856900
Fax: 6265352701
E-mail: info@idealab.com
Website: www.idealab.com

Other Offices
58-59 Haymarket
Fifth Floor
London, United Kingdom SW1Y 4QX
Phone: 20-7968-4700
Fax: 20-7930-4310

675 Avenue of the Americas
New York, NY USA 10010
Phone: 212-420-7700
Fax: 212-929-4423

380 Portage Avenue
Palo Alto, CA USA 94306
Phone: 650-251-5500
Fax: 650-251-5501

Management and Staff

Craig Chrisney, Chief Financial Officer
Marcia Goodstein, President & COO
William Gross, Chairman & CEO

Type of Firm

Private Equity Firm

Project Preferences

Type of Financing Preferred:
Early Stage
Startup

Geographical Preferences

United States Preferences:

Industry Preferences

In Internet Specific prefer:
Internet

In Computer Other prefer:
Computer Related

In Semiconductor/Electr prefer:
Electronics

In Industrial/Energy prefer:
Energy
Alternative Energy

In Transportation prefer:
Transportation

In Business Serv. prefer:
Consulting Services

Additional Information

Year Founded: 1996
Current Activity Level : Actively seeking new investments

IDEALMACHINE

Lomonosova, 9
Saint Petersburg, Russia
E-mail: info@idealmachine.ru
Website: www.idealmachine.ru

Type of Firm
Private Equity Firm

Project Preferences

Type of Financing Preferred:
Early Stage
Seed
Startup

Geographical Preferences

International Preferences:
Russia

Industry Preferences

In Computer Software prefer:
Applications Software

Additional Information

Year Founded: 2012
Current Activity Level : Actively seeking new investments

IDEASPACE FOUNDATION INC

Dela Rosa Street
10th Floor, PLDT-MGO Building
Makati, Philippines 1226
Phone: 6328880888
Website: ideaspacefoundation.org

Type of Firm
Incubator/Development Program

Project Preferences

Type of Financing Preferred:
Seed
Startup

Size of Investments Considered:
Min Size of Investment Considered (000s): $11,191
Max Size of Investment Considered (000s): $111,905

Industry Preferences

In Communications prefer:
Communications and Media
Telecommunications
Wireless Communications

In Computer Software prefer:
Software

In Medical/Health prefer:
Medical/Health

In Consumer Related prefer:
Food/Beverage

In Industrial/Energy prefer:
Energy

In Manufact. prefer:
Manufacturing

In Agr/Forestr/Fish prefer:
Agriculture related
Mining and Minerals

Additional Information

Year Founded: 2012
Current Activity Level : Actively seeking new investments

IDEASPRING CAPITAL

Millers Road
70, Grace Towers, 4th Floor
Bangalore, India 560 052
Phone: 918030789100
Fax: 91803078922
Website: www.ideaspringcap.com

Type of Firm
Private Equity Firm

Project Preferences

Type of Financing Preferred:
Early Stage
Seed

Size of Investments Considered:
Min Size of Investment Considered (000s): $452
Max Size of Investment Considered (000s): $754

Geographical Preferences

International Preferences:
India

Industry Preferences

In Computer Software prefer:
Software
Artificial Intelligence

In Internet Specific prefer:
Internet

In Computer Other prefer:
Computer Related

In Medical/Health prefer:
Health Services

Additional Information

Year Founded: 2016
Capital Under Management: $18,750,000
Current Activity Level : Actively seeking new investments

IDEIN VENTURES

B Wing 1st Floor
Bandra East
Mumbai, India
Website: ideinventures.com

Type of Firm
Private Equity Firm

Project Preferences

Type of Financing Preferred:
Early Stage
Startup

Additional Information

Year Founded: 1969
Current Activity Level : Actively seeking new investments

IDENTITY CAPITAL PARTNERS (PTY) LTD

22 Oxford Road
First Floor, Etana House
Parktown, South Africa 2193
Phone: 27113512900
Fax: 27 113518091
Website: www.identitypartners.co.za

Management and Staff

Polo Radebe, Co-Founder
Raisibe Morathi, Co-Founder
Sonja Sebotsa, Co-Founder

Type of Firm
Private Equity Firm

Pratt's Guide to Private Equity & Venture Capital Sources

Project Preferences

Type of Financing Preferred:
Leveraged Buyout
Expansion
Generalist PE
Balanced
Later Stage
Management Buyouts
Acquisition

Geographical Preferences

International Preferences:
South Africa
Africa

Industry Preferences

In Communications prefer:
Communications and Media

In Medical/Health prefer:
Health Services

In Consumer Related prefer:
Retail

In Industrial/Energy prefer:
Energy

In Transportation prefer:
Transportation

In Financial Services prefer:
Real Estate

In Agr/Forestr/Fish prefer:
Agribusiness
Mining and Minerals

Additional Information

Year Founded: 2007
Current Activity Level : Actively seeking new investments

IDEO VENTURES

100 Forest Avenue
Palo Alto, CA USA 94301
Phone: 6502893400
Fax: 6502890253
Website: www.ideo.com

Management and Staff

David Haygood, Partner

Type of Firm

Corporate PE/Venture

Additional Information

Year Founded: 1991
Current Activity Level : Actively seeking new investments

IDEOSOURCE ASIA PT

Jl. KH. Mas Mansyur No. 121
Citywalk Sudirman Bldg, #2223
Jakarta, Indonesia 10220
Phone: 62212555842
E-mail: portfolio@ideosource.com
Website: www.ideosource.com

Other Offices

Jl. KH. Mas Mansyur No. 121
Citywalk Sudirman Bldg, Cityloft, #2223
Jakarta, Indonesia 10220
Phone: 62212555842

Type of Firm

Incubator/Development Program

Project Preferences

Type of Financing Preferred:
Balanced

Additional Information

Year Founded: 2014
Current Activity Level : Actively seeking new investments

IDFC ALTERNATIVES LTD

201, Naman Chambers
C-32 G-Bk, Bandra Kurla Cplx
Mumbai, India 400 051
Phone: 912242222000
Fax: 912226523803
Website: www.idfc.com

Other Offices

No. 1, Harrington Road, Chetpet
KRM Tower, 8th Floor
Chennai, India 600031
Phone: 914445644000
Fax: 914445644022

Olof Palme Marg, Munirka
Capital Court, 2nd Floor
New Delhi, India 110 067
Phone: 91114331000
Fax: 911126713359

Yamunabai Road, Madhav Nagar Extn.,
No. 9/7, 2nd Flr., KCN Bhavan
Bengaluru, India 560 001
Phone: 918043448000
Fax: 918043448001

Management and Staff

Girish Nadkarni, Partner
Raja Parthasarathy, Partner
Rupa Vora, Chief Financial Officer
S. G. Shyam Sundar, Partner
Satish Mandhana, Managing Partner

Type of Firm

Investment Management Firm

Association Membership

Emerging Markets Private Equity Association
Indian Venture Capital Association (IVCA)

Project Preferences

Type of Financing Preferred:
Leveraged Buyout
Value-Add
Expansion
Balanced
Opportunistic
Later Stage
Other

Size of Investments Considered:
Min Size of Investment Considered (000s): $20,000
Max Size of Investment Considered (000s): $75,000

Geographical Preferences

International Preferences:
India

Industry Preferences

In Communications prefer:
Telecommunications
Wireless Communications

In Medical/Health prefer:
Medical/Health

In Consumer Related prefer:
Food/Beverage
Hotels and Resorts

In Industrial/Energy prefer:
Energy
Oil and Gas Exploration

In Transportation prefer:
Transportation

In Financial Services prefer:
Real Estate

In Business Serv. prefer:
Services
Distribution

In Agr/Forestr/Fish prefer:
Agriculture related

In Other prefer:
Environment Responsible

Additional Information

Year Founded: 2002
Capital Under Management: $1,300,000,000
Current Activity Level : Actively seeking new investments

IDFC CAPITAL (SINGAPORE) PTE LTD

Eight Marina Boulevard
05-02 Marina Bay Fin. Ctr.
Singapore, Singapore 018981
Phone: 6563381888
Fax: 6563375100

Management and Staff
Evan Gallagher, Managing Director
Veronica John, Chief Executive Officer
Vikram Raju, Managing Director

Type of Firm
Private Equity Advisor or Fund of Funds

Project Preferences

Type of Financing Preferred:
Fund of Funds

Geographical Preferences

International Preferences:
India
Asia
Africa

Additional Information
Year Founded: 2008
Capital Under Management: $50,000,000
Current Activity Level : Actively seeking new investments

IDG CAPITAL PARTNERS INC

No. 8, Jianguomeiwai Avenue
6F, Tower A, COFCO Plaza
Beijing, China 100005
Phone: 861065262400
Fax: 861065260700
E-mail: idgvc@idgvc.com.cn
Website: www.idgvc.com

Other Offices
99 Queen's Road
15/F, Unit 1509, The Center
Central, Hong Kong
Phone: 852-2529-1016
Fax: 852-2529-1619

No. 107 Zunyi Road
Room 1105, Aetna Tower
Shanghai, China 200051
Phone: 86-21-6237-5408
Fax: 86-21-6237-5899

No. 1 East Pazhoudadao
Rm 2506-2508, S. Tower, Poly Int'l Plaza
Guangzhou, China 510308
Phone: 862084120357
Fax: 862084120490

No. 3037 Jintian Road
Room 2901B, Jinzhonghuan Business Bldg.
Shenzhen, China 518048
Phone: 86-755-8280-5462
Fax: 86-755-8280-5475

Management and Staff
Alexandre Quirici, Venture Partner
Dongliang Lin, Partner
Drake Yu, Vice President
Fei Yang, Partner
Feng Li, Partner
Hugo Shong, Founder
Jeacy Yan, Partner
Jianbin Zhang, Vice President
Jianguang Li, Partner
Jianhuan Zhu, Partner
Jianping Xie, Vice President
Jingbo Wang, Vice President
Jun Ning, Partner
Justin Niu, Vice President
Kenny Hou, Vice President
Meng Lian, Vice President
Michael Mao, Partner
Michelle Ma, Vice President
Peter Zhang, Vice President
Quan Zhou, Partner
Simon Ho, Chief Financial Officer
Suyang Zhang, Partner
Xiaojun Li, Partner
Xinhua Yu, Partner
Yeshun Dong, Partner
Ying Li, Vice President
Ying Wu, Vice President
Young Guo, Partner

Type of Firm
Private Equity Firm

Association Membership
Venture Capital Association of Beijing (VCAB)
China Venture Capital Association

Project Preferences

Role in Financing:
Prefer role in deals created by others

Type of Financing Preferred:
Early Stage
Expansion
Balanced
Later Stage
Seed
Startup

Size of Investments Considered:
Min Size of Investment Considered (000s): $1,000
Max Size of Investment Considered (000s): $100,000

Geographical Preferences

International Preferences:
China
Asia

Industry Preferences

In Communications prefer:
Communications and Media
Telecommunications
Wireless Communications

In Computer Software prefer:
Software
Applications Software

In Internet Specific prefer:
Internet
Ecommerce

In Semiconductor/Electr prefer:
Semiconductor

In Medical/Health prefer:
Health Services

In Consumer Related prefer:
Consumer Products
Education Related

In Industrial/Energy prefer:
Energy

In Financial Services prefer:
Financial Services

In Business Serv. prefer:
Services
Distribution
Media

In Manufact. prefer:
Manufacturing

Additional Information
Year Founded: 1992
Capital Under Management: $3,800,000,000
Current Activity Level : Actively seeking new investments
Method of Compensation: Return on investment is of primary concern, do not charge fees

---

IDG VENTURES INDIA ADVISORS PVT LTD

One, Commissariat Road
7B, Seventh Floor, Sobha Pearl
Bangalore, India 560 025
Phone: 918040434836
Fax: 918041329226
E-mail: contact@idgvcindia.com

Other Offices
Trident Hotel, Number 1118 / 1120
Nariman Point
Mumbai, India 400 021

C/o. Int'l Financial Services Limited
IFS Court, TwentyEight, Cybercity
Ebene, Mauritius
Phone: 230-467-3000
Fax: 230-467-4000

Management and Staff
Hemir Doshi, Vice President
Manik Arora, Managing Director
Ranjith Menon, Vice President
T.C. Meenakshisundaram, Managing Director

Type of Firm
Private Equity Firm

Association Membership
Emerging Markets Private Equity Association
Indian Venture Capital Association (IVCA)

Project Preferences

Type of Financing Preferred:
Early Stage
Expansion
Balanced

Geographical Preferences

International Preferences:
India

Industry Preferences

In Communications prefer:
Wireless Communications

In Computer Software prefer:
Software

In Internet Specific prefer:
Internet

In Medical/Health prefer:
Medical Products

In Consumer Related prefer:
Consumer
Consumer Services

In Industrial/Energy prefer:
Environmental Related

In Business Serv. prefer:
Media

Additional Information
Year Founded: 2006
Capital Under Management: $150,000,000
Current Activity Level : Actively seeking new investments

IDG VENTURES USA

One Letterman Drive
Building D, Suite P 100
San Francisco, CA USA 94129
Phone: 4154394420
Fax: 4154394428
Website: www.idgvsf.com

Management and Staff
Alexander Rosen, Managing Director
Baochi Nguyen, Vice President
Lorra Stone, Chief Financial Officer
Patrick Kenealy, Managing Director
Philip Sanderson, Managing Director

Type of Firm
Private Equity Firm

Association Membership
Western Association of Venture Capitalists (WAVC)
National Venture Capital Association - USA (NVCA)

Project Preferences

Role in Financing:
Will function either as deal originator or investor in deals created by others

Type of Financing Preferred:
Early Stage

Size of Investments Considered:
Min Size of Investment Considered (000s): $1,000
Max Size of Investment Considered (000s): $5,000

Geographical Preferences

United States Preferences:

Industry Preferences

In Internet Specific prefer:
Internet
Ecommerce

In Business Serv. prefer:
Media

Additional Information
Name of Most Recent Fund: IDG Ventures USA III, L.P.
Most Recent Fund Was Raised: 02/20/2014
Year Founded: 1996
Capital Under Management: $100,000,000
Current Activity Level : Actively seeking new investments

IDI ASSET MANAGEMENT SA

18 avenue Matignon
Paris, France 75008
Phone: 0033155278000
Fax: 0033140170444
Website: www.idi.fr

Type of Firm
Investment Management Firm

Association Membership
French Venture Capital Association (AFIC)

Project Preferences

Type of Financing Preferred:
Leveraged Buyout
Early Stage
Mezzanine
Generalist PE
Public Companies
Later Stage
Acquisition

Size of Investments Considered:
Min Size of Investment Considered (000s): $6,677
Max Size of Investment Considered (000s): $40,064

Geographical Preferences

United States Preferences:

International Preferences:
United Kingdom
Europe
Asia
France

Industry Preferences

In Communications prefer:
Telecommunications

In Computer Software prefer:
Software

Additional Information
Year Founded: 1970
Capital Under Management: $284,400,000
Current Activity Level : Actively seeking new investments

IDINVEST PARTNERS SA

117, avenue des Champs Elysees
Paris, France 75008
Phone: 33158185656
Fax: 33158185689
E-mail: contact@idinvest-partners.com
Website: www.idinvest.com

Management and Staff
Alain Munoz, Venture Partner
Benoist Grossmann, Managing Director
Charles Daulon du Laurens, Partner
Christophe Simon, Partner
Francois Lacoste, Partner
Gerard Vaillant, Venture Partner
Guillaume Lautour, Partner
Jean Plamondon, Partner
Jean-Philippe Boige, Partner
Laetitia Vuitton, Partner
Laurent Dumas, Partner
Luc Maruenda, Partner
Mathieu Le Roux, Partner
Matthieu Baret, Partner
Nicolas Chaudron, Partner

Type of Firm
Insurance Firm Affiliate

Association Membership
French Venture Capital Association (AFIC)

Project Preferences

Type of Financing Preferred:
Fund of Funds
Leveraged Buyout
Early Stage
Expansion
Mezzanine
Turnaround
Later Stage
Seed
Management Buyouts
Acquisition
Startup
Fund of Funds of Second

Geographical Preferences

United States Preferences:
All U.S.

International Preferences:
Europe
Netherlands
Asia
All International
France

Industry Preferences

In Communications prefer:
Telecommunications
Data Communications

In Computer Software prefer:
Software

In Internet Specific prefer:
Internet

In Biotechnology prefer:
Biotechnology

In Medical/Health prefer:
Medical/Health

In Consumer Related prefer:
Food/Beverage

In Industrial/Energy prefer:
Energy Conservation Relat
Advanced Materials

In Transportation prefer:
Transportation

In Utilities prefer:
Utilities

In Other prefer:
Environment Responsible

Additional Information
Name of Most Recent Fund: Idinvest Secondary Fund II
Most Recent Fund Was Raised: 04/07/2014
Year Founded: 1997
Capital Under Management: $1,684,900,000
Current Activity Level : Actively seeking new investments

IDOOO SRL

Via Lodovico Il Moro, 25
Milan, Italy 20143
Phone: 39247762732
Fax: 39247762734
E-mail: info@idooo.it
Website: www.idooo.it

Type of Firm
Private Equity Firm

Project Preferences

Type of Financing Preferred:
Early Stage
Seed
Startup

Geographical Preferences

International Preferences:
Italy

Industry Preferences

In Communications prefer:
Wireless Communications
Media and Entertainment

In Internet Specific prefer:
Internet

Additional Information
Year Founded: 2011
Current Activity Level : Actively seeking new investments

IECP FUND MANAGEMENT LLC

1010 Wilshire Boulevard
Suite 206
Los Angeles, CA USA 90017
Phone: 8007304171
Fax: 6143042098
E-mail: info@iecp.com
Website: www.iecp.com

Other Offices
5965 Twin Pine Drive
New Albany, OH USA 43054
Phone: 6147431286
Fax: 6143042098

Management and Staff
Ali Osman, Partner
Calvin Harris, Chief Financial Officer
Cordis Stanfield, Partner
Khadijah Coakley, Partner
Robert Black, Partner

Type of Firm
Private Equity Firm

Project Preferences

Type of Financing Preferred:
Startup

Additional Information
Year Founded: 2014
Capital Under Management: $750,000
Current Activity Level : Actively seeking new investments

IEP FUND ADVISORS PVT LTD

Dr. Annie Besant Road
Ninth Floor, Thapar House
Mumbai, India 400 018
Phone: 912240001000
E-mail: info@iepfundadvisors.com
Website: www.iepfundadvisors.com

Other Offices
152 West 57th Street
45th Flr, Carnegie Hall Tower
New York, NY USA 10019
Phone: 212 258 9700

Dr. Annie Besant Road
505 Cee Jay House
, India 400 018

c/o Utilis Corporate Services Ltd
7th Floor, Tower 1, NeXTeracom
Cybercity, Ebene, Mauritius
Phone: 230 206 0300

Management and Staff
Abhishek Sharman, Principal
Anurag Bhargava, Managing Partner
Gaurav Mathur, Managing Director
Krishnan Iyer, Managing Director
Ravi Sampat, Chief Financial Officer
Steven Wisch, Managing Partner
Supratim Banerjee, Principal

Type of Firm
Private Equity Firm

Project Preferences

Type of Financing Preferred:
Generalist PE
Management Buyouts

Geographical Preferences

International Preferences:
India

Industry Preferences

In Medical/Health prefer:
Medical/Health

In Consumer Related prefer:
Food/Beverage
Consumer Products
Education Related

In Financial Services prefer:
Financial Services

In Business Serv. prefer:
Services
Distribution

Additional Information
Year Founded: 2007
Capital Under Management: $2,000,000,000
Current Activity Level: Actively seeking new investments

IER VENTURE CAPITAL CO LTD

No. 3039 Shennan Central Road
Inter-Cultural Building Rm2805
Shenzhen, China 518033
Phone: 8675583290633
Fax: 8675583290622

Type of Firm
Private Equity Firm

Association Membership
Shenzhen Venture Capital Association

Project Preferences

Type of Financing Preferred:
Early Stage
Balanced

Geographical Preferences

International Preferences:
China

Industry Preferences

In Biotechnology prefer:
Biotechnology

Additional Information
Year Founded: 1996
Capital Under Management: $14,746,000
Current Activity Level: Actively seeking new investments

IEUROPE CAPITAL LLC

1199 Park Avenue
Suite 19A
New York, NY USA 10028
Phone: 2128280037
Fax: 2124106196
E-mail: info@ieurope.com
Website: www.ieurope.com

Other Offices
Zugligeti ut 41.
Budapest, Hungary 1121
Phone: 36-1-200-4015
Fax: 36-1-200-5707

Management and Staff
Kristina Davison, Managing Partner
Laszlo Czirjak, Managing Partner

Type of Firm
Private Equity Firm

Project Preferences

Role in Financing:
Prefer role as deal originator but will also invest in deals created by others

Type of Financing Preferred:
Leveraged Buyout
Expansion
Generalist PE
Balanced
Acquisition

Geographical Preferences

International Preferences:
Slovenia
Hungary
Slovak Repub.
Central Europe
Czech Republic
Macedonia
Poland
Eastern Europe
Bulgaria
Estonia
Bosnia
Romania
Latvia
Lithuania

Industry Preferences

In Internet Specific prefer:
Ecommerce

In Medical/Health prefer:
Medical/Health

In Consumer Related prefer:
Consumer Products
Consumer Services

In Industrial/Energy prefer:
Alternative Energy
Industrial Products
Environmental Related

In Business Serv. prefer:
Services
Media

Additional Information
Year Founded: 2001
Current Activity Level: Actively seeking new investments

IFB INNOVATIONSSTARTER GMBH

Besenbinderhof 31
Hamburg, Germany 20097
Phone: 4940657980590
Fax: 4940657980593
Website: www.innovationsstarter.com

Management and Staff
Heiko Milde, Chief Executive Officer

Type of Firm
Government Affiliated Program

Project Preferences

Type of Financing Preferred:
Early Stage
Seed
Startup

Geographical Preferences

International Preferences:
Germany

Additional Information
Year Founded: 2011
Capital Under Management: $17,175,000
Current Activity Level: Actively seeking new investments

IFE MEZZANINE SARL

41 Avenue George Five
Paris, France 75008
Phone: 33156520240
Fax: 33147200694
E-mail: info@ifeconseil.com
Website: www.ifemezzanine.com

Management and Staff
Jean-Pascal Ley, Partner
Regis Mitjavile, Managing Partner

Type of Firm
Private Equity Firm

Association Membership
French Venture Capital Association (AFIC)
European Private Equity and Venture Capital Assoc.

Project Preferences

Role in Financing:
Will function either as deal originator or investor in deals created by others

Type of Financing Preferred:
Leveraged Buyout
Mezzanine
Management Buyouts

Size of Investments Considered:
Min Size of Investment Considered (000s): $6,831
Max Size of Investment Considered (000s): $20,495

Geographical Preferences

International Preferences:
Italy
Luxembourg
Europe
Netherlands
Switzerland
Eastern Europe
Spain
Germany
France

Industry Focus
(% based on actual investment)
Industrial/Energy 54.5%
Other Products 44.2%
Computer Software and Services 1.3%

Additional Information
Year Founded: 1998
Capital Under Management: $408,900,000
Current Activity Level : Actively seeking new investments

IFLY.VC

3150 Porter Drive
Palo Alto, CA USA 94304

Type of Firm
Private Equity Firm

Project Preferences

Type of Financing Preferred:
Early Stage

Additional Information
Year Founded: 2016
Current Activity Level : Actively seeking new investments

IFM INVESTORS PTY LTD

Two Lonsdale Street
Level 29, Casselden Place
Melbourne, Australia 3000
Phone: 61386725300
Fax: 61386725306
Website: www.ifminvestors.com

Other Offices
60 Gresham Street, Third Floor
London, United Kingdom EC2V 7BB
Phone: 442074489600
Fax: 442074489640

99 Park Avenue
19th Floor
New York, NY USA 10016
Phone: 12125751055
Fax: 12125758738

50 Pitt Street
Level Two
Sydney, Australia NSW 2000
Phone: 61280765200
Fax: 61280765201

12435 Berlin
Eichenstrabe 3A
Berlin, Germany
Phone: 4903051503802
Fax: 490305150803

1-3-1 Marunouchi, Chiyoda-ku
Level 15 Tokyo Bankers Club Building
Tokyo, Japan 100-0005
Phone: 81332167200
Fax: 81332167210

Management and Staff
Brett Himbury, Chief Executive Officer
Philip Dowman, Founder

Type of Firm
Bank Affiliated

Association Membership
New Zealand Venture Capital Association

Project Preferences

Type of Financing Preferred:
Core
Other

Geographical Preferences

United States Preferences:
North America

International Preferences:
Europe
Australia
New Zealand
Asia
All International

Industry Preferences

In Industrial/Energy prefer:
Energy
Oil and Gas Exploration

In Transportation prefer:
Transportation

In Financial Services prefer:
Real Estate

In Utilities prefer:
Utilities

Additional Information
Year Founded: 1991
Capital Under Management: $23,662,100,000
Current Activity Level : Actively seeking new investments

IG EXPANSION BUSINESS DEVELOPMENT SL

C / Velazquez 80
2nd right
Madrid, Spain 28001
Phone: 34914320253
E-mail: info@igexpansion.com
Website: www.igexpansion.com

Management and Staff
Carlos de San Pablo, Co-Founder
Jose Marin, Co-Founder

Type of Firm
Private Equity Firm

Project Preferences

Type of Financing Preferred:
Early Stage
Balanced
Later Stage
Seed
Startup

Geographical Preferences

United States Preferences:
All U.S.

International Preferences:
Europe
Spain

Additional Information
Year Founded: 2005
Current Activity Level : Actively seeking new investments

IGAN PARTNERS INC

60 Bloor Street West
Ninth Floor
Toronto, Canada M4W 3B8
Phone: 4169284349
Fax: 4169284105
E-mail: info@iGanpartners.com
Website: iganpartners.com

Management and Staff
Geoff Matus, Venture Partner
Javier Flores, Venture Partner
Kuljeev Singh, Principal
Michael Stein, Venture Partner
Michael Aron, Venture Partner
Olivier Giner, Vice President

Type of Firm
Private Equity Firm

Association Membership
Canadian Venture Capital Association

Project Preferences

Type of Financing Preferred:
Early Stage

Geographical Preferences

Canadian Preferences:
All Canada

Industry Preferences

In Computer Software prefer:
Software
Artificial Intelligence

In Internet Specific prefer:
Internet

In Medical/Health prefer:
Medical/Health

Additional Information
Name of Most Recent Fund: iGan Partners
Most Recent Fund Was Raised: 06/30/2011
Year Founded: 2010
Capital Under Management: $160,000,000
Current Activity Level: Actively seeking new investments

IGEO SPRL
41, Rue de Livourne
Brussels, Belgium B 1050
Phone: 3225343676
Website: www.koisinvest.com

Type of Firm
Private Equity Firm

Project Preferences

Type of Financing Preferred:
Early Stage
Expansion
Later Stage
Seed

Geographical Preferences

International Preferences:
India
Luxembourg
Netherlands
Belgium
France

Additional Information
Year Founded: 2010
Current Activity Level: Actively seeking new investments

IGLOBE PARTNERS LTD
Eleven Biopolis Way
Helios # 09-03
Singapore, Singapore 138667
Phone: 6564789716
Fax: 6564789717
E-mail: contact@iglobepartners.com
Website: www.iglobepartners.com

Other Offices
5201 Great America Parkway
Suite 320
Santa Clara, CA USA 95054
Phone: 4089822126
Fax: 4089822129

43D Apollo Drive
Unit 16 Mairangi Bay
Auckland, New Zealand 0632
Phone: 6499153401
Fax: 6499688431

Management and Staff
Frankie Tan, Venture Partner
Gigi Wang, Venture Partner
Jean-Philippe Sarraut, Venture Partner
Jonathan Yu, Venture Partner
Joyce Ng, Principal
Michel Birnbaum, Partner
Soo Boon Koh, Managing Partner
Trudi Schifter, General Partner

Type of Firm
Private Equity Firm

Association Membership
Singapore Venture Capital Association (SVCA)

Project Preferences

Type of Financing Preferred:
Balanced

Geographical Preferences

United States Preferences:

International Preferences:
Europe
Asia

Industry Preferences

In Communications prefer:
Communications and Media
Wireless Communications
Media and Entertainment

In Internet Specific prefer:
Internet

In Semiconductor/Electr prefer:
Semiconductor

Additional Information
Year Founded: 1999
Capital Under Management: $92,000,000
Current Activity Level: Actively seeking new investments

IGLOBE TREASURY MANAGEMENT LTD
Unit 16, 43D Apollo Drive
Mairangi Bay
Auckland, New Zealand 0632
Phone: 6499153401
Fax: 6499688431
Website: www.iglobetreasury.com

Other Offices
11 Biopolis Way
Helios Suite 09-03
Singapore, Singapore 138667
Phone: 6564789716
Fax: 656478-9717

Management and Staff
Anthony Paul Bishop, Managing Partner
Christopher Due, Venture Partner
Colin Harvey, Venture Partner
Doris Yee, General Partner
Joseph Platnick, Venture Partner
Koh Soo Boon, Managing Partner
Martin Greenberg, Venture Partner
Michael Standbridge, Venture Partner
N. Ganesan, Venture Partner
Philip Lum, General Partner
Sin Jat Lai, Partner

Type of Firm
Private Equity Firm

Association Membership
New Zealand Venture Capital Association

Project Preferences

Type of Financing Preferred:
Early Stage
Expansion
Seed
Startup

Geographical Preferences

International Preferences:
New Zealand

Industry Preferences

In Communications prefer:
Communications and Media

In Semiconductor/Electr prefer:
Electronics

In Biotechnology prefer:
Biotechnology

In Medical/Health prefer:
Medical/Health

In Consumer Related prefer:
Food/Beverage

In Industrial/Energy prefer:
Environmental Related

In Business Serv. prefer:
Media

Additional Information
Name of Most Recent Fund: iGlobe Treasury Fund
Most Recent Fund Was Raised: 06/24/2003
Year Founded: 2002
Current Activity Level : Actively seeking new investments

IGNIA PARTNERS LLC
Av. Ricardo Margain 575
Parque Corp Sta. Engracia
San Pedro Garza Garcia, Mexico 66267
Phone: 528180007280
Fax: 528180007038
E-mail: info@ignia.com.mx
Website: www.ignia.com.mx

Management and Staff
Alvaro Rodriguez Arregui, Managing Partner
Carlos Labarthe Costas, General Partner
Carlos Antonio Danel Cendoya, General Partner
Christine Kenna, Principal
Fabrice Serfati, Chief Financial Officer
Juan Jose Gutierrez Chapa, General Partner
Leon Kraig, Managing Director
Michael Chu, Managing Partner
Pablo Salazar Rojo, Principal

Type of Firm
Private Equity Firm

Project Preferences
Type of Financing Preferred:
Leveraged Buyout
Early Stage
Expansion
Balanced
Startup

Geographical Preferences
International Preferences:
Latin America
Mexico

Industry Preferences
In Medical/Health prefer:
Medical/Health

In Consumer Related prefer:
Education Related

In Utilities prefer:
Utilities

Additional Information
Year Founded: 2008
Capital Under Management: $90,000,000
Current Activity Level : Actively seeking new investments

IGNITE 100 LTD
Campus North, Sunco House
Five Carliol Square
Newcastle Upon Tyne, United Kingdom NE1 6UF
E-mail: hello@ignite100.com
Website: ignite100.com

Type of Firm
Incubator/Development Program

Project Preferences
Type of Financing Preferred:
Seed
Startup

Additional Information
Year Founded: 2011
Current Activity Level : Actively seeking new investments

IGNITE FARM LLC
1450 Maria Lane
Suite 300
Walnut Creek, CA USA 94596
Website: ignite.farm

Type of Firm
Incubator/Development Program

Project Preferences
Type of Financing Preferred:
Early Stage
Balanced
Later Stage
Startup

Industry Preferences
In Consumer Related prefer:
Food/Beverage
Consumer Products

In Business Serv. prefer:
Media

Additional Information
Year Founded: 2014
Capital Under Management: $2,300,000
Current Activity Level : Actively seeking new investments

IGNITION CAPITAL PARTNERS
1500 Fourth Avenue, Suite 200
Seattle, WA USA 98101
Phone: 2064380777
Fax: 2069715055
Website: www.igncap.com

Other Offices
11400 Southeast, 6th Street
Ste 100
BEAUX ARTS, WA USA 98004
Phone: 4257090772
Fax: 4257090798

Management and Staff
John Zagula, Founding Partner
Jon Anderson, Founding Partner
Rennie Coit, Partner
Richard Tong, Founding Partner
Shawn Bohnert, Partner
Ty Graham, Partner

Type of Firm
Private Equity Firm

Project Preferences
Type of Financing Preferred:
Expansion
Later Stage

Geographical Preferences
United States Preferences:

Industry Preferences
In Communications prefer:
Telecommunications

In Medical/Health prefer:
Medical/Health

In Consumer Related prefer:
Consumer Services

Additional Information
Name of Most Recent Fund: Ignition Growth Capital I, L.P.
Most Recent Fund Was Raised: 09/30/2007
Year Founded: 2007
Current Activity Level : Actively seeking new investments

IGNITION VENTURES MANAGEMENT LLC
350 106th Avenue Northeast
First Floor
Bellevue, WA USA 98004
Phone: 4257090772
Fax: 4257090798
E-mail: info@ignitionpartners.com
Website: ignitionpartners.com

Other Offices
421 Kipling St
PALO ALTO, CA USA 94301
Phone: 6508685553

108 First Street
LOS ALTOS HILLS, CA USA 94022
Phone: 6508256909

11400 Southeast Sixth Street
Suite 100
BEAUX ARTS, WA USA 98004

Management and Staff

Adrian Smith, Partner
Bob Kelly, Managing Partner
Brad Silverberg, Co-Founder
Cameron Myhrvold, Co-Founder
Chris Howard, Principal
Frank Artale, Managing Partner
Jack Ferry, Chief Financial Officer
John Ludwig, Co-Founder
John Connors, Managing Partner
Jonathan Roberts, Founder
Jonathan Roberts, Co-Founder
Kellan Carter, Principal
Kristina Bergmann, Principal
Michelle Goldberg, Partner
Nick Triantos, Venture Partner
Nick Sturiale, Managing Partner
Preeti Rathi, Principal
Rachel Chalmers, Principal
Richard Fade, Partner
Robert Headley, Partner
Ryan Baker, Chief Financial Officer
Steve Hooper, Co-Founder

Type of Firm

Private Equity Firm

Project Preferences

Role in Financing:
Prefer role as deal originator but will also invest in deals created by others

Type of Financing Preferred:
Early Stage
Seed

Geographical Preferences

United States Preferences:
West Coast

Industry Preferences

In Communications prefer:
Telecommunications
Data Communications

In Computer Software prefer:
Computer Services
Data Processing
Software

In Consumer Related prefer:
Consumer

Additional Information

Name of Most Recent Fund: Ignition Venture Partners V, L.P.
Most Recent Fund Was Raised: 03/29/2013
Year Founded: 2000
Capital Under Management: $4,000,000,000
Current Activity Level: Actively seeking new investments
Method of Compensation: Return on investment is of primary concern, do not charge fees

IIFL HOLDINGS LTD

Senapati Bapat Marg, Lwr Parel
9th Floor, IIFL Centre
Mumbai, India 400 013
Phone: 912246464600
Fax: 91246464700
E-mail: info@iiflcap.com
Website: www.indiainfoline.com

Management and Staff

Nipun Goel, President
Prabodh Agarwal, Chief Financial Officer
Rajamani Venkataraman, Managing Director

Type of Firm

Bank Affiliated

Project Preferences

Type of Financing Preferred:
Value-Add
Opportunistic
Seed

Geographical Preferences

International Preferences:
India

Industry Preferences

In Financial Services prefer:
Real Estate

Additional Information

Name of Most Recent Fund: IIFL Real Estate Fund (Domestic) Series 1
Most Recent Fund Was Raised: 01/25/2012
Year Founded: 2008
Capital Under Management: $100,000,000
Current Activity Level: Actively seeking new investments

IK INEKO PAT

24 Starovokzalnaya
3rd Floor
Kyiv, Ukraine 01032
Phone: 380442016417
Fax: 380442016418
E-mail: info@inekocapital.com
Website: www.ineko.com

Management and Staff

Denis Kopylov, Chief Executive Officer
Eugene Baranov, Chief Financial Officer
Oleg Morkva, Partner
Stanislav Lyudkevych, Vice President

Type of Firm

Bank Affiliated

Association Membership

European Private Equity and Venture Capital Assoc.

Project Preferences

Type of Financing Preferred:
Leveraged Buyout
Turnaround
Management Buyouts

Size of Investments Considered:
Min Size of Investment Considered (000s): $1,000
Max Size of Investment Considered (000s): $10,000

Geographical Preferences

International Preferences:
Europe
Eastern Europe
Ukraine
Russia

Industry Preferences

In Consumer Related prefer:
Food/Beverage
Hotels and Resorts

In Industrial/Energy prefer:
Energy
Materials

In Transportation prefer:
Transportation

In Financial Services prefer:
Real Estate
Financial Services

In Business Serv. prefer:
Distribution

In Manufact. prefer:
Manufacturing

Additional Information

Year Founded: 2002
Current Activity Level: Actively seeking new investments

IK INVESTMENT PARTNERS LTD

1-11, John Adam Street
London, United Kingdom WC2N 6HT
Phone: 442073044300
Fax: 442073044320
Website: www.ikinvest.com

Other Offices

1, rue de la Poudrerie
Leudelange, Luxembourg 3364
Phone: 35-22-717-2600

Birger Jarlsgatan 4
Stockholm, Sweden 114 34
Phone: 46-8-678-9500
Fax: 46-8-678-0336

350, Gustav Mahlerlaan
UN Studio, 13th Floor
Amsterdam, Netherlands 1082

6, Rue Christophe Colomb
Paris, France 75008
Phone: 33-1-4443-0660
Fax: 33-1-4443-0670

30-32 New Street, St. Helier
Charles Bisson House
Jersey, Channel Islands JE2 3RA
Phone: 44-15-3463-9380
Fax: 44-15-3463-9382

Management and Staff

Alireza Etemad, Partner
Anders Petersson, Partner
Beata Grunditz, Partner
Christopher Masek, Chief Executive Officer
Detlef Dinsel, Partner
James Yates, Partner
Kristian Kemppinen, Partner
Mads Larsen, Partner
Pierre Gallix, Partner
Remi Buttiaux, Partner
Remko Hilhorst, Partner
Thomas Klitbo, Partner

Type of Firm

Private Equity Firm

Association Membership

Finnish Venture Capital Association (FVCA)
British Venture Capital Association (BVCA)
Swedish Venture Capital Association (SVCA)
Polish Venture Capital Association (PSIC/PPEA)
European Private Equity and Venture Capital Assoc.

Project Preferences

Type of Financing Preferred:
Leveraged Buyout
Management Buyouts
Acquisition
Recapitalizations

Geographical Preferences

International Preferences:
Sweden
Luxembourg
Netherlands
Switzerland
Greenland
Austria
Iceland
Belgium
Finland
Norway
Germany
Denmark
Faroe Islands
France

Industry Focus

(% based on actual investment)
Industrial/Energy	29.5%
Other Products	27.8%
Consumer Related	21.5%
Medical/Health	9.8%
Semiconductors/Other Elect.	4.4%
Internet Specific	3.6%
Computer Software and Services	3.2%
Communications and Media	0.2%

Additional Information

Name of Most Recent Fund: IK VII Fund
Most Recent Fund Was Raised: 10/23/2013
Year Founded: 1989
Capital Under Management: $6,991,200,000
Current Activity Level : Actively seeking new investments

IKIB MITTELSTANDSFINAN-ZIERUNGS GMBH

Kolingasse 14-16
Vienna, Austria 1090
Phone: 435040040
Fax: 435040043683
E-mail: office@ikib.at
Website: www.ikib.at

Management and Staff

Andreas Huber, Managing Director

Type of Firm

Bank Affiliated

Project Preferences

Type of Financing Preferred:
Fund of Funds
Leveraged Buyout
Mezzanine
Later Stage
Management Buyouts
Acquisition
Recapitalizations

Geographical Preferences

International Preferences:
Central Europe
Switzerland
Austria
Eastern Europe
Germany

Industry Preferences

In Communications prefer:
Communications and Media

In Industrial/Energy prefer:
Machinery

In Business Serv. prefer:
Services

In Manufact. prefer:
Publishing

Additional Information

Year Founded: 1998
Capital Under Management: $58,100,000
Current Activity Level : Actively seeking new investments

IKOVE VENTURE PARTNERS LLC

1330 Kinnear Road
Suite 200
Columbus, OH USA 43212
Phone: 6148245892
Fax: 6143088992

Type of Firm

Private Equity Firm

Project Preferences

Type of Financing Preferred:
Early Stage

Additional Information

Year Founded: 2014
Current Activity Level : Actively seeking new investments

IL & FS INVESTMENT MANAGERS LTD

Bandra Kurla Complex, Bandra E
1st Flr, Plot No.C-22, G Block
Mumbai, India 400 051
Phone: 912226533333
Fax: 912226533056
Website: www.iimlindia.com

Other Offices

Al-Latheef Building, 1st Floor, No. 2,
Union Street, Off Infantry Road
Bangalore, India 560 001
Phone: 91-80-4034-3333
Fax: 91-80-4034-3310

Management and Staff
Archana Hingorani, Chief Executive Officer
Ramesh Bawa, Managing Director

Type of Firm
Private Equity Firm

Association Membership
Emerging Markets Private Equity Association
Indian Venture Capital Association (IVCA)

Project Preferences

Role in Financing:
Prefer role as deal originator but will also invest in deals created by others

Type of Financing Preferred:
Leveraged Buyout
Early Stage
Expansion
Generalist PE
Balanced
Opportunistic
Other
Seed
Recapitalizations

Size of Investments Considered:
Min Size of Investment Considered (000s): $15,000
Max Size of Investment Considered (000s): $30,000

Geographical Preferences

International Preferences:
India
Asia

Industry Focus

(% based on actual investment)
Other Products	69.2%
Industrial/Energy	13.8%
Consumer Related	5.9%
Medical/Health	4.0%
Communications and Media	1.9%
Semiconductors/Other Elect.	1.7%
Computer Software and Services	1.5%
Internet Specific	1.0%
Computer Hardware	0.7%
Biotechnology	0.3%

Additional Information
Year Founded: 1989
Capital Under Management: $3,200,000,000
Current Activity Level : Actively seeking new investments
Method of Compensation: Professional fee required whether or not deal closes

ILAB HOLDING AS

Ataturk Caddesi No. 72
Kozyatagi Daire 20
Istanbul, Turkey 34736
Phone: 902164681010
Fax: 902163028683
E-mail: info@ilab.com.tr
Website: www.ilab.com.tr

Management and Staff
Altug Inan, Chief Financial Officer
Mustafa Say, Co-Founder

Type of Firm
Private Equity Firm

Project Preferences

Type of Financing Preferred:
Early Stage
Expansion
Balanced
Later Stage

Geographical Preferences

International Preferences:
Turkey

Industry Preferences

In Computer Software prefer:
Software
Systems Software
Applications Software

In Consumer Related prefer:
Retail

In Industrial/Energy prefer:
Oil and Gas Exploration
Oil & Gas Drilling,Explor
Materials

In Financial Services prefer:
Insurance
Financial Services

In Manufact. prefer:
Manufacturing

Additional Information
Year Founded: 2000
Current Activity Level : Actively seeking new investments

ILE DE FRANCE CAPITAL SA

6 Rue de L'Isly
Paris, France 75008
Phone: 33144706161
Fax: 33144706159
E-mail: contact@idfcapital.fr
Website: www.idfcapital.fr

Management and Staff
Thomas Galloro, Chief Executive Officer

Type of Firm
Private Equity Firm

Association Membership
French Venture Capital Association (AFIC)

Project Preferences

Type of Financing Preferred:
Leveraged Buyout
Early Stage
Generalist PE
Later Stage
Management Buyouts
Acquisition

Size of Investments Considered:
Min Size of Investment Considered (000s): $130
Max Size of Investment Considered (000s): $1,300

Geographical Preferences

International Preferences:
Europe
France

Industry Preferences

In Communications prefer:
Wireless Communications

In Biotechnology prefer:
Biotechnology
Biotech Related Research

In Medical/Health prefer:
Medical/Health
Health Services

In Consumer Related prefer:
Retail

In Transportation prefer:
Transportation

In Business Serv. prefer:
Services
Distribution

Additional Information
Year Founded: 1995
Current Activity Level : Actively seeking new investments

ILIAD PARTNERS

Marina Plaza, Level 29
PO Box 392365
Dubai, Utd. Arab Em.
E-mail: info@iliad-partners.com
Website: www.iliad-partners.com

Type of Firm
Private Equity Firm

Project Preferences

Type of Financing Preferred:
Early Stage

Geographical Preferences

International Preferences:
Middle East
Africa

Industry Preferences

In Computer Software prefer:
Software

Additional Information
Year Founded: 2014
Current Activity Level : Actively seeking new investments

ILLINOIS PARTNERS LLC

60 Hazelwood Drive
Suite 226
Naperville, IL USA 60540
Phone: 3124043507
E-mail: info@illinoispartners.com
Website: www.illinoispartners.com

Management and Staff
Neil Kane, Managing Director

Type of Firm
Private Equity Firm

Project Preferences

Type of Financing Preferred:
Early Stage
Seed

Industry Preferences

In Computer Software prefer:
Software

In Industrial/Energy prefer:
Alternative Energy

Additional Information
Year Founded: 2001
Current Activity Level : Actively seeking new investments

ILLINOIS VENTURES LLC

20 North Wacker Drive
Suite 1201
Chicago, IL USA 60606
Phone: 3122510700
Fax: 3122510701
Website: www.illinoisventures.com

Other Offices
2001 South First Street
Suite 201
Champaign, IL USA 61820
Phone: 2172391950
Fax: 2172391948

Management and Staff
John Banta, CEO & Managing Director

Type of Firm
Private Equity Firm

Association Membership
Illinois Venture Capital Association

Project Preferences

Type of Financing Preferred:
Early Stage
Seed
Startup

Size of Investments Considered:
Min Size of Investment Considered (000s): $250
Max Size of Investment Considered (000s): $3,000

Geographical Preferences

United States Preferences:
Midwest
Illinois

Industry Preferences

In Semiconductor/Electr prefer:
Semiconductor

In Industrial/Energy prefer:
Energy
Alternative Energy
Advanced Materials

In Other prefer:
Environment Responsible

Additional Information
Year Founded: 2002
Capital Under Management: $40,000,000
Current Activity Level : Actively seeking new investments

ILLUMINA ACCELERATOR PROGRAM

5200 Research Place
San Diego, CA USA 92122
Phone: 8582024566
Fax: 8582024766
E-mail: info@illumina.com
Website: www.illumina.com

Type of Firm
Incubator/Development Program

Association Membership
National Venture Capital Association – USA (NVCA)

Project Preferences

Type of Financing Preferred:
Seed
Startup

Size of Investments Considered:
Min Size of Investment Considered (000s): $100
Max Size of Investment Considered (000s): $100

Industry Preferences

In Biotechnology prefer:
Biotechnology
Genetic Engineering

Additional Information
Year Founded: 2014
Capital Under Management: $40,000,000
Current Activity Level : Actively seeking new investments

ILLUMINA VENTURES

499 Illinois Street
Suite 120
San Francisco, CA USA 94158
Website: www.illuminaventures.com

Type of Firm
Private Equity Firm

Association Membership
National Venture Capital Association – USA (NVCA)

Project Preferences

Type of Financing Preferred:
Early Stage

Industry Preferences

In Medical/Health prefer:
Health Services

In Industrial/Energy prefer:
Environmental Related

In Agr/Forestr/Fish prefer:
Agriculture related

Additional Information
Year Founded: 2016
Capital Under Management: $230,000,000
Current Activity Level : Actively seeking new investments

ILLUMINATE FINANCIAL MANAGEMENT LLP

Third Floor
101 Finsbury Pavement
London, United Kingdom EC2A 1RS
Website: illuminatefinancial.com

Type of Firm
Private Equity Firm

Project Preferences

Type of Financing Preferred:
Balanced

Geographical Preferences

International Preferences:
All International

Industry Preferences

In Financial Services prefer:
Financial Services

Additional Information
Year Founded: 2014
Current Activity Level: Actively seeking new investments

ILLUMINATE VENTURES

6114 La Salle Avenue
Suite 323
Oakland, CA USA 94611
Phone: 5105316202
Fax: 5104825993
E-mail: contact@illuminate.com
Website: www.illuminate.com

Management and Staff
Jim Dai, Venture Partner
Pia Camenzind, Chief Financial Officer
Rebecca Norlander, Venture Partner

Type of Firm
Private Equity Firm

Project Preferences

Type of Financing Preferred:
Early Stage
Startup

Geographical Preferences

United States Preferences:
North America

Industry Preferences

In Communications prefer:
Wireless Communications

In Internet Specific prefer:
Internet

In Business Serv. prefer:
Media

Additional Information
Name of Most Recent Fund: Illuminate Ventures I, L.P.
Most Recent Fund Was Raised: 04/17/2012
Year Founded: 2009
Capital Under Management: $40,320,000
Current Activity Level: Actively seeking new investments

ILP III SARL

163, Rue Du Kiem
Strassen, Luxembourg L-8030
Phone: 35226384181
Fax: 35226384183
E-mail: contact@j-hirsch.lu
Website: www.ilpfunds.com

Other Offices
Steinweg 3
Frankfurt, Germany D-60313
Phone: 49-69-2992-53612
Fax: 49-69-2929-53620

Via Brera, 3
Milan, Italy I-20121
Phone: 39-2-721-1741
Fax: 39-2-7211-74219

Management and Staff
Fabrizio Rescigno, Partner
Giovanni Covati, Partner
Jean-Pierre Verlaine, Partner

Type of Firm
Private Equity Firm

Project Preferences

Type of Financing Preferred:
Leveraged Buyout
Management Buyouts
Acquisition
Recapitalizations

Size of Investments Considered:
Min Size of Investment Considered (000s): $1,314
Max Size of Investment Considered (000s): $98,529

Geographical Preferences

International Preferences:
Italy
Europe
Germany

Additional Information
Year Founded: 1997
Current Activity Level: Actively seeking new investments

ILSHIN INVESTMENT CO LTD

15-15, Yoido-Dong, Youngdeungpo
Ilshin Building
Seoul, South Korea 150010
Phone: 82237740114
Fax: 82278658914
E-mail: sjkim@ilshin.kr
Website: www.ilshin.co.kr

Other Offices
15-15, Yeouido-dong
Yeongdeungpo-gu
Seoul, South Korea 150-872

Type of Firm
Bank Affiliated

Association Membership
Korean Venture Capital Association (KVCA)

Project Preferences

Type of Financing Preferred:
Leveraged Buyout
Early Stage
Expansion
Balanced
Later Stage

Size of Investments Considered:
Min Size of Investment Considered (000s): $385
Max Size of Investment Considered (000s): $16,000

Geographical Preferences

International Preferences:
Korea, South

Industry Preferences

In Communications prefer:
Telecommunications
Media and Entertainment
Entertainment

In Computer Hardware prefer:
Computers

In Consumer Related prefer:
Consumer
Entertainment and Leisure
Retail

In Industrial/Energy prefer:
Environmental Related

In Business Serv. prefer:
Distribution
Media

In Manufact. prefer:
Manufacturing

In Other prefer:
Environment Responsible

Additional Information
Year Founded: 1951
Capital Under Management: $60,800,000
Current Activity Level: Actively seeking new investments

IMAGINARY VENTURES LLC

455 West 23rd Street
Suite 1C
New York, NY USA 10011
Phone: 9174949919

Type of Firm
Private Equity Firm

Project Preferences

Type of Financing Preferred:
Balanced

Industry Preferences

In Internet Specific prefer:
Ecommerce

In Consumer Related prefer:
Consumer Products

Additional Information

Year Founded: 2017
Current Activity Level : Actively seeking new investments

IMAGINATION CATALYST

100 McCaul Street
Toronto, Canada M5T 1W1
Website: www.ocadu.ca/research/imagination-catalyst.

Type of Firm
University Program

Project Preferences

Type of Financing Preferred:
Seed
Startup

Geographical Preferences

Canadian Preferences:
All Canada

Additional Information

Year Founded: 2014
Capital Under Management: $1,221,000
Current Activity Level : Actively seeking new investments

IMAGINE K12 LLC

395 Page Mill Road
Suite 140
Palo Alto, CA USA 94306
Website: www.imaginek12.com

Management and Staff
Alan Louie, Partner
Geoff Ralston, Partner
Tim Brady, Partner

Type of Firm
Private Equity Firm

Project Preferences

Type of Financing Preferred:
Early Stage
Seed
Startup

Size of Investments Considered:
Min Size of Investment Considered (000s): $14
Max Size of Investment Considered (000s): $100

Industry Preferences

In Consumer Related prefer:
Education Related

Additional Information

Year Founded: 2011
Current Activity Level : Actively seeking new investments

IMB DEVELOPMENT CORP

55 Exchange Place
Suite 401
New York, NY USA 10005
Phone: 6466198797
Fax: 6465064055
Website: www.imbdc.com

Management and Staff
Amber McCants, Managing Director
Jenny Machida, Managing Director
Tarrus Richardson, Chief Executive Officer

Type of Firm
Investment Management Firm

Additional Information

Year Founded: 2010
Current Activity Level : Actively seeking new investments

IMI FONDI CHIUSI SGR SPA

Via Zamboni 2
Bologna, Italy 40126
Phone: 390667124307
Fax: 390817917311
Website: www.imiinvestimenti.it

Management and Staff
Marco Cerrina Feroni, Chief Executive Officer
Sibani Leone, President

Type of Firm
Private Equity Firm

Association Membership
Italian Venture Capital Association (AIFI)
European Private Equity and Venture Capital Assoc.

Project Preferences

Type of Financing Preferred:
Leveraged Buyout
Early Stage
Expansion
Generalist PE
Later Stage
Seed
Management Buyouts
Acquisition
Recapitalizations

Geographical Preferences

International Preferences:
Italy
Europe
Israel

Industry Preferences

In Communications prefer:
Communications and Media

In Semiconductor/Electr prefer:
Electronics

In Biotechnology prefer:
Biotechnology

In Medical/Health prefer:
Medical/Health
Medical Diagnostics

In Consumer Related prefer:
Consumer

In Industrial/Energy prefer:
Industrial Products

In Transportation prefer:
Transportation

In Manufact. prefer:
Manufacturing

Additional Information

Name of Most Recent Fund: Atlante Seed
Most Recent Fund Was Raised: 04/30/2014
Year Founded: 1988
Capital Under Management: $460,000,000
Current Activity Level : Actively seeking new investments

IMI.VC

Bolshaya Tulskaya 44
Moscow, Russia
Phone: 74955454653
E-mail: info@imi.vc
Website: www.imi.vc

Other Offices
720 Market St.
San Francisco, CA USA 94102

Management and Staff
Igor Matsanyuk, Founder

Type of Firm
Private Equity Firm

Project Preferences

Type of Financing Preferred:
Early Stage
Balanced
Seed
Startup

Geographical Preferences

International Preferences:
Eastern Europe

Industry Preferences

In Communications prefer:
Entertainment

In Computer Software prefer:
Applications Software

In Internet Specific prefer:
Internet
Ecommerce

Additional Information
Year Founded: 2011
Current Activity Level : Actively seeking new investments

IMLAY INVESTMENTS

945 East Paces Ferry Road
Suite 2450
Atlanta, GA USA 30326
Phone: 4042391799
Fax: 4042391779

Management and Staff
I. Sigmund Mosley, President

Type of Firm
Private Equity Firm

Project Preferences

Role in Financing:
Will function either as deal originator or investor in deals created by others

Type of Financing Preferred:
Seed
First Stage Financing

Size of Investments Considered:
Min Size of Investment Considered (000s): $100
Max Size of Investment Considered (000s): $1,000

Geographical Preferences

United States Preferences:
Mid Atlantic
Southeast

Industry Focus
(% based on actual investment)

Computer Software and Services	46.9%
Internet Specific	35.8%
Semiconductors/Other Elect.	13.4%
Computer Hardware	1.2%
Other Products	1.1%
Biotechnology	0.7%
Consumer Related	0.6%
Communications and Media	0.4%

Additional Information
Year Founded: 1990
Current Activity Level : Actively seeking new investments
Method of Compensation: Return on investment is of primary concern, do not charge fees

IMM INVESTMENT CORP

152, Teheran-ro, Gangnam-gu
5F Gangnam Finance Center
Seoul, South Korea 135-984
Phone: 82221121777
Fax: 82221121778
Website: www.immvc.co.kr

Management and Staff
Ji Sung Bae, Chief Executive Officer
Jihun Kim, President
SangWook Kim, Managing Director
Sungbae Ji, President

Type of Firm
Private Equity Firm

Association Membership
Korean Venture Capital Association (KVCA)

Project Preferences

Type of Financing Preferred:
Fund of Funds
Leveraged Buyout
Early Stage
Expansion
Mezzanine
Generalist PE
Balanced
Management Buyouts
Startup

Geographical Preferences

International Preferences:
Korea, South

Industry Preferences

In Communications prefer:
Telecommunications
Satellite Microwave Comm.

In Internet Specific prefer:
E-Commerce Technology
Ecommerce

In Semiconductor/Electr prefer:
Semiconductor

Additional Information
Year Founded: 1999
Capital Under Management: $300,000,000
Current Activity Level : Actively seeking new investments

IMM PRIVATE EQUITY INC

737 Yeoksam-dong, Kangnam-ku
5/F, Gangnam Finance Center
Seoul, South Korea 135984
Phone: 82221121780
Fax: 82221121781
Website: www.immpe.com

Management and Staff
Chan-woo Park, Vice President
Injun Song, Chief Executive Officer
Jay Kim, Vice President
Justin Hur, Vice President
Kwan Lee, Senior Managing Director
Timothy Chang, Chief Executive Officer
Young Ho Kim, Partner

Type of Firm
Private Equity Firm

Project Preferences

Type of Financing Preferred:
Leveraged Buyout
Management Buyouts

Geographical Preferences

International Preferences:
Korea, South

Industry Preferences

In Communications prefer:
Communications and Media

In Consumer Related prefer:
Consumer
Retail
Consumer Products

In Industrial/Energy prefer:
Industrial Products

Additional Information
Year Founded: 2001
Capital Under Management: $1,150,000,000
Current Activity Level : Actively seeking new investments

IMMERSIVE CAPITAL LP

3000 El Camino Real
Building Five., Suite 225
Palo Alto, CA USA 94306
Website: www.immersive.vc

Type of Firm
Private Equity Firm

Project Preferences

Type of Financing Preferred:
Early Stage

Industry Preferences

In Computer Software prefer:
Software

Additional Information

Year Founded: 2016
Capital Under Management: $21,400,000
Current Activity Level : Actively seeking new investments

IMOG INVESTMENT AB

Berthaga Byvag 16
Eklund
Uppsala, Sweden 75260
Website: -

Type of Firm

Investment Management Firm

Project Preferences

Type of Financing Preferred:
Early Stage
Balanced
Seed

Industry Preferences

In Computer Software prefer:
Software

Additional Information

Year Founded: 2014
Current Activity Level : Actively seeking new investments

IMPACT AMERICA FUND LP

2323 Broadway
Oakland, CA USA 94612
E-mail: info@impactamericafund.com
Website: www.impactamericafund.com

Type of Firm

Private Equity Firm

Project Preferences

Type of Financing Preferred:
Early Stage

Additional Information

Year Founded: 2014
Capital Under Management: $6,750,000
Current Activity Level : Actively seeking new investments

IMPACT CAPITAL INC

171 Sully's Trail
Pittsford, NY USA 14534
Phone: 5854173710
Website: www.impactcapitalny.com

Management and Staff

Alexandra McOran-Campbell, Partner
Audrey Peters, Partner
Bruce Crager, Venture Partner
David Dunlap, Principal
Gady Shlasky, Venture Partner
Julian Henkin, Partner
Murdoch Gillespie, Partner
Myron Louisy, Partner
Rhonda Kallman, Venture Partner
Roger Kinsbourg, Venture Partner
Thomas Peters, Venture Partner
Toby Rowland-Jones, Venture Partner
Xenia Howard-Johnston, Partner

Type of Firm

Private Equity Firm

Project Preferences

Type of Financing Preferred:
Early Stage
Later Stage
Seed
Startup

Additional Information

Year Founded: 2016
Current Activity Level : Actively seeking new investments

IMPACT ENGINE LLC

222 Merchandise Mart Plaza
Suite 1212
Chicago, IL USA 60654
Website: theimpactengine.com

Type of Firm

Incubator/Development Program

Project Preferences

Type of Financing Preferred:
Seed
Startup

Industry Preferences

In Medical/Health prefer:
Medical/Health

In Consumer Related prefer:
Food/Beverage
Education Related

In Industrial/Energy prefer:
Environmental Related

In Financial Services prefer:
Financial Services

In Agr/Forestr/Fish prefer:
Agriculture related

In Other prefer:
Socially Responsible

Additional Information

Year Founded: 2011
Capital Under Management: $10,900,000
Current Activity Level : Actively seeking new investments

IMPACT FIRST INVESTMANTS LTD

51 Har Tavor street
Kfar Saba, Israel 55439
Phone: 97297673320
Fax: 972508971148
E-mail: info@impact1st.com
Website: www.impact1st.com

Management and Staff

Cecile Blilious, Managing Partner
Jordan Feder, Principal
Yoav Ben-Dror, Partner

Type of Firm

Private Equity Firm

Project Preferences

Type of Financing Preferred:
Early Stage
Expansion
Seed

Geographical Preferences

International Preferences:
Asia Pacific
Europe
Israel
All International

Industry Preferences

In Communications prefer:
Communications and Media

In Medical/Health prefer:
Health Services

In Consumer Related prefer:
Education Related

In Business Serv. prefer:
Services

In Other prefer:
Environment Responsible

Additional Information

Year Founded: 2011
Current Activity Level : Actively seeking new investments

1095

IMPACT INVESTMENT GROUP PTY LTD

11 Princes Street
St. Kilda, Australia 3182
Phone: 61385348060
Website: www.impact-group.com.au

Management and Staff
Chris Lock, Chief Executive Officer
Paul Belcher, Chief Financial Officer

Type of Firm
Investment Management Firm

Project Preferences

Type of Financing Preferred:
Generalist PE

Industry Preferences

In Industrial/Energy prefer:
Energy

In Financial Services prefer:
Real Estate

Additional Information
Year Founded: 2016
Capital Under Management: $9,730,000
Current Activity Level : Actively seeking new investments

IMPACT OPPORTUNITIES FUND LP

210 University Boulevard
Suite 650
Denver, CO USA 80206
Phone: 3038629550
Fax: 3039979833
Website: www.impactfund.com

Management and Staff
Ben Novak, Chief Financial Officer
Jason Gaede, Vice President
Tyler Tysdal, Managing Partner

Type of Firm
Private Equity Firm

Project Preferences

Type of Financing Preferred:
Leveraged Buyout
Expansion
Mezzanine
Acquisition

Industry Preferences

In Communications prefer:
Entertainment

In Medical/Health prefer:
Health Services

In Consumer Related prefer:
Consumer Products

In Manufact. prefer:
Manufacturing

In Agr/Forestr/Fish prefer:
Agribusiness
Agriculture related

Additional Information
Name of Most Recent Fund: Impact Opportunities Fund, L.P.
Most Recent Fund Was Raised: 10/06/2011
Year Founded: 2011
Capital Under Management: $6,000,000
Current Activity Level : Actively seeking new investments

IMPACT PARTENAIRES SAS

17 Avenue Gourgaud
Paris, France 75017
Phone: 33142274770
Fax: 33142274770
Website: www.impact-partenaires.fr

Management and Staff
Aziz Senni, Founder
Mathieu Cornieti, President

Type of Firm
Private Equity Firm

Association Membership
French Venture Capital Association (AFIC)

Project Preferences

Type of Financing Preferred:
Early Stage
Later Stage
Seed
Startup

Geographical Preferences

International Preferences:
Europe
France

Additional Information
Year Founded: 2007
Capital Under Management: $47,251,000
Current Activity Level : Actively seeking new investments

IMPACT VENTURE CAPITAL

801 K Street, 28th Floor
Sacramento, CA USA 95814
Phone: 8882924748
Fax: 9164045098
Website: impactvc.com

Other Offices
345 Lorton Avenue
HILLSBOROUGH, CA USA 94010
Phone: 8882924748

801 K Street
Suite 2800
SACRAMENTO, CA USA 95814
Phone: 8882924748

Management and Staff
Jack Crawford, General Partner

Type of Firm
Private Equity Firm

Project Preferences

Type of Financing Preferred:
Early Stage

Industry Preferences

In Computer Software prefer:
Software

Additional Information
Year Founded: 2017
Capital Under Management: $20,000,000
Current Activity Level : Actively seeking new investments

IMPALA CAPITAL PARTNERS SA

Calle Jorge Juan 30, 3
Madrid, Spain 28001
Phone: 34 91 411 92 90
Fax: 34 91 411 93 31

Type of Firm
Private Equity Firm

Project Preferences

Type of Financing Preferred:
Leveraged Buyout
Expansion
Management Buyouts
Recapitalizations

Size of Investments Considered:
Min Size of Investment Considered (000s): $8,754
Max Size of Investment Considered (000s): $37,642

Geographical Preferences

International Preferences:
Spain

Additional Information
Year Founded: 2000
Capital Under Management: $176,400,000
Current Activity Level : Actively seeking new investments

IMPANIX CAPITAL

202, Jhandewalan Extension
Near Videocon Tower
Delhi, India
E-mail: contact@impanixcapital.com
Website: www.impanixcapital.com

Type of Firm
Private Equity Firm

Project Preferences

Type of Financing Preferred:
Balanced
Later Stage

Additional Information
Year Founded: 2017
Current Activity Level : Actively seeking new investments

IMPAX ASSET MANAGEMENT LTD

31 Saint James's Square
Norfolk House
London, United Kingdom SW1Y 4JR
Phone: 442074341122
Fax: 442074341123

Other Offices
641 Lexington Avenue
15th Floor
New York, NY USA 10022.
Phone: 802 343 1400

Management and Staff
Bruce Jenkyn-Jones, Managing Director
Charlie Ridge, Chief Financial Officer
Daniel von Preyss, Managing Director
David Richardson, Managing Director
Hubert Aarts, Managing Director
Ian Simm, Chief Executive Officer
Nigel Taunt, Managing Director
Peter Rossbach, Managing Director

Type of Firm
Bank Affiliated

Association Membership
British Venture Capital Association (BVCA)

Project Preferences

Type of Financing Preferred:
Early Stage
Expansion
Balanced

Size of Investments Considered:
Min Size of Investment Considered (000s): $4,874
Max Size of Investment Considered (000s): $8,124

Geographical Preferences

United States Preferences:
North America

International Preferences:
United Kingdom
Europe

Industry Preferences

In Industrial/Energy prefer:
Alternative Energy
Energy Conservation Relat
Environmental Related

In Other prefer:
Socially Responsible
Environment Responsible

Additional Information
Name of Most Recent Fund: Impax Global Resource Optimization Fund, L.P.
Most Recent Fund Was Raised: 12/09/2011
Year Founded: 1994
Capital Under Management: $556,810,000
Current Activity Level : Actively seeking new investments

IMPERIAL CAPITAL CORP

200 King Street West
Suite 1701, P.O. Box 57
Toronto, Canada M5H 3T4
Phone: 4163623658
Fax: 4163628660
E-mail: icl@imperialcap.com
Website: www.imperialcap.com

Management and Staff
Christopher Harris, Vice President
Derrick Abraham, Vice President
Edward Truant, Partner
Jeffrey Rosenthal, Managing Partner
Justin MacCormack, Partner
Karen Carr, Vice President
Stephen Lister, Managing Partner

Type of Firm
Private Equity Firm

Association Membership
Canadian Venture Capital Association

Project Preferences

Type of Financing Preferred:
Leveraged Buyout
Acquisition

Geographical Preferences

United States Preferences:
North America
All U.S.

Canadian Preferences:
All Canada

Industry Preferences

In Medical/Health prefer:
Health Services

In Consumer Related prefer:
Food/Beverage
Consumer Products
Consumer Services

In Business Serv. prefer:
Services

Additional Information
Year Founded: 1989
Capital Under Management: $655,919,000
Current Activity Level : Actively seeking new investments
Method of Compensation: Return on invest. most important, but chg. closing fees, service fees, etc.

IMPETUS CAPITAL LLC

145 West 57th Street
16 Floor
New York, NY USA 10019
Phone: 2122582782
Fax: 2122582784
Website: www.impetuscapital.com

Management and Staff
Patrick Persons, Founder

Type of Firm
Private Equity Firm

Project Preferences

Type of Financing Preferred:
Leveraged Buyout
Acquisition

Geographical Preferences

United States Preferences:
All U.S.

Industry Preferences

In Medical/Health prefer:
Medical/Health
Health Services

In Consumer Related prefer:
Retail
Consumer Products

In Financial Services prefer:
Financial Services

In Business Serv. prefer:
Services
Distribution

Additional Information
Year Founded: 2010
Current Activity Level : Actively seeking new investments

IMPRESSION VENTURES
90 Eglinton Ave E
Suite 600
Toronto, Canada M4P 1A6
Phone: 6477253355
E-mail: info@impressionventures.com
Website: impression.ventures

Management and Staff
Bryan Kerdman, Managing Partner
Christian Lassonde, Managing Partner
Maor Amar, Managing Partner

Type of Firm
Private Equity Firm

Association Membership
Canadian Venture Capital Association

Project Preferences

Type of Financing Preferred:
Early Stage

Geographical Preferences

Canadian Preferences:
Quebec
Ontario

Industry Preferences

In Computer Software prefer:
Software
Applications Software

In Internet Specific prefer:
Ecommerce

Additional Information
Year Founded: 2013
Capital Under Management: $22,530,000
Current Activity Level : Actively seeking new investments

IMPRIMATUR CAPITAL HLDG LTD
Eight Tavistock Street
Hudson House
London, United Kingdom WC2E 7PP
Phone: 442031707624
Fax: 442075596501
E-mail: iw@impcap.com
Website: www.imprimaturcapital.com

Other Offices
Elizabetes, 85a
Berga Bazar, II, 19a, Second Floor
Riga, Latvia LV-1050
Phone: 371-67-365-275
Fax: 371-67-365-281

Unit 31, 39th Floor
One Exchange Square
Central, Hong Kong
Phone: 852-3101-70-90
Fax: 852-3101-75-30

Av.Jose de Souza
Campos, k550, Sala 81
Campinas, Brazil 13.092-123
Phone: 55-19-3251-8713

Level 26, 44 Market Street
Sydney, Australia NSW 2000
Phone: 612-9089-8688
Fax: 612-9089-8989

PO Box 211
Carterton, New Zealand
Phone: 64-6379-9271
Fax: 64-6379-9272

20 Cecil Street #15 - 07
Equity Plaza
Singapore, Singapore 049705
Phone: 65-6535-3454
Fax: 65-6535-3494

4 Khreschatyk
StreetSuite 20, 6th Floor
Kyiv, Ukraine 01001
Phone: 380-44-494-1898
Fax: 380-44-278-0920

Management and Staff
Ben Ferrari, Managing Director

Type of Firm
Private Equity Firm

Association Membership
Latvian Private Equity and Venture Capital Assoc

Project Preferences

Type of Financing Preferred:
Early Stage
Seed

Geographical Preferences

International Preferences:
Hungary
United Kingdom
Hong Kong
China
Brazil
Ukraine
Spain
Australia
New Zealand
Singapore
Latvia
Russia

Industry Preferences

In Communications prefer:
Communications and Media
Telecommunications

In Computer Software prefer:
Software

In Internet Specific prefer:
Internet

In Medical/Health prefer:
Medical/Health
Medical Diagnostics

In Industrial/Energy prefer:
Alternative Energy

Additional Information
Year Founded: 2002
Capital Under Management: $6,064,000
Current Activity Level : Actively seeking new investments

IMPULSE INTERNATIONAL FOR TELECOMMUNICATIONS KSCC
SHARQ, KIPCO Tower
27th Floor
Kuwait City, Kuwait
Phone: 96522598598
Fax: 96522406341
E-mail: info@impulse.com.kw
Website: www.impulse.com.kw

Type of Firm
Government Affiliated Program

Project Preferences

Type of Financing Preferred:
Later Stage

Industry Preferences

In Internet Specific prefer:
Internet

Additional Information
Year Founded: 2012
Current Activity Level : Actively seeking new investments

IMPULSEVC

Prospekt Leningradskiy 74 A
Moscow, Russia 125167
Phone: 84997023672
E-mail: start@impulsevc.com
Website: www.impulsevc.com

Type of Firm
Private Equity Firm

Project Preferences

Type of Financing Preferred:
Early Stage
Expansion
Balanced
Later Stage
Seed
Startup

Geographical Preferences

International Preferences:
Russia

Industry Preferences

In Business Serv. prefer:
Media

Additional Information
Year Founded: 2013
Current Activity Level : Actively seeking new investments

IN-Q-TEL INC

1000 Wilson Blvd
29th Floor
Arlington, VA USA 22209
Phone: 7032483000
Fax: 7032483001
E-mail: info@iqt.org
Website: www.in-q-tel.org

Management and Staff
Lisa Bader, Vice President
Steve Bowsher, Managing Partner

Type of Firm
Government Affiliated Program

Association Membership
Mid-Atlantic Venture Association
National Venture Capital Association - USA (NVCA)

Project Preferences

Type of Financing Preferred:
Early Stage
Balanced

Size of Investments Considered:
Min Size of Investment Considered (000s): $100
Max Size of Investment Considered (000s): $2,500

Geographical Preferences
United States Preferences:

Industry Preferences

In Communications prefer:
Communications and Media
Data Communications

In Computer Hardware prefer:
Computers

In Computer Software prefer:
Data Processing

In Internet Specific prefer:
Internet

Additional Information
Year Founded: 1999
Capital Under Management: $30,000,000
Current Activity Level : Actively seeking new investments

INBIO VENTURES DC LTD

10 Testovskaya
Moscow, Russia 123317
Phone: 7495988 47 95
Fax: 7495988 47 92
E-mail: info@inbiovent.com
Website: www.inbio-ventures.com

Management and Staff
Alexander Shuster, Founder
Andrei Petrov, Chief Executive Officer

Type of Firm
Private Equity Firm

Project Preferences

Type of Financing Preferred:
Early Stage

Industry Preferences

In Biotechnology prefer:
Biotechnology

In Medical/Health prefer:
Pharmaceuticals

Additional Information
Year Founded: 2013
Current Activity Level : Actively seeking new investments

INCENTIVE II MANAGEMENT LTD

Ariel Univ Center of Samaria, Building 10
Ariel, Israel 40700
Phone: 97239085000
Fax: 97239366873
Website: www.incentive-il.com

Management and Staff
Lior Shahory, Chief Executive Officer

Type of Firm
Private Equity Firm

Association Membership
Israel Venture Association

Project Preferences

Type of Financing Preferred:
Early Stage
Seed

Geographical Preferences

International Preferences:
Israel

Industry Preferences

In Computer Software prefer:
Software

In Medical/Health prefer:
Medical/Health

Additional Information
Year Founded: 1969
Current Activity Level : Actively seeking new investments

INCEPTION CAPITAL

c / Cuevas del Valle
28 - The Plantio
Madrid, Spain 28023
Phone: 34917080560
E-mail: hola@inceptioncapital.es
Website: www.inceptioncapital.es

Type of Firm
Private Equity Firm

Project Preferences

Type of Financing Preferred:
Seed

Industry Preferences

In Communications prefer:
Wireless Communications

In Internet Specific prefer:
Internet

Additional Information
Year Founded: 2013
Current Activity Level : Actively seeking new investments

INCEPTION CAPITAL MANAGEMENT LLC

5400 Carillon Point Road
Building 5000
Kirkland, WA USA 98033
E-mail: info@inceptionfunds.com
Website: www.inceptionfunds.com

Type of Firm
Private Equity Firm

Industry Preferences

In Biotechnology prefer:
Bictechnology

Additional Information
Year Founded: 2015
Capital Under Management: $1,890,000
Current Activity Level : Actively seeking new investments

INCITE CAPITAL MANAGEMENT PTY LTD

Level 9, Avaya House
123 Epping Road
North Sydney, Australia 2113
Phone: 61294845050
Fax: 61294848541
E-mail: advice@incitemg.com.au
Website: www.incitemg.com.au

Type of Firm
Private Equity Firm

Project Preferences

Type of Financing Preferred:
Early Stage
Expansion
Mezzanine
Management Buyouts
Acquisition

Size of Investments Considered:
Min Size of Investment Considered (000s): $255
Max Size of Investment Considered (000s): $1,274

Geographical Preferences

International Preferences:
Pacific

Additional Information
Year Founded: 1999
Capital Under Management: $5,200,000
Current Activity Level : Actively seeking new investments

INCITIA VENTURES AS

Lorenvangen 22
Oslo, Norway 0512
Phone: 4723137800
Fax: 4722492469
Website: www.incitia.com

Management and Staff
Asgeir Nord, Partner
Erik Sandersen, Partner
Jens Falck, Partner

Type of Firm
Private Equity Firm

Association Membership
Norwegian Venture Capital Association

Project Preferences

Type of Financing Preferred:
Early Stage
Seed
Startup

Geographical Preferences

International Preferences:
Scandanavia/Nordic Region
Norway

Industry Preferences

In Communications prefer:
Communications and Media
Telecommunications
Wireless Communications

In Computer Software prefer:
Software

In Semiconductor/Electr prefer:
Electronics
Semiconductor

In Biotechnology prefer:
Biotechnology

In Medical/Health prefer:
Pharmaceuticals

In Industrial/Energy prefer:
Energy
Oil & Gas Drilling,Explor
Alternative Energy
Energy Conservation Relat

In Other prefer:
Environment Responsible

Additional Information
Name of Most Recent Fund: Incitia Ventures II
Most Recent Fund Was Raised: 09/03/2007
Year Founded: 2001
Capital Under Management: $81,100,000
Current Activity Level : Actively seeking new investments

INCLINE MANAGEMENT CORP

625 Liberty Avenue
EQT Plaza - Suite 340
Pittsburgh, PA USA 15222
Phone: 4123157800
Fax: 4123157799
Website: inclineequity.com

Management and Staff
Deanna Barry, Chief Financial Officer
John Glover, Partner
Justin Bertram, Partner
Leon Rubinov, Partner
Wangdali Bacdayan, Partner

Type of Firm
Private Equity Firm

Project Preferences

Type of Financing Preferred:
Leveraged Buyout
Acquisition
Recapitalizations

Geographical Preferences

United States Preferences:

Canadian Preferences:
All Canada

Industry Preferences

In Industrial/Energy prefer:
Industrial Products

In Business Serv. prefer:
Services
Distribution

In Manufact. prefer:
Manufacturing

Additional Information
Year Founded: 2011
Capital Under Management: $902,120,000
Current Activity Level : Actively seeking new investments

INCTANK VENTURES

411 Massachusetts Avenue
Cambridge, MA USA 02139
Phone: 6175769555
Fax: 6175769551
Website: www.inctank.com

Other Offices
As-510, RCAST, University of Tokyo
4-6-1 Meguro-ku
Tokyo, Japan 153-8904
Phone: 81354525317
Fax: 81354525056

Management and Staff
Chad Jackson, Managing Partner
Christian Bailey, General Partner
Karl Ruping, Managing Partner
Masanobu Tsukagoshi, Venture Partner

Type of Firm
Private Equity Firm

Project Preferences

Role in Financing:
Prefer role as deal originator

Type of Financing Preferred:
Early Stage
Seed
Startup

Size of Investments Considered:
Min Size of Investment Considered (000s): $50
Max Size of Investment Considered (000s): $500

Geographical Preferences

United States Preferences:
Massachusetts

Industry Preferences

In Biotechnology prefer:
Biotechnology

In Consumer Related prefer:
Education Related

In Industrial/Energy prefer:
Materials

Additional Information
Year Founded: 1999
Current Activity Level : Actively seeking new investments

INCUBATE FUND NO1 INVESTMENT LPS

3f Arch Mori Building
1-12-32, Akasaka
Akasaka-Ku, Tokyo, Japan 107-0052
Website: incubatefund.com

Other Offices
9-5-12, Akasaka
303 Parksidesix Building
, Japan 107-0052

Management and Staff
Keisuke Wada, General Partner
Masahiko Honma, General Partner
Tohru Akaura, General Partner
Yusuke Murata, General Partner

Type of Firm
Incubator/Development Program

Association Membership
Japan Venture Capital Association

Project Preferences

Role in Financing:
Prefer role as deal originator

Type of Financing Preferred:
Early Stage
Seed
Startup

Geographical Preferences

International Preferences:
Japan

Industry Preferences

In Communications prefer:
Wireless Communications
Media and Entertainment

In Computer Software prefer:
Software

In Internet Specific prefer:
Internet
Ecommerce

In Medical/Health prefer:
Medical/Health

In Consumer Related prefer:
Entertainment and Leisure

In Financial Services prefer:
Financial Services
Real Estate

Additional Information
Year Founded: 2010
Capital Under Management: $149,710,000
Current Activity Level : Actively seeking new investments

INCUBATEUR PACA-EST

Allee Paul Ziller
1047 route des Dolines
Valbonne, France 06560
Phone: 33489866910
Fax: 33492919489
E-mail: contact@incubateurpacaest.org
Website: www.incubateurpacaest.org

Management and Staff
Gerard Giraudon, President
Jean-Pierre Laheurte, Vice President
Laurent Londeix, Vice President

Type of Firm
Incubator/Development Program

Project Preferences

Type of Financing Preferred:
Early Stage
Seed
Startup

Geographical Preferences

International Preferences:
Europe
France

Industry Preferences

In Communications prefer:
Communications and Media

In Internet Specific prefer:
Internet

In Medical/Health prefer:
Medical/Health

In Consumer Related prefer:
Food/Beverage

In Agr/Forestr/Fish prefer:
Agriculture related

In Other prefer:
Environment Responsible

Additional Information
Year Founded: 2001
Current Activity Level : Actively seeking new investments

INCUBATION FOR GROWTH SA

21 A.Tritsi street,
Building B
Thessaloniki, Greece 57001
Phone: 30-231-080-4800
Fax: 30-231-080-4810
Website: www.i4g.gr

Management and Staff
Efstathios Tavridis, Managing Director
Evi Mattheopoulou, Managing Director
Paris Kokorotsikos, Managing Director
Stathis Tavridis, Managing Director

Type of Firm
Incubator/Development Program

Association Membership
Hellenic Venture Capital Association

Project Preferences

Type of Financing Preferred:
Early Stage

Geographical Preferences

International Preferences:
Greece
Central Europe
Eastern Europe
Middle East
Africa

Additional Information
Year Founded: 2003
Current Activity Level : Actively seeking new investments

INCUBATOR LABORATORY HOLDING COMPANY SA

Konstantinou Street, 40 Ag
Aithrio Centre Suite A35
Maroussi, Greece 151-24
Phone: 302106100294
Fax: 302106178140
E-mail: info@inqlab.gr
Website: www.inqlab.gr

Type of Firm
Private Equity Firm

Project Preferences

Type of Financing Preferred:
Early Stage
Balanced
Seed
Startup

Geographical Preferences

International Preferences:
Europe

Additional Information
Year Founded: 2001
Capital Under Management: $4,600,000
Current Activity Level : Actively seeking new investments

INCUBE VENTURES LLC

2051 Ringwood Avenue
San Jose, CA USA 95131
Phone: 4084573700
Fax: 4084335440
E-mail: contact@incubevc.com
Website: www.incubevc.com

Management and Staff
Andrew Farquharson, Managing Director
Mir Imran, Founder
Wayne Roe, Managing Director
William Ringo, Venture Partner

Type of Firm
Private Equity Firm

Project Preferences

Type of Financing Preferred:
Early Stage
Expansion
Balanced
Later Stage

Industry Preferences

In Biotechnology prefer:
Biotechnology

In Medical/Health prefer:
Medical/Health
Health Services
Pharmaceuticals

Additional Information
Name of Most Recent Fund: InCube Ventures, L.P.
Most Recent Fund Was Raised: 08/28/2012
Year Founded: 2008
Capital Under Management: $88,636,000
Current Activity Level : Actively seeking new investments

INCUBIC MANAGMENT LLC

c/o 26228 Scarff Way
Los Altos, CA USA 94022
Phone: 6502792489
Fax: 6509417267
Website: www.incubic.com

Management and Staff
Milton Chang, Managing Director

Type of Firm
Private Equity Firm

Project Preferences

Type of Financing Preferred:
Early Stage
Balanced
Later Stage

Additional Information
Year Founded: 2001
Capital Under Management: $100,000,000
Current Activity Level : Actively seeking new investments

INCURAY AG

Dorfstrasse 27/29
Zurich, Switzerland 8037
Phone: 41415114503
Website: www.incuray.com

Management and Staff
Mark Berger, Co-Founder
Max Meister, Co-Founder
Oliver Walzer, Co-Founder

Type of Firm
Incubator/Development Program

Project Preferences

Type of Financing Preferred:
Early Stage
Seed
Startup

Geographical Preferences

International Preferences:
Switzerland
Western Europe

Industry Preferences

In Internet Specific prefer:
Internet

In Consumer Related prefer:
Consumer Services

Additional Information
Year Founded: 2012
Current Activity Level : Actively seeking new investments

INCUVEST PTE LTD

79 Ayer Rajah Crescent
#04-07
Singapore, Singapore 238997
Phone: 6564932468
E-mail: info@incuvestasia.com
Website: www.incuvestasia.com

Other Offices
57, Mohamed Sultan Road
#04-05
, Singapore
Phone: 6566379050

Management and Staff
Alain Arul, Partner
David Yeow, Partner
Kevin Lam, Partner
Markus Yong, Partner
Natasha Foong, Co-Founder
Ronnie Wee, Co-Founder

Type of Firm
Private Equity Firm

Project Preferences

Type of Financing Preferred:
Early Stage
Expansion
Seed

Geographical Preferences

International Preferences:
Singapore

Industry Preferences

In Medical/Health prefer:
Health Services

In Consumer Related prefer:
Entertainment and Leisure
Retail
Education Related

In Financial Services prefer:
Financial Services

Additional Information
Year Founded: 2011
Current Activity Level : Actively seeking new investments

INCWELL LLC

110 Willits Street
Birmingham, MI USA 48009
Phone: 8555276732
E-mail: info@theincwell.net
Website: www.theincwell.net

Type of Firm
Incubator/Development Program

Project Preferences

Role in Financing:
Will function either as deal originator or investor in deals created by others

Type of Financing Preferred:
Seed
Startup

Size of Investments Considered:
Min Size of Investment Considered (000s): $50
Max Size of Investment Considered (000s): $25,000

Geographical Preferences

United States Preferences:

Canadian Preferences:
All Canada

Industry Preferences

In Computer Software prefer:
Software
Applications Software

In Medical/Health prefer:
Medical/Health
Medical Products
Health Services

In Consumer Related prefer:
Consumer

In Industrial/Energy prefer:
Energy
Industrial Products
Environmental Related

In Transportation prefer:
Transportation

Additional Information
Name of Most Recent Fund: IncWell, L.P.
Most Recent Fund Was Raised: 06/11/2013
Year Founded: 2013
Capital Under Management: $10,240,000
Current Activity Level : Actively seeking new investments

INCYTE CAPITAL HOLDINGS LLC

2911 Turtle Creek Boulevard
Suite 300
Dallas, TX USA 75219
Phone: 2145239046
Fax: 2145239048
Website: www.incytecapital.com

Other Offices
845 Third Avenue
Sixth Floor
NEW YORK, NY USA 10022

Type of Firm
Private Equity Firm

Project Preferences

Role in Financing:
Prefer role as deal originator

Type of Financing Preferred:
Leveraged Buyout
Expansion
Turnaround
Management Buyouts
Recapitalizations

Geographical Preferences

United States Preferences:
North America

Industry Preferences

In Communications prefer:
Telecommunications

In Computer Software prefer:
Software

In Medical/Health prefer:
Medical/Health

In Consumer Related prefer:
Consumer Products

In Industrial/Energy prefer:
Energy

In Business Serv. prefer:
Services
Distribution

Additional Information
Year Founded: 2000
Capital Under Management: $75,000,000
Current Activity Level : Actively seeking new investments

INCYTE VENTURE PARTNERS LLC

18618 Tuscany Stone Drive
Suite 100
San Antonio, TX USA 78258
Phone: 2105588896
Fax: 2106949466
E-mail: info@incyteventures.com
Website: www.incyteventures.com

Management and Staff
Allan Dean, Senior Managing Director
Christopher Banas, Managing Partner
Paul Castella, Managing Partner

Type of Firm
Private Equity Firm

Project Preferences

Type of Financing Preferred:
Early Stage

Geographical Preferences

United States Preferences:
Alabama
Colorado
Georgia
Texas

Industry Preferences

In Biotechnology prefer:
Biotechnology
Human Biotechnology

In Medical/Health prefer:
Medical/Health
Medical Diagnostics
Medical Products
Pharmaceuticals

Additional Information
Name of Most Recent Fund: Targeted Technology Fund II, L.P.
Most Recent Fund Was Raised: 11/07/2013
Year Founded: 2009
Capital Under Management: $37,200,000
Current Activity Level : Actively seeking new investments

INDECATUR VENTURES LLC

130 North Water Street
Decatur, IL USA 62523
Fax: 217-425-8366
E-mail: inquire@indecaturventures.com

Management and Staff
Christopher Shroyer, Vice President
Larry Haab, President

Type of Firm
Private Equity Firm

Project Preferences

Role in Financing:
Will function either as deal originator or investor in deals created by others

Type of Financing Preferred:
Second Stage Financing
Early Stage
Mezzanine
Balanced
Later Stage
First Stage Financing

Size of Investments Considered:
Min Size of Investment Considered (000s): $100
Max Size of Investment Considered (000s): $1,000

Geographical Preferences

United States Preferences:
Midwest
Illinois

Industry Preferences

In Communications prefer:
Telecommunications
Wireless Communications
Data Communications

In Computer Hardware prefer:
Mainframes / Scientific
Mini and Personal/Desktop

In Computer Software prefer:
Computer Services
Data Processing
Software
Systems Software
Applications Software
Artificial Intelligence

In Internet Specific prefer:
Internet
Ecommerce

In Semiconductor/Electr prefer:
Electronics

In Biotechnology prefer:
Agricultural/Animal Bio.
Industrial Biotechnology
Biotech Related Research

In Medical/Health prefer:
Medical Diagnostics
Diagnostic Services
Diagnostic Test Products
Medical Therapeutics
Drug/Equipmt Delivery
Medical Products
Disposable Med. Products
Health Services
Pharmaceuticals

In Business Serv. prefer:
Services
Distribution

In Manufact. prefer:
Manufacturing

Additional Information
Name of Most Recent Fund: InDecatur Ventures
Most Recent Fund Was Raised: 12/31/2003
Year Founded: 2003
Capital Under Management: $3,000,000
Current Activity Level : Actively seeking new investments
Method of Compensation: Return on invest. most important, but chg. closing fees, service fees, etc.

INDEPENDENCE EQUITY MANAGEMENT LLC

2100 Sanders Road
Suite 170
Northbrook, IL USA 60062
Phone: 8477390100
Fax: 2247235071
E-mail: info@Independence-Equity.com
Website: www.independence-equity.com

Management and Staff
Donald Sackman, Managing Partner
Laurence Hayward, Partner
Michael McCullough, Partner
Michael Gruber, Partner

Type of Firm
Private Equity Firm

Project Preferences

Type of Financing Preferred:
Early Stage

Geographical Preferences

United States Preferences:
Midwest

Additional Information
Name of Most Recent Fund: Independence Equity I, L.P.
Most Recent Fund Was Raised: 01/06/2011
Year Founded: 2011
Capital Under Management: $10,990,000
Current Activity Level : Actively seeking new investments

INDEPENDENT BANKERS CAPITAL FUNDS

1700 Pacific Avenue
Suite 2740
Dallas, TX USA 75201
Phone: 2147226200
Fax: 2147226220
Website: www.ibcfund.com

Management and Staff
Barry Conrad, Founder
William Miltenberger, Principal

Type of Firm
SBIC

Association Membership
Natl Assoc of Small Bus. Inv. Co (NASBIC)

Project Preferences

Role in Financing:
Will function either as deal originator or investor in deals created by others

Type of Financing Preferred:
Leveraged Buyout
Mezzanine
Later Stage
Management Buyouts
Acquisition
Recapitalizations

Size of Investments Considered:
Min Size of Investment Considered (000s): $1,000
Max Size of Investment Considered (000s): $4,600

Geographical Preferences

United States Preferences:
Texas

Industry Preferences

In Business Serv. prefer:
Services
Distribution

In Manufact. prefer:
Manufacturing

Additional Information
Name of Most Recent Fund: Independent Bankers Capital Fund, L.P.
Most Recent Fund Was Raised: 03/31/2000
Year Founded: 2000
Capital Under Management: $133,000,000
Current Activity Level : Actively seeking new investments
Method of Compensation: Return on invest. most important, but chg. closing fees, service fees, etc.

INDEPENDENT CAPITAL AG

Am Wallgraben 99
Stuttgart, Germany 70565
Phone: 4971178284215
Fax: 4971178284229
E-mail: info@incap-ag.de
Website: www.incap-ag.de

Type of Firm
Private Equity Firm

Project Preferences

Type of Financing Preferred:
Balanced
Special Situation
Recapitalizations

Geographical Preferences

International Preferences:
Europe
Germany

Additional Information
Year Founded: 1999
Current Activity Level : Actively seeking new investments

INDEX VENTURES

2, rue de Jargonnant
Geneva, Switzerland 1207
Phone: 41227370000
Fax: 41227370099
E-mail: info@indexventures.com
Website: www.indexventures.com

Other Offices

139 Townsend Street
Suite 505
San Francisco, CA USA 94107
Phone: 14154087900
Fax: 14155439008

2nd Floor
24 Sand Street
St Helier, Jersey, United Kingdom JE2 3QF
Phone: 441534833404
Fax: 441534504444

52-53 Conduit Street
London, United Kingdom W1S 2YX
Phone: 442071542020
Fax: 442071542021

1 Seaton Place
St. Helier
Jersey, United Kingdom JEY 8Y
Phone: 441534753858
Fax: 441534605605

Management and Staff
Benjamin Holmes, Partner
Bernard Dalle, Partner
David Grainger, Venture Partner
David Rimer, Co-Founder
Dominique Vidal, Partner
Francesco de Rubertis, Partner
Gil Dibner, Principal
Giuseppe Zocco, Co-Founder
Jan Hammer, Partner
Kevin Johnson, Partner
Mark De Boer, Partner
Michele Ollier, Partner
Neil Rimer, Co-Founder
Robin Klein, Venture Partner
Roman Fleck, Principal
Shardul Shah, Principal
Simon Levene, Venture Partner

Type of Firm
Private Equity Firm

Association Membership
Swiss Venture Capital Association (SECA)
European Private Equity and Venture Capital Assoc.

Project Preferences

Type of Financing Preferred:
Early Stage
Balanced
Later Stage
Seed
Startup

Size of Investments Considered:
Min Size of Investment Considered (000s): $333
Max Size of Investment Considered (000s): $66,542

Geographical Preferences

United States Preferences:
All U.S.

International Preferences:
Italy
Sweden
United Kingdom
Europe
Netherlands
Switzerland
Jersey
Spain
Belgium
Israel
Norway
Germany
Russia
All International
Denmark
France

Industry Focus
(% based on actual investment)
Internet Specific	41.6%
Computer Software and Services	38.4%
Biotechnology	5.9%
Consumer Related	4.0%
Medical/Health	3.0%
Computer Hardware	2.8%
Other Products	1.5%
Semiconductors/Other Elect.	1.2%
Communications and Media	1.1%
Industrial/Energy	0.6%

Additional Information
Name of Most Recent Fund: Index Ventures VI
Most Recent Fund Was Raised: 06/18/2012
Year Founded: 1992
Capital Under Management: $646,100,000
Current Activity Level : Actively seeking new investments

INDIA ALTERNATIVES INVESTMENT ADVISORS PVT LTD

3rd Floor, Pinnacle House
Corner of 15th Road
Mumbai, India 400050

Management and Staff
Ashish Agarwal, Vice President
Shivani Sachdeva, Chief Executive Officer
Tariq Chinoy, Chief Financial Officer

Type of Firm
Investment Management Firm

Project Preferences

Type of Financing Preferred:
Leveraged Buyout
Acquisition

Geographical Preferences

International Preferences:
India

Additional Information
Year Founded: 1969
Current Activity Level : Actively seeking new investments

INDIA INNOVATION FUND

149 Rathna Ave,Off Richmond Rd
Karnataka
Bangalore, India 560 025
Phone: 918043356666
Fax: 918043356667
Website: www.indiainnovationfund.in

Other Offices
Genome Valley, Turkapally
Shamirpet
Hyderabad, India 500078

Management and Staff
Ashwin Raguraman, Vice President
Rajesh Rai, Chief Executive Officer

Type of Firm
Private Equity Firm

Project Preferences

Type of Financing Preferred:
Early Stage
Expansion
Seed

Size of Investments Considered:
Min Size of Investment Considered (000s): $205
Max Size of Investment Considered (000s): $1,026

Geographical Preferences

International Preferences:
India

Industry Preferences

In Communications prefer:
Communications and Media

Additional Information
Year Founded: 2009
Current Activity Level : Actively seeking new investments

INDIA VENTURE PARTNERS

75 Charles Street
Annapolis, MD USA 21404
Phone: 7039677697
Fax: 4439499938
Website: www.indiavp.com

Management and Staff
Kenneth Tighe, General Partner

Type of Firm
Private Equity Firm

Project Preferences

Type of Financing Preferred:
Early Stage

Geographical Preferences

International Preferences:
India

Industry Preferences

In Medical/Health prefer:
Medical/Health

In Consumer Related prefer:
Education Related

Additional Information
Year Founded: 2010
Current Activity Level : Actively seeking new investments

INDIAN STEPS AND BUSINESS INCUBATORS ASSOCIATION

JSSATE-STEP, C-20/1, Sector-62
Noida, India 201301
Phone: 91-12-0240-1514
Fax: 91-12-0240-0097
E-mail: mail@isba.in
Website: www.isba.in

Management and Staff
N.P. Rao, Managing Director
P. K. B. Menon, President
R. M. P. Jawahar, Vice President
Rajendra Jagdale, General Director

Type of Firm
Incubator/Development Program

Project Preferences

Type of Financing Preferred:
Start-up Financing
Seed
Startup

Geographical Preferences

International Preferences:
India
Asia

Additional Information
Year Founded: 2004
Capital Under Management: $11,700,000
Current Activity Level : Actively seeking new investments

INDIANA UNIVERSITY

1500 North State Road
46 Bypass
Bloomington, IN USA 47408
Phone: 8128558311
Fax: 8128556956
E-mail: iuf@indiana.edu
Website: www.iu.edu

Other Offices
340 West Michigan Street
Indianapolis, IN USA 46204
Phone: 3172743711
Fax: 3172748818

Management and Staff
Christopher Ritrievi, Vice President
Dee Metaj, Vice President
Paula Jenkins, Vice President

Type of Firm
University Program

Project Preferences

Type of Financing Preferred:
Fund of Funds
Early Stage
Later Stage

Geographical Preferences

United States Preferences:

Additional Information
Year Founded: 2000
Current Activity Level : Actively seeking new investments

INDICATOR VENTURES

373 Washington Street
10th Floor
Boston, MA USA 02108
Phone: 6179471984
E-mail: info@indicatorventures.com
Website: www.indicatorventures.com

Type of Firm
Private Equity Firm

Project Preferences

Type of Financing Preferred:
Early Stage

Industry Preferences

In Computer Software prefer:
Software
Systems Software
Applications Software

Additional Information
Year Founded: 2014
Capital Under Management: $14,425,000
Current Activity Level : Actively seeking new investments

INDIGO CAPITAL LLP

33 Street James's Square
London, United Kingdom SW1Y 4JS
Phone: 442073971530
Website: www.indigo-capital.co.uk

Other Offices
69 rue la Boetie
Paris, France 75008
Phone: 33-1-5688-1750
Fax: 33-1-5688-2488

Management and Staff
Anthony Grover, Partner
Christopher Howe, Co-Founder
Kevin Murphy, Co-Founder
Maria Marinas, Partner
Martin Stringfellow, Co-Founder
Richard Collins, Co-Founder

Type of Firm
Private Equity Firm

Association Membership
French Venture Capital Association (AFIC)

Project Preferences

Type of Financing Preferred:
Expansion
Mezzanine
Management Buyouts
Acquisition
Recapitalizations

Geographical Preferences

International Preferences:
Europe

Industry Focus
(% based on actual investment)

Other Products	33.2%
Communications and Media	28.0%
Computer Hardware	15.0%
Industrial/Energy	8.6%
Biotechnology	7.4%
Consumer Related	4.9%
Computer Software and Services	2.8%

Additional Information
Year Founded: 1989
Capital Under Management: $589,800,000
Current Activity Level : Actively seeking new investments

INDIGO CAPITAL PARTNERS

Povarskaya Street 10
Building 1, Office 101
Moscow, Russia 121069
Phone: 74996851420
E-mail: info@indigocapital.ru
Website: www.indigocapital.ru

Type of Firm
Private Equity Firm

Project Preferences

Type of Financing Preferred:
Leveraged Buyout
Mezzanine
Generalist PE
Balanced
Later Stage
Management Buyouts

Geographical Preferences

International Preferences:
Estonia
Latvia
Lithuania
Russia

Industry Preferences

In Communications prefer:
Media and Entertainment

In Internet Specific prefer:
Internet

In Biotechnology prefer:
Biotechnology

In Industrial/Energy prefer:
Alternative Energy

Additional Information
Year Founded: 2013
Capital Under Management: $30,000,000
Current Activity Level : Actively seeking new investments

INDIGO CAPITAL SAS

69, Rue de la Boetie
Paris, France 75008
Website: www.indigo-capital.fr

Type of Firm
Private Equity Firm

Project Preferences

Type of Financing Preferred:
Leveraged Buyout
Management Buyouts
Special Situation
Recapitalizations

Geographical Preferences

International Preferences:
Europe
France

Additional Information
Year Founded: 2011
Current Activity Level : Actively seeking new investments

INDIGO GROUP LLC

244 Fifth Avenue
Suite 2591
New York, NY USA 10001
E-mail: info@indigogroupllc.com
Website: www.indigogroupllc.com

Other Offices
65 Route Four East
River Edge, NJ USA 07661

Management and Staff
Jonathan Schechter, Principal
Thomas Foley, Founder

Type of Firm
Private Equity Firm

Project Preferences

Type of Financing Preferred:
Generalist PE
Balanced
Later Stage
Acquisition
Startup

Additional Information
Year Founded: 1969
Current Activity Level : Actively seeking new investments

INDIGO PARTNERS LLC

2525 East Camelback Road
Phoenix, AZ USA 85016
Phone: 6022241500
Fax: 6029566306

Management and Staff
William Franke, Managing Partner

Type of Firm
Private Equity Firm

Project Preferences

Type of Financing Preferred:
Early Stage
Seed

Geographical Preferences

United States Preferences:

Industry Preferences

In Transportation prefer:
Transportation
Aerospace

Additional Information
Year Founded: 2002
Current Activity Level : Actively seeking new investments

INDO-NORDIC PRIVATE EQUITY AS

P.O Box 9
Majorstuen
Oslo, Norway 0330
Phone: 47-9801-6573

Management and Staff
Suneel Regulla, Founder

Type of Firm
Private Equity Firm

Project Preferences

Type of Financing Preferred:
Balanced

Size of Investments Considered:
Min Size of Investment Considered (000s): $4,000
Max Size of Investment Considered (000s): $10,000

Geographical Preferences

International Preferences:
India

Industry Preferences

In Industrial/Energy prefer:
Energy
Oil and Gas Exploration
Oil & Gas Drilling,Explor

In Utilities prefer:
Utilities

Additional Information
Year Founded: 2008
Current Activity Level : Actively seeking new investments

INDUFIN SA

Interleuvenlaan 1515/D1
Research Park
Heverlee, Belgium 3001
Phone: 3216393040
Fax: 3216393049
E-mail: indufin@indufin.be
Website: www.indufin.be

Management and Staff
Guy Wygaerts, Managing Director
Jo Santino, Managing Director

Type of Firm
Private Equity Firm

Association Membership
Belgium Venturing Association

Project Preferences

Type of Financing Preferred:
Leveraged Buyout
Early Stage
Generalist PE
Later Stage
Management Buyouts
Acquisition

Size of Investments Considered:
Min Size of Investment Considered (000s): $3,741
Max Size of Investment Considered (000s): $12,471

Geographical Preferences

International Preferences:
Luxembourg
Europe
Belgium

Industry Preferences

In Medical/Health prefer:
Medical/Health

In Consumer Related prefer:
Consumer
Food/Beverage

In Industrial/Energy prefer:
Energy
Alternative Energy
Energy Conservation Relat

In Other prefer:
Environment Responsible

Additional Information
Year Founded: 2001
Current Activity Level : Actively seeking new investments

INDURAN VENTURES INC

150 William Street
Kingston, Canada K7L 2C9
Website: www.minkcapital.ca

Type of Firm
Private Equity Firm

Geographical Preferences

Canadian Preferences:
All Canada

Industry Preferences

In Biotechnology prefer:
Biotechnology
Biotech Related Research

Additional Information
Year Founded: 2012
Current Activity Level : Actively seeking new investments

INDUS HOLDING AG

Koelner Strasse 32
Bergisch Gladbach, Germany 51429
Phone: 49220440000
Fax: 492204400010
E-mail: indus@indus.de
Website: www.indus.de

Management and Staff
Rudolf Weichert, Chief Financial Officer

Type of Firm
Private Equity Firm

Project Preferences

Type of Financing Preferred:
Leveraged Buyout
Acquisition

Geographical Preferences

International Preferences:
Europe
Switzerland
Western Europe
Austria
Germany

Industry Preferences

In Industrial/Energy prefer:
Industrial Products
Materials
Process Control
Machinery

In Manufact. prefer:
Manufacturing

Additional Information
Year Founded: 1991
Current Activity Level : Actively seeking new investments

INDUSTRI UDVIKLING A/S

Gothersgade 175, 2nd floor
Copenhagen, Denmark 1123
Phone: 4533368999
Fax: 4533368990
E-mail: iu@industriudvikling.dk
Website: www.industriudvikling.dk

Management and Staff
Lars Blavnsfeldt, CEO & Managing Director

Type of Firm
Private Equity Firm

Project Preferences

Type of Financing Preferred:
Mezzanine
Generalist PE
Balanced
Acquisition

Size of Investments Considered:
Min Size of Investment Considered (000s): $870
Max Size of Investment Considered (000s): $3,500

Geographical Preferences

International Preferences:
Denmark

Industry Preferences

In Biotechnology prefer:
Biotech Related Research

In Consumer Related prefer:
Food/Beverage

In Industrial/Energy prefer:
Industrial Products
Advanced Materials
Factory Automation

In Business Serv. prefer:
Services

In Manufact. prefer:
Manufacturing

Additional Information
Year Founded: 1994
Capital Under Management: $36,300,000
Current Activity Level : Actively seeking new investments

INDUSTRIAL AND COMMERCIAL BANK OF CHINA LTD

No.55 Fuxingmennei Street
Xicheng District
Beijing, China 100032
Phone: 861066108608
Fax: 861066106139
Website: www.icbc.com.cn

Type of Firm
Bank Affiliated

Project Preferences

Type of Financing Preferred:
Balanced

Geographical Preferences

International Preferences:
China

Industry Preferences

In Consumer Related prefer:
Entertainment and Leisure

In Agr/Forestr/Fish prefer:
Mining and Minerals

Additional Information
Year Founded: 1984
Capital Under Management: $1,517,450,000
Current Activity Level : Actively seeking new investments

INDUSTRIAL ASSETS SPA

Via Manzoni 44
Milan, Italy 20121
Website: www.industrialassets.it

Management and Staff
Umberto Selvatico Estense, Partner

Type of Firm
Private Equity Firm

Association Membership
Italian Venture Capital Association (AIFI)

Project Preferences

Type of Financing Preferred:
Leveraged Buyout

Geographical Preferences

International Preferences:
Italy

Additional Information
Year Founded: 2008
Current Activity Level : Actively seeking new investments

INDUSTRIAL BANK OF KOREA

414 Teheran-ro Gangnam-gu
14-21F, L&B Tower
Seoul, South Korea 135080
Phone: 8215771885
Fax: 8225319789
Website: www.ibk.co.kr

Other Offices

15th Fl., Daeoh Bldg.
26-5 Yeoido-Dong Yeongdeongpo-Gu
Seoul, South Korea
Phone: 822-786-4391
Fax: 822-786-4393

6th Fl., Shinjoo Bldg.
297 Mannyeon-Dong Seo-Gu
Daejeon, South Korea
Phone: 82-42-482-2151
Fax: 82-42-482-2009

5th Fl., Boorim Bldg
42 Uljiro-1-Ga, Joong-Gu
Seoul, South Korea
Phone: 822-319-2141
Fax: 822-319-2143

14th Fl., IPIC Bldg
91-5 Boojeon-Dong Jin-Ku
Pusan, South Korea
Phone: 82-51-818-7260
Fax: 82-051-818-7259

Management and Staff
Sang Hyeon Yim, Managing Director
Yun Hui Lee, Chief Executive Officer

Type of Firm
Bank Affiliated

Project Preferences

Type of Financing Preferred:
Fund of Funds
Leveraged Buyout
Early Stage
Expansion
Balanced

Geographical Preferences

International Preferences:
Korea, South

Industry Preferences

In Computer Software prefer:
Software

In Semiconductor/Electr prefer:
Electronics

In Industrial/Energy prefer:
Industrial Products

Additional Information
Year Founded: 1961
Capital Under Management: $1,700,000
Current Activity Level : Actively seeking new investments

INDUSTRIAL GROWTH PARTNERS

100 Spear Street
Suite 1500
San Francisco, CA USA 94105
Phone: 4158824550
Fax: 4158824551
Website: www.igpequity.com

Management and Staff
Daniel Delaney, Partner
Gottfried Tittiger, Managing Director
Jeffrey Webb, Partner
Karen Greaves, Chief Financial Officer
Matthew Antaya, Partner
Michael Beaumont, Managing Director
R. Patrick Forster, Co-Founder

Type of Firm
Private Equity Firm

Project Preferences

Type of Financing Preferred:
Leveraged Buyout
Expansion
Management Buyouts
Acquisition
Recapitalizations

Geographical Preferences

United States Preferences:

Canadian Preferences:
All Canada

Industry Focus
(% based on actual investment)
Industrial/Energy	64.7%
Other Products	30.1%
Computer Hardware	5.3%

Additional Information
Name of Most Recent Fund: Industrial Growth Partners IV, L.P.
Most Recent Fund Was Raised: 06/03/2011
Year Founded: 1997
Capital Under Management: $825,000,000
Current Activity Level : Actively seeking new investments

INDUSTRIAL INNOVATION CAPITAL MANAGEMENT CO LTD

1199, Minsheng Road, Pudong
20/F, 1, Zhengdawudaokou
Shanghai, China
Phone: 862138565622
Fax: 862138565762
E-mail: contact@xyicap.com
Website: www.xyicap.com

Other Offices
No. 268, Hudong Road
16/F, Xingye Security Plaza
Fuzhou, China
Phone: 8659138281888
Fax: 8659138281550

Type of Firm
Investment Management Firm

Project Preferences

Type of Financing Preferred:
Leveraged Buyout
Expansion

Geographical Preferences

International Preferences:
China

Industry Preferences

In Communications prefer:
Telecommunications

In Internet Specific prefer:
Internet

In Medical/Health prefer:
Medical/Health

In Consumer Related prefer:
Consumer
Retail
Consumer Products

In Industrial/Energy prefer:
Energy
Energy Conservation Relat
Environmental Related

In Business Serv. prefer:
Media

In Manufact. prefer:
Manufacturing

Additional Information
Year Founded: 2010
Current Activity Level : Actively seeking new investments

INDUSTRIAL INVESTORS GROUP

Berkeley Square
Berkeley Square House, 8th Flr
London , United Kingdom W1J 6DB
Phone: 442076474000
Fax: 442076474001
E-mail: contact@industrial-investors.com
Website: www.industrial-investors.com

Type of Firm
Private Equity Firm

Additional Information
Year Founded: 2000
Current Activity Level : Actively seeking new investments

INDUSTRIAL OPPORTUNITY PARTNERS LLC

1603 Orrington Avenue
Suite 700
Evanston, IL USA 60201
Phone: 8475563460
Fax: 8475563461
Website: www.iopfund.com

Management and Staff
Adam Gottlieb, Principal
Andrew Weller, Principal
Christopher Willis, Vice President
J. Kyle Hood, Vice President
James Todd, Principal
John Colaianne, Principal
Kenneth Tallering, Managing Partner
Michael Hering, Chief Financial Officer
Nicholas Galambos, Principal
Robert Vedra, Principal
Thomas Paisley, Principal

Type of Firm
Private Equity Firm

Project Preferences

Type of Financing Preferred:
Leveraged Buyout
Turnaround
Acquisition
Recapitalizations

Industry Preferences

In Semiconductor/Electr prefer:
Electronics

In Medical/Health prefer:
Medical Products

In Industrial/Energy prefer:
Industrial Products
Advanced Materials
Machinery

In Business Serv. prefer:
Distribution

In Manufact. prefer:
Manufacturing

In Agr/Forestr/Fish prefer:
Agriculture related

Additional Information
Name of Most Recent Fund: Industrial Opportunity Partners II, L.P.
Most Recent Fund Was Raised: 02/27/2012
Year Founded: 2005
Capital Under Management: $460,000,000
Current Activity Level : Actively seeking new investments

INDUSTRIAL TECHNOLOGY INVESTMENT CORP

6/F, No 106 Ho-Ping East Rd
Section 2
Taipei, Taiwan 106
Phone: 886227377394
Fax: 886227377386
Website: www.itic.com.tw

Other Offices
R. 320, 3F, Bldg. 52, 195
Sec. 4, Chung Hsing Rd., Chutung
Hsinchu, Taiwan 310
Phone: 886-3-582-2709
Fax: 886-3-582-2983

2880 Zanker Road
Suite 109
San Jose, CA USA 95134
Phone: 408-428-9988
Fax: 408-428-9388

Management and Staff
Hanjie Luo, Vice President
Heyuan Lin, President
Jinrong Guo, Vice President
Liling Chen, Vice President
Mingyan He, Vice President
Ruizhu Li, Vice President
Sengui Zhang, Vice President
Taihe Liu, Vice President
Yihong Lin, Vice President

Type of Firm
Private Equity Firm

Association Membership
Taiwan Venture Capital Association (TVCA)

Project Preferences

Type of Financing Preferred:
Early Stage
Expansion
Balanced
Later Stage
Startup

Geographical Preferences

United States Preferences:

Canadian Preferences:
All Canada

International Preferences:
Taiwan
Israel

Industry Preferences

In Communications prefer:
Telecommunications
Wireless Communications
Data Communications

In Internet Specific prefer:
Internet

In Semiconductor/Electr prefer:
Semiconductor
Optoelectronics

In Medical/Health prefer:
Health Services

In Industrial/Energy prefer:
Energy

Additional Information
Year Founded: 1979
Capital Under Management: $11,800,000
Current Activity Level : Actively seeking new investments

INDUSTRIES ET FINANCES PARTENAIRES SAS

4 avenue Marceau
Paris, France 75008
Phone: 33158563300
Fax: 33153753300
E-mail: contact@ifpart.com
Website: www.ifpart.com

Management and Staff
Pierre Mestchersky, Co-Founder

Type of Firm
Private Equity Firm

Association Membership
French Venture Capital Association (AFIC)
European Private Equity and Venture Capital Assoc.

Project Preferences

Type of Financing Preferred:
Leveraged Buyout
Management Buyouts
Acquisition

Size of Investments Considered:
Min Size of Investment Considered (000s): $3,741
Max Size of Investment Considered (000s): $24,943

Geographical Preferences

International Preferences:
Europe
France

Additional Information
Name of Most Recent Fund: Industries et Finances Investissements III
Most Recent Fund Was Raised: 01/14/2013
Year Founded: 1999
Capital Under Management: $91,200,000
Current Activity Level : Actively seeking new investments

INDUSTRIFONDEN

Vasagatan 11
Stockholm, Sweden 111 91
Phone: 46858791900
Fax: 46858791950
E-mail: info@industrifonden.se
Website: industrifonden.com

Other Offices
Badhusgatan 5
Linkoping, Sweden 581 89

Sodra Tullgatan 4
c/o Malmohus Invest
Malmo, Sweden 211 40
Phone: 46703157290

Massans gata 18, World Trade Center
P.O. Box 5243
Gothenburg, Sweden 402 24
Phone: 4631836989
Fax: 4631812022

Management and Staff
Claes de Neergaard, Chief Executive Officer

Type of Firm
Government Affiliated Program

Association Membership
Swedish Venture Capital Association (SVCA)

Project Preferences

Type of Financing Preferred:
Early Stage
Balanced
Later Stage
Seed
Startup

Size of Investments Considered:
Min Size of Investment Considered (000s): $760
Max Size of Investment Considered (000s): $15,201

Geographical Preferences

International Preferences:
Sweden

Industry Preferences

In Communications prefer:
Telecommunications

In Computer Software prefer:
Software

In Semiconductor/Electr prefer:
Electronics

In Biotechnology prefer:
Biotechnology

In Medical/Health prefer:
Medical/Health
Pharmaceuticals

In Industrial/Energy prefer:
Industrial Products
Factory Automation

In Business Serv. prefer:
Services

In Manufact. prefer:
Manufacturing

Additional Information
Year Founded: 1979
Capital Under Management: $440,800,000
Current Activity Level : Actively seeking new investments

INDUSTRY VENTURES LLC

30 Hotaling Place
Third Floor
San Francisco, CA USA 94111
Phone: 4152734201
Fax: 4154837177
E-mail: info@industryventures.com
Website: www.industryventures.com

Other Offices

201 North Union Street
Suite 300
Alexandria, VA USA 22314
Phone: 7035193026
Fax: 7038376036

Management and Staff

Amir Malayery, Vice President
Hans Swildens, Managing Director
Ira Simkhovitch, Vice President
Jim Jones, Venture Partner
Jonathan Roosevelt, Venture Partner
Justin Burden, Managing Director
Ken Wallace, Managing Director
Lindsay Sharma, Vice President
Michael Gridley, Managing Director
Mike Gridley, Managing Director
Nate Leung, Vice President
Robert May, Chief Operating Officer
Robert May, Chief Financial Officer
Roland Reynolds, Managing Director
Victor Hwang, Managing Director
William Quist, Managing Director

Type of Firm

Private Equity Advisor or Fund of Funds

Association Membership

Mid-Atlantic Venture Association

Project Preferences

Role in Financing:
Prefer role as deal originator

Type of Financing Preferred:
Fund of Funds
Early Stage
Expansion
Balanced
Fund of Funds of Second

Geographical Preferences

United States Preferences:
Massachusetts
California

Industry Preferences

In Communications prefer:
Communications and Media
Wireless Communications

In Computer Software prefer:
Software

In Internet Specific prefer:
Internet

In Semiconductor/Electr prefer:
Electronics
Electronic Components
Semiconductor

In Medical/Health prefer:
Medical/Health

In Consumer Related prefer:
Consumer

In Industrial/Energy prefer:
Materials
Environmental Related

In Business Serv. prefer:
Services

Additional Information

Name of Most Recent Fund: Industry Ventures Special Opportunities Fund II, L.P.
Most Recent Fund Was Raised: 12/03/2013
Year Founded: 2000
Capital Under Management: $700,000,000
Current Activity Level : Actively seeking new investments
Method of Compensation: Return on invest. most important, but chg. closing fees, service fees, etc.

INE VENTURES

7th Floor, The Allman Building
1701 Walnut Street
Philadelphia, PA USA 19103
Website: ineventures.com

Type of Firm

Incubator/Development Program

Project Preferences

Type of Financing Preferred:
Early Stage
Expansion
Later Stage
Seed
Startup

Geographical Preferences

International Preferences:
Israel

Industry Preferences

In Communications prefer:
Telecommunications
Wireless Communications

In Computer Software prefer:
Software

Additional Information

Year Founded: 2013
Current Activity Level : Actively seeking new investments

INEO BETEILIGUNGS GMBH

Schwindgasse 10/Top 13
Vienna, Austria 1040
E-mail: office@ineo-capital.com

Type of Firm

Private Equity Firm

Project Preferences

Type of Financing Preferred:
Mezzanine
Balanced

Additional Information

Year Founded: 2011
Current Activity Level : Actively seeking new investments

INERJYS VENTURES INC

279 Prince Street
Montreal, Canada H3C 2N4
Phone: 5148750005
Fax: 5148759070
E-mail: info@inerjys.com

Management and Staff

Eric Ouaknine, Partner
Jigar Shah, Partner
Stephan Ouaknine, Partner
Vincent Martel, Partner

Type of Firm

Private Equity Firm

Project Preferences

Type of Financing Preferred:
Early Stage
Expansion
Balanced

Industry Preferences

In Industrial/Energy prefer:
Alternative Energy
Energy Conservation Relat

Additional Information

Year Founded: 2010
Capital Under Management: $700,000,000
Current Activity Level : Actively seeking new investments

INETWORKS LLC

870 Evergreen Avenue
Suite 202
Pittsburgh, PA USA 15209
Phone: 4129041014
Fax: 4129043983
E-mail: info@inetworksllc.com
Website: www.inetworksllc.com

Other Offices

National Technology Transfer Center
316 Washington Avenue
Wheeling, WV USA 26003

4548 Market Street
Philadelphia, PA USA 19139
Phone: 215-243-4111
Fax: 215-895-4001

Management and Staff

Anthony Tomasello, Managing Director
Anthony Lacenere, Managing Director
Charles Schliebs, Managing Director
Steven Russell, Managing Director

Type of Firm

Private Equity Firm

Project Preferences

Type of Financing Preferred:
Early Stage
Balanced
Seed

Geographical Preferences

United States Preferences:
Mid Atlantic
Pennsylvania
Michigan
West Virginia
All U.S.

Industry Preferences

In Biotechnology prefer:
Biotechnology

In Medical/Health prefer:
Medical/Health
Diagnostic Services
Drug/Equipmt Delivery
Medical Products
Health Services

In Industrial/Energy prefer:
Alternative Energy

Additional Information

Year Founded: 1999
Capital Under Management: $50,000,000
Current Activity Level : Actively seeking new investments

INFIELD CAPITAL LLC

939 Pearl Street
Suite 200
Boulder, CO USA 80302
Phone: 3034492921
Fax: 3034492936
E-mail: info@infieldcapital.com
Website: www.infieldcapital.com

Management and Staff

C. David Moll, Founder

Type of Firm

Private Equity Firm

Project Preferences

Type of Financing Preferred:
Early Stage

Geographical Preferences

United States Preferences:

Industry Preferences

In Industrial/Energy prefer:
Energy
Environmental Related

In Transportation prefer:
Transportation

Additional Information

Year Founded: 2008
Current Activity Level : Actively seeking new investments

INFINITY CAPITAL LLC

480 Cowper Street, Suite 200
Palo Alto, CA USA 94301
Phone: 6504628400
Fax: 6504628415
E-mail: info@infinityllc.com
Website: www.infinityllc.com

Management and Staff

Bruce Graham, Managing Director
Sam Lee, Founder

Type of Firm

Private Equity Firm

Project Preferences

Role in Financing:
Will function either as deal originator or investor in deals created by others

Type of Financing Preferred:
Early Stage

Size of Investments Considered:
Min Size of Investment Considered (000s): $275
Max Size of Investment Considered (000s): $10,000

Geographical Preferences

United States Preferences:

Industry Focus

(% based on actual investment)
Internet Specific	30.2%
Computer Software and Services	28.8%
Semiconductors/Other Elect.	19.2%
Communications and Media	10.9%
Computer Hardware	9.3%
Medical/Health	1.0%
Other Products	0.6%

Additional Information

Name of Most Recent Fund: Infinity Capital VF 1999
Most Recent Fund Was Raised: 09/30/1999
Year Founded: 1999
Capital Under Management: $207,500,000
Current Activity Level : Actively seeking new investments
Method of Compensation: Return on investment is of primary concern, do not charge fees

INFLECTION POINT VENTURES

30 Washington Street
Wellesley, MA USA 02481
Phone: 6175104386
Website: www.inflectpoint.com

Other Offices

7903 Sleaford Place
Bethesda, MD USA 20814
Phone: 301-656-6837
Fax: 301-656-8056

30 Washington Street
Wellesley, MA USA 02481
Phone: 781-416-5107
Fax: 781-237-6699

Management and Staff

Diane Messick, Chief Financial Officer
Jeffrey Davison, General Partner
Michael O Malley, General Partner

Type of Firm

Private Equity Firm

Project Preferences

Role in Financing:
Prefer role as deal originator

Type of Financing Preferred:
Early Stage
Seed

Size of Investments Considered:
Min Size of Investment Considered (000s): $500
Max Size of Investment Considered (000s): $2,000

Geographical Preferences

United States Preferences:
Mid Atlantic
Northeast

Industry Preferences

In Communications prefer:
Telecommunications

In Internet Specific prefer:
Ecommerce

Additional Information

Year Founded: 1998
Capital Under Management: $50,000,000
Current Activity Level : Actively seeking new investments

INFLEXION PARTNERS

12565 Research Parkway, Suite 300
Orlando, FL USA 32826
Phone: 4073812675
Fax: 4073812631
E-mail: info@inflexionvc.com
Website: www.inflexionvc.com

Management and Staff

Carolyn Ticknor, Venture Partner
Charles Resnick, Managing Partner
Daniel Rua, Managing Partner
Jim Boyle, Managing Partner
Michael Barach, Venture Partner

Type of Firm

Private Equity Firm

Project Preferences

Type of Financing Preferred:
Early Stage

Size of Investments Considered:
Min Size of Investment Considered (000s): $500
Max Size of Investment Considered (000s): $1,500

Geographical Preferences

United States Preferences:
Florida

Industry Preferences

In Computer Software prefer:
Software

Additional Information

Year Founded: 2002
Current Activity Level : Actively seeking new investments

INFLEXION PLC

9 Mandeville Place
London, United Kingdom W1G 8DX
Phone: 442074879888
Fax: 442074872774
E-mail: info@inflexion.com
Website: www.inflexion.com

Other Offices

82 King Street
Manchester, United Kingdom M2 4WQ
Phone: 44-161-935-8018
Fax: 44-161-935-8154

Management and Staff

Alistair Hamilton, Founder
Richard Swann, Partner
Tim Smallbone, Partner

Type of Firm

Private Equity Firm

Association Membership

British Venture Capital Association (BVCA)
European Private Equity and Venture Capital Assoc.

Project Preferences

Type of Financing Preferred:
Leveraged Buyout
Expansion
Management Buyouts
Acquisition

Size of Investments Considered:
Min Size of Investment Considered (000s): $2,839
Max Size of Investment Considered (000s): $14,195

Geographical Preferences

United States Preferences:
Kansas

International Preferences:
United Kingdom
Europe
Western Europe

Industry Preferences

In Communications prefer:
Communications and Media

In Internet Specific prefer:
Internet

In Computer Other prefer:
Computer Related

In Medical/Health prefer:
Medical/Health

In Consumer Related prefer:
Retail
Consumer Products
Consumer Services
Education Related

In Business Serv. prefer:
Services

Additional Information

Name of Most Recent Fund: Inflexion 2012 Co-Investment Fund
Most Recent Fund Was Raised: 08/01/2012
Year Founded: 1998
Capital Under Management: $51,100,000
Current Activity Level : Actively seeking new investments

INFLEXION POINT CAPITAL PTE. LTD

14 Robinson Road
13-00 Far East Finance Buildin
Singapore, Singapore
Website: inflexionpoint.asia

Type of Firm

Private Equity Firm

Project Preferences

Type of Financing Preferred:
Early Stage
Seed
Startup

Geographical Preferences

International Preferences:
Asia
Singapore
Japan

Industry Preferences

In Communications prefer:
Media and Entertainment
Entertainment

In Computer Software prefer:
Software
Applications Software

Additional Information

Year Founded: 2014
Capital Under Management: $15,000,000
Current Activity Level : Actively seeking new investments

INFOCOMM INVESTMENTS PTE LTD

BASH 79 Ayer Rajah Crescent
Level 3
Singapore, Singapore 139955
Phone: 6562110888
Fax: 6562112222
E-mail: info@infocomminvestments.com
Website: www.infocomminvestments.com

Other Offices

1038 Nanjing West Road
Westgate Tower 18-01
Shanghai, China 200041

Phone: 862162178822
Fax: 862162189720

Unit 06, UGF, Creator Block
International Tech Park, Whitefield Road
Bangalore, India 560066
Phone: 918041156400
Fax: 918041156104

Three Twin Dolphin Drive
Suite 260
Redwood City, CA USA 94065
Phone: 6505931716
Fax: 6505933276

Management and Staff
Kuo-Yi Lim, Chief Executive Officer

Type of Firm
Government Affiliated Program

Association Membership
Singapore Venture Capital Association (SVCA)

Project Preferences

Type of Financing Preferred:
Seed

Size of Investments Considered:
Min Size of Investment Considered (000s): $1,000
Max Size of Investment Considered (000s): $5,000

Geographical Preferences

United States Preferences:

International Preferences:
India
China
Asia
Singapore

Additional Information
Year Founded: 1996
Capital Under Management: $170,000,000
Current Activity Level : Actively seeking new investments

INFORMAL CAPITAL NETWORK BV

Sterreboslaan 3
Huizen, Netherlands 1272 PA
Phone: 31356947456
Fax: 31356321889
E-mail: info@tiincapital.nl
Website: www.informalcapital.net

Type of Firm
Private Equity Firm

Association Membership
Dutch Venture Capital Associaton (NVP)

Project Preferences

Type of Financing Preferred:
Leveraged Buyout
Early Stage
Generalist PE
Later Stage

Geographical Preferences

International Preferences:
Europe

Industry Preferences

In Medical/Health prefer:
Medical/Health

In Manufact. prefer:
Manufacturing

Additional Information
Year Founded: 2004
Capital Under Management: $8,550,000
Current Activity Level : Actively seeking new investments

INFORMATION VENTURE PARTNERS

One University Avenue
Suite 1901
Toronto, Canada M5J 2P1
Website: www.informationvp.com

Type of Firm
Private Equity Firm

Project Preferences

Type of Financing Preferred:
Early Stage
Expansion
Balanced
Later Stage

Industry Preferences

In Computer Software prefer:
Software

In Financial Services prefer:
Financial Services

Additional Information
Year Founded: 2014
Capital Under Management: $78,530,000
Current Activity Level : Actively seeking new investments

INFOTECH VENTURES CO LTD

Shanghai Platinum Blg. Room 90
233 Taicang Road
Shanghai, China 200020
Phone: 862161414788
Fax: 862161414789

Website: www.infovc.com

Other Offices
522 Cambridge Avenue
Palo Alto, CA USA 94302
Phone: 650-278-0276

Rm. 2003, Cyber Tower B
No. 2 ZhongGuanCun NanDaJie
Beijing, China 100086
Phone: 86-10-82512080
Fax: 86-10-82515186

Management and Staff
Fang Roger Li, Partner
Ning Zhou, Vice President
Terence Tan, General Partner
Tingru Liu, General Partner
Weijin Liu, Vice President

Type of Firm
Private Equity Firm

Association Membership
Venture Capital Association of Beijing (VCAB)

Project Preferences

Type of Financing Preferred:
Early Stage
Balanced
Seed

Geographical Preferences

International Preferences:
China
Asia
All International

Industry Preferences

In Communications prefer:
Data Communications
Satellite Microwave Comm.
Media and Entertainment

In Medical/Health prefer:
Medical/Health

Additional Information
Year Founded: 2000
Capital Under Management: $166,297,000
Current Activity Level : Actively seeking new investments

INFRA CAPITAL INVESTMENTS PJSC

17th Floor, Al Hana Tower
Corniche Road, Al Khaldiya
Abu Dhabi, Utd. Arab Em.
Phone: 971-2-681-1233
Fax: 971-2-681-1844
E-mail: info@adih.ae
Website: infracap.ae

Management and Staff
Emad Taha, Chief Financial Officer
Rashad Janahi, Managing Director
Wael Mattar, Chief Executive Officer

Type of Firm
Private Equity Firm

Association Membership
African Venture Capital Association (AVCA)

Project Preferences

Type of Financing Preferred:
Leveraged Buyout
Management Buyouts
Acquisition

Geographical Preferences

International Preferences:
Middle East
Asia
Africa

Industry Preferences

In Consumer Related prefer:
Consumer

Additional Information
Year Founded: 2005
Current Activity Level : Actively seeking new investments

INFRASTRUCTURE FUND THE

1000 Red River
Rm. E208
Austin, TX USA 78701
Phone: 512-344-4300
Fax: 512-344-4320
Website: www.tifb.state.tx.us

Type of Firm
Private Equity Firm

Project Preferences

Type of Financing Preferred:
Other

Additional Information
Year Founded: 2009
Current Activity Level : Actively seeking new investments

ING BELGIQUE SA

Marnixlaan 24
Brussels, Belgium 1000
Phone: 3225472232
Fax: 3225473687
E-mail: peq@ing.be
Website: www.ing.be

Type of Firm
Bank Affiliated

Association Membership
Belgium Venturing Association

Project Preferences

Type of Financing Preferred:
Leveraged Buyout
Generalist PE
Balanced
Later Stage
Management Buyouts

Geographical Preferences

International Preferences:
Luxembourg
Europe
Belgium

Industry Preferences

In Communications prefer:
Communications and Media
Commercial Communications
Telecommunications
Wireless Communications

In Computer Software prefer:
Software

In Consumer Related prefer:
Food/Beverage
Consumer Products

In Industrial/Energy prefer:
Industrial Products

In Transportation prefer:
Transportation

In Business Serv. prefer:
Services
Consulting Services

In Manufact. prefer:
Manufacturing

Additional Information
Year Founded: 1994
Capital Under Management: $98,900,000
Current Activity Level : Actively seeking new investments

ING VENTURES

888, Bijmerplein
Amsterdam, Netherlands 1102 MG

Type of Firm
Bank Affiliated

Project Preferences

Type of Financing Preferred:
Early Stage
Expansion
Later Stage
Seed

Industry Preferences

In Computer Software prefer:
Software

In Financial Services prefer:
Financial Services

Additional Information
Year Founded: 2017
Capital Under Management: $354,480,000
Current Activity Level : Actively seeking new investments

INGENIOUS HAUS GROUP

No. 3.02D, East Wing
Level 3,Suite 285, Menara BRDB
Kuala Lumpur, Malaysia 59000
Phone: 60322973618
Fax: 6032297619
E-mail: info@ingenioushaus.com
Website: www.ingenioushaus.com

Other Offices
111, North Bridge Road
Suite 27-01, Peninsula Plaza
Singapore, Singapore 179098
Phone: 65-9175-8978

Management and Staff
Judith Ng, Vice President

Type of Firm
Private Equity Firm

Association Membership
Malaysian Venture Capital Association

Project Preferences

Type of Financing Preferred:
Leveraged Buyout
Early Stage
Expansion
Generalist PE
Balanced
Later Stage
Seed
Acquisition
Startup

Geographical Preferences

International Preferences:
Asia

Industry Preferences

In Communications prefer:
Telecommunications
Wireless Communications

In Business Serv. prefer:
Media

Additional Information
Year Founded: 2004
Capital Under Management: $22,000,000
Current Activity Level : Actively seeking new investments

INGENIOUS VENTURES LP

15 Golden Square
London, United Kingdom W1F 9JG
Phone: 442073194000
Fax: 442073194001
E-mail: generalenquiries@ingeniousmedia.co.uk
Website: www.ingeniousmedia.co.uk/ventures

Management and Staff
Patrick McKenna, Chief Executive Officer

Type of Firm
Investment Management Firm

Association Membership
British Venture Capital Association (BVCA)

Project Preferences

Type of Financing Preferred:
Early Stage
Expansion
Balanced
Later Stage
Management Buyouts

Geographical Preferences

International Preferences:
United Kingdom
Europe
Western Europe
Africa

Industry Preferences

In Communications prefer:
Radio & TV Broadcasting
Media and Entertainment
Entertainment

In Internet Specific prefer:
Internet
Ecommerce

In Consumer Related prefer:
Entertainment and Leisure

In Industrial/Energy prefer:
Energy
Alternative Energy

In Business Serv. prefer:
Media

In Manufact. prefer:
Publishing

Additional Information
Year Founded: 1998
Current Activity Level : Actively seeking new investments

INGLESIDE INVESTORS LLC

12 East 49th Street
41st Floor
New York, NY USA 10017
Phone: 2126343366
E-mail: Info@inginv.com
Website: www.inglesidellc.com

Management and Staff
Greg Warner, President
James Israel, Vice President
Larry Kraus, Vice President
Mayer Rosenzweig, Managing Director

Type of Firm
Private Equity Firm

Project Preferences

Type of Financing Preferred:
Fund of Funds
Core
Leveraged Buyout
Value-Add
Generalist PE
Opportunistic
Acquisition
Special Situation

Additional Information
Year Founded: 1956
Current Activity Level : Actively seeking new investments

INGLOBO PRIVATE EQUITY

20 Denis Street
PO Box 284
Subiaco, Australia 6008
Phone: 61863636147
Fax: 61863636156
Website: www.inglobo.com.au

Management and Staff
Bruce Davis, Founder

Type of Firm
Private Equity Firm

Project Preferences

Type of Financing Preferred:
Management Buyouts

Geographical Preferences

International Preferences:
Australia

Industry Preferences

In Consumer Related prefer:
Retail

In Industrial/Energy prefer:
Oil and Gas Exploration

In Business Serv. prefer:
Distribution

In Manufact. prefer:
Manufacturing

In Agr/Forestr/Fish prefer:
Mining and Minerals

Additional Information
Year Founded: 2008
Current Activity Level : Actively seeking new investments

INHERENT GROUP LLC

510 LaGuardia Place
Fifth Floor
New York, NY USA 10012
Website: www.inherentgroup.com

Type of Firm
Investment Management Firm

Project Preferences

Type of Financing Preferred:
Later Stage

Geographical Preferences

United States Preferences:

Canadian Preferences:
All Canada

International Preferences:
Western Europe

Industry Preferences

In Consumer Related prefer:
Food/Beverage
Education Related

In Industrial/Energy prefer:
Environmental Related

In Agr/Forestr/Fish prefer:
Agriculture related

In Other prefer:
Environment Responsible

Additional Information
Year Founded: 1969
Current Activity Level : Actively seeking new investments

INITIAL FACTOR SPEED INVEST GMBH & CO KG

Spengergasse 37-39
Third Floor
Vienna, Austria 1050
Phone: 43125330338105
E-mail: pitch@initialfactor.com
Website: www.initialfactor.com

Type of Firm
Private Equity Firm

Project Preferences

Type of Financing Preferred:
Early Stage
Seed
Startup

Geographical Preferences

International Preferences:
Slovenia
Hungary
Slovak Repub.
Central Europe
Czech Republic
Switzerland
Western Europe
Austria
Eastern Europe
Croatia
Germany

Industry Preferences

In Communications prefer:
Wireless Communications

In Computer Software prefer:
Systems Software

In Internet Specific prefer:
E-Commerce Technology
Internet

Additional Information
Name of Most Recent Fund: Speedinvest I
Most Recent Fund Was Raised: 06/29/2011
Year Founded: 2009
Capital Under Management: $115,589,000
Current Activity Level : Actively seeking new investments

INITIALIZED CAPITAL

650 Delancey Street
Suite 312
San Francisco, CA USA 94107
Phone: 4154938264
Website: initialized.com

Other Offices
Former HQ: 360 Furman Street
Suite 739
BROOKLYN, NY USA 11201
Phone: 4154938264

Type of Firm
Private Equity Firm

Project Preferences

Type of Financing Preferred:
Early Stage
Startup

Additional Information
Name of Most Recent Fund: Initialized II, L.P.
Most Recent Fund Was Raised: 08/01/2013
Year Founded: 2013
Capital Under Management: $164,150,000
Current Activity Level : Actively seeking new investments

INITIATIVE & FINANCE INVESTISSEMENT SA

20, Rue Quentin Bauchart
Paris, France 75008
Phone: 33156899700
Fax: 33156899701
E-mail: infos@initiative-finance.com

Other Offices
77, rue President Edouard Herriot
Lyon, France 69002
Phone: 33478878685
Fax: 33478878500

Management and Staff
Arnaud Mendelsohn, Partner
Jean-Bernard Meurisse, President
Jean-Michel Laveu, Partner
Matthieu Douchet, Partner

Type of Firm
Bank Affiliated

Association Membership
French Venture Capital Association (AFIC)

Project Preferences

Type of Financing Preferred:
Leveraged Buyout
Management Buyouts
Acquisition

Geographical Preferences

United States Preferences:

International Preferences:
Europe
Netherlands
Belgium
Germany
France

Industry Focus
(% based on actual investment)
Other Products	33.2%
Medical/Health	25.3%
Consumer Related	23.8%
Computer Hardware	6.9%
Internet Specific	6.2%
Industrial/Energy	3.4%
Computer Software and Services	1.2%

Additional Information
Name of Most Recent Fund: Initiative & Finance FCPR 1
Most Recent Fund Was Raised: 12/01/1992
Year Founded: 1984
Capital Under Management: $204,300,000
Current Activity Level : Actively seeking new investments

INITIUM CAPITAL LLC

981 East Calle De La Cabra
Tucson, AZ USA 85702
Phone: 5205750674
Website: www.initiumcapital.com

Type of Firm
Corporate PE/Venture

Project Preferences

Type of Financing Preferred:
Early Stage
Seed

Industry Preferences

In Communications prefer:
Wireless Communications

In Computer Software prefer:
Software

In Semiconductor/Electr prefer:
Electronics
Semiconductor

In Medical/Health prefer:
Medical Products
Pharmaceuticals

In Industrial/Energy prefer:
Alternative Energy

Additional Information
Year Founded: 2003
Current Activity Level : Actively seeking new investments

INIZIATIVA GESTIONE INVESTIMENTI SGR SPA

Via Arco, 1
Milan, Italy 20123
Phone: 39236570550
Fax: 392804124
E-mail: segretaria@igisgr.it
Website: www.igisgr.it

Other Offices

Piazza Municipio, 4
Napoli, Italy 80133
Phone: 39-081-251-8111
Fax: 39-081-551-7504

Caduti del Lavoro, 40
Ancona, Italy 60131
Phone: 39-071-290-0764
Fax: 39-071-286-1891

Via Michele Scammacca, 5
Catania, Italy 95127
Phone: 39-095-722-5173
Fax: 39-095-722-1296

Mazzini 23
Vicenza, Italy 36100
Phone: 39-0444-540-403
Fax: 39-0444-324-585

Via Emilia Ponente, 317
Bologna, Italy 40125
Phone: 39-051-619-9485
Fax: 39-051-569-481

Via Abruzzi, 6
Rome, Italy
Phone: 39-06-4201-2306
Fax: 39-06-4201-0653

Viale dei Cacciatori 2
Trevisco, Italy 31100
Phone: 39-0422-580-395
Fax: 39-0422-55-199

Amendola, 172/c
Bari, Italy 70126
Phone: 39-080-546-1570
Fax: 39-080-548-1594

Corso Zanardelli 32
Brescia, Italy 25121
Phone: 39-030-280-7402
Fax: 39-030-41-050

Corso Galileo Ferraris 60
Torino, Italy
Phone: 39-011-580-6122
Fax: 39-011-500-567

Management and Staff

Giorgio Cirla, Chief Executive Officer
Matteo Cirla, Managing Partner
Paolo Merlano, Partner

Type of Firm

Private Equity Firm

Project Preferences

Role in Financing:
Will function either as deal originator or investor in deals created by others

Type of Financing Preferred:
Leveraged Buyout
Generalist PE
Balanced
Turnaround
Later Stage
Management Buyouts
First Stage Financing

Size of Investments Considered:
Min Size of Investment Considered (000s): $1,500
Max Size of Investment Considered: No Limit

Geographical Preferences

International Preferences:
Italy
Europe

Industry Preferences

In Business Serv. prefer:
Services

In Manufact. prefer:
Manufacturing

Additional Information

Year Founded: 1997
Capital Under Management: $272,700,000
Current Activity Level : Actively seeking new investments

INKEF CAPITAL BV

Symphony Offices
Gustav Mahlerplein 3
Amsterdam, Netherlands 1082 MS
Phone: 31207946060
E-mail: info@inkefcapital.com
Website: www.inkefcapital.com

Other Offices

One University Ave, Suite 1800
Toronto, Canada ON M5J 2P1
Phone: 4163693700

Management and Staff

Frank Landsberger, Senior Managing Director
Martin Eijgenhuijsen, Managing Director

Type of Firm

Private Equity Firm

Project Preferences

Type of Financing Preferred:
Early Stage
Startup

Geographical Preferences

Canadian Preferences:
All Canada

International Preferences:
Netherlands

Additional Information

Year Founded: 2010
Current Activity Level : Actively seeking new investments

INKOPO LTD

Metic House
Ripley Drive
Normanton, United Kingdom WF6 1QT
Phone: 44-192-422-7200
Fax: 44-192-489-2207
E-mail: info@inkopo.co.uk

Management and Staff

Andrew Burton, Managing Director

Type of Firm

Investment Management Firm

Project Preferences

Type of Financing Preferred:
Early Stage
Seed
Startup

Geographical Preferences

International Preferences:
United Kingdom

Industry Preferences

In Financial Services prefer:
Financial Services

Additional Information

Year Founded: 2002
Current Activity Level : Actively seeking new investments

INLANDSINNOVATION AB

Akademigatan 2
Ostersund, Sweden 831 40
Phone: 46771150180
E-mail: info@inlandsinnovation.se
Website: www.inlandsinnovation.se

Management and Staff
Barbro Ederwall, Chief Financial Officer
Gunnar Olofsson, Chief Executive Officer
Jan Nylander, Vice President

Type of Firm
Private Equity Firm

Project Preferences

Type of Financing Preferred:
Early Stage
Generalist PE
Balanced

Geographical Preferences

International Preferences:
Sweden

Industry Preferences

In Communications prefer:
Wireless Communications
Data Communications
Satellite Microwave Comm.

In Transportation prefer:
Aerospace

In Agr/Forestr/Fish prefer:
Mining and Minerals

Additional Information
Year Founded: 2011
Capital Under Management: $296,900,000
Current Activity Level : Actively seeking new investments

INNERPRODUCT PARTNERS LLC

750 Battery Street
Seventh Floor
San Francisco, CA USA 94111
Website: www.innerproductpartners.com

Type of Firm
Private Equity Firm

Project Preferences

Type of Financing Preferred:
Early Stage

Additional Information
Year Founded: 2015
Capital Under Management: $5,990,000
Current Activity Level : Actively seeking new investments

INNERVATION CAPITAL PARTNERS LTD

96 Kensington High Street
London, United Kingdom W8 4SG

Management and Staff
Jeremy Greenhalgh, Co-Founder
Sotiris Lyritzis, Co-Founder

Type of Firm
Private Equity Firm

Project Preferences

Type of Financing Preferred:
Early Stage

Geographical Preferences

United States Preferences:

International Preferences:
Europe

Additional Information
Year Founded: 2014
Current Activity Level : Actively seeking new investments

INNISFREE GROUP LTD

33 Gutter Lane
London, United Kingdom EC2V 8AS
Phone: 44-20-7367-5660
Fax: 44-20-7726-4836
E-mail: kashem@innisfree.co.uk
Website: www.innisfree.co.uk

Management and Staff
David Metter, Chief Executive Officer

Type of Firm
Private Equity Firm

Project Preferences

Type of Financing Preferred:
Fund of Funds
Special Situation

Size of Investments Considered:
Min Size of Investment Considered (000s): $6,167
Max Size of Investment Considered (000s): $98,668

Geographical Preferences

International Preferences:
United Kingdom
Europe

Industry Preferences

In Medical/Health prefer:
Medical/Health

In Consumer Related prefer:
Education Related

In Transportation prefer:
Transportation

Additional Information
Year Founded: 2002
Current Activity Level : Actively seeking new investments

INNOGEST SGR SPA

Corso Galileo Ferraris, 64
Turin, Italy 10129
Phone: 39115091411
Fax: 3911590488
E-mail: info@innogest.it
Website: www.innogest.it

Management and Staff
Claudio Giuliano, Co-Founder
Franco Rutili, Venture Partner
Giuseppe Giorgini, Venture Partner
Marco Pinciroli, Co-Founder
Paolo Cellini, Venture Partner

Type of Firm
Private Equity Firm

Association Membership
Italian Venture Capital Association (AIFI)

Project Preferences

Type of Financing Preferred:
Early Stage
Later Stage
Seed
Startup

Geographical Preferences

International Preferences:
Italy
Europe

Industry Preferences

In Medical/Health prefer:
Medical Therapeutics

Additional Information
Year Founded: 2005
Capital Under Management: $95,130,000
Current Activity Level : Actively seeking new investments

INNOSIGHT VENTURES

400 Talcott Avenue
The Arsenal on the Charles
East Watertown, MA USA 02472
Phone: 6173934500
E-mail: inquiries@innosight.com
Website: www.innosightventures.com

Other Offices

Eight Eu Tong Sen Street
Suite 15-89, The Central
Singapore 059818
Phone: 6568849375
Fax: 6568849376

No. I-SIDCO Industrial Estate
2nd Floor, Altius
Chennai, India 600032
Phone: 914442994352
Fax: 914442994300

Management and Staff

Pete Bonee, Partner
Scott Anthony, Managing Director

Type of Firm

Incubator/Development Program

Association Membership

Singapore Venture Capital Association (SVCA)

Project Preferences

Type of Financing Preferred:
Early Stage
Startup

Geographical Preferences

International Preferences:
Singapore

Additional Information

Year Founded: 2008
Current Activity Level : Actively seeking new investments

INNOSPRING INC

2901 Tasman Drive
Santa Clara, CA USA 95054
E-mail: info@innospring.net

Management and Staff

E. Zhang, President

Type of Firm

Incubator/Development Program

Project Preferences

Type of Financing Preferred:
Startup

Geographical Preferences

United States Preferences:
All U.S.

Industry Preferences

In Computer Software prefer:
Software

In Other prefer:
Socially Responsible
Environment Responsible

Additional Information

Year Founded: 2012
Capital Under Management: $5,000,000
Current Activity Level : Actively seeking new investments

INNOVA CAPITAL SP Z O O

Rondo ONZ 1
35th Floor
Warsaw, Poland 00-124
Phone: 48225449400
Fax: 48225449403
E-mail: mail@innovacap.com
Website: www.innovacap.com

Management and Staff

Andrzej Bartos, Managing Partner
Iain Haggis, Chief Financial Officer
Joanna Simonowicz, Managing Director
Krzysztof Krawczyk, Managing Partner
Krzysztof Kulig, Managing Partner
Leszek Muzyczyszyn, Partner
Robert Conn, Partner
Steven Buckley, Partner

Type of Firm

Private Equity Firm

Association Membership

Hungarian Venture Capital Association (HVCA)
Czech Venture Capital Association (CVCA)
Polish Venture Capital Association (PSIC/PPEA)
South Eastern Europes Private Equity Association
European Private Equity and Venture Capital Assoc.

Project Preferences

Role in Financing:
Prefer role as deal originator but will also invest in deals created by others

Type of Financing Preferred:
Second Stage Financing
Leveraged Buyout
Control-block Purchases
Early Stage
Expansion
Mezzanine
Balanced
Later Stage
Management Buyouts
First Stage Financing
Industry Rollups
Special Situation

Size of Investments Considered:
Min Size of Investment Considered (000s): $6,300
Max Size of Investment Considered (000s): $18,160

Geographical Preferences

International Preferences:
Hungary
Slovak Repub.
Central Europe
Czech Republic
Poland
Austria
Scandanavia/Nordic Region
Germany

Industry Preferences

In Communications prefer:
Telecommunications

In Consumer Related prefer:
Retail

In Financial Services prefer:
Financial Services

In Business Serv. prefer:
Services
Media

In Manufact. prefer:
Manufacturing

Additional Information

Name of Most Recent Fund: Innova/3 LP
Most Recent Fund Was Raised: 02/21/2002
Year Founded: 1994
Capital Under Management: $674,500,000
Current Activity Level : Actively seeking new investments

INNOVA MEMPHIS INC

20 Dudley St.
Suite 620
Memphis, TN USA 38103
Phone: 9018661466
Fax: 9018661431
Website: www.innovamemphis.com

Management and Staff

Brandon Wellford, Chief Financial Officer
Jan Bouten, Partner
Ken Woody, Partner

Type of Firm

Private Equity Firm

Project Preferences

Role in Financing:
Prefer role as deal originator but will also invest in deals created by others

Type of Financing Preferred:
Early Stage
Balanced
Later Stage
Seed
Startup

Geographical Preferences

United States Preferences:
Tennessee

Industry Preferences

In Biotechnology prefer:
Biotechnology
Agricultural/Animal Bio.

Additional Information

Year Founded: 2007
Capital Under Management: $40,000,000
Current Activity Level : Actively seeking new investments

INNOVACOM GESTION SAS

23 Rue Royale
Paris, France 75008
Phone: 33144941500
Fax: 33144941515
E-mail: info@innovacom.com
Website: www.innovacom.com

Other Offices

801 Gateway Blvd., Suite 500
South San Francisco, CA USA 94080
Phone: 650-875-3011
Fax: 415-288-0685

Birger Jarlsgatan 2
Stockholm, Sweden SE-11434
Phone: 48-6-611-2909

Management and Staff

Bruno Dizengremel, Partner
Denis Champenois, CEO & Managing Director
Frederic Humbert, Partner
Frederic Veyssiere, Venture Partner
Jerome Lecoeur, Managing Director
Vincent Deltrieu, Partner

Type of Firm

Corporate PE/Venture

Association Membership

French Venture Capital Association (AFIC)
Swedish Venture Capital Association (SVCA)

Project Preferences

Type of Financing Preferred:
Second Stage Financing
Early Stage
Start-up Financing
Seed
First Stage Financing
Startup

Size of Investments Considered:

Min Size of Investment Considered (000s): $670
Max Size of Investment Considered (000s): $13,399

Geographical Preferences

United States Preferences:
West Coast

Canadian Preferences:
All Canada
Quebec

International Preferences:
United Kingdom
Europe
Scandanavia/Nordic Region
France

Industry Focus

(% based on actual investment)
Computer Software and Services	31.8%
Internet Specific	26.0%
Communications and Media	23.1%
Semiconductors/Other Elect.	12.8%
Consumer Related	2.8%
Computer Hardware	2.7%
Industrial/Energy	0.7%
Biotechnology	0.2%

Additional Information

Year Founded: 2000
Capital Under Management: $386,900,000
Current Activity Level : Actively seeking new investments
Method of Compensation: Return on investment is of primary concern, do not charge fees

---

INNOVACORP

1400 - 1801 Hollis Street
Halifax, Canada B3J 3N4
Phone: 9024248670
Fax: 9024244679
E-mail: info@innovacorp.ca
Website: innovacorp.ca

Management and Staff

David McNamara, Vice President
Dawn House, Vice President
Jennifer Robichaud, Vice President
Patrick Keefe, Vice President

Type of Firm

Private Equity Firm

Association Membership

Canadian Venture Capital Association

Project Preferences

Type of Financing Preferred:
Early Stage
Seed
Startup

Geographical Preferences

Canadian Preferences:
All Canada
New Brunswick

Industry Preferences

In Communications prefer:
Telecommunications

In Medical/Health prefer:
Medical/Health

In Industrial/Energy prefer:
Alternative Energy
Environmental Related

Additional Information

Name of Most Recent Fund: Nova Scotia First Fund
Most Recent Fund Was Raised: 06/27/1996
Year Founded: 1995
Current Activity Level : Actively seeking new investments

INNOVAFONDS SAS

157, avenue de l'Eygala
Corenc, France 38700
Phone: 33476087946
Fax: 33469960603
E-mail: contact@innofonds.com
Website: www.innovafonds.com

Other Offices

110, rue de Richelieu
Paris, France 75002

Type of Firm

Private Equity Firm

Association Membership

French Venture Capital Association (AFIC)

Project Preferences

Type of Financing Preferred:
Leveraged Buyout
Early Stage
Expansion
Generalist PE
Later Stage
Seed
Management Buyouts
Acquisition
Startup

Geographical Preferences

International Preferences:
Europe
France

Industry Preferences

In Communications prefer:
Communications and Media
Telecommunications
Wireless Communications

In Internet Specific prefer:
Internet

In Semiconductor/Electr prefer:
Electronics

In Medical/Health prefer:
Medical/Health

In Industrial/Energy prefer:
Energy

Additional Information
Year Founded: 2008
Capital Under Management: $82,189,000
Current Activity Level : Actively seeking new investments

INNOVATE PARTNERS LLC

2211 Michelson Drive
Irvine, CA USA 92612
Phone: 9495028240
Website: www.innovatepartnersllc.com

Management and Staff
Jeff Conner, Chief Financial Officer
Richard Conn, Managing Partner
Robert Allison, Managing Partner
Simon Sollberger, Vice President

Type of Firm
Private Equity Firm

Project Preferences

Type of Financing Preferred:
Balanced

Industry Preferences

In Consumer Related prefer:
Consumer

Additional Information
Year Founded: 2014
Capital Under Management: $23,491,000
Current Activity Level : Actively seeking new investments

INNOVATECH SUD DU QUEBEC

Two Complexe Desjardins
Suite 1717, Desjardins Station
Montreal, Canada H5B 1B9
Phone: 8885223222
Fax: 5142867876
Website: www.capitalregional.com

Type of Firm
Government Affiliated Program

Project Preferences

Role in Financing:
Will function either as deal originator or investor in deals created by others

Type of Financing Preferred:
Early Stage
Research and Development
Start-up Financing
Seed
First Stage Financing

Size of Investments Considered:
Min Size of Investment Considered (000s): $83
Max Size of Investment Considered (000s): $4,153

Geographical Preferences

Canadian Preferences:
Quebec

Industry Preferences

In Communications prefer:
Telecommunications
Data Communications

In Biotechnology prefer:
Industrial Biotechnology

Additional Information
Year Founded: 1995
Capital Under Management: $58,300,000
Current Activity Level : Actively seeking new investments
Method of Compensation: Return on invest. most important, but chg. closing fees, service fees, etc.

INNOVATION CAMP INVESTMENT CONSULTING (SHANGHAI) CO LTD

128,Daxue Road,Yangpu District
Room 104
Shanghai, China
Phone: 862124556638
E-mail: info@innovation-camp.com
Website: www.innovation-camp.com

Management and Staff
Andy Wang, Partner
Jun Li, Partner
Michael Feng, Partner
Yong Wang, Partner

Type of Firm
Incubator/Development Program

Project Preferences

Type of Financing Preferred:
Seed
Startup

Size of Investments Considered:
Min Size of Investment Considered (000s): $30
Max Size of Investment Considered (000s): $50

Geographical Preferences

International Preferences:
China

Industry Preferences

In Communications prefer:
Wireless Communications

In Computer Software prefer:
Applications Software

In Internet Specific prefer:
Internet

Additional Information
Year Founded: 2011
Capital Under Management: $2,000,000
Current Activity Level : Actively seeking new investments

INNOVATION CAPITAL ADVISORS LLC

1601 Concord Pike
Suite 82
Wilmington, DE USA 19803
Phone: 3027771616
Fax: 3027771620
E-mail: info@innovationcapital.com
Website: www.innovationcapital.com

Other Offices
313 West Liberty Street
Suite 321
LANCASTER, PA USA 17603
Phone: 7173972279

Type of Firm
Private Equity Firm

Project Preferences

Type of Financing Preferred:
Early Stage
Seed
Startup

Size of Investments Considered:
Min Size of Investment Considered (000s): $25
Max Size of Investment Considered (000s): $50

Geographical Preferences

United States Preferences:
Mid Atlantic
Delaware

Industry Preferences

In Computer Software prefer:
Software

In Internet Specific prefer:
E-Commerce Technology

In Semiconductor/Electr prefer:
Electronics

In Industrial/Energy prefer:
Materials

In Financial Services prefer:
Financial Services

In Business Serv. prefer:
Services

In Manufact. prefer:
Manufacturing

Additional Information
Name of Most Recent Fund: Innovation Ventures
Most Recent Fund Was Raised: 08/18/2004
Year Founded: 1995
Capital Under Management: $10,000,000
Current Activity Level : Actively seeking new investments

INNOVATION CAPITAL ASSOCIATES PTY, LTD.

35 Lime Street
Suite 401
Sydney, Australia 2000
Phone: 61282966000
Fax: 61282966066
E-mail: info@innovationcapital.net
Website: www.innovationcapital.net

Management and Staff
Derek Kerr, Chief Financial Officer
Fiona Pak-Poy, General Partner
Ian Bund, General Partner
Michael Quinn, Managing Partner
Roger Price, General Partner

Type of Firm
Private Equity Firm

Project Preferences

Type of Financing Preferred:
Early Stage
Expansion
Turnaround
Seed
Startup

Size of Investments Considered:
Min Size of Investment Considered (000s): $458
Max Size of Investment Considered (000s): $5,500

Geographical Preferences

United States Preferences:

International Preferences:
Asia Pacific
Europe
Asia

Industry Preferences

In Communications prefer:
Telecommunications

In Biotechnology prefer:
Biotechnology

In Medical/Health prefer:
Medical Products

In Industrial/Energy prefer:
Alternative Energy

Additional Information
Name of Most Recent Fund: Innovation Capital Fund II LP
Most Recent Fund Was Raised: 04/04/2007
Year Founded: 1999
Capital Under Management: $46,600,000
Current Activity Level : Actively seeking new investments

INNOVATION CAPITAL SAS

57 Avenue
Franklin Delano Roosevelt
Paris, France 75008
Phone: 33140769900
Fax: 33145612478
Website: www.innovationcapital.fr

Management and Staff
Bertrand Limoges, Partner
Florian Reinaud, Partner
Franck Noiret, General Partner
Michel Desbard, Venture Partner
Valery Huot, Managing Partner

Type of Firm
Private Equity Firm

Association Membership
French Venture Capital Association (AFIC)
European Private Equity and Venture Capital Assoc.

Project Preferences

Type of Financing Preferred:
Early Stage
Later Stage

Geographical Preferences

International Preferences:
Central Europe
Europe
Eastern Europe
France

Industry Focus
(% based on actual investment)
Biotechnology	19.4%
Computer Hardware	17.9%
Medical/Health	15.3%
Internet Specific	14.5%
Computer Software and Services	12.4%
Semiconductors/Other Elect.	6.8%
Industrial/Energy	5.5%
Other Products	4.4%
Communications and Media	3.8%

Additional Information
Year Founded: 1999
Capital Under Management: $415,000,000
Current Activity Level : Actively seeking new investments

INNOVATION ENDEAVORS LLC

575 High Street
Suite 400
Palo Alto, CA USA 94301
E-mail: info@InnovationEndeavors.com
Website: www.innovationendeavors.com

Management and Staff
Doron Alter, Principal
Dror Berman, Managing Partner
Eric Schmidt, Partner

Type of Firm
Private Equity Firm

Project Preferences

Type of Financing Preferred:
Early Stage
Seed
Startup

Geographical Preferences

United States Preferences:

Industry Preferences

In Communications prefer:
Communications and Media
Telecommunications

In Computer Software prefer:
Software

In Internet Specific prefer:
Internet

In Computer Other prefer:
Computer Related

In Semiconductor/Electr prefer:
Electronics

In Medical/Health prefer:
Medical/Health
Health Services

In Consumer Related prefer:
Consumer

Additional Information
Year Founded: 2010
Current Activity Level : Actively seeking new investments

INNOVATION ENGINE INC

2-3-12, Shiba
3/F Shiba-Habitation Building
Minato-Ku, Tokyo, Japan 105-0014
Phone: 81357306721
Fax: 81357306722
E-mail: hpcontact@innovation-engine.co.jp
Website: www.innovation-engine.co.jp

Management and Staff
Hiroyuki Mizuno, Managing Director
Takashi Matsumoto, Partner
Tetsujiro Hayashi, Managing Director

Type of Firm
Private Equity Firm

Association Membership
Japan Venture Capital Association

Project Preferences

Role in Financing:
Prefer role as deal originator

Type of Financing Preferred:
Early Stage
Expansion
Balanced
Seed
Startup

Geographical Preferences

International Preferences:
Japan

Industry Preferences

In Semiconductor/Electr prefer:
Electronics
Semiconductor
Micro-Processing

In Medical/Health prefer:
Medical/Health

In Industrial/Energy prefer:
Energy
Advanced Materials
Environmental Related

Additional Information
Year Founded: 2001
Capital Under Management: $1,400,000
Current Activity Level : Actively seeking new investments

INNOVATION FORWARD LLC

6348 Westbrook Place
Columbus, OH USA 43085
Phone: 6145810424
Website: www.innovation4ward.com

Type of Firm
Private Equity Firm

Project Preferences

Type of Financing Preferred:
Early Stage
Balanced
Seed
Startup

Additional Information
Year Founded: 2015
Capital Under Management: $480,000
Current Activity Level : Actively seeking new investments

INNOVATION GARDEN LLC

205 Rockingham Row
Princeton, NJ USA 08540
Phone: 6096518242
Fax: 6094527212
Website: www.innovationgardennj.com

Type of Firm
Private Equity Firm

Project Preferences

Type of Financing Preferred:
Early Stage
Seed

Additional Information
Name of Most Recent Fund: Innovation Garden Accelerator Fund, L.P.
Most Recent Fund Was Raised: 03/07/2012
Year Founded: 2012
Capital Under Management: $1,200,000
Current Activity Level : Actively seeking new investments

INNOVATION GLOBAL CAPITAL LLC

555 California Street
Suite 4925
San Francisco, CA USA 94104
Phone: 4159261203O
Fax: 4156591950
E-mail: info@innovationglobal.com
Website: innovationglobal.com

Type of Firm
Private Equity Firm

Project Preferences

Type of Financing Preferred:
Expansion
Balanced
Later Stage

Industry Preferences

In Communications prefer:
Communications and Media

In Internet Specific prefer:
Ecommerce

Additional Information
Year Founded: 2016
Capital Under Management: $7,490,000
Current Activity Level : Actively seeking new investments

INNOVATION NEST SP Z O O

Ul. Ludwinowska 7/9
Cracow, Poland 30-331
E-mail: innest@innovationnest.pl
Website: www.innovationnest.pl

Management and Staff
Agnieszka Skala-Pozniak, Partner
Marek Kapturkiewicz, Chief Operating Officer
Piotr Wilam, Partner

Type of Firm
Private Equity Firm

Project Preferences

Type of Financing Preferred:
Balanced

Size of Investments Considered:
Min Size of Investment Considered (000s): $16
Max Size of Investment Considered (000s): $1,581

Geographical Preferences

International Preferences:
Poland

Industry Preferences

In Communications prefer:
Communications and Media
Wireless Communications
Media and Entertainment

In Computer Software prefer:
Software

In Internet Specific prefer:
Internet
Ecommerce
Web Aggregation/Portals

Additional Information
Year Founded: 2010
Capital Under Management: $12,600,000
Current Activity Level : Actively seeking new investments

INNOVATION NETWORK CORPORATION OF JAPAN

1-6-5, Marunouchi
22/F Marunouchi-Kitaguchi Bldg
Tokyo, Japan 100-0005
Phone: 81352187200
Fax: 81332139479
Website: www.incj.co.jp

Management and Staff
Haruyasu Asakura, Chief Operating Officer
Hidetoshi Shibata, Managing Director
Jun Hosoya, Managing Director
Kimikazu Noumi, Chief Executive Officer
Koichiro Taniyama, Managing Director
Shinichi Takahashi, Managing Director
Takeshi Sekine, Managing Director
Taro Sato, Managing Director
Tetsuro Toyota, Managing Director

Type of Firm
Government Affiliated Program

Project Preferences

Type of Financing Preferred:
Leveraged Buyout
Generalist PE
Balanced
Acquisition

Geographical Preferences

International Preferences:
Chile
Australia
Japan

Industry Preferences

In Communications prefer:
Telecommunications

In Semiconductor/Electr prefer:
Electronics

In Medical/Health prefer:
Medical/Health

In Consumer Related prefer:
Food/Beverage

In Industrial/Energy prefer:
Alternative Energy

In Business Serv. prefer:
Services

In Other prefer:
Environment Responsible

Additional Information
Year Founded: 2009
Current Activity Level : Actively seeking new investments

INNOVATION PHILADEL-PHIA

2600 Center Square West
1500 Market Street
Philadelphia, PA USA 19102
Phone: 2154968110
Fax: 2159779618
E-mail: info@innovationphiladelphia.com

Type of Firm
Incubator/Development Program

Project Preferences

Type of Financing Preferred:
Early Stage
Balanced
Seed
Startup

Geographical Preferences

United States Preferences:
Pennsylvania
Delaware
New Jersey

Additional Information
Name of Most Recent Fund: Mid-Atlantic Angel Group Fund II, L.P.
Most Recent Fund Was Raised: 04/22/2009
Year Founded: 2002
Capital Under Management: $1,100,000
Current Activity Level : Actively seeking new investments

INNOVATION SUPPORT

4773 Yonge Street
Suite 5E
Toronto, Canada M2N 0G2
Phone: 4167334200
E-mail: info@innovationsupport.ca
Website: www.innovationsupport.ca

Type of Firm
Incubator/Development Program

Project Preferences

Type of Financing Preferred:
Start-up Financing
Seed

Additional Information
Year Founded: 2013
Current Activity Level : Actively seeking new investments

INNOVATION TRANSFER CENTER - CARNEGIE MELLON UNIVERSITY

4615 Forbes Avenue
Suite 302
Pittsburgh, PA USA 15213
Phone: 4122687390
Fax: 4122687395
E-mail: innovation@cmu.edu
Website: www.cmu.edu/innovationtransfer/

Type of Firm
University Program

Project Preferences

Type of Financing Preferred:
Early Stage
Seed
Startup

Geographical Preferences

United States Preferences:

Industry Preferences

In Computer Software prefer:
Software

In Consumer Related prefer:
Education Related

Additional Information
Name of Most Recent Fund: Carnegie Mellon University
Most Recent Fund Was Raised: 12/31/1984
Year Founded: 1984
Current Activity Level : Actively seeking new investments

INNOVATION WORKS INC

2000 Technology Drive
Suite 250
Pittsburgh, PA USA 15219
Phone: 4126811520
Fax: 4126812625
Website: www.innovationworks.org

Management and Staff
Chuck Brandt, Vice President
Frank Demmler, Vice President

Type of Firm
Private Equity Firm

Project Preferences

Role in Financing:
Prefer role as deal originator

Type of Financing Preferred:
Early Stage
Balanced
Seed
Startup

Size of Investments Considered:
Min Size of Investment Considered (000s): $100
Max Size of Investment Considered (000s): $600

Geographical Preferences

United States Preferences:
Pennsylvania

Industry Preferences

In Computer Hardware prefer:
Mainframes / Scientific
Mini and Personal/Desktop
Computer Graphics and Dig
Integrated Turnkey System
Terminals
Disk Relat. Memory Device

In Computer Software prefer:
Computer Services
Data Processing
Software
Systems Software
Applications Software
Artificial Intelligence

In Internet Specific prefer:
E-Commerce Technology
Internet
Web Aggregration/Portals

In Semiconductor/Electr prefer:
Electronic Components
Semiconductor
Micro-Processing
Controllers and Sensors
Sensors
Circuit Boards
Component Testing Equipmt
Laser Related
Fiber Optics

In Biotechnology prefer:
Human Biotechnology
Industrial Biotechnology

In Medical/Health prefer:
Medical Diagnostics
Diagnostic Services
Diagnostic Test Products
Medical Therapeutics
Drug/Equipmt Delivery
Medical Products
Disposable Med. Products
Health Services
Pharmaceuticals

In Industrial/Energy prefer:
Alternative Energy
Superconductivity
Robotics

Additional Information
Name of Most Recent Fund: Riverfront Ventures LLC
Most Recent Fund Was Raised: 09/13/2013
Year Founded: 1999
Capital Under Management: $63,000,000
Current Activity Level : Actively seeking new investments
Method of Compensation: Return on investment is of primary concern, do not charge fees

INNOVATION WORKS WEISHEN (SHANGHAI) INVEST. MGMT. CONSULTING

No.2500, Siping Road., Yangpu
RB-09, F22
Shanghai, China

Type of Firm
Investment Management Firm

Project Preferences

Type of Financing Preferred:
Balanced

Geographical Preferences

International Preferences:
China

Additional Information
Year Founded: 2011
Current Activity Level : Actively seeking new investments

INNOVATIONS AND FUTURE CREATION INC

2-2-1 Marunouchi Chiyoda-ku
Kishimoto Building 6F
Tokyo, Japan 100-0005
Website: miraisozo.co.jp

Type of Firm
Incubator/Development Program

Project Preferences

Type of Financing Preferred:
Early Stage

Additional Information
Year Founded: 2014
Current Activity Level : Actively seeking new investments

INNOVATIONSKAPITAL NORDIC ADVISORS AB

Kungsportsplatsen 1
Gothenburg, Sweden 411 10
Phone: 4631609190
Fax: 4631609199
E-mail: info@innkap.se
Website: www.innkap.se

Other Offices
Birger Jarlsgatan 13
Stockholm, Sweden 111 45
Phone: 46854501490
Fax: 46854501499

P.O. Box 332
Freienbach, Switzerland 8807
Phone: 41788883547
Fax: 41434569778

Management and Staff
Gabriella Ohldin, Chief Financial Officer
Staffan Ingeborn, Founder

Type of Firm
Private Equity Firm

Association Membership
Swedish Venture Capital Association (SVCA)
European Private Equity and Venture Capital Assoc.

Project Preferences

Role in Financing:
Prefer role as deal originator but will also invest in deals created by others

Type of Financing Preferred:
Early Stage
Seed
Startup

Size of Investments Considered:
Min Size of Investment Considered (000s): $150
Max Size of Investment Considered (000s): $15,000

Geographical Preferences

International Preferences:
Scandanavia/Nordic Region

Industry Focus

(% based on actual investment)
Semiconductors/Other Elect.	23.7%
Biotechnology	19.2%
Computer Software and Services	18.9%
Industrial/Energy	11.7%
Medical/Health	9.8%
Internet Specific	7.3%
Communications and Media	6.9%
Other Products	1.8%
Computer Hardware	0.6%

Additional Information
Name of Most Recent Fund: InnKap 4 Partners
Most Recent Fund Was Raised: 10/01/2005
Year Founded: 1994
Capital Under Management: $396,700,000
Current Activity Level : Actively seeking new investments
Method of Compensation: Return on investment is of primary concern, do not charge fees

INNOVATIVE VENTURES SA

135-137 El. Venizelou Ave
Kallithea
Athens, Greece 17671
Phone: 302103319950
Fax: 302109550610
E-mail: info@nbgvc.gr
Website: www.iven.gr

Type of Firm
Incubator/Development Program

Project Preferences

Type of Financing Preferred:
Seed

Geographical Preferences

International Preferences:
Greece
Sweden
Europe

Additional Information
Year Founded: 2000
Current Activity Level : Actively seeking new investments

INNOVEN CAPITAL INDIA PVT LTD

Nariman Point
12th Floor, Express Towers
Mumbai, India 400 021
Phone: 912267446500
E-mail: contact@innovencapital.com
Website: www.innovencapital.com

Management and Staff
Ajay Hattangdi, Chief Executive Officer
Vinod Murali, Chief Executive Officer

Type of Firm
Private Equity Firm

Project Preferences

Type of Financing Preferred:
Early Stage
Distressed Debt

Geographical Preferences

International Preferences:
India
Asia
Singapore

Additional Information
Year Founded: 2008
Current Activity Level : Actively seeking new investments

INNOVENTURES CAPITAL PARTNERS

515 South 700 East, Suite 2A
Salt Lake City, UT USA 84102
Phone: 8017414200
Fax: 8017414249
Website: www.innoventurescapitalpartners.com

Management and Staff
Scott Stenberg, Chief Financial Officer

Type of Firm
Private Equity Firm

Project Preferences

Role in Financing:
Prefer role as deal originator but will also invest in deals created by others

Type of Financing Preferred:
Early Stage
Mezzanine

Size of Investments Considered:
Min Size of Investment Considered (000s): $300
Max Size of Investment Considered (000s): $500

Geographical Preferences

United States Preferences:
Utah

Industry Preferences

In Business Serv. prefer:
Services

In Manufact. prefer:
Manufacturing

Additional Information
Name of Most Recent Fund: UTFC Fund II LLC
Most Recent Fund Was Raised: 04/30/2007
Year Founded: 2001
Capital Under Management: $19,000,000
Current Activity Level : Actively seeking new investments
Method of Compensation: Return on invest. most important, but chg. closing fees, service fees, etc.

INNOVENTUS PROJECT AB

Uppsala Science Park
Dag Hammarskjolds vag 10 B
Uppsala, Sweden 752 37
Phone: 46184770470
Fax: 4618551255
E-mail: info@innoventus.se

Management and Staff
Malin Graffner Nordberg, CEO & Managing Director

Type of Firm
Incubator/Development Program

Project Preferences

Type of Financing Preferred:
Seed
Startup

Size of Investments Considered:
Min Size of Investment Considered (000s): $100
Max Size of Investment Considered (000s): $500

Geographical Preferences

International Preferences:
Sweden
Scandanavia/Nordic Region

Industry Preferences

In Biotechnology prefer:
Biotechnology

In Medical/Health prefer:
Medical Products
Pharmaceuticals

Additional Information
Year Founded: 1999
Current Activity Level : Actively seeking new investments

INNOVESTOR OY

Aleksanterinkatu 46 C
Helsinki, Finland 00100
Phone: 358103233880
E-mail: info@innovestor.fi
Website: www.innovestorgroup.com

Other Offices
Trekhprudny per. 9 bld 1
Moscow, Russia 123001
Phone: 79260398489

Type of Firm
Investment Management Firm

Geographical Preferences

International Preferences:
Europe

Additional Information
Year Founded: 2014
Current Activity Level : Actively seeking new investments

INNVOTEC LTD

52 Upper Street, Islington
Business Design Ctr., Ste. 310
London, United Kingdom N1 0QH
Phone: 442076306990
Fax: 442078288232
E-mail: info@innvotec.co.uk
Website: www.innvotec.co.uk

Pratt's Guide to Private Equity & Venture Capital Sources

Other Offices
Business Link House
Salford UBP, 35 Winders Way
Salford, United Kingdom M6 6AR
Phone: 44 161 278 2600
Fax: 44 161 278 2610

Management and Staff
Alan Mawson, Founder

Type of Firm
Private Equity Firm

Association Membership
British Venture Capital Association (BVCA)

Project Preferences

Role in Financing:
Prefer role as deal originator but will also invest in deals created by others

Type of Financing Preferred:
Early Stage
Expansion
Balanced
Start-up Financing
Seed
First Stage Financing

Size of Investments Considered:
Min Size of Investment Considered (000s): $800
Max Size of Investment Considered: No Limit

Geographical Preferences

International Preferences:
United Kingdom
Europe

Industry Focus
(% based on actual investment)
Consumer Related	23.2%
Medical/Health	20.9%
Other Products	17.3%
Communications and Media	13.7%
Semiconductors/Other Elect.	11.9%
Computer Hardware	11.3%
Internet Specific	1.6%

Additional Information
Name of Most Recent Fund: Advantage Technology Fund
Most Recent Fund Was Raised: 01/05/2001
Year Founded: 1989
Capital Under Management: $50,100,000
Current Activity Level : Actively seeking new investments
Method of Compensation: Return on investment is of primary concern, do not charge fees

INOCA CAPITAL PARTNERS LLC

321 North Clark Street, Suite 2800
Chicago, IL USA 60654
Phone: 3128574271
E-mail: info@inocacapital.com
Website: inocacapital.com

Management and Staff
Christopher Sheffert, Managing Director

Type of Firm
Private Equity Firm

Project Preferences

Type of Financing Preferred:
Leveraged Buyout
Acquisition
Recapitalizations

Geographical Preferences

United States Preferences:

Industry Preferences

In Consumer Related prefer:
Consumer Products
Consumer Services

In Business Serv. prefer:
Services

In Manufact. prefer:
Manufacturing

Additional Information
Year Founded: 2012
Current Activity Level : Actively seeking new investments

INOCAP GESTION SAS

40 rue de la Boetie
Paris, France 75008
Phone: 33145640584
E-mail: contact@inocap.fr
Website: www.inocapgestion.com

Management and Staff
Olivier Bourdelas, Chief Executive Officer
Pierrick Bauchet, Managing Partner

Type of Firm
Private Equity Firm

Association Membership
French Venture Capital Association (AFIC)

Project Preferences

Type of Financing Preferred:
Early Stage
Later Stage

Geographical Preferences

International Preferences:
Europe
France

Industry Preferences

In Communications prefer:
CATV & Pay TV Systems

In Semiconductor/Electr prefer:
Electronics
Laser Related

In Biotechnology prefer:
Agricultural/Animal Bio.

In Medical/Health prefer:
Medical/Health
Medical Diagnostics
Drug/Equipmt Delivery

In Consumer Related prefer:
Consumer Products
Education Related

In Industrial/Energy prefer:
Industrial Products

In Agr/Forestr/Fish prefer:
Mining and Minerals

Additional Information
Year Founded: 2007
Current Activity Level : Actively seeking new investments

INOVA PERSONALIZED HEALTH ACCELERATOR

c/o Inova Center
Fairfax, VA USA 22037
Website: www.inovapha.org

Type of Firm
Incubator/Development Program

Project Preferences

Type of Financing Preferred:
Early Stage

Additional Information
Year Founded: 2016
Current Activity Level : Actively seeking new investments

INOVIA CAPITAL INC

Three Place Ville-Marie
Bureau 12350
Montreal, Canada H3B 0E7
Phone: 5149822251
E-mail: info@inoviacapital.com
Website: inovia.vc

Other Offices
305 Pinnacle Ridge Place
Calgary, Canada T3Z 3N8
Phone: 4032462790

Pratt's Guide to Private Equity & Venture Capital Sources

1066 West Hastings Street
Suite 1410
Vancouver, Canada V6E 3X1

25 Taylor Street
Suite 304
SAN FRANCISCO, CA USA 94102

Eight Queen Street North
Suite One
Kitchener, Canada N2H 2G8

Three, Place Ville Marie
Office 12350
Montreal, Canada
Phone: 5149822251

151 Bloor Street West
Suite 200
Toronto, Canada M5S 2C7

1155 Rene-Levesque Boulevard
West, Suite 2701
Montreal, Canada
Phone: 5149822251

Management and Staff
Chris Arsenault, Managing Partner
Daniel Freedman, Venture Partner
David Nault, Principal
Geoffrey Judge, Partner
Karamdeep Nijjar, Partner
Kevin Swan, Venture Partner
Magaly Charbonneau, Principal
Scott Munro, Venture Partner
Shawn Abbott, Partner
Todd Simpson, Venture Partner

Type of Firm
Private Equity Firm

Association Membership
Canadian Venture Capital Association

Project Preferences

Type of Financing Preferred:
Early Stage
Seed

Geographical Preferences

United States Preferences:
North America

Canadian Preferences:
All Canada

Industry Preferences

In Communications prefer:
Communications and Media
Commercial Communications
Media and Entertainment

In Computer Software prefer:
Software
Artificial Intelligence

In Industrial/Energy prefer:
Robotics

Additional Information
Name of Most Recent Fund: iNovia Investment Fund III, LP
Most Recent Fund Was Raised: 12/16/2011
Year Founded: 2001
Capital Under Management: $450,000,000
Current Activity Level : Actively seeking new investments

INOVIS CAPITAL GMBH

Karlstrasse 35
Munich, Germany 80333
Phone: 4989452352116
Fax: 4989452352110
Website: www.inoviscapital.de

Management and Staff
Christian Wexlberger, Managing Director

Type of Firm
Investment Management Firm

Project Preferences

Type of Financing Preferred:
Later Stage
Seed
Startup

Geographical Preferences

International Preferences:
Switzerland
Austria
Germany

Industry Preferences

In Communications prefer:
Telecommunications
Wireless Communications

In Internet Specific prefer:
Internet

In Industrial/Energy prefer:
Environmental Related

Additional Information
Year Founded: 2009
Current Activity Level : Actively seeking new investments

INOVO SP Z O O

44, Twarda
Warsaw, Poland 00831
Phone: 58694829003
Website: inovo.vc

Type of Firm
Private Equity Firm

Project Preferences

Type of Financing Preferred:
Early Stage

Geographical Preferences

International Preferences:
Poland

Industry Preferences

In Computer Software prefer:
Software

In Internet Specific prefer:
Internet
Ecommerce

In Business Serv. prefer:
Media

Additional Information
Year Founded: 2010
Current Activity Level : Actively seeking new investments

INREACH VENTURES LLP

35 New Bridge Street, Fourth Floor
London, United Kingdom EC4V 6BW
Website: www.inreachventures.com

Management and Staff
Ben Smith, Co-Founder
John Mesrie, Co-Founder
Roberto Bonanzinga, Co-Founder

Type of Firm
Private Equity Firm

Project Preferences

Type of Financing Preferred:
Early Stage

Geographical Preferences

International Preferences:
Europe

Additional Information
Year Founded: 2015
Current Activity Level : Actively seeking new investments

INRETURN CAPITAL (K) LTD

Statehouse Road
Nairobi, Kenya
Phone: 254202504775
Fax: 254202658058
E-mail: info@inreturncapital.com
Website: www.inreturncapital.com

Other Offices
7, Adam Street
The Strand
London, United Kingdom WC2N 6AA
Phone: 442075209236
Fax: 442075209237

1124, Chole Road, Msasani Peninsular
Dar es Salaam, Tanzania
Phone: 254202504775

Witte Huis
23, Wijnhaven
WG Rotterdam, Netherlands NL-3011
Phone: 31102755995
Fax: 31102755999

Management and Staff
Anthony Gichini, Managing Partner
Ezra Musoke, Managing Partner

Type of Firm
Private Equity Firm

Project Preferences

Type of Financing Preferred:
Early Stage
Expansion
Balanced
Later Stage

Size of Investments Considered:
Min Size of Investment Considered (000s): $250
Max Size of Investment Considered (000s): $2,500

Geographical Preferences

International Preferences:
Uganda
Tanzania
Kenya
Africa

Additional Information
Year Founded: 2007
Current Activity Level : Actively seeking new investments

INSEED INVESTIMENTOS LTDA

Rua Amauri 286
5th Floor, Itaim
Sao Paulo, Brazil 01448000
Phone: 551125262440
E-mail: contato@inseedinvestimentos.com.br
Website: www.inseedinvestimentos.com.br

Management and Staff
Alexandre Alves, General Partner
Francisco Perez, General Partner
Gustavo Junqueira, General Partner
Paulo Tomazela, General Partner

Type of Firm
Private Equity Firm

Association Membership
Brazilian Venture Capital Association (ABCR)

Project Preferences

Type of Financing Preferred:
Early Stage
Seed
Startup

Geographical Preferences

International Preferences:
Brazil

Industry Preferences

In Biotechnology prefer:
Biotechnology

In Industrial/Energy prefer:
Energy
Alternative Energy
Environmental Related

In Other prefer:
Environment Responsible

Additional Information
Year Founded: 2008
Capital Under Management: $88,581,000
Current Activity Level : Actively seeking new investments

INSERM TRANSFERT INITIATIVE SAS

Paris BioPark
7 Rue Watt
Paris, France 75013
Phone: 33155030100
Fax: 33155030160
E-mail: contact@it-initiative.fr
Website: www.inserm-transfert-initiative.com

Management and Staff
Louis Jammayrac, President

Type of Firm
Private Equity Firm

Project Preferences

Type of Financing Preferred:
Seed
Startup

Geographical Preferences

International Preferences:
Europe
Eastern Europe
France

Industry Preferences

In Biotechnology prefer:
Human Biotechnology

Additional Information
Year Founded: 2006
Capital Under Management: $5,000,000
Current Activity Level : Actively seeking new investments

INSIGHT EQUITY HOLDINGS LLC

1400 Civic Place, Suite 250
Southlake, TX USA 76092
Phone: 8174887775
Fax: 8174887739
Website: www.insightequity.com

Other Offices
400 Madison Avenue
15th Floor
New York, NY USA 10017
Phone: 2122017899

Management and Staff
Andrew Boisseau, Principal
Ben Stolbach, Vice President
Dan Lenahan, Vice President
Daniel Davidson, Vice President
Eliot Kerlin, Partner
Jack Waterstreet, Principal
James Jackson, Vice President
Kevin Slaton, Chief Financial Officer
Victor Vescovo, Managing Partner
Warren Bonham, Partner

Type of Firm
Private Equity Firm

Project Preferences

Type of Financing Preferred:
Leveraged Buyout
Mezzanine
Management Buyouts
Recapitalizations

Geographical Preferences

United States Preferences:
North America

Industry Preferences

In Consumer Related prefer:
Consumer Products

In Industrial/Energy prefer:
Energy
Industrial Products

In Transportation prefer:
Transportation
Aerospace

In Business Serv. prefer:
Services
Distribution

In Manufact. prefer:
Manufacturing

Additional Information
Name of Most Recent Fund: Insight Equity III, L.P.
Most Recent Fund Was Raised: 12/23/2013
Year Founded: 2002
Capital Under Management: $250,000,000
Current Activity Level : Actively seeking new investments

INSIGHT VENTURE PARTNERS LLC

1114 Avenue of the Americas
36th Floor
New York, NY USA 10036
Phone: 2122309200
Fax: 2122309272
E-mail: growth@insightpartners.com
Website: www.insightpartners.com

Other Offices
FORMER HQ: 680 Fifth Avenue
Eighth Floor
NEW YORK, NY USA 10019

Management and Staff
Anika Agarwal, Vice President
Deven Parekh, Managing Director
Emmett Keeffe, Venture Partner
Gary Survis, Venture Partner
Harley Miller, Vice President
Ian Sandler, Chief Operating Officer
Jason Ewell, Venture Partner
Jeffrey Horing, Co-Founder
Jeffrey Lieberman, Managing Director
Jerry Murdock, Co-Founder
Kelly Hardeman, Vice President
Kevin Hurth, Vice President
Matt Gatto, Principal
Michael Triplett, Managing Director
Nick Sinai, Venture Partner
Peter Sobiloff, Managing Director
Philip Vorobeychik, Principal
Rachel Geller, Managing Director
Ross Devor, Managing Director
Teddie Wardi, Principal
Thilo Semmelbauer, Venture Partner

Type of Firm
Private Equity Firm

Association Membership
National Venture Capital Association - USA (NVCA)

Project Preferences

Role in Financing:
Prefer role as deal originator but will also invest in deals created by others

Type of Financing Preferred:
Expansion
Generalist PE
Balanced
Later Stage
Acquisition

Geographical Preferences

United States Preferences:
North America

International Preferences:
Asia Pacific
Europe
Eastern Europe
Middle East
Africa

Industry Focus
(% based on actual investment)

Computer Software and Services	66.4%
Internet Specific	29.3%
Computer Hardware	2.2%
Other Products	1.7%
Communications and Media	0.2%
Medical/Health	0.1%
Industrial/Energy	0.0%
Biotechnology	0.0%
Consumer Related	0.0%

Additional Information
Name of Most Recent Fund: Insight Venture Partners VIII, L.P.
Most Recent Fund Was Raised: 05/29/2013
Year Founded: 1995
Capital Under Management: $13,211,400,000
Current Activity Level : Actively seeking new investments
Method of Compensation: Return on investment is of primary concern, do not charge fees

INSIGNIA CAPITAL GROUP LP

Two Walnut Creek Center
200 Pringle Avenue, Suite 400
Point Reyes Station, CA USA 94956
Phone: 9253998900
Fax: 9252741609
Website: www.insigniacap.com

Type of Firm
Private Equity Firm

Project Preferences

Type of Financing Preferred:
Later Stage
Management Buyouts
Acquisition
Recapitalizations

Geographical Preferences

United States Preferences:
North America

Additional Information
Name of Most Recent Fund: Insignia Capital Partners, L.P.
Most Recent Fund Was Raised: 06/05/2013
Year Founded: 2011
Capital Under Management: $358,000,000
Current Activity Level : Actively seeking new investments

INSIGNIA VENTURES PARTNERS PTE LTD

#04-87 Midview City
22 Sin Ming Lane
Singapore, Singapore 573969

Type of Firm
Private Equity Firm

Project Preferences

Type of Financing Preferred:
Startup

Geographical Preferences

International Preferences:
Asia Pacific

Additional Information
Year Founded: 2017
Capital Under Management: $25,000,000
Current Activity Level : Actively seeking new investments

INSPIRATION VENTURES LLC

228 Lorton Avenue
Suite Eight
Burlingame, CA USA 94010
Website: www.inspirationventures.com

Management and Staff
Gady Nemirovsky, General Partner
Robert Fanini, General Partner

Type of Firm
Private Equity Firm

Project Preferences

Type of Financing Preferred:
Seed
Startup

Additional Information
Year Founded: 2008
Capital Under Management: $10,000,000
Current Activity Level : Actively seeking new investments

INSPIRE CORP

5-3-10 Minami-Aoyma Minato-ku
3F FROM-1st
Tokyo, Japan 107-0062
Phone: 81364181090
Fax: 81364181092
E-mail: info@inspirecorp.co.jp
Website: www.inspirecorp.co.jp

Type of Firm
Private Equity Firm

Geographical Preferences

International Preferences:
Malaysia

Additional Information
Year Founded: 2000
Capital Under Management: $46,985,000
Current Activity Level : Actively seeking new investments

INSTITUT DE DEVELOPPEMENT ECONOMIQUE DE LA BOURGOGNE SA

5 Avenue Garibaldi
BP 1449
Dijon, France 21000
Phone: 33380600800
Fax: 33380600804
Website: www.ideb.fr

Type of Firm
Private Equity Firm

Project Preferences

Type of Financing Preferred:
Leveraged Buyout
Early Stage
Generalist PE
Later Stage
Acquisition

Size of Investments Considered:
Min Size of Investment Considered (000s): $98
Max Size of Investment Considered (000s): $656

Geographical Preferences

International Preferences:
Europe
France

Additional Information
Year Founded: 1984
Current Activity Level : Actively seeking new investments

INSTITUT LORRAIN DE PARTICIPATION SA

3 rue Marconi
Batiment Ecotech
Metz, France 57070
Phone: 33387759350
Fax: 33387759351
E-mail: contact@ilp-sadepar.com
Website: www.ilp-sadepar.com

Type of Firm
Private Equity Firm

Association Membership
French Venture Capital Association (AFIC)

Project Preferences

Type of Financing Preferred:
Leveraged Buyout
Early Stage
Generalist PE
Later Stage
Seed
Acquisition
Startup

Size of Investments Considered:
Min Size of Investment Considered (000s): $129
Max Size of Investment Considered (000s): $19,412

Geographical Preferences

International Preferences:
Europe
France

Industry Preferences

In Biotechnology prefer:
Biotechnology

In Industrial/Energy prefer:
Energy

In Business Serv. prefer:
Services

In Other prefer:
Environment Responsible

Additional Information
Year Founded: 1983
Capital Under Management: $24,700,000
Current Activity Level : Actively seeking new investments

INSTITUTIONAL GLOBAL INVESTORS LLC

One Letterman Drive
Suite 200, Building C
San Francisco, CA USA 94129
Website: www.iginvestors.com

Management and Staff
John Dominguez, Co-Founder
Kirk Dizon, Co-Founder

Type of Firm
Private Equity Advisor or Fund of Funds

Project Preferences

Type of Financing Preferred:
Fund of Funds

Geographical Preferences

International Preferences:
Asia Pacific
China

Additional Information
Year Founded: 2012
Current Activity Level : Actively seeking new investments

INSTITUTIONAL VENTURE PARTNERS

3000 Sand Hill Road
Building Two, Suite 250
Menlo Park, CA USA 94025
Phone: 6508540132
Fax: 6508542009
Website: www.ivp.com

Other Offices
607 Front Street
SAN FRANCISCO, CA USA 94111
Phone: 4154324660
Fax: 4154324679

Management and Staff
Dennis Phelps, General Partner
Eric Liaw, General Partner
J. Sanford Miller, General Partner
Jules Maltz, General Partner
Norman Fogelsong, Partner
Roseanne Wincek, Principal
Somesh Dash, General Partner
Stephen Harrick, General Partner
Thomas Loverro, Principal
Todd Chaffee, General Partner
Tracy Hogan, Chief Financial Officer

Type of Firm
Private Equity Firm

Association Membership
Western Association of Venture Capitalists (WAVC)
National Venture Capital Association - USA (NVCA)

Project Preferences

Role in Financing:
Will function either as deal originator or investor in deals created by others

Type of Financing Preferred:
Expansion
Public Companies
Later Stage
Industry Rollups
Recapitalizations

Size of Investments Considered:
Min Size of Investment Considered (000s): $10,000
Max Size of Investment Considered (000s): $100,000

Geographical Preferences

United States Preferences:

Industry Focus

(% based on actual investment)
Internet Specific	40.0%
Computer Software and Services	28.0%
Communications and Media	8.7%
Medical/Health	5.6%
Computer Hardware	5.0%
Semiconductors/Other Elect.	4.7%
Biotechnology	3.0%
Other Products	2.6%
Consumer Related	2.1%
Industrial/Energy	0.3%

Additional Information
Name of Most Recent Fund: Institutional Venture Partners XIV, L.P.
Most Recent Fund Was Raised: 06/28/2012
Year Founded: 1980
Capital Under Management: $5,400,000,000
Current Activity Level : Actively seeking new investments
Method of Compensation: Return on investment is of primary concern, do not charge fees

INSTITUTO ARAGONES DE FOMENTO

Teniente Coronel Valenzuela, 9
Zaragoza, Spain 50004
Phone: 34-97-670-2100
Fax: 34-97-670-2103
E-mail: info@iaf.es
Website: www.iaf.es

Type of Firm
Private Equity Firm

Project Preferences

Type of Financing Preferred:
Expansion
Seed

Geographical Preferences

International Preferences:
Italy
Portugal
Spain
France

Industry Preferences

In Semiconductor/Electr prefer:
Electronics

In Consumer Related prefer:
Food/Beverage

In Industrial/Energy prefer:
Industrial Products

In Transportation prefer:
Transportation

In Manufact. prefer:
Manufacturing

Additional Information
Year Founded: 2004
Current Activity Level : Actively seeking new investments

INTEGRAL CAPITAL PARTNERS

2750 Sand Hill Road
Menlo Park, CA USA 94025
Phone: 6502330360
Website: www.icp.com

Other Offices
100 East Pratt Street
Suite 1520
BALTIMORE, MD USA 21202
Phone: 4438720880

Management and Staff
Brian Stansky, Managing Director
Charles Morris, Managing Director
John Powell, Managing Director
Pamela Hagenah, Managing Director

Type of Firm
Private Equity Firm

Project Preferences

Type of Financing Preferred:
Leveraged Buyout
Generalist PE
Balanced

Additional Information
Name of Most Recent Fund: Integral Capital Partners VII, L.P.
Most Recent Fund Was Raised: 05/18/2005
Year Founded: 1991
Current Activity Level : Actively seeking new investments

INTEGRAL CORP

1-11-1 Marunouchi, Chiyoda-Ku
30/F, Pacific Century Place
Tokyo, Japan 100-6230
Phone: 81362127301
Fax: 81362127302
E-mail: info@integralkk.com
Website: www.integralkk.com

Management and Staff
Aisaku Suzuki, Partner
Kensaku Mizutani, Partner
Makiko Hayase, Vice President
Nobuo Sayama, Partner
Reijiro Yamamoto, Partner
Takashi Kokubo, Vice President
Tsuyoshi Yamazaki, Vice President
Yasunari Katakura, Vice President
Yoshihiro Hemmi, Partner

Type of Firm
Private Equity Firm

Project Preferences

Type of Financing Preferred:
Leveraged Buyout
Mezzanine
Management Buyouts
Acquisition

Geographical Preferences

International Preferences:
Asia
Japan

Additional Information
Year Founded: 2007
Capital Under Management: $668,020,000
Current Activity Level : Actively seeking new investments

INTEGRAL INVESTMENT MANAGEMENT ADVISORY SHANGHAI CO LTD

333 Huaihai Middle Rd. Huangpu
Room 1110
Shanghai, China 200052
Phone: 862163866677

Type of Firm
Private Equity Firm

Project Preferences

Type of Financing Preferred:
Early Stage
Seed
Startup

Geographical Preferences

International Preferences:
China

Industry Preferences

In Internet Specific prefer:
Internet

In Medical/Health prefer:
Medical/Health

In Consumer Related prefer:
Consumer

Additional Information
Year Founded: 2011
Capital Under Management: $300,000,000
Current Activity Level : Actively seeking new investments

INTEGRATED PARTNERS

70 University Avenue
Suite 1200
Toronto, Canada M5J 2M4
Phone: 4163607667
Fax: 4163607446
E-mail: info@iamgroup.ca
Website: www.iamgroup.ca

Other Offices

130 Adelaide Street West
Suite 2200
Toronto, Canada M5H 3P5
Phone: 4163607667
Fax: 4163607446

Management and Staff

John Robertson, President & COO
Paul Patterson, Vice President
Stephen Johnson, Chief Financial Officer

Type of Firm

Bank Affiliated

Project Preferences

Type of Financing Preferred:
Leveraged Buyout
Expansion
Mezzanine
Turnaround
Opportunistic
Later Stage
Management Buyouts
Acquisition
Private Placement
Recapitalizations

Geographical Preferences

United States Preferences:
North America

Canadian Preferences:
All Canada

Industry Preferences

In Financial Services prefer:
Real Estate

Additional Information
Name of Most Recent Fund: Integrated Private Debt Fund IV, L.P.
Most Recent Fund Was Raised: 07/30/2013
Year Founded: 1998
Capital Under Management: $1,480,005,000
Current Activity Level : Actively seeking new investments

INTEL CAPITAL CORP

2200 Mission College Boulevard
RN6-37
Santa Clara, CA USA 95052
Phone: 4087658080
Fax: 4087651399
E-mail: intelcapital@intel.com
Website: www.intelcapital.com

Other Offices

88 Queensway
32 Floor Two Pacific Place
Central, Hong Kong
Phone: 852-2844-4555
Fax: 852-2868-1989

3-1-1 Marunouchi, Chiyoda-ku
Kokusai Bldg. 5F
Tokyo, Japan 100-0005
Phone: 81-3-5223-9100
Fax: 81-3-5223-9171

Al. Jerozolimskie 146c
Warszawa, Poland 02-305
Phone: 48-22-570-8130

126-130 Regent Street
Carrington House
London, United Kingdom W1B 5SE
Phone: 44-20-7292-8780

Plot No. 62, 7th Floor, Raheja Tower
G Block Bandra Kurla Complex, Bandra(E)
Mumbai, India 400 052
Phone: 91-22-659-8811
Fax: 91-22-659-8809

55/F Shun Hing Square Di Wang
5002 Shennan Road 44
Shenzhen, China 830002

#136, Airport Road
Karnataka
Bangalore, India 560017
Phone: 91-80-2507-5000

Management and Staff

Ameet Bhansali, Vice President
Anthony Lin, Managing Director
Anupam Srivastava, Managing Director
Bob Nunn, Managing Director
Bryan Wolf, Vice President
Curt Nichols, Vice President
David Flanagan, Vice President
David Thomas, Vice President
Jose-Maria Blanc, Vice President
Keith Larson, Vice President
Ken Elefant, Managing Director
Lee Sessions, Managing Director
Marc Yi, Vice President
Marcin Hejka, Vice President
Mark Lydon, Managing Director
Michael Scown, Managing Director
Mike Buckley, Managing Director
Ramamurthy Sivakumar, Vice President
Trina Van Pelt, Vice President
Wendell Brooks, President

Type of Firm

Corporate PE/Venture

Association Membership

Brazilian Venture Capital Association (ABCR)
British Venture Capital Association (BVCA)
Israel Venture Association
National Venture Capital Association - USA (NVCA)
Polish Venture Capital Association (PSIC/PPEA)

Project Preferences

Type of Financing Preferred:
Early Stage
Expansion
Balanced
Seed
Startup

Size of Investments Considered:
Min Size of Investment Considered (000s): $5,000
Max Size of Investment Considered (000s): $10,000

Geographical Preferences

United States Preferences:

International Preferences:
Latin America
India
Turkey
Europe
China
Middle East
Israel
Asia
Japan
Russia

Industry Preferences

In Communications prefer:
Communications and Media

In Computer Hardware prefer:
Computers
Mini and Personal/Desktop

In Computer Software prefer:
Software
Systems Software
Applications Software

In Internet Specific prefer:
Internet

In Semiconductor/Electr prefer:
Semiconductor

In Medical/Health prefer:
Health Services

In Consumer Related prefer:
Consumer

In Industrial/Energy prefer:
Energy Conservation Relat

In Business Serv. prefer:
Services
Media

In Manufact. prefer:
Manufacturing

In Other prefer:
Environment Responsible

Additional Information
Year Founded: 1991
Capital Under Management: $4,000,000,000
Current Activity Level: Actively seeking new investments

INTELLAGRI SA

Voie du Toec
Toulouse, France 31076
Phone: 33561153030
Fax: 33561153060

Type of Firm
Private Equity Firm

Project Preferences

Type of Financing Preferred:
Early Stage
Seed
Startup

Size of Investments Considered:
Min Size of Investment Considered (000s): $13
Max Size of Investment Considered (000s): $130

Geographical Preferences

International Preferences:
Europe
Eastern Europe
France

Industry Preferences

In Communications prefer:
Telecommunications
Wireless Communications
Data Communications

In Computer Software prefer:
Software

In Business Serv. prefer:
Services

In Agr/Forestr/Fish prefer:
Agriculture related

Additional Information
Year Founded: 1988
Current Activity Level: Actively seeking new investments

INTELLECTUAL DISCOVERY VENTURES

312, Teheran-ro, Gangnam-gu
10/F, Vision Tower
Seoul, South Korea
Phone: 8225569300
Fax: 8225560062
E-mail: info@id-vc.com
Website: www.id-vc.com

Management and Staff
Sang Gyeong Yoon, Managing Director
Seok Hwan Jang, Chief Executive Officer

Type of Firm
Private Equity Firm

Association Membership
Korean Venture Capital Association (KVCA)

Project Preferences

Type of Financing Preferred:
Early Stage
Expansion
Startup

Additional Information
Year Founded: 2012
Capital Under Management: $12,255,000
Current Activity Level: Actively seeking new investments

INTELLISYS CAPITAL LLC

187 Monroe Avenue NW Grand
Grand Rapids, MI USA 49503
Phone: 6164269284
E-mail: hello@intellisys.ai

Type of Firm
Private Equity Firm

Project Preferences

Type of Financing Preferred:
Generalist PE

Geographical Preferences

United States Preferences:

Additional Information
Year Founded: 2016
Current Activity Level: Actively seeking new investments

INTER INVEST CAPITAL SAS

40, Rue de Courcelles
Paris, France 75008
Phone: 33156620055

Type of Firm
Private Equity Firm

Project Preferences

Type of Financing Preferred:
Early Stage
Expansion
Later Stage

Geographical Preferences

International Preferences:
Europe
France

Additional Information
Year Founded: 2015
Current Activity Level: Actively seeking new investments

INTER RISCO SOCIEDADE DE CAPITAL DE RISCO SA

Avenida da Boavisa 1081
Porto, Portugal 4100129
Phone: 351220126700
Fax: 351220126718
E-mail: inter-risco@inter-risco.pt
Website: www.inter-risco.pt

Type of Firm
Bank Affiliated

Association Membership
Portuguese Venture Capital Association (APCRI)

Project Preferences

Role in Financing:
Prefer role as deal originator

Type of Financing Preferred:
Leveraged Buyout
Early Stage
Expansion
Generalist PE
Balanced
Seed
Acquisition

Size of Investments Considered:
Min Size of Investment Considered (000s): $4,338
Max Size of Investment Considered (000s): $27,259

Geographical Preferences

International Preferences:
Portugal

Industry Preferences

In Communications prefer:
Communications and Media

In Medical/Health prefer:
Medical/Health

In Industrial/Energy prefer:
Industrial Products

Additional Information

Year Founded: 1988
Capital Under Management: $70,200,000
Current Activity Level : Actively seeking new investments

INTER-AMERICAN INVESTMENT CORP

1350 New York Avenue, NW
Washington, DC USA 20577
Website: www.iic.org

Management and Staff

Steven Reed, Managing Director

Type of Firm

Incubator/Development Program

Project Preferences

Type of Financing Preferred:
Fund of Funds
Generalist PE

Geographical Preferences

International Preferences:
Latin America

Additional Information

Year Founded: 1986
Current Activity Level : Actively seeking new investments

INTERA EQUITY PARTNERS OY

Etelaesplanadi 18
Helsinki, Finland 00130
Phone: 358925252200
Fax: 358925252210
Website: www.interapartners.fi

Management and Staff

Harri Hollmen, Partner
Jokke Paananen, Partner
Martin Grotenfelt, Partner
Tuomas Lang, Managing Partner

Type of Firm

Private Equity Firm

Association Membership

Finnish Venture Capital Association (FVCA)

Project Preferences

Type of Financing Preferred:
Leveraged Buyout
Management Buyouts
Acquisition

Size of Investments Considered:
Min Size of Investment Considered (000s): $6,000
Max Size of Investment Considered (000s): $18,000

Geographical Preferences

International Preferences:
Scandanavia/Nordic Region
Finland

Industry Preferences

In Communications prefer:
Telecommunications

In Computer Other prefer:
Computer Related

In Semiconductor/Electr prefer:
Electronics

In Biotechnology prefer:
Biotechnology

In Medical/Health prefer:
Health Services
Hospitals/Clinics/Primary

In Industrial/Energy prefer:
Energy
Industrial Products

In Transportation prefer:
Transportation

In Business Serv. prefer:
Services

In Manufact. prefer:
Manufacturing

Additional Information

Name of Most Recent Fund: Intera Fund II Ky
Most Recent Fund Was Raised: 04/20/2011
Year Founded: 2007
Capital Under Management: $458,200,000
Current Activity Level : Actively seeking new investments

INTERLEADER CAPITAL LTD

18/F, 8 Wyndham Street
Central, Hong Kong
Phone: 852-2156-8876
Fax: 852-2156-8870
E-mail: info@interleadercapital.com
Website: www.interleadercapital.com

Management and Staff

Cliff Cheung, Chief Executive Officer

Type of Firm

Private Equity Firm

Association Membership

Hong Kong Venture Capital Association (HKVCA)

Project Preferences

Type of Financing Preferred:
Generalist PE

Geographical Preferences

International Preferences:
China

Industry Preferences

In Financial Services prefer:
Real Estate

Additional Information

Year Founded: 2009
Current Activity Level : Actively seeking new investments

INTERMEDIATE CAPITAL GROUP PLC

100, St Paul's Churchyard
Juxon House
London, United Kingdom EC4M 8BU
Phone: 442032017700
Fax: 442072482536
E-mail: mcr@icgplc.com
Website: www.icgam.com

Other Offices

15 Queen's Road
36th Floor, Edinburgh Tower
Central, Hong Kong
Phone: 852-2297-3080
Fax: 852-2297-3081

12. Stockwerk
An der Welle 5
Frankfurt, Germany 60322
Phone: 49-69-2549-7650
Fax: 49-69-2549-7699

88 Phillip Street
Level 18
Sydney, Australia 2000
Phone: 612-9241-5525
Fax: 612-9241-5526

Serrano, 30-3
Madrid, Spain 28001
Phone: 34-91-310-7200
Fax: 34-91-310-7201

250 Park Avenue, Suite 810
New York, NY USA 10177
Phone: 212-710-9650
Fax: 212-710-9651

Biger Jarlsgatan 13
ltr
Stockholm, Sweden 111 45
Phone: 46-8-5450-4150
Fax: 46-8-5450-4151

Paulus Potterstraat 20 II/III
Amsterdam, Netherlands 1071 DA
Phone: 31-20-305-9600
Fax: 31-20-302-9620

38 Avenue Hoche
Paris, France 75008
Phone: 33-1-4495-8686
Fax: 33-1-4495-8687

Management and Staff
Benoit Durteste, Chief Executive Officer
Philip Keller, Chief Financial Officer

Type of Firm
Private Equity Firm

Association Membership
Hong Kong Venture Capital Association (HKVCA)
French Venture Capital Association (AFIC)
European Private Equity and Venture Capital Assoc.
Singapore Venture Capital Association (SVCA)
Spanish Venture Capital Association (ASCRI)

Project Preferences

Role in Financing:
Will function either as deal originator or investor in deals created by others

Type of Financing Preferred:
Leveraged Buyout
Expansion
Mezzanine
Balanced
Turnaround
Management Buyouts

Size of Investments Considered:
Min Size of Investment Considered (000s): $4,478
Max Size of Investment Considered (000s): $298,540

Geographical Preferences

United States Preferences:

International Preferences:
United Kingdom
New Zealand
Asia
Korea, South

Industry Focus
(% based on actual investment)
Consumer Related	35.0%
Other Products	27.2%
Industrial/Energy	14.6%
Medical/Health	10.1%
Computer Software and Services	6.3%
Semiconductors/Other Elect.	4.4%
Internet Specific	2.2%
Communications and Media	0.2%
Biotechnology	0.1%

Additional Information
Name of Most Recent Fund: ICG-Longbow UK Real Estate Debt Investments III
Most Recent Fund Was Raised: 12/31/2012
Year Founded: 1989
Capital Under Management: $16,900,000
Current Activity Level : Actively seeking new investments
Method of Compensation: Return on invest. most important, but chg. closing fees, service fees, etc.

INTERNATIONAL ACCELERATOR INC

8121 Bee Cave Road Suite 150
Austin, TX USA 78746
Phone: 15122259333
Fax: 15122790964
E-mail: hello@internationalaccelerator.com
Website: www.internationalaccelerator.com

Type of Firm
Incubator/Development Program

Project Preferences

Type of Financing Preferred:
Seed
Startup

Geographical Preferences

International Preferences:
All International

Industry Preferences

In Computer Software prefer:
Artificial Intelligence

Additional Information
Year Founded: 2016
Current Activity Level : Actively seeking new investments

INTERNATIONAL BUSINESS MACHINES CORP

One New Orchard Road
Armonk, NY USA 10504
Phone: 9144991900
Website: www.ibm.com

Management and Staff
Ahuva Kamar-Vardi, Partner
Ann Scheman, Partner
Claudia Munce, Managing Director
Deborah Magid, Partner
Donna Ewart, Partner
Drew Clark, Partner
Hisashi Katsuya, Partner
Jani Byrne, Partner
Martin Kelly, Partner
Matthew Denesuk, Partner
Savitha Srinivasan, Partner
Wendy Lung, Partner

Type of Firm
Corporate PE/Venture

Association Membership
Brazilian Venture Capital Association (ABCR)
Israel Venture Association
National Venture Capital Association - USA (NVCA)

Project Preferences

Role in Financing:
Prefer role in deals created by others

Type of Financing Preferred:
Early Stage
Balanced
Fund of Funds of Second

Industry Preferences

In Communications prefer:
Communications and Media

In Computer Software prefer:
Software

In Internet Specific prefer:
Internet

In Biotechnology prefer:
Biotechnology

In Financial Services prefer:
Financial Services

Additional Information
Year Founded: 2000
Capital Under Management: $500,000,000
Current Activity Level : Actively seeking new investments

INTERNATIONAL FINANCE CORP

2121 Pennsylvania Avenue, NW
Washington, DC USA 20433
Phone: 2024733800
Fax: 2029744384
E-mail: VC@ifc.org
Website: www.ifc.org

Other Offices

14th Floor, One Pacific Place
88 Queensway, Admiralty
Hong Kong, Hong Kong
Phone: 852-2509-8100
Fax: 852-2509-9363

50-M, Shanti Path, Gate No. 3
Niti Marg, Chanakyapuri
New Delhi, India 110 021
Phone: 91-11-4111-1000
Fax: 91-11-4111-1001

Kanyon Ofis Blogu Kat 10
Levent
Istanbul, Turkey 34394
Phone: 90-212-385-3000
Fax: 90-212-385-3001

P.O. Box 41283
Craighall, South Africa 2024
Phone: 27-11-731-9000

14 Fricker Road
Illovo
Johannesburg, South Africa 2196
Phone: 27-11-731-300
Fax: 27-11-268-0074

36, Bldg. 1 Bolshaya Molchanovka St.
Third Floor
Moscow, Russia 121069
Phone: 7495-411-7555
Fax: 7495-411-7556

Management and Staff

Bernard Lauwers, Vice President
Bernie Sheahan, Vice President
Dimitris Tsitsiragos, Vice President
Hans Lankes, Vice President
James Scriven, Vice President
Jingdong Hua, Vice President
Karin Finkelston, Vice President
Mohamed Gouled, Vice President
Philippe Le Houerou, Chief Executive Officer
Saran Kebet-Koulibaly, Vice President
Stephanie von Friedeburg, Vice President

Type of Firm

Bank Affiliated

Association Membership

Gulf Venture Capital Association
Emerging Markets Private Equity Association

Project Preferences

Type of Financing Preferred:
Fund of Funds
Leveraged Buyout
Generalist PE
Balanced
Acquisition
Recapitalizations

Size of Investments Considered:
Min Size of Investment Considered (000s): $1,000
Max Size of Investment Considered (000s): $100,000

Geographical Preferences

International Preferences:
Latin America
Eastern Europe
Middle East
Asia
Africa

Industry Preferences

In Communications prefer:
Telecommunications

In Medical/Health prefer:
Medical/Health
Health Services
Hospitals/Clinics/Primary

In Consumer Related prefer:
Food/Beverage
Education Related

In Industrial/Energy prefer:
Energy
Environmental Related

In Transportation prefer:
Transportation

In Financial Services prefer:
Financial Services
Insurance
Financial Services

In Agr/Forestr/Fish prefer:
Agribusiness

In Other prefer:
Environment Responsible

Additional Information

Name of Most Recent Fund: IFC Global Infrastructure Fund
Most Recent Fund Was Raised: 04/16/2013
Year Founded: 1956
Capital Under Management: $2,450,000,000
Current Activity Level : Actively seeking new investments

INTERNATIONAL INVESTMENT AND UNDERWRITING

Custom House Quay
Int'l Fin Services Ctr House
Dublin, Ireland
Phone: 35316054444
Website: www.iiu.ie

Management and Staff

Dermot Desmond, Founder

Type of Firm

Private Equity Firm

Project Preferences

Type of Financing Preferred:
Balanced

Industry Preferences

In Consumer Related prefer:
Entertainment and Leisure
Food/Beverage

In Transportation prefer:
Transportation

Additional Information

Year Founded: 1995
Current Activity Level : Actively seeking new investments

INTERNATIONAL MAGHREB MERCHANT

87 Avenue Jugurtha
Mutuelleville
Tunis, Tunisia 1082
Phone: 21671800266
Fax: 21671800410
E-mail: imbank@imbank.com.tn
Website: www.imbank.com.tn

Management and Staff

Abderrahmen Hadjnaceur, Partner
Adel Dajani, Partner
Kacem Bousnina, Partner
Oliver Pastre, President, Founder
Reyda Ferid Benbouzid, Partner

Type of Firm

Bank Affiliated

Project Preferences

Type of Financing Preferred:
Early Stage
Later Stage

Geographical Preferences

International Preferences:
Tunisia
Algeria
Morocco
Libya

Industry Preferences

In Communications prefer:
Telecommunications
Entertainment

In Industrial/Energy prefer:
Industrial Products

Additional Information

Year Founded: 1995
Current Activity Level : Actively seeking new investments

INTERNET ATTITUDE SCRL

14, Rue de Mouhin
Waremme, Belgium 4300
Phone: 32476342990
Website: www.internet-attitude.eu

Type of Firm
Private Equity Firm

Project Preferences

Type of Financing Preferred:
Early Stage
Seed

Size of Investments Considered:
Min Size of Investment Considered (000s): $555
Max Size of Investment Considered (000s): $1,111

Geographical Preferences

International Preferences:
Europe
Belgium

Industry Preferences

In Computer Software prefer:
Software

In Internet Specific prefer:
Internet

Additional Information
Year Founded: 2010
Current Activity Level : Actively seeking new investments

INTERNET VENTURES SCANDINAVIA

Noerre Farimagsgade 13, 1. Th.
Copenhagen, Denmark 1364
Phone: 4570224020
Fax: 4570141632
E-mail: info@northcappartners.com
Website: www.northcap.vc

Other Offices

6 Arcsa Road
Richmond Bridge, East Twickenham
Middlesex, United Kingdom TW1 2TL
Phone: 44-181-408-2041

10420 Little Patuxent Parkway
Suite 301
Columbia, MD USA 21044-3636
Phone: 410-884-1700
Fax: 410-884-6171

Surenweg 6
Walchwil, Switzerland 6318
Phone: 41-417-581-422
Fax: 41-417-581-588

c/o InnovationLab
Finlandsgade 20
Arhus, Denmark 8200

Management and Staff
Benny Guld, Founder
Frank Ewald, Partner
Peter Aagaard, Partner
Preben Mejer, Partner
Soren Fogtdal, Partner
Steen Reinholdt, Founder
Sten Larsen, Chief Financial Officer
Thomas Weilby Knudsen, Chief Executive Officer

Type of Firm
Private Equity Firm

Association Membership
Danish Venture Capital Association (DVCA)

Project Preferences

Type of Financing Preferred:
Early Stage
Balanced
Seed
Startup

Size of Investments Considered:
Min Size of Investment Considered (000s): $250
Max Size of Investment Considered (000s): $2,500

Geographical Preferences

United States Preferences:

International Preferences:
Sweden
Europe
Denmark

Industry Preferences

In Communications prefer:
Commercial Communications
Telecommunications
Wireless Communications

In Computer Software prefer:
Software

In Internet Specific prefer:
Internet

Additional Information
Year Founded: 1999
Capital Under Management: $77,300,000
Current Activity Level : Actively seeking new investments

INTERSACTION VENTURES BV

7, Huizerweg
Blaricum, Netherlands 1261 AR
Phone: 31355392410
Website: http://intersection.ventures/

Type of Firm
Private Equity Firm

Project Preferences

Type of Financing Preferred:
Leveraged Buyout
Management Buyouts
Acquisition
Recapitalizations

Geographical Preferences

International Preferences:
Netherlands

Additional Information
Year Founded: 2014
Current Activity Level : Actively seeking new investments

INTERSOUTH PARTNERS

102 City Hall Plaza, Suite 200
Durham, NC USA 27701
Phone: 9194936640
Fax: 9194936649
E-mail: contact@intersouth.com
Website: www.intersouth.com

Management and Staff
Dennis Dougherty, Partner
John Glushik, Partner
Kay Burgess, Chief Financial Officer
Mitchell Mumma, Partner
Philip Tracy, Partner
Richard Kent, Partner

Type of Firm
Private Equity Firm

Association Membership
National Venture Capital Association - USA (NVCA)

Project Preferences

Role in Financing:
Prefer role as deal originator but will also invest in deals created by others

Type of Financing Preferred:
Early Stage
Seed

Size of Investments Considered:
Min Size of Investment Considered (000s): $500
Max Size of Investment Considered (000s): $12,000

Geographical Preferences

United States Preferences:
Mid Atlantic
Southeast
North Carolina
Maryland
Florida
Washington
Georgia

Industry Focus

(% based on actual investment)

Biotechnology	28.7%
Medical/Health	25.5%
Computer Software and Services	18.7%
Computer Hardware	6.7%
Internet Specific	6.4%
Semiconductors/Other Elect.	5.3%
Communications and Media	4.4%
Industrial/Energy	3.2%
Consumer Related	0.9%
Other Products	0.2%

Additional Information

Name of Most Recent Fund: Intersouth Partners VII, L.P.
Most Recent Fund Was Raised: 05/26/2006
Year Founded: 1985
Capital Under Management: $780,000,000
Current Activity Level : Actively seeking new investments
Method of Compensation: Return on investment is of primary concern, do not charge fees

INTERUNIVERSITAIR MI-CRO-ELECTRONICA CENTRUM

Kapeldreef 75
Leuven, Belgium 3001
Phone: 3216281211
Fax: 3216289400
Website: www2.imec.be

Other Offices

2225, E. Bayshore Road, Ste 209
Palo Alto, CA USA 94303
Phone: 4085514502
Fax: 4085514505

Unit A6,1F,No.1, Li-Hsin 1st Road
Hsinchu Science Park
Hsinchu City 300, Taiwan
Phone: 88635781115
Fax: 88635781551

5-4 Nibancho, Chiyoda-ku
Tokyo, Japan 102-0084
Phone: 81352105882
Fax: 81352105883

Room 701, Building 1,
Lane 500, Zhangheng Road,Pudong
Shanghai, China 201203
Phone: 862150172918
Fax: 862150192619

Management and Staff

Andre Vinck, Chief Financial Officer

Type of Firm

Incubator/Development Program

Project Preferences

Type of Financing Preferred:
Seed
Startup

Geographical Preferences

International Preferences:
Europe

Additional Information

Year Founded: 1982
Current Activity Level : Actively seeking new investments

INTERVALE CAPITAL LLC

20 University Road
Suite 360
Cambridge, MA USA 02138
Phone: 6174978282
E-mail: info@intervalecapital.com
Website: www.intervalecapital.com

Other Offices

2800 Post Oak Boulevard, Suite 5220
Houston, TX USA 77056
Phone: 713-961-0118
Fax: 713-961-0361

Management and Staff

Charles Cherington, Co-Founder
Christine Smoragiewicz, Chief Financial Officer
David Nemeskal, Principal
Erich Horsley, Partner
Jason Turowsky, Partner
Jason Arnoldy, Vice President
Patrick Conroy, Vice President
Patrick Connelly, Partner
Phil Wilson, Vice President
Sam Gurwitz, Vice President
Tuan Tran, Principal

Type of Firm

Private Equity Firm

Project Preferences

Type of Financing Preferred:
Leveraged Buyout
Expansion
Other
Acquisition
Recapitalizations

Geographical Preferences

United States Preferences:
North America
All U.S.

Canadian Preferences:
All Canada

International Preferences:
Europe

Industry Preferences

In Industrial/Energy prefer:
Energy
Oil and Gas Exploration
Oil & Gas Drilling,Explor

In Business Serv. prefer:
Services

In Manufact. prefer:
Manufacturing

Additional Information

Name of Most Recent Fund: Intervale Capital Fund III, L.P.
Most Recent Fund Was Raised: 02/25/2014
Year Founded: 2006
Capital Under Management: $25,000,000
Current Activity Level : Actively seeking new investments

INTERVEST CO LTD

Samseong-dong
1404 Trade Tower, Gangnam-gu
Seoul, South Korea 135729
Phone: 8225517340
Fax: 8225517350
E-mail: admin@intervest.co.kr

Other Offices

No.1 Science Centre Road
#08-01 The Enterprise
Singapore, Singapore 609077
Phone: 65-6822-3491
Fax: 65-3822-3490

Management and Staff

Myeng Ki Kim, Managing Director

Type of Firm

Private Equity Firm

Association Membership

Korean Venture Capital Association (KVCA)

Project Preferences

Type of Financing Preferred:
Early Stage
Expansion
Mezzanine
Balanced
Later Stage
Startup

Size of Investments Considered:
Min Size of Investment Considered (000s): $500
Max Size of Investment Considered (000s): $2,500

Geographical Preferences

International Preferences:
Asia
Singapore
Korea, South

Industry Preferences

In Communications prefer:
Telecommunications
Wireless Communications

In Computer Software prefer:
Software

In Internet Specific prefer:
Internet

In Semiconductor/Electr prefer:
Semiconductor

In Biotechnology prefer:
Biotechnology

In Industrial/Energy prefer:
Energy

Additional Information
Year Founded: 1999
Capital Under Management: $108,700,000
Current Activity Level : Actively seeking new investments

INTERWEST PARTNERS LLC

2710 Sand Hill Road, Suite 200
Menlo Park, CA USA 94025
Phone: 6508548585
Fax: 6508544706
E-mail: info@interwest.com
Website: www.interwest.com

Management and Staff
Arnie Oronsky, Managing Director
Bruce Cleveland, Managing Director
Douglas Fisher, Partner
Farah Champsi, Managing Director
Flip Gianos, Managing Director
Gilbert Kliman, General Partner
Karen Wilson, Chief Financial Officer
Keval Desai, Partner
Reza Zadno, Venture Partner
Stephen Holmes, General Partner

Type of Firm
Private Equity Firm

Association Membership
Western Association of Venture Capitalists (WAVC)
National Venture Capital Association - USA (NVCA)

Project Preferences

Role in Financing:
Prefer role as deal originator but will also invest in deals created by others

Type of Financing Preferred:
Early Stage
Balanced

Size of Investments Considered:
Min Size of Investment Considered (000s): $10,000
Max Size of Investment Considered (000s): $15,000

Industry Focus
(% based on actual investment)

Medical/Health	27.5%
Biotechnology	20.0%
Computer Software and Services	12.1%
Internet Specific	10.9%
Communications and Media	8.0%
Semiconductors/Other Elect.	7.2%
Computer Hardware	6.1%
Consumer Related	4.7%
Other Products	1.9%
Industrial/Energy	1.7%

Additional Information
Name of Most Recent Fund: InterWest Partners X, L.P.
Most Recent Fund Was Raised: 08/07/2008
Year Founded: 1979
Capital Under Management: $2,800,000,000
Current Activity Level : Actively seeking new investments
Method of Compensation: Return on investment is of primary concern, do not charge fees

INTESA SANPAOLO SPA

Piazza San Carlo 156
Torino, Italy 10121
Phone: 390115551
E-mail: info@bancaintesa.it
Website: www.group.intesasanpaolo.com

Management and Staff
Carlo Messina, Chief Executive Officer
Eliano Omar Lodesani, Chief Operating Officer
Stefano Del Punta, Chief Financial Officer

Type of Firm
Bank Affiliated

Association Membership
Italian Venture Capital Association (AIFI)

Project Preferences

Type of Financing Preferred:
Leveraged Buyout
Expansion
Turnaround
Later Stage
Startup

Geographical Preferences

International Preferences:
Italy
Russia

Additional Information
Name of Most Recent Fund: MIR Capital
Most Recent Fund Was Raised: 07/23/2012
Year Founded: 1998
Capital Under Management: $744,000,000
Current Activity Level : Actively seeking new investments

INTREPID VENTURE CAPITAL (PTY) LTD

2 Arnold Road
Rosebank, South Africa 2196
Phone: 27-11-283-0000
E-mail: shane.kidd@oba.co.uk

Type of Firm
Private Equity Firm

Project Preferences

Type of Financing Preferred:
Early Stage
Seed

Geographical Preferences

International Preferences:
South Africa

Additional Information
Year Founded: 2004
Current Activity Level : Actively seeking new investments

INTUITIS INVESTISSEURS PRIVES

16. rue de l'Abbe
Paris, France 75014
Website: www.intuitis.fr

Type of Firm
Private Equity Firm

Project Preferences

Type of Financing Preferred:
Leveraged Buyout
Management Buyouts

Geographical Preferences

International Preferences:
France

Industry Preferences

In Industrial/Energy prefer:
Energy
Industrial Products

In Transportation prefer:
Transportation

1142

In Business Serv. prefer:
Distribution

Additional Information
Year Founded: 2010
Current Activity Level : Actively seeking new investments

INTUITIVE VENTURE PARTNERS LLC

122 East, 42nd Street
Suite 1616
New York, NY USA 10168
Phone: 2126123221
Fax: 2126618786
E-mail: info@intuitivevp.com

Management and Staff
Aaron Segal, Partner
David Landskowsky, Partner
Eric Rubenstein, Partner
Scott Cardone, Partner
Timothy Herrmann, Partner
Todd Harrigan, Partner

Type of Firm
Private Equity Firm

Project Preferences

Type of Financing Preferred:
Expansion
Later Stage

Industry Preferences

In Medical/Health prefer:
Medical/Health

In Industrial/Energy prefer:
Energy

In Business Serv. prefer:
Media

Additional Information
Year Founded: 2010
Current Activity Level : Actively seeking new investments

INVENERGY FUTURE FUND MANAGER LLC

One South Wacker Drive
18th Floor
Chicago, IL USA 60606
Website: invenergyfuturefund.com

Type of Firm
Private Equity Firm

Project Preferences

Type of Financing Preferred:
Balanced

Industry Preferences

In Computer Software prefer:
Data Processing

In Industrial/Energy prefer:
Energy

In Business Serv. prefer:
Services

Additional Information
Year Founded: 2016
Current Activity Level : Actively seeking new investments

INVENI CAPITAL OY

Biomedicum Helsinki 2A
Tukholmankatu 8 A
Helsinki, Finland 00290
Website: www.invenicapital.com

Other Offices
Zweibrueckenstrasse 8
Munich, Germany 80331
Phone: 49-89-9218-5642

Management and Staff
Aki Prihti, Partner
Christina Wagner, Partner
Markku Jalkanen, Partner
Markku Fagerlund, Partner
Wolfgang Pieken, Partner

Type of Firm
Private Equity Firm

Association Membership
Finnish Venture Capital Association (FVCA)

Project Preferences

Type of Financing Preferred:
Early Stage

Geographical Preferences

International Preferences:
Europe
Finland
Germany

Industry Preferences

In Biotechnology prefer:
Biotechnology

In Medical/Health prefer:
Medical/Health
Medical Therapeutics
Pharmaceuticals

Additional Information
Year Founded: 2007
Capital Under Management: $40,400,000
Current Activity Level : Actively seeking new investments

INVENSHURE LLC

227 Colfax Avenue North
Suite 148
Minneapolis, MN USA 55405
Phone: 6125207361
E-mail: info@invenshure.com
Website: invenshure.com

Management and Staff
Mark Sylvester, Chief Financial Officer

Type of Firm
Incubator/Development Program

Project Preferences

Type of Financing Preferred:
Seed
Startup

Industry Preferences

In Communications prefer:
Wireless Communications

In Computer Software prefer:
Software

In Biotechnology prefer:
Biotech Related Research

In Medical/Health prefer:
Health Services

Additional Information
Year Founded: 2011
Current Activity Level : Actively seeking new investments

INVENT CAPITAL MX

Colonia Centro
Bucareli One, Fifth Floor
Mexico, Mexico 06600
Phone: 51283600
Website: www.capitalinvent.com

Type of Firm
Private Equity Firm

Project Preferences

Type of Financing Preferred:
Balanced

Geographical Preferences

International Preferences:
Mexico

Industry Preferences

In Communications prefer:
Telecommunications
Wireless Communications

In Internet Specific prefer:
Internet
Ecommerce

Additional Information
Year Founded: 2015
Current Activity Level : Actively seeking new investments

INVENT VENTURES INC

137 Bay Street
Suite One
Santa Monica, CA USA 90405
Phone: 7029430320
E-mail: info@invent.vc
Website: invent.vc

Management and Staff
Timothy Symington, Chief Executive Officer

Type of Firm
Incubator/Development Program

Project Preferences

Type of Financing Preferred:
Early Stage
Seed
Startup

Industry Preferences

In Communications prefer:
Communications and Media

In Internet Specific prefer:
Internet

In Biotechnology prefer:
Biotechnology

Additional Information
Year Founded: 2010
Current Activity Level : Actively seeking new investments

INVENTAGES VENTURE CAPITAL GMBH

Route de Coppet 26A
Commugny, Switzerland 1291
Phone: 41229607700
Fax: 41229607701
E-mail: contact@inventages.com
Website: www.inventages.com

Other Offices
Level 6, 2 Kitchener Street
Auckland, New Zealand 6466
Phone: 64-9-307-2562

158 Buckingham Palace Road
London, United Kingdom SW1W 9TR
Phone: 44-20-7730-0979
Fax: 44-20-7259-0386

West Bay street building 10
Office 4
Nassau, Bahamas 7532
Phone: 1-242-357-8278
Fax: 1-242-327-0096

Management and Staff
Bill Kermode, Partner
Denise DeBaun, Venture Partner
Gertrude Allen, Venture Partner
Goetz von Kalckreuth, Vice President
Herve Girsault, Venture Partner
Kees Lucas, Venture Partner
Thomas Bayerl, Venture Partner
Wolfgang Reichenberger, General Partner

Type of Firm
Private Equity Firm

Project Preferences

Type of Financing Preferred:
Early Stage
Later Stage
Seed
Startup

Geographical Preferences

United States Preferences:
All U.S.

International Preferences:
India
Europe
Switzerland
Australia
New Zealand
All International

Industry Preferences

In Biotechnology prefer:
Biotechnology
Agricultural/Animal Bio.

In Medical/Health prefer:
Medical/Health
Health Services
Pharmaceuticals

In Consumer Related prefer:
Retail
Food/Beverage

Additional Information
Year Founded: 2000
Capital Under Management: $1,500,000,000
Current Activity Level : Actively seeking new investments

INVENTURE OY

Etelaeranta Eight
Helsinki, Finland 00130
Phone: 358988601530
Fax: 358420399912

E-mail: info@inventure.fi
Website: www.inventure.fi

Management and Staff
Arve Lukander, Partner
Sami Lampinen, Managing Director
Timo Tirkkonen, Partner
Tuomas Kosonen, Partner

Type of Firm
Private Equity Firm

Association Membership
Finnish Venture Capital Association (FVCA)
European Private Equity and Venture Capital Assoc.

Project Preferences

Role in Financing:
Prefer role as deal originator

Type of Financing Preferred:
Early Stage
Seed
Startup

Size of Investments Considered:
Min Size of Investment Considered (000s): $1,300
Max Size of Investment Considered (000s): $4,200

Geographical Preferences

International Preferences:
Western Europe
Scandanavia/Nordic Region
Finland

Industry Preferences

In Communications prefer:
Communications and Media
Wireless Communications

In Computer Software prefer:
Software
Systems Software
Applications Software

In Internet Specific prefer:
Internet

In Computer Other prefer:
Computer Related

In Semiconductor/Electr prefer:
Electronics

In Manufact. prefer:
Manufacturing

Additional Information
Name of Most Recent Fund: Inventure Fund II
Most Recent Fund Was Raised: 01/07/2014
Year Founded: 2005
Capital Under Management: $137,100,000
Current Activity Level : Actively seeking new investments

INVENTURE PARTNERS

6/2 Presnenskaia Naberezhnaia
Office 608
Moscow, Russia 123317
Phone: 74956413635
Website: www.inventurepartners.com

Other Offices
96 Kensington High Street
London, United Kingdom W8 4SG

Type of Firm
Private Equity Firm

Project Preferences

Type of Financing Preferred:
Early Stage
Generalist PE
Balanced
Later Stage

Geographical Preferences

International Preferences:
Asia
Russia

Industry Preferences

In Computer Software prefer:
Software
Systems Software
Applications Software

In Internet Specific prefer:
Web Aggregation/Portals

In Computer Other prefer:
Computer Related

Additional Information
Year Founded: 2012
Current Activity Level : Actively seeking new investments

INVENTUS CAPITAL PARTNERS FUND I L P

C/o Anex Mgt. Services Ltd.
52 Cyber City
Ebene, Mauritius
Website: www.inventuscap.com

Other Offices
2735 Sand Hill Road
Menlo Park, CA USA 94025
Phone: 6502922530
Fax: 6502922570

1st Floor, G.R. Primus
69/1, 2nd Cross, Domlur
Bangalore, India 560 008
Phone: 918041256747

Management and Staff
John Dougery, Co-Founder
Kanwal Rekhi, Managing Director
Manu Rekhi, Partner
Parag Dhol, Managing Director
Rutvik Doshi, Partner
Samir Kumar, Managing Director

Type of Firm
Private Equity Firm

Association Membership
Indian Venture Capital Association (IVCA)

Project Preferences

Role in Financing:
Prefer role as deal originator but will also invest in deals created by others

Type of Financing Preferred:
Second Stage Financing
Early Stage
Expansion
First Stage Financing
Startup

Size of Investments Considered:
Min Size of Investment Considered (000s): $1,000
Max Size of Investment Considered (000s): $10,000

Geographical Preferences

United States Preferences:
California

International Preferences:
India
Asia

Industry Preferences

In Communications prefer:
Wireless Communications
Data Communications

In Computer Software prefer:
Software

In Internet Specific prefer:
Internet

In Business Serv. prefer:
Services

Additional Information
Name of Most Recent Fund: Inventus Capital Partners Fund I, L.P.
Most Recent Fund Was Raised: 11/30/2007
Year Founded: 2007
Capital Under Management: $51,000,000
Current Activity Level : Actively seeking new investments
Method of Compensation: Return on investment is of primary concern, do not charge fees

INVEREADY SEED CAPITAL SCR SA

C/ Dels Cavallers 50
Barcelona Knowledge Campus
Barcelona, Spain 08034
Phone: 34931807260
Fax: 34934473063
E-mail: info@inveready.com
Website: www.inveready.com

Management and Staff
Carlos Conti, General Partner
Ignacio Fonts Cavestany, General Partner
Javier Avellaneda Vila, Chief Operating Officer
Josep Maria Echarri i Torres, Managing Partner
Pedro Trucharte, Managing Director
Roger Pique Pijuan, General Partner
Sara Sanz, Managing Director

Type of Firm
Private Equity Firm

Association Membership
Spanish Venture Capital Association (ASCRI)

Project Preferences

Type of Financing Preferred:
Early Stage
Seed
Startup

Geographical Preferences

International Preferences:
Spain

Industry Preferences

In Communications prefer:
Commercial Communications

In Computer Software prefer:
Software

In Biotechnology prefer:
Biotechnology

In Medical/Health prefer:
Medical Products
Health Services

In Industrial/Energy prefer:
Energy
Alternative Energy

Additional Information
Year Founded: 2007
Capital Under Management: $42,598,000
Current Activity Level : Actively seeking new investments

INVERNESS GRAHAM INVESTMENTS

3811 West Chester Pike
Building 2, Suite 100
Newtown Square, PA USA 19073
Phone: 6107220300
Fax: 6102512880
Website: www.invernessgraham.com

Management and Staff
Aliya Khaydarova, Vice President
John Reilly, Chief Financial Officer
Kenneth Graham, Co-Founder
Paul Nolen, Vice President
Scott Kehoe, Co-Founder
Steven Wood, Co-Founder

Type of Firm
Private Equity Firm

Project Preferences

Role in Financing:
Prefer role as deal originator

Type of Financing Preferred:
Leveraged Buyout
Acquisition
Recapitalizations

Industry Preferences

In Business Serv. prefer:
Services

In Manufact. prefer:
Manufacturing

Additional Information
Name of Most Recent Fund: Inverness Graham Investments, L.P.
Most Recent Fund Was Raised: 01/07/2008
Year Founded: 2003
Capital Under Management: $250,000,000
Current Activity Level : Actively seeking new investments

INVERNESS MANAGEMENT LLC

21 Locust Avenue
Suite 1D
New Canaan, CT USA 06840
Phone: 2039964177
Website: www.invernessmanagement.com

Management and Staff
Brad Esson, Managing Director
Dean Anderson, Managing Director
Jacob Carmona, Chief Financial Officer
James Comis, Managing Partner
Robert Sheehy, Managing Director
W. Dunwoody, Co-Founder

Type of Firm
Private Equity Firm

Project Preferences

Role in Financing:
Prefer role as deal originator

Type of Financing Preferred:
Leveraged Buyout
Management Buyouts
Acquisition
Distressed Debt
Recapitalizations

Size of Investments Considered:
Min Size of Investment Considered (000s): $5,000
Max Size of Investment Considered (000s): $75,000

Geographical Preferences

United States Preferences:
All U.S.

Industry Focus
(% based on actual investment)
Industrial/Energy 100.0%

Additional Information
Name of Most Recent Fund: Inverness Partners II, L.P.
Most Recent Fund Was Raised: 08/27/2002
Year Founded: 1996
Capital Under Management: $400,000,000
Current Activity Level : Actively seeking new investments
Method of Compensation: Return on invest. most important, but chg. closing fees, service fees, etc.

INVERSION Y GESTION DE CAPITAL DE RIESGO DE ANDALUCIA SAU

C/Acustica, 24, Nuevo Torneo
Edificio Puerta de Indias
Sevilla, Spain 41015
Phone: 34955402400
E-mail: invercaria.igra@juntadeandalucia.es
Website: www.invercaria.es

Management and Staff
Laura Nogales Gomiz, Chief Executive Officer

Type of Firm
Government Affiliated Program

Association Membership
Spanish Venture Capital Association (ASCRI)

Project Preferences

Type of Financing Preferred:
Early Stage
Expansion
Seed
Startup

Geographical Preferences

International Preferences:
Spain
All International

Industry Preferences

In Communications prefer:
Communications and Media
Wireless Communications
Data Communications

In Biotechnology prefer:
Biotechnology
Human Biotechnology
Genetic Engineering

In Consumer Related prefer:
Food/Beverage

In Industrial/Energy prefer:
Energy
Advanced Materials
Environmental Related

In Transportation prefer:
Aerospace

In Other prefer:
Environment Responsible

Additional Information
Year Founded: 1992
Capital Under Management: $381,335,000
Current Activity Level : Actively seeking new investments

INVERSIONES GRUPO ZRISER SL

Correos 1, 3floor
Valencia, Spain 46002
Phone: 34 963 531 339
Fax: 34 963 427 720
E-mail: info@zriser.es

Type of Firm
Private Equity Firm

Project Preferences

Type of Financing Preferred:
Generalist PE

Additional Information
Year Founded: 2007
Current Activity Level : Actively seeking new investments

INVERSIONES IBERSUIZAS SA

Marques de Villamagna 3
Planta 11
Madrid, Spain 28001

Phone: 34914264380
Fax: 34914312011

Type of Firm
Private Equity Firm

Project Preferences

Type of Financing Preferred:
Leveraged Buyout
Later Stage
Management Buyouts
Acquisition

Size of Investments Considered:
Min Size of Investment Considered (000s): $13,229
Max Size of Investment Considered (000s): $132,293

Geographical Preferences

International Preferences:
Portugal
Spain

Additional Information
Year Founded: 1989
Capital Under Management: $722,200,000
Current Activity Level : Actively seeking new investments

INVERSUR CAPITAL SA

Av Providencia, 229, P3
Providence, Chile 7500768
Phone: 56222220010
E-mail: info@inversur.cl
Website: www.inversurcapital.com

Type of Firm
Private Equity Firm

Project Preferences

Type of Financing Preferred:
Early Stage
Balanced
Later Stage

Geographical Preferences

International Preferences:
Latin America
Chile

Industry Preferences

In Communications prefer:
Communications and Media
Commercial Communications

Additional Information
Year Founded: 2011
Capital Under Management: $30,000,000
Current Activity Level : Actively seeking new investments

INVESCO PRIVATE CAPITAL INC

1555 Peachtree Street, NE
Two Peachtree Pointe, Suite1800
Atlanta, GA USA 30309
Phone: 4044791095

Other Offices
30 Finsbury Square
London, United Kingdom EC2A 1AG
Phone: 415-445-3344

101 California Street
Suite 1900
San Francisco, CA USA 94111
Phone: 415-445-3344
Fax: 415-445-7549

1166 Avenue of the Americas
26th Floor
New York, NY USA 10036
Phone: 2122789000
Fax: 2122789822

Management and Staff
Amit Tiwari, Principal
Evan Jaysane-Darr, Principal
Henry Robin, General Partner
Marquette Chester, Managing Director
Mary Kelley, General Partner
Philip Shaw, General Partner
Ray Maxwell, Venture Partner

Type of Firm
Private Equity Advisor or Fund of Funds

Project Preferences

Role in Financing:
Will function either as deal originator or investor in deals created by others

Type of Financing Preferred:
Fund of Funds
Leveraged Buyout
Generalist PE
Balanced
Turnaround
Later Stage
Special Situation
Distressed Debt

Geographical Preferences

United States Preferences:

International Preferences:
Europe
Asia

Industry Focus
(% based on actual investment)
Other Products	21.6%
Medical/Health	13.9%
Internet Specific	13.3%
Communications and Media	13.3%
Computer Software and Services	12.9%
Biotechnology	11.3%
Semiconductors/Other Elect.	6.2%
Consumer Related	5.8%
Computer Hardware	1.3%
Industrial/Energy	0.4%

Additional Information
Name of Most Recent Fund: Invesco U.S. LBO & Corporate Finance Partnership Fund IV, LP
Most Recent Fund Was Raised: 06/03/2005
Year Founded: 1981
Capital Under Management: $1,600,000,000
Current Activity Level : Actively seeking new investments
Method of Compensation: Function primarily in service area, receive contingent fee in cash or equity

INVESCO REAL ESTATE, LTD.

43-45 Portman Square
1st Floor, Portman Square Hous
London, United Kingdom W1H 6LY
Phone: 442075433500
E-mail: realestate@ldn.invesco.com
Website: www.invescorealestate.co.uk

Other Offices
16-18 Rue de Londres
Paris, France 75009
Phone: 33-1-5662-4324

2001 Ross Avenue
Suite 3400
DALLAS, TX USA 75201
Phone: 9727157400

Klimentska 46
Praha City Centre
Floral Park, Czech Republic 11002
Phone: 420-227-202-420

37A, Avenue J F Kennedy
Luxembourg, Luxembourg 1855

Maffeistrasse 3
, Germany
Phone: 49-89-2060-6120

Calle Recoletos 15
Piso 1
Madrid, Spain 28001
Phone: 34-91-781-3023

Management and Staff
Andy Rofe, Managing Director

Type of Firm
Investment Management Firm

Project Preferences

Type of Financing Preferred:
Fund of Funds
Leveraged Buyout
Value-Add
Generalist PE

Geographical Preferences

International Preferences:
Asia Pacific
Europe
Asia

Industry Preferences

In Medical/Health prefer:
Medical/Health

Additional Information
Name of Most Recent Fund: Invesco Real Estate Fund III, L.P.
Most Recent Fund Was Raised: 12/12/2011
Year Founded: 1983
Capital Under Management: $744,900,000
Current Activity Level : Actively seeking new investments

INVEST DEVELOPMENT SICAR

rue Hehi Karray
Cite des sciences
Manzah, Tunisia 1004
Phone: 216-71-754-490
Fax: 216-71-754-474
E-mail: stb.invest@topnet.tn

Type of Firm
Private Equity Firm

Association Membership
Tunisian Venture Capital Association

Project Preferences

Type of Financing Preferred:
Later Stage

Size of Investments Considered:
Min Size of Investment Considered (000s): $46
Max Size of Investment Considered (000s): $796

Geographical Preferences

International Preferences:
Africa

Industry Preferences

In Communications prefer:
Telecommunications

In Internet Specific prefer:
Internet

In Biotechnology prefer:
Biotechnology

In Industrial/Energy prefer:
Industrial Products

In Manufact. prefer:
Manufacturing

Additional Information
Year Founded: 2004
Capital Under Management: $14,700,000
Current Activity Level : Actively seeking new investments

INVEST GEORGIA LLC

3423 Piedmont Road NE
Suite 555
Atlanta, GA USA 30305
Website: www.investgeorgia.net

Type of Firm
Private Equity Advisor or Fund of Funds

Project Preferences

Type of Financing Preferred:
Fund of Funds

Geographical Preferences

United States Preferences:
Georgia

Additional Information
Year Founded: 1969
Current Activity Level : Actively seeking new investments

INVEST MICHIGAN

1247 Woodward Avenue
#702
Detroit, MI USA 48226

Type of Firm
Government Affiliated Program

Project Preferences

Type of Financing Preferred:
Seed

Geographical Preferences

United States Preferences:
Michigan

Additional Information
Year Founded: 2014
Capital Under Management: $6,800,000
Current Activity Level : Actively seeking new investments

INVEST NEBRASKA CORP

4701 Innovation Drive
Suite 307
Lincoln, NE USA 68521
Phone: 4027427860
E-mail: info@investnebraska.com
Website: www.investnebraska.com

Management and Staff
Dan Hoffman, Chief Operating Officer

Type of Firm
Government Affiliated Program

Project Preferences

Type of Financing Preferred:
Seed
Startup

Geographical Preferences

United States Preferences:
Nebraska

Additional Information
Year Founded: 2013
Capital Under Management: $19,000,000
Current Activity Level : Actively seeking new investments

INVEST PME SA

9 Avenue des Montboucons
Temis Center 2
Besancon, France 25000
Phone: 33381250614
Fax: 33381250613

Type of Firm
Bank Affiliated

Project Preferences

Type of Financing Preferred:
Leveraged Buyout
Early Stage
Later Stage
Seed

Size of Investments Considered:
Min Size of Investment Considered (000s): $196
Max Size of Investment Considered (000s): $1,962

Geographical Preferences

International Preferences:
Tunisia
Algeria
Morocco

Additional Information
Year Founded: 2004
Capital Under Management: $5,288,000
Current Activity Level : Actively seeking new investments

INVEST TECH PARTICI-PACOES E INVESTIMENTOS LTDA

Rua dos Pinheiros 870
Conjunto 153 / 154
Sao Paulo, Brazil 05422
Phone: 1131992199
Website: www.investtech.com.br

Type of Firm
Private Equity Firm

Association Membership
Brazilian Venture Capital Association (ABCR)

Project Preferences

Type of Financing Preferred:
Fund of Funds
Balanced

Geographical Preferences

International Preferences:
Brazil

Industry Preferences

In Communications prefer:
Communications and Media
Telecommunications

In Medical/Health prefer:
Medical/Health

In Consumer Related prefer:
Education Related

In Agr/Forestr/Fish prefer:
Agribusiness

In Other prefer:
Environment Responsible

Additional Information
Year Founded: 2004
Capital Under Management: $339,709,000
Current Activity Level : Actively seeking new investments

INVEST UNTERNEHMENS-BETEILIGUNGS AG

Europaplatz 5a
A-4020
Linz, Austria 4020
Phone: 43-732-65962451
Fax: 43-732-65962403
E-mail: office@investag.at
Website: www.investag.at

Type of Firm
Bank Affiliated

Association Membership
Austrian PE and Venture Capital Association (AVCO)

Project Preferences

Type of Financing Preferred:
Early Stage
Mezzanine
Later Stage
Management Buyouts
Acquisition

Geographical Preferences

International Preferences:
Austria
Germany

Industry Preferences

In Consumer Related prefer:
Consumer
Retail
Consumer Products

In Financial Services prefer:
Financial Services

In Business Serv. prefer:
Services

Additional Information
Year Founded: 1994
Capital Under Management: $175,900,000
Current Activity Level : Actively seeking new investments

INVESTAMERICA VENTURE GROUP, INC.

101 Second Street Southeast
Suite 800
Cedar Rapids, IA USA 52401
Phone: 3193638249
Fax: 3193639683
Website: www.investamericaventuregroup.com

Other Offices
911 Main Street, Commerce Tower
Suite 2424
Kansas City, MO USA 64105
Phone: 816-842-0114
Fax: 816-471-7339

51 Broadway
Suite 500
Fargo, ND USA 58102
Phone: 7012980003
Fax: 7012937819

600 East Mason Street
Suite 304
Milwaukee, WI USA 53202
Phone: 414-276-3839
Fax: 414-276-1885

H.H Hall Building, Seventh Avenue
1000 Northeast, Suite 330 H
Vancouver, WA USA 98685
Phone: 3605735067
Fax: 3605737462

Management and Staff
David Schroder, President
Michael Reynoldson, Vice President

Type of Firm
Private Equity Firm

Project Preferences

Role in Financing:
Prefer role as deal originator but will also invest in deals created by others

Type of Financing Preferred:
Second Stage Financing
Leveraged Buyout
Early Stage
Expansion
Later Stage
Management Buyouts
First Stage Financing
Special Situation

Size of Investments Considered:
Min Size of Investment Considered (000s): $1,000
Max Size of Investment Considered (000s): $2,000

Geographical Preferences

United States Preferences:
Midwest
Iowa
North Dakota
Washington
Minnesota

Industry Focus
(% based on actual investment)

Other Products	21.6%
Communications and Media	18.6%
Industrial/Energy	16.6%
Internet Specific	12.2%
Consumer Related	9.2%
Semiconductors/Other Elect.	8.2%
Computer Hardware	5.5%
Biotechnology	3.2%
Medical/Health	3.2%
Computer Software and Services	1.7%

Additional Information
Name of Most Recent Fund: L&C Private Equities II, L.P.
Most Recent Fund Was Raised: 07/23/2009
Year Founded: 1959
Capital Under Management: $48,500,000
Current Activity Level : Actively seeking new investments
Method of Compensation: Return on investment is of primary concern, do not charge fees

INVESTCORP BANK BSC

PO Box 5340
Investcorp House
Manama, Bahrain
Phone: 97317532000
Fax: 97317530816
E-mail: info@investcorp.com
Website: www.investcorp.com

Other Offices

280 Park Avenue
36th Floor
NEW YORK, NY USA 10017
Phone: 212-599-4700
Fax: 212-983-7073

Management and Staff

Abbas Rizvi, Principal
Abdul Rahim Saad, Principal
Affan Ahmed, Managing Director
Aleksandra Bozic, Principal
Ali Zainal, Managing Director
Ali Alrahma, Managing Director
Anand Radhakrishnan, Managing Director
Andrea Davis, Managing Director
Andrew Fisch, Managing Director
Anthony Robinson, Chief Financial Officer
Brian Kelley, Managing Director
Carsten Hagenbuche, Managing Director
Daniel Lopez-Cruz, Managing Director
Darryl D Souza, Principal
David Tayeh, Managing Director
Deborah Smith, Managing Director
Devindra Thakur, Vice President
Dominic Elias, Managing Director
Ebrahim Ebrahim, Managing Director
F Dracos, Managing Director
Firas Al Amine, Managing Director
Firas El Amine, Managing Director
Gilbert Kamieniecky, Managing Director
Grahame Ivey, Managing Director
Herbert Myers, Managing Director
James Mahoney, Managing Director
James Sweeting, Vice President
Jennifer Cahill, Managing Director
Johannes Glas, Managing Director
John Franklin, Chief Operating Officer
Jonathan Feeney, Managing Director
Karen Van Nouhuys, Principal
Kate Evans, Principal
Kevin Nickelberry, Managing Director
Maud Brown, Managing Director
Michael O Brien, Managing Director
Mohammed Sammakia, Managing Director
Mohammed Al Shroogi, President
Mufeed Rajab, Managing Director
Najib Rahal, Principal
Neil Hasson, Managing Director
Nick Vamvakas, Managing Director
Rabih Khouri, Managing Director
Rahim Kandanuru, Vice President
Rajat Mehrotra, Vice President
Ramzi AbdelJaber, Managing Director
Rebecca Hellerstein, Managing Director
Richard Kramer, Managing Director
Sean Elliott, Principal
Sean Elliot, Principal
Sudip Dey, Principal
Thomas Best, Vice President
Yaser Bajsair, Managing Director

Type of Firm

Investment Management Firm

Association Membership

Gulf Venture Capital Association

Project Preferences

Type of Financing Preferred:
Leveraged Buyout
Value-Add
Early Stage
Generalist PE

Size of Investments Considered:
Min Size of Investment Considered (000s): $5,000
Max Size of Investment Considered: No Limit

Geographical Preferences

United States Preferences:

International Preferences:
Bahrain
Western Europe
Middle East
Africa

Industry Focus

(% based on actual investment)

Industrial/Energy	35.7%
Consumer Related	25.4%
Other Products	22.7%
Communications and Media	5.8%
Internet Specific	4.0%
Medical/Health	3.3%
Computer Software and Services	2.9%
Semiconductors/Other Elect.	0.1%

Additional Information

Year Founded: 1982
Capital Under Management: $2,800,000,000
Current Activity Level: Actively seeking new investments

INVESTCORP TECHNOLOGY INVESTMENTS GROUP

280 Park Avenue
36th Floor
New York, NY USA 10017
Phone: 2125994700
Fax: 2129837073
E-mail: info@investcorp.com
Website: www.investcorp.com

Other Offices

48 Grosvenor Street
Investcorp House
London, United Kingdom W1K 3HW
Phone: 44-20-7629-6600
Fax: 44-20-7499-0371

Management and Staff

Abbas Rizvi, Principal
Ayman Al-Arrayed, Principal
Craig Bottger, Principal
Craig Sinfield-Hain, Principal
Darryl D Souza, Principal
Deborah Botwood, Managing Director
Ebrahim Hussain Ebrahim, Principal
Elezabeth Pires, Principal
Firas El Amine, Managing Director
Grahame Ivey, Managing Director
Hasan Chehime, Managing Director
Jonathan Minor, Managing Director
Karen Van Nouhuys, Principal
Kate Evans, Principal
Michael Simatos, Principal
Mufeed Rajab, Principal
Ramzi AbdelJaber, Managing Director
Richard Kramer, Managing Director
Rishi Kapoor, Chief Financial Officer
Sean Elliott, Principal
Shahbaz Khan, Principal
Shaun Hill, Principal
Sreevatsan Rajagopalan, Principal
Stephaine Bess, Managing Director
Sudip Dey, Principal

Type of Firm

Bank Affiliated

Project Preferences

Role in Financing:
Prefer role as deal originator but will also invest in deals created by others

Type of Financing Preferred:
Leveraged Buyout
Expansion
Later Stage
Acquisition

Geographical Preferences

United States Preferences:
North America

International Preferences:
Western Europe
All International

Industry Preferences

In Communications prefer:
Communications and Media
Telecommunications
Data Communications

In Computer Software prefer:
Software

In Semiconductor/Electr prefer:
Semiconductor

In Business Serv. prefer:
Media

Additional Information

Name of Most Recent Fund: Investcorp Technology Partners III, L.P.
Most Recent Fund Was Raised: 10/11/2007
Year Founded: 1982
Current Activity Level : Actively seeking new investments

INVESTEC ASSET MANAGEMENT (PTY) LTD

36 Hans Strijdom Avenue
Foreshore
Cape Town, South Africa 8001
Phone: 27214162000
Fax: 27214162001
Website: www.investecassetmanagement.com

Other Offices

100 Grayston Drive
Sandown
Sandton, South Africa 2196

2 Gresham Street
London, United Kingdom EC2V 7QP
Phone: 44-20-7597-4000

Management and Staff

Andrew Richardson, Principal
Chris Derksen, Principal
Gerben Dijkstra, Principal
Hendrik du Toit, Chief Executive Officer
William Alexander, Principal

Type of Firm

Private Equity Firm

Association Membership

South African Venture Capital Association (SAVCA)
Emerging Markets Private Equity Association
African Venture Capital Association (AVCA)

Project Preferences

Type of Financing Preferred:
Early Stage
Expansion
Later Stage

Geographical Preferences

International Preferences:
Africa

Additional Information

Year Founded: 1991
Capital Under Management: $295,000,000
Current Activity Level : Actively seeking new investments

INVESTEC PRIVATE EQUITY

Two Gresham Street
London, United Kingdom EC2V 7QP
Phone: 442075974000
Fax: 442075974070

Other Offices

300 Middel Street
Brooklyn
Pretoria, South Africa 0075
Phone: 27-12-427-8300
Fax: 27-12-427-8310

36 Hans Strijdom Ave.
Foreshore
Cape Town, South Africa 8001
Phone: 27-21-416-1000
Fax: 27-21-416-1001

100 Grayston Drive
Sandown
Sandton, South Africa 2196
Phone: 27-11-286-7000
Fax: 27-11-286-7777

325 Smith Street
Durban, South Africa 4001
Phone: 27-31-365-4700
Fax: 27-31-365-4800

Pilot Mill House
The Quarry, Selborne
East London, South Africa 5247
Phone: 27-43-721-0660
Fax: 27-43-721-0664

Ascot Office Park, Conyngham Rd.
Green Acres
Port Elizabeth, South Africa 6045
Phone: 27-41-391-9400
Fax: 27-41-374-8346

Management and Staff

Bernard Kantor, Managing Director
Stephen Koseff, Chief Executive Officer

Type of Firm

Bank Affiliated

Association Membership

South African Venture Capital Association (SAVCA)

Project Preferences

Type of Financing Preferred:
Leveraged Buyout
Early Stage
Expansion
Mezzanine
Balanced
Later Stage
Management Buyouts
Acquisition
Recapitalizations

Geographical Preferences

United States Preferences:
All U.S.

International Preferences:
United Kingdom
Europe
Australia
Israel
Asia
South Africa

Additional Information

Name of Most Recent Fund: Guinness Mahon Venture Founders Fund
Most Recent Fund Was Raised: 12/21/1998
Year Founded: 1974
Current Activity Level : Actively seeking new investments

INVESTEC VENTURES IRELAND LTD

3 George's Dock
IFSC
Dublin, Ireland 1
Phone: 35316115611
Fax: 35316115766
E-mail: info@ncb.ie
Website: www.ncb-ventures.com

Other Offices

51 Moorgate
London, United Kingdom EC2R 6BH
Phone: 44-20-7071-5200
Fax: 44-20-7071-5202

Management and Staff

Conor O Kelly, Chief Executive Officer
Derek Crawley, Partner
Graham O Brien, Founder
John Dolan, Partner
Leo Hamill, Partner
Michael Murphy, Managing Partner
Will Prendergast, Partner

Type of Firm

Bank Affiliated

Association Membership

Irish Venture Capital Association

Project Preferences

Type of Financing Preferred:
Leveraged Buyout
Early Stage
Expansion
Later Stage
Startup

Size of Investments Considered:
Min Size of Investment Considered (000s): $1,287
Max Size of Investment Considered (000s): $6,437

Geographical Preferences

International Preferences:
Ireland
Europe

Industry Preferences

In Communications prefer:
Telecommunications
Media and Entertainment

In Computer Software prefer:
Computer Services
Software

In Semiconductor/Electr prefer:
Electronics
Semiconductor

In Biotechnology prefer:
Biotechnology

In Medical/Health prefer:
Medical Products
Health Services

In Industrial/Energy prefer:
Factory Automation
Environmental Related

Additional Information

Name of Most Recent Fund: Ulster Bank Diageo Venture Fund
Most Recent Fund Was Raised: 10/07/2008
Year Founded: 1981
Capital Under Management: $42,500,000
Current Activity Level : Actively seeking new investments

INVESTEC WENTWORTH PRIVATE EQUITY PTY LTD

Two Chifley Square
Level 23, The Chifley Tower
Sydney, Australia 2000
Phone: 61292936300
Fax: 61292936301

Other Offices

120 Collins Street
Level 49
Melbourne, Australia 3000
Phone: 61386601000

Former HQ: 2 Chifley Square, Phillip St.
Level 31, The Chifley Tower
, Australia 2000
Phone: 61292932000
Fax: 61292932002

121-129 Hutt Street
Suite Five
Adelaide, Australia 5000
Phone: 61882039102

71 Eagle Street
Level 31, Riparian Plaza
Brisbane, Australia 4000
Phone: 61730188100

62 Ord Street
Suites 9 & 10
West Perth, Australia 6005
Phone: 61892144502

Management and Staff

John Murphy, Managing Director

Type of Firm

Bank Affiliated

Association Membership

Australian Venture Capital Association (AVCAL)

Project Preferences

Role in Financing:
Will function either as deal originator or investor in deals created by others

Type of Financing Preferred:
Leveraged Buyout
Generalist PE

Size of Investments Considered:
Min Size of Investment Considered (000s): $20,000
Max Size of Investment Considered (000s): $200,000

Geographical Preferences

International Preferences:
Australia

Industry Preferences

In Consumer Related prefer:
Consumer
Food/Beverage
Education Related

In Business Serv. prefer:
Services

In Manufact. prefer:
Manufacturing

In Agr/Forestr/Fish prefer:
Mining and Minerals

Additional Information

Name of Most Recent Fund: MGB Equity Growth Unit Trust 2
Most Recent Fund Was Raised: 02/01/2004
Year Founded: 1998
Capital Under Management: $56,300,000
Current Activity Level : Actively seeking new investments
Method of Compensation: Return on invest. most important, but chg. closing fees, service fees, etc.

INVESTECO CAPITAL CORP

70 The Esplanade
Suite 400
Toronto, Canada M5E 1R2
Phone: 4163041750
Fax: 4163622387
Website: www.investeco.com

Management and Staff

Alex Chamberlain, Managing Partner
Charles Holt, Vice President
Deepak Ramachandran, Partner
John Cook, Managing Partner
Michael Curry, Managing Partner
Michael de Pencier, Co-Founder

Type of Firm

Private Equity Firm

Association Membership

Canadian Venture Capital Association

Project Preferences

Type of Financing Preferred:
Leveraged Buyout
Early Stage
Expansion
Seed
Acquisition
Startup

Geographical Preferences

United States Preferences:
North America
All U.S.

Canadian Preferences:
All Canada
Ontario

Industry Preferences

In Biotechnology prefer:
Agricultural/Animal Bio.

In Consumer Related prefer:
Food/Beverage

In Industrial/Energy prefer:
Energy
Energy Conservation Relat
Environmental Related

In Other prefer:
Environment Responsible

Additional Information

Year Founded: 2004
Capital Under Management: $3,170,000
Current Activity Level : Actively seeking new investments

INVESTEL CAPITAL CORP

200 Granville Street
Vancouver, Canada V6C 1S4
Phone: 6043985000
Fax: 8008899898
E-mail: Info@investel.com
Website: www.investel.com

Management and Staff
Benoit Laliberte, Founder

Type of Firm
Private Equity Firm

Project Preferences

Type of Financing Preferred:
Leveraged Buyout
Turnaround
Distressed Debt

Geographical Preferences

United States Preferences:

Canadian Preferences:
All Canada

Industry Preferences

In Communications prefer:
Telecommunications

Additional Information
Year Founded: 2013
Current Activity Level : Actively seeking new investments

INVESTIDOR PROFISSIONAL GESTAO DE RECURSOS LTDA

Avenida Ataulfo de Paiva 255
9th Floor, Leblon
Rio de Janeiro, Brazil 22440032
Phone: 552121040500
Fax: 552121040561
Website: www.investidorprofissional.com.br

Type of Firm
Private Equity Firm

Project Preferences

Type of Financing Preferred:
Balanced

Geographical Preferences

International Preferences:
Brazil

Additional Information
Year Founded: 1988
Capital Under Management: $12,000,000,000
Current Activity Level : Actively seeking new investments

INVESTINDUSTRIAL SERVICES LTD

180-186 Brompton Road
London, United Kingdom SW3 1HQ
Phone: 442076642121
Fax: 442076612122
E-mail: info@investindustrial.com
Website: www.investindustrial.com

Other Offices
1701 Beijing West Road
Jing An Tower
Shanghai, China 200040
Phone: 862151083529
Fax: 862161378596

51 Avenue JF Kennedy
Luxembourg, Luxembourg L-1855
Phone: 352-2609-531
Fax: 352-2609-5340

Via Nassa 5
Lugano, Switzerland 6900
Phone: 41-91-260-8300
Fax: 41-91-260-8329

375 Park Avenue
Suite 1502
New York, NY USA 10152
Phone: 2129266000
Fax: 2128721550

Edificio Zurich
Via Augusta, 200
Barcelona, Spain 08021
Phone: 34932405750
Fax: 34932405755

Management and Staff
Carlo Bonomi, Principal
Dante Razzano, Principal
Filippo Aleotti, Principal
Ignacio Arietta, Principal
John Mowinckel, Principal
Martin Del Valle, Principal
Michele Garulli, Principal
Roberto Maestroni, Principal
Salvatore Catapano, Principal

Type of Firm
Private Equity Firm

Association Membership
European Private Equity and Venture Capital Assoc.

Project Preferences

Type of Financing Preferred:
Leveraged Buyout
Mezzanine
Turnaround
Acquisition

Geographical Preferences

International Preferences:
Italy
United Kingdom
Europe
Spain

Industry Preferences

In Computer Software prefer:
Software

In Consumer Related prefer:
Consumer
Entertainment and Leisure
Retail
Food/Beverage

In Industrial/Energy prefer:
Industrial Products

In Business Serv. prefer:
Services

In Manufact. prefer:
Manufacturing

Additional Information
Year Founded: 1990
Capital Under Management: $600,000,000
Current Activity Level : Actively seeking new investments

INVESTINFUTURE BV

Stationsweg 147
Hague, The, Netherlands 2515BM
Phone: 310703699699
E-mail: info@investinfuture.nl
Website: investinfuture.nl

Management and Staff
Edgard Creemers, Managing Director

Type of Firm
Private Equity Firm

Project Preferences

Type of Financing Preferred:
Early Stage
Expansion
Mezzanine
Turnaround
Later Stage
Seed
Recapitalizations

Geographical Preferences

International Preferences:
Europe
Netherlands

Additional Information
Year Founded: 2010
Current Activity Level : Actively seeking new investments

INVESTINOR AS

Brattorkaia 17B
Trondheim, Norway 7010
Phone: 4795742000
E-mail: post@investinor.no
Website: www.investinor.no

Management and Staff
Geir Kjesbu, Chief Executive Officer
Jon Eriksen, Principal
Nils Krogstad, Principal
Tor Helmersen, Chief Financial Officer

Type of Firm
Government Affiliated Program

Association Membership
Norwegian Venture Capital Association

Project Preferences

Type of Financing Preferred:
Balanced

Geographical Preferences

International Preferences:
Norway

Industry Preferences

In Communications prefer:
Communications and Media
Wireless Communications

In Computer Software prefer:
Software
Systems Software

In Semiconductor/Electr prefer:
Electronics
Controllers and Sensors

In Medical/Health prefer:
Pharmaceuticals

In Industrial/Energy prefer:
Advanced Materials
Environmental Related

In Business Serv. prefer:
Services

Additional Information
Year Founded: 2009
Capital Under Management: $635,800,000
Current Activity Level : Actively seeking new investments

INVESTIR & + SAS

14, rue des Jeuneurs
Paris, France 75002
Website: fr.investiretplus.com

Type of Firm
Private Equity Firm

Project Preferences

Type of Financing Preferred:
Leveraged Buyout
Early Stage
Expansion
Later Stage
Management Buyouts
Acquisition

Industry Preferences

In Medical/Health prefer:
Medical/Health

In Industrial/Energy prefer:
Environmental Related

In Agr/Forestr/Fish prefer:
Agriculture related

In Utilities prefer:
Utilities

In Other prefer:
Environment Responsible

Additional Information
Year Founded: 2005
Current Activity Level : Actively seeking new investments

INVESTISSEMENT QUEBEC

600, rue de La Gauchetiere
bureau 1500
Montreal, Canada H3B 4L8
Phone: 5148734664
Fax: 5143958055
Website: www.investquebec.com

Other Offices
Former HQ: 1200 Chruch Road
Suite 500
Montreal, Canada G1V 5A3
Phone: 418643-5172

Type of Firm
Private Equity Firm

Project Preferences

Type of Financing Preferred:
Early Stage
Expansion
Generalist PE
Startup

Geographical Preferences

Canadian Preferences:
Quebec

Industry Preferences

In Industrial/Energy prefer:
Energy

In Agr/Forestr/Fish prefer:
Agriculture related
Mining and Minerals

In Other prefer:
Environment Responsible

Additional Information
Year Founded: 1998
Current Activity Level : Actively seeking new investments

INVESTISSEMENTS NOVA-CAP INC

375 Roland Therrien Boulevard
Suite 210
Longueuil, Canada J4H 4A6
Phone: 4506515000
Fax: 4506517585
E-mail: info@novacap.ca
Website: www.novacap.ca

Management and Staff
Alain Belanger, General Partner
Bruno-Etienne Duguay, Vice President
David Brassard, Vice President
Domenic Mancini, General Partner
Francois Chaurette, General Partner
Frederick Perrault, Partner
Michel Cote, General Partner
Pierre McMaster, General Partner
Stephane Blanchet, Chief Financial Officer
Stephane Tremblay, General Partner

Type of Firm
Private Equity Firm

Association Membership
Canadian Venture Capital Association

Project Preferences

Role in Financing:
Prefer role as deal originator but will also invest in deals created by others

Type of Financing Preferred:
Leveraged Buyout
Generalist PE
Balanced
Turnaround
Later Stage
Management Buyouts
Recapitalizations

Geographical Preferences

United States Preferences:
North America

Canadian Preferences:
All Canada

Industry Preferences

In Communications prefer:
Telecommunications

In Business Serv. prefer:
Services
Media

In Manufact. prefer:
Manufacturing

Additional Information
Year Founded: 1981
Capital Under Management: $1,201,000,000
Current Activity Level : Actively seeking new investments
Method of Compensation: Return on investment is of primary concern, do not charge fees

---

INVESTITIONS STRUK-TURBK RHEIN PFALZ GMBH

Holzhofstrasse 4
Mainz, Germany 55116
Phone: 49613161720
Fax: 49613161721299
E-mail: isb@isb.rlp.de
Website: isb.rlp.de

Management and Staff
Markus Engel, Vice President
Rudiger Bucher, Managing Director
Ulrich Link, Managing Director
Ulrich Dexheimer, Chief Executive Officer

Type of Firm
Bank Affiliated

Association Membership
German Venture Capital Association (BVK)

Project Preferences

Type of Financing Preferred:
Early Stage
Balanced
Later Stage
Seed
Startup

Size of Investments Considered:
Min Size of Investment Considered (000s): $131
Max Size of Investment Considered (000s): $1,312

Geographical Preferences

International Preferences:
Germany

Industry Focus
(% based on actual investment)
Computer Software and Services	76.1%
Medical/Health	12.7%
Semiconductors/Other Elect.	6.9%
Other Products	4.3%

Additional Information
Year Founded: 1993
Current Activity Level : Actively seeking new investments

INVESTITIONS UND STRUK-TURBANK RHEINLAND PFALZ ISB

Holzhofstrasse 4
Mainz, Germany 55116
Phone: 49613161720
Fax: 49613161721299
E-mail: isb-marketing(at)isb.rlp.de
Website: www.isb.rlp.de

Type of Firm
Private Equity Firm

Additional Information
Year Founded: 2016
Current Activity Level : Actively seeking new investments

INVESTLIFE EUROPAI ES TENGERENTULI TOKEBE-FEKTETO ZRT

Vaci 110
Budapest, Hungary 1133
Phone: 3612391948
Fax: 3612391949
E-mail: investlife@investlife.hu
Website: www.investlife.hu

Type of Firm
Private Equity Firm

Association Membership
Hungarian Venture Capital Association (HVCA)

Project Preferences

Type of Financing Preferred:
Leveraged Buyout
Early Stage
Generalist PE
Later Stage
Acquisition
Startup
Recapitalizations

Geographical Preferences

International Preferences:
Hungary

Additional Information
Year Founded: 1998
Capital Under Management: $100,000
Current Activity Level : Actively seeking new investments

INVESTMENT CAPITAL PARTNERS PTY LTD

Level 3, Lantos Place
80 Stamford Road
Indooroopilly, Brisbane, Australia 4068
Phone: 617-3378-6033
Fax: 617-3378-6044

Type of Firm
Private Equity Firm

Project Preferences

Type of Financing Preferred:
Balanced

Additional Information
Year Founded: 2007
Current Activity Level : Actively seeking new investments

INVESTMENT LATOUR AB

J A Wettergrens Gata 7
P.O. Box 336
Gothenburg, Sweden 401 25
Phone: 4631891790
Fax: 4631456063
E-mail: info@latour.se
Website: www.latour.se

Management and Staff
Anders Morck, Chief Financial Officer

Type of Firm
Corporate PE/Venture

Project Preferences

Type of Financing Preferred:
Balanced

Geographical Preferences

International Preferences:
Europe
Scandanavia/Nordic Region

Industry Preferences

In Industrial/Energy prefer:
Industrial Products
Materials

Additional Information
Year Founded: 1985
Current Activity Level : Actively seeking new investments

INVESTMENTS IN ATI LTD

P.O. Box 7284
Ashkelon, Israel 78172
Phone: 97286751122
Fax: 97286751113
E-mail: ati@ati.co.il
Website: www.ati.co.il

Management and Staff
Anit Portman, Chief Financial Officer
Moshe Shitrit, Chief Executive Officer

Type of Firm
Private Equity Firm

Association Membership
Israel Venture Association

Project Preferences

Type of Financing Preferred:
Early Stage
Expansion
Later Stage

Geographical Preferences

International Preferences:
Israel

Additional Information
Year Founded: 1991
Current Activity Level : Actively seeking new investments

INVESTOR GROUP, THE

727 Sapphire St Apt 116
San Diego, CA USA 92109

Type of Firm
Investment Management Firm

Project Preferences

Type of Financing Preferred:
Later Stage

Industry Preferences

In Computer Software prefer:
Software

Additional Information
Year Founded: 1969
Current Activity Level : Actively seeking new investments

INVESTOR GROWTH CAPITAL AB

Arsenalsgatan 8C
Stockholm, Sweden 103 32
Phone: 4686141800
Fax: 4686141819
Website: www.investorgrowthcapital.com

Other Offices
630 Fifth Avenue
Suite 1965
New York, NY USA 10111
Phone: 212-515-9000
Fax: 212-515-9009

Schiphol Boulevard 353
Amsterdam, Netherlands NL-1118
Phone: 31-20-577-6600
Fax: 31-20-577-6609

Unit 1603, 16F, Tower 2
No. 79 Jiangou Road
Beijing, China 100025
Phone: 86-10-6598-9118
Fax: 86-10-5866-9128

1701 Hutchison House
10 Harcourt Road
Hong Kong, Hong Kong
Phone: 852-2123-8000
Fax: 852-2123-8001

333 Middlefield Road
Suite 110
Menlo Park, CA USA 94025
Phone: 650-543-8100
Fax: 650-543-8110

Management and Staff
Abhijeet Lele, Managing Director
Albert Kim, Managing Director
Ashley Friedman, Vice President
Brian Mulvey, Vice President
Choo Jin-Hwee, Vice President
Jakob Lindberg, Vice President
Jose Suarez, Managing Director
Liza Page Nelson, Venture Partner
Neill Occhiogrosso, Vice President
Noah Walley, Managing Director
Philip Dur, Managing Director
Stephen Campe, President
Thomas Eklund, Managing Director
Xin Wang, Vice President

Type of Firm
Private Equity Firm

Association Membership
Hong Kong Venture Capital Association (HKVCA)

Project Preferences

Type of Financing Preferred:
Leveraged Buyout
Acquisition

Geographical Preferences

International Preferences:
Scandanavia/Nordic Region

Industry Focus
(% based on actual investment)

Internet Specific	25.1%
Biotechnology	22.0%
Communications and Media	16.9%
Medical/Health	11.7%
Semiconductors/Other Elect.	10.7%
Other Products	6.0%
Computer Software and Services	5.9%
Consumer Related	0.9%
Industrial/Energy	0.7%
Computer Hardware	0.2%

Additional Information
Year Founded: 1997
Capital Under Management: $321,000,000
Current Activity Level : Actively seeking new investments

INVESTOR GROWTH CAPITAL INC

One Rockefeller Plaza
Suite 2801
New York, NY USA 10020
Phone: 2125159000
Fax: 2125159009
E-mail: igc@investorab.com
Website: www.investorab.com

Other Offices
Unit 1603, 16F, Tower 2, No.79 Jianguo
China Central Place Office Building
Beijing, China 100025
Phone: 861065989118
Fax: 861065989128

Arsenalsgatan 8c
Stockholm, Sweden SE-103 32
Phone: 4686141800
Fax: 4686141819

Management and Staff
Abhijeet Lele, Managing Director
Jose Suarez, Managing Director
Michael Ricks, Managing Director
Noah Walley, Managing Director
Philip Dur, Venture Partner
Stephen Campe, President
Thomas Eklund, Managing Director
Xin Wang, Vice President

Type of Firm
Private Equity Firm

Association Membership
China Venture Capital Association

Project Preferences

Role in Financing:
Prefer role as deal originator but will also invest in deals created by others

Type of Financing Preferred:
Early Stage
Expansion
Balanced
Later Stage
Acquisition

Size of Investments Considered:
Min Size of Investment Considered (000s): $5,000
Max Size of Investment Considered (000s): $30,000

Geographical Preferences

United States Preferences:

International Preferences:
China

Industry Focus

(% based on actual investment)
Computer Software and Services	23.5%
Medical/Health	18.6%
Biotechnology	17.1%
Communications and Media	17.0%
Internet Specific	11.5%
Semiconductors/Other Elect.	4.7%
Other Products	3.0%
Computer Hardware	2.4%
Industrial/Energy	1.3%
Consumer Related	1.0%

Additional Information

Year Founded: 1995
Capital Under Management: $1,800,000,000
Current Activity Level : Actively seeking new investments
Method of Compensation: Return on investment is of primary concern, do not charge fees

INVESTORS IN PRIVATE EQUITY

1, rue Francois 1er
Paris, France 75008
Phone: 33158361550
Fax: 33158361569
E-mail: info@investors-in-private-equity.fr

Management and Staff

Philippe Nguyen, President

Type of Firm

Private Equity Firm

Project Preferences

Type of Financing Preferred:
Leveraged Buyout
Management Buyouts

Geographical Preferences

International Preferences:
Europe
France

Industry Preferences

In Communications prefer:
Entertainment

In Consumer Related prefer:
Consumer
Consumer Products

In Transportation prefer:
Transportation
Aerospace

In Agr/Forestr/Fish prefer:
Agriculture related

Additional Information

Year Founded: 2002
Current Activity Level : Actively seeking new investments

INVESTORS MANAGEMENT CORP

801 N. West Street
Raleigh, NC USA 27603
Phone: 9196537499
Fax: 9196537498
Website: www.investorsmanagement.com

Management and Staff

James Maynard, Founder
Richard Urquhart, Chief Operating Officer

Type of Firm

Investment Management Firm

Project Preferences

Type of Financing Preferred:
Leveraged Buyout
Acquisition

Additional Information

Year Founded: 1971
Current Activity Level : Actively seeking new investments

INVESTORS TOWARZYST-WO FUNDUSZY INWESTY-CYJNYCH SA

ul. Mokotowska 1
15th Floor, Zebra Tower
Warszaw, Poland 00-640
Phone: 48223789100
Fax: 48223789101
E-mail: office@investors.pl
Website: investors.pl

Management and Staff

Piotr Dziadek, Vice President
Zbigniew Wojtowicz, Vice President

Type of Firm

Private Equity Firm

Project Preferences

Type of Financing Preferred:
Leveraged Buyout

Geographical Preferences

International Preferences:
Europe

Additional Information

Year Founded: 2005
Current Activity Level : Actively seeking new investments

INVESTSUD SA

11 Rue de la Plaine, Parc
d'activites economiques du WEX
Marche-en-Famenne, Belgium 6900
Phone: 3284320520
Fax: 3284315723
E-mail: info@capitaletcroissance.be
Website: www.investsud.be

Other Offices

Rue Camille Hubert 2
Les Isnes, Belgium 5032
Phone: 3281735999

Rue de Liege 161
Verviers, Belgium 4800
Phone: 3287338339
Fax: 3287269586

Management and Staff

Benjamin Cupers, Partner
Gilles Koestel, Partner
Pierre Detrixhe, Partner
Serge De Ketelaere, Partner
Stephane Dantinne, Partner

Type of Firm

Private Equity Firm

Association Membership

Belgium Venturing Association

Project Preferences

Type of Financing Preferred:
Early Stage
Expansion
Later Stage

Geographical Preferences

International Preferences:
Luxembourg
Netherlands
Belgium
France

Industry Preferences

In Agr/Forestr/Fish prefer:
Agriculture related

Additional Information

Year Founded: 1983
Current Activity Level : Actively seeking new investments

INVESTURE LLC

126 Garrett Street
Suite J
Charlottesville, VA USA 22902
Phone: 4342200280
Fax: 4342200285
E-mail: inquiries@investure.com
Website: www.investure.com

Management and Staff

Alice Handy, President, Founder
Bruce Miller, Managing Director
Charles Cocke, Managing Director
Richard Eng, Chief Operating Officer
William West, Managing Director

Type of Firm

Private Equity Advisor or Fund of Funds

Project Preferences

Type of Financing Preferred:
Fund of Funds

Additional Information

Name of Most Recent Fund: Investure Private Partners II, L.P.
Most Recent Fund Was Raised: 05/03/2005
Year Founded: 2003
Current Activity Level : Actively seeking new investments

INVEX CAPITAL LLP

Ten Market Mews
London, United Kingdom W1J 7BZ
Phone: 442074085000
Fax: 442074085001
E-mail: info@invex.co.uk
Website: www.invex.co.uk

Type of Firm

Private Equity Firm

Project Preferences

Type of Financing Preferred:
Generalist PE

Size of Investments Considered:
Min Size of Investment Considered (000s): $6,962
Max Size of Investment Considered (000s): $139,237

Geographical Preferences

International Preferences:
United Kingdom
Europe
Asia

Additional Information

Year Founded: 2004
Current Activity Level : Actively seeking new investments

INVICO CAPITAL CORP

Bankers Hall Hollinsworth BLDG
Suite 600, 301 - Eight Ave SW
Calgary, Canada T2P1C5
Phone: 403-538-4771
Website: www.invicocapital.com

Management and Staff

Allison Taylor, Vice President
Jason Brooks, President

Type of Firm

Private Equity Firm

Project Preferences

Type of Financing Preferred:
Leveraged Buyout
Expansion
Acquisition

Additional Information

Year Founded: 2005
Capital Under Management: $6,000,000
Current Activity Level : Actively seeking new investments

INVICTO HOLDING GMBH

Gruenstrasse 24
Dusseldorf, Germany 40212
Phone: 4921117520100
Fax: 49211175201030
E-mail: info@invicto.de
Website: www.invicto.de

Type of Firm

Private Equity Firm

Project Preferences

Type of Financing Preferred:
Leveraged Buyout
Management Buyouts
Acquisition

Geographical Preferences

International Preferences:
Switzerland
Austria
Germany

Industry Preferences

In Business Serv. prefer:
Consulting Services

Additional Information

Year Founded: 2010
Current Activity Level : Actively seeking new investments

INVIMED EUROPEJSKIE CENTRUM MACIERZYNSTWA SP Z O O

No.380, Zisong Road
6/F, Zhihui Park Business Bldg
Shanghai, China 201100
Phone: 862152965210
Fax: 862152965212
E-mail: contact@istartvc.com
Website: www.istartvc.com

Management and Staff

Cun Xue, Founding Partner
Li Zha, Founding Partner

Type of Firm

Incubator/Development Program

Project Preferences

Type of Financing Preferred:
Early Stage
Seed

Geographical Preferences

International Preferences:
China

Industry Preferences

In Communications prefer:
Telecommunications
Wireless Communications

In Internet Specific prefer:
Internet

In Medical/Health prefer:
Medical/Health

In Business Serv. prefer:
Media

In Other prefer:
Environment Responsible

Additional Information

Year Founded: 2011
Capital Under Management: $31,506,000
Current Activity Level : Actively seeking new investments

INVISION AG

Grafenaustrasse 7
Zug, Switzerland 6300
Phone: 41417290101
Fax: 41417290100
E-mail: info@invision.ch
Website: www.invision.ch

Other Offices

3 The Forum Grenville Street
St. Helier
Jersey, Channel Islands JE2 4UF

Management and Staff

Gerhard Weisschaedel, Partner
Marco Martelli, Partner
Martin Staub, Partner

Type of Firm

Private Equity Firm

Association Membership

Swiss Venture Capital Association (SECA)
European Private Equity and Venture Capital Assoc.

Project Preferences

Type of Financing Preferred:
Early Stage
Acquisition

Size of Investments Considered:
Min Size of Investment Considered (000s): $6,613
Max Size of Investment Considered (000s): $66,129

Geographical Preferences

United States Preferences:

International Preferences:
Ireland
Europe
Switzerland
China
Austria
Israel
Germany
France

Industry Focus

(% based on actual investment)
Internet Specific	28.6%
Computer Software and Services	25.5%
Medical/Health	20.2%
Computer Hardware	10.4%
Consumer Related	7.1%
Other Products	5.6%
Communications and Media	1.5%
Semiconductors/Other Elect.	1.1%

Additional Information

Name of Most Recent Fund: Invision V
Most Recent Fund Was Raised: 07/23/2013
Year Founded: 1997
Capital Under Management: $41,900,000
Current Activity Level : Actively seeking new investments

INVISION CAPITAL MANAGEMENT LLC

225 West Washington Street
Suite 550
Chicago, IL USA 60606
Phone: 312-236-4600
Website: www.invisioncapitalgroup.com

Other Offices

26 Orange Blossom Circle
Suite Ten
Ladera Ranch, CA USA 92694
Phone: 949-429-7707

Management and Staff

John Devenny, Principal
Patricia Borkowski, Principal
Robert Castillo, Principal
Stephen Dorton, Principal
Thomas Harrison, Principal

Type of Firm

Private Equity Firm

Association Membership

Natl Assoc of Small Bus. Inv. Co (NASBIC)

Project Preferences

Type of Financing Preferred:
Management Buyouts
Acquisition
Recapitalizations

Industry Preferences

In Business Serv. prefer:
Services
Distribution

In Manufact. prefer:
Manufacturing

Additional Information

Name of Most Recent Fund: Invision Capital I, L.P.
Most Recent Fund Was Raised: 02/02/2010
Year Founded: 2010
Capital Under Management: $77,800,000
Current Activity Level : Actively seeking new investments

INVITALIA VENTURES SGR SPA

Via Calabria 46
Rome, Italy 00187
Phone: 3906421601
Website: www.invitaliaventures.it

Type of Firm

Government Affiliated Program

Project Preferences

Type of Financing Preferred:
Early Stage
Expansion
Later Stage
Seed
Startup

Geographical Preferences

International Preferences:
Italy

Industry Preferences

In Computer Software prefer:
Software

In Internet Specific prefer:
Internet

Additional Information

Year Founded: 2014
Capital Under Management: $178,850,000
Current Activity Level : Actively seeking new investments

INVOKE CAPITAL

33 Saint James's Square
London, United Kingdom SW1Y 4JS
Phone: 442030087611
E-mail: enquiries@invokecapital.com
Website: www.invokecapital.com

Type of Firm

Private Equity Firm

Project Preferences

Type of Financing Preferred:
Early Stage
Expansion
Balanced

Geographical Preferences

International Preferences:
United Kingdom
Europe

Industry Preferences

In Computer Software prefer:
Software

Additional Information

Year Founded: 2012
Capital Under Management: $1,000,000,000
Current Activity Level : Actively seeking new investments

INVUS GROUP LLC

750 Lexington Avenue
30th Floor
New York, NY USA 10022
Phone: 2123711717
Fax: 2123711829
E-mail: NYOffice@invus.com
Website: www.invus.com

Other Offices

275 Grove Street
Suite 2-400
Auburndale, MA USA 02466
Phone: 617-663-4917

170 Piccadillly
London, United Kingdom W1J 9EJ
Phone: 44-20-7493-9133
Fax: 44-20-7518-9629

127, Avenue des Champs
Elysees
Paris, France 75008
Phone: 33-1-5690-5000
Fax: 33-1-5690-5010

99 Queen's Road Central
66/F, The Center
Central, Hong Kong
Phone: 852-2273-5400

Management and Staff

Aflalo Guimaraes, Managing Director
Christopher Sobecki, Managing Director
Evren Bilimer, Managing Director
Francis Cukierman, Managing Director
H. Eric Chiang, Managing Director
Janet Lee, Principal
Jonas Fajgenbaum, Managing Director
Julien Sallmard, Principal
Khalil Barrage, Managing Director
Luc Ta-Ngoc, Managing Director
Philippe Amouyal, Managing Director

Type of Firm
Private Equity Firm

Association Membership
French Venture Capital Association (AFIC)

Project Preferences

Role in Financing:
Will function either as deal originator or investor in deals created by others

Type of Financing Preferred:
Leveraged Buyout

Geographical Preferences

United States Preferences:

International Preferences:
Europe

Industry Focus
(% based on actual investment)

Internet Specific	33.9%
Other Products	14.3%
Computer Software and Services	12.9%
Biotechnology	12.6%
Industrial/Energy	12.2%
Computer Hardware	7.0%
Consumer Related	4.1%
Medical/Health	1.8%
Semiconductors/Other Elect.	1.2%

Additional Information
Year Founded: 1985
Capital Under Management: $4,000,000,000
Current Activity Level : Actively seeking new investments
Method of Compensation: Return on investment is of primary concern, do not charge fees

---

INWEST INVESTMENTS LTD

8800 Glenlyon Parkway
Burnaby, Canada V5J 5K3
Phone: 604-419-1560
Fax: 604-419-1560

Type of Firm
Private Equity Firm

Project Preferences

Type of Financing Preferred:
Early Stage

Additional Information
Year Founded: 2001
Current Activity Level : Actively seeking new investments

IOWA CORN OPPORTUNITIES LLC

5505 N.W. 88th Street
Suite 100
Johnston, IA USA 50131
Fax: 5152250781
Website: www.iowacornopportunities.com

Management and Staff

Brian Jones, Chief Operating Officer
Craig Floss, Chief Executive Officer
Jon Leafstedt, President

Type of Firm
Private Equity Firm

Project Preferences

Type of Financing Preferred:
Balanced

Geographical Preferences

United States Preferences:

Industry Preferences

In Agr/Forestr/Fish prefer:
Agribusiness
Agriculture related

Additional Information
Year Founded: 2008
Current Activity Level : Actively seeking new investments

IOWA SEED FUND II LLC

230 Second Street SE
Suite 212
Cedar Rapids, IA USA 52401

Management and Staff
Curtis Nelson, President

Type of Firm
Private Equity Firm

Project Preferences

Type of Financing Preferred:
Early Stage
Expansion
Later Stage
Seed

Size of Investments Considered
Min Size of Investment Considered (000s): $100
Max Size of Investment Considered (000s): $250

Geographical Preferences

United States Preferences:
Iowa

Additional Information
Year Founded: 2011
Current Activity Level : Actively seeking new investments

IOWA STARTUP ACCELERATOR MANAGEMENT INC

4211 Glass Road NorthEast
Suite A
Cedar Rapids, IA USA 52402
Phone: 3192211667
Website: www.iowastartupaccelerator.com

Type of Firm
Incubator/Development Program

Project Preferences

Type of Financing Preferred:
Early Stage
Seed
Startup

Size of Investments Considered:
Min Size of Investment Considered (000s): $20
Max Size of Investment Considered (000s): $100

Industry Preferences

In Medical/Health prefer:
Medical/Health

In Consumer Related prefer:
Education Related

In Transportation prefer:
Transportation

In Agr/Forestr/Fish prefer:
Agriculture related

Additional Information
Year Founded: 2014
Capital Under Management: $100,000
Current Activity Level : Actively seeking new investments

IP GROUP PLC

24 Cornhill
London, United Kingdom EC3V 3ND
Phone: 448450742929
Fax: 448450742928
E-mail: enquiries@ip2ipo.com
Website: www.ipgroupplc.com

Other Offices

103 Clarendon Road
Leeds Innovation Centre
Leeds, United Kingdom LS2 9DF
Phone: 44-870-126-3200
Fax: 44-870-126-3201

West One
Suite One, Seventh Floor, Forth Banks
Newcastle Upon Tyne, United Kingdom NE1 3PA
Phone: 845-519-4112
Fax: 845-519-4113

Management and Staff
Alan Aubrey, Chief Executive Officer
David Baynes, Chief Operating Officer
Greg Smith, Chief Financial Officer

Type of Firm
University Program

Project Preferences

Type of Financing Preferred:
Balanced

Geographical Preferences

International Preferences:
United Kingdom
Europe

Industry Preferences

In Computer Software prefer:
Software

In Internet Specific prefer:
Internet

In Semiconductor/Electr prefer:
Semiconductor

In Biotechnology prefer:
Biotechnology

Additional Information
Year Founded: 2001
Capital Under Management: $170,134,000
Current Activity Level : Actively seeking new investments

IP VENTURE ADVISORS PVT LTD

Dr. Annie Besant Road, Worli
Blk A, Lvl 1, Shiv Sagar Est
Mumbai, India 400018
Phone: 912261100723
Fax: 912261100703
E-mail: info@ironpillarfund.com

Type of Firm
Private Equity Firm

Project Preferences

Type of Financing Preferred:
Early Stage
Expansion

Geographical Preferences

International Preferences:
India

Industry Preferences

In Consumer Related prefer:
Consumer Products

Additional Information
Year Founded: 1969
Capital Under Management: $20,060,000
Current Activity Level : Actively seeking new investments

IPO WACHSTUMSFONDS BETEILIGUNGS MANAGEMENT GMBH

Gross-Enzersdorferstrasse 59
Vienna, Austria 1220
Phone: 43-1-9396-03261
Fax: 43-193960493262
E-mail: office@wachstumsfonds.at
Website: www.wiener-wachstumsfonds.at

Type of Firm
Private Equity Firm

Association Membership
Austrian PE and Venture Capital Association (AVCO)

Project Preferences

Type of Financing Preferred:
Leveraged Buyout
Early Stage
Mezzanine
Later Stage
Management Buyouts
Acquisition
Startup

Size of Investments Considered:
Min Size of Investment Considered (000s): $690
Max Size of Investment Considered (000s): $6,901

Geographical Preferences

International Preferences:
Slovenia
Hungary
Slovak Repub.
Europe
Czech Republic
Austria

Industry Preferences

In Communications prefer:
Telecommunications

In Medical/Health prefer:
Medical/Health

In Industrial/Energy prefer:
Industrial Products

In Business Serv. prefer:
Services

Additional Information
Year Founded: 2005
Current Activity Level : Actively seeking new investments

IPPON CAPITAL SA

rue de Chantepoulet 7
Geneve, Switzerland 1201

Type of Firm
Private Equity Firm

Project Preferences

Type of Financing Preferred:
Early Stage
Balanced
Later Stage

Geographical Preferences

International Preferences:
United Kingdom

Industry Preferences

In Biotechnology prefer:
Biotechnology

In Medical/Health prefer:
Medical/Health
Pharmaceuticals

Additional Information

Year Founded: 2013
Current Activity Level : Actively seeking new investments

IPR.VC MANAGEMENT OY

Mannerheimintie 20 B
Meeting Park Forum
Helsinki, Finland 00100
Website: ipr.vc

Type of Firm
Private Equity Firm

Project Preferences

Type of Financing Preferred:
Early Stage
Mezzanine
Turnaround
Distressed Debt

Geographical Preferences

International Preferences:
Finland

Industry Preferences

In Communications prefer:
Telecommunications
Media and Entertainment

In Computer Software prefer:
Software

In Internet Specific prefer:
Internet
Web Aggregation/Portals

In Business Serv. prefer:
Media

In Manufact. prefer:
Publishing

Additional Information

Year Founded: 2015
Capital Under Management: $22,800,000
Current Activity Level : Actively seeking new investments

IPS INDUSTRIAL PROMOTION SERVICES LTD

60 Columbia Way
Suite 720
Markham, Canada L3R 0C9
Phone: 905-475-9400
Fax: 905-475-5003
E-mail: info@ipscanada.com
Website: www.ipscanada.com

Other Offices

Rue de la Paix One-Three
P.O. Box 2067
Geneva, Switzerland 1211
Phone: 41229097200

54/1, Sher-E-Bangla Road
PO Box 696 Hazaribagh
Dhaka, Bangladesh 1000
Phone: 8802864242

62/C, 25th Commercial Street
Tauheed Commercial Area - Phase V
Karachi, Pakistan 75600
Phone: 92215863047

1861 Avenue General
Bobozo
Kingabwa/Kinshasa, Congo BP 2340
Phone: 2431246654

Kimathi Street
P.O. Box 30500 IPS Building
Kimathi, Kenya

One - Seven Cromwell Gardens
London, United Kingdom SW7 2SL
Phone: 441718239155
Fax: 441718238084

Type of Firm
Private Equity Firm

Project Preferences

Role in Financing:
Prefer role as deal originator but will also invest in deals created by others

Type of Financing Preferred:
Leveraged Buyout
Early Stage
Expansion
Turnaround
Management Buyouts
Acquisition

Size of Investments Considered:
Min Size of Investment Considered (000s): $500
Max Size of Investment Considered: No Limit

Geographical Preferences

United States Preferences:
North America
All U.S.

Canadian Preferences:
All Canada

Industry Preferences

In Consumer Related prefer:
Food/Beverage

In Industrial/Energy prefer:
Industrial Products

In Business Serv. prefer:
Distribution

In Manufact. prefer:
Manufacturing
Publishing

In Agr/Forestr/Fish prefer:
Agribusiness
Agriculture related

Additional Information

Year Founded: 1979
Capital Under Management: $25,000,000
Current Activity Level : Actively seeking new investments
Method of Compensation: Return on invest. most important, but chg. closing fees, service fees, etc.

IPSA SAS

10 rue de la Paix
Paris, France 75002
Phone: 33147031818
Fax: 33147031839
E-mail: info@innoven-partners.com
Website: www.ipsa-pe.com

Management and Staff

Jean-Pierre Chuet, Founder
Thomas Dicker, Managing Partner

Type of Firm
Private Equity Firm

Association Membership
French Venture Capital Association (AFIC)

Project Preferences

Type of Financing Preferred:
Early Stage
Later Stage
Seed

Size of Investments Considered:
Min Size of Investment Considered (000s): $1,352
Max Size of Investment Considered (000s): $6,764

Geographical Preferences

International Preferences:
Europe
France

Industry Preferences

In Communications prefer:
Communications and Media
Telecommunications

In Computer Software prefer:
Artificial Intelligence

In Semiconductor/Electr prefer:
Electronics

In Biotechnology prefer:
Biotechnology

In Industrial/Energy prefer:
Energy

In Financial Services prefer:
Financial Services

In Business Serv. prefer:
Services

Additional Information

Year Founded: 1997
Capital Under Management: $212,700,000
Current Activity Level : Actively seeking new investments

IPT IDEYA ZAO

ul. Peterburgskaya 50
Kazan, Russia 420107
Phone: 7-843-570-68-50
Fax: 7-843-570-68-40
E-mail: info@tpidea.ru
Website: www.tpidea.ru

Management and Staff

Albert Karimov, Chief Financial Officer

Type of Firm

Government Affiliated Program

Association Membership

Russian Venture Capital Association (RVCA)

Project Preferences

Type of Financing Preferred:
Early Stage
Expansion
Seed
Startup

Geographical Preferences

International Preferences:
Russia

Additional Information

Year Founded: 2004
Current Activity Level : Actively seeking new investments

IQ CAPITAL PARTNERS LLP

85 Regent Street
Cambridge, United Kingdom CB2 1AW
Phone: 441223345616
E-mail: enquiries@iqcapital.co.uk
Website: www.iqcapital.co.uk

Management and Staff

Edward Stacey, Partner
Kerry Baldwin, Partner
Max Bautin, Partner

Type of Firm

Private Equity Firm

Association Membership

British Venture Capital Association (BVCA)
European Private Equity and Venture Capital Assoc.

Project Preferences

Type of Financing Preferred:
Early Stage
Later Stage
Seed

Geographical Preferences

International Preferences:
United Kingdom

Industry Preferences

In Communications prefer:
Communications and Media

In Industrial/Energy prefer:
Environmental Related

Additional Information

Year Founded: 2006
Capital Under Management: $70,120,000
Current Activity Level : Actively seeking new investments

IQ PARTNERS SA

Woloska 7
Fifth Floor, Mars Building
Warsaw, Poland 02 675
Phone: 48225670000
Fax: 48225670001
E-mail: info@iqpartners.pl
Website: www.iqpartners.pl

Management and Staff

Jacek Sklodowski, Chief Financial Officer

Type of Firm

Private Equity Firm

Association Membership

Polish Venture Capital Association (PSIC/PPEA)

Project Preferences

Type of Financing Preferred:
Seed
Startup

Geographical Preferences

International Preferences:
Poland

Industry Preferences

In Communications prefer:
Wireless Communications
Media and Entertainment

In Computer Software prefer:
Software

In Internet Specific prefer:
Internet
Ecommerce

Additional Information

Year Founded: 2003
Current Activity Level : Actively seeking new investments

IRDI MIDI PYRENEES SA

18, place Dupuy
BP 18008
Toulouse, France 31080
Phone: 0033581317320
Fax: 0033581317339
E-mail: contact@irdi.fr
Website: www.irdi.fr

Type of Firm

Private Equity Firm

Association Membership

French Venture Capital Association (AFIC)

Project Preferences

Type of Financing Preferred:
Leveraged Buyout
Early Stage
Expansion
Later Stage
Management Buyouts
Acquisition

Size of Investments Considered:
Min Size of Investment Considered (000s): $262
Max Size of Investment Considered (000s): $4,231

Geographical Preferences

International Preferences:
Europe
France

Additional Information

Year Founded: 1981
Capital Under Management: $129,600,000
Current Activity Level : Actively seeking new investments

IRDI SORIDEC GESTION SAS

18, Place Dominique Dupuy
Toulouse, France 31000

Type of Firm
Private Equity Firm

Project Preferences

Type of Financing Preferred:
Leveraged Buyout
Early Stage
Expansion
Later Stage
Management Buyouts
Acquisition

Geographical Preferences

International Preferences:
Europe
France

Industry Preferences

In Communications prefer:
Communications and Media

In Computer Software prefer:
Data Processing

In Biotechnology prefer:
Biotechnology

In Consumer Related prefer:
Food/Beverage

In Industrial/Energy prefer:
Industrial Products

In Business Serv. prefer:
Services

In Agr/Forestr/Fish prefer:
Agriculture related

Additional Information

Year Founded: 1983
Current Activity Level : Actively seeking new investments

IRELAND STRATEGIC INVESTMENT FUND

Treasury Building, Grand Canal
Dublin, Ireland 2
Phone: 35312384000
E-mail: info@isif.ie
Website: www.isif.ie

Type of Firm
Government Affiliated Program

Project Preferences

Type of Financing Preferred:
Generalist PE

Geographical Preferences

International Preferences:
Ireland

Additional Information

Year Founded: 1969
Current Activity Level : Actively seeking new investments

IRIS CAPITAL MANAGEMENT SAS

62, rue Pierre Charon
Paris, France 75008
Phone: 33145627373
Fax: 33145627370
E-mail: general@iriscapital.com
Website: www.iriscapital.com

Other Offices

217, Loft 2A
Dubai Media City, PO Box 502869
Dubai, Utd. Arab Em.
Phone: 97143688665

60 Spear Street
c/o Orange, 11th floor
SAN FRANCISCO, CA USA 94105
Phone: 14152836715

10/F, Raycom Infotech Park C
South Tower, n 2
Beijing, China 100190
Phone: 861082175141
Fax: 8613911339476

c/o Orange Labs, Keio Shinjuku Oiwake
Bldg 9F, Shinjuku-ku
Tokyo, Japan 160-0022
Phone: 81353128548

Office 419, Bahrain Tower
King Fahad Road
Riyadh, Saudi Arabia

Benrather Strasse 15
Dusseldorf, Germany 40213

3530 Boulevard Saint-Laurent
Bureau 300
Montreal, Canada H2X 2V1
Phone: 5142854569

Management and Staff

Alexander Wiedmer, Partner
Antoine Garrigues, Managing Partner
Curt Gunsenheimer, Partner
Erik De La Riviere, Partner
Erkan Kilicaslan, Partner
Guillaume Meulle, Partner
Guy Canali, Chief Financial Officer
Pierre de Fouquet, Managing Partner
Sophie Dingreville, Partner

Type of Firm
Investment Management Firm

Association Membership

French Venture Capital Association (AFIC)
German Venture Capital Association (BVK)
European Private Equity and Venture Capital Assoc.

Project Preferences

Type of Financing Preferred:
Leveraged Buyout
Early Stage
Generalist PE
Later Stage
Acquisition
Startup
Recapitalizations

Size of Investments Considered:

Min Size of Investment Considered (000s): $4,131
Max Size of Investment Considered (000s): $27,540

Geographical Preferences

United States Preferences:
All U.S.

Canadian Preferences:
All Canada

International Preferences:
Europe
Lebanon
France

Industry Focus

(% based on actual investment)

Computer Software and Services	38.0%
Internet Specific	27.5%
Communications and Media	17.9%
Consumer Related	6.0%
Other Products	5.3%
Semiconductors/Other Elect.	3.4%
Computer Hardware	1.8%
Medical/Health	0.2%

Additional Information

Year Founded: 1986
Capital Under Management: $508,100,000
Current Activity Level : Actively seeking new investments

IRIS CAPNAMIC MANAGEMENT GMBH

Kaiser-Wilhelm-Ring 26
Cologne, Germany 50672
Phone: 4922167781930
Fax: 4922167781931
E-mail: info@capnamic.de

Type of Firm
Private Equity Firm

Project Preferences

Type of Financing Preferred:
Early Stage
Balanced
Later Stage
Seed
Startup

Geographical Preferences

International Preferences:
Europe
Germany

Industry Preferences

In Communications prefer:
Communications and Media
Media and Entertainment

Additional Information
Year Founded: 2007
Current Activity Level : Actively seeking new investments

IRON CAPITAL LTD

1 Neathouse Place
London, United Kingdom SW1V L1H
E-mail: contact@iron-mail.co.uk
Website: irongroup.co

Type of Firm
Private Equity Firm

Project Preferences

Type of Financing Preferred:
Early Stage
Seed

Industry Preferences

In Internet Specific prefer:
E-Commerce Technology
Ecommerce

Additional Information
Year Founded: 2016
Capital Under Management: $10,860,000
Current Activity Level : Actively seeking new investments

IRON GATE CAPITAL LLC

3000 Pearl Street
Suite 201
Boulder, CO USA 80301
Phone: 3033951335
Fax: 3039571961
E-mail: info@irongatecapital.com
Website: www.irongatecapital.com

Management and Staff
Douglas Fahoury, Partner
Robert Cohen, Partner
Steve McConahey, Partner

Type of Firm
Private Equity Firm

Project Preferences

Role in Financing:
Will function either as deal originator or investor in deals created by others

Type of Financing Preferred:
Leveraged Buyout
Early Stage
Expansion
Mezzanine
Generalist PE
Balanced
Management Buyouts
Industry Rollups

Industry Preferences

In Medical/Health prefer:
Medical/Health

In Consumer Related prefer:
Retail

In Industrial/Energy prefer:
Energy

In Financial Services prefer:
Real Estate

In Business Serv. prefer:
Services

Additional Information
Name of Most Recent Fund: Iron Gate Investments VIII LLC
Most Recent Fund Was Raised: 02/29/2008
Year Founded: 2005
Capital Under Management: $1,000,000
Current Activity Level : Actively seeking new investments

IRON RANGE CAPITAL PARTNERS LLC

311 South Wacker Drive, Suite 4525
Chicago, IL USA 60606
Phone: 3124966581
Website: www.ironrangecapital.com

Type of Firm
Private Equity Firm

Project Preferences

Type of Financing Preferred:
Leveraged Buyout
Acquisition
Recapitalizations

Geographical Preferences

United States Preferences:

Industry Preferences

In Business Serv. prefer:
Services
Distribution

In Manufact. prefer:
Manufacturing

Additional Information
Year Founded: 2013
Current Activity Level : Actively seeking new investments

IRONBRIDGE CAPITAL PTY LTD

One Bligh Street, Level 17
Sydney, Australia 2000
Phone: 61292508700
Fax: 61292508777
E-mail: contact@ironbridge.com.au
Website: www.ironbridge.com.au

Other Offices

188 Quay Street
Level 27 PwC Tower
Auckland, New Zealand
Phone: 649-363-2972
Fax: 649-363-2727

88 Phillip Street
Level 39
Sydney, Australia 2000
Phone: 61292508700
Fax: 61292508777

Management and Staff
John Russell, Partner
Joshua McKean, Partner
Julian Knights, Partner
Michael Hill, Partner
Paul Evans, Chief Operating Officer
Stuart Mitchell, Chief Financial Officer

Type of Firm
Investment Management Firm

Association Membership
New Zealand Venture Capital Association
Australian Venture Capital Association (AVCAL)

Project Preferences

Role in Financing:
Will function either as deal originator or investor in deals created by others

Type of Financing Preferred:
Leveraged Buyout
Later Stage
Management Buyouts
Acquisition

Geographical Preferences

International Preferences:
Australia
New Zealand

Industry Preferences

In Medical/Health prefer:
Medical/Health
Health Services

In Financial Services prefer:
Financial Services

In Business Serv. prefer:
Services

Additional Information
Name of Most Recent Fund: Ironbridge Fund II
Most Recent Fund Was Raised: 11/01/2006
Year Founded: 2003
Capital Under Management: $1,549,500,000
Current Activity Level : Actively seeking new investments
Method of Compensation: Return on invest. most important, but chg. closing fees, service fees, etc.

IRONBRIDGE EQUITY PARTNERS MANAGEMENT LTD

22 Adelaide Street West
Suite 3520
Toronto, Canada M5H 4E3
Phone: 4168630105
Website: www.ironbridgeequity.com

Management and Staff
Andrew Walton, Partner
Andrew Mitchell, Vice President
Jeffrey Murphy, Partner
Jonathan Draycott, Vice President
Peter Samson, Managing Partner

Type of Firm
Private Equity Firm

Association Membership
Canadian Venture Capital Association

Project Preferences

Type of Financing Preferred:
Leveraged Buyout
Expansion
Management Buyouts
Recapitalizations

Geographical Preferences

Canadian Preferences:
All Canada

Industry Preferences

In Consumer Related prefer:
Consumer

In Financial Services prefer:
Real Estate
Financial Services

In Business Serv. prefer:
Services
Distribution

In Manufact. prefer:
Manufacturing

In Other prefer:
Environment Responsible

Additional Information
Year Founded: 2006
Capital Under Management: $400,000,000
Current Activity Level : Actively seeking new investments

IRONFIRE CAPITAL LLC

310 Townsend Street
San Francisco, CA USA 94107
E-mail: angel@ironfirecapital.com
Website: www.ironfirecapital.com

Type of Firm
Private Equity Firm

Project Preferences

Type of Financing Preferred:
Early Stage

Industry Preferences

In Computer Hardware prefer:
Integrated Turnkey System

In Computer Software prefer:
Software

Additional Information
Year Founded: 2013
Current Activity Level : Actively seeking new investments

IRONWOOD CAPITAL PARTNERS

116 Havelock Road
Colombo 5, Sri Lanka
Phone: 94112055730
E-mail: info@ironwoodcapitalpartners.com
Website: iwcpsl.com/

Type of Firm
Private Equity Firm

Project Preferences

Type of Financing Preferred:
Balanced

Geographical Preferences

International Preferences:
Sri Lanka

Industry Preferences

In Financial Services prefer:
Financial Services

Additional Information
Year Founded: 2014
Capital Under Management: $30,000,000
Current Activity Level : Actively seeking new investments

IRONWOOD INVESTMENT MANAGEMENT LLC

200 State Street
Fourth Floor
Boston, MA USA 02109
Phone: 6177577600
Fax: 6177577605
E-mail: info@ironwoodfunds.com
Website: www.ironwoodinvestmentmanagement.com

Other Offices
One Beacon Street
34th Floor
Boston, MA USA 02108
Phone: 6177427600
Fax: 6177427610

Management and Staff
Alex Levental, Managing Director
Carolyn Galiette, Senior Managing Director
Christopher Gabrieli, Managing Director
Dickson Suit, Managing Director
James Barra, Managing Director
M. Joshua Tolkoff, Managing Director
Marc Reich, President
Roger Roche, Senior Managing Director
Sanford Cloud, Principal
Victor Budnick, Managing Director
Zachary Luce, Chief Financial Officer

Type of Firm
SBIC

Association Membership
Natl Assoc of Small Bus. Inv. Co (NASBIC)

Project Preferences

Type of Financing Preferred:
Leveraged Buyout
Mezzanine
Balanced
Later Stage
Recapitalizations

Geographical Preferences

United States Preferences:
Mississippi
Florida
Maine

Industry Preferences

In Medical/Health prefer:
Medical/Health

In Consumer Related prefer:
Consumer Products
Education Related

In Industrial/Energy prefer:
Environmental Related

In Business Serv. prefer:
Services
Distribution
Media

In Manufact. prefer:
Manufacturing

Additional Information
Name of Most Recent Fund: Ironwood Mezzanine Fund III, L.P.
Most Recent Fund Was Raised: 10/04/2011
Year Founded: 1994
Capital Under Management: $300,000,000
Current Activity Level : Actively seeking new investments

IRONWOOD PARTNERS LLC

420 Lexington Avenue
Suite 2334
New York, NY USA 10170
Phone: 2126827100
Fax: 2126825363
E-mail: info@ironwood-partners.com
Website: www.ironwood-partners.com

Management and Staff
James Kelliher, Partner
John Cosentino, Co-Founder
Michael Jackson, Co-Founder
Paul Balser, Co-Founder

Type of Firm
Private Equity Firm

Project Preferences

Type of Financing Preferred:
Leveraged Buyout
Expansion
Recapitalizations

Geographical Preferences

United States Preferences:
North America

Industry Preferences

In Business Serv. prefer:
Distribution

In Manufact. prefer:
Manufacturing

Additional Information
Year Founded: 2003
Capital Under Management: $20,000,000
Current Activity Level : Actively seeking new investments

IRPAC DEVELOPPEMENT SA

9 bis rue des bons malades
Reims, France 51100
Phone: 33326400326
Fax: 33326883750
E-mail: contact@irpac.eu

Type of Firm
Private Equity Firm

Association Membership
French Venture Capital Association (AFIC)

Project Preferences

Type of Financing Preferred:
Leveraged Buyout
Early Stage
Generalist PE
Later Stage
Management Buyouts
Acquisition
Startup

Geographical Preferences

International Preferences:
France

Industry Preferences

In Computer Other prefer:
Computer Related

In Biotechnology prefer:
Agricultural/Animal Bio.

In Consumer Related prefer:
Consumer
Retail

In Transportation prefer:
Transportation

In Business Serv. prefer:
Services

Additional Information
Year Founded: 1984
Current Activity Level : Actively seeking new investments

IRVING PLACE CAPITAL LLC

745 Fifth Avenue
New York, NY USA 10151
Phone: 2125514500
E-mail: info@irvingplacecapital.com
Website: www.irvingplacecapital.com

Management and Staff
B. Austin, Vice President
Bob Bode, Managing Director
Brad Jacobsen, Vice President
Bret Bowerman, Principal
David Knoch, Senior Managing Director
Devraj Roy, Principal
Douglas Korn, Senior Managing Director
Eve Mongiardo, Chief Operating Officer
James McDonough, Vice President
John Howard, Chief Executive Officer
Keith Zadourian, Principal
Matthew Turner, Principal
Michael Feiner, Senior Managing Director
Philip Carpenter, Senior Managing Director
Richard Perkal, Senior Managing Director
Robert Juneja, Senior Managing Director

Type of Firm
Private Equity Firm

Association Membership
Private Equity Council (PEC)

Project Preferences

Type of Financing Preferred:
Leveraged Buyout
Recapitalizations

Geographical Preferences

United States Preferences:
North America

Industry Focus
(% based on actual investment)
Consumer Related	39.9%
Industrial/Energy	27.2%
Other Products	13.2%
Internet Specific	8.9%
Computer Software and Services	4.9%
Semiconductors/Other Elect.	2.9%
Communications and Media	2.2%
Medical/Health	0.6%
Biotechnology	0.1%
Computer Hardware	0.0%

Additional Information
Year Founded: 1983
Capital Under Management: $3,300,000,000
Current Activity Level : Actively seeking new investments

IS GIRISIM SERMAYESI YATIRIM ORTAKLIGI AS

Is Kuleleri Kule 2, Kat 2
Levent
Istanbul, Turkey 34330
Phone: 902123251744
Fax: 902122705808
E-mail: info@isgirisim.com.tr
Website: www.isgirisim.com.tr

Management and Staff
A. Murat Ozgen, Chief Executive Officer
F. Banu Gul, Managing Director
Fatma Gul, Chief Financial Officer

Type of Firm
Bank Affiliated

Project Preferences

Type of Financing Preferred:
Leveraged Buyout
Early Stage
Expansion
Generalist PE
Balanced
Later Stage
Management Buyouts
Acquisition
Startup

Geographical Preferences

International Preferences:
Turkey
Europe

Industry Preferences

In Communications prefer:
Telecommunications

In Medical/Health prefer:
Medical/Health
Health Services
Pharmaceuticals

In Consumer Related prefer:
Consumer
Retail
Food/Beverage
Education Related

In Industrial/Energy prefer:
Energy
Materials

In Business Serv. prefer:
Services
Media

Additional Information
Year Founded: 2000
Capital Under Management: $76,000,000
Current Activity Level : Actively seeking new investments

ISAI GESTION SAS

10bis, ave de la Grande Armee
Paris, France 75017
Website: www.isai.fr

Management and Staff
Geoffroy Roux de Bezieux, Co-Founder
Ouriel Ohayon, Co-Founder
Pierre Kosciusko-Morizet, Co-Founder
Stephane Treppoz, Co-Founder

Type of Firm
Private Equity Firm

Association Membership
French Venture Capital Association (AFIC)

Project Preferences

Type of Financing Preferred:
Early Stage
Later Stage
Seed
Startup

Geographical Preferences

International Preferences:
United Kingdom
Europe
France

Industry Preferences

In Internet Specific prefer:
Internet

Additional Information
Name of Most Recent Fund: ISAI Expansion FCPR
Most Recent Fund Was Raised: 06/14/2012
Year Founded: 2008
Capital Under Management: $109,582,000
Current Activity Level : Actively seeking new investments

ISATIS CAPITAL SA

23, Rue Taitbout
Paris, France 75009
Phone: 33184791730
Website: isatis-capital.fr

Type of Firm
Private Equity Firm

Project Preferences

Type of Financing Preferred:
Leveraged Buyout
Early Stage
Expansion
Generalist PE
Later Stage
Management Buyouts
Acquisition

Geographical Preferences

International Preferences:
France

Additional Information
Year Founded: 2013
Capital Under Management: $44,740,000
Current Activity Level : Actively seeking new investments

ISEED VENTURES

One Market - Spear Tower
36th Floor
San Francisco, CA USA 94105
E-mail: inquiry@iseedvc.com
Website: www.iseedvc.com

Management and Staff
Adam Lin, General Partner
Bryan Cheng, General Partner

Type of Firm
Private Equity Firm

Project Preferences

Type of Financing Preferred:
Early Stage
Balanced
Seed

Additional Information
Year Founded: 1969
Current Activity Level : Actively seeking new investments

ISELECT FUND LLC

4240 Duncan Avenue
Saint Louis, MO USA 63110
Phone: 8009635099
E-mail: curious@iselectfund.com

Management and Staff
Craig Herron, Vice President
Dan Schaub, Chief Operating Officer
Scott Prey, Venture Partner

Type of Firm
Private Equity Firm

Project Preferences

Type of Financing Preferred:
Early Stage
Balanced
Seed

Geographical Preferences

United States Preferences:

Industry Preferences

In Financial Services prefer:
Investment Groups

Additional Information
Year Founded: 2017
Current Activity Level : Actively seeking new investments

ISHERPA CAPITAL

6400 S. Fiddler's Green Circle, Suite 975
Greenwood Village, CO USA 80111
Phone: 3036450500
Fax: 3036450501
E-mail: info@isherpa.com
Website: www.isherpa.com

Management and Staff
Deepu John, Principal
Gary Rohr, Managing Partner
Nim Patel, Principal
Peter Mannetti, Managing Partner
Vipanj Patel, Managing Partner

Type of Firm
Private Equity Firm

Project Preferences

Type of Financing Preferred:
Early Stage
Seed

Geographical Preferences

United States Preferences:
All U.S.

International Preferences:
All International

Industry Preferences

In Communications prefer:
Communications and Media
Telecommunications
Wireless Communications

Additional Information
Year Founded: 2000
Capital Under Management: $31,000,000
Current Activity Level : Actively seeking new investments

ISIS VENTURE CAPITAL SL

Calle Aribau
240 8 Planta-Oficina L bis
Barcelona, Spain 08006
Phone: 34934140598
E-mail: info@isis.com
Website: www.isisve.com

Management and Staff
Angel Marquez, Co-Founder
Miguel Planas, President
Pedro Fontana, Co-Founder

Type of Firm
Incubator/Development Program

Project Preferences

Type of Financing Preferred:
Startup

Industry Preferences

In Computer Software prefer:
Software
Systems Software
Applications Software
Artificial Intelligence

In Business Serv. prefer:
Services

Additional Information
Year Founded: 1969
Current Activity Level : Actively seeking new investments

ISLAMIC DEVELOPMENT BANK

P.O. Box 5925
Jeddah, Saudi Arabia 21432
Phone: 96626361400
Fax: 96626366871

Other Offices
P.O. Box 11545
Muharraq, Bahrain
Phone: 973-536-100
Fax: 973-536-206

Management and Staff
Ahmet Tiktik, Vice President

Type of Firm
Bank Affiliated

Project Preferences

Type of Financing Preferred:
Early Stage
Balanced
Startup

Geographical Preferences

International Preferences:
Indonesia
Brunei
Middle East
Asia
Malaysia
All International

Industry Preferences

In Communications prefer:
Telecommunications

In Industrial/Energy prefer:
Energy
Oil and Gas Exploration
Coal Related
Energy Conservation Relat
Environmental Related

In Transportation prefer:
Transportation
Aerospace

In Financial Services prefer:
Financial Services

Additional Information
Year Founded: 1975
Current Activity Level : Actively seeking new investments

ISLINGTON CAPITAL PARTNERS LLC

2345 Washington Street
Suite 101
Newton Lower Falls, MA USA 02462
Phone: 6175583200
Website: www.islingtoncapital.com

Management and Staff
John Cullinane, Co-Founder
Paul Spinale, Co-Founder

Type of Firm
Private Equity Firm

Project Preferences

Role in Financing:
Prefer role as deal originator

Type of Financing Preferred:
Management Buyouts
Acquisition
Recapitalizations

Geographical Preferences

United States Preferences:
Southeast
Northeast

Additional Information

Year Founded: 2005
Current Activity Level : Actively seeking new investments

ISOMER CAPITAL LLP

100 Victoria Street
Seventh Floor
London, United Kingdom SW1E 5JL
Phone: 442079636884
E-mail: info@isomercapital.com
Website: www.isomercapital.com

Type of Firm
Private Equity Firm

Project Preferences

Type of Financing Preferred:
Fund of Funds

Geographical Preferences

International Preferences:
Europe

Additional Information
Year Founded: 2016
Current Activity Level : Actively seeking new investments

ISPRING CAPITAL SDN BHD

Jalan 13/2
Lot 2A
Petaling Jaya, Malaysia 46200
Phone: 60374955000
Fax: 60374955088

Type of Firm
Private Equity Advisor or Fund of Funds

Project Preferences

Type of Financing Preferred:
Balanced

Size of Investments Considered:
Min Size of Investment Considered (000s): $159
Max Size of Investment Considered (000s): $1,177

Geographical Preferences

International Preferences:
Asia
Malaysia

Industry Preferences

In Communications prefer:
Telecommunications
Wireless Communications
Data Communications

In Internet Specific prefer:
Internet
Ecommerce

In Semiconductor/Electr prefer:
Electronics
Semiconductor

In Medical/Health prefer:
Medical/Health

Additional Information
Year Founded: 2000
Current Activity Level : Actively seeking new investments

ISRAEL BIOTECH FUND I LP

3 Pekeris Street
Rabin Science Park
Rehovot, Israel 7670212
Phone: 972544655238
E-mail: Info@IsraelBiotechFund.com
Website: www.israelbiotechfund.com

Type of Firm
Private Equity Firm

Project Preferences

Type of Financing Preferred:
Early Stage
Seed

Geographical Preferences

International Preferences:
Israel

Industry Preferences

In Biotechnology prefer:
Biotechnology

In Medical/Health prefer:
Medical/Health
Pharmaceuticals

Additional Information
Year Founded: 2015
Current Activity Level : Actively seeking new investments

ISRAEL CLEANTECH VENTURES

Hakfar Hayarok Youth Village
Ramat Hasharon, Israel 47800
Phone: 97236446611
Fax: 97236493737
E-mail: info@israelcleantech.com
Website: www.israelcleantech.com

Management and Staff
Arnon Goldfarb, Venture Partner
Eytan Levy, Venture Partner
Glen Schwaber, Partner
Israel Kroizer, Venture Partner
Jack Levy, Partner
Lila Frenkel, Chief Financial Officer
Meir Ukeles, Partner
Yigal Stav, Venture Partner

Type of Firm
Private Equity Firm

Association Membership
Israel Venture Association

Project Preferences

Type of Financing Preferred:
Early Stage
Startup

Geographical Preferences

International Preferences:
Israel

Industry Preferences

In Industrial/Energy prefer:
Energy
Energy Conservation Relat
Environmental Related

In Agr/Forestr/Fish prefer:
Agriculture related

Additional Information
Name of Most Recent Fund: Israel Cleantech Ventures II, L.P.
Most Recent Fund Was Raised: 02/17/2011
Year Founded: 2006
Capital Under Management: $74,000,000
Current Activity Level : Actively seeking new investments

ISRAEL DISCOUNT CAPITAL MARKETS & INVESTMENTS, LTD.

23 Menahem Begin Road
Levinstein Tower, 29th floor
Tel Aviv, Israel 66182
Phone: 97237100102
Fax: 97237100100
E-mail: info@dcm.co.il
Website: www.dcm.co.il

Type of Firm
Bank Affiliated

Project Preferences

Type of Financing Preferred:
Leveraged Buyout
Early Stage
Mezzanine
Balanced
Later Stage
Acquisition
Startup

Geographical Preferences

International Preferences:
Israel

Industry Preferences

In Communications prefer:
Data Communications

In Biotechnology prefer:
Biotechnology

In Medical/Health prefer:
Medical Products

In Financial Services prefer:
Real Estate

Additional Information

Year Founded: 2000
Current Activity Level : Actively seeking new investments

ISRAEL INFINITY VENTURE CAPITAL FUND ISRAEL LP

3 Azrieli Center
42nd Floor, Triangle Tower
Tel Aviv, Israel 67023
Phone: 97236075456
Fax: 97236075455
E-mail: info@infinity-equity.com
Website: www.infinity-equity.com

Other Offices

25 Harbour Road
Unit 2001, Harbour Centre
Wan Chai, Hong Kong
Phone: 85221869016
Fax: 85221693117

No. 8 North Second Ave, Haidian District
Room 1515, Zhongguancun SOHO
Beijing, China 100080
Phone: 861059732960
Fax: 861059732965

No. 7 Shanghai Street
F22, Shangshi Building B
Harbin, China 150010

#136, Huanghe Avenue, High-tech District
Room701, Technology&Science Center
Shijiazhuang, China 050035
Phone: 8631166699011

No. 56 WenChang Road West
Room 412, Yangzhou
Jiangsu, China 225012

No. 1468 West Nanjing Road
3304 United Plaza
Shanghai, China 200040
Phone: 862162896166
Fax: 862162896133

2F, Sanlake, 345 Fengli Rd
Suzhou Industrial Park
Suzhou, China 215026
Phone: 8651266969511
Fax: 8651266969533

Southwest Airport Economic Delp Zone
Room315, Changcheng Road
Chengdu, China
Phone: 862867066688
Fax: 862867066685

33rd Floor
900 Third Avenue
New York, NY USA 10022
Phone: 2123173376
Fax: 2123173365

#9-1, East Taihu Road, Xinbei District
Room 2602
Changzhou, China

32, Dover Street
London, United Kingdom W1S 4NE
Phone: 442077589153
Fax: 442077589151

Lane 999 Yangfan Road, R&D Park
204-205, Bldg 5, National Hi-tech Zone
Ningbo, China
Phone: 8657487993880
Fax: 8657487993884

Room 704, 328 Xing Hu Street
Building 9, Suzhou Industrial Park
Jiangsu, China
Phone: 051262925886
Fax: 051262925763

2-13-1, Kakigara-cho Nihonbashi
6/F, NS Building
Tokyo, Japan 103-0014
Phone: 366598051
Fax: 366598052

Management and Staff

Ariel Poppel, Managing Director
Avishai Silvershatz, Managing Partner
Bella Ohana, Managing Director
Cao Yansong, Managing Director
Kersten Hui, Managing Director
Limei Zhao, Managing Director
Mark Chess, Venture Partner
Robert Hu, Managing Director
Steven Hsieh, Managing Director

Type of Firm

Private Equity Firm

Association Membership

Israel Venture Association

Project Preferences

Role in Financing:
Will function either as deal originator or investor in deals created by others

Type of Financing Preferred:
Early Stage
Expansion
Balanced
Later Stage
Startup

Geographical Preferences

United States Preferences:
North America

International Preferences:
China
Israel
Asia
Singapore

Industry Preferences

In Communications prefer:
Communications and Media
Wireless Communications

In Computer Software prefer:
Software

In Internet Specific prefer:
Internet

In Semiconductor/Electr prefer:
Semiconductor
Component Testing Equipmt

In Biotechnology prefer:
Biotechnology

In Medical/Health prefer:
Medical/Health

In Consumer Related prefer:
Entertainment and Leisure

In Industrial/Energy prefer:
Industrial Products
Materials

In Manufact. prefer:
Manufacturing

Additional Information
Year Founded: 1993
Capital Under Management: $700,000,000
Current Activity Level : Actively seeking new investments

ISRAEL SECONDARY LTD

8 Hachoshlim Street
6th Floor
Herzelia Pituach, Israel 4672408
Phone: 97297747070
Fax: 97299505500
E-mail: info@israelsecondary.com
Website: www.israelsecondary.com

Type of Firm
Private Equity Advisor or Fund of Funds

Geographical Preferences

International Preferences:
Israel

Additional Information
Year Founded: 2007
Capital Under Management: $100,000,000
Current Activity Level : Actively seeking new investments

ISTANBUL INVESTMENT GROUP

Buyukdere Caddesi Yapi Kredi
Plaza, B Blok, K.7
Istanbul, Turkey 34250
Phone: 902123859800
Fax: 902123859898
Website: www.iig.com.tr

Type of Firm
Private Equity Firm

Project Preferences

Type of Financing Preferred:
Leveraged Buyout
Generalist PE

Geographical Preferences

International Preferences:
Turkey

Additional Information
Year Founded: 2016
Current Activity Level : Actively seeking new investments

ISTUARY VENTURE CAPITAL INC

1125 Howe Street
Eight floor
Vancouver, Canada V6Z 2K8
Phone: 16042990388
Fax: 16042290034
Website: www.istuary.com

Other Offices
21650 Oxnard Street
Suite 1440
WOODLAND HILLS, CA USA 91367

Type of Firm
Corporate PE/Venture

Project Preferences

Type of Financing Preferred:
Balanced

Industry Preferences

In Financial Services prefer:
Financial Services

In Business Serv. prefer:
Consulting Services

Additional Information
Year Founded: 2012
Capital Under Management: $5,440,000
Current Activity Level : Actively seeking new investments

ISU VENTURE CAPITAL CO LTD

6F, ISU Building, Banpo-Dong
112-4 Seocho-Gu
Seoul, South Korea 137-040
Phone: 822-3482-2010
Fax: 822-3482-2015
Website: www.isuvc.com

Management and Staff
Yoon Chae, President

Type of Firm
Private Equity Firm

Association Membership
Korean Venture Capital Association (KVCA)

Project Preferences

Type of Financing Preferred:
Balanced

Geographical Preferences

International Preferences:
Asia

Industry Preferences

In Communications prefer:
Communications and Media
Entertainment

In Consumer Related prefer:
Entertainment and Leisure

Additional Information
Year Founded: 2000
Capital Under Management: $64,800,000
Current Activity Level : Actively seeking new investments

IT MATRIX VENTURES

1071 Post Road East
Westport, CT USA 06880
Phone: 203-226-7052
Fax: 203-226-5741

Management and Staff
Ronald Klammer, Managing Director

Type of Firm
Bank Affiliated

Project Preferences

Role in Financing:
Prefer role as deal originator

Type of Financing Preferred:
Early Stage
Seed

Geographical Preferences

United States Preferences:

Industry Preferences

In Communications prefer:
Commercial Communications
Telecommunications
Wireless Communications
Data Communications
Satellite Microwave Comm.
Other Communication Prod.

In Internet Specific prefer:
E-Commerce Technology

In Semiconductor/Electr prefer:
Electronic Components
Semiconductor
Micro-Processing
Controllers and Sensors
Sensors
Circuit Boards
Component Testing Equipmt
Laser Related
Fiber Optics
Analytic/Scientific
Optoelectronics

In Biotechnology prefer:
Biosensors

In Medical/Health prefer:
Diagnostic Test Products

In Industrial/Energy prefer:
Factory Automation
Robotics

Additional Information
Name of Most Recent Fund: IT Matrix Fund
Most Recent Fund Was Raised: 10/01/2004
Year Founded: 2004
Capital Under Management: $50,000,000
Current Activity Level : Actively seeking new investments
Method of Compensation: Professional fee required whether or not deal closes

IT-FARM CORP

6-5-1 Nishii Shinjuku
Shinjuku i-Land Tower 5F
Tokyo, Japan 1631305
Phone: 81353243531
Fax: 81353243546
E-mail: information@it-farm.com
Website: www.it-farm.com

Management and Staff
Masaaki Sekino, Partner
Morimine Kurosaki, President
Takehiro Shirai, General Partner

Type of Firm
Incubator/Development Program

Project Preferences

Type of Financing Preferred:
Early Stage
Seed
Startup

Geographical Preferences

United States Preferences:

International Preferences:
Japan

Additional Information
Year Founded: 1999
Capital Under Management: $500,000
Current Activity Level : Actively seeking new investments

IT-TRANSLATION SA

23, avenue d'Italie
Paris, France 75013
Website: it-translation.fr

Management and Staff
Laurent Kott, Chief Executive Officer
Michel Safars, Partner

Type of Firm
Private Equity Firm

Project Preferences

Type of Financing Preferred:
Early Stage
Seed

Geographical Preferences

International Preferences:
France

Industry Preferences

In Computer Hardware prefer:
Computers

In Computer Software prefer:
Software

In Internet Specific prefer:
Internet

Additional Information
Year Founded: 2011
Capital Under Management: $40,177,000
Current Activity Level : Actively seeking new investments

ITAMBY PARTICIPACAO E DESENVOLVIMENTO LTDA

Av Brigadeiro Faria Lima 2055
9th Floor, Jd Paulistano
Sao Paulo, Brazil 14899000
Phone: 551121610950
Fax: 551121610955
Website: www.itamby.com.br

Type of Firm
Private Equity Firm

Project Preferences

Type of Financing Preferred:
Early Stage
Balanced
Later Stage

Geographical Preferences

International Preferences:
Brazil

Industry Preferences

In Financial Services prefer:
Financial Services
Real Estate

Additional Information
Year Founded: 2006
Current Activity Level : Actively seeking new investments

ITAU UNIBANCO HOLDING SA

Pc Alfredo Egydio de Souza
Aranha 100
Sao Paulo, Brazil 05423-901
Phone: 5550291888
Fax: 551150291999
Website: www.itau.com.br

Management and Staff
Regina Longo Sanchez, Vice President
Roberto Setubal, Chief Executive Officer

Type of Firm
Bank Affiliated

Project Preferences

Type of Financing Preferred:
Balanced

Geographical Preferences

International Preferences:
Brazil

Additional Information
Year Founded: 1943
Current Activity Level : Actively seeking new investments

ITC HOLDINGS CORP

1791 O.G. Skinner Drive
Suite A
West Point, GA USA 31833
Phone: 7066459482
Fax: 7066455167
E-mail: info@itchold.com
Website: www.itc-holdings.com

Management and Staff
Campbell Lanier, Chairman & CEO

Type of Firm
Private Equity Firm

Additional Information
Year Founded: 1989
Current Activity Level : Actively seeking new investments

ITECHCAPITAL

Tverskoy Bulvar 16, 5
Moscow, Russia 125009
Phone: 74992771236
E-mail: info@itcap.ru
Website: www.itcap.ru

Type of Firm
Private Equity Firm

Project Preferences

Type of Financing Preferred:
Leveraged Buyout
Early Stage
Generalist PE
Later Stage
Acquisition

Geographical Preferences

International Preferences:
Russia

Industry Preferences

In Communications prefer:
Communications and Media
Commercial Communications
Telecommunications
Wireless Communications
Media and Entertainment
Entertainment

In Computer Hardware prefer:
Terminals

In Computer Software prefer:
Data Processing
Software
Systems Software
Applications Software

In Internet Specific prefer:
E-Commerce Technology
Ecommerce

Additional Information

Year Founded: 2011
Capital Under Management: $100,000,000
Current Activity Level : Actively seeking new investments

ITERATIVE INSTINCT MANAGEMENT LP

15 Broad Streeet, Suite 1601
New York, NY USA 10005
Phone: 9172885544
Website: i2.vc

Management and Staff

Brandon Buchanan, Co-Founder
Chris Dannen, Co-Founder

Type of Firm

Private Equity Firm

Project Preferences

Type of Financing Preferred:
Early Stage

Additional Information

Year Founded: 2016
Capital Under Management: $1,400,000
Current Activity Level : Actively seeking new investments

ITHMAR AL MAWARID SA

Espace les Patios
1st floor, Building 2
Rabat, Morocco
Website: www.ithmar.gov.ma

Type of Firm

Government Affiliated Program

Project Preferences

Type of Financing Preferred:
Leveraged Buyout
Early Stage
Expansion
Later Stage
Management Buyouts
Acquisition

Geographical Preferences

International Preferences:
Morocco

Industry Preferences

In Consumer Related prefer:
Entertainment and Leisure

In Transportation prefer:
Transportation

Additional Information

Year Founded: 2011
Current Activity Level : Actively seeking new investments

ITKAPITAL AB

Strandvagen 15
P.O. Box 14166
Stockholm, Sweden 104 41
Phone: 46852802200
Fax: 46852802201
E-mail: info@itkapital.se
Website: www.itkapital.se

Management and Staff

Ulf Aipel, Managing Director

Type of Firm

Private Equity Firm

Project Preferences

Type of Financing Preferred:
Seed
Startup

Size of Investments Considered:
Min Size of Investment Considered (000s): $70
Max Size of Investment Considered (000s): $700

Geographical Preferences

International Preferences:
Sweden

Industry Preferences

In Business Serv. prefer:
Services

Additional Information

Year Founded: 1997
Capital Under Management: $800,000
Current Activity Level : Actively seeking new investments

ITM VENTURES INC

39/F One Exchange Square
Central, Hong Kong
Phone: 852-2187-3200
Fax: 852-2187-2489
Website: www.trans-tele.com

Type of Firm

Corporate PE/Venture

Association Membership

Hong Kong Venture Capital Association (HKVCA)

Project Preferences

Type of Financing Preferred:
Early Stage
Expansion
Balanced
Seed

Geographical Preferences

United States Preferences:
All U.S.

International Preferences:
Taiwan
Hong Kong
China
Australia
Asia
Singapore

Industry Preferences

In Communications prefer:
Telecommunications
Wireless Communications

In Internet Specific prefer:
Internet

In Semiconductor/Electr prefer:
Electronics

In Consumer Related prefer:
Retail

Pratt's Guide to Private Equity & Venture Capital Sources

Additional Information
Year Founded: 2003
Current Activity Level : Actively seeking new investments

ITOCHU CORP

5-1, Kita-Aoyama 2-chome
Minato-ku
Tokyo, Japan 107-8077
Phone: 81334972121
Website: www.itochu.co.jp

Other Offices
1-3, Kyutaromachi 4-chome
Chuo-ku
Osaka, Japan 541-8577
Phone: 816-6241-2121

Management and Staff
Tsuyoshi Hachimura, Chief Financial Officer

Type of Firm
Corporate PE/Venture

Project Preferences

Type of Financing Preferred:
Balanced

Geographical Preferences

International Preferences:
Asia
Japan

Additional Information
Year Founded: 1949
Current Activity Level : Actively seeking new investments

ITOCHU TECHNOLOGY INC

3945 Freedom Circle
Suite 640
Santa Clara, CA USA 95054
Phone: 4087278810
Fax: 4087279391
E-mail: info@itochu.net

Other Offices
257 Park Avenue South
Eighth Floor
New York, NY USA 10010
Phone: 212-308-7800
Fax: 212-308-7886

Management and Staff
John Takita, Vice President

Type of Firm
Corporate PE/Venture

Project Preferences

Role in Financing:
Prefer role as deal originator

Type of Financing Preferred:
Early Stage
Expansion
Balanced
Later Stage

Size of Investments Considered:
Min Size of Investment Considered (000s): $500
Max Size of Investment Considered (000s): $1,000

Geographical Preferences

United States Preferences:

Industry Focus
(% based on actual investment)
Computer Software and Services	39.0%
Internet Specific	30.3%
Communications and Media	13.1%
Semiconductors/Other Elect.	11.7%
Computer Hardware	4.3%
Biotechnology	1.5%
Medical/Health	0.2%

Additional Information
Year Founded: 1984
Capital Under Management: $100,000,000
Current Activity Level : Actively seeking new investments
Method of Compensation: Return on investment is of primary concern, do not charge fees

ITQAN CAPITAL CO

PO Box 8021
Al Shatei Center Al Malik Road
Jeddah, Saudi Arabia 21482
Phone: 96622347000
Fax: 96622347222
E-mail: info@itqancapital.com
Website: www.itqancapital.com

Management and Staff
Adil Dahlawi, Chief Executive Officer
Ahmad Khalili, Chief Financial Officer
Sami Weheba, Chief Executive Officer

Type of Firm
Investment Management Firm

Project Preferences

Type of Financing Preferred:
Leveraged Buyout
Value-Add
Early Stage
Generalist PE
Later Stage
Strategic Alliances
Acquisition

Geographical Preferences

International Preferences:
Middle East

Additional Information
Year Founded: 1200
Current Activity Level : Actively seeking new investments

IVENTURECAPITAL GMBH

Wendenstrasse 21B
Hamburg, Germany 20097
Phone: 49408081250
E-mail: info@iVentureCapital.com
Website: www.iventurecapital.com

Management and Staff
Ralph Schnitzler, Managing Director

Type of Firm
Private Equity Firm

Project Preferences

Type of Financing Preferred:
Leveraged Buyout
Early Stage
Expansion
Later Stage
Acquisition

Geographical Preferences

United States Preferences:
All U.S.

International Preferences:
Europe

Industry Preferences

In Communications prefer:
Media and Entertainment
Entertainment

In Internet Specific prefer:
Internet

Additional Information
Year Founded: 2011
Current Activity Level : Actively seeking new investments

IVY CAPITAL LTD

No. 1155 Huamu Road
3803 Pudong Jialicheng
Shanghai, China 200124
Phone: 862161908111
Fax: 862161908988
E-mail: Ivycapital@ivycapital.com
Website: www.ivycapital.com

Management and Staff

Chaoyang Xia, Founder
Donghai Yin, Partner
Feng Xian, Vice President
Haiping Hu, Founder
Jiyi Weng, Founder
Lei Zhang, Founder
Lei Fu, Founder
Zurong Tang, Partner

Type of Firm

Private Equity Firm

Project Preferences

Type of Financing Preferred:
Early Stage
Balanced
Later Stage

Geographical Preferences

International Preferences:
China

Industry Preferences

In Semiconductor/Electr prefer:
Electronics

In Industrial/Energy prefer:
Energy
Alternative Energy
Environmental Related

In Business Serv. prefer:
Services
Media

Additional Information

Year Founded: 2008
Current Activity Level : Actively seeking new investments

IVYCAP VENTURES ADVISORS PVT LTD

Hiranandani Business Park
G-2, Spectra Building
Mumbai, India 400076
Phone: 912239530567
Fax: 912239530600
Website: www.ivycapventures.com

Other Offices

Former HQ: 9th Floor, Platina
Bandra Kurla Complex
Mumbai, India 400051
Phone: 912239530567
Fax: 912239530600

Management and Staff

Aakanksha Sharma, Vice President
Anju Gupta, President
Ashish Wadhwani, Managing Partner
Norbert Fernandes, Co-Founder
Prayag Mohanty, Vice President
Sonia Gupta, Vice President
Vikram Gupta, Co-Founder
Vishal Gauri, Co-Founder

Type of Firm

Private Equity Firm

Project Preferences

Type of Financing Preferred:
Early Stage
Expansion

Geographical Preferences

International Preferences:
India

Industry Preferences

In Internet Specific prefer:
Internet
Ecommerce

In Biotechnology prefer:
Biotechnology

In Medical/Health prefer:
Medical/Health
Medical Diagnostics
Medical Products
Hospitals/Clinics/Primary
Pharmaceuticals

In Consumer Related prefer:
Consumer
Food/Beverage
Education Related

In Manufact. prefer:
Manufacturing

In Agr/Forestr/Fish prefer:
Agriculture related

In Other prefer:
Environment Responsible

Additional Information

Year Founded: 2011
Capital Under Management: $42,003,000
Current Activity Level : Actively seeking new investments

IW CAPITAL LTD

42 Bruton Place
London, United Kingdom W1J 6PA
Phone: 44207015 2250
Website: www.iwcapital.co.uk

Type of Firm

Private Equity Firm

Project Preferences

Type of Financing Preferred:
Early Stage
Expansion
Balanced
Later Stage

Geographical Preferences

International Preferences:
Europe

Additional Information

Year Founded: 2014
Current Activity Level : Actively seeking new investments

IXEN PARTNERS SA

153 Rue Du Faubourg
Saint-Honore
Paris, France 75008
Phone: 33175774600
Fax: 33153754706
E-mail: contact@nixen.com
Website: www.ixen-partners.com

Management and Staff

Jean-Paul Bernardini, Chief Executive Officer
Pierre Rispoli, Managing Director
Vincent Houlot, Partner

Type of Firm

Private Equity Firm

Association Membership

French Venture Capital Association (AFIC)
European Private Equity and Venture Capital Assoc.

Project Preferences

Type of Financing Preferred:
Leveraged Buyout
Mezzanine
Later Stage
Management Buyouts
Recapitalizations

Size of Investments Considered:
Min Size of Investment Considered (000s): $13,121
Max Size of Investment Considered (000s): $65,608

Geographical Preferences

International Preferences:
Europe
France

Additional Information

Name of Most Recent Fund: FCPR iXen II
Most Recent Fund Was Raised: 06/30/2009
Year Founded: 1998
Current Activity Level : Actively seeking new investments

IXO PRIVATE EQUITY SASU

34, rue de Metz
Toulouse, France 31000
Phone: 33534417418
Fax: 33534417419
E-mail: contact@ixope.fr
Website: www.ixope.fr

Other Offices

9 Rue de Conde
Bordeaux, France 33000
Phone: 33-5-5600-1269
Fax: 33-5-5644-2351

Type of Firm

Private Equity Firm

Association Membership

French Venture Capital Association (AFIC)

Project Preferences

Type of Financing Preferred:
Fund of Funds
Early Stage
Generalist PE
Balanced
Later Stage

Size of Investments Considered:
Min Size of Investment Considered (000s): $697
Max Size of Investment Considered (000s): $13,952

Geographical Preferences

International Preferences:
Europe

Additional Information

Name of Most Recent Fund: Ixo 3 FCPI
Most Recent Fund Was Raised: 12/17/2013
Year Founded: 2003
Capital Under Management: $116,400,000
Current Activity Level : Actively seeking new investments

IXORA VENTURES PVT LTD

Lodhi Road
Suite 28, Aman Hotel
Delhi, India 110003
Phone: 911124362424
E-mail: info@ixoracapital.in
Website: www.ixoraventures.com

Management and Staff

Nikhil Mulchandani, Managing Partner
Sunder Mulchandani, General Partner

Type of Firm

Private Equity Firm

Project Preferences

Type of Financing Preferred:
Early Stage
Seed

Geographical Preferences

International Preferences:
India
Asia

Industry Preferences

In Medical/Health prefer:
Health Services

In Consumer Related prefer:
Education Related

In Transportation prefer:
Aerospace

Additional Information

Year Founded: 2011
Current Activity Level : Actively seeking new investments

IYOGIN CAPITAL CO LTD

1 Minamihoribatacho
Matsuyama, Japan 790-0006
Phone: 81899338804
Fax: 81899433443
Website: www.iyobank.co.jp

Management and Staff

Yuichi Shinoura, Chief Executive Officer

Type of Firm

Bank Affiliated

Association Membership

Japan Venture Capital Association

Project Preferences

Type of Financing Preferred:
Early Stage

Geographical Preferences

International Preferences:
Japan

Additional Information

Year Founded: 1878
Capital Under Management: $4,700,000
Current Activity Level : Actively seeking new investments

- J -

J B POINDEXTER & CO INC

600 Travis Street
Suite 200
Houston, TX USA 77002
Phone: 7136559800
Fax: 7139519038
E-mail: info@jbpco.com
Website: www.jbpoindexter.com

Management and Staff

David Nuzzo, Chief Financial Officer
Matt Marthinson, Vice President
Peter Hunt, President
Phil Schull, Vice President
Woodie Perkins, Vice President

Type of Firm

Private Equity Firm

Project Preferences

Role in Financing:
Prefer role as deal originator

Type of Financing Preferred:
Leveraged Buyout
Mezzanine
Management Buyouts
Acquisition

Size of Investments Considered:
Min Size of Investment Considered (000s): $5,000
Max Size of Investment Considered (000s): $50,000

Industry Focus

(% based on actual investment)
Other Products 84.8%
Biotechnology 15.2%

Additional Information

Year Founded: 1980
Capital Under Management: $100,000,000
Current Activity Level : Actively seeking new investments
Method of Compensation: Return on investment is of primary concern, do not charge fees

J C M B BETEILIGUNGS GMBH

Neuer Wall 46
Hamburg, Germany 20354
Phone: 4940734409890
Fax: 4940734409889
E-mail: info@jcmb.de
Website: www.jcmb.de

Management and Staff

Jurgen Uhlemann, Managing Director
Marcel Uhlemann, Managing Director

Type of Firm
Private Equity Firm

Project Preferences

Type of Financing Preferred:
Early Stage
Later Stage
Seed
Startup

Size of Investments Considered:
Min Size of Investment Considered (000s): $144
Max Size of Investment Considered (000s): $722

Geographical Preferences

International Preferences:
Switzerland
Austria
Germany

Industry Preferences

In Communications prefer:
Media and Entertainment

In Internet Specific prefer:
Internet
Ecommerce

In Business Serv. prefer:
Services

Additional Information
Year Founded: 2009
Current Activity Level : Actively seeking new investments

J WILL PARTNERS CO LTD

15F Yurakucho Denki North Bldg
1-7-1 Yurakucho, Chiyoda-ku
Tokyo, Japan 103-0027
Phone: 81362665810

Type of Firm
Private Equity Firm

Project Preferences

Type of Financing Preferred:
Leveraged Buyout

Geographical Preferences

International Preferences:
Japan

Additional Information
Year Founded: 2003
Current Activity Level : Actively seeking new investments

J-SEED VENTURES INC

2-11-7 Yaesu
Chuo-Ku, Tokyo, Japan 104-0028
Phone: 81345205424
Fax: 81362038466
E-mail: info@j-seed.com
Website: www.j-seed.com

Management and Staff
Tomoko Yoneyama, Chief Financial Officer

Type of Firm
Incubator/Development Program

Project Preferences

Type of Financing Preferred:
Seed
Startup

Geographical Preferences

International Preferences:
Japan

Industry Preferences

In Communications prefer:
Communications and Media

In Computer Software prefer:
Software

In Internet Specific prefer:
Internet

Additional Information
Year Founded: 2000
Current Activity Level : Actively seeking new investments

J-STAR CO LTD

1-12-1 Yurakucho, Chiyoda-Ku
2/F Shin-Yurakucho Bldg
Tokyo, Japan 100-0006
Phone: 81362699701
Fax: 81362699710
E-mail: info@j-star.co.jp
Website: j-star.co.jp

Management and Staff
Hideaki Sakurai, Partner
Kenichi Harada, Partner
Satoru Arakawa, Principal
Satoshi Tsuji, Principal
Tatsuya Yumoto, Partner
Tomoko Ando, Partner
Yuki Kashiyama, Partner

Type of Firm
Private Equity Firm

Project Preferences

Type of Financing Preferred:
Leveraged Buyout
Management Buyouts
Recapitalizations

Geographical Preferences

International Preferences:
Japan

Industry Preferences

In Medical/Health prefer:
Medical/Health

In Consumer Related prefer:
Consumer
Retail

In Transportation prefer:
Transportation

In Financial Services prefer:
Financial Services

In Business Serv. prefer:
Media

In Manufact. prefer:
Manufacturing

Additional Information
Year Founded: 2006
Capital Under Management: $409,934,000
Current Activity Level : Actively seeking new investments

J. F. SHEA CO INC

655 Brea Canyon Road
Walnut, CA USA 91789
Phone: 9095949500
Fax: 9095940917
Website: www.jfshea.com

Type of Firm
Corporate PE/Venture

Project Preferences

Type of Financing Preferred:
Early Stage

Geographical Preferences

United States Preferences:

Industry Focus
(% based on actual investment)

Computer Software and Services	23.6%
Communications and Media	17.6%
Internet Specific	14.5%
Semiconductors/Other Elect.	12.2%
Computer Hardware	11.4%
Industrial/Energy	9.8%
Biotechnology	2.9%
Other Products	2.9%
Medical/Health	2.8%
Consumer Related	2.3%

Additional Information
Year Founded: 1881
Capital Under Management: $50,000,000
Current Activity Level : Actively seeking new investments

J.H. WHITNEY & CO LLC

130 Main Street
New Canaan, CT USA 06840
Phone: 2037166100
Fax: 2037166122
E-mail: inquiry@whitney.com
Website: www.whitney.com

Management and Staff
Brian Cherry, Managing Director
Daniel Harknett, Vice President
James Fordyce, Managing Director
Micah Meisel, Vice President
Paul Vigano, Managing Director
Robert Williams, Managing Director
Tamara Polewik, Principal

Type of Firm
Private Equity Firm

Project Preferences

Role in Financing:
Prefer role as deal originator but will also invest in deals created by others

Type of Financing Preferred:
Leveraged Buyout
Expansion
Mezzanine
Balanced
Turnaround
Later Stage
Recapitalizations

Geographical Preferences

United States Preferences:

Industry Focus
(% based on actual investment)

Medical/Health	22.9%
Other Products	15.7%
Internet Specific	14.9%
Computer Software and Services	10.6%
Communications and Media	10.4%
Consumer Related	6.6%
Industrial/Energy	5.8%
Biotechnology	4.9%
Computer Hardware	4.7%
Semiconductors/Other Elect.	3.5%

Additional Information
Year Founded: 1946
Capital Under Management: $6,000,000,000
Current Activity Level : Actively seeking new investments
Method of Compensation: Return on invest. most important, but chg. closing fees, service fees, etc.

J.P. MORGAN (CHINA) VENTURE CAPITAL INVESTMENT CO LTD

No.7, Jinrong Street, Xicheng
20F, Winland Int'l Finance Ctr
Beijing, China 100033
Phone: 861059318500
Fax: 861059318505
Website: www.jpmorganchina.com.cn

Type of Firm
Bank Affiliated

Project Preferences

Type of Financing Preferred:
Expansion
Balanced

Geographical Preferences

International Preferences:
China

Industry Preferences

In Medical/Health prefer:
Medical/Health

In Consumer Related prefer:
Consumer Products
Education Related

In Industrial/Energy prefer:
Energy
Energy Conservation Relat
Machinery
Environmental Related

In Transportation prefer:
Transportation

In Business Serv. prefer:
Services

In Manufact. prefer:
Manufacturing

Additional Information
Year Founded: 2010
Capital Under Management: $929,028,000
Current Activity Level : Actively seeking new investments

J.W.CHILDS ASSOCIATES LP

500 Totten Pond Road
Sixth Floor
Waltham, MA USA 02451
Phone: 6177531100
Fax: 6177531101
Website: www.jwchilds.com

Management and Staff
Adam Suttin, Co-Founder
David Fiorentino, Partner
Jeffrey Teschke, Partner
Kyle Casella, Vice President
Philippe Schenk, Managing Director
Todd Fitzpatrick, Chief Financial Officer
William Watts, Partner

Type of Firm
Private Equity Firm

Project Preferences

Type of Financing Preferred:
Leveraged Buyout
Acquisition
Recapitalizations

Geographical Preferences

United States Preferences:
North America

International Preferences:
Asia

Industry Focus
(% based on actual investment)

Consumer Related	66.7%
Other Products	19.5%
Medical/Health	7.9%
Communications and Media	5.9%

Additional Information
Year Founded: 1995
Capital Under Management: $235,963,000
Current Activity Level : Actively seeking new investments

JABBAR INTERNET GROUP

3, Dubai Internet City
Dubai, Utd. Arab Em. 500253
Phone: 97144462767
Fax: 97144404843
Website: www.jabbar.com

Type of Firm
Private Equity Firm

Project Preferences

Type of Financing Preferred:
Early Stage
Seed

Geographical Preferences

International Preferences:
India
Middle East

Industry Preferences

In Internet Specific prefer:
Internet
Ecommerce

Additional Information
Year Founded: 2009
Current Activity Level : Actively seeking new investments

JABODON PT CO

111 South Wacker Drive
Suite 4000
Chicago, IL USA 60606
Phone: 3124476000
Fax: 3124476006
E-mail: info@pritzkergroup.com
Website: www.pritzkergroup.com

Other Offices
11150 Santa Monica Boulevard
Suite 1500
SAWTELLE, CA USA 90025
Phone: 3105759400
Fax: 3105759401

Management and Staff
Adam Milakofsky, Principal
Adam Koopersmith, Partner
Ceron Rhee, Principal
Chris Trick, Vice President
Christopher Girgenti, Managing Partner
David Rosen, Partner
Jeffrey Maters, Vice President
Jonathan Maschmeyer, Vice President
Kathleen Smith, Chief Financial Officer
Matt Bowman, Vice President
Matthew McCall, Partner
Michael Barzyk, Vice President
Michael Gillis, Vice President
Michael Dal Bello, Partner
Michael Nelson, Partner
Paul Carbone, Managing Partner
Richard Griffin, Partner

Type of Firm
Private Equity Firm

Association Membership
Illinois Venture Capital Association

Project Preferences

Type of Financing Preferred:
Leveraged Buyout
Acquisition
Recapitalizations

Geographical Preferences

United States Preferences:
North America

Canadian Preferences:
All Canada

Industry Preferences

In Medical/Health prefer:
Medical/Health

In Business Serv. prefer:
Services

In Manufact. prefer:
Manufacturing

Additional Information
Year Founded: 2002
Current Activity Level : Actively seeking new investments

JACANA INVEST SAS

183, rue de Courcelles
Paris, France 75017
Phone: 33146228623
E-mail: contact@jacana-invest.com
Website: jacana-invest.com

Type of Firm
Private Equity Firm

Association Membership
French Venture Capital Association (AFIC)

Project Preferences

Type of Financing Preferred:
Leveraged Buyout
Mezzanine
Management Buyouts
Acquisition

Size of Investments Considered:
Min Size of Investment Considered (000s): $3,941
Max Size of Investment Considered (000s): $6,568

Geographical Preferences

International Preferences:
Europe
France

Additional Information
Year Founded: 2013
Current Activity Level : Actively seeking new investments

JACANA PARTNERS

32-33 Gosfield Street
Third Floor
London, United Kingdom W1W 6HL
Phone: 442075209236
Website: www.jacanapartners.com

Other Offices
18, Aviation Road
PMB CT 255, Cantonments
Accra, Ghana
Phone: 233302782625
Fax: 233302782627

Statehouse Road
Opposite Gate B of Statehouse
Nairobi, Kenya 0 0100
Phone: 254 (0) 20 250 477
Fax: 254 (0) 20 265 805

Management and Staff
Anthony Gichini, Partner
Bart Meijs, Partner
Ezra Musoke, Partner
Stephen Antwi-Asimeng, Partner
Steven Otto, Partner

Type of Firm
Private Equity Firm

Project Preferences

Type of Financing Preferred:
Early Stage
Expansion
Mezzanine
Balanced
Later Stage
Acquisition

Geographical Preferences

United States Preferences:
Maryland

International Preferences:
Ethiopia
Liberia
Nigeria
Uganda
Tanzania
Ghana
Kenya
Sierra Leone
Africa

Industry Preferences

In Consumer Related prefer:
Education Related

In Financial Services prefer:
Financial Services
Insurance
Real Estate

In Business Serv. prefer:
Services

In Manufact. prefer:
Manufacturing

In Agr/Forestr/Fish prefer:
Agribusiness

Additional Information
Year Founded: 2008
Current Activity Level : Actively seeking new investments

JACKSON SQUARE VENTURES

1600 El Camino Real, Suite 280
Menlo Park, CA USA 94025
Phone: 6508531700
Fax: 6508531717
Website: www.jsv.com

Management and Staff
Melissa Alves, Chief Financial Officer

Type of Firm
Private Equity Firm

Association Membership
National Venture Capital Association - USA (NVCA)

Project Preferences

Type of Financing Preferred:
Early Stage
Expansion

Geographical Preferences

United States Preferences:
Northern California

Industry Preferences

In Communications prefer:
Wireless Communications

In Computer Software prefer:
Software
Systems Software
Applications Software

In Internet Specific prefer:
Internet

In Consumer Related prefer:
Consumer

Additional Information
Year Founded: 1969
Capital Under Management: $124,000,000
Current Activity Level : Actively seeking new investments

JACOB BALLAS CAPITAL INDIA PVT LTD

Mahipalpur, National Hi-Way 8
1F Commercial Plaza, Radisson
New Delhi, India 110037
Phone: 911143153100
Fax: 911143153111
E-mail: jbindia@jbindia.co.in
Website: www.jbindia.co.in

Other Offices
IFS Court,
TwentyEight Cybercity
Ebene, Mauritius
Phone: 230-467-3000
Fax: 230-467-4000

Management and Staff
Bharat Bakhshi, Partner
Rahul Jetley, Principal
Sandeep Goyal, Principal
Srinivas Chidambaram, Managing Director
Sunil Chawla, Partner
T. Sesha Rao, Principal

Type of Firm
Investment Management Firm

Association Membership
Emerging Markets Private Equity Association
Indian Venture Capital Association (IVCA)

Project Preferences

Type of Financing Preferred:
Expansion
Balanced
Later Stage

Size of Investments Considered:
Min Size of Investment Considered (000s): $5,000
Max Size of Investment Considered (000s): $60,000

Geographical Preferences

International Preferences:
India

Industry Preferences

In Semiconductor/Electr prefer:
Electronics

In Medical/Health prefer:
Medical/Health
Pharmaceuticals

In Consumer Related prefer:
Consumer
Retail
Consumer Products
Hotels and Resorts

In Industrial/Energy prefer:
Oil and Gas Exploration
Industrial Products

In Financial Services prefer:
Insurance
Financial Services

In Utilities prefer:
Utilities

Additional Information
Year Founded: 1995
Current Activity Level : Actively seeking new investments

JACOBS CAPITAL GROUP LLC

670 North Rosemead Boulevard
Suite 201
Pasadena, CA USA 91107
Phone: 6263513701
Fax: 6263513702
E-mail: info@jacobscapitalgroup.com
Website: www.jacobscapitalgroup.com

Management and Staff
Alexander Suh, Managing Director
William Hanna, Managing Director

Type of Firm
Private Equity Advisor or Fund of Funds

Project Preferences

Type of Financing Preferred:
Fund of Funds
Balanced

Geographical Preferences

United States Preferences:
All U.S.

International Preferences:
Europe
Asia

Additional Information
Year Founded: 2005
Current Activity Level : Actively seeking new investments

JACOBSON PARTNERS

595 Madison Avenue
31st Floor
New York, NY USA 10022
Phone: 2127584500
Fax: 2127584567

Management and Staff
Benjamin Jacobson, Managing Partner
Bernard Matte, Partner
Charles Moore, General Partner
Edmund Gaffney, General Partner
Harrison Horan, General Partner
James Morgan, General Partner
Michael Ryan, General Partner
Steven Jaffe, Vice President

Type of Firm
Bank Affiliated

Project Preferences

Type of Financing Preferred:
Leveraged Buyout
Acquisition

Industry Preferences

In Medical/Health prefer:
Medical/Health

In Consumer Related prefer:
Other Restaurants

In Manufact. prefer:
Manufacturing

Additional Information
Year Founded: 1989
Current Activity Level : Actively seeking new investments

JADE INVESTMENT CONSULTING (SHANGHAI) CO LTD

Two IFC, Level 8, Suite 818
Eight Century Avenue, Pudong
Shanghai, China 200120
Phone: 862160914400
Fax: 862160914401
E-mail: info@jadeinvest.com.cn
Website: www.jadeinvest.com.cn

Other Offices
Rashid Bin Saeed Al Maktoum St. 2
Level Ten, Al Odaid Office Tower
Abu Dhabi, Utd. Arab Em.
Phone: 97124146756
Fax: 97124146600

Former HQ: 1266 Nanjing West Road
Plaza 66, Suite 4110
Shanghai, China 200040
Phone: 86-21-6101-0060
Fax: 86-21-6101-0061

1 East Chang An Avenue
Oriental Plaza, W2 Tower 1010
Beijing, China 100738
Phone: 86-10-8518-1827
Fax: 86-10-8518-7722

Lei Shing Hong Plaza, 8 Wangjing Street
Building B, Level 15
Beijing, China 100102
Phone: 861051293258
Fax: 861084760879

Management and Staff
Dayi Sun, General Partner
Jenny Zeng, Venture Partner
Jonas Lindblad, Managing Director
Joseph Wang, Founder
Larry Ma, Venture Partner
Ludvig Nilsson, Managing Partner
Wei Zhou, Venture Partner
Zhou Wei, Venture Partner

Type of Firm
Private Equity Advisor or Fund of Funds

Association Membership
China Venture Capital Association

Project Preferences

Type of Financing Preferred:
Fund of Funds
Expansion
Fund of Funds of Second

Geographical Preferences

International Preferences:
China

Additional Information
Name of Most Recent Fund: Jade China Value Partners II, L.P.
Most Recent Fund Was Raised: 10/18/2011
Year Founded: 2005
Capital Under Management: $127,000,000
Current Activity Level : Actively seeking new investments

JADWA INVESTMENT CO SJSC

King Fahad Road
P.O. Box 60677
Riyadh, Saudi Arabia 11555
Phone: 9662791111
Fax: 9662791571
E-mail: info@jadwa.com
Website: www.jadwa.com

Management and Staff
Mohammed Ibrahim Al Issa, Founder

Type of Firm
Investment Management Firm

Project Preferences

Type of Financing Preferred:
Leveraged Buyout
Early Stage
Expansion
Generalist PE
Balanced
Later Stage
Management Buyouts
Acquisition

Geographical Preferences

International Preferences:
Utd. Arab Em.
Middle East
Saudi Arabia
Asia

Industry Preferences

In Communications prefer:
Entertainment

In Semiconductor/Electr prefer:
Electronics
Electronic Components

In Medical/Health prefer:
Medical/Health

In Consumer Related prefer:
Food/Beverage
Hotels and Resorts

In Industrial/Energy prefer:
Oil and Gas Exploration
Industrial Products
Materials

In Financial Services prefer:
Investment Groups

In Business Serv. prefer:
Distribution

In Manufact. prefer:
Manufacturing

Additional Information
Year Founded: 2006
Current Activity Level : Actively seeking new investments

JAFCO CO LTD

1-5-1 Otemachi, Chiyoda-ku
11F, Otemachi First Square
Tokyo, Japan 100-0004
Phone: 81352237536
Fax: 81352237561
E-mail: info@jafco.co.jp
Website: www.jafco.co.jp

Other Offices

No. 5 Dong San Huan Bei Lu
Room 817, Beijing Fortune Building
Beijing, China 100004
Phone: 861-6590-9730
Fax: 861-6590-9729

18 Chater Road
6th Floor, Alexandra House
Central, Hong Kong
Phone: 852-2536-1960
Fax: 852-2536-1979

159-9 Samseong-dong, Gangman-gu
18th Floor, Korea City Air Tower
Seoul, South Korea 135-973
Phone: 822-2016-6100
Fax: 822-2016-6101

505 Hamilton Avenue
Suite 310
Palo Alto, CA USA 94301
Phone: 650-463-8800
Fax: 650-463-8801

1000 Lujiazui Ring Road
Suite 42-021, 42/F, Hang Seng Bank Tower
Shanghai, China 200120
Phone: 862-1-6841-3818
Fax: 862-1-6841-3800

109 Min-Sheng East Road
14th Floor, Sec. 3
Taipei, Taiwan
Phone: 886-2-2719-0182
Fax: 886-2-2712-4930

10 Marina Boulevard
Marina Bay Financial Centre Tower 2
Singapore, Singapore 018983
Phone: 65-6224-6383
Fax: 65-6221-3690

1-5-1 Otemachi, Chiyoda-ku
11/F West Tower, Otemachi First Square
Tokyo, Japan 100-0004
Phone: 81-3-5223-7536
Fax: 81-3-5223-7561

Management and Staff

Hiroshi Yamada, Senior Managing Director
Yoshimitsu Oura, Managing Director
Yoshiyuki Shibusawa, Managing Director

Type of Firm

Private Equity Firm

Project Preferences

Role in Financing:
Will function either as deal originator or investor in deals created by others

Type of Financing Preferred:
Early Stage
Balanced
Later Stage

Geographical Preferences

United States Preferences:

International Preferences:
Europe
Asia
Japan

Industry Focus

(% based on actual investment)
Internet Specific	34.7%
Biotechnology	16.2%
Computer Software and Services	13.4%
Semiconductors/Other Elect.	9.4%
Consumer Related	9.0%
Industrial/Energy	7.7%
Medical/Health	5.7%
Communications and Media	1.8%
Other Products	1.7%
Computer Hardware	0.5%

Additional Information

Year Founded: 1973
Capital Under Management: $5,889,300,000
Current Activity Level: Actively seeking new investments
Method of Compensation: Return on investment is of primary concern, do not charge fees

JAFCO INVESTMENT (ASIA PACIFIC) LTD

10 Marina Boulevard
Suite 33-05, Marina Bay Tower 2
Singapore, Singapore 018983
Phone: 6562246383
Fax: 6562213690
E-mail: enquiry_singapore@jafcoasia.com
Website: www.jafcoasia.com

Other Offices

Room 817, Beijing Fortune Building
No.5 Dong San Huan Bei Lu
Beijing, China 100004
Phone: 86-10-6590-9730
Fax: 86-10-6590-9729

14/F, 109 Min-Sheng E. Road
Section 3
Taipei, Taiwan
Phone: 886-2-2719-0182
Fax: 886-2-2712-4930

Suite 42-021, 42/F Hang Seng Bank Tower
1000 Lujiazui Ring Road
Shanghai, China 200120
Phone: 86-21-6841-3818
Fax: 86-21-6841-3800

Former HQ: Six Battery Road
Suite 42-01
Singapore, Singapore 049909
Phone: 65-6224-6383
Fax: 65-6221-3690

6th Floor, Alexandra House
18 Chater Road
Central, Hong Kong
Phone: 6562246383
Fax: 6562213690

18/F, Korea City Air Tower
159-9 Samseong-dong Gangnam-gu
Seoul, South Korea 135-973
Phone: 82-2-2016-6100
Fax: 82-2-2016-6101

Management and Staff

Junitsu Uchikata, Managing Director
Richard Joung, Managing Director

Type of Firm

Private Equity Firm

Association Membership

Hong Kong Venture Capital Association (HKVCA)
China Venture Capital Association
Singapore Venture Capital Association (SVCA)

Project Preferences

Type of Financing Preferred:
Early Stage
Balanced
Later Stage
Seed
Startup

Geographical Preferences

International Preferences:
Asia Pacific

Industry Focus

(% based on actual investment)
Internet Specific	35.7%
Communications and Media	15.1%
Computer Software and Services	12.7%
Computer Hardware	10.6%
Semiconductors/Other Elect.	8.5%
Industrial/Energy	6.3%
Medical/Health	4.1%
Other Products	3.7%
Consumer Related	2.5%
Biotechnology	0.9%

Additional Information

Year Founded: 1990
Capital Under Management: $650,000,000
Current Activity Level: Actively seeking new investments

JAFCO VENTURES

505 Hamilton Avenue
Suite 310
Palo Alto, CA USA 94301
Phone: 6504638800
Fax: 6504638801
E-mail: info@iconventures.com
Website: www.iconventures.com

Management and Staff

Ben Shih, Partner
Dana Evan, Venture Partner
Debby Meredith, Venture Partner
Jeb Miller, General Partner
Joseph Horowitz, Managing Partner
Michael Mullany, General Partner
Paul Sallaberry, Venture Partner
Peter Yi, Principal
Takenori Sanami, Chief Financial Officer
Thomas Mawhinney, General Partner

Type of Firm

Private Equity Firm

Association Membership

Western Association of Venture Capitalists (WAVC)
National Venture Capital Association - USA (NVCA)

Project Preferences

Role in Financing:
Prefer role as deal originator but will also invest in deals created by others

Type of Financing Preferred:
Early Stage
Expansion

Size of Investments Considered:
Min Size of Investment Considered (000s): $4,000
Max Size of Investment Considered (000s): $20,000

Geographical Preferences

United States Preferences:

Industry Preferences

In Communications prefer:
Communications and Media
Wireless Communications

In Computer Software prefer:
Data Processing
Software
Applications Software

In Internet Specific prefer:
Internet

In Semiconductor/Electr prefer:
Electronic Components
Semiconductor

In Medical/Health prefer:
Medical/Health

In Consumer Related prefer:
Food/Beverage
Education Related

In Industrial/Energy prefer:
Energy

In Business Serv. prefer:
Media

In Agr/Forestr/Fish prefer:
Agriculture related

In Other prefer:
Environment Responsible

Additional Information

Name of Most Recent Fund: JAFCO Technology Partners V, L.P.
Most Recent Fund Was Raised: 05/24/2012
Year Founded: 2003
Capital Under Management: $1,046,000,000
Current Activity Level : Actively seeking new investments
Method of Compensation: Return on investment is of primary concern, do not charge fees

JAHANGIR SIDDIQUI GROUP ASSOCIATES

Block Nine, Clifton
7th Floor, The Forum
Karachi, Pakistan 75600
Phone: 92-21-583-9977
Fax: 92-21-536-1721
Website: www.js.com

Other Offices

Four Old Park Lane
London, United Kingdom W1K 1QW
Phone: 44-20-7399-4350
Fax: 44-20-7399-4351

Shaikh Zayed Road
Suite 712, The Fairmont Hotel
Dubai, Utd. Arab Em.
Phone: 971-4-312-4350
Fax: 971-4-312-4351

Management and Staff

Kamran Qadir, Chief Financial Officer
Munaf Ibrahim, Chief Executive Officer

Type of Firm

Bank Affiliated

Project Preferences

Type of Financing Preferred:
Balanced

Geographical Preferences

International Preferences:
Pakistan
Asia

Additional Information

Year Founded: 2006
Capital Under Management: $278,000,000
Current Activity Level : Actively seeking new investments

JAINA CAPITAL SASU

1 Rue Francois 1er
Paris, France 75008
Website: www.jaina.fr

Management and Staff

Angelique Lenain, Partner
Charles-Henry Tranie, Partner
Marie-Christine Levet, Partner

Type of Firm

Private Equity Firm

Project Preferences

Type of Financing Preferred:
Early Stage
Later Stage
Startup

Geographical Preferences

International Preferences:
Europe
France

Industry Preferences

In Communications prefer:
Telecommunications

In Internet Specific prefer:
Internet

In Business Serv. prefer:
Media

In Other prefer:
Environment Responsible

Additional Information

Year Founded: 2009
Current Activity Level : Actively seeking new investments

JAL VENTURES FUND LP

89E Medinat
Hayehudim St
Herzliya, Israel 4676672
E-mail: info@jalventures.com
Website: www.jalventures.com

Type of Firm

Private Equity Firm

Project Preferences

Type of Financing Preferred:
Early Stage
Expansion
Later Stage

Geographical Preferences

International Preferences:
Israel

Industry Preferences

In Computer Software prefer:
Software
Systems Software

In Internet Specific prefer:
Internet
Ecommerce

Additional Information

Year Founded: 2004
Current Activity Level : Actively seeking new investments

JAM CAPITAL PARTNERS

16 Boardwalk Plaza
Saint Simons Island, GA USA 31522
Phone: 9123997570
E-mail: info@jamcapitalpartners.net
Website: www.jamcapitalpartners.net

Type of Firm

Private Equity Firm

Project Preferences

Type of Financing Preferred:
Leveraged Buyout
Acquisition

Geographical Preferences

United States Preferences:

Additional Information

Year Founded: 2010
Current Activity Level : Actively seeking new investments

JAM EQUITY PARTNERS LLC

11 East 26th Street
Suite 1900
New York, NY USA 10010
Phone: 2122715526
Fax: 2122715525
Website: www.jampartners.com

Other Offices

2121 Rosecrans Avenue
Suite 2390
El Segundo, CA USA 90245
Phone: 3102278600
Fax: 3102278601

Type of Firm

Private Equity Firm

Project Preferences

Type of Financing Preferred:
Generalist PE

Size of Investments Considered:
Min Size of Investment Considered (000s): $2,000
Max Size of Investment Considered (000s): $10,000

Industry Preferences

In Financial Services prefer:
Financial Services

Additional Information

Name of Most Recent Fund: JAM Special Opportunities Fund III, L.P.
Most Recent Fund Was Raised: 05/06/2013
Year Founded: 2013
Capital Under Management: $90,575,000
Current Activity Level : Actively seeking new investments

JAMES & HINA CAPITAL MANAGEMENT CO LTD

Jin Shi Fang,Financial Street
C-207,Heng'ao Center, 26
Beijing, China 100033
Phone: 861066219791
Fax: 861066211311
Website: www.jhcapital.cn

Management and Staff

Zhixin Liang, Vice President

Type of Firm

Investment Management Firm

Project Preferences

Type of Financing Preferred:
Later Stage

Geographical Preferences

International Preferences:
China

Industry Preferences

In Communications prefer:
Telecommunications

In Internet Specific prefer:
Internet

In Semiconductor/Electr prefer:
Optoelectronics

In Biotechnology prefer:
Biotechnology

In Medical/Health prefer:
Pharmaceuticals

In Consumer Related prefer:
Entertainment and Leisure
Retail
Education Related

In Industrial/Energy prefer:
Alternative Energy
Energy Conservation Relat
Industrial Products
Advanced Materials

In Business Serv. prefer:
Services
Media

In Agr/Forestr/Fish prefer:
Agriculture related

In Other prefer:
Environment Responsible

Additional Information

Year Founded: 2007
Capital Under Management: $119,904,000
Current Activity Level : Actively seeking new investments

JAMJAR INVESTMENTS LLP

30 Portland Place
London, United Kingdom W1B 1LZ
Website: www.jamjarinvestments.com

Type of Firm

Private Equity Firm

Project Preferences

Type of Financing Preferred:
Early Stage
Seed
Startup

Geographical Preferences

International Preferences:
Europe

Industry Preferences

In Consumer Related prefer:
Consumer Products
Consumer Services

Additional Information

Year Founded: 2009
Current Activity Level : Actively seeking new investments

JANOM SRO

Dohnany 464
Dohnany, Slovakia 020 51
Phone: 421424710145
Fax: 421424710145
E-mail: info@janom.sk
Website: www.janom.sk

Management and Staff
Jan Miskovsky, Chief Executive Officer

Type of Firm
Private Equity Firm

Project Preferences

Type of Financing Preferred:
Later Stage
Seed

Geographical Preferences

International Preferences:
Europe

Industry Preferences

In Industrial/Energy prefer:
Alternative Energy

Additional Information
Year Founded: 2008
Current Activity Level : Actively seeking new investments

JANVEST TECHNOLOGIES LLC

6204 Waterford Blvd
Suite 7
Oklahoma City, OK USA 73118
Phone: 4258180707
Website: www.janvest.com

Type of Firm
Private Equity Firm

Project Preferences

Type of Financing Preferred:
Early Stage
Balanced
Later Stage
Seed

Geographical Preferences

International Preferences:
Israel

Industry Preferences

In Communications prefer:
Telecommunications

In Computer Software prefer:
Software

In Internet Specific prefer:
Internet

Additional Information
Year Founded: 2010
Current Activity Level : Actively seeking new investments

JAPAN ASIA INVESTMENT CO LTD

3-11 Kandanishiki-cho
Seiko Takebashi-Kyodo Building
Tokyo, Japan 101-8570
Phone: 81332598518
Fax: 81332598511
E-mail: ir@jaic-vc.co.jp
Website: www.jaic-vc.co.jp

Other Offices

02 Thi Sach Street
Room 501, Hoa Lam Building
Ho Chi Minh, Vietnam
Phone: 84-8-6291-3575
Fax: 84-8-6291-3585

8 Fleming Road, Wanchai
Room 1504, Tai Tung Building
Hong Kong, Hong Kong
Phone: 852-2509-3011
Fax: 852-2509-3025

14/F, Sumitomo Life Sendai Bldg.,
10-3 Chuo 4-Chome, Aoba-ku
Sendai, Japan 980-0021
Phone: 81-22-216-8551
Fax: 81-22-216-8550

3-1, Ofuka-cho, Kita-ku
Room K811, Grand Front Osaka North Bldg.
Osaka, Japan 530-0011
Phone: 81661363476
Fax: 81663764560

No. 1 Yue Bin Street, Shen He District
Room 302, Fang Yuan Building
Shenyang, China 110013
Phone: 862422505801

1550 New Petchburi Road
25/F, Thanapoom Tower
Bangkok, Thailand 10400
Phone: 66-2-207-0216
Fax: 66-2-207-0215

1-9, Edobori 1-chome, Nishi-ku
15/F, Higobashi Center Building
Osaka, Japan 550-0002
Phone: 81-6-6443-7770
Fax: 81-6-6443-7780

Jl. Jend. Sudirman Kav 7-8
Wisma Nugra Santana 10/F
Jakarta, Indonesia 10220
Phone: 62-21-5702-525
Fax: 62-21-5702-600

50 Raffles Place #24-03
Singapore Land Tower
Singapore, Singapore 048623
Phone: 65-6557-0511
Fax: 65-6557-0332

333 Xian Xia Road
Unit A11, 25/F, V Capital Tower
Shanghai, China 200336
Phone: 86-21-3252-8678
Fax: 86-21-3252-8677

170 Tun Hwa N. Road
Suite D, 10/F
Taipei, Taiwan 106
Phone: 886-2-8712-5818
Fax: 886-2-8712-5819

81 Jianguo Road
Room 1407, Tower 1, China Central Place
Beijing, China 100025
Phone: 86-10-6598-9549
Fax: 86-10-6598-9548

1-25 Taepyeongno, Jung-gu
9/F, Press Center Building
Seoul, South Korea 100-750
Phone: 822-3210-1855
Fax: 822-3210-1856

5th Floor, Puresuto 1-7 Building
1 Kitachijyo Nishi 7-Chome, Chuo-ku
Sapporo, Japan 060-0001
Phone: 81-11-232-3550
Fax: 81-11-232-3556

525 University Avenue, Suite 210
Palo Alto, CA USA 94301
Phone: 650-213-9011
Fax: 650-213-9012

Type of Firm
Investment Management Firm

Association Membership
Japan Venture Capital Association
Thai Venture Capital Association

Project Preferences

Role in Financing:
Prefer role as deal originator but will also invest in deals created by others

Type of Financing Preferred:
Fund of Funds
Leveraged Buyout
Early Stage
Generalist PE
Balanced
Turnaround
Later Stage
Seed
Management Buyouts
Acquisition
Recapitalizations

Geographical Preferences

United States Preferences:
All U.S.

International Preferences:
Vietnam
Asia
Japan

Industry Focus

(% based on actual investment)
Medical/Health	24.1%
Internet Specific	19.9%
Computer Hardware	15.9%
Biotechnology	15.4%
Industrial/Energy	6.2%
Consumer Related	5.1%
Computer Software and Services	4.3%
Semiconductors/Other Elect.	3.5%
Other Products	3.4%
Communications and Media	2.2%

Additional Information

Name of Most Recent Fund: DFJ-JAIC Technology Partners, L. P.
Most Recent Fund Was Raised: 10/26/2009
Year Founded: 1981
Capital Under Management: $204,300,000
Current Activity Level : Actively seeking new investments
Method of Compensation: Return on invest. most important, but chg. closing fees, service fees, etc.

JAPAN INDUSTRIAL PARTNERS INC

2-1-1 Marunouchi, Chiyoda-Ku
15F, Meiji Yasuda Life Bldg
Tokyo, Japan
Phone: 81362665781
Fax: 81362665797
E-mail: jipinc@jipinc.com
Website: www.jipinc.com

Type of Firm
Private Equity Firm

Project Preferences

Type of Financing Preferred:
Leveraged Buyout
Turnaround
Management Buyouts

Geographical Preferences

International Preferences:
Asia
Japan

Additional Information

Year Founded: 2002
Current Activity Level : Actively seeking new investments

JAPAN PRIVATE EQUITY CO LTD

1-14-21, Kudan Kita
6/F Airex Building
Chiyoda-Ku, Tokyo, Japan 102-0073
Phone: 81332381726
Fax: 81332381639
E-mail: info@private-equity.co.jp
Website: www.private-equity.co.jp

Other Offices

2-8-49, Tenjin
4/F Hulic Fukuoka Building
Fukuoka-Shi, Fukuoka, Japan
Phone: 81927252478
Fax: 81927252479

Management and Staff

Suguru Miyake, Vice President

Type of Firm
Private Equity Firm

Association Membership
Japan Venture Capital Association

Project Preferences

Type of Financing Preferred:
Leveraged Buyout
Turnaround
Management Buyouts

Geographical Preferences

International Preferences:
Japan

Industry Preferences

In Semiconductor/Electr prefer:
Electronics

In Manufact. prefer:
Manufacturing

Additional Information

Year Founded: 2000
Capital Under Management: $299,550,000
Current Activity Level : Actively seeking new investments

JARVINIAN LLC

101 Federal Street
Suite 1900
Boston, MA USA 02110
Phone: 617-342-7023
Fax: 617-395-2719
E-mail: info@jarvinian.com
Website: www.jarvinian.com

Management and Staff

Christopher Carter, Managing Director
John Dooley, Managing Director
Thomas Eddy, Managing Director

Type of Firm
Private Equity Firm

Project Preferences

Type of Financing Preferred:
Early Stage
Expansion
Mezzanine
Later Stage
Seed
Startup

Size of Investments Considered:
Min Size of Investment Considered (000s): $1,000
Max Size of Investment Considered (000s): $5,000

Industry Preferences

In Communications prefer:
Wireless Communications

In Semiconductor/Electr prefer:
Electronic Components
Semiconductor

In Business Serv. prefer:
Media

Additional Information

Year Founded: 2009
Current Activity Level : Actively seeking new investments

JASPER RIDGE PARTNERS LP

2885 Sand Hill Road
Suite 100
Menlo Park, CA USA 94025
Phone: 6504944800
E-mail: info@jasperridge.com
Website: www.jasperridge.com

Other Offices

3721 Douglas Boulevard
Roseville, CA USA 95661
Phone: 9167890600

201 Main Street
Suite 1000
Fort Worth, TX USA 76102
Phone: 8173397516

Management and Staff

Alison Diessner, Vice President
Cayman Seacrest, Vice President
Cori Duncan, Partner
David Bizer, Managing Partner
Eric Ramsay, Vice President
George Phipps, Managing Partner
Jack Muhlbeier, Chief Financial Officer
Jenny Chen, Vice President
Jeremy Wolfe, Partner
Linda Assante, Partner
Nikhilesh Tandon, Vice President
Owen DeHoff, Principal
Pamela Pavkov, Vice President
Richard Hayes, Managing Partner
Sunil Mulani, Vice President
W. Michael Hyatt, Vice President

Type of Firm

Investment Management Firm

Project Preferences

Type of Financing Preferred:
Fund of Funds
Generalist PE

Additional Information

Year Founded: 2006
Capital Under Management: $468,320,000
Current Activity Level: Actively seeking new investments

JAVELIN VENTURE PARTNERS LP

101 Spear Street
One Rincon Center, Suite 255
San Francisco, CA USA 94105
Phone: 4152025820
Fax: 4155200305
E-mail: info@javelinvp.com
Website: javelinvp.com

Management and Staff

Alex Gurevich, Partner
Jed Katz, Managing Director
Noah Doyle, Managing Director

Type of Firm

Private Equity Firm

Association Membership

Western Association of Venture Capitalists (WAVC)

Project Preferences

Type of Financing Preferred:
Early Stage
Seed
Startup

Size of Investments Considered:
Min Size of Investment Considered (000s): $250
Max Size of Investment Considered (000s): $4,000

Industry Preferences

In Communications prefer:
Wireless Communications

In Computer Hardware prefer:
Computer Graphics and Dig

In Computer Software prefer:
Software

In Internet Specific prefer:
Ecommerce
Web Aggregration/Portals

In Medical/Health prefer:
Medical/Health

In Business Serv. prefer:
Media

Additional Information

Name of Most Recent Fund: Javelin Venture Partners III, L.P.
Most Recent Fund Was Raised: 10/16/2013
Year Founded: 2008
Capital Under Management: $70,000,000
Current Activity Level: Actively seeking new investments

JAVELIN VENTURES LTD

46 Dorset Street
London, United Kingdom W1U 7NB
Phone: 442047867456
Fax: 442074867463
E-mail: info@javelin-ventures.com
Website: www.javelin-ventures.com

Type of Firm

University Program

Association Membership

British Venture Capital Association (BVCA)

Project Preferences

Type of Financing Preferred:
Early Stage
Start-up Financing
Seed
Startup

Geographical Preferences

International Preferences:
United Kingdom
Europe

Industry Preferences

In Biotechnology prefer:
Biotechnology

In Medical/Health prefer:
Medical/Health

Additional Information

Year Founded: 2002
Capital Under Management: $6,000,000
Current Activity Level: Actively seeking new investments

JAVEST INVESTMENT FUND BV

Eerste Jacob van Campenstraat 46-I
Amsterdam, Netherlands 1072 BG
Phone: 31653428711
Website: www.javestinvestment.com

Type of Firm

Private Equity Firm

Project Preferences

Type of Financing Preferred:
Early Stage
Balanced
Later Stage
Seed
Startup

Geographical Preferences

United States Preferences:
All U.S.

International Preferences:
Latin America
Europe

Industry Preferences

In Internet Specific prefer:
Internet
Web Aggregration/Portals

Additional Information

Year Founded: 2012
Current Activity Level: Actively seeking new investments

JAZZ VENTURE PARTNERS LP

2339 3rd Street
Suite 56
San Francisco, CA USA 94107
E-mail: info@jazzvp.com
Website: www.jazzvp.com

Type of Firm

Private Equity Firm

Additional Information

Year Founded: 2014
Current Activity Level: Actively seeking new investments.

JC ASIA ALPHA PRIVATE EQUITY

971 Dongfang Road, Pudong
18H, Qianjiang B/D
Shanghai, China 200122
Phone: 862168768896
Website: www.asiaalpha.com

Other Offices
161 Lujiazui East Road
China Merchant's Tower, Pudong
Shanghai, China 200120
Phone: 86-1367-181-2857
Fax: 852-9853-7778

Management and Staff
Chris Park, Managing Partner
James Hahn, Managing Partner

Type of Firm
Private Equity Firm

Project Preferences

Type of Financing Preferred:
Leveraged Buyout
Early Stage
Later Stage
Seed
Startup
Special Situation

Geographical Preferences

International Preferences:
China
Asia

Industry Preferences

In Consumer Related prefer:
Consumer
Entertainment and Leisure
Retail
Education Related

In Business Serv. prefer:
Services

In Agr/Forestr/Fish prefer:
Agriculture related

Additional Information
Year Founded: 2007
Current Activity Level : Actively seeking new investments

JC FLOWERS & CO LLC

767 Fifth Avenue
23rd Floor
New York, NY USA 10153
Phone: 2124046800
Website: jcfco.com

Other Offices
125 Old Broad Street
24th Floor
London, United Kingdom EC2N 1AR
Phone: 442077100500
Fax: 442077100519

Management and Staff
David Morgan, Managing Director
Eric Rahe, Managing Director
J. Christopher Flowers, CEO & Managing Director
John Oros, Managing Director
Jonathan Cox, Vice President
Loren Felsman, Managing Director
Michael Christner, Managing Director
Peter Yordan, Vice President
Ralph Valvano, Vice President
Thierry Porte, Managing Director
Timothy Hanford, Managing Director
Todd Freebern, Managing Director
Xiaohong Sang, Vice President

Type of Firm
Private Equity Firm

Project Preferences

Type of Financing Preferred:
Leveraged Buyout

Geographical Preferences

United States Preferences:
All U.S.

Canadian Preferences:
All Canada

International Preferences:
Europe
Mexico

Industry Preferences

In Financial Services prefer:
Financial Services

Additional Information
Name of Most Recent Fund: J.C. Flowers II, L.P.
Most Recent Fund Was Raised: 06/30/2006
Year Founded: 2000
Capital Under Management: $668,000,000
Current Activity Level : Actively seeking new investments

JC SIMMONS & ASSOCIATES

206-2187 Oak Bay Avenue
Victoria, Canada V8R1G1
Phone: 250-595-8860
Fax: 250-595-8861

Management and Staff
John Simmons, President

Type of Firm
Private Equity Firm

Project Preferences

Type of Financing Preferred:
Early Stage

Additional Information
Year Founded: 1999
Current Activity Level : Actively seeking new investments

JDRF INTERNATIONAL

26 Broadway
14th floor
New York, NY USA 10004
Phone: 8005332873
Fax: 2127859595
E-mail: info@jdrf.org
Website: jdrf.org

Management and Staff
Gil King, Vice President
Jonathan Behr, Managing Director
Julia Greenstein, Vice President
Mark Greene, Chief Financial Officer
Sridhar Thodupunoori, Vice President

Type of Firm
Endowment, Foundation or Pension Fund

Project Preferences

Type of Financing Preferred:
Early Stage

Industry Preferences

In Medical/Health prefer:
Health Services

Additional Information
Year Founded: 1970
Capital Under Management: $32,000,000
Current Activity Level : Actively seeking new investments

JEFFERIES GROUP LLC

520 Madison Avenue, Tenth Floor
New York, NY USA 10022
Phone: 2122842300
Website: www.jefferies.com

Other Offices
111 Park Place Boulevard
Suite 140
Covington, LA USA 70433
Phone: 985-845-6020

51 JFK Parkway
Third Floor
Short Hills, NJ USA 07078
Phone: 973-912-2900

Pratt's Guide to Private Equity & Venture Capital Sources

One Station Place
Three North
Stamford, CT USA 06902
Phone: 203-708-5980

One Post Office Square
Suite 3400
Boston, MA USA 02109
Phone: 617-342-7800

55 West Monroe
Suite 3500
Chicago, IL USA 60603
Phone: 312-750-4700

The Taj Mahal Palace & Tower Hotel
Suite 305, Apollo Bunder
Mumbai, India 400 001
Phone: 91-22-2287-7100

1909-1910A, CITIC Square
1168 Nanjing Road (W)
Shanghai, China 200041
Phone: 86-21-5111-8700

333 Clay Street
Suite 1000
Houston, TX USA 77002
Phone: 2817742000
Fax: 2819661851

1050 Winter Street
Suite 2400
Waltham, MA USA 02451
Phone: 781-522-8400

13355 Noel Road
Suite 1400
Dallas, TX USA 75240
Phone: 972-701-3000

650 California Street
29th Floor
San Francisco, CA USA 94108
Phone: 415-229-1400

8 rue Halevy
Paris, France 5009
Phone: 33-1-5343-6700

Hibiya Marine Building 3F
1-5-1, Yuraku-cho, Chiyoda-ku
Tokyo, Japan 100-0006
Phone: 81-3-5251-6100

3414 Peachtree Road Northeast
Suite 810
Atlanta, GA USA 30326
Phone: 404-264-5000

11100 Santa Monica
Tenth Floor
West Los Angeles, CA USA 90025
Phone: 310-445-1199

Niederlassung Frankfurt
Bockenheimer Landstrasse 24
Frankfurt am Main, Germany 60323
Phone: 49-69-719-1870

4064 Colony Road
Suite 400
Charlotte, NC USA 28211
Phone: 704-943-7400

80 Raffles Place
Suite 15-20 UOB Plaza 2
Singapore, Singapore 048624
Phone: 65-6551-3950

Vintners Place
68 Upper Thames Street
London, United Kingdom EC4V 3BJ
Phone: 44-20-7029-8000

2nd Floor, Eros Corporate Tower
Nehru Place
New Delhi, India 110019
Phone: 91-11-4059-9500

2525 West End Avenue
Suite 1150
Nashville, TN USA 37203
Phone: 615-963-8300

Uraniastrasse 12
Zurich, Switzerland 8021
Phone: 41-44-227-1600

Harborside Financial Center
34 Exchange Place, Plaza III
Jersey City, NJ USA 07311
Phone: 212-336-7000

909 Fannin Street
Suite 3100
Houston, TX USA 77010
Phone: 800-533-0072

Emirates Office Tower, Level 41
Sheikh Zayed Road
Dubai, Utd. Arab Em.
Phone: 971-4-319-7648

Management and Staff
Michael Eastwood, Managing Director
Rohit Bansal, Managing Director

Type of Firm
Bank Affiliated

Project Preferences

Role in Financing:
Prefer role as deal originator but will also invest in deals created by others

Type of Financing Preferred:
Fund of Funds
Second Stage Financing
Leveraged Buyout
Early Stage
Generalist PE
Balanced
Management Buyouts
First Stage Financing
Special Situation
Recapitalizations

Size of Investments Considered:
Min Size of Investment Considered (000s): $20,000
Max Size of Investment Considered (000s): $100,000

Geographical Preferences

United States Preferences:

International Preferences:
Europe
Asia

Industry Preferences

In Communications prefer:
Commercial Communications
Telecommunications
Wireless Communications

In Computer Software prefer:
Computer Services
Data Processing
Software
Applications Software
Artificial Intelligence

In Internet Specific prefer:
Internet
Web Aggregation/Portals

In Semiconductor/Electr prefer:
Electronic Components
Semiconductor
Laser Related
Fiber Optics

In Medical/Health prefer:
Medical/Health
Health Services
Pharmaceuticals

In Consumer Related prefer:
Other Restaurants

In Industrial/Energy prefer:
Energy
Superconductivity
Robotics

In Transportation prefer:
Transportation
Aerospace

In Business Serv. prefer:
Services
Distribution

Additional Information
Name of Most Recent Fund: Jefferies Capital Partners IV, L.P.
Most Recent Fund Was Raised: 05/26/2005
Year Founded: 1994
Capital Under Management: $600,000,000
Current Activity Level : Actively seeking new investments
Method of Compensation: Return on invest. most important, but chg. closing fees, service fees, etc.

JEFFERSON CAPITAL PARTNERS LTD

1802 Bayberry Court
Suite 301
Richmond, VA USA 23226
Phone: 8046430100
Fax: 8046439140

Management and Staff
Palmer Garson, Founder
R. Timothy O Donnell, Founder

Type of Firm
Private Equity Firm

Association Membership
Natl Assoc of Small Bus. Inv. Co (NASBIC)

Project Preferences

Type of Financing Preferred:
Leveraged Buyout
Expansion
Management Buyouts
Recapitalizations

Industry Focus
(% based on actual investment)
Computer Software and Services	39.0%
Consumer Related	27.5%
Other Products	21.2%
Internet Specific	8.6%
Medical/Health	3.7%

Additional Information
Name of Most Recent Fund: Jefferson Capital Partners II, L.P.
Most Recent Fund Was Raised: 09/01/2000
Year Founded: 1997
Capital Under Management: $108,500,000
Current Activity Level : Actively seeking new investments

JEFFERSON EDUCATION ACCELERATOR LLC

405 Emmet Street
Charlottesville, VA USA 22904
Website: www.jeauva.com

Management and Staff
Bart Epstein, CEO & Managing Director
Ileen Warner, Vice President

Type of Firm
University Program

Industry Preferences

In Consumer Related prefer:
Education Related

Additional Information
Year Founded: 2016
Current Activity Level : Actively seeking new investments

JEMISON INVESTMENT CO INC

2001 Park Place # 320
Birmingham, AL USA 35203
Phone: 2053247681
Fax: 2053247684

Management and Staff
J. David Brown, President

Type of Firm
Private Equity Firm

Additional Information
Year Founded: 2009
Current Activity Level : Actively seeking new investments

JEROME CAPITAL LLC

1260 Vallecita Drive
Santa Fe, NM USA 87501
Phone: 5059881360

Management and Staff
Halley Faust, Managing Director

Type of Firm
Private Equity Firm

Project Preferences

Role in Financing:
Prefer role as deal originator but will also invest in deals created by others

Type of Financing Preferred:
Second Stage Financing
Early Stage
Seed
First Stage Financing
Startup

Size of Investments Considered:
Min Size of Investment Considered (000s): $50,000
Max Size of Investment Considered (000s): $250,000

Geographical Preferences

United States Preferences:
New Mexico
Maryland
California
Connecticut

Industry Preferences

In Semiconductor/Electr prefer:
Laser Related

In Biotechnology prefer:
Human Biotechnology
Genetic Engineering

In Medical/Health prefer:
Medical/Health
Medical Diagnostics
Diagnostic Services
Diagnostic Test Products
Medical Therapeutics
Medical Products
Health Services
Hospitals/Clinics/Primary
Pharmaceuticals

In Consumer Related prefer:
Education Related

In Industrial/Energy prefer:
Alternative Energy

In Financial Services prefer:
Insurance

Additional Information
Year Founded: 1997
Capital Under Management: $10,000,000
Current Activity Level : Actively seeking new investments

JERUSALEM GLOBAL VENTURES

8 Hartom Street
Beck Science Building, Floor 3
Jerusalem, Israel 91481
Phone: 97225828888
Fax: 97226482451
E-mail: info@jgv.com
Website: www.jgv.com

Other Offices
Beit Hatayalet
Beitar Street 2; Floor 4
Jerusalem, Israel
Phone: 972-2-565-2220

Globus Communication Centre
Suite 220; 2nd Floor
Neve Ilan, Israel
Phone: 972-2-533-2808
Fax: 972-2-570-2352

Management and Staff

Avraham Menachem, Managing Partner
Avrom Gilbert, Principal
Dalia Megiddo, Managing Partner
Erik Grossberg, Principal
Joel Weiss, Chief Operating Officer
Jonathan Adereth, Venture Partner
Micah Avni, Partner
Michael Brous, Co-Founder
Michael Pliner, Venture Partner
Ranan Grobman, Partner
Shlomo Kalish, Partner
Shlomo Caine, Venture Partner
Yoni Hashkes, Managing Partner
Yoseph Linde, Managing Partner
Yossi Tsuria, Venture Partner

Type of Firm
Private Equity Firm

Project Preferences

Role in Financing:
Prefer role as deal originator but will also invest in deals created by others

Type of Financing Preferred:
Early Stage
Expansion
Balanced
Later Stage
Seed
Startup

Geographical Preferences

International Preferences:
Israel

Industry Preferences

In Communications prefer:
Telecommunications

In Computer Software prefer:
Software

In Internet Specific prefer:
Internet

In Computer Other prefer:
Computer Related

In Biotechnology prefer:
Biotechnology

In Medical/Health prefer:
Medical/Health
Medical Products

Additional Information

Year Founded: 1999
Capital Under Management: $117,000,000
Current Activity Level : Actively seeking new investments
Method of Compensation: Return on investment is of primary concern, do not charge fees

JESUP & LAMONT SECURITIES CORP

600 University Street
2800 One Union Square
Seattle, WA USA 98101
Phone: 2066231200
Fax: 2066232213
E-mail: seattle@broadmark.com

Management and Staff

Adam Fountain, Principal
Joseph Schocken, President

Type of Firm
Bank Affiliated

Project Preferences

Role in Financing:
Prefer role as deal originator but will also invest in deals created by others

Type of Financing Preferred:
Generalist PE

Size of Investments Considered:
Min Size of Investment Considered (000s): $5,000
Max Size of Investment Considered (000s): $100,000

Industry Focus

(% based on actual investment)
Other Products	26.2%
Communications and Media	17.3%
Computer Software and Services	17.0%
Internet Specific	14.4%
Consumer Related	14.0%
Medical/Health	5.0%
Biotechnology	4.1%
Industrial/Energy	2.1%

Additional Information

Year Founded: 1986
Capital Under Management: $20,000,000
Current Activity Level : Actively seeking new investments
Method of Compensation: Function primarily in service area, receive contingent fee in cash or equity

JFLEHMAN & CO

110 East 59th Street
27th Floor
New York, NY USA 10022
Phone: 2126340100
Fax: 2126341155
Website: www.jflpartners.com

Other Offices

2001 Jefferson Davis Highway
Suite 607
Arlington, VA USA 22202
Phone: 703-418-6095
Fax: 703-418-6099

33 Lowndes Street
5th Floor
London, United Kingdom SW1X 7HJ
Phone: 44-20-7201-5490
Fax: 44-20-7201-5499

Management and Staff

C. Alexander Harman, Partner
David Gorton, Vice President
Donald Glickman, Founding Partner
Glenn Shor, Vice President
Louis Mintz, Partner
Michael Cuff, Managing Director
Robert Lee, Vice President
Stephen Brooks, Partner
Tig Krekel, Partner

Type of Firm
Private Equity Firm

Project Preferences

Role in Financing:
Prefer role as deal originator but will also invest in deals created by others

Type of Financing Preferred:
Leveraged Buyout
Acquisition

Geographical Preferences

United States Preferences:

International Preferences:
United Kingdom

Industry Focus

(% based on actual investment)
Semiconductors/Other Elect.	68.3%
Industrial/Energy	17.2%
Other Products	10.0%
Computer Software and Services	4.5%

Additional Information

Name of Most Recent Fund: JFL Equity Investors III, L.P.
Most Recent Fund Was Raised: 09/29/2011
Year Founded: 1992
Capital Under Management: $130,000,000
Current Activity Level : Actively seeking new investments
Method of Compensation: Return on invest. most important, but chg. closing fees, service fees, etc.

JGI VENTURES INDIA PVT LTD

#34, 1st Cross, JC Road
Bangalore, India 560 027
Phone: 918043430173
E-mail: info@jgiventures.com
Website: www.jgiventures.com

Management and Staff

Hemachandra Seshadri, Chief Executive Officer

Type of Firm
Private Equity Firm

Project Preferences

Type of Financing Preferred:
Early Stage

Geographical Preferences

International Preferences:
India

Industry Preferences

In Medical/Health prefer:
Medical/Health
Health Services
Hospitals/Clinics/Primary

In Consumer Related prefer:
Education Related

In Financial Services prefer:
Financial Services

Additional Information
Year Founded: 2004
Current Activity Level : Actively seeking new investments

JH PARTNERS LLC
451 Jackson Street
San Francisco, CA USA 94111
Phone: 4153640300
E-mail: info@jhpartners.com
Website: www.jhpartners.com

Management and Staff
Jeffrey Hansen, Partner
John Hansen, Managing Partner
Michael John, Partner
Patrick Collins, Partner
Stephen Baus, Partner
Todd Forrest, Partner

Type of Firm
Private Equity Firm

Project Preferences

Type of Financing Preferred:
Leveraged Buyout
Later Stage

Geographical Preferences

International Preferences:
All International

Industry Preferences

In Consumer Related prefer:
Consumer

Additional Information
Year Founded: 1986
Capital Under Management: $1,000,000,000
Current Activity Level : Actively seeking new investments

JHP ENTERPRISES LLC
534 West Road
New Canaan, CT USA 06840
Phone: 203-652-0548
Fax: 917-591-7580
E-mail: jhpujol@jhpenter.com
Website: www.jhpenter.com

Management and Staff
Juan Pujol, President

Type of Firm
Bank Affiliated

Project Preferences

Type of Financing Preferred:
Leveraged Buyout
Management Buyouts
Recapitalizations

Geographical Preferences

United States Preferences:

International Preferences:
Latin America
Spain

Additional Information
Year Founded: 1988
Current Activity Level : Actively seeking new investments
Method of Compensation: Return on invest. most important, but chg. closing fees, service fees, etc.

JIANGSU ADDOR EQUITY INVESTMENT FUND MANAGEMENT CO LTD
No. 128, Shanxi Road
Hetai International Mansion
Nanjing, China 210009
Phone: 862566009696
Fax: 862566009900
Website: www.addorcapital.com

Management and Staff
Chunfang Zhou, Partner
Jinbai You, Partner
Liang Dong, President
Liping Fan, Partner
Tao Huang, Partner
Yunzhong Shi, Partner

Type of Firm
Private Equity Firm

Project Preferences

Type of Financing Preferred:
Leveraged Buyout
Balanced

Geographical Preferences

International Preferences:
China

Industry Preferences

In Communications prefer:
Telecommunications

In Medical/Health prefer:
Medical/Health

In Consumer Related prefer:
Consumer

In Industrial/Energy prefer:
Energy
Energy Conservation Relat
Materials

In Business Serv. prefer:
Media

Additional Information
Year Founded: 2014
Capital Under Management: $1,540,330,000
Current Activity Level : Actively seeking new investments

JIANGSU GAOTOU ZIJIN CULTURE INVESTMENT MANAGEMENT CO LTD
C/o, Govtor Capital
Jiangsu, China

Type of Firm
Government Affiliated Program

Project Preferences

Type of Financing Preferred:
Balanced

Geographical Preferences

International Preferences:
China

Industry Preferences

In Communications prefer:
Media and Entertainment

In Internet Specific prefer:
Internet

In Business Serv. prefer:
Media

Additional Information
Year Founded: 2010
Capital Under Management: $293,002,000
Current Activity Level : Actively seeking new investments

JIANGSU HIGH-TECH INVESTMENT GROUP CO LTD

No. 128, Shanxi Road
Hetai International Building
Nanjing, China 210009
Phone: 862566009999
Fax: 862566009900
Website: www.js-vc.com

Management and Staff
Wenlu Ying, Vice President

Type of Firm
Government Affiliated Program

Project Preferences

Type of Financing Preferred:
Early Stage
Expansion
Balanced
Later Stage

Geographical Preferences

International Preferences:
China

Industry Preferences

In Computer Software prefer:
Software

In Biotechnology prefer:
Biotechnology
Industrial Biotechnology

In Medical/Health prefer:
Medical/Health

In Consumer Related prefer:
Consumer Products

In Industrial/Energy prefer:
Alternative Energy
Environmental Related

In Financial Services prefer:
Financial Services

In Business Serv. prefer:
Services

In Manufact. prefer:
Manufacturing

In Agr/Forestr/Fish prefer:
Agribusiness

Additional Information
Year Founded: 1992

Capital Under Management: $193,078,000
Current Activity Level : Actively seeking new investments

JIANGSU JINMAO VENTURE CAPITAL MANAGEMENT CO LTD

No. 108 Hanzhong Road
22A Jinlun Building
Nanjing, China
Phone: 862584730307
Fax: 862584730211
E-mail: ip@jolmo.net
Website: www.jolmo.net

Other Offices
Shunde District
District Government Compound
Foshan, China
Phone: 86-757-2283-1405
Fax: 86-757-2283-1407

Management and Staff
Min Zhang, President

Type of Firm
Private Equity Firm

Project Preferences

Type of Financing Preferred:
Early Stage
Expansion
Balanced
Later Stage

Geographical Preferences

International Preferences:
China

Industry Preferences

In Biotechnology prefer:
Biotechnology

In Medical/Health prefer:
Medical/Health

In Consumer Related prefer:
Consumer

In Industrial/Energy prefer:
Energy
Alternative Energy
Energy Conservation Relat
Materials
Advanced Materials
Machinery
Environmental Related

In Transportation prefer:
Transportation

In Manufact. prefer:
Manufacturing

In Agr/Forestr/Fish prefer:
Agriculture related

In Other prefer:
Environment Responsible

Additional Information
Year Founded: 2004
Capital Under Management: $95,847,000
Current Activity Level : Actively seeking new investments

JIANGSU JIUZHOU CAPITAL CO LTD

No. 66, Guanhe East Road
23/F, Jiuzhou Huanyu Square
Changzhou, China
Phone: 8651985228901
Fax: 8651985228850
E-mail: info@jzvc.cn
Website: www.jzvc.cn

Other Offices
No. 168, Yincheng Mid Road, Lujiazui
Room 1702, East Tower, Shangyin Plaza
Shanghai, China
Phone: 862168598516
Fax: 862168595050

No. 21-27, Playing Field Road, Mong Kok
Room D, 2/F, Yuntai Plaza
Hong Kong, Hong Kong
Phone: 85224543948
Fax: 85224546580

Type of Firm
Corporate PE/Venture

Project Preferences

Role in Financing:
Prefer role in deals created by others

Type of Financing Preferred:
Early Stage
Expansion
Later Stage

Size of Investments Considered:
Min Size of Investment Considered (000s): $793
Max Size of Investment Considered (000s): $31,717

Geographical Preferences

International Preferences:
China

Industry Preferences

In Communications prefer:
Telecommunications

In Biotechnology prefer:
Biotechnology

In Medical/Health prefer:
Medical Products
Health Services
Pharmaceuticals

In Consumer Related prefer:
Consumer

In Industrial/Energy prefer:
Energy
Energy Conservation Relat
Materials
Environmental Related

In Business Serv. prefer:
Media

In Manufact. prefer:
Manufacturing

In Agr/Forestr/Fish prefer:
Agriculture related

Additional Information
Year Founded: 2004
Current Activity Level : Actively seeking new investments

JIANGSU KAITENG VENTURE CAPITAL CO LTD

Lushan Road, Jianye District
Room 755, No. 128
Nanjing, China

Type of Firm
Private Equity Firm

Project Preferences

Type of Financing Preferred:
Balanced

Geographical Preferences

International Preferences:
China

Additional Information
Year Founded: 2011
Current Activity Level : Actively seeking new investments

JIANGSU RONGZHUO INVESTMENT CO LTD

No. 100, Qinhuai Road
Haitong Bldg, Jiangning Dist
Nanjing, China

Type of Firm
Private Equity Firm

Project Preferences

Type of Financing Preferred:
Balanced

Geographical Preferences

International Preferences:
China

Industry Preferences

In Biotechnology prefer:
Biotechnology

In Medical/Health prefer:
Pharmaceuticals

In Industrial/Energy prefer:
Materials

Additional Information
Year Founded: 2011
Current Activity Level : Actively seeking new investments

JIANGSU SUDA TIANGONG VENTURE CAPITAL MANAGEMENT CO LTD

328 Xinghu St., SZ Ind. Park
101, Blk.4 Creative Ind. Park
Nanjing, China
Website: www.sudatiangong.com

Type of Firm
Incubator/Development Program

Project Preferences

Type of Financing Preferred:
Start-up Financing
Seed

Geographical Preferences

International Preferences:
China

Industry Preferences

In Industrial/Energy prefer:
Materials

Additional Information
Year Founded: 2010
Current Activity Level : Actively seeking new investments

JIANGSU XINCHENG CAPITAL CO LTD

21 Heping North Road
Zhongyin Plz, Tianning
Changzhou, China 213003
Phone: 86-519-8812
Fax: 86-519-8815

Type of Firm
Private Equity Firm

Industry Preferences

In Financial Services prefer:
Investment Groups

Additional Information
Year Founded: 2007
Current Activity Level : Actively seeking new investments

JIANGSU XINGKE VENTURE CAPITAL CO LTD

No. 5-7, Changwu Central Road
Changzhou, Jiangsu, China 213000
Phone: 8651986302528
Fax: 8651986302628
Website: www.jsxinkect.com

Type of Firm
Private Equity Firm

Project Preferences

Type of Financing Preferred:
Early Stage
Expansion

Geographical Preferences

International Preferences:
China

Industry Preferences

In Semiconductor/Electr prefer:
Electronics

In Biotechnology prefer:
Biotechnology

In Medical/Health prefer:
Medical/Health

In Industrial/Energy prefer:
Materials

Additional Information
Year Founded: 2007
Current Activity Level : Actively seeking new investments

JIANGXI COPPER BEIJING INTERNATIONAL INVESTMENT CO LTD

No. 5 Yard, Guanghua Road
Room 802, Building 1
Beijing, China
Website: www.jxcc.com

Type of Firm
Government Affiliated Program

Project Preferences

Type of Financing Preferred:
Balanced

Geographical Preferences

International Preferences:
China

Industry Preferences

In Communications prefer:
Telecommunications

In Business Serv. prefer:
Media

Additional Information

Year Founded: 2012
Current Activity Level : Actively seeking new investments

JIANGXI HIGH-TECH INDUSTRY INVESTMENT CO LTD

199 Torch Street
Hi-Tech Dev Zone
Nanchang, China 330029
Phone: 86-791-8110
Fax: 86-791-8110

Type of Firm
Government Affiliated Program

Project Preferences

Type of Financing Preferred:
Early Stage
Balanced

Industry Preferences

In Medical/Health prefer:
Pharmaceuticals

In Industrial/Energy prefer:
Alternative Energy

Additional Information

Year Founded: 2001
Capital Under Management: $8,300,000
Current Activity Level : Actively seeking new investments

JIAXING LVMINTOU EQUITY INVESTMENT FUND MANAGEMENT CO LTD

Changan St., Dongcheng Distri
Room 1910, Block E1, Dongfang
Jiaxing, China
Phone: 8601085180638
Website: www.gsxt.gov.cn

Type of Firm
Private Equity Firm

Project Preferences

Type of Financing Preferred:
Balanced

Geographical Preferences

International Preferences:
China

Additional Information

Year Founded: 2015
Current Activity Level : Actively seeking new investments

JIAXING XINGHE VENTURE CAPITAL INVESTMENT MANAGEMENT CO LTD

No.3339, Linggongtang Rd.
R226, No.2 Bldg.
Jiaxing, China

Type of Firm
Private Equity Firm

Project Preferences

Type of Financing Preferred:
Balanced

Geographical Preferences

International Preferences:
China

Additional Information

Year Founded: 2014
Current Activity Level : Actively seeking new investments

JIAXING YINRUI INVESTMENT MANAGEMENT PARTNER ENTERPRISE

Guangyi Road 705
Blk1, Intl. Trade Center
Jiaxing, China

Type of Firm
Private Equity Firm

Project Preferences

Type of Financing Preferred:
Fund of Funds
Balanced

Geographical Preferences

International Preferences:
China

Additional Information

Year Founded: 2014
Current Activity Level : Actively seeking new investments

JILIN HUIZHENG INVESTMENT CO LTD

Jilin Province
Changchun, China

Management and Staff
Wang Xitian, President

Type of Firm
Private Equity Firm

Project Preferences

Type of Financing Preferred:
Balanced

Geographical Preferences

International Preferences:
China

Industry Preferences

In Industrial/Energy prefer:
Oil and Gas Exploration

Additional Information

Year Founded: 2003
Current Activity Level : Actively seeking new investments

JILIN PROVINCE EQUITY FUND INVESTMENT CO LTD

6666 Shengtai St.,Jingyue Dist
10/F, Chuangye Service Center
Changchun, China 130119

Type of Firm
Government Affiliated Program

Project Preferences

Type of Financing Preferred:
Fund of Funds
Balanced

Geographical Preferences

International Preferences:
China

Additional Information

Year Founded: 2015
Current Activity Level : Actively seeking new investments

JILIN VENTURE CAPITAL FUND OF FUNDS MANAGEMENT CO LTD

No. 2559 Weishan Road
7/F Jilin Investment Building
Jilin, Changchun, China 130022
Phone: 8643181959791
Fax: 8643181959791
E-mail: jlvc@jl-vc.com
Website: www.jl-vc.com

Type of Firm
Private Equity Advisor or Fund of Funds

Project Preferences

Type of Financing Preferred:
Fund of Funds

Size of Investments Considered:
Min Size of Investment Considered (000s): $731
Max Size of Investment Considered (000s): $4,387

Geographical Preferences

International Preferences:
China

Industry Preferences

In Biotechnology prefer:
Biotechnology

In Medical/Health prefer:
Pharmaceuticals

In Industrial/Energy prefer:
Energy
Materials
Environmental Related

In Agr/Forestr/Fish prefer:
Agribusiness

Additional Information
Year Founded: 2007
Current Activity Level : Actively seeking new investments

JINAN HUAYUE INVESTMENT MANGEMENT CO LTD

High-Tech Zone
Jinan, China

Type of Firm
Private Equity Firm

Project Preferences

Type of Financing Preferred:
Balanced

Geographical Preferences

International Preferences:
China

Additional Information
Year Founded: 2013
Capital Under Management: $40,130,000
Current Activity Level : Actively seeking new investments

JINAN SCI-TECH VENTURE CAPITAL CO LTD

4th Floor Tech Service Center
746 Xinyu Road,Dev Zone
Jinan City, China 250101
Phone: 86-531-88879297
Fax: 86-531-88879277
E-mail: jnvc@jnvc.com.cn
Website: www.jnvc.com.cn

Type of Firm
Private Equity Firm

Project Preferences

Type of Financing Preferred:
Balanced

Geographical Preferences

International Preferences:
China

Additional Information
Year Founded: 2001
Current Activity Level : Actively seeking new investments

JINHUA HI-TECH INVESTMENT CO LTD

#8 South Street
10th Floor, No. 588
Jinhua, China 321017
Phone: 86-579-2065673
Fax: 86-579-2065674

Type of Firm
Investment Management Firm

Industry Preferences

In Business Serv. prefer:
Services

Additional Information
Year Founded: 2010
Current Activity Level : Actively seeking new investments

JINXIU ZHONGHE BEIJING CAPITAL MANAGEMENT CO LTD

No.1,Jianguomenwai Avenue
10FNo.1China World TradeCenter
Beijing, China
Phone: 861065055135
Fax: 861065055135

Type of Firm
Private Equity Firm

Project Preferences

Type of Financing Preferred:
Balanced

Geographical Preferences

International Preferences:
China

Industry Preferences

In Communications prefer:
Entertainment

In Consumer Related prefer:
Consumer
Sports

In Manufact. prefer:
Manufacturing

In Agr/Forestr/Fish prefer:
Agriculture related

Additional Information
Year Founded: 2012
Capital Under Management: $32,230,000
Current Activity Level : Actively seeking new investments

JINYINGFENG EQUITY INVESTMENT FUND SHENZHEN CO LTD

Luohu District, Shuibei Road 2
F1, Block6-8
Shenzhen, China

Type of Firm
Private Equity Firm

Project Preferences

Type of Financing Preferred:
Leveraged Buyout

Geographical Preferences

International Preferences:
China

Additional Information

Year Founded: 2011
Current Activity Level : Actively seeking new investments

JK&B CAPITAL LLC

180 North Stetson Avenue
Suite 4500, Two Prudential Pla
Chicago, IL USA 60601
Phone: 3129461200
Fax: 3129461103
E-mail: info@jkbcapital.com
Website: www.jkbcapital.com

Management and Staff

Albert DaValle, Partner
Ali Shadman, Partner
Marc Sokol, Partner
Robert Humes, Partner
Tasha Seitz, Partner
Thomas Neustaetter, Partner

Type of Firm

Private Equity Firm

Association Membership

National Venture Capital Association - USA (NVCA)

Project Preferences

Role in Financing:
Prefer role as deal originator but will also invest in deals created by others

Type of Financing Preferred:
Early Stage
Expansion
Balanced
Later Stage
Seed
Startup

Geographical Preferences

United States Preferences:

Industry Focus

(% based on actual investment)
Computer Software and Services	35.2%
Internet Specific	24.5%
Communications and Media	20.9%
Semiconductors/Other Elect.	10.7%
Computer Hardware	5.6%
Medical/Health	2.9%
Consumer Related	0.2%
Other Products	0.0%

Additional Information

Name of Most Recent Fund: JK&B Capital V, L.P.
Most Recent Fund Was Raised: 10/12/2000
Year Founded: 1996
Capital Under Management: $1,100,000,000
Current Activity Level : Actively seeking new investments
Method of Compensation: Return on invest. most important, but chg. closing fees, service fees, etc.

JKL PARTNERS, INC.

159-9 Samsung-dong, Kangnam-ku
4/F, City Airport Tower
Seoul, South Korea
Phone: 822-2016-5900
Fax: 822-2016-5912
Website: www.jklpartners.co.kr

Type of Firm

Private Equity Firm

Project Preferences

Type of Financing Preferred:
Leveraged Buyout

Geographical Preferences

International Preferences:
Korea, South

Additional Information

Year Founded: 2001
Current Activity Level : Actively seeking new investments

JLL PARTNERS INC

450 Lexington Avenue
31st Floor
New York, NY USA 10017
Phone: 2122868600
Fax: 2122868626
Website: www.jllpartners.com

Management and Staff

Alexander Castaldi, Managing Director
Andrew Goldfarb, Vice President
Dalia Cohen, Managing Director
Daniel Agroskin, Managing Director
Eugene Hahn, Managing Director
Frank Rodriguez, Managing Director
Garrett Hall, Principal
Jiten Sanghai, Vice President
Kevin Hammond, Managing Director
Michael Schwartz, Chief Financial Officer
Michel Lagarde, Managing Director
Paul Levy, Managing Director
Thomas Taylor, Managing Director
William Fradin, Vice President

Type of Firm

Private Equity Firm

Project Preferences

Type of Financing Preferred:
Leveraged Buyout
Turnaround
Management Buyouts
Acquisition
Recapitalizations

Geographical Preferences

United States Preferences:
North America

Industry Focus

(% based on actual investment)
Other Products	77.6%
Consumer Related	17.3%
Medical/Health	3.7%
Industrial/Energy	0.7%
Communications and Media	0.5%
Internet Specific	0.3%

Additional Information

Year Founded: 1988
Capital Under Management: $4,000,000,000
Current Activity Level : Actively seeking new investments

JM FINL INVEST MANAGERS LTD

141, Maker Chambers III
Nariman Point
Mumbai, India 400 021
Phone: 912266303030
Fax: 912222042137
E-mail: corporate@jmfinancial.in
Website: www.jmfinancial.in

Management and Staff

Manish Sheth, Chief Financial Officer

Type of Firm

Corporate PE/Venture

Association Membership

Indian Venture Capital Association (IVCA)

Project Preferences

Type of Financing Preferred:
Balanced

Geographical Preferences

International Preferences:
India

Additional Information

Year Founded: 2006
Current Activity Level : Actively seeking new investments

JM GALEF & CO

P.O. Box 7693
Greenwich, CT USA 06830
Phone: 203-625-8600
Fax: 203-625-8682
E-mail: admin@galef.net
Website: www.galef.net

Management and Staff

James Galef, President

Type of Firm
Private Equity Firm

Project Preferences

Role in Financing:
Prefer role as deal originator

Type of Financing Preferred:
Leveraged Buyout
Turnaround
Management Buyouts
Recapitalizations

Geographical Preferences

United States Preferences:

International Preferences:
United Kingdom
France

Additional Information
Year Founded: 1986
Current Activity Level : Actively seeking new investments
Method of Compensation: Unknown

JMC CAPITAL PARTNERS LP

125 Summer Street
Suite 1840
Boston, MA USA 02110
Phone: 6173381144
Fax: 6173385353
Website: www.jmccp.com

Management and Staff
Charlie Burckmyer, Principal
G. Lawrence Bero, Co-Founder
Michael D Amelio, Co-Founder
Scott Tucker, Vice President
Timothy Durkin, Partner
Todd Rainville, Partner

Type of Firm
Private Equity Firm

Project Preferences

Type of Financing Preferred:
Leveraged Buyout
Acquisition

Geographical Preferences

United States Preferences:
North America

Industry Preferences

In Industrial/Energy prefer:
Industrial Products

In Manufact. prefer:
Manufacturing

Additional Information
Name of Most Recent Fund: JMC Platform Fund I
Most Recent Fund Was Raised: 03/14/2014
Year Founded: 1999
Capital Under Management: $331,000,000
Current Activity Level : Actively seeking new investments

JME VENTURE CAPITAL SGEIC SA

Avenida de Europa 10
Alcobendas, Spain 28108
Website: www.jme.vc

Type of Firm
Private Equity Firm

Project Preferences

Type of Financing Preferred:
Early Stage

Geographical Preferences

United States Preferences:

International Preferences:
Europe

Additional Information
Year Founded: 2016
Current Activity Level : Actively seeking new investments

JMI MANAGEMENT INC

100 International Drive
Suite 19100
Baltimore, MD USA 21202
Phone: 4109510200
Fax: 4106378360
Website: www.jmiequity.com

Other Offices
7776 Ivanhoe Avenue
Suite 200
La Jolla, CA USA 92037
Phone: 8583629880
Fax: 8583629879

Management and Staff
Bert Winemiller, Venture Partner
Bob Nye, Principal
Bob Smith, General Partner
Bob Sywolski, Venture Partner
Brad Woloson, General Partner
Brian Hersman, Principal
Charlie Noell, Partner
David Greenberg, Principal
Harry Gruner, Founder
Jit Sinha, General Partner
Krishna Potarazu, Vice President
Larry Contrella, Principal
Lee Lesley, Principal
Matt Emery, Principal
Melissa Caslin, Vice President
Mohit Daswani, Principal
Paul Chang, Vice President
Paul Barber, Managing Partner
Peter Arrowsmith, General Partner
Robert Cesafsky, Vice President
Suken Vakil, General Partner

Type of Firm
Private Equity Firm

Association Membership
Mid-Atlantic Venture Association
National Venture Capital Association - USA (NVCA)

Project Preferences

Role in Financing:
Prefer role as deal originator but will also invest in deals created by others

Type of Financing Preferred:
Leveraged Buyout
Generalist PE
Balanced
Management Buyouts
Acquisition
Recapitalizations

Industry Preferences

In Computer Software prefer:
Software

In Internet Specific prefer:
Internet

In Medical/Health prefer:
Medical/Health

In Business Serv. prefer:
Services

Additional Information
Name of Most Recent Fund: JMI Equity Fund VII, L.P.
Most Recent Fund Was Raised: 11/30/2010
Year Founded: 1992
Capital Under Management: $3,100,000,000
Current Activity Level : Actively seeking new investments
Method of Compensation: Return on invest. most important, but chg. closing fees, service fees, etc.

JMK CONSUMER GROWTH PARTNERS LLC

379 West Broadway
New York, NY USA 10012
Website: jmkconsumer.com

Management and Staff
John Kenney, Co-Founder
Sarah Woelfel, Co-Founder

Type of Firm
Private Equity Firm

Project Preferences

Type of Financing Preferred:
Generalist PE

Industry Preferences

In Consumer Related prefer:
Food/Beverage
Consumer Products

Additional Information

Year Founded: 2014
Capital Under Management: $17,000,000
Current Activity Level : Actively seeking new investments

JNT INVESTMENT CO LTD

120-12, Samseongdong, Gangnam
4F, Aurora B/D
Seoul, South Korea
Phone: 8225382280
Fax: 8225382281

Type of Firm
Private Equity Firm

Association Membership
Korean Venture Capital Association (KVCA)

Project Preferences

Type of Financing Preferred:
Balanced

Additional Information

Year Founded: 2010
Capital Under Management: $12,885,000
Current Activity Level : Actively seeking new investments

JOBI CAPITAL

One Penn Plaza, 36th Floor
New York, NY USA 10119

Type of Firm
Private Equity Firm

Project Preferences

Type of Financing Preferred:
Early Stage
Seec

Additional Information

Year Founded: 2017
Current Activity Level : Actively seeking new investments

JOG CAPITAL INC

440 - Second Avenue South West, Suite 2370
Calgary, Canada T2P5E9
Phone: 4032323340
Fax: 4037053341
E-mail: info@jogcapital.com
Website: www.jogcapital.com

Management and Staff

Craig Golinowski, Managing Partner
Glenn Tindle, Vice President
Jason White, Managing Director
Kelvin Johnston, Managing Director
Ryan Crawford, Managing Partner

Type of Firm
Private Equity Firm

Project Preferences

Type of Financing Preferred:
Leveraged Buyout
Acquisition

Geographical Preferences

Canadian Preferences:
Alberta
Manitoba
Saskatchewan
Western Canada

Industry Preferences

In Industrial/Energy prefer:
Oil & Gas Drilling,Explor

Additional Information

Name of Most Recent Fund: JOG, L.P. VI
Most Recent Fund Was Raised: 09/18/2012
Year Founded: 2002
Capital Under Management: $1,011,300,000
Current Activity Level : Actively seeking new investments

JOHN S. AND JAMES L. KNIGHT FOUNDATION

200 South Biscayne Boulevard, Suite 3300
Miami, FL USA 33131
Phone: 3059082600
Fax: 3059082698
E-mail: web@knightfoundation.org
Website: www.knightfoundation.org

Type of Firm
Endowment, Foundation or Pension Fund

Project Preferences

Type of Financing Preferred:
Early Stage
Startup

Geographical Preferences

United States Preferences:

Industry Preferences

In Business Serv. prefer:
Media

Additional Information

Year Founded: 2010
Capital Under Management: $10,000,000
Current Activity Level : Actively seeking new investments

JOHNSON & JOHNSON INNOVATION-JJDC INC

410 George Street
New Brunswick, NJ USA 08901
Phone: 7325243218
Fax: 7322475309
Website: www.jnjinnovation.com

Management and Staff

Asish Xavier, Vice President
Brad Vale, Vice President
Dalton Einhorn, Principal
Joel Kirkston, Principal
Jun Wu, Principal
Michael Chuisano, Vice President
Rami Elghandour, Principal
Renee Ryan, Vice President
V. Kadir Kadhiresan, Principal
Zeev Zehavi, Vice President

Type of Firm
Corporate PE/Venture

Association Membership
National Venture Capital Association - USA (NVCA)

Project Preferences

Role in Financing:
Prefer role as deal originator but will also invest in deals created by others

Type of Financing Preferred:
Early Stage
Expansion
Balanced
Later Stage
Seed
Startup

Industry Focus

(% based on actual investment)

Biotechnology	44.4%
Medical/Health	40.6%
Computer Hardware	4.1%
Computer Software and Services	3.7%
Internet Specific	3.2%
Other Products	1.7%
Consumer Related	1.3%
Semiconductors/Other Elect.	0.9%
Industrial/Energy	0.1%

Additional Information

Year Founded: 1973
Capital Under Management: $16,200,000
Current Activity Level : Actively seeking new investments
Method of Compensation: Return on investment is of primary concern, do not charge fees

JOHNSTON ASSOCIATES INC

358 Wendover Drive
Princeton, NJ USA 08540
Phone: 609-924-2575
Fax: 609-924-3493
E-mail: info@jaivc.com
Website: www.jaivc.com

Management and Staff
Lynn Johnston, Vice President
Robert Johnston, President

Type of Firm
Private Equity Firm

Project Preferences

Role in Financing:
Will function either as deal originator or investor in deals created by others

Type of Financing Preferred:
Early Stage
Start-up Financing

Size of Investments Considered:
Min Size of Investment Considered (000s): $500
Max Size of Investment Considered (000s): $5,000

Geographical Preferences

United States Preferences:
Northeast

Industry Preferences

In Biotechnology prefer:
Human Biotechnology
Industrial Biotechnology

In Medical/Health prefer:
Medical Diagnostics
Pharmaceuticals

Additional Information
Year Founded: 1968
Capital Under Management: $40,000,000
Current Activity Level : Reducing investment activity
Method of Compensation: Return on investment is of primary concern, do not charge fees

JOIN CAPITAL GMBH

Muenzstrasse 19
Berlin, Germany 10178
Phone: 493023912939
Website: www.join.capital

Type of Firm
Private Equity Firm

Project Preferences

Type of Financing Preferred:
Early Stage

Additional Information
Year Founded: 2015
Current Activity Level : Actively seeking new investments

JOINT CHOICE VENTURE CAPITAL CORP

3F, No.609, Kuang-Fu Road
Section 1
Shing-Chu, Taiwan
Phone: 886-3-564-6060
Fax: 886-3-564-6099

Type of Firm
Private Equity Firm

Association Membership
Taiwan Venture Capital Association(TVCA)

Project Preferences

Type of Financing Preferred:
Early Stage
Expansion
Balanced
Seed
Startup

Geographical Preferences

International Preferences:
Taiwan

Industry Preferences

In Communications prefer:
Telecommunications

In Computer Software prefer:
Software

Additional Information
Year Founded: 1998
Capital Under Management: $36,800,000
Current Activity Level : Actively seeking new investments

JOINT POLISH INVESTMENT FUND

ul. Somiskiego 15 lok 509
Warszawau, Poland
Website: http://www.jpifund.com/

Type of Firm
Private Equity Firm

Additional Information
Year Founded: 2015
Current Activity Level : Actively seeking new investments

JOLIMONT CAPITAL PTY LTD

133 Flinders Lane
Level One
Melbourne, Australia 3000
Phone: 61381992700
Website: www.jolimontcapital.com.au

Management and Staff
Carol Sullivan, Chief Financial Officer
Charles Gillies, Co-Founder
Lex McArthur, Co-Founder
Teresa Engelhard, Managing Partner

Type of Firm
Private Equity Advisor or Fund of Funds

Project Preferences

Type of Financing Preferred:
Balanced

Size of Investments Considered:
Min Size of Investment Considered (000s): $1,042
Max Size of Investment Considered (000s): $31,263

Geographical Preferences

International Preferences:
Australia
Asia

Additional Information
Name of Most Recent Fund: Jolimont Secondaries Fund I
Most Recent Fund Was Raised: 10/24/2004
Year Founded: 2003
Capital Under Management: $123,000,000
Current Activity Level : Actively seeking new investments

JOLT

101 College Street
Suite 230
Toronto, Canada M5G 1L7
E-mail: icepractice@marsdd.com
Website: www.joltco.ca

Other Offices
101 College Street
Suite 230
Toronto, Canada M5G 1L7

Management and Staff
Sue McGill, Co-Founder

Type of Firm
Incubator/Development Program

Project Preferences

Type of Financing Preferred:
Early Stage
Seed
Startup

Geographical Preferences

Canadian Preferences:
Quebec
Ontario

Industry Preferences

In Communications prefer:
Communications and Media
Commercial Communications
Entertainment

Additional Information
Year Founded: 2012
Current Activity Level : Actively seeking new investments

JOLT CAPITAL SAS

76-78 Rue Saint-Lazare
Paris, France 75009
Phone: 331847980
E-mail: contact@jolt-tech.com
Website: www.jolt-capital.com

Management and Staff
Jean Schmitt, Managing Director

Type of Firm
Private Equity Firm

Association Membership
French Venture Capital Association (AFIC)

Project Preferences

Type of Financing Preferred:
Leveraged Buyout
Mezzanine
Generalist PE
Later Stage
Acquisition

Geographical Preferences

International Preferences:
Europe
France

Additional Information
Year Founded: 2011
Capital Under Management: $96,390,000
Current Activity Level : Actively seeking new investments

JORDAN COMPANY LP

399 Park Avenue, 30th Floor
New York, NY USA 10022
Phone: 2125720800
Fax: 2127555263

Website: www.thejordancompany.com

Other Offices
875 North Michigan Avenue
John Hancock Building Suite 4040
Chicago, IL USA 60611
Phone: 312-573-6418
Fax: 312-274-1247

CITIC Square, 1168 Nanjing Xi Lu
Floor 23, Suite 2308
Shanghai, China 200041
Phone: 86-21-5292-5566
Fax: 86-21-5292-8600

Management and Staff
A. Richard Caputo, Managing Partner
Adam Max, Managing Partner
Daniel Pezley, Vice President
Daniel Williams, Vice President
Erik Fagan, Partner
Ian Arons, Partner
Jeffrey Miller, Partner
John Straus, Vice President
John Jordan, Managing Partner
Jonathan Boucher, Managing Partner
Kristin Custar, Partner
Kristin Custar, Principal
M. Brad Wilford, Partner
Paul Rodzevik, Chief Financial Officer
Peter Suffredini, Vice President
Thomas Quinn, Managing Partner

Type of Firm
Private Equity Firm

Association Membership
Private Equity Council (PEC)

Project Preferences

Role in Financing:
Prefer role as deal originator

Type of Financing Preferred:
Leveraged Buyout
Management Buyouts
Acquisition
Recapitalizations

Industry Focus
(% based on actual investment)
Other Products	41.9%
Industrial/Energy	39.2%
Communications and Media	15.8%
Consumer Related	1.2%
Internet Specific	1.0%
Medical/Health	0.9%

Additional Information
Name of Most Recent Fund: Resolute Fund III, L.P., The
Most Recent Fund Was Raised: 10/25/2013
Year Founded: 1982
Capital Under Management: $5,000,000,000
Current Activity Level : Actively seeking new investments

Method of Compensation: Return on invest. most important, but chg. closing fees, service fees, etc.

JOSE MANUEL ENTRECA-NALES FOUNDATION

Avenida de Europa, 10
Second Floor
Madrid, Spain 28108
Phone: 34914238836
Fax: 34914238666
E-mail: info@fjme.org
Website: www.fjme.org

Type of Firm
Endowment, Foundation or Pension Fund

Project Preferences

Type of Financing Preferred:
Early Stage

Geographical Preferences

International Preferences:
Europe
Spain

Industry Preferences

In Biotechnology prefer:
Industrial Biotechnology

In Industrial/Energy prefer:
Alternative Energy
Energy Conservation Relat
Environmental Related

Additional Information
Year Founded: 2009
Current Activity Level : Actively seeking new investments

JOSHUA GREEN CORP

1425 - Fourth Avenue
Suite 420 PO Box 21829
Seattle, WA USA 98101
Phone: 2066220420
Fax: 2064671176
Website: www.joshuagreencorp.com

Type of Firm
Investment Management Firm

Project Preferences

Type of Financing Preferred:
Value-Add
Generalist PE

Geographical Preferences

United States Preferences:
Washington
All U.S.

Industry Preferences

In Financial Services prefer:
Real Estate

In Manufact. prefer:
Manufacturing

Additional Information

Year Founded: 1930
Current Activity Level : Actively seeking new investments

JOSHUA PARTNERS LLC

21 Vintage Farm Lane
Newtown, PA USA 18940
Phone: 2154979340
Fax: 2154979341
Website: www.joshuapartners.com

Type of Firm

Private Equity Firm

Project Preferences

Type of Financing Preferred:
Leveraged Buyout
Acquisition

Additional Information

Year Founded: 2007
Current Activity Level : Actively seeking new investments

JP ANDERSON (SL) LTD

Three Lamina Sankoh Street
Suite 201
Freetown, Sierra Leone 42215
Phone: 23278612380
Fax: 2328004451462
Website: jpawealth.com

Type of Firm

Investment Management Firm

Project Preferences

Type of Financing Preferred:
Generalist PE
Acquisition

Geographical Preferences

International Preferences:
Sierra Leone
Africa

Additional Information

Year Founded: 2012
Current Activity Level : Actively seeking new investments

JP MORGAN INVESTMENT MANAGEMENT INC

320 Park Avenue
15th Floor
New York, NY USA 10022
Phone: 2126482298
Fax: 2126482322
E-mail: pe.website@jpmorgan.com
Website: www.jpmorgan.com

Other Offices

C.S.T. Road
Kalina, Santacruz - East
Mumbai, India 400 098

245 Park Avenue
Third Floor
NEW YORK, NY USA 10167
Phone: 2126482298
Fax: 2126482322

Management and Staff

Ijeoma Agboti, Vice President
John Fraser, Managing Director
Julian Shles, Chief Financial Officer
Katherine Rosa, Managing Director
Lawrence Unrein, Managing Director
Meena Gandhi, Vice President
Naoko Akasaka, Vice President
Robert Cousin, Managing Director

Type of Firm

Bank Affiliated

Association Membership

Natl Assoc of Investment Cos. (NAIC)
Natl Assoc of Small Bus. Inv. Co (NASBIC)
National Venture Capital Association - USA (NVCA)

Project Preferences

Type of Financing Preferred:
Fund of Funds
Balanced

Geographical Preferences

United States Preferences:

International Preferences:
Asia

Industry Focus

(% based on actual investment)
Industrial/Energy	61.5%
Internet Specific	19.7%
Computer Hardware	7.6%
Medical/Health	4.8%
Consumer Related	2.9%
Other Products	1.8%
Computer Software and Services	1.3%
Communications and Media	0.3%
Biotechnology	0.1%

Additional Information

Name of Most Recent Fund: J.P. Morgan India Property Fund II, L.P.
Most Recent Fund Was Raised: 03/19/2013
Year Founded: 1997
Capital Under Management: $22,000,000,000
Current Activity Level : Actively seeking new investments

JPB PARTNERS LLC

8820 Columbia 100 Parkway
Suite 400
Columbia, MD USA 21045
Phone: 4108841960
E-mail: info@jpbpartners.com
Website: www.jpbe.com

Other Offices

114 Logan Lane
Suite 1-A
Santa Rosa Beach, FL USA 32459
Phone: 8502316694

Management and Staff

Allen Stott, Managing Director
Edward Harding, Managing Director
Mark Regal, Vice President
Tom Watson, Vice President

Type of Firm

Investment Management Firm

Project Preferences

Type of Financing Preferred:
Leveraged Buyout
Value-Add
Expansion
Mezzanine
Acquisition
Recapitalizations

Geographical Preferences

United States Preferences:
Mid Atlantic
Southeast

Industry Preferences

In Medical/Health prefer:
Medical/Health
Medical Products
Health Services

In Consumer Related prefer:
Retail
Consumer Products
Consumer Services
Other Restaurants

In Financial Services prefer:
Real Estate

In Business Serv. prefer:
Services
Distribution

Additional Information
Name of Most Recent Fund: JPB Capital Partners III, L.P.
Most Recent Fund Was Raised: 09/23/2013
Year Founded: 1995
Capital Under Management: $20,150,000
Current Activity Level : Actively seeking new investments

JPMORGAN CHASE & CO

270 Park Avenue
25th Floor
New York, NY USA 10017
Phone: 2122706000
Website: www.jpmorganchase.com

Other Offices

Edinburgh Tower, 15 Queen's Road
Central, Hong Kong
Phone: 852-2841-1168
Fax: 852-2973-5471

Kardinal - Faulhaber-Strasse 10
Munich, Germany 80333
Phone: 49-892-426-890
Fax: 49-8924-268-990

Av. Brigadeiro Faria Lima, 3729
andar 15
Boothbay Harbor, Brazil 04538-905
Phone: 5511-3048-3700
Fax: 5511-3048-3888

Yamato Seimei Bldg. 12F
Uchisaiwaicho, Chiyoda-ku
Tokyo , Japan 100-0011
Phone: 813-3504-2888
Fax: 813-3504-2823

333 South Hope Street
35th Floor
Los Angeles, CA USA 90071
Phone: 213-437-9278
Fax: 213-437-9365

One International Finance Centre
Suite 3003, 1 Harbour View St.
Central, Hong Kong
Phone: 852-2533-1818
Fax: 852-2868-5551

522 5th Avenue
New York, NY USA 10036
Phone: 212-837-2151
Fax: 212-837-2695

125 London Wall
London, United Kingdom EC2Y 5AJ
Phone: 44-207-777-3365
Fax: 44-207-777-4731

Walkway Level, Jardine House
One Connaught Place
Central, Hong Kong
Phone: 852-2265-1133
Fax: 852-2868-5013

Avda. Corrientes, 411
Buenos Aires, Argentina 1043
Phone: 54-11-4325-7292
Fax: 54-11-4348-7238

90 Collins Street
Eighth Floor
Melbourne, Australia 3000
Phone: 613-9631-8300
Fax: 613-9631-8333

50 California Street
29th Floor
San Francisco, CA USA 94111
Phone: 415-591-1200
Fax: 415-591-1205

Management and Staff
Marianne Lake, Chief Financial Officer
Richard Cashin, Partner

Type of Firm
Bank Affiliated

Association Membership
Hungarian Venture Capital Association (HVCA)

Project Preferences

Role in Financing:
Prefer role as deal originator but will also invest in deals created by others

Type of Financing Preferred:
Leveraged Buyout
Early Stage
Generalist PE
Balanced
Later Stage
Startup

Size of Investments Considered:
Min Size of Investment Considered (000s): $10,000
Max Size of Investment Considered (000s): $20,000

Geographical Preferences

United States Preferences:

Canadian Preferences:
All Canada

International Preferences:
Italy
United Kingdom
China
Bermuda
Spain
Australia
South Africa
Germany
Japan
All International
France

Industry Focus
(% based on actual investment)

Other Products	39.2%
Internet Specific	17.5%
Communications and Media	10.1%
Computer Software and Services	9.7%
Consumer Related	9.3%
Medical/Health	7.7%
Semiconductors/Other Elect.	3.6%
Biotechnology	1.6%
Computer Hardware	0.9%
Industrial/Energy	0.3%

Additional Information
Name of Most Recent Fund: J.P. Morgan Digital Growth Fund, L.P.
Most Recent Fund Was Raised: 02/23/2011
Year Founded: 1985
Capital Under Management: $800,000,000
Current Activity Level : Actively seeking new investments
Method of Compensation: Return on investment is of primary concern, do not charge fees

JRJ VENTURES LLP

61 Conduit Street
London, United Kingdom W1S 2GB
Phone: 442072202300
Fax: 442072202339
E-mail: enquiries@jrjgroup.com
Website: www.jrjgroup.com

Management and Staff
Jeremy Isaacs, Partner
Roger Nagioff, Partner

Type of Firm
Private Equity Firm

Project Preferences

Type of Financing Preferred:
Leveraged Buyout

Geographical Preferences

International Preferences:
Europe

Industry Preferences

In Financial Services prefer:
Financial Services

Additional Information

Year Founded: 2009
Current Activity Level : Actively seeking new investments

JSH CAPITAL OY

Honkaluodonrinne 4B
Helsinki, Finland FI-00570
Phone: 358 400 256 567
Website: www.jsh.fi

Type of Firm

Private Equity Firm

Additional Information

Year Founded: 1989
Current Activity Level : Actively seeking new investments

JUBILEE CAPITAL MANAGEMENT PTE LTD

8 Jurong Town Hall Road
#26-02, JTC Summit
Singapore, Singapore 609434
Phone: 6563161728
E-mail: info@jcmvc.com
Website: www.jtfvc.com

Type of Firm

Private Equity Firm

Geographical Preferences

United States Preferences:

International Preferences:
China

Additional Information

Year Founded: 2015
Capital Under Management: $30,000,000
Current Activity Level : Actively seeking new investments

JUBLON INVESTMENT & CONSULTANCY CO LTD

Room 508A,12A Guanghua Road
Chaoyang
Beijing, China 100020
Phone: 86-10-65810
Fax: 85-10-65810
E-mail: jublon@jublon.com
Website: www.jublon.com

Management and Staff

DS Liu, Managing Director

Type of Firm

Private Equity Firm

Project Preferences

Type of Financing Preferred:
Later Stage

Geographical Preferences

International Preferences:
Western Europe
Middle East
Asia

Additional Information

Year Founded: 2002
Current Activity Level : Actively seeking new investments

JUGGERNAUT PARTNERS LP

4445 Willard Avenue
Eleventh Floor
Chevy Chase, MD USA 20815
Phone: 3012157740
Fax: 3018412308
E-mail: info@juggernautcap.com
Website: www.juggernautcap.com

Management and Staff

Craig Hille, Managing Director
John Shulman, Managing Partner
Kevin Kuntz, Vice President

Type of Firm

Private Equity Firm

Project Preferences

Type of Financing Preferred:
Leveraged Buyout
Turnaround
Recapitalizations

Geographical Preferences

United States Preferences:

Industry Preferences

In Consumer Related prefer:
Computer Stores
Food/Beverage
Consumer Products

In Financial Services prefer:
Financial Services

In Business Serv. prefer:
Services

Additional Information

Name of Most Recent Fund: Juggernaut Capital Partners II, L.P.
Most Recent Fund Was Raised: 12/14/2012

Year Founded: 1969
Capital Under Management: $481,320,000
Current Activity Level : Actively seeking new investments

JULIP RUN CAPITAL LLC

1235 Westlakes Drive
Suite 160
Berwyn, PA USA 19312
Phone: 6102403660
Fax: 6106404981
Website: www.juliprun.com

Management and Staff

Christopher Debbas, Co-Founder
Geoffrey Warrell, Partner
Gregory Campbell, Co-Founder
James Griffiths, Co-Founder

Type of Firm

Private Equity Firm

Project Preferences

Role in Financing:
Prefer role as deal originator

Type of Financing Preferred:
Leveraged Buyout

Industry Preferences

In Business Serv. prefer:
Services

Additional Information

Year Founded: 1996
Capital Under Management: $300,000,000
Current Activity Level : Actively seeking new investments

JULZ CO LLC

1450 Raleigh Road
Suite 200
Chapel Hill, NC USA 27517
Phone: 18884913455
Website: www.julzco.com

Type of Firm

Investment Management Firm

Project Preferences

Type of Financing Preferred:
Balanced

Geographical Preferences

United States Preferences:

International Preferences:
Europe
China

Industry Preferences

In Medical/Health prefer:
Diagnostic Services
Health Services

Additional Information

Year Founded: 2012
Current Activity Level : Actively seeking new investments

JUMP CAPITAL LLC

600 West Chicago Avenue
Suite 825
Chicago, IL USA 60654
Phone: 3122058760
E-mail: info@jumpcapitalpartners.com
Website: www.jumpcapitalpartners.com

Management and Staff

Michael McMahon, Managing Director
Sach Chitnis, Managing Director

Type of Firm

Private Equity Firm

Project Preferences

Type of Financing Preferred:
Leveraged Buyout
Early Stage
Expansion
Generalist PE

Size of Investments Considered:
Min Size of Investment Considered (000s): $1,000
Max Size of Investment Considered (000s): $5,000

Industry Preferences

In Medical/Health prefer:
Medical/Health

In Financial Services prefer:
Financial Services

In Business Serv. prefer:
Services

Additional Information

Year Founded: 2012
Capital Under Management: $100,000,000
Current Activity Level : Actively seeking new investments

JUMPSTART FOUNDRY

4015 Hillsboro Pike
Nashville, TN USA 37215
E-mail: info@jumpstartfoundry.com
Website: www.jumpstartfoundry.com

Management and Staff

Marcus Whitney, Managing Director
Salil Shibad, Co-Founder
Vic Gatto, Managing Director

Type of Firm

Incubator/Development Program

Project Preferences

Type of Financing Preferred:
Early Stage
Seed
Startup

Geographical Preferences

United States Preferences:
Tennessee
All U.S.

Industry Preferences

In Communications prefer:
Wireless Communications
Data Communications

In Computer Software prefer:
Software

In Internet Specific prefer:
Internet

In Medical/Health prefer:
Medical/Health

Additional Information

Year Founded: 2010
Current Activity Level : Actively seeking new investments

JUMPSTART INC

6701 Carnegie Avenue
Suite 100
Cleveland, OH USA 44103
Phone: 2163633400
Fax: 2163633401
E-mail: info@JumpStartInc.org
Website: www.jumpstartinc.org

Management and Staff

Jerry Frantz, Venture Partner
John Dearborn, President
Raymond Leach, Chief Executive Officer
Richard Jankura, Chief Financial Officer

Type of Firm

Incubator/Development Program

Association Membership

National Venture Capital Association - USA (NVCA)

Project Preferences

Role in Financing:
Prefer role as deal originator but will also invest in deals created by others

Type of Financing Preferred:
Early Stage
Seed
Startup

Geographical Preferences

United States Preferences:
Northeast
Ohio

Industry Preferences

In Medical/Health prefer:
Medical/Health

In Consumer Related prefer:
Consumer Products
Consumer Services

In Industrial/Energy prefer:
Environmental Related

In Business Serv. prefer:
Services

Additional Information

Year Founded: 2003
Capital Under Management: $30,000,000
Current Activity Level : Actively seeking new investments
Method of Compensation: Return on investment is of primary concern, do not charge fees

JUMPSTARTUP FUND ADVISORS PVT LTD

231-236 Raheja Arcade
2nd Flr, Block 7, Koramangala
Bangalore, India 560 095
Phone: 918041305647
Fax: 91805362401
E-mail: info@jumpstartup.net
Website: www.jumpstartup.net

Other Offices

5201 Great America Parkway
Suite 320
Santa Clara, CA USA 95054
Phone: 408-562-6354
Fax: 408-562-5745

Management and Staff

K. Ganapathy Subramanian, Partner
Kiran Nadkarni, Partner
Sanjay Anandaram, Partner

Type of Firm

Private Equity Firm

Project Preferences

Type of Financing Preferred:
Early Stage
Expansion
Seed
Startup

Size of Investments Considered:
Min Size of Investment Considered (000s): $500
Max Size of Investment Considered (000s): $3,000

Geographical Preferences

United States Preferences:

International Preferences:
India

Industry Preferences

In Communications prefer:
Communications and Media
Telecommunications

In Computer Software prefer:
Software

In Internet Specific prefer:
Internet

In Computer Other prefer:
Computer Related

In Semiconductor/Electr prefer:
Electronics
Semiconductor

Additional Information
Year Founded: 2000
Capital Under Management: $40,000,000
Current Activity Level : Actively seeking new investments

JUNA EQUITY PARTNERS LP

1140 Avenue of Americas
9th Floor
New York, NY USA 10036
Website: junaequitypartners.com

Type of Firm
Private Equity Firm

Project Preferences

Type of Financing Preferred:
Leveraged Buyout
Acquisition

Additional Information
Year Founded: 2015
Capital Under Management: $100,000,000
Current Activity Level : Actively seeking new investments

JUNGLE VENTURES PTE LTD

306 Tanglin Road
Phoenix Park Office Campus
Singapore, Singapore 247973
Phone: 6564239516
Fax: 6562228916
Website: www.jungle-ventures.com

Management and Staff
Amit Anand, Co-Founder
Anurag Srivasta, Co-Founder
David Gowdey, Managing Partner
Jayesh Parekh, Managing Partner
Vaishali Cooper, Chief Financial Officer

Type of Firm
Private Equity Firm

Association Membership
Singapore Venture Capital Association (SVCA)

Project Preferences

Type of Financing Preferred:
Early Stage
Seed
Startup

Geographical Preferences

International Preferences:
India
Asia
Singapore

Industry Preferences

In Communications prefer:
Entertainment

In Computer Hardware prefer:
Integrated Turnkey System

In Computer Software prefer:
Software
Applications Software

Additional Information
Year Founded: 2011
Capital Under Management: $112,000,000
Current Activity Level : Actively seeking new investments

JUNION CAPITAL MANAGEMENT CO LTD

No.8 Haidian North 2nd Road
1218 PE Bldg Zhongguancun SOHO
Beijing, China 100080
Phone: 861082661938
Fax: 861082661938
E-mail: jcmchina@jcmchina.cn
Website: www.jcmchina.cn

Other Offices
No.8, Lujing Road, Hi-tech Zone
Room 502, 5/F, Juxing Venture Land
Changsha, China 410007
Phone: 73184481573
Fax: 73184481573

No.200, Linghu Avenue
403-B Micro-nano Sensor Park
Wuxi, China 214003
Phone: 51082700340
Fax: 51082700340

No.99, Longpan Ave, Devel Dist
Room 616, Government Affairs Center
Chuzhou, China 239000
Phone: 5503078780
Fax: 5503078780

No.75, Zhongshandong Rd
Room 408
Nanjing, China 210005
Phone: 2583703021
Fax: 2583703021

Type of Firm
Private Equity Firm

Project Preferences

Type of Financing Preferred:
Early Stage
Expansion
Later Stage

Size of Investments Considered:
Min Size of Investment Considered (000s): $1,465
Max Size of Investment Considered (000s): $14,651

Geographical Preferences

International Preferences:
China

Industry Preferences

In Communications prefer:
Commercial Communications

In Industrial/Energy prefer:
Energy
Advanced Materials

In Financial Services prefer:
Financial Services

In Business Serv. prefer:
Services

In Agr/Forestr/Fish prefer:
Agriculture related

Additional Information
Year Founded: 2010
Capital Under Management: $149,124,000
Current Activity Level : Actively seeking new investments

JUNIPER CAPITAL MANAGEMENT

3879 Maple Avenue
Suite 300
Dallas, TX USA 75219
Phone: 2124897230
Website: junipercapmgt.com

Management and Staff
Bryan Grabowsky, Founder
Lou Grabowsky, Founder

Type of Firm
Private Equity Firm

Project Preferences

Type of Financing Preferred:
Leveraged Buyout
Acquisition
Recapitalizations

Geographical Preferences

United States Preferences:

Additional Information
Year Founded: 2015
Current Activity Level: Actively seeking new investments

JUNIPER NETWORKS INC

1133 Innovation Way
Sunnyvale, CA USA 94089
Phone: 8885864737
Fax: 4087452100
Website: www.juniper.net

Management and Staff
Bjorn Liencres, Founder
Dennis Ferguson, Founder

Type of Firm
Corporate PE/Venture

Project Preferences

Type of Financing Preferred:
Early Stage

Geographical Preferences

United States Preferences:

Industry Focus
(% based on actual investment)

Computer Software and Services	31.0%
Communications and Media	28.9%
Semiconductors/Other Elect.	27.5%
Internet Specific	11.0%
Computer Hardware	1.6%

Additional Information
Year Founded: 1997
Capital Under Management: $50,000,000
Current Activity Level: Actively seeking new investments

JUNSAN CAPITAL

No. 7006 Shennan Avenue
Rm. 2101 Fuchun Dongfang Bldg.
Shenzhen, China 518040
Phone: 8675582571118
Fax: 8675582571198
E-mail: js@junsancapital.com
Website: www.junsancapital.com

Management and Staff
Shiyong Wu, Partner

Type of Firm
Private Equity Firm

Project Preferences

Type of Financing Preferred:
Balanced
Later Stage
Acquisition

Geographical Preferences

International Preferences:
Asia Pacific
China

Industry Preferences

In Communications prefer:
Entertainment

In Medical/Health prefer:
Medical/Health

In Consumer Related prefer:
Consumer

In Industrial/Energy prefer:
Energy
Materials
Environmental Related

In Financial Services prefer:
Financial Services

In Manufact. prefer:
Manufacturing

Additional Information
Year Founded: 2003
Capital Under Management: $147,441,000
Current Activity Level: Actively seeking new investments

JUNYUAN CAPITAL INVESTMENT MANAGEMENT LTD

Unit 1278, 12th Floor, Kowloon
1 Trademart Drive
Kowloon Bay, Hong Kong
Phone: 85225410862
Fax: 85235448248
E-mail: Info@junyuancapital.com
Website: www.junyuancapital.com

Management and Staff
Juyuan Liang, Chief Executive Officer

Type of Firm
Private Equity Firm

Project Preferences

Type of Financing Preferred:
Balanced

Geographical Preferences

International Preferences:
China

Industry Preferences

In Industrial/Energy prefer:
Energy
Materials

In Business Serv. prefer:
Services

In Agr/Forestr/Fish prefer:
Agribusiness

Additional Information
Year Founded: 2010
Capital Under Management: $73,257,000
Current Activity Level: Actively seeking new investments

JUPITER CAPITAL PARTNERS (PRIVATE) LTD

Suite M14, Mezzanine Floor
64, Lotus Road
Colombo, Sri Lanka
Phone: 94112380667
Fax: 94112380668
E-mail: info@jupitercapitalpartners.com
Website: www.jupitercapitalpartners.com

Type of Firm
Private Equity Firm

Project Preferences

Type of Financing Preferred:
Early Stage
Expansion
Balanced
Later Stage

Geographical Preferences

International Preferences:
Sri Lanka

Additional Information

Year Founded: 2013
Current Activity Level : Actively seeking new investments

JUPITER HOLDINGS LLC

24 Corporate Plaza
Suite 100
Newport Beach, CA USA 92660
Phone: 9497068050
Fax: 9497068051
E-mail: info@jupiterholdings.com

Type of Firm

Investment Management Firm

Project Preferences

Role in Financing:
Prefer role as deal originator

Type of Financing Preferred:
Leveraged Buyout
Expansion
Generalist PE
Opportunistic
Management Buyouts
Recapitalizations

Geographical Preferences

United States Preferences:
West Coast

Additional Information

Year Founded: 1997
Capital Under Management: $250,000,000
Current Activity Level : Actively seeking new investments
Method of Compensation: Return on investment is of primary concern, do not charge fees

JUROKU CAPITAL CO LTD

7-12 Kanda-cho
Gifu City, Japan
Phone: 81-58-264-7716
Fax: 81-58-264-7718
Website: www.juroku.co.jp

Type of Firm

Private Equity Firm

Project Preferences

Type of Financing Preferred:
Balanced

Geographical Preferences

International Preferences:
Asia
Japan

Additional Information

Year Founded: 2000
Capital Under Management: $11,700,000
Current Activity Level : Actively seeking new investments

JUURI PARTNERS OY

Urho Kekkosen katu 7 B
Helsinki, Finland 00100
Website: www.juuripartners.fi

Type of Firm

Private Equity Firm

Project Preferences

Type of Financing Preferred:
Turnaround
Management Buyouts
Acquisition
Distressed Debt

Geographical Preferences

International Preferences:
Finland

Additional Information

Year Founded: 2015
Capital Under Management: $89,110,000
Current Activity Level : Actively seeking new investments

JVAX INVESTMENT GROUP LLC

PO Box 5277
Breckenridge, Colombia 80424
Phone: 9704807669
Fax: 9707971756
E-mail: info@jvaxig.com
Website: www.jvaxig.com

Type of Firm

Private Equity Firm

Project Preferences

Type of Financing Preferred:
Expansion
Later Stage

Industry Preferences

In Medical/Health prefer:
Medical/Health

Additional Information

Year Founded: 2007
Current Activity Level : Actively seeking new investments

JVC INVESTMENT PARTNERS LLC

650 Dundee Road
Suite 380
Northbrook, IL USA 60062
Phone: 8479603840
Website: jvcmanagement.com

Type of Firm

Private Equity Firm

Project Preferences

Type of Financing Preferred:
Expansion
Balanced

Industry Preferences

In Medical/Health prefer:
Health Services

Additional Information

Year Founded: 1969
Current Activity Level : Actively seeking new investments

JVEN CAPITAL LLC

11009 Cripplegate Road
Potomac, MD USA 20854
Phone: 3012992088
Fax: 3012990555

Type of Firm

Private Equity Firm

Project Preferences

Type of Financing Preferred:
Balanced

Industry Preferences

In Biotechnology prefer:
Biotechnology

In Medical/Health prefer:
Medical Therapeutics
Medical Products

Additional Information

Year Founded: 2007
Current Activity Level : Actively seeking new investments

JVIC VENTURE CAPITAL CO LTD

5F Capital Akasaka Bldg.
1-7-19 Akasaka, MInato-ku
Tokyo, Japan 107-0052
Website: www.jvic-vc.co.jp

Management and Staff
Tetsuo Wakasa, Chief Executive Officer

Type of Firm
Private Equity Firm

Project Preferences

Type of Financing Preferred:
Balanced

Geographical Preferences

International Preferences:
Japan

Industry Preferences

In Communications prefer:
Wireless Communications

Additional Information
Year Founded: 2000
Current Activity Level : Actively seeking new investments

JVP JERUSALEM VENTURE PARTNERS ISRAEL MANAGEMENT, LTD.

24 Hebron Road
Jerusalem, Israel 93542
Phone: 972-2-640-9000
Fax: 972-2-640-9001
E-mail: info@jvpvc.com
Website: www.jvpvc.com

Other Offices
41 Madison Avenue
31st Floor
New York, NY USA 10010
Phone: 212-479-5100
Fax: 212-213-1776

Management and Staff
Agnes Touraine, Venture Partner
Alexander Ott, Venture Partner
Art Levitt, Venture Partner
Erel Margalit, Managing Partner
Fiona Darmon, Vice President
Gadi Tirosh, General Partner
Haim Kopans, Venture Partner
Kobi Rozengarten, General Partner
Noah Yago, Principal
Orit Kimmel, Vice President
Raffi Kesten, Venture Partner
Ronit Dulberg, Chief Financial Officer
Uri Adoni, Venture Partner
Yehoshua Ennis, Founder
Yoav Tzruya, Venture Partner

Type of Firm
Private Equity Firm

Association Membership
Israel Venture Association

Project Preferences

Role in Financing:
Prefer role as deal originator but will also invest in deals created by others

Type of Financing Preferred:
Early Stage
Balanced
Later Stage
Seed
Startup

Geographical Preferences

United States Preferences:
North America

International Preferences:
Europe
Israel
Asia

Industry Focus
(% based on actual investment)
Communications and Media   29.8%
Computer Software and Services   25.0%
Internet Specific   20.1%
Semiconductors/Other Elect.   15.6%
Computer Hardware   6.4%
Biotechnology   1.9%
Other Products   0.6%
Consumer Related   0.5%

Additional Information
Year Founded: 1993
Capital Under Management: $800,000,000
Current Activity Level : Actively seeking new investments

JWI CAPITAL LLC

P.O. Box 1171
Twinsburg, OH USA 44087
E-mail: info@jwicapital.com
Website: www.jwicapital.com

Management and Staff
Marc Walinsky, Managing Director
Mark Jantzen, Managing Director

Type of Firm
Private Equity Firm

Project Preferences

Type of Financing Preferred:
Leveraged Buyout
Acquisition

Geographical Preferences

United States Preferences:
Ohio

Industry Preferences

In Industrial/Energy prefer:
Energy
Industrial Products
Materials

In Transportation prefer:
Transportation
Aerospace

In Manufact. prefer:
Manufacturing

Additional Information
Year Founded: 2009
Current Activity Level : Actively seeking new investments

JXC VENTURES LTD

42 Brook Street
London, United Kingdom SW7 5JT
Phone: 440203709618
E-mail: jc@jxcventures.com
Website: www.jxcventures.com

Type of Firm
Private Equity Firm

Project Preferences

Type of Financing Preferred:
Early Stage
Balanced
Seed

Additional Information
Year Founded: 2017
Current Activity Level : Actively seeking new investments

JYNWEL CAPITAL LTD

19F, 50 Connaught Road Central
Hong Kong, Hong Kong 999077
Phone: 852 3911 2000
Fax: 852 3911 2001
E-mail: jynwel@edelman.com
Website: www.jynwelcapital.com

Management and Staff
Ker Ann Gan, Managing Director
Szen Low, Managing Director

Type of Firm
Investment Management Firm

Project Preferences

Type of Financing Preferred:
Core
Leveraged Buyout
Generalist PE
Acquisition

Industry Preferences

In Communications prefer:
Media and Entertainment

In Consumer Related prefer:
Consumer
Retail

In Industrial/Energy prefer:
Energy
Alternative Energy

In Financial Services prefer:
Real Estate

In Agr/Forestr/Fish prefer:
Mining and Minerals

In Utilities prefer:
Utilities

Additional Information
Year Founded: 1969
Current Activity Level : Actively seeking new investments

JZ CAPITAL PARTNERS LTD

Holborn Gate
26 Southampton Buildings
London, United Kingdom WC2A 1PB
Phone: 442072697175
Website: www.jzcp.com

Other Offices
767 Fifth Avenue
48th Floor
New York, NY USA 10153

Management and Staff
Emmett Mosley, Managing Director
Eric Kieras, Vice President
John Jordan, Co-Founder
Jon Gilbert, Managing Director
Matthew DeLong, Vice President
Michael Schmitz, Partner
Ole Groth, Partner
Reagan Hogerty, Managing Director
Rhett Madison, Managing Director
Todd Lanscioni, Managing Director
Torben Luth, Partner

Type of Firm
Private Equity Firm

Project Preferences

Type of Financing Preferred:
Leveraged Buyout
Mezzanine
Generalist PE
Opportunistic
Management Buyouts
Acquisition

Geographical Preferences

United States Preferences:
All U.S.

International Preferences:
Europe

Industry Preferences

In Medical/Health prefer:
Health Services

In Financial Services prefer:
Real Estate

In Manufact. prefer:
Manufacturing

Additional Information
Year Founded: 1986
Capital Under Management: $475,120,000
Current Activity Level : Actively seeking new investments

JZ INTERNATIONAL LTD

17A Curzon Street
London, United Kingdom W1J 5HS
Phone: 442074913633
E-mail: info@jzieurope.com
Website: www.jzieurope.com

Type of Firm
Private Equity Firm

Project Preferences

Type of Financing Preferred:
Leveraged Buyout
Acquisition

Geographical Preferences

International Preferences:
Italy
United Kingdom
Europe
Netherlands
Spain
Finland
Norway
Denmark

Industry Preferences

In Communications prefer:
Telecommunications

In Industrial/Energy prefer:
Energy

In Financial Services prefer:
Financial Services

In Business Serv. prefer:
Services

Additional Information
Year Founded: 1999
Current Activity Level : Actively seeking new investments

- K -

K ARIEGE S.C.

21, Cours Gabriel Faure
Foix, France 09001
Phone: 33561020321
Website: kariege.fr

Type of Firm
Government Affiliated Program

Project Preferences

Type of Financing Preferred:
Expansion
Later Stage
Management Buyouts
Acquisition

Size of Investments Considered:
Min Size of Investment Considered (000s): $22
Max Size of Investment Considered (000s): $221

Geographical Preferences

International Preferences:
France

Industry Preferences

In Industrial/Energy prefer:
Industrial Products

In Business Serv. prefer:
Services

Additional Information
Year Founded: 2013
Current Activity Level : Actively seeking new investments

K CUBE VENTURES CO LTD

726-2 Yeoksam-dong, Gangnam-gu
4F C&K Building
Seoul, South Korea
Phone: 82262430301
Fax: 8225628967
Website: kcubeventures.co.kr

Type of Firm
Private Equity Firm

Association Membership
Korean Venture Capital Association (KVCA)

Project Preferences

Type of Financing Preferred:
Early Stage

Size of Investments Considered:
Min Size of Investment Considered (000s): $92
Max Size of Investment Considered (000s): $921

Geographical Preferences

International Preferences:
Korea, South

Industry Preferences

In Communications prefer:
Wireless Communications
Entertainment

In Internet Specific prefer:
Internet

Additional Information
Year Founded: 2012
Capital Under Management: $9,950,000
Current Activity Level : Actively seeking new investments

K FUND

Nuez de Balboa 120, 28006
Madrid, Spain
Website: www.kfund.co

Type of Firm
Private Equity Firm

Project Preferences

Type of Financing Preferred:
Early Stage
Startup

Geographical Preferences

International Preferences:
Spain

Additional Information
Year Founded: 1969
Current Activity Level : Actively seeking new investments

K III SWEDEN AB

Riddargatan 13 D
Stockholm, Sweden 114 51
Phone: 46854589100
Fax: 46854589120
Website: www.karnell.se

Management and Staff
Hans Karlander, Co-Founder
Patrik Rignell, Co-Founder

Type of Firm
Private Equity Firm

Association Membership
Swedish Venture Capital Association (SVCA)

Project Preferences

Type of Financing Preferred:
Leveraged Buyout

Geographical Preferences

International Preferences:
Scandanavia/Nordic Region

Industry Preferences

In Consumer Related prefer:
Consumer
Consumer Products
Consumer Services

In Business Serv. prefer:
Services

Additional Information
Year Founded: 2009
Current Activity Level : Actively seeking new investments

K-NET INVESTMENT PARTNERS LLC

1575-3 Seocho 3 dong Seocho-ku
11/F Younghan Building
Seoul, South Korea 137-875

Type of Firm
Private Equity Firm

Association Membership
Korean Venture Capital Association (KVCA)

Project Preferences

Type of Financing Preferred:
Balanced

Additional Information
Year Founded: 2008
Capital Under Management: $33,300,000
Current Activity Level : Actively seeking new investments

K1 CAPITAL ADVISORS LLC

2141 Rosecrans Avenue, Suite 5110
El Segundo, CA USA 90245
Phone: 8003102870
E-mail: info@k1capital.com

Management and Staff
Dan Ghammachi, Managing Partner
R. Neil Malik, Managing Partner
Taylor Beaupain, Managing Partner

Type of Firm
Private Equity Firm

Project Preferences

Type of Financing Preferred:
Leveraged Buyout
Expansion
Generalist PE
Acquisition

Geographical Preferences

United States Preferences:
North America

Industry Preferences

In Computer Software prefer:
Software

In Consumer Related prefer:
Consumer Products

In Business Serv. prefer:
Services

Additional Information

Year Founded: 2011
Current Activity Level : Actively seeking new investments

K2 CAPITAL PARTNERS LLC

10435 Santa Monica Boulevard
First Floor
West Los Angeles, CA USA 90025
Website: www.k2-capital.com

Type of Firm

Private Equity Firm

Project Preferences

Type of Financing Preferred:
Leveraged Buyout

Industry Preferences

In Internet Specific prefer:
Internet

In Medical/Health prefer:
Health Services

In Transportation prefer:
Aerospace

Additional Information

Year Founded: 2015
Current Activity Level : Actively seeking new investments

K2 GLOBAL

12182 PARKER RANCH ROAD
Saratoga, CA USA 95070
Phone: 6504689060
Website: www.k2globalvc.com

Type of Firm

Private Equity Firm

Project Preferences

Type of Financing Preferred:
Later Stage

Additional Information

Year Founded: 2016
Capital Under Management: $183,000,000
Current Activity Level : Actively seeking new investments

K2 INVESTMENT PARTNERS LLC

943-24, Daechidong, Gangnamgu
#1615, Shinhan Metro Khan
Seoul, South Korea
Phone: 8225660526
Fax: 82269192465

Type of Firm

Private Equity Advisor or Fund of Funds

Association Membership

Korean Venture Capital Association (KVCA)

Project Preferences

Type of Financing Preferred:
Fund of Funds of Second

Additional Information

Year Founded: 2011
Capital Under Management: $40,130,000
Current Activity Level : Actively seeking new investments

K2 VENTURE CAPITAL CO LTD

349 Viphavadi-Rangsit Road
Ste 1902, SJ Infinite 1
Bangkok, Thailand 10900
Phone: 6621100932
E-mail: info@k2-vc.com
Website: www.k2-vc.com

Type of Firm

Private Equity Firm

Project Preferences

Type of Financing Preferred:
Balanced

Industry Preferences

In Computer Software prefer:
Data Processing
Software

In Financial Services prefer:
Insurance
Financial Services

In Agr/Forestr/Fish prefer:
Agriculture related

Additional Information

Year Founded: 2016
Current Activity Level : Actively seeking new investments

K5 ADVISORS GMBH & CO KG

Waltherstrasse 23
Munich, Germany 80337
Phone: 498951399057
Website: www.k5advisors.com

Other Offices

20/F, 8 Wyndham Street
Hong Kong, Hong Kong

Management and Staff

Gregor Von dem Knesebeck, Managing Partner
Julia Von dem Knesebeck, Managing Partner
Philipp Von dem Knesebeck, Managing Partner

Type of Firm

Private Equity Firm

Project Preferences

Type of Financing Preferred:
Early Stage
Expansion
Later Stage

Size of Investments Considered:
Min Size of Investment Considered (000s): $73
Max Size of Investment Considered (000s): $1,456

Geographical Preferences

International Preferences:
Asia Pacific
United Kingdom
Germany

Industry Preferences

In Communications prefer:
Communications and Media
Wireless Communications
Media and Entertainment
Publishing

In Internet Specific prefer:
E-Commerce Technology
Internet
Ecommerce
Web Aggregration/Portals

In Financial Services prefer:
Real Estate

Additional Information

Year Founded: 2007
Current Activity Level : Actively seeking new investments

K5 VENTURES

4590 McArthur Boulevard
Newport Beach, CA USA 92660
Website: k5ventures.com

Type of Firm
Incubator/Development Program

Project Preferences

Type of Financing Preferred:
Early Stage
Seed
Startup

Geographical Preferences

United States Preferences:
Southern California
Northern California

International Preferences:
China

Additional Information
Year Founded: 2011
Current Activity Level: Actively seeking new investments

K8 VENTURES LLC

30 East Division Street
Apartment 8C
Chicago, IL USA 60610
Phone: 3129250110
Website: www.k8.solutions

Type of Firm
Private Equity Firm

Project Preferences

Type of Financing Preferred:
Early Stage

Additional Information
Year Founded: 2016
Current Activity Level: Actively seeking new investments

K9 VENTURES LP

837 Garland Drive
P.O. Box 901
Palo Alto, CA USA 94301
E-mail: admin@k9ventures.com
Website: www.k9ventures.com

Management and Staff
Manu Kumar, Founder

Type of Firm
Private Equity Firm

Project Preferences

Type of Financing Preferred:
Early Stage
Seed
Startup

Geographical Preferences

United States Preferences:
Northern California

Industry Preferences

In Communications prefer:
Telecommunications

In Computer Software prefer:
Software

In Internet Specific prefer:
Internet

Additional Information
Name of Most Recent Fund: K9 Ventures II, L.P.
Most Recent Fund Was Raised: 07/19/2012
Year Founded: 1969
Capital Under Management: $82,000,000
Current Activity Level: Actively seeking new investments

KAE CAPITAL

802, Maker Chamber Five
Nariman Point
Mumbai, India 400 021
E-mail: info@kae-capital.com

Management and Staff
Sasha Mirchandani, Founder

Type of Firm
Private Equity Firm

Project Preferences

Type of Financing Preferred:
Early Stage
Seed

Geographical Preferences

International Preferences:
India
Asia

Industry Preferences

In Communications prefer:
Media and Entertainment

In Internet Specific prefer:
Ecommerce

In Semiconductor/Electr prefer:
Electronic Components

In Medical/Health prefer:
Medical/Health

In Business Serv. prefer:
Services

Additional Information
Year Founded: 2011
Capital Under Management: $25,000,000
Current Activity Level: Actively seeking new investments

KAEDAN CAPITAL LTD

6 Wallenberg Street
Ramat Hachayal
Tel Aviv, Israel 61131
Phone: 972772348890
Fax: 972772348880
E-mail: contact@kaedan.com
Website: www.kaedan.com

Management and Staff
Ron Tamir, Managing Partner

Type of Firm
Private Equity Firm

Project Preferences

Type of Financing Preferred:
Early Stage
Later Stage
Seed

Geographical Preferences

International Preferences:
Israel

Industry Preferences

In Communications prefer:
Media and Entertainment

In Computer Software prefer:
Applications Software

In Internet Specific prefer:
Internet

In Consumer Related prefer:
Consumer Products

Additional Information
Year Founded: 2001
Current Activity Level: Actively seeking new investments

KAGISO VENTURES

100 West Street
Wierda Valley
Sandton, South Africa 2196
Phone: 27115622500
Fax: 27115622501
E-mail: info@kti.co.za
Website: www.kagiso.com

Management and Staff
Frencel Gillion, Founder
Vuyisa Nkonyeni, Chief Executive Officer

Type of Firm
Bank Affiliated

Association Membership
South African Venture Capital Association (SAVCA)

Project Preferences

Type of Financing Preferred:
Early Stage
Expansion

Geographical Preferences

International Preferences:
Africa

Industry Preferences

In Industrial/Energy prefer:
Energy

In Financial Services prefer:
Financial Services

Additional Information
Year Founded: 1998
Capital Under Management: $51,000,000
Current Activity Level : Actively seeking new investments

KAHALA INVESTMENTS INC

8214 Westchester Drive
Suite 715
Dallas, TX USA 75225
Phone: 214-987-0077
Fax: 214-987-2332

Type of Firm
Investment Management Firm

Project Preferences

Role in Financing:
Prefer role as deal originator but will also invest in deals created by others

Type of Financing Preferred:
Leveraged Buyout
Mezzanine
Industry Rollups
Special Situation

Size of Investments Considered:
Min Size of Investment Considered (000s): $10,000
Max Size of Investment Considered: No Limit

Geographical Preferences

United States Preferences:
Southeast
Southwest

Additional Information
Year Founded: 1978
Capital Under Management: $5,000,000
Current Activity Level : Actively seeking new investments
Method of Compensation: Return on invest. most important, but chg. closing fees, service fees, etc.

KAIN CAPITAL LLC

126 East 56th Street
Floor Nine
Manhattan, NY USA 10022
Phone: 16469300930
E-mail: info@kaincap.com
Website: kaincap.com

Management and Staff
Nurbek Turdukulov, Partner

Type of Firm
Private Equity Firm

Project Preferences

Type of Financing Preferred:
Leveraged Buyout
Management Buyouts
Acquisition

Geographical Preferences

United States Preferences:

Additional Information
Year Founded: 2017
Current Activity Level : Actively seeking new investments

KAINOS CAPITAL LLC

2100 McKinney Avenue
Suite 1600
Dallas, TX USA 75201
Phone: 2147407300
Fax: 2147207888
Website: www.kainoscapital.com

Management and Staff
Andrew Rosen, Managing Partner
Daniel Hopkin, Partner
David Knickel, Chief Financial Officer
Kevin Elliott, Partner
Nirav Shah, Partner
Robert Sperry, Partner
Robin Olsson, Managing Director
Sarah Bradley, Partner

Type of Firm
Private Equity Firm

Project Preferences

Type of Financing Preferred:
Leveraged Buyout
Management Buyouts

Geographical Preferences

United States Preferences:
North America

Industry Preferences

In Consumer Related prefer:
Consumer
Food/Beverage
Consumer Products

Additional Information
Name of Most Recent Fund: Kainos Capital Partners, L.P.
Most Recent Fund Was Raised: 10/08/2013
Year Founded: 2013
Capital Under Management: $1,262,296,000
Current Activity Level : Actively seeking new investments

KAIROS VENTURE INVESTMENTS LLC

9440 S. Santa Monica Boulevard
Suite 710
Beverly Hills, CA USA 90210
E-mail: info@kairosventures.com
Website: www.kairosventures.com

Management and Staff
Carol Kachmer, Chief Financial Officer
James Jeffs, General Partner
William Powers, General Partner

Type of Firm
Private Equity Firm

Project Preferences

Type of Financing Preferred:
Early Stage

Additional Information
Year Founded: 2015
Capital Under Management: $85,150,000
Current Activity Level : Actively seeking new investments

KAISER PERMANENTE VENTURES LLC

One Kaiser Plaza
22nd Floor
Oakland, CA USA 94612
Phone: 5102677300
Fax: 5108917943
Website: www.kpventures.com

Management and Staff
Elizabeth Rockett, Principal
Sam Brasch, Senior Managing Director

Type of Firm
Corporate PE/Venture

Association Membership
National Venture Capital Association - USA (NVCA)

Project Preferences

Role in Financing:
Prefer role in deals created by others

Type of Financing Preferred:
Early Stage
Balanced
Later Stage

Industry Preferences

In Medical/Health prefer:
Medical/Health
Medical Diagnostics
Medical Therapeutics
Medical Products
Health Services

In Business Serv. prefer:
Services

Additional Information

Year Founded: 1997
Capital Under Management: $406,000,000
Current Activity Level : Actively seeking new investments
Method of Compensation: Return on investment is of primary concern, do not charge fees

KAIWU CAPITAL CO LTD

No.8, Jianguomen North Street
2301, China Resources Tower
Beijing, China 100005
Phone: 861085070088
Fax: 861085070166
E-mail: bp@kaiwucapital.com
Website: kaiwucapital.com

Other Offices

Huaihai Zhong Rd, Xuhui
Shanghai, China 200031
Phone: 862134240557
Fax: 862134240559

Management and Staff

Jianming Yao, Vice President
Qianye Liu, Partner
Qiuhu Wang, Partner
Shuhua Zhou, Managing Partner
Yibiao Chen, Partner

Type of Firm

Private Equity Firm

Project Preferences

Type of Financing Preferred:
Expansion
Balanced
Later Stage

Geographical Preferences

International Preferences:
China

Industry Preferences

In Communications prefer:
Telecommunications

In Internet Specific prefer:
Internet

In Medical/Health prefer:
Medical/Health

In Consumer Related prefer:
Consumer
Consumer Products
Education Related

In Industrial/Energy prefer:
Energy
Advanced Materials
Environmental Related

In Business Serv. prefer:
Media

Additional Information

Year Founded: 2010
Capital Under Management: $98,000,000
Current Activity Level : Actively seeking new investments

KAIZEN PRIVATE EQUITY

805 Mayuresh Chambers Plot 60
Sector 11
Mumbai, India 400 061
Phone: 912267675757
Fax: 912267675758
Website: www.kaizenpe.com

Management and Staff

Sandeep Aneja, Founder
Sim Yoong, Chief Financial Officer

Type of Firm

Private Equity Firm

Project Preferences

Type of Financing Preferred:
Leveraged Buyout
Early Stage
Expansion
Generalist PE
Balanced
Management Buyouts
Acquisition

Size of Investments Considered:
Min Size of Investment Considered (000s): $5,000
Max Size of Investment Considered (000s): $15,000

Geographical Preferences

International Preferences:
Bangladesh
Indonesia
India
Hong Kong
Sri Lanka
Asia
Singapore
Burma

Industry Preferences

In Consumer Related prefer:
Education Related

Additional Information

Year Founded: 2009
Capital Under Management: $42,000,000
Current Activity Level : Actively seeking new investments

KALAARI CAPITAL PARTNERS LLC

Intl Tech Park Whitefield Road
Ground Fl, Unit-2, Navigator
Bangalore, India 560 066
Phone: 918067159600
Fax: 918067159606
E-mail: iuvpinfo@iuvp.com
Website: www.indousventures.com

Other Offices

3945 Freedom Circle
Suite 1050
Santa Clara, CA USA 95054
Phone: 408-919-9900
Fax: 408-919-9912

Management and Staff

Kumar Shiralagi, Managing Director
Raj Chinai, Principal
Rajesh Raju, Managing Director
Sampathkumar Pudhukottai, Principal
Sumit Jain, Vice President
Vani Kola, Managing Director
Vinod Dham, Managing Director

Type of Firm

Private Equity Firm

Association Membership

Indian Venture Capital Association (IVCA)

Project Preferences

Type of Financing Preferred:
Early Stage
Expansion
Balanced

Geographical Preferences

International Preferences:
India

Industry Preferences

In Communications prefer:
Wireless Communications

In Internet Specific prefer:
Ecommerce

In Medical/Health prefer:
Health Services

In Consumer Related prefer:
Consumer Services
Education Related

In Industrial/Energy prefer:
Environmental Related

In Business Serv. prefer:
Services
Media

Additional Information

Year Founded: 2006
Capital Under Management: $440,000,000
Current Activity Level : Actively seeking new investments

KAMCO INVESTMENT CO KSCP

Khalid Bin Waleed Street
Al-Shaheed Tower
Sharq, Kuwait 13149
Phone: 965805885
Fax: 965805885
E-mail: info@kamconline.com
Website: www.kamconline.com

Management and Staff

Faisal Sarkhou, Chief Executive Officer
Hanan Abduljalil Al-Gharabally, Vice President
Harish Chopra, Vice President
Khanzada Azim, Vice President
Talal Abdullah Al-Nafisi, Vice President

Type of Firm

Investment Management Firm

Project Preferences

Type of Financing Preferred:
Early Stage
Unknown
Balanced
Later Stage
Startup
Special Situation

Geographical Preferences

International Preferences:
Tunisia
Jordan
Lebanon
Egypt
Utd. Arab Em.
Algeria
Middle East
Saudi Arabia
Morocco
Kuwait

Industry Preferences

In Communications prefer:
Communications and Media
Telecommunications
Media and Entertainment

In Medical/Health prefer:
Medical/Health

In Consumer Related prefer:
Consumer
Retail
Education Related

In Financial Services prefer:
Real Estate

In Business Serv. prefer:
Media

Additional Information

Year Founded: 1998
Current Activity Level : Actively seeking new investments

KAMYLON CAPITAL LLC

62 Walnut Street
Third Floor
Wellesley Hills, MA USA 02481
Phone: 7812637373
Fax: 7812637379
E-mail: info@kamylon.com
Website: www.kamylon.com

Management and Staff

A. Jason Brauer, Principal
David Sopp, Partner
Jeffrey Sinnett, Partner
John Lee, Principal
Richard Krause, Partner
Stephen Goddard, Partner

Type of Firm

Private Equity Firm

Project Preferences

Type of Financing Preferred:
Leveraged Buyout
Expansion

Industry Preferences

In Medical/Health prefer:
Health Services

In Consumer Related prefer:
Sports
Retail
Consumer Products
Consumer Services

In Transportation prefer:
Transportation

In Financial Services prefer:
Financial Services

In Business Serv. prefer:
Services
Distribution
Media

In Manufact. prefer:
Manufacturing
Publishing

Additional Information

Year Founded: 2006
Current Activity Level : Actively seeking new investments

KANAGAWA SCIENCE PARK INC

3-2-1 Sakado, Takatsuku
West Wing 304
Kawasaki, Japan 213-0012
Phone: 81448192001
Fax: 81448192009
Website: www.ksp.or.jp

Type of Firm

Incubator/Development Program

Project Preferences

Type of Financing Preferred:
Early Stage
Expansion
Later Stage
Seed
Startup

Geographical Preferences

International Preferences:
Asia
Japan

Additional Information

Year Founded: 1986
Capital Under Management: $56,700,000
Current Activity Level : Actively seeking new investments

KANSAS VENTURE CAPITAL INC

10601 Mission Road
Suite 250
Leawood, KS USA 66206
Phone: 9132627117
Fax: 9132623509
Website: www.kvci.com

Management and Staff
Thomas Blackburn, President

Type of Firm
SBIC

Association Membership
Natl Assoc of Small Bus. Inv. Co (NASBIC)

Project Preferences

Role in Financing:
Prefer role as deal originator but will also invest in deals created by others

Type of Financing Preferred:
Leveraged Buyout
Expansion
Turnaround
Management Buyouts
Acquisition
Recapitalizations

Geographical Preferences

United States Preferences:
Midwest

Industry Preferences

In Consumer Related prefer:
Retail

In Business Serv. prefer:
Services
Distribution

In Manufact. prefer:
Manufacturing

Additional Information
Year Founded: 1977
Capital Under Management: $50,000,000
Current Activity Level : Actively seeking new investments
Method of Compensation: Return on invest. most important, but chg. closing fees, service fees, etc.

KAOFU VENTURE AND INVESTMENT CORP

15008 Sermiamhoo Place
Surrey, Canada
Phone: 604-535-9238
Fax: 604-535-9238

Type of Firm
Private Equity Firm

Additional Information
Year Founded: 1999
Current Activity Level : Actively seeking new investments

KAPINNO SAS

30, Chemin de Saint Henri
Marseilles, France 13016
Website: kapinno.pro

Type of Firm
Private Equity Firm

Project Preferences

Type of Financing Preferred:
Early Stage
Expansion
Later Stage

Additional Information
Year Founded: 2016
Current Activity Level : Actively seeking new investments

KAPITALBETEILIGUNGS-GESELLSCHAFT NRW GMBH

Hellersbergstrasse 18
Neuss, Germany 41460
Phone: 49213151070
Fax: 4921315107333
E-mail: nfo@kbg-nrw.de
Website: www.kbg-nrw.de

Management and Staff
Christoph Bueth, Managing Director
Manfred Thivessen, Managing Director

Type of Firm
Government Affiliated Program

Association Membership
German Venture Capital Association (BVK)

Project Preferences

Type of Financing Preferred:
Early Stage
Later Stage
Management Buyouts
Startup

Geographical Preferences

International Preferences:
Germany

Additional Information
Year Founded: 1975
Current Activity Level : Actively seeking new investments

KAPOR CAPITAL

2148 Broadway
Oakland, CA USA 94612

Management and Staff
Benjamin Todd Jealous, Partner
Brian Dixon, Partner
Carolina Mendoza, Principal
Ellen Pao, Partner
Freada Kapor Klein, Partner
Mitchell Kapor, Partner
Ulili Onovakpuri, Principal

Type of Firm
Private Equity Firm

Project Preferences

Type of Financing Preferred:
Early Stage
Seed
Startup

Additional Information
Year Founded: 2010
Current Activity Level : Actively seeking new investments

KARLIN VENTURES

11755 Wilshire Boulevard
Suite 1400
Los Angeles, CA USA 90025
Phone: 3108069700
E-mail: info@karlinvc.com
Website: www.karlinvc.com

Management and Staff
TX Zhuo, Managing Partner

Type of Firm
Private Equity Firm

Project Preferences

Type of Financing Preferred:
Early Stage

Size of Investments Considered:
Min Size of Investment Considered (000s): $100
Max Size of Investment Considered (000s): $1,000

Geographical Preferences

United States Preferences:
West Coast

Industry Preferences

In Medical/Health prefer:
Health Services

In Consumer Related prefer:
Consumer Products

In Financial Services prefer:
Financial Services

In Business Serv. prefer:
Media

Additional Information
Year Founded: 2012
Current Activity Level : Actively seeking new investments

KARMA VENTURES OU

33A, Toompuiestee
Tallinn, Estonia 10149
Website: www.karma.vc

Other Offices
9, Allee Scheffer
Luxembourg, Luxembourg 2520

Management and Staff
Kristjan Laanemaa, Co-Founder
Margus Uudam, Co-Founder
Tommi Uhari, Co-Founder

Type of Firm
Private Equity Firm

Project Preferences

Type of Financing Preferred:
Early Stage
Seed

Geographical Preferences

International Preferences:
Europe

Industry Preferences

In Computer Software prefer:
Software

In Internet Specific prefer:
Internet

In Consumer Related prefer:
Education Related

In Financial Services prefer:
Financial Services

Additional Information
Year Founded: 2016
Capital Under Management: $45,120,000
Current Activity Level : Actively seeking new investments

KARMEL CAPITAL LLC

5960 Cornerstone Court West
Suite 100A
San Diego, CA USA 92121
Website: www.karmelcapital.com

Type of Firm
Private Equity Firm

Project Preferences

Type of Financing Preferred:
Leveraged Buyout
Turnaround
Acquisition

Additional Information
Year Founded: 2013
Current Activity Level : Actively seeking new investments

KARMIJN KAPITAAL MANAGEMENT BV

56, Koningin Wilhelminaplein
Amsterdam, Netherlands 1062 KS
Phone: 31202235678
E-mail: info@karmijnkapitaal.nl
Website: www.karmijnkapitaal.nl

Management and Staff
Carien van der Laan, Partner
Cilian Jansen Verplanke, Co-Founder
Desiree van Boxtel, Co-Founder
Hadewych Cels, Co-Founder

Type of Firm
Private Equity Firm

Association Membership
Dutch Venture Capital Associaton (NVP)

Project Preferences

Type of Financing Preferred:
Leveraged Buyout
Early Stage
Expansion
Later Stage
Management Buyouts
Acquisition

Size of Investments Considered:
Min Size of Investment Considered (000s): $2,207
Max Size of Investment Considered (000s): $8,277

Geographical Preferences

International Preferences:
Europe
Netherlands

Additional Information
Year Founded: 2010
Capital Under Management: $145,586,000
Current Activity Level : Actively seeking new investments

KARNATAKA INFORMATION TECHNOLOGY VENTURE CAPITAL FUND

21 Cunningham Road
403, Fourth Floor, HVS Court
Bangalore, India 560052
Phone: 08022385480
Fax: 08022386836
E-mail: info@kitven.com
Website: www.kitven.com

Management and Staff
A.R. Jayakumar, Chief Executive Officer

Type of Firm
Government Affiliated Program

Project Preferences

Type of Financing Preferred:
Early Stage
Expansion
Mezzanine
Turnaround
Later Stage
Seed
Startup

Size of Investments Considered:
Min Size of Investment Considered (000s): $5,000
Max Size of Investment Considered (000s): $15,000

Geographical Preferences

International Preferences:
India

Industry Preferences

In Communications prefer:
Communications and Media
Telecommunications

In Computer Software prefer:
Software

In Internet Specific prefer:
Internet

In Computer Other prefer:
Computer Related

In Semiconductor/Electr prefer:
Electronics
Semiconductor

In Biotechnology prefer:
Biotechnology

In Medical/Health prefer:
Medical/Health

In Manufact. prefer:
Manufacturing

In Agr/Forestr/Fish prefer:
Agriculture related

Additional Information
Year Founded: 1998
Capital Under Management: $2,200,000
Current Activity Level : Actively seeking new investments

KAROLINSKA DEVELOPMENT AB

Fogdevreten 2 A
Solna, Sweden 171 65
Phone: 46852486070
E-mail: info@karolinskadevelopment.com
Website: www.karolinskadevelopment.com

Management and Staff
Fredrik Jarrsten, Chief Financial Officer
Viktor Drvota, Chief Executive Officer

Type of Firm
Private Equity Firm

Project Preferences

Role in Financing:
Prefer role as deal originator

Type of Financing Preferred:
Early Stage
Balanced
Seed
Startup

Geographical Preferences

International Preferences:
Sweden

Industry Preferences

In Communications prefer:
Satellite Microwave Comm.

In Biotechnology prefer:
Biotechnology
Biotech Related Research

In Medical/Health prefer:
Medical/Health
Medical Therapeutics
Pharmaceuticals

Additional Information
Year Founded: 2003
Current Activity Level : Actively seeking new investments

KARPREILLY LLC

104 Field Point Road
Greenwich, CT USA 06830
Phone: 2035049900
Fax: 2035049901
Website: www.karpreilly.com

Management and Staff
Adam Burgoon, Partner
Ajay Natrajan, Chief Financial Officer
Allan Karp, Co-Founder
Andrew Keating, Partner
Billy Logan, Partner
Christopher Reilly, Co-Founder
Ed Thomas, Partner
Hank Spring, Vice President
Rich Reuter, Vice President

Type of Firm
Private Equity Firm

Project Preferences

Type of Financing Preferred:
Leveraged Buyout
Management Buyouts
Acquisition
Recapitalizations

Industry Preferences

In Consumer Related prefer:
Retail
Consumer Products
Other Restaurants

In Industrial/Energy prefer:
Industrial Products

Additional Information
Name of Most Recent Fund: KarpReilly Capital Partners II, L.P.
Most Recent Fund Was Raised: 06/05/2012
Year Founded: 2006
Capital Under Management: $500,000,000
Current Activity Level : Actively seeking new investments

KARTESIA ADVISOR LLP

14, Clifford Street
Bond Street House
London, United Kingdom W1S 4JU
Phone: 442037003330

Type of Firm
Private Equity Firm

Project Preferences

Type of Financing Preferred:
Leveraged Buyout
Management Buyouts
Acquisition

Geographical Preferences

International Preferences:
Italy
United Kingdom
Luxembourg
Europe
Netherlands
Spain
Belgium
Germany
France

Additional Information
Year Founded: 2013
Capital Under Management: $1,590,214,000
Current Activity Level : Actively seeking new investments

KASB TECHVENTURES

Seven Egerton Road
Second Floor, Associated House
Lahore, Pakistan
Phone: 92-42-630-9980
Fax: 92-42-631-1975
E-mail: info@kasbtv.com
Website: www.kasbtv.com

Management and Staff
Altaf Khan, Chief Executive Officer
Rizwan Butt, Chief Operating Officer

Type of Firm
Incubator/Development Program

Project Preferences

Type of Financing Preferred:
Startup

Size of Investments Considered:
Min Size of Investment Considered (000s): $100
Max Size of Investment Considered (000s): $100,000

Geographical Preferences

International Preferences:
Pakistan

Industry Preferences

In Communications prefer:
Telecommunications

In Computer Software prefer:
Software

In Internet Specific prefer:
Internet

In Financial Services prefer:
Financial Services

Additional Information
Year Founded: 2000
Current Activity Level : Actively seeking new investments

KASZEK VENTURES I LP

Paraguay 2141, Piso 17 Oficina
Aguada Park
Montevideo, Uruguay 11800
Phone: 5491137811525
Website: www.kaszek.com

Management and Staff
Hernan Kazah, Co-Founder
Nicolas Szekasy, Co-Founder

Type of Firm
Private Equity Firm

Association Membership
Brazilian Venture Capital Association (ABCR)

Project Preferences

Type of Financing Preferred:
Early Stage
Expansion
Balanced
Later Stage

Geographical Preferences

International Preferences:
Latin America

Additional Information
Name of Most Recent Fund: Kaszek Ventures II, L.P.
Most Recent Fund Was Raised: 01/22/2014
Year Founded: 2011
Capital Under Management: $391,375,000
Current Activity Level : Actively seeking new investments

KAWA CAPITAL MANAGEMENT INC

21500 Biscayne Boulevard
Suite 700
Aventura, FL USA 33180
Phone: 3055605200
Fax: 3055605290
E-mail: info@kawa.com
Website: www.kawa.com

Management and Staff
Alexandre Saverin, Partner
Cristina Baldim, Partner
Daniel Ades, Founder
Felipe Lemos, Partner
Luciano Lautenberg, Partner

Type of Firm
Investment Management Firm

Project Preferences

Type of Financing Preferred:
Leveraged Buyout
Acquisition

Industry Preferences

In Industrial/Energy prefer:
Energy

In Financial Services prefer:
Real Estate

Additional Information
Year Founded: 2009
Current Activity Level : Actively seeking new investments

KAYNE ANDERSON CAPITAL ADVISORS LP

1800 Avenue of the Stars
Second Floor
Los Angeles, CA USA 90067
Phone: 8006381496
Fax: 3102827900
Website: kaynecapital.com

Other Offices
200 Business Park Drive
Suite 309
Armonk, NY USA 10504
Phone: 914-273-1905

655 Madison Avenue
18th Floor
New York, NY USA 10065
Phone: 212-350-1400

717 Texas Avenue
Suite 3100
Houston, TX USA 77002
Phone: 713-493-2000

Management and Staff
Albert Rabil, Managing Partner
Daniel Weingeist, Managing Partner
David Petrucco, Managing Partner
David Walsh, Managing Partner
Edward Cerny, Managing Partner
Jeffrey Wilson, Managing Partner
John Frey, Managing Partner
John Anderson, Co-Founder
Jon Schotz, Managing Partner
Kevin McCarthy, Managing Partner
Michael Levitt, Chief Executive Officer
Paul Blank, Managing Director
Paul Stapleton, Chief Financial Officer
Terrence Quinn, Managing Partner

Type of Firm
Private Equity Firm

Association Membership
Natl Assoc of Small Bus. Inv. Co (NASBIC)

Project Preferences

Role in Financing:
Prefer role in deals created by others

Type of Financing Preferred:
Leveraged Buyout
Value-Add
Early Stage
Expansion
Generalist PE
Opportunistic
Later Stage
Management Buyouts
Acquisition

Geographical Preferences

United States Preferences:

Canadian Preferences:
All Canada

Industry Preferences

In Industrial/Energy prefer:
Energy
Oil and Gas Exploration

In Financial Services prefer:
Real Estate

Additional Information
Name of Most Recent Fund: Kayne Anderson Real Estate Partners III, L.P.
Most Recent Fund Was Raised: 06/04/2013
Year Founded: 1984
Capital Under Management: $3,783,000,000
Current Activity Level : Actively seeking new investments

KAZ CAPITAL PTY LTD

277 Sussex Street
Level 1
Sydney, Australia 2000
Phone: 61289990588
Fax: 61292660955
E-mail: info@kazcapital.com.au
Website: www.kazcapital.com.au

Management and Staff
Daniel Girgis, Managing Director

Type of Firm
Investment Management Firm

Project Preferences

Type of Financing Preferred:
Early Stage
Balanced

Geographical Preferences

International Preferences:
Australia

Industry Preferences

In Communications prefer:
Telecommunications
Wireless Communications

In Biotechnology prefer:
Biotechnology

Additional Information
Year Founded: 1988
Current Activity Level : Actively seeking new investments

KAZYNA KAPITAL MANAGEMENT AO

291/3A Dostyk Av.
2nd Floor
Almaty, Kazakhstan 050020
Phone: 77273341417
Fax: 77273341418
E-mail: info@kcm-kazyna.kz
Website: www.kcm-kazyna.kz

Management and Staff
Aidar Yegeubayev, Managing Director
Alexey Ten, Managing Director
Evgeyny Kim, Managing Director

Type of Firm
Investment Management Firm

Project Preferences

Type of Financing Preferred:
Fund of Funds
Leveraged Buyout
Generalist PE
Balanced
Turnaround
Later Stage
Acquisition
Recapitalizations

Geographical Preferences

International Preferences:
Tajikistan
Asia
Russia

Industry Preferences

In Biotechnology prefer:
Biotechnology

In Consumer Related prefer:
Food/Beverage

In Industrial/Energy prefer:
Energy
Oil and Gas Exploration
Alternative Energy
Energy Conservation Relat
Materials

In Financial Services prefer:
Financial Services

In Agr/Forestr/Fish prefer:
Agribusiness
Mining and Minerals

In Other prefer:
Environment Responsible

Additional Information
Year Founded: 2007
Capital Under Management: $400,000,000
Current Activity Level : Actively seeking new investments

KB INVESTMENT CO LTD

731 Yeongdong-daero Blvd.
Ninth Floor
Seoul, South Korea 135-953
Phone: 8225355091
Fax: 8225355092
Website: www.kbic.co.kr

Management and Staff
Han Ok Kim, Chief Executive Officer

Type of Firm
Bank Affiliated

Association Membership
Korean Venture Capital Association (KVCA)

Project Preferences

Type of Financing Preferred:
Leveraged Buyout
Early Stage
Expansion
Mezzanine
Generalist PE
Balanced
Turnaround
Later Stage
Management Buyouts
Startup
Recapitalizations

Geographical Preferences

United States Preferences:

International Preferences:
Australia
Asia
Korea, South

Industry Preferences

In Communications prefer:
Media and Entertainment

In Semiconductor/Electr prefer:
Electronics

In Biotechnology prefer:
Biotechnology

In Medical/Health prefer:
Medical/Health

In Consumer Related prefer:
Consumer
Consumer Products

In Industrial/Energy prefer:
Industrial Products

In Financial Services prefer:
Financial Services

Additional Information
Year Founded: 1990
Capital Under Management: $1,400,000,000
Current Activity Level : Actively seeking new investments

KB PARTNERS LLC

600 Central Avenue
Suite 390
Highland Park, IL USA 60035
Phone: 8476811270
Fax: 8476811370
Website: www.kbpartners.com

Management and Staff
Byron Denenberg, Managing Director
Keith Bank, Managing Director

Type of Firm
Private Equity Firm

Association Membership
Illinois Venture Capital Association

Project Preferences

Role in Financing:
Will function either as deal originator or investor in deals created by others

Type of Financing Preferred:
Early Stage
Startup

Industry Focus

(% based on actual investment)
Computer Software and Services	26.2%
Semiconductors/Other Elect.	19.0%
Internet Specific	15.3%
Communications and Media	12.9%
Medical/Health	11.4%
Biotechnology	8.0%
Industrial/Energy	5.3%
Computer Hardware	1.9%

Additional Information
Name of Most Recent Fund: KB Partners Venture Fund II, L.P.
Most Recent Fund Was Raised: 06/09/2000
Year Founded: 1996
Capital Under Management: $98,000,000
Current Activity Level : Actively seeking new investments
Method of Compensation: Return on investment is of primary concern, do not charge fees

KBL HEALTHCARE VENTURES L P

52 East 72nd Street
New York, NY USA 10021
Phone: 2123195555
Fax: 2123195591
E-mail: inquiries@kblvc.com
Website: www.kblvc.com

Management and Staff
Elijah Berk, Vice President
Marlene Krauss, Chief Executive Officer
Michael Kaswan, Chief Operating Officer

Type of Firm
Private Equity Firm

Project Preferences

Role in Financing:
Will function either as deal originator or investor in deals created by others

Type of Financing Preferred:
Early Stage
Expansion
Balanced
Later Stage
Startup

Industry Focus
(% based on actual investment)
Medical/Health	51.1%
Biotechnology	24.4%
Internet Specific	14.5%
Communications and Media	7.0%
Computer Software and Services	2.9%

Additional Information
Name of Most Recent Fund: KBL Healthcare Ventures
Most Recent Fund Was Raised: 08/06/1999
Year Founded: 1991
Capital Under Management: $100,000,000
Current Activity Level : Actively seeking new investments
Method of Compensation: Return on investment is of primary concern, do not charge fees

KBW CAPITAL PARTNERS I L P

787 7th Avenue
Sixth Floor
New York, NY USA 10019
Phone: 2128872000
Website: www.kbwam.com

Management and Staff
John Hompe, Managing Director
Peter Roth, Managing Director
Prumiys Dulger, Vice President

Type of Firm
Bank Affiliated

Project Preferences

Type of Financing Preferred:
Expansion
Generalist PE
Balanced
Later Stage
Seed
Management Buyouts
Startup
Recapitalizations

Geographical Preferences
United States Preferences:

Industry Preferences

In Financial Services prefer:
Financial Services

Additional Information
Name of Most Recent Fund: KBW Capital Partners I, L.P.
Most Recent Fund Was Raised: 04/11/2007
Year Founded: 2007
Current Activity Level : Actively seeking new investments

KC VENTURE GROUP LLC

2020 West 89th Street
Suite 320
Leawood, KS USA 66206
Phone: 9136528600
Fax: 9136526596
Website: www.kcventuregroup.com

Other Offices
800 West 47th Street
Suite 300
Kansas City, MO USA 64112
Phone: 816-753-8380
Fax: 816-753-8399

9337B Katy Freeway
Suite 323
Houston, TX USA 77024
Phone: (746) 806-5771
Fax: (713) 523-7114

Management and Staff
Paul Fingersh, Principal
Peter Engelman, Founder
Ron Nolan, Principal
Susan Pohl, Vice President

Type of Firm
Private Equity Firm

Additional Information
Year Founded: 1994
Current Activity Level : Actively seeking new investments

KCB MANAGEMENT LLC

117 E Colorado Boulevard
Suite 400
Pasadena, CA USA 91105
Phone: 6263560944
Fax: 6263560996
Website: www.kcbm.com

Management and Staff
Harvey Knell, President, Founder

Type of Firm
Private Equity Firm

Project Preferences

Type of Financing Preferred:
Acquisition

Geographical Preferences
United States Preferences:

Industry Preferences

In Consumer Related prefer:
Consumer Products
Consumer Services
Education Related

In Financial Services prefer:
Real Estate

In Business Serv. prefer:
Distribution

In Manufact. prefer:
Manufacturing

Additional Information
Name of Most Recent Fund: KCB Real Estate Fund V LP
Most Recent Fund Was Raised: 03/20/2013
Year Founded: 1986
Capital Under Management: $24,110,000
Current Activity Level : Actively seeking new investments

KCP CAPITAL LTD

Al Thuraya Tower Two
Suite 713
Dubai, Utd. Arab Em.
Phone: 97144280728
Fax: 97144280730
Website: www.kcpcapital.com

Type of Firm
Private Equity Firm

Project Preferences

Type of Financing Preferred:
Early Stage
Expansion
Start-up Financing

Industry Preferences

In Communications prefer:
Telecommunications

In Business Serv. prefer:
Media

Additional Information

Year Founded: 2001
Current Activity Level : Actively seeking new investments

KCP&L GREATER MISSOURI OPERATIONS CO

Nine East, 38th Street
12th Floor
New York, NY USA 10016
Phone: 212-813-3112
Fax: 866-734-0593
E-mail: ny@psi-world.com

Other Offices

204 Global Business Park
Tower-B
Gurgaon, India 122 002
Phone: 91-124-280-3035

Type of Firm

Investment Management Firm

Project Preferences

Type of Financing Preferred:
Early Stage
Expansion
Balanced
Seed

Geographical Preferences

United States Preferences:

International Preferences:
India
Ukraine

Industry Preferences

In Medical/Health prefer:
Pharmaceuticals

Additional Information

Year Founded: 2007
Current Activity Level : Actively seeking new investments

KCRISE FUND LLC

201 West 19th Terrace
Kansas City, MO USA 64108
Website: kcrisefund.com

Management and Staff

Darcy Howe, President

Type of Firm

Private Equity Firm

Project Preferences

Type of Financing Preferred:
Early Stage

Geographical Preferences

United States Preferences:
Kansas

Additional Information

Year Founded: 2016
Capital Under Management: $10,000,000
Current Activity Level : Actively seeking new investments

KD DD

Dunajska cesta 63
Ljubljana, Slovenia 1000
Phone: 38615826700
Fax: 38615184100
E-mail: info@kd-group.com
Website: www.kd-fd.si

Management and Staff

Janez Bojc, President

Type of Firm

Private Equity Firm

Project Preferences

Type of Financing Preferred:
Leveraged Buyout
Early Stage
Expansion
Later Stage
Management Buyouts
Acquisition
Startup

Geographical Preferences

International Preferences:
Slovenia
Europe
Czech Republic
Eastern Europe
Bulgaria
Romania

Additional Information

Year Founded: 2000
Current Activity Level : Actively seeking new investments

KDB CAPITAL CORP

KDB Capital Building
Eunhaeng-Ro 30 Yeongdeungpo-Gu
Seoul, South Korea 150740
Phone: 822-6330-0114
Website: www.kdbc.co.kr

Management and Staff

Ho Cheol Suhk, Vice President
Yeong Gi Kim, Chief Executive Officer

Type of Firm

Bank Affiliated

Project Preferences

Type of Financing Preferred:
Leveraged Buyout
Generalist PE
Balanced

Geographical Preferences

International Preferences:
Asia Pacific
No Preference
Asia
Korea, South

Industry Preferences

In Biotechnology prefer:
Agricultural/Animal Bio.

In Medical/Health prefer:
Medical/Health

In Manufact. prefer:
Manufacturing

Additional Information

Year Founded: 1972
Capital Under Management: $120,920,000
Current Activity Level : Actively seeking new investments

KDC MEDIA FUND

12 Raoul Wallenberg st
Tel Aviv, Israel
Phone: 97237677801
E-mail: bp@kdc.fund

Type of Firm

Private Equity Firm

Project Preferences

Type of Financing Preferred:
Early Stage

Geographical Preferences

International Preferences:
Israel

Industry Preferences

In Communications prefer:
Communications and Media
Data Communications

In Computer Software prefer:
Data Processing

In Business Serv. prefer:
Media

Additional Information
Year Founded: 2016
Current Activity Level : Actively seeking new investments

KDT GP LLC

306 View Street
Black Mountain, NC USA 28711

Type of Firm
Private Equity Firm

Project Preferences

Type of Financing Preferred:
Early Stage

Additional Information
Year Founded: 2017
Capital Under Management: $3,540,000
Current Activity Level : Actively seeking new investments

KEADYN

Stationsplein 45
Cambridge Innovation Center
Rotterdam, Netherlands 3013 AK
Website: keadyn.com

Type of Firm
Private Equity Firm

Project Preferences

Type of Financing Preferred:
Early Stage
Seed

Geographical Preferences

International Preferences:
Europe
Netherlands

Industry Preferences

In Computer Software prefer:
Software

In Internet Specific prefer:
Ecommerce

In Financial Services prefer:
Financial Services

Additional Information
Year Founded: 2012
Current Activity Level : Actively seeking new investments

KEANE D SOUZA VENTURE CAPITAL LLC

250 North Sunnyslope Road
Suite 245
Brookfield, WI USA 53005
Website: www.kdventurecapital.com

Management and Staff
Tim Keane, Managing Director
Trevor D Souza, Managing Director

Type of Firm
Private Equity Firm

Project Preferences

Type of Financing Preferred:
Balanced
Later Stage

Size of Investments Considered:
Min Size of Investment Considered (000s): $3,000
Max Size of Investment Considered (000s): $10,000

Geographical Preferences

United States Preferences:
Midwest

Industry Preferences

In Computer Software prefer:
Software

In Industrial/Energy prefer:
Energy
Environmental Related

In Financial Services prefer:
Financial Services

In Other prefer:
Environment Responsible

Additional Information
Year Founded: 2012
Current Activity Level : Actively seeking new investments

KEARNY VENTURE PARTNERS LP

88 Kearny Street
Suite 1800
San Francisco, CA USA 94108
Phone: 415875777
Fax: 4158757770
E-mail: info@kearnyvp.com
Website: www.kearnyvp.com

Management and Staff
Andrew Jensen, Chief Financial Officer
Anupam Dalal, Managing Director
Caley Castelein, Managing Director
James Shapiro, Managing Director
Richard Spalding, Managing Director

Type of Firm
Private Equity Firm

Project Preferences

Role in Financing:
Prefer role in deals created by others

Type of Financing Preferred:
Early Stage
Expansion
Balanced
Later Stage
Seed

Size of Investments Considered:
Min Size of Investment Considered (000s): $2,000
Max Size of Investment Considered (000s): $15,000

Industry Preferences

In Biotechnology prefer:
Biotechnology

In Medical/Health prefer:
Medical/Health
Medical Diagnostics
Medical Therapeutics
Medical Products

Additional Information
Name of Most Recent Fund: Kearny Venture Partners, L.P.
Most Recent Fund Was Raised: 09/13/2006
Year Founded: 2001
Capital Under Management: $330,000,000
Current Activity Level : Actively seeking new investments
Method of Compensation: Return on investment is of primary concern, do not charge fees

---

KEBEK MANAGEMENT NV

Romeinsesteenweg 566
Strombeek-Bever, Belgium 1853
Phone: 3226699020

Management and Staff
Ast Verbiest, Co-Founder
Floris Vansina, Co-Founder
Gerd Smeets, Co-Founder
Gert Van Huffel, Co-Founder

Type of Firm
Private Equity Firm

Project Preferences

Type of Financing Preferred:
Leveraged Buyout
Management Buyouts
Acquisition

Geographical Preferences

International Preferences:
Europe
Belgium

Additional Information
Year Founded: 2012
Capital Under Management: $28,020,000
Current Activity Level : Actively seeking new investments

KEC HOLDINGS LLC

2317 Highway 34
Suite 2B
Manasquan, NJ USA 08736
Website: www.kecholdings.com

Type of Firm
Private Equity Firm

Project Preferences

Type of Financing Preferred:
Early Stage
Balanced
Later Stage
Startup

Additional Information
Year Founded: 1999
Capital Under Management: $62,555,000
Current Activity Level : Actively seeking new investments

KEC VENTURES INC

30 Vesey Street
New York, NY USA 10013
Phone: 2125550123
Website: www.kecventures.com

Management and Staff
Brian Aoaeh, Partner
Chris Fortunato, Principal
Jeff Parkinson, Partner
Jeffrey Citron, Managing Partner
Josh Lamstein, Partner
Philip Limeri, Chief Financial Officer

Type of Firm
Private Equity Firm

Project Preferences

Type of Financing Preferred:
Early Stage
Balanced
Later Stage
Seed

Additional Information
Year Founded: 2011
Current Activity Level : Actively seeking new investments

KEEN GROWTH CAPITAL ADVISORS LLC

513 Main Street
Windermere, FL USA 34786
Phone: 4072175910
Website: keengrowthcapital.com

Management and Staff
David Comeau, Venture Partner
Jerry Bello, Co-Founder
Jonathan Smiga, Co-Founder

Type of Firm
Private Equity Firm

Project Preferences

Type of Financing Preferred:
Early Stage

Industry Preferences

In Consumer Related prefer:
Food/Beverage

Additional Information
Year Founded: 1969
Current Activity Level : Actively seeking new investments

KEEN VENTURE PARTNERS LLP

9th Floor, No. 1 Minster Court
Mincing Lane
London, United Kingdom EC3R 7AA
Phone: 2033180562
E-mail: info@keenventurepartners.com
Website: www.keenventurepartners.com

Type of Firm
Private Equity Firm

Project Preferences

Type of Financing Preferred:
Early Stage

Geographical Preferences

United States Preferences:
North America

International Preferences:
Europe

Additional Information
Year Founded: 1969
Capital Under Management: $100,360,000
Current Activity Level : Actively seeking new investments

KEENSIGHT CAPITAL SAS

64 rue de Lisbonne
Paris, France 75008
Phone: 33183798730
Fax: 33140748820
E-mail: rcm@rothschild.com
Website: www.keensightcapital.com

Management and Staff
Jean-Michel Beghin, Managing Director
Jerome Pujol, Managing Director
Pierre Remy, Managing Director

Type of Firm
Private Equity Firm

Association Membership
French Venture Capital Association (AFIC)
European Private Equity and Venture Capital Assoc.

Project Preferences

Type of Financing Preferred:
Leveraged Buyout
Generalist PE
Later Stage
Acquisition

Size of Investments Considered:
Min Size of Investment Considered (000s): $6,799
Max Size of Investment Considered (000s): $40,794

Geographical Preferences

International Preferences:
United Kingdom
Europe
Eastern Europe
France

Industry Preferences

In Communications prefer:
Communications and Media
CATV & Pay TV Systems
Telecommunications
Wireless Communications
Data Communications

In Computer Software prefer:
Software

In Semiconductor/Electr prefer:
Semiconductor

In Medical/Health prefer:
Medical/Health
Health Services

In Industrial/Energy prefer:
Energy
Oil and Gas Exploration

In Business Serv. prefer:
Services

KEGONSA CAPITAL PARTNERS LLC

5520 Nobel Drive, Suite 150
Fitchburg, WI USA 53711
Phone: 6082050100
E-mail: info@kegonsapartners.com
Website: www.kegonsapartners.com

Management and Staff
Kenneth Johnson, Managing Director

Type of Firm
Private Equity Firm

Project Preferences

Role in Financing:
Prefer role as deal originator

Type of Financing Preferred:
Early Stage
Balanced
Later Stage
Seed

Size of Investments Considered:
Min Size of Investment Considered (000s): $100
Max Size of Investment Considered (000s): $750

Geographical Preferences

United States Preferences:
Northeast
Wisconsin

Industry Preferences

In Internet Specific prefer:
Internet
Ecommerce

In Biotechnology prefer:
Biotechnology
Biotech Related Research

In Medical/Health prefer:
Medical/Health
Medical Products
Pharmaceuticals

In Industrial/Energy prefer:
Environmental Related

Additional Information
Year Founded: 2004
Capital Under Management: $11,000,000
Current Activity Level : Actively seeking new investments
Method of Compensation: Return on investment is of primary concern, do not charge fees

KEIRETSU FORUM

425 Market Street, 25th Floor
San Francisco, CA USA 94105
E-mail: info@keiretsuforum.com

Management and Staff
Judith Iglehart, Vice President
Sonja Markova, Managing Director

Type of Firm
Corporate PE/Venture

Project Preferences

Type of Financing Preferred:
Early Stage
Expansion

Geographical Preferences

United States Preferences:
North America

Canadian Preferences:
All Canada

International Preferences:
Europe
Asia

Additional Information
Year Founded: 2000
Capital Under Management: $6,100,000
Current Activity Level : Actively seeking new investments
Method of Compensation: Professional fee required whether or not deal closes

KEIRETSU VENTURES INC

1900 South Norfolk Street, Suite 135
San Mateo, CA USA 94403

Type of Firm
Incubator/Development Program

Project Preferences

Type of Financing Preferred:
Startup

Additional Information
Year Founded: 2014
Current Activity Level : Actively seeking new investments

KELSO & COMPANY LP

320 Park Avenue, 24th Floor
New York, NY USA 10022
Phone: 2127513939
Fax: 2122232379
Website: www.kelso.com

Management and Staff
Christopher Collins, Principal
Church Moore, Principal
David Wahrhaftig, Principal
Frank Bynum, Principal
Frank Loverro, Principal
George Matelich, Principal
Hank Mannix, Vice President
M. Shane Tiemann, Vice President
Matthew Edgerton, Vice President
Michael Goldberg, Principal
Philip Berney, Principal
Stanley de Osborne, Principal
Stephen Dutton, Vice President
Thomas Wall, Principal

Type of Firm
Bank Affiliated

Association Membership
Private Equity Council (PEC)

Project Preferences

Type of Financing Preferred:
Leveraged Buyout
Mezzanine
Management Buyouts
Acquisition
Recapitalizations

Geographical Preferences

United States Preferences:
North America

Canadian Preferences:
All Canada

Industry Focus
(% based on actual investment)

Other Products	41.7%
Industrial/Energy	26.2%
Consumer Related	10.7%
Communications and Media	8.8%
Medical/Health	5.3%
Semiconductors/Other Elect.	3.3%
Computer Software and Services	2.9%
Internet Specific	0.9%
Biotechnology	0.2%

Additional Information
Name of Most Recent Fund: Kelso Investment Associates VIII
Most Recent Fund Was Raised: 07/23/2007
Year Founded: 1980
Capital Under Management: $3,378,400,000
Current Activity Level : Actively seeking new investments

Additional Information (Kegonsa top)
Year Founded: 2000
Capital Under Management: $270,526,000
Current Activity Level : Actively seeking new investments

KELVIN CAPITAL LTD

163 Bath Street
Glasgow, United Kingdom G2 4QS
Phone: 1413376618
E-mail: theteam@kelvincapital.com
Website: www.kelvincapital.com

Type of Firm
Private Equity Firm

Project Preferences

Type of Financing Preferred:
Early Stage
Seed
Startup

Geographical Preferences

International Preferences:
United Kingdom

Additional Information
Year Founded: 2009
Current Activity Level: Actively seeking new investments

KENDA CAPITAL BV

Lange Kleiweg 60F
Hardenburch
Rijswijk, Netherlands 2288 GK
Phone: 31704134040
Fax: 31704134059
E-mail: info@kendacapital.com
Website: www.kendacapital.com

Other Offices
2700 Post Oak Blvd
Suite 1750
Houston, TX USA 77056
Phone: 7136235950
Fax: 7139608699

Management and Staff
Brendan Barry, Chief Financial Officer
Erik Vollebregt, Managing Director
Jason Roe, Vice President

Type of Firm
Private Equity Firm

Association Membership
European Private Equity and Venture Capital Assoc.

Project Preferences

Type of Financing Preferred:
Early Stage

Geographical Preferences

International Preferences:
Europe

Industry Preferences

In Industrial/Energy prefer:
Oil and Gas Exploration
Alternative Energy

Additional Information
Year Founded: 2007
Current Activity Level: Actively seeking new investments

KENDALL CAPITAL ASSOCIATES LLC

3715 Pomfret Lane
Charlotte, NC USA 28211
Phone: 704-366-3880
Fax: 704-366-6177
E-mail: info@kendallcap.com
Website: www.kendallcap.com

Management and Staff
James Phelps, Managing Director

Type of Firm
Bank Affiliated

Project Preferences

Type of Financing Preferred:
Leveraged Buyout
Early Stage
Mezzanine
Generalist PE
Acquisition

Geographical Preferences

United States Preferences:
Southeast

Industry Preferences

In Computer Software prefer:
Software

In Internet Specific prefer:
Ecommerce

In Semiconductor/Electr prefer:
Semiconductor

In Biotechnology prefer:
Biotechnology

In Medical/Health prefer:
Medical/Health

In Business Serv. prefer:
Distribution

In Manufact. prefer:
Manufacturing

Additional Information
Year Founded: 2000
Current Activity Level: Actively seeking new investments

KENNET PARTNERS LTD

41-46 Piccadilly
Nuffield House
London, United Kingdom W1J 0DS
Phone: 442078398020
Fax: 442074342973
E-mail: info@kennet.com
Website: www.kennet.com

Other Offices
950 Tower Lane
Suite 1710
Foster City, CA USA 94404
Phone: 650-573-8700
Fax: 650-573-8712

Management and Staff
David Carratt, Managing Director
Eric Filipek, Managing Director
Javier Rojas, Managing Director
Michael Elias, Managing Director

Type of Firm
Private Equity Firm

Association Membership
British Venture Capital Association (BVCA)

Project Preferences

Role in Financing:
Prefer role as deal originator but will also invest in deals created by others

Type of Financing Preferred:
Leveraged Buyout
Expansion
Generalist PE
Balanced
Management Buyouts
Recapitalizations

Size of Investments Considered:
Min Size of Investment Considered (000s): $10,000
Max Size of Investment Considered (000s): $100,000

Geographical Preferences

United States Preferences:
North America

International Preferences:
Europe

Industry Focus
(% based on actual investment)
Computer Software and Services 46.1%
Internet Specific 39.9%
Communications and Media 5.9%
Semiconductors/Other Elect. 3.2%
Computer Hardware 2.7%
Medical/Health 2.2%

Additional Information
Name of Most Recent Fund: Kennet II
Most Recent Fund Was Raised: 12/31/2000
Year Founded: 1997
Capital Under Management: $280,000,000
Current Activity Level : Actively seeking new investments
Method of Compensation: Return on investment is of primary concern, do not charge fees

KENSINGTON CAPITAL PARTNERS LTD

95 St. Clair Avenue West
Suite 905
Toronto, Canada M4V 1N6
Phone: 4163629000
Fax: 4163620939
E-mail: info@kcpl.ca
Website: kcpl.ca

Management and Staff
Eamonn McConnell, Managing Director
John Walker, Managing Director
Richard Nathan, Managing Director
Thomas Kennedy, Founder
William Sutherland, Principal

Type of Firm
Private Equity Firm

Association Membership
Canadian Venture Capital Association

Project Preferences

Type of Financing Preferred:
Generalist PE
Fund of Funds of Second

Geographical Preferences

Canadian Preferences:
Alberta
All Canada
British Columbia

Industry Preferences

In Industrial/Energy prefer:
Energy
Environmental Related

Additional Information
Year Founded: 1996
Capital Under Management: $341,731,000
Current Activity Level : Actively seeking new investments

KENSON VENTURES LLC

400 Hamilton Avenue, Suite 410
Palo Alto, CA USA 94301
Phone: 650-330-0322
Fax: 650-330-0577
Website: www.kensonventures.com

Management and Staff
Joseph Huang, Vice President
Yishan Li, Vice President

Type of Firm
Private Equity Firm

Project Preferences

Type of Financing Preferred:
Balanced
Seed
Startup

Size of Investments Considered:
Min Size of Investment Considered (000s): $500
Max Size of Investment Considered (000s): $3,000

Additional Information
Year Founded: 1999
Current Activity Level : Actively seeking new investments

KENTUCKY SEED CAPITAL FUND

222 South First Street
Suite 200
Louisville, KY USA 40202
Phone: 5024101652
E-mail: info@kyseed.com
Website: www.kyseed.com

Management and Staff
Andrew Mercke, Principal
George Emont, Managing Partner
Steve Gailar, Managing Partner

Type of Firm
Private Equity Firm

Project Preferences

Type of Financing Preferred:
Early Stage
Later Stage
Seed

Geographical Preferences

United States Preferences:
Louisiana
Kentucky

Industry Preferences

In Medical/Health prefer:
Medical/Health
Medical Products
Health Services

Additional Information
Year Founded: 2005
Capital Under Management: $5,000,000
Current Activity Level : Actively seeking new investments

KENYA CAPITAL PARTNERS LTD

Norfolk Towers
Kijabe Street
Nairobi, Kenya
Phone: 254-20-22-8870
Fax: 254-20-33-0120

Type of Firm
Private Equity Firm

Project Preferences

Type of Financing Preferred:
Balanced

Geographical Preferences

International Preferences:
Kenya

Additional Information
Year Founded: 2010
Current Activity Level : Actively seeking new investments

KEPHA PARTNERS

303 Wyman Street
Suite 300
Waltham, MA USA 02451
Phone: 7818397018
Website: www.kephapartners.com

Management and Staff
Eric Hjerpe, Partner
Jo Tango, Founder

Type of Firm
Private Equity Firm

Association Membership
New England Venture Capital Association

Project Preferences

Role in Financing:
Prefer role as deal originator but will also invest in deals created by others

Type of Financing Preferred:
Early Stage
Balanced
Seed
Startup

Industry Preferences

In Communications prefer:
Communications and Media

In Computer Software prefer:
Software

In Internet Specific prefer:
Internet

In Business Serv. prefer:
Media

Additional Information
Name of Most Recent Fund: Kepha Partners II, L.P.
Most Recent Fund Was Raised: 09/30/2011
Year Founded: 2006
Capital Under Management: $185,000,000
Current Activity Level : Actively seeking new investments

KERALA VENTURE CAPITAL FUND PVT LTD

604, Pioneer Towers
Marine Drive
Kochi, India 682 031
Phone: 91-484-236-1279
Fax: 91-484-237-3077
E-mail: kvcf@vsnl.in

Management and Staff
K.A. Joseph, CEO & Managing Director

Type of Firm
Government Affiliated Program

Project Preferences

Type of Financing Preferred:
Early Stage
Expansion
Mezzanine
Startup

Size of Investments Considered:
Min Size of Investment Considered (000s): $52
Max Size of Investment Considered (000s): $890

Geographical Preferences

International Preferences:
India

Industry Preferences

In Communications prefer:
Communications and Media

In Computer Software prefer:
Software

In Computer Other prefer:
Computer Related

In Semiconductor/Electr prefer:
Electronics

In Biotechnology prefer:
Biotechnology

Additional Information
Year Founded: 1999
Capital Under Management: $4,400,000
Current Activity Level : Actively seeking new investments

KERALA VENTURES

8, Place de l"opera
Paris, France 75009
Website: www.krlventures.com

Management and Staff
Antoine Freysz, Managing Director
Marc Laurent, Managing Director
Olivier Occelli, Managing Director

Type of Firm
Private Equity Firm

Project Preferences

Type of Financing Preferred:
Early Stage
Seed

Geographical Preferences

International Preferences:
France

Industry Preferences

In Communications prefer:
Wireless Communications

In Internet Specific prefer:
Internet
Ecommerce

Additional Information
Year Founded: 2014
Current Activity Level : Actively seeking new investments

KERN WHELAN CAPITAL LLC

One Letterman Drive Building C
Main Floor, Suite 200
San Francisco, CA USA 94129
Fax: 4156758794
E-mail: info@kernwhelan.com
Website: www.kernwhelan.com

Management and Staff
J.P. Whelan, Founder

Type of Firm
Private Equity Firm

Project Preferences

Type of Financing Preferred:
Balanced

Geographical Preferences

United States Preferences:

Additional Information
Year Founded: 2007

Current Activity Level : Actively seeking new investments

KERNEL CAPITAL PARTNERS

Rubicon Centre, Rossa Avenue
Bishopstown
Cork, Ireland
Phone: 353214928974
Fax: 353214928977
Website: www.kernelcapital.ie

Other Offices
15 Molesworth Street
Dublin 2, Ireland
Phone: 353-1-633-6829

Management and Staff
Daniel O Mahony, Partner
Graham Fagg, Partner
Niall Olden, Managing Partner
Seamus O Hara, Partner

Type of Firm
Private Equity Firm

Association Membership
Irish Venture Capital Association

Project Preferences

Type of Financing Preferred:
Early Stage
Expansion
Balanced
Later Stage
Seed
Management Buyouts
Startup

Size of Investments Considered:
Min Size of Investment Considered (000s): $2,974
Max Size of Investment Considered (000s): $14,872

Geographical Preferences

International Preferences:
Ireland
Europe

Industry Preferences

In Medical/Health prefer:
Medical Therapeutics

In Consumer Related prefer:
Food/Beverage

In Financial Services prefer:
Financial Services

In Other prefer:
Environment Responsible

Pratt's Guide to Private Equity & Venture Capital Sources

Additional Information
Name of Most Recent Fund: Bank of Ireland Kernel Capital Growth Fund (NI), The
Most Recent Fund Was Raised: 10/07/2013
Year Founded: 2002
Capital Under Management: $47,580,000
Current Activity Level : Actively seeking new investments

KESHIF VENTURES LLC
990 Highland Drive
Suite 314
Solana Beach, CA USA 92075

Type of Firm
Private Equity Firm

Project Preferences

Type of Financing Preferred:
Balanced

Industry Preferences

In Industrial/Energy prefer:
Energy

In Business Serv. prefer:
Media

Additional Information
Year Founded: 2016
Current Activity Level : Actively seeking new investments

KESTREL CAPITAL PTY LIMITED
5 Lime St Sydney
Suite 319
Sydney, Australia 2000
E-mail: enquiries@kestrelcapital.com.au
Website: www.kestrelcapital.com.au

Other Offices
20 Maxwell Road
#02-01 Maxwell House
Singapore, Singapore 069113

Management and Staff
Niall Cairns, Managing Director
Phillip Carter, Managing Director
Wayne Longbottom, Chief Financial Officer

Type of Firm
Private Equity Firm

Association Membership
Australian Venture Capital Association (AVCAL)

Project Preferences

Role in Financing:
Prefer role as deal originator

Type of Financing Preferred:
Expansion
Mezzanine
Later Stage

Size of Investments Considered:
Min Size of Investment Considered (000s): $1,443
Max Size of Investment Considered (000s): $2,886

Geographical Preferences

International Preferences:
Australia
New Zealand

Industry Focus
(% based on actual investment)
Other Products	38.9%
Computer Software and Services	30.5%
Consumer Related	9.5%
Semiconductors/Other Elect.	7.0%
Computer Hardware	6.1%
Industrial/Energy	5.7%
Medical/Health	2.3%

Additional Information
Name of Most Recent Fund: Nanyang Australia II, Ltd.
Most Recent Fund Was Raised: 11/16/1999
Year Founded: 1993
Capital Under Management: $78,900,000
Current Activity Level : Actively seeking new investments
Method of Compensation: Professional fee required whether or not deal closes

KEY CAPITAL PARTNERS
Mabledon Place
Hamilton House
London, United Kingdom WC1H 9BB
Phone: 442079530390
Fax: 442075548501
E-mail: london@keycapitalpartners.co.uk
Website: www.keycapitalpartners.co.uk

Other Offices
43 Temple Row
Birmingham, United Kingdom B2 5LS
Phone: 44-121-237-6008
Fax: 44-121-237-6100

Princes Exchange
Princes Square
Leeds, United Kingdom LS1 4HY
Phone: 44-113-280-5824
Fax: 44-113-280-5801

Management and Staff
James Hall, Partner
Michael Fell, Partner
Owen Trotter, Managing Partner
Peter Armitage, Partner

Type of Firm
Private Equity Firm

Association Membership
British Venture Capital Association (BVCA)

Project Preferences

Type of Financing Preferred:
Leveraged Buyout
Expansion
Generalist PE
Later Stage
Management Buyouts
Acquisition
Recapitalizations

Size of Investments Considered:
Min Size of Investment Considered (000s): $2,794
Max Size of Investment Considered (000s): $13,970

Geographical Preferences

International Preferences:
United Kingdom
Europe

Additional Information
Year Founded: 2007
Capital Under Management: $83,050,000
Current Activity Level : Actively seeking new investments

KEY VENTURE PARTNERS
225 Franklin Street
18th Floor
Boston, MA USA 02110
Phone: 6173856244
Website: www.keyvp.com

Management and Staff
John Ward, Managing Director

Type of Firm
Bank Affiliated

Project Preferences

Role in Financing:
Prefer role as deal originator but will also invest in deals created by others

Type of Financing Preferred:
Expansion
Balanced
Later Stage
Management Buyouts
Acquisition
Recapitalizations

Size of Investments Considered:
Min Size of Investment Considered (000s): $5,000
Max Size of Investment Considered (000s): $15,000

Geographical Preferences

United States Preferences:

Industry Preferences

In Computer Software prefer:
Software
Systems Software
Applications Software

In Internet Specific prefer:
E-Commerce Technology

In Medical/Health prefer:
Medical/Health

In Financial Services prefer:
Financial Services

Additional Information

Year Founded: 2003
Capital Under Management: $200,000,000
Current Activity Level: Actively seeking new investments
Method of Compensation: Return on investment is of primary concern, do not charge fees

KEYHAVEN CAPITAL PARTNERS LTD

1 Maple Place
London, United Kingdom W1T4BB
Phone: 44-20-7432-6200
Fax: 44-20-7432-6201
E-mail: info@keyhavencapital.com
Website: www.keyhavencapital.com

Management and Staff

Claus Stenbaek, Managing Director
Sasha Van de Water, Managing Director

Type of Firm

Private Equity Advisor or Fund of Funds

Association Membership

European Private Equity and Venture Capital Assoc.

Project Preferences

Type of Financing Preferred:
Fund of Funds
Leveraged Buyout

Geographical Preferences

International Preferences:
Europe

Additional Information

Year Founded: 2003
Capital Under Management: $194,610,000
Current Activity Level: Actively seeking new investments

KEYSTONE CAPITAL INC

155 North Wacker Drive
Suite 4150
Chicago, IL USA 60606
Phone: 3122197900
E-mail: info@keystonecapital.com
Website: keystonecapital.com

Management and Staff

Brian Chung, Chief Financial Officer
Chaoran Jin, Principal
David Greer, Managing Director
Dennis Howe, Vice President
Jason Van Zant, Vice President
Kent Dauten, Co-Founder
Scott Gwilliam, Co-Founder

Type of Firm

Private Equity Firm

Project Preferences

Type of Financing Preferred:
Leveraged Buyout
Later Stage
Acquisition
Special Situation
Recapitalizations

Industry Preferences

In Medical/Health prefer:
Medical Products
Health Services

In Consumer Related prefer:
Food/Beverage

In Industrial/Energy prefer:
Industrial Products

In Business Serv. prefer:
Services

In Manufact. prefer:
Manufacturing

Additional Information

Year Founded: 1994
Current Activity Level: Actively seeking new investments

KEYSTONE NATIONAL GROUP LLC

5000 Executive Parkway
Suite 445
San Ramon, CA USA 94583
Phone: 9254073120
Fax: 9254073125
E-mail: info@keystonenational.net
Website: keystonenational.net

Management and Staff

Brad Allen, Chief Financial Officer
Raymond Chan, Principal
Scott Gunter, Vice President

Type of Firm

Private Equity Advisor or Fund of Funds

Project Preferences

Type of Financing Preferred:
Fund of Funds
Leveraged Buyout

Industry Preferences

In Industrial/Energy prefer:
Energy

In Financial Services prefer:
Real Estate

Additional Information

Name of Most Recent Fund: Keystone Private Market Opportunities VI, L.P.
Most Recent Fund Was Raised: 11/19/2013
Year Founded: 2006
Capital Under Management: $250,828,000
Current Activity Level: Actively seeking new investments

KEYTONE VENTURES

No 8. Jianguomenwai Street
Room 1001 Huarun Building
Beijing, China 100005
Phone: 861085192582
Fax: 861085192584

Management and Staff

Jin Yi, Vice President
Xi Jin, Partner
Ye Tao, Vice President
Zhixiong Zhou, Founder

Type of Firm

Private Equity Firm

Project Preferences

Type of Financing Preferred:
Early Stage
Expansion
Balanced
Later Stage
Seed

Geographical Preferences

International Preferences:
China

Industry Preferences

In Consumer Related prefer:
Consumer

In Industrial/Energy prefer:
Energy
Environmental Related

In Business Serv. prefer:
Media

In Other prefer:
Environment Responsible

Additional Information
Year Founded: 2008
Capital Under Management: $20,000,000
Current Activity Level : Actively seeking new investments

KFH CAPITAL INVESTMENT CO KSCC

Safat Square Street
Baitek Tower, 32-33 Floor
Kuwait, Kuwait 13040
Phone: 96522987000
Fax: 96522491151
E-mail: info@mic.com.kw
Website: www.kfhcapital.com.kw

Type of Firm
Private Equity Firm

Project Preferences

Type of Financing Preferred:
Leveraged Buyout
Early Stage
Generalist PE

Industry Preferences

In Financial Services prefer:
Real Estate
Investment Groups

Additional Information
Year Founded: 1999
Current Activity Level : Actively seeking new investments

KFW

Palmengartenstrasse 5-9
Frankfurt am Main, Germany 60325
Phone: 496974310
Fax: 496974312944
E-mail: info@kfw.de
Website: www.kfw.de

Other Offices
Square de Meeus 37
Brussels, Belgium 1000
Phone: 32-2-233-3850
Fax: 32-2-233-3859

Charlottenstrasse 33/33a
Berlin, Germany 10117
Phone: 49-30-202-640
Fax: 49-30-202-645-188

Ludwig-Erhard-Platz 1-3
Bonn, Germany 53179
Phone: 49-228-8310
Fax: 49-228-319-500

Management and Staff
Guenther Braeunig, Chief Executive Officer

Type of Firm
Bank Affiliated

Association Membership
Brazilian Venture Capital Association (ABCR)
German Venture Capital Association (BVK)

Project Preferences

Type of Financing Preferred:
Early Stage
Turnaround
Later Stage
Seed
Startup
Recapitalizations

Geographical Preferences

International Preferences:
Germany

Industry Preferences

In Computer Software prefer:
Software
Systems Software
Applications Software

In Semiconductor/Electr prefer:
Semiconductor

In Biotechnology prefer:
Biotechnology

In Medical/Health prefer:
Medical/Health
Medical Diagnostics
Medical Therapeutics
Medical Products
Pharmaceuticals

In Industrial/Energy prefer:
Alternative Energy
Environmental Related

In Business Serv. prefer:
Services

Additional Information
Year Founded: 1948
Capital Under Management: $971,300,000
Current Activity Level : Actively seeking new investments

KGAL INVESTMENT MANAGEMENT & GMBH CO KG

Toelzer Strasse 15
Gruenwald, Germany 82031
Phone: 4989641430
Fax: 498964143150
E-mail: kgal@kgal.de
Website: www.kgal-investment-management.com

Type of Firm
Investment Management Firm

Industry Preferences

In Transportation prefer:
Aerospace

In Financial Services prefer:
Real Estate

Additional Information
Year Founded: 2016
Current Activity Level : Actively seeking new investments

KHARIS CAPITAL ADVISORY AG

ALPENSTRASSE 15
Zug, Switzerland 6300
Phone: 41417101537
Website: www.kharicapital.com

Type of Firm
Private Equity Firm

Project Preferences

Type of Financing Preferred:
Leveraged Buyout
Early Stage
Expansion
Later Stage
Management Buyouts
Acquisition

Geographical Preferences

United States Preferences:

International Preferences:
Europe

Additional Information
Year Founded: 2014
Current Activity Level : Actively seeking new investments

KHATIF HOLDING COMPANY KSC

Aljawhara Tower
18th Floor
Safat, Kuwait 13023
Phone: 96522954444
Fax: 96522954445
E-mail: info@khatif.com
Website: www.khatif.com

Management and Staff

Fatma Al-Bader, Managing Director
Osama Mohammed, Chief Executive Officer

Type of Firm

Private Equity Firm

Project Preferences

Type of Financing Preferred:
Leveraged Buyout
Early Stage
Generalist PE
Balanced
Later Stage
Seed

Acquisition
Startup

Geographical Preferences

International Preferences:
Middle East

Industry Preferences

In Financial Services prefer:
Real Estate

Additional Information

Year Founded: 2008
Current Activity Level : Actively seeking new investments

KHAZAEN VENTURE CAPITAL

Fahad Al Salem Street Awqaf
Building Fourth Floor
Kuwait City, Kuwait
Phone: 96522457420
Fax: 96522457430
E-mail: info@khazaen.com
Website: www.khazaen.com

Management and Staff

Mansour Al-Khuzam, Chief Executive Officer

Type of Firm

Private Equity Firm

Project Preferences

Type of Financing Preferred:
Early Stage
Balanced
Later Stage
Seed
Startup

Geographical Preferences

International Preferences:
Middle East
Asia
Kuwait

Industry Preferences

In Financial Services prefer:
Financial Services

Additional Information

Year Founded: 2002
Current Activity Level : Actively seeking new investments

KHAZANAH NASIONAL BHD

33th Floor, Tower 2
Petronas Twin Towers
Kuala Lumpur, Malaysia 50088
Phone: 6032034000
Fax: 60320340300
E-mail: info@khazanah.com.my
Website: www.khazanah.com.my

Other Offices

Level 14, Bangunan KWSP
No. 38 Jalan Sultan Ahmad Shah
George Town, Malaysia 10050
Phone: 60-04-2226800
Fax: 60-04-2226801

Unit 2-3, 26th Floor, Tower 2
China Central Place, No. 79 Jianguo Rd.
Beijing, China 10025
Phone: 86-10-59127300
Fax: 86-10-59127301

Management and Staff

Azman Bin Hj Mokhtar, Managing Director
Izani Ghani, Chief Financial Officer
Mohammad Zainal Shaari, Chief Operating Officer

Type of Firm

Government Affiliated Program

Project Preferences

Type of Financing Preferred:
Leveraged Buyout
Early Stage
Generalist PE
Balanced
Later Stage
Management Buyouts
Acquisition

Geographical Preferences

International Preferences:
Turkey
Asia
Malaysia

Industry Preferences

In Communications prefer:
Telecommunications

In Biotechnology prefer:
Agricultural/Animal Bio.

In Medical/Health prefer:
Medical/Health

In Industrial/Energy prefer:
Materials

In Transportation prefer:
Transportation

In Financial Services prefer:
Financial Services

Additional Information

Year Founded: 1993
Current Activity Level : Actively seeking new investments

KHK INTERROS ZAO

9 Bolshaya Yakimanka
Moscow, Russia 119049
Phone: 74957856363
Fax: 74957856364
E-mail: info@interros.ru
Website: www.interros.ru

Management and Staff

Andrei Bougrov, Managing Director
Sergey Barbashev, Chief Executive Officer
Sergey Batekhin, Vice President
Vladimir Potanin, President

Type of Firm

Investment Management Firm

Project Preferences

Type of Financing Preferred:
Generalist PE

Geographical Preferences

International Preferences:
Europe
Russia

Industry Preferences

In Industrial/Energy prefer:
Oil and Gas Exploration
Machinery

In Transportation prefer:
Transportation

In Financial Services prefer:
Financial Services
Real Estate
Financial Services

In Agr/Forestr/Fish prefer:
Mining and Minerals

Additional Information
Year Founded: 1990
Current Activity Level : Actively seeking new investments

KHOSLA VENTURES LLC

2128 Sand Hill Road
Menlo Park, CA USA 94025
Phone: 6503768500
Fax: 6509269590
E-mail: kv@khoslaventures.com
Website: www.khoslaventures.com

Management and Staff
Andrew Chung, Partner
Benjamin Ling, Partner
David Weiden, Partner
Pierre Lamond, General Partner
Samir Kaul, General Partner
Shirish Sathaye, General Partner
Vinod Khosla, Founder

Type of Firm
Private Equity Firm

Association Membership
Western Association of Venture Capitalists (WAVC)

Project Preferences

Type of Financing Preferred:
Early Stage
Balanced
Later Stage
Seed

Geographical Preferences

United States Preferences:
All U.S.

International Preferences:
Asia
All International

Industry Preferences

In Communications prefer:
Telecommunications
Wireless Communications

In Internet Specific prefer:
Internet

In Computer Other prefer:
Computer Related

In Semiconductor/Electr prefer:
Semiconductor

In Medical/Health prefer:
Medical/Health

In Consumer Related prefer:
Education Related

In Industrial/Energy prefer:
Energy
Alternative Energy
Environmental Related

In Business Serv. prefer:
Services
Media

In Agr/Forestr/Fish prefer:
Agriculture related

In Utilities prefer:
Utilities

Additional Information
Year Founded: 2004
Capital Under Management: $1,070,000,000
Current Activity Level : Actively seeking new investments

KHULA ENTERPRISE

The DTI Grp Campus, 1st Flr, G
77 Meintjie Street
Sunnyside, South Africa 0132
Phone: 27-12-394-5560
Fax: 27-12-394-6560
E-mail: helpline@khula.org.za
Website: www.khula.org.za

Type of Firm
Investment Management Firm

Project Preferences

Type of Financing Preferred:
Early Stage
Expansion

Geographical Preferences

International Preferences:
Africa

Additional Information
Year Founded: 2000
Current Activity Level : Actively seeking new investments

KI CAPITAL LTD

7 Harp Lane
London, United Kingdom EC3R 6DP
Phone: 442034881865
E-mail: in@ki.uk

Management and Staff
David Merry, Co-Founder
Michael Charalambous, Co-Founder

Type of Firm
Private Equity Firm

Project Preferences

Type of Financing Preferred:
Balanced

Industry Preferences

In Internet Specific prefer:
Internet

Additional Information
Year Founded: 1969
Current Activity Level : Actively seeking new investments

KIAN CAPITAL PARTNERS LLC

4201 Congress Street
The Rotunda, Suite 440
Charlotte, NC USA 28209
Phone: 7049432503
Fax: 7049434457

Other Offices

4201 Congress Street
Rotunda, Suite 440
CHARLOTTE, NC USA 28210
Phone: 7045265353

2970 Peachtree Road NW
Buckhead Centre, Suite 530
ATLANTA, GA USA 30305
Phone: 4047481755

Management and Staff
Caldwell Zimmerman, Vice President
Charlie Edmondson, Chief Financial Officer
Kevin McCarthy, Co-Founder
Kyle Taura, Vice President
Matt Levenson, Partner
Rick Cravey, Co-Founder
Scott Buschmann, Partner

Type of Firm
Private Equity Firm

Association Membership
Natl Assoc of Small Bus. Inv. Co (NASBIC)

Project Preferences

Type of Financing Preferred:
Mezzanine

Geographical Preferences

United States Preferences:
Southeast

Industry Preferences

In Medical/Health prefer:
Health Services

In Business Serv. prefer:
Services
Distribution

In Manufact. prefer:
Manufacturing

Additional Information

Name of Most Recent Fund: Kian Mezzanine Partners I, L.P.
Most Recent Fund Was Raised: 07/12/2011
Year Founded: 2013
Capital Under Management: $150,000,000
Current Activity Level : Actively seeking new investments

KIBO CAPITAL PARTNERS LTD

5th floor, Ebene Skies,
Rue de l'Institut
Ebene, Mauritius
Phone: 2304042200
Fax: 2304042201
E-mail: contact@kibo-capital.com
Website: www.kibo-capital.com

Type of Firm
Private Equity Firm

Association Membership
African Venture Capital Association (AVCA)

Project Preferences

Type of Financing Preferred:
Generalist PE

Geographical Preferences

International Preferences:
Africa

Industry Preferences

In Medical/Health prefer:
Health Services

In Consumer Related prefer:
Consumer
Education Related

In Financial Services prefer:
Financial Services

Additional Information
Year Founded: 2007
Capital Under Management: $100,000,000
Current Activity Level : Actively seeking new investments

KIBO VENTURES SL

Calle Zurbano 34
Madrid, Spain 28010
Phone: 34914517070
E-mail: info@kiboventures.com
Website: www.kiboventures.com

Type of Firm
Private Equity Firm

Project Preferences

Type of Financing Preferred:
Early Stage
Startup

Size of Investments Considered:
Min Size of Investment Considered (000s): $526
Max Size of Investment Considered (000s): $1,051

Geographical Preferences

International Preferences:
Latin America
Spain

Industry Preferences

In Communications prefer:
Wireless Communications

In Internet Specific prefer:
Internet

In Semiconductor/Electr prefer:
Electronics

Additional Information
Year Founded: 2011
Capital Under Management: $138,204,000
Current Activity Level : Actively seeking new investments

KICHI INVEST AB

Hoekens Gata 8
Stockholm, Sweden 116 46
Website: kichiinvest.se

Type of Firm
Private Equity Firm

Project Preferences

Type of Financing Preferred:
Balanced

Geographical Preferences

International Preferences:
Scandanavia/Nordic Region

Additional Information
Year Founded: 2017
Current Activity Level : Actively seeking new investments

KICKSTART SEED FUND LP

2795 East Cottonwoon Parkway
Suite 350
Salt Lake City, UT USA 84121
Phone: 8013080440
Fax: 8019421636
E-mail: hello@kickstartfund.com
Website: kickstartseedfund.com

Management and Staff
Alex Soffe, Chief Financial Officer
Clarke Miyasaki, General Partner
Curt Roberts, Venture Partner
Dalton Wright, Partner
Gavin Christensen, Founder

Type of Firm
Private Equity Firm

Project Preferences

Type of Financing Preferred:
Seed
Startup

Geographical Preferences

United States Preferences:

Industry Preferences

In Computer Software prefer:
Software

In Industrial/Energy prefer:
Environmental Related

Additional Information
Name of Most Recent Fund: Kickstart Seed Fund II, L.P.
Most Recent Fund Was Raised: 04/23/2013
Year Founded: 2008
Capital Under Management: $138,590,000
Current Activity Level : Actively seeking new investments

KICKSTART VENLO BV

Noorderpoort 45
Venlo, Netherlands 5916 PJ
Phone: 31630442458
Website: www.kickstartvenlo.nl

Type of Firm
Bank Affiliated

Project Preferences

Type of Financing Preferred:
Early Stage
Seed

Geographical Preferences

International Preferences:
Netherlands

Additional Information

Year Founded: 2011
Current Activity Level : Actively seeking new investments

KICKSTART VENTURES INC

Globe Telecom Plaza Tower I
Pioneer corner Madison Streets
Mandaluyong, Philippines 1552
Phone: 63 2 625 8723
Fax: 63 2 625 8718
E-mail: info@kickstart.ph
Website: www.kickstart.ph

Other Offices

55 Paseo de Roxas Avenue
Makati City, Philippines 1225

Management and Staff

Minette Navarrete, President

Type of Firm

Corporate PE/Venture

Project Preferences

Type of Financing Preferred:
Seed
Startup

Geographical Preferences

International Preferences:
Philippines

Industry Preferences

In Communications prefer:
Wireless Communications
Media and Entertainment

In Computer Hardware prefer:
Computers

In Computer Software prefer:
Software
Applications Software

In Internet Specific prefer:
Ecommerce

In Computer Other prefer:
Computer Related

In Consumer Related prefer:
Education Related

Additional Information

Year Founded: 2013
Capital Under Management: $2,400,000
Current Activity Level : Actively seeking new investments

KIDD & COMPANY LLC

1455 East Putnam Avenue
Old Greenwich, CT USA 06870
Phone: 2036610070
Fax: 2036611839
E-mail: info@kiddcompany.com

Management and Staff

Anthony Castor, Managing Director
Donald Hardie, Partner
Gerard DeBiasi, Partner
James Benedict, Principal
Kenneth Heuer, Principal
William Kidd, Partner

Type of Firm

Private Equity Firm

Association Membership

Natl Assoc of Small Bus. Inv. Co (NASBIC)

Project Preferences

Role in Financing:
Prefer role as deal originator but will also invest in deals created by others

Type of Financing Preferred:
Second Stage Financing
Leveraged Buyout
Mezzanine
First Stage Financing

Geographical Preferences

United States Preferences:
All U.S.

Additional Information

Year Founded: 1982
Capital Under Management: $60,000,000
Current Activity Level : Actively seeking new investments

KIDDAR CAPITAL

100 N Washington St
Suite 224
Falls Church, VA USA 22046
Phone: 7035320198
E-mail: info@kiddar.com
Website: kiddar.com

Type of Firm

Private Equity Firm

Geographical Preferences

International Preferences:
Rest of World

Industry Preferences

In Financial Services prefer:
Real Estate

Additional Information

Year Founded: 2007
Current Activity Level : Actively seeking new investments

KILMER CAPITAL PARTNERS LTD

King Street West Box 127
Suite 2700, Scotia Plaza
Toronto, Canada M5H 3Y2
Phone: 4166356100
Fax: 4166357697
E-mail: info@kilmercapital.com
Website: www.kilmercapital.com

Other Offices

1002 Sherbrooke Street West
Suite 2240
Montreal, Canada H3A1G3

Management and Staff

Anthony Sigel, President
Arnie Gross, Managing Partner
Doug Peel, Managing Partner
Jason Berenstein, Principal
Marie-Claude Boisvert, Principal
William Blackburn, Principal

Type of Firm

Private Equity Firm

Association Membership

Canadian Venture Capital Association

Project Preferences

Role in Financing:
Prefer role as deal originator but will also invest in deals created by others

Type of Financing Preferred:
Leveraged Buyout
Management Buyouts
Acquisition
Recapitalizations

Size of Investments Considered:
Min Size of Investment Considered (000s): $10,000
Max Size of Investment Considered (000s): $50,000

Geographical Preferences

Canadian Preferences:
All Canada

Additional Information
Year Founded: 2001
Capital Under Management: $95,800,000
Current Activity Level : Actively seeking new investments
Method of Compensation: Return on invest. most important, but chg. closing fees, service fees, etc.

KINDERHOOK INDUSTRIES LLC
521 Fifth Avenue
34th Floor
New York, NY USA 10175
Phone: 2122016780
Fax: 2122016790
Website: www.kinderhook.com

Management and Staff
Christian Michalik, Managing Director
Corwynne Carruthers, Managing Director
Lisa Schmidt, Chief Financial Officer
Lisa Clarke, Chief Financial Officer
Louis Aurelio, Principal
Michael Zoch, Vice President
Paul Cifelli, Managing Director
Robert Michalik, Managing Director
Sam Keenan, Vice President
Thomas Tuttle, Managing Director

Type of Firm
Private Equity Firm

Project Preferences

Type of Financing Preferred:
Leveraged Buyout
Management Buyouts
Acquisition

Additional Information
Year Founded: 2003
Capital Under Management: $1,270,000,000
Current Activity Level : Actively seeking new investments

KINDRED CAPITAL
144A Clerkenwell Road
Ground Floor White Bear Yard
London, United Kingdom EC1R 5DF
Website: www.kindredcapital.vc

Management and Staff
Russell Buckley, Partner

Type of Firm
Private Equity Firm

Project Preferences

Type of Financing Preferred:
Early Stage
Seed

Geographical Preferences

United States Preferences:

International Preferences:
United Kingdom

Additional Information
Year Founded: 2015
Current Activity Level : Actively seeking new investments

KINEA INVESTIMENTOS LTDA
Av. Pres Juscelino Kubitschek
1700 - 4th floor, Itaim
Sao Paulo, Brazil 04543
Phone: 551130738785
E-mail: kinea@kinea.com.br
Website: www.kinea.com.br

Management and Staff
Aymar Almeida, Co-Founder
Carlos Martins, Co-Founder
Cristiano Gioia Lauretti, Partner
Eduardo Marrachine, Partner
Marcio Verri, Co-Founder
Sergio Gabriele, Co-Founder

Type of Firm
Private Equity Firm

Association Membership
Brazilian Venture Capital Association (ABCR)

Project Preferences

Type of Financing Preferred:
Leveraged Buyout
Early Stage
Generalist PE
Balanced
Public Companies
Later Stage
Acquisition

Geographical Preferences

International Preferences:
Brazil

Industry Preferences

In Financial Services prefer:
Financial Services

Additional Information
Year Founded: 2010
Current Activity Level : Actively seeking new investments

KINETIC CAPITAL PARTNERS
1195 West Broadway
Suite 500
Vancouver, Canada V6H 3X5
Phone: 6046922530
Fax: 6046922531
Website: www.kineticcapitalpartners.com

Management and Staff
Dallas Ross, Founder
Frank Barker, Founder

Type of Firm
Private Equity Firm

Project Preferences

Type of Financing Preferred:
Early Stage
Balanced
Later Stage
Startup

Geographical Preferences

United States Preferences:

Canadian Preferences:
All Canada

Industry Preferences

In Communications prefer:
Wireless Communications

In Medical/Health prefer:
Health Services

In Consumer Related prefer:
Consumer Products

In Industrial/Energy prefer:
Industrial Products

Additional Information
Year Founded: 2001
Current Activity Level : Actively seeking new investments

KINETIC VENTURES LLC
Two Wisconsin Circle
Suite 620
Chevy Chase, MD USA 20815
Phone: 3016528066
Fax: 3016528310
E-mail: kinetic@kineticventures.com
Website: www.kineticventures.com

Other Offices
75 Fifth Street, Northwest, Suite 316
Atlanta, GA USA 30308
Phone: 404-995-8811
Fax: 404-995-4455

Management and Staff
Bernard Tarr, Managing Director
Nelson Chu, Managing Director
Sydney Shepherd, Chief Financial Officer
William Heflin, Managing Director

Type of Firm
Private Equity Firm

Association Membership
Mid-Atlantic Venture Association
National Venture Capital Association - USA (NVCA)

Project Preferences

Role in Financing:
Will function either as deal originator or investor in deals created by others

Type of Financing Preferred:
Early Stage
Expansion
Balanced
Seed

Size of Investments Considered:
Min Size of Investment Considered (000s): $2,000
Max Size of Investment Considered (000s): $7,000

Geographical Preferences

United States Preferences:
North America

Canadian Preferences:
All Canada

Industry Focus
(% based on actual investment)

Internet Specific	30.8%
Communications and Media	27.6%
Semiconductors/Other Elect.	15.9%
Computer Software and Services	14.0%
Computer Hardware	6.7%
Other Products	3.6%
Industrial/Energy	1.2%
Medical/Health	0.3%

Additional Information
Name of Most Recent Fund: Kinetic Ventures VIII, L.P.
Most Recent Fund Was Raised: 03/13/2009
Year Founded: 1984
Capital Under Management: $119,000,000
Current Activity Level : Actively seeking new investments
Method of Compensation: Return on investment is of primary concern, do not charge fees

KINETIK UK LTD
22 Arlington Street
Second Floor
London, United Kingdom SW1A 1RD
Website: www.kinetik.vc

Type of Firm
Private Equity Firm

Project Preferences

Type of Financing Preferred:
Seed
Startup

Industry Preferences

In Internet Specific prefer:
Internet

In Medical/Health prefer:
Medical/Health

In Industrial/Energy prefer:
Alternative Energy

In Transportation prefer:
Transportation

Additional Information
Year Founded: 2015
Current Activity Level : Actively seeking new investments

KING ABDULLAH UNIVERSITY OF SCIENCE AND TECHNOLOGY
Thuwal 23955-6900
Jeddah, Saudi Arabia 4700
Phone: 966128083428
Fax: 966128021027
Website: www.kaust.edu.sa

Type of Firm
University Program

Project Preferences

Type of Financing Preferred:
Early Stage
Start-up Financing
Seed

Industry Preferences

In Biotechnology prefer:
Biotechnology

In Industrial/Energy prefer:
Energy

Additional Information
Year Founded: 2009
Current Activity Level : Actively seeking new investments

KINGDOM HOLDING CO
P.O. Box One
Riyadh, Saudi Arabia 11321
Phone: 96612111111
Fax: 96612111112
E-mail: media&info@kingdom.com.sa
Website: www.kingdom.com.sa

Management and Staff
Mohamed Solaiman, Chief Financial Officer
Talal Al Maiman, Chief Executive Officer

Type of Firm
Investment Management Firm

Project Preferences

Type of Financing Preferred:
Value-Add
Early Stage
Expansion
Generalist PE
Balanced
Later Stage
Acquisition

Geographical Preferences

International Preferences:
Middle East
Saudi Arabia
Kuwait
All International

Industry Preferences

In Communications prefer:
Telecommunications
Wireless Communications
Media and Entertainment

In Medical/Health prefer:
Health Services

In Consumer Related prefer:
Consumer
Entertainment and Leisure
Food/Beverage
Other Restaurants
Hotels and Resorts

In Industrial/Energy prefer:
Industrial Products
Factory Automation

In Financial Services prefer:
Financial Services
Real Estate

In Business Serv. prefer:
Media

Additional Information
Year Founded: 1996
Current Activity Level : Actively seeking new investments

KINGFISH GROUP INC
950 Tower Lane
Suite 1050
Foster City, CA USA 94404
Phone: 6509800200

E-mail: mail@kingfishgroup.com
Website: www.kingfishgroup.com

Management and Staff
Christian Dubiel, Co-Founder
Jonathan Goldenstein, Co-Founder

Type of Firm
Private Equity Firm

Project Preferences

Type of Financing Preferred:
Leveraged Buyout

Additional Information
Year Founded: 2004
Current Activity Level : Actively seeking new investments

KINGS PARK CAPITAL LLP

35-36 Great Marlborough Street
First Floor
London, United Kingdom W1F 7JF
Phone: 442030043420
Fax: 442030043421
E-mail: contact@kingsparkcapital.com
Website: www.kpcapital.com

Management and Staff
Hugo Robinson, Co-Founder
Jason Katz, Co-Founder

Type of Firm
Private Equity Firm

Association Membership
British Venture Capital Association (BVCA)

Project Preferences

Type of Financing Preferred:
Leveraged Buyout
Acquisition

Geographical Preferences

International Preferences:
Europe

Industry Preferences

In Consumer Related prefer:
Entertainment and Leisure
Other Restaurants
Hotels and Resorts

Additional Information
Year Founded: 2007
Current Activity Level : Actively seeking new investments

KINGSBRIDGE CAPITAL PTE LTD

5 Shenton Way
09-07, UIC Building
Singapore, Singapore 068808
Phone: 65-6319-4999
Fax: 65-6226-5206
E-mail: enquiries@westcombfinancial.com
Website: www.infinitifunds.com

Management and Staff
Aw Soon Beng, Chief Executive Officer

Type of Firm
Bank Affiliated

Association Membership
Singapore Venture Capital Association (SVCA)

Project Preferences

Type of Financing Preferred:
Leveraged Buyout
Expansion

Additional Information
Year Founded: 2004
Current Activity Level : Actively seeking new investments

KINGSLEY CAPITAL PARTNERS LLP

Maddox House
1 Maddox Street
London, United Kingdom W1S 2PZ
E-mail: info@kingsleyllp.com
Website: kingsleyllp.com

Type of Firm
Private Equity Firm

Project Preferences

Type of Financing Preferred:
Leveraged Buyout
Acquisition

Geographical Preferences

International Preferences:
Europe

Industry Preferences

In Medical/Health prefer:
Health Services

In Consumer Related prefer:
Consumer
Retail

In Industrial/Energy prefer:
Industrial Products

Additional Information
Year Founded: 2016
Current Activity Level : Actively seeking new investments

KINGSMAN CAPITAL LLC

1144 West Randolph Street
Chicago, IL USA 60607
Phone: 312-320-9575
Website: www.kingsmancapital.com

Management and Staff
Keith Koeneman, Managing Partner

Type of Firm
Private Equity Firm

Project Preferences

Type of Financing Preferred:
Leveraged Buyout
Expansion
Acquisition
Industry Rollups
Recapitalizations

Geographical Preferences

United States Preferences:

Canadian Preferences:
All Canada

Industry Preferences

In Medical/Health prefer:
Health Services

In Consumer Related prefer:
Consumer Products
Consumer Services

In Industrial/Energy prefer:
Industrial Products

In Business Serv. prefer:
Services
Distribution

In Manufact. prefer:
Manufacturing

Additional Information
Year Founded: 2008
Current Activity Level : Actively seeking new investments

KINGSWAY CAPITAL LLP

24 Upper Brook Street
London, United Kingdom W1K 7QB
Phone: 442076594130
Fax: 442076594222
E-mail: info@kingswaycap.com
Website: www.kingswaycap.com

Other Offices
24 Upper Brook Street
London, United Kingdom W1K 7QB
Phone: 442076594130
Fax: 442076594222

Type of Firm
Private Equity Firm

Additional Information
Year Founded: 2013
Current Activity Level : Actively seeking new investments

KINGSWAY CAPITAL OF CANADA INC

Eight King Street East
Suite 1400
Toronto, Canada M5C1B5
Phone: 416-861-3099
Fax: 416-861-9027
E-mail: info@kingswaygroup.ca
Website: www.kingswaygroup.ca

Management and Staff
David Charnock, Vice President

Type of Firm
Corporate PE/Venture

Project Preferences

Type of Financing Preferred:
Later Stage

Additional Information
Year Founded: 2001
Current Activity Level : Actively seeking new investments

KINGSWOOD CAPITAL MANAGEMENT

11999 San Vicente Blvd
Suite 350
Los Angeles, CA USA 90049
Website: kingswood-capital.com

Type of Firm
Private Equity Firm

Project Preferences

Type of Financing Preferred:
Leveraged Buyout
Acquisition

Size of Investments Considered:
Min Size of Investment Considered (000s): $10,555
Max Size of Investment Considered (000s): $70,363

Geographical Preferences

United States Preferences:
North America

Industry Preferences

In Consumer Related prefer:
Consumer
Retail

In Industrial/Energy prefer:
Energy

Additional Information
Year Founded: 2013
Current Activity Level : Actively seeking new investments

KINLED HOLDINGS LTD

Room 902 Wilson House
19-27 Wyndham Street
Central, Hong Kong
Website: kinled.com

Type of Firm
Investment Management Firm

Project Preferences

Type of Financing Preferred:
Early Stage

Additional Information
Year Founded: 1980
Current Activity Level : Actively seeking new investments

KINNEVIK AB

P.O. Box 2094
Stockholm, Sweden SE-103 13
Phone: 46856200000
Fax: 468203774
E-mail: info@kinnevik.se
Website: www.kinnevik.com

Management and Staff
Georgi Ganev, Chief Executive Officer
Joakim Andersson, Chief Financial Officer

Type of Firm
Investment Management Firm

Project Preferences

Type of Financing Preferred:
Balanced

Industry Preferences

In Communications prefer:
Communications and Media
Entertainment

In Internet Specific prefer:
E-Commerce Technology
Ecommerce

In Financial Services prefer:
Financial Services

Additional Information
Year Founded: 1936
Current Activity Level : Actively seeking new investments

KINROT TECHNOLOGY VENTURES

Zemach
Jordan Valley, Israel 15132
Phone: 972-74-713-6666
Fax: 972-74-670-9014
E-mail: kinrot@kinrot.com
Website: www.kinrot.com

Management and Staff
Assaf Barnea, Chief Executive Officer
Micha Oberman, Chief Financial Officer

Type of Firm
Private Equity Firm

Project Preferences

Type of Financing Preferred:
Seed

Geographical Preferences

International Preferences:
Israel

Industry Preferences

In Biotechnology prefer:
Industrial Biotechnology

In Industrial/Energy prefer:
Environmental Related

In Utilities prefer:
Utilities

Additional Information
Year Founded: 1993
Current Activity Level : Actively seeking new investments

KINZIE CAPITAL PARTNERS LLC

20 North Clark Street
36th Floor
Chicago, IL USA 60602
Phone: 3128092490
Website: www.kinziecp.com

Management and Staff
David Namkung, Partner
Rodney Zech, Partner

Type of Firm
Private Equity Firm

Project Preferences

Type of Financing Preferred:
Generalist PE

Additional Information
Year Founded: 2017
Current Activity Level : Actively seeking new investments

KINZON CAPITAL

Silicon Valley
San Francisco, CA USA 94150

Type of Firm
Private Equity Firm

Project Preferences

Type of Financing Preferred:
Seed
Startup

Geographical Preferences

United States Preferences:

Industry Preferences

In Communications prefer:
Telecommunications
Entertainment

In Medical/Health prefer:
Medical/Health

In Business Serv. prefer:
Services

Additional Information
Year Founded: 2014
Capital Under Management: $100,000,000
Current Activity Level : Actively seeking new investments

KIRCHNER PRIVATE CAPITAL GROUP

36 Toronto Street
Suite 850
Toronto, Canada M5C 2C5
Phone: 416-861-9807
Fax: 954-252-2522
E-mail: info@kcpg.net
Website: www.kcpg.net

Other Offices

2618 Hopewell Place North East
Suite 340
Calgary, Canada T1Y 7J7
Phone: 403-215-5491

1155, boulevard Rene-Levesque Ouest
suite 2500
Montreal, Canada H3B 2K4
Phone: 514-868-1079

Management and Staff
Andy Agrawal, Managing Partner
Les Lyall, Managing Partner

Type of Firm
Private Equity Advisor or Fund of Funds

Association Membership
Canadian Venture Capital Association

Additional Information
Year Founded: 2009
Current Activity Level : Actively seeking new investments

KIRK & THORSEN INVEST A/S

Roms Hule 4
5th Floor
Vejle, Denmark 7100
Phone: 4572225050
E-mail: info@kirkthorsen.dk
Website: www.kirkthorsen.dk

Management and Staff
Casper Kirk Johansen, Partner
Jens Iversen, Chief Financial Officer
Peter Thorsen, Chief Executive Officer

Type of Firm
Private Equity Firm

Project Preferences

Type of Financing Preferred:
Mezzanine

Geographical Preferences

International Preferences:
Denmark

Additional Information
Year Founded: 1998
Current Activity Level : Actively seeking new investments

KISTEFOS VENTURE CAPITAL AS

Stranden 1 A
Oslo, Norway 0250
Phone: 4723117000
Fax: 4723117002
E-mail: info@kistefos.no
Website: www.kistefos.no

Management and Staff
Hege Galtung, Managing Director
Henning Jensen, Managing Director
Olav Haugland, Chief Financial Officer
Rolf Skaarberg, Managing Director

Type of Firm
Bank Affiliated

Project Preferences

Role in Financing:
Prefer role as deal originator

Type of Financing Preferred:
Leveraged Buyout
Generalist PE
Balanced
Later Stage
Acquisition

Size of Investments Considered:
Min Size of Investment Considered (000s): $835
Max Size of Investment Considered (000s): $8,353

Geographical Preferences

International Preferences:
Scandanavia/Nordic Region
Norway

Industry Preferences

In Communications prefer:
Telecommunications
Wireless Communications

In Computer Software prefer:
Software

In Industrial/Energy prefer:
Energy Conservation Relat

In Financial Services prefer:
Financial Services

Additional Information
Year Founded: 1997
Capital Under Management: $80,300,000
Current Activity Level : Actively seeking new investments

KITARA CAPITAL

PO Box 1273
Muscat, Oman 114
Phone: 96822004500
Fax: 96822004546
Website: www.kitaracapital.com

Type of Firm
Private Equity Firm

Association Membership
Indian Venture Capital Association (IVCA)

Project Preferences

Type of Financing Preferred:
Early Stage
Balanced
Seed

Size of Investments Considered:
Min Size of Investment Considered (000s): $10,000
Max Size of Investment Considered (000s): $15,000

Geographical Preferences

International Preferences:
India
Oman
Utd. Arab Em.

Industry Preferences

In Industrial/Energy prefer:
Oil and Gas Exploration
Oil & Gas Drilling,Explor
Factory Automation

In Transportation prefer:
Transportation

Additional Information
Year Founded: 2008
Current Activity Level : Actively seeking new investments

KIWI GROWTH PARTNERS LTD

57 Killarney Road
Hamilton, New Zealand
Phone: 647-848-2574
Fax: 647-848-2576
Website: www.kiwigrowthpartners.com

Management and Staff
Alvin Donovan, Founder

Type of Firm
Investment Management Firm

Project Preferences

Type of Financing Preferred:
Balanced

Geographical Preferences

International Preferences:
New Zealand
Asia

Additional Information
Year Founded: 2006
Current Activity Level : Actively seeking new investments

KIWI SPACE

Changyanggu, Yangpu District
6208-6209, Building 6
Shanghai, China
Phone: 862155833320
Website: www.kiwi1st.com

Type of Firm
Incubator/Development Program

Project Preferences

Type of Financing Preferred:
Seed
Startup

Geographical Preferences

International Preferences:
China

Industry Preferences

In Medical/Health prefer:
Medical/Health

Additional Information
Year Founded: 2015
Current Activity Level : Actively seeking new investments

KIWI VENTURE PARTNERS LLC

505 Fifth Avenue
15th Floor
New York, NY USA 10017
Phone: 6465686517
Website: www.kiwiventurepartners.com

Other Offices
3030 K Street Northwest
WASHINGTON, DC USA 20007

Management and Staff
Neal Gupta, Managing Partner
Rakesh Gupta, Managing Partner
Todd Breeden, Principal

Type of Firm
Private Equity Firm

Project Preferences

Type of Financing Preferred:
Seed
Startup

Industry Preferences

In Computer Software prefer:
Software
Applications Software

Additional Information
Year Founded: 2014
Capital Under Management: $2,500,000
Current Activity Level : Actively seeking new investments

KIWOOM INVESTMENT CO LTD

36-1, Yeouido-dong
15F Kiwoom Finance Square Bldg
Seoul, South Korea 150886
Phone: 82234304800
Fax: 82234529493
E-mail: invest@kiwoominvest.com

Management and Staff
Jong Yeon Yoon, Chief Executive Officer

Type of Firm
Corporate PE/Venture

Association Membership
Korean Venture Capital Association (KVCA)

Project Preferences

Type of Financing Preferred:
Early Stage
Expansion
Balanced
Later Stage
Startup

Geographical Preferences

International Preferences:
Korea, South

Industry Preferences

In Industrial/Energy prefer:
Environmental Related

Additional Information
Year Founded: 1999
Capital Under Management: $93,600,000
Current Activity Level : Actively seeking new investments

KIZOO TECHNOLOGY CAPITAL GMBH

Amalienbadstrasse 41
Karlsruhe, Germany 76227
Phone: 4972151600
E-mail: info@kizoo.com
Website: www.kizoo.com

Type of Firm
Private Equity Firm

Project Preferences

Type of Financing Preferred:
Early Stage
Seed
Startup

Geographical Preferences

International Preferences:
Africa

Industry Preferences

In Communications prefer:
Wireless Communications
Entertainment

In Computer Software prefer:
Software

In Internet Specific prefer:
Internet
Eccmmerce
Web Aggregation/Portals

Additional Information
Year Founded: 2008
Capital Under Management: $13,385,000
Current Activity Level : Actively seeking new investments

KJM CAPITAL LLC

3504 Lake Lynda Drive
Suite 107
Orlando, FL USA 32817
Website: www.kjmcapital.com

Management and Staff
Kenneth Meister, Founder
Roxane Kramer, Managing Director
Shahin Sazej, Managing Director

Type of Firm
Private Equity Firm

Project Preferences

Type of Financing Preferred:
Leveraged Buyout

Geographical Preferences

United States Preferences:
Rocky Mountain

Industry Preferences

In Transportation prefer:
Transportation

In Business Serv. prefer:
Services
Distribution

In Manufact. prefer:
Manufacturing

Additional Information
Year Founded: 1969
Current Activity Level : Actively seeking new investments

KK ABBALAB

3, Kanda Neribeicho, chiyoda
12F, Fujisoft Building
Tokyo, Japan 101-0023
Website: abbalab.com

Type of Firm
Private Equity Firm

Additional Information
Year Founded: 2016
Current Activity Level : Actively seeking new investments

KK BHP

2F Akatsuka Building,
1-2-8 Higashikanda, Chiyoda-ku
Tokyo, Japan 101-0031
Phone: 81-3-3862-4166
Fax: 81-3-3862-4167
E-mail: info@bhp-i.com

Management and Staff
Takeo Matsumoto, Managing Partner
Toshihiro Oguri, Managing Partner
Yuichi Iwaki, Partner

Type of Firm
Private Equity Firm

Association Membership
Japan Venture Capital Association

Project Preferences

Type of Financing Preferred:
Early Stage
Seed

Geographical Preferences

International Preferences:
Japan

Industry Preferences

In Biotechnology prefer:
Biotechnology

In Medical/Health prefer:
Health Services

Additional Information
Year Founded: 2000
Capital Under Management: $400,000
Current Activity Level : Actively seeking new investments

KK DG DAIWA VENTURES

1-9-1, Marunouchi
Chiyoda-ku
Tokyo, Japan

Type of Firm
Corporate PE/Venture

Project Preferences

Type of Financing Preferred:
Joint Ventures

Industry Preferences

In Computer Software prefer:
Artificial Intelligence

In Biotechnology prefer:
Biotechnology

Additional Information
Year Founded: 2016
Current Activity Level : Actively seeking new investments

KK FUND PTE LTD

80 Raffles Place
#32-01 UOB Plaza
Singapore, Singapore 048624
E-mail: info@kkfund.co
Website: kkfund.co

Other Offices
80 Robinson Road
Suite 10-01A
, Singapore 068898

Type of Firm
Private Equity Firm

Project Preferences

Type of Financing Preferred:
Seed

Size of Investments Considered:
Min Size of Investment Considered (000s): $100
Max Size of Investment Considered (000s): $400

Geographical Preferences

International Preferences:
Taiwan
Hong Kong
Asia

Industry Preferences

In Internet Specific prefer:
Internet

Additional Information
Year Founded: 2015
Current Activity Level : Actively seeking new investments

KK KAGAWAGIN CAPITAL

6/F KagawaginKameicho Bldg.
7-1 Kameicho
Takamatsu-shi, Japan 760-0050
Phone: 81-87-836-1310
Fax: 81-87-836-1320
Website: www.kagawabank.co.jp

Type of Firm
Bank Affiliated

Project Preferences

Type of Financing Preferred:
Leveraged Buyout
Management Buyouts
Acquisition

Geographical Preferences

International Preferences:
Japan

Additional Information
Year Founded: 1996
Current Activity Level : Actively seeking new investments

KK MIYAZAKI TAIYO CAPITAL

2-1-31 Hiroshima
Miyazaki Taiyo Bank
Miyazaki, Japan 8800806
Phone: 80985606395
Fax: 80985607092
E-mail: capital@taiyobank.co.jp
Website: www.taiyocapital.co.jp

Type of Firm
Private Equity Firm

Project Preferences

Type of Financing Preferred:
Balanced

Geographical Preferences

International Preferences:
Japan

Additional Information
Year Founded: 1996
Current Activity Level : Actively seeking new investments

KK SHIGIN CHIIKI ECONOMIC RESEARCH INSTITUTE

3F Shikoku Sogo Bldg.
1-21 Saienbamachi
Kochi-shi, Kochi-ken, Japan
Phone: 81-88-883-1152
Website: www.shikokubank.co.jp

Type of Firm
Private Equity Firm

Additional Information
Year Founded: 2007
Current Activity Level : Actively seeking new investments

KK SK VENTURES

1-11-2 Heiwadori
Shunan-shi, Japan 745-0015
Phone: 81-834-33-2661
Fax: 81-834-33-2662
E-mail: info@skv.jp
Website: www.skv.jp

Type of Firm
Bank Affiliated

Additional Information
Year Founded: 2000
Current Activity Level : Actively seeking new investments

KKR & CO LP

Nine West 57th Street
Suite 4200
New York, NY USA 10019
Phone: 2127508300
Website: www.kkr.com

Other Offices

10200 Forest Green Boulevard
Suite 112
ANCHORAGE, KY USA 40223
Phone: 5025153334

6/F, Tokyo Ginko Kyokai Building
1-3-1, Marunouchi, Chiyoda-ku
Tokyo, Japan 100-0005
Phone: 81362686000

555 California Street
50th Floor
SAN FRANCISCO, CA USA 94104
Phone: 4153153620

Levels 5 & 6, Gate Village 4
DIFC
Dubai, Utd. Arab Em. 506804
Phone: 97143781500

42 Avenue Montaigne
Paris, France 75008
Phone: 33153539600

2nd Floor, Piramal Tower, Peninsula Corp
Ganpatrao Kadam Marg, Lower Parel (West)
Mumbai, India 400 013
Phone: 912243551300

Level 56, Cheung Kong Center
2 Queen's Road
Central, Hong Kong
Phone: 85236027300

Rua Jeronimo da Veiga, 384
70 Andar, Suite 71
Sao Paulo, Brazil 04536-001

600 Travis Street
Suite 7200
HOUSTON, TX USA 77002
Phone: 7133435142

Asia Square Tower 1
8 Marina View, Suite 33-04
Singapore, Singapore 018960
Phone: 6569225800

75 St. Stephens Green
Dublin 2, Ireland
Phone: 35314757499

King Fahed Road
18F, Al Faisaliah Tower
Riyadh, Saudi Arabia 11311
Phone: 966114903767

41/F, China World Tower 3
No. 1 Jianguomenwai Street
Chaoyang District, China 100004
Phone: 861058953800

Level 42, Gateway Building
One Macquarie Place
Sydney, Australia 2000
Phone: 61282985500

335 - Eighth Avenue SW
Suite 850
Calgary, Canada T2P 1C9
Phone: 4037759244

35/F, West Tower, Mirae Asset Ctr 1 Bldg
67 Suha-dong, Jung-gu
Seoul, South Korea 100-210
Phone: 82263217700

101 Constitution Avenue N.W.
Suite 800
WASHINGTON, DC USA 20001
Phone: 2128479397

Management and Staff
Anthony Hass, Managing Director
Claire Farley, Managing Director
David Rockecharlie, Managing Director
Helenmarie Rodgers, Managing Director
Henry Hager, Principal
Henry McVey, Managing Director
Jim Burns, Partner
John Bookout, Managing Director
Kaveh Samie, Managing Director
Ralph Rosenberg, Managing Director
William Janetschek, Chief Financial Officer

Type of Firm
Private Equity Firm

Association Membership
Australian Venture Capital Association (AVCAL)
China Venture Capital Association
British Venture Capital Association (BVCA)
Emerging Markets Private Equity Association
French Venture Capital Association (AFIC)
Danish Venture Capital Association (DVCA)
German Venture Capital Association (BVK)
Swedish Venture Capital Association (SVCA)
European Private Equity and Venture Capital Assoc.
Private Equity Council (PEC)
Dutch Venture Capital Associaton (NVP)
Singapore Venture Capital Association (SVCA)
Spanish Venture Capital Association (ASCRI)
Indian Venture Capital Association (IVCA)

Project Preferences

Type of Financing Preferred:
Core
Value-Add
Generalist PE
Balanced
Management Buyouts
Acquisition
Special Situation
Distressed Debt
Recapitalizations

Geographical Preferences

United States Preferences:
North America

International Preferences:
Europe
Middle East
Australia
Asia

Industry Focus
(% based on actual investment)

Other Products	31.2%
Consumer Related	25.5%
Industrial/Energy	10.7%
Communications and Media	10.3%
Computer Software and Services	9.0%
Internet Specific	7.1%
Medical/Health	2.4%
Semiconductors/Other Elect.	2.4%
Biotechnology	1.2%
Computer Hardware	0.2%

Additional Information
Name of Most Recent Fund: KKR Special Situations Fund, L.P.
Most Recent Fund Was Raised: 12/31/2013
Year Founded: 1976
Capital Under Management: $80,379,500,000
Current Activity Level : Actively seeking new investments

KLASS CAPITAL CORP

130 Spadina Avenue
Suite 504
Toronto, Canada M5V 2L4
Phone: 4162752190

Other Offices
Former HQ: Eight Hillholm Road
Toronto, Canada M5P 1M2

Management and Staff
Daniel Klass, Founder
Jay Klein, Partner
Joel Lessem, Partner
Matthew Corrin, Partner
Oliver Centner, Partner

Type of Firm
Private Equity Firm

Association Membership
Canadian Venture Capital Association

Project Preferences

Type of Financing Preferred:
Expansion
Later Stage

Size of Investments Considered:
Min Size of Investment Considered (000s): $1,000
Max Size of Investment Considered (000s): $5,000

Geographical Preferences

Canadian Preferences:
All Canada

Industry Preferences

In Computer Software prefer:
Software

In Internet Specific prefer:
E-Commerce Technology

Additional Information
Name of Most Recent Fund: Klass Capital Fund I, L.P.
Most Recent Fund Was Raised: 02/23/2011
Year Founded: 2010
Capital Under Management: $50,703,000
Current Activity Level : Actively seeking new investments

KLAVENESS MARINE HOLDING AS

Harbitzalleen 2A
Oslo, Norway 0275
Phone: 4722398500
Fax: 4722398499
Website: www.klavenessmarine.com

Management and Staff
Carl Petter Finne, Chief Executive Officer
Henrik Falch, Chief Financial Officer
Michal Espe, Vice President
Trygve Dyrud, Vice President

Type of Firm
Investment Management Firm

Project Preferences

Type of Financing Preferred:
Generalist PE

Geographical Preferences

United States Preferences:

International Preferences:
Scandanavia/Nordic Region

Industry Preferences

In Industrial/Energy prefer:
Energy
Alternative Energy
Energy Conservation Relat

In Financial Services prefer:
Real Estate

In Other prefer:
Environment Responsible

Additional Information
Year Founded: 2011
Current Activity Level : Actively seeking new investments

KLEINER PERKINS CAUFIELD & BYERS LLC

2750 Sand Hill Road
Menlo Park, CA USA 94025
Phone: 6502332750
Fax: 6502330300
E-mail: plans@kpcb.com
Website: www.kpcb.com

Other Offices
27 South Park Street
Suite 201
SAN FRANCISCO, CA USA 94107
Phone: 16502332750
Fax: 16502330300

1273 Huai Hai Zhong Road
Unit 27 Xin Kang Garden
Shanghai, China 200031
Phone: 86-21-3383-0688
Fax: 86-21-3383-0699

No. 2 Jianguomenwai Avenue
Unit 2705, Tower C, YINTAI Centre
Beijing, China 100022
Phone: 86-10-8517-1799
Fax: 86-10-8517-1215

Middle Fuxing Road
No. 6, Lane 1350
Shanghai, China 200031
Phone: 862160252100
Fax: 862160252110

Management and Staff
Aileen Lee, Partner
Amol Deshpande, General Partner
Arielle Zuckerberg, Partner
Ben Kortlang, Partner
Beth Seidenberg, General Partner
Bill Joy, Partner
Bing Gordon, General Partner
Brook Porter, Partner
Brook Byers, Co-Founder
Chi-Hua Chien, General Partner
Christina Lee, Partner
Creighton Hicks, Partner
Dana Mead, Partner
Daniel Oros, Partner
David Mount, Partner
Dino Becirovic, Partner
Eric Feng, General Partner
Jackie Xu, Partner
John Maeda, Partner
Joseph Lacob, Partner
Juliet de Baubigny, Partner
Justin Sayarath, Partner
Lila Ibrahim, Partner
Mamoon Hamid, General Partner
Mary Meeker, General Partner
Michael Linse, Partner
Michael Abbott, General Partner
Mood Rowghani, Partner
Muzzammil Zaveri, Partner
Randy Komisar, General Partner
Ray Lane, Partner
Shabih Rizvi, Partner
Susan Biglieri, Chief Financial Officer
Swati Mylavarapu, Partner
Ted Schlein, Partner
Trae Vassallo, General Partner
Zach Barasz, Partner

Type of Firm
Private Equity Firm

Association Membership
China Venture Capital Association
Western Association of Venture Capitalists (WAVC)
National Venture Capital Association - USA (NVCA)

Project Preferences

Role in Financing:
Prefer role as deal originator but will also invest in deals created by others

Type of Financing Preferred:
Early Stage
Expansion
Balanced
Later Stage
Seed

Size of Investments Considered:
Min Size of Investment Considered (000s): $100
Max Size of Investment Considered (000s): $75,000

Geographical Preferences

United States Preferences:

International Preferences:
China

Industry Focus
(% based on actual investment)
Internet Specific	29.2%
Computer Software and Services	23.3%
Biotechnology	10.2%
Other Products	7.2%
Industrial/Energy	6.9%
Medical/Health	6.8%
Semiconductors/Other Elect.	5.4%
Communications and Media	5.0%
Computer Hardware	3.9%
Consumer Related	2.1%

Additional Information
Name of Most Recent Fund: Kleiner Perkins Caufield & Byers XV LLC
Most Recent Fund Was Raised: 05/17/2012
Year Founded: 1972
Capital Under Management: $3,400,000,000
Current Activity Level : Actively seeking new investments
Method of Compensation: Return on investment is of primary concern, do not charge fees

KLEOSS CAPITAL (PTY) LTD
2nd Floor
Office 5 3 Norwich Place
Sandton, South Africa
E-mail: info@kleosscapital.com
Website: kleosscapital.com

Management and Staff
Andile Keta, Co-Founder
Melisa Musindo, Chief Financial Officer
Zain Laher, Co-Founder

Type of Firm
Private Equity Firm

Project Preferences

Type of Financing Preferred:
Leveraged Buyout

Additional Information
Year Founded: 2016
Capital Under Management: $88,430,000
Current Activity Level : Actively seeking new investments

KLH CAPITAL LP
101 East Kennedy Boulevard
Suite 3925
Tampa, FL USA 33602
Phone: 8132220160
Fax: 8132220161
Website: www.klhcapital.com

Management and Staff
Christopher Hart, Vice President
James Darnell, Principal
John Kirtley, Principal
Kyle Madden, Vice President
P. Jeffrey Leck, Principal
William Dowden, Principal

Type of Firm
Private Equity Firm

Association Membership
Natl Assoc of Small Bus. Inv. Co (NASBIC)

Project Preferences

Type of Financing Preferred:
Expansion
Management Buyouts
Recapitalizations

Geographical Preferences

United States Preferences:

Additional Information
Year Founded: 2004
Capital Under Management: $135,000,000
Current Activity Level : Actively seeking new investments

KLINE HILL PARTNERS LLC
115 East Putnam Avenue
Floor 3
Greenwich, CT USA 06830
Phone: 12033402463
E-mail: info@klinehill.com
Website: klinehillpartners.com

Management and Staff
Jared Barlow, Partner
Michael Bego, Managing Partner

Type of Firm
Private Equity Advisor or Fund of Funds

Project Preferences

Type of Financing Preferred:
Fund of Funds of Second

Additional Information
Year Founded: 2016
Capital Under Management: $128,500,000
Current Activity Level : Actively seeking new investments

KLINGENSTEIN FIELDS VENTURE FUND LP

125 Park Avenue
Suite 1700
New York, NY USA 10017

Type of Firm
Investment Management Firm

Project Preferences

Type of Financing Preferred:
Balanced

Additional Information
Year Founded: 2017
Current Activity Level : Actively seeking new investments

KMU CAPITAL AG

Platz 6
Haus zur Rose
Herisau, Switzerland 9102

Type of Firm
Bank Affiliated

Project Preferences

Type of Financing Preferred:
Mezzanine

Additional Information
Year Founded: 1991
Current Activity Level : Actively seeking new investments

KNIGHT S BRIDGE CAPITAL CORP

Scotia Plaza, Suite 3200
40 King Street West
Toronto, Canada M5H3Y2
Phone: 4168663132
Website: www.kbcpartners.com

Management and Staff
Gary Taylor, Managing Director

Type of Firm
Private Equity Firm

Project Preferences

Type of Financing Preferred:
Leveraged Buyout
Early Stage
Generalist PE
Balanced
Later Stage
Acquisition

Geographical Preferences

United States Preferences:
North America

Canadian Preferences:
All Canada

Industry Preferences

In Internet Specific prefer:
Internet

In Consumer Related prefer:
Consumer
Consumer Products
Consumer Services

In Business Serv. prefer:
Media

Additional Information
Year Founded: 2007
Current Activity Level : Actively seeking new investments

KNOLL VENTURES ECP LLC

4550 E. Brookhaven Drive NE,
Atlanta, GA USA 30319
Website: knollventures.com

Type of Firm
Private Equity Firm

Project Preferences

Type of Financing Preferred:
Early Stage
Expansion
Later Stage
Seed

Additional Information
Year Founded: 2013
Current Activity Level : Actively seeking new investments

KNOWLEDGE HUB SP Z O O

ul. Puawska 465
Warsaw, Poland 02-844
Phone: 48 22 379 47 96
Website: knowledgehub.pl

Type of Firm
Private Equity Firm

Project Preferences

Type of Financing Preferred:
Early Stage
Expansion
Startup

Geographical Preferences

International Preferences:
Poland

Industry Preferences

In Communications prefer:
Communications and Media
Wireless Communications
Media and Entertainment

Additional Information
Year Founded: 2008
Current Activity Level : Actively seeking new investments

KOA CAPITAL PARTNERS LLC

820 West Hind Drive
Suite 1293
Honolulu, HI USA 96821
Website: koacapitalpartners.com

Type of Firm
Private Equity Firm

Project Preferences

Type of Financing Preferred:
Leveraged Buyout
Acquisition

Geographical Preferences

United States Preferences:
Hawaii

Industry Preferences

In Medical/Health prefer:
Medical/Health
Health Services

In Industrial/Energy prefer:
Industrial Products

In Business Serv. prefer:
Services

Additional Information
Year Founded: 2014
Current Activity Level : Actively seeking new investments

KOCH GENESIS LLC

4111 East 37th Street North
Wichita, KS USA 67220
Phone: 316-828-8532
Fax: 316-828-3030
E-mail: info@kochgenesis.com
Website: www.kochgenesis.com

Management and Staff
Brett Chugg, Vice President
Tim Cesarek, President

Type of Firm
Bank Affiliated

Project Preferences

Type of Financing Preferred:
Early Stage

Size of Investments Considered:
Min Size of Investment Considered (000s): $5,000
Max Size of Investment Considered (000s): $10,000

Industry Preferences

In Communications prefer:
Communications and Media

In Semiconductor/Electr prefer:
Semiconductor

In Medical/Health prefer:
Medical Products
Health Services

In Industrial/Energy prefer:
Energy

Additional Information
Current Activity Level : Actively seeking new investments

KODIAK CAPITAL GROUP LLC

260 Newport Center Drive
Newport Beach, CA USA 92660
Phone: 2122622600
E-mail: info@kodiak-capital.us
Website: www.kodiak-capital.us

Other Offices
2040 Victory Boulevard
Staten Island, NY USA 10313

16192 Coastal Highway
Lewes, DE USA 19958

Management and Staff
Ryan Hodson, Managing Director
William Newell, Managing Director

Type of Firm
Private Equity Firm

Project Preferences

Type of Financing Preferred:
Expansion
Acquisition
Recapitalizations

Geographical Preferences

United States Preferences:
North America

Industry Preferences

In Biotechnology prefer:
Biotechnology

In Consumer Related prefer:
Consumer Products

In Business Serv. prefer:
Media

In Agr/Forestr/Fish prefer:
Agriculture related

In Utilities prefer:
Utilities

Additional Information
Year Founded: 2009
Current Activity Level : Actively seeking new investments

KODIAK VENTURE PARTNERS LP

80 William St Wellesley Office
Suite 260
Wellesley, MA USA 02481
Phone: 7816722500
Fax: 7816722501
E-mail: kodiakcontact@kodiakvp.com
Website: www.kodiakvp.com

Management and Staff
Andrey Zarur, Managing Partner
Chip Meakem, Managing Partner
Louis Volpe, Managing Partner

Type of Firm
Private Equity Firm

Project Preferences

Role in Financing:
Prefer role as deal originator but will also invest in deals created by others

Type of Financing Preferred:
Early Stage
Balanced
Seed

Size of Investments Considered:
Min Size of Investment Considered (000s): $100
Max Size of Investment Considered (000s): $3,000

Geographical Preferences

United States Preferences:
Mid Atlantic
North America
Northeast
Massachusetts
New York
East Coast

Canadian Preferences:
All Canada
Eastern Canada

Industry Preferences

In Communications prefer:
Communications and Media
Wireless Communications

In Computer Software prefer:
Software

In Internet Specific prefer:
Internet

In Semiconductor/Electr prefer:
Semiconductor

In Business Serv. prefer:
Services
Media

Additional Information
Name of Most Recent Fund: Kodiak Venture Partners III, L.P.
Most Recent Fund Was Raised: 01/13/2004
Year Founded: 1999
Capital Under Management: $677,000,000
Current Activity Level : Actively seeking new investments
Method of Compensation: Return on investment is of primary concern, do not charge fees

---

KOHFOUNDERS MANAGEMENT LLC

11845 West Olympic Boulevard
#1100
Los Angeles, CA USA 90064
E-mail: team@kohfounders.com

Type of Firm
Private Equity Firm

Project Preferences

Type of Financing Preferred:
Early Stage

Industry Preferences

In Computer Software prefer:
Software
Artificial Intelligence

In Internet Specific prefer:
Internet

In Medical/Health prefer:
Health Services

In Business Serv. prefer:
Services

Additional Information
Year Founded: 2014
Current Activity Level : Actively seeking new investments

KOHLBERG & CO LLC

111 Radio Circle
Mount Kisco, NY USA 10549
Phone: 9142417430
Website: www.kohlberg.com

Other Offices
3000 Alpine Road
Suite 100
Portola Valley, CA USA 94028
Phone: 650-463-1480
Fax: 650-463-1481

Management and Staff
Ahmed Wahla, Vice President
Andrew Bonanno, Managing Director
Benjamin Mao, Partner
Christopher Anderson, Partner
Christopher Lacovara, Partner
Evan Wildstein, Partner
Jean Roberts, Vice President
Jerome Kohlberg, Partner
Michael Anderson, Vice President
Samuel Frieder, Managing Partner
Seth Hollander, Partner
Zachary Viders, Vice President

Type of Firm
Private Equity Firm

Project Preferences

Type of Financing Preferred:
Leveraged Buyout
Accuisition
Recapitalizations

Geographical Preferences

United States Preferences:
North America

Industry Focus
(% based on actual investment)
Industrial/Energy	68.7%
Other Products	12.9%
Computer Hardware	11.9%
Medical/Health	5.5%
Internet Specific	0.6%
Consumer Related	0.3%

Additional Information
Name of Most Recent Fund: Kohlberg Investors VII, L.P.
Most Recent Fund Was Raised: 09/15/2011
Year Founded: 1987
Capital Under Management: $3,946,700,000
Current Activity Level : Actively seeking new investments

KOHLBERG VENTURES LLC

3000 Alpine Road
Portola Valley, CA USA 94028
Phone: 6504631480
Fax: 6504631481
E-mail: information@kohlbergventures.com
Website: www.kohlbergventures.com

Management and Staff
Bill Youstra, Partner
Greg Shove, Partner

Type of Firm
Private Equity Firm

Project Preferences

Type of Financing Preferred:
Early Stage

Industry Preferences

In Internet Specific prefer:
Web Aggregation/Portals

In Consumer Related prefer:
Entertainment and Leisure
Food/Beverage
Consumer Products

In Industrial/Energy prefer:
Alternative Energy
Energy Conservation Relat

In Business Serv. prefer:
Media

Additional Information
Year Founded: 2009
Current Activity Level : Actively seeking new investments

KOHLI VENTURES LTD

Berkeley Square House
Ninth Floorp9
Berkeley Square, United Kingdom W1J 6DD
Phone: 4402037097085
E-mail: info@kohliventures.com
Website: www.kohliventures.com

Other Offices
Former HQ: 53 Davies Street
, United Kingdom W1K 5JH

Type of Firm
Private Equity Firm

Project Preferences

Type of Financing Preferred:
Balanced

Geographical Preferences

International Preferences:
Latin America
India
Middle East
Africa

Additional Information
Year Founded: 1969
Current Activity Level : Actively seeking new investments

KOKSA 2 AS

Martin Linges vei 25
Postboks 1
Fornebu, Norway 1330
Phone: 47-6782-7020
Fax: 47-6782-7021
E-mail: firmapost@itfi.no

Type of Firm
Incubator/Development Program

Association Membership
Norwegian Venture Capital Association

Project Preferences

Type of Financing Preferred:
Seed

Geographical Preferences

International Preferences:
Norway

Industry Preferences

In Communications prefer:
Commercial Communications

In Business Serv. prefer:
Media

Additional Information
Year Founded: 2001
Current Activity Level : Actively seeking new investments

KONGSBERG INNOVASJON AS

Kirkegardsvei 45
P.O. Box 1027
Kongsberg, Norway 3616
Phone: 4732286330
E-mail: post@k-i.no
Website: www.k-i.no

Management and Staff
Svein-Olav Toro, Chief Executive Officer

Type of Firm
Corporate PE/Venture

Project Preferences

Type of Financing Preferred:
Balanced

Geographical Preferences

International Preferences:
Norway

Industry Preferences

In Internet Specific prefer:
E-Commerce Technology

In Industrial/Energy prefer:
Energy
Machinery

Additional Information
Year Founded: 2002
Current Activity Level : Actively seeking new investments

KOPPICATCH OY

Kanavaranta 7 D
3rd Floor
Helsinki, Finland 00160
Website: www.koppicatch.com

Management and Staff
Oskari Lehtonen, Partner
Torsti Tenhunen, Partner

Type of Firm
Incubator/Development Program

Project Preferences

Type of Financing Preferred:
Seed
Startup

Size of Investments Considered:
Min Size of Investment Considered (000s): $139
Max Size of Investment Considered (000s): $1,043

Geographical Preferences

International Preferences:
Finland

Industry Preferences

In Communications prefer:
Wireless Communications
Media and Entertainment

In Computer Software prefer:
Software

In Internet Specific prefer:
Internet

In Consumer Related prefer:
Consumer Products

Additional Information
Year Founded: 2009
Current Activity Level : Actively seeking new investments

KOREA DEVELOPMENT BANK

14 Eunhaeng-ro
Yeongdeungpo-gu
Seoul, South Korea 150973
Phone: 8227876934
Fax: 8227876991
Website: www.kdb.co.kr

Type of Firm
Bank Affiliated

Project Preferences

Type of Financing Preferred:
Leveraged Buyout
Early Stage
Acquisition
Recapitalizations

Geographical Preferences

International Preferences:
Korea, South

Industry Preferences

In Biotechnology prefer:
Biotechnology

In Industrial/Energy prefer:
Environmental Related

In Transportation prefer:
Aerospace

Additional Information
Year Founded: 1954
Capital Under Management: $94,000,000
Current Activity Level : Actively seeking new investments

KOREA FINANCE CORP

22 Eunhangro, Yeouido-Dong
Yeongdeungpo-Gu
Seoul, South Korea 150-873
Phone: 8216444100
Website: www.kofc.or.kr

Type of Firm
Government Affiliated Program

Project Preferences

Type of Financing Preferred:
Balanced

Geographical Preferences

International Preferences:
Korea, South

Industry Preferences

In Industrial/Energy prefer:
Alternative Energy
Advanced Materials

Additional Information
Year Founded: 2011
Current Activity Level : Actively seeking new investments

KOREA INVESTMENT & SECURITIES CO LTD

27-1, Yeouido-Dong
Yeongdeungpo-Gu
Seoul, South Korea 150880
E-mail: truefriend@truefriend.com
Website: www.truefriend.com

Management and Staff
Seok Jin Kim, Managing Director

Type of Firm
Investment Management Firm

Project Preferences

Type of Financing Preferred:
Balanced

Geographical Preferences

International Preferences:
Asia
Korea, South

Additional Information
Year Founded: 1974
Capital Under Management: $26,250,000
Current Activity Level : Actively seeking new investments

KOREA INVESTMENT PARTNERS CO LTD

1001, ASEM Tower, Gangnam-gu
517, Yeongdong-daero
Seoul, South Korea
Phone: 82260015300
Fax: 82260015301
E-mail: dwvc@truefriend.com
Website: www.kipvc.com

Other Offices

16/F, HuaMin Empire Plaza
726 Yanan West Road
China
Phone: 86-21-6212-1522
Fax: 86-21-6212-3012

26C Huamin Empire Plaza
728 Yana West Road
Shanghai, China 20050
Phone: 862162121113
Fax: 862162123012

517 Yeongdong-daero
Floor 10, ASEM Tower
, South Korea 135798
Phone: 82260015300
Fax: 82260015301

Management and Staff

Deok-soo Ryu, Principal
Dong-hyun Song, Principal
Dong-yeong Lee, Principal
Hong Zou, Principal
Hwa-mok Chung, Principal
Hyeong-jun Park, Principal
Ji-woong Park, Principal
Jong-pil Kim, Senior Managing Director
Ke Liu, Principal
Kun-ho Kim, Principal
Kyung-sik Ho, Managing Director
Ping Wang, Principal
Sang-Ho Park, Principal
Sang-hyuk Jang, Principal
Sang-jin Lee, Principal
Sang-joon Park, Principal
Su-jin Kim, Principal
Sung-wook Yoo, Principal
Yong-kee Lim, Principal

Type of Firm

Private Equity Firm

Association Membership

Korean Venture Capital Association (KVCA)

Project Preferences

Type of Financing Preferred:
Early Stage
Expansion
Balanced
Later Stage

Geographical Preferences

International Preferences:
China
Korea, South

Industry Preferences

In Communications prefer:
Telecommunications

In Computer Software prefer:
Software

In Internet Specific prefer:
E-Commerce Technology

In Semiconductor/Electr prefer:
Electronics
Semiconductor

In Biotechnology prefer:
Biotechnology

In Consumer Related prefer:
Consumer Products
Consumer Services
Other Restaurants
Hotels and Resorts

In Industrial/Energy prefer:
Materials

In Financial Services prefer:
Financial Services
Real Estate

In Manufact. prefer:
Manufacturing

Additional Information

Year Founded: 1981
Capital Under Management: $252,000,000
Current Activity Level : Actively seeking new investments

KOREAN VENTURE FUND MANAGEMENT CO

Bigway Tower 19F, 677-25
Yeoksam-Dong, KangNam-Ku
Seoul, South Korea 135-080
Phone: 822-3452-1960
Fax: 822-3452-1690

Type of Firm

Private Equity Firm

Project Preferences

Type of Financing Preferred:
Fund of Funds
Early Stage
Expansion
Mezzanine
Balanced

Geographical Preferences

International Preferences:
Asia
Korea, South

Industry Preferences

In Communications prefer:
Communications and Media

In Computer Software prefer:
Software

In Internet Specific prefer:
Internet

In Semiconductor/Electr prefer:
Electronics
Semiconductor

In Consumer Related prefer:
Entertainment and Leisure

Additional Information

Year Founded: 2000
Current Activity Level : Actively seeking new investments

KORELYA CAPITAL SAS

87, Rue Reaumur
Paris, France 75002
Website: www.korelyacapital.com

Type of Firm

Private Equity Firm

Project Preferences

Type of Financing Preferred:
Early Stage
Seed

Geographical Preferences

International Preferences:
France

Industry Preferences

In Communications prefer:
Data Communications

In Computer Software prefer:
Data Processing
Software
Artificial Intelligence

In Internet Specific prefer:
Internet

Additional Information

Year Founded: 2016
Capital Under Management: $112,210,000
Current Activity Level : Actively seeking new investments

KORMELI LLC

25 Burlington Mall Road
Suite 301
Burlington, MA USA 01803
Phone: 7813258567
Website: kormeli.com

Management and Staff

Avner Schneur, Managing Partner

Type of Firm
Private Equity Firm

Project Preferences

Type of Financing Preferred:
Early Stage
Seed
Startup

Size of Investments Considered:
Min Size of Investment Considered (000s): $100
Max Size of Investment Considered (000s): $700

Additional Information
Year Founded: 2011
Current Activity Level : Actively seeking new investments

KORONA INVEST OY

Innopoli 1
Tekniikantie 2
Espoo, Finland 02150
Website: www.koronainvest.fi

Management and Staff
Pasi Lehtinen, Partner
Vesa Lehtomaki, Partner

Type of Firm
Private Equity Firm

Association Membership
Finnish Venture Capital Association (FVCA)

Project Preferences

Type of Financing Preferred:
Leveraged Buyout
Balanced
Later Stage
Management Buyouts
Acquisition

Size of Investments Considered:
Min Size of Investment Considered (000s): $300
Max Size of Investment Considered (000s): $3,000

Geographical Preferences

International Preferences:
Finland

Industry Preferences

In Medical/Health prefer:
Medical/Health
Health Services

Additional Information
Name of Most Recent Fund: Palvelurahasto I Ky
Most Recent Fund Was Raised: 05/10/2011
Year Founded: 2006
Capital Under Management: $78,246,000
Current Activity Level : Actively seeking new investments

KORPORATSIYA RAZVITIYA SEVERNOGO KAVKAZA AO

Pyatigorskaya Str., 139
Essentuki, Russia 357625
E-mail: info@krskfo.ru
Website: krskfo.ru

Management and Staff
Timur Charto, Managing Director

Type of Firm
Private Equity Firm

Project Preferences

Type of Financing Preferred:
Leveraged Buyout
Early Stage
Generalist PE
Later Stage
Acquisition

Geographical Preferences

International Preferences:
Kazakhstan
Azerbaijan
Russia
Georgia

Industry Preferences

In Biotechnology prefer:
Agricultural/Animal Bio.

In Industrial/Energy prefer:
Environmental Related

In Agr/Forestr/Fish prefer:
Agriculture related

Additional Information
Year Founded: 2010
Current Activity Level : Actively seeking new investments

KORYS MANAGEMENT NV

Vaucampslaan 42
Huizingen, Belgium 1654
Phone: 3228016834
E-mail: enquiries@korys.be
Website: www.korys.be

Management and Staff
Sofie Gabriels, Chief Financial Officer
Vincent Vliebergh, Chief Executive Officer

Type of Firm
Private Equity Firm

Association Membership
Belgium Venturing Association
European Private Equity and Venture Capital Assoc.

Project Preferences

Type of Financing Preferred:
Early Stage
Balanced
Later Stage
Seed
Startup

Size of Investments Considered:
Min Size of Investment Considered (000s): $655
Max Size of Investment Considered (000s): $2,622

Geographical Preferences

United States Preferences:
All U.S.

International Preferences:
Europe
Belgium

Industry Preferences

In Communications prefer:
Communications and Media
Telecommunications

In Internet Specific prefer:
Internet

In Computer Other prefer:
Computer Related

In Industrial/Energy prefer:
Energy
Alternative Energy
Energy Conservation Relat
Environmental Related

Additional Information
Year Founded: 2000
Capital Under Management: $34,500,000
Current Activity Level : Actively seeking new investments

KOTAK INVESTMENT ADVISORS LTD

CST Road , Kalina
6th Floor , INGS Point, Plot 8
Mumbai, India 400 098
Phone: 912266260500

Management and Staff
Deepshikha Dhamija, Vice President
Naozad Sirwalla, Chief Operating Officer
Raj Shah, Vice President
S. Sriniwasan, Chief Executive Officer
Shashidhar Reddy, Vice President
Sonu Jalan, Vice President
Yayati Kene, Vice President

Type of Firm
Bank Affiliated

Association Membership
Indian Venture Capital Association (IVCA)

Project Preferences

Role in Financing:
Will function either as deal originator or investor in deals created by others

Type of Financing Preferred:
Leveraged Buyout
Value-Add
Early Stage
Expansion
Generalist PE
Opportunistic
Later Stage
Other
Acquisition

Geographical Preferences

International Preferences:
India

Industry Preferences

In Communications prefer:
Media and Entertainment

In Biotechnology prefer:
Biotechnology

In Medical/Health prefer:
Medical/Health
Health Services
Pharmaceuticals

In Consumer Related prefer:
Consumer
Retail
Consumer Products

In Industrial/Energy prefer:
Energy

In Transportation prefer:
Transportation

In Financial Services prefer:
Real Estate

In Utilities prefer:
Utilities

Additional Information
Year Founded: 1985
Capital Under Management: $1,340,000,000
Current Activity Level : Actively seeking new investments

KPG VENTURES

461 Second Street, #454T
San Francisco, CA USA 94107
Phone: 4157816800
Fax: 4157816805
Website: www.kpgventures.com

Management and Staff
Julia Chang, Partner

Type of Firm
Private Equity Firm

Association Membership
National Venture Capital Association - USA (NVCA)

Project Preferences

Type of Financing Preferred:
Balanced
Later Stage

Geographical Preferences

United States Preferences:
All U.S.

Industry Preferences

In Internet Specific prefer:
Internet

Additional Information
Year Founded: 1969
Capital Under Management: $17,000,000
Current Activity Level : Actively seeking new investments

KPMG CORPORATE FINANCE INC

Bay Adelaide Centre,333 Bay St, Suite 4600
Toronto, Canada M5H2S5
Phone: 416-777-8500
Fax: 416-777-8818
Website: www.kpmg.ca

Management and Staff
Ian Shelley, Partner
Philip Reynolds, Partner

Type of Firm
Investment Management Firm

Association Membership
New Zealand Venture Capital Association
Canadian Venture Capital Association

Project Preferences

Type of Financing Preferred:
Later Stage

Additional Information
Year Founded: 1996
Current Activity Level : Actively seeking new investments

KPN VENTURES BV

Maanplein 55 TP5/6.25
The Hague, Netherlands 2516 CK
Phone: 31704517648
Fax: 31704517656

Management and Staff
Harry Hendriks, Partner
Kees Stok, Partner
Rob Langezaal, Partner
Ronald Plompen, Managing Director

Type of Firm
Corporate PE/Venture

Project Preferences

Type of Financing Preferred:
Fund of Funds
Early Stage
Balanced
Seed
Startup

Geographical Preferences

United States Preferences:
All U.S.

International Preferences:
Europe
Israel

Industry Preferences

In Communications prefer:
Communications and Media
Commercial Communications
Telecommunications

In Internet Specific prefer:
Internet

In Consumer Related prefer:
Consumer

In Business Serv. prefer:
Services
Media

Additional Information
Year Founded: 1993
Capital Under Management: $82,000,000
Current Activity Level : Actively seeking new investments

KPS CAPITAL PARTNERS LP

485 Lexington Avenue
31st Floor
New York, NY USA 10017
Phone: 2123385100
Fax: 6463077100
Website: www.kpsfund.com

Other Offices
Barckhausstrabe 1
Frankfurt, Germany D-60325
Phone: 496913814777
Fax: 496913814774

Management and Staff
Bruce Curley, Partner
Daniel Gray, Managing Director
David Shapiro, Managing Partner
David Peck, Vice President
Eugene Keilin, Co-Founder
Florian Almeling, Managing Director
Fred Spivak, Vice President
Jay Bernstein, Partner
Kevin Madden, Vice President
Michael Psaros, Managing Partner
Raquel Palmer, Partner
Ryan Baker, Vice President

Type of Firm
Private Equity Firm

Association Membership
Private Equity Council (PEC)

Project Preferences
Type of Financing Preferred:
Leveraged Buyout
Turnaround
Special Situation
Distressed Debt
Recapitalizations

Geographical Preferences
United States Preferences:
North America

Canadian Preferences:
All Canada

Industry Focus
(% based on actual investment)
Industrial/Energy	58.7%
Other Products	37.4%
Semiconductors/Other Elect.	2.5%
Consumer Related	1.3%

Additional Information
Name of Most Recent Fund: KPS Special Situations Fund IV, L.P.
Most Recent Fund Was Raised: 04/12/2013
Year Founded: 1997
Capital Under Management: $2,600,000,000
Current Activity Level : Actively seeking new investments

KRAFT GROUP LLC

One Patriot Place
Foxboro, MA USA 02035
Phone: 5085434230
E-mail: info@thekraftgroup.com
Website: www.thekraftgroup.com

Management and Staff
Jonathan Kraft, President

Type of Firm
Private Equity Firm

Project Preferences
Type of Financing Preferred:
Balanced

Geographical Preferences
United States Preferences:

Industry Preferences
In Communications prefer:
Entertainment

In Manufact. prefer:
Manufacturing

Additional Information
Year Founded: 1963
Current Activity Level : Actively seeking new investments

KRANOS CAPITAL

100 Church Street
Eighth Floor
New York, NY USA 10007
Phone: 6468457454
Fax: 6468457301
E-mail: info@kranoscapital.com
Website: www.kranoscapital.com

Type of Firm
Private Equity Firm

Project Preferences
Type of Financing Preferred:
Leveraged Buyout
Acquisition

Geographical Preferences
International Preferences:
Latin America

Industry Preferences
In Financial Services prefer:
Financial Services

Additional Information
Year Founded: 2014
Current Activity Level : Actively seeking new investments

KRC CAPITAL BV

Leidseweg 219
Voorschoten, Netherlands 2253 AE
Phone: 31715797129
Fax: 31715797452
E-mail: info@krccapital.com
Website: www.krccapital.com

Management and Staff
Rattan Chadha, President, Founder

Type of Firm
Private Equity Firm

Project Preferences
Type of Financing Preferred:
Generalist PE

Geographical Preferences
International Preferences:
Europe

Industry Preferences
In Consumer Related prefer:
Consumer
Entertainment and Leisure
Consumer Products
Hotels and Resorts

In Financial Services prefer:
Real Estate

In Business Serv. prefer:
Media

Additional Information
Year Founded: 2008
Current Activity Level : Actively seeking new investments

KREISSPARKASSE REUTLINGEN

Marktplatz 6
Reutlingen, Germany 72764
Phone: 4971213312037
Fax: 4971213312039
E-mail: wagniskapital@ksk-reutlingen.de
Website: www.ksk-reutlingen.de

Management and Staff
Joachim Pfeiffer, Managing Director
Michael Blaesius, Managing Director

Type of Firm
Bank Affiliated

Association Membership
German Venture Capital Association (BVK)

Project Preferences
Type of Financing Preferred:
Early Stage
Turnaround
Later Stage
Seed
Management Buyouts
Acquisition
Startup
Recapitalizations

Size of Investments Considered:
Min Size of Investment Considered (000s): $40,021
Max Size of Investment Considered (000s): $667,023

Geographical Preferences

International Preferences:
Germany

Additional Information

Year Founded: 2000
Current Activity Level : Actively seeking new investments

KREOS CAPITAL MANAGERS LTD

25-28 Old Burlington Street
London, United Kingdom W1S 3AN
Phone: 442075188890
Fax: 442074091034
E-mail: info@kreoscapital.com
Website: www.kreoscapital.com

Other Offices

Birger Jarlsgatan 2
Stockholm, Sweden 114 34
Phone: 4686787200
Fax: 4686780470

Six Hachoshlim Street
Sixth Floor
Herzlya Pituach, Israel 46724
Phone: 97299514434
Fax: 97299514435

Management and Staff

Luca Colciago, General Partner
Marten Vading, General Partner
Maurizio Petit Bon, General Partner
Raoul Stein, General Partner
Ross Ahlgren, General Partner

Type of Firm

Private Equity Firm

Project Preferences

Type of Financing Preferred:
Early Stage
Expansion
Balanced
Later Stage

Size of Investments Considered:
Min Size of Investment Considered (000s): $1,239
Max Size of Investment Considered (000s): $18,587

Geographical Preferences

International Preferences:
United Kingdom
Europe
Western Europe
Scandanavia/Nordic Region
Israel
Romania
Germany
France

Industry Preferences

In Communications prefer:
Communications and Media

In Computer Software prefer:
Software

In Semiconductor/Electr prefer:
Semiconductor

In Consumer Related prefer:
Consumer

In Industrial/Energy prefer:
Environmental Related

In Financial Services prefer:
Insurance

Additional Information

Name of Most Recent Fund: Kreos Capital IV
Most Recent Fund Was Raised: 01/24/2012
Year Founded: 1998
Capital Under Management: $747,477,000
Current Activity Level : Actively seeking new investments

KRG CAPITAL MANAGEMENT LP

1800 Larimer Street, Suite 2200
Denver, CO USA 80202
Phone: 3033905001
Fax: 3033905015
E-mail: info@krgcapital.com
Website: www.krgcapital.com

Management and Staff

Ben McCown, Vice President
Bennett Thompson, Managing Director
Blair Tikker, Managing Director
Bruce Rogers, Co-Founder
Charles Hamilton, Managing Director
Charles Gwirtsman, Co-Founder
Christopher Pusey, Vice President
Christopher Lane, Managing Director
Colton King, Managing Director
Dustin Jackson, Vice President
E. Sue Cho, Principal
Piotr Biezychudek, Vice President
Steven Neumann, Managing Director
Stewart Fisher, Managing Director
Ted Nark, Managing Director

Type of Firm

Private Equity Firm

Project Preferences

Role in Financing:
Prefer role as deal originator

Type of Financing Preferred:
Leveraged Buyout
Management Buyouts
Acquisition
Recapitalizations

Geographical Preferences

United States Preferences:
North America

Industry Focus

(% based on actual investment)
Medical/Health	49.6%
Other Products	44.7%
Consumer Related	2.0%
Biotechnology	1.8%
Semiconductors/Other Elect.	1.4%
Computer Software and Services	0.5%
Industrial/Energy	0.1%

Additional Information

Year Founded: 1996
Capital Under Management: $2,800,000,000
Current Activity Level : Actively seeking new investments

KRYPTON CAPITAL

Leonardo Business Center
Bohdana Khmelnytskoho 19-21
Kyiv, Ukraine
Website: krypton.capital

Management and Staff

Delzar Khalaf, Chief Operating Officer

Type of Firm

Private Equity Firm

Industry Preferences

In Computer Software prefer:
Software

In Business Serv. prefer:
Media

Additional Information

Year Founded: 1969
Current Activity Level : Actively seeking new investments

KRYSTAL FINANCIAL CORP

710 - 1050 West Pender Street
Vancouver, Canada V6E 3S7
Phone: 6046591700
Fax: 6046827394
E-mail: info@krystalfinancial.ca
Website: www.krystalfinancial.ca

Other Offices

1201 West Pender
Third Floor
, Canada V6E 2V2

Type of Firm

Private Equity Firm

KSL CAPITAL PARTNERS LLC (continued)

Project Preferences

Type of Financing Preferred:
Leveraged Buyout
Acquisition

Geographical Preferences

Canadian Preferences:
British Columbia
Western Canada

Additional Information

Year Founded: 2004
Current Activity Level: Actively seeking new investments

KSL CAPITAL PARTNERS LLC

100 Fillmore Street
Suite 600
Denver, CO USA 80206
Phone: 7202846400
Fax: 7202846401
E-mail: contact@kslcapital.com
Website: www.kslcapital.com

Other Offices

287 Bowman Avenue
3rd Floor
Purchase, NY USA 10577
Phone: 914-253-8026

Management and Staff

Adam Knox, Vice President
Bernard Siegel, Principal
Coley Brenan, Principal
Craig Henrich, Principal
Daniel Rohan, Vice President
Eric Resnick, Managing Director
Hal Shaw, Vice President
Jared Melnik, Vice President
John Ege, Principal
Martin Newburger, Partner
Michael Jo, Vice President
Michael Shannon, Managing Director
Peter McDermott, Partner
Richard Weissmann, Partner
Steven Siegel, Partner

Type of Firm

Private Equity Firm

Project Preferences

Type of Financing Preferred:
Leveraged Buyout
Management Buyouts
Acquisition

Geographical Preferences

United States Preferences:
All U.S.

Industry Preferences

In Consumer Related prefer:
Consumer

In Business Serv. prefer:
Services

Additional Information

Name of Most Recent Fund: KSL Capital Partners Credit Opportunities Fund, L.P.
Most Recent Fund Was Raised: 01/03/2014
Year Founded: 2005
Capital Under Management: $6,701,500,000
Current Activity Level: Actively seeking new investments

KT CAPITAL MANAGEMENT LLC

One Glenlake Parkway
Suite 1075
Atlanta, GA USA 30328
Phone: 7707534323
Website: www.ktcapital.net

Management and Staff

James Tapp, Principal
Peter Kacer, Principal
Robert Konrad, Principal

Type of Firm

Private Equity Firm

Project Preferences

Type of Financing Preferred:
Leveraged Buyout
Acquisition

Geographical Preferences

United States Preferences:
Southeast

Industry Preferences

In Business Serv. prefer:
Services
Distribution

In Manufact. prefer:
Manufacturing

Additional Information

Year Founded: 2008
Current Activity Level: Actively seeking new investments

KT EQUITY PARTNERS LLC

2950 SW McClure Road
Topeka, KS USA 66614

Type of Firm

Private Equity Firm

Project Preferences

Type of Financing Preferred:
Generalist PE

Industry Preferences

In Financial Services prefer:
Financial Services
Insurance

Additional Information

Year Founded: 2014
Current Activity Level: Actively seeking new investments

KTB INVESTMENT & SECURITIES CO LTD

66, Yeoui-Daero
Floor 6, KTB Building
Seoul, South Korea 150709
Phone: 82221842200
Fax: 822221842570
Website: www.ktb.co.kr

Other Offices

11/F, 88-7 Kyobo Life Building
Jungang-dong, Jung-gu
Busan, South Korea 600-014
Phone: 82-51-442-5742
Fax: 82-51-465-1136

Unit 14-16, 5Fl., China World Tower 1
No. 1 Jian Guo Men Wai Avenue
Beijing, China 100004
Phone: 86-10-6505-2583
Fax: 86-10-6505-1334

9F, Samsung Life Bldg.,
863-1 Bucheon 1 dong
Pusanjin-Ku Pusan, South Korea
Phone: 82-51-647-0051
Fax: 82-51-647-0054

Unit 03, 25F, West Tower Of Twin Towers
No.B12,Jianguomenwai, Dajie, Chaoyang Di
Beijing, China
Phone: 86-10-6568-1391
Fax: 86-10-6568-1392

720 University Avenue
Suite 100
Palo Alto, CA USA 94301
Phone: 650-324-4681
Fax: 650-324-4682

911 Iino Bldg.
2-1-1 Uchisaiwai-cho, Chiyoda-ku
Tokyo, Japan 100-0011
Phone: 81-3-3509-7588
Fax: 81-3-3509-7586

728 Yanan West Road
HuaMin Empire Plaza, Changning District
Shanghai, China
Phone: 86-10-6568-1391
Fax: 86-10-6568-1392

Management and Staff
Bon Yong Gu, Vice President
Chang Geun Lee, Vice President
Du Seung Yang, Vice President
Gyu Tae Kim, Vice President
Hui Wun Park, Managing Director
Hui Yong Choi, Managing Director
Jin Yeong Kim, Managing Director
Sang Hyun Park, Managing Director
Seung Hui Hyun, Vice President
Seung Yong Yoon, Managing Director
Yong Hwan Yoo, Managing Director

Type of Firm
Private Equity Firm

Association Membership
Korean Venture Capital Association (KVCA)

Project Preferences

Type of Financing Preferred:
Leveraged Buyout
Early Stage
Balanced
Turnaround
Acquisition
Startup
Recapitalizations

Geographical Preferences

United States Preferences:

International Preferences:
China
Asia
Korea, South

Industry Preferences

In Communications prefer:
Communications and Media
Telecommunications
Wireless Communications

In Business Serv. prefer:
Services

Additional Information
Year Founded: 1981
Capital Under Management: $1,636,500,000
Current Activity Level : Actively seeking new investments

KTB PRIVATE EQUITY CO LTD

Uiico-Ro, Yeongdongpo-Gu
66 KTB Building 12
Seoul, South Korea
Phone: 8221844100

Fax: 8221844192
Website: www.ktbpe.co.kr

Type of Firm
Private Equity Firm

Project Preferences

Type of Financing Preferred:
Leveraged Buyout

Geographical Preferences

International Preferences:
China
Singapore
Japan

Industry Preferences

In Industrial/Energy prefer:
Alternative Energy

Additional Information
Year Founded: 2012
Capital Under Management: $84,400,000
Current Activity Level : Actively seeking new investments

KTB VENTURES, INC.

One California Street, Suite 2800
San Francisco, CA USA 94111
Phone: 6503244681
Fax: 6503244682
E-mail: info@ktbvc.com
Website: www.ktbvc.com

Other Offices

23-3, Yoido-dong
Youngdeungpo-gu
Seoul, South Korea 135-080
Phone: 82-2-3466-2000
Fax: 82-2-3466-2120

1266 Nanjing West Road Jingan District
Suite 1707 Plaza 66 Tower 1
Shanghai, China 200040
Phone: 86-21-6113-5758
Fax: 86-21-6113-5759

B12 Jianguomenwai, Dajie Chaoyang Dstr.
Unit 1701B, 17F, E Tower, LG Twin Towers
Beijing, China 100022
Phone: 86-10-6568-1391
Fax: 86-10-6568-1392

2-6-10, Toranomon, Minato-ku
Ninth Floor NH Toranomon Building
Tokyo, Japan 105-0001
Phone: 81-3-3509-7588
Fax: 81-3-3509-7592

88-7 Jungang-dong, Jung-gu
11th Floor Kyobo Life Building
Busan, South Korea
Phone: 82-51-442-5742
Fax: 82-51-465-1136

50 Raffles Place
24-03 Singapore Land Tower
Singapore, Singapore 048623
Phone: 65-6557-0559
Fax: 65-6557-0332

203 Redwood Shores Parkway
Suite 610
Redwood City, CA USA 94065

Management and Staff
Ho Chan Lee, Partner
Peter Shin, Vice President
Sung Yoon, Managing Partner

Type of Firm
Private Equity Firm

Association Membership
Korean Venture Capital Association (KVCA)

Project Preferences

Role in Financing:
Will function either as deal originator or investor in deals created by others

Type of Financing Preferred:
Early Stage
Balanced

Industry Focus

(% based on actual investment)
Internet Specific	29.7%
Communications and Media	21.5%
Semiconductors/Other Elect.	13.8%
Computer Software and Services	13.2%
Consumer Related	13.2%
Medical/Health	4.1%
Other Products	3.1%
Computer Hardware	0.8%
Industrial/Energy	0.7%

Additional Information
Year Founded: 1981
Capital Under Management: $130,000,000
Current Activity Level : Actively seeking new investments
Method of Compensation: Return on investment is of primary concern, do not charge fees

KTH-CHALMERS CAPITAL KB

Birger Jarlsgatan 13
Two Tr.
Stockholm, Sweden 111 45
Phone: 4687521965
Fax: 4687516062
E-mail: info@kthchalmerscapital.se
Website: www.kthchalmerscapital.se

Other Offices
Stena Center
Holtermansgatan 1D
Goteborg, Sweden

Management and Staff
Jakob Svardstrom, Managing Partner
Jonas Rahmn, Chief Executive Officer

Type of Firm
University Program

Association Membership
Swedish Venture Capital Association (SVCA)

Project Preferences

Type of Financing Preferred:
Early Stage
Seed
Startup

Size of Investments Considered:
Min Size of Investment Considered (000s): $495
Max Size of Investment Considered (000s): $989

Geographical Preferences

International Preferences:
Sweden

Industry Preferences

In Computer Software prefer:
Systems Software

In Semiconductor/Electr prefer:
Semiconductor

In Industrial/Energy prefer:
Alternative Energy

Additional Information
Year Founded: 2003
Capital Under Management: $344,000,000
Current Activity Level : Actively seeking new investments

KUMPULAN MODAL PERDANA SDN BHD

The Gardens South Tower
Suite 7.01, Level 7
Kuala Lumpur, Malaysia 59200
Phone: 60322645288
Fax: 60322655388
E-mail: admin@modalperdana.com
Website: www.modalperdana.com

Management and Staff
Badrul Hisham Jaafar, Principal
Shahril Anwar Mohd Yunos, Chief Executive Officer

Type of Firm
Government Affiliated Program

Association Membership
Malaysian Venture Capital Association

Project Preferences

Type of Financing Preferred:
Fund of Funds
Leveraged Buyout
Expansion
Generalist PE
Later Stage
Startup

Geographical Preferences

United States Preferences:
All U.S.

International Preferences:
Malaysia

Industry Preferences

In Communications prefer:
Communications and Media
Telecommunications

In Computer Software prefer:
Software

In Semiconductor/Electr prefer:
Electronics
Semiconductor

Additional Information
Year Founded: 2001
Current Activity Level : Actively seeking new investments

KUNSHAN ACROSS STRAITS INVESTMENT ENTERPRISE, L.P.

Weiyi Road, Huaqiao Econ Dvl'p
International Finance Plaza
Kunshan, Jiangsu, China

Type of Firm
Private Equity Firm

Project Preferences

Type of Financing Preferred:
Balanced

Geographical Preferences

International Preferences:
China

Additional Information
Year Founded: 2011
Capital Under Management: $151,745,000
Current Activity Level : Actively seeking new investments

KUNWU JIUDING CAPITAL HOLDINGS CO LTD

No. 7, Finance Street
6F, Tower D, Winland Intl Ctr.
Beijing, China 100033
Phone: 861063221100
Fax: 861063221188
Website: www.jdcapital.com

Other Offices
Cuiyuan Rd.181
R1105, Shanglv Bldg. No.6
Suzhou, China

No. 1088 Yuanshen Road
25F, Gezhouba Tower
Shanghai, China 200122
Phone: 862138991533
Fax: 862138991533

No. 381, Suzhou Road East
R1105, Shanglv Bldg. No.6
Suzhou, China

1 Zhong Xin Si Road
14F, Tower One, Kerry Plaza
Shenzhen, China 518048
Phone: 8675582569395
Fax: 8675582563235

Management and Staff
Bo Yu, Partner
Lei Cai, Founder
Xiaojie Huang, President
Zhen Huang, Vice President
Zhongyi Zhao, Founder

Type of Firm
Private Equity Firm

Project Preferences

Type of Financing Preferred:
Leveraged Buyout
Expansion
Balanced
Later Stage

Geographical Preferences

International Preferences:
China

Industry Preferences

In Medical/Health prefer:
Health Services

In Consumer Related prefer:
Consumer Products

In Industrial/Energy prefer:
Energy

In Manufact. prefer:
Manufacturing

In Agr/Forestr/Fish prefer:
Agriculture related
Mining and Minerals

Additional Information
Year Founded: 2007
Capital Under Management: $856,488,000
Current Activity Level : Actively seeking new investments

KUNYOUNG INVESTMENT CO LTD

13-4 Yoido-dong
Yongdungpo-gu
Seoul, South Korea
Phone: 822-369-8484
Fax: 822-369-8489
Website: www.gyinvest.co.kr

Management and Staff
Tae In Park, President

Type of Firm
Private Equity Firm

Project Preferences

Type of Financing Preferred:
Balanced

Geographical Preferences

International Preferences:
Korea, South
Japan

Additional Information
Year Founded: 2000
Current Activity Level : Actively seeking new investments

KUO-CHUN FINANCIAL MANAGEMENT INC

3F, No. 233-1, Pao-Chiao Road
Hsin Tien
Taipei, Taiwan
Phone: 886-2-2917-7555
Fax: 386-2-2917-3789

Type of Firm
Private Equity Firm

Association Membership
Taiwan Venture Capital Association(TVCA)

Project Preferences

Type of Financing Preferred:
Expansion
Balanced
Seed
Startup

Geographical Preferences

International Preferences:
Taiwan

Industry Preferences

In Communications prefer:
Telecommunications

In Computer Software prefer:
Software

In Semiconductor/Electr prefer:
Semiconductor

In Biotechnology prefer:
Biotechnology

Additional Information
Year Founded: 1997
Capital Under Management: $14,700,000
Current Activity Level : Actively seeking new investments

KURAMO CAPITAL MANAGEMENT LLC

500 Fifth Avenue
44th Floor
New York, NY USA 10110
Phone: 2127929680
E-mail: info@kuramocapital.com
Website: kuramocapital.com

Management and Staff
Mobolaji Adeoye, Managing Director
Shaka Kariuki, Partner
Wale Adeosun, Founder

Type of Firm
Investment Management Firm

Project Preferences

Type of Financing Preferred:
Fund of Funds
Balanced

Industry Preferences

In Industrial/Energy prefer:
Energy Conservation Relat

In Financial Services prefer:
Real Estate

In Agr/Forestr/Fish prefer:
Agribusiness

Additional Information
Year Founded: 2010

Capital Under Management: $50,000,000
Current Activity Level : Actively seeking new investments

KURMA PARTNERS SA

24, Rue Royale
5th Floor
Paris, France 75008
Phone: 33158194407
E-mail: contact@kls-partners.com
Website: www.kurmapartners.com

Management and Staff
Alain Maiore, Managing Partner
Remi Droller, Partner
Thierry Laugel, Managing Partner

Type of Firm
Private Equity Firm

Association Membership
French Venture Capital Association (AFIC)

Project Preferences

Type of Financing Preferred:
Early Stage
Seed
Startup

Geographical Preferences

International Preferences:
Europe
France

Industry Preferences

In Biotechnology prefer:
Biotechnology

In Medical/Health prefer:
Medical/Health
Health Services

In Other prefer:
Environment Responsible

Additional Information
Name of Most Recent Fund: Kurma Biofund II FCPR
Most Recent Fund Was Raised: 06/20/2013
Year Founded: 2009
Capital Under Management: $94,083,000
Current Activity Level : Actively seeking new investments

KURT SALMON CAPITAL ADVISORS INC

1355 Peachtree Street
Atlanta, GA USA 30309
Phone: 404-897-7248
Fax: 404-253-0373
E-mail: services@kurtsalmon.com
Website: www.kurtsalmoncapitaladvisors.com

Management and Staff
Gary Catherman, Managing Director
O. Bradley Payme, Managing Director

Type of Firm
Private Equity Firm

Project Preferences

Role in Financing:
Prefer role as deal originator

Type of Financing Preferred:
Turnaround
Management Buyouts
Acquisition
Recapitalizations

Geographical Preferences

United States Preferences:
All U.S.

International Preferences:
Europe

Additional Information
Year Founded: 1936
Current Activity Level : Actively seeking new investments

KUWAIT FINANCE AND INVESTMENT COMPANY KSCP

Po Box 21521 Al Arabia Tower
Building No.21
Safat, Kuwait 13037
Website: www.kfic-kw.com

Management and Staff
Moataz Hegab, Chief Financial Officer

Type of Firm
Investment Management Firm

Project Preferences

Type of Financing Preferred:
Balanced

Geographical Preferences

International Preferences:
Pakistan
Bahrain
Oman
Jordan
Qatar
Lebanon
Utd. Arab Em.
Middle East
Saudi Arabia
Yemen
Kuwait

Industry Preferences

In Communications prefer:
Communications and Media
Telecommunications

In Financial Services prefer:
Insurance
Real Estate
Financial Services

Additional Information
Year Founded: 2000
Current Activity Level : Actively seeking new investments

KUWAIT FINANCIAL CENTRE KPSC

Mubarak Al-Kabeer Street
Duaij Building
Al Qiblah, Kuwait
Phone: 96522248000
Fax: 9652245828
E-mail: info@markaz.com
Website: www.markaz.com

Management and Staff
Ali Khalil, Chief Operating Officer
Basma Ghareeb, Vice President
Fahad Al Abdul Jaleel, Vice President
Leila Badine, Vice President
Manaf Al Hajeri, Chief Executive Officer

Type of Firm
Private Equity Firm

Project Preferences

Type of Financing Preferred:
Early Stage
Expansion
Unknown

Geographical Preferences

International Preferences:
Jordan
Qatar
Lebanon
Utd. Arab Em.
Middle East
Saudi Arabia

Industry Preferences

In Communications prefer:
Telecommunications

In Industrial/Energy prefer:
Energy

In Financial Services prefer:
Real Estate

In Business Serv. prefer:
Media

Additional Information
Year Founded: 1974
Current Activity Level : Actively seeking new investments

KV ASIA CAPITAL PTE LTD

Three Church Street
Suite 24-03 Samsung Hub
Singapore, Singapore 049483
Phone: 6566541280
Website: www.kvasiacapital.com

Other Offices
Jl. Jend. Sudirman Kav. 52-53
15th Floor, One Pacific Place
Jakarta, Indonesia 12190
Phone: 622125502626

Management and Staff
Vibhav Panandiker, Chief Executive Officer

Type of Firm
Private Equity Firm

Project Preferences

Type of Financing Preferred:
Management Buyouts
Acquisition

Geographical Preferences

United States Preferences:
Southeast

International Preferences:
Laos
Vietnam
Indonesia
Brunei
Thailand
Cambodia
Philippines
Singapore
Malaysia
Burma

Industry Preferences

In Communications prefer:
Telecommunications

In Medical/Health prefer:
Medical/Health

In Consumer Related prefer:
Consumer

In Industrial/Energy prefer:
Environmental Related

In Financial Services prefer:
Financial Services

In Business Serv. prefer:
Media

In Manufact. prefer:
Manufacturing

Additional Information
Year Founded: 2010
Capital Under Management: $263,000,000
Current Activity Level : Actively seeking new investments

KV PRIVATE EQUITY INC

2627 Ellwood Drive South West
Suite 108
Edmonton, Canada T6X 0P7
Phone: 7804331222
Fax: 18662291295
E-mail: info@kvprivateequity.ca
Website: www.kvprivateequity.ca

Management and Staff
Aleem Virani, President
Jonathan Herman, Chief Operating Officer
Scott Alanen, Chief Financial Officer
Shafin Kanji, Chief Executive Officer

Type of Firm
Private Equity Firm

Geographical Preferences

Canadian Preferences:
Alberta

Industry Preferences

In Consumer Related prefer:
Consumer

In Industrial/Energy prefer:
Oil & Gas Drilling,Explor
Industrial Products

In Manufact. prefer:
Manufacturing

Additional Information
Year Founded: 2014
Current Activity Level : Actively seeking new investments

KYMCO HANGZHOU VENTURE CAPITAL MANAGEMENT CO LTD

No.18 Jiaogong Road, Xihu
Oumei Center
Hangzhou, China
Phone: 8657186698010
Fax: 8657186693017
Website: www.kymcocapital.com

Type of Firm
Investment Management Firm

Project Preferences

Type of Financing Preferred:
Balanced

Geographical Preferences

International Preferences:
China

Additional Information
Year Founded: 2012
Capital Under Management: $32,000,000
Current Activity Level : Actively seeking new investments

KYUSHU JIGYO KEIZOKU BRIDGE INVESTMENT LPS

2-4-22, Daimyo, Chuo-Ku
2F Shin Nihon Building
Fukuoka-shi, Japan
Phone: 81927392311
Fax: 81927392317
E-mail: info@dogan.jp
Website: www.dogan.jp

Type of Firm
SBIC

Project Preferences

Type of Financing Preferred:
Leveraged Buyout
Early Stage
Generalist PE
Balanced
Turnaround
Seed
Management Buyouts
Acquisition
Startup
Recapitalizations

Geographical Preferences

International Preferences:
Asia
Japan

Additional Information
Year Founded: 2005
Capital Under Management: $33,033,000

- L -

L CAPITAL PARTNERS, L.P.

Ten East 53rd Street
37th Floor
New York, NY USA 10022
Phone: 2126757755
Fax: 2122069156
E-mail: info@lcapitalpartners.com
Website: www.lcapitalpartners.com

Other Offices
9 Ahad Ha'am Street
Shalom Tower
Tel-Aviv, Israel 65251
Phone: 97235108581
Fax: 97235163413

Management and Staff
Jonathan Leitersdorf, Principal

Type of Firm
Private Equity Firm

Project Preferences

Type of Financing Preferred:
Expansion
Later Stage

Geographical Preferences

United States Preferences:
East Coast

Industry Preferences

In Internet Specific prefer:
Internet

In Semiconductor/Electr prefer:
Semiconductor

In Medical/Health prefer:
Medical/Health
Medical Products
Pharmaceuticals

In Consumer Related prefer:
Entertainment and Leisure

In Industrial/Energy prefer:
Energy
Environmental Related

In Other prefer:
Environment Responsible

Additional Information
Year Founded: 2004
Capital Under Management: $170,000,000
Current Activity Level : Actively seeking new investments

1262

L CATTERTON ASIA

One Kim Seng Promenade
Suite 18-7/12, Great World City
Singapore, Singapore 237994
Phone: 6566727624
Website: www.lcapitalasia.com

Other Offices

18, Rue Francois IER
Paris, France 75008
Phone: 33144132330

Suite 3001, Plaza 66
1266, Nanjing Road West
Shanghai, China 200040
Phone: 862161332667

303, Third Floor, Tower Wing
Taj Mahal Palace, Apollo Bunder, Colaba
Mumbai, India 400001
Phone: 912261563200

Management and Staff

Anuradha Raja, Vice President
Gilbert Ong, Chief Financial Officer
Hanji Huang, Managing Director
James Tan, Vice President
Jun Wang, Vice President
Ketki Paranjpe, Vice President
Ravi Thakran, Managing Partner
Sanjay Gujral, Managing Director

Type of Firm

Private Equity Firm

Association Membership

Singapore Venture Capital Association (SVCA)

Project Preferences

Type of Financing Preferred:
Leveraged Buyout
Early Stage
Expansion
Later Stage

Geographical Preferences

International Preferences:
India
China
Asia
Singapore

Industry Preferences

In Communications prefer:
Media and Entertainment

In Consumer Related prefer:
Retail
Food/Beverage
Consumer Products

In Business Serv. prefer:
Media

Additional Information

Year Founded: 2009
Capital Under Management: $1,630,000,000
Current Activity Level : Actively seeking new investments

L CATTERTON EUROPE SAS

18, rue Francois 1er
Paris, France 75008
Phone: 33144132330
Fax: 33144134280
E-mail: lcapital@lvmh.fr
Website: www.lcapital.eu

Other Offices

Via Manzoni, 42
Milan, Italy 20121
Phone: 39-02-7626-191
Fax: 39-02-7626-1933

Almagro 1
2, 1 ZQ
Madrid, Spain 28010
Phone: 34-91-310-2748
Fax: 34-91-310-2779

Management and Staff

Andrea Ottaviano, Partner
Eduardo Velasco, Partner
Julio Babecki, Partner

Type of Firm

Corporate PE/Venture

Association Membership

French Venture Capital Association (AFIC)
European Private Equity and Venture Capital Assoc.
Spanish Venture Capital Association (ASCRI)

Project Preferences

Type of Financing Preferred:
Leveraged Buyout
Acquisition

Size of Investments Considered:
Min Size of Investment Considered (000s): $19,412
Max Size of Investment Considered (000s): $77,650

Geographical Preferences

United States Preferences:

International Preferences:
India
Europe
China
Asia
France

Industry Focus

(% based on actual investment)
Communications and Media   35.6%
Internet Specific   34.5%
Consumer Related   29.9%

Additional Information

Name of Most Recent Fund: L Capital 3 FCPR
Most Recent Fund Was Raised: 03/02/2012
Year Founded: 2001
Capital Under Management: $1,305,100,000
Current Activity Level : Actively seeking new investments

L EIGENKAPITALAGENTUR

An der RaumFabrik 10
Karlsruhe, Germany 76227
Phone: 4972113208700
Fax: 4972113208750
E-mail: kontakt@l-ea.de

Management and Staff

Heinrich Polke, Managing Director

Type of Firm

Bank Affiliated

Project Preferences

Type of Financing Preferred:
Early Stage
Seed
Management Buyouts
Startup

Size of Investments Considered:
Min Size of Investment Considered (000s): $3,332
Max Size of Investment Considered (000s): $66,631

Geographical Preferences

International Preferences:
Germany

Industry Preferences

In Communications prefer:
Communications and Media

In Biotechnology prefer:
Biotechnology

Additional Information

Year Founded: 2002
Current Activity Level : Actively seeking new investments

L SQUARED CAPITAL PARTNERS

451 West Huron
Suite 1410
Chicago, IL USA 60654
Phone: 7736299964
Website: www.lsquaredcap.com

Pratt's Guide to Private Equity & Venture Capital Sources

Type of Firm
Private Equity Firm

Project Preferences

Type of Financing Preferred:
Leveraged Buyout
Recapitalizations

Geographical Preferences

United States Preferences:
North America

Industry Preferences

In Consumer Related prefer:
Education Related

In Industrial/Energy prefer:
Industrial Products

Additional Information
Year Founded: 2014
Capital Under Management: $332,500,000
Current Activity Level: Actively seeking new investments

L&S VENTURECAPITAL CORP

944-24, Daechi-Dong, Gangam-Gu
5/F Sean Building
Seoul, South Korea 135-846
Phone: 822-501-1031
Fax: 822-501-1029

Management and Staff
Dongshik Chang, Chief Executive Officer
Shincheon Kim, President
Sunglin Ju, Partner

Type of Firm
Private Equity Firm

Association Membership
Korean Venture Capital Association (KVCA)

Project Preferences

Type of Financing Preferred:
Balanced

Geographical Preferences

International Preferences:
Korea, South

Industry Preferences

In Industrial/Energy prefer:
Environmental Related

Additional Information
Year Founded: 2006
Capital Under Management: $15,600,000
Current Activity Level: Actively seeking new investments

L'ACCELERATEUR SAS

13, Rue de Marivaux
Paris, France 75002
Website: laccelerateur.fr

Type of Firm
Incubator/Development Program

Project Preferences

Type of Financing Preferred:
Early Stage
Expansion

Geographical Preferences

International Preferences:
France

Industry Preferences

In Computer Software prefer:
Software

In Internet Specific prefer:
Internet

Additional Information
Year Founded: 2012
Current Activity Level: Actively seeking new investments

L'EXPRESS VENTURES SAS

29 rue de Chateaudun
Paris, France 75009

Type of Firm
Private Equity Firm

Project Preferences

Type of Financing Preferred:
Early Stage
Seed
Startup

Geographical Preferences

International Preferences:
Europe
France

Industry Preferences

In Communications prefer:
Media and Entertainment
Publishing

In Internet Specific prefer:
Internet
Ecommerce

Additional Information
Year Founded: 2012
Current Activity Level: Actively seeking new investments

L-GAM ADVISERS LLP

20 St James's Street
London, United Kingdom SW1A 1ES
Phone: 442070244777
E-mail: info@l-gam.com
Website: www.l-gam.com

Other Offices
2a, Rue Albert Borschette
Luxembourg, Luxembourg L-1246
Phone: 442070244765

Management and Staff
Aled Jones, Chief Financial Officer
Felipe Merry del Val, Co-Founder
Ferdinando Grimaldi, Co-Founder
Jerome Bertrand, Partner
Tito Soso, Partner
Yves Alexandre, Co-Founder

Type of Firm
Private Equity Firm

Project Preferences

Type of Financing Preferred:
Leveraged Buyout
Turnaround
Acquisition
Recapitalizations

Geographical Preferences

International Preferences:
Europe

Industry Preferences

In Medical/Health prefer:
Health Services

In Consumer Related prefer:
Consumer
Retail

In Industrial/Energy prefer:
Industrial Products

In Business Serv. prefer:
Services

Additional Information
Year Founded: 2013
Capital Under Management: $47,391,000
Current Activity Level: Actively seeking new investments

L-SPARK CORP

340 Legget Drive
Suite 110
Ottawa, Canada K2K 1Y6
Website: www.l-spark.com

Management and Staff
Leo Lax, Managing Director

Type of Firm
Incubator/Development Program

Project Preferences

Type of Financing Preferred:
Seed
Startup

Geographical Preferences

Canadian Preferences:
All Canada

Industry Preferences

In Computer Software prefer:
Software
Systems Software
Applications Software

Additional Information
Year Founded: 2014
Current Activity Level : Actively seeking new investments

L2 CAPITAL PARTNERS
259 North Radnor-Chester Road
Suite 280
Radnor, PA USA 19087
Phone: 6109224030
E-mail: info@L2Capital.net
Website: www.l2capital.net

Type of Firm
Private Equity Firm

Project Preferences

Type of Financing Preferred:
Leveraged Buyout
Acquisition
Recapitalizations

Geographical Preferences

United States Preferences:
North America

Industry Preferences

In Business Serv. prefer:
Services
Distribution

In Manufact. prefer:
Manufacturing

Additional Information
Year Founded: 2011
Current Activity Level : Actively seeking new investments

LA CHINA CAPITAL CO LTD
No.99 Hongxiang Road
Room 405, No.2 Building
Shanghai, China
E-mail: info@lachinacapital.com
Website: www.lachinacapital.com

Type of Firm
Investment Management Firm

Project Preferences

Type of Financing Preferred:
Early Stage
Expansion
Balanced
Later Stage

Geographical Preferences

International Preferences:
China

Industry Preferences

In Communications prefer:
Telecommunications
Media and Entertainment

In Medical/Health prefer:
Medical/Health
Medical Diagnostics
Medical Products

In Industrial/Energy prefer:
Energy

In Manufact. prefer:
Manufacturing

Additional Information
Year Founded: 2005
Current Activity Level : Actively seeking new investments

LA DODGERS SPORTS & ENTERTAINMENT ACCELERATOR WITH R/GA
12777 W Jefferson Blvd #101
Los Angeles, CA USA 90066
Website: www.dodgersaccelerator.com

Type of Firm
Private Equity Firm

Project Preferences

Type of Financing Preferred:
Early Stage
Seed
Startup

Geographical Preferences

United States Preferences:
California

Industry Preferences

In Communications prefer:
Media and Entertainment

In Consumer Related prefer:
Entertainment and Leisure
Sports

Additional Information
Year Founded: 2015
Current Activity Level : Actively seeking new investments

LA FAMIGLIA GMBH
Barer Strasse 65
Munich, Germany 80799
Phone: 491765683504
E-mail: ciao@lafamiglia.vc
Website: lafamiglia.vc

Type of Firm
Private Equity Firm

Project Preferences

Type of Financing Preferred:
Early Stage

Additional Information
Year Founded: 2016
Current Activity Level : Actively seeking new investments

LA FINANCIERE PATRIMONIALE D'INVESTISSEMENT SAS
24-26 rue Ballu
Paris, France 75009
Phone: 33158364490
Fax: 33158364499
E-mail: contact@lfpi.fr
Website: www.lfpi.fr

Other Offices
5, Avenue Gaston Diderich
Luxembourg, Luxembourg 1420

Rue de Rive 1
Geneva, Switzerland 1204
Phone: 41-22-319-7900
Fax: 41-22-319-7919

Management and Staff
Fabien Bismuth, President
Gilles Etrillard, President
Philippe Jonquet, Founder

Type of Firm
Private Equity Firm

Association Membership
French Venture Capital Association (AFIC)
European Private Equity and Venture Capital Assoc.

Project Preferences

Type of Financing Preferred:
Leveraged Buyout
Early Stage
Mezzanine
Generalist PE
Balanced
Public Companies
Later Stage
Management Buyouts
Acquisition

Size of Investments Considered:
Min Size of Investment Considered (000s): $3,996
Max Size of Investment Considered (000s): $66,604

Geographical Preferences

International Preferences:
Europe
Germany
France

Industry Preferences

In Communications prefer:
Entertainment

In Medical/Health prefer:
Medical/Health

In Consumer Related prefer:
Consumer
Consumer Services

In Industrial/Energy prefer:
Industrial Products

In Financial Services prefer:
Real Estate

In Business Serv. prefer:
Services
Distribution

In Manufact. prefer:
Manufacturing

Additional Information
Name of Most Recent Fund: LFPE SCA SICAR
Most Recent Fund Was Raised: 04/27/2007
Year Founded: 2002
Capital Under Management: $272,035,000
Current Activity Level : Actively seeking new investments

LA FINANZIARIA TRENTINA SPA

via Mantova, 53
38122
Trento, Italy
Phone: 39 0461 260831
Fax: 39 0461 221805
E-mail: segreteria@lafinanziariatrentina.it
Website: www.lafinanziariatrentina.it

Type of Firm
Private Equity Firm

Project Preferences

Type of Financing Preferred:
Leveraged Buyout
Acquisition

Geographical Preferences

International Preferences:
Italy

Industry Preferences

In Industrial/Energy prefer:
Energy
Industrial Products

In Transportation prefer:
Transportation

In Financial Services prefer:
Real Estate
Investment Groups

Additional Information
Year Founded: 2004
Current Activity Level : Actively seeking new investments

LABRADOR VENTURES

535 Middlefield Road
Suite 190
Menlo Park, CA USA 94025
Phone: 6503666000
Fax: 6503666430
E-mail: labrador@labrador.com
Website: www.labrador.com

Other Offices
101 University Avenue
Fourth Floor
Palo Alto, CA USA 94301

Management and Staff
Lawrence Kubal, Partner
Sean Foote, Venture Partner
Stuart Davidson, Managing Partner
Stuart Davidson, Partner

Type of Firm
Private Equity Firm

Association Membership
Western Association of Venture Capitalists (WAVC)

Project Preferences

Role in Financing:
Will function either as deal originator or investor in deals created by others

Type of Financing Preferred:
Early Stage
Seed
Startup

Size of Investments Considered:
Min Size of Investment Considered (000s): $1,000
Max Size of Investment Considered (000s): $6,000

Geographical Preferences

United States Preferences:
West Coast

Industry Preferences

In Communications prefer:
Data Communications
Satellite Microwave Comm.

In Computer Software prefer:
Software

In Computer Other prefer:
Computer Related

In Semiconductor/Electr prefer:
Semiconductor

In Industrial/Energy prefer:
Advanced Materials

In Business Serv. prefer:
Services

Additional Information
Name of Most Recent Fund: Labrador Ventures V, L.P.
Most Recent Fund Was Raised: 08/02/2002
Year Founded: 1989
Capital Under Management: $216,000,000
Current Activity Level : Actively seeking new investments
Method of Compensation: Return on investment is of primary concern, do not charge fees

LACONIA VENTURES LLC

132 W 31st Street, Suite 702
Manhattan, NY USA 10001
Website: www.laconiacapitalgroup.com

Type of Firm
Private Equity Firm

Project Preferences

Type of Financing Preferred:
Early Stage

Industry Preferences

In Communications prefer:
Communications and Media
Wireless Communications

Additional Information
Year Founded: 2013
Capital Under Management: $1,600,000
Current Activity Level : Actively seeking new investments

LACUNA LLC

1100 Spruce Street, Suite 202
Boulder, CO USA 80302
Phone: 3034471700
Fax: 3034471710
E-mail: info@lacuna.com
Website: www.lacuna.com

Management and Staff
J. Hullett, Chief Financial Officer
Rich O Leary, Partner
Wink Jones, Partner

Type of Firm
Private Equity Firm

Project Preferences

Type of Financing Preferred:
Early Stage

Size of Investments Considered:
Min Size of Investment Considered (000s): $500
Max Size of Investment Considered (000s): $3,000

Additional Information
Name of Most Recent Fund: Lacuna Venture Fund LLLP
Most Recent Fund Was Raised: 12/16/2008
Year Founded: 2006
Capital Under Management: $15,000,000
Current Activity Level : Actively seeking new investments

LAKE CAPITAL

676 North Michigan Avenue, Suite 3900
Chicago, IL USA 60611
Phone: 3126407050
Fax: 3126407051
E-mail: info@lakecapital.com
Website: www.lakecapital.com

Management and Staff
Bill Sommerschield, Vice President
Douglas Rescho, Vice President
Jonathan Westberg, Vice President
Kevin Rowe, Principal
Michael Hayes, Chief Financial Officer

Type of Firm
Private Equity Firm

Project Preferences

Role in Financing:
Prefer role as deal originator

Type of Financing Preferred:
Fund of Funds
Leveraged Buyout
Generalist PE
Acquisition
Startup

Industry Preferences

In Medical/Health prefer:
Health Services

In Consumer Related prefer:
Retail
Consumer Services

In Financial Services prefer:
Financial Services

In Business Serv. prefer:
Services
Distribution
Consulting Services

Additional Information
Name of Most Recent Fund: Lake Capital Partners II, L.P.
Most Recent Fund Was Raised: 10/08/2005
Year Founded: 1990
Capital Under Management: $1,300,000,000
Current Activity Level : Actively seeking new investments
Method of Compensation: Function primarily in service area, receive contingent fee in cash or equity

LAKEHOUSE VENTURE PARTNERS LP

1350 Avenue of the Americas, Suite 373
New York, NY USA 10019

Type of Firm
Private Equity Firm

Project Preferences

Type of Financing Preferred:
Balanced

Industry Preferences

In Consumer Related prefer:
Consumer

Additional Information
Year Founded: 2016
Current Activity Level : Actively seeking new investments

LAKESHORE CAPITAL PARTNERS CO LTD

1 S Sathorn Road, Thungmahamek
Q House Lumpini Bldg, Sathorn
Bangkok, Thailand 10120
E-mail: info@lakeshore-capital.com
Website: www.lakeshore-capital.com

Type of Firm
Private Equity Firm

Project Preferences

Type of Financing Preferred:
Management Buyouts

Industry Preferences

In Medical/Health prefer:
Medical/Health

In Consumer Related prefer:
Consumer
Retail
Food/Beverage

In Manufact. prefer:
Manufacturing

In Agr/Forestr/Fish prefer:
Agribusiness

Additional Information
Year Founded: 2011
Capital Under Management: $60,000,000
Current Activity Level : Actively seeking new investments

LAKESIDE CAPITAL MANAGEMENT LLC

50 South Sixth Street, Suite 1460
Minneapolis, MN USA 55402
Phone: 6122434400
Fax: 6122434446
E-mail: info@gmbmezz.com
Website: www.lakesidecapital.net

Management and Staff
Barry Lindquist, Co-Founder
Carleton Olmanson, Co-Founder
Daniel Hemiadan, Partner
Michael Vossen, Principal
Michael McHugh, Co-Founder
Susan Gohman, Principal
Thomas Kreimer, Chief Financial Officer

Type of Firm
Private Equity Firm

Association Membership
Natl Assoc of Small Bus. Inv. Co (NASBIC)

Project Preferences

Role in Financing:
Will function either as deal originator or investor in deals created by others

Type of Financing Preferred:
Leveraged Buyout
Expansion
Mezzanine
Management Buyouts
Acquisition
Recapitalizations

Geographical Preferences

United States Preferences:

Industry Preferences

In Industrial/Energy prefer:
Industrial Products

In Business Serv. prefer:
Services
Distribution

In Manufact. prefer:
Manufacturing

Additional Information

Name of Most Recent Fund: GMB Mezzanine Capital II, L.P.
Most Recent Fund Was Raised: 12/27/2010
Year Founded: 1997
Capital Under Management: $279,200,000
Current Activity Level : Actively seeking new investments

LAKESTAR ADVISORS GMBH

Utcquai 55
Zurich, Switzerland 8008
Phone: 41554201446
Website: www.lakestar.com

Other Offices

C\o Lakestar II G.P. LTD, PO Box 656
East Wing, Trafalgar Court, Les Banques
Saint Peter Port, United Kingdom GY1 3PP
Phone: 441481749700

Type of Firm
Private Equity Firm

Project Preferences

Type of Financing Preferred:
Early Stage
Seed
Startup

Industry Preferences

In Internet Specific prefer:
Internet

Additional Information

Year Founded: 2008
Capital Under Management: $405,750,000
Current Activity Level : Actively seeking new investments

LAKEVIEW EQUITY PARTNERS LLC

700 North Water Street
Suite 630
Milwaukee, WI USA 53202
Phone: 4147322040
Fax: 4147322041
E-mail: info@lakeviewequity.com
Website: www.lakeviewequity.com

Management and Staff

Gordon Gunnlaugsson, Principal
Joseph Cesarz, Vice President
Ted Kellner, Principal
William Abraham, Principal
William Read, Principal

Type of Firm
Private Equity Firm

Project Preferences

Type of Financing Preferred:
Leveraged Buyout
Later Stage
Management Buyouts
Acquisition
Recapitalizations

Geographical Preferences

United States Preferences:
Midwest
All U.S.

Industry Preferences

In Consumer Related prefer:
Food/Beverage

In Financial Services prefer:
Financial Services
Financial Services

In Business Serv. prefer:
Services
Distribution

In Manufact. prefer:
Manufacturing

Additional Information

Name of Most Recent Fund: Lakeview Equity Partners II, L.P.
Most Recent Fund Was Raised: 08/30/2012
Year Founded: 2005
Capital Under Management: $38,000,000
Current Activity Level : Actively seeking new investments

LAKEWEST VENTURE PARTNERS

833 N. Orleans Street
Suite 400
Chicago, IL USA 60610
Phone: 3127512777
Fax: 3127512715
Website: www.belgraviagroup.com/affiliates/lakewest

Type of Firm
Private Equity Firm

Project Preferences

Type of Financing Preferred:
Early Stage
Seed

Size of Investments Considered:
Min Size of Investment Considered (000s): $50
Max Size of Investment Considered (000s): $3,000

Geographical Preferences

United States Preferences:
Illinois

Additional Information

Year Founded: 2013
Current Activity Level : Actively seeking new investments

LAKEWOOD CAPITAL LLC

Seven Old Field Road, Suite 1001
Rowayton, CT USA 06853
Phone: 2036040863
Fax: 2036632817
E-mail: info@lakewoodcap.com
Website: www.lakewoodcap.com

Type of Firm
Private Equity Firm

Project Preferences

Type of Financing Preferred:
Leveraged Buyout

Additional Information

Year Founded: 2008
Current Activity Level : Actively seeking new investments

LAMBDA FUND MANAGEMENT INC

432 East 84th Street
New York, NY USA 10028
Phone: 2127741812
Fax: 2122887603
E-mail: alamport@lambdafund.com
Website: www.lambdafund.com

Management and Staff
Anthony Lamport, General Partner

Type of Firm
Private Equity Firm

Association Membership
National Venture Capital Association - USA (NVCA)

Project Preferences

Role in Financing:
Will function either as deal originator or investor in deals created by others

Type of Financing Preferred:
Leveraged Buyout
Early Stage

Size of Investments Considered:
Min Size of Investment Considered (000s): $100
Max Size of Investment Considered (000s): $500

Geographical Preferences

United States Preferences:
Mid Atlantic
North America
West Coast

Industry Focus
(% based on actual investment)

Biotechnology	24.7%
Computer Software and Services	14.1%
Computer Hardware	12.7%
Other Products	12.5%
Industrial/Energy	10.2%
Consumer Related	8.0%
Semiconductors/Other Elect.	7.3%
Medical/Health	4.9%
Communications and Media	3.6%
Internet Specific	2.0%

Additional Information
Year Founded: 1979
Capital Under Management: $10,000,000
Current Activity Level : Actively seeking new investments
Method of Compensation: Return on investment is of primary concern, do not charge fees

LANDA VENTURES LTD

3 Pekeris Street
Park Tamar
Rehovot, Israel 7612301
E-mail: Contact-us@landaventures.com

Type of Firm
Private Equity Firm

Project Preferences

Type of Financing Preferred:
Early Stage
Expansion
Later Stage
Seed
Startup

Geographical Preferences

International Preferences:
Israel

Industry Preferences

In Communications prefer:
Satellite Microwave Comm.

In Industrial/Energy prefer:
Energy

Additional Information
Year Founded: 2003
Current Activity Level : Actively seeking new investments

LANDIS AND GYR AG

3955 Bigelow Boulevard
Suite 100
Pittsburgh, PA USA 15213
Phone: 4125963788
Website: www.landisgyr.com

Type of Firm
Private Equity Firm

Project Preferences

Type of Financing Preferred:
Leveraged Buyout
Acquisition

Geographical Preferences

United States Preferences:

Additional Information
Year Founded: 2003
Capital Under Management: $100,000,000
Current Activity Level : Actively seeking new investments

LANDMARK CAPITAL UAB

Olimpieciu g. 1-2
Vilnius, Lithuania LT-09235
E-mail: landmark@lmcapital.lt
Website: lmcapital.lt

Management and Staff
Marijus Jarockis, Chief Executive Officer

Type of Firm
Private Equity Firm

Project Preferences

Type of Financing Preferred:
Leveraged Buyout
Value-Add
Acquisition

Geographical Preferences

International Preferences:
Lithuania

Additional Information
Year Founded: 2012
Current Activity Level : Actively seeking new investments

LANDMARK PARTNERS INC

Ten Mill Pond Lane
Simsbury, CT USA 06070
Phone: 8606519760
Fax: 8606518890
E-mail: info@landmarkpartners.com
Website: www.landmarkpartners.com

Other Offices

52 Jermyn Street
London, United Kingdom SW1Y 6LX
Phone: 442073434450
Fax: 442073434488

265 Franklin Street
18th Floor
Boston, MA USA 02110
Phone: 617-556-3910
Fax: 617-556-4266

681 Fifth Avenue
New York, NY USA 10022
Phone: 2128589760

Management and Staff
Barry Griffiths, Vice President
Chad Alfeld, Partner
Gregory Lombardi, Vice President
Ian Charles, Partner
Ibrahim Majeed, Vice President
Ira Shaw, Vice President
James McConnell, Partner
James Sunday, Partner
Jason Neal, Vice President
John Cook, Vice President
Julie Gionfriddo, Vice President
Kathryn Regan, Vice President
Michael Carrano, Vice President
Paul Giovacchini, Principal
Paul Parker, Managing Director
Paul Mehlman, Partner
Robert Dombi, Partner
Robert Shanfield, Partner
Scott Humber, Principal
Tina St. Pierre, Partner

Type of Firm
Private Equity Advisor or Fund of Funds

Project Preferences

Role in Financing:
Prefer role as deal originator

Type of Financing Preferred:
Fund of Funds
Fund of Funds of Second

Geographical Preferences

United States Preferences:
All U.S.

International Preferences:
Europe
Asia
All International

Industry Focus

(% based on actual investment)
Other Products	60.8%
Computer Software and Services	17.2%
Industrial/Energy	6.6%
Medical/Health	3.5%
Biotechnology	3.3%
Semiconductors/Other Elect.	3.0%
Computer Hardware	3.0%
Consumer Related	1.6%
Internet Specific	0.9%

Additional Information

Year Founded: 1984
Capital Under Management: $12,500,000,000
Current Activity Level : Actively seeking new investments
Method of Compensation: Other

LANDON INVESTMENTS SCR SA

Via Augusta, 200-6
Barcelona, Spain 08021
Phone: 34932405200
Fax: 34932416202
E-mail: mcaus@landon.es

Management and Staff

Antonio Gallardo Ballart, President
Julio Cazorla Aiguabella, Managing Director

Type of Firm

Private Equity Firm

Association Membership

Spanish Venture Capital Association (ASCRI)

Project Preferences

Type of Financing Preferred:
Leveraged Buyout
Early Stage
Expansion
Turnaround
Seed
Acquisition
Startup
Recapitalizations

Geographical Preferences

International Preferences:
Spain

Industry Preferences

In Consumer Related prefer:
Entertainment and Leisure
Food/Beverage
Consumer Products
Consumer Services

In Industrial/Energy prefer:
Energy
Environmental Related

In Business Serv. prefer:
Media

Additional Information

Year Founded: 2002
Current Activity Level : Actively seeking new investments

LANE FIVE VENTURES LLC

726 17th Avenue Northeast
Saint Petersburg, FL USA 33704
Phone: 727-385-7360
Fax: 813-463-1706
Website: www.lanefive.com

Management and Staff

Mark Swanson, Managing Director

Type of Firm

Private Equity Firm

Project Preferences

Type of Financing Preferred:
Startup

Geographical Preferences

United States Preferences:
All U.S.

Additional Information

Year Founded: 2008
Current Activity Level : Actively seeking new investments

LANGHOLM CAPITAL LLP

5-11 Regent Street
First Floor, Charles House
London, United Kingdom SW1Y 4LR
Phone: 442074848850
Fax: 442074848852
E-mail: info@langholm.com
Website: www.langholm.com

Management and Staff

Albert Wiegman, Founder
Anthony Sills, Partner

Type of Firm

Private Equity Firm

Association Membership

British Venture Capital Association (BVCA)
European Private Equity and Venture Capital Assoc.

Project Preferences

Role in Financing:
Prefer role as deal originator but will also invest in deals created by others

Type of Financing Preferred:
Leveraged Buyout
Management Buyouts

Geographical Preferences

International Preferences:
United Kingdom
Europe

Industry Preferences

In Consumer Related prefer:
Consumer Products

Additional Information

Name of Most Recent Fund: Langholm Capital II, L.P.
Most Recent Fund Was Raised: 01/16/2009
Year Founded: 2002
Capital Under Management: $532,800,000
Current Activity Level : Actively seeking new investments

LANKA VENTURES PLC

Ocean Lines Building
46/12, Navam Mawatha
Colombo, Sri Lanka
Phone: 94-11-243-9201
Fax: 94-11-243-9203
Website: www.acuity.lk

Management and Staff

Kanthimany Maheshwaran, Chief Executive Officer
Sumith Arangala, Chief Executive Officer

Type of Firm

Bank Affiliated

Project Preferences

Role in Financing:
Prefer role in deals created by others

Type of Financing Preferred:
Leveraged Buyout
Early Stage
Expansion
Generalist PE
Turnaround
Seed
Startup

Size of Investments Considered:
Min Size of Investment Considered (000s): $139
Max Size of Investment Considered (000s): $464

Geographical Preferences

International Preferences:
Sri Lanka

Industry Preferences

In Medical/Health prefer:
Medical/Health

In Industrial/Energy prefer:
Energy

Additional Information

Year Founded: 1992
Capital Under Management: $10,600,000
Current Activity Level: Actively seeking new investments
Method of Compensation: Return on invest. most important, but chg. closing fees, service fees, etc.

LANTERN ASSET MANAGEMENT LP

300 Crescent Court
Suite 1100
Dallas, TX USA 75201
Phone: 4695547900
Fax: 2142455882
E-mail: contact@lanternam.com

Management and Staff

Milos Brajovic, Managing Director
Thomas Schmidt, Managing Director

Type of Firm

Investment Management Firm

Project Preferences

Type of Financing Preferred:
Generalist PE

Industry Preferences

In Financial Services prefer:
Real Estate

Additional Information

Year Founded: 2010
Current Activity Level: Actively seeking new investments

LANTU INNOVATION INVESTMENT MANAGEMENT BEIJING CO LTD

No. 9 Jiuxianqiao North Road,
C7, Hengtong International Inn
Beijing, China
Phone: 861056478800
Website: www.lanfund.com.cn

Type of Firm

Investment Management Firm

Project Preferences

Type of Financing Preferred:
Balanced

Geographical Preferences

International Preferences:
China

Additional Information

Year Founded: 2014
Current Activity Level: Actively seeking new investments

LANZAME CAPITAL

Carrer de Llull, 321
Barcelona, Spain 08019
E-mail: info@lanzame.es
Website: www.lanzame.es

Type of Firm

Private Equity Firm

Project Preferences

Type of Financing Preferred:
Startup

Additional Information

Year Founded: 2012
Current Activity Level: Actively seeking new investments

LAPRADE CHAMPLIN INC

290, rue St-Joseph C.P. 607
La Tuque, Canada G9X 3P5
Phone: 819-523-2375
Fax: 819-523-7843

Type of Firm

Government Affiliated Program

Additional Information

Year Founded: 1987
Current Activity Level: Actively seeking new investments

LARIAT PARTNERS LP

1331 17th Street
Suite 812
Denver, CO USA 80202
Phone: 7205446262
E-mail: info@lariatpartners.net
Website: lariatpartners.net

Management and Staff

Jason Urband, Principal
Jay Coughlon, Co-Founder
Kevin Mitchell, Co-Founder
Matthew Amann, Chief Financial Officer

Type of Firm

Private Equity Firm

Project Preferences

Type of Financing Preferred:
Leveraged Buyout
Expansion
Later Stage
Acquisition

Industry Preferences

In Medical/Health prefer:
Health Services

In Industrial/Energy prefer:
Energy
Environmental Related

In Agr/Forestr/Fish prefer:
Agriculture related

Additional Information

Name of Most Recent Fund: Lariat Partners Fund I, L.P.
Most Recent Fund Was Raised: 10/03/2013
Year Founded: 2013
Capital Under Management: $118,000,000
Current Activity Level: Actively seeking new investments

LARSEN MACCOLL PARTNERS LP

353 West Lancaster Avenue
Radnor, PA USA 19087
Phone: 6106875045
Fax: 6105450855
E-mail: info@larsenmaccoll.com

Management and Staff

Christopher Davis, Partner
Jeff Larsen, Managing Partner
Richard Hurwitz, Managing Director
Satya Ponnuru, Partner
Tim MacColl, Managing Partner
Todd Marsteller, Partner

Type of Firm
Private Equity Firm

Project Preferences

Type of Financing Preferred:
Leveraged Buyout

Geographical Preferences

United States Preferences:

Canadian Preferences:
All Canada

Industry Preferences

In Consumer Related prefer:
Food/Beverage
Consumer Products
Consumer Services
Other Restaurants

In Industrial/Energy prefer:
Industrial Products
Advanced Materials

In Business Serv. prefer:
Services
Distribution

In Manufact. prefer:
Manufacturing

Additional Information
Name of Most Recent Fund: Larsen MacColl Partners II, L.P.
Most Recent Fund Was Raised: 12/16/2010
Year Founded: 2007
Capital Under Management: $34,247,000
Current Activity Level : Actively seeking new investments

LAS OLAS VENTURE CAPITAL

888 East Las Olas Blvd.
Suite 200
Fort Lauderdale, FL USA 33301
Website: www.lasolasvc.com

Type of Firm
Private Equity Firm

Project Preferences

Type of Financing Preferred:
Early Stage

Industry Preferences

In Computer Software prefer:
Software

In Medical/Health prefer:
Health Services

In Consumer Related prefer:
Education Related

In Business Serv. prefer:
Services

Additional Information
Year Founded: 1969
Capital Under Management: $20,680,000
Current Activity Level : Actively seeking new investments

LASALLE CAPITAL

70 West Madison Street
5710 Three First Nat'l Plaza
Chicago, IL USA 60602
Phone: 3122367041
Fax: 3122360720
E-mail: contact@lasallecapitalgroup.com
Website: www.lasallecapitalgroup.com

Management and Staff
Andrew Shackelford, Partner
Jeffrey Walters, Co-Founder
Kelly Cornelis, Partner
Naveen Neerukonda, Vice President
Nicholas Christopher, Partner
Rocco Martino, Co-Founder
Ryan Anthony, Principal

Type of Firm
Private Equity Firm

Association Membership
Illinois Venture Capital Association
Natl Assoc of Small Bus. Inv. Co (NASBIC)

Project Preferences

Role in Financing:
Prefer role as deal originator but will also invest in deals created by others

Type of Financing Preferred:
Leveraged Buyout
Expansion
Management Buyouts
Acquisition
Recapitalizations

Industry Preferences

In Consumer Related prefer:
Food/Beverage

In Business Serv. prefer:
Services
Distribution

In Manufact. prefer:
Manufacturing

Additional Information
Name of Most Recent Fund: LaSalle Capital Group II, L.P.
Most Recent Fund Was Raised: 06/07/2012
Year Founded: 1984
Capital Under Management: $330,000,000
Current Activity Level : Actively seeking new investments
Method of Compensation: Return on invest. most important, but chg. closing fees, service fees, etc.

LATERAL CAPITAL LLC

106 West 32nd
Suite 144
New York, NY USA 10001
Phone: 2126839500
Website: www.latcap.co

Type of Firm
Private Equity Firm

Project Preferences

Type of Financing Preferred:
Balanced

Geographical Preferences

International Preferences:
Africa

Additional Information
Year Founded: 2016
Current Activity Level : Actively seeking new investments

LATERAL INVESTMENT MANAGEMENT LLC

1001 Bayhill Drive
Suite 205
San Bruno, CA USA 94066
Phone: 6504896420
Fax: 7734962949
Website: www.lateralinvestors.com

Type of Firm
Investment Management Firm

Project Preferences

Type of Financing Preferred:
Leveraged Buyout
Expansion
Acquisition

Additional Information
Year Founded: 1969
Current Activity Level : Actively seeking new investments

LATIN AMERICAN PARTNERS LLC

900 17th Street, North West, Suite 910
Washington, DC USA 20006
Phone: 12025303180
E-mail: dcoffice@lapfunds.com
Website: www.latinamericanpartners.com

Other Offices

2 Avenida, Aparamentos Torrefuerte 5
Residencial La Cumbre
Tegucigalpa, Honduras
Phone: 50422321802

Durango 263, Piso 1
Colonia Roma, Mexico DF 06700
Phone: 525555338940

Type of Firm
Private Equity Firm

Project Preferences

Type of Financing Preferred:
Expansion
Mezzanine

Geographical Preferences

International Preferences:
Latin America
Mexico

Additional Information
Year Founded: 2013
Current Activity Level : Actively seeking new investments

LATIN IDEA VENTURES LLC

Paseo de las Palmas 405-601
Col. Lomas de Chapultepec
Mexico City, Mexico 11000
Phone: 525529733030
Fax: 525529733030
E-mail: info@latinidea.com
Website: www.latinidea.com

Management and Staff
Alexander Rossi, Managing Partner
Humberto Zesati, Managing Partner
Miguel Angel Davila, Managing Partner

Type of Firm
Private Equity Firm

Association Membership
Emerging Markets Private Equity Association

Project Preferences

Type of Financing Preferred:
Early Stage
Expansion
Later Stage
Seed

Size of Investments Considered:
Min Size of Investment Considered (000s): $1,000
Max Size of Investment Considered (000s): $6,000

Geographical Preferences

International Preferences:
Mexico

Industry Preferences

In Communications prefer:
Communications and Media
Telecommunications

In Business Serv. prefer:
Services
Media

Additional Information
Year Founded: 2000
Capital Under Management: $230,740,000
Current Activity Level : Actively seeking new investments

LATITUDE INVESTMENTS PTY LTD

Three Macquarie Street
Suite 75
Sydney, Australia 2000
Phone: 61292476602
Fax: 61292472990
Website: latitudeinvestments.com.au

Type of Firm
Private Equity Firm

Project Preferences

Type of Financing Preferred:
Early Stage
Seed

Geographical Preferences

International Preferences:
Australia

Industry Preferences

In Business Serv. prefer:
Distribution

In Manufact. prefer:
Manufacturing

In Agr/Forestr/Fish prefer:
Mining and Minerals

Additional Information
Year Founded: 2012
Current Activity Level : Actively seeking new investments

LATOUR CAPITAL MANAGEMENT SAS

2, Rue Washington
Paris, France 75008
Phone: 33140623000
Fax: 33140623025
Website: www.latour-capital.fr

Type of Firm
Bank Affiliated

Association Membership
French Venture Capital Association (AFIC)

Project Preferences

Type of Financing Preferred:
Later Stage

Geographical Preferences

International Preferences:
Switzerland
Belgium

Industry Preferences

In Internet Specific prefer:
Internet

In Industrial/Energy prefer:
Alternative Energy
Industrial Products

In Business Serv. prefer:
Services

In Other prefer:
Environment Responsible

Additional Information
Year Founded: 2011
Capital Under Management: $479,355,000
Current Activity Level : Actively seeking new investments

LATTERELL VENTURE PARTNERS LP

455 Market Street, Suite 2220
San Francisco, CA USA 94105
Phone: 4153999880
Fax: 4153999879
Website: www.lvpcapital.com

Management and Staff
Bob Curry, Partner
Jim Woody, Partner
Ken Widder, Partner
Patrick Latterell, Managing Partner
Peter Fitzgerald, Partner
Stephen Salmon, Partner

Type of Firm
Private Equity Firm

Project Preferences

Role in Financing:
Will function either as deal originator or investor in deals created by others

Type of Financing Preferred:
Early Stage
Startup

Size of Investments Considered:
Min Size of Investment Considered (000s): $10,000
Max Size of Investment Considered (000s): $20,000

Industry Preferences

In Biotechnology prefer:
Biotechnology

In Medical/Health prefer:
Medical/Health
Medical Diagnostics
Medical Products
Pharmaceuticals

Additional Information
Name of Most Recent Fund: Latterell Venture Partners III, L.P.
Mcst Recent Fund Was Raised: 06/23/2005
Year Founded: 2001
Capital Under Management: $96,000,000
Current Activity Level : Actively seeking new investments

LATTICE VENTURES LLC

321 W 29TH STREET
#2C
New York, NY USA 10001
Phone: 6467216368
Website: lattice.vc

Management and Staff
Brittany Gorevic, Partner
Vanessa Pestritto, Partner

Type of Firm
Private Equity Firm

Additional Information
Year Founded: 2016
Capital Under Management: $2,050,000
Current Activity Level : Actively seeking new investments

LATTICEWORK CAPITAL MANAGEMENT LLC

5950 Berkshire Lane
Suite 1401
Dallas, TX USA 75225
Phone: 2146130179
Website: latticeworkcapital.com

Type of Firm
Private Equity Firm

Project Preferences

Type of Financing Preferred:
Leveraged Buyout
Acquisition

Industry Preferences

In Medical/Health prefer:
Health Services

Additional Information
Year Founded: 2015
Current Activity Level : Actively seeking new investments

LAUDER PARTNERS LLC

88 Mercedes Loan
Menlo Park, CA USA 94027
Phone: 6503235700
Fax: 6503232171
Website: www.lauderpartners.com

Management and Staff
Gary Lauder, Managing Partner

Type of Firm
Private Equity Firm

Association Membership
Western Association of Venture Capitalists (WAVC)
National Venture Capital Association - USA (NVCA)

Project Preferences

Type of Financing Preferred:
Fund of Funds
Balanced

Geographical Preferences

United States Preferences:

Canadian Preferences:
All Canada

Industry Preferences

In Communications prefer:
Telecommunications

In Internet Specific prefer:
Internet

Additional Information
Year Founded: 1988
Capital Under Management: $10,300,000
Current Activity Level : Actively seeking new investments

LAUGHING ANGELS FOUNDATION

1344 Lexington Avenue
New York, NY USA 10128
E-mail: admin@laf-cvf.org
Website: www.winddancer.com

Type of Firm
Endowment, Foundation or Pension Fund

Project Preferences

Type of Financing Preferred:
Balanced

Industry Preferences

In Consumer Related prefer:
Education Related

In Other prefer:
Socially Responsible

Additional Information
Year Founded: 2015
Current Activity Level : Actively seeking new investments

LAUNCH FUND

3525 Eastham Drive
Culver City, CA USA 90232
Phone: 3108530743

Type of Firm
Incubator/Development Program

Project Preferences

Type of Financing Preferred:
Seed
Startup

Size of Investments Considered:
Min Size of Investment Considered (000s): $25,000
Max Size of Investment Considered (000s): $100,000

Geographical Preferences

United States Preferences:

International Preferences:
All International

Industry Preferences

In Internet Specific prefer:
Internet

In Consumer Related prefer:
Consumer Products
Consumer Services
Education Related

In Industrial/Energy prefer:
Industrial Products

Additional Information
Year Founded: 2013
Capital Under Management: $300,000
Current Activity Level : Actively seeking new investments

LAUNCH TENNESSEE

211 7th Avenue North
Suite 205
Nashville, TN USA 37219
Phone: 6156734419
Fax: 6152499949
E-mail: info@launchtn.org
Website: launchtn.org

Type of Firm
Government Affiliated Program

Project Preferences

Type of Financing Preferred:
Early Stage

Geographical Preferences

United States Preferences:
Tennessee

Additional Information
Year Founded: 1969
Capital Under Management: $29,700,000
Current Activity Level : Actively seeking new investments

LAUNCH:ALASKA

601 W 5th Ave
Floor 2
Anchorage, AK USA 99501
E-mail: info@launchalaska.com
Website: www.launchalaska.com

Type of Firm
Incubator/Development Program

Project Preferences

Type of Financing Preferred:
Seed

Additional Information
Year Founded: 2016
Capital Under Management: $120,000
Current Activity Level : Actively seeking new investments

LAUNCHCAPITAL LLC

One Mifflin Place
Suite 320
Cambridge, MA USA 02138
Website: www.launch-capital.com

Other Offices
500, Seventh Avenue
17th Floor
MIDTOWN, NY USA 10018

142 Temple Street
Suite 206
NEW HAVEN, CT USA 06510

Management and Staff
Cliff Sirlin, Managing Director
Elon Boms, Managing Director
Heather Onstott, Venture Partner
Stefan Pepe, Venture Partner
Tom Egan, Principal
Woody Benson, Venture Partner

Type of Firm
Private Equity Firm

Association Membership
New England Venture Capital Association

Project Preferences

Type of Financing Preferred:
Early Stage
Seed

Additional Information
Year Founded: 2008
Capital Under Management: $20,000,000
Current Activity Level : Actively seeking new investments

LAUNCHCYTE L L C

2403 Sidney Street
Suite 271
Pittsburgh, PA USA 15203
Phone: 4124812200
Fax: 4125920349
E-mail: info@launchcyte.com
Website: www.launchcyte.com

Management and Staff
Babs Carryer, Co-Founder

Type of Firm
Incubator/Development Program

Project Preferences

Role in Financing:
Prefer role as deal originator

Type of Financing Preferred:
Early Stage
Seed
Startup

Industry Preferences

In Biotechnology prefer:
Biotechnology

In Medical/Health prefer:
Medical Diagnostics
Medical Products
Health Services

Additional Information
Year Founded: 2000
Capital Under Management: $800,000
Current Activity Level : Actively seeking new investments

LAUNCHHOUSE

3558 Lee Road
Cleveland, OH USA 44120
Phone: 2162553070
Website: www.launchhouse.com

Type of Firm
Incubator/Development Program

Project Preferences

Type of Financing Preferred:
Early Stage
Startup

Geographical Preferences

United States Preferences:
Northeast
Ohio

Industry Preferences

In Communications prefer:
Communications and Media
Wireless Communications
Media and Entertainment

In Computer Hardware prefer:
Computers

In Computer Software prefer:
Applications Software

In Internet Specific prefer:
Internet
Ecommerce

In Medical/Health prefer:
Medical/Health
Medical Products

In Industrial/Energy prefer:
Alternative Energy
Robotics

In Business Serv. prefer:
Services

In Manufact. prefer:
Manufacturing

Additional Information
Year Founded: 2008
Current Activity Level : Actively seeking new investments

LAUNCHPAD DIGITAL HEALTH LLC

645 harrison street
suite 200
San Francisco, CA USA 94107
Website: www.launchpdh.com

Management and Staff
Mark Schwartz, Managing Director

Type of Firm
Incubator/Development Program

Project Preferences

Type of Financing Preferred:
Seed
Strategic Alliances
Startup

Size of Investments Considered:
Min Size of Investment Considered (000s): $200
Max Size of Investment Considered (000s): $400

Additional Information
Year Founded: 2014
Current Activity Level : Actively seeking new investments

LAUNCHPAD LA INC

1520 2nd Street
Santa Monica, CA USA 90401
Phone: 6504012011
E-mail: hello@launchpad.la
Website: www.launchpad.la

Management and Staff
Mark Suster, Founder
Sam Teller, Managing Director

Type of Firm
Incubator/Development Program

Project Preferences

Type of Financing Preferred:
Seed
Startup

Size of Investments Considered:
Min Size of Investment Considered (000s): $25
Max Size of Investment Considered (000s): $100

Geographical Preferences

United States Preferences:
Southern California
California

Additional Information
Year Founded: 2008
Current Activity Level : Actively seeking new investments

LAUREL CAPITAL PARTNERS

259 Radnor-Chester Road
Radnor Court, Suite 140
Wayne, PA USA 19087
Phone: 6109643313
Fax: 6109643312
Website: www.laurelcapitalpartners.com

Management and Staff
John Weber, Founding Partner
Robert Drury, Partner
Roger Braunfeld, Partner

Type of Firm
Private Equity Firm

Project Preferences

Type of Financing Preferred:
Leveraged Buyout
Expansion

Geographical Preferences

United States Preferences:
East Coast

Industry Preferences

In Medical/Health prefer:
Medical/Health
Health Services

In Transportation prefer:
Transportation

In Financial Services prefer:
Financial Services

In Manufact. prefer:
Manufacturing

Additional Information
Year Founded: 2007
Current Activity Level : Actively seeking new investments

LAURENTIAN BANK OF CANADA

1981 McGill College
Suite 1660
Montreal, Canada H3A 3K3
Phone: 514-284-3987
Fax: 514-284-3988
Website: www.laurentianbank.ca

Type of Firm
Endowment, Foundation or Pension Fund

Additional Information
Year Founded: 2009
Current Activity Level : Actively seeking new investments

LAUX CAPITAL PARTNERS

672 West Liberty Street
Medina, OH USA 44256
Phone: 330-721-0100

Management and Staff
William Laux, General Partner

Type of Firm
Private Equity Firm

Project Preferences

Type of Financing Preferred:
Mezzanine

Geographical Preferences

United States Preferences:
All U.S.

Additional Information
Year Founded: 2004
Capital Under Management: $200,000
Current Activity Level : Actively seeking new investments

LAVEER GROWTH CAPITAL LLC

450 East Waterside Drive
Suite 2803
Chicago, IL USA 60601

Type of Firm
Private Equity Firm

Project Preferences

Type of Financing Preferred:
Early Stage

Additional Information
Year Founded: 1969
Current Activity Level : Actively seeking new investments

LAVROCK VENTURES LLC

1765 Greensboro Station Place
Suite 900
McLean, VA USA 22102
Website: www.lavrockvc.com

Type of Firm
Private Equity Firm

Project Preferences

Type of Financing Preferred:
Early Stage

Industry Preferences

In Computer Software prefer:
Software

In Business Serv. prefer:
Services

Additional Information
Year Founded: 2016
Current Activity Level : Actively seeking new investments

Pratt's Guide to Private Equity & Venture Capital Sources

LAZARD AUSTRALIA PRIVATE EQUITY

One Macquarie Place
Level 44 Gateway
Sydney, Australia 2000
Phone: 61292569900
Fax: 61292569950
Website: www.lazard.com.au

Other Offices

Two Esplanade
Level 36, Exchange Plaza
, Australia WA 6000
Phone: 618-9223-0400
Fax: 618-9223-0499

101 Collins Street
Level 33
Melbourne, Australia VIC 3000
Phone: 613-9657-8400
Fax: 613-96578411

Management and Staff

Christopher Mulshine, Managing Director
John Wylie, CEO & Managing Director

Type of Firm

Private Equity Firm

Association Membership

Australian Venture Capital Association (AVCAL)

Project Preferences

Role in Financing:
Prefer role as deal originator but will also invest in deals created by others

Type of Financing Preferred:
Leveraged Buyout
Turnaround
Later Stage
Acquisition

Geographical Preferences

International Preferences:
Pacific

Industry Preferences

In Medical/Health prefer:
Medical/Health

In Industrial/Energy prefer:
Energy

In Financial Services prefer:
Financial Services

Additional Information

Name of Most Recent Fund: Lazard Australia Corporate Opportunity Fund 2
Most Recent Fund Was Raised: 11/11/2011
Year Founded: 2005
Capital Under Management: $368,000,000
Current Activity Level : Actively seeking new investments

LAZARD INDIA ADVISORS PVT LTD

Nariman Point
20th Floor Express Towers
Mumbai, India 400021
Phone: 91-22-6752-6000
Fax: 91-22-6752-6060

Type of Firm

Bank Affiliated

Project Preferences

Type of Financing Preferred:
Leveraged Buyout
Acquisition

Geographical Preferences

International Preferences:
India

Industry Preferences

In Communications prefer:
Telecommunications

In Biotechnology prefer:
Biotechnology

In Medical/Health prefer:
Health Services
Pharmaceuticals

In Consumer Related prefer:
Retail
Food/Beverage
Consumer Services
Education Related

In Industrial/Energy prefer:
Energy

In Transportation prefer:
Transportation

In Manufact. prefer:
Manufacturing

Additional Information

Year Founded: 2009
Current Activity Level : Actively seeking new investments

LAZARD TECHNOLOGY PARTNERS

30 Rockefeller Plaza
48th Floor
New York, NY USA 10020
Phone: 2126326000

Other Offices

5335 Wisconsin Avenue, Northwest
Suite 410
Washington, DC USA 20015
Phone: 2028951505
Fax: 2028951501

Type of Firm

Private Equity Firm

Project Preferences

Type of Financing Preferred:
Early Stage
Expansion
Balanced
Later Stage
Seed
Startup

Size of Investments Considered:
Min Size of Investment Considered (000s): $1,000
Max Size of Investment Considered (000s): $10,000

Geographical Preferences

United States Preferences:
Mid Atlantic
New Hampshire
Rhode Island
Vermont
Northeast
Massachusetts
Connecticut
Washington
Maine
New York

Industry Focus

(% based on actual investment)
Computer Software and Services	58.5%
Internet Specific	27.6%
Communications and Media	4.8%
Computer Hardware	4.7%
Semiconductors/Other Elect.	3.4%
Consumer Related	1.1%

Additional Information

Name of Most Recent Fund: Lazard Technology Partners II
Most Recent Fund Was Raised: 05/09/2000
Year Founded: 1998
Capital Under Management: $400,000,000
Current Activity Level : Making few, if any, new investments

LAZARUS CAPITAL PARTNERS

3300 Cahaba Road, Suite 212
Birmingham, AL USA 35223
Phone: 2058711043
Fax: 2058704502
Website: www.lazaruscap.com

1277

Management and Staff
Hewes Hull, Partner
Robert Jennings, Partner
W. Spencer South, Partner

Type of Firm
Private Equity Firm

Project Preferences

Type of Financing Preferred:
Leveraged Buyout
Early Stage
Acquisition

Geographical Preferences

United States Preferences:
Tennessee
Mississippi
Southeast
Alabama
Florida
Georgia

Industry Preferences

In Business Serv. prefer:
Services
Distribution

In Manufact. prefer:
Manufacturing

Additional Information
Name of Most Recent Fund: Lazarus Private Equity Fund II, L.P.
Most Recent Fund Was Raised: 09/10/2010
Year Founded: 1969
Capital Under Management: $10,375,000
Current Activity Level : Actively seeking new investments

LB INVESTMENT INC

512, Teheran-ro, Gangnam-gu
13Floor, Shinan Building
Seoul, South Korea 135845
Phone: 82234670500
Fax: 82234670530
Website: www.lbinvestment.com

Management and Staff
Chao Zhao, Principal
Chun Myung Park, Partner
DooSeok Chae, Partner
Geun Yeong Ahn, Vice President
JaeHyun Park, Partner
Jason Koo, Vice President
Jayna Choi, Principal
JeongGeun Park, Principal
JooWon Lee, Principal
JoungGun Park, Partner
Kyung Hoon Cho, Vice President
William Zheng, Principal
Yun Gwon Kim, General Partner

Type of Firm
Private Equity Firm

Association Membership
Korean Venture Capital Association (KVCA)

Project Preferences

Type of Financing Preferred:
Early Stage
Expansion
Mezzanine
Balanced
Seed
Startup

Size of Investments Considered:
Min Size of Investment Considered (000s): $500
Max Size of Investment Considered (000s): $3,000

Geographical Preferences

International Preferences:
China
Asia
Korea, South

Industry Preferences

In Communications prefer:
Communications and Media
Telecommunications

In Internet Specific prefer:
Internet

In Semiconductor/Electr prefer:
Semiconductor

In Biotechnology prefer:
Biotechnology
Agricultural/Animal Bio.

In Manufact. prefer:
Manufacturing

Additional Information
Year Founded: 1996
Capital Under Management: $103,400,000
Current Activity Level : Actively seeking new investments

LBBW VENTURE CAPITAL GMBH

Koenigstrasse 10 C
Stuttgart, Germany 70173
Phone: 4971130589200
Fax: 49711305892099
E-mail: Zukunft@LBBW-Venture.de
Website: www.lbbw-venture.de

Management and Staff
Harald Fuchs, Managing Director

Type of Firm
Bank Affiliated

Association Membership
German Venture Capital Association (BVK)

Project Preferences

Type of Financing Preferred:
Early Stage
Later Stage
Seed
Startup

Size of Investments Considered:
Min Size of Investment Considered (000s): $363
Max Size of Investment Considered (000s): $3,625

Geographical Preferences

International Preferences:
Switzerland
Austria
Germany

Industry Preferences

In Communications prefer:
Telecommunications

In Computer Software prefer:
Software

In Internet Specific prefer:
Internet

In Computer Other prefer:
Computer Related

In Biotechnology prefer:
Biotechnology

In Medical/Health prefer:
Medical/Health
Pharmaceuticals

In Industrial/Energy prefer:
Industrial Products

In Manufact. prefer:
Manufacturing

Additional Information
Year Founded: 2000
Current Activity Level : Actively seeking new investments

LBC CAPITAL INC

1981, avenue McGill College
Bureau 1485
Montreal, Canada H3A 3K3
Phone: 514-284-4732
Fax: 514-284-4551

Type of Firm
Investment Management Firm

Additional Information
Year Founded: 1997
Current Activity Level : Actively seeking new investments

LBC CREDIT PARTNERS INC

2929 Arch Street
Suite 1550, Cira Centre
Philadelphia, PA USA 19104
Phone: 2159728900
E-mail: info@lbccredit.com
Website: www.lbccredit.com

Other Offices

125 South Wacker Drive
Suite 1625
Chicago, IL USA 60606
Phone: 3122630312

1221 Avenue of the Americas
42nd Floor
New York, NY USA 10020
Phone: 2125425839

Management and Staff

Allan Allweiss, Managing Director
Andrew Thornton, Vice President
Christopher Calabrese, Partner
David Fraimow, Managing Director
Homyar Choksi, Managing Director
Ira Lubert, Partner
John Brignola, Managing Partner
Kevin Doogan, Managing Director
Nathaniel Cohen, Partner
Nevin Murkley, Vice President
Ryan Rassin, Managing Director

Type of Firm

Private Equity Firm

Project Preferences

Type of Financing Preferred:
Leveraged Buyout
Expansion
Mezzanine
Management Buyouts
Acquisition
Recapitalizations

Geographical Preferences

United States Preferences:
North America

Additional Information

Name of Most Recent Fund: LBC Credit Partners III, L.P.
Most Recent Fund Was Raised: 12/28/2012
Year Founded: 2005
Capital Under Management: $1,000,000,000
Current Activity Level : Actively seeking new investments

LBO FRANCE GESTION SAS

148 rue de l'Universite
Paris, France 75007
Phone: 33140627767
Fax: 33140627555
Website: www.lbofrance.com

Management and Staff

Robert Daussun, Chief Executive Officer

Type of Firm

Private Equity Firm

Association Membership

French Venture Capital Association (AFIC)
European Private Equity and Venture Capital Assoc.

Project Preferences

Type of Financing Preferred:
Leveraged Buyout
Management Buyouts
Acquisition

Geographical Preferences

International Preferences:
Fr Polynesia
Europe
Western Europe
France

Industry Focus

(% based on actual investment)
Other Products	59.2%
Consumer Related	21.1%
Industrial/Energy	17.0%
Internet Specific	1.6%
Medical/Health	0.8%
Computer Software and Services	0.2%
Semiconductors/Other Elect.	0.1%

Additional Information

Year Founded: 1985
Capital Under Management: $4,536,000,000
Current Activity Level : Actively seeking new investments

LBO ITALIA INVESTIMENTI SRL

Via Vivaio 8
Milano, Italy 20122
Phone: 390276022800
Fax: 390276022477
E-mail: lboit@lboit.com
Website: www.lboit.com

Management and Staff

Barbara Santoli, Chief Financial Officer
Giovanni Paglia, President

Type of Firm

Private Equity Firm

Project Preferences

Type of Financing Preferred:
Leveraged Buyout
Acquisition

Geographical Preferences

International Preferences:
Italy

Industry Preferences

In Medical/Health prefer:
Medical/Health
Pharmaceuticals

In Industrial/Energy prefer:
Energy

Additional Information

Year Founded: 1969
Current Activity Level : Actively seeking new investments

LCC LEGACY HOLDINGS INC

141 Adelaide Street West
Suite 770
Toronto, Canada M5H 3L5
Phone: 4162134223
Fax: 4162134232

Other Offices

303 Wyman Street
Suite 300
WALTHAM, MA USA 02451
Phone: 7815303868
Fax: 2534844262

Management and Staff

Benjamin Rovinski, Managing Director
Brian Underdown, Managing Director
Daniel Hetu, Managing Director
Gerry Brunk, Managing Director
Jacki Jenuth, Principal
Peter Van Der Velden, Managing Partner
Stephen Cummings, Chief Financial Officer

Type of Firm

Private Equity Firm

Association Membership

National Venture Capital Association - USA (NVCA)
Canadian Venture Capital Association

Project Preferences

Role in Financing:
Will function either as deal originator or investor in deals created by others

Type of Financing Preferred:
Early Stage
Balanced
Later Stage

Size of Investments Considered:
Min Size of Investment Considered (000s): $5,000
Max Size of Investment Considered (000s): $10,000

Geographical Preferences

United States Preferences:

Canadian Preferences:
All Canada

Industry Focus
(% based on actual investment)

Biotechnology	55.7%
Medical/Health	32.0%
Internet Specific	6.1%
Computer Software and Services	2.7%
Semiconductors/Other Elect.	1.3%
Communications and Media	1.0%
Consumer Related	0.7%
Industrial/Energy	0.4%
Other Products	0.1%

Additional Information
Name of Most Recent Fund: Lumira Capital II, L.P.
Most Recent Fund Was Raised: 03/26/2012
Year Founded: 1988
Capital Under Management: $1,000,000,000
Current Activity Level: Actively seeking new investments
Method of Compensation: Return on investment is of primary concern, do not charge fees

LD EQUITY

Gammeltorv 18
P.O. Box 93
Copenhagen, Denmark DK-1457
Phone: 4533387300
Fax: 4533387310
E-mail: kontakt@majinvest.com
Website: www.ldequity.dk

Management and Staff
Henrik Parkhoi, Managing Director
Jan H Sorensen, Partner
Niels Toft, Partner

Type of Firm
Private Equity Firm

Association Membership
Danish Venture Capital Association (DVCA)

Project Preferences

Type of Financing Preferred:
Leveraged Buyout
Generalist PE
Balanced
Turnaround
Management Buyouts
Acquisition

Size of Investments Considered:
Min Size of Investment Considered (000s): $10,000
Max Size of Investment Considered (000s): $30,000

Geographical Preferences

International Preferences:
Denmark

Industry Preferences

In Consumer Related prefer:
Consumer Products

In Industrial/Energy prefer:
Materials
Environmental Related

In Business Serv. prefer:
Services

Additional Information
Name of Most Recent Fund: Maj Invest Equity 4 K/S
Most Recent Fund Was Raised: 03/07/2013
Year Founded: 2005
Capital Under Management: $1,221,600,000
Current Activity Level: Actively seeking new investments

LDV PARTNERS

228 Hamilton Avenue
Third Floor
Palo Alto, CA USA 94303
Website: ldvp.com

Type of Firm
Private Equity Firm

Project Preferences

Type of Financing Preferred:
Early Stage
Later Stage

Industry Preferences

In Consumer Related prefer:
Consumer

In Industrial/Energy prefer:
Energy

In Business Serv. prefer:
Services
Media

Additional Information
Year Founded: 1969
Current Activity Level: Actively seeking new investments

LE GROUPE FORCES SENC

444, 5e Rue 2e Etase
Shawinigan, Canada G9N 1E6
Phone: 819-537-5107
Fax: 819-537-5109
Website: www.groupeforces.qc.ca

Type of Firm
Private Equity Firm

Project Preferences

Type of Financing Preferred:
Expansion

Geographical Preferences

Canadian Preferences:
Quebec

Additional Information
Year Founded: 1984
Current Activity Level: Actively seeking new investments

LEAD CAPITAL MANAGEMENT CO LTD

1-2-1 Marunouchi Chiyoda-ku
5F Tokio Marine Nichido Bldg
Tokyo, Japan 100-0005
Phone: 81332841711
Fax: 81332841885
Website: www.antcapital.jp

Type of Firm
Private Equity Firm

Project Preferences

Type of Financing Preferred:
Balanced

Geographical Preferences

International Preferences:
Japan

Additional Information
Year Founded: 2006
Capital Under Management: $100,000
Current Activity Level: Actively seeking new investments

LEAD EDGE CAPITAL

405 Lexington Avenue
32nd Floor
New York, NY USA 10174
Phone: 2129842421
Website: www.leadedgecapital.com

Type of Firm
Private Equity Firm

Project Preferences

Type of Financing Preferred:
Expansion
Balanced

Geographical Preferences

United States Preferences:

Industry Preferences

In Computer Software prefer:
Software

In Internet Specific prefer:
Internet

Additional Information

Name of Most Recent Fund: Lead Edge Ventures I, L.P.
Most Recent Fund Was Raised: 02/24/2014
Year Founded: 1969
Capital Under Management: $858,411,000
Current Activity Level : Actively seeking new investments

LEAD EQUITIES GMBH

Schwarzenbergplatz 5
Vienna, Austria 1030
Phone: 43150360860
Fax: 431503608610
E-mail: office@leadequities.at
Website: www.leadequities.at

Management and Staff

Dirk Brandis, Managing Partner
Norbert Doll, Managing Partner
Robert Wietrzyk, Chief Financial Officer
Stephan Zochling, Co-Founder

Type of Firm

Private Equity Firm

Project Preferences

Type of Financing Preferred:
Leveraged Buyout
Management Buyouts

Geographical Preferences

International Preferences:
Europe
Switzerland
Austria
Germany

Industry Preferences

In Semiconductor/Electr prefer:
Electronics

In Medical/Health prefer:
Medical/Health

In Consumer Related prefer:
Consumer
Food/Beverage

In Industrial/Energy prefer:
Machinery

In Transportation prefer:
Transportation

Additional Information

Name of Most Recent Fund: Lead Equities I
Most Recent Fund Was Raised: 01/17/2003
Year Founded: 2001
Current Activity Level : Actively seeking new investments

LEADER VENTURES LLC

3000 Sand Hill Road, 1-100
Menlo Park, CA USA 94025
Phone: 6508541800
E-mail: contact.us@leaderventures.com
Website: www.leaderventures.com

Management and Staff

Brian Best, Managing Director
Patrick Gordan, Managing Director

Type of Firm

Private Equity Firm

Project Preferences

Type of Financing Preferred:
Mezzanine

Size of Investments Considered:
Min Size of Investment Considered (000s): $1,000
Max Size of Investment Considered (000s): $5,000

Industry Preferences

In Industrial/Energy prefer:
Energy
Environmental Related

In Other prefer:
Environment Responsible

Additional Information

Year Founded: 2005
Current Activity Level : Actively seeking new investments

LEADERS FUNDS

20 Eglinton Ave W, Suite 1900
Toronto, Canada M4R 1K8
Website: leaders-fund.com

Management and Staff

David Stein, Co-Founder
Gideon Hayden, Co-Founder
Howard Gwin, Venture Partner
Stephen DeBacco, Co-Founder

Type of Firm

Private Equity Firm

Additional Information

Year Founded: 2015
Capital Under Management: $69,740,000
Current Activity Level : Actively seeking new investments

LEADING EDGE VENTURES LLC

One Innovation Way
Suite 301
Newark, DE USA 19711
Phone: 3024521120
Website: www.leading-edge-ventures.com

Other Offices

116 Research Drive
Suite 2204
Bethlehem, PA USA 18015

Type of Firm

Private Equity Firm

Project Preferences

Size of Investments Considered:
Min Size of Investment Considered (000s): $50
Max Size of Investment Considered (000s): $750

Geographical Preferences

United States Preferences:
Mid Atlantic
Delaware

Industry Preferences

In Medical/Health prefer:
Health Services

In Business Serv. prefer:
Services

Additional Information

Year Founded: 2007
Current Activity Level : Actively seeking new investments

LEADING RIDGE CAPITAL PARTNERS LLC

One Research Court
Suite 101
Rockville, MD USA 20850
Phone: 3012359020
Fax: 3012359021
E-mail: info@leadingridge.com
Website: www.leadingridge.com

Other Offices

570 Lexington Avenue
Ninth Floor
New York, NY USA 10022

Management and Staff

Pam Paladino, Vice President
Robert Mayn, Partner
Warren Coopersmith, Managing Partner
Zach Coopersmith, Partner

Type of Firm
Private Equity Firm

Project Preferences

Type of Financing Preferred:
Leveraged Buyout
Management Buyouts
Acquisition
Recapitalizations

Geographical Preferences

United States Preferences:
Mid Atlantic

Industry Preferences

In Business Serv. prefer:
Distribution

In Manufact. prefer:
Manufacturing

Additional Information
Year Founded: 2009
Current Activity Level : Actively seeking new investments

LEAF CLEAN ENERGY USA LLC

900 Seventh Street, NW
Suite 735
Washington, DC USA 20001
Phone: 2022897881
E-mail: info@leafcleanenergy.com
Website: www.leafcleanenergy.com

Management and Staff
James Potochny, Chief Financial Officer
Matthew Fedors, Principal
Yonatan Alemu, Principal

Type of Firm
Private Equity Firm

Project Preferences

Type of Financing Preferred:
Expansion
Later Stage

Size of Investments Considered:
Min Size of Investment Considered (000s): $5,000
Max Size of Investment Considered (000s): $20,000

Industry Preferences

In Industrial/Energy prefer:
Energy

Additional Information
Year Founded: 2010
Current Activity Level : Actively seeking new investments

LEAF INVESTMENTS LTD

Greenhills Road
Hibernian Industrial Estate
Dublin, Ireland 24
Phone: 353872979108
E-mail: info@leafinvestments.net
Website: www.leafinvestments.net

Management and Staff
Alan Maguire, Partner
Hugh O Driscoll, Partner
Jonny Parkes, Partner

Type of Firm
Private Equity Firm

Project Preferences

Type of Financing Preferred:
Early Stage
Expansion
Seed

Geographical Preferences

International Preferences:
Ireland
Europe

Industry Preferences

In Computer Software prefer:
Software

In Consumer Related prefer:
Education Related

Additional Information
Year Founded: 2011
Current Activity Level : Actively seeking new investments

LEAN FUND SA

Rue Emile Francqui 6/1
Mont Saint Guibert, Belgium B-1435
Website: www.leanfund.com

Type of Firm
Private Equity Firm

Project Preferences

Type of Financing Preferred:
Early Stage
Seed

Geographical Preferences

International Preferences:
Belgium

Additional Information
Year Founded: 2014
Current Activity Level : Actively seeking new investments

LEAP GLOBAL PARTNERS

3430 West Bayshore Road
Suite 104
Palo Alto, CA USA 94303
Phone: 4086577889
E-mail: info@leapglobalpartners.com
Website: www.leapglobalpartners.com

Type of Firm
Private Equity Firm

Project Preferences

Type of Financing Preferred:
Early Stage
Seed

Geographical Preferences

United States Preferences:

International Preferences:
Mexico

Additional Information
Year Founded: 2016
Current Activity Level : Actively seeking new investments

LEAP VENTURES

Beirut Digital District
BDD 1075 Bachoura
Beirut, Lebanon
Phone: 9611647888
E-mail: businessplan@leap.vc
Website: leap.vc

Other Offices
Beirut Digital District
BDD 1075 Bachoura
Beirut, Lebanon
Phone: 9611647888

Type of Firm
Private Equity Firm

Project Preferences

Type of Financing Preferred:
Early Stage

Geographical Preferences

International Preferences:
Middle East
Africa

Industry Preferences

In Computer Software prefer:
Software

In Internet Specific prefer:
Internet

LEAPFROG INVESTMENTS

One Melrose Boulevard
Unit 24, Melrose Arch
Johannesburg, South Africa
Phone: 27116842644
E-mail: info@leapfroginvest.com
Website: www.leapfroginvest.com

Management and Staff
Andrew Kuper, President
Dominic Liber, Partner
Doug Lacey, Partner
Felix Olale, Partner
Gary Herbert, Partner
Jim Roth, Co-Founder
Stewart Langdon, Partner

Type of Firm
Investment Management Firm

Association Membership
Emerging Markets Private Equity Association

Project Preferences

Type of Financing Preferred:
Generalist PE
Later Stage
Acquisition

Geographical Preferences

International Preferences:
Indonesia
Pakistan
India
Nigeria
Ghana
Kenya
Philippines
Sri Lanka
Asia
South Africa
Africa

Industry Preferences

In Financial Services prefer:
Financial Services
Insurance

Additional Information
Name of Most Recent Fund: LeapFrog Investments Fund II
Most Recent Fund Was Raised: 09/09/2013
Year Founded: 2007
Capital Under Management: $400,000,000
Current Activity Level : Actively seeking new investments

LEAPFROG VENTURES L P

830 Menlo Avenue
Suite 100
Menlo Park, CA USA 94025
E-mail: busplan@leapfrogventures.com
Website: www.leapfrogventures.com

Management and Staff
Peter Sinclair, Founder

Type of Firm
Private Equity Firm

Project Preferences

Role in Financing:
Prefer role as deal originator but will also invest in deals created by others

Type of Financing Preferred:
Seed
Startup

Size of Investments Considered:
Min Size of Investment Considered (000s): $1,000
Max Size of Investment Considered (000s): $3,000

Industry Preferences

In Communications prefer:
Communications and Media
Wireless Communications

In Computer Software prefer:
Software

In Consumer Related prefer:
Consumer

Additional Information
Name of Most Recent Fund: Leapfrog Venture II, L.P.
Most Recent Fund Was Raised: 09/29/2004
Year Founded: 1999
Capital Under Management: $100,000,000
Current Activity Level : Actively seeking new investments
Method of Compensation: Return on investment is of primary concern, do not charge fees

LEARN CAPITAL VENTURE PARTNERS LP

78 First Street
Sixth Floor
San Francisco, CA USA 94105
Phone: 8663362092
Fax: 8669017829
E-mail: info@learncapital.com

Other Offices
816 Congress Avenue
Suite 400
Austin, TX USA 78701

Additional Information
Year Founded: 2014
Capital Under Management: $71,000,000
Current Activity Level : Actively seeking new investments

Beijing Kerry Center, 11th Fl. North Twr
1 Guanghua Road, Chaoyang District
Beijing, China 100020
Phone: 86-10-6599-7941
Fax: 86-10-6599-9100

Management and Staff
Elliott Bisnow, Venture Partner
Greg Mauro, Managing Partner
Marshall Roslyn, Principal
Nathaniel Whittemore, Principal
Robert Hutter, Managing Partner
Tom Vander Ark, Managing Partner
Wade Davis, Venture Partner

Type of Firm
Private Equity Firm

Project Preferences

Type of Financing Preferred:
Early Stage
Balanced
Startup

Geographical Preferences

International Preferences:
Latin America

Industry Preferences

In Computer Software prefer:
Software

In Consumer Related prefer:
Education Related

Additional Information
Year Founded: 2008
Capital Under Management: $65,000,000
Current Activity Level : Actively seeking new investments

LEARNLAUNCHX

281 Summer Street
Floor Two
Boston, MA USA 02210
E-mail: info@learnlaunchx.com
Website: www.learnlaunchx.com

Type of Firm
Incubator/Development Program

Project Preferences

Type of Financing Preferred:
Early Stage
Seed
Startup

Industry Preferences

In Consumer Related prefer:
Education Related

Additional Information
Year Founded: 2013
Capital Under Management: $1,250,000
Current Activity Level : Actively seeking new investments

LEARNSTART LLC

119 West 24th Street
Fourth Floor
New York, NY USA 10011

Other Offices
620 Congress Avenue
Suite 200
AUSTIN, TX USA 78701

Type of Firm
Private Equity Firm

Project Preferences

Type of Financing Preferred:
Seed

Industry Preferences

In Consumer Related prefer:
Education Related

Additional Information
Year Founded: 2017
Current Activity Level : Actively seeking new investments

LEAVITT EQUITY PARTNERS LLC

299 South Main Street
Suite 2300
Salt Lake City, UT USA 84111
Phone: 8015385082
E-mail: info@leavittpartners.com
Website: leavittpartners.com

Type of Firm
Private Equity Firm

Project Preferences

Type of Financing Preferred:
Leveraged Buyout
Generalist PE
Balanced
Acquisition

Industry Preferences

In Medical/Health prefer:
Mecical/Health

Additional Information
Year Founded: 2014
Capital Under Management: $50,000,000
Current Activity Level : Actively seeking new investments

LEAWOOD VENTURES

5251 West 116th Place
Suite 200
Leawood, KS USA 66211
Phone: 9137355324
E-mail: info@leawoodventures.com
Website: www.leawoodventures.com

Type of Firm
Private Equity Firm

Project Preferences

Type of Financing Preferred:
Early Stage
Expansion

Geographical Preferences

United States Preferences:

Additional Information
Year Founded: 2017
Current Activity Level : Actively seeking new investments

LEBLON EQUITIES GESTAO DE RECURSOS LTDA

Av. Niemeyer 2, 201
Rio de Janeiro, Brazil 22450-220
Phone: 552132067300
Fax: 552132067301
E-mail: contato@leblonequities.com.br
Website: www.leblonequities.com.br

Management and Staff
Bruno Pereira, Co-Founder
Felipe Claudino, Co-Founder
George Earp, Partner
Leonardo Vazquez, Partner
Marcelo Mesquita, Co-Founder
Miguel Galvao, Partner
Pedro Chermont, Co-Founder
Pedro Rudge, Co-Founder
Victor Uebe, Partner

Type of Firm
Private Equity Firm

Project Preferences

Type of Financing Preferred:
Leveraged Buyout
Acquisition

Geographical Preferences

International Preferences:
Brazil

Additional Information
Year Founded: 2008
Current Activity Level : Actively seeking new investments

LEDRA CAPITAL LLC

228 Park Avenue
Suite 32004
New York, NY USA 10003
Phone: 8888661734
Fax: 6464175274
E-mail: info@ledracapital.com
Website: ledracapital.com

Management and Staff
Antonis Polemitis, Principal

Type of Firm
Private Equity Firm

Project Preferences

Type of Financing Preferred:
Early Stage
Balanced
Opportunistic
Other
Seed

Geographical Preferences

International Preferences:
Greece
Middle East
Africa
Cyprus

Industry Preferences

In Computer Software prefer:
Applications Software

In Consumer Related prefer:
Education Related

In Industrial/Energy prefer:
Energy

In Financial Services prefer:
Financial Services
Real Estate

In Business Serv. prefer:
Media

Additional Information
Year Founded: 2013
Current Activity Level : Actively seeking new investments

LEE EQUITY PARTNERS LLC

650 Madison Avenue
21st Floor
New York, NY USA 10022
Phone: 2128881500
Fax: 2128886388
Website: www.leeequity.com

Other Offices
767 Fifth Avenue
Sixth Floor
NEW YORK, NY USA 10022

Management and Staff
Benjamin Hochberg, Partner
Caitlyn MacDonald, Partner
Collins Ward, Partner
Daniel Rodriguez, Principal
David Morrison, Partner
Douglas Schreiber, Partner
Eric Hsu, Vice President
Geoffrey Lieberthal, Partner
Joseph Rotberg, Partner
Mark Gormley, Partner
Mark Mauceri, Vice President
Michael Bridge, Principal
Rahul Nand, Partner
Sumit Khatod, Vice President
Thomas Lee, President
Yoo Jin Kim, Partner

Type of Firm
Private Equity Firm

Project Preferences
Type of Financing Preferred:
Leveraged Buyout
Expansion
Later Stage
Acquisition
Recapitalizations

Geographical Preferences
United States Preferences:

Additional Information
Year Founded: 2006
Capital Under Management: $315,100,000
Current Activity Level : Actively seeking new investments

LEE&CO INVESTMENTS CO
Cheongbu 118-4 Cheongdam-Dong
Kangnam-Gu
Seoul, South Korea
Phone: 82-2-2088-2600
Fax: 82-2-2088-1699
E-mail: nyhwang@leenco.co.kr
Website: www.leenco.co.kr

Management and Staff
Bo-Hoi Koo, Chief Executive Officer
Hyung-Kie Kim, Managing Director
Seung-Woo Lee, Managing Director
Sung-Il Bae, Managing Director

Type of Firm
Private Equity Firm

Project Preferences
Type of Financing Preferred:
Early Stage
Balanced
Management Buyouts

Geographical Preferences
International Preferences:
No Preference
Korea, South

Additional Information
Year Founded: 2000
Capital Under Management: $8,300,000
Current Activity Level : Actively seeking new investments

LEEDS EQUITY ADVISORS INC
350 Park Avenue
23rd Floor
New York, NY USA 10022
Phone: 2128352000
Fax: 2128352020
E-mail: info@leedsequity.com
Website: www.leedsequity.com

Management and Staff
Carter Harned, Managing Director
Eric Geveda, Vice President
Jacques Galante, Managing Director
Jeffrey Leeds, President, Founder
Robert Bernstein, Senior Managing Director
Scott VanHoy, Principal

Type of Firm
Private Equity Firm

Project Preferences
Type of Financing Preferred:
Leveraged Buyout
Mezzanine
Generalist PE
Turnaround
Later Stage
Acquisition
Recapitalizations

Geographical Preferences
United States Preferences:
All U.S.

Industry Focus
(% based on actual investment)
Consumer Related	43.3%
Computer Hardware	31.7%
Computer Software and Services	15.4%
Internet Specific	9.5%

Additional Information
Name of Most Recent Fund: Leeds Weld Equity Partners IV, L.P.
Most Recent Fund Was Raised: 12/01/2002
Year Founded: 1993
Capital Under Management: $1,000,000
Current Activity Level : Actively seeking new investments

LEERINK CAPITAL PARTNERS LLC
One Federal Street
37th Floor
Boston, MA USA 02110
Phone: 8008087525
Website: leerink.com

Other Offices
255 California Street
12th Floor
SAN FRANCISCO, CA USA 94111

Type of Firm
Investment Management Firm

Project Preferences
Type of Financing Preferred:
Later Stage

Industry Preferences
In Medical/Health prefer:
Medical/Health

Additional Information
Year Founded: 2014
Capital Under Management: $505,085,000
Current Activity Level : Actively seeking new investments

LEEWARD VENTURES MANAGEMENT SA
6, rue Adolphe
B.P. 908
Luxembourg, Luxembourg 2019
Phone: 35226258711
Fax: 35224611813
E-mail: mail@leeward.lu
Website: www.leewardfund.com

Other Offices
110 Wall Street
Floor 11
New York, NY USA 10005
Phone: 1212859388
Fax: 12122084316

18 Luard Road
25/F One Capital Place
Wanchai, Hong Kong
Phone: 85230173867

Management and Staff
Peter VanderBruggen, Managing Director

Type of Firm
Private Equity Firm

Project Preferences

Type of Financing Preferred:
Leveraged Buyout
Early Stage
Mezzanine
Generalist PE
Later Stage
Management Buyouts
Acquisition
Startup
Recapitalizations

Geographical Preferences

United States Preferences:

International Preferences:
Luxembourg
Europe
Asia

Additional Information
Year Founded: 2005
Current Activity Level: Actively seeking new investments

LEGEND CAPITAL CO LTD

No. 2, Kexueyuan South Road
Tower A, Raycom Infotech
Beijing, China 100190
Phone: 861062508000
Fax: 361062509100
E-mail: er@legendcapital.com.cn
Website: www.legendcapital.com.cn

Other Offices
No. 1366 Nanjing West Road
4801B - 4802, Tower 2, Plaza 66
Shanghai, China 200040
Phone: 862162884566
Fax: 862162887455

Wuchang District
23/F Tower A, Optics Valley Intl Plaza
Wuhan, China 430000
Phone: 862787159912
Fax: 862787159916

Management and Staff
Chuanzhi Liu, Founder
Erhai Liu, Managing Director
Hao Chen, Founder
Jianqing Wang, Managing Director
Jiaqing Li, Managing Director
Jonathan Wang, Partner
Junfeng Wang, Managing Director
Lin Yang, Partner
Linan Zhu, Chief Executive Officer

Nengguang Wang, Co-Founder
Xiangyu Ouyang, Managing Director
Xiaohong Huang, Managing Director
Zehui Liu, Managing Director

Type of Firm
Corporate PE/Venture

Association Membership
Venture Capital Association of Beijing (VCAB)
China Venture Capital Association

Project Preferences

Type of Financing Preferred:
Early Stage
Expansion
Balanced
Seed
Startup

Size of Investments Considered:
Min Size of Investment Considered (000s): $2,000
Max Size of Investment Considered (000s): $10,000

Geographical Preferences

International Preferences:
China

Industry Preferences

In Communications prefer:
Telecommunications
Media and Entertainment

In Medical/Health prefer:
Medical/Health

In Consumer Related prefer:
Consumer
Consumer Products

In Business Serv. prefer:
Services
Media

In Manufact. prefer:
Manufacturing

In Other prefer:
Environment Responsible

Additional Information
Year Founded: 2001
Capital Under Management: $20,600,000
Current Activity Level: Actively seeking new investments

LEGEND PARTNERS I L P

312 Walnut Street
Suite 1151
Cincinnati, OH USA 45202
Phone: 513-651-2300
Fax: 513-651-1084
Website: www.thelegendpartners.com

Management and Staff
James Gould, Managing Partner
John Bernlohr, Partner
Mark Hauser, Managing Partner
Patrick McBride, Partner
Paul Swanson, Partner
R. Scott Barnes, Partner
Ronald Tysoe, Managing Partner

Type of Firm
Private Equity Firm

Project Preferences

Type of Financing Preferred:
Balanced

Industry Preferences

In Consumer Related prefer:
Consumer
Retail

In Business Serv. prefer:
Services

Additional Information
Year Founded: 2008
Current Activity Level: Actively seeking new investments

LEGEND STAR VENTURE INCUBATOR

No.2 Kexueyuan South Road
10/F Tower A, Raycom Info Tech
Beijing, China 100190
Phone: 861062509350
Fax: 861062561056
E-mail: ls@legendholdings.com
Website: www.legendstar.com.cn

Management and Staff
Haiqing Duan, Vice President
Lin Zhang, Vice President
Mingyao Wang, Vice President
Qing Liang, Vice President
Wei Liu, Vice President
Yameng Ding, Vice President
Yi Kuang, Vice President

Type of Firm
Incubator/Development Program

Project Preferences

Type of Financing Preferred:
Seed
Startup

Size of Investments Considered:
Min Size of Investment Considered (000s): $313
Max Size of Investment Considered (000s): $2,345

Geographical Preferences

International Preferences:
China

Industry Preferences

In Communications prefer:
Telecommunications
Wireless Communications

In Internet Specific prefer:
Internet

In Biotechnology prefer:
Biotechnology

In Medical/Health prefer:
Medical/Health
Disposable Med. Products
Pharmaceuticals

In Industrial/Energy prefer:
Alternative Energy
Energy Conservation Relat
Advanced Materials

In Business Serv. prefer:
Media

In Manufact. prefer:
Manufacturing

In Other prefer:
Environment Responsible

Additional Information

Year Founded: 2007
Current Activity Level : Actively seeking new investments

LEMHI VENTURES, INC.

315 East Lake Street, Suite 304
Wayzata, MN USA 55391
Phone: 9529089680
Fax: 9529089780
E-mail: info@lemhiventures.com
Website: www.lemhiventures.com

Management and Staff

Jodi Hubler, Managing Director
Randy Schmidt, Venture Partner
Tony Miller, Managing Partner

Type of Firm

Private Equity Firm

Project Preferences

Role in Financing:
Prefer role as deal originator but will also invest in deals created by others

Type of Financing Preferred:
Early Stage
Balanced
Startup

Geographical Preferences

United States Preferences:
All U.S.

Industry Preferences

In Medical/Health prefer:
Medical/Health
Health Services

Additional Information

Name of Most Recent Fund: Lemhi Ventures Fund II, L.P.
Most Recent Fund Was Raised: 06/22/2012
Year Founded: 2007
Capital Under Management: $150,000,000
Current Activity Level : Actively seeking new investments

LEMNOS LABS

85 Bluxome Street
Suite 101
San Francisco, CA USA 94107
E-mail: info@lemnoslabs.com
Website: lemnoslabs.com

Management and Staff

Eric Klein, Partner
Helen Zelman, Co-Founder
Jeremy Conrad, Co-Founder

Type of Firm

Incubator/Development Program

Project Preferences

Type of Financing Preferred:
Early Stage
Seed
Startup

Geographical Preferences

United States Preferences:
Northern California

Canadian Preferences:
All Canada

Industry Preferences

In Computer Hardware prefer:
Computers

Additional Information

Year Founded: 2011
Capital Under Management: $70,000,000
Current Activity Level : Actively seeking new investments

LEO GROUP LLC

One Main Street, Suite 202
Chatham, NJ USA 07928
Phone: 9736657007
Fax: 9733336823
Website: leogroupllc.com

Type of Firm

Investment Management Firm

Project Preferences

Type of Financing Preferred:
Value-Add
Expansion
Generalist PE
Acquisition
Distressed Debt

Additional Information

Year Founded: 2012
Current Activity Level : Actively seeking new investments

LEON CAPITAL

No. Four Guanghua Road
Suite 605, Tower A Oriental
Beijing, China
Phone: 861085597581
Fax: 861085597591
E-mail: mailbox@leoncapital.com
Website: www.leoncapital.com

Other Offices

Former HQ: 87 West 3rd Road North
#705, Int'l Finance & Eco Ctr
Beijing, China 100089
Phone: 86-10-8882-4906
Fax: 86-10-882-4907

6 Duddell Street, Central
17/F, Printing House
Hong Kong, Hong Kong
Phone: 852-2501-1600
Fax: 852-2147-5727

3 Hongqiao Road, Xuhui District
Unit 3506, 2 Grand Gateway
Shanghai, China 200030
Phone: 86-21-5403-2288
Fax: 86-21-5404-5399

39 Sec. 2, Jinan Road
7/Floor
Taipei, Taiwan 100
Phone: 886-2-2396-1905
Fax: 886-2-2356-7187

Type of Firm

Private Equity Firm

Project Preferences

Type of Financing Preferred:
Leveraged Buyout
Recapitalizations

Geographical Preferences

International Preferences:
Macau
Taiwan
Hong Kong
China
Singapore

Industry Preferences

In Semiconductor/Electr prefer:
Electronics
Semiconductor

In Medical/Health prefer:
Pharmaceuticals

In Consumer Related prefer:
Consumer
Retail
Food/Beverage

In Business Serv. prefer:
Services

In Manufact. prefer:
Manufacturing

Additional Information

Year Founded: 2008
Current Activity Level : Actively seeking new investments

LEONARD GREEN & PARTNERS LP

11111 Santa Monica Boulevard, Suite 2000
Los Angeles, CA USA 90025
Phone: 3109540444
Fax: 3109540404
Website: www.leonardgreen.com

Management and Staff

Adam Levyn, Principal
Alyse Wagner, Partner
Cody Franklin, Chief Financial Officer
Erika Spitzer, Principal
J. Kristofer Galashan, Partner
John Yoon, Principal
John Baumer, Partner
John Danhakl, Managing Partner
Jonathan Sokoloff, Managing Partner
Michael Solomon, Partner
Michael Gennaro, Chief Operating Officer
Michael Kirton, Principal
Timothy Flynn, Partner
Usama Cortas, Partner

Type of Firm

Private Equity Firm

Project Preferences

Role in Financing:
Prefer role as deal originator but will also invest in deals created by others

Type of Financing Preferred:
Fund of Funds
Leveraged Buyout
Management Buyouts
Acquisition
Recapitalizations

Industry Focus

(% based on actual investment)

Medical/Health	33.4%
Internet Specific	28.2%
Other Products	18.9%
Consumer Related	15.8%
Communications and Media	2.6%
Industrial/Energy	0.8%
Semiconductors/Other Elect.	0.2%
Computer Software and Services	0.1%

Additional Information

Year Founded: 1989
Capital Under Management: $9,000,000,000
Current Activity Level : Actively seeking new investments
Method of Compensation: Return on invest. most important, but chg. closing fees, service fees, etc.

LEONARDO VENTURE GMBH & CO KGAA

Augustaanlage 32
Augusta Carree
Mannheim, Germany 68165
Phone: 496214384300
Fax: 4962143843010
E-mail: kontakt@leonardoventure.de
Website: leonardoventure.com

Management and Staff

Andreas Mueller, Managing Director

Type of Firm

Private Equity Firm

Association Membership

German Venture Capital Association (BVK)

Project Preferences

Type of Financing Preferred:
Early Stage
Seed
Startup

Size of Investments Considered:
Min Size of Investment Considered (000s): $131
Max Size of Investment Considered (000s): $2,623

Geographical Preferences

International Preferences:
Switzerland
Austria
Germany

Industry Preferences

In Communications prefer:
Communications and Media
Wireless Communications

In Computer Software prefer:
Software

In Internet Specific prefer:
Internet

In Biotechnology prefer:
Biotechnology

In Medical/Health prefer:
Medical/Health

In Industrial/Energy prefer:
Industrial Products
Materials

In Other prefer:
Environment Responsible

Additional Information

Year Founded: 2000
Capital Under Management: $22,200,000
Current Activity Level : Actively seeking new investments

LEONARDOWEB GROUP SRL

Via Pignolo 16
Bergamo, Italy 40125
Phone: 3903519966064
Fax: 3903519962212
E-mail: leonardoweb@leonardoweb.it
Website: www.leonardoweb.it

Management and Staff

Enrico Levi, Partner
Roberto Vancini, Partner

Type of Firm

Private Equity Firm

Project Preferences

Type of Financing Preferred:
Second Stage Financing
Early Stage

Geographical Preferences

International Preferences:
Italy

Additional Information

Year Founded: 2002
Current Activity Level : Actively seeking new investments

LEOPARD ROCK CAPITAL PARTNERS LTD

Nine Catherine Place
London, United Kingdom SW1E 6DE
E-mail: info@leopardrockcapital.com
Website: www.leopardrockcapital.com

Management and Staff
Alastair Kerr, Co-Founder
Victor Beamish, Co-Founder

Type of Firm
Private Equity Firm

Project Preferences
Type of Financing Preferred:
Early Stage
Expansion
Later Stage

Geographical Preferences
International Preferences:
United Kingdom
Europe

Industry Preferences
In Communications prefer:
Telecommunications
Media and Entertainment

In Computer Software prefer:
Software

Additional Information
Year Founded: 2001
Current Activity Level : Actively seeking new investments

LEPE PARTNERS LLP

17 Old Court Place
London, United Kingdom W8 4PL
Phone: 2079385810
E-mail: info@lepepartners.com
Website: www.lepepartners.com

Type of Firm
Bank Affiliated

Project Preferences
Type of Financing Preferred:
Balanced

Industry Preferences
In Internet Specific prefer:
Internet

In Consumer Related prefer:
Consumer
Consumer Services

In Business Serv. prefer:
Media

Additional Information
Year Founded: 2011
Current Activity Level : Actively seeking new investments

LEREKO INVESTMENT HOLDINGS PTY LTD

39 Rivonia Road
First Floor, 3 Commerce Square
Sandhurst, South Africa 2196
Phone: 27112680755
Fax: 27112680756
E-mail: info@lereko.co.za
Website: www.lereko.co.za

Management and Staff
Cedrick Mampuru, Founder
Lulu Gwagwa, Chief Executive Officer

Type of Firm
Private Equity Firm

Association Membership
South African Venture Capital Association (SAVCA)
Emerging Markets Private Equity Association
African Venture Capital Association (AVCA)

Project Preferences
Type of Financing Preferred:
Acquisition

Size of Investments Considered:
Min Size of Investment Considered (000s): $6,175
Max Size of Investment Considered (000s): $31,710

Geographical Preferences
International Preferences:
South Africa

Industry Preferences
In Consumer Related prefer:
Food/Beverage
Consumer Products

In Manufact. prefer:
Manufacturing

In Agr/Forestr/Fish prefer:
Mining and Minerals

Additional Information
Year Founded: 2004
Current Activity Level : Actively seeking new investments

LERER VENTURES II LP

100 Crosby, Suite 308
New York, NY USA 10012
Phone: 6462374837
Website: lererhippeau.com

Management and Staff
Benjamin Lerer, Partner
Eric Ashman, Partner
Eric Hippeau, Partner
Jordan Cooper, Partner
Kenneth Lerer, Partner
Steve Schlafman, Principal

Type of Firm
Private Equity Firm

Project Preferences
Type of Financing Preferred:
Seed
Startup

Geographical Preferences
United States Preferences:
All U.S.

Industry Preferences
In Computer Software prefer:
Software

In Internet Specific prefer:
Ecommerce

In Computer Other prefer:
Computer Related

In Consumer Related prefer:
Consumer

In Financial Services prefer:
Financial Services

Additional Information
Name of Most Recent Fund: Lerer Ventures III, L.P.
Most Recent Fund Was Raised: 10/23/2012
Year Founded: 2007
Capital Under Management: $261,340,000
Current Activity Level : Actively seeking new investments

LETA GROUP ZAO

8-ya Tekstilshchikov 11, 2
Moscow, Russia
Phone: 74959842831
E-mail: info@letagroup.ru
Website: www.letagroup.ru

Type of Firm
Private Equity Firm

Project Preferences
Type of Financing Preferred:
Generalist PE

Geographical Preferences
International Preferences:
Russia

Industry Preferences

In Computer Software prefer:
Software
Systems Software
Applications Software

In Computer Other prefer:
Computer Related

Additional Information

Year Founded: 2009
Current Activity Level : Actively seeking new investments

LEVANT INVESTMENT MANAGEMENT LTD

Emirates Financial Towers
Office 1903, Dubai Int'l Fin Ct
Dubai, Utd. Arab Em.
Phone: 97143863286
Fax: 97143864874
E-mail: info@levantcapital.com
Website: www.levantcapital.com

Type of Firm
Private Equity Firm

Project Preferences

Type of Financing Preferred:
Leveraged Buyout
Early Stage
Expansion
Generalist PE
Later Stage
Acquisition
Recapitalizations

Geographical Preferences

International Preferences:
Turkey
Utd. Arab Em.
Middle East
Saudi Arabia
Africa

Industry Preferences

In Consumer Related prefer:
Retail
Consumer Products

In Industrial/Energy prefer:
Energy
Oil and Gas Exploration

In Transportation prefer:
Transportation

In Financial Services prefer:
Financial Services

Additional Information

Year Founded: 2006
Current Activity Level : Actively seeking new investments

LEVEL EQUITY MANAGEMENT LLC

140 East 45th Street
39th Floor
New York, NY USA 10017
Phone: 2126602470
E-mail: information@levelequity.com
Website: www.levelequity.com

Management and Staff
Benjamin Levin, Co-Founder
George McCulloch, Partner
Sarah Haas, Principal

Type of Firm
Private Equity Firm

Project Preferences

Type of Financing Preferred:
Balanced

Industry Preferences

In Business Serv. prefer:
Services
Media

Additional Information

Name of Most Recent Fund: Level Equity Growth Partners II, L.P.
Most Recent Fund Was Raised: 11/18/2013
Year Founded: 2010
Capital Under Management: $605,000,000
Current Activity Level : Actively seeking new investments

LEVINE LEICHTMAN CAPITAL PARTNERS INC

335 North Maple Drive
Suite 130
Beverly Hills, CA USA 90210
Phone: 3102755335
Fax: 3102751441
E-mail: Main@llcp.com
Website: www.llcp.com

Other Offices

33 Saint James's Square
London, United Kingdom SW1Y 4JS
Phone: 4402071666420
Fax: 4402071666421

200 South Wacker Drive
Suite 3100
Chicago, IL USA 60606
Phone: 312-674-4900
Fax: 312-674-4905

126 East 56th Street
31st Floor
New York, NY USA 10022
Phone: 212-600-2100
Fax: 212-355-5171

100 Crescent Court
Seventh Floor
Dallas, TX USA 75201
Phone: 214-303-0118
Fax: 214-303-0119

Management and Staff
Aaron Perlmutter, Principal
Arthur Levine, President, Founder
Brad Parish, Managing Director
Brian Stewart, Managing Director
John Romney, Managing Director
John O Neill, Managing Director
John Klinge, Managing Director
Kimberly Pollack, Principal
Lee Stern, Managing Director
Matthew Frankel, Senior Managing Director
Michael Weinberg, Managing Director
Monica Holec, Managing Director
Paul Drury, Senior Managing Director
Peter Borges, Managing Director
Robert Poletti, Principal
Robert Hays, Managing Director
Ronnie Kaplan, Managing Director
Steven Hartman, Principal
Stuart Robinson, Managing Director

Type of Firm
Private Equity Firm

Association Membership
Natl Assoc of Small Bus. Inv. Co (NASBIC)

Project Preferences

Role in Financing:
Prefer role as deal originator

Type of Financing Preferred:
Leveraged Buyout
Turnaround
Opportunistic
Management Buyouts
Acquisition
Distressed Debt
Recapitalizations

Geographical Preferences

United States Preferences:
California

International Preferences:
Europe

Industry Preferences

In Computer Software prefer:
Software

In Medical/Health prefer:
Medical Products

In Consumer Related prefer:
Food/Beverage

In Industrial/Energy prefer:
Industrial Products

In Transportation prefer:
Aerospace

In Financial Services prefer:
Financial Services

Additional Information
Name of Most Recent Fund: Levine Leichtman Capital Partners V, L.P.
Most Recent Fund Was Raised: 03/22/2013
Year Founded: 1984
Capital Under Management: $5,000,000,000
Current Activity Level : Actively seeking new investments
Method of Compensation: Return on invest. most important, but chg. closing fees, service fees, etc.

LEWIS & CLARK VENTURE CAPITAL LLC

120 South Central Avenue, Suite 1000
Saint Louis, MO USA 63105
E-mail: info@lacventures.com
Website: lewisandclarkventures.com

Management and Staff
Brian Hopcraft, Managing Director
Scott Bernstein, Vice President
Thomas Hillman, General Partner

Type of Firm
Private Equity Firm

Project Preferences

Size of Investments Considered:
Min Size of Investment Considered (000s): $3,000
Max Size of Investment Considered (000s): $10,000

Geographical Preferences

United States Preferences:
Midwest

Industry Preferences

In Medical/Health prefer:
Medical/Health

In Financial Services prefer:
Financial Services

In Agr/Forestr/Fish prefer:
Agriculture related

Additional Information
Year Founded: 2014
Capital Under Management: $124,000,000
Current Activity Level : Actively seeking new investments

LEX CAPITAL MANAGEMENT INC

2530 Sandra Schmirler Way
Regina, Canada S4W 0M7
Phone: 3067908676
E-mail: info@lexcapital.ca
Website: www.lexcapital.ca

Other Offices
#1200 - 1881 Scarth Street
Regina
Saskatchewan, Canada S4P 4K9
Phone: 3067908660

Management and Staff
Chris Olfert, Principal
Curtis Armstrong, Chief Financial Officer
Ryan Thompson, Principal

Type of Firm
Private Equity Firm

Association Membership
Canadian Venture Capital Association

Project Preferences

Type of Financing Preferred:
Other

Geographical Preferences

United States Preferences:
Southeast
Southern California

Canadian Preferences:
Saskatchewan
Western Canada

Industry Preferences

In Industrial/Energy prefer:
Energy
Oil and Gas Exploration
Oil & Gas Drilling,Explor

Additional Information
Year Founded: 2009
Capital Under Management: $290,000,000
Current Activity Level : Actively seeking new investments

LEXINGTON PARTNERS INC

660 Madison Avenue
23rd Floor
New York, NY USA 10065
Phone: 2127540411
Fax: 2127541494
E-mail: info@lexpartners.com
Website: www.lexingtonpartners.com

Other Offices
42 Berkeley Square
London, United Kingdom W1X 5DB
Phone: 44-20-7318-0888
Fax: 44-20-7318-0889

3477 Isidora Goyenechea Avenue
17th Floor, Suite 170 B
Las Condes, Chile
Phone: 56224876700

15 Queen's Road Central
5/F York House, The Landmark
Central, Hong Kong
Phone: 852-3987-1600
Fax: 852-3987-1631

111 Huntington Avenue
Suite 3020
BOSTON, MA USA 02199
Phone: 617-247-7010
Fax: 617-247-7050

Management and Staff
Anthony Garton, Principal
Bart Osman, Partner
Brent Nicklas, Managing Partner
Charles Bridgeland, Vice President
Charles Grant, Partner
Christopher Kunz, Vice President
Clark Peterson, Vice President
Craig Cook-Stevenson, Vice President
Cullen Schannep, Vice President
Daniel Klima, Vice President
David Outcalt, Partner
Donald Norton, Vice President
Duncan Chapman, Partner
Guillaume Caulier, Vice President
James Pitt, Partner
Jennifer Kheng, Principal
John Loverro, Partner
John Rudge, Partner
John Lee, Vice President
Jose Sosa del Valle, Principal
Kirk Beaton, Partner
Lee Tesconi, Partner
Lutz Fuhrmann, Vice President
Mark Andrew, Principal
Mark Fabry, Vice President
Marshall Parke, Partner
Matthew Hodan, Vice President
Nick Harris, Partner
Pal Ristvedt, Partner
Philip Smelt, Vice President
Rebecca John, Partner
Rebecca Weisel, Vice President
Ronnie Shen, Vice President
Simon Ok, Vice President
Taylor Robinson, Vice President
Timothy Huang, Principal
Tom Newby, Partner
Victor Wu, Partner
Wilson Warren, Partner

Type of Firm
Private Equity Advisor or Fund of Funds

Association Membership
Western Association of Venture Capitalists (WAVC)
European Private Equity and Venture Capital Assoc.

Project Preferences

Type of Financing Preferred:
Acquisition

Geographical Preferences

International Preferences:
Asia Pacific
Europe

Additional Information
Year Founded: 1994
Capital Under Management: $28,000,000,000
Current Activity Level : Actively seeking new investments

LFE CAPITAL LLC

319 Barry Avenue South
Suite 215
Wayzata, MN USA 55391
Phone: 612.752.1809
Fax: 6127521800
E-mail: info@lfecapital.com
Website: www.lfecapital.com

Management and Staff
Duane Harris, Partner
Laurent Frecon, Vice President

Type of Firm
Private Equity Firm

Project Preferences

Role in Financing:
Will function either as deal originator or investor in deals created by others

Type of Financing Preferred:
Leveraged Buyout
Expansion
Generalist PE
Later Stage
Acquisition
Recapitalizations

Size of Investments Considered:
Min Size of Investment Considered (000s): $2,000
Max Size of Investment Considered (000s): $10,000

Geographical Preferences

United States Preferences:
Midwest
Illinois
Southeast
Iowa
Northeast
Florida
Minnesota
New York

Industry Preferences

In Medical/Health prefer:
Medical Products
Health Services

In Consumer Related prefer:
Food/Beverage
Consumer Products
Consumer Services

In Business Serv. prefer:
Services

In Other prefer:
Women/Minority-Owned Bus.

Additional Information
Year Founded: 1999
Capital Under Management: $75,000,000
Current Activity Level : Actively seeking new investments
Method of Compensation: Return on investment is of primary concern, do not charge fees

LFM CAPITAL LLC

3016 Vanderbilt Place
Nashville, TN USA 37212
Phone: 6152099413
Website: www.lfmcapital.com

Management and Staff
Chris Lin, Vice President
Dan Shockley, Co-Founder
Rick Reisner, Co-Founder
Steve Cook, Co-Founder

Type of Firm
Private Equity Firm

Project Preferences

Type of Financing Preferred:
Leveraged Buyout
Management Buyouts
Acquisition

Geographical Preferences

United States Preferences:

Industry Preferences

In Industrial/Energy prefer:
Industrial Products

In Manufact. prefer:
Manufacturing

Additional Information
Year Founded: 2014
Capital Under Management: $110,100,000
Current Activity Level : Actively seeking new investments

LGT VENTURE PHILANTHROPY FOUNDATION SWITZERLAND

Faerberstrasse 6
Zurich, Switzerland CH-8008
Phone: 41442568110
Fax: 41442568111
E-mail: info@lgtvp.com
Website: www.lgtvp.com

Management and Staff
Alexander Leeb, President

Type of Firm
Endowment, Foundation or Pension Fund

Project Preferences

Type of Financing Preferred:
Early Stage
Mezzanine
Balanced
Later Stage
Startup

Geographical Preferences

International Preferences:
Latin America
India
United Kingdom
Europe
China
Asia
Africa

Industry Preferences

In Medical/Health prefer:
Medical/Health

In Consumer Related prefer:
Education Related

In Industrial/Energy prefer:
Energy

Additional Information
Name of Most Recent Fund: Impact Ventures UK
Most Recent Fund Was Raised: 12/09/2013
Year Founded: 2007
Capital Under Management: $34,156,000
Current Activity Level : Actively seeking new investments

LGV CAPITAL LTD

One Coleman Street
London, United Kingdom EC2R 5AA
Phone: 442031242900
Fax: 442031242546
Website: www.lgvcapital.com

Management and Staff
Ivan Heywood, Chief Executive Officer
James Dawes, Founder
Michael Mowlem, Managing Director
William Priestley, Managing Director

Type of Firm
Insurance Firm Affiliate

Association Membership
British Venture Capital Association (BVCA)

Project Preferences

Role in Financing:
Prefer role as deal originator

Type of Financing Preferred:
Leveraged Buyout
Management Buyouts
Acquisition

Geographical Preferences

International Preferences:
United Kingdom

Industry Preferences

In Biotechnology prefer:
Agricultural/Animal Bio.

In Medical/Health prefer:
Medical/Health
Health Services

In Consumer Related prefer:
Consumer
Entertainment and Leisure
Retail
Food/Beverage
Consumer Products
Consumer Services
Other Restaurants

In Business Serv. prefer:
Services
Distribution
Consulting Services

Additional Information
Year Founded: 1986
Capital Under Management: $366,300,000
Current Activity Level : Actively seeking new investments
Method of Compensation: Return on invest. most important, but chg. closing fees, service fees, etc.

LI & FUNG INVESTMENTS

18 Chater Road
33/F, Alexandria House
Central, Hong Kong
Phone: 85228441965
E-mail: enquiry@lfunginvestments.com
Website: www.fungcapitalasia.com

Other Offices
Four Embarcadero Center
Suite 3400
San Francisco, CA USA 94111
Phone: 415-315-7440

14 Savile Row
London, United Kingdom W1S 3JN
Phone: 442072879990

Management and Staff
Jose Cheng, Managing Director

Type of Firm
Corporate PE/Venture

Association Membership
British Venture Capital Association (BVCA)
Hungarian Venture Capital Association (HVCA)

Project Preferences

Role in Financing:
Prefer role as deal originator but will also invest in deals created by others

Type of Financing Preferred:
Leveraged Buyout
Early Stage
Expansion
Generalist PE
Balanced
Later Stage
Management Buyouts
Joint Ventures

Geographical Preferences

United States Preferences:
Southeast

International Preferences:
Europe
China
Japan

Industry Preferences

In Consumer Related prefer:
Retail
Consumer Products

In Business Serv. prefer:
Services
Distribution

Additional Information
Year Founded: 1982
Capital Under Management: $100,000,000
Current Activity Level : Actively seeking new investments
Method of Compensation: Return on investment is of primary concern, do not charge fees

LIANKE CHUANGYING CAPITAL MANAGEMENT CO LTD

Fengtai District
Zhongguancun Science Park
Beijing, China 100070

Type of Firm
Private Equity Firm

Project Preferences

Type of Financing Preferred:
Leveraged Buyout
Early Stage

Geographical Preferences

International Preferences:
China

Industry Preferences

In Medical/Health prefer:
Medical/Health

In Consumer Related prefer:
Sports

In Industrial/Energy prefer:
Energy
Materials

In Manufact. prefer:
Manufacturing

Additional Information
Year Founded: 2012
Capital Under Management: $14,540,000
Current Activity Level : Actively seeking new investments

LIAONING NEUSOFT VENTURE CAPITAL CO LTD

Hun Nan Industrial Area
New & Hi-tech Dev't Zone
Shenyang, China 110179
Phone: 862483668325
Fax: 862423782904

Type of Firm
Private Equity Firm

Project Preferences

Type of Financing Preferred:
Balanced

Geographical Preferences

International Preferences:
China

Industry Preferences

In Communications prefer:
Wireless Communications

Additional Information

Year Founded: 2000
Current Activity Level : Actively seeking new investments

LIAONING TECHNOLOGY VENTURE CAPITAL LIABILITY LTD CO LTD

4/F Jiahuan Building
#39 Heping South St., Heping
Shenyang, China 110003
Phone: 86-24-2322-2100
Fax: 86-24-2324-4922
E-mail: lnvc@lnvc.com.cn
Website: www.lnvc.com.cn

Type of Firm
Government Affiliated Program

Project Preferences

Type of Financing Preferred:
Early Stage
Expansion
Start-up Financing
Seed

Size of Investments Considered:
Min Size of Investment Considered (000s): $60
Max Size of Investment Considered (000s): $2,500

Geographical Preferences

International Preferences:
China

Industry Preferences

In Biotechnology prefer:
Biotechnology

In Industrial/Energy prefer:
Advanced Materials
Environmental Related

In Manufact. prefer:
Manufacturing

Additional Information

Year Founded: 2000
Capital Under Management: $24,200,000
Current Activity Level : Actively seeking new investments

LIBERTY CAPITAL MANAGEMENT CORP

1811 East Garry Avenue
Santa Ana, CA USA 92705
Phone: 949-724-8848
Fax: 949-724-8805
E-mail: info@libertycapitalmgt.com
Website: www.libertycapitalmgt.com

Management and Staff

A. Donald McCulloch, Partner
Earl Linehan, Partner
J. Eustace Wolfington, Partner
Jeffrey Levitt, Partner
Joe Zoll, Partner
Kevin Donohoe, Partner
Martin Lautman, Partner
Paul Gardi, Partner

Type of Firm
Bank Affiliated

Project Preferences

Role in Financing:
Prefer role as deal originator but will also invest in deals created by others

Type of Financing Preferred:
Leveraged Buyout
Management Buyouts
Acquisition
Recapitalizations

Geographical Preferences

United States Preferences:
All U.S.

International Preferences:
Europe
Asia

Additional Information

Year Founded: 1994
Current Activity Level : Actively seeking new investments
Method of Compensation: Return on investment is of primary concern, do not charge fees

---

LIBERTY HALL CAPITAL PARTNERS LP

350 Park Avenue
27th Floor
New York, NY USA 10022
Phone: 6462912601
Fax: 6462912632
E-mail: info@libertyhallcapital.com
Website: www.libertyhallcapital.com

Other Offices

375 Park Avenue, 26th Floor
NEW YORK, NY USA 10152

Management and Staff

Jack Nadal, Principal
Stuart Oran, Partner
Taylor Catarozoli, Principal

Type of Firm
Private Equity Firm

Project Preferences

Type of Financing Preferred:
Leveraged Buyout
Acquisition

Industry Preferences

In Transportation prefer:
Aerospace

Additional Information

Year Founded: 2011
Current Activity Level : Actively seeking new investments

LIBERTY LANE PARTNERS LLC

One Liberty Lane
Suite 100
Hampton, NH USA 03842
Phone: 6039292600
E-mail: info@libertylp.com
Website: libertylp.com

Type of Firm
Private Equity Firm

Project Preferences

Type of Financing Preferred:
Leveraged Buyout
Acquisition

Additional Information

Year Founded: 1969
Current Activity Level : Actively seeking new investments

LIBERTY MUTUAL INNOVATION

175 Berkeley Street
Boston, MA USA 02116
Phone: 6173579500
Website: www.libertymutual.com

Management and Staff

Dexter Legg, Vice President
Laurance Yahia, Vice President
Patrick Tully, Vice President

Type of Firm
Insurance Firm Affiliate

Association Membership
National Venture Capital Association – USA (NVCA)

Additional Information
Year Founded: 1997
Capital Under Management: $150,000,000
Current Activity Level : Actively seeking new investments

LIBERTY PARTNERS LTD

485 Lexington Avenue, Second Floor
New York, NY USA 10017
Phone: 2125417676
Fax: 2126496076
E-mail: info@libertypartners.com
Website: www.libertypartners.com

Management and Staff
Andrew Fleiss, Principal
Michael Fram, Managing Director
Ryan Chorazy, Vice President
Thomas Greig, Senior Managing Director

Type of Firm
Private Equity Firm

Project Preferences

Type of Financing Preferred:
Leveraged Buyout
Management Buyouts
Acquisition
Recapitalizations

Geographical Preferences

United States Preferences:
North America

International Preferences:
All International

Industry Focus
(% based on actual investment)
Industrial/Energy	29.4%
Internet Specific	21.0%
Medical/Health	19.6%
Consumer Related	12.2%
Computer Software and Services	7.2%
Other Products	5.4%
Communications and Media	4.4%
Semiconductors/Other Elect.	0.8%

Additional Information
Year Founded: 1992
Capital Under Management: $1,800,000,000
Current Activity Level : Actively seeking new investments

LIBERTY VENTURES INC

Two Commerce Square
2001 Market Street, Suite 3820
Philadelphia, PA USA 19103
Phone: 2678615692
Fax: 2678615696

Management and Staff
David Robkin, Principal
Maria Hahn, Chief Financial Officer
Thomas Morse, Principal

Type of Firm
Private Equity Firm

Project Preferences

Role in Financing:
Will function either as deal originator or investor in deals created by others

Type of Financing Preferred:
Expansion

Geographical Preferences

United States Preferences:
Mid Atlantic

Industry Focus
(% based on actual investment)
Medical/Health	43.9%
Internet Specific	27.4%
Computer Software and Services	18.6%
Semiconductors/Other Elect.	3.7%
Communications and Media	3.7%
Other Products	2.7%

Additional Information
Name of Most Recent Fund: Liberty Ventures II, L.P.
Most Recent Fund Was Raised: 12/31/1999
Year Founded: 1996
Capital Under Management: $150,000,000
Current Activity Level : Actively seeking new investments
Method of Compensation: Return on investment is of primary concern, do not charge fees

LIFE SCIENCES GREEN-HOUSE OF CENTRAL PENNSYLVANIA

225 Market Street, Suite 500
Harrisburg, PA USA 17101
Phone: 7176352100
Website: www.lsgpa.com

Type of Firm
Private Equity Firm

Association Membership
National Venture Capital Association – USA (NVCA)

Project Preferences

Role in Financing:
Prefer role as deal originator

Type of Financing Preferred:
Early Stage
Seed

Geographical Preferences

United States Preferences:
Pennsylvania

Industry Preferences

In Medical/Health prefer:
Medical/Health
Medical Diagnostics
Medical Products
Pharmaceuticals

Additional Information
Year Founded: 2002
Capital Under Management: $18,500,000
Current Activity Level : Actively seeking new investments
Method of Compensation: Return on investment is of primary concern, do not charge fees

LIFE SCIENCES PARTNERS BV

Johannes Vermeerplein 9
Amsterdam, Netherlands 1071 DV
Phone: 31206645500
Fax: 31206768810
E-mail: lspamsterdam@lspvc.com
Website: www.lspvc.com

Other Offices
Wellesley Office Park, Building 5
20 William St., Suite 160
Wellesley, MA USA 02481
Phone: 6174521000
Fax: 6174521001

Dachauer Str 65
Munich, Germany 80335
Phone: 49893306660
Fax: 498933066629

Management and Staff
Anne Portwich, Partner
Daan Ellens, Partner
Fouad Azzam, General Partner
Geraldine O Keeffe, Partner
Hans Clevers, Venture Partner
Joachim Rothe, General Partner
Joep Muijrers, Partner
Joerg Neermann, Partner
John de Koning, Partner
Manfred Ruediger, Partner
Mark Wegter, General Partner
Martijn Kleijwegt, Managing Partner
Merijn Klaassen, Chief Financial Officer
Rene Kuijten, General Partner

Type of Firm
Private Equity Firm

Association Membership
Dutch Venture Capital Associaton (NVP)

Project Preferences

Type of Financing Preferred:
Early Stage
Expansion
Balanced
Public Companies
Later Stage
Seed
Startup

Size of Investments Considered:
Min Size of Investment Considered (000s): $471
Max Size of Investment Considered (000s): $9,416

Geographical Preferences

United States Preferences:

International Preferences:
Sweden
United Kingdom
Luxembourg
Europe
Netherlands
Switzerland
Iceland
Belgium
Israel
Finland
Norway
Germany
Denmark

Industry Preferences

In Biotechnology prefer:
Biotechnology
Human Biotechnology
Agricultural/Animal Bio.

In Medical/Health prefer:
Medical/Health
Medical Diagnostics
Diagnostic Test Products
Medical Therapeutics
Drug/Equipmt Delivery
Medical Products
Health Services
Pharmaceuticals

In Consumer Related prefer:
Food/Beverage

In Agr/Forestr/Fish prefer:
Agriculture related

Additional Information

Year Founded: 1998
Capital Under Management: $541,800,000
Current Activity Level: Actively seeking new investments

LIFE.SREDA VC

Blk 79, Ayer Rajah Crescent
#05-08
Singapore, Singapore 139955
Phone: 6564932135
Website: lifesreda.com

Other Offices

c/o Probiznesbank
ulitsa Petrovka 18/2
Moscow, Russia 119285
Phone: 74959333733

Management and Staff

Aleksandr Kapelin, Partner
Roman Gavrilov, Managing Director

Type of Firm

Private Equity Firm

Project Preferences

Type of Financing Preferred:
Early Stage
Balanced
Startup

Geographical Preferences

United States Preferences:

International Preferences:
Europe
Singapore

Industry Preferences

In Computer Software prefer:
Applications Software

In Internet Specific prefer:
Internet

In Financial Services prefer:
Financial Services

Additional Information

Year Founded: 2003
Capital Under Management: $20,000,000
Current Activity Level: Actively seeking new investments

LIFELINE VENTURES GP II OY

Kalevankatu 13
Third Floor
Helsinki, Finland 00100
E-mail: info@lifelineventures.com
Website: www.lifelineventures.com

Management and Staff

Petteri Koponen, Partner
Timo Ahopelto, Partner

Type of Firm

Incubator/Development Program

Industry Preferences

In Internet Specific prefer:
Internet
Web Aggregation/Portals

In Medical/Health prefer:
Medical/Health

In Consumer Related prefer:
Entertainment and Leisure

Additional Information

Year Founded: 2009
Current Activity Level: Actively seeking new investments

LIGHT BEAM CAPITAL LLC

Ten Lawrence Avenue
Suite One
Tarrytown, NY USA 10591
Phone: 9143345220

Type of Firm

Private Equity Firm

Project Preferences

Type of Financing Preferred:
Acquisition

Geographical Preferences

United States Preferences:
All U.S.

Industry Preferences

In Computer Software prefer:
Software

In Medical/Health prefer:
Health Services

In Consumer Related prefer:
Consumer Services

In Industrial/Energy prefer:
Energy

In Financial Services prefer:
Financial Services

Additional Information

Year Founded: 2012
Current Activity Level: Actively seeking new investments

LIGHTBANK

600 West Chicago Avenue
Suite 700
Chicago, IL USA 60654
Website: www.lightbank.com

Type of Firm
Incubator/Development Program

Project Preferences

Type of Financing Preferred:
Early Stage
Seed
Startup

Size of Investments Considered:
Min Size of Investment Considered (000s): $100
Max Size of Investment Considered (000s): $5,000

Geographical Preferences

United States Preferences:
New York
East Coast

Industry Preferences

In Internet Specific prefer:
Internet
Ecommerce

In Medical/Health prefer:
Medical/Health

In Business Serv. prefer:
Media

Additional Information
Year Founded: 2010
Current Activity Level : Actively seeking new investments

LIGHTBAY CAPITAL LLC

11601 Wilshire Blvd, 11th Floor
Los Angeles, CA USA 90025
Website: www.lightbaycapital.com

Management and Staff
David Burcham, Principal
David Leeney, Managing Director
Stella Ho, Managing Director

Type of Firm
Private Equity Firm

Project Preferences

Type of Financing Preferred:
Generalist PE

Additional Information
Year Founded: 2017
Capital Under Management: $615,000,000
Current Activity Level : Actively seeking new investments

LIGHTHOUSE CAPITAL PARTNERS LP

300 Drake's Landing Road, Suite 210
Greenbrae, CA USA 94904
Phone: 4154645900
Fax: 4159253387
E-mail: info@lcpartners.com

Other Offices
3555 Alameda de las Pulgas
Suite 200
Menlo Park, CA USA 94025
Phone: 650-233-1001
Fax: 650-233-0114

20 University Road
Suite 320
Cambridge, MA USA 02138
Phone: 617-441-9192
Fax: 617-354-4374

Management and Staff
Aaron Tyler, Partner
Cristy Barnes, Managing Director
Gwill York, Co-Founder
Jeff Griffor, Managing Director
Ned Hazen, Managing Director
Richard Stubblefield, Co-Founder
Ryan Turner, Managing Director
Scott Orn, Partner

Type of Firm
Private Equity Firm

Association Membership
New England Venture Capital Association
Western Association of Venture Capitalists (WAVC)

Project Preferences

Role in Financing:
Prefer role in deals created by others

Type of Financing Preferred:
Early Stage
Expansion
Startup

Geographical Preferences

United States Preferences:
Massachusetts
California

Industry Focus
(% based on actual investment)

Internet Specific	41.8%
Communications and Media	19.1%
Semiconductors/Other Elect.	14.6%
Computer Software and Services	13.6%
Biotechnology	4.8%
Medical/Health	2.8%
Other Products	2.2%
Computer Hardware	0.5%
Consumer Related	0.5%

Additional Information
Name of Most Recent Fund: Lighthouse Capital Partners VI, L.P.
Most Recent Fund Was Raised: 02/27/2007
Year Founded: 1994
Capital Under Management: $1,000,000,000
Current Activity Level : Actively seeking new investments
Method of Compensation: Return on invest. most important, but chg. closing fees, service fees, etc.

LIGHTHOUSE EQUITY PARTNERS

1333 West Broadway
Suite 750
Vancouver, Canada V6H 4C1
Website: www.lhequitypartners.com

Type of Firm
Private Equity Firm

Project Preferences

Type of Financing Preferred:
Leveraged Buyout

Geographical Preferences

United States Preferences:
West Coast

Canadian Preferences:
Western Canada

Additional Information
Year Founded: 1969
Current Activity Level : Actively seeking new investments

LIGHTHOUSE FUND LLC

Guru Nanak Hospital Road
102-B Hallmark Business Plaza
Bandra, Mumbai, India 400 051
Phone: 912242041000
E-mail: info@lhfunds.com

Other Offices
Former HQ: 45 Rockefeller Plaza
20th Floor
NEW YORK, NY USA 10111

Management and Staff
Boris Siperstein, Partner
Mukund Krishnaswami, Partner
Sachin Bhartiya, Partner
W. Sean Sovak, Partner

Type of Firm
Private Equity Firm

Association Membership
Emerging Markets Private Equity Association
Indian Venture Capital Association (IVCA)

Project Preferences

Type of Financing Preferred:
Early Stage
Expansion
Balanced
Public Companies
Later Stage

Size of Investments Considered:
Min Size of Investment Considered (000s): $5,000
Max Size of Investment Considered (000s): $15,000

Geographical Preferences

United States Preferences:
All U.S.

International Preferences:
India

Industry Preferences

In Medical/Health prefer:
Health Services

In Consumer Related prefer:
Consumer Services
Education Related

In Agr/Forestr/Fish prefer:
Agribusiness

Additional Information
Year Founded: 2001
Capital Under Management: $138,000,000
Current Activity Level : Actively seeking new investments

LIGHTHOUSE VENTURES LLC

7525 S.E. 24th Street
Suite 180
Mercer Island, WA USA 98040
Phone: 2064329708
Fax: 2062754059
Website: www.lighthouseventuresllc.com

Management and Staff
Jim Mullen, Co-Founder

Type of Firm
Private Equity Firm

Geographical Preferences

United States Preferences:

Additional Information
Year Founded: 2015
Current Activity Level : Actively seeking new investments

LIGHTSPEED MANAGEMENT COMPANY LLC

2200 Sand Hill Road
Menlo Park, CA USA 94025
Phone: 6502348300
Fax: 6502348333
E-mail: info@lsvp.com
Website: www.lsvp.com

Other Offices

Nelson Mandela Road
1st Floor, Commercial Annex
New Delhi, India 110 070
Phone: 9111149800800

No. 223 Tai Cang Road
Suite 2207, Platinum Building
Shanghai, China 200020
Phone: 86-21-5386-6500
Fax: 86-21-5386-6668

79 Jian Guo Road
Unit 3007, Tower 2, China Central Place
Beijing, China 100025
Phone: 86-10-5969-6680
Fax: 86-10-5969-6690

50 Ramat Yam Street
Okeanus Building
Herzilya Pituach, Israel 46851
Phone: 972-9-956-1634
Fax: 972-9-954-3423

Management and Staff

Andrew Moley, Chief Financial Officer
Anshoo Sharma, Principal
Arif Janmohamed, Partner
Barry Eggers, Partner
Bipul Sinha, Venture Partner
Christopher Schaepe, Partner
David Dubick, Partner
David Chen, Partner
David Gussarsky, Partner
Dev Khare, Principal
Eric O Brien, Partner
Herry Han, Partner
Jeremy Liew, Partner
John Vrionis, Partner
Ju Zhang, Vice President
Krish Parikh, Partner
Lyon Wong, Partner
Maninder Gulati, Vice President
Michael Feldman, Partner
Michael Romano, Vice President
Nakul Mandan, Partner
Peter Nieh, Partner
Ravi Mhatre, Partner
Wei Hao, Vice President
William Kohler, Partner
Yoni Cheifetz, Partner

Type of Firm
Private Equity Firm

Association Membership
China Venture Capital Association
Israel Venture Association
Western Association of Venture Capitalists (WAVC)
National Venture Capital Association - USA (NVCA)
Canadian Venture Capital Association
Indian Venture Capital Association (IVCA)

Project Preferences

Role in Financing:
Will function either as deal originator or investor in deals created by others

Type of Financing Preferred:
Early Stage
Expansion
Balanced
Later Stage
Seed
Startup

Geographical Preferences

United States Preferences:

International Preferences:
India
China
Israel
All International

Industry Focus
(% based on actual investment)

Computer Software and Services	39.9%
Internet Specific	28.8%
Communications and Media	8.6%
Computer Hardware	6.4%
Semiconductors/Other Elect.	5.7%
Biotechnology	3.3%
Industrial/Energy	2.4%
Other Products	1.9%
Consumer Related	1.6%
Medical/Health	1.3%

Additional Information
Year Founded: 1971
Capital Under Management: $2,300,000,000
Current Activity Level : Actively seeking new investments
Method of Compensation: Return on investment is of primary concern, do not charge fees

LIGHTSPEED VENTURE PARTNERS CHINA CO LTD

No. 233, Tai Cang Road, Lu Wan
Platinum Bldg,Suite 2207,22F
Shanghai, China 200020
Phone: 862153866500
Fax: 862153866668
E-mail: info-china@lightspeedvp.com
Website: www.lightspeedvp.com

Other Offices
Ugland House, P.O. Box 309
C/O Maples Corporate Services Ltd.
Grand Cayman, Cayman Islands KY1-1104
Phone: 3459498066

No. 79, Jian Guo Road, Chaoyang District
Unit 3007, Tower 2, China Central Place
Beijing, China
Phone: 861059696680
Fax: 861059696690

Management and Staff
James Mi, Managing Director
Ron Cao, Managing Director

Type of Firm
Private Equity Firm

Association Membership
China Venture Capital Association

Project Preferences

Type of Financing Preferred:
Early Stage
Expansion

Geographical Preferences

International Preferences:
China

Industry Preferences

In Communications prefer:
Communications and Media
Wireless Communications

In Internet Specific prefer:
Internet
Ecommerce

In Semiconductor/Electr prefer:
Semiconductor

In Industrial/Energy prefer:
Environmental Related

In Business Serv. prefer:
Services

In Utilities prefer:
Utilities

Additional Information
Year Founded: 2004
Capital Under Management: $765,020,000
Current Activity Level : Actively seeking new investments

LIGHTSTONE VENTURES LP

485 Ramona Street
Palo Alto, CA USA 94301
Phone: 6503883676
Fax: 6503883675
Website: www.lightstonevc.com

Other Offices
4430 Arapahoe Avenue
Suite 220
BOULDER, CO USA 80303
Phone: 3034171604
Fax: 3034171602

Management and Staff
Adam Bruce, Chief Financial Officer
Chris Christoffersen, General Partner
Hank Plain, General Partner
Jason Lettmann, Partner
Jean George, General Partner
Jim Broderick, Partner
Mike Carusi, General Partner
Nassim Usman, Venture Partner
Richard Popp, Venture Partner
Robin Bellas, Partner
Stephen Shapiro, Venture Partner

Type of Firm
Private Equity Firm

Association Membership
National Venture Capital Association - USA (NVCA)

Project Preferences

Type of Financing Preferred:
Early Stage
Later Stage

Industry Preferences

In Biotechnology prefer:
Human Biotechnology

In Medical/Health prefer:
Medical Therapeutics
Medical Products
Pharmaceuticals

Additional Information
Year Founded: 2012
Capital Under Management: $172,000,000
Current Activity Level : Actively seeking new investments

LIGHTVIEW CAPITAL

35 Beechwood Road
Suite 2B
Summit, NJ USA 07901
Phone: 9057511500
E-mail: info@redoakgp.com
Website: www.lightviewcapital.com

Other Offices
300 Campus Drive
Suite 100
FLORHAM PARK, NJ USA 07932
Phone: 9087511500

Management and Staff
Conor Mullett, Co-Founder
Richard Erickson, Co-Founder

Type of Firm
Private Equity Firm

Project Preferences

Type of Financing Preferred:
Leveraged Buyout
Acquisition
Recapitalizations

Geographical Preferences

United States Preferences:
North America

Industry Preferences

In Computer Software prefer:
Software

In Medical/Health prefer:
Medical/Health

In Consumer Related prefer:
Consumer
Education Related

In Industrial/Energy prefer:
Industrial Products

In Financial Services prefer:
Financial Services

In Business Serv. prefer:
Services

Additional Information
Year Founded: 2013
Current Activity Level : Actively seeking new investments

LIGHTYEAR CAPITAL LLC

Nine West 57th Street
New York, NY USA 10019
Phone: 2123280555
Fax: 2123280516
E-mail: IR@lycap.com
Website: www.lycap.com

Management and Staff
Boris Rapoport, Principal
Chris Casciato, Managing Director
Daniel Freyman, Managing Director
Ellan Hayon, Chief Financial Officer
Jason Ehrlich, Vice President
Jay Comerford, Vice President
Kevin Doldan, Vice President
Laura Mothersele, Vice President
Lori Forlano, Managing Director
Mark Vassallo, Managing Partner
Max Rakhlin, Vice President
Michael Doppelt, Managing Director
Michal Petrzela, Managing Director
Stewart Gross, Managing Director
Thierry Ho, Managing Director

Type of Firm
Private Equity Firm

Project Preferences

Type of Financing Preferred:
Leveraged Buyout
Expansion
Acquisition
Recapitalizations

Industry Preferences

In Financial Services prefer:
Financial Services
Insurance

Additional Information
Name of Most Recent Fund: Lightyear Fund III, L.P.
Most Recent Fund Was Raised: 03/25/2011
Year Founded: 2000
Capital Under Management: $3,000,000,000
Current Activity Level: Actively seeking new investments

LIGURCAPITAL SPA

Piazza Dante 8/9
Genova, Italy 16162
Phone: 39-010-74-1461
Fax: 390-10-814-919
E-mail: ligur@ligurcapital.it

Type of Firm
Private Equity Firm

Project Preferences

Type of Financing Preferred:
Second Stage Financing
Seed
Startup

Geographical Preferences

International Preferences:
Italy

Additional Information
Year Founded: 1989
Capital Under Management: $12,300,000
Current Activity Level: Actively seeking new investments

LILLY ASIAN VENTURES

No. 222 Hubin Road
Room 1504, 1 Corporate Avenue
Shanghai, China 200021
Phone: 862163406188
Fax: 862163406183
E-mail: info@lillyasiaventures.com
Website: www.lillyasianventures.com

Type of Firm
Corporate PE/Venture

Project Preferences

Type of Financing Preferred:
Balanced

Geographical Preferences

United States Preferences:
Southeast

International Preferences:
China
Asia

Industry Preferences

In Biotechnology prefer:
Biotechnology

In Medical/Health prefer:
Medical/Health
Medical Diagnostics
Medical Therapeutics
Medical Products
Health Services
Pharmaceuticals

Additional Information
Year Founded: 2007
Capital Under Management: $196,678,000
Current Activity Level: Actively seeking new investments

LILLY VENTURES MANAGEMENT COMPANY LLC

115 West Washington Street,
Suite 1680 - South
Indianapolis, IN USA 46204
Phone: 3174290140
Fax: 3177592819
Website: www.lillyventures.com

Management and Staff
Armen Shanafelt, General Partner
Edward Torres, Co-Founder
Steve Hall, General Partner

Type of Firm
Private Equity Firm

Association Membership
National Venture Capital Association - USA (NVCA)

Project Preferences

Type of Financing Preferred:
Balanced

Geographical Preferences

United States Preferences:
North America

International Preferences:
Europe

Industry Preferences

In Biotechnology prefer:
Biotechnology
Biotech Related Research

In Medical/Health prefer:
Medical Diagnostics
Medical Products
Pharmaceuticals

Additional Information
Year Founded: 2009
Capital Under Management: $200,000,000
Current Activity Level: Actively seeking new investments

LIME ROCK PARTNERS LLC

274 Riverside Avenue
Westport, CT USA 06880
Phone: 2032932750
Fax: 2032932760
Website: www.lrpartners.com

Other Offices
38 Carden Place
Aberdeen, United Kingdom AB10 1UP
Phone: 44-1224-267010
Fax: 44-1224-267011

DIFC Street, Office 22
Gate Village Building 10, Level 3
Dubai, Utd. Arab Em.
Phone: 97144019261
Fax: 97143219783

20 Berkeley Square
3rd Floor
London, United Kingdom
Phone: 44-0207-5143920
Fax: 44-0207-4910087

1111 Bagby Street
Heritage Plaza, Suite 4600
Houston, TX USA 77002
Phone: 713-292-9500
Fax: 713-292-9550

Management and Staff
Anu Mehta, Vice President
Gary Sernovitz, Managing Director
Greg Highberger, Vice President
J. McLane, Managing Director
James Wallis, Vice President
Jason Smith, Vice President
Jeffrey Scofield, Managing Director
John Reynolds, Managing Director
Jonathan Farber, Managing Director
Kris Agarwal, Managing Director
Lynn Calder, Vice President
Rajat Barua, Vice President
Saad Bargach, Managing Director
Townes Pressler, Managing Director
Trevor Burgess, Managing Director

Will Franklin, Managing Director

Type of Firm
Private Equity Firm

Project Preferences

Type of Financing Preferred:
Later Stage
Other

Geographical Preferences

United States Preferences:

Canadian Preferences:
All Canada

International Preferences:
Europe
Rest of World

Industry Focus
(% based on actual investment)

Industrial/Energy	96.6%
Computer Software and Services	1.7%
Semiconductors/Other Elect.	0.8%
Consumer Related	0.4%
Communications and Media	0.3%
Other Products	0.2%

Additional Information
Name of Most Recent Fund: Lime Rock Resources III, L.P.
Most Recent Fund Was Raised: 10/08/2013
Year Founded: 1998
Capital Under Management: $3,900,000,000
Current Activity Level : Actively seeking new investments

LIMERSTON CAPITAL LLP

Two Greycoat Place
London, United Kingdom SW1P 1SB
Phone: 4402072226
E-mail: info@limerstoncap.com
Website: www.limerstoncap.com

Type of Firm
Private Equity Firm

Additional Information
Year Founded: 2014
Capital Under Management: $121,090,000
Current Activity Level : Actively seeking new investments

LINCOLN CAPITAL PARTNERS LTD

116 Harris Road
C/- B D O Spicers, Level Two
Auckland, New Zealand
Website: www.lincolncapital.co.nz

Type of Firm
Private Equity Firm

Project Preferences

Type of Financing Preferred:
Leveraged Buyout
Acquisition

Additional Information
Year Founded: 2001
Current Activity Level : Actively seeking new investments

LINCOLN FUNDS INTERNATIONAL INC

695 Town Centre Drive
First and Eight Floors
Costa Mesa, CA USA 92626
Phone: 800-918-4352
E-mail: la@lincolnfunds.com
Website: www.lincolnfunds.com

Type of Firm
Private Equity Firm

Additional Information
Year Founded: 2009
Current Activity Level : Actively seeking new investments

LINCOLN HILLS HOLDING COMPANY LLC

One N Lasalle Street
Chicago, IL USA 60602
Website: www.lincolnhillholdings.com

Type of Firm
Private Equity Firm

Project Preferences

Type of Financing Preferred:
Leveraged Buyout
Acquisition

Additional Information
Year Founded: 2017
Current Activity Level : Actively seeking new investments

LINCOLN PARK CAPITAL

440 North Wells Street
Suite 410
Chicago, IL USA 60654
Phone: 3128229300
Fax: 3128229301
E-mail: general@lpcfunds.com
Website: www.lincolnparkcapital.com

Type of Firm
Investment Management Firm

Project Preferences

Type of Financing Preferred:
Early Stage
Expansion
Generalist PE
Opportunistic
Later Stage

Industry Preferences

In Financial Services prefer:
Real Estate

Additional Information
Year Founded: 1969
Current Activity Level : Actively seeking new investments

LINCOLNSHIRE MANAGEMENT INC

780 Third Avenue
40th Floor
New York, NY USA 10017
Phone: 2123193633
Fax: 2127555457
E-mail: info@lmi780.com
Website: www.lincolnshiremgmt.com

Other Offices

1755 North Brown Road
Suite 200
Lawrenceville, GA USA 30043
Phone: 4042229585
Fax: 4042294911

10990 Wilshire Boulevard
16th Floor
Los Angeles, CA USA 90024
Phone: 3107047230
Fax: 3109432553

22 West Washington Street
15th Floor
Chicago, IL USA 60602
Phone: 3128999000
Fax: 3128999009

Management and Staff
Brian Nethercott, Managing Director
Charles Mills, Managing Director
Edwin Moss, Managing Director
George Henry, Managing Director
James Binch, Managing Director
James McLaughlin, Managing Director
John Perrachon, Managing Director
John O Connor, Managing Director
John Camp, Managing Director
Katherine Lehman, Managing Director
Michael Lyons, Senior Managing Director
Michael Forlenza, Managing Director
Nicholas Nedeau, Managing Director
Nicolo Vergani, Principal
Ottavio Serena di Lapigio, Managing Director

Patrick Coyne, Managing Director
Pieter Kodde, Managing Director
Richard Huo, Managing Director
Rick Sullivan, Principal
T.J. Maloney, President
Thomas Callahan, Managing Director
Vineet Pruthi, Senior Managing Director
William Hall, Managing Director

Type of Firm
Private Equity Firm

Project Preferences

Role in Financing:
Prefer role as deal originator

Type of Financing Preferred:
Leveraged Buyout
Management Buyouts
Acquisition
Recapitalizations

Geographical Preferences

United States Preferences:

International Preferences:
Europe
Asia

Industry Preferences

In Business Serv. prefer:
Services
Distribution

In Manufact. prefer:
Manufacturing

Additional Information
Name of Most Recent Fund: Lincolnshire Equity Fund III, L.P.
Most Recent Fund Was Raised: 09/14/2004
Year Founded: 1986
Capital Under Management: $1,800,000,000
Current Activity Level : Actively seeking new investments
Method of Compensation: Return on invest. most important, but chg. closing fees, service fees, etc.

LINDEMAN ASIA INVESTMENT CORP

2F Samik Building
720-2 Yeoksam-dong Gangnam-gu
Seoul, South Korea 135-080
Phone: 827070194001
Fax: 8225933272
Website: www.laic.kr

Management and Staff
Jean Choi, Managing Director

Type of Firm
Private Equity Firm

Association Membership
Korean Venture Capital Association (KVCA)

Project Preferences

Type of Financing Preferred:
Leveraged Buyout
Balanced

Geographical Preferences

International Preferences:
China
Korea, South

Industry Preferences

In Other prefer:
Environment Responsible

Additional Information
Year Founded: 2006
Capital Under Management: $7,400,000
Current Activity Level : Actively seeking new investments

LINDEN LLC

111 South Wacker Drive
Suite 3350
Chicago, IL USA 60606
Phone: 3125065600
Fax: 3125065601
Website: www.lindenllc.com

Management and Staff
Brian Miller, Managing Partner
Douglass VanDegrift, Chief Financial Officer
John Neal, Partner
Kamlesh Shah, Principal
Mark Sullivan, Principal
Max Gaby, Vice President
Michael Watts, Vice President
Michael Farah, Partner
Michael Bernard, Vice President
Todd Van Horn, Principal
William Drehkoff, Partner

Type of Firm
Private Equity Firm

Association Membership
Illinois Venture Capital Association

Project Preferences

Type of Financing Preferred:
Leveraged Buyout
Later Stage
Management Buyouts
Acquisition
Recapitalizations

Geographical Preferences

United States Preferences:

Canadian Preferences:
All Canada

Industry Preferences

In Medical/Health prefer:
Medical/Health
Medical Diagnostics
Medical Therapeutics
Medical Products
Health Services
Hospitals/Clinics/Primary
Pharmaceuticals

Additional Information
Year Founded: 1998
Capital Under Management: $750,000,000
Current Activity Level : Actively seeking new investments

LINDSAY GOLDBERG & BESSEMER LP

630 Fifth Avenue
30th Floor
New York, NY USA 10111
Phone: 2126511100
Fax: 2126511101
E-mail: contact@lindsaygoldbergllc.com
Website: www.lgblp.com

Other Offices

8226 Douglas Avenue
Suite 709
Dallas, TX USA 75225
Phone: 214-692-1452
Fax: 214-553-8186

5409 Maryland Way
Brentwood, TN USA 37027
Phone: 615-915-3011
Fax: 615-915-3013

415 Spruce Street
Philadelphia, PA USA 19106
Phone: 215-923-7198
Fax: 215-923-1628

132 Harbourmaster Court
Ponte Vedra Beach, FL USA 32082
Phone: 904-396-0348
Fax: 904-398-4235

253 3rd Street SE
Medicine Hat
Alberta, Canada T1A 0G4
Phone: 403-528-1095

1146 S Street
Anchorage, AK USA 99501
Phone: 907-929-7200
Fax: 907-929-7213

Ruselokkveien 26
P.O. Box 1793 Vika
Oslo, Norway 0122
Phone: 47-2201-3210
Fax: 47-2201-3211

8598 French Curve
Eden Prairie, MN USA 55347
Phone: 617-747-2497

Two Houston Center
909 Fannin, Suite 2630
Houston, TX USA 77010
Phone: 713-789-0380

Konigsallee 60A
Dusseldorf, Germany 40212
Phone: 49-211-8620-1500
Fax: 49-211-8620-1525

8065 Leesburg Pike
Suite 500
Vienna, VA USA 22182
Phone: 703-506-3902
Fax: 703-506-3905

135 South LaSalle Street
Suite 260
Chicago, IL USA 60603
Phone: 312-904-800
Fax: 312-904-6559

885 Third Avenue
20th Floor
New York, NY USA 10022
Phone: 212-230-2030
Fax: 212-758-7024

Management and Staff
Alan Goldberg, Managing Partner
Andrew Weinberg, Partner
Andrew Davis, Vice President
Ben Adams, Vice President
Brian Kelley, Partner
Eric Fry, Partner
Evan Klebe, Vice President
J. Russell Triedman, Partner
Jaime Buehl-Reichard, Principal
John Aiello, Managing Director
John Werwaiss, Partner
Krishna Agrawal, Vice President
Lance Hirt, Partner
Michael Dees, Partner
Rachael Wagner, Vice President
Robert Roriston, Partner
Robert Lindsay, Managing Partner
Ryan Miller, Principal

Type of Firm
Private Equity Firm

Association Membership
German Venture Capital Association (BVK)

Project Preferences

Type of Financing Preferred:
Leveraged Buyout
Management Buyouts
Acquisition

Additional Information
Name of Most Recent Fund: Lindsay Goldberg III, L.P.
Most Recent Fund Was Raised: 05/21/2009
Year Founded: 2001
Capital Under Management: $10,000,000,000
Current Activity Level : Actively seeking new investments

LINEAR VENTURE

Zhenbei Rd. Putuo Dist
Rm. 316, Bldg 20, No. 958
Beijing, China 200331
Website: www.linear.vc

Type of Firm
Private Equity Firm

Project Preferences

Type of Financing Preferred:
Early Stage

Geographical Preferences

International Preferences:
China

Industry Preferences

In Internet Specific prefer:
Internet

In Semiconductor/Electr prefer:
Semiconductor

In Industrial/Energy prefer:
Energy Conservation Relat

In Financial Services prefer:
Financial Services

In Business Serv. prefer:
Services
Media

Additional Information
Year Founded: 2014
Capital Under Management: $100,000,000
Current Activity Level : Actively seeking new investments

LINGFENG CAPITAL MANAGEMENT CO LTD

Third Area, An Zhen Li
5th Floor, Building 10
Beijing, China 100029
Website: www.lingfengcap.com

Type of Firm
Investment Management Firm

Project Preferences

Type of Financing Preferred:
Balanced

Geographical Preferences

International Preferences:
China

Industry Preferences

In Computer Software prefer:
Data Processing

In Consumer Related prefer:
Consumer

In Financial Services prefer:
Financial Services

Additional Information
Year Founded: 2015
Current Activity Level : Actively seeking new investments

LINGYI VENTURE CAPITAL CO LTD

No.150, Hubin Rd.,Huangpu Dist
Rm2802B,Bldg.5, Qi Ye Tian Di
Shanghai, China
Phone: 862163136288
Fax: 862163320081
E-mail: info@01vc.com
Website: www.01vc.com

Type of Firm
Private Equity Firm

Project Preferences

Type of Financing Preferred:
Early Stage

Geographical Preferences

International Preferences:
China

Industry Preferences

In Internet Specific prefer:
Internet
Ecommerce

In Consumer Related prefer:
Education Related

In Financial Services prefer:
Financial Services

Additional Information
Year Founded: 2015
Current Activity Level : Actively seeking new investments

LINK VENTURES LLLP

One Kendall Square
Building 200, Suite B2106
Cambridge, MA USA 02139
Website: www.linkventures.com

Management and Staff
Cynthia Blanco, Chief Financial Officer

Type of Firm
Private Equity Firm

Project Preferences

Type of Financing Preferred:
Early Stage

Geographical Preferences

United States Preferences:

Industry Preferences

In Internet Specific prefer:
Internet

Additional Information
Year Founded: 2007
Current Activity Level : Actively seeking new investments

LINN GROVE VENTURES LLC

5012 53rd Street South, Suite I
Fargo, ND USA 58104
Phone: 701-356-5655
Fax: 701-356-5652
E-mail: info@linngroveventures.com
Website: www.linngroveventures.com

Type of Firm
Private Equity Firm

Project Preferences

Type of Financing Preferred:
Early Stage

Geographical Preferences

United States Preferences:
South Dakota
Iowa
North Dakota
Minnesota

Canadian Preferences:
Manitoba

Industry Preferences

In Biotechnology prefer:
Agricultural/Animal Bio.

In Medical/Health prefer:
Medical/Health

In Consumer Related prefer:
Food/Beverage

In Agr/Forestr/Fish prefer:
Agriculture related

Additional Information
Name of Most Recent Fund: Linn Grove Angel Fund, L.P.
Most Recent Fund Was Raised: 12/14/2010
Year Founded: 2010
Capital Under Management: $1,115,000
Current Activity Level : Actively seeking new investments

LINSALATA CAPITAL PARTNERS INC

5900 Landerbrook Drive, Suite 280
Mayfield Heights, OH USA 44124
Phone: 4406841400
Fax: 4406840984
E-mail: info@linsalatacapital.com
Website: linsalatacapital.com

Management and Staff
Daniel DeSantis, Managing Director
Gregory Taber, Managing Director
James Guddy, Vice President
John Studdard, Principal
Michael Faremouth, Managing Director
Michael Moran, Vice President
Murad Beg, Principal

Type of Firm
Private Equity Firm

Project Preferences

Role in Financing:
Prefer role as deal originator

Type of Financing Preferred:
Leveraged Buyout
Expansion
Management Buyouts
Acquisition

Geographical Preferences

United States Preferences:

Industry Focus
(% based on actual investment)
Other Products   83.0%
Industrial/Energy   16.9%
Consumer Related   0.2%

Additional Information
Name of Most Recent Fund: Linsalata Capital Partners Fund VI, L.P.
Most Recent Fund Was Raised: 08/03/2011
Year Founded: 1984
Capital Under Management: $662,000,000
Current Activity Level : Actively seeking new investments
Method of Compensation: Return on invest. most important, but chg. closing fees, service fees, etc.

LINSE CAPITAL CP LLC

1340 Arbor Road
Menlo Park, CA USA 94025
Phone: 6507877200
E-mail: contact@linsecapital.com

Type of Firm
Private Equity Firm

Project Preferences

Type of Financing Preferred:
Later Stage

Additional Information
Year Founded: 2016
Capital Under Management: $105,430,000
Current Activity Level : Actively seeking new investments

LINX PARTNERS LLC

100 Galleria Parkway, Suite 1300
Atlanta, GA USA 30339
Phone: 7708180335
Fax: 7708189537
Website: www.linxpartners.com

Other Offices
670 White Plains Road
Suite 201
Scarsdale, NY USA 10583
Phone: 914-472-1835
Fax: 914-472-6721

Management and Staff
Barbara Henagan, Founder
Edward Leinss, Founder
Giny Mullins, Managing Director
Mark Niznik, Managing Director
Melissa Nims, Chief Financial Officer
Peter Hicks, Founder

Type of Firm
Private Equity Firm

Project Preferences

Role in Financing:
Prefer role as deal originator

Type of Financing Preferred:
Leveraged Buyout
Acquisition

Geographical Preferences

United States Preferences:

Industry Preferences

In Industrial/Energy prefer:
Industrial Products

In Business Serv. prefer:
Services
Distribution

In Manufact. prefer:
Manufacturing

Additional Information

Name of Most Recent Fund: Linx Partners III, L.P.
Most Recent Fund Was Raised: 08/02/2013
Year Founded: 1999
Capital Under Management: $188,000,000
Current Activity Level: Actively seeking new investments
Method of Compensation: Function primarily in service area, receive contingent fee in cash or equity

---

LINZOR CAPITAL PARTNERS LP

Av. Bicentenario 3883
5th Fl., Of. 502-503, Vitacura
Santiago, Chile
Phone: 5629509600
Fax: 5629509696
Website: www.linzorcapital.com

Other Offices

Carrera 9, No 80-45
Suite 801
Bogota, Colombia
Phone: 5715305177
Fax: 5715305175

Arroyo 880, Floor 6, Of. 11-12
Capital Federal (1007)
Buenos Aires, Argentina
Phone: 54-11-4328-0758
Fax: 54-11-4328-0758

Guillermo Gonzlez Camarena 1600
Of. 4B
Centro Santa Fe, Mexico 01210
Phone: 525552926448

Management and Staff

Alfredo Irigoin, Partner
Carlos Gomez, Partner
Carlos Ingham, Partner
Cipriano Santisteban, Partner
Hernan Romero, Principal
Jorge Matheu, Principal
Matias Gutierrez, Principal
Sharon Matthews, Chief Financial Officer
Tim Purcell, Managing Partner

Type of Firm

Investment Management Firm

Project Preferences

Type of Financing Preferred:
Leveraged Buyout
Acquisition
Special Situation
Distressed Debt
Recapitalizations

Geographical Preferences

International Preferences:
Latin America
Argentina
Peru
Mexico
Chile
Colombia

Industry Preferences

In Communications prefer:
Telecommunications

In Medical/Health prefer:
Medical/Health

In Consumer Related prefer:
Consumer
Retail
Education Related

In Industrial/Energy prefer:
Industrial Products

In Financial Services prefer:
Financial Services

In Business Serv. prefer:
Services
Distribution
Media

In Utilities prefer:
Utilities

Additional Information

Name of Most Recent Fund: Linzor Capital Partners II, L.P.
Most Recent Fund Was Raised: 08/06/2010
Year Founded: 2006
Capital Under Management: $1,086,000,000
Current Activity Level: Actively seeking new investments

LION CAPITAL LLP

21 Grosvenor Place
London, United Kingdom SW1X 7HF
Phone: 442072012200
Fax: 442072012222
E-mail: info@lioncapital.com
Website: www.lioncapital.com

Other Offices

888 7th Avenue
43rd Floor
NEW YORK, NY USA 10019
Phone: 12123141900
Fax: 12123141950

Management and Staff

Dominik Halstenberg, Partner
Eric Lindberg, Partner
Fabrice Chesnais, Principal
Hallie Kim, Managing Director
Jacob Capps, Partner
James Cocker, Partner
Javier Ferran, Partner
Julia van Tuyll, Vice President
Kavita Bagga, Vice President
Kelly Mayer, Partner
Lyndon Lea, Managing Partner
Mary Minnick, Partner
Matthew Wilson, Principal
Robert Darwent, Partner
Rory O Connor, Partner
Sherif Guirgis, Principal
Victor Benazech, Principal

Type of Firm

Private Equity Firm

Association Membership

British Venture Capital Association (BVCA)
European Private Equity and Venture Capital Assoc.

Project Preferences

Type of Financing Preferred:
Leveraged Buyout
Generalist PE

Geographical Preferences

International Preferences:
Europe

Industry Preferences

In Consumer Related prefer:
Consumer
Consumer Products
Consumer Services

Additional Information

Name of Most Recent Fund: Lion Capital Fund III, L.P.
Most Recent Fund Was Raised: 10/20/2010
Year Founded: 2004
Capital Under Management: $5,321,900,000
Current Activity Level: Actively seeking new investments

LION EQUITY PARTNERS LLC

3003 East Third Avenue
Suite 201
Denver, CO USA 80206
Phone: 3038474100
Fax: 3038720156
Website: www.lionequity.com

Other Offices
400 Skokie Boulevard
Suite 375
Northbrook, IL USA 60062
Phone: 3122128984
Fax: 3123618053

Management and Staff
Ari Silverman, Co-Founder
E. James Levitas, Co-Founder

Type of Firm
Private Equity Firm

Project Preferences

Type of Financing Preferred:
Leveraged Buyout
Acquisition

Geographical Preferences

United States Preferences:

Canadian Preferences:
All Canada

Industry Preferences

In Communications prefer:
Telecommunications

In Computer Software prefer:
Software

In Medical/Health prefer:
Medical/Health

In Transportation prefer:
Transportation

In Business Serv. prefer:
Services
Distribution

In Manufact. prefer:
Manufacturing

Additional Information
Year Founded: 2007
Current Activity Level : Actively seeking new investments

LION'S HEAD GLOBAL PARTNERS LLP

29-35 Old Queen Street
London, United Kingdom SW1H 9JA
Phone: 44002073400400
E-mail: info@lhgp.com
Website: www.lhgp.com

Management and Staff
Christopher Egerton-Warburton, Co-Founder
Clemens Calice, Partner
Martin Short, Managing Director

Type of Firm
Investment Management Firm

Project Preferences

Type of Financing Preferred:
Generalist PE
Later Stage

Geographical Preferences

International Preferences:
United Kingdom

Industry Preferences

In Medical/Health prefer:
Medical/Health
Health Services

In Consumer Related prefer:
Education Related

In Industrial/Energy prefer:
Energy

In Agr/Forestr/Fish prefer:
Agriculture related

Additional Information
Year Founded: 2008
Capital Under Management: $94,000,000
Current Activity Level : Actively seeking new investments

LIONBIRD VENTURES LTD

HaBarzel 25
Tel Aviv, Israel 69710
Phone: 97235333885
Fax: 97235333995
Website: lionbird.com

Other Offices
HaBarzel 25
Tel Aviv, Israel 69710
Phone: 97235333885
Fax: 97235333995

Management and Staff
Chaim Friedman, Managing Partner
Itschak Friedman, Venture Partner
Jonathan Friedman, Partner

Type of Firm
Private Equity Firm

Project Preferences

Type of Financing Preferred:
Early Stage
Seed

Size of Investments Considered:
Min Size of Investment Considered (000s): $200
Max Size of Investment Considered (000s): $750

Industry Preferences

In Communications prefer:
Wireless Communications

In Computer Software prefer:
Software

In Internet Specific prefer:
Ecommerce

In Medical/Health prefer:
Medical/Health

In Consumer Related prefer:
Retail

Additional Information
Year Founded: 2012
Capital Under Management: $45,000,000
Current Activity Level : Actively seeking new investments

LIONCOURT INVESTMENTS LTD

Carysfort House
Carysfort Avenue
Dublin, Ireland
Phone: 35316852806
E-mail: info@lioncourt.ie
Website: www.lioncourt.ie

Management and Staff
David Andrews, Co-Founder
Michael Tunney, Co-Founder

Type of Firm
Private Equity Firm

Project Preferences

Type of Financing Preferred:
Leveraged Buyout
Acquisition

Geographical Preferences

International Preferences:
Ireland
United Kingdom

Industry Preferences

In Medical/Health prefer:
Health Services

In Consumer Related prefer:
Hotels and Resorts
Education Related

Additional Information
Year Founded: 1998
Current Activity Level : Actively seeking new investments

LIONROCK CAPITAL LTD

228 Queens Road East
11/F Jonsim Place, Wanchai
Hong Kong, Hong Kong
Phone: 85228348000
E-mail: info@lionrockcapitalhk.com
Website: www.lionrockcapitalhk.com

Management and Staff
Kar Keung Tseung, Founder
Ling Low Siew, Vice President
Ned Sherwood, Managing Director

Type of Firm
Private Equity Firm

Project Preferences

Type of Financing Preferred:
Balanced

Geographical Preferences

International Preferences:
Taiwan
Hong Kong
China
Singapore

Industry Preferences

In Communications prefer:
Telecommunications

In Internet Specific prefer:
Internet

In Consumer Related prefer:
Retail
Food/Beverage
Consumer Services
Education Related

In Financial Services prefer:
Insurance

In Business Serv. prefer:
Media

Additional Information
Year Founded: 2011
Current Activity Level : Actively seeking new investments

LIQUID 2 VENTURES LP

301 MISSION ST
UNIT 41C MILLENNIUM TOWER
San Francisco, CA USA 94105
E-mail: info@liquid2.vc
Website: liquid2.vc

Management and Staff
Joe Montana, Co-Founder
Michael Ma, Co-Founder
Mike Miller, Co-Founder

Type of Firm
Private Equity Firm

Project Preferences

Type of Financing Preferred:
Early Stage
Seed

Additional Information
Year Founded: 2015
Current Activity Level : Actively seeking new investments

LIQUID REALTY PARTNERS

44 Montgomery Street
Suite 3701
San Francisco, CA USA 94104
Phone: 4158757500
Fax: 4158757550
E-mail: Corporate@LiquidRealty.com
Website: www.liquidrealty.com

Type of Firm
Private Equity Advisor or Fund of Funds

Project Preferences

Type of Financing Preferred:
Core
Value-Add
Opportunistic
Fund of Funds of Second

Geographical Preferences

United States Preferences:
North America

International Preferences:
Europe

Industry Preferences

In Financial Services prefer:
Real Estate

Additional Information
Name of Most Recent Fund: Liquid Realty Partners IV, L.P.
Most Recent Fund Was Raised: 02/12/2007
Year Founded: 2001
Capital Under Management: $158,500,000
Current Activity Level : Actively seeking new investments

LIRA VC

11205 Alpharetta Hwy
Suite G2
Roswell, GA USA 30076
Phone: 6786775496
E-mail: atlanta@liravc.com
Website: liravc.com

Type of Firm
Incubator/Development Program

Project Preferences

Type of Financing Preferred:
Early Stage
Seed

Additional Information
Year Founded: 1969
Current Activity Level : Actively seeking new investments

LIREAS HLDG

P.O. Box 10842
Johannesburg, South Africa 2000
Phone: 27-11-481-6607
Fax: 27-11-643-4245
E-mail: info@hannover-re.com
Website: www.hannover-re.co.za

Type of Firm
Corporate PE/Venture

Project Preferences

Type of Financing Preferred:
Expansion

Geographical Preferences

International Preferences:
Africa

Industry Preferences

In Financial Services prefer:
Financial Services

Additional Information
Year Founded: 2000
Capital Under Management: $3,100,000
Current Activity Level : Actively seeking new investments

LISTEN LLC
119 West Hubbard Street
Fifth Floor
Chicago, IL USA 60654
Website: listen.co

Management and Staff
Joe Silberman, Partner

Type of Firm
Private Equity Firm

Project Preferences

Type of Financing Preferred:
Seed

Additional Information
Year Founded: 2010
Capital Under Management: $15,900,000
Current Activity Level : Actively seeking new investments

LITCAPITAL ASSET MANAGEMENT UAB
Konstitucijos Pr. 7, 14th Floor
Vilnius, Lithuania 09308
Phone: 37052054479
Fax: 37052487545
E-mail: info@litcapital.lt
Website: www.litcapital.lt

Management and Staff
Arvydas Sarocka, Partner
Hanno Riismaa, Partner

Type of Firm
Private Equity Firm

Association Membership
Lithuanian Venture Capital Association

Project Preferences

Type of Financing Preferred:
Early Stage
Expansion
Balanced
Seed
Startup

Geographical Preferences

International Preferences:
Lithuania

Industry Preferences

In Industrial/Energy prefer:
Energy

Additional Information
Year Founded: 2010
Capital Under Management: $28,657,000
Current Activity Level : Actively seeking new investments

LITERA INVESTMENTS INC
720 Proudfoot Lane
London, Canada N6H 5G5
E-mail: info@literainvestments.com
Website: literainvestments.com

Type of Firm
Private Equity Firm

Project Preferences

Type of Financing Preferred:
Core
Startup

Geographical Preferences

Canadian Preferences:
Ontario

Industry Preferences

In Communications prefer:
Entertainment

In Computer Software prefer:
Systems Software

In Biotechnology prefer:
Biotechnology

In Financial Services prefer:
Real Estate

In Agr/Forestr/Fish prefer:
Agriculture related

Additional Information
Year Founded: 2014
Current Activity Level : Actively seeking new investments

LITEXCO MEDITERRANEA SURL
T. Roviralta 13
Barcelona, Spain 08022
Phone: 34934671070
E-mail: barcelona@litexco.com
Website: www.litexco.com

Other Offices
Apaca Utca 9
Gyor, Hungary 9022
Phone: 36-96-526-944
Fax: 36-96-312-302

9, Asnyka Street
Krakow, Poland 31144
Phone: 48-12-431-0576
Fax: 48-12-431-0576

Malioviza Six
Sofia, Bulgaria 1000
Phone: 35929818371

Via Cefalonia 55
Brescia, Italy 25124
Phone: 39302422016

Apiolaza S/n
Colonia Elena - C.C. 15
San Rafael - Mendoza, Argentina 5600
Phone: 5492604575726

104-106, Stirbei Voda Street
Sector 1
Bucharest, Romania
Phone: 40-21-313-6039
Fax: 40-21-313-6039

Grosslingova 56
Bratislava, Sri Lanka 811 09
Phone: 421-907-984-996
Fax: 421-2-5443-5680

Saxweg Eleven
Triesen, Liechtenstein 9495
Phone: 4232655710

Type of Firm
Private Equity Firm

Project Preferences

Type of Financing Preferred:
Early Stage
Startup

Geographical Preferences

International Preferences:
Italy
Hungary
Slovak Repub.
Latin America
Ireland
Liechtenstein
Europe
Portugal
Switzerland
Argentina
Poland
Brazil
Bulgaria
Spain
Romania

Industry Preferences

In Industrial/Energy prefer:
Alternative Energy
Environmental Related

Additional Information

Year Founded: 1989
Current Activity Level : Actively seeking new investments

LITORINA CAPITAL ADVISORS AB

Sergels Torg 12
Stockholm, Sweden 111 57
Phone: 46854518180
Fax: 46854518189
E-mail: litorina@litorina.se
Website: www.litorina.se

Other Offices

World Trade Center
Teatergatan 19
Gothenburg, Sweden 411 35
Phone: 46-8-5451-8180

Management and Staff

Harold Kaiser, Managing Partner
Jorgen Ekberg, Partner
Lars Verneholt, Partner
Paul Steene, Partner

Type of Firm

Private Equity Firm

Association Membership

Swedish Venture Capital Association (SVCA)
European Private Equity and Venture Capital Assoc.

Project Preferences

Type of Financing Preferred:
Leveraged Buyout
Management Buyouts
Acquisition

Size of Investments Considered:
Min Size of Investment Considered (000s): $1,000
Max Size of Investment Considered (000s): $10,000

Geographical Preferences

International Preferences:
Sweden
Europe
Scandanavia/Nordic Region

Industry Focus

(% based on actual investment)
Industrial/Energy	34.9%
Computer Software and Services	25.9%
Communications and Media	15.3%
Internet Specific	13.0%
Medical/Health	11.0%

Additional Information

Name of Most Recent Fund: Litorina IV, L.P.
Most Recent Fund Was Raised: 10/21/2010
Year Founded: 1998
Capital Under Management: $633,100,000
Current Activity Level : Actively seeking new investments

LITTLEBANC MERCHANT

455 Northeast
Fifth Avenue
Delray Beach, FL USA 33483
Phone: 5619223700
Website: www.lbmerchant.com

Type of Firm

Bank Affiliated

Project Preferences

Type of Financing Preferred:
Expansion
Later Stage

Industry Preferences

In Communications prefer:
Communications and Media

In Business Serv. prefer:
Services

Additional Information

Year Founded: 2009
Current Activity Level : Actively seeking new investments

LITTLEJOHN CAPITAL LLC

116 West Jones Street
Savannah, GA USA 31401
Phone: 9124720300
Website: littlejohncapital.com

Type of Firm

Private Equity Firm

Project Preferences

Type of Financing Preferred:
Leveraged Buyout
Management Buyouts
Acquisition
Recapitalizations

Industry Preferences

In Business Serv. prefer:
Services

In Manufact. prefer:
Manufacturing

Additional Information

Year Founded: 2014
Current Activity Level : Actively seeking new investments

LITTLEROCK GMBH

Goethestr. 83
Dusseldorf, Germany 40237
Website: littlerock.vc

Type of Firm

Private Equity Firm

Geographical Preferences

International Preferences:
Germany

Additional Information

Year Founded: 2015
Current Activity Level : Actively seeking new investments

LITTO INVEST SAS

1, Rue Francoise Sagan
Saint Herblain, France 44800

Type of Firm

Bank Affiliated

Project Preferences

Type of Financing Preferred:
Early Stage
Expansion
Later Stage
Seed

Geographical Preferences

International Preferences:
France

Industry Preferences

In Consumer Related prefer:
Sports
Consumer Products
Consumer Services
Hotels and Resorts

In Industrial/Energy prefer:
Alternative Energy

In Transportation prefer:
Transportation

Additional Information
Year Founded: 2014
Current Activity Level : Actively seeking new investments

LIUHE CAPITAL LLC

No. 1155, Fangdian Road
Room 3703, Jiali City
Shanghai, China 201204
Phone: 862150273377
Fax: 862150273190
Website: www.liuhecapital.com

Management and Staff
Kui Deng, Chief Financial Officer
Ye Wang, President

Type of Firm
Private Equity Firm

Project Preferences

Type of Financing Preferred:
Balanced
Public Companies

Geographical Preferences

International Preferences:
China

Industry Preferences

In Medical/Health prefer:
Medical/Health
Medical Diagnostics

In Consumer Related prefer:
Consumer Products
Consumer Services

In Industrial/Energy prefer:
Industrial Products
Materials

In Manufact. prefer:
Manufacturing

Additional Information
Year Founded: 2004
Capital Under Management: $140,306,000
Current Activity Level : Actively seeking new investments

LIVEOAK VENTURE PARTNERS

805 Las Cimas Parkway
Suite 125
Austin, TX USA 78746
Phone: 5124984900
E-mail: info@liveoakvp.com

Management and Staff
Benjamin Scott, General Partner
Krishna Srinivasan, General Partner
Venu Shamapant, General Partner

Type of Firm
Private Equity Firm

Project Preferences

Type of Financing Preferred:
Early Stage
Seed
Startup

Geographical Preferences

United States Preferences:
Southwest
Texas

Additional Information
Name of Most Recent Fund: LiveOak Venture Partners I, L.P.
Most Recent Fund Was Raised: 12/30/2013
Year Founded: 2012
Capital Under Management: $109,000,000
Current Activity Level : Actively seeking new investments

LIVONIA PARTNERS

Lacplesa Iela 20 A
Riga, Latvia LV-1011
E-mail: info@livoniapartners.com
Website: www.livoniapartners.com

Type of Firm
Private Equity Firm

Project Preferences

Type of Financing Preferred:
Leveraged Buyout
Mezzanine
Acquisition

Size of Investments Considered:
Min Size of Investment Considered (000s): $3,424
Max Size of Investment Considered (000s): $17,117

Geographical Preferences

International Preferences:
Estonia
Latvia
Lithuania

Industry Preferences

In Communications prefer:
Telecommunications

In Medical/Health prefer:
Health Services

In Consumer Related prefer:
Consumer

In Industrial/Energy prefer:
Energy

In Financial Services prefer:
Financial Services

In Business Serv. prefer:
Services
Media

In Manufact. prefer:
Manufacturing

Additional Information
Year Founded: 2016
Capital Under Management: $70,000,000
Current Activity Level : Actively seeking new investments

LIWICK INVESTMENT MANAGEMENT LTD

No. 596, Longhua Middle Road
Suite 1605, Lvdi Center East
Shanghai, China 200032
Phone: 862164185311
Fax: 862164186631
Website: liwick.cn

Type of Firm
Private Equity Firm

Project Preferences

Type of Financing Preferred:
Balanced

Geographical Preferences

International Preferences:
China

Additional Information
Year Founded: 2009
Current Activity Level : Actively seeking new investments

LIYANG HONGTU NEW ECONOMIC VENTURE CAPITAL FUND LP

Science and Education City, Wu
Room A1106, No. 1 Research & D
Changzhou, China 213000
Phone: 8651986318332

Type of Firm
Investment Management Firm

Project Preferences

Type of Financing Preferred:
Balanced

Geographical Preferences

International Preferences:
China

Additional Information
Year Founded: 2016
Current Activity Level : Actively seeking new investments

LJ2 & CO LLC

Eight Sound Shore Drive
Suite 303
Greenwich, CT USA 06830
Phone: 2035523500
Fax: 2035523550
E-mail: info@littlejohnllc.com
Website: www.littlejohnllc.com

Management and Staff
Antonio Miranda, Managing Director
Brian Ramsay, President
Brian Michaud, Vice President
David Simon, Managing Director
Drew Greenwood, Vice President
Edmund Feeley, Managing Director
Gentry Klein, Vice President
Hondo Sen, Vice President
Ichiro Osumi, Vice President
Kenneth Warren, Chief Financial Officer
Michael Kaplan, Managing Director
Michael Klein, Chief Executive Officer
Richard Maybaum, Managing Director
Robert Davis, Managing Director
Steven Kalter, Vice President
Steven Raich, Managing Director

Type of Firm
Private Equity Firm

Project Preferences

Type of Financing Preferred:
Leveraged Buyout
Management Buyouts
Acquisition
Recapitalizations

Geographical Preferences

United States Preferences:

Canadian Preferences:
All Canada

International Preferences:
Europe

Industry Focus
(% based on actual investment)
Industrial/Energy 41.0%
Internet Specific 36.9%
Other Products 15.9%
Semiconductors/Other Elect. 3.8%
Consumer Related 2.3%

Additional Information
Name of Most Recent Fund: Littlejohn Fund IV, L.P.
Most Recent Fund Was Raised: 09/14/2009
Year Founded: 1996
Capital Under Management: $2,800,000,000
Current Activity Level : Actively seeking new investments

LJH GLOBAL INVESTMENTS L L C

4851 Tamiami Trail North
Suite 302
Naples, FL USA 34103
Phone: 2394033030
Fax: 2394033031
Website: www.ljh.com

Other Offices
Former HQ: 4851 Tamiami Trail North
Suite 302
Naples, FL USA 34103

Type of Firm
Investment Management Firm

Project Preferences

Role in Financing:
Prefer role in deals created by others

Type of Financing Preferred:
Balanced

Geographical Preferences

United States Preferences:

Industry Preferences

In Communications prefer:
Communications and Media

In Computer Other prefer:
Computer Related

In Semiconductor/Electr prefer:
Electronic Components

In Financial Services prefer:
Financial Services

In Business Serv. prefer:
Distribution

Additional Information
Year Founded: 1992
Capital Under Management: $200,000,000
Current Activity Level : Actively seeking new investments

Method of Compensation: Return on investment is of primary concern, do not charge fees

LJH LINLEY CAPITAL LLC

Lexington Avenue
Suite 601, 36th Floor
New York, NY USA 10022
Phone: 6468637200
Fax: 6468637201
E-mail: info@linleycapital.com
Website: www.linleycapital.com

Management and Staff
John Jonge Poerink, Managing Partner
Robert Blabey, Chief Operating Officer

Type of Firm
Private Equity Firm

Project Preferences

Type of Financing Preferred:
Leveraged Buyout
Expansion
Management Buyouts
Recapitalizations

Geographical Preferences

United States Preferences:

Canadian Preferences:
All Canada

International Preferences:
Latin America
Europe

Industry Preferences

In Communications prefer:
Media and Entertainment

In Medical/Health prefer:
Health Services

In Consumer Related prefer:
Consumer
Retail
Food/Beverage
Consumer Products
Consumer Services
Other Restaurants

In Industrial/Energy prefer:
Energy
Industrial Products

In Transportation prefer:
Transportation
Aerospace

In Financial Services prefer:
Financial Services

In Business Serv. prefer:
Services

In Manufact. prefer:
Manufacturing

Additional Information
Year Founded: 2008
Current Activity Level : Actively seeking new investments

LKCM HEADWATER INVESTMENTS

301 Commerce Stree
Suite 1600
Fort Worth, TX USA 76102
Phone: 8173323235
Website: www.lkcmheadwater.com

Type of Firm
Private Equity Firm

Project Preferences

Type of Financing Preferred:
Leveraged Buyout
Management Buyouts
Distressed Debt
Recapitalizations

Industry Preferences

In Medical/Health prefer:
Health Services

In Industrial/Energy prefer:
Energy
Industrial Products

In Financial Services prefer:
Financial Services

Additional Information
Year Founded: 2012
Capital Under Management: $605,000,000
Current Activity Level : Actively seeking new investments

LLOYDS DEVELOPMENT CAPITAL (HOLDINGS) LTD

One Vine Street
London, United Kingdom W1J 0AH
Phone: 442077583680
Fax: 442077583681
Website: www.ldc.co.uk

Other Offices

One Forbury Square
Reading
Berkshire, United Kingdom RG1 3BB
Phone: 44-118-958-0274
Fax: 44-118-956-8991

Tithebarn Street
Mercury Court, Pall Mall House
Liverpool, United Kingdom L2 2QU
Phone: 44-151-227-5024
Fax: 44-151-236-6773

3 Temple Quay
Bristol, United Kingdom BS1 6DZ
Phone: 44-117-360-1970
Fax: 44-117-360-1971

91 Sandyford Road
P.O. Box 686, Black Horse House
Newcastle upon Tyne, United Kingdom NE99 1JW
Phone: 44-191-261-1541
Fax: 44-191-261-5934

Quay Two
139 Fountainbridge
Edinburgh, United Kingdom EH3 9QG
Phone: 44-131-257-4500
Fax: 44-131-257-4510

Edmund Street
Interchange Place
Birmingham, United Kingdom B3 2TA
Phone: 44-121-237-6500
Fax: 44-121-236-5269

33 Queens Road
Aberdeen, United Kingdom AB15 4ZN
Phone: 44-1224-261-133
Fax: 44-1224-326-023

One City Square
Leeds, United Kingdom LS1 2ES
Phone: 44-113-300-2013
Fax: 44-113-300-2601

Eight Queen's Road
26th Floor
Central, Hong Kong
Phone: 852-3416-4400
Fax: 852-3416-4401

33 Park Row
Butt Dyke House
Nottingham, United Kingdom NG1 6EE
Phone: 44-115-947-1280
Fax: 44-115-947-1290

One Marsden Street
Manchester, United Kingdom M2 1HW
Phone: 44-161-831-1720
Fax: 44-161-831-1730

Management and Staff
Chris Hurley, Managing Director
Craig Wilkinson, Managing Director
Daniel Sasaki, Managing Director
Darryl Eales, Chief Executive Officer
Martin Draper, Managing Director
Nigel Moss, Managing Director
Patrick Sellers, Chief Executive Officer
Tim Farazmand, Managing Director
Yann Souillard, Managing Director

Type of Firm
Bank Affiliated

Association Membership
British Venture Capital Association (BVCA)

Project Preferences

Type of Financing Preferred:
Leveraged Buyout
Expansion
Management Buyouts
Acquisition

Geographical Preferences

International Preferences:
United Kingdom

Industry Focus
(% based on actual investment)
Other Products	45.0%
Industrial/Energy	15.6%
Computer Software and Services	15.1%
Consumer Related	7.1%
Internet Specific	6.8%
Communications and Media	4.3%
Medical/Health	2.8%
Semiconductors/Other Elect.	2.7%
Biotechnology	0.7%

Additional Information
Name of Most Recent Fund: Henderson Unquoted Growth Equity II
Most Recent Fund Was Raised: 12/31/1994
Year Founded: 1981
Capital Under Management: $1,551,500,000
Current Activity Level : Actively seeking new investments

LLR PARTNERS INC

2929 Arch Street
Cira Centre, Suite 2700
Philadelphia, PA USA 19104
Phone: 2157172900
Fax: 2157172270
Website: www.llrpartners.com

Other Offices

3033 Wilson Boulevard
Suite 700
ARLINGTON, VA USA 22201
Phone: 7036474132

Management and Staff
Brian Radic, Vice President
Christian Bullitt, Principal
David Reuter, Partner
David Stienes, Partner
Howard Ross, Partner
Ira Lubert, Partner
Jack Slye, Partner
Justin Reger, Principal
Kristen Chang, Managing Director
Kristy DelMuto, Vice President
Michael Pantilione, Vice President
Michael Levenberg, Principal
Mitchell Hollin, Partner
Noah Becker, Chief Financial Officer
Ryan Goldenberg, Vice President
Sasank Aleti, Principal
Scott Perricelli, Partner
Seth Lehr, Partner
Zack Sigal, Vice President

Type of Firm
Private Equity Firm

Association Membership
Mid-Atlantic Venture Association

Project Preferences

Role in Financing:
Will function either as deal originator or investor in deals created by others

Type of Financing Preferred:
Leveraged Buyout
Expansion
Generalist PE
Later Stage
Management Buyouts
Acquisition

Geographical Preferences

United States Preferences:
Mid Atlantic
East Coast

Industry Preferences

In Computer Software prefer:
Software
Applications Software

In Medical/Health prefer:
Health Services

In Consumer Related prefer:
Retail
Food/Beverage
Consumer Products
Consumer Services
Other Restaurants
Education Related

In Transportation prefer:
Transportation

In Financial Services prefer:
Financial Services

In Business Serv. prefer:
Services
Consulting Services

Additional Information
Name of Most Recent Fund: LLR Equity Partners IV, L.P.
Most Recent Fund Was Raised: 09/07/2012
Year Founded: 1999
Capital Under Management: $1,400,000,000
Current Activity Level: Actively seeking new investments
Method of Compensation: Return on investment is of primary concern, do not charge fees

LNC PARTNERS
11710 Plaza America Drive
Ste 160, Plaza America Tower II
Reston, VA USA 20190
Phone: 7036512150
Fax: 7034853551
Website: www.lnc-partners.com

Management and Staff
Dan Higgins, Principal
Jon Felsher, Vice President
Kevin Cunningham, Principal
Mark Raterman, Co-Founder
Matt Kelty, Co-Founder

Type of Firm
Private Equity Firm

Project Preferences

Type of Financing Preferred:
Leveraged Buyout
Management Buyouts
Acquisition
Recapitalizations

Industry Preferences

In Medical/Health prefer:
Health Services

In Financial Services prefer:
Financial Services
Insurance

In Business Serv. prefer:
Services

In Manufact. prefer:
Manufacturing

Additional Information
Name of Most Recent Fund: Leeds Novamark Capital I, L.P.
Most Recent Fund Was Raised: 10/01/2013
Year Founded: 2013
Capital Under Management: $236,000,000
Current Activity Level: Actively seeking new investments

LNK PARTNERS LLC
81 Main Street
White Plains, NY USA 10601
Phone: 9148245900
Fax: 9148245901
E-mail: info@LNKpartners.com
Website: www.lnkpartners.com

Management and Staff
Bethany Chadwick, Chief Operating Officer
David Landau, Partner
Henry Nasella, Partner
Jeffrey Perlman, Partner
Kayvan Heravi, Managing Director
Patrick Boroian, Partner

Type of Firm
Private Equity Firm

Project Preferences

Type of Financing Preferred:
Leveraged Buyout
Expansion
Acquisition
Recapitalizations

Geographical Preferences

United States Preferences:

Industry Preferences

In Consumer Related prefer:
Consumer
Entertainment and Leisure
Retail
Franchises(NEC)
Food/Beverage
Consumer Products
Consumer Services
Other Restaurants

In Transportation prefer:
Transportation

In Manufact. prefer:
Manufacturing

Additional Information
Name of Most Recent Fund: LNK Partner
Most Recent Fund Was Raised: 11/10/20
Year Founded: 2005
Capital Under Management: $800,000
Current Activity Level: Actively seeking n

LOCALGLOBE LLP
Tileyard Road
Unit 23 Tileyard Studios
London, United Kingdom N7 9AH
Website: localglobe.vc

Pratt's Guide to Private Equity & Venture Capital Sources

Type of Firm
Private Equity Firm

Project Preferences

Type of Financing Preferred:
Seed

Additional Information
Year Founded: 2016
Current Activity Level : Actively seeking new investments

LODHA GROUP

N.M Joshi Marg
Mumbai, India 400 011
Phone: 912223024400
Fax: 912223000693
Website: www.lodhagroup.com

Type of Firm
Private Equity Firm

Project Preferences

Type of Financing Preferred:

Project Preferences

Type of Financing Preferred:
Early Stage
Seed
Strategic Alliances

Additional Information
Year Founded: 2011
Current Activity Level : Actively seeking new investments

LOGO VENTURES SA

Vouliagmenis 128
Glyfada
Athens, Greece 166 74
Phone: 30-212-112-1900
Fax: 30-211-212-1909
E-mail: info@logoventures.gr
Website: www.logoventures.gr

Management and Staff
John Pantousis, Chief Executive Officer

Type of Firm
Private Equity Firm

Association Membership
Hellenic Venture Capital Association

Project Preferences

Type of Financing Preferred:
Early Stage
Expansion
Balanced
Startup

Geographical Preferences

International Preferences:
Greece
Europe

Industry Preferences

In Industrial/Energy prefer:
Energy
Alternative Energy
Energy Conservation Relat
Environmental Related

In Other prefer:
Environment Responsible

Additional Information
Year Founded: 2002
Current Activity Level : Actively seeking new investments

LOIRE CENTRE CAPITAL SAS

Rue de Monttessuy
ris, France 75007
site: loirecentrecapital.fr

Type of Firm
Private Equity Firm

Project Preferences

Type of Financing Preferred:
Early Stage
Expansion
Later Stage
Seed
Startup

Additional Information
Year Founded: 2015
Current Activity Level : Actively seeking new investments

LOK CAPITAL

2B, Ramkishore Road
Civil Lines
New Delhi, India 110054
Phone: 911130900100
Fax: 911130900150
Website: www.lokcapital.com

Management and Staff
Donald Peck, Founder
Ganesh Rengaswamy, Partner
Gaurav Shah, Vice President
Rajiv Lall, Founder
Venky Natarajan, Managing Partner
Vishal Mehta, Partner

Type of Firm
Private Equity Firm

Project Preferences

Type of Financing Preferred:
Early Stage
Expansion
Balanced

Geographical Preferences

International Preferences:
India
Asia

Industry Preferences

In Medical/Health prefer:
Health Services

In Consumer Related prefer:
Consumer
Education Related

In Financial Services prefer:
Financial Services

Additional Information
Year Founded: 2000
Capital Under Management: $146,000,000
Current Activity Level : Actively seeking new investments

LOMBARD INVESTMENTS INC

Three Embarcadero Center
Suite 2340
San Francisco, CA USA 94111
Phone: 4153975900
Fax: 4153975820
E-mail: info@lombardinvestments.com
Website: www.lombardinvestments.com

Other Offices

87/2 Wireless Road, Phathumwan
10/F, CRC Building
Bangkok, Thailand 10330
Phone: 662-685-3599
Fax: 662-685-3588

89 Queensway, Lippo Centre
Room 2202, 22/F, Tower 1
Central, Hong Kong
Phone: 852-2878-7388
Fax: 852-2878-7288

Management and Staff

Artapong Pornahithi, Vice President
Kalaya Uahwatanasakul, Vice President
Matthew Taylor, Founder
Pote Videt, Managing Director
Thomas Smith, Managing Director

Type of Firm

Private Equity Firm

Association Membership

Thai Venture Capital Association
Hong Kong Venture Capital Association (HKVCA)
Emerging Markets Private Equity Association

Project Preferences

Role in Financing:
Prefer role as deal originator but will also invest in deals created by others

Type of Financing Preferred:
Fund of Funds
Leveraged Buyout
Early Stage
Expansion
Generalist PE
Balanced
Turnaround
Later Stage
Management Buyouts
Acquisition
Recapitalizations

Geographical Preferences

United States Preferences:
Southeast
North America
West Coast

International Preferences:
Vietnam
Indonesia
China
Thailand
Philippines
Asia

Industry Preferences

In Communications prefer:
Telecommunications
Media and Entertainment

In Medical/Health prefer:
Medical/Health
Health Services

In Consumer Related prefer:
Retail
Food/Beverage
Consumer Products
Hotels and Resorts
Education Related

In Industrial/Energy prefer:
Energy

In Financial Services prefer:
Financial Services
Real Estate

In Business Serv. prefer:
Services

In Manufact. prefer:
Manufacturing

Additional Information

Name of Most Recent Fund: Lombard Partners International LLC
Most Recent Fund Was Raised: 07/02/2001
Year Founded: 1985
Capital Under Management: $1,000,000,000
Current Activity Level : Actively seeking new investments
Method of Compensation: Return on investment is of primary concern, do not charge fees

LONE ROCK TECHNOLOGY GROUP LLC

7801 N. Capital of Texas Hwy
Suite 230
Austin, TX USA 78731
Phone: 2153701276
Fax: 8772687776
E-mail: info@lonerock.com
Website: www.lonerock.com

Management and Staff

Joel Trammell, Managing Partner
John Eckman, Managing Partner

Type of Firm

Private Equity Firm

Project Preferences

Type of Financing Preferred:
Leveraged Buyout
Acquisition

Industry Preferences

In Computer Software prefer:
Software

Additional Information

Year Founded: 2011
Current Activity Level : Actively seeking new investments

LONE STAR FUND LTD

2711 North Haskell Avenue
Suite 1700
Dallas, TX USA 75204
Phone: 2147548300
E-mail: InvestorRelations@lonestarfunds.com
Website: www.lonestarfunds.com

Other Offices

888 Seventh Avenue
Fourth Floor
NEW YORK, NY USA 10019
Phone: 212-849-9600

800 de la Gauchetiere West
South East Portal - Suite 9400
Montreal, Canada H5A 1K6
Phone: 514-879-6310

9, Boulevard de la Plaine
Brussels, Belgium B-1050
Phone: 32-2-290-2411

Hamburger Allee 14
Frankfurt, Germany D-60486
Phone: 49-69-7104-2260

1st Floor
25 - 28 Adelaide Road
Dublin, Ireland
Phone: 353-1-618-1800

1-6-5 Marunouchi Chiyoda-ku
Marunouchi Kitaguchi Building 19th Fl.
Tokyo, Japan 100-0005
Phone: 81-3-5224-5300

7 Reid Street
Washington Mall Suite 304
Hamilton, Bermuda HM11
Phone: 441-296-1754

7 Rue Robert Stumper
Luxembourg, Luxembourg L-2557
Phone: 352-27-62-431

5 Place de la Joliette
Marseille, France 13002
Phone: 33-4-2684-5824

Management and Staff
Andre Collin, Senior Managing Director
Bruno Scherrer, Senior Managing Director
John Grayken, Founder
Len Allen, Senior Managing Director
Olivier Brahin, Senior Managing Director
Takehisa Takamatsu, Senior Managing Director

Type of Firm
Investment Management Firm

Project Preferences

Type of Financing Preferred:
Leveraged Buyout
Opportunistic
Acquisition
Distressed Debt

Geographical Preferences

United States Preferences:
North America

International Preferences:
Europe
Asia

Industry Preferences

In Financial Services prefer:
Real Estate

Additional Information
Name of Most Recent Fund: Lone Star Real Estate Partners III, L.P.
Most Recent Fund Was Raised: 11/07/2013
Year Founded: 1995
Capital Under Management: $46,481,500,000
Current Activity Level : Actively seeking new investments

LONETREE CAPITAL MANAGEMENT LLC

9785 Maroon Circle
Suite 110
Englewood, CO USA 80112
Phone: 3032091905
Fax: 2172224422

Management and Staff
Charles Lillis, Co-Founder

Type of Firm
Private Equity Firm

Project Preferences

Type of Financing Preferred:
Balanced

Geographical Preferences

United States Preferences:

International Preferences:
Europe
Asia

Industry Preferences

In Communications prefer:
Communications and Media

In Internet Specific prefer:
Internet

Additional Information
Year Founded: 2001
Capital Under Management: $26,000,000
Current Activity Level : Actively seeking new investments

LONG HILL CAPITAL

1266 Nanjing West Road
Unit 2202, Plaza 66
Shanghai, China 200040
Website: www.lhcap.cn

Type of Firm
Private Equity Firm

Project Preferences

Type of Financing Preferred:
Balanced

Geographical Preferences

International Preferences:
China

Additional Information
Year Founded: 2016
Capital Under Management: $125,000,000
Current Activity Level : Actively seeking new investments

LONG LAKE PARTNERS

401 South Old Woodward Avenue
Suite 340
Birmingham, MI USA 48009
Phone: 313-247-9660
Website: www.longlake-partners.com

Other Offices
4514 Cole Avenue
Suite 600
Dallas, TX USA 75205
Phone: 214-558-0046

Management and Staff
Nicholas Kulkarni, Managing Partner
Nicholas Lardo, Managing Partner

Type of Firm
Private Equity Firm

Project Preferences

Type of Financing Preferred:
Leveraged Buyout
Later Stage
Acquisition

Geographical Preferences

United States Preferences:
Midwest

Industry Preferences

In Medical/Health prefer:
Medical/Health

In Consumer Related prefer:
Consumer
Consumer Products
Consumer Services

In Financial Services prefer:
Financial Services

In Business Serv. prefer:
Services
Consulting Services

In Manufact. prefer:
Manufacturing

Additional Information
Year Founded: 2011
Current Activity Level : Actively seeking new investments

LONG POINT CAPITAL

747 Third Avenue
22nd Floor
New York, NY USA 10022
Phone: 2125931800
Fax: 2125931888
Website: www.longpointcapital.com

Other Offices
26700 Woodward Avenue
Royal Oak, MI USA 48607
Phone: 2485916000
Fax: 2485916001

Management and Staff
Eric Von Stroh, Managing Director
Gerry Boylan, Managing Director
Ira Starr, Managing Director

Type of Firm
Private Equity Firm

Project Preferences

Role in Financing:
Prefer role as deal originator but will also invest in deals created by others

Type of Financing Preferred:
Leveraged Buyout
Management Buyouts
Acquisition
Recapitalizations

Geographical Preferences

United States Preferences:
North America

Industry Focus

(% based on actual investment)
Other Products   53.7%
Consumer Related   46.3%

Additional Information

Year Founded: 1998
Capital Under Management: $315,000,000
Current Activity Level : Actively seeking new investments
Method of Compensation: Return on invest. most important, but chg. closing fees, service fees, etc.

LONG RIDGE EQUITY PARTNERS LLC

1120 Avenue of the Americas
Suite 1807
New York, NY USA 10036
Phone: 2129518651
E-mail: info@lrepllc.com
Website: www.longridgecap.com

Management and Staff

James Brown, Managing Partner
Kevin Bhatt, Partner

Type of Firm

Private Equity Firm

Project Preferences

Type of Financing Preferred:
Leveraged Buyout
Expansion
Generalist PE
Special Situation

Geographical Preferences

United States Preferences:
All U.S.

International Preferences:
Israel

Industry Preferences

In Financial Services prefer:
Financial Services

In Business Serv. prefer:
Services

Additional Information

Name of Most Recent Fund: Long Ridge Equity Partners I, L.P.
Most Recent Fund Was Raised: 02/09/2012
Year Founded: 2007
Capital Under Management: $300,025,000
Current Activity Level : Actively seeking new investments

LONG RIVER VENTURES, INC.

Seven North Pleasant Street
Amherst, MA USA 01002
Website: www.longriverventures.com

Other Offices

148 Bartlett Street
Marlborough, MA USA 01752

470 Atlantic Avenue
Tenth Floor
Boston, MA USA 02210

Management and Staff

John Kole, Venture Partner
Joseph Steig, Chief Financial Officer
Mike Cataldo, Venture Partner
Tripp Peake, Managing Partner
William Cowen, Managing Partner

Type of Firm

Private Equity Firm

Association Membership

New England Venture Capital Association
Natl Assoc of Small Bus. Inv. Co (NASBIC)

Project Preferences

Type of Financing Preferred:
Early Stage
Seed

Size of Investments Considered:
Min Size of Investment Considered (000s): $500
Max Size of Investment Considered (000s): $1,000

Geographical Preferences

United States Preferences:
Northeast
Massachusetts
New York

Industry Preferences

In Communications prefer:
Communications and Media
Telecommunications

In Computer Software prefer:
Software

In Internet Specific prefer:
Internet

In Medical/Health prefer:
Medical/Health
Medical Diagnostics
Medical Products

Additional Information

Name of Most Recent Fund: Long River Ventures II, L.P.
Most Recent Fund Was Raised: 07/24/2007
Year Founded: 2000
Capital Under Management: $15,000,000
Current Activity Level : Actively seeking new investments

LONG ROAD INVESTMENT COUNSEL LLC

177 Broad Street
Suite 1150
Stamford, CT USA 06901
Phone: 2039671400
Fax: 2039672400

Other Offices

100 King Street West
Suite 5700
Toronto, Canada M5X 1C7
Phone: 4169154238

807 Brazos
Suite 1002
Austin, TX USA 78701
Phone: 512-236-8100
Fax: 512-236-8090

Management and Staff

Anne Whitman, Managing Director
Richard Latto, Managing Director
Steve Zambito, Managing Director

Type of Firm

Private Equity Firm

Project Preferences

Type of Financing Preferred:
Leveraged Buyout
Turnaround
Management Buyouts
Special Situation
Distressed Debt
Recapitalizations

Geographical Preferences

United States Preferences:

Canadian Preferences:
All Canada

Industry Preferences

In Consumer Related prefer:
Consumer Products

In Industrial/Energy prefer:
Energy
Industrial Products
Materials
Machinery

In Transportation prefer:
Aerospace

In Business Serv. prefer:
Services
Distribution

In Manufact. prefer:
Manufacturing

Additional Information
Year Founded: 2001
Capital Under Management: $183,000,000
Current Activity Level : Actively seeking new investments

LONGEVITY FUND, THE

1700 Owens Street
San Francisco, CA USA 94158
Phone: 6508888161
E-mail: info@longevity.vc
Website: www.longevity.vc

Type of Firm
Private Equity Firm

Project Preferences

Type of Financing Preferred:
Balanced

Industry Preferences

In Medical/Health prefer:
Medical Therapeutics

Additional Information
Year Founded: 2014
Capital Under Management: $12,550,000
Current Activity Level : Actively seeking new investments

LONGITUDE CAPITAL MANAGEMENT CO LLC

800 El Camino Real, Suite 220
Menlo Park, CA USA 94025
Phone: 6508545700
Website: www.longitudecapital.com

Other Offices
545 Steamboat Road
GREENWICH, CT USA 06830
Phone: 2037695200

Management and Staff
Andrew ElBardissi, Principal
Carolyn Helms, Chief Financial Officer
David Hirsch, Founder
David Hirsch, Founder
Douglas Foster, Founder
Elaine Erickson, Chief Financial Officer
Gregory Grunberg, Managing Director
Gregory Grunberg, Managing Director
Josh Richardson, Managing Director
Josh Richardson, Vice President
Juliet Bakker, Founder
Juliet Bakker, Founder
Marc-Henri Galletti, Founder
Marc-Henri Galletti, Founder
Oren Isacoff, Vice President
Patrick Enright, Founder
Patrick Enright, Founder
Reinaldo Diaz, Venture Partner
Sandip Agarwala, Managing Director

Type of Firm
Private Equity Firm

Association Membership
Western Association of Venture Capitalists (WAVC)
National Venture Capital Association - USA (NVCA)

Project Preferences

Role in Financing:
Will function either as deal originator or investor in deals created by others

Type of Financing Preferred:
Early Stage
Expansion
Balanced
Later Stage
Seed
Special Situation
Recapitalizations

Size of Investments Considered:
Min Size of Investment Considered (000s): $10,000
Max Size of Investment Considered (000s): $30,000

Geographical Preferences

United States Preferences:

Industry Preferences

In Medical/Health prefer:
Medical Diagnostics
Medical Products
Health Services

Additional Information
Name of Most Recent Fund: Longitude Venture Partners II, L.P.
Most Recent Fund Was Raised: 09/13/2011
Year Founded: 2006
Capital Under Management: $710,000,000
Current Activity Level : Actively seeking new investments

LONGLING CAPITAL CO LTD

Software Park
1F-B1, Block A, Huaxun Building
Xiamen, China
Website: www.longling.com

Type of Firm
Private Equity Firm

Project Preferences

Type of Financing Preferred:
Balanced

Geographical Preferences

International Preferences:
China

Industry Preferences

In Internet Specific prefer:
Internet

In Medical/Health prefer:
Medical/Health

In Consumer Related prefer:
Education Related

In Financial Services prefer:
Financial Services

Additional Information
Year Founded: 2012
Current Activity Level : Actively seeking new investments

LONGMEADOW CAPITAL PARTNERS LLC

171 Dwight Road
Suite 310
Longmeadow, MA USA 01106
Phone: 4135673366
Fax: 4135676556
Website: www.longmeadowcapital.com

Management and Staff
John Deliso, Venture Partner
Richard Steele, Founder

Type of Firm
Private Equity Firm

Project Preferences

Type of Financing Preferred:
Turnaround
Management Buyouts

Additional Information
Year Founded: 1993
Current Activity Level : Actively seeking new investments

LONGREACH GROUP LTD

1-7 Kojimachi, Chiyoda-ku
10F, Sogo Hanzomon Building
Tokyo, Japan 102-0083
Phone: 81335566740
Fax: 81335566739
E-mail: investor-relations@longreachgroup.com
Website: www.longreachgroup.com

Other Offices

18/F, Bund Center
222 Yan An East Road
Shanghai, China 200002
Phone: 86-21-6122-1015
Fax: 86-21-6122-2418

18 Chater Road
Suite 1508, Alexandra House
Central, Hong Kong
Phone: 852-3175-1700
Fax: 852-3175-1727

Management and Staff

Masamichi Yoshizawa, Partner
Tomoya Sugimoto, Partner
Wing Wong, Chief Financial Officer

Type of Firm

Private Equity Firm

Project Preferences

Type of Financing Preferred:
Leveraged Buyout
Management Buyouts
Acquisition

Geographical Preferences

International Preferences:
China
Japan

Industry Preferences

In Consumer Related prefer:
Consumer

In Industrial/Energy prefer:
Industrial Products

In Financial Services prefer:
Financial Services

In Business Serv. prefer:
Services

Additional Information

Year Founded: 2003
Capital Under Management: $400,000,000
Current Activity Level : Actively seeking new investments

LONGUEVUE CAPITAL

111 Veterans Boulevard
Suite 1020
Metairie, LA USA 70005
Phone: 5042933600
Fax: 5042933636

Other Offices

136 Heber Avenue
Suite 204
PARK CITY, UT USA 84060
Phone: 435-655-3605
Fax: 435-655-7676

410 Park Avenue
15th Floor
NEW YORK, NY USA 10022
Phone: 646-660-3994
Fax: 504-293-3636

Management and Staff

A. Peyton Bush, Vice President
Carol Hance, Managing Director
Raymond Jeandron, Vice President
Rebecca Toups, Chief Financial Officer

Type of Firm

Private Equity Firm

Association Membership

Natl Assoc of Small Bus. Inv. Co (NASBIC)

Project Preferences

Role in Financing:
Prefer role as deal originator

Type of Financing Preferred:
Leveraged Buyout
Turnaround
Management Buyouts
Recapitalizations

Industry Preferences

In Industrial/Energy prefer:
Energy

In Business Serv. prefer:
Distribution

In Manufact. prefer:
Manufacturing

Additional Information

Name of Most Recent Fund: LongueVue Capital Partners II, L.P.
Most Recent Fund Was Raised: 08/26/2011
Year Founded: 2001
Capital Under Management: $82,000,000
Current Activity Level : Actively seeking new investments
Method of Compensation: Return on investment is of primary concern, do not charge fees

LONGVIEW ASSET MANAGEMENT LTD

79 Wellington Street West
Suite 610, P.O. Box 348
Toronto, Canada M5K 1K8
Phone: 4162144800
E-mail: info@longviewassets.com
Website: www.longviewassets.com

Management and Staff

Adriana Cano, Partner
Alvin Lau, Partner
Denise Fernandes, Partner
Doug McCutcheon, President
Emily Won, Partner
James Eaton, Partner
Tom Lace, Partner

Type of Firm

Private Equity Firm

Additional Information

Year Founded: 2017
Current Activity Level : Actively seeking new investments

LONGWALL VENTURE PARTNERS LLP

The Electron Building
Fermi Avenue, Harwell
Oxford, United Kingdom OX11 0QR
Phone: 441235567352
Website: www.longwallventures.com

Management and Staff

David Denny, Founder
Matthew Frohn, Founder
Michael Penington, Founder

Type of Firm

Private Equity Firm

Project Preferences

Type of Financing Preferred:
Early Stage
Startup

Geographical Preferences

International Preferences:
United Kingdom
Europe

Industry Preferences

In Medical/Health prefer:
Medical Products

In Industrial/Energy prefer:
Industrial Products
Materials
Advanced Materials

In Transportation prefer:
Aerospace

Additional Information
Year Founded: 2011
Capital Under Management: $46,797,000
Current Activity Level : Actively seeking new investments

LONGWATER OPPORTUNITIES LLC

2519 Fairmount Street
Dallas, TX USA 75201
Phone: 469351470
Fax: 2146145126

Management and Staff
Brooks Burgum, Co-Founder
Jordan Bastable, Founding Partner

Type of Firm
Private Equity Firm

Project Preferences

Type of Financing Preferred:
Leveraged Buyout

Additional Information
Year Founded: 2009
Capital Under Management: $50,000,000
Current Activity Level : Actively seeking new investments

LONGWOOD FOUNDERS MANAGEMENT LLC

800 Boylston Street
Prudential Tower, Suite 1555
Boston, MA USA 02199
Phone: 6173512590
E-mail: info@longwoodfund.com
Website: www.longwoodfund.com

Management and Staff
Christoph Westphal, Founding Partner
Michelle Dipp, Founding Partner
Rich Aldrich, Founding Partner

Type of Firm
Private Equity Firm

Association Membership
New England Venture Capital Association

Project Preferences

Type of Financing Preferred:
Early Stage
Expansion
Balanced
Later Stage
Seed
Startup

Industry Preferences

In Biotechnology prefer:
Biotechnology

In Medical/Health prefer:
Medical/Health
Medical Products

Additional Information
Name of Most Recent Fund: Longwood Founders Fund, L.P.
Most Recent Fund Was Raised: 02/11/2010
Year Founded: 2010
Capital Under Management: $66,657,000
Current Activity Level : Actively seeking new investments

LONGWORTH VENTURE PARTNERS, L.P.

1050 Winter Street, Suite 2600
Waltham, MA USA 02451
Phone: 7816633600
Fax: 7816633619
Website: www.longworth.com

Management and Staff
David Nanto, Venture Partner
James Savage, Partner
Jim Savage, Co-Founder
Paul Margolis, Co-Founder
Peter Roberts, Partner

Type of Firm
Private Equity Firm

Association Membership
New England Venture Capital Association

Project Preferences

Role in Financing:
Will function either as deal originator or investor in deals created by others

Type of Financing Preferred:
Early Stage
Later Stage
Seed
Startup

Size of Investments Considered:
Min Size of Investment Considered (000s): $2,000
Max Size of Investment Considered (000s): $3,000

Geographical Preferences

United States Preferences:
Mid Atlantic
New Hampshire
Rhode Island
Vermont
Massachusetts
Connecticut
West Coast
Maine

Industry Preferences

In Internet Specific prefer:
Internet

In Computer Other prefer:
Computer Related

In Business Serv. prefer:
Media

Additional Information
Name of Most Recent Fund: Longworth Venture Partners III, L.P.
Most Recent Fund Was Raised: 08/03/2009
Year Founded: 1999
Capital Under Management: $139,000,000
Current Activity Level : Actively seeking new investments
Method of Compensation: Return on investment is of primary concern, do not charge fees

LONSDALE CAPITAL PARTNERS LLP

21 Upper Brook Street
London, United Kingdom W1K 7PY
Phone: 442075141800
Website: www.lonsdalepartners.com

Management and Staff
Alan Dargan, Co-Founder
David Gasparro, Partner
Ross Finegan, Co-Founder

Type of Firm
Private Equity Firm

Project Preferences

Type of Financing Preferred:
Leveraged Buyout
Acquisition

Geographical Preferences

International Preferences:
United Kingdom
Europe

Additional Information
Year Founded: 2010
Capital Under Management: $156,930,000
Current Activity Level : Actively seeking new investments

LOOKING GLASS PARTNERS LLC

777 South Flagler Drive
Suite 800
West Palm Beach, FL USA 33401
Phone: 561-515-6095
Website: www.lookingglassfund.com

Management and Staff
Luis Giralt, Principal
Nancy Cass, Principal
Shane Hackett, Principal

Type of Firm
Private Equity Firm

Project Preferences

Type of Financing Preferred:
Early Stage

Size of Investments Considered:
Min Size of Investment Considered (000s): $2,000
Max Size of Investment Considered (000s): $7,000

Industry Preferences

In Medical/Health prefer:
Health Services

In Business Serv. prefer:
Media

Additional Information
Year Founded: 2010
Current Activity Level : Actively seeking new investments

LOOKOUT CAPITAL LLC

Seven Glenwood Avenue
Raleigh, NC USA 27603
Phone: 9198251576
E-mail: info@lookoutcapital.com
Website: www.lookoutcapital.com

Type of Firm
Private Equity Firm

Project Preferences

Type of Financing Preferred:
Recapitalizations

Geographical Preferences

United States Preferences:
North Carolina

Industry Preferences

In Business Serv. prefer:
Services

Additional Information
Year Founded: 2010
Current Activity Level : Actively seeking new investments

LORRAINE CAPITAL LLC

591 Delaware Ave.
Buffalo, NY USA 14202
Phone: 7168168809
Website: lorrainecapital.com

Type of Firm
Private Equity Firm

Project Preferences

Type of Financing Preferred:
Leveraged Buyout

Geographical Preferences

United States Preferences:
New York

Industry Preferences

In Medical/Health prefer:
Medical/Health

In Consumer Related prefer:
Food/Beverage

In Industrial/Energy prefer:
Energy

In Business Serv. prefer:
Distribution

Additional Information
Year Founded: 2013
Current Activity Level : Actively seeking new investments

LOTUS INNOVATIONS LLC

19600 Fairchild Road
Suite 270
Irvine, CA USA 92612
Phone: 9494849708
E-mail: info@lotus-innovations.com
Website: lotus-innovations.com

Management and Staff
Christian Mack, Managing Director
Linda Ritchie, Managing Director

Type of Firm
Incubator/Development Program

Project Preferences

Type of Financing Preferred:
Early Stage
Seed
Startup

Industry Preferences

In Computer Software prefer:
Software

Additional Information
Year Founded: 2013
Capital Under Management: $10,000,000
Current Activity Level : Actively seeking new investments

LOTUSPOOL CAPITAL ADVISORS PVT LTD

6A, 7th Main, I Block, Koraman
II Floor, Kabra Excelsior
Bangalore, India
Phone: 918040937064
E-mail: info@lotuspoolcapital.com
Website: www.lotuspoolcapital.com

Other Offices
608 St James Court
St Denis Street
Port Louis, Mauritius
Phone: 230 210 9000
Fax: 230 210 9001

Type of Firm
Private Equity Firm

Project Preferences

Type of Financing Preferred:
Leveraged Buyout
Early Stage
Expansion
Generalist PE
Management Buyouts
Acquisition

Size of Investments Considered:
Min Size of Investment Considered (000s): $2,000
Max Size of Investment Considered (000s): $15,000

Geographical Preferences

International Preferences:
India
Asia

Industry Preferences

In Financial Services prefer:
Financial Services
Financial Services

Additional Information
Name of Most Recent Fund: LotusPool Capital Fund I
Most Recent Fund Was Raised: 10/25/2013
Year Founded: 2013
Capital Under Management: $15,000,000
Current Activity Level : Actively seeking new investments

LOUD CAPITAL LLC

629 North High Street
4th Floor
Columbus, OH USA 43215
Website: www.loudcapital.com

Management and Staff
Nathan Huang, Partner
Sriram Durvasula, Partner
Todd Whittington, Managing Partner

Type of Firm
Private Equity Firm

Project Preferences

Type of Financing Preferred:
Balanced

Additional Information
Year Founded: 1969
Current Activity Level: Actively seeking new investments

LOUDSPRING OYJ

Malminrinne 1 B
Helsinki, Finland 00100
Website: loudspring.earth

Management and Staff
Alexander Lidgren, Managing Director

Type of Firm
Private Equity Firm

Project Preferences

Type of Financing Preferred:
Early Stage
Startup

Size of Investments Considered:
Min Size of Investment Considered (000s): $1,323
Max Size of Investment Considered (000s): $2,645

Geographical Preferences

International Preferences:
Finland

Industry Preferences

In Industrial/Energy prefer:
Alternative Energy
Energy Conservation Relat

In Other prefer:
Environment Responsible

Additional Information
Year Founded: 2005
Current Activity Level: Actively seeking new investments

LOUP VENTURES

422 West Lake
Suite 214
Minneapolis, MN USA 55408
Website: loupventures.com

Management and Staff
Andrew Murphy, Managing Partner
Gene Munster, Managing Partner

Type of Firm
Private Equity Firm

Project Preferences

Type of Financing Preferred:
Early Stage

Industry Preferences

In Industrial/Energy prefer:
Robotics

Additional Information
Year Founded: 2016
Current Activity Level: Actively seeking new investments

LOVELL MINNICK PARTNERS LLC

150 North Radnor Chester Road
Suite A200
Wayne, PA USA 19087
Phone: 6109959660
Website: www.lovellminnick.com

Other Offices
2141 Rosecrans Avenue
Suite 5150
El Segundo, CA USA 90245
Phone: 3104146160

Management and Staff
Benjamin Kaplan, Vice President
Irene Edwards, Principal
John Cochran, Managing Director
Robert Belke, Managing Director
Roumi Zlateva, Vice President
Spencer Hoffman, Managing Director
Steven Pierson, President
W. Bradford Armstrong, Principal

Type of Firm
Private Equity Firm

Project Preferences

Role in Financing:
Prefer role as deal originator but will also invest in deals created by others

Type of Financing Preferred:
Leveraged Buyout
Control-block Purchases
Early Stage
Expansion
Generalist PE
Later Stage
Management Buyouts
Acquisition
Industry Rollups
Recapitalizations

Size of Investments Considered:
Min Size of Investment Considered (000s): $20,000
Max Size of Investment Considered (000s): $100,000

Geographical Preferences

Canadian Preferences:
All Canada

Additional Information
Year Founded: 1999
Capital Under Management: $839,700,000
Current Activity Level: Actively seeking new investments
Method of Compensation: Return on invest. most important, but chg. closing fees, service fees, etc.

LOW CARBON ACCELERATOR LTD

Saint Julian's Avenue
Saint Peter Port, Ogier House
Guernsey, United Kingdom GY1 1WA
E-mail: info@lowcarbonaccelerator.com

Other Offices
29 Foley Street,
2nd Floor Essel House
London, United Kingdom W1W 7TH
Phone: 44-20-7631-2630

Management and Staff
Andrew Affleck, Chief Executive Officer
Mark Shorrock, Founder

Type of Firm
Private Equity Firm

Project Preferences

Type of Financing Preferred:
Early Stage
Balanced
Later Stage
Seed

Size of Investments Considered:
Min Size of Investment Considered (000s): $39
Max Size of Investment Considered (000s): $786,600

Geographical Preferences

United States Preferences:

International Preferences:
United Kingdom
Europe

Industry Preferences

In Industrial/Energy prefer:
Energy
Alternative Energy
Environmental Related

Additional Information
Year Founded: 2006
Current Activity Level: Actively seeking new investments

LOXBRIDGE RESEARCH LLP

The Royal Institution of Great
21 Albemarle Street
London, United Kingdom W1S 4BS
Phone: 2074092992
Fax: 2076702920
Website: www.loxbridgeresearch.com

Management and Staff
Anthony Fox, Vice President
Charles Roberts, Chief Executive Officer
Mike Westby, Vice President
Robert Old, Vice President
Zoe Crookes, Chief Operating Officer

Type of Firm
Investment Management Firm

Project Preferences

Type of Financing Preferred:
Balanced

Geographical Preferences

United States Preferences:
Massachusetts
California

International Preferences:
United Kingdom
Europe

Industry Preferences

In Medical/Health prefer:
Health Services

Additional Information
Year Founded: 2008
Current Activity Level : Actively seeking new investments

LPC CAPITAL PARTNERS GMBH

Pestalozzigasse 4
Vienna, Austria 1010
Phone: 4317150404
Fax: 431714040414
Website: www.lpc-capital.at

Management and Staff
Stefan Zapotocky, Managing Partner

Type of Firm
Private Equity Firm

Association Membership
European Private Equity and Venture Capital Assoc.

Project Preferences

Type of Financing Preferred:
Leveraged Buyout
Later Stage
Management Buyouts
Acquisition

Geographical Preferences

International Preferences:
Slovenia
Slovak Repub.
Liechtenstein
Central Europe
Czech Republic
Switzerland
Austria
Eastern Europe
Germany

Industry Preferences

In Consumer Related prefer:
Consumer

In Industrial/Energy prefer:
Energy
Industrial Products

In Other prefer:
Environment Responsible

Additional Information
Year Founded: 2006
Current Activity Level : Actively seeking new investments

LR CAPITAL SIA

Republikas laukums 2A
Riga, Latvia 1010
Phone: 371 6721 2324

Type of Firm
Private Equity Firm

Project Preferences

Type of Financing Preferred:
Leveraged Buyout

Geographical Preferences

International Preferences:
Poland
Scandanavia/Nordic Region
Estonia
Germany
Latvia
Lithuania

Industry Preferences

In Computer Other prefer:
Computer Related

In Semiconductor/Electr prefer:
Electronics
Electronic Components

In Medical/Health prefer:
Medical Products

In Manufact. prefer:
Manufacturing

Additional Information
Year Founded: 2014
Current Activity Level : Actively seeking new investments

LRI VISION PARTNERS FUND I LP

2429 Queen Anne Avenue North
Seattle, WA USA 98109

Type of Firm
Private Equity Firm

Additional Information
Year Founded: 2017
Current Activity Level : Actively seeking new investments

LRM NV

Kempische Steenweg 555
Hasselt, Belgium 3500
Phone: 3211246801
Fax: 3211246850
E-mail: info@lrm.be
Website: www.lrm.be

Management and Staff
Stijn Bijnens, Chief Executive Officer
Theo Donne, Chief Financial Officer

Type of Firm
Government Affiliated Program

Association Membership
Belgium Venturing Association

Project Preferences

Type of Financing Preferred:
Leveraged Buyout
Early Stage
Mezzanine
Balanced
Start-up Financing
Later Stage
Management Buyouts
Recapitalizations

Size of Investments Considered:
Min Size of Investment Considered (000s): $188
Max Size of Investment Considered (000s): $9,416

Geographical Preferences

International Preferences:
Europe
Belgium

Industry Preferences

In Industrial/Energy prefer:
Energy
Industrial Products

In Business Serv. prefer:
Services

Additional Information

Year Founded: 1993
Capital Under Management: $105,700,000
Current Activity Level : Actively seeking new investments

LTI INVESTMENT CO LTD

1002 Daechi-dong, Gangam-gu
806 Kosmo Tower
Seoul, South Korea 135-280
Phone: 822-562-9560
Fax: 822-562-9561

Management and Staff

HS Richard Chough, Chief Executive Officer

Type of Firm

Private Equity Firm

Project Preferences

Type of Financing Preferred:
Balanced

Geographical Preferences

International Preferences:
Asia

Additional Information

Year Founded: 2008
Current Activity Level : Actively seeking new investments

LUCAS VENTURE GROUP

545 Middlefield Road
Suite 220
Menlo Park, CA USA 94025
Phone: 6505433300
Fax: 6503052319
Website: www.lucasvg.com

Management and Staff

Donald Lucas, Partner

Type of Firm

Private Equity Firm

Project Preferences

Type of Financing Preferred:
Early Stage
Balanced

Geographical Preferences

United States Preferences:
All U.S.

Additional Information

Name of Most Recent Fund: Lucas Venture Group IX LLC
Most Recent Fund Was Raised: 10/03/2011
Year Founded: 2007
Capital Under Management: $15,750,000
Current Activity Level : Actively seeking new investments

LUCOR HOLDINGS LLC

5800 North Bay Road
Suite]
Miami Beach, FL USA 33140
Phone: 3055312700
Fax: 3055315599
Website: www.lucor.net

Type of Firm

Private Equity Firm

Project Preferences

Type of Financing Preferred:
Leveraged Buyout
Mezzanine
Generalist PE
Balanced
Management Buyouts
Acquisition
Distressed Debt

Size of Investments Considered:
Min Size of Investment Considered (000s): $250
Max Size of Investment Considered (000s): $30,000

Additional Information

Year Founded: 2002
Current Activity Level : Actively seeking new investments

LUDGATE INVESTMENTS LTD

80 Cannon Street
London, United Kingdom EC4N 6HL
Phone: 442076215770
Fax: 442076215771
E-mail: info@ludgate.com
Website: www.ludgate.com

Management and Staff

Charles Sebag-Montefiore, Founder
Gijs Voskamp, Managing Director
Nick Pople, Founder

Type of Firm

Private Equity Firm

Association Membership

British Venture Capital Association (BVCA)

Project Preferences

Type of Financing Preferred:
Early Stage
Expansion
Balanced
Later Stage

Geographical Preferences

International Preferences:
United Kingdom

Industry Preferences

In Industrial/Energy prefer:
Energy
Alternative Energy
Energy Conservation Relat
Environmental Related

In Transportation prefer:
Transportation

In Other prefer:
Environment Responsible

Additional Information

Name of Most Recent Fund: Ludgate 181 (Jersey) Limited
Most Recent Fund Was Raised: 06/30/2000
Year Founded: 2001
Current Activity Level : Actively seeking new investments

LUMA CAPTIAL PARTNERS

101 5th Avenue
9th Floor
New York, NY USA 10011
Website: www.lumacapitalpartners.com

Type of Firm

Incubator/Development Program

Additional Information

Year Founded: 2015
Current Activity Level : Actively seeking new investments

LUMA INVESTMENT SA

Emilii Plater 28
Warsaw, Poland 00-688
Phone: 48226303180
E-mail: office@lumainvestment.eu
Website: lumainvestment.eu

Type of Firm

Private Equity Firm

Additional Information

Name of Most Recent Fund: Lux Ventures IV, L.P.
Most Recent Fund Was Raised: 04/02/2015
Year Founded: 2000
Capital Under Management: $995,000,000
Current Activity Level : Actively seeking new investments

LUXEMBURG CAPITAL LLC

2000 Auburn Road
Suite 330
Cleveland, OH USA 44122
Phone: 2169168476
Fax: 2169168421
E-mail: info@luxemburgcapital.com
Website: www.luxemburgcapital.com

Management and Staff

James Hummer, President

Type of Firm

Private Equity Firm

Project Preferences

Type of Financing Preferred:
Balanced

Additional Information

Year Founded: 2009
Current Activity Level : Actively seeking new investments

LUXIN VENTURE CAPITAL GROUP CO LTD

166 Jie Fang Road
Jinan,Shandong, China 250013
Phone: 865316965156
Fax: 865316969598
E-mail: sdvc@sdvc.com.cn
Website: www.600783.cn

Management and Staff

Ping Wang, Chief Financial Officer

Type of Firm

Government Affiliated Program

Project Preferences

Type of Financing Preferred:
Early Stage
Expansion
Balanced
Later Stage
Seed
Startup

Geographical Preferences

International Preferences:
China

Industry Preferences

In Communications prefer:
Telecommunications

In Semiconductor/Electr prefer:
Electronics

In Biotechnology prefer:
Biotechnology

In Medical/Health prefer:
Pharmaceuticals

In Industrial/Energy prefer:
Energy
Energy Conservation Relat
Materials
Advanced Materials
Machinery

In Manufact. prefer:
Manufacturing

In Agr/Forestr/Fish prefer:
Agribusiness
Agriculture related

In Other prefer:
Environment Responsible

Additional Information

Year Founded: 2000
Capital Under Management: $46,039,000
Current Activity Level : Actively seeking new investments

LVENTURE GROUP SPA

Via Giovanni Giolitti, 34
Rome, Italy 00185
Phone: 39 06 4547 3124
Fax: 39 06 4547 3771
E-mail: investorrelator@lventuregroup.com
Website: www.lventuregroup.com

Management and Staff

Luigi Capello, Chief Executive Officer

Type of Firm

Private Equity Firm

Project Preferences

Type of Financing Preferred:
Seed
Startup

Geographical Preferences

International Preferences:
Italy

Industry Preferences

In Internet Specific prefer:
Ecommerce
Web Aggregation/Portals

Additional Information

Year Founded: 1961
Current Activity Level : Actively seeking new investments

LYCEUM CAPITAL

Lancaster Place
Brettenham House, First Floor
London, United Kingdom WC2E 7EN
Phone: 2034361415
Fax: 2030311404
E-mail: info@lyceumcapital.co.uk

Other Offices

Former HQ: 357 Strand
Burleigh House
London, United Kingdom WC2R 0HS
Phone: 442076322480
Fax: 442078363138

Management and Staff

Anthony Greensmith, Principal
Bill McCall, Partner
Daniel Adler, Partner
David England, Partner
Gehan Talwatte, Partner
Gerry Higgins, Partner
Ian Williams, Partner
Jeremy Hand, Partner
Joe Edwards, Partner
Jonathan Bourn, Partner
Lindsay Copland, Partner
Martin Wygas, Partner
Martin Leuw, Partner
Martin Cordey, Principal
Simon Hitchcock, Partner
Steve Ashton, Partner

Type of Firm

Private Equity Firm

Association Membership

British Venture Capital Association (BVCA)

Project Preferences

Type of Financing Preferred:
Leveraged Buyout
Management Buyouts
Acquisition

Geographical Preferences

International Preferences:
United Kingdom
Europe

Industry Focus

(% based on actual investment)
Computer Software and Services	43.9%
Medical/Health	43.8%
Communications and Media	12.3%

Additional Information
Year Founded: 1999
Capital Under Management: $353,900,000
Current Activity Level : Actively seeking new investments

LYDIAN CAPITAL ADVISORS SA
Rue Du Rhone 63
Geneva, Switzerland 1204
Phone: 41227187000
Fax: 41227187001
Website: www.lydiancapitaladv.com

Management and Staff
Denis Brosnan, Founder

Type of Firm
Private Equity Firm

Project Preferences
Type of Financing Preferred:
Leveraged Buyout
Generalist PE
Turnaround
Management Buyouts
Recapitalizations

Size of Investments Considered:
Min Size of Investment Considered (000s): $11,835
Max Size of Investment Considered (000s): $59,175

Geographical Preferences
United States Preferences:

International Preferences:
Italy
United Kingdom
Spain
Germany
France

Industry Preferences
In Medical/Health prefer:
Medical/Health

In Consumer Related prefer:
Consumer
Entertainment and Leisure
Food/Beverage
Consumer Products
Consumer Services
Education Related

Additional Information
Year Founded: 2003
Current Activity Level : Actively seeking new investments

LYNX EQUITY LTD
692 Queen Street East
Unit 205
Toronto, Canada M4M 1G9
Phone: 4163233512
Fax: 4163232863
E-mail: info@lynxequity.com
Website: www.lynxequity.com

Management and Staff
Brad Nathan, President
Joanna Lipfeld, Chief Financial Officer
Marvin Pludwinski, Chief Financial Officer
Stephen Grosfield, Chief Operating Officer

Type of Firm
Private Equity Firm

Project Preferences
Type of Financing Preferred:
Leveraged Buyout
Management Buyouts
Acquisition
Recapitalizations

Geographical Preferences
United States Preferences:

Canadian Preferences:
All Canada
Ontario

Industry Preferences
In Consumer Related prefer:
Consumer Products

In Transportation prefer:
Transportation

In Business Serv. prefer:
Services

Additional Information
Year Founded: 2010
Current Activity Level : Actively seeking new investments

LYRIQUE SRRL
Route de Morges 36
St-Prex, Switzerland 1162
Phone: 41218062614
Fax: 41218062972
E-mail: info@lyrique.com
Website: www.lyrique.com

Management and Staff
Afsaneh Heyat, Venture Partner
Alexander Banz, Venture Partner
Anina Janacek, Partner
Charles Cooper, Partner
Hans Van Swaay, Partner
Jean-Noel Thelin, Partner
Kai Lu, Partner
Liqun Wang, Partner
Wen Zhang, Partner

Type of Firm
Private Equity Firm

Association Membership
European Private Equity and Venture Capital Assoc.

Project Preferences
Type of Financing Preferred:
Fund of Funds
Leveraged Buyout
Early Stage
Later Stage
Management Buyouts
Recapitalizations

Geographical Preferences
United States Preferences:
All U.S.

International Preferences:
Europe
Switzerland
Asia
Germany
France

Industry Preferences
In Medical/Health prefer:
Medical/Health

Additional Information
Year Founded: 1987
Current Activity Level : Actively seeking new investments

LYTHGOE ENTERPRISES LTD
4 Dubovskaya street
Saint Petersburg, Russia 190000
Phone: 7543834323
E-mail: rtf@fi.ru
Website: www.trtf.ru

Type of Firm
Private Equity Firm

Association Membership
Russian Venture Capital Association (RVCA)

Project Preferences

Type of Financing Preferred:
Early Stage
Balanced
Later Stage

Geographical Preferences

International Preferences:
Russia

Additional Information
Year Founded: 2000
Current Activity Level: Actively seeking new investments

- M -

M CAPITAL PARTNERS SAS

42, rue du Languedoc
CS 96804
Toulouse, France 31068
Phone: 33534320965
Fax: 33562259121
E-mail: contact@midicapital.fr
Website: www.mcapitalpartners.fr

Management and Staff
Rudy Secco, President

Type of Firm
Private Equity Firm

Association Membership
French Venture Capital Association (AFIC)

Project Preferences

Type of Financing Preferred:
Fund of Funds
Leveraged Buyout
Early Stage
Generalist PE
Balanced
Public Companies
Later Stage
Seed
Management Buyouts
Acquisition

Geographical Preferences

International Preferences:
Europe
France

Industry Preferences

In Semiconductor/Electr prefer:
Electronics

In Medical/Health prefer:
Medical/Health
Medical Diagnostics
Diagnostic Services
Diagnostic Test Products
Medical Therapeutics
Other Therapeutic
Medical Products
Health Services
Hospital/Other Instit.

In Consumer Related prefer:
Entertainment and Leisure
Consumer Products
Consumer Services
Other Restaurants

In Industrial/Energy prefer:
Energy
Alternative Energy

In Transportation prefer:
Aerospace

Additional Information
Year Founded: 2002
Capital Under Management: $157,000,000
Current Activity Level: Actively seeking new investments

M CUBE INCUBATOR GMBH

Ohlauer Strasse 43
Berlin, Germany 10999
E-mail: info@m-cube.de
Website: m-cube.de

Management and Staff
Jan Dzulko, Managing Director

Type of Firm
Incubator/Development Program

Project Preferences

Type of Financing Preferred:
Seed
Startup

Geographical Preferences

International Preferences:
Germany

Industry Preferences

In Internet Specific prefer:
Internet

Additional Information
Year Founded: 2012
Current Activity Level: Actively seeking new investments

M INVEST GMBH

Robert-Bosch-Strasse 4
Singen, Germany 78224
Phone: 4977319113220
Fax: 49773191132299
E-mail: info@m-invest.eu

Type of Firm
Private Equity Firm

Project Preferences

Type of Financing Preferred:
Early Stage
Seed
Startup

1329

Industry Preferences

In Communications prefer:
Telecommunications

In Medical/Health prefer:
Medical/Health

In Industrial/Energy prefer:
Energy

Additional Information
Year Founded: 2005
Current Activity Level : Actively seeking new investments

M SEVEN 8 LLC

6 Hedge LN
Austin, TX USA 78746
Website: www.mseven8.com

Type of Firm
Private Equity Firm

Additional Information
Year Founded: 1969
Current Activity Level : Actively seeking new investments

M&C SPA

Via Ciovasino 1 A
Milan, Italy 20121
Phone: 392727371
Fax: 39272737177
E-mail: info@management-capitali.com
Website: www.mecinv.com

Type of Firm
Private Equity Firm

Project Preferences

Type of Financing Preferred:
Turnaround

Geographical Preferences

International Preferences:
Italy
Europe

Additional Information
Year Founded: 2005
Capital Under Management: $699,300,000
Current Activity Level : Actively seeking new investments

M.P.S. MERCHANT SPA- DUCATO GESTIONI SGR P.A.

Viale Mazzini 46
Firenze, Italy
Phone: 39-55-249-8548
E-mail: info@ducatogestioni.it
Website: www.ducatogestioni.it

Type of Firm
Private Equity Firm

Project Preferences

Type of Financing Preferred:
Balanced

Geographical Preferences

International Preferences:
No Preference

Additional Information
Year Founded: 2007
Current Activity Level : Actively seeking new investments

M/C VENTURE PARTNERS LLC

75 State Street, Suite 2500
Boston, MA USA 02109
Phone: 6173457200
Fax: 6173457201
E-mail: mcp@mcpartners.com
Website: www.mcpartners.com

Other Offices

235 Pine Street
Suite 1675
San Francisco, CA USA 94104
Phone: 415-438-4875
Fax: 415-296-8901

27-29 Glasshouse Street
Fifth Floor, Venture House
London, United Kingdom W1B 5DF
Phone: 44-20-2005-8861

Management and Staff
Brian Clark, Managing Partner
David Croll, Managing Partner
David Ingraham, Vice President
Edmund Kim, Vice President
Edward Keefe, Chief Financial Officer
Gillis Cashman, Managing Partner
James Wade, Managing Partner
John Watkins, Managing Partner
Lydia Jett, Vice President
Robert Savignol, Partner
Salvatore Tirabassi, Partner

Type of Firm
Private Equity Firm

Association Membership
New England Venture Capital Association

Project Preferences

Role in Financing:
Prefer role as deal originator but will also invest in deals created by others

Type of Financing Preferred:
Leveraged Buyout
Early Stage
Expansion
Generalist PE
Balanced
Later Stage
Management Buyouts
Acquisition

Size of Investments Considered:
Min Size of Investment Considered (000s): $5,000
Max Size of Investment Considered (000s): $50,000

Geographical Preferences

United States Preferences:

Canadian Preferences:
All Canada

International Preferences:
Europe
Eastern Europe

Industry Focus
(% based on actual investment)
Communications and Media	52.7%
Internet Specific	24.5%
Computer Software and Services	10.5%
Other Products	6.2%
Consumer Related	3.4%
Semiconductors/Other Elect.	2.4%
Computer Hardware	0.2%

Additional Information
Name of Most Recent Fund: M/C Partners VII, L.P.
Most Recent Fund Was Raised: 12/31/2013
Year Founded: 1973
Capital Under Management: $550,000,000
Current Activity Level : Actively seeking new investments
Method of Compensation: Return on investment is of primary concern, do not charge fees

M13 CO

215 South La Cienega Boulevard
Suite 200
Beverly Hills, CA USA 90211
Website: m13.co

Type of Firm
Private Equity Firm

Project Preferences

Type of Financing Preferred:
Early Stage
Seed

Additional Information
Year Founded: 2016
Current Activity Level : Actively seeking new investments

M25 GROUP LLC

250 Main Street
Suite 590
Lafayette, IN USA 47901
Website: m25group.com

Management and Staff
Victor Gutwein, Managing Director

Type of Firm
Private Equity Firm

Project Preferences

Type of Financing Preferred:
Early Stage
Seed

Geographical Preferences

United States Preferences:
Midwest

Industry Preferences

In Computer Software prefer:
Software

In Internet Specific prefer:
Ecommerce

In Medical/Health prefer:
Health Services

In Consumer Related prefer:
Consumer Products
Education Related

In Financial Services prefer:
Financial Services

In Business Serv. prefer:
Media

Additional Information
Year Founded: 2015
Current Activity Level : Actively seeking new investments

M33 GROWTH LLC

545 Boyloston Street
Sixth Floor
Boston, MA USA 02116
E-mail: info@m33growth.com

Type of Firm
Private Equity Firm

Project Preferences

Type of Financing Preferred:
Generalist PE

Geographical Preferences

United States Preferences:

Industry Preferences

In Computer Software prefer:
Software

In Medical/Health prefer:
Health Services

In Business Serv. prefer:
Services

Additional Information
Year Founded: 2017
Capital Under Management: $180,000,000
Current Activity Level : Actively seeking new investments

M34 CAPITAL INC

564 Market Street
Suite 303
San Francisco, CA USA 94104
Website: www.m34capital.com

Management and Staff
Steven Blank, Co-Founder
Thomas Baruch, Co-Founder

Type of Firm
Private Equity Firm

Association Membership
National Venture Capital Association - USA (NVCA)

Project Preferences

Type of Financing Preferred:
Seed
Startup

Additional Information
Year Founded: 2015
Current Activity Level : Actively seeking new investments

M8 CAPITAL

86 Jermyn Street
Fourth Floor
Londn, United Kingdom SW1Y 6JD
Phone: 442079593460
Fax: 442079593456
E-mail: info@m8capital.com
Website: m8capital.com

Management and Staff
Joe Neale, Principal
Joseph Kim, General Partner
Laurent Souviron, Partner

Type of Firm
Private Equity Firm

Project Preferences

Type of Financing Preferred:
Early Stage
Expansion
Later Stage

Geographical Preferences

International Preferences:
Europe

Industry Preferences

In Communications prefer:
Media and Entertainment

In Internet Specific prefer:
E-Commerce Technology

In Consumer Related prefer:
Consumer
Entertainment and Leisure

In Financial Services prefer:
Financial Services

Additional Information
Year Founded: 2009
Current Activity Level : Actively seeking new investments

MAAM GP PTY LTD

1 Farrer Place
L27
Sydney, Australia 2000
Phone: 61282885555
E-mail: moelissiv@moelis.com

Type of Firm
Investment Management Firm

Project Preferences

Type of Financing Preferred:
Leveraged Buyout
Balanced
Later Stage
Acquisition

Additional Information
Year Founded: 2015
Capital Under Management: $5,500,000
Current Activity Level : Actively seeking new investments

MAAYAN VENTURES LTD

P.O. Box 3010
Omer Industrial Park
Omer, Israel 84965
Phone: 97286255888
Fax: 97286466870
E-mail: info@myv.co.il

Other Offices

3 Azrieli Center
Triangle Tower 42nd Floor
Tel Aviv, Israel 67023
Phone: 972-54-455-5219

Rotem Industrial Park
Mishor Yamin, Arava
Dimona, Israel 86800
Phone: 972-8-6558786

Type of Firm
Private Equity Firm

Project Preferences

Type of Financing Preferred:
Early Stage
Balanced
Startup

Geographical Preferences

International Preferences:
Israel
Asia

Additional Information
Year Founded: 1996
Capital Under Management: $3,300,000
Current Activity Level : Actively seeking new investments

MAB CAPITAL MANAGEMENT LLC

119 W Hubbard Avenue
Suite 113
Chicago, IL USA 60654
Phone: 3124941100
Fax: 3124941101
E-mail: contact@mabcap.com
Website: mabcap.com

Type of Firm
Private Equity Firm

Project Preferences

Type of Financing Preferred:
Early Stage
Balanced

Geographical Preferences

United States Preferences:

Industry Preferences

In Communications prefer:
Communications and Media

In Consumer Related prefer:
Entertainment and Leisure
Food/Beverage
Hotels and Resorts

Additional Information
Year Founded: 2015
Capital Under Management: $50,000,000
Current Activity Level : Actively seeking new investments

MAC6 LLC

1500 Broadway
Suite 802
New York, NY USA 10036
E-mail: info@eranyc.com
Website: www.eranyc.com

Management and Staff
Charles Kemper, Managing Director
Jonathan Axelrod, Managing Director
Murat Aktihanoglu, Managing Director

Type of Firm
Incubator/Development Program

Project Preferences

Type of Financing Preferred:
Startup

Additional Information
Name of Most Recent Fund: Entrepreneurs Roundtable Accelerator Investors I LLC
Most Recent Fund Was Raised: 06/15/2011
Year Founded: 2011
Capital Under Management: $297,000
Current Activity Level : Actively seeking new investments

MACANDREWS & FORBES INC

35 East 62nd Street
New York, NY USA 10065
Phone: 2125728600
Website: www.macandrewsandforbes.com

Type of Firm
Private Equity Firm

Additional Information
Year Founded: 1991
Current Activity Level : Actively seeking new investments

MACH VENTURES LP

203 Redwood Shores Parkway
Suite 600
Redwood City, CA USA 94065
Phone: 415-987-2273
Fax: 415-358-8564
E-mail: info@machventures.com
Website: www.machventures.com

Management and Staff
Michael Laufer, General Partner

Type of Firm
Private Equity Firm

Project Preferences

Role in Financing:
Prefer role as deal originator but will also invest in deals created by others

Type of Financing Preferred:
Early Stage
Seed
Startup

Size of Investments Considered:
Min Size of Investment Considered (000s): $50
Max Size of Investment Considered (000s): $5,000

Geographical Preferences

United States Preferences:
Northern California

Industry Preferences

In Medical/Health prefer:
Medical Products

Additional Information
Year Founded: 2006
Capital Under Management: $100,000,000
Current Activity Level : Actively seeking new investments
Method of Compensation: Return on investment is of primary concern, do not charge fees

MACKENZIE CAPITAL, SRL.

2 Daniel Danielopolu Street
TMK Business Center, 5th Floor
Bucharest, Romania 014134
Phone: 40-21-232-1844
Fax: 40-21-232-2088
E-mail: office@mackenzie.ro
Website: www.mackenzie.ro

Management and Staff
Razvan Mosoiu, Chief Operating Officer
Sorin Panturu, Chief Executive Officer

Type of Firm
Private Equity Advisor or Fund of Funds

Association Membership
South Eastern Europes Private Equity Association
European Private Equity and Venture Capital Assoc.

Project Preferences

Type of Financing Preferred:
Early Stage
Expansion
Balanced
Later Stage
Seed
Startup

Geographical Preferences

International Preferences:
Europe
Romania

Industry Preferences

In Financial Services prefer:
Real Estate
Financial Services

Additional Information

Year Founded: 2003
Capital Under Management: $35,800,000
Current Activity Level : Actively seeking new investments

MACKINNON BENNETT & COMPANY INC

0 Place Ville Marie
Suite 3438
Montreal, Canada H3B 3N6
Phone: 5148763939
Fax: 5148763956
E-mail: info@mkbandco.com
Website: www.mkbandco.com

Management and Staff

W. J. Bennett, Vice President

Type of Firm

Private Equity Firm

Industry Preferences

In Internet Specific prefer:
Internet

In Industrial/Energy prefer:
Energy

Additional Information

Year Founded: 2007
Current Activity Level : Actively seeking new investments

MACLUAN CAPITAL CORP

940 -1040 West Georgia Street
Vancour, Canada V6E 4H1
Phone: 604-688-6668
Fax: 604-688-6527
E-mail: info@macluan.com
Website: www.macluan.com

Management and Staff

Harald Ludwig, Chief Executive Officer

Type of Firm

Private Equity Firm

Project Preferences

Type of Financing Preferred:
Leveraged Buyout
Management Buyouts
Acquisition
Recapitalizations

Geographical Preferences

United States Preferences:

Additional Information

Year Founded: 2001
Current Activity Level : Actively seeking new investments

MACOMA CAPITAL GROUP

349 Broadway
Fourth Floor
New York, NY USA 10013
Phone: 3479132586
Fax: 3472447181
E-mail: info@macomacapital.com
Website: www.macomacapital.com

Type of Firm

Private Equity Firm

Project Preferences

Type of Financing Preferred:
Generalist PE
Other

Industry Preferences

In Financial Services prefer:
Real Estate

Additional Information

Year Founded: 2010
Capital Under Management: $26,335,000
Current Activity Level : Actively seeking new investments

MACQUARIE CAPITAL ALLIANCE MANAGEMENT PTY LTD

No.1 Martin Place
Sydney, Australia 2000
Phone: 61282323333
Website: www.macquarie.com

Other Offices

10 Marina Boulevard
Suite 17-01
Singapore, Singapore 018983
Phone: 6566010888

Al Sila Tower, Sowwah Square
Abu Dhabi, Utd. Arab Em.
Phone: 97125107800

Management and Staff

Anand Subramanian, Managing Director
Michael Cook, Chief Executive Officer
Nicholas Moore, CEO & Managing Director

Type of Firm

Bank Affiliated

Project Preferences

Type of Financing Preferred:
Unknown
Balanced
Other

Geographical Preferences

International Preferences:
Latin America
India
Utd. Arab Em.
Middle East
Australia
Sri Lanka
Asia
Singapore
All International

Industry Preferences

In Industrial/Energy prefer:
Energy
Oil and Gas Exploration

In Utilities prefer:
Utilities

Additional Information

Year Founded: 2005
Current Activity Level : Actively seeking new investments

MACQUARIE CAPITAL MARKETS CANADA LTD

BCE Place, 181 Bay Street
Suite 3100, P.O. Box 830
Toronto, Canada M5J2T3
Phone: 416-864-3500
Fax: 416-864-9851
Website: www.macquarie.com

Management and Staff

Anand Subramanian, Managing Director
Bill Fulton, President & COO
Doug Bell, Managing Director
Rodney Sim, Chief Executive Officer

Type of Firm

Corporate PE/Venture

Additional Information

Year Founded: 2001
Current Activity Level : Actively seeking new investments

MACQUARIE GROUP LTD

No.1 Martin Place
Sydney, Australia 2000
Phone: 6128232333
Website: www.macquarie.com.au

Other Offices
100 Wellington Street West
PO Box 234, Suite 2200
, Canada M5K 1J3
Phone: 416-607-5000
Fax: 416-607-5051

Management and Staff
Alex Harvey, Chief Financial Officer
Greg Ward, Managing Director
Nicholas Moore, Chief Executive Officer
Nicole Sorbara, Chief Operating Officer

Type of Firm
Private Equity Firm

Association Membership
Australian Venture Capital Association (AVCAL)

Project Preferences

Type of Financing Preferred:
Leveraged Buyout
Management Buyouts
Acquisition

Geographical Preferences

International Preferences:
Australia
All International

Additional Information
Year Founded: 2004
Current Activity Level : Actively seeking new investments

MACQUARIE INFRASTRUC-TURE AND REAL ASSETS (EUROPE) LTD

28 Ropemaker Street
Ropemaker Place
London, United Kingdom EC2Y 9HD
Phone: 442030372000
Website: www.macquarie.co.uk

Other Offices
Ayala Avenue
22nd Floor, 6750 Office Tower
Makati, Philippines 1226
Phone: 6328570888

Oriental Plaza
R1702, Tower E2
Beijing, China
Phone: 86106521 6000

Type of Firm
Bank Affiliated

Association Membership
Indian Venture Capital Association (IVCA)

Project Preferences

Type of Financing Preferred:
Leveraged Buyout
Generalist PE
Balanced
Other
Management Buyouts

Geographical Preferences

United States Preferences:

International Preferences:
Asia Pacific
Armenia
Belarus
United Kingdom
Kazakhstan
Europe
Portugal
Taiwan
Hong Kong
China
Tajikistan
Azerbaijan
Moldova
Chile
Philippines
Spain
Australia
Uzbekistan
Asia
Korea, South
Germany
Russia

Industry Preferences

In Communications prefer:
Communications and Media
Telecommunications

In Medical/Health prefer:
Medical/Health

In Consumer Related prefer:
Education Related

In Industrial/Energy prefer:
Energy
Oil and Gas Exploration
Alternative Energy
Energy Conservation Relat

In Transportation prefer:
Transportation

In Financial Services prefer:
Real Estate

In Business Serv. prefer:
Services

In Agr/Forestr/Fish prefer:
Agriculture related

In Utilities prefer:
Utilities

Additional Information
Year Founded: 1969
Current Activity Level : Actively seeking new investments

MACQUARIE INVESTMENT MANAGEMENT LTD

Number One Martin Place
Sydney, Australia 2000
Phone: 61282323333

Management and Staff
Greg Ward, Managing Director
Nicholas Moore, CEO & Managing Director

Type of Firm
Bank Affiliated

Association Membership
European Private Equity and Venture Capital Assoc.

Project Preferences

Role in Financing:
Prefer role as deal originator but will also invest in deals created by others

Type of Financing Preferred:
Fund of Funds
Generalist PE
Balanced

Industry Focus
(% based on actual investment)
Other Products	47.6%
Internet Specific	34.5%
Communications and Media	18.0%

Additional Information
Year Founded: 1980
Capital Under Management: $99,000,000
Current Activity Level : Actively seeking new investments
Method of Compensation: Return on investment is of primary concern, do not charge fees

MACQUARIE PRIVATE WEALTH INC

6 Wellington Street, West
Suite 5200, P.O. Box 357
Toronto, Canada M5K 1K7
Phone: 416-601-9030
Fax: 416-601-0396
Website: www.blackmont.com

Management and Staff
David Burrows, President
John Playfair, Managing Director

Type of Firm
Private Equity Firm

Additional Information
Year Founded: 1991
Current Activity Level : Actively seeking new investments

MACROCAPITALES SAFI SA

General Borgono 1156
Miraflores
Lima, Peru Lima 18
Phone: 5117022580
Website: www.macrocapitales.com

Management and Staff
Drago Kisic, President
Dulio Costa, Managing Director
Monica Com, Partner
Pablo Avendano, Managing Director
Raul Salazar, Partner

Type of Firm
Investment Management Firm

Project Preferences

Type of Financing Preferred:
Leveraged Buyout
Balanced
Acquisition

Geographical Preferences

International Preferences:
Peru

Industry Preferences

In Medical/Health prefer:
Medical/Health

In Consumer Related prefer:
Consumer Products
Education Related

In Industrial/Energy prefer:
Energy

In Business Serv. prefer:
Distribution

In Agr/Forestr/Fish prefer:
Agribusiness

Additional Information
Name of Most Recent Fund: Fortaleza Private Equity Fund
Most Recent Fund Was Raised: 07/25/2012
Year Founded: 2012
Capital Under Management: $50,000,000
Current Activity Level : Actively seeking new investments

MADISON BAY CAPITAL PARTNERS

757 Third Avenue
20th Floor
New York, NY USA 10017
Phone: 2126346485
E-mail: info@madbaycap.com
Website: madbaycap.com

Type of Firm
Private Equity Firm

Project Preferences

Type of Financing Preferred:
Early Stage
Expansion
Later Stage

Geographical Preferences

United States Preferences:

Industry Preferences

In Consumer Related prefer:
Consumer Products

In Financial Services prefer:
Financial Services

Additional Information
Year Founded: 1969
Current Activity Level : Actively seeking new investments

MADISON CAPITAL FUNDING LLC

30 South Wacker Drive
Suite 3700
Chicago, IL USA 60606
Phone: 3125966900
Fax: 3125966950
Website: www.nylinvestments.com

Management and Staff
Andrew Bucolo, Managing Director
Christopher Williams, Founder
Craig Lacy, Founder
Faraaz Kamran, Managing Director
Hugh Wade, Founder
Jeffrey Day, Managing Director
K. Thomas Klimmeck, Founder
Marcus Meyer, Managing Director
Michael Nativi, Vice President
Richard Christensen, Managing Director
Robert Douglass, Vice President
Timothy Wentink, Vice President
Trevor Clark, Chief Executive Officer
Tricia Marks, Managing Director

Type of Firm
Bank Affiliated

Project Preferences

Role in Financing:
Prefer role as deal originator but will also invest in deals created by others

Type of Financing Preferred:
Leveraged Buyout
Management Buyouts
Acquisition
Recapitalizations

Size of Investments Considered:
Min Size of Investment Considered (000s): $15,000
Max Size of Investment Considered (000s): $30,000

Geographical Preferences

United States Preferences:

Industry Preferences

In Medical/Health prefer:
Health Services

In Consumer Related prefer:
Consumer Products

In Financial Services prefer:
Financial Services

In Business Serv. prefer:
Services
Distribution

In Manufact. prefer:
Manufacturing

Additional Information
Year Founded: 2001
Current Activity Level : Actively seeking new investments

MADISON CAPITAL PARTNERS CORP

500 West Madison
Suite 3890
Chicago, IL USA 60661
Phone: 3122770156
Fax: 3122770163
Website: www.madisoncapitalpartners.net

Management and Staff
David Ball, Managing Director
George Nolen, Senior Managing Director
John Udelhofen, Chief Financial Officer
Richard Osborne, Senior Managing Director

Type of Firm
Private Equity Firm

Project Preferences

Role in Financing:
Prefer role as deal originator

1335

Type of Financing Preferred:
Leveraged Buyout
Turnaround
Management Buyouts
Acquisition
Industry Rollups

Geographical Preferences

United States Preferences:

International Preferences:
Europe

Industry Focus

(% based on actual investment)
Industrial/Energy	86.4%
Other Products	8.8%
Consumer Related	4.8%

Additional Information
Year Founded: 1994
Current Activity Level : Actively seeking new investments
Method of Compensation: Return on invest. most important, but chg. closing fees, service fees, etc.

MADISON DEARBORN PARTNERS LLC

70 West Madison
Suite 4600
Chicago, IL USA 60602
Phone: 3128951000
Fax: 3128951001
E-mail: info@mdcp.com
Website: www.mdcp.com

Management and Staff
Douglas Grissom, Managing Director
James Perry, Managing Director
Jason Shideler, Vice President
John Knutsen, Managing Director
Michael Cole, Managing Director
Michael Kreger, Vice President
Nicholas Alexos, Managing Director
Patrick Eilers, Managing Director
Robin Selati, Managing Director
Steven Russell, Vice President
Thomas Souleles, Managing Director
Timothy Sullivan, Managing Director
Vahe Dombalagian, Managing Director
Zaid Alsikafi, Managing Director

Type of Firm
Private Equity Firm

Association Membership
Illinois Venture Capital Association
Private Equity Council (PEC)

Project Preferences

Role in Financing:
Prefer role as deal originator

Type of Financing Preferred:
Leveraged Buyout
Management Buyouts
Recapitalizations

Geographical Preferences

United States Preferences:

Industry Focus

(% based on actual investment)
Other Products	45.5%
Communications and Media	16.1%
Consumer Related	10.1%
Medical/Health	8.1%
Internet Specific	7.5%
Industrial/Energy	4.4%
Computer Software and Services	3.0%
Semiconductors/Other Elect.	2.7%
Biotechnology	2.4%
Computer Hardware	0.2%

Additional Information
Year Founded: 1992
Capital Under Management: $14,000,000,000
Current Activity Level : Actively seeking new investments
Method of Compensation: Return on invest. most important, but chg. closing fees, service fees, etc.

MADISON INDIA CAPITAL MANAGEMENT CO

Les Cascades
Edith Cavell Street
Port Louis, Mauritius
Phone: 2302129800
Fax: 2302129833
E-mail: gagan@madison-india.com
Website: www.madison-india.com

Management and Staff
Nish Chawla, Managing Director
Samir Shrivastava, Vice President
Surya Chadha, Senior Managing Director

Type of Firm
Private Equity Firm

Association Membership
Indian Venture Capital Association (IVCA)

Project Preferences

Type of Financing Preferred:
Early Stage
Expansion
Balanced
Later Stage
Startup

Geographical Preferences

International Preferences:
India
Asia

Industry Preferences

In Communications prefer:
Communications and Media
Radio & TV Broadcasting
Telecommunications
Wireless Communications
Media and Entertainment
Publishing

In Business Serv. prefer:
Services

Additional Information
Year Founded: 2011
Capital Under Management: $230,000,000
Current Activity Level : Actively seeking new investments

MADISON PARKER CAPITAL LLC

680 Berkeley Avenue
Suite 100
Menlo Park, CA USA 94025
Phone: 6179100081
E-mail: info@madisonparkercapital.com
Website: www.madisonparkercapital.com

Other Offices
153 Townsend Street
Suite 9031
Daly City, CA USA 94017

Type of Firm
Private Equity Firm

Project Preferences

Type of Financing Preferred:
Leveraged Buyout
Expansion
Acquisition
Recapitalizations

Size of Investments Considered:
Min Size of Investment Considered (000s): $5,000
Max Size of Investment Considered (000s): $75,000

Geographical Preferences

United States Preferences:

Industry Preferences

In Consumer Related prefer:
Consumer
Retail
Other Restaurants

In Business Serv. prefer:
Services

In Manufact. prefer:
Manufacturing

Additional Information
Year Founded: 2007
Current Activity Level : Actively seeking new investments

MADRONA VENTURE GROUP

999 Third Avenue
34th Floor
Seattle, WA USA 98104
Phone: 2066743000
Fax: 2066748703
E-mail: information@madrona.com
Website: www.madrona.com

Other Offices
Former HQ: 1000 Second Avenue
Suite 3700
SEATTLE, WA USA 98104

Management and Staff
Daniel Weld, Venture Partner
David Rosenthal, Principal
Greg Gottesman, Venture Partner
Hope Cochran, Venture Partner
Julie Sandler, Partner
Len Jordan, Managing Director
Maria Karaivanova, Principal
Matthew McIlwain, Managing Director
Oren Etzioni, Venture Partner
Paul Goodrich, Managing Director
Scott Jacobson, Managing Director
Soma Somasegar, Managing Director
Tim Porter, Managing Director
Tom Alberg, Managing Director
Troy Cichos, Partner
William Richter, Venture Partner

Type of Firm
Private Equity Firm

Project Preferences

Role in Financing:
Will function either as deal originator or investor in deals created by others

Type of Financing Preferred:
Early Stage
Startup

Industry Focus
(% based on actual investment)
Computer Software and Services	44.9%
Internet Specific	35.4%
Semiconductors/Other Elect.	6.9%
Computer Hardware	4.4%
Consumer Related	3.3%
Other Products	2.7%
Communications and Media	2.3%
Industrial/Energy	0.1%

Additional Information
Name of Most Recent Fund: Madrona Venture Fund V, L.P.
Most Recent Fund Was Raised: 05/24/2012
Year Founded: 1995
Capital Under Management: $1,267,000,000
Current Activity Level : Actively seeking new investments
Method of Compensation: Return on investment is of primary concern, do not charge fees

MADRONE CAPITAL PARTNERS

3000 Sand Hill Road
Building Two, Suite 150
Menlo Park, CA USA 94025
Phone: 6508548300

Management and Staff
Greg Penner, General Partner
Thomas Patterson, General Partner

Type of Firm
Private Equity Firm

Project Preferences

Type of Financing Preferred:
Balanced

Geographical Preferences

United States Preferences:

Additional Information
Year Founded: 2005
Current Activity Level : Actively seeking new investments

MAGELLAN CAPITAL PARTNERS LTD

363 N. Sam Houston Parkway E.
Suite 1100
Houston, TX USA 77060
Phone: 281-405-2620
Fax: 281-405-2619
E-mail: info@magallencap.net

Management and Staff
Greg Miller, Principal
Roy Case, General Partner
Willem Timmermans, General Partner

Type of Firm
Private Equity Firm

Project Preferences

Role in Financing:
Prefer role as deal originator but will also invest in deals created by others

Type of Financing Preferred:
Leveraged Buyout
Turnaround
Acquisition

Geographical Preferences

United States Preferences:
All U.S.

Industry Preferences

In Medical/Health prefer:
Medical/Health

In Industrial/Energy prefer:
Energy

In Transportation prefer:
Aerospace

In Financial Services prefer:
Financial Services

In Manufact. prefer:
Manufacturing

Additional Information
Year Founded: 2004
Capital Under Management: $1,800,000
Current Activity Level : Actively seeking new investments

MAGHREBIA FINANCIERE

9 Rue de L`artisanat
Tunis, Tunisia 1080
Phone: 216-71-940-501
Fax: 216-71-940-528
E-mail: ufi@planet.tn

Type of Firm
Private Equity Firm

Association Membership
Tunisian Venture Capital Association

Project Preferences

Type of Financing Preferred:
Early Stage
Later Stage
Startup

Geographical Preferences

International Preferences:
Tunisia
Africa

Additional Information
Year Founded: 2004
Current Activity Level : Actively seeking new investments

Pratt's Guide to Private Equity & Venture Capital Sources

MAGIC STONE ALTERNATIVE INVESTMENT CO LTD

1 East Chang An Avenue
Room 305, 3/F, Office Tower C2
Beijing, China 100738
Phone: 861085187722
Fax: 861085187755
E-mail: info@magicstoneinvest.com
Website: www.magicstoneinvest.com

Type of Firm
Private Equity Advisor or Fund of Funds

Association Membership
China Venture Capital Association

Project Preferences

Type of Financing Preferred:
Fund of Funds

Geographical Preferences

International Preferences:
China

Additional Information
Year Founded: 2009
Current Activity Level : Actively seeking new investments

MAGILINK INVESTMENT CORP

820 Anam Tower
702-10 Yeoksam-1Dong
Seoul, South Korea 135565
Phone: 82-2-5389833
Fax: 82-2-5389844

Management and Staff
Byung Sik Cho, Chief Executive Officer

Type of Firm
Private Equity Firm

Project Preferences

Type of Financing Preferred:
Balanced

Additional Information
Year Founded: 2010
Current Activity Level : Actively seeking new investments

MAGMA PARTNERS

6443 N. Santa Monica Boulevard
Fox Point, WI USA 53217
Phone: 4143648254
Website: magmapartners.com

Type of Firm
Incubator/Development Program

Project Preferences

Type of Financing Preferred:
Seed

Geographical Preferences

International Preferences:
Latin America

Additional Information
Year Founded: 2014
Capital Under Management: $5,000,000
Current Activity Level : Actively seeking new investments

MAGNASCI VENTURES

123 North Post Oak Lane
Suite 410
Houston, TX USA 77024
Phone: 7136213111
Website: magnasciventures.com

Type of Firm
Private Equity Firm

Project Preferences

Type of Financing Preferred:
Early Stage

Additional Information
Year Founded: 2016
Capital Under Management: $10,250,000
Current Activity Level : Actively seeking new investments

MAGNE LARSEN INVESTMENTS APS

Hellerupvej 82
Hellerup, Denmark 2900

Type of Firm
Private Equity Firm

Additional Information
Year Founded: 2013
Current Activity Level : Actively seeking new investments

MAGNUM COMMUNICATIONS FUND L P

Azrieli Center 1
35th Floor
Tel Aviv, Israel 67021
Phone: 97236967285
Fax: 97236955960

Other Offices
Azrieli Center 1
35th Floor
Tel Aviv, Israel 67021
Phone: 97236967285
Fax: 97236955960

Management and Staff
Adi Yarel, Chief Financial Officer
Modi Rosen, Managing Partner
Shraga Katz, General Partner
Yahal Zilka, Managing Partner
Zvi Limon, General Partner

Type of Firm
Private Equity Firm

Association Membership
Israel Venture Association

Project Preferences

Type of Financing Preferred:
Early Stage
Balanced
Later Stage
Seed
Startup

Geographical Preferences

International Preferences:
Israel

Industry Preferences

In Communications prefer:
Communications and Media
Wireless Communications

In Computer Software prefer:
Applications Software

In Internet Specific prefer:
Internet

In Semiconductor/Electr prefer:
Semiconductor

In Business Serv. prefer:
Media

Additional Information
Name of Most Recent Fund: Magma Venture Capital III, L.P.
Most Recent Fund Was Raised: 02/18/2013
Year Founded: 1999
Capital Under Management: $500,000,000
Current Activity Level : Actively seeking new investments

MAGNUM INDUSTRIAL PARTNERS

Calle Fortuny 14, 2D
Madrid, Spain 28010
Phone: 34913106342

Fax: 34913199955
E-mail: info@magnumpartners.com
Website: www.magnumpartners.es

Other Offices

Avenida da Liberdade 249, 4
Lisbon, Portugal 1250-143
Phone: 351-213-163-730
Fax: 351-213-163-731

Management and Staff

Angel Corcostegui, Founder
Enrique de Leyva, Founder
Joao Talone, Founder
Joao Coelho Borges, Partner
Jose Manrique, Chief Financial Officer

Type of Firm

Private Equity Firm

Project Preferences

Type of Financing Preferred:
Leveraged Buyout
Acquisition

Geographical Preferences

International Preferences:
Portugal
Spain

Industry Preferences

In Industrial/Energy prefer:
Industrial Products

In Business Serv. prefer:
Services

Additional Information

Year Founded: 2006
Capital Under Management: $1,079,900,000
Current Activity Level : Actively seeking new investments

MAGNUM INDUSTRIAL PARTNERS SL

Calle Fortuny, 14, 2 D
Madrid, Spain 28010
Phone: 34913106342
Fax: 34913199955
E-mail: info@magnumpartners.com
Website: www.magnumpartners.com

Management and Staff

Alberto Bermejo, Partner
Angel Corcostegui, Co-Founder
Enrique de Leyva, Co-Founder
Joao Coelho Borges, Partner
Joao Talone, Co-Founder
Jose Manrique, Chief Financial Officer
Jose Antonio Marco, Partner

Type of Firm

Private Equity Firm

Project Preferences

Type of Financing Preferred:
Leveraged Buyout
Management Buyouts

Geographical Preferences

International Preferences:
Portugal
Spain

Additional Information

Year Founded: 2006
Current Activity Level : Actively seeking new investments

MAHON CHINA INVESTMENT MANAGEMENT LTD

14/F, Office Tower
Hong Kong-Macau Center
Beijing, China 100027
Phone: 86-10-65068908
Fax: 86-10-65012526
E-mail: info@mahonchina.com
Website: www.mahonchina.com

Type of Firm

Private Equity Firm

Project Preferences

Type of Financing Preferred:
Balanced

Geographical Preferences

International Preferences:
China
Asia

Industry Preferences

In Communications prefer:
Communications and Media

In Transportation prefer:
Transportation
Aerospace

In Manufact. prefer:
Manufacturing

Additional Information

Year Founded: 1985
Current Activity Level : Actively seeking new investments

MAIDEN LANE VENTURES

16 Maiden Lane
Suite 600
San Francisco, CA USA 94108
Website: www.maidenlane.com

Type of Firm

Private Equity Firm

Project Preferences

Type of Financing Preferred:
Early Stage
Seed
Startup

Additional Information

Year Founded: 2014
Current Activity Level : Actively seeking new investments

MAIDSTONE CAPITAL CORP

10 Saugatuck Avenue
Suite 103
Westport, CT USA 06880
Phone: 2034541888
Fax: 2066662967
E-mail: info@maidstonecapital.com
Website: www.maidstonecapital.com

Type of Firm

Private Equity Firm

Project Preferences

Type of Financing Preferred:
Leveraged Buyout
Acquisition
Recapitalizations

Additional Information

Year Founded: 2003
Current Activity Level : Actively seeking new investments

MAIF AVENIR SAS

200, Avenue Salvador Allende
Niort, France 79000
Phone: 33890391022
Website: www.maif-avenir.fr

Type of Firm

Insurance Firm Affiliate

Project Preferences

Type of Financing Preferred:
Early Stage
Seed

Geographical Preferences

International Preferences:
Europe
France

Industry Preferences

In Communications prefer:
Data Communications

In Internet Specific prefer:
Internet
Ecommerce

Additional Information

Year Founded: 2013
Capital Under Management: $12,150,000
Current Activity Level : Actively seeking new investments

MAIL.RU GROUP LTD

Leningradskiy Prospect, 47
Bldg. 2,Avion Business Center
Moscow, Russia 125167
E-mail: ir@corp.mail.ru
Website: corp.mail.ru

Other Offices

7 Kiryat Atidim
4th floor
Tel-Aviv, Israel 61580

Sachsenfeld 4
Hamburg, Germany 20097

Management and Staff

Matthew Hammond, Chief Financial Officer
Vladimir Nikolsky, Chief Operating Officer

Type of Firm

Private Equity Firm

Project Preferences

Type of Financing Preferred:
Later Stage

Geographical Preferences

International Preferences:
United Kingdom
Europe
China
Ukraine
Asia
Russia

Industry Preferences

In Communications prefer:
Media and Entertainment

In Internet Specific prefer:
E-Commerce Technology
Internet

Additional Information

Name of Most Recent Fund: DST Global II, LP
Most Recent Fund Was Raised: 06/04/2011
Year Founded: 2005
Capital Under Management: $1,700,000,000

Current Activity Level : Actively seeking new investments

MAIN CAPITAL PARTNERS BV

Paleisstraat 6
The Hague, Netherlands 2514 JA
Phone: 31703243433
Fax: 31703243093
E-mail: info@main.nl
Website: www.main.nl

Management and Staff

Charly Zwemstra, Partner
Lars Van t Hoenderdaal, Partner

Type of Firm

Private Equity Firm

Association Membership

Dutch Venture Capital Associaton (NVP)
European Private Equity and Venture Capital Assoc.

Project Preferences

Type of Financing Preferred:
Leveraged Buyout
Management Buyouts
Acquisition

Size of Investments Considered:
Min Size of Investment Considered (000s): $6,000
Max Size of Investment Considered (000s): $30,000

Geographical Preferences

International Preferences:
Luxembourg
Netherlands
Belgium
Germany

Industry Preferences

In Communications prefer:
Media and Entertainment

In Computer Software prefer:
Software

Additional Information

Year Founded: 2003
Capital Under Management: $408,000,000
Current Activity Level : Actively seeking new investments

MAIN LINE EQUITY PARTNERS LLC

16 East Lancaster Avenue, Plaza 16, Suite 202
Ardmore, PA USA 19003
Phone: 2156206993
Fax: 4136910316
E-mail: info@mainlineequity.com
Website: www.mainlineequity.com

Management and Staff

Chris Randazzo, Founder

Type of Firm

Private Equity Firm

Project Preferences

Type of Financing Preferred:
Leveraged Buyout
Mezzanine
Acquisition
Recapitalizations

Geographical Preferences

United States Preferences:
Southeast
All U.S.

Industry Preferences

In Computer Software prefer:
Software

In Medical/Health prefer:
Medical/Health

In Financial Services prefer:
Real Estate

In Manufact. prefer:
Manufacturing

Additional Information

Year Founded: 1998
Current Activity Level : Actively seeking new investments

MAIN MARKET PARTNERS LLC

39 East Market Street
Suite 403
Akron, OH USA 44308
Phone: 2169230338
Fax: 2166724474
E-mail: ccroley@mainmarketpartners.com
Website: mainmarketpartners.com

Type of Firm

Private Equity Firm

Project Preferences

Type of Financing Preferred:
Leveraged Buyout
Management Buyouts
Acquisition

Geographical Preferences

United States Preferences:

Additional Information

Year Founded: 2011
Current Activity Level : Actively seeking new investments

MAIN POST PARTNERS

One Ferry Building
Suite 350
San Francisco, CA USA 94111
Phone: 4153980770
Website: www.mainpostpartners.com

Type of Firm
Private Equity Firm

Project Preferences

Type of Financing Preferred:
Leveraged Buyout

Additional Information
Year Founded: 2014
Capital Under Management: $400,000,000
Current Activity Level : Actively seeking new investments

MAIN STREET CAPITAL CORP

1300 Post Oak Boulevard
Suite 800
Houston, TX USA 77056
Phone: 7133506000
Fax: 7133506042
Website: www.mainstcapital.com

Management and Staff
Catherine Silva, Vice President
Dwayne Hyzak, President
K. Colton Braud, Managing Director
Nicholas Meserve, Managing Director

Type of Firm
Private Equity Firm

Association Membership
Natl Assoc of Small Bus. Inv. Co (NASBIC)

Project Preferences

Role in Financing:
Prefer role as deal originator but will also invest in deals created by others

Type of Financing Preferred:
Leveraged Buyout
Expansion
Mezzanine
Later Stage
Management Buyouts
Acquisition
Recapitalizations

Geographical Preferences

United States Preferences:
Southeast
Southwest

Additional Information
Year Founded: 1997
Capital Under Management: $213,000,000
Current Activity Level : Actively seeking new investments

MAIN STREET CAPITAL HOLDINGS LLC

301 Grant Street
14th Floor, One Oxford Center
Pittsburgh, PA USA 15219
Phone: 4129044020
Fax: 4129041794
Website: www.mainstcap.com

Management and Staff
Dennis Prado, Managing Partner
Donald Jenkins, Co-Founder
W. Ryan Davis, Managing Partner

Type of Firm
Private Equity Firm

Project Preferences

Role in Financing:
Prefer role as deal originator

Type of Financing Preferred:
Leveraged Buyout
Management Buyouts
Acquisition

Geographical Preferences

United States Preferences:
East Coast

Industry Focus
(% based on actual investment)
Computer Software and Services   60.5%
Industrial/Energy   31.8%
Other Products   7.7%

Additional Information
Name of Most Recent Fund: Main Street Contessa LLC
Most Recent Fund Was Raised: 09/30/2011
Year Founded: 1994
Capital Under Management: $100,000,000
Current Activity Level : Actively seeking new investments
Method of Compensation: Return on invest. most important, but chg. closing fees, service fees, etc.

MAINSAIL PARTNERS LP

One Front Street
Suite 3000
San Francisco, CA USA 94111
Phone: 4153913150
Fax: 4157274111
Website: www.mainsailpartners.com

Management and Staff
Chris Cassidy, Partner
Lars Ahlstrom, Chief Financial Officer
Michael Anderson, Partner
Ryan Kruizenga, Vice President
Stephen Wolfe, Partner
Taylor McKinley, Chief Operating Officer
Vinay Kashyap, Vice President
William Salisbury, Chief Financial Officer

Type of Firm
Private Equity Firm

Project Preferences

Type of Financing Preferred:
Expansion
Management Buyouts
Acquisition
Recapitalizations

Geographical Preferences

United States Preferences:

Canadian Preferences:
All Canada

Industry Preferences

In Communications prefer:
Commercial Communications

In Computer Software prefer:
Applications Software

In Internet Specific prefer:
E-Commerce Technology

In Medical/Health prefer:
Health Services

In Consumer Related prefer:
Education Related

In Financial Services prefer:
Financial Services

In Business Serv. prefer:
Services
Distribution

Additional Information
Name of Most Recent Fund: Mainsail Partners III, L.P.
Most Recent Fund Was Raised: 03/14/2012
Year Founded: 2003
Capital Under Management: $160,000,000
Current Activity Level : Actively seeking new investments

MAIRDUMONT VENTURES GMBH

Marco-Polo-Str. 1
Ostfildern, Germany 73760
Phone: 4971145020
E-mail: md-ventures@mairdumont.com
Website: www.md-ventures.de

Type of Firm
Private Equity Firm

Additional Information
Year Founded: 2015
Current Activity Level : Actively seeking new investments

MAJUVEN, PTE. LTD.

36 Armenian Street
#04-05
Sinagpore, Singapore
Phone: 6562251303
Fax: 6562251305
E-mail: info@majuven.com
Website: www.majuven.com

Other Offices
175 Telok Ayer Street
, Singapore

Management and Staff
Ho Kee Lim, Managing Partner
Teck Seng Low, Managing Partner
Yoh Chie Lu, Managing Partner

Type of Firm
Private Equity Firm

Project Preferences

Type of Financing Preferred:
Early Stage
Balanced
Later Stage

Geographical Preferences

International Preferences:
Asia
Singapore

Industry Preferences

In Industrial/Energy prefer:
Alternative Energy
Environmental Related

Additional Information
Year Founded: 2011
Current Activity Level : Actively seeking new investments

MAKALANI HOLDINGS LTD

52-54 Melville Road
Ground Floor, The Reserve
Illovo, South Africa 2196
Phone: 27114280680
Fax: 27114477389
E-mail: enquiries@makalani.co.za
Website: www.makalani.co.za

Management and Staff
Keshan Pillay, Chief Executive Officer

Type of Firm
Private Equity Firm

Association Membership
South African Venture Capital Association (SAVCA)

Project Preferences

Type of Financing Preferred:
Expansion
Mezzanine

Geographical Preferences

International Preferences:
South Africa

Industry Preferences

In Communications prefer:
Telecommunications

In Medical/Health prefer:
Health Services

In Consumer Related prefer:
Consumer Services

In Industrial/Energy prefer:
Factory Automation

In Transportation prefer:
Transportation

In Financial Services prefer:
Financial Services
Real Estate

In Business Serv. prefer:
Services

In Manufact. prefer:
Manufacturing

In Agr/Forestr/Fish prefer:
Agriculture related
Mining and Minerals

Additional Information
Name of Most Recent Fund: Makalani Holdings Fund I
Most Recent Fund Was Raised: 01/12/2005
Year Founded: 2005
Current Activity Level : Actively seeking new investments

MAKARA CAPITAL

46 Kim Yam Road, Suite 05-03A
Singapore, Singapore 239351
Website: www.makaracapital.com

Type of Firm
Private Equity Firm

Project Preferences

Type of Financing Preferred:
Leveraged Buyout
Early Stage
Generalist PE

Geographical Preferences

International Preferences:
Asia Pacific

Industry Preferences

In Financial Services prefer:
Real Estate

Additional Information
Year Founded: 1969
Current Activity Level : Actively seeking new investments

MALAYSIA VENTURE CAPITAL MANAGEMENT BHD

Level 10, Menara Bank
1016 Jalan Sultan Ismail
Kuala Lumpur, Malaysia 50250
Phone: 60320503000
Fax: 60326983800
E-mail: enquiries@mavcap.com
Website: www.mavcap.com

Management and Staff
Abdul Aziz Feisal Hussein, Vice President
Effendi Abdul Jalil, Vice President
Nur Baidzurah Mohd Ali, Vice President
Renee Marcia Chandran, Vice President

Type of Firm
Government Affiliated Program

Association Membership
Malaysian Venture Capital Association

Project Preferences

Type of Financing Preferred:
Early Stage
Balanced
Later Stage
Seed
Startup

Size of Investments Considered:
Min Size of Investment Considered (000s): $300
Max Size of Investment Considered (000s): $6,008

Geographical Preferences

International Preferences:
Malaysia

Industry Preferences

In Communications prefer:
Communications and Media
Wireless Communications

In Computer Software prefer:
Software

In Consumer Related prefer:
Consumer Services

In Business Serv. prefer:
Media

Additional Information

Year Founded: 2001
Capital Under Management: $158,300,000
Current Activity Level : Actively seeking new investments

MALAYSIAN TECHNOLOGY DEVELOPMENT CORPORATION SDN BHD

Level 9, Menara Yayasan
Tun Razak, Jalan Bukit Bintag
Kuala Lumpur, Malaysia 55100
Phone: 60321726000
Fax: 60321637541
E-mail: comms@mtdc.com.my
Website: www.mtdc.com.my

Type of Firm
Government Affiliated Program

Association Membership
Malaysian Venture Capital Association

Project Preferences

Role in Financing:
Prefer role as deal originator but will also invest in deals created by others

Type of Financing Preferred:
Early Stage
Expansion
Balanced
Later Stage
Startup

Geographical Preferences

International Preferences:
Asia
Malaysia

Industry Preferences

In Communications prefer:
Communications and Media
Telecommunications
Wireless Communications

In Computer Software prefer:
Software
Applications Software

In Semiconductor/Electr prefer:
Semiconductor

In Biotechnology prefer:
Biotechnology

In Medical/Health prefer:
Medical Diagnostics
Medical Products

In Industrial/Energy prefer:
Energy
Alternative Energy
Industrial Products

In Transportation prefer:
Aerospace

In Business Serv. prefer:
Media

In Manufact. prefer:
Manufacturing

Additional Information

Year Founded: 1992
Capital Under Management: $263,700,000
Current Activity Level : Actively seeking new investments
Method of Compensation: Return on investment is of primary concern, do not charge fees

MALAZ CAPITAL COMPANY

Al Akaria III, Olaya Street
Suite 510
Riyadh, Saudi Arabia
Phone: 96614601644
Fax: 96014601644
E-mail: info@malazcapital.com
Website: www.malazcapital.com

Type of Firm
Private Equity Firm

Project Preferences

Type of Financing Preferred:
Leveraged Buyout
Early Stage
Generalist PE
Later Stage
Management Buyouts

Additional Information

Year Founded: 1969
Current Activity Level : Actively seeking new investments

MALLIN AS

Akersgaten 45
Oslo, Norway 0401
Phone: 4723100770
Fax: 4723100771
Website: mallin.no

Management and Staff
Arne Medlien, Managing Director

Type of Firm
Investment Management Firm

Association Membership
Norwegian Venture Capital Association

Project Preferences

Role in Financing:
Prefer role as deal originator but will also invest in deals created by others

Type of Financing Preferred:
Later Stage

Size of Investments Considered:
Min Size of Investment Considered (000s): $1,838
Max Size of Investment Considered (000s): $3,675

Geographical Preferences

International Preferences:
Norway

Industry Preferences

In Industrial/Energy prefer:
Alternative Energy
Energy Conservation Relat
Environmental Related

Additional Information

Year Founded: 1982
Capital Under Management: $10,000,000
Current Activity Level : Actively seeking new investments
Method of Compensation: Return on investment is of primary concern, do not charge fees

MANAGEMENT TECHNOSTARS BV

Postbus 234
Eindhoven, Netherlands 5600 AE
Phone: 3165239286
E-mail: starten@technostars.nl
Website: www.technostars.nl

Type of Firm
Private Equity Firm

Project Preferences

Type of Financing Preferred:
Early Stage
Startup

Size of Investments Considered:
Min Size of Investment Considered (000s): $129
Max Size of Investment Considered (000s): $771

Geographical Preferences

International Preferences:
Netherlands

Additional Information
Year Founded: 2006
Current Activity Level : Actively seeking new investments

MANCHESTER STORY GROUP

2116 Financial Center
Des Moines, IA USA 50309

Type of Firm
Private Equity Firm

Project Preferences

Type of Financing Preferred:
Early Stage
Expansion
Balanced
Later Stage

Size of Investments Considered:
Min Size of Investment Considered (000s): $2,500
Max Size of Investment Considered (000s): $5,000

Industry Preferences

In Computer Software prefer:
Software

In Medical/Health prefer:
Health Services

In Financial Services prefer:
Financial Services

Additional Information
Year Founded: 1969
Capital Under Management: $31,000,000
Current Activity Level : Actively seeking new investments

MANDARIN CAPITAL PARTNERS SCA SICAR

26-28, Rives de Clausen
Luxembourg, Luxembourg 2165
Phone: 352267385
E-mail: info.europe@mandarincp.com
Website: www.mandarincp.com

Other Offices
Kerry Center
1515 Nanjing Xi Lu
Shanghai, China 200040
Phone: 86-21-5298-6600

Via Brera 3
Milano, Italy 20121
Phone: 39-02-809-401

Management and Staff
Alberto Forchielli, Partner
Enrico Ricotta, Partner
Lorenzo Stanca, Partner
Michael Zheng, Vice President
Minghui Xue, Partner
Zhen Gao, Partner

Type of Firm
Private Equity Firm

Project Preferences

Type of Financing Preferred:
Leveraged Buyout
Generalist PE
Later Stage
Management Buyouts
Acquisition

Size of Investments Considered:
Min Size of Investment Considered (000s): $12,942
Max Size of Investment Considered (000s): $38,825

Geographical Preferences

International Preferences:
Italy
Europe
Switzerland
Hong Kong
China
Poland
Austria
Germany

Industry Preferences

In Industrial/Energy prefer:
Industrial Products

Additional Information
Name of Most Recent Fund: Mandarin Capital Partners II
Most Recent Fund Was Raised: 07/17/2013
Year Founded: 2007
Capital Under Management: $218,410,000
Current Activity Level : Actively seeking new investments

MANDRA CAPITAL LTD

19-20 Connaught Road
Tenth Floor, Fung House
Central, Hong Kong
Phone: 85225260668
Fax: 85231138252
Website: www.mandracapital.com

Type of Firm
Private Equity Firm

Project Preferences

Type of Financing Preferred:
Early Stage
Expansion
Balanced

Geographical Preferences

International Preferences:
Asia

Industry Preferences

In Internet Specific prefer:
Internet
Ecommerce

In Industrial/Energy prefer:
Coal Related
Environmental Related

In Agr/Forestr/Fish prefer:
Agriculture related

Additional Information
Year Founded: 2010
Current Activity Level : Actively seeking new investments

MANGROVE CAPITAL PARTNERS SA

31, Boulevard Joseph II
Luxembourg, Luxembourg 1840
Phone: 3522625341
Fax: 35226253420
Website: www.mangrove.vc

Other Offices
39 allee Scheffer
Luxembourg, Luxembourg 2520
Phone: 352 40 116 2331
Fax: 352 40 116 2331

Management and Staff
David Waroquier, Partner
Gerard Lopez, Co-Founder
Hans-Jurgen Schmitz, Co-Founder
Michael Jackson, Partner
Willibrord Ehses, Partner

Type of Firm
Private Equity Firm

Association Membership
European Private Equity and Venture Capital Assoc.

Project Preferences

Type of Financing Preferred:
Early Stage
Balanced
Later Stage
Seed
Startup

Size of Investments Considered:
Min Size of Investment Considered (000s): $500
Max Size of Investment Considered (000s): $500,000

Geographical Preferences

International Preferences:
Italy
Luxembourg
Europe
Netherlands
Spain
Belgium
Germany
Russia
France

Industry Preferences

In Communications prefer:
Communications and Media
Wireless Communications

In Computer Software prefer:
Software

In Internet Specific prefer:
Internet

In Industrial/Energy prefer:
Industrial Products

In Business Serv. prefer:
Services
Media

Additional Information
Name of Most Recent Fund: Mangrove II
Most Recent Fund Was Raised: 08/31/2006
Year Founded: 2000
Capital Under Management: $226,200,000
Current Activity Level : Actively seeking new investments

MANHATTAN VENTURE PARTNERS

Five Penn Plaza
14th Floor
New York, NY USA 10001
Website: www.mvp.vc

Type of Firm
Bank Affiliated

Project Preferences

Type of Financing Preferred:
Later Stage

Additional Information
Year Founded: 2014
Current Activity Level : Actively seeking new investments

MANIFEST INVESTMENT PARTNERS LLC

1110 Mar West Street
Suite M Belvedere
Tiburon, CA USA 94920
E-mail: info@manifestgrowth.com
Website: www.manifestgrowth.com

Type of Firm
Private Equity Firm

Project Preferences

Type of Financing Preferred:
Early Stage

Industry Preferences

In Computer Software prefer:
Software
Artificial Intelligence

In Business Serv. prefer:
Media

Additional Information
Year Founded: 2016
Capital Under Management: $20,200,000
Current Activity Level : Actively seeking new investments

MANITOBA CAPITAL FUND

2195-360 Main Street
Winnipeg, Canada R3C 3Z3
Phone: 204-925-8401
Fax: 204-949-0602
Website: www.gov.mb.ca

Management and Staff
Ken Praznuik, President

Type of Firm
Government Affiliated Program

Additional Information
Year Founded: 1996
Current Activity Level : Actively seeking new investments

MANITOBA METIS FEDERATION INC

300-150 Henry Avenue
Winnipeg, Canada R3B 0J7
Phone: 2045868474
Fax: 2049471816
Website: www.medf.ca

Type of Firm
Government Affiliated Program

Project Preferences

Type of Financing Preferred:
Balanced

Geographical Preferences

Canadian Preferences:
Manitoba

Additional Information
Year Founded: 2011
Capital Under Management: $10,023,000
Current Activity Level : Actively seeking new investments

MANOS ACCELERATOR LLC

189 West Santa Clara Street
San Jose, CA USA 95113
E-mail: info@manosaccelerator.com
Website: www.manosaccelerator.com

Type of Firm
Incubator/Development Program

Project Preferences

Type of Financing Preferred:
Early Stage
Startup

Geographical Preferences

International Preferences:
Latin America

Industry Preferences

In Communications prefer:
Wireless Communications

In Internet Specific prefer:
Internet
Web Aggregation/Portals

In Consumer Related prefer:
Consumer

Additional Information
Year Founded: 2013
Current Activity Level : Actively seeking new investments

MANSA CAPITAL MANAGEMENT LLC

500 Boylston Street
Fifth Floor
Boston, MA USA 02116
Phone: 6174244940
Fax: 6179779162
Website: mansaequity.com

Management and Staff
Caleb DesRosiers, Venture Partner
Jason Torres, Chief Operating Officer
Michael Jarjour, Venture Partner
Richard Foster, Principal
Ruben King-Shaw, Managing Partner
Stephen Agular, Venture Partner

Type of Firm
Private Equity Firm

Association Membership
Natl Assoc of Investment Cos. (NAIC)
Natl Assoc of Small Bus. Inv. Co (NASBIC)

Project Preferences

Type of Financing Preferred:
Early Stage
Expansion

Geographical Preferences

United States Preferences:
All U.S.

Industry Preferences

In Semiconductor/Electr prefer:
Electronics

In Medical/Health prefer:
Medical/Health
Medical Products
Health Services

Additional Information
Name of Most Recent Fund: Mansa Capital Fund I, L.P.
Most Recent Fund Was Raised: 09/06/2012
Year Founded: 2003
Capital Under Management: $46,073,000
Current Activity Level: Actively seeking new investments

MANTELLA VENTURE PARTNERS

488 Wellington Street
Suite 300
Toronto, Canada M5V 1E3
Phone: 14164790779
Fax: 18668758338
E-mail: info@mantellavp.com
Website: mantellavp.com

Management and Staff
Duncan Hill, General Partner
Robin Axon, General Partner

Type of Firm
Corporate PE/Venture

Association Membership
Canadian Venture Capital Association

Project Preferences

Type of Financing Preferred:
Early Stage

Geographical Preferences

Canadian Preferences:
Ontario

Industry Preferences

In Computer Software prefer:
Software

In Internet Specific prefer:
Internet

Additional Information
Year Founded: 1946
Capital Under Management: $19,704,000
Current Activity Level: Actively seeking new investments

MANTIQ INVESTIMENTOS LTDA

Av Paulista 688
6 Andar
Sao Paulo, Brazil 01310100
Phone: 551131455900
Fax: 551131455999
E-mail: info@mantiq.com.br
Website: www.mantiq.com.br

Type of Firm
Bank Affiliated

Project Preferences

Type of Financing Preferred:
Leveraged Buyout
Early Stage
Balanced
Turnaround
Later Stage
Seed
Startup
Distressed Debt

Geographical Preferences

International Preferences:
Brazil

Industry Preferences

In Communications prefer:
Telecommunications

In Computer Hardware prefer:
Terminals

In Industrial/Energy prefer:
Energy
Oil and Gas Exploration
Environmental Related

Additional Information
Year Founded: 1999
Capital Under Management: $1,200,000,000
Current Activity Level: Actively seeking new investments

MANTRA VENTURES

T4, T5 - Metrople
Third Floor
Pune, India 411001
Website: www.mantraventures.in

Type of Firm
Private Equity Firm

Project Preferences

Type of Financing Preferred:
Startup

Additional Information
Year Founded: 1969
Current Activity Level: Actively seeking new investments

MANTUCKET CAPITAL LLC

5251 DTC Parkway
Suite 995
Englewood, CO USA 80111
Phone: 3033978888
Fax: 3033978889
E-mail: info@mantucket.com
Website: mantucket.com

Management and Staff
Brian Mankwitz, Managing Director
Charlie Kettering, Vice President
Wendy Kane, President

Type of Firm
Private Equity Firm

Project Preferences

Type of Financing Preferred:
Leveraged Buyout
Value-Add
Expansion
Mezzanine
Turnaround
Opportunistic
Management Buyouts
Acquisition
Special Situation
Distressed Debt
Recapitalizations

Industry Preferences

In Computer Software prefer:
Software

In Internet Specific prefer:
Ecommerce

In Medical/Health prefer:
Health Services

In Consumer Related prefer:
Retail
Hotels and Resorts

In Industrial/Energy prefer:
Energy
Alternative Energy
Industrial Products
Environmental Related

In Financial Services prefer:
Financial Services
Real Estate

In Business Serv. prefer:
Distribution

In Manufact. prefer:
Manufacturing

In Agr/Forestr/Fish prefer:
Agriculture related

In Utilities prefer:
Utilities

In Other prefer:
Environment Responsible

Additional Information
Year Founded: 2013
Capital Under Management: $1,000,000,000
Current Activity Level : Actively seeking new investments

MANZANITA CAPITAL LTD

99-101 Regent Street
Victory House
London, United Kingdom W1B 4EZ
Phone: 442074941839
Fax: 442077344315
E-mail: info@manzanitacapital.com
Website: www.manzanitacapital.com

Type of Firm
Private Equity Firm

Project Preferences

Type of Financing Preferred:
Leveraged Buyout

Geographical Preferences

International Preferences:
Sweden
United Kingdom

Industry Preferences

In Medical/Health prefer:
Medical/Health

In Consumer Related prefer:
Consumer
Retail
Consumer Products

Additional Information
Year Founded: 2001
Current Activity Level : Actively seeking new investments

MAOZ EVEREST FUNDS MANAGEMENT LTD

21 Haarbaa Street
Tel Aviv, Israel 67134
Phone: 97236858555
Fax: 97236858557
E-mail: info@maozeverest.com
Website: www.maozeverest.com

Management and Staff
Elchanan Maoz, Founder

Type of Firm
Investment Management Firm

Project Preferences

Type of Financing Preferred:
Early Stage
Public Companies
Startup

Geographical Preferences

International Preferences:
Israel

Additional Information
Year Founded: 2000
Current Activity Level : Actively seeking new investments

MAPE ADVISORY GROUP PRIVATE LTD

211, Cunningham Road
Prestige Center Point
Bangalore, India 560052
Website: www.mapegroup.com

Management and Staff
Jacob Mathew, Co-Founder

Type of Firm
Investment Management Firm

Project Preferences

Type of Financing Preferred:
Leveraged Buyout
Early Stage
Expansion
Later Stage
Seed
Management Buyouts
Acquisition
Recapitalizations

Geographical Preferences

International Preferences:
India

Industry Preferences

In Medical/Health prefer:
Pharmaceuticals

In Consumer Related prefer:
Retail

In Financial Services prefer:
Financial Services

In Business Serv. prefer:
Media

Additional Information
Year Founded: 2001
Current Activity Level : Actively seeking new investments

MAPLE PARTNERS FINANL GROUP

79 Wellington Street West
Maritime L1life TowerSuite3500
Toronto, Canada M5K 1K7
Phone: 416-350-8200
Fax: 416-350-8222
Website: www.maplefinancialgroup.com

Management and Staff
Wolfgang Schuck, Chief Executive Officer

Type of Firm
Private Equity Firm

Additional Information
Year Founded: 1986
Current Activity Level : Actively seeking new investments

MAPLE VALLEY INVESTMENTS CO LTD

No. 1 East Changan Street
305, #2, Dongfang Plaza
Beijing, China 100738
Phone: 86-10-8518-7722
Fax: 86-10-8518-7755
E-mail: info@maplevalley.com.cn
Website: www.maplevalley.com.cn

Management and Staff
Gavin Zhang, Partner
Jenny Zeng, Founding Partner

Type of Firm
Investment Management Firm

Project Preferences

Type of Financing Preferred:
Fund of Funds
Early Stage
Balanced
Later Stage

Geographical Preferences

International Preferences:
China

Industry Preferences

In Communications prefer:
Telecommunications

In Medical/Health prefer:
Medical/Health

In Consumer Related prefer:
Consumer
Retail

In Industrial/Energy prefer:
Energy

In Financial Services prefer:
Real Estate

In Business Serv. prefer:
Media

Additional Information
Year Founded: 2005
Capital Under Management: $152,579,000
Current Activity Level : Actively seeking new investments

MAPLEWOOD PARTNERS LP

255 Aragon Avenue
Miami, FL USA 33134
Phone: 3053506800

Management and Staff
Peter Arnstein, Principal
Robert Glaser, Founder

Type of Firm
Bank Affiliated

Project Preferences

Type of Financing Preferred:
Leveraged Buyout
Mezzanine

Industry Focus
(% based on actual investment)
Other Products 87.3%
Internet Specific 12.7%

Additional Information
Year Founded: 1999
Capital Under Management: $135,000,000
Current Activity Level : Actively seeking new investments

MARANON CAPITAL LP

225 West Washington Street
Suite 200
Chicago, IL USA 60606
Phone: 3126461200
Fax: 3125780047
E-mail: info@maranoncapital.com
Website: www.maranoncapital.com

Other Offices
280 North Old Woodward Avenue, Suite 104
Birmingham, MI USA 48009
Phone: 248-220-1804

1400 E. Angela Boulevard
Unite 340
South Bend, IN USA 46617
Phone: 574-807-0714
Fax: 3125780047

Former HQ: One North Franklin Street
Suite 2700
Chicago, IL USA 60606
Phone: 3126461200

Management and Staff
Darin Schmalz, Principal
Demian Kircher, Managing Director
Greg Long, Managing Director
Greg Daniele, Vice President
Ian Larkin, Managing Director
Laura Albrecht, Principal
Richard Jander, Managing Director
Rommel Garcia, Principal
Tom Gregory, Managing Director

Type of Firm
Private Equity Firm

Project Preferences

Type of Financing Preferred:
Mezzanine
Later Stage
Acquisition
Recapitalizations

Size of Investments Considered:
Min Size of Investment Considered (000s): $5,000
Max Size of Investment Considered (000s): $30,000

Geographical Preferences

United States Preferences:
North America

Industry Preferences

In Medical/Health prefer:
Health Services

In Consumer Related prefer:
Consumer Products
Consumer Services

In Business Serv. prefer:
Services
Distribution

In Manufact. prefer:
Manufacturing

Additional Information
Name of Most Recent Fund: Maranon Mezzanine Fund II, L.P.
Most Recent Fund Was Raised: 12/20/2013
Year Founded: 2007
Capital Under Management: $557,000,000
Current Activity Level : Actively seeking new investments

MARATHON VENTURE CAPITAL

Lempesi 5-7
Athens, Greece 117 42
E-mail: info@marathon.vc
Website: marathon.vc

Type of Firm
Private Equity Firm

Project Preferences

Type of Financing Preferred:
Early Stage

Additional Information
Year Founded: 2017
Current Activity Level : Actively seeking new investments

MARCH CAPITAL PARTNERS GP LLC

725 Arizona Avenue
Suite 304
Santa Monica, CA USA 90401
Phone: 310-460-7902
Website: www.marchcp.com

Management and Staff

Dana Moraly, Chief Financial Officer
Gregory Milken, Co-Founder
Jamie Montgomery, Co-Founder
Jim Armstrong, Partner
Sumant Mandal, Partner

Type of Firm

Corporate PE/Venture

Project Preferences

Type of Financing Preferred:
Early Stage
Seed
Startup

Geographical Preferences

United States Preferences:

International Preferences:
India

Industry Preferences

In Computer Software prefer:
Software

In Internet Specific prefer:
Internet

Additional Information

Year Founded: 2014
Capital Under Management: $240,000,000
Current Activity Level : Actively seeking new investments

MARE INVESTIMENTOS LTDA

Av Ataulfo de Paiva 204
conj 901 Leblon
Rio de Janeiro, Brazil 22440333
Phone: 552135118830
E-mail: nvestors@mareinvestimentos.com.br
Website: www.mareinvestimentos.com.br

Management and Staff

Claudio Coutinho, Co-Founder
Demian Fiocca, Managing Partner
Nelson Guitti, Co-Founder
Rodolfo Landim, Managing Partner

Type of Firm

Private Equity Firm

Association Membership

Brazilian Venture Capital Association (ABCR)

Project Preferences

Type of Financing Preferred:
Leveraged Buyout
Mezzanine
Generalist PE
Balanced
Later Stage
Acquisition
Recapitalizations

Geographical Preferences

International Preferences:
Brazil

Industry Preferences

In Industrial/Energy prefer:
Oil and Gas Exploration
Oil & Gas Drilling,Explor

Additional Information

Year Founded: 2009
Capital Under Management: $397,273,000
Current Activity Level : Actively seeking new investments

MARGINXL CAPITAL PARTNERS LLC

5605 North MacArthur Boulevard
Suite 1030
Irving, TX USA 75038
Phone: 9725213060
E-mail: ignite@marginxlcapital.com
Website: www.marginxlcapital.com

Management and Staff

George Stelling, Managing Partner
Krista Stelling, Vice President

Type of Firm

Private Equity Firm

Project Preferences

Type of Financing Preferred:
Leveraged Buyout
Turnaround
Management Buyouts
Private Placement
Special Situation

Geographical Preferences

United States Preferences:

Canadian Preferences:
All Canada

Industry Preferences

In Computer Software prefer:
Software

In Consumer Related prefer:
Consumer Products
Consumer Services

In Transportation prefer:
Transportation
Aerospace

In Financial Services prefer:
Financial Services

In Business Serv. prefer:
Services

Additional Information

Year Founded: 2014
Current Activity Level : Actively seeking new investments

MARKAB CAPITAL

PO Box 39553
Kuwait City, Kuwait 73056
Fax: 96522518095
E-mail: info@markabcapital.com
Website: markabcapital.com

Type of Firm

Private Equity Firm

Project Preferences

Type of Financing Preferred:
Leveraged Buyout
Expansion
Mezzanine
Generalist PE
Acquisition

Additional Information

Year Founded: 1970
Current Activity Level : Actively seeking new investments

MARKER FINANCIAL ADVISORS LLC

130 East 59th Street
14th floor
New York, NY USA 10022
Phone: 2129379095
Website: www.marker-llc.com

Other Offices

Four Hasadnaot Street
Herzliya, Israel 46733

Management and Staff
Lluis Pedragosa, Principal
Ohad Finkelstein, Partner
Richard Scanlon, Co-Founder
Sam Zarou, Principal
Thomas Pompidou, Co-Founder
Yuval Shachar, Partner

Type of Firm
Private Equity Firm

Project Preferences

Type of Financing Preferred:
Balanced

Size of Investments Considered:
Min Size of Investment Considered (000s): $5,000
Max Size of Investment Considered (000s): $25,000

Additional Information
Year Founded: 2011
Current Activity Level : Actively seeking new investments

MARKER HILL CAPITAL LLC

1500 Wynkoop Street
Suite 200
Denver, CO USA 80202
Phone: 3037565600
Website: www.markerhillcapital.com

Management and Staff
Robert Cyman, Managing Director
Suzanne Fanch, Managing Director
Tom Juracek, Managing Director

Type of Firm
Private Equity Firm

Project Preferences

Type of Financing Preferred:
Expansion
Balanced
Later Stage

Industry Preferences

In Communications prefer:
Communications and Media

In Medical/Health prefer:
Hospitals/Clinics/Primary

In Industrial/Energy prefer:
Energy

In Financial Services prefer:
Real Estate

Additional Information
Year Founded: 2011
Current Activity Level : Actively seeking new investments

MARKET SQUARE EQUITY PARTNERS

87 Front St. E., Suite 400
Toronto, Canada M5E 1B8
Phone: 4163650060
Website: marketsquarepartners.ca

Management and Staff
Derrick Ho, Managing Partner
Matthew Hall, Managing Partner
Philip Reddon, Partner
Scott Clark, Partner

Type of Firm
Private Equity Firm

Association Membership
Canadian Venture Capital Association

Project Preferences

Type of Financing Preferred:
Leveraged Buyout
Balanced
Acquisition

Geographical Preferences

Canadian Preferences:
All Canada

Industry Preferences

In Business Serv. prefer:
Services

Additional Information
Year Founded: 2014
Current Activity Level : Actively seeking new investments

MARLIN EQUITY PARTNERS LLC

338 Pier Avenue
Hermosa Beach, CA USA 90254
Phone: 3103640100
Fax: 3103640110
E-mail: info@marlinequity.com
Website: www.marlinequity.com

Other Offices
85 Buckingham Gate
3rd Floor
London, United Kingdom SW1E 6PD
Phone: 442036680020

Management and Staff
David McGovern, Managing Partner
George Kase, Partner
Jerry Katz, Chief Operating Officer
Nick Kaiser, Partner
Peter Spasov, Partner
Steve Johnson, Principal

Type of Firm
Private Equity Firm

Project Preferences

Role in Financing:
Prefer role as deal originator but will also invest in deals created by others

Type of Financing Preferred:
Leveraged Buyout
Control-block Purchases
Public Companies
Turnaround
Management Buyouts
Acquisition
Private Placement
Industry Rollups
Special Situation
Distressed Debt
Recapitalizations

Geographical Preferences

United States Preferences:

Canadian Preferences:
All Canada

International Preferences:
Latin America
United Kingdom
Europe
Mexico
Australia
Germany
France

Industry Preferences

In Communications prefer:
Telecommunications
Data Communications

In Computer Hardware prefer:
Computers

In Computer Software prefer:
Software

In Internet Specific prefer:
Internet
Ecommerce

In Medical/Health prefer:
Medical/Health
Medical Therapeutics

In Consumer Related prefer:
Consumer
Entertainment and Leisure
Food/Beverage
Consumer Products
Consumer Services
Education Related

In Industrial/Energy prefer:
Industrial Products
Materials

In Transportation prefer:
Aerospace

In Financial Services prefer:
Financial Services

In Business Serv. prefer:
Services
Distribution
Media

In Manufact. prefer:
Manufacturing

Additional Information
Name of Most Recent Fund: Marlin Heritage, L.P.
Most Recent Fund Was Raised: 04/01/2014
Year Founded: 2005
Capital Under Management: $3,000,000,000
Current Activity Level : Actively seeking new investments

MAROC NUMERIC FUND SAS

Route De Nouaceur
Casablanca Technopark
Casablanca, Morocco 20153
Phone: 212522503033
Fax: 212522503034
E-mail: contact@mitccapital.ma
Website: www.mnf.ma

Type of Firm
Bank Affiliated

Project Preferences

Type of Financing Preferred:
Early Stage
Expansion
Startup

Size of Investments Considered:
Min Size of Investment Considered (000s): $119
Max Size of Investment Considered (000s): $950

Geographical Preferences

International Preferences:
Morocco
Africa

Industry Preferences

In Industrial/Energy prefer:
Environmental Related

In Other prefer:
Environment Responsible

Additional Information
Year Founded: 2010
Capital Under Management: $100,000,000
Current Activity Level : Actively seeking new investments

MAROCINVEST FINANCE GROUP

Rsidence les Champs d'Anfa D
Rue Bab Chellah, quartier Raci
Casablanca, Morocco 20000
Phone: 212-522-363-736
Fax: 212-522-393-959
E-mail: mig@marocinvest.com
Website: www.marocinvest.com

Type of Firm
Private Equity Firm

Association Membership
French Venture Capital Association (AFIC)

Project Preferences

Type of Financing Preferred:
Leveraged Buyout
Early Stage
Expansion
Generalist PE
Balanced
Later Stage
Acquisition
Startup

Size of Investments Considered:
Min Size of Investment Considered (000s): $800
Max Size of Investment Considered (000s): $3,300

Geographical Preferences

International Preferences:
Tunisia
Algeria
Morocco
Asia

Industry Preferences

In Communications prefer:
Communications and Media
Telecommunications

In Computer Software prefer:
Software

In Computer Other prefer:
Computer Related

In Biotechnology prefer:
Biotechnology

In Medical/Health prefer:
Medical/Health

In Consumer Related prefer:
Consumer

In Industrial/Energy prefer:
Industrial Products

In Financial Services prefer:
Financial Services

In Manufact. prefer:
Manufacturing

In Agr/Forestr/Fish prefer:
Agriculture related

Additional Information
Year Founded: 2000
Capital Under Management: $23,000,000
Current Activity Level : Actively seeking new investments

MARQUAM HILL CAPITAL LLC

20000 NorthWest Walker Road
Wilson Clark Center, Suite 450
Beaverton, OR USA 97006
Phone: 503-213-3152

Management and Staff
John Hull, Managing Director

Type of Firm
Private Equity Firm

Project Preferences

Type of Financing Preferred:
Early Stage
Startup

Industry Preferences

In Medical/Health prefer:
Medical Diagnostics

Additional Information
Year Founded: 2009
Capital Under Management: $5,000,000
Current Activity Level : Actively seeking new investments

MARQUETTE CAPITAL PARTNERS INC

60 South Sixth Street
Suite 3900
Minneapolis, MN USA 55402
Phone: 6126613990
Fax: 6126613999
Website: www.marquettecapitalpartners.com

Other Offices
222 South Riverside Plaza
29th Floor
CHICAGO, IL USA 60606
Phone: 3122391339
Fax: 3122391304

Management and Staff
Andrea Grosz, Managing Director
David Shapiro, Vice President
Greg Dames, Managing Director
Maggie Yanez, Vice President
Steven Heinen, Managing Director

Type of Firm
Investment Management Firm

Association Membership
Natl Assoc of Small Bus. Inv. Co (NASBIC)

Project Preferences

Role in Financing:
Will function either as deal originator or investor in deals created by others

Type of Financing Preferred:
Leveraged Buyout
Expansion
Mezzanine
Management Buyouts
Acquisition
Recapitalizations

Size of Investments Considered:
Min Size of Investment Considered (000s): $2,000
Max Size of Investment Considered (000s): $10,000

Geographical Preferences

United States Preferences:

Industry Preferences

In Consumer Related prefer:
Consumer
Retail

In Industrial/Energy prefer:
Industrial Products

In Business Serv. prefer:
Services
Distribution

In Manufact. prefer:
Manufacturing

Additional Information
Name of Most Recent Fund: Marquette Capital Fund II, L.P.
Most Recent Fund Was Raised: 11/02/2010
Year Founded: 1997
Capital Under Management: $170,800,000
Current Activity Level: Actively seeking new investments

MARS DISCOVERY DISTRICT

101 College St., MaRS Centre
South Tower, Suite 100
Toronto, Canada M5G 1L7
Phone: 4166738100
Fax: 4166738181
E-mail: marsdiscoverydistrict@marsdd.com
Website: www.marsdd.com

Type of Firm
Private Equity Firm

Association Membership
Canadian Venture Capital Association

Project Preferences

Type of Financing Preferred:
Early Stage
Later Stage
Seed
Startup

Geographical Preferences

Canadian Preferences:
All Canada
Ontario

Industry Preferences

In Communications prefer:
Communications and Media
Wireless Communications
Entertainment

In Computer Software prefer:
Data Processing

In Medical/Health prefer:
Medical/Health
Medical Diagnostics
Medical Therapeutics
Medical Products

In Consumer Related prefer:
Consumer
Retail
Education Related

In Industrial/Energy prefer:
Energy
Advanced Materials
Environmental Related

In Transportation prefer:
Transportation

In Financial Services prefer:
Financial Services

In Business Serv. prefer:
Services
Distribution
Media

In Manufact. prefer:
Manufacturing

In Agr/Forestr/Fish prefer:
Agriculture related

In Other prefer:
Socially Responsible

Additional Information
Year Founded: 2005
Capital Under Management: $55,500,000
Current Activity Level: Actively seeking new investments

MARS INVESTMENT ACCELERATOR FUND INC

101 College Street
Suite 125
Toronto, Canada M5G 1L7
Phone: 6472551080
Website: www.marsiaf.com

Management and Staff
Barry Gekiere, Managing Director

Type of Firm
Private Equity Firm

Association Membership
Canadian Venture Capital Association

Project Preferences

Type of Financing Preferred:
Early Stage
Start-up Financing
Seed

Geographical Preferences

Canadian Preferences:
All Canada

Industry Preferences

In Medical/Health prefer:
Health Services

Additional Information
Name of Most Recent Fund: IAF Life Sciences Investment Fund
Most Recent Fund Was Raised: 09/30/2011
Year Founded: 2008
Capital Under Management: $23,000,000
Current Activity Level: Actively seeking new investments

MARSHALL VENTURES

321 Washignton Avenue
Owensboro, KY USA 42301
Phone: 2709933766
Website: marshallventures.com

Management and Staff
John Moore, Founder

Type of Firm
Private Equity Firm

Project Preferences

Type of Financing Preferred:
Early Stage

Industry Preferences

In Financial Services prefer:
Financial Services

Additional Information

Year Founded: 2015
Capital Under Management: $1,900,000
Current Activity Level : Actively seeking new investments

MARSMAN-DRYSDALE CORP

45th Flr. Philamlife Tower
8767 Paseo de Roxas Ave.
Makati City, Philippines 1231
Phone: 632-893-0000
Fax: 632-885-0574
E-mail: mdc@marsmandrysdale.com
Website: www.marsmandrysdale.com

Other Offices

177 Bovet Rd., Suite 600
San Mateo, CA USA 94402
Phone: 1650-341-6336
Fax: 1650-341-1329

Management and Staff

Eduardo Castillo, Vice President
George Drysdale, Chief Executive Officer
Roberto Sebastian, President

Type of Firm

Private Equity Firm

Project Preferences

Type of Financing Preferred:
Leveraged Buyout
Early Stage
Startup

Geographical Preferences

International Preferences:
Asia

Industry Preferences

In Communications prefer:
Telecommunications

In Medical/Health prefer:
Medical/Health

In Consumer Related prefer:
Entertainment and Leisure
Consumer Products
Consumer Services
Hotels and Resorts

In Business Serv. prefer:
Media

In Agr/Forestr/Fish prefer:
Agriculture related

Additional Information

Year Founded: 1920
Current Activity Level : Actively seeking new investments

MARTIN COMPANIES LLC

40 Burton Hills Boulevard
Suite 100
Nashville, TN USA 37215
Phone: 6158297300

Management and Staff

Leslie Wilkinson, Managing Director

Type of Firm

Private Equity Firm

Project Preferences

Type of Financing Preferred:
Early Stage
Balanced

Geographical Preferences

United States Preferences:

Industry Preferences

In Communications prefer:
Communications and Media

In Medical/Health prefer:
Medical/Health
Health Services

Additional Information

Year Founded: 2009
Current Activity Level : Actively seeking new investments

MARUBENI CORP

4-2, Ohtemachi 1-chome
Chiyoda-ku
Tokyo, Japan 100-8088
Phone: 81332822111
Website: www.marubeni.co.jp

Management and Staff

Nobuhiro Yabe, Chief Financial Officer

Type of Firm

Corporate PE/Venture

Project Preferences

Type of Financing Preferred:
Expansion
Later Stage

Geographical Preferences

International Preferences:
China
Japan

Industry Preferences

In Semiconductor/Electr prefer:
Electronics

In Medical/Health prefer:
Pharmaceuticals

In Industrial/Energy prefer:
Machinery

Additional Information

Year Founded: 1949
Current Activity Level : Actively seeking new investments

MARVIN TRAUB LLC

885, Third Avenue
Suite 2620
New York, NY USA 10022
Phone: 6467232900
Fax: 6467232972

Management and Staff

Calvin Chou, Vice President
Geoffrey Lurie, President & COO
Kelsey Groome, Managing Director
Mortimer Singer, Chief Executive Officer

Type of Firm

Investment Management Firm

Project Preferences

Type of Financing Preferred:
Leveraged Buyout
Early Stage
Expansion
Later Stage
Management Buyouts
Acquisition

Geographical Preferences

United States Preferences:

Additional Information

Year Founded: 2015
Current Activity Level : Actively seeking new investments

MARWIT CAPITAL CORP

100 Bayview Circle
Suite 550
Newport Beach, CA USA 92660
Phone: 9498613636
Fax: 9498613637
E-mail: info@marwit.com
Website: www.marwit.com

1353

Management and Staff
Carol Farrell, Vice President
Chris Britt, Managing Partner
David Browne, Partner
Matthew Witte, Managing Partner
Rob Wendell, Principal
Sam Sippl, Vice President
Thomas Dollhopf, Partner

Type of Firm
Private Equity Firm

Project Preferences

Role in Financing:
Prefer role as deal originator but will also invest in deals created by others

Type of Financing Preferred:
Leveraged Buyout
Expansion
Management Buyouts
Acquisition
Recapitalizations

Geographical Preferences

United States Preferences:
California
West Coast

Industry Preferences

In Medical/Health prefer:
Health Services

In Consumer Related prefer:
Entertainment and Leisure
Retail
Food/Beverage
Consumer Products
Consumer Services

In Industrial/Energy prefer:
Industrial Products
Environmental Related

In Business Serv. prefer:
Services
Distribution

In Manufact. prefer:
Manufacturing

Additional Information
Name of Most Recent Fund: Marwit Capital II
Most Recent Fund Was Raised: 09/21/2007
Year Founded: 1962
Capital Under Management: $200,000,000
Current Activity Level : Actively seeking new investments
Method of Compensation: Return on invest. most important, but chg. closing fees, service fees, etc.

MARWYN INVESTMENT MANAGEMENT LLP

11 Buckingham Street
London, United Kingdom WC2N 6DF
Phone: 44-20-7004-2700
Fax: 44-20-7004-2701
E-mail: enquiries@marwyn.com
Website: www.marwyn.com

Management and Staff
Benjamin Shaw, Partner
James Corsellis, Managing Partner
Mark Watts, Managing Partner

Type of Firm
Investment Management Firm

Project Preferences

Type of Financing Preferred:
Leveraged Buyout
Acquisition
Distressed Debt

Geographical Preferences

International Preferences:
Europe

Additional Information
Year Founded: 2002
Capital Under Management: $738,100,000
Current Activity Level : Actively seeking new investments

MARYLAND DEPARTMENT OF BUSINESS AND ECONOMIC DEVELOPMENT

401 East Pratt Street
Baltimore, MD USA 21202
Phone: 4107676300
Website: www.choosemaryland.org

Management and Staff
Frank Dickson, Principal
Ovetta Moore, Chief Operating Officer
Thomas Dann, Managing Director

Type of Firm
Government Affiliated Program

Project Preferences

Type of Financing Preferred:
Early Stage
Seed

Size of Investments Considered:
Min Size of Investment Considered (000s): $100
Max Size of Investment Considered (000s): $1,000

Geographical Preferences

United States Preferences:
Maryland

Industry Preferences

In Communications prefer:
Communications and Media

In Computer Software prefer:
Software

In Medical/Health prefer:
Medical Diagnostics
Medical Therapeutics

Additional Information
Year Founded: 1994
Capital Under Management: $60,000,000
Current Activity Level : Actively seeking new investments
Method of Compensation: Return on investment is of primary concern, do not charge fees

MARYLAND TECHNOLOGY DEVELOPMENT CORP

5565 Sterrett Place
Suite 214
Columbia, MD USA 21044
Phone: 4107409442
Fax: 4107409422
E-mail: info@tedco.md
Website: tedco.md

Management and Staff
Andy Jones, Managing Director
John Wasilisin, President & COO

Type of Firm
Government Affiliated Program

Association Membership
Mid-Atlantic Venture Association

Project Preferences

Role in Financing:
Prefer role as deal originator

Type of Financing Preferred:
Early Stage
Expansion
Seed

Size of Investments Considered:
Min Size of Investment Considered (000s): $50
Max Size of Investment Considered (000s): $150

Geographical Preferences

United States Preferences:
Maryland
Virginia

Industry Preferences

In Computer Software prefer:
Computer Services

In Internet Specific prefer:
Internet

In Medical/Health prefer:
Medical/Health

In Consumer Related prefer:
Retail
Franchises(NEC)

In Industrial/Energy prefer:
Energy

In Transportation prefer:
Transportation

In Business Serv. prefer:
Services

In Manufact. prefer:
Manufacturing

Additional Information
Year Founded: 1998
Capital Under Management: $2,900,000
Current Activity Level : Actively seeking new investments
Method of Compensation: Return on investment is of primary concern, do not charge fees

---

MASDAR CAPITAL

Khalifa A City
Abu Dhabi, Utd. Arab Em.
Phone: 97126533333
Fax: 97126536002
E-mail: info@masdar.ae

Type of Firm
Investment Management Firm

Project Preferences

Type of Financing Preferred:
Balanced
Later Stage

Geographical Preferences

International Preferences:
All International

Industry Preferences

In Industrial/Energy prefer:
Alternative Energy
Energy Conservation Relat
Advanced Materials
Environmental Related

In Other prefer:
Environment Responsible

Additional Information
Name of Most Recent Fund: DB Masdar Clean Tech Fund
Most Recent Fund Was Raised: 01/18/2010
Year Founded: 2006
Capital Under Management: $290,000,000
Current Activity Level : Actively seeking new investments

MASI LTD

800 Hart Road
Suite 120
Barrington, IL USA 60010
Phone: 8479487300
Fax: 8473044480
E-mail: masi@masiltd.com
Website: www.masiltd.com

Management and Staff
Art Lyman, Managing Director
James Yuan, Managing Director
R. Charles McLravy, Managing Director

Type of Firm
Bank Affiliated

Project Preferences

Role in Financing:
Prefer role as deal originator

Type of Financing Preferred:
Leveraged Buyout
Expansion
Mezzanine
Generalist PE
Later Stage
Management Buyouts
Acquisition
Joint Ventures
Private Placement
Recapitalizations

Geographical Preferences

United States Preferences:

Canadian Preferences:
All Canada

Additional Information
Year Founded: 1984
Current Activity Level : Actively seeking new investments

MASON WELLS INC

411 East Wisconsin Avenue
Suite 1280
Milwaukee, WI USA 53202
Phone: 4147276400
Fax: 4147276410
Website: www.masonwells.com

Management and Staff
Christopher Pummill, Vice President
Greg Myers, Senior Managing Director
Jim Domach, Chief Financial Officer
Kevin Kenealey, Senior Managing Director
Thomas Smith, Managing Director

Type of Firm
Private Equity Firm

Project Preferences

Role in Financing:
Prefer role as deal originator

Type of Financing Preferred:
Leveraged Buyout
Management Buyouts
Acquisition
Recapitalizations

Geographical Preferences

United States Preferences:
Midwest

Industry Focus
(% based on actual investment)
Communications and Media	28.0%
Computer Hardware	23.0%
Other Products	16.1%
Biotechnology	13.8%
Industrial/Energy	6.7%
Medical/Health	6.2%
Computer Software and Services	5.6%
Consumer Related	0.6%

Additional Information
Name of Most Recent Fund: Mason Wells Buyout Fund II, L.P.
Most Recent Fund Was Raised: 10/07/2004
Year Founded: 1982
Capital Under Management: $500,000,000
Current Activity Level : Actively seeking new investments
Method of Compensation: Return on invest. most important, but chg. closing fees, service fees, etc.

MASS VENTURES

40 Broad Street
Suite 230
Boston, MA USA 02109
Phone: 6177234920
Fax: 6177235983
Website: mass-ventures.com

Other Offices
148 State Street
Boston, MA USA 02109
Phone: 617-723-4920

Management and Staff
Nicholas Pappas, Vice President
Walter Bird, President

Type of Firm
Incubator/Development Program

Association Membership
New England Venture Capital Association

Project Preferences

Role in Financing:
Prefer role as deal originator but will also invest in deals created by others

Type of Financing Preferred:
Early Stage
Balanced
Later Stage

Size of Investments Considered:
Min Size of Investment Considered (000s): $250
Max Size of Investment Considered (000s): $750

Geographical Preferences

United States Preferences:
Massachusetts

Industry Focus

(% based on actual investment)
Computer Software and Services	38.1%
Internet Specific	24.3%
Industrial/Energy	9.6%
Semiconductors/Other Elect.	9.4%
Medical/Health	6.6%
Computer Hardware	5.5%
Communications and Media	3.6%
Biotechnology	2.2%
Other Products	0.5%
Consumer Related	0.2%

Additional Information
Name of Most Recent Fund: Commonwealth Fund Investment Program II
Most Recent Fund Was Raised: 08/01/2000
Year Founded: 1978
Capital Under Management: $18,000,000
Current Activity Level : Actively seeking new investments
Method of Compensation: Return on invest. most important, but chg. closing fees, service fees, etc.

MASSACHUSETTS CAPITAL RESOURCE

420 Boylston Street
Fifth Floor
Boston, MA USA 02116
Phone: 6175363900
Website: www.masscapital.com

Management and Staff
Daniel Corcoran, Vice President
Paul Bolger, President
Richard Anderson, President
Suzanne Dwyer, Vice President

Type of Firm
Private Equity Firm

Project Preferences

Role in Financing:
Prefer role as deal originator but will also invest in deals created by others

Type of Financing Preferred:
Expansion
Mezzanine
Acquisition
Recapitalizations

Geographical Preferences

United States Preferences:
Massachusetts

Industry Focus

(% based on actual investment)
Industrial/Energy	23.0%
Semiconductors/Other Elect.	16.6%
Other Products	16.5%
Computer Software and Services	12.3%
Communications and Media	10.2%
Computer Hardware	8.3%
Consumer Related	7.6%
Medical/Health	2.9%
Internet Specific	2.3%
Biotechnology	0.2%

Additional Information
Year Founded: 1977
Capital Under Management: $100,000,000
Current Activity Level : Actively seeking new investments
Method of Compensation: Return on investment is of primary concern, do not charge fees

MASSACHUSETTS CLEAN ENERGY CENTER

55 Summer Street
9th Floor
Boston, MA USA 02110
Phone: 6173159355
Fax: 6173159356
E-mail: info@masscec.com
Website: www.masscec.com

Management and Staff
Alicia Barton, Chief Executive Officer

Type of Firm
Private Equity Firm

Project Preferences

Type of Financing Preferred:
Early Stage
Seed
Startup

Geographical Preferences

United States Preferences:
Massachusetts

Industry Preferences

In Industrial/Energy prefer:
Alternative Energy
Environmental Related

Additional Information
Year Founded: 2009
Current Activity Level : Actively seeking new investments

MASSACHUSETTS MUTUAL LIFE INSURANCE CO

1295 State Street
Springfield, MA USA 01111
Phone: 4137448411
Website: www.massmutual.com

Management and Staff
Susan Cicco, Vice President

Type of Firm
Insurance Firm Affiliate

Project Preferences

Size of Investments Considered:
Min Size of Investment Considered (000s): $10,000
Max Size of Investment Considered (000s): $30,000

Industry Focus

(% based on actual investment)
Other Products	52.9%
Industrial/Energy	26.2%
Consumer Related	12.3%
Internet Specific	6.0%
Medical/Health	2.0%
Communications and Media	0.6%

Additional Information
Year Founded: 1851
Current Activity Level : Actively seeking new investments

MASSENA PARTNERS SA

78 Avenue Raymond Poincare
Paris, France 75116
Phone: 33153706390
Fax: 33144050707
E-mail: e-contact@massena.fr
Website: www.massenapartners.com

Other Offices
5, rue Jacques Balmat
Geneva, Switzerland 1204
Phone: 41228394400
Fax: 41228394418

12 rue Guillaume Schneider
Luxembourg, Luxembourg 2522

Management and Staff
Claude Lutz, Chief Operating Officer
Didier Choix, Chief Executive Officer
Olivia Bernard, Chief Financial Officer
Romain Lobstein, Managing Director

Type of Firm
Private Equity Firm

Association Membership
French Venture Capital Association (AFIC)

Project Preferences

Role in Financing:
Prefer role as deal originator but will also invest in deals created by others

Type of Financing Preferred:
Leveraged Buyout
Mezzanine
Generalist PE
Later Stage

Geographical Preferences

International Preferences:
Europe
Switzerland
France

Industry Preferences

In Agr/Forestr/Fish prefer:
Agriculture related

Additional Information
Year Founded: 1990
Current Activity Level : Actively seeking new investments
Method of Compensation: Return on invest. most important, but chg. closing fees, service fees, etc.

MASSMUTUAL VENTURES LLC

470 Atlantic Avenue
Boston, MA USA 02132
Phone: 6178973500
Website: www.massmutual.com

Management and Staff
Douglas Russell, Managing Director
Eric Emmons, Managing Director
Mark Goodman, Managing Director

Type of Firm
Insurance Firm Affiliate

Project Preferences

Type of Financing Preferred:
Seed
Startup

Industry Preferences

In Computer Software prefer:
Computer Services
Applications Software

In Internet Specific prefer:
Web Aggregration/Portals

In Semiconductor/Electr prefer:
Analytic/Scientific

In Medical/Health prefer:
Health Services

In Financial Services prefer:
Financial Services

Additional Information
Year Founded: 2014
Capital Under Management: $200,000,000
Current Activity Level : Actively seeking new investments

MASTHEAD VENTURE PARTNERS

55 Cambridge Parkway
Suite 103
Cambridge, MA USA 02142
Phone: 6176213000
Fax: 6176213055
E-mail: info@mvpartners.com

Other Offices
111 Commercial Street
Suite 302
PORTLAND, ME USA 04101
Phone: 2077800905

Management and Staff
Braden Bohrmann, General Partner
Brian Owen, General Partner
Daniel Flatley, General Partner
Mary Shannon, Principal
Richard Levandov, General Partner
Stephen Smith, General Partner
Timothy Agnew, Principal

Type of Firm
Private Equity Firm

Project Preferences

Role in Financing:
Prefer role as deal originator but will also invest in deals created by others

Type of Financing Preferred:
Early Stage
Balanced
Seed
Startup

Size of Investments Considered:
Min Size of Investment Considered (000s): $1,000
Max Size of Investment Considered (000s): $8,000

Geographical Preferences

United States Preferences:
Northeast

Industry Preferences

In Communications prefer:
Communications and Media
Wireless Communications

In Computer Software prefer:
Software
Applications Software

In Internet Specific prefer:
Internet

In Medical/Health prefer:
Medical/Health

Additional Information
Year Founded: 1997
Capital Under Management: $200,000,000
Current Activity Level : Actively seeking new investments

MATADOR CAPITAL PARTNERS LLC

8750 North Central Expressway
Suite 750
Dallas, TX USA 75231
Phone: 2143695700
Fax: 2147220924
Website: www.matadorcapital.com

Management and Staff
Wicky el-Effendi, Managing Partner

Type of Firm
Private Equity Firm

Project Preferences

Type of Financing Preferred:
Leveraged Buyout
Acquisition

Geographical Preferences

United States Preferences:
All U.S.

Industry Preferences

In Consumer Related prefer:
Consumer

In Industrial/Energy prefer:
Energy

In Financial Services prefer:
Real Estate

In Business Serv. prefer:
Distribution

In Manufact. prefer:
Manufacturing

In Agr/Forestr/Fish prefer:
Agriculture related

Additional Information
Year Founded: 2016
Current Activity Level : Actively seeking new investments

MATADOR PRIVATE EQUITY AG

Untere Feldstrasse 2
Alpnach, Switzerland 6055
Phone: 41416621062
Fax: 41416610862
E-mail: office@matador-private-equity.com
Website: www.matador-private-equity.com

Type of Firm
Private Equity Firm

Project Preferences

Type of Financing Preferred:
Fund of Funds

Geographical Preferences

Canadian Preferences:
All Canada

International Preferences:
Europe
Eastern Europe
Asia

Industry Preferences

In Computer Software prefer:
Software

In Industrial/Energy prefer:
Energy
Alternative Energy

Additional Information
Year Founded: 2005
Current Activity Level : Actively seeking new investments

MATCHSTICK VENTURES

564 Saratoga Street South
Saint Paul, MN USA 55106
Website: www.matchstickventures.com

Type of Firm
Private Equity Firm

Project Preferences

Type of Financing Preferred:
Seed
Startup

Size of Investments Considered:
Min Size of Investment Considered (000s): $25
Max Size of Investment Considered (000s): $75

Geographical Preferences

United States Preferences:
Midwest

Additional Information
Year Founded: 2013
Current Activity Level : Actively seeking new investments

MATCORP HOLDING BV

Polarisavenue 136
Hoofddorp, Netherlands 2132 JX
Phone: 31235553033
Fax: 31235636079
Website: www.matcorp.nl

Management and Staff
Duncan Rooders, Chief Operating Officer

Type of Firm
Private Equity Firm

Project Preferences

Type of Financing Preferred:
Leveraged Buyout
Early Stage
Expansion
Later Stage
Seed
Acquisition

Geographical Preferences

International Preferences:
Europe

Industry Preferences

In Computer Software prefer:
Software

In Manufact. prefer:
Manufacturing

Additional Information
Year Founded: 1984
Current Activity Level : Actively seeking new investments

MATERIAL IMPACT FUND I LP

950 Winter Street
Suite 4600
Waltham, MA USA 02451
Phone: 7812900004

Type of Firm
Private Equity Firm

Additional Information
Year Founded: 2016
Current Activity Level : Actively seeking new investments

MATH VENTURE PARTNERS LP

222 W Merchandise Mart Plaza
Suite 1212
Chicago, IL USA 60654
Phone: 3124044555

Management and Staff
Mark Achler, Co-Founder
Troy Henikoff, Co-Founder

Type of Firm
Private Equity Firm

Project Preferences

Type of Financing Preferred:
Early Stage
Seed
Startup

Additional Information
Year Founded: 1969
Capital Under Management: $27,825,000
Current Activity Level : Actively seeking new investments

MATHCAPITAL MANAGEMENT LP

Four Trade Center
45th Floor
New York, NY USA 10007
Phone: 6468404200
E-mail: info@mathcapital.ventures

Type of Firm
Private Equity Advisor or Fund of Funds

Project Preferences

Type of Financing Preferred:
Early Stage

Industry Preferences

In Business Serv. prefer:
Media

Additional Information
Year Founded: 2017
Current Activity Level : Actively seeking new investments

MATHEMATICA CAPITAL MANAGEMENT LLC

Gate Five Road
75
Sausalito, CA USA 94965
Phone: 4153324051
Fax: 4153324052
E-mail: staff@mathcapm.com
Website: mathcapm.com

Type of Firm
Private Equity Firm

Geographical Preferences
United States Preferences:

Industry Preferences
In Financial Services prefer:
Financial Services

Additional Information
Year Founded: 2002
Capital Under Management: $1,500,000
Current Activity Level : Actively seeking new investments

MATIGNON INVESTISSE-MENT ET GESTION SAS

1 Rue De La Faisanderie
Paris, France 75116
Phone: 33153530123
Fax: 33145611633
E-mail: mig@matignon-gestion.fr
Website: www.matinvest.com

Type of Firm
Private Equity Firm

Association Membership
French Venture Capital Association (AFIC)

Project Preferences
Type of Financing Preferred:
Leveraged Buyout
Early Stage
Later Stage
Management Buyouts

Size of Investments Considered:
Min Size of Investment Considered (000s): $2,652
Max Size of Investment Considered (000s): $26,522

Geographical Preferences
International Preferences:
Europe
France

Industry Preferences
In Internet Specific prefer:
Internet
Ecommerce

In Financial Services prefer:
Financial Services

Additional Information
Year Founded: 1996
Current Activity Level : Actively seeking new investments

MATRIX PARTNERS, L.P.

260 Homer Avenue
Suite 201
Palo Alto, CA USA 94301
Phone: 6507981600
Fax: 6507981601
E-mail: info@matrixpartners.com
Website: www.matrixpartners.com

Other Offices
260 Homer Avenue
Suite 201
Palo Alto, CA USA 94301
Phone: 650-798-1600
Fax: 650-798-1601

Two Park Avenue
Fourth Floor
New York, NY USA 10016
Phone: 646-524-9292

No. 33 Huayuan Shiqiao Road
Suite 1001, Citigroup Tower
Shanghai, China 200120
Phone: 862161620600
Fax: 862161620660

Ceejay House #306
Annie Besant Road, Worli
Mumbai, India 400 018
Phone: 91-22-6768-0000
Fax: 91-22-6768-0001

101 Main Street
17th Floor
Cambridge, MA USA 02142
Phone: 7818902244
Fax: 7818902288

No.19A, East 3rd Ring Rd North
Suite 2901, Nexus Center
Beijing, China 100020
Phone: 861065000088
Fax: 861065000066

Management and Staff
Andrew Verhalen, General Partner
Antonio Rodriguez, General Partner
Dana Stalder, General Partner
David Skok, General Partner
Jared Fliesler, General Partner
Josh Hannah, General Partner
Paul Ferri, Founder
Paul Sherer, Venture Partner
Phyllis Doherty, Partner
Stan Reiss, General Partner
Timothy Barrows, General Partner

Type of Firm
Private Equity Firm

Association Membership
New England Venture Capital Association
Western Association of Venture Capitalists (WAVC)
National Venture Capital Association - USA (NVCA)
Indian Venture Capital Association (IVCA)

Project Preferences
Role in Financing:
Prefer role as deal originator but will also invest in deals created by others

Type of Financing Preferred:
Early Stage
Expansion
Balanced
Later Stage
Seed

Size of Investments Considered:
Min Size of Investment Considered (000s): $2,000
Max Size of Investment Considered (000s): $10,000

Geographical Preferences
United States Preferences:
Northeast
Massachusetts
California

International Preferences:
India
China

Industry Focus
(% based on actual investment)
Internet Specific	37.5%
Computer Software and Services	27.2%
Consumer Related	14.1%
Communications and Media	8.5%
Computer Hardware	4.4%
Semiconductors/Other Elect.	2.6%
Other Products	2.5%
Medical/Health	2.2%
Industrial/Energy	1.0%
Biotechnology	0.0%

Additional Information
Name of Most Recent Fund: Matrix Partners X, L.P.
Most Recent Fund Was Raised: 05/08/2013
Year Founded: 1977
Capital Under Management: $600,000,000
Current Activity Level : Actively seeking new investments
Method of Compensation: Return on investment is of primary concern, do not charge fees

Pratt's Guide to Private Equity & Venture Capital Sources

MATTER VENTURES

421 Bryant Street
San Francisco, CA USA 94107
E-mail: info@matter.vc
Website: matter.vc

Type of Firm
Incubator/Development Program

Project Preferences

Type of Financing Preferred:
Early Stage
Seed
Startup

Geographical Preferences

United States Preferences:
California

Industry Preferences

In Business Serv. prefer:
Media

Additional Information
Year Founded: 2012
Capital Under Management: $9,490,000
Current Activity Level : Actively seeking new investments

MATTHEW PRITZKER COMPANY LLC

233 South Wacker Drive
96th Floor
Chicago, IL USA 60606
Phone: 3125648800
E-mail: info@matthewpritzkercompany.com
Website: www.matthewpritzkercompany.com

Management and Staff
Don Johnson, Principal
Mio Stojkovich, Principal
Steve Strong, Principal

Type of Firm
Investment Management Firm

Project Preferences

Type of Financing Preferred:
Leveraged Buyout
Value-Add
Expansion
Mezzanine
Generalist PE
Acquisition
Recapitalizations

Geographical Preferences

United States Preferences:
All U.S.

Industry Preferences

In Financial Services prefer:
Real Estate

Additional Information
Year Founded: 2008
Current Activity Level : Actively seeking new investments

MAUI CAPITAL LTD

151 Queen Street
Level 25, IAG House
Auckland, New Zealand 1140
Phone: 6493779377
Fax: 6493779379
E-mail: info@mauicapital.co.nz
Website: www.mauicapital.co.nz

Management and Staff
John Sandford, Chief Operating Officer
Paul Chrystall, Managing Director

Type of Firm
Private Equity Firm

Association Membership
New Zealand Venture Capital Association

Project Preferences

Type of Financing Preferred:
Leveraged Buyout
Turnaround
Management Buyouts
Acquisition
Recapitalizations

Geographical Preferences

International Preferences:
Australia
New Zealand

Additional Information
Name of Most Recent Fund: Maui Capital Aqua Fund
Most Recent Fund Was Raised: 06/08/2012
Year Founded: 2008
Capital Under Management: $444,734,000
Current Activity Level : Actively seeking new investments

MAVEN CAPITAL PARTNERS UK LLP

205 West George Street
Kintyre House
Glasgow, United Kingdom G2 2LW
Phone: 01413067400
E-mail: enquiries@mavencp.com
Website: www.mavencp.com

Other Offices
9-13 St. Andrew Street
Fifth Floor
London, United Kingdom EC4A 3AF
Phone: 442031022750

Former HQ: 149 St. Vincent Street
Sutherland House
Glasgow, United Kingdom G2 5NW

5 John Dalton Street
Queens Chambers
Manchester, United Kingdom M2 6ET
Phone: 44-161-233-3500

Baskerville House
Centenary Square
Birmingham, United Kingdom B1 2ND
Phone: 44-121-503-2250

2 Walker Street
Edinburgh
Scotland, United Kingdom EH3 7LB
Phone: 44-131-306-2201

8 Albyn Terrace
Aberdeen, United Kingdom AB10 1YP
Phone: 44-1224-517-120

Management and Staff
Andrew Craig, Partner
Andrew Ferguson, Partner
Bill Kennedy, Partner
Jock Gardiner, Partner
Ramsay Duff, Partner
Stella Panu, Partner
William Nixon, Managing Partner

Type of Firm
Bank Affiliated

Association Membership
British Venture Capital Association (BVCA)

Project Preferences

Type of Financing Preferred:
Leveraged Buyout
Expansion
Mezzanine
Generalist PE
Balanced
Later Stage
Other
Seed
Management Buyouts
Acquisition

Geographical Preferences

International Preferences:
United Kingdom
Europe

Industry Preferences

In Communications prefer:
Telecommunications

In Computer Software prefer:
Software

In Medical/Health prefer:
Medical/Health

In Consumer Related prefer:
Entertainment and Leisure
Food/Beverage
Education Related

In Industrial/Energy prefer:
Energy
Advanced Materials

In Financial Services prefer:
Financial Services

In Business Serv. prefer:
Services

In Manufact. prefer:
Manufacturing

Additional Information

Name of Most Recent Fund: Scottish Loan Fund
Most Recent Fund Was Raised: 07/31/2012
Year Founded: 2009
Capital Under Management: $264,700,000
Current Activity Level : Actively seeking new investments

MAVEN VENTURE PARTNERS

155 Constitution Drive
Menlo Park, CA USA 94025
Phone: 6503245175
Website: www.mavenventurepartners.com

Management and Staff

George Richard, Managing Director
Jennifer Gill-Roberts, Managing Director
Laura Gwosden, Chief Financial Officer

Type of Firm

Private Equity Firm

Additional Information

Year Founded: 2005
Current Activity Level : Actively seeking new investments

MAVEN VENTURES GROWTH LABS

26400 Aric Lane
Los Altos, CA USA 94022
Phone: 6502182244
Website: www.mavenventures.com

Type of Firm

Incubator/Development Program

Association Membership

National Venture Capital Association - USA (NVCA)

Project Preferences

Type of Financing Preferred:
Early Stage
Seed
Startup

Industry Preferences

In Communications prefer:
Wireless Communications

In Consumer Related prefer:
Consumer

Additional Information

Year Founded: 2013
Capital Under Management: $7,000,000
Current Activity Level : Actively seeking new investments

MAVENHILL CAPITAL

100 North Main Street
Suite 430
Chagrin Falls, OH USA 44022
Phone: 4404906170
Website: mavenhillcapital.com

Management and Staff

Alex Trouten, Principal
Jay Studdard, Managing Partner
Nathan Schuster, Principal
Rhodes McKee, Managing Partner

Type of Firm

Private Equity Firm

Project Preferences

Type of Financing Preferred:
Leveraged Buyout
Acquisition
Recapitalizations

Industry Preferences

In Medical/Health prefer:
Health Services

In Industrial/Energy prefer:
Industrial Products

Additional Information

Year Founded: 2017
Current Activity Level : Actively seeking new investments

MAVERICK CAPITAL LTD

300 Crescent Court
Suite 1850
Dallas, TX USA 75201
Phone: 2148804081
Website: www.maverickcap.com

Other Offices

767 Fifth Avenue
11th Floor
New York, NY USA 10153
Phone: 212-418-6900
Fax: 212-752-5713

Management and Staff

Bill Goodell, Chief Operating Officer
David Singer, Partner
Evan Wyly, Managing Partner
Michael Moore, Managing Director

Type of Firm

Private Equity Firm

Geographical Preferences

United States Preferences:

Industry Focus

(% based on actual investment)

Medical/Health	39.4%
Internet Specific	18.3%
Computer Software and Services	17.5%
Biotechnology	16.0%
Industrial/Energy	3.0%
Semiconductors/Other Elect.	2.2%
Other Products	1.7%
Computer Hardware	1.6%
Consumer Related	0.2%

Additional Information

Year Founded: 1990
Capital Under Management: $775,000,000
Current Activity Level : Actively seeking new investments

MAVERICK CAPITAL VENTURES LLC

300 Crescent Ventures
Suite 1850
Dallas, TX USA 75201

Type of Firm

Private Equity Firm

Project Preferences

Type of Financing Preferred:
Early Stage

Industry Preferences

In Medical/Health prefer:
Health Services

Additional Information
Year Founded: 2018
Capital Under Management: $130,080,000
Current Activity Level: Actively seeking new investments

MAVERICK VENTURES ISRAEL LP

62 ROTHSCHILD BLVD
Tel Aviv, Israel 6578509
Phone: 97235342247

Management and Staff
Michelle Abadi, Co-Founder
Miguel Abadi, Co-Founder
Yaron Carni, Co-Founder

Type of Firm
Private Equity Firm

Project Preferences

Type of Financing Preferred:
Early Stage
Expansion
Balanced
Later Stage
Seed

Geographical Preferences

International Preferences:
Israel

Additional Information
Year Founded: 2013
Current Activity Level: Actively seeking new investments

MAVERIXLAB INC

177 Ocean Lane Drive
Suite 613
Key Biscayne, FL USA 33149
Phone: 7864490284
E-mail: jmorgan@maverixlab.com
Website: maverixlab.com

Type of Firm
Incubator/Development Program

Project Preferences

Type of Financing Preferred:
Seed
Startup

Geographical Preferences

United States Preferences:
Florida

Industry Preferences

In Computer Software prefer:
Software
Applications Software

In Internet Specific prefer:
Internet

In Business Serv. prefer:
Media

Additional Information
Year Founded: 2014
Current Activity Level: Actively seeking new investments

MAVERON LLC

411 First Avenue South
Suite 600
Seattle, WA USA 98104
Phone: 2062881700
Fax: 2062881777
E-mail: info@maveron.com

Other Offices
463 Pacific Avenue
San Francisco, CA USA 94133
Phone: 415-373-6250
Fax: 415-373-6255

Management and Staff
Amy Errett, Partner
Andrew Trader, Venture Partner
Ben Choi, Venture Partner
Clayton Lewis, Partner
Dan Levitan, Partner
David Wu, Venture Partner
Howard Schultz, Co-Founder
Jason Stoffer, Partner
Mark Menell, Venture Partner
Pete McCormick, Partner

Type of Firm
Private Equity Firm

Association Membership
National Venture Capital Association - USA (NVCA)

Project Preferences

Role in Financing:
Prefer role as deal originator but will also invest in deals created by others

Type of Financing Preferred:
Early Stage
Expansion
Balanced
Later Stage
Seed

Size of Investments Considered:
Min Size of Investment Considered (000s): $100
Max Size of Investment Considered (000s): $250

Geographical Preferences

United States Preferences:
Northwest

Industry Focus
(% based on actual investment)

Internet Specific	45.8%
Consumer Related	18.1%
Computer Software and Services	16.8%
Other Products	11.0%
Computer Hardware	5.1%
Communications and Media	1.1%
Medical/Health	0.9%
Industrial/Energy	0.7%
Semiconductors/Other Elect.	0.4%

Additional Information
Year Founded: 1998
Capital Under Management: $800,000,000
Current Activity Level: Actively seeking new investments
Method of Compensation: Return on investment is of primary concern, do not charge fees

MAVOR LANE LLC

2811 McKinney Avenue
Suite 230
Dallas, TX USA 75204
E-mail: info@mavorlane.com
Website: www.mavorlane.com

Type of Firm
Private Equity Firm

Project Preferences

Type of Financing Preferred:
Balanced

Geographical Preferences

United States Preferences:

Additional Information
Year Founded: 2010
Current Activity Level: Actively seeking new investments

MAX 21 AG

Robert-Koch-Strasse 9
Weiterstadt, Germany 64331
Phone: 49615190670
Fax: 4961519067299
E-mail: info@max21.de
Website: www.max21.de

Type of Firm
Private Equity Firm

Project Preferences

Type of Financing Preferred:
Leveraged Buyout
Early Stage
Expansion
Later Stage
Management Buyouts
Acquisition
Startup

Geographical Preferences

International Preferences:
Germany

Industry Preferences

In Communications prefer:
Telecommunications

In Computer Software prefer:
Software

In Business Serv. prefer:
Services

Additional Information
Year Founded: 2005
Current Activity Level : Actively seeking new investments

MAXBURG CAPITAL PARTNERS

Promenadeplatz 8
Munich, Germany 80333
Phone: 4989235135950
Fax: 4989235135979
E-mail: info@maxburg.com
Website: maxburg.com

Management and Staff
Florian Seubert, Partner
Hans Liebler, Partner
Moritz Greve, Partner

Type of Firm
Investment Management Firm

Project Preferences

Type of Financing Preferred:
Leveraged Buyout
Mezzanine
Management Buyouts
Acquisition

Geographical Preferences

International Preferences:
Switzerland
Austria
Germany

Industry Preferences

In Communications prefer:
Communications and Media
Telecommunications

In Medical/Health prefer:
Health Services

In Consumer Related prefer:
Retail
Food/Beverage

In Manufact. prefer:
Manufacturing

Additional Information
Year Founded: 2013
Current Activity Level : Actively seeking new investments

MAXIM MERCHANT CAPITAL

405 Lexington Avenue
New York, NY USA 10174
Phone: 7240761
Fax: 8953500
Website: www.maximgrp.com

Type of Firm
Private Equity Firm

Project Preferences

Type of Financing Preferred:
Early Stage
Balanced
Later Stage

Industry Preferences

In Biotechnology prefer:
Biotechnology

Additional Information
Year Founded: 2009
Current Activity Level : Actively seeking new investments

MAXIM PARTNERS LLC

105 East 1st Street
Suite 203
Hinsdale, IL USA 60521
Phone: 6302064040
Website: maximpartnersllc.com

Management and Staff
Gregory Wilson, Founder
Michael Diep, Vice President
Ryan Franco, Partner

Type of Firm
Private Equity Firm

Project Preferences

Type of Financing Preferred:
Leveraged Buyout
Acquisition

Geographical Preferences

United States Preferences:

Industry Preferences

In Consumer Related prefer:
Education Related

In Industrial/Energy prefer:
Energy

In Other prefer:
Environment Responsible

Additional Information
Year Founded: 1991
Current Activity Level : Actively seeking new investments

MAY RIVER CAPITAL LLC

191 North Wacker Drive
29th Floor
Chicago, IL USA 60606
Website: www.mayrivercapital.com

Management and Staff
Charles Grace, Partner
Daniel Barlow, Partner

Type of Firm
Private Equity Firm

Project Preferences

Type of Financing Preferred:
Leveraged Buyout
Acquisition

Additional Information
Year Founded: 2012
Capital Under Management: $165,000,000
Current Activity Level : Actively seeking new investments

MAYBAN-JAIC CAPITAL MANAGEMENT SDN BHD

20/F West Wing Menara Maybank
100 Jalan Tun Perak
Kuala Lumpur, Malaysia 50050
Phone: 603-202-2188
Fax: 603-201-2188

Type of Firm
Private Equity Firm

Project Preferences

Type of Financing Preferred:
Mezzanine
Later Stage

Geographical Preferences

International Preferences:
Vietnam
Indonesia
Thailand
Asia
Singapore
Malaysia

Industry Preferences

In Biotechnology prefer:
Biotechnology

In Consumer Related prefer:
Retail

In Transportation prefer:
Transportation

In Manufact. prefer:
Manufacturing

In Agr/Forestr/Fish prefer:
Agriculture related

Additional Information

Year Founded: 2006
Current Activity Level : Actively seeking new investments

MAYBANK VENTURE CAPITAL COMPANY SDN BHD

41st Floor, Menara Maybank
100 Jalan Tun Perak
Kuala Lumpur, Malaysia 50050
Website: www.mayban-ventures.com.my

Other Offices

41st Floor, Menara Maybank
100 Jalan Tun Perak
Kuala Lumpur, Malaysia 50050

Management and Staff

Terry Lim, Chief Executive Officer
Zaini Hj. Deni, Vice President

Type of Firm

Bank Affiliated

Association Membership

Malaysian Venture Capital Association

Project Preferences

Type of Financing Preferred:
Early Stage
Mezzanine
Balanced
Later Stage

Geographical Preferences

International Preferences:
Laos
Vietnam
Indonesia
Brunei
Thailand
Cambodia
Philippines
Singapore
Malaysia
Burma

Industry Preferences

In Consumer Related prefer:
Consumer
Consumer Products
Consumer Services

In Industrial/Energy prefer:
Alternative Energy
Environmental Related

In Manufact. prefer:
Manufacturing

Additional Information

Year Founded: 1993
Capital Under Management: $90,000,000
Current Activity Level : Actively seeking new investments

MAYFAIR EQUITY PARTNERS LLP

Eight Hanover Street
London, United Kingdom W1S 1YQ
Phone: 442037097215
E-mail: info@mayfairequity.com
Website: www.mayfairequity.com

Type of Firm

Private Equity Firm

Project Preferences

Type of Financing Preferred:
Leveraged Buyout
Acquisition

Geographical Preferences

International Preferences:
Ireland
United Kingdom

Industry Preferences

In Communications prefer:
Telecommunications
Media and Entertainment

In Consumer Related prefer:
Consumer
Consumer Products
Consumer Services

Additional Information

Year Founded: 2014
Capital Under Management: $520,680,000
Current Activity Level : Actively seeking new investments

MAYFIELD FUND

2484 Sand Hill Road
Quadrus Complex
Menlo Park, CA USA 94025
Phone: 6508545560
Fax: 6508545712
E-mail: info@mayfield.com
Website: www.mayfield.com

Other Offices

28 Cybercity
Ebene, Mauritius 742CU001
Phone: 6508545560

Management and Staff

James Beck, Chief Operating Officer
Kamini Ramani, Vice President
Navin Chaddha, Managing Director
Rajeev Batra, Partner
Robin Vasan, Managing Director
Timothy Chang, Managing Director
Ursheet Parikh, Partner
Vaneeta Varma, Chief Financial Officer

Type of Firm

Private Equity Firm

Association Membership

Western Association of Venture Capitalists (WAVC)
National Venture Capital Association - USA (NVCA)
Indian Venture Capital Association (IVCA)

Project Preferences

Role in Financing:
Prefer role as deal originator but will also invest in deals created by others

Type of Financing Preferred:
Early Stage
Startup

Geographical Preferences

United States Preferences:

International Preferences:
India
China

Industry Focus

(% based on actual investment)

Internet Specific	30.4%
Computer Software and Services	30.4%
Communications and Media	12.9%
Semiconductors/Other Elect.	8.6%
Computer Hardware	4.5%
Medical/Health	4.2%
Biotechnology	4.1%
Industrial/Energy	2.0%
Other Products	1.7%
Consumer Related	1.2%

Additional Information

Name of Most Recent Fund: Mayfield India II, Ltd.
Most Recent Fund Was Raised: 02/18/2014
Year Founded: 1969
Capital Under Management: $3,000,000,000
Current Activity Level : Actively seeking new investments
Method of Compensation: Return on investment is of primary concern, do not charge fees

MAYO MEDICAL VENTURES

200 First Avenue SouthWest
4F, Minnesota BioBusiness Ctr.
Rochester, MN USA 55905
Phone: 5072933900
Fax: 5072845410
E-mail: mayoclinicventures@mayo.edu
Website: www.mayo.edu

Management and Staff

Charles Mayo, Managing Director

Type of Firm

Corporate PE/Venture

Project Preferences

Role in Financing:
Will function either as deal originator or investor in deals created by others

Type of Financing Preferred:
Early Stage
Seed

Size of Investments Considered:
Min Size of Investment Considered (000s): $250
Max Size of Investment Considered (000s): $1,000

Geographical Preferences

United States Preferences:

Industry Focus

(% based on actual investment)

Medical/Health	72.8%
Computer Software and Services	14.9%
Biotechnology	12.3%

Additional Information

Year Founded: 1998
Capital Under Management: $25,000,000
Current Activity Level : Actively seeking new investments
Method of Compensation: Return on investment is of primary concern, do not charge fees

MAYWIC SELECT INVESTMENTS

312 Walnut Street
Suite 1151
Cincinnati, OH USA 45202
Phone: 5132411200
Fax: 5136511084
Website: www.maywic.com

Management and Staff

Chad Wick, General Partner
Frederic Mayerson, General Partner
Lawrence Horwitz, Managing Director

Type of Firm

Private Equity Firm

Project Preferences

Type of Financing Preferred:
Early Stage
Balanced

Geographical Preferences

International Preferences:
Israel

Industry Preferences

In Financial Services prefer:
Investment Groups
Financial Services

In Business Serv. prefer:
Consulting Services

Additional Information

Name of Most Recent Fund: MAYWIC Select Investments, L.P.
Most Recent Fund Was Raised: 07/23/2013
Year Founded: 2013
Capital Under Management: $5,000,000
Current Activity Level : Actively seeking new investments

MB RAHASTOT OY

Bulevardi One A
Helsinki, Finland 00100
Phone: 3589131011
Fax: 358913101310
Website: www.mbrahastot.fi

Management and Staff

Eero Niiva, Partner
Hannu Puhakka, Managing Partner
Juha Tukiainen, Partner
Kari Rytkonen, Partner
Marko Palmunen, Partner
Matti Mertsola, Partner
Mirja Sundstrom, Partner

Type of Firm

Private Equity Firm

Association Membership

Finnish Venture Capital Association (FVCA)

Project Preferences

Role in Financing:
Will function either as deal originator or investor in deals created by others

Type of Financing Preferred:
Leveraged Buyout

Size of Investments Considered:
Min Size of Investment Considered (000s): $2,858
Max Size of Investment Considered (000s): $71,439

Geographical Preferences

International Preferences:
Scandanavia/Nordic Region
Finland

Industry Focus

(% based on actual investment)

Industrial/Energy	46.3%
Other Products	35.2%
Consumer Related	9.9%
Medical/Health	7.4%
Semiconductors/Other Elect.	1.2%

Additional Information

Name of Most Recent Fund: MB Equity Fund IV
Most Recent Fund Was Raised: 09/21/2007
Year Founded: 1988
Capital Under Management: $571,500,000
Current Activity Level : Actively seeking new investments
Method of Compensation: Return on invest. most important, but chg. closing fees, service fees, etc.

MB VENTURE PARTNERS LLC

17 West Pontotoc
Suite 200
Memphis, TN USA 38103
Phone: 9013220330
Fax: 9013220339

Management and Staff

Bob Compton, Venture Partner
Charlie Federico, Venture Partner
Dick Tarr, Venture Partner
Gary Stevenson, Co-Founder
Jack Blair, Venture Partner
Larry Papasan, Venture Partner

Type of Firm

Private Equity Firm

Project Preferences

Role in Financing:
Prefer role as deal originator

Type of Financing Preferred:
Early Stage
Balanced
Later Stage
Seed

Geographical Preferences

United States Preferences:
Midwest
Southeast

Industry Preferences

In Biotechnology prefer:
Biotechnology

In Medical/Health prefer:
Medical Products

Additional Information

Name of Most Recent Fund: Memphis Biomed Ventures III, L.P.
Most Recent Fund Was Raised: 11/16/2011
Year Founded: 2001
Capital Under Management: $76,000,000
Current Activity Level : Actively seeking new investments

MBF GROUP SA

ul. Byslawska 82, office 415
Warsaw, Poland 04-994
Phone: 48223507098
Fax: 48223507013
E-mail: biuro@mbfgroup.pl
Website: www.mbfgroup.pl

Type of Firm
Service Provider

Project Preferences

Type of Financing Preferred:
Early Stage
Expansion
Later Stage
Seed

Size of Investments Considered:
Min Size of Investment Considered (000s): $27
Max Size of Investment Considered (000s): $271

Geographical Preferences

International Preferences:
Poland

Industry Preferences

In Internet Specific prefer:
Ecommerce

Additional Information

Year Founded: 2011
Current Activity Level : Actively seeking new investments

MBF HEALTHCARE PARTNERS LP

121 Alhambra Plaza
Suite 1100
Coral Gables, FL USA 33134
Phone: 3054611162
Website: www.mbfhealthcarepartners.com

Management and Staff

Isabel Pena, Chief Financial Officer
Jorge Rico, Managing Director
Luis Gonzalez, Managing Director
Marcio Cabrera, Co-Founder

Type of Firm
Private Equity Firm

Project Preferences

Type of Financing Preferred:
Leveraged Buyout
Early Stage
Expansion
Generalist PE
Balanced
Management Buyouts
Recapitalizations

Industry Preferences

In Medical/Health prefer:
Medical/Health
Health Services

Additional Information

Year Founded: 2005
Capital Under Management: $397,500,000
Current Activity Level : Actively seeking new investments

MBG BADEN-WUERTTEMBERG GMBH

Werastrasse 13-17
Stuttgart, Germany 70182
Phone: 4971116456
Fax: 497111645777
E-mail: info@buergschaftsbank.de
Website: www.mbg.de

Management and Staff

Dirk Buddensiek, Managing Director
Guy Selbherr, Managing Director

Type of Firm
Government Affiliated Program

Association Membership

German Venture Capital Association (BVK)

Project Preferences

Type of Financing Preferred:
Early Stage
Expansion
Balanced
Later Stage
Seed
Startup

Size of Investments Considered:
Min Size of Investment Considered (000s): $344
Max Size of Investment Considered (000s): $3,435

Geographical Preferences

International Preferences:
Germany

Industry Focus

(% based on actual investment)
Computer Hardware	47.4%
Biotechnology	20.6%
Computer Software and Services	11.3%
Semiconductors/Other Elect.	7.8%
Consumer Related	6.5%
Medical/Health	4.6%
Industrial/Energy	1.7%

Additional Information

Year Founded: 1971
Capital Under Management: $446,000,000
Current Activity Level : Actively seeking new investments

MBG SCHLESWIG-HOLSTEIN MBH

Lorentzendamm 21
Haus der Wirtschaft
Kiel, Germany 24103
Phone: 49431667013586
Fax: 49431667013590
E-mail: info@mbg-sh.de
Website: www.mbg-sh.de

Type of Firm
Private Equity Firm

Association Membership
German Venture Capital Association (BVK)

Project Preferences

Type of Financing Preferred:
Leveraged Buyout
Mezzanine
Later Stage
Seed
Startup

Size of Investments Considered:
Min Size of Investment Considered (000s): $32
Max Size of Investment Considered (000s): $3,172

Geographical Preferences

International Preferences:
Germany

Industry Focus

(% based on actual investment)
Internet Specific	58.9%
Medical/Health	41.1%

Additional Information

Year Founded: 1994
Current Activity Level : Actively seeking new investments

MBK PARTNERS INC

136, Sejong-daero
20F, Seoul Finance Center
Seoul, South Korea 04520
Phone: 82237068600
Fax: 82237068615

Other Offices

Two Queen's Road Central
Suite 1507, Cheung Kong Center
Hong Kong, Hong Kong
Phone: 852-2296-0000
Fax: 852-2297-0038

1-11-44 Akasaka, Minato-ku
Fourth Floor, Akasaka Intercity
Tokyo, Japan 107-0052
Phone: 813-6229-7960
Fax: 813-6229-7969

1010 Huai Hai Middle Road
Unit 3904, K. Wah Center
Shanghai, China 200031
Phone: 86-21-5404-8787
Fax: 86-21-5404-8996

Management and Staff

Dennis Wang, Vice President
Hideyuki Hidaka, Vice President
Hyukjin Kim, Vice President
In Kyung Lee, Chief Financial Officer
Jay Bu, Partner
Jeonghwan Kim, Vice President
Jong-Ha James Yoon, Partner
Kuo Chuan Kung, Partner
Kwang Il Kim, Partner
Michael Kim, Founder
Rachel Zhao, Vice President
Tae Hyun Park, Managing Director
Teck Chien Kong, Partner
Tomohiro Mochizuki, Vice President
Yonsog Choi, Vice President

Type of Firm

Private Equity Firm

Project Preferences

Type of Financing Preferred:
Leveraged Buyout
Management Buyouts

Geographical Preferences

International Preferences:
Asia Pacific
Taiwan
Hong Kong
China
Korea, South
Japan

Industry Preferences

In Communications prefer:
Telecommunications
Media and Entertainment

In Medical/Health prefer:
Pharmaceuticals

In Consumer Related prefer:
Consumer
Consumer Products

In Industrial/Energy prefer:
Industrial Products

In Financial Services prefer:
Financial Services
Financial Services

In Business Serv. prefer:
Services

Additional Information

Year Founded: 2005
Capital Under Management: $6,300,000,000
Current Activity Level : Actively seeking new investments

MBL VENTURE CAPITAL CO LTD

Nagoya Sakae Naka-ku
Building 10F 4-5-3 KDX Nagoya
Nagoya, Japan 460-0002
Phone: 81522381906
Fax: 81522381440
Website: www.mblvc.co.jp

Other Offices

Shinsei Bldg. 4F, 4-15 Uchikanada
1-chome, Chiyoda-ku
Tokyo, Japan 101-0047

Type of Firm

Private Equity Firm

Project Preferences

Type of Financing Preferred:
Balanced

Geographical Preferences

International Preferences:
Asia
Japan

Additional Information

Year Founded: 2000
Current Activity Level : Actively seeking new investments

MBLOOM LLC

77 Hookele Street
Suite 101
Kahului, HI USA 96732
Phone: 8088932400
Website: www.mbloom.com

Management and Staff

Arben Kryeziu, Co-Founder
Nick Bicanic, Co-Founder

Type of Firm

Private Equity Firm

Project Preferences

Type of Financing Preferred:
Early Stage
Startup

Geographical Preferences

United States Preferences:
Hawaii

Additional Information

Name of Most Recent Fund: mbloom Fund 1
Most Recent Fund Was Raised: 01/21/2014
Year Founded: 2014
Capital Under Management: $10,000,000
Current Activity Level : Actively seeking new investments

MBO PARTENAIRES SAS

3, rue La Boetie
Paris, France 75008
Phone: 33156641700
Fax: 33156641719
E-mail: mbo@mbopartenaires.com
Website: www.mbopartenaires.com

Other Offices

Espace Europeen, Bat G
15, chemin du Saquin
Ecully, France 69130
Phone: 33-4-7833-9710
Fax: 33-4-7833-0871

Management and Staff

Eric Dejoie, Partner
Jean-Michel Rallet, Partner
Jerome De Metz, Partner
Richard Pin, Partner

Type of Firm
Private Equity Firm

Association Membership
Emerging Markets Private Equity Association
French Venture Capital Association (AFIC)
European Private Equity and Venture Capital Assoc.

Project Preferences

Type of Financing Preferred:
Leveraged Buyout
Management Buyouts

Size of Investments Considered:
Min Size of Investment Considered (000s): $1,308
Max Size of Investment Considered (000s): $23,554

Geographical Preferences

International Preferences:
Europe
France

Additional Information
Name of Most Recent Fund: MBO Capital 3
Most Recent Fund Was Raised: 07/27/2010
Year Founded: 2002
Capital Under Management: $125,800,000
Current Activity Level: Actively seeking new investments

MBUYU CAPITAL PARTNERS LTD

43 Harwood Road
London, United Kingdom SW6 4QP
Website: www.mbuyucapital.com

Type of Firm
Private Equity Advisor or Fund of Funds

Project Preferences

Type of Financing Preferred:
Fund of Funds

Geographical Preferences

International Preferences:
Africa

Additional Information
Year Founded: 2014
Current Activity Level: Actively seeking new investments

MC3 VENTURES (FKA: MCKENNA VENTURE ACCELERATOR (MVA))

2130 Pierce Street
San Francisco, CA USA 94115
Phone: 4152905532

Other Offices
2350 W. El Camino Real, Suite 210
Mountain View, CA USA 94040

Management and Staff
David McDonnell, Managing Partner
Eric Hall, Venture Partner
Pawan Mehra, Principal
Piers Cooper, Managing Partner
Steve McGrath, Managing Partner

Type of Firm
Private Equity Firm

Project Preferences

Type of Financing Preferred:
Early Stage

Geographical Preferences

United States Preferences:

Industry Preferences

In Communications prefer:
Telecommunications
Wireless Communications

In Computer Software prefer:
Software

In Medical/Health prefer:
Medical/Health

Additional Information
Year Founded: 2000
Capital Under Management: $25,000,000
Current Activity Level: Reducing investment activity

MCB EQUITY FUND LTD

Sir Wiliam Newton Street
9th Floor, MCB Centre
Port Louis, Mauritius
Website: www.mcbcapitalmarkets.mu

Management and Staff
Ameenah Ibrahim, Managing Director
Kevin Rangasami, Managing Director
Marivonne Oxenham, Managing Director
Rony Lam, Chief Executive Officer

Type of Firm
Investment Management Firm

Project Preferences

Type of Financing Preferred:
Leveraged Buyout
Early Stage
Expansion
Later Stage
Seed
Management Buyouts
Acquisition

Size of Investments Considered:
Min Size of Investment Considered (000s): $2,500
Max Size of Investment Considered (000s): $5,000

Geographical Preferences

International Preferences:
Africa

Industry Preferences

In Medical/Health prefer:
Medical/Health

In Consumer Related prefer:
Consumer Products
Education Related

In Industrial/Energy prefer:
Industrial Products

In Manufact. prefer:
Manufacturing

In Agr/Forestr/Fish prefer:
Agribusiness

Additional Information
Year Founded: 2005
Current Activity Level: Actively seeking new investments

MCC CAPITAL PARTNERS LLC

Four Manhattanville Road
Building Four, Suite 206
Purchase, NY USA 10577
Phone: 9144375300
E-mail: contactus@mcc-cap.com
Website: www.mcc-cap.com

Management and Staff
Michael Cornell, Partner

Type of Firm
Private Equity Firm

Project Preferences

Type of Financing Preferred:
Leveraged Buyout
Acquisition

Geographical Preferences

United States Preferences:
North America

Industry Preferences

In Consumer Related prefer:
Consumer Products

Additional Information
Year Founded: 2008
Current Activity Level: Actively seeking new investments

MCCALL SPRINGER LLC

15332 Antioch Street
Suite 801
Pacific Palisades, CA USA 90272
Phone: 310-573-1172
Website: www.mccallspringer.com

Other Offices

Calle Freixa 37
4th Floor
Barcelona, Spain 08021
Phone: 34-678-49-0150

Type of Firm

Private Equity Firm

Project Preferences

Role in Financing:
Prefer role as deal originator

Type of Financing Preferred:
Leveraged Buyout
Turnaround
Later Stage

Industry Preferences

In Communications prefer:
Telecommunications

In Consumer Related prefer:
Food/Beverage
Consumer Products

In Financial Services prefer:
Real Estate
Financial Services

Additional Information

Year Founded: 1997
Current Activity Level : Actively seeking new investments
Method of Compensation: Return on invest. most important, but chg. closing fees, service fees, etc.

MCCUNE CAPITAL MANAGEMENT LLC

335 Madison Avenue
New York, NY USA 10017
E-mail: invest@mccune.vc
Website: www.mccune.vc

Management and Staff

Jason Cahill, Managing Director

Type of Firm

Private Equity Firm

Project Preferences

Type of Financing Preferred:
Early Stage
Seed

Industry Preferences

In Industrial/Energy prefer:
Energy

In Transportation prefer:
Transportation

In Manufact. prefer:
Manufacturing

In Agr/Forestr/Fish prefer:
Agriculture related

Additional Information

Year Founded: 2017
Capital Under Management: $1,500,000
Current Activity Level : Actively seeking new investments

MCG CAPITAL CORP

1001 19th Street North
10th Floor
Arlington, VA USA 22209
Phone: 8662476242
Website: www.mcgcapital.com

Management and Staff

Stephen Bacica, Chief Financial Officer

Type of Firm

Bank Affiliated

Association Membership

Natl Assoc of Small Bus. Inv. Co (NASBIC)

Project Preferences

Type of Financing Preferred:
Early Stage
Balanced
Later Stage

Additional Information

Year Founded: 1998
Capital Under Management: $7,000,000,000
Current Activity Level : Actively seeking new investments

MCH PRIVATE EQUITY ASESORES SL

Plaza de Colon 2
Torre 1, Planta 15
Madrid, Spain 28046
Phone: 34-91-426-4444
Fax: 34-91-426-4440
E-mail: mch@mch.es
Website: www.mch.es

Management and Staff

Celia Andreu, Principal
Francisco Caro, Partner
Jaime Soto, Co-Founder
Javier Herrero, Partner
Jose Maria Munoz, Co-Founder
Luis Ribed, Partner
Rafael Munoz, Principal
Ramon Nunez, Partner

Type of Firm

Private Equity Firm

Association Membership

European Private Equity and Venture Capital Assoc.
Spanish Venture Capital Association (ASCRI)

Project Preferences

Type of Financing Preferred:
Leveraged Buyout
Expansion
Later Stage
Management Buyouts
Acquisition

Geographical Preferences

International Preferences:
Europe
Portugal
Spain

Industry Preferences

In Consumer Related prefer:
Consumer Products

In Industrial/Energy prefer:
Industrial Products
Machinery

In Financial Services prefer:
Real Estate

In Business Serv. prefer:
Services
Distribution

Additional Information

Year Founded: 1998
Capital Under Management: $725,100,000
Current Activity Level : Actively seeking new investments

MCI CAPITAL SA

ul. Emilii Plater 53
21st Floor
Warsaw, Poland 00-113
Phone: 48225407380
Fax: 48225407381
E-mail: office@mci.eu
Website: mci.pl

Other Offices

ul. Bartoszowicka 3
Wroclaw, Poland 51-641
Phone: 48717591810
Fax: 48717591811

Management and Staff
Grzegorz Gromada, Venture Partner
Jacek Murawski, Venture Partner

Type of Firm
Private Equity Firm

Association Membership
Polish Venture Capital Association (PSIC/PPEA)

Project Preferences

Type of Financing Preferred:
Leveraged Buyout
Early Stage
Mezzanine
Generalist PE
Balanced
Later Stage
Startup

Geographical Preferences

International Preferences:
Eastern Europe

Industry Preferences

In Communications prefer:
Data Communications
Media and Entertainment

In Internet Specific prefer:
E-Commerce Technology
Internet

In Medical/Health prefer:
Medical Therapeutics

Additional Information
Year Founded: 1999
Capital Under Management: $245,200,000
Current Activity Level : Actively seeking new investments

MCKENNA GALE CAPITAL INC

100 King Street West
Suite 5600
Toronto, Canada M5X 1C9
Phone: 4163648884
Fax: 4163648444
E-mail: info@mckennagale.com
Website: www.mckennagale.com

Management and Staff
Gary Wade, Managing Director
Jeff Sujitno, Principal
Kevin McKenna, Managing Director
Najib Premji, Managing Director
Robert Gale, Managing Director
Stephen Stewart, Managing Director
T. Craig Ferguson, Principal

Type of Firm
Private Equity Firm

Project Preferences

Role in Financing:
Prefer role as deal originator but will also invest in deals created by others

Type of Financing Preferred:
Mezzanine

Geographical Preferences

United States Preferences:
North America

Canadian Preferences:
All Canada

Industry Focus
(% based on actual investment)
Communications and Media   44.7%
Industrial/Energy   27.7%
Consumer Related   27.6%

Additional Information
Year Founded: 1995
Capital Under Management: $600,000,000
Current Activity Level : Actively seeking new investments
Method of Compensation: Return on invest. most important, but chg. closing fees, service fees, etc.

MCLARTY CAPITAL PARTNERS

900 17th Street NW
Suite 800
Washington, DC USA 20006
Website: httwww.mclartycapital.com

Type of Firm
Investment Management Firm

Project Preferences

Type of Financing Preferred:
Leveraged Buyout
Opportunistic

Additional Information
Year Founded: 2013
Capital Under Management: $46,300,000
Current Activity Level : Actively seeking new investments

MCM CAPITAL PARTNERS L P

25201 Chagrin Boulevard, Suite 360
Cleveland, OH USA 44122
Phone: 2165141840
Fax: 2165141850
E-mail: info@mcmcapital.com
Website: www.mcmcapital.com

Management and Staff
James Poffenberger, Partner
Kevin Hayes, Chief Financial Officer
Mark Mansour, Managing Partner
Robert Kingsbury, Vice President
Steven Ross, Partner

Type of Firm
Private Equity Firm

Association Membership
Natl Assoc of Small Bus. Inv. Co (NASBIC)

Project Preferences

Role in Financing:
Prefer role as deal originator but will also invest in deals created by others

Type of Financing Preferred:
Leveraged Buyout
Management Buyouts
Acquisition
Recapitalizations

Geographical Preferences

United States Preferences:
North America

Industry Preferences

In Medical/Health prefer:
Medical Products

In Transportation prefer:
Aerospace

In Business Serv. prefer:
Services
Distribution

In Manufact. prefer:
Manufacturing

Additional Information
Year Founded: 1992
Capital Under Management: $50,000,000
Current Activity Level : Actively seeking new investments

MCNALLY CAPITAL LLC

190 South LaSalle Street, Suite 1620
Chicago, IL USA 60603
Phone: 3123573710
Website: www.mcnallycapital.com

Management and Staff
Adam Lerner, Partner
Catherine Lien, Vice President
Frank Galioto, Partner
Frank McGrew, Managing Partner
John Rompon, Managing Partner
Josh Brown, Vice President
Ravi Shah, Vice President
Ward McNally, Managing Partner

Type of Firm
Investment Management Firm

Association Membership
Natl Assoc of Small Bus. Inv. Co (NASBIC)

Project Preferences

Type of Financing Preferred:
Fund of Funds
Mezzanine

Geographical Preferences

United States Preferences:

Industry Preferences

In Medical/Health prefer:
Health Services

In Consumer Related prefer:
Consumer
Food/Beverage

In Industrial/Energy prefer:
Industrial Products

In Business Serv. prefer:
Distribution

Additional Information
Name of Most Recent Fund: McNally Capital Mezzanine Fund II, L.P.
Most Recent Fund Was Raised: 02/14/2012
Year Founded: 1969
Capital Under Management: $20,400,000
Current Activity Level : Actively seeking new investments

MCROCK CAPITAL CORP

454 Richmond Street West
Toronto, Canada M6V 1Y1
Phone: 6474789337
Website: www.mcrockcapital.com

Management and Staff
Jeremy Gilman, Principal
Scott MacDonald, Co-Founder
Whitney Rockley, Co-Founder

Type of Firm
Private Equity Firm

Association Membership
Canadian Venture Capital Association

Project Preferences

Type of Financing Preferred:
Early Stage
Later Stage

Industry Preferences

In Communications prefer:
Data Communications

In Computer Software prefer:
Data Processing
Systems Software
Artificial Intelligence

In Internet Specific prefer:
Internet

In Industrial/Energy prefer:
Industrial Products

Additional Information
Name of Most Recent Fund: McRock iNFund, L.P.
Most Recent Fund Was Raised: 12/16/2013
Year Founded: 2012
Capital Under Management: $70,000,000
Current Activity Level : Actively seeking new investments

MDB CAPITAL GROUP LLC

2425 Cedar Springs Road
Dallas, TX USA 75201
Phone: 3105265000
Fax: 3105265020
E-mail: mdb@mercomcapital.com
Website: www.mdb.com

Management and Staff
Amy Wang, Managing Director
Ankur Desai, Managing Director
Anthony DiGiandomenico, Co-Founder
Cameron Gray, Managing Director
Cary Hurwitz, Managing Director
Dan Landry, Managing Director
Daniel Nagy, Managing Director
Gary Schuman, Chief Financial Officer
George Brandon, Managing Director
Jeffrey Sun, Managing Director
Kevin Cotter, Managing Director
Robert Levande, Senior Managing Director
Robert Clifford, Senior Managing Director

Type of Firm
Bank Affiliated

Project Preferences

Type of Financing Preferred:
Early Stage
Balanced
Later Stage

Additional Information
Year Founded: 1996
Current Activity Level : Actively seeking new investments

MEAKEM BECKER VENTURE CAPITAL LLC

603 Beaver Street
Sewickley, PA USA 15143
Phone: 4127495720
Fax: 4127455721
E-mail: info@mbvc.com
Website: www.mbvc.com

Management and Staff
Alan Veeck, Principal
David Becker, Managing Director
Glen Meakem, Managing Partner
Shane Tulloch, Principal

Type of Firm
Private Equity Firm

Project Preferences

Role in Financing:
Prefer role as deal originator but will also invest in deals created by others

Type of Financing Preferred:
Early Stage
Expansion
Balanced

Geographical Preferences

United States Preferences:
Midwest
East Coast

Additional Information
Name of Most Recent Fund: Meakem Becker Venture Capital I, L.P.
Most Recent Fund Was Raised: 08/31/2006
Year Founded: 2005
Capital Under Management: $75,000,000
Current Activity Level : Actively seeking new investments
Method of Compensation: Return on investment is of primary concern, do not charge fees

---

MEC ADVISORY LTD

26/F, 100 Queen's Road Central
Central
Hong Kong, Hong Kong

Type of Firm
Investment Management Firm

Geographical Preferences

United States Preferences:
North America

Industry Preferences

In Industrial/Energy prefer:
Oil & Gas Drilling,Explor

In Agr/Forestr/Fish prefer:
Mining and Minerals

Additional Information
Year Founded: 2017
Current Activity Level : Actively seeking new investments

MED OPPORTUNITY PARTNERS LLC

Two Greenwich Office Park
Suite 300
Greenwich, CT USA 06831
Phone: 2036221333
Fax: 2036221321
Website: www.medopportunity.com

Management and Staff
James Breckenridge, Co-Founder
Robert Vaters, Partner
Vicente Trelles, Co-Founder

Type of Firm
Private Equity Firm

Project Preferences

Type of Financing Preferred:
Leveraged Buyout
Expansion
Recapitalizations

Size of Investments Considered:
Min Size of Investment Considered (000s): $5,000
Max Size of Investment Considered (000s): $40,000

Geographical Preferences

United States Preferences:

Industry Preferences

In Medical/Health prefer:
Medical/Health
Health Services
Pharmaceuticals

Additional Information
Year Founded: 2006
Current Activity Level : Actively seeking new investments

MEDALLION CAPITAL INC

3000 West Country Road
Suite 301, Road 42
Burnsville, MN USA 55337
Phone: 9528312025
Fax: 9528312945

Management and Staff
Michael Mahoney, Vice President
Paul Meyering, President

Type of Firm
SBIC

Association Membership
Natl Assoc of Small Bus. Inv. Co (NASBIC)

Project Preferences

Role in Financing:
Prefer role as deal originator but will also invest in deals created by others

Type of Financing Preferred:
Leveraged Buyout
Expansion
Mezzanine
Management Buyouts
Acquisition
Recapitalizations

Size of Investments Considered:
Min Size of Investment Considered (000s): $1,000
Max Size of Investment Considered: No Limit

Geographical Preferences

United States Preferences:
All U.S.

Industry Preferences

In Communications prefer:
CATV & Pay TV Systems
Radio & TV Broadcasting
Telecommunications

In Computer Software prefer:
Computer Services

In Semiconductor/Electr prefer:
Sensors

In Medical/Health prefer:
Other Therapeutic

In Consumer Related prefer:
Franchises(NEC)
Education Related

In Industrial/Energy prefer:
Machinery

Additional Information
Year Founded: 1987
Capital Under Management: $40,000,000
Current Activity Level : Actively seeking new investments
Method of Compensation: Return on invest. most important, but chg. closing fees, service fees, etc.

MEDCAP AB (PUBL)

Skoldungagatan 4
Stockholm, Sweden 114 27
Phone: 468347110
Fax: 468347120
E-mail: info@medcap.se
Website: www.medcap.se

Management and Staff
Hugo Petit, Chief Financial Officer
Karl Tobieson, Chief Executive Officer

Type of Firm
Private Equity Firm

Association Membership
Swedish Venture Capital Association (SVCA)

Project Preferences

Type of Financing Preferred:
Leveraged Buyout
Acquisition

Geographical Preferences

International Preferences:
Sweden

Additional Information
Year Founded: 2001
Current Activity Level : Actively seeking new investments

MEDCARE INVESTMENT FUND LTD

3322 West End Avenue, Suite 1100
Nashville, TN USA 37203
Phone: 6155159880
Fax: 6155159891
Website: www.medcarefunds.com

Other Offices
3401 West End Avenue
Suite 310
Nashville, TN USA 37203
Phone: 6155159880
Fax: 6155159891

Management and Staff
James Leininger, Co-Founder
Thomas Lyles, President
Todd Callister, Chief Financial Officer
Tom Noland, Vice President

Type of Firm
Private Equity Firm

Project Preferences

Type of Financing Preferred:
Balanced

Industry Preferences

In Medical/Health prefer:
Medical/Health
Health Services

Additional Information
Year Founded: 1993
Capital Under Management: $610,000,000
Current Activity Level : Actively seeking new investments

MEDEVICE ACCELERATOR SAS

37, Rue Cassiopee
Chavanod, France 74650
Phone: 08 92 97 73 05

Type of Firm
Private Equity Firm

Project Preferences

Type of Financing Preferred:
Early Stage
Seed

Size of Investments Considered:
Min Size of Investment Considered (000s): $589
Max Size of Investment Considered (000s): $2,355

Geographical Preferences

International Preferences:
France

Industry Preferences

In Medical/Health prefer:
Medical/Health

Additional Information
Year Founded: 2011
Current Activity Level : Actively seeking new investments

MEDFOCUS FUND LLC

13900 Alton Parkway
Suite 125
Irvine, CA USA 92618
Phone: 9495817250
Fax: 9495814761
Website: www.fund-mgmt.com

Management and Staff
Michael Henson, Founder

Type of Firm
Private Equity Firm

Project Preferences

Type of Financing Preferred:
Early Stage

Geographical Preferences

United States Preferences:

Industry Preferences

In Medical/Health prefer:
Medical Products

Additional Information
Year Founded: 2001
Current Activity Level : Actively seeking new investments

MEDHOLDINGS SA

Rue Saint-Pierre 2
Lausanne, Switzerland 1003

Type of Firm
Private Equity Firm

Project Preferences

Type of Financing Preferred:
Early Stage
Later Stage

Geographical Preferences

International Preferences:
Europe
Switzerland
Eastern Europe

Industry Preferences

In Biotechnology prefer:
Human Biotechnology

In Medical/Health prefer:
Medical/Health
Medical Therapeutics

Additional Information
Year Founded: 2010
Current Activity Level : Actively seeking new investments

MEDIA DEVELOPMENT INVESTMENT FUND INC

37 West 20th Street
Suite 801
New York, NY USA 10011
Phone: 2128071304
Fax: 2128070540
E-mail: mdif@mdif.org
Website: www.mdif.org

Other Offices
Salvatorska 10
Prague 1, Czech Republic 110 00
Phone: 420224312832
Fax: 420224315419

Management and Staff
Harlan Mandel, Chief Executive Officer
Mari Budesa, Chief Financial Officer
Marie Nemcova, Chief Operating Officer

Type of Firm
Private Equity Firm

Project Preferences

Type of Financing Preferred:
Early Stage
Seed
Startup

Geographical Preferences

International Preferences:
All International

Industry Preferences

In Business Serv. prefer:
Media

Additional Information
Year Founded: 1995
Current Activity Level : Actively seeking new investments

MEDIA DREAM WORKS

No. 178 Tiyuchang Road
Hangzhou, Zhejiang, China 31009
Phone: 8657157525200
E-mail: contact@chuangxin.com
Website: www.mediadreamworks.net

Type of Firm
Incubator/Development Program

Project Preferences

Type of Financing Preferred:
Seed
Startup

Geographical Preferences

International Preferences:
China

Industry Preferences

In Business Serv. prefer:
Media

Additional Information
Year Founded: 2011
Current Activity Level : Actively seeking new investments

MEDIA VENTURES GMBH

Wesselinger Strasse 22-30
Cologne, Germany 50999
Phone: 492236480100
Fax: 4922364801001
E-mail: info@mediaventures.de
Website: mediaventures.de

Management and Staff
Dirk Stader, Managing Partner

Type of Firm
Private Equity Firm

Project Preferences

Type of Financing Preferred:
Leveraged Buyout
Early Stage
Seed
Acquisition
Startup

Geographical Preferences

International Preferences:
Germany

Industry Preferences

In Communications prefer:
Communications and Media
Telecommunications
Wireless Communications

In Computer Software prefer:
Software

In Internet Specific prefer:
Internet
Ecommerce

In Consumer Related prefer:
Entertainment and Leisure

In Business Serv. prefer:
Media

Additional Information

Year Founded: 2000
Current Activity Level : Actively seeking new investments

MEDIAN FUND PTY LTD

Suite 416, 6 Beach Road
The Old Castle Brewery Bldg
Cape Town, South Africa 7924
Phone: 27-21-448-5945
Fax: 27-21-448-5984
E-mail: info@medianfund.com
Website: www.medianfund.com

Management and Staff

Joseph Stoltz, Chief Executive Officer
Themba Ntini, Chief Operating Officer

Type of Firm

Private Equity Firm

Project Preferences

Type of Financing Preferred:
Early Stage
Acquisition
Startup

Geographical Preferences

International Preferences:
Africa

Industry Preferences

In Communications prefer:
Publishing

In Medical/Health prefer:
Health Services
Hospitals/Clinics/Primary

Additional Information

Year Founded: 2005
Current Activity Level : Actively seeking new investments

MEDICA VENTURE PARTNERS, LTD.

4 Hasadnaot Street,
Kohav Herzliya Building
Herzlia, Israel 46728
Phone: 97299601900
Fax: 97299542266
E-mail: info@medicavp.com
Website: www.medicavp.com

Management and Staff

Ehud Geller, Managing Partner
Eli Hazum, General Partner
Henry Kay, Partner
Pennina Safer, General Partner
Yoav Waizer, Chief Financial Officer

Type of Firm

Private Equity Firm

Project Preferences

Type of Financing Preferred:
Early Stage
Expansion
Balanced
Later Stage
Seed
Startup
Special Situation

Size of Investments Considered:
Min Size of Investment Considered (000s): $500
Max Size of Investment Considered (000s): $3,000

Geographical Preferences

United States Preferences:

International Preferences:
Europe
Israel
Asia

Industry Preferences

In Biotechnology prefer:
Biotechnology

In Medical/Health prefer:
Medical Diagnostics
Diagnostic Test Products
Medical Therapeutics
Medical Products
Disposable Med. Products
Pharmaceuticals

Additional Information

Year Founded: 1995
Capital Under Management: $80,000,000
Current Activity Level : Actively seeking new investments

MEDICAL TECHNOLOGY VENTURE PARTNERS LLC

1700 4th Street
Suite 214
San Francisco, CA USA 94158
Phone: 6503088821
E-mail: info@medtechvp.com
Website: www.medtechvp.com

Type of Firm

Private Equity Firm

Project Preferences

Type of Financing Preferred:
Early Stage
Seed

Industry Preferences

In Computer Software prefer:
Artificial Intelligence

In Medical/Health prefer:
Medical/Health
Medical Therapeutics

Additional Information

Year Founded: 2017
Capital Under Management: $20,100,000
Current Activity Level : Actively seeking new investments

MEDICI INVESTMENT CO LTD

159-9,Samsung-dong, Gangnam-gu
406,4/F, Tradetower
Seoul, South Korea 135090
Phone: 82234528126
Fax: 82234528120

Type of Firm

Private Equity Firm

Association Membership

Korean Venture Capital Association (KVCA)

Project Preferences

Type of Financing Preferred:
Balanced

Geographical Preferences

International Preferences:
Korea, South

Additional Information

Year Founded: 2011
Current Activity Level : Actively seeking new investments

MEDICIS CAPITAL GMBH

Maximilianstrasse 52
Munich, Germany 80538
Phone: 4989411184520
Fax: 4989411184545
E-mail: info@medicis.de
Website: www.medicis.de

Management and Staff

Kai Deusch, Founder
Mark Adams, Managing Partner
Moritz Roever, Managing Partner
Todd Jorn, Managing Partner

Type of Firm

Private Equity Firm

Project Preferences

Type of Financing Preferred:
Early Stage
Later Stage
Seed
Startup

Geographical Preferences

International Preferences:
Switzerland
Austria
Germany

Industry Preferences

In Biotechnology prefer:
Biotechnology

In Medical/Health prefer:
Medical/Health
Medical Diagnostics
Health Services
Pharmaceuticals

Additional Information

Year Founded: 1994
Capital Under Management: $15,200,000
Current Activity Level : Actively seeking new investments

MEDICXI VENTURES (UK) LLP

3, Burlington Gardens
London, United Kingdom W1S 3EP
Phone: 442071542020
Fax: 442071542021
E-mail: info@medicxiventures.com
Website: www.medicxiventures.com

Type of Firm

Private Equity Firm

Project Preferences

Type of Financing Preferred:
Early Stage
Expansion
Later Stage
Seed

Geographical Preferences

International Preferences:
Europe

Industry Preferences

In Medical/Health prefer:
Medical/Health

Additional Information

Year Founded: 2016
Capital Under Management: $600,000,000
Current Activity Level : Actively seeking new investments

MEDIMMUNE LLC

One MedImmune Way
Gaithersburg, MD USA 20878
Phone: 3013980000
Website: www.medimmune.com

Other Offices

101 Orchard Ridge Drive
GAITHERSBURG, MD USA 20878
Phone: 3013980000

Management and Staff

Peter Greenleaf, President
Timothy Gray, Chief Financial Officer

Type of Firm

Corporate PE/Venture

Project Preferences

Type of Financing Preferred:
Early Stage
Balanced
Later Stage

Industry Preferences

In Biotechnology prefer:
Human Biotechnology

In Medical/Health prefer:
Medical/Health
Medical Products
Pharmaceuticals

Additional Information

Year Founded: 1997
Current Activity Level : Actively seeking new investments

MEDINA CAPITAL PARTNERS INC

Courvoisier Centre One
501 Brickell Key Dr, Suite 200
Miami, FL USA 33131
Phone: 3053756000
E-mail: info@medinacapital.com

Management and Staff

Adam Smith, Partner
Nelson Fonseca, Partner
Rene Rodriguez, Partner

Type of Firm

Private Equity Firm

Project Preferences

Type of Financing Preferred:
Leveraged Buyout
Early Stage
Balanced
Later Stage
Acquisition

Industry Preferences

In Computer Software prefer:
Software

Additional Information

Year Founded: 1969
Capital Under Management: $182,000,000
Current Activity Level : Actively seeking new investments

MEDIOLANUM STATE STREET SGR

Via Mazzini 2
Milan, Italy 20123
Phone: 390272147766
Fax: 390272147720
E-mail: info@fondamentasgr.com
Website: www.fondamentasgr.com

Type of Firm

Endowment, Foundation or Pension Fund

Project Preferences

Type of Financing Preferred:
Fund of Funds
Generalist PE
Joint Ventures

Geographical Preferences

International Preferences:
Italy

Industry Preferences

In Biotechnology prefer:
Biotechnology

In Medical/Health prefer:
Pharmaceuticals

In Financial Services prefer:
Real Estate

Additional Information

Year Founded: 2001
Capital Under Management: $146,152,000
Current Activity Level : Actively seeking new investments

MEDITERRA CAPITAL MANAGEMENT LTD

Sehit Halil Ibrahim
Cad. No: 39 Istinye
Sariyer Istanbul, Turkey 34460
Phone: 90 212323 54
Fax: 90 212323 54
E-mail: info@mediterracapital.com
Website: www.mediterracapital.com

Other Offices

Heritage Hall
Le Marchant Street
Guernsey, United Kingdom GY1 4HY
Phone: 441481716000

Type of Firm

Private Equity Firm

Project Preferences

Type of Financing Preferred:
Leveraged Buyout
Management Buyouts
Acquisition

Geographical Preferences

International Preferences:
Turkey
Guernsey

Industry Preferences

In Communications prefer:
Telecommunications

In Consumer Related prefer:
Consumer

Additional Information

Name of Most Recent Fund: Mediterra Capital Partners I, LP
Most Recent Fund Was Raised: 05/06/2011
Year Founded: 2010
Capital Under Management: $230,056,000
Current Activity Level : Actively seeking new investments

MEDIVATE PARTNERS LLC

1402, Boutique Monaco B Dong
397, Seocho-daero, Seocho-gu
Seoul, South Korea 06616
Phone: 8225360704
Fax: 8225360733
Website: www.medivatepartners.com

Type of Firm

Investment Management Firm

Project Preferences

Type of Financing Preferred:
Early Stage

Geographical Preferences

International Preferences:
Asia Pacific

Industry Preferences

In Medical/Health prefer:
Health Services
Pharmaceuticals

Additional Information

Year Founded: 1969
Current Activity Level : Actively seeking new investments

MEDLEY CAPITAL LLC

375 Park Avenue
Suite 3304
New York, NY USA 10152
Phone: 2127590777
Website: www.medleycapital.com

Other Offices

600 Montgomery Street
39th Floor
San Francisco, CA USA 94111
Phone: 4155682760

Management and Staff

Andrew Fentress, Partner
Brian O Reilly, Vice President
Bryan Boches, Managing Director
David DeSantis, Managing Director
Dean Crowe, Managing Director
Frank Wang, Vice President
Frank Cupido, Vice President
Jason Wong, Vice President
Jon Schroeder, Principal
Joseph Schmuckler, Partner
Joseph Princiotta, Principal
Luba Romankevich, Vice President
Mac McAulay, Principal
Richard Allorto, Chief Financial Officer
Robert Comizio, Partner
Scott Von Stein, Principal
Seth Taube, Partner
Tom Quimby, Managing Director
William Parizek, Principal

Type of Firm

Investment Management Firm

Association Membership

Natl Assoc of Small Bus. Inv. Co (NASBIC)

Project Preferences

Type of Financing Preferred:
Mezzanine

Size of Investments Considered:
Min Size of Investment Considered (000s): $7,000
Max Size of Investment Considered (000s): $100,000

Geographical Preferences

United States Preferences:
North America

Industry Preferences

In Medical/Health prefer:
Medical/Health

In Consumer Related prefer:
Consumer
Retail

In Industrial/Energy prefer:
Energy
Industrial Products
Environmental Related

In Transportation prefer:
Transportation

In Financial Services prefer:
Financial Services
Real Estate

Additional Information

Name of Most Recent Fund: Medley Opportunity Fund II, L.P.
Most Recent Fund Was Raised: 08/16/2011
Year Founded: 2009
Capital Under Management: $111,800,000
Current Activity Level : Actively seeking new investments

MEDLEY PARTNERS MANAGEMENT LLC

50 California Street
Suite 3350
San Francisco, CA USA 94111
Phone: 4153758790
E-mail: info@medleyp.com
Website: www.medley-partners.com

Type of Firm
Private Equity Advisor or Fund of Funds

Project Preferences

Type of Financing Preferred:
Fund of Funds
Fund of Funds of Second

Geographical Preferences

United States Preferences:

International Preferences:
Europe
Asia

Industry Preferences

In Financial Services prefer:
Investment Groups

Additional Information
Year Founded: 2004
Current Activity Level : Actively seeking new investments

MEDSCIENCE VENTURES LLC

745 Atlantic Avenue
Second Floor
Boston, MA USA 02111
Phone: 6175137498
Website: www.medscienceventures.com

Type of Firm
Private Equity Firm

Project Preferences

Type of Financing Preferred:
Early Stage

Geographical Preferences

United States Preferences:

International Preferences:
Asia

Industry Preferences

In Biotechnology prefer:
Biotechnology

In Medical/Health prefer:
Health Services

Additional Information
Year Founded: 2016
Capital Under Management: $4,250,000
Current Activity Level : Actively seeking new investments

MEDU CAPITAL(PTY)LTD

2 Fricker Rd, Illovo Boulevard
Illovo, Sandton
Johannesburg, South Africa 2001
Phone: 27112689140
Fax: 27112689145
Website: www.meducapital.co.za

Management and Staff
Annabelle Satterly, Chief Financial Officer
Ernest January, Co-Founder
Nhlanganiso Mkwanazi, Co-Founder
Siyabonga Nhlumayo, Principal

Type of Firm
Private Equity Firm

Association Membership
South African Venture Capital Association (SAVCA)
Emerging Markets Private Equity Association

Project Preferences

Type of Financing Preferred:
Leveraged Buyout
Expansion
Management Buyouts
Acquisition

Size of Investments Considered:
Min Size of Investment Considered (000s): $5,247
Max Size of Investment Considered (000s): $12,244

Geographical Preferences

International Preferences:
South Africa
Africa

Additional Information
Year Founded: 2003
Capital Under Management: $120,000,000
Current Activity Level : Actively seeking new investments

MEDVENTURE ASSOCIATES

5980 Horton Street
Suite 390
Emeryville, CA USA 94608
Phone: 5105977979
Fax: 5105979920
E-mail: medven@medven.com
Website: www.medven.com

Management and Staff
Annette Campbell-White, Founder
Charles Liamos, Partner
David Holbrooke, Venture Partner
Michael Laufer, Venture Partner
Philip Oyer, Venture Partner
Robert Momsen, Venture Partner
Wally Buch, Venture Partner

Type of Firm
Private Equity Firm

Association Membership
Western Association of Venture Capitalists (WAVC)

Project Preferences

Role in Financing:
Prefer role as deal originator but will also invest in deals created by others

Type of Financing Preferred:
Early Stage
Balanced
Seed

Geographical Preferences

United States Preferences:
West Coast

Industry Focus
(% based on actual investment)
Medical/Health	71.1%
Biotechnology	10.5%
Internet Specific	8.2%
Computer Software and Services	5.6%
Computer Hardware	4.5%
Communications and Media	0.2%

Additional Information
Year Founded: 1986
Capital Under Management: $325,000,000
Current Activity Level : Reducing investment activity
Method of Compensation: Return on investment is of primary concern, do not charge fees

MEGAINVESTMENT CO LTD

157-37,Samsung-dong,Gangnam-gu
4/F, Ilsong Building
Seoul, South Korea
Phone: 82234532540
Fax: 82234532539
Website: www.megainv.co.kr

Type of Firm
Private Equity Firm

Association Membership
Korean Venture Capital Association (KVCA)

Project Preferences

Type of Financing Preferred:
Balanced

Geographical Preferences

International Preferences:
Korea, South

Additional Information

Year Founded: 2012
Current Activity Level : Actively seeking new investments

MEGALE LLC

23 Mechanic Street
Red Bank, NJ USA 07701
Phone: 7324006090
Website: www.aeonfund.com

Type of Firm

Private Equity Firm

Project Preferences

Type of Financing Preferred:
Early Stage
Generalist PE
Balanced
Later Stage
Open Market
Private Placement

Additional Information

Year Founded: 2012
Capital Under Management: $29,679,000
Current Activity Level : Actively seeking new investments

MEIDLINGER PARTNERS LLC

3711 Market Street
Suite 800
Philadelphia, PA USA 19104
Phone: 2157013299
Fax: 2155570912
Website: www.meidlingerpartners.net

Management and Staff

Karen Meidlinger, Co-Founder
Kevin Brophy, Co-Founder

Type of Firm

Private Equity Firm

Project Preferences

Type of Financing Preferred:
Leveraged Buyout
Expansion
Generalist PE
Later Stage
Acquisition

Geographical Preferences

United States Preferences:

International Preferences:
Western Europe

Industry Preferences

In Industrial/Energy prefer:
Energy
Industrial Products
Environmental Related

In Utilities prefer:
Utilities

Additional Information

Year Founded: 2008
Capital Under Management: $5,000,000
Current Activity Level : Actively seeking new investments

MEKONG CAPITAL LTD

Six Thai Van Lung St., Dist. 1
Eighth Floor, Capital Place
Ho Chi Minh City, Vietnam
Phone: 84838273161
Fax: 84838273162
E-mail: info@mekongcapital.com
Website: www.mekongcapital.com

Other Offices

399 Sukhumvit Road, North Klongtoey
Level 33 Interchange 21
, Thailand 10110
Phone: 662-660 3781
Fax: 662-660-3718

12th Floor, HAREC Building
4A Lang Ha Street, Ba Dinh District
Hanoi, Vietnam
Phone: 844-772-4888
Fax: 844-772-4868

Management and Staff

Chad Ovel, Partner
Chris Freund, Founder
Giang Pham Vu, Partner
Truong Le, Partner

Type of Firm

Private Equity Firm

Association Membership

Emerging Markets Private Equity Association

Project Preferences

Type of Financing Preferred:
Expansion
Generalist PE
Balanced

Geographical Preferences

International Preferences:
Laos
Vietnam
Cambodia

Additional Information

Year Founded: 2001
Capital Under Management: $132,600,000
Current Activity Level : Actively seeking new investments

MELOY FUND I LP

1310 North Courthouse Road
Suite 110
Arlington, VA USA 22201

Type of Firm

Endowment, Foundation or Pension Fund

Project Preferences

Type of Financing Preferred:
Later Stage

Geographical Preferences

International Preferences:
Indonesia
Philippines

Industry Preferences

In Other prefer:
Environment Responsible

Additional Information

Year Founded: 2016
Capital Under Management: $10,000,000
Current Activity Level : Actively seeking new investments

MENA CAPITAL S A L

Omar Al Daouk Street
STARCO Center, Blk C
Beirut, Lebanon
Phone: 9611370222
Fax: 961370225
E-mail: info@menacapital.com.lb
Website: www.menacapital.com.lb

Type of Firm

Private Equity Firm

Project Preferences

Type of Financing Preferred:
Leveraged Buyout
Generalist PE
Later Stage
Acquisition

Industry Preferences

In Consumer Related prefer:
Food/Beverage
Consumer Products

In Financial Services prefer:
Real Estate

Additional Information

Year Founded: 2004
Current Activity Level : Actively seeking new investments

MENDEN VENTURES CONSULTING GMBH

Moltkestr, 79
Cologne, Germany 50674
Website: www.mendenventures.com

Management and Staff

Stefan Menden, Founder

Type of Firm

Private Equity Firm

Project Preferences

Type of Financing Preferred:
Seed
Startup

Geographical Preferences

International Preferences:
Germany

Industry Preferences

In Communications prefer:
Wireless Communications

In Internet Specific prefer:
Internet
Ecommerce
Web Aggregation/Portals

Additional Information

Year Founded: 2011
Current Activity Level : Actively seeking new investments

MENLO VENTURES

2884 Sand Hill Road, Suite 100
Menlo Park, CA USA 94025
Phone: 6508548540
Fax: 6508547059
E-mail: info@menloventures.com
Website: www.menloventures.com

Management and Staff

Avery More, Venture Partner
Douglas Carlisle, Partner
Douglas Carlisle, Managing Director
Greg Yap, Partner
H. DuBose Montgomery, Managing Director
H. Dubose Montgomery, Founder
Hal Calhoun, Managing Director
John Jarve, Partner
John Jarve, Managing Director
Kirsten Mello, Chief Financial Officer
Mark Siegel, Managing Director
Matt Murphy, Managing Director
Pravin Vazirani, Managing Director
Shawn Carolan, Managing Director
Shervin Pishevar, Managing Director
Sonja Perkins, Managing Director
Sunil Raman, Principal
Tyler Sosin, Principal

Type of Firm

Private Equity Firm

Association Membership

Western Association of Venture Capitalists (WAVC)
National Venture Capital Association - USA (NVCA)

Project Preferences

Role in Financing:
Prefer role as deal originator but will also invest in deals created by others

Type of Financing Preferred:
Early Stage
Balanced
Later Stage
Startup

Size of Investments Considered:
Min Size of Investment Considered (000s): $5,000
Max Size of Investment Considered (000s): $20,000

Geographical Preferences

United States Preferences:

Industry Focus

(% based on actual investment)
Computer Software and Services	31.3%
Internet Specific	27.5%
Communications and Media	15.3%
Semiconductors/Other Elect.	10.9%
Computer Hardware	6.4%
Medical/Health	4.8%
Other Products	1.9%
Consumer Related	0.9%
Biotechnology	0.7%
Industrial/Energy	0.1%

Additional Information

Year Founded: 1976
Capital Under Management: $3,900,000,000
Current Activity Level : Actively seeking new investments
Method of Compensation: Return on investment is of primary concern, do not charge fees

MENTERRA VENTURE ADVISORS PVT LTD

638, 11th Main, HAL Stage II
Indiranagar
Bangalore, India 560038
E-mail: info@menterra.com
Website: www.menterra.com

Management and Staff

Mukesh Sharma, Co-Founder
PR Ganapathy, Co-Founder
Paul Basil, Co-Founder

Type of Firm

Private Equity Firm

Project Preferences

Type of Financing Preferred:
Early Stage

Industry Preferences

In Biotechnology prefer:
Agricultural/Animal Bio.

In Medical/Health prefer:
Medical/Health

In Consumer Related prefer:
Education Related

In Industrial/Energy prefer:
Energy

Additional Information

Year Founded: 2016
Current Activity Level : Actively seeking new investments

MENTHA CAPITAL BV

Nieuwendammerdijk 538
Amsterdam, Netherlands 1023 BX
Phone: 31206363140
E-mail: info@menthacapital.com
Website: www.menthacapital.com

Management and Staff

Edo Pfennings, Partner
Gijs Botman, Managing Partner

Type of Firm

Private Equity Firm

Project Preferences

Role in Financing:
Prefer role as deal originator but will also invest in deals created by others

Type of Financing Preferred:
Leveraged Buyout
Management Buyouts
Acquisition

Geographical Preferences

International Preferences:
Luxembourg
Netherlands
Belgium

Industry Preferences

In Consumer Related prefer:
Consumer
Entertainment and Leisure
Retail

In Business Serv. prefer:
Services
Distribution

In Manufact. prefer:
Manufacturing

Additional Information
Name of Most Recent Fund: Mentha Capital Fund IV
Most Recent Fund Was Raised: 02/19/2014
Year Founded: 2006
Capital Under Management: $70,045,000
Current Activity Level : Actively seeking new investments

MENTOR CAPITAL INC

P.O. Box 1709
Ramona, CA USA 92065
Phone: 7607884700
Fax: 7607882525
Website: www.mentorcapital.com

Type of Firm
Private Equity Firm

Project Preferences

Type of Financing Preferred:
Leveraged Buyout
Acquisition
Industry Rollups

Industry Preferences

In Medical/Health prefer:
Medical Products

In Consumer Related prefer:
Consumer Products

Additional Information
Year Founded: 1994
Current Activity Level : Actively seeking new investments

MENTORTECH VENTURES LLC

3624 Market Street, Suite 300
Philadelphia, PA USA 19104
Phone: 2153824200
Website: www.mentortechventures.com

Management and Staff
Boris Kalandar, Managing Director
Brett Topche, Managing Director
Michael Aronson, Managing Director

Type of Firm
Private Equity Firm

Project Preferences

Type of Financing Preferred:
Early Stage
Seed

Geographical Preferences

United States Preferences:
Pennsylvania
New York

International Preferences:
Israel

Industry Preferences

In Medical/Health prefer:
Medical/Health

Additional Information
Name of Most Recent Fund: MentorTech Ventures III, L.P.
Most Recent Fund Was Raised: 08/16/2011
Year Founded: 2005
Capital Under Management: $10,000,000
Current Activity Level : Actively seeking new investments

MERAPAR ADVISORY BV

Wilhelminaplein 25
Eindhoven, Netherlands 5611 HG
Phone: 31408455143
Website: merapar.net

Type of Firm
Investment Management Firm

Project Preferences

Type of Financing Preferred:
Early Stage

Industry Preferences

In Communications prefer:
Telecommunications

In Internet Specific prefer:
Internet

Additional Information
Year Founded: 2013
Current Activity Level : Actively seeking new investments

MERCAPITAL SL

C/Padilla 17
Madrid, Spain 28006
Phone: 34917458484
Website: www.mercapital.com

Other Offices
Rua Casa do Ator, 1117
14th - office 144
Sao Paulo, Brazil 04546-004
Phone: 551130404330

1221 Brickell Avenue
Suite 1200
Miami, FL USA 33131
Phone: 7868711626

Management and Staff
Bruno Delgado, Partner
Carlos Barallobre, Partner
David Estefanell, Partner
Fernando De Almeida, Principal
Miguel Zurita, Partner
Nicolas Jimenez-Ugarte, Partner
Ramon Carne, Partner

Type of Firm
Private Equity Firm

Association Membership
Brazilian Venture Capital Association (ABCR)
European Private Equity and Venture Capital Assoc.

Project Preferences

Role in Financing:
Will function either as deal originator or investor in deals created by others

Type of Financing Preferred:
Leveraged Buyout
Management Buyouts

Geographical Preferences

International Preferences:
Portugal
Spain

Industry Focus
(% based on actual investment)

Other Products	42.1%
Consumer Related	24.2%
Medical/Health	17.8%
Computer Software and Services	6.8%
Communications and Media	5.7%
Industrial/Energy	3.3%
Internet Specific	0.1%

Additional Information
Name of Most Recent Fund: Mercapital Spanish Buyout Fund III
Most Recent Fund Was Raised: 11/30/2006
Year Founded: 1985

Capital Under Management: $1,977,100,000
Current Activity Level : Actively seeking new investments

MERCATO MANAGEMENT LLC

6550 South Millrock Drive
Suite 125
Salt Lake City, UT USA 84121
Phone: 8012200055
Fax: 8012200056
E-mail: info@mercatopartners.com
Website: mercatopartners.com

Management and Staff

Alan Hall, Co-Founder
Greg Warnock, Co-Founder

Type of Firm

Private Equity Firm

Project Preferences

Role in Financing:
Will function either as deal originator or investor in deals created by others

Type of Financing Preferred:
Early Stage
Expansion
Balanced
Later Stage
Recapitalizations

Geographical Preferences

United States Preferences:

Industry Preferences

In Consumer Related prefer:
Consumer

In Business Serv. prefer:
Media

Additional Information

Name of Most Recent Fund: Mercato Partners Growth III, L.P.
Most Recent Fund Was Raised: 04/04/2016
Year Founded: 2008
Capital Under Management: $15,000,000
Current Activity Level : Actively seeking new investments

MERCATOR INVESTMENTS LTD

161 Bay Street, P.O. Box 201
Suite 4520, Canada Trust Tower
Toronto, Canada M5J 2S1
Phone: 4168650003
Fax: 4168659699
E-mail: info@mercatorinvest.com
Website: www.mercatorinvest.com

Management and Staff

Peter Allen, President

Type of Firm

Private Equity Firm

Project Preferences

Type of Financing Preferred:
Early Stage
Balanced
Later Stage

Industry Preferences

In Computer Software prefer:
Software

In Computer Other prefer:
Computer Related

Additional Information

Year Founded: 1996
Current Activity Level : Actively seeking new investments

MERCER LLC

1166 Avenue of Americas
New York, NY USA 10036
Phone: 8573622000
Fax: 8573622001
Website: www.mercer.com

Other Offices

99 High Street
BOSTON, MA USA 02110
Phone: 8573622000
Fax: 8573622001

Management and Staff

Helen Shan, Chief Financial Officer
Rene Beaudoin, Chief Operating Officer

Type of Firm

Private Equity Advisor or Fund of Funds

Project Preferences

Type of Financing Preferred:
Fund of Funds

Additional Information

Name of Most Recent Fund: Mercer Private Investment Partners III, L.P.
Most Recent Fund Was Raised: 02/01/2013
Year Founded: 2013
Capital Under Management: $419,850,000
Current Activity Level : Actively seeking new investments

MERCER PRIVATE MARKETS AG

Kasernenstrasse 77b
Zurich, Switzerland 8004
Phone: 41434994949
Fax: 41434994950
E-mail: scm@scmag.com
Website: www.scmag.com

Other Offices

47, avenue John F. Kennedy
Luxembourg, Luxembourg 1855
Phone: 35224618345

17/F Aon China Building
29 Queen's Road Central
Hong Kong, Hong Kong
Phone: 85239782695
Fax: 85239782695

6th fl. Jerim Bldg
91-1 Cheongdam-dong, Kangnam-ku
Seul, South Korea 135954
Phone: 8225186550

Management and Staff

Jean-Claude Croset, Chief Financial Officer
Sascha Zeitz, Chief Operating Officer

Type of Firm

Investment Management Firm

Association Membership

Swiss Venture Capital Association (SECA)

Project Preferences

Type of Financing Preferred:
Fund of Funds
Leveraged Buyout
Early Stage
Mezzanine
Turnaround
Later Stage
Management Buyouts
Startup
Distressed Debt

Geographical Preferences

International Preferences:
Europe
Asia

Additional Information

Name of Most Recent Fund: SCM Private Equity Company Limited
Most Recent Fund Was Raised: 05/11/1998
Year Founded: 1996
Capital Under Management: $6,600,000,000
Current Activity Level : Actively seeking new investments

MERCIA FUND MANAGERS

Preston Technology Mgt. Centre
Marsh Lane
Preston, United Kingdom PR1 8UQ
Phone: 448450948886
Fax: 448450948887
Website: www.evgroup.uk.com

Other Offices

Pall Mall Court
67 King Street
Manchester, United Kingdom M2 4PD

43 Temple Row
Birmingham Office
Birmingham, United Kingdom B2 5LS

1 Whitehall
Whitehall Road
Leeds, United Kingdom LS1 4HR

Management and Staff
Jonathan Diggines, Chief Executive Officer

Type of Firm
Private Equity Firm

Association Membership
British Venture Capital Association (BVCA)

Project Preferences

Role in Financing:
Prefer role as deal originator but will also invest in deals created by others

Type of Financing Preferred:
Leveraged Buyout
Early Stage
Expansion
Mezzanine
Generalist PE
Balanced
Start-up Financing
Turnaround
Later Stage
Seed
Management Buyouts
Acquisition
Startup
Recapitalizations

Size of Investments Considered:
Min Size of Investment Considered (000s): $75
Max Size of Investment Considered (000s): $746

Geographical Preferences

International Preferences:
United Kingdom
Europe

Industry Focus
(% based on actual investment)
Industrial/Energy	20.1%
Internet Specific	14.5%
Computer Software and Services	13.5%
Other Products	12.9%
Medical/Health	10.5%
Computer Hardware	10.2%
Biotechnology	7.0%
Semiconductors/Other Elect.	5.7%
Communications and Media	3.3%
Consumer Related	2.3%

Additional Information
Name of Most Recent Fund: Coalfields Enterprise Fund
Most Recent Fund Was Raised: 05/28/2004
Year Founded: 1982
Capital Under Management: $44,800,000
Current Activity Level : Actively seeking new investments

MERCIA TECHNOLOGIES PLC

Forward House
17 High Street
Henley-in-Arden, United Kingdom B95 5AA
Website: www.merciatechnologies.com

Type of Firm
Private Equity Firm

Project Preferences

Type of Financing Preferred:
Early Stage
Balanced
Later Stage

Geographical Preferences

International Preferences:
United Kingdom

Industry Preferences

In Internet Specific prefer:
Ecommerce

In Semiconductor/Electr prefer:
Electronics

In Manufact. prefer:
Manufacturing

Additional Information
Year Founded: 2014
Current Activity Level : Actively seeking new investments

MERCK CAPITAL VENTURES LLC

101 Paragon Drive
Montvale, NJ USA 07645
Phone: 2017826060
Fax: 2017826550
Website: www.merckcapitalventures.com

Management and Staff
James Cooper, Partner

Type of Firm
Corporate PE/Venture

Project Preferences

Type of Financing Preferred:
Balanced

Size of Investments Considered:
Min Size of Investment Considered (000s): $3,000
Max Size of Investment Considered (000s): $8,000

Geographical Preferences

United States Preferences:

Industry Preferences

In Internet Specific prefer:
Internet

In Biotechnology prefer:
Biotechnology

In Medical/Health prefer:
Medical/Health
Pharmaceuticals

Additional Information
Year Founded: 2000
Capital Under Management: $100,000,000
Current Activity Level : Actively seeking new investments

MERCURIA INVESTMENT CO LTD

1-3-3 Uchisaiwaicho Chiyoda-ku
Uchisaiwaicho Daibiru Six flr
Tokyo, Japan
Phone: 81335009870
Website: www.mercuria.jp

Other Offices

No. 81 Jianguo Road
#1809 Tower 2 China Central Place
Beijing, China
Phone: 861085911811
Fax: 861085911766

Type of Firm
Investment Management Firm

Project Preferences

Type of Financing Preferred:
Leveraged Buyout
Management Buyouts
Acquisition
Startup
Recapitalizations

Geographical Preferences

United States Preferences:

International Preferences:
China
Asia
Japan

Additional Information
Year Founded: 2005
Current Activity Level : Actively seeking new investments

MERCURY CAPITAL INVESTMENTS

131 Macquarie Street
Level Five, Hudson House
Sydney, Australia 2000
Phone: 61282476700
Fax: 61292411013
E-mail: investor@mercurycapital.com.au
Website: www.mercurycapital.com.au

Management and Staff
Clark Perkins, Founder
Clark Perkins, Chief Executive Officer

Type of Firm
Private Equity Firm

Association Membership
Australian Venture Capital Association (AVCAL)
New Zealand Venture Capital Association

Project Preferences

Type of Financing Preferred:
Leveraged Buyout
Expansion
Acquisition

Geographical Preferences

International Preferences:
Australia
New Zealand

Additional Information
Year Founded: 2010
Capital Under Management: $417,000,000
Current Activity Level : Actively seeking new investments

MERCURY FUND

3737 Buffalo Speedway
Suite 1750
Houston, TX USA 77098
Phone: 7137156820
Fax: 7137156826
E-mail: info@mercuryfund.com
Website: www.mercuryfund.com

Other Offices
3925 West Braker Lane
Third Floor MCC Buildilng
BALCONES, TX USA 78759

Management and Staff
Adrian Fortino, Partner
Aziz Ahmed Gilani, Partner
Blair Garrou, Co-Founder
Dan Watkins, Co-Founder
Danny Janiak, Partner
Winston Gilpin, Chief Financial Officer

Type of Firm
Private Equity Firm

Association Membership
Illinois Venture Capital Association
National Venture Capital Association - USA (NVCA)

Project Preferences

Role in Financing:
Prefer role as deal originator but will also invest in deals created by others

Type of Financing Preferred:
Seed
Startup

Size of Investments Considered:
Min Size of Investment Considered (000s): $50
Max Size of Investment Considered (000s): $6,000

Geographical Preferences

United States Preferences:
Midwest
Rocky Mountain
Southwest
Texas

Industry Preferences

In Computer Software prefer:
Software

Additional Information
Year Founded: 2005
Capital Under Management: $225,000,000
Current Activity Level : Actively seeking new investments
Method of Compensation: Return on investment is of primary concern, do not charge fees

MERCURY VENTURES LTD

501 Park Lake Drive
McKinney, TX USA 75070
Phone: 2146540822
Fax: 2146540833
E-mail: dgoodwin@mercuryvc.com
Website: www.mercuryvc.com

Management and Staff
Don Goodwin, Partner
Kevin Howe, Partner

Type of Firm
Private Equity Firm

Project Preferences

Type of Financing Preferred:
Early Stage

Size of Investments Considered:
Min Size of Investment Considered (000s): $250
Max Size of Investment Considered (000s): $3,000

Industry Focus
(% based on actual investment)
Internet Specific   57.6%
Computer Software and Services 20.8%
Communications and Media   14.0%
Other Products   7.6%

Additional Information
Year Founded: 1999
Current Activity Level : Actively seeking new investments

MERGELANE LLC

340 18th Street
Boulder, CO USA 80302
Website: mergelane.com

Management and Staff
Elizabeth Kraus, Co-Founder

Type of Firm
Incubator/Development Program

Project Preferences

Type of Financing Preferred:
Startup

Industry Preferences

In Other prefer:
Women/Minority-Owned Bus.

Additional Information
Year Founded: 2015
Current Activity Level : Actively seeking new investments

MERGERTECH ADVISORS

4000 Executive Parkway
Suite 515
San Ramon, CA USA 94583
Phone: 9252152770
Fax: 9252152771
E-mail: info@mergertech.com
Website: www.mergertech.com

Management and Staff
Alex Howard, Managing Director
David Shohet, Managing Director
Karan Khanna, President
Lynne Turner, Managing Director
Nitin Khanna, Chief Executive Officer
Patricia Wegner, Chief Operating Officer
Philip Ma, Managing Director
Sandra Goldberg, Managing Director

Type of Firm
Bank Affiliated

Project Preferences

Type of Financing Preferred:
Early Stage
Expansion

Geographical Preferences

United States Preferences:

Industry Preferences

In Communications prefer:
Wireless Communications

In Computer Software prefer:
Data Processing

In Internet Specific prefer:
Internet

In Medical/Health prefer:
Medical/Health
Medical Products
Health Services

Additional Information
Name of Most Recent Fund: MergerTech Capital
Most Recent Fund Was Raised: 12/01/2011
Year Founded: 2011
Capital Under Management: $50,000,000
Current Activity Level : Actively seeking new investments

MERIDA CAPITAL PARTNERS LLC

6720 B Rockledge Drive
Suite 750
Crisfield, MD USA 21817
E-mail: info@meridacap.com
Website: www.meridacap.com

Management and Staff
Daniel Schmeisse, Partner
Jeffrey Monat, Partner
Justin Mullen, Partner
Kevin Gibbs, Partner
Mitch Baruchowitz, Managing Partner
Peter Kirsch, Partner
Peter Rosenberg, Partner
Stephen Ritterbush, Partner

Type of Firm
Private Equity Firm

Project Preferences

Type of Financing Preferred:
Generalist PE

Industry Preferences

In Medical/Health prefer:
Pharmaceuticals

In Consumer Related prefer:
Consumer Products

In Agr/Forestr/Fish prefer:
Agriculture related

Additional Information
Year Founded: 1969
Current Activity Level : Actively seeking new investments

MERIDIA CAPITAL PARTNERS SL

Avenida Diagonal, 640
Barcelona, Spain 08017
Phone: 34934841500
E-mail: info@meridiacapital.com
Website: www.meridiacapital.com

Management and Staff
Adrian Clarke, Vice President
Francis Muuls, Vice President

Type of Firm
Private Equity Firm

Project Preferences

Type of Financing Preferred:
Value-Add

Geographical Preferences

International Preferences:
Latin America
Europe
Spain

Industry Preferences

In Financial Services prefer:
Real Estate

Additional Information
Name of Most Recent Fund: Meridia Capital Hospitality I
Most Recent Fund Was Raised: 04/27/2007
Year Founded: 2006
Current Activity Level : Actively seeking new investments

MERIDIAN DEVELOPMENT PARTNERS LLC

280 Madison Avenue
Suite 800
New York, NY USA 10016
Phone: 2123764200
Fax: 2125329250
Website: www.meridiandp.com

Type of Firm
Private Equity Firm

Project Preferences

Type of Financing Preferred:
Leveraged Buyout
Value-Add
Expansion
Generalist PE
Opportunistic
Later Stage
Acquisition
Recapitalizations

Industry Preferences

In Biotechnology prefer:
Industrial Biotechnology

In Medical/Health prefer:
Medical/Health

In Industrial/Energy prefer:
Oil & Gas Drilling,Explor

In Financial Services prefer:
Real Estate

Additional Information
Year Founded: 1969
Current Activity Level : Actively seeking new investments

MERIDIAN GENERAL CAPITAL LLC

48 East Peninsula Center Drive
Suite 222 Rolling Hills Estate
Palos Verdes Estates, CA USA 90274
Website: www.meridiangeneral.com

Management and Staff
Peter Frank, Principal

Type of Firm
Private Equity Firm

Project Preferences

Type of Financing Preferred:
Leveraged Buyout
Acquisition

Geographical Preferences

United States Preferences:

Industry Preferences

In Communications prefer:
Communications and Media

In Computer Software prefer:
Software

In Internet Specific prefer:
Ecommerce

In Consumer Related prefer:
Entertainment and Leisure

In Transportation prefer:
Transportation
Aerospace

In Financial Services prefer:
Financial Services

Additional Information

Year Founded: 2002
Current Activity Level : Actively seeking new investments

MERIDIAN GROWTH FUND MANAGEMENT CO LTD

No. 107, Zunyi Road
1905-1907, Antai Building
Changning District, Shanghai, China 200051
Phone: 862162375090
Fax: 862162375099
Website: www.meridiancapital.com.cn

Management and Staff

Heng Zhou, Partner
Wei Ji, Partner
Xiangdong Xiong, Partner

Type of Firm

Private Equity Firm

Project Preferences

Type of Financing Preferred:
Balanced

Geographical Preferences

International Preferences:
China

Industry Preferences

In Communications prefer:
Radio & TV Broadcasting
Wireless Communications
Media and Entertainment

In Internet Specific prefer:
Internet

In Consumer Related prefer:
Entertainment and Leisure
Education Related

In Financial Services prefer:
Financial Services

In Business Serv. prefer:
Services
Media

Additional Information

Year Founded: 2010
Capital Under Management: $407,005,000
Current Activity Level : Actively seeking new investments

MERIDIAN STREET CAPITAL

11350 N. Meridian Street
Suite 420
Carmel, IN USA 46032
Phone: 3176079576
E-mail: info@meridianstreetcapital.com
Website: www.meridianstreetcapital.com

Type of Firm

Private Equity Firm

Project Preferences

Type of Financing Preferred:
Early Stage
Seed

Industry Preferences

In Medical/Health prefer:
Health Services

Additional Information

Year Founded: 2015
Capital Under Management: $10,000,000
Current Activity Level : Actively seeking new investments

MERIDIAN VENTURE PARTNERS

259 N. Radnor-Chester Road
Suite 130
Radnor, PA USA 19087
Phone: 6102542999
Fax: 6102542996

Management and Staff

Robert Brown, Managing Partner
Thomas Penn, Partner

Type of Firm

Private Equity Firm

Project Preferences

Role in Financing:
Prefer role as deal originator but will also invest in deals created by others

Type of Financing Preferred:
Leveraged Buyout
Acquisition
Recapitalizations

Geographical Preferences

United States Preferences:
Southeast

Industry Focus

(% based on actual investment)
Other Products	42.0%
Consumer Related	19.6%
Internet Specific	15.4%
Medical/Health	7.5%
Computer Software and Services	7.2%
Biotechnology	6.1%
Industrial/Energy	1.0%
Communications and Media	0.6%
Computer Hardware	0.5%

Additional Information

Name of Most Recent Fund: Meridian Venture Partners II
Most Recent Fund Was Raised: 11/01/1999
Year Founded: 1987
Capital Under Management: $110,000,000
Current Activity Level : Actively seeking new investments
Method of Compensation: Return on invest. most important, but chg. closing fees, service fees, etc.

MERIDIUS CAPITAL

349 St. Clair Avenue
Suite 111
Toronto, Canada M5P 1N3
Phone: 416-873-4219

Management and Staff

John DeHart, Partner
Richard Strafehl, Principal

Type of Firm

Private Equity Firm

Project Preferences

Type of Financing Preferred:
Later Stage

Additional Information

Year Founded: 2009
Current Activity Level : Actively seeking new investments

Pratt's Guide to Private Equity & Venture Capital Sources

MERIEUX DEVELOPPEMENT SAS

17, rue Bourgelat
Lyon, France 69002
Phone: 33478873700
Fax: 33478873702
E-mail: info@merieux-developpement.com
Website: www.merieux-developpement.com

Management and Staff
Alexandre Merieux, President
Francois Valencony, Managing Director
Valerie Calenda, Partner

Type of Firm
Private Equity Firm

Association Membership
European Private Equity and Venture Capital Assoc.

Project Preferences

Type of Financing Preferred:
Early Stage
Later Stage
Acquisition

Geographical Preferences

International Preferences:
Europe
France

Industry Preferences

In Computer Hardware prefer:
Mainframes / Scientific

In Medical/Health prefer:
Medical/Health
Medical Therapeutics
Health Services

In Business Serv. prefer:
Services

Additional Information
Year Founded: 2009
Capital Under Management: $188,250,000
Current Activity Level : Actively seeking new investments

MERIFIN CAPITAL

Place Flagey 18
Brussels, Belgium 1050
Phone: 3226462580
Fax: 3226463036
E-mail: enquiries@merifin.com
Website: www.merifin.com

Other Offices
254, Route de Lausanne
Geneva-Chambesy, Switzerland 1292
Phone: 41-22-770-0088
Fax: 41-22-758-0055

Type of Firm
Private Equity Firm

Association Membership
European Private Equity and Venture Capital Assoc.

Project Preferences

Role in Financing:
Will function either as deal originator or investor in deals created by others

Type of Financing Preferred:
Leveraged Buyout
Early Stage
Generalist PE
Turnaround
Later Stage
Management Buyouts
Private Placement

Size of Investments Considered:
Min Size of Investment Considered (000s): $250
Max Size of Investment Considered (000s): $3,000

Geographical Preferences

United States Preferences:
All U.S.

Canadian Preferences:
All Canada

International Preferences:
Italy
Latin America
United Kingdom
Europe
China
Bermuda
Eastern Europe
Spain
Australia
Asia
South Africa
Germany
France

Additional Information
Year Founded: 1980
Current Activity Level : Actively seeking new investments
Method of Compensation: Return on invest. most important, but chg. closing fees, service fees, etc.

MERION INVESTMENT PARTNERS LP

555 East Lancaster Avenue, Suite 500
Radnor, PA USA 19087
Phone: 6109925880
Fax: 6109451654
E-mail: info@merionpartners.com
Website: www.merionpartners.com

Management and Staff
Alex Rohr, Vice President
Anthony Caringi, Partner
Gayle Hughes, Partner
Samuel Brewer, Principal
William Means, Managing Partner

Type of Firm
SBIC

Association Membership
Natl Assoc of Small Bus. Inv. Co (NASBIC)

Project Preferences

Role in Financing:
Will function either as deal originator or investor in deals created by others

Type of Financing Preferred:
Leveraged Buyout
Expansion
Mezzanine
Management Buyouts
Acquisition
Industry Rollups

Geographical Preferences

United States Preferences:
Southeast
Northeast
East Coast

Industry Preferences

In Computer Software prefer:
Software

In Medical/Health prefer:
Medical Products
Health Services

In Transportation prefer:
Aerospace

In Business Serv. prefer:
Services

In Manufact. prefer:
Manufacturing

Additional Information
Year Founded: 2003
Capital Under Management: $200,000,000
Current Activity Level : Actively seeking new investments
Method of Compensation: Return on invest. most important, but chg. closing fees, service fees, etc.

MERIT CAPITAL PARTNERS IV LLC

303 West Madison Street
Suite 2100
Chicago, IL USA 60606
Phone: 3125926111
Fax: 3125926112
E-mail: mcp@meritcapital.com
Website: www.meritcapital.com

Management and Staff

Benjamin Yarbrough, Principal
Daniel Pansing, Managing Director
David Jones, Managing Director
Evan Gallinson, Managing Director
Jeremy Stump, Vice President
Joseph Polaneczky, Vice President
Lauren Hamlin, Vice President
Marc Walfish, Managing Director
Terrance Shipp, Founder
Thomas Campion, Managing Director
Timothy MacKenzie, Managing Director
Van Lam, Chief Financial Officer

Type of Firm

Private Equity Firm

Project Preferences

Role in Financing:
Will function either as deal originator or investor in deals created by others

Type of Financing Preferred:
Leveraged Buyout
Mezzanine
Later Stage
Management Buyouts
Acquisition
Recapitalizations

Geographical Preferences

United States Preferences:

Industry Focus

(% based on actual investment)
Other Products	54.0%
Industrial/Energy	23.9%
Consumer Related	13.0%
Computer Hardware	5.5%
Medical/Health	1.4%
Computer Software and Services	1.2%
Semiconductors/Other Elect.	0.5%
Internet Specific	0.5%

Additional Information

Name of Most Recent Fund: Merit Mezzanine Fund V, L.P.
Most Recent Fund Was Raised: 08/11/2010
Year Founded: 1993
Capital Under Management: $1,700,000,000
Current Activity Level : Actively seeking new investments
Method of Compensation: Return on invest. most important, but chg. closing fees, service fees, etc.

MERITAGE FUNDS

1675 Larimer Street
Suite 400
Denver, CO USA 80202
Phone: 3033522040
Fax: 3033522050

Management and Staff

David Solomon, Founder

Type of Firm

Private Equity Firm

Project Preferences

Role in Financing:
Prefer role as deal originator but will also invest in deals created by others

Type of Financing Preferred:
Leveraged Buyout
Expansion
Generalist PE
Balanced
Later Stage
Management Buyouts
Acquisition
Recapitalizations

Size of Investments Considered:
Min Size of Investment Considered (000s): $5,000
Max Size of Investment Considered (000s): $15,000

Geographical Preferences

United States Preferences:

Industry Focus

(% based on actual investment)
Computer Hardware	39.4%
Communications and Media	37.7%
Internet Specific	14.5%
Computer Software and Services	8.4%

Additional Information

Name of Most Recent Fund: Meritage Private Equity Fund III
Most Recent Fund Was Raised: 12/10/2008
Year Founded: 1998
Capital Under Management: $600,000,000
Current Activity Level : Actively seeking new investments
Method of Compensation: Return on investment is of primary concern, do not charge fees

MERITECH CAPITAL PARTNERS

245 Lytton Avenue, Suite 125
Palo Alto, CA USA 94301
Phone: 6504752200
Fax: 6504752222
E-mail: info@meritechcapital.com
Website: www.meritechcapital.com

Type of Firm

Private Equity Firm

Association Membership

National Venture Capital Association - USA (NVCA)

Project Preferences

Role in Financing:
Prefer role as deal originator but will also invest in deals created by others

Type of Financing Preferred:
Later Stage

Size of Investments Considered:
Min Size of Investment Considered (000s): $5,000
Max Size of Investment Considered (000s): $50,000

Geographical Preferences

United States Preferences:

Industry Focus

(% based on actual investment)
Computer Software and Services	42.5%
Communications and Media	24.6%
Internet Specific	22.3%
Computer Hardware	3.8%
Semiconductors/Other Elect.	2.9%
Medical/Health	2.6%
Other Products	1.0%
Biotechnology	0.4%

Additional Information

Name of Most Recent Fund: Meritech Capital Partners IV, L.P.
Most Recent Fund Was Raised: 10/27/2010
Year Founded: 1999
Capital Under Management: $2,600,000,000
Current Activity Level : Actively seeking new investments
Method of Compensation: Return on investment is of primary concern, do not charge fees

MERITUS VENTURES LP

362 Old Whitley Road
P.O. Box 1738
London, KY USA 40743
Phone: 6068645175
Fax: 6068645194
Website: www.meritusventures.com

Other Offices

1020 Commerce Park Drive
OAK RIDGE, TN USA 37830
Phone: 865-220-1715
Fax: 865-220-2024

Management and Staff

Brenda McDaniel, Chief Financial Officer
L. Ray Moncrief, General Partner

Type of Firm

SBIC

Association Membership
Community Development Venture Capital Alliance

Project Preferences

Role in Financing:
Will function either as deal originator or investor in deals created by others

Type of Financing Preferred:
Early Stage
Expansion
Balanced
Later Stage

Size of Investments Considered:
Min Size of Investment Considered (000s): $250
Max Size of Investment Considered (000s): $2,500

Geographical Preferences

United States Preferences:
Tennessee
Mississippi
Alabama
North Carolina
South Carolina
Ohio
Virginia
Georgia
Arkansas
Kentucky
West Virginia

Industry Preferences

In Computer Software prefer:
Software

In Manufact. prefer:
Manufacturing

Additional Information
Year Founded: 2006
Capital Under Management: $36,400,000
Current Activity Level : Actively seeking new investments

MERLIN NEXUS

424 West 33rd Street, Suite 330
New York, NY USA 10001
Phone: 6462275270
E-mail: invest@merlinnexus.com
Website: www.merlinnexus.com

Management and Staff
Dominique Semon, Chief Financial Officer

Type of Firm
Private Equity Firm

Project Preferences

Role in Financing:
Will function either as deal originator or investor in deals created by others

Type of Financing Preferred:
Public Companies
Later Stage

Additional Information
Name of Most Recent Fund: Merlin Nexus IV, L.P.
Most Recent Fund Was Raised: 03/06/2012
Year Founded: 2001
Capital Under Management: $175,000,000
Current Activity Level : Actively seeking new investments
Method of Compensation: Return on invest. most important, but chg. closing fees, service fees, etc.

MERRICK VENTURES LLC

200 East Randolph Street
Suite 2210
Chicago, IL USA 60601
Phone: 3129949421
E-mail: info@merrickventures.com
Website: www.merrickventures.com

Type of Firm
Private Equity Firm

Project Preferences

Type of Financing Preferred:
Balanced

Geographical Preferences

United States Preferences:
Illinois

Industry Preferences

In Internet Specific prefer:
Internet

Additional Information
Year Founded: 2007
Current Activity Level : Actively seeking new investments

MERSEYSIDE SPECIAL INVESTMENT FUND LTD

2nd Floor, One Dale Street
Exchange Court
Liverpool, United Kingdom L2 2PP
Phone: 01512364040
Fax: 01512363060
E-mail: info@msif.co.uk
Website: www.msif.co.uk

Management and Staff
Lisa Greenhalgh, Chief Operating Officer

Type of Firm
Private Equity Firm

Project Preferences

Type of Financing Preferred:
Expansion
Mezzanine
Management Buyouts
Acquisition
Startup

Geographical Preferences

International Preferences:
United Kingdom

Additional Information
Year Founded: 2010
Current Activity Level : Actively seeking new investments

MERUS CAPITAL INVESTMENT

505 Hamilton Avenue
Suite 315
Palo Alto, CA USA 94301
Phone: 6508388888
E-mail: info@meruscap.com
Website: www.meruscap.com

Management and Staff
Peter Hsing, Co-Founder
Salman Ullah, Co-Founder
Sean Dempsey, Co-Founder

Type of Firm
Private Equity Firm

Project Preferences

Role in Financing:
Prefer role as deal originator but will also invest in deals created by others

Type of Financing Preferred:
Early Stage
Seed
Startup

Geographical Preferences

United States Preferences:

Industry Preferences

In Computer Software prefer:
Software

In Internet Specific prefer:
Internet

Additional Information
Name of Most Recent Fund: Merus Capital II, L.P.
Most Recent Fund Was Raised: 04/23/2013
Year Founded: 2007
Capital Under Management: $37,000,000
Current Activity Level : Actively seeking new investments
Method of Compensation: Return on investment is of primary concern, do not charge fees

MESA VERDE VENTURE PARTNERS LP

4401 Eastgate Mall
San Diego, CA USA 92121
Phone: 8582455045
E-mail: info@mesaverdevp.com
Website: www.mesaverdevp.com

Management and Staff
Carey Ng, Principal
Daniel Wood, General Partner

Type of Firm
Private Equity Firm

Project Preferences

Type of Financing Preferred:
Early Stage

Size of Investments Considered:
Min Size of Investment Considered (000s): $250
Max Size of Investment Considered (000s): $1,500

Geographical Preferences

United States Preferences:
Southwest

Industry Preferences

In Medical/Health prefer:
Medical/Health
Diagnostic Test Products
Drug/Equipmt Delivery

Additional Information
Name of Most Recent Fund: Mesa Verde Venture Partners II, L.P.
Most Recent Fund Was Raised: 03/07/2014
Year Founded: 2006
Capital Under Management: $5,400,000
Current Activity Level : Actively seeking new investments

MESA+

85 Fifth Avenue
Suite 6
New York, NY USA 10003
Phone: 2127923950
Website: www.mesa.vc

Type of Firm
Bank Affiliated

Project Preferences

Role in Financing:
Prefer role in deals created by others

Type of Financing Preferred:
Early Stage
Seed
Startup

Geographical Preferences

United States Preferences:
New York

Industry Preferences

In Communications prefer:
Entertainment

In Internet Specific prefer:
Internet
Ecommerce

In Business Serv. prefer:
Media

Additional Information
Name of Most Recent Fund: Mesa Plus I, L.P.
Most Recent Fund Was Raised: 06/01/2012
Year Founded: 2012
Capital Under Management: $2,300,000
Current Activity Level : Actively seeking new investments

MESH VENTURES INC

Neihu District
2F, No.413, RuiGuang Road
Taipei, Taiwan 11492
Phone: 886287971707
E-mail: hello@mesh.vc
Website: www.mesh.vc

Type of Firm
Private Equity Firm

Additional Information
Year Founded: 2015
Current Activity Level : Actively seeking new investments

MESIROW FINANCIAL PRIVATE EQUITY INC

353 North Clark Street
Chicago, IL USA 60654
Phone: 3125956000
Fax: 3125954246

Management and Staff
Daniel Howell, Senior Managing Director
Jessica Marta, Vice President
Kristina Pierce, Vice President
Marc Sacks, Senior Managing Director
Robert DeBolt, Managing Director
Ryan Fedronich, Vice President
Thomas Galuhn, Senior Managing Director

Type of Firm
Investment Management Firm

Association Membership
Illinois Venture Capital Association

Project Preferences

Role in Financing:
Will function either as deal originator or investor in deals created by others

Type of Financing Preferred:
Leveraged Buyout
Value-Add
Expansion
Generalist PE
Balanced
Turnaround
Later Stage
Management Buyouts
Acquisition
Special Situation
Distressed Debt

Geographical Preferences

United States Preferences:
North America

Canadian Preferences:
All Canada

International Preferences:
Latin America
India
Western Europe

Industry Focus
(% based on actual investment)

Other Products	50.6%
Computer Software and Services	13.5%
Consumer Related	11.6%
Computer Hardware	6.8%
Communications and Media	6.5%
Internet Specific	6.0%
Industrial/Energy	1.8%
Medical/Health	1.6%
Semiconductors/Other Elect.	1.0%
Biotechnology	0.6%

Additional Information
Name of Most Recent Fund: Mesirow Financial Real Estate Value Fund II, L.P.
Most Recent Fund Was Raised: 03/10/2014
Year Founded: 1982
Capital Under Management: $800,000,000
Current Activity Level : Actively seeking new investments
Method of Compensation: Return on investment is of primary concern, do not charge fees

METALMARK CAPITAL HOLDINGS LLC

1177 Avenue of the Americas
40th Floor
New York, NY USA 10036
Phone: 2128231930
Fax: 2128231931
Website: www.metalmarkcapital.com

Management and Staff
Andrew Feller, Managing Director
David Boudo, Principal
David Battle, Vice President
Donald Gerne, Vice President
Elena McKee, Vice President
Gregory Myers, Managing Director
Jeffrey Siegal, Managing Director
Kumar Valliappan, Vice President
Leigh Abramson, Managing Director
M. Fazle Husain, Managing Director
M. Glen Itwaru, Vice President
Martin McNulty, Vice President
Michael Hoffman, Managing Director
N. Michael Farah, Vice President
Vanessa Adler, Principal
W. Russell Bennett, Vice President

Type of Firm
Private Equity Firm

Project Preferences

Type of Financing Preferred:
Leveraged Buyout
Acquisition

Industry Preferences

In Medical/Health prefer:
Medical/Health

In Industrial/Energy prefer:
Energy
Industrial Products

Additional Information
Name of Most Recent Fund: Metalmark Capital Partners II, L.P.
Most Recent Fund Was Raised: 04/15/2011
Year Founded: 2004
Capital Under Management: $3,500,000,000
Current Activity Level : Actively seeking new investments

METHOD ADVISORS LLC
192 South Street
Sixth Floor
Boston, MA USA 02111
Phone: 6174264610
Fax: 6174264614
E-mail: info@methodadvisors.com
Website: www.methodadvisors.com

Management and Staff
Christopher Welch, Managing Director
Eric Stewart, Managing Director
Jeffrey Sung, Managing Director

Type of Firm
Private Equity Advisor or Fund of Funds

Project Preferences

Type of Financing Preferred:
Fund of Funds
Fund of Funds of Second

Geographical Preferences

United States Preferences:

International Preferences:
Europe
Asia

Additional Information
Name of Most Recent Fund: Method Advisors 2012, L.P.
Most Recent Fund Was Raised: 03/20/2012
Year Founded: 2009
Capital Under Management: $114,400,000
Current Activity Level : Actively seeking new investments

METHOD CAPITAL
900 North Michigan Avenue
Suite 1600
Chicago, IL USA 60290
Phone: 3126486800
E-mail: info@kdwcventures.com
Website: http://method.capital

Type of Firm
Private Equity Firm

Project Preferences

Type of Financing Preferred:
Early Stage
Start-up Financing
Seed

Geographical Preferences

United States Preferences:
Midwest

Additional Information
Year Founded: 2015
Current Activity Level : Actively seeking new investments

METRIC CAPITAL PARTNERS LLP
Two Maddox Street
London, United Kingdom W1S 1QP
Phone: 442035401550
Fax: 442074950319
E-mail: info@metric-capital.com
Website: www.metric-capital.com

Management and Staff
David Scheurl, Principal
Giovanni Miele, Co-Founder
Ilkka Rantanen, Principal
John Sinik, Co-Founder
Peter Cornell, Partner

Type of Firm
Private Equity Firm

Project Preferences

Type of Financing Preferred:
Leveraged Buyout
Expansion
Generalist PE
Balanced
Later Stage
Management Buyouts
Acquisition
Distressed Debt

Geographical Preferences

International Preferences:
United Kingdom
Europe

Additional Information
Year Founded: 2011
Capital Under Management: $250,000,000
Current Activity Level : Actively seeking new investments

METRIX CAPITAL GROUP LLC
160 North Riverview Drive
Suite 200
Anaheim, CA USA 92808
Phone: 7148204570
Fax: 7148204599
Website: www.metrixcapitalgroup.com

Management and Staff
Jeff Brannon, Managing Director

Type of Firm
Investment Management Firm

Project Preferences

Type of Financing Preferred:
Early Stage
Balanced
Seed

Industry Preferences

In Medical/Health prefer:
Medical/Health

In Manufact. prefer:
Manufacturing

Additional Information
Year Founded: 2011
Current Activity Level : Actively seeking new investments

METRO GLOBAL VENTURES LLC

One Belmont Avenue
Suite 415
Bala Cynwyd, PA USA 19004
Phone: 484.483.3349
E-mail: info@metrogv.com
Website: metrogv.com

Type of Firm
Private Equity Firm

Project Preferences

Type of Financing Preferred:
Leveraged Buyout
Expansion
Management Buyouts
Acquisition
Distressed Debt

Additional Information
Year Founded: 2012
Current Activity Level : Actively seeking new investments

METROPOLITAN EQUITY PARTNERS LLC

70 East 55th Street
19th Floor
New York, NY USA 10022
Phone: 2125611250
Fax: 9175914289
Website: metpg.com

Other Offices
Former HQ: 590 Madison Avenue
34th Floor
MANHATTAN, NY USA 10022
Phone: 2125611257
Fax: 9175914289

Management and Staff
Eric Chasser, Chief Financial Officer
John Ioannou, President
Miles Peet, Vice President
Paul Lisiak, Managing Partner

Type of Firm
Private Equity Firm

Project Preferences

Type of Financing Preferred:
Mezzanine
Generalist PE
Other
Special Situation

Geographical Preferences

United States Preferences:

Industry Preferences

In Consumer Related prefer:
Consumer Services

In Financial Services prefer:
Financial Services

In Business Serv. prefer:
Services

Additional Information
Name of Most Recent Fund: Metropolitan EIH22, L.P.
Most Recent Fund Was Raised: 11/01/2013
Year Founded: 2008
Capital Under Management: $74,000,000
Current Activity Level : Actively seeking new investments

METROPOLITAN REAL ESTATE EQUITY MANAGEMENT LLC

650 Fifth Avenue
29th Floor
New York, NY USA 10019
Phone: 2128124950
E-mail: info@mreem.com
Website: mreem.com

Management and Staff
Alison Setterberg, Vice President
Andrew Jacobs, Managing Director
Beth-Anne Flynn, Managing Director
Christie Philbrick-Wheaton, Vice President
Christine Iijima, Vice President
David Nasaw, Co-Founder
Doug Lee, Managing Director
J.E. Taylor, Managing Director
Jeremy Ford, Managing Director
John So, Managing Director
Margaret McKnight, Managing Director
Sarah Schwarzschild, Vice President
T. Robert Burke, Co-Founder

Type of Firm
Private Equity Advisor or Fund of Funds

Project Preferences

Type of Financing Preferred:
Fund of Funds

Industry Preferences

In Financial Services prefer:
Real Estate
Investment Groups

Additional Information
Year Founded: 2002
Capital Under Management: $585,000,000
Current Activity Level : Actively seeking new investments

METROVIEW CAPITAL LLC

2217 Matthews Township Pkwy
Suite 141
Matthews, NC USA 28105
Phone: 7048824743
E-mail: info@metroviewcapital.com
Website: www.metroviewcapital.com

Type of Firm
Private Equity Firm

Project Preferences

Type of Financing Preferred:
Leveraged Buyout
Value-Add
Early Stage
Turnaround

Geographical Preferences

United States Preferences:
North America

Industry Preferences

In Medical/Health prefer:
Medical/Health

In Industrial/Energy prefer:
Alternative Energy

In Financial Services prefer:
Real Estate

Additional Information
Year Founded: 2013
Current Activity Level : Actively seeking new investments

METSOLA VENTURES OY

Visakoivuntie 20 B
Espoo, Finland 02130

Type of Firm
Private Equity Firm

Project Preferences

Type of Financing Preferred:
Early Stage
Expansion
Seed
Startup

Geographical Preferences

International Preferences:
Europe
Finland

Additional Information
Year Founded: 2010
Current Activity Level: Actively seeking new investments

MEUSINVEST SA

Rue Lambert Lombard 3
Liege, Belgium 4000
Phone: 3242216211
Fax: 3242235765
E-mail: info@meusinvest.be
Website: www.meusinvest.be

Management and Staff
Gaetan Servais, Chief Executive Officer
Josly Piette, President

Type of Firm
Private Equity Firm

Project Preferences

Type of Financing Preferred:
Leveraged Buyout
Early Stage
Generalist PE
Later Stage
Acquisition

Geographical Preferences

International Preferences:
Europe
Belgium

Additional Information
Year Founded: 1985
Capital Under Management: $135,300,000
Current Activity Level: Actively seeking new investments

MEYER VENTURES LLC

767 Fifth Avenue
18th Flr, General Motors Bldg.
New York, NY USA 10153
Phone: 2123896520
Fax: 2123896540
E-mail: info@meyerandco.com
Website: www.meyerandco.com

Type of Firm
Bank Affiliated

Project Preferences

Type of Financing Preferred:
Balanced

Industry Preferences

In Medical/Health prefer:
Health Services

In Consumer Related prefer:
Consumer Services

In Financial Services prefer:
Financial Services

In Business Serv. prefer:
Media

Additional Information
Year Founded: 2002
Current Activity Level: Actively seeking new investments

MEZZANINE CORP

11-1 Marunouchi 1-chome
Chiyoda-ku
Tokyo, Japan 100-6230
Phone: 81362127250
Fax: 81362127251
E-mail: info@mcokk.com
Website: www.mcokk.com

Management and Staff
Kengo Wada, Principal
Koji Sasayama, Managing Director
Masaaki Sato, Principal
Takao Nagata, Principal

Type of Firm
Investment Management Firm

Project Preferences

Type of Financing Preferred:
Mezzanine

Geographical Preferences

International Preferences:
Japan

Industry Preferences

In Communications prefer:
Telecommunications

In Medical/Health prefer:
Medical/Health

In Consumer Related prefer:
Retail
Food/Beverage

In Industrial/Energy prefer:
Industrial Products
Materials

In Business Serv. prefer:
Services

Additional Information
Year Founded: 2005
Current Activity Level: Actively seeking new investments

MEZZANINE MANAGEMENT FINANZ UND UNTERNEH-MENSBERATUNGSGMBH

Kohlmarkt 5/6
Vienna, Austria 1010
Phone: 4315328990
Fax: 431532899020
E-mail: office@mezzmanagement.com
Website: www.mezzmanagement.com

Other Offices
Kalman I. utca 1
Budapest, Hungary 1055
Phone: 36-1-475-1415
Fax: 36-1-475-1111

56 Roma Str.
ground floor
Bucharest 1st district, Romania
Phone: 40-21-230-3219
Fax: 40-21-230-3226

ul. Sienna 39
Warsaw, Poland 00121
Phone: 48-22-654-6415
Fax: 48-22-654-6418

B. Khmelnytskogo 52A
Kiev, Ukraine 01030
Phone: 380-44-288-0961
Fax: 380-44-288-0986

Management and Staff
Chris Buckle, Managing Director
Claudiu Corcodel, Managing Director
Przemyslaw Glebocki, Managing Director
Tomasz Kwiecien, Managing Director

Type of Firm
Private Equity Firm

Association Membership
Austrian PE and Venture Capital Association (AVCO)
Polish Venture Capital Association (PSIC/PPEA)
European Private Equity and Venture Capital Assoc.
South Eastern Europes Private Equity Association

Project Preferences

Type of Financing Preferred:
Leveraged Buyout
Mezzanine
Later Stage
Management Buyouts
Acquisition
Recapitalizations

Geographical Preferences

International Preferences:
Hungary
Slovak Repub.
Central Europe
Europe
Czech Republic
Poland
Austria
Eastern Europe
Ukraine
Bulgaria
Romania
Russia

Industry Preferences

In Communications prefer:
Commercial Communications
Radio & TV Broadcasting
Telecommunications
Wireless Communications
Media and Entertainment

In Medical/Health prefer:
Medical/Health

In Consumer Related prefer:
Consumer
Retail
Food/Beverage

In Industrial/Energy prefer:
Industrial Products
Environmental Related

In Transportation prefer:
Transportation

In Financial Services prefer:
Financial Services
Insurance
Real Estate
Financial Services

In Business Serv. prefer:
Services

In Manufact. prefer:
Manufacturing

In Agr/Forestr/Fish prefer:
Mining and Minerals

Additional Information

Name of Most Recent Fund: Accession Mezzanine Capital LP
Most Recent Fund Was Raised: 07/14/2003
Year Founded: 2000
Capital Under Management: $534,500,000
Current Activity Level : Actively seeking new investments

MEZZANINE PARTNERS (PTY) LTD

17 Melrose Blvd., Melrose Arch
3rd Floor, STANLIB Building
Johannesburg, South Africa 2196
Phone: 27114486000
Fax: 27860105395
E-mail: info@mezzpartners.com
Website: www.mezzpartners.com

Management and Staff

Walter Hirzebruch, Chief Operating Officer

Type of Firm

Private Equity Firm

Project Preferences

Type of Financing Preferred:
Leveraged Buyout
Expansion
Mezzanine
Balanced
Later Stage
Management Buyouts
Acquisition
Distressed Debt
Recapitalizations

Geographical Preferences

International Preferences:
South Africa

Additional Information

Year Founded: 2005
Current Activity Level : Actively seeking new investments

MEZZANOVE CAPITAL I

Foro Buonaparte 12
Milan, Italy 20121

Type of Firm

Private Equity Firm

Project Preferences

Type of Financing Preferred:
Mezzanine

Geographical Preferences

International Preferences:
Europe

Additional Information

Year Founded: 2006
Capital Under Management: $104,000,000
Current Activity Level : Actively seeking new investments

MFG PARTNERS LLC

900 Third Avenue
33rd Floor
New York, NY USA 10022
Phone: 2123173340
E-mail: info@mfgpartners.com
Website: mfgpartners.com

Type of Firm

Private Equity Firm

Project Preferences

Type of Financing Preferred:
Leveraged Buyout
Acquisition

Additional Information

Year Founded: 2016
Current Activity Level : Actively seeking new investments

MGI HOLDINGS INC

1601 Dodge Street
Suite 3800
Omaha, NE USA 68102
Phone: 4029328600
Fax: 4029910020
Website: www.mccarthycapital.com

Other Offices

One International Place
Seventh Floor
Boston, MA USA 02110
Phone: 617-330-9700
Fax: 617-330-9705

1601 Dodge Street
Suite 3800
Omaha, NE USA 68102
Phone: 402-932-8600
Fax: 402-991-0020

1755 Blake Street
Suite 230
Denver, CO USA 80202
Phone: 303-292-5100
Fax: 303-292-5105

Management and Staff

Michael McCarthy, Partner
Michael McGovern, Principal
Patrick Duffy, Managing Partner
Robert Emmert, Managing Partner
Robert Myers, Partner

Type of Firm

Private Equity Firm

Project Preferences

Type of Financing Preferred:
Leveraged Buyout
Later Stage
Management Buyouts
Acquisition
Recapitalizations

Size of Investments Considered:
Min Size of Investment Considered (000s): $10,000
Max Size of Investment Considered (000s): $45,000

Geographical Preferences

United States Preferences:
All U.S.

Industry Preferences

In Communications prefer:
Commercial Communications

In Computer Software prefer:
Systems Software

In Financial Services prefer:
Financial Services

In Business Serv. prefer:
Services

In Manufact. prefer:
Manufacturing

Additional Information

Name of Most Recent Fund: McCarthy Capital Fund V, L.P.
Most Recent Fund Was Raised: 06/28/2011
Year Founded: 1986
Capital Under Management: $511,000,000
Current Activity Level : Actively seeking new investments

MGM INNOVA CAPITAL LLC

1000 Brickell Avenue
Suite 900
Miami, FL USA 33131
Phone: 7864372335
E-mail: contact@mgminnovacap.com
Website: www.mgminnovacap.com

Management and Staff

Gerardo Aguilar, Senior Managing Director
Maria Pia Iannariello, Co-Founder

Type of Firm

Private Equity Firm

Project Preferences

Type of Financing Preferred:
Generalist PE

Geographical Preferences

International Preferences:
Latin America

Industry Preferences

In Industrial/Energy prefer:
Alternative Energy
Energy Conservation Relat
Environmental Related

Additional Information

Year Founded: 2010
Current Activity Level : Actively seeking new investments

MH CARNEGIE & CO PTY LTD

120B Underwood Street
Paddington, Australia 2021
Phone: 61293971400
E-mail: enquiries@mhcarnegie.com
Website: www.mhcarnegie.com

Type of Firm

Investment Management Firm

Project Preferences

Type of Financing Preferred:
Leveraged Buyout
Early Stage
Balanced
Later Stage
Seed
Acquisition

Size of Investments Considered:
Min Size of Investment Considered (000s): $250
Max Size of Investment Considered (000s): $20,000

Geographical Preferences

International Preferences:
Australia

Additional Information

Year Founded: 2010
Capital Under Management: $131,600,000
Current Activity Level : Actively seeking new investments

MHFT INVESTIMENTOS SA

Praia de Botafogo, 440-6 andar
Botafogo
Rio de Janeiro, Brazil 22250-908
Phone: 552137971000
E-mail: contact@nsgcapital.com.br
Website: www.mhftinvestimentos.com.br

Other Offices

Rua Professor Francisco Fonseca
86 - Sala 4, Bacaxa
Saquarema, Brazil 28993-000
Phone: 552226532342

Management and Staff

Aline Galant, Managing Director
Bruno Esmeraldo Torres de Oliveira, Managing Director
Jose Carlos Franco De Abreu Filho, Managing Director
Luiz Eduardo Franco de Abreu, Chief Executive Officer

Type of Firm

Private Equity Firm

Association Membership

Brazilian Venture Capital Association (ABCR)

Project Preferences

Type of Financing Preferred:
Leveraged Buyout
Management Buyouts
Acquisition
Recapitalizations

Geographical Preferences

International Preferences:
Brazil

Industry Preferences

In Industrial/Energy prefer:
Industrial Products
Advanced Materials

Additional Information

Year Founded: 2006
Current Activity Level : Actively seeking new investments

MHS CAPITAL MANAGEMENT LLC

333 Bush Street
Suite 2250
San Francisco, CA USA 94104
Phone: 4156552800
E-mail: info@mhscapital.com
Website: www.mhscapital.com

Other Offices

2201 Pacific Avenue
Suite 503
San Francisco, CA USA 94115
Phone: 4159292547

Management and Staff

Mark Sugarman, Managing Director

Type of Firm

Private Equity Firm

Project Preferences

Type of Financing Preferred:
Early Stage
Startup

Size of Investments Considered:
Min Size of Investment Considered (000s): $500
Max Size of Investment Considered (000s): $1,000

Geographical Preferences

United States Preferences:
All U.S.

International Preferences:
Latin America
Europe

Industry Preferences

In Communications prefer:
Wireless Communications

In Computer Software prefer:
Software

In Internet Specific prefer:
Ecommerce
Web Aggregation/Portals

In Medical/Health prefer:
Medical/Health

In Consumer Related prefer:
Education Related

Additional Information

Name of Most Recent Fund: MHS Capital Partners, L.P.
Most Recent Fund Was Raised: 10/26/2006
Year Founded: 2006
Capital Under Management: $74,735,000
Current Activity Level : Actively seeking new investments

MI VENTURES LLC

373 Park Avenue South
Suite 630
New York, NY USA 10016
Phone: 646257265
E-mail: info@miventuresllc.com
Website: www.miventuresllc.com

Management and Staff

Aamer Abdullah, Principal
Aaron Allon, Partner

Type of Firm

Private Equity Firm

Project Preferences

Type of Financing Preferred:
Early Stage
Seed
Startup

Geographical Preferences

United States Preferences:
All U.S.

Industry Preferences

In Computer Software prefer:
Software
Applications Software

In Internet Specific prefer:
Internet
Web Aggregation/Portals

Additional Information

Year Founded: 2010
Current Activity Level : Actively seeking new investments

MIC AG

Denisstrasse 1b
Munich, Germany 80335
Phone: 4989244192200
Fax: 4989244192230
E-mail: info@mic-ag.eu
Website: www.mic-ag.eu

Type of Firm

Private Equity Firm

Association Membership

German Venture Capital Association (BVK)

Project Preferences

Type of Financing Preferred:
Early Stage
Seed
Startup

Geographical Preferences

International Preferences:
Germany

Industry Preferences

In Communications prefer:
Communications and Media
Telecommunications

In Computer Software prefer:
Software

In Semiconductor/Electr prefer:
Optoelectronics

In Medical/Health prefer:
Medical/Health

In Industrial/Energy prefer:
Environmental Related

Additional Information

Year Founded: 2001
Current Activity Level : Actively seeking new investments

MICHEL FRAISSE GESTION ET INVESTISSEMENT SARL

4 Rue Du President Carnot
Lyon, France 69002
Website: www.mfgi.fr

Type of Firm

Private Equity Firm

Project Preferences

Type of Financing Preferred:
Leveraged Buyout
Early Stage
Expansion
Later Stage
Acquisition

Geographical Preferences

International Preferences:
France

Industry Preferences

In Semiconductor/Electr prefer:
Electronics

In Biotechnology prefer:
Agricultural/Animal Bio.

In Industrial/Energy prefer:
Industrial Products
Machinery

In Transportation prefer:
Transportation

In Agr/Forestr/Fish prefer:
Agribusiness

Additional Information

Year Founded: 1991
Current Activity Level : Actively seeking new investments

MICHIGAN ACCELERATOR FUND I MANAGEMENT LLC

140 Monroe Center Northwest
Suite 300
Grand Rapids, MI USA 49503
Phone: 6162353567
Website: www.maf-1.com

Management and Staff

Andrew Williams, Vice President
Dale Grogan, Managing Director
John Kerschen, Managing Director
Kevin Griffin, Vice President
Thomas Haan, Vice President

Type of Firm

Private Equity Firm

Project Preferences

Type of Financing Preferred:
Early Stage

Additional Information
Name of Most Recent Fund: Michigan Accelerator Fund I, L.P.
Most Recent Fund Was Raised: 08/16/2010
Year Founded: 2011
Capital Under Management: $15,100,000
Current Activity Level : Actively seeking new investments

MICHIGAN ECONOMIC DEVELOPMENT CORP

300 North Washington Square
Lansing, MI USA 48913
Phone: 5172418030
Fax: 5172410559
E-mail: medcservices@michigan.org
Website: www.michiganadvantage.org

Management and Staff
Minesh Mody, Chief Financial Officer

Type of Firm
Government Affiliated Program

Project Preferences

Role in Financing:
Will function either as deal originator or investor in deals created by others

Type of Financing Preferred:
Early Stage
Seed
Startup

Geographical Preferences

United States Preferences:
Michigan

Industry Preferences

In Industrial/Energy prefer:
Alternative Energy
Materials

In Transportation prefer:
Transportation

In Manufact. prefer:
Manufacturing

Additional Information
Year Founded: 1997
Capital Under Management: $160,000,000
Current Activity Level : Actively seeking new investments
Method of Compensation: Other

MICHIGAN VENTURE CAPITAL CO LTD

9th Floor, Daedong Building
93 Nonhyun-dong, Kangnam-Ku
Seoul, South Korea 135-010
Phone: 822-3445-1310
Fax: 822-3445-1311
E-mail: info@michiganvc.net
Website: www.michiganvc.net

Management and Staff
Don Kwon, Managing Director
Il Hyung Cho, Chief Financial Officer

Type of Firm
Corporate PE/Venture

Association Membership
Korean Venture Capital Association (KVCA)

Project Preferences

Type of Financing Preferred:
Balanced

Geographical Preferences

International Preferences:
Asia
Korea, South

Industry Preferences

In Semiconductor/Electr prefer:
Electronics

In Other prefer:
Environment Responsible

Additional Information
Year Founded: 2002
Capital Under Management: $24,000,000
Current Activity Level : Actively seeking new investments

MICROANGEL CAPITAL PARTNERS

12513 Uvalde Creek Drive
Austin, TX USA 78732
Phone: 5124613686
Website: www.microangelpartners.com

Type of Firm
Private Equity Firm

Project Preferences

Type of Financing Preferred:
Fund of Funds
Early Stage
Balanced
Later Stage
Seed
Strategic Alliances
Startup

Geographical Preferences

United States Preferences:
California
New York
Texas
All U.S.

Industry Preferences

In Communications prefer:
Wireless Communications
Media and Entertainment

In Computer Software prefer:
Applications Software

In Internet Specific prefer:
Internet

In Industrial/Energy prefer:
Alternative Energy

Additional Information
Name of Most Recent Fund: MicroAngel Startup Fund VIII
Most Recent Fund Was Raised: 09/24/2012
Year Founded: 2011
Capital Under Management: $2,975,000
Current Activity Level : Actively seeking new investments

MICROMOUNTAINS VENTURE AG

Romaeusring 4
Villingen-Schwenningen, Germany 78050
Phone: 4977212064952
Fax: 4977212064959
E-mail: info@mm-venture.de

Management and Staff
Christoph Stresing, Managing Director

Type of Firm
Private Equity Firm

Association Membership
German Venture Capital Association (BVK)

Project Preferences

Type of Financing Preferred:
Early Stage
Seed
Startup

Size of Investments Considered:
Min Size of Investment Considered (000s): $32
Max Size of Investment Considered (000s): $129

Geographical Preferences

International Preferences:
Germany

Industry Preferences

In Semiconductor/Electr prefer:
Electronics

In Medical/Health prefer:
Medical Diagnostics

In Industrial/Energy prefer:
Industrial Products
Advanced Materials
Robotics
Machinery

Additional Information
Year Founded: 2009
Current Activity Level : Actively seeking new investments

MICROVEST CAPITAL MANAGEMENT LLC

7315 Wisconsin Avenue
Suite 300W
Bethesda, MD USA 20814
Phone: 3016646680
Fax: 240380.=1028
E-mail: info@microvestfund.com
Website: www.microvestfund.com

Management and Staff
Douglas Young, Managing Director
Gilbert Crawford, Chief Executive Officer

Type of Firm
Private Equity Firm

Project Preferences

Role in Financing:
Will function either as deal originator or investor in deals created by others

Type of Financing Preferred:
Expansion
Balanced
Later Stage

Size of Investments Considered:
Min Size of Investment Considered (000s): $500
Max Size of Investment Considered (000s): $3,000

Geographical Preferences

International Preferences:
Latin America
India
Hong Kong
China
Eastern Europe
Middle East
All International

Industry Preferences

In Financial Services prefer:
Financial Services

Additional Information
Year Founded: 2003
Capital Under Management: $70,000,000
Current Activity Level : Actively seeking new investments
Method of Compensation: Return on investment is of primary concern, do not charge fees

MID ATLANTIC FINANCIAL MANAGEMENT INC

The Times Building
336 Fourth Avenue
Pittsburgh, PA USA 15222
Phone: 412-391-7077
Website: www.macg.com

Type of Firm
Private Equity Firm

Additional Information
Year Founded: 2002
Capital Under Management: $16,300,000
Current Activity Level : Actively seeking new investments

MID EUROPA PARTNERS LLP

161 Brompton Road
London, United Kingdom SW3 1EX
Phone: 442078863600
E-mail: info@mideuropa.com
Website: www.mideuropa.com

Other Offices
Bank Center, Platina Tower, 5th floor
Szabadas Ter 7
Budapest, Hungary 1054
Phone: 36-1-411-1270
Fax: 36-1-411-1271

Sair Nedim Caddesi
No. E2, Daire 9
Istanbul, Turkey 34357
Phone: 902123271240

Warsaw Financial Center, 29th Floor
Ul. Ernilii Plater 53
Warsaw, Poland 00-113
Phone: 48-22-540-7120

Management and Staff
Kerim Turkmen, Partner
Matthew Strassberg, Partner
Nikolaus Bethlen, Partner
Robert Knorr, Partner
Thierry Baudon, Managing Partner
Zbigniew Rekusz, Partner

Type of Firm
Private Equity Firm

Association Membership
Hungarian Venture Capital Association (HVCA)
Czech Venture Capital Association (CVCA)
Polish Venture Capital Association (PSIC/PPEA)
European Private Equity and Venture Capital Assoc.

Project Preferences

Type of Financing Preferred:
Leveraged Buyout
Acquisition

Geographical Preferences

International Preferences:
Turkey
Central Europe
Eastern Europe

Industry Preferences

In Communications prefer:
CATV & Pay TV Systems
Telecommunications

In Medical/Health prefer:
Medical/Health

In Consumer Related prefer:
Entertainment and Leisure
Retail
Consumer Products

In Industrial/Energy prefer:
Energy

In Transportation prefer:
Transportation

In Business Serv. prefer:
Media

Additional Information
Year Founded: 1999
Capital Under Management: $4,253,600,000
Current Activity Level : Actively seeking new investments

MID-OCEAN PARTNERS LP

320 Park Avenue
Suite 1600
New York, NY USA 10022
Phone: 2124971391
Fax: 2124971373
Website: www.midoceanpartners.com

1397

Other Offices
No.1 Grosvenor Crescent
Belgravia
London, United Kingdom SW1X 7EF
Phone: 44-20-3178-8492

Management and Staff
Andrew Gilbert, Vice President
Barrett Gilmer, Managing Director
Daniel Penn, Principal
Elias Dokas, Managing Director
Elizabeth Brewer, Vice President
Frank Schiff, Managing Director
Jonathan Marlow, Principal
Ted Virtue, Chief Executive Officer

Type of Firm
Private Equity Firm

Project Preferences

Type of Financing Preferred:
Fund of Funds
Leveraged Buyout
Management Buyouts

Geographical Preferences

United States Preferences:

Industry Preferences

In Consumer Related prefer:
Consumer
Consumer Products
Consumer Services

In Industrial/Energy prefer:
Industrial Products

In Business Serv. prefer:
Services
Media

Additional Information
Year Founded: 2003
Capital Under Management: $3,000,000,000
Current Activity Level : Actively seeking new investments

MIDAS MANAGEMENT AG

Else-Lang-Strasse 1
Cologne, Germany 50858
Phone: 492213377990
Fax: 4922133779916
E-mail: info@midasgruppe.de
Website: www.midasgruppe.de

Management and Staff
Axel Bauer, Partner
Johannes Cremer, Partner
Peter Goeke, Partner
Reiner Krug, Partner

Type of Firm
Private Equity Firm

Project Preferences

Type of Financing Preferred:
Mezzanine
Later Stage

Geographical Preferences

United States Preferences:

International Preferences:
Europe
Germany

Industry Preferences

In Computer Software prefer:
Software

In Biotechnology prefer:
Biotechnology

In Medical/Health prefer:
Medical/Health
Medical Diagnostics

In Business Serv. prefer:
Media

Additional Information
Year Founded: 2001
Current Activity Level : Actively seeking new investments

MIDCAP EQUITY PARTNERS

605 Third Avenue
Number 21
New York, NY USA 10158
Website: www.midcapequity.com

Management and Staff
Doug Hendrickson, Co-Founder
John Poppe, Co-Founder

Type of Firm
Private Equity Firm

Project Preferences

Type of Financing Preferred:
Leveraged Buyout
Management Buyouts
Acquisition

Geographical Preferences

United States Preferences:
Midwest
Northeast

Additional Information
Year Founded: 2011
Current Activity Level : Actively seeking new investments

MIDDLE BRIDGE PARTNERS LLC

1717 K Street Northwest
Suite 900
Washington, DC USA 20006
Phone: 2027855705
E-mail: info@middlebridgepartners.com
Website: www.middlebridgepartners.com

Type of Firm
Private Equity Firm

Project Preferences

Type of Financing Preferred:
Balanced

Additional Information
Year Founded: 2014
Current Activity Level : Actively seeking new investments

MIDDLE EAST & ASIA CAPITAL PARTNERS PTE LTD

50 Raffles Place
37th Flr. Singapore Land Tower
Singapore, Singapore 048623
Phone: 6568297178
Fax: 6568297294
E-mail: cleanenergy@meacp.com
Website: www.meacp.com

Type of Firm
Private Equity Firm

Project Preferences

Type of Financing Preferred:
Mezzanine
Balanced

Geographical Preferences

International Preferences:
Vietnam
Pakistan
India
Thailand
Middle East
Philippines
Asia
Malaysia

Industry Preferences

In Industrial/Energy prefer:
Energy
Environmental Related

In Business Serv. prefer:
Services

In Manufact. prefer:
Manufacturing

Additional Information
Year Founded: 2008
Capital Under Management: $150,000,000
Current Activity Level : Actively seeking new investments

MIDDLE EAST CAPITAL GROUP SAL

PO Box113
Allenby Street
Beirut, Lebanon 7310
Phone: 9611995955
E-mail: info@mecg.com.lb
Website: www.mecg.com.lb

Type of Firm
Private Equity Firm

Project Preferences

Type of Financing Preferred:
Unknown

Geographical Preferences

International Preferences:
Lebanon

Industry Preferences

In Financial Services prefer:
Real Estate

Additional Information
Year Founded: 2005
Current Activity Level : Actively seeking new investments

MIDDLE EAST VENTURE PARTNERS

Fouad Chehab Avenue, 6th Floor
Ring Building, Saifi Village
Beirut, Lebanon
Phone: 9611999605
Fax: 9611972755
E-mail: info@mevp.com
Website: www.mevp.com

Other Offices
Elie Habib, Venture Partner
1702-L Meridian Avenue
SAN JOSE, CA USA 95125
Phone: 4082293326

The Lofts Building 3
Entrance A 2nd floor
, Utd. Arab Em.
Phone: 97145584534

Management and Staff
Christina Chehade, Venture Partner
Walid Hanna, Managing Partner

Type of Firm
Private Equity Firm

Project Preferences

Type of Financing Preferred:
Early Stage
Expansion
Later Stage

Geographical Preferences

International Preferences:
Middle East

Industry Preferences

In Medical/Health prefer:
Hospitals/Clinics/Primary

In Consumer Related prefer:
Consumer
Consumer Products
Consumer Services
Other Restaurants
Hotels and Resorts

Additional Information
Name of Most Recent Fund: Middle East Venture Fund L.P.
Most Recent Fund Was Raised: 06/15/2010
Year Founded: 2009
Capital Under Management: $119,300,000
Current Activity Level : Actively seeking new investments

MIDDLEBURG CAPITAL DEVELOPMENT LTD

7 South Liberty Street
Liberty House
Middleburg, VA USA 20117
Phone: 5406877134
E-mail: info@mcapd.com
Website: mcapd.com

Management and Staff
David Sutherland, President

Type of Firm
Investment Management Firm

Project Preferences

Type of Financing Preferred:
Early Stage

Industry Preferences

In Computer Software prefer:
Data Processing

In Industrial/Energy prefer:
Environmental Related

In Business Serv. prefer:
Services

In Manufact. prefer:
Manufacturing

Additional Information
Year Founded: 1969
Current Activity Level : Actively seeking new investments

MIDDLELAND CAPITAL

888 16th Street North West
Suite 800
Washington, DC USA 20006
Phone: 2024207890
E-mail: info@middlelandcapital.com

Type of Firm
Private Equity Firm

Association Membership
Emerging Markets Private Equity Association

Project Preferences

Type of Financing Preferred:
Early Stage
Balanced
Startup

Geographical Preferences

International Preferences:
All International

Additional Information
Year Founded: 1969
Current Activity Level : Actively seeking new investments

MIDDLEMARCH PARTNERS LLC

125 Park Avenue
Suite 1700
New York, NY USA 10017
Phone: 2129139660
E-mail: info@middlemarchllc.com
Website: middlemarchllc.com

Management and Staff
Benedict Baerst, Vice President
Bruce Goldstein, Partner
Demetris Papademetriou, Founder
Sasha Gruzman, Partner

Type of Firm
Bank Affiliated

Project Preferences

Type of Financing Preferred:
Leveraged Buyout
Expansion
Generalist PE
Balanced
Acquisition

Industry Preferences

In Financial Services prefer:
Financial Services

Additional Information

Year Founded: 2015
Current Activity Level : Actively seeking new investments

MIDI PYRENEES CROISSANCE SA

18 place Dupuy
BP 18008
Toulouse, France 31080
Phone: 33581317327
Fax: 33581317339
E-mail: contact@mpcroissance.fr
Website: www.mpcroissance.fr

Management and Staff

Robert Vitrat, President

Type of Firm

Private Equity Firm

Project Preferences

Type of Financing Preferred:
Leveraged Buyout
Early Stage
Generalist PE
Later Stage
Management Buyouts
Acquisition

Geographical Preferences

International Preferences:
Europe
Eastern Europe
France

Industry Preferences

In Industrial/Energy prefer:
Energy
Industrial Products
Environmental Related

In Business Serv. prefer:
Services

Additional Information

Year Founded: 1996
Capital Under Management: $18,700,000
Current Activity Level : Actively seeking new investments

MIDINVEST MANAGEMENT OY

Kauppakatu 31 C
Jyvaskyla, Finland 40100
Phone: 358143393100
Fax: 358143393111
Website: www.midinvest.fi

Other Offices

Polttimonkatu 4
4th FL.
Tampere, Finland 33210

Management and Staff

Jukka-Pekka Nikula, Partner
Marja Kantonen, Partner
Paivi Tuulimo, Partner
Risto Jamsen, Partner

Type of Firm

Private Equity Firm

Association Membership

Finnish Venture Capital Association (FVCA)

Project Preferences

Type of Financing Preferred:
Generalist PE

Size of Investments Considered:
Min Size of Investment Considered (000s): $120
Max Size of Investment Considered (000s): $6,000

Geographical Preferences

International Preferences:
Europe
Finland

Industry Focus

(% based on actual investment)
Other Products	43.1%
Industrial/Energy	22.0%
Computer Software and Services	8.2%
Internet Specific	8.2%
Consumer Related	7.3%
Semiconductors/Other Elect.	5.2%
Communications and Media	2.9%
Computer Hardware	1.6%
Medical/Health	1.4%

Additional Information

Year Founded: 1994
Capital Under Management: $90,600,000
Current Activity Level : Actively seeking new investments

MIDMARK CAPITAL LP

177 Madison Avenue
Morristown, NJ USA 07960
Phone: 9739719960
Fax: 9739719963
E-mail: info@midmarkcapital.com
Website: www.midmarkcapital.com

Management and Staff

Denis Newman, Managing Director
Denis Newman, Co-Founder
Douglas Parker, Managing Director
Joseph Robinson, Managing Director
Matthew Finlay, Managing Director
Wayne Clevenger, Managing Director

Type of Firm

Private Equity Firm

Project Preferences

Type of Financing Preferred:
Leveraged Buyout
Expansion
Acquisition

Geographical Preferences

United States Preferences:
North America

International Preferences:
Europe
Asia

Industry Focus

(% based on actual investment)
Industrial/Energy	35.1%
Internet Specific	18.5%
Computer Hardware	16.4%
Computer Software and Services	10.4%
Consumer Related	9.5%
Semiconductors/Other Elect.	6.4%
Other Products	2.6%
Communications and Media	1.1%

Additional Information

Year Founded: 1989
Capital Under Management: $266,000,000
Current Activity Level : Actively seeking new investments

MIDSTATES CAPITAL LP

7300 West 110th Street
Suite 700
Shawnee Mission, KS USA 66210
Phone: 9139629007
Fax: 9139620699
Website: midstatescap.com

Type of Firm

SBIC

Association Membership

Natl Assoc of Small Bus. Inv. Co (NASBIC)

Project Preferences

Type of Financing Preferred:
Leveraged Buyout
Expansion
Mezzanine
Generalist PE
Later Stage
Acquisition

Geographical Preferences

United States Preferences:
Midwest

Additional Information
Year Founded: 1969
Capital Under Management: $12,120,000
Current Activity Level : Actively seeking new investments

MIDVEN LTD

39-41 Waterloo Street
Cavendish House
Birmingham, United Kingdom B2 5PP
Phone: 441217101990
Fax: 441217101999
E-mail: enquiries@midven.co.uk
Website: www.midven.com

Other Offices
15 Clarendon Street
Nottingham, United Kingdom

Management and Staff
Tony Stott, Chief Executive Officer

Type of Firm
Private Equity Firm

Association Membership
British Venture Capital Association (BVCA)

Project Preferences

Role in Financing:
Prefer role as deal originator but will also invest in deals created by others

Type of Financing Preferred:
Second Stage Financing
Leveraged Buyout
Early Stage
Expansion
Generalist PE
Balanced
Turnaround
Later Stage
Seed
Startup
Recapitalizations

Geographical Preferences

International Preferences:
United Kingdom
Europe

Industry Preferences

In Communications prefer:
Communications and Media

In Computer Other prefer:
Computer Related

In Semiconductor/Electr prefer:
Electronics

In Biotechnology prefer:
Biotechnology

In Medical/Health prefer:
Medical/Health

In Consumer Related prefer:
Consumer

In Industrial/Energy prefer:
Energy
Industrial Products
Materials

In Transportation prefer:
Transportation

In Manufact. prefer:
Manufacturing

Additional Information
Year Founded: 1990
Capital Under Management: $11,600,000
Current Activity Level : Actively seeking new investments
Method of Compensation: Return on invest. most important, but chg. closing fees, service fees, etc.

MIDVEN SA

Izbicka 28A
Warszawa, Poland 04-838
Phone: 48226158218
Fax: 48226158218
E-mail: kontakt@midven.pl
Website: midven.pl

Type of Firm
Service Provider

Project Preferences

Type of Financing Preferred:
Leveraged Buyout
Acquisition

Geographical Preferences

International Preferences:
Poland

Industry Preferences

In Computer Software prefer:
Applications Software

In Internet Specific prefer:
Ecommerce

In Medical/Health prefer:
Medical/Health

Additional Information
Year Founded: 2011
Current Activity Level : Actively seeking new investments

MIDVESTOR MANAGEMENT AS

Soren R. Thornaes Vei 10
Namsos, Norway 7800
Phone: 4747875522
Fax: 4794774839
E-mail: post@midvest.no
Website: www.midvest.no

Other Offices
Noisomhed Gard
Molde, Norway 6405

Management and Staff
Arild Aasmyr, Partner
Hakon Berg, Partner
Hakon Fredriksen, Chief Executive Officer

Type of Firm
Private Equity Firm

Association Membership
Norwegian Venture Capital Association

Project Preferences

Type of Financing Preferred:
Balanced

Geographical Preferences

International Preferences:
Norway

Industry Preferences

In Semiconductor/Electr prefer:
Electronics
Electronic Components

In Consumer Related prefer:
Consumer Products

In Industrial/Energy prefer:
Energy
Alternative Energy

Additional Information
Year Founded: 2007
Capital Under Management: $41,000,000
Current Activity Level : Actively seeking new investments

MIDWEST VENTURE ALLIANCE

7829 East Rockhill Road
Suite 307
Wichita, KS USA 67206
Phone: 316-651-5900
Fax: 866-810-6671
Website: www.midwestventure.com

Management and Staff
Dick West, Co-Founder
Eric Ferrell, Managing Partner
Gene Bicknell, Co-Founder
Patricia Brasted, Co-Founder
Stan Brannan, Co-Founder

Type of Firm
Angel Group

Project Preferences

Type of Financing Preferred:
Early Stage
Seed

Geographical Preferences

United States Preferences:
Midwest
Kansas
All U.S.

Additional Information
Name of Most Recent Fund: 2006 Ventria - I
Most Recent Fund Was Raised: 11/01/2006
Year Founded: 2005
Current Activity Level : Actively seeking new investments

MIFSUD GROUP LLC

140 Blaze Industrial Parkway
Suite 100
Berea, OH USA 44017
Phone: 2163257280
Fax: 2163257288
Website: www.mifsudgroup.com

Type of Firm
Private Equity Firm

Project Preferences

Type of Financing Preferred:
Leveraged Buyout
Acquisition

Geographical Preferences

United States Preferences:
Midwest

Industry Preferences

In Manufact. prefer:
Manufacturing

Additional Information
Year Founded: 1969
Current Activity Level : Actively seeking new investments

MIG VERWALTUNGS AG

Ismaninger Strasse 102
Munich, Germany 81675
Phone: 491805644999
Fax: 491803644999
E-mail: info@mig.ag
Website: www.mig-fonds.de

Management and Staff
Cecil Motschmann, Managing Director
Jurgen Kosch, Managing Director
Matthias Kromayer, Managing Director
Michael Motschmann, Managing Director

Type of Firm
Private Equity Firm

Association Membership
German Venture Capital Association (BVK)

Project Preferences

Type of Financing Preferred:
Leveraged Buyout
Early Stage
Later Stage
Seed
Startup

Geographical Preferences

International Preferences:
Europe
Switzerland
Austria
Eastern Europe
Germany

Industry Preferences

In Communications prefer:
Communications and Media
Telecommunications

In Semiconductor/Electr prefer:
Semiconductor

In Biotechnology prefer:
Biotechnology

In Medical/Health prefer:
Medical/Health
Pharmaceuticals

In Industrial/Energy prefer:
Energy
Alternative Energy
Industrial Products

Additional Information
Year Founded: 2004
Current Activity Level : Actively seeking new investments

MIGHTY CAPITAL MANAGEMENT LLC

419 14th Street
San Francisco, CA USA 94103

Management and Staff
SC Moatti, Founder

Type of Firm
Private Equity Firm

Project Preferences

Type of Financing Preferred:
Early Stage

Geographical Preferences

United States Preferences:
California

Industry Preferences

In Consumer Related prefer:
Consumer Products
Consumer Services

Additional Information
Year Founded: 2017
Capital Under Management: $2,600,000
Current Activity Level : Actively seeking new investments

MILAMBER VENTURES PLC

31 Harley Street
London, United Kingdom W1G 9QS
Phone: 447768875681
Website: www.milamber.co.uk

Type of Firm
Private Equity Firm

Project Preferences

Type of Financing Preferred:
Early Stage
Seed

Geographical Preferences

International Preferences:
United Kingdom

Industry Preferences

In Computer Software prefer:
Software

In Computer Other prefer:
Computer Related

Additional Information
Year Founded: 2013
Current Activity Level : Actively seeking new investments

MILBANK TWEED HADLEY & MCCLOY LLP

One Chase Manhattan Plaza
New York, NY USA 10005
Phone: 2125305000
Fax: 2125305219
Website: www.milbank.com

Other Offices

Maximilianstrasse 15
Munich, Germany 80539
Phone: 49-89-25559-3600
Fax: 49-89-25559-3700

79 Jianguo Road, China Central Place
15th Floor, Tower Two
Beijing, China 100025
Phone: 8610-5969-2700
Fax: 8610-5969-2707

601 South Figueroa Street
30th Floor
Los Angeles, CA USA 90017
Phone: 213-892-4000
Fax: 213-629-5063

Taunusanlage 15
Frankfurt am Main
Frankfurt, Germany 60325
Phone: 49-69-71914-3400
Fax: 49-69-71914-3500

10 Gresham Street
London, United Kingdom EC2V 7JD
Phone: 44-20-7615-3000
Fax: 44-20-7615-3100

9-7-1 Akasaka, Minato-ku
21st Floor, Midtown Tower
Tokyo, Japan 107-6221
Phone: 813-5410-2801
Fax: 813-5410-2891

18 Chater Road
3007 Alexandra House
Central, Hong Kong
Phone: 852-2971-4888
Fax: 852-2840-0792

Rua Colombia
325 - CEP
Sao Paolo, Brazil 01438-000
Phone: 55-11-3927-7701
Fax: 55-11-3927-7777

1850 K Street, Northwest
Suite 1100
Washington, WA USA 20006
Phone: 202-835-7500
Fax: 202-835-7586

30 Raffles Place
#14-00 Chevron House
, Singapore 048622
Phone: 65-6428-2400
Fax: 65-6428-2500

Management and Staff

Abhilash Raval, Partner
Albert Pisa, Partner
Alexander Rinne, Partner
Alexander Kaye, Partner
Allan Marks, Partner
Andrew Janszky, Partner
Andrew Walker, Partner
Andrew Leblanc, Partner
Anthony Root, Partner
Arnold Peinado, Partner
Atara Miller, Partner
Blair Tyson, Partner
Brett Goldblatt, Partner
Bruce Kayle, Partner
Cathy Marsh, Partner
Charles Conroy, Partner
Christoph Rothenfuber, Partner
Christopher Gaspar, Partner
Christopher Chalsen, Partner
Dale Ponikvar, Partner
Daniel Michalchuk, Partner
Daniel Bartfeld, Partner
Daniel Perry, Partner
Dara Panahy, Partner
David Lamb, Partner
David Gelfand, Partner
David Wolfson, Partner
David Cohen, Partner
David Zemans, Partner
David Zeltner, Partner
Deborah Festa, Partner
Deborah Ruosch-Conrad, Partner
Dennis Dunne, Partner
Dieter Yih, Partner
Douglas Henkin, Partner
Douglas Tanner, Partner
Drew Fine, Partner
Edward Kayukov, Partner
Elihu Robertson, Partner
Elizabeth Hardin, Partner
Eric Silverman, Partner
Errol Taylor, Partner
Evan Fleck, Partner
Frederick Zullow, Partner
Gary Wigmore, Partner
Georgiana Slade, Partner
Gerard Uzzi, Partner
Giles Kennedy, Partner
Glenn Gertsell, Partner
Gregory Bray, Partner
Helfried Schwarz, Partner
Jacqueline Chan, Partner
James Warbey, Partner
James Sligar, Partner
James Ball, Partner
James Benedict, Partner
James Cavoli, Partner
James Cameron, Partner
Jay Grushkin, Partner
Jerry Marks, Partner
Joel Krasnov, Partner
John Dewar, Partner
John Franchini, Partner
Jonathan Maizel, Partner
Jonathan Green, Partner
Joseph Steven Genova, Partner
Joshua Zimmerman, Partner
Julian Stait, Partner
Karen Wong, Partner
Kenneth Baronsky, Partner
Lauren Hanrahan, Partner
Laurence Jacobs, Partner
Lawrence Kass, Partner
Linda Dakin-Grimm, Partner
Marc Hanrahan, Partner
Marcus Dougherty, Partner
Mark Shinderman, Partner
Mark Stamp, Partner
Mark Mandel, Partner
Mark Scarsi, Partner
Mark Regante, Partner
Martin Erhardt, Partner
Matthew Barr, Partner
Mel Immergut, Partner
Melainie Mansfield, Partner
Michael Hirshfeld, Partner
Michael Nolan, Partner
Michael Bellucci, Partner
Michael Grace, Managing Director
Naomi Ishikawa, Partner
Neil Caddy, Partner
Neil Wertlieb, Partner
Nicholas Smith, Partner
Nicholas Spearing, Partner
Nick Angel, Partner
Norbert Rieger, Partner
Paul Aronzon, Partner
Paul Wessel, Partner
Paul Denaro, Partner
Peter Benudiz, Partner
Peter Nesgos, Partner
Peter Schwartz, Partner
Peter Nussbaum, Partner
Peter Memminger, Partner
Phillip Fletcher, Partner
Rainer Magold, Partner
Richard Sharp, Partner
Richard Gray, Partner
Robert Williams, Partner
Robert Koch, Partner
Robert Liubicic, Partner

Robert Jay Moore, Partner
Rod Miller, Partner
Roland Hlawaty, Partner
Rolf Fuger, Partner
Russell Jacobs, Partner
Russell Kestenbaum, Partner
Sander Bak, Partner
Scott Edelman, Partner
Sean Keaton, Partner
Stacey Rappaport, Partner
Stuart Harray, Partner
Suhrud Mehta, Partner
Thomas Ingenhoven, Partner
Thomas Janson, Partner
Thomas Arena, Partner
Thomas Kreller, Partner
Thomas Kleinheisterkamp, Partner
Timothy Peterson, Partner
Tobias Stirnberg, Partner
Tom Canning, Partner
Trayton Davis, Partner
Tyson Lomazow, Partner
Ulrike Friese-Dormann, Partner
Wayne Aaron, Partner
Wilbur Foster, Partner
William Bice, Partner
William Mahoney, Partner
Winthrop Brown, Partner
Young Joon Kim, Partner

Type of Firm
Investment Management Firm

Project Preferences

Type of Financing Preferred:
Generalist PE

Additional Information
Year Founded: 1866
Current Activity Level : Actively seeking new investments

MILESTONE CAPITAL MANAGEMENT LTD

No. 318, Hunan Road
Shanghai, China 200031
Phone: 862164379190
Fax: 862164379590
E-mail: info@mcmchina.com
Website: www.mcmchina.com

Other Offices
1-3 Xinyuan Nan Road
Suite A1702, Ping An Financial Centre
Beijing, China 100027
Phone: 861084971443
Fax: 861084971449

Management and Staff
Baohua Wang, Managing Director
Ke Deng, Vice President
Liping Qiu, Founder
Xing Chen, Vice President
Ying Xie, Vice President
Yinghai Xie, Managing Director
Yu Hu, Managing Director
Yunli Lou, Founder

Type of Firm
Private Equity Firm

Project Preferences

Type of Financing Preferred:
Leveraged Buyout
Expansion
Management Buyouts
Acquisition

Size of Investments Considered:
Min Size of Investment Considered (000s): $10,000
Max Size of Investment Considered (000s): $100,000

Geographical Preferences

International Preferences:
China
Asia

Additional Information
Year Founded: 2002
Capital Under Management: $268,500,000
Current Activity Level : Actively seeking new investments

MILESTONE CAPITAL PARTNERS LTD

14 Floral Street
London, United Kingdom WC2E 9DH
Phone: 442074208800
Fax: 442074208827
E-mail: info@milestone-capital.com
Website: www.milestone-capital.com

Other Offices
21 place de la Madeleine
Paris, France 75008
Phone: 33-1-8018-9160
Fax: 33-1-4924-0773

Management and Staff
Bill Robinson, Managing Partner
Erick Rinner, Managing Partner
Paul Dickson, Founder
Philip Conboy, Partner

Type of Firm
Private Equity Firm

Association Membership
British Venture Capital Association (BVCA)
French Venture Capital Association (AFIC)
Swiss Venture Capital Association (SECA)

Project Preferences

Role in Financing:
Prefer role as deal originator

Type of Financing Preferred:
Leveraged Buyout
Management Buyouts
Acquisition

Geographical Preferences

International Preferences:
Ireland
United Kingdom
Luxembourg
Netherlands
Switzerland
Western Europe
Belgium
France

Industry Focus
(% based on actual investment)
Other Products	39.2%
Medical/Health	23.5%
Consumer Related	18.2%
Computer Software and Services	17.4%
Industrial/Energy	1.6%

Additional Information
Year Founded: 1991
Capital Under Management: $454,000,000
Current Activity Level : Actively seeking new investments

MILESTONE INVESTMENT MANAGEMENT CO LTD

Guangshun Road, Changning Distr
Room 354, No. 33 building,
Shanghai, China

Type of Firm
Private Equity Firm

Project Preferences

Type of Financing Preferred:
Balanced

Geographical Preferences

International Preferences:
China

Additional Information
Year Founded: 2013
Current Activity Level : Actively seeking new investments

MILESTONE PARTNERS LP

555 East Lancaster Avenue
Suite 500
Radnor, PA USA 19087
Phone: 6105262700
Fax: 6105262701
Website: www.milestonepartners.com

Management and Staff
Adam Curtin, Principal
Brooke Hayes, Partner
Daniel Ryan, Principal
David Proctor, Partner
Geoffrey Veale, Principal
John Nowaczyk, Partner
John Shoemaker, Managing Partner
Kenneth Kummerer, Chief Financial Officer
Ric Andersen, Partner

Type of Firm
Private Equity Firm

Project Preferences

Role in Financing:
Prefer role as deal originator

Type of Financing Preferred:
Leveraged Buyout
Management Buyouts
Acquisition
Recapitalizations

Geographical Preferences

United States Preferences:
North America

Industry Focus
(% based on actual investment)
Other Products	38.9%
Consumer Related	29.9%
Internet Specific	18.6%
Computer Software and Services	6.4%
Semiconductors/Other Elect.	5.3%
Communications and Media	0.9%

Additional Information
Year Founded: 1995
Capital Under Management: $360,000,000
Current Activity Level : Actively seeking new investments
Method of Compensation: Return on invest. most important, but chg. closing fees, service fees, etc.

MILESTONE RELIGARE INVESTMENT ADVISORS PVT LTD

Tower A - 602, 6th Floor
Express Zone, Western Express
Mumbai, India 400097
Phone: 912228713773
Fax: 912242357077
E-mail: info@IBOF.in
Website: www.milestonereligare.com

Management and Staff
Anant Kulkarni, Managing Partner
Rajesh Singhal, Managing Partner
Srinivas Baratam, Managing Partner
Ved Arya, CEO & Managing Director

Type of Firm
Private Equity Firm

Association Membership
Indian Venture Capital Association (IVCA)

Project Preferences

Role in Financing:
Will function either as deal originator or investor in deals created by others

Type of Financing Preferred:
Later Stage

Size of Investments Considered:
Min Size of Investment Considered (000s): $5,000
Max Size of Investment Considered (000s): $25,000

Geographical Preferences

International Preferences:
India

Industry Preferences

In Medical/Health prefer:
Medical/Health

In Consumer Related prefer:
Education Related

Additional Information
Year Founded: 2009
Capital Under Management: $100,000,000
Current Activity Level : Actively seeking new investments

MILESTONE TURNAROUND MANAGEMENT CO LTD

3-4-1 Marunouchi, Chiyoda-Ku
8F, Shin-Kokusai Building
Tokyo, Japan 100-0005
Phone: 81368603510
Fax: 81368603511
E-mail: info@milestone-tm.co.jp
Website: www.milestone-tm.co.jp

Type of Firm
Investment Management Firm

Project Preferences

Type of Financing Preferred:
Leveraged Buyout
Turnaround

Geographical Preferences

International Preferences:
Japan

Additional Information
Year Founded: 2005
Capital Under Management: $49,316,000
Current Activity Level : Actively seeking new investments

MILESTONE VENTURE CAPITAL GMBH

Mozartstrasse 57
Hoesbach, Germany 63768
Phone: 4960215001133
Website: www.milestone-vc.com

Management and Staff
Guenther Mueller, Chief Executive Officer

Type of Firm
Private Equity Firm

Project Preferences

Type of Financing Preferred:
Early Stage
Seed
Startup

Geographical Preferences

International Preferences:
Germany

Industry Preferences

In Computer Software prefer:
Software

Additional Information
Year Founded: 2011
Current Activity Level : Actively seeking new investments

MILITELLO CAPITAL LLC

19455 Deerfield Avenue
Suite 307
Leesburg, VA USA 20176
Phone: 7033480156
E-mail: info@militellocapital.com
Website: militellocapital.com

Management and Staff
Giuliano Salvo, Chief Financial Officer
Matt Brady, Co-Founder

Type of Firm
Private Equity Firm

Project Preferences

Type of Financing Preferred:
Core

Additional Information
Year Founded: 2011
Capital Under Management: $10,229,000
Current Activity Level : Actively seeking new investments

MILL CITY CAPITAL LP

50 South Sixth Street
Suite 1390
Minneapolis, MN USA 55402
Phone: 6122389500
E-mail: Info@MillCityCapital.com
Website: millcitycapital.com

Management and Staff
Alexander Rutlin, Vice President
Darren Acheson, Co-Founder
Gary Obermiller, Co-Founder
Lisa Kro, Co-Founder
Michael Israel, Co-Founder

Type of Firm
Private Equity Firm

Project Preferences

Type of Financing Preferred:
Leveraged Buyout
Recapitalizations

Geographical Preferences

United States Preferences:
Midwest
South Dakota
Iowa
North Dakota
Wisconsin
Minnesota
All U.S.

Industry Preferences

In Consumer Related prefer:
Consumer
Retail
Food/Beverage
Consumer Products
Consumer Services
Other Restaurants

In Industrial/Energy prefer:
Oil and Gas Exploration
Alternative Energy
Industrial Products

In Transportation prefer:
Transportation
Aerospace

In Business Serv. prefer:
Distribution

In Agr/Forestr/Fish prefer:
Agribusiness

Additional Information
Year Founded: 2010
Capital Under Management: $135,078,000
Current Activity Level : Actively seeking new investments

MILL CREEK CAPITAL ADVISORS LLC

161 Washington Street
Suite 1500, 8 Tower Bridge
Conshohocken, PA USA 19428
Phone: 6109417700
Fax: 6109419792
Website: www.millcreekcap.com

Management and Staff
Brian Maxwell, Partner
Claire Kendrick, Managing Director
David Logan, Partner
Joan Straus, Vice President
Katie Thomas, Partner
Kevin Keating, Partner
Michael Jordan, Partner
Richard Stevens, Chief Executive Officer
Richard Lunsford, Chief Operating Officer
Samuel Mcfall, Vice President
Walter Harris, Partner

Type of Firm
Investment Management Firm

Project Preferences

Type of Financing Preferred:
Generalist PE

Additional Information
Year Founded: 2006
Capital Under Management: $53,000,000
Current Activity Level : Actively seeking new investments

MILL ROAD CAPITAL MANAGEMENT LLC

382 Greenwich Avenue
Suite One
Greenwich, CT USA 06830
Phone: 2039873500
Website: www.millroadcapital.com

Management and Staff
Ajay Sharma, Managing Director
Charles Goldman, Managing Director
Eric Yanagi, Vice President
James Zivin, Vice President
Justin Jacobs, Managing Director
Sarah Heberle, Vice President
Scott Scharfman, Managing Director
Thomas Lynch, Senior Managing Director

Type of Firm
Private Equity Firm

Project Preferences

Type of Financing Preferred:
Leveraged Buyout
Public Companies

Geographical Preferences

United States Preferences:

Canadian Preferences:
All Canada

Industry Preferences

In Consumer Related prefer:
Retail
Consumer Products

In Business Serv. prefer:
Services

In Manufact. prefer:
Manufacturing

Additional Information
Name of Most Recent Fund: Mill Road Capital II, L.P.
Most Recent Fund Was Raised: 06/22/2012
Year Founded: 2004
Capital Under Management: $420,000,000
Current Activity Level : Actively seeking new investments

MILL STREET & CO

7616 Yonge Street
Thornhill, Canada L4J 1V9
Phone: 9057645465
Fax: 9057648298
Website: www.millstreetco.com

Type of Firm
Private Equity Firm

Additional Information
Year Founded: 2017
Current Activity Level : Actively seeking new investments

MILLENNIAL PARTNERS & CO LLC

Millennium Plaza Office Tower
Office 2303
Dubai, Utd. Arab Em.
Phone: 97143084112
E-mail: info@millennialpartners.ae
Website: millennialpartners.ae

Type of Firm
Investment Management Firm

Project Preferences

Type of Financing Preferred:
Expansion
Seed

Geographical Preferences

International Preferences:
Bahrain
Oman
Qatar
Utd. Arab Em.
Saudi Arabia
Kuwait

Industry Preferences

In Internet Specific prefer:
Ecommerce

In Medical/Health prefer:
Health Services

In Consumer Related prefer:
Consumer
Consumer Products

Additional Information
Year Founded: 2016
Current Activity Level : Actively seeking new investments

MILLENNIUM ARK INVESTMENT CO LTD

B56 Zhongguancun South Street
Floor 13, Fangyuan Mansion
Beijing, China 100044
Phone: 861088026547
Fax: 861088026546
E-mail: ark@millenniumark.com.cn
Website: www.millenniumark.com.cn

Management and Staff
Yuming Song, President

Type of Firm
Private Equity Firm

Association Membership
Venture Capital Association of Beijing (VCAB)

Project Preferences

Type of Financing Preferred:
Balanced

Geographical Preferences

International Preferences:
China

Industry Preferences

In Medical/Health prefer:
Pharmaceuticals

In Industrial/Energy prefer:
Energy
Materials
Environmental Related

In Financial Services prefer:
Financial Services

Additional Information
Year Founded: 1999
Capital Under Management: $1,284,500,000
Current Activity Level : Actively seeking new investments

MILLENNIUM EQUITY TRADING L L C

c/o Empire Capital
One Gorham Island, Suite 201
Westport, CT USA 06880

Management and Staff
Gerald Ramdeen, Founder

Type of Firm
Private Equity Firm

Project Preferences

Type of Financing Preferred:
Leveraged Buyout

Industry Preferences

In Communications prefer:
Telecommunications

In Semiconductor/Electr prefer:
Semiconductor

Additional Information
Year Founded: 2009
Capital Under Management: $371,000,000
Current Activity Level : Actively seeking new investments

MILLENNIUM TVP MANAGEMENT CO LLC

32 Avenue of the Americas
17th Floor
New York, NY USA 10013
Phone: 6465217800
Fax: 6465217878
E-mail: info@mtvlp.com
Website: mtvlp.com

Other Offices
Former HQ: 747 Third Avenue
38th Floor
New York, NY USA 10017
Phone: 6465217800
Fax: 6465217878

Management and Staff
Daniel Burstein, Co-Founder
Daniel Borok, Partner
Jonathan Glass, Chief Financial Officer
Joseph Kao, Vice President
Max Chee, Partner
Samuel Schwerin, Co-Founder

Type of Firm
Private Equity Advisor or Fund of Funds

Project Preferences

Role in Financing:
Will function either as deal originator or investor in deals created by others

Type of Financing Preferred:
Expansion
Balanced
Fund of Funds of Second

Geographical Preferences

United States Preferences:

Industry Preferences

In Communications prefer:
Communications and Media
Wireless Communications

In Computer Software prefer:
Software

In Internet Specific prefer:
Internet

In Financial Services prefer:
Financial Services

In Business Serv. prefer:
Services
Media

Additional Information
Year Founded: 1999
Capital Under Management: $496,600,000
Current Activity Level : Actively seeking new investments

MILLER INVESTMENT MANAGEMENT LP

100 Front Street
Suite 1500
Conshohocken, PA USA 19428
Phone: 6108349820
Fax: 6108349824
E-mail: invest@millerinv.com
Website: www.millerinv.com

Type of Firm
Investment Management Firm

Project Preferences

Type of Financing Preferred:
Generalist PE
Later Stage
Acquisition

Industry Preferences

In Consumer Related prefer:
Consumer
Food/Beverage

Additional Information
Year Founded: 2007
Current Activity Level : Actively seeking new investments

MILLHOUSE INC PLC

21, John Street
London, United Kingdom WC1N2BP
Phone: 442034340091
Website: millhouse.co

Management and Staff
David Millhouse, Chief Executive Officer
Harry Charlton, Managing Director

Type of Firm
Investment Management Firm

Project Preferences

Type of Financing Preferred:
Leveraged Buyout
Early Stage
Expansion
Later Stage
Management Buyouts
Acquisition

Geographical Preferences

International Preferences:
Europe
Israel

Additional Information
Year Founded: 2010
Current Activity Level : Actively seeking new investments

MILLIWAYS VENTURES

101 University Avenue #245
Palo Alto, CA USA 94301
Website: www.milliwaysventures.com

Type of Firm
Private Equity Firm

Project Preferences

Type of Financing Preferred:
Early Stage

Additional Information
Year Founded: 2014
Current Activity Level : Actively seeking new investments

MILLPOND EQUITY PARTNERS LLC

185 North West Spanish River
Boulevard, Suite 200
Boca Raton, FL USA 33431
Phone: 5613222080
Website: millpondequity.com

Management and Staff
Jeffry Tobin, Partner
Lawrence Shagrin, Managing Partner

Type of Firm
Private Equity Firm

Project Preferences

Type of Financing Preferred:
Leveraged Buyout
Public Companies
Recapitalizations

Geographical Preferences

United States Preferences:
North America

Industry Preferences

In Consumer Related prefer:
Education Related

Additional Information
Year Founded: 1969
Current Activity Level : Actively seeking new investments

MILLSTEIN & CO LP

555 Madison Avenue
New York, NY USA 10022
Website: www.millsteinandco.com

Management and Staff
Ashley Winston, Managing Director
Brendan Hayes, Managing Director
Elizabeth Abrams, Managing Director
Jennifer Main, Chief Financial Officer
Jill Dauchy, Managing Director
Jim Wigand, Managing Director
Mark Hootnick, Managing Director
Mark Walker, Managing Director

Type of Firm
Investment Management Firm

Project Preferences

Type of Financing Preferred:
Leveraged Buyout
Special Situation

Geographical Preferences

United States Preferences:
North America

Industry Preferences

In Consumer Related prefer:
Consumer

In Financial Services prefer:
Financial Services

Additional Information
Year Founded: 2012
Current Activity Level : Actively seeking new investments

MILLSTONE CAPITAL ADVISORS LLC

7701 Forsyth Boulevard
Suite 925
Saint Louis, MO USA 63105
Phone: 3147218815
Website: www.millstoneca.com

Type of Firm
Private Equity Firm

Project Preferences

Type of Financing Preferred:
Leveraged Buyout
Expansion

Additional Information
Name of Most Recent Fund: FSM Fund I, L.P.
Most Recent Fund Was Raised: 03/20/2013
Year Founded: 2012
Capital Under Management: $19,005,000
Current Activity Level : Actively seeking new investments

MILLSTONE CAPITAL PARTNERS LLC

1515 Ormsby Station Court
Louisville, KY USA 40223
Phone: 5023151718

Type of Firm
Private Equity Firm

Project Preferences

Type of Financing Preferred:
Generalist PE
Balanced
Industry Rollups

Additional Information
Year Founded: 1969
Current Activity Level : Actively seeking new investments

MILOST GLOBAL INC

300 Vestavia Parkway
Suite 2300
Birmingham, AL USA 35216
Phone: 12057952039
E-mail: info@milostglobal.com
Website: www.milostglobal.com

Type of Firm
Private Equity Firm

Project Preferences

Type of Financing Preferred:
Leveraged Buyout
Management Buyouts
Acquisition

Additional Information
Year Founded: 2016
Current Activity Level : Actively seeking new investments

MINAS BETEILIGUNGS- U. MANAGEMENT GMBH

Passauer Platz 2/10
Vienna, Austria 1010
Phone: 43-1-533-8431
Fax: 43-1-533-843113
E-mail: office@woltron.com
Website: www.woltron.com

Management and Staff
Klaus Woltron, Chief Executive Officer

Type of Firm
Private Equity Firm

Project Preferences

Type of Financing Preferred:
Early Stage
Expansion
Balanced
Seed

Geographical Preferences

International Preferences:
Austria

Industry Preferences

In Industrial/Energy prefer:
Energy
Energy Conservation Relat

Additional Information
Year Founded: 1992
Current Activity Level : Actively seeking new investments

MINATO CAPITAL CO LTD

107-1 Ito-cho
Chuo-ku Kobe-shi
Hyogo, Japan 650-0032
Phone: 81-78-332-0451
Fax: 81-78-327-3205
Website: www.minatocp.co.jp

Type of Firm
Bank Affiliated

Project Preferences

Type of Financing Preferred:
Balanced

Geographical Preferences

International Preferences:
Japan

Additional Information
Year Founded: 2000
Capital Under Management: $12,392,000
Current Activity Level : Actively seeking new investments

MINDSET VENTURES

800 West El Camino Real
Suite 180
Mountain View, CA USA 94040
Website: www.mindset.ventures

Management and Staff
Camila Folkmann, Partner
Daniel Ibri, Partner
Ricardo Politi, Venture Partner

Type of Firm
Private Equity Firm

Project Preferences

Type of Financing Preferred:
Seed
Startup

Additional Information
Year Founded: 2016
Current Activity Level : Actively seeking new investments

MINDWORKS VENTURE

67-71 Chatham Road
Tsim Sha Tsui, Hong Kong
E-mail: info@mwsventure.com
Website: www.mwsventure.com

Type of Firm
Private Equity Firm

Project Preferences

Type of Financing Preferred:
Early Stage
Expansion
Balanced
Startup

Geographical Preferences

International Preferences:
China
Asia

Additional Information
Year Founded: 1969
Current Activity Level : Actively seeking new investments

MINELLA CAPITAL MANAGEMENT LLC

9864 Brassie Bend
Naples, FL USA 34109
Phone: 2039792776
Website: www.minellacap.com

Management and Staff
David Minella, Chief Executive Officer

Type of Firm
Private Equity Firm

Project Preferences

Type of Financing Preferred:
Leveraged Buyout

Additional Information
Year Founded: 2007
Current Activity Level : Actively seeking new investments

MINEWORKERS INVESTMENT CO

Four Eton Road
MIC Place
Parktown, South Africa 2122
Phone: 27110881800
Fax: 27110881845
E-mail: info@mic.co.za
Website: www.mic.co.za

Management and Staff
Cynthia Pongweni, Founder
Mary Bomela, Chief Executive Officer

Type of Firm
Private Equity Firm

Project Preferences

Type of Financing Preferred:
Leveraged Buyout
Expansion
Balanced
Later Stage
Acquisition

Geographical Preferences

International Preferences:
South Africa
Africa

Industry Preferences

In Consumer Related prefer:
Entertainment and Leisure

In Industrial/Energy prefer:
Oil and Gas Exploration
Industrial Products
Factory Automation

In Financial Services prefer:
Real Estate

In Business Serv. prefer:
Media

Additional Information
Year Founded: 1995
Current Activity Level : Actively seeking new investments

MINGLY CAPITAL

No. 1, East Chang An Avenue
Tower C1, Oriental Plaza
Beijing, China 100738
Phone: 861085150055
Fax: 861085150903
E-mail: info@mcgf.com.cn
Website: www.mcgf.com.cn

Other Offices

No. 11 South Street, Zhifu District
Suite 1106, YiTong International Bldg
Yantai, Shandong Province, China
Phone: 865356656505
Fax: 865356656505

525 University Avenue
Suite 225
Palo Alto, CA USA 94301
Phone: 6505666412
Fax: 6503254762

No.1266 West Nanjing Road
Suite 4605, Tower 2, Plaza 66
Shanghai, China 200040
Phone: 862162889998
Fax: 862162889166

1 Connaught Place
Suite 3701, 37/F Jardine House
Central, Hong Kong
Phone: 85221082233
Fax: 85222950292

Management and Staff
Amanda Cao, Partner
Christy Sheng, Partner
David Xu, Managing Partner
Eric Xu, Partner
Jeffrey Su, Partner
Jennifer Liang, Partner
Jianbo Yang, Partner
Katherine Xu, Partner
Ken Li, Partner
Mark Louie, Partner
Qing Huang, Partner
Rachel He, Partner
Sean Hua, Partner
Shawn Shen, Partner
Steven Du, Partner
Tony Tong, Partner

Type of Firm
Private Equity Firm

Association Membership
China Venture Capital Association

Project Preferences

Type of Financing Preferred:
Later Stage

Geographical Preferences

International Preferences:
China

Industry Preferences

In Communications prefer:
Telecommunications

In Biotechnology prefer:
Biotechnology

In Medical/Health prefer:
Medical/Health
Health Services
Pharmaceuticals

In Consumer Related prefer:
Consumer Products
Consumer Services

In Industrial/Energy prefer:
Alternative Energy

In Business Serv. prefer:
Media

In Manufact. prefer:
Manufacturing

In Agr/Forestr/Fish prefer:
Agriculture related

In Other prefer:
Environment Responsible

Additional Information
Year Founded: 2000
Capital Under Management: $20,000,000
Current Activity Level : Actively seeking new investments

MINORITY BROADCAST INVESTMENT CORPORATION

1001 Connecticut Northwest
Suite 622
Washington, DC USA 20036
Phone: 2022931166
Fax: 2028721669

Type of Firm
Private Equity Firm

Project Preferences

Role in Financing:
Will function either as deal originator or investor in deals created by others

Type of Financing Preferred:
Leveraged Buyout
Mezzanine
Special Situation

Geographical Preferences

United States Preferences:
All U.S.

Industry Preferences

In Communications prefer:
Communications and Media

Additional Information
Year Founded: 1979
Capital Under Management: $4,000,000
Current Activity Level : Actively seeking new investments
Method of Compensation: Return on invest. most important, but chg. closing fees, service fees, etc.

MINSHENG SHANGLIAN CAPITAL MANAGEMENT CO LTD

Huaqiao
Kunshan, Jiangsu, China

Type of Firm
Private Equity Firm

Project Preferences

Type of Financing Preferred:
Balanced

Pratt's Guide to Private Equity & Venture Capital Sources

Geographical Preferences

International Preferences:
China

Industry Preferences

In Industrial/Energy prefer:
Energy
Materials

Additional Information
Year Founded: 2011
Capital Under Management: $156,678,000
Current Activity Level : Actively seeking new investments

MIRABAUD ASSET MANAGEMENT FRANCE SAS

13, avenue Hoche
Paris, France 75008
Website: www.mirabaud-am.com

Type of Firm
Investment Management Firm

Project Preferences

Type of Financing Preferred:
Later Stage

Geographical Preferences

International Preferences:
Italy
Europe
Switzerland
France

Industry Preferences

In Consumer Related prefer:
Consumer Products
Consumer Services

Additional Information
Year Founded: 2017
Capital Under Management: $56,750,000
Current Activity Level : Actively seeking new investments

MIRADOR CAPITAL

52 Indian Rock Road
New Canaan, CT USA 06840
Phone: 203-966-8847
Website: www.miradorcap.com

Other Offices
95 Lilac Drive
Atherton, CA USA 94027

Management and Staff
Ken Hausman, Managing Director
Robert Young, Managing Director

Type of Firm
Private Equity Firm

Project Preferences

Type of Financing Preferred:
Fund of Funds
Balanced

Additional Information
Name of Most Recent Fund: Mirador Entreprenuers Fund II, L.P.
Most Recent Fund Was Raised: 08/02/2006
Year Founded: 2003
Capital Under Management: $7,200,000
Current Activity Level : Actively seeking new investments

MIRAE ASSET VENTURE INVESTMENT CO LTD

No. 685, Sampyeong-dong
11/F, MAVI Bldg, Bundang-gu
Seongnam, South Korea 463400
Phone: 82317801440
Website: venture.miraeasset.co.kr

Management and Staff
Eung Suk Kim, Chief Executive Officer

Type of Firm
Investment Management Firm

Association Membership
Korean Venture Capital Association (KVCA)

Project Preferences

Type of Financing Preferred:
Leveraged Buyout
Early Stage
Generalist PE
Balanced

Geographical Preferences

United States Preferences:

International Preferences:
Asia
Korea, South

Industry Preferences

In Communications prefer:
Telecommunications

In Computer Software prefer:
Software

In Semiconductor/Electr prefer:
Electronics
Electronic Components

In Biotechnology prefer:
Biotechnology

In Industrial/Energy prefer:
Materials

In Manufact. prefer:
Manufacturing

Additional Information
Year Founded: 1999
Capital Under Management: $42,600,000
Current Activity Level : Actively seeking new investments

MIRAIMON OY

Palokulmantie 22/102
Helsinki, Finland 00980
Phone: 35896852658
Fax: 358201407101

Management and Staff
Kalle Valimaa, Founder

Type of Firm
Private Equity Firm

Project Preferences

Type of Financing Preferred:
Balanced

Size of Investments Considered:
Min Size of Investment Considered (000s): $150
Max Size of Investment Considered (000s): $1,500

Geographical Preferences

International Preferences:
Scandanavia/Nordic Region
Finland

Industry Preferences

In Computer Other prefer:
Computer Related

In Semiconductor/Electr prefer:
Electronics

Additional Information
Year Founded: 2000
Capital Under Management: $9,100,000
Current Activity Level : Actively seeking new investments

MIRALTA CAPITAL INC

51 York Street
Westmount, Canada H3Z 1N7
Phone: 5144849806
E-mail: miralta@miralta.com
Website: www.miralta.com

Management and Staff
Christopher Winn, Chief Financial Officer

Type of Firm
Private Equity Firm

Project Preferences

Role in Financing:
Prefer role as deal originator

Type of Financing Preferred:
Early Stage
Expansion
Balanced
Later Stage

Size of Investments Considered:
Min Size of Investment Considered (000s): $1,000
Max Size of Investment Considered: No Limit

Geographical Preferences

Canadian Preferences:
All Canada

Industry Preferences

In Communications prefer:
Communications and Media

In Industrial/Energy prefer:
Energy Conservation Relat
Industrial Products

In Manufact. prefer:
Manufacturing

Additional Information

Year Founded: 1992
Capital Under Management: $28,000,000
Current Activity Level : Actively seeking new investments
Method of Compensation: Return on investment is of primary concern, do not charge fees

MIRAMAR VENTURE PARTNERS L P

2101 East Coast Highway
Third Floor
Corona del Mar, CA USA 92625
Phone: 9497604450
Fax: 9497604451
Website: www.miramarvp.com

Management and Staff

Bob Holmen, Managing Director
Bruce Hallett, Managing Director
Heiner Sussner, Managing Director
Rick Fink, Co-Founder

Type of Firm

Private Equity Firm

Project Preferences

Role in Financing:
Will function either as deal originator or investor in deals created by others

Type of Financing Preferred:
Early Stage
Expansion
Seed

Size of Investments Considered:
Min Size of Investment Considered (000s): $1,000
Max Size of Investment Considered (000s): $2,000

Geographical Preferences

United States Preferences:
Southern California

Industry Preferences

In Communications prefer:
Data Communications

In Computer Hardware prefer:
Disk Relat. Memory Device

In Computer Software prefer:
Software

In Internet Specific prefer:
Internet

In Computer Other prefer:
Computer Related

In Semiconductor/Electr prefer:
Semiconductor
Sensors

Additional Information

Name of Most Recent Fund: Miramar Digital Ventures, L.P.
Most Recent Fund Was Raised: 10/01/2013
Year Founded: 2001
Capital Under Management: $146,000,000
Current Activity Level : Actively seeking new investments
Method of Compensation: Return on investment is of primary concern, do not charge fees

MIRIN CAPITAL PTY, LTD.

Two Chifley Square
Level 29, Chifley Tower
Sydney, Australia NSW 2000
E-mail: info@mirin.vc
Website: www.mirin.vc

Type of Firm

Private Equity Firm

Project Preferences

Type of Financing Preferred:
Early Stage

Additional Information

Year Founded: 2012
Current Activity Level : Actively seeking new investments

MIROMA VENTURES LTD

One Cavendish Place
Secondd Floor
London, United Kingdom W1G 0QF
Phone: 44207287333
Fax: 442071994451
E-mail: info@miroma.com
Website: miromaventures.com

Type of Firm

Private Equity Firm

Project Preferences

Type of Financing Preferred:
Leveraged Buyout
Acquisition

Industry Preferences

In Consumer Related prefer:
Consumer

In Business Serv. prefer:
Media

Additional Information

Year Founded: 2009
Current Activity Level : Actively seeking new investments

MISSION BAY CAPITAL LLC

1700 Fourth Street
Suite 214
San Francisco, CA USA 94158
Phone: 4152404970
E-mail: info@missionbaycapital.com
Website: missionbaycapital.com

Management and Staff

Douglas Crawford, Managing Partner
Neena Kadaba, Partner
Regis Kelly, Managing Partner

Type of Firm

Private Equity Firm

Project Preferences

Type of Financing Preferred:
Early Stage
Seed

Geographical Preferences

United States Preferences:
North Carolina
South Carolina

Industry Preferences

In Biotechnology prefer:
Biotechnology

Additional Information

Name of Most Recent Fund: Mission Bay Capital Fund
Most Recent Fund Was Raised: 09/01/2009
Year Founded: 2009
Capital Under Management: $25,000,000
Current Activity Level : Actively seeking new investments

MISSION ENGINE LLC

128 Orchard Way
Suite 101
Berwyn, PA USA 19312
E-mail: info@missionog.com
Website: www.missionog.com

Type of Firm
Private Equity Firm

Project Preferences

Type of Financing Preferred:
Early Stage
Balanced
Later Stage

Industry Preferences

In Internet Specific prefer:
E-Commerce Technology

Additional Information

Year Founded: 2014
Capital Under Management: $24,480,000
Current Activity Level : Actively seeking new investments

MISSION VENTURES INC

3750 Carmel Mountain Road
Suite 200
San Diego, CA USA 92130
Phone: 8583502100
Fax: 8583502101
Website: www.missionventures.com

Other Offices

Former HQ: 11966 El Camino Real
Suite 450
SAN DIEGO, CA USA 92130
Phone: 8583502100
Fax: 8583502101

Management and Staff

Caroline Barberio, Chief Financial Officer
David Ryan, Managing Partner
Leo Spiegel, Managing Partner
Robert Kibble, Co-Founder
Ted Alexander, Managing Partner

Type of Firm
Private Equity Firm

Association Membership
Western Association of Venture Capitalists (WAVC)

Project Preferences

Role in Financing:
Prefer role as deal originator but will also invest in deals created by others

Type of Financing Preferred:
Early Stage

Size of Investments Considered:
Min Size of Investment Considered (000s): $2,000
Max Size of Investment Considered (000s): $10,000

Geographical Preferences

United States Preferences:
Southern California

Industry Focus

(% based on actual investment)
Computer Software and Services	30.9%
Internet Specific	28.5%
Semiconductors/Other Elect.	17.8%
Communications and Media	7.2%
Other Products	6.1%
Computer Hardware	3.6%
Consumer Related	2.4%
Industrial/Energy	1.9%
Medical/Health	1.6%

Additional Information

Name of Most Recent Fund: Mission Ventures III, L.P.
Most Recent Fund Was Raised: 09/10/2004
Year Founded: 1997
Capital Under Management: $501,000,000
Current Activity Level : Actively seeking new investments
Method of Compensation: Return on investment is of primary concern, do not charge fees

MISSIONPOINT CAPITAL PARTNERS LLC

20 Marshall Street
Suite 300
Norwalk, CT USA 06854
Phone: 2032860400
E-mail: info@missionpointcapital.com
Website: www.missionpointcapital.com

Management and Staff

Jeffrey Possick, Managing Director
Jesse Fink, Co-Founder
Leonard Nero, Chief Financial Officer
Mark Schwartz, Co-Founder
Mark Cirilli, Co-Founder

Type of Firm
Private Equity Firm

Project Preferences

Type of Financing Preferred:
Generalist PE
Later Stage
Management Buyouts
Acquisition
Joint Ventures
Recapitalizations

Industry Preferences

In Industrial/Energy prefer:
Energy
Alternative Energy
Energy Conservation Relat
Environmental Related

In Transportation prefer:
Transportation

In Financial Services prefer:
Insurance
Financial Services

In Business Serv. prefer:
Distribution

Additional Information

Name of Most Recent Fund: MissionPoint Re Community Coinvest Fund II, L.P.
Most Recent Fund Was Raised: 01/27/2012
Year Founded: 2006
Capital Under Management: $18,643,000
Current Activity Level : Actively seeking new investments

MISTLETOE INC

2-9-5, Kita-aoyama, Minato-ku
7F Stadium Place Aoyama
Tokyo, Japan 107-0061
E-mail: hello@mistletoe.co
Website: mistletoe.co

Type of Firm
Incubator/Development Program

Project Preferences

Type of Financing Preferred:
Start-up Financing
Seed

Additional Information

Year Founded: 1969
Current Activity Level : Actively seeking new investments

MISTRAL EQUITY PARTNERS LP

650 Fifth Avenue, 31st Floor
New York, NY USA 10019
Phone: 2126169600
Fax: 2126169601
E-mail: info@mistralequity.com
Website: www.mistralequity.com

Management and Staff
Andrew Heyer, CEO & Managing Director
Beth Bronner, Managing Director
Christopher Bradley, Principal
Griffin Whitney, Principal
Jeffrey Ginsberg, Managing Director
Robert Fioretti, Managing Director
William Phoenix, Managing Director

Type of Firm
Private Equity Firm

Project Preferences

Type of Financing Preferred:
Leveraged Buyout
Acquisition
Recapitalizations

Geographical Preferences

United States Preferences:
North America

Industry Preferences

In Consumer Related prefer:
Consumer

In Business Serv. prefer:
Media

Additional Information
Year Founded: 2007
Current Activity Level: Actively seeking new investments

MISTRAL VENTURE PARTNERS

100-80 Aberdeen St.
Ottawa, Canada
Website: www.mistralvp.com

Type of Firm
Private Equity Firm

Project Preferences

Type of Financing Preferred:
Early Stage
Startup

Size of Investments Considered:
Min Size of Investment Considered (000s): $50
Max Size of Investment Considered (000s): $100

Geographical Preferences

Canadian Preferences:
Ontario

Additional Information
Name of Most Recent Fund: Mistral Venture Partners Fund
Most Recent Fund Was Raised: 01/21/2013
Year Founded: 2012

Capital Under Management: $31,260,000
Current Activity Level: Actively seeking new investments

MIT SANDBOX INNOVATION FUND PROGRAM

77 Massachusetts Avenue
Cambridge, MA USA 02139
Website: andbox.mit.edu

Type of Firm
University Program

Project Preferences

Type of Financing Preferred:
Seed
Startup

Additional Information
Year Founded: 2016
Current Activity Level: Actively seeking new investments

MITHRAS CAPITAL PARTNERS LLP

53 Chandos Place
Covent Garden
London, United Kingdom WC2N 4HS
Phone: 44-20-7812-6535
Website: www.mithrascapital.com

Management and Staff
Bernie Boylan, Managing Partner
Gillian Brown, Managing Partner

Type of Firm
Private Equity Advisor or Fund of Funds

Project Preferences

Type of Financing Preferred:
Fund of Funds

Geographical Preferences

International Preferences:
United Kingdom

Additional Information
Year Founded: 2007
Current Activity Level: Actively seeking new investments

MITHRIL CAPITAL MANAGEMENT LLC

One Letterman Drive
Building C, Suite 400
San Francisco, CA USA 94129
Phone: 4152485147
Website: www.mithril.com

Management and Staff
Ajay Royan, Managing Partner

Type of Firm
Private Equity Firm

Project Preferences

Type of Financing Preferred:
Balanced
Later Stage

Additional Information
Name of Most Recent Fund: Mithril, L.P.
Most Recent Fund Was Raised: 06/18/2012
Year Founded: 2012
Capital Under Management: $1,142,300,000
Current Activity Level: Actively seeking new investments

MITSUBISHI CORP

3-1 Marunouchi 2-chome
2-6-1, Marunouchi, Chiyoda-ku
Tokyo, Japan 100-8086
Phone: 81332102121
Fax: 81332108935
Website: www.mitsubishicorp.com

Other Offices
875 North Michigan Avenue
Suite 3900
Chicago, IL USA 60611
Phone: 312-640-5621
Fax: 312-280-9271

Management and Staff
Kazuyuki Masu, Chief Financial Officer

Type of Firm
Corporate PE/Venture

Project Preferences

Type of Financing Preferred:
Leveraged Buyout
Expansion

Geographical Preferences

United States Preferences:
All U.S.

International Preferences:
Asia

Industry Preferences

In Communications prefer:
Telecommunications

In Consumer Related prefer:
Food/Beverage

In Industrial/Energy prefer:
Energy
Materials
Machinery

In Manufact. prefer:
Manufacturing

Additional Information
Year Founded: 1950
Current Activity Level : Actively seeking new investments

MITSUBISHI INTERNATIONAL CORP

655 Third Avenue
New York, NY USA 10017
Phone: 2126052000
Website: www.mitsubishicorp.com

Management and Staff
Gosuke Nakae, Vice President
Jil Galloway, Vice President
Katsuhiro Ito, Chief Financial Officer
Masakazu Horikawa, Vice President
Ryugo Izumida, Vice President
Ryuji Watanabe, Vice President
Tadashi Takasugi, Vice President
Yuzo Nouchi, Vice President

Type of Firm
Bank Affiliated

Project Preferences

Role in Financing:
Prefer role as deal originator but will also invest in deals created by others

Type of Financing Preferred:
Second Stage Financing
Mezzanine
First Stage Financing

Geographical Preferences

United States Preferences:
All U.S.

Canadian Preferences:
All Canada

International Preferences:
Asia

Industry Focus
(% based on actual investment)

Other Products	55.7%
Internet Specific	14.0%
Biotechnology	10.0%
Semiconductors/Other Elect.	5.0%
Computer Software and Services	4.6%
Communications and Media	3.6%
Computer Hardware	2.9%
Medical/Health	2.1%
Industrial/Energy	2.1%

Additional Information
Name of Most Recent Fund: Mitsubishi
Most Recent Fund Was Raised: 11/01/1988
Year Founded: 1954
Capital Under Management: $35,000,000
Current Activity Level : Actively seeking new investments

MITSUBISHI TANABE PHARMA CORP

2-6-18, Kitahama Chuo-ku
Osaka, Japan 541-8505
Phone: 81-6-6205-5555
Fax: 81-6-6205-5085
Website: www.mt-pharma.co.jp

Type of Firm
Corporate PE/Venture

Project Preferences

Type of Financing Preferred:
Balanced

Additional Information
Year Founded: 1933
Current Activity Level : Actively seeking new investments

MITSUBISHI UFJ CAPITAL CO LTD

1-7-17, Nihonbashi, Chuo-Ku
6F Nihonbashi Miyuki Bldg
Tokyo, Japan 103-0027
Phone: 81352058581
Fax: 81332735570
Website: www.mucap.co.jp

Management and Staff
Hidetsugu Hamamoto, Managing Director
Hiroshi Yamakawa, Managing Director

Type of Firm
Private Equity Firm

Association Membership
Japan Venture Capital Association

Project Preferences

Type of Financing Preferred:
Early Stage
Balanced
Later Stage
Seed

Geographical Preferences

International Preferences:
Taiwan
Hong Kong
China
Asia
Japan

Industry Preferences

In Communications prefer:
Communications and Media

In Semiconductor/Electr prefer:
Electronics

In Biotechnology prefer:
Biotechnology

In Medical/Health prefer:
Medical/Health
Medical Therapeutics
Drug/Equipmt Delivery
Medical Products
Health Services
Pharmaceuticals

In Industrial/Energy prefer:
Energy

In Manufact. prefer:
Manufacturing

Additional Information
Year Founded: 1974
Current Activity Level : Actively seeking new investments

MITSUI & CO GLOBAL INVESTMENT LTD

1-3-7, Otemachi, Chiyoda-ku
8F Nikkei Headquarters Bldg
Tokyo, Japan 100-0004
Phone: 81332853124
Fax: 81332859156
Website: www.mitsui-global.com

Other Offices

Room 3101, Kerry Centre
1515 Nanjing Rd. West
Shanghai, China 200040
Phone: 86-21-5298-5959
Fax: 86-21-5298-5177

Room 3303, China World Tower 1
Jian Guo Men wai Avenue
Beijing, China 100004
Phone: 86-10-6505-5308
Fax: 86-21-6506-3128

238 Nariman Point
77th Floor, Mafatlal Centre
Mumbai, India 400027

24 King William Street
London, United Kingdom EC4R 9AJ
Phone: 442078220422
Fax: 442071319072

535 Middlefield Road
Suite 100
Menlo Park, CA USA 94025
Phone: 6502345000
Fax: 6503231516

Management and Staff
Kanami Iga, Principal
Kinji Fuchikami, Venture Partner
Takanori Sato, Principal

Type of Firm
Corporate PE/Venture

Association Membership
Japan Venture Capital Association
Singapore Venture Capital Association (SVCA)

Project Preferences

Type of Financing Preferred:
Early Stage
Balanced

Geographical Preferences

United States Preferences:

International Preferences:
Europe
China
Japan

Industry Preferences

In Medical/Health prefer:
Medical/Health

In Industrial/Energy prefer:
Environmental Related

In Business Serv. prefer:
Services

Additional Information
Year Founded: 1995
Capital Under Management: $19,000,000
Current Activity Level : Actively seeking new investments

MITSUI & CO. GLOBAL INVESTMENT, LTD.

535 Middlefield Road
Suite 100
Menlo Park, CA USA 94025
Phone: 6502345000
Fax: 6503231516
Website: www.mitsui-global.com

Other Offices
PLATINA, C 59, G Block
Unit 704, 7th Floor
Bandra (east), India 400051
Phone: 91226774222
Fax: 912226525095

1-3-7, Otemachi, Chiyoda-ku
Tokyo, Japan 100-0004
Phone: 81332853124
Fax: 81332859156

No.1 Jianguomenwai Avenue
Chaoyang District
Beijing, China 100004
Phone: 861065055308
Fax: 861065053128

1515 Nanjing Road West
Room 3101, Kerry Center, Jingan District
Shanghai, China 200040
Phone: 862152985959
Fax: 862152985177

Management and Staff
Hiroshi Kakihira, Venture Partner
Ryuichi Mihara, Venture Partner

Type of Firm
Corporate PE/Venture

Association Membership
National Venture Capital Association - USA (NVCA)

Project Preferences

Role in Financing:
Prefer role as deal originator but will also invest in deals created by others

Type of Financing Preferred:
Early Stage
Expansion
Balanced
Later Stage
Seed
Startup

Geographical Preferences

United States Preferences:

International Preferences:
India
Europe
China
Asia
Japan

Industry Focus
(% based on actual investment)

Industrial/Energy	27.4%
Biotechnology	13.1%
Internet Specific	12.2%
Computer Software and Services	12.1%
Medical/Health	9.2%
Communications and Media	8.9%
Computer Hardware	6.6%
Semiconductors/Other Elect.	5.1%
Consumer Related	3.7%
Other Products	1.9%

Additional Information
Name of Most Recent Fund: Mitsui & Co, Ltd.
Most Recent Fund Was Raised: 12/31/1985
Year Founded: 2001
Capital Under Management: $300,000,000
Current Activity Level : Actively seeking new investments
Method of Compensation: Return on investment is of primary concern, do not charge fees

---

MITSUI SUMITOMO INSURANCE VENTURE CAPITAL CO LTD

2-2-10 Yaesu
3F, Yaesu Nagoya Bldg
Chuo-Ku, Tokyo, Japan 104-0028
Phone: 81332793672
Fax: 81332423068
E-mail: info@msivc.co.jp
Website: www.msivc.co.jp

Type of Firm
Insurance Firm Affiliate

Association Membership
Japan Venture Capital Association

Project Preferences

Type of Financing Preferred:
Balanced

Geographical Preferences

International Preferences:
Taiwan
China
Asia
Japan

Industry Focus
(% based on actual investment)

Internet Specific	50.5%
Semiconductors/Other Elect.	29.5%
Computer Software and Services	7.7%
Other Products	5.9%
Consumer Related	3.0%
Biotechnology	2.7%
Communications and Media	0.3%
Industrial/Energy	0.3%
Computer Hardware	0.1%

MITTELSTAENDISCHE BETEILIGUNGS-GESELLSCHAFT

Schwarzschildstrasse 94
Potsdam, Germany 14480
Phone: 49331649630
Fax: 493316496321
E-mail: info@mbg-bb.de
Website: www.mbg-bb.de

Management and Staff
Milos Stefanovic, Managing Director
Waltraud Wolf, Managing Director

Type of Firm
Government Affiliated Program

Association Membership
German Venture Capital Association (BVK)

Project Preferences

Type of Financing Preferred:
Early Stage
Later Stage
Seed
Management Buyouts
Startup

Geographical Preferences

International Preferences:
Germany

Industry Focus
(% based on actual investment)
Computer Software and Services   100.0%

Additional Information
Year Founded: 1993
Current Activity Level : Actively seeking new investments

MITTELSTAENDISCHE BETEILIGUNGS-GESELLSCHAFT MV MBH

Graf-Schack-Allee 12
Ludwig-Boelkow-Haus
Schwerin, Germany 19053
Phone: 49385395550
Fax: 493853955536
E-mail: info@mbm-v.de
Website: www.buergschaftsbank-mv.de

Management and Staff
Steffen Hartung, Chief Executive Officer
Thomas Drews, Chief Executive Officer

Type of Firm
Bank Affiliated

Association Membership
German Venture Capital Association (BVK)

Project Preferences

Type of Financing Preferred:
Early Stage
Later Stage
Seed
Management Buyouts
Startup

Size of Investments Considered:
Min Size of Investment Considered (000s): $73
Max Size of Investment Considered (000s): $1,452

Geographical Preferences

International Preferences:
Germany

Additional Information
Year Founded: 1993
Current Activity Level : Actively seeking new investments

MITTELSTAENDISCHE BETEILIGUNGS-GESELLSCHAFT NIEDER-SACHSEN MBH

Hildesheimer Str. 6
Hannover, Germany 30169
Phone: 495113370511
Fax: 495513370555
E-mail: info@nbb-hannover.de
Website: www.mbg-hannover.de

Type of Firm
Bank Affiliated

Association Membership
German Venture Capital Association (BVK)

Project Preferences

Type of Financing Preferred:
Early Stage
Expansion
Mezzanine
Later Stage
Seed
Startup

Size of Investments Considered:
Min Size of Investment Considered (000s): $279
Max Size of Investment Considered (000s): $1,397

Geographical Preferences

International Preferences:
Germany

Industry Preferences

In Industrial/Energy prefer:
Coal Related
Industrial Products

In Agr/Forestr/Fish prefer:
Agriculture related

Additional Information
Year Founded: 1991
Current Activity Level : Actively seeking new investments

MITTELSTAENDISCHE BETEILIGUNGS-GESELLSCHAFT SACHSEN MBH

Anton-Graff-Strasse 20
Dresden, Germany 01309
Phone: 4935144090
Fax: 493514409355
E-mail: info@mbg-sachsen.de
Website: www.mbg-sachsen.de

Management and Staff
Christian Koeppel, Managing Director
Eva Koehler, Managing Director
Markus Michalow, Managing Director
Wolf-Dieter Schwab, Managing Director

Type of Firm
Government Affiliated Program

Association Membership
German Venture Capital Association (BVK)

Project Preferences

Type of Financing Preferred:
Early Stage
Later Stage
Management Buyouts
Acquisition
Startup

Geographical Preferences

International Preferences:
Germany

Industry Focus
(% based on actual investment)
Biotechnology   51.0%
Consumer Related   24.6%
Computer Software and Services   13.2%
Internet Specific   11.3%

Additional Information
Year Founded: 1990
Capital Under Management: $31,000,000
Current Activity Level : Actively seeking new investments

MITTELSTAENDISCHE BETEILIGUNGS-GESELLSCHAFT SACHSEN-ANHALT

Grosse Diesdorfer Strasse 228
Magdeburg, Germany 39108
Phone: 49391737520
Fax: 493917375215
E-mail: info@mbg-sachsen-anhalt.de
Website: www.mbg-sachsen-anhalt.de

Management and Staff
Christian Koeppel, Managing Director
Wolf-Dieter Schwab, Managing Director

Type of Firm
Bank Affiliated

Association Membership
German Venture Capital Association (BVK)

Project Preferences

Type of Financing Preferred:
Early Stage
Later Stage
Startup

Size of Investments Considered:
Min Size of Investment Considered (000s): $32
Max Size of Investment Considered (000s): $3,181

Geographical Preferences

International Preferences:
Germany

Industry Preferences

In Consumer Related prefer:
Retail

In Industrial/Energy prefer:
Industrial Products
Materials
Machinery
Environmental Related

In Manufact. prefer:
Manufacturing

In Agr/Forestr/Fish prefer:
Agriculture related

Additional Information
Year Founded: 1992
Current Activity Level : Actively seeking new investments

MITTELSTAENDISCHE BETEILIGUNGS-GESELLSCHAFT THUERINGEN MBH

Bonifaciusstrasse 19
Erfurt, Germany 99084
Phone: 4936121350
Fax: 493612135100
E-mail: info@mbg-thueringen.de
Website: www.mbg-thueringen.de

Management and Staff
Michael Burchardt, Chief Executive Officer

Type of Firm
Government Affiliated Program

Association Membership
German Venture Capital Association (BVK)

Project Preferences

Type of Financing Preferred:
Early Stage
Later Stage
Seed
Management Buyouts
Startup

Geographical Preferences

International Preferences:
Germany

Industry Preferences

In Communications prefer:
Communications and Media

In Semiconductor/Electr prefer:
Electronics

In Consumer Related prefer:
Retail
Food/Beverage
Consumer Products

In Industrial/Energy prefer:
Industrial Products
Materials
Machinery

In Business Serv. prefer:
Services

Additional Information
Year Founded: 1993
Capital Under Management: $13,200,000
Current Activity Level : Actively seeking new investments

MIURA PRIVATE EQUITY SGEIC SA

Avenida Diagonal 399
4, 2a
Barcelona, Spain 08008
Phone: 34932723440
Fax: 34932723445
E-mail: info@miuraequity.com
Website: www.miuraequity.com

Management and Staff
Juan Eusebio Pujol, Chief Operating Officer

Type of Firm
Private Equity Firm

Association Membership
European Private Equity and Venture Capital Assoc.
Spanish Venture Capital Association (ASCRI)

Project Preferences

Type of Financing Preferred:
Leveraged Buyout
Expansion
Management Buyouts
Acquisition
Recapitalizations

Geographical Preferences

International Preferences:
Portugal
Spain

Industry Preferences

In Medical/Health prefer:
Medical/Health
Health Services

In Consumer Related prefer:
Entertainment and Leisure
Retail
Food/Beverage
Consumer Products
Consumer Services

In Industrial/Energy prefer:
Industrial Products

In Business Serv. prefer:
Services

Additional Information
Year Founded: 2007
Capital Under Management: $332,500,000
Current Activity Level : Actively seeking new investments

MIYAKO CAPITAL KK

Nihonbashu Kabuto-cho 5-1 3F
Chuo-ku
Tokyo, Japan
Website: www.miyakocapital.com

Type of Firm
Private Equity Firm

Project Preferences

Type of Financing Preferred:
Early Stage
Balanced
Seed

Industry Preferences

In Biotechnology prefer:
Biotechnology

In Industrial/Energy prefer:
Energy Conservation Relat

In Agr/Forestr/Fish prefer:
Agriculture related

Additional Information
Year Founded: 1969
Current Activity Level : Actively seeking new investments

MIZUHO CAPITAL CO LTD

1-2-1 Uchisaiwaicho Chiyoda-ku
6F Nittochi Uchisaiwaicho Bldg
Tokyo, Japan 100-0011
Phone: 81335961300
Fax: 81335961310
Website: www.mizuho-vc.co.jp

Other Offices
4-2-1 Imabashi
Chuo-ku
Osaka, Japan 541-0042
Phone: 81-6-6229-2781
Fax: 81-6-6229-2757

Management and Staff
Hiroshi Yamamoto, Managing Director
Hiroshi Suzuki, Managing Director
Masakazu Kita, Managing Director
Satoshi Akiyama, Senior Managing Director

Type of Firm
Bank Affiliated

Project Preferences

Type of Financing Preferred:
Early Stage
Expansion
Balanced
Later Stage

Geographical Preferences

International Preferences:
Japan

Industry Preferences

In Communications prefer:
Communications and Media

In Computer Software prefer:
Software

In Internet Specific prefer:
Internet

In Semiconductor/Electr prefer:
Electronics
Semiconductor

In Medical/Health prefer:
Medical/Health

In Consumer Related prefer:
Consumer

In Business Serv. prefer:
Services

Additional Information
Year Founded: 1983
Capital Under Management: $567,000,000
Current Activity Level : Actively seeking new investments

MIZUHO CAPITAL PARTNERS CO LTD

2-3-2 Marunouchi
3F YUSEN Building
Chiyoda-ku, Tokyo, Japan 100-0005
Phone: 81332841632
Website: www.mizuho-cp.co.jp

Management and Staff
Mitsuru Otawa, Managing Director

Type of Firm
Private Equity Firm

Project Preferences

Type of Financing Preferred:
Leveraged Buyout
Mezzanine
Management Buyouts

Geographical Preferences

International Preferences:
Japan

Additional Information
Year Founded: 2000
Capital Under Management: $389,540,000
Current Activity Level : Actively seeking new investments

MIZUHO GULF CAPITAL PARTNERS LTD

Level 5, The Gate Building
East Wing, DIFC
Dubai, Utd. Arab Em.
Phone: 97145528333
Website: mizuhogulf.com

Type of Firm
Private Equity Firm

Project Preferences

Type of Financing Preferred:
Generalist PE

Geographical Preferences

International Preferences:
Middle East
Japan

Industry Preferences

In Consumer Related prefer:
Food/Beverage

In Agr/Forestr/Fish prefer:
Agribusiness
Agriculture related

Additional Information
Year Founded: 2016
Current Activity Level : Actively seeking new investments

MJH GROUP LLC

6907 Mackson Drive
Temple Hills, MD USA 20748
Phone: 3014493439
Website: www.mjhgroup.com

Type of Firm
Investment Management Firm

Association Membership
Mid-Atlantic Venture Association

Project Preferences

Type of Financing Preferred:
Early Stage
Expansion
Mezzanine
Generalist PE
Later Stage
Startup

Geographical Preferences

United States Preferences:
Mid Atlantic
Maryland
Virginia
D. of Columbia

Industry Preferences

In Communications prefer:
Wireless Communications
Data Communications

In Internet Specific prefer:
E-Commerce Technology
Ecommerce

In Consumer Related prefer:
Education Related

In Industrial/Energy prefer:
Environmental Related

In Financial Services prefer:
Real Estate

In Business Serv. prefer:
Media

Additional Information

Year Founded: 1998
Current Activity Level : Actively seeking new investments

MK CAPITAL

1033 Skokie Boulevard
Suite 430
Northbrook, IL USA 60062
Phone: 3123247700
Website: www.mkcapital.com

Other Offices

535 W. William
Suite 303
Ann Arbor, MI USA 48103
Phone: 7346636500

1524F Cloverfield Boulevard
Santa Monica, CA USA 90404
Phone: 3105867400

Management and Staff

Bret Maxwell, Co-Founder
Kirk Wolfe, Partner
Mark Koulogeorge, Co-Founder
Yair Landau, Partner

Type of Firm

Private Equity Firm

Association Membership

Illinois Venture Capital Association

Project Preferences

Role in Financing:
Prefer role as deal originator but will also invest in deals created by others

Type of Financing Preferred:
Early Stage
Balanced
Later Stage

Geographical Preferences

United States Preferences:
All U.S.

Industry Preferences

In Computer Software prefer:
Data Processing
Software

In Consumer Related prefer:
Education Related

In Business Serv. prefer:
Media

Additional Information

Year Founded: 2003
Capital Under Management: $150,000,000
Current Activity Level : Actively seeking new investments

MK VENTURE CAPITAL

63 Korea Life Building
Youngdeungpo-gu
Seoul, South Korea 150-763
Phone: 822-3452-0606
Fax: 822-3452-3050

Other Offices

302 Yookeui Bldg., 376-14
Seokyo-dong, Mapo-ku
Seoul, South Korea

Type of Firm

Private Equity Firm

Association Membership

Korean Venture Capital Association (KVCA)

Project Preferences

Type of Financing Preferred:
Balanced

Geographical Preferences

International Preferences:
Korea, South

Industry Preferences

In Biotechnology prefer:
Biotechnology

Additional Information

Year Founded: 1998
Capital Under Management: $16,500,000
Current Activity Level : Actively seeking new investments

MKOBA PRIVATE EQUITY FUND

Toure Drive
Dar es Salaam, Tanzania 1820
Phone: 2550222600719
Fax: 2550222601443
E-mail: info@mkobafund.com
Website: mkobafund.com

Type of Firm

Private Equity Firm

Project Preferences

Type of Financing Preferred:
Early Stage
Balanced
Seed
Startup

Geographical Preferences

International Preferences:
Ethiopia
Rwanda
Liberia
Tanzania
Ivory Coast
Sierra Leone
Congo
Mozambique
South Africa
Africa

Industry Preferences

In Industrial/Energy prefer:
Alternative Energy

In Financial Services prefer:
Financial Services

In Manufact. prefer:
Manufacturing

In Agr/Forestr/Fish prefer:
Agriculture related

Additional Information

Year Founded: 2013
Current Activity Level : Actively seeking new investments

MMC VENTURES LTD

Two Kensington Square
London, United Kingdom W8 5EP
Phone: 020 7938 2220
Fax: 020 7938 2259
E-mail: information@mmcventures.com
Website: www.mmcventures.com

Management and Staff
Bruce Macfarlane, Co-Founder
Jonathan Coker, Managing Partner
Simon Menashy, Partner

Type of Firm
Private Equity Firm

Association Membership
British Venture Capital Association (BVCA)

Project Preferences

Role in Financing:
Prefer role as deal originator but will also invest in deals created by others

Type of Financing Preferred:
Early Stage
Balanced
Later Stage

Size of Investments Considered:
Min Size of Investment Considered (000s): $769
Max Size of Investment Considered (000s): $6,152

Geographical Preferences

International Preferences:
United Kingdom

Industry Preferences

In Computer Software prefer:
Software

In Internet Specific prefer:
Internet
Ecommerce

In Financial Services prefer:
Financial Services

In Business Serv. prefer:
Services
Media

Additional Information
Name of Most Recent Fund: MMC London Fund, The
Most Recent Fund Was Raised: 04/08/2013
Year Founded: 2000
Capital Under Management: $192,200,000
Current Activity Level : Actively seeking new investments

MMF CAPITAL MANAGEMENT LLC

55 West Monroe Street
Suite 3650
Chicago, IL USA 60603
Phone: 3122917300
Fax: 3123450665
E-mail: info@mmfcapital.com
Website: www.mmfcapital.com

Other Offices
250 Monroe Northwest
Suite 400
Grand Rapids, MI USA 49503
Phone: 6167175629
Fax: 6167175701

Management and Staff
Ana Winters, Principal
C. Michael Foster, Senior Managing Director
David Gezon, Senior Managing Director
J. Allan Kayler, Senior Managing Director
Kristin Lee, Principal
Paul Kreie, Managing Director

Type of Firm
Private Equity Firm

Association Membership
Natl Assoc of Small Bus. Inv. Co (NASBIC)

Project Preferences

Type of Financing Preferred:
Leveraged Buyout
Expansion
Mezzanine
Acquisition
Recapitalizations

Geographical Preferences

United States Preferences:

Canadian Preferences:
All Canada

Industry Focus
(% based on actual investment)
Industrial/Energy	34.4%
Other Products	32.5%
Consumer Related	30.8%
Communications and Media	2.3%

Additional Information
Name of Most Recent Fund: Midwest Mezzanine Fund V, L.P.
Most Recent Fund Was Raised: 12/11/2012
Year Founded: 1992
Capital Under Management: $269,974,000
Current Activity Level : Actively seeking new investments

MMI GROUP INC

135 Kingstreet East
Ontario, Canada M5C 1G6
Phone: 416-363-3050
Fax: 416-368-4330
E-mail: info@mmigroup.com

Type of Firm
Private Equity Firm

Additional Information
Year Founded: 2009

Current Activity Level : Actively seeking new investments

MML CAPITAL PARTNERS LLP

Grand Buildings
One to Three Strand
London, United Kingdom WC2N 5HR
Phone: 442070242200
Fax: 442070242201
Website: www.mmlcapital.com

Other Offices
46 Southfield Avenue
Suite 330, 3 Stamford Landing
Stamford, CT USA 06902
Phone: 203-323-9118
Fax: 203-323-9119

12-14 Rond-Point des Champs-Elysees
Paris, France 75008
Phone: 33-1-5353-1488
Fax: 33-1-5353-1400

92/93 St Stephens Green
Dublin, Ireland
Phone: 35314283570

Management and Staff
Balbinder Johal, Managing Partner
Henry-Louis Merieux, Managing Partner
Ian Wallis, Managing Partner
James Read, Co-Founder
Luke Jones, Partner
Parag Gandesha, Chief Operating Officer
Rory Brooks, Co-Founder

Type of Firm
Private Equity Firm

Association Membership
Irish Venture Capital Association
European Private Equity and Venture Capital Assoc.

Project Preferences

Role in Financing:
Prefer role as deal originator but will also invest in deals created by others

Type of Financing Preferred:
Leveraged Buyout
Expansion
Mezzanine
Generalist PE
Management Buyouts
Acquisition
Recapitalizations

Geographical Preferences

International Preferences:
Ireland
Central Europe
Europe

Industry Focus

(% based on actual investment)

Computer Software and Services	22.9%
Other Products	22.4%
Medical/Health	15.7%
Industrial/Energy	12.8%
Consumer Related	11.6%
Internet Specific	9.9%
Semiconductors/Other Elect.	4.7%

Additional Information

Name of Most Recent Fund: MML Growth Capital Partners Ireland
Most Recent Fund Was Raised: 11/15/2013
Year Founded: 1988
Capital Under Management: $1,250,000,000
Current Activity Level : Actively seeking new investments
Method of Compensation: Return on invest. most important, but chg. closing fees, service fees, etc.

MOBEUS EQUITY PARTNERS LLP

30 Haymarket
London, United Kingdom SW1Y 4EX
Phone: 442070247600
Fax: 442070247619
E-mail: info@mobeusequity.co.uk
Website: www.mobeusequity.co.uk

Other Offices

Dutco House, First Floor
Port Saeed, PO Box 282110
Dubai, Utd. Arab Em.
Phone: 97142942032
Fax: 97142942323

18 Walker Street
Edinburgh, United Kingdom EH3 7LP
Phone: 441312207220

Management and Staff

Ashley Broomberg, Partner
Bob Henry, Partner
Eric Tung, Partner
Jonathan Gregory, Partner
Mark Wignall, Managing Partner
Mike Walker, Partner
Rob Brittain, Partner

Type of Firm

Private Equity Firm

Association Membership

British Venture Capital Association (BVCA)

Project Preferences

Role in Financing:
Prefer role as deal originator

Type of Financing Preferred:
Leveraged Buyout
Generalist PE
Balanced
Later Stage
Management Buyouts
Acquisition
Recapitalizations

Size of Investments Considered:
Min Size of Investment Considered (000s): $3,022
Max Size of Investment Considered (000s): $15,111

Geographical Preferences

International Preferences:
United Kingdom
Europe

Industry Preferences

In Consumer Related prefer:
Food/Beverage
Consumer Products

In Business Serv. prefer:
Services
Media

In Manufact. prefer:
Manufacturing

Additional Information

Name of Most Recent Fund: Baring English Growth Fund
Most Recent Fund Was Raised: 02/01/2000
Year Founded: 2000
Capital Under Management: $196,500,000
Current Activity Level : Actively seeking new investments

MOBILE INTERNET CAPITAL INC

1-11-28 Akasaka
8F, Jowa Akasaka 1-chome Bldg
Minato-Ku, Tokyo, Japan 1070052
Phone: 81335682170
Website: www.mickk.com

Type of Firm

Private Equity Firm

Association Membership

Japan Venture Capital Association

Project Preferences

Type of Financing Preferred:
Early Stage
Balanced
Startup

Geographical Preferences

International Preferences:
Japan

Industry Preferences

In Communications prefer:
Communications and Media
Wireless Communications

In Internet Specific prefer:
Internet

In Medical/Health prefer:
Medical/Health

In Industrial/Energy prefer:
Energy
Environmental Related

Additional Information

Year Founded: 1999
Capital Under Management: $73,938,000
Current Activity Level : Actively seeking new investments

MOBILITY VENTURES LLC

16475 Dallas Parkway
Suite 620
Addison, TX USA 75001
Phone: 9729919942
Fax: 9726697873
E-mail: email@mobilityventures.com
Website: www.mobilityventures.com

Management and Staff

Arlan Harris, Partner
David Sym-Smith, Partner
Donald Yonce, Partner
Edward Fernandez, Venture Partner
Lothar Pauly, Managing Partner
Mark Fruehan, Venture Partner
Michael Buckland, Venture Partner
Roman Kikta, Managing Partner
Roy Gunter, Venture Partner
Scott Bennett, Venture Partner
Shoa-Kai Liu, Venture Partner
Stephen Lin, Venture Partner

Type of Firm

Private Equity Firm

Project Preferences

Role in Financing:
Prefer role as deal originator but will also invest in deals created by others

Type of Financing Preferred:
Early Stage
Balanced
Later Stage
Seed

Size of Investments Considered:
Min Size of Investment Considered (000s): $100
Max Size of Investment Considered (000s): $5,000

Industry Preferences

In Communications prefer:
Telecommunications
Wireless Communications

In Computer Software prefer:
Software

In Internet Specific prefer:
Ecommerce

In Semiconductor/Electr prefer:
Semiconductor

In Industrial/Energy prefer:
Alternative Energy

In Business Serv. prefer:
Services
Media

Additional Information

Year Founded: 2004
Capital Under Management: $40,000,000
Current Activity Level : Actively seeking new investments

MODARA TECHNOLOGIES SL

Calle de Sor Angela de la Cruz
Madrid, Spain 28020
E-mail: info@modara.es
Website: www.modara.es

Type of Firm

Private Equity Firm

Project Preferences

Type of Financing Preferred:
Balanced

Geographical Preferences

International Preferences:
Spain

Additional Information

Year Founded: 2009
Current Activity Level : Actively seeking new investments

MODERN AFRICA FUND MANAGERS, LLC

7 Arnold Road, Fedics House,
Rosebank
Johannesburg, South Africa 2132
Phone: 27-11-447-4834
Fax: 27-11-447-4427
Website: www.maldimix.com

Other Offices

1100 Connecticut Avenue,
Suite 500
Washington, DC USA 20036
Phone: 202-887-1772
Fax: 202-887-1788

Management and Staff

C. Timothy Wood, Managing Director
Francis Nyirjesy, Chief Financial Officer
Stephen Cashin, Managing Director

Type of Firm

Private Equity Firm

Project Preferences

Type of Financing Preferred:
Balanced
Turnaround
Later Stage
Recapitalizations

Size of Investments Considered:
Min Size of Investment Considered (000s): $3,000
Max Size of Investment Considered (000s): $15,000

Geographical Preferences

International Preferences:
Swaziland
Botswana
Namibia
Lesotho
South Africa

Industry Preferences

In Communications prefer:
Telecommunications

In Financial Services prefer:
Financial Services

In Manufact. prefer:
Manufacturing

In Agr/Forestr/Fish prefer:
Agribusiness
Agriculture related

Additional Information

Year Founded: 2010
Current Activity Level : Actively seeking new investments

MODERNE VENTURES FUND I LP

400 North Michigan Avenue
Suite 410 South
Chicago, IL USA 60611

Management and Staff

Kurt Ramirez, Vice President
Michele Conn, Principal

Type of Firm

Private Equity Firm

Project Preferences

Type of Financing Preferred:
Early Stage
Expansion
Later Stage

Industry Preferences

In Financial Services prefer:
Insurance
Real Estate
Financial Services

Additional Information

Year Founded: 1969
Capital Under Management: $33,140,000
Current Activity Level : Actively seeking new investments

MOELIS CAPITAL PARTNERS LLC

399 Park Avenue
Fifth Floor
New York, NY USA 10022
Phone: 2128833800
Fax: 2128804260
Website: www.moeliscapital.com

Management and Staff

Andy Kieffer, Principal
Gregory Share, Partner
James Johnston, Principal
Joel Killion, Principal
Kurt Larsen, Managing Partner
Lex Leeming, Principal
Stephan Oppenheimer, Partner
Ted Yun, Managing Partner

Type of Firm

Bank Affiliated

Project Preferences

Type of Financing Preferred:
Leveraged Buyout
Generalist PE
Balanced
Management Buyouts
Acquisition
Recapitalizations

Size of Investments Considered:
Min Size of Investment Considered (000s): $25,000
Max Size of Investment Considered (000s): $100,000

Geographical Preferences

United States Preferences:
All U.S.

International Preferences:
Europe

Industry Preferences

In Communications prefer:
Communications and Media
Telecommunications
Wireless Communications
Data Communications

In Computer Software prefer:
Systems Software

In Medical/Health prefer:
Medical/Health
Diagnostic Services
Health Services
Pharmaceuticals

In Consumer Related prefer:
Consumer
Retail
Food/Beverage
Consumer Products
Consumer Services
Education Related

In Transportation prefer:
Aerospace

In Financial Services prefer:
Insurance
Investment Groups
Financial Services

In Business Serv. prefer:
Services
Consulting Services

In Manufact. prefer:
Manufacturing

Additional Information
Year Founded: 2007
Current Activity Level : Actively seeking new investments

MOELLER VENTURES GMBH

Uhlandstrasse 175
Berlin, Germany 10719
Phone: 493080952040
E-mail: info@moeller-ventures.de
Website: www.moeller-ventures.de

Type of Firm
Private Equity Firm

Project Preferences

Type of Financing Preferred:
Early Stage
Expansion
Later Stage
Seed
Startup

Industry Preferences

In Internet Specific prefer:
Internet

Additional Information
Year Founded: 2011
Current Activity Level : Actively seeking new investments

MOFET B-YEHUDA TECHNOLOGICAL AND BUSINESS INCUBATOR

P.O. Box 80
Kiryat Arba, Israel 90100
Phone: 972-2-996-3880
Fax: 972-2-996-1571
E-mail: info@mofet.org.il
Website: www.mofet.org.il

Management and Staff
Yosef Ron, Chief Executive Officer

Type of Firm
Incubator/Development Program

Project Preferences

Type of Financing Preferred:
Seed

Geographical Preferences

International Preferences:
Israel

Additional Information
Year Founded: 1991
Current Activity Level : Actively seeking new investments

MOHAMMED IBRAHIM ALSUBEAEI AND SONS INVESTMENT CO

Maathar District, Makkah Road
Riyadh, Saudi Arabia 11411
Phone: 966114883388
Fax: 966114886262
Website: www.masic.com.sa

Type of Firm
Private Equity Firm

Project Preferences

Type of Financing Preferred:
Leveraged Buyout
Mezzanine
Public Companies
Acquisition

Geographical Preferences

United States Preferences:

International Preferences:
Middle East
Saudi Arabia

Industry Preferences

In Financial Services prefer:
Real Estate

Additional Information
Year Founded: 2006
Current Activity Level : Actively seeking new investments

MOHR DAVIDOW VENTURES

777 Mariners Island Boulevard
Suite 550
San Mateo, CA USA 94404
Phone: 6508547236
Fax: 6508547365
E-mail: info@mdv.com
Website: www.mdv.com

Management and Staff
Abhas Gupta, Partner
Bill Ericson, General Partner
Brett Teele, Chief Financial Officer
Bryan Stolle, General Partner
Geoffrey Moore, Venture Partner
Jim Smith, General Partner
Jon Feiber, General Partner
Joshua Green, General Partner
Joy Knox, Vice President
Katherine Barr, General Partner
Nancy Schoendorf, General Partner
Phyllis Whiteley, Venture Partner

Type of Firm
Private Equity Firm

Association Membership
Western Association of Venture Capitalists (WAVC)
National Venture Capital Association - USA (NVCA)

Project Preferences

Role in Financing:
Prefer role as deal originator but will also invest in deals created by others

Type of Financing Preferred:
Early Stage
Balanced
Later Stage
Seed

Geographical Preferences

United States Preferences:
All U.S.

Industry Focus

(% based on actual investment)
Computer Software and Services	27.5%
Internet Specific	20.1%
Biotechnology	12.5%
Semiconductors/Other Elect.	11.6%
Communications and Media	8.8%
Medical/Health	6.9%
Computer Hardware	5.0%
Industrial/Energy	4.2%
Other Products	2.7%
Consumer Related	0.8%

Additional Information

Name of Most Recent Fund: Mohr, Davidow Ventures IX
Most Recent Fund Was Raised: 08/23/2007
Year Founded: 1983
Capital Under Management: $2,000,000,000
Current Activity Level : Actively seeking new investments
Method of Compensation: Return on invest. most important, but chg. closing fees, service fees, etc.

MOLA FACTORY SL

Carretera Valldemosa 7,4
ParcBit, Edificio U, local 12
Palma de Mallorca, Spain 07121
Phone: 34971439926
E-mail: hola@mola.com
Website: www.mola.com

Management and Staff

Enrique Dubois, Founder
Francisco Gimena, Founder

Type of Firm

Incubator/Development Program

Project Preferences

Type of Financing Preferred:
Seed
Startup

Geographical Preferences

United States Preferences:
All U.S.

International Preferences:
Latin America
Spain

Industry Preferences

In Internet Specific prefer:
Internet

Additional Information

Year Founded: 2011
Current Activity Level : Actively seeking new investments

MOLASH GROUP

54 Wierda Road W,Wierda Valley
Augusta H,Inanda Greens Bus Pk
Sandton, South Africa 2196
Phone: 27118832897
Fax: 27118839462
E-mail: info@molash.co.za
Website: www.molash.co.za

Management and Staff

David Pimstein, Co-Founder
Eldon Beinart, Co-Founder
Shaun Laffer, Co-Founder

Type of Firm

Private Equity Firm

Association Membership

South African Venture Capital Association (SAVCA)

Project Preferences

Type of Financing Preferred:
Leveraged Buyout
Management Buyouts
Acquisition

Geographical Preferences

International Preferences:
South Africa
Africa

Industry Preferences

In Consumer Related prefer:
Consumer
Consumer Products

In Business Serv. prefer:
Distribution

In Manufact. prefer:
Manufacturing

Additional Information

Year Founded: 2005
Current Activity Level : Actively seeking new investments

MOMENT VENTURES LLC

385 Homer Avenue
Palo Alto, CA USA 94301
Website: www.momentventures.com

Type of Firm

Private Equity Firm

Project Preferences

Type of Financing Preferred:
Early Stage
Seed

Industry Preferences

In Computer Software prefer:
Data Processing

In Semiconductor/Electr prefer:
Sensors
Analytic/Scientific

In Industrial/Energy prefer:
Robotics

Additional Information

Year Founded: 2013
Capital Under Management: $12,500,000
Current Activity Level : Actively seeking new investments

MOMENTUM EQUITY PARTNERS LLC

260 Franklin Street
Eleventh Floor
Boston, MA USA 02110
Phone: 6174124300
Fax: 6172490140
E-mail: info@momentumequity.com
Website: www.momentumequity.com

Type of Firm

Private Equity Firm

Project Preferences

Role in Financing:
Will function either as deal originator or investor in deals created by others

Type of Financing Preferred:
Early Stage
Expansion
Balanced
Seed
Startup

Geographical Preferences

United States Preferences:

Industry Preferences

In Medical/Health prefer:
Medical/Health
Health Services

In Consumer Related prefer:
Consumer

In Industrial/Energy prefer:
Energy

Additional Information
Year Founded: 2003
Current Activity Level: Actively seeking new investments

MONARCH ALTERNATIVE CAPITAL LP

535 Madison Avenue
New York, NY USA 10022
Phone: 2125541700
Fax: 2125541701
E-mail: info@monarchlp.com
Website: www.monarchlp.com

Other Offices
52 Conduit Street
Sixth Floor
London, United Kingdom W1S 2YX

Type of Firm
Investment Management Firm

Project Preferences

Type of Financing Preferred:
Leveraged Buyout
Turnaround
Distressed Debt

Additional Information
Year Founded: 2002
Current Activity Level: Actively seeking new investments

MONASH PRIVATE CAPITAL PTY LTD

Level 14, 167 Macquarie Street
Sydney, Australia 2000
Phone: 61282783800
E-mail: contact@monashprivatecapital.com.au
Website: www.monashprivatecapital.com.au

Type of Firm
Investment Management Firm

Project Preferences

Type of Financing Preferred:
Core
Value-Add
Early Stage
Expansion
Generalist PE
Balanced
Later Stage

Geographical Preferences

United States Preferences:

International Preferences:
Europe
Israel
South Africa

Industry Preferences

In Financial Services prefer:
Real Estate

Additional Information
Year Founded: 2011
Current Activity Level: Actively seeking new investments

MONASHEES GESTAO DE INVESTIMENTOS LTDA

Rua Samuel Morse 74
Sao Paulo, Brazil 04576-060
Phone: 551155012032
E-mail: contact@monashees.com.br
Website: monashees.com.br

Management and Staff
Carlo Dapuzzo, Founder
Eric Acher, Founder
Fabio Igel, Founder

Type of Firm
Private Equity Firm

Association Membership
Brazilian Venture Capital Association (ABCR)

Project Preferences

Type of Financing Preferred:
Early Stage
Balanced
Later Stage
Seed
Startup

Geographical Preferences

International Preferences:
Brazil

Industry Preferences

In Internet Specific prefer:
Internet

In Consumer Related prefer:
Education Related

Additional Information
Name of Most Recent Fund: Monashees Capital VI, L.P.
Most Recent Fund Was Raised: 08/17/2012
Year Founded: 2005
Capital Under Management: $86,776,000

Current Activity Level: Actively seeking new investments

MONETA CAPITAL PARTNERS LTD

736- 6th Avenue South West
Suite 2050
Calgary, Canada T2P 3T7
Phone: 403-770-4150
Fax: 403-770-4151
E-mail: info@monetacapital.ca
Website: www.monetacapital.ca

Management and Staff
David Blain, Partner
Karen Hanson, Partner
Ken Hergert, Partner
Rex Kary, Managing Partner
Roy Smitshoek, Managing Partner

Type of Firm
Private Equity Firm

Project Preferences

Type of Financing Preferred:
Early Stage
Expansion
Seed
Startup

Additional Information
Year Founded: 2003
Current Activity Level: Actively seeking new investments

MONETA VENTURES LP

785 Orchard Drive
Suite 150
Folsom, CA USA 95630
Phone: 9162702700
E-mail: contact@monetaventures.com
Website: www.monetaventures.com

Type of Firm
Private Equity Firm

Project Preferences

Type of Financing Preferred:
Early Stage

Geographical Preferences

United States Preferences:
Northern California
West Coast

Industry Preferences

In Computer Software prefer:
Software

In Internet Specific prefer:
Internet

In Medical/Health prefer:
Health Services

In Consumer Related prefer:
Consumer Services

Additional Information
Year Founded: 2014
Capital Under Management: $55,000,000
Current Activity Level : Actively seeking new investments

MONHEGAN PARTNERS LLC

152 Rowayton Avenue
Norwalk, CT USA 06853
Phone: 2036553586
Website: www.moheganpartners.com

Type of Firm
Private Equity Firm

Project Preferences

Type of Financing Preferred:
Leveraged Buyout
Acquisition

Geographical Preferences

United States Preferences:

Industry Preferences

In Consumer Related prefer:
Food/Beverage
Consumer Products

In Industrial/Energy prefer:
Industrial Products
Materials

In Transportation prefer:
Transportation

In Business Serv. prefer:
Distribution

Additional Information
Year Founded: 2010
Current Activity Level : Actively seeking new investments

MONITOR CLIPPER PARTNERS LLC

116 Huntington Avenue
Ninth Floor
Boston, MA USA 02116
Phone: 6176381100
Fax: 6176381110
E-mail: mcp@monitorclipper.com
Website: www.monitorclipper.com

Other Offices
7A rue Robert Stumper
Luxembourg, Luxembourg L-2557
Phone: 3522649584294
Fax: 3522649584295

Former HQ: Two Canal Park
Fourth Floor
Cambridge, MA USA 02141
Phone: 16172522200
Fax: 16172522211

Mulebachstrasse 173
Zurich, Switzerland 8034
Phone: 41443897150
Fax: 41443897151

100 Simcoe Street
Fifth Floor
Toronto, Canada M54 3G2
Phone: 4164084800
Fax: 4164084848

Management and Staff
Adam Doctoroff, Partner
Charles Yoon, Partner
Daniel Jang, Vice President
Julia Monfrini, Vice President
Mark Thomas, Partner
Matthew Stone, Vice President
Michael Bell, Partner
Peter Laino, Partner
Samer Ezzeddine, Principal
Stephen Lehman, Partner
Travis Metz, Partner
William Young, Partner

Type of Firm
Private Equity Firm

Project Preferences

Type of Financing Preferred:
Leveraged Buyout
Expansion
Acquisition

Geographical Preferences

United States Preferences:
North America

Canadian Preferences:
All Canada

International Preferences:
Italy
Western Europe
Spain
Germany
All International
Denmark
France

Industry Focus
(% based on actual investment)
Other Products	54.0%
Consumer Related	27.8%
Internet Specific	5.3%
Communications and Media	3.8%
Computer Hardware	3.7%
Biotechnology	2.1%
Computer Software and Services	1.6%
Medical/Health	1.0%
Industrial/Energy	0.6%

Additional Information
Name of Most Recent Fund: Monitor Clipper Equity Partners IV, L.P.
Most Recent Fund Was Raised: 03/05/2014
Year Founded: 1988
Capital Under Management: $1,700,000,000
Current Activity Level : Actively seeking new investments

MONITOR VENTURE ASSOCIATES LLC

5050 El Camino Real
Suite 228
Los Altos, CA USA 94022
Phone: 6504757300
Website: www.monitorventures.com

Other Offices
1888 Century Park East
Suite 520
LOS ANGELES, CA USA 90067
Phone: 3105959600

Management and Staff
Fern Mandelbaum, Partner
Jerome Engel, General Partner
Jerry Engel, General Partner
Neal Bhadkamkar, Managing Partner
Teymour Boutros-Ghali, Co-Founder

Type of Firm
Private Equity Firm

Project Preferences

Type of Financing Preferred:
Early Stage

Geographical Preferences

United States Preferences:
All U.S.

Additional Information
Name of Most Recent Fund: Monitor Venture Partners, L.P.
Most Recent Fund Was Raised: 09/01/2004
Year Founded: 2002
Capital Under Management: $29,300,000
Current Activity Level : Actively seeking new investments

MONK'S HILL VENTURES PTE LTD

32 Pekin Street #04-01
Far East Square
Singapore, Singapore 048762
Phone: 6565140015
E-mail: reach.us@monkshill.com
Website: www.monkshill.com

Management and Staff
Kuo-Yi Lim, Partner
Peng Ong, Partner
Stefan Jung, Partner

Type of Firm
Private Equity Firm

Project Preferences

Type of Financing Preferred:
Early Stage
Startup

Geographical Preferences

United States Preferences:
Southeast

Industry Preferences

In Communications prefer:
Wireless Communications
Data Communications

In Computer Software prefer:
Software

Additional Information
Year Founded: 2014
Capital Under Management: $159,195,000
Current Activity Level : Actively seeking new investments

MONOGRAM CAPITAL PARTNERS

8383 Wilshire Boulevard
Suite 430
West Hollywood, CA USA 90069
Website: monogramcapital.com

Type of Firm
Private Equity Firm

Project Preferences

Type of Financing Preferred:
Leveraged Buyout
Acquisition

Industry Preferences

In Consumer Related prefer:
Consumer
Retail
Food/Beverage
Consumer Products
Other Restaurants

Additional Information
Year Founded: 2014
Current Activity Level : Actively seeking new investments

MONOMOY CAPITAL PARTNERS LLC

142 West 57th Street
17th Floor
New York, NY USA 10019
Phone: 2126994000
Fax: 2126994010
E-mail: info@mcpfunds.com
Website: www.mcpfunds.com

Management and Staff
Andrea Cipriani, Chief Financial Officer
Ashley Johansen, Managing Director
Daniel Collin, Founder
David Robbins, Managing Director
John Stewart, Partner
Justin Hillenbrand, Founder
Kareem Akhtar, Vice President
Phillip Arra, Managing Director
Stephen Presser, Founder

Type of Firm
Private Equity Firm

Project Preferences

Type of Financing Preferred:
Leveraged Buyout
Turnaround
Acquisition
Distressed Debt
Recapitalizations

Geographical Preferences

United States Preferences:
North America

International Preferences:
India
Europe
China
Brazil
Asia

Industry Preferences

In Consumer Related prefer:
Consumer Products

In Industrial/Energy prefer:
Industrial Products

In Business Serv. prefer:
Distribution

In Manufact. prefer:
Manufacturing

Additional Information
Year Founded: 2005
Capital Under Management: $1,167,000,000
Current Activity Level : Actively seeking new investments

MONROE CAPITAL LLC

311 South Wacker Drive
Suite 6400
Chicago, IL USA 60606
Phone: 3122588300
Fax: 3122588350
E-mail: info@monroecap.com
Website: www.monroecap.com

Management and Staff
Aaron Peck, Managing Director
Alex Franky, Managing Director
Andrew Cozewith, Managing Director
Ben Marzouk, Managing Director
Cesar Gueikian, Managing Director
David Jacobson, Chief Financial Officer
Jeffrey Cupples, Vice President
Jeffrey Kolke, Managing Director
Jeremy VanDerMeid, Managing Director
Joe Rodgers, Managing Director
Kyle Asher, Vice President
Laura Kraus, Managing Director
Marc Adelson, Managing Director
Mark Solovy, Managing Director
Nathan Harrel, Vice President
Patrick White, Managing Director
Steve Hinrichs, Managing Director
T. David McKee, Managing Director
Thomas Aronson, Managing Director
Ty Dealy, Managing Director
Warren Woo, Managing Director
Zia Uddin, Managing Director

Type of Firm
Private Equity Firm

Association Membership
Natl Assoc of Small Bus. Inv. Co (NASBIC)
Illinois Venture Capital Association

Project Preferences

Type of Financing Preferred:
Leveraged Buyout
Expansion
Mezzanine
Acquisition
Recapitalizations

Geographical Preferences

United States Preferences:

Canadian Preferences:
All Canada

Industry Preferences

In Communications prefer:
Telecommunications

In Computer Software prefer:
Software

In Medical/Health prefer:
Medical/Health

In Consumer Related prefer:
Entertainment and Leisure
Retail
Consumer Products
Education Related

In Industrial/Energy prefer:
Energy

In Business Serv. prefer:
Services
Distribution
Media

In Manufact. prefer:
Manufacturing
Publishing

In Other prefer:
Women/Minority-Owned Bus.

Additional Information
Name of Most Recent Fund: Monroe Capital Partners Fund II, L.P.
Most Recent Fund Was Raised: 02/13/2014
Year Founded: 1969
Capital Under Management: $1,569,658,000
Current Activity Level : Actively seeking new investments

MONTA VISTA CAPITAL LP

415 Oakmead Pkwy
Sunnyvale, CA USA 94085

Management and Staff
Mark Greenough, Chief Financial Officer
Nimish Mehta, Partner
Prashant Shah, Partner
Venktesh Shukla, Partner

Type of Firm
Private Equity Firm

Project Preferences

Type of Financing Preferred:
Early Stage

Additional Information
Year Founded: 2014
Current Activity Level : Actively seeking new investments

MONTAGE PARTNERS INC

6720 North Scottsdale Road
Suite 230
Paradise Valley, AZ USA 85253
Fax: 4803469696
Website: montagepartnersinc.com

Management and Staff
Jordan Tate, Managing Partner
Robert Wolfman, Managing Partner

Type of Firm
Private Equity Firm

Project Preferences

Type of Financing Preferred:
Leveraged Buyout
Acquisition
Recapitalizations

Geographical Preferences

United States Preferences:
Rocky Mountain
West Coast
Southwest

Additional Information
Year Founded: 2004
Current Activity Level : Actively seeking new investments

MONTAGE VENTURES

364 University Avenue
Second Floor
Palo Alto, CA USA 94301
Phone: 6502852382
E-mail: info@montageventures.com
Website: montageventures.com

Type of Firm
Private Equity Firm

Project Preferences

Type of Financing Preferred:
Early Stage
Expansion
Startup

Geographical Preferences

United States Preferences:
Illinois
California
New York

Industry Preferences

In Internet Specific prefer:
E-Commerce Technology
Ecommerce

In Medical/Health prefer:
Medical/Health
Health Services

In Financial Services prefer:
Financial Services

Additional Information
Year Founded: 2013
Capital Under Management: $11,325,000
Current Activity Level : Actively seeking new investments

MONTAGU PRIVATE EQUITY LLP

Two More London Riverside
London, United Kingdom SE1 2AP
Phone: 442073369955
Fax: 442073369961
E-mail: ir@montagu.com
Website: www.montagu.com

Other Offices

Aleje Ujazdowskie 41
Warsaw Financial Center
Warsaw, Poland 00-540
Phone: 48222058600
Fax: 48222058620

Junghofstrabe 22/24
Frankfurt am Main, Germany 60311
Phone: 4969365069850
Fax: 4969365069899

Tower 12, Level 10, 18/22 Bridge Street
The Avenue, North Spinningfields
Manchester, United Kingdom M3 3BZ
Phone: 44-16-1233-6660
Fax: 44-12-1233-6666

Management and Staff
Jason Gatenby, Chief Executive Officer

Type of Firm
Bank Affiliated

Association Membership
British Venture Capital Association (BVCA)
French Venture Capital Association (AFIC)
Danish Venture Capital Association (DVCA)
German Venture Capital Association (BVK)
Swedish Venture Capital Association (SVCA)
Polish Venture Capital Association (PSIC/PPEA)
European Private Equity and Venture Capital Assoc.

Project Preferences

Role in Financing:
Prefer role as deal originator but will also invest in deals created by others

Type of Financing Preferred:
Leveraged Buyout
Management Buyouts

Geographical Preferences

International Preferences:
United Kingdom

Industry Preferences

In Medical/Health prefer:
Medical/Health
Health Services
Pharmaceuticals

In Industrial/Energy prefer:
Environmental Related

In Transportation prefer:
Transportation

In Business Serv. prefer:
Services

In Manufact. prefer:
Manufacturing

Additional Information

Year Founded: 1968
Capital Under Management: $5,960,000,000
Current Activity Level : Actively seeking new investments
Method of Compensation: Return on invest. most important, but chg. closing fees, service fees, etc.

MONTANA CAPITAL PARTNERS AG

Haldenstrasse 1
Baar, Switzerland 6342
Phone: 41415117950
E-mail: info@mcp.eu
Website: www.montana-capital-partners.eu

Management and Staff

Christian Diller, Co-Founder
Marco Wulff, Co-Founder

Type of Firm

Private Equity Advisor or Fund of Funds

Association Membership

European Private Equity and Venture Capital Assoc.

Project Preferences

Type of Financing Preferred:
Fund of Funds
Fund of Funds of Second

Additional Information

Name of Most Recent Fund: Annual Secondary Program
Most Recent Fund Was Raised: 07/02/2013
Year Founded: 2011
Capital Under Management: $675,805,000
Current Activity Level : Actively seeking new investments

MONTAUK TRIGUARD MANAGEMENT INC

300 Spectrum Center Drive
Suite 880
Irvine, CA USA 92618
Phone: 949-398-0000
Fax: 949-398-0001
E-mail: investorrelations@triguardpartners.com
Website: www.montauktriguard.com

Management and Staff

Bryan Smith, Principal
Edgar Pfohl, Principal
Ronn Cornelius, Co-Founder
Samuel Tang, Principal

Type of Firm

Private Equity Advisor or Fund of Funds

Project Preferences

Type of Financing Preferred:
Fund of Funds
Fund of Funds of Second

Additional Information

Name of Most Recent Fund: Montauk TriGuard Fund V, L.P.
Most Recent Fund Was Raised: 07/01/2011
Year Founded: 1969
Capital Under Management: $750,000,000
Current Activity Level : Actively seeking new investments

MONTECO LTD

2 Saint Clair Avenue
West # 2100
Toronto, Canada
E-mail: info@monteco.com
Website: monteco.com

Type of Firm

Private Equity Firm

Geographical Preferences

Canadian Preferences:
All Canada

Additional Information

Year Founded: 1995
Current Activity Level : Actively seeking new investments

MONTEFIORE INVESTMENT SAS

17 rue de Miromesnil
Paris, France 75008
Phone: 33158186868
Fax: 3315883027
E-mail: contact@montefiore.fr
Website: www.montefiore.fr

Other Offices

37 Rue de Surene
Paris, France 75008
Phone: 33-1-5318-6868
Fax: 33-1-5818-3027

Management and Staff

Alexandre Bonnecuelle, Principal
Daniel Elalouf, Partner
Jean-Marc Espalioux, Partner

Type of Firm

Private Equity Firm

Association Membership

French Venture Capital Association (AFIC)

Project Preferences

Type of Financing Preferred:
Leveraged Buyout
Generalist PE
Later Stage

Size of Investments Considered:
Min Size of Investment Considered (000s): $10,482
Max Size of Investment Considered (000s): $26,205

Geographical Preferences

United States Preferences:
All U.S.

International Preferences:
Europe
France

Industry Preferences

In Medical/Health prefer:
Health Services

In Consumer Related prefer:
Entertainment and Leisure
Consumer Services
Hotels and Resorts

In Transportation prefer:
Transportation

In Business Serv. prefer:
Services
Distribution
Consulting Services

In Other prefer:
Socially Responsible

Additional Information
Name of Most Recent Fund: Montefiore Investment III
Most Recent Fund Was Raised: 09/17/2012
Year Founded: 2005
Capital Under Management: $778,672,000
Current Activity Level : Actively seeking new investments

MONTEREY VENTURE PARTNERS LLC
2818 Congress Road
Pebble Beach, CA USA 93953
Phone: 831-658-0800
E-mail: info@montereyvp.com
Website: www.montereyvp.com

Management and Staff
Barbara Bellissimo, Partner
David Worrell, Partner
Marshall Frank, Partner
Peter Townshend, Partner
William Manby, Partner

Type of Firm
Private Equity Advisor or Fund of Funds

Project Preferences
Type of Financing Preferred:
Early Stage
Startup

Geographical Preferences
United States Preferences:
California

Industry Preferences
In Consumer Related prefer:
Food/Beverage

In Industrial/Energy prefer:
Energy

In Other prefer:
Environment Responsible

Additional Information
Year Founded: 2001
Current Activity Level : Actively seeking new investments

MONTERREY CAPITAL PARTNERS
Av. Gomez Morin 285 Sur 3 Piso
Valle del Campestre
Monterrey, Mexico 66265
Phone: 52-818-1737303
Fax: 52-818-1737315

Management and Staff
Luis Porras, Principal

Type of Firm
Bank Affiliated

Project Preferences
Type of Financing Preferred:
Expansion

Geographical Preferences
International Preferences:
Mexico

Industry Preferences
In Communications prefer:
Telecommunications

In Medical/Health prefer:
Medical/Health

In Business Serv. prefer:
Media

Additional Information
Year Founded: 2000
Current Activity Level : Actively seeking new investments

MONTERRO INVESTMENT AB
Birger Jarlsgatan 2
Stockholm, Sweden SE-114 34

Type of Firm
Private Equity Firm

Project Preferences
Type of Financing Preferred:
Balanced
Later Stage

Size of Investments Considered:
Min Size of Investment Considered (000s): $3,057
Max Size of Investment Considered (000s): $15,286

Geographical Preferences
International Preferences:
Scandanavia/Nordic Region

Industry Preferences
In Computer Software prefer:
Software
Systems Software

Additional Information
Year Founded: 2012
Capital Under Management: $147,626,000
Current Activity Level : Actively seeking new investments

MONTGOMERY & CO LLC
1660 Stanford Street
Santa Monica, CA USA 90401
Phone: 3102606006
Fax: 3102606095
E-mail: info@monty.com
Website: www.monty.com

Other Offices
Two Embarcadero Center
Suite 2900
San Francisco, CA USA 94111
Phone: 4159624560
Fax: 4159624567

Management and Staff
Brad Floering, Vice President
Christopher Park, Vice President
Eric Wagner, Managing Director
Greg Dietrick, Principal
J.T Cecchini, Principal
James Min, Managing Director
Joe Morgan, Principal
John Roediger, Managing Director
Kevin Higgins, Chief Financial Officer
Michael Montgomery, President
Penelope Linge, Vice President
Sandra Grinker, Principal
Yale Yee, Principal

Type of Firm
Bank Affiliated

Project Preferences
Type of Financing Preferred:
Expansion
Balanced
Later Stage

Industry Preferences
In Internet Specific prefer:
Internet

In Business Serv. prefer:
Media

Additional Information
Year Founded: 1986
Capital Under Management: $35,000,000
Current Activity Level : Actively seeking new investments

MONTIS CAPITAL LLC
2595 Canyon Boulevard
Suite 410
Boulder, CO USA 80302
Phone: 3034403352
Fax: 3034495626
E-mail: info@montiscapital.com
Website: www.montiscapital.com

Management and Staff
Adam Kimberly, Managing Partner
Andrew Morley, Managing Partner

Type of Firm
Private Equity Firm

Project Preferences

Role in Financing:
Prefer role as deal originator but will also invest in deals created by others

Type of Financing Preferred:
Leveraged Buyout
Expansion
Management Buyouts
Acquisition
Recapitalizations

Size of Investments Considered:
Min Size of Investment Considered (000s): $500,000
Max Size of Investment Considered: No Limit

Geographical Preferences

United States Preferences:
All U.S.

Industry Preferences

In Communications prefer:
Telecommunications

In Consumer Related prefer:
Consumer Products

In Industrial/Energy prefer:
Energy
Environmental Related

In Transportation prefer:
Transportation

In Business Serv. prefer:
Services
Distribution
Media

In Manufact. prefer:
Manufacturing

Additional Information
Year Founded: 2007
Capital Under Management: $8,000,000
Current Activity Level : Actively seeking new investments

MONTLAKE CAPITAL LLC

1200 Fifth Avenue
Suite 1800
Seattle, WA USA 98101
Phone: 2069560898
E-mail: montlake@montlakecapital.com
Website: www.montlakecapital.com

Other Offices
910 Technology Boulevard
Suite A
BOZEMAN, MT USA 59718
Phone: 4065818779

2041 Silver Creek Land
BOISE, ID USA 83706
Phone: 2088631027

1120 Northwest Couch Street
Suite 450
PORTLAND, OR USA 97209

Management and Staff
Andrew Dale, Managing Director
Dale Vogel, Managing Director
Michael Luce, Partner
Noel de Turenne, Principal
Tom Kealey, Managing Director

Type of Firm
Private Equity Firm

Project Preferences

Role in Financing:
Prefer role as deal originator but will also invest in deals created by others

Type of Financing Preferred:
Early Stage
Generalist PE

Industry Preferences

In Consumer Related prefer:
Consumer Products
Consumer Services

In Financial Services prefer:
Financial Services

In Business Serv. prefer:
Services

Additional Information
Name of Most Recent Fund: Montlake Capital II, L.P.
Most Recent Fund Was Raised: 08/03/2006
Year Founded: 1999
Capital Under Management: $93,000,000
Current Activity Level : Actively seeking new investments
Method of Compensation: Return on invest. most important, but chg. closing fees, service fees, etc.

MONTREUX EQUITY PARTNERS

One Ferry Building
Sutie 255
San Francisco, CA USA 94111
Phone: 6502341200
Fax: 6502341250
E-mail: info@mepvc.com
Website: www.mepvc.com

Other Offices
3000 Sand Hill Road
Suite 260, Building One
MENLO PARK, CA USA 94025
Phone: 6502341200
Fax: 6502341250

One Ferry Building
Suite 255
SAN FRANCISCO, CA USA 94111

Management and Staff
Daniel Turner, Founder
Jessica Hou, Principal
Matt Lambert, Principal
Michael Matly, Managing Director
Thomas Fremd, Chief Financial Officer

Type of Firm
Private Equity Firm

Association Membership
Western Association of Venture Capitalists (WAVC)
National Venture Capital Association - USA (NVCA)

Project Preferences

Role in Financing:
Will function either as deal originator or investor in deals created by others

Type of Financing Preferred:
Early Stage
Balanced
Later Stage
Seed
Startup

Geographical Preferences

United States Preferences:
West Coast

Industry Focus
(% based on actual investment)

Medical/Health	71.6%
Biotechnology	13.5%
Computer Software and Services	7.6%
Consumer Related	5.0%
Internet Specific	1.8%
Communications and Media	0.6%
Other Products	0.0%

Additional Information
Name of Most Recent Fund: Montreux Equity Partners IV, L.P.
Most Recent Fund Was Raised: 09/01/2006
Year Founded: 1993
Capital Under Management: $500,000,000
Current Activity Level : Actively seeking new investments
Method of Compensation: Return on invest. most important, but chg. closing fees, service fees, etc.

MOONRISE VENTURE PARTNERS, L.P.

404 North Maple Avenue
Greenwich, CT USA 06830

Type of Firm
Private Equity Firm

Project Preferences

Type of Financing Preferred:
Early Stage

Additional Information
Year Founded: 2016
Capital Under Management: $90,000,000
Current Activity Level : Actively seeking new investments

MOONSAIL PARTNERS LP

1511 Avenue Ponce de Leon
Suite K
San Juan, PR USA 00909
Phone: 9172871751

Management and Staff
Rafael Ortiz, Managing Director

Type of Firm
Private Equity Firm

Additional Information
Year Founded: 2017
Capital Under Management: $27,500,000
Current Activity Level : Actively seeking new investments

MOONSHOTS CAPITAL

3300 Park Hills Drive
Austin, TX USA 78746
Website: www.moonshotscapital.com

Management and Staff
Craig Cummings, Co-Founder
Kelly Perdew, Co-Founder

Type of Firm
Private Equity Firm

Project Preferences

Type of Financing Preferred:
Early Stage
Seed

Additional Information
Year Founded: 2014
Current Activity Level : Actively seeking new investments

MOOR&MOOR AB

Malmskillnadsgatan 32
Stockholm, Sweden 111 51
E-mail: ideas@moorcap.com
Website: moorcap.com

Type of Firm
Investment Management Firm

Project Preferences

Type of Financing Preferred:
Early Stage
Expansion
Seed
Startup

Geographical Preferences

International Preferences:
Sweden
Europe

Additional Information
Year Founded: 2014
Current Activity Level : Actively seeking new investments

MOORFIELD GROUP LTD

65 Curzon Street
Nightingale House
London, United Kingdom W1J 8PE
Phone: 442073991900
Fax: 442074992114
E-mail: enquiry@moorfield.com
Website: www.moorfield.com

Management and Staff
Marc Gilbard, Chief Executive Officer

Type of Firm
Private Equity Firm

Association Membership
British Venture Capital Association (BVCA)
European Private Equity and Venture Capital Assoc.

Project Preferences

Type of Financing Preferred:
Value-Add
Opportunistic

Geographical Preferences

International Preferences:
United Kingdom
Europe

Industry Preferences

In Financial Services prefer:
Real Estate

Additional Information
Name of Most Recent Fund: Moorfield Real Estate Fund III
Most Recent Fund Was Raised: 04/05/2013
Year Founded: 1983
Capital Under Management: $4,906,800,000
Current Activity Level : Actively seeking new investments

MOORIM CAPITAL CO LTD

110, Sogong-dong,
10/F, Hanhwa Bldg, Jung-gu
Seoul, South Korea 100070
Phone: 82237098800
Fax: 82237098890
Website: www.moorimcapital.co.kr

Management and Staff
Jun Yong Goh, Chief Executive Officer

Type of Firm
Private Equity Firm

Project Preferences

Type of Financing Preferred:
Generalist PE

Additional Information
Year Founded: 2009
Current Activity Level : Actively seeking new investments

MORADO VENTURE MANAGEMENT LLC

27765 Lupine Road
Los Altos, CA USA 94022
Phone: 4082426780
Website: www.moradoventures.com

Other Offices
455B Portage Avenue
Palo Alto, CA USA 94306

Management and Staff
Ash Patel, Co-Founder
Michael Marquez, Co-Founder

Type of Firm
Private Equity Firm

Project Preferences

Type of Financing Preferred:
Seed
Startup

Geographical Preferences

United States Preferences:
Northern California
West Coast
Washington
New York

Industry Preferences

In Communications prefer:
Wireless Communications

In Computer Software prefer:
Software

In Internet Specific prefer:
Internet

In Consumer Related prefer:
Consumer

Additional Information

Name of Most Recent Fund: Morado Venture Partners, L.P.
Most Recent Fund Was Raised: 12/08/2010
Year Founded: 2010
Current Activity Level : Actively seeking new investments

MORGAN CREEK CAPITAL MANAGEMENT LLC

301 West Barbee Chapel Road, Suite 200
Chapel Hill, NC USA 27517
Phone: 9199334004
Fax: 9199334048
Website: www.morgancreekcap.com

Other Offices

8 Century Avenue
Unit 2305-06, Phase 2, IFC
Shanghai, China 200120
Phone: 862160751688
Fax: 862160752558

100 Park Avenue
28th Floor
New York, NY USA 10017
Phone: 212-692-8660
Fax: 212-692-8661

10 Collyer Quay
Level 40, Ocean Financial Centre
Singapore, Singapore 049315
Phone: 6568086192

Management and Staff

Andrea Szigethy, Principal
Anna Bickley, Vice President
Bradford Briner, Managing Director
David Kim, Managing Director
Eileen Mancera, Managing Director
Jason Zhang, Managing Director
Jim Patrick, Vice President
Joseph Gil, Managing Director
Josh Tilley, Principal
Mark Morris, Managing Director
Mark Yusko, Chief Executive Officer
Michael Hennessy, Managing Director
Nirav Kachalia, Managing Director
Peter Gutrich, Managing Director
Sameh DeRosa-Farag, Managing Director

Type of Firm
Private Equity Advisor or Fund of Funds

Project Preferences

Type of Financing Preferred:
Fund of Funds
Fund of Funds of Second

Geographical Preferences

United States Preferences:

International Preferences:
China
Asia

Additional Information

Name of Most Recent Fund: Morgan Creek Partners Venture Access Fund, L.P.
Most Recent Fund Was Raised: 03/22/2012
Year Founded: 2004
Capital Under Management: $492,815,000
Current Activity Level : Actively seeking new investments

MORGAN NOBLE LLC

2445 M Street Northwest
Washington, DC USA 20037
Website: www.morgannoble.com

Management and Staff

Navid Farzad, Partner
Robert Haft, Managing Partner

Type of Firm
Private Equity Firm

Project Preferences

Type of Financing Preferred:
Generalist PE
Balanced

Industry Preferences

In Medical/Health prefer:
Health Services

Additional Information

Year Founded: 1997
Current Activity Level : Actively seeking new investments

MORGAN STANLEY ALTERNATIVE INVESTMENT PARTNERS LP

1585 Broadway
New York, NY USA 10036
Phone: 8884543965

Other Offices

222 Yan An Road (East)
Unit 702A & 703, 7/F, Bund Center
Shanghai, China 200002
Phone: 862123260000
Fax: 862123260001

No. 5, Sector 30, Athena, Building
Mindspace, Goregaon West
Mumbai, India 400 090
Phone: 912266411000
Fax: 912266411001

101 Collins Street
Level 53
Melbourne, Australia 3000
Phone: 61392568900
Fax: 61392568951

Al Ma'ather Street
Al Rashid Tower, Floor 10
Riyadh, Saudi Arabia 11586
Phone: 96612187000
Fax: 96612187003

Hovslagargatan 5A
Stockholm, Sweden 111 48
Phone: 4686789600
Fax: 4686789601

100 Front Street
One Tower Bridge
West Conshohocken, PA USA 19428
Phone: 6109405000
Fax: 6102607093

207, Tun Hwa South Road, Sec. 2
22/F, Taipei Metro
Taipei, Taiwan 106
Phone: 886227302800
Fax: 886227302810

Venezia 16
Palazzo Serbelloni Corso
Milan, Italy 20121

Phone: 39276331
Fax: 392783057

Two Chifley Square
Level 39, Chifley Tower
Sydney, Australia 2000
Phone: 61297701111
Fax: 61297701101

181 Bay Street
Suite 3700, Brookfield Place
Toronto, Canada M5J 2T3
Phone: 4169438400
Fax: 4169438444

140 - 4th Avenue Southwest
Suite 2740, Sun Life Plaza, North Tower
Calgary, Canada T2P 3N3
Phone: 4035091033

23 Church Street
#16-01 Capital Square
Singapore, Singapore 049481
Phone: 6568346888
Fax: 6568346806

12 Place de la Fusterie
Geneva, Switzerland CH-1204
Phone: 41223198000
Fax: 41223198033

Bahnhofstrasse 92
Zurich, Switzerland CH-8021
Phone: 41442209901
Fax: 41442209911

The Gate, Level 5, West Wing
Dubai, Utd. Arab Em.
Phone: 97143634800
Fax: 97143634848

440 South LaSalle Street
Suite 3800
Chicago, IL USA 60605
Phone: 3127064000

3424 Peachtree Road, Northeast
Suite 800
Atlanta, GA USA 30326
Phone: 4048461300

One Austin Road West
Level 46, International Commerce Center
Hong Kong, Hong Kong
Phone: 85228485200
Fax: 85222397805

61, rue de Monceau
Paris, France 75008
Phone: 33142907000
Fax: 33172907099

Av. Alicia Moreau de Justo 740
2nd Floor, Office 6
Buenos Aires, Argentina
Phone: 541143490700
Fax: 541143490707

Paseo de Tamarindos 90 Torre 1 Piso 29
Bosques de las Lomas, Cuajimalpa
Mexico, Mexico 05120
Phone: 525552826700
Fax: 525552829200

21 1st Tverskaya-Yamskaya Street
Moscow, Russia 125047
Phone: 74952872100
Fax: 74952872101

999/9 Rama I Road, Kwaeng Pathumwan
Level 29, The Offices of Centralwood
Bangkok, Thailand 10330
Phone: 6622072323
Fax: 6622072345

2 Merchant Place
Cnr Fredman & Rivonia Drive
Sandton, South Africa 2196
Phone: 27115870800
Fax: 27115870801

One International Place
13th Floor
Boston, MA USA 02110
Phone: 6178568700
Fax: 6178568020

18 Taipingqiao Street
11F, Tower 1, Fortune Resources Intl Ctr
Beijing, China 100032
Phone: 861083563188
Fax: 861083563168

7-11 Sir John Rogerson Quay
The Observatory
Dublin, Ireland 2
Phone: 35317998700

1999 Avenue of the Stars
Suite 2400
Los Angeles, CA USA 90067
Phone: 3107882000
Fax: 3107882048

222 Yan An Road (East)
22/F, Bund Center
Shanghai, China 200002
Phone: 862123212345
Fax: 862123212346

4-20-3 Ebisu, Shibuya-ku
Yebisu Garden Place Tower
Tokyo, Japan 150-6008
Phone: 81354245000
Fax: 81357235000

18 Taipingqiao Street
12F, Tower 1, Fortune Resources Intl Ctr
Beijing, China 100032
Phone: 861083563800
Fax: 861083563801

226 Shinmunro 1ga, Chongro-Gu
12F/22F/23F Heungkuk Life Insurance Bldg
Seoul, South Korea 110-061
Phone: 8223994848
Fax: 8223994842

No. 188 Jingshan Road, Jida
28/F and G2, Yuecai Building
Guangdong, China 519015
Phone: 867563212188
Fax: 867563212168

17 HaArba'ah Street
19th Floor
Tel Aviv, Israel 64739
Phone: 97236236300
Fax: 97236236399

200 Burrard Street
Suite 610, Waterfront Center
Vancouver, Canada V6C 3L6
Phone: 6046588100

2725 Sand Hill Road
Suite 200
Menlo Park, CA USA 94025
Phone: 6502345500

Junghofstrasse 13-15
Frankfurt, Germany 60311
Phone: 496921662900
Fax: 496921662099

Elphinstone Road, One Indiabulls Center
18F/19F, Tower 2, Jupiter Mills Compound
Mumbai, India 400 013
Phone: 912261181000
Fax: 912261181011

Avenida Brigadeiro Faria Lima 3600
6th Floor
Sao Paulo, Brazil 04538-132
Phone: 551130486000
Fax: 551130486099

30 Hickson Road
Level 2, The Bond
Sydney, Australia 2000
Phone: 61297752222

350 7th Avenue Southwest
Suite 2800, First Canadian Center
Calgary, Canada T2P 3N9

Ayala Triangle, Ayala Avenue
6th Floor, Ayala Tower One
Makati City, Philippines 1226
Phone: 6328569716
Fax: 6328569761

Jalan Jendral Sudirman Kav 54-55
21st Floor, Plaza Bapindo, Mandiri Tower
Jakarta, Indonesia 12190
Phone: 62215266575
Fax: 62215266585

59A Ly Thai To Street, Hoan Kiem Street
Suite 607. 6th Floor, Hanoi Press Club
Hanoi, Vietnam
Phone: 84439368075
Fax: 84439368069

Serrano 55
Madrid, Spain 28006
Phone: 34914181200
Fax: 34914181222

25 Cabot Square
Canary Wharf
London, United Kingdom E14 4QA
Phone: 442074258000
Fax: 442074258990

555 California Street
San Francisco, CA USA 94104
Phone: 4155762000
Fax: 4159824907

2000 Westchester Avenue
Purchase, NY USA 10577
Phone: 9142255510
Fax: 9142256770

401 9th Street Northwest
Suite 630
Washington, DC USA 20004

Prannerstrasse 10
Munich, Germany 80333
Phone: 498924212022
Fax: 498924212199

Lechner Odon fasor 8
Business and Technology Center
Budapest, Hungary 1095
Phone: 3618814000
Fax: 3618892700

700 Wellington Street
Suite 3000
Montreal, Canada H3C 3S4
Phone: 5148765700

Amstelplein 1 1096 HA
Rembrandt Tower 11th Floor
Amsterdam, Netherlands
Phone: 31204621300
Fax: 31204621310

Financial Park Labuan Complex
Unit Level 3J (1), Main Office Tower
Labuan, Malaysia 87000
Phone: 6087423878
Fax: 6087424878

55 Douglas Street
The Cerium Building
Glasgow, United Kingdom G2 7NP
Phone: 441412458000
Fax: 441412457493

200 South Biscayne Boulevard
51st Floor
Miami, FL USA 33131
Phone: 7864374950

5002 T-Rex Avenue
Suite 300
Boca Raton, FL USA 33431
Phone: 5613948600
Fax: 5613948660

600 Travis Street
Suite 3700
Houston, TX USA 77002
Phone: 7135124400
Fax: 7135124559

Management and Staff
Arthur Lev, Managing Director
Brian Ksenak, Vice President
Christina Han, Vice President
Christopher Morser, Managing Director
Damon Wu, Vice President
Daniel Spear, Vice President
David Boyle, Managing Director
Dima Skvortsov, Vice President
Donna Phillips, Vice President
Geoffrey Mullen, Managing Director
James Sperans, Managing Director
Jarrod Quigley, Managing Director
John Wolak, Managing Director
John Mecca, Vice President
Jon Sandstrom, Vice President
Jonathan Costello, Managing Director
Jonathan Pistilli, Vice President
Jose Gonzalez-Heres, Managing Director
Joseph McDonnell, Managing Director
Kenneth Michlitsch, Vice President
Lisa Shaposhnick, Vice President
Mark van der Zwan, Managing Director
Maryellen Fazzino, Vice President
Matthew Graver, Managing Director
Mercedes Elias, Vice President
Michael Dyer, Vice President
Michelle Schepis, Vice President
Mustafa Jama, Managing Director
Nash Waterman, Vice President
Neil Harper, Managing Director
Nej Hanna, Vice President
Nicole Wiley, Vice President
Pamela Fung, Vice President
Paresh Bhatt, Managing Director
Paul Vosper, Managing Director
Peter Vasiliadis, Managing Director
Ping Chen, Vice President
Robert Rafter, Vice President
Ryan Meredith, Managing Director
Satya Prasad, Vice President
Sean Ondish, Vice President
Silva Sevdalian, Vice President
Stephanie Girshovich, Vice President
Stephen Davidson, Vice President
Steven Shin, Vice President
Thomas Clarkson, Vice President
Thomas Dorr, Managing Director

Type of Firm
Private Equity Advisor or Fund of Funds

Association Membership
Emerging Markets Private Equity Association

Project Preferences

Type of Financing Preferred:
Fund of Funds
Fund of Funds of Second

Geographical Preferences

United States Preferences:

International Preferences:
Europe
All International

Additional Information
Name of Most Recent Fund: AIP Private Markets Fund VI, L.P.
Most Recent Fund Was Raised: 12/30/2013
Year Founded: 2000
Capital Under Management: $813,400,000
Current Activity Level : Actively seeking new investments

MORGAN STANLEY CREDIT PARTNERS LP

1585 Broadway, 39th Floor
New York, NY USA 10036
Phone: 212-761-6422
E-mail: credit.partners@morganstanley.com
Website: www.morganstanley.com/creditpartners

Management and Staff
Debra Abramovitz, Chief Operating Officer
Hank D Alessandro, Managing Director
Jeff Levin, Vice President

Type of Firm
Bank Affiliated

Project Preferences

Type of Financing Preferred:
Leveraged Buyout
Mezzanine
Later Stage
Acquisition
Recapitalizations

Geographical Preferences

United States Preferences:

International Preferences:
Western Europe

Additional Information
Name of Most Recent Fund: Morgan Stanley Credit Partners, L.P.
Most Recent Fund Was Raised: 12/30/2009
Year Founded: 2009
Capital Under Management: $1,000,000,000
Current Activity Level : Actively seeking new investments

MORGAN STANLEY ENERGY PARTNERS

522 Fifth Avenue
New York, NY USA 10036
Phone: 8553325306
Website: www.morganstanley.com

Type of Firm
Private Equity Firm

Project Preferences

Type of Financing Preferred:
Leveraged Buyout

Geographical Preferences

United States Preferences:
North America

Industry Preferences

In Industrial/Energy prefer:
Energy

Additional Information
Year Founded: 1969
Current Activity Level : Actively seeking new investments

MORGAN STANLEY EXPANSION CAPITAL

1585 Broadway
39th Floor
New York, NY USA 10036
Phone: 2127617070
Website: www.morganstanley.com

Management and Staff
Peter Chung, Managing Director

Type of Firm
Investment Management Firm

Association Membership
National Venture Capital Association - USA (NVCA)

Project Preferences

Type of Financing Preferred:
Later Stage

Industry Preferences

In Medical/Health prefer:
Health Services

In Consumer Related prefer:
Consumer

In Business Serv. prefer:
Media

Additional Information
Name of Most Recent Fund: Morgan Stanley Expansion Capital, L.P.
Most Recent Fund Was Raised: 06/13/2011
Year Founded: 2011
Capital Under Management: $144,080,000
Current Activity Level : Actively seeking new investments

MORGAN STANLEY MULTICULTURAL INNOVATION LAB

1585 Broadway
Times Square, NY USA 10036

Type of Firm
Incubator/Development Program

Project Preferences

Type of Financing Preferred:
Early Stage
Startup

Additional Information
Year Founded: 2017
Current Activity Level : Actively seeking new investments

MORGAN STANLEY PRIVATE EQUITY

1585 Broadway
38th Floor
New York, NY USA 10036
Phone: 2127614000
E-mail: private.equity@morganstanley.com
Website: www.morganstanley.com

Other Offices

Grand Hyatt Plaza, Unit E
Western Express Highway, Santa Cruz-East
Mumbai, India 400 055

30/F Three Exchange Square
Central
Hong Kong, Hong Kong
Phone: 852-2848-5200
Fax: 852-2848-5282

37/F, Yebisu Garden Tower
4-20-3 Ebisu, Shibuya ku
, Japan 150-6001

20 Bank Street
Canary Wharf
London, United Kingdom E14 4AD
Phone: 44-207-425-8000
Fax: 44-207-425-4691

Unit 3A & 3B, 12/F, Tower 1
18 Taipingqiao Street, Xicheng District
Beijing, China 100032

46, Intl Commerce Center
1 Austin Rd
Kowloon, Hong Kong
Phone: 85228485200
Fax: 85222397805

22nd Floor, Hungkuk Life Insurance Bldg
226 Shinmun-ro 1-Ga, Chongro-Gu
Seoul, South Korea 110-061

Management and Staff
Bill Wang, Vice President
David Thompson, Vice President
David Cook, Vice President
Eric Kanter, Managing Director
Eric Fry, Managing Director
Gary Matthews, Managing Director
Mark Bye, Managing Director
Robert Lee, Managing Director
Ryan Jordan, Vice President

Type of Firm
Bank Affiliated

Association Membership
Hungarian Venture Capital Association (HVCA)

Project Preferences

Type of Financing Preferred:
Leveraged Buyout
Expansion
Generalist PE
Management Buyouts
Acquisition
Recapitalizations

Geographical Preferences

United States Preferences:
North America

International Preferences:
India
Europe
Taiwan
Asia

Industry Focus

(% based on actual investment)

Other Products	64.3%
Internet Specific	10.5%
Industrial/Energy	5.7%
Consumer Related	4.7%
Communications and Media	4.1%
Semiconductors/Other Elect.	3.8%
Computer Software and Services	2.9%
Computer Hardware	1.6%
Medical/Health	1.4%
Biotechnology	1.0%

Additional Information
Name of Most Recent Fund: Morgan Stanley Capital Partners V, L.P.
Most Recent Fund Was Raised: 11/20/2008
Year Founded: 1935
Capital Under Management: $6,371,400,000
Current Activity Level : Actively seeking new investments

MORGENTHALER VENTURES

2710 Sand Hill Road
Suite 100
Menlo Park, CA USA 94025
Phone: 6503887600
Fax: 6503887601
Website: www.morgenthaler.com

Other Offices

222 Berkeley Street
20th Floor
BOSTON, MA USA 02116
Phone: 617-587-7800
Fax: 617-587-7801

One Liberty Square
Suite 620
BOSTON, MA USA 02109
Phone: 6175877800
Fax: 6175877801

4430 Arapahoe Avenue
Suite 220
BOULDER, CO USA 80303
Phone: 303-417-1604
Fax: 303-417-1602

600 Superior Avenue East
Suite 2500, Fifth Third Center
CLEVELAND, OH USA 44114
Phone: 2164167500
Fax: 2164167501

Management and Staff

Ching Wu, Vice President
Gary Little, Partner
Gary Morgenthaler, Partner
Rebecca Lynn, Partner

Type of Firm

Private Equity Firm

Association Membership

Western Association of Venture Capitalists (WAVC)
National Venture Capital Association - USA (NVCA)

Project Preferences

Role in Financing:
Prefer role as deal originator

Type of Financing Preferred:
Leveraged Buyout
Early Stage
Generalist PE
Balanced
Later Stage
Management Buyouts
Acquisition
Recapitalizations

Size of Investments Considered:
Min Size of Investment Considered (000s): $5,000
Max Size of Investment Considered (000s): $15,000

Geographical Preferences

United States Preferences:
North America

Industry Focus

(% based on actual investment)
Semiconductors/Other Elect.   19.2%
Medical/Health   16.8%
Biotechnology   15.2%
Computer Software and Services   12.6%
Communications and Media   11.6%
Internet Specific   11.0%
Industrial/Energy   5.6%
Other Products   3.6%
Computer Hardware   3.2%
Consumer Related   1.3%

Additional Information

Name of Most Recent Fund: Morgenthaler Venture Partners IX, L.P.
Most Recent Fund Was Raised: 06/24/2008
Year Founded: 1968
Capital Under Management: $3,000,000,000
Current Activity Level : Actively seeking new investments
Method of Compensation: Return on investment is of primary concern, do not charge fees

MORNINGSIDE VENTURE CAPITAL

380 Wuyuan Rd, Xuhui District
Shanghai, China
Phone: 862164380260
Fax: 862164380267
Website: www.morningsidevc.com

Type of Firm

Private Equity Firm

Project Preferences

Type of Financing Preferred:
Early Stage

Additional Information

Year Founded: 2007
Current Activity Level : Actively seeking new investments

MORPHEUS

109 Fifth Main, Sixth Cross
RK Layout, Padmanabhanagar
Bangalore, India 560070
E-mail: neo@themorpheus.com
Website: www.themorpheus.com

Type of Firm

Private Equity Firm

Project Preferences

Type of Financing Preferred:
Early Stage
Expansion
Seed

Geographical Preferences

International Preferences:
India

Additional Information

Year Founded: 2009
Capital Under Management: $783,000
Current Activity Level : Actively seeking new investments

MORPHEUS CAPITAL ADVISORS LLC

100 Park Avenue
Eleventh Floor
New York, NY USA 10017
Phone: 2125579700
Website: www.morpheuscap.com

Management and Staff

Mitchell Gordon, President
Morgan St, John, Partner

Type of Firm

Investment Management Firm

Project Preferences

Type of Financing Preferred:
Early Stage
Expansion
Mezzanine
Later Stage
Distressed Debt

Additional Information

Year Founded: 2008
Current Activity Level : Actively seeking new investments

MORRIS CAPITAL MANAGEMENT LLC

1200 Mountain Creek Road
Suite 230
Chattanooga, TN USA 37405
Phone: 4238700800
Fax: 4238700805
Website: morriscapitalmanagement.com

Management and Staff

Larry Hughes, Partner
Ricky Sanders, Partner
Tim Morris, Partner

Type of Firm

Private Equity Firm

Project Preferences

Type of Financing Preferred:
Leveraged Buyout
Turnaround
Acquisition
Recapitalizations

Geographical Preferences

United States Preferences:
All U.S.

Additional Information

Year Founded: 2002
Current Activity Level : Actively seeking new investments

MORRISON & FOERSTER LLP

755 Page Mill Road
Palo Alto, CA USA 94304
Phone: 6508135600
Fax: 6504940792
E-mail: info@mofo.com
Website: www.mofo.com

Other Offices

5200 Republic Plaza
370 Seventeenth Street
Denver, CO USA 80202
Phone: 303-592-1500
Fax: 303-592-1510

555 West Fifth Street
Suite 3500
Los Angeles, CA USA 90013
Phone: 213-892-5200
Fax: 213-892-5454

101 Ygnacio Valley Road
Suite 450
Walnut Creek, CA USA 94596
Phone: 925-295-3300
Fax: 925-946-9912

15 Queen's Road
41/F Edinburgh Tower
Central, Hong Kong
Phone: 852-2585-0888
Fax: 852-2585-0800

One Ropemaker Street
CityPoint
London, United Kingdom EC2Y 9AW
Phone: 4420-7920-4000
Fax: 4420-7496-8500

400 Capitol Mail
Suite 2600
Sacramento, CA USA 95814
Phone: 916-448-3200
Fax: 916-448-3222

12531 High Bluff Drive
Suite 100
San Diego, CA USA 92130
Phone: 858-720-5100
Fax: 858-720-5125

1650 Tysons Boulevard
Suite 400
McLean, VA USA 22102
Phone: 703-760-7700
Fax: 703-760-7777

Yan An East Road No.222
Suite 3501, Bund Center
Shanghai, China 200002
Phone: 86-21-6335-2290
Fax: 86-21-6335-2290

Avenue Moliere 262
Brussels, Belgium 1180
Phone: 322-347-0400
Fax: 322-347-1824

50 Collyer Quay
Suite 12-01 OUE Bayfront
Singapore, Singapore 049321
Phone: 6569222000
Fax: 6569222008

No. 1 Jianguomenwai Avenue
Suite 3408, China World Tower 2
Beijing, China
Phone: 86-10-6505-9090
Fax: 86-10-6505-9090

5-1 Marunouchi 1-chrome, Chiyodaku
29th Floor Shin-Marunouchi Building
Tokyo, Japan 100-6529
Phone: 813-3214-6522
Fax: 813-3214-6512

1290 Avenue of the Americas
New York, NY USA 10101
Phone: 212-468-8000
Fax: 212-468-7900

425 Market Street
San Francisco, CA USA 94105
Phone: 415-268-7000
Fax: 415-268-7522

2000 Pennsylvania Avenue Northwest
Suite 5500
Washington, DC USA 20006
Phone: 202-887-1500
Fax: 202-887-0763

Management and Staff

Adam Hoffinger, Partner
Alan Johnston, Partner
Alan Owens, Partner
Alex Chartove, Partner
Alexander Hadjis, Partner
Alison Tucher, Partner
Alistair Maughan, Partner
Anders Aannestad, Partner
Andrew Thorpe, Partner
Andrew Monach, Partner
Andrew Morrison, Partner
Andrew Smith, Partner
Andrew David Muhback, Partner
Andrew William Winden, Partner
Ann Bevitt, Partner
Anna Pinedo, Partner
Anna Erickson White, Partner
Anthony Press, Partner
Anthony Princi, Partner
Arturo Gonzalez, Partner
Barbara Mendelson, Partner
Benjamin Fox, Partner
Bernie Pistillo, Partner
Bill Veatch, Partner
Bita Rahebi, Partner
Bradley Lui, Partner
Brandon Parris, Partner
Brett Miller, Partner
Brian Matsui, Partner
Brian Bates, Partner
Brian Kramer, Partner
Brooks Beard, Partner
Bryan Wilson, Partner
Carl Loewenson, Partner
Cassandra Swain, Partner
Catherine Polizzi, Partner
Cedric Chao, Partner
Charles Horn, Partner
Charles Barquist, Partner
Charles Cole, Partner
Charles Chau, Partner
Charles Comey, Partner
Charles Farman, Partner
Charles Katz, Partner
Charles Kerr, Partner
Chie Yakura, Partner
Chris Ford, Partner
Chris Carr, Partner
Chris Coulter, Partner
Christine Lyon, Partner
Christopher Delson, Partner
Christopher Eide, Partner
Christopher Forrester, Partner
Craig Fields, Partner
Craig Martin, Partner
Craig Celniker, Partner
Craig Schloss, Partner
Craig Etlin, Partner
D. Anthony Rodriguez, Partner
D. Reed Freeman, Partner
Dale Araki, Partner
Dale Caldwell, Partner
Dan Marmalefsky, Partner
Daniel Levison, Partner
Daniel Leventhal, Partner
Daniel Westman, Partner
Darryl Rains, Partner
David Doyle, Partner
David Lipkin, Partner
David Lynn, Partner
David McDowell, Partner
David Meyer, Partner

Pratt's Guide to Private Equity & Venture Capital Sources

David Strong, Partner
David Gold, Partner
David Fehrman, Partner
David Fioccola, Partner
David Kaufman, Partner
David Murphy, Partner
David Slotkin, Partner
Deanne Maynard, Partner
Dennis Orr, Partner
Derek Foran, Partner
Don Rushing, Partner
Dorothy Fernandez, Partner
Douglas Hendricks, Partner
Dwight Smith, Partner
Edward Lukins, Partner
Elana Hahn, Partner
Emily Evans, Partner
Eric Acker, Partner
Eric Walters, Partner
Eric McCrath, Partner
Eric Roose, Partner
Eric Coffill, Partner
Eric Piesner, Partner
Eric Akira Tate, Partner
Erik Olson, Partner
Erin Bosman, Partner
Eugene Illovsky, Partner
Ezra Levine, Partner
Frederick Jenney, Partner
Fuyuo Mitomi, Partner
G. Brian Busey, Partner
Gabriel Meister, Partner
Gary Maeder, Partner
Gary Lee, Partner
Gary Mitchel Smith, Partner
Gavin Grover, Partner
George Harris, Partner
Glenn Kubota, Partner
Gordon Milner, Partner
Grant Esposito, Partner
Greg Giammittorio, Partner
Gregory Tan, Partner
Gregory Dresser, Partner
Gregory Koltun, Partner
Gregory Feihong Wang, Partner
Harold McWlhinny, Partner
Hector Gallegos, Partner
Hendrick Jordaan, Partner
Henry Fields, Partner
Hillel Cohn, Partner
Hollis Hyans, Partner
Ivan Smallwood, Partner
J. Alexander Lawrence, Partner
Jack Londen, Partner
Jack Lewis, Partner
Jackie Liu, Partner
James Bennett, Partner
James Bergin, Partner
James Huston, Partner
James Mullen, Partner
James Schurz, Partner
James Hough, Partner
James Tanenbaum, Partner
James McGuire, Partner
Jamie Levitt, Partner
Jana Mansour, Partner
Janet Xiao, Partner
Janie Schulman, Partner
Jason Crotty, Partner
Jason Bartlett, Partner
Jay Ponazecki, Partner
Jay Baris, Partner
Jay De Groot, Partner
Jeff Jaeckel, Partner
Jeffrey Temple, Partner
Jeffrey Bell, Partner
Jennifer Mink, Partner
Jennifer Lee Taylor, Partner
Jeremy Jennings-Mares, Partner
Jeremy Hunt, Partner
Jie Zhou, Partner
Jill Feldman, Partner
Jim McCabe, Partner
Joel Friley, Partner
Joel Haims, Partner
John Moore, Partner
John Rafferty, Partner
John McCarthy, Partner
John Campbell, Partner
John Delaney, Partner
John Harper, Partner
John Hempill, Partner
Jonathan Melmed, Partner
Jonathan Gowdy, Partner
Jonathan Bockman, Partner
Jonathan Edward Wheeler, Partner
Jordan Eth, Partner
Judson Lobdell, Partner
Julian Thurston, Partner
Justin Michael Stock, Partner
Karen Kubin, Partner
Karen Hagberg, Partner
Karin Retzer, Partner
Karl Kramer, Partner
Kathryn Johnstone, Partner
Katsuhiko Fujihira, Partner
Keisuke Mochizuki, Partner
Ken Muller, Partner
Kenneth Siegel, Partner
Kenneth Kuwayti, Partner
Kevin Roberts, Partner
Kimberly Van Voorhis, Partner
Kristin Yohannan Moore, Partner
Kyle Mooney, Partner
Larry Engel, Partner
Lawrence Bard, Partner
Lawrence Yanowitch, Partner
Lawrence Gerschwer, Partner
Linda Shostak, Partner
Linda Lane, Partner
Lindsay Thomas, Partner
Lisa Ann Boychenko, Partner
Lloyd Harmetz, Partner
Lorenzo Marinuzzi, Partner
Louise Stoupe, Partner
M. Andrew Woodmansee, Partner
Marc Young, Partner
Marc Pernick, Partner
Marc David Peters, Partner
Mark Zebrowski, Partner
Mark Ungerman, Partner
Mark Foster, Partner
Mark Edelstein, Partner
Mark Danis, Partner
Mark McDonald, Partner
Mark Wicker, Partner
Mark Ladner, Partner
Mark David McPherson, Partner
Masato Hayakawa, Partner
Matthew D Amore, Partner
Matthew Kreeger, Partner
Max Olson, Partner
Mehran Arjomand, Partner
Melody He-Chen, Partner
Mia Mazza, Partner
Michael Ward, Partner
Michael Miller, Partner
Michael Cohen, Partner
Michael Braun, Partner
Michael Doherty, Partner
Michael Agoglia, Partner
Michael Frank, Partner
Michael Graffagna, Partner
Michael O Donnell, Partner
Michael O Bryan, Partner
Michael Jacobs, Partner
Michael O Donnell, Partner
Michael Jacob Steel, Partner
Michele Corash, Partner
Mika Mayer, Partner
Miriam Wugmeister, Partner
Mitchell Newmark, Partner
Mitsutoshi Uchida, Partner
Motonori Araki, Partner
Narutake Takasu, Partner
Nicholas Spiliotes, Partner
Nicole Smith, Partner
Norman Rosenbaum, Partner
Obrea Poindexter, Partner
Oliver Ireland, Partner
Otis Littlefield, Partner
Pamela Reed, Partner
Pat Cavaney, Chief Operating Officer
Patricia Martone, Partner
Patrick McCabe, Partner
Paul Lion, Partner
Paul McKenzie, Partner
Paul Friedman, Partner
Paul Borden, Partner
Paul Flum, Partner
Paul Jahn, Partner
Penelope Preovolos, Partner
Peng Chen, Partner
Peter Pfister, Partner
Peter Stern, Partner
Peter Yim, Partner
Peter Hsiao, Partner
Peter Green, Partner
Peter Aitelli, Partner
Peter Dopsch, Partner
R. Gregory Roberts, Partner
Rachel Krevans, Partner
Randall Fons, Partner
Randy Steven Laxer, Partner
Rebekah Kaufman, Partner

Remmelt Reigersman, Partner
Rich Kim, Partner
Richard Hung, Partner
Rick Fischer, Partner
Rick Vacura, Partner
Robert Cudd, Partner
Robert Mattson, Partner
Robert Salerno, Partner
Robert Townsend, Partner
Robert Hubbell, Partner
Robert Stern, Partner
Robert Falk, Partner
Robert Hollingshead, Partner
Roger Fones, Partner
Ronald White, Partner
Rony Gerrits, Partner
Rosemary Tarlton, Partner
Rudy Kim, Partner
Russell Weiss, Partner
Ruth Borenstein, Partner
Ryan Hassanein, Partner
Ryugo Yoshimura, Partner
Saori Nakamura, Partner
Scott Stanton, Partner
Scott Moore, Partner
Scott Oliver, Partner
Scott McPhee, Partner
Scott Llewellyn, Partner
Sean Gates, Partner
Sean Prosser, Partner
Sharon Parella, Partner
Sherry Yin, Partner
Somnath Chatterjee, Partner
Spencer Klein, Partner
Stanley Yukevich, Partner
Stefan Engelhardt, Partner
Stephen Thau, Partner
Stephen Freccero, Partner
Stephen Colangelo, Partner
Stephen Feldman, Partner
Steve Rowles, Partner
Steven Comer, Partner
Stuart Plunkett, Partner
Stuart Beraha, Partner
Susan Mac Cormac, Partner
Suzanne Graeser, Partner
Sylvia Rivera, Partner
Taylor Stevens, Partner
Tessa Schwartz, Partner
Theodore Seltzer, Partner
Thomas Humphreys, Partner
Thomas McGovern, Partner
Thomas Steele, Partner
Thomas Fileti, Partner
Thomas Devaney, Partner
Thomas Chou, Partner
Thomas Knox, Partner
Tiffany Cheung, Partner
Timothy Harris, Partner
Timothy Blakely, Partner
Todd Goren, Partner
Tom Wilson, Partner
Tom McQuail, Partner
Tony Grundy, Partner
Trevor James, Partner

Van Ellis, Partner
Venantius Tan, Partner
Vincent Belusko, Partner
Vivian Hanson, Partner
W. Stephen Smith, Partner
Wendy Garbers, Partner
Wesley Overson, Partner
Whitney Holmes, Partner
William Schwartz, Partner
William O Connor, Partner
William Choe, Partner
William Stern, Partner
William Tarantino, Partner
William Sloan, Partner
Xiaohu Ma, Partner
Yukako Wagatsuma, Partner
Yukihiro Terazawa, Partner
Zane Gresham, Partner

Type of Firm
Corporate PE/Venture

Association Membership
Mid-Atlantic Venture Association
Israel Venture Association

Project Preferences

Type of Financing Preferred:
Other

Additional Information
Year Founded: 1883
Current Activity Level : Actively seeking new investments

MOSAIC CAPITAL CORP

Fourth Street Southwest
400, 2424
Calgary, Canada T2S 2T4
Phone: 4032186500
E-mail: info@mosaiccapitalcorp.com
Website: www.mosaiccapitalcorp.com

Management and Staff
Barclay Laughland, Vice President
Mark Gardhouse, Chief Executive Officer
Monty Balderston, Chief Financial Officer
Richard Pearce, Chief Operating Officer

Type of Firm
Investment Management Firm

Association Membership
Canadian Venture Capital Association

Project Preferences

Type of Financing Preferred:
Generalist PE
Acquisition

Geographical Preferences

United States Preferences:

Canadian Preferences:
All Canada

Industry Preferences

In Industrial/Energy prefer:
Oil and Gas Exploration

In Financial Services prefer:
Real Estate

In Manufact. prefer:
Publishing

Additional Information
Year Founded: 2011
Capital Under Management: $40,000,000
Current Activity Level : Actively seeking new investments

MOSAIC CAPITAL LLC

15165 Ventura Boulevard
Suite 425
Sherman Oaks, CA USA 91403
Phone: 310-432-6777
Fax: 310-432-6779
E-mail: info@mosaiccapital.com
Website: www.mosaiccapital.com

Management and Staff
Gordon Gregory, Managing Director

Type of Firm
Private Equity Firm

Project Preferences

Type of Financing Preferred:
Leveraged Buyout
Expansion
Management Buyouts
Acquisition
Recapitalizations

Industry Focus
(% based on actual investment)
Internet Specific	78.0%
Industrial/Energy	22.0%

Additional Information
Year Founded: 1996
Capital Under Management: $25,000,000
Current Activity Level : Actively seeking new investments

MOSAIC CAPITAL PARTNERS LLC

4101 Lake Boone Trail, Suite 120
Raleigh, NC USA 27607
Phone: 7046258840
Website: www.mosaic-cp.com

Management and Staff
Dabney Smith, Managing Partner
Joseph Strycharz, Managing Partner
Keith Butcher, Managing Partner
Stephen Buchanan, Managing Partner
William Hayes, Managing Partner

Type of Firm
Private Equity Firm

Association Membership
Natl Assoc of Small Bus. Inv. Co (NASBIC)

Project Preferences
Type of Financing Preferred:
Mezzanine

Geographical Preferences
United States Preferences:
Midwest

Industry Preferences
In Medical/Health prefer:
Medical/Health

In Consumer Related prefer:
Retail
Food/Beverage

In Industrial/Energy prefer:
Energy
Materials
Advanced Materials
Environmental Related

In Business Serv. prefer:
Distribution

In Manufact. prefer:
Manufacturing

In Agr/Forestr/Fish prefer:
Mining and Minerals

Additional Information
Name of Most Recent Fund: Mosaic Capital Investors I, L.P.
Most Recent Fund Was Raised: 08/08/2013
Year Founded: 1989
Capital Under Management: $165,000,000
Current Activity Level : Actively seeking new investments

MOSAIC PRIVATE EQUITY LTD

Three Hardman Street
10th Floor, Spinningfields
Manchester, United Kingdom M3 3HF
Phone: 441619321475
Website: www.mosaicpe.com

Management and Staff
Mike Rogan, Co-Founder
Paul Newton, Co-Founder

Type of Firm
Private Equity Firm

Association Membership
British Venture Capital Association (BVCA)

Project Preferences
Type of Financing Preferred:
Expansion
Generalist PE
Management Buyouts
Acquisition

Size of Investments Considered:
Min Size of Investment Considered (000s): $3,186
Max Size of Investment Considered (000s): $15,732

Geographical Preferences
International Preferences:
United Kingdom

Additional Information
Year Founded: 2006
Current Activity Level : Actively seeking new investments

MOSAIC VENTURE PARTNERS

65 Front Street East
Suite 200
Toronto, Canada M5E 1B5
Phone: 4163672888
Fax: 4163678146
Website: www.mosaicvp.com

Management and Staff
David Samuel, Managing Director
Vernon Lobo, Managing Director

Type of Firm
Private Equity Firm

Project Preferences
Type of Financing Preferred:
Early Stage
Balanced

Geographical Preferences
United States Preferences:

Canadian Preferences:
All Canada

Industry Preferences
In Internet Specific prefer:
Internet

Additional Information
Year Founded: 1998
Current Activity Level : Actively seeking new investments

MOSAIC VENTURES LTD

One Heddon Street
London, United Kingdom W1B 4BD
Website: www.mosaicventures.com

Type of Firm
Private Equity Firm

Project Preferences
Type of Financing Preferred:
Early Stage
Startup

Geographical Preferences
International Preferences:
Europe

Industry Preferences
In Computer Software prefer:
Software

In Internet Specific prefer:
Ecommerce

In Medical/Health prefer:
Medical/Health

In Consumer Related prefer:
Education Related

In Financial Services prefer:
Financial Services

Additional Information
Year Founded: 2014
Current Activity Level : Actively seeking new investments

MOSAIK PARTNERS LLC

555 California Street, 18th Floor
San Francisco, CA USA 94104
Phone: 7072664840
E-mail: info@mosaikpartners.com
Website: www.mosaikpartners.com

Management and Staff
E. Miles Kilburn, Co-Founder
Howard Mergelkamp, Co-Founder

Type of Firm
Private Equity Firm

Project Preferences
Type of Financing Preferred:
Early Stage
Balanced
Later Stage

Size of Investments Considered:
Min Size of Investment Considered (000s): $2,000
Max Size of Investment Considered (000s): $7,000

Geographical Preferences

United States Preferences:

Industry Preferences

In Internet Specific prefer:
Ecommerce

Additional Information
Year Founded: 2014
Capital Under Management: $45,400,000
Current Activity Level : Actively seeking new investments

MOSAIX VENTURES LLC

1822 North Mohawk Street
Chicago, IL USA 60614
Phone: 3122740988
Fax: 7739132792

Management and Staff
Germano Giuliani, Founder

Type of Firm
Private Equity Firm

Project Preferences

Role in Financing:
Will function either as deal originator or investor in deals created by others

Type of Financing Preferred:
Early Stage
Expansion

Size of Investments Considered:
Min Size of Investment Considered (000s): $1,000
Max Size of Investment Considered (000s): $4,000

Geographical Preferences

United States Preferences:
West Coast

Industry Preferences

In Medical/Health prefer:
Medical Products
Health Services

Additional Information
Year Founded: 2000
Capital Under Management: $60,000,000
Current Activity Level : Actively seeking new investments
Method of Compensation: Return on investment is of primary concern, do not charge fees

---

MOSLEY VENTURES

75 Fifth Street North West
Suite 328
Atlanta, GA USA 30308
E-mail: info@mosleyventures.com
Website: www.mosleyventures.com

Type of Firm
Private Equity Firm

Project Preferences

Type of Financing Preferred:
Early Stage
Startup

Geographical Preferences

United States Preferences:

Industry Preferences

In Communications prefer:
Communications and Media
Wireless Communications
Data Communications

In Computer Software prefer:
Software
Applications Software

In Internet Specific prefer:
Internet

In Medical/Health prefer:
Health Services

Additional Information
Year Founded: 1990
Capital Under Management: $30,000,000
Current Activity Level : Actively seeking new investments

MOTALA VERKSTAD GROUP AB

Sodergatan 3
Malmo, Sweden 211 34
Phone: 4620210999
E-mail: info@qeepventures.com
Website: mvg.se

Type of Firm
Private Equity Firm

Project Preferences

Type of Financing Preferred:
Balanced

Geographical Preferences

International Preferences:
Hungary
Sweden
Norway
Germany
Denmark

Industry Preferences

In Consumer Related prefer:
Food/Beverage

In Industrial/Energy prefer:
Machinery

In Business Serv. prefer:
Consulting Services

Additional Information
Year Founded: 2009
Current Activity Level : Actively seeking new investments

MOTILAL OSWAL PVT EQUITY ADVISORS PVT LTD

Nariman Point
Third Floor, Hoechst House
Mumbai, India 400 021
Phone: 912239825500
Fax: 912222823499
E-mail: info@motilaloswal.com
Website: www.motilaloswal.com

Management and Staff
Prakash Dhoot, Vice President
Prakash Bagla, Vice President
Vishal Gupta, Principal

Type of Firm
Bank Affiliated

Association Membership
Indian Venture Capital Association (IVCA)

Project Preferences

Type of Financing Preferred:
Leveraged Buyout
Value-Add
Early Stage
Expansion
Later Stage
Acquisition

Industry Preferences

In Communications prefer:
Media and Entertainment

In Consumer Related prefer:
Consumer
Entertainment and Leisure
Retail
Food/Beverage
Education Related

1443

In Transportation prefer:
Transportation

In Financial Services prefer:
Financial Services
Financial Services

In Business Serv. prefer:
Distribution

In Agr/Forestr/Fish prefer:
Agribusiness

Additional Information

Name of Most Recent Fund: India Realty Excellence Fund II
Most Recent Fund Was Raised: 03/05/2014
Year Founded: 2006
Capital Under Management: $125,000,000
Current Activity Level : Actively seeking new investments

MOTION EQUITY PARTNERS LLP

Ten Lower Grosvenor Place
Second Floor
London, United Kingdom SW1W 0EN
Phone: 4407709332652
Website: www.motionequitypartners.com

Other Offices

47, avenue George V
Paris, France 75008
Phone: 33-1-5383-7910
Fax: 33-1-5383-7920

Via Saffi 25
Milano, Italy 20123
Phone: 39-2-888-9001
Fax: 39-2-8889-0040

Management and Staff

Cedric Rays, Partner
Charles St. John, Partner
Edward Koopman, Partner
Giovanna Voltolina, Principal
Jonathan Musselwhite, Partner
Mathew James, Chief Financial Officer
Maurizio Bianco, Partner
Nigel McConnell, Partner
Patrick Eisenchteter, Managing Partner

Type of Firm

Private Equity Firm

Association Membership

British Venture Capital Association (BVCA)
French Venture Capital Association (AFIC)
German Venture Capital Association (BVK)
European Private Equity and Venture Capital Assoc.

Project Preferences

Type of Financing Preferred:
Leveraged Buyout
Management Buyouts
Acquisition

Geographical Preferences

International Preferences:
Europe

Industry Focus

(% based on actual investment)
Other Products	45.1%
Consumer Related	34.5%
Industrial/Energy	14.3%
Semiconductors/Other Elect.	3.8%
Medical/Health	1.8%
Internet Specific	0.5%

Additional Information

Name of Most Recent Fund: Cognetas Fund II
Most Recent Fund Was Raised: 07/25/2005
Year Founded: 2000
Capital Under Management: $2,424,200,000
Current Activity Level : Actively seeking new investments

MOTIVE PARTNERS GP LLC

401 Broadway
Suite 1412
New York, NY USA 10012
Phone: 6463489500
Website: motivepartners.com

Type of Firm

Private Equity Firm

Project Preferences

Type of Financing Preferred:
Early Stage

Industry Preferences

In Financial Services prefer:
Financial Services

Additional Information

Year Founded: 2017
Current Activity Level : Actively seeking new investments

MOTOROLA SOLUTIONS VENTURE CAPITAL

1303 East Algonquin Road
Sixth Floor
Schaumburg, IL USA 60196
Phone: 8475765000
E-mail: motorolaventures@motorola.com
Website: www.motorolasolutions.com

Type of Firm

Corporate PE/Venture

Association Membership

New England Venture Capital Association
Illinois Venture Capital Association
National Venture Capital Association - USA (NVCA)

Project Preferences

Role in Financing:
Will function either as deal originator or investor in deals created by others

Type of Financing Preferred:
Early Stage
Expansion
Balanced
Later Stage
Startup

Industry Focus

(% based on actual investment)
Communications and Media	23.5%
Computer Software and Services	21.3%
Internet Specific	19.2%
Semiconductors/Other Elect.	15.9%
Computer Hardware	10.0%
Medical/Health	4.9%
Other Products	3.7%
Biotechnology	0.9%
Industrial/Energy	0.3%
Consumer Related	0.2%

Additional Information

Year Founded: 1999
Capital Under Management: $400,000,000
Current Activity Level : Actively seeking new investments
Method of Compensation: Return on investment is of primary concern, do not charge fees

MOTSENG INVESTMENT HOLDINGS (PTY) LTD

204 Rivonia Road, Rivonia
Motseng House
Johannesburg, South Africa 2010
Phone: 27112822500
Fax: 27112822525
E-mail: contact@motseng.co.za

Management and Staff

Andries Smit, Managing Director
Dewald Van Staden, Managing Director
Ipeleng Mkhari, Chief Operating Officer
Merafe Moloto, Managing Director
Prosper Nkosi, Managing Director

Type of Firm

Investment Management Firm

Project Preferences

Type of Financing Preferred:
Leveraged Buyout
Management Buyouts
Acquisition

Geographical Preferences

International Preferences:
South Africa
Africa

Industry Preferences

In Communications prefer:
Communications and Media

In Industrial/Energy prefer:
Oil and Gas Exploration

In Transportation prefer:
Transportation

In Financial Services prefer:
Financial Services
Real Estate

In Business Serv. prefer:
Services

In Manufact. prefer:
Manufacturing

Additional Information

Year Founded: 1998
Current Activity Level : Actively seeking new investments

MOTU VENTURES MANAGEMENT GMBH

Kurfuerstendamm 54/55
Berlin, Germany 10707
Phone: 493088713233
Fax: 493088713221
Website: motuventures.com

Type of Firm
Private Equity Firm

Project Preferences

Type of Financing Preferred:
Early Stage
Start-up Financing
Seed

Industry Preferences

In Computer Software prefer:
Software

Additional Information

Year Founded: 2014
Current Activity Level : Actively seeking new investments

MOTUS MITTELSTANDSKAPITAL GMBH

Rankestrasse 5/6
Berlin, Germany 10789
Phone: 493088572644
Fax: 493088572645
E-mail: info@motus-kapital.de
Website: www.motus-kapital.de

Management and Staff
Ralf Baumeister, Chief Executive Officer

Type of Firm
Private Equity Firm

Association Membership
German Venture Capital Association (BVK)

Project Preferences

Type of Financing Preferred:
Expansion
Mezzanine
Management Buyouts
Acquisition

Geographical Preferences

International Preferences:
Germany

Additional Information

Year Founded: 2008
Current Activity Level : Actively seeking new investments

MOTUS VENTURES

541 Jefferson Avenue
Suite 100
Redwood City, CA USA 94063
Phone: 6502834402
E-mail: info@transportationtechnologyventures.com

Management and Staff
James DiSanto, Managing Director
Robert Seidl, Managing Director

Type of Firm
Incubator/Development Program

Project Preferences

Type of Financing Preferred:
Early Stage
Seed

Geographical Preferences

United States Preferences:

Industry Preferences

In Computer Software prefer:
Software

In Transportation prefer:
Transportation

Additional Information

Year Founded: 2012
Current Activity Level : Actively seeking new investments

MOUNT KELLETT CAPITAL HONG KONG LTD

1 Harbour View Street
One International Finance Ctr.
Central, Hong Kong
Phone: 85239008000
Fax: 85239008080
E-mail: info@mountkellett.com
Website: www.mountkellett.com

Other Offices

One Harbour View Street
Suites 505-510, Fifth Floor
Central, Hong Kong, Hong Kong
Phone: 85239008000
Fax: 85239008080

Berger House, 36-38 Berkeley Square
Seconf Floor
New York, United Kingdom W1J 5AE
Phone: 442076472050
Fax: 442076472060

Maker Maxity, Bandra Kurla Complex, East
Units 61&62, 6th Flr, Bldg. 3, N. Avenue
, India 400 051
Phone: 912242158888
Fax: 912242158877

Management and Staff
Jason Maynard, Founder
Mark McGoldrick, Founder

Type of Firm
Private Equity Firm

Project Preferences

Type of Financing Preferred:
Leveraged Buyout
Turnaround
Acquisition
Distressed Debt

Geographical Preferences

United States Preferences:
North America

International Preferences:
Asia Pacific
India
Europe
Hong Kong
China

Additional Information

Year Founded: 2008
Capital Under Management: $7,443,600,000
Current Activity Level : Actively seeking new investments

MOUNT YALE ASSET MANAGEMENT LLC

8000 Norman Center Drive
Suite 630
Minneapolis, MN USA 55437
Phone: 9528975390
Fax: 9528975391

Other Offices
1125 Seventeenth Street
Suite 1400
Denver, CO USA 80202
Phone: 3033822880
Fax: 3033822888

Management and Staff
Brian McLean, Senior Managing Director
Roger Bowden, President

Type of Firm
Private Equity Advisor or Fund of Funds

Project Preferences

Type of Financing Preferred:
Fund of Funds
Fund of Funds of Second

Geographical Preferences

United States Preferences:

Additional Information
Name of Most Recent Fund: MYPE Partners, L.P.
Most Recent Fund Was Raised: 09/27/2010
Year Founded: 1999
Capital Under Management: $17,700,000
Current Activity Level : Actively seeking new investments

MOUNTAIN CLEANTECH AG

Fuhrstrasse 12
Unterer Leihof
Waedenswil, Switzerland 8820
Phone: 41447838041
Fax: 41447838040
E-mail: contact@mountain-cleantech.ch
Website: www.mountain-cleantech.ch

Management and Staff
Alexander von Hutten, Managing Partner
Daniel Koppelkamm, Principal
Juergen Habichler, Managing Partner
Marc Dietrich, Venture Partner
Patrik Soderlund, Venture Partner

Type of Firm
Private Equity Firm

Project Preferences

Type of Financing Preferred:
Later Stage
Management Buyouts
Special Situation

Geographical Preferences

United States Preferences:
All U.S.

International Preferences:
Sweden
Switzerland
Austria
Middle East
Asia
Finland
Norway
Germany
Denmark

Industry Preferences

In Industrial/Energy prefer:
Alternative Energy
Materials
Environmental Related

In Other prefer:
Environment Responsible

Additional Information
Name of Most Recent Fund: Mountain Cleantech Fund II
Most Recent Fund Was Raised: 10/20/2011
Year Founded: 2007
Capital Under Management: $31,694,000
Current Activity Level : Actively seeking new investments

MOUNTAIN DO BRASIL PARTICIPACOES LTDA

R Sampaio Vidal
1140, Pinheiros
Sao Paulo, Brazil 01452
Website: www.mountaindobrasil.com.br

Type of Firm
Private Equity Firm

Project Preferences

Type of Financing Preferred:
Early Stage
Seed

Geographical Preferences

International Preferences:
Brazil

Industry Preferences

In Communications prefer:
Wireless Communications

In Internet Specific prefer:
Ecommerce
Web Aggregation/Portals

Additional Information
Year Founded: 1969
Current Activity Level : Actively seeking new investments

MOUNTAIN GROUP CAPITAL LLC

1600 Division Street
Suite 580
Nashville, TN USA 37203
Phone: 6158439100
Fax: 6153139996
Website: mgcfund.com

Management and Staff
Byron Smith, Principal
Joseph Cook, Co-Founder
Steven Singleton, Co-Founder

Type of Firm
Private Equity Firm

Project Preferences

Type of Financing Preferred:
Leveraged Buyout
Early Stage
Expansion
Balanced
Later Stage
Seed

Geographical Preferences

United States Preferences:
Tennessee
Southeast
North America

Industry Preferences

In Communications prefer:
Communications and Media

In Medical/Health prefer:
Medical/Health
Medical Diagnostics
Medical Products

In Consumer Related prefer:
Consumer

In Business Serv. prefer:
Services
Distribution

In Manufact. prefer:
Manufacturing

Additional Information
Name of Most Recent Fund: MGC Venture Partners 2013, L.P.

Most Recent Fund Was Raised: 03/26/2013
Year Founded: 2002
Capital Under Management: $21,451,000
Current Activity Level : Actively seeking new investments

MOUNTAIN KEJORA VENTURES

Barito Pacific Plaza Tower A
Level Six
Jakarta, Indonesia 11410
Website: www.mkv.vc

Type of Firm
Private Equity Firm

Project Preferences

Type of Financing Preferred:
Seed
Startup

Geographical Preferences

United States Preferences:
Southeast

Additional Information
Year Founded: 2013
Capital Under Management: $25,000,000
Current Activity Level : Actively seeking new investments

MOUNTAIN PARTNERS AG

Poststrasse 17
St. Gallen, Switzerland 9001
Phone: 41447838030
Fax: 41447838040
Website: mountain.partners.ch

Management and Staff
Christine Schmitz-Riol, Founder

Type of Firm
Private Equity Firm

Project Preferences

Type of Financing Preferred:
Leveraged Buyout
Early Stage
Generalist PE
Later Stage
Seed
Startup

Geographical Preferences

International Preferences:
Europe
Switzerland
Austria
Germany

Industry Preferences

In Communications prefer:
Media and Entertainment

In Computer Software prefer:
Software

In Internet Specific prefer:
Internet

In Biotechnology prefer:
Biotechnology

In Medical/Health prefer:
Medical/Health

In Industrial/Energy prefer:
Alternative Energy
Industrial Products
Materials
Environmental Related

In Financial Services prefer:
Financial Services

In Other prefer:
Environment Responsible

Additional Information
Year Founded: 2002
Current Activity Level : Actively seeking new investments

MOUNTAIN RIDGE CAPITAL LLC

6500 South Quebec Street
Suite 300
Englewood, CO USA 80002
Phone: 7206086090
E-mail: info@mountainridgecapital.com
Website: www.mountainridgecapital.com

Management and Staff
Boris Katsnelson, Founder

Type of Firm
Private Equity Firm

Project Preferences

Type of Financing Preferred:
Leveraged Buyout
Acquisition

Additional Information
Year Founded: 2014
Current Activity Level : Actively seeking new investments

MOUNTAINEER CAPITAL, L.P.

107 Capitol Street
Suite 300
Charleston, WV USA 25301
Phone: 3043477519
Fax: 3043470072
E-mail: info@mountaineercapital.com
Website: www.mountaineercapital.com

Management and Staff
Bruce Merrifield, Chief Executive Officer
J. Rudy Henley, Partner
William Taylor, Managing Partner

Type of Firm
SBIC

Association Membership
Community Development Venture Capital Alliance
Natl Assoc of Small Bus. Inv. Co (NASBIC)

Project Preferences

Role in Financing:
Will function either as deal originator or investor in deals created by others

Type of Financing Preferred:
Leveraged Buyout
Early Stage
Expansion
Balanced

Geographical Preferences

United States Preferences:
Mid Atlantic
West Virginia

Additional Information
Name of Most Recent Fund: Mountaineer Capital, L.P. - SBIC
Most Recent Fund Was Raised: 04/01/2000
Year Founded: 2000
Capital Under Management: $17,000,000
Current Activity Level : Actively seeking new investments
Method of Compensation: Return on invest. most important, but chg. closing fees, service fees, etc.

MOUNTAINGATE CAPITAL MANAGEMENT LP

1800 Larimer Street
Suite 2200
Denver, CO USA 80202
Phone: 3033905001
Fax: 3033905015
Website: mountaingatecap.com

Management and Staff
Ben McCown, Vice President
Bennett Thompson, Managing Director
Bruce Rogers, Managing Director
Colton King, Managing Director
Piotr Biezychudek, Vice President
Stewart Fisher, Managing Director
Sue Cho, Principal

Type of Firm
Private Equity Firm

Project Preferences

Type of Financing Preferred:
Leveraged Buyout

Industry Preferences

In Business Serv. prefer:
Services
Distribution

In Manufact. prefer:
Manufacturing

Additional Information
Year Founded: 2015
Capital Under Management: $395,000,000
Current Activity Level: Actively seeking new investments

MOVIDA JAPAN INC

9-5-12, Parkside 6 Suite 301
Minato-Ku, Akasaka
Tokyo, Japan 107-0052
Phone: 81368633782
E-mail: info@movidainc.com
Website: www.movidainc.com

Management and Staff
Shin Matsumura, Chief Operating Officer
Toshiyuki Oma, Chief Financial Officer

Type of Firm
Incubator/Development Program

Association Membership
Japan Venture Capital Association

Project Preferences

Type of Financing Preferred:
Seed
Startup

Geographical Preferences

International Preferences:
Asia
Japan

Industry Preferences

In Communications prefer:
Wireless Communications

In Computer Hardware prefer:
Integrated Turnkey System

In Internet Specific prefer:
Internet

Additional Information
Year Founded: 2009
Current Activity Level: Actively seeking new investments

MOVIPART BV

De Gorzen 5
Groot-Ammers, Netherlands 2964 AA
Phone: 31184661266
Fax: 31184661785

Type of Firm
Private Equity Firm

Project Preferences

Type of Financing Preferred:
Balanced

Size of Investments Considered:
Min Size of Investment Considered (000s): $352,063
Max Size of Investment Considered: No Limit

Geographical Preferences

International Preferences:
Netherlands

Additional Information
Year Founded: 2004
Current Activity Level: Reducing investment activity

MP HEALTHCARE VENTURE MANAGEMENT INC

33 Arch Street
Suite 2202
Boston, MA USA 02110
Phone: 6177374690
Fax: 6177374695
E-mail: MPH-Web@mp-healthcare.com
Website: www.mp-healthcare.com

Management and Staff
Jeffrey Moore, President
Tak Mukohira, President

Type of Firm
Private Equity Firm

Project Preferences

Type of Financing Preferred:
Early Stage
Balanced
Later Stage
Seed

Geographical Preferences

United States Preferences:
North America

International Preferences:
Europe

Industry Preferences

In Medical/Health prefer:
Medical Diagnostics
Medical Products

Additional Information
Year Founded: 2006
Capital Under Management: $100,000,000
Current Activity Level: Actively seeking new investments

MPK EQUITY PARTNERS LLC

3000 Turtle Creek Boulevard
Dallas, TX USA 75219
Fax: 2142385800
Website: www.mpkequitypartners.com

Management and Staff
Douglas Kennealey, Managing Partner
Nick Huerta, Vice President
Patrick McGee, Managing Partner

Type of Firm
Private Equity Firm

Project Preferences

Type of Financing Preferred:
Early Stage
Generalist PE
Later Stage

Geographical Preferences

United States Preferences:

Additional Information
Year Founded: 2017
Current Activity Level: Actively seeking new investments

MPM CAPITAL LLC

450 Kendall Street
Cambridge, MA USA 02142
Phone: 6174259200
Fax: 6174259201
Website: www.mpmcapital.com

Other Offices
1901 Olathe Boulevard
MPM Heartland House
ROSEDALE, KS USA 66103

Promenadeplatz 12
Munich, Germany 80333
Phone: 49-89-43597568
Fax: 49-89-211128-128

747 SW 2nd Ave.
Suite 201
GAINESVILLE, FL USA 32601
Phone: 352-294-2715

Management and Staff
Ansbert Gadicke, Managing Director
Bard Geesaman, Managing Director
Briggs Morrison, Managing Director
Corey McCann, Principal
David Stack, Managing Director
Elizabeth Stoner, Managing Director
Gary Patou, Managing Director
George Daley, Venture Partner
Gregory Sieczkiewicz, Managing Director
H. Robert Horvitz, Venture Partner
James Scopa, Managing Director
John Vander Vort, Chief Operating Officer
Kazumi Shiosaki, Managing Director
Lauren Cauley, Chief Financial Officer
Luke Evnin, Managing Director
Mirko Scherer, Managing Director
Phil Gutry, Principal
Robert Millman, Managing Director
Sebastian Meier-Ewert, Managing Director
Todd Foley, Managing Director
Vaughn Kailian, Managing Director
William Greene, Venture Partner

Type of Firm
Private Equity Firm

Association Membership
New England Venture Capital Association
National Venture Capital Association - USA (NVCA)

Project Preferences

Type of Financing Preferred:
Early Stage
Balanced

Geographical Preferences

United States Preferences:

International Preferences:
Europe
Asia

Industry Focus
(% based on actual investment)
Biotechnology	58.0%
Medical/Health	40.8%
Computer Software and Services	0.8%
Internet Specific	0.4%
Other Products	0.0%

Additional Information
Name of Most Recent Fund: MPM SunStates Fund, L.P.
Most Recent Fund Was Raised: 02/01/2012
Year Founded: 1996
Capital Under Management: $2,581,000,000
Current Activity Level : Actively seeking new investments
Method of Compensation: Return on investment is of primary concern, do not charge fees

MPOOL BETEILIGUNGEN GMBH
Kieshecker Weg 240
Duesseldorf, Germany 40468
Phone: 492114361760
Fax: 4921143617619
E-mail: investment@mpool-group.de
Website: www.mpool-investments.de

Type of Firm
Private Equity Firm

Project Preferences

Type of Financing Preferred:
Leveraged Buyout
Acquisition
Special Situation

Additional Information
Year Founded: 2002
Current Activity Level : Actively seeking new investments

MPOWER VENTURES, L.P.
C/o MPOWER Labs
323 Congress Avenue
Austin, TX USA 78701
Phone: 512-391-9998
Website: www.mpowerlabs.com

Management and Staff
Bertrand Sosa, Partner
Jorge Vergara Madrigal, Founder

Type of Firm
Incubator/Development Program

Project Preferences

Type of Financing Preferred:
Early Stage
Seed
Startup

Geographical Preferences

International Preferences:
Bolivia
Peru
Mexico
Brazil
Colombia

Industry Preferences

In Communications prefer:
Wireless Communications

In Semiconductor/Electr prefer:
Electronics

In Financial Services prefer:
Financial Services

Additional Information
Year Founded: 2006
Capital Under Management: $15,000,000
Current Activity Level : Actively seeking new investments

MR INVESTMENT PARTNERS
845 Third Avenue
Sixth Floor
New York, NY USA 10022
Phone: 646-290-5091
Fax: 646-290-5001
Website: www.mrinvestpartners.com

Management and Staff
Christopher Roden, Principal
Richard McGinn, Principal

Type of Firm
Private Equity Firm

Project Preferences

Type of Financing Preferred:
Balanced

Industry Preferences

In Communications prefer:
Communications and Media
Media and Entertainment

Additional Information
Year Founded: 2010
Current Activity Level : Actively seeking new investments

MRM CAPITAL INC
201 East 5th street, 1201
Cincinnati, OH USA 45202
Phone: 15139290500
E-mail: info@mrmcapitalllc.com
Website: www.mrmcapitalllc.com

Type of Firm
Private Equity Firm

Project Preferences

Type of Financing Preferred:
Value-Add
Balanced

Geographical Preferences

United States Preferences:
Nevada
Arizona
Oregon
California
Colorado
Washington
Texas

Industry Preferences

In Financial Services prefer:
Real Estate

Additional Information

Year Founded: 2002
Current Activity Level : Actively seeking new investments

MSD CAPITAL LP

645 Fifth Avenue
21st Floor
New York, NY USA 10022
Phone: 2123031650
Fax: 2123031634
E-mail: investments@msdcapital.com
Website: www.msdcapital.com

Other Offices

29-30 St James's Street
London, United Kingdom SW1A 1HB
Phone: 442070702550
Fax: 442070702551

100 Wilshire Boulevard
Suite 1700
Santa Monica, CA USA 90401
Phone: 3104583600
Fax: 3104583619

Management and Staff

Andrew Hee, Partner
Barry Sholem, Partner
Brian Frank, Partner
Daniel Shuchman, Partner
Douglas Londal, Partner
Eric Rosen, Partner
Glenn Fuhrman, Managing Partner
Howard Berk, Partner
John Phelan, Managing Partner
Marc Lisker, Partner
Mei-Ying Tsai, Partner
Michael Dell, Founder
Robert Platek, Partner

Type of Firm

Investment Management Firm

Project Preferences

Type of Financing Preferred:
Leveraged Buyout
Mezzanine
Management Buyouts
Acquisition

Additional Information

Year Founded: 1998
Current Activity Level : Actively seeking new investments

MSI CAPITAL PARTNERS LLC

555 Michelle Lane
Collegeville, PA USA 19426

Type of Firm

Private Equity Firm

Project Preferences

Type of Financing Preferred:
Leveraged Buyout
Recapitalizations

Geographical Preferences

United States Preferences:
North America

Additional Information

Year Founded: 2017
Current Activity Level : Actively seeking new investments

MSOUTH EQUITY PARTNERS LLC

3050 Peachtree Road NorthWest
Suite 550, Two Buckhead Plaza
Atlanta, GA USA 30305
Phone: 4048163255
Fax: 4048163258
E-mail: info@msouth.com
Website: www.msouth.com

Management and Staff

Barry Boniface, Partner
Bart McLean, Co-Founder
Mark Feidler, Co-Founder
Michael Long, Co-Founder
Peter Pettit, Partner
Wanda Morgan, Chief Financial Officer

Type of Firm

Private Equity Firm

Project Preferences

Type of Financing Preferred:
Leveraged Buyout
Recapitalizations

Geographical Preferences

United States Preferences:
Southeast

Industry Preferences

In Business Serv. prefer:
Services

In Manufact. prefer:
Manufacturing

Additional Information

Name of Most Recent Fund: MSouth Equity Partners II, L.P.
Most Recent Fund Was Raised: 08/03/2011
Year Founded: 2006
Capital Under Management: $700,000,000
Current Activity Level : Actively seeking new investments

MTH VENTURES

c/o Macdonald T. Haskell
Ponte Vedra Beach, FL USA 32004
Website: www.phoenixbiotechnology.com/board_of_directors

Type of Firm

Private Equity Firm

Additional Information

Year Founded: 2015
Current Activity Level : Actively seeking new investments

MTI PARTNERS LTD

Victoria Street
2 Victoria Square
St. Albans, United Kingdom AL1 3TF
Phone: 44177884985
Fax: 441923247783
E-mail: headoffice@mtifirms.com
Website: www.mtifirms.com

Other Offices

303 Wyman Street
Suite 300
WALTHAM, MA USA 02451
Phone: 1 781 530 3777
Fax: 1 781 530 3600

Manchester Incubator Building
48 Grafton Street
Manchester, United Kingdom M13 9XX
Phone: 44 161 603 7769
Fax: 44 161 241 5411

Management and Staff

David Holbrook, General Partner
David Ward, Managing Partner
Jayne Chase, Venture Partner
Ray Sangster, Venture Partner
Richard Henderson, Managing Partner

Type of Firm

Private Equity Firm

Association Membership

British Venture Capital Association (BVCA)

Project Preferences

Role in Financing:
Prefer role as deal originator but will also invest in deals created by others

Type of Financing Preferred:
Early Stage
Balanced
Seed

Geographical Preferences

United States Preferences:

International Preferences:
United Kingdom
Europe

Industry Focus

(% based on actual investment)
Computer Software and Services	30.6%
Industrial/Energy	27.1%
Medical/Health	12.3%
Semiconductors/Other Elect.	12.3%
Communications and Media	8.2%
Internet Specific	7.2%
Biotechnology	2.1%
Other Products	0.1%

Additional Information

Name of Most Recent Fund: Orion Fund, The
Most Recent Fund Was Raised: 02/01/2012
Year Founded: 1983
Capital Under Management: $359,000,000
Current Activity Level : Actively seeking new investments
Method of Compensation: Return on invest. most important, but chg. closing fees, service fees, etc.

MTM CAPITAL PARTNERS LTD

42 Brook Street
London, United Kingdom W1K 5DB
Phone: 44-207-144-1155
Fax: 44-207-629-6966
E-mail: mail@mtmcapital.com
Website: www.mtmcapital.com

Management and Staff

James Adams, Managing Director
Michael Acland, Managing Director

Type of Firm

Private Equity Firm

Project Preferences

Type of Financing Preferred:
Balanced

Geographical Preferences

International Preferences:
China

Industry Preferences

In Industrial/Energy prefer:
Energy
Environmental Related

Additional Information

Year Founded: 2003
Current Activity Level : Actively seeking new investments

MTN CAPITAL PARTNERS LLC

489 Fifth Avenue
21st Floor
New York, NY USA 10017
Phone: 2124002670
Fax: 2129861781
Website: www.mtncapital.com

Management and Staff

Dan Negrea, Managing Partner
Ivan Lustig, Managing Director
Olivier Trouveroy, Co-Founder
Pierre Dahmani, Managing Director
Steven Ross, Managing Director
Wendy Gallagher, Vice President

Type of Firm

Private Equity Firm

Project Preferences

Type of Financing Preferred:
Leveraged Buyout
Distressed Debt

Geographical Preferences

United States Preferences:
North America

International Preferences:
Aruba

Industry Preferences

In Communications prefer:
Telecommunications

In Consumer Related prefer:
Food/Beverage
Consumer Products

In Business Serv. prefer:
Services
Media

In Manufact. prefer:
Manufacturing

Additional Information

Year Founded: 2003
Current Activity Level : Actively seeking new investments

MTS HEALTH PARTNERS LP

623 Fifth Avenue, 14th Floor
New York, NY USA 10022
Phone: 2128872100
Fax: 2128872111
E-mail: info@mtspartners.com
Website: www.mtspartners.com

Other Offices

3200 Park Center Drive
Suite 1160
Costa Mesa, CA USA 92626
Phone: 714-427-0499
Fax: 714-427-0409

Management and Staff

Alexander Buzik, Principal
Andrew Weisenfeld, Senior Managing Director
Andrew Fineberg, Managing Director
Beth Steinberg, Chief Operating Officer
Bradley Sitko, Vice President
Christopher Burnes, Vice President
Curtis Lane, Senior Managing Director
Jay Shiland, Senior Managing Director
Kazuki Kusaka, Partner
Margarita Cervone, Chief Financial Officer
Mark Epstein, Senior Managing Director
Oliver Moses, Senior Managing Director
Peter Collum, Managing Director
Peter Crowley, Senior Managing Director
Sooin Kwon, Managing Director
Vince Lambert, Senior Managing Director
Vishal Gandhi, Vice President
William Stitt, Partner

Type of Firm

Bank Affiliated

Project Preferences

Role in Financing:
Will function either as deal originator or investor in deals created by others

Type of Financing Preferred:
Leveraged Buyout
Later Stage
Management Buyouts
Acquisition
Recapitalizations

Size of Investments Considered:
Min Size of Investment Considered (000s): $1,500
Max Size of Investment Considered (000s): $1,500

Geographical Preferences

United States Preferences:

Industry Focus

(% based on actual investment)
Medical/Health	90.7%
Internet Specific	9.3%

Additional Information

Name of Most Recent Fund: MTS Health Investors III, L.P.
Most Recent Fund Was Raised: 02/27/2013
Year Founded: 2000
Capital Under Management: $80,000,000
Current Activity Level : Actively seeking new investments
Method of Compensation: Return on invest. most important, but chg. closing fees, service fees, etc.

MUBADALA INFRASTRUCTURE PARTNERS LTD

PO Box 45023, Al Sila Tower 1
15th Floor Sowah Square
Abu Dhabi, Utd. Arab Em.
Phone: 97124174200
Fax: 97124174300
E-mail: info@mip.ae
Website: www.mip.ae

Management and Staff
Abdul Karim Al Jazzar, Principal
Oluwakemi Abdul, Principal
Osman Qureshi, Chief Financial Officer
Philip Haddad, Chief Executive Officer

Type of Firm
Private Equity Firm

Project Preferences

Type of Financing Preferred:
Unknown

Geographical Preferences

International Preferences:
Turkey
Middle East
Africa

Industry Preferences

In Communications prefer:
Telecommunications

In Industrial/Energy prefer:
Energy

In Transportation prefer:
Transportation

Additional Information
Year Founded: 2009
Capital Under Management: $500,000,000
Current Activity Level : Actively seeking new investments

MUCKERLAB LLC

202 Bicknell Avenue
Santa Monica, CA USA 90405
Phone: 6508435000

Management and Staff
Erik Rannala, Co-Founder
William Hsu, Co-Founder

Type of Firm
Incubator/Development Program

Project Preferences

Type of Financing Preferred:
Early Stage
Seed
Startup

Geographical Preferences

United States Preferences:
Nevada
Southern California
California

Industry Preferences

In Communications prefer:
Wireless Communications
Media and Entertainment

In Computer Software prefer:
Software
Systems Software
Applications Software

In Internet Specific prefer:
Internet
Ecommerce

In Financial Services prefer:
Financial Services

In Business Serv. prefer:
Media

Additional Information
Year Founded: 2011
Capital Under Management: $45,400,000
Current Activity Level : Actively seeking new investments

MUELLER MOEHL GROUP

Weinplatz 10
Zurich, Switzerland 8022
Phone: 41433446666
Fax: 41433446660
E-mail: e-mail@mm-grp.com
Website: www.mm-grp.com

Management and Staff
Christophe Rouvinez, Chief Executive Officer

Type of Firm
Private Equity Firm

Association Membership
Swiss Venture Capital Association (SECA)

Project Preferences

Type of Financing Preferred:
Balanced
Acquisition

Geographical Preferences

International Preferences:
Italy
Switzerland
Austria
Germany
France

Industry Preferences

In Consumer Related prefer:
Education Related

In Other prefer:
Socially Responsible
Women/Minority-Owned Bus.

Additional Information
Year Founded: 2000
Current Activity Level : Actively seeking new investments

MULLER & MONROE ASSET MANAGEMENT LLC

180 North Stetson Avenue
Suite 1320
Chicago, IL USA 60601
Phone: 312-782-7771
Fax: 312-782-9290
E-mail: info@m2am.com
Website: www.m2am.com

Management and Staff
Alfred Sharp, Principal
Andre Rice, President, Founder
Marcia Markowitz, Principal
Shannon Warland, Chief Financial Officer

Type of Firm
Private Equity Advisor or Fund of Funds

Association Membership
Natl Assoc of Investment Cos. (NAIC)

Project Preferences

Type of Financing Preferred:
Fund of Funds
Fund of Funds of Second

Additional Information
Name of Most Recent Fund: M2 Private Equity Fund-of-Funds II, L.P.
Most Recent Fund Was Raised: 03/10/2014
Year Founded: 1999
Capital Under Management: $302,510,000
Current Activity Level : Actively seeking new investments

MULTICAPITAL DO BRASIL CONSULTORIA E PARTICIPACOES

Rua Visconde de Piraja 414
Sala 401
Rio de Janeiro, Brazil 22410002
Phone: 552122877819
Fax: 552122876921
Website: www.multi-k.com

Other Offices
Avenida Reboucas
1511, sl 83
Sao Paulo - SP, Brazil 05401-200
Phone: 55-11-3062-7915

Management and Staff
Roberto Hesketh, Managing Director

Type of Firm
Private Equity Firm

Project Preferences

Type of Financing Preferred:
Expansion
Acquisition
Startup

Geographical Preferences

International Preferences:
Brazil

Industry Preferences

In Computer Other prefer:
Computer Related

In Biotechnology prefer:
Biotechnology

In Medical/Health prefer:
Medical/Health

In Industrial/Energy prefer:
Energy

Additional Information
Year Founded: 1987
Current Activity Level : Actively seeking new investments

MULTICROISSANCE SAS

33-43 avenue Georges Pompidou
Balma, France 31135
Phone: 33561614401
Website: multicroissance.fr

Other Offices
Avenue Maryse Bastie
Camp La Courbisie
Cahors, France 46000

Type of Firm
Bank Affiliated

Association Membership
French Venture Capital Association (AFIC)

Project Preferences

Type of Financing Preferred:
Leveraged Buyout
Generalist PE
Later Stage
Acquisition

Geographical Preferences

International Preferences:
Europe
France

Additional Information
Year Founded: 1987
Current Activity Level : Actively seeking new investments

MULTIPLES ALTERNATE ASSET MANAGEMENT PVT LTD

Dr Annie Besant Road, Worli
7F 701A Poonam Chambers B Wing
Mumbai, India 400 018
Phone: 912266245500
E-mail: info@multiplesequity.com
Website: www.multiplesequity.com

Management and Staff
Renuka Ramnath, Founder

Type of Firm
Private Equity Firm

Association Membership
Indian Venture Capital Association (IVCA)

Project Preferences

Type of Financing Preferred:
Leveraged Buyout
Later Stage
Management Buyouts
Acquisition

Geographical Preferences

International Preferences:
India

Industry Preferences

In Medical/Health prefer:
Medical/Health

In Consumer Related prefer:
Retail
Other Restaurants

In Transportation prefer:
Transportation

In Financial Services prefer:
Financial Services

Additional Information
Year Founded: 2009
Capital Under Management: $1,410,600,000
Current Activity Level : Actively seeking new investments

MULTIPLIER CAPITAL LP

815 Moraga Drive
Brentwood, CA USA 90049
Website: www.multipliercapital.com

Other Offices
2 Wisconsin Circle
Suite 700
Chevy Chase, MD USA 20815

444 Madison Avenue
Suite 1800
New York, NY USA 10022

Management and Staff
Ezra Friedberg, General Partner
Henry O Connor, General Partner
Kevin Sheehan, Co-Founder
Ray Boone, Co-Founder

Type of Firm
Private Equity Firm

Project Preferences

Type of Financing Preferred:
Mezzanine

Size of Investments Considered:
Min Size of Investment Considered (000s): $3,000
Max Size of Investment Considered (000s): $15,000

Industry Preferences

In Communications prefer:
Communications and Media

In Internet Specific prefer:
Internet
Ecommerce

In Consumer Related prefer:
Consumer Products
Consumer Services

Additional Information
Year Founded: 2012
Capital Under Management: $497,512,000
Current Activity Level : Actively seeking new investments

1453

MULVERHILL ASSOCIATES

PO Box 31303
Dubai, Utd. Arab Em.
Phone: 971-4-319-9235
E-mail: info@mulverhillassociates.com
Website: www.mulverhillassociates.com

Management and Staff
Jonathan Hall, Founder

Type of Firm
Investment Management Firm

Project Preferences

Type of Financing Preferred:
Early Stage
Balanced
Later Stage
Seed

Geographical Preferences

International Preferences:
Middle East
Africa

Industry Preferences

In Financial Services prefer:
Investment Groups

In Business Serv. prefer:
Consulting Services

Additional Information
Year Founded: 2010
Current Activity Level : Actively seeking new investments

MUNHWA INVESTMENT

93-52 Buckchang-dong
2/F, JinheungKumgo Bldg.
Gwangju, South Korea 506-050
Phone: 82-2-773-6810
Fax: 82-2-773-6818
Website: www.munhwainvest.com

Other Offices
93-52, Bukchang-Dong, Jung-Gu
Seoul, South Korea

Management and Staff
Un Tae Kim, President

Type of Firm
Bank Affiliated

Association Membership
Korean Venture Capital Association (KVCA)

Project Preferences

Type of Financing Preferred:
Early Stage
Mezzanine
Balanced
Turnaround
Acquisition

Geographical Preferences

International Preferences:
Korea, South

Industry Preferences

In Communications prefer:
Telecommunications

In Internet Specific prefer:
Internet

In Semiconductor/Electr prefer:
Electronics
Semiconductor

In Biotechnology prefer:
Biotechnology
Human Biotechnology

In Medical/Health prefer:
Medical/Health

Additional Information
Year Founded: 1987
Current Activity Level : Actively seeking new investments

MURCIA EMPRENDE SCR DE REGIMEN SIMPLIFICADO SA

C/ Jacobo de las Leyes n 12
planta baja
Murcia, Spain 30001
Phone: 34-968-205-051
Fax: 34-968-205-052
Website: www.murciaemprende.com

Type of Firm
Private Equity Firm

Association Membership
Spanish Venture Capital Association (ASCRI)

Project Preferences

Type of Financing Preferred:
Balanced
Later Stage

Size of Investments Considered:
Min Size of Investment Considered (000s): $60
Max Size of Investment Considered (000s): $150

Geographical Preferences

International Preferences:
Europe
No Preference
Spain

Additional Information
Year Founded: 2006
Capital Under Management: $5,521,000
Current Activity Level : Actively seeking new investments

MUREX INVESTMENTS, INC.

4700 Wissahickon Avenue
Suite 126
Philadelphia, PA USA 19144
Phone: 2159517200
Website: www.murexinvests.com

Management and Staff
Jacob Gray, Managing Partner
Joel Steiker, Managing Partner
Michael Forman, Founder

Type of Firm
SBIC

Association Membership
Community Development Venture Capital Alliance

Project Preferences

Role in Financing:
Will function either as deal originator or investor in deals created by others

Type of Financing Preferred:
Early Stage
Expansion
Balanced

Size of Investments Considered:
Min Size of Investment Considered (000s): $500
Max Size of Investment Considered (000s): $2,000

Geographical Preferences

United States Preferences:
Mid Atlantic

Industry Preferences

In Computer Software prefer:
Software

In Industrial/Energy prefer:
Energy

In Financial Services prefer:
Financial Services

Additional Information
Year Founded: 2003
Capital Under Management: $13,800,000

Current Activity Level : Actively seeking new investments
Method of Compensation: Return on investment is of primary concern, do not charge fees

MURPHREE VENTURE PARTNERS

1100 Louisiana
Suite 5005
Houston, TX USA 77002
Phone: 7136558500
Fax: 7136558503
Website: www.murphreeventures.com

Other Offices

2005 10th Street
Suite D
BOULDER, CO USA 80302
Phone: 303-413-1264
Fax: 303-413-1266

820 Shades Creek Parkway
Suite 3100
BIRMINGHAM, AL USA 35209
Phone: 205-870-8050
Fax: 205-870-8052

9600 Great Hills Trail
Suite 300E
BALCONES, TX USA 78759
Phone: 512-241-8100
Fax: 512-241-8001

Management and Staff

Dennis Murphree, Managing Partner
John White, General Partner
Steven Dauphin, General Partner

Type of Firm

Private Equity Firm

Project Preferences

Role in Financing:
Prefer role as deal originator but will also invest in deals created by others

Type of Financing Preferred:
Early Stage
Balanced
Start-up Financing
Seed
First Stage Financing

Size of Investments Considered:
Min Size of Investment Considered (000s): $2,000
Max Size of Investment Considered (000s): $10,000

Geographical Preferences

United States Preferences:
Southeast
Southwest

Industry Focus

(% based on actual investment)
Computer Software and Services 34.4%
Industrial/Energy 33.5%
Internet Specific 13.8%
Semiconductors/Other Elect. 13.2%
Consumer Related 2.3%
Medical/Health 2.2%
Computer Hardware 0.3%
Biotechnology 0.2%
Communications and Media 0.1%

Additional Information

Name of Most Recent Fund: MVP Growth Equity Fund II, L.P.
Most Recent Fund Was Raised: 06/13/2008
Year Founded: 1989
Capital Under Management: $46,400,000
Current Activity Level : Actively seeking new investments
Method of Compensation: Return on investment is of primary concern, do not charge fees

MURRAY CAPITAL LTD

Murray + Company House
5th Floor, 133 Victoria Street
Christchurch, New Zealand 8013
Phone: 6433778838
Fax: 6433778839
E-mail: info@murrays.co.nz
Website: www.murraycapital.co.nz

Management and Staff

Justin Murray, Managing Director

Type of Firm

Bank Affiliated

Project Preferences

Type of Financing Preferred:
Leveraged Buyout
Mezzanine
Management Buyouts
Acquisition
Recapitalizations

Geographical Preferences

International Preferences:
New Zealand

Additional Information

Name of Most Recent Fund: Rakaia Fund
Most Recent Fund Was Raised: 12/18/2009
Year Founded: 2009
Capital Under Management: $15,000,000
Current Activity Level : Actively seeking new investments

MURU-D

Level 9, 175 Liverpool Street
Sydney, Australia 2000
Website: muru-d.com

Type of Firm

Incubator/Development Program

Project Preferences

Type of Financing Preferred:
Startup

Geographical Preferences

International Preferences:
Australia
Singapore

Additional Information

Year Founded: 2014
Current Activity Level : Actively seeking new investments

MUSHARAKA VENTURE MANAGEMENT SDN BHD

9-2, Platinum Walk
2 Jalan Langkawi, Setapak
Kuala Lumpur, Malaysia 53300
Phone: 603-4142-7285
Fax: 603-4143-6346

Management and Staff

Encik Nor Idzam Yaakub, Managing Director

Type of Firm

Government Affiliated Program

Project Preferences

Type of Financing Preferred:
Early Stage
Expansion
Mezzanine
Generalist PE
Management Buyouts
Acquisition
Startup

Geographical Preferences

International Preferences:
Malaysia

Industry Preferences

In Communications prefer:
Communications and Media

Additional Information

Year Founded: 2008
Capital Under Management: $10,800,000
Current Activity Level : Actively seeking new investments

MUSTANG GROUP LLC

339 Auburn Street
Suite 12
Auburndale, MA USA 02466
Phone: 6174676800
Fax: 6174676801
E-mail: info@mustanggroup.com
Website: www.mustanggroup.com

Management and Staff
Ben Coes, Managing Partner
Bob Crowley, Managing Partner
Carson Biederman, Managing Partner
Stephen Owen, Principal

Type of Firm
Private Equity Firm

Project Preferences

Type of Financing Preferred:
Expansion
Later Stage
Management Buyouts
Recapitalizations

Industry Preferences

In Communications prefer:
Communications and Media

In Consumer Related prefer:
Entertainment and Leisure
Retail
Consumer Products
Consumer Services

In Transportation prefer:
Transportation

In Financial Services prefer:
Financial Services

In Manufact. prefer:
Manufacturing

Additional Information
Year Founded: 2003
Current Activity Level : Actively seeking new investments

MUSTARD SEED IMPACT LTD

13 Cope Place
London, United Kingdom W8 6AA
E-mail: info@mustardseedimpact.com

Type of Firm
Private Equity Firm

Project Preferences

Type of Financing Preferred:
Early Stage
Seed

Additional Information
Year Founded: 1969
Current Activity Level : Actively seeking new investments

MUTARES AG

Uhlandstrasse 3
Munich, Germany 80336
Phone: 498992927760
Fax: 4989929277622
Website: www.mutares.de

Management and Staff
Mark Friedrich, Chief Financial Officer
Wolf Cornelius, Chief Operating Officer

Type of Firm
Private Equity Firm

Association Membership
German Venture Capital Association (BVK)

Project Preferences

Type of Financing Preferred:
Leveraged Buyout
Acquisition

Geographical Preferences

International Preferences:
Europe
Germany
Africa
France

Additional Information
Year Founded: 2008
Current Activity Level : Actively seeking new investments

MUTUAL CAPITAL PARTNERS

5805 Bridge Avenue
Cleveland, OH USA 44102
Phone: 2169281908
Website: www.mutualcapitalpartners.com

Management and Staff
Wayne Wallace, Co-Founder
William Trainor, Co-Founder

Type of Firm
Private Equity Firm

Project Preferences

Role in Financing:
Will function either as deal originator or investor in deals created by others

Type of Financing Preferred:
Early Stage
Expansion
Balanced
Later Stage

Geographical Preferences

United States Preferences:
Midwest

Industry Preferences

In Computer Software prefer:
Software

In Medical/Health prefer:
Medical/Health

Additional Information
Name of Most Recent Fund: Mutual Capital Partners Fund II, L.P.
Most Recent Fund Was Raised: 02/04/2011
Year Founded: 2005
Capital Under Management: $40,263,900,000
Current Activity Level : Actively seeking new investments

MV HOLDING AS

Gulbahar sokak, No:14 Kat:10
KVK Plaza, Bayar caddesi
Istanbul, Turkey 34742
Website: www.mvholding.com.tr

Type of Firm
Private Equity Firm

Project Preferences

Type of Financing Preferred:
Balanced

Geographical Preferences

International Preferences:
Turkey

Industry Preferences

In Communications prefer:
Telecommunications

In Medical/Health prefer:
Hospital/Other Instit.

In Industrial/Energy prefer:
Energy

In Business Serv. prefer:
Media

Additional Information
Year Founded: 1993
Current Activity Level : Actively seeking new investments

MVC CAPITAL INC

287 Bowman Avenue
Second Floor
Purchase, NY USA 10577
Phone: 9147010310
Fax: 9147010315
Website: www.mvccapital.com

Management and Staff

Christopher Sullivan, Managing Director
Jaclyn Shapiro-Rothchild, Vice President
James Lynch, Managing Director
James O Connor, Managing Director
John Kelly, Vice President
Puneet Sanan, Managing Director
Scott Schuenke, Chief Financial Officer
Shivani Khurana, Managing Director

Type of Firm

Incubator/Development Program

Association Membership

Illinois Venture Capital Association

Project Preferences

Role in Financing:
Prefer role as deal originator but will also invest in deals created by others

Type of Financing Preferred:
Leveraged Buyout
Expansion
Balanced
Public Companies
Turnaround
Management Buyouts
Acquisition
Recapitalizations

Size of Investments Considered:
Min Size of Investment Considered (000s): $3,000
Max Size of Investment Considered (000s): $25,000

Geographical Preferences

United States Preferences:
All U.S.

Industry Focus

(% based on actual investment)

Industry	%
Internet Specific	37.0%
Other Products	24.9%
Computer Software and Services	15.6%
Medical/Health	6.5%
Communications and Media	5.8%
Consumer Related	5.2%
Industrial/Energy	3.6%
Computer Hardware	1.5%

Additional Information

Year Founded: 1999
Capital Under Management: $117,000,000
Current Activity Level: Actively seeking new investments

MVI ITALIA SRL

Via Santa Marta 19
Milan, Italy 20123
Phone: 39-02720-93833
Fax: 39-02720-15230
E-mail: info@mvi.it

Type of Firm

Private Equity Firm

Project Preferences

Size of Investments Considered:
Min Size of Investment Considered (000s): $191
Max Size of Investment Considered (000s): $6,351

Additional Information

Year Founded: 2006
Capital Under Management: $1,600,000
Current Activity Level: Actively seeking new investments

MVI SUPPORT SA

Master Samuelsgatan 42
4th floor
Stockholm, Sweden 11157
E-mail: assist@mvisupport.ch

Other Offices

19-20 Woodstock Street
London, United Kingdom W1C 2AN
Phone: 44-207-016-5242
Fax: 44-207-491-1935

Fredrikinkatu 48 A
11th FL.
Helsinki, Finland 00100
Phone: 358-9-6869-2250
Fax: 358-9-6869-2241

Kungstradgarden
Stockholm, Sweden 111 47
Phone: 46-8-5246-3104

Type of Firm

Private Equity Firm

Project Preferences

Type of Financing Preferred:
Leveraged Buyout
Later Stage
Management Buyouts

Size of Investments Considered:
Min Size of Investment Considered (000s): $739
Max Size of Investment Considered (000s): $5,914

Geographical Preferences

International Preferences:
Sweden
United Kingdom
Europe
Switzerland
Scandanavia/Nordic Region

Industry Preferences

In Consumer Related prefer:
Consumer Products
Consumer Services

Additional Information

Year Founded: 1984
Current Activity Level: Actively seeking new investments

MVM PARTNERS LLP

Six Henrietta Street
London, United Kingdom WC2E 8PU
Phone: 442075577500
Fax: 442075577501
Website: www.mvm.com

Other Offices

45 School Street
Old City Hall
Boston, MA USA 02108
Phone: 617-383-2101
Fax: 617-383-2106

Management and Staff

Alexander Pasteur, Partner
Bosun Hau, Partner
Eric Bednarski, Partner
Hugo Harrod, Partner
Martin Murphy, Partner
Neil Akhurst, Partner
Stephen Reeders, Partner
Thomas Casdagli, Partner

Type of Firm

Private Equity Firm

Project Preferences

Type of Financing Preferred:
Early Stage
Balanced
Later Stage

Size of Investments Considered:
Min Size of Investment Considered (000s): $8,123
Max Size of Investment Considered (000s): $24,369

Geographical Preferences

United States Preferences:
All U.S.

International Preferences:
Europe
Israel

Industry Preferences

In Biotechnology prefer:
Biotechnology
Biotech Related Research

In Medical/Health prefer:
Medical/Health
Medical Diagnostics
Drug/Equipmt Delivery
Medical Products
Pharmaceuticals

Additional Information

Year Founded: 1997
Capital Under Management: $500,000,000
Current Activity Level : Actively seeking new investments

MVP CAPITAL LLC

244 Jackson Street
Fourth Floor
San Francisco, CA USA 94111
Phone: 4153914877
Fax: 4153914912
Website: www.mvpcapital.com

Other Offices

1800 Baltimore Avenue
Suite 300
Kansas City, MO USA 64108
Phone: 816-817-0570
Fax: 816-820-0169

75 State Street
Suite 2500
Boston, MA USA 02109
Phone: 617-345-7316
Fax: 617-507-5667

2033 11th Street
Suite Six
Boulder, CO USA 80301
Phone: 303-284-3965
Fax: 303-484-2943

Management and Staff

Bill Fanning, Vice President
Brian Pryor, Managing Director
Elliot Evers, Managing Director
Greg Widroe, Managing Director
Jason Hill, Managing Director
Jason Nicolay, Vice President
Paul Stapleton, Managing Director
R. Clayton Funk, Managing Director
Tim Beach, Vice President

Type of Firm

Bank Affiliated

Project Preferences

Role in Financing:
Prefer role as deal originator but will also invest in deals created by others

Type of Financing Preferred:
Balanced

Geographical Preferences

United States Preferences:

Industry Preferences

In Communications prefer:
Telecommunications

In Business Serv. prefer:
Media

Additional Information

Year Founded: 1987
Current Activity Level : Actively seeking new investments
Method of Compensation: Return on investment is of primary concern, do not charge fees

MVP MANAGEMENT GMBH

Hansastrasse 40
Munich, Germany 80686
Phone: 498920001230
Fax: 4989200012329
E-mail: info@munichvp.com
Website: www.munichvp.de

Management and Staff

Martin Kroener, Partner
Michael Sailer, Chief Financial Officer
Rolf Nagel, Partner
Soenke Mehrgardt, Partner
Walter Grassl, Partner

Type of Firm

Private Equity Firm

Project Preferences

Type of Financing Preferred:
Early Stage
Later Stage
Seed
Startup

Geographical Preferences

International Preferences:
Germany

Industry Preferences

In Communications prefer:
Communications and Media

In Semiconductor/Electr prefer:
Semiconductor

In Industrial/Energy prefer:
Energy
Materials
Environmental Related

Additional Information

Name of Most Recent Fund: Munich Venture Partners II
Most Recent Fund Was Raised: 06/28/2011
Year Founded: 2005
Capital Under Management: $100,575,000
Current Activity Level : Actively seeking new investments

MW CAPITAL INC

800 Fifth Avenue
Suite 101-588
Seattle, WA USA 98104
Phone: 2063742753
E-mail: BusinessPlan@MWCapital.net
Website: www.mwcapital.net

Other Offices

Dun Hua South Road, Section 2
13F-1, No. 76
Taipei, China 106
Phone: 886-2-2701-2878
Fax: 886-2-2702-1169

Management and Staff

Sherry Wangli, Chief Executive Officer

Type of Firm

Private Equity Firm

Project Preferences

Type of Financing Preferred:
Balanced
Later Stage

Geographical Preferences

United States Preferences:
West Coast

International Preferences:
Taiwan
China

Industry Preferences

In Communications prefer:
Wireless Communications

In Semiconductor/Electr prefer:
Semiconductor

In Medical/Health prefer:
Medical Products
Health Services

In Industrial/Energy prefer:
Environmental Related

Additional Information

Year Founded: 1998
Current Activity Level : Actively seeking new investments

MYO CAPITAL ADVISERS LTD

9/F, The Workstation
43 Lyndhurst Terrace
Central, Hong Kong
E-mail: info@myocap.com
Website: www.myocap.com

Type of Firm
Investment Management Firm

Project Preferences

Type of Financing Preferred:
Special Situation
Distressed Debt

Geographical Preferences

International Preferences:
Indonesia
China
Australia
Asia

Additional Information
Year Founded: 2010
Capital Under Management: $150,000,000
Current Activity Level : Actively seeking new investments

MYONIC HOLDING GMBH

Koenigstrasse 10c
Stuttgart, Germany 70173
Phone: 49711892007200
Fax: 49711892007501
E-mail: info@suedbg.de

Management and Staff
Christian Vogel, Managing Director
Joachim Hug, Managing Director
Joachim Erdle, Managing Director
Juergen Prockl, Managing Director

Type of Firm
Bank Affiliated

Association Membership
German Venture Capital Association (BVK)

Project Preferences

Type of Financing Preferred:
Fund of Funds
Early Stage
Turnaround
Later Stage
Seed
Management Buyouts
Startup
Recapitalizations

Geographical Preferences

International Preferences:
Germany

Additional Information
Year Founded: 2009
Current Activity Level : Actively seeking new investments

MYRISOPH CAPITAL

Dubai Healthcare City
Al Razi Complex 64
Dubai, Utd. Arab Em.
E-mail: info@myrisoph.com
Website: www.myrisophcapital.com

Other Offices
Dubai Healthcare City
Al Razi Complex 64
Dubai, Utd. Arab Em.

Type of Firm
Private Equity Firm

Project Preferences

Type of Financing Preferred:
Generalist PE

Geographical Preferences

International Preferences:
Saudi Arabia

Industry Preferences

In Medical/Health prefer:
Health Services

Additional Information
Year Founded: 2016
Current Activity Level : Actively seeking new investment

- N -

9MILE LABS LLC

821 2nd Avenue, Suite 800
Seattle, WA USA 98104
Website: www.9milelabs.com

Type of Firm
Incubator/Development Program

Project Preferences

Type of Financing Preferred:
Early Stage
Startup

Geographical Preferences

United States Preferences:
Northwest
All U.S.

Industry Preferences

In Computer Hardware prefer:
Integrated Turnkey System

In Computer Software prefer:
Software
Systems Software
Applications Software

Additional Information
Year Founded: 2013
Capital Under Management: $2,130,000
Current Activity Level : Actively seeking new investments

9TH STREET INVESTMENTS

700 12th Street
Golden, CO USA 80401
Phone: 7203289055
Website: 9thstreetinvestments.com

Management and Staff
Andrew Coors, Chief Financial Officer
Doug Coors, President
Mark Petty, Vice President

Type of Firm
Private Equity Firm

Project Preferences

Type of Financing Preferred:
Fund of Funds
Balanced
Acquisition

Industry Preferences

In Industrial/Energy prefer:
Advanced Materials
Environmental Related

In Manufact. prefer:
Manufacturing

Additional Information
Year Founded: 2011
Current Activity Level : Actively seeking new investments

N D B CAPITAL HOLDINGS PLC

40, NDB Building
Nawam Mawatha
Colombo, Sri Lanka 02
Phone: 941-243-7701
Fax: 941-234-1047
E-mail: boc@boc.lk
Website: www.boc.lk

Management and Staff
Joseph Cooray, Vice President
Kusal Jayawardana, Chief Operating Officer
Senaka Kakiriwaragodage, Vice President
Waruna Singappuli, Vice President

Type of Firm
Bank Affiliated

Project Preferences

Role in Financing:
Prefer role as deal originator but will also invest in deals created by others

Type of Financing Preferred:
Second Stage Financing
Balanced
Start-up Financing
First Stage Financing

Size of Investments Considered:
Min Size of Investment Considered (000s): $300
Max Size of Investment Considered (000s): $500

Geographical Preferences

International Preferences:
Pacific Rim

Industry Preferences

In Communications prefer:
Communications and Media
Telecommunications

In Computer Software prefer:
Computer Services
Systems Software

In Internet Specific prefer:
Internet

In Semiconductor/Electr prefer:
Electronic Components

In Biotechnology prefer:
Biotechnology

In Medical/Health prefer:
Health Services

In Consumer Related prefer:
Consumer Services
Education Related

In Industrial/Energy prefer:
Energy
Industrial Products
Materials
Environmental Related

In Business Serv. prefer:
Media

In Manufact. prefer:
Manufacturing

Additional Information
Year Founded: 1983
Capital Under Management: $8,100,000
Current Activity Level : Actively seeking new investments
Method of Compensation: Return on investment is of primary concern, do not charge fees

NAB VENTURES

National Australia Bank
800 Bourke St
Melbourne, Australia 3008
Website: www.nab.com.au

Type of Firm
Bank Affiliated

Project Preferences

Type of Financing Preferred:
Startup

Additional Information
Year Founded: 2016
Capital Under Management: $50,000,000
Current Activity Level : Actively seeking new investments

NADATHUR ESTATES PVT LTD

Plot No. 23, 8th Main Road
3rd Floor, Nadathur Place
Bangalore, India 560 011
Phone: 918066709900
Fax: 918066709901
E-mail: info@nadathur.com
Website: www.nadathur.com

Other Offices
71A Amoy Street
Singapore, Singapore 069890
Phone: 65-6595-9350
Fax: 65-6220-3642

Management and Staff
Nadathur Raghavan, Founder
Vishal Jain, Chief Executive Officer

Type of Firm
Private Equity Firm

Project Preferences

Type of Financing Preferred:
Early Stage
Start-up Financing
Later Stage
Seed

Geographical Preferences

International Preferences:
India

Industry Preferences

In Communications prefer:
Wireless Communications

In Computer Software prefer:
Software

In Internet Specific prefer:
Web Aggregation/Portals

In Biotechnology prefer:
Biotechnology

In Medical/Health prefer:
Health Services

In Consumer Related prefer:
Education Related

In Transportation prefer:
Aerospace

Additional Information
Year Founded: 2000
Current Activity Level : Actively seeking new investments

NAGOYA SMALL & MEDIUM BUSINESS INVESTMENT & CONSULTATION CO.

1-16-30, Meieki Minami
7F, Tokai Building
Nagoya, Japan 450-0003
Phone: 81525819541
Fax: 81525838501
Website: www.sbic-cj.co.jp

Type of Firm
Private Equity Firm

Project Preferences

Type of Financing Preferred:
Balanced

Geographical Preferences

International Preferences:
Japan

Additional Information
Year Founded: 1963
Capital Under Management: $166,600,000
Current Activity Level : Actively seeking new investments

NALA INVESTMENTS LLC

2016 Broadway Place
Santa Monica, CA USA 90404
Phone: 3102642555
Website: nalainvestments.com

Other Offices
Bosque de Alisos 47-B 5to piso
Mexico, Mexico 05120

Type of Firm
Private Equity Firm

Project Preferences

Type of Financing Preferred:
Early Stage
Expansion
Balanced
Later Stage
Seed
Startup

Geographical Preferences

International Preferences:
Latin America

Industry Preferences

In Business Serv. prefer:
Media

Additional Information
Year Founded: 2012
Current Activity Level : Actively seeking new investments

NALANDA CAPITAL PTE LTD

65 Chulia Street
#37-03/04 OCBC Centre
Singapore, Singapore 049513
Phone: 6826 9100
Fax: 6826 9101
E-mail: bek.soh@nalandacapital.com
Website: www.nalandacapital.com

Type of Firm
Private Equity Firm

Project Preferences

Type of Financing Preferred:
Balanced

Geographical Preferences

International Preferences:
India

Additional Information
Year Founded: 2007
Current Activity Level : Actively seeking new investments

NAMUR INVEST SA

160 Avenue des Champs Elysees
Namur, Belgium 5000
Phone: 3281225903
Fax: 3281231146
E-mail: info@namurinvest.be
Website: www.namurinvest.be

Management and Staff
Jean Kluyskens, Vice President
Jean-Paul Feldbusch, President
Jean-Pierre Grimoux, Founder

Type of Firm
Private Equity Firm

Project Preferences

Type of Financing Preferred:
Early Stage
Later Stage

Geographical Preferences

International Preferences:
Europe
Belgium

Industry Preferences

In Communications prefer:
Entertainment

In Semiconductor/Electr prefer:
Electronics
Electronic Components

In Medical/Health prefer:
Medical/Health
Medical Products
Pharmaceuticals

In Consumer Related prefer:
Consumer
Food/Beverage
Consumer Services

In Agr/Forestr/Fish prefer:
Agriculture related

In Other prefer:
Environment Responsible

Additional Information
Year Founded: 2004
Current Activity Level : Actively seeking new investments

NANCY CREEK CAPITAL

2849 Paces Ferry Road
Overlook I, Suite 160
Atlanta, GA USA 30339
Phone: 6783844520
Fax: 6783844521
E-mail: info@nancycreek.com
Website: www.nancycreekcapital.com

Management and Staff

Barrington Branch, Partner
Charles Shelton, Partner
Edgar Sims, Partner
O. Scott Barfield, Principal
Steven Brannon, Principal

Type of Firm
Private Equity Firm

Project Preferences

Role in Financing:
Prefer role as deal originator but will also invest in deals created by others

Type of Financing Preferred:
Mezzanine

Size of Investments Considered:
Min Size of Investment Considered (000s): $1,000
Max Size of Investment Considered (000s): $5,000

Geographical Preferences

United States Preferences:
Southeast

Industry Preferences

In Medical/Health prefer:
Medical/Health

In Consumer Related prefer:
Consumer
Other Restaurants

In Industrial/Energy prefer:
Industrial Products

In Business Serv. prefer:
Distribution

In Manufact. prefer:
Manufacturing

Additional Information

Name of Most Recent Fund: Nancy Creek Capital II, L.P.
Most Recent Fund Was Raised: 10/26/2005
Year Founded: 2005
Capital Under Management: $70,000,000
Current Activity Level : Actively seeking new investments

NANJING HEDING VENTURE CAPITAL MANAGEMENT CO LTD

No. 268 Zhongshan Road
23/F Hui Jie Square
Nanjing, China 210008
Phone: 86-25-8657-9659
Fax: 86-25-8657-9660

Type of Firm
Private Equity Firm

Project Preferences

Type of Financing Preferred:
Expansion
Later Stage

Geographical Preferences

International Preferences:
China

Industry Preferences

In Semiconductor/Electr prefer:
Electronics

In Biotechnology prefer:
Biotechnology

In Medical/Health prefer:
Medical/Health

In Consumer Related prefer:
Education Related

In Industrial/Energy prefer:
Energy
Materials
Environmental Related

In Financial Services prefer:
Financial Services

In Business Serv. prefer:
Media

In Agr/Forestr/Fish prefer:
Agribusiness

Additional Information

Year Founded: 2009
Capital Under Management: $80,000,000
Current Activity Level : Actively seeking new investments

NANJING JUSHI VENTURE CAPITAL CO LTD

No.8 DaZhong Ting
Gu Lou Area
Nanjing, China 210008
Phone: 8683367888
Fax: 8683367377

Type of Firm
Bank Affiliated

Project Preferences

Type of Financing Preferred:
Balanced

Geographical Preferences

International Preferences:
China

Additional Information

Year Founded: 2012
Current Activity Level : Actively seeking new investments

NANJING SHARELINK INVESTMENT MANAGEMENT CO LTD

No.188, Yangtze River Rd.
F7, Deji Mansion
Nanjing, China
Phone: 862586816820
Fax: 862586816826
E-mail: vc@sharelink-vc.com
Website: www.sharelink-vc.com

Type of Firm
Private Equity Firm

Project Preferences

Type of Financing Preferred:
Leveraged Buyout
Early Stage
Seed
Startup

Geographical Preferences

International Preferences:
China

Industry Preferences

In Internet Specific prefer:
Internet

In Biotechnology prefer:
Biotechnology

In Medical/Health prefer:
Medical/Health
Diagnostic Services
Pharmaceuticals

In Consumer Related prefer:
Consumer Products
Consumer Services

In Industrial/Energy prefer:
Energy
Materials

In Manufact. prefer:
Manufacturing

Additional Information

Year Founded: 2009
Current Activity Level : Actively seeking new investments

NANJING TONGREN BODA INVESTMENT MANAGEMENT CO LTD

No. 359 Jiangdong Middle Rd.,
Room 208 Section B Block 1, Gu
Nanjing, China

Type of Firm
Investment Management Firm

Project Preferences

Type of Financing Preferred:
Balanced

Geographical Preferences

International Preferences:
China

Additional Information

Year Founded: 2015
Current Activity Level : Actively seeking new investments

NANJING WEIZHONGXIANG EQUITY INVESTMENT FUND MANAGEMENT CO

Zhujiang Road, Xuanwu District
4F, No. 280
Nanjing, China

Type of Firm
Private Equity Firm

Project Preferences

Type of Financing Preferred:
Balanced

Geographical Preferences

International Preferences:
China

Industry Preferences

In Internet Specific prefer:
Internet

In Financial Services prefer:
Financial Services

Additional Information

Year Founded: 2015
Current Activity Level : Actively seeking new investments

NANJING ZIJIN SCIENCE & TECHNOLOGY VENTURE INVESTMENT GROUP

No.8,Yulan Rd.,Yuhuatai Dist.
3 Floor, Guozi Dasha
Nanjing, China 210012
Phone: 862586579688

Type of Firm
Private Equity Firm

Project Preferences

Type of Financing Preferred:
Seed
Startup

Geographical Preferences

International Preferences:
China

Industry Preferences

In Financial Services prefer:
Financial Services

Additional Information

Year Founded: 2011
Capital Under Management: $78,700,000
Current Activity Level : Actively seeking new investments

NANODIMENSION MANAGEMENT LTD

23 Lime Tree Bay Avenue
Governor's Square, 3-213-6
Grand Cayman, Cayman Islands KY1-1302
Phone: 3459465556
Fax: 3459465558
E-mail: info@nanodimension.com
Website: www.nanodimension.com

Other Offices

Schoffelgasse 3
Zurich, Switzerland CH-8001
Phone: 41442717580
Fax: 41442717581

880 Santa Cruz Avenue, Suite 200
Menlo Park, CA USA 94025
Phone: 6502411155
Fax: 6504621155

Management and Staff
Kelly Sallin, Chief Operating Officer

Type of Firm
Private Equity Firm

Project Preferences

Type of Financing Preferred:
Early Stage
Expansion
Balanced
Later Stage
Seed
Startup

Geographical Preferences

United States Preferences:
North America

International Preferences:
Europe

Industry Preferences

In Semiconductor/Electr prefer:
Electronics

In Industrial/Energy prefer:
Energy
Materials

Additional Information

Year Founded: 2002
Capital Under Management: $50,000,000
Current Activity Level : Actively seeking new investments

NANTONG WOOFOO JINXIN INVESTMENT MANAGEMENT CO LTD

Pudong New District, Shanghai
Room 702, Block B, Changtai Pl
Shanghai, China
Website: www.woofoocapital.com

Type of Firm
Private Equity Firm

Project Preferences

Type of Financing Preferred:
Early Stage
Expansion

Geographical Preferences

International Preferences:
China

Industry Preferences

In Communications prefer:
Communications and Media

In Internet Specific prefer:
Internet

In Financial Services prefer:
Financial Services

1463

NAPIER PARK GLOBAL CAPITAL (US) LP

280 Park Avenue
Third Floor
New York, NY USA 10022
Phone: 2122350700
E-mail: IR@napierparkglobal.com
Website: www.napierparkglobal.com

Other Offices
DIFC Gate Building
5th Floor
Dubai, Utd. Arab Em.

Bahnhofstrasse One
Pfaffikon, Switzerland 8808

Management and Staff
James M. OBrien, Chief Executive Officer
Joseph Lane, Managing Director

Type of Firm
Investment Management Firm

Project Preferences

Type of Financing Preferred:
Leveraged Buyout
Generalist PE
Later Stage
Acquisition
Special Situation
Distressed Debt
Recapitalizations

Industry Preferences

In Financial Services prefer:
Financial Services

Additional Information
Name of Most Recent Fund: Financial Partners Fund I, L.P.
Most Recent Fund Was Raised: 11/19/2013
Year Founded: 2013
Capital Under Management: $50,995,000
Current Activity Level : Actively seeking new investments

NARODNY HOLDINGOVY FOND SRO

Nevadzova 5
Bratislava, Slovakia 821 01
Phone: 421248287413
Fax: 421248287413
E-mail: fondfondov@fondfondov.sk
Website: www.nhfond.sk

Additional Information
Year Founded: 2015
Current Activity Level : Actively seeking new investments

Other Offices
Rudohorska 33
Banska Bystrica, Slovakia 974 11
Phone: 421-48-471-6489
Fax: 421-48-471-6414

Type of Firm
Private Equity Firm

Project Preferences

Type of Financing Preferred:
Early Stage
Seed
Startup

Geographical Preferences

International Preferences:
Slovak Repub.

Industry Preferences

In Consumer Related prefer:
Consumer
Hotels and Resorts

In Industrial/Energy prefer:
Industrial Products

In Transportation prefer:
Transportation

In Business Serv. prefer:
Services

Additional Information
Year Founded: 1994
Capital Under Management: $3,500,000
Current Activity Level : Actively seeking new investments

NARRA VENTURE CAPITAL

Filinvest Corporate City
Unit 2202, 22F Asian Star Bldg
Alabang, Muntinlupa, Philippines 1781
Phone: 6325521175
Fax: 6325521177
E-mail: info@narravc.com
Website: www.narravc.com

Management and Staff
Paco Sandejas, Managing Partner

Type of Firm
Private Equity Firm

Project Preferences

Type of Financing Preferred:
Balanced

Geographical Preferences

United States Preferences:

International Preferences:
Philippines
Asia

Industry Preferences

In Communications prefer:
Communications and Media

In Computer Software prefer:
Software

In Semiconductor/Electr prefer:
Electronics
Semiconductor

Additional Information
Year Founded: 2002
Current Activity Level : Actively seeking new investments

NASCENT VENTURES BV

39, Langegracht
Maarssen, Netherlands 3601 AJ
Website: nascentventures.nl

Type of Firm
Private Equity Firm

Project Preferences

Type of Financing Preferred:
Early Stage
Seed

Geographical Preferences

International Preferences:
Netherlands

Industry Preferences

In Semiconductor/Electr prefer:
Circuit Boards
Optoelectronics

In Biotechnology prefer:
Biotechnology

In Industrial/Energy prefer:
Advanced Materials
Robotics

Additional Information
Year Founded: 2017
Current Activity Level : Actively seeking new investments

NATCITY INVESTMENTS INC

1900 East 9th Street
20th Floor
Cleveland, OH USA 44114
Phone: 216-222-2000
E-mail: resourcecenter@nationalcity.com

Management and Staff

Herbert Martens, President
Sean Dorsey, Senior Managing Director
William Haggerty, Senior Managing Director

Type of Firm

Bank Affiliated

Project Preferences

Type of Financing Preferred:
Management Buyouts
Acquisition
Recapitalizations

Geographical Preferences

United States Preferences:
Midwest

International Preferences:
All International

Additional Information

Year Founded: 1937
Current Activity Level : Actively seeking new investments

NATIONAL CITY EQUITY PARTNERS INC

1900 East Ninth Street
17th Floor
Cleveland, OH USA 44114
Phone: 2162223763
Website: www.pncerieview.com

Management and Staff

Carl Baldassarre, Managing Director
Edward Pentecost, President
Eric Morgan, Managing Director
Jay Freund, Managing Director
Steven Pattison, Managing Director

Type of Firm

Bank Affiliated

Project Preferences

Role in Financing:
Will function either as deal originator or investor in deals created by others

Type of Financing Preferred:
Expansion
Mezzanine
Generalist PE
Later Stage
Acquisition
Recapitalizations

Geographical Preferences

United States Preferences:
Midwest
North America

Industry Focus

(% based on actual investment)
Industrial/Energy	25.7%
Other Products	22.4%
Semiconductors/Other Elect.	15.3%
Consumer Related	14.4%
Internet Specific	10.1%
Medical/Health	4.6%
Biotechnology	4.1%
Communications and Media	3.2%
Computer Hardware	0.1%

Additional Information

Year Founded: 1979
Capital Under Management: $1,000,000,000
Current Activity Level : Actively seeking new investments
Method of Compensation: Return on invest. most important, but chg. closing fees, service fees, etc.

NATIONAL CORN GROWERS ASSOCIATION

632 Cepi Drive
Chesterfield, MO USA 63005
Phone: 636-733-9004
Fax: 636-733-9005
Website: www.ncga.com

Other Offices

122 C Street Northwest, Suite 510
Washington, DC USA 20001
Phone: 202-628-7001
Fax: 202-628-1933

Type of Firm

Private Equity Firm

Project Preferences

Type of Financing Preferred:
Balanced

Additional Information

Year Founded: 2004
Current Activity Level : Actively seeking new investments

NATIONAL DEVELOPMENT FUND EXECUTIVE YUAN

7F., No. 49, Guancian Rd.
Jhongjheng District, Taipei100
Taiwan, Taiwan
Phone: 886223890633
Fax: 886223890636
Website: www.df.gov.tw

Type of Firm

Government Affiliated Program

Project Preferences

Type of Financing Preferred:
Balanced

Geographical Preferences

International Preferences:
Taiwan

Additional Information

Year Founded: 1973
Current Activity Level : Actively seeking new investments

NATIONAL ENDOWMENT FOR SCIENCE TECHNOLOGY AND THE ARTS

1 Plough Place
London, United Kingdom EC4A 1DE
Phone: 442074382500
Fax: 442074382501
E-mail: information@nesta.org.uk
Website: www.nesta.org.uk

Management and Staff

Geoff Mulgan, Chief Executive Officer
Matthew Mead, Chief Financial Officer

Type of Firm

Endowment, Foundation or Pension Fund

Association Membership

British Venture Capital Association (BVCA)
European Private Equity and Venture Capital Assoc.

Project Preferences

Role in Financing:
Prefer role as deal originator

Type of Financing Preferred:
Early Stage
Later Stage
Seed
Startup

Geographical Preferences

International Preferences:
United Kingdom
Europe

Industry Preferences

In Communications prefer:
Entertainment

In Biotechnology prefer:
Human Biotechnology

In Medical/Health prefer:
Medical/Health
Diagnostic Test Products
Drug/Equipmt Delivery
Medical Products
Health Services

In Consumer Related prefer:
Ecucation Related

In Industrial/Energy prefer:
Environmental Related

In Other prefer:
Socially Responsible

Additional Information

Name of Most Recent Fund: Nest Social Investment Fund
Most Recent Fund Was Raised: 10/23/2012
Year Founded: 1998
Capital Under Management: $22,800,000
Current Activity Level : Actively seeking new investments

NATIONAL HEALTHCARE SERVICES

320 Golden Shore Avenue, Suite 120
Long Beach, CA USA 90802
Phone: 5624320047
Fax: 5624320091
Website: www.nationalhealthcareservices.com

Management and Staff

Brant Heise, Managing Director

Type of Firm

Private Equity Firm

Project Preferences

Type of Financing Preferred:
Early Stage
Later Stage

Industry Preferences

In Biotechnology prefer:
Biotechnology

In Medical/Health prefer:
Medical/Health
Medical Products
Health Services

Additional Information

Year Founded: 2002
Capital Under Management: $25,000,000
Current Activity Level : Actively seeking new investments

NATIONAL ICT R&D FUND

Jinnah Avenue, Blue Area
Sixth Floor, HBL Towers
Islamabad, Pakistan 44000
Phone: 92519215360
Fax: 92519215366
Website: www.ictrdf.org.pk

Management and Staff

Fawad Younus, Chief Executive Officer

Type of Firm

Government Affiliated Program

Project Preferences

Type of Financing Preferred:
Early Stage
Start-up Financing

Geographical Preferences

International Preferences:
Pakistan

Industry Preferences

In Communications prefer:
Telecommunications
Wireless Communications
Data Communications

Additional Information

Year Founded: 2011
Current Activity Level : Actively seeking new investments

NATIONAL INNOVATION COUNCIL

Parliament Street, Suite 125, Yojana Bhawan
New Delhi, India 110001
Phone: 911123096622
Website: www.innovationcouncil.gov.in

Type of Firm

Government Affiliated Program

Project Preferences

Type of Financing Preferred:
Early Stage
Expansion
Seed

Geographical Preferences

International Preferences:
India

Industry Preferences

In Semiconductor/Electr prefer:
Electronics

In Medical/Health prefer:
Health Services

In Consumer Related prefer:
Education Related

In Agr/Forestr/Fish prefer:
Agribusiness

Additional Information

Year Founded: 2012
Capital Under Management: $75,456,000
Current Activity Level : Actively seeking new investments

NATIONAL INVESTMENTS CO KSCP

P.O. Box 25667
Safat, Kuwait 13117
Phone: 96522266666
Fax: 96522494748
E-mail: nic@nic.com.kw
Website: www.nic.com.kw

Management and Staff

Fahad Al Mukhaizim, Chief Executive Officer

Type of Firm

Private Equity Firm

Project Preferences

Type of Financing Preferred:
Leveraged Buyout
Early Stage
Generalist PE

Industry Preferences

In Communications prefer:
Telecommunications

In Medical/Health prefer:
Hospitals/Clinics/Primary

In Financial Services prefer:
Financial Services

Additional Information

Year Founded: 1987
Current Activity Level : Actively seeking new investments

NATIONAL NET VENTURES

No 7656, Prince Mus'ad A. St.
Riyadh, Saudi Arabia 11393
Phone: 966114774245
Fax: 96612923272
Website: www.n2v.com

Management and Staff
Rashid Al Ballaa, Chief Executive Officer
Shadi Qishta, Chief Financial Officer

Type of Firm
Private Equity Firm

Association Membership
Gulf Venture Capital Association

Project Preferences

Type of Financing Preferred:
Early Stage
Balanced
Later Stage
Startup

Geographical Preferences

International Preferences:
Utd. Arab Em.
Middle East
Saudi Arabia
Asia

Industry Preferences

In Internet Specific prefer:
Internet
Web Aggregation/Portals

Additional Information
Year Founded: 2008
Current Activity Level : Actively seeking new investments

NATIONAL RESEARCH COUNCIL CANADA

1200 Montreal Road
Building M-58
Ottawa, Canada K1A 0R6
Phone: 613-993-9101
Fax: 613-952-9907
E-mail: info@nrc-cnrc.gc.ca
Website: www.nrc-cnrc.gc.ca

Type of Firm
Government Affiliated Program

Project Preferences

Type of Financing Preferred:
Expansion
Later Stage

Geographical Preferences

Canadian Preferences:
Quebec

Additional Information
Year Founded: 2004
Current Activity Level : Actively seeking new investments

NATIONS FUNDS INC

8540 Colonnade Center Drive, Suite 401
Raleigh, NC USA 27615
Phone: 9198462324
Fax: 9198463433

Management and Staff
David Perkins, Chief Executive Officer
J. Michael Fields, Chief Operating Officer
Lance Baker, Chief Financial Officer
Robert Worthington, President

Type of Firm
Investment Management Firm

Project Preferences

Type of Financing Preferred:
Fund of Funds
Leveraged Buyout
Generalist PE
Balanced
Distressed Debt

Geographical Preferences

United States Preferences:
All U.S.

International Preferences:
Europe
Asia

Additional Information
Name of Most Recent Fund: Hatteras Global Private Equity Fund II LLC
Most Recent Fund Was Raised: 06/14/2012
Year Founded: 2003
Capital Under Management: $14,389,000
Current Activity Level : Actively seeking new investments

NATIONWIDE MUTUAL CAPITAL LLC

One Nationwide Plaza
Mail Code 1-24-15
Columbus, OH USA 43215
Website: www.nationwide.com

Management and Staff
Ryan Helon, Managing Director

Type of Firm
Insurance Firm Affiliate

Project Preferences

Role in Financing:
Will function either as deal originator or investor in deals created by others

Type of Financing Preferred:
Early Stage
Balanced
Later Stage
Seed

Size of Investments Considered:
Min Size of Investment Considered (000s): $1,000
Max Size of Investment Considered (000s): $4,000

Geographical Preferences

United States Preferences:

International Preferences:
United Kingdom
Europe

Industry Preferences

In Computer Software prefer:
Data Processing
Software
Systems Software
Applications Software

In Internet Specific prefer:
Ecommerce
Web Aggregation/Portals

In Medical/Health prefer:
Health Services

In Financial Services prefer:
Financial Services
Insurance

Additional Information
Year Founded: 2002
Capital Under Management: $40,000,000
Current Activity Level : Actively seeking new investments
Method of Compensation: Return on investment is of primary concern, do not charge fees

---

NATIONWIDE VENTURES LLC

One Nationwide Plaza
Columbus, OH USA 43215
Phone: 18776696877

Management and Staff
Brian Anderson, Principal

Type of Firm
Private Equity Firm

Project Preferences

Type of Financing Preferred:
Balanced

Pratt's Guide to Private Equity & Venture Capital Sources

Geographical Preferences

United States Preferences:

Additional Information
Year Founded: 2017
Current Activity Level : Actively seeking new investments

NATIVE AMERICAN VENTURE FUND LLC

7380 Spout Spring Road Ste 210, Suite 209
Flowery Branch, GA USA 30542
Phone: 2126344300
Website: www.nativeamericanventurefund.com

Type of Firm
Private Equity Firm

Project Preferences

Type of Financing Preferred:
Early Stage
Seed

Geographical Preferences

United States Preferences:

Industry Preferences

In Consumer Related prefer:
Sports

In Industrial/Energy prefer:
Environmental Related

In Financial Services prefer:
Real Estate

Additional Information
Year Founded: 2015
Current Activity Level : Actively seeking new investments

NATIVE VENTURE CAPITAL CO., LTD.

21 Artist View Pointe, Box 7
Site 25, RR12
Calgary, Canada T3E 6W3
Phone: 903-208-5380

Type of Firm
Private Equity Firm

Project Preferences

Role in Financing:
Prefer role as deal originator but will also invest in deals created by others

Type of Financing Preferred:
Second Stage Financing
Leveraged Buyout
Start-up Financing
Seed
First Stage Financing

Size of Investments Considered:
Min Size of Investment Considered (000s): $300
Max Size of Investment Considered: No Limit

Geographical Preferences

Canadian Preferences:
Western Canada

Additional Information
Year Founded: 1981
Capital Under Management: $10,000,000
Current Activity Level : Actively seeking new investments
Method of Compensation: Return on invest. most important, but chg. closing fees, service fees, etc.

NATIXIS PRIVATE EQUITY SA

5/7 rue de Monttessuy
Paris, France 75340
Phone: 33158192000
Fax: 33158192020
E-mail: contact@natexis-pe.com
Website: www.privateequity.natixis.com

Other Offices

745 Fifth Avenue
28th Floor
NEW YORK, NY USA 10151
Phone: 212-703-0300

52 B, Avenue Francois Giroud
Dijon, France 21000
Phone: 33380702610

Management and Staff

Bernard Mizandjian, Managing Director
David Manjarres, Managing Director
Dominique Sabassier, Chief Executive Officer
Jimmy Hsu, Managing Director
Kit Jong Tan, Managing Director
Lay Hong Lee, Managing Director
Satyan Malhotra, President
Sheryl Schwartz, Managing Director

Type of Firm
Bank Affiliated

Association Membership
French Venture Capital Association (AFIC)
European Private Equity and Venture Capital Assoc.

Project Preferences

Type of Financing Preferred:
Fund of Funds
Leveraged Buyout
Early Stage
Mezzanine
Generalist PE
Public Companies
Later Stage
Management Buyouts
Recapitalizations

Geographical Preferences

United States Preferences:
Southern California
North America

International Preferences:
Europe
Brazil
Asia
Germany
France

Industry Focus
(% based on actual investment)

Other Products	83.9%
Computer Software and Services	4.7%
Communications and Media	3.5%
Internet Specific	3.5%
Industrial/Energy	2.1%
Computer Hardware	1.1%
Semiconductors/Other Elect.	0.8%
Medical/Health	0.4%
Consumer Related	0.0%

Additional Information
Name of Most Recent Fund: Caspian Private Equity II, L.P.
Most Recent Fund Was Raised: 12/07/2012
Year Founded: 1997
Capital Under Management: $3,460,000,000
Current Activity Level : Actively seeking new investments

NATURAL GAS PARTNERS

5221 North O'Connor Boulevard, Suite 1100
Irving, TX USA 75039
Phone: 9724321440
Fax: 9724321441
E-mail: inquiries@ngptrs.com
Website: www.naturalgaspartners.com

Other Offices

1266 East Main Street
Sixth Floor
STAMFORD, CT USA 06902
Phone: 203-504-5072
Fax: 203-504-5073

1401 McKinney Suite 1025
Five Houston Center
HOUSTON, TX USA 77010
Phone: 713-579-5700
Fax: 713579-5740

Pratt's Guide to Private Equity & Venture Capital Sources

Management and Staff
Brian Minnehan, Managing Director
Christopher Carter, Managing Director
Christopher Ray, Senior Managing Director
Craig Glick, Senior Managing Director
Daniel Goodman, Principal
David Hayes, Managing Director
James Wallis, Partner
Jesse Bomer, Principal
John Foster, Managing Director
Joseph Looke, Principal
Kenneth Hersh, Chief Executive Officer
Patrick McWilliams, Managing Director
Richard Covington, Managing Director
Robert Edwards, Managing Director
Roy Aneed, Managing Director
Scott Gieselman, Managing Director
Tomas Ackerman, Managing Director
Tony Weber, Chief Operating Officer

Type of Firm
Private Equity Firm

Project Preferences

Role in Financing:
Prefer role as deal originator

Type of Financing Preferred:
Leveraged Buyout
Other

Industry Focus
(% based on actual investment)

Industrial/Energy	95.7%
Other Products	4.1%
Computer Software and Services	0.1%
Internet Specific	0.1%
Semiconductors/Other Elect.	0.0%
Medical/Health	0.0%

Additional Information
Name of Most Recent Fund: NGP Natural Resources X, L.P.
Most Recent Fund Was Raised: 06/02/2011
Year Founded: 1988
Capital Under Management: $3,000,000,000
Current Activity Level : Actively seeking new investments
Method of Compensation: Return on invest. most important, but chg. closing fees, service fees, etc.

NAUSICAA VENTURES SCA

1, Rue de Rodeuhaie
Louvain-la-Neuve, Belgium B-1348
Website: nausicaa-ventures.be

Type of Firm
Private Equity Firm

Project Preferences

Type of Financing Preferred:
Early Stage

Size of Investments Considered:
Min Size of Investment Considered (000s): $1,093
Max Size of Investment Considered (000s): $4,373

Geographical Preferences

International Preferences:
Belgium

Industry Preferences

In Communications prefer:
Data Communications

In Medical/Health prefer:
Medical/Health

In Industrial/Energy prefer:
Alternative Energy
Energy Conservation Relat

In Manufact. prefer:
Manufacturing

Additional Information
Year Founded: 2009
Current Activity Level : Actively seeking new investments

NAUTA CAPITAL SL

Avenida Diagonal, 593, 8th Floor
Barcelona, Spain 08014
Phone: 34935035900
Fax: 34935035901
E-mail: info@nautacapital.com
Website: www.nautacapital.com

Other Offices
Eight Faneuil Hall Marketplace
Third Floor
BOSTON, MA USA 02109
Phone: 6179735082

Management and Staff
Al Sisto, Venture Partner
Carles Ferrer, General Partner
Daniel Sanchez, General Partner
Dominic Endicott, General Partner
Ferran Soriano, Venture Partner
Hamilton Sekino, General Partner
Javier Rubio, General Partner
Jordi Vinas, General Partner
Marcel Rafart, General Partner

Type of Firm
Private Equity Firm

Association Membership
European Private Equity and Venture Capital Assoc.
Spanish Venture Capital Association (ASCRI)

Project Preferences

Type of Financing Preferred:
Early Stage
Seed

Size of Investments Considered:
Min Size of Investment Considered (000s): $628
Max Size of Investment Considered (000s): $7,539

Geographical Preferences

United States Preferences:

International Preferences:
Europe

Industry Preferences

In Communications prefer:
Communications and Media
Wireless Communications

In Computer Software prefer:
Software

In Internet Specific prefer:
Internet
Ecommerce

Additional Information
Year Founded: 2004
Capital Under Management: $166,170,000
Current Activity Level : Actively seeking new investments

NAUTIC PARTNERS LLC

50 Kennedy Plaza
12th Floor
Providence, RI USA 02903
Phone: 4012786770
Fax: 4012786387
Website: www.nautic.com

Management and Staff
Allan Petersen, Vice President
Bernie Buonanno, Managing Director
Charles Bartolini, Chief Financial Officer
Chris Corey, Managing Director
Chris Pierce, Managing Director
Chris Crosby, Managing Director
Douglas Hill, Managing Director
Habib Gorgi, Managing Director
Jim Beakey, Managing Director
Scott Hilinski, Managing Director

Type of Firm
Private Equity Firm

Project Preferences

Role in Financing:
Prefer role as deal originator but will also invest in deals created by others

Type of Financing Preferred:
Leveraged Buyout
Expansion
Management Buyouts
Acquisition
Recapitalizations

1469

Pratt's Guide to Private Equity & Venture Capital Sources

Size of Investments Considered:
Min Size of Investment Considered (000s): $5,000
Max Size of Investment Considered (000s): $75,000

Geographical Preferences

United States Preferences:
North America

Industry Focus

(% based on actual investment)
Communications and Media	25.6%
Other Products	22.0%
Computer Software and Services	12.6%
Internet Specific	11.0%
Consumer Related	10.9%
Medical/Health	8.3%
Semiconductors/Other Elect.	4.9%
Industrial/Energy	3.7%
Computer Hardware	1.0%

Additional Information

Name of Most Recent Fund: Nautic Partners VII, L.P.
Most Recent Fund Was Raised: 06/05/2013
Year Founded: 1986
Capital Under Management: $2,500,000,000
Current Activity Level : Actively seeking new investments
Method of Compensation: Return on invest. most important, but chg. closing fees, service fees, etc.

NAV.VC

11911 Freedom Drive, Suite 1080
Reston, VA USA 20190
Phone: 7035634100
Fax: 7035634111
Website: nav.vc

Other Offices

One Broadway
14th Floor
CAMBRIDGE, MA USA 02142
Phone: 617-758-4275
Fax: 617-758-4101

Management and Staff

John Backus, Co-Founder
Mel Davidson, Chief Financial Officer
Scott Johnson, Co-Founder
Thanasis Delistathis, Co-Founder
Timothy Rowe, Venture Partner
Todd Hixon, Co-Founder

Type of Firm

Private Equity Firm

Association Membership

Mid-Atlantic Venture Association
New England Venture Capital Association
National Venture Capital Association - USA (NVCA)

Project Preferences

Role in Financing:
Will function either as deal originator or investor in deals created by others

Type of Financing Preferred:
Early Stage
Later Stage
Seed

Size of Investments Considered:
Min Size of Investment Considered (000s): $250
Max Size of Investment Considered (000s): $3,000

Industry Focus

(% based on actual investment)
Internet Specific	49.6%
Computer Software and Services	33.8%
Communications and Media	7.2%
Medical/Health	3.8%
Semiconductors/Other Elect.	2.1%
Other Products	1.7%
Computer Hardware	0.8%
Industrial/Energy	0.7%
Consumer Related	0.3%

Additional Information

Name of Most Recent Fund: New Atlantic Venture Fund IV, L.P.
Most Recent Fund Was Raised: 12/21/2012
Year Founded: 1999
Capital Under Management: $372,000,000
Current Activity Level : Actively seeking new investments
Method of Compensation: Return on investment is of primary concern, do not charge fees

---

NAVAM CAPITAL LTD

15A Hemanta Basu Sarani
Continental Chambers, 4th Flr.
Calcutta, India 700001
Website: www.navamcapital.com

Type of Firm

Private Equity Firm

Project Preferences

Type of Financing Preferred:
Early Stage
Seed

Industry Preferences

In Medical/Health prefer:
Medical/Health

In Industrial/Energy prefer:
Energy

Additional Information

Year Founded: 2010
Current Activity Level : Actively seeking new investments

NAVASOTA GROUP

1-7-2 Otemachi, Chiyoda-Ku
27th Floor, Tokyo Sankei Bldg.
Tokyo, Japan 100-0004
Phone: 81345789700
Fax: 81345789716
E-mail: contact@navasotagroup.com
Website: www.navasotagroup.com

Management and Staff

Akio Tsuyoshi, Chief Financial Officer
Arnold Conway, Chief Executive Officer
Hiro Navasota, Co-Founder

Type of Firm

Private Equity Firm

Project Preferences

Type of Financing Preferred:
Early Stage
Balanced
Later Stage
Seed

Industry Preferences

In Biotechnology prefer:
Biotechnology

In Medical/Health prefer:
Medical Diagnostics
Medical Products

In Industrial/Energy prefer:
Oil and Gas Exploration
Oil & Gas Drilling,Explor
Alternative Energy
Industrial Products

In Agr/Forestr/Fish prefer:
Agriculture related
Mining and Minerals

Additional Information

Year Founded: 2003
Capital Under Management: $800,000,000
Current Activity Level : Actively seeking new investments

NAVIGATION CAPITAL PARTNERS INC

3060 Peachtree Road NorthWest
One Buckhead Plaza, Suite 780
Atlanta, GA USA 30305
Phone: 4042649180
Fax: 4042649305
E-mail: deals@navigationcapital.com
Website: www.navigationcapital.com

Management and Staff
Darlene Clott, Chief Financial Officer
David Panton, Co-Founder
Eerik Giles, Co-Founder
John Richardson, Co-Founder
Lawrence Mock, Co-Founder
Mark Downs, Co-Founder

Type of Firm
Private Equity Firm

Project Preferences

Type of Financing Preferred:
Leveraged Buyout
Management Buyouts
Acquisition
Recapitalizations

Geographical Preferences

United States Preferences:
Southeast
Texas

Industry Preferences

In Transportation prefer:
Transportation

In Financial Services prefer:
Financial Services

In Business Serv. prefer:
Services
Distribution
Media

Additional Information
Year Founded: 2006
Capital Under Management: $294,000,000
Current Activity Level : Actively seeking new investments

NAVIGATOR EQUITY PARTNERS LLC

428 Springfield Avenue
Second Floor
Summit, NJ USA 07901
Phone: 9082737733
Fax: 9082735566
Website: www.navigatorequity.com

Management and Staff
Bernard Markey, Managing Partner
W. Joseph Imhoff, Managing Partner

Type of Firm
Private Equity Firm

Project Preferences

Role in Financing:
Will function either as deal originator or investor in deals created by others

Type of Financing Preferred:
Leveraged Buyout
Management Buyouts
Acquisition

Geographical Preferences

United States Preferences:
Mid Atlantic
Northeast

Industry Focus
(% based on actual investment)
Other Products 53.4%
Medical/Health 46.1%
Industrial/Energy 0.5%

Additional Information
Year Founded: 1999
Capital Under Management: $80,000,000
Current Activity Level : Actively seeking new investments
Method of Compensation: Return on invest. most important, but chg. closing fees, service fees, etc.

NAVIMED CAPITAL ADVISORS LLC

1333 H Street NorthWest, Suite 400 West
Washington, DC USA 20005
Phone: 2025686476
E-mail: info@navimed.com
Website: navimed.com

Management and Staff
Bijan Salehizadeh, Managing Director
Brian Canann, Managing Director
Ryan Schwarz, Managing Director

Type of Firm
Private Equity Firm

Project Preferences

Type of Financing Preferred:
Expansion
Later Stage

Industry Preferences

In Medical/Health prefer:
Medical Diagnostics
Medical Products
Health Services

Additional Information
Name of Most Recent Fund: NaviMed Partners, L.P.
Most Recent Fund Was Raised: 02/15/2013
Year Founded: 2011
Capital Under Management: $107,881,000
Current Activity Level : Actively seeking new investments

NAVIS MANAGEMENT SDN BHD

9, Jalan Stesen Sentral V
Level 17, Axiata Tower
Kuala Lumpur, Malaysia 50470
Phone: 60323023888
Fax: 60323023883
Website: www.naviscapital.com

Other Offices
#10-01, Tung Center
20, Collyer Quay
Singapore, Singapore 049319
Phone: 6564380711
Fax: 6564380721

No. 201 Century Avenue
Rm. 539, 5F, Standard Chartered Bank
Shanghai, China 200120
Phone: 862161826785
Fax: 862161826777

The IL&FS Financial Center
Quadrant C, 1F, Bandra Kurla Complex
Mumbai, India 400051
Phone: 912267676565
Fax: 912226533596

88 Queensway, Suite 1508, 15/F, One Pacific Place
Hong Kong, Hong Kong
Phone: 85225260238
Fax: 85225260308

56 Pitt Street
Level Eight
Sydney, Australia 2000
Phone: 61280247800
Fax: 61280247878

Management and Staff
Bruno Seghin, Partner
David Ireland, Partner
Jean-Christophe Marti, Partner
Michael Octoman, Partner
Nicholas Bloy, Partner
Philip Latham, Partner
Richard Foyston, Partner
Rik Muilwijk, Partner
Rodney Muse, Partner
Thomas Beecroft, Partner
Timothy McKinlay, Partner

Type of Firm
Private Equity Firm

Association Membership
Australian Venture Capital Association (AVCAL)
Thai Venture Capital Association
Hong Kong Venture Capital Association (HKVCA)
Malaysian Venture Capital Association
Singapore Venture Capital Association (SVCA)

Project Preferences

Type of Financing Preferred:
Leveraged Buyout
Recapitalizations

Geographical Preferences

International Preferences:
Hong Kong
Australia
Asia

Industry Focus

(% based on actual investment)
Other Products 43.9%
Consumer Related 34.3%
Medical/Health 11.3%
Computer Software and Services 5.7%
Industrial/Energy 4.8%

Additional Information

Year Founded: 1998
Capital Under Management: $285,500,000
Current Activity Level : Actively seeking new investments

NAVITAS CAPITAL

1751 Harbor Bay Parkway, Suite 200
Alameda, CA USA 94502

Other Offices

11990 San Vicente Boulevard, Suite 350
Los Angeles, CA USA 90049

Type of Firm

Private Equity Firm

Project Preferences

Type of Financing Preferred:
Early Stage

Industry Preferences

In Industrial/Energy prefer:
Environmental Related

In Other prefer:
Environment Responsible

Additional Information

Name of Most Recent Fund: Navitas Capital I, L.P.
Most Recent Fund Was Raised: 04/17/2009
Year Founded: 2008
Capital Under Management: $60,000,000
Current Activity Level : Actively seeking new investments

NAVITAS MANAGEMENT BV

Raoul Wallenbergplein 25A
Alphen aan den Rijn, Netherlands 2404 ND
Phone: 31172448388
Fax: 31172448389
E-mail: info@navitascapital.nl
Website: www.navitascapital.nl

Management and Staff

Rense Jonk, Managing Director

Type of Firm

Private Equity Firm

Association Membership

Dutch Venture Capital Associaton (NVP)

Project Preferences

Type of Financing Preferred:
Public Companies
Later Stage
Management Buyouts

Geographical Preferences

International Preferences:
Netherlands

Additional Information

Year Founded: 1967
Current Activity Level : Actively seeking new investments

NAVUS VENTURES BV

Oostgaag 49
Maasland, Netherlands 3155 CE
Phone: 31647358074
Website: www.navusventures.nl

Type of Firm

Private Equity Firm

Project Preferences

Type of Financing Preferred:
Early Stage
Balanced
Later Stage
Seed

Geographical Preferences

International Preferences:
Netherlands

Industry Preferences

In Industrial/Energy prefer:
Energy
Alternative Energy
Environmental Related

In Other prefer:
Environment Responsible

Additional Information

Year Founded: 2013
Current Activity Level : Actively seeking new investments

NAXICAP PARTNERS SA

5-7 rue de Monttessuy
Paris, France 75340
Phone: 33158192220
Fax: 33158192230
E-mail: contact.paris@naxicap.fr
Website: www.naxicap.fr

Other Offices

1 place Aristide Briand
Nantes, France 44000
Phone: 33-2-5189-6890
Fax: 33-2-5189-6899

5, rue Genty Magre
BP 30534
Toulouse, France 31005
Phone: 33-5-3441-3141
Fax: 33-5-6162-6863

10 rue Saint Odile
Strasbourg, France 67000
Phone: 33-3-8824-2098
Fax: 33-3-8824-6201

Management and Staff

Alban Sarie, General Partner
Bruno Denis, Managing Partner
Jacques Vachelard, Managing Partner
Marc Le Gallais, Managing Partner
Nadine Michotey, Managing Partner
Nathalie Triolet, General Partner
Virginie Lambert, Managing Partner

Type of Firm

Private Equity Firm

Association Membership

French Venture Capital Association (AFIC)

Project Preferences

Type of Financing Preferred:
Leveraged Buyout
Early Stage
Expansion
Research and Development
Generalist PE
Later Stage
Management Buyouts
Acquisition
Startup

Size of Investments Considered:

Min Size of Investment Considered (000s): $1,297
Max Size of Investment Considered (000s): $84,317

Geographical Preferences

International Preferences:
Europe
France

Additional Information
Year Founded: 1982
Capital Under Management: $1,246,800,000
Current Activity Level : Actively seeking new investments

NAXOS CAPITAL PARTNERS
No. 44
Chelsea Park Gardens
London, United Kingdom SW3 6AB
E-mail: info@naxoscapital.com

Type of Firm
Private Equity Firm

Project Preferences

Type of Financing Preferred:
Leveraged Buyout
Acquisition

Industry Preferences

In Communications prefer:
Communications and Media

In Business Serv. prefer:
Services
Media

In Manufact. prefer:
Manufacturing

Additional Information
Year Founded: 2009
Current Activity Level : Actively seeking new investments

NAXURI CAPITAL
425 Broadway Street
Redwood City, CA USA 94062
E-mail: info@naxuricapital.com
Website: www.naxuricapital.com

Management and Staff
Enrico Beltramini, Managing Director
Patrick Chung, Managing Director

Type of Firm
Private Equity Firm

Project Preferences

Type of Financing Preferred:
Seed

Size of Investments Considered:
Min Size of Investment Considered (000s): $250
Max Size of Investment Considered (000s): $2,000

Industry Preferences

In Consumer Related prefer:
Consumer
Retail

Additional Information
Year Founded: 2013
Current Activity Level : Actively seeking new investments

NAYA VENTURES LLC
222 West Las Colinas Boulevard, Suite 1410 North
Irving, TX USA 75039
Phone: 2146301480
Fax: 2146301481

Other Offices
A Block, Software Units Layout
Ground Floor, Unit 18, iLabs Center
Hyderabad, India 500081
Phone: 914066545466
Fax: 914066545410

710 Second Avenue, Suite 400
Seattle, WA USA 98104
Phone: 14256384500
Fax: 14256384700

Management and Staff
Alan Buehler, Chief Financial Officer
Dayakar Puskoor, General Partner
Gary Himes, Managing Director
Prabhakar Reddy, Managing Partner

Type of Firm
Private Equity Firm

Project Preferences

Type of Financing Preferred:
Early Stage
Later Stage

Geographical Preferences

United States Preferences:

International Preferences:
India

Industry Preferences

In Communications prefer:
Wireless Communications
Data Communications

In Computer Software prefer:
Software

Additional Information
Name of Most Recent Fund: Naya Ventures Fund I, L.P.
Most Recent Fund Was Raised: 10/03/2012
Year Founded: 2009
Capital Under Management: $4,550,000
Current Activity Level : Actively seeking new investments

NAZCA CAPITAL SGEIC SA
Calle Fortuny 37
3o Derecha
Madrid, Spain 28010
Phone: 34917000501
E-mail: info@nazca.es
Website: www.nazca.es

Management and Staff
Alvaro Mariategui, Managing Partner
Carlos Perez de Jauregui, Partner
Carlos Carbo, Managing Partner
Celia Perez-Beato, Partner

Type of Firm
Bank Affiliated

Association Membership
Spanish Venture Capital Association (ASCRI)

Project Preferences

Type of Financing Preferred:
Leveraged Buyout
Management Buyouts
Acquisition
Recapitalizations

Geographical Preferences

International Preferences:
Spain

Additional Information
Year Founded: 2001
Capital Under Management: $112,200,000
Current Activity Level : Actively seeking new investments

NAZCA VENTURES
Juana Azurduy 2440
Buenos Aires, Argentina C1429BZJ
E-mail: info@nazcaventures.com
Website: www.nazcaventures.com

Management and Staff
Alan Farcas, Managing Partner
Eduardo Amadeo, Partner
Felipe Meyer, Partner
Santiago Bengolea, Partner

Type of Firm
Private Equity Firm

Project Preferences

Type of Financing Preferred:
Early Stage

Size of Investments Considered:
Min Size of Investment Considered (000s): $150
Max Size of Investment Considered (000s): $750

Pratt's Guide to Private Equity & Venture Capital Sources

Geographical Preferences

International Preferences:
Latin America

Industry Preferences

In Communications prefer:
Wireless Communications

In Computer Software prefer:
Software

In Internet Specific prefer:
Internet
Ecommerce

In Consumer Related prefer:
Consumer
Education Related

In Business Serv. prefer:
Media

Additional Information

Year Founded: 2013
Current Activity Level: Actively seeking new investments

NB DISTRESSED DEBT INVESTMENT FUND LTD

190 South LaSalle Street
23rd Floor
Chicago, IL USA 60603
Phone: 3126098426
E-mail: NBDistressedDebt@nb.com
Website: www.nbddif.com

Management and Staff

Michael Holmberg, Managing Director
Patrick Flynn, Managing Director

Type of Firm

Investment Management Firm

Project Preferences

Type of Financing Preferred:
Special Situation
Distressed Debt

Geographical Preferences

United States Preferences:
North America

Industry Preferences

In Industrial/Energy prefer:
Energy

In Transportation prefer:
Aerospace

Additional Information

Name of Most Recent Fund: NB Distressed Debt Fund, L.P.
Most Recent Fund Was Raised: 01/13/2011
Year Founded: 1939
Capital Under Management: $7,500,000
Current Activity Level: Actively seeking new investments

NB PRIVATE EQUITY PARTNERS LTD

325 North St. Paul Street, Suite 4900
Dallas, TX USA 75219
Phone: 214-647-9593
Fax: 214-647-9501
E-mail: IR_NBPE@nb.com
Website: www.nbprivateequitypartners.com

Other Offices

Le Marchant Street
Heritage Hall, St. Peter Port
Guernsey, Channel Islands GY1 4HY
Phone: 441481716000
Fax: 441481728452

Management and Staff

Anthony Tutrone, Managing Director
Brien Smith, Managing Director
David Stoneberg, Managing Director
Jonathan Shofet, Managing Director
Joseph Malick, Managing Director

Type of Firm

Private Equity Advisor or Fund of Funds

Project Preferences

Type of Financing Preferred:
Fund of Funds
Fund of Funds of Second

Additional Information

Name of Most Recent Fund: Lehman Brothers Crossroads XVII, L.P.
Most Recent Fund Was Raised: 07/28/2005
Year Founded: 1984
Capital Under Management: $5,800,000,000
Current Activity Level: Actively seeking new investments

NBC CAPITAL PTY LTD

493 Ipswich Road
Level One
Annerley, Australia 4103
Phone: 61732339200
Fax: 61732339223
E-mail: info@nbccapital.com.au

Management and Staff

Bruce Scott, Managing Director
Shane Lawrence, General Partner
Tony Keating, Chief Financial Officer

Type of Firm

Private Equity Firm

Project Preferences

Type of Financing Preferred:
Leveraged Buyout
Expansion
Generalist PE
Later Stage
Acquisition

Industry Preferences

In Consumer Related prefer:
Retail
Franchises(NEC)
Food/Beverage
Consumer Services

In Transportation prefer:
Transportation

In Business Serv. prefer:
Services

Additional Information

Year Founded: 1999
Capital Under Management: $174,400,000
Current Activity Level: Actively seeking new investments

NBD SANA CAPITAL LTD

P.O. Box 777
Dubai, Utd. Arab Em.
Phone: 971-4-229-8155
Fax: 971-4-224-8157
Website: www.nbdsana.com

Management and Staff

Abdullah Qassem, Chief Operating Officer
Rick Pudner, Chief Executive Officer

Type of Firm

Bank Affiliated

Project Preferences

Type of Financing Preferred:
Leveraged Buyout
Expansion
Generalist PE
Turnaround

Geographical Preferences

International Preferences:
Turkey
Middle East
Asia
Africa

Industry Preferences

In Communications prefer:
Communications and Media
Telecommunications
Media and Entertainment

In Medical/Health prefer:
Medical/Health
Health Services
Pharmaceuticals

In Consumer Related prefer:
Consumer
Retail
Consumer Services

In Industrial/Energy prefer:
Energy

Additional Information
Year Founded: 2007
Capital Under Management: $170,000,000
Current Activity Level : Actively seeking new investments

NBGI PRIVATE EQUITY LTD

128 Queen Victoria Street
Old Change House
London, United Kingdom EC4V 4BJ
Phone: 442076615678
Fax: 442076615667
Website: www.nbgipe.com

Other Offices
37, rue la Perouse
Paris, France 75116
Phone: 33158561895

Cad. No. 30, D:6 Zincirkuyu, Nisantasi
Istanbul Liaison Office Shitleri
Istanbul, Turkey
Phone: 902122245902
Fax: 902122245981

Management and Staff
Alex Borg, Chief Financial Officer

Type of Firm
Bank Affiliated

Association Membership
British Venture Capital Association (BVCA)
French Venture Capital Association (AFIC)
European Private Equity and Venture Capital Assoc.

Project Preferences

Type of Financing Preferred:
Core
Leveraged Buyout
Expansion
Generalist PE
Turnaround
Later Stage
Management Buyouts
Acquisition
Recapitalizations

Size of Investments Considered:
Min Size of Investment Considered (000s): $6,349
Max Size of Investment Considered (000s): $63,492

Geographical Preferences

International Preferences:
United Kingdom
Turkey
Central Europe
Europe
Eastern Europe
France

Industry Preferences

In Communications prefer:
Communications and Media

In Internet Specific prefer:
Internet

In Medical/Health prefer:
Medical Products
Health Services

In Consumer Related prefer:
Retail
Food/Beverage
Consumer Products

In Financial Services prefer:
Real Estate

In Business Serv. prefer:
Services
Distribution
Media

In Manufact. prefer:
Manufacturing

Additional Information
Name of Most Recent Fund: NBGI SEE Energy Fund, L.P.
Most Recent Fund Was Raised: 11/20/2008
Year Founded: 2000
Capital Under Management: $128,000,000
Current Activity Level : Actively seeking new investments

NBI INVESTORS BV

Laan van Kronenburg 14
Amstelveen, Netherlands 1183 AS
Phone: 31203032071
Website: www.nbi-investors.nl

Type of Firm
Private Equity Firm

Project Preferences

Type of Financing Preferred:
Early Stage
Expansion
Later Stage

Geographical Preferences

International Preferences:
Europe
Netherlands

Industry Preferences

In Biotechnology prefer:
Agricultural/Animal Bio.

In Medical/Health prefer:
Medical/Health

In Industrial/Energy prefer:
Environmental Related

In Manufact. prefer:
Manufacturing

In Agr/Forestr/Fish prefer:
Agribusiness

In Other prefer:
Environment Responsible

Additional Information
Name of Most Recent Fund: Mainport Innovation Fund BV
Most Recent Fund Was Raised: 12/31/2009
Year Founded: 2014
Capital Under Management: $21,790,000
Current Activity Level : Actively seeking new investments

NBK CAPITAL PARTNERS LTD

PO Box 4950
Safat, Kuwait 13050
Phone: 96522246901
Fax: 96522246904
E-mail: info.request@nbkcapital.com
Website: www.nbkcapital.com

Other Offices
PO Box 506506
Dubai, Utd. Arab Em.
Phone: 971-4-365-2800
Fax: 971-4-365-2805

2 Wadi El-Nile Street
Mohandeseen, 12th Floor
Giza, Egypt
Phone: 202-3302-6004
Fax: 202-3302-6008

34398 Sisli
Istanbul, Turkey 34398
Phone: 90-212-276-5400
Fax: 90-212-276-541

Management and Staff
Anand Hariharan, Chief Financial Officer
Isam Al-Sager, Chairman & CEO
Yaser Moustafa, Senior Managing Director

Type of Firm
Bank Affiliated

Association Membership
Gulf Venture Capital Association

Project Preferences

Type of Financing Preferred:
Leveraged Buyout
Expansion
Mezzanine
Generalist PE
Balanced
Turnaround
Management Buyouts
Acquisition
Recapitalizations

Geographical Preferences

International Preferences:
Bahrain
Oman
Turkey
Qatar
Egypt
Utd. Arab Em.
Middle East
Saudi Arabia
Asia
Kuwait
Africa

Industry Preferences

In Medical/Health prefer:
Medical/Health
Health Services

In Consumer Related prefer:
Food/Beverage
Consumer Products
Education Related

In Transportation prefer:
Transportation

In Financial Services prefer:
Investment Groups
Financial Services

In Manufact. prefer:
Manufacturing

In Utilities prefer:
Utilities

Additional Information
Year Founded: 2005
Capital Under Management: $875,000,000
Current Activity Level : Actively seeking new investments

NBT CAPITAL CORP

52 South Broad Street
Norwich, NY USA 13815
Phone: 607-337-6810
Fax: 607-336-6545

Management and Staff
Duke Crandall, Managing Director
Michael Chewens, Chief Financial Officer

Type of Firm
Private Equity Firm

Project Preferences

Type of Financing Preferred:
Second Stage Financing
Early Stage
Expansion
Mezzanine
Later Stage
Management Buyouts

Geographical Preferences

United States Preferences:
Mid Atlantic
Pennsylvania
Northeast
New York

Industry Preferences

In Computer Hardware prefer:
Computers

In Computer Software prefer:
Computer Services

In Biotechnology prefer:
Biotechnology

In Manufact. prefer:
Manufacturing

Additional Information
Year Founded: 1998
Capital Under Management: $5,000,000
Current Activity Level : Actively seeking new investments

NCA PARTNERS INC

1200 Westlake Avenue North, Suite 600
Seattle, WA USA 98109
Phone: 2066895615
Fax: 2066895614
Website: www.nwcap.com

Management and Staff
Bradford Creswell, Partner
John Jacobs, Partner

Type of Firm
Private Equity Firm

Project Preferences

Role in Financing:
Prefer role as deal originator but will also invest in deals created by others

Type of Financing Preferred:
Leveraged Buyout
Expansion
Turnaround
Acquisition
Recapitalizations

Geographical Preferences

United States Preferences:
Northwest
North America

Industry Focus
(% based on actual investment)
Industrial/Energy   100.0%

Additional Information
Name of Most Recent Fund: Northwest Capital Appreciation Fund I, L.P.
Most Recent Fund Was Raised: 01/01/1996
Year Founded: 1992
Capital Under Management: $190,000,000
Current Activity Level : Actively seeking new investments
Method of Compensation: Return on invest. most important, but chg. closing fees, service fees, etc.

NCB CAPITAL DIFC LTD

Level 13 Park Place
Sheikh Zayed Road
Dubai, Utd. Arab Em.
Phone: 97143297171
Fax: 97143297272
E-mail: info@eastgategroup.com

Management and Staff
Ghazi Al-Rawi, Managing Director
Nasr-Eddine Benaissa, Managing Director
Sanjay Agarwal, Chief Financial Officer
Yusuf Ozdalga, Vice President

Type of Firm
Bank Affiliated

Association Membership
Gulf Venture Capital Association

Project Preferences

Type of Financing Preferred:
Leveraged Buyout
Early Stage
Expansion
Generalist PE
Later Stage
Acquisition

Geographical Preferences

International Preferences:
Asia Pacific
India
Turkey
China
Egypt
Utd. Arab Em.
Algeria
Eastern Europe
Middle East
Saudi Arabia
Asia
Russia
Africa

Industry Preferences

In Financial Services prefer:
Real Estate
Financial Services

In Manufact. prefer:
Manufacturing

Additional Information
Year Founded: 2006
Current Activity Level : Actively seeking new investments

NCH CAPITAL INC

452 Fifth Avenue
24th Floor
New York, NY USA 10018
Phone: 2126413200
Fax: 2126413201
Website: www.nchcapital.com

Other Offices

Wilmington-Sucursala Bucuresti
Bd. Pierre de Coubertin, nr. 3-5
Bucharest, Romania 021902

27-T Degtyarevskaya Street
2nd Floor
Kyiv, Ukraine 04119

67-B Hose de San Martin Street
Sofia, Bulgaria 1111

Krzhizhanovskogo Street, 14
Building 3, 5th Floor
Moscow, Russia 117218

SkyTower, Number 72
Rr. Deshmoret e 4 Shkurtit
Tirana, Albania

Armiansky Per. 1/8
BUilding 3
Moscow, Russia 101000

Baznicas 20/22
Riga, Latvia LV 1143

Skytower Office Center, 4F, Office E
63, Vlaicu Pircalab Street
Chisinau, Moldova MD-2012

138 Obvodny Canal Embankment, Bldg. 101
Treugolink Business Center, 3rd Floor
St. Petersburg, Russia 190020

Management and Staff

Andi Ballta, Managing Director
Andrew Radchenko, Vice President
Chris Abbott, Managing Director
Edna Beaudette, Managing Director
George Rohr, Managing Partner
Joseph Bond, Managing Director
Mikhail Vasiliev, Vice President
Moris Tabacinic, Managing Partner
Nikola Zikatanov, Vice President
Patrick Ghidirim, Managing Director
Victor Popusoi, Vice President

Type of Firm
Private Equity Firm

Project Preferences

Type of Financing Preferred:
Balanced

Geographical Preferences

International Preferences:
Russia

Industry Preferences

In Biotechnology prefer:
Agricultural/Animal Bio.

In Financial Services prefer:
Real Estate

Additional Information
Year Founded: 1993
Capital Under Management: $100,940,000
Current Activity Level : Actively seeking new investments

NCI SAS

57, avenue de Bretagne
Rouen, France 76100
Phone: 33232186302
Fax: 33232186393
E-mail: infos@ncigestion.com
Website: www.n-ci.com

Management and Staff
Gerard Lissot, President

Type of Firm
Private Equity Firm

Association Membership
French Venture Capital Association (AFIC)

Project Preferences

Type of Financing Preferred:
Leveraged Buyout
Early Stage
Generalist PE
Later Stage
Management Buyouts
Acquisition
Startup

Size of Investments Considered:
Min Size of Investment Considered (000s): $387
Max Size of Investment Considered (000s): $6,443

Geographical Preferences

International Preferences:
Europe
France

Industry Preferences

In Computer Software prefer:
Software

In Internet Specific prefer:
Internet

In Biotechnology prefer:
Biotechnology
Agricultural/Animal Bio.

In Consumer Related prefer:
Consumer

In Business Serv. prefer:
Services

In Agr/Forestr/Fish prefer:
Agriculture related

Additional Information
Year Founded: 2000
Capital Under Management: $125,048,000
Current Activity Level : Actively seeking new investments

NCK CAPITAL LLC

6440 North Central Expy, Suite 100
Dallas, TX USA 75206
Website: www.nckcapital.com

Management and Staff
Grant Kornman, Managing Partner
Michael Kornman, Managing Partner

Type of Firm
Private Equity Firm

Project Preferences

Type of Financing Preferred:
Leveraged Buyout
Management Buyouts
Acquisition
Recapitalizations

Geographical Preferences

United States Preferences:
Texas

Industry Preferences

In Medical/Health prefer:
Medical/Health

In Consumer Related prefer:
Food/Beverage

In Industrial/Energy prefer:
Energy

In Financial Services prefer:
Financial Services

Additional Information
Year Founded: 2013
Current Activity Level : Actively seeking new investments

NCT VENTURES LLC

274 Marconi Boulevard
One Marconi Place, Suite 400
Columbus, OH USA 43215
Phone: 6147942732
Fax: 6142282737
E-mail: info@nctventures.com
Website: www.nctventures.com

Management and Staff
JT Kreager, Managing Director
Michael Butler, Venture Partner
Richard Langdale, Managing Director
Rick Milenthal, Venture Partner

Type of Firm
Private Equity Firm

Association Membership
Natl Assoc of Small Bus. Inv. Co (NASBIC)
National Venture Capital Association - USA (NVCA)

Project Preferences

Type of Financing Preferred:
Early Stage
Balanced
Seed

Geographical Preferences

United States Preferences:
Ohio

Industry Preferences

In Consumer Related prefer:
Retail

In Business Serv. prefer:
Distribution
Media

Additional Information
Name of Most Recent Fund: NCT Ventures Fund I, L.P.
Most Recent Fund Was Raised: 06/03/2008
Year Founded: 1986
Capital Under Management: $58,000,000
Current Activity Level : Actively seeking new investments

NDUSAGE PARTNERS

Justice Ramaswammy Street
Kasthuriba Nagar, Adyar
Tamil Nadu, India
Phone: 914443504050
Fax: 914443504932
E-mail: info@indusage.com
Website: www.indusage.com

Type of Firm
Private Equity Firm

Project Preferences

Type of Financing Preferred:
Early Stage

Geographical Preferences

United States Preferences:

International Preferences:
India

Additional Information
Year Founded: 2015
Current Activity Level : Actively seeking new investments

NEBRASKA GLOBAL

151 North 8th Street, Suite 300
Lincoln, NE USA 68508
Phone: 4023251525
Fax: 4023251524
E-mail: contact@nebraskaglobal.com
Website: www.nebraskaglobal.com

Type of Firm
Private Equity Firm

Project Preferences

Type of Financing Preferred:
Early Stage
Expansion
Balanced
Later Stage
Seed
Startup

Geographical Preferences

United States Preferences:
All U.S.

Industry Preferences

In Computer Software prefer:
Software

Additional Information
Year Founded: 2010
Current Activity Level : Actively seeking new investments

NEDVEST CAPITAL BEHEER BV

Hygieastraat 10
Amsterdam, Netherlands 1076 RM
Phone: 31205711554
E-mail: info@nedvest.nl
Website: www.nedvest.nl

Type of Firm
Private Equity Firm

Project Preferences

Type of Financing Preferred:
Leveraged Buyout
Acquisition

Geographical Preferences

International Preferences:
Europe
Netherlands

Additional Information
Year Founded: 2013
Current Activity Level : Actively seeking new investments

NEF INVESTISSEMENT SA

26 rue Carnot
Levallois Perret, France 92300

Type of Firm
Private Equity Firm

Association Membership
French Venture Capital Association (AFIC)

Project Preferences

Type of Financing Preferred:
Balanced

Geographical Preferences

International Preferences:
Europe
France

Additional Information
Year Founded: 2007
Current Activity Level : Actively seeking new investments

NEO CAPITAL LLP

36-38, Wigmore Street
442072589800
London, United Kingdom W1U 2LJ
Phone: 442072589800
Fax: 42074874393
Website: www.neo-cap.com

Management and Staff

David Belhassen, Founder

Type of Firm

Private Equity Firm

Project Preferences

Type of Financing Preferred:
Leveraged Buyout
Management Buyouts
Acquisition

Geographical Preferences

International Preferences:
United Kingdom
Europe

Industry Preferences

In Consumer Related prefer:
Consumer
Retail
Food/Beverage
Consumer Services
Education Related

In Business Serv. prefer:
Services

Additional Information

Name of Most Recent Fund: NEO Capital Private Equity Fund II, L.P.
Most Recent Fund Was Raised: 08/01/2013
Year Founded: 2004
Capital Under Management: $50,421,000
Current Activity Level : Actively seeking new investments

NEO CAPITAL MANAGEMENT GROUP CO LTD

Caitianlijiaoqiao, North Ring
43/F,Blk.A, Xinhao E Du
Shenzhen, China
Phone: 8675582760370
Website: www.xiaoniu66.com

Type of Firm

Investment Management Firm

Project Preferences

Type of Financing Preferred:
Leveraged Buyout
Mezzanine
Balanced

Geographical Preferences

International Preferences:
China

Additional Information

Year Founded: 2013
Current Activity Level : Actively seeking new investments

NEO INVESTMENT PARTNERS LLP

36-38 Wigmore Street
London, United Kingdom W1U 2LJ
Website: www.neoinvestmentpartners.com

Management and Staff

Alain Mikli, Partner
Alexandre Mattiussi, Partner
David Holder, Partner
Delphine Plisson, Partner
Francis Holder, Partner
Lionel Giraud, Partner
Olivier Bon, Partner
Pierre Marcolini, Partner
Pierre-Charles Cros, Partner
Romee Goriainoff, Partner
Sara Ferrero, Partner
Sarah Rotheram, Partner
Silvio Ursini, Partner
Tom Dixon, Partner

Type of Firm

Investment Management Firm

Project Preferences

Type of Financing Preferred:
Leveraged Buyout
Acquisition

Geographical Preferences

International Preferences:
Europe

Industry Preferences

In Consumer Related prefer:
Consumer Products

Additional Information

Year Founded: 2004
Current Activity Level : Actively seeking new investments

NEOMED MANAGEMENT AS

Parkveien 55
Oslo, Norway 0256
Phone: 4722545940
Fax: 4722545941
Website: neomed.net

Other Offices

13 Castle Street
St. Helier
Jersey, Channel Islands JE4 5UT
Phone: 441534722787

7, Place du Molard
Geneva, Switzerland 1204
Phone: 41225667802

Management and Staff

Claudio Nessi, Partner
Dina Chaya, Partner
Thomas Goebel, Principal

Type of Firm

Private Equity Firm

Association Membership

Norwegian Venture Capital Association
European Private Equity and Venture Capital Assoc.

Project Preferences

Role in Financing:
Will function either as deal originator or investor in deals created by others

Type of Financing Preferred:
Early Stage
Balanced
Later Stage
Seed
Startup

Geographical Preferences

United States Preferences:

International Preferences:
Europe
Scandanavia/Nordic Region
Norway
All International

Industry Preferences

In Biotechnology prefer:
Biotechnology
Human Biotechnology
Biosensors
Biotech Related Research

In Medical/Health prefer:
Medical/Health
Medical Diagnostics
Medical Therapeutics
Medical Products
Health Services
Pharmaceuticals

Additional Information
Name of Most Recent Fund: NeoMed Innovation V L.P.
Most Recent Fund Was Raised: 06/18/2012
Year Founded: 1997
Capital Under Management: $125,000,000
Current Activity Level : Actively seeking new investments
Method of Compensation: Return on investment is of primary concern, do not charge fees

NEOPLUX CO LTD
18-12, Euljiro 6-ga, Junggu
15/F, Doosan Tower
Seoul, South Korea 100730
Phone: 82233981070
Fax: 82233981071
E-mail: neoplux@neoplux.com
Website: www.neoplux.co.kr

Management and Staff
Il-Chun Kim, Managing Director
Ja-deug Ku, Managing Director
Jong Gap Lee, Chief Executive Officer
Jung-hyun Kim, Managing Director
Kyung-Min Min, Vice President
Tae-joon Chin, Managing Director

Type of Firm
Corporate PE/Venture

Association Membership
Korean Venture Capital Association (KVCA)

Project Preferences

Type of Financing Preferred:
Leveraged Buyout
Early Stage
Expansion
Mezzanine
Balanced
Turnaround
Management Buyouts
Startup
Recapitalizations

Size of Investments Considered:
Min Size of Investment Considered (000s): $500
Max Size of Investment Considered (000s): $3,000

Geographical Preferences

International Preferences:
Asia
Korea, South

Industry Preferences

In Communications prefer:
Telecommunications

In Computer Software prefer:
Software

In Semiconductor/Electr prefer:
Electronics
Semiconductor

In Biotechnology prefer:
Biotechnology

In Business Serv. prefer:
Media

Additional Information
Year Founded: 2000
Capital Under Management: $78,900,000
Current Activity Level : Actively seeking new investments

NEOTECH CAPITAL
64 Prince Street
Second Floor
Montreal, Canada H3C 2M8
Phone: 5149075388
Website: www.minkcapital.ca

Type of Firm
Private Equity Firm

Industry Preferences

In Internet Specific prefer:
Internet
Web Aggregation/Portals

In Business Serv. prefer:
Media

Additional Information
Year Founded: 2002
Current Activity Level : Actively seeking new investments

NEOTENY LABS PTE LTD
One Raffles Quay
Level 25, North Tower
Singapore, Singapore 048583
Website: www.neotenylabs.com

Management and Staff
Andrew Huang, Venture Partner
James Chan, Principal
Joichi Ito, General Partner

Type of Firm
Private Equity Firm

Project Preferences

Type of Financing Preferred:
Early Stage
Seed
Startup

Geographical Preferences

International Preferences:
Asia
Singapore

Industry Preferences

In Internet Specific prefer:
Internet

Additional Information
Year Founded: 2009
Current Activity Level : Actively seeking new investments

NEOTRIBE MANAGEMENT COMPANY, LLC
3340 Hillview Avenue
Palo Alto, CA USA 94304
Website: www.neotribe.vc

Type of Firm
Private Equity Firm

Project Preferences

Type of Financing Preferred:
Early Stage

Additional Information
Year Founded: 2017
Capital Under Management: $113,500,000
Current Activity Level : Actively seeking new investments

NEOWING CAPITAL
No. 258 Weihai Road
16/F,South Zhaoshang Plaza
Shanghai, China 200041
Phone: 86-21-61935782
Fax: 86-21-61935785
E-mail: bp@neowingvc.com
Website: www.neowingvc.com

Type of Firm
Service Provider

Project Preferences

Type of Financing Preferred:
Balanced

Geographical Preferences

International Preferences:
China

Additional Information
Year Founded: 2008
Current Activity Level : Actively seeking new investments

NEREUS CAPITAL

Bandra Kurla Complex, Trident, Suite 736, C-56 G Block
Mumbai, India 400098
E-mail: info@nereuscap.com
Website: www.nereuscap.com

Management and Staff
C Rajesh, Managing Director

Type of Firm
Private Equity Firm

Project Preferences

Type of Financing Preferred:
Balanced
Turnaround
Seed
Startup

Geographical Preferences

International Preferences:
Indonesia
India
Asia

Industry Preferences

In Industrial/Energy prefer:
Energy
Alternative Energy
Energy Conservation Relat

In Transportation prefer:
Transportation

Additional Information
Year Founded: 2012
Capital Under Management: $120,000,000
Current Activity Level : Actively seeking new investments

NES PARTNER HOLDING APS

Norre Farimagsgade 13
First floor
Copenhagen, Denmark 1364
Phone: 4533936300
E-mail: mmo@nespartners.dk
Website: www.nespartnersweb.dk

Management and Staff
Mads Moller, Partner
Poul Erik Schou-Petersen, Managing Partner

Type of Firm
Private Equity Firm

Association Membership
Danish Venture Capital Association (DVCA)

Project Preferences

Type of Financing Preferred:
Early Stage
Later Stage

Geographical Preferences

International Preferences:
Ireland
United Kingdom
Netherlands
Switzerland
Austria
Scandanavia/Nordic Region
Denmark

Industry Preferences

In Industrial/Energy prefer:
Energy
Alternative Energy

Additional Information
Year Founded: 2002
Current Activity Level : Actively seeking new investments

NEST

143-145 Bonham Strand
16/F Chaos Building
Sheung Wan, Hong Kong
Phone: 85236203885
E-mail: contact@nest.vc
Website: nest.vc

Type of Firm
Incubator/Development Program

Project Preferences

Type of Financing Preferred:
Seed
Startup

Additional Information
Year Founded: 2014
Current Activity Level : Actively seeking new investments

NEST VENTURES LLC

3104 East Camelback Road, Suite 144
Phoenix, AZ USA 85016
Phone: 480-675-7703
Fax: 480-675-8751
E-mail: info@nestventures.com
Website: www.nestventures.com

Type of Firm
Private Equity Firm

Industry Preferences

In Communications prefer:
Communications and Media
Wireless Communications

In Computer Software prefer:
Software

In Biotechnology prefer:
Biotechnology

In Industrial/Energy prefer:
Energy

In Business Serv. prefer:
Media

Additional Information
Year Founded: 2000
Current Activity Level : Actively seeking new investments

NEST-TN LLC

414 Wilson Avenue, Suite 102
Tullahoma, TN USA 37388
Phone: 9314550155
Fax: 9314554375
Website: www.nest-tn.com

Management and Staff
Fran Marcum, Managing Partner

Type of Firm
Private Equity Firm

Project Preferences

Type of Financing Preferred:
Early Stage
Seed
Startup

Geographical Preferences

United States Preferences:
Tennessee

Industry Preferences

In Computer Hardware prefer:
Computer Graphics and Dig

In Internet Specific prefer:
Internet

In Computer Other prefer:
Computer Related

In Industrial/Energy prefer:
Energy
Advanced Materials
Environmental Related

In Business Serv. prefer:
Media

In Manufact. prefer:
Manufacturing

Additional Information
Name of Most Recent Fund: Nest-USA, L.P.
Most Recent Fund Was Raised: 07/29/2011
Year Founded: 2009
Capital Under Management: $4,640,000
Current Activity Level : Actively seeking new investments

NESTA BRAND CO INC

343 Preston Street, 11th Floor
Ottawa, Canada K1S 1N4
Phone: 3432911153
Website: www.nesta.co

Type of Firm
Private Equity Firm

Geographical Preferences

United States Preferences:
North America

International Preferences:
Europe

Additional Information
Year Founded: 2015
Current Activity Level : Actively seeking new investments

NETCIRQ

One Market Street
36th Floor Spear Tower
San Francisco, CA USA 94105
Phone: 415-293-8310
Fax: 415-293-8001
Website: www.netcirq.com

Type of Firm
Private Equity Firm

Association Membership
National Venture Capital Association - USA (NVCA)

Additional Information
Year Founded: 2000
Capital Under Management: $7,000,000
Current Activity Level : Actively seeking new investments

NETHERLANDS DEVELOPMENT FINANCE COMPANY NV

Anna van Saksenlaan 71
The Hague, Netherlands 2593 HW
Phone: 31703149696
Fax: 31703246187
E-mail: info@fmo.nl
Website: www.fmo.nl

Management and Staff
Nanno Kleiterp, Chief Executive Officer
Nico K.G. Pijl, Chief Financial Officer

Type of Firm
Private Equity Firm

Association Membership
Dutch Venture Capital Associaton (NVP)

Project Preferences

Type of Financing Preferred:
Balanced

Size of Investments Considered:
Min Size of Investment Considered (000s): $1,283
Max Size of Investment Considered (000s): $19,247

Geographical Preferences

International Preferences:
Africa

Industry Preferences

In Consumer Related prefer:
Consumer Products
Consumer Services

In Industrial/Energy prefer:
Energy

In Financial Services prefer:
Financial Services

In Business Serv. prefer:
Services

Additional Information
Year Founded: 1970
Capital Under Management: $2,951,100,000
Current Activity Level : Actively seeking new investments

NETWORK FINANCES SAS

13, rue Saint-Lazare
Paris, France 75009
Website: www.network-finances.com

Type of Firm
Private Equity Firm

Project Preferences

Type of Financing Preferred:
Early Stage
Later Stage
Seed
Startup

Size of Investments Considered:
Min Size of Investment Considered (000s): $224
Max Size of Investment Considered (000s): $672

Geographical Preferences

International Preferences:
Europe
France

Industry Preferences

In Communications prefer:
Communications and Media
Wireless Communications

In Internet Specific prefer:
Internet
Ecommerce

Additional Information
Year Founded: 2012
Current Activity Level : Actively seeking new investments

NETWORK VENTURES

220 North Green Street
Chicago, IL USA 60607
E-mail: info@networkventures.vc
Website: www.networkventures.vc

Type of Firm
Private Equity Firm

Project Preferences

Type of Financing Preferred:
Early Stage

Additional Information
Year Founded: 2016
Current Activity Level : Actively seeking new investments

NEUBERGER BERMAN LLC

605 Third Avenue, 36th Floor
New York, NY USA 10158
Phone: 8002236448
Website: www.nb.com

Other Offices
100 Century Avenue, Suite Number 6551
Shanghai, China 200120
Phone: 862138996000
Fax: 38996001

Room3543-49 Level35
Citic Square,Nanjing Road West
Shanghai, China

Number Six Largo Richini
Italy
Phone: 390258215502

Symphony Building
Gustav Mahlerpleon 109-111
Netherlands 1082
Phone: 31207085870

Shin-Marunouchi Building
10th Floor, 1-5-1 Marunouchi, Chiyoda-ku
Tokyo, Japan 100-6510
Phone: 81-3-5218-1930

Lansdowne House
57 Berkeley Square
London, United Kingdom W1J 6ER
Phone: 44-20-3214-9000

Cheung Kong Center, Suite 4701, 2 Queen's Road Central
Central, Hong Kong
Phone: 852-3664-8800

Dreikonigstrasse 31a
Zurich, Switzerland 8002
Phone: 41-44-208-3773

Jardine House, One Connaught Place
20th Floor, Suites 2010- 2020
, Hong Kong
Phone: 85236648800

333 Collins Street
Level 25
, Australia 3000

5 Temasek Boulevard, Suite 11-01 Suntec Tower Five
Singapore, Singapore 038985

Seoul Finance Center, 84 Taepyeongro
21st Floor, Suite 40A
Seoul, South Korea 100-768

10 Collyer Quay, Ocean Financial Centre, Suite 15-05/06
, Singapore 049315
Phone: 6566453760

Messeturm, Friedrich-Ebert-Anlage 49
25th Floor
, Germany 60308
Phone: 4969509565648

Piso Two
Castex 3123
, Argentina C1425CDA

Management and Staff
Bill Arnold, Chief Financial Officer
David Morse, Managing Director
David Stonberg, Managing Director
Harold Newman, Partner
John Buser, Managing Director
Kent Chen, Managing Director
Patricia Miller, Managing Director
Susan Kasser, Managing Director

Type of Firm
Bank Affiliated

Association Membership
Natl Assoc of Investment Cos. (NAIC)

Project Preferences

Type of Financing Preferred:
Leveraged Buyout
Expansion
Mezzanine
Balanced
Other
Fund of Funds of Second

Geographical Preferences

United States Preferences:
All U.S.

International Preferences:
All International

Additional Information
Name of Most Recent Fund: NB Secondary Opportunities Fund III, L.P.
Most Recent Fund Was Raised: 03/18/2013
Year Founded: 1939
Capital Under Management: $15,032,870,000
Current Activity Level : Actively seeking new investments

NEUFLIZE OBC CINEMA SCA SICAR

3, avenue Hoche
France, France 75008
Phone: 33156217000

Type of Firm
Bank Affiliated

Project Preferences

Type of Financing Preferred:
Seed
Startup

Geographical Preferences

International Preferences:
Europe
France

Industry Preferences

In Communications prefer:
Radio & TV Broadcasting
Media and Entertainment
Entertainment

In Consumer Related prefer:
Entertainment and Leisure

Additional Information
Year Founded: 2012
Capital Under Management: $19,830,000
Current Activity Level : Actively seeking new investments

NEUHAUS PARTNERS GMBH

Jungfernstieg 30
Hamburg, Germany 20354
Phone: 49403552820
Fax: 494035528239
E-mail: info@neuhauspartners.com
Website: www.neuhauspartners.com

Management and Staff
Gottfried Neuhaus, Managing Partner
Matthias Grychta, Managing Partner
Peter Gombert, Chief Financial Officer

Type of Firm
Private Equity Firm

Association Membership
German Venture Capital Association (BVK)

Project Preferences

Role in Financing:
Prefer role as deal originator but will also invest in deals created by others

Type of Financing Preferred:
Early Stage
Later Stage
Seed
Startup

Size of Investments Considered:
Min Size of Investment Considered (000s): $700
Max Size of Investment Considered (000s): $4,194

Geographical Preferences

International Preferences:
Europe
Scandanavia/Nordic Region
Germany

Industry Preferences

In Communications prefer:
Communications and Media
Commercial Communications
Wireless Communications

In Computer Software prefer:
Software

In Internet Specific prefer:
Internet

In Semiconductor/Electr prefer:
Electronics

In Industrial/Energy prefer:
Industrial Products
Factory Automation

Additional Information
Name of Most Recent Fund: Neuhaus III
Most Recent Fund Was Raised: 01/01/2008

Year Founded: 1998
Capital Under Management: $182,700,000
Current Activity Level : Actively seeking new investments

NEUROVENTURES CAPITAL LLC

Zero Court Square
Charlottesville, VA USA 22902
Phone: 4342971000
Fax: 4342971001
E-mail: info@neuroventures.com
Website: www.neuroventures.com

Management and Staff

Daniel O Connell, Managing Partner
Mark Cochran, Partner

Type of Firm

Private Equity Firm

Project Preferences

Role in Financing:
Prefer role as deal originator but will also invest in deals created by others

Type of Financing Preferred:
Early Stage
First Stage Financing
Startup

Size of Investments Considered:
Min Size of Investment Considered (000s): $200
Max Size of Investment Considered (000s): $2,000

Geographical Preferences

United States Preferences:

Industry Preferences

In Biotechnology prefer:
Human Biotechnology

In Medical/Health prefer:
Medical Therapeutics
Drug/Equipmt Delivery
Pharmaceuticals

Additional Information

Name of Most Recent Fund: NeuroVentures Fund, L.P.
Most Recent Fund Was Raised: 03/05/2001
Year Founded: 2000
Capital Under Management: $16,000,000
Current Activity Level : Actively seeking new investments
Method of Compensation: Return on investment is of primary concern, do not charge fees

NEW 2ND CAPITAL ADVISORS LP

205 East 42nd Street
20th Floor
New York, NY USA 10017
E-mail: info@new2ndcapital.com

Type of Firm

Private Equity Firm

Project Preferences

Type of Financing Preferred:
Leveraged Buyout
Acquisition

Geographical Preferences

United States Preferences:
North America

Additional Information

Year Founded: 1969
Current Activity Level : Actively seeking new investments

NEW ACCESS CAPITAL

No. 212, Jiangning Road
14D-1, Kaidike Building
Shanghai, China 200041
Phone: 862152895201
Fax: 862152895210
E-mail: chinadeals@newaccess.com.cn
Website: www.newaccess.com.cn

Management and Staff

Andy Lu, Venture Partner
Breaux Walker, Managing Partner
Wei Zhang, Partner
Zhihu Tan, Partner

Type of Firm

Private Equity Firm

Project Preferences

Type of Financing Preferred:
Balanced

Geographical Preferences

International Preferences:
China

Industry Preferences

In Medical/Health prefer:
Medical/Health

In Consumer Related prefer:
Consumer

In Industrial/Energy prefer:
Energy
Alternative Energy
Environmental Related

In Business Serv. prefer:
Media

In Other prefer:
Environment Responsible

Additional Information

Year Founded: 2003
Capital Under Management: $66,383,000
Current Activity Level : Actively seeking new investments

NEW ALPHA ASSET MANAGEMENT SAS

128, Boulevard Raspail
Paris, France 75006
Phone: 33144561000
Fax: 33144561100
Website: www.newalpha.net

Type of Firm

Investment Management Firm

Project Preferences

Type of Financing Preferred:
Fund of Funds
Early Stage
Expansion
Later Stage

Geographical Preferences

International Preferences:
France

Industry Preferences

In Financial Services prefer:
Financial Services
Financial Services

Additional Information

Year Founded: 2003
Capital Under Management: $63,510,000
Current Activity Level : Actively seeking new investments

NEW AMSTERDAM GROWTH CAPITAL LLC

299 Park Avenue
2nd Floor
New York, NY USA 10171
Phone: 212-763-5674
E-mail: info@nagrowth.com
Website: www.nagrowth.com

Type of Firm

Private Equity Firm

Project Preferences

Type of Financing Preferred:
Leveraged Buyout
Early Stage
Later Stage

Geographical Preferences

United States Preferences:
New York
East Coast

Industry Preferences

In Communications prefer:
Communications and Media

In Internet Specific prefer:
Internet

Additional Information
Year Founded: 2013
Current Activity Level : Actively seeking new investments

NEW ANGLIA CAPITAL LTD

The Walpole Suite
Ketteringham Hall
Wymondham, United Kingdom NR18 9RS
Phone: 1603510070
E-mail: info@newanglia.co.uk
Website: www.newanglia.co.uk

Type of Firm
Private Equity Firm

Project Preferences

Type of Financing Preferred:
Early Stage
Seed

Industry Preferences

In Medical/Health prefer:
Health Services

In Industrial/Energy prefer:
Energy

In Manufact. prefer:
Manufacturing

Additional Information
Year Founded: 2015
Current Activity Level : Actively seeking new investments

NEW ASIA PARTNERS LLC

12/F, Shui On Plaza
333 Huai Hai Zhong Road
Shanghai, China 2000021
Website: www.newasiapartners.com

Other Offices
705 Kinwick Centre
32 Hollywood Road
Central, Hong Kong 1801-03
Phone: 852-2851-9836
Fax: 852-2544-9816

US Bancorp Center, Suite 2690, 800 Nicollet Mall
Minneapolis, MN USA 55402

Management and Staff
Dennis Nguyen, Chief Executive Officer
Dwight Clark, Managing Director
Gregory Grego, Chief Financial Officer

Type of Firm
Private Equity Firm

Project Preferences

Type of Financing Preferred:
Early Stage
Balanced
Seed

Geographical Preferences

International Preferences:
Hong Kong
China

Industry Preferences

In Biotechnology prefer:
Biotechnology

In Medical/Health prefer:
Medical/Health
Pharmaceuticals

In Consumer Related prefer:
Consumer
Retail

In Industrial/Energy prefer:
Energy
Environmental Related

Additional Information
Year Founded: 2002
Current Activity Level : Actively seeking new investments

NEW BRAND VENTURES LLC

5104 North Lockwood Ridge Road, Suite 303C
Sarasota, FL USA 34234
Phone: 2036353098

Type of Firm
Incubator/Development Program

Project Preferences

Type of Financing Preferred:
Early Stage
Later Stage
Seed
Startup

Industry Preferences

In Communications prefer:
Telecommunications
Media and Entertainment

In Internet Specific prefer:
Ecommerce

In Medical/Health prefer:
Medical/Health

In Consumer Related prefer:
Food/Beverage
Consumer Products
Consumer Services

In Financial Services prefer:
Financial Services

Additional Information
Year Founded: 2013
Current Activity Level : Actively seeking new investments

NEW BRUNSWICK INNOVATION FOUNDATION

440 King Street, Suite 602, KingTower
Fredicton, Canada E3B 5H8
Phone: 5064522884
Fax: 5064522886
E-mail: info@nbif.ca
Website: www.nbif.ca

Type of Firm
Government Affiliated Program

Association Membership
Canadian Venture Capital Association

Project Preferences

Type of Financing Preferred:
Early Stage
Expansion
Later Stage
Seed
Startup

Geographical Preferences

Canadian Preferences:
All Canada
New Brunswick

Additional Information
Name of Most Recent Fund: Startup Investment Fund
Most Recent Fund Was Raised: 10/23/2013
Year Founded: 2003

Capital Under Management: $60,000,000
Current Activity Level: Actively seeking new investments

NEW CANAAN FUNDING

21 Locust Avenue, Suite 1C
New Canaan, CT USA 06840
Phone: 2039661071
Fax: 2039661081
Website: www.newcanaanfunding.com

Other Offices

20 Danada Square West, Suite 205
Wheaton, IL USA 60187
Phone: 6306907768
Fax: 2039661081

Management and Staff

Gregory Kopchinsky, Founder
Mark Thies, Founder
Sharon Fitzpatrick, Vice President

Type of Firm

Private Equity Firm

Association Membership

Natl Assoc of Small Bus. Inv. Co (NASBIC)

Project Preferences

Type of Financing Preferred:
Leveraged Buyout
Expansion
Mezzanine
Recapitalizations

Geographical Preferences

United States Preferences:

Industry Preferences

In Business Serv. prefer:
Services

In Manufact. prefer:
Manufacturing

Additional Information

Name of Most Recent Fund: New Canaan Funding Mezzanine V, L.P.
Most Recent Fund Was Raised: 06/30/2011
Year Founded: 1995
Capital Under Management: $172,080,000
Current Activity Level: Actively seeking new investments

NEW CAPITAL MANAGEMENT INC

2100 Freedom Road, Suite A
Little Chute, WI USA 54140
Phone: 9207315777
Fax: 9202246357

Management and Staff

Charlie Goff, President
David Gitter, Managing Director
Robert DeBruin, Managing Director
Steve Predayna, Managing Director

Type of Firm

Private Equity Firm

Project Preferences

Type of Financing Preferred:
Early Stage
Balanced
Seed

Size of Investments Considered:
Min Size of Investment Considered (000s): $500
Max Size of Investment Considered (000s): $150,000

Geographical Preferences

United States Preferences:
Wisconsin

Industry Preferences

In Manufact. prefer:
Manufacturing

In Agr/Forestr/Fish prefer:
Agriculture related

Additional Information

Year Founded: 2006
Capital Under Management: $25,000,000
Current Activity Level: Actively seeking new investments

NEW CAPITAL PARTNERS

2900 First Avenue South, Suite 200
Birmingham, AL USA 35233
Phone: 2059398400
Fax: 2059398402
E-mail: info@newcapitalpartners.com
Website: www.newcapitalpartners.com

Other Offices

2101 Cedar Springs Road, Suite 1201
Dallas, TX USA 75201
Phone: 214-871-5408
Fax: 214-871-5401

Management and Staff

Adam Cranford, Principal
James Outland, Managing Partner
Jim Little, Managing Partner
Paul Pless, Principal
Seton Marshall, Principal
Will Matthews, Partner

Type of Firm

Private Equity Firm

Project Preferences

Role in Financing:
Prefer role as deal originator but will also invest in deals created by others

Type of Financing Preferred:
Early Stage
Expansion
Balanced
Later Stage

Size of Investments Considered:
Min Size of Investment Considered (000s): $500
Max Size of Investment Considered (000s): $3,000

Geographical Preferences

United States Preferences:
Southeast
Southwest
Texas
All U.S.

Industry Preferences

In Communications prefer:
Commercial Communications
Telecommunications
Wireless Communications
Data Communications

In Computer Software prefer:
Software
Systems Software
Applications Software

In Internet Specific prefer:
Internet

In Medical/Health prefer:
Medical Diagnostics
Diagnostic Services
Diagnostic Test Products
Drug/Equipmt Delivery
Medical Products
Disposable Med. Products
Health Services

In Industrial/Energy prefer:
Energy

In Financial Services prefer:
Financial Services
Insurance
Financial Services

In Business Serv. prefer:
Services
Distribution

In Utilities prefer:
Utilities

In Other prefer:
Environment Responsible

Additional Information

Name of Most Recent Fund: New Capital Partners Private Equity Fund II, L.P.
Most Recent Fund Was Raised: 07/24/2008
Year Founded: 2000
Capital Under Management: $232,000,000
Current Activity Level : Actively seeking new investments
Method of Compensation: Return on invest. most important, but chg. closing fees, service fees, etc.

NEW CHINA CAPITAL MANAGEMENT LP

One Dock Street
Stamford, CT USA 06902
Phone: 2033281800
Fax: 2033281801
E-mail: info@cathay-capital.com
Website: www.cathay-capital.com

Other Offices

17 Financial Street, Suite 708, China Life Center
Beijing, China 100140
Phone: 861066220509
Fax: 861066220081

33 Garden Road
14th Floor, St. John's Building
Hong Kong, Hong Kong
Phone: 85225302212
Fax: 85221475050

Management and Staff

Ling Liu, Managing Director

Type of Firm

Private Equity Firm

Project Preferences

Type of Financing Preferred:
Expansion
Balanced
Later Stage
Acquisition

Size of Investments Considered:
Min Size of Investment Considered (000s): $8,000
Max Size of Investment Considered (000s): $80,000

Geographical Preferences

International Preferences:
China

Industry Preferences

In Communications prefer:
Wireless Communications
Media and Entertainment

In Medical/Health prefer:
Pharmaceuticals

In Consumer Related prefer:
Food/Beverage
Consumer Products

In Industrial/Energy prefer:
Industrial Products
Environmental Related

In Transportation prefer:
Transportation

In Financial Services prefer:
Financial Services
Real Estate
Financial Services

In Business Serv. prefer:
Services
Media

In Manufact. prefer:
Manufacturing

In Agr/Forestr/Fish prefer:
Agriculture related

Additional Information

Year Founded: 1992
Capital Under Management: $193,750,000
Current Activity Level : Actively seeking new investments

NEW COAST VENTURES LLC

116 West Illinois Street, Suite 5E
Chicago, IL USA 60654
Phone: 8474364229
E-mail: info@newcoastventures.com
Website: www.newcoastventures.com

Type of Firm

Private Equity Firm

Project Preferences

Type of Financing Preferred:
Early Stage
Seed

Additional Information

Year Founded: 2014
Current Activity Level : Actively seeking new investments

NEW CYCLE CAPITAL LLC

410 Jessie Street, Suite 501
San Francisco, CA USA 94103
Phone: 4156150130
Fax: 4153733828
E-mail: info@newcyclecapital.com

Management and Staff

Benjamin Black, General Partner
Josh Becker, General Partner

Type of Firm

Private Equity Firm

Project Preferences

Type of Financing Preferred:
Early Stage

Geographical Preferences

United States Preferences:

Industry Preferences

In Other prefer:
Socially Responsible
Environment Responsible

Additional Information

Year Founded: 2007
Current Activity Level : Actively seeking new investments

NEW ECONOMY DEVELOPMENT FUND SA

12 Amerikis Street
6th & 7th Floor
Athens, Greece 10671
Phone: 30-210-338-7110
Fax: 30-210-338-7116
E-mail: info@taneo.gr
Website: www.taneo.gr

Management and Staff

Nikolaos Haritakis, Chief Executive Officer

Type of Firm

Private Equity Advisor or Fund of Funds

Association Membership

Hellenic Venture Capital Association

Project Preferences

Type of Financing Preferred:
Fund of Funds

Geographical Preferences

International Preferences:
Greece

Industry Preferences

In Computer Software prefer:
Computer Services
Software

In Biotechnology prefer:
Human Biotechnology

In Industrial/Energy prefer:
Machinery

In Agr/Forestr/Fish prefer:
Agribusiness

In Utilities prefer:
Utilities

Additional Information
Year Founded: 2000
Capital Under Management: $260,900,000
Current Activity Level : Actively seeking new investments

NEW ENERGY CAPITAL CORP

53 South Main Street
Third Floor
Hanover, NH USA 03755
Phone: 603-643-8885
Fax: 603-653-7524
E-mail: info@newenergycapital.com
Website: www.newenergycapital.com

Management and Staff
Adam Bernstein, Principal
Curt Whittaker, Managing Partner
Ian Marcus, Principal
Jeph Shaw, Principal
Patrick Fox, Partner
Scott Brown, Managing Partner
Thomas Naughton, Chief Financial Officer

Type of Firm
Private Equity Firm

Association Membership
China Venture Capital Association

Project Preferences

Type of Financing Preferred:
Later Stage
Acquisition

Size of Investments Considered:
Min Size of Investment Considered (000s): $10,000
Max Size of Investment Considered (000s): $200,000

Geographical Preferences

United States Preferences:
All U.S.

Industry Preferences

In Biotechnology prefer:
Industrial Biotechnology

In Industrial/Energy prefer:
Energy
Alternative Energy
Energy Conservation Relat

Additional Information
Name of Most Recent Fund: New Energy Capital Fund I, L.P.
Most Recent Fund Was Raised: 05/09/2005
Year Founded: 2003
Capital Under Management: $400,000
Current Activity Level : Actively seeking new investments

NEW ENGLAND CAPITAL PARTNERS

One Gateway Center, Suite 405
Newton, MA USA 02458
Phone: 6179647300
Fax: 6179647301
E-mail: info@necapitalpartners.com
Website: www.necapitalpartners.com

Management and Staff
Robert Winneg, President

Type of Firm
Private Equity Firm

Project Preferences

Type of Financing Preferred:
Acquisition

Geographical Preferences

United States Preferences:
Northeast
All U.S.

Industry Preferences

In Consumer Related prefer:
Consumer Services

In Business Serv. prefer:
Services
Distribution

In Manufact. prefer:
Manufacturing

Additional Information
Year Founded: 2004
Current Activity Level : Actively seeking new investments

NEW ENTERPRISE ASSOCIATES INC

2855 Sand Hill Road
Menlo Park, CA USA 94025
Phone: 6508549499
Fax: 6508549397
Website: www.nea.com

Other Offices
1954 Greenspring Drive, Suite 600
Lutherville-Timonium, MD USA 21093
Phone: 4102440115
Fax: 4107527721

C-59, G Block
First Floor, Platina
Mumbai, India 400 051
Phone: 912242235600

Prestige Omega, No. 104, Suite 212, Second Floor
Bangalore, India 560 066
Phone: 918040600801
Fax: 918040600700

No. 19 Financial Street
Room B1706, Focus Place
Beijing, China 100140
Phone: 861066575566
Fax: 861066573553

44 West 28th Street
Eighth Floor
MANHATTAN, NY USA 10001

1266 Nanjing West Road
Unit 2202, Plaza 66
Shanghai, China 200040
Phone: 862161381000
Fax: 862161381010

Management and Staff
A. Jay Graf, Venture Partner
Aaron Jacobson, Partner
Ali Behbahani, Principal
Amit Mukherjee, Partner
Andrew Schoen, Principal
Anthony Florence, General Partner
Ben Narasin, Venture Partner
Blake Wu, Principal
Carol Gallagher, Partner
David Mott, General Partner
Dayna Grayson, Partner
Edward Mathers, Partner
Forest Baskett, General Partner
Frank Torti, Principal
Harry Weller, General Partner
Hilarie Koplow-McAdams, Venture Partner
Jake Nunn, Partner
Jon Sakoda, Partner
Joshua Makower, Venture Partner
Kavita Patel, Venture Partner
Krishna Kolluri, General Partner
Matt Sacks, Principal
Mohamad Makhzoumi, General Partner
Peter Sonsini, General Partner
Peter Barris, Managing Partner
Ravi Viswanathan, General Partner
Robert Croce, Venture Partner
Ronald Bernal, Venture Partner
Sara Nayeem, Partner
Scott Sandell, General Partner
Suzanne King, Partner
Timothy Schaller, Chief Financial Officer
Vanessa Larco, Partner

Type of Firm
Private Equity Firm

Association Membership
Mid-Atlantic Venture Association
New England Venture Capital Association
Western Association of Venture Capitalists (WAVC)
National Venture Capital Association - USA (NVCA)
Indian Venture Capital Association (IVCA)

Project Preferences

Role in Financing:
Prefer role as deal originator but will also invest in deals created by others

Type of Financing Preferred:
Early Stage
Balanced
Later Stage
Seed
Startup

Geographical Preferences

United States Preferences:

International Preferences:
India
China

Industry Focus

(% based on actual investment)
Computer Software and Services	22.9%
Medical/Health	17.2%
Internet Specific	16.2%
Communications and Media	13.0%
Biotechnology	10.9%
Other Products	6.2%
Semiconductors/Other Elect.	5.4%
Computer Hardware	4.1%
Industrial/Energy	3.6%
Consumer Related	0.7%

Additional Information

Name of Most Recent Fund: New Enterprise Associates 14, L.P.
Most Recent Fund Was Raised: 05/09/2012
Year Founded: 1978
Capital Under Management: $14,000,000,000
Current Activity Level : Actively seeking new investments
Method of Compensation: Return on investment is of primary concern, do not charge fees

NEW ENTERPRISE EAST INVESTMENTS

Cassells Ghantoot Resort
Ghantoot, 3rd Floor
Abu Dhabi, Utd. Arab Em.
Phone: 971-2-562-9114
Fax: 971-2-562-9115
Website: www.ip-venturepartners.com

Other Offices

1001 Pennsylvania Avenue, Suite 600 South
Washington, WA USA 20004
Phone: 202-756-2263
Fax: 202-756-7323

Management and Staff

Harvey Klyce, Managing Director
Jack Roepers, Managing Director

Type of Firm
Private Equity Firm

Project Preferences

Type of Financing Preferred:
Early Stage

Size of Investments Considered:
Min Size of Investment Considered (000s): $2,000
Max Size of Investment Considered (000s): $100,000

Geographical Preferences

International Preferences:
Bahrain
Oman
Qatar
Iran
Utd. Arab Em.
Saudi Arabia
Kuwait
Iraq

Industry Preferences

In Communications prefer:
Wireless Communications

In Industrial/Energy prefer:
Alternative Energy
Energy Conservation Relat
Environmental Related

In Financial Services prefer:
Financial Services
Real Estate

Additional Information

Year Founded: 2008
Capital Under Management: $40,000,000
Current Activity Level : Actively seeking new investments

NEW ENTERPRISE INVESTMENT CO LTD

B-12 Jianguomenwai Avenue
1703, East Tower, Twin Towers
Beijing, China
Phone: 861085185285
Fax: 861085184966

Management and Staff

Yangyu Xiao, Founder

Type of Firm
Private Equity Firm

Association Membership

Hong Kong Venture Capital Association (HKVCA)
Emerging Markets Private Equity Association
China Venture Capital Association

Project Preferences

Type of Financing Preferred:
Expansion
Generalist PE

Size of Investments Considered:
Min Size of Investment Considered (000s): $10,000
Max Size of Investment Considered (000s): $50,000

Geographical Preferences

International Preferences:
China

Industry Preferences

In Medical/Health prefer:
Medical/Health

In Consumer Related prefer:
Retail
Consumer Products
Consumer Services

In Industrial/Energy prefer:
Environmental Related

In Manufact. prefer:
Manufacturing

In Agr/Forestr/Fish prefer:
Agribusiness

Additional Information

Year Founded: 2006
Capital Under Management: $113,000,000
Current Activity Level : Actively seeking new investments

NEW EQUITY VENTURE INTERNATIONAL AB

Birger Jarlsgatan 18 A
Stockholm, Sweden 10243
E-mail: ir@newequityventure.com
Website: www.newequityventure.com

Type of Firm
Private Equity Firm

Geographical Preferences

International Preferences:
Sweden
All International

Additional Information

Year Founded: 2013
Current Activity Level : Actively seeking new investments

NEW EUROPE VENTURE EQUITY

53B N.J. Vaptzarov Boulevard
4/F,Ofc 12,Mandarin Ofc Ctr.
Sofia, Bulgaria 1407
Phone: 35929587665
Fax: 35929587666
E-mail: office@neveq.com
Website: www.neveq.com

Management and Staff
Konstantin Petrov, Co-Founder
Pavel Ezekiev, Co-Founder
Peter Safran, Partner

Type of Firm
Private Equity Firm

Project Preferences

Type of Financing Preferred:
Early Stage
Expansion
Balanced
Later Stage
Seed
Startup

Size of Investments Considered:
Min Size of Investment Considered (000s): $691
Max Size of Investment Considered (000s): $6,907

Geographical Preferences

United States Preferences:
All U.S.

International Preferences:
United Kingdom
Turkey
Argentina
Macedonia
Brazil
Bulgaria
Spain
Romania

Industry Preferences

In Communications prefer:
Communications and Media

In Internet Specific prefer:
E-Commerce Technology
Ecommerce

Additional Information
Year Founded: 2006
Capital Under Management: $39,500,000
Current Activity Level : Actively seeking new investments

NEW FRONTIER PARTNERS CO LTD

2-31-19, Shiba, Minato-ku
7F, Banzai Building
Tokyo, Japan 105-0014
Phone: 81345036400
Fax: 81345036491
E-mail: info@nf-partners.co.jp
Website: www.nf-partners.co.jp

Type of Firm
Private Equity Firm

Project Preferences

Type of Financing Preferred:
Early Stage
Balanced

Geographical Preferences

International Preferences:
No Preference
Western Europe
Japan

Additional Information
Year Founded: 1985
Capital Under Management: $114,900,000
Current Activity Level : Actively seeking new investments

NEW GROUND VENTURES

20 Ketchum Street
Westport Inovation Hub
Westport, CT USA 06880
Website: ngv.us

Type of Firm
Private Equity Firm

Project Preferences

Type of Financing Preferred:
Balanced
Later Stage
Seed

Industry Preferences

In Medical/Health prefer:
Medical/Health

In Consumer Related prefer:
Food/Beverage
Education Related

In Financial Services prefer:
Financial Services

Additional Information
Year Founded: 2013
Capital Under Management: $34,555,000
Current Activity Level : Actively seeking new investments

NEW HARBOR CAPITAL MANAGEMENT LLC

Ten South Wacker Drive, Suite 3175
Chicago, IL USA 60606
Phone: 3128768605
Fax: 3128763854
Website: newharborcap.com

Type of Firm
Private Equity Firm

Project Preferences

Type of Financing Preferred:
Leveraged Buyout
Expansion
Management Buyouts
Recapitalizations

Industry Preferences

In Medical/Health prefer:
Health Services

In Consumer Related prefer:
Education Related

In Business Serv. prefer:
Services

Additional Information
Year Founded: 2013
Capital Under Management: $396,000,000
Current Activity Level : Actively seeking new investments

NEW HERITAGE CAPITAL LLC

800 Boylston Street, Suite 1535, Prudential Tower
Boston, MA USA 02199
Phone: 6174390688
Fax: 6174390689
Website: www.newheritagecapital.com

Management and Staff
Charles Gifford, General Partner
Judson Samuels, Principal
Mark Jrolf, Managing Partner
Melissa Barry, Principal
Nickie Norris, General Partner

Type of Firm
Private Equity Firm

Project Preferences

Role in Financing:
Prefer role as deal originator

Type of Financing Preferred:
Leveraged Buyout
Acquisition
Recapitalizations

Geographical Preferences

United States Preferences:
All U.S.

Industry Focus

(% based on actual investment)
Medical/Health	57.6%
Other Products	28.8%
Consumer Related	8.6%
Industrial/Energy	4.5%
Internet Specific	0.3%
Semiconductors/Other Elect.	0.3%

Additional Information

Name of Most Recent Fund: New Heritage Capital Fund, L.P.
Most Recent Fund Was Raised: 09/27/2013
Year Founded: 1987
Capital Under Management: $1,433,000,000
Current Activity Level : Reducing investment activity
Method of Compensation: Return on investment is of primary concern, do not charge fees

NEW HILL MANAGEMENT LLC

225 Franklin Street
Boston, MA USA 02110
Phone: 6172172770
E-mail: contact@newhillmgt.com
Website: www.newhillmgt.com

Other Offices

23 Berkeley Square
London, United Kingdom W1J 6HE
Phone: 4402033728600

Type of Firm

Private Equity Firm

Project Preferences

Type of Financing Preferred:
Expansion
Later Stage

Geographical Preferences

International Preferences:
United Kingdom

Additional Information

Year Founded: 2009
Current Activity Level : Actively seeking new investments

NEW HORIZON CAPITAL

89 Jin Bao Street, Suite 1008, Jin Bao Tower
Beijing, China 100005
Phone: 861089508400
Fax: 861089508401
E-mail: enquiry@nhfund.com
Website: www.nhfund.com

Other Offices

Eigth Connaught Place, Suite 1702-03, One Exchange Square
Central, Hong Kong
Phone: 85228016988
Fax: 85228014882

Management and Staff

Jianming Yu, President
Xin Wang, Vice President

Type of Firm

Private Equity Firm

Project Preferences

Type of Financing Preferred:
Early Stage
Balanced
Later Stage

Geographical Preferences

International Preferences:
China

Industry Preferences

In Medical/Health prefer:
Medical/Health

In Consumer Related prefer:
Consumer Products
Consumer Services

In Industrial/Energy prefer:
Energy

In Manufact. prefer:
Manufacturing

Additional Information

Year Founded: 2005
Capital Under Management: $1,050,000,000
Current Activity Level : Actively seeking new investments

NEW HORIZON CAPITAL CO LTD

2-8-6, Nishinbashi, Minato-ku
4/F, Sumitomo Fudosan Hibiya
Tokyo, Japan 105-0003
Phone: 81-3-3519-1260
Fax: 81-3-3519-1261
Website: www.newhorizon.jp

Management and Staff

Akiyo Arai, Partner
Hajime Nakamura, Partner
Naoko Hatakeyama, Partner
Yasushi Ando, Chief Executive Officer
Yoichiro Kurosawa, Partner

Type of Firm

Private Equity Firm

Project Preferences

Type of Financing Preferred:
Leveraged Buyout
Turnaround
Management Buyouts
Recapitalizations

Geographical Preferences

International Preferences:
Japan

Industry Preferences

In Business Serv. prefer:
Services

In Manufact. prefer:
Manufacturing

Additional Information

Year Founded: 2006
Current Activity Level : Actively seeking new investments

NEW HORIZONS VENTURE CAPITAL LLC

1808 Eye Street, Northwest, Suite 200
Washington, DC USA 20006
Phone: 2029557965
Fax: 2029557966
E-mail: info@newhorizonsvc.com
Website: www.newhorizonsvc.com

Type of Firm

Private Equity Firm

Project Preferences

Role in Financing:
Prefer role as deal originator but will also invest in deals created by others

Type of Financing Preferred:
Early Stage
Startup

Size of Investments Considered:
Min Size of Investment Considered (000s): $1,000
Max Size of Investment Considered (000s): $4,000

Geographical Preferences

United States Preferences:
Mid Atlantic

Industry Focus

(% based on actual investment)
Internet Specific	48.4%
Consumer Related	21.2%
Computer Hardware	17.0%
Computer Software and Services	8.1%
Semiconductors/Other Elect.	5.2%

Additional Information
Year Founded: 1999
Capital Under Management: $200,000,000
Current Activity Level : Actively seeking new investments

NEW JERSEY ECONOMIC DEVELOPMENT AUTHORITY

36 West State Steet
Trenton, NJ USA 08625
Phone: 6098586700
Website: www.njeda.com

Other Offices
Gateway One, Suite 900
NEWARK, NJ USA 07102
Phone: 973-648-4130

Management and Staff
Melissa Orsen, Chief Executive Officer
Timothy Lizura, President & COO

Type of Firm
Government Affiliated Program

Project Preferences

Type of Financing Preferred:
Early Stage
Startup

Size of Investments Considered:
Min Size of Investment Considered (000s): $100
Max Size of Investment Considered (000s): $1,000

Geographical Preferences

United States Preferences:
New Jersey
All U.S.

Additional Information
Year Founded: 2006
Current Activity Level : Actively seeking new investments

NEW LEAF VENTURE PARTNERS LLC

Times Square Tower
Seven Times Square, Suite 3502
New York, NY USA 10036
Phone: 6468716400
Fax: 6468716450
E-mail: info@nlvpartners.com
Website: www.nlvpartners.com

Other Offices
2500 Sand Hill Road, Suite 203
Menlo Park, CA USA 94025
Phone: 650-234-2700
Fax: 650-234-2704

1200 Park Place, Suite 300
San Mateo, CA USA 94403
Phone: 6502342700
Fax: 6502342704

Management and Staff
Craig Slutzkin, Chief Financial Officer
James Niedel, Managing Director
Jeani Delagardelle, Managing Director
Kathleen LaPorte, Partner
Liam Ratcliffe, General Partner
Mark Charest, Vice President
Michael Dybbs, Principal
Philippe Chambon, Managing Director
Ronald Hunt, Managing Director
Srinivas Akkaraju, Managing Director
Vijay Lathi, Managing Director

Type of Firm
Private Equity Firm

Association Membership
National Venture Capital Association - USA (NVCA)

Project Preferences

Role in Financing:
Prefer role as deal originator but will also invest in deals created by others

Type of Financing Preferred:
Fund of Funds
Early Stage
Expansion
Balanced
Later Stage
Seed
Startup

Geographical Preferences

United States Preferences:

Industry Preferences

In Biotechnology prefer:
Biotechnology
Biotech Related Research

In Medical/Health prefer:
Medical/Health
Medical Diagnostics
Medical Therapeutics
Drug/Equipmt Delivery
Medical Products
Health Services
Hospitals/Clinics/Primary
Pharmaceuticals

Additional Information
Name of Most Recent Fund: New Leaf Ventures II, L.P.
Most Recent Fund Was Raised: 10/18/2007
Year Founded: 2005
Capital Under Management: $766,000,000
Current Activity Level : Actively seeking new investments

NEW LEGACY CAPITAL LLC

122 East 42nd Street
8th Floor
New York, NY USA 10168
Phone: 2126168020
Website: www.newlegacy.com

Management and Staff
Adam Geiger, President
Elisa Mailman, Managing Director

Type of Firm
Private Equity Firm

Project Preferences

Type of Financing Preferred:
Generalist PE

Additional Information
Year Founded: 2015
Capital Under Management: $26,460,000
Current Activity Level : Actively seeking new investments

NEW MAGELLAN VENTURE PARTNERS LLC

1212 New York Avenue, NW, Suite 700
Washington, DC USA 20005
Phone: 2027839320
Fax: 2027839329
E-mail: info@newmagellan.com
Website: www.newmagellan.com

Management and Staff
Kathryn Kaufman, Partner
Mark Walker, Partner
Melvin Richmond, Partner
Michael Finnegan, Partner
Richard Lawless, Partner

Type of Firm
Investment Management Firm

Project Preferences

Type of Financing Preferred:
Early Stage

Geographical Preferences

United States Preferences:
All U.S.

International Preferences:
Asia Pacific

Industry Preferences

In Industrial/Energy prefer:
Energy

In Transportation prefer:
Transportation
Aerospace

In Financial Services prefer:
Real Estate

Additional Information
Year Founded: 2009
Current Activity Level : Actively seeking new investments

NEW MAINSTREAM CAPITAL

77 Water Street, Suite 2602
New York, NY USA 10005
Phone: 2124227099
Website: www.nms-capital.com

Other Offices
300 Crescent Court, Suite 1700
Dallas, TX USA 75201
Phone: 2148718350

Management and Staff
James Wilson, Partner
Kevin Jordan, Co-Founder
Martin Chavez, Co-Founder
Wyche Walton, Partner

Type of Firm
Private Equity Firm

Association Membership
Natl Assoc of Investment Cos. (NAIC)

Project Preferences

Type of Financing Preferred:
Leveraged Buyout
Acquisition

Geographical Preferences

United States Preferences:

Industry Preferences

In Medical/Health prefer:
Health Services

In Consumer Related prefer:
Food/Beverage
Consumer Products
Consumer Services

In Business Serv. prefer:
Services

Additional Information
Name of Most Recent Fund: NMS Fund II, L.P.
Most Recent Fund Was Raised: 09/06/2013
Year Founded: 2010
Capital Under Management: $225,600,000
Current Activity Level : Actively seeking new investments

NEW MARKETS VENTURE PARTNERS

8161 Maple Lawn Boulevard, Suite 350
Fulton, MD USA 20759
Phone: 3013625511
Fax: 3013625517
Website: www.newmarketsvp.com

Management and Staff
Donald Spero, General Partner
Elizabeth Chou, Principal
Frank Bonsal, Venture Partner
Frank Bonsal, Partner
Mark Grovic, General Partner
Robb Doub, General Partner

Type of Firm
Private Equity Firm

Association Membership
Community Development Venture Capital Alliance
Mid-Atlantic Venture Association

Project Preferences

Role in Financing:
Prefer role as deal originator but will also invest in deals created by others

Type of Financing Preferred:
Early Stage
Balanced
Later Stage
Seed

Geographical Preferences

United States Preferences:
Mid Atlantic

Industry Preferences

In Consumer Related prefer:
Education Related

In Business Serv. prefer:
Services

Additional Information
Year Founded: 2003
Capital Under Management: $20,000,000
Current Activity Level : Actively seeking new investments
Method of Compensation: Return on investment is of primary concern, do not charge fees

NEW MEDIA INNOVATION CENTRE

590 - 515 W Hastings Street
Vancouver, Canada V6B 5K3
Phone: 604-268-7968
Fax: 604-268-7967
Website: www.newmic.com

Management and Staff
Fred Lake, Chief Financial Officer

Type of Firm
Private Equity Firm

Project Preferences

Type of Financing Preferred:
Startup

Geographical Preferences

Canadian Preferences:
Western Canada

Additional Information
Year Founded: 2009
Current Activity Level : Actively seeking new investments

NEW MEXICO COMMUNITY CAPITAL

801 University Boulevard, Suite 102
Albuquerque, NM USA 87106
Phone: 5059242820
Fax: 5052130333
E-mail: info@nmccap.org
Website: www.nmccap.org

Management and Staff
J. Michael Schafer, Managing Director
Leslie Elgood, Chief Executive Officer
Mike Emerson, Vice President

Type of Firm
Government Affiliated Program

Association Membership
Community Development Venture Capital Alliance

Project Preferences

Type of Financing Preferred:
Early Stage
Seed
Startup

Geographical Preferences

United States Preferences:
New Mexico

Industry Preferences

In Medical/Health prefer:
Medical/Health

In Industrial/Energy prefer:
Energy
Environmental Related

In Agr/Forestr/Fish prefer:
Agriculture related

Additional Information
Name of Most Recent Fund: NMCC LP Fund I
Most Recent Fund Was Raised: 05/01/2005
Year Founded: 2004
Capital Under Management: $14,700,000
Current Activity Level : Actively seeking new investments

NEW MOUNTAIN CAPITAL I LLC

787 Seventh Avenue
49th Floor
New York, NY USA 10019
Phone: 2127200300
Fax: 2125822277
Website: www.newmountaincapital.com

Management and Staff
Alok Singh, Managing Director
Beth Grafstrom, Vice President
Christopher Noelcke, Vice President
Daniel Riley, Managing Director
David Frost, Managing Director
David Coquillette, Managing Director
Douglas Londal, Managing Director
Harris Kealey, Vice President
Jack Qian, Vice President
John Kline, Managing Director
Joshua Hirschhorn, Vice President
Krish Daftary, Vice President
Lars Johansson, Vice President
Laura Holson, Vice President
Linda Chiu, Vice President
Mathew Lori, Managing Director
Matthew Holt, Managing Director
Michael Ajouz, Managing Director
Peter Masucci, Managing Director
Robert Mulcare, Vice President
Robert Hamwee, Managing Director
Sunil Mishra, Managing Director
Teddy Kaplan, Managing Director
Thomas Morgan, Managing Director

Type of Firm
Private Equity Firm

Association Membership
Private Equity Council (PEC)

Project Preferences

Type of Financing Preferred:
Leveraged Buyout
Acquisition

Geographical Preferences

United States Preferences:
North America

Industry Focus
(% based on actual investment)
Other Products	48.7%
Industrial/Energy	18.3%
Internet Specific	14.9%
Computer Software and Services	10.0%
Biotechnology	4.7%
Consumer Related	3.4%

Additional Information
Year Founded: 1999
Capital Under Management: $8,500,000,000
Current Activity Level : Actively seeking new investments

NEW PROTEIN CAPITAL PTE LTD

44 A Amoy Street
Singapore, Singapore 069870
Phone: 6567182570
Website: www.newproteincapital.com

Type of Firm
Private Equity Firm

Project Preferences

Type of Financing Preferred:
Balanced

Industry Preferences

In Consumer Related prefer:
Food/Beverage

In Agr/Forestr/Fish prefer:
Agriculture related

Additional Information
Year Founded: 2015
Current Activity Level : Actively seeking new investments

NEW RICHMOND VENTURES

1801 East Cary Street
Studio 100
Richmond, VA USA 23223
E-mail: contact@newrichmondventures.com
Website: newrichmondventures.com

Type of Firm
Private Equity Firm

Project Preferences

Type of Financing Preferred:
Startup

Geographical Preferences

United States Preferences:
Virginia

Additional Information
Year Founded: 2011
Capital Under Management: $33,000,000
Current Activity Level : Actively seeking new investments

NEW SCIENCE VENTURES LLC

610 Fifth Avenue, Suite 305
New York, NY USA 10020
Phone: 2126613498
Fax: 2123089196
E-mail: info@newscienceventures.com
Website: newscienceventures.com

Management and Staff
Somasundaram Subramaniam, Managing Partner
Thomas Lavin, Chief Financial Officer

Type of Firm
Private Equity Firm

Project Preferences

Type of Financing Preferred:
Early Stage
Balanced
Later Stage

Geographical Preferences

United States Preferences:
All U.S.

International Preferences:
India
Europe
China

Industry Preferences

In Semiconductor/Electr prefer:
Semiconductor

In Biotechnology prefer:
Biotechnology

In Medical/Health prefer:
Medical Products
Pharmaceuticals

In Industrial/Energy prefer:
Advanced Materials

Additional Information
Year Founded: 2004
Capital Under Management: $2,500,000
Current Activity Level : Actively seeking new investments

NEW SILK ROUTE PARTNERS, LLC

540 Madison Avenue
30th Floor
New York, NY USA 10022
Phone: 2127105221
Fax: 6467440331
Website: www.nsrpartners.com

Other Offices

205 Ceejay House
Shivsagar Estate, Dr. Annie Besant Road
Mumbai, India 400 018
Phone: 91-22-6618-0964
Fax: 91-22-6615-0901

33 Promenade Road
Lone Star, 1st Floor
Bangalore, India 560005
Phone: 91-80-4022-4103
Fax: 91-80-4022-4033

Sheikh Zayed Road
Office Tower, 7th Flr., Shangri-la Hotel
Dubai, Utd. Arab Em.
Phone: 971-4-321-1772
Fax: 971-4-321-1773

Management and Staff

Abdul Hafeez Shaikh, General Partner
Anand Dorairaj, Partner
Arvind Malhan, Principal
Darius Pandole, Partner
Harsha Misra, Principal
Jacob Kurian, Partner
Jens Yahya Zimmermann, Partner
Jens Yahya Zimmermann, Partner
Nithin Kaimal, Principal
Rajan Singh, Vice President
Shantanu Nalavadi, Partner
Sumit Sharma, Vice President
Supratim Bose, Partner
Vivek Sett, Partner

Type of Firm

Private Equity Firm

Association Membership

Gulf Venture Capital Association
Indian Venture Capital Association (IVCA)

Project Preferences

Type of Financing Preferred:
Leveraged Buyout
Expansion

Geographical Preferences

International Preferences:
Bangladesh
Pakistan
India
Middle East
Sri Lanka
Asia

Industry Preferences

In Communications prefer:
Telecommunications

In Consumer Related prefer:
Consumer Services

In Financial Services prefer:
Financial Services

In Business Serv. prefer:
Media

In Manufact. prefer:
Manufacturing

Additional Information

Year Founded: 2006
Capital Under Management: $1,400,000,000
Current Activity Level : Actively seeking new investments

NEW SOUTH CAPITAL PTY LTD

Three Spring Street
Sydney, Australia NSW 2000
Phone: 61280767699
Website: www.newsouth.com.au

Management and Staff

Tom Beecroft, Managing Director

Type of Firm

Private Equity Firm

Association Membership

Australian Venture Capital Association (AVCAL)

Project Preferences

Type of Financing Preferred:
Leveraged Buyout
Turnaround
Management Buyouts
Acquisition

Geographical Preferences

International Preferences:
Asia Pacific
Australia

Industry Preferences

In Communications prefer:
Communications and Media
Media and Entertainment

In Medical/Health prefer:
Health Services

In Consumer Related prefer:
Entertainment and Leisure
Retail
Food/Beverage
Hotels and Resorts
Education Related

In Industrial/Energy prefer:
Environmental Related

In Business Serv. prefer:
Distribution
Media

Additional Information

Year Founded: 2005
Capital Under Management: $15,000,000
Current Activity Level : Actively seeking new investments

NEW STATE CAPITAL PARTNERS LLC

1890 Palmer Avenue, Suite 402
Larchmont, NY USA 10538
Phone: 2126751600
E-mail: info@newstatecp.com
Website: www.newstatecp.com

Management and Staff

David Blechman, Founder

Type of Firm

Private Equity Firm

Project Preferences

Type of Financing Preferred:
Leveraged Buyout
Later Stage
Acquisition
Special Situation

Industry Preferences

In Medical/Health prefer:
Health Services

In Industrial/Energy prefer:
Industrial Products

In Business Serv. prefer:
Services

Additional Information

Year Founded: 2013
Capital Under Management: $128,570,000
Current Activity Level : Actively seeking new investments

NEW VALUE CAPITAL

1389 Center Dr
#200
Park City, UT USA 84098
Phone: 4352520545
Website: www.newvaluecapital.com

Type of Firm
Private Equity Firm

Additional Information
Year Founded: 2011
Current Activity Level : Actively seeking new investments

NEW VANTAGE GROUP

1616 Anderson Road, Suite 323
McLean, VA USA 22102
E-mail: info@newvantagegroup.com
Website: www.newvantagegroup.com

Management and Staff
John May, Managing Partner

Type of Firm
Private Equity Firm

Project Preferences

Role in Financing:
Will function either as deal originator or investor in deals created by others

Type of Financing Preferred:
Early Stage

Size of Investments Considered:
Min Size of Investment Considered (000s): $250
Max Size of Investment Considered (000s): $1,000

Geographical Preferences

United States Preferences:
Mid Atlantic

Industry Preferences

In Communications prefer:
Telecommunications
Wireless Communications
Data Communications

In Computer Software prefer:
Computer Services
Software
Systems Software
Applications Software

In Internet Specific prefer:
Internet
Ecommerce
Web Aggregation/Portals

In Semiconductor/Electr prefer:
Micro-Processing
Controllers and Sensors
Laser Related
Fiber Optics

In Biotechnology prefer:
Human Biotechnology

In Medical/Health prefer:
Diagnostic Test Products
Medical Products

In Consumer Related prefer:
Education Related

In Financial Services prefer:
Financial Services

Additional Information
Year Founded: 1999
Capital Under Management: $30,000,000
Current Activity Level : Actively seeking new investments
Method of Compensation: Return on investment is of primary concern, do not charge fees

NEW VENTURE DEVELOPMENT SPA

Via Asti 12
Turin, Italy 10015
Phone: 39 0125 64 1183
Fax: 39 0125 48 772
E-mail: info@nvd.it
Website: www.nvd.it

Management and Staff
Mario Ciofalo, Partner

Type of Firm
Private Equity Firm

Project Preferences

Type of Financing Preferred:
Early Stage
Expansion
Seed

Geographical Preferences

International Preferences:
Italy

Additional Information
Year Founded: 1999
Current Activity Level : Actively seeking new investments

NEW VENTURE PARTNERS LLC

430 Mountain Avenue
Murray Hill, NJ USA 07974
Phone: 9084640900
Fax: 9084648131
E-mail: info@nvpllc.com
Website: www.nvpllc.com

Management and Staff
Andrew Garman, Co-Founder
Stephen Socolof, Managing Partner
Thomas Uhlman, Co-Founder

Type of Firm
Private Equity Firm

Association Membership
National Venture Capital Association - USA (NVCA)

Project Preferences

Type of Financing Preferred:
Early Stage
Balanced
Seed

Geographical Preferences

United States Preferences:

Industry Preferences

In Communications prefer:
Telecommunications
Data Communications
Satellite Microwave Comm.

In Computer Software prefer:
Data Processing
Software
Systems Software

In Semiconductor/Electr prefer:
Electronics
Semiconductor

In Industrial/Energy prefer:
Materials
Environmental Related

In Business Serv. prefer:
Services

Additional Information
Name of Most Recent Fund: NV Partners IV, L.P.
Most Recent Fund Was Raised: 12/29/2005
Year Founded: 1997
Capital Under Management: $700,000,000
Current Activity Level : Actively seeking new investments

NEW VENTURES LLC

3500 Pacific Avenue
Virginia Beach, VA USA 23451
Phone: 7574911200

Type of Firm
Private Equity Firm

Project Preferences

Type of Financing Preferred:
Early Stage

Industry Preferences

In Medical/Health prefer:
Health Services

Additional Information
Year Founded: 2016
Capital Under Management: $7,250,000
Current Activity Level : Actively seeking new investments

NEW WATER CAPITAL LP

2424 North Federal Highway, Suite 418
Boca Raton, FL USA 33431
Phone: 5612357310
Fax: 5619104052
Website: www.newwatercap.com

Management and Staff
Andrew Ravenna, Vice President
Brian McGee, Partner
Jason Neimark, Partner
John Disa, Partner
Mark Becker, Partner

Type of Firm
Private Equity Firm

Project Preferences

Type of Financing Preferred:
Leveraged Buyout
Turnaround
Acquisition
Recapitalizations

Geographical Preferences

United States Preferences:
North America

Industry Preferences

In Consumer Related prefer:
Retail
Consumer Products

In Business Serv. prefer:
Services

In Manufact. prefer:
Manufacturing

Additional Information
Year Founded: 2014
Capital Under Management: $406,000,000
Current Activity Level : Actively seeking new investments

NEW WORLD ANGELS, INC.

8130 Glades Rd, Suite 293
Boca Raton, FL USA 33431
Phone: 5613726309
Fax: 5615845211
E-mail: info@newworldangels.com
Website: www.newworldangels.com

Management and Staff
Carl Treleaven, Vice President
John Clark, Vice President
Jonathan Cole, Vice President
Rhys Williams, President
Ryan Morgan, Vice President
Steve Hara, President
Tom Cardy, Vice President

Type of Firm
Angel Group

Project Preferences

Type of Financing Preferred:
Early Stage

Geographical Preferences

United States Preferences:
Florida

Additional Information
Year Founded: 2005
Current Activity Level : Actively seeking new investments

NEW WORLD PRIVATE EQUITY PARTNERS LLP

64 New Cavendish Street
London, United Kingdom W1G8TB
Phone: 442076121888
Fax: 442076121889
Website: www.nwpep.com

Management and Staff
Nigel Berger, Co-Founder
Stephen Altman, Co-Founder

Type of Firm
Private Equity Firm

Project Preferences

Type of Financing Preferred:
Expansion
Generalist PE
Balanced
Later Stage
Management Buyouts
Acquisition
Recapitalizations

Geographical Preferences

International Preferences:
United Kingdom

Industry Preferences

In Consumer Related prefer:
Entertainment and Leisure
Retail
Consumer Services
Other Restaurants

In Financial Services prefer:
Financial Services

Additional Information
Year Founded: 2010
Current Activity Level : Actively seeking new investments

NEW YORK BUSINESS DEVELOPMENT CORP

50 Beaver Street, Suite 600
Albany, NY USA 12207
Phone: 18009898504
Website: www.nybdc.com

Other Offices
534 Broadhollow Road, Suite 430
Melville, NY USA 11747
Phone: 516-845-2700
Fax: 516-845-2705

300 International Boulevard, Suite 126
Williamsville, NY USA 14221
Phone: 716-626-3423
Fax: 716-626-3001

215 Washington Street, Suite 102
Watertown, NY USA 13601
Phone: 315-755-2700
Fax: 518-694-8551

290 Elwood Davis Road
Executive Office Suite 20
Liverpool, NY USA 13088
Phone: 315-453-8195
Fax: 315-453-8197

Five Hanover Square, Suite 1003
New York, NY USA 10004
Phone: 212-785-5642
Fax: 212-785-5987

70 Linden Oaks
Third Floor
Rochester, NY USA 14625
Phone: 585-662-4150
Fax: 585-662-4151

Management and Staff
Audrey Tomlinson, Vice President
Curt Solomon, Vice President
Irvin Nash, Vice President
John King, Vice President
Michael Zihal, Vice President
R. Thomas Faughnan, Vice President
Richard Champion, Vice President
Sarah Halliday, Vice President
Sean O Connor, Vice President

Type of Firm
Investment Management Firm

Project Preferences

Type of Financing Preferred:
Early Stage
Expansion
Balanced
Later Stage
Startup

Geographical Preferences

United States Preferences:
New York

Additional Information
Year Founded: 1973
Capital Under Management: $500,000
Current Activity Level : Actively seeking new investments

NEW YORK CITY ECONOMIC DEVELOPMENT CORP

110 William Street
New York, NY USA 10038
Phone: 2126195000
Website: www.nycedc.com

Management and Staff
Alejandro Baquero-Cifuentes, Vice President
Chris Leng Smith, Vice President
Kyle Kimball, Chief Financial Officer
Seth Pinsky, President

Type of Firm
Government Affiliated Program

Project Preferences

Type of Financing Preferred:
Balanced

Geographical Preferences

United States Preferences:
New York

Additional Information
Year Founded: 2012
Capital Under Management: $22,000,000
Current Activity Level : Actively seeking new investments

NEW YORK DIGITAL HEALTH ACCELERATOR

40 Worth Street
5th Floor
New York, NY USA 10013
E-mail: info@digitalhealthaccelerator.com
Website: www.digitalhealthaccelerator.com

Type of Firm
Incubator/Development Program

Project Preferences

Type of Financing Preferred:
Early Stage
Later Stage

Size of Investments Considered:
Min Size of Investment Considered (000s): $100
Max Size of Investment Considered (000s): $300

Geographical Preferences

United States Preferences:
New York

Industry Preferences

In Medical/Health prefer:
Medical/Health
Health Services

Additional Information
Year Founded: 2012
Current Activity Level : Actively seeking new investments

NEW YORK TIMES CO

620 Eighth Avenue
New York, NY USA 10018
Phone: 2125561234
Website: www.nytco.com

Management and Staff
David Perpich, President
Joseph Garbus, Vice President
Philip Ciuffo, Vice President
Susan Murphy, Vice President
Vincenzo DiMaggio, Vice President

Type of Firm
Corporate PE/Venture

Additional Information
Year Founded: 1896
Current Activity Level : Actively seeking new investments

NEW ZEALAND VENTURE INVESTMENT FUND, LTD.

93-95 Ascot Avenue
Unit 1B, Ascot Office Park
Auckland, New Zealand
Phone: 6499510170
Fax: 6499510171
E-mail: venture@nzvif.co.nz
Website: www.nzvif.com

Management and Staff
Franceska Banga, Chief Executive Officer

Type of Firm
Government Affiliated Program

Association Membership
New Zealand Venture Capital Association

Project Preferences

Type of Financing Preferred:
Fund of Funds
Early Stage
Expansion
Seed
Startup

Geographical Preferences

International Preferences:
New Zealand

Additional Information
Year Founded: 2002
Capital Under Management: $164,500,000
Current Activity Level : Actively seeking new investments

NEWABLE INVESTMENTS LTD

Dirac Crescent, Emersons Green
Bristol and Bath Science Park
Bristol, United Kingdom BS16 7FR
Phone: 4411737077470
E-mail: info@yfmep.com

Other Offices
Berkeley Square House
Berkeley Square
London, United Kingdom W1J 6BD
Phone: 44-20-7887-7522
Fax: 44-20-7887-7563

New Bailey Street
Third Floor, Cloister House
Manchester, United Kingdom M3 5AP
Phone: 44-16-1832-7603
Fax: 44-16-1819-3192

The Hart Shaw Building, Europa Link, Suite 1, SO Offices
Sheffield, United Kingdom S9 1XU
Phone: 441142800160

100 Old Hall Street
The Plaza
Liverpool, United Kingdom L3 9QJ
Phone: 44-15-1600-5134

210-212 Chapeltown Road
Saint Martins House
Leeds, United Kingdom LS7 4HZ
Phone: 44-11-3294-5000
Fax: 441132945002

Management and Staff
David Hall, Managing Director
David Best, Managing Director

Type of Firm
Private Equity Firm

Association Membership
British Venture Capital Association (BVCA)

Project Preferences

Role in Financing:
Prefer role as deal originator but will also invest in deals created by others

Type of Financing Preferred:
Leveraged Buyout
Early Stage
Expansion
Generalist PE
Balanced
Management Buyouts

Geographical Preferences

International Preferences:
United Kingdom
Europe

Industry Focus

(% based on actual investment)
Computer Software and Services	34.7%
Other Products	14.5%
Communications and Media	9.6%
Computer Hardware	9.6%
Consumer Related	7.1%
Medical/Health	6.6%
Internet Specific	5.5%
Industrial/Energy	4.8%
Biotechnology	4.5%
Semiconductors/Other Elect.	3.1%

Additional Information
Year Founded: 1982
Capital Under Management: $605,000,000
Current Activity Level : Actively seeking new investments
Method of Compensation: Return on invest. most important, but chg. closing fees, service fees, etc.

NEWABLE PRIVATE INVESTING

c/o Newable Ltd
140 Aldersgate Street
London, United Kingdom EC1A 4HY
Phone: 442070892330
E-mail: privateinvesting@newable.co.uk
Website: www.newable.co.uk/private-investing

Type of Firm
Private Equity Firm

Project Preferences

Type of Financing Preferred:
Early Stage

Additional Information
Year Founded: 1969
Current Activity Level : Actively seeking new investments

NEWBROOK CAPITAL MANAGEMENT INC

245 Fifth Avenue
25th Floor
New York, NY USA 10016
Phone: 2122139614
Fax: 2122139607

Type of Firm
Private Equity Advisor or Fund of Funds

Project Preferences

Type of Financing Preferred:
Fund of Funds

Geographical Preferences

United States Preferences:

International Preferences:
Europe

Additional Information
Name of Most Recent Fund: Independence Venture and Technology Fund, L.P.
Most Recent Fund Was Raised: 05/01/2001
Year Founded: 1999
Capital Under Management: $50,000,000
Current Activity Level : Actively seeking new investments

NEWBURY PARTNERS LLC

100 First Stamford Place
Stamford, CT USA 06902
Phone: 2034283600
Fax: 2034283601
Website: www.newbury-partners.com

Management and Staff
Andrew Levy, Managing Director
Brian Kapetanis, Vice President
David Shyu, Vice President
David Overton, Vice President
Gerry Esposito, Chief Financial Officer
Richard Lichter, Managing Director
Warren Symon, Vice President

Type of Firm
Private Equity Advisor or Fund of Funds

Project Preferences

Type of Financing Preferred:
Fund of Funds of Second

Geographical Preferences

United States Preferences:
North America

International Preferences:
Latin America
Europe
Middle East
Australia
Asia

Additional Information
Name of Most Recent Fund: Newbury Equity Partners III, L.P.
Most Recent Fund Was Raised: 08/01/2013
Year Founded: 2006
Capital Under Management: $2,369,900,000
Current Activity Level : Actively seeking new investments

NEWBURY PIRET & CO INC

400 Totten Pond Road
First Floor
North Waltham, MA USA 02451
Phone: 617-367-7300
Fax: 617-367-7301
Website: www.newburypiret.com

Type of Firm
Investment Management Firm

Project Preferences

Role in Financing:
Prefer role as deal originator but will also invest in deals created by others

Type of Financing Preferred:
Leveraged Buyout
Acquisition
Special Situation

Size of Investments Considered:
Min Size of Investment Considered (000s): $3,000
Max Size of Investment Considered: No Limit

Geographical Preferences

United States Preferences:
All U.S.

Canadian Preferences:
All Canada

International Preferences:
Italy
United Kingdom
China
Bermuda
Spain
Germany
Japan
France

Industry Preferences

In Communications prefer:
Communications and Media

In Medical/Health prefer:
Medical/Health

In Industrial/Energy prefer:
Energy
Environmental Related

In Financial Services prefer:
Financial Services

In Business Serv. prefer:
Services
Distribution

In Manufact. prefer:
Manufacturing

In Other prefer:
Socially Responsible

Additional Information

Year Founded: 1981
Current Activity Level : Actively seeking new investments
Method of Compensation: Function primarily in service area, receive contingent fee in cash or equity

NEWBURY VENTURES

255 Shoreline Drive, Suite 520
Redwood City, CA USA 94065
Phone: 6504862444
E-mail: info@risingtidefund.com
Website: www.newburyventures.com

Other Offices

350 Terry Fox Drive, Suite 350
Kanata, Canada K2K 2W5
Phone: 613-271-1005
Fax: 613-271-0066

90 Avenue Henri Martin
Paris, France 75016
Phone: 33-8-70-38-2467
Fax: 33-1-45-04-9616

Management and Staff

Bruce Bauer, Venture Partner
Ossama Hassanein, Partner
Roham Gharegozlou, Partner
Tamer Hassanein, Partner
Youssri Helmy, Partner

Type of Firm

Private Equity Firm

Project Preferences

Role in Financing:
Prefer role as deal originator

Type of Financing Preferred:
Early Stage
Expansion
Balanced
Later Stage

Industry Focus

(% based on actual investment)

Computer Software and Services	22.3%
Semiconductors/Other Elect.	19.2%
Communications and Media	14.1%
Computer Hardware	12.9%
Medical/Health	12.9%
Internet Specific	12.4%
Industrial/Energy	5.4%
Biotechnology	0.5%
Consumer Related	0.2%

Additional Information

Name of Most Recent Fund: Newbury Ventures III, LP
Most Recent Fund Was Raised: 04/05/2001
Year Founded: 1992
Capital Under Management: $300,000,000
Current Activity Level : Actively seeking new investments
Method of Compensation: Return on investment is of primary concern, do not charge fees

NEWCAP PARTNERS INC

5777 West Century Boulevard, Suite 1135
Los Angeles, CA USA 90045
Phone: 310-645-7900
Fax: 310-215-1025
E-mail: info@newcap.com
Website: www.newcap.com

Other Offices

Vasagatan 11
Stockholm, Sweden 10139
Phone: 46-8545-13250
Fax: 46-8545-13369

460 Bush Street, Suite 200
San Francisco, CA USA 94108
Phone: 4152640054
Fax: 4156279079

2082 Michelson Drive #212
Irvine, CA USA 92612
Phone: 9496601919
Fax: 9496601922

1122 Bristol Street
Costa Mesa, CA USA 92626
Phone: 7142418686
Fax: 7144369055

2716 Wemberly Drive
Belmont, CA USA 94002
Phone: 6506310787
Fax: 6502644040

36 Bei Sanhuan East
Room 1908, Building A
Chaoyang District, China 100013
Phone: 861058257001
Fax: 861058257055

Management and Staff

Dan Stanford, Principal
Danny Piper, Principal
David Kuo, Principal
Gary Hultguist, Principal
Kenneth Epstein, Principal
Valerio Giannini, Principal

Type of Firm

Bank Affiliated

Project Preferences

Type of Financing Preferred:
Balanced

Industry Preferences

In Computer Other prefer:
Computer Related

In Semiconductor/Electr prefer:
Semiconductor

In Medical/Health prefer:
Medical/Health

In Consumer Related prefer:
Consumer Products

In Industrial/Energy prefer:
Industrial Products

In Business Serv. prefer:
Distribution

In Other prefer:
Environment Responsible

Additional Information

Year Founded: 2002
Current Activity Level : Actively seeking new investments

NEWFUND MANAGEMENT SA

124, Boulevard Haussmann
Paris, France 75008
E-mail: contact@newfund.fr
Website: newfundcap.com

Type of Firm
Private Equity Firm

Association Membership
French Venture Capital Association (AFIC)

Project Preferences

Type of Financing Preferred:
Later Stage
Recapitalizations

Geographical Preferences

International Preferences:
Europe
France

Industry Preferences

In Communications prefer:
Entertainment

In Consumer Related prefer:
Retail

Additional Information
Year Founded: 2007
Capital Under Management: $248,100,000
Current Activity Level : Actively seeking new investments

NEWGATE CAPITAL PARTNERS LLC

601 North New York Avenue, Suite 220
Winter Park, FL USA 32789
Phone: 4076478752
Website: www.newgatecapitalpartners.com

Type of Firm
Investment Management Firm

Project Preferences

Type of Financing Preferred:
Leveraged Buyout
Value-Add
Early Stage
Balanced
Public Companies
Later Stage
Seed
Startup
Recapitalizations

Geographical Preferences

United States Preferences:
All U.S.

Canadian Preferences:
All Canada

International Preferences:
Europe

Industry Preferences

In Communications prefer:
Communications and Media
Telecommunications

In Computer Software prefer:
Software

In Biotechnology prefer:
Biotechnology

In Medical/Health prefer:
Medical Products
Health Services

In Consumer Related prefer:
Consumer
Retail
Consumer Products

In Financial Services prefer:
Financial Services
Real Estate

Additional Information
Year Founded: 2012
Current Activity Level : Actively seeking new investments

NEWGEN CAPITAL II LP

624 University Avenue
Palo Alto, CA USA 94301
Website: www.newgencap.com

Management and Staff
Yuen Homan, Managing Partner

Type of Firm
Private Equity Firm

Project Preferences

Type of Financing Preferred:
Early Stage

Industry Preferences

In Internet Specific prefer:
Internet
Ecommerce

Additional Information
Year Founded: 2016
Current Activity Level : Actively seeking new investments

NEWGEN VENTURE PARTNERS

624 University Avenue
Palo Alto, CA USA 94301
Website: www.newgenvc.com

Type of Firm
Private Equity Firm

Project Preferences

Type of Financing Preferred:
Early Stage
Seed

Industry Preferences

In Computer Other prefer:
Computer Related

In Biotechnology prefer:
Biotech Related Research

In Medical/Health prefer:
Medical Products

Additional Information
Year Founded: 2015
Current Activity Level : Actively seeking new investments

NEWGLOBE CAPITAL PARTNERS LLP

55 Park Lane, Suite 14a
London, United Kingdom W1K 1NA
Phone: 442076291306
E-mail: info@newglobecapital.com
Website: www.newglobecapital.com

Other Offices
20th Floor
40, West 57th Street
New York, NY USA 10022
Phone: 12122313955

Management and Staff
Christophe Browne, Founder
Ricardo Lombardi, Principal

Type of Firm
Private Equity Advisor or Fund of Funds

Project Preferences

Type of Financing Preferred:
Fund of Funds
Recapitalizations

Geographical Preferences

International Preferences:
United Kingdom
Europe

Additional Information
Year Founded: 2012
Current Activity Level : Actively seeking new investments

NEWGROWTH FUND
Juan Salvador Agraz 97
Oficina 4-D, Edificio Paragon
Cuajimalpa, Mexico 05330
Phone: 525552921691
Website: www.newgrowthfund.com

Management and Staff
Rene Fernandez, Managing Partner

Type of Firm
Private Equity Firm

Project Preferences

Type of Financing Preferred:
Generalist PE

Geographical Preferences

International Preferences:
Mexico

Industry Preferences

In Medical/Health prefer:
Medical/Health

In Consumer Related prefer:
Consumer Products
Education Related

In Business Serv. prefer:
Services

In Other prefer:
Environment Responsible

Additional Information
Year Founded: 2010
Current Activity Level : Actively seeking new investments

NEWION INVESTMENTS BV
Businesspark Friesland W 27B
Nijehaske, Netherlands 8466 SL
Phone: 31513640633
Fax: 31513640871
E-mail: info@newion-investments.com

Other Offices
Businesspark Friesland West 27B
Nijehaske, Netherlands 8466

Management and Staff
Jaap Van Barneveld, Managing Partner
Patrick Polak, Managing Partner

Type of Firm
Private Equity Firm

Association Membership
European Private Equity and Venture Capital Assoc.
Dutch Venture Capital Associaton (NVP)

Project Preferences

Type of Financing Preferred:
Early Stage
Generalist PE
Balanced
Later Stage
Management Buyouts
Acquisition

Geographical Preferences

International Preferences:
Luxembourg
Europe
Netherlands
Belgium

Industry Preferences

In Communications prefer:
Communications and Media

In Computer Software prefer:
Software

In Internet Specific prefer:
Internet

In Semiconductor/Electr prefer:
Electronic Components

Additional Information
Year Founded: 2000
Capital Under Management: $123,300,000
Current Activity Level : Actively seeking new investments

NEWLIN INVESTMENT COMPANY LP
428 Beaver Street, Second Floor
Sewickley, PA USA 15143
Phone: 4127410630
Fax: 4127410657
Website: www.newlininvestment.com

Type of Firm
Private Equity Firm

Project Preferences

Type of Financing Preferred:
Generalist PE

Industry Preferences

In Consumer Related prefer:
Retail

Additional Information
Year Founded: 1969
Current Activity Level : Actively seeking new investments

NEWQUEST CAPITAL ADVISORS HK LTD
Eight Wyndham Street
26th Floor
Central, Hong Kong
Phone: 82539053600
Fax: 85221857300
E-mail: info@nqcap.com
Website: www.nqcap.com

Management and Staff
Amit Gupta, Chief Operating Officer
Bonnie Lo, Partner
Darren Massara, Managing Partner
Min Lin, Partner

Type of Firm
Private Equity Advisor or Fund of Funds

Project Preferences

Type of Financing Preferred:
Leveraged Buyout
Expansion
Fund of Funds of Second

Geographical Preferences

United States Preferences:
Southeast

International Preferences:
Asia Pacific
India
Taiwan
China
Australia
Singapore
Korea, South
Japan

Industry Preferences

In Communications prefer:
Telecommunications

In Medical/Health prefer:
Medical/Health

In Consumer Related prefer:
Consumer

In Industrial/Energy prefer:
Energy
Industrial Products

In Financial Services prefer:
Financial Services
Financial Services

In Business Serv. prefer:
Media

In Other prefer:
Environment Responsible

Pratt's Guide to Private Equity & Venture Capital Sources

Additional Information
Name of Most Recent Fund: NewQuest Asia Fund II, L.P.
Most Recent Fund Was Raised: 02/16/2013
Year Founded: 2011
Capital Under Management: $1,155,100,000
Current Activity Level : Actively seeking new investments

NEWROAD CAPITAL PARTNERS LLC

102 East Central Avenue
Bentonville, AR USA 72712
Phone: 4796572100
Website: newroadcp.com

Management and Staff
Clete Brewer, Managing Partner
Doug Degn, Partner
Jeremy Wilson, Managing Partner
Steve Brooks, Partner

Type of Firm
Private Equity Firm

Industry Preferences

In Medical/Health prefer:
Health Services

In Consumer Related prefer:
Retail
Consumer Products

In Manufact. prefer:
Manufacturing

Additional Information
Year Founded: 2016
Capital Under Management: $90,000,000
Current Activity Level : Actively seeking new investments

NEWSCHOOLS VENTURE FUND

1970 Broadway, Suite 350
Oakland, CA USA 94612
Phone: 4156156860
Fax: 4156156861
E-mail: info@newschools.org
Website: www.newschools.org

Other Offices
1638 R Street, NW, Suite 300
Washington, DC USA 20009
Phone: 2026098150
Fax: 2025248786

211 Congress Street
Tenth Floor
Boston, MA USA 02110
Phone: 6175899447
Fax: 6175899448

Management and Staff
Deborah McGriff, Partner
Gloria Lee, Chief Operating Officer
Jennifer Carolan, Partner
Jim Peyser, Partner
Jonathan Schorr, Partner
Julie Mikuta, Partner
Kristi Ransick, Principal
Lauren Kushman, Principal
Maura Marino, Principal
Rick Crandall, Partner
Sandra Becker, Chief Financial Officer
Shauntel Poulson, Partner
Stacey Childress, Chief Executive Officer

Type of Firm
Private Equity Firm

Project Preferences

Type of Financing Preferred:
Early Stage
Seed
Startup

Geographical Preferences

United States Preferences:
All U.S.

Industry Preferences

In Consumer Related prefer:
Education Related

Additional Information
Name of Most Recent Fund: NewSchools Seed Fund
Most Recent Fund Was Raised: 02/19/2014
Year Founded: 1998
Capital Under Management: $20,000,000
Current Activity Level : Actively seeking new investments

NEWSION VENTURE CAPITAL CO., LTD.

No.18, Cuiyu South Rd, Gubei
Shanghai, China 201103
E-mail: contact@newsionvc.com
Website: www.newsionvc.com

Other Offices
B, Jiahua Bldg, Shangdi 3rd Rd
Beijing, China 100085

Type of Firm
Private Equity Firm

Project Preferences

Type of Financing Preferred:
Early Stage
Balanced
Seed

Geographical Preferences

International Preferences:
China

Industry Preferences

In Business Serv. prefer:
Services

Additional Information
Year Founded: 2011
Current Activity Level : Actively seeking new investments

NEWSPRING CAPITAL

555 East Lancaster Avenue
Radnor Financial Ctr, Ste 444
Radnor, PA USA 19087
Phone: 6105672380
Fax: 6105672388
E-mail: info@newspringventures.com
Website: www.newspringcapital.com

Other Offices
100 West Road, Suite 325 Towson, Maryland
EUDOWOOD, MD USA 21204
Phone: 4108327586
Fax: 6105672388

655 Fifteenth Street
Northwest 2nd Floor
WASHINGTON, DC USA 20005
Phone: 6105672380
Fax: 6105672388

101 JFK Parkway
Fourth Floor
SHORT HILLS, NJ USA 07078
Phone: 973-467-1133
Fax: 973-467-3007

Management and Staff
Andrew Panzo, General Partner
Anne Schoemaker-Vazquez, Partner
Brian Kim, Principal
Brian Murphy, General Partner
Bruce Downey, Partner
Chris Bodine, Venture Partner
Eric Jensen, Principal
Glenn Rieger, General Partner
Gregory Barger, General Partner
James Ashton, General Partner
Justin Brock, Vice President
Kapila Ratnam, Partner
Kristin Lee, Principal
Lee Garber, Principal
Marc Lederman, General Partner
Michael DiPiano, Managing Partner
Skip Maner, General Partner
Steven Hobman, General Partner

Type of Firm
Private Equity Firm

Pratt's Guide to Private Equity & Venture Capital Sources

Association Membership
Natl Assoc of Small Bus. Inv. Co (NASBIC)
National Venture Capital Association - USA (NVCA)

Project Preferences

Role in Financing:
Will function either as deal originator or investor in deals created by others

Type of Financing Preferred:
Leveraged Buyout
Expansion
Mezzanine
Generalist PE
Balanced
Later Stage
Management Buyouts
Strategic Alliances
Acquisition
Recapitalizations

Size of Investments Considered:
Min Size of Investment Considered (000s): $5,000
Max Size of Investment Considered (000s): $50,000

Geographical Preferences

United States Preferences:
Mid Atlantic
Illinois
Pennsylvania
Delaware
North Carolina
Northeast
Massachusetts
Ohio
New Jersey
New York

Industry Preferences

In Communications prefer:
Wireless Communications
Data Communications

In Computer Hardware prefer:
Computers

In Computer Software prefer:
Computer Services
Data Processing
Software

In Internet Specific prefer:
E-Commerce Technology
Ecommerce

In Computer Other prefer:
Computer Related

In Semiconductor/Electr prefer:
Electronics
Optoelectronics

In Biotechnology prefer:
Biotechnology

In Medical/Health prefer:
Medical/Health
Medical Diagnostics
Medical Therapeutics
Drug/Equipmt Delivery
Medical Products
Health Services
Pharmaceuticals

In Consumer Related prefer:
Consumer
Consumer Products
Consumer Services
Education Related

In Financial Services prefer:
Financial Services

In Business Serv. prefer:
Services
Distribution
Consulting Services
Media

In Manufact. prefer:
Manufacturing

Additional Information
Name of Most Recent Fund: NewSpring Growth Capital III, L.P.
Most Recent Fund Was Raised: 03/31/2012
Year Founded: 1999
Capital Under Management: $1,000,000,000
Current Activity Level : Actively seeking new investments
Method of Compensation: Return on investment is of primary concern, do not charge fees

NEWSTONE CAPITAL PARTNERS LLC

11111 Santa Monica Boulevard, Suite 1100
Los Angeles, CA USA 90025
Phone: 310-689-1710
Fax: 3106891722
Website: www.newstonecapital.com

Other Offices
2501 North Harwood Street, Suite 1250
Dallas, TX USA 75201
Phone: 2147534300
Fax: 2147534399

Management and Staff
Grant Johnson, Managing Director
Jeff Morales, Managing Director
John Rocchio, Managing Director
Jordan Sebold, Vice President
Michael Tait, Vice President
Robert Brougham, Managing Director
Timothy Costello, Managing Director

Type of Firm
Private Equity Firm

Project Preferences

Type of Financing Preferred:
Leveraged Buyout
Mezzanine
Later Stage
Recapitalizations

Industry Preferences

In Computer Software prefer:
Software

In Medical/Health prefer:
Medical/Health

In Consumer Related prefer:
Consumer Products

In Business Serv. prefer:
Services

In Manufact. prefer:
Manufacturing

Additional Information
Year Founded: 2006
Capital Under Management: $800,000,000
Current Activity Level : Actively seeking new investments

NEWTEN VENTURES GMBH

Jaegerstrasse 34
Berlin, Germany 10117
Phone: 49302464799
Fax: 49302464799
E-mail: ventures@newten.com
Website: www.newten.com

Management and Staff
Birgit Stroebel, Partner
Karsten Wulf, Partner
Lutz Grimm, Partner
Rainer Bormann, Managing Partner
Rene Gurka, Managing Partner

Type of Firm
Private Equity Firm

Project Preferences

Type of Financing Preferred:
Early Stage
Seed
Startup

Geographical Preferences

International Preferences:
Europe
Germany

Industry Preferences

In Internet Specific prefer:
Internet

Pratt's Guide to Private Equity & Venture Capital Sources

Additional Information
Year Founded: 2012
Current Activity Level : Actively seeking new investments

NEWWORLD CAPITAL GROUP LLC

444 Madison Avenue
31st Floor
New York, NY USA 10022
Phone: 2124863400
E-mail: info@newworldcapital.net
Website: www.newworldcapital.net

Management and Staff
Ali Iz, Co-Founder
Bob Kennedy, Chief Financial Officer
Evereth Smith, Co-Founder
Louis Schick, Co-Founder
Silda Spitzer, Principal
William Hallisey, Co-Founder

Type of Firm
Private Equity Firm

Project Preferences

Type of Financing Preferred:
Leveraged Buyout
Early Stage
Expansion
Balanced
Later Stage

Geographical Preferences

United States Preferences:

Canadian Preferences:
All Canada

International Preferences:
Europe

Industry Preferences

In Industrial/Energy prefer:
Energy
Alternative Energy
Energy Conservation Relat
Environmental Related

In Utilities prefer:
Utilities

In Other prefer:
Environment Responsible

Additional Information
Name of Most Recent Fund: NWC Investment Partnership II, L.P.
Most Recent Fund Was Raised: 09/23/2011
Year Founded: 2009
Capital Under Management: $42,690,000
Current Activity Level : Actively seeking new investments

NEX CUBED LLC

325 Pacific Avenue, Suite B
San Francisco, CA USA 94111
Website: nex3.com

Management and Staff
Kelsey Morgan, Co-Founder
Kip Quackenbush, Co-Founder

Type of Firm
Incubator/Development Program

Project Preferences

Type of Financing Preferred:
Startup

Industry Preferences

In Computer Software prefer:
Artificial Intelligence

In Computer Other prefer:
Computer Related

In Industrial/Energy prefer:
Robotics
Machinery

Additional Information
Year Founded: 2016
Current Activity Level : Actively seeking new investments

NEXIT VENTURES OY

Kaisaniemenkatu Two B
Helsinki, Finland 00100
Phone: 35896818910
Fax: 358968189117
E-mail: info@nexitventures.com
Website: www.nexitventures.com

Other Offices
Norrmalmstorg 14
Stockholm, Sweden 111 46
Phone: 46852509020
Fax: 46855114101

Management and Staff
Artturi Tarjanne, General Partner
Michael Mandahl, General Partner
Michel Wendell, General Partner
Patrice Peyret, Venture Partner
Pekka Salonoja, General Partner
Risto Yli-Tainio, Chief Financial Officer
Tarja Jyrkas, Chief Financial Officer

Type of Firm
Private Equity Firm

Association Membership
Finnish Venture Capital Association (FVCA)

Project Preferences

Type of Financing Preferred:
Early Stage
Seed
Startup

Size of Investments Considered:
Min Size of Investment Considered (000s): $1,300
Max Size of Investment Considered (000s): $13,000

Geographical Preferences

United States Preferences:

International Preferences:
Scandanavia/Nordic Region
Asia

Industry Preferences

In Communications prefer:
Communications and Media
Commercial Communications
Wireless Communications
Data Communications

In Computer Software prefer:
Software
Systems Software
Applications Software

In Internet Specific prefer:
Internet

Additional Information
Name of Most Recent Fund: Nexit Infocom II
Most Recent Fund Was Raised: 03/03/2008
Year Founded: 1999
Capital Under Management: $211,300,000
Current Activity Level : Actively seeking new investments

NEXO CAPITAL PARTNERS

68 South Main Street
8th Floor
Salt Lake City, UT USA 84101
Phone: 4356021467
E-mail: contact@nexocapitalpartners.com
Website: www.nexocapitalpartners.com

Management and Staff
A. Bradley Randall, Partner
Andrew Sloop, Managing Partner
Joshua Tandy, Partner
Kurt West, Principal
Sujal Bhalakia, Partner

Type of Firm
Private Equity Firm

Project Preferences

1505

Type of Financing Preferred:
Turnaround
Management Buyouts
Distressed Debt
Recapitalizations

Industry Preferences

In Industrial/Energy prefer:
Environmental Related

Additional Information

Year Founded: 2015
Capital Under Management: $200,000
Current Activity Level : Actively seeking new investments

NEXOS CAPITAL PARTNERS

99 Park Avenue, Suite 1560
New York, NY USA 10016
Phone: 2129071450
Fax: 2129071451
E-mail: info@nexoscapital.com
Website: www.nexoscapital.com

Other Offices

30211 Avenida de las Banderas, Suite 200
Rancho Santa Margarita, CA USA 92688
Phone: 949-766-6733
Fax: 949-766-6734

Management and Staff

Eduardo Bohorquez, Principal
John McIntire, Principal
Joseph Vadapalas, Principal
Justo Frias, Principal

Type of Firm
Private Equity Firm

Project Preferences

Type of Financing Preferred:
Later Stage

Geographical Preferences

United States Preferences:

Industry Preferences

In Consumer Related prefer:
Consumer Products

In Business Serv. prefer:
Services
Distribution

Additional Information

Year Founded: 2008
Capital Under Management: $225,000,000
Current Activity Level : Actively seeking new investments

NEXPHASE CAPITAL LLC

399 Park Avenue
6th Floor
New York, NY USA 10022
Phone: 2128786000
Fax: 2128804260
E-mail: info@nexphase.com
Website: www.nexphase.com

Management and Staff

Andrew Goldfarb, Chief Financial Officer
Andy Kieffer, Partner
George Zahringer, Principal
Jamie Kaufman, Principal
Jim Johnston, Partner
Joel Killion, Partner
Kurt Larsen, Managing Partner
Lex Leeming, Partner
Robert Gartland, Vice President
Ted Yun, Managing Partner

Type of Firm
Private Equity Firm

Project Preferences

Type of Financing Preferred:
Leveraged Buyout

Industry Preferences

In Computer Software prefer:
Software

In Medical/Health prefer:
Medical/Health

In Consumer Related prefer:
Consumer

In Industrial/Energy prefer:
Industrial Products

Additional Information

Year Founded: 2016
Capital Under Management: $310,380,000
Current Activity Level : Actively seeking new investments

NEXT CANADA

130 Bloor Street West, Suite 702
Toronto, Canada M5S 2C7
Phone: 6472598943
E-mail: info@thenext36.ca
Website: www.thenext36.ca

Management and Staff

Ajay Agrawal, Co-Founder
Claudia Hepburn, Co-Founder
Reza Satchu, Co-Founder
Tim Hodgson, Co-Founder

Type of Firm
Incubator/Development Program

Project Preferences

Type of Financing Preferred:
Seed
Startup

Geographical Preferences

Canadian Preferences:
All Canada

Industry Preferences

In Communications prefer:
Wireless Communications

Additional Information

Year Founded: 2010
Current Activity Level : Actively seeking new investments

NEXT CAPITAL PARTNERS SGECR SA

C/ Deportistas Hermanos Torres, Suite Four
Alicante, Spain 03016
Phone: 34965266800
Website: www.nextcapital.es

Management and Staff

Manuel Gomez Del Rio, Chief Executive Officer

Type of Firm
Private Equity Firm

Association Membership
Spanish Venture Capital Association (ASCRI)

Project Preferences

Type of Financing Preferred:
Leveraged Buyout
Acquisition

Geographical Preferences

International Preferences:
Spain

Additional Information

Year Founded: 2009
Current Activity Level : Actively seeking new investments

NEXT CAPITAL PTY LTD

25 Bligh Street, Level 30/31
GPO Box 4076
Sydney, Australia 2000
Phone: 61282225555
Fax: 61282225556
E-mail: info@nextcapital.com.au
Website: www.nextcapital.com.au

Type of Firm
Private Equity Firm

Association Membership
New Zealand Venture Capital Association
Australian Venture Capital Association (AVCAL)

Project Preferences

Role in Financing:
Will function either as deal originator or investor in deals created by others

Type of Financing Preferred:
Leveraged Buyout
Generalist PE
Later Stage
Management Buyouts

Geographical Preferences

International Preferences:
Australia
New Zealand

Additional Information
Name of Most Recent Fund: Next Capital Fund II
Most Recent Fund Was Raised: 06/30/2008
Year Founded: 2005
Capital Under Management: $678,000,000
Current Activity Level : Actively seeking new investments

NEXT COAST VENTURES LLC

3600 North Capital of texas Hi
Building B Suite 250
Austin, TX USA 78746
Phone: 6508149469
Website: www.nextcoastventures.com

Management and Staff
Jim Dunham, Venture Partner
Mike Smerklo, Co-Founder
Paul Rogers, Venture Partner
Thomas Ball, Co-Founder
Zeynep Young, Venture Partner

Type of Firm
Private Equity Firm

Project Preferences

Type of Financing Preferred:
Balanced

Additional Information
Year Founded: 2016
Capital Under Management: $87,920,000
Current Activity Level : Actively seeking new investments

NEXT EQUITIES

6602 45th Street
Leduc, Canada
Phone: 7809860095
Fax: 7809801300
E-mail: info@nextequities.com
Website: www.nextequities.com

Type of Firm
Private Equity Firm

Association Membership
Canadian Venture Capital Association

Project Preferences

Type of Financing Preferred:
Leveraged Buyout
Acquisition

Geographical Preferences

Canadian Preferences:
Western Canada

Industry Preferences

In Industrial/Energy prefer:
Process Control

In Transportation prefer:
Transportation

In Financial Services prefer:
Financial Services

In Manufact. prefer:
Manufacturing

Additional Information
Year Founded: 2010
Current Activity Level : Actively seeking new investments

NEXT FRONTIER CAPITAL

201 S. Wallace Avenue, Suite B3F
Bozeman, MT USA 59715
Phone: 4062099743
Fax: 4067940384
Website: www.nextfrontiercapital.com

Type of Firm
Private Equity Firm

Association Membership
National Venture Capital Association - USA (NVCA)

Project Preferences

Size of Investments Considered:
Min Size of Investment Considered (000s): $200
Max Size of Investment Considered (000s): $1,500

Geographical Preferences

United States Preferences:
Montana

Industry Preferences

In Computer Software prefer:
Software

In Semiconductor/Electr prefer:
Fiber Optics

In Medical/Health prefer:
Medical/Health

Additional Information
Year Founded: 2015
Capital Under Management: $43,200,000
Current Activity Level : Actively seeking new investments

NEXT FRONTIER CAPITAL LLC

700 North Sacramento Boulevard, Suite 130
Chicago, IL USA 60612
Phone: 773-822-0320
Fax: 773-822-0308
E-mail: info@chiventures.org
Website: www.chiventures.org

Management and Staff
Kathleen Wilkerson, Managing Director
Lauren Robinson, Managing Director

Type of Firm
Corporate PE/Venture

Project Preferences

Type of Financing Preferred:
Balanced

Size of Investments Considered:
Min Size of Investment Considered (000s): $250
Max Size of Investment Considered (000s): $2,500

Geographical Preferences

United States Preferences:
Illinois

Industry Preferences

In Other prefer:
Women/Minority-Owned Bus.

Additional Information
Year Founded: 2004
Current Activity Level : Actively seeking new investments

NEXT GENERATION FINANCE INVEST AG

Baarerstrasse 79
Zug, Switzerland 6300
Phone: 41417122353
Fax: 41417122354
E-mail: investors@nextgfi.com
Website: www.nextgfi.com

Type of Firm
Private Equity Firm

Association Membership
Swiss Venture Capital Association (SECA)

Project Preferences

Type of Financing Preferred:
Early Stage
Seed
Startup

Geographical Preferences

International Preferences:
United Kingdom
Europe
Switzerland
Germany

Industry Preferences

In Financial Services prefer:
Financial Services
Insurance

Additional Information
Year Founded: 2009
Current Activity Level : Actively seeking new investments

NEXT LEVEL VENTURES LLC

666 Walnut Street, Suite 1280
Des Moines, IA USA 50309
Phone: 5153692600
E-mail: info@nextlevelvc.com
Website: www.nextlevelvc.com

Management and Staff
Duane Harris, Principal
Scott Hoekman, Principal

Type of Firm
Private Equity Firm

Project Preferences

Type of Financing Preferred:
Early Stage
Balanced
Later Stage

Size of Investments Considered:
Min Size of Investment Considered (000s): $1,000
Max Size of Investment Considered (000s): $4,000

Geographical Preferences

United States Preferences:
Iowa

Industry Preferences

In Biotechnology prefer:
Biotechnology

In Manufact. prefer:
Manufacturing

Additional Information
Name of Most Recent Fund: Next Level Ventures Fund I, L.L.L.P.
Most Recent Fund Was Raised: 01/16/2014
Year Founded: 2014
Capital Under Management: $38,100,000
Current Activity Level : Actively seeking new investments

NEXT ORBIT VENTURES PVT LTD

Cardinal Gracias Road, Andheri, Suite 609 Inizio Building
Mumbai, India 400099
Phone: 919167540972
E-mail: contactus@nextorbitventures.com
Website: www.nextorbitventures.com

Management and Staff
Anil Goyal, Managing Partner

Type of Firm
Private Equity Firm

Additional Information
Year Founded: 2015
Current Activity Level : Actively seeking new investments

NEXT POINT CAPITAL CORP

10866 Wilshire Boulevard, Suite 400
Los Angeles, CA USA 90064
Phone: 8889576398
Website: nextpointcapital.com

Management and Staff
Mark Mickelson, Partner

Type of Firm
Private Equity Firm

Project Preferences

Type of Financing Preferred:
Leveraged Buyout
Expansion
Mezzanine
Management Buyouts
Acquisition
Recapitalizations

Geographical Preferences

United States Preferences:
Midwest
California

Additional Information
Year Founded: 1969
Current Activity Level : Actively seeking new investments

NEXT SECTOR CAPITAL

2530 Meridian Parkway, Suite 2001
Cary, NC USA 27513
Phone: 9196364610
Website: www.nextsectorcapital.com

Type of Firm
Investment Management Firm

Project Preferences

Type of Financing Preferred:
Early Stage
Expansion
Later Stage

Industry Preferences

In Medical/Health prefer:
Health Services

In Consumer Related prefer:
Food/Beverage

Additional Information
Year Founded: 2016
Capital Under Management: $5,000,000
Current Activity Level : Actively seeking new investments

NEXT VENTURE INVESTMENT CORP

18th Floor, ASEM Tower, 159-1
Samsung-dong, Kangnam-Gu
Seoul, South Korea 135-798
Phone: 822-6001-7700
Fax: 822-6001-7709
Website: www.nextvic.com

Management and Staff
Injun Nam, Chief Executive Officer
Jaehwan Song, Vice President

Type of Firm
Private Equity Firm

Project Preferences

Type of Financing Preferred:
Balanced

Geographical Preferences

International Preferences:
Korea, South

Additional Information
Year Founded: 2000
Capital Under Management: $37,200,000
Current Activity Level : Actively seeking new investments

NEXT WAVE FUNDS

P.O. Box 1403
Washington, CT USA 06793
Phone: 860-868-2021
Fax: 860-868-7967
Website: www.nextwavefunds.com

Other Offices

Klostertern 10
Hamburg, Germany 20149
Phone: 49-40-4809-2910
Fax: 49-40-4609-5705

Management and Staff

Elliott Davis, Managing Partner
Gerlach Wecken, General Partner

Type of Firm

Private Equity Firm

Project Preferences

Type of Financing Preferred:
Fund of Funds
Early Stage
Expansion

Geographical Preferences

International Preferences:
Europe

Additional Information

Year Founded: 1999
Current Activity Level : Actively seeking new investments

NEXT WAVE PARTNERS LLP

42 Wigmore Street
London, United Kingdom W1U 2RY
Phone: 442030057535
E-mail: enquiries@nextwavepartners.co.uk
Website: www.nextwavepartners.co.uk

Management and Staff

Carolyn Maddox, Partner
Jonathan Brod, Managing Partner
Stephen Walls, Partner

Type of Firm

Private Equity Firm

Association Membership

British Venture Capital Association (BVCA)
European Private Equity and Venture Capital Assoc.

Project Preferences

Type of Financing Preferred:
Leveraged Buyout
Acquisition

Size of Investments Considered:
Min Size of Investment Considered (000s): $3,968
Max Size of Investment Considered (000s): $39,680

Geographical Preferences

International Preferences:
United Kingdom
Europe

Industry Preferences

In Consumer Related prefer:
Entertainment and Leisure
Retail
Food/Beverage
Other Restaurants
Education Related

In Industrial/Energy prefer:
Energy Conservation Relat

In Business Serv. prefer:
Services
Media

Additional Information

Year Founded: 2006
Capital Under Management: $42,115,000
Current Activity Level : Actively seeking new investments

NEXT WORLD CAPITAL LLC

836 Montgomery Street
San Francisco, CA USA 94133
Phone: 4152025450
Fax: 4153588233
Website: www.nextworldcap.com

Other Offices

Avenue Louise, 480
Brussels, Belgium 1050
Phone: 413226261020
Fax: 413226261030

Eleven Avenue Myron Herrick
Paris, France 75008
Phone: 33155359920
Fax: 33145636098

Management and Staff

Ben Fu, General Partner
Colin Paton, Chief Financial Officer
Craig Hanson, Co-Founder
Sebastien Lepinard, Co-Founder
Tarun Kalra, Principal
Thorsten Claus, Principal
Tom Rikert, Partner

Type of Firm

Investment Management Firm

Project Preferences

Type of Financing Preferred:
Expansion
Balanced
Later Stage

Geographical Preferences

United States Preferences:

International Preferences:
Europe

Industry Preferences

In Communications prefer:
Wireless Communications

In Computer Software prefer:
Software

In Internet Specific prefer:
Internet

In Consumer Related prefer:
Consumer
Retail

Additional Information

Year Founded: 2008
Capital Under Management: $200,000,000
Current Activity Level : Actively seeking new investments

NEXTECH INVEST LTD

Scheuchzerstrasse 35
Zurich, Switzerland 8006
Phone: 41443666611
Fax: 41443666610
E-mail: info@nextechinvest.com
Website: www.nextechinvest.com

Management and Staff

Roland Ruckstuhl, Chief Financial Officer
Rudolf Gygax, Managing Partner

Type of Firm

Investment Management Firm

Association Membership

Swiss Venture Capital Association (SECA)
European Private Equity and Venture Capital Assoc.

Project Preferences

Role in Financing:
Prefer role as deal originator but will also invest in deals created by others

Type of Financing Preferred:
Early Stage
Later Stage
Seed
Startup

Size of Investments Considered:
Min Size of Investment Considered (000s): $430
Max Size of Investment Considered (000s): $8,601

Geographical Preferences

United States Preferences:
All U.S.

International Preferences:
Europe
Asia

Industry Preferences

In Biotechnology prefer:
Human Biotechnology
Biotech Related Research

In Medical/Health prefer:
Medical/Health
Medical Diagnostics
Medical Therapeutics
Pharmaceuticals

Additional Information

Name of Most Recent Fund: Nextech III Oncology
Most Recent Fund Was Raised: 04/29/2010
Year Founded: 1998
Capital Under Management: $25,800,000
Current Activity Level : Actively seeking new investments

NEXTENERGY CAPITAL LTD

23 Hanover Square
London, United Kingdom W1S 1JB
Phone: 442037148945
E-mail: info@nextenergycapital.com
Website: www.nextenergycapital.com

Other Offices

Corso Vittorio Emanuele II, 30
Milan, Italy 20122
Phone: 390236706201

Management and Staff

Abid Kazim, Managing Director
Carlos Javier, Vice President
Davide Nielsen, Vice President
Gianluca Boccanera, Managing Director
Martina De Luca, Vice President
Michael Bonte-Friedheim, Chief Executive Officer
Rodolfo Bigolin, Vice President
Ross Grier, Principal

Type of Firm

Investment Management Firm

Project Preferences

Type of Financing Preferred:
Early Stage
Expansion
Acquisition

Industry Preferences

In Industrial/Energy prefer:
Energy
Alternative Energy
Energy Conservation Relat
Environmental Related

In Other prefer:
Socially Responsible

Additional Information

Year Founded: 2011
Capital Under Management: $168,140,000
Current Activity Level : Actively seeking new investments

NEXTEQUITY PARTNERS LLC

3000 Sand Hill Road, Suite 4-140
Menlo Park, CA USA 94025
Phone: 6506876800
E-mail: info@nextequity.com

Type of Firm

Private Equity Firm

Project Preferences

Type of Financing Preferred:
Early Stage
Later Stage
Startup

Industry Preferences

In Business Serv. prefer:
Media

Additional Information

Year Founded: 1969
Current Activity Level : Actively seeking new investments

NEXTGEN GROWTH PARTNERS LLC

443 N. Clark Street, Suite 400
Chicago, IL USA 60654
Website: nextgengp.com

Management and Staff

Josh Dennis, Founder

Type of Firm

Private Equity Firm

Project Preferences

Type of Financing Preferred:
Leveraged Buyout
Acquisition

Additional Information

Year Founded: 2016
Capital Under Management: $38,430,000
Current Activity Level : Actively seeking new investments

NEXTGEN VENTURE PARTNERS LLC

One Thomas Circle, Suite 801
Washington, DC USA 20005
Website: nextgenvp.com

Other Offices

1400 Key Boulevard, Suite 100
ARLINGTON, VA USA 22209
Phone: 4043242222

Management and Staff

Brett Gibson, Managing Partner
Brian Vahaly, Chief Operating Officer
Chris Keller, Managing Partner
Jon Bassett, Managing Partner
Lisa Cuesta, Vice President

Type of Firm

Private Equity Firm

Additional Information

Year Founded: 2016
Capital Under Management: $15,960,000
Current Activity Level : Actively seeking new investments

NEXTSTAGE CAPITAL LP

2570 Boulevard of the Generals
Building 100, Second Floor
Audubon, PA USA 19403
Phone: 6105392297
Website: www.nextstagecapital.com

Management and Staff

Daniel McKinney, Co-Founder
Rob Adams, Co-Founder
Terry Williams, Co-Founder

Type of Firm

Private Equity Firm

Project Preferences

Role in Financing:
Prefer role as deal originator but will also invest in deals created by others

Type of Financing Preferred:
Early Stage
Seed

Size of Investments Considered:
Min Size of Investment Considered (000s): $250
Max Size of Investment Considered (000s): $1,000

Geographical Preferences

United States Preferences:

Industry Preferences

In Communications prefer:
Communications and Media
Telecommunications

In Computer Software prefer:
Software

In Medical/Health prefer:
Health Services

In Financial Services prefer:
Financial Services

In Business Serv. prefer:
Services

Additional Information
Year Founded: 2004
Capital Under Management: $17,000,000
Current Activity Level : Actively seeking new investments
Method of Compensation: Return on investment is of primary concern, do not charge fees

NEXTVIEW VENTURES LP

179 Lincoln Street
#404
Boston, MA USA 02111
Website: nextviewventures.com

Other Offices
Former: 186 South Street
BOSTON, MA USA 02111

Management and Staff
David Beisel, Partner
Lee Hower, Partner
Melody Koh, Venture Partner
Robert Go, Partner

Type of Firm
Private Equity Firm

Association Membership
New England Venture Capital Association

Project Preferences

Type of Financing Preferred:
Early Stage
Seed
Startup

Size of Investments Considered:
Min Size of Investment Considered (000s): $250
Max Size of Investment Considered (000s): $500

Geographical Preferences

United States Preferences:
East Coast

Industry Preferences

In Computer Software prefer:
Software

In Internet Specific prefer:
Internet

Additional Information
Name of Most Recent Fund: NextView Ventures, L.P.
Most Recent Fund Was Raised: 03/31/2011
Year Founded: 2010
Capital Under Management: $110,798,000
Current Activity Level : Actively seeking new investments

NEXUS MEDICAL PARTNERS

400 Crown Colony Drive, Suite 104
Quincy, MA USA 02169
Phone: 6174722805
Fax: 6174723531
E-mail: contact@nmtcapital.com
Website: www.nexusmp.com

Other Offices
12, rue Eugene Ruppert
Luxembourg, Luxembourg L-2453

411 University Ridge, Suite A, Next Center
Greenville, SC USA 29601
Phone: 8647515061

Management and Staff
Gregory Zaic, Principal
Robert Fleming, Principal
Thomas Hancock, Principal

Type of Firm
Private Equity Firm

Project Preferences

Type of Financing Preferred:
Balanced

Geographical Preferences

United States Preferences:
All U.S.

International Preferences:
Europe

Industry Preferences

In Communications prefer:
Data Communications

In Computer Software prefer:
Software

In Biotechnology prefer:
Biotechnology

In Medical/Health prefer:
Medical Products
Pharmaceuticals

In Industrial/Energy prefer:
Advanced Materials

Additional Information
Year Founded: 2004
Current Activity Level : Actively seeking new investments

NEXUS VENTURE PARTNERS

2200 Sand Hill Road, Suite 100
Menlo Park, CA USA 94025
Phone: 6502330700
Website: www.nexusvp.com

Other Offices
100, Dr. Annie Besant Road
G-2, Sarjan Plaza
Mumbai, India 400018
Phone: 912266260000
Fax: 912266260001

No. 1&2, Murphy Road, Suite 1001, 10/F, Tower B,
RMZ Millenia
Bangalore, India 560 008
Phone: 918049456600

Management and Staff
Jishnu Bhatacharjee, Managing Director
K. G. Subramanian, Chief Financial Officer
Narendra Gupta, Co-Founder
Sandeep Singhal, Co-Founder
Suvir Sujan, Co-Founder

Type of Firm
Private Equity Firm

Association Membership
Indian Venture Capital Association (IVCA)

Project Preferences

Type of Financing Preferred:
Early Stage
Later Stage
Seed

Geographical Preferences

United States Preferences:

International Preferences:
India

Industry Preferences

In Internet Specific prefer:
Internet

In Consumer Related prefer:
Consumer

In Business Serv. prefer:
Services
Media

In Agr/Forestr/Fish prefer:
Agriculture related

Additional Information
Year Founded: 2006
Capital Under Management: $320,000,000
Current Activity Level : Actively seeking new investments

NEXUSS GROUP SAC

Carlos Villaran 140, Piso 19
La Victoria
Lima, Peru L13
Phone: 5116114733

Management and Staff
Alejandro Ponce, Managing Partner
Carlos Rodriguez-Pastor, Managing Partner
Juan Carlos Vallejo, Managing Partner

Type of Firm
Private Equity Firm

Project Preferences

Type of Financing Preferred:
Leveraged Buyout

Geographical Preferences

International Preferences:
Ecuador
Bolivia
Peru
Colombia
Venezuela

Additional Information
Name of Most Recent Fund: NG Capital Partners II, L.P.
Most Recent Fund Was Raised: 03/05/2013
Year Founded: 1969
Capital Under Management: $920,000,000
Current Activity Level : Actively seeking new investments

NEXXUS CAPITAL SA DE CV

Av. Vasco de Quiroga No. 3880
2nd Floor, Santa Fe
Mexico City, Mexico 05300
Phone: 525552923400
E-mail: infonexxus@nexxuscapital.com
Website: www.nexxuscapital.com

Management and Staff
Alejandro Oliver, Managing Director
Alejandro Saiz, Vice President
Arturo Saval Perez, Senior Managing Director
Enrique Castillo Badia, Managing Director
Juan Carlos Gavito, Vice President
Luis Alberto Harvey MacKissack, Founder
Roberto Terrazas de la Cerda, Managing Director

Type of Firm
Private Equity Firm

Project Preferences

Type of Financing Preferred:
Leveraged Buyout
Expansion
Acquisition

Geographical Preferences

International Preferences:
Mexico

Industry Preferences

In Medical/Health prefer:
Medical/Health

In Consumer Related prefer:
Entertainment and Leisure
Retail
Consumer Products
Consumer Services
Hotels and Resorts
Education Related

In Financial Services prefer:
Financial Services

In Business Serv. prefer:
Services

In Manufact. prefer:
Manufacturing

Additional Information
Name of Most Recent Fund: Nexxus Capital VI
Most Recent Fund Was Raised: 11/20/2013
Year Founded: 1995
Capital Under Management: $1,078,096,000
Current Activity Level : Actively seeking new investments

NF HOLDINGS LTD

27-35 Grainger Street
Fifth Floor, Maybrook House
Newcastle upon Tyne, United Kingdom NE1 5JE
Phone: 441912292770
Fax: 441912292789
E-mail: enquiries@northstarventures.co.uk
Website: www.northstarventures.co.uk

Other Offices
One St James' Gate
Ground Floor
Newcastle upon Tyne, United Kingdom NE1 4AD
Phone: 441912112300
Fax: 441912112323

Management and Staff
Andrew Mitchell, Chief Executive Officer
Jason Hobbs, Founder

Type of Firm
Private Equity Firm

Project Preferences

Type of Financing Preferred:
Early Stage
Expansion
Seed

Geographical Preferences

United States Preferences:
Northeast

International Preferences:
United Kingdom

Industry Preferences

In Communications prefer:
Entertainment

In Consumer Related prefer:
Retail

In Industrial/Energy prefer:
Alternative Energy

In Transportation prefer:
Transportation

In Financial Services prefer:
Financial Services
Real Estate

In Business Serv. prefer:
Distribution

In Manufact. prefer:
Manufacturing

In Agr/Forestr/Fish prefer:
Agriculture related

Additional Information
Year Founded: 2003
Capital Under Management: $64,600,000
Current Activity Level : Actively seeking new investments

NFACTORY INVEST SAS

20, Place Saint Marc
Rouen, France 76000
Website: nfactory.io

Type of Firm
Incubator/Development Program

Project Preferences

Type of Financing Preferred:
Early Stage
Seed

Geographical Preferences

International Preferences:
Europe
France

Industry Preferences

In Computer Software prefer:
Software

In Internet Specific prefer:
Internet
Ecommerce

In Consumer Related prefer:
Consumer
Consumer Products

Additional Information
Year Founded: 2016
Current Activity Level : Actively seeking new investments

NFQ VENTURES

468 Wellington Street, Suite 400A
Toronto, Canada M5V 1E3
Phone: 4163606663
Fax: 4163606563
E-mail: info@NFQventures.com
Website: www.nfqventures.com

Type of Firm
Private Equity Firm

Additional Information
Year Founded: 2011
Current Activity Level : Actively seeking new investments

NFT VENTURES AB

Eriksbergsgatan 8A
Stockholm, Sweden 11430
Phone: 46739880422
E-mail: info@nftventures.com
Website: www.nftventures.com

Type of Firm
Private Equity Firm

Project Preferences

Type of Financing Preferred:
Early Stage
Startup

Geographical Preferences

International Preferences:
Sweden
United Kingdom
Luxembourg
Netherlands
Belgium
Norway
Germany
Denmark

Industry Preferences

In Financial Services prefer:
Financial Services

Additional Information
Year Founded: 2015
Current Activity Level : Actively seeking new investments

NGEN PARTNERS LLC

1114 State Street, Suite 247
Santa Barbara, CA USA 93101
Phone: 8055643156
Fax: 8055641669
Website: www.ngenpartners.com

Other Offices
720 University Avenue, Suite 200
Palo Alto, CA USA 94301
Phone: 650-321-4100

733 Third Avenue
18th Floor
New York, NY USA 10017
Phone: 212-450-9700

Management and Staff
John Robison, Principal
Peter Grubstein, Founder
Robb McLarty, Principal
Rosemary Ripley, Managing Director
Steve Parry, Managing Director

Type of Firm
Private Equity Firm

Association Membership
National Venture Capital Association - USA (NVCA)

Project Preferences

Role in Financing:
Will function either as deal originator or investor in deals created by others

Type of Financing Preferred:
Early Stage
Expansion
Balanced
Later Stage

Size of Investments Considered:
Min Size of Investment Considered (000s): $5,000
Max Size of Investment Considered (000s): $25,000

Geographical Preferences

United States Preferences:

Canadian Preferences:
All Canada

Industry Preferences

In Industrial/Energy prefer:
Energy
Alternative Energy
Energy Conservation Relat
Environmental Related

In Agr/Forestr/Fish prefer:
Agriculture related

In Other prefer:
Environment Responsible

Additional Information
Name of Most Recent Fund: NGEN Partners Fund III
Most Recent Fund Was Raised: 08/14/2008
Year Founded: 2001
Capital Under Management: $145,400,000
Current Activity Level : Actively seeking new investments
Method of Compensation: Return on investment is of primary concern, do not charge fees

NGN CAPITAL LLC

369 Lexington Avenue
17th Floor
New York, NY USA 10017
Phone: 2129720077
Fax: 2129720080
E-mail: investorrelations@ngncapital.com
Website: www.ngncapital.com

Other Offices
c/o Oracle Partners
200 Greenwich Avenue
Greenwich, CT USA 06830
Phone: 2038627900
Fax: 2038621613

Bergheimer Strasse 89a
Heidelberg, Germany 69115
Phone: 49-62-2189-3760
Fax: 4962218937625

Management and Staff
Bernard Peperstraete, Partner
Ivica Cerina, Partner
John Costantino, Managing Partner
Kenneth Abramowitz, Co-Founder
Kenneth Gorelick, Venture Partner
Leon Recanati, Venture Partner
Leonard Hirsch, Chief Financial Officer
Loren Busby, Partner
Noah Kroloff, Partner
Peter Johann, Managing Partner

Type of Firm
Private Equity Firm

Project Preferences

Type of Financing Preferred:
Early Stage
Later Stage

Geographical Preferences

United States Preferences:

International Preferences:
Europe

Industry Preferences

In Biotechnology prefer:
Biotechnology

In Medical/Health prefer:
Medical/Health
Medical Products
Health Services
Pharmaceuticals

Additional Information
Year Founded: 2004
Capital Under Management: $430,000,000
Current Activity Level : Actively seeking new investments

NGP CAPITAL

418 Florence Street
Palo Alto, CA USA 94301

Other Offices

No. 5 Donghuan Zhonglu
Beijing Economic Technological Devt Area
Beijing, China 100027
Phone: 8613910938937

12 Avenue des Morgines
1213 Petit-Lancy
Geneva, Switzerland

Keilalahdentie 2-4
Espoo
Helsinki, Finland 02150
Phone: 358504821277

Chaowai Street, Vantone Center, Jia # 6
Rm. 2627, Tower D-26f, Chaoyang District
Beijing, China

Industrial Plot # 243
Udyog Vihar Phase-1
Gurgaon, India 122016
Phone: 911244833000

Management and Staff
Anupam Rastogi, Principal
Bo Ilsoe, Partner
Guo Lu, Principal
John Gardner, Partner
Mary Bedegi, Chief Financial Officer
Monica Johnson, Chief Financial Officer
Paul Asel, Managing Partner
Tang David, Partner
Upal Basu, Partner
Walter Masalin, Partner

Type of Firm
Private Equity Firm

Project Preferences

Role in Financing:
Will function either as deal originator or investor in deals created by others

Type of Financing Preferred:
Fund of Funds
Early Stage
Balanced

Size of Investments Considered:
Min Size of Investment Considered (000s): $5,000
Max Size of Investment Considered (000s): $15,000

Geographical Preferences

International Preferences:
All International

Industry Preferences

In Communications prefer:
Telecommunications
Wireless Communications
Media and Entertainment

In Business Serv. prefer:
Services
Media

Additional Information
Name of Most Recent Fund: Nokia Growth Partners III S.C.A.
Most Recent Fund Was Raised: 09/07/2012
Year Founded: 2004
Capital Under Management: $600,000,000
Current Activity Level : Actively seeking new investments
Method of Compensation: Return on investment is of primary concern, do not charge fees

NHN INVESTMENT CO LTD

Daechi-dong, Kangnam-gu
7th FL., Cosmo Tower
Seoul, South Korea 135549
Phone: 82221364500
E-mail: invinfo@nhninv.com
Website: www.nhninv.com

Type of Firm
Private Equity Firm

Project Preferences

Type of Financing Preferred:
Balanced

Geographical Preferences

International Preferences:
Korea, South

Industry Preferences

In Communications prefer:
Commercial Communications

In Internet Specific prefer:
Internet

In Semiconductor/Electr prefer:
Semiconductor

In Biotechnology prefer:
Genetic Engineering

In Industrial/Energy prefer:
Materials
Environmental Related

Additional Information
Year Founded: 2010
Current Activity Level : Actively seeking new investments

NIBC PRINCIPAL INVESTMENTS BV

Carnegieplein 4
The Hague, Netherlands 2517 KJ
Phone: 31703425425
Fax: 31703651071
E-mail: info@nibc.com
Website: www.nibc.com

Other Offices

1095 Avenue of the Americas
26th floor
New York, NY USA 10036
Phone: 1-212-461-6400
Fax: 1-212-461-6498

Wetenschapsstraat 41
Brussels, Belgium 1040
Phone: 32-2-235-8803
Fax: 32-2-235-8809

1 Finlayson Green #15-01
Singapore, Singapore 049246
Phone: 65-65-380-736
Fax: 65-65-382-510

Neue Mainzer Strasse 52
Frankfurt, Germany D - 60311
Phone: 49-69-5050-6550
Fax: 49-69-5050-2183

125 Old Broad Street
11th Floor
London, United Kingdom EC2N 1AR
Phone: 44-20-7375-7777
Fax: 44-20-7588-6483

Management and Staff
Alfred Tulp, Managing Director
C.M. Vermeulen, Managing Director
Charly Zwemstra, Partner
Christian M. Bachle, Partner
Darren Kyte, Chief Executive Officer
E.J. Van Der Burg, Managing Director
Ernest Lambers, Partner
Gerard Burgers, Managing Director
Hilde Famaey, Partner
J.H. Vermeulen, Managing Director
Joris de Meester, Partner
Niels Ruigrok, Partner
Patrick Paardenkooper, Partner
Paul de Klerk, Managing Partner
Paul Zekveld, Partner
Piet Serrure, Partner

Type of Firm
Bank Affiliated

Project Preferences
Role in Financing:
Prefer role as deal originator but will also invest in deals created by others

Type of Financing Preferred:
Second Stage Financing
Leveraged Buyout
Value-Add
Mezzanine
Management Buyouts
Special Situation

Size of Investments Considered:
Min Size of Investment Considered (000s): $13,114
Max Size of Investment Considered (000s): $52,459

Geographical Preferences
International Preferences:
Western Europe

Industry Focus
(% based on actual investment)
Other Products   100.0%

Additional Information
Name of Most Recent Fund: European CMBS Opportunity Fund
Most Recent Fund Was Raised: 09/05/2008
Year Founded: 1994
Capital Under Management: $1,392,000,000
Current Activity Level : Actively seeking new investments

NIBIRU CAPITAL MANAGEMENT LTD

130 King Street West, Suite 1800
Toronto, Canada M5X 1E3
Phone: 905-319-2548
Fax: 905-332-4499
E-mail: info@nibiru.ca
Website: www.nibiru.ca

Management and Staff
Dave Smardon, Managing Partner
Norm Kirkpatrick, Managing Partner
P. Jelf Caruso, Managing Partner
Roger Wright, Venture Partner

Type of Firm
Private Equity Firm

Project Preferences
Type of Financing Preferred:
Early Stage
Expansion
Recapitalizations

Geographical Preferences
Canadian Preferences:
All Canada

Industry Preferences
In Communications prefer:
Wireless Communications

In Semiconductor/Electr prefer:
Semiconductor

In Medical/Health prefer:
Medical Therapeutics
Medical Products
Health Services

In Industrial/Energy prefer:
Alternative Energy

In Transportation prefer:
Aerospace

Additional Information
Year Founded: 1990
Current Activity Level : Actively seeking new investments

NICOLET CAPITAL PARTNERS LLC

1603 Orrington Avenue, Suite 815
Evanston, IL USA 60201
Phone: 8475635377
Fax: 2535402700
Website: www.nicoletcap.com

Management and Staff
Brett Snyder, President

Type of Firm
Private Equity Firm

Project Preferences
Type of Financing Preferred:
Leveraged Buyout
Acquisition

Size of Investments Considered:
Min Size of Investment Considered (000s): $15,000
Max Size of Investment Considered (000s): $50,000

Geographical Preferences
United States Preferences:

Industry Preferences
In Consumer Related prefer:
Consumer

In Business Serv. prefer:
Services
Distribution

In Manufact. prefer:
Manufacturing

Additional Information
Year Founded: 2007
Current Activity Level : Actively seeking new investments

NIIGATA VENTURE CAPITAL CO LTD

3-1-46 Yoneyama, Chuo-Ku
Niigata-Shi, Niigata, Japan 950-0961
Phone: 81252506306
E-mail: info@niigata-vc.co.jp
Website: www.niigata-vc.co.jp

Type of Firm
Private Equity Firm

Project Preferences
Type of Financing Preferred:
Balanced
Seed

Geographical Preferences
International Preferences:
Japan

Additional Information
Year Founded: 2010
Current Activity Level : Actively seeking new investments

NIKOIL INVESTMENT BANK

8 Efremova Street
Moscow, Russia 119048
Phone: 74957059039
Fax: 74957457010

Type of Firm
Bank Affiliated

Project Preferences
Type of Financing Preferred:
Balanced

Geographical Preferences

International Preferences:
Russia

Industry Preferences

In Communications prefer:
Commercial Communications

In Computer Software prefer:
Software

In Industrial/Energy prefer:
Oil & Gas Drilling,Explor

In Manufact. prefer:
Manufacturing

Additional Information

Year Founded: 1993
Current Activity Level : Actively seeking new investments

NIKORRINVEST CO LTD

7 Korovyi val
Office 155
Moscow, Russia 119049
Phone: 74957204578
E-mail: uk@nicor-vc.ru
Website: www.nicor.ru

Type of Firm
Government Affiliated Program

Association Membership
Russian Venture Capital Association (RVCA)

Project Preferences

Type of Financing Preferred:
Early Stage
Seed
Startup

Geographical Preferences

International Preferences:
Russia

Industry Preferences

In Communications prefer:
Communications and Media

In Biotechnology prefer:
Biotechnology

In Industrial/Energy prefer:
Alternative Energy

Additional Information

Year Founded: 2005
Current Activity Level : Actively seeking new investments

NINGBO ANGEL CAPITAL GUIDING FUND CO LTD

Yangfan Road, Ningbo National
Room 213, Block B3, Lane 999
Ningbo, China 315040
Phone: 86574-27960377
Website: www.nbstf.org.cn

Type of Firm
Government Affiliated Program

Project Preferences

Type of Financing Preferred:
Early Stage
Seed
Startup

Geographical Preferences

International Preferences:
China

Industry Preferences

In Medical/Health prefer:
Health Services

In Industrial/Energy prefer:
Energy
Advanced Materials
Environmental Related

Additional Information

Year Founded: 2013
Current Activity Level : Actively seeking new investments

NINGBO CHENHAI LING-BI EQUITY INVESTMENT PARNER ENTERPRISE

No.1, Meishan Yanchang
R173, Office No.11
Ningbo, China

Type of Firm
Private Equity Firm

Project Preferences

Type of Financing Preferred:
Early Stage
Expansion
Later Stage

Geographical Preferences

International Preferences:
China

Industry Preferences

In Internet Specific prefer:
Internet

In Consumer Related prefer:
Consumer
Retail

In Financial Services prefer:
Financial Services

In Business Serv. prefer:
Services

Additional Information

Year Founded: 2015
Capital Under Management: $115,220,000
Current Activity Level : Actively seeking new investments

NINGBO GAOXIN DISTRICT JIAXIN EQUITY INVT MGMT CO LTD

No.66 Yuanshi Road, High-tech
Room 4-21-2, Venture Mansion
Ningbo, China 200050
Phone: 862152675899

Type of Firm
Private Equity Firm

Project Preferences

Type of Financing Preferred:
Balanced

Geographical Preferences

International Preferences:
China

Additional Information

Year Founded: 2009
Current Activity Level : Actively seeking new investments

NINGBO JIAMING HAOC-HUN INVESTMENT MANAGEMENT CO LTD

No.1168 Nanjing West Road
Room 4208, Building 42
Shanghai, China 200041
Phone: 862151178985
Fax: 862152524616
Website: www.dongtinglakeinvestment.com

Type of Firm
Investment Management Firm

Project Preferences

Type of Financing Preferred:
Generalist PE

Geographical Preferences

International Preferences:
China

Industry Preferences

In Computer Software prefer:
Software

In Internet Specific prefer:
Internet

Additional Information

Year Founded: 2015
Current Activity Level : Actively seeking new investments

NINGBO JUNRUN EQUITY INVESTMENT MANAGEMENT CO LTD

Essence Road 188
High-tech Zone
Ningbo, China 315103
Phone: 8657487915090
Fax: 8657487915077
Website: www.jrcapital.com.cn

Management and Staff

Huichang Jiang, President

Type of Firm

Private Equity Firm

Project Preferences

Type of Financing Preferred:
Generalist PE
Balanced

Geographical Preferences

International Preferences:
China

Additional Information

Year Founded: 2009
Capital Under Management: $6,091,000
Current Activity Level : Actively seeking new investments

NINGBO JUNRUN VENTURE CAPITAL INVESTMENT MGMT CO LTD

No.587, Juxian Road
15F,Bldg. A3, Lvchengyanfayuan
Ningbo, China 315048
Phone: 8657487863106
Fax: 8657487863109
E-mail: junrun@jrcapital.com.cn
Website: www.jrcapital.com.cn

Management and Staff

Chunlin Fan, Vice President

Type of Firm

Private Equity Firm

Project Preferences

Type of Financing Preferred:
Balanced

Geographical Preferences

International Preferences:
China

Additional Information

Year Founded: 2010
Current Activity Level : Actively seeking new investments

NINGBO RONGYIN EQUITY INVESTMENT PARTNERSHIP LP

Beilun District, Ningbo
Room 1025, Building 18, Busine
Ningbo, China

Type of Firm

Private Equity Firm

Project Preferences

Type of Financing Preferred:
Balanced

Geographical Preferences

International Preferences:
China

Additional Information

Year Founded: 2016
Current Activity Level : Actively seeking new investments

NINTH STREET CAPITAL PARTNERS LLC

2000 Auburn Drive, Suite 200-2022
Cleveland, OH USA 44122
Phone: 2163730925
Fax: 2162236287
E-mail: info@ninthstreetcapital.com
Website: www.ninthstreetcapital.com

Type of Firm

Private Equity Firm

Project Preferences

Type of Financing Preferred:
Leveraged Buyout
Expansion
Later Stage
Acquisition

Industry Preferences

In Medical/Health prefer:
Health Services

In Industrial/Energy prefer:
Energy

In Business Serv. prefer:
Services

In Manufact. prefer:
Manufacturing

Additional Information

Year Founded: 2009
Current Activity Level : Actively seeking new investments

NIPPON ANGELS INVESTMENT CO LTD

2F Akasaka Hananoki Bldg.
1-5-25 Moto-Akasaka, Minato-ku
Tokyo, Japan 107-0051
Phone: 81-3-5770-6301
Fax: 81-3-5770-6302
E-mail: info@naic.co.jp
Website: www.naic.co.jp

Type of Firm

Angel Group

Project Preferences

Type of Financing Preferred:
Balanced

Additional Information

Year Founded: 2000
Current Activity Level : Actively seeking new investments

NIPPON SANGYO SUISHIN KIKO LTD

2-5-1 Atago Minato-ku
17FMORITower Atago Green Hill
Tokyo, Japan 105-6217
Phone: 81354015600
Fax: 81354015620
Website: www.nsskjapan.com

Type of Firm

Private Equity Firm

Project Preferences

Type of Financing Preferred:
Leveraged Buyout
Expansion
Generalist PE
Balanced
Acquisition

Geographical Preferences

International Preferences:
Japan

Industry Preferences

In Consumer Related prefer:
Entertainment and Leisure

Additional Information

Year Founded: 2014
Capital Under Management: $532,320,000
Current Activity Level : Actively seeking new investments

NIPPON TECHNOLOGY VENTURE PARTNERS LTD

Akihabara Dai Bldg. 8F 804
1-18-13, Sotokanda
Tokyo, Japan 101-0021
Phone: 813-3526-3131
Fax: 813-3526-3555
Website: www.ntvp.com

Management and Staff

Kazutaka Muraguchi, Chief Executive Officer

Type of Firm

Private Equity Firm

Project Preferences

Type of Financing Preferred:
Early Stage

Geographical Preferences

International Preferences:
Japan

Industry Preferences

In Computer Hardware prefer:
Computers

In Internet Specific prefer:
Internet

In Semiconductor/Electr prefer:
Semiconductor

In Financial Services prefer:
Financial Services

Additional Information

Year Founded: 1998
Capital Under Management: $26,400,000
Current Activity Level : Actively seeking new investments

NIPPON VENTURE CAPITAL CO LTD

2-4-1 Marunouchi
Chiyoda-ku
Tokyo, Japan 107-0052
Phone: 81362560230
Fax: 81362560231
E-mail: info@nvcc.co.jp
Website: www.nvcc.co.jp

Other Offices

3-2-20, Imahashi
2/F Kouan Nissei Building
Chuo-Ku, Osaka, Japan 541-0042
Phone: 81662312112
Fax: 81662312050

Type of Firm

Private Equity Firm

Association Membership

Japan Venture Capital Association

Project Preferences

Type of Financing Preferred:
Balanced

Geographical Preferences

International Preferences:
Asia
Japan

Industry Preferences

In Communications prefer:
Commercial Communications

In Biotechnology prefer:
Biotechnology

In Industrial/Energy prefer:
Robotics
Environmental Related

Additional Information

Year Founded: 1996
Capital Under Management: $26,400,000
Current Activity Level : Actively seeking new investments

NIRVANA VENTURE ADVISORS PVT LTD

604 Regent Chambers
Nariman Point
Mumbai, India 400-021
Phone: 912243471430
Fax: 912243471437
E-mail: info@nirvanaventures.in
Website: www.nirvanaventures.in

Management and Staff

Rajan Mehra, Managing Director

Type of Firm

Private Equity Firm

Association Membership

Indian Venture Capital Association (IVCA)

Project Preferences

Type of Financing Preferred:
Early Stage
Expansion
Seed
Startup

Size of Investments Considered:
Min Size of Investment Considered (000s): $500
Max Size of Investment Considered (000s): $4,000

Geographical Preferences

International Preferences:
India

Industry Preferences

In Communications prefer:
Communications and Media
Data Communications

In Computer Software prefer:
Data Processing

In Internet Specific prefer:
E-Commerce Technology
Internet
Ecommerce

In Transportation prefer:
Transportation

Additional Information

Year Founded: 2011
Capital Under Management: $30,000,000
Current Activity Level : Actively seeking new investments

NISCHER PROPERTIES AB

Kungsgatan 30
Stockholm, Sweden 111 35
Phone: 4687896175
Fax: 4687896170
Website: www.nischer.se

Management and Staff

Roger Blomqvist, Chief Executive Officer
Urban Larsson, Chief Executive Officer

Type of Firm

Private Equity Firm

Project Preferences

Type of Financing Preferred:
Balanced

Size of Investments Considered:
Min Size of Investment Considered (000s): $531
Max Size of Investment Considered (000s): $5,310

Geographical Preferences

International Preferences:
Scandanavia/Nordic Region

Industry Preferences

In Internet Specific prefer:
Internet

In Business Serv. prefer:
Media

Additional Information

Year Founded: 2000
Capital Under Management: $37,200,000
Current Activity Level : Actively seeking new investments

NISSAY CAPITAL CO LTD

2-4-8, Nagatacho, Chiyoda-ku
8F Nissay Nagatacho Building
Tokyo, Japan 100-0014
Phone: 81335016644
Fax: 81335016640
Website: www.nissay-cap.co.jp

Type of Firm
Private Equity Firm

Association Membership
Japan Venture Capital Association

Project Preferences

Type of Financing Preferred:
Early Stage
Balanced
Later Stage
Startup

Geographical Preferences

International Preferences:
Asia
Japan

Industry Preferences

In Biotechnology prefer:
Biotechnology

In Manufact. prefer:
Manufacturing

Additional Information

Year Founded: 1991
Capital Under Management: $37,800,000
Current Activity Level : Actively seeking new investments

NITTANY LION VENTURE CAPITAL

220 Business Building
University Park, PA USA 16802
Phone: 703-405-9602

Management and Staff
Jason Sandusky, Managing Director
Robert Sanders, Managing Director

Type of Firm
Private Equity Firm

Project Preferences

Type of Financing Preferred:
Balanced

Geographical Preferences

United States Preferences:
All U.S.

Additional Information

Year Founded: 2005
Capital Under Management: $5,000,000
Current Activity Level : Actively seeking new investments

NIVELINVEST SA

Rue Louis de Geer, 2
Louvain la Neuve, Belgium 1348
Phone: 3210884646
Fax: 3210884650
E-mail: invest@nivelinvest.be
Website: nivelinvest.be

Management and Staff
Corinne Estie Venart, Founder
Guy Zone, President
Philippe Remy, Managing Director

Type of Firm
Government Affiliated Program

Association Membership
Belgium Venturing Association

Project Preferences

Type of Financing Preferred:
Early Stage
Later Stage
Startup

Geographical Preferences

International Preferences:
Europe
Belgium

Industry Preferences

In Industrial/Energy prefer:
Industrial Products

In Business Serv. prefer:
Services

Additional Information

Year Founded: 1987
Current Activity Level : Actively seeking new investments

NJTC VENTURE FUND

96 Albany Street
New Brunswick, NJ USA 08901
Phone: 18562736800
Fax: 19084648131
E-mail: info@njtcvc.com
Website: www.njtcvc.com

Management and Staff
James Gunton, Co-Founder
Joseph Falkenstein, General Partner
Maxine Ballen, Co-Founder
Robert Chefitz, General Partner

Type of Firm
Private Equity Firm

Project Preferences

Role in Financing:
Will function either as deal originator or investor in deals created by others

Type of Financing Preferred:
Early Stage
Seed
Startup

Geographical Preferences

United States Preferences:
New Jersey

Industry Preferences

In Biotechnology prefer:
Biotechnology

In Industrial/Energy prefer:
Energy
Advanced Materials

Additional Information

Year Founded: 2001
Capital Under Management: $80,000,000
Current Activity Level : Actively seeking new investments
Method of Compensation: Return on investment is of primary concern, do not charge fees

NM INVESTMENTS LTD

Grosvenor Business Tower
Office 1912
Dubai, Utd. Arab Em.
Phone: 97144227272
Fax: 97144227422
E-mail: info@nm-invest.com
Website: www.nm-invest.com

Type of Firm
Private Equity Firm

Project Preferences

Type of Financing Preferred:
Early Stage
Expansion
Mezzanine
Seed

Additional Information
Year Founded: 1969
Current Activity Level : Actively seeking new investments

NMP MANAGEMENT CORP

3284 Northside Parkway, NW, Suite 525
Atlanta, GA USA 30327
Phone: 4042331966
Website: www.noromoseley.com

Management and Staff
Alan Taetle, General Partner
Allen Moseley, General Partner
John Ale, Vice President
Michael Elliott, Managing Partner
Spence McClelland, Partner

Type of Firm
Private Equity Firm

Association Membership
National Venture Capital Association - USA (NVCA)
Natl Assoc of Small Bus. Inv. Co (NASBIC)

Project Preferences

Role in Financing:
Prefer role as deal originator but will also invest in deals created by others

Type of Financing Preferred:
Early Stage
Expansion
Generalist PE
Balanced

Size of Investments Considered:
Min Size of Investment Considered (000s): $2,000
Max Size of Investment Considered (000s): $7,000

Geographical Preferences

United States Preferences:
Southeast
Virginia
Texas

Industry Focus
(% based on actual investment)
Computer Software and Services	25.4%
Internet Specific	24.1%
Medical/Health	14.5%
Other Products	12.6%
Communications and Media	7.7%
Consumer Related	5.8%
Computer Hardware	4.1%
Semiconductors/Other Elect.	3.3%
Industrial/Energy	1.3%
Biotechnology	1.2%

Additional Information
Name of Most Recent Fund: Noro-Moseley Partners VII, L.P.
Most Recent Fund Was Raised: 09/16/2013
Year Founded: 1983
Capital Under Management: $660,000,000
Current Activity Level : Actively seeking new investments
Method of Compensation: Return on investment is of primary concern, do not charge fees

NMS CAPITAL PARTNERS

433 North Camden Drive
Fourth Floor
Beverly Hills, CA USA 90210
Phone: 8007162080
Website: www.nmscapital.com

Other Offices
620 Newport Center Drive, Suite 1100
Newport Beach, CA USA 92660
Phone: 8007162080

18101 Von Karman Avenue, Suite 300
Irvine, CA USA 92612
Phone: 8883335853

80 Raffles Place
Level 36-01, UOB Plaza 1
, Singapore 048624
Phone: Singapore

14 Wall Street
20th Floor
New York, NY USA 10005
Phone: 8007162080

2810 Bank of America Tower
No. 12 Harcourt Road
Central, Hong Kong

3rd Floor Kingsbury House
15/17 King Street, St Jamess
London, United Kingdom SW1Y 6QU

Al Mussalla Commercial Tower
17th Floor
Dubai, Utd. Arab Em.

Haus zum Schwert
Weinplatz 10
Zurich, Switzerland 8001

Management and Staff
James Miller, Managing Director
Michael Nahass, Managing Director
Schad Brannon, Managing Director
Tyler Spring, Managing Director

Type of Firm
Investment Management Firm

Project Preferences

Type of Financing Preferred:
Early Stage
Expansion
Balanced

Additional Information
Year Founded: 2011
Current Activity Level : Actively seeking new investments

NOAH PRIVATE WEALTH MANAGEMENT CENTRE CO LTD

#68 Middle Yincheng Road
6/F One Lujiazui
Shanghai, China 200120
Phone: 86-21-3860-2301
Fax: 86-21-3860-2300

Other Offices
#4011 Shennan Road
Room 1402A, Zhonglu Building
Shenzhen, China 518031
Phone: 86-755-8256-2922
Fax: 86-755-8256-6628

#25 Tongxin Street
45F, Dalian World Trade Building
Dalian, Liaoning, China 116001
Phone: 86-411-3986-9299
Fax: 86-411-3986-9255

#55 Hongwu North Road, Xuanwu District
Rm 1901-1902, Zhidi Square
Nanjing, Jiangsu, China 210005
Phone: 86-25-6859-8488
Fax: 86-25-6859-8484

#5-1 Middle Chengjiang Road
Room 1004, Dongdu Int'l Tower
Jiangyin, Jiangsu, China 214400
Phone: 86-510-8166-6900
Fax: 86-510-8166-6898

#51, North Nanhai Avenue
Room 1310, Caihui Building
Foshan, Guangdong, China 528200
Phone: 86-757-8632-6277
Fax: 86-757-8632-6378

#36, Xianggang Zhong Road
Room 2206, Zhaoyin Building
Qingdao, Shandong, China 266071
Phone: 86-532-8667-8668
Fax: 86-532-8667-8669

#118 Xinhua Zhong Road
Room C, 15/F, Xiangming Building
Zhongshan, Guangdong, China 528415
Phone: 86-760-8982-3388
Fax: 86-760-8982-3000

Wusi Road
1811-1812, 19/F, Huangqiu Square
Fuzhou, Fujian, China 350000
Phone: 86-591-3811-8697
Fax: 86-591-3811-8610

#1 Chengmentou West Road
Room 1201-02, 12/F Global Int'l Square
Foshan, China 528000
Phone: 86-757-8236-3416
Fax: 86-757-8236-3416

#38, East Sanhuan North Road
Room 703, Tower 4, Beijing Int'l Center
Beijing, China 100026
Phone: 86-10-8587-9698
Fax: 86-10-8587-9689

#18 Weijin Road
Rm 605-606, Block A, Xindu Building
Tianjin, China 300073
Phone: 86-22-2777-8905
Fax: 86-22-2777-8915

#901 Baizhang East Road
Room 18-2, 18-3 Xinye Building
Ningbo, Zhejiang, China 315040
Phone: 86-574-8781-5252
Fax: 86-574-8781-5226

Jinfuyuan Zhubao Building
Room 1002, 1003, 1005, Block A
Yiwu, Zhejiang, China 320000
Phone: 86-579-8565-8908
Fax: 86-579-8565-8890

#371-375 Huangshi Street
Room 1113-1117 World Trade Center
Guangzhou, China 510060
Phone: 86-20-5775-1189
Fax: 86-20-8775-1219

#343 Zhongshan Road
9/F, Block A, Dongfang Square
Wuxi, Zhejiang, China 214000
Phone: 86-510-8118-9099
Fax: 86-510-8118-9079

#819 Shixin Zhong Road
Room 2102, Ludu World Trade Square Bldg
Hangzhou, Zhejiang, China 311203
Phone: 86-571-5712-8002
Fax: 86-571-5712-8015

#1277 Development Avenue
Room 1307, Xiangge Tower
Cixi, Zhejiang, China 315300
Phone: 86-574-2345-0282
Fax: 86-574-2345-0283

#34 West Chengxi Road
Room 702, Guibin Int'l Bell Tower
Yixing, Jiangsu, China 214200
Phone: 86-510-8733-9788
Fax: 86-510-8733-6909

#205 Zhaohui Road, Xiacheng District
Room 2305, Shenlan Square Building
Hangzhou, Zhejiang, China 310014
Phone: 86-571-5689-9994
Fax: 86-571-5689-9997

#2 Zongfu Road
Room 907, Block A, Times Square
Chengdu, China 610016
Phone: 86-28-8671-0878
Fax: 86-28-8671-0690

#228 Aibandeng Road
713, European City Ctr Dept Store Bldg
Wenzhou, Zhejiang, China 325000
Phone: 86-577-8986-6829
Fax: 86-577-8986-6812

Dalianxingui Road
Room 513, Block 1, Mingri Square
Foshan, China 528300
Phone: 86-757-2809-3900
Fax: 86-757-2809-3901

#2 Suhua Road, Suzhou Ind'l Park
17/F, International Building
Suzhou, Jiangsu, China 215000
Phone: 86-512-6280-5880
Fax: 86-512-6280-5955

Taizhou Economic Development Zone
C Area, 12F, New Taizhou Building
Taizhou, Zhejiang, China 318000
Phone: 86-576-8187-1160
Fax: 86-576-8187-1161

#112, Jinkeqiao Avenue
15/F Jinggong Building
Shaoxing, Zhejiang, China 312030
Phone: 86-575-8118-9501
Fax: 86-575-8118-9502

Management and Staff

Song Ying, Chief Operating Officer
Tao Wu, Chief Financial Officer

Type of Firm

Investment Management Firm

Project Preferences

Type of Financing Preferred:
Balanced

Geographical Preferences

International Preferences:
China

Additional Information

Year Founded: 2003
Current Activity Level: Actively seeking new investments

NOBLE (BEIJING) FUND MANAGEMENT INC

No. 19, Jianguomenwai Street
Rm 702, A, Interantional Plaza
Beijing, China
Phone: 861085261055
Fax: 861085263529
E-mail: noble@6nfund.com
Website: www.6nfund.com

Other Offices

Changsha Furong District Wuyi Avenue
Room 11049, Zhongtian Plaza Building
Hunan, China
Phone: 8673185837366
Fax: 8673189850696

Management and Staff

Chi Pan, Chief Financial Officer
Donghong Xiong, Vice President
Fei Chen, Vice President
Hongqiang Liu, Managing Partner
Xingdong Miao, Partner
Yanhua Zhang, Vice President
Yongqing Zhou, Partner

Type of Firm

Corporate PE/Venture

Project Preferences

Role in Financing:
Prefer role in deals created by others

Type of Financing Preferred:
Early Stage
Expansion
Generalist PE
Later Stage

Geographical Preferences

International Preferences:
China

Industry Preferences

In Medical/Health prefer:
Medical/Health

In Industrial/Energy prefer:
Energy
Environmental Related

In Financial Services prefer:
Real Estate

In Business Serv. prefer:
Media

Additional Information
Year Founded: 2010
Current Activity Level : Actively seeking new investments

NOBLE FOUR PARTNERS LLC

230 Park Avenue, Suite 1000
New York, NY USA 10169
Phone: 6465685220
E-mail: info@noblefourpartnersllc.com
Website: www.noblefourpartnersllc.com

Management and Staff
Mark Tomassini, Partner
Robert Schimmel, Vice President
Stephen Merchant, Partner

Type of Firm
Private Equity Firm

Project Preferences

Type of Financing Preferred:
Generalist PE

Additional Information
Year Founded: 2017
Current Activity Level : Actively seeking new investments

NOE BETEILIGUNGSFINAN-ZIERUNGEN GMBH

Seidengasse 9-11
Top 3.1.
Vienna, Austria 1030
Phone: 4317105210
Fax: 431710521040
E-mail: office@noebeg.at
Website: www.noebeg.at

Other Offices
Niederoesterreichring 2
Haus B, 4. Stock
St. Poelten, Austria 3100
Phone: 43-2742-9000-19325
Fax: 43-2742-9000-19330

Type of Firm
Government Affiliated Program

Project Preferences

Type of Financing Preferred:
Leveraged Buyout
Early Stage
Later Stage
Seed
Management Buyouts
Startup

Size of Investments Considered:
Min Size of Investment Considered (000s): $145
Max Size of Investment Considered (000s): $2,175

Geographical Preferences

International Preferences:
Austria

Industry Preferences

In Communications prefer:
Telecommunications

In Biotechnology prefer:
Agricultural/Animal Bio.

In Medical/Health prefer:
Medical/Health

In Consumer Related prefer:
Consumer
Entertainment and Leisure
Sports
Retail
Food/Beverage
Hotels and Resorts

In Industrial/Energy prefer:
Industrial Products
Materials
Environmental Related

Additional Information
Year Founded: 1979
Capital Under Management: $60,200,000
Current Activity Level : Actively seeking new investments

NOMO VENTURES MANAGEMENT LLC

100 Broadway
San Francisco, CA USA 94111

Type of Firm
Private Equity Firm

Project Preferences

Type of Financing Preferred:
Balanced

Additional Information
Year Founded: 2016
Current Activity Level : Actively seeking new investments

NOMURA CHINA ASSET MANAGEMENT CO LTD

No.1, Qianwan First Road
Room 201, Building A
Shenzhen, China

Type of Firm
Private Equity Firm

Project Preferences

Type of Financing Preferred:
Leveraged Buyout
Generalist PE
Balanced

Geographical Preferences

International Preferences:
China

Additional Information
Year Founded: 2014
Current Activity Level : Actively seeking new investments

NOMURA CO LTD

2 World Financial Center B
18th Floor
New York, NY USA 10281
Phone: 212-667-1414
Fax: 212-667-1460
Website: www.nomurakougei.co.jp

Management and Staff
Kiyoshi Yoshimoto, Managing Director
Takeshi Masuda, Managing Director
Yoshinobu Tominaga, Senior Managing Director

Type of Firm
Private Equity Firm

Additional Information
Year Founded: 1969
Current Activity Level : Actively seeking new investments

NONAME VENTURES LLC

915 Wilshire Boulevard, Suite 1750
Los Angeles, CA USA 90017
Website: www.noname.ventures

Type of Firm
Private Equity Firm

Pratt's Guide to Private Equity & Venture Capital Sources

Project Preferences

Type of Financing Preferred:
Early Stage

Additional Information

Year Founded: 1969
Current Activity Level : Actively seeking new investments

NONGGU INVESTMENT CO LTD

No.28 Changning Avenue
Dongbao District
Jingmen, China
Phone: 867242295197
Fax: 867242295197
Website: ng-inv.com.cn

Type of Firm

Government Affiliated Program

Project Preferences

Type of Financing Preferred:
Balanced

Geographical Preferences

International Preferences:
China

Industry Preferences

In Agr/Forestr/Fish prefer:
Agriculture related

Additional Information

Year Founded: 2015
Capital Under Management: $74,130,000
Current Activity Level : Actively seeking new investments

NORD CAPITAL PARTE-NAIRES SAS

77 rue Nationale
Lille, France 59000
Phone: 33361582600
Fax: 33361582609
Website: www.nord-cp.com

Management and Staff

Benoit Pastour, Vice President
Frederic Kuhlmann, Founder
Olivier Motte, President

Type of Firm

Bank Affiliated

Project Preferences

Type of Financing Preferred:
Leveraged Buyout
Early Stage
Expansion
Generalist PE
Later Stage
Seed
Management Buyouts
Acquisition

Geographical Preferences

International Preferences:
France

Industry Preferences

In Internet Specific prefer:
E-Commerce Technology
Ecommerce

In Medical/Health prefer:
Medical/Health
Health Services

In Consumer Related prefer:
Hotels and Resorts

In Industrial/Energy prefer:
Industrial Products

In Business Serv. prefer:
Services
Distribution

In Agr/Forestr/Fish prefer:
Agribusiness

In Other prefer:
Environment Responsible

Additional Information

Year Founded: 2010
Capital Under Management: $43,000,000
Current Activity Level : Actively seeking new investments

NORD EUROPE PARTENARIAT SA

2 rue Andrei Dimitri Sakharov
Mont ST Aignan, France 76130
Phone: 33320128537
Fax: 33320128724

Type of Firm

Bank Affiliated

Project Preferences

Type of Financing Preferred:
Leveraged Buyout
Generalist PE
Later Stage
Acquisition
Recapitalizations

Size of Investments Considered:
Min Size of Investment Considered (000s): $174
Max Size of Investment Considered (000s): $929

Geographical Preferences

International Preferences:
Europe
France

Additional Information

Year Founded: 1988
Current Activity Level : Actively seeking new investments

NORD FRANCE AMORCAGE SASU

151, Avenue du Hoover
Lille, France 59000

Type of Firm

Government Affiliated Program

Project Preferences

Type of Financing Preferred:
Leveraged Buyout
Early Stage
Expansion
Later Stage
Management Buyouts
Acquisition

Size of Investments Considered:
Min Size of Investment Considered (000s): $32
Max Size of Investment Considered (000s): $648

Geographical Preferences

International Preferences:
France

Additional Information

Year Founded: 2012
Current Activity Level : Actively seeking new investments

NORD HOLDING UN-TERNEHMENSBETEILIGU-NGSGESELLSCHAFT MBH

Walderseestrasse 23
Villa Venture
Hannover, Germany 30177
Phone: 495112704150
Fax: 495112704155
E-mail: info@nordholding.de
Website: nordholding.de

Management and Staff

Matthias Kues, Chief Executive Officer
Rainer Effinger, Managing Director
Thomas Bagusch, Managing Director

1523

Type of Firm
Bank Affiliated

Association Membership
German Venture Capital Association (BVK)

Project Preferences

Type of Financing Preferred:
Fund of Funds
Leveraged Buyout
Early Stage
Mezzanine
Turnaround
Later Stage
Management Buyouts
Acquisition
Recapitalizations

Geographical Preferences

International Preferences:
Switzerland
Austria
Germany

Industry Focus
(% based on actual investment)
Computer Software and Services 51.2%
Industrial/Energy 48.8%

Additional Information
Year Founded: 1969
Capital Under Management: $334,485,000
Current Activity Level : Actively seeking new investments

NORD KAPITALFORVALT-NING AS

Fredrik Langes Gate 20
2nd floor
Tromso, Norway 9008
Website: www.nordkapital.no

Management and Staff
Bjorn Hesthamar, Partner
Fredrik Borch, Partner
Kurt Jan Jensen, Managing Partner
Tove Sundstrom, Chief Financial Officer

Type of Firm
Private Equity Firm

Association Membership
European Private Equity and Venture Capital Assoc.

Project Preferences

Type of Financing Preferred:
Generalist PE
Turnaround
Recapitalizations

Geographical Preferences

International Preferences:
Norway

Industry Preferences

In Biotechnology prefer:
Biotechnology

In Industrial/Energy prefer:
Energy
Oil and Gas Exploration
Industrial Products

In Financial Services prefer:
Real Estate

In Business Serv. prefer:
Services

Additional Information
Year Founded: 2011
Capital Under Management: $74,700,000
Current Activity Level : Actively seeking new investments

NORDEST MERCHANT SPA

Viale Mazzini 77/D
Vicenza, Italy 36100
Phone: 39-444-235-479
Fax: 39-444-544-754
E-mail: vicenza@nordest-merchant.it

Type of Firm
Bank Affiliated

Project Preferences

Type of Financing Preferred:
Leveraged Buyout
Expansion
Management Buyouts

Geographical Preferences

International Preferences:
Italy
Europe

Additional Information
Year Founded: 1978
Current Activity Level : Actively seeking new investments

NORDIAN CAPITAL BV

Prince Bernhardplein 200
1097 JB
Amsterdam, Netherlands
Phone: 31207518550
E-mail: info@nordian.nl
Website: www.nordian.nl

Management and Staff
Minou Janus, Chief Financial Officer

Type of Firm
Private Equity Firm

Project Preferences

Type of Financing Preferred:
Leveraged Buyout
Acquisition

Geographical Preferences

International Preferences:
Europe

Additional Information
Year Founded: 2012
Current Activity Level : Actively seeking new investments

NORDIC CAPITAL

Master Samuelsgatan 21
9th floor
Stockholm, Sweden SE-111 44
Phone: 4684405050
Fax: 4686117998
E-mail: investor@nordiccapital.je
Website: www.nordiccapital.com

Other Offices
Berkeley Square House
Berkeley Square
London, United Kingdom W1J 6BY
Phone: 44-20-7355-5700
Fax: 44-20-7355-5749

Bygdoey Alle 9
Oslo, Norway 0257
Phone: 47-2255-0290
Fax: 47-2255-0291

Ulmenstrasse 37-39
Frankfurt, Germany 60325
Phone: 49-69-9726-6940
Fax: 49-69-972-669-429

Sankt Annae Plads 11
Copenhagen, Denmark 1250
Phone: 45-3344-7750
Fax: 45-3344-7755

26 Esplanade
St. Helier
Jersey, Channel Islands JE2 3QA
Phone: 44-534-605-100
Fax: 44-534-605-199

Management and Staff
Anders Hultin, Partner
Andrew Bennett, Managing Director
Bo Soderberg, Partner
Fredrik Naslund, Partner
Hans Eckerstrom, Partner
Joakim Karlsson, Partner
Klas Tikkanen, Chief Financial Officer
Kristoffer Melinder, Partner
Lars Terney, Partner
Morgan Olsson, Partner
Peter Hansson, Partner
Robert Andreen, Partner
Robert Furuhjelm, Partner
Sonke Bastlein, Partner
Tom Rygh, Partner
Toni Weitzberg, Partner

Type of Firm
Private Equity Firm

Association Membership
Finnish Venture Capital Association (FVCA)
Danish Venture Capital Association (DVCA)
Norwegian Venture Capital Association
Swedish Venture Capital Association (SVCA)
European Private Equity and Venture Capital Assoc.

Project Preferences

Role in Financing:
Prefer role as deal originator

Type of Financing Preferred:
Leveraged Buyout
Turnaround
Management Buyouts

Size of Investments Considered:
Min Size of Investment Considered (000s): $30,000
Max Size of Investment Considered (000s): $150,000

Geographical Preferences

International Preferences:
Europe
Switzerland
Western Europe
Austria
Scandanavia/Nordic Region
Germany

Industry Focus
(% based on actual investment)
Other Products	80.8%
Industrial/Energy	7.0%
Computer Software and Services	4.9%
Medical/Health	3.1%
Biotechnology	2.3%
Communications and Media	1.0%
Consumer Related	0.7%
Internet Specific	0.1%

Additional Information
Name of Most Recent Fund: Nordic Capital Fund VIII LP
Most Recent Fund Was Raised: 12/30/2013
Year Founded: 1989
Capital Under Management: $12,851,200,000
Current Activity Level : Actively seeking new investments

NORDIC EYE K/S
Nyhavn 16
Copenhagen , Denmark 1051
Website: nordiceye.com

Type of Firm
Private Equity Firm

Project Preferences

Type of Financing Preferred:
Early Stage

Geographical Preferences

International Preferences:
Europe

Additional Information
Year Founded: 2016
Current Activity Level : Actively seeking new investments

NORDIC MAKERS IVS
C.F. Richsvej 136, 1 tv
Frederiksberg, Denmark 2000

Type of Firm
Angel Group

Project Preferences

Type of Financing Preferred:
Early Stage
Balanced
Later Stage
Startup

Geographical Preferences

International Preferences:
Scandanavia/Nordic Region

Additional Information
Year Founded: 2016
Current Activity Level : Actively seeking new investments

NORDIC MEZZANINE LTD
Mikonkatu Four B
Helsinki, Finland 00100
Phone: 35896840640
Fax: 358968406410
Website: www.nordicmezzanine.com

Management and Staff
Kimmo Kallioniemi, Chief Financial Officer
Vesa Suurmunne, Chief Executive Officer

Type of Firm
Private Equity Firm

Association Membership
Estonian Private Equity and Venture Capital Assoc
Finnish Venture Capital Association (FVCA)
European Private Equity and Venture Capital Assoc.

Project Preferences

Role in Financing:
Prefer role in deals created by others

Type of Financing Preferred:
Leveraged Buyout
Mezzanine
Acquisition

Geographical Preferences

International Preferences:
Luxembourg
Switzerland
Austria
Scandanavia/Nordic Region
Belgium
Germany

Industry Focus
(% based on actual investment)
Other Products	58.6%
Industrial/Energy	26.1%
Consumer Related	13.5%
Internet Specific	1.9%

Additional Information
Year Founded: 1999
Capital Under Management: $709,800,000
Current Activity Level : Actively seeking new investments

NORDIC OPTION OY
Isokatu 32 B
Oulu, Finland 90100
Phone: 35888873300
Fax: 35888873310
E-mail: info@teknoventure.fi

Management and Staff
Ilkka Lukkariniemi, Managing Director
Kaarina Pekkinen, Partner
Kari Italahti, Partner
Mauri Visuri, Partner
Tuulikki Marjomaa, Partner

Type of Firm
Private Equity Firm

Project Preferences

Type of Financing Preferred:
Balanced

Size of Investments Considered:
Min Size of Investment Considered (000s): $200
Max Size of Investment Considered (000s): $2,000

Geographical Preferences

International Preferences:
Finland

Industry Preferences

In Communications prefer:
Telecommunications

In Computer Other prefer:
Computer Related

In Semiconductor/Electr prefer:
Optoelectronics

In Biotechnology prefer:
Biotechnology

In Medical/Health prefer:
Medical/Health
Medical Products

In Consumer Related prefer:
Consumer Products

In Industrial/Energy prefer:
Industrial Products

In Financial Services prefer:
Financial Services

In Manufact. prefer:
Manufacturing

In Agr/Forestr/Fish prefer:
Mining and Minerals

Additional Information

Year Founded: 1991
Capital Under Management: $70,800,000
Current Activity Level : Actively seeking new investments

NORDIC VENTURE PARTNERS APS

Amagertorv 1, 3rd floor
Copenhagen, Denmark 1160
Phone: 4533307880
Fax: 4533307889
Website: www.nordic.com

Other Offices

Bulevardi 1A
Helsinki, Finland 00100
Phone: 358-9-4282-6100
Fax: 358-9-4282-6110

Birger Jarlsgatan 14, 1st floor
Stockholm, Sweden S-114 34
Phone: 46-8-611-0703
Fax: 46-8-611-0704

Management and Staff

Claus Andersen, General Partner
Henrik Albertsen, Managing Partner
Thomas Tofte Hansen, General Partner

Type of Firm
Bank Affiliated

Project Preferences

Type of Financing Preferred:
Balanced

Geographical Preferences

International Preferences:
United Kingdom
Western Europe
Scandanavia/Nordic Region

Industry Preferences

In Communications prefer:
Telecommunications
Wireless Communications
Data Communications
Entertainment

In Computer Software prefer:
Software

In Internet Specific prefer:
Internet

In Consumer Related prefer:
Education Related

Additional Information

Name of Most Recent Fund: Nordic Venture Partners Fund II LLC
Most Recent Fund Was Raised: 06/08/2012
Year Founded: 2004
Capital Under Management: $439,400,000
Current Activity Level : Actively seeking new investments

NORDIKA ASSET MANAGEMENT AS

Radhusgaten 25
Postboks 1464 Vika
Oslo, Norway 0158
Phone: 47-22-936-820
Fax: 47-22-936-821

Type of Firm
Private Equity Firm

Project Preferences

Type of Financing Preferred:
Balanced

Geographical Preferences

International Preferences:
Norway

Additional Information

Year Founded: 2004
Current Activity Level : Actively seeking new investments

NORDKAPP GESTION SGIIC SA

Plaza Marques de Salamanca, 3-4
Madrid, Spain 28006
Phone: 55-91-432-39-10
Fax: 55-91-576-66-60
E-mail: madrid@nordkapp.es
Website: nordkapp.es

Other Offices

Avenida Carlos III, 13-15, 4a
Pamplona, Spain 31002
Phone: 55-948-20-30-70
Fax: 55-948-20-30-71

Pascual y Genis, 1, 9a
Valencia, Spain 46002
Phone: 55-96-351-13-12
Fax: 55- 96-394-25-31

Management and Staff
Enrique Lucas Romani, President

Type of Firm
Private Equity Firm

Project Preferences

Type of Financing Preferred:
Early Stage
Expansion
Later Stage
Seed
Startup

Geographical Preferences

International Preferences:
Europe
Spain

Additional Information
Year Founded: 2003
Current Activity Level : Actively seeking new investments

NORDSTJERNAN AB

Stureplan Three
Stockholm, Sweden 103 75
Phone: 4687885000
Fax: 4687885010
E-mail: info@nordstjernan.se
Website: www.nordstjernan.se

Management and Staff
Angela Langemar Olsson, Chief Financial Officer
Tomas Billing, Chief Executive Officer

Type of Firm
Private Equity Firm

Project Preferences

Type of Financing Preferred:
Leveraged Buyout
Generalist PE
Later Stage
Management Buyouts
Acquisition

Size of Investments Considered:
Min Size of Investment Considered (000s): $100
Max Size of Investment Considered (000s): $100,000

Geographical Preferences

International Preferences:
Scandanavia/Nordic Region

Industry Focus

(% based on actual investment)
Industrial/Energy   79.5%
Medical/Health   15.7%
Other Products   4.8%

Additional Information

Year Founded: 1890
Capital Under Management: $382,300,000
Current Activity Level : Actively seeking new investments

NORFUND

Stoperigata 2
Oslo, Norway 0250
Phone: 4722019393
Fax: 4722019394
E-mail: post@norfund.no
Website: www.norfund.no

Other Offices

Sureste de Multiplaza, Piso 4
San Jose, Costa Rica 721-1000
Phone: 506-2201-9292
Fax: 506-2201-5028

1016 Oakhill, Fourways Golf Park
Roos Street, Fourways 2055
Johannesburg, South Africa 2196
Phone: 27-11-467-4070
Fax: 27-11-467-4079

7th floor Pirshottam Place
Museum Hill
Nairobi, Kenya 00800
Phone: 254-203-601-820

Management and Staff

Kjell Roland, Managing Director

Type of Firm

Government Affiliated Program

Project Preferences

Type of Financing Preferred:
Generalist PE
Balanced
Turnaround
Management Buyouts

Size of Investments Considered:
Min Size of Investment Considered (000s): $400
Max Size of Investment Considered (000s): $20,000

Geographical Preferences

United States Preferences:

International Preferences:
Latin America
Rwanda
Europe
Uganda
Zambia
Tanzania
Botswana
Kenya
Pacific
Asia
Mozambique
Zimbabwe
Africa

Industry Preferences

In Biotechnology prefer:
Agricultural/Animal Bio.

In Industrial/Energy prefer:
Energy
Industrial Products
Advanced Materials

In Financial Services prefer:
Financial Services

In Manufact. prefer:
Manufacturing

Additional Information

Year Founded: 1997
Capital Under Management: $460,000,000
Current Activity Level : Actively seeking new investments

NORINNOVA FORVALTNING AS

Forskningsparken
Research Park
Tromso, Norway 9294
Phone: 4790559001
E-mail: post@norinnovaforvaltning.no
Website: www.norinnovaforvaltning.no

Management and Staff

January Kristoffersen, Partner
Karl-Johan Jakola, Managing Partner

Type of Firm

Private Equity Firm

Association Membership

Norwegian Venture Capital Association

Project Preferences

Type of Financing Preferred:
Early Stage
Later Stage
Seed
Startup

Geographical Preferences

International Preferences:
Norway

Industry Preferences

In Biotechnology prefer:
Biotechnology

In Medical/Health prefer:
Medical/Health
Medical Products
Pharmaceuticals

In Industrial/Energy prefer:
Energy

Additional Information

Year Founded: 2007
Current Activity Level : Actively seeking new investments

NORMANDIE PARTICIPATIONS SASU

Place Reine Mathilde
Abbaye Aux Dames
Caen, France 14000
Website: www.normandie-participations.fr

Type of Firm

Government Affiliated Program

Project Preferences

Type of Financing Preferred:
Early Stage
Expansion
Later Stage
Seed

Geographical Preferences

International Preferences:
France

Additional Information

Year Founded: 2016
Current Activity Level : Actively seeking new investments

NORRIS EQUITY PARTNERS

1251 N. Eddy Street, Suite 200
South Bend, IN USA 46617
Website: www.norrisequitypartners.com

Type of Firm
Private Equity Firm

Project Preferences

Type of Financing Preferred:
Leveraged Buyout

Geographical Preferences

United States Preferences:
Indiana

Additional Information
Year Founded: 2016
Capital Under Management: $3,500,000
Current Activity Level : Actively seeking new investments

NORRLANDS

Kopmansgatan 40
P.O. Box 56
Lulea, Sweden 971 03
Phone: 46920244250
Fax: 46920244269
E-mail: info@norrlandsfonden.se
Website: www.norrlandsfonden.se

Other Offices
Storgatan 31
Sundsvall, Sweden 852 30
Phone: 46-920-244-250
Fax: 46-60-123-103

Type of Firm
Private Equity Firm

Project Preferences

Type of Financing Preferred:
Seed
Startup

Size of Investments Considered:
Min Size of Investment Considered (000s): $100
Max Size of Investment Considered (000s): $1,000

Geographical Preferences

International Preferences:
Sweden

Industry Preferences

In Business Serv. prefer:
Services

In Manufact. prefer:
Manufacturing

Additional Information
Year Founded: 1961
Capital Under Management: $98,800,000
Current Activity Level : Actively seeking new investments

NORSELAB HOLDING AS

Karenslyst All 9A
Oslo, 0278
E-mail: hello@norselab.com
Website: www.norselab.com

Type of Firm
Incubator/Development Program

Additional Information
Year Founded: 2009
Current Activity Level : Actively seeking new investments

NORTH ATLANTIC CAPITAL

Two City Center
Fifth Floor
Portland, ME USA 04101
Phone: 2077724470
Fax: 2077723257
Website: www.northatlanticcapital.com

Management and Staff
Cheryl Hallett, Chief Financial Officer
David Coit, Managing Director
Kimberley Niles, Chief Financial Officer
Mark Morrissette, Managing Director

Type of Firm
Private Equity Firm

Association Membership
Natl Assoc of Small Bus. Inv. Co (NASBIC)

Project Preferences

Role in Financing:
Will function either as deal originator or investor in deals created by others

Type of Financing Preferred:
Early Stage
Expansion
Balanced
Later Stage

Size of Investments Considered:
Min Size of Investment Considered (000s): $4,000
Max Size of Investment Considered (000s): $8,000

Geographical Preferences

United States Preferences:
Northeast

Industry Focus
(% based on actual investment)
Internet Specific	30.0%
Computer Software and Services	14.6%
Communications and Media	13.3%
Other Products	10.4%
Computer Hardware	8.5%
Semiconductors/Other Elect.	7.6%
Consumer Related	6.5%
Industrial/Energy	5.6%
Medical/Health	3.0%
Biotechnology	0.5%

Additional Information
Name of Most Recent Fund: North Atlantic SBIC IV
Most Recent Fund Was Raised: 12/31/2006
Year Founded: 1986
Capital Under Management: $198,000,000
Current Activity Level : Actively seeking new investments
Method of Compensation: Return on investment is of primary concern, do not charge fees

NORTH BAY EQUITY PARTNERS

1111 Brickell Avenue
Eleventh Floor
Miami, FL USA 33131
Phone: 3059137160
Fax: 3059134101
E-mail: info@northbayequity.com
Website: www.northbayequity.com

Management and Staff
Alfredo Gutierrez, Partner
Matthew Cole, Partner

Type of Firm
Bank Affiliated

Project Preferences

Role in Financing:
Prefer role as deal originator

Type of Financing Preferred:
Expansion
Later Stage
Management Buyouts

Size of Investments Considered:
Min Size of Investment Considered (000s): $10,000
Max Size of Investment Considered (000s): $25,000

Geographical Preferences

United States Preferences:
Southwest

International Preferences:
Latin America
Mexico
Brazil

Industry Preferences

In Communications prefer:
Commercial Communications
CATV & Pay TV Systems
Radio & TV Broadcasting
Telecommunications
Wireless Communications
Data Communications
Satellite Microwave Comm.
Other Communication Prod.

In Internet Specific prefer:
E-Commerce Technology

In Biotechnology prefer:
Agricultural/Animal Bio.

In Transportation prefer:
Transportation

In Business Serv. prefer:
Media

Additional Information
Year Founded: 2001
Current Activity Level : Actively seeking new investments
Method of Compensation: Function primarily in service area, receive contingent fee in cash or equity

NORTH BRANCH CAPITAL LP

200 South Wacker Drive, Suite 3100
Chicago, IL USA 60606
Website: www.northbranchcap.com

Management and Staff
Bill Huber, Partner
Dan Bauman, Partner
Jonathan Leiman, Partner

Type of Firm
Private Equity Firm

Project Preferences

Type of Financing Preferred:
Leveraged Buyout
Acquisition

Industry Preferences

In Business Serv. prefer:
Services

In Manufact. prefer:
Manufacturing

Additional Information
Year Founded: 2014
Current Activity Level : Actively seeking new investments

NORTH CASTLE PARTNERS LLC

183 East Putnam Avenue
Greenwich, CT USA 06830
Phone: 2038623200
Fax: 2038623270
Website: www.northcastlepartners.com

Management and Staff
Alison Minter, Managing Director
Alyse Skidmore, Chief Financial Officer
Charles Baird, Founder
Jay Galluzzo, Managing Director
Jonathan Canarick, Managing Director
Louis Marinaccio, Managing Director

Type of Firm
Private Equity Firm

Project Preferences

Type of Financing Preferred:
Leveraged Buyout
Expansion
Acquisition

Geographical Preferences

United States Preferences:
North America

Industry Focus
(% based on actual investment)

Consumer Related	88.5%
Internet Specific	7.8%
Medical/Health	2.2%
Biotechnology	1.0%
Computer Hardware	0.5%

Additional Information
Name of Most Recent Fund: North Castle Partners V, L.P.
Most Recent Fund Was Raised: 11/27/2012
Year Founded: 1997
Capital Under Management: $470,400,000
Current Activity Level : Actively seeking new investments

NORTH COAST ANGEL FUND L L C

5875 Landerbrook Drive, Suite 300
Mayfield Heights, OH USA 44124
Phone: 8009755846
Fax: 8009755846
E-mail: Info@northcoastangelfund.com

Type of Firm
Angel Group

Project Preferences

Type of Financing Preferred:
Early Stage

Geographical Preferences

United States Preferences:
Ohio

Industry Preferences

In Semiconductor/Electr prefer:
Electronics

In Biotechnology prefer:
Biotechnology

In Industrial/Energy prefer:
Energy
Advanced Materials

Additional Information
Name of Most Recent Fund: North Coast Venture Fund, L.P.
Most Recent Fund Was Raised: 02/24/2014
Year Founded: 2006
Capital Under Management: $13,370,000
Current Activity Level : Actively seeking new investments

NORTH COAST TECHNOLOGY INVESTORS, L.P.

206 South Fifth Avenue, Suite 550
Ann Arbor, MI USA 48104
Phone: 7346627667
Fax: 7346626261
E-mail: partners@northcoastvc.com
Website: www.northcoastvc.com

Other Offices
300 Rodd Street, Suite 201
Midland, MI USA 48640
Phone: 989-832-2300
Fax: 989-832-2301

Management and Staff
Hugo Braun, Co-Founder
Lindsay Aspergren, Co-Founder

Type of Firm
Private Equity Firm

Project Preferences

Role in Financing:
Will function either as deal originator or investor in deals created by others

Type of Financing Preferred:
Balanced

Additional Information
Name of Most Recent Fund: NCTI II, L.P.
Most Recent Fund Was Raised: 12/21/2009
Year Founded: 1998
Capital Under Management: $79,000,000
Current Activity Level : Actively seeking new investments
Method of Compensation: Return on investment is of primary concern, do not charge fees

NORTH HILL VENTURES LP

535 Boylston Street
6th Floor
Boston, MA USA 02116
Phone: 6176007050
Website: www.northhillventures.com

Management and Staff
Ben Malka, General Partner
Brett Rome, General Partner
Shamez Kanji, General Partner

Type of Firm
Private Equity Firm

Project Preferences

Role in Financing:
Will function either as deal originator or investor in deals created by others

Type of Financing Preferred:
Early Stage

Size of Investments Considered:
Min Size of Investment Considered (000s): $2,000
Max Size of Investment Considered (000s): $3,000

Industry Preferences

In Financial Services prefer:
Financial Services
Financial Services

In Business Serv. prefer:
Services

Additional Information
Year Founded: 1999
Capital Under Management: $70,000,000
Current Activity Level: Actively seeking new investments
Method of Compensation: Return on investment is of primary concern, do not charge fees

NORTH IOWA VENTURE CAPITAL FUND II LLC

500 College Drive
John Papajohn Entrepreneurial
Mason City, IA USA 50401
Website: www.niacc.edu/pappajohn

Type of Firm
Private Equity Firm

Additional Information
Year Founded: 2016
Current Activity Level: Actively seeking new investments

NORTH RIVER CAPITAL LLC

5642 Coventry Lane
Fort Wayne, IN USA 46804
Phone: 2604322233
Fax: 2604363047
E-mail: info@northrivercapital.net
Website: www.northrivercapital.net

Management and Staff
Daniel Rifkin, Partner
Gary Rohrs, Partner
Grant Schultz, Partner
Jennifer Wilson, Partner
Martin Rifkin, Partner
Richard Rifkin, Partner

Type of Firm
Private Equity Firm

Project Preferences

Type of Financing Preferred:
Leveraged Buyout
Management Buyouts
Acquisition

Geographical Preferences

United States Preferences:
Indiana

Industry Preferences

In Industrial/Energy prefer:
Industrial Products

In Financial Services prefer:
Real Estate
Investment Groups

In Manufact. prefer:
Manufacturing

Additional Information
Year Founded: 2008
Current Activity Level: Actively seeking new investments

NORTH SKY CAPITAL LLC

33 South Sixth Street, Suite 4646
Minneapolis, MN USA 55402
Phone: 6124357150
Fax: 6124357151
Website: www.northskycapital.com

Other Offices
100 Crescent Court, Suite 700
Dallas, TX USA 75201
Phone: 2144593133
Fax: 2144357163

Management and Staff
Danny Zouber, Managing Director
Denise Galvin, Chief Financial Officer
Mark Austin, Managing Director
Megan McElroy, Vice President
Mike Pohlen, Managing Director
Phil Ebner, Vice President
Scott Barrington, CEO & Managing Director

Type of Firm
Private Equity Firm

Project Preferences

Type of Financing Preferred:
Fund of Funds
Leveraged Buyout
Expansion
Generalist PE
Later Stage
Management Buyouts
Distressed Debt

Geographical Preferences

United States Preferences:

Industry Preferences

In Medical/Health prefer:
Medical/Health

In Consumer Related prefer:
Consumer
Retail

In Industrial/Energy prefer:
Energy
Alternative Energy
Industrial Products
Advanced Materials
Environmental Related

In Transportation prefer:
Transportation

In Business Serv. prefer:
Services

In Agr/Forestr/Fish prefer:
Agriculture related

Additional Information
Year Founded: 2000
Capital Under Management: $811,400,000
Current Activity Level: Actively seeking new investments

NORTHBRIDGE CAPITAL PARTNERS

100 Pinebush Road
Cambridge, Canada N1R 8J8
Phone: 5197217144
Fax: 5196235654
E-mail: info@northspringcapitalpartners.com
Website: www.northspringcapitalpartners.com

Other Offices
445 Thompson Drive
Cambridge, Canada N1T 2K7

Former HQ: 70 Cowansview Road
Cambridge, Canada N1R 7N3
Phone: 5197217144
Fax: 5196235654

Management and Staff
Brian Hunter, President

Type of Firm
Private Equity Firm

Project Preferences

Type of Financing Preferred:
Leveraged Buyout
Expansion
Mezzanine
Management Buyouts
Recapitalizations

Geographical Preferences

Canadian Preferences:
Ontario

Industry Preferences

In Business Serv. prefer:
Services
Distribution

In Manufact. prefer:
Manufacturing

Additional Information
Year Founded: 2009
Current Activity Level : Actively seeking new investments

NORTHCAP PARTNERS APS

Noerre Farimagsgade 13, 1. Th.
Copenhagen, Denmark 1364
Phone: 4570224020
Fax: 4570141632
E-mail: info@northcappartners.com
Website: www.northcap.vc

Management and Staff
Jacob Pedersen, General Partner
Kim Wiencken, General Partner
Soren Nielsen, General Partner
Thomas Knudsen, General Partner

Type of Firm
Private Equity Firm

Association Membership
Danish Venture Capital Association (DVCA)

Project Preferences

Type of Financing Preferred:
Balanced
Seed
Startup

Geographical Preferences

International Preferences:
Sweden
Scandanavia/Nordic Region
Denmark

Industry Preferences

In Communications prefer:
Communications and Media
Telecommunications
Wireless Communications

In Computer Software prefer:
Software

In Internet Specific prefer:
Internet
Ecommerce
Web Aggregation/Portals

Additional Information
Year Founded: 2007
Current Activity Level : Actively seeking new investments

NORTHCREEK MEZZANINE

255 East Fifth Street, Suite 3010
Cincinnati, OH USA 45202
Phone: 513-985-6601
Fax: 513-985-6603
Website: www.northcreekmezzanine.com

Management and Staff
Barry Peterson, Managing Partner
K.Rodger Davis, Managing Partner
Steven Touvelle, Partner

Type of Firm
SBIC

Association Membership
Natl Assoc of Small Bus. Inv. Co (NASBIC)

Project Preferences

Role in Financing:
Will function either as deal originator or investor in deals created by others

Type of Financing Preferred:
Leveraged Buyout
Expansion
Mezzanine
Acquisition
Recapitalizations

Size of Investments Considered:
Min Size of Investment Considered (000s): $1,000
Max Size of Investment Considered (000s): $8,000

Geographical Preferences

United States Preferences:
Midwest

Additional Information
Name of Most Recent Fund: Northcreek Mezzanine Fund II, L.P.
Most Recent Fund Was Raised: 02/13/2014
Year Founded: 2010
Capital Under Management: $111,400,000
Current Activity Level : Actively seeking new investments

NORTHEDGE CAPITAL LLP

Fourways House
57 Hilton Street
Manchester, United Kingdom M1 2EJ
Website: northedgecapital.com

Management and Staff
Dan Wright, Chief Operating Officer
Grant Berry, Managing Partner
John Rastrick, Partner
Prem Raj, Chief Financial Officer
Raymond Stenton, Partner

Type of Firm
Private Equity Firm

Project Preferences

Type of Financing Preferred:
Leveraged Buyout
Generalist PE
Management Buyouts
Acquisition

Geographical Preferences

International Preferences:
United Kingdom

Additional Information
Year Founded: 2011
Capital Under Management: $774,785,000
Current Activity Level : Actively seeking new investments

NORTHERN CAPITAL MANAGEMENT GROUP

8 Wangjing East Road
Tower 2, Suite 1422-1423
Beijing, China 100102
Phone: 861065980950
Fax: 861065980953
E-mail: info@ncmg.com.cn
Website: www.ncmg.com.cn

Other Offices
88 Queensway
One Pacific Place, Suite 805
Hong Kong, Hong Kong

106 Stone Cliff Road
Princeton, NJ USA 08540
Phone: 609-716-1800
Fax: 609-945-3509

Former HQ: No. 5 Wanhong Road, Suite A-211,
Lonsdale Ctr
New York, China 100015
Phone: 86-10-6434-9090
Fax: 86-10-6438-7908

Type of Firm
Investment Management Firm

Project Preferences

Type of Financing Preferred:
Balanced

Geographical Preferences

United States Preferences:

International Preferences:
China

Additional Information
Year Founded: 1997
Current Activity Level : Actively seeking new investments

NORTHERN LIGHT VENTURE CAPITAL DEVELOPMENT LTD

Ten Harcourt Road, Suite 1720, Hutchison House
Central, Hong Kong
Phone: 85222816200
Fax: 85225373299
E-mail: info@nlvc.com
Website: www.nlvc.com

Other Offices
Hai De San Dao, East Coast
Unit 1407, Coastal Building
Shenzhen, China 518054
Phone: 8675536992780
Fax: 8675536882155

1266 Nanjing West Road, Suite 2207A, Plaza 66
Shanghai, China 200040
Phone: 862161034800
Fax: 862161381010

79 Jianguo Road
China Central Place
Beijing, China 100025
Phone: 861057696500
Fax: 861059696185

No.345 Fengli Street, Industrial Park
A101, Building 1
Suzhou, China 215026
Phone: 8651266969911
Fax: 8651266969916

2855 Sand Hill Road
Menlo Park, CA USA 94025
Phone: 6505855450
Fax: 6505855451

Management and Staff
Elton Jiang, Managing Director
Feng Deng, Managing Director
Han Shen, Vice President
He Huang, Vice President
Jeffrey Lee, Managing Director & CFO
John Wu, Venture Partner
Lixin Li, Managing Director
Ray Yang, Managing Director
Tony Wu, Vice President
Yan Ke, Managing Director
Ying Wang, Vice President
Zhi Tan, Venture Partner

Type of Firm
Private Equity Firm

Association Membership
China Venture Capital Association
Western Association of Venture Capitalists (WAVC)
National Venture Capital Association - USA (NVCA)

Project Preferences

Role in Financing:
Prefer role as deal originator but will also invest in deals created by others

Type of Financing Preferred:
Early Stage
Expansion
Balanced
Later Stage

Geographical Preferences

United States Preferences:
California

International Preferences:
China
Asia

Industry Preferences

In Communications prefer:
Communications and Media
Telecommunications
Wireless Communications

In Computer Software prefer:
Software

In Internet Specific prefer:
E-Commerce Technology
Internet

In Medical/Health prefer:
Medical/Health
Medical Diagnostics
Medical Products
Health Services
Pharmaceuticals

In Consumer Related prefer:
Consumer
Consumer Products
Consumer Services

In Industrial/Energy prefer:
Energy
Alternative Energy
Energy Conservation Relat
Environmental Related

In Manufact. prefer:
Manufacturing

Additional Information
Name of Most Recent Fund: Northern Light Venture Fund, L.P.
Most Recent Fund Was Raised: 12/12/2005
Year Founded: 2005
Capital Under Management: $1,000,000,000
Current Activity Level : Actively seeking new investments

NORTHERN LIGHTS CAPITAL GROUP LLC

818 Stewart Street, Suite 910
Seattle, WA USA 98101
Phone: 2069658879
E-mail: info@nlcg.com
Website: www.northernlightsventures.com

Other Offices
1498 Pacific Avenue, Suite 515
Tacoma, WA USA 98402
Phone: 2532380417

44 Cook Street, Suite 1020
Denver, CO USA 80206
Phone: 3033219900

Management and Staff
Andrew Turner, Co-Founder
Jack Swift, Managing Director
Paul Greenwood, Co-Founder
Timothy Carver, Co-Founder
Trent Erickson, Chief Financial Officer

Type of Firm
Private Equity Firm

Project Preferences

Role in Financing:
Prefer role as deal originator but will also invest in deals created by others

Type of Financing Preferred:
Expansion
Later Stage

Industry Preferences

In Financial Services prefer:
Investment Groups
Financial Services

Additional Information
Name of Most Recent Fund: Northern Lights Capital Partners, LLC
Most Recent Fund Was Raised: 01/24/2007

Year Founded: 2005
Capital Under Management: $1,000,000,000
Current Activity Level : Actively seeking new investments
Method of Compensation: Return on investment is of primary concern, do not charge fees

NORTHERN PACIFIC GROUP LLC

315 East Lake Street, Suite 301
Wayzata, MN USA 55391
Website: www.northernpacificgroup.com

Type of Firm
Private Equity Firm

Project Preferences

Type of Financing Preferred:
Leveraged Buyout
Acquisition

Geographical Preferences

United States Preferences:
Midwest

Industry Preferences

In Business Serv. prefer:
Services

Additional Information
Year Founded: 2012
Capital Under Management: $28,950,000
Current Activity Level : Actively seeking new investments

NORTHERN PLAINS CAPITAL LTD

304-8th Avenue SouthWest, Suite 504
Calgary, Canada T2P 1C2
Phone: 403-503-5251
Website: www.northernplains.ca

Other Offices
9622-42nd Avenue, Suite 307
Edmonton, Canada T6E 5Y4

Management and Staff
Dustin Owen, Vice President
Miles Lich, Managing Director
Rod Graham, Managing Director
Terry Freeman, Managing Director

Type of Firm
Private Equity Firm

Project Preferences

Type of Financing Preferred:
Leveraged Buyout
Early Stage
Expansion

Geographical Preferences

Canadian Preferences:
All Canada

Industry Preferences

In Industrial/Energy prefer:
Energy
Oil and Gas Exploration

Additional Information
Name of Most Recent Fund: NPC Fund III
Most Recent Fund Was Raised: 10/03/2008
Year Founded: 2005
Capital Under Management: $102,051,000
Current Activity Level : Actively seeking new investments

NORTHERN TRUST CORP

50 South LaSalle Street
Chicago, IL USA 60603
Phone: 3126306000
Website: www.northerntrust.com

Other Offices
300 Atlantic Street
Stamford, CT USA 06901
Phone: 2033518700

Management and Staff
Bob Morgan, Managing Director

Type of Firm
Private Equity Advisor or Fund of Funds

Association Membership
Illinois Venture Capital Association

Project Preferences

Type of Financing Preferred:
Fund of Funds

Geographical Preferences

United States Preferences:

Industry Preferences

In Financial Services prefer:
Financial Services

Additional Information
Name of Most Recent Fund: Northern Trust Global Venture Capital Fund V, L.P.
Most Recent Fund Was Raised: 01/24/2013
Year Founded: 1971
Capital Under Management: $1,260,354,000
Current Activity Level : Actively seeking new investments

NORTHGATE CAPITAL LLC

649 San Ramon Valley Boulevard
Danville, CA USA 94526
Phone: 9258209970
Fax: 9258209994
E-mail: info@northgate.com
Website: www.northgatecapital.com

Other Offices
50 Pall Mall
London, United Kingdom SW1Y 5JH
Phone: 442079688100
Fax: 442079688111

D3, P3B, District Centre, Saket
New Delhi, India 110017
Phone: 911139125000

Paseo de la Reforma 115
Fourth Floor
Mexico, Mexico 11000
Phone: 525580007545

8 Connaught Place, Suite 2601, 26/F, Two Exchange Square
Central, Hong Kong
Phone: 85239239517

Avenida Ricardo Margain 575
Parque Santa Engracia
Garza Garcia, Mexico 66267
Phone: 528180201547

Management and Staff
Alejandro Medina, Principal
Alfredo Alfaro, Managing Partner
Allan Chou, Partner
Brent Jones, Managing Director
Eduardo Mapes, Partner
Gabriel Mizrahi, Partner
Georg Mende, Partner
Guillermo Carmona, Principal
Hosein Khajey-Hosseiny, Managing Director
Hosein Khajeh-Hosseiny, Chief Executive Officer
Ian Walker, Principal
Mark Harris, Managing Director
Mauricio Moral, Partner
Nicole Connolly, Principal
Oscar Alvarado, Partner
Thomas Vardell, Managing Director
Thorsten Claus, Partner
Tomas Mathe, Partner

Type of Firm
Private Equity Advisor or Fund of Funds

Project Preferences

Type of Financing Preferred:
Fund of Funds
Expansion

Geographical Preferences

United States Preferences:
North America

International Preferences:
Latin America
Europe
Asia
Japan
All International

Industry Preferences

In Communications prefer:
Communications and Media

In Medical/Health prefer:
Health Services

In Consumer Related prefer:
Education Related

In Financial Services prefer:
Financial Services

In Manufact. prefer:
Manufacturing

Additional Information
Name of Most Recent Fund: Northgate Mexico, L.P.
Most Recent Fund Was Raised: 07/11/2012
Year Founded: 2000
Capital Under Management: $184,400,000
Current Activity Level : Actively seeking new investments

NORTHILL CAPITAL LLP

83 Piccadilly
London, United Kingdom W1J 8QA
Phone: 442070164040
E-mail: info@northill.com
Website: northill.com

Management and Staff
Cathy Jones, Partner
Jeremy Bassil, Partner
Jonathan Little, Co-Founder
Rick Potter, Partner

Type of Firm
Private Equity Firm

Project Preferences

Type of Financing Preferred:
Leveraged Buyout
Early Stage
Balanced
Seed
Acquisition

Geographical Preferences

International Preferences:
United Kingdom
Europe

Additional Information
Year Founded: 2010
Current Activity Level : Actively seeking new investments

NORTHLANE CAPITAL PARTNERS LLC

2 Bethesda Metro Center
14th Floor
Bethesda, MD USA 20814
Website: northlanecapital.com

Type of Firm
Private Equity Firm

Project Preferences

Type of Financing Preferred:
Leveraged Buyout

Geographical Preferences

United States Preferences:
North America

Industry Preferences

In Biotechnology prefer:
Industrial Biotechnology

In Medical/Health prefer:
Health Services

In Business Serv. prefer:
Services

Additional Information
Year Founded: 2014
Capital Under Management: $1,100,000,000
Current Activity Level : Actively seeking new investments

NORTHLEAF CAPITAL PARTNERS LTD

79 Wellington Street West
Sixth Floor Box 120
Toronto, Canada M5K 1N9
Phone: 8669644141
Fax: 4163040195
E-mail: investors@northleafcapital.com
Website: www.northleafcapital.com

Other Offices
14 Waterloo Square
Fourth Floor
London, United Kingdom SW1Y 4AR
Phone: 4402073215750
Fax: 4402079307171

3000 Sand Hill Road
Building One - Suite 230
Menlo Park, CA USA 94025
Phone: 6502349810
Fax: 6502349859

Management and Staff
Anthony Paniccia, Vice President
Daniel Dupont, Managing Director
Elaine Shiu, Vice President
George Zakem, Managing Director
Jamie Storrow, Managing Director
Jared Waldron, Vice President
Jeanette White, Vice President
Jeffrey Pentland, Managing Director
Kathleen Ffrench, Vice President
Kaushik Ramki, Vice President
Lauren Harris, Vice President
Matthew Woodeson, Managing Director
Melissa McJannet, Managing Director
Michael Bowman, Vice President
Michael Flood, Managing Director
Nadim Vasanji, Vice President
Neil Marcovitz, Vice President
Phillippa Perkins, Vice President
Stuart Waugh, Managing Partner
Susie Lee, Vice President
Todd Papau, Vice President

Type of Firm
Private Equity Firm

Association Membership
Canadian Venture Capital Association

Project Preferences

Type of Financing Preferred:
Fund of Funds
Leveraged Buyout
Balanced
Other

Geographical Preferences

United States Preferences:
North America
All U.S.

Canadian Preferences:
All Canada

International Preferences:
Europe
Asia
All International

Industry Preferences

In Industrial/Energy prefer:
Industrial Products

Additional Information
Year Founded: 1968
Capital Under Management: $200,000,000
Current Activity Level : Actively seeking new investments

NORTHPORT INVESTMENTS

One Northfield Plaza, Suite 300
Northfield, IL USA 60093
Phone: 8477841815
Fax: 8476372062
E-mail: contact@NorthportInvestments.com
Website: www.northportinvestments.com

Management and Staff
David Shelby, Founder
Josh Shelby, Managing Partner
Tyson Morgan, Managing Partner

Type of Firm
Private Equity Firm

Project Preferences

Type of Financing Preferred:
Later Stage

Additional Information
Name of Most Recent Fund: Northport XIX Private Equity LLC
Most Recent Fund Was Raised: 09/13/2010
Year Founded: 1996
Current Activity Level : Actively seeking new investments

NORTHROCK CAPITAL PARTNERS

448 Glenlake Avenue
Toronto, Canada M6P 1G8
Phone: 416-760-8819
Fax: 416-760-8427
E-mail: ntownsend@northrockcapital.com
Website: www.northrockcapital.com

Type of Firm
Private Equity Firm

Project Preferences

Type of Financing Preferred:
Leveraged Buyout
Expansion
Management Buyouts
Acquisition
Recapitalizations

Geographical Preferences

Canadian Preferences:
All Canada
Ontario

Additional Information
Year Founded: 2006
Current Activity Level : Actively seeking new investments
Method of Compensation: Return on invest. most important, but chg. closing fees, service fees, etc.

NORTHSTAR CAPITAL LLC

2310 Plaza VII
45 South Seventh Street
Minneapolis, MN USA 55402
Phone: 6123715700
Fax: 6123715710
Website: www.northstarcapital.com

Management and Staff
Brent McVay, Principal
Brian Schneider, Partner
Charles Schroeder, Managing Partner
Douglas Mark, Managing Partner
Jeffrey Dennis, Partner
Scott Becker, Managing Partner

Type of Firm
Private Equity Firm

Project Preferences

Type of Financing Preferred:
Mezzanine

Industry Focus
(% based on actual investment)
Other Products	36.9%
Industrial/Energy	28.4%
Consumer Related	18.7%
Medical/Health	7.2%
Internet Specific	6.2%
Computer Software and Services	2.0%
Computer Hardware	0.6%

Additional Information
Name of Most Recent Fund: Northstar Mezzanine Partners VI, L.P.
Most Recent Fund Was Raised: 06/28/2013
Year Founded: 1993
Capital Under Management: $300,300,000
Current Activity Level : Actively seeking new investments

NORTHWATER CAPITAL MANAGEMENT INC

181 Bay St., Brookfield Place, Suite 4700, Bay Wellington Twr
Toronto, Canada M5J2T3
Phone: 4163605435
Fax: 4153600671
E-mail: info@northwatercapital.com
Website: www.northwatercapital.com

Management and Staff
Annie Theriault, Vice President
Daniel Mills, Managing Director
Frances Kordyback, Managing Director
Jennifer Schwartz, Vice President
Jonathan Piurko, Managing Director
Shauna Cassidy, Vice President
Steve Redmond, Vice President

Type of Firm
Private Equity Firm

Association Membership
Canadian Venture Capital Association

Project Preferences

Type of Financing Preferred:
Balanced

Additional Information
Name of Most Recent Fund: Northwater Intellectual Property Fund, L.P. II
Most Recent Fund Was Raised: 10/30/2008
Year Founded: 1989
Current Activity Level : Actively seeking new investments

NORTHWEST TECHNOLOGY VENTURES

663 North West Compton Loop
Murdock Building, Room 515
Beaverton, OR USA 97006
Website: www.nwtechventures.com

Management and Staff
G. Hoffman, Managing Director
William Newman, Managing Director

Type of Firm
Private Equity Firm

Project Preferences

Role in Financing:
Will function either as deal originator or investor in deals created by others

Type of Financing Preferred:
Early Stage
Seed

Geographical Preferences

United States Preferences:
Oregon

Industry Focus
(% based on actual investment)
Semiconductors/Other Elect.	30.8%
Biotechnology	27.0%
Computer Software and Services	16.2%
Medical/Health	7.8%
Computer Hardware	7.0%
Other Products	4.7%
Consumer Related	4.6%
Industrial/Energy	1.9%

Additional Information
Name of Most Recent Fund: Northwest Technology Ventures
Most Recent Fund Was Raised: 06/01/2002
Year Founded: 1987
Capital Under Management: $20,000,000

Current Activity Level : Actively seeking new investments
Method of Compensation: Return on investment is of primary concern, do not charge fees

NORTHWESTERN MUTUAL CAPITAL LLC

720 East Wisconsin Avenue
Milwaukee, WI USA 53202
Phone: 4146655499
Fax: 4146657124
Website: www.northwesternmutualcapital.com

Other Offices

17-19 Maddox Street
First Floor
London, United Kingdom W1S 2QH
Phone: 442073186670

Management and Staff

David Barras, Managing Director
Howard Stern, Managing Director
Jeffrey Lueken, President
Jerome Baier, Managing Director
Mark Kishler, Managing Director
Randal Ralph, Managing Director
Richard Strait, Managing Director
Timothy Collins, Managing Director

Type of Firm

Insurance Firm Affiliate

Project Preferences

Type of Financing Preferred:
Leveraged Buyout
Mezzanine
Later Stage
Distressed Debt

Geographical Preferences

United States Preferences:

International Preferences:
Europe
Asia

Additional Information

Name of Most Recent Fund: Northwestern Mutual Capital Strategic Equity Fund III, L.P.
Most Recent Fund Was Raised: 11/06/2012
Year Founded: 1978
Capital Under Management: $205,000,000
Current Activity Level : Actively seeking new investments

NORTHWOOD VENTURES

485 Underhill Boulevard, Suite 205
Syosset, NY USA 11791
Phone: 5163645544
Fax: 5163640879
Website: www.northwoodventures.com

Management and Staff

Henry Wilson, Managing Partner
James Schiff, Vice President
Paul Homer, Principal
Peter Schiff, Managing Partner

Type of Firm

Private Equity Firm

Project Preferences

Role in Financing:
Will function either as deal originator or investor in deals created by others

Type of Financing Preferred:
Leveraged Buyout
Early Stage
Expansion
Balanced
Turnaround
Later Stage
Seed
Management Buyouts
Acquisition
Startup
Special Situation
Recapitalizations

Size of Investments Considered:
Min Size of Investment Considered (000s): $2,000
Max Size of Investment Considered (000s): $8,000

Geographical Preferences

United States Preferences:
All U.S.

International Preferences:
All International

Industry Focus

(% based on actual investment)
Communications and Media	48.9%
Consumer Related	16.8%
Internet Specific	14.5%
Other Products	9.4%
Biotechnology	4.4%
Industrial/Energy	2.8%
Computer Software and Services	1.5%
Semiconductors/Other Elect.	1.3%
Computer Hardware	0.4%

Additional Information

Name of Most Recent Fund: Northwood Ventures
Most Recent Fund Was Raised: 12/31/1982
Year Founded: 1983
Capital Under Management: $200,000,000
Current Activity Level : Actively seeking new investments
Method of Compensation: Return on investment is of primary concern, do not charge fees

NORTHZONE VENTURES

Bygdoy Alle 2
Oslo, Norway 0105
Phone: 4722125010
Fax: 4722125011
E-mail: info@northzone.com
Website: www.northzone.com

Other Offices

33 W 17th Street, 5th floor
NEW YORK, NY USA 10011

42, Master Samuelsgatan
Stockholm, Sweden 111 57

6-8 Kingly Court
London, United Kingdom W1B 5PW

Strandvejen 100, 4th floor
Hellerup, Denmark 2900
Phone: 45-7022-2475

Management and Staff

Bjorn Stray, General Partner
Hans Otterling, General Partner
Jeppe Zink, General Partner
Jessica Nilsson, Partner
Marta Sjogren, Principal
Michiel Kotting, General Partner
Par-Jorgen Parson, General Partner
Tellef Thorleifsson, Founding Partner

Type of Firm

Private Equity Firm

Association Membership

British Venture Capital Association (BVCA)
Danish Venture Capital Association (DVCA)
Norwegian Venture Capital Association
Swedish Venture Capital Association (SVCA)
European Private Equity and Venture Capital Assoc.

Project Preferences

Type of Financing Preferred:
Early Stage
Balanced
Later Stage
Seed
Startup

Size of Investments Considered:
Min Size of Investment Considered (000s): $900
Max Size of Investment Considered (000s): $9,000

Geographical Preferences

United States Preferences:

International Preferences:
United Kingdom
Europe
Western Europe
Scandanavia/Nordic Region

Industry Preferences

In Communications prefer:
Telecommunications
Wireless Communications
Entertainment

In Computer Software prefer:
Software

In Computer Other prefer:
Computer Related

In Semiconductor/Electr prefer:
Semiconductor

In Biotechnology prefer:
Biotechnology

In Consumer Related prefer:
Consumer

Additional Information

Name of Most Recent Fund: Northzone VII
Most Recent Fund Was Raised: 12/05/2013
Year Founded: 1994
Capital Under Management: $1,188,000,000
Current Activity Level : Actively seeking new investments

NORVESTIA OYJ

Pohjoisesplanadi 35 E
Helsinki, Finland FI-00100
Phone: 35896226380
Fax: 35896222080
E-mail: info@norvestia.fi
Website: www.norvestia.fi

Management and Staff

Juha Kasanen, Chief Executive Officer

Type of Firm

Investment Management Firm

Project Preferences

Type of Financing Preferred:
Fund of Funds
Expansion
Mezzanine
Acquisition
Distressed Debt

Geographical Preferences

International Preferences:
Scandanavia/Nordic Region

Additional Information

Year Founded: 2000
Current Activity Level : Actively seeking new investments

NORVESTOR EQUITY AS

Roald Amundsensgata 6
P.O Box 1223, Vika
Oslo, Norway 0110
Phone: 4723000700
Fax: 4723000701
E-mail: contact@norvestor.com
Website: www.norvestor.no

Management and Staff

Christian Sontum, Partner
Fredrik Korterud, Partner
Henning Vold, Partner

Type of Firm

Private Equity Firm

Association Membership

Norwegian Venture Capital Association
Swedish Venture Capital Association (SVCA)
European Private Equity and Venture Capital Assoc.

Project Preferences

Type of Financing Preferred:
Leveraged Buyout

Size of Investments Considered:
Min Size of Investment Considered (000s): $15,000
Max Size of Investment Considered (000s): $60,000

Geographical Preferences

International Preferences:
Sweden
Scandanavia/Nordic Region
Norway

Industry Preferences

In Communications prefer:
Communications and Media
Telecommunications

In Computer Software prefer:
Software

In Consumer Related prefer:
Retail
Food/Beverage
Consumer Services

In Industrial/Energy prefer:
Energy
Oil & Gas Drilling,Explor

In Manufact. prefer:
Manufacturing

Additional Information

Name of Most Recent Fund: Norvestor VI, L.P.
Most Recent Fund Was Raised: 03/28/2012
Year Founded: 1997
Capital Under Management: $471,200,000
Current Activity Level : Actively seeking new investments

NORWEST EQUITY PARTNERS

80 South Eighth Street, Suite 3600
Minneapolis, MN USA 55402
Phone: 6122151600
Fax: 6122151601
Website: www.nep.com

Other Offices

375 Park Avenue, Suite 1009
NEW YORK, NY USA 10152
Phone: 212-380-9300
Fax: 212-380-9301

Management and Staff

Andrew Cantwell, Partner
Jason Sondell, Principal
John Whaley, Partner
John Lindahl, Managing Partner
Taylor Moore, Principal
Thomas Schauerman, Partner
Timothy Kuehl, Partner
Timothy DeVries, Managing Partner
Todd Solow, Partner

Type of Firm

Private Equity Firm

Project Preferences

Role in Financing:
Prefer role as deal originator but will also invest in deals created by others

Type of Financing Preferred:
Leveraged Buyout
Mezzanine
Management Buyouts
Acquisition
Recapitalizations

Geographical Preferences

United States Preferences:
All U.S.

Industry Preferences

In Medical/Health prefer:
Medical/Health
Health Services

In Consumer Related prefer:
Consumer Products
Consumer Services

In Industrial/Energy prefer:
Industrial Products

In Business Serv. prefer:
Services
Distribution

In Manufact. prefer:
Manufacturing

In Agr/Forestr/Fish prefer:
Agriculture related

Additional Information

Name of Most Recent Fund: Norwest Equity Partners VII, L.P.
Most Recent Fund Was Raised: 10/27/1999
Year Founded: 1961
Capital Under Management: $4,600,000,000
Current Activity Level : Actively seeking new investments
Method of Compensation: Return on investment is of primary concern, do not charge fees

NORWEST MEZZANINE PARTNERS

80 South Eighth Street, Suite 3600
Minneapolis, MN USA 55320
Phone: 6122151600
Fax: 6122151602
Website: www.nmp.com

Management and Staff

Carter Balfour, Partner
John Whaley, Partner
John Hogan, Partner
Sean Stevens, Partner
Shani Graber, Principal
Timothy DeVries, Managing Partner

Type of Firm

Private Equity Firm

Project Preferences

Type of Financing Preferred:
Leveraged Buyout
Mezzanine
Acquisition
Recapitalizations

Geographical Preferences

United States Preferences:
All U.S.

Industry Preferences

In Medical/Health prefer:
Medical/Health

In Consumer Related prefer:
Consumer Products

In Business Serv. prefer:
Distribution

In Manufact. prefer:
Manufacturing

In Agr/Forestr/Fish prefer:
Agriculture related

Additional Information

Name of Most Recent Fund: Norwest Mezzanine Partners II, L.P.
Most Recent Fund Was Raised: 06/15/2004
Year Founded: 2000
Capital Under Management: $1,400,000,000
Current Activity Level : Actively seeking new investments

NORWEST VENTURE PARTNERS

525 University Avenue, Suite 800
Palo Alto, CA USA 94301
Phone: 6503218000
Fax: 6503218010
Website: www.nvp.com

Other Offices

2800 Piper Jaffray Tower
222 S. Ninth Street
MINNEAPOLIS, MN USA 55402
Phone: 6126671650
Fax: 6126671660

UB City, 1 Vittal Mallya Rd.
15th Floor, Concorde Towers
Bengaluru, India 560001
Phone: 91-80-4030-0456

701/705 Dalamal House
Nariman Point
Mumbai, India 400021
Phone: 91-22-6150-1111

6 Hachoshlim Street
7th Floor
Herzelia, Israel 46724
Phone: 972-77-410-7090

Management and Staff

Ashutosh Sharma, Vice President
Casper De Clercq, General Partner
Conrad Shang, Vice President
David Su, Partner
Dror Nahumi, General Partner
Edward Yip, Vice President
Ethel Chen, Vice President
George Still, Partner
Jared Hyatt, Vice President
Jeffrey Crowe, Managing Partner
Jon Kossow, General Partner
Josh Goldman, General Partner
Katie Belding, Partner
Lisa Wu, Vice President
Matthew Howard, Managing Partner
Parker Barrile, Partner
Promod Haque, Managing Partner
Rama Sekhar, Partner
Ran Ding, Vice President
Robert Arditi, Partner
Robert Mittendorff, Partner
Robert Abbott, General Partner
Ryan Harris, General Partner
Sean Jacobsohn, Partner
Sergio Monsalve, Partner
Sharon McKenzie, Partner
Shiv Chaudhary, Vice President
Sohil Chand, Managing Director
Sonya Brown, General Partner
Stewart Campbell, Vice President
Teri McFadden, Vice President
Vab Goel, General Partner

Type of Firm

Private Equity Firm

Association Membership

Israel Venture Association
Western Association of Venture Capitalists (WAVC)
National Venture Capital Association - USA (NVCA)
Indian Venture Capital Association (IVCA)

Project Preferences

Role in Financing:
Prefer role as deal originator but will also invest in deals created by others

Type of Financing Preferred:
Leveraged Buyout
Early Stage
Generalist PE
Balanced
Later Stage
Management Buyouts
Acquisition
Special Situation
Recapitalizations

Size of Investments Considered:
Min Size of Investment Considered (000s): $10,000
Max Size of Investment Considered (000s): $15,000

Geographical Preferences

United States Preferences:

International Preferences:
India
China
Israel

Industry Focus

(% based on actual investment)

Computer Software and Services	35.8%
Internet Specific	35.4%
Communications and Media	8.3%
Other Products	6.2%
Semiconductors/Other Elect.	5.1%
Medical/Health	5.0%
Computer Hardware	2.5%
Industrial/Energy	0.9%
Consumer Related	0.5%
Biotechnology	0.2%

Additional Information

Name of Most Recent Fund: Norwest Venture Partners XI, LP.
Most Recent Fund Was Raised: 11/17/2009
Year Founded: 1961
Capital Under Management: $5,000,000,000
Current Activity Level : Actively seeking new investments
Method of Compensation: Return on investment is of primary concern, do not charge fees

NORWICH VENTURES

1601 Trapelo Road, Suite 145
North Waltham, MA USA 02451
Phone: 7818902161
Fax: 7818902162

Other Offices
1601 Trapelo Road, Suite 145
North Waltham, MA USA 02451
Phone: 7818902161
Fax: 7818902162

Management and Staff
Aaron Sandoski, Co-Founder
Marlin Miller, Co-Founder

Type of Firm
Private Equity Firm

Association Membership
New England Venture Capital Association

Project Preferences
Type of Financing Preferred:
Early Stage
Balanced
Seed

Geographical Preferences
United States Preferences:
Mid Atlantic
Northeast

Industry Preferences
In Medical/Health prefer:
Medical/Health

Additional Information
Year Founded: 2005
Capital Under Management: $30,000,000
Current Activity Level : Actively seeking new investments

NOSON LAWEN PARTNERS LLC

19 West 44th Street, Suite 812
New York, NY USA 10036
Phone: 2123022435
E-mail: info@nosonlp.com
Website: www.nosonlawen.com

Other Offices
558 West Uwchlan Avenue
Lionvile, PA USA 19341
Phone: 610-995-9280

Management and Staff
Earl Macomber, Partner
Ted Carroll, Partner

Type of Firm
Private Equity Firm

Project Preferences
Type of Financing Preferred:
Leveraged Buyout
Later Stage

Geographical Preferences
United States Preferences:
All U.S.

Industry Preferences
In Communications prefer:
CATV & Pay TV Systems
Radio & TV Broadcasting
Media and Entertainment
Publishing

In Consumer Related prefer:
Education Related

In Business Serv. prefer:
Media

Additional Information
Name of Most Recent Fund: Noson Lawen Partners, L.P.
Most Recent Fund Was Raised: 02/15/2007
Year Founded: 2007
Current Activity Level : Actively seeking new investments

NOTION CAPITAL PARTNERS LLP

8a Ledbury Mews North
London, United Kingdom W11 2AF
Phone: 448454989393
E-mail: Info@notioncapital.com

Other Offices
Montpellier Drive, Suite 101, Eagle Tower
Cheltenham, United Kingdom GL50 1TA

Management and Staff
Ben White, Co-Founder
Chris Tottman, Co-Founder
Chrys Chrysanthou, Partner
Ian Milbourn, Co-Founder
Jos White, Co-Founder
Patrick Norris, Partner
Stephen Chandler, Co-Founder

Type of Firm
Private Equity Firm

Project Preferences
Type of Financing Preferred:
Early Stage
Expansion
Balanced
Later Stage
Seed
Startup

Geographical Preferences
International Preferences:
United Kingdom
Europe

Industry Preferences
In Computer Software prefer:
Software
Systems Software
Applications Software

In Internet Specific prefer:
Internet

Additional Information
Name of Most Recent Fund: Notion Capital Fund-2
Most Recent Fund Was Raised: 04/17/2012
Year Founded: 2009
Capital Under Management: $320,000,000
Current Activity Level : Actively seeking new investments

NOVA CAPITAL MANAGEMENT, LTD.

30 Buckingham Gate
First Floor, Cayzer House
London, United Kingdom SW1E 6NN
Phone: 442079011760
Fax: 442079011761
E-mail: info@nova-cap.com
Website: www.nova-cap.com

Other Offices
172, Bethridge Road
Toronto, Canada M9W 1N3
Phone: 17789858834

885 West Georgia Street, Suite 1500
Vancouver, Canada V6C 3E8
Phone: 6046012092

P.O. Box 820
Lenoir City, TN USA 37771
Phone: 8656211402

John Hancock Center
875, N Michigan Avenue, Suite 3100
Chicago, IL USA 60611
Phone: 13123733895
Fax: 13123733894

Management and Staff
David Jacobs, Partner
Jonathan Seal, Partner
Kathryn Jones, Partner
Michael Kelly, Managing Director
Mike Nevin, Partner
Ralph Forster, Partner
Simon Smith, Partner
Simon Bliss, Chief Financial Officer
Tom Leader, Partner

Type of Firm
Private Equity Firm

Association Membership
British Venture Capital Association (BVCA)

Project Preferences

Type of Financing Preferred:
Leveraged Buyout
Expansion
Generalist PE
Balanced
Management Buyouts
Acquisition

Geographical Preferences

United States Preferences:
North America

Canadian Preferences:
All Canada

International Preferences:
United Kingdom
Europe

Industry Focus
(% based on actual investment)

Medical/Health	58.9%
Internet Specific	18.0%
Other Products	10.5%
Computer Software and Services	9.5%
Communications and Media	3.1%

Additional Information
Year Founded: 2002
Capital Under Management: $768,000,000
Current Activity Level : Actively seeking new investments

NOVA FOUNDERS CAPITAL

Chao's Building, 18th floor
143-145 Bonham Strand
Hong Kong, Hong Kong
E-mail: info@novafounders.com
Website: www.novafounders.com

Type of Firm
Private Equity Firm

Project Preferences

Type of Financing Preferred:
Balanced

Industry Preferences

In Internet Specific prefer:
Internet

In Financial Services prefer:
Financial Services

Additional Information
Year Founded: 1969
Current Activity Level : Actively seeking new investments

NOVA GESTAO DE RECURSOS LTDA

Praca XV de Novembro 34
10 Andar, Centro
Rio de Janeiro, Brazil 20010010
Phone: 552121148400
Fax: 552121148420
E-mail: contato@novainv.com.br

Management and Staff
Fabio Santos, Partner
Frederico Robalinho, Chief Executive Officer
Leonardo Pimenta, Co-Founder
Mauro Passini, Co-Founder
Pedro Robalinho, Co-Founder
Raphael Fraga, Co-Founder

Type of Firm
Private Equity Firm

Association Membership
Brazilian Venture Capital Association (ABCR)

Project Preferences

Type of Financing Preferred:
Leveraged Buyout
Mezzanine
Generalist PE
Balanced
Later Stage
Other
Acquisition
Recapitalizations

Geographical Preferences

International Preferences:
Brazil

Industry Preferences

In Industrial/Energy prefer:
Energy

In Agr/Forestr/Fish prefer:
Mining and Minerals

Additional Information
Year Founded: 2010
Current Activity Level : Actively seeking new investments

NOVA TECHNOLOGY MANAGEMENT LTD

20 Castle Terrace
Fourth Floor, Saltire Court
Edinburgh, United Kingdom EH1 2EN
Phone: 44-1463-732-559
Fax: 44-1224-705-481
Website: www.novafund.co.uk

Type of Firm
Private Equity Firm

Project Preferences

Type of Financing Preferred:
Second Stage Financing
Early Stage
Expansion

Geographical Preferences

International Preferences:
United Kingdom

Industry Preferences

In Industrial/Energy prefer:
Oil and Gas Exploration
Oil & Gas Drilling,Explor

Additional Information
Year Founded: 2000
Capital Under Management: $7,100,000
Current Activity Level : Actively seeking new investments

NOVABASE CAPITAL SOCIEDADE DE CAPITAL DE RISCO SA

Avenida D. Joao II, 34
Parque das Nacoes
Lisboa, Portugal 1998031
Phone: 351213836300
Fax: 351213836301
E-mail: info@novabase.pt
Website: www.novabasecapital.pt

Other Offices
Edificio Olympus II
Av. D. Afonso Henriques, 1462
Matosinhos, Portugal 4450-013
Phone: 351-22-608-5100
Fax: 351-22-608-5101

7 andar - Vila Olimpia
Av. Dr. Cardoso de Melo, 1450
Sao Paulo, Brazil
Phone: 55-11-3848-5120
Fax: 55-11-3848-5122

Carrera de San Jeronimo, 15 - 2 piso
Palacio de Miraflores
Madrid, Spain 28014
Phone: 34-91-454-7248
Fax: 34-91-454-7247

Type of Firm
Corporate PE/Venture

Association Membership
Portuguese Venture Capital Association (APCRI)

Project Preferences

Type of Financing Preferred:
Early Stage
Seed
Startup

Geographical Preferences

International Preferences:
Portugal

Industry Preferences

In Computer Software prefer:
Software

In Internet Specific prefer:
Internet

In Computer Other prefer:
Computer Related

Additional Information
Year Founded: 1989
Capital Under Management: $30,000,000
Current Activity Level : Actively seeking new investments

NOVAK BIDDLE VENTURE PARTNERS LP

7501 Wisconsin Avenue, Suite 1380-E
Bethesda, MD USA 20814
Phone: 2404971910
Fax: 2402230255
E-mail: info@novakbiddle.com
Website: www.novakbiddle.com

Management and Staff
A.G.W. Biddle, Co-Founder
E. Rogers Novak, Co-Founder
Janet Yang, Partner
Joy Binford, Chief Financial Officer
Philip Bronner, Venture Partner
Prashanth Boccasam, General Partner
Sean Glass, Venture Partner
Simita Bose, Partner
Thomas Scholl, Venture Partner

Type of Firm
Private Equity Firm

Association Membership
Mid-Atlantic Venture Association
National Venture Capital Association - USA (NVCA)

Project Preferences

Role in Financing:
Will function either as deal originator or investor in deals created by others

Type of Financing Preferred:
Early Stage
Later Stage

Size of Investments Considered:
Min Size of Investment Considered (000s): $100
Max Size of Investment Considered (000s): $10,000

Geographical Preferences

United States Preferences:
Mid Atlantic

Industry Focus
(% based on actual investment)
Computer Software and Services   36.3%
Internet Specific   26.7%
Semiconductors/Other Elect.   15.4%
Communications and Media   9.8%
Computer Hardware   6.5%
Consumer Related   2.4%
Other Products   1.5%
Industrial/Energy   1.3%

Additional Information
Year Founded: 1997
Capital Under Management: $580,000,000
Current Activity Level : Actively seeking new investments
Method of Compensation: Return on investment is of primary concern, do not charge fees

---

NOVAQUEST INFOSYSTEMS INC

4208 Six Forks Road, Suite 920
Raleigh, NC USA 27609
Phone: 9194598620
Website: www.webvision.com

Management and Staff
Daisuke Makino, Principal
Jonathan Tunnicliffe, Partner
Manabu Ikegami, Principal
Matt Bullard, Principal
Michael Bologna, Principal
Robert Hester, Chief Financial Officer
Ronald Wooten, Managing Partner
William Robb, Partner

Type of Firm
Private Equity Firm

Project Preferences

Type of Financing Preferred:
Early Stage
Expansion
Balanced
Later Stage
Seed
Startup

Industry Preferences

In Biotechnology prefer:
Biotechnology

In Medical/Health prefer:
Pharmaceuticals

Additional Information
Name of Most Recent Fund: NovaQuest Co-Investment Fund I, L.P.
Most Recent Fund Was Raised: 05/02/2013
Year Founded: 2006
Capital Under Management: $748,880,000
Current Activity Level : Actively seeking new investments

NOVARTIS VENTURE FUNDS

Novartis International AG
Forum 1-3.73 P.O. Box
Basel, Sweden CH-4002
Phone: 41613243267
Fax: 41613248679
Website: www.nvfund.com

Other Offices
Five Cambridge Center
Cambridge, MA USA 02142
Phone: 617-871-3536
Fax: 617-871-7788

Former HQ: 608 Fifth Avenue
New York, NY USA 10020
Phone: 2123071122
Fax: 2122460185

Management and Staff
Anja Koenig, Managing Director
Campbell Murray, Managing Director
Florent Gros, Managing Director
Giovanni Ferrara, Venture Partner
Henry Skinner, Managing Director
Lauren Silverman, Managing Director
Markus Goebel, Managing Director
Steve Weinstein, Managing Director

Type of Firm
Corporate PE/Venture

Association Membership
New England Venture Capital Association
National Venture Capital Association - USA (NVCA)

Project Preferences

Type of Financing Preferred:
Early Stage
Balanced
Startup

Size of Investments Considered:
Min Size of Investment Considered (000s): $15,000
Max Size of Investment Considered (000s): $20,000

Geographical Preferences

United States Preferences:

Canadian Preferences:
All Canada

International Preferences:
Asia Pacific
Latin America
Sweden
Europe
Western Europe
Korea, South

Industry Focus
(% based on actual investment)
Biotechnology	75.3%
Medical/Health	19.9%
Computer Software and Services	4.0%
Internet Specific	0.8%

Additional Information
Year Founded: 1997
Capital Under Management: $725,000,000
Current Activity Level : Actively seeking new investments

NOVASTAR VENTURES
PO Box 339-00502
Nairobi, Kenya
Phone: 254723930
Website: www.novastarventures.com

Type of Firm
Private Equity Firm

Project Preferences

Type of Financing Preferred:
Balanced

Geographical Preferences

International Preferences:
Africa

Additional Information
Year Founded: 2016
Current Activity Level : Actively seeking new investments

NOVATOR PARTNERS LLP
25 Park Lane
Mayfair
London, United Kingdom W1K 1RA
Phone: 442076471500
Fax: 442076471520
E-mail: info@novator.co.uk
Website: www.novator.co.uk

Type of Firm
Investment Management Firm

Project Preferences

Type of Financing Preferred:
Generalist PE

Geographical Preferences

International Preferences:
United Kingdom

Industry Preferences

In Communications prefer:
Telecommunications

In Medical/Health prefer:
Pharmaceuticals

In Industrial/Energy prefer:
Energy

Additional Information
Year Founded: 2003
Current Activity Level : Actively seeking new investments

NOVAX AB
Villagatan 6
Stockholm, Sweden 100 41
Phone: 4687006660
E-mail: info@novax.se
Website: www.novax.se

Management and Staff
Anders Slettengren, Chief Executive Officer
Veronica Nilsson, Chief Financial Officer

Type of Firm
Corporate PE/Venture

Association Membership
Swedish Venture Capital Association (SVCA)

Project Preferences

Type of Financing Preferred:
Later Stage

Size of Investments Considered:
Min Size of Investment Considered (000s): $300
Max Size of Investment Considered (000s): $1,500

Geographical Preferences

International Preferences:
Sweden

Industry Preferences

In Consumer Related prefer:
Consumer Products
Consumer Services

In Business Serv. prefer:
Services

Additional Information
Year Founded: 1999
Capital Under Management: $32,100,000
Current Activity Level : Actively seeking new investments

NOVERRA CONSULTING AND CAPITAL PARTNERS
701 West Georgia, Suite 1460
Vancouver, Canada V7Y 1E4
Website: www.noverra.com

Management and Staff
Hasmukh Patel, Partner
Kabir Jivraj, Partner
Omar Ladak, Partner
Steve Lux, Partner
Suzanne Boyd, Partner

Type of Firm
Private Equity Firm

Additional Information
Year Founded: 2011
Current Activity Level : Actively seeking new investments

NOVITAS CAPITAL LP
435 Devon Park Drive, Suite 801
Wayne, PA USA 19087
Phone: 6102934075
Fax: 6102544240
E-mail: info@novitascapital.com
Website: www.novitascapital.com

Other Offices
1085 Van Voorhis Road
The United Center, Suite 390
Morgantown, WV USA 26507
Phone: 304-599-1032
Fax: 304-599-4272

15 Bonnie Way
Allendale, NJ USA 07401
Phone: 610-254-4286
Fax: 610-254-4240

100 Technology Drive, Suite 400
Pittsburgh, PA USA 15219
Phone: 412-770-1636
Fax: 412-770-1638

Management and Staff
Lisa Melvin-Joswick, Chief Financial Officer
Michael Bolton, Founder
Paul Schmitt, Managing Director

Type of Firm
Private Equity Firm

Project Preferences

Role in Financing:
Will function either as deal originator or investor in deals created by others

Type of Financing Preferred:
Early Stage
Seed
Startup

Industry Focus

(% based on actual investment)
Internet Specific	35.7%
Biotechnology	22.3%
Computer Software and Services	16.2%
Semiconductors/Other Elect.	11.9%
Other Products	7.4%
Medical/Health	2.9%
Communications and Media	2.7%
Industrial/Energy	0.6%
Consumer Related	0.4%

Additional Information

Year Founded: 1997
Capital Under Management: $237,500,000
Current Activity Level : Actively seeking new investments
Method of Compensation: Return on investment is of primary concern, do not charge fees

NOVO HOLDINGS A/S

Tuborg Havnevej 19
Hellerup, Denmark 2900
Phone: 4535276500
Fax: 4535276510
Website: www.novo.dk

Other Offices

1700 Owens Street, Suite 540
SAN FRANCISCO, CA USA 94158

Management and Staff

Bobby Soni, Principal
Casper Tind Hansen, Principal
Heath Lukatch, Partner
Henrik Gurtler, Chief Executive Officer
Jack Nielsen, Partner
Kim Dueholm, Partner
Peter Bisgaard, Partner
Peter Moldt, Partner
Soren Carlsen, Managing Partner
Thorkil Christensen, Chief Financial Officer
Tiba Aynechi, Principal
Ulrik Spork, Managing Partner

Type of Firm

Corporate PE/Venture

Association Membership

Danish Venture Capital Association (DVCA)
National Venture Capital Association - USA (NVCA)
European Private Equity and Venture Capital Assoc.

Project Preferences

Role in Financing:
Will function either as deal originator or investor in deals created by others

Type of Financing Preferred:
Early Stage
Later Stage
Seed
First Stage Financing
Startup

Geographical Preferences

United States Preferences:

Canadian Preferences:
All Canada

International Preferences:
Europe
Scandanavia/Nordic Region
Denmark

Industry Preferences

In Biotechnology prefer:
Biotechnology
Human Biotechnology
Industrial Biotechnology
Biotech Related Research

In Medical/Health prefer:
Medical/Health
Medical Diagnostics
Drug/Equipmt Delivery
Pharmaceuticals

In Consumer Related prefer:
Food/Beverage

In Industrial/Energy prefer:
Environmental Related

Additional Information

Year Founded: 1999
Capital Under Management: $553,500,000
Current Activity Level : Actively seeking new investments
Method of Compensation: Return on investment is of primary concern, do not charge fees

NOVO HORIZONTE INVES-TIMENTOS E CONSULTO-RIA LTDA

Father R Carvalho 295
Sao Paulo, Brazil 05427100
Phone: 551134763093
E-mail: contato@nhinvestimentos.com.br
Website: www.nhinvestimentos.com.br

Type of Firm

Private Equity Firm

Project Preferences

Type of Financing Preferred:
Early Stage
Seed
Startup

Geographical Preferences

International Preferences:
Brazil

Industry Preferences

In Internet Specific prefer:
E-Commerce Technology

In Medical/Health prefer:
Medical/Health

In Consumer Related prefer:
Education Related

In Financial Services prefer:
Financial Services
Financial Services

Additional Information

Year Founded: 1999
Current Activity Level : Actively seeking new investments

NOVO TELLUS CAPITAL PARTNERS PTE LTD

43 Mosque Street, Suite Four-Three
Singapore, Singapore 059521
Phone: 6564388074
Fax: 6562236216
E-mail: info@novotellus.com
Website: www.novotellus.com

Management and Staff

Andrew Yeo, Managing Director
James Toh, Founder
Newell Cotton, Vice President
Wai San Loke, Managing Director

Type of Firm

Investment Management Firm

Project Preferences

Type of Financing Preferred:
Leveraged Buyout
Balanced
Management Buyouts
Acquisition

Industry Preferences

In Other prefer:
Environment Responsible

Additional Information

Year Founded: 2011
Capital Under Management: $20,000,000

Current Activity Level : Actively seeking new investments

NOVOTECH INVESTMENT LTD

Holland Drive
Block B, Holland Park
Newcastle, United Kingdom NE2 4LD

Type of Firm
Private Equity Firm

Project Preferences

Type of Financing Preferred:
Balanced

Additional Information
Year Founded: 2006
Current Activity Level : Actively seeking new investments

NOVUS BIOTECHNOLOGY FUND

241 East Michigan Avenue
Kalamazoo, MI USA 49007
Phone: 8888951030
Website: www.novusvc.com

Type of Firm
Investment Management Firm

Project Preferences

Type of Financing Preferred:
Early Stage
Startup

Geographical Preferences

United States Preferences:

Industry Preferences

In Biotechnology prefer:
Biotechnology
Human Biotechnology
Agricultural/Animal Bio.
Industrial Biotechnology
Biosensors
Biotech Related Research
Biotech Related Research

Additional Information
Year Founded: 2014
Capital Under Management: $2,000,000
Current Activity Level : Actively seeking new investments

NOVUS VIA LLC

774 Mays Boulevard
#10-588
Incline Village, NV USA 89451

Website: novusviafund.com

Type of Firm
Private Equity Firm

Project Preferences

Type of Financing Preferred:
Early Stage

Industry Preferences

In Medical/Health prefer:
Health Services

In Industrial/Energy prefer:
Energy

Additional Information
Year Founded: 2012
Capital Under Management: $14,680,000
Current Activity Level : Actively seeking new investments

NPM CAPITAL NV

Breitnerstraat 1
Amsterdam, Netherlands 1077 BL
Phone: 31205705555
Fax: 31204706454
E-mail: mails@npm-capital.com
Website: www.npm-capital.com

Other Offices
Snelliuslaan 10
Hilversum, Netherlands 1222 TE
Phone: 31356265587
Fax: 31356265555

Rue de Ligne 13
Brussels, Belgium 1000
Phone: 3222106090
Fax: 3222196719

Management and Staff
Jan Baud, Managing Director

Type of Firm
Private Equity Firm

Association Membership
Belgium Venturing Association
European Private Equity and Venture Capital Assoc.
Dutch Venture Capital Associaton (NVP)

Project Preferences

Role in Financing:
Prefer role as deal originator but will also invest in deals created by others

Type of Financing Preferred:
Leveraged Buyout
Mezzanine
Generalist PE
Management Buyouts
Acquisition
Recapitalizations

Size of Investments Considered:
Min Size of Investment Considered (000s): $26,864
Max Size of Investment Considered (000s): $268,636

Geographical Preferences

International Preferences:
Ireland
Luxembourg
Europe
Netherlands
Belgium
Germany
France

Industry Focus
(% based on actual investment)

Internet Specific	39.8%
Industrial/Energy	21.7%
Other Products	14.3%
Computer Software and Services	10.2%
Semiconductors/Other Elect.	8.3%
Computer Hardware	2.3%
Medical/Health	1.6%
Biotechnology	1.1%
Consumer Related	0.7%

Additional Information
Year Founded: 1948
Capital Under Management: $921,300,000
Current Activity Level : Actively seeking new investments
Method of Compensation: Return on invest. most important, but chg. closing fees, service fees, etc.

NRD CAPITAL MANAGEMENT LLC

4170 Ashford Dunwoody Road, Suite 390
Atlanta, GA USA 30319
Website: nrdcapital.com

Management and Staff
Anwar Bhayani, Chief Financial Officer
Harrison Price, Partner

Type of Firm
Private Equity Firm

Project Preferences

Type of Financing Preferred:
Leveraged Buyout
Acquisition

Industry Preferences

In Medical/Health prefer:
Health Services

In Consumer Related prefer:
Consumer Products
Consumer Services
Other Restaurants

Additional Information

Year Founded: 2015
Capital Under Management: $104,000,000
Current Activity Level : Actively seeking new investments

NRDC EQUITY PARTNERS

Three Manhattanville Road
Purchase, NY USA 10577
Phone: 914-272-8067
Fax: 914-696-1229
Website: www.nrdcequity.com

Management and Staff

Francis Casale, Managing Director

Type of Firm

Private Equity Firm

Project Preferences

Type of Financing Preferred:
Leveraged Buyout
Acquisition

Size of Investments Considered:
Min Size of Investment Considered (000s): $50,000
Max Size of Investment Considered (000s): $750,000

Geographical Preferences

United States Preferences:
All U.S.

Industry Preferences

In Consumer Related prefer:
Entertainment and Leisure
Retail
Consumer Services

In Financial Services prefer:
Real Estate

Additional Information

Year Founded: 2005
Current Activity Level : Actively seeking new investments

NRW BANK

Kavalleriestrasse 22
Duesseldorf, Germany 40213
Phone: 49211917410
Fax: 49211917411800
E-mail: info@nrwbank.de
Website: www.nrwbank.de

Other Offices

Friedrichstrasse 1
Muenster, Germany 48145
Phone: 49-251-917-410
Fax: 49-251-917-412-921

Type of Firm

Bank Affiliated

Association Membership

German Venture Capital Association (BVK)
European Private Equity and Venture Capital Assoc.

Project Preferences

Type of Financing Preferred:
Leveraged Buyout
Early Stage
Mezzanine
Seed
Management Buyouts
Acquisition
Startup

Geographical Preferences

International Preferences:
Europe
Western Europe
Germany

Industry Preferences

In Communications prefer:
Communications and Media

In Computer Software prefer:
Software

In Semiconductor/Electr prefer:
Micro-Processing

In Biotechnology prefer:
Biotechnology

In Medical/Health prefer:
Medical/Health

In Consumer Related prefer:
Consumer
Consumer Products

In Industrial/Energy prefer:
Alternative Energy
Factory Automation
Robotics
Machinery
Environmental Related

Additional Information

Year Founded: 2002
Current Activity Level : Actively seeking new investments

NSBI VENTURE CAPITAL

1800 Argyle Street, Suite 701
Halifax, Canada B3J 3N8
Phone: 9024246650
Fax: 9024245739
E-mail: info@nsbi.ca
Website: www.novascotiabusiness.com

Management and Staff

Harvey Doane, Managing Director
Lisa Bugden, Vice President
Peter MacAskill, Vice President

Type of Firm

Government Affiliated Program

Association Membership

Canadian Venture Capital Association

Geographical Preferences

Canadian Preferences:
Nova Scotia

Additional Information

Year Founded: 2001
Current Activity Level : Actively seeking new investments

NSI VENTURES

6 Battery Road
Unit #35-05
Singapore, Singapore 049909
Phone: 6565333210
Fax: 6565333211
Website: nsi.vc

Management and Staff

Anvesh Ramineni, Vice President
Hian Goh, Co-Founder
Ian Sikora, Vice President
Shane Chesson, Co-Founder

Type of Firm

Private Equity Firm

Project Preferences

Type of Financing Preferred:
Balanced
Acquisition

Geographical Preferences

International Preferences:
Asia

Industry Preferences

In Communications prefer:
Telecommunications

In Consumer Related prefer:
Consumer
Retail

In Industrial/Energy prefer:
Environmental Related

In Financial Services prefer:
Financial Services

In Business Serv. prefer:
Consulting Services

Additional Information
Year Founded: 2015
Capital Under Management: $89,000,000
Current Activity Level : Actively seeking new investments

NTH POWER LLC

One Embarcadero Center, Suite 1550
San Francisco, CA USA 94111
Phone: 4159839983
Fax: 4159839984
E-mail: info@nthpower.com
Website: www.nthpower.com

Management and Staff
Bryant Tong, Managing Director
Elaine Erickson, Chief Financial Officer
Matt Jones, Partner
Nancy Floyd, Co-Founder
Tim Woodward, Managing Director

Type of Firm
Private Equity Firm

Project Preferences

Role in Financing:
Will function either as deal originator or investor in deals created by others

Type of Financing Preferred:
Balanced
Startup

Size of Investments Considered:
Min Size of Investment Considered (000s): $1,000
Max Size of Investment Considered (000s): $5,000

Industry Focus
(% based on actual investment)

Industry	%
Industrial/Energy	57.6%
Semiconductors/Other Elect.	11.6%
Other Products	9.6%
Computer Software and Services	9.6%
Internet Specific	7.3%
Communications and Media	3.3%
Computer Hardware	1.0%

Additional Information
Name of Most Recent Fund: Nth Power Technologies Fund IV, L.P.
Most Recent Fund Was Raised: 06/13/2006
Year Founded: 1993

Capital Under Management: $347,000,000
Current Activity Level : Actively seeking new investments
Method of Compensation: Return on investment is of primary concern, do not charge fees

NTT FINANCE CORP

1-2-1, Shibaura
Seavans N, Minato-Ku
Tokyo, Japan 105-6791
Phone: 81354455400
Website: www.ntt-finance.co.jp

Management and Staff
Akihiko Okada, Managing Director
Masataka Isaji, Managing Director
Takahiro Mitsushima, Managing Director

Type of Firm
Investment Management Firm

Project Preferences

Type of Financing Preferred:
Early Stage
Expansion
Balanced
Later Stage
Seed

Geographical Preferences

United States Preferences:

International Preferences:
Europe
China
Japan

Industry Preferences

In Communications prefer:
Telecommunications

In Computer Software prefer:
Software

Additional Information
Year Founded: 1997
Current Activity Level : Actively seeking new investments

NUCLEUS VENTURE PARTNERS LTD

13 Webworks, Forster Street
Galway, Ireland
Phone: 35391396505
E-mail: info@nucleusvp.com
Website: www.nucleusvp.com

Type of Firm
Private Equity Firm

Project Preferences

Type of Financing Preferred:
Early Stage
Expansion
Seed

Geographical Preferences

International Preferences:
United Kingdom

Industry Preferences

In Communications prefer:
Telecommunications

In Computer Software prefer:
Software

In Industrial/Energy prefer:
Environmental Related

Additional Information
Year Founded: 2010
Current Activity Level : Actively seeking new investments

NUETERRA CAPITAL

11221 Roe Avenue, Suite 210
Leawood, KS USA 66211
Phone: 9133870510
Website: www.nueterra.com

Type of Firm
Investment Management Firm

Industry Preferences

In Medical/Health prefer:
Medical/Health

Additional Information
Year Founded: 2016
Current Activity Level : Actively seeking new investments

NV INDUSTRIEBANK LIOF

Boschstaat 76
Maastricht, Netherlands 6211 AX
Phone: 31433280280
Fax: 31433280200
E-mail: info@liof.nl
Website: www.liof.nl

Other Offices
Sint Jansweg 15
Venlo, Netherlands 5928 RC
Phone: 31773208108
Fax: 31773208100

Management and Staff
Thomas Verhagen, Managing Director

Type of Firm
Government Affiliated Program

Association Membership
Dutch Venture Capital Associaton (NVP)

Project Preferences

Type of Financing Preferred:
Early Stage
Later Stage
Seed
Startup

Geographical Preferences

International Preferences:
Netherlands

Industry Preferences

In Communications prefer:
Communications and Media

In Computer Other prefer:
Computer Related

In Semiconductor/Electr prefer:
Electronics

In Biotechnology prefer:
Biotechnology

In Medical/Health prefer:
Medical/Health

In Consumer Related prefer:
Consumer

In Industrial/Energy prefer:
Energy
Industrial Products

In Manufact. prefer:
Manufacturing

Additional Information
Year Founded: 1975
Capital Under Management: $89,100,000
Current Activity Level : Actively seeking new investments

NV NOM

Paterswoldseweg 810
Groningen, Netherlands 9728 BM
Phone: 31505214444
Fax: 31505214400
E-mail: info@nom.nl
Website: www.nom.nl

Management and Staff
Siem Jansen, Managing Director

Type of Firm
Private Equity Firm

Association Membership
Dutch Venture Capital Associaton (NVP)

Project Preferences

Type of Financing Preferred:
Early Stage
Later Stage

Geographical Preferences

International Preferences:
Netherlands

Industry Preferences

In Semiconductor/Electr prefer:
Sensors

In Biotechnology prefer:
Agricultural/Animal Bio.

In Consumer Related prefer:
Consumer

In Industrial/Energy prefer:
Energy
Alternative Energy
Environmental Related

In Business Serv. prefer:
Services
Consulting Services

In Other prefer:
Environment Responsible

Additional Information
Year Founded: 2004
Current Activity Level : Actively seeking new investments

NVM PE LTD

Rotterdam House
116 Quayside
Newcastle upon Tyne, United Kingdom NE1 3DY
Phone: 441912446000
E-mail: newcastle@nvm.co.uk
Website: www.nvm.co.uk

Other Offices

Forbury Court
12 Forbury Road
Reading, United Kingdom RG1 1SB
Phone: 44-118-951-7000
Fax: 44-118-951-7001

Rotterdam House
116 Quayside
Newcastle upon Tyne, United Kingdom NE1 3DY
Phone: 1912446000

82 King Street
Manchester, United Kingdom M2 4WQ
Phone: 1619358419

Management and Staff
Alastair Conn, Co-Founder
Christopher Mellor, Partner
Martin Green, Managing Partner

Type of Firm
Bank Affiliated

Association Membership
British Venture Capital Association (BVCA)

Project Preferences

Role in Financing:
Prefer role as deal originator but will also invest in deals created by others

Type of Financing Preferred:
Early Stage
Generalist PE
Balanced
Later Stage
Management Buyouts
Acquisition

Size of Investments Considered:
Min Size of Investment Considered (000s): $3,202
Max Size of Investment Considered (000s): $16,008

Geographical Preferences

International Preferences:
United Kingdom

Industry Focus
(% based on actual investment)
Other Products	34.1%
Industrial/Energy	21.2%
Computer Software and Services	14.7%
Consumer Related	11.0%
Medical/Health	5.8%
Biotechnology	5.7%
Semiconductors/Other Elect.	2.7%
Computer Hardware	1.9%
Internet Specific	1.8%
Communications and Media	1.1%

Additional Information
Year Founded: 1987
Capital Under Management: $442,100,000
Current Activity Level : Actively seeking new investments
Method of Compensation: Return on invest. most important, but chg. closing fees, service fees, etc.

NVM PRIVATE EQUITY LLP

Time Central 32 Gallowgate
Newcastle Upon , United Kingdom TYNE NE1
Website: www.nvm.co.uk

Type of Firm
Private Equity Firm

Project Preferences

Type of Financing Preferred:
Management Buyouts

Additional Information

Year Founded: 1984
Current Activity Level : Actively seeking new investments

NWK NORDWEST KAPITALBETEILIGUNGSGESELLSCHAFT DER SPARKASSE

Am Brill 1-3
Bremen, Germany 28195
Phone: 49-4211792043
Fax: 494211791464
E-mail: info@nwk-nwu.de
Website: www.nwk-nwu.de

Management and Staff

Ralf Paslack, Managing Director
Ralf Kubitz, Managing Director

Type of Firm

Bank Affiliated

Association Membership

German Venture Capital Association (BVK)

Project Preferences

Type of Financing Preferred:
Early Stage
Mezzanine
Turnaround
Later Stage
Management Buyouts
Startup

Size of Investments Considered:
Min Size of Investment Considered (000s): $657
Max Size of Investment Considered (000s): $3,939

Geographical Preferences

International Preferences:
Germany

Industry Preferences

In Consumer Related prefer:
Retail
Food/Beverage
Consumer Services

In Industrial/Energy prefer:
Industrial Products

Additional Information

Year Founded: 2005
Current Activity Level : Actively seeking new investments

NXT CAPITAL VENTURE FINANCE

191 North Wacker Drive, Suite 1200
Chicago, IL USA 60606
Phone: 3124508000
Fax: 3124508100
Website: www.nxtcapital.com

Other Offices

500 Edgewater Drive, Suite 509
Wakefield, MA USA 01880

2105 Woodside Road, Suite B
Redwood City, CA USA 94062

Management and Staff

Anurag Chandra, Managing Director
Jan Haas, Senior Managing Director
Peter Fair, Managing Director
Stacia Kopplin, Managing Director

Type of Firm

Investment Management Firm

Project Preferences

Type of Financing Preferred:
Early Stage
Expansion
Balanced
Later Stage
Seed
Acquisition
Startup
Recapitalizations

Size of Investments Considered:
Min Size of Investment Considered (000s): $1,000
Max Size of Investment Considered (000s): $20,000

Geographical Preferences

United States Preferences:

Industry Preferences

In Communications prefer:
Data Communications

In Computer Software prefer:
Data Processing
Software

In Internet Specific prefer:
Internet

In Medical/Health prefer:
Medical/Health
Medical Products
Health Services

In Industrial/Energy prefer:
Environmental Related

In Business Serv. prefer:
Services

Additional Information

Year Founded: 2011
Current Activity Level : Actively seeking new investments

NXT VENTURES FUND 1 LLC

5 Sewall Street
Marblehead, MA USA 01945
Phone: 7816394774
Website: nxtventures.com

Management and Staff

Barry Turkanis, Managing Director
Kacey Muldoon, Chief Financial Officer
Raymond Chang, Managing Director

Type of Firm

Private Equity Firm

Project Preferences

Type of Financing Preferred:
Startup

Geographical Preferences

United States Preferences:

International Preferences:
Asia

Additional Information

Year Founded: 1969
Current Activity Level : Actively seeking new investments

NXTP LABS SRL

1/2 Piso, Palermo Soho
Malabia 1720
Buenos Aires, Argentina B6443
Phone: 541152783248
E-mail: infolabs@nextperience.net
Website: www.nxtplabs.com

Management and Staff

Ariel Arrieta, Co-Founder

Type of Firm

Incubator/Development Program

Project Preferences

Type of Financing Preferred:
Seed
Startup

Geographical Preferences

International Preferences:
Latin America
Argentina

Industry Preferences

In Communications prefer:
Wireless Communications
Media and Entertainment

In Computer Software prefer:
Software

In Internet Specific prefer:
Internet
Web Aggregration/Portals

In Semiconductor/Electr prefer:
Electronics

In Consumer Related prefer:
Retail

In Business Serv. prefer:
Services

Additional Information

Year Founded: 2011
Current Activity Level : Actively seeking new investments

NYC SEED LLC

Six MetroTech Center
Brooklyn, NY USA 11201
Phone: 7074693669
Website: www.nycseed.com

Management and Staff

Owen Davis, Managing Director

Type of Firm

Private Equity Firm

Project Preferences

Type of Financing Preferred:
Seed
Startup

Geographical Preferences

United States Preferences:
New York

Industry Preferences

In Computer Software prefer:
Software

Additional Information

Year Founded: 2010
Current Activity Level : Actively seeking new investments

NYCA PARTNERS

485 Madison Avenure
12th Floor
New York, NY USA 10017
Phone: 2128931168
E-mail: info@nycapartners.com
Website: www.nycapartners.com

Type of Firm

Private Equity Firm

Project Preferences

Type of Financing Preferred:
Seed
Startup

Size of Investments Considered:
Min Size of Investment Considered (000s): $10,000
Max Size of Investment Considered (000s): $15,000

Industry Preferences

In Financial Services prefer:
Financial Services

Additional Information

Year Founded: 2014
Capital Under Management: $155,000,000
Current Activity Level : Actively seeking new investments

NYSKOPUNARSJODUR

Kringlunni 7
3rd floor
Reykjavik, Iceland 103
Phone: 3545101800
Fax: 3545101809
E-mail: nsa@nsa.is
Website: www.nsa.is

Management and Staff

Helga Valfells, Chief Executive Officer
Smari Thorarinsson, Chief Financial Officer

Type of Firm

Government Affiliated Program

Association Membership

European Private Equity and Venture Capital Assoc.

Project Preferences

Type of Financing Preferred:
Early Stage
Seed
Startup

Size of Investments Considered:
Min Size of Investment Considered (000s): $400
Max Size of Investment Considered (000s): $2,000

Geographical Preferences

International Preferences:
Iceland

Industry Preferences

In Communications prefer:
Wireless Communications

In Biotechnology prefer:
Biotechnology

In Medical/Health prefer:
Medical/Health

In Consumer Related prefer:
Consumer

In Industrial/Energy prefer:
Energy

Additional Information

Year Founded: 1998
Capital Under Management: $60,000,000
Current Activity Level : Actively seeking new investments

NYSTAR

633 Third Avenue
31st Floor
New York, NY USA 10017
Phone: 2128033100
Fax: 2128033131
Website: www.nystar.state.ny.us

Management and Staff

Divjot Narang, Managing Director
Frances Walton, Chief Financial Officer
Harvey Cohen, Vice President
Jen McCormick, Vice President

Type of Firm

Government Affiliated Program

Project Preferences

Role in Financing:
Will function either as deal originator or investor in deals created by others

Type of Financing Preferred:
Early Stage

Size of Investments Considered:
Min Size of Investment Considered (000s): $100
Max Size of Investment Considered (000s): $500

Geographical Preferences

United States Preferences:
New York

Industry Preferences

In Biotechnology prefer:
Biotechnology

Additional Information

Year Founded: 1981
Capital Under Management: $25,000,000
Current Activity Level : Actively seeking new investments
Method of Compensation: Return on invest. most important, but chg. closing fees, service fees, etc.

- O -

1&12 VENTURES BV

Science Park 105
Amsterdam, Netherlands 1098 XG
Phone: 31615549726
Fax: 31629523813
E-mail: info@1and12.biz
Website: www.1and12.biz

Management and Staff

Chatib Sjarbaini, Managing Director
Hans Roeland Poolman, Managing Director

Type of Firm

Private Equity Firm

Project Preferences

Type of Financing Preferred:
Early Stage
Start-up Financing
Seed

Size of Investments Considered:
Min Size of Investment Considered (000s): $123
Max Size of Investment Considered (000s): $617

Geographical Preferences

International Preferences:
Europe

Additional Information

Year Founded: 2009
Current Activity Level : Actively seeking new investments

101 SEEDS

Carrer Pic de Peguera, 15
Girona, Spain 17003
E-mail: info@101startups.com
Website: www.101seeds.com

Type of Firm

Incubator/Development Program

Project Preferences

Type of Financing Preferred:
Seed
Startup

Industry Preferences

In Communications prefer:
Wireless Communications

In Internet Specific prefer:
Internet

Additional Information

Year Founded: 1969
Current Activity Level : Actively seeking new investments

10X VENTURE PARTNERS LLC

21 Continental Boulevard
Merrimack, NH USA 03054
Website: www.10xvp.com

Management and Staff

Art Garofalo, Partner
Charlie Northrup, Partner
James Alvarez, Partner
John Gargasz, Partner
Matt Pierson, Partner
Tony Giroti, Partner

Type of Firm

Private Equity Firm

Project Preferences

Type of Financing Preferred:
Early Stage
Balanced
Later Stage
Seed

Size of Investments Considered:
Min Size of Investment Considered (000s): $50
Max Size of Investment Considered (000s): $500

Geographical Preferences

United States Preferences:
Northeast

Industry Preferences

In Communications prefer:
Telecommunications
Wireless Communications

In Internet Specific prefer:
Internet

In Medical/Health prefer:
Medical/Health

In Other prefer:
Environment Responsible

Additional Information

Year Founded: 2012
Current Activity Level : Actively seeking new investments

123 INVESTMENT MANAGERS SA

94, Rue de la Victoire
Paris, France 75009
Phone: 33149269800
Fax: 33149269819
E-mail: info@123venture.com
Website: www.123-im.com

Type of Firm

Private Equity Firm

Association Membership

French Venture Capital Association (AFIC)

Project Preferences

Type of Financing Preferred:
Fund of Funds
Leveraged Buyout
Early Stage
Expansion
Mezzanine
Research and Development
Generalist PE
Balanced
Later Stage
Seed
Startup

Size of Investments Considered:
Min Size of Investment Considered (000s): $2,741
Max Size of Investment Considered (000s): $4,569

Geographical Preferences

International Preferences:
Europe
France

Industry Preferences

In Biotechnology prefer:
Biotechnology

In Medical/Health prefer:
Hospital/Other Instit.

In Consumer Related prefer:
Hotels and Resorts

In Industrial/Energy prefer:
Energy
Alternative Energy
Environmental Related

In Financial Services prefer:
Real Estate

In Other prefer:
Environment Responsible

Additional Information

Year Founded: 2000
Capital Under Management: $16,200,000
Current Activity Level : Actively seeking new investments

1315 CAPITAL LLC

3020 Market Street, Suite 104
Philadelphia, PA USA 19104
Phone: 9145891769
Fax: 2156894648
Website: www.1315capital.com

Management and Staff
Adele Oliva, Founder
Brian Schwenk, Chief Financial Officer
Edward Chan, Principal
Matthew Reber, Partner
Michael Koby, Partner

Type of Firm
Private Equity Firm

Project Preferences

Type of Financing Preferred:
Expansion
Later Stage

Size of Investments Considered:
Min Size of Investment Considered (000s): $10,000
Max Size of Investment Considered (000s): $20,000

Industry Preferences

In Medical/Health prefer:
Medical/Health
Health Services
Pharmaceuticals

Additional Information
Year Founded: 2015
Capital Under Management: $200,000,000
Current Activity Level : Actively seeking new investments

1337 VENTURES SDN BHD

Megan Avenue One
E-9-1 Block E
Kuala Lumpur, Malaysia
Website: 1337accelerator.com

Management and Staff
Bikesh Lakhmichand, Chief Executive Officer

Type of Firm
Incubator/Development Program

Project Preferences

Type of Financing Preferred:
Early Stage
Seed
Startup

Geographical Preferences

International Preferences:
Malaysia

Industry Preferences

In Computer Software prefer:
Applications Software

Additional Information
Year Founded: 2013
Current Activity Level : Actively seeking new investments

137 VENTURES LP

26 O' Farrell Street
San Francisco, CA USA 94108
Phone: 4155135222
E-mail: info@137ventures.com
Website: 137ventures.com

Management and Staff
Alda Leu Dennis, Managing Partner
Andrew Hansen, Chief Financial Officer
Andrew Laszlo, Managing Partner
Justin Fisher-Wolfson, Co-Founder
Kathy Chan, Co-Founder
S. Alexander Jacobson, Co-Founder

Type of Firm
Private Equity Firm

Industry Preferences

In Computer Software prefer:
Software

In Medical/Health prefer:
Medical/Health

In Financial Services prefer:
Financial Services

Additional Information
Year Founded: 2010
Capital Under Management: $187,952,000
Current Activity Level : Actively seeking new investments

1517 FUND

5519 McMillan Street
Oakland, CA USA 94618
Website: www.1517fund.com

Type of Firm
Private Equity Firm

Project Preferences

Type of Financing Preferred:
Seed

Additional Information
Year Founded: 2015
Capital Under Management: $6,400,000
Current Activity Level : Actively seeking new investments

17 CAPITAL LLP

7 Curzon Street
London, United Kingdom W1J 5HG
Phone: 44-20-7493-2462
Fax: 44-20-7529-1908
E-mail: contact@17capital.com
Website: www.17capital.com

Management and Staff
Augustin Duhamel, Co-Founder
Pierre-Antoine De Selancy, Co-Founder
Robert De Corainville, Vice President

Type of Firm
Private Equity Advisor or Fund of Funds

Association Membership
French Venture Capital Association (AFIC)
European Private Equity and Venture Capital Assoc.

Project Preferences

Type of Financing Preferred:
Fund of Funds
Leveraged Buyout
Early Stage
Expansion
Mezzanine
Generalist PE
Balanced
Later Stage
Acquisition

Size of Investments Considered:
Min Size of Investment Considered (000s): $13,996
Max Size of Investment Considered (000s): $69,979

Geographical Preferences

International Preferences:
United Kingdom
Europe
Western Europe

Additional Information
Year Founded: 2008
Capital Under Management: $2,548,793,000
Current Activity Level : Actively seeking new investments

1717 PARTNERS

1717 East Cary Street
Richmond, VA USA 23223

Type of Firm
Private Equity Firm

Project Preferences

Type of Financing Preferred:
Early Stage

Additional Information
Year Founded: 2016
Current Activity Level : Actively seeking new investments

1776

1133 15th Street
Washington, DC USA 20005
E-mail: info@1776.vc
Website: www.1776.vc

Pratt's Guide to Private Equity & Venture Capital Sources

Type of Firm
Incubator/Development Program

Project Preferences

Type of Financing Preferred:
Seed
Startup

Geographical Preferences

United States Preferences:
Washington

Industry Preferences

In Medical/Health prefer:
Medical/Health

In Consumer Related prefer:
Education Related

In Industrial/Energy prefer:
Energy
Energy Conservation Relat

Additional Information
Year Founded: 2013
Capital Under Management: $12,500,000
Current Activity Level : Actively seeking new investments

180 DEGREE CAPITAL CORP

1450 Broadway, 24th Floor
New York, NY USA 10018
Phone: 2125820900
Fax: 2125829563
E-mail: admin@tinytechvc.com
Website: www.180degreecapital.com

Other Offices

420 Florence Street, Suite 200
Palo Alto, CA USA 94301
Phone: 650-321-2668
Fax: 650-321-1561

Management and Staff

Blake Stevens, Vice President
Daniel Wolfe, President
Misti Ushio, Managing Director

Type of Firm
Private Equity Firm

Project Preferences

Role in Financing:
Will function either as deal originator or investor in deals created by others

Type of Financing Preferred:
Early Stage
Start-up Financing
First Stage Financing
Startup

Size of Investments Considered:
Min Size of Investment Considered (000s): $100
Max Size of Investment Considered (000s): $6,000

Geographical Preferences

United States Preferences:

Industry Preferences

In Semiconductor/Electr prefer:
Electronics
Electronic Components
Laser Related
Analytic/Scientific
Optoelectronics

In Biotechnology prefer:
Biotechnology
Human Biotechnology
Agricultural/Animal Bio.
Industrial Biotechnology
Biosensors
Biotech Related Research

In Medical/Health prefer:
Medical Diagnostics
Medical Therapeutics
Medical Products
Pharmaceuticals

In Industrial/Energy prefer:
Energy
Alternative Energy
Coal Related
Energy Conservation Relat
Materials

Additional Information
Year Founded: 1983
Capital Under Management: $48,000,000
Current Activity Level : Actively seeking new investments
Method of Compensation: Return on investment is of primary concern, do not charge fees

1847 HOLDINGS LLC

590 Madison Avenue
21st Floor New York
New York, NY USA 10022
Website: www.1847holdings.com

Management and Staff
Edward Tobin, Managing Director

Type of Firm
Private Equity Firm

Project Preferences

Type of Financing Preferred:
Leveraged Buyout
Recapitalizations

Geographical Preferences

United States Preferences:
North America

Industry Preferences

In Consumer Related prefer:
Retail
Consumer Products
Consumer Services

In Financial Services prefer:
Financial Services

In Business Serv. prefer:
Services
Distribution

Additional Information
Year Founded: 2013
Current Activity Level : Actively seeking new investments

1984 VENTURES LP

44 Tehama Street
San Francisco, CA USA 94105
Phone: 4084209220
E-mail: team@1984.vc

Type of Firm
Private Equity Firm

Additional Information
Year Founded: 2017
Current Activity Level : Actively seeking new investments

1CONFIRMATION

1840 Green Street, Suite 2
San Francisco, CA USA 94123
Website: www.1confirmation.com

Type of Firm
Private Equity Firm

Project Preferences

Type of Financing Preferred:
Balanced

Additional Information
Year Founded: 2017
Current Activity Level : Actively seeking new investments

O'BRIEN CAPITAL LLC

7700 Forsyth Boulevard, Suite 1230
Saint Louis, MO USA 63105
E-mail: info@obcapllc.com
Website: www.obcapllc.com

Type of Firm
Private Equity Firm

Project Preferences

Type of Financing Preferred:
Leveraged Buyout
Expansion
Generalist PE
Turnaround
Later Stage

Industry Preferences

In Manufact. prefer:
Manufacturing

Additional Information

Year Founded: 2008
Current Activity Level : Actively seeking new investments

O'MELVENY & MYERS LLP

400 South Hope Street
Los Angeles, CA USA 90071
Phone: 2134306000
Fax: 2134306407
E-mail: omminfo@omm.com
Website: www.omm.com

Other Offices

The Plaza Office Tower
41st Floor, JI.M.H.Thamrin Kavling 28-30
Jakarta, Indonesia 10350
Phone: 622129921988
Fax: 622129928198

Seven Times Square
Times Square Tower
New York, NY USA 10036
Phone: 212-326-2000
Fax: 212-326-2061

610 Newport Center Drive
17th Floor
Newport Beach, CA USA 92660
Phone: 949-760-9600
Fax: 949-823-6994

1266 Nanjing Road West
Plaza 66, Tower 1, 37th Floor
Shanghai, China 200040
Phone: 86-21-2307-7000
Fax: 86-21-2307-7300

1999 Avenue of the Stars
Seventh Floor
Los Angeles, CA USA 90067
Phone: 310-553-6700
Fax: 310-246-6779

1 Connaught Road Central
31st Floor, AIA Central
Central, Hong Kong
Phone: 85235122300
Fax: 85225221760

2-1-1, Marunouchi, Chiyoda-ku
Meiji Yasuda Seimei Bldg., 11th Floor
Tokyo, Japan
Phone: 81-3-5293-2700
Fax: 81-3-5293-2780

No.2 Jianguomenwai Avenue
Yin Tai Center, Office Tower, 37th Floor
Beijing, China 100022
Phone: 86-10-6563-4200
Fax: 86-10-6563-4201

1625 Eye Street Northwest
Washington, DC USA 20006
Phone: 202-383-5300
Fax: 202-383-5414

5 Paternoster Square
Warwick Court
London, United Kingdom EC4M 7DX
Phone: 44-20-7088-0000
Fax: 44-20-7088-0001

2765 Sand Hill Road
Menlo Park, CA USA 94025
Phone: 650-473-2600
Fax: 650-473-2601

Nine Raffles Place, Republic Plaza One
22-01/02
Singapore, Singapore 048619
Phone: 6565931800
Fax: 6565931801

Tqo Embarcadero Center
28th Floor
San Francisco, CA USA 94111
Phone: 415-984-8700
Fax: 415-984-8701

Avenue Louise 326
Blue Tower
Brussels, Belgium 1050
Phone: 32-2-642-4100
Fax: 32-2-642-4190

Management and Staff

Carol Mays, Managing Director
George Demos, Chief Operating Officer
Jeffrey Rovner, Managing Director
Keith Whitman, Managing Director
Majory Appel, Managing Director
Michelle Egan, Managing Director
Paul Covey, Managing Director
Ron Hofmeister, Chief Financial Officer
Teresa Doremus, Managing Director

Type of Firm

Service Provider

Association Membership

Emerging Markets Private Equity Association

Project Preferences

Role in Financing:
Other

Type of Financing Preferred:
Fund of Funds

Geographical Preferences

United States Preferences:

Additional Information

Year Founded: 1885
Current Activity Level : Actively seeking new investments
Method of Compensation: Return on investment is of primary concern, do not charge fees

---

O'REILLY ALPHATECH VENTURES LLC

One Lombard Street, Suite 303
San Francisco, CA USA 94111
Phone: 4156930200
E-mail: plans@oatv.com
Website: www.oatv.com

Management and Staff

Bryce Roberts, Co-Founder
Mark Jacobsen, Managing Director

Type of Firm

Private Equity Firm

Project Preferences

Role in Financing:
Will function either as deal originator or investor in deals created by others

Type of Financing Preferred:
Early Stage
Seed

Size of Investments Considered:
Min Size of Investment Considered (000s): $1,000
Max Size of Investment Considered (000s): $2,000

Geographical Preferences

United States Preferences:

Industry Preferences

In Communications prefer:
Communications and Media

In Computer Software prefer:
Systems Software

In Internet Specific prefer:
E-Commerce Technology
Internet
Ecommerce

In Computer Other prefer:
Computer Related

Additional Information

Name of Most Recent Fund: OATV III, L.P.
Most Recent Fund Was Raised: 11/16/2012
Year Founded: 2005
Capital Under Management: $195,000,000
Current Activity Level : Actively seeking new investments

O2 INVESTMENT PARTNERS LLC

40900 Woodward Avenue, Suite 200
Bloomfield Hills, MI USA 48304
Phone: 2485544227
Fax: 2485407280
Website: o2investment.com

Management and Staff

Gregg Orley, Partner
Larry Lax, Partner
Rob Orley, Partner
Todd Fink, Partner

Type of Firm

Private Equity Firm

Project Preferences

Type of Financing Preferred:
Leveraged Buyout
Turnaround
Management Buyouts
Acquisition
Special Situation
Recapitalizations

Geographical Preferences

United States Preferences:
Midwest
Illinois
Pennsylvania
Michigan
Iowa
Ohio
Wisconsin
Indiana
Kentucky
Minnesota

Canadian Preferences:
Ontario

Industry Preferences

In Medical/Health prefer:
Medical/Health

In Industrial/Energy prefer:
Environmental Related

In Financial Services prefer:
Financial Services
Real Estate

In Business Serv. prefer:
Services
Distribution

In Manufact. prefer:
Manufacturing

Additional Information

Year Founded: 2010
Current Activity Level : Actively seeking new investments

O3 CAPITAL ADVISORS PVT LTD

27, Magrath Road
o3 House
Bangalore, India 560025
Phone: 918042410000
Website: www.o3capital.com

Other Offices

Former: 5367 Grand Hyatt
Santa Cruz (East)
, India 400055
Phone: 912232626264

901, Piramal Towers
Peninsula Corporate Park
Mumbai, India 400 013
Phone: 912261115700

635 Madison Avenue
1th Floor
New York, NY USA 10022
Phone: 2128260303

Management and Staff

Adam Larkey, President
Amol Bhabal, Vice President
Deepesh Garg, Managing Director
Gaurav Khungar, Managing Director
Gautam Jaggi, Vice President
Gawir Baig, Vice President
Prashant Jain, Vice President
Shiraz Bugwadia, Managing Director
Shyam Shenthar, Chief Executive Officer
T.R. Srinivas, Co-Founder
Vishal Katkoria, Vice President

Type of Firm

Investment Management Firm

Project Preferences

Type of Financing Preferred:
Leveraged Buyout
Acquisition
Special Situation

Geographical Preferences

International Preferences:
India

Industry Preferences

In Medical/Health prefer:
Medical/Health

In Consumer Related prefer:
Retail
Food/Beverage
Consumer Products
Consumer Services
Education Related

Additional Information

Year Founded: 2007
Current Activity Level : Actively seeking new investments

OAK BRIDGE HOLDING, INC.

279 King Street West, Suite 201
Kitchener, Canada N2G 3X9
Phone: 519-745-4050

Type of Firm

Private Equity Firm

Project Preferences

Type of Financing Preferred:
Leveraged Buyout
Recapitalizations

Geographical Preferences

Canadian Preferences:
All Canada
Ontario

Industry Preferences

In Manufact. prefer:
Manufacturing

Additional Information

Year Founded: 2002
Current Activity Level : Actively seeking new investments

OAK CAPITAL CORP

8-10-24 Akasaka, Minato-ku
6FSumitomoFudosan Akasaka Bldg
Tokyo, Japan 107-0052
Phone: 81354127700
Fax: 81354128811
E-mail: irinfo2@oakcapital.jp
Website: www.oakcapital.jp

Type of Firm

Bank Affiliated

Project Preferences

Type of Financing Preferred:
Leveraged Buyout
Early Stage
Expansion
Generalist PE
Public Companies
Later Stage
Private Placement

Geographical Preferences

International Preferences:
Asia
Japan

Additional Information

Year Founded: 1918
Current Activity Level : Actively seeking new investments

OAK HC/FT PARTNERS LP

Three Pickwick Plaza, Suite 302
Greenwich, CT USA 06830

Management and Staff

Andrew Adams, General Partner
Anil Aggarwal, Venture Partner
Annie Lamont, Managing Partner
Chris Price, Venture Partner
David Black, Partner
Ezekiel Emanuel, Venture Partner
Jonathan Weiner, Venture Partner
Matthew Streisfeld, Principal
Michael Heller, Venture Partner
Michelle Daubar, Principal
Nancy Brown, Venture Partner
Patricia Kemp, General Partner

Type of Firm

Private Equity Firm

Project Preferences

Type of Financing Preferred:
Balanced

Geographical Preferences

United States Preferences:

Industry Preferences

In Medical/Health prefer:
Health Services

In Financial Services prefer:
Financial Services

Additional Information

Year Founded: 2014
Capital Under Management: $1,100,000,000
Current Activity Level : Actively seeking new investments

OAK HILL ADVISORS LP

1114 Avenue of the Americas
27th Floor
New York, NY USA 10036
Phone: 2123261500
E-mail: ir@oakhilladvisors.com
Website: www.oakhilladvisors.com

Other Offices

83 Pall Mall
6th Floor
London, United Kingdom SW1Y 5ES
Phone: 44-20-7968-3670

50 Bridge Street
Level 34, AMP Centre
Sydney, Australia 2000
Phone: 61280060478

201 Main Street, Suite 1250
Fort Worth, TX USA 76102
Phone: 817-338-8311

Management and Staff

Adam Kertzner, Partner
Alan Schrager, Partner
Alexandra Jung, Partner
Carl Wernicke, Managing Director
Christopher Cereghino, Managing Director
Dalia Cohen, Managing Director
Declan Tiernan, Managing Director
Doug Henderson, Partner
Eitan Arbeter, Principal
Eric Storch, Managing Director
Fritz Thomas, Managing Director
Goran Puljic, Managing Director
Jason Epstein, Principal
Jason Serrano, Managing Director
Jeffrey Kirt, Managing Director
Jennifer Schultz Cohen, Managing Director
Justin Tasso, Managing Director
Nadav Braun, Principal
Nicholas Mah, Principal
Richard Munn, Managing Director
Scott Snell, Principal
Steven Wayne, Managing Director
T.K. Narayan, Managing Director
Thomas Wong, Partner
William Bohnsack, President

Type of Firm

Investment Management Firm

Project Preferences

Type of Financing Preferred:
Leveraged Buyout
Turnaround
Distressed Debt

Geographical Preferences

United States Preferences:

Additional Information

Name of Most Recent Fund: OHA European Strategic Credit Fund, L.P.
Most Recent Fund Was Raised: 10/16/2011
Year Founded: 1991
Capital Under Management: $1,350,000,000
Current Activity Level : Actively seeking new investments

OAK HILL CAPITAL MANAGEMENT INC

263 Tresser Boulevard
15th Floor, One Stamford Plaza
Stamford, CT USA 06901
Phone: 2033281600
Website: www.oakhillcapital.com

Other Offices

2775 Sand Hill Road, Suite 220
Menlo Park, CA USA 94025
Phone: 6502340500

65 East 55th Street
32nd Floor
New York, NY USA 10022
Phone: 2125278400

Management and Staff

Benjamin Diesbach, Partner
Christopher Williams, Vice President
David Scott, Principal
Denis Nayden, Managing Partner
Douglas Kaden, Partner
Harry Eichelberger, Principal
J. Taylor Crandall, Managing Partner
John Rachwalski, Principal
Jonathan Friesel, Partner
Kevin Mailender, Principal
Lorie Coulombe, Vice President
Michael Green, Partner
Michael Warren, Principal
Robert Morse, Partner
Scott Kauffman, Principal
Scott Baker, Principal
Shawn Hessing, Chief Financial Officer
Steven Gruber, Managing Partner
Stratton Heath, Partner
Ted Dardani, Partner
Tyler Wolfram, Partner
William Pade, Partner

Type of Firm

Private Equity Firm

Project Preferences

Role in Financing:
Prefer role as deal originator but will also invest in deals created by others

Type of Financing Preferred:
Leveraged Buyout
Turnaround
Management Buyouts
Acquisition

Geographical Preferences

United States Preferences:

Industry Focus
(% based on actual investment)

Other Products	35.5%
Consumer Related	28.4%
Industrial/Energy	26.6%
Communications and Media	3.4%
Internet Specific	3.2%
Medical/Health	2.1%
Computer Software and Services	0.7%
Computer Hardware	0.2%

Additional Information
Name of Most Recent Fund: Oak Hill Capital Partners III, L.P.
Most Recent Fund Was Raised: 10/29/2007
Year Founded: 1992
Capital Under Management: $8,000,000,000
Current Activity Level : Actively seeking new investments
Method of Compensation: Return on invest. most important, but chg. closing fees, service fees, etc.

OAK INVESTMENT PARTNERS

Three Pickwick Plaza, Suite 302
Greenwich, CT USA 06830
Phone: 2032268346
Fax: 2038460282
Website: www.oakinv.com

Other Offices

525 University Avenue, Suite 1300
PALO ALTO, CA USA 94301
Phone: 650-614-3700
Fax: 650-328-6345

901 Main Avenue, Suite 600
NORWALK, CT USA 06851

Management and Staff
Allan Kwan, Venture Partner
Andrew Adams, General Partner
Annie Lamont, Managing Partner
Bandel Carano, Managing Partner
Brian Hinman, Venture Partner
Frederic Harman, Managing Partner
Gerald Gallagher, General Partner
H. Eugene Lockhart, Venture Partner
Iftikar Ahmed, General Partner
John Beletic, Venture Partner
Ranjan Chak, Venture Partner
Ren Riley, General Partner
Robert Majteles, Venture Partner
Roy Rodrigues, Venture Partner
Scot Jarvis, Venture Partner
Thomas Huseby, Venture Partner
Tony Downer, Venture Partner

Type of Firm
Private Equity Firm

Association Membership
National Venture Capital Association - USA (NVCA)

Project Preferences

Role in Financing:
Will function either as deal originator or investor in deals created by others

Type of Financing Preferred:
Early Stage
Balanced
Public Companies
Later Stage

Geographical Preferences

United States Preferences:
All U.S.

International Preferences:
United Kingdom
Western Europe
Israel
Asia
France

Industry Focus
(% based on actual investment)

Internet Specific	21.3%
Computer Software and Services	19.7%
Other Products	13.8%
Communications and Media	13.6%
Semiconductors/Other Elect.	10.7%
Medical/Health	7.1%
Computer Hardware	5.2%
Consumer Related	3.5%
Industrial/Energy	3.1%
Biotechnology	1.9%

Additional Information
Year Founded: 1978
Capital Under Management: $8,400,000,000
Current Activity Level : Actively seeking new investments
Method of Compensation: Return on investment is of primary concern, do not charge fees

OAKCREST CAPITAL PARTNERS LLC

600 13th Street NorthWest, Suite 790
Washington, DC USA 20005
Phone: 2023154250
Fax: 2023154251
Website: www.oakcrestcapital.com

Management and Staff
J. C. Watts, Founder
Miguel Lambert, Vice President

Type of Firm
Private Equity Firm

Project Preferences

Type of Financing Preferred:
Later Stage
Management Buyouts
Acquisition
Recapitalizations

Geographical Preferences

United States Preferences:
North America

Industry Preferences

In Medical/Health prefer:
Medical/Health

In Consumer Related prefer:
Consumer Products
Consumer Services

In Transportation prefer:
Transportation

In Business Serv. prefer:
Services
Media

In Manufact. prefer:
Manufacturing

Additional Information
Year Founded: 2006
Current Activity Level : Actively seeking new investments

OAKFIELD CAPITAL PARTNERS LLP

23-24 George Street
Greyhound House
Surrey, United Kingdom TW9 1HY
Phone: 442070847272
Fax: 442089488057
E-mail: info@oakfieldcapital.co.uk
Website: www.oakfieldcapital.co.uk

Management and Staff
David Pitman, Partner
Michael Patton, Co-Founder
Roy Merritt, Co-Founder
Timothy Woodcock, Co-Founder

Type of Firm
Private Equity Firm

Project Preferences

Type of Financing Preferred:
Early Stage
Acquisition

Geographical Preferences

International Preferences:
United Kingdom

Industry Preferences

In Communications prefer:
Telecommunications

In Consumer Related prefer:
Entertainment and Leisure

In Industrial/Energy prefer:
Industrial Products

In Business Serv. prefer:
Services
Media

Additional Information

Name of Most Recent Fund: Oakfield UK Special Situations Fund
Most Recent Fund Was Raised: 05/20/2013
Year Founded: 2008
Capital Under Management: $9,154,000
Current Activity Level : Actively seeking new investments

OAKHOUSE PARTNERS LLC

201 Mission Street
12th Floor
San Francisco, CA USA 94105
Phone: 4158511625
Website: oakhousepartners.com

Type of Firm

Private Equity Firm

Project Preferences

Type of Financing Preferred:
Balanced

Additional Information

Year Founded: 2016
Current Activity Level : Actively seeking new investments

OAKLAND ENERGY & WATER VENTURES

38955 Hills Tech Drive
Farmington Hills, MI USA 48331
Website: www.oaklandewv.com

Type of Firm

Private Equity Firm

Project Preferences

Type of Financing Preferred:
Early Stage
Expansion
Balanced
Startup

Industry Preferences

In Industrial/Energy prefer:
Alternative Energy
Energy Conservation Relat

Additional Information

Year Founded: 2013
Current Activity Level : Actively seeking new investments

OAKLAND STANDARD CO

300 Park Suite, Suite 380
Birmingham, MI USA 48009
Website: oaklandstandard.com

Type of Firm

Private Equity Firm

Project Preferences

Type of Financing Preferred:
Leveraged Buyout

Recapitalizations

Geographical Preferences

United States Preferences:

Canadian Preferences:
All Canada

Industry Preferences

In Industrial/Energy prefer:
Industrial Products

Additional Information

Year Founded: 2012
Current Activity Level : Actively seeking new investments

OAKLEY CAPITAL INVESTMENTS LTD

Eight Par-la-Ville Road
Third Floor
Hamilton, Bermuda HM08
Phone: 4415426330
Fax: 4415426724
Website: www.oakleycapitalinvestments.com

Type of Firm

Private Equity Firm

Project Preferences

Type of Financing Preferred:
Leveraged Buyout
Early Stage
Expansion
Mezzanine
Generalist PE
Balanced
Turnaround
Later Stage
Management Buyouts
Acquisition
Recapitalizations

Geographical Preferences

International Preferences:
United Kingdom
Europe

Additional Information

Name of Most Recent Fund: Oakley Capital Private Equity II-B, L.P.
Most Recent Fund Was Raised: 10/03/2013
Year Founded: 2007
Capital Under Management: $344,400,000
Current Activity Level : Actively seeking new investments

OAKLEY CAPITAL LTD

Three Cadogan Gate
London, United Kingdom SW1X 0AS
Phone: 4402077666900
E-mail: enquiries@oakleycapital.com
Website: www.oakleycapital.com

Management and Staff

Alexander Collins, Partner
Arthur Mornington, Partner
David Brickell, Managing Director
David Till, Co-Founder
Del Huse, Managing Director
Mark Joseph, Partner
Peter Dubens, Co-Founder
Ralf Schremper, Partner
Stewart Porter, Chief Operating Officer

Type of Firm

Investment Management Firm

Project Preferences

Type of Financing Preferred:
Leveraged Buyout
Mezzanine
Later Stage

Geographical Preferences

International Preferences:
United Kingdom
Western Europe

Industry Preferences

In Communications prefer:
Telecommunications

In Internet Specific prefer:
Ecommerce

In Consumer Related prefer:
Entertainment and Leisure
Consumer Products
Education Related

In Business Serv. prefer:
Services
Media

Additional Information

Year Founded: 2002
Current Activity Level : Actively seeking new investments

OAKSTONE VENTURE PARTNERS LLC

260 Sheridan Avenue, Suite 400
Palo Alto, CA USA 94306
Phone: 9259373307
Fax: 6504751401

Other Offices

100 Sopris Drive
P.O. Box 4358
Basalt, CO USA 81621
Phone: 970-927-8761
Fax: 775-259-0254

Management and Staff

Frank Robles, Founder
Peter Kaminski, Founder
Peter Hawkins, General Partner

Type of Firm

Private Equity Firm

Project Preferences

Type of Financing Preferred:
Balanced

Geographical Preferences

United States Preferences:
All U.S.

Additional Information

Year Founded: 1999
Current Activity Level : Actively seeking new investments

OAKTREE CAPITAL MANAGEMENT LP

333 South Grand Avenue, 28th Floor
Los Angeles, CA USA 90071
Phone: 2138306300
Fax: 2138306293
E-mail: contactus@oaktreecapital.com
Website: www.oaktreecapital.com

Other Offices

27 Knightsbridge
London, United Kingdom SW1X 7LY
Phone: 44-207-201-4600
Fax: 44-207-201-4601

Atago Green Hills, Mori Tower 37th Floor
2-5-1 Atago Minato-ku
Tokyo, Japan 105-6237
Phone: 813-5776-6760
Fax: 813-5776-6761

680 Washington Boulevard
Sixth Floor
Stamford, CT USA 06901
Phone: 203-363-3200
Fax: 203-363-3210

1301 Avenue of the Americas
34th Floor
New York, NY USA 10019
Phone: 212-284-1900
Fax: 212-284-1901

80 Raffles Place
#51-03 UOB Plaza 1
Singapore, Singapore 048624
Phone: 6563056550
Fax: 6563056551

Frankfurter Welle
An der Welle 3, Ninth Floor
Frankfurt, Germany 60322
Phone: 49692443393000
Fax: 49692443393199

11611 San Vicente Boulevard, Suite 710
Brentwood, CA USA 90049
Phone: 3104420542
Fax: 3104420540

No. 1 Jianguomenwai Avenue
China World Office 1,Suite 8, 14th Floor
Beijing, China 100020
Phone: 861065350208
Fax: 861065350209

Jan van Goyenkade 8
Amsterdam, Netherlands 1075 HP
Phone: 31205792128
Fax: 31205792129

26A, boulevard Royal
Seventh Floor
Luxembourg, Luxembourg L-2449
Phone: 3522663254700
Fax: 35226632599

44, rue de Lisbonne
Paris, France 75008
Phone: 331-4299-1515
Fax: 331-4299-1511

1 Connaught Road Central, Suite 2001, AIA Central
Central, Hong Kong
Phone: 852-3655-6800
Fax: 852-3655-6900

67-8 Yangiae I-dong, Seocho-gu
Sixth Floor Pangaea B/D
Seoul, South Korea 137-889
Phone: 82221918000
Fax: 82221918080

Management and Staff

Aaron Bendikson, Managing Director
Abraham Ofer, Managing Director
Adrian Lorimer, Vice President
Alan Adler, Managing Director
Alap Shah, Vice President
Alejandro Cano, Vice President
Alex De Borja, Vice President
Ambrose Fisher, Managing Director
Amy Rice, Vice President
Andrew Watts, Managing Director
Andrew Osler, Managing Director
Andrew Robinson, Vice President
Anthony Shackleton, Managing Director
Arnold Estanislao, Vice President
Art Galan, Managing Director
Atif Chaudhry, Vice President
Baptiste Vaissie, Vice President
Barry Broomberg, Vice President
Bill Casperson, Managing Director
Bill Santangelo, Managing Director
Bradford Forth, Managing Director
Brett McKeone, Vice President
Brian Seidman, Vice President
Brian Laibow, Managing Director
Brian Beck, Managing Director
Brian Grefsrud, Managing Director
Brook Hinchman, Vice President
Caleb Kramer, Managing Director
Carl Johan Kask, Vice President
Carolyn O Brien, Managing Director
Carolyn Fair-Tis, Vice President
Carrie Armenta, Vice President
Charlotte Liu, Vice President
Chip Cushman, Managing Director
Chris Vermette, Vice President
Chris Boehringer, Managing Director
Christina Lee, Vice President
Christopher Huisken, Managing Director
Colin Bekemeyer, Managing Director
Craig Borcherding, Vice President
Cynthia Rocco, Vice President
Dale Ruby, Managing Director
Dan Robinson, Managing Director
Dan Levine, Vice President
Daniel von Rothenburg, Managing Director
David Kirchheimer, Chief Financial Officer
David Brookman, Vice President
David DeMilt, Vice President

Pratt's Guide to Private Equity & Venture Capital Sources

David Park, Vice President
David Johnston, Vice President
David Orkin, Managing Director
David Rosenberg, Managing Director
David Yee, Managing Director
David Tanner, Managing Director
Debra Huber, Vice President
Derek Smith, Managing Director
Desmund Shirazi, Managing Director
Donna Barnes, Vice President
Ed Vazquez, Vice President
Edgar Lee, Managing Director
Emily Stephens, Managing Director
Eric Speicher, Vice President
Eric Livingstone, Managing Director
Eva Ly, Vice President
Eyal Malinger, Vice President
Felix Shabashevich, Vice President
Flynn Ravner, Vice President
Frances Nelson, Managing Director
Francoise Giacalone, Managing Director
Frank Carroll, Managing Director
Geoff Greulich, Managing Director
George Leiva, Managing Director
Gerlinde Thompson, Vice President
Guillaume Bayol, Vice President
Guy Clark, Vice President
Harry Smith, Vice President
Heiko Keppler, Vice President
Hermann Dambach, Managing Director
Hideya Takahashi, Vice President
Hillary Cookler, Vice President
Hiroshi Nakamura, Managing Director
Ian Schapiro, Managing Director
Iris Fein, Managing Director
James Turner, Managing Director
James Lee, Vice President
Jameson Weber, Vice President
Jane Yau, Vice President
Janet Wang, Managing Director
Janis Henneberg, Vice President
Jared Lazarus, Vice President
Jason Keller, Managing Director
Jay Daryanani, Vice President
Jean-Paul Nedelec, Managing Director
Jeff Arnold, Managing Director
Jeffrey Nordhaus, Managing Director
Jeffrey Joseph, Vice President
Jelmar De Jong, Managing Director
Jennifer Loew, Vice President
Jesse Clapham, Vice President
Jim Ford, Managing Director
Jim Van Steenkiste, Managing Director
Joe Fergus, Managing Director
John Edwards, Managing Director
John Brady, Managing Director
Jonas Mitzschke, Vice President
Jordon Kruse, Managing Director
Julio Herrera, Managing Director
Justin Guichard, Managing Director
Justin Bickle, Managing Director
Justin Tucker, Vice President
Karim Khairallah, Managing Director
Katherine Ho, Vice President
Keith Gollenberg, Managing Director

Kenneth Lee, Vice President
Kenneth Liang, Managing Director
Kentaro Takao, Vice President
Kevin Clayton, Principal
Kevin Burnett, Vice President
Kimberly Johnson, Vice President
Kiyohiko Tsukada, Managing Director
Laura Randolph, Vice President
Lawrence Keele, Principal
Lee Nemchek, Vice President
Lesley Chao, Vice President
Liam McGuinness, Vice President
Lisa Arakaki, Managing Director
Lowell Hill, Managing Director
Luan Bui, Vice President
Madelaine Jones, Managing Director
Maged Marcus, Vice President
Mark Chesler, Managing Director
Mark Jacobs, Managing Director
Martin Graham, Vice President
Mary Knobler, Managing Director
Mathieu Guillemin, Managing Director
Mati Adler, Vice President
Matthew Wilson, Managing Director
Mel Carlisle, Managing Director
Michael Phillips, Vice President
Michael Harmon, Managing Director
Mukya Porter, Vice President
Naeem Arastu, Vice President
Nael Khatoun, Managing Director
Naina Ghelani, Vice President
Narman Murtaza, Vice President
Neel Shah, Vice President
Nicolas Ducarre, Vice President
Nicole Adrien, Managing Director
Odette Rose, Vice President
Oren Peleg, Managing Director
Pablo Velez, Vice President
Pablo Acuna, Vice President
Paras Vira, Vice President
Paul Deitch, Managing Director
Paulina Yap Ho, Vice President
Pearlyn Chong, Managing Director
Pedro Urquidi, Managing Director
Perry Chan, Vice President
Peter DiMartino, Vice President
Peter Deschner, Vice President
Peter Raketic, Vice President
Philip Hofmann, Managing Director
Rachel Chao, Vice President
Raghav Khanna, Vice President
Raj Makam, Managing Director
Rajath Shourie, Managing Director
Ramzi Habibi, Vice President
Randi Becker, Vice President
Raymond Gong, Vice President
Regan Scott, Managing Director
Renee Kemp, Vice President
Rengasamy Velu, Vice President
Richa Gulati, Vice President
Richard Goldstein, Managing Director
Robert Sullivan, Vice President
Robert O Leary, Managing Director
Robert Dupree, Vice President
Robert Perelson, Managing Director

Robert Self, Vice President
Ronald Beck, Managing Director
Russ Romero, Vice President
Ryan Fowlkes, Vice President
Sam Rotondo, Managing Director
Samuele Cappelletti, Vice President
Sanjay Rathod, Vice President
Sava Savov, Vice President
Savan Shah, Vice President
Scott Joerger, Vice President
Scott Levy, Managing Director
Scott Beltz, Managing Director
Scott Graves, Managing Director
Sebastian Eiseler, Vice President
Shannon Ward, Managing Director
Shant Babikian, Vice President
Sheldon Stone, Principal
Shun Maki, Vice President
Sibil Lin, Vice President
Soichiro Tabu, Vice President
Stacie Nemetz, Vice President
Stacy Ripley, Vice President
Stefano Mazzoli, Vice President
Stephanie Chi, Vice President
Stephen Collins, Vice President
Steve Kaplan, Principal
Steve Choi, Managing Director
Steven Prado, Managing Director
Stuart Spangler, Managing Director
Suzette Ramirez-Carr, Managing Director
Taejo Kim, Vice President
Thomas Casarella, Vice President
Timothy Jensen, Managing Director
Todd Liker, Managing Director
Tom Jaggers, Vice President
Tom Beck, Managing Director
Tony Best, Vice President
Tony Harrington, Managing Director
Toshi Kuroda, Managing Director
Tracy Freeman, Vice President
Troy Campbell, Vice President
Ulysses Fowler, Vice President
Umang Bhavsar, Vice President
Victoria Park, Vice President
Vuk Nikcevic, Vice President
Wende Lee, Vice President
William Sacher, Managing Director
William Kerins, Managing Director
William Melanson, Vice President
Yen Li Chew, Vice President
Young In, Vice President
Yusef Kudsi, Vice President
Zenobia Walji, Vice President

Type of Firm
Investment Management Firm

Project Preferences

Role in Financing:
Will function either as deal originator or investor in deals created by others

Type of Financing Preferred:
Leveraged Buyout
Value-Add
Early Stage
Mezzanine
Generalist PE
Turnaround
Opportunistic
Other
Distressed Debt
Recapitalizations

Geographical Preferences

United States Preferences:

Canadian Preferences:
All Canada

International Preferences:
Europe
Asia
All International

Industry Focus

(% based on actual investment)

Other Products	60.2%
Consumer Related	11.9%
Industrial/Energy	11.8%
Semiconductors/Other Elect.	4.7%
Internet Specific	4.1%
Communications and Media	3.6%
Computer Software and Services	1.5%
Medical/Health	1.5%
Biotechnology	0.8%

Additional Information

Name of Most Recent Fund: Oaktree Principal Fund VI, L.P.
Most Recent Fund Was Raised: 03/25/2014
Year Founded: 1995
Capital Under Management: $40,281,000,000
Current Activity Level : Actively seeking new investments
Method of Compensation: Other

OAKWOOD MEDICAL INVESTORS

10411 Clayton Road, Suite 302
Saint Louis, MO USA 63131
Phone: 3149917979
Fax: 3149917914
E-mail: info@oakwoodmedical.com
Website: www.oakwoodmedical.com

Management and Staff

Daniel Burkhardt, Managing Director
Raul Perez, President

Type of Firm

Private Equity Firm

Project Preferences

Role in Financing:
Will function either as deal originator or investor in deals created by others

Type of Financing Preferred:
Balanced

Industry Preferences

In Biotechnology prefer:
Biotechnology

In Medical/Health prefer:
Medical Products
Health Services
Pharmaceuticals

Additional Information

Year Founded: 1997
Capital Under Management: $77,000,000
Current Activity Level : Actively seeking new investments
Method of Compensation: Return on investment is of primary concern, do not charge fees

---

OASIS CAPITAL GHANA LTD

No. 4A Charlotteville
OIC Road
East Legon, Ghana
Phone: 233302522624
Fax: 233302544011
E-mail: info@oasiscapitalghana.com
Website: oasiscapitalghana.com

Type of Firm

Private Equity Firm

Project Preferences

Type of Financing Preferred:
Balanced

Geographical Preferences

International Preferences:
Africa

Industry Preferences

In Medical/Health prefer:
Health Services

In Consumer Related prefer:
Food/Beverage
Education Related

In Financial Services prefer:
Financial Services

Additional Information

Year Founded: 2010
Capital Under Management: $37,000,000
Current Activity Level : Actively seeking new investments

OASIS CAPITAL PARTNERS LLC

1001 Avenue of the Americas
Fourth Floor
New York, NY USA 10001
Phone: 212-302-4525
Fax: 212-279-1804
Website: oasiscapital.net

Management and Staff

Cathy Ross, Managing Director
Joseph Lucchese, Managing Director
Wilford Adkins, Managing Director

Type of Firm

Bank Affiliated

Project Preferences

Role in Financing:
Prefer role as deal originator but will also invest in deals created by others

Type of Financing Preferred:
Leveraged Buyout
Expansion
Turnaround
Management Buyouts
Industry Rollups
Recapitalizations

Geographical Preferences

United States Preferences:
All U.S.

International Preferences:
Latin America

Additional Information

Year Founded: 1997
Current Activity Level : Actively seeking new investments
Method of Compensation: Return on invest. most important, but chg. closing fees, service fees, etc.

OBELYSK INC

Canada Trust Tower Brookfield, Suite 2300
Toronto, Canada M5J 2S1
Phone: 416361125
Fax: 4163616018
E-mail: info@obelysk.com
Website: www.obelysk.com

Type of Firm

Private Equity Firm

Additional Information

Year Founded: 2017
Current Activity Level : Actively seeking new investments

OBEROESTERREICHISCHE UNTERNEHMENSBETEILI-GUNGS GMBH

Bethlehemstrasse 3
Linz, Austria 4020
Phone: 43732777800
Fax: 4373277780040
E-mail: info@kgg-ubg.at
Website: www.kgg-ubg.at

Management and Staff
Friedrich Filzmoser, Chief Executive Officer
Konrad Remplbauer, Chief Executive Officer

Type of Firm
Private Equity Firm

Project Preferences

Type of Financing Preferred:
Early Stage
Later Stage
Seed
Startup

Size of Investments Considered:
Min Size of Investment Considered (000s): $26
Max Size of Investment Considered (000s): $10,492

Geographical Preferences

International Preferences:
Austria

Industry Preferences

In Medical/Health prefer:
Medical/Health

In Consumer Related prefer:
Consumer
Entertainment and Leisure
Other Restaurants
Hotels and Resorts

In Industrial/Energy prefer:
Industrial Products

In Manufact. prefer:
Manufacturing

Additional Information
Year Founded: 1996
Current Activity Level : Actively seeking new investments

OBVIOUS VENTURES MANAGEMENT LLC

220 Halleck Street, Suite 120
San Francisco, CA USA 94129
Website: www.obvious.com

Management and Staff
Andrew Beebe, Managing Director
Evan Williams, Co-Founder
James Joaquin, Co-Founder
Nan Li, Principal
Sami Inkinen, Venture Partner
Vishal Vasishth, Co-Founder

Type of Firm
Private Equity Firm

Project Preferences

Type of Financing Preferred:
Early Stage
Startup

Additional Information
Year Founded: 2014
Capital Under Management: $301,857,000
Current Activity Level : Actively seeking new investments

OC COVE FUND I LLC

5141 California Avenue
Irvine, CA USA 92617

Type of Firm
Private Equity Firm

Project Preferences

Type of Financing Preferred:
Seed

Geographical Preferences

United States Preferences:
California

Additional Information
Year Founded: 2015
Capital Under Management: $5,620,000
Current Activity Level : Actively seeking new investments

OCA VENTURES

351 West Hubbard Street, Suite 600
Chicago, IL USA 60654
Phone: 3123278400
Fax: 3125428952
Website: www.ocaventures.com

Management and Staff
David Zyer, General Partner
Ian Drury, General Partner
Imran Ahmad, Principal
James Dugan, Chief Executive Officer
John Dugan, Co-Founder
Peter Ianello, Co-Founder
Robert Saunders, General Partner
Tamim Majid, Vice President

Type of Firm
Private Equity Firm

Association Membership
National Venture Capital Association – USA (NVCA)
Illinois Venture Capital Association

Project Preferences

Role in Financing:
Prefer role as deal originator but will also invest in deals created by others

Type of Financing Preferred:
Early Stage
Balanced
Seed

Size of Investments Considered:
Min Size of Investment Considered (000s): $1,000
Max Size of Investment Considered (000s): $4,000

Geographical Preferences

United States Preferences:

Industry Preferences

In Medical/Health prefer:
Medical/Health

In Consumer Related prefer:
Education Related

In Financial Services prefer:
Financial Services

In Business Serv. prefer:
Services

Additional Information
Name of Most Recent Fund: OCA Ventures II
Most Recent Fund Was Raised: 09/30/2008
Year Founded: 1999
Capital Under Management: $90,000,000
Current Activity Level : Actively seeking new investments
Method of Compensation: Return on investment is of primary concern, do not charge fees

OCBC CAPITAL MANAGEMENT

65 Chulia Street
#23-02 OCBC Center
Singapore, Singapore 049513
Phone: 65-6530-1688
Fax: 65-6536-7485
E-mail: ocms@pacific.net.sg
Website: www.ocbc.com

Other Offices
No. 1155 Yuanshen Road
Pudong New District
Shanghai, China 200135
Phone: 862120831246
Fax: 862158300657

Management and Staff
David Conner, Chief Executive Officer
Wei Hong Ching, Chief Financial Officer

Type of Firm
Bank Affiliated

Association Membership
Singapore Venture Capital Association (SVCA)

Project Preferences

Type of Financing Preferred:
Leveraged Buyout
Expansion
Mezzanine
Balanced
Management Buyouts
Acquisition

Size of Investments Considered:
Min Size of Investment Considered (000s): $581
Max Size of Investment Considered (000s): $8,712

Geographical Preferences

International Preferences:
Indonesia
China
Asia
Singapore
Malaysia

Industry Preferences

In Medical/Health prefer:
Health Services

In Consumer Related prefer:
Consumer Products
Consumer Services

In Industrial/Energy prefer:
Machinery

In Manufact. prefer:
Manufacturing

In Agr/Forestr/Fish prefer:
Agribusiness

In Other prefer:
Environment Responsible

Additional Information
Year Founded: 1995
Current Activity Level: Actively seeking new investments

OCCIDENT GROUP AG

Bahnhofstrasse 10
Zug, Switzerland 6300
Phone: 41415113280
E-mail: Office@Occident.Group
Website: www.occident.group

Type of Firm
Investment Management Firm

Additional Information
Year Founded: 1993
Current Activity Level: Actively seeking new investments

OCEAN ACCELERATOR INC

3450 Madison Road
Cincinnati, OH USA 45209
Phone: 5133512345
Website: www.oceanaccelerator.com

Type of Firm
Incubator/Development Program

Project Preferences

Type of Financing Preferred:
Early Stage

Additional Information
Year Founded: 2014
Current Activity Level: Actively seeking new investments

OCEAN AVENUE CAPITAL PARTNERS LP

401 Wilshire Boulevard, Suite 230
Santa Monica, CA USA 90401
Phone: 4242380730
Fax: 4242380728
Website: www.oceanavenuecapital.com

Management and Staff
Duran Curis, Co-Founder
Jacques Youssefmir, Co-Founder
Jeff Ennis, Co-Founder
Peter Notz, Principal

Type of Firm
Private Equity Firm

Project Preferences

Type of Financing Preferred:
Turnaround
Acquisition
Recapitalizations

Geographical Preferences

United States Preferences:

Canadian Preferences:
All Canada

Additional Information
Name of Most Recent Fund: Ocean Avenue Fund II, L.P.
Most Recent Fund Was Raised: 03/27/2014
Year Founded: 2010
Capital Under Management: $354,500,000
Current Activity Level: Actively seeking new investments

OCEAN PARTICIPATIONS SAS

34 rue Leandre Merlet
La Roche-sur-Yon, France 85000
Phone: 33251475440
Fax: 33251475307

Management and Staff
Dominique Michel Ren Jacquinet, Chief Executive Officer

Type of Firm
Private Equity Firm

Project Preferences

Type of Financing Preferred:
Leveraged Buyout
Early Stage
Generalist PE
Later Stage
Acquisition

Geographical Preferences

International Preferences:
Europe
France

Additional Information
Year Founded: 1988
Capital Under Management: $8,600,000
Current Activity Level: Actively seeking new investments

OCEAN TOMO CAPITAL L L C

200 West Madison
37th Floor
Chicago, IL USA 60606
Phone: 312-327-4400
Fax: 312-327-4401
Website: www.oceantomo.com

Other Offices

126 Sea View Avenue
Palm Beach, FL USA 33480
Phone: 561-309-0011
Fax: 561-835-0003

19990 MacArthur Blvd, Suite 1150
Irvine, CA USA 92612
Phone: 888-295-7007
Fax: 949-222-1265

125 Summer Street
7th Floor
Boston, MA USA 02110
Phone: 617-345-3824
Fax: 617-812-3077

101 Montgomery Street, Suite 2100
San Francisco, CA USA 94104
Phone: 415-946-2600

4630 Montgomery Ave
3rd Floor
Bethesda, MD USA 20814

7475 Wisconsin Avenue, Suite 525
Bethesda, MD USA 20814
Phone: 240-482-8200

251 Kearny Street
8th Floor
San Francisco, CA USA 94108
Phone: 415-946-2600
Fax: 415-946-2601

19200 Von Karman Avenue, Suite 600
Irvine, CA USA 92612
Phone: 949-648-7340

340 Royal Poinciana Way, Suite 317
Palm Beach, FL USA 33480
Phone: 786-266-8989

Two Sound View Drive
Greenwich, CT USA 06830
Phone: 203-602-3901
Fax: 203-602-3902

Management and Staff
Andrew Carter, Managing Director

Type of Firm
Bank Affiliated

Project Preferences

Type of Financing Preferred:
Leveraged Buyout
Mezzanine

Additional Information
Year Founded: 2005
Current Activity Level : Actively seeking new investments

OCEANBRIDGE PARTNERS LLC

570 Lexington Avenue
42nd Floor
New York, NY USA 10022
Phone: 6465583170
Website: www.ocbrpartners.com

Other Offices
Three Matthew Parker Street
Number 38
London, United Kingdom SW1H 9NE
Phone: 646558138

Management and Staff
Martin Clarke, Founder
Michael Dugan, Founder
Nicholas Hewitt, Partner
Philippe Robert, Founder
Robert MacKenzie, Partner

Type of Firm
Investment Management Firm

Project Preferences

Type of Financing Preferred:
Leveraged Buyout
Expansion
Generalist PE
Later Stage
Acquisition
Distressed Debt
Recapitalizations

Geographical Preferences

United States Preferences:
New York

International Preferences:
United Kingdom

Additional Information
Year Founded: 2012
Current Activity Level : Actively seeking new investments

OCEANIA CAPITAL PARTNERS LTD

50 Pitt Street, Suite Three, Level Three
Sydney, Australia 2000
Phone: 61282432200
Fax: 61282432222
E-mail: info@oceaniacapital.com.au
Website: www.oceaniacapital.com.au

Type of Firm
Private Equity Firm

Project Preferences

Type of Financing Preferred:
Leveraged Buyout
Public Companies
Distressed Debt

Additional Information
Year Founded: 2004
Current Activity Level : Actively seeking new investments

OCEANIC PARTNERS INC

526 Northern Avenue
Mill Valley, CA USA 94941

Management and Staff
Max Morgunov, Vice President
Tim Sullivan, Chief Executive Officer

Type of Firm
Private Equity Firm

Project Preferences

Type of Financing Preferred:
Balanced

Additional Information
Year Founded: 2014
Current Activity Level : Actively seeking new investments

OCH-ZIFF CAPITAL MANAGEMENT GROUP LLC

Nine West 57th Street
39th Floor
New York, NY USA 10019
Phone: 2127900041
Website: www.ozcap.com

Other Offices
40 Argyll Street
London, United Kingdom W1F 7EB
Phone: 44-20-7758-4400

No 6 Jia Jianguomenwai Avenue
Chao Yang District, Rm 5, 35F, SK Tower
Beijing, China 100022
Phone: 861085679987

Bandra Kurla Complex, Bandra (E)
Unit 1079, Level 1, Trade Centre
Mumbai, India 400 051
Phone: 912240700443

Cheung Kong Center, Suite 2003A
2 Queens Road
Central, Hong Kong
Phone: 852-2297-2595

Management and Staff
Alesia Haas, Chief Financial Officer
Wayne Cohen, Chief Operating Officer

Type of Firm
Investment Management Firm

Project Preferences

Type of Financing Preferred:
Leveraged Buyout
Generalist PE
Opportunistic
Other
Acquisition
Special Situation
Distressed Debt

Geographical Preferences

United States Preferences:
North America

Industry Preferences

In Industrial/Energy prefer:
Energy

In Financial Services prefer:
Real Estate

Additional Information
Name of Most Recent Fund: Och-Ziff Energy Fund, L.P.
Most Recent Fund Was Raised: 01/04/2011
Year Founded: 1994
Capital Under Management: $22,300,000
Current Activity Level : Actively seeking new investments

OCP ASIA HONG KONG LTD

12-16 Des Voeux Road
34F,Gloucester Tw,The Landmark
Central, Hong Kong
Phone: 85222360557
Fax: 85222360600
Website: www.ocpasia.com

Other Offices
12-01/03 Shaw House
350, Orchard Road
Singapore, Singapore 238868
Phone: 6564039880
Fax: 656403 9878

Management and Staff
Stuart Wilson, Co-Founder
Teall Edds, Co-Founder

Type of Firm
Private Equity Firm

Project Preferences

Type of Financing Preferred:
Leveraged Buyout
Expansion
Generalist PE
Acquisition

Geographical Preferences

International Preferences:
Asia Pacific
Hong Kong
Singapore

Additional Information
Year Founded: 2004
Current Activity Level : Actively seeking new investments

OCROMA INVESTIMENTOS E GESTAO LTDA

Rua Ferreira de Araujo 221
Cj. 105
Sao Paulo, Brazil 05428000
Phone: 551135884800
Website: www.ocroma.com

Management and Staff
Leonardo Ribeiro, Partner
Ricardo Kanitz, Partner

Type of Firm
Private Equity Advisor or Fund of Funds

Project Preferences

Type of Financing Preferred:
Fund of Funds
Fund of Funds of Second

Geographical Preferences

International Preferences:
Latin America
Brazil

Additional Information
Year Founded: 2008
Current Activity Level : Actively seeking new investments

OCTALFA SAS

15 Chemin Du Saquin
Espace Europeen - Bat G
Ecully, France 69130
Phone: 33437498720
Fax: 33478333629
Website: initiative-octalfa.eu

Management and Staff
Gilles Alberici, President

Type of Firm
Private Equity Firm

Project Preferences

Type of Financing Preferred:
Early Stage
Seed

Geographical Preferences

International Preferences:
France

Industry Preferences

In Biotechnology prefer:
Biotech Related Research

In Medical/Health prefer:
Pharmaceuticals

Additional Information
Year Founded: 2006
Current Activity Level : Actively seeking new investments

OCTOPUS VENTURES LTD

20 Old Bailey
London, United Kingdom EC4M 7AN
Phone: 448003162349
E-mail: info@octopusventures.com
Website: www.octopusventures.com

Management and Staff
Alliott Cole, Principal
Eyal Rabinovich, Venture Partner
Frederic Lardieg, Principal
George Whitehead, Venture Partner
Luke Hakes, Principal
Stephen Morana, Venture Partner

Type of Firm
Private Equity Firm

Project Preferences

Type of Financing Preferred:
Early Stage
Expansion
Balanced
Public Companies
Later Stage

Size of Investments Considered:
Min Size of Investment Considered (000s): $411
Max Size of Investment Considered (000s): $8,217

Geographical Preferences

International Preferences:
United Kingdom
Europe

Industry Preferences

In Biotechnology prefer:
Biotechnology

In Medical/Health prefer:
Pharmaceuticals

Additional Information
Name of Most Recent Fund: Eclipse VCT
Most Recent Fund Was Raised: 12/31/2004
Year Founded: 2000
Capital Under Management: $61,900,000
Current Activity Level : Actively seeking new investments

OCV INVESTORS LLC

525 West Monroe Street, Suite 1600
Chicago, IL USA 60661
Phone: 3129025254

Type of Firm
Private Equity Firm

Project Preferences

Type of Financing Preferred:
Other

Additional Information

Year Founded: 2002
Capital Under Management: $4,000,000
Current Activity Level : Actively seeking new investments

ODDO BHF ASSET MANAGEMENT SAS

12 Boulevard de la Madeleine
Paris, France 75440
Phone: 33144518500
Fax: 33144518510
E-mail: information_oam@oddo.fr
Website: am.oddo-bhf.com

Type of Firm
Investment Management Firm

Association Membership
French Venture Capital Association (AFIC)

Project Preferences

Type of Financing Preferred:
Fund of Funds
Early Stage
Later Stage

Geographical Preferences

International Preferences:
Europe
Eastern Europe
France

Industry Preferences

In Computer Software prefer:
Software

In Internet Specific prefer:
E-Commerce Technology
Internet

In Medical/Health prefer:
Medical/Health

In Industrial/Energy prefer:
Energy
Alternative Energy
Environmental Related

In Business Serv. prefer:
Consulting Services

Additional Information
Year Founded: 1987
Current Activity Level: Actively seeking new investments

ODEON CAPITAL PARTNERS LP

747 Third Avenue
24th Floor, Suite A
New York, NY USA 10017
Phone: 2127851300
Fax: 2127853159
Website: www.odeoncapital.com

Management and Staff
Jeffrey Finkle, Managing Partner
Marc Aronstein, Partner
Matthew Smith, Managing Partner
Qayyum Hafeez, Principal

Type of Firm
Private Equity Firm

Project Preferences

Type of Financing Preferred:
Balanced
Other

Size of Investments Considered:
Min Size of Investment Considered (000s): $10,000
Max Size of Investment Considered (000s): $15,000

Geographical Preferences

United States Preferences:

Industry Focus
(% based on actual investment)
Internet Specific   55.6%
Computer Software and Services   40.7%
Other Products   3.7%

Additional Information
Year Founded: 1999
Capital Under Management: $115,000,000
Current Activity Level : Actively seeking new investments

ODERC AS

Stortingsgaten 22
Third Floor
Oslo, Norway 0124
Phone: 4723100650
Fax: 4723100651
E-mail: info@credopartners.no
Website: www.credopartners.no

Management and Staff
Christian Sorum, Partner
Ellen Hanetho, Partner

Type of Firm
Private Equity Firm

Association Membership
Norwegian Venture Capital Association

Project Preferences

Type of Financing Preferred:
Leveraged Buyout

Geographical Preferences

International Preferences:
Europe
Norway

Industry Preferences

In Biotechnology prefer:
Agricultural/Animal Bio.

In Consumer Related prefer:
Consumer

In Industrial/Energy prefer:
Industrial Products

In Agr/Forestr/Fish prefer:
Agriculture related

Additional Information
Year Founded: 1991
Current Activity Level : Actively seeking new investments

ODEWALD & COMPAGNIE FUER BETEILIGUNGEN GMBH

Franzoesische Strasse 8
Berlin, Germany 10117
Phone: 49302017230
Fax: 493020172360
E-mail: ocie@odewald.com
Website: www.odewald.com

Management and Staff
Andreas Fetting, Managing Director
Ernst-Moritz Lipp, Managing Director
Klaus Eierhoff, Managing Director
Torsten Krumm, Managing Director

Type of Firm
Private Equity Firm

Association Membership
German Venture Capital Association (BVK)

Project Preferences

Role in Financing:
Prefer role as deal originator

Type of Financing Preferred:
Leveraged Buyout
Later Stage
Management Buyouts

Size of Investments Considered:
Min Size of Investment Considered (000s): $7,061
Max Size of Investment Considered (000s): $127,101

Geographical Preferences

International Preferences:
Switzerland
Austria
Germany

Industry Preferences

In Medical/Health prefer:
Medical/Health

In Consumer Related prefer:
Food/Beverage

In Industrial/Energy prefer:
Energy
Machinery

In Business Serv. prefer:
Services

Additional Information

Year Founded: 1997
Capital Under Management: $1,392,800,000
Current Activity Level : Actively seeking new investments

ODIN EQUITY PARTNERS K/S

Avderodvej 27C
Vintappergarden
Kokkedal, Denmark 2980
Phone: 4548401200
Fax: 4548481213
E-mail: info@odinequity.dk
Website: www.odinequity.dk

Management and Staff

Bernd Petersen, Founder
Erik Boyter, Partner
Esben Bay Jorgensen, Founder
Jacob Bergenholtz, Partner
Jesper Wadum Nielsen, Partner
Soren Friis, Chief Financial Officer

Type of Firm

Private Equity Firm

Association Membership

Danish Venture Capital Association (DVCA)

Project Preferences

Type of Financing Preferred:
Leveraged Buyout
Turnaround
Acquisition

Geographical Preferences

International Preferences:
Denmark

Industry Preferences

In Medical/Health prefer:
Medical/Health

In Consumer Related prefer:
Consumer Products

In Industrial/Energy prefer:
Industrial Products
Advanced Materials

In Transportation prefer:
Transportation
Aerospace

In Business Serv. prefer:
Services

Additional Information

Year Founded: 2005
Current Activity Level : Actively seeking new investments

ODLANDER FREDRIKSON & CO AB

Strandvagen 5B
Stockholm, Sweden 114 51
Phone: 4684425850
Fax: 4684425879

Other Offices

18 Avenue D'Ouchy
Lausanne, Switzerland 1006
Phone: 41-21-614-3500
Fax: 41-21-601-5544

Management and Staff

Anki Forsberg, Partner
Bjorn Odlander, Founder
Carl-Johan Dalsgaard, Partner
Eugen Steiner, Partner
Jacob Gunterberg, Partner
Johan Christenson, Partner
Marten Steen, Partner
Peder Fredrikson, Partner
Per Samuelsson, Partner
Staffan Lindstrand, Partner

Type of Firm

Private Equity Firm

Association Membership

Swedish Venture Capital Association (SVCA)
European Private Equity and Venture Capital Assoc.

Project Preferences

Type of Financing Preferred:
Leveraged Buyout
Early Stage
Generalist PE
Balanced
Later Stage
Acquisition

Geographical Preferences

United States Preferences:
All U.S.

International Preferences:
Europe
Eastern Europe

Industry Preferences

In Biotechnology prefer:
Biotechnology

In Medical/Health prefer:
Medical/Health
Medical Diagnostics
Medical Therapeutics
Medical Products
Pharmaceuticals

Additional Information

Name of Most Recent Fund: HealthCap VI, L.P.
Most Recent Fund Was Raised: 04/04/2012
Year Founded: 1996
Capital Under Management: $1,121,800,000
Current Activity Level : Actively seeking new investments

ODYSSEE VENTURE SAS

26 Rue de Berri
Paris, France 75008
Phone: 33171181150
Fax: 33171181160
E-mail: entrepreneurs@odysseeventure.com
Website: www.odyssee-venture.com

Management and Staff

Anne Tilly, Partner

Type of Firm

Private Equity Firm

Association Membership

French Venture Capital Association (AFIC)

Project Preferences

Type of Financing Preferred:
Fund of Funds
Leveraged Buyout
Early Stage
Mezzanine
Generalist PE
Turnaround
Later Stage
Startup

Size of Investments Considered:
Min Size of Investment Considered (000s): $696
Max Size of Investment Considered (000s): $9,753

Geographical Preferences

International Preferences:
Europe
France

Industry Preferences

In Computer Software prefer:
Software

In Biotechnology prefer:
Biotechnology

In Medical/Health prefer:
Medical/Health

Additional Information

Year Founded: 1999
Capital Under Management: $134,100,000
Current Activity Level : Actively seeking new investments

ODYSSEY INVESTMENT PARTNERS LLC

280 Park Avenue
38th Floor, West Tower
New York, NY USA 10017
Phone: 2123517900
Fax: 2123517925
E-mail: info@odysseyinvestment.com
Website: www.odysseyinvestment.com

Other Offices

21650 Oxnard Street, Suite 1650
Woodland Hills, CA USA 91367
Phone: 8187371111
Fax: 8187371101

Management and Staff

Brian Zaumeyer, Principal
Dennis Moore, Principal
Jason Cowett, Vice President
Jonathan Place, Vice President
Micah Levin, Vice President
Peter Cureton, Principal
Robert Aikman, Principal
Ross Rodrigues, Principal
Thomas Zanios, Vice President
William Bishop, Vice President

Type of Firm

Private Equity Firm

Project Preferences

Type of Financing Preferred:
Leveraged Buyout
Expansion
Acquisition
Recapitalizations

Geographical Preferences

United States Preferences:
All U.S.

Industry Focus
(% based on actual investment)

Consumer Related	30.1%
Industrial/Energy	25.0%
Other Products	21.2%
Semiconductors/Other Elect.	7.5%
Medical/Health	7.4%
Internet Specific	7.3%
Communications and Media	1.4%
Computer Software and Services	0.1%
Biotechnology	0.0%

Additional Information

Year Founded: 1982
Capital Under Management: $2,000,000,000
Current Activity Level : Actively seeking new investments

ODYSSEY VENTURE PARTNERS SINGLE MEMBER PRIVATE COMPANY

60, Kifissias Avenue
Maroussi
Athens, Greece 15125
Phone: 302112103086
E-mail: info@odysseyvp.com
Website: odysseyvp.com

Type of Firm

Private Equity Firm

Project Preferences

Type of Financing Preferred:
Early Stage
Seed
Startup

Geographical Preferences

International Preferences:
Greece
Europe

Industry Preferences

In Communications prefer:
Communications and Media

Additional Information

Year Founded: 2013
Current Activity Level : Actively seeking new investments

OESTJYSK INNOVATION A/S

Aabogade 15
Aarhus, Denmark 8200
Phone: 45 4676 0850
E-mail: http://www.capnova.dk
Website: www.oei.dk

Type of Firm

Incubator/Development Program

Project Preferences

Type of Financing Preferred:
Seed

Size of Investments Considered:
Min Size of Investment Considered (000s): $34
Max Size of Investment Considered (000s): $126

Geographical Preferences

International Preferences:
Denmark

Industry Preferences

In Semiconductor/Electr prefer:
Electronics

In Biotechnology prefer:
Biotechnology

In Medical/Health prefer:
Medical/Health

In Consumer Related prefer:
Food/Beverage

In Industrial/Energy prefer:
Materials

In Agr/Forestr/Fish prefer:
Agriculture related

In Other prefer:
Environment Responsible

Additional Information

Year Founded: 1998
Capital Under Management: $4,300,000
Current Activity Level : Actively seeking new investments
Method of Compensation: Return on invest. most important, but chg. closing fees, service fees, etc.

OFER HI TECH LTD

40 Einstein St., Ramat Aviv
Ramat Aviv Towers, Sixth Floor
Tel Aviv, Israel 69102
Phone: 97237456000
Fax: 97237604355
Website: www.oferhitech.com

Management and Staff

Shay Dubi, Vice President
Shelly Aharonovitch, Founder
Yoav Doppelt, Chief Executive Officer
Yoav Sebba, Vice President

Type of Firm

Private Equity Firm

Association Membership

Israel Venture Association

Project Preferences

Type of Financing Preferred:
Early Stage
Expansion
Balanced
Later Stage
Seed
Startup

Geographical Preferences

International Preferences:
No Preference
Israel

Industry Preferences

In Communications prefer:
Commercial Communications

In Computer Software prefer:
Software

In Biotechnology prefer:
Bictechnology

In Medical/Health prefer:
Medical Products

Additional Information

Year Founded: 1997
Current Activity Level : Actively seeking new investments

OFFICE OF SMALL AND MEDIUM ENTERPRISES PROMOTION

21 Viphavadi-Rungsit Rd
G, 15, 17-20, 23 Flr, TST Twr.
Bangkok, Thailand 10900
Phone: 66022788800
Fax: 66022738850
E-mail: info@sme.go.th
Website: www.sme.go.th

Type of Firm
Government Affiliated Program

Association Membership
Thai Venture Capital Association

Project Preferences

Type of Financing Preferred:
Balanced

Geographical Preferences

International Preferences:
Asia Pacific
Thailand

Industry Preferences

In Communications prefer:
Media and Entertainment

In Consumer Related prefer:
Food/Beverage
Hotels and Resorts

In Industrial/Energy prefer:
Energy
Machinery

Additional Information

Year Founded: 2008
Current Activity Level : Actively seeking new investments

OGDON VENTURES

28311 Shadow Mountain Drive
Conifer, CO USA 80433
Website: www.ogdonventures.com

Type of Firm
Private Equity Firm

Project Preferences

Type of Financing Preferred:
Leveraged Buyout

Industry Preferences

In Business Serv. prefer:
Services
Distribution

In Manufact. prefer:
Manufacturing

Additional Information

Year Founded: 2017
Current Activity Level : Actively seeking new investments

OGI VENTURE CAPITAL CO LTD

1-Chome, 3-24 Ebie
Fukushima
Osaka, Japan 532-0003
Phone: 81661318025
Fax: 81661318026
Website: www.ogi-capital.com

Management and Staff
Shigeo Miyazato, President

Type of Firm
Private Equity Firm

Association Membership
Japan Venture Capital Association

Project Preferences

Type of Financing Preferred:
Balanced

Geographical Preferences

International Preferences:
Japan

Additional Information

Year Founded: 1999
Current Activity Level : Actively seeking new investments

OHIO INNOVATION FUND

1120 Chester Avenue, Suite 418
Cleveland, OH USA 44114
Phone: 2165332351
Fax: 3306593270
Website: www.oifventures.com

Management and Staff
Jeff Hanson, Partner
Timothy Biro, Managing Partner

Type of Firm
Private Equity Firm

Project Preferences

Role in Financing:
Prefer role as deal originator but will also invest in deals created by others

Type of Financing Preferred:
Early Stage

Size of Investments Considered:
Min Size of Investment Considered (000s): $250
Max Size of Investment Considered (000s): $1,000

Geographical Preferences

United States Preferences:
Midwest

Industry Preferences

In Communications prefer:
Telecommunications

In Computer Software prefer:
Software
Systems Software
Applications Software

In Internet Specific prefer:
E-Commerce Technology

In Semiconductor/Electr prefer:
Semiconductor
Micro-Processing
Sensors
Analytic/Scientific

In Biotechnology prefer:
Human Biotechnology

In Medical/Health prefer:
Medical Diagnostics
Medical Therapeutics
Pharmaceuticals

Additional Information
Year Founded: 1997
Capital Under Management: $12,600,000
Current Activity Level : Actively seeking new investments
Method of Compensation: Return on investment is of primary concern, do not charge fees

OHIO TECH ANGELS

1275 Kinnear Road
Columbus, OH USA 43212
Phone: 6144873700
Website: www.ohiotechangels.com

Type of Firm
Angel Group

Association Membership
National Venture Capital Association - USA (NVCA)

Project Preferences

Type of Financing Preferred:
Early Stage
Seed
Startup

Geographical Preferences

United States Preferences:
Ohio

Industry Preferences

In Medical/Health prefer:
Medical/Health

In Industrial/Energy prefer:
Advanced Materials

Additional Information
Current Activity Level : Actively seeking new investments

OITA VENTURE CAPITAL CO LTD

No. 9 2-chome, Chuo-cho
Major Building 2F, Suite 24
Oita, Japan
Phone: 81-97-536-7525
Fax: 81-97-536-7532
E-mail: infomail@oita-vc.co.jp
Website: www.oita-vc.co.jp

Type of Firm
Bank Affiliated

Project Preferences

Type of Financing Preferred:
Early Stage
Expansion
Balanced
Later Stage

Geographical Preferences

International Preferences:
Japan

Industry Preferences

In Industrial/Energy prefer:
Energy
Alternative Energy
Energy Conservation Relat

In Financial Services prefer:
Financial Services

Additional Information
Year Founded: 1997
Capital Under Management: $650,900,000
Current Activity Level : Actively seeking new investments

OJAS VENTURE PARTNERS

Peripheral Road, Koramangala
No. 772, Third Floor, 8oft
Bangalore, India 560 034
Phone: 918040610300
Fax: 918041425476
E-mail: pingus@ojasventures.com
Website: www.ojasventures.com

Management and Staff
Gautam Balijepalli, Partner
Pavan Krishnamurthy, Partner
Raghu Batta, Partner
Rajesh Srivathsa, Managing Partner

Type of Firm
Private Equity Firm

Association Membership
Indian Venture Capital Association (IVCA)

Project Preferences

Type of Financing Preferred:
Early Stage
Seed

Size of Investments Considered:
Min Size of Investment Considered (000s): $750
Max Size of Investment Considered (000s): $3,000

Geographical Preferences

International Preferences:
India

Industry Preferences

In Communications prefer:
Telecommunications
Wireless Communications

Additional Information
Year Founded: 2007
Capital Under Management: $35,000,000
Current Activity Level : Actively seeking new investments

OKAPI VENTURE CAPITAL LLC

1590 South Coast Highway, Suite Ten
Laguna Beach, CA USA 92651
Phone: 9497155555
Fax: 9497155556

Management and Staff
B. Marc Averitt, Co-Founder
Sharon Stevenson, Co-Founder

Type of Firm
Private Equity Firm

Association Membership
National Venture Capital Association - USA (NVCA)

Project Preferences

Role in Financing:
Prefer role as deal originator

Type of Financing Preferred:
Early Stage
Seed

Size of Investments Considered:
Min Size of Investment Considered (000s): $500
Max Size of Investment Considered (000s): $2,000

Geographical Preferences

United States Preferences:
California

Industry Preferences

In Computer Software prefer:
Software

In Internet Specific prefer:
Internet

In Semiconductor/Electr prefer:
Semiconductor

In Biotechnology prefer:
Biotechnology

In Medical/Health prefer:
Medical Diagnostics
Health Services

Additional Information
Name of Most Recent Fund: Okapi Ventures II, L.P.
Most Recent Fund Was Raised: 03/09/2012
Year Founded: 2005
Capital Under Management: $46,500,000
Current Activity Level : Actively seeking new investments
Method of Compensation: Return on investment is of primary concern, do not charge fees

OKASAN VENTURE CAPITAL CO LTD

9-9 Koamicho
Nihonbashi,Chuo-ku
Tokyo, Japan 103-0016
Phone: 81-3-3665-1011

Management and Staff
Yoshida Takashi, President

Type of Firm
Bank Affiliated

Additional Information
Year Founded: 1983
Current Activity Level : Actively seeking new investments

OKINAWA HUMAN CAPITAL INC

503 1831-1 Koroku
Okinawa Industry Support Ctr.
Naha, Japan 901-0152
Phone: 81988518517
Fax: 81988518518
Website: www.okinawa-hc.com

Management and Staff
Wako Kaneshiro, President

Type of Firm
Private Equity Firm

Project Preferences

Type of Financing Preferred:
Balanced

Geographical Preferences

International Preferences:
Japan

Additional Information
Year Founded: 2006
Current Activity Level : Actively seeking new investments

OKLAHOMA EQUITY PARTNERS LLC

301 Northwest 63rd Street, Suite 500
Oklahoma City, OK USA 73116
Phone: 4058489456
Website: www.oepvc.com

Management and Staff
David Humphrey, Chief Operating Officer

Type of Firm
Private Equity Firm

Project Preferences

Type of Financing Preferred:
Balanced
Acquisition

Geographical Preferences

United States Preferences:
All U.S.

Additional Information
Year Founded: 2006
Current Activity Level : Actively seeking new investments

OKLAHOMA LIFE SCIENCE FUND LLC

100 West Fifth Street
Tulsa, OK USA 74103
Phone: 9185840440
Website: www.olsfventures.com

Type of Firm
Private Equity Firm

Project Preferences

Type of Financing Preferred:
Early Stage

Geographical Preferences

United States Preferences:
Oklahoma

Additional Information
Name of Most Recent Fund: Oklahoma Life Science Fund II LLC
Most Recent Fund Was Raised: 04/27/2007
Year Founded: 2000
Current Activity Level : Actively seeking new investments

OLD MUTUAL PLC

Two Lambeth Hill
Fifth Floor, Old Mutual Place
London, United Kingdom EC4V 4GG
Phone: 442070027000
Fax: 442070027200
E-mail: contact@oldmutual.com
Website: www.oldmutualplc.com

Other Offices
Old Mutual Square, Grayston Drive
Sandton
Johannesburg, South Africa 2196

Jan Smuts Drive
Pinelands
Cape Town, South Africa 7405

Management and Staff
Jonathan Hemphill, Chief Executive Officer
Tim Tookey, Chief Financial Officer

Type of Firm
Bank Affiliated

Association Membership
South African Venture Capital Association (SAVCA)

Project Preferences

Type of Financing Preferred:
Generalist PE
Balanced

Geographical Preferences

International Preferences:
Europe
South Africa

Industry Preferences

In Medical/Health prefer:
Medical/Health

In Industrial/Energy prefer:
Energy
Oil and Gas Exploration
Oil & Gas Drilling,Explor
Industrial Products
Environmental Related

In Manufact. prefer:
Manufacturing

Additional Information
Year Founded: 1998
Current Activity Level : Actively seeking new investments

OLIMPIA PARTNERS GESTAO DE RECURSOS SA

Rua Joaquim Floriano, 960
Sixth floor, Itaim Bibi
Sao Paulo, Brazil 04534-004
Phone: 551135081100
Fax: 551135081115
E-mail: info@olimpiapartners.com.br
Website: www.olimpiapartners.com.br

Management and Staff
Richard Rainer, Founder

Type of Firm
Investment Management Firm

Project Preferences

Type of Financing Preferred:
Leveraged Buyout
Acquisition

Geographical Preferences

International Preferences:
Brazil

Industry Preferences

In Medical/Health prefer:
Medical/Health
Health Services

In Consumer Related prefer:
Consumer
Retail
Consumer Products

In Business Serv. prefer:
Services

Additional Information
Year Founded: 2011
Current Activity Level : Actively seeking new investments

OLMA CAPITAL MANAGEMENT LTD

7 Seville Place
Dublin, Ireland
Phone: 442074845462
E-mail: info@olmafund.com

Management and Staff
George Guthrie, Partner
Jeremy Barnes, Managing Partner
Ludovic Maulucci, Partner
Nicolas Salmon, Partner
Peter Bennett, Partner
Philippe Der Megreditchian, Managing Partner
Stephane Petrossian, Partner

Type of Firm
Private Equity Firm

Additional Information
Year Founded: 2012
Current Activity Level : Actively seeking new investments

OLYMPIC VALLEY CAPITAL LLC

100 Pine Street, Suite 1250
San Francisco, CA USA 94111
Phone: 4157637402
Fax: 5103730165
E-mail: contact@olympicvalleycapital.com
Website: olympicvalleycapital.com

Type of Firm
Private Equity Firm

Project Preferences

Type of Financing Preferred:
Leveraged Buyout
Management Buyouts
Acquisition
Recapitalizations

Industry Preferences

In Medical/Health prefer:
Medical/Health

In Consumer Related prefer:
Consumer Products

In Industrial/Energy prefer:
Materials

In Transportation prefer:
Aerospace

In Business Serv. prefer:
Services
Distribution

In Manufact. prefer:
Manufacturing

Additional Information
Year Founded: 2013
Current Activity Level : Actively seeking new investments

OLYMPUS CAPITAL HOLDINGS ASIA HONG KONG LTD

One Exchange Square, Suite 3406
Central, Hong Kong
Phone: 85221400500
Fax: 85221400555
E-mail: info@olympuscap.com
Website: www.olympuscap.com

Other Offices
South City - I
4th Floor, Tower B, Signature Towers
New Delhi, India 122 002
Phone: 91-124-451-7000
Fax: 91-124-451-7015

17/F The Tokyo Ginko Kyokai Building
1-3-1 Marunouchi, Chiyoda-ku
Tokyo, Japan 100-0005
Phone: 813-5288-6721
Fax: 813-5288-6722

12 Yeoido-Dong, Youngdungpo-Ku
Nineth Floor CCMM Building
Seoul, South Korea 150-869
Phone: 8227865060
Fax: 8227865655

485 Madison Avenue
18th Floor
New York, NY USA 10022
Phone: 212-201-8533
Fax: 212-201-8532

No. One Hongqiao Road Xuhui District, Suite 4108
Grand Gateway
Shanghai, China 200030
Phone: 86-21-6447-0066
Fax: 86-21-6447-6299

Management and Staff
Alex Lui, Managing Director
Daniel Mintz, Co-Founder
David Shen, Managing Director
Edan Lee, Managing Director
Etsuko Matsuoka, Vice President
Frederick Long, Co-Founder
Gaurav Malik, Managing Director
Lawrence Miao, Co-Founder
Pankaj Ghai, Vice President
Peter Cimmet, Managing Director
Rahul Mukim, Vice President
Stephen Dai, Vice President
Takayuki Nakazato, Vice President
Timothy Koo, Vice President

Type of Firm
Private Equity Firm

Association Membership
Indian Venture Capital Association (IVCA)

Project Preferences

Type of Financing Preferred:
Early Stage
Expansion
Balanced
Later Stage
Seed
Startup

Geographical Preferences

United States Preferences:
Southeast

Pratt's Guide to Private Equity & Venture Capital Sources

International Preferences:
Vietnam
Indonesia
India
Hong Kong
China
Thailand
Philippines
Australia
Asia
Singapore
Korea, South
Japan
Malaysia

Industry Preferences

In Industrial/Energy prefer:
Alternative Energy
Energy Conservation Relat
Environmental Related

In Financial Services prefer:
Financial Services

In Business Serv. prefer:
Services

In Agr/Forestr/Fish prefer:
Agribusiness

In Other prefer:
Environment Responsible

Additional Information

Year Founded: 1997
Capital Under Management: $500,000,000
Current Activity Level : Actively seeking new investments

OLYMPUS PARTNERS

Metro Center
One Station Place
Stamford, CT USA 06902
Phone: 2033535900
Fax: 2033535910
Website: www.olympuspartners.com

Management and Staff

Chase Ormond, Vice President
David Haddad, Principal
Evan Eason, Partner
James Conroy, Partner
Jason Miller, Principal
L. David Cardenas, Partner
Louis Mischianti, Managing Partner
Manu Bettegowda, Partner
Michael Horgan, Partner
Paul Rubin, Partner
Peter Tedesco, Vice President
Robert Morris, Managing Partner

Type of Firm

Private Equity Firm

Project Preferences

Role in Financing:
Prefer role as deal originator but will also invest in deals created by others

Type of Financing Preferred:
Leveraged Buyout
Expansion
Generalist PE
Later Stage
Management Buyouts
Acquisition

Size of Investments Considered:
Min Size of Investment Considered (000s): $20,000
Max Size of Investment Considered (000s): $300,000

Industry Focus

(% based on actual investment)
Other Products	42.6%
Consumer Related	26.7%
Medical/Health	10.5%
Industrial/Energy	6.5%
Communications and Media	5.1%
Internet Specific	4.3%
Computer Software and Services	2.1%
Semiconductors/Other Elect.	1.7%
Computer Hardware	0.6%

Additional Information

Name of Most Recent Fund: Olympus Growth Fund VI, L.P.
Most Recent Fund Was Raised: 05/14/2013
Year Founded: 1988
Capital Under Management: $3,000,000,000
Current Activity Level : Actively seeking new investments

OMAN INDIA JOINT INVESTMENT FUND

Senapati Bapat Marg
One Indiabulls Centre Tower 2A
Mumbai, India 400 013
Phone: 912224210760
E-mail: contact@oijif.com
Website: www.oijif.com

Type of Firm

Private Equity Firm

Project Preferences

Type of Financing Preferred:
Leveraged Buyout
Acquisition

Geographical Preferences

International Preferences:
India

Additional Information

Year Founded: 2011
Capital Under Management: $320,000,000
Current Activity Level : Actively seeking new investments

OMBU LTD

79 Knightsbridge
London, United Kingdom SW1X 7RB
Phone: 442077520865
E-mail: ombu@ombugroup.com
Website: www.ombugroup.com

Management and Staff

Jonathan Fish, Chief Operating Officer

Type of Firm

Private Equity Firm

Project Preferences

Type of Financing Preferred:
Leveraged Buyout
Early Stage
Expansion
Balanced
Acquisition

Geographical Preferences

International Preferences:
United Kingdom
Europe

Industry Preferences

In Industrial/Energy prefer:
Energy
Industrial Products
Environmental Related

Additional Information

Year Founded: 2011
Current Activity Level : Actively seeking new investments

OMEGA CAPITAL MANAGEMENT LLC

4124 South Rockford Avenue, Suite 201
Tulsa, OK USA 74105
Phone: 9182933925
Fax: 9182933926
Website: www.omegacapital.com

Management and Staff

Jason Martin, President, Founder

Type of Firm

Private Equity Firm

Project Preferences

Type of Financing Preferred:
Leveraged Buyout
Management Buyouts
Acquisition
Recapitalizations

Geographical Preferences

United States Preferences:
Oklahoma

Industry Preferences

In Medical/Health prefer:
Medical/Health

In Consumer Related prefer:
Food/Beverage

In Industrial/Energy prefer:
Energy
Industrial Products
Machinery

In Transportation prefer:
Aerospace

Additional Information

Year Founded: 2013
Capital Under Management: $30,000,000
Current Activity Level : Actively seeking new investments

OMEGA FUND MANAGEMENT LLC

185 Dartmouth Street, Suite 502
Boston, MA USA 02116
E-mail: info@omegafunds.net
Website: www.omegafunds.net

Management and Staff

Anne-Mari Paster, Chief Financial Officer
Otello Stampacchia, Partner
Richard Lim, Partner
Vincent Ossipow, Venture Partner

Type of Firm

Private Equity Firm

Association Membership

European Private Equity and Venture Capital Assoc.

Project Preferences

Type of Financing Preferred:
Leveraged Buyout
Generalist PE
Later Stage

Geographical Preferences

United States Preferences:
All U.S.

International Preferences:
Europe

Industry Preferences

In Biotechnology prefer:
Biotechnology
Human Biotechnology

In Medical/Health prefer:
Medical/Health
Medical Diagnostics
Diagnostic Services
Medical Therapeutics
Medical Products
Health Services

Additional Information

Year Founded: 2004
Capital Under Management: $481,875,000
Current Activity Level : Actively seeking new investments

OMERS INFRASTRUCTURE

200 Bay Street
Royal Bank Plaza, South Tower
Toronto, Canada M5J 2J2
Phone: 4163611011
E-mail: info@borealisinfrastructure.com
Website: www.borealisinfrastructure.com

Other Offices

Ernst & Young Tower
440 - 2nd Avenue South West, Suite 700
Calgary, Canada T2P 5E9
Phone: 403-206-6529

Management and Staff

Bruce Crane, Vice President
Darren Soanes, Vice President
Jim Woods, Vice President
John Guccione, Vice President
Mark Murphy, Vice President
Mary-Jo Hewat, Vice President
Michael Holland, Vice President
Paul Manias, Vice President
Peter-Paul Bloemen, Vice President
Philippe Busslinger, Vice President
Reena Sagoo, Chief Financial Officer
Robert Deutschmann, Vice President
Ryan Doersam, Vice President
Tenio Evangelista, Vice President

Type of Firm

Private Equity Firm

Project Preferences

Type of Financing Preferred:
Leveraged Buyout

Geographical Preferences

United States Preferences:
All U.S.

Canadian Preferences:
All Canada

Industry Preferences

In Industrial/Energy prefer:
Energy

Additional Information

Year Founded: 2003
Current Activity Level : Actively seeking new investments

OMERS PRIVATE EQUITY INC

200 Bay St., Royal Bank Plaza
South Tower, Suite 2010
Toronto, Canada M5J 2J2
Phone: 4168643200
Fax: 4168643255
E-mail: contactus@omerspe.com
Website: www.omerspe.com

Other Offices

6 New Street Square
New Fetter Lane
London, United Kingdom EC4A 3BF
Phone: 442078228300
Fax: 442078228325

320 Park Avenue
17th Floor
New York, NY USA 10022
Phone: 2129867500
Fax: 2129867510

Management and Staff

Chantal Thibault, Managing Director
Eric Haley, Managing Director
Jim Orlando, Managing Director
Mark Dolfato, Managing Director
Mark Redman, Senior Managing Director
Martin Day, Managing Director
Martin Le Huray, Managing Director
Michael Lank, Senior Managing Director
Michael Graham, Senior Managing Director
Phil Mauchel, Senior Managing Director
Robert Hedges, Chief Financial Officer
Tim Patterson, Senior Managing Director

Type of Firm

Private Equity Firm

Association Membership

Canadian Venture Capital Association
European Private Equity and Venture Capital Assoc.

Project Preferences

Role in Financing:
Will function either as deal originator or investor in deals created by others

Type of Financing Preferred:
Leveraged Buyout
Mezzanine
Later Stage
Management Buyouts

Pratt's Guide to Private Equity & Venture Capital Sources

Geographical Preferences

United States Preferences:
North America

Canadian Preferences:
All Canada

International Preferences:
All International

Industry Preferences

In Communications prefer:
Communications and Media
Wireless Communications

In Computer Software prefer:
Software

In Consumer Related prefer:
Retail
Food/Beverage
Consumer Products
Education Related

In Industrial/Energy prefer:
Industrial Products

In Transportation prefer:
Transportation

In Financial Services prefer:
Financial Services

In Manufact. prefer:
Manufacturing

Additional Information

Year Founded: 1996
Current Activity Level : Actively seeking new investments

OMERS VENTURES

200 Bay Street, Suite 1410
Toronto, Canada M5J 2J2
Phone: 4163693720
Fax: 4163693721
E-mail: info@omersventures.com
Website: omersventures.com

Management and Staff

Damien Steel, Managing Director
Derek Smyth, Managing Director
Howard Gwin, Venture Partner
John Ruffolo, Chief Executive Officer
Kent Thexton, Managing Director
Kevin Kimsa, Venture Partner

Type of Firm

Endowment, Foundation or Pension Fund

Association Membership

Canadian Venture Capital Association

Project Preferences

Type of Financing Preferred:
Early Stage
Expansion
Balanced
Later Stage
Seed

Size of Investments Considered:
Min Size of Investment Considered (000s): $495
Max Size of Investment Considered (000s): $29,694

Geographical Preferences

United States Preferences:
All U.S.

Canadian Preferences:
All Canada

International Preferences:
Europe

Industry Preferences

In Communications prefer:
Telecommunications

In Business Serv. prefer:
Media

In Other prefer:
Environment Responsible

Additional Information

Year Founded: 2011
Capital Under Management: $470,000,000
Current Activity Level : Actively seeking new investments

OMIDYAR NETWORK COMMONS LLC

1991 Broadway Street, Suite 200
Redwood City, CA USA 94063
Phone: 6504822500
Fax: 6504822525
E-mail: info@omidyar.com
Website: www.omidyar.com

Other Offices

61B, 2 North Avenue
Maker Maxity, Bandra-Kurla Complex
Mumbai, India 400 051
Phone: 9102261187300

1333 New Hampshire Avenue NW, Suite 730
Washington, DC USA 20036
Phone: 2024484505

47- 49 Charlotte Road
Charlotte House, 1st Floor
London, United Kingdom EC2A 3QT
Phone: 442077299997

Management and Staff

Amy Klement, Vice President
Badri Pillapakkam, Principal
David Sasaki, Principal
Jayant Sinha, Partner
Mallika Singh, Principal
Matthew Bannick, Managing Partner
Pam Omidyar, Co-Founder
Pierre Omidyar, Partner
Sal Giambanco, Partner
Stephanie Cohn-Rupp, Principal
Stephen King, Partner
Susan Phillips, Vice President
Todor Tashev, Partner

Type of Firm

Private Equity Firm

Association Membership

Emerging Markets Private Equity Association
National Venture Capital Association - USA (NVCA)
Indian Venture Capital Association (IVCA)
African Venture Capital Association (AVCA)

Project Preferences

Type of Financing Preferred:
Fund of Funds
Second Stage Financing
Mezzanine
Generalist PE
Balanced
Seed
First Stage Financing

Geographical Preferences

United States Preferences:

International Preferences:
Latin America
Europe
Asia
Africa

Industry Preferences

In Communications prefer:
Wireless Communications

In Computer Software prefer:
Software

In Internet Specific prefer:
Internet

In Consumer Related prefer:
Consumer

Additional Information

Year Founded: 2004
Capital Under Management: $200,000,000
Current Activity Level : Actively seeking new investments

OMIDYAR TECHNOLOGY VENTURES LLC

1991 Broadway Street, Suite 301
Redwood City, CA USA 94063
Website: www.omidyarventures.com

Management and Staff
Christopher Bishko, Partner
Pearl Chan, Principal
Todor Tashev, Managing Partner

Type of Firm
Private Equity Firm

Project Preferences

Type of Financing Preferred:
Early Stage

Additional Information
Year Founded: 2015
Current Activity Level : Actively seeking new investments

OMNES CAPITAL SAS

37-41 rue de Rocher
Paris, France 75008
Phone: 33180487900
Fax: 33142934855
E-mail: cape.contact@ca-privateequity.fr
Website: www.omnescapital.com

Other Offices

1, boulevard Vivier-Merle
Tour Suisse
Lyon, France 69443
Phone: 33-4-3756-1363
Fax: 33-1-3756-1365

3 Azrieli Towers
Tel Aviv, Israel
Phone: 972-52-648-3936

Piazza del Duomo, 17
Milano, Italy 20121

Management and Staff
Bertrand Tissot, Partner
Eric Rey, Partner
Laurent Perret, Principal
Ludovic Valentin-Pereira, Principal
Philippe Zurawski, Partner

Type of Firm
Bank Affiliated

Association Membership
French Venture Capital Association (AFIC)
European Private Equity and Venture Capital Assoc.

Project Preferences

Type of Financing Preferred:
Fund of Funds
Leveraged Buyout
Early Stage
Mezzanine
Generalist PE
Balanced
Later Stage
Other
Management Buyouts
Strategic Alliances
Startup
Special Situation
Fund of Funds of Second

Size of Investments Considered:
Min Size of Investment Considered (000s): $1,372
Max Size of Investment Considered (000s): $68,595

Geographical Preferences

United States Preferences:
Alaska
All U.S.

International Preferences:
Europe
Eastern Europe
France

Industry Focus
(% based on actual investment)
Consumer Related	29.2%
Other Products	15.1%
Industrial/Energy	13.5%
Biotechnology	13.0%
Computer Software and Services	10.9%
Medical/Health	8.5%
Internet Specific	7.0%
Communications and Media	1.9%
Computer Hardware	1.4%
Semiconductors/Other Elect.	-0.5%

Additional Information
Year Founded: 1999
Capital Under Management: $586,400,000
Current Activity Level : Actively seeking new investments

OMNI CAPITAL GROUP LLC

800 West Main Street, Suite 204
Freehold, NJ USA 07728
Phone: 9084976807
Fax: 9085020424
E-mail: info@omnivc.com
Website: www.omnivc.com

Management and Staff
Arun Netravali, Managing Partner
Bill Gourgey, Venture Partner
Douglas Eby, Venture Partner
Jim Brewington, Venture Partner
Jon Harrington, Venture Partner

Type of Firm
Private Equity Firm

Project Preferences

Role in Financing:
Prefer role in deals created by others

Type of Financing Preferred:
Early Stage
Later Stage
Seed
Startup

Size of Investments Considered:
Min Size of Investment Considered (000s): $2,000
Max Size of Investment Considered (000s): $8,000

Geographical Preferences

United States Preferences:
Washington
East Coast

Industry Preferences

In Communications prefer:
Communications and Media
Commercial Communications
Wireless Communications

In Internet Specific prefer:
E-Commerce Technology
Internet

In Medical/Health prefer:
Medical/Health

In Industrial/Energy prefer:
Energy

In Financial Services prefer:
Financial Services

Additional Information
Name of Most Recent Fund: OmniCapital Fund, L.P.
Most Recent Fund Was Raised: 05/10/2006
Year Founded: 2006
Capital Under Management: $25,000,000
Current Activity Level : Actively seeking new investments

OMNIMEDIA LIVE SA DE CV

Lazaro Cardenas 2400 Pte
Garza Garcia, Mexico 66260
Phone: 528180444500
E-mail: info@naranya.com

Management and Staff
Marcela Gutierrez, Managing Director

Type of Firm
Incubator/Development Program

Project Preferences

Type of Financing Preferred:
Startup

Industry Preferences

In Communications prefer:
Wireless Communications
Entertainment

In Internet Specific prefer:
Internet
Ecommerce

Additional Information
Year Founded: 2013
Current Activity Level : Actively seeking new investments

OMNIVORE CAPITAL MANAGEMENT ADVISORS PVT LTD

Pirojshanagar, Eastern Express
Vikhroli
Mumbai, India 400 079
Phone: 912225194490
E-mail: info@omnivore.vc
Website: www.omnivore.vc

Type of Firm
Private Equity Firm

Project Preferences

Type of Financing Preferred:
Early Stage

Geographical Preferences

International Preferences:
India

Industry Preferences

In Biotechnology prefer:
Agricultural/Animal Bio.

Additional Information
Year Founded: 1969
Current Activity Level : Actively seeking new investments

OMOS EQUITYPARTNERS GMBH

Mommsenstrasse 55
Berlin, Germany 10289
Phone: 493031998932
Fax: 493043727660
E-mail: info@omos-equitypartners.de
Website: omos-equitypartners.com

Management and Staff
Christoph Schroeder, Managing Director
Richard Markus, Managing Director

Type of Firm
Private Equity Firm

Project Preferences

Type of Financing Preferred:
Leveraged Buyout
Acquisition
Recapitalizations

Industry Preferences

In Semiconductor/Electr prefer:
Electronics
Component Testing Equipmt

In Medical/Health prefer:
Medical/Health
Medical Therapeutics

Additional Information
Year Founded: 2014
Current Activity Level : Actively seeking new investments

OMPHALOS VENTURE PARTNERS LLC

100 Fuller Street South, Suite 230
Shakopee, MN USA 55379
Phone: 9526575561
Website: www.omphalosventures.com

Type of Firm
Private Equity Firm

Additional Information
Year Founded: 1969
Current Activity Level : Actively seeking new investments

OMRON ADVANCED SYSTEMS INC

3945 Freedom Circle, Suite 1070
Santa Clara, CA USA 95054
Phone: 408-970-1150
Fax: 408-727-5540

Management and Staff
Kimihiko Iwamura, President

Type of Firm
Corporate PE/Venture

Additional Information
Year Founded: 2002
Current Activity Level : Actively seeking new investments

OMRON VENTURES CO LTD

Shiokoji,Shimogyo-ku
Omron Kyoto Center Building
Kyoto, Japan 600-8530
Phone: 86753447000
Fax: 86753447001
E-mail: ovc_info@omron.co.jp
Website: www.omron.co.jp

Type of Firm
Private Equity Firm

Project Preferences

Type of Financing Preferred:
Start-up Financing

Industry Preferences

In Computer Software prefer:
Software

In Business Serv. prefer:
Services

Additional Information
Year Founded: 2014
Current Activity Level : Actively seeking new investments

ON CAPITAL LTD

Five Guanghua Road
21/F, Tower 2, Prosper Center
Chaoyang, Beijing, China
Phone: 861085875899
E-mail: info@onccf.com
Website: www.onccf.com

Management and Staff
Alain Fontaine, General Partner
Dennis Ip, General Partner
Eugene Wong, General Partner
Laurie Kan, General Partner

Type of Firm
Private Equity Firm

Association Membership
China Venture Capital Association

Project Preferences

Type of Financing Preferred:
Leveraged Buyout
Acquisition

Geographical Preferences

International Preferences:
China

Industry Preferences

In Communications prefer:
Telecommunications

In Consumer Related prefer:
Retail

In Industrial/Energy prefer:
Energy
Environmental Related

In Financial Services prefer:
Financial Services

In Business Serv. prefer:
Media

Additional Information
Year Founded: 2004
Current Activity Level : Actively seeking new investments

ONA CAPITAL PRIVAT, SCR DE R.S., S.A.

Via Ausetania 13 - 1a planta
Manlleu
Barcelona, Spain 08560
Phone: 938510099
Fax: 938511647
E-mail: info@onacapital.com
Website: www.onacapital.com

Type of Firm
Private Equity Firm

Association Membership
Spanish Venture Capital Association (ASCRI)

Project Preferences

Type of Financing Preferred:
Early Stage

Geographical Preferences

International Preferences:
Spain

Industry Preferences

In Industrial/Energy prefer:
Alternative Energy

Additional Information
Year Founded: 2006
Capital Under Management: $4,299,000
Current Activity Level : Actively seeking new investments

ONCAP INVESTMENT PARTNERS L P

161 Bay Street
48th Floor
Toronto, Canada M5J 2S1
Phone: 4162144300
Fax: 4162146106
E-mail: info@oncap.com
Website: www.oncap.com

Management and Staff
Gregory Baylin, Managing Director
Jeremy Thompson, Managing Director
Mark MacTavish, Managing Director
Mark Gordon, Managing Director
Michael Lay, Managing Partner

Type of Firm
Investment Management Firm

Association Membership
Canadian Venture Capital Association

Project Preferences

Type of Financing Preferred:
Leveraged Buyout
Management Buyouts
Acquisition

Geographical Preferences

United States Preferences:
North America

Additional Information
Name of Most Recent Fund: ONCAP III, L.P.
Most Recent Fund Was Raised: 09/29/2011
Year Founded: 1999
Capital Under Management: $1,848,550,000
Current Activity Level : Actively seeking new investments
Method of Compensation: Return on invest. most important, but chg. closing fees, service fees, etc.

ONDERNEMEND TWENTE PARTICIPATIES BV

Hengelosestraat 585
Enschede, Netherlands 7500 GM
Phone: 31534849843
Fax: 31534849838
E-mail: info@ondernemendtwente.nl
Website: www.ondernemendtwente.nl

Type of Firm
Private Equity Firm

Project Preferences

Type of Financing Preferred:
Early Stage
Startup

Size of Investments Considered:
Min Size of Investment Considered (000s): $102,739
Max Size of Investment Considered (000s): $616,438

Geographical Preferences

International Preferences:
Netherlands

Industry Preferences

In Medical/Health prefer:
Hospitals/Clinics/Primary

In Consumer Related prefer:
Retail

In Financial Services prefer:
Financial Services
Insurance

Additional Information
Year Founded: 2004
Current Activity Level : Actively seeking new investments

ONE EARTH CAPITAL LLC

P.O. Box 1565
Felton, CA USA 95018
Phone: 8886115515
E-mail: info@oneearthcapital.com
Website: www.oneearthcapital.com

Management and Staff
Chris Berkner, Managing Director
Joe Hudson, Managing Director

Type of Firm
Private Equity Firm

Project Preferences

Type of Financing Preferred:
Early Stage
Seed

Industry Preferences

In Industrial/Energy prefer:
Environmental Related

Additional Information
Year Founded: 2007
Capital Under Management: $2,640,000
Current Activity Level : Actively seeking new investments

ONE EQUITY PARTNERS LLC

510 Madison Avenue
19th Floor
New York, NY USA 10022
Phone: 2122771500
Fax: 2122771533
E-mail: oep.info@oneequity.com
Website: www.oneequity.com

Other Offices
Av. Brigadeiro Faria Lima 2179
So Paulo, Spain 01452-000

330 N Wabash, Suite 3750
CHICAGO, IL USA 60611
Phone: 3125173750

Neue Mainzer
Str. 84
Frankfurt am Main, Germany 60311
Phone: 496950607470
Fax: 49695060174740

8 Connaught Road Central
Chater House, 20/F
Hong Kong, Hong Kong
Phone: 852-2800-0185

575 Market Street
Floor 35
SAN FRANCISCO, CA USA 94105
Phone: 4158560490
Fax: 4158560494

Opernring 17
Vienna, Austria 1010

Management and Staff
Andrew Dunn, Managing Director
Andrew Oliver, Managing Director
Ante Kusurin, Vice President
Brad Coppens, Managing Director
Carlo Padovano, Managing Director
Chip Schorr, Senior Managing Director
Christoph Giulini, Senior Managing Director
David Lippin, Managing Director
David Han, Senior Managing Director
Erin Hill, Chief Financial Officer
Greg Belinfanti, Senior Managing Director
Inna Etinberg, Vice President
JB Cherry, Senior Managing Director
James Koven, Senior Managing Director
Jessica Marion, Chief Financial Officer
Joerg Zirener, Managing Director
Johann-Melchior von Peter, Senior Managing Director
Joseph Huffsmith, Managing Director
Lee Gardner, Managing Director
Richard Cashin, President

Type of Firm
Private Equity Firm

Association Membership
German Venture Capital Association (BVK)

Project Preferences

Role in Financing:
Prefer role as deal originator

Type of Financing Preferred:
Leveraged Buyout
Acquisition

Geographical Preferences

United States Preferences:
North America

International Preferences:
Europe
Asia

Industry Focus
(% based on actual investment)
Computer Software and Services 37.1%
Communications and Media 19.3%
Medical/Health 11.2%
Consumer Related 10.5%
Industrial/Energy 7.3%
Other Products 5.4%
Internet Specific 5.3%
Computer Hardware 3.0%
Biotechnology 0.8%

Additional Information
Year Founded: 2001
Capital Under Management: $4,500,000,000
Current Activity Level : Actively seeking new investments

ONE LINE PARTNERS LLC

69 Charlton Street
First Floor
New York, NY USA 10014
Phone: 9177276859
Website: www.onelinepartners.com

Management and Staff
Alex Ginsberg, Co-Founder
Woody Baum, Co-Founder

Type of Firm
Private Equity Firm

Project Preferences

Type of Financing Preferred:
Leveraged Buyout
Acquisition

Geographical Preferences

United States Preferences:

Canadian Preferences:
All Canada

International Preferences:
Mexico

Industry Preferences

In Computer Software prefer:
Software

In Financial Services prefer:
Financial Services

In Business Serv. prefer:
Services

Additional Information
Year Founded: 2014
Current Activity Level : Actively seeking new investments

ONE PEAK PARTNERS LLP

1 Babmaes Street
James House 1st Floor
London, United Kingdom SW1Y 6HD
Phone: 442038378280
E-mail: info@onepeakpartners.com
Website: www.onepeakpartners.com

Management and Staff
Christoph Mayer, Principal
David Klein, Co-Founder
Humbert De Liedekerke, Co-Founder

Type of Firm
Private Equity Firm

Project Preferences

Type of Financing Preferred:
Generalist PE

Additional Information
Year Founded: 2015
Current Activity Level : Actively seeking new investments

ONE ROCK CAPITAL PARTNERS LLC

655 Third Avenue
21st Floor
New York, NY USA 10017
Phone: 2126052535
E-mail: info@onerockcapital.com
Website: www.onerockcapital.com

Management and Staff
Scott Spielvogel, Managing Director
Tony Lee, Managing Director

Type of Firm
Private Equity Firm

Association Membership
Natl Assoc of Investment Cos. (NAIC)

Project Preferences

Type of Financing Preferred:
Leveraged Buyout

Additional Information
Name of Most Recent Fund: One Rock Capital Partners, L.P.
Most Recent Fund Was Raised: 11/19/2012
Year Founded: 2012
Capital Under Management: $1,395,500,000
Current Activity Level : Actively seeking new investments

ONE STONE ENERGY PARTNERS

730 Fifth Avenue
New York, NY USA 10019
Website: 1stone-llc.com

Type of Firm
Private Equity Firm

Project Preferences

Type of Financing Preferred:
Leveraged Buyout
Acquisition

Geographical Preferences

United States Preferences:
North America

International Preferences:
Europe
Africa

Industry Preferences

In Industrial/Energy prefer:
Oil and Gas Exploration
Environmental Related

Additional Information
Year Founded: 2012
Capital Under Management: $109,000,000
Current Activity Level : Actively seeking new investments

ONE WAY VENTURES MANAGEMENT PBC INC

One Marina Park Drive, Suite 900
Boston, MA USA 02210
E-mail: info@onewayvc.com

Type of Firm
Private Equity Firm

Project Preferences

Type of Financing Preferred:
Seed

Geographical Preferences

United States Preferences:

Additional Information
Year Founded: 2017
Capital Under Management: $16,320,000
Current Activity Level : Actively seeking new investments

ONEACCORD CAPITAL LLC

1018 Market Street
Kirkland, WA USA 98033
Phone: 4252500883
Website: www.oneaccordcapital.com

Management and Staff
Dean Kato, Principal
Eric Lind, Principal
Glenn Hansen, Partner
John Kaminski, Partner
Max Clough, Principal
Richard Brune, Partner
Todd Ostrander, Partner

Type of Firm
Private Equity Firm

Additional Information
Year Founded: 2016
Current Activity Level : Actively seeking new investments

ONEGATE CAPITAL

233 Tai Cang Road
12/F Platinum Building
Shanghai, China 200020
Phone: 86-21-5178-5090
E-mail: inquiries@onegatecapital.com
Website: www.onegatecapital.com

Management and Staff
Leon Lin, Founding Partner

Type of Firm
Private Equity Firm

Project Preferences

Type of Financing Preferred:
Leveraged Buyout
Balanced
Later Stage
Acquisition

Geographical Preferences

International Preferences:
China

Industry Preferences

In Biotechnology prefer:
Biotechnology

In Medical/Health prefer:
Pharmaceuticals

In Consumer Related prefer:
Consumer

In Industrial/Energy prefer:
Energy
Environmental Related

In Manufact. prefer:
Manufacturing

In Agr/Forestr/Fish prefer:
Agriculture related

In Utilities prefer:
Utilities

Additional Information
Year Founded: 2010
Capital Under Management: $292,737,000
Current Activity Level : Actively seeking new investments

ONELIFE ADVISORS SA

Via Cantonale One
Lugano, Switzerland 6900
Phone: 41919242400
Fax: 41919242402
E-mail: info@onelife.ch
Website: www.onelife.ch

Type of Firm
Investment Management Firm

Association Membership
Swiss Venture Capital Association (SECA)

Project Preferences

Type of Financing Preferred:
Early Stage
Balanced
Later Stage
Startup

Geographical Preferences

International Preferences:
Switzerland

Industry Preferences

In Biotechnology prefer:
Biotechnology

In Medical/Health prefer:
Medical/Health
Pharmaceuticals

Additional Information
Year Founded: 2006
Current Activity Level : Actively seeking new investments

ONEVENTURES PTY LTD

179 Elizabeth Street
Level 13
Sydney, Australia 2000
Phone: 61282057379
Fax: 61292479181
E-mail: enquiries@one-ventures.com
Website: one-ventures.com.au

Pratt's Guide to Private Equity & Venture Capital Sources

Other Offices
145 Eagle Street
Level Three
Brisbane, Australia 4000

Management and Staff
Anne-Marie Birkill, General Partner
Michelle Deaker, Founder
Paul Kelly, General Partner

Type of Firm
Private Equity Firm

Association Membership
Australian Venture Capital Association (AVCAL)

Project Preferences

Type of Financing Preferred:
Early Stage
Seed

Size of Investments Considered:
Min Size of Investment Considered (000s): $361
Max Size of Investment Considered (000s): $7,215

Geographical Preferences

International Preferences:
Australia

Industry Preferences

In Communications prefer:
Communications and Media

In Medical/Health prefer:
Medical/Health

In Industrial/Energy prefer:
Environmental Related

In Business Serv. prefer:
Media

In Other prefer:
Environment Responsible

Additional Information
Name of Most Recent Fund: OneVentures Fund (IIF)
Most Recent Fund Was Raised: 05/03/2010
Year Founded: 2006
Capital Under Management: $129,600,000
Current Activity Level : Actively seeking new investments

ONEX CORP

161 Bay Street
Toronto, Canada M5J 2S1
Phone: 4163627711
Fax: 4163625765
E-mail: info@onex.com
Website: www.onex.com

Other Offices
712 Fifth Avenue
40th Floor
New York, NY USA 10019
Phone: 212-582-2211
Fax: 2125820909

17 Duke of York Street
London, United Kingdom SW1Y 6LB
Phone: 4402073891540

Management and Staff
Adam Reinmann, Principal
Amir Motamedi, Managing Director
Andrew Lapham, Principal
Anthony Munk, Senior Managing Director
Christine Donaldson, Managing Director
Christopher Govan, Chief Financial Officer
David Hirsch, Managing Director
David Mansell, Managing Director
David Copeland, Managing Director
Ewout Heersink, Senior Managing Director
Joshua Hausman, Managing Director
Konstantin Gilis, Managing Director
Kosty Gilis, Managing Director
Manish Srivastava, Managing Director
Matthew Ross, Managing Director
Nehal Abdel Hakim, Managing Director
Nigel Wright, Managing Director
Robert Le Blanc, Senior Managing Director
Seth Mersky, Senior Managing Director
Tawfiq Popatia, Managing Director
Timothy A. Duncanson, Managing Director
Todd Clegg, Managing Director
Tony Morgan, Managing Director

Type of Firm
Investment Management Firm

Association Membership
Canadian Venture Capital Association

Project Preferences

Role in Financing:
Prefer role as deal originator but will also invest in deals created by others

Type of Financing Preferred:
Leveraged Buyout
Acquisition

Geographical Preferences

United States Preferences:
North America

Additional Information
Name of Most Recent Fund: Onex Partners IV, L.P.
Most Recent Fund Was Raised: 12/18/2013
Year Founded: 1980
Capital Under Management: $420,000,000
Current Activity Level : Actively seeking new investments
Method of Compensation: Return on invest. most important, but chg. closing fees, service fees, etc.

ONICS GMBH

Georgiring 1-3
Leipzig, Germany 04103
Phone: 493413556666
Fax: 493413556667
Website: www.onics.de

Type of Firm
Private Equity Firm

Project Preferences

Type of Financing Preferred:
Leveraged Buyout
Management Buyouts
Acquisition

Additional Information
Year Founded: 2008
Current Activity Level : Actively seeking new investments

ONLINE SOLUTIONS VENTURES GMBH

Grillparzerstrasse 8
Munich, Germany 81675
Phone: 49892557428
Fax: 4989943992010
E-mail: info@online-solutions-ventures.de
Website: www.online-solutions-ventures.de

Management and Staff
Florian Mueller, Founder
Malte Daun, Chief Executive Officer

Type of Firm
Private Equity Firm

Project Preferences

Type of Financing Preferred:
Early Stage
Seed

Additional Information
Year Founded: 2012
Current Activity Level : Actively seeking new investments

ONONDAGA VENTURE CAPITAL FUND LLC

241 West Fayette Street
Syracuse, NY USA 13202
Phone: 3154780157
Fax: 3154780158
Website: www.ovcfund.com

Management and Staff
Michael Schattner, President

Type of Firm
Private Equity Firm

Project Preferences

Role in Financing:
Will function either as deal originator or investor in deals created by others

Type of Financing Preferred:
Second Stage Financing
Early Stage
Expansion

Size of Investments Considered:
Min Size of Investment Considered (000s): $50
Max Size of Investment Considered (000s): $300

Geographical Preferences

United States Preferences:
Northeast

Industry Preferences

In Communications prefer:
Commercial Communications
Wireless Communications

In Computer Software prefer:
Software

In Semiconductor/Electr prefer:
Electronic Components
Sensors

In Biotechnology prefer:
Industrial Biotechnology
Biosensors

In Medical/Health prefer:
Medical Diagnostics
Drug/Equipmt Delivery
Medical Products
Disposable Med. Products
Health Services

In Consumer Related prefer:
Consumer

In Manufact. prefer:
Manufacturing

In Agr/Forestr/Fish prefer:
Agriculture related

Additional Information
Name of Most Recent Fund: Onondaga Venture Capital
Most Recent Fund Was Raised: 03/31/1985
Year Founded: 1985
Capital Under Management: $2,500,000
Current Activity Level : Actively seeking new investments
Method of Compensation: Return on invest. most important, but chg. closing fees, service fees, etc.

ONPOINT TECHNOLOGIES
270 West New England Ave
Winter Park, FL USA 32789
Phone: 4078381401
Fax: 4076590447
E-mail: info@onpoint.us

Management and Staff
David Odom, Principal
Dennis Behm, Principal
Henry Huey, Principal
Jason Rottenberg, Managing Director
John Trbovich, Principal

Type of Firm
Government Affiliated Program

Project Preferences

Role in Financing:
Will function either as deal originator or investor in deals created by others

Type of Financing Preferred:
Early Stage
Balanced

Size of Investments Considered:
Min Size of Investment Considered (000s): $500
Max Size of Investment Considered (000s): $2,000

Geographical Preferences

United States Preferences:

Industry Preferences

In Semiconductor/Electr prefer:
Electronic Components

In Industrial/Energy prefer:
Energy
Alternative Energy

Additional Information
Year Founded: 2003
Capital Under Management: $48,000,000
Current Activity Level : Actively seeking new investments
Method of Compensation: Return on investment is of primary concern, do not charge fees

ONRAMP
117 W 9th Street, Suite 1009
Los Angeles, CA USA 90015
E-mail: info@onrampfund.com
Website: www.onrampfund.com

Type of Firm
Incubator/Development Program

Project Preferences

Type of Financing Preferred:
Early Stage
Seed
Startup

Additional Information
Year Founded: 2015
Capital Under Management: $10,000,000
Current Activity Level : Actively seeking new investments

ONSET VENTURES
2490 Sand Hill Road, Suite 150
Menlo Park, CA USA 94025
Phone: 6505290700
Fax: 6505290777
E-mail: mp@onset.com
Website: www.onset.com

Management and Staff
David Lane, Partner
John Ryan, Partner
Leslie Bottorff, Partner
Raman Khanna, Partner
Richard Schell, Venture Partner
Robert Kuhling, Partner
Shomit Ghose, Partner
Stephen Bernardez, Principal
Steve LaPorte, Venture Partner
Steven Laporte, Venture Partner
Terry Opdendyk, Founder

Type of Firm
Private Equity Firm

Association Membership
Western Association of Venture Capitalists (WAVC)
National Venture Capital Association - USA (NVCA)

Project Preferences

Role in Financing:
Prefer role as deal originator but will also invest in deals created by others

Type of Financing Preferred:
Early Stage
Expansion
Balanced
Later Stage
Seed
Startup

Industry Focus
(% based on actual investment)

Medical/Health	33.9%
Computer Software and Services	30.6%
Internet Specific	15.0%
Communications and Media	8.1%
Computer Hardware	4.9%
Biotechnology	4.6%
Semiconductors/Other Elect.	1.9%
Other Products	0.7%
Industrial/Energy	0.3%

Pratt's Guide to Private Equity & Venture Capital Sources

Additional Information

Name of Most Recent Fund: ONSET VI, L.P.
Most Recent Fund Was Raised: 10/27/2008
Year Founded: 1984
Capital Under Management: $1,000,000,000
Current Activity Level : Actively seeking new investments
Method of Compensation: Return on investment is of primary concern, do not charge fees

ONTARIO CAPITAL GROWTH CORP

393 University Avenue, Suite 1701
Toronto, Canada M5G 1E6
Phone: 4163256874
Fax: 4162120794
Website: www.ocgc.gov.on.ca

Type of Firm

Government Affiliated Program

Project Preferences

Type of Financing Preferred:
Early Stage
Balanced

Geographical Preferences

Canadian Preferences:
Ontario

Industry Preferences

In Other prefer:
Environment Responsible

Additional Information

Year Founded: 2008
Current Activity Level : Actively seeking new investments

ONTARIO CENTRES OF EX-CELLENCE

156 Front Street West, Suite 200
Toronto, Canada M5J 2L6
Phone: 4168611092
Fax: 8667596014
Website: www.oce-ontario.org

Management and Staff

Barry Gekiere, Managing Director
Don Duval, Vice President
Ilse Treurnicht, Chief Executive Officer
Joanne Thomsen, Vice President
Michael Heilbronn, Chief Financial Officer
Michael Harvey, Vice President
Tony Redpath, Vice President

Type of Firm

Government Affiliated Program

Project Preferences

Type of Financing Preferred:
Early Stage
Seed
Startup

Geographical Preferences

Canadian Preferences:
All Canada
Ontario

Industry Preferences

In Semiconductor/Electr prefer:
Sensors

In Industrial/Energy prefer:
Alternative Energy
Energy Conservation Relat
Environmental Related

In Other prefer:
Environment Responsible

Additional Information

Year Founded: 2000
Capital Under Management: $8,455,000
Current Activity Level : Actively seeking new investments

ONTARIO PRIVATE EQUITY LTD

291 Sprite Avenue
Pretoria, South Africa 0081
Phone: 27123617492
Fax: 27866801633
E-mail: info@ontariope.co.za
Website: www.ontariope.co.za

Type of Firm

Private Equity Firm

Project Preferences

Type of Financing Preferred:
Leveraged Buyout
Recapitalizations

Additional Information

Year Founded: 2010
Current Activity Level : Actively seeking new investments

ONTARIO TEACHERS' PENSION PLAN

5650 Yonge Street
Toronto, Canada M2M 4H5
Phone: 4162285900
Fax: 4167305082
E-mail: inquiry@otpp.com
Website: www.otpp.com

Other Offices

375 Park Avenue, Suite 3508
New York, NY USA 10152
Phone: 212-888-5799
Fax: 212-838-2549

Curzon Street, Mayfair
Leconfield House, 4th Floor
London, United Kingdom W1J 5JA
Phone: 442076594450
Fax: 442076594451

Management and Staff

Bogdan Cenanovic, Vice President
Charles Thomazi, Managing Director
Chris Schindler, Vice President
Dale Burgess, Vice President
Gillian Brown, Managing Director
Glen Silvestri, Vice President
Jacqueline Beaurivage, Vice President
Jason Chang, Vice President
Jeff Clark, Managing Director
Jo Taylor, Vice President
Jonathan Hausman, Vice President
Kevin Duggan, Vice President
Lee Sienna, Vice President
Leslie Lefebvre, Vice President
Michael Murray, Vice President
Nicole Musicco, Vice President
Olivia Steedman, Vice President
Robert De Santis, Vice President
Rosemarie McClean, Chief Operating Officer
Sandra McEwen, Vice President
Steve Faraone, Vice President
Tamara Finch, Managing Director
Tanya Carmichael, Managing Director
William Royan, Vice President
Ziad Hindo, Vice President

Type of Firm

Endowment, Foundation or Pension Fund

Association Membership

Emerging Markets Private Equity Association
Canadian Venture Capital Association

Project Preferences

Type of Financing Preferred:
Fund of Funds
Leveraged Buyout
Early Stage
Expansion
Generalist PE
Balanced
Later Stage
Management Buyouts
Acquisition
Recapitalizations

Geographical Preferences

United States Preferences:
North America

International Preferences:
United Kingdom
Europe
Middle East
Africa

Industry Preferences

In Communications prefer:
Telecommunications

In Medical/Health prefer:
Medical/Health

In Consumer Related prefer:
Consumer
Retail

In Industrial/Energy prefer:
Energy
Industrial Products

In Financial Services prefer:
Financial Services

In Business Serv. prefer:
Media

Additional Information
Year Founded: 1989
Current Activity Level : Actively seeking new investments

ONTARIO VENTURE CAPITAL FUND INC

79 Wellington Street West
Sixth Floor
Toronto, Canada M5K 1N9
Phone: 8669644141
Fax: 4163040195
E-mail: ovcf@northleafcapital.com

Type of Firm
Private Equity Advisor or Fund of Funds

Project Preferences

Type of Financing Preferred:
Fund of Funds

Geographical Preferences

Canadian Preferences:
All Canada
Ontario

Additional Information
Year Founded: 2008
Current Activity Level : Actively seeking new investments

ONWAVE VENTURES

88 Dunn Street, Suite 402
Oakville, Canada L6J 3C7
Website: www.onwaveventures.com

Management and Staff
Vlad Ilchuk, Managing Partner

Type of Firm
Private Equity Firm

Project Preferences

Type of Financing Preferred:
Balanced

Geographical Preferences

United States Preferences:

Canadian Preferences:
All Canada

Industry Preferences

In Internet Specific prefer:
Internet

In Financial Services prefer:
Financial Services

Additional Information
Year Founded: 2016
Current Activity Level : Actively seeking new investments

ONZA CAPITAL

Cuevas del Valle 28
Madrid, Spain 28023
Phone: 34911256710
E-mail: hola@onzacapital.com
Website: www.onzacapital.com

Type of Firm
Private Equity Firm

Project Preferences

Type of Financing Preferred:
Early Stage
Balanced

Geographical Preferences

International Preferences:
Spain

Industry Preferences

In Computer Software prefer:
Applications Software

In Internet Specific prefer:
Internet
Web Aggregation/Portals

In Business Serv. prefer:
Media

Additional Information
Year Founded: 2014
Capital Under Management: $24,865,000

Current Activity Level : Actively seeking new investments

OOE HIGHTECHFONDS GMBH

Bethlehemstrasse 3
Linz, Austria 4020
Phone: 43732777800
Fax: 4373277780040
E-mail: office@hightechfonds.at
Website: www.hightechfonds.at

Type of Firm
Private Equity Firm

Project Preferences

Type of Financing Preferred:
Early Stage
Seed
Startup

Geographical Preferences

International Preferences:
Austria

Additional Information
Year Founded: 2011
Current Activity Level : Actively seeking new investments

OPCAPITA LLP

173-176 Sloane Street
London, United Kingdom SW1X 9QG
E-mail: info@opcapita.com
Website: www.opcapita.com

Other Offices
1 Royal Plaza
Royal Avenue
GUERNSEY, United Kingdom GY1 2HL

Management and Staff
Chris McDermott, Principal
David Hamid, Co-Founder
Joshua Spoerri, Managing Director
Simon Millerchip, Chief Financial Officer

Type of Firm
Private Equity Firm

Project Preferences

Type of Financing Preferred:
Leveraged Buyout
Turnaround
Acquisition

Geographical Preferences

1583

International Preferences:
Italy
Sweden
United Kingdom
Luxembourg
Europe
Netherlands
Greenland
Iceland
Spain
Belgium
Finland
Norway
Germany
Denmark
Faroe Islands
France

Industry Preferences

In Internet Specific prefer:
Internet

In Medical/Health prefer:
Medical/Health

In Consumer Related prefer:
Consumer
Entertainment and Leisure
Retail
Food/Beverage

In Transportation prefer:
Transportation

Additional Information
Year Founded: 2006
Capital Under Management: $393,920,000
Current Activity Level: Actively seeking new investments

OPEN CNP SASU

4, Place Raoul Dautry
Paris, France 75015

Type of Firm
Insurance Firm Affiliate

Project Preferences

Type of Financing Preferred:
Early Stage
Expansion
Later Stage

Industry Preferences

In Computer Software prefer:
Software

In Internet Specific prefer:
Internet

In Medical/Health prefer:
Medical/Health

In Financial Services prefer:
Financial Services

Additional Information
Year Founded: 2016
Current Activity Level: Actively seeking new investments

OPEN FIELD CAPITAL LLC

1140 Ave of the Americas
9th Floor
New York, NY USA 10036
Phone: 2129139515
E-mail: info@ofcap.com
Website: www.ofcap.com

Management and Staff
Michael Sandifer, Principal
Robert Griffin, Principal

Type of Firm
Investment Management Firm

Additional Information
Year Founded: 2015
Current Activity Level: Actively seeking new investments

OPEN NETWORK LAB INC

3-5-7, Ebisu
11F, Daikanyama DG Bldg
Tokyo, Japan 150-0022
Website: onlab.jp

Type of Firm
Incubator/Development Program

Project Preferences

Type of Financing Preferred:
Seed

Geographical Preferences

International Preferences:
Japan

Additional Information
Year Founded: 2011
Current Activity Level: Actively seeking new investments

OPEN OCEAN CAPITAL OY

Pohjois-Esplanadi 31
Helsinki, Finland 00100
Phone: 358405075024
E-mail: info@openoceancapital.com
Website: www.openoceancapital.com

Management and Staff
Patrik Backman, Managing Partner
Ralf Wahlsten, Partner
Tom Henriksson, Partner

Type of Firm
Private Equity Firm

Association Membership
Finnish Venture Capital Association (FVCA)
European Private Equity and Venture Capital Assoc.

Project Preferences

Type of Financing Preferred:
Early Stage
Expansion
Seed
Startup

Geographical Preferences

International Preferences:
Europe
Finland

Industry Preferences

In Communications prefer:
Wireless Communications

In Computer Software prefer:
Software
Applications Software

In Internet Specific prefer:
Internet
Web Aggregation/Portals

Additional Information
Name of Most Recent Fund: Open Ocean Fund Three Ky
Most Recent Fund Was Raised: 05/25/2011
Year Founded: 2008
Capital Under Management: $177,419,000
Current Activity Level: Actively seeking new investments

OPEN PRAIRIE VENTURES

400 East Jefferson
Effingham, IL USA 62401
Phone: 2173471000
Fax: 2173471001
E-mail: info@OpenPrairie.com
Website: www.openprairie.com

Other Offices
18001 West 100th Street, Suite 125
Olathe, KS USA 66061
Phone: 913-317-1548
Fax: 913-317-1505

2001 South First Street, Suite 209A
Champaign, IL USA 61820
Phone: 217-337-7700
Fax: 217-347-1001

Management and Staff
Jason Wrone, Vice President
Jim Budzynski, Venture Partner
Michael Peck, General Partner
Pat Morand, Partner
Sam Hogg, Venture Partner

Type of Firm
Private Equity Firm

Project Preferences

Role in Financing:
Will function either as deal originator or investor in deals created by others

Type of Financing Preferred:
Early Stage
Later Stage
Seed

Geographical Preferences

United States Preferences:
Midwest

Industry Preferences

In Communications prefer:
Telecommunications
Wireless Communications
Data Communications

In Computer Software prefer:
Applications Software

In Semiconductor/Electr prefer:
Electronics
Semiconductor
Micro-Processing
Circuit Boards
Component Testing Equipmt
Fiber Optics

In Biotechnology prefer:
Biotechnology
Human Biotechnology
Agricultural/Animal Bio.
Biosensors

In Medical/Health prefer:
Drug/Equipmt Delivery
Medical Products
Pharmaceuticals

In Consumer Related prefer:
Food/Beverage
Consumer Products

In Industrial/Energy prefer:
Energy

In Agr/Forest/Fish prefer:
Agriculture related

Additional Information
Year Founded: 1997
Capital Under Management: $63,000,000

Current Activity Level : Actively seeking new investments
Method of Compensation: Return on invest. most important, but chg. closing fees, service fees, etc.

OPENAIR EQUITY PARTNERS

4520 Main Street, Suite 1400
Kansas City, MO USA 64111
Phone: 9133621111
E-mail: info@openairep.com

Management and Staff
Kathy Walker, Managing Director
Lance LeMay, Managing Director
Ronald LeMay, Managing Director
Scott Ford, Managing Director

Type of Firm
Private Equity Firm

Project Preferences

Type of Financing Preferred:
Leveraged Buyout
Early Stage
Expansion
Balanced
Later Stage

Industry Preferences

In Communications prefer:
Wireless Communications

Additional Information
Year Founded: 2010
Current Activity Level : Actively seeking new investments

OPENINCUBATE

c/o Austin Ventures
Austin, TX USA 78701
E-mail: info@openincubate.com
Website: www.openincubate.com

Type of Firm
Incubator/Development Program

Project Preferences

Type of Financing Preferred:
Seed
Startup

Industry Preferences

In Computer Software prefer:
Software
Applications Software

In Computer Other prefer:
Computer Related

Additional Information
Year Founded: 2013
Current Activity Level : Actively seeking new investments

OPENVIEW VENTURE PARTNERS LP

303 Congress Street
Seventh Floor
Boston, MA USA 02210
Phone: 6174787500
Fax: 6174787501
E-mail: info@openviewpartners.com
Website: openviewpartners.com

Management and Staff
Adam Marcus, Managing Partner
Blake Bartlett, Partner
Bonnie Lewis, Chief Financial Officer
Daniel Demmer, Managing Partner
Devon McDonald, Partner
Elizabeth Cain, Vice President
George Roberts, Venture Partner
James Baum, Venture Partner
Mackey Craven, Partner
Ricky Pelletier, Partner
Scott Maxwell, Founder

Type of Firm
Private Equity Firm

Project Preferences

Role in Financing:
Prefer role as deal originator

Type of Financing Preferred:
Expansion
Later Stage

Size of Investments Considered:
Min Size of Investment Considered (000s): $5,000
Max Size of Investment Considered (000s): $20,000

Geographical Preferences

United States Preferences:
North America

Industry Preferences

In Computer Software prefer:
Software
Systems Software
Applications Software

Additional Information
Name of Most Recent Fund: OpenView Venture Partners III, L.P.
Most Recent Fund Was Raised: 12/22/2011
Year Founded: 2006
Capital Under Management: $445,000,000
Current Activity Level : Actively seeking new investments
Method of Compensation: Return on investment is of primary concern, do not charge fees

OPERATIVE CAPITAL GP LLC

30 Liberty Ship Way, Suite 3325
Sausalito, CA USA 94965
Phone: 4154257496
Website: www.operativecapital.com

Type of Firm
Private Equity Firm

Project Preferences

Type of Financing Preferred:
Early Stage

Industry Preferences

In Internet Specific prefer:
E-Commerce Technology

Additional Information
Year Founded: 2015
Current Activity Level : Actively seeking new investments

OPPORTUNITIES NB

250 King Street
Place 2000
Fredericton, Canada E3B 9M9
Phone: 15064535471
Fax: 15064444277
E-mail: info@onbcanada.ca
Website: onbcanada.ca

Type of Firm
Government Affiliated Program

Project Preferences

Type of Financing Preferred:
Early Stage
Seed

Geographical Preferences

Canadian Preferences:
New Brunswick

Additional Information
Year Founded: 2017
Current Activity Level : Actively seeking new investments

OPT VENTURES INC

6, Yonban-Cho, Chiyoda-Ku
Tokyu Banmachi Bldg.
Tokyo, Japan 102-0081
Website: www.opt-ventures.co.jp

Type of Firm
Private Equity Firm

Project Preferences

Type of Financing Preferred:
Balanced

Additional Information
Year Founded: 2015
Current Activity Level : Actively seeking new investments

OPTICS VALLEY CREATIVE INDUSTRY BASE CONSTRUCTION INVEST CO.

No. 20, Guanshan 1st Road
Donghu New Tech Dist
Wuhan, Hubei, China
Phone: 862787767888
Website: www.ovcreative.com

Type of Firm
Incubator/Development Program

Project Preferences

Type of Financing Preferred:
Early Stage
Expansion
Balanced

Geographical Preferences

International Preferences:
China

Industry Preferences

In Consumer Related prefer:
Entertainment and Leisure

Additional Information
Year Founded: 2009
Current Activity Level : Actively seeking new investments

OPTIMA INVESTMENTS BV

41, Hendrik van Borsselenkade
Amsterdam, Netherlands 1181 AZ
Phone: 31642303646
Website: www.optimainvests.com

Type of Firm
Private Equity Firm

Project Preferences

Type of Financing Preferred:
Early Stage

Industry Preferences

In Communications prefer:
Telecommunications

In Internet Specific prefer:
Internet

In Business Serv. prefer:
Media

Additional Information
Year Founded: 2005
Current Activity Level : Actively seeking new investments

OPTIMUM TECHNOLOGY FUND LP

118 8th Avenue Southwest
200
Calgary, Canada T2P 1G4
Phone: 15873326826
E-mail: info@optimumtechfund.com
Website: www.optimumtechfund.com

Management and Staff
Neal Gledhil, Partner
Patrick Barrington, Managing Partner
Ross Bricker, Managing Partner

Type of Firm
Private Equity Firm

Project Preferences

Type of Financing Preferred:
Early Stage
Balanced
Later Stage

Geographical Preferences

United States Preferences:
Northwest

Canadian Preferences:
All Canada

Industry Preferences

In Communications prefer:
Communications and Media
Wireless Communications

Additional Information
Year Founded: 2014
Current Activity Level : Actively seeking new investments

OPTRUST PRIVATE MARKETS GROUP

1 Adelaide Street East, Suite 1100
Toronto, Canada M5C 3A7
Phone: 14166813033
Fax: 14166813040
Website: www.optrust.com/investments/private-markets.asp

Management and Staff
Douglas Michael, Chief Financial Officer
Tim Shortill, Vice President

Type of Firm
Investment Management Firm

Project Preferences

Type of Financing Preferred:
Leveraged Buyout
Generalist PE
Balanced
Acquisition
Special Situation

Additional Information
Year Founded: 2006
Current Activity Level : Actively seeking new investments

OPUS CAPITAL

2730 Sand Hill Road, Suite 150
Menlo Park, CA USA 94025
Phone: 6505432900
Fax: 6505619570
E-mail: contact@opuscapital.com
Website: www.opuscapitalllc.com

Management and Staff
Carl Showalter, General Partner
Dan Avida, General Partner
Gill Cogan, General Partner
Philip Greer, Partner
Serge Plotkin, Venture Partner

Type of Firm
Private Equity Firm

Project Preferences

Type of Financing Preferred:
Balanced
Later Stage
Seed
Startup

Industry Preferences

In Communications prefer:
Commercial Communications
Wireless Communications

In Computer Software prefer:
Applications Software

In Internet Specific prefer:
Internet

In Semiconductor/Electr prefer:
Semiconductor

Additional Information
Name of Most Recent Fund: Opus Capital Venture Partners VI, L.P.
Most Recent Fund Was Raised: 06/16/2009
Year Founded: 1963
Capital Under Management: $1,000,000,000
Current Activity Level : Actively seeking new investments

OQUENDO CAPITAL SL

Calle Maria de Molina 40
4th Center
Madrid, Spain 28006
Phone: 34912976454
Fax: 34912976464
E-mail: info@oquendocapital.com
Website: www.oquendocapital.com

Type of Firm
Private Equity Firm

Association Membership
Spanish Venture Capital Association (ASCRI)

Project Preferences

Type of Financing Preferred:
Leveraged Buyout
Expansion
Mezzanine
Fund of Funds of Second
Recapitalizations

Geographical Preferences

International Preferences:
Portugal
Spain

Additional Information
Year Founded: 2005
Capital Under Management: $402,030,000
Current Activity Level : Actively seeking new investments

ORACLE CAPITAL PARTNERS LLC

500 Griswold Avenue
The Guardian Bldg., Suite 2450
Detroit, MI USA 48226
Phone: 3139659950
Fax: 3139659956
E-mail: info@oracle-capital.com
Website: www.oracle-capital.com

Management and Staff
David Morris, Managing Director
Henry Brandon, Managing Director

Type of Firm
Private Equity Firm

Project Preferences

Type of Financing Preferred:
Balanced
Later Stage

Geographical Preferences

United States Preferences:
Michigan

Industry Preferences

In Medical/Health prefer:
Health Services

In Consumer Related prefer:
Consumer Products

In Business Serv. prefer:
Services

In Manufact. prefer:
Manufacturing

Additional Information
Name of Most Recent Fund: Oracle Capital Fund, L.P.
Most Recent Fund Was Raised: 12/21/2005
Year Founded: 2005
Current Activity Level : Actively seeking new investments

ORANGEWOOD PARTNERS LLC

9 West 57th Street
33rd Floor
New York, NY USA 10019
Website: www.orangewoodpartners.com

Type of Firm
Private Equity Firm

Project Preferences

Type of Financing Preferred:
Leveraged Buyout

Additional Information
Year Founded: 2015
Current Activity Level : Actively seeking new investments

ORAXYS SA

41 Avenue de la Gare
Bertrange, Luxembourg 1611
Phone: 3526311840
Fax: 3526311841
E-mail: contact@oraxys.com
Website: www.oraxys.com

Type of Firm
Private Equity Firm

Project Preferences

Type of Financing Preferred:
Leveraged Buyout
Early Stage
Generalist PE
Later Stage
Acquisition

Size of Investments Considered:
Min Size of Investment Considered (000s): $1,339
Max Size of Investment Considered (000s): $20,083

Geographical Preferences

International Preferences:
Luxembourg
Swaziland
Netherlands
Switzerland
Belgium
France

Industry Preferences

In Computer Software prefer:
Software

In Medical/Health prefer:
Medical/Health
Medical Products

In Consumer Related prefer:
Consumer
Food/Beverage
Consumer Products

In Industrial/Energy prefer:
Energy
Materials
Environmental Related

Additional Information
Year Founded: 2008
Current Activity Level : Actively seeking new investments

ORBE INVESTIMENTOS E PARTICIPACOES LTDA

Rua Wisard 308
Vila Madalena
Sao Paulo, Brazil 05434-000
Phone: 551134655600
Fax: 551134655601
E-mail: orbe@orbeinvestimentos.com
Website: www.orbeinvestimentos.com

Type of Firm
Private Equity Firm

Project Preferences

Type of Financing Preferred:
Early Stage
Balanced
Public Companies
Later Stage

Additional Information
Year Founded: 2002
Current Activity Level : Actively seeking new investments

ORBIMED ADVISORS LLC

601 Lexington Avenue
54th Floor
New York, NY USA 10022
Phone: 2127396400
E-mail: info@orbimed.com
Website: www.orbimed.com

Other Offices
268 Xizang Middle Road
Unit 4706, Raffles City Shanghai Office
Shanghai, China 200001
Phone: 862163351700

89 Medinat HaYehudim street
Build E, 11th Floor
Herzliya, Israel 46766
Phone: 972-73-2822600

, Suite F 8E, Grand Hyatt Plaza
Santacruz
Mumbai, India 400055
Phone: 912261403000

455 Mission Bay Boulevard South, Suite 555
San Francisco, CA USA 94158
Phone: 4152948740

Management and Staff
Anat Naschitz, Managing Director
Aya Jakobovits, Venture Partner
C. Scotland Stevens, Partner
Chau Khuong, Principal
Daniel Zhou, Vice President
David Wang, Senior Managing Director
David Bonita, Principal
Erez Chimovits, Managing Director
Evan Sotiriou, Chief Financial Officer
Geoffrey Hsu, Partner
Jonathan Wang, Senior Managing Director
Jonathan Silverstein, General Partner
Klaus Veitinger, Venture Partner
Matthew Rizzo, Managing Director
Matthew Wotiz, Principal
Michael Sheffery, Partner
Mona Ashiya, Vice President
Nissim Darvish, Senior Managing Director
Peter Thompson, Venture Partner
Rajesh Dalal, Venture Partner
Richard Klemm, Partner
Rishi Gupta, Partner
Samuel Isaly, Managing Partner
Sunny Sharma, Senior Managing Director
Sven Borho, Partner
Tadd Wessel, Managing Director
Trevor Polischuk, Partner
Vince Burgess, Venture Partner
W. Carter Neild, Partner
William Sawyer, Partner

Type of Firm
Private Equity Firm

Project Preferences

Role in Financing:
Prefer role as deal originator but will also invest in deals created by others

Type of Financing Preferred:
Leveraged Buyout
Early Stage
Expansion
Generalist PE
Balanced
Later Stage
Seed
Management Buyouts

Geographical Preferences

United States Preferences:
North America

International Preferences:
Europe
Israel
Asia

Industry Focus
(% based on actual investment)
Biotechnology	49.7%
Medical/Health	47.0%
Computer Software and Services	2.6%
Consumer Related	0.3%
Internet Specific	0.2%
Computer Hardware	0.2%

Additional Information
Name of Most Recent Fund: OrbiMed Private Investments V, L.P.
Most Recent Fund Was Raised: 10/31/2013
Year Founded: 1989
Capital Under Management: $75,000,000,000
Current Activity Level : Actively seeking new investments
Method of Compensation: Return on investment is of primary concern, do not charge fees

ORCHARD FIRST SOURCE INC

2850 West Golf Road
5th Floor
Rolling Meadows, IL USA 60008
Phone: 8477342000
Fax: 8477347910
E-mail: info@ofsmanagement.com
Website: www.ofscapital.com

Management and Staff
David Quon, Managing Director
Kathi Inorio, Senior Managing Director

Type of Firm
Private Equity Advisor or Fund of Funds

Project Preferences

Size of Investments Considered:
Min Size of Investment Considered (000s): $10,000
Max Size of Investment Considered (000s): $86,000

Additional Information
Year Founded: 2000
Current Activity Level : Actively seeking new investments

ORCHARD HOLDINGS GROUP LLC

6847 Cintas Boulevard, Suite 120
Mason, OH USA 45040
Phone: 5137543500
Fax: 5137543595
Website: www.orchardholdings.com

Management and Staff
Pete Boylan, Managing Director
Phil Collins, Managing Director

Type of Firm
Private Equity Firm

Project Preferences

Type of Financing Preferred:
Leveraged Buyout
Expansion
Mezzanine
Later Stage
Special Situation
Recapitalizations

Additional Information
Name of Most Recent Fund: Orchard Tosca Investment Partners, L.P.
Most Recent Fund Was Raised: 08/14/2012
Year Founded: 1969
Capital Under Management: $21,929,000
Current Activity Level : Actively seeking new investments

ORCHESTRA MEDICAL VENTURES LLC

142 West 57th Street, Suite 4A
New York, NY USA 10019
Phone: 6463675900
E-mail: info@orchestramv.com
Website: www.orchestramv.com

Management and Staff
Darren Sherman, Managing Partner
David Hochman, Managing Partner
John Brancaccio, Chief Financial Officer
Steven Camp, Vice President
Yuval Binur, Managing Partner

Type of Firm
Private Equity Firm

Project Preferences

Type of Financing Preferred:
Balanced

Industry Preferences

In Medical/Health prefer:
Medical/Health
Health Services

Additional Information
Year Founded: 2011
Current Activity Level : Actively seeking new investments

ORCHID ASIA GROUP MANAGEMENT LTD

99 Queen's Road Central, Suite 6211-12, 62/F,The Center
Central, Hong Kong
Phone: 85221158810
Fax: 85221158120
Website: www.orchidasia.com

Other Offices
1228 Middle Yan'an Road, Kerry Center
Unit 2103, 21/F, Tower 3 Jing An
Shanghai, China 200040
Phone: 862152986222
Fax: 862152985210

3-15 Linhexi Road, Tianhe District, Suite 1002, China Shine Plaza
Guangzhou, China 510610
Phone: 862038396155
Fax: 862038396126

Unit 2502, Tower 2, China Central Place
No. 79 Jianguo Road, Chaoyang District
Beijing, China 100025
Phone: 861065989160
Fax: 861065989166

Management and Staff
Aaron Wen, Vice President
Gabriel Li, Managing Director
Peter Joost, President, Founder
Steven Kwok, Partner

Type of Firm
Private Equity Firm

Project Preferences

Role in Financing:
Prefer role as deal originator

Type of Financing Preferred:
Expansion
Balanced
Later Stage

Geographical Preferences

International Preferences:
China
Asia

Industry Preferences

In Medical/Health prefer:
Health Services

In Consumer Related prefer:
Consumer Products
Consumer Services

In Business Serv. prefer:
Services

In Manufact. prefer:
Manufacturing

Additional Information
Year Founded: 1997
Capital Under Management: $700,000,000
Current Activity Level : Actively seeking new investments

ORE VENTURES LLC

22 West 21st
7th Fl
New York, NY USA 10010
E-mail: info@ore.vc
Website: ore.vc

Type of Firm
Private Equity Firm

Project Preferences

Type of Financing Preferred:
Early Stage
Seed

Industry Preferences

In Business Serv. prefer:
Media

Additional Information
Year Founded: 2016
Current Activity Level : Actively seeking new investments

ORESA VENTURES SP Z OO

Al. Ujazdowskie 41
Warsaw, Poland 00-540
Phone: 48223195630
Fax: 48223195633
E-mail: infopl@oresaventures.com
Website: www.oresaventures.com

Other Offices
Pietermaai 15
Curaao, Neth. Antilles

Baneasa Business & Technology Park
42-44 Bucuresti -Ploiesti St.
Bucharest 1, Romania 013696
Phone: 40213610562
Fax: 40213610565

Type of Firm
Private Equity Firm

Association Membership
Polish Venture Capital Association (PSIC/PPEA)
South Eastern Europes Private Equity Association
European Private Equity and Venture Capital Assoc.

Project Preferences

Role in Financing:
Prefer role as deal originator but will also invest in deals created by others

Type of Financing Preferred:
Leveraged Buyout
Generalist PE
Balanced
Management Buyouts
Acquisition

Geographical Preferences

International Preferences:
Central Europe
Poland
Eastern Europe
Romania

Industry Preferences

In Medical/Health prefer:
Medical/Health
Pharmaceuticals

In Consumer Related prefer:
Consumer
Consumer Products
Education Related

In Industrial/Energy prefer:
Materials

In Financial Services prefer:
Financial Services

In Business Serv. prefer:
Distribution

Additional Information
Year Founded: 1995
Capital Under Management: $75,000,000
Current Activity Level : Actively seeking new investments
Method of Compensation: Return on investment is of primary concern, do not charge fees

ORGONE CAPITAL I L L C

1140 Edmer Avenue
Oak Park, IL USA 60302
Phone: 773-858-9263
Website: www.orgonecapital.com

Other Offices
Bosque de Acacias 61-B
Bosques de las Lomas, Mexico DF- 11700
Phone: 52-55-3098-2908

Management and Staff
Rafael Escobar, Founder

Type of Firm
Private Equity Firm

Project Preferences

Type of Financing Preferred:
Later Stage

Additional Information
Year Founded: 2009
Current Activity Level : Actively seeking new investments

ORICA CAPITAL CO LTD

Jintian Road
No.1708, Rongchaojinmao Center
Shenzhen, China
Phone: 8675583515166
Fax: 8675582789371
Website: www.orica.com.cn

Other Offices
No.1717, Sichuan North Rd.
F27, Jiajie Intl. Plaza
Shanghai, China 200080
Phone: 8602163845349
Fax: 8602153064128

Management and Staff
Longjiu Liu, Vice President
Zhidong Kan, President

Type of Firm
Private Equity Firm

Association Membership
Shenzhen Venture Capital Association

Project Preferences

Type of Financing Preferred:
Balanced

Geographical Preferences

International Preferences:
China

Industry Preferences

In Biotechnology prefer:
Biotechnology

In Medical/Health prefer:
Medical/Health
Pharmaceuticals

In Industrial/Energy prefer:
Alternative Energy
Coal Related
Machinery

In Transportation prefer:
Transportation

In Business Serv. prefer:
Services
Media

In Agr/Forestr/Fish prefer:
Mining and Minerals

Additional Information
Year Founded: 2005
Capital Under Management: $153,582,000
Current Activity Level : Actively seeking new investments

ORIENS CAPITAL

PO Box 13477
Tauranga Central, New Zealand 3141
Website: www.orienscapital.co.nz

Management and Staff
David Bell, Chief Financial Officer
James Beale, Chief Executive Officer
Peter Tinholt, Chief Operating Officer

Type of Firm
Private Equity Firm

Project Preferences

Type of Financing Preferred:
Generalist PE

Industry Preferences

In Consumer Related prefer:
Food/Beverage

In Transportation prefer:
Transportation

In Agr/Forestr/Fish prefer:
Agriculture related

Additional Information
Year Founded: 2016
Capital Under Management: $30,000,000
Current Activity Level : Actively seeking new investments

ORIENS IM HUNGARY SZOLGALTATO KFT

Jozsef Attila utca 1
1 em 2
Budapest, Hungary 1051
Phone: 3614290195
Fax: 3614290194
E-mail: info@oriensim.com
Website: www.oriensim.com

Other Offices

2A Saborna Street
Sofia 1000
Bulgaria, Bulgaria
Phone: 359-888-530870

Str. Caimatei, nr. 20
Sec. 2, Bucuresti
Romania, Romania
Phone: 40-744-290795

Management and Staff

Krisztian Orban, Managing Partner
Peter Holtzer, Partner
Tamas Vojnits, Partner

Type of Firm

Investment Management Firm

Project Preferences

Type of Financing Preferred:
Leveraged Buyout
Early Stage
Expansion
Generalist PE
Balanced
Later Stage
Management Buyouts
Acquisition

Geographical Preferences

International Preferences:
Hungary
Eastern Europe
Bulgaria
Romania

Industry Preferences

In Medical/Health prefer:
Medical/Health

In Consumer Related prefer:
Retail

In Industrial/Energy prefer:
Energy
Environmental Related

In Financial Services prefer:
Real Estate
Financial Services

Additional Information

Year Founded: 2007
Capital Under Management: $29,900,000
Current Activity Level : Actively seeking new investments

ORIGAMI CAPITAL PARTNERS, LLC

191 North Wacker Drive, Suite 2350
Chicago, IL USA 60606
Phone: 3122637800
Fax: 3122637806
E-mail: info@origamicapital.com
Website: origamicapital.com

Other Offices

17 Old Court Place
Lexicon House
London, United Kingdom W8 4PL
Phone: 442037139182

Management and Staff

Darren OBrien, Managing Director
Jeff Young, Managing Partner
Joelle Kellam, Chief Financial Officer
Julie Klaff, Vice President
Matthew Miller, Vice President
Richard Olson, Managing Director
Thomas Elden, Managing Partner

Type of Firm

Private Equity Firm

Project Preferences

Type of Financing Preferred:
Value-Add
Mezzanine
Generalist PE
Other
Recapitalizations

Size of Investments Considered:
Min Size of Investment Considered (000s): $10,000
Max Size of Investment Considered (000s): $50,000

Geographical Preferences

United States Preferences:
North America

International Preferences:
Europe

Industry Preferences

In Industrial/Energy prefer:
Energy

In Financial Services prefer:
Real Estate

Additional Information

Year Founded: 2008
Capital Under Management: $371,000,000
Current Activity Level : Actively seeking new investments

ORIGIN CAPITAL LTD

26-32 Voltaire Road
7A
London, United Kingdom SW4 6DH
E-mail: info@origingroup.co.uk
Website: www.origingroup.co.uk

Type of Firm

Private Equity Firm

Project Preferences

Type of Financing Preferred:
Early Stage

Industry Preferences

In Computer Software prefer:
Software

In Consumer Related prefer:
Consumer Products

In Financial Services prefer:
Financial Services

In Business Serv. prefer:
Media

In Manufact. prefer:
Manufacturing

Additional Information

Year Founded: 1998
Current Activity Level : Actively seeking new investments

ORIGIN VENTURES LLC

549 W Randolph, Suite 601
Chicago, IL USA 60661
Phone: 8479193546
Fax: 8479193547
E-mail: inquire@originventures.com
Website: www.originventures.com

Management and Staff

Brent Hill, Partner
Bruce Barron, Co-Founder
Jason Heltzer, Partner
Jason Heltzer, Partner
Steven Miller, Co-Founder

Type of Firm

Private Equity Firm

Association Membership

Illinois Venture Capital Association

Project Preferences

Role in Financing:
Will function either as deal originator or investor in deals created by others

Type of Financing Preferred:
Early Stage

Size of Investments Considered:
Min Size of Investment Considered (000s): $1,000
Max Size of Investment Considered (000s): $3,000

Geographical Preferences

United States Preferences:
Midwest
New York

Industry Preferences

In Communications prefer:
Wireless Communications

In Computer Software prefer:
Software

In Internet Specific prefer:
Internet
Ecommerce

In Biotechnology prefer:
Human Biotechnology

In Medical/Health prefer:
Mecical Products

In Business Serv. prefer:
Media

Additional Information
Name of Most Recent Fund: Origin Ventures III, L.P.
Most Recent Fund Was Raised: 02/21/2013
Year Founded: 1999
Capital Under Management: $62,200,000
Current Activity Level : Actively seeking new investments
Method of Compensation: Return on investment is of primary concern, do not charge fees

ORIGINATE VENTURES

205 Webster Street
Bethlehem, PA USA 18015
Phone: 6108665588
Fax: 6108665688
Website: www.originateventures.com

Management and Staff
Eric Arnson, Managing Partner
Glen Bressner, Managing Partner
Mike Gausling, Managing Partner

Type of Firm
Private Equity Firm

Project Preferences

Type of Financing Preferred:
Second Stage Financing
Early Stage
Expansion
Turnaround
Management Buyouts
Private Placement
Special Situation

Geographical Preferences

United States Preferences:
Mid Atlantic
Pennsylvania
Northeast

Industry Preferences

In Communications prefer:
Telecommunications

In Computer Software prefer:
Software
Systems Software
Applications Software

In Internet Specific prefer:
E-Commerce Technology
Internet
Web Aggregation/Portals

In Semiconductor/Electr prefer:
Fiber Optics

In Medical/Health prefer:
Medical/Health
Medical Diagnostics
Diagnostic Services
Diagnostic Test Products
Medical Therapeutics
Drug/Equipmt Delivery
Medical Products
Disposable Med. Products
Health Services

In Consumer Related prefer:
Consumer
Consumer Products

In Business Serv. prefer:
Distribution

Additional Information
Name of Most Recent Fund: Originate Growth Fund I
Most Recent Fund Was Raised: 03/10/2009
Year Founded: 2006
Capital Under Management: $5,000,000
Current Activity Level : Actively seeking new investments

ORIGO PARTNERS PLC

No. 8, Dongdaqiao Road
Bldg. A, N Tower, SOHO Shangdu
Beijing, China 100020
Phone: 861059002770
Fax: 861059002776
E-mail: contact@origoplc.com
Website: www.origoplc.com

Management and Staff
Alan Matthews, Managing Director
Jian Cao, Managing Director
Niklas Ponnert, Chief Financial Officer
Sig Dugal, Managing Director

Type of Firm
Private Equity Firm

Association Membership
China Venture Capital Association

Project Preferences

Type of Financing Preferred:
Leveraged Buyout
Early Stage
Expansion
Generalist PE
Balanced
Management Buyouts
Acquisition

Size of Investments Considered:
Min Size of Investment Considered (000s): $3,000
Max Size of Investment Considered (000s): $20,000

Geographical Preferences

International Preferences:
China
Asia

Industry Preferences

In Consumer Related prefer:
Consumer

In Industrial/Energy prefer:
Oil & Gas Drilling,Explor
Alternative Energy
Coal Related
Energy Conservation Relat
Environmental Related

In Business Serv. prefer:
Media

Additional Information
Year Founded: 2010
Capital Under Management: $340,000,000
Current Activity Level : Actively seeking new investments

ORION HEALTHCARE EQUITY PARTNERS

The Pilot House
Sixth Floor, Lewis Wharf
Boston, MA USA 02110
Phone: 6173264150
Fax: 6173264141
Website: www.orhep.com

Type of Firm
Private Equity Firm

Association Membership
New England Venture Capital Association

Project Preferences

Type of Financing Preferred:
Early Stage
Balanced

Geographical Preferences

United States Preferences:
All U.S.

International Preferences:
Europe

Industry Preferences

In Biotechnology prefer:
Biotechnology

Additional Information
Year Founded: 2007
Current Activity Level : Actively seeking new investments

ORIUM SAS

17 boulevard Malesherbes
Paris, France 75008
Phone: 33144117020
Fax: 33144117029
E-mail: orium@orium.fr
Website: www.orium.fr

Management and Staff
Guy Van Der Mersbrugghe, President
Olivier Moreau, President, Founder

Type of Firm
Private Equity Firm

Association Membership
French Venture Capital Association (AFIC)

Project Preferences

Type of Financing Preferred:
Leveraged Buyout
Generalist PE
Balanced
Later Stage
Management Buyouts

Geographical Preferences

International Preferences:
Italy
Europe
Portugal
Switzerland
Spain
Germany
France

Industry Preferences

In Communications prefer:
Media and Entertainment

In Internet Specific prefer:
Internet

In Consumer Related prefer:
Consumer Products

Additional Information
Year Founded: 1996
Current Activity Level : Actively seeking new investments

ORIX MEZZANINE & PRIVATE EQUITY

1717 Main Street, Suite 1100
Dallas, TX USA 75201
Website: www.orix.com

Type of Firm
Bank Affiliated

Project Preferences

Type of Financing Preferred:
Leveraged Buyout
Mezzanine
Management Buyouts
Acquisition
Recapitalizations

Geographical Preferences

United States Preferences:

Additional Information
Year Founded: 2012
Current Activity Level : Actively seeking new investments

ORIX VENTURE FINANCE

245 Park Avenue
19th Floor
New York, NY USA 10167
Phone: 8008876781
E-mail: info@orixventures.com

Other Offices
100 Pearl Street
14th Floor
HARTFORD, CT USA 06103
Phone: 8602497111

1717 Main Street, Suite 1100
DALLAS, TX USA 75201
Phone: 2142372000

Two Wisconsin Circle, Suite 575
CHEVY CHASE, MD USA 20815
Phone: 2404830679

300 Hamilton Avenue, Suite 400
PALO ALTO, CA USA 94301
Phone: 6503525000

Management and Staff
Kevin Sheehan, Chief Executive Officer
Michael David, Managing Director

Type of Firm
Private Equity Firm

Association Membership
Mid-Atlantic Venture Association
Western Association of Venture Capitalists (WAVC)

Project Preferences

Type of Financing Preferred:
Leveraged Buyout
Later Stage
Acquisition
Recapitalizations

Geographical Preferences

United States Preferences:

Canadian Preferences:
All Canada

Industry Preferences

In Communications prefer:
Telecommunications
Wireless Communications
Data Communications
Media and Entertainment

In Computer Software prefer:
Data Processing
Software

In Internet Specific prefer:
Internet

In Medical/Health prefer:
Medical/Health
Medical Products
Health Services

In Consumer Related prefer:
Consumer

In Industrial/Energy prefer:
Energy
Environmental Related

In Business Serv. prefer:
Services

ORIZA VENTURES

3300 Central Expy, Suite A
Santa Clara, CA USA 95050
E-mail: info@orizaventures.com
Website: www.orizaventures.com

Type of Firm
Private Equity Firm

Project Preferences

Type of Financing Preferred:
Early Stage

Geographical Preferences

United States Preferences:

Additional Information
Year Founded: 2015
Current Activity Level : Actively seeking new investments

ORIZZONTE SGR SPA

Piazza Sallustio, 9
Rome, Italy 00187
Phone: 39642011629
Fax: 39642814495
E-mail: info@orizzontesgr.it
Website: www.orizzontesgr.it

Management and Staff
Aldo Naples, Chief Executive Officer
Sergio Duke, President

Type of Firm
Private Equity Firm

Geographical Preferences

International Preferences:
Italy

Industry Preferences

In Computer Hardware prefer:
Terminals

In Industrial/Energy prefer:
Alternative Energy

In Transportation prefer:
Transportation
Aerospace

In Financial Services prefer:
Financial Services

Additional Information
Year Founded: 2001
Current Activity Level : Actively seeking new investments

ORKILA CAPITAL LLC

134 Spring Street
#301
New York, NY USA 10012
Phone: 2122301604
E-mail: contact@orkilacapital.com
Website: orkilacapital.com

Management and Staff
Jesse Du Bey, Co-Founder

Type of Firm
Private Equity Firm

Project Preferences

Type of Financing Preferred:
Early Stage
Balanced
Later Stage

Industry Preferences

In Consumer Related prefer:
Consumer
Entertainment and Leisure

In Business Serv. prefer:
Media

Additional Information
Year Founded: 2013
Capital Under Management: $148,525,000
Current Activity Level : Actively seeking new investments

ORKOS CAPITAL SAS

2 rue Flechier
Paris, France 75009
Phone: 33175442250
E-mail: info@orkoscapital.com
Website: www.orkoscapital.com

Management and Staff
Christian Borie, Partner
Dominique Rencurel, Partner
Jean-Jacques Bertrand, Partner
Pierre-Eric Leibovici, Partner
Pierre-Yves Meerschman, Partner

Type of Firm
Investment Management Firm

Association Membership
French Venture Capital Association (AFIC)

Additional Information
Year Founded: 2007
Capital Under Management: $240,400,000
Current Activity Level : Actively seeking new investments

Project Preferences

Type of Financing Preferred:
Leveraged Buyout
Generalist PE
Later Stage
Acquisition

Geographical Preferences

International Preferences:
Europe
France

Industry Preferences

In Communications prefer:
Communications and Media
Commercial Communications
Telecommunications
Data Communications

In Computer Hardware prefer:
Computers

In Computer Software prefer:
Data Processing
Software

In Internet Specific prefer:
Ecommerce

In Business Serv. prefer:
Services

Additional Information
Year Founded: 2006
Current Activity Level : Actively seeking new investments

ORLANDO MANAGEMENT AG

Platzl 4
Orlando-Haus
Munich, Germany 80331
Phone: 498929004850
Fax: 498929004899
E-mail: info@orlandofund.com
Website: www.orlandofund.com

Other Offices
Pfingstweidstrasse 60
Zurich, Switzerland 8005
Phone: 41442715550
Fax: 41442715554

Management and Staff
Florian Pape, Co-Founder
Georg Madersbacher, Co-Founder
Hans Gottwald, Co-Founder
Henrik Fastrich, Co-Founder
Stephan Rosarius, Managing Partner

Type of Firm
Private Equity Firm

Association Membership
Swiss Venture Capital Association (SECA)

Project Preferences

Type of Financing Preferred:
Leveraged Buyout
Turnaround
Special Situation
Recapitalizations

Geographical Preferences

International Preferences:
Switzerland
Austria
Germany

Industry Preferences

In Consumer Related prefer:
Consumer
Retail
Food/Beverage

In Industrial/Energy prefer:
Industrial Products
Materials

In Transportation prefer:
Transportation

In Financial Services prefer:
Financial Services

In Business Serv. prefer:
Services

In Manufact. prefer:
Manufacturing

Additional Information
Name of Most Recent Fund: Special Situations Venture Partners III, L.P.
Most Recent Fund Was Raised: 11/09/2011
Year Founded: 2001
Capital Under Management: $306,529,000
Current Activity Level : Actively seeking new investments

ORLANDO NORDICS AB

Birger Jarlsgatan 10
Stockholm, Sweden 114 34
Phone: 46084121280
Website: www.orlandofund.com

Type of Firm
Private Equity Firm

Project Preferences

Type of Financing Preferred:
Leveraged Buyout
Turnaround
Management Buyouts

Geographical Preferences

International Preferences:
Sweden
Finland
Norway
Denmark

Additional Information
Year Founded: 2014
Current Activity Level : Actively seeking new investments

ORLANDO VENTURE CAPITAL INC

P.O.Box 1529
Daytona Beach, FL USA 32115
Phone: 407-234-1336
Website: www.orlandoventurecapital.com

Type of Firm
Private Equity Firm

Project Preferences

Type of Financing Preferred:
Early Stage

Geographical Preferences

United States Preferences:
Florida

Industry Preferences

In Semiconductor/Electr prefer:
Laser Related
Fiber Optics

Additional Information
Year Founded: 2001
Current Activity Level : Actively seeking new investments

ORTHOGONAL PARTNERS LLP

9 Queen Anne Street
London, United Kingdom W1G 9HW
Phone: 44-20-7436-9462
Fax: 44-20-7436-9428

Management and Staff
Ahmet Ismael, Founding Partner
Daniel Gore, Founding Partner
Romek Pawlowicz, Founding Partner

Type of Firm
Private Equity Firm

Project Preferences

Type of Financing Preferred:
Fund of Funds

Geographical Preferences

International Preferences:
Europe

Additional Information
Year Founded: 2006
Current Activity Level : Actively seeking new investments

ORYX PARTNER SARL

34, quai Charles de Gaulle
Lyon, France 69006
Phone: 33472823737
Fax: 33472823739
E-mail: info@oryxpartner.fr
Website: www.oryxpartner.fr

Management and Staff
Jerome Pignard, President

Type of Firm
Private Equity Firm

Project Preferences

Type of Financing Preferred:
Leveraged Buyout
Management Buyouts

Geographical Preferences

International Preferences:
France

Additional Information
Year Founded: 1996
Current Activity Level : Actively seeking new investments

OSAGE UNIVERSITY PARTNERS

50 Monument Road, Suite 201
Bala Cynwyd, PA USA 19004
Phone: 4844342255
Fax: 4844342256
Website: osagepartners.com/osage-university-partners/

Type of Firm
Private Equity Firm

Project Preferences

Type of Financing Preferred:
Balanced

Size of Investments Considered:
Min Size of Investment Considered (000s): $5,000
Max Size of Investment Considered (000s): $10,000

Industry Preferences

In Industrial/Energy prefer:
Energy

Additional Information
Year Founded: 2014
Capital Under Management: $215,000,000
Current Activity Level : Actively seeking new investments

OSAGE VENTURE PARTNERS

50 Monument Road, Suite 201
Bala Cynwyd, PA USA 19004
Phone: 4844342255
Fax: 4844342256
E-mail: investorrelations@osagepartners.com
Website: osagepartners.com/osage-ventures-partners/

Other Offices
10 County Line Road
SOMERVILLE, NJ USA 08876
Phone: 4844342255
Fax: 4844342256

Management and Staff
John Lee, Principal
Marc Singer, Managing Partner
Matthew Cohen, Principal
Robert Adelson, Co-Founder
Sean Dowling, Vice President
William Harrington, Managing Partner

Type of Firm
Private Equity Firm

Association Membership
Mid-Atlantic Venture Association

Project Preferences

Role in Financing:
Prefer role as deal originator but will also invest in deals created by others

Type of Financing Preferred:
Early Stage

Size of Investments Considered:
Min Size of Investment Considered (000s): $1,000
Max Size of Investment Considered (000s): $3,000

Geographical Preferences

United States Preferences:
East Coast

Industry Preferences

In Computer Software prefer:
Software

Additional Information
Name of Most Recent Fund: Osage Venture Partners III, L.P.
Most Recent Fund Was Raised: 08/24/2011
Year Founded: 1990
Capital Under Management: $139,600,000
Current Activity Level : Actively seeking new investments
Method of Compensation: Return on investment is of primary concern, do not charge fees

OSAKA SMALL & MEDIUM BUSINESS INVESTMENT & CONSULTATION CO.

3-3-23 Nakanoshima
28/F Nakanoshima Dai Building
Osaka, Japan 530-6128
Phone: 81664591700
Fax: 81664591703
Website: www.sbic-wj.co.jp

Other Offices
2-14-13 Tenjin
6/F Tenjin Mitsui Building
Chuo-Ku, Fukuoka, Japan 810-0001
Phone: 81927240651
Fax: 81927240657

Type of Firm
Private Equity Firm

Project Preferences

Type of Financing Preferred:
Balanced

Geographical Preferences

International Preferences:
Japan

Additional Information
Year Founded: 1963
Current Activity Level : Actively seeking new investments

OSCEOLA CAPITAL MANAGEMENT LLC

40 Ranch Road
Thonotosassa, FL USA 33592
Phone: 8139865788
Fax: 8139863123
Website: osceolacapitalmgmt.com

Management and Staff
Benjamin Moe, Venture Partner
Harold Babb, Managing Partner
Michael Babb, Managing Partner
Robert Thomas, Managing Partner
Robert Collins, Venture Partner
Tony Umholtz, Venture Partner

Type of Firm
Private Equity Firm

Project Preferences

Type of Financing Preferred:
Leveraged Buyout
Acquisition

Additional Information
Year Founded: 2015
Capital Under Management: $9,025,000
Current Activity Level : Actively seeking new investments

OSK VENTURES INTERNATIONAL BHD

Plaza OSK, Jalan Ampang
15th floor
Kuala Lumpur, Malaysia 50450
Phone: 60321753388
Fax: 60321753391
E-mail: corp.finance@osk.com.my
Website: www.oskvi.com

Management and Staff
Chee Wai Yee, Chief Operating Officer
Choo Chee Beng, Chief Financial Officer
Patrick Yee Chee Wai, Chief Operating Officer
Shew Sze Ong, Chief Financial Officer

Type of Firm
Bank Affiliated

Association Membership
Malaysian Venture Capital Association

Project Preferences

Role in Financing:
Prefer role as deal originator

Type of Financing Preferred:
Leveraged Buyout
Mezzanine
Balanced
Later Stage

Geographical Preferences

International Preferences:
Asia
Malaysia

Industry Preferences

In Communications prefer:
Communications and Media

In Biotechnology prefer:
Biotechnology

In Manufact. prefer:
Manufacturing

Additional Information
Year Founded: 2003
Capital Under Management: $26,000,000
Current Activity Level : Actively seeking new investments

OSPREY CAPITAL LTD

Exchange Flags
Fifth Floor, Horton House
Liverpool, United Kingdom L2 3PF
Phone: 447941140629
E-mail: info@osprey-capital.co.uk
Website: www.osprey-capital.co.uk

Type of Firm
Private Equity Firm

Project Preferences

Type of Financing Preferred:
Early Stage
Expansion
Later Stage
Seed
Startup

Geographical Preferences

International Preferences:
United Kingdom

Industry Preferences

In Consumer Related prefer:
Retail

In Financial Services prefer:
Financial Services

In Business Serv. prefer:
Services

Additional Information
Year Founded: 2008
Current Activity Level : Actively seeking new investments

OTIUM CAPITAL SARL

19 Avenue Dubonnet
Courbevoie, France 92400
Phone: 33170840100
Fax: 33170840215
Website: www.otiumcapital.com

Management and Staff
Antoine Freysz, Managing Director
Christian Raisson, Chief Financial Officer

Type of Firm
Private Equity Firm

Project Preferences

Type of Financing Preferred:
Early Stage
Later Stage
Seed
Startup

Geographical Preferences

International Preferences:
Italy
United Kingdom
Europe
Netherlands
Spain
Australia
France

Industry Preferences

In Communications prefer:
Telecommunications

In Computer Software prefer:
Software
Applications Software

In Internet Specific prefer:
Internet

In Consumer Related prefer:
Entertainment and Leisure

Additional Information
Year Founded: 2009
Current Activity Level : Actively seeking new investments

OTTER CAPITAL LLC

755 Page Mill Road, Suite A200
Palo Alto, CA USA 94304
Phone: 6504935263
Website: ottercapital.com

Management and Staff
John Pasquesi, Founder

Type of Firm
Private Equity Firm

Project Preferences

Type of Financing Preferred:
Balanced

Geographical Preferences

United States Preferences:

Industry Preferences

In Internet Specific prefer:
Ecommerce

In Consumer Related prefer:
Food/Beverage

In Financial Services prefer:
Financial Services

Additional Information
Year Founded: 2000
Current Activity Level : Actively seeking new investments

OUEST ANGELS DEVELOPPEMENT SAS

8 rue de Gorges - place Royale
Nantes, France 79035
Phone: 33240356942
Fax: 33251720207
E-mail: contact@ouestangels.org
Website: www.ouestangels.org

Management and Staff
Gilles Gergaud, President

Type of Firm
Private Equity Firm

Project Preferences

Type of Financing Preferred:
Early Stage
Seed

Size of Investments Considered:
Min Size of Investment Considered (000s): $63
Max Size of Investment Considered (000s): $251

Geographical Preferences

International Preferences:
Europe
France

Industry Preferences

In Communications prefer:
Commercial Communications
Telecommunications
Media and Entertainment

In Internet Specific prefer:
Internet
Ecommerce

In Semiconductor/Electr prefer:
Electronics

In Medical/Health prefer:
Medical/Health
Health Services

In Industrial/Energy prefer:
Industrial Products

In Business Serv. prefer:
Services

Additional Information
Year Founded: 2010
Current Activity Level : Actively seeking new investments

OUEST CROISSANCE SAS

3 Impasse Claude Nougard Bat D
D2 ZAC Armor Plaza
Saint-Herblain, France 44812
Phone: 33240586219

Fax: 33240586203
Website: www.ouest-croissance.com

Management and Staff
Didier Chaboche, Founder
Olivier Philippon, Founder
Stephane Michel, Founder

Type of Firm
Bank Affiliated

Association Membership
French Venture Capital Association (AFIC)

Project Preferences

Type of Financing Preferred:
Leveraged Buyout
Early Stage
Generalist PE
Later Stage
Acquisition

Size of Investments Considered:
Min Size of Investment Considered (000s): $141
Max Size of Investment Considered (000s): $7,086

Geographical Preferences

International Preferences:
Europe
France

Industry Preferences

In Biotechnology prefer:
Agricultural/Animal Bio.

In Industrial/Energy prefer:
Industrial Products

In Business Serv. prefer:
Services

In Manufact. prefer:
Manufacturing

In Agr/Forestr/Fish prefer:
Agriculture related

Additional Information
Year Founded: 1987
Current Activity Level : Actively seeking new investments

OURCROWD INVESTMENT IN SHOPIAL LP

14 Rabbi Akiva Street
Jerusalem, Israel 9102301
Phone: 97226369303

Type of Firm
Private Equity Firm

Project Preferences

Type of Financing Preferred:
Early Stage
Expansion
Balanced
Later Stage

Geographical Preferences

International Preferences:
Israel
Asia

Additional Information
Year Founded: 2012
Current Activity Level : Actively seeking new investments

OUTBOUND VENTURES LLC

1460 Broadway
New York, NY USA 10036
E-mail: hello@outboundventures.com
Website: outboundventures.com

Type of Firm
Private Equity Firm

Project Preferences

Type of Financing Preferred:
Balanced

Additional Information
Year Founded: 2016
Current Activity Level : Actively seeking new investments

OUTLIER VENTURES LTD

3 Churchgates The Wilderness
Berkhamsted
Hertfordshire, United Kingdom

Management and Staff
Stephan Apel, Managing Partner
Walther Doernte, Partner

Type of Firm
Private Equity Firm

Project Preferences

Type of Financing Preferred:
Balanced

Industry Preferences

In Computer Software prefer:
Software

In Industrial/Energy prefer:
Robotics

Additional Information
Year Founded: 2014
Current Activity Level : Actively seeking new investments

OUTLOOK VENTURES

3000F Danville Boulevard, Suite 110
Alamo, CA USA 94507
Phone: 4155470000
Website: www.outlookventures.com

Management and Staff
Carl Nichols, Managing Director
Randy Haykin, Managing Director

Type of Firm
Private Equity Firm

Project Preferences

Role in Financing:
Prefer role as deal originator but will also invest in deals created by others

Type of Financing Preferred:
Early Stage
Expansion
Balanced

Size of Investments Considered:
Min Size of Investment Considered (000s): $1,000
Max Size of Investment Considered (000s): $10,000

Geographical Preferences

United States Preferences:
West Coast

Industry Focus
(% based on actual investment)
    Computer Software and Services 50.8%
    Internet Specific 38.1%
    Other Products 10.4%
    Computer Hardware 0.6%

Additional Information
Name of Most Recent Fund: Outlook Ventures III
Most Recent Fund Was Raised: 10/10/2002
Year Founded: 1996
Capital Under Management: $225,000,000
Current Activity Level : Actively seeking new investments
Method of Compensation: Return on investment is of primary concern, do not charge fees

OUTPOST CAPITAL LLC

220 Monroe Drive
Mountain View, CA USA 94040
Phone: 7182882654
Website: www.outpostvc.com

Type of Firm
Private Equity Firm

Project Preferences

Type of Financing Preferred:
Early Stage

Geographical Preferences

United States Preferences:

International Preferences:
China

Industry Preferences

In Computer Software prefer:
Artificial Intelligence

Additional Information

Year Founded: 2017
Capital Under Management: $5,000,000
Current Activity Level : Actively seeking new investments

OVAL PARTNERS

201 Spear Street, Suite 1750
San Francisco, CA USA 94105
E-mail: info@OvalPartners.com
Website: www.ovalpartners.com

Management and Staff

Dan Ruhl, Co-Founder
Jake Mizrahi, Co-Founder
John Knoll, Co-Founder

Type of Firm

Private Equity Firm

Additional Information

Year Founded: 2015
Current Activity Level : Actively seeking new investments

OVERALL CAPITAL PARTNERS

306 Dartmouth Street, Suite 204
Boston, MA USA 02116
E-mail: info@overallcapital.com
Website: www.overallcapital.com

Type of Firm

Private Equity Firm

Project Preferences

Type of Financing Preferred:
Leveraged Buyout
Expansion
Generalist PE
Later Stage

Additional Information

Year Founded: 1969
Current Activity Level : Actively seeking new investments

OVERLAKE CAPITAL LLC

11900 NorthEast 1st streeet, Suite 300
Bellevue, WA USA 98005
E-mail: info@overlake.com
Website: www.overlake.com

Type of Firm

Investment Management Firm

Project Preferences

Type of Financing Preferred:
Value-Add
Balanced

Industry Preferences

In Financial Services prefer:
Real Estate

Additional Information

Year Founded: 2009
Current Activity Level : Actively seeking new investments

OVERSEAS PRIVATE INVESTMENT CORP

1100 New York Avenue
Washington, DC USA 20527
Phone: 2023368400
Fax: 2023367949
E-mail: info@opic.gov
Website: www.opic.gov

Management and Staff

Allan Villabroza, Chief Financial Officer
John Moran, Vice President
John Morton, Vice President
Judith Pryor, Vice President

Type of Firm

Government Affiliated Program

Association Membership

Emerging Markets Private Equity Association

Project Preferences

Type of Financing Preferred:
Fund of Funds
Balanced

Geographical Preferences

International Preferences:
Latin America
Eastern Europe
Middle East
Asia
Africa

Industry Preferences

In Biotechnology prefer:
Agricultural/Animal Bio.

In Medical/Health prefer:
Medical/Health

In Other prefer:
Socially Responsible

Additional Information

Year Founded: 1911
Current Activity Level : Actively seeking new investments

OVERTURE CAPITAL PARTNERS (AKA: OVERTURE)

205 - 5th Avenue Southwest
Ste 3400, Bow Valley Square II
Calgary, Canada T2P 2V7
Phone: 403-770-4800
Fax: 403-770-4850
Website: www.overlordfinancial.com

Type of Firm

Bank Affiliated

Project Preferences

Type of Financing Preferred:
Early Stage

Geographical Preferences

Canadian Preferences:
All Canada

Industry Preferences

In Industrial/Energy prefer:
Energy
Oil and Gas Exploration

Additional Information

Year Founded: 2003
Current Activity Level : Actively seeking new investments

OVO FUND LLC

235 Alma Street
Palo Alto, CA USA 94301
E-mail: info@ovofund.com
Website: www.ovofund.com

Type of Firm

Private Equity Firm

Project Preferences

Type of Financing Preferred:
Early Stage
Seed

Additional Information
Year Founded: 2014
Capital Under Management: $17,210,000
Current Activity Level : Actively seeking new investments

OWL VENTURES LP

400 Pacific Ave
San Francisco, CA USA 94133
Phone: 4152770300
Fax: 4152770301
E-mail: info@owlvc.com
Website: www.owlvc.com

Management and Staff
Amit Patel, Principal
Ashley Bittner, Principal
Jed Smith, Co-Founder
Tom Costin, Principal
Tory Patterson, Co-Founder

Type of Firm
Private Equity Firm

Project Preferences

Type of Financing Preferred:
Balanced

Industry Preferences

In Consumer Related prefer:
Education Related

Additional Information
Year Founded: 2015
Current Activity Level : Actively seeking new investments

OWNER RESOURCE GROUP LLC

600 Congress Avenue, Suite 200
Austin, TX USA 78701
Phone: 5125054180
E-mail: info@orgroup.com

Management and Staff
Jonathan Gormin, Managing Director
Lee Walker, Managing Director
Will Burnett, Managing Director

Type of Firm
Private Equity Firm

Association Membership
Natl Assoc of Small Bus. Inv. Co (NASBIC)

Project Preferences

Type of Financing Preferred:
Leveraged Buyout
Management Buyouts
Acquisition

Industry Preferences

In Business Serv. prefer:
Services
Distribution

In Manufact. prefer:
Manufacturing

Additional Information
Name of Most Recent Fund: ORG Opportunity Fund II, L.P.
Most Recent Fund Was Raised: 06/24/2013
Year Founded: 2009
Capital Under Management: $153,600,000
Current Activity Level : Actively seeking new investments

OWW CAPITAL PARTNERS PTE LTD

65 Chulia Street, Suite 39-01 OCBC Center
Singapore, Singapore 049513
Phone: 6565381220
Fax: 6565380544
E-mail: corporate@oww.com.sg
Website: www.oww.com.sg

Other Offices
Number 969 Zhong Shan Nan Road
Room 1001 Gu Tai Bin Jiang Plaza
Shanghai, China 200010
Phone: 86-21-5150-8802
Fax: 86-21-5150-8801

Management and Staff
Bien Chuan Tan, Co-Founder
Meng Yiau Lye, Vice President

Type of Firm
Private Equity Firm

Project Preferences

Type of Financing Preferred:
Early Stage
Expansion
Balanced
Later Stage
Seed
Startup

Size of Investments Considered:
Min Size of Investment Considered (000s): $500
Max Size of Investment Considered (000s): $10,000

Geographical Preferences

United States Preferences:
Southeast

International Preferences:
China
Asia

Industry Preferences

In Communications prefer:
Telecommunications

In Medical/Health prefer:
Medical/Health

In Consumer Related prefer:
Consumer Services
Education Related

In Financial Services prefer:
Financial Services

In Business Serv. prefer:
Distribution

Additional Information
Year Founded: 1991
Capital Under Management: $140,000,000
Current Activity Level : Actively seeking new investments

OXEON PARTNERS

330 Hudson Street, Suite 300
New York, NY USA 10013
Phone: 6465032200
E-mail: info.oxeonpartners.com
Website: www.oxeonpartners.com

Management and Staff
JIA JIA YE, Chief Operating Officer

Type of Firm
Private Equity Firm

Project Preferences

Type of Financing Preferred:
Early Stage

Industry Preferences

In Medical/Health prefer:
Health Services

In Business Serv. prefer:
Services

Additional Information
Year Founded: 2011
Current Activity Level : Actively seeking new investments

OXER CAPITAL INC

2523 BRENTWOOD ROAD
Columbus, OH USA 43209
Website: www.oxercapital.com

Management and Staff
Michael O Brien, Partner

Type of Firm
Private Equity Firm

Project Preferences

Type of Financing Preferred:
Leveraged Buyout
Mezzanine
Acquisition
Recapitalizations

Geographical Preferences

United States Preferences:
North America

Additional Information
Year Founded: 2016
Capital Under Management: $122,000,000
Current Activity Level : Actively seeking new investments

OXFORD BIOSCIENCE PARTNERS

535 Boylston Street, Suite 402
Boston, MA USA 02116
Phone: 6173577474
Fax: 6173577476
Website: www.oxbio.com

Other Offices

191 Post Road West, Suite 69
Westport, CT USA 06880
Phone: 203-341-3300
Fax: 203-341-3309

30765 Pacific Coast Highway, Suite 427
Malibu, CA USA 90265
Phone: 310-589-0025
Fax: 310-589-0099

Management and Staff

Alan Walton, General Partner
B. Christopher Kim, Partner
Cornelius Ryan, Founder
Dan Cole, Venture Partner
Douglas Fambrough, Venture Partner
Edmund Olivier, General Partner
Jonathan Fleming, Managing Partner
Matthew Gibbs, General Partner
Raymond Charest, Chief Financial Officer

Type of Firm
Private Equity Firm

Association Membership
New England Venture Capital Association

Project Preferences

Role in Financing:
Prefer role as deal originator but will also invest in deals created by others

Type of Financing Preferred:
Early Stage
Balanced
Seed
Startup

Size of Investments Considered:
Min Size of Investment Considered (000s): $1,000
Max Size of Investment Considered (000s): $10,000

Geographical Preferences

United States Preferences:

International Preferences:
North Korea
Korea, South

Industry Focus
(% based on actual investment)

Biotechnology	51.9%
Medical/Health	39.7%
Computer Software and Services	2.2%
Industrial/Energy	2.0%
Internet Specific	1.5%
Semiconductors/Other Elect.	1.5%
Consumer Related	0.9%
Other Products	0.2%

Additional Information
Year Founded: 1992
Capital Under Management: $1,000,000,000
Current Activity Level : Actively seeking new investments
Method of Compensation: Return on investment is of primary concern, do not charge fees

OXFORD CAPITAL PARTNERS HOLDINGS LTD

201 Cumnor Hill
Oxford, United Kingdom OX2 9PJ
Phone: 441865860760
Fax: 441865860761
E-mail: info@oxcp.com
Website: www.oxcp.com

Other Offices

18 Harcourt Road
2802 Admiralty Centre Tower 1
, Hong Kong
Phone: 852-3748-3715
Fax: 44-0-1865-860-761

Six route de Malagnou
Geneva, Switzerland 1208
Phone: 41-22-347-7933
Fax: 41-22-346-4110

Management and Staff
Edward Mott, Chief Executive Officer

Type of Firm
Bank Affiliated

Association Membership
British Venture Capital Association (BVCA)

Project Preferences

Type of Financing Preferred:
Early Stage
Expansion
Balanced
Seed
Startup

Geographical Preferences

International Preferences:
United Kingdom
Europe

Industry Preferences

In Communications prefer:
Telecommunications
Wireless Communications
Data Communications

In Computer Software prefer:
Software

In Internet Specific prefer:
Internet

In Biotechnology prefer:
Biotechnology

In Medical/Health prefer:
Medical/Health
Pharmaceuticals

In Industrial/Energy prefer:
Advanced Materials

Additional Information
Year Founded: 1999
Capital Under Management: $73,400,000
Current Activity Level : Actively seeking new investments

OXFORD EARLY INVESTMENTS

Oxford Centre For Innovation
Mill Street
Oxford, United Kingdom OX2 0JX
Phone: 441865261490
E-mail: contact@oxei.co.uk
Website: www.oxei.co.uk

Type of Firm
Angel Group

Project Preferences

Type of Financing Preferred:
Early Stage

Size of Investments Considered:
Min Size of Investment Considered (000s): $80
Max Size of Investment Considered (000s): $399

Geographical Preferences

International Preferences:
United Kingdom
Western Europe

Additional Information

Year Founded: 2004
Current Activity Level : Actively seeking new investments

OXFORD TECHNOLOGY MANAGEMENT LTD

1 Robert Robinson Avenue
Magdalen Centre
Oxford, United Kingdom OX4 4GA
Phone: 441865784466
Fax: 441865784430
Website: www.oxfordtechnology.com

Management and Staff

Lucius Cary, Managing Director

Type of Firm

Private Equity Firm

Project Preferences

Role in Financing:
Prefer role as deal originator but will also invest in deals created by others

Type of Financing Preferred:
Early Stage
Balanced
Later Stage
Seed

Size of Investments Considered:
Min Size of Investment Considered (000s): $160
Max Size of Investment Considered (000s): $3,191

Geographical Preferences

International Preferences:
United Kingdom

Industry Focus

(% based on actual investment)
Medical/Health	47.0%
Biotechnology	26.6%
Internet Specific	11.1%
Industrial/Energy	5.7%
Computer Software and Services	3.7%
Semiconductors/Other Elect.	1.9%
Other Products	1.9%
Communications and Media	1.2%
Computer Hardware	0.8%

Additional Information

Name of Most Recent Fund: Oxford Technology 4 VCT
Most Recent Fund Was Raised: 08/31/2004
Year Founded: 1983
Capital Under Management: $18,100,000

Current Activity Level : Actively seeking new investments
Method of Compensation: Return on invest. most important, but chg. closing fees, service fees, etc.

OXX LTD

20-22 Bedford Row
London, United Kingdom WC1R 4JS
Website: oxx.vc

Type of Firm

Private Equity Firm

Project Preferences

Type of Financing Preferred:
Balanced

Industry Preferences

In Computer Software prefer:
Software

Additional Information

Year Founded: 2017
Current Activity Level : Actively seeking new investments

OXY CAPITAL SOCIEDADE DE CAPITAL DE RISCO SA

Avenida Engenheiro Duarte Pach
Tower 2, 15Th Floor
Lisbon, Portugal 1070102
Phone: 351218200010
E-mail: info@oxycapital.com
Website: www.oxycapital.com

Type of Firm

Private Equity Firm

Project Preferences

Type of Financing Preferred:
Leveraged Buyout
Expansion
Mezzanine
Generalist PE
Balanced
Later Stage
Acquisition
Recapitalizations

Geographical Preferences

International Preferences:
Europe
Portugal

Additional Information

Year Founded: 2011
Capital Under Management: $96,850,000
Current Activity Level : Actively seeking new investments

OXYGEN VENTURES LTD

L13, Ten Queens Road
Melbourne, Australia 3004
Phone: 61398689936
E-mail: hello@oxygenventures.com.au
Website: www.oxygenventures.com.au

Type of Firm

Private Equity Firm

Association Membership

Australian Venture Capital Association (AVCAL)

Project Preferences

Type of Financing Preferred:
Early Stage
Startup

Additional Information

Year Founded: 2012
Capital Under Management: $38,900,000
Current Activity Level : Actively seeking new investments

OYSTER CAPITAL PARTNERS

Oyster Point, Temple Road
Blackrock
Dublin, Ireland
Phone: 35312799549
Fax: 35312799589

Management and Staff

Martin Scully, Chief Executive Officer

Type of Firm

Private Equity Firm

Project Preferences

Type of Financing Preferred:
Early Stage
Startup

Geographical Preferences

International Preferences:
Ireland

Additional Information

Year Founded: 2000
Current Activity Level : Actively seeking new investments

- P -

P FACTORY SAS

Rue Joseph Biaggi
Chez EMD
Marseilles, France 13331
Website: pfactory.co

Type of Firm
Incubator/Development Program

Project Preferences

Type of Financing Preferred:
Early Stage
Seed

Geographical Preferences

International Preferences:
France

Additional Information
Year Founded: 2014
Current Activity Level : Actively seeking new investments

P SCHOENFELD ASSET MANAGEMENT LP

1350 Avenue of the Americas
21st Floor
New York, NY USA 10019
Phone: 2126499500
Fax: 2126499540
E-mail: info@psam.com
Website: www.psamllc.com

Other Offices
Ten Bruton Street
Second Floor
London, United Kingdom W1J 6PX

Management and Staff
Louis Friedman, President

Type of Firm
Investment Management Firm

Project Preferences

Type of Financing Preferred:
Acquisition
Special Situation
Distressed Debt

Industry Focus
(% based on actual investment)
Computer Software and Services	92.8%
Other Products	7.2%

Additional Information
Year Founded: 1997

P&S CAPITAL DOO

Slovenska 56
Ljubljana, Slovenia SI-1000
Phone: 38612343300
Fax: 38612343333
E-mail: info@p-s.com
Website: www.p-s.si

Other Offices
11 Stefan Karadzha Street
entrance B, 3rd floor
Sofia, Bulgaria 1000

B-dul Unirii, bloc 15
Scara 7, 1st floor, Suite #19, Sector 5
Bucharest, Romania

Tolstogo 41, of. 3, 5
Kiev, Ukraine 01032

82 St. John Street
London, United Kingdom EC 1M 4JN

65 Boulevard de la Grand-Duchesse Charlotte
, Luxembourg L-1331

Management and Staff
Dean Mikolic, Managing Partner

Type of Firm
Service Provider

Project Preferences

Type of Financing Preferred:
Leveraged Buyout
Management Buyouts
Acquisition

Geographical Preferences

International Preferences:
Europe
Eastern Europe
Ukraine
Bulgaria
Romania

Industry Preferences

In Communications prefer:
Telecommunications

In Medical/Health prefer:
Medical/Health
Pharmaceuticals

In Consumer Related prefer:
Entertainment and Leisure

Capital Under Management: $300,000,000
Current Activity Level : Actively seeking new investments

In Industrial/Energy prefer:
Environmental Related

In Transportation prefer:
Transportation
Aerospace

In Financial Services prefer:
Financial Services

In Business Serv. prefer:
Services

Additional Information
Year Founded: 1989
Current Activity Level : Actively seeking new investments

P39 CAPITAL LP

350 Rhode Island Street, Suite 420
San Francisco, CA USA 94103
Website: www.p39capital.com

Type of Firm
Private Equity Firm

Project Preferences

Type of Financing Preferred:
Startup

Geographical Preferences

United States Preferences:
Northern California

International Preferences:
India

Additional Information
Year Founded: 2015
Current Activity Level : Actively seeking new investments

P4G CAPITAL MANAGEMENT LLC

455 Market Street, Suite 620
San Francisco, CA USA 94105
Phone: 4155102160
E-mail: info@p4gcap.com
Website: www.p4gcap.com

Management and Staff
Hugh Browne, Managing Director
Mark Allums, Vice President
Rachel Lehman, Managing Director
Shamus Dailey, Vice President
Todd Meyerrose, Vice President

Type of Firm
Private Equity Firm

Project Preferences

Type of Financing Preferred:
Generalist PE

Industry Preferences

In Industrial/Energy prefer:
Energy

In Transportation prefer:
Aerospace

In Manufact. prefer:
Manufacturing

Additional Information
Year Founded: 2017
Current Activity Level : Actively seeking new investments

PAC-LINK MANAGEMENT CORP

2. Tun Hwa South Road, Sec. 2
14F
Taipei, Taiwan
Phone: 886227555000
Fax: 886227552000
E-mail: info@paclink.com.tw
Website: www.paclink.com.tw

Other Offices

20/F 8 Xingyi Road
Shanghai Maxdo Center
Shanghai, China
Phone: 86-21-5208-2929
Fax: 86-21-5208-1369

2445 Faber Place, Suite 102
Palo Alto, CA USA 94303
Phone: 650-857-0686
Fax: 650-857-0682

Management and Staff

Allen Hsu, General Partner
Ben Feng, General Partner
Jessica Huang, Partner
Le-Chun Wang, Partner
Ming Hsu, General Partner
Neil Wu, Partner

Type of Firm
Private Equity Firm

Association Membership
Taiwan Venture Capital Association (TVCA)

Project Preferences

Type of Financing Preferred:
Expansion
Mezzanine
Balanced
Seed
Startup

Geographical Preferences

United States Preferences:
North America

International Preferences:
Taiwan
China
Asia

Industry Preferences

In Communications prefer:
Telecommunications

In Computer Software prefer:
Software

In Semiconductor/Electr prefer:
Semiconductor
Optoelectronics

In Biotechnology prefer:
Biotechnology

In Industrial/Energy prefer:
Advanced Materials
Factory Automation
Process Control
Machinery
Environmental Related

In Transportation prefer:
Transportation

Additional Information
Year Founded: 1998
Capital Under Management: $205,700,000
Current Activity Level : Actively seeking new investments

PACIFIC ADVANTAGE CAPITAL LTD

29 Queen's Road
17/F Aon China Building
Hong Kong, Hong Kong
Phone: 852-3978-2321
E-mail: info@pac-partners.com
Website: www.pac-partners.com

Management and Staff
David Zezza, Partner
James White, Partner
Joseph Draper, Partner

Type of Firm
Private Equity Firm

Project Preferences

Type of Financing Preferred:
Leveraged Buyout
Expansion
Generalist PE
Turnaround
Opportunistic
Acquisition
Distressed Debt

Geographical Preferences

International Preferences:
Hong Kong

Industry Preferences

In Medical/Health prefer:
Medical/Health
Diagnostic Services
Health Services
Pharmaceuticals

Additional Information
Year Founded: 2008
Current Activity Level : Actively seeking new investments

PACIFIC AGRI CAPITAL LTD

Three Pickering Street, Suite 02-11 Nankin Row
China Square Central, Singapore 048660
Phone: 6562244873
Fax: 6562244874
Website: pacificagricapital.com

Management and Staff
Bill Randall, Managing Director

Type of Firm
Private Equity Firm

Association Membership
Emerging Markets Private Equity Association

Project Preferences

Type of Financing Preferred:
Early Stage
Expansion
Later Stage

Geographical Preferences

International Preferences:
Peru
Asia
Singapore
Malaysia

Industry Preferences

In Consumer Related prefer:
Food/Beverage

In Agr/Forestr/Fish prefer:
Agribusiness
Agriculture related

In Other prefer:
Environment Responsible

Additional Information
Year Founded: 2011
Current Activity Level : Actively seeking new investments

PACIFIC ALLIANCE CAPITAL GROUP LTD

Nine Queen's Road Central, Suite 2501, 25th Floor
Hong Kong, Hong Kong
Phone: 85228101399
E-mail: pag@pacgrp.com
Website: www.pacgrp.com

Management and Staff
Cecilia Mak, Managing Director
Jacky Soong, Chief Operating Officer
Kevin Murphy, Managing Director

Type of Firm
Private Equity Firm

Project Preferences

Type of Financing Preferred:
Early Stage
Balanced
Later Stage
Startup

Geographical Preferences

International Preferences:
Asia Pacific
Hong Kong
Asia

Additional Information
Year Founded: 1991
Current Activity Level : Actively seeking new investments

PACIFIC ALLIANCE GROUP LTD

1 Connaught Road Central
32nd Floor, AIA Central
Hong Kong, Hong Kong
Phone: 85229180088
Fax: 85229180081
E-mail: info@pagasia.com
Website: www.pagasia.com

Other Offices
1 Connaught Road Central
15/F, AIA Central
Hong Kong, Hong Kong
Phone: 85229180088
Fax: 85229180881

226 Shinmunro, 1-Ga, Jongro-Gu
14/F Hungkuk Life Insurance Bldg
Seoul, South Korea 110-786
Phone: 82267420100
Fax: 82267420110

1366 Nanjing Road (West)
45/F, Unit 01, Tower 2, Plaza 66
Shanghai, China 200040
Phone: 862162883788
Fax: 862162889272

79 Jianguo Road
24/F, Unit 05, Tower 2, China Central
Beijing, China 100025
Phone: 861085882998
Fax: 861085882996

15, Tolstoy Marg,
8/F, Tolstoy House
New Delhi, India 110001
Phone: 911143094309
Fax: 911143094310

4-1-28 Toranomon, Minato-ku
20/F, Toranomon Towers Office
Tokyo, Japan 105-6033
Phone: 81364303511
Fax: 81364303521

Management and Staff
Anthony Miller, Partner
Christopher Gradel, Managing Partner
J-P Toppino, Managing Partner
Jack Keese, Managing Director
Weijian Shan, Chief Executive Officer

Type of Firm
Investment Management Firm

Association Membership
China Venture Capital Association
Hong Kong Venture Capital Association (HKVCA)

Project Preferences

Type of Financing Preferred:
Leveraged Buyout
Value-Add

Geographical Preferences

International Preferences:
China

Industry Preferences

In Medical/Health prefer:
Medical/Health

In Industrial/Energy prefer:
Energy
Industrial Products

In Transportation prefer:
Transportation

In Financial Services prefer:
Financial Services
Real Estate

Additional Information
Year Founded: 2002
Capital Under Management: $6,056,410,000
Current Activity Level : Actively seeking new investments

PACIFIC CAPITAL SARL

28, Boulevard d'Avranches
Luxembourg, Luxembourg L-1160
Phone: 35226262925
Fax: 35224611653
E-mail: info@pacific-capital.lu
Website: www.pacific-capital.lu

Other Offices
255-257 Gloucester Road, Suite 1703, Sino Plaza
Causeway Bay, Hong Kong
Phone: 85228400222
Fax: 85228931860

Type of Firm
Private Equity Firm

Project Preferences

Type of Financing Preferred:
Leveraged Buyout
Early Stage
Generalist PE
Public Companies
Later Stage
Seed
Management Buyouts
Acquisition

Geographical Preferences

International Preferences:
Luxembourg
Europe
Germany

Industry Preferences

In Communications prefer:
Communications and Media
Telecommunications
Wireless Communications
Media and Entertainment

In Industrial/Energy prefer:
Energy Conservation Relat
Environmental Related

In Other prefer:
Environment Responsible

Additional Information
Year Founded: 2007
Current Activity Level : Actively seeking new investments

PACIFIC COMMUNITY VENTURES LLC

51 Federal Street, Suite 402
San Francisco, CA USA 94107
Phone: 4154424300
Fax: 4154424313
E-mail: information@pcvfund.com
Website: www.pacificcommunityventures.org

Management and Staff
Eduardo Rallo, Managing Partner
Peter Mehrberg, Managing Partner
Yolanda Ruiz, Partner

Type of Firm
Private Equity Firm

Association Membership
Community Development Venture Capital Alliance

Project Preferences

Role in Financing:
Will function either as deal originator or investor in deals created by others

Type of Financing Preferred:
Expansion
Generalist PE
Balanced
Management Buyouts
Recapitalizations

Size of Investments Considered:
Min Size of Investment Considered (000s): $1,000
Max Size of Investment Considered (000s): $4,000

Geographical Preferences

United States Preferences:
California

Industry Preferences

In Communications prefer:
Radio & TV Broadcasting

In Consumer Related prefer:
Consumer

In Business Serv. prefer:
Services
Distribution

In Manufact. prefer:
Manufacturing

In Other prefer:
Socially Responsible
Women/Minority-Owned Bus.

Additional Information
Name of Most Recent Fund: Pacific Community Ventures III, LLC
Most Recent Fund Was Raised: 01/09/2007
Year Founded: 1999
Capital Under Management: $60,000,000
Current Activity Level: Actively seeking new investments
Method of Compensation: Return on invest. most important, but chg. closing fees, service fees, etc.

PACIFIC ENTERPRISE CAPITAL LLC

CITIC Building, Suite 2504
19 Jianguomenwai Ave.
Beijing, China 100004
Phone: 86-10-8526-1255
Fax: 86-10-8526-1277
E-mail: info@pecgroup.com
Website: www.pecgroup.com

Other Offices
1840 Gateway Drive, Suite 200
San Mateo, CA USA 94404
Phone: 650-378-1465
Fax: 650-378-1399

Management and Staff
Henry Sun, Managing Director

Type of Firm
Private Equity Firm

Project Preferences

Type of Financing Preferred:
Early Stage
Balanced

Size of Investments Considered:
Min Size of Investment Considered (000s): $2,000
Max Size of Investment Considered (000s): $8,000

Geographical Preferences

International Preferences:
China

Industry Preferences

In Medical/Health prefer:
Health Services

In Financial Services prefer:
Financial Services

In Business Serv. prefer:
Media

Additional Information
Year Founded: 1999
Current Activity Level: Actively seeking new investments

PACIFIC EQUITY PARTNERS PTY LTD

126 Phillip Street
Level 31
Sydney, Australia 2000
Phone: 61282382600
Fax: 61282382690
E-mail: information@pep.com.au
Website: www.pep.com.au

Management and Staff
Cameron Blanks, Managing Director
David Grayce, Managing Director
David Brown, Managing Director
Geoff Hutchinson, Managing Director
Jake Haines, Managing Director
Paul McCullagh, Founder
Rickard Gardell, Managing Director
Shannon Wolfers, Managing Director
Simon Pillar, Managing Director
Tim Sims, Founder
Tony Duthie, Managing Director

Type of Firm
Private Equity Firm

Association Membership
New Zealand Venture Capital Association
Australian Venture Capital Association (AVCAL)

Project Preferences

Role in Financing:
Will function either as deal originator or investor in deals created by others

Type of Financing Preferred:
Leveraged Buyout
Later Stage

Geographical Preferences

International Preferences:
Australia
New Zealand

Industry Preferences

In Consumer Related prefer:
Entertainment and Leisure
Consumer Products

In Industrial/Energy prefer:
Energy
Industrial Products

In Financial Services prefer:
Financial Services

Additional Information
Year Founded: 1998
Capital Under Management: $6,404,600,000
Current Activity Level: Actively seeking new investments
Method of Compensation: Return on invest. most important, but chg. closing fees, service fees, etc.

PACIFIC GENERAL VENTURES LLC

99 Belbrook Way
Atherton, CA USA 94027
Phone: 6509269599
E-mail: information@pacgenvc.com
Website: www.pacgenvc.com

Management and Staff
Nersi Nazari, Founder

Type of Firm
Private Equity Firm

Project Preferences

Type of Financing Preferred:
Early Stage

Industry Preferences

In Semiconductor/Electr prefer:
Semiconductor

Additional Information
Year Founded: 2003
Current Activity Level : Actively seeking new investments

PACIFIC GROWTH INVESTORS LLC

21515 Hawthorne Boulevard, Suite 940
Torrance, CA USA 90503
Phone: 3103590456
Website: www.pacificgrowthinvestors.com

Type of Firm
Private Equity Firm

Project Preferences

Type of Financing Preferred:
Management Buyouts
Acquisition
Recapitalizations

Geographical Preferences

United States Preferences:
West Coast

Industry Preferences

In Medical/Health prefer:
Medical Diagnostics

In Industrial/Energy prefer:
Industrial Products

In Transportation prefer:
Aerospace

Additional Information
Year Founded: 2017
Current Activity Level : Actively seeking new investments

PACIFIC HORIZON VENTURES LLC

800 Fifth Avenue, Suite 4120
Seattle, WA USA 98104
Phone: 2066821181
Fax: 2066828077
E-mail: phv@pacifichorizon.com
Website: www.pacifichorizon.com

Management and Staff
Donald Elmer, Managing Partner

Type of Firm
Private Equity Firm

Project Preferences

Role in Financing:
Will function either as deal originator or investor in deals created by others

Type of Financing Preferred:
Early Stage
Expansion
Balanced

Geographical Preferences

United States Preferences:
Northwest
North America

Industry Focus
(% based on actual investment)

Biotechnology	80.0%
Medical/Health	8.5%
Industrial/Energy	4.4%
Computer Software and Services	4.1%
Internet Specific	2.0%
Communications and Media	1.2%

Additional Information
Name of Most Recent Fund: Koronis Antiviral Partners III, L.P.
Most Recent Fund Was Raised: 01/09/2012
Year Founded: 1993
Capital Under Management: $73,000,000
Current Activity Level : Actively seeking new investments
Method of Compensation: Return on investment is of primary concern, do not charge fees

PACIFIC INVESTMENTS MANAGEMENT LTD

124 Sloane Street
London, United Kingdom SW1X 9BW
Phone: 44-207-225-2250
Fax: 44-207-591-1650
E-mail: bvca@beckwithlondon.com
Website: www.pacificinvestments.com

Type of Firm
Bank Affiliated

Association Membership
British Venture Capital Association (BVCA)

Project Preferences

Type of Financing Preferred:
Fund of Funds
Second Stage Financing
Leveraged Buyout
Early Stage
Expansion
Mezzanine
Generalist PE
Balanced
Seed
Startup

Industry Preferences

In Medical/Health prefer:
Medical/Health

In Consumer Related prefer:
Entertainment and Leisure

In Financial Services prefer:
Financial Services

In Business Serv. prefer:
Media

Additional Information
Year Founded: 1999
Current Activity Level : Actively seeking new investments

PACIFIC PARTNERS

601 Montgomery Street, Suite 1207
San Francisco, CA USA 94111
Phone: 4152170052
Fax: 4152170053
E-mail: info@PacificPartnersLP.com

Management and Staff
Gordon Rubenstein, Managing Director
Max Kay, Vice President
Travis Nelson, Managing Director

Type of Firm
Private Equity Firm

Project Preferences

Type of Financing Preferred:
Early Stage
Balanced

Size of Investments Considered:
Min Size of Investment Considered (000s): $2,000
Max Size of Investment Considered (000s): $10,000

Industry Preferences

In Computer Software prefer:
Software
Systems Software
Applications Software

Additional Information

Year Founded: 2000
Capital Under Management: $35,000,000
Current Activity Level : Actively seeking new investments

PACIFIC ROAD CAPITAL MANAGEMENT PTY LTD

88 George Street
Level 2
Sydney, Australia 2000
Phone: 61292411000
Fax: 61292412255
Website: www.pacroad.com.au

Other Offices

Eight Rebelo Lane
NOVATO, CA USA 94947
Phone: 415-895-5494
Fax: 415-897-7070

Management and Staff

Lee Graber, Vice President

Type of Firm

Investment Management Firm

Association Membership

Australian Venture Capital Association (AVCAL)

Project Preferences

Role in Financing:
Will function either as deal originator or investor in deals created by others

Type of Financing Preferred:
Expansion
Generalist PE
Other
Management Buyouts
Private Placement

Geographical Preferences

International Preferences:
Australia
Asia
Africa

Industry Preferences

In Business Serv. prefer:
Services

Additional Information

Year Founded: 2006
Capital Under Management: $593,900,000

Current Activity Level : Actively seeking new investments

PACIFIC VENTURE PARTNERS CO LTD

No. 351 Yangguang Street
Floor 8
Taipei, Taiwan 114
Phone: 886227979877
Fax: 886227970377

Other Offices

6/F, No. 26 Xinghai Street
Suzhou Industrial Park
Jiangsu, China 215021
Phone: 86-512-6762-3400
Fax: 65-512-6762-3466

38C, No.7, Lane 500
Chang De Road
Shanghai, China 200041
Phone: 86-21-5292-5811
Fax: 86-21-5292-5822

Management and Staff

Jacob Almagor, Co-Founder
Joan Wang, Vice President
Pang-yien Yang, President
Paul Wang, Founder
Rigdon Currie, Co-Founder

Type of Firm

Private Equity Firm

Association Membership

Taiwan Venture Capital Association(TVCA)

Project Preferences

Type of Financing Preferred:
Early Stage
Expansion
Balanced
Later Stage
Startup

Size of Investments Considered:
Min Size of Investment Considered (000s): $3,000
Max Size of Investment Considered (000s): $50,000

Geographical Preferences

United States Preferences:

International Preferences:
Taiwan
Asia

Industry Preferences

In Communications prefer:
Telecommunications

In Computer Software prefer:
Software

In Internet Specific prefer:
Internet

In Semiconductor/Electr prefer:
Electronics
Semiconductor
Optoelectronics

In Biotechnology prefer:
Biotechnology

In Industrial/Energy prefer:
Machinery

In Manufact. prefer:
Manufacturing

Additional Information

Year Founded: 1990
Capital Under Management: $800,000,000
Current Activity Level : Actively seeking new investments

PACIFIC VIEW ASSET MANAGEMENT LLC

600 Montgomery Street
5th Floor
San Francisco, CA USA 94111
Phone: 4153185800
Fax: 4153185801
Website: www.pacviewam.com

Management and Staff

Brendan Contant, President
Tracey Daly, Vice President

Type of Firm

Investment Management Firm

Project Preferences

Type of Financing Preferred:
Later Stage

Additional Information

Year Founded: 2012
Current Activity Level : Actively seeking new investments

PACIFIC WIRLESS VENTURES LLC

5603 Eleventh Avenue, NE
Seattle, WA USA 98105

Type of Firm

Private Equity Firm

Project Preferences

Type of Financing Preferred:
Balanced
Later Stage

Geographical Preferences

United States Preferences:
Northeast

Industry Preferences

In Communications prefer:
Communications and Media

In Internet Specific prefer:
Web Aggregration/Portals

Additional Information

Year Founded: 2012
Current Activity Level : Actively seeking new investments

PACKARD PLACE PROPERTIES LLC

222 South Church Street, Suite 100
Charlotte, NC USA 28202
Phone: 7042485660
E-mail: info@packardplace.us

Type of Firm

Incubator/Development Program

Project Preferences

Type of Financing Preferred:
Seed
Startup

Geographical Preferences

United States Preferences:
North Carolina

Additional Information

Year Founded: 2010
Current Activity Level : Actively seeking new investments

PACT RESEARCH FUND

855-2nd Street, South West, Suite 1220
Calgary, Canada T2P 4J7
Phone: 403-303-1583
Fax: 403-294-1196

Management and Staff

Maury Parsons, Managing Partner

Type of Firm

Private Equity Firm

Project Preferences

Type of Financing Preferred:
Later Stage

Additional Information

Year Founded: 2009
Current Activity Level : Actively seeking new investments

PACTINVEST SA

Diligentei 7
Bucharest, Romania

Type of Firm

Private Equity Firm

Project Preferences

Type of Financing Preferred:
Leveraged Buyout
Early Stage
Expansion
Generalist PE
Later Stage
Seed
Management Buyouts
Acquisition
Startup

Geographical Preferences

International Preferences:
Europe
Romania

Additional Information

Year Founded: 2002
Current Activity Level : Actively seeking new investments

PAEAN ADVISORS PTY LTD

PO Box 1094
Gallo Manor, South Africa 2052
Phone: 27828828000
Website: www.paean-privateequity.co.za

Management and Staff

Dave Stadler, Chief Executive Officer
Laurence Green, Co-Founder

Type of Firm

Private Equity Firm

Association Membership

South African Venture Capital Association (SAVCA)
South Eastern Europes Private Equity Association

Project Preferences

Type of Financing Preferred:
Leveraged Buyout
Expansion
Generalist PE
Balanced
Later Stage
Management Buyouts
Acquisition

Geographical Preferences

International Preferences:
South Africa
Africa

Industry Preferences

In Consumer Related prefer:
Entertainment and Leisure
Retail

In Industrial/Energy prefer:
Industrial Products

In Transportation prefer:
Transportation

In Agr/Forestr/Fish prefer:
Mining and Minerals

Additional Information

Year Founded: 2011
Current Activity Level : Actively seeking new investments

PAGODA INVESTMENT ADVISORS S PTE LTD

China World Trade Center Offic
Room 3701, Tower 1
Beijing, China 100004
Website: www.pagodainv.com

Type of Firm

Private Equity Firm

Project Preferences

Type of Financing Preferred:
Leveraged Buyout
Expansion

Geographical Preferences

International Preferences:
China

Industry Preferences

In Communications prefer:
Telecommunications
Media and Entertainment

In Medical/Health prefer:
Medical/Health

In Consumer Related prefer:
Consumer
Education Related

Additional Information

Year Founded: 2015
Current Activity Level : Actively seeking new investments

PAI PARTNERS SAS

232, rue de Rivoli
Paris, France 75054
Phone: 33143166300
Fax: 330143166389
E-mail: pai.paris@paipartners.com
Website: www.paipartners.com

Other Offices

4 Albemarle Street
4th floor
London, United Kingdom W1S 4GA
Phone: 44-20-7297-4660
Fax: 44-20-7297-4679

Luisenstrasse 14
Munich, Germany 80333
Phone: 49-89-5151-4650
Fax: 49-89-5151-46510

12 rue Guillaume Schneider
Luxembourg, Luxembourg L2522
Phone: 35-226-2697-7177
Fax: 35-226-2697-3000

Calle Jose Ortega y Gasset
21, 3 Derecha
Madrid, Spain 28006
Phone: 34-91-590-2250
Fax: 34-91-590-2258

Nyhavn 63A, 1st floor
Copenhagen, Denmark 1051
Phone: 45-3330-0630
Fax: 44-3311-1102

Via della Posta 8
Milan, Italy 20123
Phone: 39-2-854-5151
Fax: 39-2-867-300

Management and Staff

Alex Kessler, Principal
Blaise Duault, Principal
Charles Bouaziz, Partner
Colm O Sullivan, Partner
Edward Chandler, Partner
Eleanor Chambers, Principal
Fabrice Fouletier, Partner
Federico Conchillo, Principal
Franck Temam, Principal
Frederic Stevenin, Partner
Gaelle d Engremont, Principal
Ivan Massonnat, Principal
Jean-Michel Dalmasso, Principal
Laurent Rivoire, Partner
Mathieu Paillat, Principal
Mirko Meyer-Schoenherr, Partner
Nicolas Holzman, Partner
Olivier de Vregille, Partner
Patrick Mouterde, Partner
Raffaele Vitale, Partner
Ragnar Hellenius, Principal
Ricardo de Serdio, Partner
Richard Howell, Partner
Roberto Ferraresi, Principal
Sophie Lombard, Partner
Stefano Drago, Principal
Stephane Roussilhe, Principal
Violaine Grison, Principal
Yannis Josse, Chief Financial Officer

Type of Firm
Private Equity Firm

Association Membership
Italian Venture Capital Association (AIFI)
French Venture Capital Association (AFIC)
German Venture Capital Association (BVK)
Swedish Venture Capital Association (SVCA)
European Private Equity and Venture Capital Assoc.

Project Preferences

Size of Investments Considered:
Min Size of Investment Considered (000s): $9,416
Max Size of Investment Considered (000s): $188,320

Geographical Preferences

International Preferences:
Europe
Western Europe
France

Industry Focus
(% based on actual investment)
Other Products 41.1%
Consumer Related 34.1%
Communications and Media 10.9%
Internet Specific 7.5%
Semiconductors/Other Elect. 3.0%
Computer Software and Services 2.1%
Biotechnology 0.7%
Medical/Health 0.6%

Additional Information
Name of Most Recent Fund: PAI Europe V
Most Recent Fund Was Raised: 08/20/2007
Year Founded: 1872
Capital Under Management: $3,892,636,000
Current Activity Level: Actively seeking new investments

PAINE SCHWARTZ PARTNERS LLC

One Franklin Parkway
Building 910, Suite 120
San Mateo, CA USA 94403
Phone: 6503937100
Fax: 6503937150
E-mail: info@painepartners.com
Website: www.painepartners.com

Other Offices

461 Fifth Avenue
17th Floor
NEW YORK, NY USA 10017
Phone: 212-379-7200
Fax: 212-379-7235

71 South Wacker Drive, Suite 1875
CHICAGO, IL USA 60606
Phone: 312-564-5300
Fax: 312-564-5400

Management and Staff

Adam Fless, Managing Director
Alexander Corbacho, Principal
Andrew Freeman, Partner
Angelos Dassios, Partner
David Buckeridge, Partner
Gerald Adler, Chief Operating Officer
Justin Kern, Principal
Kevin Schwartz, Chief Executive Officer
Mark Fuller, Principal
Robert Meyer, Chief Financial Officer
William Keesler, Principal

Type of Firm
Private Equity Firm

Project Preferences

Type of Financing Preferred:
Leveraged Buyout
Management Buyouts
Acquisition
Recapitalizations

Industry Preferences

In Consumer Related prefer:
Food/Beverage

In Industrial/Energy prefer:
Energy
Industrial Products

In Financial Services prefer:
Financial Services

In Agr/Forestr/Fish prefer:
Agribusiness

Additional Information
Name of Most Recent Fund: Paine & Partners Fund III, L.P.
Most Recent Fund Was Raised: 04/17/2006
Year Founded: 2006
Capital Under Management: $2,700,000,000
Current Activity Level: Actively seeking new investments

PAK OMAN INVESTMENT COMPANY LTD

Shahra-e-Faisal, Tower A
1/F Finance and Trade Center
Karachi, Pakistan
Phone: 92-21-3563-0971
Fax: 92-21-3563-0969
E-mail: info@pakoman.com
Website: pakoman.com

Other Offices

Ruwi
Office No. 505, P- Floor, Fahd Plaza
Muscat, Oman
Phone: 968-2481-8523
Fax: 968-2481-2565

Eigth Floo Markaz
Room 201 & 202 Khayal Plaza
Islamabad, Pakistan
Phone: 92-51-228-2615
Fax: 92-51-225-5038

72 Main Boulevard, Gulberg II
No. 207, 2nd Flr., Siddique Trade Center
Lahore, Pakistan
Phone: 92-42-3578-1893
Fax: 92-42-3578-1892

Port Road West Bay
Gwadar, Pakistan
Phone: 92-86-421-2020

Management and Staff

Agha Ahmed Shah, Chief Executive Officer
Jehangir Shah, Managing Director
Mohammad Jamal Nasir, Chief Financial Officer

Type of Firm

Government Affiliated Program

Project Preferences

Type of Financing Preferred:
Balanced

Geographical Preferences

International Preferences:
Pakistan
Oman
Utd. Arab Em.

Industry Preferences

In Industrial/Energy prefer:
Industrial Products

In Business Serv. prefer:
Services

In Agr/Forestr/Fish prefer:
Agribusiness
Agriculture related

Additional Information

Year Founded: 2001
Current Activity Level : Actively seeking new investments

PALA INVESTMENTS

Gotthardstrasse 26
Zug, Switzerland 6300
Phone: 41415609070
Fax: 41415609071
E-mail: info@pala.com
Website: www.pala.com

Management and Staff

Jan Castro, Chief Executive Officer
Michael Barton, Managing Director
Paul Bosma, Vice President

Type of Firm

Private Equity Firm

Project Preferences

Type of Financing Preferred:
Leveraged Buyout
Early Stage
Public Companies
Management Buyouts
Acquisition

Geographical Preferences

United States Preferences:
All U.S.

Canadian Preferences:
All Canada

International Preferences:
India
Australia
All International

Industry Preferences

In Industrial/Energy prefer:
Coal Related
Materials

In Agr/Forestr/Fish prefer:
Mining and Minerals

Additional Information

Year Founded: 2006
Current Activity Level : Actively seeking new investments

PALAASH VENTURES PVT LTD

38, Okhla Industrial Estate
New Delhi, India
Phone: 911148900000
E-mail: info@palaashventures.com
Website: www.palaashventures.com

Type of Firm

Private Equity Firm

Project Preferences

Type of Financing Preferred:
Early Stage
Expansion
Seed

Geographical Preferences

International Preferences:
India

Additional Information

Year Founded: 2013
Current Activity Level : Actively seeking new investments

PALACE VENTURES LTD

Eight Grafton Street
London, United Kingdom W1S 4EL
Phone: 44-20-317-0864
E-mail: info@palaceventures.com
Website: www.palaceventures.com

Management and Staff

Andrew Halsall, Managing Director

Type of Firm

Private Equity Firm

Project Preferences

Type of Financing Preferred:
Generalist PE
Balanced

Geographical Preferences

United States Preferences:
All U.S.

International Preferences:
United Kingdom
Europe
Middle East
Asia

Industry Preferences

In Communications prefer:
Communications and Media
Telecommunications

Additional Information

Year Founded: 2004
Current Activity Level : Actively seeking new investments

PALADIN CAPITAL MANAGEMENT LLC

2020 K Street Northwest, Suite 400
Washington, DC USA 20006
Phone: 2022935590
Fax: 2022935597
Website: www.paladincapgroup.com

Other Offices

75 Rockefeller Plaza
14th Floor
NEW YORK, NY USA 10019
Phone: 212-350-8206

Dubai International Financial Centre
Level 15, Suite 48
Dubai, Utd. Arab Em.
Phone: 971-4-401-9703
Fax: 971-4-401-9578

525 University Avenue, Suite 230
PALO ALTO, CA USA 94301

2, rue Jean Monnet
Luxembourg, Luxembourg 2180

295 Madison Avenue
12th Floor
MANHATTAN, NY USA 10017
Phone: 2022935590

Management and Staff
Alf Andreassen, Managing Director
Brenda Chia, Venture Partner
Chris Inglis, Managing Director
Christopher Steed, Managing Director
Colin Bryant, Vice President
E. Kenneth Pentimonti, Principal
E. Kenneth Pentimonti, Principal
Gibb Witham, Vice President
H. Lee Buchanan, Venture Partner
Kenneth Minihan, Managing Director
Mark Maloney, Co-Founder
Matt Bigge, Venture Partner
Michael Moniz, Managing Director
Mourad Yesayan, Principal
Niloofar Howe, Managing Director
Paul Conley, Managing Director
Philip Eliot, Principal
Philip Eliot, Managing Director
William Reinisch, Venture Partner

Type of Firm
Private Equity Firm

Association Membership
Mid-Atlantic Venture Association

Project Preferences

Type of Financing Preferred:
Early Stage
Expansion
Balanced
Later Stage
Acquisition

Additional Information
Name of Most Recent Fund: Paladin III, L.P.
Most Recent Fund Was Raised: 08/20/2007
Year Founded: 2001
Capital Under Management: $740,000,000
Current Activity Level : Actively seeking new investments

PALAMON CAPITAL PARTNERS LP
33 King Street
Cleveland House
London, United Kingdom SW1Y 6RJ
Phone: 442077662000
Fax: 442077662002
Website: www.palamon.com

Management and Staff
A. Michael Hoffman, Co-Founder
Alexandre Rahmatollahi, Partner
Daan Knottenbelt, Partner
Daniel Mytnik, Partner
Fabio Massimo Giuseppetti, Partner
Gary Pritchard, Partner
Jean Bonnavion, Partner
John David, Managing Director
Julian Carreras, Principal
Louis Elson, Co-Founder
Michael Beetz, Principal
Mina Mutafchieva, Principal
Olivia Roberts, Principal
Pascal Noth, Partner
Philippe Arbour, Managing Director
Ricardo Caupers, Partner

Type of Firm
Private Equity Firm

Association Membership
British Venture Capital Association (BVCA)
European Private Equity and Venture Capital Assoc.

Project Preferences

Type of Financing Preferred:
Leveraged Buyout
Early Stage
Turnaround
Acquisition
Recapitalizations

Geographical Preferences

International Preferences:
Italy
United Kingdom
Luxembourg
Europe
Netherlands
Western Europe
Scandanavia/Nordic Region
Spain
Belgium
Germany
France

Industry Preferences

In Communications prefer:
Communications and Media

In Computer Software prefer:
Software

In Medical/Health prefer:
Medical/Health

In Consumer Related prefer:
Entertainment and Leisure
Retail

In Financial Services prefer:
Financial Services

In Business Serv. prefer:
Services

Additional Information
Name of Most Recent Fund: Palamon Auxiliary Partnership 2013, L.P.
Most Recent Fund Was Raised: 09/30/2013
Year Founded: 1999
Capital Under Management: $1,423,000,000
Current Activity Level : Actively seeking new investments

PALAPA VENTURES
500 Third Street, Suite 515
San Francisco, CA USA 94104
Website: www.palapavc.com

Type of Firm
Private Equity Firm

Project Preferences

Type of Financing Preferred:
Early Stage
Seed

Geographical Preferences

United States Preferences:

International Preferences:
Indonesia

Industry Preferences

In Communications prefer:
Telecommunications

In Computer Software prefer:
Software

Additional Information
Year Founded: 2017
Current Activity Level : Actively seeking new investments

PALATINE PRIVATE EQUITY LLP

17 Marble Street
11th Floor, Lowry House
Manchester, United Kingdom M2 3AW
Phone: 441612144730
Fax: 441618392816
E-mail: info@zeusprivateequity.co.uk
Website: www.palatinepe.com

Other Offices

Venturers House
King Street
Bristol, United Kingdom BS1 4PB
Phone: 44-0117-915-4017
Fax: 44-0117-915-4088

Four Park Place
London, United Kingdom SW1A 1LP
Phone: 44-20-7661-9196
Fax: 44-20-3178-4120

Management and Staff

Andy Lees, Partner
Ed Fazakerley, Partner
Tony Dickin, Founder

Type of Firm

Private Equity Firm

Association Membership

British Venture Capital Association (BVCA)

Project Preferences

Type of Financing Preferred:
Leveraged Buyout
Management Buyouts
Acquisition
Recapitalizations

Geographical Preferences

International Preferences:
United Kingdom
Europe

Industry Preferences

In Medical/Health prefer:
Health Services

In Consumer Related prefer:
Retail
Consumer Products

In Industrial/Energy prefer:
Industrial Products

In Financial Services prefer:
Financial Services

Additional Information

Name of Most Recent Fund: Palatine Private Equity Fund II, L.P.
Most Recent Fund Was Raised: 01/04/2012
Year Founded: 2005
Capital Under Management: $704,141,000
Current Activity Level : Actively seeking new investments

PALERO CAPITAL GMBH

Maximilianstrasse 12-14
Munich, Germany 80539
Phone: 4989889887100
E-mail: contact@palero-capital.de
Website: palero.de

Management and Staff

Christian Daumann, Managing Director
Conny Wuppermann, Managing Director
Felix Frohn-Bernau, Managing Director

Type of Firm

Private Equity Firm

Association Membership

German Venture Capital Association (BVK)

Project Preferences

Type of Financing Preferred:
Leveraged Buyout
Turnaround
Acquisition
Special Situation
Recapitalizations

Geographical Preferences

International Preferences:
United Kingdom
Switzerland
Austria
Germany

Industry Preferences

In Semiconductor/Electr prefer:
Electronics

Additional Information

Year Founded: 2010
Current Activity Level : Actively seeking new investments

PALIO CAPITAL PARTNERS LLP

42 Brook Street
London, United Kingdom W1K 5DB
Phone: 442031787425
E-mail: info@paliocap.com
Website: paliocapitalpartners.com

Management and Staff

Darren Gibson, Chief Operating Officer

Type of Firm

Private Equity Firm

Project Preferences

Type of Financing Preferred:
Leveraged Buyout
Mezzanine
Management Buyouts
Acquisition

Size of Investments Considered:
Min Size of Investment Considered (000s): $1,585
Max Size of Investment Considered (000s): $15,849

Geographical Preferences

International Preferences:
United Kingdom
Europe
Asia

Additional Information

Year Founded: 2010
Current Activity Level : Actively seeking new investments

PALISADE CAPITAL MANAGEMENT LLC

One Bridge Plaza, Suite 695
Fort Lee, NJ USA 07024
Phone: 2015857733
Fax: 2015859798
E-mail: info@palcap.com
Website: www.palisadecapital.com

Other Offices

515 North Flagler Drive, Suite 808
West Palm Beach, FL USA 33401
Phone: 5618323558

1225 Camino Del Mar
Del Mar, CA USA 92014
Phone: 201-346-5740

Management and Staff

Bernard Picchi, Managing Director
Brian Fern, Chief Financial Officer
Brian Deitelzweig, Managing Director
Elliot Stiefel, Managing Director
James Marrone, Managing Director
James Boothby, Vice President
James Jahnke, Managing Director
Jason Rich, Vice President
Jeffrey Serkes, Chief Operating Officer
Jeffrey Weekes, Vice President
Jonathan Masarof, Vice President
Judith Keilp, Vice President
Mahendra Misir, Managing Director
Michael Feiler, Vice President
Michael Chizmar, Vice President
Michael Appleton, Vice President
Sammy Oh, Managing Director
Wendy Popowich, Managing Director
William Potter, Managing Director

Type of Firm
Private Equity Advisor or Fund of Funds

Project Preferences

Type of Financing Preferred:
Leveraged Buyout
Early Stage
Later Stage
Acquisition
Special Situation

Additional Information
Year Founded: 1995
Current Activity Level : Actively seeking new investments

PALISADES VENTURES

11726 San Vicente Boulevard, Suite 450
Los Angeles, CA USA 90049
Phone: 3105716214
E-mail: info@palisadesventures.com
Website: www.palisadesventures.com

Management and Staff
Anders Richardson, Co-Founder
Henry Lichstein, Venture Partner
Paul D Addario, Co-Founder

Type of Firm
Private Equity Firm

Project Preferences

Type of Financing Preferred:
Expansion
Balanced
Later Stage

Size of Investments Considered:
Min Size of Investment Considered (000s): $2,500
Max Size of Investment Considered (000s): $7,000

Industry Preferences

In Communications prefer:
Wireless Communications

In Computer Software prefer:
Software

In Business Serv. prefer:
Services
Media

Additional Information
Name of Most Recent Fund: Palisades Ventures
Most Recent Fund Was Raised: 09/01/2002
Year Founded: 2000
Capital Under Management: $75,000,000
Current Activity Level : Actively seeking new investments

PALLADIAN CAPITAL PARTNERS LLC

420 Lexington Avenue
New York, NY USA 10170
Phone: 2128802400
Fax: 2126821538
E-mail: info@palladianadvisors.com
Website: www.palladiancap.com

Management and Staff
B. Andrew Spence, Managing Director
Carl Glaeser, Co-Founder
John Gordon, Co-Founder

Type of Firm
Private Equity Firm

Project Preferences

Type of Financing Preferred:
Leveraged Buyout
Management Buyouts
Acquisition
Joint Ventures
Industry Rollups
Recapitalizations

Industry Preferences

In Computer Software prefer:
Software

In Consumer Related prefer:
Retail
Consumer Products

In Business Serv. prefer:
Services
Distribution

In Manufact. prefer:
Manufacturing

Additional Information
Year Founded: 2004
Current Activity Level : Actively seeking new investments

PALLADIN CAPITAL GROUP INC

200 Clarendon Street
26th Floor
Boston, MA USA 02116
Phone: 6175853800
E-mail: info@pcrp.com
Website: www.pcrp.com

Management and Staff
David Chin, Vice President
George Aggouras, Chief Financial Officer
Mark Schwartz, Chief Executive Officer
Tobias Nanda, Principal

Type of Firm
Private Equity Firm

Project Preferences

Type of Financing Preferred:
Leveraged Buyout
Balanced
Later Stage

Geographical Preferences

United States Preferences:
North America

International Preferences:
Europe

Industry Preferences

In Consumer Related prefer:
Retail
Consumer Products

Additional Information
Year Founded: 2000
Current Activity Level : Actively seeking new investments

PALLADIO HOLDING SPA

Strada Statale Padana Verso
Verona 6
Vicenza, Italy 36100
Phone: 39444650500
Fax: 39444650580
E-mail: vicenza@palladiofinanziaria.it
Website: www.pfh.eu

Management and Staff
Giorgio Drago, Managing Director

Type of Firm
Investment Management Firm

Project Preferences

Type of Financing Preferred:
Leveraged Buyout
Early Stage
Expansion
Later Stage

Geographical Preferences

International Preferences:
Italy

Additional Information
Year Founded: 2000
Current Activity Level : Actively seeking new investments

PALLADION PARTNERS GESELLSCHAFT FUER PRIVATE EQUITY MBH

Taunusanlage 21
Frankfurt am Main, Germany 60325
Phone: 49692429870
Fax: 496924298787
E-mail: info@palladion-partners.de
Website: www.palladion.de

Management and Staff
Hans-Dieter von Meibom, Founder

Type of Firm
Private Equity Firm

Project Preferences

Type of Financing Preferred:
Leveraged Buyout
Public Companies
Later Stage
Management Buyouts
Recapitalizations

Geographical Preferences

International Preferences:
Europe
Switzerland
Austria
Germany

Additional Information
Year Founded: 1988
Capital Under Management: $94,200,000
Current Activity Level : Actively seeking new investments

PALLADIUM EQUITY PARTNERS LLC

1270 Avenue of the Americas
Rockefeller Center, Suite 2200
New York, NY USA 10020
Phone: 2122185150
Fax: 2122185155
Website: www.palladiumequity.com

Management and Staff
Adam Shebitz, Managing Director
Alejandro Ventosa, Managing Director
Caleb Clark, Managing Director
Chris Allen, Principal
Daniel Ilundain, Managing Director
David Perez, President & COO
Erik Scott, Managing Director
Justin Green, Managing Director
Kevin Reymond, Chief Financial Officer
Leon Brujis, Principal
Luis Zaldivar, Senior Managing Director
Marcos Rodriguez, Founder
Rafael Ortiz, Principal
Yue Bonnet, Principal

Type of Firm
Private Equity Firm

Association Membership
Natl Assoc of Investment Cos. (NAIC)

Project Preferences

Role in Financing:
Prefer role as deal originator but will also invest in deals created by others

Type of Financing Preferred:
Leveraged Buyout
Expansion
Management Buyouts
Recapitalizations

Geographical Preferences

United States Preferences:

Industry Focus
(% based on actual investment)

Consumer Related	34.2%
Other Products	21.5%
Computer Software and Services	20.6%
Industrial/Energy	10.9%
Internet Specific	9.1%
Medical/Health	3.5%
Biotechnology	0.3%

Additional Information
Name of Most Recent Fund: Palladium Equity Partners IV, L.P.
Most Recent Fund Was Raised: 07/26/2012
Year Founded: 1997
Capital Under Management: $936,000,000
Current Activity Level : Actively seeking new investments

PALM BEACH CAPITAL MANAGEMENT LLC

505 South Flagler Drive, Suite 1400
West Palm Beach, FL USA 33401
Phone: 5616599022
Fax: 5616599055
Website: www.pbcap.com

Other Offices
5001 Lemon Street
Tampa, FL USA 33609
Phone: 8136234041
Fax: 8136234034

Management and Staff
Adam Klein, Chief Financial Officer
Michael Schmickle, Partner
Nathan Ward, Co-Founder
Richard Schlanger, Co-Founder
Shaun McGruder, Co-Founder

Type of Firm
Private Equity Firm

Project Preferences

Type of Financing Preferred:
Leveraged Buyout
Expansion
Recapitalizations

Additional Information
Name of Most Recent Fund: Palm Beach Capital Fund III, L.P.
Most Recent Fund Was Raised: 03/25/2011
Year Founded: 2001
Capital Under Management: $182,850,000
Current Activity Level : Actively seeking new investments

PALM DRIVE VENTURES LLC

424 Broadway
Unit 602
New York, NY USA 10013
E-mail: info@palmdrive.vc
Website: www.palmdrive.vc

Type of Firm
Private Equity Firm

Project Preferences

Type of Financing Preferred:
Balanced

Geographical Preferences

United States Preferences:

Industry Preferences

In Computer Software prefer:
Software

Additional Information
Year Founded: 2015
Current Activity Level : Actively seeking new investments

PALM VENTURES LLC

400 North McCarthy Boulvard
Milpitas, CA USA 95035
Phone: 408-503-7000
Fax: 408-503-2750
E-mail: kgarrigus@arpartners.com
Website: www.palmventures.com

Management and Staff
Greg Millhauser, Vice President
Hank Boot, Managing Director
Harold Levy, Managing Director
Jason Woody, Managing Director
Jeremy Friedman, Managing Director
Joshua Horowitz, Managing Director
Michael Koby, Managing Director

Type of Firm
Private Equity Firm

Project Preferences

Type of Financing Preferred:
Early Stage
Balanced

Size of Investments Considered:
Min Size of Investment Considered (000s): $1,000
Max Size of Investment Considered (000s): $5,000

Geographical Preferences

United States Preferences:

Industry Preferences

In Communications prefer:
Telecommunications

Additional Information
Year Founded: 1992
Capital Under Management: $50,000,000
Current Activity Level : Actively seeking new investments

PALO ALTO INVESTORS LLC

470 University Avenue
Palo Alto, CA USA 94301
Phone: 6503250772
Fax: 6503255028
Website: www.pa-investors.com

Management and Staff
Joon Yun, President
Scott Smith, Chief Operating Officer
William Edwards, Founder

Type of Firm
Investment Management Firm

Project Preferences

Type of Financing Preferred:
Balanced

Geographical Preferences

United States Preferences:

Industry Preferences

In Medical/Health prefer:
Medical/Health
Health Services

In Industrial/Energy prefer:
Energy

Additional Information
Year Founded: 1989
Capital Under Management: $1,200,000,000
Current Activity Level : Actively seeking new investments

PALO ALTO VENTURE PARTNERS

300 Hamilton Avenue
Fourth Floor
Palo Alto, CA USA 94301
Phone: 6504621221
Fax: 6504621227
Website: www.pavp.com

Management and Staff
Peter Ziebelman, Founder

Type of Firm
Private Equity Firm

Project Preferences

Role in Financing:
Prefer role as deal originator but will also invest in deals created by others

Type of Financing Preferred:
Early Stage
Balanced
Startup

Size of Investments Considered:
Min Size of Investment Considered (000s): $1,000
Max Size of Investment Considered (000s): $10,000

Industry Focus
(% based on actual investment)

Internet Specific	50.5%
Computer Software and Services	33.0%
Communications and Media	6.9%
Consumer Related	4.6%
Semiconductors/Other Elect.	2.2%
Other Products	2.1%
Biotechnology	0.6%

Additional Information
Name of Most Recent Fund: 21VC Fund II
Most Recent Fund Was Raised: 10/02/1999
Year Founded: 1996
Capital Under Management: $150,000,000
Current Activity Level : Actively seeking new investments
Method of Compensation: Return on investment is of primary concern, do not charge fees

PALO ALTO VENTURE SCIENCE LLC

501 Forest Avenue, Suite 703
Palo Alto, CA USA 94301
Phone: 6505300040
E-mail: info@venture-science.com
Website: pavs-public.sharepoint.com

Type of Firm
Private Equity Firm

Project Preferences

Type of Financing Preferred:
Early Stage
Seed
Startup

Industry Preferences

In Communications prefer:
Wireless Communications

In Internet Specific prefer:
Ecommerce

In Medical/Health prefer:
Medical/Health

In Consumer Related prefer:
Consumer
Consumer Products
Education Related

Additional Information
Year Founded: 2013
Current Activity Level : Actively seeking new investments

PALOMAR VENTURES

233 Wilshire Boulevard, Suite 900
Santa Monica, CA USA 90401
Phone: 3102606050
Fax: 3105106836

Other Offices
18881 Von Karman Avenue, Suite 960
Irvine, CA USA 92612
Phone: 9494759455
Fax: 9494759456

1200 Park Place, Suite 300
San Mateo, CA USA 94403
Phone: 6505661100

Management and Staff
Amanda Reed, Partner
Bob Obuch, Partner
Bryn Davis, Venture Partner
Jim Gauer, Managing Director
Lisa Riedmiller, Chief Financial Officer

Type of Firm
Private Equity Firm

Project Preferences

Role in Financing:
Prefer role as deal originator but will also invest in deals created by others

Type of Financing Preferred:
Early Stage
Seed
Startup

Geographical Preferences

United States Preferences:
Northern California
West Coast
Southwest
All U.S.

Industry Focus
(% based on actual investment)
Computer Software and Services	37.2%
Communications and Media	29.4%
Internet Specific	18.6%
Semiconductors/Other Elect.	9.4%
Consumer Related	2.0%
Biotechnology	2.0%
Computer Hardware	1.5%

Additional Information
Year Founded: 1999
Capital Under Management: $2,000,000
Current Activity Level : Actively seeking new investments
Method of Compensation: Return on investment is of primary concern, do not charge fees

PALUEL MARMONT CAPITAL SASU

24, rue Murillo
Paris, France 75008
Phone: 33144299823
Fax: 33144299850
Website: www.paluel-marmont-capital.fr

Type of Firm
Bank Affiliated

Association Membership
French Venture Capital Association (AFIC)

Project Preferences

Type of Financing Preferred:
Leveraged Buyout
Management Buyouts

Geographical Preferences

International Preferences:
Europe
France

Additional Information
Year Founded: 1991
Current Activity Level : Actively seeking new investments

PAMA VENTURA INDONESIA PT

Wisma GKBI, Suite 3901
lantai 39] . Jend. Sudirman
Jakarta, Indonesia 10210
Phone: 62-21-5799-8173
Fax: 62-21-5799-8174

Management and Staff
Nang Yong Tan, President

Type of Firm
Private Equity Firm

Project Preferences

Type of Financing Preferred:
Balanced

Geographical Preferences

International Preferences:
Asia

Additional Information
Year Founded: 2000
Current Activity Level : Actively seeking new investments

PAMICA NV

Rouaansekaai 1
Antwerp, Belgium 2000
E-mail: peggy.salien@pamica.be
Website: www.pamica.be

Type of Firm
Private Equity Firm

Geographical Preferences

International Preferences:
Europe

Additional Information
Year Founded: 2014
Current Activity Level : Actively seeking new investments

PAMLICO CAPITAL MANAGEMENT LP

150 North College Street, Suite 2400
Charlotte, NC USA 28202
Phone: 7044147150
Website: www.pamlicocapital.com

Management and Staff
Arthur Roselle, Partner
Courtney McCarthy, Principal
D. Neal Morrison, Partner
Eric Wilkins, Partner
Frederick Eubank, Managing Partner
L. Watts Hamrick, Managing Partner
Scott Perper, Managing Partner
Scott Stevens, Partner
Stuart Christhilf, Partner
Tracey Chaffin, Chief Financial Officer
Walker Simmons, Partner

Type of Firm
Private Equity Firm

Project Preferences

Role in Financing:
Will function either as deal originator or investor in deals created by others

Type of Financing Preferred:
Fund of Funds
Leveraged Buyout
Early Stage
Expansion
Mezzanine
Generalist PE
Management Buyouts
Acquisition

Size of Investments Considered:
Min Size of Investment Considered (000s): $20,000
Max Size of Investment Considered (000s): $100,000

Geographical Preferences

United States Preferences:
North America

Industry Focus
(% based on actual investment)
Other Products	29.9%
Internet Specific	27.5%
Communications and Media	19.2%
Consumer Related	7.0%
Computer Software and Services	6.6%
Medical/Health	5.9%
Industrial/Energy	2.3%
Semiconductors/Other Elect.	1.2%
Computer Hardware	0.2%

Additional Information
Name of Most Recent Fund: Pamlico Capital III, L.P.
Most Recent Fund Was Raised: 03/21/2013
Year Founded: 1988

PAMPLONA CAPITAL MANAGEMENT LLP

25 Park Lane
London, United Kingdom W1K 1RA
Phone: 442070798000
Fax: 442074953909
E-mail: info@pamplonafunds.com
Website: www.pamplonafunds.com

Other Offices

Triq I-Abate Rigord
Level 5, Marina Business Center
Ta'Xbiex, Malta XBX 1127
Phone: 35620909000
Fax: 35620909001

375 Park Avenue
23rc Floor
New York, NY USA 10152
Phone: 2122076820
Fax: 2122078821

Management and Staff

Brian Byrne, Chief Operating Officer
Brian Ratzan, Partner
David Lang, Principal
Eric Bidinger, Vice President
John Halsted, Managing Partner
Justin Perreault, Partner
Kevin O Flaherty, Chief Financial Officer
Markku Lonnqvist, Partner
Markus Noe-Nordberg, Partner
Martin Schwab, Partner
Michael Rosen, Principal
Nick Gordon Smith, Managing Partner
Paul Thompson, Partner
Robert Warden, Partner
Selahattin Zoralioglu, Principal

Type of Firm
Private Equity Firm

Project Preferences

Type of Financing Preferred:
Leveraged Buyout
Management Buyouts

Geographical Preferences

United States Preferences:
North America

International Preferences:
United Kingdom
Europe

Additional Information
Year Founded: 2005

Capital Under Management: $900,000,000
Current Activity Level : Actively seeking new investments
Method of Compensation: Return on investment is of primary concern, do not charge fees

PAN AFRICAN CAPITAL GROUP LLC

1100 Connecticut Avenue, NW, Suite 330
Washington, DC USA 20036
Phone: 2028871772
Fax: 2028871788
E-mail: info@panafricancapital.com
Website: www.panafricancapital.com

Type of Firm
Bank Affiliated

Association Membership
Emerging Markets Private Equity Association

Project Preferences

Type of Financing Preferred:
Leveraged Buyout
Acquisition

Geographical Preferences

International Preferences:
Africa

Industry Preferences

In Communications prefer:
Telecommunications

In Industrial/Energy prefer:
Materials

In Financial Services prefer:
Financial Services

In Manufact. prefer:
Manufacturing

In Agr/Forestr/Fish prefer:
Agribusiness

Additional Information
Year Founded: 2004
Current Activity Level : Actively seeking new investments

Capital Under Management: $11,144,091,000
Current Activity Level : Actively seeking new investments

PANACEA CAPITAL ADVISORS INC

3 Bethesda Metro Center, Suite 700
Bethesda, MD USA 20814
Phone: 3019611592
Website: www.panaceacap.com

Management and Staff
Samuel Rubenstein, President, Founder

Type of Firm
Private Equity Firm

Project Preferences

Type of Financing Preferred:
Early Stage

Geographical Preferences

United States Preferences:
All U.S.

Industry Preferences

In Communications prefer:
Media and Entertainment

In Internet Specific prefer:
Ecommerce

In Consumer Related prefer:
Food/Beverage

In Industrial/Energy prefer:
Energy

In Financial Services prefer:
Financial Services

Additional Information
Year Founded: 2016
Current Activity Level : Actively seeking new investments

PANAKES PARTNERS SGR SPA

Via Boscovich 31
Milan, Italy 20124
Website: www.panakes.it

Type of Firm
Private Equity Firm

Project Preferences

Type of Financing Preferred:
Early Stage
Expansion
Startup

Geographical Preferences

International Preferences:
Italy
Europe
Israel

Industry Preferences

In Biotechnology prefer:
Biotechnology
Human Biotechnology

In Medical/Health prefer:
Diagnostic Test Products
Health Services

PANASONIC VENTURE GROUP

10900 North Tantau Avenue
Cupertino, CA USA 95014
Phone: 4088613900
Fax: 4088613990
E-mail: info@vc.panasonic.com
Website: www.panasonicventures.com

Management and Staff

Dilip Sampath, Venture Partner
Patrick Suel, Venture Partner

Type of Firm

Corporate PE/Venture

Project Preferences

Type of Financing Preferred:
Early Stage
Balanced
Startup

Size of Investments Considered:
Min Size of Investment Considered (000s): $1,000
Max Size of Investment Considered (000s): $3,000

Geographical Preferences

United States Preferences:

Industry Preferences

In Communications prefer:
Satellite Microwave Comm.

In Semiconductor/Electr prefer:
Electronics
Semiconductor
Fiber Optics

In Medical/Health prefer:
Medical/Health

In Industrial/Energy prefer:
Environmental Related

Additional Information

Year Founded: 1998
Capital Under Management: $100,000,000
Current Activity Level : Actively seeking new investments

PANDA CAPITAL ASIA LTD

Unit 706, Lu Plaza
2 Wing Yip Street, Kowloon
Hong Kong, Hong Kong
Phone: 852-2799-3733
Fax: 852-2798-6254
Website: www.pandacapital.cn

Other Offices

Huafu Tiandi, Room1602, Building 3
222 Ma Dang Road
Shanghai, China 200020
Phone: 86-21-5306-7202
Fax: 86-21-5306-7251

7, Lane 333, DunHua North Road
Taipei, Taiwan
Phone: 886-2-2718-9908
Fax: 886-2-2719-4765

222 Yan An Road (East), Suite 4104, Bund Center
Shanghai, China
Phone: 86-21-6335-0305
Fax: 86-21-6335-0306

Management and Staff

Andreas Schwyn, Managing Partner
Arfen Hsu, Managing Partner
Harry Sprecher, Partner

Type of Firm

Private Equity Firm

Project Preferences

Type of Financing Preferred:
Expansion

Geographical Preferences

International Preferences:
China

Additional Information

Year Founded: 2007
Current Activity Level : Actively seeking new investments

PANGAEA VENTURES LTD

1500 West Georgia Street, Suite 1520
Vancouver, Canada V6G 2Z6
Phone: 6048000411
E-mail: info@pangaeaventures.com
Website: www.pangaeaventures.com

Other Offices

10A prospect 60-letia Oktyabrya
Office 450-455
Moscow, Russia 117036

Management and Staff

Andrew Haughian, General Partner
Keith Gillard, General Partner
Purnesh Seegopaul, General Partner

Type of Firm

Private Equity Firm

Association Membership

National Venture Capital Association - USA (NVCA)
Canadian Venture Capital Association

Project Preferences

Type of Financing Preferred:
Early Stage

Geographical Preferences

United States Preferences:
North America

Canadian Preferences:
All Canada
British Columbia

International Preferences:
Europe
Russia

Industry Preferences

In Industrial/Energy prefer:
Energy
Alternative Energy
Energy Conservation Relat
Environmental Related

Additional Information

Year Founded: 2000
Capital Under Management: $133,000,000
Current Activity Level : Actively seeking new investments

PANGEA S EDGE HOLDINGS LTD

2245 Keller Way, Suite 340
Carrollton, TX USA 75006
Phone: 9722367633
Website: www.pangeasedge.com

Type of Firm

Private Equity Firm

Project Preferences

Role in Financing:
Prefer role in deals created by others

Type of Financing Preferred:
Leveraged Buyout
Generalist PE
Balanced
Seed

Industry Preferences

In Industrial/Energy prefer:
Energy

In Financial Services prefer:
Real Estate

Additional Information

Year Founded: 1969
Current Activity Level : Actively seeking new investments

PANORAMA POINT PARTNERS LLC

13030 Pierce Street, Suite 300
Omaha, NE USA 68144

Management and Staff
Brian Radermacher, Chief Financial Officer
Clarey Castner, Co-Founder
Mark Stafford, Managing Director

Type of Firm
Private Equity Firm

Project Preferences

Type of Financing Preferred:
Leveraged Buyout
Generalist PE
Balanced

Additional Information
Year Founded: 2014
Current Activity Level : Actively seeking new investments

PANORAMIC GROWTH EQUITY (FUND MANAGEMENT) LLP

35 Old Jewry
6th Floor, Becket House
London, United Kingdom EC2V 6EB
Phone: 442071003715
E-mail: team@pgequity.com
Website: www.pgequity.com

Other Offices
140 West George Street
First Floor
Glasgow, United Kingdom G2 2HG
Phone: 441413315100

Management and Staff
David Wilson, Partner
Malcolm Kpedekpo, Partner
Stephen Campbell, Partner

Type of Firm
Private Equity Firm

Project Preferences

Type of Financing Preferred:
Expansion
Balanced
Management Buyouts
Acquisition

Size of Investments Considered:
Min Size of Investment Considered (000s): $817
Max Size of Investment Considered (000s): $5,553

Geographical Preferences

International Preferences:
United Kingdom

Industry Preferences

In Communications prefer:
Communications and Media
Telecommunications

In Medical/Health prefer:
Medical/Health
Health Services

In Industrial/Energy prefer:
Energy

In Business Serv. prefer:
Media

Additional Information
Name of Most Recent Fund: Panoramic Enterprise Capital Fund I
Most Recent Fund Was Raised: 06/14/2010
Year Founded: 2009
Capital Under Management: $93,610,000
Current Activity Level : Actively seeking new investments

PANOSTAJA OYJ

Postitorvenkatu 16
P.O. Box 783
Tampere, Finland 33101
Phone: 35832634300
Fax: 358102173232
E-mail: panostaja@panostaja.fi
Website: www.panostaja.fi

Management and Staff
Juha Sarsama, Chief Executive Officer
Tapio Tommila, Chief Financial Officer

Type of Firm
Private Equity Firm

Project Preferences

Type of Financing Preferred:
Leveraged Buyout
Acquisition

Geographical Preferences

International Preferences:
Central Europe
Western Europe
Eastern Europe
Scandanavia/Nordic Region
Finland

Industry Preferences

In Computer Software prefer:
Computer Services

In Consumer Related prefer:
Consumer Products
Consumer Services

In Industrial/Energy prefer:
Industrial Products

In Other prefer:
Environment Responsible

Additional Information
Year Founded: 1984
Current Activity Level : Actively seeking new investments

PANTERA CAPITAL MANAGEMENT LP

One Market Plaza, Spear Tower, Suite 4050
San Francisco, CA USA 94105
Phone: 4153603600
E-mail: info@panteracapital.com
Website: www.panteracapital.com

Type of Firm
Private Equity Firm

Project Preferences

Type of Financing Preferred:
Early Stage
Expansion
Balanced

Industry Preferences

In Financial Services prefer:
Financial Services

Additional Information
Year Founded: 2003
Capital Under Management: $24,880,000
Current Activity Level : Actively seeking new investments

PANTHEON VENTURES (UK) LLP

10 Finsbury Square
Fourth Floor
London, United Kingdom EC2A 1AF
Phone: 442033561800
Website: http://pantheon.com

Other Offices
1095 Avenue of the Americas
32nd Floor
NEW YORK, NY USA 10036
Phone: 2122052000
Fax: 2122052099

Eight Connaught Place
Ste 3001-3, 30th Flr
Hong Kong, Hong Kong
Phone: 85228108063
Fax: 85225260218

Management and Staff

Alec Brown, Vice President
Alexander Wilmerding, Principal
Alexander Scott, Partner
Amanda McCrystal, Principal
Andres Reibel, Vice President
Andrew Sherriff, Vice President
Andrew Lebus, Partner
Bing Wong, Vice President
Brett Johnson, Partner
Brian Lim, Partner
Brian Buenneke, Partner
Carsten Huwendiek, Principal
Cecile Ross, Vice President
Charlotte Morris, Vice President
Chris Meads, Partner
Clem Geraghty, Principal
Daniela Konrath, Partner
Dennis McCrary, Partner
Dinesh Ramasamy, Vice President
Dushy Sivanithy, Principal
Elly Livingstone, Partner
Erik Wong, Principal
Evan Corley, Partner
Francesco Di Valmarana, Partner
Heiko Schupp, Principal
Helen Steers, Partner
Jaime Londono, Principal
Jeff Lumbard, Principal
Jeff Miller, Principal
Jeffrey Reed, Principal
John Morgan, Partner
Jonathan Spalter, Principal
Kathryn Leaf Wilmes, Partner
Kevin Albert, Partner
Kevin Dunwoodie, Vice President
Kunal Sood, Vice President
Leon Hadass, Principal
Lois Towers, Principal
Londono Jaime, Principal
Matt Garfunkle, Partner
Matthew Jones, Partner
Maureen Downey, Principal
Michael Riak, Principal
Nik Morandi, Principal
Paul Ward, Managing Partner
Paul Jones, Principal
Ralph Guenther, Partner
Rebeca Ehrnrooth, Principal
Richard Sem, Partner
Rob Barr, Partner
Robert Amis, Partner
Robin Bailey, Partner
Samayita Das, Vice President
Sara Lonergan, Vice President
Sheldon Chang, Partner
Sibing Huang, Vice President
Susan McAndrews, Partner
Tatjana Van Vloten, Vice President

Type of Firm
Private Equity Advisor or Fund of Funds

Association Membership
Australian Venture Capital Association (AVCAL)
Hong Kong Venture Capital Association (HKVCA)
Emerging Markets Private Equity Association
German Venture Capital Association (BVK)
European Private Equity and Venture Capital Assoc.
African Venture Capital Association (AVCA)

Project Preferences

Role in Financing:
Prefer role in deals created by others

Type of Financing Preferred:
Fund of Funds
Leveraged Buyout
Other
Fund of Funds of Second

Geographical Preferences

United States Preferences:
North America

International Preferences:
Latin America
Europe
Australia
Asia
Africa

Industry Preferences

In Communications prefer:
Communications and Media

In Medical/Health prefer:
Medical/Health

In Consumer Related prefer:
Consumer Products

In Industrial/Energy prefer:
Energy

In Transportation prefer:
Transportation

In Business Serv. prefer:
Services

In Manufact. prefer:
Manufacturing

In Utilities prefer:
Utilities

Additional Information
Name of Most Recent Fund: BVK Private Equity 2014, L.P.
Most Recent Fund Was Raised: 01/22/2014
Year Founded: 1982
Capital Under Management: $24,500,000,000
Current Activity Level : Actively seeking new investments
Method of Compensation: Return on investment is of primary concern, do not charge fees

PANTHERA CAPITAL GROUP

34 Fuxingxi Lu
Shanghai, China 200031
Phone: 86-21-6431-9126
Fax: 86-21-6431-9709

Management and Staff
Fu Zhong, Venture Partner
Jim Preissier, Managing Partner
Richard Hui, Managing Partner
San Eng, Managing Partner

Type of Firm
Private Equity Firm

Project Preferences

Type of Financing Preferred:
Expansion
Balanced
Later Stage

Geographical Preferences

International Preferences:
Asia

Additional Information
Year Founded: 2007
Current Activity Level : Actively seeking new investments

PAPILLON CAPITAL LLC

8000 Westpark Drive, Suite 250
McLean, VA USA 22102
Website: www.papillon.vc

Management and Staff
John Cibinic, Co-Founder
Kartik Kumaramangalam, Co-Founder

Type of Firm
Private Equity Firm

Project Preferences

Type of Financing Preferred:
Early Stage

Geographical Preferences

International Preferences:
India
Asia

Additional Information
Year Founded: 2014
Current Activity Level : Actively seeking new investments

PAPPAS VENTURES

2520 Meridian Parkway, Suite 400
Durham, NC USA 27713
Phone: 9199983300
Fax: 9199983301
Website: www.pappasventures.com

Management and Staff

Arthur Pappas, Managing Partner
Ernest Mario, Venture Partner
Ford Worthy, Partner
Franz Humer, Venture Partner
Michael Grey, Venture Partner
Scott Weiner, Partner

Type of Firm
Private Equity Firm

Association Membership
National Venture Capital Association - USA (NVCA)

Project Preferences

Role in Financing:
Will function either as deal originator or investor in deals created by others

Type of Financing Preferred:
Early Stage
Balanced
Later Stage

Geographical Preferences

United States Preferences:
North America

Industry Focus

(% based on actual investment)
Biotechnology	64.8%
Medical/Health	33.6%
Computer Software and Services	1.2%
Industrial/Energy	0.3%
Internet Specific	0.1%

Additional Information

Name of Most Recent Fund: A.M. Pappas Life Science Ventures IV, L.P.
Most Recent Fund Was Raised: 11/21/2008
Year Founded: 1994
Capital Under Management: $353,000,000
Current Activity Level : Actively seeking new investments
Method of Compensation: Return on investment is of primary concern, do not charge fees

PAR CAPITAL MANAGEMENT INC

200 Clarendon Street
48th Floor
Boston, MA USA 02116
Website: www.parcapital.com

Type of Firm
Private Equity Firm

Project Preferences

Type of Financing Preferred:
Generalist PE

Additional Information
Year Founded: 1990
Current Activity Level : Actively seeking new investments

PAR EQUITY LLP

3A Dublin Meuse
Edinburgh, United Kingdom EH3 6NW
Phone: 441315560044
E-mail: info@parequity.com
Website: www.parequity.com

Management and Staff

Andrew Castell, Partner
Paul Munn, Partner
Paul Atkinson, Partner
Robert Higginson, Partner

Type of Firm
Private Equity Firm

Project Preferences

Type of Financing Preferred:
Balanced

Size of Investments Considered:
Min Size of Investment Considered (000s): $813
Max Size of Investment Considered (000s): $4,063

Geographical Preferences

International Preferences:
Europe

Additional Information
Year Founded: 2009
Current Activity Level : Actively seeking new investments

PARAGON ADVISORS INC

20820 Chagrin Boulevard
Chagrin Corporate Center
Cleveland, OH USA 44122
Phone: 216-491-3990
Fax: 216-495-3995
E-mail: paragon@paragonadvisors.net
Website: paragonadvisors.net

Type of Firm
Investment Management Firm

Project Preferences

Type of Financing Preferred:
Leveraged Buyout
Value-Add
Mezzanine
Other

Industry Preferences

In Industrial/Energy prefer:
Energy

In Financial Services prefer:
Real Estate

Additional Information
Name of Most Recent Fund: Real Estate Capital Fund 2013 LLC
Most Recent Fund Was Raised: 08/07/2013
Year Founded: 1996
Capital Under Management: $15,158,000
Current Activity Level : Actively seeking new investments

PARAGON PARTNERS

175 CST Road, Kalina
901, Grande Palladium
Mumbai, India 400098
Website: www.paragonpartners.in

Type of Firm
Private Equity Firm

Project Preferences

Type of Financing Preferred:
Later Stage

Size of Investments Considered:
Min Size of Investment Considered (000s): $10,000
Max Size of Investment Considered (000s): $20,000

Geographical Preferences

International Preferences:
India

Industry Preferences

In Biotechnology prefer:
Industrial Biotechnology

In Medical/Health prefer:
Health Services

In Consumer Related prefer:
Consumer

In Industrial/Energy prefer:
Industrial Products

In Financial Services prefer:
Financial Services

In Manufact. prefer:
Manufacturing

Additional Information
Year Founded: 2015
Capital Under Management: $120,000,000
Current Activity Level : Actively seeking new investments

PARAGON PARTNERS GMBH

Leopoldstrasse 10
Munich, Germany 80802
Phone: 49893888700
Fax: 498938887015
E-mail: info@paragon-partners.de
Website: www.paragon.de

Management and Staff
Edin Hadzic, Co-Founder
Krischan von Moeller, Co-Founder
Marco Attolini, Partner
Stefan Winterling, Co-Founder

Type of Firm
Private Equity Firm

Project Preferences

Role in Financing:
Prefer role as deal originator

Type of Financing Preferred:
Turnaround
Management Buyouts
Acquisition

Geographical Preferences

International Preferences:
Liechtenstein
Switzerland
Western Europe
Austria
Germany

Industry Preferences

In Communications prefer:
Communications and Media

In Medical/Health prefer:
Medical/Health

In Consumer Related prefer:
Education Related

In Industrial/Energy prefer:
Industrial Products

In Financial Services prefer:
Financial Services

In Business Serv. prefer:
Services

Additional Information
Year Founded: 2004
Capital Under Management: $715,400,000
Current Activity Level : Actively seeking new investments

PARAKLETOS@VENTURES MILLENIUM FUND LP

175 Nortech Parkway, Suite 200
San Jose, CA USA 95134
Phone: 4089417000
Fax: 4089417001
E-mail: info@parakletos.com

Management and Staff
Alan Hsia, Principal

Type of Firm
Private Equity Firm

Project Preferences

Type of Financing Preferred:
Early Stage
Balanced

Geographical Preferences

United States Preferences:
California

International Preferences:
India
China
Korea, South

Industry Preferences

In Communications prefer:
Communications and Media
Telecommunications

In Semiconductor/Electr prefer:
Semiconductor

In Financial Services prefer:
Financial Services

Additional Information
Year Founded: 1999
Capital Under Management: $30,000,000
Current Activity Level : Actively seeking new investments

PARALLAX CAPITAL PARTNERS LLC

23332 Mill Creek Drive, Suite 155
Laguna Hills, CA USA 92653
Phone: 9492964800
Fax: 9492964801
E-mail: info@parallaxcap.com
Website: www.parallaxcap.com

Management and Staff
Brad Clark, Principal
Chris Kanaley, Vice President
James McGarry, Principal
James Hale, Managing Partner
John Baldwin, Partner
Lisa Hale, Partner
Michael Zazulak, Vice President
Mike Hale, Principal
Murray Snowden, Vice President
Pam Wood, Vice President
Richard Campbell, Chief Financial Officer
Scott Lencz, Partner

Type of Firm
Private Equity Firm

Project Preferences

Type of Financing Preferred:
Leveraged Buyout
Turnaround
Management Buyouts
Acquisition
Recapitalizations

Geographical Preferences

United States Preferences:
North America

Canadian Preferences:
All Canada

International Preferences:
Asia Pacific
Europe
Asia

Industry Preferences

In Communications prefer:
Telecommunications

In Computer Hardware prefer:
Computers

In Computer Software prefer:
Software

In Computer Other prefer:
Computer Related

In Semiconductor/Electr prefer:
Semiconductor

In Medical/Health prefer:
Medical/Health
Pharmaceuticals

In Business Serv. prefer:
Media

Additional Information
Name of Most Recent Fund: Parallax Capital Fund, L.P.
Most Recent Fund Was Raised: 12/28/2012
Year Founded: 2003
Capital Under Management: $115,500,000
Current Activity Level : Actively seeking new investments

PARALLEL49 EQUITY

1111 West Hastings Street, Suite 200
Vancouver, Canada V6E 2J3
Phone: 6046887669
Fax: 6046887649
E-mail: info@tricorpacific.com
Website: www.p49equity.com

Other Offices
One Westminster Place, Suite 100
Lake Forest, IL USA 60045
Phone: 8472954410
Fax: 8472954243

Management and Staff
Bradley Seaman, Managing Director
David Barkwell, Vice President
David Rowntree, Managing Director
J. Trevor Johnstone, Managing Director
Jeremy Billan, Vice President
Nicholas Peters, Managing Director
Rob Wildeman, Managing Director
Roderick Senft, Managing Director
Scott Daum, Managing Director

Type of Firm
Private Equity Firm

Project Preferences

Type of Financing Preferred:
Leveraged Buyout
Management Buyouts
Acquisition
Recapitalizations

Geographical Preferences

United States Preferences:

Canadian Preferences:
All Canada

Industry Preferences

In Consumer Related prefer:
Consumer
Consumer Products

In Business Serv. prefer:
Services
Distribution

In Manufact. prefer:
Manufacturing

Additional Information
Name of Most Recent Fund: Parallel49 Equity Fund V
Most Recent Fund Was Raised: 12/28/2013
Year Founded: 1996
Capital Under Management: $1,000,000,000
Current Activity Level: Actively seeking new investments

PARAMPARA CAPITAL & MANAGEMENT CONSULTANTS LLP

504, Image Garden Lane
5th Floor, Fortune Chambers
Hyderabad, India 500081
Website: www.paramparas.com

Management and Staff
Jatin Desai, General Partner
Sridhar Rampalli, General Partner
Venkat Vallabhaneni, General Partner

Type of Firm
Private Equity Firm

Project Preferences

Type of Financing Preferred:
Early Stage
Expansion
Later Stage

Geographical Preferences

International Preferences:
India

Industry Preferences

In Consumer Related prefer:
Consumer

In Industrial/Energy prefer:
Industrial Products

In Financial Services prefer:
Financial Services

Additional Information
Year Founded: 2014
Capital Under Management: $16,000,000
Current Activity Level: Actively seeking new investments

PARAS VENTURES LLC

4545 Connecticut Avenue NW, Suite 26
Washington, DC USA 20008
Phone: 877-505-6317
Fax: 877-505-6317
E-mail: info@parasventures.com
Website: www.parasventures.com

Type of Firm
Private Equity Firm

Project Preferences

Type of Financing Preferred:
Early Stage

Geographical Preferences

United States Preferences:

Industry Preferences

In Computer Software prefer:
Software

In Internet Specific prefer:
Internet

In Biotechnology prefer:
Biotechnology

Additional Information
Year Founded: 2001
Current Activity Level: Actively seeking new investments

PARIS BUSINESS ANGELS

16, rue de Turbigo
Paris, France 75002
Phone: 33144827773
Fax: 33144827776
E-mail: contact@parisbusinessangels.com
Website: www.parisbusinessangels.com

Type of Firm
Angel Group

Association Membership
French Venture Capital Association (AFIC)

Project Preferences

Type of Financing Preferred:
Early Stage
Seed
Startup

Geographical Preferences

International Preferences:
France

Industry Preferences

In Communications prefer:
Telecommunications
Media and Entertainment

In Internet Specific prefer:
E-Commerce Technology
Internet

In Medical/Health prefer:
Medical/Health
Medical Diagnostics
Medical Therapeutics
Medical Products
Health Services

In Industrial/Energy prefer:
Industrial Products

In Business Serv. prefer:
Services

In Other prefer:
Environment Responsible

Additional Information
Year Founded: 2004
Current Activity Level : Actively seeking new investments

PARK SQUARE CAPITAL LLP

Seventh Floor, Stratton House
Five Stratton Street
London, United Kingdom W1J 8LA
Phone: 44-20-7529-1800
Fax: 44-20-7529-1810
Website: www.parksquarecapital.com

Other Offices
50, Avenue de la Liberte
Fifth Floor
Luxembourg, Luxembourg L-1930
Phone: 352-26-897-418
Fax: 352-26-897-894

Le Bordage, St. Peter Port
Second Floor
Guernsey, United Kingdom GY1 6HJ
Phone: 44-14-8174-9700
Fax: 44-14-8174-9749

Management and Staff
Brandon Bradkin, Partner
David Cottam, Partner
Franck Duhamel, Partner
Joanna Hislop, Partner
Klaus Petersen, Partner
Osvaldo Pereira, Principal
Robin Doumar, Managing Partner
Rudiger Blank, Principal

Type of Firm
Private Equity Firm

Project Preferences

Type of Financing Preferred:
Leveraged Buyout
Balanced
Special Situation
Distressed Debt

Geographical Preferences

International Preferences:
Europe

Industry Preferences

In Computer Other prefer:
Computer Related

Additional Information
Year Founded: 2004
Capital Under Management: $3,300,000
Current Activity Level : Actively seeking new investments

PARK STREET CAPITAL LLC

125 High Street
23rd Floor
Boston, MA USA 02110
Phone: 6178979200
Fax: 6178979201
E-mail: info@parkstreetcapital.com
Website: www.parkstreetcapital.com

Other Offices
500 Washington Street, Suite 325
San Francisco, CA USA 94111
Phone: 4152734208
Fax: 4158206101

Management and Staff
Dorr Begnal, Managing Director
Heather Foley, Chief Financial Officer
John Fantozzi, Managing Director
Kenneth Smith, Managing Director
Kristine Dailey, Managing Director
Robert Segel, Managing Director

Type of Firm
Private Equity Advisor or Fund of Funds

Project Preferences

Geographical Preferences

United States Preferences:

Additional Information
Name of Most Recent Fund: Park Street Capital Private Equity Fund XI, L.P.
Most Recent Fund Was Raised: 01/15/2014
Year Founded: 1997
Capital Under Management: $2,900,900,000
Current Activity Level : Actively seeking new investments
Method of Compensation: Other

PARKERGALE LP

222 Wes Merchandise Mart Plaza, Suite 1212
Chicago, IL USA 60654
Website: www.parkergale.com

Type of Firm
Private Equity Firm

Project Preferences

Type of Financing Preferred:
Leveraged Buyout
Acquisition

Geographical Preferences

United States Preferences:

Additional Information
Year Founded: 2015
Capital Under Management: $240,000,000
Current Activity Level : Actively seeking new investments

PARKVIEW CAPITAL PRATNERS

105 Bedford Road
Toronto, Canada M5R 2K4
Phone: 4169470123
Fax: 4169471877
Website: www.parkviewcapital.com

Type of Firm
Private Equity Firm

Additional Information
Year Founded: 1993
Current Activity Level : Actively seeking new investments

PARKWALK ADVISORS LTD

University House
11-13, Lower Grosvenor Place
London, United Kingdom SW1W 0EX
Phone: 442077592285
E-mail: enquiries@parkwalkadvisors.com
Website: parkwalkadvisors.com

Other Offices
Atenas 2
Pozuelo de Alarcon
Madrid, Spain 28224
Phone: 34917091130

Type of Firm
Private Equity Firm

Project Preferences

Type of Financing Preferred:
Early Stage
Expansion
Balanced
Later Stage

Size of Investments Considered:
Min Size of Investment Considered (000s): $738
Max Size of Investment Considered (000s): $14,762

Geographical Preferences

International Preferences:
United Kingdom
Europe

Industry Preferences

In Computer Software prefer:
Software

In Biotechnology prefer:
Biotechnology
Human Biotechnology
Industrial Biotechnology

Additional Information

Year Founded: 2009
Current Activity Level : Actively seeking new investments

PARTECH INTERNATIONAL

200 California Street, Suite 500
San Francisco, CA USA 94111
Phone: 4157882929
Fax: 4157886763
E-mail: contact@partechventures.com
Website: www.partechvc.com

Other Offices

Gipsstrasse 3
Berlin, Germany 10119

442 Rue de Kaolack PointE
Dakar, Senegal
Phone: 153656553

Management and Staff

Andreas Schlenker, General Partner
Christell Pariat, Chief Financial Officer
Emmanuel Delaveau, General Partner
Jai Choi, Venture Partner
Jean-Marc Patouillaud, General Partner
Nicholas El Baze, General Partner
Philippe Collombel, General Partner
Puyu Li, Chief Financial Officer
Reza Malekzadeh, General Partner
Scott Matson, Chief Financial Officer
Timothy Wilson, General Partner

Type of Firm

Private Equity Firm

Association Membership

French Venture Capital Association (AFIC)
Western Association of Venture Capitalists (WAVC)
German Venture Capital Association (BVK)

Project Preferences

Role in Financing:
Will function either as deal originator or investor in deals created by others

Type of Financing Preferred:
Early Stage
Balanced
Later Stage
Seed
Startup

Size of Investments Considered:
Min Size of Investment Considered (000s): $250
Max Size of Investment Considered (000s): $10,000

Geographical Preferences

United States Preferences:

Industry Focus

(% based on actual investment)
Computer Software and Services	35.1%
Internet Specific	30.6%
Semiconductors/Other Elect.	9.1%
Communications and Media	7.2%
Consumer Related	7.0%
Computer Hardware	3.8%
Medical/Health	3.5%
Other Products	1.5%
Industrial/Energy	1.3%
Biotechnology	0.7%

Additional Information

Name of Most Recent Fund: Partech Growth Fund
Most Recent Fund Was Raised: 01/26/2015
Year Founded: 1982
Capital Under Management: $880,000,000
Current Activity Level : Actively seeking new investments
Method of Compensation: Return on investment is of primary concern, do not charge fees

PARTHENON CAPITAL LLC

One Federal Street, 21st Floor
Boston, MA USA 02110
Phone: 6179604000
Fax: 6179604010
E-mail: info@parthenoncapital.com
Website: www.parthenoncapital.com

Other Offices

Four Embarcadero Center, Suite 3610
San Francisco, CA USA 94111
Phone: 415-913-3900
Fax: 415-913-3913

Management and Staff

Andrew Dodson, Partner
Brian Golson, Managing Partner
David Ament, Managing Partner
Eli Berlin, Vice President
H. Bradley Sloan, Principal
John Rutherford, Partner
Kurt Brumme, Vice President
William Kessinger, Managing Partner
William Winterer, Partner
Zachary Sadek, Partner

Type of Firm

Private Equity Firm

Project Preferences

Role in Financing:
Prefer role as deal originator but will also invest in deals created by others

Type of Financing Preferred:
Leveraged Buyout
Expansion
Management Buyouts
Acquisition
Recapitalizations

Geographical Preferences

United States Preferences:

Industry Focus

(% based on actual investment)
Other Products	54.2%
Communications and Media	10.6%
Consumer Related	9.8%
Internet Specific	8.2%
Industrial/Energy	5.6%
Semiconductors/Other Elect.	5.5%
Computer Hardware	2.6%
Medical/Health	2.2%
Computer Software and Services	1.4%

Additional Information

Name of Most Recent Fund: Parthenon Investors IV, L.P.
Most Recent Fund Was Raised: 10/12/2011
Year Founded: 1998
Capital Under Management: $2,200,000,000
Current Activity Level : Actively seeking new investments

PARTHENON TRUST SA

32 Amalias Avenue
Athens, Greece 10558
Phone: 30-210-331-3000
Fax: 30-210-331-3800

Management and Staff

Zaharias Palexas, Co-Founder

Type of Firm

Bank Affiliated

Association Membership

Hellenic Venture Capital Association

Project Preferences

Type of Financing Preferred:
Early Stage
Balanced
Later Stage
Startup

Geographical Preferences

International Preferences:
Europe

Additional Information

Year Founded: 2004
Current Activity Level : Actively seeking new investments

PARTICIPATIEMAATSCHAPPIJ INNOVATIONQUARTER BV

Prinses Margrietplantsoen 32
WTC The Hague
The Hague, Netherlands 2595BR
Phone: 31884747255
Website: www.innovationquarter.nl

Type of Firm
Government Affiliated Program

Project Preferences

Type of Financing Preferred:
Early Stage

Geographical Preferences

International Preferences:
Netherlands

Industry Preferences

In Medical/Health prefer:
Medical/Health

In Industrial/Energy prefer:
Environmental Related

In Agr/Forestr/Fish prefer:
Agribusiness

Additional Information
Year Founded: 2013
Current Activity Level : Actively seeking new investments

PARTICIPATIEMAATSCHAPPIJ OOST NEDERLAND NV

Hengelosestraat 585
Ondernemingshuis Twente
Enschede, Netherlands 7521 AG
Phone: 31538516851
Fax: 31538516868
E-mail: info@ppmoost.nl
Website: www.ppmoost.nl

Other Offices
Meander 601
Bedrijvenpark IJsseloord 2
Arnhem, Netherlands 7521 AG
Phone: 31263844222
Fax: 31263844244

Management and Staff
Marius Prins, President
Ron Willems, Vice President

Type of Firm
Government Affiliated Program

Association Membership
Dutch Venture Capital Associaton (NVP)

Project Preferences

Type of Financing Preferred:
Early Stage
Balanced
Later Stage

Geographical Preferences

International Preferences:
Europe
Netherlands

Industry Preferences

In Biotechnology prefer:
Agricultural/Animal Bio.

In Medical/Health prefer:
Medical/Health
Health Services

In Consumer Related prefer:
Food/Beverage

In Industrial/Energy prefer:
Energy
Environmental Related

In Other prefer:
Socially Responsible

Additional Information
Year Founded: 2003
Capital Under Management: $67,500,000
Current Activity Level : Actively seeking new investments

PARTICIPATIEMAATSCHAPPIJ VLAANDEREN NV

Oude Graanmarkt 63
Brussels, Belgium 1000
Phone: 3222295230
Fax: 3222295231
E-mail: info@pmv.eu
Website: www.pmv.eu

Type of Firm
Private Equity Firm

Association Membership
Belgium Venturing Association
European Private Equity and Venture Capital Assoc.

Project Preferences

Type of Financing Preferred:
Fund of Funds
Early Stage
Mezzanine
Generalist PE
Later Stage
Seed
Acquisition
Startup

Geographical Preferences

International Preferences:
Luxembourg
Europe
Netherlands
Belgium

Industry Preferences

In Communications prefer:
Communications and Media
Commercial Communications
Media and Entertainment
Entertainment
Publishing

In Computer Hardware prefer:
Computer Graphics and Dig

In Computer Other prefer:
Computer Related

In Biotechnology prefer:
Biotechnology
Industrial Biotechnology
Biotech Related Research

In Medical/Health prefer:
Medical/Health
Medical Diagnostics
Medical Products

In Consumer Related prefer:
Entertainment and Leisure
Sports
Education Related

In Industrial/Energy prefer:
Energy
Alternative Energy
Energy Conservation Relat

In Financial Services prefer:
Real Estate

In Business Serv. prefer:
Media

In Other prefer:
Environment Responsible

Additional Information
Year Founded: 1995
Capital Under Management: $298,681,000
Current Activity Level : Actively seeking new investments

PARTICIPEX GESTION SAS

1 rue Esquermoise
Place du Theatre
Lille, France 59800
Phone: 33320219380
Fax: 33320219389
E-mail: participex@participex.fr

Type of Firm
Private Equity Firm

Association Membership
French Venture Capital Association (AFIC)

Project Preferences

Type of Financing Preferred:
Leveraged Buyout
Early Stage
Generalist PE
Later Stage
Management Buyouts
Acquisition

Size of Investments Considered:
Min Size of Investment Considered (000s): $402
Max Size of Investment Considered (000s): $13,394

Geographical Preferences

International Preferences:
Europe
Belgium
France

Additional Information
Year Founded: 1980
Capital Under Management: $41,200,000
Current Activity Level : Actively seeking new investments

PARTISAN MANAGEMENT GROUP INC

7026 Timbers Drive
Evergreen, CO USA 80439
Phone: 3036701413
Website: www.partisanmgmt.com

Other Offices

293 Pearl Street
BOULDER, CO USA 80302
Phone: 3034448983
Fax: 3034440038

Six Ocean Club Drive
FERNANDINA, FL USA 32034
Phone: 9044918619

Management and Staff
Karen Cassidy, Principal
Norman Weldon, Principal

Type of Firm
Private Equity Firm

Project Preferences

Role in Financing:
Prefer role as deal originator

Type of Financing Preferred:
Early Stage
Balanced

Industry Preferences

In Medical/Health prefer:
Medical Products

Additional Information
Year Founded: 1987
Capital Under Management: $10,000,000
Current Activity Level : Actively seeking new investments
Method of Compensation: Return on investment is of primary concern, do not charge fees

PARTNER ONE CAPITAL

505 Maisonneuve West, Suite 400
Montreal, Canada H3A 3C2
E-mail: info@partneronecapital.com
Website: partneronecapital.com

Other Offices
Banner Bank Building
950 West Bannock Street
BOISE, ID USA 83702
Phone: 8556972786

Type of Firm
Private Equity Firm

Project Preferences

Type of Financing Preferred:
Core
Early Stage
Expansion
Generalist PE
Balanced
Later Stage
Acquisition
Startup

Industry Preferences

In Communications prefer:
Communications and Media

In Financial Services prefer:
Real Estate

In Business Serv. prefer:
Media

Additional Information
Year Founded: 1995
Current Activity Level : Actively seeking new investments

PARTNERINVEST OVRE NORRLAND AB

Storgatan 74
Pitea, Sweden 941 32
Website: www.partnerinvestnorr.se

Type of Firm
Private Equity Firm

Project Preferences

Type of Financing Preferred:
Later Stage

Size of Investments Considered:
Min Size of Investment Considered (000s): $297
Max Size of Investment Considered (000s): $594

Geographical Preferences

International Preferences:
Sweden

Industry Preferences

In Communications prefer:
Communications and Media
Commercial Communications
Wireless Communications

In Computer Software prefer:
Software

In Internet Specific prefer:
Internet

In Semiconductor/Electr prefer:
Electronics

In Biotechnology prefer:
Biotechnology

In Medical/Health prefer:
Medical/Health
Medical Diagnostics

In Industrial/Energy prefer:
Alternative Energy
Energy Conservation Relat

In Other prefer:
Environment Responsible

Additional Information
Year Founded: 2009
Capital Under Management: $31,600,000
Current Activity Level : Actively seeking new investments

PARTNERS CAPITAL INVESTMENT GROUP HOLDINGS LLC

50 Rowes Wharf
Fourth Floor
Boston, MA USA 02110
Phone: 617-292-2570
Fax: 617-292-2571
E-mail: enquiries@partners-cap.com
Website: www.partners-cap.com

Other Offices

5 Young Street
London, United Kingdom W8 5EH
Phone: 44-20-7938-5200
Fax: 44-20-7938-5201

Eight Connaught Place
Level 8, Two Exchange Square
Central, Hong Kong
Phone: 85222972467
Fax: 85222972490

Management and Staff

Brendan Corcoran, Partner
David Shusan, Partner
Euan Finlay, Partner
Richard Scarinci, Partner
Stan Miranda, Chief Executive Officer
Toby Joll, Partner

Type of Firm

Private Equity Firm

Project Preferences

Type of Financing Preferred:
Turnaround
Acquisition
Distressed Debt

Industry Preferences

In Financial Services prefer:
Real Estate

Additional Information

Name of Most Recent Fund: Partners Capital Condor Fund VII, L.P.
Most Recent Fund Was Raised: 12/06/2013
Year Founded: 2001
Capital Under Management: $9,300,000
Current Activity Level : Actively seeking new investments

PARTNERS FOR GROWTH INC

1660 Tiburon Boulevard, Suite D
Belvedere Tiburon, CA USA 94920
Phone: 4159125894
Website: www.pfgrowth.com

Management and Staff

Rita Kim, Chief Executive Officer

Type of Firm

Private Equity Firm

Project Preferences

Type of Financing Preferred:
Leveraged Buyout
Mezzanine
Generalist PE
Later Stage
Management Buyouts
Acquisition

Geographical Preferences

United States Preferences:

Additional Information

Year Founded: 2004
Capital Under Management: $276,000,000
Current Activity Level : Actively seeking new investments

PARTNERS GROUP HOLDING AG

Zugerstrasse 57
Baar, Switzerland 6341
Phone: 41417846000
Fax: 41417846001
E-mail: partnersgroup@partnersgroup.com
Website: www.partnersgroup.com

Other Offices

1114 Avenue of the Americas
37th Floor
NEW YORK, NY USA 10036
Phone: 2129082600
Fax: 2129082601

First Angel Court
19th Floor
London, United Kingdom EC2R 7HJ
Phone: 44-20-7260-1700
Fax: 44-20-7260-1701

Office No. 24, Level 3, Gate Village 10
P.O. BOX 125115
Dubai, Utd. Arab Em.
Phone: 971-4-401-9143
Fax: 971-4-401-9142

#3026 Floor ASEM Tower
159-1 Samsung-dong, Gangnamgu
Seoul, South Korea 135-798
Phone: 82-2-6001-2913
Fax: 82-2-6001-3186

5847 San Feliper Street, Suite 1730
HOUSTON, TX USA 77057
Phone: 17138211622
Fax: 1713821162

Daido Seimei Kasumigaseki Bldg. 5F
1-4-2 Kasumigaseki, Chiyoda-ku
Tokyo, Japan 100-0013
Phone: 81-3-5532-2030
Fax: 81-3-5532-2040

150 Spear Street
18th Floor
SAN FRANCISCO, CA USA 94105
Phone: 415-537-8585
Fax: 415-537-8558

Number 6 Wudinghou Street
#1105 Excel Center
Beijing, China 100033
Phone: 86-10-8356-1600
Fax: 86-10-8356-1601

450 Lexington Avenue
39th Floor
MANHATTAN, NY USA 10017
Phone: 212-763-4700
Fax: 212-763-4701

Rua Joaquim Floriano
1052 Conj. 142, CEP 04534-014
Sao Paulo, Brazil
Phone: 551130740346
Fax: 551130740349

10 rue Labie
Paris, France 75017
Phone: 33145036084

114, Dr. E Moses Road, Worli, Suite 1106
Mumbai, India 400 018
Phone: 912224818750
Fax: 91224818756

55 avenue de la gare
Luxembourg, Luxembourg 1611
Phone: 352-27-48281
Fax: 352-27-482-828

Gundelindenstrasse 2
Munich, Germany 80805
Phone: 49-89-3838-920
Fax: 49-89-3838-9299

61 Robinson Road
#16-01 Robinson Centre
Singapore, Singapore 068893
Phone: 65-62-48-3535
Fax: 65-62-48-3536

AMP Center
L34, 50 Bridge Street
Sydney, Australia 2000
Phone: 61-2-8216-0885
Fax: 61-2-8216-0883

Management and Staff
Alex Cho, Managing Director
Andreas Knecht, Chief Operating Officer
Armin Weiland, Partner
Brooks Lindberg, Partner
Christian Ebert, Managing Director
Cyrill Wipfli, Chief Financial Officer
Cyrus Driver, Managing Director
Hans-Ulrich Mueller, Partner
Henning Eckermann, Partner
Jochen Weirich, Partner
Josef Bieri, Partner
Juergen Diegruber, Partner
Manuel Martiny, Partner
Marc Weiss, Partner
Marcel Erni, Co-Founder
Marcel Wieduwilt, Partner
Mark Rowe, Partner
Michael Barben, Partner
Nan Leake, Partner
Nori Lietz, Partner
Robert Collins, Managing Director
Roland Roffler, Partner
Sandra Pajarola, Partner
Scott Higbee, Partner
Thomas Staubli, Partner
Walter Keller, Partner

Type of Firm
Investment Management Firm

Association Membership
Brazilian Venture Capital Association (ABCR)
Australian Venture Capital Association (AVCAL)
China Venture Capital Association
Swiss Venture Capital Association (SECA)
European Private Equity and Venture Capital Assoc.
Singapore Venture Capital Association (SVCA)

Project Preferences

Type of Financing Preferred:
Fund of Funds
Value-Add
Expansion
Mezzanine
Management Buyouts
Recapitalizations

Size of Investments Considered:
Min Size of Investment Considered (000s): $5,000
Max Size of Investment Considered (000s): $20,000

Geographical Preferences

United States Preferences:
All U.S.

International Preferences:
Sweden
United Kingdom
Western Europe
Asia
Germany
France

Industry Preferences

In Communications prefer:
Communications and Media
Telecommunications

In Medical/Health prefer:
Health Services

In Consumer Related prefer:
Consumer

In Industrial/Energy prefer:
Energy
Alternative Energy
Industrial Products
Materials

In Financial Services prefer:
Financial Services
Real Estate

In Business Serv. prefer:
Media

Additional Information
Name of Most Recent Fund: Partners Group Kingdom, L.P. Inc.
Most Recent Fund Was Raised: 02/05/2014
Year Founded: 1996
Capital Under Management: $57,000,000,000
Current Activity Level : Actively seeking new investments

PARTNERS INNOVATION FUND LLC

215 First Street, Suite 500
Cambridge, MA USA 02142
Phone: 8573072400
Website: innovation.partners.org

Management and Staff
Carl Berke, Partner
Richard Wilmot, Principal
Roger Kitterman, Managing Partner

Type of Firm
Private Equity Firm

Association Membership
New England Venture Capital Association

Project Preferences

Type of Financing Preferred:
Early Stage
Balanced

Industry Preferences

In Biotechnology prefer:
Biotechnology

Additional Information
Year Founded: 2008
Capital Under Management: $166,100,000
Current Activity Level : Actively seeking new investments

PARTNERS VENTURE CAPITAL CO LTD

11F, Eunseong Building
53-8 Cheongdam-dong Gangnam-gu
Seoul, South Korea 135-763
Phone: 822-6248-7600
Fax: 822-6248-7612
E-mail: partners@partners.com
Website: www.partnersventure.com

Type of Firm
Private Equity Firm

Project Preferences

Type of Financing Preferred:
Leveraged Buyout
Balanced
Management Buyouts
Acquisition

Geographical Preferences

International Preferences:
Asia
Korea, South

Industry Preferences

In Communications prefer:
Entertainment

In Biotechnology prefer:
Agricultural/Animal Bio.

Additional Information
Year Founded: 2000
Capital Under Management: $46,900,000
Current Activity Level : Actively seeking new investments

PARTNERSHIP CAPITAL GROWTH LLC

One Embarcadero Center, Suite 3810
San Francisco, CA USA 94111
Phone: 4157058008
Fax: 4157055279

Management and Staff
Brent Knudsen, Managing Partner
Brian Smith, Principal
Christopher Spahr, Partner
Eric Schiller, Vice President
Nathan Belden, Partner
Tripp Baird, Principal

Type of Firm
Investment Management Firm

Project Preferences

Type of Financing Preferred:
Expansion
Balanced
Later Stage
Distressed Debt

Industry Preferences

In Communications prefer:
Communications and Media

In Medical/Health prefer:
Medical/Health
Medical Products
Health Services
Hospital/Other Instit.

In Consumer Related prefer:
Consumer
Entertainment and Leisure
Sports
Retail
Food/Beverage
Consumer Products
Other Restaurants

In Industrial/Energy prefer:
Alternative Energy
Energy Conservation Relat
Environmental Related

In Utilities prefer:
Utilities

Additional Information

Year Founded: 1969
Capital Under Management: $61,300,000
Current Activity Level: Actively seeking new investments

PARTNERSHIP FUND FOR NEW YORK CITY

One Battery Park Plaza
5th Floor
New York, NY USA 10004
Phone: 2124937400
Fax: 2123443344
Website: pfnyc.org

Management and Staff

Anthony Giugliano, Chief Financial Officer

Type of Firm

Private Equity Firm

Association Membership

Community Development Venture Capital Alliance

Project Preferences

Role in Financing:
Will function either as deal originator or investor in deals created by others

Type of Financing Preferred:
Early Stage
Balanced
Later Stage
Seed
Startup

Size of Investments Considered:
Min Size of Investment Considered (000s): $1,000
Max Size of Investment Considered (000s): $5,000

Geographical Preferences

United States Preferences:
New York

Industry Preferences

In Communications prefer:
Communications and Media
Telecommunications
Wireless Communications
Media and Entertainment

In Computer Software prefer:
Software

In Internet Specific prefer:
Internet

In Biotechnology prefer:
Biotechnology

In Consumer Related prefer:
Retail
Food/Beverage
Education Related

In Industrial/Energy prefer:
Energy
Alternative Energy

In Transportation prefer:
Transportation

In Other prefer:
Socially Responsible
Women/Minority-Owned Bus.

Additional Information

Name of Most Recent Fund: New York Small Business Venture Fund III
Most Recent Fund Was Raised: 11/17/2005
Year Founded: 1996
Capital Under Management: $114,000,000
Current Activity Level: Actively seeking new investments
Method of Compensation: Return on investment is of primary concern, do not charge fees

---

PARTNERSHIPS UK PLC

10 Great George Street
London, United Kingdom SW1P 3AE
Phone: 442033017105
E-mail: info@partenershipsuk.org.uk
Website: www.partnershipsuk.org.uk

Management and Staff

Michael Gerrard, Chief Executive Officer

Type of Firm

Government Affiliated Program

Association Membership

British Venture Capital Association (BVCA)

Project Preferences

Type of Financing Preferred:
Early Stage
Expansion
Balanced

Geographical Preferences

International Preferences:
United Kingdom
Europe
Western Europe

Industry Preferences

In Communications prefer:
Communications and Media

In Medical/Health prefer:
Medical/Health
Health Services

In Consumer Related prefer:
Education Related

In Industrial/Energy prefer:
Energy Conservation Relat

In Transportation prefer:
Transportation

In Business Serv. prefer:
Services

In Other prefer:
Environment Responsible

Additional Information

Year Founded: 2000
Current Activity Level: Actively seeking new investments

PARVILLA SASU

42, Avenue Montaigne
Paris, France 75008
E-mail: office@parvilla.com
Website: www.parvilla.com

Management and Staff

Jean-Marie Fabre, Chief Executive Officer

Type of Firm

Private Equity Firm

Association Membership

French Venture Capital Association (AFIC)
European Private Equity and Venture Capital Assoc.

Project Preferences

Type of Financing Preferred:
Fund of Funds
Leveraged Buyout

Geographical Preferences

International Preferences:
Sweden
United Kingdom
Luxembourg
Europe
Netherlands
Belgium
Finland
Norway
Denmark
France

Additional Information

Name of Most Recent Fund: Fonds Parvilla II
Most Recent Fund Was Raised: 10/05/2012
Year Founded: 2006
Capital Under Management: $26,069,000
Current Activity Level : Actively seeking new investments

PASADENA ANGELS, INC.

2400 North Lincoln Avenue
Altadena, CA USA 91001
E-mail: info@pasadenaangels.com
Website: www.pasadenaangels.com

Type of Firm

Angel Group

Project Preferences

Type of Financing Preferred:
Early Stage
Seed

Size of Investments Considered:
Min Size of Investment Considered (000s): $100
Max Size of Investment Considered (000s): $1,500

Geographical Preferences

United States Preferences:
Southern California

Additional Information

Year Founded: 2001
Current Activity Level : Actively seeking new investments

PASSION CAPITAL INVESTMENTS LLP

144a Clerkenwell Road
Fieldwood House
London, United Kingdom EC1R 5DF
Phone: 442078333373
Website: www.passioncapital.com

Management and Staff

Eileen Burbidge, Partner
Stefan Glaenzer, Founder

Type of Firm

Investment Management Firm

Project Preferences

Type of Financing Preferred:
Early Stage
Seed
Startup

Geographical Preferences

International Preferences:
United Kingdom

Industry Preferences

In Communications prefer:
Communications and Media
Media and Entertainment

Additional Information

Year Founded: 2011
Capital Under Management: $127,414,000
Current Activity Level : Actively seeking new investments

PASSPORT CAPITAL LLC

30 Hotaling Place, Suite 300
San Francisco, CA USA 94111
Phone: 4153214600
Fax: 4153214620
Website: www.passportcapital.com

Management and Staff

Elizabeth Mahon, Chief Financial Officer
Joanne Poile, Chief Operating Officer
John Moran, President

Type of Firm

Investment Management Firm

Project Preferences

Type of Financing Preferred:
Later Stage

Geographical Preferences

International Preferences:
Middle East
Africa

Industry Preferences

In Medical/Health prefer:
Health Services

In Consumer **Related prefer:**
Consumer

In Industrial/Energy prefer:
Energy
Oil and Gas Exploration
Industrial Products
Materials

In Financial Services prefer:
Financial Services

In Agr/Forestr/Fish prefer:
Agriculture related

Additional Information

Year Founded: 2000
Current Activity Level : Actively seeking new investments

PATAGONIA CAPITAL PARTNERS, LLC

Somellera 726 Adrogue
Buenos Aires, Argentina 1846
Website: www.patagoniacp.com

Type of Firm

Private Equity Firm

Geographical Preferences

United States Preferences:
All U.S.

International Preferences:
Europe
Argentina
Mexico

Additional Information

Year Founded: 2017
Capital Under Management: $480,000
Current Activity Level : Actively seeking new investments

PATHBREAKER VENTURES

221 Kearny Street
Fifth Floor
San Francisco, CA USA 94108
Website: www.pathbreakervc.com

Other Offices

165 Jordan Avenue
Apt Four
SAN FRANCISCO, CA USA 94118
Phone: 6782322664

Type of Firm

Private Equity Firm

Project Preferences

Type of Financing Preferred:
Early Stage
Expansion
Later Stage

Pratt's Guide to Private Equity & Venture Capital Sources

Additional Information
Year Founded: 2015
Capital Under Management: $12,910,000
Current Activity Level : Actively seeking new investments

PATHENA SA

Praca do Bom Sucesso 131
Edificio Peninsula, sala 506
Porto, Portugal 4150-456
Phone: 351225430707
E-mail: info@pathena.com
Website: www.pathena.com

Type of Firm
Private Equity Firm

Association Membership
Portuguese Venture Capital Association (APCRI)

Project Preferences

Type of Financing Preferred:
Early Stage
Expansion
Seed
Startup

Geographical Preferences

International Preferences:
Europe
Portugal

Additional Information
Year Founded: 2007
Capital Under Management: $65,317,000
Current Activity Level : Actively seeking new investments

PATHFINDER INVESTMENT CO

153 A Law College Road
Second Floor, Varun Complex
Pune, India 411004
Phone: 91-20-2565-1833
Fax: 91-20-2565-1846
E-mail: pathfind@vsnl.com

Management and Staff
N.K. Prasad, Chairman & Managing Director

Type of Firm
Private Equity Firm

Project Preferences

Role in Financing:
Prefer role as deal originator but will also invest in deals created by others

Type of Financing Preferred:
Second Stage Financing
Expansion
Mezzanine
Later Stage

Geographical Preferences

International Preferences:
India

Industry Preferences

In Communications prefer:
Commercial Communications
Telecommunications

In Computer Hardware prefer:
Integrated Turnkey System

In Computer Software prefer:
Computer Services
Systems Software
Applications Software

In Computer Other prefer:
Computer Related

In Semiconductor/Electr prefer:
Electronic Components
Analytic/Scientific

In Medical/Health prefer:
Medical/Health
Diagnostic Services
Medical Products
Disposable Med. Products
Hospital/Other Instit.
Pharmaceuticals

In Consumer Related prefer:
Consumer
Franchises(NEC)
Food/Beverage
Consumer Products
Consumer Services
Hotels and Resorts
Education Related

In Industrial/Energy prefer:
Alternative Energy
Energy Conservation Relat
Industrial Products
Materials
Factory Automation
Machinery
Environmental Related

In Financial Services prefer:
Financial Services

In Business Serv. prefer:
Services
Consulting Services

In Manufact. prefer:
Manufacturing
Publishing

Additional Information
Year Founded: 1993
Current Activity Level : Actively seeking new investments
Method of Compensation: Return on investment is of primary concern, do not charge fees

PATRIOT CAPITAL FUNDING INC

509 South Exeter Street, Suite 210
Baltimore, MD USA 21202
Phone: 4435733010
Fax: 4435733020
E-mail: patriotpartners@patriot-capital.com
Website: www.patcapfunding.com

Other Offices
225 West Washington, Suite 2200
Chicago, IL USA 60606
Phone: 847-867-1299
Fax: 847-574-1285

750 North Saint Paul Street, Suite 1600
Dallas, TX USA 75201
Phone: 2146795034
Fax: 2147468811

Management and Staff
Charles McCusker, Co-Founder
Chris Royston, Co-Founder
Daniel Yardley, Managing Director
Patrick Hamner, Managing Director
Stacey Wittelsberger, Vice President
Thomas Holland, Co-Founder
Thomas Holland, Managing Partner
Thomas Neale, Managing Partner
Tom Kurtz, Managing Director

Type of Firm
Private Equity Firm

Association Membership
Illinois Venture Capital Association
Natl Assoc of Small Bus. Inv. Co (NASBIC)

Project Preferences

Type of Financing Preferred:
Expansion
Mezzanine
Management Buyouts
Acquisition
Recapitalizations

Geographical Preferences

United States Preferences:
Mid Atlantic
Midwest
Southeast
Southwest

Industry Preferences

In Communications prefer:
Telecommunications

In Computer Software prefer:
Applications Software

In Internet Specific prefer:
Ecommerce

In Consumer Related prefer:
Consumer
Consumer Products
Consumer Services
Education Related

In Transportation prefer:
Transportation

In Financial Services prefer:
Financial Services

In Business Serv. prefer:
Services
Distribution

In Manufact. prefer:
Manufacturing

Additional Information

Name of Most Recent Fund: Patriot Capital III SBIC, L.P.
Most Recent Fund Was Raised: 07/09/2013
Year Founded: 2003
Capital Under Management: $150,000,000
Current Activity Level : Actively seeking new investments

PATRIOT FINANCIAL PARTNERS LP

2929 Arch Street
Cira Centre
Philadelphia, PA USA 19104
Phone: 2153994650
E-mail: info@patriotfp.com
Website: www.patriotfp.com

Management and Staff

Conor McDonnell, Vice President
Ira Lubert, Partner
James Lynch, Managing Partner
Kevin Kooman, Principal
M. Katherine Lynch, Principal
W. Kirk Wycoff, Managing Partner
Wilson Smith, Principal

Type of Firm

Private Equity Firm

Project Preferences

Type of Financing Preferred:
Leveraged Buyout
Generalist PE
Later Stage

Size of Investments Considered:
Min Size of Investment Considered (000s): $10,000
Max Size of Investment Considered (000s): $25,000

Geographical Preferences

United States Preferences:
All U.S.

Industry Preferences

In Financial Services prefer:
Financial Services

Additional Information

Name of Most Recent Fund: Patriot Financial Partners II, L.P.
Most Recent Fund Was Raised: 09/09/2013
Year Founded: 2007
Capital Under Management: $390,605,000
Current Activity Level : Actively seeking new investments

PATRON CAPITAL ADVISERS LLP

Seven Hanover Square
London, United Kingdom W1S 1HQ
Phone: 442076299417
Fax: 442076299418
E-mail: uk@patroncapital.com
Website: www.patroncapital.com

Other Offices

Via Santo Spirito, 5
Milan, Italy 20121
Phone: 39-2-798-416
Fax: 39-2-7601-2090

Passeig de Gracia 74
Barcelona, Spain 08007
Phone: 34-93-467-9100
Fax: 34-93-467-9101

5, Rue Guillaume Kroll
Luxembourg, Luxembourg L-1637
Phone: 352-2627-0391
Fax: 352-2627-0390

Management and Staff

Johannes Kalker, Managing Director
Keith Breslauer, Managing Director
Luigi Capuano, Managing Director
Mark Parnell, Founder
Pedro Barcelo, Managing Director
Shane Law, Chief Operating Officer

Type of Firm

Private Equity Firm

Project Preferences

Type of Financing Preferred:
Value-Add
Opportunistic

Size of Investments Considered:
Min Size of Investment Considered (000s): $35,409
Max Size of Investment Considered (000s): $106,227

Geographical Preferences

International Preferences:
Europe

Industry Focus

(% based on actual investment)
Other Products 65.7%
Consumer Related 31.8%
Industrial/Energy 2.5%

Additional Information

Name of Most Recent Fund: Patron Capital, L.P. IV
Most Recent Fund Was Raised: 10/27/2011
Year Founded: 1999
Capital Under Management: $2,900,000,000
Current Activity Level : Actively seeking new investments

PAUA VENTURES GMBH

Linienstrasse 157
Berlin, Germany 10115
E-mail: info@pauaventures.com
Website: www.pauaventures.com

Management and Staff

Christian Buchenau, Managing Director
Christophe Defforey, Managing Director

Type of Firm

Private Equity Firm

Project Preferences

Type of Financing Preferred:
Early Stage
Seed
Startup

Geographical Preferences

International Preferences:
Europe
Poland
Germany

Industry Preferences

In Computer Software prefer:
Software

In Internet Specific prefer:
Ecommerce

Additional Information

Year Founded: 2010
Capital Under Management: $45,000,000
Current Activity Level : Actively seeking new investments

PAVILION ALTERNATIVES GROUP LTD

20 Grosvenor Place
London, United Kingdom SW1X 7HN
Phone: 442078387640
Fax: 442078387699
E-mail: information@altius-associates.com
Website: www.altius-associates.com

Other Offices
Ocean Financial Centre
10 Collyer Quay
, Singapore
Phone: 65 6232 2980
Fax: 65 6232 2888

6641 West Broad Street, Suite 402
Richmond, VA USA 23230
Phone: 1 804 282 9000
Fax: 1 804 282 6767

Management and Staff
Bradford Young, Partner
Catherine Mountjoy, Partner
Charles Magnay, Partner
Chason Beggerow, Partner
Doug Moore, Partner
Elvire Perrin, Partner
Eric Warner, Partner
Harry Olieman, Co-Founder
Jay Yoder, Partner
Jenny Fenton, Co-Founder
Joachim Suter, Partner
Rajesh Mehmi, Principal
Rhonda Ryan, Partner
William Charlton, Partner

Type of Firm
Private Equity Advisor or Fund of Funds

Association Membership
Emerging Markets Private Equity Association

Project Preferences

Type of Financing Preferred:
Fund of Funds
Generalist PE

Geographical Preferences

International Preferences:
Armenia
United Kingdom
Europe
Australia

Additional Information
Name of Most Recent Fund: ALTIUS REAL ASSETS FUND, LP
Most Recent Fund Was Raised: 10/10/2012
Year Founded: 2012
Capital Under Management: $92,395,000
Current Activity Level : Actively seeking new investments

PAVONIS GROUP LLC

4501 Cartwright Road, Suite 204
Missouri City, TX USA 77459
Website: www.pavonisgroup.com

Management and Staff
Demetrios Louziotis, Co-Founder
Mark Kingston, Co-Founder
Soh Har Pang, Co-Founder

Type of Firm
Private Equity Firm

Project Preferences

Type of Financing Preferred:
Early Stage
Generalist PE
Balanced
Opportunistic
Later Stage

Industry Preferences

In Communications prefer:
Data Communications

In Financial Services prefer:
Real Estate

Additional Information
Year Founded: 2013
Current Activity Level : Actively seeking new investments

PBM CAPITAL GROUP LLC

200 Garrett Street, Suite O
Charlottesville, VA USA 22902
Phone: 4349808100
Fax: 4349808199
Website: www.pbmcap.com

Management and Staff
Angelo LaMascolo, Principal
Damian deGoa, Managing Director
Sean Stalfort, Partner

Type of Firm
Private Equity Firm

Project Preferences

Type of Financing Preferred:
Leveraged Buyout
Generalist PE
Turnaround
Seed
Acquisition
Startup

Geographical Preferences

United States Preferences:

International Preferences:
Sweden

Industry Preferences

In Medical/Health prefer:
Medical/Health
Medical Diagnostics
Medical Products
Pharmaceuticals

In Consumer Related prefer:
Consumer Products
Consumer Services

Additional Information
Year Founded: 2010
Current Activity Level : Actively seeking new investments

PC CAPITAL SAPI DE CV

Bosque de Ciruelos 304
Second Floor
Mexico, Mexico DF CP11700
Phone: 525552518279
Fax: 525552450557
E-mail: info@pc-capital.com
Website: www.pc-capital.com

Management and Staff
Gabriel Araujo, Vice President
Pablo Cervantes, Partner
Pablo Coballasi, Partner

Type of Firm
Private Equity Firm

Project Preferences

Type of Financing Preferred:
Early Stage
Expansion
Later Stage

Geographical Preferences

International Preferences:
Mexico

Industry Preferences

In Consumer Related prefer:
Retail
Education Related

In Industrial/Energy prefer:
Environmental Related

In Financial Services prefer:
Financial Services

Pratt's Guide to Private Equity & Venture Capital Sources

Additional Information
Year Founded: 2012
Capital Under Management: $5,000,000
Current Activity Level : Actively seeking new investments

PC-CAPITAL OY

Keskuskatu 1 B
Helsinki, Finland 00100
Phone: 35896877170
Fax: 358968771745

Type of Firm
Investment Management Firm

Project Preferences

Type of Financing Preferred:
Balanced

Size of Investments Considered:
Min Size of Investment Considered (000s): $400
Max Size of Investment Considered (000s): $2,000

Geographical Preferences

International Preferences:
Finland

Industry Preferences

In Industrial/Energy prefer:
Alternative Energy
Energy Conservation Relat

In Financial Services prefer:
Real Estate

In Other prefer:
Environment Responsible

Additional Information
Year Founded: 2000
Current Activity Level : Actively seeking new investments

PCGI LLC

616 High Street, North West, Suite 450
Washington, DC USA 20001
Phone: 202-824-1600
Fax: 202-824-4300
E-mail: info@pcgi.net
Website: www.pcgi.net

Management and Staff
Bernard McGuire, Managing Director
Charles Toy, Managing Director
Gene Pohren, Managing Director
Stephen O Neill, Managing Director
Steve Cowan, Managing Director

Type of Firm
Private Equity Advisor or Fund of Funds

Geographical Preferences

International Preferences:
All International

Additional Information
Year Founded: 2005
Current Activity Level : Actively seeking new investments

PCM COMPANIES LLC

2600 Eagan Woods Drive, Suite 150
Eagan, MN USA 55121
Phone: 6514520212
Website: www.pcmmgmt.com

Management and Staff
Brian Smith, President
Dean Bachmeier, Principal
Michael Davies, Principal

Type of Firm
Investment Management Firm

Project Preferences

Type of Financing Preferred:
Leveraged Buyout
Acquisition

Additional Information
Year Founded: 1998
Current Activity Level : Actively seeking new investments

PCP CAPITAL PARTNERS LLP

31Hill St
London, United Kingdom W1J 5LS

Type of Firm
Private Equity Firm

Project Preferences

Type of Financing Preferred:
Unknown

Additional Information
Year Founded: 2016
Current Activity Level : Actively seeking new investments

PEAK CAPITAL BV

Johannes Vermeerstraat 23
Amsterdam, Netherlands 1016 HH
Website: www.peakcapital.nl

Other Offices
Prinsengracht 270
Amsterdam, Netherlands 1016 HH

Management and Staff
Christiaan Alberdingk Thijm, Partner
Hans De Rooij, Partner
Hein Siemerink, Partner
Heleen Van Oord, Partner
Johan Van Mil, Partner
Menno Kenter, Partner

Type of Firm
Private Equity Firm

Project Preferences

Type of Financing Preferred:
Early Stage
Seed

Size of Investments Considered:
Min Size of Investment Considered (000s): $267
Max Size of Investment Considered (000s): $1,067

Geographical Preferences

International Preferences:
Europe
Netherlands

Industry Preferences

In Communications prefer:
Telecommunications
Media and Entertainment

In Computer Software prefer:
Software

In Internet Specific prefer:
Internet

Additional Information
Year Founded: 2007
Current Activity Level : Actively seeking new investments

PEAK ROCK CAPITAL LLC

13413 Galleria Circle, Suite Q-300
Austin, TX USA 78738
Phone: 5127656520
E-mail: info@PeakRockCapital.com
Website: peakrockcapital.com

Management and Staff
Anthony DiSimone, CEO & Managing Director
Carsten Beck, Principal
Jung Choi, Chief Financial Officer
Peter Leibman, Managing Director
Robert Pistilli, Vice President
Steven Martinez, Managing Director
Tiffany Kosch, Managing Director
William Kuntz, Principal

Type of Firm
Private Equity Firm

Project Preferences

Type of Financing Preferred:
Leveraged Buyout
Mezzanine
Management Buyouts
Special Situation
Recapitalizations

Industry Preferences

In Communications prefer:
Commercial Communications

In Medical/Health prefer:
Medical/Health
Health Services

In Consumer Related prefer:
Consumer

In Industrial/Energy prefer:
Energy
Industrial Products
Materials

In Transportation prefer:
Transportation

In Business Serv. prefer:
Services
Distribution
Media

In Manufact. prefer:
Manufacturing

Additional Information

Name of Most Recent Fund: Peak Rock Capital Fund, L.P.
Most Recent Fund Was Raised: 06/17/2013
Year Founded: 2012
Capital Under Management: $2,000,000,000
Current Activity Level : Actively seeking new investments

PEAKEQUITY PARTNERS

555 East Lancaster Ave, Suite 500
Radnor, PA USA 19087
Phone: 4842530002
Website: www.peakequity.com

Management and Staff

Gregory Case, Founding Partner

Type of Firm

Private Equity Firm

Project Preferences

Type of Financing Preferred:
Leveraged Buyout
Expansion
Recapitalizations

Industry Preferences

In Computer Software prefer:
Software

Additional Information

Year Founded: 2014
Capital Under Management: $137,000,000
Current Activity Level : Actively seeking new investments

PEAKSPAN CAPITAL LLC

1424 Chapin Avenue
Burlingame, CA USA 94010
Phone: 6503532588
Website: peakspancapital.com

Management and Staff

Brian Mulvey, Co-Founder
Matt Melymuka, Co-Founder
Philip Dur, Co-Founder

Type of Firm

Private Equity Firm

Industry Preferences

In Computer Software prefer:
Software

In Consumer Related prefer:
Retail

In Financial Services prefer:
Financial Services

Additional Information

Year Founded: 2014
Capital Under Management: $150,000,000
Current Activity Level : Actively seeking new investments

PEAR VENTURES

320 High Street
Palo Alto, CA USA 94306
Phone: 6506780123
E-mail: info@pejmanmar.com
Website: www.pear.vc

Management and Staff

Ajay Kamat, Partner
Mar Hershenson, Co-Founder
Neda Blocho, Partner
Pejman Nozad, Co-Founder

Type of Firm

Private Equity Firm

Project Preferences

Type of Financing Preferred:
Early Stage
Balanced

Industry Preferences

In Computer Software prefer:
Software
Applications Software

Additional Information

Year Founded: 2014
Capital Under Management: $129,920,000
Current Activity Level : Actively seeking new investments

PEARL STREET CAPITAL GROUP

1401 Pearl Street, Suite 400
Boulder, CO USA 80302
Phone: 3033394800
Fax: 3033394801
E-mail: info@pearlcap.com
Website: www.pearlcap.com

Other Offices

Ten Derne Street
Boston, MA USA 02114

Management and Staff

Brian Koeller, Managing Director
Craig Caukin, Managing Director
Gordon Reinert, Managing Director
Jeffrey Hiller, Chief Financial Officer

Type of Firm

Private Equity Firm

Geographical Preferences

United States Preferences:
Colorado

Additional Information

Year Founded: 2002
Current Activity Level : Actively seeking new investments

PEATE VENTURES LLC

505 Poli Street, Suite 301
Ventura, CA USA 93001
Website: www.peateventures.com

Management and Staff

Dan Peate, Founder

Type of Firm

Private Equity Firm

Project Preferences

Type of Financing Preferred:
Early Stage
Seed

1637

Geographical Preferences

United States Preferences:
West Coast

Additional Information

Name of Most Recent Fund: Buenaventura Fund, L.P.
Most Recent Fund Was Raised: 08/26/2013
Year Founded: 2013
Capital Under Management: $4,780,000
Current Activity Level : Actively seeking new investments

PECHEL INDUSTRIES SAS

162, Rue Du Faubourg
Saint Honore
Paris, France 75008
Phone: 33156597959
Fax: 33156597956
E-mail: contact@pechel.com
Website: www.pechel.com

Management and Staff

Bertrand Hainguerlot, Managing Director
Jean Gore, Managing Director
Philippe Renie, Managing Partner

Type of Firm

Private Equity Firm

Association Membership

French Venture Capital Association (AFIC)

Project Preferences

Type of Financing Preferred:
Leveraged Buyout
Early Stage
Generalist PE
Later Stage
Management Buyouts
Acquisition

Geographical Preferences

International Preferences:
Luxembourg
Europe
Switzerland
Eastern Europe
Belgium
France

Industry Preferences

In Industrial/Energy prefer:
Industrial Products

In Business Serv. prefer:
Services

Additional Information

Year Founded: 1997
Capital Under Management: $174,220,000
Current Activity Level : Actively seeking new investments

PECUNIANO GMBH

Residenzstrasse 18
Munich, Germany 80333
Phone: 49892919580
Fax: 498929195858
E-mail: info@nordwindcapital.com
Website: www.nordwindcapital.com

Management and Staff

Anton Schneider, Managing Director
Hans Albrecht, Founder
Martin Beck, Managing Director
Tom Harder, Managing Director

Type of Firm

Private Equity Firm

Project Preferences

Type of Financing Preferred:
Turnaround
Later Stage
Recapitalizations

Geographical Preferences

International Preferences:
Switzerland
Austria
Germany

Additional Information

Year Founded: 2002
Capital Under Management: $377,000,000
Current Activity Level : Actively seeking new investments

PEEPUL CAPITAL LLC

Saint Louis Business Centre
Cnr Desroches St. Louis Street
Port Louis, Mauritius
Phone: 2302031100
Fax: 2302031150
E-mail: contact@peepulcapital.com
Website: www.peepulcapital.com

Other Offices

62/14, ABM Avenue
Boat Club, R.A. Puram
Chennai, India 600 028
Phone: 91-44-4223-5000
Fax: 91-44-4507-0404

Building No.3, # 18
Software Units Layout, Madhapur
Hydrabad, India
Phone: 91-40-3048-4444
Fax: 91-40-3048-4445

08-14, 10A Mount Sophia
Singapore, Singapore 228463

Management and Staff

P. Sridhar, Principal
Sandeep Reddy, Managing Director
Srini Raju, Managing Director

Type of Firm

Private Equity Firm

Project Preferences

Type of Financing Preferred:
Leveraged Buyout
Early Stage
Expansion
Recapitalizations

Size of Investments Considered:
Min Size of Investment Considered (000s): $15,000
Max Size of Investment Considered (000s): $25,000

Geographical Preferences

International Preferences:
India
Asia

Additional Information

Year Founded: 2000
Capital Under Management: $325,000,000
Current Activity Level : Actively seeking new investments

PEERAGE CAPITAL INC

1325 Lawrence Avenue East, Suite 200
Toronto, Canada M3A 1C6
E-mail: info@peeragecapital.com
Website: www.peeragecapital.com

Management and Staff

Miles Nadal, Founder

Type of Firm

Private Equity Firm

Project Preferences

Type of Financing Preferred:
Acquisition

Additional Information

Year Founded: 2015
Current Activity Level : Actively seeking new investments

PEESH VENTURE CAPITAL

422 Morris Avenue Summit
Summit, NJ USA 07901
Website: peeshvc.com

Other Offices

35 Mirage Point 80 Feet Road
Bangalore, India 560034

91M, Connaught Place
Delhi, India 110001

Type of Firm
Private Equity Firm

Project Preferences

Type of Financing Preferred:
Early Stage
Startup

Geographical Preferences

United States Preferences:

International Preferences:
India

Industry Preferences

In Computer Software prefer:
Software

In Internet Specific prefer:
Internet
Ecommerce

In Consumer Related prefer:
Education Related

Additional Information
Year Founded: 2015
Capital Under Management: $50,000,000
Current Activity Level : Actively seeking new investments

PEF (BEIJING) INVESTMENT CONSULTATION LTD

151,Zhongguancun North Road
507,Resource Building
Bejing, China
Phone: 861062756962
Fax: 861062753856
Website: www.pefchina.com

Type of Firm
Service Provider

Association Membership
Venture Capital Association of Beijing (VCAB)

Project Preferences

Type of Financing Preferred:
Balanced

Geographical Preferences

International Preferences:
China

Industry Preferences

In Semiconductor/Electr prefer:
Electronics

In Biotechnology prefer:
Biotechnology

In Medical/Health prefer:
Pharmaceuticals

In Consumer Related prefer:
Education Related

In Industrial/Energy prefer:
Alternative Energy
Energy Conservation Relat
Advanced Materials

In Business Serv. prefer:
Services

In Agr/Forestr/Fish prefer:
Agriculture related

In Other prefer:
Environment Responsible

Additional Information
Year Founded: 2007
Current Activity Level : Actively seeking new investments

PEGASUS CAPITAL ADVISORS LP

99 River Road
Cos Cob, CT USA 06807
Phone: 12038694400
Fax: 12038696940
Website: www.pcalp.com

Other Offices
505 Park Avenue
21st Floor
New York, NY USA 10022
Phone: 2127102500
Fax: 2123552303

Management and Staff
Alec Machiels, Partner
Andrew Cooper, Partner
Daniel Stencel, Chief Financial Officer
Daniel Gross, Managing Director
Eric Gribetz, Managing Partner
Joel Haney, Vice President
Mitchell Zucker, Vice President

Type of Firm
Private Equity Firm

Project Preferences

Role in Financing:
Prefer role as deal originator

Type of Financing Preferred:
Leveraged Buyout
Other
Management Buyouts
Acquisition

Industry Focus
(% based on actual investment)
Other Products	37.3%
Industrial/Energy	18.3%
Consumer Related	17.5%
Semiconductors/Other Elect.	14.2%
Communications and Media	7.7%
Internet Specific	3.6%
Medical/Health	0.8%
Computer Software and Services	0.7%
Biotechnology	0.0%

Additional Information
Name of Most Recent Fund: Pegasus Partners V, L.P.
Most Recent Fund Was Raised: 08/16/2011
Year Founded: 1995
Capital Under Management: $1,800,000,000
Current Activity Level : Actively seeking new investments
Method of Compensation: Return on invest. most important, but chg. closing fees, service fees, etc.

PEGASUS CAPITAL GROUP INC

3250 Ocean Park Boulevard, Suite 203
Santa Monica, CA USA 90405
Phone: 3103929100
Fax: 3103929101
E-mail: info@pegasuscapgroup.com
Website: www.pegasusmgmt.com

Type of Firm
Private Equity Firm

Project Preferences

Type of Financing Preferred:
Leveraged Buyout
Acquisition

Geographical Preferences

United States Preferences:

Canadian Preferences:
All Canada

Industry Preferences

In Industrial/Energy prefer:
Industrial Products
Advanced Materials
Machinery

In Business Serv. prefer:
Services
Distribution

In Manufact. prefer:
Manufacturing

Additional Information
Year Founded: 2005
Current Activity Level : Actively seeking new investments

PEI FUNDS LLC

505 Park Avenue
Fourth Floor
New York, NY USA 10022
Phone: 2127501228
Fax: 2127502685
E-mail: info@peifunds.com
Website: www.peifunds.com

Management and Staff

Benjamin Wilson, Managing Director
Chuck Stetson, Managing Director
David Parshall, Managing Director
David Parshall, Co-Founder
Gunnar Fremuth, Managing Director
Gunnar Fremuth, Managing Director
Lucien Ruby, Managing Director
Richard Vietor, Venture Partner

Type of Firm

Private Equity Advisor or Fund of Funds

Association Membership

National Venture Capital Association - USA (NVCA)

Project Preferences

Role in Financing:
Prefer role as deal originator but will also invest in deals created by others

Type of Financing Preferred:
Fund of Funds
Fund of Funds of Second

Geographical Preferences

United States Preferences:

Industry Focus

(% based on actual investment)
Biotechnology	37.7%
Computer Hardware	30.4%
Semiconductors/Other Elect.	25.2%
Communications and Media	4.9%
Computer Software and Services	1.7%

Additional Information

Name of Most Recent Fund: Private Equity Investment Fund IV, L.P.
Most Recent Fund Was Raised: 03/21/2005
Year Founded: 1992
Capital Under Management: $110,000,000
Current Activity Level : Actively seeking new investments
Method of Compensation: Return on investment is of primary concern, do not charge fees

PEKAO INVESTMENT BANKING SA

ul. Emilii Plater 53
Warsaw, Poland 00113
Phone: 48225862999
Fax: 48225862852
E-mail: office.poland@caib.unicreditgroup.eu
Website: pekaoib.pl

Management and Staff

Jacek Radziwilski, Managing Director
Tomasz Witczak, Managing Director

Type of Firm

Bank Affiliated

Project Preferences

Type of Financing Preferred:
Early Stage
Later Stage

Size of Investments Considered:
Min Size of Investment Considered (000s): $3,103
Max Size of Investment Considered (000s): $12,414

Geographical Preferences

International Preferences:
Central Europe
Poland
Eastern Europe

Industry Preferences

In Consumer Related prefer:
Retail
Consumer Products

In Industrial/Energy prefer:
Industrial Products

In Manufact. prefer:
Manufacturing

Additional Information

Year Founded: 2003
Current Activity Level : Actively seeking new investments

PELICAN POINT INVESTMENT GROUP LLC

660 Newport Center Drive, Suite 710
Newport Beach, CA USA 92660
Phone: 9497067888
Website: pelicanpointinvestments.com

Management and Staff

Adam Chaudhary, President

Type of Firm

Private Equity Firm

Project Preferences

Type of Financing Preferred:
Leveraged Buyout
Balanced
Later Stage
Acquisition

Industry Preferences

In Communications prefer:
Entertainment

In Biotechnology prefer:
Biotech Related Research

In Medical/Health prefer:
Health Services

In Industrial/Energy prefer:
Energy

In Financial Services prefer:
Financial Services
Real Estate

In Business Serv. prefer:
Media

Additional Information

Year Founded: 2016
Current Activity Level : Actively seeking new investments

PELION VENTURE PARTNERS

2755 East Cottonwood Parkway, Suite 600
Salt Lake City, UT USA 84121
Phone: 8013650262
Fax: 8013650233
E-mail: info@pelionvp.com
Website: www.pelionvp.com

Management and Staff

Benjamin Dahl, Partner
Blake Modersitzki, Managing Director
Carl Ledbetter, Managing Director
Chad Packard, Partner
Chris Cooper, Partner
James Dreyfous, Partner
Jaquie McKay, Chief Financial Officer

Type of Firm

Private Equity Firm

Association Membership

National Venture Capital Association - USA (NVCA)

Project Preferences

Role in Financing:
Will function either as deal originator or investor in deals created by others

Type of Financing Preferred:
Early Stage
Seed
Startup

Geographical Preferences

United States Preferences:
West Coast

Industry Focus

(% based on actual investment)

Computer Software and Services	50.7%
Internet Specific	22.5%
Medical/Health	8.5%
Communications and Media	6.5%
Computer Hardware	6.2%
Biotechnology	5.3%
Semiconductors/Other Elect.	0.2%
Industrial/Energy	0.1%

Additional Information

Name of Most Recent Fund: Pelion Ventures V, L.P.
Most Recent Fund Was Raised: 08/03/2012
Year Founded: 1986
Capital Under Management: $200,000,000
Current Activity Level : Actively seeking new investments
Method of Compensation: Return on investment is of primary concern, do not charge fees

PELORUS VENTURE CAPITAL LTD

30 Harvey Road, Suite 2
St. John's, Canada A1C-2G1
Website: www.pelorusventure.com

Type of Firm
Private Equity Firm

Project Preferences

Type of Financing Preferred:
Seed

Geographical Preferences

Canadian Preferences:
Newfoundland

Additional Information
Year Founded: 2014
Capital Under Management: $10,520,000
Current Activity Level : Actively seeking new investments

PELOTON EQUITY LLC

Ten Glenville Street
Greenwich, CT USA 06831
Website: www.pelotonequity.com

Management and Staff
Carlos Ferrer, Partner
Justin Yang, Principal
Nicole Sansone, Chief Financial Officer
Theodore Lundberg, Partner

Type of Firm
Private Equity Firm

Project Preferences

Type of Financing Preferred:
Leveraged Buyout
Acquisition

Industry Preferences

In Medical/Health prefer:
Medical/Health

Additional Information
Year Founded: 2014
Capital Under Management: $48,090,000
Current Activity Level : Actively seeking new investments

PEMBANGUNAN EKUITI SDN BHD

Level 11, Menara SME Bank
Jalan Sultan Ismail
Kuala Lumpur, Malaysia 50250
Phone: 60-326-973-324
Fax: 60-326-073-343
Website: www.pekuiti.com

Management and Staff
Jasmani Abbas, Chief Executive Officer
Tairuddin Yusoff, Chief Operating Officer

Type of Firm
Private Equity Firm

Association Membership
Malaysian Venture Capital Association

Project Preferences

Type of Financing Preferred:
Balanced

Geographical Preferences

International Preferences:
Asia
Malaysia

Industry Preferences

In Communications prefer:
Communications and Media
Wireless Communications

In Consumer Related prefer:
Food/Beverage
Consumer Services

In Industrial/Energy prefer:
Oil and Gas Exploration
Oil & Gas Drilling,Explor
Industrial Products

In Manufact. prefer:
Manufacturing

Additional Information
Year Founded: 2009
Current Activity Level : Actively seeking new investments

PEMBROKE VCT PLC

Three Cadogan Gate
London, United Kingdom SW1X 0AS
Phone: 442077666900
E-mail: info@pembrokevct.com
Website: www.pembrokevct.com

Type of Firm
Private Equity Firm

Project Preferences

Type of Financing Preferred:
Leveraged Buyout
Early Stage
Balanced
Later Stage
Acquisition

Geographical Preferences

International Preferences:
United Kingdom

Additional Information
Year Founded: 2012
Current Activity Level : Actively seeking new investments

PENCARROW PRIVATE EQUITY LTD

1-3 Willeston Street
Level 14, Pencarrow House
Wellington, New Zealand 6143
Phone: 6444999190
Fax: 6444727687
E-mail: email@pencarrowpe.co.nz

Management and Staff
Leah Anderson, Chief Financial Officer

Type of Firm
Private Equity Firm

Association Membership
New Zealand Venture Capital Association

Project Preferences

Role in Financing:
Prefer role as deal originator

Type of Financing Preferred:
Leveraged Buyout
Expansion
Management Buyouts
Acquisition

Geographical Preferences

International Preferences:
New Zealand

Industry Focus
(% based on actual investment)
Consumer Related	46.8%
Other Products	41.3%
Industrial/Energy	12.0%

Additional Information
Name of Most Recent Fund: Pencarrow IV Investment Fund
Most Recent Fund Was Raised: 12/09/2011
Year Founded: 1993
Capital Under Management: $118,600,000
Current Activity Level : Actively seeking new investments

PENDER WEST CAPITAL PARTNERS, INC.

1111 West Hastings Street, Suite 200
Vancouver, Canada V6E 2J3
Phone: 6046691500
Website: www.penderwest.com

Management and Staff
Bruce Hodge, Managing Director
John Zaplatynsky, Managing Director
Wade Flemons, Managing Director

Type of Firm
Private Equity Firm

Project Preferences
Type of Financing Preferred:
Leveraged Buyout
Management Buyouts
Acquisition
Recapitalizations

Geographical Preferences
United States Preferences:
All U.S.

Canadian Preferences:
All Canada

Additional Information
Year Founded: 2009
Current Activity Level : Actively seeking new investments

PENFUND PARTNERS INC

333 Bay Street, Suite 610
Toronto, Canada M5H 2R2
Phone: 4168650707
Fax: 4163644149
Website: www.penfund.com

Management and Staff
Adam Breslin, Partner
Barry Yontef, Partner
John Bradlow, Partner
Richard Bradlow, Partner

Type of Firm
Private Equity Firm

Association Membership
Canadian Venture Capital Association

Project Preferences
Role in Financing:
Will function either as deal originator or investor in deals created by others

Type of Financing Preferred:
Leveraged Buyout
Mezzanine
Management Buyouts
Acquisition
Recapitalizations

Geographical Preferences
United States Preferences:
North America

Canadian Preferences:
All Canada

Industry Focus
(% based on actual investment)
Consumer Related	47.6%
Medical/Health	28.5%
Other Products	13.3%
Biotechnology	8.6%
Computer Software and Services	1.9%

Additional Information
Name of Most Recent Fund: Penfund Capital Fund IV
Most Recent Fund Was Raised: 03/07/2012
Year Founded: 1979
Capital Under Management: $1,012,084,000
Current Activity Level : Actively seeking new investments
Method of Compensation: Return on investment is of primary concern, do not charge fees

PENINSULA CAPITAL ADVISORS LLP

10 Brook Street
London, United Kingdom

Management and Staff
Carlos Lapique, Partner
Nicola Colavito, Partner
Ramon Soria, Partner

Type of Firm
Private Equity Firm

Project Preferences
Type of Financing Preferred:
Leveraged Buyout
Public Companies
Turnaround
Recapitalizations

Geographical Preferences
International Preferences:
Latin America
Europe

Industry Preferences
In Communications prefer:
Telecommunications

In Medical/Health prefer:
Health Services

In Consumer Related prefer:
Consumer

In Financial Services prefer:
Financial Services

In Business Serv. prefer:
Media

Additional Information
Year Founded: 2015
Current Activity Level : Actively seeking new investments

PENINSULA CAPITAL PARTNERS LLC

500 Woodward Avenue, Suite 2800, One Detroit Center
Detroit, MI USA 48226
Phone: 3132375100
Fax: 3132375111
Website: www.peninsulafunds.com

Management and Staff
Christopher Gessner, Vice President
Hector Bultynck, Partner
Hector Bultynck, Partner
James Illikman, Partner
Karl LaPeer, Partner
Steven Beckett, Partner

Type of Firm
Private Equity Firm

Project Preferences
Role in Financing:
Prefer role in deals created by others

Type of Financing Preferred:
Leveraged Buyout
Expansion
Mezzanine
Management Buyouts
Acquisition
Special Situation
Recapitalizations

Geographical Preferences
Canadian Preferences:
All Canada

Industry Focus

(% based on actual investment)
Other Products	29.1%
Industrial/Energy	25.1%
Consumer Related	17.3%
Internet Specific	16.5%
Semiconductors/Other Elect.	7.4%
Computer Hardware	2.2%
Communications and Media	1.2%
Computer Software and Services	0.9%
Medical/Health	0.3%

Additional Information

Name of Most Recent Fund: Peninsula Fund V, L.P.
Most Recent Fund Was Raised: 12/22/2009
Year Founded: 1995
Capital Under Management: $1,200,000,000
Current Activity Level : Actively seeking new investments
Method of Compensation: Return on invest. most important, but chg. closing fees, service fees, etc.

PENINSULA PACIFIC STRATEGIC PARTNERS LLC

10250 Constellation Blvd, Suite 2230
Los Angeles, CA USA 90067
Phone: 4242810700
E-mail: info@peninsulapacific.com
Website: www.peninsulapacific.com

Management and Staff

Joshua Phillips, Managing Partner
Matthew Homme, Principal
Stephen Alarcon, Vice President

Type of Firm

Private Equity Firm

Project Preferences

Type of Financing Preferred:
Leveraged Buyout
Turnaround
Acquisition
Special Situation
Recapitalizations

Industry Preferences

In Medical/Health prefer:
Medical/Health

In Consumer Related prefer:
Food/Beverage
Consumer Products

In Industrial/Energy prefer:
Energy
Industrial Products
Materials

In Transportation prefer:
Transportation
Aerospace

In Business Serv. prefer:
Services
Distribution

In Manufact. prefer:
Manufacturing

In Agr/Forestr/Fish prefer:
Mining and Minerals

Additional Information

Year Founded: 2014
Current Activity Level : Actively seeking new investments

PENINSULA VENTURES

201 Redwood Shores Parkway, Suite 100
Redwood City, CA USA 94065
Phone: 6505171900
Fax: 6505171999
E-mail: info@peninsulaventures.com
Website: www.peninsulaventures.com

Other Offices

2670 SW Corona Avenue
Portland, OR USA 97201
Phone: 6505171900

Management and Staff

Bob Patterson, Managing Director
Brian Smith, Managing Director
Gregory Ennis, Managing Director
Gregory Robinson, Partner
Gregory Robinson, Managing Director

Type of Firm

Private Equity Firm

Association Membership

Western Association of Venture Capitalists (WAVC)

Project Preferences

Role in Financing:
Will function either as deal originator or investor in deals created by others

Type of Financing Preferred:
Early Stage

Geographical Preferences

United States Preferences:
West Coast

Industry Preferences

In Computer Software prefer:
Software

Additional Information

Name of Most Recent Fund: Peninsula-KCG, L.P.
Most Recent Fund Was Raised: 02/05/2013
Year Founded: 2001
Capital Under Management: $100,000,000
Current Activity Level : Actively seeking new investments

PENN SQUARE REAL ESTATE GROUP LLC

150 North Radnor-Chester Road, Suite A110
Radnor, PA USA 19087
Phone: 6109432321
E-mail: info@pennsquare.com
Website: www.pennsquare.com

Management and Staff

Jon Albro, Managing Partner

Type of Firm

Private Equity Advisor or Fund of Funds

Project Preferences

Type of Financing Preferred:
Fund of Funds

Geographical Preferences

United States Preferences:
North America

International Preferences:
Asia Pacific
Latin America
India
Central Europe
Europe
Western Europe
China
Mexico
Eastern Europe
Middle East
Brazil
Asia
Germany
Japan
Africa

Industry Preferences

In Financial Services prefer:
Insurance
Real Estate

Additional Information

Name of Most Recent Fund: TownSquare Real Estate Fund I, L.P.
Most Recent Fund Was Raised: 08/28/2012
Year Founded: 2006
Capital Under Management: $157,030,000
Current Activity Level : Actively seeking new investments

PENN VENTURE PARTNERS, L.P.

132 State Street, Suite 200
Harrisburg, PA USA 17101
Phone: 7172362300
Fax: 7172362350
Website: www.pennventures.com

Management and Staff
Dean Kline, Managing Director
Robert Graham, Managing Director
Thomas Penn, Managing Director

Type of Firm
Private Equity Firm

Association Membership
Community Development Venture Capital Alliance

Project Preferences

Role in Financing:
Will function either as deal originator or investor in deals created by others

Type of Financing Preferred:
Leveraged Buyout
Expansion
Later Stage
Acquisition

Size of Investments Considered:
Min Size of Investment Considered (000s): $500
Max Size of Investment Considered (000s): $2,000

Geographical Preferences

United States Preferences:
Pennsylvania

Additional Information
Year Founded: 2003
Capital Under Management: $25,000,000
Current Activity Level : Actively seeking new investments
Method of Compensation: Return on investment is of primary concern, do not charge fees

PENNANTPARK INVESTMENT CORPORATION

590 Madison Avenue, 15 Floor
New York, NY USA 10022
Phone: 2129051000
Fax: 2129051075
Website: www.pennantpark.com

Type of Firm
SBIC

Project Preferences

Type of Financing Preferred:
Mezzanine

Size of Investments Considered:
Min Size of Investment Considered (000s): $10,000
Max Size of Investment Considered (000s): $50,000

Geographical Preferences

United States Preferences:

Additional Information
Year Founded: 2010
Current Activity Level : Actively seeking new investments

PENTA CAPITAL LLP

150 Saint Vincent Street
Glasgow, United Kingdom G2 5NE
Phone: 441415727300
Fax: 441415727310
E-mail: info@pentacapital.com
Website: www.pentacapital.com

Other Offices
90 Long Acre
Seventh Floor
London, United Kingdom WC2E 4RA
Phone: 442033260350
Fax: 442033260360

Management and Staff
David Calder, Founder
Mark Phillips, Partner
Paul Cassidy, Partner
Steven Scott, Partner
Torquil MacNaughton, Partner

Type of Firm
Private Equity Firm

Association Membership
British Venture Capital Association (BVCA)

Project Preferences

Type of Financing Preferred:
Leveraged Buyout
Management Buyouts
Acquisition

Geographical Preferences

International Preferences:
United Kingdom

Industry Preferences

In Communications prefer:
Telecommunications

In Consumer Related prefer:
Consumer
Entertainment and Leisure

In Financial Services prefer:
Financial Services

In Business Serv. prefer:
Services

Additional Information
Name of Most Recent Fund: Penta Fund 1
Most Recent Fund Was Raised: 05/04/2000
Year Founded: 1999
Capital Under Management: $324,100,000
Current Activity Level : Actively seeking new investments

PENTA INVESTMENTS LTD

Agias Fylaxeos & Polygnostou
212 C&I Center
Limassol, Cyprus 3082
Phone: 35725733104
Fax: 35725733135
E-mail: limassol@pentainvestments.com
Website: www.pentainvestments.com

Other Offices
Krizkova 9
Bratislava, Slovakia 81104
Phone: 421-257-788-111
Fax: 421-257-788-055

Na Prikope 15
Praha 1, Czech Republic 110 00
Phone: 420-210-083-111
Fax: 420-210-083-160

Strawinskylaan 1223, World Trade Center
Tower A/ Level 12
Amsterdam, Netherlands 1077
Phone: 31-2-0333-1166
Fax: 31-2-0333-1160

Nowogrodzka 21
Warsaw, Poland 00-511
Phone: 48-22-502-3233
Fax: 48-22-502-3223

M. Sukharevskaya pl. 12
Business Center Sadovaya Gallery
Moscow, Russia 125047
Phone: 7-495-937-8573
Fax: 7-495-937-8571

Management and Staff
Eduard Matak, Managing Partner
Iain Child, Partner
Jaroslav Hascak, Managing Partner
Jozef Oravkin, Managing Partner
Marek Dospiva, Partner
Martin Kusik, Partner

Type of Firm
Private Equity Firm

Project Preferences

Type of Financing Preferred:
Leveraged Buyout
Expansion
Balanced
Later Stage
Acquisition
Recapitalizations

Geographical Preferences

International Preferences:
Hungary
Slovak Repub.
Europe
Czech Republic
Poland

Industry Preferences

In Communications prefer:
Telecommunications

In Medical/Health prefer:
Medical/Health

In Consumer Related prefer:
Retail

In Industrial/Energy prefer:
Industrial Products

In Financial Services prefer:
Financial Services

In Agr/Forestr/Fish prefer:
Mining and Minerals

In Utilities prefer:
Utilities

Additional Information
Year Founded: 1994
Capital Under Management: $607,500,000
Current Activity Level : Actively seeking new investments

PENTA MEZZANINE FUND

20 North Orange Avenue, Suite 1550
Orlando, FL USA 32801
Phone: 4076485097
Fax: 4076419286
Website: www.pentamezz.com

Type of Firm
Private Equity Firm

Association Membership
Natl Assoc of Small Bus. Inv. Co (NASBIC)

Project Preferences

Type of Financing Preferred:
Expansion
Mezzanine
Management Buyouts
Acquisition
Recapitalizations

Geographical Preferences

United States Preferences:

Additional Information
Name of Most Recent Fund: Penta Mezzanine Fund I, L.P.
Most Recent Fund Was Raised: 05/17/2012
Year Founded: 2012

Capital Under Management: $27,400,000
Current Activity Level : Actively seeking new investments

PENTAHOLD NV

72, Xavier De Cocklaan
Deurle, Belgium 9831
Phone: 3293351880
Website: www.pentahold.eu

Type of Firm
Private Equity Firm

Project Preferences

Type of Financing Preferred:
Leveraged Buyout
Early Stage
Expansion
Later Stage
Management Buyouts
Acquisition
Recapitalizations

Size of Investments Considered:
Min Size of Investment Considered (000s): $2,802
Max Size of Investment Considered (000s): $22,419

Additional Information
Year Founded: 1999
Current Activity Level : Actively seeking new investments

PENTALABBS SAS

1, Rue des Hauts
La Chapelle Saint-Mesmin, France 45380
Phone: 3323825303
Website: www.pentalabbs-incubateur.fr

Type of Firm
Incubator/Development Program

Project Preferences

Type of Financing Preferred:
Early Stage
Seed

Geographical Preferences

International Preferences:
Europe
France

Industry Preferences

In Computer Software prefer:
Software

In Internet Specific prefer:
Internet

In Consumer Related prefer:
Consumer Services

In Financial Services prefer:
Financial Services

In Business Serv. prefer:
Media

Additional Information
Year Founded: 2015
Current Activity Level : Actively seeking new investments

PENTECH VENTURES LLP

39 Melville Street
Edinburgh, United Kingdom EH3 7JF
Phone: 441312408280
E-mail: info@pentechvc.com
Website: www.pentechvc.com

Other Offices
One Alfred Place
London, United Kingdom WC1E 7EB
Phone: 44-203-128-7473

Management and Staff
Craig Anderson, Partner
Derek Gray, Partner
Eddie Anderson, Partner
Ian Ritchie, Partner
Karen Slatford, Partner
Marc Moens, Partner
Mike Ramsay, Partner
Nick Felisiak, Partner
Robert Thomson, Partner
Sandy McKinnon, Partner

Type of Firm
Private Equity Firm

Association Membership
British Venture Capital Association (BVCA)

Project Preferences

Type of Financing Preferred:
Early Stage
Later Stage

Geographical Preferences

International Preferences:
Ireland
United Kingdom

Industry Preferences

In Communications prefer:
Communications and Media
Telecommunications
Wireless Communications

In Computer Software prefer:
Software
Systems Software
Applications Software

In Internet Specific prefer:
Internet

In Business Serv. prefer:
Media

Additional Information
Name of Most Recent Fund: Pentech Fund I
Most Recent Fund Was Raised: 11/06/2001
Year Founded: 2001
Capital Under Management: $154,260,000
Current Activity Level : Actively seeking new investments

PEOPLE FUND LLC

26027 Huntington Lane, Suite A
Valencia, CA USA 91355
Website: www.thepeoplefund.net

Management and Staff
Chris McCarty, Partner
John Maly, Managing Partner

Type of Firm
Private Equity Firm

Project Preferences

Type of Financing Preferred:
Balanced

Industry Preferences

In Biotechnology prefer:
Biotechnology

In Medical/Health prefer:
Health Services

In Consumer Related prefer:
Retail
Food/Beverage
Education Related

In Industrial/Energy prefer:
Energy
Industrial Products

In Manufact. prefer:
Manufacturing

Additional Information
Year Founded: 2008
Current Activity Level : Actively seeking new investments

PEPPERMINT VEN-TUREPARTNERS GMBH

Kurfuerstendamm 21
Neues Kranzler Eck
Berlin, Germany 10719
Phone: 4930590064412
Fax: 4930590064401
E-mail: info@peppermint-vp.com
Website: www.peppermint-vp.com

Management and Staff
Ingeborg Neumann, Founder
Joachim Rautter, Founder
Klaus Stoeckemann, Founder
Magnus Holm, Venture Partner

Type of Firm
Private Equity Firm

Association Membership
German Venture Capital Association (BVK)

Project Preferences

Type of Financing Preferred:
Early Stage
Turnaround
Later Stage
Seed
Startup

Geographical Preferences

International Preferences:
Switzerland
Austria
Germany

Industry Preferences

In Computer Software prefer:
Software

In Internet Specific prefer:
Internet

In Semiconductor/Electr prefer:
Electronics
Micro-Processing

In Biotechnology prefer:
Biotechnology

In Medical/Health prefer:
Medical/Health
Medical Diagnostics
Diagnostic Services
Pharmaceuticals

In Industrial/Energy prefer:
Materials

Additional Information
Name of Most Recent Fund: Charite Biomedical Fund
Most Recent Fund Was Raised: 04/26/2011
Year Founded: 1996
Capital Under Management: $22,300,000
Current Activity Level : Actively seeking new investments

PEPPERTREE CAPITAL MANAGEMENT INC

86 West Street
Chagrin Falls, OH USA 44022
Phone: 4405280333
Fax: 4405280334
Website: www.peppertreecapital.com

Other Offices
3550 Lander Road, Suite 300
Mayfield Heights, OH USA 44124
Phone: 2165144949
Fax: 2165144959

Management and Staff
Cynthia Debevec, Chief Financial Officer
F. Howard Mandel, President
Jeffrey Howard, Co-Founder
Jeffrey Milius, Co-Founder
Kevin McGinty, Co-Founder
Ryan Lepene, Managing Director

Type of Firm
Private Equity Firm

Project Preferences

Role in Financing:
Prefer role in deals created by others

Type of Financing Preferred:
Fund of Funds
Leveraged Buyout
Early Stage
Expansion
Generalist PE
Later Stage
Seed
Management Buyouts
Recapitalizations

Geographical Preferences

United States Preferences:

Industry Preferences

In Communications prefer:
Communications and Media
Telecommunications
Wireless Communications

In Business Serv. prefer:
Services
Media

Additional Information
Year Founded: 2000
Capital Under Management: $183,000,000
Current Activity Level : Actively seeking new investments
Method of Compensation: Return on investment is of primary concern, do not charge fees

PEPPERWOOD PARTNERS LLC

5420 LBJ Freeway
Two Lincoln Center, Suite 535
Dallas, TX USA 75240
Phone: 9724998000
Fax: 9724991114
E-mail: info@PepperwoodPartners.com
Website: www.pepperwoodpartners.com

Management and Staff

Eugene Terekhov, Partner
Michael O Donnell, Managing Partner
Mike Willingham, Partner
Patrick Seaman, Partner
R. Dale Appleby, Partner
Rick Spitz, Partner

Type of Firm
Bank Affiliated

Project Preferences

Type of Financing Preferred:
Leveraged Buyout
Mezzanine
Turnaround
Acquisition

Industry Preferences

In Internet Specific prefer:
Internet

In Consumer Related prefer:
Retail
Consumer Products

In Industrial/Energy prefer:
Alternative Energy

Additional Information
Year Founded: 2012
Current Activity Level : Actively seeking new investments

PERA CAPITAL PARTNERS ADVISORY LTD

Insirah Cad. Cemre Sok. No : 1
Istanbul, Turkey 34342
Phone: 902122595222
Fax: 902122595228
Website: peracap.com

Management and Staff

Kerim Yalman, Co-Founder
Louis Negre, Co-Founder
Robert Romain, Co-Founder

Type of Firm
Private Equity Firm

Project Preferences

Type of Financing Preferred:
Leveraged Buyout
Generalist PE
Management Buyouts
Acquisition

Geographical Preferences

International Preferences:
Turkey
Europe

Additional Information
Year Founded: 2011
Current Activity Level : Actively seeking new investments

PERCEPTIVE ADVISORS LLC

51 Astor Place
Tenth Floor
New York, NY USA 10003
Phone: 6462055340
Website: www.perceptivelife.com

Management and Staff
Joseph Edelman, Chief Executive Officer

Type of Firm
Private Equity Firm

Project Preferences

Type of Financing Preferred:
Early Stage
Balanced

Industry Preferences

In Medical/Health prefer:
Medical/Health
Medical Products

Additional Information
Year Founded: 2000
Current Activity Level : Actively seeking new investments

PERCEVA SAS

31, avenue de l'Opera
Paris, France 75001
Phone: 33142971990
Fax: 33142971991
E-mail: perceva@percevacapital.com
Website: www.perceva.fr

Management and Staff
Christophe Ambrosi, Partner
Franck Kelif, Partner
Jean-Louis Grevet, Managing Partner
Veronique Cayrol Darnaudet, Chief Financial Officer
Xavier Lepine, Partner

Type of Firm
Private Equity Firm

Association Membership
French Venture Capital Association (AFIC)

Project Preferences

Type of Financing Preferred:
Leveraged Buyout
Generalist PE
Public Companies
Turnaround
Later Stage
Management Buyouts
Acquisition
Recapitalizations

Geographical Preferences

International Preferences:
Europe
France

Additional Information
Year Founded: 2007
Current Activity Level : Actively seeking new investments

PERCIPIENT CAPITAL

55 Bryanston Street
8th Flr, Marble Arch Tower
London, United Kingdom W1H 7AA
Website: www.percipientcapital.com

Type of Firm
Private Equity Firm

Project Preferences

Type of Financing Preferred:
Later Stage

Additional Information
Year Founded: 2010
Current Activity Level : Actively seeking new investments

PEREG VENTURES LLC

295 Madison Avenue
22nd Floor
New York, NY USA 10017
Phone: 19177273734
E-mail: info@peregventures.com
Website: www.peregventures.com

Management and Staff
Claudia Iannazzo, Chief Executive Officer

Type of Firm
Private Equity Firm

Project Preferences

Type of Financing Preferred:
Early Stage
Balanced
Later Stage
Startup

Geographical Preferences

United States Preferences:

International Preferences:
Israel

Industry Preferences

In Consumer Related prefer:
Consumer

In Business Serv. prefer:
Media

Additional Information

Name of Most Recent Fund: Pereg Venture Fund I, L.P.
Most Recent Fund Was Raised: 12/20/2012
Year Founded: 2012
Capital Under Management: $25,055,000
Current Activity Level : Actively seeking new investments

PERELLA WEINBERG PARTNERS LP

767 Fifth Avenue
New York, NY USA 10153
Phone: 2122873200
Fax: 2122873201
Website: www.pwpartners.com

Other Offices

401 Congress Avenue, Suite 3000
Austin, TX USA 78701
Phone: 5122877100
Fax: 5122877101

20 Grafton Street
London, United Kingdom W1S 4DZ
Phone: 442072682800
Fax: 442072682900

Mohammed Bin Khalifa Street (15th St.)
Level 4 Building B Al Mamoura
Abu Dhabi, Utd. Arab Em.
Phone: 97126594080
Fax: 97126594083

No. 6 Wudinghou Street
1106, Beijing Excel Center
Beijing, China 100140
Phone: 861057985388
Fax: 861057985366

One California Street, Suite 2250
San Francisco, CA USA 94111
Phone: 4156714532
Fax: 4156714503

7979 East Tufts Avenue, Suite 700
Denver, CO USA 80237
Phone: 3038137913
Fax: 3034845790

Management and Staff

Aaron Hood, Chief Financial Officer
Alex Tracy, Managing Director
Amr Nosseir, Partner
Andrew Dym, Partner
Andrew Bednar, Partner
Arnaud Dassy, Partner
Bernard Gault, Partner
Cem Koray, Partner
Charles Ward, Partner
Chip Krotee, Partner
Chip Baird, Partner
Christopher O Connor, Partner
Christopher Bittman, Partner
Claus Becker, Partner
Cory Hill, Managing Director
Daniel Arbess, Partner
David Landman, Partner
David Ferguson, Partner
David Azema, Partner
David Schiff, Partner
Derron Slonecker, Partner
Emile Westergaard, Partner
Gary Barancik, Partner
Graham Davidson, Partner
Ihsan Essaid, Partner
Jameel Akhrass, Partner
Jeffrey Silverman, Partner
John Hale, Partner
John Cesarz, Managing Director
John Varughese, Partner
Joseph Lovell, Managing Partner
Joseph Perella, Partner
Joshua Scherer, Partner
Kent Muckel, Partner
Klaus Wulfing, Partner
Leon Bressler, Partner
Mal Durkee, Partner
Marie-Helene McAndrew, Managing Director
Mark McGreenery, Partner
Mauro Rossi, Managing Director
Michael Kramer, Partner
Michael Dickman, Partner
Nabil Lahham, Partner
Paulo Pereira, Partner
Peter Weinberg, Partner
Philip Yates, Partner
Riccardo Benedetti, Partner
Richard Sherlund, Partner
Richard Shinder, Partner
Robert Maguire, Partner
Rod Parsley, Partner
Scott Bruckner, Partner
Stefan Jentzsch, Partner
Steven Asciutto, Partner

Susan Soh, Partner
Tarek Abdel-Meguid, Partner
Titus Leung, Partner
Trey Thompson, Partner
Victor Consoli, Partner
William Johnson, Partner
William Kourakos, Partner
Woody Young, Partner

Type of Firm

Investment Management Firm

Project Preferences

Type of Financing Preferred:
Leveraged Buyout
Value-Add
Opportunistic
Later Stage
Management Buyouts
Acquisition

Geographical Preferences

United States Preferences:
All U.S.

International Preferences:
United Kingdom
Europe

Industry Preferences

In Consumer Related prefer:
Consumer
Consumer Services

In Industrial/Energy prefer:
Industrial Products

In Financial Services prefer:
Real Estate

In Business Serv. prefer:
Services

Additional Information

Year Founded: 2006
Capital Under Management: $2,128,008,000
Current Activity Level : Actively seeking new investments

PERFECTIS PRIVATE EQUITY SA

41-43 rue Saint Dominique
Paris, France 75007
Phone: 33153059444
Fax: 33153059445
Website: www.perfectis.eu

Management and Staff

Gabriel Fossorier, Co-Founder
Jean-Marie Lavirotte, Co-Founder

Type of Firm

Insurance Firm Affiliate

Association Membership
French Venture Capital Association (AFIC)

Project Preferences

Type of Financing Preferred:
Leveraged Buyout
Later Stage
Management Buyouts
Acquisition

Size of Investments Considered:
Min Size of Investment Considered (000s): $2,678
Max Size of Investment Considered (000s): $24,106

Geographical Preferences

International Preferences:
Europe
France

Industry Focus
(% based on actual investment)
Industrial/Energy   40.7%
Other Products   38.5%
Consumer Related   20.7%

Additional Information
Year Founded: 2000
Capital Under Management: $95,800,000
Current Activity Level : Actively seeking new investments

PERFORMA INVESTIMENTOS LTDA

Avenida Paulista 2001
8 Andar cj 809
Sao Paolo, Brazil
Phone: 551132630577
Website: www.performainvestimentos.com.br

Management and Staff
Eduardo Grytz, Partner
Felipe Teixeira Favaro, Partner
Humberto Matsuda, Founder

Type of Firm
Private Equity Firm

Association Membership
Brazilian Venture Capital Association (ABCR)

Project Preferences

Type of Financing Preferred:
Early Stage
Seed

Geographical Preferences

International Preferences:
Latin America
Brazil

Industry Preferences

In Biotechnology prefer:
Biotechnology

In Industrial/Energy prefer:
Oil and Gas Exploration
Oil & Gas Drilling,Explor
Alternative Energy
Environmental Related

In Other prefer:
Environment Responsible

Additional Information
Year Founded: 2005
Capital Under Management: $8,531,000
Current Activity Level : Actively seeking new investments

PERFORMANCE EQUITY MANAGEMENT LLC

Two Pickwick Plaza, Suite 310
Greenwich, CT USA 06830
Phone: 2037422400
E-mail: info@peqm.com
Website: www.peqm.com

Management and Staff
Alex Rogers, Vice President
Charles Froland, Chief Executive Officer
Frank Brenninkmeyer, Managing Director
James Tybur, Principal
Jeff Reals, Managing Director
Jeffrey Chang, Principal
Jeffrey Barman, Managing Director
John Clark, Managing Director
Jon deKlerk, Chief Operating Officer
Marcia Haydel, Managing Director
S. Lawrence Rusoff, Managing Director
Scott Koeber, Chief Financial Officer

Type of Firm
Private Equity Advisor or Fund of Funds

Project Preferences

Type of Financing Preferred:
Fund of Funds
Expansion

Geographical Preferences

United States Preferences:

International Preferences:
Asia Pacific
Europe

Additional Information
Name of Most Recent Fund: Performance Venture Capital III, L.P.
Most Recent Fund Was Raised: 03/11/2014
Year Founded: 2005
Capital Under Management: $11,000,000,000
Current Activity Level : Actively seeking new investments

PERION KOCKAZATI TOKEALAP KEZELO ZRT

Honved utca 20
Budapest, Hungary 1055
Website: www.perion.hu

Type of Firm
Private Equity Firm

Project Preferences

Type of Financing Preferred:
Early Stage
Balanced

Geographical Preferences

International Preferences:
Hungary
Europe

Industry Preferences

In Medical/Health prefer:
Health Services

Additional Information
Year Founded: 2009
Current Activity Level : Actively seeking new investments

PERISCOPE EQUITY LLC

One North Wacker Drive, Suite 4050
Chicago, IL USA 60606
Phone: 3122816205
Website: periscopeequity.com

Management and Staff
John Findlay, Vice President
S. Brian Mukherjee, Partner
Steve Jarmel, Principal

Type of Firm
Private Equity Firm

Project Preferences

Type of Financing Preferred:
Leveraged Buyout
Acquisition

Additional Information
Year Founded: 2014
Current Activity Level : Actively seeking new investments

PERLE VENTURES PTY LTD

52 Martin Place
Level 24
Sydney, Australia 2000
Website: perleventures.com

Management and Staff
Michael An, Co-Founder
Shayne Smyth, Co-Founder

Type of Firm
Private Equity Firm

Project Preferences

Type of Financing Preferred:
Early Stage
Expansion
Later Stage
Seed
Startup

Additional Information
Year Founded: 1969
Current Activity Level : Actively seeking new investments

PERMIRA ADVISERS LLP

80, Pall Mall
London, United Kingdom SW1Y 5ES
Phone: 442076321000
Fax: 442079303185
E-mail: London@permira.com
Website: www.permira.com

Other Offices

PO Box 503, Trafalgar Court
Les Banques, St. Peter Port
Guernsey, United Kingdom GY1 6DJ
Phone: 44-1481-743-200
Fax: 44-1481-743-201

320 Park Avenue
33rd Floor
New York, NY USA
Phone: 1-212-386-7480
Fax: 1-212-386-7481

Plaza del Marques de Salamanca, 10
Primero Izquierda
Madrid, Spain 28006
Phone: 34-91-418-2499
Fax: 34-91-426-1193

64 Willow Place, Suite 101
MENLO PARK, CA USA 94025
Phone: 650-681-4701
Fax: 650-853-0180

8 Connaught Place, Central Hong Kong
Exchange Square One
Central Hong Kong, Hong Kong
Phone: 852-3972-0800
Fax: 852-2111-1148

Birger Jarlsgatan 12
Stockholm, Sweden 114 34
Phone: 46-8-5031-2200
Fax: 46-8-5031-2299

Akasaka Intercity Building 3F
1-11-44 Akasaka, Minato-ku
Tokyo, Japan 107-0052
Phone: 81-3-6230-2051
Fax: 81-3-6230-2052

6, rue Halevy
2nd floor
Paris, France 75001
Phone: 33-1-4286-6378
Fax: 44-20-7497-2174

80 Pall Mall
London, United Kingdom SW1Y 5ES
Phone: 44-20-7632-1000
Fax: 44-20-7930-3185

282, route de Longwy
Luxembourg, Luxembourg L-1940
Phone: 352-26-86-811
Fax: 352-26-86-8181

Management and Staff
Alexandre Margoline, Principal
Andrew Young, Principal
Benoit Vauchy, Partner
Brian Ruder, Partner
Carlos Mallo, Partner
Cheryl Potter, Partner
Chris North, Principal
Chris Pell, Principal
Chris Davison, Partner
Christian Paul, Principal
Dipan Patel, Partner
Elisabetta Frontini, Principal
Fabrizio Carretti, Partner
Federico Saruggia, Partner
Francesco Pascalizi, Principal
Francesco de Mojana, Partner
Francesco De Mojana, Partner
Henry Minello, Principal
James Fraser, Partner
John Coyle, Partner
Jorg Rockenhauser, Partner
Michail Zekkos, Partner
Mubasher Sheikh, Partner
Nic Volpi, Partner
Nicola Volpi, Partner
Ola Nordquist, Partner
Paul Armstrong, Principal
Pedro Lopez, Principal
Peter Gibbs, Principal
Phil Guinand, Partner
Philip Muelder, Partner
Richard Carey, Partner
Richard Sanders, Partner
Roberto Biondi, Partner
Robin Bell-Jones, Partner
Sebastian Hoffmann, Principal
Silvia Oteri, Partner
Stefan Dziarski, Principal
Tara Alhadeff, Principal
Torsten Vogt, Partner
Ulrich Gasse, Partner

Type of Firm
Private Equity Firm

Association Membership
Italian Venture Capital Association (AIFI)
British Venture Capital Association (BVCA)
Swedish Venture Capital Association (SVCA)
European Private Equity and Venture Capital Assoc.
Dutch Venture Capital Associaton (NVP)
Spanish Venture Capital Association (ASCRI)

Project Preferences

Type of Financing Preferred:
Leveraged Buyout
Turnaround
Management Buyouts
Acquisition

Industry Focus
(% based on actual investment)

Other Products	25.0%
Industrial/Energy	21.1%
Consumer Related	17.9%
Computer Software and Services	17.4%
Medical/Health	12.5%
Communications and Media	4.8%
Internet Specific	0.8%
Semiconductors/Other Elect.	0.3%
Biotechnology	0.2%

Additional Information
Year Founded: 1985
Capital Under Management: $33,860,000,000
Current Activity Level : Actively seeking new investments

PERMIRA DEBT MANAGERS LTD

80 Pall Mall
London, United Kingdom SW1Y 5ES
Phone: 442076321000
Fax: 442079303185
Website: www.permiradebtmanagers.com

Other Offices

3000 Sand Hill Road
Building 1 Suite 260
Menlo Park, CA USA 94025
Phone: 16506814701
Fax: 16508530180

320 Park Avenue
33rd Floor
New York, NY USA 10022
Phone: 12123867480
Fax: 12123867481

Management and Staff
Robin Bell-Jones, Partner

Type of Firm
Investment Management Firm

Project Preferences

Type of Financing Preferred:
Mezzanine

Geographical Preferences

International Preferences:
Europe

Industry Preferences

In Medical/Health prefer:
Health Services

In Consumer Related prefer:
Consumer

In Industrial/Energy prefer:
Industrial Products

In Financial Services prefer:
Financial Services

Additional Information

Year Founded: 1985
Capital Under Management: $3,619,185,000
Current Activity Level : Actively seeking new investments

PERPETUAL CAPITAL MANAGEMENT LTD

1358 Eruera Street
Rotorua, New Zealand 3010
Phone: 6473476239
Fax: 6473476305
Website: www.perpetualcapital.co.nz

Type of Firm
Private Equity Firm

Association Membership
New Zealand Venture Capital Association

Project Preferences

Type of Financing Preferred:
Leveraged Buyout
Expansion
Generalist PE
Balanced
Later Stage
Acquisition

Size of Investments Considered:
Min Size of Investment Considered (000s): $939
Max Size of Investment Considered (000s): $3,756

Geographical Preferences

International Preferences:
New Zealand

Additional Information

Year Founded: 2002
Capital Under Management: $119,000,000
Current Activity Level : Actively seeking new investments

PERPETUAL CAPITAL PARTNERS LLC

1000 Wilson Boulevard, Suite 2700
Arlington, VA USA 22209
Phone: 7036478700
E-mail: info@perpetualcap.com
Website: www.perpetualcap.com

Type of Firm
Private Equity Firm

Project Preferences

Type of Financing Preferred:
Leveraged Buyout
Acquisition

Geographical Preferences

United States Preferences:

Additional Information

Year Founded: 1969
Current Activity Level : Actively seeking new investments

PERSEUS LLC

2099 Pennsylvania Avenue, NW
Ninth Floor
Washington, DC USA 20006
Phone: 2024520101
Fax: 2024290588
E-mail: info@perseusllc.com
Website: www.perseusllc.com

Other Offices

Schumannstrasse Four
Munich, Germany D-81679
Phone: 49-1890-8810
Fax: 49-1890-8850

Management and Staff

Anjali Jolly, Managing Director
Joanne Shea, Vice President
John Fox, Senior Managing Director
Kristin Milone, Vice President
Michael Miller, Managing Director
Susan Inouye Tarter, Chief Financial Officer

Type of Firm
Private Equity Firm

Project Preferences

Role in Financing:
Prefer role as deal originator

Type of Financing Preferred:
Leveraged Buyout
Expansion
Generalist PE
Balanced
Turnaround
Acquisition
Recapitalizations

Geographical Preferences

United States Preferences:

Canadian Preferences:
All Canada

International Preferences:
Western Europe

Industry Focus

(% based on actual investment)
Biotechnology	21.3%
Consumer Related	21.1%
Industrial/Energy	12.5%
Other Products	12.3%
Semiconductors/Other Elect.	10.1%
Internet Specific	9.2%
Communications and Media	6.5%
Computer Software and Services	5.0%
Computer Hardware	1.1%
Medical/Health	0.9%

Additional Information

Name of Most Recent Fund: Perseus Partners VII, L.P.
Most Recent Fund Was Raised: 04/26/2006
Year Founded: 1995
Capital Under Management: $1,600,000,000
Current Activity Level : Actively seeking new investments
Method of Compensation: Return on invest. most important, but chg. closing fees, service fees, etc.

PERSHING SQUARE CAPITAL MANAGEMENT LP

888 Seventh Avenue
42nd Floor
New York, NY USA 10019
Phone: 2128133700
Fax: 2122861133

Management and Staff

Nicholas Botta, Chief Financial Officer
Paul Hilal, Partner
Roy Katzovicz, Partner
Timothy Barefield, Chief Operating Officer
William Ackman, Founder

Type of Firm
Private Equity Firm

Project Preferences

Type of Financing Preferred:
Leveraged Buyout

Additional Information
Year Founded: 2004
Current Activity Level : Actively seeking new investments

PERSISTENCE CAPITAL PARTNERS LP

500 Sherbrooke Street West, Suite 500
Montreal, Canada H3A 3C6
Phone: 5144992778
Fax: 5148459178
E-mail: info@persistencecapital.com
Website: www.persistencecapital.com

Management and Staff
John Trang, Principal
Lloyd Segal, Partner
Philippe Couillard, Partner
Sheldon Elman, Managing Partner
Stuart Elman, Managing Partner

Type of Firm
Private Equity Firm

Association Membership
Canadian Venture Capital Association

Project Preferences

Type of Financing Preferred:
Leveraged Buyout
Later Stage
Management Buyouts
Distressed Debt
Recapitalizations

Size of Investments Considered:
Min Size of Investment Considered (000s): $4,833
Max Size of Investment Considered (000s): $19,331

Geographical Preferences

Canadian Preferences:
All Canada

Industry Preferences

In Medical/Health prefer:
Medical/Health
Hospitals/Clinics/Primary
Hospital/Other Instit.

Additional Information
Name of Most Recent Fund: Persistence Capital Partners II, L.P.
Most Recent Fund Was Raised: 05/22/2013
Year Founded: 2008
Capital Under Management: $86,789,000
Current Activity Level : Actively seeking new investments

PERSISTENCE PARTNERS, L.P.

610 Anacapa Street
Santa Barbara, CA USA 93101
Phone: 8059661000
Fax: 8054132019
E-mail: info@persistencepartners.com
Website: www.persistencepartners.com

Management and Staff
David Gross, Managing Partner
Jason Spievak, Venture Partner
Rusty Reed, Managing Partner

Type of Firm
Private Equity Firm

Project Preferences

Role in Financing:
Prefer role as deal originator but will also invest in deals created by others

Type of Financing Preferred:
Early Stage

Geographical Preferences

United States Preferences:
California

Additional Information
Name of Most Recent Fund: Great Pacific Capital Partners I, L.P.
Most Recent Fund Was Raised: 07/05/2007
Year Founded: 2005
Capital Under Management: $15,000,000
Current Activity Level : Reducing investment activity
Method of Compensation: Return on investment is of primary concern, do not charge fees

PERUSA GMBH

Theatinerstrasse 40
Munich, Germany 80333
Phone: 4989238887890
Fax: 4989238878950
E-mail: info@perusa.de
Website: www.perusa-partners.de

Type of Firm
Private Equity Firm

Association Membership
German Venture Capital Association (BVK)

Project Preferences

Type of Financing Preferred:
Leveraged Buyout
Turnaround
Later Stage
Management Buyouts
Acquisition
Special Situation

Geographical Preferences

International Preferences:
Europe
Switzerland
Austria
Germany

Industry Preferences

In Consumer Related prefer:
Consumer

In Industrial/Energy prefer:
Industrial Products
Machinery

Additional Information
Name of Most Recent Fund: Perusa Partners 2 LP
Most Recent Fund Was Raised: 11/29/2011
Year Founded: 2007
Capital Under Management: $350,000,000
Current Activity Level : Actively seeking new investments

PERWYN LLLP

Anchor House
15-19 Britten St
London, United Kingdom SW3 3TY
Phone: 442073689209
Website: www.perwyn.co.uk

Type of Firm
Investment Management Firm

Project Preferences

Type of Financing Preferred:
Leveraged Buyout
Management Buyouts

Additional Information
Year Founded: 2013
Current Activity Level : Actively seeking new investments

PETERSON PARTNERS LP

2755 East Cottonwood Parkway, Suite 400
Salt Lake City, UT USA 84121
Phone: 8014170748
Fax: 8013657212
E-mail: contact@petersonpartners.com
Website: petersonpartners.com

Management and Staff
Aaron Gabbart, Vice President
Ben Capell, Partner
Brandon Cope, Partner
Clint Peterson, Managing Partner
Eric Noble, Chief Financial Officer
Joel Peterson, Founder
Matthew Day, Partner
Nick Jean-Baptiste, Principal
Spencer Clawson, Vice President

Type of Firm
Private Equity Firm

Project Preferences

Type of Financing Preferred:
Leveraged Buyout
Expansion
Management Buyouts
Acquisition
Recapitalizations

Geographical Preferences

United States Preferences:

Canadian Preferences:
All Canada

International Preferences:
Brazil

Additional Information
Name of Most Recent Fund: Peterson Partners VII, L.P.
Most Recent Fund Was Raised: 01/11/2013
Year Founded: 1995
Capital Under Management: $100,000,000
Current Activity Level : Actively seeking new investments

PETERSON VENTURES LLC

2825 East Cottonwood Parkway, Suite 400
Salt Lake City, UT USA 84121
Phone: 8013650180
Fax: 8013650181
E-mail: info@petersonventures.com
Website: www.petersonventures.com

Management and Staff
Brandon Cope, Partner
Dan Peterson, Partner
Joel Peterson, Founder
Valarie Ballein, Chief Financial Officer

Type of Firm
Private Equity Firm

Project Preferences

Type of Financing Preferred:
Early Stage
Balanced
Later Stage

Size of Investments Considered:
Min Size of Investment Considered (000s): $100
Max Size of Investment Considered (000s): $1,000

Geographical Preferences

United States Preferences:
West Coast
East Coast

Additional Information
Name of Most Recent Fund: Peterson Ventures IV, L.P.
Most Recent Fund Was Raised: 05/08/2012
Year Founded: 2008
Capital Under Management: $15,050,000
Current Activity Level : Actively seeking new investments

PETIT POUCET SAS

9 Rue Guyton de Morveau
Paris, France 75013
Phone: 33145659228
Fax: 33145652588
E-mail: info@petitpoucet.fr
Website: www.petitpoucet.fr

Management and Staff
Mathias Monribot, Founder

Type of Firm
Private Equity Firm

Project Preferences

Type of Financing Preferred:
Early Stage
Later Stage

Size of Investments Considered:
Min Size of Investment Considered (000s): $65
Max Size of Investment Considered (000s): $647

Geographical Preferences

International Preferences:
Europe
France

Additional Information
Year Founded: 2002
Current Activity Level : Actively seeking new investments

PETRA CAPITAL PARTNERS LLC

3825 Bedford Avenue, Suite 101
Nashville, TN USA 37215
Phone: 6153135999
Fax: 6153135990
Website: www.petracapital.com

Management and Staff
David Fitzgerald, General Partner
Douglas Owen, Principal
Fitzgerald David, Partner
Robert Smith, Co-Founder

Type of Firm
Private Equity Firm

Association Membership
Natl Assoc of Small Bus. Inv. Co (NASBIC)

Project Preferences

Role in Financing:
Prefer role as deal originator but will also invest in deals created by others

Type of Financing Preferred:
Leveraged Buyout
Expansion
Mezzanine
Generalist PE
Later Stage
Acquisition
Recapitalizations

Geographical Preferences

United States Preferences:

Industry Focus
(% based on actual investment)

Medical/Health	39.3%
Computer Software and Services	23.2%
Other Products	15.1%
Internet Specific	9.2%
Communications and Media	5.8%
Consumer Related	4.4%
Computer Hardware	1.7%
Biotechnology	0.7%
Semiconductors/Other Elect.	0.6%

Additional Information
Name of Most Recent Fund: Petra Growth Fund III
Most Recent Fund Was Raised: 05/13/2013
Year Founded: 1996
Capital Under Management: $456,000,000
Current Activity Level : Actively seeking new investments
Method of Compensation: Return on investment is of primary concern, do not charge fees

PETRICHOR HEALTHCARE CAPITAL MANAGEMENT LP

399 Park Avenue
Sixth Floor
New York, NY USA 10022
Website: petrichorcap.com

Type of Firm
Private Equity Firm

Project Preferences

Type of Financing Preferred:
Generalist PE

Industry Preferences

In Medical/Health prefer:
Health Services

Additional Information

Year Founded: 2017
Capital Under Management: $100,000,000
Current Activity Level : Actively seeking new investments

PETROS PARTNERS

300 West Sixth Street, Suite 1540
Austin, TX USA 78701
Phone: 5125999022
Fax: 5125510448
Website: www.petrospartners.com

Other Offices

175 Atlantic Street
Stamford, CT USA 06901

170 East Broadway, Suite 100A
Jackson Hole, WY USA 83001

Type of Firm

Private Equity Firm

Project Preferences

Type of Financing Preferred:
Generalist PE

Additional Information

Year Founded: 2014
Capital Under Management: $23,000,000
Current Activity Level : Actively seeking new investments

PFINGSTEN PARTNERS LLC

300 North LaSalle Street, Suite 5400
Chicago, IL USA 60654
Phone: 3122228707
Fax: 3122228708
E-mail: pfingsten@pfingsten.com
Website: www.pfingsten.com

Other Offices

Second Road, Zhendi District
5th Floor, Lucky Commercial Building
Guangdong, China 523850
Phone: 8676981663655

335, Udyog Vihar
Phase IV
Gurgoan, Haryana, India 122015
Phone: 911244308204

Management and Staff

Alex Gregor, Vice President
Brenda Lee Lally, Vice President
Christopher Siebert, Vice President
Craig Tompkins, Vice President
David Johnston, Vice President
Denio Bolzan, Managing Director
James Norton, Senior Managing Director
Jeffrey Cote, Chief Financial Officer
John Underwood, Senior Managing Director
John Starcevich, Managing Director
Jonathan Leiman, Vice President
Ken Hessevick, Vice President
Lawrence Taylor, Vice President
Marc Mar-Yohana, Vice President
Matthew Schloop, Vice President
Micah Wickersheim, Vice President
Phillip Bronsteatter, Vice President
Robert Gladden, Principal
Scott Gilbertson, Principal
Scott Finegan, Managing Director
Thomas Bagley, Founder
Tina Tromiczak, Vice President

Type of Firm

Private Equity Firm

Project Preferences

Role in Financing:
Prefer role as deal originator

Type of Financing Preferred:
Leveraged Buyout
Management Buyouts
Acquisition
Special Situation
Recapitalizations

Geographical Preferences

United States Preferences:
Mid Atlantic
Midwest

Industry Preferences

In Business Serv. prefer:
Services
Distribution

In Manufact. prefer:
Manufacturing

Additional Information

Name of Most Recent Fund: Pfingsten Executive Fund III, L.P.
Most Recent Fund Was Raised: 04/11/2003
Year Founded: 1989
Capital Under Management: $1,200,000,000
Current Activity Level : Actively seeking new investments
Method of Compensation: Return on investment is *of primary concern, do not charge fees*

PFIZER VENTURE INVESTMENTS

235 East 42nd Street
New York, NY USA 10017
Phone: 2127332323
E-mail: VentureInvestments@pfizer.com

Management and Staff

Barbara Dalton, Vice President
Elaine Jones, Chief Executive Officer
Ian Read, Chief Executive Officer
Ilya Oshman, Vice President

Type of Firm

Corporate PE/Venture

Association Membership

National Venture Capital Association - USA (NVCA)

Project Preferences

Role in Financing:
Will function either as deal originator or investor in deals created by others

Type of Financing Preferred:
Fund of Funds
Balanced
Public Companies

Geographical Preferences

United States Preferences:
All U.S.

Industry Preferences

In Medical/Health prefer:
Medical/Health
Medical Diagnostics
Diagnostic Services
Diagnostic Test Products
Drug/Equipmt Delivery
Pharmaceuticals

Additional Information

Year Founded: 2004
Capital Under Management: $50,000,000
Current Activity Level : Actively seeking new investments

PFM CAPITAL INC

1925 Victoria Avenue
2nd Floor, The Assiniboia Club
Regina, Canada S4P 0R3
Phone: 3067914855
Fax: 3067914848
E-mail: pfm@pfm.ca
Website: www.pfm.ca

Management and Staff
Chris Selness, Vice President
Mike Merth, Chief Financial Officer
Rob Duguid, Vice President

Type of Firm
Private Equity Firm

Association Membership
Canadian Venture Capital Association

Project Preferences

Type of Financing Preferred:
Leveraged Buyout
Early Stage
Expansion
Generalist PE
Management Buyouts
Acquisition
Startup
Recapitalizations

Geographical Preferences

Canadian Preferences:
Saskatchewan

Industry Preferences

In Medical/Health prefer:
Medical/Health

In Consumer Related prefer:
Retail

In Industrial/Energy prefer:
Oil & Gas Drilling,Explor

In Agr/Forestr/Fish prefer:
Agriculture related

Additional Information
Year Founded: 1989
Capital Under Management: $51,714,000
Current Activity Level : Actively seeking new investments

PHARMA CAPITAL VENTURES

600 East Crescent Avenue, Suite 205
Upper Saddle River, NJ USA 07458
Phone: 973-629-3777
E-mail: PCV@pharmacapitalventures.com
Website: www.pharmacapitalventures.com

Management and Staff
Gary Lubin, Managing Director
Jeff Tarlowe, Managing Director
Per Lofberg, Co-Founder

Type of Firm
Private Equity Firm

Project Preferences

Type of Financing Preferred:
Balanced

Industry Preferences

In Biotechnology prefer:
Biotechnology

In Medical/Health prefer:
Medical/Health

Additional Information
Year Founded: 2009
Current Activity Level : Actively seeking new investments

PHAROS CAPITAL GROUP LLC

300 Crescent Court, Suite 1380
Dallas, TX USA 75201
Phone: 2148550194
Fax: 2148551230
E-mail: info@pharosfunds.com
Website: www.pharosfunds.com

Other Offices
112 Enfield Road
Baltimore, MD USA 21212
Phone: 4103231105
Fax: 4103231677

8 Cadillac Drive, Suite 180
Brentwood, TN USA 37027
Phone: 6152345522
Fax: 6152630234

Management and Staff
Anna Kovalkova, Partner
D. Robert Crants, Co-Founder
Jim Phillips, Partner
Joel Goldberg, Partner
Joseph Acevedo, Principal
Kimberly Futrell, Chief Financial Officer
Kneeland Youngblood, Co-Founder
Michael Devlin, Co-Founder
Ryan Shelton, Vice President

Type of Firm
Private Equity Firm

Association Membership
Natl Assoc of Investment Cos. (NAIC)
Natl Assoc of Small Bus. Inv. Co (NASBIC)

Project Preferences

Role in Financing:
Prefer role as deal originator

Type of Financing Preferred:
Leveraged Buyout
Expansion
Generalist PE
Later Stage
Management Buyouts
Acquisition
Recapitalizations

Geographical Preferences

United States Preferences:

Industry Preferences

In Medical/Health prefer:
Medical/Health

In Business Serv. prefer:
Services

Additional Information
Name of Most Recent Fund: Pharos Capital Partners III, L.P.
Most Recent Fund Was Raised: 07/09/2012
Year Founded: 1998
Capital Under Management: $600,000,000
Current Activity Level : Actively seeking new investments
Method of Compensation: Return on investment is of primary concern, do not charge fees

PHASE4 VENTURES LTD

1 St. Martin's-le-Grand
Nomura House
London, United Kingdom EC1A 4NP
Phone: 44-20-7521-2386
Fax: 44-20-7521-2386
Website: www.nomura.com

Management and Staff
Alastair MacKinnon, Principal
Charles Sermon, Partner
Jennifer Hamilton, Venture Partner
John Westwater, Principal
Jonathan Jones, Principal
Naveed Siddiqi, Partner

Type of Firm
Bank Affiliated

Project Preferences

Type of Financing Preferred:
Second Stage Financing
Early Stage
Expansion

Size of Investments Considered:
Min Size of Investment Considered (000s): $10,000
Max Size of Investment Considered (000s): $40,000

Geographical Preferences

United States Preferences:
All U.S.

International Preferences:
Europe

Industry Preferences

In Biotechnology prefer:
Biotech Related Research

In Medical/Health prefer:
Medical/Health
Medical Products
Pharmaceuticals

Additional Information

Year Founded: 2004
Current Activity Level : Actively seeking new investments

PHATISA GROUP LTD

Suite 510 Fifth Floor Barkly
Wharf Le Caudan Waterfront
Port Louis, Mauritius

Type of Firm
Private Equity Firm

Association Membership
South African Venture Capital Association (SAVCA)

Project Preferences

Type of Financing Preferred:
Fund of Funds
Leveraged Buyout
Early Stage
Expansion
Generalist PE
Balanced
Later Stage
Management Buyouts
Acquisition
Startup
Fund of Funds of Second

Geographical Preferences

International Preferences:
Zambia
Tanzania
Ghana
Kenya
South Africa
Africa

Industry Preferences

In Consumer Related prefer:
Food/Beverage

In Agr/Forestr/Fish prefer:
Agriculture related

Additional Information
Name of Most Recent Fund: AAF SME Fund, The
Most Recent Fund Was Raised: 02/13/2012
Year Founded: 2005

Capital Under Management: $279,040,000
Current Activity Level : Actively seeking new investments

PHD EQUITY PARTNERS LLP

7700 Daresbury Park
Daresbury
Cheshire, United Kingdom WA4 4BS
Phone: 441928715700
Fax: 441928751839
Website: www.phdequitypartners.com

Management and Staff
Andy Dodd, Partner
Craig Richardson, Partner
James Dow, Managing Partner
Jon Schofield, Partner
Mark Watts, Partner
Philip Price, Partner

Type of Firm
Private Equity Firm

Project Preferences

Type of Financing Preferred:
Expansion
Turnaround
Management Buyouts
Acquisition
Recapitalizations

Geographical Preferences

International Preferences:
United Kingdom

Industry Preferences

In Medical/Health prefer:
Health Services

In Consumer Related prefer:
Consumer

In Financial Services prefer:
Financial Services

In Manufact. prefer:
Manufacturing

Additional Information
Year Founded: 2008
Capital Under Management: $25,808,000
Current Activity Level : Actively seeking new investments

PHENOMEN VENTURES

Paveletskaya Square 2
Paveletskaya Plaza
Moscow, Russia
E-mail: info@phenomenvc.com
Website: www.phenomenvc.com

Other Offices
Azrieli Business Center, Round Tower
Floor 32
Tel-Aviv, Israel 67021

Type of Firm
Private Equity Firm

Project Preferences

Type of Financing Preferred:
Early Stage
Balanced
Later Stage
Seed
Startup

Industry Preferences

In Internet Specific prefer:
Internet

Additional Information
Year Founded: 2012
Current Activity Level : Actively seeking new investments

PHENOMENELLE ANGELS MANAGEMENT LLC

510 Charmany, Suite 175B
Madison, WI USA 53719
Phone: 6084418315
E-mail: info@phenomenelleangels.com
Website: www.phenomenelleangels.com

Management and Staff
Dedee Wojtal, General Partner
Joseph Hildebrandt, Co-Founder
Lauren Flanagan, Co-Founder
Tiffany Wilke, General Partner
Valerie Wulf, General Partner

Type of Firm
Private Equity Firm

Project Preferences

Role in Financing:
Prefer role as deal originator but will also invest in deals created by others

Type of Financing Preferred:
Early Stage

Size of Investments Considered:
Min Size of Investment Considered (000s): $100
Max Size of Investment Considered (000s): $500

Geographical Preferences

United States Preferences:
Midwest
Wisconsin

Industry Preferences

In Communications prefer:
Communications and Media

In Biotechnology prefer:
Biotechnology

In Consumer Related prefer:
Consumer Products

In Other prefer:
Women/Minority-Owned Bus.

Additional Information

Name of Most Recent Fund: Phenomenelle Angels Fund I, L.P.
Most Recent Fund Was Raised: 05/09/2006
Year Founded: 2006
Current Activity Level : Actively seeking new investments

PHI CAPITAL HOLDINGS INC

17011 Beach Boulevard, Suite 1230
Huntington Beach, CA USA 92647
Phone: 714-843-5450
Fax: 714-843-5452

Management and Staff

Benjamin Tran, Managing Director
Tan Phuong, Chief Operating Officer

Type of Firm

Bank Affiliated

Project Preferences

Type of Financing Preferred:
Expansion
Later Stage
Acquisition
Industry Rollups

Geographical Preferences

International Preferences:
Vietnam

Additional Information

Year Founded: 2000
Current Activity Level : Actively seeking new investments

PHI INDUSTRIAL ACQUISI-TIONS SL

Calle Lagasca, 121-1 Centro
Madrid, Spain 28006
Phone: 34915613371
E-mail: info@phi-industrial.com
Website: www.phi-industrial.com

Management and Staff

Alexander Wit, Managing Partner
Elena Mialdea, Founder
Jordi Bricio, Managing Partner
Jorge Beschinsky, Managing Director
Lluis - Maria Munne, Managing Director
Manuel Alonso, Managing Director

Type of Firm

Private Equity Firm

Project Preferences

Type of Financing Preferred:
Turnaround
Acquisition
Special Situation
Recapitalizations

Geographical Preferences

International Preferences:
Europe

Additional Information

Year Founded: 2006
Current Activity Level : Actively seeking new investments

PHILLIMORE INVESTISSE-MENT SAS

14 Avenue de l'Opera
Paris, France 75001
Phone: 33147030814
Fax: 33147030817
E-mail: contact@phillimore.fr
Website: www.phillimore.fr

Management and Staff

Anne-Sophie Vinet, Partner
Cyril Tramon, President, Founder
Frederic Arnaud, Partner

Type of Firm

Private Equity Firm

Association Membership

French Venture Capital Association (AFIC)

Project Preferences

Type of Financing Preferred:
Leveraged Buyout
Mezzanine
Generalist PE
Later Stage
Management Buyouts
Acquisition

Geographical Preferences

United States Preferences:
Alaska

International Preferences:
Europe
Eastern Europe
France

Industry Preferences

In Communications prefer:
Communications and Media

In Internet Specific prefer:
Ecommerce

In Business Serv. prefer:
Distribution
Media

In Manufact. prefer:
Manufacturing

Additional Information

Year Founded: 2003
Current Activity Level : Actively seeking new investments

PHILLIP PRIVATE EQUITY PTE LTD

250 North Bridge Road
06-00 Raffles City Tower
Singapore, Singapore 179 101
Phone: 65336001
E-mail: enquiry@phillipprivateequity.com
Website: www.phillipprivateequity.com

Management and Staff

Timothy Chan, Vice President

Type of Firm

Insurance Firm Affiliate

Association Membership

Singapore Venture Capital Association (SVCA)

Project Preferences

Role in Financing:
Prefer role in deals created by others

Type of Financing Preferred:
Expansion
Mezzanine
Balanced
Seed
Startup
Special Situation

Geographical Preferences

United States Preferences:
California
All U.S.

International Preferences:
Pacific Rim
Eastern Europe
Asia
Singapore
All International

Industry Preferences

In Communications prefer:
Communications and Media
Radio & TV Broadcasting
Telecommunications

In Internet Specific prefer:
Internet

In Computer Other prefer:
Computer Related

In Semiconductor/Electr prefer:
Electronic Components

In Biotechnology prefer:
Biotechnology

In Medical/Health prefer:
Medical/Health
Pharmaceuticals

In Consumer Related prefer:
Entertainment and Leisure
Food/Beverage
Consumer Services

In Transportation prefer:
Transportation

In Financial Services prefer:
Financial Services

Additional Information

Year Founded: 1993
Capital Under Management: $30,200,000
Current Activity Level : Actively seeking new investments
Method of Compensation: Return on investment is of primary concern, do not charge fees

PHITRUST IMPACT INVESTORS SA

34 Avenue De La Motte- Picquet
Paris, France 75007
Phone: 33156883200
Fax: 33156883209
E-mail: info@lc-capital.com
Website: www.phitrustimpactinvestors.com

Other Offices

34 Avenue de la Motte- Picquet
Paris, France 75007
Phone: 33-1-5688-3200
Fax: 33-1-5688-3209

Management and Staff

Jean-Claude Leveque, Co-Founder
Jean-Marie Chauvet, Co-Founder

Type of Firm

Private Equity Firm

Association Membership

French Venture Capital Association (AFIC)

Project Preferences

Role in Financing:
Will function either as deal originator or investor in deals created by others

Type of Financing Preferred:
Early Stage
Later Stage

Geographical Preferences

International Preferences:
United Kingdom
Europe
Spain
France

Industry Preferences

In Communications prefer:
Telecommunications

In Computer Software prefer:
Software

In Biotechnology prefer:
Biotechnology

In Medical/Health prefer:
Medical/Health

Additional Information

Year Founded: 2003
Current Activity Level : Actively seeking new investments
Method of Compensation: Return on investment is of primary concern, do not charge fees

PHOENICIAN FUNDS

Selim Bustrs street
7th floor, Dakdouk building
Beirut, Lebanon 16-5048
Phone: 9611328233
Fax: 9611325200
E-mail: info@phoenicianfunds.com
Website: phoenicianfunds.com

Other Offices

Selim Bustrs street
7th floor, Dakdouk building
Beirut, Lebanon
Phone: 9611328233
Fax: 9611325200

Type of Firm

Private Equity Firm

Project Preferences

Type of Financing Preferred:
Early Stage
Seed

Geographical Preferences

International Preferences:
Middle East
Africa

Industry Preferences

In Computer Software prefer:
Software

In Internet Specific prefer:
Internet

In Financial Services prefer:
Financial Services

Additional Information

Year Founded: 2015
Capital Under Management: $26,000,000
Current Activity Level : Actively seeking new investments

PHOENIX ASSET MANAGEMENT CO LTD

No. 3, South Xinyuan Road
Ping'an Inte'l Finance Ctr.
Beijing, China 100027
Phone: 861059892311
Fax: 861059892333
Website: www.phoenixassetcn.com

Management and Staff

Chong Tang, President

Type of Firm

Investment Management Firm

Project Preferences

Type of Financing Preferred:
Balanced

Geographical Preferences

International Preferences:
China

Industry Preferences

In Industrial/Energy prefer:
Materials
Environmental Related

In Financial Services prefer:
Financial Services

Additional Information
Year Founded: 2009
Current Activity Level : Actively seeking new investments

PHOENIX CAPITAL CO LTD

2-2-1 Marunouchi
9F, Kishimoto Bldg
Tokyo, Japan 1000005
Phone: 81332153260
Fax: 81332153261
Website: www.phoenixcapital.co.jp

Type of Firm
Private Equity Firm

Project Preferences

Type of Financing Preferred:
Leveraged Buyout
Mezzanine
Turnaround
Management Buyouts
Recapitalizations

Geographical Preferences

International Preferences:
Japan

Additional Information
Year Founded: 2002
Capital Under Management: $9,702,000
Current Activity Level : Actively seeking new investments

PHOENIX CONTACT INNO-VATION VENTURES GMBH

Flachsmarktstrasse 8
Blomberg, Germany 32825
Phone: 495235300
E-mail: contact@phoenixinnovation.de
Website: www.phoenixcontact.com

Type of Firm
Private Equity Firm

Project Preferences

Type of Financing Preferred:
Early Stage

Additional Information
Year Founded: 2015
Current Activity Level : Actively seeking new investments

PHOENIX EQUITY PART-NERS LTD

25 Bedford Street
London, United Kingdom WC2E 9ES
Phone: 442074346999
Fax: 442030041496
E-mail: enquiries@phoenix-equity.com
Website: www.phoenix-equity.com

Other Offices
73-79 King Street
3rd Floor, The Pinnacle
Manchester, United Kingdom M2 4NG
Phone: 441618173360
Fax: 441618173369

Victoria Avenue
Clarendon House
Harrogate, United Kingdom HG1 1JD
Phone: 44-1423-789-080
Fax: 44-1423-538-293

Former HQ: 33 Glasshouse Street
London, United Kingdom W1B 5DG
Phone: 442074346999
Fax: 442074346998

Management and Staff
Adam Corbett, Principal
Barry Robinson, Principal
David Burns, Managing Partner
James Thomas, Managing Partner
John Rastrick, Partner
Kevin Keck, Partner
Mark Sargeant, Principal
Richard Daw, Managing Partner
Timothy Dunn, Partner
William Skinner, Principal

Type of Firm
Private Equity Firm

Association Membership
British Venture Capital Association (BVCA)

Project Preferences

Role in Financing:
Prefer role as deal originator but will also invest in deals created by others

Type of Financing Preferred:
Leveraged Buyout
Management Buyouts
Acquisition

Geographical Preferences

International Preferences:
United Kingdom

Industry Focus
(% based on actual investment)

Industry	%
Other Products	39.7%
Consumer Related	33.0%
Communications and Media	9.7%
Medical/Health	6.7%
Internet Specific	5.9%
Biotechnology	2.8%
Computer Software and Services	1.8%
Industrial/Energy	0.3%
Semiconductors/Other Elect.	0.2%

Additional Information
Year Founded: 1984
Capital Under Management: $714,200,000
Current Activity Level : Actively seeking new investments
Method of Compensation: Return on invest. most important, but chg. closing fees, service fees, etc.

PHOENIX PARTNERS

8225 Mayrand
Montreal, Canada H4P 2C7
E-mail: info@phoenix-partners.ca
Website: www.phoenix-partners.ca

Type of Firm
Private Equity Firm

Project Preferences

Type of Financing Preferred:
Leveraged Buyout
Acquisition

Additional Information
Year Founded: 2012
Current Activity Level : Actively seeking new investments

PHOENIX STRATEGY IN-VESTMENTS LLC

21 King Charles Drive
Portsmouth, RI USA 02871
Website: phoenixstrategy.com

Other Offices
12720 Hillcrest Road, Suite 650
Dallas, TX USA 75230

Type of Firm
Private Equity Firm

Project Preferences

Type of Financing Preferred:
Leveraged Buyout
Acquisition
Recapitalizations

Geographical Preferences

United States Preferences:
Southeast
Northeast
West Coast
Southwest

Industry Preferences

In Medical/Health prefer:
Medical/Health

In Consumer Related prefer:
Franchises(NEC)
Consumer Services

In Financial Services prefer:
Financial Services

In Business Serv. prefer:
Services
Distribution

In Manufact. prefer:
Manufacturing

Additional Information
Year Founded: 2002
Current Activity Level : Actively seeking new investments

PHOENIX VENTURE FUND LLC

110 East 59th Street
New York, NY USA 10022
Phone: 2127591909

Management and Staff
Andrea Goran, Managing Director

Type of Firm
Private Equity Firm

Project Preferences

Type of Financing Preferred:
Later Stage

Additional Information
Year Founded: 2004
Current Activity Level : Actively seeking new investments

PHOENIX VENTURE PARTNERS LLC

1700 South El Camino Real, Suite 355
San Mateo, CA USA 94402
Phone: 6503493467
E-mail: info@phoenix-vp.com

Other Offices
35 Spinelli Place
CAMBRIDGE, MA USA 02138

16 Nanyang Drive
Innovation Center #01-110
, Singapore 637722

Management and Staff
Avinash Kant, Venture Partner
David Soane, Founder
Frank Levinson, Founder
Jennifer Wang, Chief Financial Officer

Type of Firm
Private Equity Firm

Project Preferences

Type of Financing Preferred:
Early Stage
Balanced
Seed
Startup

Industry Preferences

In Semiconductor/Electr prefer:
Electronics

In Medical/Health prefer:
Drug/Equipmt Delivery

In Consumer Related prefer:
Consumer

In Industrial/Energy prefer:
Energy
Energy Conservation Relat
Advanced Materials

In Manufact. prefer:
Manufacturing

In Other prefer:
Environment Responsible

Additional Information
Name of Most Recent Fund: Phoenix Venture Partners L.P.
Most Recent Fund Was Raised: 08/16/2010
Year Founded: 2010
Capital Under Management: $116,500,000
Current Activity Level : Actively seeking new investments

PHYSIC VENTURES LLC

200 California Street
Fifth Floor
San Francisco, CA USA 94111
Phone: 4153544901
Fax: 4153544915
E-mail: info@physicventures.com
Website: www.physicventures.com

Management and Staff
Andrew Williamson, Partner
Andy Donner, Partner
Dion Madsen, Co-Founder
Stacy Feld, Partner
William Rosenzweig, Co-Founder

Type of Firm
Private Equity Firm

Project Preferences

Type of Financing Preferred:
Early Stage
Expansion
Seed

Geographical Preferences

United States Preferences:
North America

Industry Preferences

In Medical/Health prefer:
Medical Products
Health Services

In Consumer Related prefer:
Consumer Products

In Industrial/Energy prefer:
Alternative Energy
Materials

In Transportation prefer:
Transportation

In Agr/Forestr/Fish prefer:
Agriculture related

In Other prefer:
Environment Responsible

Additional Information
Name of Most Recent Fund: Physic Ventures, L.P.
Most Recent Fund Was Raised: 03/28/2007
Year Founded: 2007
Capital Under Management: $185,000,000
Current Activity Level : Actively seeking new investments

PHYTO PARTNERS

2080 NW Boca Raton Boulevard, Suite Six
Boca Raton, FL USA 33431
Phone: 5615426090
Website: www.phytopartners.com

Type of Firm
Private Equity Firm

Project Preferences

Type of Financing Preferred:
Early Stage
Balanced

Industry Preferences

In Medical/Health prefer:
Health Services

Additional Information
Year Founded: 2015
Capital Under Management: $2,200,000
Current Activity Level : Actively seeking new investments

PI LABS LTD

14 Bedford Square
Fitzrovia
London, United Kingdom WC1B 3JA
E-mail: info@pilabs.co.uk
Website: pilabs.co.uk

Type of Firm
Private Equity Firm

Project Preferences

Type of Financing Preferred:
Early Stage

Additional Information
Year Founded: 2016
Current Activity Level : Actively seeking new investments

PICARDIE INVESTISSEMENTS SA

18, Rue Lamartine
Amiens, France 80005
Phone: 33322917020
Fax: 33322916670
E-mail: contacts@picardie-investissement.fr
Website: www.picardie-investissement.fr

Management and Staff
Patrick Colin, President

Type of Firm
Private Equity Firm

Association Membership
French Venture Capital Association (AFIC)

Project Preferences

Type of Financing Preferred:
Leveraged Buyout
Early Stage
Generalist PE
Later Stage
Other
Management Buyouts
Acquisition

Geographical Preferences

International Preferences:
Europe
France

Industry Preferences

In Biotechnology prefer:
Agricultural/Animal Bio.

In Medical/Health prefer:
Medical/Health
Medical Diagnostics
Medical Therapeutics
Medical Products
Health Services
Pharmaceuticals

In Industrial/Energy prefer:
Energy
Industrial Products

In Business Serv. prefer:
Services
Distribution

Additional Information
Year Founded: 1985
Current Activity Level : Actively seeking new investments

PICUS CAPITAL GMBH

Tuerkenstrasse 7
Munich, Germany 80333

Type of Firm
Private Equity Firm

Project Preferences

Type of Financing Preferred:
Early Stage

Additional Information
Year Founded: 2017
Current Activity Level : Actively seeking new investments

PIEDMONT PARTNERS GROUP VENTURES LLC

The Wakefield Building
426 17th Street, 8th Floor
Oakland, CA USA 94612
Website: www.piedmontpartnersgroup.com

Type of Firm
Private Equity Firm

Project Preferences

Type of Financing Preferred:
Leveraged Buyout
Acquisition
Recapitalizations

Industry Preferences

In Medical/Health prefer:
Medical/Health

In Consumer Related prefer:
Consumer

In Financial Services prefer:
Financial Services

In Business Serv. prefer:
Services

In Other prefer:
Environment Responsible

Additional Information
Year Founded: 2009
Current Activity Level : Actively seeking new investments

PIERPOINT CAPITAL LLC

575 Madison Avenue
16th Floor
New York, NY USA 10022
Phone: 2129406490
E-mail: info@pierpointcap.com
Website: pierpointcap.com

Management and Staff
Jarret Fass, Co-Founder
Richard Krupp, Co-Founder

Type of Firm
Private Equity Firm

Project Preferences

Type of Financing Preferred:
Leveraged Buyout
Generalist PE
Balanced

Size of Investments Considered:
Min Size of Investment Considered (000s): $1,000
Max Size of Investment Considered (000s): $5,000

Geographical Preferences

United States Preferences:

International Preferences:
Israel

Additional Information
Year Founded: 2013
Current Activity Level : Actively seeking new investments

PII INVESTIMENTOS IMOBILIARIOS LTDA

Av Brigadeiro Faria Lima, 2055
7 Andar
Sao Paulo, Brazil 01452-001
Phone: 551130399000
Fax: 551130399001
Website: www.patriainvestimentos.com.br

Management and Staff
Marco Nicola D Ippolito, Principal
Ricardo Scavazza, Principal

Type of Firm
Investment Management Firm

Association Membership
Brazilian Venture Capital Association (ABCR)

Project Preferences

Type of Financing Preferred:
Leveraged Buyout
Value-Add
Opportunistic
Other
Management Buyouts
Acquisition

Geographical Preferences

International Preferences:
Latin America
Rest of World
Brazil

Industry Preferences

In Medical/Health prefer:
Medical/Health

In Consumer Related prefer:
Consumer
Retail

In Industrial/Energy prefer:
Oil and Gas Exploration
Oil & Gas Drilling,Explor

In Transportation prefer:
Transportation

In Financial Services prefer:
Real Estate

In Utilities prefer:
Utilities

Additional Information
Name of Most Recent Fund: P2 Brasil Private Infrastructure Fund II, L.P.
Most Recent Fund Was Raised: 02/28/2011
Year Founded: 1994
Capital Under Management: $250,000,000
Current Activity Level : Actively seeking new investments

PILGRIM BAXTER

210 West Tenth Street
Kansas City, MO USA 64102

Type of Firm
Corporate PE/Venture

Project Preferences

Type of Financing Preferred:
Balanced

Additional Information
Year Founded: 1999
Current Activity Level : Actively seeking new investments

PILGRIM CAPITAL PARTNERS LLC

163 Oldfield Road
The Harbor House
Fairfield, CT USA 06824
Phone: 2032926616
Fax: 2032926673
Website: www.pilgrimcap.com

Management and Staff
Christopher Daley, Partner
Christopher Wright, Partner

Type of Firm
Private Equity Firm

Additional Information
Year Founded: 2006
Current Activity Level : Actively seeking new investments

PILLAR COMPANIES MANAGEMENT LLC

One Marina Park Drive, Suite 900
Boston, MA USA 02210
E-mail: contact@pillar.vc
Website: pillar.vc

Management and Staff
Robert May, Venture Partner
Russ Wilcox, Partner

Type of Firm
Private Equity Firm

Project Preferences

Type of Financing Preferred:
Early Stage

Additional Information
Year Founded: 2016
Current Activity Level : Actively seeking new investments

PILLSMAN PARTNERS LLC

45 East Putnam Avenue, Suite 118
Greenwich, CT USA 06830
Website: www.pillsmanpartners.com

Management and Staff
Chris Eichmann, Managing Partner
Edwin Burke, Managing Partner

Type of Firm
Private Equity Firm

Project Preferences

Type of Financing Preferred:
Leveraged Buyout
Acquisition

Industry Preferences

In Industrial/Energy prefer:
Industrial Products

Additional Information
Year Founded: 2011
Current Activity Level : Actively seeking new investments

PILOT GROUP LP

75 Rockefeller Plaza
23rd Floor
New York, NY USA 10019
Phone: 2124864446

Management and Staff
Marshall Cohen, Partner
Mayo Stuntz, Co-Founder
Paul McNichol, Principal
Robert Pittman, Principal

Type of Firm
Private Equity Firm

Project Preferences

Type of Financing Preferred:
Turnaround
Later Stage

Industry Preferences

In Communications prefer:
Communications and Media

In Consumer Related prefer:
Consumer

In Business Serv. prefer:
Services

Additional Information
Year Founded: 2003
Current Activity Level : Actively seeking new investments

PILOT GROWTH EQUITY PARTNERS

44 Montgomery Street, Suite 1500
San Francisco, CA USA 94104
Website: www.pilotgrowth.com

Type of Firm
Private Equity Firm

Project Preferences

Type of Financing Preferred:
Later Stage

Additional Information
Year Founded: 1969
Current Activity Level : Actively seeking new investments

PILOT HOUSE VENTURES GROUP, LLC

The Pilot House
Lewis Wharf
Boston, MA USA 02110
Phone: 6178543318
E-mail: phv@pilothouse.com
Website: www.pilothouseventures.com

Management and Staff
Margaret Lawrence, Partner
Stephen Van Beaver, General Partner

Type of Firm
Private Equity Firm

Project Preferences

Role in Financing:
Prefer role in deals created by others

Type of Financing Preferred:
Early Stage
Balanced
Seed

Size of Investments Considered:
Min Size of Investment Considered (000s): $2,000
Max Size of Investment Considered (000s): $10,000

Geographical Preferences

United States Preferences:
Northeast

Industry Preferences

In Communications prefer:
Communications and Media
Telecommunications
Wireless Communications
Data Communications

In Computer Software prefer:
Software

In Internet Specific prefer:
Internet

In Business Serv. prefer:
Services

Additional Information
Year Founded: 1999
Current Activity Level : Actively seeking new investments

PILOT WALL GROUP LLC

2801 Via Fortuna, Suite 660
Austin, TX USA 78746
Phone: 5122125331
E-mail: inquiries@PilotWallGroup.com
Website: pilotwallgroup.com

Type of Firm
Private Equity Firm

Project Preferences

Type of Financing Preferred:
Early Stage

Industry Preferences

In Medical/Health prefer:
Health Services

In Financial Services prefer:
Insurance

Additional Information
Year Founded: 1969
Current Activity Level : Actively seeking new investments

PINE BROOK ROAD PARTNERS LLC

60 East 42nd Street
50th Floor
New York, NY USA 10165
Phone: 2128474333
Fax: 2128474334
E-mail: info@pinebrookpartners.com
Website: www.pinebrookpartners.com

Other Offices
1301 McKinney Street, Suite 3550
Houston, TX USA 77010
Phone: 8329249950
Fax: 8329249940

Management and Staff
Andre Burba, Managing Director
Benjamin Johnston, Principal
Bharath Srikrishnan, Managing Director
Craig Jarchow, Managing Director
Dan Ballen, Vice President
Edward Donkor, Principal
Ganesh Betanabhatla, Vice President
Grace Kim, Principal
Guillermo Bron, Managing Director
James Rutherfurd, Managing Director
Kristin Gilbert, Principal
Lawrence Marsiello, Managing Director
Matthew Zales, Vice President
Michael McMahon, Managing Director
Nicholaos Krenteras, Managing Director
Oliver Goldstein, Managing Director
Richard Aube, Managing Director
Robert Glanville, Managing Director
Scott Schaen, Principal
Ted Maa, Principal
William Spiegel, Managing Director

Type of Firm
Private Equity Firm

Association Membership
National Venture Capital Association - USA (NVCA)

Project Preferences

Type of Financing Preferred:
Leveraged Buyout
Early Stage
Expansion
Generalist PE
Balanced
Management Buyouts
Acquisition

Industry Preferences

In Industrial/Energy prefer:
Energy
Oil and Gas Exploration
Oil & Gas Drilling,Explor

In Transportation prefer:
Transportation

In Financial Services prefer:
Financial Services
Insurance

Additional Information
Year Founded: 2006
Capital Under Management: $1,400,000,000
Current Activity Level : Actively seeking new investments

PINE STREET CAPITAL PARTNERS LP

Eleven North Pearl Street, Suite 1700
Albany, NY USA 12207
Phone: 5184499070
Website: www.pinecap.com

Other Offices
572 Washington Street, Suite 16, The Rotunda Building
Wellesley, MA USA 02482
Phone: 7812370005

45 Broadway
26th Floor
New York, NY USA 10006
Phone: 212-785-4377

Management and Staff
David Morris, Managing Partner
Michael Lasch, Managing Partner
Timothy Welles, Managing Partner

Type of Firm
Bank Affiliated

Association Membership
Natl Assoc of Small Bus. Inv. Co (NASBIC)

Project Preferences

Type of Financing Preferred:
Leveraged Buyout
Expansion
Mezzanine
Management Buyouts
Acquisition
Recapitalizations

Size of Investments Considered:
Min Size of Investment Considered (000s): $2,000
Max Size of Investment Considered (000s): $6,000

Geographical Preferences

United States Preferences:
Mid Atlantic
Northeast

Industry Preferences

In Medical/Health prefer:
Medical/Health

In Consumer Related prefer:
Consumer Products

In Business Serv. prefer:
Services
Media

In Manufact. prefer:
Manufacturing

Additional Information
Name of Most Recent Fund: Pine Street Capital Partners II, L.P.
Most Recent Fund Was Raised: 09/22/2010
Year Founded: 2004
Capital Under Management: $25,000,000
Current Activity Level : Actively seeking new investments

PINE TREE EQUITY MANAGEMENT LP

777 Brickell Avenue, Suite 1070
Miami, FL USA 33131
Phone: 3058089820
Fax: 3058089821
E-mail: info@pinetreeequity.com
Website: pinetreeequity.com

Management and Staff
Gregory Diem, Managing Director
Jeff Settembrino, Managing Partner
R. Evan Horton, Vice President
Roberto Canto, Managing Director

Type of Firm
Private Equity Firm

Project Preferences

Type of Financing Preferred:
Leveraged Buyout
Management Buyouts
Recapitalizations

Industry Preferences

In Consumer Related prefer:
Franchises(NEC)
Consumer Products
Consumer Services

In Financial Services prefer:
Financial Services

In Business Serv. prefer:
Services

In Manufact. prefer:
Manufacturing

Additional Information
Name of Most Recent Fund: Pine Tree Equity III, L.P.
Most Recent Fund Was Raised: 04/16/2013
Year Founded: 2006
Capital Under Management: $150,000,000
Current Activity Level : Actively seeking new investments

PINEBRIDGE INVESTMENTS LLC

399 Park Avenue
Fourth Floor
New York, NY USA 10022
Phone: 6468578000
Website: www.pinebridge.com

Other Offices
Blvd. Manuel A. Camacho #76, Piso 8
Col. Lomas de Chapultepec
Mexico, Mexico
Phone: 52-55-4739-3800

Minchuan East Road
10/F,144
Taipei, Taiwan 10436

11100 Santa Monica Blvd, Suite 550
West Los Angeles, CA USA 90025

Cerro El Plomo 5630
Torre 8, Office 1503
, Chile 7560742
Phone: 56-2-411-1002

33 St Mary Axe
Exchequer Court
London, United Kingdom EC3A 8AA
Phone: 44-020-7398-6000

50 Market Street
Level 2
Melbourne, Australia VIC 3000

Peninsula Corporate Park
6th Floor, Peninsula Tower
Mumbai, India 400 013

64-5 Chungmuro-2-ga
10F, Shinil building
Seoul, South Korea 100-012

Otemachi 1-chomeme
JA Building, 3-1
Tokyo, Japan 100-6813
Phone: 81-3-5208-5800

Seefeldstrasse 69
Zurich, Switzerland 8008

2929 Allen Parkway
Houston, TX USA 77019

Bahrain Financial Harbour District
GBCORP Tower, 13th Floor
Manama, Bahrain
Phone: 973-17111888

1 Queen's Road East
Level 31, Three Pacific Place
, Hong Kong
Phone: 852-3970-3970

1 Robinson Road
#21-01 AIA Tower
, Singapore 048542

Management and Staff
Brian McLoone, Senior Managing Director
David Jiang, Chief Executive Officer
George Hornig, Chief Operating Officer
Hans Danielsson, Senior Managing Director
W. Michael Verge, Chief Financial Officer

Type of Firm
Investment Management Firm

Association Membership
Czech Venture Capital Association (CVCA)

Project Preferences

Type of Financing Preferred:
Fund of Funds
Leveraged Buyout
Early Stage
Mezzanine
Generalist PE
Balanced
Later Stage
Acquisition
Fund of Funds of Second
Recapitalizations

Geographical Preferences

International Preferences:
Africa

Additional Information

Name of Most Recent Fund: PineBridge Secondary Partners III, L.P.
Most Recent Fund Was Raised: 07/16/2013
Year Founded: 1990
Capital Under Management: $12,700,000,000
Current Activity Level : Actively seeking new investments

PINEBRIDGE INVESTMENTS MIDDLE EAST BSCC

13th Floor, GBCORP Tower
Bahrain Financial Harbour Dist
Manama, Bahrain
Phone: 97317111888
Fax: 97317111020
Website: www.pinebridge.com

Type of Firm

Private Equity Firm

Project Preferences

Type of Financing Preferred:
Core
Leveraged Buyout
Turnaround
Management Buyouts
Acquisition
Recapitalizations

Geographical Preferences

International Preferences:
Bahrain
Oman
Turkey
Qatar
Utd. Arab Em.
Middle East
Saudi Arabia
Kuwait
Africa

Industry Preferences

In Medical/Health prefer:
Hospitals/Clinics/Primary
Hospital/Other Instit.

In Financial Services prefer:
Real Estate
Investment Groups

Additional Information

Year Founded: 2014
Capital Under Management: $140,000,000
Current Activity Level : Actively seeking new investments

PINETREE CAPITAL LTD

130 King Street West
The Exchange Tower, Suite 2500
Toronto, Canada M5X 2A2
Phone: 4169419600
Fax: 4169411090
E-mail: ir@pinetreecapital.com
Website: www.pinetreecapital.com

Management and Staff

Damien Leonard, Chief Executive Officer
Jamie Levy, Vice President
Susan Fox, Chief Financial Officer

Type of Firm

Investment Management Firm

Project Preferences

Type of Financing Preferred:
Early Stage
Generalist PE
Acquisition
Startup

Geographical Preferences

Canadian Preferences:
All Canada

Industry Preferences

In Industrial/Energy prefer:
Oil & Gas Drilling,Explor

In Agr/Forestr/Fish prefer:
Mining and Minerals

Additional Information

Year Founded: 1992
Current Activity Level : Actively seeking new investments

PING AN BRIGHT FORTUNE INVESTMENT MANAGEMENT CO

Ba Gua No. 3 Road
c/o Ping An Insurance Group
Shenzhen, China 518029
Phone: 8675582262888
Fax: 8675582414817

Type of Firm

Insurance Firm Affiliate

Project Preferences

Type of Financing Preferred:
Early Stage
Expansion
Later Stage

Geographical Preferences

International Preferences:
China

Additional Information

Year Founded: 2007
Current Activity Level : Actively seeking new investments

PING AN LIFE INSURANCE CO OF CHINA LTD

Ba Gua No. 3 Road
Ping An Building
Shenzhen, China 518040
Website: about.pingan.com

Management and Staff

Bo Yao, Chief Financial Officer

Type of Firm

Insurance Firm Affiliate

Project Preferences

Type of Financing Preferred:
Early Stage
Balanced
Seed

Geographical Preferences

International Preferences:
China

Industry Preferences

In Communications prefer:
Wireless Communications

In Computer Software prefer:
Data Processing

In Medical/Health prefer:
Medical/Health

In Consumer Related prefer:
Consumer

In Transportation prefer:
Transportation

In Financial Services prefer:
Financial Services

In Business Serv. prefer:
Media

Additional Information

Year Founded: 1988
Capital Under Management: $156,723,000
Current Activity Level : Actively seeking new investments

PING AN VENTURES

Lujiazui Ring Road
Pudong New District
Shanghai, China
Website: www.pinganventures.com

Type of Firm
Insurance Firm Affiliate

Project Preferences

Type of Financing Preferred:
Startup

Geographical Preferences

International Preferences:
All International

Additional Information
Year Founded: 2012
Capital Under Management: $154,030,000
Current Activity Level : Actively seeking new investments

PINNACLE CAPITAL

161 Bay Street, BCE Place, Suite 3930, TD Canada Trust
Toronto, Canada M5J 2S1
Phone: 4166012270
Fax: 4166012280
E-mail: info@pincap.com
Website: www.pincap.com

Management and Staff
Arif Bhalwani, Founder
Stuart Ross, Principal

Type of Firm
Private Equity Firm

Association Membership
Canadian Venture Capital Association

Project Preferences

Type of Financing Preferred:
Early Stage

Industry Preferences

In Communications prefer:
Telecommunications

In Biotechnology prefer:
Biotechnology

In Industrial/Energy prefer:
Energy

In Financial Services prefer:
Financial Services

In Business Serv. prefer:
Media

In Manufact. prefer:
Manufacturing

Additional Information
Year Founded: 1998
Current Activity Level : Actively seeking new investments

PINNACLE FINANCIAL PARTNERS INC

150 Third Avenue South, Suite 900
Nashville, TN USA 37201
Phone: 18002643613
Website: www.pnfp.com

Other Offices
150 Third Avenue South, Suite 900
Nashville, TN USA
Phone: 18002643613

Management and Staff
Harold Carpenter, Chief Financial Officer

Type of Firm
Private Equity Firm

Project Preferences

Type of Financing Preferred:
Unknown

Geographical Preferences

International Preferences:
No Preference

Additional Information
Year Founded: 1990
Current Activity Level : Actively seeking new investments

PINNACLE GROUP

145 Northfield Drive
Waterloo, Canada N2L 5J3
Phone: 519-746-3080
Fax: 519-888-6183

Type of Firm
Private Equity Firm

Additional Information
Year Founded: 1983
Current Activity Level : Actively seeking new investments

PINNACLE VENTURES

1600 El Camino Real, Suite 250
Menlo Park, CA USA 94025
Phone: 6509267800
Website: www.pinnacleven.com

Management and Staff
Arun Ramamoorthy, Partner
Donal Delaney, Chief Financial Officer
Kenneth Pelowski, Co-Founder
Robert Savoie, Co-Founder
Ted Wilson, Principal

Type of Firm
Private Equity Firm

Association Membership
Western Association of Venture Capitalists (WAVC)

Project Preferences

Type of Financing Preferred:
Early Stage
Expansion
Later Stage

Geographical Preferences

United States Preferences:

International Preferences:
Brazil

Industry Preferences

In Computer Software prefer:
Software

In Medical/Health prefer:
Medical/Health

In Industrial/Energy prefer:
Alternative Energy

Additional Information
Year Founded: 2002
Capital Under Management: $300,000,000
Current Activity Level : Actively seeking new investments

PINOVA CAPITAL GMBH

Rindermarkt 7
Munich, Germany 80331
Phone: 4989189425440
Fax: 4989189425469
Website: www.pinovacapital.com

Management and Staff
Joern Pelzer, Founder
Katrin Broekelmann, Founder
Marko Maschek, Founder
Martin Olbort, Founder

Type of Firm
Private Equity Firm

Association Membership
German Venture Capital Association (BVK)

Project Preferences

Type of Financing Preferred:
Leveraged Buyout
Turnaround
Later Stage
Recapitalizations

Size of Investments Considered:
Min Size of Investment Considered (000s): $3,873
Max Size of Investment Considered (000s): $19,367

Geographical Preferences

International Preferences:
Switzerland
Austria
Germany

Industry Preferences

In Medical/Health prefer:
Medical/Health

In Industrial/Energy prefer:
Industrial Products
Materials

In Transportation prefer:
Transportation

In Business Serv. prefer:
Services

In Other prefer:
Environment Responsible

Additional Information
Year Founded: 2007
Capital Under Management: $189,330,000
Current Activity Level : Actively seeking new investments

PINPOINT FUND

#33 Hua Yuan Shi Qiao Road
Room 1515, Citigroup Tower
Shanghai, China
Phone: 86-21-61682250
Fax: 86-21-61682256
E-mail: services@pinpointfund.com
Website: www.pinpointfund.com

Other Offices
3A Chater Road, Central, Suite 802-803, The Hong Kong Club Bldg.
Hong Kong, China
Phone: 852-25235990
Fax: 852-25235993

Type of Firm
Investment Management Firm

Project Preferences

Type of Financing Preferred:
Balanced

Geographical Preferences

International Preferences:
China

Industry Preferences

In Semiconductor/Electr prefer:
Electronic Components

In Industrial/Energy prefer:
Energy

In Transportation prefer:
Transportation

In Financial Services prefer:
Financial Services

Additional Information
Year Founded: 1999
Capital Under Management: $2,661,000
Current Activity Level : Actively seeking new investments

PIONEER BEIJING INVESTMENT FUND CO LTD

7 East Third Ring Middlle Road
3705 Tower A Fortune Plaza
Beijing, China 100010
Phone: 861065361255
Fax: 861065361256
E-mail: ktz@ktzpe.com
Website: www.ktzpe.com

Type of Firm
Private Equity Firm

Project Preferences

Type of Financing Preferred:
Leveraged Buyout

Geographical Preferences

International Preferences:
China

Industry Preferences

In Financial Services prefer:
Real Estate

In Business Serv. prefer:
Media

In Agr/Forestr/Fish prefer:
Mining and Minerals

Additional Information
Year Founded: 2012
Capital Under Management: $80,400,000
Current Activity Level : Actively seeking new investments

PIONEER CAPITAL PARTNERS AS

Heather Street
Parnell
Auckland, New Zealand 1052
Phone: 6493040870
Fax: 6493040871
Website: www.pioneercapital.co.nz

Other Offices
Level 14 Forsyth Barr House
764 Colombo Street
Christchurch, New Zealand

Management and Staff
Matthew Houtman, Managing Director
Randal Barrett, Managing Director

Type of Firm
Private Equity Firm

Association Membership
New Zealand Venture Capital Association

Project Preferences

Type of Financing Preferred:
Early Stage
Expansion
Balanced

Geographical Preferences

International Preferences:
New Zealand

Industry Preferences

In Manufact. prefer:
Manufacturing

Additional Information
Name of Most Recent Fund: Pioneer Capital Partners II
Most Recent Fund Was Raised: 07/01/2013
Year Founded: 1969
Capital Under Management: $211,246,000
Current Activity Level : Actively seeking new investments

PIONEER POINT PARTNERS LLP

12 Princes Street
Hanover Square
London, United Kingdom W1B 2LL
Phone: 442076293908
E-mail: info@pioneer-point.com
Website: www.pioneer-point.com

Management and Staff
Giuseppe Curatolo, Partner
Sam Abboud, Partner
Terrence Tehranian, Partner

Type of Firm
Private Equity Firm

Project Preferences

Type of Financing Preferred:
Leveraged Buyout
Expansion
Acquisition

Geographical Preferences

International Preferences:
United Kingdom
Europe

Industry Preferences

In Communications prefer:
Telecommunications
Media and Entertainment

In Industrial/Energy prefer:
Energy

Additional Information
Year Founded: 2008
Current Activity Level : Actively seeking new investments

PIONEER VENTURE PARTNERS LLC

520 Pike Street, Suite 2200
Seattle, WA USA 98101
E-mail: info@pvpartners.com
Website: www.pvpartners.com

Management and Staff
Ben Goux, Chief Financial Officer

Type of Firm
Private Equity Firm

Project Preferences

Type of Financing Preferred:
Early Stage
Seed

Geographical Preferences

United States Preferences:
Northwest

Industry Preferences

In Internet Specific prefer:
Web Aggregation/Portals

Additional Information
Year Founded: 1998
Current Activity Level : Actively seeking new investments

PIPELINE CAPITAL PARTNERS

2882 Sand Hill Road, Suite 150
Menlo Park, CA USA 94025
Phone: 2533366465
Website: www.pipeline.vc

Type of Firm
Private Equity Firm

Project Preferences

Type of Financing Preferred:
Seed

Additional Information
Year Founded: 2016
Capital Under Management: $17,590,000
Current Activity Level : Actively seeking new investments

PIPER JAFFRAY VENTURES INC

800 Nicollet Mall, Suite 800
Minneapolis, MN USA 55402
Phone: 6123036000
Fax: 6123031350

Other Offices

633 West Fifth Street, Suite 2800
Los Angeles, CA USA 90013

345 California Street, Suite 2400
San Francisco, CA USA 94104

2626 Cole Street, Suite 500
Dallas, TX USA 75204

140 Glastonbury Boulevard
Second Floor, Suite Ten
Glastonbury, CT USA 06033

1100 South Coast, Suite 300A, Highway
Laguna Beach, CA USA 92651

100 North 18th Street, Suite 1820, Two Logan Square
Philadelphia, PA USA 19103

750 East Mulberry Avenue, Suite 301, Trinity Plaza I
San Antonio, TX USA 78212

18 Division Street, Suite 301
Saratoga Springs, NY USA 12866

265 Franklin Street, Suite 710
Boston, MA USA 02110

101 South Tryon Street, Suite 2450
Charlotte, NC USA 28280

3900 Ingersoll Avenue, Suite 110
Des Moines, IA USA 50312

11150 Overbrook Road, Suite 310, One Hailbrook Place
Shawnee Mission, KS USA 66211

3200 West End Avenue, Suite 500
Nashville, TN USA 37203

601 Union Street, Suite 5010, Two Union Square
Seattle, WA USA 98101

159 Crocker Park Boulevard, Suite 416
Westlake, OH USA 44145

503 Martindale Street
Seventh Floor
Pittsburgh, PA USA 15212

88 Queensway, Admiralty, Suite 1308, 13/F, Two Pacific Place
Hong Kong, Hong Kong
Phone: 85237552288

111 Southwest Fifth Avenue, Suite 1900
Portland, OR USA 97204

101 West Ohio Street, Suite 2000
Indianapolis, IN USA 46204

One South Place
Fifth Floor
London, United Kingdom EC2M 2RB

8235 Forsyth Boulevard, Suite 600
Clayton, MO USA 63105

71 South Wacker Drive
24th Floor, Hyatt Center
Chicago, IL USA 60606

2525 East Camelback Road, Suite 925
Phoenix, AZ USA 85016

770 L Street, Suite 950, Pacific Business Centers
Sacramento, CA USA 95814

3238 Players Club Circle, Suite 59
Memphis, TN USA 38125

222 East Erie Street, Suite 230
Milwaukee, WI USA 53202

1200 17th Street, Suite 1250, Tabor Center
Denver, CO USA 80202

1100 Louisiana Avenue, Suite 4425
Houston, TX USA 77002

4250 Lakeside Drive, Suite 216
Jacksonville, FL USA 32210.

2321 Rosecrans Avenue, Suite 3200
El Segundo, CA USA 90245

345 Park Avenue, Suite 1200
New York, NY USA 10154

1950 University Avenue, Suite 200
East Palo Alto, CA USA 94303

Claridenstrasse 20
Zurich, Switzerland CH-8002

Management and Staff
Brad Winges, Managing Director
Brien O Brien, Managing Director
Chad Abraham, Managing Director
Christine Esckilsen, Managing Director
Francis Fairman, Managing Director
Jason Harkness, Managing Director
Jeffrey Klinefelter, Managing Director
Scott LaRue, Managing Director
Shawn Quant, Managing Director
Thomas Smith, Managing Director

Type of Firm
Private Equity Firm

Project Preferences

Role in Financing:
Prefer role as deal originator but will also invest in deals created by others

Type of Financing Preferred:
Fund of Funds
Leveraged Buyout
Mezzanine
Generalist PE
Balanced
Later Stage
Management Buyouts
Acquisition
Recapitalizations

Geographical Preferences

United States Preferences:

International Preferences:
All International

Industry Focus
(% based on actual investment)

Medical/Health	36.7%
Computer Software and Services	32.4%
Internet Specific	10.8%
Industrial/Energy	6.4%
Other Products	5.3%
Semiconductors/Other Elect.	4.2%
Consumer Related	2.0%
Biotechnology	1.3%
Computer Hardware	0.8%
Communications and Media	0.2%

Additional Information
Name of Most Recent Fund: Piper Jaffray Venture Fund IV, L.P.
Most Recent Fund Was Raised: 03/10/2009
Year Founded: 1895
Capital Under Management: $245,000,000
Current Activity Level : Actively seeking new investments
Method of Compensation: Return on investment is of primary concern, do not charge fees

PIPER PE LLP

182-184 Campden Hill Road
Eardley House
London, United Kingdom W8 7AS
Phone: 442077273842
Fax: 442077278969
E-mail: info@piperprivateequity.com
Website: www.piperprivateequity.com

Management and Staff
Christopher Curry, Managing Partner
George Adams, Partner
Libby Gibson, Co-Founder
Peter Kemp-Welch, Partner

Type of Firm
Private Equity Firm

Association Membership
British Venture Capital Association (BVCA)

Project Preferences

Type of Financing Preferred:
Second Stage Financing
Leveraged Buyout
Expansion
Management Buyouts
Acquisition

Size of Investments Considered:
Min Size of Investment Considered (000s): $4,694
Max Size of Investment Considered (000s): $23,468

Geographical Preferences

International Preferences:
United Kingdom
Europe

Industry Focus
(% based on actual investment)

Consumer Related	69.3%
Internet Specific	24.4%
Other Products	6.3%

Additional Information
Year Founded: 1988
Capital Under Management: $14,300,000
Current Activity Level : Actively seeking new investments

PITANGO VENTURE CAPITAL MANAGEMENT ISRAEL, LTD.

11 HaMenofim Street,
Building B
Herzliya, Israel 46725
Phone: 97299718100
Fax: 97299718102
E-mail: mail@pitango.com
Website: www.pitango.com

Other Offices
2929 Campus Drive, Suite 410
SAN MATEO, CA USA 94403
Phone: 650-357-9080
Fax: 650-357-9088

Management and Staff
Aaron Mankovski, Managing General Partner
Bruce Crocker, General Partner
Chemi Peres, Managing General Partner
David Israeli, Venture Partner
Eitan Bek, Partner
Isaac Hillel, Managing General Partner
Ittai Harel, Partner
Merav Weinryb, Principal
Rami Kalish, Managing General Partner
Rami Beracha, Managing General Partner
Rona Segev-Gal, General Partner
Ruti Alon, General Partner

Type of Firm
Private Equity Firm

Association Membership
Israel Venture Association
Western Association of Venture Capitalists (WAVC)

Project Preferences

Role in Financing:
Prefer role as deal originator but will also invest in deals created by others

Type of Financing Preferred:
Expansion
Later Stage
Seed

Geographical Preferences

United States Preferences:

International Preferences:
Asia Pacific
Europe
Israel
All International

Industry Focus
(% based on actual investment)

Computer Software and Services	31.5%
Internet Specific	15.3%
Medical/Health	15.0%
Semiconductors/Other Elect.	14.2%
Communications and Media	11.8%
Biotechnology	5.1%
Computer Hardware	4.1%
Industrial/Energy	1.7%
Other Products	0.7%
Consumer Related	0.6%

Additional Information
Name of Most Recent Fund: Pitango Venture Capital Fund VI, L.P.

Most Recent Fund Was Raised: 09/02/2012
Year Founded: 1993
Capital Under Management: $1,400,000,000
Current Activity Level : Actively seeking new investments

PITON CAPITAL LLP

27-29 Glasshouse Street
Fifth Floor, Venture House
London, United Kingdom W1B 5DF
Phone: 442074080451
Fax: 442072906699
E-mail: info@pitoncap.com
Website: pitoncap.com

Type of Firm
Private Equity Firm

Project Preferences

Type of Financing Preferred:
Later Stage
Seed

Geographical Preferences

International Preferences:
United Kingdom
Europe

Industry Preferences

In Communications prefer:
Communications and Media
Media and Entertainment

In Internet Specific prefer:
Internet

In Business Serv. prefer:
Services

Additional Information
Year Founded: 2011
Current Activity Level : Actively seeking new investments

PITT CAPITAL PARTNERS LTD

160 Pitt Street Mall, Level 2
Sydney, Australia 2000
Phone: 61292107000
Fax: 61292107099
E-mail: info@pittcapitalpartners.com.au
Website: www.pittcapitalpartners.com.au

Other Offices
459 Collins Street, Level 11
Melbourne, Australia 3000
Phone: 61-3-8669-0260
Fax: 61-3-8669-0264

Management and Staff
Hugh Williams, Managing Director
Jaime Pinto, Chief Financial Officer
Todd Barlow, Managing Director

Type of Firm
Bank Affiliated

Project Preferences

Role in Financing:
Will function either as deal originator or investor in deals created by others

Type of Financing Preferred:
Leveraged Buyout
Expansion
Generalist PE
Balanced
Recapitalizations

Size of Investments Considered:
Min Size of Investment Considered (000s): $381
Max Size of Investment Considered (000s): $15,254

Geographical Preferences

International Preferences:
Australia
New Zealand
Asia

Additional Information
Year Founded: 2002
Capital Under Management: $112,600,000
Current Activity Level : Actively seeking new investments
Method of Compensation: Return on invest. most important, but chg. closing fees, service fees, etc.

PITTSBURGH EQUITY PARTNERS LP

6507 Wilkins Avenue, Suite 209
Pittsburgh, PA USA 15217
Phone: 4122651325
E-mail: info@pghpep.com
Website: www.pghpep.com

Management and Staff
Edward Engler, Managing Partner
Stephen Robinson, Managing Partner

Type of Firm
Private Equity Firm

Project Preferences

Type of Financing Preferred:
Early Stage
Startup

Geographical Preferences

United States Preferences:
Pennsylvania
Ohio

Additional Information
Name of Most Recent Fund: Pittsburgh Equity Partners, L.P.
Most Recent Fund Was Raised: 04/01/2009
Year Founded: 2009
Capital Under Management: $6,500,000
Current Activity Level : Actively seeking new investments

PITTSBURGH LIFE SCIENCES GREENHOUSE

2425 Sidney Street
Pittsburgh, PA USA 15203
Phone: 4122017370
Fax: 4127701276
E-mail: info@plsg.com
Website: www.plsg.com

Management and Staff
Alan West, Venture Partner
John Brooks, Venture Partner
Lynn Banaszak Brusco, Vice President
Samuel Straface, Venture Partner

Type of Firm
Private Equity Firm

Association Membership
National Venture Capital Association - USA (NVCA)

Project Preferences

Type of Financing Preferred:
Early Stage
Balanced
Seed
Startup

Size of Investments Considered:
Min Size of Investment Considered (000s): $100
Max Size of Investment Considered (000s): $500

Geographical Preferences

United States Preferences:
Pennsylvania

Industry Preferences

In Biotechnology prefer:
Biotechnology

In Medical/Health prefer:
Medical/Health
Medical Diagnostics
Diagnostic Services
Medical Therapeutics
Other Therapeutic
Medical Products

Additional Information
Name of Most Recent Fund: PLSG Accelerator Fund LLC
Most Recent Fund Was Raised: 01/07/2011
Year Founded: 2002
Capital Under Management: $5,000,000
Current Activity Level : Actively seeking new investments

PIUMOC INVERSIONS SCR DE REGIMEN SIMPLIFICADO SA

Paseo De Barcelona, 6
Oficina 15
Girona, Spain 17800

Type of Firm
Private Equity Firm

Project Preferences

Type of Financing Preferred:
Balanced

Additional Information
Year Founded: 2013
Current Activity Level : Actively seeking new investments

PIVOT INVESTMENT PARTNERS LLC

25 Broadway, Suite 9019
New York, NY USA 10004
Phone: 6466813710
Website: pivotinvestment.com

Management and Staff
Akbar Poonawala, Partner
Dinkar Jetley, Partner

Type of Firm
Private Equity Firm

Project Preferences

Type of Financing Preferred:
Early Stage
Expansion

Geographical Preferences

United States Preferences:

International Preferences:
Europe

Industry Preferences

In Computer Software prefer:
Software

In Financial Services prefer:
Financial Services
Insurance

In Business Serv. prefer:
Services

Additional Information
Year Founded: 2014
Current Activity Level : Actively seeking new investments

PIVOTAL BIOVENTURE PARTNERS LLC

1700 Owens Street, Suite 595
San Francisco, CA USA 94158
Phone: 4156971002
E-mail: info@pivotalbiovp.com
Website: pivotalbiovp.com

Management and Staff
Karoly Nikoloch, Venture Partner
Tracy Saxton, Managing Partner
Vincent Cheung, Managing Partner

Type of Firm
Private Equity Firm

Project Preferences

Type of Financing Preferred:
Early Stage

Industry Preferences

In Biotechnology prefer:
Biotechnology

In Medical/Health prefer:
Medical/Health
Medical Therapeutics

Additional Information
Year Founded: 2017
Capital Under Management: $300,000,000
Current Activity Level : Actively seeking new investments

PIVOTAL CAPITAL PARTNERS LLC

2882 Sand Hill Rd
#100
Menlo Park, CA USA 94025
E-mail: contact@pivotalcp.com
Website: www.pivotalcp.com

Type of Firm
Private Equity Firm

Project Preferences

Type of Financing Preferred:
Early Stage

Additional Information
Year Founded: 2016
Current Activity Level : Actively seeking new investments

PIVOTAL GROUP INC

3200 East Camelback Road, Suite 295
Phoenix, AZ USA 85018
Phone: 6029567200
Fax: 6029562313
Website: www.pivotalgroupinc.com

Management and Staff
Ayman Zameli, Managing Director
Jerry Pence, Managing Director
Rich Sonntag, Managing Director
Richard Garner, Chief Financial Officer
Scott Knauer, Managing Director

Type of Firm
Private Equity Firm

Project Preferences

Type of Financing Preferred:
Leveraged Buyout
Value-Add
Acquisition
Recapitalizations

Geographical Preferences

United States Preferences:
West Coast
Southwest

Industry Preferences

In Communications prefer:
Telecommunications

In Transportation prefer:
Aerospace

In Financial Services prefer:
Financial Services
Real Estate

In Business Serv. prefer:
Services
Media

Additional Information
Year Founded: 2011
Current Activity Level : Actively seeking new investments

PIVOTAL INVESTMENTS LLC

108 North West Ninth Avenue, Suite 201
Portland, OR USA 97209
Phone: 5035390294
Website: www.pivotal-investments.com

Management and Staff
Bradley Zenger, Co-Founder
John Miner, Managing Director

Type of Firm
Private Equity Firm

Project Preferences

Role in Financing:
Prefer role as deal originator but will also invest in deals created by others

Pratt's Guide to Private Equity & Venture Capital Sources

Type of Financing Preferred:
Early Stage
Seed

Geographical Preferences

United States Preferences:
Northwest
Idaho
Washington
Montana

Canadian Preferences:
All Canada

Industry Preferences

In Industrial/Energy prefer:
Materials

In Other prefer:
Environment Responsible

Additional Information
Name of Most Recent Fund: Pivotal Investments I, LP
Most Recent Fund Was Raised: 06/16/2010
Year Founded: 2008
Capital Under Management: $17,250,000,000
Current Activity Level : Actively seeking new investments

PIVOTNORTH CAPITAL

3000 Sand Hill Road, Suite 230, Building 3
Menlo Park, CA USA 94025
Phone: 6502068068
Website: www.pivotnorth.com

Management and Staff
Timothy Conners, Managing Partner

Type of Firm
Private Equity Firm

Project Preferences

Type of Financing Preferred:
Early Stage
Seed

Size of Investments Considered:
Min Size of Investment Considered (000s): $100
Max Size of Investment Considered (000s): $3,000

Geographical Preferences

United States Preferences:

Industry Preferences

In Computer Software prefer:
Software

In Consumer Related prefer:
Consumer

Additional Information
Name of Most Recent Fund: PivotNorth Fund I, L.P.
Most Recent Fund Was Raised: 03/31/2011
Year Founded: 2010
Capital Under Management: $35,000,000
Current Activity Level : Actively seeking new investments

PIX VINE CAPITAL PTE LTD

30 Toh Guan Road East
Unit 2, Enterprise Hub
Singapore, Singapore 608577
Phone: 6565594640
E-mail: contact@pixvc.com
Website: www.pixvc.com

Management and Staff
Fang Soong Chou, General Partner
Patrick De Silva, Partner

Type of Firm
Private Equity Firm

Project Preferences

Type of Financing Preferred:
Early Stage

Geographical Preferences

International Preferences:
Asia Pacific
Israel
Asia

Industry Preferences

In Medical/Health prefer:
Medical/Health

Additional Information
Year Founded: 2007
Current Activity Level : Actively seeking new investments

PLATAFORMA CAPITAL PARTNERS GESTAO DE INVESTIMENTOS LTDA

Av. Dr. Cardoso de Melo 1460, 12th Floor
Sao Paulo, Brazil 04548005
Phone: 551130474647
Fax: 551130474646
E-mail: info@pcapital.com.br
Website: www.pcapital.com.br

Other Offices
Olimpia Sao Paulo
Georgetown, Spain 04548

Management and Staff
Anibal Messa, Managing Partner
Antonio Henrique Prado, Partner
Franco Pontillo, Partner

Type of Firm
Private Equity Firm

Project Preferences

Type of Financing Preferred:
Early Stage
Seed
Startup

Geographical Preferences

International Preferences:
Brazil

Industry Preferences

In Communications prefer:
Communications and Media

In Computer Hardware prefer:
Computers

In Computer Software prefer:
Software

In Semiconductor/Electr prefer:
Electronics
Electronic Components

Additional Information
Year Founded: 1999
Current Activity Level : Actively seeking new investments

PLATFORM PARTNERS INVESTMENT COMPANY LLC

600 Travis, Suite 6160
Houston, TX USA 77002
Phone: 7133352300
Fax: 7133352310
Website: www.platformllc.com

Management and Staff
Frederick Brazelton, President
Scott Nichols, Vice President

Type of Firm
Private Equity Firm

Project Preferences

Type of Financing Preferred:
Leveraged Buyout
Management Buyouts
Acquisition
Recapitalizations

Geographical Preferences

United States Preferences:

Industry Preferences

In Communications prefer:
Radio & TV Broadcasting
Telecommunications

In Consumer Related prefer:
Retail

In Industrial/Energy prefer:
Industrial Products

In Financial Services prefer:
Financial Services

In Business Serv. prefer:
Distribution
Media

Additional Information
Year Founded: 2006
Current Activity Level : Actively seeking new investments

PLATINA FINANCE, LTD.

20 Manchester Square
London, United Kingdom W1U 3PZ
Phone: 442070429600
Fax: 442070429601
E-mail: info@platinapartners.com
Website: www.platinapartners.com

Other Offices
3 Via Ulrico Hoepli
Milan, Italy 20121
Phone: 390236515075
Fax: 390236518517

32 Rue La Boetie
Paris, France 75008
Phone: 33176773500
Fax: 33176773535

Management and Staff
Alexandre Labouret, Partner
Emma Collins, Managing Partner
Fabien Castello, Managing Partner
Jerome Girszyn, Partner
Mikael Schoultz, Partner
Riccardo Cirillo, Partner
Thomas Rottner, Managing Partner

Type of Firm
Private Equity Firm

Association Membership
French Venture Capital Association (AFIC)
European Private Equity and Venture Capital Assoc.

Project Preferences

Type of Financing Preferred:
Leveraged Buyout
Early Stage
Balanced
Other
Management Buyouts

Geographical Preferences

International Preferences:
Europe

Industry Preferences

In Industrial/Energy prefer:
Energy
Alternative Energy

Additional Information
Year Founded: 2002
Capital Under Management: $490,800,000
Current Activity Level : Actively seeking new investments

PLATINUM EQUITY LLC

360 North Crescent Drive
Beverly Hills, CA USA 90210
Phone: 3107121850
Fax: 3107121848
Website: www.platinumequity.com

Other Offices
Berkeley Square House
2nd Floor
London, United Kingdom W1J 6BD
Phone: 44-20-7887-7877

52 Vanderbilt Avenue,
21st Floor
New York, NY USA 10017
Phone: 212-905-0010

Management and Staff
Adam Cooper, Principal
Bastian Lueken, Principal
Bryan Kelln, Partner
Dan Krasner, Principal
Dave Aroesty, Principal
Eric Worley, Principal
Eva Kalawski, Partner
Jacok Kotzubei, Partner
Jason Leach, Principal
Johnny Lopez, Founder
Louis Samson, Partner
Luke Johnson, Principal
Mark Barnhill, Partner
Mark Wiesenthal, Principal
Mary Sigler, Chief Financial Officer
Matt Young, Principal
Mike Scott, Principal
Paul Bridwell, Principal
Robert Wymbs, Principal
Robert Klap, Principal
Roger House, Principal
Scott McCarthy, Principal
Steve Zollo, Principal

Type of Firm
Private Equity Firm

Project Preferences

Type of Financing Preferred:
Leveraged Buyout
Turnaround
Acquisition

Geographical Preferences

United States Preferences:
North America

International Preferences:
Western Europe

Industry Focus
(% based on actual investment)
Other Products	66.8%
Consumer Related	10.8%
Computer Software and Services	8.1%
Industrial/Energy	7.7%
Communications and Media	3.4%
Computer Hardware	2.8%
Internet Specific	0.4%

Additional Information
Year Founded: 1995
Capital Under Management: $10,250,000,000
Current Activity Level : Actively seeking new investments

PLATTE RIVER VENTURES LLC

200 Fillmore Street, Suite 200
Denver, CO USA 80206
Phone: 3032927300
Fax: 3032927310
E-mail: info@platteriverventures.com
Website: www.platteriverequity.com

Management and Staff
Andrew Gustin, Principal
Derria Banta, Managing Director
Edward Hutcheson, Managing Director
Gregory Sissel, Managing Director
J. Landis Martin, Founder
James Moore, Vice President
Kristian Whalen, Managing Director
Mark Brown, Principal
Michelle Eidson, Vice President
Peter Calamari, Managing Director
Timothy Grein, Principal
William Robb, Managing Director

Type of Firm
Private Equity Firm

Project Preferences

Type of Financing Preferred:
Leveraged Buyout
Management Buyouts
Acquisition
Recapitalizations

Size of Investments Considered:
Min Size of Investment Considered (000s): $5,000
Max Size of Investment Considered (000s): $40,000

Industry Preferences

In Industrial/Energy prefer:
Alternative Energy
Industrial Products
Materials

In Transportation prefer:
Aerospace

In Business Serv. prefer:
Services

In Manufact. prefer:
Manufacturing

Additional Information
Name of Most Recent Fund: Platte River Equity III, L.P.
Most Recent Fund Was Raised: 08/15/2012
Year Founded: 2005
Capital Under Management: $75,000,000
Current Activity Level : Actively seeking new investments

PLAYGROUND GLOBAL LLC

380 Portage Avenue
Palo Alto, CA USA 94306
Phone: 6504270000
Website: playground.global

Management and Staff
Bruce Leak, Co-Founder
Jory Bell, Vice President
Kristin Beach, Chief Financial Officer
Matt Hershenson, Co-Founder

Type of Firm
Incubator/Development Program

Project Preferences

Type of Financing Preferred:
Seed

Industry Preferences

In Computer Software prefer:
Software

Additional Information
Year Founded: 2015
Capital Under Management: $54,000,000
Current Activity Level : Actively seeking new investments

PLAYGROUND VENTURES GP LLC

399 Main Street
Los Altos, CA USA 94022
Phone: 6504270000
Website: www.playground.global

Management and Staff
Kristin Beach, Chief Financial Officer
Mark Valdez, Principal

Type of Firm
Private Equity Firm

Association Membership
National Venture Capital Association – USA (NVCA)

Project Preferences

Type of Financing Preferred:
Balanced

Additional Information
Year Founded: 2015
Capital Under Management: $800,000,000
Current Activity Level : Actively seeking new investments

PLAZA VENTURES LTD

Ten Wanless Avenue, Suite 201
Toronto, Canada M4N 1V6
Phone: 4164812222
Fax: 4164818000
Website: www.plazaventures.ca

Management and Staff
Daniel Brothman, Co-Founder
Jesse Kaplan, Partner
Matthew Leibowitz, Partner
Robert Richards, Managing Partner

Type of Firm
Private Equity Firm

Project Preferences

Type of Financing Preferred:
Seed

Geographical Preferences

Canadian Preferences:
Quebec

Industry Preferences

In Internet Specific prefer:
Internet

In Business Serv. prefer:
Media

Additional Information
Year Founded: 1998
Current Activity Level : Actively seeking new investments

PLEASANT BAY CAPITAL PARTNERS LLC

265 Franklin Street
Boston, MA USA 02110
Phone: 6173143911
Website: www.pleasantbaycp.com

Management and Staff
James Vandervelden, Founder
Scott Fisher, Managing Director

Type of Firm
Bank Affiliated

Project Preferences

Type of Financing Preferred:
Leveraged Buyout
Acquisition
Recapitalizations

Industry Preferences

In Computer Software prefer:
Software

In Medical/Health prefer:
Medical/Health
Medical Products
Health Services

In Consumer Related prefer:
Consumer

In Business Serv. prefer:
Services

Additional Information
Year Founded: 2012
Current Activity Level : Actively seeking new investments

PLEIADE INVESTISSEMENT SAS

29 rue de Miromesnil
Paris, France 75008
Phone: 0033142256485
Fax: 0033142256465
Website: www.pleiadeventure.com

Type of Firm
Private Equity Firm

Association Membership
French Venture Capital Association (AFIC)

Project Preferences

Type of Financing Preferred:
Early Stage
Later Stage
Acquisition
Startup

Geographical Preferences

International Preferences:
Europe
France

Industry Preferences

In Consumer Related prefer:
Consumer Products
Consumer Services

Additional Information

Year Founded: 1999
Current Activity Level : Actively seeking new investments

PLENIUM PARTNERS SL

Velazquez 47
7th Floor
Madrid, Spain 28001
Phone: 34914449980
Fax: 34914364910
Website: www.pleniumpartners.com

Type of Firm
Bank Affiliated

Project Preferences

Type of Financing Preferred:
Leveraged Buyout
Acquisition

Industry Preferences

In Communications prefer:
Communications and Media

In Industrial/Energy prefer:
Energy

In Transportation prefer:
Transportation

In Business Serv. prefer:
Services

Additional Information

Year Founded: 2007
Current Activity Level : Actively seeking new investments

PLEXUS CAPITAL LLC

200 Providence Road
Second Floor, Suite 210
Charlotte, NC USA 28207
Phone: 7049276245
Fax: 7049276255
Website: www.plexuscap.com

Other Offices

4601 Six Forks Road, Suite 528
Raleigh, NC USA 27609
Phone: 919-256-6340
Fax: 919-256-6350

Management and Staff

Alex Bean, Vice President
Bob Anders, Co-Founder
Kel Landis, Co-Founder
Michael Painter, Managing Partner
Michael Becker, Co-Founder
Robert Gefaell, Co-Founder
Ronda Penn, Chief Financial Officer
Will Anders, Vice President

Type of Firm
Private Equity Firm

Association Membership
Natl Assoc of Small Bus. Inv. Co (NASBIC)

Project Preferences

Type of Financing Preferred:
Leveraged Buyout
Management Buyouts
Acquisition
Recapitalizations

Geographical Preferences

United States Preferences:
Mid Atlantic
Southeast

Industry Preferences

In Consumer Related prefer:
Consumer Services

In Business Serv. prefer:
Distribution

In Manufact. prefer:
Manufacturing

Additional Information

Name of Most Recent Fund: Plexus Fund III, L.P.
Most Recent Fund Was Raised: 03/07/2013
Year Founded: 2005
Capital Under Management: $26,900,000
Current Activity Level : Actively seeking new investments

PLUG AND PLAY TECH CENTER

440 N Wolfe Road
Sunnyvale, CA USA 94085
Phone: 4085241400
Website: www.plugandplaytechcenter.com

Type of Firm
Incubator/Development Program

Project Preferences

Type of Financing Preferred:
Early Stage
Startup

Geographical Preferences

United States Preferences:

International Preferences:
All International

Additional Information

Year Founded: 2006
Current Activity Level : Actively seeking new investments

PLUS EIGHT CAPITAL MANAGEMENT LLC

214 E 24th Street
New York, NY USA 10010
E-mail: info@plus8equity.com
Website: plus8equity.com

Management and Staff

John Acquaviva, Co-Founder
Rishi Patel, Co-Founder

Type of Firm
Private Equity Firm

Project Preferences

Type of Financing Preferred:
Early Stage

Industry Preferences

In Semiconductor/Electr prefer:
Electronic Components

Additional Information

Year Founded: 2014
Current Activity Level : Actively seeking new investments

PLYMOUTH VENTURE PARTNERS

717 East Huron Street, Suite 2E
Ann Arbor, MI USA 48104
Phone: 7347479401
Fax: 7349291811
E-mail: info@plymouthventurepartners.com

Other Offices

100 Main Street
NORTHWOOD, OH USA 43605
Phone: 4192059000
Fax: 8666961492

Management and Staff

Bob Savage, Partner
Christopher Frick, Chief Financial Officer
Evan Ufer, Partner
Jeff Barry, Partner
Jeffery Barry, Partner
Kevin Terrasi, Partner

Pratt's Guide to Private Equity & Venture Capital Sources

Type of Firm
Private Equity Firm

Project Preferences

Role in Financing:
Will function either as deal originator or investor in deals created by others

Type of Financing Preferred:
Expansion
Later Stage

Size of Investments Considered:
Min Size of Investment Considered (000s): $1,000
Max Size of Investment Considered (000s): $5,000

Geographical Preferences

United States Preferences:
Illinois
Pennsylvania
Michigan
Ohio
Wisconsin
Indiana
Minnesota
New York

Additional Information
Name of Most Recent Fund: Plymouth Venture Partners III, L.P.
Most Recent Fund Was Raised: 03/31/2014
Year Founded: 2002
Capital Under Management: $149,500,000
Current Activity Level : Actively seeking new investments
Method of Compensation: Return on invest. most important, but chg. closing fees, service fees, etc.

PM & PARTNERS SPA

via Senato,12
Milan, Italy 20121
Phone: 3927249041
Fax: 39272490440
E-mail: pmp@pm-partners.it
Website: www.pm-partners.it

Other Offices
via Campania, n 59
Roma, Italy 00187
Phone: 39-6-420-3621
Fax: 39-6-4203-6240

Management and Staff
Andrea Mugnai, Co-Founder
Massimo Grasselli, Managing Partner
Riccardo Rainone, Partner

Type of Firm
Private Equity Firm

Project Preferences

Type of Financing Preferred:
Leveraged Buyout
Acquisition

Geographical Preferences

International Preferences:
Italy

Industry Focus
(% based on actual investment)
Other Products 49.4%
Computer Software and Services 45.5%
Medical/Health 5.1%

Additional Information
Year Founded: 2000
Capital Under Management: $291,900,000
Current Activity Level : Actively seeking new investments

PNC EQUITY MANAGEMENT CORP

620 Liberty Avenue
22nd Floor, Two PNC Plaza
Pittsburgh, PA USA 15222
Phone: 4127622289
Fax: 4127053669

Management and Staff
David Mcl. Hillman, President
John Glover, Partner
Justin Bertram, Founder
Leon Rubinov, Principal
Wangdali Bacdayan, Partner

Type of Firm
Bank Affiliated

Project Preferences

Role in Financing:
Will function either as deal originator or investor in deals created by others

Type of Financing Preferred:
Leveraged Buyout
Mezzanine
Generalist PE
Balanced
Later Stage
Acquisition
Recapitalizations

Geographical Preferences

United States Preferences:

Canadian Preferences:
All Canada

Industry Focus
(% based on actual investment)
Other Products 31.1%
Communications and Media 22.3%
Industrial/Energy 15.1%
Medical/Health 11.2%
Internet Specific 8.1%
Consumer Related 7.6%
Computer Software and Services 3.2%
Semiconductors/Other Elect. 1.0%
Biotechnology 0.2%
Computer Hardware 0.2%

Additional Information
Name of Most Recent Fund: PNC Mezzanine Partners III, L.P.
Most Recent Fund Was Raised: 10/14/2005
Year Founded: 1982
Capital Under Management: $972,000,000
Current Activity Level : Actively seeking new investments

POALIM ASIA DIRECT LTD

4 Guanghua Road,Chaoyang Dist
1806, A, Oriental Media Center
Beijing, China 100026
Phone: 861065818018
Fax: 861065818028
E-mail: sean@pcmasiadirect.com
Website: www.pcmasiadirect.com

Other Offices
46 Rothschild Blvd.
Alrov Tower
Tel Aviv, Israel
Phone: 97235675959
Fax: 97235675760

Type of Firm
Bank Affiliated

Project Preferences

Type of Financing Preferred:
Early Stage
Expansion
Generalist PE
Turnaround
Later Stage
Distressed Debt

Geographical Preferences

International Preferences:
China

Industry Preferences

In Medical/Health prefer:
Drug/Equipmt Delivery

In Consumer Related prefer:
Consumer Products

In Industrial/Energy prefer:
Alternative Energy
Materials
Environmental Related

In Transportation prefer:
Transportation

In Financial Services prefer:
Financial Services

In Agr/Forestr/Fish prefer:
Agriculture related

Additional Information
Year Founded: 2001
Current Activity Level : Actively seeking new investments

POALIM CAP MARK TECH, LTD.

46 Rothschild Boulevard
Al Rov Tower
Tel Aviv, Israel 66883
Phone: 97235675333
Fax: 97235675760
E-mail: info@pcm.co.il
Website: www.pcm.co.il

Management and Staff
Ami Samuels, Managing Director
Dan Cohen, Founder
Eran Gersht, Managing Director
Hannah Feuer, Chief Financial Officer
Oren Yahav, Managing Director
Roy David, Managing Director

Type of Firm
Bank Affiliated

Association Membership
Israel Venture Association

Project Preferences

Type of Financing Preferred:
Leveraged Buyout
Value-Add
Early Stage
Expansion
Mezzanine
Generalist PE
Balanced
Turnaround
Later Stage
Distressed Debt
Recapitalizations

Size of Investments Considered:
Min Size of Investment Considered (000s): $3,000
Max Size of Investment Considered (000s): $7,000

Geographical Preferences

International Preferences:
Czech Republic
Rest of World
Eastern Europe
Israel
Romania

Industry Preferences

In Medical/Health prefer:
Health Services

In Industrial/Energy prefer:
Alternative Energy

In Financial Services prefer:
Real Estate

Additional Information
Year Founded: 1990
Capital Under Management: $1,500,000,000
Current Activity Level : Actively seeking new investments

POIBOS VENTURE CAPITAL

120-8, Samseong 2-dong
2/F, Haepyeong Bldg, Gangnam
Seoul, South Korea 135509
Phone: 8225643635
Fax: 8225643675

Type of Firm
Corporate PE/Venture

Project Preferences

Type of Financing Preferred:
Balanced

Geographical Preferences

International Preferences:
Asia

Industry Preferences

In Communications prefer:
Entertainment

Additional Information
Year Founded: 1999
Capital Under Management: $10,800,000
Current Activity Level : Actively seeking new investments

POINCARE GESTION SAS

7, Rue De Serre
Nancy, France 54000
Phone: 33383324837
Fax: 33383320321
E-mail: contact@fonds-gei.com
Website: www.fonds-gei.com

Management and Staff
Serge Peiffer, President

Type of Firm
Private Equity Firm

Project Preferences

Type of Financing Preferred:
Leveraged Buyout
Early Stage
Generalist PE
Later Stage
Management Buyouts
Acquisition

Geographical Preferences

International Preferences:
Europe
France

Industry Preferences

In Industrial/Energy prefer:
Energy
Alternative Energy
Industrial Products
Environmental Related

In Business Serv. prefer:
Services

In Other prefer:
Environment Responsible

Additional Information
Year Founded: 2010
Capital Under Management: $73,187,000
Current Activity Level : Actively seeking new investments

POINT B CAPITAL LLC

300 East Pine Street
Seattle, WA USA 98122
Phone: 2065777221
E-mail: info@pointbcap.com
Website: www.pointb.com

Management and Staff
Brian Armstrong, Partner
Dennin Brasch, Managing Director
Henry Lin, Managing Director
John Bjornson, President
Joseph Piper, Managing Director

Type of Firm
Private Equity Firm

Project Preferences

Type of Financing Preferred:
Early Stage
Generalist PE
Seed
Acquisition

Additional Information
Year Founded: 2011
Current Activity Level : Actively seeking new investments

POINT GUARD VENTURES LLC

One First Street, Suite 16
Los Altos, CA USA 94022
Phone: 6508435000
E-mail: info@pointguardventures.com
Website: www.pointguardventures.com

Type of Firm
Private Equity Firm

Project Preferences

Type of Financing Preferred:
Early Stage

Additional Information
Year Founded: 2014
Capital Under Management: $50,000,000
Current Activity Level : Actively seeking new investments

POINT JUDITH CAPITAL

211 Congress Street, Suite 210
Boston, MA USA 02110
Phone: 6176006260
E-mail: info@pointjudithcapital.com
Website: www.pointjudithcapital.com

Management and Staff
David Mixer, Co-Founder
David Martirano, Co-Founder
Sean Marsh, Co-Founder
Zaid Ashai, General Partner

Type of Firm
Private Equity Firm

Association Membership
New England Venture Capital Association
National Venture Capital Association - USA (NVCA)

Project Preferences

Role in Financing:
Prefer role as deal originator but will also invest in deals created by others

Type of Financing Preferred:
Early Stage

Size of Investments Considered:
Min Size of Investment Considered (000s): $500
Max Size of Investment Considered (000s): $3,000

Industry Preferences

In Computer Software prefer:
Software

In Internet Specific prefer:
Internet

In Medical/Health prefer:
Medical/Health

In Industrial/Energy prefer:
Energy

In Business Serv. prefer:
Services

Additional Information
Name of Most Recent Fund: Point Judith Venture Fund III, L.P.
Most Recent Fund Was Raised: 12/11/2012
Year Founded: 2001
Capital Under Management: $96,000,000
Current Activity Level : Actively seeking new investments
Method of Compensation: Return on investment is of primary concern, do not charge fees

POINTBREAK PRIVATE EQUITY

99 Jip de Jager Drive
Vineyards Office Estate
Bellville, South Africa 7536
Phone: 27-21-912-4000
Fax: 27-21-912-4040
E-mail: info@pointbreak.co.za
Website: www.pointbreak.co.za

Other Offices
Sam Nujoma Drive
1st Floor, Woerman Brock Mall
Swakopmund, Namibia
Phone: 264-64-405-164

24 Orban Street
Klein Windhoek
Windhoek, Namibia
Phone: 264-61-371-660

Management and Staff
John Hamman, Founding Partner
Pieter Laubscher, Founding Partner
Rein Van Veen, Founder

Type of Firm
Private Equity Firm

Project Preferences

Type of Financing Preferred:
Leveraged Buyout
Early Stage
Balanced
Seed
Management Buyouts
Startup

Size of Investments Considered:
Min Size of Investment Considered (000s): $37
Max Size of Investment Considered (000s): $622

Geographical Preferences

International Preferences:
South Africa
Africa

Additional Information
Year Founded: 2000
Current Activity Level : Actively seeking new investments

POITOU CHARENTES EXPANSION SAS

8 Rue du Pre- Medard
Saint- Benoit, France 86280
Phone: 33549525809
Fax: 33549504895
E-mail: P.C.E@wanadoo.fr

Type of Firm
Private Equity Firm

Project Preferences

Type of Financing Preferred:
Leveraged Buyout
Early Stage
Generalist PE
Later Stage
Acquisition

Geographical Preferences

International Preferences:
Europe
France

Industry Preferences

In Medical/Health prefer:
Medical/Health

In Industrial/Energy prefer:
Energy
Environmental Related

In Business Serv. prefer:
Services

In Other prefer:
Environment Responsible

Additional Information
Year Founded: 1994
Capital Under Management: $8,200,000
Current Activity Level : Actively seeking new investments

POITOU-CHARENTES INNOVATION SAS

3, Rue Raoul Follereau
Poitiers, France 86000
Website: www.bpifrance.fr

Type of Firm
Government Affiliated Program

Project Preferences

Type of Financing Preferred:
Early Stage
Seed

Size of Investments Considered:
Min Size of Investment Considered (000s): $207
Max Size of Investment Considered (000s): $690

Geographical Preferences

International Preferences:
France

Industry Preferences

In Biotechnology prefer:
Biotechnology

In Consumer Related prefer:
Consumer Services

In Industrial/Energy prefer:
Energy
Environmental Related

In Other prefer:
Environment Responsible

Additional Information
Year Founded: 1998
Current Activity Level : Actively seeking new investments

POLAR CAPITAL INVESTMENTS

401 Bay Street, Suite 1900, PO Box 19
Toronto, Canada M5H 2Y4
Phone: 4163674364
E-mail: info@polarcapital.com
Website: www.polarcapital.com

Other Offices
205 - 5th Avenue SW, Suite 3710, Bow Valley Square 2
Calgary, Canada T2P 2V7
Phone: 4037057300

Management and Staff
Jerry Jackson, Partner
Richard Vaughan, Principal
Steve Mulherin, Partner

Type of Firm
Private Equity Firm

Project Preferences

Type of Financing Preferred:
Leveraged Buyout
Expansion
Generalist PE
Turnaround
Acquisition

Size of Investments Considered:
Min Size of Investment Considered (000s): $2,000
Max Size of Investment Considered (000s): $15,000

Geographical Preferences

United States Preferences:

Canadian Preferences:
All Canada

International Preferences:
United Kingdom

Industry Preferences

In Computer Software prefer:
Applications Software

In Medical/Health prefer:
Health Services

In Industrial/Energy prefer:
Alternative Energy
Industrial Products

In Business Serv. prefer:
Services

In Manufact. prefer:
Manufacturing

Additional Information
Year Founded: 1995
Current Activity Level : Actively seeking new investments

POLARIS CAPITAL GROUP CO LTD

2-4-1, Yaesu, Chuo-Ku
7F, Jowa Yaesu Building
Tokyo, Japan 1040028
Phone: 81362255040
E-mail: info@polaris-cg.com
Website: www.polaris-cg.com

Management and Staff
Sotaro Inose, Managing Director

Type of Firm
Private Equity Firm

Project Preferences

Type of Financing Preferred:
Leveraged Buyout
Expansion
Generalist PE
Recapitalizations

Geographical Preferences

International Preferences:
Japan

Industry Preferences

In Communications prefer:
Entertainment

In Consumer Related prefer:
Retail
Consumer Products

In Transportation prefer:
Transportation

In Financial Services prefer:
Financial Services

In Business Serv. prefer:
Services
Media

In Manufact. prefer:
Manufacturing

Additional Information
Year Founded: 2004
Capital Under Management: $1,700,000
Current Activity Level : Actively seeking new investments

POLARIS MANAGEMENT A/S

Malmogade 3
Copenhagen, Denmark 2100
Phone: 4535263574
Fax: 4535263594
E-mail: polaris@polarisequity.dk
Website: www.polarisequity.dk

Management and Staff
Allan Bach Pedersen, Partner
Jan Dahlqvist, Partner
Jan Kuhl, Managing Partner
Niels Worning, Partner
Peter Ankerst, Partner

Type of Firm
Private Equity Firm

Association Membership
Danish Venture Capital Association (DVCA)
Swedish Venture Capital Association (SVCA)
European Private Equity and Venture Capital Assoc.

Project Preferences

Role in Financing:
Prefer role as deal originator but will also invest in deals created by others

Type of Financing Preferred:
Leveraged Buyout
Turnaround
Management Buyouts
Recapitalizations

Size of Investments Considered:
Min Size of Investment Considered (000s): $20,599
Max Size of Investment Considered (000s): $205,987

Industry Focus
(% based on actual investment)
Consumer Related	59.1%
Medical/Health	37.6%
Internet Specific	3.3%

Additional Information
Year Founded: 1998
Capital Under Management: $842,900,000
Current Activity Level : Actively seeking new investments

POLARIS VENTURE PARTNERS

One Marina Park Drive
Tenth Floor
Boston, MA USA 02210
Website: www.polarispartners.com

Other Offices

Grand Canal Dock, The Warehouse
35 Barrow Street
Dublin, Ireland
Phone: 353.1.901.0336

One Marina Park Drive
Tenth Floor
BOSTON, MA USA 02210
Phone: 8557873500

One Letterman Drive
Building C, Suite C3600
SAN FRANCISCO, CA USA 94129
Phone: 8557873500

1000 Winter Street, Suite 3350
WALTHAM, MA USA 02451

Management and Staff
Alan Spoon, General Partner
Alan Crane, General Partner
Amir Nashat, General Partner
Brian Chee, General Partner
Bryce Youngren, General Partner
David Barrett, General Partner
George Conrades, Venture Partner
Jason Trevisan, General Partner
John Gannon, General Partner
Jonathan Flint, Co-Founder
Kevin Bitterman, Principal
Peter Flint, General Partner
Robert Metcalfe, General Partner
Ryan Spoon, Principal
Ryan Woodley, Principal

Stephen Arnold, Venture Partner
Terrance McGuire, Co-Founder

Type of Firm
Private Equity Firm

Association Membership
New England Venture Capital Association
National Venture Capital Association - USA (NVCA)

Project Preferences

Role in Financing:
Prefer role as deal originator but will also invest in deals created by others

Type of Financing Preferred:
Leveraged Buyout
Early Stage
Expansion
Balanced
Later Stage
Seed

Industry Focus
(% based on actual investment)
Internet Specific	25.5%
Computer Software and Services	22.1%
Biotechnology	20.5%
Medical/Health	17.2%
Consumer Related	3.8%
Semiconductors/Other Elect.	3.2%
Communications and Media	2.8%
Other Products	1.8%
Computer Hardware	1.7%
Industrial/Energy	1.4%

Additional Information
Name of Most Recent Fund: Polaris Venture Partners VI, L.P.
Most Recent Fund Was Raised: 06/07/2010
Year Founded: 1996
Capital Under Management: $3,500,000,000
Current Activity Level : Actively seeking new investments
Method of Compensation: Return on investment is of primary concern, do not charge fees

POLE CAPITAL SAS

Three, Rue Paul Cezanne
Paris, France 75008
Phone: 33153059444
E-mail: info@polecapital.com
Website: www.polecapital.com

Management and Staff
Andre Raoul, President, Founder

Type of Firm
Private Equity Firm

Project Preferences

Type of Financing Preferred:
Early Stage
Later Stage

Geographical Preferences

International Preferences:
Europe
France

Industry Preferences

In Communications prefer:
Telecommunications

In Internet Specific prefer:
Internet

In Consumer Related prefer:
Entertainment and Leisure

In Industrial/Energy prefer:
Alternative Energy
Environmental Related

In Business Serv. prefer:
Media

In Other prefer:
Environment Responsible

Additional Information
Year Founded: 2010
Current Activity Level : Actively seeking new investments

POLYTECH VENTURES & CIE SCPC

Parc scientifique EPFL
Batiment E
Ecublens, Switzerland 1015
Phone: 41216939210
E-mail: info@polytechventures.ch
Website: www.polytechventures.ch

Type of Firm
Private Equity Firm

Project Preferences

Type of Financing Preferred:
Early Stage
Startup

Geographical Preferences

International Preferences:
Switzerland

Industry Preferences

In Communications prefer:
Communications and Media

In Medical/Health prefer:
Medical/Health

Additional Information
Year Founded: 2008
Capital Under Management: $40,000,000
Current Activity Level : Actively seeking new investments

POND VENTURE PARTNERS LTD

102-104 Sheen Rd, The Monaco, Suite, G/F, Grand Prix House
London, United Kingdom TW9 1UF
Phone: 442089401001
Fax: 442089406792
E-mail: office@pondventures.com
Website: www.pondventures.com

Other Offices
11, Hamenofim Street
Building B, 5th floor, Ackerstein Towers
, Israel 46120
Phone: 972-9-971-6010

2033 Gateway Place, Suite 600
San Jose, CA USA 95110
Phone: 408-467-3806

Management and Staff
Charles Irving, Co-Founder
James Urquhart, Venture Partner
Kent Godfrey, General Partner
Richard Irving, Co-Founder

Type of Firm
Private Equity Firm

Association Membership
British Venture Capital Association (BVCA)

Project Preferences

Type of Financing Preferred:
Early Stage
Startup

Geographical Preferences

United States Preferences:

Industry Preferences

In Communications prefer:
Telecommunications
Wireless Communications

In Computer Software prefer:
Software

In Internet Specific prefer:
Internet

In Semiconductor/Electr prefer:
Semiconductor

In Medical/Health prefer:
Medical/Health

In Industrial/Energy prefer:
Energy

Additional Information
Name of Most Recent Fund: Pond Ventures III
Most Recent Fund Was Raised: 06/30/2005
Year Founded: 1998
Capital Under Management: $70,000,000
Current Activity Level : Actively seeking new investments

PONOI CAPITAL LP

1700 Owens Street, Suite 500
San Francisco, CA USA 94158

Management and Staff
James Evangelista, Chief Financial Officer

Type of Firm
Private Equity Firm

Project Preferences

Type of Financing Preferred:
Balanced

Additional Information
Year Founded: 2017
Current Activity Level : Actively seeking new investments

PONTIFAX MANAGEMENT COMPANY LTD

Eight Hamenofim Street
Herzliya Pituach
Herzelia, Israel 46725
Phone: 97299725617
Fax: 97299725618
Website: www.pontifax.com

Other Offices
2400 BROADWAY, SUITE D-270
Santa Monica, CA USA 90404
Phone: 14242267770

Management and Staff
Tomer Kariv, Managing Partner

Type of Firm
Private Equity Firm

Project Preferences

Type of Financing Preferred:
Early Stage
Expansion
Balanced
Later Stage

Geographical Preferences

International Preferences:
Israel

Industry Preferences

In Medical/Health prefer:
Pharmaceuticals

Additional Information
Name of Most Recent Fund: Pontifax III Fund
Most Recent Fund Was Raised: 11/03/2011
Year Founded: 2004
Capital Under Management: $88,000,000
Current Activity Level : Actively seeking new investments

POPLAR CAPITAL PARTNERS LLC

255 West 36th Street, Suite 1502
New York, NY USA 10018
Phone: 6465863060
E-mail: info@poplarpartners.com
Website: www.poplarpartners.com

Type of Firm
Private Equity Firm

Project Preferences

Type of Financing Preferred:
Leveraged Buyout
Acquisition

Geographical Preferences

United States Preferences:

International Preferences:
Asia Pacific

Industry Preferences

In Computer Software prefer:
Data Processing
Systems Software

In Medical/Health prefer:
Medical/Health

In Business Serv. prefer:
Services

Additional Information
Year Founded: 2013
Current Activity Level : Actively seeking new investments

POPLAR VENTURES LLC

1800 Casselberry Road
Louisville, KY USA 40205
E-mail: info@poplarventures.com
Website: poplarventures.com

Type of Firm
Private Equity Firm

Project Preferences

Type of Financing Preferred:
Early Stage
Expansion
Balanced
Later Stage

Industry Preferences

In Computer Software prefer:
Software
Systems Software
Applications Software

In Medical/Health prefer:
Medical/Health

Additional Information
Year Founded: 1969
Current Activity Level : Actively seeking new investments

PORT-MONNAIE VENTURE AB

Stortorget 17
Malmo, Sweden 211 22

Management and Staff
Joakim Falk, Co-Founder
Pouyan Kasraian, Co-Founder
Staffan Gestrelius, Co-Founder

Type of Firm
Private Equity Firm

Project Preferences

Type of Financing Preferred:
Balanced

Geographical Preferences

International Preferences:
Sweden

Additional Information
Year Founded: 2013
Current Activity Level : Actively seeking new investments

PORTAG3 VENTURES INC GP

77 King Street West
Toronto, Canada M5K 0A1
Phone: 15142866270
E-mail: info@p3vc.com
Website: p3vc.com

Management and Staff
Francois Lafortune, Managing Partner
Ronald Close, Managing Partner
Samuel Robinson, Managing Partner

Type of Firm
Private Equity Firm

Project Preferences

Type of Financing Preferred:
Early Stage

Additional Information
Year Founded: 2016
Current Activity Level : Actively seeking new investments

PORTAL CAPITAL LLC

2000 Auburn Road, Suite 221
Beachwood, OH USA 44122
Phone: 2163787688
Website: www.aditfunds.com

Management and Staff
John Zak, Partner
William Kilroy, Managing Partner

Type of Firm
Private Equity Firm

Project Preferences

Type of Financing Preferred:
Leveraged Buyout
Early Stage
Generalist PE
Balanced
Later Stage
Acquisition
Recapitalizations

Size of Investments Considered:
Min Size of Investment Considered (000s): $250
Max Size of Investment Considered (000s): $10,000

Geographical Preferences

United States Preferences:
All U.S.

Industry Preferences

In Medical/Health prefer:
Medical Diagnostics
Diagnostic Test Products
Medical Products
Health Services

Additional Information
Year Founded: 2008
Current Activity Level : Actively seeking new investments

PORTBANK CAPITAL GESTORA DE RECURSOS SA

R Dr Renato Paes de Barros 750
6 Andar, Itaim Bibi
Sao Paulo, Brazil 04530001
Phone: 551130742366
E-mail: portbank@portbank.com.br
Website: www.portbank.com.br

Type of Firm
Private Equity Firm

Association Membership
Brazilian Venture Capital Association (ABCR)

Project Preferences

Type of Financing Preferred:
Early Stage
Balanced
Later Stage
Seed
Startup

Geographical Preferences

International Preferences:
Brazil

Industry Preferences

In Transportation prefer:
Aerospace

Additional Information
Year Founded: 2009
Capital Under Management: $55,043,000
Current Activity Level : Actively seeking new investments

PORTCHESTER EQUITY LTD

20 Jewry Street
Hampshire, United Kingdom
Website: portchesterequity.com

Type of Firm
Private Equity Firm

Project Preferences

Type of Financing Preferred:
Leveraged Buyout
Acquisition
Recapitalizations

Geographical Preferences

International Preferences:
United Kingdom
Europe

Industry Preferences

In Business Serv. prefer:
Services

In Manufact. prefer:
Manufacturing

Additional Information
Year Founded: 2010
Current Activity Level : Actively seeking new investments

PORTFOLIO ADVISORS, LLC

Nine Old Kings Highway South
Darien, CT USA 06820
Phone: 2036623456
Fax: 2036620013
E-mail: info@portad.com
Website: www.portad.com

Other Offices
18 Harbour Road
Level 69, Central Plaza
Wan Chai, Hong Kong

Seefeldstrasse 35
Zurich, Switzerland 8008
Phone: 41-44-200-3500
Fax: 41-44-200-3501

Management and Staff
Adam Clemens, Managing Director
Brian Murphy, Managing Director
Christopher Ruder, Managing Director
Gregory Garrett, Managing Director
Harry Pierandri, Managing Director
Jonathan Murphy, Senior Managing Director
Kenneth Wisdom, Managing Director
Kenneth Jarvis, Vice President
Michael Galbreath, Managing Director
Michael Trinkaus, Chief Financial Officer
Paul Crotty, Managing Director
Ryan Butler, Vice President
Todd Hughes, Managing Director
William Walsh, Managing Director
William Indelicato, Managing Director

Type of Firm
Investment Management Firm

Association Membership
Swiss Venture Capital Association (SECA)
European Private Equity and Venture Capital Assoc.

Project Preferences

Type of Financing Preferred:
Fund of Funds
Leveraged Buyout
Value-Add
Early Stage
Mezzanine
Generalist PE
Opportunistic
Later Stage
Seed
Special Situation
Fund of Funds of Second

Additional Information
Name of Most Recent Fund: Portfolio Advisors Asia Fund IV, L.P.
Most Recent Fund Was Raised: 07/02/2013
Year Founded: 1994

Capital Under Management: $145,000,000
Current Activity Level: Actively seeking new investments

PORTFOLION KOCKAZATI TOKEALAP KEZELO ZRT

Bebr u 7
Budapest, Hungary 1131
Phone: 3612983367
Fax: 3612983303
E-mail: info@portfolion.hu
Website: portfolion.hu

Other Offices
Bebr u 7
Budapest, Hungary 1131
Phone: 3612983367
Fax: 3612983303

Type of Firm
Private Equity Firm

Association Membership
Hungarian Venture Capital Association (HVCA)

Project Preferences

Type of Financing Preferred:
Early Stage
Expansion
Balanced
Later Stage
Seed
Startup

Geographical Preferences

International Preferences:
Hungary
Europe

Industry Preferences

In Biotechnology prefer:
Biotechnology
Industrial Biotechnology

In Medical/Health prefer:
Medical Diagnostics

In Consumer Related prefer:
Consumer
Sports
Food/Beverage
Consumer Products

In Industrial/Energy prefer:
Alternative Energy
Energy Conservation Relat
Environmental Related

In Financial Services prefer:
Financial Services

Additional Information
Year Founded: 2010

Capital Under Management: $1,160,000
Current Activity Level: Actively seeking new investments

PORTLAND HOLDINGS INC

1375 Kerns Road, Suite 100
Ontario, Canada L7P 4V7
Phone: 9053314292
Website: www.portlandholdings.com

Other Offices
1375 Kerns Road, Suite 1000
Burlington, Canada
Phone: 905.331.4292

Type of Firm
Private Equity Firm

Project Preferences

Type of Financing Preferred:
Leveraged Buyout
Acquisition

Industry Preferences

In Communications prefer:
Telecommunications
Media and Entertainment

In Medical/Health prefer:
Medical/Health
Health Services

In Financial Services prefer:
Financial Services

Additional Information
Year Founded: 1987
Current Activity Level: Actively seeking new investments

PORTLAND PRIVATE EQUITY LP

P.O. Box 5104
Burlington, Canada L7R 0B8
Phone: 9053314250
Website: portlandpe.com

Management and Staff
Doug Hewson, Partner
Joe Vescio, Managing Partner
Kip Thompson, Managing Partner
Mark McIntosh, Vice President
Robert Almeida, Managing Partner

Type of Firm
Private Equity Firm

Project Preferences

Type of Financing Preferred:
Leveraged Buyout
Acquisition

Geographical Preferences

United States Preferences:

International Preferences:
Dominican Rep.

Additional Information
Name of Most Recent Fund: AIC Caribbean Fund
Most Recent Fund Was Raised: 06/12/2007
Year Founded: 2007
Capital Under Management: $20,000,000
Current Activity Level : Actively seeking new investments

PORTO CAPITAL GESTORA DE RECURSOS SA

Al Ribeiro da Silva 275
Campos Eliseos
Sao Paulo, Brazil 01217-011
Phone: 551133668085

Type of Firm
Insurance Firm Affiliate

Project Preferences

Type of Financing Preferred:
Early Stage
Expansion
Balanced
Later Stage
Seed
Startup

Geographical Preferences

International Preferences:
Brazil

Industry Preferences

In Medical/Health prefer:
Health Services

In Consumer Related prefer:
Consumer
Education Related

In Financial Services prefer:
Financial Services
Financial Services

Additional Information
Year Founded: 2016
Current Activity Level : Actively seeking new investments

PORTOBELLO CAPITAL ADVISORS SL

Serrano 30, 2
Madrid, Spain 28001
Phone: 34914318071
Fax: 3491431452
E-mail: info@portobellocapital.es
Website: www.portobellocapital.es

Management and Staff
Fernando Chinchurreta, Partner
Inigo Sanchez-Asiain, Partner
Juan Ramirez, Partner
Luis Penarrocha, Partner
Ramon Cerdeiras, Partner

Type of Firm
Private Equity Firm

Association Membership
Spanish Venture Capital Association (ASCRI)

Project Preferences

Type of Financing Preferred:
Leveraged Buyout
Management Buyouts
Acquisition

Geographical Preferences

International Preferences:
Portugal
Spain

Additional Information
Year Founded: 2005
Capital Under Management: $485,186,000
Current Activity Level : Actively seeking new investments

PORTUGAL CAPITAL VENTURES SGPS SA

Av Dr Antunes Guimaraes 103
Oporto, Portugal 4100079
Phone: 351226165390
Fax: 351226102089
E-mail: contact@portugalventures.pt
Website: www.portugalventures.pt

Other Offices
Pastor of Bom Sucesso, 127/131
Peninsula Building 5 - room 507
Porto, Portugal 4150-146
Phone: 351-226-079-270
Fax: 351-226-062-519

Type of Firm
Government Affiliated Program

Association Membership
Portuguese Venture Capital Association (APCRI)
New England Venture Capital Association

Project Preferences

Type of Financing Preferred:
Early Stage
Expansion
Balanced
Seed
Startup

Geographical Preferences

International Preferences:
Italy
Europe
Portugal

Industry Preferences

In Communications prefer:
Communications and Media
Telecommunications

In Computer Other prefer:
Computer Related

In Consumer Related prefer:
Consumer
Entertainment and Leisure

In Industrial/Energy prefer:
Energy
Alternative Energy
Industrial Products

Additional Information
Year Founded: 1988
Capital Under Management: $733,900,000
Current Activity Level : Actively seeking new investments

POSEIDON ASSET MANAGEMENT LLC

130 Frederick Street, Suite 102
San Francisco, CA USA 94117
Website: poseidonassetmanagement.com

Type of Firm
Investment Management Firm

Project Preferences

Type of Financing Preferred:
Early Stage

Industry Preferences

In Medical/Health prefer:
Medical/Health

Additional Information
Year Founded: 2013
Current Activity Level : Actively seeking new investments

POST CAPITAL PARTNERS LLC

805 Third Avenue
8th Floor
New York, NY USA 10022
Phone: 2128885700
Fax: 2062222518
Website: www.postcp.com

Management and Staff
Michael Pfeffer, Managing Director
Mitchell Davidson, Co-Founder
Zuri Briscoe, Vice President

Type of Firm
Private Equity Firm

Project Preferences

Type of Financing Preferred:
Leveraged Buyout
Management Buyouts
Acquisition
Recapitalizations

Size of Investments Considered:
Min Size of Investment Considered (000s): $5,000
Max Size of Investment Considered (000s): $50,000

Geographical Preferences

United States Preferences:
All U.S.

Industry Preferences

In Medical/Health prefer:
Health Services

In Consumer Related prefer:
Consumer Products
Consumer Services

In Industrial/Energy prefer:
Industrial Products

In Transportation prefer:
Transportation

In Financial Services prefer:
Financial Services
Insurance

In Business Serv. prefer:
Services
Media

In Manufact. prefer:
Manufacturing
Publishing

Additional Information
Year Founded: 2004
Capital Under Management: $25,000,000
Current Activity Level : Actively seeking new investments

POST-PRIVATIZATION FOUNDATION

46-48 Calea Plevnei
Bucharest, Romania 010233
Phone: 40-31-100-0719
Fax: 40-31-100-0720
E-mail: info@postprivatizare.ro
Website: www.postprivatizare.ro

Type of Firm
Government Affiliated Program

Project Preferences

Type of Financing Preferred:
Leveraged Buyout
Early Stage
Expansion
Generalist PE
Balanced
Seed
Management Buyouts
Acquisition
Startup

Geographical Preferences

International Preferences:
Europe
Romania

Additional Information
Year Founded: 1996
Current Activity Level : Actively seeking new investments

POTENZA CAPITAL, LLC

111 Eight Avenue
New York, NY USA 10011
E-mail: info@potenzacap.com
Website: potenzacap.com

Type of Firm
Private Equity Firm

Project Preferences

Type of Financing Preferred:
Generalist PE

Additional Information
Year Founded: 2015
Current Activity Level : Actively seeking new investments

POTOMAC ENERGY FUND LP

Five South Market Street
Fourth Floor
Frederick, MD USA 21701
Phone: 3016959229
Fax: 3016959597
E-mail: info@potomacenergyfund.com
Website: www.potomacenergyfund.com

Management and Staff
Christopher Weir, Chief Financial Officer
Dan Nadash, Managing Director
Goodloe Byron, Managing Partner
Mahesh Konduru, Principal
Matt Klinger, Principal

Type of Firm
Private Equity Firm

Project Preferences

Type of Financing Preferred:
Expansion
Later Stage

Industry Preferences

In Industrial/Energy prefer:
Environmental Related

Additional Information
Year Founded: 2008
Current Activity Level : Actively seeking new investments

POTOMAC EQUITY PARTNERS LLC

5111 Yuma Place North West, Suite 200
Washington, DC USA 20016
Phone: 2025053050
Website: www.potomacequitypartners.com

Management and Staff
Christopher Blythe, Principal
John Bates, Founder
Michael Platt, Partner
Pascal Denis, Principal
Peter Masanotti, Partner
Raymond Smith, Partner
Robert Christie, Partner
Tony Coelho, Partner

Type of Firm
Private Equity Firm

Project Preferences

Type of Financing Preferred:
Leveraged Buyout
Acquisition

Geographical Preferences

United States Preferences:
North America

Industry Preferences

In Computer Software prefer:
Software

In Medical/Health prefer:
Health Services

In Consumer Related prefer:
Education Related

In Business Serv. prefer:
Services

Additional Information
Year Founded: 2015
Current Activity Level : Actively seeking new investments

POUSCHINE COOK CAPITAL MANAGEMENT LLC

375 Park Avenue, Suite 3408
New York, NY USA 10152
Phone: 2127840620
Fax: 2127840621
Website: www.pouschinecook.com

Management and Staff
Bonnie Harland, Vice President
Everett Cook, Co-Founder
Geoffrey Teillon, Managing Director
John Minner, Chief Financial Officer
John Pouschine, Co-Founder
Robert Jenkins, Managing Director

Type of Firm
Private Equity Firm

Project Preferences

Role in Financing:
Prefer role as deal originator

Type of Financing Preferred:
Leveraged Buyout
Management Buyouts
Acquisition
Recapitalizations

Geographical Preferences

United States Preferences:

Industry Preferences

In Medical/Health prefer:
Health Services

In Consumer Related prefer:
Retail
Consumer Products
Consumer Services
Other Restaurants
Education Related

In Industrial/Energy prefer:
Industrial Products
Advanced Materials
Environmental Related

In Financial Services prefer:
Financial Services

In Business Serv. prefer:
Services
Media

In Manufact. prefer:
Manufacturing

Additional Information
Name of Most Recent Fund: Pouschine Cook Capital Partners II, L.P.
Most Recent Fund Was Raised: 05/05/2005
Year Founded: 1999
Capital Under Management: $261,500,000
Current Activity Level : Actively seeking new investments
Method of Compensation: Return on invest. most important, but chg. closing fees, service fees, etc.

POWER FINANCE CORPORATION LTD

Urjanidhi, One Barakhamba Lane
Connaught Place
New Delhi, India 110 001
Phone: 91-11-2345-6000
Website: www.pfcindia.com

Other Offices
New No.185, Old No.137, Anna Salai
First Floor, SPS Building
Chennai, India 600 002
Phone: 91-44-2860-2431

158 Maharishi Karve Road, Churchgate
Ground Floor, Moonlight Building
Mumbai, India 400 020
Phone: 91-22-2288-2440

Type of Firm
Government Affiliated Program

Project Preferences

Type of Financing Preferred:
Other

Geographical Preferences

International Preferences:
India

Industry Preferences

In Industrial/Energy prefer:
Energy

Additional Information
Year Founded: 1986
Current Activity Level : Actively seeking new investments

POWERHOUSE

Building DG7
Dovedale Village
Ilam, New Zealand 8540
Phone: 6439282282
E-mail: info@powerhouse-ventures.co.nz
Website: www.powerhouse-ventures.co.nz

Type of Firm
Incubator/Development Program

Project Preferences

Type of Financing Preferred:
Early Stage
Seed
Startup

Additional Information
Year Founded: 1969
Current Activity Level : Actively seeking new investments

POWERONE CAPITAL MARKETS LTD

130 King Street West, Suite 2210, The Exchange Tower
Toronto, Canada M5X 1E4
Phone: 4163624157
Fax: 4163627360
Website: www.poweronecapital.com

Management and Staff
David D Onofrio, Chief Financial Officer
Pasquale DiCapo, Founder

Type of Firm
Bank Affiliated

Project Preferences

Type of Financing Preferred:
Early Stage

Additional Information
Year Founded: 2003
Current Activity Level : Actively seeking new investments

POWERPLANT LLC

600 South Lake Avenue
Pasadena, CA USA 91106
Phone: 3239429426

Type of Firm
Private Equity Firm

Project Preferences

Type of Financing Preferred:
Balanced

Industry Preferences

In Agr/Forestr/Fish prefer:
Agriculture related

Additional Information

Year Founded: 2015
Capital Under Management: $42,000,000
Current Activity Level : Actively seeking new investments

PPF INVESTMENTS LTD

Whiteley Chambers
Don Street, Saint Helier
Jersey, United Kingdom JE4 9WG
E-mail: info@ppfinvestments.com
Website: www.ppfinvestments.com

Other Offices

50 Liangmaqiao Road, Chaoyang District
Beijing Lufthansa Center, C 312A
Beijing, China 100016
Phone: 86-10-6463-8682
Fax: 86-10-6264-2448

Management and Staff

Miroslav Nosal, Chief Executive Officer

Type of Firm

Private Equity Firm

Project Preferences

Type of Financing Preferred:
Balanced

Geographical Preferences

International Preferences:
Central Europe
Eastern Europe
Asia

Additional Information

Year Founded: 2006
Current Activity Level : Actively seeking new investments

PPF PARTNERS AS

Hirzel Street, St. Peter Port
Generali House
Guernsey, Channel Islands GY1 4PA
Phone: 441481754950
Fax: 441481703092
E-mail: info@ppfpartners.com
Website: www.ppf.com

Other Offices

PPF GATE, Evropska 2690/17
P.O. Box 177
Prague 6, Czech Republic 160 41
Phone: 420-224-174-900
Fax: 420-224-174-625

Management and Staff

Katerina Jiraskova, Chief Financial Officer
Tomas Brzobohaty, Chairman & CEO

Type of Firm

Private Equity Firm

Association Membership

European Private Equity and Venture Capital Assoc.

Project Preferences

Type of Financing Preferred:
Leveraged Buyout
Early Stage
Generalist PE

Geographical Preferences

International Preferences:
Central Europe
Eastern Europe

Industry Preferences

In Consumer Related prefer:
Entertainment and Leisure

In Industrial/Energy prefer:
Oil and Gas Exploration

In Business Serv. prefer:
Media

In Other prefer:
Environment Responsible

Additional Information

Year Founded: 2008
Current Activity Level : Actively seeking new investments

PPM AMERICA CAPITAL PARTNERS LLC

225 West Wacker Drive, Suite 1200
Chicago, IL USA 60606
Phone: 3126342500
Fax: 3126340050

Other Offices

300 North Martingale Road, Suite 440
Schaumburg, IL USA 60173
Phone: 8474138500
Fax: 8474133240

750 Lexington Avenue
Tenth Floor
New York, NY USA 10022
Phone: 2125837300
Fax: 2125837311

Management and Staff

Austin Krumpfes, Partner
Bruce Gorchow, President
Champ Raju, Partner
Claudia Baron, Partner
Craig Radis, Principal
Kevin Keefe, Principal
Mark Staub, Principal
Ray Zhang, Principal
Robert O Rourke, Partner

Type of Firm

Bank Affiliated

Association Membership

Illinois Venture Capital Association

Project Preferences

Role in Financing:
Will function either as deal originator or investor in deals created by others

Type of Financing Preferred:
Fund of Funds
Leveraged Buyout
Expansion
Management Buyouts
Acquisition
Special Situation
Recapitalizations

Geographical Preferences

United States Preferences:

Canadian Preferences:
All Canada

Industry Focus

(% based on actual investment)
Other Products	75.0%
Internet Specific	14.2%
Computer Hardware	3.6%
Medical/Health	3.5%
Consumer Related	2.6%
Communications and Media	0.7%
Computer Software and Services	0.4%

Additional Information

Name of Most Recent Fund: PPM America Private Equity Fund V, L.P.
Most Recent Fund Was Raised: 02/10/2014
Year Founded: 1990
Capital Under Management: $620,500,000
Current Activity Level : Actively seeking new investments
Method of Compensation: Return on investment is of primary concern, do not charge fees

PRACTICA CAPITAL UAB

Naugarduko g. 3
Vilnius, Lithuania 03231
Phone: 37052603159
E-mail: info@practica.lt
Website: www.practica.lt

Type of Firm

Private Equity Firm

Association Membership
Lithuanian Venture Capital Association

Project Preferences

Type of Financing Preferred:
Early Stage
Later Stage
Seed
Startup

Size of Investments Considered:
Min Size of Investment Considered (000s): $4
Max Size of Investment Considered (000s): $3,994

Geographical Preferences

International Preferences:
Europe
Eastern Europe
Lithuania

Industry Preferences

In Computer Software prefer:
Software
Systems Software

In Internet Specific prefer:
E-Commerce Technology

In Computer Other prefer:
Computer Related

Additional Information
Name of Most Recent Fund: Practica Venture Capital Fund
Most Recent Fund Was Raised: 07/26/2012
Year Founded: 2011
Capital Under Management: $26,648,000
Current Activity Level : Actively seeking new investments

PRAEDIUM MANAGEMENT CO SL

Moll de Ronda, Port Forum
St. Adri de Besos
Barcelona, Spain 08930
Phone: 34932240330
E-mail: contact@praediumglobal.com
Website: www.praedium.es

Other Offices
Maria de Molina, 40
Madrid, Spain 28006

Type of Firm
Private Equity Firm

Project Preferences

Type of Financing Preferred:
Leveraged Buyout
Generalist PE
Balanced
Other

Industry Preferences

In Consumer Related prefer:
Consumer
Retail

In Industrial/Energy prefer:
Energy
Industrial Products

In Financial Services prefer:
Financial Services
Real Estate

In Business Serv. prefer:
Services
Distribution

Additional Information
Year Founded: 1992
Current Activity Level : Actively seeking new investments

PRAESIDIAN CAPITAL

419 Park Avenue South
New York, NY USA 10016
Phone: 2125202600
Fax: 2125202601
E-mail: info@praesidian.com

Other Offices
12 Blandford Street
London, United Kingdom W1U 4AZ

Management and Staff
Anthony Brennan, Partner
Christian Heidl, Partner
Jason Drattell, Founder

Type of Firm
Private Equity Firm

Association Membership
Natl Assoc of Small Bus. Inv. Co (NASBIC)

Project Preferences

Type of Financing Preferred:
Leveraged Buyout
Mezzanine
Generalist PE
Balanced
Management Buyouts
Acquisition
Recapitalizations

Size of Investments Considered:
Min Size of Investment Considered (000s): $5,000
Max Size of Investment Considered (000s): $20,000

Geographical Preferences

United States Preferences:

Industry Preferences

In Business Serv. prefer:
Services
Distribution

In Manufact. prefer:
Manufacturing

Additional Information
Year Founded: 2002
Capital Under Management: $89,600,000
Current Activity Level : Actively seeking new investments

PRAGATI INDIA FUND PVT LTD

#436, Regus Business Centre
Commercial Complex
New Delhi, India
E-mail: info@pragatifund.com

Type of Firm
Private Equity Firm

Project Preferences

Type of Financing Preferred:
Early Stage
Expansion
Seed

Geographical Preferences

International Preferences:
India

Additional Information
Year Founded: 2011
Capital Under Management: $70,001,000
Current Activity Level : Actively seeking new investments

PRAGMA CAPITAL SA

13 Avenue Hoche
Paris, France 75008
Phone: 33158364950
Fax: 33158364951
E-mail: accueil.pragma@pragma-capital.com
Website: www.pragmacapital.fr

Management and Staff
Christophe Ramoisy, Partner
Gilles Gramat, Partner
Jean-Pierre Creange, Partner
Pascal Gagna, Founder
Stephane Monmousseau, Partner

Type of Firm
Private Equity Firm

Association Membership
French Venture Capital Association (AFIC)

Project Preferences

Type of Financing Preferred:
Leveraged Buyout
Management Buyouts
Acquisition

Size of Investments Considered:
Min Size of Investment Considered (000s): $13,680
Max Size of Investment Considered (000s): $47,880

Geographical Preferences

International Preferences:
Europe
France

Additional Information
Year Founded: 2002
Capital Under Management: $370,300,000
Current Activity Level : Actively seeking new investments

PRAGUE STARTUP CENTRE

36/31, Jungmannova
Prague, Czech Republic 110 00
Phone: 42602297287
Website: www.praguestartupcentre.cz

Type of Firm
Incubator/Development Program

Project Preferences

Type of Financing Preferred:
Early Stage
Seed

Geographical Preferences

International Preferences:
Czech Republic

Additional Information
Year Founded: 2016
Current Activity Level : Actively seeking new investments

PRAIRIE CAPITAL, L.P.

191 North Wacker Drive, Suite 800
Chicago, IL USA 60606
Phone: 3123601133
Fax: 3123601193
Website: www.prairie-capital.com

Management and Staff
Bryan Daniels, Partner
Christopher Killackey, Partner
D.J. Lipke, Vice President
Darren Snyder, Partner
Holly Lane, Chief Financial Officer
John Mayfield, Managing Director
Nathan Good, Managing Director
Ron Huberman, Chief Operating Officer
Sean McNally, Managing Director
Stephen King, Partner
Steven Groya, Managing Director

Type of Firm
Private Equity Firm

Association Membership
Natl Assoc of Small Bus. Inv. Co (NASBIC)
Illinois Venture Capital Association

Project Preferences

Role in Financing:
Will function either as deal originator or investor in deals created by others

Type of Financing Preferred:
Leveraged Buyout
Mezzanine
Acquisition
Recapitalizations

Geographical Preferences

United States Preferences:

Industry Focus
(% based on actual investment)
Other Products	37.0%
Consumer Related	29.3%
Computer Software and Services	28.3%
Communications and Media	4.9%
Medical/Health	0.5%

Additional Information
Name of Most Recent Fund: Prairie Capital III, L.P.
Most Recent Fund Was Raised: 09/15/2003
Year Founded: 1997
Capital Under Management: $390,000,000
Current Activity Level : Actively seeking new investments
Method of Compensation: Return on invest. most important, but chg. closing fees, service fees, etc.

PRAIRIE CREST CAPITAL LLC

317 6th Avenue, Suite #700
Des Moines, IA USA 50309
Phone: 5153934555

Type of Firm
Private Equity Firm

Project Preferences

Type of Financing Preferred:
Early Stage

Industry Preferences

In Agr/Forestr/Fish prefer:
Agriculture related

Additional Information
Year Founded: 2016
Current Activity Level : Actively seeking new investments

PRAIRIE OAK CAPITAL LLC

5465 Mills Civic Parkway, Suite 400
Newton, IA USA 50208
Phone: 5155647603
Website: www.prairieoakcapital.com

Management and Staff
Jim Kurtenbach, General Partner

Type of Firm
Private Equity Firm

Project Preferences

Type of Financing Preferred:
Balanced

Geographical Preferences

United States Preferences:
All U.S.

Industry Preferences

In Medical/Health prefer:
Medical/Health

In Manufact. prefer:
Manufacturing

Additional Information
Year Founded: 2007
Capital Under Management: $7,500,000
Current Activity Level : Actively seeking new investments

PRAIRIE VENTURES LLC

2323 South 171 Street, Suite 202
Omaha, NE USA 68130
Phone: 4023982200
E-mail: info@prairieventures.net
Website: www.prairieventures.net

Type of Firm
Private Equity Firm

Project Preferences

Type of Financing Preferred:
Early Stage
Balanced
Seed
Startup

Geographical Preferences

United States Preferences:
All U.S.

Canadian Preferences:
All Canada

Industry Preferences

In Medical/Health prefer:
Medical/Health

In Consumer Related prefer:
Consumer

In Financial Services prefer:
Financial Services
Real Estate

In Manufact. prefer:
Manufacturing

In Agr/Forestr/Fish prefer:
Agriculture related

Additional Information

Year Founded: 2000
Current Activity Level : Actively seeking new investments

PRAIRIEGOLD VENTURE PARTNERS

5708 South Remington Place, Suite 600
Sioux Falls, SD USA 57108
Phone: 6052752999
E-mail: info@pgvp.com
Website: www.pgvp.com

Management and Staff

Michael Jerstad, Partner
Paul Batcheller, Partner
Susan Simko, Chief Financial Officer

Type of Firm

Private Equity Firm

Association Membership

Community Development Venture Capital Alliance

Project Preferences

Type of Financing Preferred:
Early Stage

Geographical Preferences

United States Preferences:
Midwest

Industry Preferences

In Industrial/Energy prefer:
Alternative Energy
Environmental Related

In Other prefer:
Environment Responsible

Additional Information

Name of Most Recent Fund: PrairieGold VenCap Fund II, LP

Most Recent Fund Was Raised: 04/14/2008
Year Founded: 2003
Current Activity Level : Actively seeking new investments

PRAX CAPITAL MANAGEMENT CO

333 Huai Hai Zhong Road, Suite 1701, Shui On Plaza
Shanghai, China 200021
Phone: 862163850606
Fax: 862162376709
E-mail: info@praxcapital.com
Website: www.praxcapital.com

Other Offices

1001 Brickell Bay Drive, Suite 2402
Miami, FL USA 33131
Phone: 305-358-9696
Fax: 305-358-9797

Diagonal 605, 7 - 3
Barcelona, Spain 08028
Phone: 34-93-363-3320
Fax: 34-93-419-1042

Level 25, Bank Of China Tower
1 Garden Road
Central Hong Kong, Hong Kong
Phone: 852-2251-8652
Fax: 852-2251-8656

Management and Staff

Fernando Vila, Partner
Guowei Chen, Partner
Jiping Yao, Managing Partner
Ke Jia, Vice President
Kun Zhang, Vice President
Lei Xu, Partner
Meilan Gan, Managing Partner
Renjie Li, Partner
Wenrong Xu, Chief Financial Officer
Zhenmu Wang, Vice President
Zhigang Lai, Vice President

Type of Firm

Private Equity Firm

Project Preferences

Type of Financing Preferred:
Expansion
Balanced
Later Stage

Size of Investments Considered:
Min Size of Investment Considered (000s): $10,000
Max Size of Investment Considered (000s): $30,000

Geographical Preferences

International Preferences:
China

Industry Preferences

In Consumer Related prefer:
Consumer Services

In Industrial/Energy prefer:
Industrial Products
Environmental Related

In Financial Services prefer:
Real Estate

In Business Serv. prefer:
Services

In Manufact. prefer:
Manufacturing

Additional Information

Year Founded: 2003
Current Activity Level : Actively seeking new investments

PRAXIS CAPITAL PARTNERS CO LTD

312 Teheran-ro, Gangnam-gu
Vision Tower 17th Floor
Seoul, South Korea
Phone: 25425666
Website: praxiscp.com

Type of Firm

Private Equity Firm

Project Preferences

Type of Financing Preferred:
Generalist PE
Balanced
Acquisition
Industry Rollups

Additional Information

Year Founded: 2013
Current Activity Level : Actively seeking new investments

PRC VENTURE PARTNERS LLC

88 Jianguo Road, Chaoyang Dist
B-1803 Soho City
Beijing, China 100022
Phone: 86-21-85894857
Fax: 86-21-85898387

Other Offices

195 Field Point Road
Greenwich, CT USA 06830
Phone: 203-869-5540
Fax: 203-869-5564

Type of Firm

Private Equity Firm

Pratt's Guide to Private Equity & Venture Capital Sources

Industry Preferences

In Communications prefer:
Communications and Media

In Medical/Health prefer:
Medical/Health

In Financial Services prefer:
Financial Services

Additional Information

Year Founded: 2010
Current Activity Level : Actively seeking new investments

PRE MANAGEMENT AS

Kronprinsesse Marthas plass 1
P.O. Box 1988
Oslo, Norway 0160
Phone: 4722478820
Fax: 4722478830
Website: www.pre-management.com

Management and Staff

Erik Dahl, Chief Executive Officer

Type of Firm
Investment Management Firm

Project Preferences

Type of Financing Preferred:
Balanced

Geographical Preferences

International Preferences:
China

Industry Preferences

In Financial Services prefer:
Insurance

Additional Information

Year Founded: 2007
Current Activity Level : Actively seeking new investments

PRE-SEED INNOVATION A/S

Diplomvej 381
Kongens Lyngby, Denmark 2800
Phone: 4577340755
Fax: 4588708090
E-mail: dsi@seedcapital.dk
Website: www.dtusymbioninnovation.dk

Management and Staff

Carsten Schou, General Partner
Jakob Fuglede Nielsen, Chief Financial Officer
Steen Halbye, Partner
Ulla Brockenhuus-Schack, Chief Executive Officer

Type of Firm
University Program

Project Preferences

Type of Financing Preferred:
Early Stage
Seed
Startup

Geographical Preferences

International Preferences:
Denmark

Industry Preferences

In Communications prefer:
Wireless Communications

In Computer Software prefer:
Software

In Biotechnology prefer:
Biotechnology

In Medical/Health prefer:
Medical Diagnostics
Medical Therapeutics
Pharmaceuticals

In Consumer Related prefer:
Entertainment and Leisure
Food/Beverage

In Industrial/Energy prefer:
Energy

In Financial Services prefer:
Financial Services

In Business Serv. prefer:
Services

Additional Information

Year Founded: 1998
Current Activity Level : Actively seeking new investments

PRECISION CAPITAL ADVISORS LLC

399 Park Avenue
37th Floor
New York, NY USA 10022
Phone: 2124769300
Fax: 2123553250
E-mail: investorrelations@precisioncapital.com
Website: www.precisioncapital.com

Management and Staff

Gina LaVersa, Partner
Rob Goodman, Vice President
Todd Kesselman, Partner

Type of Firm
Private Equity Advisor or Fund of Funds

Project Preferences

Type of Financing Preferred:
Fund of Funds

Additional Information

Name of Most Recent Fund: Special Opportunities Fund V, L.P.
Most Recent Fund Was Raised: 04/05/2013
Year Founded: 2013
Capital Under Management: $329,735,000
Current Activity Level : Actively seeking new investments

PRECURSOR VENTURES

170 Grant Avenue
Fourth Floor
San Francisco, CA USA 94108

Type of Firm
Private Equity Firm

Project Preferences

Type of Financing Preferred:
Seed

Industry Preferences

In Computer Software prefer:
Software

Additional Information

Year Founded: 2015
Capital Under Management: $15,180,000
Current Activity Level : Actively seeking new investments

PREIPO CAPITAL PARTNERS LTD

No. 832 Huamu Road
5th Floor
Shanghai, China 201204
Phone: 86-21-50591378
E-mail: info@preipo.cn
Website: www.preipo.cn

Management and Staff

Fen Xiong, Vice President
Scott Zheng, Managing Director
Tian Zhao, Vice President

Type of Firm
Private Equity Firm

Project Preferences

Role in Financing:
Will function either as deal originator or investor in deals created by others

1691

Type of Financing Preferred:
Expansion
Balanced
Later Stage

Size of Investments Considered:
Min Size of Investment Considered (000s): $1,000
Max Size of Investment Considered (000s): $50,000

Geographical Preferences

International Preferences:
China

Industry Preferences

In Computer Other prefer:
Computer Related

In Biotechnology prefer:
Biotechnology

In Medical/Health prefer:
Medical/Health
Health Services

In Consumer Related prefer:
Retail
Consumer Products

In Industrial/Energy prefer:
Energy
Materials

In Transportation prefer:
Transportation

In Financial Services prefer:
Financial Services

In Business Serv. prefer:
Services
Media

In Manufact. prefer:
Manufacturing

In Agr/Forestr/Fish prefer:
Agriculture related

Additional Information
Year Founded: 1999
Capital Under Management: $15,472,000
Current Activity Level : Actively seeking new investments

PRELUDE PARTNERS

7700 Irvine Center Dr., Suite 255
Irvine, CA USA 92618
Phone: 9493227187
E-mail: ta@prelude.partners
Website: www.prelude.partners

Type of Firm
Investment Management Firm

Additional Information
Year Founded: 2016

Current Activity Level : Actively seeking new investments

PRELUDE VENTURES LLC

One Ferry Building, Suite 300
San Francisco, CA USA 94111
Phone: 4157291270
Website: www.preludeventures.com

Management and Staff
Gabriel Kra, Founder
Mark Cupta, Principal
Tim Woodward, Managing Director

Type of Firm
Private Equity Firm

Association Membership
National Venture Capital Association - USA (NVCA)

Project Preferences

Type of Financing Preferred:
Balanced

Industry Preferences

In Industrial/Energy prefer:
Energy

In Other prefer:
Environment Responsible

Additional Information
Year Founded: 2014
Current Activity Level : Actively seeking new investments

PREMIER PARTNERS LLC

1002 Daechi-dong, Kangnam-ku
Kosmo Tower, Seventh Floor
Seoul, South Korea 135-549
Phone: 8225540030
Fax: 8225546442
E-mail: premier@premiervp.co.kr
Website: www.premierpartners.co.kr

Management and Staff
Jay Song, Partner
Jong Ho Lee, Managing Director
Joonyoun Cho, Principal
Seong Kim, Partner
Seung-Wook Cheon, Managing Director
Tai-Seung Oh, Partner

Type of Firm
Private Equity Firm

Association Membership
Korean Venture Capital Association (KVCA)

Geographical Preferences

United States Preferences:

International Preferences:
Asia
Korea, South

Industry Preferences

In Semiconductor/Electr prefer:
Electronics

Additional Information
Year Founded: 2005
Capital Under Management: $54,600,000
Current Activity Level : Actively seeking new investments

PREMIUM EQUITY PARTNERS GMBH

Siesmayerstrasse 21
Frankfurt, Germany 60323
Phone: 496971449946
Website: www.premium-equity.com

Management and Staff
Eckart Kottkamp, Partner
Manfred Krunnies, Partner
Marcel Van Wijk, Partner
Peter-Paul Schmidt-Fischer, Co-Founder
Thomas Duhnkrack, Co-Founder
Thomas Stoek, Partner
Wolf-Dietrich Loose, Partner
Wolfgang Jeblonski, Partner

Type of Firm
Private Equity Firm

Project Preferences

Type of Financing Preferred:
Leveraged Buyout
Acquisition

Geographical Preferences

International Preferences:
Germany

Industry Preferences

In Industrial/Energy prefer:
Industrial Products

Additional Information
Year Founded: 2011
Current Activity Level : Actively seeking new investments

PRESIDIO INVESTORS LLC

101 California Street, Suite 1200
San Francisco, CA USA 94111
Phone: 4154491000

Other Offices

9533 West Pico Boulevard
Second Floor, Suite A
Los Angeles, CA USA 90035
Phone: 310-407-7901
Fax: 310-407-7906

100 Crescent Court, Suite 550
Dallas, TX USA 75201
Phone: 214-855-2200
Fax: 214-855-2219

Management and Staff

Barry Rudolph, Managing Director
Brodie Cobb, CEO & Managing Director
Karl Schade, Managing Director
Victor Masaya, Vice President

Type of Firm

Bank Affiliated

Project Preferences

Type of Financing Preferred:
Leveraged Buyout
Expansion
Management Buyouts
Acquisition
Recapitalizations

Size of Investments Considered:
Min Size of Investment Considered (000s): $3,000
Max Size of Investment Considered (000s): $2,000

Industry Preferences

In Computer Software prefer:
Software

In Financial Services prefer:
Financial Services
Real Estate

In Business Serv. prefer:
Services

Additional Information

Name of Most Recent Fund: Presidio Investors Fund I, L.P.
Most Recent Fund Was Raised: 04/30/2008
Year Founded: 2008
Current Activity Level : Actively seeking new investments

PRESIDIO PARTNERS

One Letterman Drive
Building C, Suite CM500
San Francisco, CA USA 94129

Type of Firm

Private Equity Firm

Project Preferences

Type of Financing Preferred:
Balanced

Additional Information

Year Founded: 2014
Capital Under Management: $140,357,000
Current Activity Level : Actively seeking new investments

PRESIDIO VENTURES INC

3979 Freedom Circle, Suite 340
Santa Clara, CA USA 95054
Phone: 4088459458
E-mail: info@presidio-ventures.com
Website: www.presidio-ventures.com

Management and Staff

Lee Pantuso, Chief Financial Officer
Peter Gajdos, Managing Director

Type of Firm

Corporate PE/Venture

Association Membership

National Venture Capital Association - USA (NVCA)

Project Preferences

Role in Financing:
Will function either as deal originator or investor in deals created by others

Type of Financing Preferred:
Early Stage
Startup

Geographical Preferences

United States Preferences:

International Preferences:
Asia
Japan

Industry Preferences

In Computer Software prefer:
Software
Systems Software

In Internet Specific prefer:
Internet

In Semiconductor/Electr prefer:
Semiconductor

In Industrial/Energy prefer:
Materials
Environmental Related

In Business Serv. prefer:
Services
Media

Additional Information

Year Founded: 1998
Current Activity Level : Actively seeking new investments
Method of Compensation: Return on investment is of primary concern, do not charge fees

---

PRETTYBROOK PARTNERS LLC

174 Nassau Street, Suite 320
Princeton, NJ USA 08542
E-mail: info@prettybrookpartners.com
Website: www.prettybrookpartners.com

Management and Staff

Erin Enright, Co-Founder

Type of Firm

Private Equity Firm

Project Preferences

Type of Financing Preferred:
Leveraged Buyout
Acquisition

Industry Preferences

In Medical/Health prefer:
Health Services

Additional Information

Year Founded: 1969
Current Activity Level : Actively seeking new investments

PREVIZ VENTURES LTD

Ackerstein Towers, Building D
12 Abba Eban Av.
Herzeliya, Israel 46725
Phone: 97299720467
Fax: 97299520732
Website: www.previzv.com

Management and Staff

Dan Baruchi, Managing Partner
Eliav Azulay-Oz, Managing Partner

Type of Firm

Private Equity Firm

Project Preferences

Type of Financing Preferred:
Early Stage

Geographical Preferences

International Preferences:
Israel
Asia

Industry Preferences

In Computer Software prefer:
Software

In Medical/Health prefer:
Medical/Health

Additional Information
Year Founded: 1969
Current Activity Level : Actively seeking new investments

PRICOA CAPITAL GROUP LTD

180 North Stetson Avenue, Suite 5600
Chicago, IL USA 60601
Website: www.pricoacapital.com

Other Offices
47 King William Street
Sixth Floor
London, United Kingdom EC4R 9AF
Fax: 44-20-7621-8448

Bleichstrae 52
Frankfurt, Germany 60313
Fax: 496995528799

54-56 Avenue Hoche
Paris, France 75008
Fax: 33156605581

Management and Staff
Bruno Wanske, Managing Partner

Type of Firm
Insurance Firm Affiliate

Project Preferences

Type of Financing Preferred:
Leveraged Buyout
Expansion
Mezzanine
Later Stage
Management Buyouts
Acquisition
Private Placement
Recapitalizations

Geographical Preferences

United States Preferences:

International Preferences:
Europe
Australia

Industry Focus
(% based on actual investment)
Other Products	45.9%
Consumer Related	34.9%
Computer Software and Services	10.5%
Internet Specific	7.3%
Communications and Media	1.5%

Additional Information
Name of Most Recent Fund: PRICOA Private Capital Partners II
Most Recent Fund Was Raised: 11/01/2000
Year Founded: 1985
Capital Under Management: $800,000,000
Current Activity Level : Actively seeking new investments

PRIDE INVESTMENTS GROUP LTD

99 Queen's Road
3606, The Center
Central, Hong Kong
Phone: 852-2110-3129
Fax: 852-2110-0616
E-mail: info@prideinvestmentsgroup.com

Other Offices
Rm. 408 No. 538 Shangyin Road Intl.
Finance Plaza Huaqiao Economic Dev. Zone
Kunshan, Jiangsu, PRC, China 215332

1007A, No. 1 Central Fuxing Road Shenerg
International Building
Shanghai, PRC, China 200021
Phone: 862133765565
Fax: 862162270239

Cricket Square, Hutchins Drive
P.O. Box 2681
Grand Cayman, Cayman Islands KY1-1111

2702, 2 Grand Gateway
No. 3 Hongqiao Road
Shanghai, China
Phone: 86-21-3353-0081
Fax: 86-21-6227-0239

Units 2306-7, Cosco Tower,
183 Queen's Road
Central, Hong Kong

Management and Staff
BoBo Tang, Chief Executive Officer
Jue Qi, Managing Director

Type of Firm
Investment Management Firm

Association Membership
Hong Kong Venture Capital Association (HKVCA)

Project Preferences

Type of Financing Preferred:
Early Stage
Expansion
Balanced
Later Stage

Geographical Preferences

International Preferences:
Hong Kong
China

Industry Preferences

In Consumer Related prefer:
Consumer

In Industrial/Energy prefer:
Environmental Related

In Financial Services prefer:
Financial Services

In Manufact. prefer:
Manufacturing

Additional Information
Year Founded: 2007
Capital Under Management: $47,003,000
Current Activity Level : Actively seeking new investments

PRIDES CROSSING CAPITAL LP

701 Edgewater Drive, Suite 130
Wakefield, MA USA 01880
Phone: 7817165830
Fax: 7817165835
Website: www.pridescrossingcapital.com

Type of Firm
Private Equity Firm

Project Preferences

Type of Financing Preferred:
Mezzanine

Additional Information
Year Founded: 2013
Capital Under Management: $50,570,000
Current Activity Level : Actively seeking new investments

PRIMAL CAPITAL

2-23-1 Akasaka
ARK Hills Front Tower 705
Minato-ku, Japan 107-0052
Website: primalcap.com

Type of Firm
Incubator/Development Program

Project Preferences

Type of Financing Preferred:
Seed
Startup

Geographical Preferences

International Preferences:
Asia
Japan

Additional Information
Year Founded: 2012
Current Activity Level : Actively seeking new investments

PRIMARY CAPITAL LTD

Augustine House
Austin Friars
London, United Kingdom EC2N 2HA
Phone: 442079204800
Fax: 442079204801
E-mail: primary@primaryeurope.com
Website: www.primaryeurope.com

Other Offices
Clarence House
Clarence Street
Manchester, United Kingdom M2 4DW
Phone: 4401616411000

Management and Staff
Iain Wolstenholme, Partner
Neil Wallace, Chief Executive Officer

Type of Firm
Private Equity Firm

Association Membership
British Venture Capital Association (BVCA)
European Private Equity and Venture Capital Assoc.

Project Preferences

Type of Financing Preferred:
Leveraged Buyout
Expansion
Turnaround
Later Stage
Management Buyouts

Geographical Preferences

International Preferences:
United Kingdom
Western Europe
Germany

Industry Focus
(% based on actual investment)
Other Products	79.4%
Consumer Related	16.9%
Computer Hardware	2.8%
Computer Software and Services	1.0%

Additional Information
Name of Most Recent Fund: Primary Capital II
Most Recent Fund Was Raised: 03/18/2002
Year Founded: 1995
Capital Under Management: $585,900,000
Current Activity Level : Actively seeking new investments

PRIMARY CARE INNOVATION FUND

c/o PCOM
4170 City Avenue
Philadelphia, PA USA 19131

Type of Firm
Endowment, Foundation or Pension Fund

Project Preferences

Type of Financing Preferred:
Expansion

Geographical Preferences

United States Preferences:
All U.S.

Industry Preferences

In Medical/Health prefer:
Health Services

Additional Information
Year Founded: 2016
Capital Under Management: $5,000,000
Current Activity Level : Actively seeking new investments

PRIMARY VENTURE PARTNERS

900 Broadway, Suite 203
New York, NY USA 12180
Phone: 5187203087
Fax: 5187203091
E-mail: info@hpvp.com
Website: www.hpvp.com

Management and Staff
Bela Musits, Venture Partner
Bradley Svrluga, Co-Founder
Mark Davis, Venture Partner
Rahul Gandhi, Principal
Russell Howard, Co-Founder

Type of Firm
Private Equity Firm

Project Preferences

Role in Financing:
Prefer role as deal originator but will also invest in deals created by others

Type of Financing Preferred:
Early Stage
Seed
Startup

Size of Investments Considered:
Min Size of Investment Considered (000s): $50
Max Size of Investment Considered (000s): $500

Geographical Preferences

United States Preferences:
Northeast
New York

Industry Preferences

In Computer Software prefer:
Software

In Internet Specific prefer:
Ecommerce

In Medical/Health prefer:
Medical Products

Additional Information
Name of Most Recent Fund: High Peaks Seed Ventures NY, L.P.
Most Recent Fund Was Raised: 09/20/2010
Year Founded: 2004
Capital Under Management: $46,000,000
Current Activity Level : Actively seeking new investments

PRIMAVERA CAPITAL

No. 1 Jianguomenwai Street
48/F, China World Tower 3
Beijing, China 100004
Phone: 861085598988
Fax: 861085598989
E-mail: contact@primavera-capital.com

Other Offices
8 Finance Street, Central, Suite 5801 Two International Finance Ctr
Hong Kong, Hong Kong
Phone: 85237675000
Fax: 85237675001

Management and Staff
Jie Lian, Partner

Type of Firm
Private Equity Firm

Project Preferences

Type of Financing Preferred:
Leveraged Buyout
Expansion
Turnaround
Special Situation
Distressed Debt

Geographical Preferences

International Preferences:
China

Additional Information
Year Founded: 2011
Capital Under Management: $2,520,367,000
Current Activity Level : Actively seeking new investments

PRIME MONT VENTURE CAPITAL CO LTD

Eight Gongti N Rd., Chaoyang
18/F Tower C, Sanlitun SOHO
Beijing, China 100027
Phone: 861065959696
Fax: 861085900608
E-mail: contact@primemontvc.com
Website: www.primemontvc.com

Management and Staff
Hairuo Zheng, Partner
Yu Lu, Managing Partner

Type of Firm
Private Equity Firm

Project Preferences

Type of Financing Preferred:
Early Stage
Expansion
Balanced
Later Stage

Geographical Preferences

International Preferences:
China

Industry Preferences

In Communications prefer:
Telecommunications
Media and Entertainment

In Biotechnology prefer:
Biotechnology

In Medical/Health prefer:
Pharmaceuticals

In Consumer Related prefer:
Consumer
Entertainment and Leisure
Retail

In Industrial/Energy prefer:
Alternative Energy
Advanced Materials

In Business Serv. prefer:
Services

In Manufact. prefer:
Manufacturing

In Agr/Forestr/Fish prefer:
Agriculture related

Additional Information
Year Founded: 2010
Current Activity Level: Actively seeking new investments

PRIME TECHNOLOGY VENTURES NV

Museumplein 5A
Amsterdam, Netherlands 1071 DJ
Phone: 31202050820
Fax: 31202050819
E-mail: info@primeventures.com

Other Offices
Wellington House, East Road, Suite 217
Cambridge, United Kingdom CB1 1BH
Phone: 441223451007
Fax: 441223451100

Management and Staff
Alexander Ribbink, Partner
Jelto Kromwijk Smits, Partner
Joost Holleman, Partner
Monish Suri, Partner
Roel De Hoop, Partner
Sake Bosch, Managing Partner
Sandeep Kapadia, Venture Partner

Type of Firm
Private Equity Firm

Association Membership
Dutch Venture Capital Associaton (NVP)
European Private Equity and Venture Capital Assoc.

Project Preferences

Type of Financing Preferred:
Early Stage
Balanced
Later Stage
Seed
Startup

Size of Investments Considered:
Min Size of Investment Considered (000s): $652
Max Size of Investment Considered (000s): $32,586

Geographical Preferences

International Preferences:
United Kingdom
Luxembourg
Europe
Netherlands
Western Europe
Scandanavia/Nordic Region
Belgium

Industry Preferences

In Communications prefer:
Communications and Media
Commercial Communications
Telecommunications
Data Communications
Media and Entertainment

In Computer Software prefer:
Software

In Internet Specific prefer:
Internet
Ecommerce

In Computer Other prefer:
Computer Related

In Semiconductor/Electr prefer:
Electronics
Semiconductor

In Industrial/Energy prefer:
Energy
Alternative Energy
Energy Conservation Relat

In Business Serv. prefer:
Consulting Services

In Other prefer:
Environment Responsible

Additional Information
Year Founded: 1999
Capital Under Management: $358,400,000
Current Activity Level: Actively seeking new investments

PRIME VALUE CAPITAL MANAGEMENT LTD

100 Balizhuang Xili, Chaoyang
A70 One Zhubang 2000
Beijing, China
Phone: 861085868816
Fax: 861085868385
E-mail: lqchen@primevaluecm.com
Website: www.primevaluecm.com

Management and Staff
Chaoming Zhang, Vice President
Chenhui Wen, Partner
Jianbo Wang, Partner
Rongliang Gu, Managing Director
Tangfeng Yan, Partner
Yansong Chen, Partner

Type of Firm
Investment Management Firm

Project Preferences

Type of Financing Preferred:
Balanced

Geographical Preferences

International Preferences:
China
All International

Industry Preferences

In Biotechnology prefer:
Biotechnology

In Medical/Health prefer:
Medical/Health

In Consumer Related prefer:
Retail

In Industrial/Energy prefer:
Environmental Related

Additional Information
Year Founded: 2009
Current Activity Level : Actively seeking new investments

PRIME VENTURE PARTNERS

Boulevard Plaza, Tower 1
Sheikh Mohammed Bin
Dubai, Utd. Arab Em.
Phone: 971503563778
Website: primeventurepartners.com

Type of Firm
Private Equity Firm

Project Preferences

Type of Financing Preferred:
Early Stage

Geographical Preferences

International Preferences:
Middle East

Additional Information
Year Founded: 2016
Current Activity Level : Actively seeking new investments

PRIMERA CAPITAL

8598 South Miller
Littleton, CO USA 80127
E-mail: info@primeracapital.com
Website: www.primeracapital.com

Management and Staff
Mohanbir Gyani, Partner
Oren Zeev, Partner
Ori Sasson, Partner
Sharam Sasson, Partner

Type of Firm
Private Equity Firm

Project Preferences

Type of Financing Preferred:
Early Stage

Industry Preferences

In Communications prefer:
Telecommunications
Wireless Communications

In Computer Software prefer:
Software
Applications Software

In Internet Specific prefer:
Internet

Additional Information
Year Founded: 2008
Current Activity Level : Actively seeking new investments

PRIMUS CAPITAL

5900 Landerbrook Drive, Suite 200
Cleveland, OH USA 44124
Phone: 4406847300
Fax: 4406847342
E-mail: info@primuscapital.com
Website: www.primuscapital.com

Management and Staff
Jonathan Dick, Managing Director
L Wilson, Managing Director
Phillip Molner, Managing Director
Ronald Hess, Principal
Scott Harper, Managing Director
William Mulligan, Managing Director

Type of Firm
Private Equity Firm

Project Preferences

Role in Financing:
Prefer role as deal originator but will also invest in deals created by others

Type of Financing Preferred:
Leveraged Buyout
Expansion
Generalist PE
Balanced
Management Buyouts
Acquisition
Recapitalizations

Size of Investments Considered:
Min Size of Investment Considered (000s): $15,000
Max Size of Investment Considered (000s): $40,000

Geographical Preferences

United States Preferences:

Canadian Preferences:
All Canada

Industry Focus
(% based on actual investment)
Communications and Media	32.4%
Computer Software and Services	17.6%
Other Products	16.2%
Medical/Health	11.4%
Consumer Related	7.5%
Internet Specific	6.3%
Biotechnology	3.7%
Industrial/Energy	2.9%
Computer Hardware	1.3%
Semiconductors/Other Elect.	0.7%

Additional Information
Name of Most Recent Fund: Primus Capital Fund VII, L.P.
Most Recent Fund Was Raised: 03/06/2012
Year Founded: 1983
Capital Under Management: $625,000,000
Current Activity Level : Actively seeking new investments
Method of Compensation: Return on investment is of primary concern, do not charge fees

PRIMUS CAPITAL PARTNERS LLC

Marvany Utca 16
Budapest, Hungary 1012
Phone: 3612251162
Fax: 3612251163
E-mail: info@primuscapital.hu

Management and Staff
Zoltan Bruckner, Managing Partner

Type of Firm
Private Equity Firm

Association Membership
Hungarian Venture Capital Association (HVCA)

Project Preferences

Type of Financing Preferred:
Early Stage
Expansion
Balanced

Size of Investments Considered:
Min Size of Investment Considered (000s): $50
Max Size of Investment Considered (000s): $500

Geographical Preferences

International Preferences:
Hungary
Slovak Repub.
Central Europe
Europe
Czech Republic

Industry Preferences

In Communications prefer:
Telecommunications

In Computer Software prefer:
Software

In Semiconductor/Electr prefer:
Electronics

In Biotechnology prefer:
Biotechnology

In Medical/Health prefer:
Pharmaceuticals

In Financial Services prefer:
Real Estate

Additional Information
Year Founded: 2003
Current Activity Level : Actively seeking new investments

PRINCETON BIOPHARMA CAPITAL PARTNERS LLC

750 Route 202, Suite 620
Bridgewater, NJ USA 08807
Website: www.princetonbcp.com

Management and Staff
Barry Levinson, Managing Director
George Parise, Managing Director
Michael Wells, Managing Director

Type of Firm
Investment Management Firm

Project Preferences

Type of Financing Preferred:
Early Stage
Expansion
Later Stage

Industry Preferences

In Medical/Health prefer:
Health Services

Additional Information
Year Founded: 1969
Current Activity Level : Actively seeking new investments

PRINCETON GROWTH VENTURES LLC

1185 Sixth Avenue
Third Floor
New York, NY USA 10036
E-mail: info@princetongv.com
Website: www.princetongv.com

Management and Staff
Varoon Raghavan, President

Type of Firm
Private Equity Firm

Project Preferences

Type of Financing Preferred:
Generalist PE

Geographical Preferences

International Preferences:
Latin America
India
China
Asia

Industry Preferences

In Communications prefer:
Telecommunications

In Business Serv. prefer:
Media

Additional Information
Year Founded: 2017
Current Activity Level : Actively seeking new investments

PRINCETON UNIVERSITY INVESTMENT CO

22 Chambers Street, Suite 400
Princeton, NJ USA 08544
Phone: 6092584136

Management and Staff
Andrew Golden, President
Dan Feder, Managing Director

Type of Firm
Private Equity Firm

Project Preferences

Type of Financing Preferred:
Generalist PE

Additional Information
Year Founded: 2001
Current Activity Level : Actively seeking new investments

PRINCETON VENTURES MANAGEMENT LLC

254 Witherspoon Street
Princeton, NJ USA 08542
Phone: 6099453961
Fax: 6099453962
E-mail: info@princetonventures.com
Website: princetonventures.com

Management and Staff
Alexander Harrison, Partner
James Waskovich, Co-Founder
Michael Swackhamer, Vice President
Robert Lerner, Venture Partner
William Martin, Co-Founder

Type of Firm
Private Equity Firm

Project Preferences

Type of Financing Preferred:
Leveraged Buyout
Expansion
Acquisition
Recapitalizations

Industry Preferences

In Communications prefer:
Media and Entertainment

In Internet Specific prefer:
Internet

In Medical/Health prefer:
Medical/Health
Health Services

In Consumer Related prefer:
Consumer
Education Related

In Financial Services prefer:
Financial Services

In Business Serv. prefer:
Services
Media

Additional Information
Year Founded: 2000
Current Activity Level : Actively seeking new investments

PRINCEVILLE GLOBAL PARTNERS LTD

101 Natoma Street
Second Floor
San Francisco, CA USA 94105
Phone: 4154328880
E-mail: inquiries@pvglobal.com
Website: www.princevilleglobal.com

Type of Firm
Private Equity Firm

Project Preferences

Type of Financing Preferred:
Balanced

Industry Preferences

In Computer Software prefer:
Software

Additional Information
Year Founded: 2017
Current Activity Level : Actively seeking new investments

PRINCIPLE CAPITAL LTD

No. 360 Pudong South Road
26F, New Shanghai Int Building
Shanghai, China 200120
Phone: 862168862466
Fax: 862168862467
E-mail: dhwang@principle-capital.com
Website: www.principle-capital.com

Management and Staff
Feng Yin, Vice President
Hui Chen, Vice President
Ligao Huang, Vice President
Lin Lin Zhou, Chief Executive Officer
Ping Wu, Vice President
Zhongren Jin, Vice President

Type of Firm
Private Equity Firm

Project Preferences

Type of Financing Preferred:
Leveraged Buyout
Balanced
Acquisition

Geographical Preferences

International Preferences:
China

Industry Preferences

In Biotechnology prefer:
Biotechnology

In Medical/Health prefer:
Medical/Health
Pharmaceuticals

In Consumer Related prefer:
Food/Beverage
Consumer Products

In Industrial/Energy prefer:
Energy
Materials

Additional Information
Year Founded: 2002
Current Activity Level : Actively seeking new investments

PRISM VENTUREWORKS

75 Second Avenue, Suite 210
Needham, MA USA 02494
Phone: 7813024000
Fax: 7813024040
E-mail: ir@prismventure.com
Website: www.prismventure.com

Management and Staff
Anthony Natale, Venture Partner
Brendan O Leary, Managing Director
Jim Counihan, Managing Director
John Brooks, Co-Founder
Robert Fleming, Co-Founder
Steven Benson, Managing Director

Type of Firm
Private Equity Firm

Association Membership
New England Venture Capital Association

Project Preferences

Role in Financing:
Prefer role as deal originator but will also invest in deals created by others

Type of Financing Preferred:
Early Stage
Expansion
Startup

Geographical Preferences

United States Preferences:

Canadian Preferences:
All Canada

Industry Focus
(% based on actual investment)
Medical/Health	32.0%
Internet Specific	22.9%
Communications and Media	15.5%
Computer Software and Services	13.5%
Biotechnology	5.5%
Computer Hardware	5.0%
Semiconductors/Other Elect.	4.7%
Industrial/Energy	0.8%
Consumer Related	0.2%

Additional Information
Year Founded: 1996
Capital Under Management: $1,250,000,000
Current Activity Level : Actively seeking new investments
Method of Compensation: Return on investment is of primary concern, do not charge fees

---

PRITZKER GROUP VENTURE CAPITAL

111 South Wacker Drive, Suite 4000
Chicago, IL USA 60606
Phone: 3124476000
Fax: 3124476006
Website: www.pritzkergroup.com

Other Offices
11111 Santa Monica Boulevard, Suite 1650
West Los Angeles, CA USA 90025
Phone: 3105759400

Management and Staff
Adam Koopersmith, Partner
Brad West, Principal
Carter Cast, Venture Partner
Christopher Girgenti, Managing Partner
David Habiger, Venture Partner
Gabe Greenbaum, Partner
J.B. Pritzker, Founder
Jeffrey Maters, Vice President
Kevin Willer, Venture Partner
Matthew McCall, Partner
Peter Liu, Vice President
Sonia Sahney Nagar, Vice President
Tony Pritzker, Partner

Type of Firm
Private Equity Firm

Association Membership
Illinois Venture Capital Association
National Venture Capital Association - USA (NVCA)

Project Preferences

Role in Financing:
Prefer role as deal originator but will also invest in deals created by others

Type of Financing Preferred:
Early Stage
Later Stage

Size of Investments Considered:
Min Size of Investment Considered (000s): $3,000
Max Size of Investment Considered (000s): $7,000

Geographical Preferences

United States Preferences:
Illinois

Industry Focus
(% based on actual investment)
Internet Specific	53.1%
Computer Software and Services	43.7%
Computer Hardware	1.4%
Communications and Media	1.3%
Consumer Related	0.6%

Additional Information
Year Founded: 1996
Capital Under Management: $75,000,000
Current Activity Level : Actively seeking new investments
Method of Compensation: Return on investment is of primary concern, do not charge fees

---

PRIVATE ADVISORS LLC

901 East Byrd Street
Riverfront Plaza West
Richmond, VA USA 23219
Phone: 8042896000
Fax: 8042896001
Website: www.privateadvisors.com

Other Offices

4/5 Grosvenor Place
Ground Floor A (Front South)
London, United Kingdom SW1X 7HJ
Phone: 44-779-556-0525

1660 West 2nd Street, Suite 940
Cleveland, OH USA 44113

1290 Avenue of the Americas
34th Floor
New York, NY USA 10104

Management and Staff

Amy Gray, Chief Financial Officer
Charles Johnson, Partner
Charles Honey, Managing Director
Christopher Mackay, Partner
Christopher Stringer, Partner
Craig Truitt, Partner
Gregory Ciaverelli, Managing Director
James Shannon, Chief Operating Officer
Jennifer Buckley, Managing Director
Jens Bisgaard-Frantzen, Partner
John Davenport, Partner
Kee Rabb, Managing Director
Laura Baird, Vice President
Louis Moelchert, Managing Partner
Louise Smith, Vice President
Macon Clarkson, Vice President
Matthew Baker, Managing Director
Michael Fuller, Partner
Peter Fink, Managing Director
Rafael Astruc, Partner
Rickard Fischerstrom, Managing Director
Robert Voeks, Partner
S.S. Taliaferro, Managing Director
Scott Crenshaw, Vice President
T. Scott White, Vice President
Timothy Berry, Partner
Tod Childress, Partner
Todd Milligan, Vice President

Type of Firm

Private Equity Advisor or Fund of Funds

Project Preferences

Type of Financing Preferred:
Fund of Funds
Leveraged Buyout
Expansion
Fund of Funds of Second

Geographical Preferences

United States Preferences:
North America

International Preferences:
Europe
All International

Additional Information

Name of Most Recent Fund: Private Advisors Small Company Private Equity Fund VI, L.P.
Most Recent Fund Was Raised: 01/09/2014
Year Founded: 1997
Capital Under Management: $1,000,000,000
Current Activity Level : Actively seeking new investments

PRIVATE EQUITY INVEST AG

Bahnhofstrasse 69
Zurich, Switzerland 8001
Phone: 41 44 215 70 00
Fax: 41 44 215 70 01
E-mail: info@pei.ch
Website: www.pei.ch

Management and Staff

Aleksander Nunlist, Partner
Cem Yilmaz, Partner
Markus Ritter, Partner

Type of Firm

Private Equity Firm

Association Membership

Swiss Venture Capital Association (SECA)

Project Preferences

Type of Financing Preferred:
Leveraged Buyout
Mezzanine

Geographical Preferences

International Preferences:
Europe
Switzerland

Additional Information

Year Founded: 2000
Current Activity Level : Actively seeking new investments

PRIVATE EQUITY INVESTMENTS II BV

Schiphol Boulevard 375
WTC Schiphol Airport
Schiphol Airport, Netherlands 1118 BJ
Phone: 31206587500
E-mail: info@parcomcapital.com
Website: www.parcomcapital.com

Other Offices

19, Avenue de l'Opera
Paris, France 75001
Phone: 33170086090
Fax: 33142969820

Ludwigstrasse 7
Munich, Georgia 80539
Phone: 49892000380
Fax: 4989200038111

Management and Staff

Anouar Noudari, Partner
Piet-Hein de Jager, Partner

Type of Firm

Corporate PE/Venture

Association Membership

European Private Equity and Venture Capital Assoc.
Dutch Venture Capital Associaton (NVP)

Project Preferences

Type of Financing Preferred:
Fund of Funds
Leveraged Buyout
Generalist PE
Later Stage
Management Buyouts
Acquisition

Size of Investments Considered:
Min Size of Investment Considered (000s): $13,410
Max Size of Investment Considered (000s): $67,051

Geographical Preferences

International Preferences:
Europe
Netherlands

Industry Preferences

In Computer Software prefer:
Software

In Consumer Related prefer:
Consumer

In Industrial/Energy prefer:
Oil and Gas Exploration
Industrial Products

In Business Serv. prefer:
Services

Additional Information

Year Founded: 1982
Capital Under Management: $1,489,900,000
Current Activity Level : Actively seeking new investments

PRIVATE EQUITY PARTNERS SPA

Via Degli Omenoni, 2
Milan, Italy 20121
Phone: 39028052171
Fax: 39028052321
E-mail: info@privateequitypartners.com
Website: www.privateequitypartners.com

Other Offices

Wielicka Street 36, Suite 9
Warsaw, Poland 02-657
Phone: 48-22-853-1085
Fax: 48-22-853-1085

Pratt's Guide to Private Equity & Venture Capital Sources

25a Bolshoy Strochenosky lane
Moscow, Russia 123100
Phone: 7-495-980-88-77
Fax: 7-495-98-88-77

Fairlink Centre, C.T.S. No. 701
Village Oshiwara, Off New Link Road
Mumbai, India 400 053
Phone: 91-022-22-40933701
Fax: 91-022-4016-8369

Rua Madre Mazzarello 331
Fairfax, VT USA
Phone: 55-1130236166
Fax: 55-1130236166

2809 China insurance Building
166 Lu Jia Zui East Road
Shanghai, China 200120
Phone: 86-21-5879-5600
Fax: 86-21-5879-5699

Management and Staff
Giovanni Campolo, Founder
Leonardo Bruzzichesi, Partner

Type of Firm
Bank Affiliated

Association Membership
European Private Equity and Venture Capital Assoc.

Project Preferences

Role in Financing:
Prefer role as deal originator but will also invest in deals created by others

Type of Financing Preferred:
Leveraged Buyout
Later Stage
Management Buyouts
Acquisition

Size of Investments Considered:
Min Size of Investment Considered (000s): $900
Max Size of Investment Considered: No Limit

Geographical Preferences

International Preferences:
Italy
India
China
Russia

Industry Focus
(% based on actual investment)
Industrial/Energy	60.4%
Computer Software and Services	20.9%
Other Products	15.3%
Consumer Related	3.0%
Internet Specific	0.4%

Additional Information
Year Founded: 1989
Capital Under Management: $706,100,000

Current Activity Level : Actively seeking new investments

PRIVEQ CAPITAL FUNDS
1500 Don Mills Road, Suite 711
Toronto, Canada M3B 3K4
Phone: 4164473330
Fax: 4164473331
Website: www.priveq.ca

Management and Staff
Bradley Ashley, Managing Partner
Lee Grunberg, Partner

Type of Firm
Private Equity Firm

Association Membership
Canadian Venture Capital Association

Project Preferences

Role in Financing:
Prefer role as deal originator but will also invest in deals created by others

Type of Financing Preferred:
Leveraged Buyout
Expansion
Turnaround
Management Buyouts
Acquisition
Recapitalizations

Geographical Preferences

United States Preferences:

Canadian Preferences:
All Canada

Industry Preferences

In Business Serv. prefer:
Services
Distribution

In Manufact. prefer:
Manufacturing

Additional Information
Year Founded: 1994
Capital Under Management: $73,700,000
Current Activity Level : Actively seeking new investments
Method of Compensation: Return on investment is of primary concern, do not charge fees

PRIVEQ PARTNERS AB
Humlegardsgatan 20
Box 5295
Stockholm, Sweden 102 46
Phone: 4684596760
Fax: 468203566
E-mail: info@priveq.se

Website: www.priveq.se

Management and Staff
Helena Ekstrand, Chief Financial Officer
Mikael Selin, Co-Founder

Type of Firm
Private Equity Firm

Association Membership
Swedish Venture Capital Association (SVCA)
European Private Equity and Venture Capital Assoc.

Project Preferences

Type of Financing Preferred:
Leveraged Buyout
Acquisition

Size of Investments Considered:
Min Size of Investment Considered (000s): $5,400
Max Size of Investment Considered (000s): $13,500

Geographical Preferences

International Preferences:
Sweden
Scandanavia/Nordic Region

Industry Preferences

In Semiconductor/Electr prefer:
Electronics

In Medical/Health prefer:
Medical/Health
Medical Products
Disposable Med. Products
Pharmaceuticals

In Consumer Related prefer:
Sports
Consumer Products

In Industrial/Energy prefer:
Environmental Related

In Manufact. prefer:
Manufacturing

Additional Information
Name of Most Recent Fund: Priveq Investment Fund IV
Most Recent Fund Was Raised: 05/02/2011
Year Founded: 1983
Capital Under Management: $157,900,000
Current Activity Level : Actively seeking new investments

PRIVET CAPITAL LLP
35 Bruton Street
London, United Kingdom W1J 6QY
Phone: 442071933382
Website: www.privetcapital.co.uk

Management and Staff
Stephen Keating, Founder

Type of Firm
Private Equity Firm

Project Preferences

Type of Financing Preferred:
Turnaround
Distressed Debt
Recapitalizations

Geographical Preferences

International Preferences:
United Kingdom

Additional Information
Year Founded: 2009
Current Activity Level : Actively seeking new investments

PROA CAPITAL DE INVERSIONES SGEIC SA

Fortuny 5 4B
Madrid, Spain 28010
Phone: 34913911309
Fax: 34913915151
E-mail: info@proacapital.com
Website: proacapital.com

Management and Staff
Alberto Yanci, Partner
Fernando Ortiz-Vaamonde, Managing Director
Santiago Gomez, Partner

Type of Firm
Private Equity Firm

Association Membership
Spanish Venture Capital Association (ASCRI)

Project Preferences

Type of Financing Preferred:
Leveraged Buyout
Management Buyouts

Size of Investments Considered:
Min Size of Investment Considered (000s): $12,199
Max Size of Investment Considered (000s): $60,998

Geographical Preferences

International Preferences:
Portugal
Spain

Additional Information
Year Founded: 2007
Capital Under Management: $327,175,000
Current Activity Level : Actively seeking new investments

PROBING SHANGHAI VENTURE CAPITAL PARTNERSHIP ENTERPRISE LP

288 Xiang Cheng Rd, Pudong Xin
Room 1107, SOHO Century Plaza
Shanghai, China 200120
Phone: 862158309168
Fax: 862158303168
Website: www.probingvc.com

Type of Firm
Private Equity Firm

Project Preferences

Type of Financing Preferred:
Early Stage
Seed
Startup

Geographical Preferences

International Preferences:
China

Industry Preferences

In Communications prefer:
Telecommunications
Media and Entertainment

Additional Information
Year Founded: 2014
Current Activity Level : Actively seeking new investments

PROBITAS PARTNERS INC

425 California Street, Suite 2300
San Francisco, CA USA 94104
Phone: 4154020700
Fax: 4154020052
E-mail: info@probitaspartners.com
Website: www.probitaspartners.com

Other Offices
3 Garden Road
21/F ICBC Tower Citibank Plaza
Central, Hong Kong
Phone: 852-2273-5143
Fax: 852-2273-5999

1251 Avenue of the Americas, 44th Floor, Suite 2390
New York, NY USA 10020
Phone: 212-403-3662
Fax: 212-403-3537

36-38 Southampton Street
1st Floor Dudley House
London, United Kingdom WC2E 7HF
Phone: 44-20-7845-5400
Fax: 44-20-7240-3339

Management and Staff
Adam Frieman, Partner
Alan Bear, Principal
Charles Phillips, Vice President
Christopher Mayo, Vice President
Craig Marmer, Founder
Dale Meyer, Partner
David Dinerman, Chief Financial Officer
Greg Hausler, Managing Director
Jack Wills, Managing Director
Jane Harris, Vice President
Jeffrey Mills, Principal
Jenny West, Vice President
John Murphy, Chief Financial Officer
Jonathan Jameson, Principal
Kelly DePonte, Managing Director
Michael Hoffmann, President
Nam Hoang, Vice President
Ray Tsao, Vice President
Reidan Cruz, Partner
Robert Hofeditz, Partner
Stacy Kincaid, Vice President
Stephen Salyer, Vice President

Type of Firm
Private Equity Firm

Association Membership
Hong Kong Venture Capital Association (HKVCA)

Project Preferences

Type of Financing Preferred:
Balanced

Geographical Preferences

United States Preferences:
All U.S.

Industry Preferences

In Financial Services prefer:
Financial Services

Additional Information
Year Founded: 2001
Current Activity Level : Actively seeking new investments

PROCURITAS PARTNERS KB

Linnegatan 9-11
Stockholm, Sweden 114 47
Phone: 46850614300
Fax: 46850614344
E-mail: procuritas@procuritas.se

Other Offices
Langwisstrasse 32
Zumikon, Switzerland 8126
Phone: 41449183917

Management and Staff
Bjorn Lindberg, Partner
Erik Fougner, Partner
Hans Wikse, Managing Partner
Mattias Feiff, Partner
Mikael Ahlstrom, Partner
Tomas Johansson, Partner

Type of Firm
Private Equity Firm

Association Membership
Swedish Venture Capital Association (SVCA)

Project Preferences

Role in Financing:
Prefer role as deal originator

Type of Financing Preferred:
Leveraged Buyout
Management Buyouts

Geographical Preferences

International Preferences:
Scandanavia/Nordic Region

Additional Information
Name of Most Recent Fund: Procuritas Capital Investors V, L.P.
Most Recent Fund Was Raised: 06/28/2012
Year Founded: 1986
Capital Under Management: $100,000,000
Current Activity Level : Actively seeking new investments
Method of Compensation: Return on invest. most important, but chg. closing fees, service fees, etc.

PROCYON VENTURES

745 Atlantic Avenue
Boston, MA USA 02110
E-mail: contact@procyonventures.com
Website: www.procyonventures.com

Type of Firm
Private Equity Firm

Project Preferences

Type of Financing Preferred:
Early Stage

Industry Preferences

In Semiconductor/Electr prefer:
Sensors

Additional Information
Year Founded: 1969
Current Activity Level : Actively seeking new investments.

PRODIGY CAPITAL MANAGEMENT LLC

Park 80 West, Plaza II, Suite 200
Saddle Brook, NJ USA 07663
Phone: 201-291-2707
Fax: 201-368-1944
Website: www.prodigycapitalmgmt.com

Management and Staff
Cheol Hee Lee, General Partner

Type of Firm
Private Equity Advisor or Fund of Funds

Project Preferences

Type of Financing Preferred:
Fund of Funds
Expansion
Later Stage

Geographical Preferences

United States Preferences:
North America

International Preferences:
China
North Korea
Korea, South
Japan

Industry Preferences

In Communications prefer:
Wireless Communications

In Biotechnology prefer:
Biotechnology

In Medical/Health prefer:
Medical Products

In Business Serv. prefer:
Media

Additional Information
Name of Most Recent Fund: Prodigy Capital Partners LLC
Most Recent Fund Was Raised: 09/24/2010
Year Founded: 2007
Capital Under Management: $6,800,000
Current Activity Level : Actively seeking new investments

PROEQUITA FUND LLC

101 Convention Center Drive, Suite 1005
Las Vegas, NV USA 89109
Phone: 8772432113
E-mail: info@proequita.com
Website: www.proequita.com

Type of Firm
Private Equity Firm

Project Preferences

Type of Financing Preferred:
Leveraged Buyout
Value-Add
Early Stage
Acquisition
Distressed Debt

Industry Preferences

In Industrial/Energy prefer:
Energy

In Financial Services prefer:
Financial Services
Real Estate

Additional Information
Year Founded: 2014
Capital Under Management: $48,000
Current Activity Level : Actively seeking new investments

PROFOUNDERS CAPITAL LTD

3 Cadogan Gate
Chelsea
London, United Kingdom SW1X 0AS
Phone: 442077666900
E-mail: contact@profounderscapital.com

Management and Staff
Andrew Phillipps, Partner
Brent Hoberman, Partner
Daniel Bergmann, Partner
George Coelho, Partner
Johan Brenner, Partner
Jon Wood, Partner
Jonathan Goodwin, Partner
Karen Hanton, Partner
Mark Zaleski, Partner
Matthew Eames, Partner
Matthew Stillman, Partner
Michael Birch, Partner
Mike Danson, Partner
Peter Dubens, Partner
Rogan Angelini-Hurll, General Partner
Russel Glenister, Partner
Sean Seton-Rogers, General Partner
Torben Majgaard, Partner

Type of Firm
Private Equity Firm

Project Preferences

Type of Financing Preferred:
Early Stage

Size of Investments Considered:
Min Size of Investment Considered (000s): $797
Max Size of Investment Considered (000s): $3,984

Pratt's Guide to Private Equity & Venture Capital Sources

Geographical Preferences

International Preferences:
Europe

Industry Preferences

In Business Serv. prefer:
Media

Additional Information

Year Founded: 2009
Capital Under Management: $50,150,000
Current Activity Level : Actively seeking new investments

PROFURA AB

Lilla Bommen 1
Gothenburg, Sweden SE 411 04
Phone: 46317009880
Fax: 46317009885
E-mail: info@profura.se
Website: www.profura.se

Management and Staff

Ola Cronholm, Chief Financial Officer

Type of Firm

Private Equity Firm

Project Preferences

Type of Financing Preferred:
Leveraged Buyout
Value-Add
Generalist PE
Acquisition

Geographical Preferences

International Preferences:
Sweden

Industry Preferences

In Industrial/Energy prefer:
Industrial Products
Materials
Process Control

In Transportation prefer:
Transportation

In Financial Services prefer:
Real Estate

In Business Serv. prefer:
Services

Additional Information

Year Founded: 1994
Current Activity Level : Actively seeking new investments

PROGRAMMA 101 SRL

Via Chiossetto, 1
Milan, Italy 20122
Phone: 3902 36595255
Fax: 3902 49533650
E-mail: info@p101.it
Website: www.p101.it

Management and Staff

Giuseppe Donvito, Partner
Glenda Grazioli, Partner

Type of Firm

Private Equity Firm

Association Membership

Italian Venture Capital Association (AIFI)

Additional Information

Year Founded: 2014
Current Activity Level : Actively seeking new investments

PROGRESS EQUITY PARTNERS LTD

2200 Ross Avenue, Suite 3838
Dallas, TX USA 75201
Phone: 2149783838
Fax: 2149783848
Website: www.progressequity.com

Other Offices

7887 East Belleview Avenue, Suite 1100
GREENWOOD VILLAGE, CO USA 80111
Phone: 303-297-1701
Fax: 303-557-0677

Management and Staff

Carolina Hensley, Vice President
Melanie Barton, Vice President
Michael Bailey, Co-Founder
Paul Yeoham, Co-Founder
Ralph Manning, Co-Founder
Stephen Sangalis, Co-Founder

Type of Firm

Private Equity Firm

Project Preferences

Role in Financing:
Prefer role as deal originator

Type of Financing Preferred:
Leveraged Buyout
Management Buyouts
Acquisition
Recapitalizations

Geographical Preferences

United States Preferences:

Industry Preferences

In Communications prefer:
Communications and Media

In Medical/Health prefer:
Health Services
Pharmaceuticals

In Consumer Related prefer:
Franchises(NEC)
Food/Beverage

In Business Serv. prefer:
Services

Additional Information

Year Founded: 1993
Current Activity Level : Actively seeking new investments

PROGRESS INVESTMENT MANAGEMENT CO

33 New Montgomery Street
19th Floor
San Francisco, CA USA 94105
Phone: 4155123480
Fax: 4155123475
E-mail: mcs@progressinvestment.com
Website: progressinvestment.com

Management and Staff

Samuel Molinaro, President

Type of Firm

Private Equity Firm

Project Preferences

Type of Financing Preferred:
Fund of Funds

Geographical Preferences

United States Preferences:

Additional Information

Year Founded: 1990
Capital Under Management: $65,000,000
Current Activity Level : Actively seeking new investments

PROGRESS VENTURES INC

One Broadway
14th Floor
Cambridge, MA USA 02142
Phone: 6174012711
Website: progressventures.com

Other Offices
245 Park Avenue
27th Floor
New York, NY USA 10167
Phone: 6174012711

Type of Firm
Investment Management Firm

Project Preferences

Type of Financing Preferred:
Early Stage

Industry Preferences

In Communications prefer:
Media and Entertainment

In Internet Specific prefer:
Internet

In Business Serv. prefer:
Media

Additional Information
Name of Most Recent Fund: Progress Ventures Fund II, L.P.
Most Recent Fund Was Raised: 12/05/2013
Year Founded: 2008
Capital Under Management: $21,000,000
Current Activity Level : Actively seeking new investments

PROGRESSIO SGR SPA

Piazza Diaz, No. 7
Milan, Italy
Phone: 390272141245
Fax: 390272141299
E-mail: segreteria@progressiosgr.it
Website: www.progressiosgr.it

Management and Staff
Angelo Catapano, Partner
Angelo Piero La Runa, Partner
Filippo Gaggini, Managing Partner
Guido De Vivo, Managing Partner
Nino Mascellaro, Partner
Stefania Petruccioli, Partner

Type of Firm
Private Equity Firm

Project Preferences

Type of Financing Preferred:
Leveraged Buyout
Balanced

Geographical Preferences

International Preferences:
Italy
Europe

Industry Preferences

In Consumer Related prefer:
Retail
Consumer Products

Additional Information
Year Founded: 2004
Capital Under Management: $295,171,000
Current Activity Level : Actively seeking new investments

PROGRESSION CAPITAL AFRICA LTD.

Haven Court Block B Unit 6
Waiyaki Way Westland
Nairobi, Kenya 00606
Phone: 2302129800
Fax: 2302129833
Website: www.progressioncapitalafrica.com

Type of Firm
Private Equity Firm

Project Preferences

Type of Financing Preferred:
Generalist PE

Geographical Preferences

International Preferences:
Kenya

Additional Information
Year Founded: 2016
Current Activity Level : Actively seeking new investments

PROGRESSUS MANAGEMENT AS

Klubbgaten 1
2nd floor
Stavanger, Norway 4013
Phone: 4790504400
Fax: 4794750040
E-mail: progressus@progressus.no
Website: www.progressus.no

Management and Staff
Per Jensen, Partner
Rune Jensen, Managing Partner

Type of Firm
Private Equity Firm

Association Membership
Norwegian Venture Capital Association

Project Preferences

Type of Financing Preferred:
Leveraged Buyout

Size of Investments Considered:
Min Size of Investment Considered (000s): $3,329
Max Size of Investment Considered (000s): $19,973

Geographical Preferences

International Preferences:
Norway

Industry Preferences

In Industrial/Energy prefer:
Energy

In Manufact. prefer:
Manufacturing

Additional Information
Year Founded: 2006
Capital Under Management: $82,300,000
Current Activity Level : Actively seeking new investments

PROJECT 11 VENTURES, L.P.

Six Dexter Road
Lexington, MA USA 02420
Phone: 6175289011
Website: www.project11.com

Type of Firm
Private Equity Firm

Project Preferences

Type of Financing Preferred:
Early Stage

Additional Information
Year Founded: 2010
Current Activity Level : Actively seeking new investments

PROJECT A VENTURES GMBH & CO KG

Julie-Wolfthorn-Strasse 1
Berlin, Germany 10115
Phone: 4930340606300
Fax: 4930340606399
E-mail: info@project-a.com
Website: www.project-a.com

Management and Staff
Christian Weiss, Managing Director
Thies Sander, Managing Director
Uwe Horstmann, Managing Director

Type of Firm
Incubator/Development Program

Project Preferences

Type of Financing Preferred:
Early Stage
Seed
Startup

Geographical Preferences

International Preferences:
Germany

Industry Preferences

In Communications prefer:
Wireless Communications

In Internet Specific prefer:
Internet

Additional Information
Year Founded: 2012
Capital Under Management: $260,000,000
Current Activity Level : Actively seeking new investments

PROLOG VENTURES

7701 Forsyth Boulevard, Suite 1095
Saint Louis, MO USA 63105
Phone: 3147432400
Fax: 3147432403
Website: www.prologventures.com

Management and Staff
Brian Clevinger, Managing Director
Daniel Broderick, Venture Partner
Gregory Johnson, Managing Director
Ilya Nykin, Managing Director
John Steuart, Managing Director

Type of Firm
Private Equity Firm

Project Preferences

Role in Financing:
Will function either as deal originator or investor in deals created by others

Type of Financing Preferred:
Early Stage
Startup

Industry Preferences

In Industrial/Energy prefer:
Environmental Related

Additional Information
Name of Most Recent Fund: Prolog Capital IV, L.P.
Most Recent Fund Was Raised: 07/24/2013
Year Founded: 2001
Capital Under Management: $120,000,000
Current Activity Level : Actively seeking new investments

PROLOGIS INC

2-7-3, Marunouchi, Chiyoda-ku
Tokyo Building, 21st Floor
Tokyo, Japan 105-7104
Phone: 81-3-6860-9090
Fax: 81-3-6860-9050
Website: www.prologis.co.jp

Other Offices
Former HQ: 4F Shiodome City Center, 1-5-
Higashi-Shimbashi, Minato-ku
Tokyo, Japan 105-7104
Phone: 81-3-6215-9099
Fax: 81-3-6215-8490

2-2-22, Umeda, Kita-ku
HERBIS ENT Office Tower, 9F
Osaka, Japan 530-0001
Phone: 81-6-7664-9000
Fax: 81-6-7664-9010

Type of Firm
Corporate PE/Venture

Project Preferences

Type of Financing Preferred:
Opportunistic

Geographical Preferences

International Preferences:
Japan

Industry Preferences

In Financial Services prefer:
Real Estate

Additional Information
Year Founded: 1999
Current Activity Level : Actively seeking new investments

PROMECAP SA DE CV

Bosque de Alisos No. 47A-3
Bosques de las Lomas
Mexico City, Mexico 05120
Phone: 525511050800
Website: www.promecap.com

Type of Firm
Private Equity Firm

Project Preferences

Type of Financing Preferred:
Leveraged Buyout
Mezzanine
Acquisition
Special Situation

Additional Information
Name of Most Recent Fund: Promecap
Most Recent Fund Was Raised: 08/05/2010
Year Founded: 1997
Capital Under Management: $199,168,000
Current Activity Level : Actively seeking new investments

PROMETHEAN INVESTMENTS FUND LP

5 Old Bailey
2nd Floor
London, United Kingdom EC4M 7BA
Phone: 442072462590

Management and Staff
Michael Burt, Partner
Michael Biddulph, Partner

Type of Firm
Private Equity Firm

Project Preferences

Type of Financing Preferred:
Early Stage
Expansion
Balanced
Public Companies
Seed
Special Situation
Distressed Debt

Geographical Preferences

International Preferences:
United Kingdom

Additional Information
Year Founded: 2005
Capital Under Management: $30,307,000
Current Activity Level : Actively seeking new investments

PROMETHEUS CAPITAL CO LTD

No. 93, Jianguo Road
A, Wanda Plaza, Chaoyang Dist
Beijing, China 100022
Website: www.pusicapital.com

Type of Firm
Private Equity Firm

Project Preferences

Type of Financing Preferred:
Early Stage
Expansion
Startup

Geographical Preferences

International Preferences:
China

Industry Preferences

In Medical/Health prefer:
Medical Products
Health Services

In Consumer Related prefer:
Consumer Products

In Industrial/Energy prefer:
Energy
Energy Conservation Relat
Advanced Materials

In Manufact. prefer:
Manufacturing

In Agr/Forestr/Fish prefer:
Agriculture related

In Other prefer:
Environment Responsible

Additional Information

Year Founded: 2009
Current Activity Level : Actively seeking new investments

PROMON VENTURES(PROMON)

Av. Pres. Juscelino Kubitschek
1830
Sao Paulo, Brazil 04543-900
Phone: 551138474488
Fax: 551138474890
E-mail: ventures@promon.com.br

Other Offices

Rod. SP - 340 (Campinas-Mogi), km 118,5
Building 9A
Campinas, Brazil 13086-902
Phone: 55-19-3707-3400

Av. Abiurana, 449 - Block 1
Manaus , Brazil 69075-010
Phone: 55-92-3616-9201

Praia do Flamengo, 154
Rio de Janeiro, Brazil 22210-906
Phone: 55-21-3235-1200

Type of Firm
Private Equity Firm

Project Preferences

Type of Financing Preferred:
Balanced

Geographical Preferences

International Preferences:
Brazil

Industry Preferences

In Communications prefer:
Telecommunications

In Consumer Related prefer:
Education Related

In Industrial/Energy prefer:
Energy
Oil and Gas Exploration

In Transportation prefer:
Transportation

In Agr/Forestr/Fish prefer:
Mining and Minerals

Additional Information
Year Founded: 1960
Current Activity Level : Actively seeking new investments

PROMOTORA DE PROYECTOS SA

Carrera 35A, Edificio Prisma
Ste 15B-35,Ofc 401,Piso 4 Sur
Medellin, Colombia
Phone: 5744484511
Fax: 5743113903
E-mail: infopro@promotora.com.co
Website: www.promotora.com.co

Management and Staff
Rafael Yepes, Managing Partner

Type of Firm
Private Equity Firm

Project Preferences

Type of Financing Preferred:
Early Stage
Expansion
Balanced
Later Stage

Geographical Preferences

International Preferences:
Peru
Mexico
Chile
Colombia

Industry Preferences

In Communications prefer:
Communications and Media

In Biotechnology prefer:
Biotechnology

In Medical/Health prefer:
Medical/Health

In Industrial/Energy prefer:
Materials
Advanced Materials
Environmental Related

Additional Information
Year Founded: 2009
Capital Under Management: $78,000,000
Current Activity Level : Actively seeking new investments

PROMUS EQUITY PARTNERS

30 South Wacker Drive, Suite 1600
Chicago, IL USA 60606
Phone: 3127843990
Fax: 3127843991
Website: www.promusequity.com

Other Offices
Former HQ: Ten South Wacker Drive, Suite 2250
Chicago, IL USA 60606
Phone: 3127843990
Fax: 3127843991

Management and Staff
Andrew Code, Partner
Sarah Wuellner, Partner
Steven Brown, Partner

Type of Firm
Investment Management Firm

Project Preferences

Type of Financing Preferred:
Leveraged Buyout
Expansion
Management Buyouts
Acquisition
Recapitalizations

Industry Preferences

In Consumer Related prefer:
Consumer
Food/Beverage
Consumer Products

In Industrial/Energy prefer:
Industrial Products

In Business Serv. prefer:
Services
Distribution

In Manufact. prefer:
Manufacturing

Additional Information
Year Founded: 2010
Capital Under Management: $500,000,000
Current Activity Level : Actively seeking new investments

PROMUS VENTURES

30 South Wacker Drive, Suite 1600
Chicago, IL USA 60606
Website: www.promusventures.com

Type of Firm
Private Equity Firm

Project Preferences

Type of Financing Preferred:
Early Stage

Industry Preferences

In Computer Software prefer:
Software

Additional Information
Year Founded: 1969
Capital Under Management: $14,720,000
Current Activity Level : Actively seeking new investments

PROOF VENTURES LLC

625 Second Street, Suite 102
San Francisco, CA USA 94107
E-mail: info@proofventures.com
Website: proofventures.com

Type of Firm
Private Equity Firm

Project Preferences

Type of Financing Preferred:
Early Stage
Balanced
Later Stage

Geographical Preferences

United States Preferences:

International Preferences:
North Korea
Korea, South

Additional Information
Year Founded: 2013
Current Activity Level : Actively seeking new investments

PROPARCO SA

151 Rue Saint Honore
Paris, France 75001
Phone: 33153443108
Fax: 33153443838
E-mail: proparco@proparco.fr
Website: www.proparco.fr

Management and Staff
Etienne Viard, Chief Executive Officer
Marie Sennequier, Chief Financial Officer

Type of Firm
Private Equity Firm

Association Membership
Emerging Markets Private Equity Association

Project Preferences

Type of Financing Preferred:
Fund of Funds
Leveraged Buyout
Early Stage
Mezzanine
Generalist PE
Later Stage
Management Buyouts
Acquisition
Startup

Size of Investments Considered:
Min Size of Investment Considered (000s): $626
Max Size of Investment Considered (000s): $25,053

Geographical Preferences

International Preferences:
Asia
Africa

Industry Preferences

In Communications prefer:
Communications and Media

In Biotechnology prefer:
Agricultural/Animal Bio.

In Industrial/Energy prefer:
Industrial Products

In Financial Services prefer:
Financial Services

In Manufact. prefer:
Manufacturing

Additional Information
Year Founded: 1977
Capital Under Management: $118,400,000
Current Activity Level : Actively seeking new investments

PROPEL EQUITY PARTNERS LLC

10 Glenville Street
Greenwich, CT USA 06831
Phone: 9146974855
Fax: 9146974854
E-mail: info@mcc-cap.com
Website: propelequity.com

Management and Staff
John Belniak, Partner
Michael Cornell, Partner
Robert Farinholt, Partner

Type of Firm
Private Equity Firm

Project Preferences

Type of Financing Preferred:
Later Stage
Management Buyouts
Recapitalizations

Size of Investments Considered:
Min Size of Investment Considered (000s): $5,000
Max Size of Investment Considered (000s): $15,000

Geographical Preferences

United States Preferences:
North America

Industry Preferences

In Consumer Related prefer:
Entertainment and Leisure
Consumer Products

In Financial Services prefer:
Financial Services

In Business Serv. prefer:
Distribution

In Manufact. prefer:
Manufacturing

Additional Information
Year Founded: 2012
Current Activity Level : Actively seeking new investments

PROPEL VENTURE PARTNERS

55 2nd Street, Suite 1900
San Francisco, CA USA 94105
E-mail: hello@propel.vc
Website: www.propel.vc

Type of Firm
Private Equity Firm

Project Preferences

Type of Financing Preferred:
Early Stage
Expansion
Later Stage

Industry Preferences

In Financial Services prefer:
Financial Services

PROPHET EQUITY LLC

1460 Main Street, Suite 200
Southlake, TX USA 76092
Phone: 8178981500
Fax: 8178981509
E-mail: info@prophetequity.com
Website: www.prophetequity.com

Management and Staff

Ben Eakes, Principal
Michael Sullivan, Vice President
Pelham Smith, Managing Director
Trevor Cohen, Vice President

Type of Firm

Private Equity Firm

Project Preferences

Type of Financing Preferred:
Leveraged Buyout
Turnaround
Acquisition
Special Situation
Recapitalizations

Industry Preferences

In Medical/Health prefer:
Medical/Health

In Consumer Related prefer:
Consumer Products
Consumer Services

In Industrial/Energy prefer:
Energy

In Transportation prefer:
Transportation
Aerospace

In Financial Services prefer:
Financial Services

In Business Serv. prefer:
Distribution

In Manufact. prefer:
Manufacturing

Additional Information

Year Founded: 2007
Capital Under Management: $300,000,000
Current Activity Level : Actively seeking new investments

PROPHETES DD

Koprska ulica 108 A
Ljubljana, Slovenia 1000
Phone: 38612443870
Fax: 38612443871
E-mail: info@prophetes.com
Website: www.prophetes.com

Type of Firm

Private Equity Firm

Project Preferences

Type of Financing Preferred:
Early Stage
Expansion
Balanced
Later Stage
Startup

Geographical Preferences

International Preferences:
Slovenia
Europe

Industry Preferences

In Medical/Health prefer:
Medical Products

In Consumer Related prefer:
Consumer Products

Additional Information

Year Founded: 1999
Current Activity Level : Actively seeking new investments

PROPRIUM CAPITAL PARTNERS LP

One Landmark Square
19th Floor
Stamford, CT USA 06901
Phone: 2038830355
E-mail: info@proprium.com
Website: proprium.com

Management and Staff

Anthony Kingsley, Partner
Frank Shu, Principal
J. Timothy Morris, Co-Founder
Javier Lecumberri, Principal
John Clingan, Principal
John Curran, Chief Financial Officer
Jonathan Harper, Chief Operating Officer
Philipp Westermann, Partner
Rajat Tandon, Managing Director
Rajul Patel, Principal
Siddharth Sangal, Vice President
Thomas Wong, Partner
Thomas Carey, Managing Director
Tony Martin, Partner

Additional Information

Year Founded: 2016
Capital Under Management: $150,000,000
Current Activity Level : Actively seeking new investments

Willem De Geus, Co-Founder
Yash Ravel, Principal

Type of Firm

Private Equity Firm

Project Preferences

Type of Financing Preferred:
Leveraged Buyout
Opportunistic
Management Buyouts
Acquisition

Industry Preferences

In Financial Services prefer:
Real Estate

Additional Information

Year Founded: 1969
Current Activity Level : Actively seeking new investments

PROPULSION VENTURES INC

1250 Rene-Levesque Boulevard
38th Floor
Montreal, Canada H3B 4W8
Phone: 5143979797
Fax: 5143978451

Management and Staff

Denis Sirois, Vice President
Jean-Paul Tardif, Vice President
Michel Cordeau, Vice President

Type of Firm

Private Equity Firm

Project Preferences

Type of Financing Preferred:
Early Stage
Expansion
Seed
Startup

Size of Investments Considered:
Min Size of Investment Considered (000s): $1,000
Max Size of Investment Considered (000s): $3,000

Geographical Preferences

United States Preferences:

Canadian Preferences:
All Canada
Quebec
Ontario

Industry Preferences

In Computer Software prefer:
Software

In Internet Specific prefer:
Internet

Additional Information
Name of Most Recent Fund: Propulsion Ventures III, L.P.
Most Recent Fund Was Raised: 12/19/2004
Year Founded: 1995
Capital Under Management: $200,000,000
Current Activity Level : Actively seeking new investments

PROQUEST INVESTMENTS

2430 Vanderbilt Beach Road, Suite 108 - 190
Naples, FL USA 34109
Phone: 6099193560
Fax: 6099193570
Website: www.proquestvc.com

Other Offices
12626 High Bluff Drive, Suite 325
San Diego, CA USA 92130
Phone: 858-847-0315
Fax: 858-847-0316

380 Rue St-Antoine Ouest
Bureau 2020
Montreal, Canada H2Y 3X7
Phone: 514-842-1625
Fax: 514-842-1379

Management and Staff
Alain Schreiber, Partner
Jay Moorin, Partner
Jee Shin, Principal
Karen Hong, Principal
Pasquale DeAngelis, Chief Financial Officer
Steven Ratoff, Venture Partner
Wendy Johnson, Venture Partner

Type of Firm
Private Equity Firm

Project Preferences

Role in Financing:
Will function either as deal originator or investor in deals created by others

Type of Financing Preferred:
Early Stage
Expansion
Balanced
Later Stage
Seed

Size of Investments Considered:
Min Size of Investment Considered (000s): $250
Max Size of Investment Considered (000s): $25,000

Geographical Preferences

United States Preferences:

Canadian Preferences:
All Canada

International Preferences:
Western Europe

Industry Focus
(% based on actual investment)
Biotechnology 51.9%
Medical/Health 46.5%
Internet Specific 1.6%

Additional Information
Name of Most Recent Fund: ProQuest Investments IV, L.P.
Most Recent Fund Was Raised: 12/08/2006
Year Founded: 1998
Capital Under Management: $900,000,000
Current Activity Level : Actively seeking new investments
Method of Compensation: Return on invest. most important, but chg. closing fees, service fees, etc.

PROREGIO MITTELSTANDS-FINANZIERUNGS AG

Gruber & Kaja Strasse 1
St. Marien, Austria 4502
Phone: 437229804002800
Fax: 437229804002880

Management and Staff
Karlheinz Wintersberger, Managing Director
Nikolaus Kretz, Managing Director

Type of Firm
Private Equity Firm

Project Preferences

Type of Financing Preferred:
Later Stage

Geographical Preferences

International Preferences:
Austria

Industry Preferences

In Communications prefer:
Communications and Media

In Consumer Related prefer:
Food/Beverage

In Industrial/Energy prefer:
Industrial Products

Additional Information
Year Founded: 2003
Capital Under Management: $10,600,000
Current Activity Level : Actively seeking new investments

PROSEED VENTURE CAPITAL FUND, LTD.

85 Yehuda Halevi Street
Tel Aviv, Israel 65796
Phone: 97235661284
Fax: 97235661285
Website: www.proseed.co.il

Management and Staff
Dalit Shifron, Chief Financial Officer
Moshe Shai Levy, Chief Executive Officer

Type of Firm
Private Equity Firm

Project Preferences

Type of Financing Preferred:
Early Stage
Seed

Geographical Preferences

International Preferences:
Israel

Industry Preferences

In Communications prefer:
Telecommunications
Wireless Communications
Data Communications

In Computer Software prefer:
Software

In Internet Specific prefer:
Internet

In Medical/Health prefer:
Medical Products

In Industrial/Energy prefer:
Alternative Energy

Additional Information
Year Founded: 2000
Capital Under Management: $10,000,000
Current Activity Level : Actively seeking new investments

PROSPECT PARTNERS LLC

200 West Madison Street, Suite 2710
Chicago, IL USA 60606
Phone: 3127827400
Fax: 3127827410
Website: www.prospect-partners.com

Management and Staff
Bradley O Dell, Principal
Brett Holcomb, Principal
Erik Maurer, Principal
Louis Kenter, Co-Founder
Maneesh Chawla, Principal
Phillip Brennan, Vice President
Richard Tuttle, Co-Founder
William Glastris, Co-Founder
William Lump, Chief Financial Officer

Type of Firm
Private Equity Firm

Association Membership
Illinois Venture Capital Association

Project Preferences

Role in Financing:
Prefer role as deal originator

Type of Financing Preferred:
Leveraged Buyout
Management Buyouts
Acquisition
Recapitalizations

Geographical Preferences

United States Preferences:

Industry Focus
(% based on actual investment)
Other Products	82.6%
Industrial/Energy	7.1%
Consumer Related	5.8%
Semiconductors/Other Elect.	4.4%

Additional Information
Name of Most Recent Fund: Prospect Partners III, L.P.
Most Recent Fund Was Raised: 08/31/2010
Year Founded: 1998
Capital Under Management: $270,000,000
Current Activity Level : Actively seeking new investments
Method of Compensation: Return on invest. most important, but chg. closing fees, service fees, etc.

PROSPECT STREET VENTURES

10 East 40th Street
42nd Floor
New York, NY USA 10016
Phone: 2124480702
Fax: 2124489652
E-mail: InvestorRelations@prospectstreet.com
Website: www.prospectstreet.com

Management and Staff
Bart de Bie, Managing Director
Benton Cummings, Managing Director
Brian Oswald, Chief Financial Officer
David Belzer, Managing Director
Jason Wilson, Principal
John Barry, Chairman & CEO
M.Grier Eliasek, President & COO
Mark Hull, Vice President
Richard Carratu, Managing Director
Steven Devloo, Principal

Type of Firm
Private Equity Firm

Project Preferences

Role in Financing:
Prefer role as deal originator but will also invest in deals created by others

Type of Financing Preferred:
Leveraged Buyout
Mezzanine
Generalist PE
Later Stage
Acquisition
Recapitalizations

Geographical Preferences

United States Preferences:

Canadian Preferences:
All Canada

Industry Focus
(% based on actual investment)
Computer Software and Services	38.4%
Industrial/Energy	26.5%
Other Products	18.2%
Internet Specific	13.0%
Communications and Media	2.3%
Medical/Health	1.5%
Consumer Related	0.3%

Additional Information
Year Founded: 1988
Capital Under Management: $206,000,000
Current Activity Level : Actively seeking new investments
Method of Compensation: Return on invest. most important, but chg. closing fees, service fees, etc.

PROSPECT VENTURE PARTNERS

435 Tasso Street, Suite 200
Palo Alto, CA USA 94301
Phone: 6503278800
Fax: 6503248838
Website: www.prospectventures.com

Management and Staff
David Schnell, Founder
Rebecca Lucia, Chief Financial Officer
Russell Hirsch, Managing Director

Type of Firm
Private Equity Firm

Project Preferences

Role in Financing:
Prefer role as deal originator but will also invest in deals created by others

Type of Financing Preferred:
Second Stage Financing
Early Stage
Expansion
Balanced
Later Stage
Seed

Size of Investments Considered:
Min Size of Investment Considered (000s): $500
Max Size of Investment Considered (000s): $20,000

Geographical Preferences

United States Preferences:

Industry Focus
(% based on actual investment)
Medical/Health	56.8%
Biotechnology	39.7%
Other Products	1.3%
Computer Software and Services	1.1%
Semiconductors/Other Elect.	0.6%
Consumer Related	0.5%

Additional Information
Name of Most Recent Fund: Prospect Venture Partners III, L.P.
Most Recent Fund Was Raised: 12/09/2004
Year Founded: 1997
Capital Under Management: $1,000,000,000
Current Activity Level : Actively seeking new investments
Method of Compensation: Return on invest. most important, but chg. closing fees, service fees, etc.

PROSPER CAPITAL CORP

Kungsgatan 12-14
P.O. Box 3356
Stockholm, Sweden 103 67
Phone: 4684540650
Fax: 4684540671

Type of Firm
Private Equity Firm

Project Preferences

Type of Financing Preferred:
Early Stage

Geographical Preferences

United States Preferences:

International Preferences:
Scandanavia/Nordic Region

Additional Information
Year Founded: 2012
Current Activity Level : Actively seeking new investments

PROSPER CAPITAL LLC

P.O. Box 170051
Saint Louis, MO USA 63117
Website: www.prosperstl.com

Type of Firm
Incubator/Development Program

Project Preferences

Type of Financing Preferred:
Early Stage
Startup

Industry Preferences

In Medical/Health prefer:
Medical/Health

In Consumer Related prefer:
Consumer Products

In Other prefer:
Environment Responsible
Women/Minority-Owned Bus.

Additional Information
Year Founded: 2015
Capital Under Management: $1,100,000
Current Activity Level : Actively seeking new investments

PROSTAR INVESTMENTS PTE LTD

Level 37, Ocean Financial Cent
10, Collyer Quay
Singapore, Singapore 049315
E-mail: info@prostarcapital.com
Website: www.prostarcapital.com

Other Offices
Level 19, Governor Macquarie Tower
1, Farrer Place
Sydney, Australia 2000
, Suite 410, 1700 East Putnam Avenue
Old Greenwich, CT USA 06870

Management and Staff
Alan Young, Partner
David Noakes, Partner
John Troy, Partner
Steve Bickerton, Managing Partner

Type of Firm
Private Equity Firm

Project Preferences

Type of Financing Preferred:
Leveraged Buyout
Other
Acquisition

Geographical Preferences

United States Preferences:
North America

International Preferences:
Asia Pacific
Australia
Asia
Singapore

Industry Preferences

In Industrial/Energy prefer:
Energy
Oil and Gas Exploration
Alternative Energy

Additional Information
Year Founded: 2010
Capital Under Management: $200,000,000
Current Activity Level : Actively seeking new investments

PROSTOR CAPITAL

2 Europe Square
Slavyanskaya Hotel
Moscow, Russia
Phone: +74956385082
E-mail: info@prostor-capital.ru
Website: www.prostor-capital.ru

Type of Firm
Private Equity Firm

Association Membership
Russian Venture Capital Association (RVCA)

Project Preferences

Type of Financing Preferred:
Early Stage
Balanced
Later Stage

Geographical Preferences

International Preferences:
Europe
Russia

Industry Preferences

In Communications prefer:
Wireless Communications

In Computer Software prefer:
Software
Systems Software
Applications Software

In Medical/Health prefer:
Medical/Health

In Consumer Related prefer:
Education Related

Additional Information
Year Founded: 2011
Current Activity Level : Actively seeking new investments

PROTEKTUS AG

Grunewaldstrasse 22
Berlin, Germany 12065
Phone: 49302190880
Fax: 493021908890
E-mail: info@protektus.ag

Type of Firm
Private Equity Firm

Project Preferences

Type of Financing Preferred:
Early Stage
Balanced
Later Stage
Startup

Geographical Preferences

International Preferences:
Germany

Industry Preferences

In Communications prefer:
Communications and Media

In Semiconductor/Electr prefer:
Electronics

In Biotechnology prefer:
Biotechnology

In Medical/Health prefer:
Medical/Health

In Industrial/Energy prefer:
Energy

In Other prefer:
Environment Responsible

Additional Information
Year Founded: 1998
Current Activity Level : Actively seeking new investments

PROTERRA INVESTMENT PARTNERS LP

9320 Excelsior Boulevard
MS 143-5-2
Hopkins, MN USA 55343
Phone: 9529843232
Website: www.proterrapartners.com

Management and Staff
Charlie Plummer, Chief Financial Officer
Sheri Bebb, Vice President

Type of Firm
Investment Management Firm

Project Preferences

Type of Financing Preferred:
Leveraged Buyout
Acquisition

Industry Preferences

In Biotechnology prefer:
Agricultural/Animal Bio.

In Consumer Related prefer:
Food/Beverage

In Agr/Forestr/Fish prefer:
Agriculture related
Mining and Minerals

Additional Information
Year Founded: 2016
Capital Under Management: $2,100,000,000
Current Activity Level : Actively seeking new investments

PROTO INVESTMENT PARTNERS PTY LTD

66 Hunter Street
Level Four
Sydney, Australia 2000
Phone: 61290374144
Website: www.protoinvest.com

Other Offices
281 Brunswick Street
Studio 4, Level 1
Fitzroy, Australia 3065
Phone: 61392889444

Management and Staff
Jeremy Colless, Managing Director

Type of Firm
Private Equity Firm

Project Preferences

Type of Financing Preferred:
Early Stage
Seed
Startup

Size of Investments Considered:
Min Size of Investment Considered (000s): $100
Max Size of Investment Considered (000s): $500

Geographical Preferences

International Preferences:
Australia

Industry Preferences

In Internet Specific prefer:
Internet

Additional Information
Year Founded: 2010
Current Activity Level : Actively seeking new investments

PROTON ENTERPRISES LLC

1150 Central Avenue
Naples, FL USA 34102
Website: www.protonenterprises.com

Type of Firm
Incubator/Development Program

Project Preferences

Type of Financing Preferred:
Early Stage
Startup

Geographical Preferences

United States Preferences:

Industry Preferences

In Internet Specific prefer:
Internet
Ecommerce

In Consumer Related prefer:
Retail

In Transportation prefer:
Transportation

Additional Information
Year Founded: 2012
Current Activity Level : Actively seeking new investments

PROTOS VENTURE CAPITAL SP Z O O

Wilcza 28/5
Warsaw, Poland 05-544
Website: www.protos.vc

Type of Firm
Private Equity Firm

Project Preferences

Type of Financing Preferred:
Early Stage
Seed

Geographical Preferences

International Preferences:
Europe
Poland

Industry Preferences

In Internet Specific prefer:
Internet

In Consumer Related prefer:
Consumer Services

Additional Information
Year Founded: 2012
Current Activity Level : Actively seeking new investments

PROVCO GROUP

795 East Lancaster Avenue, Suite 200
Villanova, PA USA 19085
Phone: 6105202010
Fax: 6105201905
Website: www.provcogroup.com

Management and Staff
Gary DiLella, Vice President
Jerry Holtz, Principal
Richard Caruso, Founder

Type of Firm
Investment Management Firm

Project Preferences

Role in Financing:
Prefer role as deal originator but will also invest in deals created by others

Type of Financing Preferred:
Leveraged Buyout
Generalist PE
Balanced
Other

Size of Investments Considered:
Min Size of Investment Considered (000s): $1,000
Max Size of Investment Considered (000s): $10,000

Geographical Preferences

United States Preferences:

Industry Preferences

In Industrial/Energy prefer:
Energy

In Financial Services prefer:
Real Estate

In Manufact. prefer:
Manufacturing

Additional Information
Year Founded: 1978
Capital Under Management: $100,000,000
Current Activity Level : Actively seeking new investments
Method of Compensation: Return on investment is of primary concern, do not charge fees

PROVENANCE VENTURES

3143 Donald Douglas Loop South
Santa Monica, CA USA 90405
Phone: 3104405080
Website: www.provenanceventures.com

Management and Staff
Bryan Biniak, Managing Director

Type of Firm
Private Equity Firm

Project Preferences

Type of Financing Preferred:
Early Stage
Balanced
Seed

Geographical Preferences

United States Preferences:

Industry Preferences

In Communications prefer:
Communications and Media
Media and Entertainment

Additional Information
Year Founded: 2006
Current Activity Level : Actively seeking new investments

PROVENTURE MANAGEMENT AS

Havnegata Nine
Trondheim, Norway 7010
Phone: 4773545002
Fax: 4773545059
E-mail: post@proventure.no
Website: www.proventure.no

Management and Staff
Hans Torsen, Partner
Herbjorn Skjervold, Managing Partner
Ingvar Katmo, Partner
Thor Egil Five, Partner

Type of Firm
Private Equity Firm

Association Membership
Norwegian Venture Capital Association

Project Preferences

Type of Financing Preferred:
Seed
Startup

Geographical Preferences

International Preferences:
Norway

Industry Preferences

In Industrial/Energy prefer:
Energy
Materials

In Transportation prefer:
Transportation

Additional Information
Year Founded: 2006
Capital Under Management: $61,100,000
Current Activity Level : Actively seeking new investments

PROVIDENCE EQUITY PARTNERS LLC

50 Kennedy Plaza
18th Floor
Providence, RI USA 02903
Phone: 4017511700
Fax: 4017511790
E-mail: contact@provequity.com
Website: www.provequity.com

Other Offices

28 St. George Street
London, United Kingdom W1S 2FA
Phone: 44-207-514-8800
Fax: 44-207-629-2778

100 Queen's Road
Ninth Floor, Suite 902
Hong Kong, Hong Kong
Phone: 852-3653-3800
Fax: 852-3653-3900

Nine West 57th Street, Suite 4700
New York, NY USA 10019
Phone: 212-588-6700
Fax: 212-588-6701

25 Barakhamba Road
6th Floor, Birla Tower
New Delhi, India 110 001
Phone: 91-11-3041-9000
Fax: 91-11-3041-9090

No.1 Jianguomenwai Avenue
47th Floor, China World Trade Center
Beijing, China 100004
Phone: 86-10-5706-1300
Fax: 86-10-5706-1400

Nine Battery Road
Straits Trading Building 08-02
Singapore, Singapore 049910
Phone: 6568051600
Fax: 6564915423

Management and Staff
Albert Dobron, Managing Director
Alexander Evans, Managing Director
Andrew Tisdale, Managing Director
Ankur Kumar, Vice President
Biswajit Subramanian, Managing Director
Blair Faulstich, Managing Director
Charles Gottdiener, Managing Director
Christian Rammer, Vice President
Christopher Halpin, Managing Director
David Ren, Managing Director
Elena Rochelli, Vice President
Emily DeGrado, Vice President
Glenn Creamer, Senior Managing Director
Gustavo Schwed, Managing Director
James Ko, Vice President
Jessica Huang, Vice President
John Hahn, Managing Director
Jonathan Nelson, Chief Executive Officer
Julie Fisher, Managing Director
Julie Richardson, Managing Director
Karim Tabet, Managing Director
Louise Tabbiner, Vice President
Mark Masiello, Managing Director
Mary Bertke, Vice President
Mary Kate Bertke, Vice President
Matthew Nelson, Managing Director
Michael Paasche, Managing Director
Michael Dominguez, Managing Director
Michael Song, Vice President
Ming Jin, Vice President
Nadim Nsouli, Managing Director
Oliver Wriedt, Managing Director
Paul Salem, Senior Managing Director
Peter Wilde, Managing Director
Piers Dennison, Managing Director
R. Scott Farden, Managing Director
Renee Beaumont, Managing Director
Robert Hull, Chief Financial Officer
Robert Sudo, Vice President
Roderik Schlosser, Vice President
Scott Marimow, Vice President
ShanMae Teo, Vice President
Stephen Mahedy, Managing Director
Tao Sun, Managing Director
Thomas Gahan, President
Varun Laul, Vice President
William Hughes, Vice President
Wooseok Jun, Vice President

Type of Firm
Private Equity Firm

Association Membership
British Venture Capital Association (BVCA)
Hong Kong Venture Capital Association (HKVCA)
Private Equity Council (PEC)
European Private Equity and Venture Capital Assoc.
Indian Venture Capital Association (IVCA)

Project Preferences

Role in Financing:
Prefer role as deal originator

Type of Financing Preferred:
Mezzanine
Turnaround
Management Buyouts
Acquisition
Recapitalizations

Geographical Preferences

United States Preferences:
North America

International Preferences:
Europe
Asia

Industry Focus

(% based on actual investment)
Communications and Media	42.0%
Computer Software and Services	36.7%
Other Products	8.0%
Internet Specific	7.3%
Medical/Health	3.0%
Semiconductors/Other Elect.	1.6%
Consumer Related	0.8%
Computer Hardware	0.5%
Biotechnology	0.0%

Additional Information

Year Founded: 1989
Capital Under Management: $40,000,000,000
Current Activity Level : Actively seeking new investments

PROVIDENCE VENTURES LLC

1801 Lind Avenue South West
Renton, WA USA 98057
Phone: 4255253355
Website: www2.providence.org

Management and Staff

Aaron Martin, Managing Partner

Type of Firm

Endowment, Foundation or Pension Fund

Project Preferences

Type of Financing Preferred:
Early Stage

Industry Preferences

In Medical/Health prefer:
Medical/Health
Medical Diagnostics
Health Services
Hospitals/Clinics/Primary

Additional Information

Year Founded: 2014
Capital Under Management: $150,000,000
Current Activity Level : Actively seeking new investments

PROVIDENT HEALTHCARE PARTNERS

260 Franklin Street
16th Floor
Boston, MA USA 02110
Website: www.providenthp.com

Management and Staff

Justin Hand, Managing Director
Kevin Palamara, Managing Director
Michael Patton, Managing Director
Rebecca Leiba, Managing Director
Steven Aguiar, Managing Director

Type of Firm

Private Equity Firm

Project Preferences

Type of Financing Preferred:
Generalist PE

Industry Preferences

In Medical/Health prefer:
Health Services

Additional Information

Year Founded: 2016
Current Activity Level : Actively seeking new investments

PROVIDENT HEALTHCARE VENTURES LLC

183 State Street
Boston, MA USA 02109
Phone: 617-367-5000
Fax: 617-742-9810
Website: www.providenthv.com

Management and Staff

Robert Ciardi, Managing Partner
William Shepard, Managing Director

Type of Firm

Private Equity Firm

Project Preferences

Type of Financing Preferred:
Early Stage
Balanced

Size of Investments Considered:
Min Size of Investment Considered (000s): $250
Max Size of Investment Considered (000s): $3,000

Industry Preferences

In Medical/Health prefer:
Medical/Health
Diagnostic Services
Medical Therapeutics
Health Services
Pharmaceuticals

Additional Information

Year Founded: 2010
Capital Under Management: $25,000,000
Current Activity Level : Actively seeking new investments

PROXY VENTURES UK LTD

Unit G10, Clerkenwell Workshop
27-31 Clerkenwell Close
London, United Kingdom EC1R 0AT
Website: proxyventures.com

Management and Staff

Aapo Bovellan, Founder
Miia Bovellan, Founder

Type of Firm

Private Equity Firm

Project Preferences

Type of Financing Preferred:
Early Stage
Seed
Startup

Additional Information

Year Founded: 2014
Current Activity Level : Actively seeking new investments

PRUDENTIAL CAPITAL GROUP LP

180 North Stetson Avenue, Suite 5600, 2 Prudential Plaza
Chicago, IL USA 60601
Phone: 3125404235
Fax: 3125404219
E-mail: prudentialcapitalgroup@prudential.com
Website: www.prudentialcapitalgroup.com

Other Offices

100 Mulberry Street
Gateway Center Three, 18th Floor
Newark, NJ USA 07102
Phone: 973-802-6000

Four Embarcadero Center, Suite 2700
San Francisco, CA USA 94111
Phone: 415-398-7310

1114 Avenue of the Americas
30th Floor
New York, NY USA 10036
Phone: 212-626-2071

2200 Ross Avenue, Suite 4200E
Dallas, TX USA 75201
Phone: 214-720-6200

1170 Peachtree Street, Suite 500
Atlanta, GA USA 30309
Phone: 404-870-3740

2029 Century Park East, Suite 710
Los Angeles, CA USA 90067
Phone: 310-295-5000

Management and Staff
Albert Trank, Managing Director
Allen Weaver, Senior Managing Director
Billy Greer, Managing Director
Brian Thomas, Managing Director
Charles King, Managing Director
Jeffrey Dickson, Managing Director
Julia Buthman, Managing Director
Marie Fioramonti, Managing Director
Mark Hoffmeister, Managing Director
Mathew Douglass, Managing Director
Mitchell Reed, Managing Director
P.Scott Von Fischer, Managing Director
Paul Meiring, Managing Director
Paul Price, Managing Director
Randall Kob, Managing Director
Ric Abel, Managing Director
Robert Derrick, Managing Director
Robert Penfold, Managing Director
Stephen DeMartini, Managing Director
William Engelking, Managing Director

Type of Firm
Insurance Firm Affiliate

Project Preferences
Role in Financing:
Will function either as deal originator or investor in deals created by others

Type of Financing Preferred:
Leveraged Buyout
Expansion
Mezzanine
Balanced
Management Buyouts
Private Placement
Recapitalizations

Size of Investments Considered:
Min Size of Investment Considered (000s): $10,000
Max Size of Investment Considered: No Limit

Geographical Preferences
United States Preferences:
North America

Industry Focus
(% based on actual investment)
Industrial/Energy 24.9%
Semiconductors/Other Elect. 19.5%
Other Products 14.4%
Communications and Media 13.7%
Medical/Health 12.0%
Internet Specific 5.9%
Computer Hardware 5.2%
Consumer Related 4.5%

Additional Information
Name of Most Recent Fund: Prudential Capital Partners IV, L.P.
Most Recent Fund Was Raised: 12/20/2012
Year Founded: 1969
Capital Under Management: $31,000,000,000
Current Activity Level : Actively seeking new investments
Method of Compensation: Return on invest. most important, but chg. closing fees, service fees, etc.

PS 27 VENTURES LLC

7841 Bayberry Road
Jacksonville, FL USA 32256
E-mail: info@PS27ventures.com
Website: ps27ventures.com

Management and Staff
James Stallings, Managing Partner

Type of Firm
Private Equity Firm

Project Preferences
Type of Financing Preferred:
Early Stage
Startup

Industry Preferences
In Medical/Health prefer:
Medical/Health

In Consumer Related prefer:
Consumer Products

In Business Serv. prefer:
Services

Additional Information
Year Founded: 1969
Current Activity Level : Actively seeking new investments

PS SEED II L L C

101 California Street
36th Floor
San Francisco, CA USA 94111
Phone: 415-352-7100

Type of Firm
Private Equity Firm

Project Preferences
Type of Financing Preferred:
Seed

Geographical Preferences
United States Preferences:
All U.S.

Additional Information
Name of Most Recent Fund: PS Seed II, LLC
Most Recent Fund Was Raised: 08/13/2004
Year Founded: 2004
Capital Under Management: $8,900,000
Current Activity Level : Actively seeking new investments

PSILOS GROUP MANAGERS LLC

140 Broadway
51st Floor
New York, NY USA 10005
Phone: 2122428844
Fax: 2122428855
Website: www.psilos.com

Other Offices
21 Tamal Vista Boulevard, Suite 194
Corte Madera, CA USA 94925
Phone: 415-945-7010
Fax: 415-945-7011

100 North Guadalupe Street, Suite 203
Santa Fe, NM USA 87501
Phone: 505-995-8500
Fax: 505-995-8501

Management and Staff
Albert Waxman, Founder
Stephen Krupa, Chief Operating Officer

Type of Firm
Private Equity Firm

Project Preferences
Type of Financing Preferred:
Expansion
Balanced
Later Stage

Size of Investments Considered:
Min Size of Investment Considered (000s): $8,000
Max Size of Investment Considered (000s): $15,000

Geographical Preferences
United States Preferences:

Industry Focus

(% based on actual investment)
Medical/Health	39.7%
Computer Software and Services	38.1%
Internet Specific	16.3%
Biotechnology	3.5%
Other Products	2.2%
Consumer Related	0.2%

Additional Information

Name of Most Recent Fund: Psilos IV Growth Equity, L.P.
Most Recent Fund Was Raised: 12/23/2010
Year Founded: 1998
Capital Under Management: $580,000,000
Current Activity Level : Actively seeking new investments

PSP CAPITAL PARTNERS LLC

300 North LaSalle, Suite 1500
Chicago, IL USA 60654
Website: www.pspcapital.com

Management and Staff

John Kevin Poorman, President
Penny Pritzker, Founder

Type of Firm

Private Equity Firm

Project Preferences

Type of Financing Preferred:
Leveraged Buyout
Mezzanine
Turnaround
Other
Acquisition
Recapitalizations

Geographical Preferences

United States Preferences:
All U.S.

Industry Preferences

In Consumer Related prefer:
Entertainment and Leisure
Food/Beverage

In Financial Services prefer:
Real Estate

In Business Serv. prefer:
Distribution

In Manufact. prefer:
Manufacturing

In Agr/Forestr/Fish prefer:
Agribusiness

Additional Information

Year Founded: 2010
Current Activity Level : Actively seeking new investments

PT CAPITAL LLC

188 West Northern Lights Blvd., Suite 920
Anchorage, AK USA 99503
Phone: 9074336600
Fax: 9074336650
E-mail: info@ptcapital.com
Website: ptcapital.com

Management and Staff

Andrew Mack, Managing Director
Francisco Sanchez, Senior Managing Director
Mead Treadwell, President
Richard Monroe, Managing Director

Type of Firm

Private Equity Firm

Geographical Preferences

United States Preferences:
Alaska

Additional Information

Year Founded: 2015
Capital Under Management: $125,000,000
Current Activity Level : Actively seeking new investments

PT CELEBES ARTHA VENTURA

Wisma Millenia 2nd Floor
Jl. MT Haryono Kav 16
Jakarta , Indonesia 12810
Phone: 0218319828
Fax: 0218319028
Website: www.celebescapital.com

Type of Firm

Private Equity Firm

Industry Preferences

In Financial Services prefer:
Financial Services
Insurance

In Agr/Forestr/Fish prefer:
Agriculture related
Mining and Minerals

Additional Information

Year Founded: 1996
Current Activity Level : Actively seeking new investments

PTI VENTURES

47485 Seabridge Drive
Fremont, CA USA 94538
Phone: 510-743-2888
Fax: 510-743-2889
E-mail: info@ptiventures.com
Website: www.ptiventures.com

Other Offices

106, 3F, #30 Sec.
3 Ren-Ai Road
Taipei, Taiwan
Phone: 886-2-2700-4333
Fax: 8862-2706-2282

Management and Staff

Tom Wang, Venture Partner
Y Tsay, General Partner

Type of Firm

Private Equity Firm

Project Preferences

Type of Financing Preferred:
Early Stage
Later Stage

Size of Investments Considered:
Min Size of Investment Considered (000s): $500
Max Size of Investment Considered (000s): $2,000

Geographical Preferences

United States Preferences:

International Preferences:
Taiwan
China
Asia
Japan

Industry Preferences

In Communications prefer:
Communications and Media

In Computer Software prefer:
Software

In Internet Specific prefer:
Internet

In Computer Other prefer:
Computer Related

In Semiconductor/Electr prefer:
Semiconductor

In Business Serv. prefer:
Services

Additional Information

Year Founded: 1997
Current Activity Level : Actively seeking new investments

PTV HEALTHCARE CAPITAL

3600 N. Capital of Texas Hwy, Suite B180
Austin, TX USA 78746
Phone: 5128724000
Fax: 5128724012
E-mail: ptv@ptvsciences.com
Website: ptvhc.com

Other Offices

1000 Main, Suite 3250
HOUSTON, TX USA 77002
Phone: 7132097555
Fax: 7132097599

Management and Staff

Barton Sachs, Venture Partner
Ben Streetman, Venture Partner
Clay Cockerell, Venture Partner
Dimitris Lagoudas, Venture Partner
Evan Melrose, Managing Director
Gordon Mills, Venture Partner
Matthew Crawford, Managing Director
Rick Anderson, Managing Director
Rod Rohrich, Venture Partner
Stephen Slade, Venture Partner
Stephen Spann, Venture Partner
Steve Whitlock, Venture Partner
Steven McKnight, Venture Partner
Wei-Kan Chu, Venture Partner
William Cohn, Venture Partner

Type of Firm
Private Equity Firm

Association Membership
National Venture Capital Association - USA (NVCA)

Project Preferences

Type of Financing Preferred:
Early Stage
Expansion
Generalist PE
Balanced
Later Stage
Seed

Geographical Preferences

United States Preferences:
Southwest
Texas
All U.S.

Industry Preferences

In Communications prefer:
Wireless Communications

In Semiconductor/Electr prefer:
Electronic Components
Semiconductor

In Biotechnology prefer:
Biotechnology
Human Biotechnology

In Medical/Health prefer:
Medical/Health
Medical Diagnostics
Medical Therapeutics
Medical Products
Health Services
Hospitals/Clinics/Primary
Pharmaceuticals

Additional Information
Name of Most Recent Fund: PTV Special Opportunities I, L.P.
Most Recent Fund Was Raised: 10/22/2013
Year Founded: 2003
Capital Under Management: $390,000,000
Current Activity Level : Actively seeking new investments

PUBLIC AUTHORITY FOR INVESTMENT PROMOTION&EXPORT DEVELOPMENT

P.O. Box 25
Wadi Kabir P.C. 117
Sultanate of Oman, Oman
Phone: 96824826699
Fax: 96824810890
E-mail: info@ociped.com
Website: www.paiped.com

Management and Staff
Salim Ben Nasser Al Ismaily, Chief Executive Officer

Type of Firm
Government Affiliated Program

Project Preferences

Type of Financing Preferred:
Early Stage
Balanced
Later Stage
Seed
Startup

Geographical Preferences

International Preferences:
Oman

Industry Preferences

In Semiconductor/Electr prefer:
Electronics

In Industrial/Energy prefer:
Energy

Additional Information
Year Founded: 1996
Capital Under Management: $135,000,000
Current Activity Level : Actively seeking new investments

PUBLIC PENSION CAPITAL LLC

500 Park Avenue
Fourth Floor
New York, NY USA 10022
Phone: 2127684554
Website: ppcenterprises.com

Type of Firm
Private Equity Firm

Project Preferences

Type of Financing Preferred:
Generalist PE

Size of Investments Considered:
Min Size of Investment Considered (000s): $25,000
Max Size of Investment Considered (000s): $75,000

Geographical Preferences

United States Preferences:
All U.S.

Industry Preferences

In Medical/Health prefer:
Health Services

In Financial Services prefer:
Financial Services

In Business Serv. prefer:
Services

Additional Information
Year Founded: 2014
Capital Under Management: $640,000,000
Current Activity Level : Actively seeking new investments

PUBLIC SECTOR PENSION INVESTMENT BOARD

One Rideau Street
7th floor
Montreal, Canada K1N 8S7
Phone: 6137823095
Fax: 5149373155
E-mail: info@investpsp.ca
Website: www.investpsp.ca

Type of Firm
Endowment, Foundation or Pension Fund

Project Preferences

Type of Financing Preferred:
Leveraged Buyout
Acquisition

Industry Preferences

In Communications prefer:
Communications and Media
Telecommunications

In Consumer Related prefer:
Consumer

In Industrial/Energy prefer:
Energy

In Financial Services prefer:
Financial Services

In Manufact. prefer:
Manufacturing

Additional Information
Year Founded: 2004
Current Activity Level : Actively seeking new investments

PUJI HOLDING INC

No.1601, Nanjing West Road, Suite 3703, Park Place
Shanghai, China 200040
Phone: 862132518822
Fax: 862132525893
Website: www.pujicn.com

Type of Firm
Private Equity Firm

Project Preferences

Type of Financing Preferred:
Expansion

Geographical Preferences

International Preferences:
China

Industry Preferences

In Consumer Related prefer:
Entertainment and Leisure
Retail
Consumer Products
Other Restaurants
Education Related

In Industrial/Energy prefer:
Energy
Environmental Related

In Financial Services prefer:
Real Estate

In Business Serv. prefer:
Media

In Agr/Forestr/Fish prefer:
Agriculture related

Additional Information
Year Founded: 2012
Current Activity Level : Actively seeking new investments

PULSAR ECOSYSTEM LLC

Peterburgskaia, 50
Kazan, Russia 420107
Phone: 78432274027
E-mail: info@pulsar.vc
Website: pulsar.vc

Other Offices
Sheikh Zayed Road 2302
Single Business Tower, Business Bay
Dubai, Utd. Arab Em.

Guinness Enterprise Centre
Taylor's Ln, Ushers
Dublin, Ireland 8

Management and Staff
Gadir Shiraliyev, Partner
Leonard Grayver, Partner
Pavel Korloev, Chief Executive Officer
Sergei Mitrofanov, Managing Partner

Type of Firm
Private Equity Firm

Project Preferences

Type of Financing Preferred:
Early Stage
Seed
Startup

Geographical Preferences

International Preferences:
Russia

Industry Preferences

In Computer Software prefer:
Software

In Semiconductor/Electr prefer:
Electronic Components

In Other prefer:
Environment Responsible

Additional Information
Year Founded: 2009
Current Activity Level : Actively seeking new investments

PULSE EQUITY PARTNERS LLC

777 Third Avenue
25th Floor
New York, NY USA 10017
Phone: 2122575901
Fax: 2122575913
E-mail: info@pulsequity.com
Website: www.pulsequity.com

Other Offices
909 Third Avenue
27th Floor
MANHATTAN, NY USA 10022
Phone: 2127358639
Fax: 2127358708

Management and Staff
Arden Miller, Vice President
Ira Brind, Partner
JD Friedland, Principal
John Thomson, Partner

Type of Firm
Private Equity Firm

Project Preferences

Type of Financing Preferred:
Leveraged Buyout
Management Buyouts
Acquisition

Geographical Preferences

United States Preferences:

Industry Preferences

In Medical/Health prefer:
Health Services

In Consumer Related prefer:
Food/Beverage

Additional Information
Year Founded: 2010
Current Activity Level : Actively seeking new investments

PULTE CAPITAL PARTNERS LLC

3707 West Maple Road
Bloomfield Township, MI USA 48301
Phone: 2486476549
Fax: 2486444526
Website: pultecapital.com

Management and Staff
William Pulte, Chief Executive Officer

Type of Firm
Private Equity Firm

Project Preferences

Type of Financing Preferred:
Leveraged Buyout
Management Buyouts
Acquisition
Recapitalizations

Geographical Preferences

United States Preferences:

Industry Preferences

In Industrial/Energy prefer:
Industrial Products
Advanced Materials
Environmental Related

In Business Serv. prefer:
Distribution

In Manufact. prefer:
Manufacturing

Additional Information
Year Founded: 2011
Current Activity Level : Actively seeking new investments

PUMMERIN INVESTMENTS LLC

952 Echo Lane, Suite 410
Houston, TX USA 77024
Phone: 8327673100
Website: www.pummerininvestments.com

Type of Firm
Private Equity Firm

Project Preferences

Type of Financing Preferred:
Leveraged Buyout
Expansion
Acquisition
Recapitalizations

Industry Preferences

In Consumer Related prefer:
Consumer
Retail

In Industrial/Energy prefer:
Industrial Products

In Financial Services prefer:
Financial Services

In Manufact. prefer:
Manufacturing

Additional Information
Year Founded: 2010
Current Activity Level : Actively seeking new investments

PUNAKAIKI FUND LTD

188 Quay Street
PricewaterhouseCoopers Tower
Auckland, New Zealand 1140
Phone: 6421526239
E-mail: investor@punakaikifund.co.nz
Website: punakaikifund.co.nz

Type of Firm
Private Equity Firm

Project Preferences

Type of Financing Preferred:
Expansion
Balanced
Later Stage
Seed

Size of Investments Considered:
Min Size of Investment Considered (000s): $50
Max Size of Investment Considered (000s): $2,000

Industry Preferences

In Computer Hardware prefer:
Computer Graphics and Dig

In Computer Software prefer:
Software

Additional Information
Year Founded: 2013
Current Activity Level : Actively seeking new investments

PUNJAB VENTURE CAPITAL LTD

Udyog Bhawan, 18-Himalaya Marg
Sector 17
Chandigarh, India 160017
Phone: 91-172-270-3693
Fax: 91-172-270-4145

Other Offices
2nd Florr, Udyog Bhawan
18, Himalaya Marg, Sector - 17
Chandigarh , India 160017
Phone: 91-172-2703-963

Management and Staff
R.K. Bhandari, Chief Executive Officer

Type of Firm
Private Equity Firm

Project Preferences

Type of Financing Preferred:
Early Stage
Expansion
Seed
Startup

Size of Investments Considered:
Min Size of Investment Considered (000s): $1
Max Size of Investment Considered (000s): $508

Geographical Preferences

International Preferences:
India

Industry Preferences

In Computer Hardware prefer:
Computers

In Computer Software prefer:
Software

Additional Information
Year Founded: 2000
Capital Under Management: $2,200,000
Current Activity Level : Actively seeking new investments

PURA VIDA INVESTMENTS LLC

888 Seventh Ave
6th Floor
New York, NY USA 10106
Website: www.puravidainvestments.com

Type of Firm
Private Equity Firm

Project Preferences

Type of Financing Preferred:
Expansion
Balanced

Geographical Preferences

International Preferences:
Israel

Industry Preferences

In Biotechnology prefer:
Biotechnology

In Medical/Health prefer:
Medical Products
Health Services
Pharmaceuticals

Additional Information
Year Founded: 2016
Current Activity Level : Actively seeking new investments

PURETECH VENTURES

500 Boylston Street, Suite 1600
Boston, MA USA 02116
Phone: 6174822333
Fax: 6174823337
E-mail: info@puretechventures.com

Pratt's Guide to Private Equity & Venture Capital Sources

Management and Staff
Bernat Olle, Principal
Daphne Zohar, Founder
David Steinberg, Partner
Eric Elenko, Partner
John Zabriskie, Co-Founder
Robert Langer, Co-Founder
Stephen Muniz, Partner

Type of Firm
Private Equity Firm

Project Preferences

Type of Financing Preferred:
Early Stage
Seed

Geographical Preferences

United States Preferences:

International Preferences:
Israel

Industry Preferences

In Communications prefer:
Communications and Media

Additional Information
Year Founded: 2001
Capital Under Management: $10,000,000
Current Activity Level : Actively seeking new investments

PURPLE HORSE FUND

No.9 Middle of E.3rd Ring Road
31F Fuer Building
Beijing, China 100020
Phone: 861085910855
Fax: 861085910853
E-mail: service@purplehorsefund.com
Website: www.purplehorsefund.com

Management and Staff
Xueqing Tang, President

Type of Firm
Private Equity Advisor or Fund of Funds

Association Membership
Beijing Private Equity Association (BPEA)

Project Preferences

Type of Financing Preferred:
Fund of Funds

Geographical Preferences

International Preferences:
China

Industry Preferences

In Industrial/Energy prefer:
Energy

In Financial Services prefer:
Real Estate
Financial Services

Additional Information
Year Founded: 2012
Capital Under Management: $4,800,000
Current Activity Level : Actively seeking new investments

PURPLETALK, INC.

1263 Oakmead Parkway
Second Floor
Sunnyvale, CA USA 94085
Phone: 408-625-3711
E-mail: info@purpleTalk.com
Website: www.purpletalk.com

Other Offices
Sanali InfoPark
8-2-120/113, Road No. 2, Banjara Hills
Hyderabad, India 500 034

Management and Staff
Bharath Lingam, Chief Executive Officer

Type of Firm
Incubator/Development Program

Project Preferences

Type of Financing Preferred:
Seed
Startup

Geographical Preferences

International Preferences:
India

Industry Preferences

In Communications prefer:
Wireless Communications

In Computer Software prefer:
Applications Software

Additional Information
Year Founded: 2010
Current Activity Level : Actively seeking new investments

PURVI CAPITAL LLC

184 Fifth Avenue
Fourth Floor
New York, NY USA 10010
Website: purvicapital.com

Type of Firm
Private Equity Firm

Project Preferences

Type of Financing Preferred:
Early Stage

Additional Information
Year Founded: 2015
Capital Under Management: $2,900,000
Current Activity Level : Actively seeking new investments

PV VENTURES LLC

630 Southpointe Court, Suite 220
Colorado Springs, CO USA 80906
E-mail: info@pvstrat.com
Website: www.pvventuresllc.com

Type of Firm
Private Equity Firm

Project Preferences

Type of Financing Preferred:
Early Stage
Seed

Geographical Preferences

United States Preferences:
Colorado

Additional Information
Year Founded: 2014
Capital Under Management: $4,850,000
Current Activity Level : Actively seeking new investments

PYLON CAPITAL LLC

12100 Wilshire Boulevard, Suite 800
West Los Angeles, CA USA 90025
E-mail: info@pyloncap.com
Website: www.pyloncap.com

Management and Staff
Chris Lueck, Co-Founder
Tom Tzakis, Co-Founder

Type of Firm
Private Equity Firm

Project Preferences

Type of Financing Preferred:
Leveraged Buyout
Expansion
Acquisition

Industry Preferences

In Computer Software prefer:
Software

In Internet Specific prefer:
Ecommerce

In Medical/Health prefer:
Health Services

In Financial Services prefer:
Financial Services

In Business Serv. prefer:
Services

Additional Information
Year Founded: 2010
Current Activity Level : Actively seeking new investments

PYMBLE HOLDINGS INC

Box 1239
Lambeth, Canada N0L 1S0
Phone: 519-652-5675
Fax: 519-652-6450

Type of Firm
Private Equity Firm

Additional Information
Year Founded: 1983
Current Activity Level : Actively seeking new investments

PYRENEES GASCOGNE DEVELOPPEMENT SASU

Chemin de Devezes
Serres Castet, France 64121
Phone: 33559127575
Website: www.ca-pyrenees-gascogne.fr

Type of Firm
Bank Affiliated

Project Preferences

Type of Financing Preferred:
Leveraged Buyout
Early Stage
Expansion
Later Stage
Management Buyouts
Acquisition

Geographical Preferences

International Preferences:
France

Additional Information
Year Founded: 2007
Current Activity Level : Actively seeking new investments

- Q -

Q CAPITAL PARTNERS CO LTD

890-16, Daechi-dong
10/F Hiliving Bldg, Gangnam-gu
Seoul, South Korea 135280
Phone: 8225382411
Fax: 8225381583
E-mail: qcp1@qcapital.co.kr
Website: www.qcapital.co.kr

Management and Staff
Hyoung Jun Cho, Managing Director
Min Soo Ahn, Vice President
Min Su Ahn, Vice President
Yeong Hwan Song, Vice President

Type of Firm
Private Equity Firm

Association Membership
Korean Venture Capital Association (KVCA)

Project Preferences

Role in Financing:
Prefer role as deal originator but will also invest in deals created by others

Type of Financing Preferred:
Leveraged Buyout
Early Stage
Expansion
Generalist PE
Balanced
Turnaround
Later Stage
Management Buyouts
Distressed Debt
Recapitalizations

Geographical Preferences

United States Preferences:

International Preferences:
Asia
Korea, South
Japan

Industry Preferences

In Biotechnology prefer:
Biotechnology

In Medical/Health prefer:
Medical/Health
Medical Therapeutics
Medical Products
Health Services

In Industrial/Energy prefer:
Energy

In Manufact. prefer:
Manufacturing

In Utilities prefer:
Utilities

Additional Information
Year Founded: 1982
Capital Under Management: $96,000,000
Current Activity Level : Actively seeking new investments
Method of Compensation: Return on investment is of primary concern, do not charge fees

QALAA HOLDINGS SAE

Four Seasons Nile Blaza Bldg
1089 Corniche El-Nil
Cairo, Egypt 1089
Phone: 20227914440
Fax: 20227914448
E-mail: info@citadelcapital.com
Website: www.qalaaholdings.com

Other Offices
1 Amar Souiki Street
El-Biar
Algiers, Algeria 1600
Phone: 213-21-691-161
Fax: 213-21-694-356

Management and Staff
Abdullah El Ebiary, Managing Director
Ahmed El Shamy, Managing Director & CFO
Ahmed El Sharkawy, Managing Director
Ahmed El Houssieny, Managing Director
Alaa El-Afifi, Managing Director
Hisham Al Khazendar, Managing Director
Hisham El Khazindar, Managing Director
Karim Badr, Managing Director
Karim Sadek, Managing Director
Karim Sadeq, Managing Director
Marwan Elaraby, Managing Director
Mohammed Abdullah, Managing Director
Mohsen Mansour, Principal
Mostafa Sowelem, Managing Director
Raouf Tawfik, Managing Director
Tariq Atteya, Managing Director
Yaser Gamali, Managing Director

Type of Firm
Private Equity Firm

Association Membership
Gulf Venture Capital Association
Emerging Markets Private Equity Association
African Venture Capital Association (AVCA)

Project Preferences

Type of Financing Preferred:
Leveraged Buyout
Expansion
Balanced
Turnaround
Distressed Debt

Pratt's Guide to Private Equity & Venture Capital Sources

Geographical Preferences

International Preferences:
Egypt
Algeria
Middle East
Libya
Africa

Industry Preferences

In Consumer Related prefer:
Food/Beverage

In Industrial/Energy prefer:
Oil and Gas Exploration
Alternative Energy
Materials
Advanced Materials
Environmental Related

In Transportation prefer:
Transportation

In Financial Services prefer:
Financial Services

In Business Serv. prefer:
Services

In Manufact. prefer:
Manufacturing

In Agr/Forestr/Fish prefer:
Agribusiness
Agriculture related

In Utilities prefer:
Utilities

Additional Information
Year Founded: 2004
Capital Under Management: $9,000,000,000
Current Activity Level : Actively seeking new investments

QAT INVESTMENTS SA

Keizerinlaan 66
Brussels, Belgium 1000
Phone: 3225671788
Fax: 3225671789
Website: www.qatinvestments.com

Other Offices

Bd de l'Imperatrice 66
Keizerinlaan 66
Brussel, Belgium B-1000
Phone: 32-2567-1788
Fax: 32-2567-1789

Schiphol Boulevard 249
World Trade Center Schiphol
BH Luchthaven Schiphol, Netherlands NL-1118

Management and Staff

Yves Van Sante, Chief Executive Officer

Type of Firm
Private Equity Firm

Association Membership
Belgium Venturing Association
Dutch Venture Capital Associaton (NVP)
European Private Equity and Venture Capital Assoc.

Project Preferences

Type of Financing Preferred:
Early Stage
Generalist PE

Geographical Preferences

International Preferences:
Luxembourg
Europe
Netherlands
Belgium

Industry Preferences

In Communications prefer:
Telecommunications
Entertainment

In Medical/Health prefer:
Medical/Health
Medical Products

In Industrial/Energy prefer:
Environmental Related

In Other prefer:
Environment Responsible

Additional Information
Name of Most Recent Fund: QAT III
Most Recent Fund Was Raised: 11/09/2011
Year Founded: 2002
Capital Under Management: $27,064,000
Current Activity Level : Actively seeking new investments

QATAR FIRST BANK LLC

Suhaim Bin Hamad St
PO Box 28028
Doha, Qatar
Phone: 97444483333
Fax: 97444483560
E-mail: information@qfib.com.qa
Website: www.qfb.com.qa

Management and Staff

Hani Katra, Chief Financial Officer
Nayeem Khan, Chief Operating Officer
Ziad Makkawi, Chief Executive Officer

Type of Firm
Bank Affiliated

Project Preferences

Type of Financing Preferred:
Leveraged Buyout
Early Stage
Expansion
Generalist PE
Balanced
Later Stage
Acquisition

Geographical Preferences

International Preferences:
Middle East

Industry Preferences

In Medical/Health prefer:
Medical/Health
Health Services

In Industrial/Energy prefer:
Energy Conservation Relat
Industrial Products

In Financial Services prefer:
Financial Services
Real Estate
Financial Services

Additional Information
Year Founded: 2008
Current Activity Level : Actively seeking new investments

QATAR HOLDING LLC

Q-Tel Tower, Diplomatic Area
West Bay PO Box 23224
Doha, Qatar

Management and Staff

Ahmad Al-Sayed, CEO & Managing Director

Type of Firm
Private Equity Firm

Project Preferences

Type of Financing Preferred:
Leveraged Buyout
Early Stage
Generalist PE
Balanced
Later Stage
Seed
Acquisition
Startup

Geographical Preferences

International Preferences:
Europe
Asia

Industry Preferences

In Communications prefer:
Telecommunications

In Consumer Related prefer:
Consumer
Retail
Consumer Products
Consumer Services

In Financial Services prefer:
Financial Services
Real Estate

In Agr/Forestr/Fish prefer:
Agriculture related

Additional Information
Year Founded: 2006
Current Activity Level: Actively seeking new investments

QATAR INVESTMENT AUTHORITY

PO Box 23224
Doha, Qatar
Phone: 97444995919
E-mail: contactus@qia.qa
Website: www.qia.qa

Management and Staff
Hamad Al Thani, Chief Executive Officer

Type of Firm
Government Affiliated Program

Project Preferences

Type of Financing Preferred:
Unknown

Geographical Preferences

International Preferences:
Qatar

Additional Information
Year Founded: 2004
Current Activity Level: Actively seeking new investments

QATARI FORTIS INVESTMENT MANAGEMENT

c/o Qinvest LLC QIB Building,
1st Floor, Al Sadd Street
Doha, Qatar
Phone: 9744246666
Fax: 9744448446

Type of Firm
Bank Affiliated

Project Preferences

Type of Financing Preferred:
Mezzanine

Geographical Preferences

International Preferences:
Qatar
Middle East

Industry Preferences

In Transportation prefer:
Transportation

In Financial Services prefer:
Investment Groups

Additional Information
Year Founded: 2009
Current Activity Level: Actively seeking new investments

QB1 VENTURES LLC

950 3rd Avenue
New York, NY USA 10022
Phone: 12127355260
Website: www.qb1ventures.com

Type of Firm
Private Equity Firm

Project Preferences

Type of Financing Preferred:
Early Stage

Geographical Preferences

United States Preferences:
All U.S.

International Preferences:
Israel

Additional Information
Year Founded: 1969
Current Activity Level: Actively seeking new investments

QED GLOBAL

17/F China Hong Kong Tower
8-12 Hennessy Road
Hennesy, Hong Kong
Phone: 85231028700
Fax: 85231029010
E-mail: info@qedglobal.com
Website: www.qedglobal.com

Management and Staff
Helen Wong, Co-Founder
Patrick Cheung, Co-Founder

Type of Firm
Private Equity Firm

Project Preferences

Type of Financing Preferred:
Balanced

Geographical Preferences

International Preferences:
Indonesia
India
China
Asia

Industry Preferences

In Internet Specific prefer:
Internet

Additional Information
Year Founded: 2000
Current Activity Level: Actively seeking new investments

QIANHAI FUND OF FUNDS EQUITY INVESTMENT SHENZHEN CO LTD

Qianhai SZ HK Cooperation Zone
Rm 201, Bldg A, No. 1, Qianwan
Shenzhen, China

Type of Firm
Private Equity Advisor or Fund of Funds

Project Preferences

Type of Financing Preferred:
Fund of Funds

Geographical Preferences

International Preferences:
China

Additional Information
Year Founded: 2016
Capital Under Management: $3,260,930,000
Current Activity Level: Actively seeking new investments

QIANHAI GREAT WALL FUND MANAGEMENT SHENZHEN CO LTD

Gaoxin South 1st Road
Hatching Base
Shenzhen, China
Phone: 8675526983433
Website: greatwallfund.cn

Type of Firm
Private Equity Firm

Project Preferences

Type of Financing Preferred:
Balanced

Geographical Preferences

International Preferences:
China

Industry Preferences

In Medical/Health prefer:
Medical/Health

In Industrial/Energy prefer:
Energy

Additional Information

Year Founded: 2015
Capital Under Management: $31,380,000
Current Activity Level : Actively seeking new investments

QIANHAI INDUSTRY UNIVERSITY RESEARCH FUND MANAGEMENT CO LTD

Futian District
31/F, CEB Building, Zhuzilin
Shenzhen, China
Phone: 864000616156
Website: www.urifund.com

Type of Firm

Investment Management Firm

Project Preferences

Type of Financing Preferred:
Leveraged Buyout
Seed

Geographical Preferences

International Preferences:
China

Additional Information

Year Founded: 2013
Current Activity Level : Actively seeking new investments

QIANHE VENTURE MANAGEMENT LTD

Shenzhen Chanyeyan Bldg
Rm. B815, Nanshan District
Shenzhen, China

Type of Firm

Investment Management Firm

Project Preferences

Type of Financing Preferred:
Balanced

Geographical Preferences

International Preferences:
China

Additional Information

Year Founded: 2012
Capital Under Management: $1,600,000
Current Activity Level : Actively seeking new investments

QIFUND PARTNERS NV

Kranenberg 6
Research Park
Zellik, Belgium B-1731
Phone: 32478318840
Fax: 3222564300
Website: www.qifund.com

Management and Staff

Carlo Van Dyck, Partner
Dirk Deceuninck, Partner

Type of Firm

Private Equity Firm

Project Preferences

Type of Financing Preferred:
Early Stage
Startup

Geographical Preferences

International Preferences:
Europe
Belgium

Industry Preferences

In Communications prefer:
Communications and Media

In Business Serv. prefer:
Services

Additional Information

Year Founded: 2001
Current Activity Level : Making few, if any, new investments

QIMING VENTURE PARTNERS II LP

No. 88, Century Boulevard Ave.
Room 3906, Jinmao Tower
Shanghai, China 200121
Phone: 862161016522
Fax: 862161016512

Other Offices

No.1 Jianguomenwai Street
Unit 13-17, 24th floor, CWTC Tower 1
Beijing, China 100004
Phone: 861059611188
Fax: 861059611288

350 106th Avenue NE
First Floor
BELLEVUE, WA USA 98004
Phone: 4257090772

345 Fengli Street
Block Two, San Lake Square
Jiangsu, China
Phone: 862165883308

Queen's Road East
Unit 11, level 3, Three Pacific Place 1
Hong Kong, Hong Kong
Phone: 85228556848
Fax: 85228556800

Management and Staff

Bin Hu, Partner
Chivas Lam, Venture Partner
Fengzhi Wu, Vice President
Jia Yu, Partner
Jianping Gan, Managing Partner
John Zagula, Co-Founder
Qi Wang, Vice President
Rich Tong, Co-Founder
Robert Headley, Managing Director
Ruikun Sun, Partner
Shihao Tong, Managing Partner
Shuxian Lee, Chief Financial Officer
William Hu, Managing Partner
Yang Peng, Venture Partner
Yingyu Liang, Partner
Yong Zhang, Partner

Type of Firm

Private Equity Firm

Association Membership

China Venture Capital Association

Project Preferences

Type of Financing Preferred:
Early Stage
Expansion
Balanced

Geographical Preferences

International Preferences:
China

Industry Preferences

In Internet Specific prefer:
Internet

In Medical/Health prefer:
Medical/Health

In Consumer Related prefer:
Consumer
Retail

In Industrial/Energy prefer:
Environmental Related

In Business Serv. prefer:
Media

In Other prefer:
Environment Responsible

Additional Information
Year Founded: 2006
Capital Under Management: $2,500,000,000
Current Activity Level : Actively seeking new investments

QINGDAO HAILI FANGZHOU EQUITY INVESTMENT MANAGEMENT CO LTD

Huoju Road, High-Tech Zone
Room 301, Tower A, Panguchuang
Qingdao, China

Type of Firm
Investment Management Firm

Project Preferences

Type of Financing Preferred:
Balanced

Geographical Preferences

International Preferences:
China

Additional Information
Year Founded: 2015
Current Activity Level : Actively seeking new investments

QINGDAO HAIYINDA VENTURE CAPITAL CO LTD

Hi-tech Ind Dev Zone
Qingdao, China

Type of Firm
Private Equity Firm

Association Membership
Shenzhen Venture Capital Association

Project Preferences

Type of Financing Preferred:
Early Stage
Expansion
Later Stage

Size of Investments Considered:
Min Size of Investment Considered (000s): $793
Max Size of Investment Considered (000s): $7,933

Geographical Preferences

International Preferences:
China

Industry Preferences

In Communications prefer:
Telecommunications

In Semiconductor/Electr prefer:
Semiconductor

In Consumer Related prefer:
Consumer Products

In Industrial/Energy prefer:
Energy
Materials
Environmental Related

In Manufact. prefer:
Manufacturing

Additional Information
Year Founded: 2009
Capital Under Management: $15,900,000
Current Activity Level : Actively seeking new investments

QINGDAO HUATONG JIANLI VENTURE CAPITAL CO LTD

National High-Tech Ind'l Zone
Qingdao, China

Type of Firm
Private Equity Firm

Project Preferences

Type of Financing Preferred:
Later Stage

Geographical Preferences

International Preferences:
China

Additional Information
Year Founded: 2010
Capital Under Management: $10,000,000
Current Activity Level : Actively seeking new investments

QINGDAO HUAYAO CAPITAL MANAGEMENT CENTER LP

No.118 Liaoyang West Road, Qin
Room 903, Xingye Building
Qingdao, China
Website: www.horusvc.com

Type of Firm
Private Equity Firm

Project Preferences

Type of Financing Preferred:
Leveraged Buyout
Balanced

Geographical Preferences

International Preferences:
China

Industry Preferences

In Biotechnology prefer:
Biotechnology

In Medical/Health prefer:
Medical/Health

In Industrial/Energy prefer:
Energy Conservation Relat
Materials

In Other prefer:
Environment Responsible

Additional Information
Year Founded: 2012
Capital Under Management: $1,000,000,000
Current Activity Level : Actively seeking new investments

QINGDAO MORNING CAPITAL MANAGEMENT CO LTD

Ningxia Road , Southern Distri
Room 801, Building 1, 288 Sout
Qingdao, China
Phone: 0532-85920511
Website: morningcapital.cn

Type of Firm
Private Equity Firm

Project Preferences

Type of Financing Preferred:
Balanced

Geographical Preferences

International Preferences:
China

Industry Preferences

In Internet Specific prefer:
Internet

In Biotechnology prefer:
Biotechnology

In Medical/Health prefer:
Medical/Health

In Industrial/Energy prefer:
Energy Conservation Relat
Advanced Materials

In Other prefer:
Environment Responsible

Additional Information
Year Founded: 2011
Current Activity Level : Actively seeking new investments

QINGSONG FUND

Jingan District, Shanghai
Room 3902, SOHO Donghai Plaza,
Shenzhen, China 518057
Phone: 8675533326333
Fax: 8675533303333
Website: www.qingsongfund.com

Type of Firm
Private Equity Firm

Project Preferences

Type of Financing Preferred:
Early Stage
Seed
Startup

Geographical Preferences

International Preferences:
China

Industry Preferences

In Internet Specific prefer:
Internet

Additional Information
Year Founded: 2012
Capital Under Management: $128,900,000
Current Activity Level : Actively seeking new investments

QINHUANGDAO SCIENCE TECHNOLOGY INVESTMENT CO LTD

7 Yingbin Road
Haigang
Qinhuangdao, China
Phone: 86-335-3067
Fax: 86-335-3067
E-mail: qhdktgs@sina.com

Type of Firm
Government Affiliated Program

Additional Information
Year Founded: 2000
Capital Under Management: $12,100,000
Current Activity Level : Actively seeking new investments

QINO FLAGSHIP AG

Rothusstrasse 21
Huenenberg, Switzerland 6331
Phone: 41417665333
Fax: 41417665334

Type of Firm
Investment Management Firm

Project Preferences

Type of Financing Preferred:
Balanced

Geographical Preferences

International Preferences:
Europe

Industry Preferences

In Computer Software prefer:
Software

Additional Information
Year Founded: 2000
Capital Under Management: $46,800,000
Current Activity Level : Actively seeking new investments

QINVEST LTD

Tornado Tower, 39th Floor
West Bay
Doha, Qatar
Phone: 974-405-6666
Fax: 974-444-8446
E-mail: info@qinvest.com
Website: qinvest.com.au

Management and Staff
Balaji Krishnamurthy, Chief Operating Officer
Shahzad Shahbaz, Chief Executive Officer

Type of Firm
Investment Management Firm

Project Preferences

Type of Financing Preferred:
Generalist PE

Geographical Preferences

International Preferences:
Turkey
Middle East
Asia
Africa
All International

Industry Preferences

In Financial Services prefer:
Financial Services

Additional Information
Year Founded: 2007
Capital Under Management: $750,000,000
Current Activity Level : Actively seeking new investments

QIWI AO

Northern Chertanovo, d. 1A
Building 1
Moscow, Russia 117648
Phone: 74957835959
E-mail: universe@qiwi.ru
Website: universe.qiwi.com

Type of Firm
Corporate PE/Venture

Project Preferences

Type of Financing Preferred:
Start-up Financing
Seed

Geographical Preferences

International Preferences:
Russia

Additional Information
Year Founded: 2004
Current Activity Level : Actively seeking new investments

QLEAP ACCELERATORS LTD

Suite 1204, 12F, Wing On House
71 Des Voeux Road Central
Hong Kong, Hong Kong
Phone: 852-2116-3218
Fax: 852-2116-9186
E-mail: business@qleap.com.hk
Website: www.qleap.com.hk

Management and Staff
Wilton Chau, Managing Partner
Yaw-Nam Yong, Partner

Type of Firm
Private Equity Firm

Project Preferences

Type of Financing Preferred:
Expansion
Balanced
Later Stage

Geographical Preferences

United States Preferences:

International Preferences:
Hong Kong
China
Asia
Singapore

Industry Preferences

In Communications prefer:
Wireless Communications

In Semiconductor/Electr prefer:
Electronics
Semiconductor

In Industrial/Energy prefer:
Advanced Materials
Environmental Related

Additional Information
Year Founded: 2007
Current Activity Level : Actively seeking new investments

QUABBIN CAPITAL INC

160 Federal Street
Boston, MA USA 02110
Phone: 6173309041
Fax: 6173309047
E-mail: info@quabbincapital.com
Website: www.quabbincapital.com

Management and Staff
John Snow, President
Robert Hannon, Chief Financial Officer
Steven Leese, Managing Director

Type of Firm
Investment Management Firm

Association Membership
Natl Assoc of Small Bus. Inv. Co (NASBIC)

Project Preferences

Type of Financing Preferred:
Mezzanine
Generalist PE
Balanced

Geographical Preferences

United States Preferences:
All U.S.

International Preferences:
All International

Industry Preferences

In Biotechnology prefer:
Biotechnology

In Industrial/Energy prefer:
Energy

In Financial Services prefer:
Real Estate
Financial Services

In Manufact. prefer:
Manufacturing

Additional Information
Year Founded: 1974
Current Activity Level : Actively seeking new investments

QUAD VENTURES LLC

570 Lexington Avenue
36th Floor
New York, NY USA 10022
Phone: 2127242200
E-mail: quad@quadpartners.com
Website: www.quadventures.com

Other Offices
895 Dove Street
Third Floor
Newport Beach, CA USA 92660
Phone: 949-851-6450

Management and Staff
Andrew Kaplan, General Partner
Daniel Neuwirth, General Partner
Lincoln Frank, Managing Partner
Russell Dritz, Principal
Stephen Spahn, Partner
Thomas Kean, Partner
William Bernard, Chief Financial Officer

Type of Firm
Private Equity Firm

Project Preferences

Type of Financing Preferred:
Leveraged Buyout
Generalist PE
Later Stage
Acquisition
Recapitalizations

Geographical Preferences

United States Preferences:
All U.S.

Industry Focus
(% based on actual investment)
Consumer Related	80.7%
Computer Software and Services	15.6%
Internet Specific	3.7%

Additional Information
Year Founded: 2000
Capital Under Management: $400,000,000
Current Activity Level : Actively seeking new investments

QUAD-C MANAGEMENT INC

200 Garrett Street, Suite M
Charlottesville, VA USA 22902
Phone: 4349792070
Fax: 4349791145
E-mail: info@qc-inc.com
Website: www.quadcmanagement.com

Management and Staff
Anthony Ignaczak, Managing Partner
Frank Winslow, Partner
Jack Walker, Vice President
Michael Brooks, Principal
Nina Myers, Chief Financial Officer
Rob Reistetter, Principal
Steve Burns, Managing Partner
Thad Jones, Partner
Timothy Billings, Partner
Tom Hickey, Partner

Type of Firm
Private Equity Firm

Project Preferences

Role in Financing:
Prefer role as deal originator

Type of Financing Preferred:
Leveraged Buyout
Management Buyouts
Acquisition
Industry Rollups
Recapitalizations

Size of Investments Considered:
Min Size of Investment Considered (000s): $35,000
Max Size of Investment Considered (000s): $125,000

Geographical Preferences

United States Preferences:

Canadian Preferences:
All Canada

Industry Focus
(% based on actual investment)
Consumer Related	46.6%
Medical/Health	30.4%
Other Products	11.6%
Industrial/Energy	7.1%
Internet Specific	3.6%
Communications and Media	0.7%

Additional Information
Name of Most Recent Fund: Quad-C Partners VIII, L.P.
Most Recent Fund Was Raised: 07/07/2011
Year Founded: 1989
Capital Under Management: $650,000,000
Current Activity Level : Actively seeking new investments
Method of Compensation: Return on invest. most important, but chg. closing fees, service fees, etc.

QUADIA SA

Rue du Conseil-General 20
Geneva, Switzerland 1205
Phone: 41228881200
Fax: 41228881201
E-mail: contact@quadia.ch
Website: www.quadia.ch

Type of Firm
Investment Management Firm

Additional Information
Year Founded: 2015
Current Activity Level : Actively seeking new investments

QUADRANGLE GROUP LLC

1065 Avenue of the Americas
New York, NY USA 10018
Phone: 2124181700
Fax: 2124181701
E-mail: info@quadranglegroup.com
Website: www.quadranglegroup.com

Other Offices
16/F, One Exchange Square
8 Connaught Place
Central, Hong Kong
Phone: 852-3656-6300
Fax: 852-3656-6301

Management and Staff
Alfheidur Saemundsson, Vice President
Bret Oettmeier, Vice President
Puneet Gulati, Chief Financial Officer

Type of Firm
Private Equity Firm

Association Membership
Hong Kong Venture Capital Association (HKVCA)

Project Preferences

Role in Financing:
Prefer role as deal originator but will also invest in deals created by others

Type of Financing Preferred:
Leveraged Buyout
Turnaround
Acquisition
Distressed Debt

Geographical Preferences

United States Preferences:

International Preferences:
Western Europe

Industry Focus
(% based on actual investment)
Communications and Media	57.4%
Other Products	14.1%
Semiconductors/Other Elect.	11.9%
Consumer Related	11.3%
Internet Specific	5.3%

Additional Information
Name of Most Recent Fund: Quadrangle Capital Partners II, L.P.
Most Recent Fund Was Raised: 04/01/2005
Year Founded: 2000
Capital Under Management: $920,000,000
Current Activity Level : Actively seeking new investments
Method of Compensation: Return on invest. most important, but chg. closing fees, service fees, etc.

QUADRANT MEZZANINE PARTNERS LLC

8333 Douglas Avenue, Suite 1350
Dallas, TX USA 75225
Phone: 2145400528
Fax: 2148558858
Website: www.quadrantcapital.com

Management and Staff
Grant Garlock, Vice President
Michael Young, Co-Founder
Randy Fleisher, Co-Founder
Roddy O Neal, Managing Director

Type of Firm
Private Equity Firm

Project Preferences

Type of Financing Preferred:
Mezzanine

Industry Preferences

In Financial Services prefer:
Real Estate

Additional Information
Year Founded: 2016
Capital Under Management: $10,000,000
Current Activity Level : Actively seeking new investments

QUADRANT PRIVATE EQUITY

126 Phillip Street
Level 30
Sydney, Australia 2000
Phone: 61292213044
Fax: 61292218447
E-mail: quadrant@quadrantpe.com.au
Website: www.quadrantpe.com.au

Management and Staff
Alex Eady, Partner
Emily Kaveney, Chief Financial Officer
Jonathon Pearce, Partner
Justin Ryan, Managing Partner
Marcus Darville, Managing Partner

Type of Firm
Bank Affiliated

Association Membership
Australian Venture Capital Association (AVCAL)

Project Preferences

Type of Financing Preferred:
Leveraged Buyout
Expansion
Mezzanine
Generalist PE
Later Stage
Management Buyouts

Geographical Preferences

International Preferences:
Australia
New Zealand

Additional Information
Name of Most Recent Fund: Quadrant Private Equity Fund No. 4
Most Recent Fund Was Raised: 02/27/2014
Year Founded: 1996
Capital Under Management: $1,731,500,000
Current Activity Level : Actively seeking new investments

QUADRIA CAPITAL INVESTMENT ADVISORS PVT LTD

80 Raffles Place
11-20, UOB Plaza 2
Singapore, Singapore 048 624
Phone: 6566452844
Website: www.quadriacapital.com

Other Offices
Level Three, D-Three
District Center Saket
New Delhi, India 110 017
Phone: 911139126211
Fax: 911139126241

Management and Staff
Abrar Mir, Managing Partner
Amit Varma, Managing Partner
Anne Kim, Vice President

Type of Firm
Private Equity Firm

Project Preferences

Type of Financing Preferred:
Leveraged Buyout

Geographical Preferences

United States Preferences:
Southeast

International Preferences:
Vietnam
Indonesia
India
Thailand
Philippines
Sri Lanka
Malaysia

Industry Preferences

In Medical/Health prefer:
Medical/Health
Pharmaceuticals

Additional Information

Year Founded: 2012
Capital Under Management: $604,000,000
Current Activity Level : Actively seeking new investments

QUADRILLE CAPITAL SAS

16, Place de la Madeleine
Paris, France 75008
Phone: 33179742340
Website: www.quadrillecapital.com

Management and Staff

David Shu, Chief Financial Officer
Florent Illat, Vice President
Henri de Perignon, Partner
Jerome Chevalier, Partner

Type of Firm

Private Equity Firm

Association Membership

French Venture Capital Association (AFIC)

Project Preferences

Type of Financing Preferred:
Leveraged Buyout
Generalist PE
Later Stage
Management Buyouts
Acquisition

Industry Preferences

In Industrial/Energy prefer:
Oil and Gas Exploration
Alternative Energy
Energy Conservation Relat
Environmental Related

Additional Information

Year Founded: 2001
Capital Under Management: $78,693,000
Current Activity Level : Actively seeking new investments

QUADRIVIO SGR SPA

Via G. Mazzini, 2
Milan, Italy 20123
Phone: 39276317693
Fax: 39229014008
E-mail: info@quadriviosgr.it
Website: www.quadriviosgr.it

Other Offices

1 Duddel Street
Room 901, 9/F
Central Hong Kong, Hong Kong
Phone: 85223593600

535 Madison Avenue
4th Floor
New York, NY USA 10022
Phone: 2123559938

Type of Firm

Private Equity Firm

Association Membership

Italian Venture Capital Association (AIFI)

Project Preferences

Type of Financing Preferred:
Second Stage Financing
Leveraged Buyout
Generalist PE
Later Stage

Size of Investments Considered:
Min Size of Investment Considered (000s): $3,995
Max Size of Investment Considered (000s): $19,976

Geographical Preferences

International Preferences:
Italy
Europe

Industry Preferences

In Consumer Related prefer:
Consumer
Retail
Food/Beverage

In Financial Services prefer:
Financial Services

In Business Serv. prefer:
Services

Additional Information

Year Founded: 2001
Capital Under Management: $68,600,000
Current Activity Level : Actively seeking new investments

QUAESTUS PRIVATE EQUITY DOO

Radnicka Cesta 52/R2
Zagreb, Croatia 10000
Phone: 38514880900
Fax: 38514870159
E-mail: quaestus@quaestus.hr
Website: www.quaestus.hr

Management and Staff

Borislav Skegro, Partner
Tomislav Matic, Partner
Vjenceslav Terzic, Managing Director
Zeljko Lukac, Partner

Type of Firm

Investment Management Firm

Project Preferences

Type of Financing Preferred:
Early Stage
Generalist PE
Acquisition
Startup
Recapitalizations

Size of Investments Considered:
Min Size of Investment Considered (000s): $500
Max Size of Investment Considered (000s): $16,417

Geographical Preferences

International Preferences:
Macedonia
Eastern Europe
Croatia
Bosnia

Industry Preferences

In Communications prefer:
Telecommunications

In Biotechnology prefer:
Agricultural/Animal Bio.

In Medical/Health prefer:
Medical/Health

In Consumer Related prefer:
Food/Beverage

Additional Information

Name of Most Recent Fund: Quaestus Private Equity Kapital
Most Recent Fund Was Raised: 03/07/2006
Year Founded: 2003
Capital Under Management: $144,300,000
Current Activity Level : Actively seeking new investments

QUAKER PARTNERS MANAGEMENT LP

2929 Arch Street
Cira Centre
Philadelphia, PA USA 19104
Phone: 2159886800
Fax: 2159886801
E-mail: info@quakerpartners.com

Management and Staff

Adele Oliva, Partner
Adele Oliva, Partner
Andrew Khouri, Vice President
Brenda Gavin, Founder
Brenda Gavin, Partner
Brian Schwenk, Chief Financial Officer
David King, Venture Partner
Eric Emrich, Chief Financial Officer
Ira Lubert, Partner
Ira Lubert, Founder
Matthew Rieke, Partner
P. Sherrill Neff, Founder
P. Sherrill Neff, Partner
Richard Kollender, Partner
Sanjay Mistry, Vice President
Wesley Kaupinen, Principal

Type of Firm

Private Equity Firm

Association Membership

National Venture Capital Association - USA (NVCA)

Project Preferences

Role in Financing:
Will function either as deal originator or investor in deals created by others

Type of Financing Preferred:
Early Stage
Balanced
Later Stage

Size of Investments Considered:
Min Size of Investment Considered (000s): $5,000
Max Size of Investment Considered (000s): $25,000

Geographical Preferences

United States Preferences:
East Coast

Industry Preferences

In Biotechnology prefer:
Biotechnology

In Medical/Health prefer:
Medical/Health
Medical Diagnostics
Medical Therapeutics
Medical Products
Health Services
Pharmaceuticals

Additional Information

Name of Most Recent Fund: Quaker BioVentures II, L.P.
Most Recent Fund Was Raised: 04/02/2007
Year Founded: 2002
Capital Under Management: $700,000,000
Current Activity Level : Actively seeking new investments

QUALCOMM VENTURES

5775 Morehouse Drive
San Diego, CA USA 92121
Website: qualcommventures.com

Other Offices

EPIP II Phase, Whitefield
G/F Part A 1st & 2nd floor
Bangalore, India 560 066

Nahum Het Street, Tirat Hacarmel
4th Floor, Omega Building
Haifa, Israel 31905

Av. Eng. Luis Carlos Berrini, 550
8th Floor
Sao Paulo, Brazil 04571-000

No.1 Guanghua Road
Beijing Kerry Centre
Beijing, China 100020
Phone: 86-10-8285-6030
Fax: 86-10-8285-6218

566 Chiswick High Road
Building 4 3rd floor
London, United Kingdom W4 5YE

1303-22 Seocho-4Dong
Kyobo Tower, B-14th Floor
Seoul, South Korea 137-920

Management and Staff

Adam Schwenker, Vice President
Carlos Kokron, Managing Director
James Shen, Vice President
Karthee Madasamy, Managing Director
Miles Kirby, Managing Director
Quinn Li, Vice President

Type of Firm

Corporate PE/Venture

Association Membership

Brazilian Venture Capital Association (ABCR)
China Venture Capital Association
National Venture Capital Association - USA (NVCA)

Project Preferences

Role in Financing:
Prefer role in deals created by others

Type of Financing Preferred:
Early Stage
Seed
Startup

Geographical Preferences

United States Preferences:
North America

International Preferences:
India
Europe
Western Europe
China
Eastern Europe
Brazil
Korea, South

Industry Preferences

In Communications prefer:
Communications and Media

In Computer Software prefer:
Software
Applications Software

In Internet Specific prefer:
Internet
Ecommerce

In Semiconductor/Electr prefer:
Semiconductor

In Medical/Health prefer:
Medical/Health
Drug/Equipmt Delivery
Health Services

In Consumer Related prefer:
Education Related

Additional Information

Name of Most Recent Fund: Qualcomm Life Fund
Most Recent Fund Was Raised: 12/05/2011
Year Founded: 2000
Capital Under Management: $250,000,000
Current Activity Level : Actively seeking new investments

QUALITAS EQUITY PARTNERS SGECR SA

Calle Serrano 26, 6 planta
Madrid, Spain 28001
Phone: 34914238270
Fax: 34914238275
E-mail: info@qualitasequity.com
Website: www.qualitasequity.com

Management and Staff

Eric Halverson, Partner
Inigo Olaguibel, Partner
Sergio Perez, Partner

1731

Type of Firm
Private Equity Firm

Association Membership
Spanish Venture Capital Association (ASCRI)

Project Preferences

Type of Financing Preferred:
Leveraged Buyout
Expansion
Management Buyouts
Acquisition

Geographical Preferences

International Preferences:
Spain

Industry Preferences

In Industrial/Energy prefer:
Alternative Energy

Additional Information
Year Founded: 2001
Current Activity Level : Actively seeking new investments

QUALIUM INVESTISSEMENT SAS

41 avenue de Friedland
Paris, France 75008
Phone: 33158509091
Website: www.qualium-investissement.com

Management and Staff
Jacques Pancrazi, Managing Director
Marc Auberger, Chief Operating Officer
Martin Massot, Chief Financial Officer
Paul Costa de Beauregard, Managing Director
Rudolf Mouradian, Managing Partner

Type of Firm
Bank Affiliated

Association Membership
French Venture Capital Association (AFIC)
European Private Equity and Venture Capital Assoc.

Project Preferences

Type of Financing Preferred:
Fund of Funds
Leveraged Buyout
Early Stage
Generalist PE
Later Stage
Recapitalizations

Size of Investments Considered:
Min Size of Investment Considered (000s): $1,000
Max Size of Investment Considered: No Limit

Geographical Preferences

United States Preferences:
All U.S.

International Preferences:
Europe
France

Industry Focus
(% based on actual investment)
Other Products	86.9%
Consumer Related	5.1%
Biotechnology	4.5%
Computer Software and Services	0.9%
Internet Specific	0.9%
Semiconductors/Other Elect.	0.9%
Communications and Media	0.5%
Industrial/Energy	0.2%
Medical/Health	0.2%

Additional Information
Name of Most Recent Fund: Qualium Fund VI FCPR
Most Recent Fund Was Raised: 07/20/2011
Year Founded: 1985
Capital Under Management: $1,455,000,000
Current Activity Level : Actively seeking new investments

QUAM ASSET MANAGEMENT LTD

Rm 1008, 10/F, Man Yee Bldg
68 Des Voeux Rd
Central, Hong Kong
Phone: 852-2847222
E-mail: quamlimited@quamgroup.com
Website: www.quamfunds.com

Management and Staff
Chris Choy, Managing Director

Type of Firm
Private Equity Firm

Project Preferences

Type of Financing Preferred:
Generalist PE

Geographical Preferences

International Preferences:
China

Additional Information
Year Founded: 2010
Current Activity Level : Actively seeking new investments

QUAN VENTURES LP

8 Avenue Peschier
Geneva, Switzerland 1206
Phone: 940274040
Website: www.quanvc.com

Type of Firm
Private Equity Firm

Project Preferences

Role in Financing:
Will function either as deal originator or investor in deals created by others

Type of Financing Preferred:
Balanced

Size of Investments Considered:
Min Size of Investment Considered (000s): $50
Max Size of Investment Considered (000s): $5,000

Geographical Preferences

United States Preferences:

International Preferences:
Europe

Industry Preferences

In Communications prefer:
Commercial Communications
Telecommunications
Wireless Communications
Data Communications
Satellite Microwave Comm.

In Computer Hardware prefer:
Computer Graphics and Dig

In Internet Specific prefer:
E-Commerce Technology

In Semiconductor/Electr prefer:
Electronics
Semiconductor
Laser Related
Fiber Optics
Optoelectronics

Additional Information
Year Founded: 1996
Capital Under Management: $11,000,000
Current Activity Level : Actively seeking new investments
Method of Compensation: Return on investment is of primary concern, do not charge fees

---

QUANTICA SGR SPA

Via Quintino Sella 3
Milan, Italy 20121
Phone: 39236589750
Fax: 39236589779
E-mail: info@principiasgr.it
Website: www.quanticasgr.it

Management and Staff
Stefano Peroncini, Partner

Type of Firm
Private Equity Firm

Association Membership
Italian Venture Capital Association (AIFI)

Project Preferences

Type of Financing Preferred:
Expansion
Balanced

Geographical Preferences

International Preferences:
No Preference

Additional Information
Year Founded: 2005
Capital Under Management: $90,000,000
Current Activity Level : Actively seeking new investments

QUANTUM CAPITAL

161 Bay Street
27th Floor
Toronto, Canada M5J 2S1
Phone: 4165722070
Fax: 6463492994
Website: www.quantumcapital.com

Management and Staff
Andrew Blott, Co-Founder
Jack Cowin, Partner
John Drake, Partner
Lawrence Stuart, Co-Founder

Type of Firm
Private Equity Firm

Project Preferences

Type of Financing Preferred:
Acquisition
Distressed Debt
Recapitalizations

Additional Information
Year Founded: 2004
Current Activity Level : Actively seeking new investments

QUANTUM CAPITAL PARTNERS AG

Ludwigstrasse 10
Munich, Germany 80539
Phone: 498945213290
E-mail: info@quantum-capital-partners.com
Website: www.quantum-capital-partners.com

Management and Staff
Murat Bekiroglu, Chief Operating Officer
Steffen Goerig, President

Type of Firm
Private Equity Firm

Project Preferences

Type of Financing Preferred:
Leveraged Buyout
Management Buyouts
Acquisition

Geographical Preferences

International Preferences:
Western Europe
Germany

Additional Information
Year Founded: 2008
Capital Under Management: $72,216,000
Current Activity Level : Actively seeking new investments

QUANTUM VALLEY INVESTMENTS

485 Wes Graham Way
Waterloo, Canada N2L 0A7
E-mail: contact@quantumvalleyinvestments.com
Website: quantumvalleyinvestments.com

Management and Staff
Douglas Fregin, Co-Founder
Michael Lazaridis, Co-Founder

Type of Firm
Incubator/Development Program

Project Preferences

Type of Financing Preferred:
Seed
Startup

Geographical Preferences

Canadian Preferences:
All Canada
Ontario

Additional Information
Year Founded: 2013
Capital Under Management: $98,242,000
Current Activity Level : Actively seeking new investments

QUARK VENTURE

1075 West Georgia Street, Suite 2500
Vancouver, Canada V6E 2M6
Phone: 7782388766
E-mail: info@quarkventure.com
Website: www.quarkventure.com

Type of Firm
Private Equity Firm

Project Preferences

Type of Financing Preferred:
Balanced

Industry Preferences

In Biotechnology prefer:
Biotech Related Research

In Medical/Health prefer:
Health Services

Additional Information
Year Founded: 2016
Capital Under Management: $100,000,000
Current Activity Level : Actively seeking new investments

QUARK VENTURES LLC

2255 Glades Road, Suite 324A
Boca Raton, FL USA 33431
Phone: 15617055659
E-mail: us@quarkventures.com
Website: www.quarkvc.com

Management and Staff
Adrian Dzielnicki, Partner
Andrew Filipek, Partner
David Waldman, Partner
Karimah Es Sabar, Chief Executive Officer
Larry Wolf, Partner
Tomasz Zastawny, Partner
Wojciech Gudaszewski, Partner

Type of Firm
Private Equity Firm

Project Preferences

Type of Financing Preferred:
Early Stage
Expansion
Later Stage
Seed

Geographical Preferences

United States Preferences:
North America

Industry Preferences

In Other prefer:
Environment Responsible

Additional Information
Year Founded: 2012
Current Activity Level : Actively seeking new investments

QUARTET VENTURES

Governor Phillip Tower, Suite 3 Level 44, 1 Farrer Pla
Sydney, Australia
Website: www.quartetventures.com.au

QUASAR BUILDERS

Avenida del Libertador 6810
Pizo 16
Buenos Aires, Argentina
E-mail: info@quasarb.com
Website: www.quasarbuilders.com

Type of Firm
Incubator/Development Program

Project Preferences

Type of Financing Preferred:
Early Stage
Seed

Geographical Preferences

International Preferences:
Argentina
Brazil

Industry Preferences

In Communications prefer:
Data Communications

In Computer Software prefer:
Software

In Internet Specific prefer:
Internet
Ecommerce

Additional Information
Year Founded: 2012
Current Activity Level: Actively seeking new investments

QUEBEC EQUITY & CAPITAL CO

1010 Rue Sherbrooke Ouest, Suite 2210
Montreal, Canada H3A 2R7

Type of Firm
Private Equity Firm

Project Preferences

Type of Financing Preferred:
Early Stage

Industry Preferences

In Consumer Related prefer:
Education Related

Additional Information
Year Founded: 2015
Current Activity Level: Actively seeking new investments

QUEBECOR FUND

1030, Rue Cherrier, Suite 503
Montreal, Canada H2L 1H9
Phone: 5148422497
Fax: 5145249192
E-mail: info@fondsquebecor.ca
Website: www.fondsquebecor.ca

Type of Firm
Private Equity Firm

Additional Information
Year Founded: 2002
Current Activity Level: Actively seeking new investments

QUEENSBRIDGE VENTURE PARTNERS LLC

1801 Century Park East, Suite 1132
Los Angeles, CA USA 90067
Phone: 3105533300
E-mail: info@qbvpfund.com
Website: www.qbvpfund.com

Type of Firm
Private Equity Firm

Project Preferences

Type of Financing Preferred:
Startup

Additional Information
Year Founded: 1969
Current Activity Level: Actively seeking new investments

QUEENSLAND BIOCAPITAL FUNDS LD PTY

66 Eagle Street
Level 6 Central Plaza II
Brisbane, Australia 4001
Phone: 61730096850
Fax: 61730096851

Other Offices

71 High Holborn
Level 9 MidCity Place
London, United Kingdom WC1V 6EA
Phone: 44270928200
Fax: 44270928201

52 Martin Place
Level 34
Sydney, Australia NSW 1225
Phone: 61293473300
Fax: 61293473399

222 North Sepulveda Boulevard, Suite 2350
El Segundo, CA USA 90245
Phone: 13109551670
Fax: 13109551701

80 Collins Street
Level 46
Melbourne, Australia VIC 3000
Phone: 61386814900
Fax: 61386814901

One Maritime Plaza, Suite 1000
San Francisco, CA USA 94111
Phone: 14156331111
Fax: 14156331112

Management and Staff
Claire Blake, Chief Financial Officer
Damien Frawley, Chief Executive Officer
Paul Leitch, Chief Operating Officer

Type of Firm
Government Affiliated Program

Association Membership
European Private Equity and Venture Capital Assoc.

Project Preferences

Type of Financing Preferred:
Leveraged Buyout
Expansion
Generalist PE
Balanced
Other

Geographical Preferences

United States Preferences:
All U.S.

International Preferences:
Europe
Pacific
Australia
Asia
All International

Industry Preferences

In Biotechnology prefer:
Biotechnology

In Medical/Health prefer:
Medical/Health
Pharmaceuticals

In Financial Services prefer:
Financial Services

Additional Information
Year Founded: 2002
Capital Under Management: $121,300,000
Current Activity Level : Actively seeking new investments

QUEST CAPITAL INC

2344 Washington Street
Newton, MA USA 02462
Phone: 617-332-7227
Fax: 617-332-3113
Website: www.questcapcorp.com

Management and Staff
Ed Slade, Co-Founder
John Bello, Co-Founder

Type of Firm
Private Equity Firm

Project Preferences

Type of Financing Preferred:
Early Stage

Industry Preferences

In Consumer Related prefer:
Consumer
Retail
Food/Beverage
Consumer Products

Additional Information
Year Founded: 2003
Current Activity Level : Actively seeking new investments

QUEST FOR GROWTH NV

Lei 19, Box 3
Leuven, Netherlands 3000
Phone: 32016284128
Fax: 32016284129
E-mail: quest@questforgrowth.com
Website: www.questforgrowth.com

Type of Firm
Private Equity Firm

Association Membership
Belgium Venturing Association

Project Preferences

Type of Financing Preferred:
Public Companies
Later Stage

Geographical Preferences

International Preferences:
Europe

Industry Preferences

In Computer Software prefer:
Software

In Semiconductor/Electr prefer:
Electronics
Electronic Components
Semiconductor

In Biotechnology prefer:
Biotechnology
Human Biotechnology

In Medical/Health prefer:
Medical/Health
Health Services
Pharmaceuticals

In Industrial/Energy prefer:
Alternative Energy
Materials
Environmental Related

Additional Information
Year Founded: 1998
Current Activity Level : Actively seeking new investments

QUEST INVESTMENT CORP

1103 - 1166 Alberni Street
Vancouver, Canada V6E 3Z3
Phone: 604-688-3410
Fax: 604-683-2235

Type of Firm
Private Equity Firm

Additional Information
Year Founded: 2001
Current Activity Level : Actively seeking new investments

QUEST VENTURE PARTNERS LLC

101 Jefferson Drive
Menlo Park, CA USA 94025
E-mail: info@questvp.com

Type of Firm
Private Equity Firm

Project Preferences

Type of Financing Preferred:
Early Stage
Startup

Size of Investments Considered:
Min Size of Investment Considered (000s): $100
Max Size of Investment Considered (000s): $1,500

Additional Information
Year Founded: 2007
Current Activity Level : Actively seeking new investments

QUESTA CAPITAL MANAGEMENT LLC

750 Battery Street
Seveth Floor
San Francisco, CA USA 94111
Website: questacapital.com

Management and Staff
Bradley Sloan, Managing Director
Justin Kirkpatrick, Vice President
Ryan Drant, Founder
Shawn Conway, Chief Operating Officer

Type of Firm
Private Equity Firm

Project Preferences

Type of Financing Preferred:
Later Stage

Industry Preferences

In Biotechnology prefer:
Biotech Related Research

In Medical/Health prefer:
Medical/Health
Medical Diagnostics
Health Services

Additional Information
Year Founded: 2016
Capital Under Management: $99,750,000
Current Activity Level : Actively seeking new investments

QUESTMARK PARTNERS LP

2850 Quarry Lake Drive, Suite 301
Baltimore, MD USA 21209
Phone: 4108955800
Fax: 4108955808
Website: www.questmarkpartners.com

Other Offices
One South Street, Suite 800
Baltimore, MD USA 21202
Phone: 4108955800
Fax: 4108955808

Management and Staff
Benjamin Schapiro, Founder
Brian Matthews, Principal
Jason Sydow, Partner
Mike Ward, Partner
Nick Superina, Partner
Timothy Krongard, Partner

Type of Firm
Private Equity Firm

Association Membership
National Venture Capital Association - USA (NVCA)

Project Preferences

Role in Financing:
Prefer role as deal originator but will also invest in deals created by others

Type of Financing Preferred:
Expansion
Later Stage

Size of Investments Considered:
Min Size of Investment Considered (000s): $5,000
Max Size of Investment Considered (000s): $15,000

Geographical Preferences

United States Preferences:

Industry Focus

(% based on actual investment)
Computer Software and Services	41.0%
Internet Specific	15.5%
Medical/Health	13.7%
Semiconductors/Other Elect.	7.6%
Consumer Related	7.5%
Communications and Media	5.3%
Biotechnology	4.4%
Computer Hardware	3.5%
Industrial/Energy	1.1%
Other Products	0.3%

Additional Information

Name of Most Recent Fund: QuestMark Partners III, L.P.
Most Recent Fund Was Raised: 06/15/2007
Year Founded: 1998
Capital Under Management: $750,000,000
Current Activity Level : Actively seeking new investments
Method of Compensation: Return on investment is of primary concern, do not charge fees

QUESTOR PARTNERS HOLDINGS INC

101 Southfield Road
Second Floor
Birmingham, MI USA 48009
Phone: 2485931930
Fax: 2487233907
Website: www.questor.com

Management and Staff

Jay Alix, Founder
Robert Denious, Managing Director
Wallace Rueckel, Managing Director

Type of Firm

Private Equity Firm

Project Preferences

Type of Financing Preferred:
Leveraged Buyout
Turnaround
Special Situation

Geographical Preferences

United States Preferences:

International Preferences:
All International

Industry Focus

(% based on actual investment)
Other Products	45.1%
Industrial/Energy	21.6%
Communications and Media	18.4%
Consumer Related	6.7%
Medical/Health	5.8%
Computer Software and Services	2.0%
Semiconductors/Other Elect.	0.5%

Additional Information

Name of Most Recent Fund: Questor Partners Fund II, L.P.
Most Recent Fund Was Raised: 01/20/1999
Year Founded: 1995
Capital Under Management: $1,200,000,000
Current Activity Level : Actively seeking new investments

QUICKSILVER VENTURES

14375 Saratoga Avenue, Suite 104
Saratoga, CA USA 95070
Phone: 4088650685
Fax: 4088651055
Website: www.qtvcapital.com

Management and Staff

Randall Meals, Managing Director
Steve Schlossareck, Managing Director

Type of Firm

Private Equity Firm

Project Preferences

Type of Financing Preferred:
Balanced

Industry Preferences

In Computer Software prefer:
Software
Applications Software

In Consumer Related prefer:
Consumer

In Business Serv. prefer:
Services

Additional Information

Year Founded: 2000
Current Activity Level : Actively seeking new investments

QUILVEST PRIVATE EQUITY SCA SICAR

84, Grand-Rue
Luxembourg, Luxembourg L-1660
Phone: 352473885
Fax: 352226056
E-mail: quilvestprivateequity@quilvest.com
Website: www.quilvest.com

Other Offices

598 Madison Avenue
8th Floor
New York, NY USA 10022
Phone: 2129203800
Fax: 2129203850

Stockerstrasse 23
Zurich, Switzerland 8002
Phone: 41442244444
Fax: 41442244400

7, rue Thomas Edison
PO Box 131
Strassen, Luxembourg 1445
Phone: 352270271
Fax: 35227027275

1-3 Pedder Street, Central Building
Level 9, room 977
Hong Kong, Hong Kong
Phone: 8523972822

243, boulevard Saint-Germain
Paris, France 75007
Phone: 33140620762
Fax: 33147052471

Gate Village 4 - DIFC
1st floor- Office 5
Dubai, Utd. Arab Em.
Phone: 97143231664
Fax: 97143231667

25 de Mayo 444 of. 301
CP
Montevideo, Uruguay 11000
Phone: 59829161285
Fax: 59829172053

9 Raffles Place 16-20
Republic Plaza 2
Singapore, Singapore 048619
Phone: 6565368868
Fax: 6565362923

Ed. Arroba 2, Local 004
Zonamerica - Ruta 8 Km. 17,500
Montevideo, Uruguay 91600
Phone: 59825184800
Fax: 59825184804

46 Albemarle Street
London, United Kingdom W1S4JN
Phone: 442072901710
Fax: 442072901720

Management and Staff
F. Michel Abouchalache, Chief Executive Officer

Type of Firm
Private Equity Firm

Project Preferences

Type of Financing Preferred:
Fund of Funds
Leveraged Buyout
Early Stage
Generalist PE
Opportunistic
Later Stage
Acquisition
Startup

Geographical Preferences

United States Preferences:
All U.S.

International Preferences:
Central Europe
Europe
Western Europe
Asia

Industry Preferences

In Communications prefer:
Commercial Communications

In Internet Specific prefer:
Internet

In Biotechnology prefer:
Biotechnology

In Medical/Health prefer:
Medical/Health
Medical Products

In Consumer Related prefer:
Retail

In Industrial/Energy prefer:
Energy
Oil and Gas Exploration
Oil & Gas Drilling,Explor
Alternative Energy
Coal Related
Energy Conservation Relat

In Financial Services prefer:
Financial Services
Real Estate

In Other prefer:
Environment Responsible

Additional Information
Name of Most Recent Fund: QS Capital Strategies
Most Recent Fund Was Raised: 05/23/2013
Year Founded: 1972
Capital Under Management: $537,000,000
Current Activity Level : Actively seeking new investments

QUILVEST USA INC
527 Madison Avenue
Eleventh Floor
New York, NY USA 10022
Phone: 2129203800
Fax: 2129203850
Website: www.quilvest.com

Type of Firm
Private Equity Firm

Association Membership
Emerging Markets Private Equity Association
Natl Assoc of Small Bus. Inv. Co (NASBIC)

Project Preferences

Type of Financing Preferred:
Fund of Funds
Acquisition
Fund of Funds of Second

Additional Information
Year Founded: 1983
Current Activity Level : Actively seeking new investments

QUMRA CAPITAL ISRAEL I LTD
4 Hanevi'im Street
Tel Aviv, Israel 64356
Phone: 97236055205
Fax: 97236058789
E-mail: info@qumracapital.com
Website: www.qumracapital.com

Other Offices
4 Hanevi'im Street
Tel Aviv, Israel 64356
Phone: 97236055205
Fax: 97236058789

Management and Staff
Boaz Dinte, Managing Partner
Daniel Slutzky, Chief Financial Officer
Erez Shachar, Managing Partner
Sivan Dahan, Partner

Type of Firm
Private Equity Firm

Project Preferences

Type of Financing Preferred:
Expansion
Later Stage

Geographical Preferences

International Preferences:
Israel

Additional Information
Year Founded: 2012
Current Activity Level : Actively seeking new investments

QUONA CAPITAL MANAGEMENT LTD
1101 15th Street Northwest, Suite 401
Washington, DC USA 20005
Phone: 2027065886
E-mail: info@quona.com
Website: www.quona.com

Management and Staff
Ganesh Rengaswamy, Partner
Jonathan Whittle, Partner
Miguel Herrera, Partner
Monica Engel, Partner
Pat Wilson, Vice President

Type of Firm
Private Equity Firm

Project Preferences

Type of Financing Preferred:
Early Stage
Expansion
Later Stage

Industry Preferences

In Communications prefer:
Commercial Communications

In Internet Specific prefer:
E-Commerce Technology

In Consumer Related prefer:
Consumer Products

In Business Serv. prefer:
Distribution

Additional Information
Year Founded: 2014
Capital Under Management: $141,000,000
Current Activity Level : Actively seeking new investments

QVENTURES MANAGEMENT GMBH
Am Pilgerrain 17
Bad Homburg, Germany 61352
Phone: 4961724020
Fax: 496172402119
E-mail: qventures@quandt.de

Pratt's Guide to Private Equity & Venture Capital Sources

Management and Staff
David Pierce, Managing Director

Type of Firm
Bank Affiliated

Project Preferences

Type of Financing Preferred:
Early Stage
Later Stage

Geographical Preferences

International Preferences:
Italy
Israel
Germany

Industry Preferences

In Communications prefer:
Telecommunications
Wireless Communications

In Computer Software prefer:
Software

In Internet Specific prefer:
E-Commerce Technology

In Semiconductor/Electr prefer:
Laser Related

In Medical/Health prefer:
Medical/Health
Medical Products
Pharmaceuticals

Additional Information
Year Founded: 2000
Current Activity Level : Actively seeking new investments

- R -

R&D ADVISORY SRL

3, Via Brera
Milano, Italy 20121
Phone: 39-02-80-9401
Fax: 39-028-699-8148

Management and Staff
Alberto Camaggi, Partner
Enrico Ricotta, Managing Director

Type of Firm
Private Equity Firm

Project Preferences

Type of Financing Preferred:
Leveraged Buyout
Expansion
Recapitalizations

Geographical Preferences

International Preferences:
Italy
Europe

Additional Information
Year Founded: 2005
Capital Under Management: $118,400,000
Current Activity Level : Actively seeking new investments

R/GA VENTURES

350 West 39th
New York, NY USA 10018

Type of Firm
Incubator/Development Program

Project Preferences

Type of Financing Preferred:
Early Stage

Additional Information
Year Founded: 2014
Current Activity Level : Actively seeking new investments

R204 PARTNERS SPA

Via Crucifix, 6
Milan, Italy 20122
Phone: 3902582881
E-mail: info@r204partners.com
Website: www.r204partners.com

Type of Firm
Private Equity Firm

Project Preferences

Type of Financing Preferred:
Balanced

Additional Information
Year Founded: 2015
Current Activity Level : Actively seeking new investments

R301 CAPITAL

Via Ciani 16/a
Lugano, Italy 6900
E-mail: alessandro@r301capital.com
Website: www.r301capital.com

Management and Staff
Alessandro Rivetti, Managing Director
Nader Sabbaghian, Managing Director

Type of Firm
Private Equity Firm

Project Preferences

Type of Financing Preferred:
Early Stage

Geographical Preferences

International Preferences:
Europe

Industry Preferences

In Computer Software prefer:
Software

In Internet Specific prefer:
E-Commerce Technology
Ecommerce

Additional Information
Year Founded: 2015
Current Activity Level : Actively seeking new investments

R72 PARTNERS

Corso Magenta 10
Milan, Italy 20123
Phone: 39-2-8889-0511
Fax: 39-2-8058-1087
E-mail: info@R72partners.com
Website: www.r72partners.com

Type of Firm
Private Equity Advisor or Fund of Funds

Project Preferences

Type of Financing Preferred:
Recapitalizations

Geographical Preferences

International Preferences:
Italy

Additional Information

Year Founded: 2005
Current Activity Level : Actively seeking new investments

RA CAPITAL MANAGEMENT LLC

20 Park Plaza, Suite 1200
Boston, MA USA 02116
Website: www.racap.com

Management and Staff

Amanda Daniels, Chief Operating Officer
Andrew Levin, Managing Director
Kai Wu, Chief Financial Officer
Peter Kolchinsky, Managing Director
Rajeev Shah, Managing Director

Type of Firm

Private Equity Firm

Project Preferences

Type of Financing Preferred:
Early Stage

Geographical Preferences

United States Preferences:

Industry Preferences

In Biotechnology prefer:
Biotechnology

In Medical/Health prefer:
Medical/Health
Pharmaceuticals

Additional Information

Name of Most Recent Fund: RA Capital Healthcare Fund, L.P.
Most Recent Fund Was Raised: 09/12/2008
Year Founded: 2002
Capital Under Management: $250,000,000
Current Activity Level : Actively seeking new investments

RABO INDIA FINANCE LTD

DLF Cyber City Phase - III
GF/A-03B Ground Flr. DLF Bldg
Gurgaon, India 122 022
Phone: 911242713000
Fax: 911242713004
E-mail: india@rabobank.com
Website: www.rabobank.com

Other Offices

Forbes Building, 2nd Floor
Charanjit Rai Marg
Mumbai, India 400 001
Phone: 91-22-2203-4567
Fax: 91-22-2203-5544

Management and Staff

Kaushik Modak, Managing Director
Nalin Kumar, Managing Director
Surojit Shome, CEO & Managing Director

Type of Firm

Bank Affiliated

Project Preferences

Type of Financing Preferred:
Early Stage
Expansion
Balanced
Later Stage

Geographical Preferences

International Preferences:
India

Industry Preferences

In Medical/Health prefer:
Pharmaceuticals

In Consumer Related prefer:
Food/Beverage

In Industrial/Energy prefer:
Alternative Energy

In Agr/Forestr/Fish prefer:
Agribusiness
Agriculture related

Additional Information

Year Founded: 1998
Capital Under Management: $100,000,000
Current Activity Level : Actively seeking new investments

RABO PARTICIPATIES BV

Mondriaantoren, Amstelplein 6-8
Third Floor
Amsterdam, Netherlands 1096 BC
Phone: 31887200100
Fax: 31887200117
E-mail: info@raboprivateequity.nl

Other Offices

Rubens 2000 Blok D
Uitbreidingsstraat 86 bus 3
Berchem, Belgium 2600
Phone: 32-3-290-1719
Fax: 32-3-290-1798

Management and Staff

Adam Anders, Managing Director
Joost Verbeek, Managing Director
Marcel Wijnen, Chief Financial Officer

Type of Firm

Bank Affiliated

Association Membership

Dutch Venture Capital Associaton (NVP)
Indian Venture Capital Association (IVCA)

Project Preferences

Type of Financing Preferred:
Fund of Funds
Leveraged Buyout
Early Stage
Generalist PE
Turnaround
Later Stage
Management Buyouts
Acquisition
Startup

Geographical Preferences

International Preferences:
Europe
Netherlands
Belgium

Industry Preferences

In Biotechnology prefer:
Biotechnology

Additional Information

Name of Most Recent Fund: Rabo Ventures
Most Recent Fund Was Raised: 12/31/2009
Year Founded: 2002
Capital Under Management: $139,200,000
Current Activity Level : Actively seeking new investments

RAC I SA

10, rue du Chateau d'eau
Champagne au Mont d'Or, France 69410
Phone: 33472523939
Fax: 33472523930
E-mail: info@r-a-c.fr
Website: www.r-a-c.fr

Management and Staff

Guy Rigaud, Chief Executive Officer

Type of Firm

Private Equity Firm

Project Preferences

Type of Financing Preferred:
Early Stage
Seed
Startup

Size of Investments Considered:
Min Size of Investment Considered (000s): $138
Max Size of Investment Considered (000s): $413

Geographical Preferences

International Preferences:
France

Industry Preferences

In Biotechnology prefer:
Biotechnology
Industrial Biotechnology

In Business Serv. prefer:
Services

Additional Information
Year Founded: 1990
Capital Under Management: $60,641,000
Current Activity Level : Actively seeking new investments

RADAR CAPITAL INC

150 King Street West, Suite 1702
Toronto, Canada M5H 1J9
Phone: 4168006733
Fax: 4168622498
E-mail: info@radarcapital.ca
Website: www.radarcapital.ca

Management and Staff
Mark Lerohl, President

Type of Firm
Private Equity Firm

Project Preferences

Type of Financing Preferred:
Balanced
Later Stage

Geographical Preferences

Canadian Preferences:
All Canada

Additional Information
Year Founded: 1969
Current Activity Level : Actively seeking new investments

RADAR PARTNERS LLC

737 Bryant Street
Palo Alto, CA USA 94301
Phone: 6505663300

Management and Staff
Douglas Mackenzie, Co-Founder
J. Andrew Bugas, Partner
Kevin Compton, Co-Founder

Type of Firm
Private Equity Firm

Project Preferences

Type of Financing Preferred:
Seed
Startup

Additional Information
Year Founded: 2005
Current Activity Level : Actively seeking new investments

RADIAL CAPITAL PARTNERS GMBH & CO KG

Sendlinger Strasse 33A
Munich, Germany 80331
Phone: 4989122234750
Fax: 4989122234754
E-mail: info@radialcapital.com
Website: radialcapital.com

Type of Firm
Private Equity Firm

Project Preferences

Type of Financing Preferred:
Later Stage

Geographical Preferences

International Preferences:
Western Europe
Brazil

Additional Information
Year Founded: 2014
Current Activity Level : Actively seeking new investments

RADIANT CAPITAL

16 Old Queen Street
London, United Kingdom SW1H 9HP
Phone: 44-20-7100-3540
Fax: 44-20-7100-3550
E-mail: uk@radiantcapital.com
Website: radiantcapital.com

Other Offices
Clarendon House
2 Church Street
Hamilton, Bermuda HM11

19, 20 Centrum Plaza
Sector - 53, Golf Course Road
Gurgaon, India 122002
Phone: 91-124-421-3070
Fax: 91-124-421-3075

Management and Staff
Vishal Gulati, Managing Director

Type of Firm
Private Equity Firm

Project Preferences

Type of Financing Preferred:
Early Stage
Expansion
Seed

Size of Investments Considered:
Min Size of Investment Considered (000s): $5,000
Max Size of Investment Considered (000s): $20,000

Geographical Preferences

International Preferences:
India
United Kingdom
Europe

Industry Preferences

In Medical/Health prefer:
Health Services

In Consumer Related prefer:
Education Related

In Industrial/Energy prefer:
Energy
Coal Related
Energy Conservation Relat

In Business Serv. prefer:
Services

In Manufact. prefer:
Manufacturing

Additional Information
Year Founded: 2006
Current Activity Level : Actively seeking new investments

RADIANT CAPITAL LLC

915 Broadway, Suite 904
New York, NY USA 10010
Phone: 6468381127
Website: www.radiancapital.com

Type of Firm
Private Equity Firm

Project Preferences

Type of Financing Preferred:
Balanced

Industry Preferences

In Computer Software prefer:
Software

RADICLE ACCELERATOR

4365 Executive Drive, Suite 1500
San Diego, CA USA 92121
Website: radiclellc.com

Type of Firm
Incubator/Development Program

Project Preferences

Type of Financing Preferred:
Early Stage

Industry Preferences

In Agr/Forestr/Fish prefer:
Agriculture related

Additional Information
Year Founded: 2016
Capital Under Management: $6,000,000
Current Activity Level : Actively seeking new investments

RADICLE IMPACT

1438 Webster Street
Oakland, CA USA 94612
Website: www.radicleimpact.com

Management and Staff
Becca Levin, Managing Partner
Dan Skaff, Managing Partner

Type of Firm
Private Equity Firm

Project Preferences

Type of Financing Preferred:
Early Stage
Balanced

Geographical Preferences

United States Preferences:
West Coast

Industry Preferences

In Consumer Related prefer:
Food/Beverage
Consumer Services

In Industrial/Energy prefer:
Energy
Environmental Related

In Financial Services prefer:
Financial Services

Additional Information
Year Founded: 2003
Capital Under Management: $36,000,000
Current Activity Level : Actively seeking new investments

RADIUS VENTURES LLC

400 Madison Avenue
Eighth Floor
New York, NY USA 10017
Phone: 2128977778
Fax: 2123972656
E-mail: info@radiusventures.com
Website: www.radiusventures.com

Management and Staff
Daniel Lubin, Co-Founder
Floyd Loop, Venture Partner
George Milne, Venture Partner
James Mead, Venture Partner
Jordan Davis, Co-Founder
Kathleen Regan, Venture Partner
Vincent Conti, Venture Partner

Type of Firm
Private Equity Firm

Association Membership
National Venture Capital Association - USA (NVCA)

Project Preferences

Role in Financing:
Prefer role as deal originator but will also invest in deals created by others

Type of Financing Preferred:
Expansion
Later Stage

Size of Investments Considered:
Min Size of Investment Considered (000s): $100
Max Size of Investment Considered (000s): $10,000

Industry Preferences

In Biotechnology prefer:
Biotechnology

In Medical/Health prefer:
Medical/Health
Medical Diagnostics
Diagnostic Services
Diagnostic Test Products
Medical Therapeutics
Drug/Equipmt Delivery
Medical Products
Disposable Med. Products
Health Services
Pharmaceuticals

In Business Serv. prefer:
Services

Additional Information
Name of Most Recent Fund: Eagle Cliff Reinvestment Fund, L.P.
Most Recent Fund Was Raised: 07/10/2013
Year Founded: 2013
Capital Under Management: $20,100,000
Current Activity Level : Actively seeking new investments

RADY SCHOOL OF MANAGEMENT

9500 Gilman Drive
MC 0554
La Jolla, CA USA 92093
Phone: 8585349000
Website: rady.ucsd.edu

Type of Firm
University Program

Project Preferences

Role in Financing:
Prefer role in deals created by others

Type of Financing Preferred:
Early Stage
Seed

Size of Investments Considered:
Min Size of Investment Considered (000s): $75
Max Size of Investment Considered (000s): $150

Geographical Preferences

United States Preferences:
California

Industry Preferences

In Communications prefer:
Commercial Communications

In Biotechnology prefer:
Biotechnology

In Medical/Health prefer:
Medical Diagnostics
Diagnostic Test Products
Medical Products

In Other prefer:
Environment Responsible

Additional Information
Name of Most Recent Fund: Radius Venture Partners III, L.P.
Most Recent Fund Was Raised: 01/08/2007
Year Founded: 1997
Capital Under Management: $128,000,000
Current Activity Level : Actively seeking new investments
Method of Compensation: Return on investment is of primary concern, do not charge fees

Additional Information
Year Founded: 2001
Capital Under Management: $200,000
Current Activity Level : Actively seeking new investments

RAED VENTURES

2881 King Fahd Rd
AlFaisaliyah
Dammam, Saudi Arabia
E-mail: info@raed.vc
Website: raed.vc

Type of Firm
Private Equity Firm

Project Preferences

Type of Financing Preferred:
Early Stage
Seed
Startup

Geographical Preferences

International Preferences:
Middle East
Saudi Arabia

Industry Preferences

In Communications prefer:
Entertainment

In Computer Software prefer:
Software

In Medical/Health prefer:
Health Services

In Consumer Related prefer:
Retail
Education Related

In Industrial/Energy prefer:
Industrial Products

In Transportation prefer:
Transportation

In Financial Services prefer:
Financial Services

Additional Information
Year Founded: 2015
Current Activity Level : Actively seeking new investments

RAF INDUSTRIES, INC.

165 Township Line Road
One Pitcairn Place, Suite 2100
Jenkintown, PA USA 19046
Phone: 2155720738
Fax: 2155761640
E-mail: acquisitions@rafind.com
Website: www.rafind.com

Management and Staff
Andrew Souder, Vice President
John Piree, Vice President
Richard Horowitz, President & COO

Type of Firm
Private Equity Firm

Project Preferences

Type of Financing Preferred:
Leveraged Buyout
Management Buyouts
Acquisition

Geographical Preferences

United States Preferences:
All U.S.

Industry Preferences

In Consumer Related prefer:
Consumer
Entertainment and Leisure
Consumer Products
Consumer Services

In Business Serv. prefer:
Services

In Utilities prefer:
Utilities

Additional Information
Year Founded: 1979
Current Activity Level : Actively seeking new investments

RAGING BULL PTE LTD

73 AYER RAJAH CRESCENT, Suite 02-03/04
Singapore, Singapore 139952

Type of Firm
Private Equity Firm

Project Preferences

Type of Financing Preferred:
Balanced

Industry Preferences

In Internet Specific prefer:
Internet

In Medical/Health prefer:
Health Services

Additional Information
Year Founded: 2002
Current Activity Level : Actively seeking new investments

RAIFFEISENLANDESBANK OBEROESTERREICH AG

Europaplatz 1a
Linz, Austria 4020
Phone: 4373265960
Fax: 4373265962739
E-mail: internet@rlbooe.at
Website: www.rlbooe.at

Management and Staff
Hans Schilcher, Chief Executive Officer

Type of Firm
Bank Affiliated

Project Preferences

Type of Financing Preferred:
Later Stage
Management Buyouts

Geographical Preferences

International Preferences:
Austria
Germany

Additional Information
Year Founded: 1974
Current Activity Level : Actively seeking new investments

RAIN SOURCE CAPITAL, INC.

1600 University Avenue West, Suite 401
Saint Paul, MN USA 55104
Phone: 6516322140
Fax: 6516322145
E-mail: info@rainsourcecapital.com
Website: www.rainsourcecapital.com

Management and Staff
Clifford Smith, President
Peter Birkeland, Chief Financial Officer
Ron Leaf, Vice President

Type of Firm
Private Equity Firm

Association Membership
Community Development Venture Capital Alliance

Project Preferences

Role in Financing:
Will function either as deal originator or investor in deals created by others

Type of Financing Preferred:
Second Stage Financing
Leveraged Buyout
Early Stage
Expansion
Mezzanine
Generalist PE
Balanced
Later Stage
Management Buyouts
First Stage Financing
Private Placement
Startup
Special Situation
Recapitalizations

Size of Investments Considered:
Min Size of Investment Considered (000s): $250
Max Size of Investment Considered (000s): $2,000

Geographical Preferences

United States Preferences:
South Dakota
Iowa
North Dakota
Oregon
Idaho
Washington
Minnesota
Montana
All U.S.

Industry Preferences

In Communications prefer:
Communications and Media

In Computer Hardware prefer:
Computers

In Semiconductor/Electr prefer:
Electronics

In Biotechnology prefer:
Biotechnology

In Medical/Health prefer:
Medical/Health

In Consumer Related prefer:
Consumer
Food/Beverage
Education Related

In Industrial/Energy prefer:
Energy
Industrial Products
Superconductivity
Process Control
Robotics
Machinery

In Transportation prefer:
Transportation

In Business Serv. prefer:
Distribution

In Manufact. prefer:
Manufacturing

In Agr/Forestr/Fish prefer:
Agriculture related

In Other prefer:
Socially Responsible
Environment Responsible
Women/Minority-Owned Bus.

Additional Information
Year Founded: 1998
Capital Under Management: $16,000,000
Current Activity Level : Actively seeking new investments

Method of Compensation: Return on invest. most important, but chg. closing fees, service fees, etc.

RAINE GROUP LLC, THE
810 Seventh Avenue
39th Floor
New York, NY USA 10019
Phone: 2126035500
Fax: 2126035501
Website: www.raine.com

Other Offices
435 Tasso Street, Suite 305
Palo Alto, CA USA 94301
Phone: 6053884200
Fax: 6053884201

One Dongsanhuan Zhong Road, Suite 403, East Tower
Beijing, China 100020
Phone: 861057381086
Fax: 861059817598

9560 Wilshire Boulevard
Penthouse
Beverly Hills, CA USA 90212
Phone: 3109877700
Fax: 3109877701

Management and Staff
Jeffrey Sine, Founder
Joseph Ravitch, Founder

Type of Firm
Investment Management Firm

Project Preferences

Type of Financing Preferred:
Balanced

Size of Investments Considered:
Min Size of Investment Considered (000s): $40,000
Max Size of Investment Considered (000s): $80,000

Industry Preferences

In Communications prefer:
Communications and Media
Media and Entertainment

In Internet Specific prefer:
Ecommerce

In Consumer Related prefer:
Sports

Additional Information
Name of Most Recent Fund: Raine Partners II, L.P.
Most Recent Fund Was Raised: 01/15/2014
Year Founded: 2010
Capital Under Management: $1,032,675,000
Current Activity Level : Actively seeking new investments

RAINMAKER INVESTMENTS GMBH
Waltherstrasse 23
Munich, Germany 80337
E-mail: office@ri.de
Website: ri.de

Type of Firm
Private Equity Firm

Project Preferences

Type of Financing Preferred:
Early Stage
Seed
Startup

Additional Information
Year Founded: 2009
Current Activity Level : Actively seeking new investments

RAINMATTER
4th Cross, JP Nagar 4th Phase
No: 153/154
Bangalore, India
E-mail: talk@rainmatter.com
Website: rainmatter.com

Type of Firm
Incubator/Development Program

Project Preferences

Type of Financing Preferred:
Seed
Startup

Size of Investments Considered:
Min Size of Investment Considered (000s): $100
Max Size of Investment Considered (000s): $500

Geographical Preferences

International Preferences:
India

Industry Preferences

In Financial Services prefer:
Financial Services

Additional Information
Year Founded: 2015
Current Activity Level : Actively seeking new investments

RAJASTHAN ASSET MANAGEMENT CO PVT LTD

Bapu Nagar, Tonk Road
7th Floor, Ganga Heights
Jaipur, India 302005
Phone: 911414071680
Fax: 911414071683
E-mail: ravi@rvcf.org
Website: www.rvcf.org

Management and Staff
Girish Gupta, Chief Executive Officer

Type of Firm
Government Affiliated Program

Association Membership
Indian Venture Capital Association (IVCA)

Project Preferences

Type of Financing Preferred:
Leveraged Buyout
Early Stage
Expansion
Mezzanine
Turnaround
Seed
Startup

Size of Investments Considered:
Min Size of Investment Considered (000s): $814
Max Size of Investment Considered (000s): $2,443

Geographical Preferences

International Preferences:
India

Industry Preferences

In Computer Other prefer:
Computer Related

In Biotechnology prefer:
Biotechnology

In Medical/Health prefer:
Medical/Health

In Consumer Related prefer:
Entertainment and Leisure
Retail
Hotels and Resorts
Education Related

In Industrial/Energy prefer:
Industrial Products

In Transportation prefer:
Transportation

In Business Serv. prefer:
Services

Additional Information
Year Founded: 2002
Capital Under Management: $1,800,000
Current Activity Level : Actively seeking new investments

RALLY CAPITAL LLC

2365 Carillon Point
Kirkland, WA USA 98033
Phone: 4258894333

Type of Firm
Private Equity Firm

Project Preferences

Type of Financing Preferred:
Balanced

Additional Information
Year Founded: 2004
Current Activity Level : Actively seeking new investments

RALLY VENTURES

850 Oak Grove Avenue
Menlo Park, CA USA 94025
Phone: 6508541200
Fax: 6508541202
Website: www.rallyventures.com

Other Offices
601 Carlson Parkway, Suite 1160
Minnetonka, MN USA 55305
Phone: 9529957450
Fax: 9599957493

Type of Firm
Private Equity Firm

Project Preferences

Type of Financing Preferred:
Early Stage
Seed

Size of Investments Considered:
Min Size of Investment Considered (000s): $100
Max Size of Investment Considered (000s): $4,000

Industry Preferences

In Communications prefer:
Wireless Communications

In Computer Software prefer:
Systems Software

Additional Information
Name of Most Recent Fund: Icon Venture Partners, L.P.
Most Recent Fund Was Raised: 11/06/2013
Year Founded: 2013
Capital Under Management: $100,000,000
Current Activity Level : Actively seeking new investments

RAMPERSAND

105-115 Dover Street
Cremorne
Melbourne, Australia
Website: www.rampersand.com

Type of Firm
Private Equity Firm

Project Preferences

Type of Financing Preferred:
Early Stage
Balanced
Later Stage
Seed
Startup

Geographical Preferences

International Preferences:
Australia

Industry Preferences

In Communications prefer:
Communications and Media

Additional Information
Year Founded: 2013
Capital Under Management: $5,632,000
Current Activity Level : Actively seeking new investments

RAMPHASTOS INVESTMENTS MANAGEMENT BV

Grebbeweg 111
Rhenen , Netherlands 3911 AV
Phone: 3103177227
Fax: 3103177227
E-mail: info@ramphastos.com
Website: www.ramphastosinvestments.com

Type of Firm
Private Equity Firm

Additional Information
Year Founded: 1994
Current Activity Level : Actively seeking new investments

RANCH CREEK PARTNERS LLC

2157 N. Northlake Way, Suite 230
Seattle, WA USA 98103
E-mail: info@ranchcreekllc.com
Website: www.ranchcreekllc.com

Type of Firm
Private Equity Firm

Pratt's Guide to Private Equity & Venture Capital Sources

Project Preferences

Type of Financing Preferred:
Leveraged Buyout

Additional Information

Year Founded: 2015
Current Activity Level : Actively seeking new investments

RAND CAPITAL CORP

2200 Rand Building
Buffalo, NY USA 14203
Phone: 7168530802
Fax: 7168548480
Website: www.randcapital.com

Type of Firm

Private Equity Firm

Association Membership

Natl Assoc of Small Bus. Inv. Co (NASBIC)

Project Preferences

Role in Financing:
Will function either as deal originator or investor in deals created by others

Type of Financing Preferred:
Early Stage
Balanced
Later Stage

Size of Investments Considered:
Min Size of Investment Considered (000s): $500
Max Size of Investment Considered (000s): $1,500

Geographical Preferences

United States Preferences:
West Coast
New York

Industry Focus

(% based on actual investment)
Industrial/Energy	14.9%
Computer Software and Services	12.3%
Medical/Health	12.0%
Internet Specific	11.4%
Other Products	10.7%
Consumer Related	9.2%
Biotechnology	8.4%
Communications and Media	7.4%
Semiconductors/Other Elect.	7.0%
Computer Hardware	6.7%

Additional Information

Name of Most Recent Fund: Rand Capital Corporation
Most Recent Fund Was Raised: 12/21/1998
Year Founded: 1969
Capital Under Management: $25,000,000
Current Activity Level : Actively seeking new investments
Method of Compensation: Return on invest. most important, but chg. closing fees, service fees, etc.

RANGATIRA LTD

Level Ten SolNet House
70 The Terrace
Wellington, New Zealand
Phone: 6444720251
Fax: 6444732685
E-mail: info@rangatira.co.nz
Website: rangatira.co.nz

Management and Staff

Ian Frame, Chief Executive Officer

Type of Firm

Private Equity Firm

Project Preferences

Type of Financing Preferred:
Leveraged Buyout
Expansion
Acquisition

Geographical Preferences

International Preferences:
Australia
New Zealand

Additional Information

Year Founded: 1937
Current Activity Level : Actively seeking new investments

RANGE LIGHT LLC

2795 Pearl Street, Suite 200
Boulder, CO USA 80302
Phone: 3034444420
Website: www.rangelightllc.com

Type of Firm

Private Equity Firm

Project Preferences

Type of Financing Preferred:
Balanced

Size of Investments Considered:
Min Size of Investment Considered (000s): $1,000
Max Size of Investment Considered (000s): $20,000

Industry Preferences

In Consumer Related prefer:
Food/Beverage

Additional Information

Year Founded: 2017
Current Activity Level : Actively seeking new investments

RANTUM CAPITAL MANAGEMENT GMBH

Guiollettstrasse 25
Frankfurt am Main, Germany 60325
Phone: 496997776790
E-mail: info@rantumcapital.de
Website: rantumcapital.de

Management and Staff

Dirk Notheis, Managing Director
Fritz Koop, Managing Director
Marc Pahlow, Managing Director

Type of Firm

Bank Affiliated

Project Preferences

Type of Financing Preferred:
Leveraged Buyout
Mezzanine
Acquisition

Geographical Preferences

International Preferences:
Germany

Additional Information

Year Founded: 2013
Capital Under Management: $110,742,000
Current Activity Level : Actively seeking new investments

RAPS FINANCE (PTY) LTD

224 Loristo Street
Pretorius Park
Pretoria, South Africa 0010
Phone: 27-12-998-8280
Fax: 27-12-998-8401
E-mail: info@raps.co.za
Website: www.raps.co.za

Type of Firm

Private Equity Firm

Project Preferences

Type of Financing Preferred:
Balanced

Geographical Preferences

International Preferences:
South Africa

Industry Preferences

In Industrial/Energy prefer:
Energy

Additional Information

Year Founded: 2003
Current Activity Level : Actively seeking new investments

RAPTOR CAPITAL MANAGEMENT LP

280 Congress Street
12th Floor
Boston, MA USA 02210
Phone: 6177724600
Website: www.raptorcapitalmanagement.com

Other Offices

401 West, 14th Street
Fourth Floor
New York, NY USA 10014
Phone: (212) 266-6900

50 Rowes Wharf
Sixth Floor
Boston, MA USA 02110

Management and Staff

Andrew Spellman, Managing Director
Harry DeMott, Managing Director
John Burns, Managing Director
Michael Ryan, Vice President
Peter Monaco, Managing Director
Richie Notar, Managing Director
Robert Needham, Chief Financial Officer
Sara Christensen, Vice President

Type of Firm

Investment Management Firm

Project Preferences

Type of Financing Preferred:
Balanced
Later Stage

Industry Preferences

In Consumer Related prefer:
Consumer
Consumer Products
Consumer Services

Additional Information

Name of Most Recent Fund: Raptor Consumer Partners Fund I, L.P.
Most Recent Fund Was Raised: 12/20/2012
Year Founded: 2011
Capital Under Management: $54,660,000
Current Activity Level : Actively seeking new investments

RATIONALWAVE CAPITAL PARTNERS LLC

230 Park Avenue, Suite 928
New York, NY USA 10169

Type of Firm

Private Equity Firm

Project Preferences

Type of Financing Preferred:
Early Stage
Expansion

Geographical Preferences

United States Preferences:

Additional Information

Year Founded: 2003
Current Activity Level : Actively seeking new investments

RATOS AB

Drottninggatan 2
P.O. Box 1661
Stockholm, Sweden 111 96
Phone: 4687001700
Fax: 468102559
E-mail: info@ratos.se
Website: www.ratos.se

Type of Firm

Private Equity Firm

Association Membership

Danish Venture Capital Association (DVCA)
Swedish Venture Capital Association (SVCA)

Project Preferences

Type of Financing Preferred:
Leveraged Buyout
Acquisition

Size of Investments Considered:
Min Size of Investment Considered (000s): $45,000
Max Size of Investment Considered (000s): $750,000

Geographical Preferences

International Preferences:
Scandanavia/Nordic Region

Industry Focus

(% based on actual investment)
Consumer Related	23.2%
Industrial/Energy	20.4%
Other Products	19.8%
Internet Specific	10.1%
Communications and Media	9.4%
Medical/Health	7.6%
Semiconductors/Other Elect.	5.1%
Biotechnology	2.8%
Computer Software and Services	1.6%

Additional Information

Year Founded: 1934
Capital Under Management: $1,198,500,000
Current Activity Level : Actively seeking new investments

RAVEN CAPITAL PTY LTD

Seven Ridge Street, Suite Five
North Sydney, Australia 2060
Phone: 0294604534
Fax: 0299649299
E-mail: info@ravencapital.com.au
Website: www.ravencapital.com.au

Management and Staff

Kristian Blaszczynsk, Co-Founder
Philip Sheridan, Co-Founder
Ross Hopkins, Co-Founder

Type of Firm

Investment Management Firm

Project Preferences

Type of Financing Preferred:
Early Stage
Seed

Additional Information

Year Founded: 2011
Current Activity Level : Actively seeking new investments

RB CAPITAL SASU

62-64, Rue de Lisbonne
Paris, France 75008
Phone: 33153670950
Website: www.b-and-capital.com

Type of Firm

Private Equity Firm

Project Preferences

Type of Financing Preferred:
Leveraged Buyout
Management Buyouts
Acquisition

Geographical Preferences

International Preferences:
France

Industry Preferences

In Medical/Health prefer:
Medical/Health

In Industrial/Energy prefer:
Industrial Products
Environmental Related

In Business Serv. prefer:
Services
Distribution

Additional Information

Year Founded: 2016
Current Activity Level : Actively seeking new investments

RB WEBBER AND COMAPNY INC

2121 South El Camino Real, Suite 700
San Mateo, CA USA 94403
Phone: 6502927100
Fax: 6502927110

Management and Staff
Jeffrey Webber, Partner
Joseph Brilando, Partner
Katharine Boshkoff, Partner
Mark Hamilton, Principal
Rob Meinhardt, Principal
Robert Lauridsen, Partner
Stephen Plume, Partner
Stephen Jordan, Partner
Todd Keleher, Principal

Type of Firm
Private Equity Firm

Project Preferences

Type of Financing Preferred:
Early Stage

Geographical Preferences

United States Preferences:
All U.S.

Industry Preferences

In Communications prefer:
Wireless Communications

In Computer Software prefer:
Software

In Internet Specific prefer:
E-Commerce Technology

Additional Information
Name of Most Recent Fund: Entrepreneurs Fund III, L.P.
Most Recent Fund Was Raised: 08/23/2007
Year Founded: 1991
Capital Under Management: $8,200,000
Current Activity Level : Actively seeking new investments

RBC CAPITAL PARTNERS

333 Bay Street, Suite 1640, P.O. Box 21
Toronto, Canada M5H 2R2
Phone: 4163672440
Fax: 4163674604
Website: www.rbccm.com

Other Offices

One East Weaver Street
3rd Floor
Greenwich, CT USA 06831
Phone: 212-428-6902
Fax: 212-428-3069

, Suite 1340 - B.C. Gas Building
1111 West Georgia Street
Vancouver, Canada V6C 2X8
Phone: 604-665-0460
Fax: 604-665-8699

One Place Ville Marie
Fourth Floor, North Wing
Montreal, Canada H3C 3A9
Phone: 514-874-5081
Fax: 514-874-2294

Two Embarcadero Center, Suite 1200
San Francisco, CA USA 94111
Phone: 415-633-8619

75 Fifth Street, NW, Suite 900
Atlanta, GA USA 30308
Phone: 404-495-6060

Management and Staff
David Unsworth, Partner
Kevin Talbot, Managing Partner
Robert Antoniades, Partner
Tony Manastersky, Managing Partner

Type of Firm
Bank Affiliated

Association Membership
Canadian Venture Capital Association

Project Preferences

Role in Financing:
Prefer role as deal originator but will also invest in deals created by others

Type of Financing Preferred:
Second Stage Financing
Leveraged Buyout
Early Stage
Expansion
Mezzanine
Balanced
Seed
First Stage Financing
Acquisition
Startup

Size of Investments Considered:
Min Size of Investment Considered (000s): $3,000
Max Size of Investment Considered (000s): $50,000

Geographical Preferences

United States Preferences:
All U.S.

Canadian Preferences:
All Canada

Industry Focus
(% based on actual investment)
Computer Software and Services 24.9%
Communications and Media 18.9%
Biotechnology 16.0%
Medical/Health 10.7%
Internet Specific 8.7%
Other Products 6.2%
Semiconductors/Other Elect. 5.1%
Industrial/Energy 4.9%
Consumer Related 4.7%

Additional Information
Year Founded: 1969
Capital Under Management: $800,000,000
Current Activity Level : Actively seeking new investments
Method of Compensation: Return on invest. most important, but chg. closing fees, service fees, etc.

RBV CAPITAL

10 Testovskaya Street
North Tower
Moscow, Russia
Phone: 74957822342
E-mail: info@rbvcapital.com
Website: rbvcapital.com

Type of Firm
Private Equity Firm

Project Preferences

Type of Financing Preferred:
Balanced

Geographical Preferences

United States Preferences:

International Preferences:
Russia

Industry Preferences

In Biotechnology prefer:
Biotechnology

Additional Information
Year Founded: 2017
Current Activity Level : Actively seeking new investments

RCAPITAL LTD

24 Old Bond Street
Fifth Floor, Mayfair
London, United Kingdom W1K4LS
Phone: 448452939888
Fax: 448452939889
E-mail: info@rcapital.co.uk
Website: www.rcapital.co.uk

Management and Staff
Peter Ward, Co-Founder

Pratt's Guide to Private Equity & Venture Capital Sources

Type of Firm
Private Equity Firm

Project Preferences

Type of Financing Preferred:
Turnaround
Distressed Debt

Geographical Preferences

International Preferences:
United Kingdom

Additional Information
Year Founded: 2004
Current Activity Level : Actively seeking new investments

RCF MANAGEMENT LLC

1400 Sixteenth Street, Suite 200
Denver, CO USA 80202
Phone: 7209461444
Fax: 7209461450
Website: www.resourcecapitalfunds.com

Other Offices

24 Kings Park Road
Level 3
West Perth, Australia 6005
Phone: 610894761900
Fax: 610894852779

224 Wall Street, Suite 202
Huntington, NY USA 11743
Phone: 6316929111
Fax: 6316929119

25 York Street, Suite 610
Toronto, Canada M5J 2V5
Phone: 6477260642102

224 Wall Street Huntington, Suite 202
Huntington, NY USA 11743
Phone: 6316929111
Fax: 6316929119

25 York Street, Suite 610
London, United Kingdom M5J 2V5
Phone: 6477260642

Management and Staff
Brian Dolan, Partner
Chris Corbett, Principal
Glen Parrott, Vice President
Henderson Tuten, Partner
James McClements, Managing Partner
Jasper Bertisen, Principal
Mason Hills, Partner
Peter Nicholson, Partner
Quinn Roussel, Principal
Raul Borrastero, Vice President
Ross Bhappu, Partner
Russ Cranswick, Partner
Sherry Croasdale, Chief Financial Officer

Type of Firm
Private Equity Firm

Association Membership
Australian Venture Capital Association (AVCAL)

Project Preferences

Type of Financing Preferred:
Leveraged Buyout
Later Stage
Acquisition
Distressed Debt

Industry Preferences

In Agr/Forestr/Fish prefer:
Mining and Minerals

Additional Information
Name of Most Recent Fund: Resource Capital Fund VI, L.P.
Most Recent Fund Was Raised: 02/21/2013
Year Founded: 1998
Capital Under Management: $1,800,000,000
Current Activity Level : Actively seeking new investments

RCP ADVISORS LLC

100 North Riverside Plaza, Suite 2400
Chicago, IL USA 60606
Phone: 3122667300
Fax: 3122667433
E-mail: rcp@rcpadvisors.com
Website: www.rcpadvisors.com

Other Offices

949 South Coast Drive, Suite 550
COSTA MESA, CA USA 92626
Phone: 949-335-5000
Fax: 949-266-9156

1111 Bayside Drive, Suite 270
CORONA DEL MAR, CA USA 92625
Phone: 9493355000
Fax: 9492669156

Management and Staff
Andrew Nelson, Principal
David McCoy, Principal
Jon Madorsky, Principal
Michael Feinglass, Principal
Nell Blatherwick, Principal

Type of Firm
Private Equity Advisor or Fund of Funds

Association Membership
Illinois Venture Capital Association
Natl Assoc of Small Bus. Inv. Co (NASBIC)

Project Preferences

Role in Financing:
Other

Type of Financing Preferred:
Fund of Funds
Other
Special Situation

Geographical Preferences

United States Preferences:
North America

Additional Information
Name of Most Recent Fund: RCP Fund IX, L.P.
Most Recent Fund Was Raised: 03/31/2014
Year Founded: 2006
Capital Under Management: $4,300,000,000
Current Activity Level : Actively seeking new investments

RE SOURCES CAPITAL SAS

53, Avenue de Flandre
Marcq en Baroeul, France 59700
Website: www.re-sources-capital.fr

Type of Firm
Private Equity Firm

Project Preferences

Type of Financing Preferred:
Management Buyouts

Geographical Preferences

International Preferences:
Luxembourg
France

Additional Information
Year Founded: 2014
Current Activity Level : Actively seeking new investments

REACH CAPITAL

532 Emerson Street
Palo Alto, CA USA 94301
Website: www.reachcap.com

Type of Firm
Private Equity Firm

Project Preferences

Type of Financing Preferred:
Early Stage
Later Stage
Seed
Startup

Industry Preferences

In Consumer Related prefer:
Education Related

Additional Information
Year Founded: 2015
Current Activity Level : Actively seeking new investments

REAKTOR VENTURES LTD

Mannerheimintie 2
Helsinki, Finland 00100
Phone: 358941520200
Fax: 358941520201
E-mail: polte@reaktor.fi
Website: www.reaktor.vc

Type of Firm
Private Equity Firm

Project Preferences

Type of Financing Preferred:
Seed
Startup

Geographical Preferences

International Preferences:
Finland

Industry Preferences

In Communications prefer:
Communications and Media
Wireless Communications

In Computer Software prefer:
Software

In Internet Specific prefer:
Internet

Additional Information
Year Founded: 2013
Current Activity Level : Actively seeking new investments

REAL VENTURES

51 Sherbrooke Street West
Maison Notman House
Montreal, Canada H2X 1X2
E-mail: hello@realventures.com
Website: www.realventures.com

Management and Staff
Alan MacIntosh, General Partner
Charles Seely, Venture Partner
Isaac Souweine, Partner
Janet Bannister, General Partner
Jean-Sebastien Cournoyer, Co-Founder
John Stokes, General Partner
Mike Shaver, General Partner
Omar Dhalla, Venture Partner
Sam Haffar, Partner
Sylvain Carle, General Partner

Type of Firm
Private Equity Firm

Association Membership
Canadian Venture Capital Association

Project Preferences

Type of Financing Preferred:
Early Stage
Seed
Startup

Industry Preferences

In Communications prefer:
Wireless Communications
Data Communications
Entertainment

In Computer Software prefer:
Software

In Internet Specific prefer:
Internet
Ecommerce
Web Aggregation/Portals

Additional Information
Name of Most Recent Fund: Real Ventures III
Most Recent Fund Was Raised: 04/12/2014
Year Founded: 2007
Capital Under Management: $308,455,000
Current Activity Level : Actively seeking new investments

REALZA CAPITAL SGECR SA

Paseo de la Castellana
15-3 dcha
Madrid, Spain 28046
Phone: 34917820982
Fax: 34917820983
E-mail: bv@realzacapital.com
Website: www.realzacapital.com

Management and Staff
Alfredo Zavala, Partner
Martin Gonzalez del Valle, Partner
Sonsoles Manglano, Chief Financial Officer

Type of Firm
Private Equity Firm

Association Membership
Spanish Venture Capital Association (ASCRI)

Project Preferences

Role in Financing:
Prefer role as deal originator but will also invest in deals created by others

Type of Financing Preferred:
Leveraged Buyout
Acquisition

Geographical Preferences

International Preferences:
Portugal
Spain

Industry Preferences

In Industrial/Energy prefer:
Energy

In Financial Services prefer:
Financial Services

Additional Information
Name of Most Recent Fund: Realza Capital Fondo FCR
Most Recent Fund Was Raised: 09/19/2007
Year Founded: 2007
Capital Under Management: $364,500,000
Current Activity Level : Actively seeking new investments

REAYA HOLDING

Kheriji Plaza, Madinah Road, Suite 3007, 3rd Flr.
Jeddah, Saudi Arabia 21352
Phone: 96626676777
Fax: 96626634884
Website: www.reayaholding.com

Management and Staff
Ahmad Emara, Chief Executive Officer

Type of Firm
Private Equity Firm

Association Membership
Gulf Venture Capital Association

Project Preferences

Type of Financing Preferred:
Leveraged Buyout
Early Stage
Generalist PE
Balanced
Later Stage
Acquisition
Startup

Geographical Preferences

International Preferences:
Middle East
Saudi Arabia

Industry Preferences

In Medical/Health prefer:
Medical/Health
Medical Products
Health Services

Additional Information
Year Founded: 2009
Current Activity Level : Actively seeking new investments

REBRIGHT PARTNERS INC

30-1-2 Kudan-minami
Tokyo, Japan 102-0074
Website: rebrightpartners.com

Type of Firm
Private Equity Firm

Project Preferences

Type of Financing Preferred:
Seed
Startup

Geographical Preferences

International Preferences:
Vietnam
Indonesia
India
Thailand
Philippines
Singapore
Malaysia

Industry Preferences

In Communications prefer:
Wireless Communications
Media and Entertainment

In Internet Specific prefer:
E-Commerce Technology
Internet
Ecommerce

In Business Serv. prefer:
Media

Additional Information
Year Founded: 2007
Current Activity Level : Actively seeking new investments

RECIPROCAL VENTURE MANAGEMENT LLC

475 Park Avenue South
32nd Floor
New York, NY USA 10016
E-mail: info@recinv.com
Website: recvc.com

Type of Firm
Private Equity Firm

Project Preferences

Type of Financing Preferred:
Early Stage
Seed

Geographical Preferences

United States Preferences:

International Preferences:
United Kingdom
Europe
Israel

Industry Preferences

In Financial Services prefer:
Financial Services

Additional Information
Year Founded: 2017
Capital Under Management: $25,000,000
Current Activity Level : Actively seeking new investments

RECRUIT STRATEGIC PARTNERS INC

530 Lytton Avenue, Suite 231
Palo Alto, CA USA 94301
E-mail: contact@recruitstrategicpartners.com
Website: www.recruitstrategicpartners.com

Other Offices
156 2nd Street
San Francisco, CA USA 94105

Management and Staff
Akihiko Okamoto, President

Type of Firm
Private Equity Firm

Project Preferences

Type of Financing Preferred:
Seed
Startup

Geographical Preferences

United States Preferences:
All U.S.

Industry Preferences

In Communications prefer:
Media and Entertainment

In Internet Specific prefer:
Ecommerce

In Consumer Related prefer:
Entertainment and Leisure
Food/Beverage

In Financial Services prefer:
Real Estate

In Business Serv. prefer:
Services

Additional Information
Year Founded: 1969
Current Activity Level : Actively seeking new investments

RED & BLUE VENTURES LLC

3401 Grays Ferry Avenue
Pennovation Center Bldg 176
Philadelphia, PA USA 19146
Website: www.redandblue.vc

Type of Firm
Private Equity Firm

Project Preferences

Type of Financing Preferred:
Early Stage
Seed

Geographical Preferences

United States Preferences:
Pennsylvania
Washington
New York

Industry Preferences

In Computer Software prefer:
Software

In Internet Specific prefer:
Ecommerce

Additional Information
Year Founded: 2016
Capital Under Management: $13,920,000
Current Activity Level : Actively seeking new investments

RED ARTS CAPITAL LLC

180 North Jefferson
Apt. 401
Chicago, IL USA 60601
E-mail: info@redartscapital.com
Website: www.redartscapital.com

Management and Staff
Nicholas Antoine, Partner

Type of Firm
Private Equity Firm

Additional Information
Year Founded: 2016
Current Activity Level : Actively seeking new investments

RED BANYAN CAPITAL MANAGEMENT CO LTD

No. 1366 Qianjiang Road
46F, Building B, China Resourc
Hangzhou, China
Phone: 8657181101063
Website: www.hr-invest.com

Type of Firm
Investment Management Firm

Project Preferences

Type of Financing Preferred:
Balanced

Geographical Preferences

International Preferences:
Asia

Additional Information
Year Founded: 2015
Current Activity Level : Actively seeking new investments

RED CEDAR VENTURES LLC

2727 Alliance Drive, Suite C
Lansing, MI USA 48910
Phone: 5173539268
Fax: 5173539215
E-mail: msuf@msu.edu
Website: www.msufoundation.org

Type of Firm
Incubator/Development Program

Project Preferences

Type of Financing Preferred:
Seed
Startup

Additional Information
Year Founded: 2016
Capital Under Management: $5,000,000
Current Activity Level : Actively seeking new investments

RED DIAMOND CAPITAL

655 Third Avenue
New York, NY USA 10017
Phone: 212-605-2300
Fax: 212-605-1977

Type of Firm
Private Equity Firm

Project Preferences

Type of Financing Preferred:
Leveraged Buyout
Management Buyouts
Recapitalizations

Geographical Preferences

United States Preferences:
North America

Industry Preferences

In Business Serv. prefer:
Distribution

In Manufact. prefer:
Manufacturing

Additional Information
Year Founded: 2002
Current Activity Level : Actively seeking new investments

RED RIVER WEST SASU

12, rue Francois 1er
Paris, France 75008
Website: www.redriverwest.com

Type of Firm
Investment Management Firm

Project Preferences

Type of Financing Preferred:
Early Stage
Expansion
Later Stage
Seed

Size of Investments Considered:
Min Size of Investment Considered (000s): $5,682
Max Size of Investment Considered (000s): $56,818

Geographical Preferences

International Preferences:
France

Industry Preferences

In Communications prefer:
Data Communications

In Computer Software prefer:
Data Processing
Software

In Internet Specific prefer:
E-Commerce Technology
Internet
Ecommerce

In Business Serv. prefer:
Media

Additional Information
Year Founded: 2017
Capital Under Management: $113,400,000
Current Activity Level : Actively seeking new investments

RED ROCK VENTURES

530 Lytton Avenue
Second Floor
Palo Alto, CA USA 94301
Phone: 6503253111
Website: www.redrockventures.com

Management and Staff
Curtis Myers, Partner
Laura Gwosden, Chief Financial Officer
Peter Dumanian, Partner
Robert Todd, Partner

Type of Firm
Private Equity Firm

Project Preferences

Role in Financing:
Will function either as deal originator or investor in deals created by others

Type of Financing Preferred:
Early Stage
Seed

Industry Focus
(% based on actual investment)
Computer Software and Services	60.7%
Internet Specific	34.1%
Communications and Media	4.7%
Medical/Health	0.5%

Additional Information
Name of Most Recent Fund: Red Rock Ventures III, L.P.
Most Recent Fund Was Raised: 10/01/2000
Year Founded: 1997
Capital Under Management: $223,000,000
Current Activity Level : Actively seeking new investments

REDALPINE VENTURE PARTNERS AG

Pfingstweidstrasse 60
Zurich, Switzerland 8005
Phone: 41442711530
Fax: 41442711532
E-mail: info@redalpine.com
Website: www.redalpine.com

Other Offices
Linstows Gate 6
Oslo, Norway 0166

Management and Staff
Maya Lalive D Epinay, Partner
Michael Sidler, General Partner
Nicolas Berg, General Partner
Peter Niederhauser, General Partner

Type of Firm
Private Equity Firm

Association Membership
Swiss Venture Capital Association (SECA)

Project Preferences

Type of Financing Preferred:
Early Stage
Seed
Startup

Size of Investments Considered:
Min Size of Investment Considered (000s): $148
Max Size of Investment Considered (000s): $2,707

Geographical Preferences

International Preferences:
Italy
Switzerland
Scandanavia/Nordic Region
Norway
Germany

Industry Preferences

In Communications prefer:
Communications and Media
Wireless Communications
Media and Entertainment
Entertainment

In Internet Specific prefer:
Internet

In Biotechnology prefer:
Biotechnology

In Medical/Health prefer:
Medical/Health

In Consumer Related prefer:
Entertainment and Leisure
Food/Beverage

In Industrial/Energy prefer:
Environmental Related

Additional Information
Year Founded: 2007
Current Activity Level : Actively seeking new investments

REDBIRD CAPITAL PARTNERS PLATFORM LP

667 Madison Avenue
16th Floor
New York, NY USA 10065
Phone: 2122351000
E-mail: info@redbirdcap.com
Website: www.redbirdcap.com

Management and Staff
Andrew Lauck, Vice President
Gerry Cardinale, Chief Executive Officer
Hunter Carpenter, Partner
Jason Young, Chief Financial Officer
Michael Zabik, Vice President
Tyler Alexander, Vice President

Type of Firm
Private Equity Firm

Project Preferences

Type of Financing Preferred:
Balanced

Additional Information
Year Founded: 2014
Capital Under Management: $139,980,000
Current Activity Level : Actively seeking new investments

REDBUS INVESTMENTS

16-18 Berners Street
Fifth Floor, Orwell House
London, United Kingdom W1T 3LN
Phone: 44-20-7299-8844
Fax: 44-20-7299-8840
E-mail: info@redbus.co.uk
Website: www.redbus.co.uk

Management and Staff
Dean Dorrell, Chief Executive Officer

Type of Firm
Private Equity Firm

Project Preferences

Type of Financing Preferred:
Early Stage
Balanced
Seed
Acquisition

Geographical Preferences

International Preferences:
United Kingdom

Additional Information
Year Founded: 1998
Capital Under Management: $24,700,000
Current Activity Level : Actively seeking new investments

REDCLAYS CAPITAL PVT LTD

81/A, Sixth Main, 18th Cross
Malleshwaram (West)
Bangalore, India 560055
Website: www.redclays.com

Type of Firm
Private Equity Firm

Association Membership
Indian Venture Capital Association (IVCA)

Project Preferences

Type of Financing Preferred:
Leveraged Buyout
Early Stage
Expansion
Generalist PE
Balanced
Later Stage

Geographical Preferences

International Preferences:
India

Industry Preferences

In Communications prefer:
Media and Entertainment

In Semiconductor/Electr prefer:
Semiconductor

In Consumer Related prefer:
Consumer

In Industrial/Energy prefer:
Industrial Products
Environmental Related

In Financial Services prefer:
Real Estate

Additional Information
Year Founded: 2006
Current Activity Level : Actively seeking new investments

REDCLIFFE CAPITAL

One Fore Street
London, United Kingdom EC2Y 5EJ
Phone: 8700201656
E-mail: getintouch@redcliffecapital.com
Website: www.redcliffecapital.com

Type of Firm
Private Equity Firm

Project Preferences

REDFIRE INVESTMENTS PTY LTD

Level 2, 217 Queen Street
Melbourne, Australia 3000
Phone: 613-8610-2527
Fax: 613-9670-6495
E-mail: info@redfireinvestments.com.au

Management and Staff
Geoff Drucker, Co-Founder
Gordon Crosbie-Walsh, Co-Founder

Type of Firm
Private Equity Firm

Project Preferences

Type of Financing Preferred:
Early Stage
Later Stage

Geographical Preferences

International Preferences:
Australia
Asia

Industry Preferences

In Industrial/Energy prefer:
Environmental Related

Additional Information
Year Founded: 2008
Capital Under Management: $10,000,000
Current Activity Level : Actively seeking new investments

REDHILLS VENTURES LLC

2620 Regatta Drive, Suite 208
Las Vegas, NV USA 89128
Phone: 702-233-2160
Fax: 702-233-2167
E-mail: info@redhillsventures.com
Website: www.redhillsventures.com

Other Offices
908 Trophy Hills Drive
Las Vegas, NV USA 89134

Type of Firm
Private Equity Firm

Type of Financing Preferred:
Leveraged Buyout
Early Stage
Seed

Additional Information
Year Founded: 2008
Current Activity Level : Actively seeking new investments

REDMONT VENTURE PARTNERS

3104 Blue Lake Drive
Vestavia Hills, AL USA 35243
Phone: 2059435646
Fax: 2059434748
Website: www.redmontvp.com

Management and Staff
Michael Humber, Principal
Philip Hodges, Managing Partner
Roddy Clark, Managing Partner

Type of Firm
Private Equity Firm

Project Preferences

Role in Financing:
Will function either as deal originator or investor in deals created by others

Type of Financing Preferred:
Early Stage
Expansion
Mezzanine

Size of Investments Considered:
Min Size of Investment Considered (000s): $500
Max Size of Investment Considered (000s): $2,500

Geographical Preferences

United States Preferences:
Southeast
Alabama

Industry Preferences

In Medical/Health prefer:
Medical/Health

Association Membership
National Venture Capital Association - USA (NVCA)

Project Preferences

Size of Investments Considered:
Min Size of Investment Considered (000s): $125
Max Size of Investment Considered (000s): $7,000

Industry Preferences

In Medical/Health prefer:
Health Services

In Financial Services prefer:
Real Estate

Additional Information
Year Founded: 2002
Capital Under Management: $10,000,000
Current Activity Level : Actively seeking new investments

REDPOINT EVENTURES CONSULTORIA EMPRESARIAL LTDA

Rochavera Marble Tower
Av. das Nacoes Unidas
Sao Paulo, Brazil 14171
E-mail: contact@rpev.com.br
Website: rpev.com.br

Management and Staff
Anderson Thees, Co-Founder
Jeffrey Brody, Partner
Mathias Schilling, Managing Partner
Yann De Vries, Partner

Type of Firm
Private Equity Firm

Association Membership
Brazilian Venture Capital Association (ABCR)

Project Preferences

Type of Financing Preferred:
Early Stage

Geographical Preferences

International Preferences:
Brazil

Industry Preferences

In Communications prefer:
Telecommunications
Wireless Communications

In Computer Software prefer:
Applications Software

In Internet Specific prefer:
Internet
Ecommerce

In Industrial/Energy prefer:
Industrial Products

In Financial Services prefer:
Financial Services

In Business Serv. prefer:
Services

In Manufact. prefer:
Manufacturing

Additional Information
Name of Most Recent Fund: Enhanced Alabama Issuer II LLC
Most Recent Fund Was Raised: 06/24/2008
Year Founded: 1997
Capital Under Management: $33,700,000
Current Activity Level : Actively seeking new investments
Method of Compensation: Return on investment is of primary concern, do not charge fees

In Consumer Related prefer:
Consumer

In Business Serv. prefer:
Media

Additional Information
Name of Most Recent Fund: Redpoint e.ventures
Most Recent Fund Was Raised: 07/19/2012
Year Founded: 2012
Capital Under Management: $130,000,000
Current Activity Level : Actively seeking new investments

REDPOINT VENTURES

3000 Sand Hill Road
Building Two, Suite 290
Menlo Park, CA USA 94025
Phone: 6509265600
Fax: 6508545762
Website: www.redpoint.com

Other Offices

1366 Nanjin Road West
Plaza 66, Tower 2, Suite 2904
Shanghai, China 200040
Phone: 86-21-6288-7757
Fax: 86-21-6288-7797

Management and Staff

Alex Zhang, Vice President
Alex Bard, Partner
Allen Beasley, Partner
Andy Rubin, Venture Partner
Chris Moore, Partner
David Yuan, Partner
Elliot Geidt, Principal
Geoffrey Yang, Partner
Jamie Davidson, Partner
Jeffrey Brody, Partner
John Walecka, Partner
Kyle Liu, Vice President
Lenny Pruss, Principal
Mahesh Vellanki, Vice President
Reggie Zhang, Partner
Ryan Sarver, Partner
Satish Dharmaraj, Partner
Scott Raney, Partner
Timothy Haley, Partner
Tom Dyal, Partner
Tomasz Tunguz, Partner
Tony Wu, Partner

Type of Firm
Private Equity Firm

Association Membership
Western Association of Venture Capitalists (WAVC)
National Venture Capital Association - USA (NVCA)

Project Preferences

Type of Financing Preferred:
Early Stage
Balanced
Later Stage
Seed
Startup

Size of Investments Considered:
Min Size of Investment Considered (000s): $1,000
Max Size of Investment Considered (000s): $10,000

Geographical Preferences

United States Preferences:
All U.S.

International Preferences:
China

Industry Focus

(% based on actual investment)
Internet Specific	34.9%
Computer Software and Services	27.6%
Communications and Media	15.7%
Semiconductors/Other Elect.	7.6%
Industrial/Energy	6.5%
Computer Hardware	4.0%
Other Products	2.0%
Consumer Related	1.3%
Medical/Health	0.3%

Additional Information
Name of Most Recent Fund: Redpoint Ventures V, L.P.
Most Recent Fund Was Raised: 01/03/2013
Year Founded: 1999

Capital Under Management: $2,000,000,000
Current Activity Level : Actively seeking new investments

REDROCK CAPITAL VENTURE LTD

No. 1 East Chang An Avenue
Room 1208, Oriental Plaza
Beijing, China 100738
Phone: 861085189669
Fax: 861085189797
Website: www.sunredrock.com

Management and Staff
Kenin Hui, Vice President

Type of Firm
Investment Management Firm

Project Preferences

Type of Financing Preferred:
Balanced

Geographical Preferences

International Preferences:
China

Industry Preferences

In Communications prefer:
Telecommunications

In Biotechnology prefer:
Biotechnology

In Medical/Health prefer:
Medical/Health
Drug/Equipmt Delivery
Medical Products

In Industrial/Energy prefer:
Energy
Environmental Related

In Business Serv. prefer:
Media

In Agr/Forestr/Fish prefer:
Mining and Minerals

Additional Information
Year Founded: 2007
Current Activity Level : Actively seeking new investments

REDSEED SRL

Via Giacomo Puccini 3
Milano, Italy I-20121
Phone: 39 02 8708 4855
Fax: 39 02 8708 4874
E-mail: info@redseed.it
Website: www.redseed.it

Type of Firm
Private Equity Firm

Project Preferences

Type of Financing Preferred:
Early Stage
Startup

Industry Preferences

In Computer Software prefer:
Software

Additional Information
Year Founded: 2014
Current Activity Level : Actively seeking new investments

REDSHIFT CAPITAL LLC

7055 Veterans Boulevard
Unit A
Burr Ridge, IL USA 60527
Phone: 6303211333
Fax: 6303211321
E-mail: growth@redshft.com
Website: www.redshift.us.com

Type of Firm
Private Equity Firm

Project Preferences

Type of Financing Preferred:
Core
Leveraged Buyout
Generalist PE
Other

Industry Preferences

In Industrial/Energy prefer:
Alternative Energy

In Financial Services prefer:
Real Estate

In Business Serv. prefer:
Services

In Manufact. prefer:
Manufacturing

Additional Information
Year Founded: 2006
Current Activity Level : Actively seeking new investments

REDSHIFT VENTURES MANAGEMENT INC

5425 Wisconsin Avenue, Suite 704
Chevy Chase, MD USA 20815
Phone: 7039049800
Fax: 703-904-0571
Website: www.redshiftventures.com

Other Offices
3057 Nutley Street, Suite 562
Fairfax, VA USA 22031
Phone: 7039049800

Management and Staff
Mark Frantz, Venture Partner
Srinivas Mirmira, Partner

Type of Firm
Private Equity Firm

Project Preferences

Role in Financing:
Will function either as deal originator or investor in deals created by others

Type of Financing Preferred:
Early Stage
Later Stage

Size of Investments Considered:
Min Size of Investment Considered (000s): $1,000
Max Size of Investment Considered (000s): $4,000

Geographical Preferences

United States Preferences:

Industry Focus
(% based on actual investment)
Computer Software and Services	29.8%
Communications and Media	27.5%
Internet Specific	18.1%
Semiconductors/Other Elect.	17.5%
Industrial/Energy	6.3%
Other Products	0.8%

Additional Information
Name of Most Recent Fund: RedShift Ventures III, L.P.
Most Recent Fund Was Raised: 04/18/2001
Year Founded: 1991
Capital Under Management: $222,000,000
Current Activity Level : Actively seeking new investments
Method of Compensation: Return on invest. most important, but chg. closing fees, service fees, etc.

REDSTONE CAPITAL INVESTMENT MANAGEMENT CO LTD

No. 8, Yongzhong Road
Red Stone Plaza
Wenzhou, China
Phone: 8657785982222
Fax: 8657786867070
Website: www.redstone.cc

Type of Firm
Private Equity Firm

Project Preferences

Type of Financing Preferred:
Expansion
Later Stage

Geographical Preferences

International Preferences:
China

Industry Preferences

In Medical/Health prefer:
Drug/Equipmt Delivery

In Consumer Related prefer:
Education Related

In Industrial/Energy prefer:
Alternative Energy
Energy Conservation Relat
Materials

In Manufact. prefer:
Manufacturing

In Agr/Forestr/Fish prefer:
Agriculture related

Additional Information
Year Founded: 2011
Capital Under Management: $77,316,000
Current Activity Level : Actively seeking new investments

REDWOOD CAPITAL INVESTMENTS LLC

7301 Parkway Drive
Hanover, MD USA 21076
E-mail: info@redcapinv.com
Website: www.redcapinv.com

Management and Staff
David Watson, Principal
Kevin Loden, Vice President
Patrick Sissman, Vice President
Ryan Mostrom, Vice President

Type of Firm
Private Equity Firm

Project Preferences

Type of Financing Preferred:
Leveraged Buyout
Management Buyouts

Additional Information
Year Founded: 2006
Current Activity Level : Actively seeking new investments

REDWOOD CAPITAL, INC.

4115 Blackhawk Plaza Circle, Suite 20
Danville, CA USA 94506
Phone: 925-648-2080
Fax: 925-648-2081
Website: www.redwoodcapinc.com

Other Offices
No.39, Dong San Huan Zhong Lu
Jianwai SOHO Building 10, Suite 1605
Beijing, China 100022
Phone: 86-10-5869-1336
Fax: 86-10-5869-5527

Management and Staff
Matthew Totty, Managing Director
Richard Chiang, Managing Director

Type of Firm
Bank Affiliated

Project Preferences

Type of Financing Preferred:
Later Stage

Geographical Preferences

United States Preferences:
North America
California

International Preferences:
China

Industry Preferences

In Consumer Related prefer:
Food/Beverage
Consumer Products
Education Related

In Industrial/Energy prefer:
Energy
Industrial Products
Materials
Environmental Related

In Business Serv. prefer:
Services
Media

Additional Information
Year Founded: 2010
Capital Under Management: $50,000,000
Current Activity Level : Actively seeking new investments

REDWOOD VENTURE PARTNERS

4984 El Camino Real, Suite 200
Los Altos, CA USA 94022
Phone: 6503351111
Fax: 6503351110
Website: www.redwoodvp.com

Management and Staff
Bill Glazier, Venture Partner
Raj Singh, Managing Director

Type of Firm
Investment Management Firm

Project Preferences

Role in Financing:
Will function either as deal originator or investor in deals created by others

Type of Financing Preferred:
Early Stage
Startup

Size of Investments Considered:
Min Size of Investment Considered (000s): $1,000
Max Size of Investment Considered (000s): $10,000

Geographical Preferences

United States Preferences:

Industry Preferences

In Communications prefer:
Telecommunications
Wireless Communications
Data Communications

In Computer Software prefer:
Software

In Internet Specific prefer:
Internet

In Semiconductor/Electr prefer:
Semiconductor

Additional Information
Name of Most Recent Fund: Redwood Ventures IV LLP
Most Recent Fund Was Raised: 09/29/2000
Year Founded: 1997
Capital Under Management: $150,000,000
Current Activity Level : Actively seeking new investments
Method of Compensation: Return on investment is of primary concern, do not charge fees

REED ELSEVIER INC

1-3 The Strand
London, United Kingdom WC2N 5JR
Phone: 442071665665

Other Offices
201 Mission Street
San Francisco, CA USA 94105
Phone: 4156164420

Management and Staff
Anthony Askew, General Partner
Kevin Brown, General Partner

Type of Firm
Corporate PE/Venture

Project Preferences

Role in Financing:
Will function either as deal originator or investor in deals created by others

Type of Financing Preferred:
Early Stage
Expansion
Balanced
Later Stage
Seed

Size of Investments Considered:
Min Size of Investment Considered (000s): $250
Max Size of Investment Considered (000s): $5,000

Geographical Preferences

United States Preferences:

International Preferences:
Europe
Israel

Industry Preferences

In Communications prefer:
Wireless Communications

In Computer Software prefer:
Data Processing
Software
Applications Software

In Internet Specific prefer:
Internet

In Semiconductor/Electr prefer:
Analytic/Scientific

In Medical/Health prefer:
Medical/Health

In Business Serv. prefer:
Media

Additional Information
Year Founded: 2000
Capital Under Management: $250,000,000
Current Activity Level : Actively seeking new investments

REEF CAPITAL VENTURES LLC

1110 Nuuanu Avenue
Honolulu, HI USA 96817
Website: reef.vc

Type of Firm
Private Equity Firm

Project Preferences

Type of Financing Preferred:
Balanced

Geographical Preferences

United States Preferences:
Hawaii

Additional Information
Year Founded: 2015
Capital Under Management: $20,000,000
Current Activity Level : Actively seeking new investments

REFACTOR CAPITAL LP

330 Primrose Road, Suite 201
Burlingame, CA USA 94010
Phone: 6508435000

Management and Staff
David Lee, Managing Partner
Rick Barber, Venture Partner
Zal Bilimoria, Managing Partner

Type of Firm
Private Equity Firm

Project Preferences

Type of Financing Preferred:
Early Stage
Seed

Industry Preferences

In Medical/Health prefer:
Health Services

In Transportation prefer:
Aerospace

In Financial Services prefer:
Financial Services

In Agr/Forestr/Fish prefer:
Agriculture related

Additional Information
Year Founded: 2016
Current Activity Level : Actively seeking new investments

REFLEX CAPITAL SE

Rasinovo Waterfront 2000
Prague, Czech Republic 120 00
Phone: 420603194892
E-mail: info@reflexcapital.com
Website: www.spread-capital.cz

Type of Firm
Private Equity Firm

Project Preferences

Type of Financing Preferred:
Balanced

Additional Information
Year Founded: 2012
Current Activity Level : Actively seeking new investments

REGARD VENTURE SOLUTIONS

1640, Fifth Street, Suite 206
Santa Monica, CA USA 90401
E-mail: info@regardventures.com
Website: www.regardventures.com

Type of Firm
Private Equity Firm

Project Preferences

Type of Financing Preferred:
Seed
Startup

Additional Information
Year Founded: 1994
Current Activity Level : Actively seeking new investments

REGENT LP

9720 Wilshire Blvd
Beverly Hills, CA USA 90212
Website: www.regent.co

Type of Firm
Private Equity Firm

Project Preferences

Type of Financing Preferred:
Leveraged Buyout
Acquisition

Additional Information
Year Founded: 2013
Current Activity Level : Actively seeking new investments

REGIMEN CAPITAL PARTNERS

1285 West Pender Street, Suite 570
Vancouver, Canada V6E 4B1
Phone: 7783791000
E-mail: info@regimencapital.com
Website: www.regimenpartners.com

Other Offices
638 Broughton Street, Suite 320
Vancouver, Canada V6G 3K3

Management and Staff
James Livingstone, President

Type of Firm
Private Equity Firm

Association Membership
Canadian Venture Capital Association

Project Preferences

Type of Financing Preferred:
Leveraged Buyout
Acquisition

Geographical Preferences

Canadian Preferences:
All Canada

Industry Preferences

In Industrial/Energy prefer:
Energy

In Business Serv. prefer:
Services
Distribution

Additional Information
Year Founded: 2014
Current Activity Level : Actively seeking new investments

REITEN & CO AS

Haakon VIIs gt. 1, 3rd floor
P.O. Box 1531 Vika
Oslo, Norway 0117
Phone: 4723113700
Fax: 4723113721
E-mail: post@reitenco.no
Website: www.reitenco.no

Management and Staff
Bard Brath Ingero, Partner
Christian Melby, Partner
John Bjerkan, Partner
Kathryn Moore Baker, Partner
Narve Reiten, Partner
Per Wien, Chief Financial Officer
Terje Bakken, Partner

Type of Firm
Private Equity Firm

Association Membership
Norwegian Venture Capital Association
European Private Equity and Venture Capital Assoc.

Project Preferences

Type of Financing Preferred:
Leveraged Buyout
Generalist PE
Balanced
Management Buyouts

Size of Investments Considered:
Min Size of Investment Considered (000s): $14,000
Max Size of Investment Considered (000s): $84,000

Geographical Preferences

International Preferences:
Scandanavia/Nordic Region

Industry Preferences

In Computer Other prefer:
Computer Related

In Medical/Health prefer:
Medical/Health

In Consumer Related prefer:
Consumer
Consumer Products
Consumer Services

In Industrial/Energy prefer:
Energy

In Transportation prefer:
Transportation

In Financial Services prefer:
Financial Services
Insurance
Real Estate

In Business Serv. prefer:
Services

Additional Information
Name of Most Recent Fund: Reiten & Co Capital Partners VII, L.P.
Most Recent Fund Was Raised: 10/25/2007
Year Founded: 1996
Capital Under Management: $622,500,000
Current Activity Level : Actively seeking new investments

REITER CAPITAL CO LTD

No. 66, Nanlishi Road
1002, Jianwei Building
Beijing, China 100045
Phone: 861068080108
Fax: 861083907861
Website: www.reitercapital.com

Type of Firm
Private Equity Firm

Project Preferences

Type of Financing Preferred:
Early Stage
Expansion
Balanced
Later Stage

Geographical Preferences

International Preferences:
China

Industry Preferences

In Communications prefer:
Wireless Communications

In Biotechnology prefer:
Biotechnology

In Medical/Health prefer:
Pharmaceuticals

In Consumer Related prefer:
Consumer Products
Consumer Services

In Industrial/Energy prefer:
Materials
Machinery
Environmental Related

In Business Serv. prefer:
Services

In Manufact. prefer:
Manufacturing

Additional Information
Year Founded: 2007
Capital Under Management: $14,650,000
Current Activity Level : Actively seeking new investments

RELATIVITY CAPITAL LLC

1300 17th Street, North, Suite 750
Arlington, VA USA 22209
Phone: 7038123020
E-mail: info@relativitycapitalllc.com
Website: www.relativitycapitalllc.com

Other Offices
825 Third Avenue
36th floor
New York, NY USA 10022
Phone: 212-350-1540

180 High Oak Road, Suite 100
Bloomfield Hills, MI USA 48304
Phone: 2482581623

Management and Staff
Andrew Lodge, Principal
Brian Kirschbaum, Vice President
Brian Lee, Principal
David Miller, Vice President
James Riepe, Principal
Jennifer Versaw, Chief Financial Officer
Joyce Johnson-Miller, Senior Managing Director
Leslie Armitage, Senior Managing Director

Type of Firm
Private Equity Firm

Project Preferences

Type of Financing Preferred:
Leveraged Buyout
Acquisition
Distressed Debt

Geographical Preferences

United States Preferences:
North America

Industry Preferences

In Medical/Health prefer:
Medical/Health

In Consumer Related prefer:
Consumer

In Transportation prefer:
Transportation
Aerospace

In Financial Services prefer:
Financial Services

In Business Serv. prefer:
Services
Consulting Services

In Manufact. prefer:
Manufacturing

Additional Information
Year Founded: 2005
Current Activity Level : Actively seeking new investments

RELAY VENTURES

333 Bay St., Bay Adelaide Ctr., Suite 1130
Toronto, Canada M5H 2R2
Phone: 4163672440
Fax: 4163674604
E-mail: toronto@relayventures.com
Website: www.relayventures.com

Other Offices
3000 Sand Hill Road
Building 2, Suite 180
MENLO PARK, CA USA 94025
Phone: 6506277749
Fax: 6507277755

Management and Staff
Alex Baker, Partner
Irfhan Rawji, Venture Partner
Jeannette Wiltse, Chief Financial Officer
John Occhipinti, Partner
John Albright, Co-Founder
Kevin Talbot, Co-Founder
Tawfiq Arafat, Partner

Type of Firm
Private Equity Firm

Association Membership
Canadian Venture Capital Association
National Venture Capital Association - USA (NVCA)

Project Preferences

Role in Financing:
Prefer role as deal originator

Type of Financing Preferred:
Early Stage
Balanced
Seed

Industry Preferences

In Communications prefer:
Wireless Communications

In Medical/Health prefer:
Medical/Health

In Consumer Related prefer:
Education Related

Additional Information
Name of Most Recent Fund: Relay Ventures Fund II
Most Recent Fund Was Raised: 03/21/2012
Year Founded: 2008
Capital Under Management: $650,000,000
Current Activity Level : Actively seeking new investments
Method of Compensation: Return on invest. most important, but chg. closing fees, service fees, etc.

RELEVANCE CAPITAL INC

414 Wilson Avenue, Suite 102
Tullahoma, TN USA 37388
Phone: 6153450450
Fax: 6153018617
E-mail: info@relevancecapital.com
Website: relevancecapital.com

Management and Staff
Fran Marcum, Chief Executive Officer

Type of Firm
Private Equity Firm

Project Preferences

Type of Financing Preferred:
Early Stage
Startup

Industry Preferences

In Computer Software prefer:
Software

In Medical/Health prefer:
Medical/Health

Additional Information
Year Founded: 2000
Capital Under Management: $4,220,000
Current Activity Level : Actively seeking new investments

RELIANCE CAPITAL VENTURES LTD

11th Floor, One Indiabulls Ctr
841, Jupiter Mills Lower Parel
Mumbai, India 400 013
Phone: 912230957200
Fax: 912230957203
Website: fairwinds.in

Management and Staff
Prakash Iyer, Partner
Rahul Manek, Partner
Rajiv Sharma, Chief Financial Officer
Snehal Shah, Partner

Type of Firm
Corporate PE/Venture

Association Membership
Indian Venture Capital Association (IVCA)

Project Preferences

Role in Financing:
Will function either as deal originator or investor in deals created by others

Type of Financing Preferred:
Leveraged Buyout
Expansion
Balanced
Opportunistic
Later Stage
Management Buyouts
Acquisition

Geographical Preferences

International Preferences:
India

Industry Preferences

In Medical/Health prefer:
Health Services

In Consumer Related prefer:
Consumer

In Transportation prefer:
Transportation

In Financial Services prefer:
Real Estate
Financial Services

In Business Serv. prefer:
Services
Media

In Manufact. prefer:
Manufacturing

Additional Information
Year Founded: 2004
Capital Under Management: $484,800,000
Current Activity Level : Actively seeking new investments
Method of Compensation: Return on investment is of primary concern, do not charge fees

REMBRANDT VENTURE MANAGEMENT LLC

600 Montgomery Street, 44th Floor
San Francisco, CA USA 94111
Phone: 4155282900
Fax: 4155282901
Website: www.rembrandtvc.com

Other Offices
2440 Sand Hill Road, Suite 100
Menlo Park, CA USA 94025
Phone: 6503267070
Fax: 6503263780

Management and Staff
Clara Yee, Chief Financial Officer
Douglas Schrier, General Partner
Gerald Casilli, General Partner
In Sik Rhee, General Partner
Michael Baum, Venture Partner
Richard Ling, Venture Partner
Scott Irwin, General Partner

Type of Firm
Private Equity Firm

Association Membership
Western Association of Venture Capitalists (WAVC)

Project Preferences

Type of Financing Preferred:
Early Stage
Seed
Startup

Geographical Preferences

United States Preferences:
California

Industry Preferences

In Communications prefer:
Communications and Media
Wireless Communications

In Computer Software prefer:
Software
Applications Software

In Internet Specific prefer:
Internet

In Business Serv. prefer:
Media

Additional Information
Year Founded: 2004
Capital Under Management: $307,000,000
Current Activity Level : Actively seeking new investments

REMEDITEX VENTURES LLC

2501 Cedar Springs Road
Dallas, TX USA 75201
Phone: 2145062662
E-mail: innovation@remeditex.com
Website: remeditex.com

Management and Staff
Brett Ringle, President
Claire Aldridge, Vice President
John Creecy, Chief Executive Officer

Type of Firm
Incubator/Development Program

Project Preferences

Type of Financing Preferred:
Early Stage
Seed

Geographical Preferences

United States Preferences:
Texas

Pratt's Guide to Private Equity & Venture Capital Sources

Industry Preferences

In Biotechnology prefer:
Biotechnology

Additional Information

Year Founded: 2011
Current Activity Level : Actively seeking new investments

REMIGES BIOPHARMA FUND LP

404 Underhill Road
Scarsdale, NY USA 10583
Phone: 9142632303

Type of Firm
Private Equity Firm

Project Preferences

Type of Financing Preferred:
Balanced

Industry Preferences

In Biotechnology prefer:
Biotechnology

Additional Information

Year Founded: 2014
Capital Under Management: $80,000,000
Current Activity Level : Actively seeking new investments

REMORA PARTNERS SA

Rue du Petit-Chene 12
Lausanne, Switzerland 1003
Phone: 41213110376
Fax: 41215441201
E-mail: info@remora-partners.ch
Website: www.remora-partners.ch

Management and Staff

Carsten Laue, Principal
Gerald Neuville, Co-Founder
Jean-Marc Le Doussal, Co-Founder
Pierre Huygues-Despointes, Principal

Type of Firm
Private Equity Firm

Association Membership
Swiss Venture Capital Association (SECA)

Project Preferences

Type of Financing Preferred:
Early Stage
Balanced
Later Stage

Geographical Preferences

International Preferences:
Europe

Industry Preferences

In Medical/Health prefer:
Medical/Health
Health Services

In Consumer Related prefer:
Food/Beverage

Additional Information

Year Founded: 2011
Current Activity Level : Actively seeking new investments

RENAISSANCE VENTURES L L C

33 South 13th Street
3rd Floor, P.O. Box 2157
Richmond, VA USA 23219
Phone: 8046435500
Fax: 8046435322
E-mail: info@renventures.com

Management and Staff
Herbert Jackson, Managing Director

Type of Firm
Private Equity Firm

Project Preferences

Type of Financing Preferred:
Early Stage
Seed

Geographical Preferences

International Preferences:
Europe

Industry Preferences

In Biotechnology prefer:
Biotechnology

Additional Information

Name of Most Recent Fund: Renaissance Ventures, L.P.
Most Recent Fund Was Raised: 03/18/1998
Year Founded: 1995
Capital Under Management: $12,000,000
Current Activity Level : Actively seeking new investments

RENEGADE CAPITAL LP

3200 Southwest Freeway, Suite 3120
Houston, TX USA 77027
Phone: 7133751300
E-mail: info@riverrockgrp.com
Website: www.renegadecap.com

Management and Staff
James Hickey, Managing Director

Type of Firm
Private Equity Firm

Project Preferences

Type of Financing Preferred:
Leveraged Buyout
Early Stage
Generalist PE
Turnaround
Distressed Debt

Geographical Preferences

United States Preferences:
Texas

Industry Preferences

In Medical/Health prefer:
Health Services

In Consumer Related prefer:
Consumer Products
Consumer Services

In Financial Services prefer:
Financial Services

In Business Serv. prefer:
Services
Distribution

Additional Information

Name of Most Recent Fund: RiverRock Investment Fund IV, L.P.
Most Recent Fund Was Raised: 06/03/2013
Year Founded: 2009
Capital Under Management: $23,566,000
Current Activity Level : Actively seeking new investments

RENEW RURAL IOWA

5400 University Avenue
West Des Moines, IA USA 50266
Website: www.renewruraliowa.com

Type of Firm
Government Affiliated Program

Additional Information

Year Founded: 2016
Current Activity Level : Actively seeking new investments

RENEWAL PARTNERS

500-163 West Hastings Street
Tides Renewal Center
Vancouver, Canada V6B 1H5
Phone: 6048447474
Fax: 6048447441

Management and Staff
Carol Newell, Co-Founder
Pamela Chaloult, Managing Director
Paul Richardson, Chief Executive Officer

Type of Firm
Private Equity Firm

Project Preferences

Type of Financing Preferred:
Early Stage
Expansion
Later Stage

Geographical Preferences

United States Preferences:
North America

Canadian Preferences:
All Canada
British Columbia

Industry Preferences

In Consumer Related prefer:
Food/Beverage

In Industrial/Energy prefer:
Environmental Related

In Agr/Forestr/Fish prefer:
Agriculture related

In Other prefer:
Socially Responsible
Environment Responsible

Additional Information
Name of Most Recent Fund: Renewal3
Most Recent Fund Was Raised: 02/28/2014
Year Founded: 2008
Capital Under Management: $130,000,000
Current Activity Level : Actively seeking new investments

RENFEI INVESTMENT MANAGEMENT SHANGHAI CO LTD

No.2077, YanAn West Road
Jinqiao Building
Shanghai, China

Type of Firm
Private Equity Firm

Project Preferences

Type of Financing Preferred:
Early Stage

Size of Investments Considered:
Min Size of Investment Considered (000s): $77
Max Size of Investment Considered (000s): $774

Geographical Preferences

International Preferences:
China

Additional Information
Year Founded: 2015
Current Activity Level : Actively seeking new investments

RENOVO CAPITAL LLC

14241 Dallas Parkway, Suite 475
Dallas, TX USA 75254
Phone: 2146994960
Website: renovocapital.com

Other Offices
700 Rangeview Drive
Littleton, CO USA 80120
Phone: 303-953-9543

Management and Staff
Don Jungerman, Co-Founder
Mark Barbeau, Co-Founder
Scott Lavie, Co-Founder

Type of Firm
Private Equity Firm

Project Preferences

Type of Financing Preferred:
Leveraged Buyout
Turnaround
Management Buyouts
Special Situation
Distressed Debt

Geographical Preferences

United States Preferences:
North America

Industry Preferences

In Business Serv. prefer:
Services
Distribution

In Manufact. prefer:
Manufacturing

Additional Information
Name of Most Recent Fund: Renwood Opportunities Fund I
Most Recent Fund Was Raised: 10/08/2010
Year Founded: 2008
Capital Under Management: $182,000,000
Current Activity Level : Actively seeking new investments

RENOVUS CAPITAL PARTNERS LP

308 East Lancaster Avenue
Wynnewood, PA USA 19096
Phone: 4844160856
Fax: 4844160857
E-mail: info@renovuscapital.com
Website: www.renovuscapital.com

Management and Staff
Atif Gilani, Partner
Brad Whitman, Partner
Jesse Serventi, Partner
William Landman, Partner

Type of Firm
SBIC

Association Membership
Natl Assoc of Small Bus. Inv. Co (NASBIC)

Project Preferences

Type of Financing Preferred:
Leveraged Buyout
Mezzanine
Later Stage
Management Buyouts
Acquisition

Industry Preferences

In Consumer Related prefer:
Education Related

In Business Serv. prefer:
Services

Additional Information
Name of Most Recent Fund: Renovus Capital Partners, L.P.
Most Recent Fund Was Raised: 01/21/2011
Year Founded: 2010
Capital Under Management: $300,000,000
Current Activity Level : Actively seeking new investments

REPUBLIC ALLEY SA

320 Rue Saint Honore
Paris, France 75011
Phone: 33147001234
Fax: 33147001514
E-mail: info@republicalley.com

Management and Staff
Arnaud Gougne, Partner
Brahim Hamdouni, Partner
Charles Madeline, Partner
Gilles Labossiere, President

Type of Firm
Incubator/Development Program

Project Preferences

Role in Financing:
Prefer role as deal originator

Type of Financing Preferred:
Seed
Startup

Geographical Preferences

International Preferences:
Europe
France

Industry Preferences

In Internet Specific prefer:
Internet

Additional Information

Name of Most Recent Fund: Republic Alley
Most Recent Fund Was Raised: 02/01/2001
Year Founded: 2000
Capital Under Management: $6,000,000
Current Activity Level : Actively seeking new investments

RESEARCH CORPORATION TECHNOLOGIES

5210 East Williams Circle, Suite 240
Tucson, AZ USA 85711
Phone: 5207484400
Fax: 5207480025
E-mail: attention@rctech.com
Website: www.rctech.com

Management and Staff

Chad Souvignier, Managing Director
Christopher Martin, Chief Financial Officer
Paul Grand, Managing Director

Type of Firm

Incubator/Development Program

Association Membership

National Venture Capital Association - USA (NVCA)

Project Preferences

Type of Financing Preferred:
Early Stage
Balanced
Startup

Geographical Preferences

United States Preferences:
All U.S.

Canadian Preferences:
All Canada

International Preferences:
United Kingdom
Australia

Industry Preferences

In Biotechnology prefer:
Biotechnology

In Medical/Health prefer:
Medical/Health
Medical Therapeutics
Medical Products
Pharmaceuticals

Additional Information

Year Founded: 1987
Capital Under Management: $50,000,000
Current Activity Level : Actively seeking new investments

RESEARCH PARTNERS LTD

17 State Street
Seventh Floor
New York, NY USA 10004
Phone: 212-785-3611
Fax: 212-785-3616
E-mail: info@researchpartnersltd.com
Website: www.researchpartnersltd.com

Management and Staff

Antal Foldi, Chief Financial Officer
Arie Abecassis, Managing Director
Arthur Rosenzweig, Founder
Lisa Warren, Managing Director
Peter Arnold, Managing Director

Type of Firm

Private Equity Firm

Project Preferences

Type of Financing Preferred:
Balanced

Industry Preferences

In Computer Other prefer:
Computer Related

In Financial Services prefer:
Financial Services

Additional Information

Year Founded: 1994
Current Activity Level : Actively seeking new investments

RESERVOIR CAPITAL GROUP LLC

650 Madison Avenue
26th Floor
New York, NY USA 10022
Phone: 2126109000
E-mail: info@reservoircap.com
Website: www.reservoircap.com

Management and Staff

Craig Huff, Managing Director
Daniel Stern, Chief Executive Officer
Gregg Zeitlin, Managing Director
Norman Katzwer, Chief Financial Officer

Type of Firm

Private Equity Firm

Project Preferences

Type of Financing Preferred:
Leveraged Buyout
Generalist PE
Balanced
Other

Geographical Preferences

United States Preferences:

International Preferences:
All International

Industry Focus

(% based on actual investment)
Other Products	83.6%
Industrial/Energy	10.4%
Consumer Related	2.9%
Computer Software and Services	2.0%
Medical/Health	1.2%

Additional Information

Year Founded: 1998
Capital Under Management: $768,228,000
Current Activity Level : Actively seeking new investments

RESERVOIR VENTURE PARTNERS 2 LP

400 West Wilson Bridge Road, Suite 310
Columbus, OH USA 43085
Phone: 6148467241
Fax: 6148467267
E-mail: info@reservoirvp.com

Management and Staff

Curtis Crocker, Managing Partner
Steven Jaffee, General Partner
William Tanner, Chief Financial Officer

Type of Firm

Private Equity Firm

Project Preferences

Type of Financing Preferred:
Early Stage

Size of Investments Considered:
Min Size of Investment Considered (000s): $500
Max Size of Investment Considered (000s): $1,000

Geographical Preferences

United States Preferences:
Ohio

Industry Preferences

In Communications prefer:
Wireless Communications

In Computer Software prefer:
Software

In Biotechnology prefer:
Biotechnology

In Medical/Health prefer:
Medical/Health
Medical Diagnostics
Drug/Equipmt Delivery
Medical Products

In Industrial/Energy prefer:
Energy
Advanced Materials

Additional Information

Name of Most Recent Fund: Reservoir Venture Partners (FKA: Battelle Technology Fund)
Most Recent Fund Was Raised: 11/01/2001
Year Founded: 2003
Capital Under Management: $28,000,000
Current Activity Level : Actively seeking new investments

RESIDEX BV

Van Golsteinlaan 26
Apeldoorn, Netherlands 7339 GT
Phone: 31555260800
Fax: 31555260808
E-mail: office@residex.nl
Website: www.residex.nl

Type of Firm
Private Equity Firm

Association Membership
Dutch Venture Capital Associaton (NVP)

Project Preferences

Type of Financing Preferred:
Fund of Funds
Early Stage
Balanced
Later Stage
Seed
Startup

Size of Investments Considered:
Min Size of Investment Considered (000s): $500
Max Size of Investment Considered (000s): $500,000

Geographical Preferences

International Preferences:
Netherlands

Industry Preferences

In Medical/Health prefer:
Medical/Health
Medical Diagnostics
Diagnostic Test Products
Health Services
Hospitals/Clinics/Primary
Hospital/Other Instit.

In Consumer Related prefer:
Retail

In Industrial/Energy prefer:
Industrial Products

Additional Information
Year Founded: 1999
Capital Under Management: $306,900,000
Current Activity Level : Actively seeking new investments

RESILIENCE CAPITAL PARTNERS LLC

25101 Chagrin Boulevard, Suite 350
Cleveland, OH USA 44122
Phone: 2162920200
Fax: 2162924750
E-mail: info@resiliencecapital.com
Website: www.resiliencecapital.com

Management and Staff
Bassem Mansour, Managing Partner
David Glickman, Partner
George Ammar, Chief Financial Officer
Malachi Mixon, Partner
Megan McPherson, Vice President
Michael Cavanaugh, Partner
Robert Potokar, Partner
Ron Cozean, Partner
Theodore Laufik, Chief Financial Officer
Ulf Buergel, Partner

Type of Firm
Private Equity Firm

Project Preferences

Type of Financing Preferred:
Leveraged Buyout
Turnaround
Management Buyouts
Acquisition
Recapitalizations

Size of Investments Considered:
Min Size of Investment Considered (000s): $5,000
Max Size of Investment Considered (000s): $20,000

Geographical Preferences

United States Preferences:
North America

Industry Preferences

In Consumer Related prefer:
Consumer Products

In Industrial/Energy prefer:
Oil & Gas Drilling,Explor
Industrial Products

In Transportation prefer:
Transportation
Aerospace

In Business Serv. prefer:
Distribution

In Manufact. prefer:
Manufacturing

Additional Information
Name of Most Recent Fund: Resilience Fund III, L.P.
Most Recent Fund Was Raised: 06/07/2011
Year Founded: 2001
Capital Under Management: $75,000,000
Current Activity Level : Actively seeking new investments

RESOLUTE CAPITAL PARTNERS FUND IV LP

20 Burton Hill Boulevard, Suite 430
Nashville, TN USA 37215
Phone: 6156653636
E-mail: info@resolutecap.com

Type of Firm
Private Equity Firm

Project Preferences

Type of Financing Preferred:
Mezzanine
Acquisition

Geographical Preferences

United States Preferences:

Additional Information
Name of Most Recent Fund: Resolute Capital Partners Fund III, L.P.
Most Recent Fund Was Raised: 07/15/2011
Year Founded: 2011
Capital Under Management: $140,780,000
Current Activity Level : Actively seeking new investments

RESOLUTE.VC

100 Winter Street, Suite 3350
North Waltham, MA USA 02451
Phone: 7815226729
Website: www.resolute.vc

Management and Staff
Michael Hirshland, Founder

Type of Firm
Private Equity Firm

Project Preferences

Role in Financing:
Prefer role as deal originator

Type of Financing Preferred:
Seed
Startup

Size of Investments Considered:
Min Size of Investment Considered (000s): $50
Max Size of Investment Considered (000s): $750

Geographical Preferences

United States Preferences:
California

Industry Preferences

In Computer Software prefer:
Software

In Internet Specific prefer:
Internet
Ecommerce

Additional Information
Year Founded: 2011
Capital Under Management: $65,000,000
Current Activity Level : Actively seeking new investments

RESONANT VENTURE PARTNERS

617 Detroit Street, Suite 110
Ann Arbor, MI USA 48104
Phone: 7342772054
E-mail: info@resonantvc.com
Website: www.resonantvc.com

Management and Staff
Jason Townsend, Managing Director
Michael Godwin, Managing Director

Type of Firm
Private Equity Firm

Project Preferences

Type of Financing Preferred:
Seed

Geographical Preferences

United States Preferences:
Michigan

Industry Preferences

In Industrial/Energy prefer:
Alternative Energy

In Manufact. prefer:
Manufacturing

Additional Information
Name of Most Recent Fund: Resonant Fund I, L.P.
Most Recent Fund Was Raised: 08/25/2010
Year Founded: 2010
Capital Under Management: $7,550,000
Current Activity Level : Actively seeking new investments

RESONETICS LLC

Ten East 40th Street, Suite 3210
New York, NY USA 10016
Phone: 2122602743
Fax: 2122602748
E-mail: info@corporatefuelpartners.com
Website: corporatefuel.com

Management and Staff
Alan Breitman, Managing Director
Cathleen Cote, Vice President
Charles Lachman, Partner
Eric Haley, Vice President
John Simons, Partner
John Bolebruch, Managing Director
Kevin Bodnar, Managing Partner
Marc Hirschfield, Vice President
Russ Fein, Managing Director
Stephen Tisdell, Managing Director

Type of Firm
Investment Management Firm

Project Preferences

Role in Financing:
Prefer role as deal originator

Type of Financing Preferred:
Leveraged Buyout
Expansion
Management Buyouts
Acquisition
Recapitalizations

Geographical Preferences

United States Preferences:
New Hampshire
Rhode Island
Vermont
Massachusetts
Connecticut
Maine
New York

Additional Information
Year Founded: 2005
Capital Under Management: $25,000,000
Current Activity Level : Actively seeking new investments
Method of Compensation: Return on invest. most important, but chg. closing fees, service fees, etc.

RESOURCE FINANCIAL CORP

550 West Van Buren Street, Suite 1410
Chicago, IL USA 60607
Phone: 312-525-2600
Fax: 312-525-2610
Website: www.resource-financial.com

Other Offices
111 East Kilbourn, Suite 1725
Milwaukee, WI USA 53202
Phone: 414-224-7000
Fax: 414-224-7015

Management and Staff
Mark Teufel, Managing Director

Type of Firm
Bank Affiliated

Project Preferences

Role in Financing:
Prefer role as deal originator but will also invest in deals created by others

Type of Financing Preferred:
Leveraged Buyout
Early Stage
Expansion
Generalist PE
Turnaround
Management Buyouts
Acquisition
Special Situation
Distressed Debt
Recapitalizations

Size of Investments Considered:
Min Size of Investment Considered (000s): $5,000
Max Size of Investment Considered: No Limit

Geographical Preferences

United States Preferences:

Canadian Preferences:
All Canada

International Preferences:
Italy
Latin America
India
United Kingdom
Luxembourg
Netherlands
Portugal
Mexico
Spain
Australia
Belgium
New Zealand
Germany
All International
France

RESOURCE PARTNERS SP ZOO

Mokotowska One
Zebra Tower
Warsaw, Poland 00-640
Phone: 48223777900
Fax: 48223777901
E-mail: office@resourcepartners.eu
Website: www.resourcepartners.eu

Management and Staff
Aleksander Kacprzyk, Managing Partner
Piotr Nocen, Managing Partner
Ryszard Wojtkowski, Managing Partner

Type of Firm
Private Equity Firm

Association Membership
Polish Venture Capital Association (PSIC/PPEA)

Project Preferences

Type of Financing Preferred:
Leveraged Buyout
Expansion

Geographical Preferences

International Preferences:
Central Europe
Poland
Eastern Europe

Industry Preferences

In Medical/Health prefer:
Medical/Health

In Consumer Related prefer:
Consumer Products

In Manufact. prefer:
Manufacturing

Additional Information
Year Founded: 2009
Capital Under Management: $139,798,000
Current Activity Level: Actively seeking new investments

RESPONDER VENTURES LLC

500 South Australian Avenue, Suite 523
West Palm Beach, FL USA 33401
Phone: 8779669455
E-mail: info@responderventures.com
Website: www.responderventures.com

Management and Staff
Bryce Stirton, Vice President
Dennis Weiner, Co-Founder
Nathanial Wish, Co-Founder

Type of Firm
Private Equity Firm

Project Preferences

Type of Financing Preferred:
Early Stage
Startup

Geographical Preferences

United States Preferences:

Additional Information
Year Founded: 2017
Current Activity Level: Actively seeking new investments

RESURGENS TECHNOLOGY PARTNERS LLC

1075 Peachtree Street NE, Suite 2200
Atlanta, GA USA 30309
Phone: 6788941447
Website: www.resurgenstech.com

Management and Staff
Adi Filipovic, Co-Founder
Fred Sturgis, Co-Founder
John Baumstark, Co-Founder

Type of Firm
Private Equity Firm

Project Preferences

Type of Financing Preferred:
Generalist PE

Industry Preferences

In Computer Software prefer:
Software

In Semiconductor/Electr prefer:
Analytic/Scientific

Additional Information
Year Founded: 2017
Current Activity Level: Actively seeking new investments

RETHINK EDUCATION LP

707 Westchester Avenue, Suite 401
White Plains, NY USA 10604
Phone: 9146838474
E-mail: info@rteducation.com
Website: www.rteducation.com

Management and Staff
Brandon Avrutin, Vice President
Matt Greenfield, Managing Director
Michael Walden, Venture Partner
Rick Segal, Managing Director

Type of Firm
Private Equity Firm

Project Preferences

Type of Financing Preferred:
Early Stage

Industry Preferences

In Computer Other prefer:
Computer Related

In Consumer Related prefer:
Education Related

Additional Information
Name of Most Recent Fund: Rethink Education, L.P.
Most Recent Fund Was Raised: 08/09/2012
Year Founded: 2012
Capital Under Management: $92,180,000
Current Activity Level: Actively seeking new investments

RETHINK IMPACT MANAGEMENT LLC

707 Westchester Avenue, Suite 401
West Harrison, NY USA 10604
Phone: 9142690938
Website: rethinkimpact.com

Management and Staff
Heidi Patel, Partner
Shakawat Chowdhury, Chief Financial Officer

Type of Firm
Private Equity Firm

Project Preferences

Type of Financing Preferred:
Early Stage
Balanced

Industry Preferences

In Medical/Health prefer:
Health Services

In Consumer Related prefer:
Education Related

In Industrial/Energy prefer:
Environmental Related

In Other prefer:
Environment Responsible

(continued from previous entry)

Additional Information
Year Founded: 2001
Current Activity Level: Actively seeking new investments
Method of Compensation: Professional fee required whether or not deal closes

RETRO VENTURE PARTNERS L P

3000 Sand Hill Road
Building Two, Suite 150
Menlo Park, CA USA 94025
Phone: 6505438999
Fax: 6508544715
Website: www.retrovp.com

Management and Staff
Lawrence Mohr, Managing Director
Salvador Gutierrez, Managing Director

Type of Firm
Private Equity Firm

Project Preferences

Type of Financing Preferred:
Balanced

Size of Investments Considered:
Min Size of Investment Considered (000s): $500
Max Size of Investment Considered (000s): $1,500

Additional Information
Name of Most Recent Fund: Retro Venture Partners, L.P.
Most Recent Fund Was Raised: 05/13/2008
Year Founded: 2008
Capital Under Management: $30,000,000
Current Activity Level : Actively seeking new investments

REV VENTURE PARTNERS LTD

One Strand Trafalgar Square
London, United Kingdom WC2N 5JR
Phone: 4402071665665
Website: rev.vc

Management and Staff
Kevin Brown, Co-Founder
Tony Askew, Co-Founder

Type of Firm
Private Equity Firm

Project Preferences

Type of Financing Preferred:
Early Stage

Industry Preferences

In Semiconductor/Electr prefer:
Analytic/Scientific

Additional Information
Year Founded: 2016
Capital Under Management: $2,750,000
Current Activity Level : Actively seeking new investments

REVEL PARTNERS LLC

250 Hudson Street
Fourth Floor
New York, NY USA 10013
Phone: 6467200500

Management and Staff
Charlie Kemper, Partner
Chris Young, Partner
John Vincent, Partner
Joseph Apprendi, Partner
Thomas Falk, Partner

Type of Firm
Private Equity Firm

Project Preferences

Type of Financing Preferred:
Early Stage
Expansion
Balanced

Geographical Preferences

United States Preferences:
New York

International Preferences:
Europe

Industry Preferences

In Internet Specific prefer:
Internet

In Business Serv. prefer:
Media

Additional Information
Year Founded: 2011
Capital Under Management: $20,640,000
Current Activity Level : Actively seeking new investments

REVELRY BRANDS LLC

2737 Mapleton Avenue
Boulder, CO USA 80304
E-mail: info@revelrybrands.com
Website: revelrybrands.com

Management and Staff
Gil Fronzaglia, Chief Operating Officer
Megan Reimers, Managing Director
Seth Beers, Chief Financial Officer

Type of Firm
Private Equity Firm

Project Preferences

Type of Financing Preferred:
Leveraged Buyout
Acquisition

Industry Preferences

In Consumer Related prefer:
Food/Beverage
Consumer Products

Additional Information
Year Founded: 2009
Current Activity Level : Actively seeking new investments

REVELSTOKE CAPITAL PARTNERS LLC

3033 East First Avenue, Suite 501
Denver, CO USA 80206
Website: www.revelstokecp.com

Management and Staff
Andrew Welch, Vice President
Arion Robbins, Vice President
Dale Meyer, Co-Founder
Eric Shuey, Managing Director
Mark King, Chief Executive Officer
Simon Bachleda, Co-Founder

Type of Firm
Private Equity Firm

Project Preferences

Type of Financing Preferred:
Leveraged Buyout
Management Buyouts
Acquisition

Industry Preferences

In Medical/Health prefer:
Medical/Health
Medical Products
Health Services

In Industrial/Energy prefer:
Energy
Industrial Products

In Transportation prefer:
Transportation

In Financial Services prefer:
Financial Services
Insurance

In Business Serv. prefer:
Services
Distribution
Consulting Services

Additional Information
Year Founded: 2013
Capital Under Management: $303,000,000
Current Activity Level : Actively seeking new investments

REVERENCE CAPITAL PARTNERS LLC

399 Park Avenue
Sixth Floor
New York, NY USA 10022

Type of Firm
Investment Management Firm

Project Preferences

Type of Financing Preferred:
Leveraged Buyout
Acquisition

Industry Preferences

In Financial Services prefer:
Financial Services

Additional Information
Year Founded: 2013
Capital Under Management: $228,400,000
Current Activity Level : Actively seeking new investments

REVO CAPITAL MANAGEMENT BV

Prins Bernhardplein 200
Amsterdam, Netherlands 1097 JB
Website: www.revo.vc

Type of Firm
Private Equity Firm

Project Preferences

Type of Financing Preferred:
Early Stage

Geographical Preferences

International Preferences:
Turkey

Industry Preferences

In Communications prefer:
Telecommunications

In Computer Software prefer:
Software

In Internet Specific prefer:
Internet

In Consumer Related prefer:
Retail

In Business Serv. prefer:
Media

Additional Information
Year Founded: 2013
Current Activity Level : Actively seeking new investments

REVOLUTION

1717 Rhode Island Avenue NW, Suite 1000
Washington, DC USA 20036
Phone: 2027761400
E-mail: info@revolution.com
Website: www.revolutionworld.com

Management and Staff
Allyson Burns, Vice President
David Hall, Vice President
Donn Davis, Co-Founder
Evan Morgan, Partner
John Sabin, Chief Financial Officer
Steve Murray, Managing Partner
Tige Savage, Co-Founder
Todd Klein, Partner

Type of Firm
Private Equity Firm

Project Preferences

Type of Financing Preferred:
Early Stage
Expansion
Balanced

Size of Investments Considered:
Min Size of Investment Considered (000s): $20,000
Max Size of Investment Considered (000s): $50,000

Geographical Preferences

United States Preferences:
East Coast

Industry Preferences

In Communications prefer:
Media and Entertainment

In Financial Services prefer:
Real Estate

Additional Information
Year Founded: 2007
Capital Under Management: $150,000,000
Current Activity Level : Actively seeking new investments

REVOLUTION CAPITAL GROUP LLC

1999 Avenue of the Stars, Suite 3430
Los Angeles, CA USA 90067
Phone: 3102290800
Fax: 3102290808
E-mail: info@revolutionpe.com
Website: www.revolutionpe.com

Other Offices
26 York Street
London, United Kingdom W1U 6PZ
Phone: 44-207-873-2215
Fax: 44-207-873-2216

1385 Broadway, Suite 914
New York, NY USA 10018
Phone: 2127761827
Fax: 2126964565

Management and Staff
Aman Bajaj, Managing Director
Cyrus Nikou, Partner
Gary Alcock, Managing Director
Jeff Gray, Managing Director
Rick Bigelow, Managing Director

Type of Firm
Private Equity Firm

Project Preferences

Type of Financing Preferred:
Leveraged Buyout
Management Buyouts
Recapitalizations

Industry Preferences

In Communications prefer:
Telecommunications

In Computer Software prefer:
Software

In Medical/Health prefer:
Medical/Health

In Consumer Related prefer:
Entertainment and Leisure

In Industrial/Energy prefer:
Oil & Gas Drilling,Explor
Industrial Products

In Transportation prefer:
Transportation

In Business Serv. prefer:
Services
Distribution

In Manufact. prefer:
Manufacturing

Additional Information
Year Founded: 2009
Current Activity Level : Actively seeking new investments

REVOLUTION VENTURES LLC

11682 El Camino Real, Suite 100
San Diego, CA USA 92130
Phone: 8584502842
Fax: 8778819192
Website: revolution.com/revolution-ventures

Other Offices
1717 Rhode Island Avenue NW
Washington, DC USA 20036
Phone: 2027761400

Management and Staff
David Golden, Managing Director
Tige Savage, Managing Director

Type of Firm
Private Equity Firm

Project Preferences

Type of Financing Preferred:
Early Stage

Industry Preferences

In Communications prefer:
Entertainment

In Consumer Related prefer:
Consumer

In Business Serv. prefer:
Media

Additional Information
Name of Most Recent Fund: Revolution Ventures II, L.P.
Most Recent Fund Was Raised: 09/30/2013
Year Founded: 2000
Capital Under Management: $1,175,000,000
Current Activity Level : Actively seeking new investments

REVTECH LABS

C/o Packard Place
222 South Church Street
Charlotte, NC USA 28202
E-mail: info@packardplace.us
Website: www.revtechlabs.com

Type of Firm
Incubator/Development Program

Project Preferences

Type of Financing Preferred:
Early Stage
Seed
Startup

Geographical Preferences

United States Preferences:
North Carolina

Industry Preferences

In Communications prefer:
Wireless Communications

In Computer Software prefer:
Software

In Internet Specific prefer:
Internet

Additional Information
Year Founded: 1969
Current Activity Level : Actively seeking new investments

REXITER CAPITAL MANAGEMENT LTD

80 Cannon Street
London, United Kingdom EC4N 6HL
Phone: 442076986400
Fax: 442076986410
E-mail: contactus@rexiter.com
Website: www.rexiter.co.uk

Other Offices
84, Taepyungro 1-ka, Chung-Ku
15th Floor, Seoul Finance Center Buildin
Seoul, South Korea 100-768
Phone: 82237064600
Fax: 82237064646

One International Place
25th Floor
Boston, MA USA 02110
Phone: 6176646005
Fax: 6176642939

15A Duxton Hill
, Singapore 089598
Phone: 6565001310
Fax: 6565001359

Kwanghwamun Bldg., 13/F
64-8 Taepyung-ro 1 ka, Chung-ku
Seoul, South Korea
Phone: 822-399-3736
Fax: 822-399-3749

21 St. James's Square
London, United Kingdom SW1Y 4SS
Phone: 44-20-7698-6401
Fax: 44-20-7698-6410

Management and Staff
Christopher Vale, Managing Director

Type of Firm
Bank Affiliated

Project Preferences

Type of Financing Preferred:
Early Stage
Expansion
Mezzanine
Private Placement

Geographical Preferences

International Preferences:
Korea, South
All International

Additional Information
Year Founded: 1997
Current Activity Level : Actively seeking new investments

REYNOLDS & COMPANY VENTURE PARTNERS LLC

84 Main Street
Cold Spring Harbor, NY USA 11724
Phone: 6316927009
E-mail: submissions@rcvpartners.com
Website: rcvpartners.com

Type of Firm
Private Equity Firm

Project Preferences

Type of Financing Preferred:
Expansion
Later Stage

Size of Investments Considered:
Min Size of Investment Considered (000s): $50
Max Size of Investment Considered (000s): $2,000

Geographical Preferences

United States Preferences:

Additional Information
Year Founded: 2012
Current Activity Level : Actively seeking new investments

REZON8 CAPITAL & ADVISORY GROUP LLC

9888 Windy Hollow Road
Great Falls, VA USA 22066
E-mail: info@rezon8capital.com
Website: rezon8capital.com

Management and Staff
Anjuli Singh, Principal
K. Paul Singh, CEO & Managing Director

Type of Firm
Private Equity Firm

Additional Information

Year Founded: 2011
Current Activity Level : Actively seeking new investments

REZVEN PARTNERS LLC

220 Newport Center Drive, Suite 11-220
Newport Beach, CA USA 92660
Phone: 9493821400
Fax: 9493821401
Website: www.rezven.com

Management and Staff

Anderee Berengian, Co-Founder

Type of Firm

Private Equity Firm

Project Preferences

Type of Financing Preferred:
Expansion

Industry Preferences

In Communications prefer:
Media and Entertainment

In Computer Software prefer:
Software

Additional Information

Year Founded: 2007
Current Activity Level : Actively seeking new investments

RFE INVESTMENT PARTNERS

36 Grove Street
New Canaan, CT USA 06840
Phone: 2039662800
E-mail: info@freip.com
Website: rfeip.com

Management and Staff

James Parsons, Managing Director
Jeffrey Zolman, Vice President
Michael Rubel, Principal
Michael Foster, Managing Director
Ned Truslow, Managing Director
Paul Schilpp, Principal
R. Peter Reiter, Managing Director

Type of Firm

Private Equity Firm

Project Preferences

Role in Financing:
Will function either as deal originator or investor in deals created by others

Type of Financing Preferred:
Leveraged Buyout
Generalist PE
Balanced
Later Stage
Management Buyouts
Acquisition

Industry Focus

(% based on actual investment)
Other Products	37.2%
Medical/Health	18.6%
Industrial/Energy	16.8%
Consumer Related	9.2%
Computer Software and Services	7.5%
Computer Hardware	4.5%
Communications and Media	3.5%
Semiconductors/Other Elect.	2.6%
Biotechnology	0.1%

Additional Information

Name of Most Recent Fund: RFE Investment Partners VIII, L.P.
Most Recent Fund Was Raised: 08/26/2011
Year Founded: 1979
Capital Under Management: $600,000,000
Current Activity Level : Actively seeking new investments
Method of Compensation: Return on invest. most important, but chg. closing fees, service fees, etc.

RHEA GIRISIM SERMAYESI YATIRIM ORTAKLIGI AS

Iran Caddesi No 21
Karum Is Merkezi Kat 3
Ankara, Turkey
Phone: 903124668450
Fax: 903124668449
E-mail: gsyo@rheagirisim.com
Website: www.rheagirisim.com.tr

Management and Staff

Abdullah Kefeli, Chief Financial Officer

Type of Firm

Bank Affiliated

Project Preferences

Type of Financing Preferred:
Leveraged Buyout
Early Stage
Expansion
Generalist PE
Balanced
Later Stage

Geographical Preferences

International Preferences:
Turkey
Europe

Industry Preferences

In Computer Hardware prefer:
Integrated Turnkey System

In Computer Software prefer:
Computer Services
Software

In Internet Specific prefer:
E-Commerce Technology
Internet

In Medical/Health prefer:
Diagnostic Test Products
Disposable Med. Products
Pharmaceuticals

In Consumer Related prefer:
Education Related

In Industrial/Energy prefer:
Energy
Energy Conservation Relat

In Financial Services prefer:
Insurance
Financial Services

In Business Serv. prefer:
Media

Additional Information

Year Founded: 1996
Capital Under Management: $5,000,000
Current Activity Level : Actively seeking new investments

RHEINGAU FOUNDERS GMBH

Oranienstrasse 185
Berlin, Germany 10999
Phone: 493069535800
Fax: 4930722399112
E-mail: contact@rheingau-ventures.com
Website: www.rheingau-ventures.com

Management and Staff

Kai Hansen, Partner
Philipp Hartmann, Managing Partner

Type of Firm

Incubator/Development Program

Project Preferences

Type of Financing Preferred:
Early Stage
Seed
Startup

Geographical Preferences

International Preferences:
Germany

Industry Preferences

In Communications prefer:
Communications and Media
Wireless Communications

In Internet Specific prefer:
Internet
Ecommerce

Additional Information

Year Founded: 2011
Current Activity Level: Actively seeking new investments

RHO CAPITAL PARTNERS INC

152 West 57th Street
23rd Floor, Carnegie Hall Twr
New York, NY USA 10019
Phone: 2127516677
Fax: 2127513613
Website: www.rho.com

Other Offices

525 University Avenue, Suite 1350
PALO ALTO, CA USA 94301
Phone: 650-463-0300
Fax: 650-463-0311

1800 McGill College Avenue, Suite 840
Montreal, Canada H3A 3J6
Phone: 514-844-5605
Fax: 514-844-9004

Management and Staff

David Carlick, Venture Partner
Douglas McCormick, Venture Partner
Habib Kairouz, Managing Partner
Haider Akmal, Principal
Hugh Browne, Principal
John Parker, Venture Partner
Joshua Ruch, Managing Partner
Mark Leschly, Managing Partner
Martin Vogelbaum, Partner
Medha Vedaprakash, Principal
Nicholas Darby, Venture Partner
Patrick Wack, Venture Partner
Paul Bartlett, Partner
Peter Kalkanis, Chief Financial Officer

Type of Firm

Private Equity Firm

Association Membership

Canadian Venture Capital Association
National Venture Capital Association - USA (NVCA)

Project Preferences

Role in Financing:
Prefer role as deal originator but will also invest in deals created by others

Type of Financing Preferred:
Fund of Funds
Early Stage
Balanced
Later Stage
Seed
Fund of Funds of Second

Geographical Preferences

United States Preferences:
North America

Canadian Preferences:
All Canada

International Preferences:
Europe

Industry Focus

(% based on actual investment)

Internet Specific	31.3%
Biotechnology	14.1%
Communications and Media	13.1%
Computer Software and Services	12.7%
Industrial/Energy	9.2%
Medical/Health	8.2%
Semiconductors/Other Elect.	6.1%
Other Products	2.6%
Computer Hardware	2.5%
Consumer Related	0.2%

Additional Information

Year Founded: 1981
Capital Under Management: $2,500,000,000
Current Activity Level: Actively seeking new investments

RHODIUM LTD

91 Medinat Hayehudim Street
Hertzeliya Pituach
Herzliya, Israel 46140
Phone: 97299606900
Fax: 97299606910
E-mail: info@rhodium.co.il
Website: www.rhodium.co.il

Type of Firm

Private Equity Firm

Project Preferences

Type of Financing Preferred:
Early Stage
Expansion
Startup

Geographical Preferences

International Preferences:
Israel

Industry Preferences

In Communications prefer:
Communications and Media

In Internet Specific prefer:
Internet

In Business Serv. prefer:
Media

Additional Information

Year Founded: 2009
Current Activity Level: Actively seeking new investments

RHONE ALPES PME GESTION SA

139 Rue Vendome
Lyon, France 69006
Phone: 33472832323
Fax: 33472832040

Management and Staff

Cyril Fromager, Chief Executive Officer

Type of Firm

Private Equity Firm

Project Preferences

Type of Financing Preferred:
Leveraged Buyout
Early Stage
Later Stage
Acquisition

Geographical Preferences

International Preferences:
Europe
France

Additional Information

Year Founded: 1999
Current Activity Level: Actively seeking new investments

RHONE CAPITAL LLC

630 Fifth Avenue
27th Floor
New York, NY USA 10111
Phone: 2122186770
Fax: 2122186789
Website: www.rhonegroup.com

Other Offices

40 Bruton Street
London, United Kingdom W1J 6QZ

72 Rue Du Faubourg Saint Honore
Paris, France 75008

Management and Staff
Andrew Sweet, Managing Director
Colin Hall, Partner
Elaine Eng, Chief Financial Officer
Ferdinand Groos, Partner
M. Steven Langman, Managing Director
Nancy Cooper, Partner
Robert Agostinelli, Partner

Type of Firm
Private Equity Firm

Geographical Preferences
United States Preferences:
All U.S.

Industry Focus
(% based on actual investment)
Consumer Related	50.4%
Industrial/Energy	24.3%
Other Products	21.3%
Communications and Media	2.2%
Biotechnology	1.8%

Additional Information
Name of Most Recent Fund: Rhone Partners IV, L.P.
Most Recent Fund Was Raised: 06/27/2011
Year Founded: 1997
Capital Under Management: $350,000,000
Current Activity Level : Actively seeking new investments

RHONE DAUPHINE DEVEL-OPPEMENT SA

19 rue des Berges
Polytec
Grenoble, France 38000
Phone: 33476414928
Fax: 33476908257

Management and Staff
Thierry Uring, Vice President

Type of Firm
Private Equity Firm

Project Preferences

Type of Financing Preferred:
Leveraged Buyout
Early Stage
Later Stage

Geographical Preferences
International Preferences:
Europe
France

Industry Preferences

In Industrial/Energy prefer:
Industrial Products

In Business Serv. prefer:
Services

Additional Information
Year Founded: 1988
Current Activity Level : Actively seeking new investments

RHV CAPITAL LLC

600 Anchor Rode Drive
Naples, FL USA 34103
Website: www.rhvcapital.com

Type of Firm
Private Equity Firm

Project Preferences

Type of Financing Preferred:
Leveraged Buyout
Acquisition
Recapitalizations

Additional Information
Year Founded: 2008
Current Activity Level : Actively seeking new investments

RIBBIT CAPITAL LP

364 University Avenue
Palo Alto, CA USA 94301
E-mail: info@ribbitcap.com
Website: ribbitcap.com

Management and Staff
Meyer Malka, Founder

Type of Firm
Private Equity Firm

Project Preferences

Type of Financing Preferred:
Early Stage

Industry Preferences

In Financial Services prefer:
Financial Services
Financial Services

Additional Information
Year Founded: 2012
Capital Under Management: $224,725,000
Current Activity Level : Actively seeking new investments

RICHARDSON CAPITAL LTD

3100 One Lombard Place
Winnipeg, Canada R3B 0H3
Phone: 2049537969
Fax: 2049490731
E-mail: info@richardsoncapital.com
Website: www.richardsoncapital.com

Management and Staff
David Brown, Chief Executive Officer
Hartley Richardson, Managing Director
James McCallum, Managing Director
Mark Gray, Principal
Robert Puchniak, Managing Director
Sandy Riley, Managing Director
Stephen Boyd, Vice President

Type of Firm
Private Equity Firm

Project Preferences

Type of Financing Preferred:
Leveraged Buyout
Expansion
Later Stage
Management Buyouts
Acquisition

Geographical Preferences
Canadian Preferences:
All Canada

Industry Preferences

In Communications prefer:
Telecommunications

In Biotechnology prefer:
Biotechnology

In Medical/Health prefer:
Medical Products

In Industrial/Energy prefer:
Alternative Energy

In Transportation prefer:
Aerospace

Additional Information
Year Founded: 2003
Current Activity Level : Actively seeking new investments

RICHLINK INTERNATIONAL CAPITAL CO LTD

No. 77 Jianguo Road
2501A Tower 3, China Ctr Place
Beijing, China 100025
Phone: 861059695599
Fax: 861059696269
E-mail: Service@richlink.com.cn
Website: www.richlink.com.cn

Other Offices
No. 17 Santaiyun House
Hangzhou, China 310000
Phone: 86-571-8798-0837
Fax: 86-571-8798-0839

Jianguo West Road 568
Shanghai, China
Phone: 86-21-64728518
Fax: 86-21-64336781

45 Wu Lan District, Kun Shan
Bei Guo Cheng Office Building
Baotou, China
Phone: 86-472-2119666
Fax: 86-472-2166500

39 Dongshui East Road
Pubilish Tower
Henan, China
Phone: 86-371-56611297
Fax: 86-371-56611297

268 Des Voeux Road
13th Floor, Shum Tower
Hong Kong, Hong Kong
Phone: 852-28514722
Fax: 852-25456693

Management and Staff
Bei Wang, Partner
Hong Zhou, Partner
Qi Qiao, Partner
Shujun Lan, Partner
Yingzhe Sun, Partner
Yuan Gong, Partner

Type of Firm
Investment Management Firm

Project Preferences

Type of Financing Preferred:
Generalist PE
Opportunistic

Geographical Preferences

International Preferences:
Hong Kong
China
Asia

Industry Preferences

In Biotechnology prefer:
Biotechnology

In Medical/Health prefer:
Medical/Health

In Consumer Related prefer:
Consumer

In Industrial/Energy prefer:
Energy Conservation Relat
Environmental Related

In Financial Services prefer:
Real Estate

In Business Serv. prefer:
Services
Media

Additional Information
Name of Most Recent Fund: Chongqing Richlink Real Estate Private Equity Fund
Most Recent Fund Was Raised: 03/07/2013
Year Founded: 2004
Capital Under Management: $16,077,000
Current Activity Level : Actively seeking new investments

RICHMOND ASSET MANAGEMENT

Yeouido-dong, Yeongdeungpo-gu
13F 63 Bldg
Seoul, South Korea
Phone: 82262763000
Fax: 82262763086
Website: www.richmondam.com

Type of Firm
Investment Management Firm

Project Preferences

Type of Financing Preferred:
Generalist PE

Geographical Preferences

International Preferences:
Korea, South

Additional Information
Year Founded: 2007
Current Activity Level : Actively seeking new investments

RICHMOND CAPITAL (PTY) LTD

Tannery Park, 21 Belmont Road
Ground Flr,W. Block,Rondebosch
Cape Town, South Africa 7700
Phone: 27216895841
Fax: 27216895842
Website: www.richmondcapital.co.za

Type of Firm
Private Equity Firm

Project Preferences

Type of Financing Preferred:
Leveraged Buyout
Expansion
Later Stage
Management Buyouts
Acquisition

Geographical Preferences

International Preferences:
South Africa

Additional Information
Year Founded: 2009

Current Activity Level : Actively seeking new investments

RICHMOND GLOBAL

15500 New Barn Road, Suite 104
Miami Lakes, FL USA 33014
Phone: 8552973369
E-mail: info@rglobal.com
Website: www.rglobal.com

Other Offices
No. 211, Shi Men Yi Road
Media Zone Jing An 20F
Shanghai, China 200041

900 Third Avenue, Suite 1401
New York, NY USA 10022

181 Fremont Street
Floor one
San Francisco, CA USA 94105

Management and Staff
Andras Forgacs, Managing Director
Justin Rockefeller, Principal

Type of Firm
Private Equity Firm

Project Preferences

Type of Financing Preferred:
Early Stage
Seed

Geographical Preferences

United States Preferences:

International Preferences:
Rest of World

Industry Preferences

In Communications prefer:
Wireless Communications

In Internet Specific prefer:
Internet
Ecommerce

In Business Serv. prefer:
Media

Additional Information
Year Founded: 1999
Capital Under Management: $67,680,000
Current Activity Level : Actively seeking new investments

RICHMOND PARK PARTNERS LLP

One Grosvenor Place
London, United Kingdom SW1X 7JH
Phone: 442072017970
Fax: 442072017971
E-mail: rpp@richmondparkpartners.com
Website: www.richmondparkpartners.com

Management and Staff
Andrew Pisker, Co-Founder
Bruno Cappuccini, Partner
Gunnar Palm, Partner
Nirav Hathi, Managing Director
Pascal Maeter, Partner
Peter Dailey, Partner
Scott Mead, Co-Founder
Werner Grub, Co-Founder

Type of Firm
Private Equity Firm

Project Preferences

Type of Financing Preferred:
Leveraged Buyout
Expansion
Generalist PE

Geographical Preferences

United States Preferences:

International Preferences:
United Kingdom
Europe

Additional Information
Year Founded: 2009
Current Activity Level : Actively seeking new investments

RICHMOND VIEW VENTURES GMBH

Schlesische Strasse 26
Berlin, Germany 10997
Website: www.rvv.tv

Type of Firm
Private Equity Firm

Industry Preferences

In Internet Specific prefer:
Internet

Additional Information
Year Founded: 2007
Current Activity Level : Actively seeking new investments

RICHWISE INTERNATIONAL INVESTMENT HLDG LTD

Sea Meadow House
Blackburne Highway, Road Town
Tortola, Br. Virgin I.

Type of Firm
Private Equity Firm

Project Preferences

Type of Financing Preferred:
Generalist PE

Additional Information
Year Founded: 2004
Current Activity Level : Actively seeking new investments

RICO HARVEST (SHANGHAI) PRIVATE EQUITY MANAGEMENT LTD.

No. 488 Middle Yincheng Road, Suite 1103A,11/F,
Taping Tower
Shanghai, China 200120
Phone: 862160752908
Fax: 862160752907
E-mail: info@ricoharvest.com
Website: www.ricoharvest.com

Management and Staff
Chengjie Yao, Vice President
Kenny Yap Kean Chong, President
Rong Fan, Vice President

Type of Firm
Private Equity Firm

Project Preferences

Type of Financing Preferred:
Expansion
Balanced
Public Companies
Later Stage

Size of Investments Considered:
Min Size of Investment Considered (000s): $4,689
Max Size of Investment Considered (000s): $7,816

Geographical Preferences

International Preferences:
China

Industry Preferences

In Medical/Health prefer:
Medical/Health
Medical Diagnostics

In Consumer Related prefer:
Consumer
Retail
Franchises(NEC)

In Industrial/Energy prefer:
Energy
Alternative Energy
Energy Conservation Relat
Environmental Related

In Agr/Forestr/Fish prefer:
Agribusiness
Agriculture related

In Other prefer:
Environment Responsible

Additional Information
Year Founded: 2008
Capital Under Management: $29,298,000
Current Activity Level : Actively seeking new investments

RIDGE CAPITAL PARTNERS LLC

9 North Liberty Street
P.O. Box 2056
Middleburg, VA USA 20118
Phone: 5406878161
Fax: 5406878164
Website: www.ridgecapital.com

Management and Staff
Clark F. Davis, Partner
J. Bradley Davis, Managing Partner
Jeffrey Webb, Vice President
Nancy Kendal-Ward, Chief Financial Officer
Ross Posner, Partner

Type of Firm
Bank Affiliated

Project Preferences

Role in Financing:
Prefer role as deal originator

Type of Financing Preferred:
Leveraged Buyout
Management Buyouts
Special Situation

Industry Preferences

In Consumer Related prefer:
Consumer Products

In Business Serv. prefer:
Services
Distribution

In Manufact. prefer:
Manufacturing

1773

Additional Information

Name of Most Recent Fund: Ridge Capital Fund II, L.P.
Most Recent Fund Was Raised: 12/01/2000
Year Founded: 1989
Capital Under Management: $70,000,000
Current Activity Level : Actively seeking new investments
Method of Compensation: Return on invest. most important, but chg. closing fees, service fees, etc.

RIDGELIFT VENTURES

P.O. Box 620405
Woodside, CA USA 94062
Phone: 650-331-0092
Fax: 650-529-1788
E-mail: info@ridgelift.com
Website: www.ridgelift.com

Other Offices

155 Constitution Drive
Menlo Park, CA USA 94025
Phone: 650-331-0092
Fax: 650-529-1788

Management and Staff

David Newman, Managing Director
Kendall Cooper, Chief Financial Officer
Robert Goldberg, Managing Director
Stuart Phillips, Managing Director

Type of Firm

Private Equity Firm

Project Preferences

Type of Financing Preferred:
Early Stage
Seed

Geographical Preferences

United States Preferences:

Additional Information

Year Founded: 2006
Current Activity Level : Actively seeking new investments

RIDGEMONT PARTNERS MANAGEMENT LLC

150 North College Street, Suite 2500
Charlotte, NC USA 28202
Phone: 7049440914
Fax: 7049440973
Website: www.ridgemontep.com

Management and Staff

Cay Wylie, Vice President
David Lavins, Vice President
Donny Harrison, Partner
Ed Balogh, Chief Operating Officer
George Morgan, Partner
J. Travis Hain, Partner
Jack Purcell, Principal
John Shimp, Partner
Kelly Brennan, Vice President
Kurt Leedy, Vice President
Rob Edwards, Partner
Scott Poole, Partner
Tim Dillon, Vice President
Trey Sheridan, Partner
Walker Poole, Partner
Yeatts Anderson, Vice President

Type of Firm

Private Equity Firm

Project Preferences

Type of Financing Preferred:
Acquisition

Industry Preferences

In Communications prefer:
Telecommunications
Wireless Communications

In Computer Software prefer:
Software

In Medical/Health prefer:
Medical/Health
Health Services
Pharmaceuticals

In Industrial/Energy prefer:
Oil & Gas Drilling,Explor
Industrial Products
Materials

In Transportation prefer:
Transportation

In Business Serv. prefer:
Services
Distribution
Media

In Manufact. prefer:
Manufacturing

In Utilities prefer:
Utilities

In Other prefer:
Environment Responsible

Additional Information

Name of Most Recent Fund: Ridgemont Equity Partners I, L.P.
Most Recent Fund Was Raised: 04/11/2012
Year Founded: 1993
Capital Under Management: $2,050,000,000
Current Activity Level : Actively seeking new investments

RIDGEWOOD CAPITAL MANAGEMENT LLC

14 Philips Parkway
Montvale, NJ USA 07645
Phone: 2014479000
Fax: 2014470474
E-mail: onlineservices@ridgewoodcapital.com
Website: www.ridgewoodcapital.com

Other Offices

1254 Enclave Parkway
HOUSTON, TX USA 77079
Phone: 8009425550

Management and Staff

Elton Sherwin, Senior Managing Director
Jeffrey Strasberg, Chief Financial Officer
Leslie Golden, Managing Director
Matthew Swanson, Vice President
Mirna Valdes, Vice President

Type of Firm

Private Equity Firm

Project Preferences

Role in Financing:
Will function either as deal originator or investor in deals created by others

Type of Financing Preferred:
Early Stage
Balanced
Later Stage

Geographical Preferences

United States Preferences:

Industry Focus

(% based on actual investment)
Internet Specific	27.6%
Semiconductors/Other Elect.	22.9%
Communications and Media	17.9%
Computer Software and Services	16.7%
Industrial/Energy	8.1%
Other Products	3.1%
Computer Hardware	3.1%
Biotechnology	0.7%

Additional Information

Year Founded: 1998
Capital Under Management: $290,000,000
Current Activity Level : Actively seeking new investments
Method of Compensation: Return on investment is of primary concern, do not charge fees

RIFT VALLEY EQUITY PARTNERS LLC

250 Greenwich Street
7 World Trade Center, 46th Flr
New York, NY USA 10007
Phone: 2122660131
Fax: 9176334446
E-mail: info@riftvalleyequity.com
Website: www.riftvalleyequity.com

Management and Staff
Mark Woolgar, Partner
Oliver Ong, Partner

Type of Firm
Private Equity Firm

Project Preferences

Type of Financing Preferred:
Leveraged Buyout

Geographical Preferences

United States Preferences:
North America

Industry Preferences

In Consumer Related prefer:
Retail
Consumer Products
Consumer Services

In Industrial/Energy prefer:
Industrial Products

In Business Serv. prefer:
Services

Additional Information
Year Founded: 2014
Current Activity Level : Actively seeking new investments

RIGHT CLICK CAPITAL

Seven Bridge Street
Level Two
Sydney, Australia 2000
Phone: 61299678800
E-mail: info@rightclickcapital.com

Management and Staff
Ari Klinger, Partner
Benjamin Chong, Partner
Garry Visontay, Partner

Type of Firm
Private Equity Firm

Project Preferences

Type of Financing Preferred:
Early Stage
Seed

Size of Investments Considered:
Min Size of Investment Considered (000s): $50
Max Size of Investment Considered (000s): $10,000

Industry Preferences

In Internet Specific prefer:
Internet

Additional Information
Year Founded: 2013
Current Activity Level : Actively seeking new investments

RIGHT SIDE CAPITAL MANAGEMENT LLC

649 Mission Street
Fifth Floor
San Francisco, CA USA 94105
Phone: 4156554965
Website: www.rightsidecapital.com

Type of Firm
Private Equity Firm

Project Preferences

Type of Financing Preferred:
Seed
Startup

Additional Information
Year Founded: 2012
Capital Under Management: $10,320,000
Current Activity Level : Actively seeking new investments

RINCON VENTURE PARTNERS L P

803 Chapala Street
Santa Barbara, CA USA 93101
Phone: 8059695484
Fax: 8058452270

Other Offices
1520 2nd Street
SANTA MONICA, CA USA 90401

Management and Staff
Brian Kelly, General Partner
Jim Andelman, Managing Partner
John Greathouse, General Partner

Type of Firm
Private Equity Firm

Project Preferences

Type of Financing Preferred:
Early Stage
Seed

Size of Investments Considered:
Min Size of Investment Considered (000s): $500
Max Size of Investment Considered (000s): $1,250

Geographical Preferences

United States Preferences:
Southern California

Industry Preferences

In Communications prefer:
Communications and Media

In Internet Specific prefer:
Internet

In Industrial/Energy prefer:
Alternative Energy

Additional Information
Name of Most Recent Fund: Rincon Venture Partners, L.P.
Most Recent Fund Was Raised: 05/03/2007
Year Founded: 2005
Current Activity Level : Actively seeking new investments

RINGLEADER VENTURES LLC

111 Adell Place
Elmhurst, IL USA 60126
Phone: 3127157405
E-mail: info@ringleaderventures.com
Website: www.ringleaderventures.com

Management and Staff
Jeff Hart, Co-Founder
Jordan Buller, Principal
Mike Maddock, Co-Founder
Mike Bechtel, Managing Partner

Type of Firm
Private Equity Firm

Project Preferences

Type of Financing Preferred:
Balanced

Additional Information
Year Founded: 2014
Current Activity Level : Actively seeking new investments

RIO TECHNOLOGY PARTNERS

Boulevard Plaza Tower 1
Level 14, Emaar Boulevard
Dubai, Utd. Arab Em.
Website: www.rioafrica.com

1775

Type of Firm
Private Equity Firm

Project Preferences

Type of Financing Preferred:
Early Stage
Seed

Geographical Preferences

International Preferences:
Ghana
Africa

Industry Preferences

In Communications prefer:
Telecommunications
Media and Entertainment

In Internet Specific prefer:
E-Commerce Technology

Additional Information
Year Founded: 2014
Current Activity Level : Actively seeking new investments

RIORDAN LEWIS & HADEN

10900 Wilshire Boulevard, Suite 850
Los Angeles, CA USA 90024
Phone: 3104057200
Fax: 3104057222
Website: www.rlhequity.com

Other Offices

18300 Von Karman Avenue, Suite 730
Irvine, CA USA 92612
Phone: 949-428-2200
Fax: 949-428-2210

Management and Staff

Kevin Cantrell, Managing Director
Michel Glouchevitch, Managing Director
Murray Rudin, Managing Director
Navid Gharavi, Vice President
Richard Riordan, Co-Founder
Robert Zielinski, Managing Director
Robert Rodin, Managing Director
Ryan Smiley, Principal
Stefan Jensen, Vice President
John Lewis, Co-Founder

Type of Firm
Private Equity Firm

Project Preferences

Type of Financing Preferred:
Leveraged Buyout
Acquisition
Recapitalizations

Industry Preferences

In Semiconductor/Electr prefer:
Analytic/Scientific

In Medical/Health prefer:
Medical/Health
Pharmaceuticals

In Financial Services prefer:
Financial Services

In Business Serv. prefer:
Services
Distribution
Consulting Services

In Manufact. prefer:
Manufacturing

Additional Information
Year Founded: 1982
Capital Under Management: $700,000,000
Current Activity Level : Actively seeking new investments

RIPPLEWOOD HOLDINGS LLC

One Rockefeller Plaza
32nd Floor
New York, NY USA 10020
Phone: 2125826700
Fax: 2125824110

Management and Staff

Masamoto Yashiro, Partner
Paul Liska, Partner
Robert Berner, Managing Director
Timothy Collins, Chief Executive Officer

Type of Firm
Private Equity Firm

Project Preferences

Type of Financing Preferred:
Leveraged Buyout
Turnaround
Management Buyouts

Geographical Preferences

United States Preferences:

International Preferences:
Japan

Industry Focus
(% based on actual investment)
Other Products	89.4%
Consumer Related	6.6%
Communications and Media	3.6%
Internet Specific	0.3%
Industrial/Energy	0.1%

Additional Information
Name of Most Recent Fund: Ripplewood Partners II, L.P.
Most Recent Fund Was Raised: 12/22/2000
Year Founded: 1995
Current Activity Level : Actively seeking new investments

RISE CAPITAL MANAGEMENT LLC

One Ferry Building, Suite 255
San Francisco, CA USA 94111
Phone: 4156775450
E-mail: info@risecapital.com
Website: risecapital.com

Type of Firm
Private Equity Firm

Project Preferences

Type of Financing Preferred:
Expansion
Later Stage

Industry Preferences

In Internet Specific prefer:
Internet

Additional Information
Year Founded: 2015
Capital Under Management: $59,550,000
Current Activity Level : Actively seeking new investments

RISIKOKAPITAL FONDS ALLGAEU GMBH & CO KG

21 King Street
Kempten, Germany 87435
Phone: 498312051176
Fax: 498312051254

Management and Staff

Rochus Weber, Managing Director
Wolfgang Obermeyer, Managing Director

Type of Firm
Bank Affiliated

Project Preferences

Type of Financing Preferred:
Early Stage
Seed
Startup

Geographical Preferences

International Preferences:
Germany

Additional Information
Year Founded: 2001
Current Activity Level : Actively seeking new investments

RISING JAPAN EQUITY INC
1-7-2, Ohtenomachi
27F MetroSquare, Chiyoda
Tokyo, Japan
Phone: 81345009590
Website: rje.jp

Management and Staff
Jun Hayase, Partner
Katsuyuki Sakauchi, Partner
Tetsuo Maruyama, President
Toshiyasu Horie, Partner

Type of Firm
Private Equity Firm

Project Preferences

Type of Financing Preferred:
Leveraged Buyout
Management Buyouts
Acquisition

Geographical Preferences

International Preferences:
Japan

Additional Information
Year Founded: 2010
Current Activity Level : Actively seeking new investments

RISING STAR AG
Seestrasse 46
Bottighofen, Switzerland 8598
Phone: 41716869400
Fax: 41716869415
E-mail: info@risingstar.ch
Website: www.risingstar.ch

Type of Firm
Private Equity Advisor or Fund of Funds

Project Preferences

Type of Financing Preferred:
Fund of Funds
Leveraged Buyout
Balanced

Geographical Preferences

United States Preferences:
All U.S.

International Preferences:
Asia Pacific
Latin America
Central Europe
Europe
Eastern Europe
Asia
Africa

Industry Preferences

In Financial Services prefer:
Real Estate

Additional Information
Name of Most Recent Fund: STAR Private Equity VI Asia Pacific
Most Recent Fund Was Raised: 06/30/2008
Year Founded: 2001
Current Activity Level : Actively seeking new investments

RISING VENTURES SA
Rua Virglio Correia 26C
Lisbon, Portugal 1600-223
Phone: 351211362900
E-mail: geral@risingventures.pt
Website: www.risingventures.pt

Management and Staff
Joaquim Oliveira, Co-Founder
Miguel Caldas, Managing Director
Rolando Oliveira, Co-Founder

Type of Firm
Private Equity Firm

Project Preferences

Type of Financing Preferred:
Early Stage
Seed
Startup

Geographical Preferences

International Preferences:
Brazil

Industry Preferences

In Computer Software prefer:
Software

Additional Information
Year Founded: 2014
Current Activity Level : Actively seeking new investments

RISK CAPITAL PARTNERS LTD
31 North Row
London, United Kingdom W1K 6DA
Phone: 442070160700
Fax: 442076297195
Website: www.riskcapitalpartners.co.uk

Management and Staff
Ben Redmond, Co-Founder
Luke Johnson, Co-Founder

Type of Firm
Private Equity Firm

Association Membership
British Venture Capital Association (BVCA)

Project Preferences

Type of Financing Preferred:
Expansion
Mezzanine
Generalist PE
Public Companies
Turnaround
Management Buyouts
Acquisition

Size of Investments Considered:
Min Size of Investment Considered (000s): $5,013
Max Size of Investment Considered (000s): $16,711

Geographical Preferences

International Preferences:
United Kingdom

Industry Preferences

In Communications prefer:
Media and Entertainment

In Medical/Health prefer:
Medical/Health

In Consumer Related prefer:
Consumer
Entertainment and Leisure
Retail
Food/Beverage

In Transportation prefer:
Transportation

In Financial Services prefer:
Financial Services

In Business Serv. prefer:
Services

Additional Information
Year Founded: 2001
Capital Under Management: $107,000,000
Current Activity Level : Actively seeking new investments

RIT CAPITAL PARTNERS PLC
27 St. James's Place
London, United Kingdom SW1A 1NR
Phone: 442074938111
Fax: 442074935765
E-mail: investorrelations@ritcap.co.uk
Website: www.ritcap.com

Management and Staff
Andrew Jones, Chief Financial Officer

Type of Firm
Private Equity Firm

Project Preferences

Type of Financing Preferred:
Balanced
Public Companies

Additional Information
Year Founded: 1987
Current Activity Level : Actively seeking new investments

RIVA Y GARCIA PRIVATE EQUITY

Casa Berenguer
Diputacion, 246 principal
Barcelona, Spain 08007
Phone: 34932701212
Fax: 34932701213
E-mail: bcn@rivaygarcia.es
Website: www.rivaygarcia.es

Other Offices
Villa 28, Cite des Moudjahidines
Cheraga, Algiers
Algeria, Spain 2132136837

39, Rue Normandie Racine
Casablanca Anfa
Marruecos, Morocco 20100

Immeuble Victoria
Bloc C, Les Berges du Lac
Tunisia, Spain
Phone: 21671962469
Fax: 21621184384

Prncipe, 9 2
Vigo
Pontevedra, Spain 36202
Phone: 34986227969
Fax: 34986220810

Avda. Carlos III, 7 1 C
Pamplona, Spain 31002

39, Rue Normandie Racine
Casablanca Anfa, Morocco 20100
Phone: 212522790940
Fax: 21222369772

Serrano, 1;
3, B
Madrid, Spain 28006
Phone: 34913600639
Fax: 34913600860

Conde de Montornes, 1, Pral.
Valencia, Spain 46003
Phone: 34961042250
Fax: 34961042250

Type of Firm
Investment Management Firm

Association Membership
Spanish Venture Capital Association (ASCRI)

Project Preferences

Type of Financing Preferred:
Early Stage
Expansion
Generalist PE
Balanced
Later Stage
Seed
Management Buyouts
Startup
Special Situation

Geographical Preferences

International Preferences:
Tunisia
Europe
Algeria
Spain
Morocco

Industry Preferences

In Communications prefer:
Wireless Communications

In Computer Software prefer:
Applications Software

In Internet Specific prefer:
Internet

In Business Serv. prefer:
Media

Additional Information
Year Founded: 1999
Capital Under Management: $218,100,000
Current Activity Level : Actively seeking new investments

RIVE PRIVATE INVESTMENT SWITZERLAND SA

1 place Saint-Gervais
Geneva, Switzerland 1201
Phone: 41225936998
Fax: 41225936994
E-mail: contact@rive-investment.com
Website: www.rive-investment.com

Type of Firm
Private Equity Firm

Project Preferences

Type of Financing Preferred:
Leveraged Buyout
Mezzanine
Generalist PE
Other

Geographical Preferences

United States Preferences:

International Preferences:
Europe

Industry Preferences

In Industrial/Energy prefer:
Energy
Energy Conservation Relat
Environmental Related

In Other prefer:
Environment Responsible

Additional Information
Year Founded: 2013
Current Activity Level : Actively seeking new investments

RIVER ASSOCIATES LLC

633 Chestnut Street, Suite 1640
Chattanooga, TN USA 37450
Phone: 4237550888
Fax: 4237550870
Website: www.riverassociatesllc.com

Management and Staff
J. Mark Jones, Partner
James Baker, Managing Partner
W. Craig Baker, Partner

Type of Firm
Private Equity Firm

Project Preferences

Role in Financing:
Will function either as deal originator or investor in deals created by others

Type of Financing Preferred:
Leveraged Buyout
Management Buyouts
Acquisition
Recapitalizations

Geographical Preferences

United States Preferences:

Canadian Preferences:
All Canada

Industry Preferences

In Industrial/Energy prefer:
Industrial Products

In Business Serv. prefer:
Services
Distribution

In Manufact. prefer:
Manufacturing

Additional Information
Name of Most Recent Fund: River V, L.P.
Most Recent Fund Was Raised: 07/08/2005
Year Founded: 1989
Capital Under Management: $100,000,000
Current Activity Level : Actively seeking new investments
Method of Compensation: Return on invest. most important, but chg. closing fees, service fees, etc.

RIVER CAPITAL PTY LTD

Level 15
644 Chapel Street
South Yarra, Australia 3141
Phone: 613-9825-5111
Fax: 613-9825-5110
E-mail: info@rivercapital.com.au
Website: rivercapital.com.au

Management and Staff
Barry Carp, Managing Director

Type of Firm
Private Equity Firm

Project Preferences

Type of Financing Preferred:
Balanced

Geographical Preferences

International Preferences:
Pacific

Additional Information
Year Founded: 2000
Current Activity Level : Actively seeking new investments

RIVER CITIES CAPITAL FUND LP

221 East Fourth Street, Suite 2400
Cincinnati, OH USA 45202
Phone: 5136219700
E-mail: info@rccf.com
Website: rccf.com

Management and Staff
Adrienne Vannarsdall, Chief Financial Officer
Britney Hamberg, Vice President
Daniel Fleming, Managing Director
David Kereiakes, Principal
Edward McCarthy, Managing Director
J. Carter McNabb, Managing Director
Parag Rathi, Vice President
Patrick Dunnigan, Principal
R. Glen Mayfield, Founder
Robert Heimann, Managing Director
Rurik Vandevenne, Managing Director
Walker Fuller, Vice President

Type of Firm
Private Equity Firm

Association Membership
Mid-Atlantic Venture Association
Illinois Venture Capital Association
National Venture Capital Association - USA (NVCA)

Project Preferences

Role in Financing:
Will function either as deal originator or investor in deals created by others

Type of Financing Preferred:
Expansion
Balanced
Later Stage

Geographical Preferences

United States Preferences:
Midwest
Southeast

Industry Preferences

In Communications prefer:
Telecommunications

In Computer Software prefer:
Software

In Medical/Health prefer:
Medical/Health
Medical Products
Health Services

In Business Serv. prefer:
Services

In Manufact. prefer:
Manufacturing

Additional Information
Year Founded: 1994
Capital Under Management: $500,000,000
Current Activity Level : Actively seeking new investments
Method of Compensation: Return on investment is of primary concern, do not charge fees

RIVER GLEN PRIVATE CAPITAL LLC

2600 Westown Parkway, Suite 346
West Des Moines, IA USA 50266
Phone: 5154229040
Website: riverglencapital.com

Type of Firm
Private Equity Firm

Additional Information
Year Founded: 2010
Current Activity Level : Actively seeking new investments

RIVER HOLLOW PARTNERS LLC

437 Madison Avenue
36th Floor
New York, NY USA 10022
E-mail: info@riverhollowpartners.com
Website: www.riverhollowpartners.com

Management and Staff
Adam Deutsch, Vice President
Amy Wolf, Partner
Charlie Baynes-Reid, Partner
Kevin Charlton, Managing Partner

Type of Firm
Private Equity Firm

Project Preferences

Type of Financing Preferred:
Leveraged Buyout
Acquisition

Geographical Preferences

United States Preferences:
All U.S.

Industry Preferences

In Consumer Related prefer:
Retail
Consumer Products

In Industrial/Energy prefer:
Oil and Gas Exploration
Oil & Gas Drilling,Explor

In Manufact. prefer:
Manufacturing

Additional Information
Year Founded: 2013
Capital Under Management: $2,500,000
Current Activity Level : Actively seeking new investments

RIVER STREET MANAGEMENT LLC

1025 Cherry Road
Memphis, TN USA 38117
Phone: 9018180910

Management and Staff
Stephen Roberts, Partner

Type of Firm
Private Equity Firm

Association Membership
National Venture Capital Association - USA (NVCA)

Project Preferences

Type of Financing Preferred:
Expansion
Balanced
Later Stage

Geographical Preferences

United States Preferences:
North America

Additional Information
Year Founded: 1969
Current Activity Level : Actively seeking new investments

RIVERIA INVESTMENT GROUP

99 Park Avenue
Third Floor
New York, NY USA 10016
Phone: 2122038319
Fax: 6465372655
E-mail: info@riveriagroup.com
Website: www.riveriagroup.com

Management and Staff
TJ Gupta, Managing Partner

Type of Firm
Private Equity Firm

Project Preferences

Type of Financing Preferred:
Leveraged Buyout
Management Buyouts
Acquisition
Recapitalizations

Geographical Preferences

United States Preferences:

Industry Preferences

In Communications prefer:
Media and Entertainment

In Medical/Health prefer:
Medical/Health

In Consumer Related prefer:
Retail
Consumer Products
Education Related

In Industrial/Energy prefer:
Industrial Products

In Business Serv. prefer:
Services
Distribution

In Manufact. prefer:
Manufacturing

Additional Information
Year Founded: 2010
Current Activity Level : Actively seeking new investments

RIVERLAKE PARTNERS LLC

1000 Southwest Broadway, Suite 1010
Portland, OR USA 97205
Phone: 5032287100
Fax: 5032287105
Website: www.riverlakepartners.com

Management and Staff
Greg Tansey, Principal
Tom Zupan, Chief Financial Officer
Victor Petroff, Partner

Type of Firm
Private Equity Firm

Project Preferences

Role in Financing:
Prefer role as deal originator

Type of Financing Preferred:
Leveraged Buyout
Acquisition

Industry Preferences

In Consumer Related prefer:
Consumer
Education Related

In Industrial/Energy prefer:
Industrial Products

In Business Serv. prefer:
Services

In Manufact. prefer:
Manufacturing

Additional Information
Year Founded: 2003
Capital Under Management: $90,100,000
Current Activity Level : Actively seeking new investments
Method of Compensation: Return on invest. most important, but chg. closing fees, service fees, etc.

RIVERROCK EUROPEAN CAPITAL PARTNERS LLP

15 Wrights Lane
London, United Kingdom W8 5SL
Phone: 442078427650
Website: www.riverrock.eu

Other Offices
Via Caradosso, 12
Milan, Italy 20123
Phone: 390240741179

63 Avenue des Champs-Elysees
Paris, France 75008
Phone: 3317577300

Management and Staff
Michel Peretie, Chief Executive Officer
Mikael Mallion, Managing Director
Roberto Ippolito, Managing Partner
Ugo Fiaccadori, Managing Partner

Type of Firm
Investment Management Firm

Project Preferences

Type of Financing Preferred:
Leveraged Buyout
Early Stage
Expansion
Acquisition
Startup
Distressed Debt

Geographical Preferences

International Preferences:
Italy
United Kingdom
Western Europe
France

Additional Information
Year Founded: 2009
Capital Under Management: $328,361,000
Current Activity Level : Actively seeking new investments

RIVERS CAPITAL PARTNERS LTD

Two Collingwood Street
Third Floor
Newcastle upon Tyne, United Kingdom NE1 1JF
Phone: 441912306370
E-mail: info@riverscap.com
Website: www.riverscap.com

Other Offices
16-18 Hood Street
Newcastle upon Tyne, United Kingdom NE1 6JQ

Management and Staff
Iain Coward, Founder
John White, Chief Executive Officer

Type of Firm
Private Equity Firm

Project Preferences
Type of Financing Preferred:
Early Stage
Expansion
Startup

Geographical Preferences
International Preferences:
United Kingdom

Additional Information
Year Founded: 2009
Capital Under Management: $12,126,000
Current Activity Level: Actively seeking new investments

RIVERSIDE CO

630 Fifth Avenue, Suite 2400, 45 Rockefeller Ctr
New York, NY USA 10111
Phone: 2122656575
Fax: 2122656478
E-mail: riverside@riversidecompany.com
Website: www.riversidecompany.com

Other Offices
3131 McKinney Avenue, Suite 160
DALLAS, TX USA 75204
Phone: 214-871-9640
Fax: 214-871-9620

Level 9, Kamiyacho Prime Place
4-1-17, Toranomon, Minatoku
Tokyo, Japan 105-0001
Phone: 81-3-3242-6198
Fax: 81-3-3242-6336

Riverside Kft.
Batthyany u.
Budapest, Hungary 1015
Phone: 36-1-224-9050
Fax: 36-1-224-9051

46A Avenue, J.F. Kennedy
Luxembourg, Luxembourg L-1855
Phone: 3522717291
Fax: 35227172999

2746 Dover Road
ATLANTA, GA USA 30327
Phone: 770-948-4256
Fax: 770-948-6881

45 Rockefeller Center, 630 Fifth Avenue, Suite 2400
NEW YORK, NY USA 10111
Phone: 212-265-6575
Fax: 212-265-6478

Blasieholmsgatan 4A
Stockholm, Sweden 114 48
Phone: 46-8-5450-3030
Fax: 46-8-5450-3035

c/o Horvat Capital Corporation
3400-666 Burrard Street
Vancouver, Canada V6C 2X8
Phone: 604-639-3139
Fax: 604-688-1320

ul. Zielna 37/c
Warszaw, Poland 00-108
Phone: 48-22-320-4820
Fax: 48-22-320-4828

Serrano 120-3 dcha
Madrid, Spain 28006
Phone: 34-91-590-1337
Fax: 34-91-561-1606

10 Hagestraat 5-B
Eindhoven, Netherlands 5611 EG
Phone: 31-40-203-4710
Fax: 31-40-203-4715

140 William Street
Level 35
Melbourne, Australia 3000
Phone: 61396789145
Fax: 4153489561

4545 North Hermitage Avenue
CHICAGO, IL USA 60640
Phone: 773-334-7518
Fax: 773-334-7103

Vaclavske namesti 832/19
Praha 1
Prague, Czech Republic 110 00
Phone: 420-224-890-166
Fax: 420-224-890-164

21FL, Seoul Finance Center
Taepyeongro 1-ga, Jung-gu
Seoul, South Korea 100-768
Phone: 82-2-3782-6820
Fax: 82-2-3782-6824

1 Matheson St., Shell Tower
Room 2912, Times Square
Causeway Bay, Hong Kong
Phone: 852-2159-7492
Fax: 852-2159-7493

Level 9, Kamiyacho Prime Place
4-1-17, Toranomon, Minatoku
Tokyo, Japan 105-0001
Phone: 81-3-5408-1230
Fax: 81-3-5408-1231

7 Avenue
Lloyd George
Brussels, Belgium B-1000
Phone: 32-2-626-2121
Fax: 32-2-626-2122

303 Collins Street
Level 28
Melbourne, Australia 3000
Phone: 61-3-9678-9145
Fax: 415-348-9561

455 Market Street, Suite 1520
SAN FRANCISCO, CA USA 94105
Phone: 415-348-9560
Fax: 415-348-9561

Alter Hof 5
Munich, Germany 80331
Phone: 49-89-2422-4890
Fax: 49-89-2422-4899

Management and Staff
Adam Pietruszkiewicz, Principal
Alan Peyrat, Partner
Amy Margolis, Principal
Anne Hayes, Partner
Antonio Cabral, Managing Partner
Bela Schwartz, Chief Financial Officer
Brad Roberts, Principal
Brad Resnick, Vice President
Brian Bunker, Managing Director
Damien Gaudin, Vice President
David Reiss, Managing Director
Dorte Hoppner, Chief Operating Officer
Drew Flanigan, Vice President
Graham Hearns, Managing Director
Hiro Wakashita, Vice President
Hunter Peterson, Partner
Ivica Turza, Managing Director
Jason Fulton, Vice President
Jeroen Lenssen, Vice President
Joe Manning, Partner
Jonathan Kinney, Managing Director
Karen Pajarillo, Partner
Kristin Newhall, Partner
Lars Eriksson, Managing Director
Loren Schlachet, Managing Partner
Martin Scott, Partner
Meranee Phing, Partner
Michael Weber, Partner
Molly O Neill, Vice President
Nicholas Speer, Partner

Peter Tsang, Partner
Peter Schaberger, Partner
Ron Sansom, Managing Partner
Ryan Richards, Principal
Sarah Roth, Partner
Stephen Rice, Vice President
Steven Spiteri, Partner
Stuart Baxter, Managing Partner
Suzanne Kriscunas, Managing Partner
Tim Gosline, Partner

Type of Firm
Private Equity Firm

Association Membership
Australian Venture Capital Association (AVCAL)
Belgium Venturing Association
Czech Venture Capital Association (CVCA)
German Venture Capital Association (BVK)
Natl Assoc of Small Bus. Inv. Co (NASBIC)
Polish Venture Capital Association (PSIC/PPEA)
Swedish Venture Capital Association (SVCA)
Private Equity Council (PEC)
European Private Equity and Venture Capital Assoc.
Dutch Venture Capital Associaton (NVP)
Spanish Venture Capital Association (ASCRI)

Project Preferences

Role in Financing:
Prefer role as deal originator but will also invest in deals created by others

Type of Financing Preferred:
Management Buyouts
Acquisition

Geographical Preferences

United States Preferences:
North America

International Preferences:
Asia Pacific
Europe
Asia

Industry Focus
(% based on actual investment)

Other Products	47.4%
Medical/Health	21.1%
Internet Specific	12.3%
Industrial/Energy	8.2%
Consumer Related	4.5%
Semiconductors/Other Elect.	2.9%
Communications and Media	2.1%
Computer Software and Services	1.4%

Additional Information
Name of Most Recent Fund: Riverside Micro-Cap Fund III, L.P.
Most Recent Fund Was Raised: 03/25/2014
Year Founded: 1988
Capital Under Management: $6,200,000,000
Current Activity Level : Actively seeking new investments
Method of Compensation: Return on invest. most important, but chg. closing fees, service fees, etc.

RIVERSIDE PARTNERS LLC

699 Boylston Street
14th Floor, One Exeter Plaza
Boston, MA USA 02116
Phone: 6173512800
Fax: 6173512801
Website: www.riversidepartners.com

Management and Staff
Brian Guthrie, General Partner
Christopher Ryan, Principal
Craig Stern, Principal
David Del Papa, Partner
David Belluck, General Partner
Frank Do, General Partner
Ian Blasco, General Partner
Jon Lemelman, General Partner
Kevin Sullivan, Chief Financial Officer
Max Osofsky, General Partner
Michelle Noon, General Partner
Patrick Dooling, Principal
Philip Borden, General Partner
Shahan Zafar, Vice President
Steve Kaplan, General Partner

Type of Firm
Private Equity Firm

Project Preferences

Role in Financing:
Prefer role as deal originator but will also invest in deals created by others

Type of Financing Preferred:
Leveraged Buyout
Expansion
Recapitalizations

Industry Focus
(% based on actual investment)

Other Products	49.7%
Computer Software and Services	22.8%
Medical/Health	18.9%
Communications and Media	4.1%
Industrial/Energy	3.4%
Internet Specific	0.6%
Computer Hardware	0.5%
Semiconductors/Other Elect.	0.1%

Additional Information
Name of Most Recent Fund: Riverside Fund V, L.P.
Most Recent Fund Was Raised: 03/26/2012
Year Founded: 1988
Capital Under Management: $96,000,000
Current Activity Level : Actively seeking new investments

RIVERSTONE HOLDINGS LLC

712 Fifth Avenue
36th Floor
New York, NY USA 10019
Phone: 2129930076
Fax: 2129930077
Website: www.riverstonellc.com

Other Offices
1000 Louisiana, Suite 1000
Houston, TX USA 77002
Phone: 7133571400
Fax: 7133571399

Javier Barros Sierra 540
Piso 5 Colonia Lomas de Santa Fe
, Mexico 01210

Three Burlington Gardens
London, United Kingdom W1S 3EP
Phone: 442032066300
Fax: 442032066301

Management and Staff
Alfredo Marti, Principal
Andrew Ward, Partner
Baran Tekkora, Managing Director
Brett Staffieri, Principal
Brian Iversen, Vice President
Carl Williams, Principal
Christopher Hunt, Managing Director
Daniel Sailors, Vice President
David Leuschen, Founder
E. Bartow Jones, Managing Director
Ed Arulanandam, Vice President
Elizabeth Weymouth, Partner
Ernst Sack, Vice President
Haroun van Hoevell, Managing Director
James Hackett, Partner
John Staudinger, Vice President
Joshua Sanger, Vice President
Kenneth Ryan, Managing Director
Lord Browne, Partner
M. Cliff Ryan, Vice President
Mark Papa, Partner
Michael Hoffman, Partner
N. John Lancaster, Partner
Olivia Wassenaar, Principal
Patrick Connell, Vice President
Peter Coneway, Managing Director
Pierre Lapeyre, Founder
Ralph Alexander, Managing Director
Robert Tichio, Managing Director
Robin Duggan, Principal
Stephen Schaefer, Partner

Type of Firm
Private Equity Firm

Project Preferences

Role in Financing:
Prefer role as deal originator but will also invest in deals created by others

Type of Financing Preferred:
Other

Geographical Preferences

International Preferences:
Latin America
Asia
Africa

Industry Preferences

In Industrial/Energy prefer:
Energy
Oil and Gas Exploration
Alternative Energy

Additional Information

Name of Most Recent Fund: Riverstone PVR Strategic, L.P.
Most Recent Fund Was Raised: 05/21/2012
Year Founded: 2000
Capital Under Management: $17,104,000,000
Current Activity Level : Actively seeking new investments
Method of Compensation: Return on investment is of primary concern, do not charge fees

---

RIVERVEST VENTURE PARTNERS LLC

101 S. Hanley Road, Suite 1850
Saint Louis, MO USA 63105
Phone: 13147266700
Fax: 13147266715
E-mail: info@rivervest.com
Website: www.rivervest.com

Other Offices

11000 Cedar Avenue, Suite 100
CLEVELAND, OH USA 44106
Phone: 216-658-3982

Management and Staff

Jay Schmelter, Co-Founder
John McKearn, Managing Director
Karen Mullis, Venture Partner
Karen Spilizewski, Vice President
Nancy Hong, Managing Director
Niall O Donnell, Managing Director
Thomas Melzer, Co-Founder

Type of Firm

Private Equity Firm

Association Membership

National Venture Capital Association - USA (NVCA)

Project Preferences

Role in Financing:
Will function either as deal originator or investor in deals created by others

Type of Financing Preferred:
Early Stage
Balanced
Later Stage

Additional Information

Name of Most Recent Fund: 3x5 Special Opportunity Fund, L.P.
Most Recent Fund Was Raised: 09/12/2012
Year Founded: 2000
Capital Under Management: $321,000,000
Current Activity Level : Actively seeking new investments
Method of Compensation: Return on investment is of primary concern, do not charge fees

---

RIVERWOOD CAPITAL GROUP LLC

70 Willow Road, Suite 100
Menlo Park, CA USA 94025
Phone: 6506187300
E-mail: info@rwcm.com
Website: www.riverwoodcapital.com

Other Offices

399 Park Avenue, Fifth Floor
New York, NY USA 10022
Phone: 2129076041

Management and Staff

Augustin Hong, Principal
Chris Varelas, Founder
Francisco Alvarez-Demalde, Founder
Harish Belur, Vice President
Jeffrey Parks, Founder
Michael Marks, Founder
Nicholas Brathwaite, Founder
Scott Ransenberg, Principal
Sean McArthur, Principal
Thomas Smach, Founder

Type of Firm

Private Equity Firm

Project Preferences

Type of Financing Preferred:
Leveraged Buyout
Expansion
Balanced
Acquisition
Industry Rollups
Recapitalizations

Geographical Preferences

United States Preferences:
North America

International Preferences:
Latin America
Europe
Eastern Europe
Asia

Industry Preferences

In Computer Software prefer:
Software
Applications Software

In Semiconductor/Electr prefer:
Electronics
Electronic Components
Semiconductor

In Consumer Related prefer:
Consumer

In Business Serv. prefer:
Services
Consulting Services

Additional Information

Name of Most Recent Fund: Riverwood Capital Partners II L.P.
Most Recent Fund Was Raised: 01/10/2014
Year Founded: 2007
Capital Under Management: $2,342,900,000
Current Activity Level : Actively seeking new investments

RIVET VENTURES MANAGEMENT LLC

330 Townsend Street, Suite One
San Francisco, CA USA 94107
Website: www.rivetventures.com/

Management and Staff

Christina Brodbeck, Co-Founder
Rebeca Hwang, Co-Founder
Shadi Mehraein, Co-Founder

Type of Firm

Private Equity Firm

Project Preferences

Type of Financing Preferred:
Startup

Industry Preferences

In Consumer Related prefer:
Consumer

In Other prefer:
Women/Minority-Owned Bus.

Additional Information

Year Founded: 2014
Current Activity Level : Actively seeking new investments

RIVIERA GESTORA DE RECURSOS LTDA

Ave Brigadeiro Faria Lima 1355
Jardim Paulistano
Sao Paulo, Brazil 01452-002
Phone: 551132992138
E-mail: riviera@rivierainvestimentos.com.br
Website: rivierainvestimentos.com.br

Type of Firm

Private Equity Firm

Project Preferences

Type of Financing Preferred:
Leveraged Buyout
Acquisition

Geographical Preferences

International Preferences:
Brazil

Industry Preferences

In Industrial/Energy prefer:
Industrial Products

In Financial Services prefer:
Financial Services
Real Estate

In Agr/Forestr/Fish prefer:
Agribusiness

Additional Information
Year Founded: 2008
Current Activity Level : Actively seeking new investments

RIYAD CAPITAL LLC

6775 Takhassusi Street Olaya
Riyadh, Saudi Arabia
Phone: 966920012299
Website: www.riyadcapital.com

Other Offices
6775 Takhassusi Street Olaya
Riyadh, Saudi Arabia
Phone: 966920012299

Type of Firm
Investment Management Firm

Project Preferences

Type of Financing Preferred:
Early Stage

Geographical Preferences

International Preferences:
Saudi Arabia
All International

Industry Preferences

In Communications prefer:
Telecommunications

In Financial Services prefer:
Real Estate

Additional Information
Year Founded: 2008
Capital Under Management: $450,000,000
Current Activity Level : Actively seeking new investments

RIYADH VALLEY CO

King Saud University
Innovation Tower
Riyadh, Saudi Arabia
Phone: 966114693219
E-mail: info@rvc.com.sa
Website: rvc.com.sa

Type of Firm
Private Equity Firm

Project Preferences

Type of Financing Preferred:
Leveraged Buyout
Early Stage
Expansion
Later Stage
Acquisition
Startup

Geographical Preferences

International Preferences:
Saudi Arabia

Industry Preferences

In Industrial/Energy prefer:
Energy
Alternative Energy
Energy Conservation Relat
Environmental Related

Additional Information
Year Founded: 2016
Current Activity Level : Actively seeking new investments

RIZK VENTURES LLC

1540 Broadway
New York, NY USA 10036
Phone: 2129800100
E-mail: info@rizkventures.com
Website: www.rizkventures.com

Management and Staff
Barry Lefkowitz, Managing Partner
Brain Taylor, Principal
Ernie Liang, Managing Partner
Geoffrey Rizk, Managing Partner
Jack Lyden, Managing Partner
James Wiley, Principal
Klaus Lederer, Managing Partner
Leo Nolan, Vice President
Linda Rizk, Co-Founder
Michael Gervasio, Principal
Roger Thomas, Managing Partner

Type of Firm
Private Equity Firm

Project Preferences

Type of Financing Preferred:
Leveraged Buyout
Value-Add
Mezzanine
Generalist PE
Balanced

Additional Information
Year Founded: 2013
Current Activity Level : Actively seeking new investments

RIZVI TRAVERSE MANAGEMENT LLC

260 East Brown Street, Suite 380
Birmingham, MI USA 48009
Phone: 2485944751
Fax: 2485944754
Website: www.rizvitraverse.com

Other Offices
1999 Avenue of the Stars, Suite 3030
Los Angeles, CA USA 90067
Phone: 3107867443

Three Juliano Drive, Suite 207
Oxford, CT USA 06478
Phone: 2035754555

Management and Staff
Ben Kohn, Partner
John Giampetroni, Co-Founder
Suhail Rizvi, Co-Founder
Todd Knowles, Chief Financial Officer
Viq Shariff, Partner

Type of Firm
Private Equity Firm

Project Preferences

Type of Financing Preferred:
Leveraged Buyout
Expansion
Generalist PE
Public Companies
Turnaround
Later Stage
Management Buyouts
Acquisition
Recapitalizations

Geographical Preferences

United States Preferences:
All U.S.

Industry Preferences

In Communications prefer:
Telecommunications

1784

In Semiconductor/Electr prefer:
Electronics

In Financial Services prefer:
Financial Services

In Business Serv. prefer:
Media

In Manufact. prefer:
Manufacturing

Additional Information
Name of Most Recent Fund: Rizvi Opportunistic Equity Fund III, L.P.
Most Recent Fund Was Raised: 09/23/2013
Year Founded: 2004
Capital Under Management: $183,750,000
Current Activity Level : Actively seeking new investments

RJD PARTNERS LTD
8-9 Well Court
Bow Lane
London, United Kingdom EC4M 9DN
Phone: 442070506868
Fax: 442070506869
Website: www.rjdpartners.com

Management and Staff
Alexander Hay, Partner
Francis Bulman, Partner
John Dillon, Co-Founder
Richard Caston, Co-Founder

Type of Firm
Private Equity Firm

Association Membership
British Venture Capital Association (BVCA)

Project Preferences

Type of Financing Preferred:
Leveraged Buyout
Management Buyouts
Acquisition

Geographical Preferences

International Preferences:
United Kingdom

Industry Focus
(% based on actual investment)
Other Products	64.5%
Consumer Related	14.1%
Medical/Health	11.7%
Internet Specific	9.7%

Additional Information
Name of Most Recent Fund: Royal London Private Equity (RLPE)
Most Recent Fund Was Raised: 04/28/2003
Year Founded: 2001
Current Activity Level : Actively seeking new investments

RLG CAPITAL LLC
2750 Rasmussen Road, Suite 107
Park City, UT USA 84098
Phone: 4355651272
E-mail: greg@rlgcap.com
Website: www.rlgcap.com

Management and Staff
Greg Robinson, Co-Founder
Mark Lisonbee, Co-Founder

Type of Firm
Private Equity Firm

Project Preferences

Type of Financing Preferred:
Leveraged Buyout

Additional Information
Year Founded: 2013
Current Activity Level : Actively seeking new investments

RLJ EQUITY PARTNERS LLC
Three Bethesda Metro Center, Suite 1000
Bethesda, MD USA 20814
Phone: 2407447856
Fax: 2407447857
E-mail: epteam@rljequity.com
Website: www.rljequitypartners.com

Management and Staff
Jerry Johnson, Managing Director
Nigel Howard, Vice President
Rufus Rivers, Managing Partner
Salo Aizenberg, Managing Director
Seth Friedman, Managing Director
T. Otey Smith, Vice President

Type of Firm
Private Equity Firm

Association Membership
Natl Assoc of Investment Cos. (NAIC)
Natl Assoc of Small Bus. Inv. Co (NASBIC)

Project Preferences

Type of Financing Preferred:
Leveraged Buyout
Expansion
Mezzanine
Acquisition
Recapitalizations

Geographical Preferences

United States Preferences:
North America
West Coast

Industry Preferences

In Communications prefer:
Telecommunications

In Consumer Related prefer:
Consumer
Retail

In Industrial/Energy prefer:
Industrial Products

In Transportation prefer:
Transportation
Aerospace

In Business Serv. prefer:
Services
Media

Additional Information
Name of Most Recent Fund: RLJ Credit Opportunity Fund I, L.P.
Most Recent Fund Was Raised: 07/06/2012
Year Founded: 2006
Capital Under Management: $199,000,000
Current Activity Level : Actively seeking new investments

RMB CORVEST (PTY) LIMITED
54 Melville Road, Illovo
Second Floor The Reserve
Johannesburg, South Africa 2196
Phone: 27113808300
Fax: 27113808310
E-mail: info@rmbcorvest.co.za
Website: www.rmbcorvest.co.za

Other Offices
P O Box 411024
Craighall, South Africa 2024

Management and Staff
Neil Page, Managing Director

Type of Firm
Bank Affiliated

Association Membership
South African Venture Capital Association (SAVCA)

Project Preferences

Type of Financing Preferred:
Leveraged Buyout
Management Buyouts

Geographical Preferences

International Preferences:
South Africa
Africa

Industry Focus
(% based on actual investment)
Other Products 100.0%

Additional Information
Year Founded: 1989
Current Activity Level : Actively seeking new investments

RMB INVESTMENT ADVISORY PTY LTD

60 Castlereagh Street
Level 13
Sydney, Australia 2000
Phone: 61292566245
Fax: 61292566293
E-mail: info@rmbcapital.com.au
Website: www.rmbcapital.com.au

Management and Staff
Mark Summerhayes, Managing Director
Nicholas Batchelor, Managing Director

Type of Firm
Bank Affiliated

Association Membership
South African Venture Capital Association (SAVCA)
Australian Venture Capital Association (AVCAL)

Project Preferences

Type of Financing Preferred:
Leveraged Buyout
Management Buyouts
Acquisition

Geographical Preferences

International Preferences:
Australia
New Zealand

Additional Information
Year Founded: 1998
Capital Under Management: $309,400,000
Current Activity Level : Actively seeking new investments

ROADMAP CAPITAL INC

130 Bloor Street West, Suite 603
Toronto, Canada M5S 1N5
E-mail: info@roadmapcapitalinc.com
Website: roadmapcapitalinc.com

Type of Firm
Private Equity Firm

Association Membership
Canadian Venture Capital Association

Project Preferences

Type of Financing Preferred:
Balanced

Additional Information
Year Founded: 2013
Current Activity Level : Actively seeking new investments

ROARK CAPITAL GROUP INC

1180 Peachtree Street NE, Suite 2500
Atlanta, GA USA 30309
Phone: 4045915200
Fax: 4045915201
Website: www.roarkcapital.com

Management and Staff
Anthony Scotto, Managing Director
David Lee, Principal
Erik Morris, Managing Director
Ezra Field, Managing Director
Geoff Hill, Vice President
Jeffrey Keenan, President
Matthew Kaelin, Vice President
Michael Lee, Vice President
Neal Aronson, Managing Partner
Robert Chambers, Managing Director
Robert Bryant, Vice President
Robert Sheft, Managing Director
Steve Romaniello, Managing Director
Timothy Armstrong, Managing Director
Tracy Haas, Chief Financial Officer

Type of Firm
Private Equity Firm

Project Preferences

Type of Financing Preferred:
Leveraged Buyout
Management Buyouts
Acquisition
Recapitalizations

Industry Preferences

In Consumer Related prefer:
Consumer
Retail
Franchises(NEC)
Food/Beverage
Consumer Products
Consumer Services
Other Restaurants

In Industrial/Energy prefer:
Environmental Related

In Business Serv. prefer:
Services

Additional Information
Name of Most Recent Fund: Roark Capital Partners III, L.P.
Most Recent Fund Was Raised: 04/12/2012
Year Founded: 2001
Capital Under Management: $3,000,000,000
Current Activity Level : Actively seeking new investments

ROBECO PRIVATE EQUITY

Coolsingel 120
Rotterdam, Netherlands 3011 AG
Phone: 31102241224
Fax: 31104115288
E-mail: cc@robeco.nl
Website: www.robeco.com

Other Offices
27F Man Yee Bldng
Room 2707
Central, Hong Kong
Phone: 85237197400
Fax: 85225305696

909 Third Avenue
New York, NY USA 10022
Phone: 212-908-9576
Fax: 212-908-9672

Taunusanlage 17
Frankfurt am Main, Germany 60325
Phone: 49-69-959-0858
Fax: 49-69-959-0850

Paseo de la Castellana 41-6B
Madrid, Spain 28046
Phone: 34-91-702-0705
Fax: 34-91-702-0671

21, Boulevard de la Madeleine
Paris Cedex 01, France 75039
Phone: 33-1-5535-4500
Fax: 33-1-5535-4501

Uraniastrasse 12
Zurich, Switzerland 8001
Phone: 41-44-227-7272
Fax: 41-44-227-7222

ul. Grzybowska 12/14
office B-3
Warszawa, Poland 00-132
Phone: 48-22-374-7666
Fax: 48-22-405-2750

6-12, Place d' Armes
Luxembourg, Luxembourg 1136

Thames Court One Queenhithe
London, United Kingdom EC4V 3RL
Phone: 44-207-334-9199
Fax: 44-207-334-9187

Avenue de Tervuren, 273
Brussels, Belgium 1150
Phone: 32-2-761-1040
Fax: 32-2-762-5140

Management and Staff
Jurgen Stegmann, Chief Financial Officer
Leni Boeren, Chief Operating Officer
Roderick Munsters, Chief Executive Officer

Type of Firm
Bank Affiliated

Association Membership
European Private Equity and Venture Capital Assoc.

Project Preferences

Type of Financing Preferred:
Fund of Funds
Leveraged Buyout
Early Stage
Balanced
Later Stage

Geographical Preferences

United States Preferences:
All U.S.

International Preferences:
Europe
Western Europe
Eastern Europe
Israel
Asia
Japan
All International

Industry Focus
(% based on actual investment)

Other Products	35.2%
Industrial/Energy	21.6%
Computer Hardware	11.5%
Consumer Related	11.4%
Communications and Media	8.0%
Computer Software and Services	5.1%
Medical/Health	4.2%
Biotechnology	1.3%
Semiconductors/Other Elect.	1.2%
Internet Specific	0.5%

Additional Information
Name of Most Recent Fund: WPG Corporate Development Associates V, LP
Most Recent Fund Was Raised: 10/27/1997
Year Founded: 1929
Capital Under Management: $430,000,000
Current Activity Level : Actively seeking new investments

ROBECO TEDA TIANJIN INVESTMENT MANAGEMENT CO LTD

Tianjin Economic Tech Dev'l
Binhai New Area
Tianjin, China

Type of Firm
Bank Affiliated

Project Preferences

Type of Financing Preferred:
Balanced

Geographical Preferences

International Preferences:
China

Industry Preferences

In Industrial/Energy prefer:
Energy Conservation Relat
Environmental Related

Additional Information
Year Founded: 2009
Current Activity Level : Actively seeking new investments

ROBIN HOOD VENTURES

3711 Market Street
8th Floor
Philadelphia, PA USA 19104
Phone: 2159666220
Fax: 4842140114
E-mail: info@robinhoodventures.com
Website: www.robinhoodventures.com

Management and Staff
George Marks, Co-Founder
Lawrence Brotzge, General Partner
Tim Flatley, Founder

Type of Firm
Angel Group

Project Preferences

Role in Financing:
Prefer role as deal originator but will also invest in deals created by others

Type of Financing Preferred:
Early Stage
Balanced

Size of Investments Considered:
Min Size of Investment Considered (000s): $250
Max Size of Investment Considered (000s): $1,000

Geographical Preferences

United States Preferences:
Mid Atlantic

Industry Preferences

In Internet Specific prefer:
Ecommerce

Additional Information
Year Founded: 1999
Capital Under Management: $9,800,000
Current Activity Level : Actively seeking new investments
Method of Compensation: Return on investment is of primary concern, do not charge fees

ROBOTICS HUB SPV 1 LLC

4618 Henry Street
Pittsburgh, PA USA 15213
Website: www.roboticshub.io

Type of Firm
Private Equity Firm

Project Preferences

Type of Financing Preferred:
Early Stage
Seed

Industry Preferences

In Industrial/Energy prefer:
Robotics

Additional Information
Year Founded: 2017
Capital Under Management: $2,550,000
Current Activity Level : Actively seeking new investments

ROBSON CAPITAL PARTNERS CORP

W. Georgia Street, Suite 800 - 1040
Vancouver, Canada V6E 4H3
E-mail: info@robsoncapital.ca
Website: www.robsoncapital.ca

Management and Staff
Colin Robson, Co-Founder
Ryan Cheung, Managing Partner

Type of Firm
Investment Management Firm

Additional Information
Year Founded: 2015
Current Activity Level : Actively seeking new investments

ROBUR CAPITAL NV

45, Industrieweg
Roeselare, Belgium 8800
Phone: 3251240600
Website: www.roburcapital.be

Type of Firm
Private Equity Firm

Project Preferences

Type of Financing Preferred:
Early Stage
Expansion
Later Stage
Management Buyouts
Acquisition

Geographical Preferences

International Preferences:
United Kingdom
Luxembourg
Netherlands
Belgium
Germany
France

Additional Information
Year Founded: 2016
Current Activity Level : Actively seeking new investments

ROC CAPITAL PTY LTD

259 George Street
Level 38
Sydney, Australia
E-mail: info@rocp.com
Website: www.rocp.com

Type of Firm
Investment Management Firm

Project Preferences

Type of Financing Preferred:
Fund of Funds

Geographical Preferences

International Preferences:
Asia Pacific
Australia

Additional Information
Year Founded: 2016
Capital Under Management: $150,760,000
Current Activity Level : Actively seeking new investments

ROCH CAPITAL INC

50 Applied Card Way
Glen Mills, PA USA 19342
Website: www.rochcap.com

Type of Firm
Private Equity Firm

Project Preferences

Type of Financing Preferred:
Leveraged Buyout
Value-Add
Generalist PE

Industry Preferences

In Financial Services prefer:
Real Estate

Additional Information
Year Founded: 2014
Current Activity Level : Actively seeking new investments

ROCK CREEK CAPITAL LLC

9995 Gate Pkwy North, Suite 330
Jacksonville, FL USA 32246

Management and Staff
Arthur Cahoon, Chief Executive Officer
Bill Schroeder, Managing Director
James Dahl, Founder
John Drilling, Chief Financial Officer
Kenneth Criss, Vice President
M. Ashton Hudson, President

Type of Firm
Private Equity Firm

Project Preferences

Type of Financing Preferred:
Early Stage
Balanced
Later Stage

Industry Preferences

In Medical/Health prefer:
Medical/Health

In Financial Services prefer:
Financial Services

In Business Serv. prefer:
Services

In Manufact. prefer:
Manufacturing

Additional Information
Year Founded: 2015
Current Activity Level : Actively seeking new investments

ROCK HEALTH

455 Mission Bay Boulevard S, Suite 124
San Francisco, CA USA 94158
Phone: 6174592712
E-mail: hello@rockhealth.org
Website: www.rockhealth.com

Type of Firm
Incubator/Development Program

Project Preferences

Type of Financing Preferred:
Seed
Startup

Geographical Preferences

United States Preferences:

Additional Information
Year Founded: 2010
Capital Under Management: $5,700,000
Current Activity Level : Actively seeking new investments

ROCK HILL CAPITAL GROUP LLC

2777 Allen Parkway, Suite 850
Houston, TX USA 77019
Phone: 7137157510
Fax: 7137157520
E-mail: info@rockhillcap.com
Website: www.rockhillcap.com

Management and Staff
James Wilson, Managing Director
Jeffrey Christman, Managing Director
Randall Hale, Founder

Type of Firm
Private Equity Firm

Project Preferences

Type of Financing Preferred:
Leveraged Buyout
Expansion
Management Buyouts
Acquisition
Recapitalizations

Geographical Preferences

United States Preferences:
Southeast
Southwest

International Preferences:
Soviet Union

Industry Preferences

In Industrial/Energy prefer:
Energy
Industrial Products

In Business Serv. prefer:
Distribution

Additional Information
Year Founded: 2008
Capital Under Management: $238,275,000
Current Activity Level : Actively seeking new investments

ROCK RIVER CAPITAL LLC

1302 South Union
Rock Rapids, IA USA 51246
Phone: 712-472-2531

Type of Firm
Angel Group

Project Preferences

Type of Financing Preferred:
Startup

Geographical Preferences

United States Preferences:
South Dakota
Iowa
Minnesota

Additional Information
Year Founded: 2005
Capital Under Management: $500,000
Current Activity Level : Actively seeking new investments

ROCK RIVER CAPITAL PARTNERS

111 North Fairchild Street, Suite 240
Madison, WI USA 53703
E-mail: info@rockrivercapital.com
Website: www.rockrivercapital.com

Type of Firm
Private Equity Firm

Project Preferences

Type of Financing Preferred:
Early Stage

Industry Preferences

In Computer Software prefer:
Data Processing
Software

Additional Information
Year Founded: 2017
Current Activity Level : Actively seeking new investments

ROCK SPRINGS CAPITAL MANAGEMENT LP

650 South Exeter Street, Suite 1070
Baltimore, MD USA 21202
E-mail: info@rockspringscapital.com
Website: www.rockspringscapital.com

Type of Firm
Private Equity Firm

Project Preferences

Type of Financing Preferred:
Early Stage
Balanced
Later Stage

Additional Information
Year Founded: 1969
Current Activity Level : Actively seeking new investments

ROCKAWAY CAPITAL SE

Na Hrebenech II 1718/8
Prague, Czech Republic 14000
E-mail: info@rockaway.cz
Website: www.rockawaycapital.com

Management and Staff
Jan Jirovec, Chief Operating Officer
Jaromir Svihovsky, Chief Financial Officer

Type of Firm
Private Equity Firm

Project Preferences

Type of Financing Preferred:
Leveraged Buyout
Early Stage
Expansion
Later Stage
Seed
Acquisition

Additional Information
Year Founded: 2013
Current Activity Level : Actively seeking new investments

ROCKBRIDGE GROWTH EQUITY LLC

1070 Woodward Avenue
One Campus Martius
Detroit, MI USA 48226
Phone: 3133737000
E-mail: info@rbequity.com
Website: www.rbequity.com

Management and Staff
Brian Hermelin, Founder
Daniel Gilbert, Founder
Kevin Prokop, Founder
Steve Linden, Vice President

Type of Firm
Private Equity Firm

Project Preferences

Type of Financing Preferred:
Leveraged Buyout
Expansion
Acquisition

Size of Investments Considered:
Min Size of Investment Considered (000s): $15,000
Max Size of Investment Considered (000s): $40,000

Geographical Preferences

United States Preferences:

Industry Preferences

In Consumer Related prefer:
Consumer
Entertainment and Leisure
Sports

In Financial Services prefer:
Financial Services

In Business Serv. prefer:
Services
Media

Additional Information
Year Founded: 2007
Current Activity Level : Actively seeking new investments

ROCKET INTERNET AG

Johannisstrasse 20
Berlin, Germany 10117
Phone: 4930300131800
Fax: 4930300131899
E-mail: info@rocket-internet.de
Website: www.rocket-internet.de

Management and Staff
Arnt Jeschke, Managing Director
Eyad Alkassar, Managing Director
Heavent Malhotra, Managing Director
Jeremy Hodara, Managing Director
Sacha Poignonnec, Managing Director

Type of Firm
Private Equity Firm

Project Preferences

Type of Financing Preferred:
Leveraged Buyout
Early Stage
Seed
Acquisition
Startup

Geographical Preferences

International Preferences:
Germany

Industry Preferences

In Internet Specific prefer:
Internet

Additional Information
Year Founded: 1999
Capital Under Management: $1,000,000,000
Current Activity Level : Actively seeking new investments

ROCKET VENTURES

2200 Sand Hill Road, Suite 240
Menlo Park, CA USA 94025
Phone: 6505619100
Fax: 6505619183
Website: www.rocketventures.com

Management and Staff
David Adams, Managing Director

Type of Firm
Private Equity Firm

Association Membership
National Venture Capital Association - USA (NVCA)

Project Preferences

Type of Financing Preferred:
Early Stage
Balanced
Seed
Startup

Size of Investments Considered:
Min Size of Investment Considered (000s): $1,000
Max Size of Investment Considered (000s): $8,000

Geographical Preferences

United States Preferences:
California
West Coast

Industry Preferences

In Communications prefer:
Communications and Media

In Computer Software prefer:
Software

In Internet Specific prefer:
Internet

In Semiconductor/Electr prefer:
Semiconductor

In Consumer Related prefer:
Consumer Services

In Business Serv. prefer:
Media

Additional Information
Name of Most Recent Fund: Rocket Ventures II, L.P.
Most Recent Fund Was Raised: 03/01/2000
Year Founded: 1998
Capital Under Management: $13,500,000
Current Activity Level : Actively seeking new investments

ROCKET VENTURES LLC

2600 Dorr Street
Toledo, OH USA 43606
Phone: 4195306230
Website: rocketventures.org

Type of Firm
Private Equity Firm

Project Preferences

Role in Financing:
Will function either as deal originator or investor in deals created by others

Type of Financing Preferred:
Early Stage

Geographical Preferences

United States Preferences:
Ohio

Additional Information
Name of Most Recent Fund: Rocket Venture Fund, LLC
Most Recent Fund Was Raised: 12/31/2008
Year Founded: 2007
Current Activity Level : Actively seeking new investments

ROCKETSHIP.VC

101 University Avenue, Suite 245
Palo Alto, CA USA 94301
Website: www.rocketship.vc

Type of Firm
Private Equity Firm

Project Preferences

Type of Financing Preferred:
Early Stage
Expansion
Later Stage

Additional Information
Year Founded: 2016
Capital Under Management: $40,140,000
Current Activity Level : Actively seeking new investments

ROCKLEY GROUP

Belsyre Court
57 Woodstock Road
Oxford, United Kingdom OX2 6HJ
Phone: 441672511022
Fax: 441672511002
Website: rockleygroup.com

Other Offices
Room 1502, 15/FL, China World Trade Ctr
Tower 3, No. 1 Jianguomenwai Avenue
Beijing, China 100004
Phone: 861057372518
Fax: 861057372627

Management and Staff
Robert Rickman, Partner

Type of Firm
Private Equity Firm

Project Preferences

Type of Financing Preferred:
Expansion
Balanced
Later Stage

Geographical Preferences

International Preferences:
Europe
China

Industry Preferences

In Communications prefer:
Media and Entertainment

In Computer Hardware prefer:
Computers

In Computer Software prefer:
Data Processing

In Medical/Health prefer:
Medical/Health

In Industrial/Energy prefer:
Energy
Industrial Products

In Financial Services prefer:
Financial Services

In Other prefer:
Environment Responsible

ROCKPOINT CAPITAL LTD

419 S. San Antonio Road, Suite 212
Los Altos, CA USA 94022
E-mail: info@rpcap.com
Website: rpcap.com

Type of Firm
Private Equity Firm

Project Preferences

Type of Financing Preferred:
Balanced

Industry Preferences

In Computer Software prefer:
Software

In Consumer Related prefer:
Consumer Products

Additional Information
Year Founded: 2014
Current Activity Level : Actively seeking new investments

ROCKPOOL INVESTMENTS LLP

45 Pall Mall
Times Place
London, United Kingdom SW1Y 5JG
Phone: 442070152150
Website: www.rockpool.uk.com

Management and Staff
Alan Armstrong, Partner
Gary Robins, Partner
Graham Brown, Partner
Matthew Taylor, Managing Partner
Richard King, Partner

Type of Firm
Private Equity Firm

Project Preferences

Type of Financing Preferred:
Leveraged Buyout
Early Stage
Expansion
Generalist PE
Balanced
Later Stage
Management Buyouts
Acquisition

Additional Information
Year Founded: 2009
Capital Under Management: $200,000,000
Current Activity Level : Actively seeking new investments

Size of Investments Considered:
Min Size of Investment Considered (000s): $3,120
Max Size of Investment Considered (000s): $15,599

Geographical Preferences

International Preferences:
United Kingdom

Additional Information
Year Founded: 2011
Current Activity Level : Actively seeking new investments

ROCKPORT CAPITAL PARTNERS

160 Federal Street
18th Floor
Boston, MA USA 02110
Phone: 6179121420
Fax: 6179121449
Website: www.rockportcap.com

Other Offices
539 Bryant Street, Suite 306
SAN FRANCISCO, CA USA 94107
Phone: 4157809900
Fax: 4157809907

Management and Staff
Abe Yokell, Partner
Alexander Ellis, General Partner
Charles McDermott, General Partner
David Prend, Co-Founder
Janet James, General Partner
Stoddard Wilson, General Partner
William James, Co-Founder

Type of Firm
Private Equity Firm

Association Membership
Western Association of Venture Capitalists (WAVC)

Project Preferences

Role in Financing:
Will function either as deal originator or investor in deals created by others

Type of Financing Preferred:
Early Stage
Expansion
Balanced
Later Stage
Seed
Startup

Size of Investments Considered:
Min Size of Investment Considered (000s): $500
Max Size of Investment Considered (000s): $25,000

Industry Preferences

In Consumer Related prefer:
Consumer
Consumer Products
Consumer Services

In Industrial/Energy prefer:
Energy
Oil and Gas Exploration
Alternative Energy
Energy Conservation Relat
Industrial Products
Advanced Materials
Environmental Related

In Transportation prefer:
Transportation

Additional Information
Name of Most Recent Fund: RockPort Capital Partners III, L.P.
Most Recent Fund Was Raised: 06/17/2008
Year Founded: 1998
Capital Under Management: $850,000,000
Current Activity Level : Actively seeking new investments
Method of Compensation: Return on investment is of primary concern, do not charge fees

ROCKSPRING

Station Road, 20
307 CB1 Business
Cambridge, United Kingdom CB1 2JD
E-mail: contact@rockspring.co.uk
Website: www.rockspring.co.uk

Type of Firm
Private Equity Firm

Project Preferences

Type of Financing Preferred:
Early Stage
Seed
Startup

Additional Information
Year Founded: 2014
Current Activity Level : Actively seeking new investments

ROCKSTEAD CAPITAL PTE., LTD.

24, Raffles Place
Clifford Centre
Singapore, Singapore 048621
Phone: 6565352684
Fax: 6565352654
E-mail: enquiries@rockstead.com
Website: www.rockstead.com

Other Offices

3304, Zuoyue Business District Centre
3rd Fuhua Road
Shenzhen, China 518048
Phone: 8675523910258
Fax: 8675523910358

168, Tibet Road
City Headquarters Building
Shanghai, China 200001
Phone: 862151798641
Fax: 862151798618

Type of Firm
Private Equity Firm

Project Preferences

Type of Financing Preferred:
Leveraged Buyout
Early Stage
Expansion
Generalist PE
Balanced
Later Stage
Management Buyouts
Acquisition

Geographical Preferences

International Preferences:
China
Asia
Singapore

Additional Information
Year Founded: 1999
Current Activity Level : Actively seeking new investments

ROCKWOOD EQUITY PARTNERS LLC

730 Fifth Avenue
15th Floor
New York, NY USA 10019
Phone: 2122188284
Fax: 2122188207
Website: www.rockwoodequity.com

Other Offices

3201 Enterprise Parkway, Suite 370
Beachwood, OH USA 44122
Phone: 2163421790
Fax: 2163421799

Management and Staff
Brett Keith, Co-Founder
H. Josef Merrill, Partner
Steve Demko, Chief Financial Officer
Vince Nardy, Partner

Type of Firm
Private Equity Firm

Association Membership
Natl Assoc of Small Bus. Inv. Co (NASBIC)

Project Preferences

Type of Financing Preferred:
Leveraged Buyout
Recapitalizations

Geographical Preferences

United States Preferences:
North America
All U.S.

Canadian Preferences:
All Canada

Industry Preferences

In Semiconductor/Electr prefer:
Electronic Components

In Medical/Health prefer:
Medical/Health

In Industrial/Energy prefer:
Energy
Industrial Products

In Business Serv. prefer:
Services
Distribution

In Manufact. prefer:
Manufacturing

In Utilities prefer:
Utilities

Additional Information
Year Founded: 1999
Capital Under Management: $74,120,000
Current Activity Level : Actively seeking new investments

ROCKY MOUNTAIN INNOVATION INITIATIVE INC

320 East Vine Drive, Suite 101
Fort Collins, CO USA 80524
Phone: 9702211301
Website: innosphere.org

Management and Staff
Mike Freeman, Chief Executive Officer

Type of Firm
Incubator/Development Program

Association Membership
Community Development Venture Capital Alliance

Project Preferences

Type of Financing Preferred:
Early Stage
Startup

Geographical Preferences

United States Preferences:
Colorado

Industry Preferences

In Industrial/Energy prefer:
Energy Conservation Relat
Environmental Related

Additional Information
Year Founded: 1999
Capital Under Management: $5,000,000
Current Activity Level : Actively seeking new investments

RODA GROUP, THE

918 Parker Street
Berkeley, CA USA 94710
Phone: 5106491900
E-mail: info@rodagroup.com

Management and Staff
Daniel Miller, Managing Director
Marty Reed, Principal

Type of Firm
Private Equity Firm

Project Preferences

Role in Financing:
Will function either as deal originator or investor in deals created by others

Type of Financing Preferred:
Early Stage
Balanced
Seed

Industry Preferences

In Industrial/Energy prefer:
Alternative Energy
Environmental Related

In Other prefer:
Environment Responsible

Additional Information
Name of Most Recent Fund: Roda Group Investment Fund XX LLC, The
Most Recent Fund Was Raised: 05/12/2010
Year Founded: 1997
Capital Under Management: $2,845,000
Current Activity Level : Actively seeking new investments
Method of Compensation: Return on invest. most important, but chg. closing fees, service fees, etc.

ROGERS VENTURES LTD

350 Bloor Street East
Toronto, Canada M4W 0A1
Phone: 4167642000
E-mail: contact@rogersventures.ca

Management and Staff
Mike Lee, Vice President

Type of Firm
Corporate PE/Venture

Association Membership
National Venture Capital Association - USA (NVCA)
Canadian Venture Capital Association

Project Preferences

Type of Financing Preferred:
Early Stage
Seed
Startup

Geographical Preferences

Canadian Preferences:
All Canada

Additional Information
Year Founded: 2009
Current Activity Level : Actively seeking new investments

ROMULUS CAPITAL LLC

90 Broadway
Cambridge, MA USA 02142
Phone: 6309308828
Website: www.romuluscap.com

Other Offices
104 Hancock Street, Suite Six
Cambridge, MA USA 02139

Management and Staff
Anantshree Chaturvedi, Co-Founder
Cankut Durgun, Co-Founder
Krishna Gupta, Co-Founder
Neil Chheda, Co-Founder

Type of Firm
Private Equity Firm

Project Preferences

Role in Financing:
Prefer role as deal originator but will also invest in deals created by others

Type of Financing Preferred:
Early Stage
Seed
Startup

Size of Investments Considered:
Min Size of Investment Considered (000s): $100
Max Size of Investment Considered (000s): $4,000

Geographical Preferences

United States Preferences:
East Coast

International Preferences:
India
United Kingdom
Israel

Additional Information
Name of Most Recent Fund: Romulus Capital II, L.P.
Most Recent Fund Was Raised: 11/13/2012
Year Founded: 2008
Capital Under Management: $1,000,000,000
Current Activity Level : Actively seeking new investments

RONGXIN CAPITAL FUND MANAGEMENT LTD

No. 5 Chaoyangmenwai Street
2/F, B, 5th Plaza
Beijing, China 100010
Phone: 86-10-8399-3788
Fax: 86-10-8399-3083
Website: www.rongxincapital.com

Other Offices
No. 287-291 Des Voeux Road
Room 1501 Champion Building
Hong Kong, Hong Kong
Phone: 852-2541-8442
Fax: 852-2544-5684

Management and Staff
Changbo Xiao, Founding Partner
Jie Yu, Founding Partner
Liang Wang, Founding Partner
Qun Ma, Partner

Type of Firm
Bank Affiliated

Project Preferences

Type of Financing Preferred:
Leveraged Buyout
Generalist PE
Later Stage

Geographical Preferences

International Preferences:
China

Industry Preferences

In Biotechnology prefer:
Biotechnology

In Industrial/Energy prefer:
Energy
Materials
Environmental Related

In Financial Services prefer:
Real Estate

In Agr/Forestr/Fish prefer:
Agriculture related
Mining and Minerals

Additional Information
Year Founded: 2000
Current Activity Level : Actively seeking new investments

RONGYIN CAPITAL INVESTMENT MANAGEMENT CO LTD

No. 11, Caihefang Road
18F, Huayi Hldg Bldg
Beijing, China
Phone: 861082871118
Fax: 861082871117
E-mail: mxy@ry-capital.com
Website: www.ry-capital.com

Type of Firm
Investment Management Firm

Project Preferences

Type of Financing Preferred:
Balanced
Later Stage

Geographical Preferences

International Preferences:
China

Industry Preferences

In Industrial/Energy prefer:
Energy
Energy Conservation Relat
Advanced Materials
Machinery

In Business Serv. prefer:
Services

In Manufact. prefer:
Manufacturing

In Agr/Forestr/Fish prefer:
Agriculture related

In Other prefer:
Environment Responsible

Additional Information
Year Founded: 2010
Capital Under Management: $8,100,000
Current Activity Level : Actively seeking new investments

RONGZHONG CAPITAL INVESTMENT GROUP CO LTD

568 Xinshe Dadao
50/F New World Trade Building
Wuhan, China 430022
Phone: 86-27-8555-8008
Fax: 86-27-8555-8190
Website: www.rongzhong.cn

Management and Staff
Hai Tao Zhang, Vice President

Type of Firm
Bank Affiliated

Project Preferences

Type of Financing Preferred:
Mezzanine
Generalist PE
Balanced

Geographical Preferences

International Preferences:
China

Industry Preferences

In Medical/Health prefer:
Medical/Health

In Industrial/Energy prefer:
Energy

In Transportation prefer:
Transportation

In Financial Services prefer:
Financial Services
Real Estate

In Business Serv. prefer:
Media

In Manufact. prefer:
Manufacturing

Additional Information
Year Founded: 2005
Capital Under Management: $16,200,000
Current Activity Level : Actively seeking new investments

RONOC

10 Merrion Square
Second Floor
Dublin, Ireland
Phone: 35316615100
E-mail: info@ronoc.ie
Website: www.ronoc.ie

Type of Firm
Private Equity Firm

Project Preferences

Type of Financing Preferred:
Leveraged Buyout
Expansion
Generalist PE
Balanced
Later Stage
Acquisition

Geographical Preferences

International Preferences:
Ireland
United Kingdom
Europe

Industry Preferences

In Communications prefer:
Commercial Communications

In Financial Services prefer:
Financial Services
Financial Services

Additional Information
Year Founded: 2007
Current Activity Level : Actively seeking new investments

ROOGREEN VENTURES LLP

Centurion House
129, Deansgate
Manchester, United Kingdom M3 3WR
Phone: 441616312751
E-mail: info@roogreenllp.com
Website: roogreenventures.com

Management and Staff
Brian Davidson, Chief Executive Officer

Type of Firm
Private Equity Firm

Project Preferences

Type of Financing Preferred:
Leveraged Buyout
Early Stage
Expansion
Generalist PE
Balanced
Turnaround
Later Stage
Management Buyouts
Acquisition
Recapitalizations

Geographical Preferences

International Preferences:
United Kingdom
Europe

Additional Information
Year Founded: 2006
Current Activity Level : Actively seeking new investments

ROOT CAPITAL LLP

20 Farringdon Road, Clerkenwel
5th Floor Farringdon Place
London, United Kingdom EC1M 3HE
Phone: 442030961970
Fax: 447966369642
E-mail: info@rootcapital.co.uk
Website: www.rootcapital.co.uk

Management and Staff
Frank Hyman, Partner

Type of Firm
Private Equity Firm

Association Membership
British Venture Capital Association (BVCA)

Project Preferences

Type of Financing Preferred:
Leveraged Buyout
Expansion
Turnaround
Industry Rollups

Geographical Preferences

International Preferences:
United Kingdom
Europe

Industry Preferences

In Communications prefer:
Telecommunications

In Computer Software prefer:
Software

In Internet Specific prefer:
Internet

In Financial Services prefer:
Financial Services

In Business Serv. prefer:
Services
Consulting Services
Media

In Manufact. prefer:
Publishing

Additional Information
Year Founded: 2002
Capital Under Management: $318,700,000
Current Activity Level : Actively seeking new investments
Method of Compensation: Return on invest. most important, but chg. closing fees, service fees, etc.

ROOT VENTURES

2525 Third Street
San Francisco, CA USA 94107
Website: www.root.vc

Management and Staff
Avidan Ross, Partner

Type of Firm
Private Equity Firm

Project Preferences

Type of Financing Preferred:
Early Stage

Size of Investments Considered:
Min Size of Investment Considered (000s): $25
Max Size of Investment Considered (000s): $500

Industry Preferences

In Computer Hardware prefer:
Computers

In Computer Other prefer:
Computer Related

Additional Information
Year Founded: 2012
Capital Under Management: $31,416,000
Current Activity Level : Actively seeking new investments

ROSE PARK ADVISORS LLC

200 State Street
Boston, MA USA 02109
Phone: 6178499265
E-mail: info@roseparkadvisors.com
Website: www.roseparkadvisors.com

Management and Staff
Clayton Christensen, Co-Founder
Kirk Allen, Managing Director
Matthew Christensen, Chief Executive Officer

Type of Firm
Private Equity Firm

Project Preferences

Type of Financing Preferred:
Early Stage

Additional Information
Year Founded: 2006
Current Activity Level : Actively seeking new investments

ROSE TECH VENTURES LLC

158 West 29th Street
Eleventh Floor
New York, NY USA 10001
Phone: 2122288770
Fax: 2122289911
E-mail: info@rose.vc
Website: www.rose.vc

Management and Staff
David Rose, Managing Partner

Type of Firm
Private Equity Firm

Project Preferences

Type of Financing Preferred:
Early Stage
Seed

Additional Information
Year Founded: 2007
Capital Under Management: $10,000,000
Current Activity Level : Actively seeking new investments

ROSECLIFF VENTURE PARTNERS LP

245 Fifth Avenue
14th Floor
New York, NY USA 10016
Phone: 2124923000
Fax: 2125867695
Website: www.rosecliffvc.com

Management and Staff
Michael Caso, Principal

Type of Firm
Private Equity Firm

Project Preferences

Type of Financing Preferred:
Early Stage
Startup

Additional Information
Year Founded: 2016
Capital Under Management: $19,680,000
Current Activity Level : Actively seeking new investments

ROSEMONT INVESTMENT PARTNERS LLC

300 Conshohocken State Road, Suite 680
West Conshohocken, PA USA 19428
Phone: 6108341370
Fax: 6108321265
E-mail: info@rosemontpartnersllc.com

Management and Staff
Charles Burkhart, Founder
David Silvera, Managing Director
Genie Logue, Principal
Sam Schecter, Chief Financial Officer
Thomas Balderston, Principal

Type of Firm
Private Equity Firm

Project Preferences

Role in Financing:
Prefer role as deal originator

Type of Financing Preferred:
Leveraged Buyout
Early Stage
Generalist PE
Management Buyouts
Acquisition
Startup
Recapitalizations

Industry Focus
(% based on actual investment)
Other Products 74.0%
Computer Software and Services 26.0%

Additional Information
Name of Most Recent Fund: Rosemont Partners III, L.P.
Most Recent Fund Was Raised: 03/01/2012
Year Founded: 2000
Capital Under Management: $168,000,000
Current Activity Level : Actively seeking new investments
Method of Compensation: Return on investment is of primary concern, do not charge fees

ROSEMONT SENECA TECHNOLOGY PARTNERS

44 Montgomery Street, Suite 1500
San Francisco, CA USA 94104
Phone: 4157671280
Website: www.rstp.com

Other Offices
One Market, Spear Tower
36th Floor
SAN FRANCISCO, CA USA 94105

Management and Staff
John DeLoche, Managing Director
Neil Callahan, Managing Director

Type of Firm
Private Equity Firm

Project Preferences

Type of Financing Preferred:
Expansion

Additional Information
Name of Most Recent Fund: RSTP LLC
Most Recent Fund Was Raised: 01/10/2012
Year Founded: 2012
Capital Under Management: $29,625,000
Current Activity Level : Actively seeking new investments

ROSEPAUL INVESTMENTS LLC

214 W 29th St
New York, NY USA 10001

Type of Firm
Private Equity Firm

Project Preferences

Type of Financing Preferred:
Seed

Industry Preferences

In Computer Software prefer:
Software

Additional Information
Year Founded: 2011
Current Activity Level : Actively seeking new investments

ROSETTA CAPITAL LTD

New Broad Street House
35 New Broad Street
London, United Kingdom EC2M 1NH
Phone: 442071948080
Fax: 441462896781
E-mail: info@rosettacapital.com
Website: www.rosettacapital.com

Other Offices
10-12 Allington Street
Elliot House
London, United Kingdom SW1E 5EH

Management and Staff
Graham Fagg, Partner
Jonathan Hepple, Partner
Michael Forer, Partner
Torsten Goesch, Partner

Type of Firm
Private Equity Firm

Project Preferences

Type of Financing Preferred:
Early Stage
Balanced
Later Stage
Seed
Startup

Geographical Preferences

Canadian Preferences:
All Canada

International Preferences:
United Kingdom
Europe
Switzerland
Germany

Industry Preferences

In Biotechnology prefer:
Biotechnology

In Medical/Health prefer:
Health Services

Additional Information
Name of Most Recent Fund: Rosetta Capital IV, L.P.
Most Recent Fund Was Raised: 03/15/2013
Year Founded: 2001
Capital Under Management: $43,980,000
Current Activity Level : Actively seeking new investments

ROSEWOOD CAPITAL LLC

One Maritime Plaza, Suite 1575
San Francisco, CA USA 94111
Phone: 4153625526
Fax: 4153621192
Website: www.rosewoodcap.com

Management and Staff
Byron Adams, Managing Director
Kyle Anderson, Managing Director
Peter Breck, Managing Director
Timothy Burke, Managing Director
Trevor Ashley, Vice President

Type of Firm
Private Equity Firm

Project Preferences

Role in Financing:
Prefer role as deal originator but will also invest in deals created by others

Type of Financing Preferred:
Leveraged Buyout
Later Stage

Industry Focus
(% based on actual investment)

Consumer Related	53.6%
Internet Specific	22.9%
Computer Software and Services	10.3%
Other Products	5.6%
Communications and Media	4.6%
Biotechnology	3.0%

Additional Information
Name of Most Recent Fund: Rosewood Capital V, L.P.
Most Recent Fund Was Raised: 10/31/2005
Year Founded: 1985
Capital Under Management: $600,000,000
Current Activity Level : Actively seeking new investments
Method of Compensation: Return on investment is of primary concern, do not charge fees

ROSNANOMEDINVEST OOO

29, 1st Brestskaya Street
Business-center Capital Tower
Moscow, Russia
Phone: 74955453912
Website: rmi.com.ru

Type of Firm
Private Equity Firm

Project Preferences

Type of Financing Preferred:
Early Stage
Expansion
Balanced
Later Stage
Startup

Geographical Preferences

United States Preferences:

International Preferences:
Russia

Industry Preferences

In Biotechnology prefer:
Biotechnology
Human Biotechnology
Genetic Engineering
Biotech Related Research

In Medical/Health prefer:
Medical Diagnostics
Medical Therapeutics
Medical Products
Health Services
Pharmaceuticals

Additional Information
Year Founded: 2012
Current Activity Level : Actively seeking new investments

ROSSER CAPITAL PARTNERS

33 Benedict Place
Greenwich, CT USA 06830
Phone: 2033405100
Fax: 2033405111
E-mail: info@rossercapitalpartners.com
Website: www.rossercapitalpartners.com

Management and Staff
Harold Rosser, Managing Partner
Jacob Organek, Partner
Luke Rosser, Vice President

Type of Firm
Private Equity Firm

Project Preferences

Type of Financing Preferred:
Leveraged Buyout
Acquisition

Industry Preferences

In Consumer Related prefer:
Consumer
Retail
Food/Beverage
Consumer Products
Consumer Services
Other Restaurants

Additional Information

Year Founded: 2012
Current Activity Level : Actively seeking new investments

ROSSIISKAIA KORPORATSIIA NANOTEKHNOLOGII GK

10A Prospekt 60-letiya
Oktyabrya
Moscow, Russia 117036
Phone: 74959885388
Fax: 74959885399
E-mail: info@rusnano.com
Website: www.rusnano.com

Other Offices

3000 Sand Hill Road
1-145
Menlo Park, CA USA 94025

Management and Staff

Alexander Kondrashov, Managing Director
Dmitriy Lisenkov, Managing Director
Dmitry Pimkin, Managing Director
Georgiy Kolpachev, Managing Director
Konstantin Demetriou, Managing Director
Olga Shpichko, Managing Director
Sergey Polikarpov, Managing Director

Type of Firm

Government Affiliated Program

Association Membership

National Venture Capital Association - USA (NVCA)
Russian Venture Capital Association (RVCA)

Project Preferences

Type of Financing Preferred:
Leveraged Buyout
Early Stage
Expansion
Balanced
Later Stage
Seed
Acquisition
Distressed Debt

Geographical Preferences

International Preferences:
Asia
Russia

Industry Preferences

In Biotechnology prefer:
Industrial Biotechnology

In Medical/Health prefer:
Health Services

In Consumer Related prefer:
Education Related

In Industrial/Energy prefer:
Energy
Alternative Energy
Energy Conservation Relat

In Financial Services prefer:
Investment Groups

Additional Information

Year Founded: 2007
Current Activity Level : Actively seeking new investments

ROSSIYSKAYA VENCHURNAYA KOMPANIYA OAO

3-1 Kapranova lane
Moscow, Russia 123242
Phone: 74957770104
Fax: 74957770106
E-mail: rusventure.ru@info
Website: www.rusventure.ru

Other Offices

420 Boylston Street
6th Floor
Boston, MA USA 02115
Phone: 8572847220
Fax: 8573503240

Management and Staff

Igor Agamirzyan, Chief Executive Officer
Nikolay Korolev, Chief Operating Officer

Type of Firm

Private Equity Advisor or Fund of Funds

Association Membership

Russian Venture Capital Association (RVCA)

Project Preferences

Type of Financing Preferred:
Fund of Funds
Early Stage
Seed
Startup

Geographical Preferences

International Preferences:
Russia

Additional Information

Year Founded: 2006
Capital Under Management: $113,280,000
Current Activity Level : Actively seeking new investments

ROSSLYN CAPITAL PARTNERS OOD SOFIA

13 Slavyanska Street
Sofia, Bulgaria 1000
Phone: 35929158010
Fax: 35929818512
Website: www.rosslyncp.com

Management and Staff

Daniel Alexandrov, Managing Director

Type of Firm

Private Equity Firm

Project Preferences

Type of Financing Preferred:
Fund of Funds
Leveraged Buyout

Geographical Preferences

International Preferences:
Europe
Switzerland
Bulgaria

Industry Preferences

In Communications prefer:
Telecommunications

In Consumer Related prefer:
Food/Beverage

In Industrial/Energy prefer:
Alternative Energy

In Financial Services prefer:
Real Estate

In Manufact. prefer:
Manufacturing

In Agr/Forestr/Fish prefer:
Agriculture related

Additional Information

Year Founded: 2002
Current Activity Level : Actively seeking new investments

ROTH CAPITAL PARTNERS LLC

888 San Clemente Drive
Newport Beach, CA USA 92660
Phone: 8006789147
Fax: 9497207215
E-mail: invest@rothcp.com
Website: www.roth.com

Other Offices

12626 High Bluff Drive, Suite 370
San Diego, CA USA 92130
Phone: 800-957-2788
Fax: 858-720-9081

809 Presido Ave, Suite B
Santa Barbara, CA USA 93101
Phone: 800-873-4886
Fax: 805-966-5205

999 Third Avenue, Suite 2424
Seattle, WA USA 98104
Phone: 800-960-2788
Fax: 206-667-9028

11100 Santa Monica Blvd, Suite 800
West Los Angeles, CA USA 90025
Phone: 800-991-2788
Fax: 310-235-0525

Management and Staff

Aaron Gurewitz, Managing Director
Bill Davenport, Managing Director
Byron Roth, Chairman & CEO
Don Bordelon, Managing Director
Joe Schimmelpfennig, Managing Director
John Ma, Managing Director
John Weber, Managing Director
Richard DeNey, Managing Director
Ted Roth, President

Type of Firm
Bank Affiliated

Project Preferences

Type of Financing Preferred:
Fund of Funds
Later Stage

Industry Preferences

In Communications prefer:
Communications and Media

In Computer Software prefer:
Software

In Internet Specific prefer:
Internet

In Medical/Health prefer:
Medical/Health

In Consumer Related prefer:
Consumer Products

Additional Information
Year Founded: 1998
Capital Under Management: $552,591,000
Current Activity Level : Actively seeking new investments

ROTHSCHILD & CO SCA

23 bis Avenue de Messine
Paris, France 75008
Phone: 33153776510
Fax: 33145638528
E-mail: contact@paris-orleans.com
Website: www.rothschildandco.com

Other Offices

1, Place d'Armes
Luxembourg, Luxembourg L-1136
Phone: 3522749721

Type of Firm
Private Equity Firm

Association Membership
Emerging Markets Private Equity Association

Project Preferences

Role in Financing:
Will function either as deal originator or investor in deals created by others

Type of Financing Preferred:
Fund of Funds
Acquisition
Recapitalizations

Geographical Preferences

International Preferences:
Western Europe
France

Industry Preferences

In Computer Software prefer:
Software

In Medical/Health prefer:
Medical/Health

In Consumer Related prefer:
Consumer Services
Education Related

Additional Information
Name of Most Recent Fund: Five Arrows Credit Solutions Fund
Most Recent Fund Was Raised: 05/16/2013
Year Founded: 1838
Capital Under Management: $1,852,183,000
Current Activity Level : Actively seeking new investments

ROTUNDA CAPITAL PARTNERS LLC

4800 Hampden Lane, Suite 200
Bethesda, MD USA 20814
Phone: 2404820612
Fax: 2404823759
Website: www.rotundacapital.com

Management and Staff

Bob Wickham, Partner
Corey Whisner, Partner
Dan Lipson, Co-Founder
John Fruehwirth, Co-Founder

Type of Firm
Private Equity Firm

Project Preferences

Type of Financing Preferred:
Leveraged Buyout
Expansion
Acquisition

Industry Preferences

In Consumer Related prefer:
Consumer
Retail

In Financial Services prefer:
Financial Services
Insurance

In Business Serv. prefer:
Services

In Manufact. prefer:
Manufacturing

Additional Information
Year Founded: 2008
Current Activity Level : Actively seeking new investments

ROUGE RIVER CAPITAL

46 Wellington Street East
Toronto, Canada L4G 1H5
Phone: 9057132220
Website: rougerivercapital.com

Type of Firm
Bank Affiliated

Project Preferences

Type of Financing Preferred:
Leveraged Buyout
Turnaround
Special Situation
Recapitalizations

Geographical Preferences

United States Preferences:
Northeast

Canadian Preferences:
All Canada

Industry Preferences

In Transportation prefer:
Transportation

In Business Serv. prefer:
Distribution

In Manufact. prefer:
Manufacturing

Additional Information
Year Founded: 2008
Current Activity Level : Actively seeking new investments

ROUND HILL MUSIC ROYALTY FUND LP

400 Madison Avenue
18th Floor
New York, NY USA 10017
Phone: 2123800080
E-mail: info@rhmusicroyaltypartners.com

Management and Staff
Jennifer Scher, Chief Financial Officer
Mark Brown, Vice President
Michael Lau, Chief Operating Officer
Neil Gillis, President
Tami Lester, Vice President

Type of Firm
Private Equity Firm

Project Preferences

Type of Financing Preferred:
Balanced

Industry Preferences

In Communications prefer:
Entertainment

Additional Information
Year Founded: 2011
Capital Under Management: $465,000,000
Current Activity Level : Actively seeking new investments

ROUND13 CAPITAL

55 Mill Street, Suite 301
Toronto, Canada M5A 3C4
E-mail: contact@round13capital.com
Website: www.round13capital.com

Management and Staff
Bruce Croxon, Co-Founder
John Eckert, Co-Founder

Type of Firm
Private Equity Firm

Association Membership
Canadian Venture Capital Association

Project Preferences

Type of Financing Preferred:
Balanced

Geographical Preferences

United States Preferences:
All U.S.

Canadian Preferences:
Quebec
Ontario

Industry Preferences

In Communications prefer:
Communications and Media
Commercial Communications
Entertainment

Additional Information
Name of Most Recent Fund: Round13 Capital
Most Recent Fund Was Raised: 08/15/2017
Year Founded: 2012
Capital Under Management: $74,500,000
Current Activity Level : Actively seeking new investments

ROUNDTABLE HEALTHCARE PARTNERS LP

272 East Deerpath Road, Suite 350
Lake Forest, IL USA 60045
Phone: 8477393200
Fax: 8474829215
Website: www.roundtablehp.com

Management and Staff
Andrew Hochman, Principal
G. Adam Hentze, Vice President
Greg Baumli, Principal
Jack McGinley, Partner
Joseph Damico, Partner
Lester Knight, Partner
Olga Zorc, Vice President
Todd Warnock, Partner

Type of Firm
Private Equity Firm

Association Membership
Illinois Venture Capital Association

Project Preferences

Type of Financing Preferred:
Leveraged Buyout
Mezzanine

Industry Focus
(% based on actual investment)
Medical/Health   100.0%

Additional Information
Year Founded: 2001
Capital Under Management: $1,675,250,000
Current Activity Level : Actively seeking new investments

ROUTE 66 VENTURES LLC

118 King Street
Second Floor
Alexandria, VA USA 22314
Phone: 7038284198
Fax: 7039977479
Website: route66ventures.com

Management and Staff
Ben Britt, Vice President
Jim Rothberg, Partner
Michael Meyer, Managing Partner
Pascal Bouvier, Partner

Type of Firm
Private Equity Firm

Association Membership
Mid-Atlantic Venture Association

Project Preferences

Type of Financing Preferred:
Early Stage
Expansion
Mezzanine
Balanced
Later Stage

Industry Preferences

In Financial Services prefer:
Real Estate
Financial Services

Additional Information
Year Founded: 1969
Current Activity Level : Actively seeking new investments

ROUTER VENTURES LP

1905 Harney Street
Omaha, NE USA 68102
Website: www.routerventures.com

Type of Firm
Private Equity Firm

Pratt's Guide to Private Equity & Venture Capital Sources

Project Preferences

Type of Financing Preferred:
Early Stage
Expansion
Later Stage

Additional Information

Year Founded: 2015
Capital Under Management: $1,000,000
Current Activity Level : Actively seeking new investments

ROWAN UNIVERSITY FOUNDATION INC

201 Mullica Road
Glassboro, NJ USA 08028
Phone: 8562564000
Website: www.rufoundation.org

Type of Firm

University Program

Project Preferences

Type of Financing Preferred:
Early Stage

Additional Information

Year Founded: 2014
Capital Under Management: $5,000,000
Current Activity Level : Actively seeking new investments

ROYAL BRIDGE INVESTMENT CO LTD

3/F,Hyeong Deok Building
1714-32Seocho-dong
Seoul, South Korea
Phone: 82-2-5351411
Fax: 82-2-5351422
E-mail: yongkyu@naver.com
Website: www.royalbridgeinvest.com

Type of Firm

Private Equity Firm

Project Preferences

Type of Financing Preferred:
Balanced

Additional Information

Year Founded: 2009
Current Activity Level : Actively seeking new investments

ROYAL DUTCH SHELL PLC

Carel van Bylandtlaan 16
The Hague, Netherlands 2596 HR
Phone: 31703779111
Fax: 31703773115
E-mail: info@shell.com
Website: www.shell.com

Management and Staff

Ben van Beurden, Chief Executive Officer
Jessica Uhl, Chief Financial Officer

Type of Firm

Corporate PE/Venture

Project Preferences

Type of Financing Preferred:
Later Stage

Geographical Preferences

United States Preferences:
All U.S.

International Preferences:
United Kingdom
Europe
Netherlands

Industry Preferences

In Consumer Related prefer:
Consumer

In Industrial/Energy prefer:
Energy
Oil and Gas Exploration
Alternative Energy
Coal Related

In Business Serv. prefer:
Services
Distribution

Additional Information

Year Founded: 2002
Current Activity Level : Actively seeking new investments

ROYAL STREET INVESTMENT AND INNOVATION CENTER LLC

7620 ROYAL ST, Suite 203
Park City, UT USA 84060
Website: www.royalstreet.vc

Management and Staff

Ben Rifkin, Venture Partner
Jeff Stowell, Founder
Laura Brady, Partner
Stephanie Spong, Venture Partner

Type of Firm

Private Equity Firm

Project Preferences

Type of Financing Preferred:
Early Stage
Seed

Size of Investments Considered:
Min Size of Investment Considered (000s): $500
Max Size of Investment Considered (000s): $2,000

Geographical Preferences

United States Preferences:
Midwest
California

Additional Information

Year Founded: 2016
Current Activity Level : Actively seeking new investments

ROYALTON PARTNERS

Na Prikope 15
Prague, Czech Republic 110 00
Phone: 420236073000
Fax: 420236073001
Website: www.royalton-partners.com

Other Offices

59, Zlota
SkyLight Zlote Tarasy
Warsaw, Poland 00-120
Phone: 48222865100

3, Avenue Monterey
Luxembourg, Luxembourg
Phone: 35226470320

Na Prikope 15
Prague, Czech Republic 11000
Phone: 420236073000
Fax: 420236073001

Management and Staff

Gabriella Huber, Chief Financial Officer
Ivan Vohlmuth, Partner
Marcin Benbenek, Partner
Nigel Williams, Managing Partner
Przemyslaw Bielicki, Partner

Type of Firm

Private Equity Firm

Association Membership

Polish Venture Capital Association (PSIC/PPEA)
European Private Equity and Venture Capital Assoc.

Project Preferences

Type of Financing Preferred:
Leveraged Buyout

Size of Investments Considered:
Min Size of Investment Considered (000s): $10,120
Max Size of Investment Considered (000s): $23,920

Geographical Preferences

International Preferences:
Hungary
Slovak Repub.
Czech Republic
Poland
Eastern Europe
Croatia
Bulgaria
Estonia
Romania
Latvia
Lithuania

Industry Preferences

In Communications prefer:
Commercial Communications
Telecommunications
Media and Entertainment

In Consumer Related prefer:
Retail
Education Related

In Industrial/Energy prefer:
Energy
Alternative Energy
Energy Conservation Relat

In Financial Services prefer:
Financial Services
Insurance

In Business Serv. prefer:
Services

Additional Information
Name of Most Recent Fund: Royalton Capital Investors II, L.P.
Most Recent Fund Was Raised: 11/07/2007
Year Founded: 1996
Capital Under Management: $142,500,000
Current Activity Level : Actively seeking new investments

ROYNAT CAPITAL INC

40 King Street West
26th Floor
Toronto, Canada M5H 1H1
Phone: 4169331441
Fax: 4169332783
Website: www.scotiabank.com

Other Offices

525 North Tryon Street., Suite 1600
Charlotte, NC USA 28202
Phone: 7043313935
Fax: 7043345719

181 West Madison Street, Suite 3700
Chicago, IL USA 60602
Phone: 3122014110
Fax: 3122014063

Management and Staff
Russ Andrew, Managing Director

Type of Firm
Bank Affiliated

Association Membership
Canadian Venture Capital Association

Project Preferences

Role in Financing:
Prefer role as deal originator but will also invest in deals created by others

Type of Financing Preferred:
Leveraged Buyout
Expansion
Mezzanine
Balanced
Later Stage

Size of Investments Considered:
Min Size of Investment Considered (000s): $3,000
Max Size of Investment Considered (000s): $10,000

Geographical Preferences

United States Preferences:

Canadian Preferences:
All Canada

Industry Preferences

In Medical/Health prefer:
Medical/Health

In Consumer Related prefer:
Education Related

In Business Serv. prefer:
Distribution

In Manufact. prefer:
Manufacturing

Additional Information
Year Founded: 1962
Capital Under Management: $78,000,000
Current Activity Level : Actively seeking new investments
Method of Compensation: Return on invest. most important, but chg. closing fees, service fees, etc.

ROZVOJOVY FOND PRE MALE A STREDNE PODNIKANIE AS

Nevadzova 5
Bratislava, Slovakia
Website: www.fondfondov.sk

Type of Firm
Private Equity Firm

Project Preferences

Type of Financing Preferred:
Seed

Geographical Preferences

International Preferences:
Europe

Additional Information
Year Founded: 2004
Current Activity Level : Actively seeking new investments

RPM VENTURES MANAGEMENT LLC

320 North Main Street, Suite 400
Ann Arbor, MI USA 48104
Phone: 7343321700
Fax: 7343321900
E-mail: info@rpmvc.com
Website: rpmvc.com

Management and Staff
Adam Boyden, Managing Director
Anthony Grover, Managing Director
Marc Weiser, Managing Director
Tony Grover, Managing Director

Type of Firm
Private Equity Firm

Project Preferences

Role in Financing:
Will function either as deal originator or investor in deals created by others

Type of Financing Preferred:
Early Stage
Seed

Geographical Preferences

United States Preferences:
North America

Industry Preferences

In Computer Software prefer:
Software

In Internet Specific prefer:
Ecommerce

In Semiconductor/Electr prefer:
Semiconductor

In Transportation prefer:
Transportation

In Business Serv. prefer:
Media

Additional Information
Name of Most Recent Fund: RPM Ventures II, L.P.
Most Recent Fund Was Raised: 02/08/2008
Year Founded: 2000
Capital Under Management: $15,000,000
Current Activity Level : Actively seeking new investments

RRE VENTURES LLC

130 East 59th Street
17th Floor
New York, NY USA 10022
Phone: 2124185100
E-mail: info@rre.com
Website: www.rre.com

Management and Staff
Adam Ludwin, Principal
Eric Wiesen, General Partner
James Robinson, General Partner
James Robinson, Co-Founder
John Hass, Partner
M. Michel Orban, Founder
Stuart Ellman, Co-Founder
Thomas Loverro, Principal
William Porteous, General Partner

Type of Firm
Private Equity Firm

Association Membership
National Venture Capital Association - USA (NVCA)

Project Preferences
Role in Financing:
Will function either as deal originator or investor in deals created by others

Type of Financing Preferred:
Early Stage
Balanced
Later Stage
Seed
Startup

Geographical Preferences
United States Preferences:
New York

International Preferences:
All International

Industry Focus
(% based on actual investment)
Internet Specific	42.4%
Computer Software and Services	29.0%
Other Products	10.8%
Computer Hardware	5.9%
Communications and Media	5.8%
Industrial/Energy	3.1%
Semiconductors/Other Elect.	2.5%
Consumer Related	0.5%
Medical/Health	0.2%

Additional Information
Name of Most Recent Fund: RRE Ventures V, L.P.
Most Recent Fund Was Raised: 08/03/2011
Year Founded: 1994
Capital Under Management: $850,000,000
Current Activity Level : Actively seeking new investments

Method of Compensation: Return on invest. most important, but chg. closing fees, service fees, etc.

RRJ CAPITAL FUND

68 Des Voeux Road
1201-02, Man Yee Building
Central, Hong Kong
Phone: 85239156222
Fax: 85221857498
E-mail: enquiry@rrjcap.com

Management and Staff
Richard Ong, Chairman & CEO

Type of Firm
Private Equity Firm

Project Preferences
Type of Financing Preferred:
Leveraged Buyout
Value-Add
Early Stage
Expansion
Balanced
Later Stage
Management Buyouts
Acquisition

Geographical Preferences
International Preferences:
Laos
Hong Kong
Brunei
China
Thailand
Cambodia
Philippines
Asia
Singapore
Malaysia
Burma

Industry Preferences
In Consumer Related prefer:
Food/Beverage
Consumer Products

In Financial Services prefer:
Real Estate
Financial Services

In Agr/Forestr/Fish prefer:
Agriculture related

Additional Information
Year Founded: 2011
Capital Under Management: $6,562,000,000
Current Activity Level : Actively seeking new investments

RSE VENTURES

423 West 55th Street
11th Floor
New York, NY USA 10019
Phone: 2125065849
E-mail: info@rseventures.com
Website: www.rseventures.com

Type of Firm
Incubator/Development Program

Project Preferences
Type of Financing Preferred:
Early Stage
Seed

Industry Preferences
In Computer Software prefer:
Applications Software

In Consumer Related prefer:
Entertainment and Leisure

In Business Serv. prefer:
Media

Additional Information
Year Founded: 2012
Capital Under Management: $25,000,000
Current Activity Level : Actively seeking new investments

RSVP CAPITAL

912 North Main Street, Suite 111
Ann Arbor, MI USA 48104
Phone: 7342373210
E-mail: info@rsvpcapital.com
Website: www.rsvpcapital.com

Management and Staff
Kevin Wittrup, Managing Director
Paul Vlasic, Partner
Raymond Spencer, Partner

Type of Firm
Private Equity Firm

Project Preferences
Type of Financing Preferred:
Early Stage
Balanced

Industry Preferences
In Medical/Health prefer:
Medical/Health

In Industrial/Energy prefer:
Alternative Energy
Environmental Related

Additional Information
Year Founded: 1969
Current Activity Level: Actively seeking new investments

RT-INVEST OOO
Presnenskaya naberezhnaya
dom 10, 14 etazh
Moscow, Russia 123317
Phone: 74957488674
E-mail: info@rt-invest.com
Website: rt-invest.com

Management and Staff
Andrey Shipelov, Chief Executive Officer
Anton Storchak, Chief Executive Officer
Sergey Bubnov, Managing Director
Tatiana Olifirova, Chief Executive Officer

Type of Firm
Private Equity Firm

Project Preferences
Type of Financing Preferred:
Leveraged Buyout

Geographical Preferences
International Preferences:
Russia

Industry Preferences
In Medical/Health prefer:
Medical/Health
Pharmaceuticals

In Industrial/Energy prefer:
Advanced Materials
Environmental Related

In Financial Services prefer:
Financial Services

Additional Information
Year Founded: 2012
Current Activity Level: Actively seeking new investments

RTAVENTURES VC SP Z O O SK
ul. Podbipiety 52
Warsaw, Poland 02-732
Phone: 48225591360
Fax: 48225591361
E-mail: venture.capital@rtaventures.com
Website: rtaventures.com

Management and Staff
Lubomir Jurczak, Managing Partner
Piotr Kulesza, Managing Partner

Type of Firm
Private Equity Firm

Project Preferences
Type of Financing Preferred:
Balanced

Geographical Preferences
International Preferences:
Europe
Poland

Industry Preferences
In Communications prefer:
Wireless Communications

In Medical/Health prefer:
Health Services

Additional Information
Year Founded: 2011
Capital Under Management: $3,200,000
Current Activity Level: Actively seeking new investments

RTW INVESTMENTS
80 State Street
Albany, NY USA 12207
Website: www.rtwfunds.com

Type of Firm
Investment Management Firm

Project Preferences
Type of Financing Preferred:
Early Stage
Balanced

Industry Preferences
In Medical/Health prefer:
Medical/Health

Additional Information
Year Founded: 2017
Current Activity Level: Actively seeking new investments

RU-NET VENTURES
B. Ovchinnikovsky Per.,16
Fourth Floor, Office 402
Moscow, Russia 115184
Phone: 74957979763
Fax: 74957754905
E-mail: info@ru-net.ru
Website: www.ru-net.ru

Other Offices
900 Third Avenue
25th floor
New York, NY USA 10022

Type of Firm
Investment Management Firm

Project Preferences
Type of Financing Preferred:
Early Stage
Expansion
Startup

Geographical Preferences
United States Preferences:
North America

International Preferences:
Europe
Asia
Russia

Industry Preferences
In Communications prefer:
Commercial Communications
Entertainment

In Computer Software prefer:
Software

In Internet Specific prefer:
E-Commerce Technology
Internet
Ecommerce

In Computer Other prefer:
Computer Related

In Industrial/Energy prefer:
Energy

Additional Information
Year Founded: 1999
Capital Under Management: $700,000,000
Current Activity Level: Actively seeking new investments

RUBICON TECHNOLOGY PARTNERS LLC
2800 Sand Hill Road, Suite 170
Menlo Park, CA USA 94025
Phone: 6506879770
E-mail: info@rubicontp.com
Website: www.rubicontp.com

Other Offices
One Dock Street, Suite 112
Stamford, CT USA 06902
Phone: 2039307770

Type of Firm
Private Equity Firm

Project Preferences

Type of Financing Preferred:
Leveraged Buyout
Recapitalizations

Industry Preferences

In Communications prefer:
Communications and Media

In Computer Software prefer:
Software

In Business Serv. prefer:
Services

Additional Information
Year Founded: 2013
Capital Under Management: $835,265,000
Current Activity Level : Actively seeking new investments

RUDYARD PARTNERS

33 Bradford Street
2nd Floor
Concord, MA USA 01742
Phone: 9782870007
Website: www.rudyardpartners.com

Type of Firm
Private Equity Firm

Project Preferences

Type of Financing Preferred:
Early Stage

Industry Preferences

In Consumer Related prefer:
Consumer Products

Additional Information
Year Founded: 2008
Current Activity Level : Actively seeking new investments

RUFFENA CAPITAL LTD

11-14 Grafton Street, Mayfair
The Clubhouse
London, United Kingdom W1S 4EW
Website: www.ruffena.co.uk

Type of Firm
Private Equity Firm

Project Preferences

Type of Financing Preferred:
Early Stage
Expansion
Balanced
Later Stage
Seed

Additional Information
Year Founded: 2013
Current Activity Level : Actively seeking new investments

RUMSON CAPITAL ADVISORS

Five Independence Way, Suite 300
Princeton, NJ USA 08540

Management and Staff
Alex Bangash, Founder

Type of Firm
Private Equity Advisor or Fund of Funds

Project Preferences

Type of Financing Preferred:
Fund of Funds

Additional Information
Year Founded: 2003
Current Activity Level : Actively seeking new investments

RUN CAPITAL

Spiridonovka, 4
Building 2
Moscow, Russia
E-mail: info@runcapital.ru
Website: www.runcapital.ru

Type of Firm
Private Equity Firm

Project Preferences

Type of Financing Preferred:
Seed
Startup

Additional Information
Year Founded: 2014
Current Activity Level : Actively seeking new investments

RUNA CAPITAL

Tsvetnoy Boulevard, 11
Building 6, 6th Floor
Moscow, Russia 127051
Phone: 74959849703
E-mail: info@runacap.com
Website: www.runacap.com

Other Offices
128 King Street
San Francisco, CA USA 94107

Greifswalder Strasse 207
Berlin, Germany 10405
Phone: 493020689720

Management and Staff
Alexey Vernigora, Vice President
Andre Bliznyuk, Partner
Dmitry Chikhachev, Managing Partner
Vera Shokina, Partner

Type of Firm
Private Equity Firm

Project Preferences

Type of Financing Preferred:
Early Stage
Expansion
Balanced
Start-up Financing
Later Stage
Seed

Geographical Preferences

United States Preferences:

International Preferences:
Asia Pacific
Turkey
Central Europe
Western Europe
Eastern Europe
Israel

Industry Preferences

In Computer Software prefer:
Software
Applications Software

In Internet Specific prefer:
Internet

Additional Information
Name of Most Recent Fund: Runa Capital Fund I L.P.
Most Recent Fund Was Raised: 02/03/2011
Year Founded: 2010
Capital Under Management: $70,000,000
Current Activity Level : Actively seeking new investments

RUNZE YUNNENG (BEIJING) INVESTMENT MANAGEMENT CO., LTD.

Unit 08, Area B, No. 26
Zhenhai Road, Simin District
Xiamen, China 361000

Type of Firm
Private Equity Firm

Project Preferences

Type of Financing Preferred:
Balanced

Geographical Preferences

International Preferences:
China

Additional Information

Year Founded: 2015
Current Activity Level : Actively seeking new investments

RURAL AMERICAN FUND LP

115 South LaSalle Street, Suite 2920
Chicago, IL USA 60603
Phone: 3127500662
Fax: 3127500672
Website: www.raflp.com

Management and Staff

Mia Koch, Co-Founder
Paul Smith, Principal
Thomas Karlson, Co-Founder

Type of Firm

Private Equity Firm

Project Preferences

Type of Financing Preferred:
Leveraged Buyout

Geographical Preferences

United States Preferences:

Industry Preferences

In Business Serv. prefer:
Services

In Agr/Forestr/Fish prefer:
Agriculture related

Additional Information

Year Founded: 2007
Capital Under Management: $50,000,000
Current Activity Level : Actively seeking new investments

RUSNANO USA INC

3000 Sand Hill Rd, Suite 240
Menlo Park, CA USA 94025
Phone: 6506810747
Website: www.rusnano.com

Type of Firm

Private Equity Firm

Association Membership

National Venture Capital Association - USA (NVCA)

Project Preferences

Type of Financing Preferred:
Early Stage

Geographical Preferences

United States Preferences:

International Preferences:
Russia

Industry Preferences

In Communications prefer:
Wireless Communications

In Semiconductor/Electr prefer:
Semiconductor

In Industrial/Energy prefer:
Alternative Energy

Additional Information

Year Founded: 2011
Current Activity Level : Actively seeking new investments

RUSSELL SQUARE PARTNERS INC

Two St. Clair Avenue W, Suite 1004
Toronto, Canada M4V 1L5
Website: russellsquarepartners.com

Management and Staff

Andy Burgess, Co-Founder
Daniel Baum, Co-Founder

Type of Firm

Private Equity Firm

Project Preferences

Type of Financing Preferred:
Leveraged Buyout
Management Buyouts
Acquisition
Recapitalizations

Geographical Preferences

Canadian Preferences:
All Canada

Additional Information

Year Founded: 2014
Current Activity Level : Actively seeking new investments

RUSSKIYE FONDY ZAO

6 Pervyi Polutvinskiy Pereulok
Moscow, Russia 119180
Phone: 74957255515
Fax: 74957255616
E-mail: mailbox@rusfund.ru
Website: www.rusfund.ru

Management and Staff

Konstantin A. Beirit, Chief Executive Officer

Type of Firm

Private Equity Firm

Project Preferences

Type of Financing Preferred:
Early Stage
Balanced
Later Stage

Geographical Preferences

International Preferences:
Europe

Industry Preferences

In Financial Services prefer:
Financial Services

Additional Information

Year Founded: 1999
Current Activity Level : Actively seeking new investments

RUSTARS VENTURES

Nauchnyi proezd, 17
Moscow, Russia 105122
E-mail: JOIN@RUSTARSVENTURES.RU
Website: www.rustarsventures.ru

Type of Firm

Private Equity Firm

Project Preferences

Type of Financing Preferred:
Seed
Startup

Geographical Preferences

International Preferences:
Russia

Additional Information

Year Founded: 2012
Current Activity Level : Actively seeking new investments

RUSTIC PARTNERS LP

100 Wilshire Boulevard, Suite 200
Santa Monica, CA USA 90401
Phone: 3109988000
E-mail: ideas@rusticcanyon.com
Website: www.rusticcanyon.com

Other Offices

Former HQ: 2425 Olympic Boulevard, Suite 6050
West
Santa Monica, CA USA 90404
Phone: 3109988000
Fax: 3109988001

475 Sansome Street, Suite 1880
San Francisco, CA USA 94111
Phone: 6506548503

Management and Staff
David Travers, Partner
John Babcock, Venture Partner
Mike Jones, Venture Partner
Nate Redmond, Managing Partner
Neal Hansch, Partner
Thomas Unterman, Partner

Type of Firm
Private Equity Firm

Project Preferences

Role in Financing:
Prefer role as deal originator but will also invest in deals created by others

Type of Financing Preferred:
Early Stage
Balanced
Later Stage

Size of Investments Considered:
Min Size of Investment Considered (000s): $1,000
Max Size of Investment Considered (000s): $10,000

Industry Focus
(% based on actual investment)
Internet Specific	40.2%
Computer Software and Services	21.2%
Other Products	10.5%
Semiconductors/Other Elect.	7.8%
Communications and Media	7.1%
Industrial/Energy	6.3%
Consumer Related	6.0%
Computer Hardware	1.0%

Additional Information
Name of Most Recent Fund: Rustic Canyon Ventures III, L.P.
Most Recent Fund Was Raised: 06/06/2007
Year Founded: 1999
Capital Under Management: $610,000,000
Current Activity Level : Actively seeking new investments

RUTBERG AND CO LLC

351 California Street, Suite 1100
San Francisco, CA USA 94104
Phone: 415-371-1186
Fax: 415-317-1187
E-mail: info@rutbergco.com
Website: www.rutbergco.com

Other Offices
800 Boylston Street
16th Floor
Boston, MA USA 02199
Phone: 6172626694

Management and Staff
Bryan Rutberg, Chief Executive Officer
Christopher Greer, Senior Managing Director
Eric Risley, Senior Managing Director
John Mecklenburg, Managing Director

Type of Firm
Bank Affiliated

Project Preferences

Type of Financing Preferred:
Balanced

Geographical Preferences

United States Preferences:

Industry Preferences

In Communications prefer:
Communications and Media
Wireless Communications

Additional Information
Year Founded: 2001
Current Activity Level : Actively seeking new investments

RUTLAND PARTNERS LLP

15 Regent Street
Cunard House
London, United Kingdom SW1Y 4LR
Phone: 442074510700
Fax: 442074510701
E-mail: info@rutlandpartners.com
Website: www.rutlandpartners.com

Management and Staff
Ben Slatter, Partner
David Wingfield, Partner
Michael Harris, Partner
Nicholas Morrill, Managing Partner
Oliver Jones, Partner
Paul Cartwright, Managing Partner

Type of Firm
Private Equity Firm

Association Membership
British Venture Capital Association (BVCA)

Project Preferences

Type of Financing Preferred:
Leveraged Buyout
Turnaround
Later Stage
Management Buyouts
Special Situation
Recapitalizations

Geographical Preferences

International Preferences:
United Kingdom

Additional Information
Name of Most Recent Fund: Rutland Fund
Most Recent Fund Was Raised: 11/02/2000
Year Founded: 2000
Capital Under Management: $363,000,000
Current Activity Level : Actively seeking new investments

RUVENTO VENTURES PTE LTD

Blk 71 Ayer Rajah Cres, Suite 06-11
Singapore, Singapore 139951
E-mail: info@ruvento.com
Website: ruvento.com

Management and Staff
Gene Berger, Managing Partner
Slava Solonitsyn, Managing Partner
Tim Shishkin, Partner

Type of Firm
Private Equity Firm

Project Preferences

Type of Financing Preferred:
Startup

Geographical Preferences

International Preferences:
Indonesia
China
Singapore
Russia

Industry Preferences

In Communications prefer:
Communications and Media
Data Communications

In Computer Software prefer:
Data Processing
Software
Systems Software

In Computer Other prefer:
Computer Related

Additional Information
Year Founded: 1969
Current Activity Level : Actively seeking new investments

RW CAPITAL PARTNERS LLC

9595 Wilshire Boulevard, Suite 900
Beverly Hills, CA USA 90212
Phone: 3104924322
Fax: 3103004480
Website: www.rwcplp.com

Pratt's Guide to Private Equity & Venture Capital Sources

Other Offices
101 California Street, Suite 2450
San Francisco, CA USA 94111
Phone: 415-550-1025
Fax: 310-300-4480

Management and Staff
Ellery Roberts, Managing Partner
Michael Wingard, Managing Partner

Type of Firm
SBIC

Project Preferences

Type of Financing Preferred:
Leveraged Buyout
Expansion
Turnaround
Management Buyouts
Acquisition
Recapitalizations

Size of Investments Considered:
Min Size of Investment Considered (000s): $2,000
Max Size of Investment Considered (000s): $10,000

Geographical Preferences

United States Preferences:
West Coast
All U.S.

Industry Preferences

In Consumer Related prefer:
Consumer Products
Consumer Services

Additional Information
Year Founded: 2010
Current Activity Level : Actively seeking new investments

RYERSON FUTURES INC

10 Dundas Street East
Dundas Square
Toronto, Canada
Website: www.ryersonfutures.ca

Management and Staff
Alan Lysne, Managing Director
Matthew Saunders, President

Type of Firm
Incubator/Development Program

Project Preferences

Type of Financing Preferred:
Seed
Startup

Additional Information
Year Founded: 2013
Current Activity Level : Actively seeking new investments

- S -

6 DIMENSIONS CAPITAL LLC

PO Box 309
Ugland House
Grand Cayman, Cayman Islands KY1-1104
Phone: 3459498066

Type of Firm
Private Equity Firm

Project Preferences

Type of Financing Preferred:
Balanced

Geographical Preferences

United States Preferences:

International Preferences:
China

Industry Preferences

In Medical/Health prefer:
Health Services

Additional Information
Year Founded: 2017
Current Activity Level : Actively seeking new investments

---

6 PACIFIC GROUP

10940 Wilshire Boulevard, Suite 1600
Westwood, CA USA 90024
Phone: 3107465421
Fax: 3108811910
Website: www.6pacificpartners.com

Other Offices
4955 Riverside Drive East, Suite 902
Windsor, Canada N8Y583
Phone: 3122123636

Type of Firm
Investment Management Firm

Project Preferences

Type of Financing Preferred:
Generalist PE

Size of Investments Considered:
Min Size of Investment Considered (000s): $2,000
Max Size of Investment Considered (000s): $5,000

Industry Preferences

In Consumer Related prefer:
Food/Beverage
Consumer Products

Additional Information
Year Founded: 1998
Current Activity Level : Actively seeking new investments

---

645 VENTURES

401 Park Avenue South
10th Floor
New York, NY USA 10013
Website: www.645ventures.com

Type of Firm
Private Equity Firm

Project Preferences

Type of Financing Preferred:
Early Stage
Expansion

Geographical Preferences

United States Preferences:

Industry Preferences

In Computer Software prefer:
Computer Services
Software

In Internet Specific prefer:
Internet

Additional Information
Year Founded: 2014
Capital Under Management: $4,380,000
Current Activity Level : Actively seeking new investments

---

654 ADVISORS LLC

One Montgomery Street
33rd Floor
San Francisco, CA USA 94104
Phone: 415-374-8122
Fax: 415-374-8124
Website: 654advisors.com

Type of Firm
Private Equity Firm

Industry Preferences

In Medical/Health prefer:
Medical/Health

Additional Information
Year Founded: 2001
Capital Under Management: $8,100,000
Current Activity Level : Actively seeking new investments

7 GATE VENTURES

1080 Mainland Street
Vancouver, Canada V6B 2T4
E-mail: info@7gateventures.com
Website: 7gateventures.com

Type of Firm
Private Equity Firm

Project Preferences

Type of Financing Preferred:
Early Stage
Startup

Additional Information
Year Founded: 2017
Current Activity Level : Actively seeking new investments

7 HEALTH VENTURES

Shenkar 16/b
P.O.Box 12327
Herzeliya Pituach, Israel 46733
Phone: 97299520200
Fax: 97299520201
E-mail: info@7-main.com

Management and Staff
Amir Zaidman, Principal
Dalia Megiddo, Managing Partner
Ephraim Heller, Partner
Limor Sandach, Partner

Type of Firm
Private Equity Firm

Project Preferences

Type of Financing Preferred:
Expansion
Balanced
Later Stage
Seed
Startup

Geographical Preferences

International Preferences:
Israel

Additional Information
Year Founded: 2007
Current Activity Level : Actively seeking new investments

747 CAPITAL LLC

880 Third Avenue
17th Floor
New York, NY USA 10022
Phone: 2127477474
E-mail: info@747capital.com

Management and Staff
Gijs van Thiel, Managing Partner
Joshua Sobeck, Partner
Marc Der Kinderen, Managing Partner

Type of Firm
Private Equity Advisor or Fund of Funds

Association Membership
Natl Assoc of Small Bus. Inv. Co (NASBIC)

Project Preferences

Type of Financing Preferred:
Fund of Funds

Geographical Preferences

United States Preferences:

Canadian Preferences:
All Canada

Industry Preferences

In Financial Services prefer:
Financial Services

Additional Information
Year Founded: 2005
Capital Under Management: $146,920,000
Current Activity Level : Actively seeking new investments

777 PARTNERS

600 Brickwell Avenue
19th Floor
Miami, FL USA 33131
Phone: 8004949145
E-mail: info@777part.com
Website: www.777part.com

Type of Firm
Private Equity Firm

Project Preferences

Type of Financing Preferred:
Leveraged Buyout
Acquisition
Recapitalizations

Industry Preferences

In Consumer Related prefer:
Consumer

Additional Information
Year Founded: 2017
Current Activity Level : Actively seeking new investments

79 VENTURES

555 California Street, Suite 4925
San Francisco, CA USA 94104
Phone: 4156591882
E-mail: info@79ven.com
Website: www.79ven.com

Type of Firm
Private Equity Firm

Project Preferences

Type of Financing Preferred:
Early Stage
Seed
Startup

Additional Information
Year Founded: 2016
Current Activity Level : Actively seeking new investments

7BRIDGE CAPITAL PARTNERS LTD

10 Chater Road, Suite 1524, Prince's Building
Central, Hong Kong
Phone: 852-2110-9200
Fax: 852-2110-9983
E-mail: hongkong@7bridge.com
Website: www.7bridge.com

Other Offices
1662 West Petunia
Tucson, AZ USA 85737

616 - 1489 Marine Drive
West Vancouver, Canada V7T 1B8
Phone: 604-725-8022
Fax: 778-737-4775

Management and Staff
Alan Chan, Vice President
Cherry Lim, Partner
Richard Clarke, Partner

Type of Firm
Private Equity Firm

Project Preferences

Type of Financing Preferred:
Leveraged Buyout
Early Stage
Generalist PE

Geographical Preferences

United States Preferences:
All U.S.

Canadian Preferences:
All Canada

International Preferences:
India
Taiwan
Hong Kong
Malaysia

Industry Preferences

In Communications prefer:
Telecommunications

In Computer Hardware prefer:
Computers

In Internet Specific prefer:
Internet

In Biotechnology prefer:
Biotechnology

Additional Information

Year Founded: 2007
Current Activity Level : Actively seeking new investments

7VIZHN OOO

13 Pyatnitskaya
Moscow, Russia 125009
E-mail: plan@kiteventures.com
Website: www.kiteventures.com

Management and Staff

Edward Shenderovich, Founder
Vera Loginova, Chief Financial Officer

Type of Firm

Private Equity Firm

Project Preferences

Type of Financing Preferred:
Early Stage
Startup

Geographical Preferences

International Preferences:
Europe
Russia

Industry Preferences

In Internet Specific prefer:
Internet
Ecommerce

In Business Serv. prefer:
Media

Additional Information

Year Founded: 2008
Current Activity Level : Actively seeking new investments

7WIRE VENTURES

444 North Michigan Avenue, Suite 2880
Chicago, IL USA 60611
Phone: 3123575450
Website: 7wireventures.com

Type of Firm

Private Equity Firm

Project Preferences

Type of Financing Preferred:
Early Stage
Expansion
Balanced

Geographical Preferences

United States Preferences:
All U.S.

Industry Preferences

In Medical/Health prefer:
Medical/Health

In Consumer Related prefer:
Education Related

Additional Information

Year Founded: 2011
Capital Under Management: $49,490,000
Current Activity Level : Actively seeking new investments

S CUBED CAPITAL LLC

2061 Avy Avenue
Menlo Park, CA USA 94025
Website: www.scubedcap.com

Management and Staff

Mark A. STEVENS, Managing Partner

Type of Firm

Private Equity Firm

Project Preferences

Type of Financing Preferred:
Balanced

Industry Preferences

In Financial Services prefer:
Financial Services
Real Estate

In Agr/Forestr/Fish prefer:
Agribusiness

Additional Information

Year Founded: 1969
Current Activity Level : Actively seeking new investments

S KAP UNTERNEHMENS-BETEILIGUNGS GMBH & CO KG

Poststrasse 3
Pforzheim, Germany 75172
Phone: 4907231139960
Fax: 49072311399629
E-mail: info@s-kap.de
Website: www.s-kap.de

Management and Staff

Daniel Zeiler, Managing Director
Hans Neuweiler, Managing Director
Herbert Mueller, Managing Director
Scholl Stephan, Managing Director

Type of Firm

Bank Affiliated

Association Membership

German Venture Capital Association (BVK)

Project Preferences

Type of Financing Preferred:
Early Stage
Mezzanine
Later Stage
Startup

Geographical Preferences

International Preferences:
Germany

Industry Preferences

In Medical/Health prefer:
Medical/Health

In Consumer Related prefer:
Consumer
Food/Beverage

In Industrial/Energy prefer:
Alternative Energy
Industrial Products

Additional Information

Year Founded: 2008
Current Activity Level : Actively seeking new investments

S PARTNER KAPITAL AG

Karolinenplatz 1
Munich, Germany 80333
Phone: 498954801880
Fax: 4989548018890
E-mail: info@partnerkapital-ag.de

Management and Staff

Werner Stockner, Managing Director

Type of Firm
Bank Affiliated

Association Membership
German Venture Capital Association (BVK)

Project Preferences

Type of Financing Preferred:
Leveraged Buyout
Early Stage
Mezzanine
Later Stage
Management Buyouts
Acquisition

Size of Investments Considered:
Min Size of Investment Considered (000s): $342
Max Size of Investment Considered (000s): $2,735

Geographical Preferences

International Preferences:
Germany

Industry Preferences

In Business Serv. prefer:
Services

Additional Information
Year Founded: 2002
Current Activity Level : Actively seeking new investments

S REFIT AG

Sedanstrasse 15
Regensburg, Germany 93055
Phone: 49941695560
Fax: 499416955611
E-mail: info@s-refit.de
Website: www.s-refit.de

Other Offices
Henkestrasse 91
Erlangen, Germany 91052
Phone: 49-941-695-5625
Fax: 49-941-695-5613

Management and Staff
Peter Terhardt, Chief Executive Officer

Type of Firm
Bank Affiliated

Association Membership
German Venture Capital Association (BVK)
European Private Equity and Venture Capital Assoc.

Project Preferences

Type of Financing Preferred:
Leveraged Buyout
Early Stage
Mezzanine
Later Stage
Seed
Management Buyouts
Startup

Geographical Preferences

International Preferences:
Germany

Industry Preferences

In Communications prefer:
Communications and Media

In Semiconductor/Electr prefer:
Electronics

In Biotechnology prefer:
Biotechnology

In Medical/Health prefer:
Medical/Health
Pharmaceuticals

In Industrial/Energy prefer:
Materials
Machinery

In Business Serv. prefer:
Services

Additional Information
Year Founded: 1990
Capital Under Management: $35,500,000
Current Activity Level : Actively seeking new investments

S UBG AG

Markt 45-47
Aachen, Germany 52062
Phone: 49241470560
Fax: 492414705620
E-mail: info@s-ubg.de
Website: www.s-ubg.de

Management and Staff
Harald Heidemann, Managing Director

Type of Firm
Bank Affiliated

Association Membership
German Venture Capital Association (BVK)

Project Preferences

Type of Financing Preferred:
Early Stage
Mezzanine
Turnaround
Later Stage
Seed
Management Buyouts
Startup
Recapitalizations

Size of Investments Considered:
Min Size of Investment Considered (000s): $481
Max Size of Investment Considered (000s): $2,407

Geographical Preferences

International Preferences:
Germany

Industry Preferences

In Communications prefer:
Communications and Media

In Computer Software prefer:
Software

In Semiconductor/Electr prefer:
Electronics

In Biotechnology prefer:
Biotechnology

In Medical/Health prefer:
Medical/Health

In Industrial/Energy prefer:
Environmental Related

In Manufact. prefer:
Manufacturing

Additional Information
Year Founded: 1988
Capital Under Management: $43,600,000
Current Activity Level : Actively seeking new investments

S+R INVESTIMENTI E GESTIONI SGR SPA

Via Armorari, 14
Milan, Italy 20123
Phone: 39028053753
Fax: 39028052415

Type of Firm
Bank Affiliated

Project Preferences

Type of Financing Preferred:
Balanced

Additional Information
Year Founded: 2007
Current Activity Level : Actively seeking new investments

S-BETEILIGUNGS-GESELLSCHAFT DER SPARKASSE FREIBURG

Unterlinden 9
Freiburg, Germany 79098
Phone: 497612153030
Fax: 497612153039
E-mail: info@s-beteiligung.de
Website: www.s-beteiligung.de

Management and Staff

Hermann Dittmers, Chief Executive Officer

Type of Firm

Bank Affiliated

Project Preferences

Role in Financing:
Will function either as deal originator or investor in deals created by others

Type of Financing Preferred:
Early Stage
Mezzanine
Later Stage
Management Buyouts
Startup

Geographical Preferences

International Preferences:
Germany

Additional Information

Year Founded: 1998
Capital Under Management: $2,300,000
Current Activity Level : Actively seeking new investments

S-UNTERNEHMENSBETEILIGUNGSGESELLSCHAFT DER SPARKASSE LEIPZIG

Nordstrasse 27
Leipzig, Germany 04105
Phone: 493419867241
Fax: 493419867249
E-mail: info@s-beteiligungen.de
Website: www.s-beteiligungen.de

Management and Staff

Reik Hesselbarth, Managing Director

Type of Firm

Bank Affiliated

Project Preferences

Type of Financing Preferred:
Early Stage
Later Stage
Seed
Startup

Size of Investments Considered:
Min Size of Investment Considered (000s): $68
Max Size of Investment Considered (000s): $1,022

Geographical Preferences

International Preferences:
Germany

Industry Preferences

In Communications prefer:
Media and Entertainment
Entertainment

In Computer Software prefer:
Software

In Medical/Health prefer:
Medical/Health
Pharmaceuticals

In Consumer Related prefer:
Consumer
Retail
Food/Beverage

In Industrial/Energy prefer:
Industrial Products
Machinery

In Financial Services prefer:
Financial Services

In Business Serv. prefer:
Services

Additional Information

Year Founded: 1999
Current Activity Level : Actively seeking new investments

S2G VENTURES LLC

110 N W Second Street, Suite 30
Bentonville, AR USA 72712
Website: s2gventures.com

Management and Staff

Chuck Templeton, Managing Director
Sanjeev Krishnan, Managing Director
Victor Friedberg, Co-Founder

Type of Firm

Private Equity Firm

Project Preferences

Type of Financing Preferred:
Balanced

Geographical Preferences

United States Preferences:

Industry Preferences

In Agr/Forestr/Fish prefer:
Agriculture related

Additional Information

Year Founded: 2015
Capital Under Management: $180,000,000
Current Activity Level : Actively seeking new investments

S3 VENTURES LLC

6300 Bridgepoint Parkway
Building One, Suite 405
Austin, TX USA 78730
Phone: 5122581759
Website: www.s3vc.com

Management and Staff

Brian Smith, Managing Director
Charlie Plauche, Vice President
Rajiv Bala, Vice President
Stephen Banks, Venture Partner

Type of Firm

Private Equity Firm

Association Membership

National Venture Capital Association - USA (NVCA)

Project Preferences

Role in Financing:
Will function either as deal originator or investor in deals created by others

Type of Financing Preferred:
Early Stage
Expansion
Balanced
Later Stage
Startup

Geographical Preferences

United States Preferences:

Industry Preferences

In Medical/Health prefer:
Medical Products

Additional Information

Name of Most Recent Fund: S3 Ventures Fund V, L.P.
Most Recent Fund Was Raised: 06/10/2013
Year Founded: 2006
Capital Under Management: $185,000,000
Current Activity Level : Actively seeking new investments

SA FRAMTAK GP EHF

Laugavegi 7
Reykjavik, Iceland 101
Phone: 3545717373
Website: www.saframtak.is

Type of Firm
Private Equity Firm

Project Preferences

Type of Financing Preferred:
Expansion
Startup

Geographical Preferences

International Preferences:
Iceland

Industry Preferences

In Computer Software prefer:
Software

In Internet Specific prefer:
Internet

In Biotechnology prefer:
Biotechnology

In Consumer Related prefer:
Food/Beverage

In Industrial/Energy prefer:
Energy

Additional Information
Year Founded: 2015
Capital Under Management: $31,416,000
Current Activity Level : Actively seeking new investments

SAAD INVESTMENTS

Salahuddin Al-Ayoubi Street
Golden Belt Area
Al-Khobar, Saudi Arabia 31952
Phone: 96638822220
Fax: 96638827989
E-mail: info@saad.com.sa

Type of Firm
Private Equity Firm

Project Preferences

Type of Financing Preferred:
Early Stage
Balanced
Seed
Startup

Additional Information
Year Founded: 2008
Current Activity Level : Actively seeking new investments

SAAMA CAPITAL LLC

19 Cybercity
4th Floor, Raffles Tower
Ebene, Mauritius
Website: www.saamacapital.vc

Management and Staff
Ash Lilani, Managing Partner
Monica Brand, Managing Partner

Type of Firm
Private Equity Firm

Project Preferences

Type of Financing Preferred:
Early Stage
Later Stage
Seed

Geographical Preferences

International Preferences:
India

Additional Information
Year Founded: 2006
Capital Under Management: $1,590,000
Current Activity Level : Actively seeking new investments

SAARLANDISCHE WAG-NISFINANZIERUNGS-GESELLSCHAFT MBH (AKA SWG)

Franz-Josef-Roeder-Strasse 17
Saarbruecken, Germany 66119
Phone: 4968130330
Fax: 496813033100
E-mail: info@swgmbh.de

Management and Staff
Armin Reinke, Chief Executive Officer

Type of Firm
Bank Affiliated

Association Membership
German Venture Capital Association (BVK)

Project Preferences

Type of Financing Preferred:
Early Stage
Seed
Startup

Size of Investments Considered:
Min Size of Investment Considered (000s): $169
Max Size of Investment Considered (000s): $1,353

Geographical Preferences

International Preferences:
Germany

Industry Preferences

In Communications prefer:
Communications and Media

In Biotechnology prefer:
Biotechnology

In Medical/Health prefer:
Medical/Health
Pharmaceuticals

In Industrial/Energy prefer:
Industrial Products
Materials
Machinery

Additional Information
Year Founded: 1997
Current Activity Level : Actively seeking new investments

SAASTR FUND

555 Bryant Street, Suite 928
Palo Alto, CA USA 94301
Phone: 6507205650
Website: www.saastrfund.com

Management and Staff
Gretchen DeKnikker, Chief Operating Officer

Type of Firm
Private Equity Firm

Project Preferences

Type of Financing Preferred:
Seed

Additional Information
Year Founded: 2016
Capital Under Management: $68,220,000
Current Activity Level : Actively seeking new investments

SABADELL CAPITAL

Sena, 12, Pol. Ind.
Can Sant Joan
Barcelona, Spain 08008
Phone: 34937281200
E-mail: InvestorRelations@bancsabadell.com

Type of Firm
Bank Affiliated

Association Membership
Spanish Venture Capital Association (ASCRI)

Project Preferences

Type of Financing Preferred:
Leveraged Buyout
Expansion
Generalist PE
Later Stage
Acquisition

Size of Investments Considered:
Min Size of Investment Considered (000s): $13,153
Max Size of Investment Considered (000s): $65,734

Industry Preferences

In Industrial/Energy prefer:
Energy

Additional Information

Name of Most Recent Fund: Aurica XXI SCR SA
Most Recent Fund Was Raised: 09/20/2000
Year Founded: 2000
Capital Under Management: $149,700,000
Current Activity Level : Actively seeking new investments

SABAN CAPITAL GROUP INC

10100 Santa Monica Boulevard
Los Angeles, CA USA 90067
Phone: 3105575100
Website: www.saban.com

Other Offices

Saban Capital Group (Asia) Pte Ltd.
Singapore, Singapore

Kreab Gavin Anderson
, Hong Kong
Phone: 852 2218 9910

Management and Staff

Adam Chesnoff, President & COO
Adam Weene, Managing Director
Joel Andryc, Managing Director
Richard Yen, Managing Director

Type of Firm

Private Equity Firm

Project Preferences

Role in Financing:
Will function either as deal originator or investor in deals created by others

Type of Financing Preferred:
Leveraged Buyout
Early Stage
Expansion
Generalist PE
Management Buyouts
Acquisition

Geographical Preferences

United States Preferences:

International Preferences:
China
Asia

Industry Preferences

In Communications prefer:
Communications and Media
Telecommunications
Wireless Communications
Media and Entertainment

In Internet Specific prefer:
E-Commerce Technology
Internet
Ecommerce

In Business Serv. prefer:
Media

Additional Information

Year Founded: 2001
Capital Under Management: $100,000,000
Current Activity Level : Actively seeking new investments

SABRE PARTNERS INDIA ADVISORS PVT LTD

86 Free Press House
Nariman Point
Mumbai, India 400 021
Phone: 912266178800
Fax: 912266178888
E-mail: info@sabre-partners.com
Website: www.sabre-partners.com

Management and Staff

Sukesh Khandelwal, Chief Financial Officer

Type of Firm

Private Equity Firm

Project Preferences

Type of Financing Preferred:
Leveraged Buyout
Early Stage
Expansion
Later Stage

Geographical Preferences

International Preferences:
Asia Pacific
India

Industry Preferences

In Biotechnology prefer:
Biotechnology

In Medical/Health prefer:
Health Services
Pharmaceuticals

In Financial Services prefer:
Real Estate

Additional Information

Year Founded: 2002
Current Activity Level : Actively seeking new investments

SABVEST LTD

39 Rivonia Road
Four Commerce Square
Sandhurst, South Africa
Phone: 27-11-268-2400
Fax: 27-11-268-2422
E-mail: ho@sabvest.com
Website: www.sabvest.co.za

Management and Staff

Christopher Seabrooke, Chief Executive Officer
Raymond Pleaner, Chief Financial Officer

Type of Firm

Private Equity Firm

Project Preferences

Type of Financing Preferred:
Balanced

Geographical Preferences

International Preferences:
No Preference
South Africa

Additional Information

Year Founded: 1998
Current Activity Level : Actively seeking new investments

SACHS CAPITAL LLC

10516 Tulip Lane
Potomac, MD USA 20854
Phone: 3016107603
Fax: 3016107608
E-mail: info@sachscapital.com
Website: www.sachscapital.com

Type of Firm

Private Equity Firm

Project Preferences

Type of Financing Preferred:
Leveraged Buyout

Size of Investments Considered:
Min Size of Investment Considered (000s): $3,000
Max Size of Investment Considered (000s): $10,000

Pratt's Guide to Private Equity & Venture Capital Sources

Geographical Preferences

United States Preferences:
Mid Atlantic

Additional Information
Name of Most Recent Fund: Sachs Capital Fund I LLC
Most Recent Fund Was Raised: 07/12/2007
Year Founded: 2007
Capital Under Management: $3,000,000
Current Activity Level : Actively seeking new investments

SAENTIS CAPITAL INVESTMENT AG

Hintere Oberdorfstrasse 17
Herisau, Switzerland 9100
Phone: 41713527240
Fax: 41713527244
Website: www.saentis-investment.ch

Management and Staff
Torsten Petersen, Chief Executive Officer

Type of Firm
Private Equity Firm

Project Preferences

Type of Financing Preferred:
Mezzanine
Later Stage

Geographical Preferences

United States Preferences:
All U.S.

International Preferences:
Liechtenstein
Switzerland
Austria
Germany

Additional Information
Year Founded: 2000
Current Activity Level : Actively seeking new investments

SAFANAD INC

500 Fifth Avenue
38th Floor
New York, NY USA 10110
Website: safanad.com

Management and Staff
Ahmed Farid, President
Brett Owen, Vice President
Michael Kramer, Vice President
Mitchell Oh, Vice President
Vincent Pica, Managing Partner
Ziad Dannaoui, Managing Director

Type of Firm
Investment Management Firm

Project Preferences

Type of Financing Preferred:
Generalist PE

Industry Preferences

In Financial Services prefer:
Real Estate

Additional Information
Year Founded: 2009
Current Activity Level : Actively seeking new investments

SAFEGUARD SCIENTIFICS INC

70 North Radnor-Chester Road, Suite 200
Wayne, PA USA 19087
Phone: 6102930600
Fax: 6102930601
Website: www.safeguard.com

Management and Staff
Brian Sisko, Chief Operating Officer
Wei Zhang, Principal

Type of Firm
Corporate PE/Venture

Association Membership
National Venture Capital Association - USA (NVCA)

Project Preferences

Role in Financing:
Will function either as deal originator or investor in deals created by others

Type of Financing Preferred:
Leveraged Buyout
Early Stage
Expansion
Generalist PE
Balanced
Later Stage
Management Buyouts
Recapitalizations

Geographical Preferences

United States Preferences:

Industry Focus
(% based on actual investment)

Industry	%
Computer Software and Services	32.2%
Internet Specific	31.4%
Medical/Health	15.8%
Biotechnology	11.1%
Communications and Media	5.4%
Other Products	2.7%
Semiconductors/Other Elect.	0.7%
Computer Hardware	0.7%

Additional Information
Name of Most Recent Fund: Eastern Technology Fund
Most Recent Fund Was Raised: 08/17/2000
Year Founded: 1953
Capital Under Management: $420,000,000
Current Activity Level : Actively seeking new investments
Method of Compensation: Return on invest. most important, but chg. closing fees, service fees, etc.

SAFFELBERG INVESTMENTS SA

Oplombeekstraat Six
Gooik, Belgium 1755
Phone: 3227932550
Fax: 3227932559
Website: www.saffelberg.com

Type of Firm
Private Equity Firm

Project Preferences

Type of Financing Preferred:
Leveraged Buyout
Early Stage
Mezzanine
Later Stage
Management Buyouts
Acquisition

Geographical Preferences

International Preferences:
Europe
Belgium

Industry Preferences

In Medical/Health prefer:
Pharmaceuticals

In Industrial/Energy prefer:
Industrial Products

Additional Information
Year Founded: 2007
Current Activity Level : Actively seeking new investments

SAGACITY VENTURES SAS

11, rue Eugene Labiche
Paris, France 75116

Type of Firm
Private Equity Firm

Project Preferences

Type of Financing Preferred:
Early Stage
Expansion
Later Stage

Geographical Preferences

International Preferences:
Europe
France

Industry Preferences

In Internet Specific prefer:
Internet
Ecommerce

In Financial Services prefer:
Financial Services

In Business Serv. prefer:
Media

Additional Information
Year Founded: 2015
Current Activity Level : Actively seeking new investments

SAGAMORE CAPITAL GROUP LLC

750 Lexington Avenue
15th Floor
New York, NY USA 10022
Phone: 2124466980
E-mail: info@sagamorecap.com
Website: www.sagamorecap.com

Management and Staff
David Brand, Managing Director
Eric Zahler, Managing Director

Type of Firm
Private Equity Firm

Project Preferences

Type of Financing Preferred:
Leveraged Buyout
Management Buyouts
Acquisition

Industry Preferences

In Semiconductor/Electr prefer:
Electronics

In Industrial/Energy prefer:
Industrial Products

In Business Serv. prefer:
Services

Additional Information
Year Founded: 2011
Current Activity Level : Actively seeking new investments

SAGARD SAS

24/32 Rue Jean Goujon
Paris, France 75008
Phone: 33153833000
Fax: 33153833030
E-mail: contact@sagard.com
Website: www.sagard.com

Management and Staff
Antoine Ernoult-Dairaine, Partner
Frederic Stolar, Co-Founder
Jocelyn Lefebvre, Co-Founder
Mariane Le Bourdiec, Chief Financial Officer
Rik Battey, Partner
Saik Paugam, Partner

Type of Firm
Private Equity Firm

Association Membership
French Venture Capital Association (AFIC)

Project Preferences

Type of Financing Preferred:
Leveraged Buyout
Generalist PE
Later Stage
Management Buyouts
Acquisition

Geographical Preferences

International Preferences:
Europe
Switzerland
Belgium
France

Additional Information
Year Founded: 2002
Capital Under Management: $424,130,000
Current Activity Level : Actively seeking new investments

SAGE ROAD CAPITAL

2121 Sage Road, Suite 325
Houston, TX USA 77056
Phone: 7133641400
Website: www.sagerc.com

Type of Firm
Private Equity Firm

Project Preferences

Type of Financing Preferred:
Leveraged Buyout
Acquisition

Geographical Preferences

United States Preferences:
Northwest

Industry Preferences

In Industrial/Energy prefer:
Energy
Oil and Gas Exploration

Additional Information
Year Founded: 2013
Capital Under Management: $74,500,000
Current Activity Level : Actively seeking new investments

SAGEVIEW CAPITAL LP

245 Lytton Avenue, Suite 250
Palo Alto, CA USA 94301
Phone: 6504735400
Fax: 6504735401
E-mail: Info@sageviewcapital.com
Website: www.sageviewcapital.com

Other Offices
55 Railroad Avenue
Greenwich, CT USA 06830
Phone: 203-625-4200
Fax: 203-625-4201

Management and Staff
Andrew Campelli, Principal
Andrew Korn, Principal
Dean Nelson, Partner
Dino Verardo, Chief Financial Officer
Edward Gilhuly, Managing Partner
Fredrik Sjodin, Principal
Jeffrey Klemens, Principal
Laura Sims, Principal
Sasank Chary, Principal
Scott Stuart, Managing Partner

Type of Firm
Private Equity Firm

Project Preferences

Type of Financing Preferred:
Leveraged Buyout
Public Companies
Acquisition

Geographical Preferences

United States Preferences:
North America

International Preferences:
Europe

Additional Information
Year Founded: 2005
Capital Under Management: $1,045,000,000
Current Activity Level : Actively seeking new investments

SAGIN CAPITAL & CONSULTING CO LTD

7-17 Aikei machi
Saga shi, Japan 840-0812
Phone: 81-95-229-7658
Fax: 81-95-229-8052
Website: www.sagin-capital.co.jp

Type of Firm
Private Equity Firm

Project Preferences

Type of Financing Preferred:
Balanced

Geographical Preferences

International Preferences:
Japan

Additional Information
Year Founded: 1991
Capital Under Management: $14,700,000
Current Activity Level : Actively seeking new investments

SAGRI DEVELOPMENT AB

Hovslagargatan 5 B
2nd Floor
Stockholm, Sweden 111 48
Phone: 46854504410
Fax: 4686784730

Type of Firm
Corporate PE/Venture

Project Preferences

Type of Financing Preferred:
Balanced

Geographical Preferences

International Preferences:
Sweden

Additional Information
Year Founded: 2006
Current Activity Level : Actively seeking new investments

SAHA FUND

No. 70, 2nd Floor, Grace Tower
Millers Road
Bangalore, India 560052
Website: www.sahafund.com

Type of Firm
Private Equity Firm

Project Preferences

Type of Financing Preferred:
Balanced

Geographical Preferences

International Preferences:
India

Industry Preferences

In Computer Software prefer:
Software

In Internet Specific prefer:
Internet
Ecommerce

In Medical/Health prefer:
Health Services

In Consumer Related prefer:
Food/Beverage
Education Related

Additional Information
Year Founded: 2013
Current Activity Level : Actively seeking new investments

SAIC VENTURE CAPITAL CORPORATION

7455 West Washington Avenue, Suite 290
Las Vegas, NV USA 89128
Phone: 7023288495
Fax: 7028395630
E-mail: lauren.a.presti@saic.com

Type of Firm
Corporate PE/Venture

Project Preferences

Type of Financing Preferred:
Balanced

Geographical Preferences

United States Preferences:
All U.S.

Industry Preferences

In Communications prefer:
Telecommunications

In Internet Specific prefer:
Internet

Additional Information
Year Founded: 2000
Current Activity Level : Actively seeking new investments

SAIF PARTNERS

Suites 2516-2520
2 Pacific Place, 88 Queensway
Hong Kong, Hong Kong
Phone: 85229182200
Fax: 85222349116
E-mail: info@sbaif.com
Website: www.sbaif.com

Other Offices

DBS Business Center
Raheja Chambers, 213, Nariman Point
Mumbai, India 400021

6A, Jianguomenwai Avenue
Twr C, Central Int'l Trade Ct
Beijing, China 100022
Phone: 861065630202
Fax: 861065630252

No.1, Haier Road
Haier Industrial Park
Qingdao, China

Shanghai Hong Qiao State Guest Hotel
1591 Hong Qiao Road, Villa +16
Shanghai, China
Phone: 86-21-6295-2768
Fax: 86-21-6295-2783

5F, 1 Labs Ctr, Plot No. 18
Software Units Layout, Madhapu
Hyderabad, India 500081
Phone: 91-98-6646-1770
Fax: 91-22-6645-9581

Time Tower, MG Road
Unit 511, 5th Floor
Gurgaon, India 122002
Phone: 91-98-6646-1770
Fax: 91-22-6645-9581

C/O One97 Communications (P) Limited
1st Floor, Devika Tower, Nehru Place
New Delhi, India 110 019
Phone: 91-98-1019-4624

Management and Staff

Alma Ge, Vice President
Andrew Yan, Managing Partner
Annie Li, Chief Financial Officer
Ben Ng, Partner
Brandon Lin, Partner
Chris Jin, Principal
D.C. Lee, Venture Partner
Daniel Yang, Partner
Flora Zhao, Vice President
Hang Xu, Partner
Hao Lu, Venture Partner
Janson Law, Chief Financial Officer
Jason So, Partner
Joanna Li, Vice President
Jun Ye, Venture Partner

Ken Tucker, Managing Director
Kenneth Lee, Principal
Lynda Lau, Principal
Scott Cai, Vice President
Sherman Sheng, Vice President
Song Ge, Venture Partner
Stanley Wang, Vice President
Xiaohua Qian, Venture Partner
Yeung Heung Yeung, Venture Partner
Yong Hong Xu, Venture Partner
Yudan Jin, Partner

Type of Firm
Private Equity Firm

Association Membership
China Venture Capital Association

Project Preferences

Type of Financing Preferred:
Early Stage
Expansion
Balanced
Later Stage
Seed
Startup

Size of Investments Considered:
Min Size of Investment Considered (000s): $10,000
Max Size of Investment Considered (000s): $100,000

Geographical Preferences

International Preferences:
India
Taiwan
Hong Kong
China

Industry Preferences

In Communications prefer:
Telecommunications
Wireless Communications

In Internet Specific prefer:
Internet

In Medical/Health prefer:
Medical/Health

In Consumer Related prefer:
Consumer
Entertainment and Leisure
Consumer Products
Consumer Services
Education Related

In Industrial/Energy prefer:
Industrial Products

In Financial Services prefer:
Financial Services
Financial Services

In Manufact. prefer:
Manufacturing

In Agr/Forestr/Fish prefer:
Agriculture related

In Other prefer:
Environment Responsible

Additional Information
Year Founded: 2001
Capital Under Management: $3,500,000,000
Current Activity Level: Actively seeking new investments

SAIGON FUND MANAGEMENT JSC

172 Hai Ba Trung Street
12th Floor, TMS Building
Ho Chi Minh, Vietnam
Phone: 84854043488
Fax: 84854043487
E-mail: info@saigonam.com
Website: www.saigoncapital.com.vn

Management and Staff
Peter Dinning, Senior Managing Director

Type of Firm
Investment Management Firm

Project Preferences

Type of Financing Preferred:
Public Companies
Later Stage

Geographical Preferences

International Preferences:
Vietnam

Additional Information
Year Founded: 2007
Current Activity Level: Actively seeking new investments

SAIL CAPITAL PARTNERS LLC

3161 Michelson Drive, Suite 750
Irvine, CA USA 92612
Phone: 9493985100
Fax: 9493985101
E-mail: info@sailvc.com
Website: www.sailcapital.com

Other Offices
1441 Canal Street, Suite 324
NEW ORLEANS, LA USA 70112
Phone: 5045985244

79 Wellington Street West
21st Floor
Toronto, Canada M5K1B7

30 Rockefeller Plaza, Suite 3108
NEW YORK, NY USA 10112
Phone: 917-612-2620

Management and Staff
Chris Rhoades, Partner
Chuck Swanson, Chief Financial Officer
F. Henry Habicht, Managing Partner
F. Henry Habicht, Managing Partner
John Elstrott, Partner
Louis Freeman, Partner
Marcia Bateson, Chief Financial Officer
Michael Hammons, Partner
Michael Hammons, Partner
Peter Polydor, Vice President
R. Foster Duncan, Managing Partner
Walter Schindler, Managing Director

Type of Firm
Private Equity Firm

Project Preferences

Role in Financing:
Prefer role as deal originator

Type of Financing Preferred:
Early Stage
Expansion
Balanced
Later Stage

Geographical Preferences

United States Preferences:
Louisiana

Canadian Preferences:
Ontario

Industry Preferences

In Consumer Related prefer:
Food/Beverage

In Industrial/Energy prefer:
Energy
Alternative Energy
Energy Conservation Relat
Environmental Related

In Other prefer:
Environment Responsible

Additional Information
Name of Most Recent Fund: SAIL Sustainable Louisiana II
Most Recent Fund Was Raised: 09/12/2012
Year Founded: 2002
Capital Under Management: $200,000,000
Current Activity Level: Actively seeking new investments

SAINTS VENTURES

2020 Union Street
San Francisco, CA USA 94123
Phone: 4157732080
Fax: 4158355970
E-mail: info@saintscapital.com
Website: www.saintscapital.com

Other Offices

23 Berkeley Square
Palladium
London, United Kingdom W1J 6HE
Phone: 44-20-7993-6852

Management and Staff

Amar Senan, Managing Director
David Quinlivan, Managing Director
Ghia Griarte, Managing Director
Joseph Yang, Venture Partner
Kenneth Sawyer, Managing Director
Marc Friend, Venture Partner
Mike Boggs, Vice President
Mike Callaghan, Venture Partner
Neal Hansch, Principal
Pete Peterson, Vice President
Robert Keppler, Chief Financial Officer
Robert Simon, Venture Partner
Scott Halsted, Managing Director

Type of Firm

Private Equity Firm

Project Preferences

Role in Financing:
Will function either as deal originator or investor in deals created by others

Type of Financing Preferred:
Leveraged Buyout
Early Stage
Generalist PE
Later Stage
Fund of Funds of Second

Geographical Preferences

United States Preferences:
All U.S.

Industry Preferences

In Communications prefer:
Wireless Communications

In Computer Software prefer:
Software
Systems Software

In Internet Specific prefer:
Internet
Ecommerce

In Medical/Health prefer:
Medical/Health

In Business Serv. prefer:
Services

Additional Information

Name of Most Recent Fund: Saints Capital V, L.P.
Most Recent Fund Was Raised: 09/12/2005
Year Founded: 2000
Capital Under Management: $707,000,000
Current Activity Level : Actively seeking new investments

SAKORNINVEST NORD AS

Sjogata 15/17
Postboks 521
Bodo, Norway 8001
Phone: 47-9260-5601
Fax: 47-7556-0056
Website: www.sinas.no

Management and Staff

Kristin Ingebrigtsen, Chief Executive Officer

Type of Firm

Private Equity Firm

Project Preferences

Type of Financing Preferred:
Seed
Startup

Geographical Preferences

International Preferences:
Norway

Additional Information

Year Founded: 1999
Capital Under Management: $13,600,000
Current Activity Level : Actively seeking new investments

SALEM CAPITAL PARTNERS, LP (FKA: VENTURE CAPITAL SOLUTIONS)

112 Cambridge Plaza Drive
Winston-Salem, NC USA 27104
Phone: 3367689343
Fax: 3367686471
E-mail: inquiry@salemcapital.com

Other Offices

600 Paces Summit
2410 Paces Ferry Road
Atlanta, GA USA 30339
Phone: 770-805-2320
Fax: 770-805-2185

Management and Staff

Kevin Jessup, Principal
Phillip Martin, Principal
W. Spalding White, Principal

Type of Firm

Private Equity Firm

Association Membership

Natl Assoc of Small Bus. Inv. Co (NASBIC)

Project Preferences

Type of Financing Preferred:
Leveraged Buyout
Early Stage
Expansion
Mezzanine
Management Buyouts
Acquisition
Recapitalizations

Size of Investments Considered:
Min Size of Investment Considered (000s): $750
Max Size of Investment Considered (000s): $2,000

Geographical Preferences

United States Preferences:
Tennessee
Southeast
Alabama
North Carolina
South Carolina
Maryland
Virginia
Florida
Georgia

Industry Preferences

In Business Serv. prefer:
Services
Distribution

In Manufact. prefer:
Manufacturing

Additional Information

Name of Most Recent Fund: Salem Investment Partners III, L.P.
Most Recent Fund Was Raised: 06/19/2012
Year Founded: 1999
Capital Under Management: $40,000,000
Current Activity Level : Actively seeking new investments

SALEM PARTNERS LLC

11111 Santa Monica Boulevard, Suite 2250
Los Angeles, CA USA 90025
Website: www.salempartners.com

Management and Staff

John Dyett, Founder
Stephen Prough, Founder

Type of Firm

Investment Management Firm

Project Preferences

Type of Financing Preferred:
Early Stage
Expansion
Later Stage

Additional Information

Year Founded: 1997
Current Activity Level : Actively seeking new investments

SALIX VENTURES LP

23 Bancroft Place
Nashville, TN USA 37215
Phone: 6156651409
Fax: 6156652912
Website: www.salixventures.com

Management and Staff
Christopher Grant, Co-Founder
David Ward, Co-Founder

Type of Firm
Private Equity Firm

Project Preferences

Role in Financing:
Will function either as deal originator or investor in deals created by others

Type of Financing Preferred:
Early Stage
Expansion
Later Stage

Size of Investments Considered:
Min Size of Investment Considered (000s): $5,000
Max Size of Investment Considered (000s): $7,000

Geographical Preferences

United States Preferences:

Industry Focus

(% based on actual investment)
Medical/Health	60.9%
Computer Software and Services	15.8%
Internet Specific	8.2%
Biotechnology	3.9%
Consumer Related	3.4%
Computer Hardware	3.2%
Other Products	2.3%
Communications and Media	2.3%

Additional Information
Name of Most Recent Fund: Salix Ventures II, L.P.
Most Recent Fund Was Raised: 04/03/2000
Year Founded: 1997
Capital Under Management: $190,000,000
Current Activity Level : Reducing investment activity
Method of Compensation: Return on investment is of primary concern, do not charge fees

SALKANTAY PARTNERS SAC

Torre Real 6, Suite 606, San Isidro
Lima, Peru
Phone: 6508046100
E-mail: info@salkap.com
Website: www.salkantaypartners.com

Management and Staff
Guillermo Miro Quesada, Managing Director
Luis Fernando Miranda, Managing Director
Martin Aspillaga, Managing Director

Type of Firm
Private Equity Firm

Project Preferences

Type of Financing Preferred:
Leveraged Buyout
Expansion
Management Buyouts
Acquisition

Geographical Preferences

International Preferences:
Latin America
Peru

Industry Preferences

In Communications prefer:
Entertainment

In Medical/Health prefer:
Health Services

In Consumer Related prefer:
Consumer
Retail
Education Related

In Industrial/Energy prefer:
Industrial Products

In Financial Services prefer:
Real Estate

Additional Information
Year Founded: 2012
Current Activity Level : Actively seeking new investments

SALMON RIVER CAPITAL LLC

126 East 56th Street
25th Floor
New York, NY USA 10022
Phone: 6462918831
Website: www.salmonrivercapital.com

Management and Staff
Joshua Lewis, Founder

Type of Firm
Private Equity Firm

Project Preferences

Type of Financing Preferred:
Balanced

Industry Preferences

In Computer Software prefer:
Software
Applications Software

In Consumer Related prefer:
Education Related

In Financial Services prefer:
Financial Services

Additional Information
Name of Most Recent Fund: Salmon River Capital II, L.P.
Most Recent Fund Was Raised: 10/20/2005
Year Founded: 2005
Capital Under Management: $20,000,000
Current Activity Level : Actively seeking new investments

SALT CREEK CAPITAL MANAGEMENT LLC

1001 O'Brien Drive
Menlo Park, CA USA 94025
E-mail: info@saltcreekcap.com
Website: www.saltcreekcap.com

Management and Staff
Dan Mytels, Managing Director
Daniel Phelps, Founder

Type of Firm
Private Equity Firm

Project Preferences

Type of Financing Preferred:
Leveraged Buyout
Expansion
Management Buyouts
Acquisition
Recapitalizations

Geographical Preferences

United States Preferences:

Industry Preferences

In Consumer Related prefer:
Franchises(NEC)
Consumer Services

In Industrial/Energy prefer:
Energy

In Financial Services prefer:
Financial Services

In Business Serv. prefer:
Services
Distribution

In Manufact. prefer:
Manufacturing

Additional Information
Year Founded: 2009
Current Activity Level : Actively seeking new investments

SALVEO CAPITAL

180 North LaSalle Street, Suite 3700
Chicago, IL USA 60601
Phone: 3129810991
Website: www.salveocap.com

Type of Firm
Private Equity Firm

Project Preferences

Type of Financing Preferred:
Early Stage

Geographical Preferences

United States Preferences:

Industry Preferences

In Computer Software prefer:
Software

In Medical/Health prefer:
Medical Therapeutics
Medical Products

Additional Information
Year Founded: 2015
Capital Under Management: $1,690,000
Current Activity Level : Actively seeking new investments

SALZBURGER UNTERNEH-MENSBETEILIGUNGS-GE-SELLSCHAFT MBH IN LIQU

Julius-Raab-Platz 1
Salzburg, Austria 5027
Phone: 436628888556
Fax: 436628888678
E-mail: office@subg-skgg.at
Website: www.subg-skgg.at

Management and Staff
Guido Piekarz, Managing Director
Manfred Werndl, Managing Director

Type of Firm
Private Equity Firm

Project Preferences

Type of Financing Preferred:
Early Stage
Later Stage
Seed
Startup

Size of Investments Considered:
Min Size of Investment Considered (000s): $109
Max Size of Investment Considered (000s): $1,088

Geographical Preferences

International Preferences:
Austria

Industry Preferences

In Consumer Related prefer:
Consumer
Entertainment and Leisure

In Industrial/Energy prefer:
Industrial Products

In Transportation prefer:
Transportation

Additional Information
Year Founded: 1999
Capital Under Management: $5,300,000
Current Activity Level : Actively seeking new investments

SAM PRIVATE EQUITY AG

Josefstrasse 218
Zurich, Switzerland 8005
Phone: 41446531010
Fax: 41446531080
E-mail: info@robecosam.com
Website: www.robecosam.com

Other Offices
909 Third Avenue
New York, NY USA 10022
Phone: 2129089768
Fax: 9176799950

Management and Staff
Michael Baldinger, Chief Executive Officer
Stefan Gordijn, Chief Operating Officer

Type of Firm
Private Equity Firm

Project Preferences

Type of Financing Preferred:
Fund of Funds
Generalist PE
Fund of Funds of Second

Geographical Preferences

United States Preferences:
All U.S.

International Preferences:
Europe
Pacific

Industry Preferences

In Industrial/Energy prefer:
Alternative Energy
Environmental Related

Additional Information
Year Founded: 1995
Current Activity Level : Actively seeking new investments

SAMA FUND LLC

1500 Market Street
12th Floor, East Tower
Philadelphia, PA USA 19102
Phone: 2672462046

Type of Firm
Private Equity Firm

Project Preferences

Type of Financing Preferred:
Balanced

Additional Information
Year Founded: 2010
Current Activity Level : Actively seeking new investments

SAMAIPATA VENTURES

18 Velazquez Street
2 Izquierda
Madrid, Spain 28001
Phone: 914346544
Website: samaipataventures.com

Type of Firm
Private Equity Firm

Geographical Preferences

International Preferences:
Europe

Industry Preferences

In Internet Specific prefer:
Ecommerce

Additional Information
Year Founded: 1969
Current Activity Level : Actively seeking new investments

SAMARA CAPITAL MANAGEMENT LTD

135, 13th Fl,215 Nariman Point
Free Press House
Mumbai, India 400 021
Phone: 912222886661
E-mail: info@samaracapital.com
Website: www.samaracapital.com

Other Offices

International Financial Services Ltd
IFS Court Twenty Eight Cybercity
Ebene, Mauritius
Phone: 230 467 3000

Eros Corporate Tower, 15th Floor
Nehru Place
New Delhi , India 110 019
Phone: 91-11-4223-5091

Management and Staff

Gautam Gode, Managing Director
Sanjay Bhargava, Managing Director
Sumeet Narang, Managing Partner

Type of Firm

Private Equity Firm

Project Preferences

Type of Financing Preferred:
Leveraged Buyout
Balanced
Acquisition

Geographical Preferences

International Preferences:
India
Asia

Industry Preferences

In Communications prefer:
Telecommunications

In Medical/Health prefer:
Medical/Health
Health Services
Pharmaceuticals

In Consumer Related prefer:
Retail
Consumer Products
Consumer Services

In Financial Services prefer:
Financial Services
Financial Services

In Manufact. prefer:
Manufacturing

Additional Information

Year Founded: 2006
Capital Under Management: $125,125,000
Current Activity Level : Actively seeking new investments

SAMBRINVEST SA

Av Georges Lemaitre 62
Aeropole
Gosselies, Belgium 6041
Phone: 3271259494
Fax: 3271259499
E-mail: sambrinvest@sambrinvest.be
Website: www.sambrinvest.be

Management and Staff

Michel Marlot, President

Type of Firm

Private Equity Firm

Association Membership

Belgium Venturing Association

Project Preferences

Type of Financing Preferred:
Early Stage
Mezzanine
Balanced
Start-up Financing
Later Stage
Seed

Geographical Preferences

International Preferences:
Belgium

Industry Preferences

In Computer Software prefer:
Software

In Computer Other prefer:
Computer Related

In Biotechnology prefer:
Biotechnology

In Consumer Related prefer:
Retail

In Industrial/Energy prefer:
Factory Automation

In Transportation prefer:
Transportation

In Business Serv. prefer:
Services

In Other prefer:
Environment Responsible

Additional Information

Year Founded: 1985
Capital Under Management: $5,000,000
Current Activity Level : Actively seeking new investments

SAMENA CAPITAL MANAGEMENT LLP

21-22 Grosvenor Street
London, United Kingdom W1K4QJ
Phone: 442073197600
Fax: 442073197699
E-mail: info@samenacapital.com
Website: www.samenacapital.com

Other Offices

8, Queen's Road Central
Hong Kong, Hong Kong
Phone: 85235836000
Fax: 85235719400

14th Floor, South Tower
Emirates Financial Towers,DIFC
Dubai, Utd. Arab Em.
Phone: 97144364900
Fax: 97144364901

Management and Staff

Manoj Kulkarni, Vice President
Mudit Bali, Vice President
Peter Litvin, Chief Financial Officer
Philip Young, Vice President
Ramiz Hasan, Co-Founder
Roshan Banka, Vice President
Shirish Saraf, Chief Executive Officer
Simon Wong, Co-Founder

Type of Firm

Private Equity Firm

Project Preferences

Type of Financing Preferred:
Leveraged Buyout
Early Stage
Expansion
Generalist PE
Balanced
Public Companies
Later Stage
Acquisition
Private Placement

Geographical Preferences

International Preferences:
Asia Pacific
Bahrain
United Kingdom
Europe
Hong Kong
Middle East
Asia
Africa

Industry Preferences

In Industrial/Energy prefer:
Oil & Gas Drilling,Explor

In Transportation prefer:
Transportation

In Agr/Forestr/Fish prefer:
Agriculture related

Additional Information

Year Founded: 2008
Capital Under Management: $1,000,000,000
Current Activity Level : Actively seeking new investments

SAMOS INVESTMENTS ADVISORY LTD

22 Charing Cross Road
London, United Kingdom WC2H 0HS
Phone: 442076322520
E-mail: contact@samos.uk.com
Website: www.samos.uk.com

Type of Firm
Private Equity Firm

Project Preferences

Type of Financing Preferred:
Leveraged Buyout
Early Stage
Expansion
Balanced
Management Buyouts
Acquisition

Geographical Preferences

International Preferences:
United Kingdom
Europe

Industry Preferences

In Internet Specific prefer:
Ecommerce

In Biotechnology prefer:
Human Biotechnology

In Consumer Related prefer:
Retail

In Industrial/Energy prefer:
Energy
Environmental Related

In Financial Services prefer:
Financial Services

In Business Serv. prefer:
Media

Additional Information
Year Founded: 2008
Current Activity Level : Actively seeking new investments

SAMSARA BIOCAPITAL LP

565 Everett Avenue
Palo Alto, CA USA 94301

Management and Staff
Srinivas Akkaraju, General Partner

Type of Firm
Private Equity Firm

Project Preferences

Type of Financing Preferred:
Balanced

Additional Information
Year Founded: 2017
Current Activity Level : Actively seeking new investments

SAMSUNG VENTURE INVESTMENT CORP

Seocho 2 dong, Seocho-gu
29F,Samsung Electronics seocho
Seoul, South Korea 132010
Phone: 8222550299
Website: www.samsungventure.co.kr

Other Offices
85 West Tasman Drive
San Jose, CA USA 95134
Phone: 408-544-4470
Fax: 409-544-4976

Type of Firm
Corporate PE/Venture

Association Membership
Korean Venture Capital Association (KVCA)

Project Preferences

Role in Financing:
Will function either as deal originator or investor in deals created by others

Type of Financing Preferred:
Balanced

Geographical Preferences

United States Preferences:

International Preferences:
Korea, South

Industry Preferences

In Communications prefer:
Communications and Media
Telecommunications
Wireless Communications
Media and Entertainment
Entertainment

In Computer Software prefer:
Software

In Internet Specific prefer:
Internet

In Semiconductor/Electr prefer:
Electronics
Semiconductor

In Biotechnology prefer:
Biotechnology

In Medical/Health prefer:
Medical Products

Additional Information
Year Founded: 1999
Capital Under Management: $452,000,000
Current Activity Level : Actively seeking new investments
Method of Compensation: Return on investment is of primary concern, do not charge fees

SAMURAI INCUBATE INC

2-2-28, Higashishinagawa
2F Samurai Startup Island
Tokyo, Japan 1400002
Website: www.samurai-incubate.asia

Management and Staff
Hayato Ikegami, Chief Operating Officer
Kentaro Sakakibara, Chief Executive Officer

Type of Firm
Incubator/Development Program

Project Preferences

Type of Financing Preferred:
Early Stage
Seed
Startup

Geographical Preferences

United States Preferences:

International Preferences:
Europe
Israel
Japan

Industry Preferences

In Communications prefer:
Commercial Communications

In Computer Software prefer:
Software

In Internet Specific prefer:
E-Commerce Technology

In Computer Other prefer:
Computer Related

In Business Serv. prefer:
Services

Additional Information
Year Founded: 2008
Capital Under Management: $8,046,000
Current Activity Level : Actively seeking new investments

SAN FRANCISCO EQUITY PARTNERS LP

50 California Street, Suite 1320
San Francisco, CA USA 94111
Phone: 4157381200
Fax: 4152961162
E-mail: info@sfequitypartners.com
Website: www.sfequitypartners.com

Management and Staff
Chris Sargent, Vice President
David Mannix, Vice President
Julie Bell, Partner

Type of Firm
Private Equity Firm

Project Preferences

Type of Financing Preferred:
Leveraged Buyout
Generalist PE
Later Stage
Recapitalizations

Size of Investments Considered:
Min Size of Investment Considered (000s): $10,000
Max Size of Investment Considered (000s): $20,000

Industry Preferences

In Medical/Health prefer:
Medical/Health

In Consumer Related prefer:
Consumer
Retail
Food/Beverage

Additional Information
Name of Most Recent Fund: San Francisco Equity Partners III, L.P.
Most Recent Fund Was Raised: 02/02/2011
Year Founded: 2005
Capital Under Management: $80,000,000
Current Activity Level : Actively seeking new investments

SAN JOAQUIN CAPITAL LLC

1155 W Sahw Avenue, Suite 102
Fresno, CA USA 93711

Management and Staff
Eric Hanson, Co-Founder
Eric Nasalroad, Co-Founder
Tim Goetz, Co-Founder

Type of Firm
Private Equity Firm

Project Preferences

Type of Financing Preferred:
Early Stage
Expansion
Later Stage

Additional Information
Year Founded: 2015
Capital Under Management: $4,000,000
Current Activity Level : Actively seeking new investments

SAN SHAN CAPITAL PARTNERS LTD

Cheung Kong Centre
Central, Hong Kong

Management and Staff
John Thornton, Venture Partner
Zhimin Wen, Vice President

Type of Firm
Private Equity Firm

Additional Information
Year Founded: 2008
Current Activity Level : Actively seeking new investments

SAND HILL GROUP LLC

3450 Sacramento Street, Suite 615
San Francisco, CA USA 94118
Phone: 4159229802
Fax: 4159229806
Website: www.sandhill.com

Management and Staff
Constantin Delivanis, Co-Founder
M.R. Rangaswami, Co-Founder

Type of Firm
Private Equity Firm

Project Preferences

Type of Financing Preferred:
Early Stage
Balanced
Startup

Additional Information
Year Founded: 2005
Current Activity Level : Actively seeking new investments

SAND OAK CAPITAL PARTNERS LLC

900 Third Avenue
33rd Floor
New York, NY USA 10022
Phone: 2123173340
E-mail: info@sandoak.com
Website: www.sandoak.com

Management and Staff
Jeffrey Mizrahi, Partner
Jeremy Schwimmer, Partner

Type of Firm
Private Equity Firm

Project Preferences

Type of Financing Preferred:
Leveraged Buyout
Turnaround
Acquisition
Recapitalizations

Industry Preferences

In Medical/Health prefer:
Drug/Equipmt Delivery

In Consumer Related prefer:
Consumer Products

In Industrial/Energy prefer:
Materials
Superconductivity
Process Control
Machinery
Environmental Related

In Transportation prefer:
Aerospace

In Agr/Forestr/Fish prefer:
Mining and Minerals

Additional Information
Year Founded: 2009
Current Activity Level : Actively seeking new investments

SANDBOX & CO LTD

WeWork South Bank
22 Upper Ground
London, United Kingdom SE1 9PD
E-mail: hello@sandboxandco.com
Website: www.sandboxandco.com

Management and Staff
Abhi Arya, Partner
Miki Chojnacka, Partner

Type of Firm
Private Equity Firm

Project Preferences

Type of Financing Preferred:
Leveraged Buyout
Acquisition

Additional Information
Year Founded: 2014
Current Activity Level : Actively seeking new investments

SANDBOX INDUSTRIES LLC

213 North Racine Avenue, Suite 102
Chicago, IL USA 60607
Phone: 3122434100
Fax: 3122434110
E-mail: info@sandboxindustries.com
Website: www.sandboxindustries.com

Management and Staff

Anna Haghgooie, Managing Director
Bob Shapiro, Managing Director
Drew Turitz, Managing Director
Matthew Downs, Managing Director
Millie Tadewaldt, Managing Director
Nick Rosa, Managing Director
Nina Nashif, Managing Director
Paul Brown, Managing Director
Steve Engelberg, Managing Director
Tom Hawes, Managing Director

Type of Firm

Private Equity Firm

Association Membership

Illinois Venture Capital Association

Project Preferences

Type of Financing Preferred:
Early Stage
Balanced
Seed
Startup

Size of Investments Considered:
Min Size of Investment Considered (000s): $25
Max Size of Investment Considered (000s): $15,000

Geographical Preferences

United States Preferences:
Michigan

Industry Preferences

In Agr/Forestr/Fish prefer:
Agribusiness

Additional Information

Name of Most Recent Fund: Cultivian Sandbox Food & Agriculture Fund II, L.P.
Most Recent Fund Was Raised: 06/18/2013
Year Founded: 2003
Capital Under Management: $355,000,000
Current Activity Level : Actively seeking new investments

SANDBRIDGE CAPITAL LLC

725 Fifth Avenue
23rd Floor
New York, NY USA 10022
Phone: 2122927870
E-mail: info@sandbridgecap.com
Website: sandbridgecap.com

Management and Staff

David Fife, Managing Partner
Jeff Palmese, Principal
Richard Henry, Vice President

Type of Firm

Private Equity Firm

Project Preferences

Type of Financing Preferred:
Leveraged Buyout
Management Buyouts
Acquisition

Industry Preferences

In Consumer Related prefer:
Consumer
Retail
Food/Beverage
Consumer Products
Consumer Services

Additional Information

Year Founded: 2013
Capital Under Management: $30,775,000
Current Activity Level : Actively seeking new investments

SANDERLING VENTURES

400 South El Camino Real, Suite 1200
San Mateo, CA USA 94402
Phone: 6504012000
Fax: 6503757077
E-mail: info@sanderling.com
Website: www.sanderling.com

Management and Staff

Fred Middleton, Managing Director
Paulette Taylor, Principal
Peter McWilliams, Managing Director
Robert McNeil, Founder
Timothy Wollaeger, Managing Director
Timothy Mills, Managing Director

Type of Firm

Private Equity Firm

Association Membership

National Venture Capital Association - USA (NVCA)

Project Preferences

Role in Financing:
Prefer role as deal originator but will also invest in deals created by others

Type of Financing Preferred:
Early Stage
Balanced
Later Stage
Seed
Startup

Geographical Preferences

United States Preferences:
West Coast

Canadian Preferences:
All Canada

Industry Focus

(% based on actual investment)
Medical/Health	51.4%
Biotechnology	41.8%
Industrial/Energy	3.0%
Computer Software and Services	1.8%
Internet Specific	1.0%
Communications and Media	0.4%
Semiconductors/Other Elect.	0.3%
Other Products	0.2%
Computer Hardware	0.1%
Consumer Related	0.0%

Additional Information

Name of Most Recent Fund: Sanderling Ventures VII, L.P.
Most Recent Fund Was Raised: 09/05/2013
Year Founded: 1979
Capital Under Management: $1,005,000,000
Current Activity Level : Actively seeking new investments
Method of Compensation: Return on invest. most important, but chg. closing fees, service fees, etc.

SANDLEIGH VENTURES LLC

9433 Bee Caves Road Building 3, Suite 101--A
Austin, TX USA 78733
Phone: 5122632423
Fax: 5128709438
Website: www.sandleighventures.com

Management and Staff

Lorne Abony, Partner
Russell Geyser, Partner

Type of Firm

Private Equity Firm

Project Preferences

Type of Financing Preferred:
Balanced

Additional Information

Year Founded: 1969
Current Activity Level : Actively seeking new investments

SANDLER CAPITAL MANAGEMENT

711 Fifth Avenue, 15th Floor
New York, NY USA 10022
Phone: 2127548100
Fax: 2128260280
Website: www.sandlercap.com

Management and Staff
Adi Dehejia, Managing Director
Farah Khan, Vice President
John Tinker, Managing Director
Michael Tully, Vice President
Michael Marocco, Managing Director
William Bianco, Managing Director

Type of Firm
Private Equity Firm

Project Preferences

Role in Financing:
Prefer role as deal originator but will also invest in deals created by others

Type of Financing Preferred:
Leveraged Buyout
Expansion
Mezzanine
Acquisition

Industry Focus
(% based on actual investment)
Internet Specific	46.5%
Communications and Media	38.1%
Computer Software and Services	5.9%
Other Products	4.5%
Consumer Related	1.8%
Medical/Health	1.7%
Semiconductors/Other Elect.	1.4%

Additional Information
Year Founded: 1980
Capital Under Management: $1,500,000,000
Current Activity Level: Actively seeking new investments
Method of Compensation: Return on investment is of primary concern, do not charge fees

---

SANDPIPER DIGITAL PAYMENTS AG

Dufourstrasse 121
St. Gallen, Switzerland 9001
Phone: 41447838030
Fax: 41447838040
E-mail: contact@super-angel.ch
Website: www.sandpiper.ch

Management and Staff
Alexander Schuemperli, Chief Operating Officer
Cornelius Boersch, President
Manfred Rietzler, Vice President

Type of Firm
Angel Group

Project Preferences

Type of Financing Preferred:
Leveraged Buyout
Early Stage
Later Stage
Seed
Special Situation
Distressed Debt
Recapitalizations

Size of Investments Considered:
Min Size of Investment Considered (000s): $142
Max Size of Investment Considered (000s): $1,418

Geographical Preferences

International Preferences:
Switzerland
Austria
Germany

Industry Preferences

In Communications prefer:
Communications and Media
Telecommunications
Media and Entertainment
Entertainment

In Internet Specific prefer:
Internet

In Medical/Health prefer:
Medical/Health

Additional Information
Year Founded: 2007
Capital Under Management: $55,500,000
Current Activity Level: Actively seeking new investments

SANDS CAPITAL MANAGEMENT LLC

1000 Wilson Blvd, Suite 3000
Arlington, VA USA 22209
Phone: 7035624000
Fax: 7035624006
Website: sandscapital.com

Management and Staff
David Kluger, Managing Director
David Levanson, Managing Director
Michael Hotchkiss, Managing Director
Robert Hancock, Chief Operating Officer
Sharon Kedar, Managing Director
Thomas Ricketts, Managing Director

Type of Firm
Investment Management Firm

Project Preferences

Type of Financing Preferred:
Expansion
Balanced

Industry Preferences

In Biotechnology prefer:
Biotechnology

In Medical/Health prefer:
Medical/Health
Health Services

Additional Information
Year Founded: 1992
Capital Under Management: $167,445,000
Current Activity Level: Actively seeking new investments

SANDTON CAPITAL LP

25 West 45th Street, Suite 1205
New York, NY USA 10036
Phone: 2124447200
Website: www.sandtoncapital.com

Type of Firm
Private Equity Firm

Project Preferences

Type of Financing Preferred:
Turnaround
Special Situation
Distressed Debt
Recapitalizations

Geographical Preferences

United States Preferences:

International Preferences:
Europe

Additional Information
Year Founded: 2009
Current Activity Level: Actively seeking new investments

SANDWITH VENTURES LLC

3612 Webster Street
San Francisco, CA USA 94123
Phone: 4152187940
Fax: 4152762340
Website: www.sandwithventures.com

Other Offices
2101 Market Street, Suite 2106
Philadelphia, PA USA 19103

Management and Staff
Colin Evans, Managing Partner

Type of Firm
Private Equity Firm

Project Preferences

Type of Financing Preferred:
Early Stage
Seed

Geographical Preferences

United States Preferences:
Pennsylvania
California
East Coast

Industry Preferences

In Internet Specific prefer:
E-Commerce Technology
Internet

In Consumer Related prefer:
Consumer
Retail

Additional Information
Year Founded: 2007
Current Activity Level : Actively seeking new investments

SANED EQUITY PARTNERS LTD

Sofil Center Block C,
9th Floor, Charles Malek Avenue
Beirut, Lebanon
Phone: 9611201773
Fax: 9611216533
E-mail: info@sanedpartners.com
Website: sanedpartners.com

Other Offices
Sofil Center Block C,
9th Floor, Charles Malek Avenue
Beirut, Lebanon
Phone: 9611201773
Fax: 9611216533

Management and Staff
George Salhab, Partner
Mu taz Sawwaf, Partner
Talal Idriss, Partner
Walid Attieh, Partner

Type of Firm
Private Equity Firm

Project Preferences

Type of Financing Preferred:
Early Stage
Later Stage

Geographical Preferences

International Preferences:
Jordan
Lebanon
Utd. Arab Em.
Middle East
Africa

Industry Preferences

In Communications prefer:
Telecommunications

In Consumer Related prefer:
Food/Beverage
Consumer Services

In Business Serv. prefer:
Media

In Manufact. prefer:
Manufacturing

Additional Information
Year Founded: 2014
Capital Under Management: $7,500,000
Current Activity Level : Actively seeking new investments

SANGAMON INDUSTRIES LLC

520 Lake Cook Road, Suite 375
Deerfield, IL USA 60015
Phone: 847-374-9140
Fax: 847-347-9150
Website: www.sangamonindustries.com

Management and Staff
Mark Essig, Chief Executive Officer

Type of Firm
Private Equity Firm

Project Preferences

Type of Financing Preferred:
Management Buyouts
Distressed Debt
Recapitalizations

Geographical Preferences

United States Preferences:
All U.S.

Industry Preferences

In Business Serv. prefer:
Distribution

In Manufact. prefer:
Manufacturing

Additional Information
Year Founded: 2009
Current Activity Level : Actively seeking new investments

SANGO CAPITAL MANAGEMENT

One Monte Casino Boulevard
Block E, The Pivot
Johannesburg, South Africa
Website: www.sangocapitalmanagement.com

Type of Firm
Private Equity Advisor or Fund of Funds

Association Membership
African Venture Capital Association (AVCA)

Project Preferences

Type of Financing Preferred:
Fund of Funds

Geographical Preferences

International Preferences:
South Africa
Africa

Additional Information
Name of Most Recent Fund: Sango Capital Partners, L.P.
Most Recent Fund Was Raised: 11/05/2012
Year Founded: 2012
Capital Under Management: $109,500,000
Current Activity Level : Actively seeking new investments

SANLAM PRIVATE EQUITY

Two Strand Road
Bellville, South Africa 2196
Phone: 27117786613
Fax: 27117786651
E-mail: intouch@spe.sanlam.com
Website: www.sanlam.co.za

Management and Staff
Alton Solomons, Chief Executive Officer
Raymond Simao, Principal
Rene Schutte, Principal

Type of Firm
Private Equity Firm

Association Membership
South African Venture Capital Association (SAVCA)

Project Preferences

Type of Financing Preferred:
Fund of Funds
Leveraged Buyout
Expansion
Mezzanine
Generalist PE
Balanced
Later Stage
Other

Geographical Preferences

International Preferences:
South Africa
Africa

Industry Preferences

In Industrial/Energy prefer:
Alternative Energy

In Agr/Forestr/Fish prefer:
Agribusiness
Agriculture related

Additional Information

Year Founded: 1996
Capital Under Management: $553,500,000
Current Activity Level : Actively seeking new investments

SANOFI-SUNRISE

640 Memorial Drive
Cambridge, MA USA 02139
Phone: 6176654516
Website: www.sanofi-sunrise.com

Management and Staff

Brian Bronk, Principal
Stuart Pollard, Vice President

Type of Firm

Private Equity Firm

Project Preferences

Type of Financing Preferred:
Early Stage

Industry Preferences

In Biotechnology prefer:
Biotechnology

In Medical/Health prefer:
Medical/Health
Medical Therapeutics

Additional Information

Year Founded: 2013
Current Activity Level : Actively seeking new investments

SANSEI CAPITAL INVESTMENT CO LTD

1-9-2, Honcho, Nihonbashi
Mitsui Life Nihonbashi Bldg
Tokyo, Japan 1030023
Phone: 81332720181
Fax: 81332720184
E-mail: info@sanseicapital.com
Website: www.sanseicapital.com

Type of Firm

Private Equity Firm

Association Membership

Japan Venture Capital Association

Project Preferences

Type of Financing Preferred:
Balanced

Geographical Preferences

International Preferences:
Japan

Additional Information

Year Founded: 1991
Capital Under Management: $27,400,000
Current Activity Level : Actively seeking new investments

SANTE VENTURES

401 Congress Avenue, Suite 2950, Frost Bank Tower
Austin, TX USA 78701
Phone: 5127211200
Website: santeventures.com

Other Offices

6500 Main Street, Suite 1010
HOUSTON, TX USA 77030
Phone: 7139041782

Management and Staff

Billy Cohn, Venture Partner
Douglas French, Co-Founder
James Eadie, Principal
Jim Graham, Principal
Joe Cunningham, Co-Founder
Kevin Lalande, Co-Founder
Steven Seach, Chief Operating Officer

Type of Firm

Private Equity Firm

Association Membership

National Venture Capital Association - USA (NVCA)

Project Preferences

Type of Financing Preferred:
Early Stage
Later Stage
Seed

Size of Investments Considered:
Min Size of Investment Considered (000s): $2,000
Max Size of Investment Considered (000s): $12,000

Geographical Preferences

United States Preferences:

Industry Preferences

In Medical/Health prefer:
Medical/Health
Medical Products
Health Services

Additional Information

Name of Most Recent Fund: Sante Health Ventures II, L.P.
Most Recent Fund Was Raised: 03/14/2011
Year Founded: 2006
Capital Under Management: $260,000,000
Current Activity Level : Actively seeking new investments

SAPHIR CAPITAL PARTNERS SA

35a, Avenue John F. Kennedy
Luxembourg, Luxembourg L-1855
Phone: 352278438
E-mail: contact@saphircapitalpartners.com
Website: www.saphircapitalpartners.com

Other Offices

1512A Ocean Centre
223-231 Canton Road
Tsimshatsui, Hong Kong

42 Brook Street
London, United Kingdom W1K 5DB
Phone: 442034276364

Management and Staff

Maxime Ray, Principal
Raffaele Levi-Minzi, Principal

Type of Firm

Private Equity Firm

Project Preferences

Type of Financing Preferred:
Leveraged Buyout
Acquisition

Geographical Preferences

International Preferences:
Europe
France

Industry Preferences

In Consumer Related prefer:
Retail
Consumer Products
Consumer Services

Additional Information

Year Founded: 2010
Current Activity Level : Actively seeking new investments

SAPIENT CAPITAL MANAGEMENT LLC

4020 Lake Creek Drive
P.O. Box 1590
Wilson, WY USA 83014
Phone: 3077333806
Fax: 3077334630
E-mail: contact@sapientcapital.com
Website: www.sapientcapital.com

Management and Staff

Mitchell Dann, Principal

Type of Firm

Private Equity Firm

Project Preferences

Role in Financing:
Will function either as deal originator or investor in deals created by others

Type of Financing Preferred:
Early Stage
Balanced
Seed
Startup

Size of Investments Considered:
Min Size of Investment Considered (000s): $2,000
Max Size of Investment Considered (000s): $3,000

Geographical Preferences

United States Preferences:

Industry Preferences

In Medical/Health prefer:
Medical/Health
Medical Products

Additional Information

Year Founded: 2000
Capital Under Management: $26,000,000
Current Activity Level : Actively seeking new investments
Method of Compensation: Return on investment is of primary concern, do not charge fees

SAPIENVENTURES LLP

One Farrer Place
Level 23, Governor Phillip Tow
Sydney, Australia 2000
Phone: 61280911847
E-mail: hello@sapienventures.vc
Website: www.sapienventures.vc

Type of Firm

Private Equity Firm

Project Preferences

Type of Financing Preferred:
Early Stage

Geographical Preferences

International Preferences:
Australia

Industry Preferences

In Computer Software prefer:
Software

Additional Information

Year Founded: 2015
Current Activity Level : Actively seeking new investments

SAPLING FUND LP

8917 South Old State Road, Suite 106
Lewis Center, OH USA 43035
Website: www.saplingfund.com

Type of Firm

Private Equity Firm

Project Preferences

Type of Financing Preferred:
Early Stage

Additional Information

Year Founded: 2014
Capital Under Management: $50,000,000
Current Activity Level : Actively seeking new investments

SAPPHIRE CAPITAL PARTNERS LLP

34 South Molton Street
London, United Kingdom W1K 5RG
Phone: 4408000545070
Website: www.sapphirecapitalpartners.co.uk

Type of Firm

Investment Management Firm

Additional Information

Year Founded: 2016
Current Activity Level : Actively seeking new investments

SAPPHIRE VENTURES LLC

3408 Hillview Avenue
Building Five
Palo Alto, CA USA 94304
Phone: 6508493950
E-mail: info@sapphireventures.com
Website: sapphireventures.com

Management and Staff

Anders Ranum, Venture Partner
Andreas Weiskam, Managing Director
Anthony Matusich, Chief Financial Officer
David Hartwig, Managing Director
Doug Higgins, Managing Director
Elizabeth Clarkson, Managing Director
Gaurav Tewari, Managing Director
Jai Das, Managing Director
Kevin Diestel, Principal
Kevin Diestal, Vice President
Nino Marakovic, CEO & Managing Director
Rajeev Dham, Vice President
Rami Branitzky, Managing Director
Steve Abbott, Managing Director
Steven Abbott, Managing Director
Winter Mead, Vice President

Type of Firm

Private Equity Firm

Association Membership

National Venture Capital Association - USA (NVCA)

Project Preferences

Role in Financing:
Prefer role as deal originator but will also invest in deals created by others

Type of Financing Preferred:
Fund of Funds
Early Stage
Expansion
Balanced
Later Stage
Startup

Size of Investments Considered:
Min Size of Investment Considered (000s): $5,000
Max Size of Investment Considered (000s): $20,000

Geographical Preferences

United States Preferences:
All U.S.

International Preferences:
India
Europe
China
Brazil

Industry Preferences

In Communications prefer:
Data Communications

In Computer Software prefer:
Software

Additional Information

Year Founded: 1996
Capital Under Management: $1,400,000,000
Current Activity Level : Actively seeking new investments

SAPPORO HOKUYO LEASE CO LTD

3/F Hokuyo Sapporo South Bldg.
8 West 3 South 2, Chuo-ku
Sapporo-shi, Japan 060-0062
Phone: 81-11-231-7135
Website: www.shls.co.jp

Management and Staff
Toshihiko Aoyama, President

Type of Firm
Private Equity Firm

Additional Information
Year Founded: 2006
Current Activity Level : Actively seeking new investments

SARATOGA INVESTAMA SEDAYA TBK PT

Jl. H.R. Rasuna Said Block X-5
Kav. 1-2, Menara Karya, 15th F
Jakarta, Indonesia 12950
Phone: 622157944355
Fax: 622157944365
E-mail: info@saratoga-investama.com
Website: www.saratoga-investama.com

Other Offices
Jl. H.R. Rasuna Said Block X-5 Kav. 1-2
Menara Karya, 15th Floor
Jakarta, Indonesia 12950
Phone: 622157944355
Fax: 622157944365

Management and Staff
Michael William P. Soeryadjaya, President

Type of Firm
Private Equity Firm

Project Preferences

Type of Financing Preferred:
Early Stage
Expansion
Acquisition
Special Situation

Geographical Preferences

International Preferences:
Indonesia

Industry Preferences

In Consumer Related prefer:
Consumer

In Industrial/Energy prefer:
Environmental Related

Additional Information
Year Founded: 1992
Current Activity Level : Actively seeking new investments

SARATOGA PARTNERS LP

535 Madison Avenue
4th Floor
New York, NY USA 10022
Phone: 2129067800
Fax: 2127503343
E-mail: saratoga@saratogapartners.com
Website: www.saratogapartners.com

Management and Staff
Richard Petrocelli, Managing Director

Type of Firm
Private Equity Firm

Project Preferences

Type of Financing Preferred:
Leveraged Buyout
Turnaround
Acquisition
Special Situation
Distressed Debt
Recapitalizations

Geographical Preferences

United States Preferences:

Industry Focus
(% based on actual investment)
Communications and Media	34.5%
Other Products	34.2%
Industrial/Energy	16.8%
Consumer Related	10.8%
Medical/Health	3.8%

Additional Information
Name of Most Recent Fund: Saratoga Partners IV, L.P.
Most Recent Fund Was Raised: 09/01/1999
Year Founded: 1984
Current Activity Level : Actively seeking new investments

SARATOGA VENTURES, L.P.

5201 Great America Parkway, Suite 3302
Santa Clara, CA USA 95054
Phone: 6508151942
Fax: 4087163142
Website: www.saratogavc.com

Management and Staff
Gwen Watanabe, General Partner
Richard Ferrari, Founder

Type of Firm
Private Equity Firm

Project Preferences

Role in Financing:
Prefer role in deals created by others

Type of Financing Preferred:
Early Stage
Seed

Size of Investments Considered:
Min Size of Investment Considered (000s): $100
Max Size of Investment Considered (000s): $1,000

Industry Preferences

In Medical/Health prefer:
Medical Products

Additional Information
Name of Most Recent Fund: Saratoga Ventures VI, L.P.
Most Recent Fund Was Raised: 03/27/2007
Year Founded: 1997
Capital Under Management: $18,500,000
Current Activity Level : Actively seeking new investments
Method of Compensation: Return on invest. most important, but chg. closing fees, service fees, etc.

SARONA ASSET MANAGEMENT INC

110 Frobisher Drive
1B
Waterloo, Canada N2V 2G7
Phone: 5198837557
E-mail: sarona@saronafund.com
Website: www.saronafund.com

Management and Staff
Amie McPhee, Chief Financial Officer
Serge LeVert-Chiasson, Chief Operating Officer

Type of Firm
Investment Management Firm

Association Membership
Emerging Markets Private Equity Association

Project Preferences

Type of Financing Preferred:
Fund of Funds
Early Stage
Fund of Funds of Second

Geographical Preferences

International Preferences:
India
Mexico
Brazil
Cameroon

Industry Preferences

In Medical/Health prefer:
Medical/Health

In Industrial/Energy prefer:
Energy
Environmental Related

In Financial Services prefer:
Real Estate

In Agr/Forestr/Fish prefer:
Agribusiness

In Other prefer:
Environment Responsible

Additional Information
Name of Most Recent Fund: Sarona Frontier Markets U.S. Fund 2 L.P.
Most Recent Fund Was Raised: 07/08/2013
Year Founded: 2009
Capital Under Management: $180,375,000
Current Activity Level : Actively seeking new investments

SARSIA SEED MANAGEMENT AS

Thormohlensgate 51
Vitensenteret, Marineholmen, 2/F
Bergen, Norway 5006
Phone: 4755595949
Fax: 4755595948
E-mail: contact@sarsiaseed.com
Website: www.sarsiaseed.com

Management and Staff
Erlend Skagseth, Partner
Farzad Abdi-Dezfuli, Partner
Jon Berg, Partner
Oivind Enger, Partner
Sveinung Hole, Managing Partner

Type of Firm
Private Equity Firm

Association Membership
Norwegian Venture Capital Association

Project Preferences

Type of Financing Preferred:
Early Stage
Startup

Size of Investments Considered:
Min Size of Investment Considered (000s): $168
Max Size of Investment Considered (000s): $841

Geographical Preferences

International Preferences:
Norway

Industry Preferences

In Biotechnology prefer:
Biotechnology

In Industrial/Energy prefer:
Oil and Gas Exploration
Alternative Energy

Additional Information
Year Founded: 2007
Capital Under Management: $59,100,000
Current Activity Level : Actively seeking new investments

SASFIN PRIVATE EQUITY FUND MANAGERS PTY LTD

29 Scott Street
Waverley, South Africa 2090
Phone: 27-11-809-7500
E-mail: info@sasfin.com
Website: www.sasfin.co.za

Type of Firm
Private Equity Firm

Association Membership
South African Venture Capital Association (SAVCA)

Project Preferences

Type of Financing Preferred:
Leveraged Buyout
Early Stage
Expansion
Management Buyouts
Acquisition

Size of Investments Considered:
Min Size of Investment Considered (000s): $511
Max Size of Investment Considered (000s): $5,113

Geographical Preferences

International Preferences:
South Africa
Africa

Additional Information
Year Founded: 2005
Current Activity Level : Actively seeking new investments

SASKATCHEWAN OPPORTUNITIES CORP

114-15 Innovation Boulevard
Saskatoon, Canada S7N 2X8
Phone: 306-933-6295
Fax: 306-933-8215
E-mail: saskatoon@innovationplace.com
Website: www.soco.sk.ca

Management and Staff
Austin Beggs, Vice President
Lorne Vinish, Vice President

Type of Firm
Government Affiliated Program

Additional Information
Year Founded: 1994
Current Activity Level : Actively seeking new investments

SATOR SPA

Via G. Carissimi, 41
Rome, Italy 00198
Phone: 396858291
Fax: 390685829301
E-mail: info@satorgroup.com
Website: www.satorgroup.it

Management and Staff
Matteo Arpe, Chief Executive Officer

Type of Firm
Investment Management Firm

Project Preferences

Type of Financing Preferred:
Leveraged Buyout

Geographical Preferences

International Preferences:
Italy
Europe

Industry Preferences

In Industrial/Energy prefer:
Industrial Products

In Financial Services prefer:
Financial Services
Real Estate

Additional Information
Year Founded: 2007
Current Activity Level : Actively seeking new investments

SATORI CAPITAL LLC

2501 North Harwood Street
20th Floor
Dallas, TX USA 75201
Phone: 8889728674
E-mail: investorrelations@satoricapital.com
Website: www.satoricapital.com

Other Offices
2821 West Seventh Street, Suite 525
Fort Worth, TX USA 76107

Management and Staff

Christiana Wyly, Venture Partner
Jon Gard, Vice President
Randall Hunt, Vice President
Randy Eisenman, Co-Founder
Rugger Burke, Principal
Sunny Vanderbeck, Co-Founder

Type of Firm

Private Equity Firm

Project Preferences

Type of Financing Preferred:
Leveraged Buyout
Acquisition

Geographical Preferences

United States Preferences:
Colorado
Southwest
Texas

Industry Preferences

In Communications prefer:
Telecommunications

In Computer Software prefer:
Software

In Internet Specific prefer:
Ecommerce

In Medical/Health prefer:
Medical Products

In Consumer Related prefer:
Consumer Products

In Financial Services prefer:
Financial Services

In Business Serv. prefer:
Services

In Manufact. prefer:
Manufacturing

Additional Information

Name of Most Recent Fund: Satori Capital Strategic Opportunities, L.P.
Most Recent Fund Was Raised: 05/14/2012
Year Founded: 2008
Capital Under Management: $279,367,000
Current Activity Level : Actively seeking new investments

SATURN MANAGEMENT LLC

75 Federal Street, Suite 1320
Boston, MA USA 02110
Phone: 6175743330
Fax: 6175743331
Website: www.saturnpartnersvc.com

Management and Staff

Edward Lafferty, Chief Financial Officer
Robert Chicoski, Partner
Susan Antonio, Partner
William Guttman, Partner

Type of Firm

Private Equity Firm

Association Membership

New England Venture Capital Association

Project Preferences

Type of Financing Preferred:
Early Stage

Geographical Preferences

United States Preferences:

Industry Preferences

In Biotechnology prefer:
Biotechnology

In Financial Services prefer:
Financial Services

Additional Information

Year Founded: 1994
Current Activity Level : Actively seeking new investments

SATYA CAPITAL LTD

35 Portman Square
London, United Kingdom W1H 6LR
Phone: 442075355080
Fax: 442075355081
E-mail: info@satyacapital.com

Management and Staff

Elom Lassey, Principal
Jide Olanrewaju, Partner
Justin Abbott, Managing Partner
Matthew Hodgkinson, Principal
Moez Daya, Managing Partner
Nick Levi-Gardes, Principal
Tsega Gebreyes, Managing Partner

Type of Firm

Private Equity Firm

Project Preferences

Type of Financing Preferred:
Expansion
Later Stage

Geographical Preferences

International Preferences:
South Africa
Africa

Industry Preferences

In Communications prefer:
Telecommunications

In Medical/Health prefer:
Medical/Health

In Consumer Related prefer:
Consumer Products

In Financial Services prefer:
Financial Services

In Business Serv. prefer:
Services
Media

In Manufact. prefer:
Manufacturing

Additional Information

Year Founded: 2009
Capital Under Management: $30,000,000
Current Activity Level : Actively seeking new investments

SAUDI ARABIAN INVESTMENT CO

Abraj Tower, 11Th Floor,
King Fahed Street, Al Olaya
Riyadh, Saudi Arabia
Phone: 966112180044
Fax: 966112181313
Website: www.sanabil.com

Type of Firm

Private Equity Firm

Project Preferences

Type of Financing Preferred:
Leveraged Buyout
Balanced
Management Buyouts

Geographical Preferences

International Preferences:
Africa

Industry Preferences

In Communications prefer:
Telecommunications
Data Communications

In Consumer Related prefer:
Consumer Services
Education Related

In Industrial/Energy prefer:
Industrial Products
Materials

In Financial Services prefer:
Financial Services

In Other prefer:
Environment Responsible

Additional Information
Year Founded: 2009
Current Activity Level : Actively seeking new investments

SAUDI TECHNOLOGY DEVELOPMENT AND INVESTMENT CO

Olaya Street,
P.O. Box 87211
Riyadh, Saudi Arabia 11642
Phone: 966112211111
Fax: 966112681111
Website: www.taqnia.com

Type of Firm
Government Affiliated Program

Project Preferences

Type of Financing Preferred:
Early Stage
Startup

Geographical Preferences

United States Preferences:

International Preferences:
Europe
Middle East
Saudi Arabia

Additional Information
Year Founded: 2011
Current Activity Level : Actively seeking new investments

SAUGATUCK CAPITAL CO

187 Danbury Road
Wilton, CT USA 06897
Phone: 2033486669
Fax: 2033246995
E-mail: saugatuck@saugatuckcapital.com
Website: www.saugatuckcapital.com

Management and Staff
Frank Hawley, Founder
Gary Goldberg, Managing Director
Joseph Solari, Managing Director
Stuart Hawley, Managing Director
Thomas Berardino, Managing Director

Type of Firm
Investment Management Firm

Project Preferences

Role in Financing:
Prefer role as deal originator

Type of Financing Preferred:
Leveraged Buyout
Expansion
Management Buyouts
Acquisition
Recapitalizations

Industry Focus
(% based on actual investment)
Other Products	33.9%
Medical/Health	16.7%
Consumer Related	14.8%
Communications and Media	11.4%
Industrial/Energy	9.0%
Semiconductors/Other Elect.	6.1%
Computer Hardware	3.8%
Computer Software and Services	2.8%
Internet Specific	1.4%

Additional Information
Year Founded: 1982
Capital Under Management: $125,000,000
Current Activity Level : Actively seeking new investments
Method of Compensation: Return on invest. most important, but chg. closing fees, service fees, etc.

SAVVIS INC

One Savvis Parkway
Town & Country
Chesterfield, MO USA 63017
Phone: 3146287000
Fax: 3147192499
Website: www.centurylinktechnology.com

Management and Staff
Brian Klingbeil, Chief Operating Officer
Daniel Patton, Vice President
Jeffrey Von Deylen, President
Mark Smith, Managing Director
Neil Cresswell, Managing Director

Type of Firm
Corporate PE/Venture

Additional Information
Year Founded: 2002
Current Activity Level : Actively seeking new investments

SAW MILL CAPITAL LLC

555 Pleasantville Road
South Building, Suite 220
Briarcliff Manor, NY USA 10510
Phone: 9147411300
Fax: 9147419099
E-mail: info@sawmillcapital.com
Website: www.sawmillcapital.com

Management and Staff
Blinn Cirella, Chief Financial Officer
Howard Unger, Managing Partner
J. Peter Coyne, Vice President
Jason Mueller, Vice President
John Shaia, Partner
Scott Budoff, Partner
Scott Rivard, Principal
Timothy Nelson, Principal
William Gerstner, Partner

Type of Firm
Private Equity Firm

Project Preferences

Role in Financing:
Prefer role as deal originator but will also invest in deals created by others

Type of Financing Preferred:
Leveraged Buyout
Acquisition

Size of Investments Considered:
Min Size of Investment Considered (000s): $10,000
Max Size of Investment Considered (000s): $75,000

Geographical Preferences

United States Preferences:
North America

Industry Focus
(% based on actual investment)
Other Products	64.7%
Industrial/Energy	35.3%

Additional Information
Name of Most Recent Fund: Saw Mill Capital Partners, L.P.
Most Recent Fund Was Raised: 12/22/2006
Year Founded: 1997
Capital Under Management: $325,000,000
Current Activity Level : Actively seeking new investments
Method of Compensation: Return on invest. most important, but chg. closing fees, service fees, etc.

SAWARI VENTURES LLC

One Dr. Mohamed Sobhy St, Giza, Suite Nine
Cairo, Egypt 00202
Phone: 2020235701802
Fax: 202035734496
E-mail: info@sawariventures.com
Website: www.sawariventures.com

Other Offices
5505 Connecticut Ave, NW # 260
Washington, DC USA 20015
Phone: 202-370-7807
Fax: 202-204-6344

Management and Staff
Hany Al Sonbaty, Managing Partner
Leslie Jump, Partner

Type of Firm
Private Equity Firm

Project Preferences

Type of Financing Preferred:
Early Stage
Balanced
Later Stage

Size of Investments Considered:
Min Size of Investment Considered (000s): $250
Max Size of Investment Considered (000s): $5,000

Geographical Preferences

International Preferences:
Middle East
Africa

Industry Preferences

In Communications prefer:
Telecommunications

In Computer Software prefer:
Software

In Internet Specific prefer:
E-Commerce Technology

In Financial Services prefer:
Financial Services

In Business Serv. prefer:
Media

Additional Information
Year Founded: 2010
Capital Under Management: $50,000,000
Current Activity Level : Actively seeking new investments

SAYBROOK CAPITAL LLC

11400 W. Olympic Boulevard, Suite 1400
Cheviot Hills, CA USA 90064
Phone: 3108999200
Fax: 3108999101

Other Offices

303 Twin Dolphin Drive, Suite 600
Redwood City, CA USA 94065
Phone: 6506324522
Fax: 6506324530

Former HQ: 401 Wilshire Boulevard, Suite 850
Santa Monica, CA USA 90401
Phone: 3108999200
Fax: 3108999101

Management and Staff
Brieanne Nikrandt, Vice President
Dan Hayes, Principal
Dave Rodriguez, Vice President
John O Hare, Managing Director
Jonathan Thomas, Partner
Leonard Dunn, Vice President
M. Leigh Austin, Principal
Scott Bayliss, Managing Director

Type of Firm
Investment Management Firm

Project Preferences

Type of Financing Preferred:
Leveraged Buyout
Turnaround
Distressed Debt
Recapitalizations

Geographical Preferences

United States Preferences:

Canadian Preferences:
All Canada

Additional Information
Name of Most Recent Fund: Saybrook Corporate Opportunity Fund II, L.P.
Most Recent Fund Was Raised: 09/27/2012
Year Founded: 1998
Capital Under Management: $100,690,000
Current Activity Level : Actively seeking new investments

SB CAPITAL PARTNERS LTD

Berkeley Square House
Berkeley Square
London, United Kingdom W1J 6BD
Phone: 4402071837183
Fax: 4402076385587
E-mail: ir@sbcappartners.com
Website: www.sbcapital-partners.com

Management and Staff
Gintas Karpavicius, Vice President
Jason Knox, Vice President
Sanjeet Bhavnani, Managing Director

Type of Firm
Private Equity Firm

Project Preferences

Type of Financing Preferred:
Leveraged Buyout
Acquisition
Recapitalizations

Geographical Preferences

United States Preferences:

Industry Preferences

In Consumer Related prefer:
Consumer Services

In Financial Services prefer:
Financial Services
Insurance
Real Estate

In Manufact. prefer:
Manufacturing

Additional Information
Year Founded: 2008
Current Activity Level : Actively seeking new investments

SBCVC FUND II L P

728 YanAn Road
15A-C, HuaMin Empire Plaza
Shanghai, China 200050
Phone: 862152534888
Fax: 862152400366
E-mail: contact@sbcvc.com

Management and Staff
Alan Song, Managing Partner
Chauncey Shey, President
Peter Hua, Managing Partner
Tim Liu, Managing Partner

Type of Firm
Private Equity Firm

Project Preferences

Type of Financing Preferred:
Early Stage
Expansion
Balanced
Later Stage
Seed

Size of Investments Considered:
Min Size of Investment Considered (000s): $500
Max Size of Investment Considered (000s): $10,000

Geographical Preferences

International Preferences:
China
Asia

Industry Preferences

In Communications prefer:
Telecommunications
Wireless Communications
Media and Entertainment

In Computer Software prefer:
Software

In Internet Specific prefer:
Internet

In Computer Other prefer:
Computer Related

In Medical/Health prefer:
Medical/Health
Pharmaceuticals

In Consumer Related prefer:
Consumer
Retail

1833

In Industrial/Energy prefer:
Energy
Alternative Energy
Materials
Advanced Materials
Environmental Related

In Business Serv. prefer:
Media

In Other prefer:
Environment Responsible

Additional Information
Year Founded: 2000
Capital Under Management: $94,207,000
Current Activity Level : Actively seeking new investments

SBG SAECHSISCHE BETEILIGUNGS-GESELLSCHAFT MBH

Pirnaische Strasse 9
Dresden, Germany 01069
Phone: 49035149105474
Fax: 49035149105489
E-mail: servicecenter@sbg.sachsen.de
Website: www.sbg.sachsen.de

Type of Firm
Bank Affiliated

Project Preferences

Type of Financing Preferred:
Mezzanine
Turnaround
Later Stage
Management Buyouts
Special Situation

Geographical Preferences

International Preferences:
Germany

Industry Preferences

In Communications prefer:
Telecommunications

In Semiconductor/Electr prefer:
Electronics

In Biotechnology prefer:
Biotechnology

In Industrial/Energy prefer:
Machinery

In Business Serv. prefer:
Services

In Manufact. prefer:
Manufacturing

Additional Information
Year Founded: 1997
Current Activity Level : Actively seeking new investments

SBI - BMI

Avenue de Tervueren 168
bte 9
Brussels, Belgium 1150
Phone: 3227760100
Fax: 3227706638
E-mail: info@bmi-sbi.be
Website: www.bmi-sbi.be

Management and Staff
Michel Van Hecke, President

Type of Firm
Private Equity Firm

Association Membership
Belgium Venturing Association

Project Preferences

Type of Financing Preferred:
Early Stage
Mezzanine
Later Stage

Size of Investments Considered:
Min Size of Investment Considered (000s): $668
Max Size of Investment Considered (000s): $3,338

Geographical Preferences

United States Preferences:
All U.S.

International Preferences:
Latin America
Europe
Western Europe
Eastern Europe
Asia
Africa

Industry Preferences

In Communications prefer:
Communications and Media

In Semiconductor/Electr prefer:
Electronics

In Biotechnology prefer:
Biotechnology

In Medical/Health prefer:
Medical/Health

In Consumer Related prefer:
Food/Beverage
Consumer Products
Consumer Services

In Industrial/Energy prefer:
Energy
Environmental Related

In Transportation prefer:
Transportation

In Manufact. prefer:
Manufacturing

In Agr/Forestr/Fish prefer:
Agriculture related

Additional Information
Year Founded: 1971
Current Activity Level : Actively seeking new investments

SBI CAPITAL VENTURES

202, Maker Tower E
Cuffe Parade
Mumbai, India 400 005
Phone: 912222178300
Fax: 912222188832
E-mail: corporate.office@sbicaps.com
Website: www.sbicaps.com

Other Offices
World Trade Tower
6th Floor, Barakhamba Lane
New Delhi, India 110 001
Phone: 91-11-2341-8460
Fax: 91-11-2341-8773

1, Middleton Street,
Jeevandeep Bldg., 9th floor,
Kolkata, India 700 071
Phone: 91-33-2288-6602
Fax: 91-33-2288-6608

Municipal No: 6-3-648/301,
III Floor, Somajiguda,
Hyderabad, India 500 482
Phone: 91-40-2332-1605
Fax: 91-40-2331-6800

Almas Centre, 6th Floor
87, M. G. Road,
Bangalore, India 560 001
Phone: 91-80-2558-5471
Fax: 91-80-2558-5478

Zodiac Avenue, 4th Floor,
Netaji Road
Ahmedabad, India 380 006
Phone: 91-79-2656-0122
Fax: 91-79-2656-5718

Circle Top House, Gr. Flr.,
Aparna Complex, 16, College Lane,
Chennai, India 600 006
Phone: 91-44-2821-3801
Fax: 91-44-2825-6244

Management and Staff
A. Verma, CEO & Managing Director
Rajeev Krishnan, President & COO
S. Vishvanathan, CEO & Managing Director

Type of Firm
Bank Affiliated

Project Preferences

Type of Financing Preferred:
Early Stage
Expansion
Balanced
Startup

Geographical Preferences

International Preferences:
India

Industry Preferences

In Biotechnology prefer:
Biotechnology

In Medical/Health prefer:
Pharmaceuticals

In Business Serv. prefer:
Services

In Manufact. prefer:
Manufacturing

Additional Information
Year Founded: 2006
Current Activity Level : Actively seeking new investments

SBI INVESTMENT CO LTD

1-6-1, Roppongi, Minato-ku
19F Izumi Garden Tower
Tokyo, Japan 105-0003
Phone: 81355012711
Fax: 81355012718
E-mail: info@sbinvestment.co.jp
Website: www.sbinvestment.co.jp

Management and Staff
Takashi Nakagawa, Chief Operating Officer
Yoshitaka Kitao, Chief Executive Officer

Type of Firm
Bank Affiliated

Project Preferences

Type of Financing Preferred:
Early Stage
Balanced
Later Stage
Seed

Geographical Preferences

International Preferences:
Taiwan
All International

Industry Preferences

In Communications prefer:
Communications and Media
Wireless Communications

In Internet Specific prefer:
Internet

In Biotechnology prefer:
Biotechnology

In Consumer Related prefer:
Food/Beverage

In Industrial/Energy prefer:
Energy
Environmental Related

In Business Serv. prefer:
Services
Media

Additional Information
Year Founded: 1996
Capital Under Management: $1,513,700,000
Current Activity Level : Actively seeking new investments

SBI INVESTMENT KOREA CO LTD

143-40, Samseong-Dong
3F, 15F, Hyundai Swiss Tower
Seoul, South Korea 135090
Phone: 82221399200
Fax: 82221126260
Website: www.sbik.co.kr

Other Offices
2180 Sand Hill Road, Suite 450
Menlo Park, CA USA 94025
Phone: 650-321-3899

Management and Staff
Seok Jin Yoo, Vice President
Yoshimi Takahashi, Chief Executive Officer

Type of Firm
Private Equity Firm

Association Membership
Korean Venture Capital Association (KVCA)

Project Preferences

Type of Financing Preferred:
Leveraged Buyout
Early Stage
Expansion
Balanced
Later Stage
Management Buyouts
Startup
Distressed Debt

Geographical Preferences

International Preferences:
Europe
Middle East
Asia
Korea, South

Industry Preferences

In Communications prefer:
Communications and Media
Telecommunications
Media and Entertainment

In Computer Hardware prefer:
Computers

In Semiconductor/Electr prefer:
Electronics

In Biotechnology prefer:
Biotechnology

In Medical/Health prefer:
Medical/Health

In Consumer Related prefer:
Entertainment and Leisure

In Industrial/Energy prefer:
Industrial Products

In Business Serv. prefer:
Services

In Manufact. prefer:
Manufacturing

Additional Information
Year Founded: 1986
Capital Under Management: $122,100,000
Current Activity Level : Actively seeking new investments

SBI VEN CAPITAL PTE LTD

No. 18-03 One Raffles Place
Singapore, Singapore 048616
Phone: 65-6536-6123
Fax: 65-6536-6983
E-mail: general@sbivencapital.com.sg
Website: www.sbivencapital.com.sg

Type of Firm
Private Equity Firm

Association Membership
Singapore Venture Capital Association (SVCA)

Project Preferences

Type of Financing Preferred:
Expansion
Balanced
Later Stage

Geographical Preferences

International Preferences:
Vietnam
Bangladesh
Indonesia
India
Taiwan
China
Cambodia
Philippines
Sri Lanka
Asia
Singapore

Industry Preferences

In Communications prefer:
Commercial Communications

In Internet Specific prefer:
Internet

In Biotechnology prefer:
Biotechnology

In Medical/Health prefer:
Health Services

In Consumer Related prefer:
Consumer
Education Related

In Industrial/Energy prefer:
Industrial Products
Environmental Related

In Financial Services prefer:
Financial Services

Additional Information
Year Founded: 2010
Capital Under Management: $60,000,000
Current Activity Level : Actively seeking new investments

SBT VENTURE CAPITAL

1 East Poultry Avenue
London, United Kingdom EC1A 9PT
Website: www.sbt-vc.com

Management and Staff
Matteo Rizzi, Partner
Mircea Mihaescu, Partner

Type of Firm
Bank Affiliated

Project Preferences

Type of Financing Preferred:
Early Stage
Later Stage
Startup

Geographical Preferences

United States Preferences:

International Preferences:
Western Europe
Russia

Industry Preferences

In Computer Software prefer:
Systems Software

In Financial Services prefer:
Financial Services

Additional Information
Year Founded: 2013
Current Activity Level : Actively seeking new investments

SC CAPITAL MANAGEMENT LLC

712 Fifeth Avenue
11th Floor
New York, NY USA 10019
Phone: 212-245-1719

Management and Staff
Srini Conjeevaram, Managing Director

Type of Firm
Private Equity Firm

Project Preferences

Type of Financing Preferred:
Balanced

Additional Information
Year Founded: 2008
Current Activity Level : Actively seeking new investments

SCALE CAPITAL APS

Carolinevej 2 A
Hellerup, Denmark 2900
Phone: 4570301101
Website: www.scalecapital.com

Management and Staff
Kenneth Grunow, Partner
Lars Jensen, Partner

Type of Firm
Private Equity Firm

Project Preferences

Type of Financing Preferred:
Early Stage

Geographical Preferences

International Preferences:
Denmark

Industry Preferences

In Communications prefer:
Communications and Media

In Computer Software prefer:
Software

In Internet Specific prefer:
E-Commerce Technology

Additional Information
Year Founded: 2013
Current Activity Level : Actively seeking new investments

SCALE UP VENTURE CAPITAL

20 Trevor Square
Knightsbridge
London, United Kingdom SW7 1DZ
E-mail: info@scale-up.vc
Website: www.scale-up.vc

Other Offices
2916 Ramona Street
Palo Alto, CA USA 94306
Phone: 6504600427

Type of Firm
Private Equity Firm

Project Preferences

Type of Financing Preferred:
Start-up Financing
Seed

Industry Preferences

In Computer Software prefer:
Software

Additional Information
Year Founded: 2015
Current Activity Level : Actively seeking new investments

SCALE VENTURE PARTNERS

950 Tower Lane, Suite 1150
Foster City, CA USA 94404
Phone: 6503786000
Fax: 6503786040
Website: www.scalevp.com

Management and Staff

Alexander Niehenke, Partner
Andy Vitus, Partner
Ariel Tseitlin, Partner
Benson Fu, Principal
Cack Wilhem, Principal
Dale Chang, Vice President
Eric Anderson, Principal
Jaime Lovejoy, Vice President
Katherine Mitchell, Co-Founder
Mark Brooks, Venture Partner
Mary Denten, Chief Financial Officer
Robert Herb, Venture Partner
Rory O Driscoll, Co-Founder
Sharon Wienbar, Venture Partner
Stacey Bishop, Partner
Susan Liu, Principal

Type of Firm
Private Equity Firm

Association Membership
Western Association of Venture Capitalists (WAVC)
National Venture Capital Association - USA (NVCA)

Project Preferences

Role in Financing:
Prefer role as deal originator

Type of Financing Preferred:
Early Stage
Expansion
Balanced
Later Stage
Startup

Size of Investments Considered:
Min Size of Investment Considered (000s): $5,000
Max Size of Investment Considered (000s): $25,000

Geographical Preferences

United States Preferences:

Industry Focus
(% based on actual investment)

Industry	%
Computer Software and Services	35.3%
Internet Specific	19.9%
Biotechnology	10.9%
Medical/Health	10.8%
Semiconductors/Other Elect.	6.9%
Computer Hardware	5.3%
Communications and Media	4.4%
Other Products	3.2%
Industrial/Energy	2.5%
Consumer Related	0.8%

Additional Information
Name of Most Recent Fund: Scale Venture Partners IV, L.P.
Most Recent Fund Was Raised: 05/03/2013
Year Founded: 1995
Capital Under Management: $1,200,000,000
Current Activity Level : Actively seeking new investments
Method of Compensation: Return on investment is of primary concern, do not charge fees

SCALE VENTURES PVT LTD

D38, Hauz Khas, Near E-Block
New Delhi, India 110016
E-mail: scale@scalegroup.in
Website: scaleventures.in

Type of Firm
Private Equity Firm

Project Preferences

Type of Financing Preferred:
Seed

Additional Information
Year Founded: 2016
Current Activity Level : Actively seeking new investments

SCALEWORKS INC

118 Broadway, Suite 627
San Antonio, TX USA 78205
Website: www.scaleworks.com

Management and Staff
Ed Byrne, General Partner
Lew Moorman, General Partner

Type of Firm
Private Equity Firm

Industry Preferences

In Computer Software prefer:
Software

Additional Information
Year Founded: 2016
Capital Under Management: $60,000,000
Current Activity Level : Actively seeking new investments

SCANDINAVIAN LIFE SCIENCE VENTURE

Norrlandsgatan 16
Stockholm, Sweden 111 43
E-mail: info@slsinvest.com

Other Offices
Norregade 21
Copenhagen, Denmark 1165
Phone: 4520203687

Management and Staff
Ingelise Saunders, Chief Executive Officer
Mikael Mortensen, Chief Financial Officer

Type of Firm
Private Equity Firm

Project Preferences

Type of Financing Preferred:
Balanced

Size of Investments Considered:
Min Size of Investment Considered (000s): $1,300
Max Size of Investment Considered (000s): $13,000

Geographical Preferences

International Preferences:
Scandanavia/Nordic Region

Industry Preferences

In Biotechnology prefer:
Biotechnology

In Medical/Health prefer:
Medical/Health
Medical Diagnostics
Medical Products
Pharmaceuticals

Additional Information
Year Founded: 2000
Capital Under Management: $209,800,000
Current Activity Level : Actively seeking new investments

SCF PARTNERS LP

600 Travis, Suite 6600
Houston, TX USA 77002
Phone: 7132277888
Fax: 7132277850
Website: www.scfpartners.com

Other Offices
3430 Canterra Tower
400-3rd Avenue South West
Calgary, Canada T2P 4H2
Phone: 403-244-7888
Fax: 403-234-7829

15 Rubislaw Terrace
Aberdeen
Scotland, United Kingdom AB10 IXE
Phone: 44-11-4465-6930
Fax: 44-11-4465-6931

Management and Staff
Andrew Waite, Managing Director
Ann Fox, Vice President
David Baldwin, Managing Director
John Geddes, Managing Director
L. E. Simmons, President, Founder
Nicholas Drake, Vice President
Theresa Eaton, Vice President
W. Patrick Connelly, Vice President

Type of Firm
Private Equity Firm

Project Preferences

Type of Financing Preferred:
Other

Geographical Preferences

United States Preferences:

Canadian Preferences:
All Canada

Industry Preferences

In Industrial/Energy prefer:
Energy
Oil and Gas Exploration
Oil & Gas Drilling,Explor
Industrial Products

In Business Serv. prefer:
Services

In Manufact. prefer:
Manufacturing

Additional Information

Name of Most Recent Fund: SCF-VIII, L.P.
Most Recent Fund Was Raised: 12/19/2012
Year Founded: 1989
Capital Under Management: $1,000,000,000
Current Activity Level : Actively seeking new investments

SCHILLING UNTERNEH-MENSBETEILIGUNG GMBH

Erdbergstrasse 8
Vienna, Austria 1030
Phone: 43124280
Fax: 43124280209
E-mail: office@saminvest.at
Website: www.saminvest.at

Management and Staff

Horst Neuhauser, Managing Director
Josef Schroll, Managing Director
Karl E. Surma, Managing Director

Type of Firm

Private Equity Firm

Project Preferences

Type of Financing Preferred:
Early Stage
Seed
Startup

Geographical Preferences

International Preferences:
Austria

Industry Preferences

In Communications prefer:
Telecommunications

In Biotechnology prefer:
Biotechnology

In Medical/Health prefer:
Medical/Health

In Industrial/Energy prefer:
Energy
Industrial Products

In Business Serv. prefer:
Services
Consulting Services

Additional Information

Year Founded: 2004
Current Activity Level : Actively seeking new investments

SCHOONER CAPITAL LLC

60 South Street, Suite 1120
Boston, MA USA 02111
Phone: 6179635200
Fax: 6179635201
E-mail: info@schoonercapital.com
Website: www.schoonercapital.com

Other Offices

745 Atlantic Avenue
11th Floor
Boston, MA USA 02111

Management and Staff

Peter Binas, Managing Director
Scott Yaphe, Managing Director
Ted Henderson, Managing Director

Type of Firm

Investment Management Firm

Association Membership

New England Venture Capital Association

Project Preferences

Role in Financing:
Prefer role as deal originator

Type of Financing Preferred:
Early Stage
Balanced
Later Stage

Geographical Preferences

United States Preferences:

Additional Information

Year Founded: 1971
Capital Under Management: $300,000,000
Current Activity Level : Actively seeking new investments

SCHRODERS PLC

31 Gresham Street
London, United Kingdom EC2V 7QA
Phone: 442076586000
Fax: 442076586965
Website: www.schroders.com

Other Offices

Montes Urales 760 Desp. 101
Col. Lomas de Chapultepec
Mexico, Mexico 11000
Phone: 52-55-1100-1030
Fax: 52-55-1100-1039

Eight Century Avenue
Unit 1101, 11/F, Shanghai IFC Phase I
Shanghai, China 200120
Phone: 86-21-5012-0580
Fax: 86-21-5012-0586

131 Front Street
Hamilton, Bermuda HM 12
Phone: 441-292-4995
Fax: 441-292-2437

520 Walnut Street, Suite 1150
Philadelphia, PA USA 19106
Phone: 215-861-0997
Fax: 215-861-0989

88 Queensway, Suites 3301, Level 33, Two Pacific Place
Hong Kong, Hong Kong
Phone: 852-2521-1633
Fax: 852-2530-9095

1-8-3 Marunouchi
21st Floor Marunouchi Trust Tower Main
Tokyo, Japan 100-0005

108, Sec.5, Hsin-Yi Road
2F, Suite B1, Hsin-YI District
Taipei, Taiwan 11047
Phone: 886-2-2722-1868
Fax: 886-2-2722-3899

Taunustor 2
Frankfurt, Germany 60311
Phone: 49-69-9757-170
Fax: 49-69-9757-17302

5, rue Hohenhof
Senningerberg, Luxembourg L-1736
Phone: 352-341-342-212
Fax: 352-341-342-342

De entree 260
18th Floor
Amsterdam, Netherlands 1101 EE
Phone: 31-20-301-6560
Fax: 31-20-301-6561

Dubai International Financial Center
1st Floor, Gate Village Six
Dubai, Utd. Arab Em.
Phone: 971-4-701-9100
Fax: 971-4-323-0306

Via della Spiga 30
Milan, Italy 20121
Phone: 39-2-763-771
Fax: 39-2-7637-7600

2-6 Church Street
St. Helier
Jersey, Cayman Islands JE4 9WB
Phone: 44-15-3475-6600
Fax: 44-15-3475-6601

100 – Cjtos 141 / 142
Itaim Bibi
Sao Paulo, Brazil 04534-000
Phone: 55-11-3054-5155
Fax: 55-11-3054-5173

P.O. Box 1040GT
Harbour Center
Grand Cayman, Cayman Islands
Phone: 345-949-2849
Fax: 345-949-5409

84 Taepyungro 1ga, Chung-gu
15th Floor, Seoul Finance Center
Seoul, South Korea 100-768
Phone: 822-3783-0500
Fax: 822-3783-0503

24 College Lane
Gibraltar, Cayman Islands
Phone: 350-200-77760
Fax: 350-200-77742

P.O. Box 334, Regency Court
Glategny Esplanade, St. Peter Port
Guernsey, Cayman Islands GY1 3UF
Phone: 44-14-8170-3700
Fax: 44-14-8170-3600

123 Pitt Street
Level 20, Angel Place
Sydney, Australia 2000
Phone: 61-2-9210-9200
Fax: 61-2-9231-1119

Jl. Jend. Sudirman Kav. 52-53
Tower 2, 31st Floor.
Jakarta, Indonesia 12190
Phone: 62-21-515-0101
Fax: 62-21-515-0505

Store Strandstraede 21
Copenhagen, Denmark 1255
Phone: 45-3315-1822
Fax: 45-3315-0650

Sveavagen 9
Stockholm, Sweden SE-111 57
Phone: 46-8-678-4010
Fax: 46-8-678-4410

875 Third Avenue
22nd Floor
New York, NY USA 10022
Phone: 212-641-3830
Fax: 212-641-3985

Seven Finance Street
Room 926, Winland Int'l Finance Center
Beijing, China 100033
Phone: 86-10-6655-5388
Fax: 86-10-6655-5398

Central 2
Zurich, Switzerland CH-8001
Phone: 41-44-250-1111
Fax: 41-44-250-1312

11 Beach Road
#06-01
Singapore, Singapore 189675
Phone: 65-6507-0123
Fax: 65-6507-0122

Ing. Enrique Butty 220, Piso 12
Buenos Aires, Argentina C1001AFB
Phone: 54-11-4317-1300
Fax: 54-11-4317-1313

65 Chulia Street
46-00, OCBC Center
Singapore, Singapore 049513
Phone: 65-6535-3411
Fax: 65-6535-3486

8-10 rue Lamennais
Paris, France 75008
Phone: 33-1-5385-8585
Fax: 33-1-5385-8586

Management and Staff
Peter Harrison, Chief Executive Officer
Richard Keers, Chief Financial Officer

Type of Firm
Investment Management Firm

Project Preferences

Type of Financing Preferred:
Fund of Funds
Value-Add
Early Stage
Generalist PE
Balanced
Later Stage

Geographical Preferences

United States Preferences:

International Preferences:
Europe
Middle East
Asia

Industry Preferences

In Financial Services prefer:
Real Estate

Additional Information
Year Founded: 2000
Capital Under Management: $36,000,000,000
Current Activity Level : Actively seeking new investments
Method of Compensation: Return on invest. most important, but chg. closing fees, service fees, etc.

SCHULTZ INVESTMENT CO

P.O. Box 218
Effingham, IL USA 62401
Phone: 2173424100
Fax: 2173420800
E-mail: bschultz@schultzusa.com
Website: www.schultzusa.com

Type of Firm
Private Equity Firm

Project Preferences

Type of Financing Preferred:
Expansion
Balanced
Startup

Geographical Preferences

United States Preferences:
Illinois

Additional Information
Year Founded: 1969
Current Activity Level : Actively seeking new investments

SCIENTIFIC HEALTH DEVELOPMENT

2305 Cedar Springs Road, Suite 240
Dallas, TX USA 75201
Phone: 2143031540
Fax: 2143031597
E-mail: info@shdpartners.com
Website: www.shdpartners.com

Management and Staff
Carter Meyer, Chief Executive Officer
Philip Romano, Co-Founder
Stuart Fitts, Co-Founder

Pratt's Guide to Private Equity & Venture Capital Sources

Type of Firm
Investment Management Firm

Project Preferences

Type of Financing Preferred:
Early Stage
Balanced

Industry Preferences

In Medical/Health prefer:
Medical/Health
Health Services

Additional Information
Name of Most Recent Fund: Scientific Health Development II, Ltd.
Most Recent Fund Was Raised: 03/02/2010
Year Founded: 2006
Capital Under Management: $15,500,000
Current Activity Level : Actively seeking new investments

SCIENTIPOLE ILE DE FRANCE CAPITAL SAS

Centre Scientifique d'Orsay
Batiment 503
Orsay, France 91893
E-mail: fcadereau@scientipolecapital.fr
Website: www.scientipolecapital.fr

Type of Firm
Private Equity Firm

Project Preferences

Type of Financing Preferred:
Early Stage
Seed
Startup

Size of Investments Considered:
Min Size of Investment Considered (000s): $195
Max Size of Investment Considered (000s): $650

Geographical Preferences

International Preferences:
Europe
France

Industry Preferences

In Computer Software prefer:
Software

In Biotechnology prefer:
Biotechnology

In Medical/Health prefer:
Medical/Health

In Industrial/Energy prefer:
Environmental Related

In Other prefer:
Environment Responsible

Additional Information
Year Founded: 2006
Current Activity Level : Actively seeking new investments

SCIFI VC

140 Second Street
Third Floor
Daly City, CA USA 94015
E-mail: info@scifi.vc
Website: scifi.vc

Type of Firm
Incubator/Development Program

Project Preferences

Type of Financing Preferred:
Seed

Industry Preferences

In Computer Software prefer:
Software

In Financial Services prefer:
Financial Services

Additional Information
Year Founded: 1969
Current Activity Level : Actively seeking new investments

SCIVANTAGE FINTECH INCUBATOR PROGRAM

499 Washington Boulevard
11th Floor
Jersey City, NJ USA 07310
Website: www.scivantageincubator.com

Other Offices
186 Lincoln Street, Suite 801
Boston, MA USA 02111

Type of Firm
Incubator/Development Program

Project Preferences

Type of Financing Preferred:
Early Stage
Seed

Industry Preferences

In Communications prefer:
Wireless Communications

In Computer Software prefer:
Software

In Internet Specific prefer:
Ecommerce

In Financial Services prefer:
Financial Services

In Business Serv. prefer:
Services

Additional Information
Year Founded: 2014
Current Activity Level : Actively seeking new investments

SCOPE CAPITAL ADVISORY AB

Kungsgatan 30
Stockholm, Sweden 111 35
Phone: 46850606200
Fax: 46850606210
E-mail: contact@scope.se
Website: www.scope.se

Other Offices
Place de la Taconnerie 3
Geneva, Switzerland CH-1204
Phone: 41223186039

Management and Staff
Andreas Ossmark, Partner
Frederik Oweson, Partner
Jonas Palmquist, Partner
Kristina Patek, Partner
Mikael Kamras, Co-Founder
Monalotte Theorell Christofferson, Partner

Type of Firm
Private Equity Firm

Association Membership
Swedish Venture Capital Association (SVCA)

Project Preferences

Type of Financing Preferred:
Balanced
Seed
Startup

Size of Investments Considered:
Min Size of Investment Considered (000s): $3,098
Max Size of Investment Considered (000s): $15,484

Geographical Preferences

International Preferences:
Europe
Scandanavia/Nordic Region

Industry Preferences

In Communications prefer:
Communications and Media

In Internet Specific prefer:
E-Commerce Technology
Ecommerce

In Medical/Health prefer:
Medical/Health

In Consumer Related prefer:
Consumer
Sports

In Financial Services prefer:
Financial Services

In Business Serv. prefer:
Services
Consulting Services

Additional Information
Year Founded: 2001
Capital Under Management: $189,200,000
Current Activity Level : Actively seeking new investments

SCOPUS VENTURES LLC

12100 Wilshire Boulevard, Suite 1960
Los Angeles, CA USA 90025
E-mail: info@scopusventures.com
Website: www.scopusventures.com

Type of Firm
Private Equity Firm

Project Preferences

Type of Financing Preferred:
Early Stage
Startup

Additional Information
Year Founded: 2017
Current Activity Level : Actively seeking new investments

SCORPION CAPITAL PARTNERS LP

11 East 26th Street
15th Floor
New York, NY USA 10010
Phone: 2122139190
Fax: 2122139607
E-mail: info@scorpioncap.com
Website: www.scorpioncap.com

Management and Staff
Kevin McCarthy, Co-Founder
Nuno Brandolini, Co-Founder
Robert Schoff, Chief Financial Officer

Type of Firm
SBIC

Project Preferences

Type of Financing Preferred:
Leveraged Buyout
Generalist PE
Later Stage
Management Buyouts
Acquisition
Recapitalizations

Additional Information
Year Founded: 2004
Capital Under Management: $18,300,000
Current Activity Level : Actively seeking new investments

SCOTIABANK PVT EQUITY

40 King Street West
Scotia Plaza
Toronto, Canada M5W 2X6
Phone: 4168637411
Fax: 4168623052
Website: www.scotiabank.com

Management and Staff
Peter Adamek, Managing Director

Type of Firm
Investment Management Firm

Association Membership
Canadian Venture Capital Association

Project Preferences

Type of Financing Preferred:
Leveraged Buyout
Expansion
Management Buyouts
Acquisition
Startup

Geographical Preferences

United States Preferences:
All U.S.

Canadian Preferences:
All Canada

Industry Preferences

In Consumer Related prefer:
Consumer Products

In Financial Services prefer:
Financial Services
Financial Services

In Business Serv. prefer:
Services

In Manufact. prefer:
Manufacturing

Additional Information
Year Founded: 2000
Current Activity Level : Actively seeking new investments

SCOTTISH ENTERPRISE GLASGOW

50 Waterloo Street
Atrium Court
Glasgow, United Kingdom G2 6HQ
Phone: 44-1412487700
Fax: 44-1412282045
E-mail: enquiries@scotent.co.uk
Website: www.scottish-enterprise.com

Other Offices

Tinwald Downs Road
Dumfries Enterprise Park, Solway House
Dumfries, United Kingdom DG1 3SJ
Phone: 441387254000
Fax: 441387246224

Spectrum House
Clydebank Business Park
Glasgow, United Kingdom G81 2DR
Phone: 441419512121
Fax: 441419511907

99 Haymarket Terrace
Apex House
Edinburgh, United Kingdom EH12 5HD
Phone: 441313134000
Fax: 441313134231

Three Greenmarket
Enterprise House
Dundee, United Kingdom DD1 4QB
Phone: 441382223100
Fax: 441382201319

17/19 Hill Street
Kilmarnock
Ayrshire, United Kingdom KA3 1HA
Phone: 441563526623
Fax: 441563543636

Kingdom House
Saltire Centre
Glenrothes, United Kingdom KY6 2AQ
Phone: 441592623000
Fax: 44159262314

27 Causeyside Street
Paisley, United Kingdom PA1 1UL
Phone: 441418480101
Fax: 441418486930

27 Albyn Place
Aberdeen, United Kingdom AB10 1DB
Phone: 441224252000
Fax: 441224213417

New Lanarkshire House
Dove Wynd, Strathclyde Business Park
United Kingdom ML4 3AD
Phone: 441698745454
Fax: 441698842211

Laurel House
Larelhill Business Park
Stirling, United Kingdom FK7 9JQ
Phone: 441786451919
Fax: 441786478123

Bridge Street
Galashiels, United Kingdom TD1 1SW
Phone: 441896758991
Fax: 441896758625

Type of Firm
Government Affiliated Program

Project Preferences

Type of Financing Preferred:
Early Stage
Balanced
Later Stage
Seed

Geographical Preferences

International Preferences:
United Kingdom
Europe

Additional Information
Year Founded: 2004
Current Activity Level : Actively seeking new investments

SCOTTISH EQUITY PARTNERS LLP

29 St George Street
London, United Kingdom W1S2FA
Phone: 44207758 5900
Fax: 44207758 5901
E-mail: enquiries@sep.co.uk
Website: www.sep.co.uk

Other Offices

29 St. George Street
London, United Kingdom W1S 2FA
Phone: 4402077585900
Fax: 4402077585901

Management and Staff
Andrew Davison, Partner
Brian Kerr, Partner
Calum Paterson, Co-Founder
David Sneddon, Partner
Fearghal O Riordain, Partner
Gary Le Sueur, Partner
Jan Rutherford, Partner
Lorna Foy, Chief Financial Officer
Richard Sparrow, Co-Founder
Stuart Paterson, Partner

Type of Firm
Private Equity Firm

Association Membership
British Venture Capital Association (BVCA)
European Private Equity and Venture Capital Assoc.

Project Preferences

Role in Financing:
Prefer role as deal originator but will also invest in deals created by others

Type of Financing Preferred:
Early Stage
Expansion
Balanced
Later Stage
Other
Seed

Size of Investments Considered:
Min Size of Investment Considered (000s): $6,511
Max Size of Investment Considered (000s): $26,042

Geographical Preferences

International Preferences:
United Kingdom
Europe

Industry Focus
(% based on actual investment)

Computer Software and Services	21.9%
Internet Specific	21.5%
Semiconductors/Other Elect.	15.4%
Communications and Media	9.6%
Industrial/Energy	9.4%
Biotechnology	8.7%
Consumer Related	4.4%
Medical/Health	3.8%
Other Products	3.3%
Computer Hardware	2.0%

Additional Information
Name of Most Recent Fund: Scottish Equity Partners Fund IV
Most Recent Fund Was Raised: 09/19/2011
Year Founded: 2000
Capital Under Management: $887,300,000
Current Activity Level : Actively seeking new investments

SCOTTISH MICROELECTRONICS CENTRE

West Mains Road
The King's Buildings
Edinburgh, United Kingdom EH9 3JF
Phone: 44-131-650-7474
Fax: 44-131-650-7475
E-mail: enquiries@scotmicrocentre.co.uk
Website: www.scotmicrocentre.co.uk

Management and Staff
Ian Hyslop, Chief Executive Officer

Type of Firm
Incubator/Development Program

Project Preferences

Type of Financing Preferred:
Seed
Startup

Geographical Preferences

International Preferences:
United Kingdom

Industry Preferences

In Semiconductor/Electr prefer:
Electronics

Additional Information
Year Founded: 2000
Current Activity Level : Actively seeking new investments

SCOUT VENTURES LLC

47 Murray Street
Lower Level
New York, NY USA 10007
Website: www.scoutventures.com

Management and Staff
Bradley Harrison, Managing Partner
Brendan Syron, Principal
John Ryu, Partner
John Ryu, Principal
Mitchell Kleinhandler, Venture Partner

Type of Firm
Private Equity Firm

Project Preferences

Type of Financing Preferred:
Balanced
Startup

Industry Preferences

In Communications prefer:
Media and Entertainment

In Computer Software prefer:
Computer Services

In Internet Specific prefer:
Internet

Additional Information
Name of Most Recent Fund: BHV Entrepreneurship Fund, L.P.
Most Recent Fund Was Raised: 07/06/2011
Year Founded: 2009
Capital Under Management: $18,000,000
Current Activity Level : Actively seeking new investments

SCP III LP

28 Havemeyer Place
Greenwich, CT USA 06830
Phone: 2034858550
Website: www.shumwaycapital.com

Type of Firm
Private Equity Firm

Project Preferences

Type of Financing Preferred:
Generalist PE

Additional Information
Year Founded: 2011
Current Activity Level : Actively seeking new investments

SCP PRIVATE EQUITY PARTNERS

7 Great Valley Parkway, Suite 190
Malvern, PA USA 19355
Phone: 6109952900
Fax: 6109759546
E-mail: info@scppartners.com
Website: www.scppartners.com

Other Offices
74 Grand Avenue
ENGLEWOOD, NJ USA 07631
Phone: 201-541-1080
Fax: 201-541-1084

1200 Liberty Ridge Drive, Suite 300
WAYNE, PA USA 19087

Management and Staff
Dennis Ferry, Chief Financial Officer
Jim Evans, Venture Partner
John Keane, Venture Partner
Richard Sherman, Venture Partner
Robert Yablunsky, Venture Partner
Roger Carolin, Venture Partner
Thomas Rebar, Partner
Wayne Weisman, Partner
Yaron Eitan, Partner

Type of Firm
Private Equity Firm

Association Membership
Israel Venture Association

Project Preferences

Type of Financing Preferred:
Early Stage
Expansion
Balanced
Later Stage

Size of Investments Considered:
Min Size of Investment Considered (000s): $2,000
Max Size of Investment Considered (000s): $50,000

Industry Focus
(% based on actual investment)
Computer Software and Services	32.9%
Internet Specific	31.4%
Medical/Health	16.2%
Other Products	6.0%
Biotechnology	4.9%
Communications and Media	2.9%
Semiconductors/Other Elect.	2.7%
Consumer Related	2.5%
Computer Hardware	0.5%

Additional Information
Name of Most Recent Fund: SCP Vitalife Partners II, L.P.
Most Recent Fund Was Raised: 04/23/2007
Year Founded: 1996
Capital Under Management: $828,300,000
Current Activity Level : Actively seeking new investments

SCRONCE AND ASSOCIATES LLC

302-A South Stratford Road, Suite 18
Winston-Salem, NC USA 27103
Website: scronceandassociates.com

Management and Staff
Timothy Scronce, Founder

Type of Firm
Private Equity Firm

Project Preferences

Type of Financing Preferred:
Leveraged Buyout
Acquisition

Geographical Preferences

United States Preferences:
Southeast

Industry Preferences

In Business Serv. prefer:
Services
Distribution

In Manufact. prefer:
Manufacturing

Additional Information
Year Founded: 2005
Current Activity Level : Actively seeking new investments

SCRUM VENTURES LLC

717 Market Street, Suite 100
San Francisco, CA USA 94103
E-mail: contact@scrumventures.co
Website: scrum.vc

Management and Staff
Takuya Miyata, Founder

Type of Firm
Private Equity Firm

Project Preferences

Type of Financing Preferred:
Startup

Geographical Preferences

United States Preferences:
California

Industry Preferences

In Communications prefer:
Telecommunications

Additional Information
Year Founded: 2013
Capital Under Management: $27,900,000
Current Activity Level : Actively seeking new investments

SCS CAPITAL SDN BHD

Level 40 Petronas Twin Towers
Twr. 2, Kuala Lumpur City Ctr.
Kuala Lumpur, Malaysia 50088
Phone: 603-2168-4740
Fax: 603-2168-4201
Website: www.scscapital.com

Other Offices
30th Floor Shinjuku Park Tower
3-7-1 Nishi-Shinjuku
Shinjuku-ku, Tokyo, Japan 163-1030
Phone: 813-5326-3625
Fax: 813-5326-3001

29th Floor One Canada Square
Canary Wharf
London, United Kingdom E14 5DY
Phone: 44-207-712-1591
Fax: 44-207-712-1501

14 Wall Street
20th Floor, New York
New York, NY USA 100050
Phone: 212-618-1255
Fax: 212-618-1705

Type of Firm
Private Equity Firm

Project Preferences

Type of Financing Preferred:
Balanced

Geographical Preferences

International Preferences:
No Preference
Malaysia

Additional Information

Year Founded: 2005
Current Activity Level : Actively seeking new investments

SDIC INNOVATION INVESTMENT MANAGEMENT LTD

6-6, Fuchengmen N St, Xicheng
Tower A, Int'l Investment Bldg
Beijing, China 100034
Phone: 861088006412
Fax: 861088006415
Website: www.sdicfund.com

Management and Staff

Dazhong Lu, Managing Director
Guoguang Bai, Managing Director
Guohua Gao, President

Type of Firm

Government Affiliated Program

Project Preferences

Type of Financing Preferred:
Expansion
Generalist PE
Balanced

Geographical Preferences

International Preferences:
China

Industry Preferences

In Medical/Health prefer:
Medical/Health

In Industrial/Energy prefer:
Energy
Energy Conservation Relat
Materials
Environmental Related

In Business Serv. prefer:
Services
Media

In Manufact. prefer:
Manufacturing

In Agr/Forestr/Fish prefer:
Agriculture related
Mining and Minerals

Additional Information

Year Founded: 2009
Capital Under Management: $924,200,000
Current Activity Level : Actively seeking new investments

SDL VENTURES LLC

480 San Antonio Road, Suite 200
Mountain View, CA USA 94040
Phone: 6505599355
Fax: 6505599353
Website: www.sdlcapital.com

Management and Staff

Donald Scifres, Managing Director
Michael Foster, Partner

Type of Firm

Private Equity Firm

Project Preferences

Type of Financing Preferred:
Early Stage

Industry Preferences

In Communications prefer:
Commercial Communications

In Internet Specific prefer:
Internet

In Semiconductor/Electr prefer:
Fiber Optics

In Biotechnology prefer:
Biotechnology

In Medical/Health prefer:
Medical/Health

In Industrial/Energy prefer:
Environmental Related

In Business Serv. prefer:
Media

Additional Information

Year Founded: 2003
Current Activity Level : Actively seeking new investments

SE BLUE HOLDING A/S

Jupitervej 2
Kolding, Denmark 6000
Website: www.seblueequity.dk

Management and Staff

Christian Moller, Managing Partner
Thomas Bonde, Partner

Type of Firm

Private Equity Firm

Association Membership

Danish Venture Capital Association (DVCA)

Project Preferences

Type of Financing Preferred:
Leveraged Buyout

Geographical Preferences

International Preferences:
Denmark

Industry Preferences

In Industrial/Energy prefer:
Alternative Energy
Energy Conservation Relat

In Other prefer:
Environment Responsible

Additional Information

Year Founded: 2012
Current Activity Level : Actively seeking new investments

SE CAPITAL LLC

30 South Wacker Drive, Suite 2200
Chicago, IL USA 60606
Phone: 3124252787
E-mail: info@secapital.com
Website: www.secapital.com

Type of Firm

Private Equity Firm

Project Preferences

Type of Financing Preferred:
Leveraged Buyout

Additional Information

Year Founded: 2001
Current Activity Level : Actively seeking new investments

SEA CHANGE MANAGEMENT LLC

423 Washington Street
Fourth Floor
San Francisco, CA USA 94111
Phone: 4154214213
Fax: 4159827989
E-mail: info@seachangefund.com
Website: www.seachangemanagement.com

Type of Firm

Private Equity Firm

Project Preferences

Type of Financing Preferred:
Balanced

Industry Preferences

In Consumer Related prefer:
Food/Beverage
Other Restaurants

In Industrial/Energy prefer:
Environmental Related

In Other prefer:
Environment Responsible

Additional Information
Year Founded: 2005
Current Activity Level : Actively seeking new investments

SEA EQUITY LTD

23 Hanover Square
London, United Kingdom W1S 1JB
Website: www.seaequity.com

Management and Staff
Elliott Nicholson, Founder
Stani Schmidt-Chiari, Partner

Type of Firm
Private Equity Firm

Project Preferences

Type of Financing Preferred:
Leveraged Buyout

Geographical Preferences

International Preferences:
United Kingdom
Europe

Industry Preferences

In Industrial/Energy prefer:
Industrial Products

In Business Serv. prefer:
Services

In Manufact. prefer:
Manufacturing

Additional Information
Year Founded: 2013
Current Activity Level : Actively seeking new investments

SEABRIGHT ASSET MANAGEMENT LTD

16 Harcourt Road
36th Floor, Far East Finance C
Hong Kong, China
Phone: 852-253-7668
Fax: 852-252-6991

Type of Firm
Investment Management Firm

Additional Information
Year Founded: 2010
Current Activity Level : Actively seeking new investments

SEABURY VENTURE PARTNERS LLC

345 Lorton Avenue, Suite 401
Burlingame, CA USA 94010
Phone: 650-373-1030
Fax: 650-373-1031
E-mail: info@seaburypartners.com
Website: www.seaburypartners.com

Management and Staff
Mark Olhoeft, Chief Financial Officer
Michael Fitzpatrick, General Partner
Patricia Fitzpatrick, General Partner

Type of Firm
Private Equity Firm

Project Preferences

Type of Financing Preferred:
Balanced

Geographical Preferences

United States Preferences:
All U.S.

Industry Preferences

In Communications prefer:
Telecommunications

In Semiconductor/Electr prefer:
Optoelectronics

Additional Information
Year Founded: 2000
Current Activity Level : Actively seeking new investments

SEACLIFF PRIVATE EQUITY

305-1788 5th Ave West
Vancouver, Canada V6J 1P2
Website: seacliffgroup.com

Management and Staff
Stephen Curran, Managing Director

Type of Firm
Private Equity Firm

Geographical Preferences

Canadian Preferences:
All Canada
Western Canada

Industry Preferences

In Consumer Related prefer:
Food/Beverage
Consumer Services

In Industrial/Energy prefer:
Energy

In Financial Services prefer:
Financial Services

In Manufact. prefer:
Manufacturing

Additional Information
Year Founded: 1988
Current Activity Level : Actively seeking new investments

SEACOAST CAPITAL

55 Ferncroft Road, Suite 110
Danvers, MA USA 01923
Phone: 9787501300
Fax: 9787501301
Website: www.seacoastcapital.com

Other Offices
One Bush Street, Suite 650
San Francisco, CA USA 94104
Phone: 4159561400
Fax: 4159561459

Management and Staff
Eben Moulton, Partner
James Donelan, Vice President
Jeffrey Holland, Partner
Thomas Ley, Principal
Thomas Gorman, Partner
Timothy Fay, Partner
Walter Leonard, Partner

Type of Firm
SBIC

Association Membership
Natl Assoc of Small Bus. Inv. Co (NASBIC)

Project Preferences

Role in Financing:
Prefer role as deal originator but will also invest in deals created by others

Type of Financing Preferred:
Leveraged Buyout
Mezzanine
Management Buyouts
Acquisition

Size of Investments Considered:
Min Size of Investment Considered (000s): $3,000
Max Size of Investment Considered (000s): $12,000

1845

Geographical Preferences

United States Preferences:

Industry Focus

(% based on actual investment)
Other Products	35.1%
Consumer Related	14.1%
Industrial/Energy	11.4%
Semiconductors/Other Elect.	11.4%
Internet Specific	9.2%
Computer Software and Services	8.2%
Medical/Health	6.3%
Computer Hardware	4.2%

Additional Information

Name of Most Recent Fund: Seacoast Capital Partners III, L.P.
Most Recent Fund Was Raised: 02/27/2013
Year Founded: 1994
Capital Under Management: $300,000,000
Current Activity Level : Actively seeking new investments
Method of Compensation: Return on invest. most important, but chg. closing fees, service fees, etc.

SEAFORT ADVISORS GMBH

Alsterarkaden 20
Hamburg, Germany 20354
Phone: 494086624095
Fax: 494086624096
Website: www.seafort.de

Management and Staff

Johann Herstatt, Co-Founder
Patrick Hennings-Huep, Co-Founder

Type of Firm
Private Equity Firm

Project Preferences

Type of Financing Preferred:
Leveraged Buyout
Acquisition

Geographical Preferences

International Preferences:
Western Europe
Germany

Industry Preferences

In Industrial/Energy prefer:
Environmental Related

In Business Serv. prefer:
Services

In Manufact. prefer:
Manufacturing

Additional Information

Year Founded: 2012
Current Activity Level : Actively seeking new investments

SEAFORT CAPITAL INC

1809 Barrington Street, Suite 701, CIBC Building
Halifax, Canada B3J 3k8

Management and Staff

Robert Normandeau, President

Type of Firm
Private Equity Firm

Association Membership

Canadian Venture Capital Association

Project Preferences

Type of Financing Preferred:
Generalist PE

Geographical Preferences

Canadian Preferences:
All Canada

Industry Preferences

In Business Serv. prefer:
Distribution

In Manufact. prefer:
Manufacturing

Additional Information

Year Founded: 2012
Current Activity Level : Actively seeking new investments

SEAFRONT CAPITAL LLC

80 Liberty Ship Way, Suite 25
Sausalito, CA USA 94965
Phone: 14159671965
Website: www.seafrontcap.com

Type of Firm
Private Equity Firm

Project Preferences

Type of Financing Preferred:
Expansion
Later Stage

Geographical Preferences

United States Preferences:

Additional Information

Year Founded: 2017
Capital Under Management: $2,180,000
Current Activity Level : Actively seeking new investments

SEAL ROCK PARTNERS

712 Fifth Avenue, 12th Floor
New York, NY USA 10019
E-mail: info@sealrockpartners.com
Website: www.sealrockpartners.com

Type of Firm
Private Equity Firm

Project Preferences

Type of Financing Preferred:
Later Stage
Acquisition
Recapitalizations

Additional Information

Year Founded: 1969
Current Activity Level : Actively seeking new investments

SEALAND INNOVATION CAPITAL INVESTMENT MANAGEMENT CO LTD

Zhuzilin 4th Rd., Futian Dist.
China Everbright Bank
Nanning, China 518000

Type of Firm
Bank Affiliated

Project Preferences

Type of Financing Preferred:
Balanced

Geographical Preferences

International Preferences:
China

Industry Preferences

In Communications prefer:
Telecommunications

In Medical/Health prefer:
Medical/Health

In Business Serv. prefer:
Media

In Manufact. prefer:
Manufacturing

In Other prefer:
Environment Responsible

Additional Information

Year Founded: 2012
Current Activity Level : Actively seeking new investments

SEALINK CAPITAL PARTNERS

1st Floor, Trade Center
Bandra Kurla Complex
Mumbai, India 400 051
E-mail: info@sealinkcap.com
Website: www.sealinkcap.com

Management and Staff
Heramb Hajarnavis, Managing Partner
Rahul Sanghavi, Vice President
Ravi Sampat, Chief Financial Officer

Type of Firm
Private Equity Firm

Project Preferences

Type of Financing Preferred:
Leveraged Buyout

Industry Preferences

In Medical/Health prefer:
Health Services
Pharmaceuticals

In Consumer Related prefer:
Consumer
Retail

In Financial Services prefer:
Financial Services

In Manufact. prefer:
Manufacturing

Additional Information
Year Founded: 2015
Current Activity Level : Actively seeking new investments

SEAPOINT VENTURES

719 Second Avenue, Suite 1405
Seattle, WA USA 98104
Phone: 2064381880
Fax: 2064381886
E-mail: info@seapointventures.com
Website: www.seapointventures.com

Management and Staff
Melissa Widner, General Partner

Type of Firm
Private Equity Firm

Project Preferences

Role in Financing:
Prefer role as deal originator but will also invest in deals created by others

Type of Financing Preferred:
Early Stage
Seed

Geographical Preferences

United States Preferences:

Industry Focus
(% based on actual investment)
Internet Specific	36.1%
Computer Software and Services	23.9%
Communications and Media	18.7%
Computer Hardware	18.6%
Other Products	1.8%
Biotechnology	0.8%

Additional Information
Name of Most Recent Fund: Seapoint Ventures II, L.P.
Most Recent Fund Was Raised: 03/31/2001
Year Founded: 1997
Capital Under Management: $68,000,000
Current Activity Level : Actively seeking new investments
Method of Compensation: Return on investment is of primary concern, do not charge fees

---

SEAPORT CAPITAL LLC

40 Fulton Street
27th Floor
New York, NY USA 10038
Phone: 2128478900
Fax: 2124251420
E-mail: info@seaportcapital.com
Website: www.seaportcapital.com

Management and Staff
Bob Tamashunas, Principal
James Collis, Partner
Jim Collis, Co-Founder
Justin Choi, Vice President
Scott McCormack, Partner
William Luby, Partner
William Luby, Co-Founder

Type of Firm
Private Equity Firm

Project Preferences

Role in Financing:
Prefer role as deal originator but will also invest in deals created by others

Type of Financing Preferred:
Leveraged Buyout
Expansion
Mezzanine
Management Buyouts
Acquisition
Recapitalizations

Geographical Preferences

United States Preferences:
All U.S.

Industry Focus
(% based on actual investment)
Internet Specific	56.8%
Communications and Media	30.3%
Other Products	8.5%
Computer Hardware	3.1%
Computer Software and Services	1.4%
Consumer Related	0.0%

Additional Information
Year Founded: 1997
Capital Under Management: $550,000,000
Current Activity Level : Actively seeking new investments
Method of Compensation: Return on investment is of primary concern, do not charge fees

---

SEARCHLIGHT CAPITAL PARTNERS LLC

745 Fifth Avenue
32nd Floor
New York, NY USA 10151
Phone: 2122933730
E-mail: ir@searchlightcap.com
Website: www.searchlightcap.com

Other Offices
181 Bay Street
28th Floor
Toronto, Canada M5J 2T3
Phone: 4166876590

Berkeley Square House, Fifth Floor
Berkeley Square
London, United Kingdom W1J 6BR
Phone: 4402072907910

Management and Staff
Eric Zinterhofer, Partner
Erol Uzumeri, Partner
Oliver Haarmann, Partner

Type of Firm
Private Equity Firm

Association Membership
Canadian Venture Capital Association

Project Preferences

Type of Financing Preferred:
Leveraged Buyout
Generalist PE
Later Stage
Acquisition
Recapitalizations

Geographical Preferences

United States Preferences:
North America

International Preferences:
Europe

Industry Preferences

In Communications prefer:
Communications and Media
Telecommunications
Media and Entertainment

In Internet Specific prefer:
Internet

In Consumer Related prefer:
Consumer Products
Consumer Services
Education Related

In Industrial/Energy prefer:
Industrial Products

In Financial Services prefer:
Financial Services

In Business Serv. prefer:
Services

Additional Information
Name of Most Recent Fund: Searchlight Co-Investment, L.P.
Most Recent Fund Was Raised: 07/29/2011
Year Founded: 2010
Capital Under Management: $900,000
Current Activity Level : Actively seeking new investments

SEARS CAPITAL MANAGEMENT, INC.

20370 Town Center Lane, Suite 120
Cupertino, CA USA 95014
Phone: 4088650000
E-mail: info@searscapital.net
Website: www.searscapital.net

Management and Staff
Lowell Sears, Chairman & CEO

Type of Firm
Private Equity Firm

Project Preferences

Type of Financing Preferred:
Early Stage
Seed

Industry Preferences

In Medical/Health prefer:
Medical Products
Pharmaceuticals

Additional Information
Year Founded: 1994
Current Activity Level : Actively seeking new investments

SEAS CAPITAL PARTNERS LLC

P.O. Box 700560
Plymouth, MI USA 48170
E-mail: info@seascapitalpartners.com
Website: www.seascapitalpartners.com

Type of Firm
Private Equity Firm

Project Preferences

Type of Financing Preferred:
Leveraged Buyout
Expansion

Industry Preferences

In Industrial/Energy prefer:
Industrial Products

Additional Information
Year Founded: 2012
Current Activity Level : Actively seeking new investments

SEAVEST CAPITAL PARTNERS LLC

707 Westchester Avenue, Suite 401
White Plains, NY USA 10604
Phone: 9146838474
Fax: 9146815182
E-mail: info@seavestcp.com
Website: www.seavestcp.com

Management and Staff
Michael Walden, Chief Operating Officer
Richard Segal, Chairman & CEO

Type of Firm
Private Equity Firm

Project Preferences

Type of Financing Preferred:
Early Stage
Expansion
Balanced

Size of Investments Considered:
Min Size of Investment Considered (000s): $2,000
Max Size of Investment Considered (000s): $4,000

Industry Preferences

In Medical/Health prefer:
Medical/Health

In Consumer Related prefer:
Consumer
Education Related

In Business Serv. prefer:
Media

Additional Information
Year Founded: 1981
Current Activity Level : Actively seeking new investments

SEAVI ADVENT CORPORATION LTD

331 North Bridge Road
#05-04/05 Odeon Towers
Singapore, Singapore 188720
Phone: 6563399090
Fax: 6563398247
E-mail: info@seavi.com.sg
Website: www.seavi.com.sg

Other Offices
500 Zhangyang Road
28th Floor, Unit B
Shanghai, China 200122
Phone: 862161090673
Fax: 862161090679
, Suite 1520, 15F, One Corporate Avenue
222 Hubin Road, Luwan District
Shanghai, China 200021
Phone: 86-21-6122-1136
Fax: 86-21-6122-2418

Room 1312, 13th Floor, Ocean Centre
5 Canton Road, Tsimshatsui West
Kowloon, Hong Kong
Phone: 852-2376-0606
Fax: 852-2375-9666

Central International Trade Center
6A Jian Guo Men Wai St., Chaoyang Dist.
Beijing, China 100022
Phone: 86-10-6563-9815
Fax: 86-10-6563-9833

Management and Staff
Henry Yao Wei Min, Partner
Hoe Boon Kwee, Chief Financial Officer
Kevin Chan, Partner
Meow Chan Lee, Managing Partner
Tan Keng Boon, Managing Partner
Teo Yi-Dar, Partner
Yong Wah Ling, Partner

Type of Firm
Private Equity Firm

Association Membership
Hong Kong Venture Capital Association (HKVCA)
China Venture Capital Association
Singapore Venture Capital Association (SVCA)

Project Preferences

Role in Financing:
Prefer role as deal originator but will also invest in deals created by others

Type of Financing Preferred:
Leveraged Buyout
Early Stage
Expansion
Mezzanine
Generalist PE
Later Stage
Management Buyouts
Acquisition
Recapitalizations

Size of Investments Considered:
Min Size of Investment Considered (000s): $10,000
Max Size of Investment Considered (000s): $25,000

Geographical Preferences

United States Preferences:
Southeast

International Preferences:
Indonesia
Hong Kong
China
Thailand
Philippines
Asia
Singapore
Malaysia

Industry Preferences

In Communications prefer:
Telecommunications

In Semiconductor/Electr prefer:
Electronics

In Biotechnology prefer:
Genetic Engineering

In Medical/Health prefer:
Health Services

In Consumer Related prefer:
Consumer
Retail
Consumer Services

In Industrial/Energy prefer:
Energy
Alternative Energy
Industrial Products
Materials
Environmental Related

In Business Serv. prefer:
Services

Additional Information

Year Founded: 1984
Capital Under Management: $50,000,000

Current Activity Level : Actively seeking new investments

SEAYA CAPITAL GESTION SGECR SA

Calle Salamanca 17
Madrid, Spain 28020

Type of Firm
Private Equity Firm

Project Preferences

Type of Financing Preferred:
Balanced

Industry Preferences

In Communications prefer:
Wireless Communications

In Internet Specific prefer:
E-Commerce Technology

In Biotechnology prefer:
Biotechnology
Human Biotechnology
Industrial Biotechnology

Additional Information

Year Founded: 2012
Capital Under Management: $52,880,000
Current Activity Level : Actively seeking new investments

SEB INVEST GMBH

Sveavagen 8
Stockholm, Sweden 106 40
Phone: 4687635000

Management and Staff
Lars Lundquist, Chief Financial Officer

Type of Firm
Private Equity Advisor or Fund of Funds

Project Preferences

Type of Financing Preferred:
Fund of Funds

Geographical Preferences

International Preferences:
All International

Additional Information

Year Founded: 1978
Current Activity Level : Actively seeking new investments

SEBRINA HOLDINGS LTD

38 Beach Road, Suite 16-12
Singapore, Singapore 189767

Management and Staff
Harold Gan, Chief Financial Officer

Type of Firm
Private Equity Firm

Project Preferences

Type of Financing Preferred:
Generalist PE

Geographical Preferences

International Preferences:
Asia

Industry Preferences

In Internet Specific prefer:
Internet

In Financial Services prefer:
Real Estate

Additional Information

Year Founded: 1995
Current Activity Level : Actively seeking new investments

SECOND ALPHA PARTNERS LLC

330 Madison Avenue
Ninth Floor
New York, NY USA 10017
Phone: 1212446160
Website: secondalpha.com

Management and Staff
Eugene Galantini, Chief Financial Officer
Jim Sanger, Co-Founder
Richard Brekka, Co-Founder

Type of Firm
Private Equity Advisor or Fund of Funds

Association Membership
New England Venture Capital Association
National Venture Capital Association - USA (NVCA)

Project Preferences

Type of Financing Preferred:
Fund of Funds of Second

Geographical Preferences

United States Preferences:

Canadian Preferences:
All Canada

International Preferences:
All International

Industry Preferences

In Communications prefer:
Telecommunications

In Business Serv. prefer:
Media

Additional Information

Name of Most Recent Fund: Second Alpha Partners II, L.P.
Most Recent Fund Was Raised: 12/04/2013
Year Founded: 2012
Capital Under Management: $20,825,000
Current Activity Level : Actively seeking new investments

SECOND AVENUE PARTNERS

1301 Second Avenue, Suite 2850
Seattle, WA USA 98101
Phone: 2063321200
Fax: 2063221201

Management and Staff

Frank Higgins, Partner
Keith Grinstein, Partner
Michael Slade, Co-Founder
Nicolas Hanauer, Co-Founder

Type of Firm

Private Equity Firm

Project Preferences

Type of Financing Preferred:
Early Stage
Balanced

Industry Preferences

In Internet Specific prefer:
Internet

Additional Information

Year Founded: 2000
Current Activity Level : Actively seeking new investments

SECOND CENTURY VENTURES LLC

430 North Michigan Avenure
Fifth Floor
Chicago, IL USA 60611
Phone: 3123298524
E-mail: Info@SecondCenturyVentures.com
Website: www.secondcenturyventures.com

Management and Staff

Constance Freedman, Managing Director
Dale Stinton, President

Type of Firm

Private Equity Firm

Association Membership

National Venture Capital Association - USA (NVCA)

Project Preferences

Type of Financing Preferred:
Balanced

Additional Information

Year Founded: 2009
Capital Under Management: $20,000,000
Current Activity Level : Actively seeking new investments

SECOND CITY CAPITAL PARTNERS

1075 West Georgia Street, Suite 2600
Vancouver, Canada V6E 3C9
Phone: 6048063350
Fax: 6046614873
E-mail: info@secondcitycapital.com
Website: www.secondcitycapital.com

Management and Staff

Colin Bosa, Managing Director
Gregory Tylee, Managing Director
James Farrar, Managing Director
Ryan Chan, Chief Financial Officer
Ryan Dunfield, Vice President
Samuel Belzberg, Partner

Type of Firm

Private Equity Firm

Project Preferences

Type of Financing Preferred:
Leveraged Buyout
Value-Add

Geographical Preferences

United States Preferences:

Canadian Preferences:
All Canada

Industry Preferences

In Industrial/Energy prefer:
Energy
Oil and Gas Exploration
Materials

In Financial Services prefer:
Real Estate

In Business Serv. prefer:
Services

Additional Information

Name of Most Recent Fund: Second City Capital Partners II, L.P.
Most Recent Fund Was Raised: 06/14/2011
Year Founded: 2004
Capital Under Management: $153,975,000

Current Activity Level : Actively seeking new investments

SECTION 32 LLC

2033 San Elijo Avenue, Suite 565
Cardiff, CA USA 92007
Website: www.section32.com

Management and Staff

Bill Maris, Founder

Type of Firm

Private Equity Firm

Project Preferences

Type of Financing Preferred:
Balanced

Industry Preferences

In Medical/Health prefer:
Health Services

In Agr/Forestr/Fish prefer:
Agriculture related

Additional Information

Year Founded: 2017
Capital Under Management: $151,300,000
Current Activity Level : Actively seeking new investments

SECTORAL ASSET MANAGEMENT INC

1000 Sherbrooke St. West, Suite 2120
Montreal, Canada H3A 3G4
Phone: 5148498777
Fax: 5148496777
E-mail: info@sectoral.com
Website: www.sectoral.com

Other Offices

Seven Rue du Marche
Geneva, Switzerland 1204
Phone: 41223166633
Fax: 41223166631

Type of Firm

Investment Management Firm

Project Preferences

Type of Financing Preferred:
Generalist PE
Public Companies

Geographical Preferences

United States Preferences:
North America

International Preferences:
Europe
Rest of World
Asia

Industry Focus
(% based on actual investment)
Biotechnology 64.8%
Medical/Health 35.2%

Additional Information
Year Founded: 2000
Capital Under Management: $1,500,000,000
Current Activity Level : Actively seeking new investments

SECURITY GROWTH PARTNERS

450 Seventh Avenue, Suite 2100
New York, NY USA 10123
Phone: 2128751210
E-mail: info@securitygrowth.com
Website: www.securitygrowth.com

Type of Firm
Private Equity Firm

Project Preferences

Type of Financing Preferred:
Early Stage

Geographical Preferences

United States Preferences:
All U.S.

Industry Preferences

In Communications prefer:
Wireless Communications

In Computer Software prefer:
Software

Additional Information
Year Founded: 2006
Current Activity Level : Actively seeking new investments

SECUS ASSET MANAGEMENT SA

ul. Paderewskiego 32c
Katowice, Poland 40-282
Phone: 48-32-352-0013
Fax: 48-32-352-0014
E-mail: kontakt@secus.pl
Website: www.secus.pl

Other Offices
ul. Wspolna 50A
Warsaw, Poland 00-684
Phone: 48-22-403-60-40
Fax: 48-22-403-60-50

Type of Firm
Private Equity Firm

Association Membership
Polish Venture Capital Association (PSIC/PPEA)

Project Preferences

Type of Financing Preferred:
Balanced
Later Stage

Geographical Preferences

International Preferences:
Poland

Industry Preferences

In Industrial/Energy prefer:
Energy

In Financial Services prefer:
Financial Services

Additional Information
Year Founded: 2004
Current Activity Level : Actively seeking new investments

SEDCO CAPITAL CO

King Abdulaziz (Malik) Road
Morgan District
Jeddah, Saudi Arabia
Phone: 96622151500
Website: www.sedcocapital.com

Type of Firm
Private Equity Firm

Project Preferences

Type of Financing Preferred:
Leveraged Buyout
Expansion
Generalist PE

Industry Preferences

In Medical/Health prefer:
Health Services

In Industrial/Energy prefer:
Energy Conservation Relat

Additional Information
Year Founded: 2010
Current Activity Level : Actively seeking new investments

SEDCO HOLDING

Precinct Bldg. No 4, Level 5,, Suite 501
Dubai, Utd. Arab Em.
Phone: 97143637166
Fax: 97143637164
E-mail: dig@sedco.com
Website: www.sedco.com

Type of Firm
Investment Management Firm

Association Membership
Gulf Venture Capital Association

Project Preferences

Type of Financing Preferred:
Later Stage
Management Buyouts
Acquisition

Size of Investments Considered:
Min Size of Investment Considered (000s): $20,000
Max Size of Investment Considered (000s): $40,000

Geographical Preferences

International Preferences:
Vietnam
Indonesia
Pakistan
India
Turkey
Thailand
Middle East
Asia
Singapore
Malaysia

Additional Information
Year Founded: 1976
Current Activity Level : Actively seeking new investments

SEED & SPEED GMBH

Hindenburgstrasse 42
Hannover, Germany 30175
Phone: 4951147353390
Fax: 4951147353397
E-mail: info@seedandspeed.de
Website: seedandspeed.de

Type of Firm
Private Equity Firm

Project Preferences

Type of Financing Preferred:
Early Stage
Seed

Geographical Preferences

International Preferences:
Germany

Additional Information
Year Founded: 2016
Current Activity Level : Actively seeking new investments

SEED CAPITAL DE BIZKAIA SGEIC SA

c/Elcano 9 - 10 Izqda
Bilbao, Spain 48008
Phone: 34944162223
Fax: 34944160223
E-mail: seedcapitalbizkaia@bizkaia.net

Type of Firm
Private Equity Firm

Association Membership
European Private Equity and Venture Capital Assoc.
Spanish Venture Capital Association (ASCRI)

Project Preferences

Type of Financing Preferred:
Startup

Geographical Preferences

International Preferences:
Spain

Additional Information
Year Founded: 1999
Capital Under Management: $1,800,000
Current Activity Level : Actively seeking new investments

SEED CAPITAL MANAGEMENT I/S

Diplomvej 381
Kongens Lyngby, Denmark 2800
Phone: 4577340755
Fax: 4570141515
E-mail: info@seedcapital.dk
Website: www.seedcapital.dk

Management and Staff
Anne Cathrine Wilhjelm, Partner
Carsten Schou, General Partner
Lars Andersen, General Partner
Peter Torstensen, Chief Executive Officer
Ulla Brockenhuus-Schack, Managing Partner

Type of Firm
Investment Management Firm

Association Membership
Danish Venture Capital Association (DVCA)

Project Preferences

Type of Financing Preferred:
Early Stage
Seed
Startup

Size of Investments Considered:
Min Size of Investment Considered (000s): $176
Max Size of Investment Considered (000s): $3,521

Geographical Preferences

United States Preferences:
All U.S.

International Preferences:
Sweden
Scandanavia/Nordic Region
Denmark

Industry Preferences

In Communications prefer:
Communications and Media
Commercial Communications
CATV & Pay TV Systems
Telecommunications

In Computer Software prefer:
Software

In Medical/Health prefer:
Medical/Health
Medical Diagnostics
Medical Therapeutics
Medical Products
Pharmaceuticals

In Consumer Related prefer:
Entertainment and Leisure

In Industrial/Energy prefer:
Industrial Products
Advanced Materials

In Business Serv. prefer:
Services

Additional Information
Name of Most Recent Fund: SEED Capital Denmark II K/S
Most Recent Fund Was Raised: 02/03/2010
Year Founded: 2004
Capital Under Management: $3,350,100,000
Current Activity Level : Actively seeking new investments

SEED CAPITAL PARTNERS

3008 Taylor Street
Dallas, TX USA 75226
Phone: 2144325817
Fax: 2146511862
E-mail: info2@seedcap.com
Website: www.seedcap.com

Other Offices
585 Massachusetts Avenue
Fourth Floor
Cambridge, MA USA 02139
Phone: 617-299-2740
Fax: 617-299-2749

Type of Firm
Bank Affiliated

Project Preferences

Role in Financing:
Prefer role as deal originator

Type of Financing Preferred:
Early Stage
Seed

Size of Investments Considered:
Min Size of Investment Considered (000s): $250
Max Size of Investment Considered (000s): $2,500

Geographical Preferences

United States Preferences:
Northeast

Canadian Preferences:
Quebec
Ontario

International Preferences:
Israel

Industry Focus
(% based on actual investment)

Internet Specific	33.6%
Computer Software and Services	25.7%
Communications and Media	20.2%
Industrial/Energy	9.0%
Biotechnology	5.7%
Semiconductors/Other Elect.	4.0%
Computer Hardware	1.7%

Additional Information
Year Founded: 1999
Capital Under Management: $58,000,000
Current Activity Level : Actively seeking new investments
Method of Compensation: Return on investment is of primary concern, do not charge fees

SEED EQUITY CAPITAL PARTNERS LLC

4640 S. Holladay Village Plaza
Suite 206
Holladay, UT USA 84117
Phone: 8444387333
Fax: 3852757225
E-mail: info@seedequitypartners.com
Website: www.seedequitypartners.com

Type of Firm
Private Equity Firm

Project Preferences

Type of Financing Preferred:
Early Stage
Startup

Size of Investments Considered:
Min Size of Investment Considered (000s): $100
Max Size of Investment Considered (000s): $500

Industry Preferences

In Computer Software prefer:
Software

In Consumer Related prefer:
Consumer Services

In Financial Services prefer:
Financial Services

Additional Information
Year Founded: 2014
Current Activity Level : Actively seeking new investments

SEED SYNDICATES SL

C / Gandia 1
Madrid, Spain 28007
Website: seedsyndicates.com

Type of Firm
Incubator/Development Program

Project Preferences

Type of Financing Preferred:
Startup

Industry Preferences

In Internet Specific prefer:
E-Commerce Technology
Internet
Ecommerce

Additional Information
Year Founded: 1969
Current Activity Level : Actively seeking new investments

SEEDCAMP INVESTMENTS LLP

4-5 Bonhill Street
London, United Kingdom EC2A 4BX
E-mail: info@seedcamp.com

Management and Staff
Carlos Espinal, Partner
Reshma Sohoni, Co-Founder

Type of Firm
Incubator/Development Program

Project Preferences

Type of Financing Preferred:
Early Stage
Seed
Startup

Geographical Preferences

United States Preferences:
All U.S.

International Preferences:
Europe

Additional Information
Name of Most Recent Fund: Seedcamp Fund II
Most Recent Fund Was Raised: 11/16/2010
Year Founded: 2007
Capital Under Management: $78,590,000
Current Activity Level : Actively seeking new investments

SEEDCAPITAL DORTMUND & GMBH CO KG

Freistuhl 2
Dortmund, Germany 44137
Phone: 49023118334201
Fax: 49023118334299
E-mail: info@seed-do.de
Website: www.seedcapital-dortmund.de

Type of Firm
Private Equity Firm

Association Membership
German Venture Capital Association (BVK)

Project Preferences

Type of Financing Preferred:
Early Stage
Seed
Startup

Geographical Preferences

International Preferences:
Europe
Western Europe
Germany

Additional Information
Year Founded: 2006
Current Activity Level : Actively seeking new investments

SEEDER FUND SA

Allee de la Recherche 12
Bruxelles, Belgium 1070
Phone: 3225295967
Fax: 32473354598
E-mail: info@seederfund.be
Website: www.seederfund.be

Type of Firm
Incubator/Development Program

Geographical Preferences

International Preferences:
Europe
Belgium

Additional Information
Year Founded: 2016

Capital Under Management: $13,080,000
Current Activity Level : Actively seeking new investments

SEEDFUND

Shakti Mills Lane, E Moses Rd.
3 Turf Estate
Mahalaxmi, Mumbai, India 400 011
Phone: 912224902201
Fax: 912224902205
E-mail: info@seedfund.in

Management and Staff
Bharati Jacob, Partner
Mahesh Murthy, Partner
Pravin Gandhi, Partner
Sanjay Anandaram, Venture Partner

Type of Firm
Private Equity Firm

Association Membership
Indian Venture Capital Association (IVCA)

Project Preferences

Type of Financing Preferred:
Early Stage
Seed
Startup

Size of Investments Considered:
Min Size of Investment Considered (000s): $220
Max Size of Investment Considered (000s): $1,101

Geographical Preferences

International Preferences:
India

Industry Preferences

In Communications prefer:
Wireless Communications

In Internet Specific prefer:
Internet

In Consumer Related prefer:
Retail

In Business Serv. prefer:
Media

Additional Information
Year Founded: 2006
Current Activity Level : Actively seeking new investments

SEEDINVEST TECHNOLOGY LLC

116 West Houston, Sixth Floor
New York, NY USA 10012
E-mail: contactus@seedinvest.com
Website: www.seedinvest.com

Type of Firm
Private Equity Firm

Project Preferences

Type of Financing Preferred:
Early Stage

Industry Preferences

In Financial Services prefer:
Financial Services

Additional Information
Year Founded: 2012
Capital Under Management: $200,000
Current Activity Level : Actively seeking new investments

SEEDSTARTUP

Emirates Tower
Level 41
Dubai, Utd. Arab Em.
Phone: 97143199069
Website: www.seedstartup.com

Management and Staff
Rony El-Nashar, Managing Partner
Salem Al Noaimi, Partner

Type of Firm
Private Equity Firm

Project Preferences

Type of Financing Preferred:
Early Stage
Seed
Startup

Industry Preferences

In Internet Specific prefer:
Web Aggregation/Portals

Additional Information
Year Founded: 1969
Current Activity Level : Actively seeking new investments

SEEK CAPITAL LLC

1230 Peachtree Street NE, Suite 2445
Atlanta, GA USA 30309
Phone: 4045497890
E-mail: info@seekcap.com
Website: www.seekcap.com

Management and Staff
Jeffrey Koebler, Managing Partner

Type of Firm
Investment Management Firm

Project Preferences

Type of Financing Preferred:
Generalist PE

Additional Information
Year Founded: 2007
Current Activity Level : Actively seeking new investments

SEGULAH ADVISOR AB

Ostermalmstorg 1
Stockholm, Sweden 114 84
Phone: 4684028700
Fax: 4684028799
E-mail: info@segulah.se
Website: www.segulah.se

Management and Staff
Christian Tegenmark, Partner
Christian Sievert, Partner
Erik Thornell, Partner
Jorgen Centerman, Partner
Lennart Kalen, Partner
Marcus Jansson, Partner
Marcus Planting-Bergloo, Partner
Percy Calissendorff, Partner
Peter Elving, Partner
Sebastian Ehrnrooth, Managing Partner

Type of Firm
Private Equity Firm

Association Membership
Swedish Venture Capital Association (SVCA)
European Private Equity and Venture Capital Assoc.

Project Preferences

Role in Financing:
Prefer role as deal originator

Type of Financing Preferred:
Leveraged Buyout

Geographical Preferences

International Preferences:
Western Europe
Scandanavia/Nordic Region

Industry Focus
(% based on actual investment)
Industrial/Energy	44.3%
Other Products	32.4%
Computer Software and Services	13.1%
Medical/Health	10.1%
Internet Specific	0.0%
Consumer Related	0.0%
Communications and Media	0.0%

Additional Information
Name of Most Recent Fund: Segulah IV, L.P.
Most Recent Fund Was Raised: 10/23/2007
Year Founded: 1994
Capital Under Management: $1,365,200,000
Current Activity Level : Actively seeking new investments

SEIDLER EQUITY PARTNERS

4640 Admiralty Way, Suite 1200
Marina del Rey, CA USA 90292
Phone: 2136834622
Fax: 2136240691
E-mail: info@sepfunds.com
Website: www.sepfunds.com

Management and Staff
Christopher Eastland, Partner
Eric Kutsenda, Managing Partner
Leonard Lee, Partner
Matt Seidler, Partner
Peter Seidler, Managing Partner
Robert Seidler, Managing Partner
Tobin Ryan, Partner
Troy Smildzins, Partner

Type of Firm
Private Equity Firm

Project Preferences

Type of Financing Preferred:
Leveraged Buyout
Later Stage
Management Buyouts
Acquisition
Recapitalizations

Geographical Preferences

United States Preferences:

Additional Information
Name of Most Recent Fund: Seidler Equity Partners III, L.P.
Most Recent Fund Was Raised: 02/15/2006
Year Founded: 2000
Capital Under Management: $891,000,000
Current Activity Level : Actively seeking new investments

SEIR VENTURE CAPITAL

2/F, 12-20 Jamwon-dong
Seocho-ku
Seoul, South Korea 137-903
Phone: 82-2-547-2300
Fax: 82-2-547-8477

Management and Staff
Hyun Joo Choi, President

Type of Firm
Private Equity Firm

Project Preferences

Type of Financing Preferred:
Balanced

Geographical Preferences

International Preferences:
Korea, South

Additional Information

Year Founded: 2007
Current Activity Level : Actively seeking new investments

SEJIN TS CO LTD

#561-1 Jimoon-Ri, Wongok-Myun
Kyungki-Do
Ansung, South Korea 456-810
Phone: 82-31-650-3700
Fax: 82-31-692-3700
E-mail: thpark@sejints.co.kr

Management and Staff

Dal-je Kim, President

Type of Firm

Private Equity Firm

Project Preferences

Type of Financing Preferred:
Balanced

Geographical Preferences

International Preferences:
Korea, South

Additional Information

Year Founded: 1990
Current Activity Level : Actively seeking new investments

SELECT CAPITAL VENTURES

4718 Old Gettysburg Road, Suite 405
Mechanicsburg, PA USA 17055
Phone: 7179721304
Fax: 7179721050
E-mail: general@selectcapitalventures.com
Website: www.selectcapitalventures.com

Management and Staff

Debra Hellyer, Chief Financial Officer
Robert Ortenzio, Co-Founder
Rocco Ortenzio, Co-Founder

Type of Firm

Private Equity Firm

Project Preferences

Role in Financing:
Will function either as deal originator or investor in deals created by others

Type of Financing Preferred:
Early Stage
Expansion
Seed

Size of Investments Considered:
Min Size of Investment Considered (000s): $500
Max Size of Investment Considered (000s): $2,700

Geographical Preferences

United States Preferences:
Mid Atlantic

Industry Preferences

In Computer Software prefer:
Software

In Medical/Health prefer:
Medical/Health
Medical Products
Pharmaceuticals

In Consumer Related prefer:
Consumer Services

In Financial Services prefer:
Financial Services

Additional Information

Name of Most Recent Fund: Select Capital Ventures I, L.P.
Most Recent Fund Was Raised: 06/30/2002
Year Founded: 2002
Capital Under Management: $14,000,000
Current Activity Level : Actively seeking new investments

SELECT VENTURE PARTNERS LLC

159 Lichfield Boulevard, Suite 101
Fredericksburg, VA USA 22406
E-mail: info@selectvp.com
Website: www.selectvp.com

Management and Staff

Adam Slovik, Managing Partner
Jonathan Zhukovsky, Managing Partner
Michael Pratt, Co-Founder
Sameer Shalaby, Co-Founder
Sol Zlotchenko, Managing Partner

Type of Firm

Private Equity Firm

Project Preferences

Type of Financing Preferred:
Early Stage
Seed
Startup

Geographical Preferences

United States Preferences:
Pennsylvania
Massachusetts
Utah
Washington
New York
East Coast

Industry Preferences

In Computer Software prefer:
Software
Applications Software

In Internet Specific prefer:
Ecommerce

In Semiconductor/Electr prefer:
Analytic/Scientific

Additional Information

Year Founded: 2014
Current Activity Level : Actively seeking new investments

SELIGMAN PRIVATE EQUITY SELECT LLP

37 Upper Brook Street
2nd Floor
London, United Kingdom W1K 7PR
Phone: 442073550590
E-mail: gk@seligmanselect.com
Website: www.seligmanselect.com

Type of Firm

Private Equity Advisor or Fund of Funds

Project Preferences

Type of Financing Preferred:
Fund of Funds
Fund of Funds of Second

Geographical Preferences

International Preferences:
Europe

Additional Information

Year Founded: 2003
Capital Under Management: $29,472,000
Current Activity Level : Actively seeking new investments

SELVAAG INVEST AS

Lorenvangen 22
Oslo, Norway 0580
Phone: 4723137000
Fax: 4722492469
E-mail: selvaag.invest@selvaag.no

Type of Firm

Corporate PE/Venture

Project Preferences

Type of Financing Preferred:
Balanced

Size of Investments Considered:
Min Size of Investment Considered (000s): $1,800
Max Size of Investment Considered (000s): $5,400

Geographical Preferences

International Preferences:
Norway

Industry Preferences

In Communications prefer:
Communications and Media

In Computer Software prefer:
Software

In Biotechnology prefer:
Biotechnology

In Industrial/Energy prefer:
Energy
Oil and Gas Exploration

In Transportation prefer:
Transportation

In Financial Services prefer:
Financial Services

In Agr/Forestr/Fish prefer:
Agriculture related

Additional Information

Year Founded: 1984
Current Activity Level : Actively seeking new investments

SELWAY PARTNERS L L C

900 Third Avenue
19th Floor
New York, NY USA 10022
Phone: 6464216666
E-mail: info@selwaycapital.com
Website: www.selway.com

Other Offices

100 Bomont Place
Totowa, NJ USA 07512
Phone: 973-785-1774
Fax: 973-785-8628

Management and Staff

Randy Illig, Venture Partner

Type of Firm

Private Equity Firm

Project Preferences

Type of Financing Preferred:
Balanced

Industry Preferences

In Communications prefer:
Communications and Media

In Consumer Related prefer:
Education Related

In Business Serv. prefer:
Services

Additional Information

Year Founded: 2009
Current Activity Level : Actively seeking new investments

SEM GENOPOLE SAEM

5, Rue Henri Desbrueres
Evry, France 91030
Phone: 33160878300
Fax: 33160878301
E-mail: presse@genopole.fr
Website: www.semgenopole.com

Management and Staff

Pierre Tambourin, Chief Executive Officer
Thierry Mandon, President

Type of Firm

Corporate PE/Venture

Project Preferences

Type of Financing Preferred:
Early Stage
Seed
Startup

Geographical Preferences

International Preferences:
Europe
Eastern Europe
France

Industry Preferences

In Biotechnology prefer:
Biotechnology
Human Biotechnology
Genetic Engineering
Industrial Biotechnology
Biotech Related Research

Additional Information

Year Founded: 1998
Current Activity Level : Actively seeking new investments

SEMBAWANG CAPITAL PTE LTD

No. 143 Cecil Street
09-01
Singapore, Singapore 069542
Phone: 65-6226-3383
Fax: 65-6221-9579

Management and Staff

Boon Wah Tan, Vice President

Type of Firm

Corporate PE/Venture

Project Preferences

Type of Financing Preferred:
Expansion
Start-up Financing

Geographical Preferences

International Preferences:
Asia

Industry Preferences

In Medical/Health prefer:
Medical/Health

Additional Information

Year Founded: 1997
Current Activity Level : Actively seeking new investments

SENAHILL INVESTMENT GROUP LLC

115 Broadway
New York, NY USA 10006
Phone: 2127308544
Website: senahill.com

Type of Firm

Investment Management Firm

Project Preferences

Type of Financing Preferred:
Early Stage

Industry Preferences

In Financial Services prefer:
Financial Services

Additional Information

Year Founded: 2015
Current Activity Level : Actively seeking new investments

SENDERO CAPITAL PARTNERS INC

800 Rockmead, Suite 136
Kingwood, TX USA 77339
Phone: 2817138912
Fax: 2817138913
Website: www.sendero.biz

Type of Firm

Private Equity Firm

Project Preferences

Type of Financing Preferred:
Leveraged Buyout
Management Buyouts
Acquisition
Recapitalizations

Geographical Preferences

United States Preferences:

Industry Preferences

In Industrial/Energy prefer:
Energy
Oil and Gas Exploration

Additional Information

Year Founded: 2011
Current Activity Level : Actively seeking new investments

SENECA PARTNERS INC

300 Park Street, Suite 400
Birmingham, MI USA 48009
Phone: 2487236650
Fax: 2487236651
E-mail: info@senecapartners.com
Website: www.senecapartners.com

Other Offices

2201 Waukegan Road, Suite 245
Bannockburn, IL USA 60015
Phone: 8472827040
Fax: 8472827043

121 West Washington Street, Suite 400
Ann Arbor, MI USA 48104
Phone: 7349964434
Fax: 8889259867

Management and Staff

Alfred Robertson, Vice President
Anthony Zambelli, Managing Director
Michael Skaff, Managing Director
Rajesh Kothari, Managing Director

Type of Firm

Bank Affiliated

Project Preferences

Role in Financing:
Will function either as deal originator or investor in deals created by others

Type of Financing Preferred:
Early Stage
Balanced
Later Stage
Seed

Size of Investments Considered:
Min Size of Investment Considered (000s): $500
Max Size of Investment Considered (000s): $2,500

Geographical Preferences

United States Preferences:
Midwest

Industry Preferences

In Medical/Health prefer:
Medical/Health
Medical Products
Health Services

Additional Information

Year Founded: 2005
Capital Under Management: $20,000,000
Current Activity Level : Actively seeking new investments
Method of Compensation: Return on investment is of primary concern, do not charge fees

SENECA PARTNERS LTD

12 The Parks
Merseyside, United Kingdom WA12 0JQ
E-mail: enquiries@senecapartners.co.uk
Website: senecapartners.co.uk

Management and Staff

David Thomas, Partner
Melanie Hird, Founder

Type of Firm

Investment Management Firm

Project Preferences

Type of Financing Preferred:
Leveraged Buyout
Turnaround
Management Buyouts
Acquisition
Special Situation
Distressed Debt

Geographical Preferences

International Preferences:
United Kingdom

Additional Information

Year Founded: 2012
Current Activity Level : Actively seeking new investments

SENOVO GMBH

Amalienstrasse 62
Muenchen, Germany 80799
Phone: 4989416176250
Fax: 4989416176259
Website: www.senovo.de

Type of Firm

Private Equity Firm

Association Membership

European Private Equity and Venture Capital Assoc.

Project Preferences

Type of Financing Preferred:
Early Stage
Balanced
Later Stage
Seed
Startup

Geographical Preferences

International Preferences:
Germany

Industry Preferences

In Computer Software prefer:
Applications Software

In Internet Specific prefer:
E-Commerce Technology

Additional Information

Year Founded: 2011
Current Activity Level : Actively seeking new investments

SENSHU IKEDA CAPITAL CO LTD

18-14 Chaya-machi,Kita-ku
4F Osaka Umeda Ikegin Bldg
Osaka, Japan 530-0013
Phone: 81663757204
Fax: 81363757214
E-mail: info@ikegin-c.jp
Website: www.ikegin-c.jp

Type of Firm

Bank Affiliated

Association Membership

Japan Venture Capital Association

Additional Information

Year Founded: 1989
Current Activity Level : Actively seeking new investments

SENTICA PARTNERS OY

Bulevardi One
Helsinki, Finland 00100
Phone: 358207529610
Fax: 358207529637
Website: www.sentica.fi

Other Offices

TietoTeknia House
P.O. Box 1750, Savilahdentie 6
Kuopio, Finland 70211
Phone: 358207529610

Kelloportinkatu 1 B
Tampere, Finland 33100
Phone: 358207529610

Management and Staff
Christer Niemi, Partner
Eero Leskinen, Partner
Johan Wentzel, Partner
Lasse Gronlund, Partner
Marjatta Rytomaa, Partner
Mika Uotila, Managing Partner
Pentti Tuunala, Partner

Type of Firm
Private Equity Firm

Association Membership
Finnish Venture Capital Association (FVCA)

Project Preferences

Type of Financing Preferred:
Leveraged Buyout
Generalist PE
Balanced
Management Buyouts

Size of Investments Considered:
Min Size of Investment Considered (000s): $1,300
Max Size of Investment Considered (000s): $13,000

Geographical Preferences

International Preferences:
Scandanavia/Nordic Region
Finland

Industry Preferences

In Computer Software prefer:
Software

In Medical/Health prefer:
Medical/Health
Health Services

In Consumer Related prefer:
Consumer Products

In Industrial/Energy prefer:
Industrial Products
Materials

In Business Serv. prefer:
Services
Consulting Services

In Manufact. prefer:
Manufacturing

Additional Information
Name of Most Recent Fund: Sentica Buyout IV
Most Recent Fund Was Raised: 02/07/2013
Year Founded: 1998
Capital Under Management: $228,800,000
Current Activity Level : Actively seeking new investments

SENTIENT GROUP LTD

64 Earth Close
First Floor, Landmark Square
Grand Cayman, Cayman Islands KY1-1007
Website: www.thesentientgroup.com

Other Offices
1001 Square Victoria, Suite 450, Montreal Herald Building
Montreal, Canada H2Z 2B1

264 George St., Australia Square Tower, Suite 24, Level 24
Sydney, Australia 2000
Phone: 61282432900
Fax: 61282432990

Management and Staff
Colin Maclean, Founder
Mike De Leeuw, Chief Financial Officer

Type of Firm
Private Equity Firm

Industry Preferences

In Industrial/Energy prefer:
Energy
Environmental Related

In Agr/Forestr/Fish prefer:
Mining and Minerals

Additional Information
Name of Most Recent Fund: Sentient Global Resources Fund IV, L.P.
Most Recent Fund Was Raised: 05/18/2011
Year Founded: 2001
Capital Under Management: $1,300,000,000
Current Activity Level : Actively seeking new investments

SENTINEL ADVISORS L L C

1516 Foxford Road
Greeneville, TN USA 37743
Phone: 8779050957
E-mail: info@SentinelAdvisors.com
Website: www.sentineladvisors.com

Other Offices
546 Fifth Avenue
New York, NY USA 10036
Phone: 212-391-1818
Fax: 212-391-4323

Type of Firm
Private Equity Firm

Additional Information
Year Founded: 1999
Current Activity Level : Actively seeking new investments

SENTINEL CAPITAL PARTNERS LLC

330 Madison Avenue, 27th Floor
New York, NY USA 10017
Phone: 2126883100
Fax: 2126886513
E-mail: info@sentinelpartners.com
Website: www.sentinelpartners.com

Management and Staff
C. Scott Perry, Principal
David Lobel, Managing Partner
Douglas Levy, Chief Financial Officer
Eric Bommer, Partner
Graham Schena, Principal
James Coady, Partner
John McCormack, Partner
John Van Sickle, Vice President
Michael Purcell, Vice President
Michael Fabian, Principal
Paul Murphy, Partner

Type of Firm
Private Equity Firm

Project Preferences

Role in Financing:
Prefer role as deal originator but will also invest in deals created by others

Type of Financing Preferred:
Leveraged Buyout
Turnaround
Management Buyouts
Acquisition
Special Situation
Recapitalizations

Geographical Preferences

United States Preferences:
North America

Canadian Preferences:
All Canada

Industry Focus
(% based on actual investment)

Medical/Health	48.7%
Other Products	22.7%
Consumer Related	14.8%
Industrial/Energy	6.9%
Internet Specific	4.9%
Communications and Media	2.0%

Additional Information
Name of Most Recent Fund: Sentinel Capital Partners V, L.P.
Most Recent Fund Was Raised: 08/01/2013
Year Founded: 1995
Capital Under Management: $1,300,000,000
Current Activity Level : Actively seeking new investments
Method of Compensation: Return on investment is of primary concern, do not charge fees

SEQUEL VENTURE PARTNERS

4430 Arapahoe Avenue, Suite 220
Boulder, CO USA 80303
Phone: 3035460400
Fax: 3035469728
Website: www.sequelvc.com

Management and Staff
Christopher Scoggins, Venture Partner
Daniel Mitchell, Co-Founder
John Greff, Co-Founder
Kinney Johnson, Co-Founder
Thomas Washing, Co-Founder
Tim Connor, Partner

Type of Firm
Private Equity Firm

Project Preferences

Role in Financing:
Prefer role as deal originator but will also invest in deals created by others

Type of Financing Preferred:
Early Stage

Geographical Preferences

United States Preferences:
Rocky Mountain
Colorado

Industry Focus
(% based on actual investment)

Internet Specific	31.7%
Computer Software and Services	30.3%
Medical/Health	13.1%
Biotechnology	9.8%
Semiconductors/Other Elect.	4.3%
Other Products	3.3%
Communications and Media	3.3%
Industrial/Energy	2.4%
Computer Hardware	1.7%

Additional Information
Year Founded: 1996
Capital Under Management: $409,000,000
Current Activity Level : Actively seeking new investments

SEQUOIA APPS LLC

11180 Sunrise Valley Drive, Suite 110
Reston, VA USA 20191
Phone: 5712677945
Fax: 5713138630
Website: www.sequoia-apps.com

Type of Firm
Incubator/Development Program

Project Preferences

Type of Financing Preferred:
Early Stage
Seed

Additional Information
Year Founded: 2015
Current Activity Level : Actively seeking new investments

SEQUOIA CAPITAL INDIA

77 Town Ctr Off Hal Airport Rd
6F East Wing Block B
Bangalore, India 560037
Phone: 918041245880
Fax: 918041245884
Website: www.sequoiacap.com

Other Offices
2 Nelson Mandela Road
First Floor The Grand Hotel Gate 1
New Delhi, India 110070
Phone: 911149567200
Fax: 911149567201

902 Nicholas Piramai Towers
Peninsula Corporate Park
Mumbai, India 400013
Phone: 91-22-4074-7272
Fax: 91-22-4074-7271

Management and Staff
Abhay Pandey, Managing Director
Abheek Anand, Principal
Anjana Sasidharan, Principal
Bharat Singh, Chief Financial Officer
G.V. Ravishankar, Managing Director
GV Ravishankar, Managing Director
Gautam Mago, Principal
Mohit Bhatnagar, Managing Director
Nipun Mehra, Vice President
Pieter Kemps, Vice President
Rohit Bhat, Vice President
Shailendra Singh, Managing Director
Shailendra Jit Singh, Managing Director
Shailesh Lakhani, Principal
V.T. Bharadwaj, Managing Director
VT Bharadwaj, Managing Director
Yinglan Tan, Venture Partner

Type of Firm
Private Equity Firm

Association Membership
Indian Venture Capital Association (IVCA)

Project Preferences

Role in Financing:
Prefer role as deal originator but will also invest in deals created by others

Type of Financing Preferred:
Early Stage
Balanced
Later Stage
Seed

Geographical Preferences

International Preferences:
Asia Pacific
India
Asia

Industry Preferences

In Medical/Health prefer:
Health Services

In Consumer Related prefer:
Consumer

Additional Information
Year Founded: 2000
Capital Under Management: $350,000,000
Current Activity Level : Actively seeking new investments
Method of Compensation: Return on investment is of primary concern, do not charge fees

SEQUOIA CAPITAL OPERATIONS LLC

3000 Sand Hill Road
Building Four, Suite 250
Menlo Park, CA USA 94025
Phone: 6508543927
Fax: 6508542977
Website: www.sequoiacap.com

Other Offices
1366 Nanjing West Road
Room 4603,Plaza 66, Tower 2 Jingan Dist.
Shanghai, China 200040
Phone: 86-21-6288-4222
Fax: 86-21-6288-4350

Peninsula Corporate Park
902 Nicholas Piramal Towers
Mumbai, India 400013
Phone: 91-22-407-47272
Fax: 91-22-407-47271
, Suite 235, Hyatt Regency
Bhikaji Cama Place
New Delhi, India 110067
Phone: 91-11-4165-8040
Fax: 91-11-4165-8046

Jianguo Road
Room 3606, China Cntrl Tower 3
Beijing, China 100025
Phone: 86-10-8447-5668
Fax: 86-10-84475-669

88 Queensway Road
Two Pacific Place Suite 2215, 22nd Floor
Hong Kong, Hong Kong
Phone: 852-2501-8989
Fax: 852-2501-5249

One and Two Murphy Road, Ulsoor
The Millenia Tower A, 11th Floor
Bangalore, India 560025
Phone: 91-80-4124-5880
Fax: 91-80-4124-5884

The Grand Hotel, Gate 1, 1st Floor
2, Nelson Mandela Road Vasant Kunj Ph II
New Delhi, India 110070
Phone: 91-11-4956-7200
Fax: 91-11-4956-7201

Management and Staff
Donald Valentine, Founder
Gaurav Garg, Partner
Jess Lee, Partner
Joe Dobrenski, Partner
Mark Dempster, Partner
Mark Kvamme, Partner
Melinda Dunn, Chief Financial Officer
Mike Vernal, Partner
Todd Cozzens, Partner
William Coughran, Partner

Type of Firm
Private Equity Firm

Association Membership
Israel Venture Association
Western Association of Venture Capitalists (WAVC)
National Venture Capital Association - USA (NVCA)

Project Preferences

Role in Financing:
Will function either as deal originator or investor in deals created by others

Type of Financing Preferred:
Early Stage
Expansion
Balanced
Later Stage
Seed

Size of Investments Considered:
Min Size of Investment Considered (000s): $100
Max Size of Investment Considered (000s): $10,000

Industry Focus
(% based on actual investment)
Internet Specific	39.8%
Computer Software and Services	32.7%
Other Products	6.4%
Semiconductors/Other Elect.	4.5%
Communications and Media	4.1%
Consumer Related	3.2%
Computer Hardware	3.1%
Biotechnology	2.6%
Medical/Health	2.4%
Industrial/Energy	1.2%

Additional Information
Name of Most Recent Fund: Sequoia Capital U.S. Venture Fund XIV, L.P.
Most Recent Fund Was Raised: 08/15/2013
Year Founded: 1972
Capital Under Management: $4,000,000,000
Current Activity Level : Actively seeking new investments
Method of Compensation: Return on investment is of primary concern, do not charge fees

SERAFIN UNTERNEHMENS-GRUPPE GMBH

Sendlinger Strasse 10
Munich, Germany 80331
Phone: 498930906690
Fax: 4989309066911
Website: www.serafin-gruppe.de

Management and Staff
Dino Kitzinger, Managing Director
Falk Daum, Managing Director
Philipp Haindl, Managing Director

Type of Firm
Private Equity Firm

Project Preferences

Type of Financing Preferred:
Leveraged Buyout
Turnaround
Management Buyouts

Geographical Preferences

International Preferences:
Europe

Industry Preferences

In Consumer Related prefer:
Consumer

In Industrial/Energy prefer:
Industrial Products
Machinery

Additional Information
Year Founded: 2010
Current Activity Level : Actively seeking new investments

SERAPH GROUP

530 Piedmont Avenue, Northeast, Suite 209
Atlanta, GA USA 30308
Phone: 6789197191
Fax: 6789197242
E-mail: contact@seraphgroup.net
Website: www.seraphgroup.net

Other Offices
2000 University Avenue
East Palo Alto, CA USA 94303
Phone: 650-292-0893
Fax: 678-919-7242

Management and Staff
Tuff Yen, President, Founder

Type of Firm
Angel Group

Project Preferences

Type of Financing Preferred:
Early Stage
Seed

Additional Information
Name of Most Recent Fund: Seraph Partners IV, L.P.
Most Recent Fund Was Raised: 09/09/2008
Year Founded: 2005
Capital Under Management: $3,560,000
Current Activity Level : Actively seeking new investments

SERAPHIM CAPITAL (GENERAL PARTNER) LLP

Berkeley Square House
2nd Floor, Berkeley Square
London, United Kingdom W1J 6BD
Phone: 442070892318
Fax: 442070892301
E-mail: info@seraphimcapital.co.uk
Website: www.seraphimcapital.co.uk

Management and Staff
Anthony Clarke, Managing Partner
Mark Boggett, Managing Partner
Michael Jones, Managing Partner
Paul Thomas, Managing Partner

Type of Firm
Private Equity Firm

Association Membership
British Venture Capital Association (BVCA)

Project Preferences

Type of Financing Preferred:
Early Stage
Expansion
Balanced
Start-up Financing
Turnaround
Seed

Geographical Preferences

International Preferences:
Europe

Additional Information
Year Founded: 2006
Capital Under Management: $130,200,000
Current Activity Level : Actively seeking new investments

SERENA CAPITAL SAS

21 rue Auber
Paris, France 75009
Phone: 33177373030
Fax: 33177352515
E-mail: contact@serenacapital.com
Website: www.serenacapital.com

Management and Staff
Marc Fournier, Managing Partner
Philippe Hayat, Managing Partner
Xavier Lorphelin, Venture Partner

Type of Firm
Private Equity Firm

Association Membership
French Venture Capital Association (AFIC)
European Private Equity and Venture Capital Assoc.

Project Preferences

Type of Financing Preferred:
Early Stage
Later Stage

Size of Investments Considered:
Min Size of Investment Considered (000s): $3,972
Max Size of Investment Considered (000s): $10,594

Geographical Preferences

International Preferences:
Europe
France

Industry Preferences

In Communications prefer:
Commercial Communications
Telecommunications
Wireless Communications

In Computer Software prefer:
Software

In Business Serv. prefer:
Services
Media

Additional Information
Name of Most Recent Fund: Serena II FCPR
Most Recent Fund Was Raised: 09/16/2013
Year Founded: 2008
Capital Under Management: $354,500,000
Current Activity Level : Actively seeking new investments

SERENDIPITY IXORA AB (PUBL)

STUREPLAN 15
STOCKHOLM, Sweden SE-111

Type of Firm
Private Equity Firm

Project Preferences

Type of Financing Preferred:
Early Stage
Expansion

Geographical Preferences

International Preferences:
All International

Industry Preferences

In Biotechnology prefer:
Biotech Related Research

In Medical/Health prefer:
Medical/Health

In Industrial/Energy prefer:
Advanced Materials
Environmental Related

Additional Information
Year Founded: 2011
Current Activity Level : Actively seeking new investments

SERENE CAPITAL MANAGEMENT LLC

7033 East Greenway Parkway, Suite 220
Scottsdale, AZ USA 85254
Phone: 4084786960
Fax: 4804786961
Website: www.serenecapitalmgmt.com

Management and Staff
Scott Lavinia, Managing Partner

Type of Firm
Private Equity Firm

Project Preferences

Type of Financing Preferred:
Leveraged Buyout
Mezzanine
Management Buyouts

Industry Preferences

In Consumer Related prefer:
Consumer
Retail

In Industrial/Energy prefer:
Energy

In Business Serv. prefer:
Services

In Manufact. prefer:
Manufacturing

Additional Information
Year Founded: 2012
Current Activity Level : Actively seeking new investments

SERENT CAPITAL LLC

One Embarcadero Center, Suite 1680
San Francisco, CA USA 94111
Phone: 4153431050
Fax: 4153431051
E-mail: info@serentcapital.com
Website: www.serentcapital.com

Management and Staff
Aaron Dupuis, Principal
Andrew Peix, Vice President
Chris Choi, Principal
David Kennedy, Founding Partner
Jon Cheek, Vice President
Kevin Frick, Founding Partner
Lance Fenton, Principal
Mark Shang, Chief Financial Officer
Nadim Homsany, Vice President

Type of Firm
Private Equity Firm

Project Preferences

Type of Financing Preferred:
Leveraged Buyout
Management Buyouts
Recapitalizations

Industry Preferences

In Business Serv. prefer:
Services
Distribution

SEROBA KERNEL LIFE SCIENCES LTD

15 Molesworth Street
Dublin, Ireland
Phone: 35316334028
Fax: 35316779388
Website: www.seroba-kernel.com

Management and Staff

Alan O Connell, Partner
Andrew Duignan, Chief Financial Officer
Daniel O Mahony, Partner
Peter Sandys, Co-Founder

Type of Firm
Private Equity Firm

Association Membership
Irish Venture Capital Association
European Private Equity and Venture Capital Assoc.

Project Preferences

Role in Financing:
Prefer role as deal originator but will also invest in deals created by others

Type of Financing Preferred:
Early Stage
Expansion
Balanced

Geographical Preferences

International Preferences:
Ireland
United Kingdom
Europe
Western Europe

Industry Preferences

In Medical/Health prefer:
Medical Diagnostics
Medical Therapeutics
Medical Products

Additional Information
Name of Most Recent Fund: Seroba Kernel Life Sciences Fund II, L.P.
Most Recent Fund Was Raised: 02/09/2009
Year Founded: 2001
Capital Under Management: $97,600,000
Current Activity Level : Actively seeking new investments

Additional Information
Name of Most Recent Fund: Serent Capital II, L.P.
Most Recent Fund Was Raised: 01/30/2013
Year Founded: 2008
Capital Under Management: $600,000,000
Current Activity Level : Actively seeking new investments

SERPENT VENTURE CAPITAL LP

220 Cedar St
Petal, MS USA 39465
Phone: 6015224576

Type of Firm
Private Equity Firm

Additional Information
Year Founded: 2015
Current Activity Level : Actively seeking new investments

SERRA VENTURES LLC

2021 South First Street, Suite 206
Champaign, IL USA 61820
Phone: 2178195200
Fax: 2178195205
E-mail: info@serraventures.com
Website: serraventures.com

Management and Staff
Dennis Beard, Principal
Karin O Connor, Venture Partner
Tim Hoerr, Chief Executive Officer

Type of Firm
Private Equity Firm

Project Preferences

Type of Financing Preferred:
Early Stage
Expansion
Balanced
Later Stage
Seed
Startup

Geographical Preferences

United States Preferences:
Illinois
California
Texas

Industry Preferences

In Computer Software prefer:
Software

In Industrial/Energy prefer:
Materials
Environmental Related

In Agr/Forestr/Fish prefer:
Agriculture related

In Other prefer:
Environment Responsible

Additional Information
Name of Most Recent Fund: Serra Capital II, L.P.
Most Recent Fund Was Raised: 12/06/2013
Year Founded: 1998
Capital Under Management: $52,770,000
Current Activity Level : Actively seeking new investments

SERVE CAPITAL PARTNERS LLC

2901 Via Fortuna
Building 6, Suite 550
Austin, TX USA 78746
Phone: 5125054153
Website: www.servecapitalpartners.com

Type of Firm
SBIC

Additional Information
Year Founded: 2016
Capital Under Management: $52,180,000
Current Activity Level : Actively seeking new investments

SERVICE PROVIDER CAPITAL LLC

601 16th Street, Suite C - Suite 270
Golden, CO USA 80401
Phone: 4154654295
E-mail: founders@serviceprovidercapital.com
Website: www.serviceprovidercapital.com

Type of Firm
Private Equity Firm

Project Preferences

Type of Financing Preferred:
Seed

Additional Information
Year Founded: 2014
Current Activity Level : Actively seeking new investments

SET VENTURE PARTNERS BV

Keizersgracht 756
Amsterdam, Netherlands 1017 EZ
Phone: 31203200104
Fax: 31203200107
E-mail: info@chrysalixset.com
Website: www.setvp.com

Management and Staff
Wouter Jonk, Managing Partner
Yvette Go, Partner

Type of Firm
Private Equity Firm

Association Membership
European Private Equity and Venture Capital Assoc.

Project Preferences

Type of Financing Preferred:
Early Stage
Balanced

Size of Investments Considered:
Min Size of Investment Considered (000s): $739
Max Size of Investment Considered (000s): $7,390

Geographical Preferences

International Preferences:
Europe

Industry Preferences

In Industrial/Energy prefer:
Alternative Energy
Energy Conservation Relat
Environmental Related

In Other prefer:
Environment Responsible

Additional Information

Year Founded: 2007
Capital Under Management: $73,900,000
Current Activity Level: Actively seeking new investments

SEVEN MILE CAPITAL PARTNERS LP

515 Madison Avenue
15th Floor
New York, NY USA 10022
Phone: 2122074945
Fax: 6467371939
E-mail: info@sevenmilecp.com
Website: www.sevenmilecp.com

Management and Staff

Alec Brown, Vice President
Chris Papadopoulos, Chief Financial Officer
Kevin Kruse, Partner
Vincent Fandozzi, Managing Partner

Type of Firm

Private Equity Firm

Project Preferences

Type of Financing Preferred:
Leveraged Buyout
Acquisition

Industry Preferences

In Consumer Related prefer:
Consumer Products

In Industrial/Energy prefer:
Industrial Products

In Financial Services prefer:
Financial Services

In Business Serv. prefer:
Services

Additional Information

Name of Most Recent Fund: Seven Mile Capital Partners II, L.P.
Most Recent Fund Was Raised: 12/18/2013
Year Founded: 2011
Capital Under Management: $26,120,000
Current Activity Level: Actively seeking new investments

SEVEN PEAKS VENTURES

1001 Southwest Emkay Drive, Suite 140
Bend, OR USA 97702
Website: www.sevenpeaksventures.com

Type of Firm

Private Equity Firm

Project Preferences

Type of Financing Preferred:
Early Stage
Seed

Additional Information

Name of Most Recent Fund: Seven Peaks Ventures Fund I, L.P.
Most Recent Fund Was Raised: 06/28/2013
Year Founded: 2013
Capital Under Management: $3,130,000
Current Activity Level: Actively seeking new investments

SEVEN POINT EQUITY PARTNERS LLC

36 Church Lane
Westport, CT USA 06880
Website: sevenpointpartners.com

Management and Staff

Mark Kammert, Partner
Thomas Burchill, Managing Partner

Type of Firm

Private Equity Firm

Project Preferences

Type of Financing Preferred:
Leveraged Buyout

Additional Information

Year Founded: 2011
Current Activity Level: Actively seeking new investments

SEVEN SEAS PARTNERS

3000 Sand Hill Road
4-100
Menlo Park, CA USA 94025
Website: www.7seasvc.com

Management and Staff

Jack Yao, Partner
Jack Xu, Managing Partner
Jeff Xiong, Managing Partner
Li Ivy, Partner
Meng Henry, Partner
Tsang Justin, Partner

Type of Firm

Private Equity Firm

Project Preferences

Type of Financing Preferred:
Balanced

Geographical Preferences

United States Preferences:

International Preferences:
China

Additional Information

Year Founded: 1969
Capital Under Management: $69,500,000
Current Activity Level: Actively seeking new investments

SEVENTURE PARTNERS SA

5-7, rue de Monttessuy
Paris, France 75340
Phone: 33158192270
Fax: 33158192280
E-mail: contact@seventure.fr
Website: www.seventure.fr

Other Offices

67, Brunnenstrasse
Baldham, Germany 85598
Phone: 49-8-9878-0686
Fax: 49-898-7806-8699

Management and Staff

Bruno Rivet, General Partner
Catherine Buisson, Chief Financial Officer
Didier Piccino, Partner
Emmanuel Fiessinger, General Partner
Isabelle de Cremoux, CEO & Managing Director
Marion Aubry, Partner
Pierre Aumenier, Chief Financial Officer

Type of Firm

Bank Affiliated

Association Membership

French Venture Capital Association (AFIC)
German Venture Capital Association (BVK)

Project Preferences

Type of Financing Preferred:
Generalist PE

Geographical Preferences

International Preferences:
France

Industry Preferences

In Communications prefer:
Communications and Media
Wireless Communications

In Computer Software prefer:
Software

In Internet Specific prefer:
E-Commerce Technology

In Semiconductor/Electr prefer:
Semiconductor
Micro-Processing

In Biotechnology prefer:
Biotech Related Research

In Medical/Health prefer:
Medical Therapeutics
Medical Products
Pharmaceuticals

In Other prefer:
Environment Responsible

Additional Information

Name of Most Recent Fund: Masseran Innovation IV FCPI
Most Recent Fund Was Raised: 01/09/2012
Year Founded: 1997
Capital Under Management: $785,100,000
Current Activity Level : Actively seeking new investments

SEVENTY SIX CAPITAL

100 Four Falls, Suite 101 West
West Conshohocken, PA USA 19428
Phone: 6108250250
E-mail: info@artistsandinstigators.com
Website: www.seventysixcapital.com

Type of Firm
Private Equity Firm

Association Membership
National Venture Capital Association – USA (NVCA)

Project Preferences

Role in Financing:
Prefer role as deal originator but will also invest in deals created by others

Type of Financing Preferred:
Early Stage
Balanced

Geographical Preferences

United States Preferences:

Industry Preferences

In Internet Specific prefer:
Internet

In Medical/Health prefer:
Medical/Health
Health Services

In Consumer Related prefer:
Entertainment and Leisure
Food/Beverage

In Transportation prefer:
Transportation

In Business Serv. prefer:
Services
Media

Additional Information

Name of Most Recent Fund: ETF Venture Fund II, L.P.
Most Recent Fund Was Raised: 07/01/2007
Year Founded: 2000
Capital Under Management: $45,000,000
Current Activity Level : Actively seeking new investments

SEVIN ROSEN FUNDS

13455 Noel Road, Suite 1670, Two Galleria Tower
Dallas, TX USA 75240
Phone: 9727021100
Fax: 9727021103
E-mail: info@srfunds.com
Website: www.srfunds.com

Other Offices

6300 Bridgepoint Parkway
Building One, Suite 500
Austin, TX USA 78730
Phone: 512-745-5336
Fax: 512-795-5849

421 Kipling Street
Palo Alto, CA USA 94301
Phone: 650-326-0550
Fax: 650-326-0707

Management and Staff

Alan Buehler, Chief Financial Officer
Alan Schuele, General Partner
Charles Phipps, General Partner
David McLean, General Partner
Jackie Kimzey, General Partner
John Oxaal, General Partner
John Jaggers, General Partner
Jon Bayless, General Partner
Stephen Domenik, General Partner
Stephen Dow, General Partner
William Paiva, Partner

Type of Firm
Private Equity Firm

Project Preferences

Role in Financing:
Prefer role as deal originator

Type of Financing Preferred:
Early Stage
Balanced
Later Stage

Size of Investments Considered:
Min Size of Investment Considered (000s): $100
Max Size of Investment Considered (000s): $10,000

Geographical Preferences

United States Preferences:

Industry Focus

(% based on actual investment)

Communications and Media	38.8%
Computer Software and Services	18.4%
Internet Specific	15.0%
Semiconductors/Other Elect.	12.0%
Computer Hardware	6.9%
Biotechnology	3.7%
Medical/Health	2.0%
Industrial/Energy	1.9%
Consumer Related	0.9%
Other Products	0.3%

Additional Information

Name of Most Recent Fund: Sevin Rosen Fund IX
Most Recent Fund Was Raised: 10/11/2004
Year Founded: 1981
Capital Under Management: $1,535,000,000
Current Activity Level : Making few, if any, new investments
Method of Compensation: Return on investment is of primary concern, do not charge fees

---

SEYEN CAPITAL LLC

150 North Wacker Drive,, Suite 660
Chicago, IL USA 60606
Phone: 3128954564
Fax: 3128272281

Management and Staff

Ellen Carnahan, Managing Director

Type of Firm
Private Equity Firm

Project Preferences

Type of Financing Preferred:
Expansion
Balanced
Later Stage

Size of Investments Considered:
Min Size of Investment Considered (000s): $5,000
Max Size of Investment Considered (000s): $25,000

Industry Preferences

In Consumer Related prefer:
Consumer

In Financial Services prefer:
Financial Services

Additional Information
Year Founded: 2012
Current Activity Level : Actively seeking new investments

SF HOLDING CORP

111 Center Street, Suite 2400
Little Rock, AR USA 72201
Phone: 5013772000
Fax: 5013772470
Website: www.stephens.com

Other Offices

3700 Buffalo Speedway, Suite 900
Houston, TX USA 77098
Phone: 713-993-4200

65 East 55th Street
22nd Floor
New York, NY USA 10022
Phone: 212-891-1700
Fax: 212-891-1750

601 Pennsylvania Avenue North West, Suite 720
South Building
Washington, DC USA 20004
Phone: 202-628-6668

Crescent Boulevard, Suite 203
Ridgeland, MS USA 39157
Phone: 601-605-5660
Fax: 601-605-5670

161 Television Hill Road
Hot Springs, AR USA 71913
Phone: 501-609-4100
Fax: 501-609-4115

100 North Broadway, Suite 1850
Oklahoma City, OK USA 73102
Phone: 405-231-4445
Fax: 405-231-4466

100 Congress Avenue, Suite 750
Austin, TX USA 78701
Phone: 512-542-3200
Fax: 512-542-3275

175 Federal Street
Ninth Floor
Boston, MA USA 02110
Phone: 617-237-7500
Fax: 617-239-7546

703 Chestnut
Conway, AR USA 72032
Phone: 501-328-4000
Fax: 501-328-4090

909 Davis Street, Suite 260
Evanston, IL USA 60201
Phone: 847-563-5500
Fax: 847-563-5507

9100 South Dadeland Boulevard, Suite 1500
Miami, FL USA 33156
Phone: 786-497-7233

3100 West End Avenue, Suite 630
Nashville, TN USA 37203
Phone: 615-279-4300
Fax: 615-279-4365

195 Church Street, 15th Floor
New Haven, CT USA 06510
Phone: 203-747-3600
Fax: 203-747-3610

Westerre III Building
3900 Westerre Parkway, Suite 204
Richmond, VA USA 23233
Phone: 804-727-6200
Fax: 804-727-6250

950 East Paces Ferry Road, Suite 2850
Atlanta, GA USA 30326
Phone: 404-461-5100
Fax: 404-461-5135

445 North Boulevard
City Plaza, Suite 802
Baton Rouge, LA USA 70802
Phone: 225-214-4883
Fax: 225-214-4898

3425 North Futrall Drive, Suite 201
Fayetteville, AR USA 72703
Phone: 479-718-7400
Fax: 479-718-7490

1320 Main Street, Suite 550
Columbia, SC USA 29201
Phone: 803-343-0100
Fax: 803-343-0110

300 Crescent Court, Suite 600
Dallas, TX USA 75201
Phone: 214-258-2700
Fax: 214-258-2740

6075 Poplar Avenue, Suite 200
Memphis, TN USA 38119
Phone: 901-681-1300
Fax: 901-681-1375

4521 Sharon Road, Suite 200
Charlotte, NC USA 28211
Phone: 704-442-5000
Fax: 704-442-5055

63 Saint James' Street
London, United Kingdom

150 Second Avenue North, Suite 700
Saint Petersburg, FL USA 33701
Phone: 727-502-3500
Fax: 727-502-3550

Management and Staff
Douglas Martin, Senior Managing Director
Kathy Bryant, Chief Financial Officer
Kevin Wilcox, Managing Director
Kevin Eckert, Managing Director
Mark Doramus, Chief Financial Officer
Noel Strauss, Managing Director
Richard Blank, Managing Director
Robert Janes, Managing Director
Stephen Dearing, Managing Director

Type of Firm
Bank Affiliated

Project Preferences

Role in Financing:
Will function either as deal originator or investor in deals created by others

Type of Financing Preferred:
Leveraged Buyout
Control-block Purchases
Mezzanine
Generalist PE
Later Stage
Management Buyouts
Acquisition
Private Placement
Special Situation

Size of Investments Considered:
Min Size of Investment Considered (000s): $1,000
Max Size of Investment Considered (000s): $100,000

Geographical Preferences

United States Preferences:

Industry Focus
(% based on actual investment)

Computer Software and Services	21.5%
Consumer Related	20.2%
Industrial/Energy	18.3%
Other Products	12.1%
Communications and Media	7.5%
Medical/Health	7.5%
Biotechnology	6.3%
Internet Specific	3.4%
Semiconductors/Other Elect.	3.2%

Additional Information
Name of Most Recent Fund: Center Street Capital Partners
Most Recent Fund Was Raised: 08/12/1994
Year Founded: 1933
Current Activity Level : Actively seeking new investments
Method of Compensation: Return on investment is of primary concern, do not charge fees

Pratt's Guide to Private Equity & Venture Capital Sources

SFP CAPITAL LLC

790 Ritchie Highway, Suite E36
Severna Park, MD USA 21146
E-mail: info@sfpcapital.com
Website: sfpcapital.com

Management and Staff

Lisa Clark, Vice President
Paul Intlekofer, President

Type of Firm

Private Equity Firm

Project Preferences

Type of Financing Preferred:
Early Stage
Seed

Additional Information

Year Founded: 2013
Current Activity Level : Actively seeking new investments

SFW CAPITAL PARTNERS LLC

22 Elm Place
Rye, NY USA 10580
Phone: 9145108910
Fax: 9145108911
E-mail: info@sfwcap.com
Website: www.sfwcap.com

Other Offices

615 Club Drive
Aurora, OH USA 44202
Phone: 3306558850

Management and Staff

Ahmad Sheikh, Partner
Andrew Cialino, Vice President
David Webb, Partner
Nora Mende, Chief Financial Officer
Norman Wells, Partner
Omair Sarwar, Vice President
Paresh Vaish, Partner
Roger Freeman, Partner
Sean Mooney, Partner
Terry Smith, Chief Financial Officer
Thomas Salice, Partner

Type of Firm

Private Equity Firm

Project Preferences

Type of Financing Preferred:
Acquisition
Recapitalizations

Industry Preferences

In Computer Software prefer:
Software
Systems Software
Applications Software

In Semiconductor/Electr prefer:
Sensors
Analytic/Scientific

In Medical/Health prefer:
Medical Products
Health Services

In Business Serv. prefer:
Services
Media

Additional Information

Year Founded: 2005
Capital Under Management: $300,000,000
Current Activity Level : Actively seeking new investments

SG VC, L.P.

9665 Wilshire Boulevard, Suite 430
Beverly Hills, CA USA 90212
Website: www.sg-vc.com

Type of Firm

Private Equity Firm

Project Preferences

Type of Financing Preferred:
Early Stage
Balanced
Later Stage

Additional Information

Year Founded: 2011
Capital Under Management: $50,100,000
Current Activity Level : Actively seeking new investments

SGH CAPITAL SA

37, Val Saint Andre
Luxembourg, Luxembourg L-1128
Website: www.sghcapital.ch

Other Offices

10, Avenue Roosevelt
Paris, France 75008

Type of Firm

Private Equity Firm

Project Preferences

Type of Financing Preferred:
Leveraged Buyout
Early Stage
Expansion
Later Stage
Management Buyouts
Acquisition

Geographical Preferences

United States Preferences:

International Preferences:
Europe
Iran

Industry Preferences

In Internet Specific prefer:
Internet

In Biotechnology prefer:
Biotechnology

In Medical/Health prefer:
Medical/Health

In Consumer Related prefer:
Retail
Hotels and Resorts

In Transportation prefer:
Transportation

Additional Information

Year Founded: 2013
Capital Under Management: $70,000,000
Current Activity Level : Actively seeking new investments

SHAANXI CULTURAL INDUSTRY INVESTMENT MANAGEMENT CO LTD

300-9 Yanta South Road
Shaanxi Cultural Bldg,Block B
Shaanxi, China 710061
Phone: 862985358099
Fax: 862985358000
Website: www.shanwentou.com.cn

Type of Firm

Investment Management Firm

Project Preferences

Type of Financing Preferred:
Balanced

Geographical Preferences

International Preferences:
China

Industry Preferences

In Consumer Related prefer:
Entertainment and Leisure

Additional Information
Year Founded: 2009
Capital Under Management: $47,486,000
Current Activity Level : Actively seeking new investments

SHAANXI GUANTIAN XIXIAN EQUITY INVESTMENT MANAGEMENT CO LTD

No.1, Jinye Road, Gaoxin Dist.
1119, Building B, City Door
Xi'an, China
Phone: 862965691008
Website: www.guantiancapital.com.cn

Type of Firm
Private Equity Firm

Project Preferences

Type of Financing Preferred:
Balanced
Start-up Financing
Seed

Geographical Preferences

International Preferences:
China

Additional Information
Year Founded: 2011
Capital Under Management: $8,030,000
Current Activity Level : Actively seeking new investments

SHAANXI HAISHI VENTURE INVESTMENT CO LTD

Xiaozhai Shizi Trade Building
10th Floor
Xian, China
Phone: 86-29-8538-1677
Fax: 86-29-8538-1676

Type of Firm
Private Equity Firm

Project Preferences

Type of Financing Preferred:
Early Stage
Expansion
Balanced
Later Stage

Geographical Preferences

International Preferences:
China

Industry Preferences

In Communications prefer:
Wireless Communications

In Internet Specific prefer:
Internet

In Biotechnology prefer:
Biotechnology

In Consumer Related prefer:
Retail

In Industrial/Energy prefer:
Energy

In Financial Services prefer:
Real Estate

In Business Serv. prefer:
Services

Additional Information
Year Founded: 2003
Current Activity Level : Actively seeking new investments

SHAANXI HARLYN INVESTMENT MANAGEMENT CO LTD

Shanxi Guoye Bureau
Xi'an, China
Phone: 862989292405

Type of Firm
Private Equity Firm

Project Preferences

Type of Financing Preferred:
Balanced

Geographical Preferences

International Preferences:
China

Industry Preferences

In Biotechnology prefer:
Agricultural/Animal Bio.

In Consumer Related prefer:
Food/Beverage

Additional Information
Year Founded: 2012
Capital Under Management: $80,062,000
Current Activity Level : Actively seeking new investments

SHAANXI HIGH-TECH INVESTMENT CO LTD

Tang Yan Rd., Suite 45
Xi'an, China 710075
Website: www.china-hics.com

Type of Firm
Government Affiliated Program

Project Preferences

Type of Financing Preferred:
Balanced

Geographical Preferences

International Preferences:
China

Industry Preferences

In Biotechnology prefer:
Biotechnology

In Industrial/Energy prefer:
Materials

Additional Information
Year Founded: 1999
Current Activity Level : Actively seeking new investments

SHAANXI TECHNOLOGY VENTURE CAPITAL MANAGEMENT CO LTD

Zhangbawu Road
Technology Resources Center
Shaanxi, China
Website: www.cycn.net

Type of Firm
Private Equity Firm

Project Preferences

Type of Financing Preferred:
Balanced

Geographical Preferences

International Preferences:
China

Additional Information
Year Founded: 2012
Current Activity Level : Actively seeking new investments

SHAANXI ZENISUN VENTURE CAPITAL CO LTD

Xian Hi-tech Road, Building 31
9th Floor, Enterasys
Xi'an, China 710065
Phone: 86-29-88255097
Fax: 86-29-88255097
E-mail: 21-vc@163.com
Website: www.21-vc.com

Management and Staff
Fan Hao, Co-Founder
Liu Wen Meeting, Co-Founder

Type of Firm
Government Affiliated Program

Project Preferences

Type of Financing Preferred:
Balanced

Additional Information
Year Founded: 2010
Current Activity Level : Actively seeking new investments

SHACKLETON VENTURES LTD

14-15 Jewry Street
Winchester, United Kingdom SO23 8RZ
Phone: 441962842621
Fax: 448703836626
E-mail: info@shackletonventures.com

Management and Staff
Deborah Hudson, Partner
Hugh Stewart, Managing Partner
Michael Low, Partner
Steve Burton, Partner

Type of Firm
Private Equity Advisor or Fund of Funds

Association Membership
British Venture Capital Association (BVCA)

Project Preferences

Type of Financing Preferred:
Leveraged Buyout
Balanced

Geographical Preferences

International Preferences:
United Kingdom
Europe
All International

Industry Preferences

In Communications prefer:
Communications and Media

In Medical/Health prefer:
Medical/Health
Health Services

In Consumer Related prefer:
Consumer Products

In Industrial/Energy prefer:
Energy

In Financial Services prefer:
Financial Services

In Other prefer:
Environment Responsible

Additional Information
Year Founded: 2006
Current Activity Level : Actively seeking new investments

SHAKED GLOBAL GROUP

85A Medinat Hayehudim Street
Herzliya Pituach, Israel 46140
Phone: 972732565555
Fax: 972792565551
E-mail: info@shaked-global.com
Website: www.shaked-global.com

Management and Staff
Guy Regev, Chief Executive Officer
Ohad Shaked, Founder

Type of Firm
Private Equity Firm

Project Preferences

Type of Financing Preferred:
Expansion
Later Stage

Geographical Preferences

International Preferences:
All International

Industry Preferences

In Industrial/Energy prefer:
Alternative Energy
Environmental Related

In Other prefer:
Environment Responsible

Additional Information
Year Founded: 2007
Current Activity Level : Actively seeking new investments

SHAMROCK CAPITAL ADVISORS LLC

1100 Glendon Avenue, Suite 1600
Westwood, CA USA 90024
Phone: 3109746600
Fax: 3109746601
E-mail: contact@shamrockcap.com
Website: www.shamrockcap.com

Management and Staff
Alan Resnikoff, Principal
Andrew Howard, Partner
Jason Sklar, Managing Director
Laura Held, Vice President
Michael LaSalle, Partner
Peter Rivera, Chief Financial Officer
Robert Perille, Partner
Stephen Royer, Partner
Timothy Bluth, Vice President
William Wynperle, Partner

Type of Firm
Private Equity Firm

Project Preferences

Type of Financing Preferred:
Leveraged Buyout
Expansion
Management Buyouts
Acquisition
Recapitalizations

Geographical Preferences

United States Preferences:

International Preferences:
Western Europe
Israel

Industry Preferences

In Communications prefer:
Communications and Media
Media and Entertainment
Entertainment

In Business Serv. prefer:
Media

Additional Information
Name of Most Recent Fund: Shamrock Capital Growth Fund III, L.P.
Most Recent Fund Was Raised: 01/05/2011
Year Founded: 1978
Capital Under Management: $700,000,000
Current Activity Level : Actively seeking new investments

SHANDONG JIAHUA SHENGYU VENTURE CAPITAL CO LTD

No. 11, Nandajie Street
1811, 18/F,Yitong Int'l Bdg
Yantai,Shandong, China
Phone: 865356869999
Fax: 865356871999
Website: www.jhsytz.com

Type of Firm
Private Equity Firm

Project Preferences

Type of Financing Preferred:
Balanced

Geographical Preferences

International Preferences:
China

Industry Preferences

In Biotechnology prefer:
Agricultural/Animal Bio.

In Medical/Health prefer:
Drug/Equipmt Delivery

In Industrial/Energy prefer:
Alternative Energy
Advanced Materials

In Other prefer:
Environment Responsible

Additional Information
Year Founded: 2009
Current Activity Level : Actively seeking new investments

SHANDONG KEXIN VENTURE CAPITAL CO LTD

No.669, Bohai 18 Huanghe 6 Rd
Bingzhou, China

Type of Firm
Private Equity Firm

Project Preferences

Type of Financing Preferred:
Early Stage

Geographical Preferences

International Preferences:
China

SHANGHAI AIYUN VENTURE CAPITAL MANAGEMENT CO LTD

No.1452 Hongqiao Road
8F, Unit 1, Changning Dist
Shanghai, China 200030
Phone: 862152989370
Fax: 862152989391
E-mail: peivy@peivy.com
Website: www.peivy.com

Type of Firm
Private Equity Firm

Project Preferences

Type of Financing Preferred:
Early Stage
Expansion

Geographical Preferences

International Preferences:
China

Industry Preferences

In Computer Software prefer:
Software

In Semiconductor/Electr prefer:
Circuit Boards

Additional Information
Year Founded: 2011
Capital Under Management: $31,765,000
Current Activity Level : Actively seeking new investments

SHANGHAI ALLIANCE INVESTMENT LTD

19 Gaoyou Roadd
Shanghai, China 200031
Phone: 86-21-64714
Fax: 86-21-64746

Industry Preferences

In Biotechnology prefer:
Biotechnology

In Industrial/Energy prefer:
Energy
Energy Conservation Relat
Materials
Environmental Related

Additional Information
Year Founded: 2006
Capital Under Management: $17,000,000
Current Activity Level : Actively seeking new investments

Type of Firm
Government Affiliated Program

Project Preferences

Type of Financing Preferred:
Generalist PE

Geographical Preferences

International Preferences:
China

Industry Preferences

In Biotechnology prefer:
Genetic Engineering

In Medical/Health prefer:
Pharmaceuticals

In Industrial/Energy prefer:
Alternative Energy
Materials

In Financial Services prefer:
Financial Services

In Business Serv. prefer:
Services

In Agr/Forestr/Fish prefer:
Agribusiness

In Other prefer:
Women/Minority-Owned Bus.

Additional Information
Year Founded: 1994
Current Activity Level : Actively seeking new investments

SHANGHAI AMARA EQUITY INVESTMENT MANAGEMENT CO LTD

No. 1515 Nanjing Road West
1806, Shanghai Kerry Centre
Shanghai, China 200040
Phone: 86-21-5298-6955
Fax: 86-21-5298-6956
E-mail: info@shanghai-amara.com.cn
Website: www.shanghai-amara.com.cn

Other Offices

330 Bay Street, Suite 820
Toronto, Canada M5H 2S8

29-30, St. James's Street
2/F, Stanmore House
London, United Kingdom SW1A 1HB

Sheikh Zayed Road
The Fairmont Building
Dubai, Utd. Arab Em.

60 Wyndham Street
12/F, The Centrium
Central, Hong Kong

Management and Staff
Tony Zhou, Managing Director

Type of Firm
Investment Management Firm

Project Preferences

Type of Financing Preferred:
Balanced

Geographical Preferences

International Preferences:
China

Industry Preferences

In Consumer Related prefer:
Consumer

In Industrial/Energy prefer:
Energy
Environmental Related

In Business Serv. prefer:
Services

In Manufact. prefer:
Manufacturing

In Agr/Forestr/Fish prefer:
Agribusiness

Additional Information
Year Founded: 2010
Current Activity Level : Actively seeking new investments

SHANGHAI AMPLE HARVEST FINANCIAL SERVICES CO LTD

Luoshan Road
R203-1, No.13, 1502 Long
Shanghai, China

Type of Firm
Investment Management Firm

Project Preferences

Type of Financing Preferred:
Leveraged Buyout
Balanced

Geographical Preferences

International Preferences:
China

Additional Information
Year Founded: 2013
Current Activity Level : Actively seeking new investments

SHANGHAI ATLAS CAPITAL LTD

No.160 Taiyuan Road
No.3 Building
Shanghai, China 200031
Phone: 862161709170
Fax: 862161709171
Website: www.atlas-venture.com

Management and Staff
Bernard Ho, Venture Partner
Feng Yu, Partner
Frank Chen, Partner

Type of Firm
Government Affiliated Program

Project Preferences

Type of Financing Preferred:
Early Stage
Expansion
Balanced
Later Stage

Geographical Preferences

International Preferences:
China

Industry Preferences

In Semiconductor/Electr prefer:
Electronics

In Industrial/Energy prefer:
Alternative Energy
Advanced Materials

In Manufact. prefer:
Manufacturing

In Utilities prefer:
Utilities

In Other prefer:
Environment Responsible

Additional Information
Year Founded: 2010
Capital Under Management: $158,300,000
Current Activity Level : Actively seeking new investments

SHANGHAI BANGMING INVESTMENT MANAGEMENT CO LTD

University of Economy, Yangpu
Room 703-707, No.198 Wudong Rd
Shanghai, China 200434
Phone: 862165105827
Fax: 862165105827
Website: www.bmc-sh.com

Type of Firm
Private Equity Firm

Project Preferences

Type of Financing Preferred:
Early Stage
Expansion

Size of Investments Considered:
Min Size of Investment Considered (000s): $762
Max Size of Investment Considered (000s): $4,574

Geographical Preferences

International Preferences:
China

Industry Preferences

In Medical/Health prefer:
Medical/Health

In Industrial/Energy prefer:
Energy Conservation Relat
Materials

In Business Serv. prefer:
Services

In Other prefer:
Environment Responsible

Additional Information
Year Founded: 2010
Current Activity Level : Actively seeking new investments

SHANGHAI BEYOND BINGHONG EQUITY INVESTMENT MANAGEMENT CO LTD

No.2277, Longyang Road
Shanghai, China
Phone: 862133842992
Fax: 862133842992
Website: www.beyondfund.com

Other Offices

No.13, Shangwuwaihuan
28F, Lvdi Fenghui Tianxia
Zhengzhou, China
Phone: 8637169190135
Fax: 8637169190135

No.8, Haidian North 2 Street, Haidian
Unit 701, Zhongguancun Soho
Beijing, China
Phone: 861082483542
Fax: 861082484305

Management and Staff
Bing Yang, Partner
Jun Zhou, Vice President
Qiang Kong, Founder
Xiao ou Zhu, Partner
Xiaoou Zhu, Partner
Yun Zhou, Partner
Zhenhe Li, Vice President
Zhenwu Sun, Vice President

Type of Firm
Private Equity Firm

Project Preferences
Type of Financing Preferred:
Early Stage
Expansion
Balanced
Later Stage

Geographical Preferences
International Preferences:
China

Industry Preferences
In Biotechnology prefer:
Industrial Biotechnology

In Medical/Health prefer:
Pharmaceuticals

In Industrial/Energy prefer:
Energy
Energy Conservation Relat

In Business Serv. prefer:
Media

In Manufact. prefer:
Manufacturing

In Agr/Forestr/Fish prefer:
Mining and Minerals

Additional Information
Year Founded: 2008
Capital Under Management: $147,000,000
Current Activity Level : Actively seeking new investments

SHANGHAI BOJIANG INVESTMENT MANAGEMENT CO LTD

Chaoyang North Road,Chaoyang
No.99 building, 21 Floor
Beijing, China
Phone: 861057151970
Website: www.bojcf.com

Type of Firm
Private Equity Firm

Project Preferences
Type of Financing Preferred:
Balanced

Geographical Preferences
International Preferences:
China

Industry Preferences
In Communications prefer:
Telecommunications
Data Communications
Media and Entertainment

In Computer Software prefer:
Artificial Intelligence

In Semiconductor/Electr prefer:
Semiconductor

In Biotechnology prefer:
Biotechnology

In Industrial/Energy prefer:
Robotics

Additional Information
Year Founded: 2005
Current Activity Level : Actively seeking new investments

SHANGHAI BROAD RESOURCES INVESTMENT MANAGEMENT CO LTD

#166, East Lujiazui Road
2702, China Insurance Building
Shanghai, China 200120
Phone: 862168419101
Fax: 862168419102
E-mail: info@broadresources.com
Website: www.broadresources.com

Other Offices
#3850, Jiangnan Road, Binjiang District
9th Floor, Chuangxin Plaza
Hangzhou, China 310053
Phone: 8657187110733
Fax: 8657186661202

Donghu Development District, Hi-Tech Rd
5th Floor-B1, Guanggu Shengwu Building
Wuhan, China 200120
Phone: 862787205916
Fax: 862787205929

#2, South Guangdong Street
2701, West Tower, Van Palance
Beijing, China 100020
Phone: 861065610486
Fax: 861065610136

Management and Staff
Pei Zhang, Vice President
Xinyi Hua, Vice President
Yuliang Chen, Vice President

Type of Firm
Investment Management Firm

Project Preferences
Type of Financing Preferred:
Expansion
Balanced
Later Stage

Geographical Preferences
International Preferences:
China

Industry Preferences
In Biotechnology prefer:
Biotechnology

In Medical/Health prefer:
Pharmaceuticals

In Consumer Related prefer:
Entertainment and Leisure
Consumer Products

In Industrial/Energy prefer:
Alternative Energy
Energy Conservation Relat
Advanced Materials
Machinery

In Business Serv. prefer:
Services

In Manufact. prefer:
Manufacturing

In Other prefer:
Environment Responsible

Additional Information
Year Founded: 2007
Capital Under Management: $23,662,000
Current Activity Level : Actively seeking new investments

SHANGHAI BROADVIEW CAPITAL MANAGEMENT CO LTD

567, Weihai Road, Jing'an Dist
The 4th Building
Shanghai, China
Phone: 862162889018
Fax: 862162889330
E-mail: info@bviewcapital.com
Website: bviewcapital.com

Management and Staff
Gang Kong, Partner
Guangyu Wu, Partner
Han Xu, Partner
Jiantao Zhang, Partner
Jim Ye, Partner

Type of Firm
Private Equity Firm

Project Preferences

Type of Financing Preferred:
Leveraged Buyout
Later Stage

Geographical Preferences

International Preferences:
China

Industry Preferences

In Communications prefer:
Telecommunications

In Biotechnology prefer:
Biotechnology

In Medical/Health prefer:
Pharmaceuticals

In Consumer Related prefer:
Consumer Products

In Industrial/Energy prefer:
Energy
Energy Conservation Relat
Materials
Environmental Related

In Financial Services prefer:
Real Estate

In Business Serv. prefer:
Services
Media

In Manufact. prefer:
Manufacturing

In Agr/Forestr/Fish prefer:
Agriculture related
Mining and Minerals

Additional Information
Year Founded: 2011
Current Activity Level : Actively seeking new investments

SHANGHAI BUTTONWOOD CAPITAL CO LTD

No. 45 Nanchang Road, Huangpu
8A, Chenghui Mansion
Shanghai, China 200020
Phone: 862153089513
Fax: 862154660968

Website: purpleskycap.com

Type of Firm
Private Equity Firm

Project Preferences

Type of Financing Preferred:
Early Stage
Balanced
Seed
Startup

Geographical Preferences

International Preferences:
China

Industry Preferences

In Biotechnology prefer:
Biotechnology

In Consumer Related prefer:
Consumer

In Industrial/Energy prefer:
Energy
Materials
Environmental Related

In Business Serv. prefer:
Media

In Manufact. prefer:
Manufacturing

In Agr/Forestr/Fish prefer:
Agriculture related

Additional Information
Year Founded: 2011
Current Activity Level : Actively seeking new investments

SHANGHAI CCI INVESTMENT CO LTD

No. 333, North Caoxi Road
6F, CCI Inte'l Plaza
Shanghai, China 201103
Phone: 862162089257
Fax: 862162950475
E-mail: ccifund@ccig.com
Website: www.ccifund.com

Management and Staff
Gao Ming Jiang, Chief Executive Officer

Type of Firm
Investment Management Firm

Project Preferences

Type of Financing Preferred:
Expansion
Later Stage

Size of Investments Considered:
Min Size of Investment Considered (000s): $4,642
Max Size of Investment Considered (000s): $15,472

Geographical Preferences

International Preferences:
China

Industry Preferences

In Medical/Health prefer:
Medical/Health

In Industrial/Energy prefer:
Machinery
Environmental Related

In Business Serv. prefer:
Services
Media

In Manufact. prefer:
Manufacturing

In Agr/Forestr/Fish prefer:
Agriculture related

Additional Information
Year Founded: 1997
Current Activity Level : Actively seeking new investments

SHANGHAI CENOVA VENTURES MANAGEMENT CO LTD

No. 53 GaoYou Road
XuHui District
Shanghai, China 200031
Phone: 862164662333
Fax: 862164375623
E-mail: info@cenovaventures.com
Website: www.cenovaventures.com

Management and Staff
Huatao Liu, Partner
Ruihua Yuan, Partner
Yi Huang, Partner

Type of Firm
Private Equity Firm

Project Preferences

Type of Financing Preferred:
Early Stage
Balanced

Geographical Preferences

International Preferences:
China

Industry Preferences

In Biotechnology prefer:
Biotechnology

In Medical/Health prefer:
Medical/Health
Medical Diagnostics
Diagnostic Services
Medical Products
Pharmaceuticals

Additional Information

Year Founded: 2010
Capital Under Management: $91,615,000
Current Activity Level : Actively seeking new investments

SHANGHAI CHENG FENG INVESTMENT CO LTD

1468 Nanjing West Road
2006-2007,ZhongXin Businss Ctr
Shanghai, China 200040
Phone: 862151086958
Fax: 862168590901
E-mail: cf@cf-capital.cn
Website: www.cf-capital.cn

Other Offices

No.86 East Shanghai Road
Unit 1518, Fortune Tower
Suzhou, China
Phone: 8651253511798
Fax: 8651253511798

Management and Staff

Gang Wang, Managing Partner
Rong Guo, Managing Partner

Type of Firm

Private Equity Firm

Project Preferences

Type of Financing Preferred:
Balanced

Geographical Preferences

International Preferences:
China

Industry Preferences

In Biotechnology prefer:
Biotechnology

In Medical/Health prefer:
Pharmaceuticals

In Consumer Related prefer:
Retail
Consumer Products
Consumer Services

In Industrial/Energy prefer:
Alternative Energy
Advanced Materials

In Agr/Forestr/Fish prefer:
Agriculture related

Additional Information

Year Founded: 2011
Capital Under Management: $79,300,000
Current Activity Level : Actively seeking new investments

SHANGHAI CHESSBOARD INVESTMENT MANAGEMENT CO LTD

No. 1591, Hongqiao Road
Extra 9 Villa
Shanghai, China 200336
Phone: 8621-62957277
Fax: 8621-62957517
Website: www.laomaoffice.com

Type of Firm

Private Equity Firm

Project Preferences

Type of Financing Preferred:
Acquisition

Geographical Preferences

International Preferences:
China

Additional Information

Year Founded: 2007
Current Activity Level : Actively seeking new investments

SHANGHAI CHINA SUMMIT CAPITAL CO., LTD.

780 Cailun Road, Pudong
201 Suite
Shanghai, China
E-mail: info@chinasummit.com.cn
Website: www.chinasummit.com.cn

Type of Firm

Private Equity Firm

Project Preferences

Type of Financing Preferred:
Balanced

Geographical Preferences

International Preferences:
China

Industry Preferences

In Medical/Health prefer:
Medical/Health

Additional Information

Year Founded: 2013
Current Activity Level : Actively seeking new investments

SHANGHAI CORUN VENTURE CAPITAL CO LTD

Ste. G, 9F, Shuangge Plz
438 Pudian Rd,Pudong New Area
Shanghai, China 200120

Type of Firm

Private Equity Firm

Additional Information

Year Founded: 2000
Current Activity Level : Actively seeking new investments

SHANGHAI CURA INVESTMENT & MANAGEMENT CO LTD

500 Hongqiao Rd., Xuhui Dist.
8/F, Cura International Center
Shanghai, China 200030
Phone: 862138870996
Fax: 862158820669
Website: www.curafund.com

Type of Firm

Investment Management Firm

Project Preferences

Type of Financing Preferred:
Core
Mezzanine
Generalist PE
Balanced

Geographical Preferences

International Preferences:
China

Additional Information

Year Founded: 2002
Current Activity Level : Actively seeking new investments

SHANGHAI DECENT INVESTMENT GROUP CO LTD

No. 3806, Zhuoyue Time Plaza
Futian District
Shenzhen, China 518048
Phone: 8675523994021
Fax: 8675523994020
Website: www.decent-china.com

Type of Firm
Private Equity Firm

Project Preferences

Type of Financing Preferred:
Seed
Startup

Geographical Preferences

International Preferences:
China

Industry Preferences

In Communications prefer:
Wireless Communications
Entertainment

In Internet Specific prefer:
Internet

Additional Information
Year Founded: 2007
Current Activity Level : Actively seeking new investments

SHANGHAI DINGHUI INVESTMENT MANAGEMENT CO LTD

No. 37, 2188 Alley
Hongqiao Road
Shanghai, China 200336
Phone: 86-21-6862-0000
Fax: 86-21-6251-0980
E-mail: zj198@zj198.com
Website: www.d-hui.com

Type of Firm
Investment Management Firm

Project Preferences

Type of Financing Preferred:
Balanced

Geographical Preferences

International Preferences:
China

Industry Preferences

In Internet Specific prefer:
Internet

In Medical/Health prefer:
Medical/Health

In Industrial/Energy prefer:
Environmental Related

In Financial Services prefer:
Financial Services
Real Estate

Additional Information
Year Founded: 2003
Current Activity Level : Actively seeking new investments

SHANGHAI DINGJIA VENTURES CO LTD

No. 350 Chunxiao Road
Zhangjiang Gaokeji Park
Shanghai, China 201203
Phone: 86-21-5080-0508
Fax: 86-21-5080-1918
E-mail: zj-vc@zj-vc.com
Website: www.zj-vc.com

Management and Staff
Jiwei Hu, Partner
Kang Gu, Partner
Xiaohua Yang, Partner
Yongxiang Jiang, Partner

Type of Firm
Private Equity Firm

Project Preferences

Type of Financing Preferred:
Early Stage
Balanced
Later Stage
Startup

Geographical Preferences

International Preferences:
China

Industry Preferences

In Communications prefer:
Telecommunications

In Biotechnology prefer:
Biotechnology

In Industrial/Energy prefer:
Alternative Energy
Materials

In Business Serv. prefer:
Services
Media

Additional Information
Year Founded: 2003
Current Activity Level : Actively seeking new investments

SHANGHAI DIVINE INVESTMENT MANAGEMENT CO LTD

No. 58, Changliu Road
Rm. 1106, Zhengdalifang Bldg.
Shanghai, China
Phone: 862133926483
Fax: 862133926423
E-mail: contact@divinecapital.com.cn
Website: www.divinecapital.net

Management and Staff
Danyang Bian, Partner
Jiang Lin, Partner
Jin Bian, Partner
Mushun Lin, Partner
Yan Zhou, Partner
Yidong Liu, Partner
Yu Zheng, Partner
Zhen Li, Partner

Type of Firm
Private Equity Firm

Project Preferences

Type of Financing Preferred:
Balanced
Later Stage

Geographical Preferences

International Preferences:
China

Additional Information
Year Founded: 2009
Capital Under Management: $30,341,000
Current Activity Level : Actively seeking new investments

SHANGHAI DONFCESHENG ASSET MANAGEMENT CO LTD

No.248 Yanshupu Road
23F
Shanghai, China 200082
Phone: 862165465036

Type of Firm
Private Equity Firm

Project Preferences

Type of Financing Preferred:
Balanced

Geographical Preferences

International Preferences:
China

Additional Information

Year Founded: 2015
Current Activity Level : Actively seeking new investments

SHANGHAI DONG XI INVESTMENT DEVELOPMENT CO LTD

No. 1591 Hongqiao Road, Changn
Building 35, Hongqiao Guest Ho
Shanghai, China
Phone: 862162197237
Website: www.ewc.org.cn

Type of Firm
Private Equity Firm

Project Preferences

Type of Financing Preferred:
Balanced

Geographical Preferences

International Preferences:
China

Industry Preferences

In Communications prefer:
Media and Entertainment

In Internet Specific prefer:
Internet

In Medical/Health prefer:
Medical/Health

In Industrial/Energy prefer:
Energy Conservation Relat

In Agr/Forestr/Fish prefer:
Agriculture related

In Other prefer:
Environment Responsible

Additional Information

Year Founded: 2010
Current Activity Level : Actively seeking new investments

SHANGHAI DONGKAI JINGXU VENTURE CAPITAL MANAGEMENT CO LTD

958, Zhenbei Rd., Putuo Dist.
Room 1551, Block 20
Shanghai, China

Type of Firm
Private Equity Firm

Project Preferences

Type of Financing Preferred:
Balanced

Geographical Preferences

International Preferences:
China

Industry Preferences

In Medical/Health prefer:
Medical/Health

Additional Information

Year Founded: 2015
Current Activity Level : Actively seeking new investments

SHANGHAI DONGZHEN INVESTMENT CO LTD

589 Gucao Road, Pudong
Room 603
Shanghai, China 201209

Type of Firm
Investment Management Firm

Additional Information

Year Founded: 2010
Current Activity Level : Actively seeking new investments

SHANGHAI EVER BRIGHT INVESTMENT MANAGEMENT CO LTD

No. 3131, Hongmei Road
Buiilding 36, Fuhong Garden
Shanghai, China 201103
Phone: 862152277200
Fax: 862164028699
E-mail: info@ebigroup.cn
Website: www.ebigroup.cn

Type of Firm
Private Equity Firm

Project Preferences

Type of Financing Preferred:
Expansion
Balanced

Geographical Preferences

International Preferences:
China

Industry Preferences

In Communications prefer:
Telecommunications

In Consumer Related prefer:
Education Related

In Industrial/Energy prefer:
Energy
Energy Conservation Relat
Environmental Related

In Financial Services prefer:
Financial Services
Real Estate

In Business Serv. prefer:
Services
Media

In Manufact. prefer:
Manufacturing

Additional Information

Year Founded: 2004
Capital Under Management: $2,000,000,000
Current Activity Level : Actively seeking new investments

SHANGHAI FENGSHANG INVESTMENT MANAGEMENT CO LTD

Belle In'l Plaza
6/F
Shanghai, China 200235
Website: www.fengshion.com

Type of Firm
Investment Management Firm

Project Preferences

Type of Financing Preferred:
Balanced

Geographical Preferences

International Preferences:
China

Industry Preferences

In Communications prefer:
Entertainment

In Medical/Health prefer:
Medical/Health

Additional Information

Year Founded: 2015
Current Activity Level : Actively seeking new investments

SHANGHAI FENYI INVESTMENT MANAGEMENT CONSULTING CO LTD

No. 55 Huiyuan Road, Jiading I
Room 2107, Block A, 2F, Buildi
Shanghai, China

Type of Firm
Bank Affiliated

Project Preferences

Type of Financing Preferred:
Early Stage

Geographical Preferences

International Preferences:
China

Industry Preferences

In Communications prefer:
Media and Entertainment

In Medical/Health prefer:
Medical/Health

In Consumer Related prefer:
Education Related

Additional Information
Year Founded: 2015
Current Activity Level : Actively seeking new investments

SHANGHAI FORTE AUSPICIOUS INVESTMENT MANAGEMENT PARTNERS ENT

Julu Road, Jing An District
No. 8, Lane 687
Shanghai, China 200040
Phone: 862154047968

Type of Firm
Private Equity Firm

Project Preferences

Type of Financing Preferred:
Balanced

Geographical Preferences

International Preferences:
China

Additional Information
Year Founded: 2011
Current Activity Level : Actively seeking new investments

SHANGHAI FORTUNE UNITED INVESTMENT GROUP CO LTD

No.1568 Shiji Avenue
Rm 1701 Zhongjian Bldg.
Shanghai, China 200122
Phone: 862161652500
Fax: 862161652511
E-mail: master@panlincap.com
Website: www.panlincap.com

Management and Staff
Huidong Tan, Partner
Libo Wang, Managing Partner
Mengjun Xue, Partner
Xi Lin, Venture Partner
Yuheng Liu, Partner
Yuhui Li, General Partner

Type of Firm
Private Equity Firm

Project Preferences

Type of Financing Preferred:
Leveraged Buyout
Expansion
Balanced

Geographical Preferences

International Preferences:
China

Industry Preferences

In Medical/Health prefer:
Medical/Health
Drug/Equipmt Delivery

In Consumer Related prefer:
Consumer
Education Related

In Industrial/Energy prefer:
Energy
Energy Conservation Relat
Materials
Environmental Related

In Transportation prefer:
Transportation

In Business Serv. prefer:
Media

In Agr/Forestr/Fish prefer:
Agriculture related

Additional Information
Year Founded: 2010
Capital Under Management: $24,211,000
Current Activity Level : Actively seeking new investments

SHANGHAI FORWARD TECHNOLOGY VENTURE CO LTD

No. 333, Huaihai Middle Road
20/F, Ruian Square
Shanghai, China 200021
Phone: 862163872288
Fax: 862163869700

Type of Firm
University Program

Project Preferences

Type of Financing Preferred:
Balanced

Geographical Preferences

International Preferences:
China

Additional Information
Year Founded: 2000
Current Activity Level : Actively seeking new investments

SHANGHAI FOSUN CAPITAL INVESTMENT MANAGEMENT CO LTD

No. 28 Zhongshan South Road
27F, Jiushi Building
Shanghai, China 200010
Phone: 862163335067
Fax: 862163335033
E-mail: capital@fosun.com
Website: www.fosuncapital.com

Management and Staff
Bin Tang, President
Dachun Zhang, Chief Financial Officer

Type of Firm
Corporate PE/Venture

Project Preferences

Type of Financing Preferred:
Generalist PE
Balanced
Public Companies
Later Stage
Recapitalizations

Geographical Preferences

International Preferences:
Europe
China
All International

Industry Preferences

In Consumer Related prefer:
Consumer
Consumer Products

In Industrial/Energy prefer:
Energy
Energy Conservation Relat
Advanced Materials
Machinery
Environmental Related

In Transportation prefer:
Transportation
Aerospace

In Financial Services prefer:
Financial Services
Insurance

In Business Serv. prefer:
Services

In Manufact. prefer:
Manufacturing

In Agr/Forestr/Fish prefer:
Agriculture related
Mining and Minerals

In Other prefer:
Environment Responsible

Additional Information

Year Founded: 2007
Capital Under Management: $3,000,000,000
Current Activity Level : Actively seeking new investments

SHANGHAI FUHAI WANSHENG INVESTMENT MANAGEMENT CO LTD

No. 16, Boyang Road, Yangpu
Room 2611, 2F, Building 8
Shanghai, China

Type of Firm
Private Equity Firm

Project Preferences

Type of Financing Preferred:
Balanced

Geographical Preferences

International Preferences:
China

Additional Information

Year Founded: 2013
Current Activity Level : Actively seeking new investments

SHANGHAI FUYUAN YINKONG INVESTMENT MANAGEMENT CO LTD

Huangpu District
Shanghai, China

Type of Firm
Private Equity Firm

Project Preferences

Type of Financing Preferred:
Balanced

Geographical Preferences

International Preferences:
China

Industry Preferences

In Financial Services prefer:
Investment Groups

In Business Serv. prefer:
Services

Additional Information

Year Founded: 2011
Current Activity Level : Actively seeking new investments

SHANGHAI GMALL VENTURE CAPITAL MANAGEMENT CO LTD

No. 3398 North Di Road
Shanghai Minhang District
Beijing, China
Phone: 86-21-5976-3893
Fax: 86-21-5976-6651

Management and Staff
Jing Zhao, Chief Operating Officer

Type of Firm
Private Equity Firm

Industry Preferences

In Communications prefer:
Telecommunications

In Industrial/Energy prefer:
Energy

In Financial Services prefer:
Real Estate
Financial Services

Additional Information

Year Founded: 2007
Current Activity Level : Actively seeking new investments

SHANGHAI GRAND YANGTZE CAPITAL INVESTMENT MANAGEMENT CO LTD

210 Century Ave., Pudong
Rm.1601, 21st Century Mansion
Shanghai, China 200120
Phone: 862160475959
Fax: 862160476533
E-mail: serve@grandyangtze.com
Website: www.grandyangtze.com

Management and Staff
Chunyi Li, President

Type of Firm
Investment Management Firm

Project Preferences

Type of Financing Preferred:
Early Stage
Expansion
Later Stage

Geographical Preferences

International Preferences:
China

Industry Preferences

In Medical/Health prefer:
Medical/Health
Drug/Equipmt Delivery
Health Services
Pharmaceuticals

In Industrial/Energy prefer:
Energy Conservation Relat

In Business Serv. prefer:
Services

In Manufact. prefer:
Manufacturing

In Other prefer:
Environment Responsible

Additional Information

Year Founded: 2012
Capital Under Management: $146,044,000
Current Activity Level : Actively seeking new investments

SHANGHAI GUANGZHIYUAN INVESTMENT MANAGEMENT CO LTD

210 21st Century Ave., Pudong
6018 21st Century Center Bldg.
Shanghai, China 200000
Website: www.lighthousecap.cn

Type of Firm
Private Equity Firm

Project Preferences

Type of Financing Preferred:
Start-up Financing
Seed

Geographical Preferences

International Preferences:
China

Industry Preferences

In Communications prefer:
Telecommunications

In Business Serv. prefer:
Media

Additional Information
Year Founded: 2014
Current Activity Level : Actively seeking new investments

SHANGHAI GUOHE CAPITAL

No. 1318, Lujiazui Ring Road
19F, Xingzhan Bank Building
Shanghai, China 200121
Phone: 862128931818
Fax: 862128931819
E-mail: info@guohecapital.com
Website: www.guohecapital.com

Other Offices

No. 18, Taipingqiao St, Xicheng District
16/F, Fengrong International Plaza
Beijing, China 10032
Phone: 861058377015
Fax: 861058377025

Management and Staff
Dezhen Zhu, President

Type of Firm
Private Equity Firm

Project Preferences

Type of Financing Preferred:
Balanced

Geographical Preferences

International Preferences:
China

Industry Preferences

In Medical/Health prefer:
Medical/Health

In Consumer Related prefer:
Consumer
Consumer Services

In Industrial/Energy prefer:
Energy Conservation Relat

In Financial Services prefer:
Financial Services

In Business Serv. prefer:
Services
Media

In Other prefer:
Environment Responsible

Additional Information
Year Founded: 2009
Capital Under Management: $760,900,000
Current Activity Level : Actively seeking new investments

SHANGHAI GUOSHENG GROUP CO LTD

No 1320, Yuyuan Road
Changning District
Shanghai, China 200050
Phone: 862152388000
Fax: 862162407121
E-mail: info@sh-gsg.com
Website: www.sh-gsg.com

Type of Firm
Investment Management Firm

Project Preferences

Type of Financing Preferred:
Balanced

Geographical Preferences

International Preferences:
China

Industry Preferences

In Agr/Forestr/Fish prefer:
Agriculture related

Additional Information
Year Founded: 2007
Capital Under Management: $1,565,600,000
Current Activity Level : Actively seeking new investments

SHANGHAI HAIJI INVESTMENT DEVELOPMENT CO LTD

390 Panyu Road Changning
Shanghai, China 200052
Phone: 862162941007

Type of Firm
Private Equity Firm

Project Preferences

Type of Financing Preferred:
Generalist PE

Additional Information
Year Founded: 2007
Current Activity Level : Actively seeking new investments

SHANGHAI HANTAN INVESTMENT MANAGEMENT CO LTD

No.7 Pubei RD., Xuhui District
Room 2101, ZStar Plaza
Shanghai, China
E-mail: information@hantancapital.com
Website: www.hantancapital.com

Type of Firm
Private Equity Firm

Project Preferences

Type of Financing Preferred:
Early Stage
Seed
Startup

Geographical Preferences

International Preferences:
China

Industry Preferences

In Internet Specific prefer:
Internet

Additional Information
Year Founded: 2013
Current Activity Level : Actively seeking new investments

SHANGHAI HEDUO INVESTMENT MANAGEMENT CO LTD

Southeast corner, Ciyun Bridge
Room 1906, Block A
Beijing, China
E-mail: BP@Pre-Angel.com
Website: www.pre-angel.com

Type of Firm
Private Equity Firm

Project Preferences

Type of Financing Preferred:
Early Stage
Seed
Startup

Geographical Preferences

International Preferences:
China

Industry Preferences

In Internet Specific prefer:
E-Commerce Technology
Internet

In Medical/Health prefer:
Medical Products

Additional Information

Year Founded: 2011
Capital Under Management: $4,550,000
Current Activity Level : Actively seeking new investments

SHANGHAI HEJING LEYI INVESTMENT ADVISORY CO LTD

Longshui South Road 188-15
Shanghai, China
Website: www.whalescapital.com

Type of Firm

Private Equity Firm

Project Preferences

Type of Financing Preferred:
Balanced

Geographical Preferences

International Preferences:
China

Additional Information

Year Founded: 2014
Current Activity Level : Actively seeking new investments

SHANGHAI HONGZHANG INVESTMENT MANAGEMENT CO LTD

Pudong New Area
Room 1005, Block A0201
Shanghai, China
Website: chinaconsumer.com.cn

Management and Staff

Yinuo Weng, Partner

Type of Firm

Private Equity Firm

Project Preferences

Type of Financing Preferred:
Leveraged Buyout
Balanced

Geographical Preferences

International Preferences:
China

Industry Preferences

In Internet Specific prefer:
Internet

In Consumer Related prefer:
Consumer
Retail

Additional Information

Year Founded: 2011
Current Activity Level : Actively seeking new investments

SHANGHAI HUAQIANG EQUITY INVESTMENT MANAGEMENT CO LTD

No. 698 Hualing Road, Baoshan
Shanghai, China 200442
Phone: 862166340070

Type of Firm

Investment Management Firm

Project Preferences

Type of Financing Preferred:
Balanced

Geographical Preferences

International Preferences:
China

Additional Information

Year Founded: 2015
Current Activity Level : Actively seeking new investments

SHANGHAI HUITONG TIANXIA EQUITY INVESTMENT CO LTD

c/o Greater China Int'l Group
Greater China International
Shenzhen, China

Management and Staff

Donglin Zhong, Managing Partner

Type of Firm

Private Equity Firm

Project Preferences

Type of Financing Preferred:
Balanced
Later Stage

Geographical Preferences

International Preferences:
China
Asia

Additional Information

Year Founded: 2009
Capital Under Management: $292,800,000
Current Activity Level : Actively seeking new investments

SHANGHAI INCUFORTUNE VENTURE CAPITAL MANAGEMENT CO LTD

335 National Road
Building 2, Room 1508
Shanghai, China
Phone: 21-65651178
Fax: 86 -21-65650817
Website: www.incufortune.com

Type of Firm

Incubator/Development Program

Project Preferences

Type of Financing Preferred:
Later Stage
Seed

Geographical Preferences

International Preferences:
China

Industry Preferences

In Biotechnology prefer:
Biotechnology

In Medical/Health prefer:
Medical/Health

In Industrial/Energy prefer:
Alternative Energy
Energy Conservation Relat
Advanced Materials
Environmental Related

In Manufact. prefer:
Manufacturing

Additional Information

Year Founded: 2010
Capital Under Management: $45,551,000
Current Activity Level : Actively seeking new investments

SHANGHAI INESA VENTURE CAPITAL CO LTD

No. 25 Cangwu Road
2/F, Building 1
Shanghai, China 200233
Phone: 862154266377
Fax: 862154266376
Website: www.inesavc.com

Type of Firm
Private Equity Firm

Project Preferences

Type of Financing Preferred:
Early Stage
Expansion

Geographical Preferences

International Preferences:
China

Industry Preferences

In Internet Specific prefer:
Internet

In Medical/Health prefer:
Medical Therapeutics

In Consumer Related prefer:
Education Related

In Transportation prefer:
Transportation

Additional Information
Year Founded: 2013
Current Activity Level : Actively seeking new investments

SHANGHAI JIAHAO CAPITAL CO LTD

Pudong New District, Shanghai
Room 302, Block 7, Hengtai Pla
Shanghai, China
Phone: 862162187515
Website: www.jiahaocapital.com

Type of Firm
Investment Management Firm

Project Preferences

Type of Financing Preferred:
Balanced

Geographical Preferences

International Preferences:
China

Industry Preferences

In Communications prefer:
Telecommunications
Media and Entertainment

In Consumer Related prefer:
Sports

Additional Information
Year Founded: 2014
Current Activity Level : Actively seeking new investments

SHANGHAI JIANMING ASSET MANAGEMENT CO LTD

Pudong New Area
518, Xiukang Rd
Shanghai, China
Phone: 862158523466
Fax: 862158523466
Website: www.jmcapital.com.cn

Type of Firm
Private Equity Firm

Project Preferences

Type of Financing Preferred:
Expansion
Later Stage

Geographical Preferences

International Preferences:
China

Industry Preferences

In Communications prefer:
Entertainment

In Internet Specific prefer:
Internet

Additional Information
Year Founded: 2014
Current Activity Level : Actively seeking new investments

SHANGHAI LANGCHENG INVESTMENT MANAGEMENT CO LTD

No. 2272, Hongqiao Road
Tower M, 7F, Hongqiao Business
Shanghai, China 201103
Phone: 8621-62951100
Fax: 8621-62952310

Type of Firm
Private Equity Firm

Project Preferences

Type of Financing Preferred:
Balanced

Geographical Preferences

International Preferences:
China

Industry Preferences

In Internet Specific prefer:
Internet

In Medical/Health prefer:
Medical/Health

In Industrial/Energy prefer:
Energy Conservation Relat

In Financial Services prefer:
Financial Services

In Manufact. prefer:
Manufacturing

In Other prefer:
Environment Responsible

Additional Information
Year Founded: 2007
Current Activity Level : Actively seeking new investments

SHANGHAI LEADING CAPITAL CO LTD

No.8, Xingyi Road
Rm 912-913, Maxdo Tower
Shanghai, China 200036
Phone: 862162091156
Fax: 862162082927
Website: www.leadingcapital.com.cn

Management and Staff
Fengyong Gao, Chief Executive Officer
Lei Duan, Partner
Shaohuan Song, Partner

Type of Firm
Private Equity Firm

Project Preferences

Type of Financing Preferred:
Leveraged Buyout
Balanced

Geographical Preferences

International Preferences:
China

Industry Preferences

In Communications prefer:
Wireless Communications

In Internet Specific prefer:
Internet

In Medical/Health prefer:
Medical/Health
Pharmaceuticals

In Consumer Related prefer:
Consumer
Consumer Products
Consumer Services

In Industrial/Energy prefer:
Energy
Energy Conservation Relat
Environmental Related

In Business Serv. prefer:
Media

In Manufact. prefer:
Manufacturing

In Other prefer:
Environment Responsible

Additional Information
Year Founded: 2007
Capital Under Management: $214,295,000
Current Activity Level : Actively seeking new investments

SHANGHAI LIANXIN EQUITY INVESTMENT MANAGEMENT CENTER LP

Dongchuan Rd., Minxing Dist.
R2059, Bldg Yi
Shanghai, China

Type of Firm
Private Equity Firm

Project Preferences

Type of Financing Preferred:
Balanced

Geographical Preferences

International Preferences:
China

Industry Preferences

In Agr/Forestr/Fish prefer:
Agriculture related

Additional Information
Year Founded: 2012
Current Activity Level : Actively seeking new investments

SHANGHAI LIANXIN INVESTMENT MANAGEMENT CO LTD

No. 381, Huaihai Middle Road
Room 2617, Central Plaza
Shanghai, China 200020
Phone: 8621161703999
Fax: 862161703998
E-mail: zhangting@nac-capital.com
Website: www.nac-capital.com

Management and Staff
Bin Geng, Partner
Fei Li, Partner
Hai Xu, Partner
Jian Zhou, Partner
Jing Li, Partner
Kai Di, Partner
Lei Cai, Partner
Lie Wang, Partner
Nan Zhang, Partner
Wei Liu, Partner
Yin Zhu, Partner
Zhijun Guo, Partner
Zonghe Wu, Partner

Type of Firm
Private Equity Firm

Project Preferences

Type of Financing Preferred:
Expansion
Balanced

Geographical Preferences

International Preferences:
China

Industry Preferences

In Communications prefer:
Entertainment

In Computer Hardware prefer:
Computers

In Consumer Related prefer:
Sports
Consumer Products

In Industrial/Energy prefer:
Energy
Environmental Related

In Business Serv. prefer:
Services
Media

Additional Information
Year Founded: 2008
Current Activity Level : Actively seeking new investments

SHANGHAI LINNAI INDUSTRIAL INVESTMENT CENTER LP

Qingpu District, Shanghai
Room 385, Section C, 3F, Block
Shanghai, China
Phone: 862164721053

Type of Firm
Private Equity Firm

Project Preferences

Type of Financing Preferred:
Balanced

Geographical Preferences

International Preferences:
China

Additional Information
Year Founded: 2007
Current Activity Level : Actively seeking new investments

SHANGHAI LIYI INVESTMENT MANAGEMENT PARTNERSHIP LP

No.700 Jiahao Rd.,Jiading Dist
Room 1409, Block 2
Shanghai, China 200021
Phone: 862163406188

Type of Firm
Private Equity Firm

Project Preferences

Type of Financing Preferred:
Balanced

Geographical Preferences

International Preferences:
China

Additional Information
Year Founded: 2014
Capital Under Management: $32,380,000
Current Activity Level : Actively seeking new investments

SHANGHAI LONYER HOLDING CO LTD

No. 710 Tomson Commercial Bldg
Dongfang Road
Shanghai, China 200122
Phone: 86-21-5830-1681
Fax: 86-21-5830-1682
E-mail: invest@lonyer.com
Website: www.lonyer.cn

Type of Firm
Corporate PE/Venture

Project Preferences

Type of Financing Preferred:
Balanced

Geographical Preferences

International Preferences:
No Preference
China

Industry Preferences

In Biotechnology prefer:
Biotechnology

In Industrial/Energy prefer:
Advanced Materials

In Other prefer:
Environment Responsible

Additional Information
Year Founded: 1999
Current Activity Level : Actively seeking new investments

SHANGHAI MAITENG YONGLIAN VENTURE INVESTMENT MANAGEMENT

Lane 822, Zhennan Rd., Putuo
Rm. 109, Bldg 3, Lane 129
Shanghai, China
Phone: 862166080180
Website: www.mytechchina.com

Type of Firm
Private Equity Firm

Project Preferences

Type of Financing Preferred:
Expansion
Start-up Financing
Seed

Geographical Preferences

International Preferences:
China

Industry Preferences

In Internet Specific prefer:
Internet

Additional Information
Year Founded: 2014
Current Activity Level : Actively seeking new investments

SHANGHAI MEFUND ASSETS MANAGEMENT CO LTD

Lonnghua East Rd., Huangpu
Rm.703,Blk.B,No.858
Shanghai, China 200023
Phone: 862163269680
Fax: 862163269661
Website: www.me-fund.cn

Type of Firm
Investment Management Firm

Project Preferences

Type of Financing Preferred:
Generalist PE

Geographical Preferences

International Preferences:
China

Industry Preferences

In Communications prefer:
Entertainment

In Medical/Health prefer:
Medical/Health

In Consumer Related prefer:
Consumer

In Industrial/Energy prefer:
Energy Conservation Relat

In Financial Services prefer:
Financial Services

In Other prefer:
Environment Responsible

Additional Information
Year Founded: 2014
Capital Under Management: $1,000,000,000
Current Activity Level : Actively seeking new investments

SHANGHAI MILESTONE ASSET MANAGEMENT CO LTD

No.58, Changliu Road, Pudong
R2203, Zengdai Cube Edifice
Shanghai, China 200135
Phone: 0860216854581
Fax: 0860216854517
E-mail: milestone@smilestone.com.cn
Website: www.smilestone.com.cn

Type of Firm
Investment Management Firm

Project Preferences

Type of Financing Preferred:
Leveraged Buyout

Geographical Preferences

International Preferences:
China

Industry Preferences

In Communications prefer:
Telecommunications

In Medical/Health prefer:
Medical/Health

In Consumer Related prefer:
Consumer

In Business Serv. prefer:
Media

In Manufact. prefer:
Manufacturing

Additional Information
Year Founded: 2007
Capital Under Management: $66,075,000
Current Activity Level : Actively seeking new investments

SHANGHAI MULTIMEDIA PARK VENTURE CAPITAL CO LTD

Rm 1003, 10/F,Zhaofeng Plz
1027 Changning Rd
Shanghai, China 200050
Phone: 86-21-52385488
Fax: 86-21-52385489
E-mail: contact@mpvc.cn
Website: www.mpvc.cn

Other Offices
15th Floor, Huamin Empire Plaza,
728 Yan An Road
Shanghai, China 200050
Phone: 86-21-52385488
Fax: 86-21-52385489

Type of Firm
Government Affiliated Program

Project Preferences

Type of Financing Preferred:
Early Stage

Geographical Preferences

International Preferences:
China

Additional Information
Year Founded: 2003
Current Activity Level : Actively seeking new investments

SHANGHAI NCE VENTURE CAPITAL MANAGEMENT CO LTD

Yinhang Road, Yangpu District
Room 114, Number 751
Shanghai, China

Management and Staff
Qiwei Chen, Partner
Yilu Chen, Partner
Yuwei Qi, Founder

Type of Firm
Private Equity Firm

Project Preferences

Type of Financing Preferred:
Early Stage
Seed

Geographical Preferences

International Preferences:
China

Industry Preferences

In Medical/Health prefer:
Pharmaceuticals

In Industrial/Energy prefer:
Alternative Energy
Materials
Environmental Related

Additional Information
Year Founded: 2008
Current Activity Level : Actively seeking new investments

SHANGHAI NEWGEN VENTURE CAPITAL CENTER LP

298 Lianzhen Road
D221, Builidng 4
Shanghai, China

E-mail: contact@newgenpartners.com
Website: www.newgenvc.com

Type of Firm
Private Equity Firm

Project Preferences

Type of Financing Preferred:
Early Stage
Seed

Size of Investments Considered:
Min Size of Investment Considered (000s): $15
Max Size of Investment Considered (000s): $436

Geographical Preferences

United States Preferences:

International Preferences:
United Kingdom
Hong Kong
China

Industry Preferences

In Communications prefer:
Communications and Media

In Internet Specific prefer:
Internet

In Biotechnology prefer:
Biotechnology

In Medical/Health prefer:
Medical/Health
Pharmaceuticals

Additional Information
Year Founded: 2012
Current Activity Level : Actively seeking new investments

SHANGHAI NEWMARGIN VENTURES CO LTD

No. 78, Xingguo Road
Villa 11, Radisson Plaza
Shanghai, China 200052
Phone: 862162123000
Fax: 862162123900
E-mail: info@newmargin.com
Website: www.newmargin.com

Other Offices
No. 33 Beishan Road
Xi Hu District
Hangzhou, China 310007
Phone: 8657128130555
Fax: 8657128137909

Zui Xiang Road, Xingfu Meilin
Jinjiang District
Chengdu, China 610000
Phone: 862884675195
Fax: 862884675185

No. 35 Qin Lao Hutong
Dong Cheng District
Beijing, China 100080
Phone: 86-10-840-22999
Fax: 86-10-840-20555

Management and Staff
Di Ai, Managing Partner
Hanjie Xu, Managing Partner
Huan Ma, Managing Partner
Junqi He, Managing Partner
Kevin Yip, Managing Partner
Shuiwen Zhou, Managing Partner
Tao Feng, Chief Executive Officer
Yongkai Zhou, Managing Partner
Yuze Han, Managing Partner

Type of Firm
Private Equity Firm

Project Preferences

Type of Financing Preferred:
Leveraged Buyout
Early Stage
Expansion
Balanced
Later Stage
Seed
Startup

Geographical Preferences

International Preferences:
China
Asia

Industry Preferences

In Communications prefer:
Telecommunications
Wireless Communications

In Semiconductor/Electr prefer:
Fiber Optics

In Biotechnology prefer:
Biotechnology

In Medical/Health prefer:
Medical/Health
Pharmaceuticals

In Industrial/Energy prefer:
Alternative Energy

In Other prefer:
Environment Responsible

Additional Information
Year Founded: 1999
Capital Under Management: $120,000,000
Current Activity Level : Actively seeking new investments

SHANGHAI NSR WEALTH INVESTMENT MANAGEMENT CO LTD

No. 1088 Yuanshen Rd.
5F, Pingan Wealth Building
Shanghai, China 200122
Website: www.nsrwm.com

Type of Firm
Private Equity Firm

Project Preferences

Type of Financing Preferred:
Generalist PE

Geographical Preferences

International Preferences:
China

Industry Preferences

In Industrial/Energy prefer:
Energy
Energy Conservation Relat

In Manufact. prefer:
Manufacturing

Additional Information
Year Founded: 2015
Current Activity Level : Actively seeking new investments

SHANGHAI PANASIA STRATEGY INVESTMENT CO LTD

2558 Yan'an Road West
#8 Building
Shanghai, China 201103
Phone: 86-21-62959
Fax: 86-21-62958
Website: www.psi.net.cn

Type of Firm
Investment Management Firm

Additional Information
Year Founded: 2009
Capital Under Management: $18,100,400
Current Activity Level : Actively seeking new investments

SHANGHAI PEELI INVESTMENT MANAGEMENT CO LTD

No. 2299, Yan An Road West, Suite 2812, Shanghai Mart
Shanghai, China 200336
Phone: 862162362188
Fax: 862162361936
E-mail: info@peeliventures.com
Website: www.peeliventures.com

Management and Staff
Harry Qin, Managing Partner
Sharon Zhang, Partner

Type of Firm
Private Equity Firm

Project Preferences

Type of Financing Preferred:
Early Stage
Expansion

Geographical Preferences

International Preferences:
China

Industry Preferences

In Internet Specific prefer:
Internet

In Consumer Related prefer:
Consumer Products
Education Related

In Business Serv. prefer:
Services
Media

Additional Information
Year Founded: 2014
Current Activity Level : Actively seeking new investments

SHANGHAI PLINTH CAPITAL MANAGEMENT CO LTD

88 Century Avenue, Pudong
47/F, Jinmao Tower
Shanghai, China 200121
Phone: 862150477908
Fax: 862150477905
E-mail: info@plinth-capital.com
Website: www.plinth-capital.com

Type of Firm
Private Equity Firm

Project Preferences

Type of Financing Preferred:
Early Stage
Expansion
Later Stage
Startup

Geographical Preferences

International Preferences:
China

Industry Preferences

In Medical/Health prefer:
Medical/Health

In Consumer Related prefer:
Consumer
Education Related

In Industrial/Energy prefer:
Energy
Materials
Machinery

In Business Serv. prefer:
Services
Media

In Agr/Forestr/Fish prefer:
Agriculture related

Additional Information
Year Founded: 2010
Current Activity Level : Actively seeking new investments

SHANGHAI PROVIDENCE EQUITY INVEST. MGMT. PATNER ENTERPRISE

No.9, 2351 Lane, Wangyuan Road
Room 212
Shanghai, China 200052
Phone: 862162262179

Type of Firm
Private Equity Firm

Project Preferences

Type of Financing Preferred:
Balanced

Geographical Preferences

International Preferences:
China

Additional Information
Year Founded: 2012
Current Activity Level : Actively seeking new investments

SHANGHAI PUDONG SCIENCE AND TECHNOLOGY INVESTMENT CO LTD

No. 439 Chunxiao Road
13/F Zhangjiang High-tech Dist
Shanghai, China 201203
Phone: 862150276328
Fax: 862150276385
E-mail: info@pdsti.com
Website: www.pdsti.com

Type of Firm
Government Affiliated Program

Project Preferences

Type of Financing Preferred:
Fund of Funds
Expansion
Balanced
Later Stage

Geographical Preferences

International Preferences:
China

Industry Preferences

In Computer Software prefer:
Software

In Semiconductor/Electr prefer:
Semiconductor

In Biotechnology prefer:
Biotechnology

In Industrial/Energy prefer:
Energy
Materials

In Agr/Forestr/Fish prefer:
Agriculture related

Additional Information
Year Founded: 1999
Capital Under Management: $37,936,000
Current Activity Level : Actively seeking new investments

SHANGHAI PUDONG VENTURE CAPITAL CO LTD

351 Guoshoujin Road
Zhangjiang High-tech Park
Shanghai, China 201203
Phone: 86-21-50800118
Fax: 86-21-50800216

Type of Firm
Private Equity Firm

Project Preferences

Type of Financing Preferred:
Early Stage
Later Stage

Geographical Preferences

International Preferences:
China

Industry Preferences

In Computer Hardware prefer:
Mainframes / Scientific
Integrated Turnkey System

In Computer Software prefer:
Software
Applications Software

In Medical/Health prefer:
Medical Diagnostics
Medical Products
Pharmaceuticals

Additional Information
Year Founded: 2010
Current Activity Level : Actively seeking new investments

SHANGHAI QIANLONG YUHAN INVESTMENT MANAGEMENT CO LTD

1299, Minsheng Road, Pudong
Dingxiang Intel Business Cent
Shanghai, China

Type of Firm
Private Equity Firm

Project Preferences

Type of Financing Preferred:
Balanced

Geographical Preferences

International Preferences:
China

Industry Preferences

In Medical/Health prefer:
Medical/Health

Additional Information
Year Founded: 2015
Capital Under Management: $800,000,000
Current Activity Level : Actively seeking new investments

SHANGHAI QINGCONG ASSET MANAGEMENT CO LTD

No.507,Huajing Rd., Xuhui Dist
Room 158, Block 5
Shanghai, China 200000
Website: qingcongcapital.cn

Type of Firm
Private Equity Firm

Project Preferences

Type of Financing Preferred:
Seed
Startup

Geographical Preferences

International Preferences:
China

Industry Preferences

In Internet Specific prefer:
Internet

In Consumer Related prefer:
Consumer

Additional Information
Year Founded: 2014
Current Activity Level : Actively seeking new investments

SHANGHAI QINGKE HUAGAI INVESTMENT MANAGEMENT CO LTD

No. 4988, Caoan Rd, Jiading
Room 2008, Tower 6
Shanghai, China

Type of Firm
Private Equity Firm

Project Preferences

Type of Financing Preferred:
Balanced

Geographical Preferences

International Preferences:
China

Additional Information
Year Founded: 2015
Current Activity Level : Actively seeking new investments

SHANGHAI REALEADER INVESTMENT FUND MANAGEMENT CO LTD

No.950 Dalian Road
1909 Room, Yangpu District
Shanghai, China
Fax: 862133770799
Website: www.realeader.com.cn

Management and Staff
Bin Qin, Managing Partner
Hongguang Qiiu, Partner
Rongguo Wu, Partner

Type of Firm
Private Equity Firm

Project Preferences

Type of Financing Preferred:
Balanced

Geographical Preferences

International Preferences:
China

Additional Information
Year Founded: 2011
Current Activity Level : Actively seeking new investments

SHANGHAI RELIANCE CAPITAL MANAGEMENT CO LTD

Changjiang Farm, Chongming Cou
Room 102, 1F, East of Huanghe
Shanghai, China
Phone: 8621-55510309

Type of Firm
Private Equity Firm

Project Preferences

Type of Financing Preferred:
Balanced

Geographical Preferences

International Preferences:
China

Industry Preferences

In Biotechnology prefer:
Biotechnology

In Medical/Health prefer:
Medical/Health

In Consumer Related prefer:
Consumer
Retail

In Industrial/Energy prefer:
Environmental Related

Additional Information
Year Founded: 2008
Current Activity Level : Actively seeking new investments

SHANGHAI RONGXI VENTURE CAPITAL INVESTMENT MANAGEMENT CO LTD

Building 2, No. 770
Yishan Road, Xuhui District
Shanghai, China 200233
Phone: 862154223827

Type of Firm
Investment Management Firm

Project Preferences

Type of Financing Preferred:
Balanced

Geographical Preferences

International Preferences:
China

Additional Information
Year Founded: 2009
Current Activity Level : Actively seeking new investments

SHANGHAI RUIQI SCIENCE & TECHNOLOGY DEVELOPMENT CO LTD

No. 270, Songhu Road, Yangpu
B1, Blk3, Zhichuang Tiandi
Shanghai, China
Phone: 862155225009
E-mail: innospace@qq.com
Website: www.innospace.com.cn

Management and Staff
Ruigang Li, Founder

Type of Firm
Private Equity Firm

Project Preferences

Type of Financing Preferred:
Early Stage
Seed
Startup

Geographical Preferences

International Preferences:
China

Industry Preferences

In Internet Specific prefer:
Internet

Additional Information
Year Founded: 2012
Current Activity Level : Actively seeking new investments

SHANGHAI SAITIAN INVESTMENT MANAGEMENT CO LTD

No. 196 Ouyang Rd., Hongkou Di
Room 317, Block 10
Shanghai, China

Type of Firm
Investment Management Firm

Project Preferences

Type of Financing Preferred:
Balanced

Geographical Preferences

International Preferences:
China

Industry Preferences

In Computer Software prefer:
Artificial Intelligence

In Semiconductor/Electr prefer:
Sensors

In Industrial/Energy prefer:
Energy
Materials

Additional Information
Year Founded: 2011
Current Activity Level : Actively seeking new investments

SHANGHAI SCIENCE & TECHNOLOGY INVESTMENT HOLDING CO LTD

No. 285 West Jianguo Road
Xuhui District
Shanghai, China
Website: www.sstic.com.cn

Type of Firm
Private Equity Firm

Project Preferences

Type of Financing Preferred:
Early Stage
Balanced
Later Stage

Geographical Preferences

International Preferences:
China

Industry Preferences

In Biotechnology prefer:
Biotechnology

In Medical/Health prefer:
Medical/Health

In Industrial/Energy prefer:
Energy
Energy Conservation Relat
Materials
Environmental Related

In Business Serv. prefer:
Services

Additional Information

Year Founded: 1993
Current Activity Level : Actively seeking new investments

SHANGHAI SEASONAL CAPITAL CO LTD

3A-B
433 Zhaojiabang Rd
Shanghai, China 200030
Phone: 86-21-64049702
Fax: 86-21-64178726
Website: www.seasonalcapital.com

Other Offices

433 Zhaojiabang No. 3A-B
Shanghai, China 200030
Phone: 021-640-49702
Fax: 021-641-78786

Type of Firm

Private Equity Firm

Additional Information

Year Founded: 2010
Current Activity Level : Actively seeking new investments

SHANGHAI SEEINFRONT NETWORK TECHNOLOGY LTD

No.1236 Zhaixi Road, Huangpu
3F, Bldg 2
Shanghai, China
Phone: 862163317151
Website: www.seeinfront.com

Type of Firm

Investment Management Firm

Project Preferences

Type of Financing Preferred:
Balanced

Additional Information

Year Founded: 2015
Current Activity Level : Actively seeking new investments

SHANGHAI SHANGCHUANG JUNQIANG INVESTMENT MANAGEMENT CO LTD

Alley 320, Tianping Road
Room 401, Ouxi'ai Center
Shanghai , China 200030
Phone: 862180238661

Type of Firm

Private Equity Firm

Project Preferences

Type of Financing Preferred:
Balanced

Geographical Preferences

International Preferences:
China

Additional Information

Year Founded: 2010
Current Activity Level : Actively seeking new investments

SHANGHAI SHANGQI INVESTMENT MGMT PARTNERSHIP ENTERPRISE

No. 741, 745,747, Lingshi Road
Room 510, Floor 5
Shanghai, China

Other Offices

Yangtze River North Rd. 471
Yangzhou, China

Type of Firm

Private Equity Firm

Project Preferences

Type of Financing Preferred:
Leveraged Buyout

Geographical Preferences

International Preferences:
China

Additional Information

Year Founded: 2012
Current Activity Level : Actively seeking new investments

SHANGHAI SHANLAN INVESTMENT MANAGEMENT CO LTD CO LTD

No.1502 Lane No.14Luoshan Road
Room 303-4
Shanghai, China

Type of Firm

Investment Management Firm

Project Preferences

Type of Financing Preferred:
Early Stage
Expansion
Balanced
Later Stage

Geographical Preferences

International Preferences:
China

Industry Preferences

In Medical/Health prefer:
Medical/Health

Additional Information

Year Founded: 2014
Capital Under Management: $8,260,000
Current Activity Level : Actively seeking new investments

SHANGHAI SHENGDIAN YINGHUA INVESTMENT CO LTD

Maoming South Rd.Huangpu Dist.
Floor 2, No 3 Lane 163
Shanghai, China 200020
Phone: 862164330532
Fax: 862163906570
Website: www.s-mediafund.com

Type of Firm

Private Equity Firm

Project Preferences

Type of Financing Preferred:
Balanced

Geographical Preferences

International Preferences:
China

Industry Preferences

In Communications prefer:
Entertainment

Additional Information
Year Founded: 2011
Current Activity Level : Actively seeking new investments

SHANGHAI SHENGHU INVESTMENT MANAGEMENT CO LTD

8, Xiushan Rd, Chengming Town
Room 2025, Zone U, 3F, Block 3
Shanghai, China 202155

Type of Firm
Private Equity Firm

Project Preferences

Type of Financing Preferred:
Balanced

Geographical Preferences

International Preferences:
China

Additional Information
Year Founded: 2015
Capital Under Management: $58,840,000
Current Activity Level : Actively seeking new investments

SHANGHAI SHIBEI TECHNOLOGY VENTURE CAPITAL CO LTD

c/o, SSTI
Shanghai, China

Type of Firm
Private Equity Firm

Project Preferences

Type of Financing Preferred:
Early Stage
Expansion
Balanced

Geographical Preferences

International Preferences:
China

Industry Preferences

In Industrial/Energy prefer:
Alternative Energy
Advanced Materials

Additional Information
Year Founded: 2011
Current Activity Level : Actively seeking new investments

SHANGHAI SINOHEAD CAPITAL CO LTD

877 Dongfang Road, Pudong Area
20th Floor, # 1
Shanghai, China 200122
Phone: 86-21-68671262
Fax: 86-21-58305390
Website: www.sinohead.com

Management and Staff
Axin Lin, President
Wenhui Pan, Vice President

Type of Firm
Private Equity Firm

Additional Information
Year Founded: 2006
Capital Under Management: $2,500,000
Current Activity Level : Actively seeking new investments

SHANGHAI SMC CAPITAL CO LTD

1168 West Nanjing Road
Unit 1410 CITIC Square
Shanghai, China 200041
Phone: 862131001885
Fax: 862153752208
E-mail: info@smc-capital.com
Website: cn.smc-capital.com

Other Offices
879 Hongqiao Road
19th Floor
Wuxi, Jiangsu, China
Phone: 8651085898583
Fax: 8651085817557

2 Queen's Road Central
3601 Cheung Kong Center
Hong Kong, Hong Kong
Phone: 85225011339
Fax: 85228385130

24 Queen Anne's Gate
London, United Kingdom SW1H9AA
Phone: 442077998800
Fax: 442077998808

9-1, 1-chome Yurakucho Chiyoda
Tokyo, Japan 100-0006
Phone: 1352225316
Fax: 81352223788

2 Zhong Shan Square
Dalian, Liaoning, China
Phone: 8641186508888
Fax: 8641186508888

Management and Staff
Alexandre Xing, Partner
Hamilton Tang, Chief Executive Officer
Norman Lui, Venture Partner
San Eng, Partner
Simon Mackinnon, Venture Partner
Waisum Fan, Partner

Type of Firm
Investment Management Firm

Project Preferences

Type of Financing Preferred:
Expansion
Balanced
Later Stage
Startup

Size of Investments Considered:
Min Size of Investment Considered (000s): $2,000
Max Size of Investment Considered (000s): $20,000

Geographical Preferences

International Preferences:
China

Industry Preferences

In Biotechnology prefer:
Biotechnology

In Medical/Health prefer:
Health Services

In Consumer Related prefer:
Consumer

In Industrial/Energy prefer:
Energy
Alternative Energy
Industrial Products
Environmental Related

In Manufact. prefer:
Manufacturing

Additional Information
Year Founded: 1997
Capital Under Management: $106,973,000
Current Activity Level : Actively seeking new investments

SHANGHAI SOVA CAPITAL CO LTD

No. 500 Southeast Road
16/F, National Dev'l Bank Bldg
Shanghai, China 200120
Phone: 862158400138
Fax: 862158400132
E-mail: shengwan@sova.cn
Website: www.sova.cn

Management and ...
Dan Zhou, Founding Partner
Xiaoqiu He, Founding Part...

Type of Firm
Service Provider

Project Pr...

Type of F...
Balanced
Later S...

G...

/Fish prefer:
...tated

...onal Information
Founded: 2004
...pital Under Management: $31,332,000
Current Activity Level : Actively seeking new investments

SHANGHAI STONE CAPITAL CO LTD

163-4, South Maoming Road
Shanghai, China
Phone: 862160758996
Website: www.stonecapital.com.cn

Type of Firm
Private Equity Firm

Project Preferences

Type of Financing Preferred:
Early Stage
Expansion
Balanced
Later Stage

Geographical Preferences

International Preferences:
China

Industry Preferences

In Consumer Related prefer:
Consumer
Retail

In Industrial/Energy prefer:
Energy
Energy Conservation Relat
Machinery

In Manufact. prefer:
Manufacturing

In Other prefer:
Environment Responsible

Additional Information
Year Founded: 2008
Capital Under Management: $48,154,000
Current Activity Level : Actively seeking new investments

SHANGHAI SUN TERRA CAPITAL MANAGEMENT CO LTD

Room 809-17,8/F, Central Plaza
No. 281, Huaihai Zhong Rd
Shanghai, China
Phone: 02163916608
E-mail: Xudh@sunterra-capital.com
Website: www.sunterra-capital.com

Type of Firm
Private Equity Firm

Industry Preferences

In Biotechnology prefer:
Biotechnology

Additional Information
Year Founded: 1969
Current Activity Level : Actively seeking new investments

SHANGHAI TAOSHI INVESTMENT MANAGEMENT PARTNER ENTERPRISE LP

No.1056, Yangshupu Rd.
R709. No.1 Bldg.
Shanghai, China
Website: www.taoshicapital.com

Type of Firm
Private Equity Firm

Project Preferences

Type of Financing Preferred:
Balanced

Geographical Preferences

International Preferences:
China

Industry Preferences

In Internet Specific prefer:
Internet

In Financial Services prefer:
Financial Services

Additional Information
Year Founded: 2014
Current Activity Level : Actively seeking new investments

SHANGHAI TECHNOLOGY VENTURE CAPITAL GROUP CO LTD

No.1634 Huaihai Middle Road
Shanghai, China
Phone: 862164311988
Fax: 862164312336
Website: www.shvc.com.cn

Type of Firm
Government Affiliated Program

Project Preferences

Type of Financing Preferred:
Early Stage
Seed
Startup

Geographical Preferences

International Preferences:
China

Industry Preferences

In Computer Software prefer:
Software

In Semiconductor/Electr prefer:
Semiconductor

In Biotechnology prefer:
Biotechnology

In Industrial/Energy prefer:
Energy
Energy Conservation Relat
Advanced Materials

Additional Information
Year Founded: 2014
Capital Under Management: $12,000,000,000
Current Activity Level : Actively seeking new investments

SHANGHAI TIANCHENG INVESTMENT CENTRE LP

No.5885 Jinhai Road
Room3575
Shanghai, China

Type of Firm
Private Equity Firm

Project Preferences

Type of Financing Preferred:
Balanced

Geographical Preferences

International Preferences:
China

Additional Information
Year Founded: 2011
Current Activity Level : Actively seeking new investments

SHANGHAI TIANDI RENHE VENTURE CAPITAL CO

No.161, Lujiazui E Road
2101, Pudong New District
Shanghai, China

Type of Firm
Private Equity Firm

Project Preferences

Type of Financing Preferred:
Early Stage

Geographical Preferences

International Preferences:
China

Industry Preferences

In Industrial/Energy prefer:
Energy Conservation Relat
Advanced Materials

In Other prefer:
Environment Responsible

Additional Information
Year Founded: 2012
Capital Under Management: $63,554,000
Current Activity Level : Actively seeking new investments

SHANGHAI TIANYI INDUSTRIAL HOLDING GROUP CO LTD

No.2018, Huashan Road
North Building, HuiYin Square
Shanghai, China 200030
Phone: 862154070999
Fax: 862154070655
Website: www.tyi.cn

Type of Firm
Private Equity Firm

Project Preferences

Type of Financing Preferred:
Leveraged Buyout
Early Stage
Expansion
Balanced

Geographical Preferences

International Preferences:
China

Industry Preferences

In Communications prefer:
Media and Entertainment
Other Communication Prod.

In Internet Specific prefer:
Internet

In Biotechnology prefer:
Biotechnology

In Medical/Health prefer:
Medical/Health
Health Services
Pharmaceuticals

In Consumer Related prefer:
Education Related

In Industrial/Energy prefer:
Energy
Energy Conservation Relat
Materials
Advanced Materials

In Financial Services prefer:
Financial Services

In Business Serv. prefer:
Services

In Other prefer:
Environment Responsible

Additional Information
Year Founded: 1998
Capital Under Management: $313,900,000
Current Activity Level : Actively seeking new investments

SHANGHAI ... VESTMEN... CO LTD

No. 19 Wuning Road
12/F Lijing Yangguang
Shanghai, China
Phone: 862160957088
Fax: 862160957099
Website: www.ch-tj.com

Management and S...
Baoguo Zhang, President & Cha...

Type of Firm
Investment Management Firm

Project Preferences

Type of Financing Preferred:
Early Stage

Geographical Preferences

International Preferences:
China

Additional Information
Year Founded: 2011
Current Activity Level : Actively seeking new investment

SHANGHAI TRIUMPH INVESTMENT MANAGEMENT CO LTD

No.1142, Kongjiang Road
F6136, No.23 Building
Shanghai, China

Type of Firm
Investment Management Firm

Project Preferences

Type of Financing Preferred:
Fund of Funds
Leveraged Buyout
Balanced

Geographical Preferences

International Preferences:
China

Industry Preferences

In Communications prefer:
Telecommunications

In Business Serv. prefer:
Media

Pratt's Guide to Private Equity & Venture Capital Sources

Additional Information
Year Founded: 2014
Current Activity Level : Actively seeking new investments

SHANGHAI TRONFUND MANAGEMENT CO LTD
No.161 Songhu Road
16th Floor
Shanghai, China 200433
Phone: 862155661370
Fax: 862155665521
E-mail: contact@tronfund.com
Website: www.tronfund.com

Management and Staff
Jihao Chen, Partner
Ke Zhang, Partner
Sucheng Lin, Partner
Zhen Peng, Managing Partner
Zhengqing Li, Partner

Type of Firm
Private Equity Firm

Project Preferences
Type of Financing Preferred:
Expansion
Balanced
Opportunistic

Geographical Preferences
International Preferences:
China

Industry Preferences
In Medical/Health prefer:
Medical/Health

In Consumer Related prefer:
Consumer Products

In Industrial/Energy prefer:
Energy

In Financial Services prefer:
Real Estate

In Manufact. prefer:
Manufacturing

In Agr/Forestr/Fish prefer:
Agriculture related

Additional Information
Year Founded: 2011
Capital Under Management: $321,300,000
Current Activity Level : Actively seeking new investments

SHANGHAI TRUSTBRIDGE PARTNERS INVESTMENT MANAGEMENT CO LTD
50 Connaught Road
Unit 2001, ABC Tower
Central, Hong Kong
Phone: 862150106188
Website: www.trustbridgepartners.com

Management and Staff
Donglei Zhou, Co-Founder
Shujun Li, Partner
Yi Zhang, Partner

Type of Firm
Private Equity Firm

Association Membership
Hong Kong Venture Capital Association (HKVCA)

Project Preferences
Type of Financing Preferred:
Expansion
Balanced
Later Stage

Geographical Preferences
International Preferences:
China

Industry Preferences
In Communications prefer:
Communications and Media
Telecommunications

In Internet Specific prefer:
Internet

In Consumer Related prefer:
Retail
Consumer Products

In Business Serv. prefer:
Media

Additional Information
Year Founded: 2006
Capital Under Management: $1,391,735,000
Current Activity Level : Actively seeking new investments

SHANGHAI VISINO INVESTMENT MANAGEMENT CO LTD
No.471, Guiping Road
F4, Building 8
Shanghai, China
Phone: 862164956850
Fax: 862164956001
Website: www.visino.org

Type of Firm
Private Equity Firm

Project Preferences
Type of Financing Preferred:
Start-up Financing
Seed

Geographical Preferences
International Preferences:
China

Industry Preferences
In Communications prefer:
Telecommunications

In Medical/Health prefer:
Medical/Health

In Consumer Related prefer:
Consumer

In Business Serv. prefer:
Media

In Agr/Forestr/Fish prefer:
Agriculture related

Additional Information
Year Founded: 2015
Current Activity Level : Actively seeking new investments

SHANGHAI VOLCANICS INVESTMENT MANAGEMENT CO LTD
No.26, 28, Jiangchang 3rd Road
Room 217
Shanghai, China

Type of Firm
Private Equity Firm

Project Preferences
Type of Financing Preferred:
Balanced

Geographical Preferences
International Preferences:
China

Additional Information
Year Founded: 2016
Current Activity Level : Actively seeking new investments

SHANGHAI VSTONE CAPITAL CO., LTD

No.1, Yanan East Road
F4, Vstone Building
Shanghai, China
Website: www.vstone.com.cn

Type of Firm
Private Equity Firm

Project Preferences

Type of Financing Preferred:
Leveraged Buyout
Balanced

Geographical Preferences

International Preferences:
China

Additional Information
Year Founded: 2009
Current Activity Level: Actively seeking new investments

SHANGHAI WIN CAPITAL PTE LTD

855 South Pudong Road
10th Floor, World Plaza
Shanghai, China
Phone: 86-21-5840-3608
Fax: 86-21-6859-8125

Type of Firm
Private Equity Firm

Project Preferences

Type of Financing Preferred:
Balanced

Industry Preferences

In Industrial/Energy prefer:
Energy
Environmental Related

Additional Information
Year Founded: 2008
Capital Under Management: $146,000,000
Current Activity Level: Actively seeking new investments

SHANGHAI WUQIONG VENTURE CAPITAL MANAGEMENT CO LTD

200 Guoding E. Rd., Yangpu
Room 602-10, Block 2
Shanghai, China

Type of Firm
Private Equity Firm

Project Preferences

Type of Financing Preferred:
Start-up Financing
Seed

Size of Investments Considered:
Min Size of Investment Considered (000s): $770
Max Size of Investment Considered (000s): $3,080

Geographical Preferences

International Preferences:
China

Industry Preferences

In Communications prefer:
Telecommunications
Entertainment

In Business Serv. prefer:
Media

Additional Information
Year Founded: 2015
Current Activity Level: Actively seeking new investments

SHANGHAI XIANGCAI STRING INVESTMENT MANAGEMENT CO LTD

139 Yincheng East Rd, Lujiazui
19/F, Huaneng United
Shanghai, China
Phone: 86-21-68634
Fax: 86-21-68866

Type of Firm
Private Equity Firm

Industry Preferences

In Other prefer:
Environment Responsible

Additional Information
Year Founded: 2001
Current Activity Level: Actively seeking new investments

SHANGHAI XINXIN INVESTMENT CO LTD

118 Ruijin Second Road
Tower G, Ruijin Hotel
Shanghai, China
Phone: 86-21-64670010
Fax: 86-21-64670

Type of Firm
Private Equity Firm

Additional Information
Year Founded: 2001
Current Activity Level: Actively seeking new investments

SHANGHAI XINYOU INVESTMENT MANAGEMENT CO LTD

Pudong Ave., Pudong New Dist.
Building 21, No.2123
Shanghai, China 200135

Type of Firm
Private Equity Firm

Project Preferences

Type of Financing Preferred:
Early Stage

Geographical Preferences

International Preferences:
China

Industry Preferences

In Communications prefer:
Entertainment

In Internet Specific prefer:
Internet

Additional Information
Year Founded: 2014
Current Activity Level: Actively seeking new investments

SHANGHAI XIYU ASSET MANAGEMENT CO LTD

Pudong New District
2F, Block 1, No. 777 Fangdian
Shanghai, China
Website: www.allycapital.cn

Type of Firm
Investment Management Firm

Project Preferences

Type of Financing Preferred:
Balanced

Geographical Preferences

International Preferences:
China

Industry Preferences

In Internet Specific prefer:
Internet

In Financial Services prefer:
Financial Services

Additional Information
Year Founded: 2015
Current Activity Level : Actively seeking new investments

SHANGHAI XUHUI VENTURE CAPITAL LTD

Zhao Jia Bang Rd., Xuhui Dist.
Lane Room 1709, No. A
Shanghai, China 200030
Phone: 863367707
Fax: 8333680013
E-mail: xhvc@xhvc.net
Website: www.xhvc.net

Type of Firm
Private Equity Firm

Project Preferences

Type of Financing Preferred:
Balanced

Geographical Preferences

International Preferences:
China

Industry Preferences

In Communications prefer:
Telecommunications

In Biotechnology prefer:
Biotechnology

In Industrial/Energy prefer:
Materials

In Business Serv. prefer:
Media

Additional Information
Year Founded: 1998
Current Activity Level : Actively seeking new investments

SHANGHAI YABAO FANGHE INVESTMENT MANAGEMENT CENTER LP

No. 146, Fute East 1st Road
Room F099, F Zone, 2F, Block 3
Shanghai, China
Website: www.sigmasquare.com

Type of Firm
Private Equity Firm

Project Preferences

Type of Financing Preferred:
Early Stage
Expansion

Size of Investments Considered:
Min Size of Investment Considered (000s): $2,906
Max Size of Investment Considered (000s): $7,264

Geographical Preferences

International Preferences:
China

Industry Preferences

In Internet Specific prefer:
Internet

In Medical/Health prefer:
Medical/Health

In Consumer Related prefer:
Consumer

In Financial Services prefer:
Financial Services

Additional Information
Year Founded: 2015
Current Activity Level : Actively seeking new investments

SHANGHAI YANGPU HIGH-TECH VENTURE CENTER CO LTD

No. 335 Guoding Road
Shanghai, China 200433
Phone: 86-21-5566-3061
Fax: 86-21-6511-6218
Website: www.ypbase.com

Type of Firm
Incubator/Development Program

Project Preferences

Type of Financing Preferred:
Early Stage
Expansion
Seed

Geographical Preferences

International Preferences:
China

Industry Preferences

In Biotechnology prefer:
Biotechnology

In Medical/Health prefer:
Medical/Health

In Industrial/Energy prefer:
Energy
Materials
Environmental Related

In Manufact. prefer:
Manufacturing

Additional Information
Year Founded: 1997
Capital Under Management: $14,600,000
Current Activity Level : Actively seeking new investments

SHANGHAI YIDEZENG EQUITY INVESTMENT MANAGEMENT CENTER GP

No.80, Moling Road
Room 603H, Building 2
Shanghai, China

Type of Firm
Private Equity Firm

Project Preferences

Type of Financing Preferred:
Early Stage
Expansion
Balanced

Geographical Preferences

International Preferences:
China

Additional Information
Year Founded: 2010
Capital Under Management: $127,456,000
Current Activity Level : Actively seeking new investments

SHANGHAI YIFAN INVESTMENT MANAGEMENT CO LTD

Xinshi North Road, Hongkou
Rm.601, No.32, Lane 1508
Shanghai, China 200080
Phone: 862160340201

Type of Firm
Private Equity Firm

Project Preferences

Type of Financing Preferred:
Balanced

Geographical Preferences

International Preferences:
China

Additional Information
Year Founded: 2012
Current Activity Level : Actively seeking new investments

SHANGHAI YIJIN INVESTMENT MANAGEMENT CO LTD

Lane 299,Jiangchang W. Road
Zhongtiezhonghuan Plaza
Shanghai, China

Type of Firm
Private Equity Firm

Project Preferences

Type of Financing Preferred:
Balanced

Geographical Preferences

International Preferences:
China

Industry Preferences

In Industrial/Energy prefer:
Energy Conservation Relat
Environmental Related

In Business Serv. prefer:
Media

In Manufact. prefer:
Manufacturing

Additional Information
Year Founded: 2009
Current Activity Level : Actively seeking new investments

SHANGHAI YINLAI INVESTMENT GROUP CO LTD

No.710 Dongfang Road Pudongxin
24F Tangchen Financial Buildin
Shanghai, China 200120
Phone: 862131005555
Website: www.yinland.com.cn

Type of Firm
Investment Management Firm

Project Preferences

Type of Financing Preferred:
Leveraged Buyout
Generalist PE
Balanced

Geographical Preferences

International Preferences:
China

Industry Preferences

In Communications prefer:
Telecommunications

In Medical/Health prefer:
Medical/Health

In Financial Services prefer:
Real Estate

In Business Serv. prefer:
Media

In Agr/Forestr/Fish prefer:
Agriculture related

In Other prefer:
Environment Responsible

Additional Information
Year Founded: 2006
Current Activity Level : Actively seeking new investments

SHANGHAI YONGHUA CAPITAL MANAGEMENT CO LTD

No. 1088, Fangdian Road
Room 1505, Zizhu Inte'l Bldg.
Shanghai, China 201204
Phone: 862150158708
Fax: 862150158661
E-mail: Yonghua@yonghuacapital.com.cn
Website: www.yonghuacapital.com.cn

Other Offices
No. 27, Financial Street, Xicheng Dist
11/F, Tower B, Investment Plaza
Beijing, China 100140
Phone: 861066220651
Fax: 861066212180

Management and Staff
Dong Gao, Managing Director
Yang Li, Vice President

Type of Firm
Private Equity Firm

Project Preferences

Type of Financing Preferred:
Early Stage
Balanced
Later Stage

Geographical Preferences

International Preferences:
China

Additional Information
Year Founded: 1994
Current Activity Level : Actively seeking new investments

SHANGHAI YUANHE VENTURE CAPITAL INVESTMENT CENTRE LP

Room 701, Building 5
No.200 Guoding East Road
Shanghai, China
Phone: 86-21-65055235
Fax: 86-21-65055235

Type of Firm
Private Equity Firm

Project Preferences

Type of Financing Preferred:
Early Stage
Seed
Startup

Size of Investments Considered:
Min Size of Investment Considered (000s): $76
Max Size of Investment Considered (000s): $762

Geographical Preferences

International Preferences:
China

Industry Preferences

In Communications prefer:
Entertainment

In Internet Specific prefer:
Internet

In Consumer Related prefer:
Consumer

In Industrial/Energy prefer:
Materials

Additional Information
Year Founded: 2012
Current Activity Level : Actively seeking new investments

SHANGHAI ZHANGJIANG BIOMEDICAL INDUSTRY FUND

Zhangjiang High-Tech Park
Shanghai, China

Type of Firm
Government Affiliated Program

Project Preferences

Type of Financing Preferred:
Balanced

Geographical Preferences

International Preferences:
China

Industry Preferences

In Biotechnology prefer:
Biotechnology

In Medical/Health prefer:
Medical/Health
Pharmaceuticals

Additional Information
Year Founded: 2009
Capital Under Management: $146,772,000
Current Activity Level : Actively seeking new investments

SHANGHAI ZHANGJIANG TECHNOLGY VENTURE INVESTMENT CO LTD

Zhangjiang High Tech Park
Rm.305, Blk.C, Bldg.16
Shanghai, China 201203
Phone: 862150800601
Website: www.zjventure.com

Type of Firm
Private Equity Firm

Project Preferences

Type of Financing Preferred:
Balanced

Geographical Preferences

International Preferences:
China

Industry Preferences

In Medical/Health prefer:
Medical/Health

Additional Information
Year Founded: 2004
Current Activity Level : Actively seeking new investments

SHANGHAI ZHANGJIANG TORCH VENTURE PARK INVESTMENT DVLP.

No.1158, Zhangdong Road
R618, No.3 Building
Shanghai, China
Website: zjhjf.com

Type of Firm
Government Affiliated Program

Project Preferences

Type of Financing Preferred:
Start-up Financing
Seed

Geographical Preferences

International Preferences:
China

Additional Information
Year Founded: 2008
Current Activity Level : Actively seeking new investments

SHANGHAI ZHENGSAILIAN VENTURE CAPITAL MANAGEMENT CO LTD

690,Bibo Road,Pudong District
Room 201C, Building 2
Shanghai, China 201203
Phone: 862120249811
Fax: 862120248711
Website: www.cacfund.com

Management and Staff
Cun Nan, Co-Founder
Xidong Sun, Co-Founder

Type of Firm
Private Equity Firm

Project Preferences

Type of Financing Preferred:
Balanced

Geographical Preferences

International Preferences:
China

Industry Preferences

In Semiconductor/Electr prefer:
Electronics

In Manufact. prefer:
Manufacturing

Additional Information
Year Founded: 2010
Capital Under Management: $80,576,000
Current Activity Level : Actively seeking new investments

SHANGHAI ZHIYI CHENGXI ASSET MANAGEMENT CO LTD

Beiqing Road 9138
Room 350, Building 1
Shanghai, China

Type of Firm
Private Equity Firm

Project Preferences

Type of Financing Preferred:
Balanced

Geographical Preferences

International Preferences:
China

Additional Information
Year Founded: 2014
Current Activity Level : Actively seeking new investments

SHANGHAI ZHONGBO CAPITAL CO LTD

Room 706, Mingshen Plaza
400 Caobao Rd
Shanghai, China 200233
Phone: 86-21-5116-8681
Fax: 86-21-5116-8505
E-mail: master@chinavc.cn
Website: www.chinavc.cn

Type of Firm
Government Affiliated Program

Project Preferences

Type of Financing Preferred:
Early Stage
Balanced

Geographical Preferences

International Preferences:
China

Industry Preferences

In Communications prefer:
Wireless Communications

In Internet Specific prefer:
E-Commerce Technology

In Biotechnology prefer:
Biotechnology

In Industrial/Energy prefer:
Alternative Energy
Materials
Environmental Related

Additional Information
Year Founded: 2010
Current Activity Level : Actively seeking new investments

SHANGHAI ZHONGLU (GROUP) CO LTD

Pudong New Area
No.832 Hua Mu Road
Shanghai, China 201204
Phone: 862150591378
Fax: 862138763256
Website: www.zhonglu.com.cn

Type of Firm
Private Equity Firm

Project Preferences

Type of Financing Preferred:
Generalist PE

Geographical Preferences

International Preferences:
China

Industry Preferences

In Computer Software prefer:
Software

In Semiconductor/Electr prefer:
Electronic Components

In Biotechnology prefer:
Biotechnology

In Medical/Health prefer:
Medical/Health

In Industrial/Energy prefer:
Energy
Materials
Environmental Related

In Financial Services prefer:
Financial Services

In Agr/Forestr/Fish prefer:
Agriculture related

Additional Information
Year Founded: 1998
Current Activity Level : Actively seeking new investments

SHANGHAI ZHONGMI INVESTMENT MANAGEMENT CO LTD

No. 584, Zhizaoju Road
2F-3F, Building F
Shanghai, China
Phone: 862133302128
Fax: 862160932685

Type of Firm
Private Equity Firm

Project Preferences

Type of Financing Preferred:
Seed
Startup

Geographical Preferences

International Preferences:
China

Industry Preferences

In Communications prefer:
Data Communications
Media and Entertainment

In Computer Software prefer:
Artificial Intelligence

In Consumer Related prefer:
Sports

Additional Information
Year Founded: 2013
Current Activity Level : Actively seeking new investments

SHANGHAI ZHONGXIN TECHNOLOGY INVESTMENT CO LTD

1634 Huaihai Middle Road
Shanghai, China

Type of Firm
Private Equity Firm

Additional Information
Year Founded: 2010
Current Activity Level : Actively seeking new investments

SHANGHAI ZHONGYI ZHIJIAO EQUITY INVESTMENT CO., LTD.

Yangpu District
Room 801, No.6, Weide Rd.
Shanghai, China

Type of Firm
Investment Management Firm

Project Preferences

Type of Financing Preferred:
Early Stage
Seed
Startup

Geographical Preferences

International Preferences:
China

Industry Preferences

In Consumer Related prefer:
Education Related

In Business Serv. prefer:
Media

Additional Information
Year Founded: 2016
Current Activity Level : Actively seeking new investments

SHANGHAI ZHONGZHI VENTURE CAPITAL CO LTD

16/F World Plaza A
855 South Pudong Road
Shanghai, China 200120
Phone: 86-21-6887-3258
Fax: 86-21-6887-3257
Website: www.chdhvc.com

Management and Staff
Michael Lee, Managing Director

Type of Firm
Private Equity Firm

Project Preferences

Type of Financing Preferred:
Early Stage
Expansion
Seed

Geographical Preferences

International Preferences:
Macau
Taiwan
Hong Kong
China

Industry Preferences

In Biotechnology prefer:
Biotechnology

In Medical/Health prefer:
Pharmaceuticals

In Industrial/Energy prefer:
Energy Conservation Relat
Environmental Related

Additional Information
Year Founded: 2007
Current Activity Level : Actively seeking new investments

SHANGHAI ZHULU INVESTMENT MANAGEMENT CO LTD

No.600 Yunling West Road Putuo
3F No.6 Jinhuan Building
Shanghai, China
Website: www.zhulu.vc

Type of Firm
Private Equity Firm

Project Preferences

Type of Financing Preferred:
Seed
Startup

Geographical Preferences

International Preferences:
China

Industry Preferences

In Communications prefer:
Telecommunications
Media and Entertainment

Additional Information
Year Founded: 2014
Current Activity Level : Actively seeking new investments

SHANGHAI ZHUOPU INVESTMENT MANAGEMENT CENTER LP

Xiaomuqiao Road
Room 201-29
Shanghai, China
Website: www.zhuopucapital.com

Type of Firm
Investment Management Firm

Project Preferences

Type of Financing Preferred:
Balanced

Geographical Preferences

International Preferences:
China

Additional Information
Year Founded: 2011
Current Activity Level : Actively seeking new investments

SHANGHAI ZHUOZHONG INVESTMENT MANAGEMENT CO LTD CO LTD

No.89 Yunling East Road
Room 1601
Shanghai, China
Website: www.preotc.cn

Type of Firm
Investment Management Firm

Project Preferences

Type of Financing Preferred:
Balanced

Geographical Preferences

International Preferences:
China

Industry Preferences

In Communications prefer:
Telecommunications
Media and Entertainment

In Computer Software prefer:
Artificial Intelligence

In Medical/Health prefer:
Medical/Health

In Consumer Related prefer:
Consumer

In Industrial/Energy prefer:
Energy Conservation Relat
Materials
Robotics

In Manufact. prefer:
Manufacturing

In Other prefer:
Environment Responsible

Additional Information
Year Founded: 2014
Capital Under Management: $149,600,000
Current Activity Level : Actively seeking new investments

SHANGHAI ZIJIANG VENTURE CAPITAL CO LTD

No. 5481 Humin Road
Minxing District
Shanghai, China

Type of Firm
Private Equity Firm

Project Preferences

Type of Financing Preferred:
Balanced

Geographical Preferences

International Preferences:
China

Industry Preferences

In Biotechnology prefer:
Biotechnology
Biotech Related Research

In Industrial/Energy prefer:
Energy
Materials

In Other prefer:
Environment Responsible

Additional Information
Year Founded: 2000
Current Activity Level : Actively seeking new investments

SHANGHAI ZONGQUAN INVESTMENT MANAGEMENT CO LTD

733 Fuxing Eastern Road, Suite 1503
Shanghai, China 200010
Phone: 862158206488
Fax: 862160911253
Website: www.ric-cap.com

Type of Firm
Investment Management Firm

Project Preferences

Type of Financing Preferred:
Leveraged Buyout
Early Stage
Expansion

Geographical Preferences

International Preferences:
Asia

Additional Information
Year Founded: 2009
Current Activity Level : Actively seeking new investments

SHANGHAI ZUHE INVESTMENT MANAGEMENT CO LTD

No. 715, Sanshuang Road
Room 207, Building 1
Shanghai, China

Type of Firm
Private Equity Firm

Project Preferences

Type of Financing Preferred:
Fund of Funds
Leveraged Buyout

Geographical Preferences

International Preferences:
China

Additional Information
Year Founded: 2014
Capital Under Management: $49,556,000
Current Activity Level : Actively seeking new investments

SHANNON CAPITAL MANAGEMENT LLC

511 Union Street, Suite 2700
Nashville, TN USA 37219
Phone: 6153731714
Fax: 6152446804
Website: www.shannoncap.com

Type of Firm
Investment Management Firm

Project Preferences

Type of Financing Preferred:
Turnaround
Distressed Debt
Recapitalizations

Geographical Preferences

United States Preferences:
All U.S.

Industry Preferences

In Medical/Health prefer:
Medical/Health

In Financial Services prefer:
Financial Services

In Business Serv. prefer:
Distribution

In Manufact. prefer:
Manufacturing

Additional Information
Year Founded: 2013
Current Activity Level : Actively seeking new investments

SHAPE CAPITAL AG IN LIQUIDATION

Wolleraustrasse 41a
Freienbach, Switzerland 8807
Phone: 41585961296
Fax: 41585961297
E-mail: info@shape-capital.com

Type of Firm
Private Equity Advisor or Fund of Funds

Association Membership
Swiss Venture Capital Association (SECA)

Project Preferences

Type of Financing Preferred:
Fund of Funds
Leveraged Buyout
Later Stage
Special Situation

Geographical Preferences

United States Preferences:
All U.S.

International Preferences:
Europe
All International

Additional Information
Year Founded: 2001
Capital Under Management: $80,400,000
Current Activity Level : Actively seeking new investments

SHARD CAPITAL PARTNERS LLP

20 Fenchurch Street
23rd Floor
London, United Kingdom EC3M 3BY
Phone: 4402071869900
Fax: 440)207 186 997
E-mail: info@shardcapital.com
Website: shardcapital.com

Management and Staff
Alastair Brown, Partner
Chris Woods, Partner
Dick Durrant, Partner
Greg Lomas, Partner
Jose Benedicto, Partner
Michael Hollings, Partner
Ronnie Alder, Partner
Toby Raincock, Chief Executive Officer

Type of Firm
Private Equity Firm

Project Preferences

Type of Financing Preferred:
Balanced

Industry Preferences

In Computer Software prefer:
Software

In Financial Services prefer:
Financial Services

Additional Information
Year Founded: 2010
Capital Under Management: $25,000,000
Current Activity Level : Actively seeking new investments

SHARE CAPITAL PARTNERS LP

Haide 3rd Avenue
Hai'an City, Nanshan District
Shenzhen, China 518054
Phone: 8675586331929
Fax: 8675586331909
E-mail: maggie@sharecapital.cn
Website: www.sharecapital.cn

Type of Firm
Private Equity Firm

Project Preferences

Type of Financing Preferred:
Early Stage
Expansion
Balanced
Later Stage

Geographical Preferences

International Preferences:
China

Industry Preferences

In Internet Specific prefer:
Internet

In Industrial/Energy prefer:
Energy

In Business Serv. prefer:
Services

Additional Information
Year Founded: 2007
Capital Under Management: $128,288,000
Current Activity Level : Actively seeking new investments

SHARESPOST FINANCIAL CORP

1150 Bayhill Drive, Suite 300
San Bruno, CA USA 94066
Phone: 6504926870
Fax: 6504926871
E-mail: info@sharespost.com
Website: welcome.sharespost.com

Management and Staff
Sven Weber, President

Type of Firm
Investment Management Firm

Project Preferences

Type of Financing Preferred:
Later Stage

Industry Preferences

In Computer Software prefer:
Software

In Internet Specific prefer:
Web Aggregration/Portals

In Biotechnology prefer:
Biotechnology

In Medical/Health prefer:
Health Services

In Industrial/Energy prefer:
Energy

Additional Information
Year Founded: 2014
Current Activity Level : Actively seeking new investments

SHAREWIN EQUITY FUND MANAGEMENT CO LTD

No. 391, Guiping Road
Xincaohejing Inte'l Trade Ctr.
Shanghai, China 200233
Phone: 862133563256
Fax: 862133563258
E-mail: xiangms@sharewin-sh.com
Website: www.sharewin-sh.com

Management and Staff
Jianbing Zhang, Vice President
Xiaoyong Wang, Vice President

Type of Firm
Private Equity Firm

Project Preferences

Type of Financing Preferred:
Early Stage
Expansion
Balanced
Later Stage

Geographical Preferences

International Preferences:
China

Industry Preferences

In Computer Software prefer:
Software

In Semiconductor/Electr prefer:
Semiconductor

In Medical/Health prefer:
Pharmaceuticals

In Consumer Related prefer:
Consumer

In Industrial/Energy prefer:
Materials

In Manufact. prefer:
Manufacturing

Additional Information
Year Founded: 2008
Capital Under Management: $410,200,000
Current Activity Level : Actively seeking new investments

SHARK BITES SPA

Via Olmetto 1
Milan, Italy 20123
Website: sharkbites.co

Type of Firm
Private Equity Firm

Additional Information
Year Founded: 2015
Current Activity Level : Actively seeking new investments

SHASTA VENTURES LP

2440 Sand Hill Road, Suite 300
Menlo Park, CA USA 94025
Phone: 6505431700
Fax: 6505431799
Website: www.shastaventures.com

Other Offices
27 South Park Street, Suite 101
SAN FRANCISCO, CA USA 94107

Management and Staff
Austin Grose, Chief Financial Officer
Catherine Norman, Vice President
Douglas Pepper, Managing Director
Jacob Mullins, Principal
Jason Pressman, Managing Director
Jayaram Bhat, Venture Partner
Nikhil Trivedi, Principal
Nitin Chopra, Principal
Phil Fernandez, Venture Partner
Ravi Mohan, Managing Director
Robert Coneybeer, Managing Director
Sean Flynn, Managing Director
Tod Francis, Managing Director

Type of Firm
Private Equity Firm

Association Membership
Western Association of Venture Capitalists (WAVC)
National Venture Capital Association - USA (NVCA)

Project Preferences

Type of Financing Preferred:
Early Stage
Startup

Size of Investments Considered:
Min Size of Investment Considered (000s): $250
Max Size of Investment Considered (000s): $12,000

Geographical Preferences

United States Preferences:

Industry Preferences

In Communications prefer:
Wireless Communications

In Computer Software prefer:
Software
Systems Software
Applications Software

In Internet Specific prefer:
Internet

In Consumer Related prefer:
Consumer

Additional Information
Name of Most Recent Fund: Shasta Ventures III, L.P.
Most Recent Fund Was Raised: 09/20/2011
Year Founded: 2004
Capital Under Management: $460,000,000
Current Activity Level : Actively seeking new investments

SHATTER FUND

950 Battery Street
Fourth Floor
San Francisco, CA USA 94111
E-mail: information@shatterfund.com
Website: shatterfund.com

Type of Firm
Private Equity Firm

Pratt's Guide to Private Equity & Venture Capital Sources

Project Preferences

Type of Financing Preferred:
Early Stage

Industry Preferences

In Other prefer:
Women/Minority-Owned Bus.

Additional Information

Year Founded: 1969
Current Activity Level : Actively seeking new investments

SHAW KWEI & PARTNERS

13 Connaught Road Central
1601 Euro Trade Center
Hong Kong, Hong Kong
Phone: 85231628479
Fax: 85231628499
E-mail: info@shawkwei.com
Website: www.shawkwei.com

Management and Staff

Allen Huie, Managing Director
Christoph Mueller, Managing Director
Kyle Shaw, Managing Director
Peter Ko, Managing Director
Sung Lam Tsui, Managing Director

Type of Firm

Private Equity Firm

Project Preferences

Role in Financing:
Prefer role as deal originator but will also invest in deals created by others

Type of Financing Preferred:
Leveraged Buyout
Management Buyouts
Acquisition
Recapitalizations

Geographical Preferences

United States Preferences:
Southeast

International Preferences:
China
Asia

Additional Information

Year Founded: 1999
Capital Under Management: $100,000,000
Current Activity Level : Actively seeking new investments

SHAW VENTURE PARTNERS

3438 SW Brentwood Drive
Portland, OR USA 97201
Phone: 503-228-4884
Fax: 503-212-0547

Management and Staff

Gayle Kovacs, Chief Financial Officer
Ralph Shaw, General Partner

Type of Firm

Private Equity Firm

Project Preferences

Role in Financing:
Will function either as deal originator or investor in deals created by others

Type of Financing Preferred:
Second Stage Financing
Leveraged Buyout
Early Stage
Balanced
Start-up Financing
Seed
First Stage Financing

Geographical Preferences

United States Preferences:
Northwest
West Coast

Industry Focus

(% based on actual investment)
Communications and Media	29.5%
Computer Software and Services	17.8%
Industrial/Energy	10.8%
Semiconductors/Other Elect.	10.5%
Consumer Related	7.6%
Internet Specific	6.8%
Computer Hardware	6.6%
Biotechnology	5.4%
Medical/Health	3.5%
Other Products	1.3%

Additional Information

Name of Most Recent Fund: Shaw Venture Partners IV
Most Recent Fund Was Raised: 01/01/1995
Year Founded: 1982
Capital Under Management: $80,000,000
Current Activity Level : Reducing investment activity
Method of Compensation: Return on investment is of primary concern, do not charge fees

SHENGSHANG CAPITAL MANAGEMENT CO LTD

Haidian District, Beijing
6F, Junma International Buildi
Beijing, China
Phone: 4008235999
Website: sscap.cn

Type of Firm

Private Equity Firm

Project Preferences

Type of Financing Preferred:
Balanced

Geographical Preferences

International Preferences:
China

Industry Preferences

In Communications prefer:
Telecommunications
Media and Entertainment

In Medical/Health prefer:
Medical/Health

In Consumer Related prefer:
Education Related

In Industrial/Energy prefer:
Energy Conservation Relat
Materials

Additional Information

Year Founded: 2013
Current Activity Level : Actively seeking new investments

SHENGYANG INVESTMENT AND FINANCING MANAGEMENT CENTER

Shenhe District
No.78, North Street
Shenyang, China 110014

Type of Firm

Government Affiliated Program

Project Preferences

Type of Financing Preferred:
Early Stage
Expansion
Balanced
Seed
Startup

Geographical Preferences

International Preferences:
China

Industry Preferences

In Business Serv. prefer:
Services
Media

In Manufact. pref
Manufacturing

In Agr/Fore
Agriculture

...000
...new investments

Addi...
Yea...

...MENT
...O LTD

...o.cn
...z.com

...nt and Staff
...hief Financial Officer

...ype of Firm
Investment Management Firm

Project Preferences

Type of Financing Preferred:
Leveraged Buyout
Later Stage
Acquisition

Geographical Preferences

International Preferences:
China

Additional Information
Year Founded: 2010
Current Activity Level : Actively seeking new investments

SHENZHEN AEROSPACE HI-TECH INVESTMENT MANAGEMENT CO LTD

West of Beichang'an Street
Renmin Road, Songling Town
Wujiang, Jiangsu, China

Type of Firm
Private Equity Firm

Project Preferences

Type of Financing Preferred:
Early Stage
Expansion
Balanced

Geographical Preferences

International Preferences:
China

Industry Preferences

In Transportation prefer:
Aerospace

Additional Information
Year Founded: 2011
Capital Under Management: $158,358,000
Current Activity Level : Actively seeking new investments

SHENZHEN ANZHUOXIN VENTURE CAPITAL INVESTMENT CO LTD

No.8, Kefa Road, Nanshan
6B, Building 1
Shenzhen, China

Type of Firm
Private Equity Firm

Project Preferences

Type of Financing Preferred:
Early Stage
Expansion
Later Stage

Geographical Preferences

International Preferences:
China

Industry Preferences

In Communications prefer:
Commercial Communications
Other Communication Prod.

In Internet Specific prefer:
Internet

In Biotechnology prefer:
Biotechnology

In Medical/Health prefer:
Medical Therapeutics
Pharmaceuticals

In Consumer Related prefer:
Education Related

In Industrial/Energy prefer:
Materials

Additional Information
Year Founded: 2007
Current Activity Level : Actively seeking new investments

SHENZHEN BORI VENTURE CAPITAL CO LTD

Tian'an Digital Plaza
2/F, Block CD
Shenzhen, Guangdong, China
Phone: 86075583562657
Fax: 86075583562711
E-mail: boricapital@boricapital.com
Website: www.boricapital.com

Type of Firm
Private Equity Firm

Association Membership
Shenzhen Venture Capital Association

Project Preferences

Type of Financing Preferred:
Leveraged Buyout
Early Stage
Expansion
Balanced

Geographical Preferences

International Preferences:
China

Additional Information
Year Founded: 2010
Capital Under Management: $47,500,000
Current Activity Level : Actively seeking new investments

SHENZHEN CAPITAL FORTUNE INVESTMENT CO LTD

4009 Shennan Ave., Futian Dist
03B Zone,2/F,Investment Bldg.
Shenzhen, China 518048
Phone: 8675583882057
Fax: 8675583882073
Website: www.szpema.com

Type of Firm
Private Equity Firm

Project Preferences

Type of Financing Preferred:
Leveraged Buyout
Balanced

Pratt's Guide to Private Equity & Venture Capital Sources

Geographical Preferences

International Preferences:
China

Industry Preferences

In Business Serv. prefer:
Consulting Services

Additional Information

Year Founded: 2013
Current Activity Level : Actively seeking new investments

SHENZHEN CAPITAL GROUP CO LTD

No. 4009, Shennan Rd
11F, Investment Building
Shenzhen, China 518048
Phone: 8675582912888
Fax: 8675592912880
Website: www.szvc.com.cn

Other Offices

No. 8 Shichang Avenue
514, Weihai State-Owned Assets Bldg
Weihai, China 264200
Phone: 866315231709
Fax: 866315285097

No. 37 Technology Road
1715, Tower A, Haixing City Plaza
Xi an, China 710075
Phone: 862988348859
Fax: 862988348867

No. 3 Zhongguancun South Street
Room 902, Haidian Science Bldg
Beijing, China 100081
Phone: 861068943958
Fax: 861068948819

No. 966 North Tianfu Avenue
Room 222, Tower 2
Chengdu, China 610041
Phone: 862885336920
Fax: 862885336922

No. 768 Minzhu Road
Room 2106, Huayin Building
Wuhan, China 430071
Phone: 862787339802
Fax: 862787339809

No. 166 Lujiazui Loop
26/F, Tower C, Future Assets Bldg.
Shanghai, China 200120
Phone: 862161001305
Fax: 862161001310

Management and Staff

Anping Shi, Vice President
Bo Liu, Chief Financial Officer
Dongsheng Sun, Vice President
Lian Zhong, Vice President
Wanshou Li, President
Wenzheng Chen, Vice President

Type of Firm

Private Equity Firm

Project Preferences

Type of Financing Preferred:
Early Stage
Expansion
Balanced
Later Stage

Geographical Preferences

International Preferences:
China
Asia

Industry Preferences

In Computer Software prefer:
Data Processing

In Internet Specific prefer:
Internet

In Semiconductor/Electr prefer:
Electronics
Optoelectronics

In Biotechnology prefer:
Biotechnology

In Medical/Health prefer:
Pharmaceuticals

In Consumer Related prefer:
Consumer
Sports
Consumer Products

In Industrial/Energy prefer:
Energy
Energy Conservation Relat
Materials
Advanced Materials
Machinery
Environmental Related

In Transportation prefer:
Transportation

In Business Serv. prefer:
Distribution
Media

In Manufact. prefer:
Manufacturing

In Agr/Forestr/Fish prefer:
Agriculture related

Additional Information

Year Founded:
Capital Under
Current Activity: $63,000,000
Actively seeking new investments

SHENZHEN CO LTD

Middle Shennan Road
Room 1209, Qiushi Buil
Shenzhen, China 518040
Phone: 8675583189608
Website: www.cdfcn.com

Management and Staff

Angsheng Jin, Partner
Jin Pan, Partner
Ming Zeng, Partner
Wei Wu, Partner
Yunfeng Lin, Partner

Type of Firm

Private Equity Firm

Association Membership

Venture Capital Association of Beijing (VCAB)

Project Preferences

Type of Financing Preferred:
Early Stage
Balanced
Seed

Geographical Preferences

International Preferences:
China

Industry Preferences

In Communications prefer:
Communications and Media

In Internet Specific prefer:
E-Commerce Technology
Internet

In Biotechnology prefer:
Biotechnology

In Medical/Health prefer:
Medical/Health

In Consumer Related prefer:
Entertainment and Leisure
Education Related

In Industrial/Energy prefer:
Energy
Materials
Environmental Related

In Business Serv. prefer:
Services
Media

In Manufact. prefer:
Manufacturing

In Agr/Forestr/Fish prefer:
Agriculture related

Additional Information
Year Founded: 2007
Capital Under Management: $119,600,000
Current Activity Level : Actively seeking new investments

SHENZHEN CENTERGATE VC MGMT CO

Shangbao Road, Futian
18/F, Olympic Building
Shenzhen, China 518034
Phone: 86-755-8352869
Fax: 86-755-83522204

Management and Staff
Xiangxiong Deng, Vice President

Type of Firm
Private Equity Firm

Additional Information
Year Founded: 2001
Current Activity Level : Actively seeking new investments

SHENZHEN CHANGRUN LIANHE ASSET MANAGEMENT CO LTD

No. 399, Fuhua Road, Futian
Room 808, Zhonghai Mansion
Shenzhen, China

Type of Firm
Private Equity Firm

Project Preferences

Type of Financing Preferred:
Leveraged Buyout

Geographical Preferences

International Preferences:
China

Additional Information
Year Founded: 2014
Current Activity Level : Actively seeking new investments

SHENZHEN CHINA MERCHANTS QIHANG INTNT INVSTMT MNGMT CO LTD

No. 22 Yanshan Road, Shekou, N
Torch Entrepreneurship Mansion
Shenzhen, China 518067
Phone: 8675521617757
Website: www.cmfhk.com/cmfh_fund_cn_qh.html

Type of Firm
Incubator/Development Program

Project Preferences

Type of Financing Preferred:
Early Stage
Seed
Startup

Geographical Preferences

International Preferences:
China

Industry Preferences

In Computer Software prefer:
Artificial Intelligence

In Internet Specific prefer:
Internet
Ecommerce

In Medical/Health prefer:
Medical/Health

In Financial Services prefer:
Financial Services

In Manufact. prefer:
Manufacturing

Additional Information
Year Founded: 2000
Current Activity Level : Actively seeking new investments

SHENZHEN CHUANGTONG JIALI INVESTMENT PARTNERSHIP LP

Futian Subdistrict, Futian Dis
Rm 3201, Zhuoyue Times Square
Shenzhen, China 518028

Type of Firm
Private Equity Firm

Project Preferences

Type of Financing Preferred:
Balanced

Geographical Preferences

International Preferences:
China

Additional Information
Year Founded: 2016
Current Activity Level : Actively seeking new investments

SHENZHEN CLASSICS VENTURE CAPITAL CO LTD

Jin Tian Road, Futian Dist.
3605Golden Ctr Hotel Main Bldg
Shenzhen, China 518000
Phone: 8675582562211
Fax: 8575582562216
E-mail: vc@classicsvc.com
Website: www.classicsvc.com

Type of Firm
Private Equity Firm

Association Membership
Shenzhen Venture Capital Association

Project Preferences

Type of Financing Preferred:
Leveraged Buyout
Early Stage

Geographical Preferences

International Preferences:
China

Industry Preferences

In Communications prefer:
Telecommunications

In Medical/Health prefer:
Medical/Health

In Industrial/Energy prefer:
Alternative Energy
Advanced Materials
Environmental Related

In Business Serv. prefer:
Media

In Manufact. prefer:
Manufacturing

In Agr/Forestr/Fish prefer:
Agriculture related

Additional Information
Year Founded: 2008
Current Activity Level : Actively seeking new investments

SHENZHEN CO-POWER VENTURE CAPITAL CO LTD

Overseas Chinese Town, Nanshan, Suite 1104,
Hantang Plaza
Shenzhen, China 518053
Phone: 86-755-26935145
Fax: 86-755-26935158
E-mail: am@chinacopower.com
Website: www.chinacopower.com

Type of Firm
Private Equity Firm

Association Membership
Shenzhen Venture Capital Association

Project Preferences

Type of Financing Preferred:
Expansion
Balanced

Geographical Preferences

International Preferences:
China
Asia

Industry Preferences

In Consumer Related prefer:
Consumer Products

In Industrial/Energy prefer:
Alternative Energy
Machinery

In Financial Services prefer:
Insurance
Financial Services

Additional Information
Year Founded: 2007
Capital Under Management: $74,708,000
Current Activity Level : Actively seeking new investments

SHENZHEN CO-WIN VENTURE CAPITAL INVESTMENTS LTD

No. 168, Fuhua 3rd Rd, Futian
2702 Int'l Shanghui Center
Shenzhen, China
Phone: 8675582877508
Fax: 8675582879025
E-mail: cowin@cowincapital.com
Website: www.cowincapital.com

Other Offices
166 East Lujiazui Road
China Insurance Building, 14th Floor
Shanghai, China
Phone: 862161089969
Fax: 862161089828

Haidian District, Zhongguancun
SOHO Building, Room 1216
Beijing, China
Phone: 861059718380
Fax: 861059718389

Management and Staff
Baoyu Ding, Managing Director
Boxiao Zhang, Vice President
Li Huang, Managing Director
Ping Tongzi, Vice President
Qing Zhu, Vice President
Wei Wang, Vice President
Xiao Zhang, Vice President
Zhongcheng Tang, Partner

Type of Firm
Private Equity Firm

Association Membership
China Venture Capital Association

Project Preferences

Type of Financing Preferred:
Early Stage
Expansion
Balanced
Later Stage
Startup

Geographical Preferences

International Preferences:
China

Industry Preferences

In Communications prefer:
Telecommunications
Wireless Communications

In Internet Specific prefer:
E-Commerce Technology
Internet

In Semiconductor/Electr prefer:
Electronics

In Biotechnology prefer:
Biotechnology

In Medical/Health prefer:
Medical/Health
Pharmaceuticals

In Consumer Related prefer:
Consumer
Retail
Consumer Products
Consumer Services

In Industrial/Energy prefer:
Energy
Alternative Energy
Energy Conservation Relat
Materials
Environmental Related

In Transportation prefer:
Transportation

In Business Serv. prefer:
Services
Media

In Agr/Forestry/Fish prefer:
Agriculture related

In Other prefer:
Environment Responsible

Additional Information
Year Founded: 2000
Capital Under Management: $450,313,000
Current Activity Level : Actively seeking new investments

SHENZHEN CORNERSTONE OF ENTREPRENEURIAL CCI CAPITAL LTD

Futian District
3 Lunuo De Main Bldg 35F
Shenzhen, China 518026
Phone: 75582792366
Fax: 75582792416
Website: www.stonevc.com

Other Offices
No. 12, North Street, Dongcheng District
Tianchen Building 23
Beijing, China 100020
Phone: 1065550080
Fax: 1065550081

Former HQ: No. 1 China Phoenix Mansion
Futian District
Shenzhen, China 518046
Phone: 8675582792357
Fax: 8675582792416

No. 56-62 Changliu Road
Zendai Cube Tower, Rm. 907
Shanghai, China 200135
Phone: 50309096
Fax: 2133901577

Management and Staff
Jun Shao, Vice President
Ling Lin, Partner
Qiwen Wang, President
Tao Tao, Partner
Tao Chen, Managing Director
Weibin Yu, Vice President
Weibin Xu, Vice President
Xunjun Zhang, Vice President
Yangwen Qin, Partner
Yanli Chen, Partner
Zaiwu Han, Partner

Type of Firm
Private Equity Firm

Project Preferences

Type of Financing Preferred:
Early Stage
Expansion
Balanced
Later Stage

Geographical Preferences

International Preferences:
China

Industry Preferences

In Communications prefer:
Communications and Media

In Computer Software prefer:
Software

In Internet Specific prefer:
Internet
Ecommerce

In Semiconductor/Electr prefer:
Electronics

In Biotechnology prefer:
Biotechnology

In Medical/Health prefer:
Medical/Health
Health Services
Pharmaceuticals

In Consumer Related prefer:
Consumer Products

In Industrial/Energy prefer:
Energy
Alternative Energy
Materials

In Financial Services prefer:
Financial Services

In Business Serv. prefer:
Services
Distribution
Media

In Manufact. prefer:
Manufacturing

In Agr/Forestr/Fish prefer:
Agriculture related

Additional Information
Year Founded: 2000
Capital Under Management: $229,400,000
Current Activity Level : Actively seeking new investments

SHENZHEN CUICAN INNOVATION CAPITAL CO LTD
Keyuan Road 1002
Room 902, Music Building
Shenzhen, China
Phone: 8675586572755
Website: www.brightvc.com

Type of Firm
Private Equity Firm

Project Preferences

Type of Financing Preferred:
Early Stage
Expansion

Geographical Preferences

International Preferences:
China

Industry Preferences

In Communications prefer:
Telecommunications
Media and Entertainment

In Medical/Health prefer:
Medical/Health

In Manufact. prefer:
Manufacturing

Additional Information
Year Founded: 2017
Current Activity Level : Actively seeking new investments

SHENZHEN DARWIN CAPITAL MANAGEMENT CO LTD
Futian District
Shenzhen, China
Website: www.darwin-capital.com

Type of Firm
Private Equity Firm

Project Preferences

Type of Financing Preferred:
Balanced

Geographical Preferences

International Preferences:
China

Industry Preferences

In Internet Specific prefer:
Internet

In Financial Services prefer:
Financial Services

Additional Information
Year Founded: 2015
Current Activity Level : Actively seeking new investments

SHENZHEN DEZHENG JIACHENG INVESTMENT FUND PARTNERSHIP LP
Shengang Cooperation District
Room 201, Block A, No. 1 Qianw
Shenzhen, China
Phone: 8675583337288

Type of Firm
Investment Management Firm

Project Preferences

Type of Financing Preferred:
Balanced

Geographical Preferences

International Preferences:
China

Additional Information
Year Founded: 2015
Current Activity Level : Actively seeking new investments

SHENZHEN DG CAPITAL MANAGEMENT CO LTD
No.88 Fuhua3rd Rd, Futian Dist
49F, Times Fortune Mansion
Shenzhen, China 518026
Phone: 8675533363322
Fax: 8675533363262
Website: www.daogecapital.com

Type of Firm
Private Equity Firm

Project Preferences

Type of Financing Preferred:
Generalist PE

1905

Geographical Preferences

International Preferences:
China

Additional Information

Year Founded: 2016
Current Activity Level : Actively seeking new investments

SHENZHEN DINGXIN CAPITAL MANAGEMENT CO LTD

Yuehai Ave., Nanshan District
Room 803-804, East Block Costa
Shenzhen, China 518000
Phone: 8675582766866
Website: www.dingxin-capital.com

Type of Firm
Investment Management Firm

Project Preferences

Type of Financing Preferred:
Early Stage

Geographical Preferences

International Preferences:
China

Industry Preferences

In Medical/Health prefer:
Medical/Health

In Business Serv. prefer:
Consulting Services

Additional Information

Year Founded: 2015
Current Activity Level : Actively seeking new investments

SHENZHEN DINOVA CAPITAL INVESTMENT MANAGEMENT PARTNER LP

4068 Yitian Rd., Futian Dist.
3908 Zhuoyue Time Square
Shenzhen, China
Phone: 8675588606000
Website: www.dinovacapital.com

Type of Firm
Private Equity Firm

Project Preferences

Type of Financing Preferred:
Early Stage
Expansion

Geographical Preferences

International Preferences:
China

Industry Preferences

In Medical/Health prefer:
Medical/Health

Additional Information

Year Founded: 2011
Current Activity Level : Actively seeking new investments

SHENZHEN DONGFANG SHENGFU VENTURE CAPITAL MANAGEMENT CO LTD

Fuhua 1st Street
Shenzhen Central Business Bldg
Futian, Shenzhen, China
Phone: 8675582038388
Fax: 8675582033138
Website: www.shengfuvc.com

Management and Staff
Jian Wang, Partner

Type of Firm
Private Equity Firm

Project Preferences

Type of Financing Preferred:
Expansion
Mezzanine
Balanced
Later Stage

Geographical Preferences

International Preferences:
China

Industry Preferences

In Medical/Health prefer:
Medical/Health

In Consumer Related prefer:
Consumer
Food/Beverage
Consumer Products
Education Related

In Industrial/Energy prefer:
Alternative Energy
Energy Conservation Relat
Advanced Materials
Environmental Related

In Business Serv. prefer:
Services

In Manufact. prefer:
Manufacturing

In Agr/Forestr/Fish prefer:
Agriculture related

Additional Information

Year Founded: 2010
Capital Under Management: $19,417,000
Current Activity Level : Actively seeking new investments

SHENZHEN DONGSHENG VENTURE CAPITAL CO LTD

No. 3008, Yitian Road
Rm. 2209, 3#, Huangdu Square
Shenzhen, China 518048
Phone: 8675588251556

Type of Firm
Private Equity Firm

Project Preferences

Type of Financing Preferred:
Balanced

Geographical Preferences

International Preferences:
China

Additional Information

Year Founded: 2000
Current Activity Level : Actively seeking new investments

SHENZHEN EFUNG VENTURE CAPITAL CO LTD

No.4019, Shennan Avenue
Rm610Space A bldg, Futian Dist
Shenzhen, China 518048
Phone: 8675533992623
Fax: 8675533992621
E-mail: info@efung.cc
Website: www.efung.cc

Type of Firm
Private Equity Firm

Association Membership
Shenzhen Venture Capital Association

Project Preferences

Type of Financing Preferred:
Early Stage
Expansion

Size of Investments Considered:
Min Size of Investment Considered (000s): $792
Max Size of Investment Considered (000s): $7,922

Geographical Preferences

International Preferences:
China

Industry Preferences

In Biotechnology prefer:
Biotechnology

In Medical/Health prefer:
Medical/Health
Medical Products
Pharmaceuticals

In Industrial/Energy prefer:
Energy
Materials
Environmental Related

Additional Information

Year Founded: 2007
Current Activity Level : Actively seeking new investments

SHENZHEN FORTUNE CAIZHI VENTURE CAPITAL MANAGEMENT CO LTD

Shennan Avenue, Futian
2303, Baoye Building
Shenzhen, China

Type of Firm
Private Equity Firm

Project Preferences

Type of Financing Preferred:
Balanced

Geographical Preferences

International Preferences:
China

Additional Information

Year Founded: 2008
Capital Under Management: $402,804,000
Current Activity Level : Actively seeking new investments

SHENZHEN FORTUNE LINK VENTURE CAPITAL MANAGEMENT CO LTD

Jintian Road, Futian District
1708, Rongchao Jingmao Centre
Shenzhen, China 518035
Phone: 867558351566
Fax: 8675582789371
Website: www.orica.com.cn

Management and Staff
Zhidong Kan, President

Type of Firm
Private Equity Firm

Project Preferences

Type of Financing Preferred:
Expansion
Balanced

Geographical Preferences

International Preferences:
China

Industry Preferences

In Semiconductor/Electr prefer:
Electronics

In Biotechnology prefer:
Biotechnology

In Medical/Health prefer:
Pharmaceuticals

In Consumer Related prefer:
Consumer Products

In Industrial/Energy prefer:
Energy
Alternative Energy
Materials
Advanced Materials
Machinery
Environmental Related

In Manufact. prefer:
Manufacturing

In Agr/Forestr/Fish prefer:
Agriculture related

Additional Information

Year Founded: 2005
Capital Under Management: $266,234,000
Current Activity Level : Actively seeking new investments

SHENZHEN FU SI ER WAN INVESTMENT PARTNERSHIP LP

No. 210 Century Avenue, Pudon
Room 1606, 21th Century Plaza
Shenzhen, China 200120
Phone: 862150431866

Type of Firm
Private Equity Firm

Project Preferences

Type of Financing Preferred:
Balanced

Geographical Preferences

International Preferences:
China

Additional Information

Year Founded: 2015
Current Activity Level : Actively seeking new investments

SHENZHEN FUHAI YINTAO VENTURE CAPITAL CO LTD

No. 118, Meilin 8th Road
8F, Dingye Building, Futian
Shenzhen, China 518049
Phone: 8675582588062

Management and Staff
Bo Jiang, President
Chenglin Mao, Vice President
Chengyu Cui, Vice President

Type of Firm
Investment Management Firm

Project Preferences

Type of Financing Preferred:
Early Stage
Balanced
Later Stage

Geographical Preferences

International Preferences:
China

Industry Preferences

In Medical/Health prefer:
Medical/Health

In Consumer Related prefer:
Retail
Food/Beverage
Consumer Products

In Industrial/Energy prefer:
Energy
Materials

In Financial Services prefer:
Financial Services

In Business Serv. prefer:
Media

In Manufact. prefer:
Manufacturing

Additional Information

Year Founded: 2007
Current Activity Level : Actively seeking new investments

SHENZHEN G STREET CAPITAL CO LTD

No. 5033 Yitian Road, Futian D
85F, PingAn Financial Building
Shenzhen, China 518033
Phone: 8675521244105
Website: www.gstreetcap.com

Type of Firm
Private Equity Firm

Project Preferences

Type of Financing Preferred:
Expansion
Later Stage

Geographical Preferences

International Preferences:
China

Industry Preferences

In Communications prefer:
Media and Entertainment

In Internet Specific prefer:
Internet
Ecommerce

In Medical/Health prefer:
Medical/Health

In Financial Services prefer:
Financial Services

In Manufact. prefer:
Manufacturing

Additional Information
Year Founded: 2017
Current Activity Level : Actively seeking new investments

SHENZHEN GAOZHANG CAPITAL INVESTMENT CO LTD

Fuzhong Rd, Futian Dist
1009, New World Center
Shenzhen, China
Website: www.gaozhangcap.cn

Type of Firm
Private Equity Firm

Project Preferences

Type of Financing Preferred:
Balanced

Geographical Preferences

International Preferences:
China

Industry Preferences

In Communications prefer:
Media and Entertainment

In Internet Specific prefer:
Internet

Additional Information
Year Founded: 2015
Current Activity Level : Actively seeking new investments

SHENZHEN GOLD MATCH SILVER FUND MANAGEMENT CO LTD

No. 1036, Bao'an South Road
905 Dingfeng Building
Shenzhen, China 518000
Phone: 8675522204176
Fax: 867552220376
Website: www.jinsaiyin.com

Management and Staff
Jiaming Wang, Vice President

Type of Firm
Investment Management Firm

Project Preferences

Type of Financing Preferred:
Leveraged Buyout
Generalist PE

Geographical Preferences

International Preferences:
China

Industry Preferences

In Consumer Related prefer:
Entertainment and Leisure

In Agr/Forestr/Fish prefer:
Agriculture related

Additional Information
Year Founded: 2011
Capital Under Management: $333,656,000
Current Activity Level : Actively seeking new investments

SHENZHEN GOLDPORT CAPITAL MANAGEMENT CO LTD

Fuhua 1st Road, Futian Distric
1905, Zhuoyue Mansion
Shenzhen, China 518048
Phone: 8675582874950
Fax: 8675582028719
Website: www.goldportcapital.com

Type of Firm
Private Equity Firm

Project Preferences

Type of Financing Preferred:
Balanced

Geographical Preferences

International Preferences:
China

Additional Information
Year Founded: 2014
Current Activity Level : Actively seeking new investments

SHENZHEN GREEN PINE CAPITAL PARTNERS CO LTD

No. 3039 Shennan Zhong Road
Rm. 2805 Int'l Culture Bldg.
Shenzhen, China 518033
Phone: 8675583290633
Fax: 8675583290622
E-mail: pinevc@pinevc.com.cn

Other Offices

No.19 Haitian 1st Rd
4A1102, Software Industry Base
Shenzhen, China

No. 161, Linhe West Road, Tianhe Dist
A1202, 12/F, Zhongtai Int'l Plaza Tower
Guangzhou, China 510630
Phone: 862038213316
Fax: 862038258873

South Street No.1, Zhongguancun, Haidian
Room 64042, Yayuan Apartment
Beijing, China 100873
Phone: 861068948141
Fax: 861068948128

No.1, Lane 6, Gaoan Road, Xuhui District
Shanghai, China 200030
Phone: 862164661567
Fax: 862164664839

No. 966, Tianfu Avenue North Section
Room 103, Tower 2, Admistrative center
Chengdu, China 610042
Phone: 862885987088
Fax: 862885987089

No.345 Fengli Street
2A104-2, Shahu Venture Center
Suzhou, China 215000
Phone: 8675583290509

Management and Staff

Binxian Tan, Managing Director
Chen Sun, Managing Director
Dan Qiu, Managing Director
Fan Hu, Managing Director
Fei Luo, Chairman & Managing Director
Fengzhi Wu, Managing Director
Hao Liu, Managing Director
Hua Xiao, Managing Director
Huaming Guan, Managing Director
Jingfei Yue, Managing Director
Liqing Sun, Managing Director
Lixin Xu, Partner
Mengling Li, Managing Director
Shijun Chen, Managing Director
Tianyang Wang, Managing Director
Wei Li, Managing Director
Xiaoyu Zeng, Managing Director
Xueyong Lu, Managing Director
Yong Wang, Managing Partner
Zhaoping Tong, Managing Director
Zhiliang Lin, Managing Director
Zhiwei Feng, Managing Director

Type of Firm

Private Equity Firm

Project Preferences

Type of Financing Preferred:
Balanced

Geographical Preferences

International Preferences:
China

Industry Preferences

In Communications prefer:
Communications and Media
Telecommunications

In Internet Specific prefer:
Internet
Ecommerce

In Medical/Health prefer:
Pharmaceuticals

In Industrial/Energy prefer:
Materials
Machinery

In Business Serv. prefer:
Media

Additional Information

Year Founded: 2008
Capital Under Management: $39,721,000
Current Activity Level : Actively seeking new investments

SHENZHEN GTJA INVESTMENT GROUP CO LTD

No. 3, Haide Road
15F, Tiley Central Plaza
Shenzhen, China 518054
Phone: 8675586332999
Fax: 8675586332710
Website: www.szgig.com

Other Offices

Torch Ave., Hi-Tech Dist.
R407, Jiangshan Mansion A
Jiangxi, China

Management and Staff

Huang Yu, President
Jiehui Guo, Partner
Yu Huang, President

Type of Firm

Private Equity Firm

Industry Preferences

In Communications prefer:
Telecommunications

In Computer Software prefer:
Software

In Medical/Health prefer:
Medical/Health
Pharmaceuticals

In Consumer Related prefer:
Consumer

In Industrial/Energy prefer:
Advanced Materials

In Business Serv. prefer:
Services

Additional Information

Year Founded: 2001
Capital Under Management: $30,000,000
Current Activity Level : Actively seeking new investments

SHENZHEN GUANGLIANG CAILVE INVESTMENT MANAGEMENT CO LTD

Futian Dist
601, Rongchao Intl
Shenzhen, China

Type of Firm

Private Equity Firm

Project Preferences

Type of Financing Preferred:
Balanced

Geographical Preferences

International Preferences:
China

Industry Preferences

In Communications prefer:
Telecommunications
Media and Entertainment

In Manufact. prefer:
Manufacturing

Additional Information

Year Founded: 2014
Current Activity Level : Actively seeking new investments

SHENZHEN GUOCHENG VENTURE CAPITAL LTD

6008 Shennan Road
Special Zone Press Tower
Shenzhen, China 518009
Phone: 8675583516448
Fax: 867558351944
E-mail: info@szgcvc.com
Website: www.szgcvc.com

Type of Firm

Private Equity Firm

Project Preferences

Type of Financing Preferred:
Balanced

Geographical Preferences

International Preferences:
China

Additional Information

Year Founded: 1997
Current Activity Level : Actively seeking new investments

SHENZHEN GUOZHONG VENTURE CAPITAL MANAGEMENT CO LTD

Shenzhen Fuhua Rd., Futian Dis
19F Galaxy Development Centre
Shenzhen, China
Phone: 8675582562906
Website: www.gzvcm.com

Type of Firm

Private Equity Firm

Project Preferences

Type of Financing Preferred:
Balanced

Geographical Preferences

International Preferences:
China

Industry Preferences

In Communications prefer:
Telecommunications
Media and Entertainment

In Biotechnology prefer:
Biotechnology

In Industrial/Energy prefer:
Energy Conservation Relat
Materials

In Manufact. prefer:
Manufacturing

In Other prefer:
Environment Responsible

Additional Information

Year Founded: 2015
Current Activity Level : Actively seeking new investments

SHENZHEN HEHUI XINDA INVESTMENT CO LTD

No. 6008, Shennandadao Road
Tequbaoye Bldg
Shenzhen, China 518009
Website: www.hbtscapital.com

Type of Firm
Private Equity Firm

Project Preferences

Type of Financing Preferred:
Balanced

Geographical Preferences

International Preferences:
China

Additional Information

Year Founded: 2010
Current Activity Level : Actively seeking new investments

SHENZHEN HENGTAI-HUASHENG ASSET MANAGEMENT CO LTD

No.32, Road, Baoshui Zone
4/F, Xin Rui Ke Ke Ji Da Sha
Shenzhen, China 518045
Phone: 8675523950088
Website: www.hths-capital.com

Type of Firm
Private Equity Firm

Project Preferences

Type of Financing Preferred:
Mezzanine
Balanced
Public Companies

Geographical Preferences

International Preferences:
China

Additional Information

Year Founded: 2013
Current Activity Level : Actively seeking new investments

SHENZHEN HIGH TECH INVESTMENT GROUP CO LTD

7028, Shennan Avenue, Futian
22/23/F, Times Tech Building
Shenzhen, China 518040
Phone: 8675582852588
Fax: 8675582852555
E-mail: rjgsyw1@szhti.com.cn
Website: www.szhti.com.cn

Type of Firm
Private Equity Firm

Project Preferences

Type of Financing Preferred:
Balanced

Geographical Preferences

International Preferences:
China

Additional Information

Year Founded: 1994
Current Activity Level : Actively seeking new investments

SHENZHEN HONGCHOU INVESTMENT CO LTD

Xinghua Rd, Shekou, Nanshan
Rm. 301, Section 1, Haibin Com
Shenzhen, China
Phone: 86-755-26820636
Fax: 86-755-26820456
Website: szhc.cn

Type of Firm
Private Equity Firm

Project Preferences

Type of Financing Preferred:
Balanced

Geographical Preferences

International Preferences:
China

Additional Information

Year Founded: 1997
Current Activity Level : Actively seeking new investments

SHENZHEN HONGSHISAN CAPITAL CO LTD

Bldg 5, No. 5, Qiongyu Road
Nanshan Technology Zone
Shenzhen, Guangdong, China 518057
Website: www.red13.com.cn

Management and Staff

Baohua Chen, Partner
Chungang Zheng, Partner
Dekun Fu, Partner
Haiying Huang, Partner
Hua Zeng, Partner
Jianhe Kong, Partner
Jungeng Sun, Partner
Junping Yang, Partner
Shengli Zhou, Partner
Yanwen Kong, Partner
Yuqing Zhang, Partner
Zhi Li, Partner

Type of Firm
Private Equity Firm

Project Preferences

Type of Financing Preferred:
Balanced

Additional Information

Year Founded: 2011
Capital Under Management: $183,522,000
Current Activity Level : Actively seeking new investments

SHENZHEN HONGXIU CAPITAL MANAGEMENT CO LTD

Soft Park Base, Nanshan
Building 5 E Tower
Shenzhen, China
Phone: 8675586681221
Website: www.hongxiuvc.com

Type of Firm
Private Equity Firm

Project Preferences

Type of Financing Preferred:
Balanced

Geographical Preferences

International Preferences:
China

Industry Preferences

In Communications prefer:
Telecommunications
Media and Entertainment

In Medical/Health prefer:
Medical/Health

In Consumer Related prefer:
Consumer
Education Related

Additional Information

Year Founded: 2015
Current Activity Level : Actively seeking new investments

SHENZHEN HUAXIN VENTURE CAPITAL CO LTD

Zhenxin Road
Huamei Building, Rm 530
Shenzhen, China 518031
Phone: 8675583276308
Fax: 8675583326104

Type of Firm
Private Equity Firm

Association Membership
Shenzhen Venture Capital Association

Project Preferences

Type of Financing Preferred:
Balanced

Geographical Preferences

International Preferences:
China

Industry Preferences

In Medical/Health prefer:
Medical/Health

In Industrial/Energy prefer:
Energy Conservation Relat
Materials
Environmental Related

Additional Information

Year Founded: 2011
Current Activity Level : Actively seeking new investments

SHENZHEN HUITOU CAPITAL CO LTD

Keyuan Ave, Nanshan Dist
Rm 901, Bldg 2, Xunmei Tech
Shenzhen, China 518003
Phone: 8675526656239
Fax: 8675586968314
Website: www.huitouziben.com

Type of Firm
Investment Management Firm

Project Preferences

Type of Financing Preferred:
Balanced

Geographical Preferences

International Preferences:
China

Additional Information

Year Founded: 2015
Current Activity Level : Actively seeking new investments

SHENZHEN HUOCHENG ACCELERATOR CO LTD

Shennan West Road, Shatou St
2501, Main Bldg
Shenzhen, China
Website: www.maxcapital.cn

Type of Firm
Incubator/Development Program

Project Preferences

Type of Financing Preferred:
Seed
Startup

Geographical Preferences

International Preferences:
China

Industry Preferences

In Communications prefer:
Telecommunications
Media and Entertainment

In Computer Software prefer:
Artificial Intelligence

In Internet Specific prefer:
Internet

In Consumer Related prefer:
Consumer

Additional Information

Year Founded: 2016
Current Activity Level : Actively seeking new investments

SHENZHEN INNOVATION CENTER CO. LTD.

5/F, Block 2, Cybercity
Hi-tech Industry Park
Shenzhen, China
Phone: 86-755-671-6698
E-mail: sic@sicvc.com
Website: www.sicvc.com

Type of Firm
Bank Affiliated

Project Preferences

Type of Financing Preferred:
Balanced
Seed
Startup

Geographical Preferences

International Preferences:
No Preference
China

Industry Preferences

In Computer Software prefer:
Software

In Semiconductor/Electr prefer:
Electronics

In Biotechnology prefer:
Biotechnology

In Industrial/Energy prefer:
Energy
Advanced Materials
Environmental Related

Additional Information

Year Founded: 2003
Current Activity Level : Actively seeking new investments

SHENZHEN JIAHE ASSET MANAGEMENT CO LTD

Shengang Cooperation District
Room 201, Block A, No. 1 Qianw
Shenzhen, China

Type of Firm
Investment Management Firm

Project Preferences

Type of Financing Preferred:
Balanced

Geographical Preferences

International Preferences:
China

Additional Information

Year Founded: 2015
Current Activity Level : Actively seeking new investments

SHENZHEN JIAQIAO INVESTMENT CO LTD

No.4068 Futian District
Room2401ZhuoyuePlaza
Shenzhen, China
Phone: 8675588315078
Fax: 8675588313048
Website: www.bridgecap.cn

Type of Firm

Private Equity Firm

Project Preferences

Type of Financing Preferred:
Generalist PE

Geographical Preferences

International Preferences:
China

Industry Preferences

In Computer Software prefer:
Artificial Intelligence

In Consumer Related prefer:
Consumer

Additional Information

Year Founded: 2009
Capital Under Management: $449,400,000
Current Activity Level : Actively seeking new investments

SHENZHEN JIDI XINTIAN VENTURE INVESTMENT CO LTD

Qiaoxiang Road 4068, Nanshan
Block B, Zhihui Square
Shenzhen, China
Phone: 8675586667539
Fax: 8675526904650
E-mail: yangt@avcapital.cn
Website: www.avcapital.cn

Management and Staff

Junxi Zhang, Partner
Xiaoyu Zhang, Chief Operating Officer
Yujie Jiang, Partner

Type of Firm

Private Equity Firm

Project Preferences

Type of Financing Preferred:
Early Stage

Geographical Preferences

International Preferences:
China

Industry Preferences

In Internet Specific prefer:
Internet

Additional Information

Year Founded: 2014
Current Activity Level : Actively seeking new investments

SHENZHEN JIEAO FUND MANAGEMENT CO LTD

No. 9 Langshan Road, Xili Neig
502, 5F, Dongjiang Environment
Shenzhen, China

Type of Firm

Investment Management Firm

Project Preferences

Type of Financing Preferred:
Balanced

Geographical Preferences

International Preferences:
China

Additional Information

Year Founded: 2011
Current Activity Level : Actively seeking new investments

SHENZHEN JIESHIBO CAPITAL MANAGEMENT CO LTD

No.1, Qianwan 1st Road
Room 201, Building A
Shenzhen, China

Type of Firm

Private Equity Firm

Project Preferences

Type of Financing Preferred:
Balanced

Geographical Preferences

International Preferences:
China

Additional Information

Year Founded: 2014
Current Activity Level : Actively seeking new investments

SHENZHEN JIN SHENG SHUO INDUSTRY ASSET MANAGEMENT CO., LTD.

Rongchao Trading Center
Room 3002, 30 Floor
Shenzhen, China 518038
Phone: 8675523607705
Fax: 8675523901096
E-mail: info@jsfof.com
Website: www.jsfof.com

Management and Staff

Jia Wang, Partner

Type of Firm

Private Equity Advisor or Fund of Funds

Project Preferences

Type of Financing Preferred:
Fund of Funds

Geographical Preferences

International Preferences:
China

Additional Information

Year Founded: 2011
Capital Under Management: $163,000,000
Current Activity Level : Actively seeking new investments

SHENZHEN JIUPAI CAPITAL MANAGEMENT CO LTD

Haisong Mansion
Room 505B, Tower B
Shenzhen, China 518040
Phone: 8675523981646
Fax: 8675523981415
Website: www.jiupaicapital.com

Management and Staff

Shaohong Wu, Partner
Yanxin Yu, Partner
Yunshan Chen, Partner

Type of Firm

Bank Affiliated

Project Preferences

Type of Financing Preferred:
Leveraged Buyout

Geographical Preferences

International Preferences:
China

Additional Information

Year Founded: 2014
Current Activity Level : Actively seeking new investments

SHENZHEN JIZHI EQUITY INVESTMENT CO LTD

Tianhe District, Guangzhou
Room 3504, Block 1, Taiguhui,
Shenzhen, China
Phone: 862038088109

Type of Firm

Private Equity Firm

Project Preferences

Type of Financing Preferred:
Balanced

Geographical Preferences

International Preferences:
China

Additional Information

Year Founded: 2016
Current Activity Level : Actively seeking new investments

SHENZHEN LEAGUER VENTURE CAPITAL CO LTD

S High-Tech Industrial Park
3F B Tsinghua University
Shenzhen, China 518057
Phone: 8675526551416
Fax: 8675526551372
E-mail: info@leaguer.com.cn
Website: www.leaguer.com.cn

Type of Firm

University Program

Association Membership

Shenzhen Venture Capital Association

Project Preferences

Type of Financing Preferred:
Early Stage

Industry Preferences

In Communications prefer:
Data Communications

In Semiconductor/Electr prefer:
Electronics

Additional Information

Year Founded: 1999
Current Activity Level : Actively seeking new investments

SHENZHEN LEPRO ENTERTAINMENT TECHNOLOGY CO LTD

No. 9 South Road, Haidan Dist.
Building Four
Beijing, China 100048
Phone: 861088568881
Fax: 861088568883
E-mail: zktz@leprogroup.com
Website: www.leprogroup.com

Type of Firm

Investment Management Firm

Association Membership

Venture Capital Association of Beijing (VCAB)

Project Preferences

Type of Financing Preferred:
Expansion
Later Stage

Geographical Preferences

International Preferences:
China

Industry Preferences

In Medical/Health prefer:
Pharmaceuticals

In Industrial/Energy prefer:
Alternative Energy
Energy Conservation Relat
Advanced Materials

In Business Serv. prefer:
Media

In Agr/Forestr/Fish prefer:
Mining and Minerals

In Other prefer:
Environment Responsible

Additional Information

Year Founded: 2007
Current Activity Level : Actively seeking new investments

SHENZHEN LIANGKE VENTURE CAPITAL CO LTD

Zhogngqing Road, Luohu District
Rm 2102, Waimao Group Bldg
Shenzhen, Guangdong Province, China

Type of Firm

Bank Affiliated

Project Preferences

Type of Financing Preferred:
Early Stage
Expansion
Later Stage
Seed

Geographical Preferences

International Preferences:
China

Industry Preferences

In Biotechnology prefer:
Biotechnology

In Industrial/Energy prefer:
Environmental Related

Additional Information

Year Founded: 2000
Current Activity Level : Actively seeking new investments

SHENZHEN LIHE QINGYUAN VENTURE CAPITAL MANAGEMENT CO., LTD.

High Tech Industry Park, South
A308, Qinghua Research Bldg
Shenzhen, Guangdong, China
Phone: 8675526551410
Fax: 8675586363823
E-mail: info@leaguercapital.com
Website: www.leaguercapital.com

Other Offices

No.1, Xihu Road, Wujin Dist
Rm 116, Wujin Hi-tech Com
Changzhou, China
Phone: 8651986220118
Fax: 8651986220118

No. 10, East Ring Mid Road, Chaoyang
903B, Nanhang Business Hotel
Beijing, China
Phone: 861065661251

Zhihui Road, Huishan Economic Dvlp Zone
Room 611, Qinghua Innovation Plaza
Wuxi, China
Phone: 8651083590287
Fax: 8651083590286

Management and Staff

Haifeng Pan, Partner
Jianyun Liu, President
Qing Hao, Partner
Yuzhe Lu, Partner

Type of Firm
Private Equity Firm

Association Membership
Shenzhen Venture Capital Association

Project Preferences

Type of Financing Preferred:
Expansion

Geographical Preferences

International Preferences:
China

Industry Preferences

In Communications prefer:
Telecommunications

In Computer Software prefer:
Software

In Internet Specific prefer:
Internet

In Semiconductor/Electr prefer:
Electronics
Circuit Boards
Optoelectronics

In Biotechnology prefer:
Biotechnology

In Medical/Health prefer:
Pharmaceuticals

In Consumer Related prefer:
Consumer
Education Related

In Industrial/Energy prefer:
Energy
Materials
Environmental Related

In Business Serv. prefer:
Services
Media

In Manufact. prefer:
Manufacturing

In Other prefer:
Environment Responsible

Additional Information
Year Founded: 2010
Capital Under Management: $174,800,000
Current Activity Level : Actively seeking new investments

SHENZHEN LITONG INDUSTRY INVESTMENT FUND CO LTD

Yue Hing Road 2
Wuhan University
Shenzhen, China

Type of Firm
Private Equity Firm

Project Preferences

Type of Financing Preferred:
Balanced

Geographical Preferences

International Preferences:
China

Additional Information
Year Founded: 2013
Current Activity Level : Actively seeking new investments

SHENZHEN MAISON CAPITAL MANAGEMENT CO LTD

No. 1, Zhongxin Road
Tower 1, Kerry Plaza
Shenzhen, China
Phone: 8675588266877
Fax: 8675588266884
Website: www.maisoncapital.com

Type of Firm
Private Equity Firm

Industry Preferences

In Medical/Health prefer:
Medical/Health

In Consumer Related prefer:
Consumer
Retail

Additional Information
Year Founded: 2004
Current Activity Level : Actively seeking new investments

SHENZHEN MAIXING INVESTMENT CO LTD

Shangbu Road, Futian District
Room 807,Sichuan Bilding
Shenzhen, Guangdong, China

Type of Firm
Private Equity Firm

Project Preferences

Type of Financing Preferred:
Expansion
Balanced

Geographical Preferences

International Preferences:
China

Industry Preferences

In Computer Software prefer:
Software

In Medical/Health prefer:
Health Services

In Consumer Related prefer:
Retail
Consumer Products
Consumer Services

Additional Information
Year Founded: 2005
Current Activity Level : Actively seeking new investments

SHENZHEN MALIANG EQUITY INVESMENT MANAGEMENT CO LTD

No. 3037 Jintian Road, Futian
Room 3201, Jinzhonghuan Intern
Shenzhen, China
Phone: 8675523992794

Type of Firm
Investment Management Firm

Project Preferences

Type of Financing Preferred:
Generalist PE

Geographical Preferences

International Preferences:
China

Industry Preferences

In Medical/Health prefer:
Medical/Health

In Industrial/Energy prefer:
Energy Conservation Relat
Materials

Additional Information
Year Founded: 2014
Current Activity Level : Actively seeking new investments

SHENZHEN MERCHANTS BUREAU TECHNOLOGY INVESTMENT CO LTD

Shekou nanhai DadaoNo.1077
5FBeikeChuanyeBldg.
Shenzhen, China
Phone: 8675526888600
Fax: 8675526888628

Type of Firm
Government Affiliated Program

Project Preferences

Type of Financing Preferred:
Balanced

Geographical Preferences

International Preferences:
China

Additional Information
Year Founded: 1995
Current Activity Level : Actively seeking new investments

SHENZHEN NALANDA INVESTMENT FUND MANAGEMENT COLTD

Qiaoxiang Road
Zhihui Building
Shenzhen, China

Type of Firm
Private Equity Firm

Project Preferences

Type of Financing Preferred:
Balanced

Geographical Preferences

International Preferences:
China

Additional Information
Year Founded: 2010
Current Activity Level : Actively seeking new investments

SHENZHEN ORIENTAL FORTUNE CAPITAL CO LTD

Tian'an Cyber Park, Futian
Room 2602 Cybertimes Tower A
Shenzhen, China 518040
Phone: 8675588836399
Fax: 8675583475799
E-mail: bp@ofcapital.com
Website: www.ofcapital.com

Other Offices
No. 1, Duchun Road, Jinghu
3/F, Capital CBD
Wuhu, China 241000
Phone: 865533850671
Fax: 865533852752

No. 1777 Century Avenue
7/F, D, East Hope Plaza
Shanghai, China 200122
Phone: 862150581867
Fax: 862150581867

A-19 North Dong Sanhuan Road
Room 2911, NEXUS CENTER
Beijing, China 100020
Phone: 861065865653
Fax: 861065865653

Management and Staff
Houbo Cheng, President, Founder
Hui Zhao, Partner
Jian Mei, Partner
Juanhuan Diao, Partner
Qing Liu, Partner
Wenqing Tan, Partner

Type of Firm
Private Equity Firm

Project Preferences

Type of Financing Preferred:
Early Stage
Expansion
Balanced
Later Stage
Seed
Startup

Geographical Preferences

International Preferences:
China

Industry Preferences

In Medical/Health prefer:
Medical/Health

In Consumer Related prefer:
Consumer Products

In Industrial/Energy prefer:
Energy
Materials

Additional Information
Year Founded: 2006
Capital Under Management: $7,000,000,000
Current Activity Level : Actively seeking new investments

SHENZHEN PING AN NEW CAPITAL INVESTMENT CO LTD

Bagua 3 Road
Ping'an Bldg, Futian District
Shenzhen, China 518000

Type of Firm
Private Equity Firm

Project Preferences

Type of Financing Preferred:
Balanced

Additional Information
Year Founded: 1992
Current Activity Level : Actively seeking new investments

SHENZHEN PINQING CAPITAL MANAGEMENT CO LTD

Fuxingmennei Avenue, Xicheng
F305, Yuanyang Mansion, No.158
Shenzhen, China 100031
Phone: 86400-650-6857
Website: www.pinqingcapital.com

Type of Firm
Investment Management Firm

Project Preferences

Type of Financing Preferred:
Balanced

Geographical Preferences

International Preferences:
China

Additional Information
Year Founded: 2015
Current Activity Level : Actively seeking new investments

SHENZHEN PUHE ASSETS MANAGEMENT CO LTD

Qianhai Rd, Nanshan Dist
3103, Zhenye Intl Busi Center
Shenzhen, China
Phone: 8675523999376
Fax: 8675523999511
Website: www.puhecapital.com

Type of Firm
Private Equity Firm

Project Preferences

Type of Financing Preferred:
Generalist PE

Geographical Preferences

International Preferences:
China

Additional Information

Year Founded: 2016
Capital Under Management: $77,020,000
Current Activity Level : Actively seeking new investments

SHENZHEN QF CAPITAL MANAGEMENT CO LTD

No.9, High-tech South Branch
F26, Zhongke Building
Shenzhen, China
Phone: 8675586700021
E-mail: public@qfcapital.com.cn
Website: www.qfvc.cn

Other Offices

Lanyue Road 80
Technical Innovation Base
Guangzhou, China

Management and Staff

Changzhen Wang, Partner
Kai Gu, Partner
Xin Peng, Partner
Yuanyuan Chen, Partner
Yunxia Long, Partner
Zheng Zeng, Partner

Type of Firm

Private Equity Firm

Project Preferences

Type of Financing Preferred:
Early Stage
Expansion
Balanced
Seed
Startup

Geographical Preferences

International Preferences:
China

Industry Preferences

In Communications prefer:
Telecommunications

In Industrial/Energy prefer:
Materials

In Business Serv. prefer:
Services
Media

Additional Information

Year Founded: 2013
Capital Under Management: $49,556,000
Current Activity Level : Actively seeking new investments

SHENZHEN QIANHAI ANXING ASSETS MANAGEMENT CO LTD

No.5016 Shennan East Road
Jingji 100 Building
Shenzhen, China

Type of Firm

Private Equity Firm

Project Preferences

Type of Financing Preferred:
Mezzanine
Generalist PE
Balanced

Geographical Preferences

International Preferences:
China

Industry Preferences

In Communications prefer:
Telecommunications
Media and Entertainment

In Medical/Health prefer:
Medical/Health

In Industrial/Energy prefer:
Energy Conservation Relat

In Transportation prefer:
Transportation

In Financial Services prefer:
Real Estate

Additional Information

Year Founded: 2013
Current Activity Level : Actively seeking new investments

SHENZHEN QIANHAI BAINUO INTERNATIONAL BUYOUT INVEST MGMT LTD

No.1, Qianwanyilu
Room 201, Block A
Shenzhen, China

Type of Firm

Private Equity Firm

Project Preferences

Type of Financing Preferred:
Leveraged Buyout

Geographical Preferences

International Preferences:
China

Additional Information

Year Founded: 2015
Current Activity Level : Actively seeking new investments

SHENZHEN QIANHAI CREATION VENTURE PARTNERS MANAGEMENT

No.15, Keyuan Road
Kexing Science Park
Shenzhen, China
Phone: 8675586653799
Website: www.creationventure.com

Type of Firm

Private Equity Firm

Project Preferences

Type of Financing Preferred:
Early Stage
Start-up Financing
Seed

Geographical Preferences

International Preferences:
China

Industry Preferences

In Communications prefer:
Entertainment

Additional Information

Year Founded: 2014
Current Activity Level : Actively seeking new investments

SHENZHEN QIANHAI DAYI INVESTMENT FUND MANAGEMENT CO LTD

60 Xizhimen North Street
Haidian District
Beijing, China
Phone: 861082290166
Fax: 861082290166
Website: www.dayitouzi.com

Type of Firm

Private Equity Firm

Project Preferences

Type of Financing Preferred:
Early Stage
Expansion
Start-up Financing
Seed

Geographical Preferences

International Preferences:
China

Industry Preferences

In Industrial/Energy prefer:
Energy

Additional Information

Year Founded: 2013
Current Activity Level : Actively seeking new investments

SHENZHEN QIANHAI GUOTAI FUND MANAGEMENT CO LTD

Room 201, Building A, No. 1
Qianwan First Road
Shenzhen, China 518000

Type of Firm

Private Equity Firm

Project Preferences

Type of Financing Preferred:
Balanced

Geographical Preferences

International Preferences:
China

Additional Information

Year Founded: 2015
Current Activity Level : Actively seeking new investments

SHENZHEN QIANHAI HARSUN CAPITAL MANAGEMENT CO LTD

Taoyuan Road, Nanshan District
Room 08-10, 35F, Tower A
Shenzhen, China
Phone: 86-755-86716958
Fax: 86-755-86716959
Website: www.harsun.cn

Type of Firm

Private Equity Firm

Project Preferences

Type of Financing Preferred:
Generalist PE

Geographical Preferences

International Preferences:
China

Industry Preferences

In Medical/Health prefer:
Medical/Health

In Industrial/Energy prefer:
Coal Related

In Manufact. prefer:
Manufacturing

In Agr/Forestr/Fish prefer:
Agriculture related

In Other prefer:
Environment Responsible

Additional Information

Year Founded: 2014
Current Activity Level : Actively seeking new investments

SHENZHEN QIANHAI HENGXING ASSET MANAGEMENT CO LTD

No. 1, Qianwan 1st Road, Qianh
(Settled at Shenzhen Qianhai B
Shenzhen, China 518000

Type of Firm

Private Equity Firm

Project Preferences

Type of Financing Preferred:
Balanced

Geographical Preferences

International Preferences:
China

Additional Information

Year Founded: 2014
Current Activity Level : Actively seeking new investments

SHENZHEN QIANHAI HUINENG FINANCIAL HOLDINGS GROUP CO LTD

Fuhua 3th Road, Futian Dist.
F17, Huanggang Business Center
Shenzhen, China
Fax: 8675583700820
Website: www.qhhn-fund.com

Type of Firm

Investment Management Firm

Project Preferences

Type of Financing Preferred:
Balanced

Geographical Preferences

International Preferences:
China

Additional Information

Year Founded: 2013
Current Activity Level : Actively seeking new investments

SHENZHEN QIANHAI HUIZHONG DONGLU INVST MGMT PARTNERSHIP LP

Fuhua Road, Futian District
Room 1803-1805, Tower B
Shenzhen, China 518000

Type of Firm

Private Equity Firm

Project Preferences

Type of Financing Preferred:
Balanced

Geographical Preferences

International Preferences:
China

Additional Information

Year Founded: 2015
Current Activity Level : Actively seeking new investments

SHENZHEN QIANHAI HUXING ASSET MANAGEMENT CO LTD

Qianhai Shenzhen-Hong Kong Coo
Room 201, Block A, No. 1 Qianw
Shenzhen, China
Phone: 8675583360578

Type of Firm

Investment Management Firm

Project Preferences

Type of Financing Preferred:
Balanced

Geographical Preferences

International Preferences:
China

Additional Information

Year Founded: 2015
Current Activity Level : Actively seeking new investments

SHENZHEN QIANHAI JOINT WIN INVESTMENT MANAGEMENT CO LTD

Qianwan Road, Qianhai Port
Room 201, A Building
Shenzhen, China

Type of Firm
Investment Management Firm

Project Preferences

Type of Financing Preferred:
Balanced

Geographical Preferences

International Preferences:
China

Additional Information

Year Founded: 2015
Current Activity Level : Actively seeking new investments

SHENZHEN QIANHAI MASS EAGLE VENTURE CAPITAL INVESTMENT LTD

Room 201, Tower A
Qianhai Shengang Cooperative
Shenzhen, China

Type of Firm
Private Equity Firm

Project Preferences

Type of Financing Preferred:
Balanced

Geographical Preferences

International Preferences:
China

Industry Preferences

In Internet Specific prefer:
Ecommerce

Additional Information

Year Founded: 2014
Current Activity Level : Actively seeking new investments

SHENZHEN QIANHAI MIDDAY CAPITAL MANAGEMENT CO LTD

Ganli 2nd Rd, Longgang Dis
10F, Block B, Jinpingguo
Shenzhen, China 518112
Phone: 8675589325888
Website: www.middaycapital.com

Type of Firm
Investment Management Firm

Project Preferences

Type of Financing Preferred:
Balanced

Geographical Preferences

International Preferences:
China

Additional Information

Year Founded: 2015
Current Activity Level : Actively seeking new investments

SHENZHEN QIANHAI QIANYUANKUNYI EQUITY INVST FUND MGMT CO LTD

Zhongshihua Building
191 Tiyu West Road
Shenzhen, China

Type of Firm
Private Equity Firm

Project Preferences

Type of Financing Preferred:
Balanced

Geographical Preferences

International Preferences:
China

Additional Information

Year Founded: 2014
Current Activity Level : Actively seeking new investments

SHENZHEN QIANHAI QINZHI INTERNATIONAL CAPITAL MNGMT CO LTD

Shennan Avenue 2012
Shenzhen Stock Exchange Square
Shenzhen, China
Website: www.triwise.cn

Type of Firm
Private Equity Firm

Project Preferences

Type of Financing Preferred:
Generalist PE

Geographical Preferences

International Preferences:
China

Additional Information

Year Founded: 2015
Current Activity Level : Actively seeking new investments

SHENZHEN QIANHAI SEQUOIA GUANGJING INVESTMENT MANAGEMENT

Qianwan 1st Road
Room 201, Tower A, No.1
Shenzhen, China

Type of Firm
Investment Management Firm

Project Preferences

Type of Financing Preferred:
Leveraged Buyout

Geographical Preferences

International Preferences:
China

Additional Information

Year Founded: 2014
Current Activity Level : Actively seeking new investments

SHENZHEN QIANHAI SHOURUN INVESTMENT MANAGEMENT CO LTD

No.2012, Shennan Road
Shenzhen Stock Exchange Square
Shenzhen, China
Phone: 8675588662908
Website: szqhsr.com

Type of Firm
Private Equity Firm

Project Preferences

Type of Financing Preferred:
Leveraged Buyout

Geographical Preferences

International Preferences:
China

Additional Information

Year Founded: 2015
Current Activity Level : Actively seeking new investments

SHENZHEN QIANHAI XING-WANG INVESTMENT MANAGEMENT CO LTD

Keyuan Road 1001
Room 1603
Shenzhen, China
Phone: 862168581980
Fax: 862150498882
Website: www.xwinvest.com.cn

Type of Firm
Private Equity Firm

Project Preferences

Type of Financing Preferred:
Balanced

Geographical Preferences

International Preferences:
China

Industry Preferences

In Communications prefer:
Telecommunications
Media and Entertainment

In Medical/Health prefer:
Medical/Health

In Consumer Related prefer:
Consumer
Education Related

Additional Information

Year Founded: 2015
Capital Under Management: $3,000,000,000
Current Activity Level : Actively seeking new investments

SHENZHEN QIANHAI YUN-TAI EQUITY INVT FUND MGMT CO., LTD.

Room 201, building A, No. 1
, Qianwan First Road
Shenzhen, China
Phone: 861084783288
Fax: 861084783133
Website: www.yuntaifund.com

Type of Firm
Private Equity Firm

Project Preferences

Type of Financing Preferred:
Generalist PE

Geographical Preferences

International Preferences:
China

Industry Preferences

In Internet Specific prefer:
Internet

In Medical/Health prefer:
Medical/Health

In Consumer Related prefer:
Consumer Products

In Industrial/Energy prefer:
Energy

Additional Information

Year Founded: 2015
Current Activity Level : Actively seeking new investments

SHENZHEN QIUSHI ASSET MANAGEMENT CO LTD

No.1, Qianwan Road
R201, Builing A
Shenzhen, China

Type of Firm
Investment Management Firm

Project Preferences

Type of Financing Preferred:
Leveraged Buyout

Geographical Preferences

International Preferences:
China

Additional Information

Year Founded: 2014
Capital Under Management: $24,778,000
Current Activity Level : Actively seeking new investments

SHENZHEN READYSUN INVESTMENT GROUP CO LTD

No.4018 Jintian Road, Futian
2103 Room, Anlian Building A
Shenzhen, China
Phone: 8675533368600
Fax: 8575533368601
Website: www.readysun.net

Type of Firm
Investment Management Firm

Project Preferences

Type of Financing Preferred:
Generalist PE

Geographical Preferences

International Preferences:
China

Industry Preferences

In Medical/Health prefer:
Medical/Health

In Industrial/Energy prefer:
Robotics

Additional Information

Year Founded: 2007
Capital Under Management: $449,200,000
Current Activity Level : Actively seeking new investments

SHENZHEN RICHLAND INVESTMENT CO LTD

Enping Street, OCT, Nanshan
2nd Building
Shenzhen, China 518053
Phone: 8675588311638
Fax: 8675588312178
Website: www.rlequities.com

Other Offices

No. 766 Wuyi Avenue
21033-21034 Zhongtian Plaza
Changsha, China 410005
Phone: 8673189793256
Fax: 8673189793207

No. 345 Xianxia Road, Changning Dist
11D-1
Shanghai, China 200336
Phone: 862162337132
Fax: 862162341673

A19 East 3 rd Ring North Road
Room 3311, Jiasheng Center
Beijing, China 100027
Phone: 861059670702
Fax: 861059670702616

No. 62 Xingguang Ave.
1-1 2F, C Neptune Tech. Bldg
Chongqing, China 401121
Phone: 862367030567
Fax: 862367030600

No. 41 Gannuo Middle Avenue, Central
Rm 33 15 F, Yingzhi Bldg
Hong Kong, Hong Kong
Phone: 85237579783
Fax: 85237579401

Management and Staff

Baojie Liu, Partner
Bo Liu, Partner
Dong Liang, Partner
Hongwei Tang, Partner
Jiawu Hu, Partner
Lin Jiang, Partner
Qunyi Jiang, Partner
Tong Liang, Partner

Type of Firm

Private Equity Firm

Project Preferences

Type of Financing Preferred:
Leveraged Buyout
Early Stage
Expansion
Balanced
Later Stage

Geographical Preferences

International Preferences:
China

Industry Preferences

In Communications prefer:
Media and Entertainment

In Computer Hardware prefer:
Integrated Turnkey System
Terminals

In Computer Software prefer:
Software

In Biotechnology prefer:
Biotechnology

In Medical/Health prefer:
Medical/Health
Pharmaceuticals

In Consumer Related prefer:
Consumer

In Industrial/Energy prefer:
Energy
Alternative Energy
Energy Conservation Relat
Advanced Materials
Machinery
Environmental Related

In Transportation prefer:
Transportation

In Business Serv. prefer:
Services

In Manufact. prefer:
Manufacturing

In Agr/Forestr/Fish prefer:
Agriculture related

In Other prefer:
Environment Responsible

Additional Information

Year Founded: 1999
Capital Under Management: $78,562,000
Current Activity Level : Actively seeking new investments

SHENZHEN RONGCHUANG VENTURE CAPITAL CO LTD

No. 4013, Shennan Ave., Futian
Rm. 708, Xingye Bank Bldg.
Shenzhen, China
Phone: 8675582934214
Fax: 8675582934234
E-mail: mail.szrci.com
Website: www.szrci.com

Management and Staff

Enpei Wang, Partner
Junfeng Zhao, Founder
Lidong Li, Partner
Xiaoping Dai, Partner
Xuefei Lin, Vice President
Yanfeng Zhu, Partner

Type of Firm

Private Equity Firm

Project Preferences

Type of Financing Preferred:
Early Stage
Expansion
Later Stage

Geographical Preferences

International Preferences:
China

Industry Preferences

In Communications prefer:
Telecommunications

In Biotechnology prefer:
Biotechnology

In Medical/Health prefer:
Medical/Health

In Consumer Related prefer:
Consumer

In Industrial/Energy prefer:
Materials

In Business Serv. prefer:
Media

In Manufact. prefer:
Manufacturing

In Agr/Forestr/Fish prefer:
Agriculture related

Additional Information

Year Founded: 2004
Capital Under Management: $79,100,000
Current Activity Level : Actively seeking new investments

SHENZHEN RUIYING ZHUOYUE CAPITAL MANAGEMENT PARTNERSHIP (LP)

No.6023 Shennan Road, Fudian
902-903,Yaohuachuangjian Plaza
Shenzhen, China
Phone: 8675583186955
Fax: 8675523600883
Website: www.bestpe.cn

Management and Staff

Caiqin Yang, Founder
Hui Sun, Co-Founder

Type of Firm

Private Equity Firm

Project Preferences

Type of Financing Preferred:
Balanced

Geographical Preferences

International Preferences:
China

Additional Information

Year Founded: 2011
Current Activity Level : Actively seeking new investments

SHENZHEN SANGEL VENTURE CAPITAL CO LTD

Nanshan District
2401/2402, Venture Capital Bui
Shenzhen, China
Phone: 8675526069007
Fax: 8675526069007
Website: www.sangelvc.com

Type of Firm

Private Equity Firm

Project Preferences

Type of Financing Preferred:
Balanced

Geographical Preferences

International Preferences:
China

Industry Preferences

In Medical/Health prefer:
Medical/Health

Additional Information

Year Founded: 2012
Current Activity Level : Actively seeking new investments

SHENZHEN SCINFO VENTURE CAPITAL MANAGEMENT CO LTD

807, Excellence Times Square
Yitian Rd.,Futian CBD.
Shenzhen, China 518048
Phone: 86-755-83066610
Fax: 86-755-23996480
E-mail: info@sivc.com.cn
Website: www.sivc.com.cn

Type of Firm
Private Equity Firm

Association Membership
Shenzhen Venture Capital Association

Project Preferences

Type of Financing Preferred:
Early Stage
Balanced

Geographical Preferences

International Preferences:
China

Additional Information

Year Founded: 1994
Current Activity Level : Actively seeking new investments

SHENZHEN SHENGTAI INVESTMENT MANAGEMENT CO LTD

Shennan Road
Block B
Shenzhen, China 6009
Phone: 8675583363199
Fax: 8675583363299
Website: www.shengtaitouzi.com

Type of Firm
Investment Management Firm

Project Preferences

Type of Financing Preferred:
Leveraged Buyout
Expansion
Mezzanine
Turnaround
Later Stage
Management Buyouts

Geographical Preferences

International Preferences:
China

Industry Preferences

In Communications prefer:
Telecommunications

In Internet Specific prefer:
Internet

In Biotechnology prefer:
Biotechnology

In Medical/Health prefer:
Health Services
Pharmaceuticals

In Consumer Related prefer:
Consumer Products

In Industrial/Energy prefer:
Energy
Advanced Materials

In Transportation prefer:
Aerospace

In Agr/Forestr/Fish prefer:
Agriculture related
Mining and Minerals

In Other prefer:
Environment Responsible

Additional Information

Year Founded: 2010
Capital Under Management: $2,800,000
Current Activity Level : Actively seeking new investments

SHENZHEN SILVER STAR INVESTMENT GROUP CO LTD

No. 1301, Guanguang Road
Yinxing Building, Guanlan Town
Shenzhen, China
Website: www.szyxjt.com

Type of Firm
Incubator/Development Program

Project Preferences

Type of Financing Preferred:
Seed
Startup

Geographical Preferences

International Preferences:
China

Additional Information

Year Founded: 2012
Current Activity Level : Actively seeking new investments

SHENZHEN SINO PACIFIC CAPITAL MANAGEMENT CO LTD

No.138 Fuhua 1st Road
28F, Tower A
Shenzhen, China
Phone: 8675583681186
Website: www.zhonghaicapital.com

Type of Firm
Private Equity Firm

Project Preferences

Type of Financing Preferred:
Balanced

Geographical Preferences

International Preferences:
China

Industry Preferences

In Communications prefer:
Telecommunications
Media and Entertainment

In Medical/Health prefer:
Medical/Health

In Manufact. prefer:
Manufacturing

Additional Information

Year Founded: 2015
Current Activity Level : Actively seeking new investments

SHENZHEN SUVC GUIGUXING FUND MANAGEMENT ENTERPRISE LP

No.1003 Keyuan Road
NanshanDistrict
Shenzhen, China
Website: www.sinousvc.com

Pratt's Guide to Private Equity & Venture Capital Sources

Type of Firm
Private Equity Firm

Project Preferences

Type of Financing Preferred:
Early Stage
Expansion
Seed
Startup

Size of Investments Considered:
Min Size of Investment Considered (000s): $304
Max Size of Investment Considered (000s): $3,042

Geographical Preferences

United States Preferences:
All U.S.

International Preferences:
China

Industry Preferences

In Communications prefer:
Telecommunications
Media and Entertainment

In Internet Specific prefer:
Internet
Ecommerce

Additional Information
Year Founded: 2014
Capital Under Management: $76,100,000
Current Activity Level : Actively seeking new investments

SHENZHEN TEAM-TOP INVESTMENT MANAGEMENT CO LTD

Fuzhong 3rd Road
Lunuode Finance Center
Shenzhen, Guangdong, China
Fax: 8675588263350
Website: www.team-top.com.cn

Management and Staff
Tao Huang, Chief Executive Officer
Xiaoshuang Wei, Vice President

Type of Firm
Private Equity Firm

Project Preferences

Type of Financing Preferred:
Balanced

Geographical Preferences

International Preferences:
China

Industry Preferences

In Medical/Health prefer:
Medical/Health
Pharmaceuticals

In Consumer Related prefer:
Consumer Products

Additional Information
Year Founded: 2004
Current Activity Level : Actively seeking new investments

SHENZHEN TEMPUS WU-TONG INVESTMENT CO LTD

No.9, Taohua Road, Futian
Section C, 6F
Shenzhen, China

Type of Firm
Private Equity Firm

Project Preferences

Type of Financing Preferred:
Leveraged Buyout

Geographical Preferences

International Preferences:
China

Industry Preferences

In Communications prefer:
Entertainment

In Computer Software prefer:
Data Processing

In Financial Services prefer:
Financial Services
Financial Services

Additional Information
Year Founded: 2014
Current Activity Level : Actively seeking new investments

SHENZHEN TIANTU CAPITAL MANAGEMENT CENTER LP

No.4068, Qiaoxiang Road
Tower 1, Bldg. B, Zhihui Plaza
Shenzhen, China 518053
Phone: 8675536909866
Fax: 8675536909834
Website: www.tiantu.com.cn

Other Offices
3 South Street
Room 1501, Haidian Capital Center
Beijing, China 100081
Phone: 86-10-6894-2112

Management and Staff
Haiyan Zhang, Partner
Xiangdong Chen, Partner
Xiaoyi Li, Partner
Zhimin Tang, Partner

Type of Firm
Private Equity Firm

Association Membership
Shenzhen Venture Capital Association

Project Preferences

Type of Financing Preferred:
Balanced

Geographical Preferences

International Preferences:
China

Industry Preferences

In Communications prefer:
Telecommunications

In Medical/Health prefer:
Medical/Health

In Consumer Related prefer:
Consumer

In Industrial/Energy prefer:
Environmental Related

In Transportation prefer:
Transportation

In Business Serv. prefer:
Media

Additional Information
Year Founded: 2002
Capital Under Management: $770,886,000
Current Activity Level : Actively seeking new investments

SHENZHEN TIMESBOLE VENTURE CAPITAL INVESTMENT MGMT. CO., LTD

No.6002 Shennan Avenue, Futian
F17,Renmin Building
Shenzhen, China
Phone: 8675583065000
Fax: 8675583067481
Website: www.timesbole.cn

Other Offices
Linggongtang Road
Comprehensive building
Jiaxing, China

Type of Firm
Private Equity Firm

Project Preferences

Type of Financing Preferred:
Balanced

Geographical Preferences

International Preferences:
China

Industry Preferences

In Communications prefer:
Telecommunications

In Medical/Health prefer:
Medical/Health

In Consumer Related prefer:
Consumer Services

In Industrial/Energy prefer:
Materials
Environmental Related

In Business Serv. prefer:
Media

Additional Information

Year Founded: 2011
Capital Under Management: $33,038,000
Current Activity Level : Actively seeking new investments

SHENZHEN WANHAI INVESTMENT MANAGEMENT CO LTD

Qianhai Shenzhen-Hong kong Coo
Room 201, Block A, No. 1 Qianw
Shenzhen, China

Type of Firm

Private Equity Firm

Project Preferences

Type of Financing Preferred:
Early Stage
Seed
Startup

Geographical Preferences

International Preferences:
China

Industry Preferences

In Internet Specific prefer:
Internet

In Medical/Health prefer:
Health Services

In Consumer Related prefer:
Consumer

Additional Information

Year Founded: 2014
Current Activity Level : Actively seeking new investments

SHENZHEN WARANTY ASSET MANAGEMENT CO LTD

11 Shangbao E. Rd., Futian
29/F,Yinglong Commercial Bldg.
Shenzhen, China 518034
Phone: 8675582798608
Fax: 8675582072923
Website: www.waranty.com.cn

Type of Firm

Investment Management Firm

Project Preferences

Type of Financing Preferred:
Leveraged Buyout
Balanced

Geographical Preferences

International Preferences:
China

Industry Preferences

In Biotechnology prefer:
Biotechnology

In Medical/Health prefer:
Pharmaceuticals

In Other prefer:
Environment Responsible

Additional Information

Year Founded: 2009
Current Activity Level : Actively seeking new investments

SHENZHEN WEIGUANG QIMING INVESTMENT MANAGEMENT CO LTD

Hong Li Xi Road
16B, Building A
Shenzhen, China
Phone: 8675582963771
Website: welightcapital.com

Type of Firm

Private Equity Firm

Project Preferences

Type of Financing Preferred:
Early Stage
Expansion

Geographical Preferences

International Preferences:
China

Industry Preferences

In Internet Specific prefer:
Internet
Ecommerce

In Financial Services prefer:
Financial Services

Additional Information

Year Founded: 2015
Current Activity Level : Actively seeking new investments

SHENZHEN WEILIDA FUND MANAGEMENT CO LTD

6003-4,Yitian Rd.,Futian Dist.
Floor 21, Tower B
Shenzhen, China
Website: www.we-leader.com

Type of Firm

Private Equity Firm

Project Preferences

Type of Financing Preferred:
Leveraged Buyout

Additional Information

Year Founded: 2015
Capital Under Management: $72,657,000
Current Activity Level : Actively seeking new investments

SHENZHEN WEIXI INVESTMENT PARTNERSHIP CO LTD

Yiongmei Park, Meihua Hill
No.2 Villia
Shenzhen, China
Phone: 8675585203344
E-mail: 9999999@qq.com
Website: www.weixivc.com

Management and Staff

Dansong Tang, Managing Partner
Gaopan Wu, Managing Partner
Gaoyuan Wu, Founder
Ke Zhou, Managing Partner
Tianyi Huang, Managing Partner
Xin Zhou, Managing Partner
Zhibo Zhou, Managing Partner

Type of Firm

Private Equity Firm

Project Preferences

Type of Financing Preferred:
Early Stage
Seed
Startup

Geographical Preferences

International Preferences:
China

Industry Preferences

In Internet Specific prefer:
Internet

Additional Information
Year Founded: 2014
Current Activity Level : Actively seeking new investments

SHENZHEN WINKING VENTURE CAPITAL MANAGEMENT CO LTD

Rm 1511, Unit A, United Plz
5022 Binghe Rd,Futian
Shenzhen, China
Phone: 86-755-2901
Fax: 86-755-2901
Website: www.winking.com.cn

Type of Firm
Private Equity Firm

Project Preferences

Type of Financing Preferred:
Balanced

Geographical Preferences

International Preferences:
China

Additional Information
Year Founded: 1997
Current Activity Level : Actively seeking new investments

SHENZHEN XINHENG LIDA CAPITAL MANAGEMENT CO LTD

3rd Fuzhong Road
27B, Noble Financial Center
Shenzhen, China
Phone: 8675583718558
Fax: 8675583717558
E-mail: xhld@cnxhld.com
Website: www.cnxhld.com

Type of Firm
Private Equity Firm

Project Preferences

Type of Financing Preferred:
Expansion
Later Stage

Geographical Preferences

International Preferences:
China

Industry Preferences

In Internet Specific prefer:
Internet

In Medical/Health prefer:
Medical/Health

In Industrial/Energy prefer:
Energy
Alternative Energy
Materials

Additional Information
Year Founded: 2013
Current Activity Level : Actively seeking new investments

SHENZHEN YUANZHENG INVESTMENT DEVELOPMENT CO LTD

Room 1518, 15F, Songpingshan
Hi-tech Zone, Nanshan
Shenzhen, China
Phone: 8675586530186
Fax: 518057
E-mail: thyx@thyx.com

Type of Firm
Private Equity Firm

Project Preferences

Type of Financing Preferred:
Early Stage
Seed
Startup

Geographical Preferences

International Preferences:
China

Industry Preferences

In Communications prefer:
Entertainment

In Computer Software prefer:
Software

In Internet Specific prefer:
Internet

In Biotechnology prefer:
Biotechnology

In Medical/Health prefer:
Medical/Health
Drug/Equipmt Delivery

In Consumer Related prefer:
Education Related

In Industrial/Energy prefer:
Energy
Energy Conservation Relat

Additional Information
Year Founded: 1994
Current Activity Level : Actively seeking new investments

SHENZHEN YUANZHI INVESTMENT CO LTD

No. 4009 Shennan Ave., Futian
Section B-C, 14F, Investment B
Shenzhen, China 518000
Phone: 8675583883660
Website: www.szcapital.com.cn

Type of Firm
Government Affiliated Program

Project Preferences

Type of Financing Preferred:
Generalist PE

Geographical Preferences

International Preferences:
China

Additional Information
Year Founded: 2007
Current Activity Level : Actively seeking new investments

SHENZHEN YUESHANGZHIFU ASSET MANAGEMENT CO LTD

Tairan 8th Road, Chegongmiao
18F, West Tower, Shengtang
Shenzhen, China 510623
Phone: 8675582783012
Fax: 8675523614547
Website: www.yueshangzhifu.com

Type of Firm
Private Equity Firm

Project Preferences

Type of Financing Preferred:
Generalist PE

Geographical Preferences

International Preferences:
China

SHENZHEN YUNCHUANG CAPITAL INVESTMENT MANAGEMENT CO LTD

Intersection of Keyuan Rd. and
Room 1606, Satellite Building
Shenzhen, China 518000
Website: www.corerain.com/zh

Type of Firm
Investment Management Firm

Project Preferences

Type of Financing Preferred:
Balanced

Geographical Preferences

International Preferences:
Asia

Industry Preferences

In Communications prefer:
Telecommunications

In Internet Specific prefer:
Internet

In Business Serv. prefer:
Media

Additional Information
Year Founded: 2015
Current Activity Level : Actively seeking new investments

SHENZHEN ZHENGXUAN INVESTMENT LTD

Yitian Road 6001
Taiping financial Building
Shenzhen, China
Website: http://www.zxholdings.com/

Type of Firm
Investment Management Firm

Project Preferences

Type of Financing Preferred:
Balanced

Geographical Preferences

International Preferences:
China

Industry Preferences

In Internet Specific prefer:
Internet

In Financial Services prefer:
Real Estate

Additional Information
Year Founded: 2003
Current Activity Level : Actively seeking new investments

SHENZHEN ZHONGJIAXING INVESTMENT CO LTD

No. 6, South Keji Rd, Nanshan
20F, Maikelong Building
Shenzhen, China
Phone: 8675586510811

Type of Firm
Private Equity Firm

Project Preferences

Type of Financing Preferred:
Balanced

Geographical Preferences

International Preferences:
China

Industry Preferences

In Internet Specific prefer:
Internet

In Medical/Health prefer:
Medical/Health

In Consumer Related prefer:
Consumer

In Industrial/Energy prefer:
Energy
Energy Conservation Relat
Environmental Related

In Business Serv. prefer:
Services
Media

In Agr/Forestr/Fish prefer:
Agriculture related

Additional Information
Year Founded: 2011
Capital Under Management: $78,622,000
Current Activity Level : Actively seeking new investments

SHENZHEN ZHONGJINFU VENTURE CAPITAL MANAGEMENT CO LTD

3rd Haide Avenue, Nanshan
1114, East Tower, Hai'an Bldg
Shenzhen, China 518059
Phone: 8675586271801
Fax: 8675586290055
Website: www.zjfvc.com

Type of Firm
Investment Management Firm

Association Membership
Shenzhen Venture Capital Association

Project Preferences

Type of Financing Preferred:
Expansion
Public Companies
Later Stage

Geographical Preferences

International Preferences:
China

Industry Preferences

In Internet Specific prefer:
Ecommerce

In Medical/Health prefer:
Medical Products
Pharmaceuticals

In Consumer Related prefer:
Consumer Products
Education Related

In Industrial/Energy prefer:
Energy
Energy Conservation Relat

In Agr/Forestr/Fish prefer:
Agriculture related

In Utilities prefer:
Utilities

Additional Information
Year Founded: 2009
Current Activity Level : Actively seeking new investments

SHENZHEN ZHONGSHI FUND MANAGEMENT CO LTD

No.88 Haide 1st Rd, Nanshan
C,33F,Zhongzhou Intl Financial
Shenzhen, China 518000
Phone: 8675586281188
Website: zsfunds.cn

Other Offices
No.88 Haide 1st Rd, Nanshan District
C,33F,Zhongzhou Intl Financial Center
, China 518000
Phone: 8675586281188

Type of Firm
Investment Management Firm

Project Preferences

Type of Financing Preferred:
Balanced

Geographical Preferences

International Preferences:
China

Industry Preferences

In Medical/Health prefer:
Medical/Health

In Industrial/Energy prefer:
Energy Conservation Relat

In Other prefer:
Environment Responsible

Additional Information
Year Founded: 2015
Current Activity Level : Actively seeking new investments

SHENZHEN ZHONGYI ASSETS MANAGEMENT CO LTD

Dongcheng District
51105, 11F, Yinhe SOHO
Beijing, China
Phone: 861053801210
Fax: 861059576595
Website: www.zycvc.com

Type of Firm
Private Equity Firm

Project Preferences

Type of Financing Preferred:
Ba.anced

Geographical Preferences

International Preferences:
China

Additional Information
Year Founded: 2013
Capital Under Management: $149,800,000
Current Activity Level : Actively seeking new investments

SHEPHERD VENTURES LP

11722 Sorrento Valley Rd., Suite G-2,
San Diego, CA USA 92130
Phone: 8585094744
Fax: 8585093662
E-mail: info@shepherdventures.com
Website: www.shepherdventures.com

Management and Staff
Frederick Lawrence, Venture Partner
George Kenney, Managing Director
George Kenney, Co-Founder
John Nelson, Venture Partner
Richard Kuntz, Managing Director
Tom Siegel, Co-Founder
Tom Siegel, Managing Director

Type of Firm
Private Equity Firm

Project Preferences

Role in Financing:
Will function either as deal originator or investor in deals created by others

Type of Financing Preferred:
Early Stage
Balanced
Later Stage
Seed
Startup

Size of Investments Considered:
Min Size of Investment Considered (000s): $500
Max Size of Investment Considered (000s): $3,000

Geographical Preferences

United States Preferences:
Southern California
Northern California
West Coast
Southwest

Industry Preferences

In Communications prefer:
Commercial Communications
Wireless Communications
Data Communications

In Computer Hardware prefer:
Computer Graphics and Dig

In Computer Software prefer:
Computer Services
Software
Applications Software

In Biotechnology prefer:
Biotechnology

In Medical/Health prefer:
Medical/Health
Medical Diagnostics
Medical Therapeutics
Medical Products

Additional Information
Year Founded: 2001
Capital Under Management: $80,500,000
Current Activity Level : Actively seeking new investments
Method of Compensation: Return on investment is of primary concern, do not charge fees

SHERBROOKE CAPITAL

2344 Washington Street
Newton Lower Falls, MA USA 02462
Phone: 6173327227
Fax: 6173323113
E-mail: info@sherbrookecapital.com

Management and Staff
Cory Comstock, General Partner
John Giannuzzi, Managing General Partner
John Bello, General Partner

Type of Firm
Private Equity Firm

Project Preferences

Role in Financing:
Will function either as deal originator or investor in deals created by others

Type of Financing Preferred:
Expansion
Balanced
Later Stage

Industry Preferences

In Internet Specific prefer:
Ecommerce

In Biotechnology prefer:
Agricultural/Animal Bio.

In Medical/Health prefer:
Medical/Health
Medical Diagnostics
Medical Products

In Consumer Related prefer:
Consumer
Food/Beverage
Consumer Products
Consumer Services
Education Related

In Business Serv. prefer:
Services

Additional Information
Name of Most Recent Fund: Sherbrooke Health And Wellness Fund II, L.P.
Most Recent Fund Was Raised: 02/26/2007
Year Founded: 1998
Capital Under Management: $183,000,000
Current Activity Level : Actively seeking new investments
Method of Compensation: Return on investment is of primary concern, do not charge fees

SHERIDAN CAPITAL PARTNERS

400 N. Michigan Avenue, Suite 900
Chicago, IL USA 60611
Website: www.sheridancp.com

Management and Staff
Jonathan Lewis, Founder
Michael Allietta, Partner
Timothy Danis, Partner

Type of Firm
Private Equity Firm

Project Preferences

Type of Financing Preferred:
Leveraged Buyout
Management Buyouts
Acquisition
Recapitalizations

Geographical Preferences

United States Preferences:

Canadian Preferences:
All Canada

Industry Preferences

In Medical/Health prefer:
Medical Products
Health Services

In Consumer Related prefer:
Consumer Products
Consumer Services

In Business Serv. prefer:
Services
Distribution

Additional Information
Year Founded: 2011
Current Activity Level : Actively seeking new investments

SHERPA CAPITAL

800 Market Street
Eighth Floor
San Francisco, CA USA 94102
Phone: 4158058486
E-mail: sherpaventures.com
Website: www.sherpa.com

Type of Firm
Private Equity Firm

Project Preferences

Type of Financing Preferred:
Startup

Additional Information
Year Founded: 2013
Capital Under Management: $624,000,000
Current Activity Level : Actively seeking new investments

SHERPA CAPITAL GESTION

Orense 25
Paseo Alameda 35 Bis
Madrid, Spain
Phone: 34-90-270-2526
E-mail: info@sherpacapital.es

Other Offices
Hermosilla Street, 11
Madrid, Spain

Alameda Street 35, bis.
Valencia, Spain

Type of Firm
Private Equity Firm

Association Membership
Spanish Venture Capital Association (ASCRI)

Project Preferences

Type of Financing Preferred:
Leveraged Buyout
Turnaround
Management Buyouts
Acquisition
Special Situation
Distressed Debt
Recapitalizations

Geographical Preferences

International Preferences:
United Kingdom
Europe

Additional Information
Year Founded: 2010
Capital Under Management: $179,018,000
Current Activity Level : Actively seeking new investments

SHERPA PARTNERS LLC

5775 Wayzata Boulevard, Suite 955
Saint Louis Park, MN USA 55416
E-mail: info@sherpapartners.com
Website: www.sherpapartners.com

Management and Staff
C. McKenzie Lewis, Founder
Richard Brimacomb, Partner
Steven Pederson, General Partner

Type of Firm
Private Equity Firm

Project Preferences

Role in Financing:
Will function either as deal originator or investor in deals created by others

Type of Financing Preferred:
Early Stage
Seed

Size of Investments Considered:
Min Size of Investment Considered (000s): $250
Max Size of Investment Considered (000s): $1,000

Geographical Preferences

United States Preferences:
Minnesota

Industry Preferences

In Communications prefer:
Telecommunications
Wireless Communications

In Computer Software prefer:
Software
Systems Software

Additional Information
Name of Most Recent Fund: Sherpa Trek Fund I
Most Recent Fund Was Raised: 01/14/2001
Year Founded: 1997
Capital Under Management: $13,000,000
Current Activity Level : Actively seeking new investments
Method of Compensation: Return on investment is of primary concern, do not charge fees

SHERPALO VENTURES

2725 Sand Hill Road, Suite 120
Menlo Park, CA USA 94025
Phone: 6503192220
Fax: 6503192221
E-mail: info@sherpalo.com
Website: www.sherpalo.com

Management and Staff
Ram Shiram, Founder
Sandeep Murthy, Partner

Type of Firm
Private Equity Firm

Project Preferences

Type of Financing Preferred:
Early Stage

Geographical Preferences

United States Preferences:
All U.S.

Industry Preferences

In Internet Specific prefer:
Internet

In Consumer Related prefer:
Consumer

In Business Serv. prefer:
Services

Additional Information
Year Founded: 2000
Current Activity Level : Actively seeking new investments

SHIHEZI HAOYU PE INVESTMENT MANAGEMENT CO LTD

No.37 Sidong Road, Dev Zone
Room 2-224
Shihezi, China

Type of Firm
Private Equity Firm

Project Preferences

Type of Financing Preferred:
Balanced

Geographical Preferences

International Preferences:
China

Additional Information
Year Founded: 2016
Capital Under Management: $308,070,000
Current Activity Level : Actively seeking new investments

SHIKATA VENTURE FUND

19F Hilton Plaza West Office
2-2-2 Umeda, Kita-ku
Osaka, Japan 530-0001

Management and Staff
Osamu Shikata, President

Type of Firm
Private Equity Firm

Additional Information
Year Founded: 2005
Current Activity Level : Reducing investment activity

SHIN POONG VENTURE CAPITAL

1/F Shinpoong Building, 733-23
Yeongsam-2-dong, Kangnam-gu
Seoul, South Korea
Phone: 822-563-3121
Fax: 822-563-3124

Management and Staff
Yong Taek Chang, President

Type of Firm
Private Equity Firm

Project Preferences

Type of Financing Preferred:
Balanced

Geographical Preferences

International Preferences:
Korea, South

Additional Information
Year Founded: 2000
Current Activity Level : Actively seeking new investments

SHINHAN PRIVATE EQUITY INC

Deakyung B/D, 120.2-Ga
Taepyung-ro, jung-Gu
Seoul, South Korea 100-102
Phone: 0263603000
Fax: 027771883
Website: www.shinhangroup.co.kr

Management and Staff
Jin Yong Lee, Chief Executive Officer

Type of Firm
Bank Affiliated

Project Preferences

Type of Financing Preferred:
Leveraged Buyout
Balanced

Geographical Preferences

International Preferences:
Korea, South

Industry Preferences

In Industrial/Energy prefer:
Energy

Additional Information
Year Founded: 2004
Current Activity Level : Actively seeking new investments

SHINHAN VENTURE CAPITAL CO LTD

6F Inhee Building,
52-1 Cheong, Gangnam-Gu
Seoul, South Korea 135-100
Phone: 8225461414
Fax: 8225461405

Management and Staff
Dongseung Yu, Chief Executive Officer

Type of Firm
Private Equity Firm

Project Preferences

Type of Financing Preferred:
Balanced

Geographical Preferences

International Preferences:
No Preference
Korea, South

Additional Information
Year Founded: 1998
Current Activity Level : Actively seeking new investments

SHINKIN CAPITAL CO LTD

Bldg No. 3, No. 6 Sun 6 land
Chuo-ku
Tokyo, Japan 980-0804
Phone: 0352994356
Website: www.shinkin-vc.co.jp

Type of Firm
Private Equity Firm

Association Membership
Japan Venture Capital Association

Project Preferences

Type of Financing Preferred:
Early Stage
Expansion
Balanced
Later Stage
Startup

Geographical Preferences

International Preferences:
Japan

Additional Information
Year Founded: 2001
Current Activity Level : Actively seeking new investments

SHINSEI BANK LTD

9-7, Otemachi 1-chome
16F Otemachi Financial City
Tokyo, Japan 100-0004
Phone: 81368609660
Website: www.shinseibank.com

Management and Staff
Masayuki Nankoin, Chief Financial Officer

Type of Firm
Bank Affiliated

Project Preferences

Type of Financing Preferred:
Leveraged Buyout
Mezzanine
Later Stage
Management Buyouts
Recapitalizations

Additional Information
Year Founded: 1952
Capital Under Management: $457,600,000
Current Activity Level : Actively seeking new investments

SHINWA VENTURE CAPITAL CO LTD

6F Shinwa Bank Bldg. Annex
10-12 Shimanose-cho
Nagasaki, Japan 857-0806
Phone: 81-956-24-6165
Fax: 81-956-24-6165
Website: www.fukuoka-fg.com

Management and Staff
Mitsukazu Iwasa, President

Type of Firm
Bank Affiliated

Additional Information
Year Founded: 1996
Current Activity Level : Actively seeking new investments

SHINWON VENTURE CAPITAL CO LTD

532 Tohwa-dong Mapo-ku
Seoul, South Korea
Phone: 822-3274-7474
Fax: 822-3274-7479

Management and Staff
Ki Han Song, President

Type of Firm
Private Equity Firm

Project Preferences

Type of Financing Preferred:
Balanced

Geographical Preferences

International Preferences:
Korea, South

Additional Information
Year Founded: 1990
Current Activity Level : Actively seeking new investments

SHIPROCK CAPITAL LLC

396 Washington Street, Suite 148
Wellesley, MA USA 02481
Phone: 7817721229
E-mail: info@shiprock.com
Website: www.shiprock.com

Management and Staff
Nicholas Harvey, Managing Director
Richard Shipley, Founder

Type of Firm
Private Equity Firm

Project Preferences

Type of Financing Preferred:
Early Stage
Expansion
Balanced

Industry Preferences

In Semiconductor/Electr prefer:
Electronics

Additional Information
Year Founded: 1957
Current Activity Level : Actively seeking new investments

SHIYU CAPITAL

Jinshifang Street, Xicheng
Room 505-506, No. 35
Beijing, China 100034
Phone: 86 10 83064550
Website: www.shiyucapital.com

Type of Firm
Private Equity Firm

Project Preferences

Type of Financing Preferred:
Balanced

Geographical Preferences

International Preferences:
China

Industry Preferences

In Medical/Health prefer:
Medical/Health

In Consumer Related prefer:
Consumer

Additional Information
Year Founded: 2014
Capital Under Management: $143,760,000
Current Activity Level : Actively seeking new investments

SHIZUOKA CAPITAL CO LTD

1-13-10 Kusanagi, Shimizu-ku
Shizuoka Bank Kusanagi Office
Shizuoka, Japan
Phone: 81543472210
Website: www.shizuokabank.co.jp

Type of Firm
Bank Affiliated

Association Membership
Japan Venture Capital Association

Project Preferences

Type of Financing Preferred:
Leveraged Buyout

Geographical Preferences

International Preferences:
Japan

Additional Information
Year Founded: 1984
Current Activity Level : Actively seeking new investments

SHK FUND MANAGEMENT LTD

33 Hysan Avenue
42/F, The Lee Gardens
Causeway Bay, Hong Kong
Phone: 85239202866
E-mail: funds@shkf.com
Website: www.shkfunds.com

Other Offices
9 Raffles Place
Level 18 Republic Plaza II
Singapore, Singapore 048619
Phone: 6565131918

Management and Staff
Christine Wong, Founder
Christophe Lee, Chief Executive Officer
Ken Wong, Managing Director
Rizal Wijono, Managing Director

Type of Firm
Investment Management Firm

Project Preferences

Type of Financing Preferred:
Balanced

Geographical Preferences

International Preferences:
Asia

Additional Information
Year Founded: 1989
Current Activity Level : Actively seeking new investments

SHORE CAPITAL PARTNERS LLC

70 East Lake Street, Suite 520
Chicago, IL USA 60601
Phone: 3123487580
Fax: 3123487669
E-mail: info@shorecp.com
Website: www.shorecp.com

Management and Staff
John Hennegan, Vice President
Justin Ishbia, Managing Partner
Michael Cooper, Vice President
Ryan Kelley, Partner

Type of Firm
Private Equity Firm

Association Membership
Illinois Venture Capital Association

Project Preferences

Type of Financing Preferred:
Leveraged Buyout
Management Buyouts
Acquisition
Recapitalizations

Geographical Preferences

United States Preferences:
North America

Industry Preferences

In Biotechnology prefer:
Human Biotechnology

In Medical/Health prefer:
Medical Diagnostics
Medical Therapeutics
Medical Products
Health Services
Pharmaceuticals

Additional Information
Year Founded: 2009
Capital Under Management: $30,000,000
Current Activity Level : Actively seeking new investments

SHORE POINTS CAPITAL MANAGEMENT LLC

1221 Avenue of the Americas
42nd Floor
New York, NY USA 10020
Website: www.shorepointscapital.com

Type of Firm
Private Equity Firm

Project Preferences

Type of Financing Preferred:
Leveraged Buyout
Acquisition

Geographical Preferences

United States Preferences:
North America

Industry Preferences

In Computer Software prefer:
Software

In Business Serv. prefer:
Services
Distribution

In Manufact. prefer:
Manufacturing

Additional Information
Year Founded: 2006
Current Activity Level : Actively seeking new investments

SHOREBANK CAPITAL CORP

7936 S. Cottage Grove
Chicago, IL USA 60619
Phone: 773-371-7060
Fax: 773-371-7035

Management and Staff
David Shryock, Chief Executive Officer

Type of Firm
SBIC

Project Preferences

Type of Financing Preferred:
Balanced

Geographical Preferences

International Preferences:
Vietnam
Bangladesh
Indonesia
Pakistan
India
China
Thailand
Philippines
Sri Lanka

Additional Information
Name of Most Recent Fund: ShoreCap II, Ltd.
Most Recent Fund Was Raised: 02/01/2010
Year Founded: 1978
Capital Under Management: $4,300,000
Current Activity Level : Actively seeking new investments

SHOREHILL CAPITAL LLC

Ten South Wacker Drive, Suite 3175
Chicago, IL USA 60606
Phone: 312876267
E-mail: info@shorehillcapital.com
Website: www.shorehillcapital.com

Management and Staff
Brian Simmons, Co-Founder
David Hawkins, Co-Founder
Doug Knoch, Managing Director
Michelle Eidson, Managing Director
Robert Hogan, Managing Director
Ronelle DeShazer, Vice President
Todd Schneider, Chief Financial Officer

Type of Firm
Private Equity Firm

Project Preferences

Type of Financing Preferred:
Leveraged Buyout

Geographical Preferences

United States Preferences:
North America

Industry Preferences

In Industrial/Energy prefer:
Industrial Products

In Business Serv. prefer:
Distribution

Additional Information
Year Founded: 1969
Capital Under Management: $128,450,000
Current Activity Level : Actively seeking new investments

SHORELINE VENTURE MANAGEMENT, LLC

850 Gateway Drive, Suite 600
San Mateo, CA USA 94404
Phone: 6508546685
Fax: 4153896757
E-mail: info@shorelineventures.com

Other Offices
675 Mariners Island Boulevard, Suite 109
San Mateo, CA USA 94404

Management and Staff
Barry Lynn, General Partner
Peter Craddock, Managing Director
Rich Miller, Venture Partner
Rich Freyberg, Venture Partner
Robert Spears, Co-Founder

Type of Firm
Private Equity Firm

Project Preferences

Type of Financing Preferred:
Early Stage
Seed

Size of Investments Considered:
Min Size of Investment Considered (000s): $3,000
Max Size of Investment Considered (000s): $5,000

Geographical Preferences

Canadian Preferences:
All Canada

International Preferences:
Europe

Industry Preferences

In Computer Software prefer:
Software

In Medical/Health prefer:
Medical/Health
Medical Diagnostics
Medical Therapeutics

Additional Information
Year Founded: 1998
Capital Under Management: $8,100,000
Current Activity Level : Actively seeking new investments

SHORENSTEIN CO LLC

235 Montgomery Street
16th Floor
San Francisco, CA USA 94104
Phone: 4157727000
Website: www.shorenstein.com

Other Offices
850 Third Avenue
17th Floor
New York, NY USA 10022
Phone: 212-986-2100

Management and Staff
Andrew Friedman, Managing Director
Anthony Calabrese, Vice President
Brandon Shorenstein, Managing Director
Caitlin Simon, Vice President
Glenn Shannon, President
Jed Brush, Vice President
John Boynton, Vice President
Mark Portner, Managing Director
Mark McCarthy, Managing Director
Matthew Knisely, Managing Director
Meg Spriggs, Managing Director
Russell Cooper, Managing Director
Thomas Holt, Vice President

Type of Firm
Private Equity Firm

Project Preferences

Type of Financing Preferred:
Opportunistic

Geographical Preferences

United States Preferences:
Illinois
Oregon
Massachusetts
Virginia
California
Florida
Washington
D. of Columbia
Georgia
New York
Texas

Industry Preferences

In Financial Services prefer:
Real Estate

Additional Information
Name of Most Recent Fund: Shorenstein Realty Investors Ten, L.P.
Most Recent Fund Was Raised: 10/14/2010
Year Founded: 1992
Capital Under Management: $494,900,000
Current Activity Level : Actively seeking new investments

SHOREVIEW INDUSTRIES

222 South Ninth Street, Suite 3130
Minneapolis, MN USA 55402
Phone: 6124364280
Fax: 6124360576
E-mail: info@shoreviewindustries.com
Website: www.shoreviewindustries.com

Management and Staff
Adam Reeves, Vice President
Brett Habstritt, Partner
Jeffrey Mudge, Managing Partner
Peter Zimmerman, Principal
Scott Gage, Partner
Thomas D Ovidio, Partner

Type of Firm
Private Equity Firm

Project Preferences

Type of Financing Preferred:
Leveraged Buyout
Management Buyouts
Acquisition
Recapitalizations

Geographical Preferences

United States Preferences:
North America

Industry Preferences

In Consumer Related prefer:
Consumer Products

In Industrial/Energy prefer:
Industrial Products

In Business Serv. prefer:
Services
Distribution

In Manufact. prefer:
Manufacturing

Additional Information
Year Founded: 1995
Capital Under Management: $600,000,000
Current Activity Level : Actively seeking new investments

SHOUTAI JINXIN EQUITY INVESTMENT FUND MANAGEMENT CO LTD

No2, 3rd East Ring Road East
F23, 27B03
Chaoyang, Beijing, China

Type of Firm
Investment Management Firm

Project Preferences

Type of Financing Preferred:
Generalist PE
Balanced

Geographical Preferences

International Preferences:
China

Industry Preferences

In Financial Services prefer:
Real Estate

In Business Serv. prefer:
Media

Additional Information

Year Founded: 2011
Capital Under Management: $78,395,000
Current Activity Level : Actively seeking new investments

SHS GESELLSCHAFT FUER BETEILIGUNGSMANAGE-MENT MBH

Bismarckstrasse 12
Tuebingen, Germany 72072
Phone: 49707191690
Fax: 4970719169190
E-mail: tuebingen@shsvc.net
Website: www.shs-capital.eu

Management and Staff

Andre Zimmerman, Partner
Bernhard Schirmers, Co-Founder
Hubertus Leonhardt, Partner
Rainer Miller, Partner
Reinhilde Spatscheck, Co-Founder
Uwe Steinbacher, Partner
Volker Pfahlert, Partner

Type of Firm

Private Equity Firm

Association Membership

German Venture Capital Association (BVK)
European Private Equity and Venture Capital Assoc.

Project Preferences

Role in Financing:
Prefer role as deal originator

Type of Financing Preferred:
Leveraged Buyout
Early Stage
Expansion
Generalist PE
Balanced
Seed
Acquisition
Startup

Size of Investments Considered:
Min Size of Investment Considered (000s): $5,000
Max Size of Investment Considered (000s): $15,000

Geographical Preferences

International Preferences:
Western Europe
Germany

Industry Preferences

In Medical/Health prefer:
Medical/Health
Pharmaceuticals

Additional Information

Name of Most Recent Fund: SHS IV Medtech Investments GmbH & Co KG
Most Recent Fund Was Raised: 12/31/2013
Year Founded: 1993
Capital Under Management: $229,100,000
Current Activity Level : Actively seeking new investments

SI TECHNOLOGY VENTURE CAPITAL

26/F, Harcourt House
39 Gloucester Road, Wanchai
Hong Kong, Hong Kong
Phone: 852-2529-5652
Fax: 852-2520-0128
Website: www.sihl.com.hk

Management and Staff

Yutian Cai, Chief Executive Officer

Type of Firm

Private Equity Firm

Project Preferences

Type of Financing Preferred:
Balanced

Geographical Preferences

International Preferences:
Asia

Additional Information

Year Founded: 2000
Current Activity Level : Actively seeking new investments

SI2 FUND CVBA

42, Rue Ducale
Brussels, Belgium 1000
Phone: 3222740750
Website: www.si2fund.com

Type of Firm

Private Equity Firm

Project Preferences

Type of Financing Preferred:
Early Stage
Later Stage

Geographical Preferences

International Preferences:
Belgium

Industry Preferences

In Medical/Health prefer:
Health Services

In Industrial/Energy prefer:
Environmental Related

In Business Serv. prefer:
Services

Additional Information

Year Founded: 2012
Current Activity Level : Actively seeking new investments

SIAS AMIDI US-CHINA STARTUPS INCUBATION CENTER

Xinzheng
No. 168, Renmin Road
Zhengzhou, China 451150
Phone: 8637162607676
Fax: 8637162607677
E-mail: info@siasincubator.com
Website: www.siasincubator.com

Type of Firm

Incubator/Development Program

Project Preferences

Type of Financing Preferred:
Early Stage
Startup

Geographical Preferences

International Preferences:
China

Industry Preferences

In Communications prefer:
Entertainment

In Biotechnology prefer:
Biotechnology

In Consumer Related prefer:
Education Related

In Business Serv. prefer:
Media

Additional Information

Year Founded: 2012
Current Activity Level : Actively seeking new investments

SIAULIU BANKAS AB

149 Tilzes Street
Siauliai, Lithuania 76348
Phone: 37041522117
Fax: 37041430774

E-mail: info@sb.lt
Website: www.sb.lt

Management and Staff
Daiva Soriene, Chief Executive Officer
Donatas Savickas, Chief Executive Officer
Vytautas Sinius, Chief Executive Officer

Type of Firm
Bank Affiliated

Project Preferences

Type of Financing Preferred:
Balanced

Geographical Preferences

International Preferences:
Eastern Europe
Lithuania

Industry Preferences

In Financial Services prefer:
Financial Services
Real Estate
Investment Groups

In Business Serv. prefer:
Consulting Services

Additional Information
Year Founded: 1992
Current Activity Level : Actively seeking new investments

SIB INNOVATIONS UND BETEILIGUNGS-GESELLSCHAFT MBH

Elsasser Strasse 6
Dresden, Germany 01307
Phone: 493518474280
Fax: 4935184742829
E-mail: info@sib-dresden.de
Website: www.sib-dresden.de

Management and Staff
Herr Kampwerth, Managing Director

Type of Firm
Bank Affiliated

Association Membership
German Venture Capital Association (BVK)

Project Preferences

Type of Financing Preferred:
Early Stage
Mezzanine
Balanced
Later Stage
Seed
Startup

Geographical Preferences

International Preferences:
Western Europe
Germany

Industry Preferences

In Biotechnology prefer:
Biotechnology

In Industrial/Energy prefer:
Machinery

Additional Information
Year Founded: 1999
Current Activity Level : Actively seeking new investments

SIBLING CAPITAL LLC

18313 Calle La Serra
Rancho Santa Fe, CA USA 92091
Website: www.siblingcapital.com

Other Offices
1441 Canal Street, Suite 422
New Orleans, LA USA 70112

Management and Staff
Brian Isern, Vice President
Sandra Coufal, President, Founder

Type of Firm
Private Equity Firm

Project Preferences

Type of Financing Preferred:
Later Stage

Additional Information
Year Founded: 2012
Current Activity Level : Actively seeking new investments

SICHUAN DINGXIANG EQUITY INVESTMENT FUND CO LTD

No. 1700 North Section of Tian E1-11F, Global Center
Sichuan, China
Phone: 862885343188
Fax: 862885343188
Website: www.dinxcapital.com

Type of Firm
Private Equity Firm

Project Preferences

Type of Financing Preferred:
Generalist PE

Geographical Preferences

International Preferences:
China

Industry Preferences

In Communications prefer:
Communications and Media

In Computer Software prefer:
Artificial Intelligence

In Medical/Health prefer:
Medical/Health

In Consumer Related prefer:
Consumer
Entertainment and Leisure

Additional Information
Year Founded: 2014
Capital Under Management: $800,000,000
Current Activity Level : Actively seeking new investments

SICHUAN SHUXIANG INVESTMENT CO LTD

488 Shuahan Road
2F, Strait Building
Chengdu, China 610036
Phone: 862887570330
Fax: 862887530542
E-mail: pe@shuxianginvestment.com
Website: www.shuxianginvestment.com

Type of Firm
Private Equity Firm

Industry Preferences

In Semiconductor/Electr prefer:
Electronics

In Biotechnology prefer:
Biotechnology
Agricultural/Animal Bio.

In Medical/Health prefer:
Medical/Health
Pharmaceuticals

In Consumer Related prefer:
Consumer Products
Education Related

In Industrial/Energy prefer:
Energy
Energy Conservation Relat
Materials
Advanced Materials
Machinery
Environmental Related

In Financial Services prefer:
Financial Services

In Business Serv. prefer:
Media

In Manufact. prefer:
Manufacturing

In Agr/Forestr/Fish prefer:
Agriculture related

In Utilities prefer:
Utilities

In Other prefer:
Environment Responsible

Additional Information
Year Founded: 2009
Capital Under Management: $391,019,000
Current Activity Level: Actively seeking new investments

SICHUAN YINZHENG JIA-HUA EQUITY INVEST FUND MGMT CO., LTD.

No.6 Xiaman St., Qingyang Dist
15F Tianfulvzhou
Chengdu, China 610041
Phone: 862885924900
Fax: 862885924900
Website: www.scyzfund.com

Type of Firm
Investment Management Firm

Project Preferences

Type of Financing Preferred:
Balanced

Geographical Preferences

International Preferences:
China

Additional Information
Year Founded: 2012
Current Activity Level: Actively seeking new investments

SICHUAN YUEHUA INVESTMENT MANAGEMENT CO LTD

No. 177, Jiaozi Avenue
Zhonghai International Center
Chengdu, China 610000

Type of Firm
Investment Management Firm

Project Preferences

Type of Financing Preferred:
Leveraged Buyout

Geographical Preferences

International Preferences:
China

Industry Preferences

In Communications prefer:
Telecommunications

In Medical/Health prefer:
Medical/Health

In Industrial/Energy prefer:
Energy
Energy Conservation Relat

In Financial Services prefer:
Financial Services

In Business Serv. prefer:
Media

Additional Information
Year Founded: 2015
Current Activity Level: Actively seeking new investments

SICHUAN YUNKUN INVESTMENT MANAGEMENT CO LTD

No.539 Jincheng Avenue
Room 1302, Floor 13
Chengdu, China
Website: www.yunzb.cn

Type of Firm
Private Equity Firm

Project Preferences

Type of Financing Preferred:
Balanced

Geographical Preferences

International Preferences:
China

Additional Information
Year Founded: 2015
Capital Under Management: $8,037,000
Current Activity Level: Actively seeking new investments

SID R BASS ASSOCIATES LP

201 Main Street, Suite 3200
Fort Worth, TX USA 76102
Phone: 8173908820
Fax: 8173908821

Type of Firm
Private Equity Firm

Project Preferences

Role in Financing:
Will function either as deal originator or investor in deals created by others

Type of Financing Preferred:
Early Stage
Balanced
Later Stage

Size of Investments Considered:
Min Size of Investment Considered (000s): $1,000
Max Size of Investment Considered (000s): $10,000

Geographical Preferences

United States Preferences:

Industry Preferences

In Communications prefer:
Communications and Media
Wireless Communications

In Computer Software prefer:
Software

In Consumer Related prefer:
Consumer

In Business Serv. prefer:
Services
Media

Additional Information
Year Founded: 2004
Capital Under Management: $300,000,000
Current Activity Level: Actively seeking new investments
Method of Compensation: Return on investment is of primary concern, do not charge fees

SIDBI VENTURE CAPITAL LTD

MSME Development Center, C-11
G Block, Bandra Kurla Complex
Mumbai, India 400 051
Phone: 912226527124
Fax: 912226527126
E-mail: info@sidbiventure.co.in
Website: www.sidbiventure.co.in

Management and Staff
Harsh Kaul, Chief Executive Officer
R.V. Dilip Kumar, Vice President
Sailendra Narain, Managing Director
Sajit Kumar, Vice President
Vipul Mankad, President

Type of Firm
Bank Affiliated

Association Membership
Indian Venture Capital Association (IVCA)

Pratt's Guide to Private Equity & Venture Capital Sources

Project Preferences

Type of Financing Preferred:
Early Stage
Expansion
Balanced
Startup

Size of Investments Considered:
Min Size of Investment Considered (000s): $111
Max Size of Investment Considered (000s): $1,110

Geographical Preferences

International Preferences:
India
Asia

Industry Preferences

In Computer Software prefer:
Software

In Internet Specific prefer:
Internet

In Computer Other prefer:
Computer Related

In Semiconductor/Electr prefer:
Electronics
Semiconductor

In Biotechnology prefer:
Agricultural/Animal Bio.

In Medical/Health prefer:
Medical/Health

In Consumer Related prefer:
Retail
Food/Beverage

In Industrial/Energy prefer:
Energy
Environmental Related

In Financial Services prefer:
Financial Services

In Manufact. prefer:
Manufacturing

In Agr/Forestr/Fish prefer:
Agribusiness
Agriculture related

Additional Information

Year Founded: 1999
Capital Under Management: $33,300,000
Current Activity Level : Actively seeking new investments

SIDCO SICAR

Avenue Imam Sahnoun
Immeuble Dar El Fallah
Kairouan, Tunisia 3100
Phone: 216-77-233-660
Fax: 216-77-233-660
E-mail: sidco.sicar@gnet.tn
Website: www.sidco-sicar.com

Management and Staff

Riadh Abida, Chief Executive Officer

Type of Firm

Private Equity Firm

Association Membership

Tunisian Venture Capital Association

Project Preferences

Type of Financing Preferred:
Balanced
Startup

Size of Investments Considered:
Min Size of Investment Considered (000s): $68
Max Size of Investment Considered (000s): $344

Geographical Preferences

International Preferences:
Tunisia

Industry Preferences

In Industrial/Energy prefer:
Industrial Products

In Business Serv. prefer:
Services

In Agr/Forestr/Fish prefer:
Agriculture related

Additional Information

Year Founded: 1991
Current Activity Level : Actively seeking new investments

SIDE CAPITAL

62, Rue Jean Jacques Rousseau
Paris, France 75001
Website: www.side-capital.com

Type of Firm

Private Equity Firm

Project Preferences

Type of Financing Preferred:
Early Stage
Seed

Size of Investments Considered:
Min Size of Investment Considered (000s): $326
Max Size of Investment Considered (000s): $652

Geographical Preferences

International Preferences:
Europe
France

Industry Preferences

In Computer Software prefer:
Software

In Internet Specific prefer:
Internet

Additional Information

Year Founded: 2015
Current Activity Level : Actively seeking new investments

SIDER ISRA'EL IYE`UTS KALKALI BE`AM

9 Keren Hayesod Street
PO Box 505
Herzelia, Israel 46105
Phone: 97299577227
Fax: 97299577228
E-mail: info@cedarfund.com
Website: www.cedarfund.com

Management and Staff

Allen Bernardo, Partner
Amnon Shoham, Founder
Dorin Miller, Venture Partner
Gal Israely, Co-Founder
Moshe Tur, Venture Partner
Yuval Ruhama, Chief Financial Officer

Type of Firm

Private Equity Firm

Association Membership

Israel Venture Association

Project Preferences

Type of Financing Preferred:
Early Stage
Seed

Geographical Preferences

International Preferences:
Israel
Asia

Industry Preferences

In Communications prefer:
Communications and Media
Telecommunications

In Computer Software prefer:
Software

In Internet Specific prefer:
Internet

Additional Information

Year Founded: 1997
Capital Under Management: $50,000,000
Current Activity Level : Actively seeking new investments

SIDEREAL CAPITAL GROUP LLC

18 Washington Avenue
Chatham, NJ USA 07928
Website: www.sideealcapital.com

Management and Staff
A. Jabbar Abdi, Managing Partner
E.J. Sloboda, Managing Partner
R. Kenneth Bryant, Managing Partner

Type of Firm
Private Equity Firm

Project Preferences

Type of Financing Preferred:
Leveraged Buyout

Additional Information
Year Founded: 2015
Current Activity Level: Actively seeking new investments

SIDEX LP

360, rue Saint-Jacques, Suite 1700
Montreal, Canada H2Y 1P5
Phone: 5143832612
Fax: 5148505449
E-mail: info@sidex.ca
Website: www.sidex.ca

Management and Staff
Michel Champagne, Chief Executive Officer

Type of Firm
Government Affiliated Program

Project Preferences

Type of Financing Preferred:
Leveraged Buyout
Acquisition
Private Placement

Geographical Preferences

Canadian Preferences:
Quebec

Industry Preferences

In Agr/Forestr/Fish prefer:
Mining and Minerals

Additional Information
Year Founded: 2001
Current Activity Level: Actively seeking new investments

SIEMENS TECHNOLOGY ACCELERATOR GMBH

Otto-Hahn-Ring 6
Munich, Germany 81739
Phone: 498963635853
Fax: 498963635856
Website: www.sta.siemens.com

Management and Staff
Christian Wiesinger, Chief Financial Officer
Rudolf Freytag, Chief Executive Officer

Type of Firm
Corporate PE/Venture

Project Preferences

Type of Financing Preferred:
Seed
Startup

Geographical Preferences

United States Preferences:
All U.S.

International Preferences:
United Kingdom
Europe
Germany

Industry Preferences

In Communications prefer:
Communications and Media

In Computer Software prefer:
Software

In Semiconductor/Electr prefer:
Sensors

In Medical/Health prefer:
Medical/Health

In Industrial/Energy prefer:
Energy
Materials
Environmental Related

In Manufact. prefer:
Manufacturing

Additional Information
Year Founded: 2000
Current Activity Level: Actively seeking new investments

SIEMENS VENTURE CAPITAL GMBH

Otto-Hahn-Ring 6
Munich, Germany 81739
Phone: 498963633585
Fax: 498963634884
E-mail: communications.sfs@siemens.com
Website: finance.siemens.de

Other Offices
801 Boylston Street
5th Floor
Boston, MA USA 02116
Phone: 617-531-2901
Fax: 617-531-2908

5th Floor, Electric Mansion
1086, Appasaheb Marathe Marg Prabhadevi
Mumbai, India 400 025
Phone: 91-22-6757-2203
Fax: 91-22-6757-2260

435 Tasso Street, Suite 315
Palo Alto, CA USA 94301
Phone: 650-463-1700
Fax: 650-289-9108

13 Hamelacha Street
Afeq Industrial Park
Rosh Ha'ayin, Israel 48091
Phone: 972-3-915-1536
Fax: 972-3-915-1551

No.7 Wangjing Zhonghuan Nanlu
Chaoyang District
Beijing, China 100102
Phone: 86-10-6476-8890
Fax: 86-10-6476-4984

Management and Staff
Andrew Jay, Partner
Anupendra Sharma, Partner
Detlef Pohl, Partner
Doris Blasel, Managing Partner
Eric Emmons, Partner
Gerd Goette, Partner
Jackie Hoffmann, Partner
Klaus Gruenfelder, Chief Financial Officer
Madeline Song, Partner
Michael Sears, Partner
Mike Majors, Partner
Ralf Schnell, Chief Executive Officer
Rudolf Ohnesorge, Partner
Susanne Von Gueltlingen, Partner

Type of Firm
Corporate PE/Venture

Association Membership
National Venture Capital Association - USA (NVCA)
European Private Equity and Venture Capital Assoc.

Project Preferences

Role in Financing:
Will function either as deal originator or investor in deals created by others

Type of Financing Preferred:
Fund of Funds
Early Stage
Expansion
Balanced
Later Stage
Seed
Startup

Geographical Preferences

United States Preferences:
All U.S.

International Preferences:
India
Europe
China
Israel
Asia
Germany

Industry Focus

(% based on actual investment)
Computer Software and Services	30.6%
Internet Specific	14.4%
Communications and Media	14.4%
Industrial/Energy	11.0%
Medical/Health	9.6%
Semiconductors/Other Elect.	9.5%
Other Products	6.0%
Biotechnology	3.7%
Computer Hardware	0.8%

Additional Information

Name of Most Recent Fund: Industry of the Future Fund
Most Recent Fund Was Raised: 02/17/2014
Year Founded: 2006
Capital Under Management: $800,000,000
Current Activity Level : Actively seeking new investments
Method of Compensation: Return on investment is of primary concern, do not charge fees

SIERRA MADRE MANAGERS

1F First Lucky Place Place
2259 Pasong Tamo Extension
Makati, Philippines 1231
Phone: 6327720340
Website: www.sierramadre-pe.com

Type of Firm

Private Equity Firm

Project Preferences

Type of Financing Preferred:
Generalist PE

Industry Preferences

In Medical/Health prefer:
Health Services

In Consumer Related prefer:
Consumer
Consumer Services
Education Related

In Transportation prefer:
Transportation

Additional Information

Year Founded: 2016
Capital Under Management: $50,000,000
Current Activity Level : Actively seeking new investments

SIERRA VENTURES

1400 Fashion Island Blvd., Suite 1010
Foster City, CA USA 94404
Phone: 6508541000
Fax: 6508545593
E-mail: info@sierraventures.com
Website: www.sierraventures.com

Management and Staff

Aaron Tong, Partner
Ayden Ye, Principal
Ben Yu, Managing Director
David Schwab, Managing Director
Mark Fernandes, Managing Director
Martha Clarke Adamson, Chief Financial Officer
Peter Wendell, Managing Director
Steven Williams, Managing Director
Tim Guleri, Managing Director

Type of Firm

Private Equity Firm

Association Membership

Western Association of Venture Capitalists (WAVC)
National Venture Capital Association - USA (NVCA)

Project Preferences

Role in Financing:
Prefer role as deal originator but will also invest in deals created by others

Type of Financing Preferred:
Early Stage
Expansion
Balanced
Later Stage
Seed

Size of Investments Considered:
Min Size of Investment Considered (000s): $500
Max Size of Investment Considered (000s): $25,000

Geographical Preferences

United States Preferences:
North America

International Preferences:
India
Europe
China

Industry Focus

(% based on actual investment)
Computer Software and Services	38.7%
Internet Specific	20.2%
Communications and Media	9.5%
Semiconductors/Other Elect.	9.0%
Biotechnology	5.9%
Other Products	4.2%
Computer Hardware	3.9%
Medical/Health	3.7%
Industrial/Energy	3.5%
Consumer Related	1.3%

Additional Information

Name of Most Recent Fund: Sierra Ventures X, L.P.
Most Recent Fund Was Raised: 12/21/2012
Year Founded: 1982
Capital Under Management: $1,590,000,000
Current Activity Level : Actively seeking new investments
Method of Compensation: Return on investment is of primary concern, do not charge fees

SIERRA WASATCH CAPITAL

11170 Alder Drive
Truckee, CA USA 96160
Website: www.sierrawasatch.com

Type of Firm

Private Equity Firm

Project Preferences

Type of Financing Preferred:
Early Stage

Industry Preferences

In Business Serv. prefer:
Media

Additional Information

Year Founded: 2016
Capital Under Management: $5,700,000
Current Activity Level : Actively seeking new investments

SIERRACONSTELLATION PARTNERS LLC

333 South Hope Street, Suite 3500
Los Angeles, CA USA 90071
Phone: 2132899060
Fax: 2132323285
E-mail: info@sierraconstellation.com
Website: www.sierraconstellation.com

Type of Firm

Private Equity Advisor or Fund of Funds

Project Preferences

Pratt's Guide to Private Equity & Venture Capital Sources

Type of Financing Preferred:
Leveraged Buyout
Turnaround
Management Buyouts
Special Situation

Industry Preferences

In Consumer Related prefer:
Food/Beverage
Consumer Products

In Industrial/Energy prefer:
Materials
Advanced Materials

In Transportation prefer:
Aerospace

In Business Serv. prefer:
Services
Distribution

In Manufact. prefer:
Manufacturing

In Agr/Forestr/Fish prefer:
Agriculture related

Additional Information

Year Founded: 2013
Current Activity Level : Actively seeking new investments

SIFEM AG

Bubenbergplatz 11
Bern, Switzerland 3011
Phone: 41313100930
Fax: 41313100939
Website: www.sifem.ch

Management and Staff

Claude Barras, CEO & Managing Director

Type of Firm

Private Equity Firm

Association Membership

Community Development Venture Capital Alliance
African Venture Capital Association (AVCA)

Project Preferences

Type of Financing Preferred:
Fund of Funds
Leveraged Buyout
Mezzanine

Geographical Preferences

International Preferences:
Armenia
Indonesia
Latin America
Belarus
Macedonia
Kyrgyzstan
Tajikistan
Azerbaijan
Moldova
Ukraine
Asia
Bosnia
Malaysia
Africa
All International
Georgia

Additional Information

Year Founded: 2005
Capital Under Management: $196,000,000
Current Activity Level : Actively seeking new investments

SIG ASIA INVESTMENTS LLLP

222 Hu Bin Road, Suite 1705-09, Corporate Ave.
Shanghai, China 200021
Phone: 862161222888
Fax: 862161223488
E-mail: Info@sig-china.com
Website: www.sig-china.com

Other Offices

B12 Jianguomenwai Da Jie, Suite 1908, Twin Towers
Beijing, China 100022
Phone: 861065666882
Fax: 861065666881

101 California Street, Suite 3250
San Francisco, CA USA 94111
Phone: 4154036510
Fax: 6106173896

Management and Staff

Andrew Frost, Founder
Arthur Dantchik, Founder

Type of Firm

Bank Affiliated

Association Membership

China Venture Capital Association

Project Preferences

Type of Financing Preferred:
Early Stage
Expansion
Balanced
Later Stage

Geographical Preferences

International Preferences:
China

Industry Preferences

In Communications prefer:
Wireless Communications
Media and Entertainment

In Internet Specific prefer:
Internet

In Medical/Health prefer:
Medical/Health

In Consumer Related prefer:
Consumer
Retail
Consumer Services

In Business Serv. prefer:
Services
Media

In Manufact. prefer:
Manufacturing

In Agr/Forestr/Fish prefer:
Agriculture related

Additional Information

Year Founded: 2004
Current Activity Level : Actively seeking new investments

SIG CAPITAL PARTNERS LTD

No. 1010 Huaihai Zhong Rd.
Unit3701, K.Wah Center
Shanghai, China 200031
Phone: 862161611777
Fax: 862154035580

Management and Staff

Jiong Jin, Managing Partner
Xin Guan, Managing Partner

Type of Firm

Private Equity Firm

Project Preferences

Type of Financing Preferred:
Leveraged Buyout
Expansion
Generalist PE

Geographical Preferences

International Preferences:
China

Industry Preferences

In Medical/Health prefer:
Health Services

In Consumer Related prefer:
Entertainment and Leisure
Consumer Products
Consumer Services
Education Related

In Transportation prefer:
Transportation

In Business Serv. prefer:
Media

Additional Information
Year Founded: 2004
Current Activity Level : Actively seeking new investments

SIGEFI ITALIA PRIVATE EQUITY SPA

Via San Senatore 10
Milan, Italy 20122
Phone: 39-28-969-14-77
Fax: 39-28-969-14-83
E-mail: b.metais@siparex.com
Website: www.siparex.com

Type of Firm
Private Equity Firm

Association Membership
Italian Venture Capital Association (AIFI)

Project Preferences

Type of Financing Preferred:
Expansion

Geographical Preferences

International Preferences:
Europe

Industry Preferences

In Financial Services prefer:
Financial Services

Additional Information
Year Founded: 2009
Current Activity Level : Actively seeking new investments

SIGHTLINE PARTNERS LLC

8500 Normandale Lake Boulevard, Suite 1070
Minneapolis, MN USA 55437
Phone: 9526410300
Fax: 9526410310
Website: www.sightlinepartners.com

Management and Staff
Buzz Benson, Managing Director
Joe Biller, Managing Director
Scott Ward, Venture Partner

Type of Firm
Private Equity Firm

Project Preferences

Role in Financing:
Will function either as deal originator or investor in deals created by others

Type of Financing Preferred:
Balanced
Later Stage

Geographical Preferences

United States Preferences:

Industry Preferences

In Medical/Health prefer:
Medical/Health
Medical Diagnostics
Diagnostic Test Products
Medical Therapeutics
Drug/Equipmt Delivery
Medical Products
Disposable Med. Products

Additional Information
Name of Most Recent Fund: SightLine Healthcare Opportunity Fund II, L.P.
Most Recent Fund Was Raised: 02/14/2013
Year Founded: 1992
Capital Under Management: $300,000,000
Current Activity Level : Actively seeking new investments

SIGMA GESTION SA

59 Avenue d'Iena
Paris, France 75016
Phone: 33147039842
Fax: 33149269111
E-mail: infos@sigmagestion.com
Website: www.sigmagestion.com

Management and Staff
Emmanuel Simonneau, President
Phillippe Cholet, Founder

Type of Firm
Private Equity Firm

Association Membership
French Venture Capital Association (AFIC)

Project Preferences

Type of Financing Preferred:
Early Stage
Expansion
Balanced
Later Stage

Geographical Preferences

International Preferences:
Europe
France

Industry Preferences

In Communications prefer:
Telecommunications
Other Communication Prod.

In Semiconductor/Electr prefer:
Electronics

In Industrial/Energy prefer:
Energy
Alternative Energy
Industrial Products

In Business Serv. prefer:
Services
Distribution

Additional Information
Year Founded: 1993
Current Activity Level : Actively seeking new investments

SIGMA PARTNERS

156 Diablo Road, Suite 320
Danville, CA USA 94526
Phone: 6508531700
Fax: 6508531717
Website: www.sigmapartners.com

Management and Staff
Bob Spinner, Managing Director
Clifford Haas, Managing Director
Fahri Diner, Managing Director
Gardner Hendrie, Partner
Gregory Gretsch, Managing Director
John Mandile, Managing Director
Lawrence Finch, Managing Director
Melissa Alves, Chief Financial Officer
Paul Flanagan, Managing Director
Peter Solvik, Managing Director
Richard Dale, Principal
Robert Davoli, Managing Director
Wade Woodson, Managing Director

Type of Firm
Private Equity Firm

Association Membership
Western Association of Venture Capitalists (WAVC)

Project Preferences

Role in Financing:
Prefer role as deal originator but will also invest in deals created by others

Type of Financing Preferred:
Early Stage
Startup

Geographical Preferences

United States Preferences:

Industry Focus

(% based on actual investment)
Computer Software and Services	47.0%
Internet Specific	20.3%
Semiconductors/Other Elect.	14.0%
Communications and Media	5.4%
Other Products	4.5%
Computer Hardware	3.7%
Industrial/Energy	2.8%
Medical/Health	1.5%
Biotechnology	0.5%
Consumer Related	0.2%

Additional Information

Name of Most Recent Fund: Sigma Partners 8, L.P.
Most Recent Fund Was Raised: 08/18/2007
Year Founded: 1984
Capital Under Management: $2,229,000,000
Current Activity Level : Actively seeking new investments
Method of Compensation: Return on investment is of primary concern, do not charge fees

SIGMA PRIME VENTURES LLC

20 Custom House Street, Suite 830
Boston, MA USA 02110
Phone: 6173307872
Website: www.sigmaprime.com

Management and Staff

Andrea Boyer, Chief Financial Officer
Andrew Rollins, Venture Partner
John Simon, Managing Director
John Mandile, Managing Director
Melissa Alves, Chief Financial Officer
Paul Flanagan, Managing Director
Raju Rishi, Venture Partner
Robert Davoli, Managing Director

Type of Firm
Private Equity Firm

Association Membership
New England Venture Capital Association
National Venture Capital Association - USA (NVCA)

Project Preferences

Type of Financing Preferred:
Early Stage

Geographical Preferences

United States Preferences:
Massachusetts
Alaska
New York
East Coast

Industry Preferences

In Business Serv. prefer:
Services

Additional Information
Name of Most Recent Fund: Sigma Prime Partners IX, L.P.
Most Recent Fund Was Raised: 06/25/2013
Year Founded: 1969
Capital Under Management: $115,585,000
Current Activity Level : Actively seeking new investments

SIGNAL HILL EQUITY PARTNERS

Two Carlton Street, Suite 1700
Toronto, Canada M5B 1J3
Phone: 4168471502
Website: www.signalhillequity.com

Management and Staff

Andrew Walton, Partner
Arun Thathachari, Vice President
Claire Duckworth, Chief Financial Officer
David Dolan, Managing Director
Hai Tran-Viet, Vice President
James Burnham, Managing Partner
Matthew Fiore, Managing Director

Type of Firm
Private Equity Firm

Association Membership
Mid-Atlantic Venture Association
Canadian Venture Capital Association

Project Preferences

Type of Financing Preferred:
Leveraged Buyout

Geographical Preferences

United States Preferences:

Canadian Preferences:
All Canada

Industry Preferences

In Consumer Related prefer:
Consumer Products

In Financial Services prefer:
Financial Services

In Business Serv. prefer:
Services
Distribution

In Manufact. prefer:
Manufacturing

Additional Information

Year Founded: 1969
Capital Under Management: $116,844,000
Current Activity Level : Actively seeking new investments

SIGNAL LAKE MANAGEMENT LLC

606 Post Road East, Suite 667
Westport, CT USA 06880
Phone: 2034541133
Fax: 2034547142
E-mail: info@signallake.com
Website: www.signallake.com

Management and Staff

Bart Stuck, Managing Director
Barton Stuck, Co-Founder

Type of Firm
Private Equity Firm

Project Preferences

Role in Financing:
Will function either as deal originator or investor in deals created by others

Type of Financing Preferred:
Leveraged Buyout
Early Stage
Expansion
Mezzanine
Balanced
Later Stage
Seed
Acquisition

Size of Investments Considered:
Min Size of Investment Considered (000s): $100
Max Size of Investment Considered (000s): $100,000

Geographical Preferences

United States Preferences:
Mid Atlantic
Northwest
Northern California
Southwest

International Preferences:
Europe
Pacific
Asia

Industry Focus

(% based on actual investment)
Communications and Media	39.8%
Internet Specific	22.3%
Computer Hardware	16.9%
Semiconductors/Other Elect.	14.1%
Computer Software and Services	6.9%

Additional Information

Year Founded: 1998
Capital Under Management: $300,000,000
Current Activity Level : Actively seeking new investments
Method of Compensation: Return on investment is of primary concern, do not charge fees

SIGNAL PEAK VENTURES

2795 East Cottonwood Parkway, Suite 360
Salt Lake City, UT USA 84121
Phone: 8019428999
Fax: 8019421636
E-mail: info@signalpeakvc.com
Website: www.signalpeakvc.com

Management and Staff
Brandon Tidwell, Managing Director
Dinesh Patel, Managing Director
Lisa Dunlea, Venture Partner
Ronald Heinz, Managing Director
Scott Petty, Managing Director
Travis Heath, Chief Financial Officer

Type of Firm
Private Equity Firm

Project Preferences

Type of Financing Preferred:
Balanced
Later Stage

Size of Investments Considered:
Min Size of Investment Considered (000s): $250
Max Size of Investment Considered (000s): $10,000

Geographical Preferences

United States Preferences:
Rocky Mountain

Industry Preferences

In Computer Software prefer:
Software

In Medical/Health prefer:
Drug/Equipmt Delivery

Additional Information
Name of Most Recent Fund: Signal Peak Technology Ventures, L.P.
Most Recent Fund Was Raised: 08/08/2011
Year Founded: 2011
Capital Under Management: $500,000,000
Current Activity Level : Actively seeking new investments

SIGNALFIRE LLC

333 Bryant Street, Suite 190
San Francisco, CA USA 94107
Website: www.signalfire.com

Type of Firm
Private Equity Firm

Project Preferences

Type of Financing Preferred:
Early Stage
Seed

Industry Preferences

In Communications prefer:
Media and Entertainment

In Internet Specific prefer:
Ecommerce

In Consumer Related prefer:
Consumer

Additional Information
Year Founded: 2015
Capital Under Management: $151,070,000
Current Activity Level : Actively seeking new investments

SIGNATURE CAPITAL LLC

400 R Street, Suite 1080
Sacramento, CA USA 95814
Phone: 8009525210

Type of Firm
Private Equity Firm

Project Preferences

Type of Financing Preferred:
Balanced

Additional Information
Year Founded: 1969
Current Activity Level : Actively seeking new investments

SIGNATURE CAPITAL LLC

100 Commercial Street, Suite 414
Portland, ME USA 04101
Phone: 2077738123
Fax: 8778452775
E-mail: info@sigcap.com

Management and Staff
Nina Garrisson, Vice President
William Turner, Managing Director

Type of Firm
Private Equity Firm

Project Preferences

Role in Financing:
Prefer role as deal originator

Type of Financing Preferred:
Early Stage

Geographical Preferences

United States Preferences:
Mid Atlantic
Midwest
Southeast
Northeast
Southwest

Industry Preferences

In Communications prefer:
Telecommunications

In Internet Specific prefer:
Internet
Ecommerce

In Semiconductor/Electr prefer:
Semiconductor
Micro-Processing
Circuit Boards

In Biotechnology prefer:
Human Biotechnology

In Medical/Health prefer:
Medical Products

In Business Serv. prefer:
Services
Distribution

Additional Information
Year Founded: 1997
Current Activity Level : Actively seeking new investments
Method of Compensation: Return on invest. most important, but chg. closing fees, service fees, etc.

SIGNATURE FINANCIAL MANAGEMENT INC

150 West Main Street, Suite 1550
Norfolk, VA USA 23510
Phone: 757-625-7670
Fax: 757-625-7673
E-mail: info@sigfin.com
Website: www.sigfin.com

Other Offices
410 East Water Street, Suite 500
Charlottesville, VA USA 22902
Phone: 4342953191

Management and Staff
Anne Shumadine, President
Susan Colpitts, Chief Financial Officer

Type of Firm
Private Equity Advisor or Fund of Funds

Project Preferences

Type of Financing Preferred:
Fund of Funds

Geographical Preferences

United States Preferences:
All U.S.

Additional Information
Year Founded: 1994
Capital Under Management: $172,100,000
Current Activity Level : Actively seeking new investments

SIGNET HEALTHCARE PARTNERS

152 West 57th Street
19F Carnegie Hall Towers
New York, NY USA 10019
Phone: 6468404990
Fax: 2124193956
Website: www.signethealthcarepartners.com

Other Offices

3100 Chase Tower
Houston, TX USA 77002
Phone: 713-993-4690
Fax: 713-993-4699

Management and Staff

Al Hansen, Managing Director
James Gale, Founder
Joyce Erony, Managing Director
Joyce Erony, Managing Director
Martin Zeiger, Partner
Samuel Altman, Partner
Todd Sone, Managing Director

Type of Firm

Private Equity Firm

Project Preferences

Role in Financing:
Prefer role as deal originator but will also invest in deals created by others

Type of Financing Preferred:
Leveraged Buyout
Expansion
Balanced
Later Stage

Geographical Preferences

United States Preferences:

International Preferences:
Europe
Asia
All International

Industry Preferences

In Medical/Health prefer:
Medical/Health
Diagnostic Services
Diagnostic Test Products
Drug/Equipmt Delivery
Medical Products
Health Services
Pharmaceuticals

In Other prefer:
Environment Responsible

Additional Information

Year Founded: 1998
Capital Under Management: $200,000,000

Current Activity Level: Actively seeking new investments

SIGULER GUFF & COMPANY LP

825 Third Avenue
Tenth Floor
New York, NY USA 10022
Phone: 2123325100
Fax: 2123325120
E-mail: info@sigulerguff.com
Website: www.sigulerguff.com

Other Offices

Stoleshnikov Per. 14
Second Floor
Moscow, Russia 107031
Phone: 7-495-234-3095
Fax: 7-495-234-3099

150 North Wacker Drive, Suite 1740
CHICAGO, IL USA 60606
Phone: 3122799300
Fax: 3122799301

One Boston Place
27th Floor
BOSTON, MA USA 02108
Phone: 6176482100
Fax: 6176482121

2205 CITIC Square
1168 West Nanjing Road
Shanghai, China 200040
Phone: 86-21-5292-5256
Fax: 86-21-5292-5575

, Suite 8FB, Grand Hyatt Plaza
Santacruz East
Mumbai, India 400055
Phone: 91-22-4215-4830

Av. Pres. Juscelino Kubistcheck 1726
Conjunto 203, Itaim
Sao Paulo, Brazil 04543-000
Phone: 551134769992

Management and Staff

Ally Zhang, Managing Director
Andrew Guff, Founder
Angela Yang, Vice President
Anthony Cusano, Managing Director
Anthony Corriggio, Managing Director
Ashley Freger, Vice President
Aviral Jain, Principal
Bradley Bennett, Vice President
C. Driessen, Vice President
Cesar Collier, Managing Director
Christopher Barbier, Principal
Clifford Yonce, Managing Director
Daniel Whitcomb, Principal
David Boal, Managing Director
Donald Spencer, Founder
Douglas Loveland, Principal
Evgeniy Gorkov, Managing Director
Fernando Arakaki, Vice President
Florian Lahnstein, Managing Director
George Siguler, Founder
Hamid Tabib, Vice President
Helen Tang, Vice President
Huwaida Hassan, Vice President
Ilomai Kurrik, Principal
Jacqueline Battista, Vice President
James Corl, Managing Director
James Gereghty, Managing Director
Jarrad Krulick, Principal
Jason Mundt, Principal
Jay Koh, Partner
Jonathan Wilson, Managing Director
Jun Isoda, Principal
Kathryn Kantarian, Principal
Kenneth Burns, Partner
Kevin Kester, Managing Director
Kyungoh Kook, Managing Director
Langdon Mitchell, Vice President
Leon Zilber, Principal
Mark Denomme, Managing Director
Matthew Brewer, Vice President
Michael Markman, Vice President
Neil Fowler, Principal
Nestor Weigand, Principal
Praneet Singh, Managing Director
Ralph Jaeger, Managing Director
Remy Kawkabani, Managing Director
Roman Simonov, Managing Director
Ryan Mason, Principal
Ryan Stuckert, Vice President
Sandip Kakar, Managing Director
Scott Berger, Vice President
Sean Greene, Managing Director
Sean MacDonald, Vice President
Stephen Faughnan, Principal
Vladimir Andrienko, Managing Director

Type of Firm

Private Equity Firm

Association Membership

Brazilian Venture Capital Association (ABCR)
Emerging Markets Private Equity Association
Natl Assoc of Small Bus. Inv. Co (NASBIC)
European Private Equity and Venture Capital Assoc.
African Venture Capital Association (AVCA)

Project Preferences

Role in Financing:
Will function either as deal originator or investor in deals created by others

Type of Financing Preferred:
Fund of Funds
Leveraged Buyout
Early Stage
Mezzanine
Generalist PE
Balanced
Opportunistic
Later Stage
Other
Special Situation

Geographical Preferences

United States Preferences:
North America

International Preferences:
Europe

Industry Preferences

In Financial Services prefer:
Real Estate

Additional Information

Name of Most Recent Fund: Siguler Guff Distressed Real Estate Opportunities Fund II,LP
Most Recent Fund Was Raised: 09/12/2013
Year Founded: 1995
Capital Under Management: $10,964,700,000
Current Activity Level : Actively seeking new investments
Method of Compensation: Return on investment is of primary concern, do not charge fees

SIGVION CAPITAL

1970 North Halsted Street
3rd Floor
Chicago, IL USA 60614
E-mail: info@orchardvc.com
Website: www.orchardvc.com

Management and Staff

Josh Fairbank, Partner
Michael Pape, Partner

Type of Firm

Private Equity Firm

Project Preferences

Type of Financing Preferred:
Early Stage

Geographical Preferences

United States Preferences:

Industry Preferences

In Medical/Health prefer:
Medical Therapeutics
Drug/Equipmt Delivery
Pharmaceuticals

Additional Information

Name of Most Recent Fund: Sigvion Fund I, L.P.
Most Recent Fund Was Raised: 03/08/2006
Year Founded: 2004
Current Activity Level : Actively seeking new investments

SILAS CAPITAL LLC

45 Rockefeller Plaza, Suite 2000
New York, NY USA 10111
Phone: 2122186893
E-mail: info@silascapital.com
Website: www.silascapital.com

Type of Firm

Private Equity Firm

Project Preferences

Type of Financing Preferred:
Early Stage

Size of Investments Considered:
Min Size of Investment Considered (000s): $500
Max Size of Investment Considered (000s): $4,000

Geographical Preferences

United States Preferences:
New York

Industry Preferences

In Internet Specific prefer:
Internet

In Consumer Related prefer:
Retail
Consumer Products

Additional Information

Year Founded: 2011
Current Activity Level : Actively seeking new investments

SILCON VALLEY DATA CAPITAL MANAGEMENT LLC

150 West Evelyn Avenue, Suite 100
Mountain View, CA USA 94041

Type of Firm

Private Equity Firm

Project Preferences

Type of Financing Preferred:
Balanced

Additional Information

Year Founded: 2016
Capital Under Management: $38,270,000
Current Activity Level : Actively seeking new investments

SILICON BADIA

123, Zahran Street
Amman, Jordan 11181
E-mail: info@siliconbadia.com
Website: www.siliconbadia.com

Management and Staff

Emile Cubeisy, Managing Partner
Hagop Taminian, Principal

Type of Firm

Private Equity Firm

Project Preferences

Type of Financing Preferred:
Early Stage
Balanced
Later Stage
Seed
Startup

Geographical Preferences

United States Preferences:

International Preferences:
Jordan
Middle East

Industry Preferences

In Communications prefer:
Wireless Communications

In Computer Other prefer:
Computer Related

Additional Information

Year Founded: 2011
Capital Under Management: $17,000,000
Current Activity Level : Actively seeking new investments

SILICON OASIS FOUNDERS FZCO

PO Box 341110
Dubai, Utd. Arab Em.
Phone: 97143821300
Fax: 97145015200
E-mail: bizplan@dso.ae
Website: www.siliconoasisfounders.com

Type of Firm

Incubator/Development Program

Project Preferences

Type of Financing Preferred:
Early Stage
Seed
Startup

Geographical Preferences

International Preferences:
Utd. Arab Em.
Asia

Industry Preferences

In Communications prefer:
Telecommunications
Wireless Communications

Additional Information

Year Founded: 2014
Current Activity Level : Actively seeking new investments

SILICON VALLEY BANCVENTURES LP

2400 Hanover Street
Palo Alto, CA USA 94304
Phone: 6503201100
Fax: 6503200016
Website: www.svb.com/svbcapital

Other Offices

2770 Sand Hill Road
MENLO PARK, CA USA 94025
Phone: 6509260440
Fax: 6502348292

275 Grove Street, Suite Two-200
AUBURNDALE, MA USA 02466
Phone: 6176304100
Fax: 6179695849

38 Technology Drive West, Suite 150
IRVINE, CA USA 92618
Phone: 9497540800
Fax: 9497909007

3000 Sand Hill Road
Building Three, Suite 150
MENLO PARK, CA USA 94025
Phone: 6502337420
Fax: 6502336611

Management and Staff

Aaron Gershenberg, Managing Partner
John Otterson, Partner
Katie Knepley, Principal
Ken Loveless, Managing Director
Kenneth Wilcox, Chief Executive Officer
Larry Zahn, Partner
Sulu Mamdani, Managing Director
Sven Weber, Managing Director
Thorben Hett, Principal
Vincent Williams, Partner
Yeh Ming, Managing Director

Type of Firm
Private Equity Advisor or Fund of Funds

Association Membership
Mid-Atlantic Venture Association
New England Venture Capital Association
Western Association of Venture Capitalists (WAVC)
National Venture Capital Association - USA (NVCA)
Indian Venture Capital Association (IVCA)

Project Preferences

Role in Financing:
Prefer role as deal originator but will also invest in deals created by others

Type of Financing Preferred:
Fund of Funds
Early Stage
Expansion

Geographical Preferences

United States Preferences:

International Preferences:
India
United Kingdom
China
Israel

Industry Focus
(% based on actual investment)
Internet Specific	43.2%
Computer Software and Services	24.4%
Communications and Media	8.0%
Semiconductors/Other Elect.	7.8%
Other Products	6.8%
Computer Hardware	4.6%
Consumer Related	2.6%
Biotechnology	1.4%
Medical/Health	0.8%
Industrial/Energy	0.3%

Additional Information
Name of Most Recent Fund: Qualified Investors Fund III LLC
Most Recent Fund Was Raised: 10/23/2013
Year Founded: 2000
Capital Under Management: $56,000,000
Current Activity Level : Actively seeking new investments
Method of Compensation: Return on invest. most important, but chg. closing fees, service fees, etc.

SILICON VALLEY FUTURE CAPITAL

1059 East Meadow Circle
Palo Alto, CA USA 94303
Phone: 6506665568
Website: svfcapital.com

Type of Firm
Private Equity Firm

Project Preferences

Type of Financing Preferred:
Early Stage

Industry Preferences

In Computer Software prefer:
Artificial Intelligence

In Biotechnology prefer:
Biotechnology

In Industrial/Energy prefer:
Robotics

Additional Information
Year Founded: 2018
Current Activity Level : Actively seeking new investments

SILICON VALLEY GROWTH SYNDICATE

1370 Willow Road
Menlo Park, CA USA 94025
Phone: 6505427725
Fax: 6505427768
E-mail: seeking@siliconvalleygrowth.com
Website: www.siliconvalleygrowth.com

Type of Firm
Private Equity Firm

Project Preferences

Type of Financing Preferred:
Early Stage

Size of Investments Considered:
Min Size of Investment Considered (000s): $10
Max Size of Investment Considered (000s): $50

Geographical Preferences

United States Preferences:
Northern California

Industry Preferences

In Communications prefer:
Wireless Communications

In Computer Software prefer:
Software
Applications Software

In Internet Specific prefer:
Ecommerce

Additional Information
Name of Most Recent Fund: Silicon Valley Growth Syndicate Fund I, L.P.
Most Recent Fund Was Raised: 11/20/2013
Year Founded: 2013
Capital Under Management: $600,000
Current Activity Level : Actively seeking new investments

SILICON VALLEY PARADISE VENTURE INVESTMENT CO., LTD.

Zhongguancun South Street
12 Huan Tai Bldg
Beijing, China 100081
Phone: 86-10-6212-5588
Fax: 86-10-6210-9119
Website: www.ggttvc.com

Other Offices

Renmin South Road, New Hope, Building 1
Sec 45, Room 1707
Chengdu, China 610041
Phone: 2885257989
Fax: 2885256209

Jintian Road Rongchao Trade Cente
3208-3209
Shenzhen, China 518035
Phone: 75533226099
Fax: 75533226069

Song of the Art and Cultural Center
A District
Wuhan, China 430050
Phone: 2784842218
Fax: 2784842228

Jinye Road
Block B, Toom 809
Xi'an, China 710065
Phone: 2987997799
Fax: 2968596825

Chunxiao Road
Building 9, Number 439
Shanghai, China 201203
Phone: 2150274986
Fax: 215025016

Type of Firm
Private Equity Firm

Project Preferences

Type of Financing Preferred:
Generalist PE
Balanced

Geographical Preferences

International Preferences:
China

Additional Information
Year Founded: 2000
Current Activity Level : Actively seeking new investments

SILK INVEST LTD

145 Leadenhall Street
London, United Kingdom EC3V 4QT
Phone: 442079338610
Website: www.silkinvest.com

Other Offices
DIFC
Gate Village 10, Level 3
Dubai, Utd. Arab Em. 125115
Phone: 971 4 4019789

TAYA. Lotissement les Arnes
Rue N2. 3eme Etage
Casablanca, Morocco MAARIF 201
Phone: 212 522991056

Eden Square
Chiromo Road
Nairobi, Kenya
Phone: 254 20 367 3000

37 Kingfisher Drive
Hartebeespoort, South Africa 0240
Phone: 27 122 441 110

24 Iskandar Al-Akbar Street
11341 Heliopolice
Cairo, Egypt
Phone: 202 2417 6826

Management and Staff
Abdeltif Stitou, Chief Operating Officer
Baldwin Berges, Managing Partner
Daniel Broby, Chief Executive Officer
Waseem Khan, Managing Partner
Zin Bekkali, Chief Executive Officer

Type of Firm
Private Equity Firm

Project Preferences

Type of Financing Preferred:
Leveraged Buyout
Early Stage
Generalist PE
Management Buyouts

Industry Preferences

In Consumer Related prefer:
Food/Beverage

Additional Information
Year Founded: 2008
Current Activity Level : Actively seeking new investments

SILK ROAD MANAGEMENT

12 Jamiyangun Street, Suite 65, Grand Office Center
Ulaanbaatar, Mongolia 14240
Phone: 97670130078
E-mail: info@silkroadm.com
Website: www.silkroadm.com

Management and Staff
Alisher Ali, Managing Partner

Type of Firm
Investment Management Firm

Project Preferences

Type of Financing Preferred:
Leveraged Buyout
Early Stage
Expansion
Generalist PE
Balanced
Management Buyouts
Acquisition

Geographical Preferences

International Preferences:
Mongolia
Asia
Burma

Industry Preferences

In Communications prefer:
Data Communications

In Medical/Health prefer:
Medical/Health

In Consumer Related prefer:
Education Related

In Financial Services prefer:
Financial Services
Real Estate

In Business Serv. prefer:
Media

Additional Information
Year Founded: 2011
Capital Under Management: $55,000,000
Current Activity Level : Actively seeking new investments

SILK VENTURES LTD

One Canada Square
London, United Kingdom E14 5AB
Phone: 4402037257593
E-mail: hello@silk-ventures.com
Website: silk-ventures.com

Management and Staff
Angelica Anton, Partner
Edward Zeng, Partner
Ian Foley, Venture Partner

Type of Firm
Private Equity Firm

Project Preferences

Type of Financing Preferred:
Early Stage
Expansion

Geographical Preferences

United States Preferences:

International Preferences:
United Kingdom
China

Industry Preferences

In Computer Software prefer:
Artificial Intelligence

In Medical/Health prefer:
Health Services

Additional Information
Year Founded: 2017

Capital Under Management: $500,000,000
Current Activity Level : Actively seeking new investments

SILKROAD EQUITY LLC

20 West Kinzie Street, Suite 1420
Chicago, IL USA 60654
Phone: 8478402356
Fax: 8479193514
E-mail: info@silkroadequity.com
Website: www.silkroadequity.com

Management and Staff
Matthew Roszak, Co-Founder

Type of Firm
Private Equity Firm

Project Preferences

Type of Financing Preferred:
Leveraged Buyout
Early Stage
Generalist PE
Balanced
Later Stage
Seed
Acquisition
Startup

Size of Investments Considered:
Min Size of Investment Considered (000s): $1,000
Max Size of Investment Considered (000s): $20,000

Geographical Preferences

United States Preferences:
All U.S.

Industry Preferences

In Communications prefer:
Telecommunications
Media and Entertainment

In Consumer Related prefer:
Retail

In Business Serv. prefer:
Services

In Manufact. prefer:
Manufacturing

Additional Information
Year Founded: 2003
Current Activity Level : Actively seeking new investments

SILVER CREEK VENTURES CORP

5949 Sherry Lane, Suite 1450
Dallas, TX USA 75225
Phone: 2142652020
Fax: 2146926233

Website: silvercreekfund.com

Management and Staff
Bob Mosteller, Chief Financial Officer
John Adler, General Partner
Mark Masur, General Partner
Michael Segrest, General Partner

Type of Firm
Private Equity Firm

Project Preferences

Role in Financing:
Prefer role as deal originator but will also invest in deals created by others

Type of Financing Preferred:
Early Stage
Balanced
Later Stage
Seed

Size of Investments Considered:
Min Size of Investment Considered (000s): $500
Max Size of Investment Considered (000s): $10,000

Geographical Preferences

United States Preferences:
Rocky Mountain
California
Colorado
West Coast
Southwest
Texas

Industry Focus
(% based on actual investment)
Communications and Media	45.2%
Computer Hardware	26.8%
Computer Software and Services	16.5%
Semiconductors/Other Elect.	6.2%
Internet Specific	3.6%
Consumer Related	1.3%
Other Products	0.4%

Additional Information
Year Founded: 1989
Capital Under Management: $139,600,000
Current Activity Level : Actively seeking new investments
Method of Compensation: Return on investment is of primary concern, do not charge fees

SILVER INVESTMENT PARTNERS GMBH & CO KG

Wilhelm-Bonn-Strasse 12a
Kronberg, Germany 61476
Phone: 496917537000
Fax: 4969175370099
E-mail: info@silver-ip.com
Website: www.silver-ip.com

Management and Staff
Mark Elborn, Managing Partner
Oliver Kolbe, Managing Partner
Philipp Amereller, Managing Partner

Type of Firm
Private Equity Firm

Association Membership
German Venture Capital Association (BVK)

Project Preferences

Type of Financing Preferred:
Leveraged Buyout
Balanced
Turnaround
Later Stage

Geographical Preferences

International Preferences:
Switzerland
Austria
Germany

Industry Preferences

In Medical/Health prefer:
Medical/Health

In Industrial/Energy prefer:
Environmental Related

In Business Serv. prefer:
Services

In Manufact. prefer:
Manufacturing

Additional Information
Year Founded: 2009
Current Activity Level : Actively seeking new investments

SILVER LAKE PARTNERS LP

9 West 57th Street
32nd Floor
New York, NY USA 10019
Phone: 2129815600
Fax: 2129813535
Website: www.silverlake.com

Other Offices
1717 West Nanjing Road
25th Floor, Wheelock Square
Shanghai, China 200040
Phone: 86-21-6157-5164
Fax: 86-21-6157-5390

Marunouchi, Chiyoda-ku
Yusen Building Seventh Floor, 2-3-2
Tokyo, Japan 100-0005
Phone: 81-3-5219-6260
Fax: 81-3-5219-6274

Broadbent House
65 Grosvenor Street
London, United Kingdom W1K 3JH
Phone: 44-20-3205-8400
Fax: 44-20-3205-8401

One Market Plaza, Steuart Tower
Tenth Floor, Suite 1000
SAN FRANCISCO, CA USA 94105
Phone: 415-293-4355
Fax: 415-293-4365

10080 North Wolfe Road, Suite SW3-190
CUPERTINO, CA USA 95014
Phone: 408-454-4732
Fax: 408-454-4734

Eight Finance Street
33rd Floor Two IFC
Hong Kong, Hong Kong
Phone: 852-3664-3300
Fax: 852-3664-3456

Management and Staff

Christian Lucas, Managing Director
David Roux, Co-Founder
Egon Durban, Managing Partner
Frank Walters, Principal
Geoffrey Oltmans, Managing Director
Glenn Hutchins, Co-Founder
Gregory Mondre, Managing Partner
James Davidson, Co-Founder
Joe Osnoss, Managing Director
John Rudella, Principal
Karol Niewiadomski, Principal
Kenneth Hao, Managing Partner
Kyle Paster, Principal
Mark Zhu, Principal
Mark Beith, Principal
Michael Korzinstone, Principal
Mike Widmann, Principal
Mike Bingle, Managing Partner
Ryan Bone, Principal
Samuel Powell, Principal
Simon Patterson, Managing Director
Stephen Evans, Managing Director
Ulf Pagenkopf, Principal
Yingqi Li, Principal
Zheng Wang, Managing Director

Type of Firm

Private Equity Firm

Association Membership

Private Equity Council (PEC)

Project Preferences

Type of Financing Preferred:
Leveraged Buyout
Acquisition

Geographical Preferences

United States Preferences:

Industry Focus

(% based on actual investment)
Semiconductors/Other Elect.	74.8%
Computer Software and Services	12.7%
Internet Specific	10.2%
Computer Hardware	0.9%
Other Products	0.6%
Industrial/Energy	0.5%
Communications and Media	0.2%

Additional Information

Year Founded: 1999
Capital Under Management: $5,900,000,000
Current Activity Level : Actively seeking new investments

SILVER OAK SERVICES PARTNERS

1560 Sherman Avenue, Suite 1200
Evanston, IL USA 60201
Phone: 8473320400
Fax: 8474921717
E-mail: info@silveroaksp.com
Website: www.silveroaksp.com

Management and Staff

Daniel Gill, Managing Partner
David Bornhoeft, Vice President
Gregory Barr, Managing Partner
Jeffrey Mann, Chief Financial Officer
Wade Glisson, Vice President

Type of Firm

Private Equity Firm

Project Preferences

Type of Financing Preferred:
Leveraged Buyout
Acquisition
Recapitalizations

Size of Investments Considered:
Min Size of Investment Considered (000s): $10,000
Max Size of Investment Considered (000s): $30,000

Geographical Preferences

United States Preferences:
All U.S.

Industry Preferences

In Computer Software prefer:
Software

In Medical/Health prefer:
Health Services

In Consumer Related prefer:
Entertainment and Leisure
Consumer Services

In Business Serv. prefer:
Services
Distribution

Additional Information

Name of Most Recent Fund: Silver Oak Services Partners II, L.P.
Most Recent Fund Was Raised: 07/18/2012
Year Founded: 2006
Capital Under Management: $541,000,000
Current Activity Level : Actively seeking new investments

SILVER POINT CAPITAL LLC

Two Greenwich Plaza
Greenwich, CT USA 06830
Phone: 2035424230
E-mail: info@silverpointcapital.com
Website: www.silverpointcapital.com

Type of Firm

Private Equity Firm

Project Preferences

Type of Financing Preferred:
Turnaround
Distressed Debt

Additional Information

Year Founded: 2002
Current Activity Level : Actively seeking new investments

SILVER POINT VENTURES BV

Rapenburg 27
Leiden, Netherlands 2311 VT
Website: www.silverpointventures.com

Type of Firm

Private Equity Firm

Project Preferences

Type of Financing Preferred:
Early Stage
Seed

Geographical Preferences

International Preferences:
Europe
Netherlands

Industry Preferences

In Computer Software prefer:
Software

In Internet Specific prefer:
Internet

Additional Information

Year Founded: 2015
Current Activity Level : Actively seeking new investments

SILVER SAIL CAPITAL LLC

200 S Barrington Avenue
#286
Brentwood, CA USA 90049
Phone: 13106940618
Fax: 13105640045
Website: www.silversailcapital.com

Type of Firm
Private Equity Firm

Project Preferences

Type of Financing Preferred:
Leveraged Buyout

Geographical Preferences

United States Preferences:
North America

Industry Preferences

In Consumer Related prefer:
Food/Beverage
Consumer Products

In Industrial/Energy prefer:
Industrial Products

In Manufact. prefer:
Manufacturing

Additional Information
Year Founded: 2012
Current Activity Level : Actively seeking new investments

SILVERFERN GROUP INC

599 Lexington Avenue
47th Floor
New York, NY USA 10022
Phone: 2122098860
Fax: 2122098861

Other Offices
Achterom 7
Blaricum, Netherlands 1261EE
Phone: 31356954601

An der Welle 4
Frankfurt am Main, Germany 60322
Phone: 491732537465

Level 29, Chifley Tower
2 Chifley Square
Sydney, Australia 2000
Phone: 61299605883

Management and Staff
Andrew Isikoff, Managing Director
Brooks Klimley, Managing Director
Christopher Marlowe, Managing Director
Clive Holmes, Co-Founder
Deepak Ghosh, Managing Director
Edward Rimland, Managing Director
Kees-Jan Van Uchelen, Managing Director
Marino Marin, Managing Director
Mark Baldassarre, Managing Director
Paul Schroder, Managing Director
Reeta Holmes, Co-Founder
Richard Facioni, Managing Director
Rist Brouwer, Managing Director
Robert Raciti, Managing Director
Stephen Greene, Managing Director
Terence Bruyn, Managing Director

Type of Firm
Investment Management Firm

Project Preferences

Type of Financing Preferred:
Leveraged Buyout
Value-Add
Opportunistic
Acquisition
Recapitalizations

Size of Investments Considered:
Min Size of Investment Considered (000s): $25,000
Max Size of Investment Considered (000s): $150,000

Geographical Preferences

United States Preferences:
All U.S.

International Preferences:
Asia Pacific
Europe

Industry Preferences

In Communications prefer:
Telecommunications

In Consumer Related prefer:
Consumer
Food/Beverage

In Industrial/Energy prefer:
Energy
Environmental Related

In Financial Services prefer:
Financial Services

Additional Information
Year Founded: 2001
Current Activity Level : Actively seeking new investments

SILVERFLEET CAPITAL PARTNERS LLP

One Carter Lane
London, United Kingdom EC4V 5ER
Phone: 442078221000
Fax: 442078221001
E-mail: investor.relations@silverfleetcapital.com

Other Offices
Oberanger 28
Munich, Germany D-80331
Phone: 49-89-238-8960
Fax: 49-89-2388-9699

46 avenue Kleber
Paris, France 75116
Phone: 33-1-5689-1414
Fax: 33-1-5689-1429

Management and Staff
Adrian Yurkwich, Partner
Alexandre Lefebvre, Partner
Alfa Chan, Partner
Andreas Holtschneider, Principal
Darren Jordan, Partner
David MacKenzie, Partner
Gareth Whiley, Partner
Geraldine Kennell, Partner
Guido May, Partner
Ian Oxley, Partner
Jean Chatillon, Partner
Joachim Braun, Partner
Kay Ashton, Partner
Klaus Maurer, Partner
Maire Deslandes, Partner
Mark Piasecki, Partner
Neil MacDougall, Managing Partner

Type of Firm
Private Equity Firm

Association Membership
Hong Kong Venture Capital Association (HKVCA)
British Venture Capital Association (BVCA)
French Venture Capital Association (AFIC)
European Private Equity and Venture Capital Assoc.

Project Preferences

Role in Financing:
Prefer role as deal originator but will also invest in deals created by others

Type of Financing Preferred:
Leveraged Buyout
Expansion
Management Buyouts
Acquisition

Geographical Preferences

United States Preferences:

International Preferences:
United Kingdom
Luxembourg
Netherlands
Scandanavia/Nordic Region
Belgium
Germany
All International
France

Industry Focus

(% based on actual investment)

Consumer Related	48.6%
Other Products	26.0%
Medical/Health	8.4%
Internet Specific	7.0%
Communications and Media	3.7%
Industrial/Energy	3.2%
Computer Software and Services	2.6%
Computer Hardware	0.4%
Biotechnology	0.0%

Additional Information

Name of Most Recent Fund: Silverfleet Capital Fund, L.P.
Most Recent Fund Was Raised: 12/18/2007
Year Founded: 1984
Capital Under Management: $2,183,600,000
Current Activity Level : Actively seeking new investments
Method of Compensation: Return on invest. most important, but chg. closing fees, service fees, etc.

SILVERHAWK CAPITAL PARTNERS LLC

140 Greenwich Avenue, Suite 200
Greenwich, CT USA 06830
Phone: 2038612905
Fax: 2038612903
E-mail: info@silverhawkcp.com
Website: www.silverhawkcapitalpartners.com

Other Offices

5605 Carnegie Boulevard, Suite 420
Charlotte, NC USA 28209
Phone: 7044093334
Fax: 7044093330

10955 Lowell Avenue, Suite 600
Shawnee Mission, KS USA 66210
Phone: 9132532202

Management and Staff

David Scanlan, Co-Founder
James Cook, Co-Founder
Mark Demetree, Co-Founder
Matthew Sheehy, Principal
Ted Gardner, Co-Founder

Type of Firm

Private Equity Firm

Project Preferences

Type of Financing Preferred:
Leveraged Buyout
Mezzanine
Management Buyouts
Acquisition

Size of Investments Considered:
Min Size of Investment Considered (000s): $10,000
Max Size of Investment Considered (000s): $35,000

Geographical Preferences

International Preferences:
Europe
Eastern Europe

Industry Preferences

In Medical/Health prefer:
Medical/Health

In Consumer Related prefer:
Consumer Services

In Industrial/Energy prefer:
Energy
Oil and Gas Exploration
Industrial Products

In Business Serv. prefer:
Services
Distribution

In Manufact. prefer:
Manufacturing

Additional Information

Name of Most Recent Fund: Silverhawk Capital Partners II, L.P.
Most Recent Fund Was Raised: 01/25/2010
Year Founded: 2005
Capital Under Management: $46,300,000
Current Activity Level : Actively seeking new investments

SILVERSMITH CAPITAL PARTNERS LLC

177 Huntington Avenue
25th Floor
Boston, MA USA 02115
Phone: 617-359-1286
E-mail: nfo@silversmithcapital.com

Management and Staff

Brian Peterson, Vice President
Jeffrey Crisan, Managing Partner
Jim Quagliaroli, Co-Founder
Lori Whelan, Co-Founder
Marc Munfa, Principal
Sri Rao, Vice President
Todd MacLean, Co-Founder

Type of Firm

Private Equity Firm

Project Preferences

Type of Financing Preferred:
Later Stage

Industry Preferences

In Computer Software prefer:
Systems Software
Applications Software

In Medical/Health prefer:
Health Services

Additional Information

Year Founded: 2015
Capital Under Management: $460,000,000
Current Activity Level : Actively seeking new investments

SILVERSTREAM CAPITAL LLC

4747 Executive Drive, Suite 1010
San Diego, CA USA 92121
Phone: 8587905850
Website: www.silverstreamcapital.com

Management and Staff

Anand Gowda, Managing Partner
Brett Doyle, Principal
Cary Devore, Managing Director
David Keane, Chief Financial Officer
George Goldstein, Managing Director
Matt Simas, Managing Director
Patrick Cook, Vice President

Type of Firm

Private Equity Firm

Project Preferences

Type of Financing Preferred:
Leveraged Buyout
Expansion
Recapitalizations

Geographical Preferences

United States Preferences:
North America

International Preferences:
Europe

Industry Preferences

In Computer Software prefer:
Software

In Medical/Health prefer:
Medical/Health

Additional Information

Year Founded: 1969
Current Activity Level : Actively seeking new investments

SILVERSTREET CAPITAL LLP

33, St. James' Square
London, United Kingdom SW1Y 4JS
Phone: 442073314320
Website: www.silverstreetcapital.com

Other Offices
6, Rue Gabriel Lippmann
Munsbach, Luxembourg 5365

Type of Firm
Private Equity Firm

Project Preferences

Type of Financing Preferred:
Balanced

Geographical Preferences

International Preferences:
Zambia
Tanzania
Africa

Industry Preferences

In Agr/Forestr/Fish prefer:
Agribusiness
Agriculture related

Additional Information
Year Founded: 2010
Current Activity Level : Actively seeking new investments

SILVERTON PARTNERS

1000 Rio Grande Street
Austin, TX USA 78701
Phone: 5124766700
Fax: 5124770025
Website: www.silvertonpartners.com

Type of Firm
Private Equity Firm

Association Membership
Canadian Venture Capital Association

Project Preferences

Type of Financing Preferred:
Early Stage
Seed
Startup

Size of Investments Considered:
Min Size of Investment Considered (000s): $200
Max Size of Investment Considered (000s): $2,000

Geographical Preferences

United States Preferences:
Texas

Industry Preferences

In Computer Software prefer:
Software

In Internet Specific prefer:
Internet

Additional Information
Name of Most Recent Fund: Silverton Partners IV, L.P.
Most Recent Fund Was Raised: 11/07/2013
Year Founded: 2000
Capital Under Management: $75,000,000
Current Activity Level : Actively seeking new investments

SIMA CAPITAL HOLDING COMPANY KSCC

Rakan Tower 19th Floor
Fahad Al Salem Street
Kuwait City, Kuwait
Phone: 96522412369
Fax: 96522401429
E-mail: investor@simacap.com

Type of Firm
Private Equity Firm

Project Preferences

Type of Financing Preferred:
Early Stage
Balanced
Later Stage
Seed
Strategic Alliances

Geographical Preferences

International Preferences:
Middle East
Asia

Industry Preferences

In Communications prefer:
Telecommunications

In Consumer Related prefer:
Consumer
Retail
Food/Beverage

In Transportation prefer:
Transportation

In Financial Services prefer:
Real Estate

Additional Information
Year Founded: 2009
Current Activity Level : Actively seeking new investments

SIMAKH INVEST ZAO

Tvardovskogo Street
Building Eight
Moscow, Russia 123458
Phone: 74952255809
E-mail: info@geneziscap.com
Website: geneziscap.com

Type of Firm
Private Equity Firm

Project Preferences

Type of Financing Preferred:
Early Stage
Balanced
Later Stage
Seed

Size of Investments Considered:
Min Size of Investment Considered (000s): $0
Max Size of Investment Considered (000s): $20,000

Geographical Preferences

United States Preferences:

International Preferences:
Europe
Asia
Russia

Industry Preferences

In Biotechnology prefer:
Biotechnology

In Industrial/Energy prefer:
Alternative Energy
Robotics
Environmental Related

Additional Information
Year Founded: 2012
Current Activity Level : Actively seeking new investments

SIMFONEC CO

Cass Business School
106 Bunhill Row
London, United Kingdom EC1Y 8TZ
Phone: 44-20-7040-8726
Fax: 44-20-7040-8882
E-mail: info@simfonec.co.uk
Website: www.simfonec.co.uk

Type of Firm
University Program

Project Preferences

Type of Financing Preferred:
Early Stage
Seed
Startup

Geographical Preferences

International Preferences:
United Kingdom
Europe

Industry Preferences

In Biotechnology prefer:
Biotechnology

In Medical/Health prefer:
Medical/Health
Pharmaceuticals

Additional Information

Year Founded: 2003
Current Activity Level : Actively seeking new investments

SIMILE VENTURE PARTNERS

68/70 Butyrskiy Val Street
Building 9
Moscow, Russia 127055
Phone: 74959677376
Fax: 74957907528
Website: www.simileventure.com

Type of Firm
Private Equity Firm

Project Preferences

Type of Financing Preferred:
Early Stage
Seed
Startup

Geographical Preferences

International Preferences:
Europe
Russia

Industry Preferences

In Communications prefer:
Media and Entertainment

In Internet Specific prefer:
Internet

Additional Information
Year Founded: 2012
Current Activity Level : Actively seeking new investments

SIMMONS & COMPANY INTERNATIONAL

700 Louisiana, Suite 1900
Houston, TX USA 77002
Phone: 713-236-9999
Fax: 713-223-7800
E-mail: info@simmonsco-intl.com
Website: www.simmonsco-intl.com

Other Offices
Simmons House
22 Waverley Place
Aberdeen, United Kingdom AB10 1XP
Phone: 44-12-2420-2300
Fax: 44-12-2420-2303

Type of Firm
SBIC

Project Preferences

Type of Financing Preferred:
Leveraged Buyout
Expansion
Other
Acquisition

Geographical Preferences

International Preferences:
Asia Pacific
Europe
Australia
Asia
Africa

Industry Preferences

In Industrial/Energy prefer:
Energy
Oil & Gas Drilling,Explor
Alternative Energy

Additional Information
Year Founded: 1979
Capital Under Management: $66,961,000
Current Activity Level : Actively seeking new investments

SIMON EQUITY PARTNERS LLC

101 Mission St., Suite 1115
San Francisco, CA USA 94105
Phone: 4158560569
E-mail: info@simonequity.com
Website: www.simonequity.com

Management and Staff
Jonathan Rosenbaum, Managing Partner
Stephen Simon, Co-Founder

Type of Firm
Private Equity Firm

Additional Information
Year Founded: 2014
Current Activity Level : Actively seeking new investments

SIMPLEPITCH VENTURES

3404 Via Lido, Suite B
Newport Beach, CA USA 92663
Website: www.thesimplepitch.com

Type of Firm
Private Equity Firm

Project Preferences

Type of Financing Preferred:
Balanced
Later Stage
Startup

Additional Information
Year Founded: 1969
Current Activity Level : Actively seeking new investments

SINCLAIR VENTURES INC

10706 Beaver Dam Road
Hunt Valley, MD USA 21030
Phone: 4105681500
Fax: 4105681533
Website: www.sbgi.net/business/ventures.shtml

Management and Staff
Donald Thompson, Vice President
Frederick Smith, Vice President
James Smith, Vice President
Paul Nesterovsky, Vice President
Thomas Waters, Vice President

Type of Firm
Corporate PE/Venture

Project Preferences

Type of Financing Preferred:
Second Stage Financing
Early Stage
First Stage Financing

Size of Investments Considered:
Min Size of Investment Considered (000s): $500
Max Size of Investment Considered (000s): $5,000

Geographical Preferences

United States Preferences:

Industry Preferences

In Communications prefer:
Radio & TV Broadcasting
Wireless Communications
Media and Entertainment

In Computer Software prefer:
Software

In Internet Specific prefer:
Internet

In Consumer Related prefer:
Consumer Services

In Financial Services prefer:
Investment Groups

In Business Serv. prefer:
Media

Additional Information
Year Founded: 1999
Capital Under Management: $40,000,000
Current Activity Level : Actively seeking new investments

SINDICATUM CARBON CAPITAL LTD

5th Floor
18 Hanover Square
London, United Kingdom W1S 1HX
Phone: 44-20-3008-8602
Fax: 44-20-3008-4752
E-mail: info@sindicatum.com

Other Offices
69 Road 161
PO box 2
Cairo, Egypt 11431
Phone: 2-2-528-3693

Rua Sao Tome
86-11th floor
Sao Paulo, Brazil 04551-080
Phone: 55-11-3055-2050
Fax: 55-11-3055-2050

Culiacan 123 Col.
Hipodromo Condesa C.P
Mexico, Mexico
Phone: 52-55-5265-1230
Fax: 52-55-5265-1246

Tengda Building No 168
Xiwai Street
Beijing, China 100044
Phone: 86-10-8857-6830

Wisma 46 Kota BNI
Jalan Jendral Sudirman Kav. 1
Jakarta, Indonesia 10220
Phone: 62-817-076-9030
Fax: 62-21-251-4719

598 Madison Avenue
9th floor
New York, NY USA 10022
Phone: 212-508-3620
Fax: 212-508-3629

138 Rue du Faubourg St. Honore
Paris, France 75008
Phone: 33-1-5353-0808
Fax: 33-1-5353-0800

IBC Building F
Seimyniskiu g. 3
Vilnius, Lithuania 09310
Phone: 370-5-263-8787
Fax: 370-5-263-6242

6 Duke Street
London, United Kingdom W1U 3EN
Phone: 44-20-7224-7555
Fax: 44-20-7224-7333

Management and Staff
Assaad Razzouk, Chief Executive Officer
David Carew, Co-Founder
Susan Wood, Chief Executive Officer

Type of Firm
Bank Affiliated

Project Preferences

Type of Financing Preferred:
Balanced

Geographical Preferences

International Preferences:
Europe

Industry Preferences

In Industrial/Energy prefer:
Energy

Additional Information
Year Founded: 2002
Current Activity Level : Actively seeking new investments

SINGAPORE POWER GROUP

111 Somerset Road
#16-01
Singapore, Singapore 238164
Phone: 6823-8888
Fax: 6823-8188
Website: www.singaporepower.com

Type of Firm
Private Equity Firm

Additional Information
Year Founded: 2001
Current Activity Level : Actively seeking new investments

SINGAPORE TECHNOLOGIES KINETICS LTD

5 Portsdown Road
Singapore, Singapore 139296
Website: www.stengg.com

Type of Firm
Private Equity Firm

Project Preferences

Type of Financing Preferred:
Balanced

Additional Information
Year Founded: 2001
Current Activity Level : Actively seeking new investments

SINGAPORE TECHNOLOGIES TELEMEDIA PTE LTD

1 Temasek Avenue
#33-01 Millenia Tower
Singapore, Singapore 039192
Phone: 6567238777
Fax: 6567207266
Website: www.sttelemedia.com

Type of Firm
Investment Management Firm

Project Preferences

Type of Financing Preferred:
Balanced

Geographical Preferences

International Preferences:
Singapore

Industry Preferences

In Communications prefer:
Telecommunications
Wireless Communications
Data Communications

In Internet Specific prefer:
Internet

Additional Information
Year Founded: 1994
Current Activity Level : Actively seeking new investments

SINGLE OAK VENTURES LP

25240 Hancock Avenue, Suite 405
Murrieta, CA USA 92562
Phone: 8666036484
E-mail: info@singleoakvc.com
Website: www.singleoakvc.com

Management and Staff
Bennett Yankowitz, Managing Partner
James Smythe, Partner
Louis Petrossi, Partner
Ralph Williams, Founder
Stephen Espinosa, Founder
Tom Jones, Partner

Type of Firm
Private Equity Firm

Project Preferences

Type of Financing Preferred:
Fund of Funds

Additional Information
Year Founded: 2015
Capital Under Management: $250,000
Current Activity Level : Actively seeking new investments

SINGULARITEAM LTD

Berkovitz Four
18th Floor
Tel Aviv, Israel
E-mail: info@singulariteam.com
Website: www.singulariteam.com

Management and Staff
Kenges Rakishev, Managing Partner

Type of Firm
Private Equity Firm

Project Preferences

Type of Financing Preferred:
Early Stage
Start-up Financing
Seed
Startup

Geographical Preferences

International Preferences:
Israel

Industry Preferences

In Communications prefer:
Wireless Communications

In Computer Software prefer:
Artificial Intelligence

In Industrial/Energy prefer:
Robotics

Additional Information
Year Founded: 2012
Capital Under Management: $202,000,000
Current Activity Level : Actively seeking new investments

SINGULARITY INVESTMENTS LLC

3529 Marquette Street
Dallas, TX USA 75225
E-mail: InfoNA@SingularityInvest.com
Website: singularityinvest.com

Management and Staff
Issam Darwish, Principal
Mohamad Darwish, Principal

Type of Firm
Private Equity Firm

Project Preferences

Type of Financing Preferred:
Early Stage

Geographical Preferences

United States Preferences:

International Preferences:
Africa

Additional Information
Year Founded: 2016
Current Activity Level : Actively seeking new investments

SINO H & B PRIVATE EQUITY FUND CO LTD

No. 7 Jinrong Street
Rm 901, Winland Int'l Center
Beijing, China 100033
Phone: 861064088105
Fax: 861064088155
E-mail: info@surelandcap.com
Website: www.surelandcap.com

Type of Firm
Private Equity Firm

Association Membership
Venture Capital Association of Beijing (VCAB)

Project Preferences

Type of Financing Preferred:
Balanced

Geographical Preferences

International Preferences:
China

Industry Preferences

In Consumer Related prefer:
Consumer Services

In Industrial/Energy prefer:
Environmental Related

In Financial Services prefer:
Financial Services

In Manufact. prefer:
Manufacturing

Additional Information
Year Founded: 2007
Current Activity Level : Actively seeking new investments

SINO IC CAPITAL CO LTD

Economic and Technological Dev
Room 707, 7F, Block 52, No. 2
Beijing, China

Type of Firm
Government Affiliated Program

Project Preferences

Type of Financing Preferred:
Balanced

Geographical Preferences

International Preferences:
China

Industry Preferences

In Semiconductor/Electr prefer:
Circuit Boards

Additional Information
Year Founded: 2014
Capital Under Management: $14,231,970,000
Current Activity Level : Actively seeking new investments

SINO RESOURCES INVESTMENT CO LTD

9A Financial Street Center
Room 301
Beijing, China
Phone: 86-10-66013895
Fax: 86-10-66014585

Management and Staff
Hongtao Yang, President
Liang Zhou, Vice President

Type of Firm
Bank Affiliated

Additional Information
Year Founded: 2010
Current Activity Level : Actively seeking new investments

SINO-CAN HARVEST CAPITAL CO LTD

No. 91 Jianguo Road
3201-3207, Gemdale Plaza A
Beijing, China 100022
Phone: 01085597685
Fax: 01085597686
Website: www.scharvestcap.com

Management and Staff
Dawei Xu, Partner
Xiongzhi Wu, Vice President

Type of Firm
Private Equity Firm

Project Preferences

Type of Financing Preferred:
Expansion
Balanced
Later Stage

Geographical Preferences

International Preferences:
China

Industry Preferences

In Semiconductor/Electr prefer:
Electronics

In Medical/Health prefer:
Medical/Health

In Consumer Related prefer:
Entertainment and Leisure
Retail
Food/Beverage
Education Related

In Industrial/Energy prefer:
Energy
Materials
Machinery
Environmental Related

In Business Serv. prefer:
Services
Media

In Agr/Forestr/Fish prefer:
Agriculture related

In Other prefer:
Environment Responsible

Additional Information

Year Founded: 2008
Capital Under Management: $560,800,000
Current Activity Level : Actively seeking new investments

SINOLATIN CAPITAL

No. 1518-A, Min Sheng Lu, Suite 703A, Building A
Shanghai, China 200135
Phone: 862161099568
Fax: 862161099570
E-mail: info@sinolatincapital.com
Website: www.sinolatincapital.com

Management and Staff

Erik Bethel, Partner
Jorge Barreda, Partner
Luis Gomez Cobo, Partner
Mei Lu, Partner

Type of Firm

Bank Affiliated

Project Preferences

Type of Financing Preferred:
Leveraged Buyout
Acquisition

Geographical Preferences

International Preferences:
Latin America

Industry Preferences

In Industrial/Energy prefer:
Energy
Industrial Products

In Agr/Forestr/Fish prefer:
Agribusiness
Mining and Minerals

Additional Information

Year Founded: 2009
Current Activity Level : Actively seeking new investments

SINOVATION VENTURES LTD

10F, Office Building,Block A
No. 3, Haidian Street, Haidian
Beijing, China 100080
Phone: 861057525200
E-mail: contact@chuangxin.com
Website: www.sinovationventures.com

Management and Staff

Chris Evdemon, Partner
Christine Lang, Partner
Grace Xu, Vice President
John Qiu, Partner
Tina Tao, Chief Operating Officer
Xiuping Liu, Chief Financial Officer
Ye Wang, Founder

Type of Firm

Incubator/Development Program

Project Preferences

Type of Financing Preferred:
Early Stage
Balanced
Seed

Geographical Preferences

International Preferences:
China

Industry Preferences

In Internet Specific prefer:
E-Commerce Technology
Internet

Additional Information

Year Founded: 2009
Capital Under Management: $415,922,000
Current Activity Level : Actively seeking new investments

SINTEF MRB

Kongens plass 5
Kristiansund, Norway 6501
Phone: 4771573330
Fax: 4771573311

Type of Firm

Private Equity Firm

Project Preferences

Type of Financing Preferred:
Early Stage
Seed
Startup

Geographical Preferences

International Preferences:
Norway

Industry Preferences

In Communications prefer:
Wireless Communications

In Consumer Related prefer:
Food/Beverage

In Industrial/Energy prefer:
Alternative Energy
Energy Conservation Relat

In Business Serv. prefer:
Services

In Other prefer:
Environment Responsible

Additional Information

Year Founded: 2007
Capital Under Management: $28,900,000
Current Activity Level : Actively seeking new investments

SIPADAN CAPITAL

50 Broad Street
New York, NY USA 10004
Phone: 2125949861
Website: www.sipadancapital.com

Type of Firm

Private Equity Firm

Project Preferences

Type of Financing Preferred:
Early Stage
Expansion
Later Stage
Seed
Acquisition

1954

Industry Preferences

In Consumer Related prefer:
Consumer Products

Additional Information

Year Founded: 2017
Current Activity Level : Actively seeking new investments

SIPAREX GROUP

139, rue Vendome
Lyon, France 69006
Phone: 33472832323
Fax: 33472832300
E-mail: siparex@siparex.com
Website: www.siparex.com

Other Offices

1400 Fashion Island Boulevard, Suite 600
SAN MATEO, CA USA 94404
Phone: 650-522-0085
Fax: 650-522-0087

Via San Maurilio
Milan, Italy 20123
Phone: 39-02-3655-5373
Fax: 39-02-805-5252

37/41, rue de la Barre
Lille, France 59005
Phone: 33-3-2017-6600
Fax: 33-3-2014-2131

10 Rue Schimper
Strasbourg, France 67000
Phone: 33-03-8823-6168
Fax: 33-3-8823-6326

9, Avenue des Montboucons
Temis Center 2
Besancon, France 25000
Phone: 33-3-8125-0614
Fax: 33-3-2125-0613

27, Boulevard de la Corderie
Limousin, France 87031
Phone: 33587310012

27, rue Marbeuf
Paris, France 75008
Phone: 33-1-5393-0220
Fax: 33-1-5393-0230

Calle Serrano 88
Madrid, Spain 28006
Phone: 34-91-400-5464
Fax: 39-41-435-3593

Management and Staff

Antonie Krug, Managing Director
Bertrand Rambaud, Chief Executive Officer
Bertrand Robert, Managing Director
Dominique Nouvellet, Founder
Florent Lauzet, Managing Director
Jerome Burtin, Managing Partner
Olivier Richard, Managing Director
Patric Blasselle, Managing Director
Pierre Bordeaux Montrieux, Managing Director
Thierry Candelier, Managing Director
Valerie Gerbet, Chief Financial Officer

Type of Firm

Private Equity Firm

Association Membership

French Venture Capital Association (AFIC)
European Private Equity and Venture Capital Assoc.

Project Preferences

Type of Financing Preferred:
Second Stage Financing
Leveraged Buyout
Early Stage
Expansion
Generalist PE
Later Stage
Management Buyouts
Acquisition
Startup
Recapitalizations

Size of Investments Considered:
Min Size of Investment Considered (000s): $1,271
Max Size of Investment Considered (000s): $25,432

Geographical Preferences

United States Preferences:

International Preferences:
Italy
Europe
Portugal
Spain
Belgium
France

Industry Focus

(% based on actual investment)
Other Products	23.7%
Consumer Related	17.6%
Internet Specific	15.3%
Industrial/Energy	11.8%
Semiconductors/Other Elect.	10.1%
Computer Software and Services	7.5%
Medical/Health	5.4%
Biotechnology	3.7%
Communications and Media	2.6%
Computer Hardware	2.3%

Additional Information

Year Founded: 1977
Capital Under Management: $1,113,100,000
Current Activity Level : Actively seeking new investments

SIPAREX PROXIMITE INNOVATION SAS

27 Rue Marbeuf
Paris, France 75008
Phone: 33144561000
Fax: 33144561100
E-mail: contact-ufgpe@groupe-ufg.com
Website: xange.biz

Other Offices

17 rue de Marigan
Paris, France 75008
Phone: 33-1-7300-7300
Fax: 33-1-7300-7301

Management and Staff

Alain Wicker, Vice President
Alain Grec, Managing Director
Alain Gerbaldi, Managing Director
Guy Lepage, Managing Director
Jean-Marc Coly, Managing Director
Marc Bertrand, Managing Director
Partick Riviere, Managing Director
Pascale Auclair, Managing Director
Philippe Verdier, Managing Director

Type of Firm

Private Equity Firm

Association Membership

French Venture Capital Association (AFIC)

Project Preferences

Type of Financing Preferred:
Fund of Funds
Leveraged Buyout
Early Stage
Generalist PE
Later Stage
Management Buyouts
Acquisition

Geographical Preferences

United States Preferences:
All U.S.

International Preferences:
Italy
Sweden
Luxembourg
Europe
Switzerland
Monaco
Spain
Belgium
Asia
Finland
Norway
Germany
Denmark
France

Industry Preferences

In Communications prefer:
Wireless Communications

In Consumer Related prefer:
Retail

In Industrial/Energy prefer:
Alternative Energy
Advanced Materials

In Business Serv. prefer:
Media

Additional Information

Year Founded: 2004
Capital Under Management: $253,400,000
Current Activity Level : Actively seeking new investments

SIPPL MACDONALD VENTURES

1422 El Camino Real
Menlo Park, CA USA 94025
Phone: 6505666860
Fax: 6503264404
Website: www.sipmac.com

Management and Staff

Glenn Myers, Chief Financial Officer
Jacqueline Macdonald, Partner
Roger Sippl, Partner

Type of Firm

Private Equity Firm

Project Preferences

Type of Financing Preferred:
Early Stage
Expansion
Later Stage

Size of Investments Considered:
Min Size of Investment Considered (000s): $200
Max Size of Investment Considered (000s): $750

Geographical Preferences

United States Preferences:
California
West Coast

Industry Focus

(% based on actual investment)
Computer Software and Services	84.4%
Internet Specific	14.6%
Communications and Media	0.5%
Other Products	0.4%

Additional Information

Name of Most Recent Fund: Sippl Macdonald Ventures II, L.P.
Most Recent Fund Was Raised: 11/01/1997
Year Founded: 1995

Capital Under Management: $30,000,000
Current Activity Level : Actively seeking new investments

SIRAJ FUND MANAGEMENT CO

P.O. Box 1218
Ramallah, Israel
Phone: 972-2-240-9108
Fax: 972-2-240-9752
E-mail: info@siraj.ps
Website: www.siraj.ps

Management and Staff

Bashar Masri, Founder
Samir Hulileh, Chief Executive Officer

Type of Firm

Private Equity Firm

Project Preferences

Type of Financing Preferred:
Leveraged Buyout
Early Stage
Expansion
Research and Development
Balanced
Later Stage
Seed
Acquisition
Startup
Distressed Debt

Geographical Preferences

International Preferences:
Israel

Industry Preferences

In Biotechnology prefer:
Agricultural/Animal Bio.

In Medical/Health prefer:
Health Services

In Consumer Related prefer:
Education Related

In Transportation prefer:
Transportation

In Financial Services prefer:
Financial Services

In Manufact. prefer:
Manufacturing

In Agr/Forestr/Fish prefer:
Agriculture related

Additional Information

Name of Most Recent Fund: Siraj Palestine Fund I
Most Recent Fund Was Raised: 02/03/2011
Year Founded: 2011
Capital Under Management: $60,000,000

Current Activity Level : Actively seeking new investments

SIRIS CAPITAL GROUP LLC

601 Lexington Avenue
59th Floor
New York, NY USA 10022
Phone: 2122310095
Fax: 2122312680
Website: www.siriscapital.com

Management and Staff

Ciara Roche, Chief Operating Officer
Elias Mendoza, Managing Director
Frank Baker, Co-Founder
Ian Silverman, Chief Financial Officer
Jeffrey Hendren, Co-Founder
Jerry Stapp, Vice President
Peter Berger, Co-Founder
Philip Lo, Vice President

Type of Firm

Private Equity Firm

Project Preferences

Type of Financing Preferred:
Leveraged Buyout
Acquisition
Special Situation

Geographical Preferences

United States Preferences:
North America

Industry Preferences

In Communications prefer:
Telecommunications
Data Communications

In Medical/Health prefer:
Medical/Health

In Business Serv. prefer:
Services

Additional Information

Name of Most Recent Fund: Siris Partners II, L.P.
Most Recent Fund Was Raised: 09/26/2011
Year Founded: 2011
Capital Under Management: $2,291,068,000
Current Activity Level : Actively seeking new investments

SIRIUS VENTURE CONSULTING PTE LTD

30 Cecil Street
#15-00 Prudential Tower
Singapore, Singapore 049712
Phone: 6562322742
Fax: 6562322888
E-mail: general@sirius.com.sg
Website: www.sirius.com.sg

Other Offices

555 Bryant Street, Suite 190
Palo Alto, CA USA 94301

Kamiyacho MT Building, 14th Floor
4-3-20 Toranomon Minato-ku
Tokyo, Japan 105-0001
Phone: 813-4496-4481
Fax: 813-4496-4481

489 Hennessy Road
Unit 2202, Causeway Bay Plaza I
Causeway Bay, Hong Kong
Phone: 852-3588-1759
Fax: 852-2536-0804

Management and Staff

Eugene Wong, Managing Director
Rosita Wu, Partner

Type of Firm

Service Provider

Association Membership

Singapore Venture Capital Association (SVCA)

Project Preferences

Role in Financing:
Prefer role as deal originator but will also invest in deals created by others

Type of Financing Preferred:
Early Stage
Expansion
Later Stage
Seed
Startup
Recapitalizations

Geographical Preferences

United States Preferences:
All U.S.

International Preferences:
Indonesia
China
Singapore
Japan

Industry Preferences

In Semiconductor/Electr prefer:
Electronics

In Consumer Related prefer:
Consumer
Food/Beverage

In Industrial/Energy prefer:
Energy
Environmental Related

In Transportation prefer:
Transportation

In Business Serv. prefer:
Services

In Manufact. prefer:
Manufacturing

Additional Information

Year Founded: 2002
Current Activity Level : Actively seeking new investments

SIRIUS VENTURE PARTNERS GMBH

Biebricher Allee 22
Wiesbaden, Germany 65187
Phone: 496116966990
Fax: 4961169669990
E-mail: info@sirius-venture.com
Website: www.sirius-venture.com

Other Offices

Merowingerplatz 1
Dusseldorf, Germany 40225
Phone: 49-211-542-1530
Fax: 49-211-5421-5390

Management and Staff

Ernst Mayer, Managing Partner
Friedrich von Diest, Managing Partner

Type of Firm

Private Equity Firm

Association Membership

German Venture Capital Association (BVK)

Project Preferences

Type of Financing Preferred:
Early Stage
Later Stage
Seed
Startup

Size of Investments Considered:
Min Size of Investment Considered (000s): $196
Max Size of Investment Considered (000s): $1,957

Geographical Preferences

International Preferences:
Switzerland
Austria
Germany

Industry Preferences

In Communications prefer:
Communications and Media

In Biotechnology prefer:
Biotechnology

In Medical/Health prefer:
Medical/Health

In Industrial/Energy prefer:
Energy
Alternative Energy
Energy Conservation Relat
Materials
Environmental Related

In Business Serv. prefer:
Services

In Other prefer:
Environment Responsible

Additional Information

Name of Most Recent Fund: Sirius EcoTech Fonds Duesseldorf GmbH & Co. KG
Most Recent Fund Was Raised: 08/30/2009
Year Founded: 2004
Current Activity Level : Actively seeking new investments

SISTEMA INVESTIMENTI SPA

Via Santa Maria di Betlem 18
Catania, Italy 95131
E-mail: info@sistemainvestimenti.com
Website: www.sistemainvestimenti.com

Type of Firm

Private Equity Firm

Additional Information

Year Founded: 2014
Current Activity Level : Actively seeking new investments

SIX SQUARED CAPITAL

3300 Bloor Street West
Toronto, Canada
Website: www.sixsquaredcapital.com

Type of Firm

Private Equity Firm

Project Preferences

Type of Financing Preferred:
Early Stage
Seed

Geographical Preferences

Canadian Preferences:
Ontario

Industry Preferences

In Computer Software prefer:
Systems Software

In Medical/Health prefer:
Medical/Health

Additional Information
Year Founded: 2014
Current Activity Level : Actively seeking new investments

SIX THIRTY

911 Washington Ave, Suite 801
Saint Louis, MO USA 63101
Phone: 3146696803
E-mail: hello@sixthirty.co
Website: www.sixthirty.co

Management and Staff
Jim McKelvey, Managing Director
Kasey Joyce, Principal
Matt Menietti, Venture Partner

Type of Firm
Incubator/Development Program

Project Preferences

Type of Financing Preferred:
Early Stage
Startup

Geographical Preferences

United States Preferences:
All U.S.

Industry Preferences

In Financial Services prefer:
Financial Services

Additional Information
Year Founded: 2013
Capital Under Management: $1,000,000
Current Activity Level : Actively seeking new investments

SIXPOINT PARTNERS LLC

830 Third Avenue
8th Floor
New York, NY USA 10022
Phone: 7518690
Fax: 7510197
E-mail: info@sixpointpartners.com
Website: www.sixpointpartners.com

Management and Staff
Ben Wiley, Partner
Bobby Farina, Partner
Eric Zoller, Founder
Joan Tan, Managing Director
Laurence Smith, Partner
Matthew Thornton, Partner
Ryan Carey, Vice President
Sean Joffe, Vice President
Shawn Schestag, Managing Director
Werner Albeseder, Partner

Type of Firm
Private Equity Firm

Project Preferences

Type of Financing Preferred:
Generalist PE

Additional Information
Year Founded: 2007
Current Activity Level : Actively seeking new investments

SIXTH SWEDISH NATIONAL PENSION

Ostra Hamngatan 18
Gothenburg, Sweden 411 09
Phone: 46317411000
Fax: 46317411098
E-mail: info@apfond6.se
Website: www.apfond6.se

Management and Staff
Henrik Dahl, Chief Financial Officer
Karl Swartling, Chief Executive Officer

Type of Firm
Endowment, Foundation or Pension Fund

Association Membership
Swedish Venture Capital Association (SVCA)
European Private Equity and Venture Capital Assoc.

Project Preferences

Type of Financing Preferred:
Fund of Funds
Balanced

Geographical Preferences

International Preferences:
Scandanavia/Nordic Region

Industry Preferences

In Communications prefer:
Communications and Media
Telecommunications
Wireless Communications

In Computer Software prefer:
Software

In Semiconductor/Electr prefer:
Electronics

In Biotechnology prefer:
Biotechnology

In Medical/Health prefer:
Medical/Health
Pharmaceuticals

In Industrial/Energy prefer:
Industrial Products

In Transportation prefer:
Transportation

In Financial Services prefer:
Real Estate

Additional Information
Year Founded: 1996
Capital Under Management: $3,068,700,000
Current Activity Level : Actively seeking new investments

SJ PARTNERS LLC

250 Park Avenue South
7th Floor
New York, NY USA 10019
Phone: 2123621530
Website: www.sjpartners.com

Type of Firm
Private Equity Firm

Project Preferences

Type of Financing Preferred:
Leveraged Buyout
Acquisition

Industry Preferences

In Consumer Related prefer:
Consumer
Sports
Food/Beverage

In Transportation prefer:
Aerospace

In Business Serv. prefer:
Services

Additional Information
Year Founded: 2001
Current Activity Level : Actively seeking new investments

SJF VENTURES

200 North Magnum Street, Suite 203
Durham, NC USA 27701
Phone: 9195301177
Fax: 9195301178
Website: www.sjfventures.com

Other Offices

885 Third Avenue
20th Floor
NEW YORK, NY USA 10022
Phone: 2122093063
Fax: 2123715500

700 Larkspur Landing Circle, Suite 199
LARKSPUR, CA USA 94939
Phone: 4156598277

101 California Street, Suite 2450
SAN FRANCISCO, CA USA 94111
Phone: 4156598277

Management and Staff
Alan Kelley, Managing Director
Arrun Kapoor, Managing Director
Cody Nystrom, Managing Director
David Kirkpatrick, Co-Founder
David Griest, Managing Director
Rick Defieux, Founder

Type of Firm
Private Equity Firm

Association Membership
Community Development Venture Capital Alliance
Natl Assoc of Small Bus. Inv. Co (NASBIC)

Project Preferences

Role in Financing:
Will function either as deal originator or investor in deals created by others

Type of Financing Preferred:
Early Stage
Expansion
Balanced

Size of Investments Considered:
Min Size of Investment Considered (000s): $1,000
Max Size of Investment Considered (000s): $10,000

Geographical Preferences

United States Preferences:

Industry Preferences

In Medical/Health prefer:
Medical/Health

In Consumer Related prefer:
Consumer
Consumer Products

In Industrial/Energy prefer:
Alternative Energy

In Business Serv. prefer:
Services
Media

In Other prefer:
Socially Responsible
Environment Responsible
Women/Minority-Owned Bus.

Additional Information
Name of Most Recent Fund: SJF Ventures III, L.P.
Most Recent Fund Was Raised: 03/07/2012
Year Founded: 1999
Capital Under Management: $90,000,000
Current Activity Level : Actively seeking new investments
Method of Compensation: Return on investment is of primary concern, do not charge fees

SK CAPITAL PARTNERS LP
400 Park Avenue, Suite 810
New York, NY USA 10022
Phone: 2128262700
Fax: 2128674525
E-mail: inquiries@skcapitalpartners.com
Website: www.skcapitalpartners.com

Other Offices
1515 North Federal Highway, Suite 405
Boca Raton, FL USA 33432
Phone: (561) 362-6370
Fax: (561) 362-6353

Management and Staff
Aaron Davenport, Managing Director
Barry Siadat, Managing Director
Carrie Fischer, Chief Financial Officer
Edward Donkor, Principal
Ian McKelvie, Vice President
Jack Norris, Managing Director
James Marden, Managing Director
Jamshid Keynejad, Managing Director
Stephen d Incelli, Principal

Type of Firm
Private Equity Firm

Project Preferences

Type of Financing Preferred:
Leveraged Buyout

Geographical Preferences

United States Preferences:

International Preferences:
Europe
Asia

Industry Preferences

In Medical/Health prefer:
Medical/Health

In Industrial/Energy prefer:
Industrial Products
Materials

Additional Information
Name of Most Recent Fund: SK Capital Partners IV, L.P.
Most Recent Fund Was Raised: 12/02/2014
Year Founded: 2007
Capital Under Management: $1,500,000,000
Current Activity Level : Actively seeking new investments

SK TELECOM CO LTD
11, Euljiro, 2-ga, Jung-gu
Jung-gu
Seoul, South Korea 100999
Phone: 82-2-61002114
E-mail: press@sktelecom.com
Website: www.sktelecom.com

Type of Firm
Private Equity Firm

Additional Information
Year Founded: 1984
Current Activity Level : Actively seeking new investments

SK VENTURES LLC
6547 Midnight Pass Road, Suite 39
Siesta Key, FL USA 34242
Phone: 6508435294
Website: www.skvcap.com

Management and Staff
Paul Kedrosky, General Partner

Type of Firm
Private Equity Firm

Project Preferences

Type of Financing Preferred:
Seed

Geographical Preferences

United States Preferences:
All U.S.

Additional Information
Name of Most Recent Fund: SK Ventures I, L.P.
Most Recent Fund Was Raised: 05/17/2011
Year Founded: 2011
Capital Under Management: $1,120,000
Current Activity Level : Actively seeking new investments

SKAGERAK VENTURE CAPITAL AS
Markens gate 9
Kristiansand, Norway 4610
Phone: 4721002700
E-mail: post@svc.no
Website: www.svc.no

Other Offices
Tordenskioldsgate 6 B
Oslo, Norway 0160
Phone: 4791519207

Storgata 8
Kongsberg, Norway 3611
Phone: 4795270739

Management and Staff
Andre Edvardsen, Chief Financial Officer
Erik Toennesen, Managing Partner
Jorn Lindtvedt, Partner
Terje Berg-Utby, Partner

Type of Firm
Private Equity Firm

Association Membership
Norwegian Venture Capital Association

Project Preferences

Type of Financing Preferred:
Early Stage
Later Stage
Seed

Geographical Preferences

International Preferences:
Scandanavia/Nordic Region

Industry Preferences

In Communications prefer:
Communications and Media
Wireless Communications

In Computer Software prefer:
Software

In Industrial/Energy prefer:
Alternative Energy
Industrial Products

In Manufact. prefer:
Manufacturing

Additional Information
Year Founded: 2006
Capital Under Management: $7,200,000
Current Activity Level : Actively seeking new investments

SKANDIA INNOVATION AB

Sveavagen 44
Stockholm, Sweden 103 50
Phone: 4687881000
Fax: 4687883080

Other Offices

Bosque de Ciruelos 162
1er piso Col.
Bosques de las Lomas, Mexico
Phone: 52-55-5093-0200
Fax: 52-55-5245-1272

Flat C-1, Floor 24, JiuShi FuXing Mansio
No. 918, Huai Hai Road (M)
Shanghai, China 200020
Phone: 86-21-6415-8145
Fax: 86-21-6415-8146

Postfach 10
Wildpretmarkt 2-4
Vienna, Austria 1013
Phone: 43-1-536-640
Fax: 43-1-535-1662

Via Fatebenefratelli 3
Milan, Italy I-20121
Phone: 39-02-623-1161
Fax: 39-02-655-4576

PL 1129 FIN-00101
Bulevardi 2-4A
Helsinki, Finland FIN-00120
Phone: 358-9-680-3260
Fax: 358-9-644-194

One Corporate Drive
PO Box 883
Shelton, CT USA 06484-0883
Phone: 203-926-1888

C/. Ruiz de Alarcon 11
Madrid, Spain E-28014
Phone: 34-91-524-3400
Fax: 34-91-524-3401

Office 102, Alastor Building
23 Armenias Avenue
Nicosia, Cyprus
Phone: 357-22-315-380
Fax: 357-22-315-254

Level 18
1 Castlereagh Street
Sydney, Australia 2000
Phone: 61-2-8226-8900
Fax: 61-2-9232-1433

Av. da Liberdade
180 E 1 dto
Lisbon, Portugal
Phone: 351-211-210-000
Fax: 351-211-210-009

Stenersgt. 2
Postboks 731 Sentrum
Oslo, Norway
Phone: 47-23-15-9800
Fax: 47-23-15-9801

Tour Areva
1, place de la Coupole
Paris, France 92084
Phone: 33-1-479-667-00
Fax: 33-1-479-667-01

Centro Skandia Avenida 19, 113-30
Apartado Aereo 103 970
Bogota D.C., Colombia
Phone: 57-1-620-5566
Fax: 57-1-612-9105

Migdalowa 4
Warsaw, Poland
Phone: 48-22-332-1700
Fax: 48-22-332-1701

Magdalena 121
Las Condes
Santiago, Chile
Phone: 56-428-7000
Fax: 56-374-2137

Stamholmen 151
Hvidovre, Denmark
Phone: 45-70-12-4747
Fax: 45-70-12-4748

Kaiserin-Augusta-Allee 108
Berlin, Germany 10553
Phone: 49-30-31-0070
Fax: 49-30-31-007-2888

Management and Staff
Jenny Rosberg, Vice President

Type of Firm
Bank Affiliated

Project Preferences

Type of Financing Preferred:
Early Stage
Seed
Startup

Geographical Preferences

United States Preferences:

International Preferences:
Europe
Scandanavia/Nordic Region

Industry Preferences

In Financial Services prefer:
Financial Services

Additional Information
Year Founded: 2000
Current Activity Level : Actively seeking new investments

SKANDINAVISKA ENSKILDA BANKEN AB

Kungstradgardsgatan 8
Merchant Banking
Stockholm, Sweden SE-106 40
Phone: 46771621000
E-mail: info@seb.com
Website: www.seb.se

Other Offices

Jogailos g. 10
Vilnius, Lithuania 01116
Phone: 37052682407

Scandinavian House
2-6 Cannon Street
London, United Kingdom EC4M6XX
Phone: 442072464000

Management and Staff
Johan Torgeby, President
Magnus Carlsson, Chief Executive Officer

Type of Firm
Bank Affiliated

Association Membership
Swedish Venture Capital Association (SVCA)

Project Preferences

Type of Financing Preferred:
Early Stage
Balanced
Later Stage
Startup

Size of Investments Considered:
Min Size of Investment Considered (000s): $200
Max Size of Investment Considered (000s): $12,000

Geographical Preferences

International Preferences:
United Kingdom
Eastern Europe
Scandanavia/Nordic Region
Lithuania

Industry Focus

(% based on actual investment)
Other Products	34.9%
Internet Specific	20.4%
Medical/Health	14.6%
Computer Software and Services	13.7%
Biotechnology	10.5%
Semiconductors/Other Elect.	3.0%
Communications and Media	1.3%
Industrial/Energy	1.1%
Consumer Related	0.5%
Computer Hardware	0.0%

Additional Information
Year Founded: 1995
Capital Under Management: $52,000,000
Current Activity Level : Actively seeking new investments

SKIDMORE GROUP

8658 Commerce Court
Burnaby, Canada V5A 4N6
Phone: 6044381000
Fax: 6044387923
Website: skidmoregroup.com

Type of Firm
Private Equity Firm

Project Preferences

Type of Financing Preferred:
Leveraged Buyout
Management Buyouts

Industry Preferences

In Medical/Health prefer:
Health Services

In Consumer Related prefer:
Retail

Additional Information
Year Founded: 2017
Current Activity Level : Actively seeking new investments

SKY 9 CAPITAL

1027 Changning Road, Suite 2408
Shanghai, China 200050
Phone: 8621523836
Website: www.sky9capital.com

Type of Firm
Private Equity Firm

Project Preferences

Type of Financing Preferred:
Early Stage
Balanced

Geographical Preferences

International Preferences:
China

Industry Preferences

In Internet Specific prefer:
Internet

In Consumer Related prefer:
Consumer

Additional Information
Year Founded: 2016
Current Activity Level : Actively seeking new investments

SKY INVESTMENT

153-55 Samseong 1(il)-dong
Floor 5, Sim Seu Building
Gyeonggi-do, South Korea 135878
Phone: 825087980
Fax: 825087983
Website: www.skyvc.co.kr

Type of Firm
Private Equity Firm

Association Membership
Korean Venture Capital Association (KVCA)

Project Preferences

Type of Financing Preferred:
Balanced

Geographical Preferences

International Preferences:
Korea, South

Industry Preferences

In Biotechnology prefer:
Biotech Related Research

In Industrial/Energy prefer:
Energy

Additional Information
Year Founded: 2007
Current Activity Level : Actively seeking new investments

SKY VENTURES INTERNATIONAL LLC

100 Hight Street
Boston, MA USA 02110
Phone: 6176789766
E-mail: contact@sky-ventures.com
Website: www.sky-ventures.com

Type of Firm
Private Equity Firm

Project Preferences

Type of Financing Preferred:
Early Stage

Additional Information
Year Founded: 2014
Current Activity Level : Actively seeking new investments

SKYLAKE INVESTMENT & CO

517-10, Dogok-Dong, Gangnam-Gu
4/F, KAIST Digital Media Lab
Seoul, South Korea 135270
Phone: 8225795511
Fax: 8225795441
E-mail: info@skylakeincuvest.com
Website: www.skylakeincuvest.com

Other Offices
1801 Page Mill, Suite 270
Palo Alto, CA USA 94304

Management and Staff
Don Suh, Managing Director
Harry Kim, Managing Director
Hyeon Gi Min, Managing Director
Kang Seok Lee, Managing Director
Seung Wu Choi, Managing Director
Young-min Kim, Vice President

Type of Firm
Private Equity Firm

Project Preferences

Type of Financing Preferred:
Leveraged Buyout
Early Stage
Expansion
Generalist PE
Public Companies
Seed

Geographical Preferences

International Preferences:
Asia
Korea, South

Industry Preferences

In Communications prefer:
Communications and Media
Commercial Communications
Telecommunications
Wireless Communications
Data Communications

Additional Information

Year Founded: 2006
Current Activity Level : Actively seeking new investments

SKYLAND VENTURES

1-1-10 Ohkubo, Shinjuku-ku
Gunkan Higashi Shinjuku Bldg
Tokyo, Japan 169-0072
E-mail: info@skyland.vc
Website: skyland.vc

Management and Staff

Yoshihiko Kinoshita, Partner

Type of Firm

Incubator/Development Program

Project Preferences

Type of Financing Preferred:
Seed
Startup

Geographical Preferences

International Preferences:
Japan

Additional Information

Year Founded: 2012
Current Activity Level : Actively seeking new investments

SKYLINE VENTURES INC

525 University Avenue, Suite 601
Palo Alto, CA USA 94301
Phone: 6504625800
Fax: 6503291090
Website: www.skylineventures.com

Other Offices

263 Tresser Boulevard, Suite 902 One Stamford Plaza
Stamford, CT USA 06901
Phone: 203-564-1596
Fax: 203-564-1402

303 Wyman Street, Suite 300
Waltham, MA USA 02451
Phone: 781-530-3600
Fax: 781-530-6805

Management and Staff

Eric Gordon, Co-Founder
John Freund, Co-Founder
Yasunori Kaneko, Managing Director

Type of Firm

Private Equity Firm

Project Preferences

Type of Financing Preferred:
Early Stage
Startup

Size of Investments Considered:
Min Size of Investment Considered (000s): $15,000
Max Size of Investment Considered (000s): $25,000

Geographical Preferences

United States Preferences:

Industry Focus

(% based on actual investment)
Biotechnology	59.0%
Medical/Health	35.0%
Computer Software and Services	4.5%
Internet Specific	1.5%

Additional Information

Name of Most Recent Fund: Skyline Venture Partners V, L.P.
Most Recent Fund Was Raised: 11/12/2007
Year Founded: 1997
Capital Under Management: $800,000,000
Current Activity Level : Actively seeking new investments

SKYPOINT VENTURES LLC

601 South Saginaw Street, Suite 500
Flint, MI USA 48502
Phone: 8105475591
Website: skypointventures.com

Management and Staff

Bryce Moe, Managing Director
David Ollila, Vice President
Jocelyn Hagerman, Co-Founder
Philip Hagerman, Co-Founder

Type of Firm

Private Equity Firm

Additional Information

Year Founded: 2014
Current Activity Level : Actively seeking new investments

SKYSTAR VENTURES

Jalan Scientia Boulevard
New Media Tower Lv. 12
Tangerang, Indonesia 15811
Phone: 622154220808
E-mail: skystarventures@umn.ac.id

Other Offices

Jalan Scientia Boulevard
New Media Tower Lv. 12
Tangerang, Indonesia 15811
Phone: 622154220808

Type of Firm

Private Equity Firm

Project Preferences

Type of Financing Preferred:
Early Stage
Startup

Industry Preferences

In Internet Specific prefer:
Internet

In Consumer Related prefer:
Education Related

Additional Information

Year Founded: 1969
Current Activity Level : Actively seeking new investments

SKYTREE CAPITAL PARTNERS LP

8515 Edna Avenue, Suite 210
Las Vegas, NV USA 89117
E-mail: info@skytreepartners.com
Website: www.skytreepartners.com

Management and Staff

Darrick Cole, Co-Founder
Luke Stanton, Managing Partner
Matthew Neely, Co-Founder

Type of Firm

Private Equity Firm

Project Preferences

Type of Financing Preferred:
Generalist PE

Industry Preferences

In Medical/Health prefer:
Health Services

In Industrial/Energy prefer:
Energy

In Agr/Forestr/Fish prefer:
Agriculture related

Additional Information
Year Founded: 2016
Current Activity Level : Actively seeking new investments

SKYVEN ASSET MANAGEMENT PTE LTD

2 Alexandra Road
#06-02 Delta House
Singapore, Singapore 159919
Phone: 65-6371-7088
Fax: 65-6272-0602
E-mail: info@skyven.com
Website: www.skyven.com

Management and Staff
Peter Tan, Managing Partner

Type of Firm
Private Equity Firm

Association Membership
Singapore Venture Capital Association (SVCA)

Project Preferences

Type of Financing Preferred:
Expansion
Later Stage

Size of Investments Considered:
Min Size of Investment Considered (000s): $1,000
Max Size of Investment Considered (000s): $5,000

Geographical Preferences

United States Preferences:
All U.S.

International Preferences:
Asia Pacific
India
China
Singapore

Industry Preferences

In Medical/Health prefer:
Medical Products
Health Services

In Consumer Related prefer:
Retail
Food/Beverage
Consumer Products
Consumer Services

In Industrial/Energy prefer:
Energy
Oil and Gas Exploration
Environmental Related

In Financial Services prefer:
Real Estate

In Business Serv. prefer:
Services

In Manufact. prefer:
Manufacturing

In Agr/Forestr/Fish prefer:
Agriculture related

Additional Information
Year Founded: 2000
Current Activity Level : Actively seeking new investments

SKYVIEW CAPITAL LLC

9777 Wilshire Boulevard
Seventh Floor
Beverly Hills, CA USA 90210
Phone: 3102736000
Fax: 3102736006
E-mail: info@skyviewcapital.com
Website: www.skyviewcapital.com

Management and Staff
Christopher Aye, Vice President
Jeffrey White, Vice President
Krishna Viswanadham, Vice President
Matt Thompson, Vice President

Type of Firm
Private Equity Firm

Project Preferences

Type of Financing Preferred:
Leveraged Buyout
Acquisition

Geographical Preferences

United States Preferences:
All U.S.

International Preferences:
Latin America
Europe

Industry Preferences

In Communications prefer:
Telecommunications

In Computer Software prefer:
Software
Systems Software

Additional Information
Year Founded: 2005
Current Activity Level : Actively seeking new investments

SKYWOOD VENTURES LLC

140 Sunrise Drive
Woodside, CA USA 94062
E-mail: info@skywood.com
Website: www.skywood.com

Other Offices
2436 Devotion Ridge Drive
Henderson, NV USA 89052-5674

Management and Staff
Jared Anderson, Principal
Jerry Anderson, Managing Partner
L. Curtis Widdoes, Venture Partner
L. John Lloyd, Venture Partner
Steve White, Venture Partner

Type of Firm
Private Equity Firm

Project Preferences

Type of Financing Preferred:
Early Stage
Seed
Startup

Industry Preferences

In Medical/Health prefer:
Medical Products

Additional Information
Year Founded: 1998
Current Activity Level : Actively seeking new investments

SL CAPITAL PARTNERS LLP

One George Street
Edinburgh, United Kingdom EH2 2LL
Phone: 441312450055
Fax: 441312456105
Website: www.slcapital.com

Other Offices
One Beacon Street
34th Floor
Boston, MA USA 02108
Phone: 617-720-7900

Management and Staff
Craig Williamson, Partner
Graeme Gunn, Partner
Ian Harris, Chief Operating Officer
Mark Nicolson, Partner
Patrick Knechtli, Partner
Peter McKellar, Partner
Roger Pim, Partner
Roland Brinkman, Partner
Stewart Hay, Partner

Type of Firm
Private Equity Advisor or Fund of Funds

Association Membership
British Venture Capital Association (BVCA)
Hong Kong Venture Capital Association (HKVCA)
European Private Equity and Venture Capital Assoc.

Project Preferences

Role in Financing:
Prefer role as deal originator but will also invest in deals created by others

Type of Financing Preferred:
Fund of Funds
Fund of Funds of Second

Geographical Preferences

United States Preferences:
North America

International Preferences:
United Kingdom
Europe

Industry Focus
(% based on actual investment)

Industrial/Energy	68.6%
Other Products	14.5%
Consumer Related	9.5%
Medical/Health	4.9%
Communications and Media	1.4%
Computer Software and Services	1.1%

Additional Information
Name of Most Recent Fund: SL Capital SOF I, L.P.
Most Recent Fund Was Raised: 08/09/2013
Year Founded: 1998
Capital Under Management: $11,017,600,000
Current Activity Level : Actively seeking new investments
Method of Compensation: Return on investment is of primary concern, do not charge fees

---

SL INVESTMENT CO LTD

737, Yeoksam 1-dong, Gangnam
25/F, Gangnam Finance Center
Seoul, South Korea 135081
Phone: 82262415400
Fax: 82262415412

Other Offices
501 Orchard Road
Wheelock Place, 13-02
Singapore, Singapore 238880
Phone: 65-6820-9665
Fax: 65-6820-9700

Type of Firm
Private Equity Firm

Association Membership
Korean Venture Capital Association (KVCA)

Project Preferences

Type of Financing Preferred:
Leveraged Buyout
Early Stage
Expansion
Mezzanine
Turnaround
Recapitalizations

Geographical Preferences

International Preferences:
Asia
Korea, South

Industry Preferences

In Communications prefer:
Telecommunications

In Computer Software prefer:
Software

In Computer Other prefer:
Computer Related

In Semiconductor/Electr prefer:
Electronics
Semiconductor

In Biotechnology prefer:
Biotechnology

In Industrial/Energy prefer:
Energy

In Manufact. prefer:
Manufacturing

Additional Information
Year Founded: 2000
Capital Under Management: $30,800,000
Current Activity Level : Actively seeking new investments

SLATE CAPITAL GROUP LLC

Two East Read Street
The Latrobe Bldg., Third Floor
Baltimore, MD USA 21202
Phone: 4105603572
Fax: 6302148572
E-mail: contact@slatecap.com
Website: www.slatecap.com

Management and Staff
Erik Ginsberg, Founder
Parker Davis, Partner
Rick Corcoran, Founder

Type of Firm
Private Equity Firm

Project Preferences

Type of Financing Preferred:
Leveraged Buyout
Expansion
Generalist PE

Geographical Preferences

United States Preferences:
Mid Atlantic

Industry Preferences

In Computer Software prefer:
Software

In Medical/Health prefer:
Medical/Health

In Consumer Related prefer:
Consumer
Retail
Education Related

In Business Serv. prefer:
Services
Distribution

In Manufact. prefer:
Manufacturing

Additional Information
Year Founded: 2004
Current Activity Level : Actively seeking new investments

SLATER TECHNOLOGY FUND INC

Three Davol Square, Suite A340
Providence, RI USA 02903
Phone: 4018316633
Fax: 4018310022
E-mail: info@slaterfund.com
Website: www.slaterfund.com

Management and Staff
Richard Horan, Senior Managing Director
Thorne Sparkman, Managing Director

Type of Firm
Government Affiliated Program

Association Membership
National Venture Capital Association - USA (NVCA)

Project Preferences

Role in Financing:
Will function either as deal originator or investor in deals created by others

Type of Financing Preferred:
Early Stage
Seed
Startup

Geographical Preferences

United States Preferences:
New Hampshire
Rhode Island
Vermont
Massachusetts
Connecticut
Maine

Industry Preferences

In Computer Software prefer:
Software

In Internet Specific prefer:
Internet

In Biotechnology prefer:
Biotechnology

In Industrial/Energy prefer:
Energy

In Business Serv. prefer:
Media

In Other prefer:
Environment Responsible

Additional Information
Year Founded: 1997
Capital Under Management: $28,000,000
Current Activity Level : Actively seeking new investments

SLEEPZ AG

Schlueterstrasse 38
Berlin, Germany 10629
Phone: 4930203050
Fax: 493020305555
E-mail: bmp@bmp.com
Website: www.sleepz.com

Type of Firm
Private Equity Firm

Project Preferences

Role in Financing:
Prefer role as deal originator but will also invest in deals created by others

Type of Financing Preferred:
Seed
Startup

Size of Investments Considered:
Min Size of Investment Considered (000s): $706
Max Size of Investment Considered (000s): $7,061

Geographical Preferences

International Preferences:
Poland
Germany

Industry Focus
(% based on actual investment)

Other Products	31.7%
Internet Specific	20.9%
Medical/Health	16.7%
Biotechnology	14.9%
Computer Software and Services	13.9%
Communications and Media	1.0%
Industrial/Energy	0.7%
Computer Hardware	0.3%

Additional Information
Name of Most Recent Fund: BFB Fruehphasenfonds Brandenburg GmbH
Most Recent Fund Was Raised: 03/25/2010
Year Founded: 1997
Capital Under Management: $29,100,000
Current Activity Level : Actively seeking new investments

SLINGSHOT MANAGEMENT BV

24, Weteringschans
Amsterdam, Netherlands 1017 SG

Type of Firm
Private Equity Firm

Project Preferences

Type of Financing Preferred:
Early Stage
Expansion
Later Stage
Seed

Size of Investments Considered:
Min Size of Investment Considered (000s): $561
Max Size of Investment Considered (000s): $3,923

Industry Preferences

In Computer Software prefer:
Software

In Internet Specific prefer:
E-Commerce Technology
Internet
Ecommerce

In Consumer Related prefer:
Consumer Services

Additional Information
Year Founded: 2015
Current Activity Level : Actively seeking new investments

SLOVENSKI PODJETNISKI SKLAD

Trubarjeva ulica 11
Maribor, Slovenia SI-2000
Phone: 38622341260
Fax: 38622341282
E-mail: info@podjetniskisklad.si
Website: www.podjetniskisklad.si

Management and Staff
Boris Pfeifer, Managing Director

Type of Firm
Government Affiliated Program

Project Preferences

Type of Financing Preferred:
Early Stage
Mezzanine
Generalist PE
Later Stage
Seed
Startup

Geographical Preferences

International Preferences:
Slovak Repub.
Europe

Additional Information
Year Founded: 1992
Current Activity Level : Actively seeking new investments

SLOW VENTURES LLC

775 East Blithedale Avenue, Suite 515
San Francisco, CA USA 94101
Phone: 4153710098
Website: slowventures.com

Type of Firm
Private Equity Firm

Project Preferences

Type of Financing Preferred:
Seed

Additional Information
Year Founded: 1969
Capital Under Management: $210,000,000
Current Activity Level : Actively seeking new investments

SMALL BUSINESS GUARANTEE AND FINANCE CORPORATION

17 & 18F, 139 Corporate Center
139 Valero St, Salcedo Village
Makati, Philippines 1227
Phone: 63-2-751-1888
Fax: 63-2-813-5726
Website: www.sbgfc.org.ph

Other Offices

Unit 76, 7F, Landco Corporate Center
JP Laurel Avenue, Bajada
Davao, Philippines
Phone: 63-82-221-1488
Fax: 63-82-221-0858

Unit 802-B, Keppel Center
Cebu Business Park
Cebu City, Philippines
Phone: 63-32-232-1200
Fax: 63-32-234-4500

Management and Staff

Alfredo Dimaculangan, Vice President
Alice Sy, Vice President
Daniel Gonzales, Vice President
Hector Olmedillo, Vice President
Melvin Abanto, Vice President
Modesto Butalid, Vice President
Peter Pizarro, Vice President
Virgilio Angelo, Chairman & CEO

Type of Firm

Government Affiliated Program

Project Preferences

Type of Financing Preferred:
Balanced

Geographical Preferences

International Preferences:
No Preference
Philippines

Additional Information

Year Founded: 1991
Current Activity Level : Actively seeking new investments

SMALL CAP PARTNERS MANAGEMENT I MALMO AB

Hans Michelsensgatan 9
Malmo, Sweden 21120
Phone: 040-660 04 00
Website: www.smallcappartners.se

Type of Firm

Private Equity Firm

Project Preferences

Type of Financing Preferred:
Leveraged Buyout
Management Buyouts

Geographical Preferences

International Preferences:
Sweden

Additional Information

Year Founded: 2016
Current Activity Level : Actively seeking new investments

SMALL ENTERPRISE ASSISTANCE FUNDS

1500 K Street NorthWest, Suite 375
Washington, DC USA 20005
Phone: 2027378463
Fax: 2027375536
E-mail: contactus@seaf.com
Website: seaf.com

Other Offices

Baltic Small Equity Fund
29-2 Lacplesa St., Suite 9
Riga, Latvia 1011
Phone: 371-728-9500
Fax: 371-728-9547

Trans-Balkan Bulgaria Fund
22 Zlaten Rog St, 8th Floor
Sofia, Bulgaria 1407
Phone: 359-2-917-4950
Fax: 359-2-917-4951

Sichuan Small Investment Fund
Building Office 2307, 45 Zhongfu Road
Chengdu, China 610016
Phone: 86-28-8290-3508
Fax: 86-28-8625-5325

CASEF
Kabanbai Batyr 76
Almaty, Kazakhstan 050012
Phone: 7-3272-587-593
Fax: 7-3272-587-595

St. Orce Nikolov 188-2/4
Skopje, Macedonia 1000
Phone: 38923091337
Fax: 38923217025

TBRF, Strada Octavian Goga 4,
Bloc M26, Parter, Sector 3
Bucharest, Romania 030982
Phone: 4021-326-7340
Fax: 4021-326 7337

Baltic Small Equity Fund/CEE Growth Fund
Parnu mnt 142, 6th Floor
Tallinn, Estonia 11317
Phone: 372-651-2690
Fax: 372-651-2693

SEAF-Croatia
Britanski trg 5/11
Zagreb, Croatia 10000
Phone: 385-1-481-1912
Fax: 385-1-482-3558

CASEF
Rakatboshi Street #27
Tashkent, Uzbekistan 70031
Phone: 998-71-139-1620
Fax: 998-71-139-1680

Ed. Eduardo Abaroa, Planta Baja,
Sanchez Lima esq. Belisario
Salinas, La Paz, Bolivia
Phone: 591-2-242-4788
Fax: 591-2-242-4788

Carrera 12 No. 89-28
Office 402
Bogota, Colombia
Phone: 5716352399
Fax: 5716212374

SEAF-Macedonia
Metropolit Teodosij Gologanov 28
Skopje, Macedonia 1000
Phone: 389-2-3079-611
Fax: 389-2-3079-612

CARESBAC
ul. Polna 40
Warsaw, Poland 00-635
Phone: 48-22-825-6205
Fax: 48-22-825-4650

Stichting-SEAF
Valeriusstraat 124-boven
Amsterdam, Netherlands 1075 GD
Phone: 31-641-385-111
Fax: 31-348-424-652

Equipetrol Calle 7
Oeste #16
Santa Cruz, Bolivia
Phone: 591-3-332-5392
Fax: 591-3-332-5392

Transandian Fund
Calle Martir Olaya 129, Miraflores
Lima, Peru 18
Phone: 51-1-444-2020
Fax: 51-1-444-2009

No. 30-31, Shubhadha Building B Wing
Pochkhanwala Road Worli
Mumbai, India 400 020
Phone: 91-22-2494-0399
Fax: 91-98102-74483

7 North Nikoladze Street
Second Floor
Tbilisi, Georgia 0108
Phone: 995322998115

Management and Staff

Armands Fomicevs, Managing Director
Donald Lubreski, Chief Financial Officer
Donald Nicholson, Managing Director
Esben Emborg, Managing Director
Gary Dodge, Managing Director

George Zhang, Managing Director
Harry Schuster, Managing Director
Hector Cateriano, Managing Director
Hemendra Mathur, Managing Director
Mustafa Kazem, Managing Director
Nikola Stefanovic, Managing Director
Oliver Kosturanov, Managing Director
Partha Choudhury, Managing Director
Piotr Kalaman, Managing Director
Richard Russell, Managing Director
Zia Ahmed, Managing Director

Type of Firm
Incubator/Development Program

Association Membership
Community Development Venture Capital Alliance

Project Preferences

Type of Financing Preferred:
Fund of Funds
Leveraged Buyout
Early Stage
Expansion
Balanced
Later Stage
Acquisition

Size of Investments Considered:
Min Size of Investment Considered (000s): $500
Max Size of Investment Considered (000s): $3,000

Geographical Preferences

International Preferences:
Slovenia
Vietnam
Greece
Slovak Repub.
Czech Republic
Bolivia
Macedonia
China
Peru
Poland
Kyrgyzstan
Croatia
Tajikistan
Turkmenistan
Bulgaria
Estonia
Colombia
Romania
Latvia
Lithuania

Industry Preferences

In Communications prefer:
CATV & Pay TV Systems
Telecommunications
Media and Entertainment

In Computer Software prefer:
Software

In Internet Specific prefer:
Internet

In Semiconductor/Electr prefer:
Electronics

In Medical/Health prefer:
Pharmaceuticals

In Consumer Related prefer:
Retail
Food/Beverage
Consumer Products

In Industrial/Energy prefer:
Industrial Products

In Business Serv. prefer:
Services
Distribution
Media

In Agr/Forestr/Fish prefer:
Agriculture related

In Other prefer:
Women/Minority-Owned Bus.

Additional Information
Year Founded: 1989
Capital Under Management: $130,000,000
Current Activity Level : Actively seeking new investments

SMALL VENTURES USA LP

3050 Post Oak Boulevard, Suite 460
Houston, TX USA 77056
Phone: 7133417916
Fax: 7135839206
E-mail: info@smallventuresusa.com
Website: www.smallventuresusa.com

Management and Staff
Eddie Hernandez, Partner
Kayla Bruzzese, Chief Financial Officer
William Perkins, President, Founder

Type of Firm
Private Equity Firm

Project Preferences

Type of Financing Preferred:
Early Stage
Balanced

Industry Preferences

In Communications prefer:
Entertainment

In Industrial/Energy prefer:
Energy

Additional Information
Year Founded: 2008
Current Activity Level : Actively seeking new investments

SMALL WORLD GROUP INCUBATOR PTE LTD

71 Ayer Rajah Crescent
Singapore, Singapore 139951
Website: smallworldgroup.com

Management and Staff
Cindy Calderon, Partner
David Young, Partner
Dean Haritos, Partner
Kent Pavey, Partner

Type of Firm
Incubator/Development Program

Association Membership
Singapore Venture Capital Association (SVCA)

Project Preferences

Type of Financing Preferred:
Early Stage
Later Stage
Seed

Additional Information
Year Founded: 1969
Current Activity Level : Actively seeking new investments

SMART VENTURES INC

1720 Arezzo Circle
Boynton Beach, FL USA 33436
Phone: 9177278656
E-mail: management@smartventuresinc.com

Management and Staff
Roger Smith, Chief Executive Officer

Type of Firm
Private Equity Firm

Project Preferences

Type of Financing Preferred:
Early Stage
Later Stage
Acquisition

Geographical Preferences

United States Preferences:

Canadian Preferences:
All Canada

Industry Preferences

In Medical/Health prefer:
Medical/Health

In Industrial/Energy prefer:
Oil and Gas Exploration
Oil & Gas Drilling,Explor

Additional Information
Year Founded: 2006
Current Activity Level : Actively seeking new investments

SMARTCAP AS
Rotermanni 8
Tallinn, Estonia 10111
Phone: 3726161100
E-mail: info@smartcap.ee
Website: www.smartcap.ee

Management and Staff
Seppo Sneck, Chief Executive Officer

Type of Firm
Private Equity Firm

Project Preferences

Type of Financing Preferred:
Early Stage
Balanced
Later Stage
Seed

Geographical Preferences

International Preferences:
Estonia

Industry Preferences

In Internet Specific prefer:
E-Commerce Technology

In Biotechnology prefer:
Biotechnology

In Industrial/Energy prefer:
Alternative Energy

In Manufact. prefer:
Manufacturing

Additional Information
Year Founded: 2011
Current Activity Level : Actively seeking new investments

SMARTFIN CAPITAL NV
37 A, Hanswijkstraat
Mechelen, Belgium B-2800
Website: smartfincapital.com

Type of Firm
Private Equity Firm

Project Preferences

Type of Financing Preferred:
Expansion
Later Stage

Size of Investments Considered:
Min Size of Investment Considered (000s): $1,093
Max Size of Investment Considered (000s): $10,933

Geographical Preferences

International Preferences:
United Kingdom
Europe
Belgium

Industry Preferences

In Communications prefer:
Data Communications

In Computer Software prefer:
Software

In Internet Specific prefer:
E-Commerce Technology

Additional Information
Year Founded: 2014
Current Activity Level : Actively seeking new investments

SMARTFOREST VENTURES
P.O. Box 9085
Portland, OR USA 97207
Phone: 5039430904
Fax: 5032222834
E-mail: contactus@smartforest.com
Website: www.smartforest.com

Management and Staff
Debi Coleman, Managing Partner
Hugh Mackworth, Managing Partner
Huoy-Ming Yeh, Partner
Thomas Toy, General Partner

Type of Firm
SBIC

Project Preferences

Role in Financing:
Prefer role as deal originator but will also invest in deals created by others

Type of Financing Preferred:
Seed

Geographical Preferences

United States Preferences:
Northwest

Additional Information
Year Founded: 2000
Capital Under Management: $75,000,000
Current Activity Level : Actively seeking new investments
Method of Compensation: Return on investment is of primary concern, do not charge fees

SMARTHUB OOO
Kutuzova 34
Kaliningrad, Russia 236010
Website: smarthub.ru

Management and Staff
Bogdan Yarovoy, Managing Partner
Olga Dorofeeva, Managing Partner

Type of Firm
Private Equity Firm

Project Preferences

Type of Financing Preferred:
Early Stage
Seed
Startup

Geographical Preferences

International Preferences:
United Kingdom
Hong Kong
Russia

Industry Preferences

In Financial Services prefer:
Financial Services

Additional Information
Year Founded: 2015
Current Activity Level : Actively seeking new investments

SMBC VENTURE CAPITAL CO LTD
1-13-12, Kayaba-cho, Nihonbashi
Sakura, Nihonbashi Bldg
Tokyo, Japan 103-0025
Phone: 81362311580
Website: www.smbc-vc.co.jp

Management and Staff
Masahiro Yamaguchi, Managing Director
Oharu Furuta, Managing Director

Type of Firm
Bank Affiliated

Project Preferences

Type of Financing Preferred:
Balanced

Geographical Preferences

International Preferences:
Japan

Industry Preferences

In Communications prefer:
Telecommunications

In Semiconductor/Electr prefer:
Electronic Components

In Medical/Health prefer:
Medical/Health

In Industrial/Energy prefer:
Environmental Related

Additional Information

Year Founded: 2005
Capital Under Management: $6,100,000
Current Activity Level : Actively seeking new investments

SMEDVIG CAPITAL LTD

20, St. James's Street
London, United Kingdom SW1A 1ES
Phone: 442074512100
Fax: 442074512101
E-mail: enquiries@smedvigcapital.com
Website: www.smedvigcapital.com

Other Offices

Finnestadveien 28
PO Box 110
Stavanger, Norway 4001
Phone: 47 5150 9900
Fax: 47 5150 9688

Management and Staff

Alistair Cairns, Managing Director
Cristian Young, Chief Financial Officer
Jonathan Lerner, Principal
Jordan Mayo, Managing Director
Robert Toms, Managing Director

Type of Firm
Private Equity Firm

Association Membership
British Venture Capital Association (BVCA)

Project Preferences

Type of Financing Preferred:
Early Stage
Expansion
Generalist PE
Seed
Management Buyouts
Acquisition
Startup

Geographical Preferences

International Preferences:
Europe

Additional Information
Year Founded: 1996

Capital Under Management: $600,000,000
Current Activity Level : Actively seeking new investments

SMG GROUP SA

16/18 impasse d'Antin
Paris, France 75008
Phone: 33153239800
Fax: 33153239801
E-mail: smg@smg.fr
Website: www.smg.fr

Management and Staff
Xavier-Jacques Gondel, Founder

Type of Firm
Private Equity Firm

Project Preferences

Type of Financing Preferred:
Seed
Startup

Geographical Preferences

International Preferences:
Europe
France

Industry Preferences

In Internet Specific prefer:
Internet

In Biotechnology prefer:
Biotechnology

Additional Information
Year Founded: 1993
Current Activity Level : Actively seeking new investments

SMILEGATE INVESTMENT INC

220 Pangyoyeok-ro Bundang-gu
3F Ancheolsu R&D Center
Seongnam-si, South Korea 135010
Phone: 823180179620
Fax: 823180179710
Website: www.smilegateinvestment.com

Management and Staff
Gi Mun Nam, Chief Executive Officer
Jong Hyeok Park, Partner
Yeong Gwon Gu, Vice President

Type of Firm
Private Equity Firm

Association Membership
Korean Venture Capital Association (KVCA)

Project Preferences

Type of Financing Preferred:
Fund of Funds
Early Stage
Expansion
Balanced
Seed
Startup

Geographical Preferences

International Preferences:
China
Korea, South

Industry Preferences

In Communications prefer:
Wireless Communications

In Internet Specific prefer:
Internet

In Semiconductor/Electr prefer:
Semiconductor

In Biotechnology prefer:
Biotechnology

In Medical/Health prefer:
Medical/Health
Medical Products

In Industrial/Energy prefer:
Alternative Energy

Additional Information
Year Founded: 2000
Capital Under Management: $95,500,000
Current Activity Level : Actively seeking new investments

SMS PRIVATE EQUITY FUND MANAGEMENT CO LTD

Jingan District
Shanghai, China

Type of Firm
Private Equity Firm

Project Preferences

Type of Financing Preferred:
Fund of Funds
Balanced

Geographical Preferences

International Preferences:
China

Industry Preferences

In Consumer Related prefer:
Consumer
Food/Beverage

Additional Information
Year Founded: 2010
Current Activity Level : Actively seeking new investments

SMV MANAGEMENT A/S

Marselis Tvrvej 4
Aarhus, Denmark 8000
Website: www.smvinvest.dk.linux42.unoeuro-server.com

Type of Firm
Investment Management Firm

Project Preferences

Type of Financing Preferred:
Leveraged Buyout
Management Buyouts

Geographical Preferences

International Preferences:
Denmark

Additional Information
Year Founded: 2013
Current Activity Level : Actively seeking new investments

SNIPER INVESTMENTS NV

Hanswijkstraat 37 A
Mechelen, Belgium 2800
Phone: 3215287880
Fax: 3215287889
E-mail: info@sniperinvestments.com
Website: www.sniperinvestments.com

Type of Firm
Private Equity Firm

Project Preferences

Type of Financing Preferred:
Early Stage
Seed

Geographical Preferences

International Preferences:
Europe
Belgium

Additional Information
Year Founded: 2011
Current Activity Level : Actively seeking new investments

SNOW PHIPPS GROUP LLC

667 Madison Avenue
18th Floor
New York, NY USA 10065
Phone: 2125083300
Fax: 2125083301
Website: www.snowphipps.com

Management and Staff
Alan Mantel, Partner
Brandon Kiss, Vice President
Gerald Sheehan, Vice President
Ian Snow, Chief Executive Officer
John Pless, Principal
Ogden Phipps, Partner
Sean Epps, Partner
Steven Schwinger, Chief Financial Officer
Townsend Bancroft, Vice President

Type of Firm
Private Equity Firm

Project Preferences

Type of Financing Preferred:
Leveraged Buyout
Acquisition
Recapitalizations

Geographical Preferences

United States Preferences:
North America

Additional Information
Year Founded: 2005
Capital Under Management: $809,500,000
Current Activity Level : Actively seeking new investments

SNOWBIRD CAPITAL INC

11921 Freedom Drive, Suite 1120, Reston Town Center
Reston, VA USA 20190
Phone: 7039554471
Fax: 7032592401
E-mail: investments@snowbirdcapital.com
Website: www.snowbirdcapital.com

Management and Staff
Christine Piorkowski, Chief Financial Officer
John Carbonell, Managing Director

Type of Firm
Private Equity Firm

Project Preferences

Type of Financing Preferred:
Leveraged Buyout
Expansion
Mezzanine
Management Buyouts
Recapitalizations

Geographical Preferences

United States Preferences:

Additional Information
Year Founded: 2004
Current Activity Level : Actively seeking new investments

SOARING PINE CAPITAL MANAGEMENT

335 Maple Road
Birmingham, MI USA 48009
Phone: 3136623691
Website: www.soaringpine.com

Type of Firm
Private Equity Firm

Additional Information
Year Founded: 2014
Current Activity Level : Actively seeking new investments

SOBERA CAPITAL GMBH

Markgrafenstrasse 33
Berlin, Germany 10117
Phone: 4930577088370
Fax: 4930577088379
Website: sobera-capital.com

Management and Staff
Johannes Rabini, Co-Founder
Stefan Beil, Co-Founder

Type of Firm
Private Equity Advisor or Fund of Funds

Association Membership
German Venture Capital Association (BVK)

Project Preferences

Type of Financing Preferred:
Fund of Funds of Second

Geographical Preferences

United States Preferences:
All U.S.

International Preferences:
Europe
Germany

Additional Information
Year Founded: 2010
Current Activity Level : Actively seeking new investments

SOC CAPITAL RISQUE PROVENCALE ET CORSE SAS

247, Avenue du Prado
Marseille, France 13008

Type of Firm
Bank Affiliated

Project Preferences

Type of Financing Preferred:
Early Stage
Expansion
Later Stage
Seed

Geographical Preferences

International Preferences:
France

Additional Information
Year Founded: 2004
Current Activity Level : Actively seeking new investments

SOCADIF

26 quai de la Rapee
Paris, France 75012
Phone: 33144732638
Fax: 33144731523
E-mail: socadif@ca-socadif.fr

Type of Firm
Bank Affiliated

Association Membership
French Venture Capital Association (AFIC)

Project Preferences

Type of Financing Preferred:
Leveraged Buyout
Early Stage
Later Stage
Management Buyouts

Geographical Preferences

International Preferences:
Europe
France

Additional Information
Year Founded: 1990
Current Activity Level : Actively seeking new investments

SOCIAL DISCOVERY VENTURES

589 8th Ave
23rd floor
New York, NY USA 10018
Website: sdventures.com

Type of Firm
Private Equity Firm

Additional Information
Year Founded: 1993
Current Activity Level : Actively seeking new investments

SOCIAL INTERNET FUND, THE

120 Broadway
27th Floor
New York, NY USA 10271

Type of Firm
Private Equity Firm

Project Preferences

Type of Financing Preferred:
Early Stage
Strategic Alliances
Startup

Geographical Preferences

United States Preferences:
California
All U.S.

Industry Preferences

In Internet Specific prefer:
Internet

Additional Information
Year Founded: 2012
Current Activity Level : Actively seeking new investments

SOCIAL LEVERAGE LLC

5110 North 40th Street, Suite 108
Phoenix, AZ USA 85018
Phone: 6023159966

Management and Staff
Thomas Peterson, Chief Executive Officer

Type of Firm
Private Equity Firm

Project Preferences

Type of Financing Preferred:
Early Stage

Size of Investments Considered:
Min Size of Investment Considered (000s): $100
Max Size of Investment Considered (000s): $500

Geographical Preferences

United States Preferences:

Additional Information
Year Founded: 2000
Current Activity Level : Actively seeking new investments

SOCIAL+CAPITAL PARTNERSHIP

120 Hawthorne Avenue
Palo Alto, CA USA 94301
Phone: 6505219007
E-mail: inbox@s23p.com

Other Offices
475 Embarcadero Road
PALO ALTO, CA USA 94301

Management and Staff
Adam Nelson, Partner
Arjun Sethi, Partner
Ashley Carroll, Partner
Ashley Mayer, Partner
Carl Anderson, Partner
Jay Zaveri, Partner
Mamoon Hamid, Co-Founder
Sakya Duvvuru, Partner
Sandhya Venkatachalam, Partner
Ted Maidenberg, Co-Founder

Type of Firm
Private Equity Firm

Geographical Preferences

United States Preferences:
All U.S.

Industry Preferences

In Medical/Health prefer:
Medical/Health

In Consumer Related prefer:
Education Related

In Financial Services prefer:
Financial Services

Additional Information
Year Founded: 2011
Capital Under Management: $875,000,000
Current Activity Level : Actively seeking new investments

SOCIEDAD DE DESARROLLO DE NAVARRA SL

Avenida Carlos III el Noble
36, 1 Dcha.
Pamplona, Spain 31003
Phone: 34848421942
Fax: 34848421943
E-mail: info@sodena.com
Website: www.sodena.com

Management and Staff
Jose Maria Riog Aldasoro, President

Type of Firm
Incubator/Development Program

Association Membership
Spanish Venture Capital Association (ASCRI)

Project Preferences

Type of Financing Preferred:
Expansion
Balanced
Seed
Startup

Geographical Preferences

International Preferences:
Spain

Industry Preferences

In Communications prefer:
Telecommunications

In Computer Other prefer:
Computer Related

In Semiconductor/Electr prefer:
Electronics

In Biotechnology prefer:
Biotechnology

In Medical/Health prefer:
Medical Products
Pharmaceuticals

In Consumer Related prefer:
Entertainment and Leisure
Food/Beverage

In Industrial/Energy prefer:
Energy
Alternative Energy
Materials
Environmental Related

In Transportation prefer:
Transportation

In Business Serv. prefer:
Services

In Agr/Forestr/Fish prefer:
Agriculture related

Additional Information
Year Founded: 1984
Capital Under Management: $450,000,000
Current Activity Level : Actively seeking new investments

SOCIEDAD PARA EL DESARROLLO DE LAS COMARCAS MINERAS SA

C/La Union, 21
La Felguera (Asturias), Spain 33930
Phone: 34-985-691-446
Fax: 34-985-682-962
E-mail: sodeco@las.es
Website: www.sodeco.es

Type of Firm
Private Equity Firm

Association Membership
Spanish Venture Capital Association (ASCRI)

Project Preferences

Role in Financing:
Prefer role in deals created by others

Type of Financing Preferred:
Second Stage Financing
Start-up Financing
First Stage Financing
Startup

Geographical Preferences

International Preferences:
Europe
Spain

Additional Information
Year Founded: 1988
Capital Under Management: $40,000,000
Current Activity Level : Actively seeking new investments
Method of Compensation: Return on invest. most important, but chg. closing fees, service fees, etc.

SOCIETA FINANZIARIA LAZIALE DI SVILUPPO FILAS SPA

Via della Conciliazione 22
Rome, Italy 00193
Phone: 39-06-328851
Fax: 39-06-3600-6808
E-mail: info@filas.it
Website: www.filas.eu

Type of Firm
Private Equity Firm

Association Membership
Italian Venture Capital Association (AIFI)

Project Preferences

Type of Financing Preferred:
Early Stage
Expansion
Generalist PE
Seed
Startup

Geographical Preferences

International Preferences:
Italy
Spain

Industry Preferences

In Biotechnology prefer:
Agricultural/Animal Bio.

In Transportation prefer:
Transportation

In Financial Services prefer:
Financial Services
Real Estate

Additional Information
Year Founded: 1975
Current Activity Level : Actively seeking new investments

SOCIETA FINANZIARIA REGIONE SARDEGNA SPA

Via S. Margherita 4
Cagliari, Italy 09124
Phone: 39-070-679-791
Fax: 39-070-663-213
E-mail: sfirs@tin.it
Website: www.sfirs.it

Type of Firm
Government Affiliated Program

Project Preferences

Type of Financing Preferred:
Second Stage Financing
Leveraged Buyout
Expansion
Startup

Geographical Preferences

International Preferences:
Italy

Additional Information
Year Founded: 2002
Current Activity Level : Actively seeking new investments

SOCIETATEA DE INVESTITII FINANCIARE BANAT CRISANA SA

35A Calea Victoriei
Arad, Romania 310158
Phone: 40257234473
Fax: 40257230370
E-mail: sifbc@sif1.ro
Website: www.sif1.ro

Other Offices

Piata Muzeului nr. 1
Cluj-Napoca, Romania 400019

Bulevard Regina Elisabeta nr. 54
Sector 5
Bucharest, Romania 050014

Street Maresal Averescu nr. 3
Appartment 37
Satu Mare, OH USA 440042

No. 23 General Grigore Balan Street
Bistrita, Romania 420094
Phone: 40263218551
Fax: 40263218551

Management and Staff

Radu Straut, Chief Executive Officer

Type of Firm

Private Equity Firm

Association Membership

European Private Equity and Venture Capital Assoc.

Project Preferences

Type of Financing Preferred:
Early Stage
Balanced
Seed
Startup

Geographical Preferences

International Preferences:
Europe
Romania

Additional Information

Year Founded: 1992
Current Activity Level : Actively seeking new investments

SOCIETATEA DE INVESTITII FINANCIARE TRANSILVANIA SA

2, Nicolae Iorga Street
Brasov, Romania 2200
Phone: 40268413752
Fax: 40268473215
E-mail: marketing@transif.ro
Website: www.transif.ro

Management and Staff

Adriana Boian, Chief Financial Officer
Iulian Stan, Chief Executive Officer

Type of Firm

Private Equity Firm

Association Membership

European Private Equity and Venture Capital Assoc.

Project Preferences

Type of Financing Preferred:
Public Companies
Later Stage

Geographical Preferences

International Preferences:
Romania

Industry Preferences

In Communications prefer:
Telecommunications

In Semiconductor/Electr prefer:
Electronics

In Consumer Related prefer:
Entertainment and Leisure
Food/Beverage
Consumer Products
Consumer Services
Other Restaurants
Hotels and Resorts

In Industrial/Energy prefer:
Industrial Products
Materials
Machinery

In Transportation prefer:
Transportation

In Financial Services prefer:
Financial Services
Insurance

In Business Serv. prefer:
Consulting Services

In Agr/Forestr/Fish prefer:
Agriculture related

Additional Information

Year Founded: 1996
Current Activity Level : Actively seeking new investments

SOCIETE ANTILLES GUYANE D INVESTISSEMENT ET PARTICIPATIONS

ZAC de Houelbourg Sud II
Baie Mahahault, France 97122
Phone: 33590944548
Fax: 33590944545
E-mail: contact@sagipar.com
Website: www.cdcentreprises.fr

Type of Firm

Private Equity Firm

Project Preferences

Type of Financing Preferred:
Leveraged Buyout
Early Stage
Generalist PE
Later Stage
Acquisition

Geographical Preferences

International Preferences:
Martinque
France

Industry Preferences

In Industrial/Energy prefer:
Energy

In Other prefer:
Environment Responsible

Additional Information

Year Founded: 1989
Current Activity Level : Actively seeking new investments

SOCIETE D INVESTISSEMENT A CAPITAL RISQUE DU GROUPE STB

Centre Urbain Nord
Imm. EL IMTIEZ
Tunis, Tunisia 1082
Phone: 21671238729
Fax: 21671234411
E-mail: info@stbsicar.com.tn
Website: www.stbsicar.com.tn

Type of Firm

Private Equity Firm

Association Membership

Tunisian Venture Capital Association

Project Preferences

Type of Financing Preferred:
Leveraged Buyout
Early Stage
Generalist PE
Public Companies
Later Stage
Acquisition
Startup

Geographical Preferences

International Preferences:
Tunisia

Industry Preferences

In Consumer Related prefer:
Hotels and Resorts

In Industrial/Energy prefer:
Industrial Products

In Business Serv. prefer:
Services

In Agr/Forestr/Fish prefer:
Agriculture related

Additional Information

Year Founded: 1998
Current Activity Level : Actively seeking new investments

SOCIETE D'ASSISTANCE ET DE GESTION DES FONDS D'ESSAIMAGE

Imm.Mark Crown - Rue lac Leman
Les Berges du Lac
Tunis, Tunisia 1053
Phone: 21671961993
Fax: 21671961983

Type of Firm
Investment Management Firm

Association Membership
Tunisian Venture Capital Association

Project Preferences

Type of Financing Preferred:
Leveraged Buyout
Early Stage
Expansion
Later Stage
Acquisition
Startup

Geographical Preferences

International Preferences:
Tunisia
Europe
Africa

Industry Preferences

In Industrial/Energy prefer:
Energy
Environmental Related

In Business Serv. prefer:
Services

In Manufact. prefer:
Manufacturing

In Agr/Forestr/Fish prefer:
Mining and Minerals

In Utilities prefer:
Utilities

Additional Information

Year Founded: 2006
Capital Under Management: $4,996,000
Current Activity Level : Actively seeking new investments

SOCIETE D'INVESTISSEMENTS ET DE PARTICIPATIONS SICAR

Rue Hedi Nouira
Tunis, Tunisia 1002
Phone: 21671834968
Fax: 21671801731
E-mail: sicar.invest@planet.tn

Type of Firm
Private Equity Firm

Association Membership
Tunisian Venture Capital Association

Project Preferences

Type of Financing Preferred:
Early Stage
Later Stage

Geographical Preferences

International Preferences:
Tunisia
Africa

Additional Information

Year Founded: 1997
Current Activity Level : Making few, if any, new investments

SOCIETE DE DEVELOPPEMENT ET D'INVESTISSEMENT DU NORD-OUEST

Av.Taieb M'hiri
Batiment Societe de la foire
Siliana, Tunisia 6100
Phone: 216-71-795-688
Fax: 216-71-797-513
E-mail: sodino.sicar@hexabyte.tn

Type of Firm
Private Equity Firm

Project Preferences

Type of Financing Preferred:
Early Stage
Expansion
Balanced
Later Stage

Geographical Preferences

International Preferences:
Tunisia

Industry Preferences

In Industrial/Energy prefer:
Industrial Products

In Business Serv. prefer:
Services

In Agr/Forestr/Fish prefer:
Agriculture related

Additional Information

Year Founded: 1992
Current Activity Level : Actively seeking new investments

SOCIETE DE L'INVESTISSEMENT MODERNE

67, Rue Alain Savary
Cite les jardins immeuble B
Tunis, Tunisia 1002
Phone: 21671781955
Fax: 21671846675
E-mail: simsicar@wanadoo.tn
Website: www.sim-sicar.com

Type of Firm
Private Equity Firm

Association Membership
Tunisian Venture Capital Association

Project Preferences

Role in Financing:
Will function either as deal originator or investor in deals created by others

Type of Financing Preferred:
Early Stage
Later Stage
Seed
Startup

Size of Investments Considered:
Min Size of Investment Considered (000s): $12
Max Size of Investment Considered (000s): $3,753

Geographical Preferences

International Preferences:
Tunisia
Africa

Industry Preferences

In Manufact. prefer:
Manufacturing

In Agr/Forestr/Fish prefer:
Agriculture related

Additional Information

Name of Most Recent Fund: FONDS FILIALES
Most Recent Fund Was Raised: 12/31/2005
Year Founded: 1997
Capital Under Management: $66,100,000
Current Activity Level : Actively seeking new investments

SOCIETE FINANCIERE LORIENT DEVELOPPEMENT SA

12, avenue de La Perriere
Lorient Cedex, France 56324
Phone: 33297882251
Fax: 33297882240
E-mail: contact@sfld.fr
Website: www.sfld.fr

Management and Staff

Bruno Le Jossec, Partner

Type of Firm

Private Equity Firm

Project Preferences

Type of Financing Preferred:
Leveraged Buyout
Early Stage
Expansion
Generalist PE
Later Stage
Seed
Management Buyouts
Startup

Geographical Preferences

International Preferences:
Europe
France

Additional Information

Year Founded: 1991
Current Activity Level : Actively seeking new investments

SOCIETE GENERALE CAPITAL PARTENAIRES SAS

17 Cours Valmy
Puteaux, France 92800
Phone: 33299787055
Fax: 33299787060
Website: capitalpartenaires.societegenerale.com

Management and Staff

Jean-Pierre Flais, Chief Operating Officer

Type of Firm

Bank Affiliated

Association Membership

French Venture Capital Association (AFIC)

Project Preferences

Type of Financing Preferred:
Leveraged Buyout
Early Stage
Later Stage
Management Buyouts
Startup

Size of Investments Considered:
Min Size of Investment Considered (000s): $403
Max Size of Investment Considered (000s): $10,771

Geographical Preferences

International Preferences:
Europe
France

Additional Information

Year Founded: 1973
Capital Under Management: $630,900,000
Current Activity Level : Actively seeking new investments

SOCIETE REGIONALE D'INVESTISSEMENT DE WALLONIE SA

13, Avenue Maurice Destenay
Liege, Belgium 40000
Phone: 3242219811
Fax: 3241219999
E-mail: info@sriw.be
Website: www.sriw.be

Type of Firm

Private Equity Firm

Association Membership

Belgium Venturing Association
European Private Equity and Venture Capital Assoc.

Project Preferences

Type of Financing Preferred:
Second Stage Financing
Early Stage
Later Stage
Startup

Geographical Preferences

International Preferences:
Europe
Belgium

Industry Preferences

In Communications prefer:
Telecommunications

In Semiconductor/Electr prefer:
Electronics

In Biotechnology prefer:
Biotechnology

In Consumer Related prefer:
Food/Beverage
Consumer Services
Hotels and Resorts

In Industrial/Energy prefer:
Materials

In Transportation prefer:
Aerospace

In Financial Services prefer:
Real Estate

In Business Serv. prefer:
Services

In Agr/Forestr/Fish prefer:
Agriculture related

In Other prefer:
Environment Responsible

Additional Information

Year Founded: 1979
Capital Under Management: $106,032,000
Current Activity Level : Actively seeking new investments

SOCIT D INVESTISSEMENT TREMPLIN 2000, INC.

2, Complexe Desjardins
bureau 1717
Montreal, Canada H5B 1B8
Phone: 514-281-7131
Fax: 514-281-7808

Type of Firm

Private Equity Advisor or Fund of Funds

Additional Information
Year Founded: 1987
Current Activity Level : Actively seeking new investments

SOCIUS CAPITAL GROUP LLC

6505 East Dorado Place
Greenwood Village
Englewood, CO USA 80111
Website: www.yournewpartner.com

Other Offices
3701 Sacramento Street, Suite 185
San Francisco, CA USA 94118
Phone: 4159229421
Fax: 4159229424

Management and Staff
David Woodward, Co-Founder
Jeffrey Lamb, Co-Founder
John Katzenberg, Managing Partner
Stephen Hill, Managing Partner

Type of Firm
Private Equity Firm

Project Preferences

Type of Financing Preferred:
Leveraged Buyout
Acquisition
Recapitalizations

Geographical Preferences

United States Preferences:
West Coast

Industry Preferences

In Business Serv. prefer:
Services
Distribution

In Manufact. prefer:
Manufacturing

Additional Information
Year Founded: 2010
Current Activity Level : Actively seeking new investments

SODERO PARTICIPATIONS SAS

13 rue la Perouse
BP 31715
Nantes, France 44017
Phone: 33240415216
Fax: 33240485987

Other Offices
20 quai Duguay Trouin
Rennes, France 35000
Phone: 33-2-9967-9769
Fax: 33-2-9967-4600

Management and Staff
Didier Patault, President

Type of Firm
Corporate PE/Venture

Association Membership
French Venture Capital Association (AFIC)

Project Preferences

Type of Financing Preferred:
Leveraged Buyout
Early Stage
Expansion
Generalist PE
Balanced
Later Stage
Recapitalizations

Size of Investments Considered:
Min Size of Investment Considered (000s): $131
Max Size of Investment Considered (000s): $1,958

Geographical Preferences

International Preferences:
Europe
Faroe Islands
France

Industry Preferences

In Communications prefer:
Wireless Communications

In Industrial/Energy prefer:
Energy
Industrial Products
Environmental Related

In Business Serv. prefer:
Services

Additional Information
Name of Most Recent Fund: Loire Bretagne Expansion 6 FIP
Most Recent Fund Was Raised: 06/30/2010
Year Founded: 2000
Capital Under Management: $9,300,000
Current Activity Level : Actively seeking new investments

SODICA SASU

100 boulevard du Montparnasse
Paris, France 75682
Phone: 33143232424
Fax: 33143236582
Website: www.sodica-midcaps.fr

Management and Staff
Arnaud Pradier, Partner
Karine Gras, Chief Financial Officer
Karine Gras, Chief Financial Officer

Type of Firm
Bank Affiliated

Association Membership
French Venture Capital Association (AFIC)

Project Preferences

Type of Financing Preferred:
Leveraged Buyout
Early Stage
Later Stage
Acquisition

Geographical Preferences

International Preferences:
France

Industry Preferences

In Consumer Related prefer:
Food/Beverage

In Agr/Forestr/Fish prefer:
Agriculture related

Additional Information
Year Founded: 2004
Current Activity Level : Actively seeking new investments

SODICAL SCR

Jacinto Benavente No. 2
Arroyo de la Encomienda
Valladolid, Spain 47195
Phone: 34983343811
Fax: 34983330702
E-mail: sodical@sodical.es
Website: www.sodical.es

Management and Staff
Fernando Calleja Merino, Chief Financial Officer

Type of Firm
Private Equity Firm

Association Membership
Spanish Venture Capital Association (ASCRI)

Project Preferences

Type of Financing Preferred:
Expansion
Balanced
Seed
Startup

Geographical Preferences

International Preferences:
Europe
Spain

Industry Preferences

In Industrial/Energy prefer:
Materials

In Agr/Forestr/Fish prefer:
Agribusiness
Agriculture related

In Other prefer:
Environment Responsible

Additional Information

Year Founded: 2007
Current Activity Level: Actively seeking new investments

SODICAMAN CASTILLA LA MANCHA

Avda. De Castilla, 12-1
Guadalajara, Spain 19002
Phone: 34949229121
Fax: 34949215555
E-mail: sodicaman@sodicaman.com
Website: www.icmf.es

Type of Firm

Private Equity Firm

Association Membership

Spanish Venture Capital Association (ASCRI)

Project Preferences

Type of Financing Preferred:
Early Stage
Balanced
Later Stage

Geographical Preferences

International Preferences:
Spain

Additional Information

Year Founded: 1999
Capital Under Management: $14,600,000
Current Activity Level: Actively seeking new investments

SODIEX SA

Avda. Ruta de la Plata, 13
Apdo. de correo
Caceres, Spain 10001
Phone: 34-92422-4878
Fax: 927243304
E-mail: sodiex@sodiex.es
Website: www.sodiex.es

Management and Staff

Pablo Gonzalez, President

Type of Firm

Government Affiliated Program

Association Membership

Spanish Venture Capital Association (ASCRI)

Project Preferences

Type of Financing Preferred:
Early Stage
Expansion
Startup

Size of Investments Considered:
Min Size of Investment Considered (000s): $30,000
Max Size of Investment Considered (000s): $900,000

Geographical Preferences

International Preferences:
Europe
Spain

Industry Preferences

In Communications prefer:
Commercial Communications

In Computer Software prefer:
Software

In Semiconductor/Electr prefer:
Electronics

In Biotechnology prefer:
Biotechnology

In Medical/Health prefer:
Health Services

In Consumer Related prefer:
Food/Beverage
Consumer Products
Consumer Services
Hotels and Resorts

In Industrial/Energy prefer:
Energy
Industrial Products
Environmental Related

In Transportation prefer:
Transportation
Aerospace

In Financial Services prefer:
Financial Services

In Business Serv. prefer:
Media

In Agr/Forestr/Fish prefer:
Agribusiness

Additional Information

Year Founded: 2004
Current Activity Level: Actively seeking new investments

SODIS SICAR SA

Building Ettanmia
Medenine, Tunisia 4119
Phone: 21675642628
Fax: 21675640593
Website: www.sodis-sicar.com

Type of Firm

Private Equity Firm

Project Preferences

Type of Financing Preferred:
Early Stage
Balanced
Later Stage

Geographical Preferences

International Preferences:
Tunisia

Industry Preferences

In Biotechnology prefer:
Agricultural/Animal Bio.

In Consumer Related prefer:
Entertainment and Leisure

In Financial Services prefer:
Financial Services

In Business Serv. prefer:
Services

Additional Information

Year Founded: 1966
Current Activity Level: Actively seeking new investments

SOFILARO GESTION SAS

Avenue du Montpellieret
Lattes, France 34970
Website: www.sofilaro.fr

Type of Firm

Bank Affiliated

Project Preferences

Type of Financing Preferred:
Early Stage
Expansion
Later Stage
Seed
Management Buyouts
Acquisition

Geographical Preferences

International Preferences:
France

Additional Information
Year Founded: 2002
Current Activity Level : Actively seeking new investments

SOFIMAC INNOVATION SAS

23 Avenue D'Iena
Paris, France 75116
Phone: 33145014646
Fax: 33145014660
E-mail: info@isourcevc.com
Website: www.isourcevc.com

Management and Staff
Didier Moret, Co-Founder
Jean-Philippe Zoghbi, Managing Partner
Nicolas Landrin, Managing Partner
Nicolas Boulay, Principal

Type of Firm
Private Equity Firm

Association Membership
French Venture Capital Association (AFIC)
European Private Equity and Venture Capital Assoc.

Project Preferences

Type of Financing Preferred:
Early Stage
Balanced
Seed
Startup

Size of Investments Considered:
Min Size of Investment Considered (000s): $676
Max Size of Investment Considered (000s): $2,029

Geographical Preferences

International Preferences:
Europe
Western Europe
France

Industry Preferences

In Communications prefer:
Communications and Media
Telecommunications
Other Communication Prod.

In Computer Software prefer:
Software

In Internet Specific prefer:
Internet

In Computer Other prefer:
Computer Related

In Medical/Health prefer:
Medical/Health

In Industrial/Energy prefer:
Environmental Related

In Business Serv. prefer:
Services
Media

Additional Information
Name of Most Recent Fund: Angel Source FCPR
Most Recent Fund Was Raised: 12/11/2012
Year Founded: 1998
Capital Under Management: $200,000,000
Current Activity Level : Actively seeking new investments

SOFIMAC PARTNERS SA

24 avenue de l'Agriculture
Clermont-Ferrand, France 63100
Phone: 33473745757
Fax: 33473745758
E-mail: info@sofimacpartners.com
Website: www.sofimacpartners.com

Other Offices

19, rue de l'arbre sec
Lyon, France 69001
Phone: 33-4-3726-2090
Fax: 33-4-7207-7038

38 rue de la Marine de Loire
Orleans, France 45100
Phone: 33-2-3822-3060
Fax: 33-2-3856-6225

Type of Firm
Private Equity Firm

Project Preferences

Type of Financing Preferred:
Leveraged Buyout
Early Stage
Mezzanine
Generalist PE
Later Stage
Seed
Acquisition
Startup

Geographical Preferences

International Preferences:
Europe
France

Industry Preferences

In Computer Software prefer:
Software

In Internet Specific prefer:
Ecommerce

In Biotechnology prefer:
Biotechnology

In Medical/Health prefer:
Medical/Health
Pharmaceuticals

In Consumer Related prefer:
Retail

In Industrial/Energy prefer:
Energy
Industrial Products
Materials
Advanced Materials

In Transportation prefer:
Aerospace

In Business Serv. prefer:
Services
Distribution

In Other prefer:
Environment Responsible

Additional Information
Year Founded: 1977
Capital Under Management: $34,100,000
Current Activity Level : Actively seeking new investments

SOFINA SA

Rue de l'Industrie, 31
Brussels, Belgium 1040
Phone: 403219397
Website: www.sofina.be

Management and Staff
Harold Boel, Chief Executive Officer
Jean-Francois Lambert, Chief Operating Officer

Type of Firm
Investment Management Firm

Project Preferences

Type of Financing Preferred:
Leveraged Buyout
Balanced
Acquisition

Geographical Preferences

United States Preferences:

International Preferences:
Europe
Asia

Industry Preferences

In Internet Specific prefer:
E-Commerce Technology

Additional Information
Year Founded: 1956
Current Activity Level : Actively seeking new investments

SOFINDEV MANAGEMENT NV

Lambroekstraat 5 D
Green Square
Diegem, Belgium 1831
Phone: 3227207007
Fax: 3227214352
E-mail: info@sofindev.be
Website: www.sofindev.be

Management and Staff
Eric Van Droogenbroeck, Managing Partner

Type of Firm
Investment Management Firm

Association Membership
Belgium Venturing Association

Project Preferences

Role in Financing:
Prefer role as deal originator but will also invest in deals created by others

Type of Financing Preferred:
Leveraged Buyout
Mezzanine
Generalist PE
Later Stage
Management Buyouts
Acquisition

Geographical Preferences

International Preferences:
Belgium
France

Industry Focus
(% based on actual investment)
Biotechnology   56.1%
Other Products   34.1%
Computer Software and Services 9.8%

Additional Information
Year Founded: 1982
Capital Under Management: $96,700,000
Current Activity Level: Actively seeking new investments
Method of Compensation: Return on investment is of primary concern, do not charge fees

SOFINIM NV

Begijnenvest 113
Antwerpen, Belgium 2000
Phone: 3232318770
Fax: 3232252533
E-mail: info@avh.be

Other Offices
Avenue de Tervueren 72
Brussels, Belgium B-1040
Phone: 3222370701
Fax: 3222370800

Management and Staff
Andre Cooreman, Chief Operating Officer
Tom Bamelis, Founder

Type of Firm
Corporate PE/Venture

Association Membership
Belgium Venturing Association
European Private Equity and Venture Capital Assoc.

Project Preferences

Role in Financing:
Prefer role as deal originator but will also invest in deals created by others

Type of Financing Preferred:
Fund of Funds
Leveraged Buyout
Control-block Purchases
Mezzanine
Balanced
Public Companies
Turnaround
Later Stage
Management Buyouts
Acquisition
Private Placement
Industry Rollups
Recapitalizations

Size of Investments Considered:
Min Size of Investment Considered (000s): $3,000
Max Size of Investment Considered (000s): $146,007

Geographical Preferences

International Preferences:
Luxembourg
Netherlands
Belgium
France

Industry Focus
(% based on actual investment)
Consumer Related   48.6%
Other Products   44.2%
Internet Specific   4.0%
Medical/Health   1.8%
Biotechnology   1.4%

Additional Information
Year Founded: 1988
Capital Under Management: $463,100,000
Current Activity Level: Actively seeking new investments
Method of Compensation: Return on invest. most important, but chg. closing fees, service fees, etc.

SOFINNOVA PARTNERS SAS

16-18, Rue du Quatre Septembre
Paris, France 75002
Phone: 33153054100
Fax: 33153054129
E-mail: info@sofinnova.fr
Website: www.sofinnova.fr

Management and Staff
Alain Tingaud, Venture Partner
Alessio Beverina, Partner
Antoine Papiernik, Managing Partner
Gerard Hascoet, Venture Partner
Graziano Seghezzi, Partner
Jean-Claude Martinez, Venture Partner
Maina Bhaman, Partner
Olivier Sichel, Partner
Rafaele Tordjman, Partner
Rob Woodman, Principal

Type of Firm
Private Equity Firm

Association Membership
French Venture Capital Association (AFIC)
European Private Equity and Venture Capital Assoc.

Project Preferences

Type of Financing Preferred:
Early Stage
Turnaround
Seed
Startup
Recapitalizations

Size of Investments Considered:
Min Size of Investment Considered (000s): $2,824
Max Size of Investment Considered (000s): $28,245

Geographical Preferences

United States Preferences:

International Preferences:
Europe
France

Industry Preferences

In Communications prefer:
Commercial Communications
Telecommunications
Wireless Communications

In Internet Specific prefer:
E-Commerce Technology
Internet

In Semiconductor/Electr prefer:
Semiconductor

In Biotechnology prefer:
Biotechnology
Human Biotechnology
Industrial Biotechnology

In Medical/Health prefer:
Medical/Health
Medical Diagnostics
Medical Therapeutics
Drug/Equipmt Delivery
Pharmaceuticals

In Industrial/Energy prefer:
Energy
Alternative Energy
Environmental Related

In Other prefer:
Environment Responsible

Additional Information
Name of Most Recent Fund: Sofinnova Green Seed Fund
Most Recent Fund Was Raised: 12/11/2012
Year Founded: 1997
Capital Under Management: $1,624,800,000
Current Activity Level : Actively seeking new investments

SOFINNOVA VENTURES INC

3000 Sand Hill Road
Building Four, Suite 250
Menlo Park, CA USA 94025
Phone: 6506818420
Fax: 6503222037
Website: www.sofinnova.com

Other Offices
1250 Prospect Street
Ocean Level - 4
LA JOLLA, CA USA 92037
Phone: 858-551-4880
Fax: 858-459-0466

Fitzwilliam Hall, Fitzwilliam Place
Dublin, Ireland 94568
Phone: 35301669662
Fax: 35301669474

Management and Staff
Anand Mehra, General Partner
Cory Freedland, Principal
Goro Takeda, Venture Partner
James Healy, General Partner
Michael Powell, General Partner
Sunil Agarwal, Partner

Type of Firm
Private Equity Firm

Association Membership
French Venture Capital Association (AFIC)
Western Association of Venture Capitalists (WAVC)
National Venture Capital Association - USA (NVCA)

Project Preferences

Role in Financing:
Prefer role as deal originator but will also invest in deals created by others

Type of Financing Preferred:
Early Stage
Later Stage
Seed
Startup

Size of Investments Considered:
Min Size of Investment Considered (000s): $100
Max Size of Investment Considered (000s): $30,000

Geographical Preferences

United States Preferences:
West Coast

International Preferences:
India
Western Europe

Industry Focus
(% based on actual investment)
Biotechnology	56.0%
Medical/Health	23.0%
Computer Software and Services	5.6%
Internet Specific	5.4%
Communications and Media	4.2%
Semiconductors/Other Elect.	3.6%
Computer Hardware	2.1%
Industrial/Energy	0.0%

Additional Information
Name of Most Recent Fund: Sofinnova Venture Partners VIII, L.P.
Most Recent Fund Was Raised: 10/14/2011
Year Founded: 1974
Capital Under Management: $1,000,000,000
Current Activity Level : Actively seeking new investments
Method of Compensation: Return on investment is of primary concern, do not charge fees

SOFIPACA SA

25 Chemin des Trois Cypres
Aix En Provence, France 13097
Phone: 33442192990
E-mail: sofipaca@wanadoo.fr
Website: www.sofipaca.fr

Management and Staff
Yves Besset, Chief Executive Officer

Type of Firm
Bank Affiliated

Association Membership
French Venture Capital Association (AFIC)

Project Preferences

Type of Financing Preferred:
Balanced
Later Stage
Recapitalizations

Geographical Preferences

International Preferences:
France

Additional Information
Year Founded: 1984
Capital Under Management: $35,300,000
Current Activity Level : Actively seeking new investments

SOFTBANK CAPITAL PARTNERS L P

38 Glen Avenue
Newton, MA USA 02459
Phone: 6179289300
Fax: 6179289304
E-mail: contactus@softbank.com
Website: www.softbankvc.com

Other Offices
One Circle Star Way
Fourth Floor
SAN CARLOS, CA USA 94070
Phone: 6179289300
Fax: 6179289304

130 West 25th Street
8th Floor
MANHATTAN, NY USA 10001
Phone: 617-928-9300
Fax: 617-928-9304

One News Plaza, Suite 10
BUFFALO, NY USA 14203
Phone: 716-845-7520
Fax: 716-845-7539

Management and Staff
Eric Hippeau, Partner
Joe Medved, Partner
Jordan Levy, Partner
Josh Guttman, Partner
Josh Lubov, Chief Financial Officer
Kabir Misra, Managing Partner
Matt Krna, Partner
Michael Perlis, Partner
Phil Shevrin, Vice President
Ron Schreiber, Partner
Ronald Fisher, Managing Partner
Scarlett O Sullivan, Partner
Steve Murray, Partner

Type of Firm
Corporate PE/Venture

Association Membership

New England Venture Capital Association
National Venture Capital Association - USA (NVCA)

Project Preferences

Role in Financing:
Prefer role as deal originator but will also invest in deals created by others

Type of Financing Preferred:
Early Stage
Expansion
Balanced
Later Stage
Startup

Geographical Preferences

United States Preferences:

International Preferences:
China
Asia
Japan

Industry Focus

(% based on actual investment)
Internet Specific	54.7%
Computer Software and Services	24.3%
Consumer Related	10.8%
Communications and Media	5.9%
Computer Hardware	2.1%
Semiconductors/Other Elect.	1.3%
Other Products	0.9%
Industrial/Energy	0.0%

Additional Information

Name of Most Recent Fund: SOFTBANK Capital Technology New York Fund II, L.P.
Most Recent Fund Was Raised: 05/30/2013
Year Founded: 1994
Capital Under Management: $3,300,000,000
Current Activity Level : Making few, if any, new investments
Method of Compensation: Return on investment is of primary concern, do not charge fees

---

SOFTBANK CHINA & INDIA HOLDINGS LTD

No. 1515, West Nanjing Road, Suite 802, Shanghai Kerry Ctr.
Shanghai, China 200040
E-mail: info@softbankci.com
Website: www.softbankci.com

Management and Staff

Anil Viakara, Partner
Anna Lo, Co-Founder
Kabir Misra, President
Scarlett O Sullivan, Chief Operating Officer
William Bao Bean, Partner

Type of Firm
Corporate PE/Venture

Project Preferences

Type of Financing Preferred:
Early Stage
Mezzanine

Geographical Preferences

International Preferences:
India
China
Asia

Industry Preferences

In Communications prefer:
Telecommunications
Media and Entertainment

In Computer Software prefer:
Software

In Internet Specific prefer:
Internet

In Medical/Health prefer:
Health Services

In Consumer Related prefer:
Consumer Services

In Financial Services prefer:
Financial Services

Additional Information
Year Founded: 2006
Current Activity Level : Actively seeking new investments

SOFTBANK GROUP CORP

1-9-1, Higashi-shimbashi
Tokyo Shiodome Bldg
Tokyo, Japan 105-7303
Phone: 81368892000
Fax: 81368892000
Website: www.softbank.co.jp

Other Offices

14 Flood Walk
London, United Kingdom SW3 5RG
Phone: 44-20-7881-2700
Fax: 44-20-7881-2701
, Suites 2115-2118, Two Pacific Place
88 Queensway
Admiralty, Hong Kong
Phone: 852-2918-2206
Fax: 852-2234-9116

Type of Firm
Corporate PE/Venture

Project Preferences

Type of Financing Preferred:
Early Stage
Balanced
Startup

Geographical Preferences

United States Preferences:

International Preferences:
Latin America
Ireland
United Kingdom
Europe
China
Asia
Korea, South
Japan
All International

Industry Focus

(% based on actual investment)
Computer Software and Services	46.7%
Internet Specific	42.8%
Other Products	8.2%
Communications and Media	1.3%
Consumer Related	0.4%
Medical/Health	0.3%
Biotechnology	0.2%
Industrial/Energy	0.1%

Additional Information
Year Founded: 1956
Current Activity Level : Actively seeking new investments

SOFTBANK VENTURES KOREA INC

8th Floor, Shinyoung Building
68-5 Chungdam-dong, Gangnam-gu
Seoul, South Korea 135-100
Phone: 82234849000
Fax: 82234849010
Website: ventures.softbank.co.kr

Management and Staff

Greg Moon, Chief Executive Officer
Steve Lee, Managing Director
Sungwoon Yu, Principal

Type of Firm
Corporate PE/Venture

Association Membership
Korean Venture Capital Association (KVCA)

Project Preferences

Type of Financing Preferred:
Early Stage
Balanced
Later Stage
Seed
Recapitalizations

Geographical Preferences

United States Preferences:
Southeast

International Preferences:
Asia
Korea, South

Industry Preferences

In Communications prefer:
Wireless Communications
Data Communications

In Computer Software prefer:
Software

In Internet Specific prefer:
Internet

In Consumer Related prefer:
Education Related

Additional Information
Year Founded: 2000
Capital Under Management: $95,400,000
Current Activity Level : Actively seeking new investments

SOGAL VENTURES

630 Childs Way
Los Angeles, CA USA 90089
E-mail: deals@sogalventures.com
Website: sogalventures.com

Type of Firm
Private Equity Firm

Project Preferences

Type of Financing Preferred:
Early Stage
Startup

Geographical Preferences

United States Preferences:

International Preferences:
Asia

Additional Information
Year Founded: 2017
Current Activity Level : Actively seeking new investments

SOLACE CAPITAL PARTNERS LLC

11111 Santa Monica Boulevard, Suite 1275
West Los Angeles, CA USA 90025
Phone: 3105972888
Fax: 3109195402
Website: solacecap.com

Other Offices
299 Park Avenue
Sixth Floor
New York, NY USA 10171
Phone: 2122561108
Fax: 3109195402

Management and Staff
Brett Wyard, Managing Partner
Brian Moody, Managing Director
Christopher Brothers, Managing Partner
Vincent Cebula, Managing Partner

Type of Firm
Private Equity Firm

Project Preferences

Type of Financing Preferred:
Leveraged Buyout
Acquisition
Recapitalizations

Geographical Preferences

United States Preferences:

Canadian Preferences:
All Canada

Industry Preferences

In Communications prefer:
Telecommunications
Media and Entertainment
Entertainment

In Consumer Related prefer:
Consumer Products
Consumer Services

In Industrial/Energy prefer:
Energy
Industrial Products

In Transportation prefer:
Transportation
Aerospace

In Financial Services prefer:
Financial Services

In Manufact. prefer:
Manufacturing

Additional Information
Year Founded: 2014
Capital Under Management: $576,000,000

Current Activity Level : Actively seeking new investments

SOLAMERE GROUP LLC

137 Newbury Street
Seventh Floor
Boston, MA USA 02116
Phone: 8573629205
E-mail: investorrelations@solameregroup.com
Website: www.solameregroup.com

Management and Staff
Allan Dowds, Chief Financial Officer
Kearney Shanahan, Vice President

Type of Firm
Private Equity Firm

Project Preferences

Type of Financing Preferred:
Fund of Funds
Generalist PE

Additional Information
Year Founded: 2008
Capital Under Management: $425,950,000
Current Activity Level : Actively seeking new investments

SOLARIS ENERGY CAPITAL LLC

9811 Katy Freeway, Suite 900
Houston, TX USA 77024
Phone: 2815013070
Website: solarisenergycapital.com

Management and Staff
Chris Work, Chief Financial Officer
Jonathan Scheiner, Vice President
Kyle Ramachandran, Vice President
William Zartler, Managing Partner

Type of Firm
Private Equity Firm

Project Preferences

Type of Financing Preferred:
Generalist PE

Geographical Preferences

United States Preferences:
North America

Industry Preferences

In Industrial/Energy prefer:
Oil & Gas Drilling,Explor

Additional Information
Year Founded: 1969
Current Activity Level : Actively seeking new investments

SOLAS BIOVENTURES (AEGEA) LLC

835 Georgia Ave, Suite 800
Chattanooga, TN USA 37402

Type of Firm
Private Equity Firm

Additional Information
Year Founded: 1969
Current Activity Level : Actively seeking new investments

SOLBORN VENTURE INVESTMENT CO LTD

66-4, Cheongdam-dong
1/F, Cheongdam Spopia, Gangnam
Seoul, South Korea 135953
Phone: 8225467722
Fax: 8225469959
Website: www.solbornvi.com

Type of Firm
Corporate PE/Venture

Association Membership
Korean Venture Capital Association (KVCA)

Project Preferences
Type of Financing Preferred:
Balanced

Geographical Preferences
International Preferences:
Korea, South

Industry Preferences
In Biotechnology prefer:
Biotechnology

Additional Information
Year Founded: 2000
Capital Under Management: $8,100,000
Current Activity Level : Actively seeking new investments

SOLIC CAPITAL PARTNERS LLC

1603 Orrington Avenue, Suite 1600
Evanston, IL USA 60201
Phone: 8475831618
E-mail: info@soliccapital.com
Website: www.soliccapital.com

Type of Firm
Bank Affiliated

Project Preferences
Type of Financing Preferred:
Distressed Debt
Recapitalizations

Geographical Preferences
United States Preferences:
North America

Industry Preferences
In Medical/Health prefer:
Medical/Health

In Consumer Related prefer:
Consumer
Retail

In Industrial/Energy prefer:
Energy

In Financial Services prefer:
Financial Services
Real Estate
Financial Services

In Manufact. prefer:
Manufacturing

Additional Information
Year Founded: 2012
Capital Under Management: $35,000,000
Current Activity Level : Actively seeking new investments

SOLID VENTURES BV

Postbus 14816
Amsterdam, Netherlands 1001 LH
Phone: 31655325873
E-mail: info@solidventures.nl
Website: www.solidventures.nl

Management and Staff
Floris Van Alkemade, Partner
Herman DeLatte, Partner
Robert Wilhelm, Partner

Type of Firm
Private Equity Firm

Project Preferences
Type of Financing Preferred:
Early Stage
Balanced
Later Stage

Size of Investments Considered:
Min Size of Investment Considered (000s): $129
Max Size of Investment Considered (000s): $3,214

Geographical Preferences
International Preferences:
Luxembourg
Netherlands
Belgium

Industry Preferences
In Computer Software prefer:
Software

In Internet Specific prefer:
Internet

In Business Serv. prefer:
Media

Additional Information
Name of Most Recent Fund: Solid Capital ICT Fund III
Most Recent Fund Was Raised: 03/30/2005
Year Founded: 2004
Current Activity Level : Actively seeking new investments

SOLID WOOD SHANGHAI INVESTMENT MANAGEMENT CO LTD

Huashen Road
Room 419, 4F, Block 1, No. 180
Shanghai, China

Type of Firm
Private Equity Firm

Project Preferences
Type of Financing Preferred:
Balanced

Industry Preferences
In Communications prefer:
Media and Entertainment

In Internet Specific prefer:
Internet

In Biotechnology prefer:
Industrial Biotechnology

In Medical/Health prefer:
Medical/Health

In Industrial/Energy prefer:
Materials

Additional Information
Year Founded: 2015
Current Activity Level : Actively seeking new investments

Pratt's Guide to Private Equity & Venture Capital Sources

SOLIDARITY FUND QFL

545, boul cremazie Est
Bureau 200
Montreal, Canada H2M 2W4
Phone: 5143833663
Fax: 5143832501
E-mail: infoinvestissement@fondsftq.com
Website: www.fondsftq.com

Management and Staff
Chantal Dore, Vice President
Maurice Prudhomme, Vice President
Raymond Bachand, President
Richard Cloutier, Principal

Type of Firm
Private Equity Firm

Association Membership
Canadian Venture Capital Association

Project Preferences

Role in Financing:
Will function either as deal originator or investor in deals created by others

Type of Financing Preferred:
Leveraged Buyout
Mezzanine
Generalist PE
Balanced

Geographical Preferences

Canadian Preferences:
Quebec

Industry Preferences

In Communications prefer:
Telecommunications

In Computer Hardware prefer:
Computer Graphics and Dig

In Industrial/Energy prefer:
Energy Conservation Relat
Industrial Products

In Agr/Forestr/Fish prefer:
Agribusiness

Additional Information
Year Founded: 1994
Capital Under Management: $5,631,200,000
Current Activity Level : Actively seeking new investments
Method of Compensation: Return on invest. most important, but chg. closing fees, service fees, etc.

SOLIDUS COMPANY, L.P.

4015 Hillsboro Pike, Suite 214
Nashville, TN USA 37215
Phone: 6156653818
Website: www.solidus.com

Management and Staff
Brad Reed, Partner
Vic Gatto, Partner

Type of Firm
Private Equity Firm

Project Preferences

Type of Financing Preferred:
Early Stage
Seed

Industry Preferences

In Medical/Health prefer:
Health Services

In Business Serv. prefer:
Media

Additional Information
Name of Most Recent Fund: Solidus-TNInvestco
Most Recent Fund Was Raised: 08/04/2010
Year Founded: 1997
Capital Under Management: $20,000,000
Current Activity Level : Actively seeking new investments

SOLIDUS INVESTMENT CO LTD

Yeoksam-dong, Gangnam-gu
Seoul, South Korea 135907
Phone: 82234683341
Website: www.solidusvc.com

Type of Firm
Private Equity Firm

Association Membership
Korean Venture Capital Association (KVCA)

Project Preferences

Type of Financing Preferred:
Balanced

Geographical Preferences

International Preferences:
Korea, South

Industry Preferences

In Biotechnology prefer:
Agricultural/Animal Bio.

In Medical/Health prefer:
Medical/Health

In Consumer Related prefer:
Food/Beverage

In Agr/Forestr/Fish prefer:
Agribusiness

Additional Information
Year Founded: 2011
Current Activity Level : Actively seeking new investments

SOLIS CAPITAL PARTNERS LLC

23 Corporate Plaza, Suite 215
Newport Beach, CA USA 92660
Phone: 9492962440
Fax: 9497204675
Website: www.soliscapital.com

Other Offices
3371 Calle Tres Vistas, Suite 100
Encinitas, CA USA 92024
Phone: 7603099436

Management and Staff
Craig Dupper, Partner
Dan Lubeck, Managing Director
Josh Harmsen, Principal

Type of Firm
Private Equity Firm

Project Preferences

Type of Financing Preferred:
Leveraged Buyout
Management Buyouts
Acquisition
Recapitalizations

Geographical Preferences

United States Preferences:
California
West Coast
All U.S.

Industry Preferences

In Computer Software prefer:
Software

In Business Serv. prefer:
Services
Distribution

In Manufact. prefer:
Manufacturing

Additional Information
Name of Most Recent Fund: Solis Capital Partners II, L.P.
Most Recent Fund Was Raised: 02/10/2012
Year Founded: 2006
Capital Under Management: $61,000,000
Current Activity Level : Actively seeking new investments

SOLITAIRE CAPITAL ADVISORS PVT LTD

112, 113 Charmwood Plaza
Suraj Kund Road, Eros Garden
Faridabad, India 121 009
Phone: 91-29-411-8193
Fax: 91-29-411-8194
E-mail: solitaire@solitairecapital.com
Website: www.solitairecapital.com

Other Offices

3A Margate Road
Singapore, Singapore 438076
Phone: 65-6536-8915
Fax: 65-6536-8914

241, Okhla Industrial Estate
Phase III
New Delhi, India 110 019
Phone: 91-11-4100-0861

Management and Staff

Sanjiv Ahuja, Chief Executive Officer

Type of Firm

Private Equity Firm

Project Preferences

Type of Financing Preferred:
Balanced

Geographical Preferences

International Preferences:
India

Industry Preferences

In Financial Services prefer:
Real Estate

Additional Information

Year Founded: 2005
Current Activity Level : Actively seeking new investments

SOLOMON GLOBAL HOLDINGS INC

88 East Broad Street
Floor 15 Key Bank Building
Columbus, OH USA 43215
Phone: 6147324906
Fax: 6148552823
E-mail: info@solomongh.com
Website: www.solomonglobalholdings.com

Management and Staff

Darren Jordan, Chief Operating Officer
Ryan Retcher, Chief Financial Officer
William Sudeck, Managing Director

Type of Firm

Investment Management Firm

Project Preferences

Type of Financing Preferred:
Leveraged Buyout
Acquisition

Industry Preferences

In Communications prefer:
Telecommunications

In Consumer Related prefer:
Consumer Products

In Industrial/Energy prefer:
Energy

In Financial Services prefer:
Financial Services
Real Estate

In Business Serv. prefer:
Consulting Services

Additional Information

Year Founded: 2011
Current Activity Level : Actively seeking new investments

SOLSTICE CAPITAL

81 Washington Street, Suite 303
Salem, MA USA 01970
Phone: 6175237733
E-mail: info@solcap.com
Website: www.solcap.com

Management and Staff

Harry George, Managing Partner
Henry Newman, General Partner

Type of Firm

Private Equity Firm

Project Preferences

Role in Financing:
Will function either as deal originator or investor in deals created by others

Type of Financing Preferred:
Early Stage
Seed
Startup

Size of Investments Considered:
Min Size of Investment Considered (000s): $500
Max Size of Investment Considered (000s): $1,000

Geographical Preferences

United States Preferences:
Arizona
Northwest
Northeast
Southwest

Industry Focus

(% based on actual investment)
Computer Software and Services	31.8%
Biotechnology	25.5%
Medical/Health	15.2%
Industrial/Energy	10.7%
Internet Specific	6.5%
Computer Hardware	4.7%
Semiconductors/Other Elect.	4.2%
Communications and Media	1.1%
Consumer Related	0.3%

Additional Information

Name of Most Recent Fund: Solstice Capital II, L.P.
Most Recent Fund Was Raised: 05/22/2001
Year Founded: 1995
Capital Under Management: $85,000,000
Current Activity Level : Actively seeking new investments
Method of Compensation: Professional fee required whether or not deal closes

SOLSTRA CAPITAL PARTNERS A/S

Lautrupsgade Seven, Three
Copenhagen, Denmark 2100
Phone: 4539139100
Website: www.solstracapital.com

Other Offices

47 Park Lane
London, United Kingdom W1K 1PR
Phone: 442076476640

Management and Staff

Johan Ewald Lorentzen, Founder
Oscar Crohn, Founder

Type of Firm

Investment Management Firm

Project Preferences

Type of Financing Preferred:
Value-Add
Generalist PE

Geographical Preferences

International Preferences:
Scandanavia/Nordic Region

Additional Information

Year Founded: 2012
Capital Under Management: $1,679,400,000
Current Activity Level : Actively seeking new investments

SOMA CAPITAL MANAGEMENT LLC

301 Mission Street, Suite 603
San Francisco, CA USA 94105
E-mail: info@somacapital.io
Website: www.somacapital.io

Type of Firm
Private Equity Firm

Project Preferences

Type of Financing Preferred:
Balanced

Additional Information
Year Founded: 1969
Current Activity Level : Actively seeking new investments

SONAE INVESTMENT MANAGEMENT SOFTWARE AND TECHNOLOGY SGPS SA

Rua Henrique Pousao 432
Senhora Da Hora, Portugal 4460841
Phone: 351229572000
Website: www.sonaeim.com

Type of Firm
Private Equity Firm

Project Preferences

Type of Financing Preferred:
Early Stage
Expansion
Balanced
Later Stage
Seed
Startup

Geographical Preferences

International Preferences:
Latin America
United Kingdom
Europe
Portugal
Spain
Israel
Germany

Industry Preferences

In Communications prefer:
Telecommunications

In Internet Specific prefer:
Ecommerce

In Consumer Related prefer:
Retail

Additional Information
Year Founded: 2000
Current Activity Level : Actively seeking new investments

SONANZ GMBH

Franz-Joseph-Strasse 12
Munich, Germany 80801
Phone: 49894115115
E-mail: info@sonanz.com
Website: www.sonanz.com

Type of Firm
Private Equity Advisor or Fund of Funds

Project Preferences

Type of Financing Preferred:
Fund of Funds
Early Stage
Expansion
Later Stage

Industry Preferences

In Industrial/Energy prefer:
Environmental Related

In Other prefer:
Socially Responsible
Environment Responsible

Additional Information
Year Founded: 2015
Capital Under Management: $8,200,000
Current Activity Level : Actively seeking new investments

SONAR VENTURES SL

Lopez de Hoyos 327, 5 -3
Madrid, Spain 28043
Phone: 34917219277
E-mail: info@sonarventures.com
Website: www.sonarventures.com

Type of Firm
Incubator/Development Program

Project Preferences

Type of Financing Preferred:
Startup

Additional Information
Year Founded: 2014
Current Activity Level : Actively seeking new investments

SONOMA BRANDS

153 W. Napa Street
Sonoma, CA USA 95476
E-mail: hello@sonomabrands.co
Website: www.sonomabrands.co

Type of Firm
Incubator/Development Program

Project Preferences

Type of Financing Preferred:
Early Stage

Industry Preferences

In Consumer Related prefer:
Food/Beverage

Additional Information
Year Founded: 2015
Capital Under Management: $60,000,000
Current Activity Level : Actively seeking new investments

SONOMA MANAGEMENT PARTNERS PVT LTD

134/1, I.T.I. Road, Aundh
Fourth floor, Plexus complex
Pune, India 411007
Phone: 912041315656
E-mail: contact@smpequity.com
Website: www.sonomamgmt.com

Management and Staff
Indroneel Dutt, Partner
Jagmeet Lamba, Vice President
Pravin Jain, Chief Executive Officer
Rahul Gupta, President

Type of Firm
Private Equity Firm

Project Preferences

Type of Financing Preferred:
Leveraged Buyout
Acquisition

Geographical Preferences

International Preferences:
India

Additional Information
Year Founded: 2008
Capital Under Management: $16,100,000
Current Activity Level : Actively seeking new investments

SOOCHOW VENTURE CAPITAL CO LTD

No.181, Cuiyuan Road
Suzhou Industrial Zone
Suzhou, Jiangsu, China 215028
Phone: 8651233396288
Fax: 8651265581101
E-mail: sms05058@gsjq.com.cn
Website: www.dwjq.com.cn

Type of Firm
Bank Affiliated

Project Preferences

Type of Financing Preferred:
Balanced

Geographical Preferences

International Preferences:
China

Industry Preferences

In Industrial/Energy prefer:
Advanced Materials

In Business Serv. prefer:
Services

Additional Information
Year Founded: 2010
Current Activity Level : Actively seeking new investments

SOPARTEC SA

Chemin du Cyclotron 6
Louvain-la-Neuve, Belgium 1348
Phone: 3210390021
Fax: 3210390029
E-mail: secretariat@sopartec.com
Website: www.sopartec.com

Management and Staff
Philippe Durieux, Chief Executive Officer
Vivian Capart, Chief Financial Officer

Type of Firm
University Program

Association Membership
Belgium Venturing Association
European Private Equity and Venture Capital Assoc.

Project Preferences

Type of Financing Preferred:
Early Stage
Seed
Startup

Geographical Preferences

International Preferences:
Europe
Netherlands
Belgium
France

Industry Preferences

In Communications prefer:
Communications and Media

In Computer Other prefer:
Computer Related

In Biotechnology prefer:
Biotechnology
Biotech Related Research

In Medical/Health prefer:
Medical/Health

In Industrial/Energy prefer:
Energy

In Other prefer:
Environment Responsible

Additional Information
Year Founded: 1992
Capital Under Management: $34,000,000
Current Activity Level : Actively seeking new investments

SOPROMEC PARTICIPATIONS SA

19 rue du Quatre Septembre
Paris, France 75002
Phone: 33144779480
Fax: 33144778977
E-mail: contact@sopromec.com
Website: www.sopromec.fr

Type of Firm
Private Equity Firm

Association Membership
French Venture Capital Association (AFIC)

Project Preferences

Type of Financing Preferred:
Leveraged Buyout
Generalist PE
Later Stage
Acquisition

Geographical Preferences

International Preferences:
Europe
France

Industry Preferences

In Industrial/Energy prefer:
Industrial Products
Materials

In Business Serv. prefer:
Services
Distribution

In Manufact. prefer:
Manufacturing

Additional Information
Year Founded: 1964
Current Activity Level : Actively seeking new investments

SORENSON CAPITAL PARTNERS LP

3400 North Ashton Boulevard, Suite 400
Lehi, UT USA 84043
Phone: 8014078400
Fax: 8014078411
E-mail: info@sorensoncap.com
Website: www.sorensoncapital.com

Management and Staff
Bert Roberts, Vice President
Brian Dunn, Chief Financial Officer
Curtis Toone, Managing Director
D. Fraser Bullock, Managing Director
David Dame, Managing Director
Jay Suel, Vice President
Jerry Henley, Vice President
John Bennion, Vice President
LeGrand Lewis, Managing Director
Lee Rowe, Vice President
Len Blackwell, Managing Director
Luke Sorenson, Managing Director
Mark Ludwig, Managing Director
Matt Lehman, Managing Director
Peter Sturgeon, Managing Director
Ronald Mika, Managing Director
Tim Layton, Managing Director
Tommy Macdonald, Vice President

Type of Firm
Private Equity Firm

Project Preferences

Type of Financing Preferred:
Leveraged Buyout
Expansion
Generalist PE
Balanced

Geographical Preferences

United States Preferences:
Rocky Mountain
West Coast

Additional Information
Name of Most Recent Fund: Sorenson Capital Partners II, L.P.
Most Recent Fund Was Raised: 01/07/2008
Year Founded: 2002
Current Activity Level : Actively seeking new investments

SORIDEC INGENIERIE SARL

954, Avenue Jean Mermoz
Residence l 'Acropole
Montpellier, France 34000
Phone: 33499233240
E-mail: contact@soridec.fr
Website: www.soridec.fr

Pratt's Guide to Private Equity & Venture Capital Sources

Type of Firm
Private Equity Firm

Project Preferences

Type of Financing Preferred:
Leveraged Buyout
Early Stage
Expansion
Generalist PE
Later Stage
Seed
Management Buyouts
Acquisition
Startup

Size of Investments Considered:
Min Size of Investment Considered (000s): $129
Max Size of Investment Considered (000s): $3,220

Geographical Preferences

International Preferences:
Europe
Eastern Europe
France

Industry Preferences

In Communications prefer:
Communications and Media

In Computer Software prefer:
Data Processing

In Biotechnology prefer:
Biotechnology

In Consumer Related prefer:
Food/Beverage

In Industrial/Energy prefer:
Industrial Products

In Business Serv. prefer:
Services

In Agr/Forestr/Fish prefer:
Agriculture related

Additional Information
Year Founded: 1983
Current Activity Level : Actively seeking new investments

SOROS STRATEGIC PARTNERS LP

888 Seventh Avenue
33rd Floor
New York, NY USA 10106
Phone: 2122626300
Fax: 2122455154

Management and Staff
Abbas Zuaiter, Chief Financial Officer
Alex Fridlyand, Principal
George Soros, Founder
Srdjan Vukovic, Vice President

Type of Firm
Private Equity Firm

Project Preferences

Type of Financing Preferred:
Leveraged Buyout
Expansion
Generalist PE
Acquisition
Startup

Additional Information
Year Founded: 2000
Current Activity Level : Actively seeking new investments

SOUNDCORE CAPITAL PARTNERS LLC

600 Madison Avenue
20th Floor
New York, NY USA 10022
Phone: 2128121180
Fax: 2124464900
E-mail: info@soundcorecap.com
Website: www.soundcorecap.com

Other Offices
601 Lexington Avenue
40th Floor
MANHATTAN, NY USA 10022
Phone: 2123904223

Type of Firm
Private Equity Firm

Project Preferences

Type of Financing Preferred:
Leveraged Buyout

Size of Investments Considered:
Min Size of Investment Considered (000s): $4,000
Max Size of Investment Considered (000s): $30,000

Geographical Preferences

United States Preferences:
All U.S.

Industry Preferences

In Medical/Health prefer:
Health Services

In Consumer Related prefer:
Food/Beverage
Consumer Products

In Industrial/Energy prefer:
Energy
Materials
Machinery

In Transportation prefer:
Transportation

In Business Serv. prefer:
Services
Distribution

In Manufact. prefer:
Manufacturing

Additional Information
Year Founded: 2015
Current Activity Level : Actively seeking new investments

SOURCE CAPITAL LLC

75 Fourteenth Street, Suite 2700
Atlanta, GA USA 30309
Phone: 8669491381
Fax: 4044104019
Website: www.source-cap.com

Other Offices
150 Spear Street, Suite 950
San Francisco, CA USA 94105
Phone: 4159860165
Fax: 6308397008

Former HQ: 1776 Peachtree Road, Suite 220 South
Atlanta, GA USA 30309
Phone: 8669491381
Fax: 7702344152

Management and Staff
Chad Riedel, Managing Director
Greg Cohn, Managing Director
Katherine Harbin, Managing Director
Thomas Harbin, Managing Director

Type of Firm
Private Equity Firm

Project Preferences

Type of Financing Preferred:
Leveraged Buyout
Expansion
Mezzanine
Management Buyouts
Acquisition
Recapitalizations

Geographical Preferences

United States Preferences:

Canadian Preferences:
All Canada

Industry Preferences

In Medical/Health prefer:
Medical/Health

In Consumer Related prefer:
Consumer Products
Consumer Services

In Business Serv. prefer:
Services
Distribution

In Manufact. prefer:
Manufacturing

Additional Information
Name of Most Recent Fund: Source Capital Mezzanine Fund I, LP
Most Recent Fund Was Raised: 01/27/2011
Year Founded: 2002
Capital Under Management: $40,280,000
Current Activity Level : Actively seeking new investments

SOUTH SUEZ CAPITAL LTD

Suite 104 Grand Baie Office
Park
Grand Baie, Mauritius
Phone: 2302631491
Fax: 2302632087
E-mail: info@southsuez.com
Website: www.southsuez.com

Type of Firm
Private Equity Advisor or Fund of Funds

Association Membership
South African Venture Capital Association (SAVCA)
Emerging Markets Private Equity Association
African Venture Capital Association (AVCA)

Project Preferences

Type of Financing Preferred:
Fund of Funds
Balanced
Fund of Funds of Second

Geographical Preferences

International Preferences:
Nigeria
Senegal
Ghana
Kenya
Togo
South Africa
Zimbabwe
Africa

Industry Preferences

In Communications prefer:
Telecommunications

In Consumer Related prefer:
Retail

In Industrial/Energy prefer:
Oil and Gas Exploration

In Transportation prefer:
Transportation

In Financial Services prefer:
Insurance
Real Estate
Financial Services

In Business Serv. prefer:
Services

In Agr/Forestr/Fish prefer:
Agribusiness

Additional Information
Name of Most Recent Fund: South Suez Africa Fund
Most Recent Fund Was Raised: 12/31/2011
Year Founded: 2011
Capital Under Management: $278,000,000
Current Activity Level : Actively seeking new investments

SOUTH VENTURES

104 Crandon Boulevard
Key Biscayne, FL USA 33149
Phone: 7864085625
E-mail: info@sthventures.com
Website: sthventures.com

Type of Firm
Private Equity Firm

Project Preferences

Type of Financing Preferred:
Startup

Geographical Preferences

United States Preferences:

International Preferences:
Ireland
Brazil
Spain
Colombia

Industry Preferences

In Internet Specific prefer:
E-Commerce Technology
Ecommerce

Additional Information
Year Founded: 2013
Current Activity Level : Actively seeking new investments

SOUTHBRIDGE CAPITAL INC

150 Water Street South
Cambridge, Canada N1R 3E2
Phone: 519-621-8886
Fax: 519-621-8144
E-mail: contact@southbridgeinc.com
Website: southbridgecapitalinc.com

Management and Staff
Bob Yoanidis, Partner
Linda King, Partner
Mike Petersen, Managing Partner

Type of Firm
Private Equity Firm

Project Preferences

Type of Financing Preferred:
Leveraged Buyout

Additional Information
Year Founded: 1997
Current Activity Level : Actively seeking new investments

SOUTHEAST EUROPE EQUITY FUND

C/O 45, Oborishte Street
P.O. Box 147
Sofia, Bulgaria 1504
Phone: 35929434417
Fax: 35929434979

Type of Firm
Private Equity Firm

Project Preferences

Type of Financing Preferred:
Balanced

Geographical Preferences

International Preferences:
Europe
No Preference

Additional Information
Year Founded: 2005
Current Activity Level : Actively seeking new investments

SOUTHERN AFRICA ENTERPRISE DEVELOPMENT FUND

Rosewood House, 1st Flr.
33 Ballyclare Drive
Bryanston, South Africa
Phone: 27-11-367-0900
Fax: 27-11-367-0949
E-mail: info@saedf.com
Website: www.net.co.za

Other Offices

P.O. Box 2241
Saxonwold, South Africa 2132

1825 Eye Street,
International Square, N.W. Suite 400
Washington, DC USA 20006
Phone: 202-587-4749
Fax: 202-466-2693

Management and Staff

Emmanuel Qua-Enoo, Chief Financial Officer

Type of Firm
Government Affiliated Program

Project Preferences

Type of Financing Preferred:
Leveraged Buyout
Expansion
Generalist PE
Turnaround
Management Buyouts
Private Placement

Size of Investments Considered:
Min Size of Investment Considered (000s): $1,000
Max Size of Investment Considered (000s): $5,000

Geographical Preferences

International Preferences:
Angola
Malawi
Swaziland
Zambia
Tanzania
Botswana
Namibia
Lesotho
Mozambique
South Africa

Additional Information

Year Founded: 1994
Capital Under Management: $100,000,000
Current Activity Level : Actively seeking new investments

SOUTHERN CAPITAL GROUP PTE LTD

501 Orchard Road, Suite 17-01 Wheelock Place
Singapore, Singapore 238880
Phone: 6568368600
Fax: 6568368601
E-mail: information@southerncapitalgroup.com
Website: www.southerncapitalgroup.com

Management and Staff

Boh Sang Wei, Vice President
Eiichi Isozaki, Managing Director
Eugene Lai, Managing Director
Jennivine Yuwono, Managing Director
Kenneth Tan, Managing Director
Ming Tze Tjia, Vice President
Ong Guan Hin, Managing Director
Wong Chin Toh, Principal

Type of Firm
Private Equity Firm

Association Membership
Singapore Venture Capital Association (SVCA)

Project Preferences

Type of Financing Preferred:
Leveraged Buyout
Management Buyouts

Geographical Preferences

International Preferences:
Laos
Vietnam
Indonesia
Brunei
China
Thailand
Cambodia
Philippines
Asia
Singapore
Korea, South
Malaysia

Industry Preferences

In Medical/Health prefer:
Medical/Health

In Consumer Related prefer:
Food/Beverage
Consumer Products

In Financial Services prefer:
Financial Services

In Manufact. prefer:
Manufacturing

Additional Information

Year Founded: 2007
Capital Under Management: $400,000,000
Current Activity Level : Actively seeking new investments

SOUTHERN CAPITOL VENTURES LLC

21 Glenwood Avenue, Suite 105
Raleigh, NC USA 27603
Phone: 9198587580
Fax: 9198632394
E-mail: info@southerncapitolventures.com
Website: www.southerncapitolventures.com

Management and Staff

Al Childers, Venture Partner
Ben Brooks, Partner
Dave Murray, General Partner
David Jones, Partner
Jason Caplain, General Partner

Type of Firm
Private Equity Firm

Project Preferences

Role in Financing:
Will function either as deal originator or investor in deals created by others

Type of Financing Preferred:
Early Stage
Later Stage
Seed

Size of Investments Considered:
Min Size of Investment Considered (000s): $35
Max Size of Investment Considered (000s): $1,500

Geographical Preferences

United States Preferences:
Mid Atlantic
Southeast

Industry Preferences

In Communications prefer:
Wireless Communications

In Computer Software prefer:
Software

In Internet Specific prefer:
Ecommerce

In Business Serv. prefer:
Media

Additional Information

Year Founded: 2000
Capital Under Management: $20,000,000
Current Activity Level : Actively seeking new investments
Method of Compensation: Return on investment is of primary concern, do not charge fees

SOUTHERN CROSS CAPITAL MANAGEMENT SA

Av. Libertador 602 Piso 5
Buenos Aires, Argentina C1001ABT
Phone: 541148165054
Fax: 541148162469
Website: www.southerncrossgroup.com

Other Offices

El Regidor 66 Piso 16
Las Condes
Santiago, Chile
Phone: 5625825715
Fax: 5625825180

Av. Brigadeiro Faria Lima, 2277
Conjunto 604 - Jd. Paulistano
Sao Paolo, Brazil 01452-000
Phone: 551130398050
Fax: 551130398052

41 West Putnam Avenue
Second Floor
Greenwich, CT USA 06830
Phone: 2036298272
Fax: 2036298370

Boulevard Manuel Avila Camacho N 40
Edificio Esmeralda I. Piso 18 - 1802
Col. Lomas de Chapultepec, Mexico 11000
Phone: 525580009200
Fax: 525580009202

300 5th Ave. So., Suite 203D
Naples, FL USA 34102
Phone: 239 353-0661

Cra 9 # 77-67 Of 1001
Bogot, Colombia
Phone: 57 1 702-8876

Management and Staff

Angel Uribe, Managing Director
Cesar Perez Barnes, Managing Director
Diego Acevedo, Partner
Diego Stark, Principal
Gonzalo Dulanto, Managing Director
Horacio Reyser, Partner
Marcos Mulcahy, Principal
Norberto Morita, Founder
Raul Sotomayor, Partner
Ricardo Rodriguez, Founder
Rodrigo Lowndes, Managing Director
Sebastian Villa, Partner

Type of Firm

Private Equity Firm

Association Membership

Brazilian Venture Capital Association (ABCR)

Project Preferences

Type of Financing Preferred:
Leveraged Buyout

Geographical Preferences

International Preferences:
Uruguay
Latin America
Argentina
Bolivia
Paraguay
Peru
Mexico
Brazil
Chile

Additional Information

Name of Most Recent Fund: Southern Cross Latin America Private Equity Fund IV, L.P.
Most Recent Fund Was Raised: 05/27/2010
Year Founded: 1998
Capital Under Management: $2,195,810,000
Current Activity Level : Actively seeking new investments

SOUTHERN CROSS VENTURE PARTNERS PTY LTD

80 Mount Street, Level Five
Sydney, Australia 2060
Phone: 61283147400
Fax: 61299576399
E-mail: investmentteam@sxvp.com
Website: www.sxvp.com

Other Offices

285 Hamilton Avenue, Suite 240
PALO ALTO, CA USA 94301
Phone: 6505617150

Management and Staff

Gareth Dando, Co-Founder
Jo Hume, Venture Partner
John Scull, Co-Founder
Jonathan Whitehouse, Chief Financial Officer
Mark Bonnar, Managing Director
Mark Gill, Venture Partner
Robert Christiansen, Co-Founder
William Bartee, Co-Founder

Type of Firm

Private Equity Firm

Association Membership

Australian Venture Capital Association (AVCAL)

Project Preferences

Type of Financing Preferred:
Early Stage
Expansion
Later Stage
Seed
Startup

Size of Investments Considered:
Min Size of Investment Considered (000s): $100
Max Size of Investment Considered (000s): $10,000

Geographical Preferences

International Preferences:
Pacific
Australia

Industry Preferences

In Communications prefer:
Telecommunications

In Computer Software prefer:
Software
Systems Software

In Semiconductor/Electr prefer:
Electronics
Semiconductor

In Industrial/Energy prefer:
Energy
Materials
Environmental Related

In Agr/Forestr/Fish prefer:
Agriculture related

In Other prefer:
Environment Responsible

Additional Information

Year Founded: 2006
Capital Under Management: $427,500,000
Current Activity Level : Actively seeking new investments

SOUTHERN RAYTAI FUND MANAGEMENT CO LTD

No.3 Fuhua Road
3401, ZhuoyueCentry 1st Center
Shenzhen, China
Phone: 8675582778151
Fax: 8675582778151
Website: www.southernraytai.com

Management and Staff

Bingshi Wang, Vice President
Ying Jin, Chief Financial Officer

Type of Firm

Investment Management Firm

Project Preferences

Type of Financing Preferred:
Leveraged Buyout
Balanced

Geographical Preferences

International Preferences:
China

Industry Preferences

In Medical/Health prefer:
Medical/Health
Pharmaceuticals

In Industrial/Energy prefer:
Energy

In Manufact. prefer:
Manufacturing

In Agr/Forestr/Fish prefer:
Agriculture related

Additional Information

Year Founded: 2013
Capital Under Management: $80,256,000
Current Activity Level : Actively seeking new investments

SOUTHFIELD CAPITAL ADVISORS LLC

53 Greenwich Avenue
Second Floor
Greenwich, CT USA 06830
Phone: 2038134100
Fax: 2038134141
E-mail: info@southfieldcapital.com
Website: www.southfieldcapital.com

Other Offices

9900 Corporate Campus Drive, Suite 3000
Louisville, KY USA 40223
Phone: 5026576088
Fax: 5026576089

Management and Staff

A. Andrew Levison, Managing Partner
Andrew Cook, Principal
Eric Sloane, Partner
Heb James, Principal
Jonathan Goldstein, Chief Financial Officer
Steven Axel, Partner
Vincent Tyra, Managing Partner

Type of Firm

Private Equity Firm

Association Membership

Natl Assoc of Small Bus. Inv. Co (NASBIC)

Project Preferences

Type of Financing Preferred:
Leveraged Buyout
Opportunistic
Management Buyouts
Acquisition
Industry Rollups
Recapitalizations

Size of Investments Considered:
Min Size of Investment Considered (000s): $10,000
Max Size of Investment Considered (000s): $40,000

Geographical Preferences

United States Preferences:
All U.S.

Canadian Preferences:
All Canada

Industry Preferences

In Communications prefer:
Media and Entertainment

In Medical/Health prefer:
Medical/Health

In Consumer Related prefer:
Retail
Consumer Products
Consumer Services

In Industrial/Energy prefer:
Energy

In Financial Services prefer:
Financial Services
Financial Services

In Business Serv. prefer:
Services
Distribution

In Manufact. prefer:
Manufacturing

In Utilities prefer:
Utilities

Additional Information

Name of Most Recent Fund: Southfield Partners II, L.P.
Most Recent Fund Was Raised: 03/29/2012
Year Founded: 2005
Capital Under Management: $283,350,000
Current Activity Level : Actively seeking new investments

SOUTHLAKE EQUITY GROUP

1121 South Carroll Avenue, Suite 230
Grapevine, TX USA 76092
Phone: 8173283600
Fax: 8173283601
Website: www.southlakeequity.com

Type of Firm

Bank Affiliated

Project Preferences

Type of Financing Preferred:
Leveraged Buyout
Management Buyouts
Recapitalizations

Geographical Preferences

United States Preferences:
Southwest
Texas

Industry Preferences

In Consumer Related prefer:
Consumer Products

In Industrial/Energy prefer:
Industrial Products

In Business Serv. prefer:
Services

In Manufact. prefer:
Manufacturing

Additional Information

Year Founded: 2007
Current Activity Level : Actively seeking new investments

SOUTHMORE CAPITAL PTY LTD

147 Pirie Street, Suite 715
Adelaide, Australia
Website: www.southmore.com.au

Type of Firm

Private Equity Firm

Project Preferences

Type of Financing Preferred:
Early Stage

Additional Information

Year Founded: 2006
Capital Under Management: $35,000,000
Current Activity Level : Actively seeking new investments

SOUTHPAC PARTNERS INC

513 1540 West Second Avenue
Vancouver, Canada V6J 1H2
Phone: 6046470001
Website: www.southpacpartners.com

Management and Staff

Christopher Charlwood, Managing Partner
Jeremy South, Managing Partner

Type of Firm

Private Equity Firm

Project Preferences

Type of Financing Preferred:
Management Buyouts
Special Situation

Geographical Preferences

Canadian Preferences:
All Canada

Industry Preferences

In Consumer Related prefer:
Consumer

In Financial Services prefer:
Financial Services
Real Estate

Additional Information

Year Founded: 2017
Current Activity Level : Actively seeking new investments

SOUTHPOINTE VENTURES LLC

3525 Piedmont Road
Eight Piedmont Center
Atlanta, GA USA 30305
Website: www.southpointeventures.com

Type of Firm
Private Equity Firm

Project Preferences

Type of Financing Preferred:
Leveraged Buyout
Acquisition

Additional Information
Year Founded: 2003
Current Activity Level : Actively seeking new investments

SOUTHPORT LANE MANAGEMENT LLC

350 Madison Avenue
21st Floor
New York, NY USA 10017
Phone: 2127293247
Fax: 2127291147
E-mail: info@southportlane.com
Website: www.southportlane.com

Other Offices
George Town
Grand Cayman
Cayman, Cayman Islands

1221 East Pike Street, Suite 205
Seattle, WA USA 98122

Management and Staff
Andrew Scherr, Chief Financial Officer
Brian Lessig, President
Kevin Adler, Chief Executive Officer

Type of Firm
Investment Management Firm

Project Preferences

Type of Financing Preferred:
Leveraged Buyout
Mezzanine
Turnaround
Management Buyouts
Acquisition
Distressed Debt
Recapitalizations

Industry Preferences

In Consumer Related prefer:
Consumer

Additional Information
Year Founded: 2010
Current Activity Level : Actively seeking new investments

SOUTHWEST MIDDLE MARKET M&A

712 Main Street, Suite 2500
Houston, TX USA 77002
Phone: 2814456611
Fax: 2814454298
Website: www.growth-capital.com

Other Offices
Two Sound View Drive, Suite 100
Greenwich, CT USA 06830
Phone: 203-622-3916
Fax: 203-622-3917

9600 Crumley Ranch Road
Austin, TX USA 78738
Phone: 512-263-2938
Fax: 512-263-2864

2626 Cole Avenue, Suite 240
Dallas, TX USA 75204
Phone: 214-303-1177
Fax: 214-303-1172

Management and Staff
Andrew Oshman, Vice President
Charles Stephenson, Co-Founder
Dallin Westwood, Managing Director
Edward DiPaolo, Partner
Ivonne Chiok, Vice President
James Rebello, Managing Director
John Grimes, Managing Director
John Bresnahan, Managing Director
Sean Flinn, Vice President
W.A Williamson, Managing Director

Type of Firm
Bank Affiliated

Project Preferences

Type of Financing Preferred:
Expansion
Mezzanine
Management Buyouts
Acquisition
Recapitalizations

Size of Investments Considered:
Min Size of Investment Considered (000s): $1,000
Max Size of Investment Considered (000s): $5,000

Geographical Preferences

United States Preferences:
Southwest

Additional Information
Name of Most Recent Fund: Southwest Mezzanine Investments II, L.P.
Most Recent Fund Was Raised: 07/29/2005
Year Founded: 1992
Capital Under Management: $78,000,000
Current Activity Level : Actively seeking new investments

SOUTHWESTERN GROWTH PARTNERS LLC

141 East Palace Avenue
Santa Fe, NM USA 87501
Website: www.swgrowth.com

Type of Firm
Private Equity Firm

Project Preferences

Type of Financing Preferred:
Leveraged Buyout
Management Buyouts
Acquisition
Recapitalizations

Geographical Preferences

United States Preferences:
New Mexico
Oklahoma
Arizona
Colorado
Utah
Southwest
Texas

Industry Preferences

In Medical/Health prefer:
Medical Diagnostics

In Industrial/Energy prefer:
Oil and Gas Exploration
Oil & Gas Drilling,Explor

In Business Serv. prefer:
Services

In Agr/Forestr/Fish prefer:
Agribusiness
Agriculture related

Additional Information
Year Founded: 1969
Current Activity Level : Actively seeking new investments

SOVEREIGN CAPITAL LTD

25 Victoria Street
London, United Kingdom SW1H 0EX
Phone: 442073408800
Fax: 442073408811
E-mail: info@sovereigncapital.co.uk

Management and Staff
David Myers, Partner
Dominic Dalli, Partner
Kevin Whittle, Partner
Matthew Owen, Partner
Michael Needley, Partner

Type of Firm
Private Equity Firm

Association Membership
British Venture Capital Association (BVCA)

Project Preferences

Role in Financing:
Prefer role as deal originator but will also invest in deals created by others

Type of Financing Preferred:
Leveraged Buyout
Expansion
Generalist PE
Balanced
Acquisition

Geographical Preferences

International Preferences:
United Kingdom

Industry Preferences

In Medical/Health prefer:
Health Services

In Consumer Related prefer:
Entertainment and Leisure
Education Related

In Financial Services prefer:
Financial Services

In Business Serv. prefer:
Services

In Other prefer:
Environment Responsible

Additional Information
Name of Most Recent Fund: Sovereign Capital Limited Partnership II
Most Recent Fund Was Raised: 05/11/2005
Year Founded: 2001
Capital Under Management: $1,015,000,000
Current Activity Level : Actively seeking new investments
Method of Compensation: Return on invest. most important, but chg. closing fees, service fees, etc.

SOVEREIGN'S CAPITAL LP

201 West Main Street, Suite 100, No. 107
Durham, NC USA 27701
E-mail: info@sovereignscapital.com
Website: sovereignscapital.com

Other Offices
Jalan Jend. Sudirman kav. 52-53
Level 11, One Pacific Place SCBD Area
Jakarta, Indonesia 12190
Phone: 622129859606

Type of Firm
Private Equity Firm

Project Preferences

Type of Financing Preferred:
Early Stage

Size of Investments Considered:
Min Size of Investment Considered (000s): $250
Max Size of Investment Considered (000s): $2,000

Geographical Preferences

United States Preferences:
Southeast

International Preferences:
Indonesia

Industry Preferences

In Medical/Health prefer:
Medical/Health

In Consumer Related prefer:
Consumer Products
Consumer Services

Additional Information
Name of Most Recent Fund: Sovereign's Capital, L.P.
Most Recent Fund Was Raised: 09/19/2012
Year Founded: 2012
Capital Under Management: $12,012,000
Current Activity Level : Actively seeking new investments

SOZO VENTURES LLC

855 El Camino Real, Suite 12
Palo Alto, CA USA 94301
Phone: 4088923401

Type of Firm
Private Equity Firm

Project Preferences

Type of Financing Preferred:
Balanced

Geographical Preferences

United States Preferences:
Northern California

Additional Information
Name of Most Recent Fund: Sozo Ventures - TrueBridge Fund I, L.P.
Most Recent Fund Was Raised: 01/08/2013
Year Founded: 2013
Capital Under Management: $244,000,000
Current Activity Level : Actively seeking new investments

SP AKTIF

Barinors Vineyard South
The Vineyards Office Estate
Bellville, South Africa 7530
Phone: 27-21-913-8950
Fax: 27-21-913-8954
E-mail: office@sp-aktif.com
Website: www.sp-aktif.com

Other Offices
P. O. Box 3395
TygerValley, South Africa 7536

Type of Firm
Private Equity Firm

Association Membership
African Venture Capital Association (AVCA)

Project Preferences

Type of Financing Preferred:
Fund of Funds
Balanced

Geographical Preferences

International Preferences:
Africa

Industry Preferences

In Communications prefer:
Communications and Media

In Consumer Related prefer:
Entertainment and Leisure
Food/Beverage

In Business Serv. prefer:
Distribution

In Agr/Forestr/Fish prefer:
Agriculture related

Pratt's Guide to Private Equity & Venture Capital Sources

Additional Information
Year Founded: 2010
Capital Under Management: $209,791,000
Current Activity Level: Actively seeking new investments

SP VENTURES GESTORA DE RECURSOS SA

Rua Helena 309
Vila Olimpia
Sao Paulo, Brazil
Phone: 1125948774
E-mail: contato@spventures.com.br
Website: www.spventures.com.br

Management and Staff
Francisco Jardim, Co-Founder
Patrick Schechtmann, Co-Founder

Type of Firm
Private Equity Firm

Project Preferences

Type of Financing Preferred:
Early Stage
Seed
Startup

Geographical Preferences

International Preferences:
Brazil

Industry Preferences

In Biotechnology prefer:
Biotechnology
Agricultural/Animal Bio.

In Medical/Health prefer:
Medical/Health

In Industrial/Energy prefer:
Advanced Materials

In Agr/Forestr/Fish prefer:
Agriculture related

Additional Information
Year Founded: 2013
Capital Under Management: $48,840,000
Current Activity Level: Actively seeking new investments

SPANOS BARBER JESSE & CO LLC

One Market, Spear Tower
36th Floor
San Francisco, CA USA 94105
E-mail: info@sbjcap.com
Website: sbjcap.com

Other Offices
1350 Treat Boulevard, Suite 400
WALNUT CREEK, CA USA 94597

4311 Oak Lawn Avenue, Suite 620
DALLAS, TX USA 75219

Management and Staff
Bill Jesse, Managing Director
Dack LaMarque, Vice President
Gus Spanos, Managing Director
Matt Cole, Vice President
Tom Barber, Managing Director

Type of Firm
Private Equity Firm

Project Preferences

Type of Financing Preferred:
Leveraged Buyout
Acquisition
Distressed Debt
Recapitalizations

Geographical Preferences

United States Preferences:

Industry Preferences

In Medical/Health prefer:
Health Services

In Consumer Related prefer:
Consumer
Retail
Food/Beverage
Consumer Products

In Business Serv. prefer:
Services
Media

Additional Information
Year Founded: 2014
Capital Under Management: $204,000,000
Current Activity Level: Actively seeking new investments

SPARK CAPITAL

137 Newbury Street
Eighth Floor
Boston, MA USA 02116
Phone: 6178302000
E-mail: Info@sparkcapital.com
Website: www.sparkcapital.com

Other Offices
138 Spring Street
Sixth Floor
New York, NY USA 10012
Phone: 9172434200

74 Langton Street
San Francisco, CA USA 94103

Management and Staff
Alexander Finkelstein, General Partner
Andrew Parker, General Partner
Bijan Sabet, General Partner
Mo Koyfman, General Partner
Nabeel Hyatt, Venture Partner
Paul Conway, Co-Founder
Santo Politi, Co-Founder
Todd Dagres, Co-Founder

Type of Firm
Private Equity Firm

Association Membership
New England Venture Capital Association

Project Preferences

Type of Financing Preferred:
Early Stage
Balanced
Later Stage
Seed
Startup

Size of Investments Considered:
Min Size of Investment Considered (000s): $500
Max Size of Investment Considered (000s): $25,000

Geographical Preferences

United States Preferences:
All U.S.

International Preferences:
Europe

Industry Preferences

In Communications prefer:
Commercial Communications
Wireless Communications
Data Communications
Media and Entertainment

In Computer Software prefer:
Data Processing
Software

In Internet Specific prefer:
E-Commerce Technology
Internet
Ecommerce
Web Aggregation/Portals

In Computer Other prefer:
Computer Related

In Business Serv. prefer:
Services

Additional Information
Name of Most Recent Fund: Spark Capital Founders' Fund IV, L.P.
Most Recent Fund Was Raised: 02/24/2014
Year Founded: 2005
Capital Under Management: $260,000,000
Current Activity Level: Actively seeking new investments

1995

SPARK IMPACT LTD

131 Mount Pleasant
Liverpool Science Park
Liverpool, United Kingdom L3 5TF
Phone: 441517053416
Fax: 441517053425
Website: www.sparkimpact.co.uk

Management and Staff
Andrew Carruthers, Managing Director

Type of Firm
Private Equity Firm

Project Preferences

Type of Financing Preferred:
Early Stage
Expansion
Mezzanine
Seed

Geographical Preferences

International Preferences:
United Kingdom
Europe

Industry Preferences

In Biotechnology prefer:
Biotechnology
Biotech Related Research

In Medical/Health prefer:
Diagnostic Services
Pharmaceuticals

Additional Information
Year Founded: 1988
Current Activity Level : Actively seeking new investments

SPARK VENTURE CAPITAL CO LTD

10F, Internet Financial Center
Danliang Street, Haidian
Beijing, China 100080
Phone: 864000571177
Website: www.vcspark.com

Type of Firm
Private Equity Firm

Project Preferences

Type of Financing Preferred:
Balanced

Geographical Preferences

International Preferences:
China

Industry Preferences

In Communications prefer:
Telecommunications

In Internet Specific prefer:
Internet

In Medical/Health prefer:
Medical/Health

In Consumer Related prefer:
Consumer Services

In Business Serv. prefer:
Media

In Agr/Forestr/Fish prefer:
Agriculture related

In Other prefer:
Environment Responsible

Additional Information
Year Founded: 2014
Current Activity Level : Actively seeking new investments

SPARKASSENBETEILIGUNGS HEILBRONN FRANKEN GMBH & CO KG

Am Wollhaus 14
Heilbronn, Germany 74072
Phone: 49713163810684
Fax: 49713163820684
E-mail: info@sparkassen-beteiligung.de
Website: www.sparkassen-beteiligung.de

Management and Staff
Rolf Schiller, Managing Director

Type of Firm
Bank Affiliated

Project Preferences

Type of Financing Preferred:
Leveraged Buyout
Early Stage
Later Stage
Management Buyouts
Acquisition
Startup

Size of Investments Considered:
Min Size of Investment Considered (000s): $67
Max Size of Investment Considered (000s): $334

Geographical Preferences

International Preferences:
Germany

Industry Preferences

In Semiconductor/Electr prefer:
Electronics

In Industrial/Energy prefer:
Industrial Products
Environmental Related

Additional Information
Year Founded: 2000
Current Activity Level : Actively seeking new investments

SPARKLABKC

215 West Pershing Road
Kansas City, MO USA 64108
Website: www.sparklabkc.com

Type of Firm
Incubator/Development Program

Project Preferences

Type of Financing Preferred:
Early Stage
Seed
Startup

Size of Investments Considered:
Min Size of Investment Considered (000s): $6
Max Size of Investment Considered (000s): $18

Geographical Preferences

United States Preferences:
D. of Columbia
New York
East Coast

Industry Preferences

In Communications prefer:
Telecommunications

In Internet Specific prefer:
Internet

In Medical/Health prefer:
Medical/Health

In Industrial/Energy prefer:
Energy

In Agr/Forestr/Fish prefer:
Agriculture related

Additional Information
Year Founded: 2013
Current Activity Level : Actively seeking new investments

SPARKLABS

343-1, Yatab-dong
Bundang-gu
Seongnam, South Korea
Phone: 823115442233
Website: www.sparklabs.co.kr

Management and Staff
Awy Julianto, General Partner
Bernard Moon, Co-Founder
Han Ju Lee, Co-Founder
Ho Min Kim, Co-Founder
Jay McCarthy, General Partner

Type of Firm
Incubator/Development Program

Project Preferences

Type of Financing Preferred:
Seed
Startup

Geographical Preferences

International Preferences:
Korea, South

Industry Preferences

In Communications prefer:
Wireless Communications

In Internet Specific prefer:
Internet
Ecommerce

Additional Information
Year Founded: 2012
Current Activity Level : Actively seeking new investments

SPARKLAND CAPITAL

385 River Oaks Parkway
San Jose, CA USA 95134
Website: www.sparkland-capital.com

Management and Staff
Dong Guo, Partner
Jing Sun, Managing Partner
Sichao Chen, Managing Partner
Tony Wu, Partner

Type of Firm
Private Equity Firm

Project Preferences

Type of Financing Preferred:
Early Stage
Start-up Financing

Additional Information
Year Founded: 2015
Current Activity Level : Actively seeking new investments

SPARKLING PARTNERS SAS

12, Rue des Tours
Lille, France 59800
Website: www.sparkling-partners.com

Type of Firm
Private Equity Firm

Project Preferences

Type of Financing Preferred:
Early Stage
Seed

Geographical Preferences

International Preferences:
Europe
France

Industry Preferences

In Communications prefer:
Data Communications

In Computer Software prefer:
Software

In Internet Specific prefer:
E-Commerce Technology
Internet

Additional Information
Year Founded: 2012
Current Activity Level : Actively seeking new investments

SPARX CAPITAL PARTNERS CO LTD

16F East TW. Gate City Ohsaki
1-11-12 Ohsaki, Shinagawa-ku
Tokyo, Japan 141-0032
Phone: 81-3-54357-9800
Fax: 81-3-54357-9801
Website: www.sparx.co.jp

Management and Staff
Shinji Naito, Senior Managing Director
Shuhei Abe, Founder

Type of Firm
Private Equity Firm

Project Preferences

Type of Financing Preferred:
Balanced

Geographical Preferences

International Preferences:
Japan

Additional Information
Year Founded: 2006
Capital Under Management: $111,090,000
Current Activity Level : Actively seeking new investments

SPECIAL SITUATIONS FUND ADVISORS, INC.

527 Madison Avenue, Suite 2600
New York, NY USA 10022
Phone: 2123196670
Website: www.ssfund.com

Other Offices
153 East 53rd Street
55th Floor
New York, NY USA 10022
Phone: 2122076500
Fax: 2122076515

Type of Firm
Private Equity Firm

Project Preferences

Type of Financing Preferred:
Generalist PE
Opportunistic
Other

Additional Information
Name of Most Recent Fund: Special Situations Technology Fund, L.P.
Most Recent Fund Was Raised: 12/20/2006
Year Founded: 1999
Capital Under Management: $162,200,000
Current Activity Level : Actively seeking new investments

SPECTRO INVESTOR GROUP LLC

Seven Sapir
Ness Ziona, Israel 74071

Type of Firm
Private Equity Firm

Project Preferences

Type of Financing Preferred:
Early Stage
Balanced
Later Stage
Seed

Additional Information
Year Founded: 2012
Current Activity Level : Actively seeking new investments

SPECTRUM 28

855 El Camino Real 13A-328
Palo Alto, CA USA 94301
Website: spectrum28.com

Type of Firm
Private Equity Firm

Project Preferences

Type of Financing Preferred:
Early Stage
Expansion
Later Stage

Additional Information
Year Founded: 2015
Capital Under Management: $169,700,000
Current Activity Level : Actively seeking new investments

SPECTRUM EQUITY INVESTORS LP

One International Place
35th Floor
Boston, MA USA 02110
Phone: 6174644600
Fax: 6174644601

Other Offices
333 Middlefield Road, Suite 200
Menlo Park, CA USA 94025
Phone: 415-464-4600
Fax: 415-464-4601

Management and Staff
Adam Margolin, Principal
Benjamin Spero, Managing Director
Brion Applegate, Founder
Christopher Mitchell, Managing Director
Jake Heller, Vice President
James Quagliaroli, Managing Director
Jeffrey Haywood, Vice President
Julia Kuo, Vice President
Michael Kennealy, Managing Director
Michael Farrell, Managing Director
Peter Jensen, Principal
Stephen LeSieur, Principal
Victor Parker, Managing Director
William Collatos, Senior Managing Director

Type of Firm
Private Equity Firm

Association Membership
New England Venture Capital Association
National Venture Capital Association - USA (NVCA)

Project Preferences

Role in Financing:
Prefer role as deal originator but will also invest in deals created by others

Type of Financing Preferred:
Leveraged Buyout
Balanced
Acquisition
Recapitalizations

Geographical Preferences

United States Preferences:
North America

International Preferences:
Western Europe
Australia

Industry Focus
(% based on actual investment)
Internet Specific	27.1%
Communications and Media	24.8%
Computer Software and Services	24.4%
Other Products	13.3%
Consumer Related	4.0%
Medical/Health	2.6%
Computer Hardware	2.5%
Semiconductors/Other Elect.	1.4%

Additional Information
Year Founded: 1994
Capital Under Management: $4,019,100,000
Current Activity Level : Actively seeking new investments
Method of Compensation: Return on investment is of primary concern, do not charge fees

SPECTRUM HEALTHCARE FUND LLC

555 Mission Street
23rd Floor
San Francisco, CA USA 94105
Phone: 4153625800
Fax: 4155205656
E-mail: info@healthevolutionpartners.com
Website: www.healthevolutionpartners.com

Other Offices
888 Seventh Avenue
43rd Floor
NEW YORK, NY USA 10019
Phone: 212-660-8070
Fax: 415-520-5656

Management and Staff
Braden Kelly, Partner
Carl Zimmerman, Vice President
Christopher McFadden, Managing Partner
David Brailer, Chief Executive Officer
Erin Harrell, Partner
Jay Rose, Principal
Joshua Saipe, Principal
Kay Yun, Partner
Ned Brown, Partner

Type of Firm
Private Equity Firm

Project Preferences

Type of Financing Preferred:
Fund of Funds
Leveraged Buyout
Generalist PE
Later Stage
Management Buyouts

Industry Preferences

In Internet Specific prefer:
Internet

In Biotechnology prefer:
Biotech Related Research

In Medical/Health prefer:
Medical/Health
Medical Diagnostics
Medical Therapeutics
Medical Products
Health Services
Hospitals/Clinics/Primary
Pharmaceuticals

In Consumer Related prefer:
Consumer Products
Consumer Services

In Business Serv. prefer:
Media

Additional Information
Year Founded: 2007
Current Activity Level : Actively seeking new investments

SPEED@BDD SAL

Beirut Digital District
Bechara El Khoury Street
Beirut , Lebanon 1294
Phone: 9611649555
E-mail: fo@speedlebanon.com
Website: www.speedlebanon.com

Type of Firm
Private Equity Firm

Project Preferences

Type of Financing Preferred:
Early Stage
Seed
Startup

Geographical Preferences

International Preferences:
Lebanon
Middle East

Industry Preferences

In Computer Software prefer:
Software

In Internet Specific prefer:
Web Aggregration/Portals

Additional Information
Year Founded: 2014
Capital Under Management: $6,000,000
Current Activity Level : Actively seeking new investments

SPEEDUP IQBATOR SP Z O O

Sadowa 32
Poznan, Poland 64-657
Phone: 48618270999
Website: www.speedupiqbator.pl

Management and Staff
Bartlomiej Gola, Managing Partner
Michal Lehmann, Managing Partner
Rene Xavier Gerard, Managing Partner

Type of Firm
Private Equity Firm

Project Preferences

Type of Financing Preferred:
Seed
Startup

Geographical Preferences

International Preferences:
Poland

Industry Preferences

In Communications prefer:
Communications and Media
Wireless Communications

In Computer Software prefer:
Software

In Internet Specific prefer:
E-Commerce Technology
Internet
Web Aggregration/Portals

Additional Information
Year Founded: 2009
Capital Under Management: $8,965,000
Current Activity Level : Actively seeking new investments

SPELL CAPITAL PARTNERS LLC

222 South Ninth Street, Suite 2880
Minneapolis, MN USA 55402
Phone: 6123719650
Fax: 6123719651
Website: www.spellcapital.com

Management and Staff
Andrea Nelson, Managing Director
Bruce Richard, General Partner
Dobson West, Senior Managing Director
James Rikkers, Managing Director
Kristin Waddell, Vice President
Stephan Jones, Senior Managing Director
William Spell, President

Type of Firm
Private Equity Firm

Association Membership
Natl Assoc of Small Bus. Inv. Co (NASBIC)

Project Preferences

Role in Financing:
Prefer role as deal originator but will also invest in deals created by others

Type of Financing Preferred:
Leveraged Buyout
Expansion
Mezzanine
Acquisition
Recapitalizations

Geographical Preferences

United States Preferences:
Midwest

Industry Focus
(% based on actual investment)
   Semiconductors/Other Elect.   56.7%
   Industrial/Energy   43.3%

Additional Information
Name of Most Recent Fund: Spell Capital Mezzanine Partners SBIC, L.P.
Most Recent Fund Was Raised: 09/14/2012
Year Founded: 1988
Capital Under Management: $110,000,000
Current Activity Level : Actively seeking new investments
Method of Compensation: Return on invest. most important, but chg. closing fees, service fees, etc.

SPENCER TRASK VENTURES INC

750 Third Avenue
11th Floor
New York, NY USA 10017
Phone: 8006227078
E-mail: inquiries@spencertrask.com
Website: www.spencertraskventures.com

Other Offices
One Rotary Center
1560 Sherman Avenue, Suite 803
Evanston, IL USA 60201
Phone: 3123805300

1700 East Putnam Avenue, Suite 401
Old Greenwich, CT USA 06870
Phone: 8006227078

Management and Staff
Adam Stern, Managing Director
Joseph Marinelli, Chief Financial Officer
Michael Siek, President
Michael Turillo, Chief Operating Officer
Roger Baumberger, Managing Director

Type of Firm
Private Equity Firm

Project Preferences

Role in Financing:
Prefer role as deal originator

Type of Financing Preferred:
Second Stage Financing
Early Stage
Start-up Financing
First Stage Financing

Size of Investments Considered:
Min Size of Investment Considered (000s): $1,000
Max Size of Investment Considered (000s): $20,000

Geographical Preferences

United States Preferences:
All U.S.

Additional Information
Name of Most Recent Fund: Spencer Trask Private Equity Fund I
Most Recent Fund Was Raised: 03/31/2001
Year Founded: 1991
Current Activity Level : Actively seeking new investments
Method of Compensation: Function primarily in service area, receive contingent fee in cash or equity

SPEYSIDE EQUITY LLC

1741 Tomlinson Road
Philadelphia, PA USA 19116
Website: www.speysideequity.com

Management and Staff
Jeffrey Stone, Partner
Kevin Daugherty, Partner
Oliver Maier, Partner
Robert Sylvester, Partner

Type of Firm
Private Equity Firm

Project Preferences

Type of Financing Preferred:
Leveraged Buyout
Acquisition

Size of Investments Considered:
Min Size of Investment Considered (000s): $20,000
Max Size of Investment Considered (000s): $200,000

Geographical Preferences

United States Preferences:

International Preferences:
Europe

Additional Information
Year Founded: 2004
Capital Under Management: $130,000,000
Current Activity Level : Actively seeking new investments

SPH PLUG AND PLAY

79 Ayer Rajah
Crescent
Singapore, Singapore
E-mail: info@sphplugandplay.com
Website: www.sphplugandplay.com

Type of Firm
Incubator/Development Program

Project Preferences

Type of Financing Preferred:
Early Stage
Start-up Financing

Geographical Preferences

International Preferences:
Singapore

Industry Preferences

In Business Serv. prefer:
Media

Additional Information
Year Founded: 2015
Current Activity Level : Actively seeking new investments

SPICE PRIVATE EQUITY AG

Industriestrasse 13C
Zug, Switzerland 6304
Phone: 41417107060
Fax: 41417107064
E-mail: info@apen.ch
Website: www.spice-private-equity.com

Management and Staff
David Salim, Chief Executive Officer
Guido Cornella, Chief Financial Officer

Type of Firm
Private Equity Advisor or Fund of Funds

Association Membership
Swiss Venture Capital Association (SECA)
European Private Equity and Venture Capital Assoc.

Project Preferences

Type of Financing Preferred:
Fund of Funds
Leveraged Buyout
Mezzanine

Geographical Preferences

United States Preferences:
All U.S.

Canadian Preferences:
All Canada

International Preferences:
Europe

Additional Information
Year Founded: 1999
Current Activity Level : Actively seeking new investments

SPILTAN INVESTMENT AB

Grevgatan 39
Stockholm, Sweden 114 53
Phone: 46854581340
Fax: 46854581348
E-mail: spiltan@spiltan.se
Website: www.spiltan.se

Management and Staff
Anja Diedrichs, Chief Financial Officer

Type of Firm
Private Equity Firm

Project Preferences

Type of Financing Preferred:
Early Stage
Seed
Startup

Size of Investments Considered:
Min Size of Investment Considered (000s): $500
Max Size of Investment Considered (000s): $1,500

Geographical Preferences

International Preferences:
Scandanavia/Nordic Region

Industry Preferences

In Biotechnology prefer:
Biotechnology

In Medical/Health prefer:
Medical/Health
Medical Therapeutics
Pharmaceuticals

In Financial Services prefer:
Financial Services

In Business Serv. prefer:
Services

Additional Information
Year Founded: 1985
Capital Under Management: $30,000,000
Current Activity Level : Actively seeking new investments

SPINDLETOP CAPITAL MANAGEMENT LLC

3571 Far West Boulevard
PMB 108
Austin, TX USA 78731
Phone: 5129614633
Fax: 5125908729
E-mail: admin@spindletopcapital.com
Website: www.spindletopcapital.com

Management and Staff
Doug Ulman, Venture Partner
Erik Lundh, Venture Partner
Evan Melrose, Managing Director
Harry Zimmerman, Venture Partner
Jon Foster, Venture Partner
Paul Tirjan, Venture Partner
Richard Hawkins, Venture Partner
Robert McDonald, Venture Partner
Rodney Altman, Venture Partner
Steve Basta, Venture Partner
Todd Fruchterman, Venture Partner

Type of Firm
Private Equity Firm

Project Preferences

Type of Financing Preferred:
Expansion
Later Stage
Management Buyouts
Industry Rollups
Recapitalizations

Size of Investments Considered:
Min Size of Investment Considered (000s): $10,000
Max Size of Investment Considered (000s): $50,000

Geographical Preferences

United States Preferences:
Texas

Industry Preferences

In Biotechnology prefer:
Biotechnology

In Medical/Health prefer:
Medical/Health
Medical Diagnostics
Medical Products
Health Services
Pharmaceuticals

In Business Serv. prefer:
Distribution

Additional Information
Year Founded: 2011
Capital Under Management: $50,500,000
Current Activity Level : Actively seeking new investments

SPINNAKER CAPITAL GROUP

6 Grosvenor Street
London, United Kingdom W1K 4DJ
Phone: 44-20-7903-2900
Fax: 44-20-7903-2999
Website: www.spinnakercapital.com

Other Offices

16 Collyer Quay #34-02
Hitachi Tower
Singapore, Singapore 049318
Phone: 65-6303-9900
Fax: 65-6303-9919

Alameda Santos, 1940
14 degree andar
Sao Paulo, Brazil 01418-200
Phone: 55-11-4505-2255
Fax: 55-11-3284-4600

#901 Pacific Place 9th Floor
Jl. Jend. Sudirman Kav. 52-53
Jakarta, Indonesia 12190
Phone: 62-21-5797-3370
Fax: 62-21-5797-3373

Level 3, Gate Village 10
Dubai International Financial Centre
Dubai, Utd. Arab Em.
Phone: 971-4-4019678
Fax: 971-4-4019676

Room 231, DBS Business Centre
Raheja Chambers, 2FL, Nariman Point
Mumbai, India 400 021
Phone: 91-22-4050-9231
Fax: 91-22-2287-6240

, Suite 4208 Two Exchange Square
8 Connaught Place
Hong Kong, Hong Kong
Phone: 852-2867-7808
Fax: 852-2867-7800

Type of Firm
Private Equity Firm

Project Preferences

Type of Financing Preferred:
Expansion
Balanced
Later Stage

Geographical Preferences

International Preferences:
Europe
Middle East
Asia

Additional Information
Year Founded: 2005
Current Activity Level : Actively seeking new investments

SPINNAKER GROWTH PARTNERS (PTY) LTD

82, Maude Street
Sandton
Johannesburg, South Africa 2196
Phone: 27100200265
E-mail: info@spinnakergrowth.com
Website: www.spinnakergrowth.com

Other Offices

5, Wandel Street
Dunkley Squar
Cape Tow, South Africa 8000

Management and Staff

Evan Rice, Co-Founder
Hlumelo Biko, Co-Founder
Manie Wessels, Co-Founder
Marc Van Olst, Co-Founder

Type of Firm
Private Equity Firm

Association Membership
South African Venture Capital Association (SAVCA)

Project Preferences

Type of Financing Preferred:
Leveraged Buyout
Early Stage
Expansion
Generalist PE
Balanced
Later Stage
Management Buyouts
Acquisition

Geographical Preferences

International Preferences:
South Africa
Africa

Industry Preferences

In Biotechnology prefer:
Industrial Biotechnology

In Medical/Health prefer:
Health Services

In Consumer Related prefer:
Retail
Education Related

In Industrial/Energy prefer:
Energy

In Transportation prefer:
Transportation

In Agr/Forestr/Fish prefer:
Agribusiness

Additional Information
Year Founded: 2012
Current Activity Level : Actively seeking new investments

SPINNAKER VENTURES

582 Market Street, Suite 307
San Francisco, CA USA 94104
Phone: 415-374-2700
Fax: 415-374-2707
E-mail: information@spinnakerventures.com
Website: www.spinnakerventures.com

Type of Firm
Private Equity Firm

Project Preferences

Role in Financing:
Prefer role in deals created by others

Type of Financing Preferred:
Expansion
Later Stage

Size of Investments Considered:
Min Size of Investment Considered (000s): $200
Max Size of Investment Considered (000s): $200

Geographical Preferences

United States Preferences:

International Preferences:
Latin America

Industry Preferences

In Communications prefer:
Telecommunications
Wireless Communications
Data Communications

In Computer Software prefer:
Software
Applications Software

In Internet Specific prefer:
Internet

In Semiconductor/Electr prefer:
Semiconductor
Micro-Processing
Fiber Optics

In Medical/Health prefer:
Diagnostic Test Products
Medical Products
Disposable Med. Products

In Industrial/Energy prefer:
Energy

In Financial Services prefer:
Financial Services

Additional Information
Year Founded: 1997
Capital Under Management: $53,500,000
Current Activity Level : Actively seeking new investments
Method of Compensation: Return on investment is of primary concern, do not charge fees

SPINTOP PRIVATE PARTNERS AB

Skeppsbron 5
Third Floor
Malmo, Sweden
Website: www.spintopventures.com

Management and Staff
Erik Wenngren, Founder
Finn Persson, Partner
Mats Johansson, Partner

Type of Firm
Private Equity Firm

Association Membership
Swedish Venture Capital Association (SVCA)

Project Preferences

Type of Financing Preferred:
Early Stage

Geographical Preferences

International Preferences:
Sweden
Scandanavia/Nordic Region

Industry Preferences

In Communications prefer:
Communications and Media
Wireless Communications
Media and Entertainment

Additional Information
Year Founded: 2010
Current Activity Level : Actively seeking new investments

SPIRAL SUN VENTURES LLC

435 North LaSalle, Suite 201
Chicago, IL USA 60654

Management and Staff
Mark Thomann, Co-Founder
Michael Kaplan, Co-Founder
Shaun OBrien, Principal
Steve Gaither, Principal

Type of Firm
Private Equity Firm

Project Preferences

Type of Financing Preferred:
Early Stage
Seed

Industry Preferences

In Medical/Health prefer:
Medical/Health

In Consumer Related prefer:
Consumer Products

In Other prefer:
Environment Responsible
Women/Minority-Owned Bus.

Additional Information
Year Founded: 2017
Capital Under Management: $1,020,000
Current Activity Level : Actively seeking new investments

SPIRE CAPITAL PARTNERS LP

1500 Broadway, Suite 1811
New York, NY USA 10036
Phone: 2122185454
Fax: 2122185455
Website: www.spirecapital.com

Other Offices
100 Front Street, One Tower Bridge, Suite 1310
Conshohocken, PA USA 19428

300 Barr Harbor Drive, Suite 720, Five Tower Bridge
West Conshohocken, PA USA 19428
Phone: 6103971700
Fax: 6103971014

Management and Staff
Andrew Armstrong, Co-Founder
Anthony Cassano, Principal
Benjamin Meyer, Principal
Bruce Hernandez, Co-Founder
David Schaible, Partner
Donald Stewart, Chief Financial Officer
Michael Grady, Vice President
Richard Patterson, Co-Founder
Sean White, Partner

Type of Firm
Private Equity Firm

Project Preferences

Role in Financing:
Prefer role as deal originator but will also invest in deals created by others

Type of Financing Preferred:
Leveraged Buyout
Acquisition

Size of Investments Considered:
Min Size of Investment Considered (000s): $15,000
Max Size of Investment Considered (000s): $40,000

Geographical Preferences

United States Preferences:
North America

Industry Focus
(% based on actual investment)
Communications and Media	44.0%
Consumer Related	15.3%
Internet Specific	14.4%
Other Products	9.7%
Computer Software and Services	8.4%
Semiconductors/Other Elect.	8.1%

Additional Information
Name of Most Recent Fund: Spire Capital Partners III, L.P.
Most Recent Fund Was Raised: 05/15/2013
Year Founded: 2000
Capital Under Management: $260,000,000
Current Activity Level : Actively seeking new investments
Method of Compensation: Return on investment is of primary concern, do not charge fees

SPIRE VENTURES, LTD.

60 Grosvenor Street
London, United Kingdom W1K 3HZ
Phone: 442073996700
E-mail: info@spireventures.co.uk
Website: www.spireventures.co.uk

Management and Staff
Tristan Ramus, Managing Director

Type of Firm
Private Equity Firm

Project Preferences

Type of Financing Preferred:
Leveraged Buyout
Generalist PE
Balanced

Industry Preferences

In Communications prefer:
Media and Entertainment

In Financial Services prefer:
Financial Services
Real Estate

In Business Serv. prefer:
Services

Additional Information
Year Founded: 2004
Current Activity Level : Actively seeking new investments

SPIRIT CAPITAL (PTY) LTD

DM Kisch House, Inanda Greens
Business Park, 54 Wierda Road
Sandton, South Africa 2196
Phone: 27-11-784-1712
Fax: 27-11-784-4755
E-mail: info@spiritcapital.co.za
Website: www.spiritcapital.co.za

Type of Firm
Private Equity Firm

Project Preferences

Type of Financing Preferred:
Leveraged Buyout
Expansion
Management Buyouts
Acquisition

Additional Information
Year Founded: 2002
Current Activity Level : Actively seeking new investments

SPIRIT CAPITAL PARTNERS LLP

Two Wellington Place
Fifth Floor
London, United Kingdom SW1W 0AU
Phone: 441133662045
Fax: 441133662001
E-mail: info@spiritcapital.co.uk
Website: www.spiritcapital.co.uk

Other Offices
2 Wellington Place
5th Floor
Leeds, United Kingdom LS1 4AP
Phone: 441133662045
Fax: 441133662001

Management and Staff
Andrew Glennon, Partner
Colin Stirling, Partner
Francesco Santinon, Managing Partner

Type of Firm
Private Equity Firm

Association Membership
British Venture Capital Association (BVCA)

Project Preferences

Role in Financing:
Prefer role as deal originator but will also invest in deals created by others

Type of Financing Preferred:
Leveraged Buyout
Later Stage
Management Buyouts
Acquisition
Recapitalizations

Geographical Preferences

International Preferences:
United Kingdom

Industry Focus
(% based on actual investment)
Other Products	52.9%
Industrial/Energy	31.1%
Computer Hardware	11.9%
Consumer Related	4.0%

Additional Information
Year Founded: 2008
Capital Under Management: $477,300,000
Current Activity Level : Actively seeking new investments

SPIRITS CAPITAL PARTNERS LLC

2 Wellington Place Leeds
5th Floor
Dallas, GA USA 30157
E-mail: info@spiritcapital.co.uk
Website: www.spiritscapital.com

Type of Firm
Private Equity Firm

Project Preferences

Type of Financing Preferred:
Balanced

Size of Investments Considered:
Min Size of Investment Considered (000s): $5,000
Max Size of Investment Considered (000s): $25,000

Additional Information
Year Founded: 2015
Current Activity Level : Actively seeking new investments

SPK CAPITAL LLC

10877 Wilshire Boulevard, Suite 1605
Westwood, CA USA 90024

Type of Firm
Private Equity Firm

Project Preferences

Type of Financing Preferred:
Generalist PE

Additional Information
Year Founded: 1969
Current Activity Level : Actively seeking new investments

SPLIT ROCK PARTNERS LLC

10400 Viking Drive, Suite 550
Eden Prairie, MN USA 55344
Phone: 9529957474
Fax: 9529957475
Website: www.splitrock.com

Management and Staff
Dave Stassen, Founder
Jim Simons, Founder
Joshua Baltzell, Venture Partner
Leo de Luna, Principal
Michael Gorman, Founder
Steve Schwen, Chief Financial Officer

Type of Firm
Private Equity Firm

Project Preferences

Role in Financing:
Will function either as deal originator or investor in deals created by others

Type of Financing Preferred:
Early Stage
Balanced

Geographical Preferences

United States Preferences:
Midwest
West Coast

Industry Preferences

In Computer Software prefer:
Software

In Internet Specific prefer:
Internet

In Medical/Health prefer:
Medical/Health
Medical Diagnostics
Medical Therapeutics
Medical Products
Pharmaceuticals

In Consumer Related prefer:
Consumer Services

In Business Serv. prefer:
Services

Additional Information

Name of Most Recent Fund: Split Rock Partners II, L.P.
Most Recent Fund Was Raised: 05/07/2008
Year Founded: 2004
Capital Under Management: $1,000,000,000
Current Activity Level : Actively seeking new investments

SPONSOR CAPITAL OY

Mannerheimintie Four
Helsinki, Finland 00100
Phone: 35896803300
Fax: 3589643252
Website: www.sponsor.fi

Management and Staff

Ari Jokelainen, Partner
Juhani Kalliovaara, Partner
Juuso Kivinen, Partner
Kaj Hagglund, Managing Partner
Mikael von Frenckell, Partner
Olli Anttila, Partner
Sami Heikkila, Partner

Type of Firm
Private Equity Firm

Association Membership
Finnish Venture Capital Association (FVCA)

Project Preferences

Type of Financing Preferred:
Leveraged Buyout
Turnaround
Management Buyouts

Geographical Preferences

International Preferences:
Sweden
Finland

Industry Focus

(% based on actual investment)
Consumer Related	59.0%
Other Products	41.0%

Additional Information

Year Founded: 1997
Capital Under Management: $67,800,000
Current Activity Level : Actively seeking new investments

SPORTSNET 360 MEDIA INC

1605 Main Street West
Hamilton, Canada L8S 1E6
Phone: 905-522-4269
Fax: 905-522-9744
Website: www.scoremedia.com

Other Offices

1605 Main Street West
Hamilton, Canada L8S 1E6
Phone: 905-522-4269
Fax: 905-522-9744

Management and Staff

Benjamin Levy, Chief Operating Officer
Thomas Hearne, Chief Financial Officer

Type of Firm
Private Equity Firm

Project Preferences

Type of Financing Preferred:
Early Stage
Startup

Geographical Preferences

Canadian Preferences:
All Canada

Additional Information

Year Founded: 2000
Current Activity Level : Actively seeking new investments

SPRAY VENTURE PARTNERS

2330 Washington Street
Newton, MA USA 02462
Phone: 6173326060
Fax: 6173326070
E-mail: info@spraypartners.com
Website: www.spraypartners.com

Management and Staff

J. Daniel Cole, General Partner
Kevin Connors, Partner

Type of Firm
Private Equity Firm

Project Preferences

Role in Financing:
Will function either as deal originator or investor in deals created by others

Type of Financing Preferred:
Early Stage

Geographical Preferences

United States Preferences:

Industry Focus

(% based on actual investment)
Medical/Health	91.7%
Biotechnology	7.0%
Internet Specific	1.3%

Additional Information

Name of Most Recent Fund: Spray Venture Partners II, L.P.
Most Recent Fund Was Raised: 12/01/2003
Year Founded: 1996
Capital Under Management: $52,000,000
Current Activity Level : Actively seeking new investments
Method of Compensation: Return on investment is of primary concern, do not charge fees

SPRING BAY COMPANIES

816 A1A North, Suite 201
Ponte Vedra Beach, FL USA 32082
Phone: 9042738755
Fax: 9042738745
Website: www.spring-bay.com

Management and Staff

Daniel Ryan, Managing Director
Frederick Sontag, President
Matthew Miller, Vice President

Type of Firm
Private Equity Firm

Project Preferences

Type of Financing Preferred:
Leveraged Buyout
Generalist PE
Acquisition
Recapitalizations

Size of Investments Considered:
Min Size of Investment Considered (000s): $1,000
Max Size of Investment Considered (000s): $10,000

Geographical Preferences

United States Preferences:

Additional Information

Year Founded: 2004
Current Activity Level : Actively seeking new investments

SPRING CAPITAL ASIA LTD

30 Queen's Road
27/F Entertainment Building
Central, Hong Kong
Phone: 85236677787
Fax: 85236677789
Website: www.springcapasia.com

Other Offices

1000 Lu Jia Zui Ring Road
Hang Seng Bank Tower
Shanghai, China 200120
Phone: 862153752065
Fax: 862153752070

Management and Staff
Brian Ho, Chief Financial Officer
Lei Tang, Vice President
Wenzhong Jia, Managing Director

Type of Firm
Private Equity Firm

Association Membership
Hong Kong Venture Capital Association (HKVCA)

Project Preferences

Type of Financing Preferred:
Leveraged Buyout
Early Stage
Expansion
Acquisition

Size of Investments Considered:
Min Size of Investment Considered (000s): $4,000
Max Size of Investment Considered (000s): $25,000

Geographical Preferences

International Preferences:
China

Industry Preferences

In Medical/Health prefer:
Medical/Health

In Consumer Related prefer:
Retail
Consumer Products

In Industrial/Energy prefer:
Industrial Products
Environmental Related

In Business Serv. prefer:
Services

In Manufact. prefer:
Manufacturing

In Other prefer:
Environment Responsible

Additional Information
Year Founded: 2007
Capital Under Management: $184,000,000
Current Activity Level : Actively seeking new investments

SPRING CAPITAL PARTNERS

2330 West Joppa Road
The Foxleigh Bldg., Suite 340
Lutherville, MD USA 21093
Phone: 4106858000
Fax: 4105450015
Website: www.springcap.com

Other Offices
100 Matsonford Road
Five Radnor Corporate Center, Suite 520
Radnor, PA USA 19087
Phone: 6109647972
Fax: 6109770119

Management and Staff
Brian McDaid, Vice President
F. Stuart Knott, Vice President
John Acker, General Partner
Michael Donoghue, Co-Founder
Michael Donoghue, General Partner
Peter Orthwein, Vice President
Robert Stewart, General Partner

Type of Firm
Private Equity Firm

Association Membership
Natl Assoc of Small Bus. Inv. Co (NASBIC)

Project Preferences

Role in Financing:
Will function either as deal originator or investor in deals created by others

Type of Financing Preferred:
Leveraged Buyout
Expansion
Mezzanine
Later Stage
Management Buyouts
Acquisition

Geographical Preferences

United States Preferences:
East Coast

Industry Preferences

In Computer Software prefer:
Software

In Medical/Health prefer:
Health Services

In Consumer Related prefer:
Consumer Products

In Business Serv. prefer:
Services

In Manufact. prefer:
Manufacturing

Additional Information
Name of Most Recent Fund: Spring Capital Partners III, L.P.
Most Recent Fund Was Raised: 09/11/2013
Year Founded: 1999
Capital Under Management: $187,000,000
Current Activity Level : Actively seeking new investments
Method of Compensation: Return on invest. most important, but chg. closing fees, service fees, etc.

SPRING LANE CAPITAL FUND I LP

50 Milk Street
16th Floor
Boston, MA USA 02109
Phone: 6173910252

Type of Firm
Private Equity Firm

Project Preferences

Type of Financing Preferred:
Generalist PE

Additional Information
Year Founded: 2017
Current Activity Level : Actively seeking new investments

SPRING MILL VENTURE PARTNERS

11611 North Meridian Street, Suite 310
Carmel, IN USA 46032
Phone: 3177137550
E-mail: info@springmillvp.com

Other Offices
Historic Hirons Building
555 N. Morton Street
Bloomington, IN USA 47404

Management and Staff
Dave Wortman, Venture Partner
David Mann, Managing Partner
Jane Martin, General Partner
Ken Green, Managing Partner

Type of Firm
Private Equity Firm

Project Preferences

Type of Financing Preferred:
Early Stage
Seed

Geographical Preferences

United States Preferences:
Midwest
Indiana

Industry Preferences

In Communications prefer:
Wireless Communications

Additional Information
Year Founded: 2000
Current Activity Level : Actively seeking new investments

SPRING MOUNTAIN CAPITAL LP

650 Madison Avenue
20th Floor
New York, NY USA 10022
Phone: 2122928300
Website: www.springmountaincapital.com

Management and Staff
Andrew Fiore, Vice President
Gregory Ho, President
Jamie Weston, Managing Director
Jason Orchard, Managing Director
Jeffrey Lee, Vice President
John Gu, Vice President
John Steffens, Founder
Lauren Brueggen, Principal
Lucianne Painter, Managing Director
Raymond Wong, Managing Director

Type of Firm
Investment Management Firm

Project Preferences
Type of Financing Preferred:
Fund of Funds
Generalist PE

Industry Preferences
In Financial Services prefer:
Investment Groups

Additional Information
Name of Most Recent Fund: SMC Holdings II, L.P.
Most Recent Fund Was Raised: 03/29/2012
Year Founded: 2001
Capital Under Management: $164,294,000
Current Activity Level : Actively seeking new investments

SPRING SEEDS CAPITAL PTE, LTD.

One Fusionopolis Walk
One-Two South Tower, Solaris
Singapore, Singapore 138628
Phone: 6562786666
Fax: 6562786667
E-mail: SEEDS@spring.gov.sg
Website: www.spring.gov.sg

Management and Staff
Mok Lee Chew, Chief Executive Officer

Type of Firm
Government Affiliated Program

Project Preferences
Type of Financing Preferred:
Startup

Geographical Preferences
International Preferences:
Singapore

Industry Preferences
In Communications prefer:
Commercial Communications

In Business Serv. prefer:
Services
Media

Additional Information
Year Founded: 2001
Current Activity Level : Actively seeking new investments

SPRINGBOARD VENTURE FUND LLC

2100 Foxhall Road
Washington, DC USA 20003
Website: springboardfund.co

Management and Staff
Amy Wildstein, Co-Founder
John Minner, Chief Financial Officer
Kay Koplovitz, Co-Founder

Type of Firm
Incubator/Development Program

Project Preferences
Type of Financing Preferred:
Early Stage
Seed
Startup

Additional Information
Year Founded: 2016
Current Activity Level : Actively seeking new investments

SPRINGFONDET MANAGEMENT AS

Gaustadalleen 21
Oslo, Norway 0349
Phone: 4722958500
Fax: 4722604427
E-mail: post@springfondet.no
Website: www.springfondet.no

Management and Staff
Bente Loe, Partner
Johan Gjesdahl, Managing Partner

Type of Firm
Private Equity Firm

Association Membership
Norwegian Venture Capital Association

Project Preferences
Type of Financing Preferred:
Early Stage
Balanced
Later Stage
Seed
Startup

Geographical Preferences
International Preferences:
Europe
Norway
Germany

Industry Preferences
In Communications prefer:
Communications and Media

In Industrial/Energy prefer:
Oil and Gas Exploration

In Transportation prefer:
Transportation

In Agr/Forestr/Fish prefer:
Mining and Minerals

Additional Information
Name of Most Recent Fund: Springfondet II
Most Recent Fund Was Raised: 07/11/2011
Year Founded: 2009
Capital Under Management: $18,147,000
Current Activity Level : Actively seeking new investments

SPRINGROCK VENTURES LLC

2001 6th Avenue, Suite 3400
Seattle, WA USA 98121
Website: springrockventures.com

Type of Firm
Private Equity Firm

Project Preferences
Type of Financing Preferred:
Early Stage
Expansion
Balanced
Later Stage

Geographical Preferences
United States Preferences:
North America

Industry Preferences
In Computer Software prefer:
Software

In Medical/Health prefer:
Medical/Health
Health Services

Additional Information
Year Founded: 2015
Current Activity Level : Actively seeking new investments

SPRINGSTAR GMBH

Rosa-Luxemburg-Str. Two
Berlin, Germany 10178
Phone: 49360985739
Fax: 49397894187
E-mail: info@springstar.com
Website: www.springstar.com

Management and Staff
Jonathan Teklu, Managing Partner
Klaus Hommels, Partner
Manu Gupta, Partner
Mark Schmitz, Partner
Michael Stunkel, Partner
Oliver Jung, Partner
Shantanu Mathur, Managing Partner

Type of Firm
Incubator/Development Program

Project Preferences

Type of Financing Preferred:
Seed
Startup

Geographical Preferences

United States Preferences:
All U.S.

Canadian Preferences:
All Canada

International Preferences:
India
Turkey
Europe
Switzerland
Utd. Arab Em.
Mexico
Middle East
Brazil
Australia
Germany
Russia
All International

Industry Preferences

In Internet Specific prefer:
Internet
Ecommerce

Additional Information
Year Founded: 2010
Current Activity Level : Actively seeking new investments

SPRINGWATER CAPITAL LLC

345 West 600 South, Suite 104
Heber City, UT USA 84032
Phone: 18014264786
Fax: 18014371925
Website: www.springwatercapital.org

Other Offices
6-8 Place de Longemalle
Geneva, Switzerland 1204
Phone: 41225950777
Fax: 41225950760

Management and Staff
Martin Gruschka, Managing Director

Type of Firm
Private Equity Firm

Project Preferences

Type of Financing Preferred:
Turnaround

Geographical Preferences

International Preferences:
Europe

Additional Information
Year Founded: 2011
Current Activity Level : Actively seeking new investments

SPRITA STARTUPS

Calle Escritora Gertrudis
Gomez de Avellaneda, 28
Malaga, Spain 29196
Phone: 34952178597
Website: www.sprita-startups.es

Other Offices
Avenida Juan Lopez Penalver, 21
Andalusia Technology Park
Malaga, Spain 29590

Type of Firm
Incubator/Development Program

Project Preferences

Type of Financing Preferred:
Seed
Startup

Geographical Preferences

International Preferences:
Spain

Additional Information
Year Founded: 1969
Current Activity Level : Actively seeking new investments

SPROTT RESOURCE CORP

200 Bay Street
Royal Bank Plaza, Suite 2750
Toronto, Canada M5J 2J2
Phone: 4169777333
Fax: 4169779555
E-mail: info@sprottresource.com
Website: www.sprottresource.com

Management and Staff
Andrew Stronach, Managing Director
Michael Staresinic, Chief Financial Officer
Peter Grosskopf, Managing Director
Steve Yuzpe, Chief Financial Officer

Type of Firm
Private Equity Firm

Project Preferences

Type of Financing Preferred:
Generalist PE

Industry Preferences

In Industrial/Energy prefer:
Oil and Gas Exploration
Oil & Gas Drilling,Explor

In Agr/Forestr/Fish prefer:
Agriculture related

Additional Information
Year Founded: 2007
Current Activity Level : Actively seeking new investments

SPROUTX PTY LTD

459 Little Collins Street
Level 1
Melbourne, Australia
Website: sproutx.com.au

Type of Firm
Incubator/Development Program

Project Preferences

Type of Financing Preferred:
Early Stage
Seed

Industry Preferences

In Agr/Forestr/Fish prefer:
Agriculture related

Additional Information
Year Founded: 2016
Capital Under Management: $7,680,000
Current Activity Level : Actively seeking new investments

SPRUCE CAPITAL PARTNERS LLC

100 Montgomery Street, Suite 2190
San Francisco, CA USA 94104
Website: www.sprucecp.com

Management and Staff
Ganesh Kishore, Managing Partner
Greg Young, Managing Partner
Roger Wyse, Managing Partner

Type of Firm
Private Equity Firm

Project Preferences

Type of Financing Preferred:
Balanced

Industry Preferences

In Biotechnology prefer:
Biotechnology
Industrial Biotechnology

In Agr/Forestr/Fish prefer:
Agriculture related

Additional Information
Year Founded: 2017
Current Activity Level : Actively seeking new investments

SQUADRON CAPITAL LLC

18 Hartford Avenue
Box 223
Granby, CT USA 06035
Phone: 8604139875
Fax: 8604139872
E-mail: ahoskins@sqdncap.com
Website: www.sqdncap.com

Type of Firm
Private Equity Firm

Project Preferences

Type of Financing Preferred:
Leveraged Buyout

Geographical Preferences

United States Preferences:

International Preferences:
All International

Industry Preferences

In Medical/Health prefer:
Medical/Health
Drug/Equipmt Delivery
Medical Products

In Industrial/Energy prefer:
Machinery

In Manufact. prefer:
Manufacturing

Additional Information
Year Founded: 2008
Current Activity Level : Actively seeking new investments

SQUARE 1 VENTURES

406 Blackwell Street, Suite 240
Durham, NC USA 27701
Phone: 9193541275
Fax: 9193141285
E-mail: info@square1ventures.com
Website: www.square1ventures.com

Other Offices
2420 Sand Hill Road, Suite 100
Menlo Park, CA USA 94025
Phone: 650-543-2700
Fax: 650-543-2780

225 Arizona Avenue, Suite 200
Santa Monica, CA USA 90401
Phone: 310-264-1050

890 Winter Street, Suite 110
North Waltham, MA USA 02451
Phone: 7815470847
Fax: 7815470848

901 South Mopac Expressway
Barton Oaks Plaza Two, Suite 420
Austin, TX USA 78746
Phone: 512-439-2830
Fax: 512-439-2829

1801 13th Street, Suite 204
Boulder, CO USA 80302
Phone: 3039383097
Fax: 3039383097

403 Columbia Street, Suite 410
Seattle, WA USA 98104
Phone: 2068124254
Fax: 2068124253

12481 High Bluff Drive, Suite 350
San Diego, CA USA 92130
Phone: 8584363500
Fax: 8584363501

1420 Beverly Road, Suite 350
McLean, VA USA 22101
Phone: 703-962-6630
Fax: 703-448-1849

500 Fifth Avenue, 46th Floor
New York, NY USA 10110
Phone: 6467709380
Fax: 6463364961

Management and Staff
Adrian Wilson, President
Richard Casey, Founder
Wiley Becker, Principal

Type of Firm
Bank Affiliated

Association Membership
Mid-Atlantic Venture Association
Natl Assoc of Small Bus. Inv. Co (NASBIC)
Illinois Venture Capital Association

Project Preferences

Role in Financing:
Prefer role in deals created by others

Type of Financing Preferred:
Fund of Funds
Expansion
Mezzanine
Later Stage

Size of Investments Considered:
Min Size of Investment Considered (000s): $2,000
Max Size of Investment Considered (000s): $10,000

Geographical Preferences

United States Preferences:
All U.S.

Additional Information
Year Founded: 2010
Capital Under Management: $54,000,000
Current Activity Level : Actively seeking new investments

SR ONE LTD

161 Washington Street, Suite 500, Eight Tower Bridge
Conshohocken, PA USA 19428
Phone: 6105671000
Fax: 6105671039
Website: www.srone.com

Other Offices
1700 Owens Street, Suite 530
SAN FRANCISCO, CA USA 94101

One Broadway
Fourth Floor
CAMBRIDGE, MA USA 02142

29 Farm Street
Office Suite 3.10
London, United Kingdom W1J5RL
Phone: 442080472610

Management and Staff
Brian Gallagher, Partner
Deborah Harland, Partner
Jens Eckstein, President
Matthew Foy, Partner
Rajeev Dadoo, Partner
Simeon George, Partner
Vikas Goyal, Principal

Type of Firm
Corporate PE/Venture

Association Membership
New England Venture Capital Association
National Venture Capital Association - USA (NVCA)

Project Preferences

Role in Financing:
Prefer role as deal originator but will also invest in deals created by others

Type of Financing Preferred:
Early Stage

Industry Focus
(% based on actual investment)
Biotechnology	72.9%
Medical/Health	18.8%
Other Products	3.9%
Computer Software and Services	3.3%
Internet Specific	0.8%
Consumer Related	0.3%

Additional Information
Name of Most Recent Fund: GSK Canada Life Sciences Innovation Fund
Most Recent Fund Was Raised: 11/10/2011
Year Founded: 1985
Capital Under Management: $500,000,000
Current Activity Level : Actively seeking new investments
Method of Compensation: Return on investment is of primary concern, do not charge fees

---

SRI CAPITAL
Road No.92, Jubilee Hills
Plot No. 564-A-26-III
Hyderabad, India 500 033
Website: sricapital.in

Type of Firm
Private Equity Firm

Project Preferences

Type of Financing Preferred:
Early Stage
Expansion
Seed

Size of Investments Considered:
Min Size of Investment Considered (000s): $225
Max Size of Investment Considered (000s): $450

Geographical Preferences

International Preferences:
India

Additional Information
Year Founded: 2007
Current Activity Level : Actively seeking new investments

SRI INTERNATIONAL
333 Ravenswood Avenue
Menlo Park, CA USA 94025
Phone: 650-859-2000
Website: www.sri.com

Other Offices
1100 Wilson Boulevard, Suite 2800, 28th floor
ARLINGTON, VA USA 22209
Phone: 703-524-2053
Fax: 703-247-8569

Sondrestrom Research Facility
Kellyville Radar
Kangerlussuaq, Greenland 3910

2 Ichibancho, Chiyoda-ku, Tokyo
Park Side House 8th Floor
Tokyo, Japan 102-0082
Phone: 81-3-5211-8511
Fax: 81-3-5211-8524

210 Kumkok-Dong, Bundang-Ku, Suite 2412, Kolon-Tripolis Building "B"
Sungnam City, South Korea 463-943
Phone: 82-31-728-3781
Fax: 82-31-728-3782

Management and Staff
Manish Kothari, Vice President
Norman Winarsky, Vice President

Type of Firm
Service Provider

Association Membership
National Venture Capital Association - USA (NVCA)

Additional Information
Year Founded: 1946
Capital Under Management: $40,000,000
Current Activity Level : Actively seeking new investments

SRIB
Rue de Stassart 32
Brussels, Belgium 1050
Phone: 3225482211
Fax: 3225489074
E-mail: info@srib.be

Management and Staff
Serege Vilain, President

Type of Firm
Government Affiliated Program

Association Membership
Belgium Venturing Association

Project Preferences

Role in Financing:
Prefer role as deal originator but will also invest in deals created by others

Type of Financing Preferred:
Second Stage Financing
Early Stage
Expansion
Mezzanine
Later Stage
First Stage Financing
Startup

Size of Investments Considered:
Min Size of Investment Considered (000s): $100
Max Size of Investment Considered (000s): $100,000

Geographical Preferences

International Preferences:
Europe
Belgium

Industry Preferences

In Communications prefer:
Communications and Media
Commercial Communications
CATV & Pay TV Systems
Telecommunications
Data Communications
Satellite Microwave Comm.

In Computer Hardware prefer:
Computer Graphics and Dig

In Computer Software prefer:
Systems Software
Applications Software
Artificial Intelligence

In Internet Specific prefer:
Internet

In Semiconductor/Electr prefer:
Electronic Components

In Biotechnology prefer:
Biotechnology
Industrial Biotechnology
Biotech Related Research

In Medical/Health prefer:
Medical Diagnostics
Medical Therapeutics
Hospitals/Clinics/Primary
Hospital/Other Instit.

In Consumer Related prefer:
Retail
Food/Beverage
Consumer Products
Consumer Services

In Industrial/Energy prefer:
Industrial Products
Factory Automation
Machinery
Environmental Related

In Transportation prefer:
Transportation

In Financial Services prefer:
Financial Services
Real Estate

In Business Serv. prefer:
Services
Consulting Services

Additional Information
Year Founded: 1984
Capital Under Management: $1,800,000
Current Activity Level : Actively seeking new investments
Method of Compensation: Return on investment is of primary concern, do not charge fees

SSC FUND CO LTD

Beihuayuan St, Chaoyang
423, 4F, Bldg No1, No1 Yard
Beijing, China 100020
Phone: 861056258577
Website: www.sscfund.cn

Type of Firm
Private Equity Firm

Project Preferences

Type of Financing Preferred:
Early Stage
Expansion
Seed
Startup

Geographical Preferences

International Preferences:
China

Industry Preferences

In Communications prefer:
Entertainment

In Internet Specific prefer:
Internet
Ecommerce

In Business Serv. prefer:
Services

In Agr/Forestr/Fish prefer:
Agriculture related

Additional Information
Year Founded: 2015
Current Activity Level : Actively seeking new investments

SSG CAPITAL MANAGEMENT HONG KONG LTD

Center 99 Queen's Road Central
SSG Capital Management Suite
Hong Kong, Hong Kong
Phone: 85239098888
Fax: 85239098808
E-mail: info@ssgasia.com
Website: www.ssgasia.com

Type of Firm
Private Equity Firm

Project Preferences

Type of Financing Preferred:
Leveraged Buyout
Turnaround
Acquisition
Special Situation
Distressed Debt
Recapitalizations

Geographical Preferences

United States Preferences:
Southeast

International Preferences:
Asia Pacific
Indonesia
India
China

Additional Information
Year Founded: 2012
Capital Under Management: $1,365,000,000
Current Activity Level : Actively seeking new investments

SSM PARTNERS LP

6075 Poplar Avenue, Suite 560
Memphis, TN USA 38119
Phone: 9017671131
Fax: 9017671135
Website: www.ssmpartners.com

Management and Staff
Casey West, Partner
David Swenson, Venture Partner
Hunter Witherington, Vice President
Jim Witherington, Managing Partner
R. Wilson Orr, Managing Partner

Type of Firm
Private Equity Firm

Project Preferences

Role in Financing:
Prefer role as deal originator but will also invest in deals created by others

Type of Financing Preferred:
Leveraged Buyout
Expansion
Balanced
Acquisition
Recapitalizations

Geographical Preferences

United States Preferences:
Southeast

Industry Focus
(% based on actual investment)

Computer Software and Services	34.6%
Internet Specific	24.3%
Medical/Health	12.1%
Communications and Media	11.3%
Other Products	7.5%
Consumer Related	5.0%
Computer Hardware	2.8%
Semiconductors/Other Elect.	2.4%

Additional Information
Name of Most Recent Fund: SSM Partners IV, L.P.
Most Recent Fund Was Raised: 09/11/2009
Year Founded: 1973
Capital Under Management: $215,500,000
Current Activity Level : Actively seeking new investments
Method of Compensation: Return on investment is of primary concern, do not charge fees

ST BAKER ENERGY INNOVATION FUND

99 Creek Street
Level 4
Brisbane, Australia 4000
Website: stbenergy.com.au

Type of Firm
Private Equity Firm

Project Preferences

Type of Financing Preferred:
Early Stage

Industry Preferences

In Industrial/Energy prefer:
Energy

Additional Information
Year Founded: 1969
Current Activity Level : Actively seeking new investments

ST CLOUD CAPITAL LLC

10866 Wilshire Boulevard, Suite 1450
Los Angeles, CA USA 90024
Phone: 3104752700
Fax: 3104750550
Website: www.stcloudcapital.com

Management and Staff
Benjamin Hom, Managing Partner
James Hays, Chief Financial Officer
Jeremy May, Principal
Kacy Rozelle, Co-Founder
Kevin Tom, Vice President
Marshall Geller, Co-Founder
Robert Lautz, Co-Founder

Type of Firm
Private Equity Firm

Association Membership
Natl Assoc of Small Bus. Inv. Co (NASBIC)

Project Preferences

Type of Financing Preferred:
Leveraged Buyout
Mezzanine
Management Buyouts
Acquisition
Recapitalizations

Geographical Preferences

United States Preferences:

Additional Information
Year Founded: 2001
Capital Under Management: $200,000,000
Current Activity Level : Actively seeking new investments

ST GEORGE BANK VENTURE CAPITAL

Locked Bag 1
Kogarah, Australia 1485
Phone: 61295535333
Website: www.stgeorge.com.au

Type of Firm
Bank Affiliated

Project Preferences

Type of Financing Preferred:
Balanced

Geographical Preferences

International Preferences:
Pacific
Australia

Additional Information
Year Founded: 1996

Current Activity Level : Actively seeking new investments

ST PAUL VENTURE CAPITAL INC

10400 Viking Drive, Suite 550
Eden Prairie, MN USA 55344
Phone: 9529957474
Fax: 9529957475

Other Offices
601 Carlson Parkway, Suite 1160
HOPKINS, MN USA 55305
Phone: 952-995-7468
Fax: 952-995-7493

Management and Staff
Steve Schwen, Chief Financial Officer

Type of Firm
Private Equity Firm

Project Preferences

Role in Financing:
Prefer role as deal originator but will also invest in deals created by others

Type of Financing Preferred:
Early Stage

Size of Investments Considered:
Min Size of Investment Considered (000s): $2,000
Max Size of Investment Considered (000s): $40,000

Geographical Preferences

United States Preferences:
Massachusetts
California
Minnesota
All U.S.

Industry Focus
(% based on actual investment)

Computer Software and Services	20.5%
Communications and Media	19.4%
Internet Specific	19.0%
Medical/Health	18.6%
Semiconductors/Other Elect.	8.8%
Consumer Related	7.1%
Other Products	2.2%
Computer Hardware	2.2%
Biotechnology	1.2%
Industrial/Energy	1.1%

Additional Information
Name of Most Recent Fund: St. Paul Venture Capital VI
Most Recent Fund Was Raised: 10/18/2000
Year Founded: 1988
Capital Under Management: $3,000,000,000
Current Activity Level : Actively seeking new investments
Method of Compensation: Return on investment is of primary concern, do not charge fees

ST. MARTIN LAND CO

115 Third Street SE, Suite 806, P.O. Box 2529
Cedar Rapids, IA USA 52401
Phone: 3193828654
E-mail: info@stmartinland.com
Website: stmartinland.com

Type of Firm
Investment Management Firm

Project Preferences

Type of Financing Preferred:
Generalist PE
Later Stage

Geographical Preferences

United States Preferences:
Iowa
Louisiana

Additional Information
Year Founded: 1969
Current Activity Level : Actively seeking new investments

STADIA VENTURES LLC

911 Washington Avenue
Saint Louis, MO USA 63101
Website: www.stadiaventures.com

Management and Staff
Art Chou, Co-Founder
Tim Hayden, Co-Founder

Type of Firm
Incubator/Development Program

Project Preferences

Type of Financing Preferred:
Early Stage

Geographical Preferences

United States Preferences:

Additional Information
Year Founded: 2015
Current Activity Level : Actively seeking new investments

STAFFORD TIMBERLAND LTD

24 Old Bond Street
Fourth Floor
London, United Kingdom W1S 4AW
Phone: 442075354915
Website: www.staffordtimberland.net

Other Offices
One Main Street, Suite Five
Lyme, NH USA 03768
Phone: 603-795-4460
Fax: 603-795-4465

66 Gloucester Street, The Rocks
Terrace 1
Sydney, Australia NSW 2000
Phone: 61292416188

33 South Main Street
Hanover, NH USA 03755
Phone: 16032779951

Management and Staff
Geoff Norman, Co-Founder
Richard Bowley, Co-Founder
Tom Goodrich, Principal

Type of Firm
Private Equity Advisor or Fund of Funds

Project Preferences

Type of Financing Preferred:
Fund of Funds

Geographical Preferences

United States Preferences:

Canadian Preferences:
All Canada

International Preferences:
Uruguay
Latin America
Brazil
Chile
Australia
New Zealand

Industry Preferences

In Agr/Forestr/Fish prefer:
Agribusiness

Additional Information
Year Founded: 2002
Capital Under Management: $250,000,000
Current Activity Level : Actively seeking new investments

STAGE 1 VENTURES LLC

1000 Winter Street, Suite 2000
Waltham, MA USA 02451
Phone: 7817721010
Fax: 9418477121
E-mail: info@stage1ventures.com
Website: www.stage1ventures.com

Other Offices
5580 La Jolla Boulevard
Unit 80
La Jolla, CA USA 92037
Phone: 6503363778

2F 242 Yang-Guang Street
Neihu
Taipei, Taiwan 11491
Phone: 886975726772

Management and Staff
David Baum, Managing Director
Jonathan Gordon, Managing Director

Type of Firm
Private Equity Firm

Project Preferences

Type of Financing Preferred:
Early Stage
Balanced

Geographical Preferences

United States Preferences:

Industry Preferences

In Communications prefer:
Commercial Communications
Wireless Communications

In Computer Software prefer:
Software

In Internet Specific prefer:
Internet

Additional Information
Year Founded: 2007
Current Activity Level : Actively seeking new investments

STAGE CAPITAL LLP

128 Queen Victoria Street
Old Change House
London, United Kingdom EC4V 4BJ
Phone: 2076615656

Type of Firm
Private Equity Firm

Project Preferences

Type of Financing Preferred:
Leveraged Buyout
Value-Add
Early Stage
Expansion
Generalist PE
Later Stage
Seed
Acquisition

Geographical Preferences

International Preferences:
United Kingdom

Additional Information
Year Founded: 1969
Current Activity Level : Actively seeking new investments

STAGE FUND, THE

1732 Wazee Street, Suite 202
Denver, CO USA 80202
Website: www.thestagefund.com

Type of Firm
Private Equity Firm

Project Preferences

Type of Financing Preferred:
Leveraged Buyout
Acquisition

Additional Information
Year Founded: 2009
Current Activity Level : Actively seeking new investments

STAGE VENTURE PARTNERS LLC

1888 Century Park East
Ninth Floor
Los Angeles, CA USA 90067

Management and Staff
Alex Rubalcava, Co-Founder
Rob Vickery, Co-Founder

Type of Firm
Private Equity Firm

Project Preferences

Type of Financing Preferred:
Early Stage

Industry Preferences

In Computer Software prefer:
Software

Additional Information
Year Founded: 2016
Capital Under Management: $14,600,000
Current Activity Level : Actively seeking new investments

STAGE1FUNDING LLC

301 East Pine St., Suite 850
Orlando, FL USA 32801
Website: stageonefunding.com

Type of Firm
Private Equity Firm

Project Preferences

Type of Financing Preferred:
Generalist PE

Industry Preferences

In Financial Services prefer:
Financial Services
Real Estate

Additional Information
Year Founded: 2016
Current Activity Level : Actively seeking new investments

STAGEONE VENTURES

39 Ha'masger Street
Tel Aviv, Israel
Phone: 97236494000
Fax: 97236495000
E-mail: contact@stageonevc.com
Website: www.stageonevc.com

Other Offices
39 Ha'masger Street
Tel Aviv, Israel
Phone: 97236494000
Fax: 97236495000

Management and Staff
Tal Jacobi, Chief Financial Officer
Yuval Cohen, Managing Partner

Type of Firm
Private Equity Firm

Project Preferences

Type of Financing Preferred:
Early Stage
Startup

Geographical Preferences

International Preferences:
Israel

Industry Preferences

In Communications prefer:
Communications and Media
Commercial Communications
Telecommunications

In Computer Software prefer:
Software

In Internet Specific prefer:
Internet

In Business Serv. prefer:
Media

Additional Information
Year Founded: 2001
Capital Under Management: $65,000,000
Current Activity Level : Actively seeking new investments

STAGWELL GROUP LLC

1700 K Street NW, Suite 750
Washington, DC USA 20006
Phone: 2025244365
Website: www.stagwellgroup.com

Management and Staff
Beth Sidhu, Chief Operating Officer
Jason Reid, Vice President
Jay Leveton, Partner
Mark Penn, President
Ryan Greene, Chief Financial Officer

Type of Firm
Investment Management Firm

Project Preferences

Type of Financing Preferred:
Leveraged Buyout

Industry Preferences

In Business Serv. prefer:
Services

Additional Information
Year Founded: 2015
Current Activity Level : Actively seeking new investments

STAIRWAY CAPITAL MANAGEMENT

519 RXR Plaza
Uniondale, NY USA 11556
Phone: 5166293478
Fax: 5166293481
Website: www.stairwaycapital.com

Management and Staff
Alex Verba, Vice President
Chris Leheny, Chief Operating Officer
John Rijo, Principal

Type of Firm
Private Equity Firm

Project Preferences

Type of Financing Preferred:
Leveraged Buyout
Acquisition
Recapitalizations

Additional Information
Name of Most Recent Fund: Stairway Capital Management III, L.P.
Most Recent Fund Was Raised: 04/01/2011

Year Founded: 2005
Capital Under Management: $90,300,000
Current Activity Level : Actively seeking new investments

STALEY CAPITAL MANAGEMENT LLC

950 Winter Street, Suite 1701
North Waltham, MA USA 02451
Phone: 7814872222
Fax: 7814870033
E-mail: info@staleycapital.com

Management and Staff
Amit Basak, General Partner
Renny Smith, Managing Partner

Type of Firm
Private Equity Firm

Project Preferences

Type of Financing Preferred:
Leveraged Buyout
Expansion
Generalist PE
Recapitalizations

Size of Investments Considered:
Min Size of Investment Considered (000s): $10,000
Max Size of Investment Considered (000s): $100,000

Industry Preferences

In Business Serv. prefer:
Services

Additional Information
Name of Most Recent Fund: Staley Capital Fund I, L.P.
Most Recent Fund Was Raised: 04/06/2010
Year Founded: 1969
Capital Under Management: $22,500,000
Current Activity Level : Actively seeking new investments

STANDARD CHARTERED PRIVATE EQUITY LTD

22/F, Standard Chartered Bank
4-4A, Des Voeux Road
Central, Hong Kong
Phone: 85228410275
Fax: 85228685430
Website: www.wholesalebanking.standardchartered.com

Other Offices
17F, SCFB HQ Building
47 Jongno, Jongro-gu
Seoul, South Korea 110702
Phone: 822-700-1300
Fax: 822-722-8236

2013

4/F, Standard Chartered Building
23-25 Mahatma Gandhi Road
Mumbai, India 400001
Phone: 91-22-6735-5613
Fax: 91-22-2202-2580

Marina Bay Financial Centre (Tower 1)
Level 23, 8 Marina Boulevard
Singapore, Singapore 018981
Phone: 65-6596-4527
Fax: 65-6634-9560

22/F Standard Chartered Bank Building
4-4A Des Voeux Road
Central, Hong Kong
Phone: 852 2841 0275
Fax: 852 2868 5430

Menara Standard Chartered, 8/F
Jl. Prof. DR. Satrio No. 164
Jakarta Selatan, Indonesia 12930
Phone: 62 21 2555 1698

3rd Floor, Marsh Building
No. 4 Sandown Valley Crescent
Sandton, South Africa 2196
Phone: 27-11-217-6885
Fax: 27-11-217-6801

Unit 5, 12th Floor, Standard Chartered
No. 1 East Third Ring Middle Road
Beijing, China 100020
Phone: 86-10-5918-6111
Fax: 86-10-5918-6100

Building No. 7A 2nd floor,
DLF Cyber City Sector 24, 25 & 25A
Gurgaon, India 122002
Phone: 91 124 4876075

Management and Staff
Alastair Morrison, Managing Director
Andrew Dawson, Chief Operating Officer
Charles Huh, Managing Director
Kanad Virk, Managing Director
Kim Taeyub, Managing Director
Marlon Chingwende, Managing Director
Rahul Raisurana, Managing Director
Rajiv Maliwal, Managing Director
Taimoor Labib, Managing Director
Wei Zhu, Managing Director
Zhu Wei, Managing Director

Type of Firm
Bank Affiliated

Association Membership
Hong Kong Venture Capital Association (HKVCA)
Singapore Venture Capital Association (SVCA)
Indian Venture Capital Association (IVCA)

Project Preferences

Type of Financing Preferred:
Leveraged Buyout
Early Stage
Expansion
Mezzanine
Generalist PE
Balanced
Turnaround
Later Stage
Management Buyouts
Acquisition
Distressed Debt

Geographical Preferences

International Preferences:
Europe
Middle East
Singapore
Korea, South

Additional Information
Year Founded: 2002
Capital Under Management: $3,900,000,000
Current Activity Level : Actively seeking new investments

STANDARD INVESTMENT BV

Leidsegracht 3
Amsterdam, Netherlands 1017 NA
Phone: 312033575430
Website: www.standard.nl

Management and Staff
Guido Grobbink, Partner
Hendrik Jan Ten Have, Partner
Idgar Van Kippersluis, Partner

Type of Firm
Private Equity Firm

Project Preferences

Type of Financing Preferred:
Leveraged Buyout
Acquisition

Geographical Preferences

International Preferences:
Netherlands
Belgium

Industry Preferences

In Business Serv. prefer:
Distribution

In Manufact. prefer:
Manufacturing

Additional Information
Year Founded: 2005
Current Activity Level : Actively seeking new investments

STANHOPE CAPITAL LLP

35 Portman Square
London, United Kingdom W1H 6LR
Phone: 4402077251800
Fax: 4402077251801
Website: www.stanhopecapital.com

Management and Staff
Daniel Pinto, Chief Executive Officer

Type of Firm
Investment Management Firm

Project Preferences

Type of Financing Preferred:
Leveraged Buyout

Additional Information
Year Founded: 2017
Capital Under Management: $105,250,000
Current Activity Level : Actively seeking new investments

STANMORE MEDICAL INVESTMENTS

319 Clematis Street, Suite 1008
West Palm Beach, FL USA 33401
Phone: 5617760911
E-mail: info@stanmoremedical.com
Website: www.stanmoremedical.com

Other Offices
PO Box 3228
West Palm Beach, FL USA 33402

Type of Firm
Private Equity Firm

Project Preferences

Type of Financing Preferred:
Early Stage
Mezzanine

Size of Investments Considered:
Min Size of Investment Considered (000s): $250
Max Size of Investment Considered (000s): $2,000

Industry Preferences

In Medical/Health prefer:
Medical Products

Additional Information
Name of Most Recent Fund: Medvest Fund, L.P.
Most Recent Fund Was Raised: 07/12/2013
Year Founded: 2013
Capital Under Management: $2,000,000
Current Activity Level : Actively seeking new investments

STAPLE STREET CAPITAL LLC

888 Seventh Avenue
29th Floor
New York, NY USA 10019
Phone: 2126133100
Fax: 2126133142
E-mail: info@staplestreetcapital.com
Website: www.staplestreetcapital.com

Management and Staff
Hootan Yaghoobzadeh, Co-Founder
Stephen Owens, Co-Founder

Type of Firm
Private Equity Firm

Project Preferences

Type of Financing Preferred:
Leveraged Buyout
Turnaround
Management Buyouts
Acquisition
Recapitalizations

Industry Preferences

In Communications prefer:
Communications and Media
Wireless Communications

In Computer Software prefer:
Software

In Consumer Related prefer:
Consumer
Retail

In Industrial/Energy prefer:
Energy
Industrial Products

In Business Serv. prefer:
Services
Distribution

In Manufact. prefer:
Manufacturing

Additional Information
Year Founded: 2009
Current Activity Level : Actively seeking new investments

STAR AVENUE CAPITAL LLC

277 Park Avenue
39th Floor
New York, NY USA 10172
Phone: 2125514500
Website: www.staravenuecapital.com

Management and Staff
Chi-Chien Hou, Vice President
Craig Elson, Managing Director
Drew Baird, Vice President
Paul Lattanzio, President

Type of Firm
Private Equity Firm

Project Preferences

Type of Financing Preferred:
Leveraged Buyout
Later Stage
Acquisition
Recapitalizations

Geographical Preferences

United States Preferences:
North America

Industry Preferences

In Medical/Health prefer:
Medical/Health

In Consumer Related prefer:
Consumer
Sports
Retail
Food/Beverage

Additional Information
Year Founded: 2010
Current Activity Level : Actively seeking new investments

STAR CAPITAL MANAGEMENT INC

3363 North East 163rd Street, Suite 707
Miami, FL USA 33160
Phone: 3055171811
E-mail: info@starcapitalfund.com
Website: www.starcapitalmanagement.net

Type of Firm
Private Equity Firm

Project Preferences

Type of Financing Preferred:
Balanced

Geographical Preferences

United States Preferences:

Additional Information
Year Founded: 1969
Current Activity Level : Actively seeking new investments

STAR CAPITAL PARTNERS LTD

52-55 Piccadilly
Third Floor, Colette House
London, United Kingdom W1G 0PW
Phone: 442070168500
Fax: 442070168501
E-mail: mail@star-capital.com
Website: www.star-capital.com

Other Offices
33 Cavendish Square
Sixth Floor
London, United Kingdom W1G 0PW
Phone: 442070168500
Fax: 442070168501

Management and Staff
Mike Williams, Chief Financial Officer
Paul Gough, Partner
Roy Mani, Partner
Tony Mallin, Chief Executive Officer
Uniti Bhalla, Partner

Type of Firm
Bank Affiliated

Association Membership
British Venture Capital Association (BVCA)

Project Preferences

Type of Financing Preferred:
Leveraged Buyout
Management Buyouts
Acquisition

Geographical Preferences

International Preferences:
Western Europe

Industry Preferences

In Communications prefer:
Telecommunications

In Medical/Health prefer:
Medical/Health

In Industrial/Energy prefer:
Energy
Oil and Gas Exploration

In Transportation prefer:
Transportation

Additional Information
Year Founded: 2000
Capital Under Management: $1,813,400,000
Current Activity Level : Actively seeking new investments

STAR CAPITAL SGR SPA

Via P. Paleocapa 6
Milan, Italy 20121
Phone: 39028858541l
Fax: 39028052505
E-mail: info@starcapital.it

Management and Staff
Giorgio Drago, Managing Director

Type of Firm
Private Equity Firm

Association Membership
Italian Venture Capital Association (AIFI)

Project Preferences
Type of Financing Preferred:
Leveraged Buyout
Generalist PE

Geographical Preferences
International Preferences:
Italy

Additional Information
Name of Most Recent Fund: Star III
Most Recent Fund Was Raised: 08/06/2012
Year Founded: 2002
Capital Under Management: $220,700,000
Current Activity Level : Actively seeking new investments

STAR MOUNTAIN CAPITAL LLC

Tower 57 at 135 East 57th St
25th Floor
New York, NY USA 10022
Phone: 2128109044
Fax: 8008044278
E-mail: info@starmountaincapital.com
Website: www.starmountaincapital.com

Management and Staff
Brett Hickey, Chief Executive Officer
Christopher Gimbert, Chief Operating Officer
Christopher Layden, Managing Director
Daniel Small, Managing Director
David DiPaolo, Managing Director
David Christopher, Managing Director
John McCarty, Managing Director
Rakesh Jain, Managing Director
Robert Long, President
Robert Golding, Managing Director
Ryan McGovern, Managing Director

Type of Firm
SBIC

Project Preferences
Type of Financing Preferred:
Fund of Funds
Mezzanine
Generalist PE

Additional Information
Year Founded: 2015
Capital Under Management: $29,020,000
Current Activity Level : Actively seeking new investments

STARBOARD CAPITAL PARTNERS LLC

30 Jelliff Lane
Southport, CT USA 06890
Phone: 2032598855
Fax: 2032598287
E-mail: info@starboardcapital.net
Website: www.starboardcapital.net

Management and Staff
Peter Smith, Managing Director
Ridgely Cromwell, Managing Director
Ward Urban, Managing Director

Type of Firm
Private Equity Firm

Project Preferences
Type of Financing Preferred:
Leveraged Buyout
Acquisition
Recapitalizations

Industry Preferences
In Internet Specific prefer:
Ecommerce

In Medical/Health prefer:
Medical/Health

In Consumer Related prefer:
Consumer Products

In Industrial/Energy prefer:
Industrial Products

In Financial Services prefer:
Financial Services
Real Estate

In Business Serv. prefer:
Distribution

In Manufact. prefer:
Manufacturing

Additional Information
Year Founded: 2004
Current Activity Level : Actively seeking new investments

STARBRIGHT INVEST AB

Gjuterigatan 9
Jonkoping, Sweden 553 18
Phone: 46704210404
Website: www.starbrightinvest.com

Management and Staff
Hans Borjesson, Co-Founder
Patric Bottne, Co-Founder

Type of Firm
Private Equity Firm

Project Preferences
Type of Financing Preferred:
Early Stage
Seed

Industry Preferences
In Computer Software prefer:
Software

In Internet Specific prefer:
Internet
Ecommerce

Additional Information
Year Founded: 2017
Current Activity Level : Actively seeking new investments

STARBURST ACCELERATOR SARL

130 Rue de Lourmel
75015 Paris-15E-Arrondissement
Paris, France
Website: starburst.aero

Other Offices
721 N Douglas Street
EL SEGUNDO, CA USA 90245

Blk 79 Ayer Rajah Crescent
#04-01
, Singapore 139955

Type of Firm
Incubator/Development Program

Project Preferences
Type of Financing Preferred:
Balanced

Industry Preferences
In Transportation prefer:
Aerospace

Additional Information
Year Founded: 2016
Capital Under Management: $200,000,000
Current Activity Level : Actively seeking new investments

STARFISH VENTURES PTY LTD

120 Jolimont Road
Level One
East Melbourne, Australia 3002
Phone: 61396542121
Fax: 61396542922
E-mail: admin@starfishvc.com
Website: www.starfishvc.com

Management and Staff
Eve Burgess, Chief Financial Officer
John Dyson, Principal
Michael Panaccio, Principal

Type of Firm
Private Equity Firm

Project Preferences

Role in Financing:
Prefer role as deal originator but will also invest in deals created by others

Type of Financing Preferred:
Early Stage
Balanced
Later Stage
Seed
Startup

Size of Investments Considered:
Min Size of Investment Considered (000s): $72
Max Size of Investment Considered (000s): $7,216

Geographical Preferences

International Preferences:
Australia

Industry Preferences

In Communications prefer:
Telecommunications

In Computer Software prefer:
Software

In Biotechnology prefer:
Biotechnology

In Medical/Health prefer:
Medical Products

In Industrial/Energy prefer:
Energy
Alternative Energy

In Other prefer:
Environment Responsible

Additional Information
Name of Most Recent Fund: Starfish IIFF Trust
Most Recent Fund Was Raised: 12/31/2009
Year Founded: 2001
Capital Under Management: $418,600,000
Current Activity Level : Actively seeking new investments

STARLING INTERNATIONAL MANAGEMENT LTD (DUBAI BRANCH)

Dubai World Trade Centre,
27th Floor
Dubai, Utd. Arab Em.
Phone: 97143322772
Fax: 97143318817
E-mail: info@starlinggroup.com
Website: www.starlinggroup.com

Management and Staff
Ahmed Jawa, President
Ravi Mehta, Chief Financial Officer

Type of Firm
Private Equity Firm

Project Preferences

Type of Financing Preferred:
Leveraged Buyout
Early Stage
Generalist PE
Later Stage

Additional Information
Year Founded: 1986
Current Activity Level : Actively seeking new investments

STARQUEST ISF SAS

154 Bd Haussmann
Paris, France 75008
Phone: 33180481230
Fax: 33180481231
E-mail: contact@starquest-capital.com
Website: www.starquest-capital.com

Type of Firm
Private Equity Firm

Project Preferences

Type of Financing Preferred:
Early Stage
Later Stage

Geographical Preferences

International Preferences:
Europe
Eastern Europe
France

Additional Information
Year Founded: 2009
Current Activity Level : Actively seeking new investments

STARR INTERNATIONAL COMPANY INC

19 Par la Ville Road
Hamilton, Bermuda HM11
Phone: 4412789313
Website: www.starrcompanies.com

Other Offices
Central Plaza, 18 Harbour Road
Unit 1901, 19th Floor
Wanchai, Hong Kong
Phone: 852-3765-5333

399 Park Avenue
MANHATTAN, NY USA 10022
Phone: 646-227-6600

140 Leadenhall Street
3rd Floor
London, United Kingdom EC3V 4QT
Phone: 441) 278-9313

Management and Staff
Joseph Johnson, President

Type of Firm
Insurance Firm Affiliate

Project Preferences

Type of Financing Preferred:
Generalist PE
Balanced

Geographical Preferences

International Preferences:
All International

Industry Preferences

In Biotechnology prefer:
Biotechnology

In Medical/Health prefer:
Health Services

In Consumer Related prefer:
Consumer Products
Consumer Services

In Industrial/Energy prefer:
Energy

In Financial Services prefer:
Real Estate
Financial Services

Additional Information
Year Founded: 1943
Current Activity Level : Actively seeking new investments

Pratt's Guide to Private Equity & Venture Capital Sources

START GREEN FUND BV

Linnaeusstraat 35F
Amsterdam, Netherlands 1093 EE
Phone: 31205682060
E-mail: info@startgreen.nl
Website: www.startgreen.nl

Management and Staff

Coenraad De Vries, Managing Director
Laura Rooseboom, Managing Partner

Type of Firm

Private Equity Firm

Association Membership

Dutch Venture Capital Associaton (NVP)

Project Preferences

Type of Financing Preferred:
Early Stage
Later Stage
Seed
Startup

Size of Investments Considered:
Min Size of Investment Considered (000s): $375,658
Max Size of Investment Considered (000s): $3,005

Geographical Preferences

International Preferences:
Europe
Netherlands

Industry Preferences

In Biotechnology prefer:
Agricultural/Animal Bio.

In Industrial/Energy prefer:
Alternative Energy

In Other prefer:
Environment Responsible

Additional Information

Year Founded: 2007
Current Activity Level : Actively seeking new investments

START GROUP LLC

1121 Delano Street
Houston, TX USA 77003
Phone: 2814074731
E-mail: contact@starthouston.com
Website: www.starthouston.com

Management and Staff

Apurva Sanghavi, Co-Founder
Gaurav Khandelwal, Co-Founder

Type of Firm

Incubator/Development Program

Project Preferences

Type of Financing Preferred:
Early Stage
Seed
Startup

Geographical Preferences

United States Preferences:
Texas

Industry Preferences

In Computer Software prefer:
Software

In Internet Specific prefer:
Internet

Additional Information

Year Founded: 2012
Current Activity Level : Actively seeking new investments

START SMART LABS

350 Cambridge Avenue, Suite 250
Palo Alto, CA USA 94306
Phone: 6504279026
E-mail: info@startsmartlabs.com
Website: www.startsmartlabs.com

Management and Staff

Ellen Salisbury, Co-Founder
Nanda Krish, General Partner
Raymie Stata, Co-Founder
Vijay Babu, Managing Director

Type of Firm

Incubator/Development Program

Project Preferences

Type of Financing Preferred:
Seed

Industry Preferences

In Computer Software prefer:
Data Processing

Additional Information

Year Founded: 2017
Current Activity Level : Actively seeking new investments

STARTA CAPITAL

Zemlianoi val, 9
Moscow, Russia 105064
Website: www.startacapital.com

Type of Firm

Private Equity Firm

Project Preferences

Type of Financing Preferred:
Early Stage
Seed
Startup

Geographical Preferences

International Preferences:
Russia

Additional Information

Year Founded: 2011
Current Activity Level : Actively seeking new investments

STARTCAPS VENTURES

199 Marina Boulevard
San Francisco, CA USA 94123
Phone: 6502231959
E-mail: info@startcaps.com
Website: www.startcaps.com

Type of Firm

Private Equity Firm

Project Preferences

Type of Financing Preferred:
Early Stage
Seed
Startup

Size of Investments Considered:
Min Size of Investment Considered (000s): $100
Max Size of Investment Considered (000s): $150

Geographical Preferences

United States Preferences:

International Preferences:
Latin America
Europe

Industry Preferences

In Communications prefer:
Wireless Communications
Entertainment

In Computer Software prefer:
Data Processing

In Medical/Health prefer:
Medical/Health

In Consumer Related prefer:
Education Related

Additional Information

Year Founded: 2011
Capital Under Management: $350,000
Current Activity Level : Actively seeking new investments

STARTKAPITAL FONDS AUGSBURG GMBH

Stettenstrasse 1+3
Augsburg, Germany 86150
Phone: 49082190785876
Fax: 49082178472678
E-mail: ska@schwaben.ihk.de
Website: www.startkapitalfonds.de

Type of Firm
Incubator/Development Program

Project Preferences

Type of Financing Preferred:
Seed
Startup

Geographical Preferences

International Preferences:
Germany

Industry Preferences

In Computer Software prefer:
Software

In Biotechnology prefer:
Biotechnology

In Industrial/Energy prefer:
Environmental Related

Additional Information
Year Founded: 1997
Current Activity Level : Actively seeking new investments

STARTKAPITAL I NORR AB

Storgatan 11
Lulea, Sweden 972 38
Website: www.startkapitalinorr.se

Type of Firm
Private Equity Firm

Project Preferences

Type of Financing Preferred:
Early Stage
Seed
Startup

Geographical Preferences

International Preferences:
Sweden

Additional Information
Year Founded: 2011
Current Activity Level : Actively seeking new investments

STARTUP AVENUE SAS

102 bis rue de Miromesnil
Paris, France 75008
Phone: 33149296676
Fax: 33153014810
E-mail: info@startupavenue.com
Website: www.startupavenue.com

Management and Staff
Fabrice Laurence, Chief Operating Officer

Type of Firm
Private Equity Firm

Project Preferences

Type of Financing Preferred:
Early Stage
Seed
Startup

Geographical Preferences

International Preferences:
Europe
France

Industry Preferences

In Communications prefer:
Communications and Media
CATV & Pay TV Systems
Radio & TV Broadcasting
Wireless Communications
Publishing

In Computer Software prefer:
Software

In Internet Specific prefer:
Internet

In Consumer Related prefer:
Sports

Additional Information
Year Founded: 1999
Capital Under Management: $2,000,000
Current Activity Level : Actively seeking new investments

STARTUP CANADA WOMEN FOUNDERS FUND

56 Sparks Street, Suite 300
Ottawa, Canada K1P 5A9
Website: www.startupcan.ca

Type of Firm
Investment Management Firm

Industry Preferences

In Other prefer:
Women/Minority-Owned Bus.

Additional Information
Year Founded: 2016
Current Activity Level : Actively seeking new investments

STARTUP CAPITAL VENTURES LP

535 Middlefield Road, Suite 280
Menlo Park, CA USA 94025
Phone: 6504618100
Fax: 6504618101
Website: www.startupcv.com

Other Offices
Fuhua Road 3 CBD Futian District
Rm 1605A 16F Int'l Chamber of Commerce
Shenzhen, China 518048

125 University Avenue, Suite 88
Palo Alto, CA USA 94301

2800 Woodlawn Drive, Suite 265
Honolulu, HI USA 96822

20 Westland Road, Quarry Bay
Room 2101, 21/F Westlands Center
Hong Kong, Hong Kong
Phone: 85229604611
Fax: 85229600185

Management and Staff
Agnes Ngo, Venture Partner
Danny Lui, Managing Partner
John Dean, Managing Partner
Pia Camenzind, Chief Financial Officer
Robert Rees, General Partner
Timothy Dick, General Partner

Type of Firm
Private Equity Firm

Project Preferences

Role in Financing:
Will function either as deal originator or investor in deals created by others

Type of Financing Preferred:
Early Stage

Size of Investments Considered:
Min Size of Investment Considered (000s): $250
Max Size of Investment Considered (000s): $1,000

Geographical Preferences

United States Preferences:
Oklahoma
Hawaii
Northern California
Texas

International Preferences:
China

Pratt's Guide to Private Equity & Venture Capital Sources

Industry Preferences

In Computer Software prefer:
Software

Additional Information
Name of Most Recent Fund: Startup Capital Ventures, L.P.
Most Recent Fund Was Raised: 04/27/2005
Year Founded: 2005
Capital Under Management: $25,500,000
Current Activity Level : Actively seeking new investments

STARTUP FACTORY

Norrlandsgatan 22
Stockholm, Sweden 103 86
Phone: 46854553200
Fax: 46854553211

Other Offices
Strawinskylaan 1159
WTC
Amsterdam, Netherlands 1077 XX
Phone: 31-20-577-6600

Management and Staff
Staffan Helgesson, Chief Executive Officer
Ulf Brandels, Managing Director

Type of Firm
Incubator/Development Program

Project Preferences

Type of Financing Preferred:
Early Stage
Seed
Startup

Geographical Preferences

United States Preferences:

International Preferences:
Scandanavia/Nordic Region

Industry Preferences

In Communications prefer:
Communications and Media
Commercial Communications
Telecommunications

In Computer Software prefer:
Software

In Internet Specific prefer:
Internet

In Computer Other prefer:
Computer Related

In Semiconductor/Electr prefer:
Electronics

Additional Information
Year Founded: 1969
Capital Under Management: $53,100,000
Current Activity Level : Actively seeking new investments

STARTUP YARD LTD

2 Woodberry Grove
Winnington House
London, United Kingdom N12 0DR
Website: www.startup-yard.com

Other Offices
Lomnickeho 1705/7
Prague, Czech Republic 140 79

Management and Staff
Lukas Hudecek, Founder
Petr Ocasek, Founder

Type of Firm
Incubator/Development Program

Project Preferences

Type of Financing Preferred:
Seed

Geographical Preferences

International Preferences:
Slovak Repub.
Czech Republic

Industry Preferences

In Communications prefer:
Wireless Communications

In Internet Specific prefer:
E-Commerce Technology
Internet

Additional Information
Year Founded: 2011
Current Activity Level : Actively seeking new investments

STARTUPBOOTCAMP IOT LTD

1, St. katherine's Way
International House Rainmaki
London, United Kingdom E1W 1UN

Other Offices
2b, Via Ludovico di Savoia
Spazio M3
Rome, Italy 00185

Type of Firm
Incubator/Development Program

Project Preferences

Type of Financing Preferred:
Seed

Geographical Preferences

United States Preferences:

International Preferences:
Turkey
Europe
Singapore

Industry Preferences

In Computer Software prefer:
Software

In Internet Specific prefer:
Ecommerce

In Medical/Health prefer:
Medical/Health

In Consumer Related prefer:
Food/Beverage

In Transportation prefer:
Transportation

In Financial Services prefer:
Financial Services

Additional Information
Year Founded: 2010
Current Activity Level : Actively seeking new investments

STARTUPHIGHWAY

5 Galvydzio
Vilnius, Latvia
Website: www.startuphighway.com

Management and Staff
Indre Milukaite, Co-Founder
Rokas Tamoiunas, Co-Founder

Type of Firm
Incubator/Development Program

Project Preferences

Type of Financing Preferred:
Seed

Geographical Preferences

International Preferences:
Central Europe
Eastern Europe

Additional Information
Year Founded: 2011
Current Activity Level : Actively seeking new investments

STARTUPRUNNER CAPITAL LLC

701 Brazos Street, Suite 1616
Austin, TX USA 78701
Phone: 5122225536
Website: startuprunner.com

Type of Firm
Private Equity Firm

Project Preferences

Type of Financing Preferred:
Seed
Startup

Geographical Preferences

United States Preferences:

Industry Preferences

In Financial Services prefer:
Financial Services

In Business Serv. prefer:
Consulting Services

Additional Information
Year Founded: 2015
Current Activity Level : Actively seeking new investments

STARTUPXSEED VENTURES LLP

Opposite to Mini Forest
JP Nagar, 3rd Phase
Bangalore, India 560078
Phone: 918041501409
Website: www.startupxseed.in

Type of Firm
Private Equity Firm

Project Preferences

Type of Financing Preferred:
Seed

Geographical Preferences

International Preferences:
India

Additional Information
Year Founded: 2015
Capital Under Management: $7,540,000
Current Activity Level : Actively seeking new investments

STARTX

450 Serra Mall
Stanford, CA USA 94305
Website: www.startx.stanford.edu

Type of Firm
University Program

Project Preferences

Type of Financing Preferred:
Early Stage

Geographical Preferences

United States Preferences:
California

Industry Preferences

In Medical/Health prefer:
Medical/Health

In Consumer Related prefer:
Consumer

Additional Information
Year Founded: 2013
Current Activity Level : Actively seeking new investments

STARVEST PARTNERS LP

750 Lexington Ave, 59th Street
15th Floor
New York, NY USA 10022
Phone: 2128632500
Fax: 2128632520
E-mail: info@starvestpartners.com
Website: www.starvestpartners.com

Management and Staff
Deborah Farrington, General Partner
Jeanne Sullivan, Co-Founder
Laura Sachar, General Partner
Liza Boyd, Venture Partner
Liza Benson, Venture Partner
Robert Kelly, Chief Financial Officer

Type of Firm
Private Equity Firm

Project Preferences

Role in Financing:
Prefer role as deal originator but will also invest in deals created by others

Type of Financing Preferred:
Early Stage
Expansion
Balanced
Later Stage
Startup

Geographical Preferences

United States Preferences:
Illinois
Arizona
New York
Texas

Industry Preferences

In Communications prefer:
Telecommunications
Media and Entertainment

In Computer Software prefer:
Software
Systems Software
Applications Software

In Internet Specific prefer:
E-Commerce Technology
Internet
Ecommerce
Web Aggregation/Portals

In Computer Other prefer:
Computer Related

In Consumer Related prefer:
Retail
Consumer Products

In Financial Services prefer:
Financial Services

In Business Serv. prefer:
Services

Additional Information
Name of Most Recent Fund: StarVest Partners II, L.P.
Most Recent Fund Was Raised: 05/01/2007
Year Founded: 1998
Capital Under Management: $400,000,000
Current Activity Level : Actively seeking new investments
Method of Compensation: Return on investment is of primary concern, do not charge fees

STARWOOD CAPITAL GROUP I LP

591 West Putnam Avenue
Greenwich, CT USA 06830
Phone: 2034227700
Fax: 2034227784
Website: www.starwoodcapital.com

Other Offices
52 Conduit Street
1st Floor
London, United Kingdom W1S 2YX
Phone: 44-207-434-8570

129, Turner Road
Fifth Floor, Gayatri Plaza
Mumbai, India 400050
Phone: 91-22-6781-9000

2021

50, Place de l'Ellipse
Village 5
France, United Kingdom 92081
Phone: 33-1-4291-4500

Av. Brig. Faria Lima, 3.729 - 5o andar
Sao Paulo, Brazil 04538-905
Phone: 5511-3443-6313

6, rue Julien Vesque
, Luxembourg L-2688
Phone: 352-26-64-5120

455 Market Street, Suite 2200
San Francisco, CA USA 94105
Phone: 415-247-1220

400 Galleria Parkway, Suite 1450
Atlanta, GA USA 30339
Phone: 770-541-9046

3-2-6 Kasumigaseki, Chiyoda-ku
Tokyo Club Building 11th Floor
Tokyo, Japan 100-0013
Phone: 81-3-4577-3300

1255 23rd Street North West, Suite 675
Washington, DC USA 20037
Phone: 202-470-1546

Management and Staff
Himanshu Saxena, Chief Executive Officer

Type of Firm
Private Equity Firm

Project Preferences

Type of Financing Preferred:
Opportunistic
Other

Geographical Preferences

United States Preferences:
North America

Canadian Preferences:
All Canada

International Preferences:
Europe

Industry Preferences

In Industrial/Energy prefer:
Energy

In Financial Services prefer:
Real Estate

Additional Information
Name of Most Recent Fund: Starwood Energy Infrastructure Fund II
Most Recent Fund Was Raised: 01/07/2014
Year Founded: 1991
Capital Under Management: $17,342,930,000

Current Activity Level : Actively seeking new investments

STATA VENTURE PARTNERS
197 First Avenue
Needham, MA USA 02494
Phone: 7815915210

Management and Staff
Leonard Barbieri, Managing Director
Raymond Stata, Founder

Type of Firm
Private Equity Firm

Project Preferences

Type of Financing Preferred:
Early Stage

Geographical Preferences

United States Preferences:

International Preferences:
Ireland
Israel
All International

Industry Preferences

In Communications prefer:
Telecommunications

In Semiconductor/Electr prefer:
Semiconductor

Additional Information
Name of Most Recent Fund: Stata Venture Partners III LLC
Most Recent Fund Was Raised: 12/30/2008
Year Founded: 1999
Current Activity Level : Actively seeking new investments

STATE DEVELOPMENT & INVESTMENT CORP LTD
6-6 Fuchengmen North Street
International Investment Plaza
Beijing, China 100034
Phone: 861088006880
Fax: 861066579035
E-mail: sdic@sdic.com.cn
Website: www.sdic.com.cn

Other Offices
No.1, Qianwan Road One
R201, Building A
Shenzhen, China

Management and Staff
Bing Li, Vice President
Dechun Chen, Vice President
Hongxiang Shi, Vice President
Hua Zhang, Chief Financial Officer
Meng Qian, Vice President
Ming Qin, Vice President

Type of Firm
Government Affiliated Program

Project Preferences

Type of Financing Preferred:
Balanced

Geographical Preferences

International Preferences:
China

Industry Preferences

In Communications prefer:
Telecommunications
Wireless Communications

In Computer Software prefer:
Software

In Internet Specific prefer:
Internet
Ecommerce

In Semiconductor/Electr prefer:
Electronics

In Biotechnology prefer:
Biotechnology

In Medical/Health prefer:
Medical/Health

In Industrial/Energy prefer:
Materials

In Transportation prefer:
Transportation

In Business Serv. prefer:
Media

Additional Information
Year Founded: 1995
Capital Under Management: $390,380,000
Current Activity Level : Actively seeking new investments

STATE OF MIND VENTURES
Ha-Menofim Street 1
Herzliyya, Israel
Phone: 97297888000
Fax: 97298339901
E-mail: info@stateofmind.ventures
Website: www.somv.com

Other Offices
Ha-Menofim Street 1
Herzliyya, Israel
Phone: 097888000

Type of Firm
Private Equity Firm

Project Preferences

Type of Financing Preferred:
Early Stage
Seed

Geographical Preferences

International Preferences:
Israel

Industry Preferences

In Computer Software prefer:
Software

In Internet Specific prefer:
Internet

Additional Information
Year Founded: 2015
Capital Under Management: $75,000,000
Current Activity Level : Actively seeking new investments

STATE OF WISCONSIN INVESTMENT BOARD

121 East Wilson Street
P.O. Box 7842
Madison, WI USA 53703
Phone: 6082662381
Fax: 6082662436
E-mail: info@swib.state.wi.us
Website: www.swib.state.wi.us

Other Offices
330 North Orchard Street, Suite B1254C
Madison, WI USA 53715

Management and Staff
Charles Carpenter, Managing Director
Ronald Mensink, Managing Director

Type of Firm
Government Affiliated Program

Project Preferences

Type of Financing Preferred:
Early Stage
Balanced
Seed
Startup

Geographical Preferences

United States Preferences:
Wisconsin

Additional Information
Year Founded: 1951
Capital Under Management: $30,000,000
Current Activity Level : Actively seeking new investments

STATKRAFT VENTURES GMBH

Derendorfer Allee 2a
Dusseldorf, Germany 40476
Phone: 4921160244000
Fax: 4921160244199
E-mail: info@statkraftventures.com
Website: www.statkraftventures.com

Management and Staff
Matthias Dill, Managing Director
Stefan-Joerg Goebel, Managing Director

Type of Firm
Private Equity Firm

Project Preferences

Type of Financing Preferred:
Early Stage

Geographical Preferences

International Preferences:
Europe

Industry Preferences

In Industrial/Energy prefer:
Energy

Additional Information
Year Founded: 2015
Current Activity Level : Actively seeking new investments

STE AMEN INVESTISSEMENT SA

Rue du Lac NEUCHATEL
Immeuble Amen Invest. 9
Tunis, Tunisia 1053
Phone: 21671965410
Fax: 21671965426
Website: www.ameninvest.com.tn

Type of Firm
Investment Management Firm

Project Preferences

Type of Financing Preferred:
Early Stage

Geographical Preferences

International Preferences:
Tunisia

Industry Preferences

In Industrial/Energy prefer:
Industrial Products

Additional Information
Year Founded: 1994
Capital Under Management: $3,718,000
Current Activity Level : Actively seeking new investments

STE DE DEVELOPPEMENT ECONOMIQUE KASSERINE SA

Av. Habib Bourguiba
en Face de la B.C.T
Kasserine, Tunisia 1200
Phone: 21677478680
Fax: 21677478710
E-mail: sodek.sicar@topnet.tn
Website: www.invest-in-kasserine.tn

Other Offices
Avenue Suffeitula
Cite Ezzhours
Kasserine, Tunisia 1279
Phone: 21677478680
Fax: 21677478710

Type of Firm
Private Equity Firm

Association Membership
Tunisian Venture Capital Association

Project Preferences

Role in Financing:
Will function either as deal originator or investor in deals created by others

Type of Financing Preferred:
Early Stage
Later Stage

Geographical Preferences

International Preferences:
Tunisia
Africa

Industry Preferences

In Consumer Related prefer:
Entertainment and Leisure

In Industrial/Energy prefer:
Industrial Products

In Business Serv. prefer:
Services

In Agr/Forestr/Fish prefer:
Agriculture related

Additional Information
Year Founded: 1997
Current Activity Level : Actively seeking new investments

STE HOLDING FINANCIERE DE PARTICIPATION ET D'INVESTISSEMENTS

Place Moulay El Hassan
Rabat, Morocco
Phone: 212537669151
Fax: 212537669010
Website: www.fipar.ma

Type of Firm
Private Equity Firm

Project Preferences

Type of Financing Preferred:
Leveraged Buyout
Early Stage
Generalist PE
Later Stage
Seed
Acquisition
Startup

Geographical Preferences

International Preferences:
Morocco
Africa

Industry Preferences

In Consumer Related prefer:
Consumer Services

In Financial Services prefer:
Financial Services
Financial Services

In Business Serv. prefer:
Services

Additional Information
Year Founded: 1989
Current Activity Level : Actively seeking new investments

STE INVES PART SICAR

Rue Hedi Nouira
Residence le Palace NASR II
Tunis, Tunisia 2037
Phone: 216-71-828-992
Fax: 216-71-828-972
E-mail: simpar@planet.tn

Type of Firm
Bank Affiliated

Association Membership
Tunisian Venture Capital Association

Project Preferences

Role in Financing:
Will function either as deal originator or investor in deals created by others

Type of Financing Preferred:
Early Stage
Later Stage
Startup
Special Situation

Geographical Preferences

International Preferences:
Tunisia
Africa

Additional Information
Year Founded: 2004
Current Activity Level : Actively seeking new investments

STEADFAST CAPITAL GMBH

Myliusstrasse 47
Frankfurt am Main, Germany 60323
Phone: 4969506850
Fax: 496950685100
E-mail: info@steadfastcapital.de
Website: www.steadfastcapital.de

Management and Staff
Andrea Scheerer, Founder
Brian James Veitch, Managing Partner
Clemens Busch, Managing Partner
James Homer, Chief Financial Officer
Kay Buschmann, Principal
Marco Bernecker, Partner
Markus Geiger, Principal
Nicholas Money-Kyrle, Managing Partner

Type of Firm
Private Equity Firm

Association Membership
German Venture Capital Association (BVK)
European Private Equity and Venture Capital Assoc.

Project Preferences

Type of Financing Preferred:
Leveraged Buyout
Later Stage
Management Buyouts

Geographical Preferences

International Preferences:
Luxembourg
Europe
Netherlands
Switzerland
Austria
Belgium
Germany

Industry Preferences

In Consumer Related prefer:
Food/Beverage

In Industrial/Energy prefer:
Energy
Industrial Products
Materials
Factory Automation
Machinery
Environmental Related

Additional Information
Name of Most Recent Fund: Steadfast Capital Fund III
Most Recent Fund Was Raised: 06/27/2011
Year Founded: 2001
Capital Under Management: $435,000,000
Current Activity Level : Actively seeking new investments

STEAMBOAT VENTURES

801 North Boulevard, Suite 665
Glendale, CA USA 91203
Phone: 8185537900
Fax: 8186962686
E-mail: svmail@steamboatvc.com
Website: www.steamboatvc.com

Other Offices
One Matheson Street
20th Floor, Shell Tower
Causeway Bay, Hong Kong
Phone: 85222032300
Fax: 852220318000

513 Hennessy Rd
20/F, Wellable Commercial Bldg
Causeway Bay, Hong Kong SAR
Phone: 85235119276

222 Hu Bin Road
Unit 1002-1004, One Corporate Aven
, China
Phone: 862123081800
Fax: 862123081999

Management and Staff
Perry Chui, General Partner
Sidney Wen, Principal

Type of Firm
Corporate PE/Venture

Association Membership
Hong Kong Venture Capital Association (HKVCA)
National Venture Capital Association - USA (NVCA)

Project Preferences

Role in Financing:
Will function either as deal originator or investor in deals created by others

2024

Type of Financing Preferred:
Early Stage
Balanced
Later Stage

Size of Investments Considered:
Min Size of Investment Considered (000s): $2,000
Max Size of Investment Considered (000s): $20,000

Industry Preferences

In Communications prefer:
Communications and Media

In Consumer Related prefer:
Consumer

Additional Information
Name of Most Recent Fund: Steamboat Ventures V, L.P.
Most Recent Fund Was Raised: 12/14/2012
Year Founded: 2000
Capital Under Management: $660,000,000
Current Activity Level : Actively seeking new investments

STEEL PIER CAPITAL ADVISORS LLC

750 Lexington Avenue
22nd Floor
New York, NY USA 10022
Phone: 2129949861
E-mail: info@spcfund.com

Management and Staff
Gene Salkind, Managing Partner
Johnathan Weigand, Vice President
Mark Burgess, Chief Financial Officer

Type of Firm
Investment Management Firm

Project Preferences

Type of Financing Preferred:
Leveraged Buyout
Expansion
Management Buyouts
Acquisition
Recapitalizations

Industry Preferences

In Medical/Health prefer:
Medical/Health

In Consumer Related prefer:
Consumer
Retail

In Industrial/Energy prefer:
Industrial Products
Environmental Related

In Business Serv. prefer:
Services
Media

In Manufact. prefer:
Manufacturing

Additional Information
Year Founded: 2011
Current Activity Level : Actively seeking new investments

STEELHEAD CAPITAL MANAGEMENT

1401 Foch Street, Suite 140
Westover Hills, TX USA 76107
Phone: 8179845964
E-mail: jfucci@steelheadcm.com
Website: steelheadcm.com

Type of Firm
Private Equity Firm

Project Preferences

Type of Financing Preferred:
Generalist PE
Later Stage
Seed

Industry Preferences

In Medical/Health prefer:
Pharmaceuticals

In Consumer Related prefer:
Consumer

In Industrial/Energy prefer:
Energy

Additional Information
Year Founded: 2017
Current Activity Level : Actively seeking new investments

STEELHEAD VENTURES LLC

44 Tehama Street
San Francisco, CA USA 94105

Type of Firm
Private Equity Firm

Project Preferences

Type of Financing Preferred:
Early Stage
Start-up Financing

Additional Information
Year Founded: 2014
Current Activity Level : Actively seeking new investments

STEELHOUSE VENTURES LTD

London Road
Tubs Hill House
Sevenoaks, United Kingdom TN13 IBL
E-mail: admin@steelhouse-ventures.com
Website: www.steelhouse-ventures.com

Other Offices
Sundgauer Strasse 105c
Berlin, Germany 14169
Phone: 4930221608199

Management and Staff
Mark Conway, Co-Founder
Peter Bryant, Co-Founder
Roger Turner, Co-Founder

Type of Firm
Private Equity Firm

Project Preferences

Type of Financing Preferred:
Early Stage
Expansion
Balanced

Geographical Preferences

International Preferences:
United Kingdom
Europe

Industry Preferences

In Communications prefer:
Wireless Communications
Data Communications

In Industrial/Energy prefer:
Energy

Additional Information
Year Founded: 1990
Current Activity Level : Actively seeking new investments

STEELPOINT CAPITAL PARTNERS LP

420 Stevens Avenue, Suite 370
Solana Beach, CA USA 92075
Phone: 8587648700
Fax: 8587648701
E-mail: info@steelpointcp.com
Website: www.steelpointcp.com

Other Offices
Former HQ: One Penn Palaza, Suite 2207
New York, NY USA 10119
Phone: 2129123800

Management and Staff
Garrett Potter, Managing Director

Type of Firm
Private Equity Firm

Project Preferences

Type of Financing Preferred:
Leveraged Buyout
Generalist PE
Balanced
Later Stage
Recapitalizations

Size of Investments Considered:
Min Size of Investment Considered (000s): $5,000
Max Size of Investment Considered (000s): $30,000

Geographical Preferences

United States Preferences:

Industry Preferences

In Communications prefer:
Telecommunications

In Medical/Health prefer:
Health Services

In Business Serv. prefer:
Media

Additional Information
Year Founded: 2003
Current Activity Level : Actively seeking new investments

STEFNIR ASSET MANAGEMENT COMPANY HF

Borgartuni 19
Reykjavik, Iceland 105
Phone: 3544447400
E-mail: info@stefnir.is
Website: www.stefnir.is

Management and Staff
Floki Halldorsson, Managing Director

Type of Firm
Bank Affiliated

Project Preferences

Type of Financing Preferred:
Balanced

Additional Information
Year Founded: 1996
Current Activity Level : Actively seeking new investments

STELLA MARIS PARTNERS

Jimenez 465, Piso 2
Monterrey, Mexico
Phone: 528120865596
E-mail: info@stellamaris.mx
Website: www.stellamaris.mx

Type of Firm
Private Equity Firm

Project Preferences

Type of Financing Preferred:
Balanced

Additional Information
Year Founded: 1969
Current Activity Level : Actively seeking new investments

STELLA POINT CAPITAL LLC

444 Madison Avenue, Suite 302
New York, NY USA 10022
Phone: 2122350200
E-mail: info@stellapoint.com
Website: stellapoint.com

Type of Firm
Private Equity Firm

Project Preferences

Type of Financing Preferred:
Leveraged Buyout

Industry Preferences

In Consumer Related prefer:
Consumer

In Industrial/Energy prefer:
Industrial Products

In Business Serv. prefer:
Services

Additional Information
Year Founded: 1969
Current Activity Level : Actively seeking new investments

STELLARIS VENTURE PARTNERS

Stratup Warehouse
Diamond District
Domlur, Bangalore, India
Website: stellarisvp.com

Management and Staff
Alok Goyal, Partner
Rahul Chowdhri, Partner
Ritesh Banglani, Partner

Type of Firm
Private Equity Firm

Project Preferences

Type of Financing Preferred:
Early Stage

Additional Information
Year Founded: 2016
Capital Under Management: $50,000,000
Current Activity Level : Actively seeking new investments

STELLEX CAPITAL MANAGEMENT LP

900 Third Avenue
22nd Floor
New York, NY USA 10022
Phone: 2127102323
Website: www.stellexcapitalmanagement.com

Management and Staff
Michael Stewart, Managing Partner
Raymond Whiteman, Managing Partner
Tony Braddock, Chief Financial Officer

Type of Firm
Private Equity Firm

Project Preferences

Type of Financing Preferred:
Leveraged Buyout
Turnaround
Special Situation
Distressed Debt

Geographical Preferences

United States Preferences:

International Preferences:
Europe

Industry Preferences

In Communications prefer:
Communications and Media

In Consumer Related prefer:
Consumer Services

In Transportation prefer:
Aerospace

In Financial Services prefer:
Financial Services

In Business Serv. prefer:
Services
Consulting Services

Additional Information
Year Founded: 2014
Capital Under Management: $870,000,000
Current Activity Level : Actively seeking new investments

STELLUS CAPITAL MANAGEMENT LLC

4400 Post Oak Parkway, Suite 2200
Houston, TX USA 77027
Phone: 7132925400
Website: www.stelluscapital.com

Other Offices
4520 East West Highway, Suite 630
Bethesda, MD USA 20814
Phone: 3016343000

411 Theodore Fremd Avenue, Suite 206 South
Rye, NY USA 10580
Phone: 9149253466

Management and Staff
Adam Pollock, Principal
Dean D Angelo, Partner
Debra Blank, Vice President
Derek Crevello, Principal
Eric Madry, Vice President
Gavin Roseman, Vice President
Joshua Davis, Partner
Kenneth Debow, Principal
Robert Collins, Principal
Stephen Bernier, Principal
Todd Huskinson, Chief Financial Officer
Todd Overbergen, Partner
Victoria Garcia, Vice President
Vivek Shah, Principal

Type of Firm
Private Equity Firm

Association Membership
Natl Assoc of Small Bus. Inv. Co (NASBIC)

Project Preferences

Type of Financing Preferred:
Leveraged Buyout
Expansion
Mezzanine
Turnaround
Other
Acquisition
Distressed Debt
Recapitalizations

Geographical Preferences

United States Preferences:

Canadian Preferences:
All Canada

Industry Preferences

In Computer Software prefer:
Software

In Medical/Health prefer:
Medical/Health

In Industrial/Energy prefer:
Energy
Oil & Gas Drilling,Explor
Industrial Products

In Financial Services prefer:
Financial Services

In Business Serv. prefer:
Services

Additional Information
Year Founded: 1988
Current Activity Level : Actively seeking new investments

STENTON LEIGH GROUP, INC.

2888 East Oakland Park Blvd.
Fort Lauderdale, FL USA 33306
Phone: 561-361-1866
Fax: 561-361-1867
E-mail: info@stentonleighgroup.com
Website: www.stentonleighgroup.com

Management and Staff
Milton Barbarosh, Chief Executive Officer

Type of Firm
Bank Affiliated

Project Preferences

Role in Financing:
Will function either as deal originator or investor in deals created by others

Type of Financing Preferred:
Leveraged Buyout
Control-block Purchases
Expansion
Mezzanine
Later Stage
Management Buyouts
Acquisition
Recapitalizations

Size of Investments Considered:
Min Size of Investment Considered (000s): $500
Max Size of Investment Considered (000s): $100,000

Geographical Preferences

United States Preferences:

Canadian Preferences:
All Canada
Quebec
Ontario

Additional Information
Year Founded: 1989
Capital Under Management: $20,000,000
Current Activity Level : Actively seeking new investments
Method of Compensation: Return on invest. most important, but chg. closing fees, service fees, etc.

STEPSTONE GROUP LP

505 Fifth Avenue
17th Floor
New York, NY USA 10017
Phone: 2123516100
Fax: 2123516101
E-mail: ir@stepstoneglobal.com
Website: www.stepstonellc.com

Other Offices
Albemarle House, One Albemarle Street
Fourth Floor
London, United Kingdom W1S4HA
Phone: 4402076477550
Fax: 4402076477599

4350 La Jolla Village Drive, Suite 800
San Diego, CA USA 92122
Phone: 8585589700
Fax: 8585589701

One Guang Hua Road, Beijing Kerry Centre
North Tower, 20th Floor, Suite 2005-2007
Beijing, China 100020
Phone: 861085298784
Fax: 861085298447

Management and Staff
Aiyu Yuan, Vice President
Andy Tsai, Managing Director
Anupam Gupta, Managing Director
Darren Friedman, Partner
David Jeffrey, Partner
Geoffrey Dolan, Vice President
Ian Aaker, Vice President
James Gamett, Partner
Jason Ment, Partner
Jay Morgan, Managing Director
Jay Rose, Partner
Joe Topley, Managing Director
John Kettnich, Vice President
John Coelho, Partner
Johnny Randel, Partner
Jose Fernandez, Founder
Kristin DePlatchett, Vice President
Lindsay Creedon, Principal
Mark Maruszewski, Partner
Michael McCabe, Partner
Monte Brem, Chief Executive Officer
Mrinalini Lhila, Vice President
Rohit Malhotra, Managing Director
Scott Hart, Partner
Shin Kim, Managing Director
Timothy Weld, Principal
Tom Bradley, Partner
Tom Keck, Founder

Vincent Hsu, Vice President
Vita Gorkova, Vice President
Weichou Su, Partner

Type of Firm
Private Equity Firm

Association Membership
China Venture Capital Association
European Private Equity and Venture Capital Assoc.

Project Preferences

Type of Financing Preferred:
Fund of Funds
Leveraged Buyout
Value-Add
Mezzanine
Generalist PE
Other
Acquisition
Joint Ventures
Special Situation
Distressed Debt
Fund of Funds of Second
Recapitalizations

Geographical Preferences

United States Preferences:
North America

International Preferences:
Latin America
Europe
Middle East
Australia
Asia
Africa

Industry Preferences

In Industrial/Energy prefer:
Energy
Oil and Gas Exploration

In Financial Services prefer:
Real Estate

Additional Information
Name of Most Recent Fund: StepStone Tactical Growth Fund, L.P.
Most Recent Fund Was Raised: 10/04/2013
Year Founded: 2003
Capital Under Management: $1,441,680,000
Current Activity Level : Actively seeking new investments

STEREO CAPITAL

530 Lytton Avenue
Second Floor
Palo Alto, CA USA 94301
E-mail: contacts@stereocap.vc
Website: www.stereocap.vc

Type of Firm
Private Equity Firm

Project Preferences

Type of Financing Preferred:
Expansion

Industry Preferences

In Computer Software prefer:
Software

In Medical/Health prefer:
Health Services

In Financial Services prefer:
Financial Services

Additional Information
Year Founded: 2013
Current Activity Level : Actively seeking new investments

STERLING GROUP LP

Nine Greenway Plaza, Suite 2400
Houston, TX USA 77046
Phone: 7138778257
Fax: 7138771824
E-mail: info@sterling-group.com
Website: sterling-group.com

Management and Staff
Bradley Staller, Partner
Brian Henry, Managing Director
C. Kevin Garland, Partner
Francis Carr, Managing Director
Frank Hevrdejs, Founder
Gary Rosenthal, Partner
Gregory Elliott, Partner
Hunter Nelson, Partner
John Hawkins, Partner
Reymond Wallace, Partner
Shirley Jefferies, Chief Financial Officer
William Oehmig, Partner

Type of Firm
Private Equity Firm

Project Preferences

Role in Financing:
Prefer role as deal originator

Type of Financing Preferred:
Leveraged Buyout
Management Buyouts
Acquisition
Recapitalizations

Geographical Preferences

United States Preferences:

Canadian Preferences:
All Canada

Industry Focus
(% based on actual investment)

Industrial/Energy	56.7%
Other Products	38.8%
Biotechnology	3.3%
Consumer Related	1.2%

Additional Information
Name of Most Recent Fund: Sterling Group Partners III, L.P.
Most Recent Fund Was Raised: 11/13/2009
Year Founded: 1982
Capital Under Management: $1,300,000,000
Current Activity Level : Actively seeking new investments

STERLING INVESTMENT PARTNERS II LP

285 Riverside Avenue, Suite 300
Westport, CT USA 06880
Phone: 2032268711
Fax: 2034545780
Website: www.sterlinglp.com

Management and Staff
Charles Santoro, Co-Founder
Douglas Newhouse, Co-Founder
James Soldano, Principal
Joseph Gault, Principal
M. William Macey, Co-Founder
Michael Barr, Partner
William Selden, Co-Founder
William Russell, Partner

Type of Firm
Private Equity Firm

Project Preferences

Role in Financing:
Prefer role as deal originator but will also invest in deals created by others

Type of Financing Preferred:
Leveraged Buyout
Management Buyouts
Acquisition
Recapitalizations

Geographical Preferences

United States Preferences:

Industry Focus
(% based on actual investment)

Other Products	85.8%
Computer Software and Services	11.3%
Internet Specific	2.3%
Industrial/Energy	0.6%

Additional Information
Name of Most Recent Fund: Sterling Investment Partners III, L.P.
Most Recent Fund Was Raised: 01/11/2013
Year Founded: 1991
Capital Under Management: $1,000,000,000
Current Activity Level : Actively seeking new investments
Method of Compensation: Return on invest. most important, but chg. closing fees, service fees, etc.

STERLING JOHNSTON CAPITAL MANAGEMENT LP

50 California Street, Suite 3325
San Francisco, CA USA 94111
Phone: 415-477-2300
Fax: 415-477-2334
E-mail: info@sterlingjohnston.com

Type of Firm
Private Equity Firm

Project Preferences

Type of Financing Preferred:
Leveraged Buyout
Later Stage

Additional Information
Year Founded: 1985
Current Activity Level : Actively seeking new investments

STERLING PARTNERS GP LLC

650 South Exeter Street, Suite 1000
Baltimore, MD USA 21202
Phone: 4437031700
Fax: 4437031750

Other Offices
401 N. Michigan Ave., Suite 3300
Chicago, IL USA 60611
Phone: 3124657000

701 Brickell Avenue, Suite 1700
Miami, FL USA 33131
Phone: 3058082970

Management and Staff
Alan Macksey, Managing Director
Andy Colmone, Vice President
Brandon Labrum, Vice President
Brennan Barthelemy, Principal
Chris Hoehn-Saric, Co-Founder
Daniel Hosler, Principal
Daniel Rosenberg, Managing Director
Eric Becker, Co-Founder
Garrick Rice, Managing Director
Jason Rosenberg, Principal
Jeffrey Elburn, Founder
John Ebersole, Principal
Julie Stacey, Vice President
Kevin McAllister, Principal
Kim Moffat, Principal
Matt Hankins, Vice President
Michael Drai, Principal
Ricardo Prado, Vice President
Rick Elfman, Senior Managing Director
Shoshana Vernick, Principal
Steve Chang, Principal
Todd Miller, Vice President
Tom Wippman, Managing Director
William Gonzalez, Vice President

Type of Firm
Private Equity Firm

Association Membership
Illinois Venture Capital Association
Private Equity Council (PEC)

Project Preferences

Role in Financing:
Will function either as deal originator or investor in deals created by others

Type of Financing Preferred:
Leveraged Buyout
Generalist PE
Later Stage
Management Buyouts
Acquisition
Industry Rollups

Industry Preferences

In Medical/Health prefer:
Medical/Health

In Consumer Related prefer:
Education Related

In Business Serv. prefer:
Services

Additional Information
Name of Most Recent Fund: Sterling Capital Partners IV, L.P.
Most Recent Fund Was Raised: 06/30/2011
Year Founded: 1983
Capital Under Management: $4,000,000,000
Current Activity Level : Actively seeking new investments
Method of Compensation: Return on invest. most important, but chg. closing fees, service fees, etc.

STERN PARTNERS INC

650 West Georgia Street, Suite 2900 - P.O Box 11583
Vancouver, Canada V6B 4N8
Phone: 6046818817
Fax: 6046818861
E-mail: info@sternpartners.com
Website: sternpartners.com

Management and Staff
Chris Tsoromocos, Vice President
Keith Van Apeldoorn, Vice President
Norm Drewlo, Vice President
Ronald Stern, President

Type of Firm
Private Equity Firm

Project Preferences

Type of Financing Preferred:
Leveraged Buyout
Turnaround
Management Buyouts
Recapitalizations

Additional Information
Year Founded: 2007
Current Activity Level : Actively seeking new investments

STEWART CAPITAL MANAGEMENT LLC

19154 Mohawk Street
Stilwell, KS USA 66085
E-mail: Info@StewartCapitalManagement.com
Website: stewartcapitalmanagement.com

Management and Staff
Jon Strombom, Vice President
Paul Pickard, Managing Director

Type of Firm
Private Equity Firm

Project Preferences

Type of Financing Preferred:
Leveraged Buyout
Expansion
Management Buyouts
Acquisition
Recapitalizations

Geographical Preferences

United States Preferences:
North America

Industry Preferences

In Consumer Related prefer:
Retail
Other Restaurants

In Business Serv. prefer:
Services
Distribution

In Manufact. prefer:
Manufacturing

Additional Information
Year Founded: 1969
Current Activity Level : Actively seeking new investments

STG CAPITAL LLC

780 Third Avenue
45th Floor
New York, NY USA 10017
Phone: 212-833-9975

Management and Staff
Steven Glass, Managing Partner

Type of Firm
Other

Industry Preferences

In Communications prefer:
Telecommunications
Media and Entertainment

Additional Information
Year Founded: 2002
Capital Under Management: $3,600,000
Current Activity Level : Actively seeking new investments

STIC INVESTMENT INC

11F, MSA Bldg.,
12, Teheran-ro 78-gil, Gangnam
Seoul, South Korea 135840
Phone: 82234047800
Fax: 82234047890
E-mail: info@stic.co.kr
Website: www.stic.co.kr

Other Offices

9 Fl., No.51, Sec. 2
Keelung Rd., Xinyi District
Taipei, Taiwan
Phone: 886277185198
Fax: 886277180100

228 Hamilton Avenue, Suite 210
Palo Alto, CA USA 94301
Phone: 650-330-7350
Fax: 650-330-7351

Unit 2406, 24 Fl. Shanghai Times Square
93 Huai Hai Zhong Road
Shanghai, China 200021
Phone: 862163406660
Fax: 862163406670

, Suite 908, 9FI, Sun Wah Tower
115 Nguyen Hue Blvd. Dist. 1
Ho Chi Minh, Vietnam
Phone: 84-8-3827-8491
Fax: 84-8-3827-8492

402 Centun Venure Town
No. 1475 U-dong, Haeundae-gu
Busan, South Korea 612-020
Phone: 82-51-731-2195
Fax: 82-51-731-2197

Suite 2002, Nexxus Building
41 Connaught Road
Central, Hong Kong
Phone: 852-2901-2300
Fax: 852-2973-0013

Management and Staff
Andy Chang, Managing Partner
Chang Suk Kim, Managing Director
Dae Hwan Kwag, Managing Director
Daniel Lee, Managing Director
David Jeong, Managing Director
Hans Jung, Managing Partner
Hoang Duy Ly, Principal
Hyung Gun Park, Managing Partner
Jong Chan Lee, Managing Director
Kyeong-Cheol Koo, Managing Partner
Minsik Park, Managing Director
Sam Lee, Managing Partner
Seon Bae, Managing Director
Seongkyu Lee, Managing Partner
Sung-Que Koh, Managing Director

Type of Firm
Private Equity Firm

Association Membership
Hong Kong Venture Capital Association (HKVCA)
Korean Venture Capital Association (KVCA)

Project Preferences

Type of Financing Preferred:
Leveraged Buyout
Generalist PE
Balanced
Later Stage
Fund of Funds of Second
Recapitalizations

Size of Investments Considered:
Min Size of Investment Considered (000s): $3,000
Max Size of Investment Considered (000s): $15,000

Geographical Preferences

International Preferences:
Asia
Korea, South

Industry Preferences

In Communications prefer:
Telecommunications

In Computer Other prefer:
Computer Related

In Semiconductor/Electr prefer:
Electronics

In Medical/Health prefer:
Medical Products
Hospitals/Clinics/Primary

In Consumer Related prefer:
Entertainment and Leisure
Retail
Consumer Products
Consumer Services

In Transportation prefer:
Transportation

In Financial Services prefer:
Financial Services

In Business Serv. prefer:
Services
Media

In Manufact. prefer:
Manufacturing

Additional Information
Year Founded: 1999
Capital Under Management: $247,900,000
Current Activity Level : Actively seeking new investments

STICHTING BEWAARDER AMSTERDAMS KLIMAAT & ENERGIEFONDS

Pedro de Medinalaan 11
Amsterdam, Netherlands 1086XK
Website: www.akef.nl

Type of Firm
Government Affiliated Program

Project Preferences

Type of Financing Preferred:
Leveraged Buyout
Early Stage
Expansion
Later Stage
Management Buyouts
Acquisition

Geographical Preferences

International Preferences:
Netherlands

Industry Preferences

In Industrial/Energy prefer:
Alternative Energy
Energy Conservation Relat

Additional Information
Year Founded: 2013
Current Activity Level : Actively seeking new investments

STIRLING SQUARE CAPITAL PARTNERS LP

127-131 Sloane Street
Liscarton House, Fourth Floor
London, United Kingdom SW1X 9AS
Phone: 442078084130
Fax: 442078084131
E-mail: info@stirlingsquare.com

Other Offices

11 - 15 Seaton Place
St. Helier
Jersey, Channel Islands JE4 0QH
Phone: 44-153-483-3000
Fax: 44-1534-833-033

Management and Staff

Bolaji Odunsi, Partner
Enrico Biale, Partner
Gregorio Napoleone, Partner
Jakob Forschner, Partner
Par Petterson, Partner
Robert Swift, Partner
Stefano Bonfiglio, Partner
Stuyvie Comfort, Partner

Type of Firm

Private Equity Firm

Association Membership

European Private Equity and Venture Capital Assoc.

Project Preferences

Type of Financing Preferred:
Leveraged Buyout
Expansion
Acquisition

Geographical Preferences

United States Preferences:

International Preferences:
Italy
United Kingdom
Europe
Scandanavia/Nordic Region
Germany
France

Industry Preferences

In Communications prefer:
Communications and Media

In Computer Software prefer:
Software

In Semiconductor/Electr prefer:
Electronics
Semiconductor

In Medical/Health prefer:
Medical Products

In Consumer Related prefer:
Consumer
Food/Beverage
Consumer Products
Education Related

In Industrial/Energy prefer:
Industrial Products

In Financial Services prefer:
Financial Services

In Business Serv. prefer:
Services

Additional Information

Year Founded: 1988
Capital Under Management: $1,162,277,000
Current Activity Level : Actively seeking new investments

STOCKHOLM INNOVATION & GROWTH AB

Isafjordsgatan 39B
Growhouse
Kista, Sweden 164 40
Phone: 46705789562
E-mail: info@stingcapital.com
Website: www.stockholminnovation.com

Management and Staff

Par Hedberg, Chief Executive Officer

Type of Firm

Private Equity Firm

Association Membership

Swedish Venture Capital Association (SVCA)

Project Preferences

Type of Financing Preferred:
Early Stage
Seed
Startup

Size of Investments Considered:
Min Size of Investment Considered (000s): $70
Max Size of Investment Considered (000s): $600

Geographical Preferences

International Preferences:
Sweden
Europe

Industry Preferences

In Biotechnology prefer:
Biotechnology

In Medical/Health prefer:
Medical/Health
Disposable Med. Products
Health Services
Pharmaceuticals

In Consumer Related prefer:
Entertainment and Leisure

In Industrial/Energy prefer:
Energy

Additional Information

Year Founded: 2005
Capital Under Management: $12,600,000
Current Activity Level : Actively seeking new investments

STONE ARCH CAPITAL LLC

800 Nicollet Mall, Suite 1150
Minneapolis, MN USA 55402
Phone: 6123172980
Fax: 6123172988
E-mail: info@stonearchcapital.com
Website: www.stonearchcapital.com

Management and Staff

Charlie Lannin, Partner
Dean Wikenheiser, Vice President
F. Clayton Miller, Partner
Kelly Horner, Chief Financial Officer
Peter Grant, Partner
Peter Offenhauser, Principal

Type of Firm

Private Equity Firm

Project Preferences

Role in Financing:
Prefer role as deal originator

Type of Financing Preferred:
Leveraged Buyout
Acquisition
Recapitalizations

Size of Investments Considered:
Min Size of Investment Considered (000s): $20,000
Max Size of Investment Considered (000s): $100,000

Geographical Preferences

United States Preferences:
Midwest
Illinois
Michigan
Nebraska
South Dakota
Iowa
North Dakota
Kansas
Ohio
Wisconsin
Missouri
Indiana
Minnesota

Industry Preferences

In Business Serv. prefer:
Services

In Manufact. prefer:
Manufacturing

Additional Information
Year Founded: 2004
Capital Under Management: $150,000,000
Current Activity Level : Actively seeking new investments
Method of Compensation: Return on invest. most important, but chg. closing fees, service fees, etc.

STONE CANYON INDUSTRIES LLC

1250 4th Street
Santa Monica, CA USA 90401
Phone: 4243162061
Fax: 4243162062
Website: stonecanyonllc.com

Management and Staff
Damien Lim, Managing Director
Jin Cheah, Managing Director
Michael Neumann, President
Peter Tan, Chief Executive Officer

Type of Firm
Private Equity Firm

Project Preferences

Type of Financing Preferred:
Leveraged Buyout
Acquisition

Additional Information
Year Founded: 2014
Current Activity Level : Actively seeking new investments

STONE CANYON VENTURE PARTNERS

150 South Barrington Place
Los Angeles, CA USA 90049
Phone: 3104325180
Fax: 3104325181
E-mail: info@scvp.com
Website: www.stonecanyonvp.com

Management and Staff
John Matise, Managing Director
John Davis, Managing Director
Kenneth Kilroy, Managing Director
Michael Seibert, Managing Director
Philip Smith, Managing Director
Wendy Seretan, Chief Financial Officer

Type of Firm
Private Equity Firm

Project Preferences

Role in Financing:
Will function either as deal originator or investor in deals created by others

Type of Financing Preferred:
Early Stage

Geographical Preferences

United States Preferences:
Southern California
Northern California

Industry Preferences

In Communications prefer:
CATV & Pay TV Systems
Radio & TV Broadcasting
Other Communication Prod.

In Internet Specific prefer:
E-Commerce Technology

In Medical/Health prefer:
Diagnostic Services
Medical Therapeutics
Medical Products
Health Services
Hospitals/Clinics/Primary

In Consumer Related prefer:
Consumer
Entertainment and Leisure
Retail
Franchises(NEC)
Food/Beverage
Hotels and Resorts

In Business Serv. prefer:
Media

Additional Information
Name of Most Recent Fund: Stone Canyon Venture Partners SBIC Fund
Most Recent Fund Was Raised: 01/09/2001
Year Founded: 2002
Capital Under Management: $85,000,000
Current Activity Level : Actively seeking new investments
Method of Compensation: Return on investment is of primary concern, do not charge fees

STONE DRUM CAPITAL LTD

134-136 Des Voeux Road
2/F., Bocg Insurance Tower
Hong Kong, China
Phone: 86-852-2568065
Fax: 86-852-2568035

Type of Firm
Private Equity Advisor or Fund of Funds

Additional Information
Year Founded: 2010
Current Activity Level : Actively seeking new investments

STONE POINT CAPITAL LLC

20 Horseneck Lane
Greenwich, CT USA 06830
Phone: 2038622900
Fax: 2036258357
Website: www.stonepoint.com

Management and Staff
Agha Khan, Principal
Andrew Reutter, Vice President
Charles Davis, Chief Executive Officer
Christopher Doody, Principal
Darran Baird, Principal
Emanuel Citron, Principal
Eric Rosenzweig, Vice President
Fayez Muhtadie, Vice President
Jacqueline Giammarco, Vice President
James Matthews, Principal
Kurt Bolin, Principal
Michael Gregorich, Principal
Peter Mundheim, Principal
Stephen Levey, Vice President

Type of Firm
Private Equity Firm

Project Preferences

Type of Financing Preferred:
Leveraged Buyout
Early Stage
Balanced
Acquisition

Size of Investments Considered:
Min Size of Investment Considered (000s): $50,000
Max Size of Investment Considered (000s): $400,000

Geographical Preferences

United States Preferences:

International Preferences:
Western Europe
All International

Industry Focus
(% based on actual investment)

Other Products	80.9%
Computer Software and Services	10.6%
Medical/Health	4.4%
Internet Specific	2.6%
Semiconductors/Other Elect.	0.6%
Computer Hardware	0.4%
Communications and Media	0.4%
Consumer Related	0.0%

Additional Information
Name of Most Recent Fund: Trident Fund V, L.P.
Most Recent Fund Was Raised: 03/12/2010
Year Founded: 2005
Capital Under Management: $9,730,880,000
Current Activity Level : Actively seeking new investments

STONE POINTE LLC

55 South Main Street, Suite 335
Naperville, IL USA 60540
Phone: 6306964175
Fax: 6306964176
Website: www.stonepointeinvest.com

Management and Staff
Lee Vandermyde, Partner

Type of Firm
Private Equity Firm

Project Preferences

Type of Financing Preferred:
Leveraged Buyout
Management Buyouts
Recapitalizations

Industry Preferences

In Consumer Related prefer:
Consumer Products

In Industrial/Energy prefer:
Industrial Products

Additional Information
Year Founded: 2007
Current Activity Level : Actively seeking new investments

STONE-GOFF PARTNERS LLC

900 Third Avenue
33rd Floor
New York, NY USA 10022
Website: www.stonegoff.com

Other Offices
177 Huntington Avenue, Suite 1708
BOSTON, MA USA 02108
Phone: 8572775118

Management and Staff
Hannah Craven, Co-Founder
Jin Kim, Vice President
Laurens Goff, Co-Founder
Robert Rob, Managing Director

Type of Firm
Private Equity Firm

Project Preferences

Type of Financing Preferred:
Leveraged Buyout
Acquisition

Size of Investments Considered:
Min Size of Investment Considered (000s): $6,000
Max Size of Investment Considered (000s): $20,000

Industry Preferences

In Communications prefer:
Communications and Media
Media and Entertainment
Entertainment

In Internet Specific prefer:
Ecommerce

In Consumer Related prefer:
Consumer
Retail
Consumer Services

In Business Serv. prefer:
Media

Additional Information
Year Founded: 2010
Capital Under Management: $50,000,000
Current Activity Level : Actively seeking new investments

STONEBRIDGE CAPITAL INC

Yeoksam-Dong
2F F&F Building, Gangnam-gu
Seoul, South Korea 135-913
Phone: 82234966600
E-mail: info@stonebridge.co.kr
Website: www.stonebridge.co.kr

Management and Staff
In Ho Son, Vice President

Type of Firm
Private Equity Firm

Association Membership
Korean Venture Capital Association (KVCA)

Project Preferences

Type of Financing Preferred:
Early Stage
Generalist PE
Management Buyouts

Geographical Preferences

International Preferences:
China
Korea, South
Japan

Industry Preferences

In Medical/Health prefer:
Medical/Health

In Consumer Related prefer:
Consumer Products

In Industrial/Energy prefer:
Oil and Gas Exploration

In Financial Services prefer:
Financial Services

Additional Information
Year Founded: 2008
Current Activity Level : Actively seeking new investments

STONEBRIDGE PARTNERS LP

81 Main Street, Suite 505
White Plains, NY USA 10601
Phone: 9146822700
Fax: 9146820834
E-mail: info@stonebridgepartners.com
Website: www.stonebridgepartners.com

Management and Staff
Andrew Thomas, General Partner
David Schopp, General Partner
Michael Steinback, General Partner
Michael Bruno, Managing Partner
Richard Heggelund, Principal
Stephen Hanna, Principal
William Connors, Principal

Type of Firm
Private Equity Firm

Project Preferences

Role in Financing:
Prefer role as deal originator

Type of Financing Preferred:
Leveraged Buyout
Management Buyouts
Acquisition

Size of Investments Considered:
Min Size of Investment Considered (000s): $30,000
Max Size of Investment Considered (000s): $200,000

Geographical Preferences

United States Preferences:

Canadian Preferences:
All Canada

Industry Focus
(% based on actual investment)
    Other Products   60.7%
    Industrial/Energy   20.4%
    Communications and Media   11.8%
    Consumer Related   6.7%
    Internet Specific   0.4%

Additional Information
Year Founded: 1986
Capital Under Management: $550,000,000
Current Activity Level : Actively seeking new investments
Method of Compensation: Return on invest. most important, but chg. closing fees, service fees, etc.

STONECALIBRE LLC

1801 Avenue of the Stars, Suite 905
Los Angeles, CA USA 90067
Phone: 3107740014
Website: www.stonecalibre.com

Type of Firm
Private Equity Firm

Project Preferences

Type of Financing Preferred:
Leveraged Buyout
Mezzanine
Turnaround
Later Stage
Seed
Special Situation
Distressed Debt

Industry Preferences

In Communications prefer:
Telecommunications

In Computer Software prefer:
Software

In Transportation prefer:
Transportation

In Business Serv. prefer:
Services

In Manufact. prefer:
Manufacturing

Additional Information
Year Founded: 2012
Current Activity Level : Actively seeking new investments

STONECREEK CAPITAL

18500 Von Karman Avenue, Suite 590
Irvine, CA USA 92612
Phone: 9497524580
Fax: 9497524585
E-mail: info@stonecreekcapital.com
Website: www.stonecreekcapital.com

Management and Staff
Bruce Lipian, Managing Director
David Sincich, Vice President
Drew Adams, President

Type of Firm
Bank Affiliated

Project Preferences

Role in Financing:
Will function either as deal originator or investor in deals created by others

Type of Financing Preferred:
Leveraged Buyout
Acquisition
Recapitalizations

Geographical Preferences

United States Preferences:
West Coast

Canadian Preferences:
All Canada

Industry Focus
(% based on actual investment)
Medical/Health	46.5%
Consumer Related	36.1%
Other Products	17.3%

Additional Information
Name of Most Recent Fund: Gordon & Morris Group Investment Partnership
Most Recent Fund Was Raised: 10/05/1994
Year Founded: 1992
Current Activity Level : Actively seeking new investments

STONEGATE CAPITAL GROUP LLC

222 Pitkin Street
East Hartford, CT USA 06108
Phone: 860-899-1181
Fax: 860-899-1491
Website: www.stonegatecapitalgroup.com

Other Offices
Former HQ: 185 Asylum Street
CityPlace II, 17th Floor
Hartford, CT USA 06103
Phone: 860-678-7800
Fax: 860-899-1491

Management and Staff
Claudia Horn, Vice President
Joel Hartstone, Managing Director

Type of Firm
Private Equity Firm

Project Preferences

Type of Financing Preferred:
Leveraged Buyout

Geographical Preferences

United States Preferences:

Additional Information
Year Founded: 1982
Current Activity Level : Actively seeking new investments

STONEHAMMER CAPITAL LLC

301 Carlson Parkway, Suite 110
Hopkins, MN USA 55305
Phone: 9529602478
E-mail: info@stonehammercapital.com
Website: stonehammercapital.com

Type of Firm
Private Equity Firm

Project Preferences

Type of Financing Preferred:
Seed

Additional Information
Year Founded: 2016
Current Activity Level : Actively seeking new investments

STONEHENGE GROWTH CAPITAL LLC

236 Third Street
Baton Rouge, LA USA 70801
Phone: 2254083000
Fax: 2254083090
Website: www.stonehengegrowthcapital.com

Other Offices
8000 Maryland Avenue, Suite 1190
Saint Louis, MO USA 63105
Phone: 314-721-5707
Fax: 314-721-5135

7887 East Belleview Avenue, Suite 1100
Englewood, CO USA 80111
Phone: 720-956-0235
Fax: 720-956-0209

152 West 57th Street
20th Floor
New York, NY USA 10019
Phone: 212-265-9380
Fax: 212-656-1344

191 West Nationwide Boulevard, Suite 600
Columbus, OH USA 43215
Phone: 614-246-2456
Fax: 614-246-2461

3424 North Shepard Avenue
Milwaukee, WI USA 53211
Phone: 414-906-1702
Fax: 414-906-1703

2001 Park Place, Suite 320
Birmingham, AL USA 35203
Phone: 205-458-2778
Fax: 866-539-9881

3625 North Hall Street, Suite 615
Dallas, TX USA 75219
Phone: 214-599-8850
Fax: 214-442-5626

1020 Highland Colony Parkway, Suite 1400
Ridgeland, MS USA 39157
Phone: 6019485711

707 West Azeele Street
Tampa, FL USA 33606
Phone: 813-221-4413
Fax: 813-221-6453

Management and Staff
Ari Kocen, Managing Director
Brent Sacha, Vice President
Charles Haberkorn, Managing Director
David Webber, Managing Director
Nemesio Viso, Managing Director
Stephen Bennett, Managing Director

Type of Firm
Investment Management Firm

Association Membership
Natl Assoc of Small Bus. Inv. Co (NASBIC)

Project Preferences

Role in Financing:
Will function either as deal originator or investor in deals created by others

Type of Financing Preferred:
Other

Size of Investments Considered:
Min Size of Investment Considered (000s): $3,000
Max Size of Investment Considered (000s): $7,000

Geographical Preferences

United States Preferences:
Pennsylvania
Southeast
Alabama
North Carolina
Northeast
Connecticut
Florida
Louisiana
New Jersey
Georgia
Texas

Industry Focus
(% based on actual investment)

Other Products	24.1%
Industrial/Energy	16.4%
Computer Software and Services	14.0%
Internet Specific	11.0%
Communications and Media	8.6%
Consumer Related	8.3%
Medical/Health	7.0%
Semiconductors/Other Elect.	5.4%
Biotechnology	3.6%
Computer Hardware	1.7%

Additional Information
Name of Most Recent Fund: Stonehenge Capital Fund Nevada I LLC
Most Recent Fund Was Raised: 02/05/2014
Year Founded: 1999
Capital Under Management: $677,000,000
Current Activity Level : Actively seeking new investments
Method of Compensation: Return on invest. most important, but chg. closing fees, service fees, etc.

STONEHENGE PARTNERS INC

191 W. Nationwide Boulevard, Suite 600
Columbus, OH USA 43215
Phone: 6142462500
Fax: 6142462431
E-mail: info@stonehengepartners.com
Website: www.stonehengepartners.com

Management and Staff
Keith Bishop, Managing Director
Michael Arguelles, Managing Director
Nathan McGill, Vice President
Nicholas Ulrich, Managing Director
Peter Davies, Managing Partner
Robert Eversole, Managing Partner
Stephen Kimpel, Managing Partner
Thomas Utgard, Managing Partner

Type of Firm
Private Equity Firm

Project Preferences

Type of Financing Preferred:
Leveraged Buyout
Expansion
Mezzanine
Later Stage
Management Buyouts
Acquisition
Recapitalizations

Geographical Preferences

United States Preferences:
Midwest

Industry Preferences

In Medical/Health prefer:
Health Services

In Business Serv. prefer:
Services
Distribution

In Manufact. prefer:
Manufacturing

Additional Information
Year Founded: 1999
Capital Under Management: $700,000,000
Current Activity Level : Actively seeking new investments

STONETREE CAPITAL MANAGEMENT LLC

500 Lake Cook Road, Suite 350
Deerfield, IL USA 60015
Phone: 8479457355
Website: www.stonetreemgt.com

Management and Staff
Robert Placek, Chief Financial Officer
Robert Murray, Managing Director
Robert Brady, Managing Director

Type of Firm
Private Equity Advisor or Fund of Funds

Project Preferences

Type of Financing Preferred:
Fund of Funds

Additional Information
Name of Most Recent Fund: Stonetree Capital Fund IV, L.P.
Most Recent Fund Was Raised: 05/02/2011
Year Founded: 2011
Capital Under Management: $50,000,000
Current Activity Level : Actively seeking new investments

STONEWAY CAPITAL LC

4290 North Vintage Circle
Provo, UT USA 84604
Website: stonewaycapital.com

Management and Staff
Warren Osborn, Managing Director

Type of Firm
Private Equity Firm

Project Preferences

Type of Financing Preferred:
Balanced

Additional Information
Year Founded: 1969
Current Activity Level : Actively seeking new investments

STONEWOOD CAPITAL MANAGEMENT INC

209 Fourth Avenue
Pittsburgh, PA USA 15222
Phone: 4123910300
Fax: 4123910500
E-mail: info@stonewoodcapital.com
Website: www.stonewoodcapital.com

Other Offices
Former HQ: Three Gateway Center, 13 East
Pittsburgh, PA USA 15222
Phone: 4123910300
Fax: 4123910500

Management and Staff
J. Kenneth Moritz, President
John Tippins, Managing Director
Peter Muth, Vice President

Type of Firm
Private Equity Firm

Project Preferences

Type of Financing Preferred:
Leveraged Buyout
Early Stage
Generalist PE
Turnaround
Management Buyouts
Acquisition
Recapitalizations

Size of Investments Considered:
Min Size of Investment Considered (000s): $100
Max Size of Investment Considered (000s): $1,000

Geographical Preferences

United States Preferences:
Northeast

Canadian Preferences:
All Canada

Industry Focus
(% based on actual investment)

Communications and Media	36.6%
Computer Software and Services	30.5%
Medical/Health	26.8%
Semiconductors/Other Elect.	6.1%

Additional Information
Year Founded: 1993
Current Activity Level : Actively seeking new investments

STOREHILL CAPITAL LLC

10 South Wacker Drive, Suite 3175
Chicago, IL USA 60606
Phone: 3128767267
E-mail: info@StorehillCapital.com
Website: www.shorehillcapital.com

Management and Staff
Doug Knoch, Managing Director
Rob Hogan, Managing Director

Type of Firm
Private Equity Firm

Project Preferences

Type of Financing Preferred:
Leveraged Buyout
Management Buyouts
Distressed Debt
Recapitalizations

Geographical Preferences

United States Preferences:
North America

Industry Preferences

In Industrial/Energy prefer:
Industrial Products

In Business Serv. prefer:
Distribution

Additional Information
Year Founded: 2013
Capital Under Management: $173,820,000
Current Activity Level : Actively seeking new investments

STORM VENTURES INC

3000 Sand Hill Road
Bldg 4, Suite 210
Menlo Park, CA USA 94025
Phone: 6509268800
Fax: 6509268888
E-mail: generalinfo@stormventures.com
Website: www.stormventures.com

Management and Staff
Alex Mendez, Co-Founder
Anshu Sharma, Venture Partner
Arun Penmetsa, Principal
Josef Friedman, Venture Partner
Kevin Melia, Chief Financial Officer
Ryan Floyd, Co-Founder
Sanjay Subhedar, Co-Founder
Tae Hea Nahm, Co-Founder
Timothy Danford, General Partner

Type of Firm
Private Equity Firm

Association Membership
Western Association of Venture Capitalists (WAVC)

Project Preferences

Role in Financing:
Prefer role as deal originator but will also invest in deals created by others

Type of Financing Preferred:
Early Stage
Balanced
Seed

Size of Investments Considered:
Min Size of Investment Considered (000s): $100
Max Size of Investment Considered (000s): $3,000

Geographical Preferences

United States Preferences:
West Coast

Industry Preferences

In Communications prefer:
Telecommunications
Wireless Communications

In Computer Software prefer:
Software

In Internet Specific prefer:
Internet

In Business Serv. prefer:
Services

Additional Information
Name of Most Recent Fund: Storm Ventures Fund IV, L.P.
Most Recent Fund Was Raised: 09/27/2011
Year Founded: 1997
Capital Under Management: $812,000,000
Current Activity Level : Actively seeking new investments
Method of Compensation: Return on investment is of primary concern, do not charge fees

STORNOWAY PORTFOLIO MANAGEMENT INC

30 St Clair Ave West, Suite 901
Toronto, Canada M4V 3A1
Website: www.stornowayportfolio.com

Type of Firm
Investment Management Firm

Project Preferences

Type of Financing Preferred:
Turnaround
Distressed Debt

STORY VENTURES LLC

555 Park Avenue
Apartmetn 5E
New York, NY USA 10021

Type of Firm
Private Equity Firm

Project Preferences

Type of Financing Preferred:
Early Stage
Seed

Industry Preferences

In Computer Software prefer:
Applications Software

Additional Information
Year Founded: 2016
Current Activity Level : Actively seeking new investments

STRAIGHTFORWARD CAPITAL MANAGEMENT OY

Hiilikatu 3
Helsinki, Finland 00180
E-mail: info@straightforward.vc
Website: straightforward.vc

Type of Firm
Private Equity Firm

Project Preferences

Type of Financing Preferred:
Early Stage

Additional Information
Year Founded: 2016
Current Activity Level : Actively seeking new investments

STRAIT LANE CAPITAL PARTNERS LLC

8333 Douglas Avenue, Suite 1010
Dallas, TX USA 75225
Phone: 2142959574
Fax: 2143906225
E-mail: info@straitlanecapital.com.
Website: www.straitlanecapital.com

Management and Staff
Richard Diamond, Partner
Warren Edwards, President

Type of Firm
Private Equity Firm

Project Preferences

Type of Financing Preferred:
Leveraged Buyout

Additional Information
Year Founded: 2009
Current Activity Level : Actively seeking new investments

STRAND EQUITY PARTNERS LLC

One North Wacker Drive, Suite 3605
Chicago, IL USA 60606
Website: strandequity.com

Management and Staff
David Vennettilli, Vice President
Seth Rodsky, Co-Founder
Theodore Schwartz, Co-Founder
Todd Schwartz, Partner
Tracy Ward, Partner

Type of Firm
Private Equity Firm

Project Preferences

Type of Financing Preferred:
Balanced

Industry Preferences

In Consumer Related prefer:
Consumer
Food/Beverage

Additional Information
Year Founded: 2012
Current Activity Level : Actively seeking new investments

STRAND VENTURES LTD

Nine South Street
London, United Kingdom W1K 2XA
Phone: 442079078500
Fax: 442079078509
E-mail: email@strandpartners.co.uk
Website: www.strandpartners.co.uk

Type of Firm
Bank Affiliated

Project Preferences

Type of Financing Preferred:
Early Stage
Expansion

Geographical Preferences

International Preferences:
United Kingdom
Africa

Industry Preferences

In Medical/Health prefer:
Health Services

In Industrial/Energy prefer:
Energy

In Agr/Forestr/Fish prefer:
Agriculture related

In Other prefer:
Environment Responsible

Additional Information
Year Founded: 2009
Current Activity Level : Actively seeking new investments

STRATEGIC ADVISORY GROUP INC

253 Main Street
P.O. Box 773
Sag Harbor, NY USA 11963
Phone: 6317257746
Fax: 6317257739
Website: www.strategicadvisorygroup.com

Other Offices
94 Mohegan Drive
West Hartford, CT USA 06117
Phone: 203-523-4257
Fax: 203-523-4530

Management and Staff
Carol Hance, Managing Director
Pierce Hance, Managing Director

Type of Firm
Service Provider

Project Preferences

Role in Financing:
Prefer role as deal originator

Type of Financing Preferred:
Mezzanine
Management Buyouts
Private Placement
Recapitalizations

Size of Investments Considered:
Min Size of Investment Considered (000s): $500
Max Size of Investment Considered (000s): $50,000

Geographical Preferences

United States Preferences:
All U.S.

Additional Information

Year Founded: 1992
Current Activity Level : Actively seeking new investments
Method of Compensation: Professional fee required whether or not deal closes

STRATEGIC CAPITAL PARTNERS

1-6-15 Nishi-Shinbashi, Minato
2F Aiko Building
Tokyo, Japan 105-0003
Phone: 81352515577

Type of Firm
SBIC

Additional Information
Year Founded: 2006
Current Activity Level : Actively seeking new investments

STRATEGIC CYBER VENTURES LLC

1717 Pennsylvania Ave
Washington, DC USA 20006
Phone: 2027334719
E-mail: info@scvgroup.net
Website: scvgroup.net

Type of Firm
Private Equity Firm

Project Preferences

Type of Financing Preferred:
Early Stage
Expansion

Industry Preferences

In Computer Software prefer:
Software

Additional Information
Year Founded: 2016
Current Activity Level : Actively seeking new investments

STRATEGIC INVESTMENTS, L.P.

50 Fountain Plaza, Suite 1350
Buffalo, NY USA 14202
Phone: 7168576000
Fax: 7168576490
E-mail: info@sihi.net
Website: www.sihi.net

Management and Staff
David Zebro, Principal
Gary Brost, Principal
John Dunbar, Principal

Type of Firm
Private Equity Firm

Project Preferences

Role in Financing:
Prefer role as deal originator

Type of Financing Preferred:
Leveraged Buyout
Expansion
Turnaround
Management Buyouts
Acquisition
Recapitalizations

Geographical Preferences

United States Preferences:
Pennsylvania
West Coast
New York

Canadian Preferences:
All Canada

Additional Information
Year Founded: 1983
Capital Under Management: $150,000,000
Current Activity Level : Actively seeking new investments
Method of Compensation: Return on invest. most important, but chg. closing fees, service fees, etc.

STRATEGIC VALUE CAPITAL PARTNERS MANAGEMENT GMBH

Vinzenzstrasse 36
Bornheim, Germany 53332
Phone: 49222791420
Fax: 492227914210
E-mail: svcp@svcp.eu
Website: www.svcp.eu

Management and Staff
Erwin Diesler, Managing Director

Type of Firm
Private Equity Firm

Association Membership
German Venture Capital Association (BVK)

Project Preferences

Type of Financing Preferred:
Leveraged Buyout
Acquisition

Geographical Preferences

International Preferences:
Luxembourg
Netherlands
Switzerland
Austria
Belgium
Germany

Additional Information
Year Founded: 1991
Current Activity Level : Actively seeking new investments

STRATEGIC VALUE PARTNERS LLC

100 West Putnam Avenue
Greenwich, CT USA 06830
Phone: 2036183500
Fax: 2037244683
Website: www.svpglobal.com

Other Offices

Marunouchi Building 24F
2-4-1 Marunouchi
Tokyo, Japan
Phone: 81352182900

5 Saville Row
London, United Kingdom W1S 3PD
Phone: 44-20-7758-7800

22 Grand Rue
Luxembourg, Luxembourg L 1660
Phone: 352-262-070-5200

Taunusanlage 1
Frankfurt, Germany 60329
Phone: 49-69-808062200

Management and Staff
Albert Shin, Managing Director
Benjamin Young, Managing Director
Edward Kelly, Chief Operating Officer
H. Jumbo Tanaka, Managing Director
HJ Woltery, Managing Director
Jason Clarke, Managing Director
Jean-Louise Lelogeais, Senior Managing Director
Kevin Lydon, Managing Director
Robert Adler, Managing Director
Steve McGuinness, Senior Managing Director

Type of Firm
Investment Management Firm

Association Membership
European Private Equity and Venture Capital Assoc.

Project Preferences

Type of Financing Preferred:
Leveraged Buyout
Turnaround
Special Situation
Distressed Debt

Geographical Preferences

United States Preferences:
North America

International Preferences:
Europe
Western Europe

Additional Information

Name of Most Recent Fund: Strategic Value Special Situations Fund III, L.P.
Most Recent Fund Was Raised: 12/20/2013
Year Founded: 2001
Capital Under Management: $2,626,740,000
Current Activity Level : Actively seeking new investments

STRATEJIK YONETIM HIZMETLERI AS

Kizilserce Sokak No. 30
Anadolu Hisari
Istanbul, Turkey 34810
Phone: 902165160100
Fax: 902165160101
E-mail: info@acteragroup.com

Management and Staff

Isak Antika, Co-Founder
Murat Cavusoglu, Co-Founder
Selmi Haleva, Partner
Turker Tekten, Chief Financial Officer
Yagiz Cekin, Partner

Type of Firm

Private Equity Firm

Project Preferences

Type of Financing Preferred:
Leveraged Buyout
Early Stage
Expansion
Generalist PE
Balanced
Later Stage
Management Buyouts
Acquisition

Geographical Preferences

International Preferences:
Turkey
Europe

Industry Preferences

In Communications prefer:
Commercial Communications

In Computer Hardware prefer:
Integrated Turnkey System

In Consumer Related prefer:
Sports
Food/Beverage

In Business Serv. prefer:
Media

Additional Information

Name of Most Recent Fund: Actera Partners II L.P
Most Recent Fund Was Raised: 02/15/2012
Year Founded: 2006
Capital Under Management: $1,519,520,000
Current Activity Level : Actively seeking new investments

STRATHSPEY CROWN LLC

4040 Macarthur Boulevard, Suite 210
Newport Beach, CA USA 92660
Phone: 9492601700
Fax: 9492601705
Website: www.strathspeycrown.com

Management and Staff

Todd Watts, Senior Managing Director
Vikram Malik, Managing Partner

Type of Firm

Private Equity Firm

Project Preferences

Type of Financing Preferred:
Leveraged Buyout
Later Stage

Industry Preferences

In Medical/Health prefer:
Medical/Health

Additional Information

Name of Most Recent Fund: Strathspey Crown LLC
Most Recent Fund Was Raised: 05/01/2012
Year Founded: 2012
Capital Under Management: $1,450,000
Current Activity Level : Actively seeking new investments

STRATIM CAPITAL LLC

333 Bush Street, Suite 2250
San Francisco, CA USA 94104
Phone: 4156745800
E-mail: investors@stratimcapital.com
Website: www.stratimcapital.com

Management and Staff

Craig Such, Partner
Nicholas Van Loan, Principal
Tom Thompson, Chief Financial Officer
Zachary Abrams, Managing Partner

Type of Firm

Private Equity Firm

Project Preferences

Type of Financing Preferred:
Fund of Funds
Leveraged Buyout
Generalist PE
Later Stage
Fund of Funds of Second

Size of Investments Considered:
Min Size of Investment Considered (000s): $3,000
Max Size of Investment Considered (000s): $5,000

Geographical Preferences

United States Preferences:
All U.S.

Industry Preferences

In Consumer Related prefer:
Consumer

In Financial Services prefer:
Financial Services

In Business Serv. prefer:
Services

Additional Information

Year Founded: 2006
Current Activity Level : Actively seeking new investments

STRATTAM CAPITAL LLC

106 East Sixth Street, Suite 900
Austin, TX USA 78701
E-mail: info@strattam.com
Website: strattam.com

Management and Staff

Hilary Fleischer, Principal
Kyle Reesing, Principal

Type of Firm

Private Equity Firm

Project Preferences

Type of Financing Preferred:
Leveraged Buyout

Additional Information

Year Founded: 2014
Capital Under Management: $157,000,000
Current Activity Level : Actively seeking new investments

STRATUM WLL

NBB Tower, 13th Floor
Government Avenue
Manama, Bahrain
Phone: 973-17-221-515
Fax: 973-17-224-166
E-mail: info@stratumwll.com
Website: www.stratumwll.com

Management and Staff
Ahmad Al Umran, Co-Founder
Marwan Tabbara, Co-Founder
Waleed Dhaduk, Partner
Walid Dhaduk, Partner

Type of Firm
Private Equity Firm

Project Preferences

Type of Financing Preferred:
Early Stage
Balanced

Geographical Preferences

United States Preferences:
East Coast

International Preferences:
Asia

Industry Preferences

In Communications prefer:
Telecommunications

In Financial Services prefer:
Real Estate
Financial Services

In Manufact. prefer:
Manufacturing

Additional Information
Year Founded: 2003
Current Activity Level : Actively seeking new investments

STRATUS INVESTIMENTOS LTDA

Rua Funchal 418
28Th Floor, Vila Olimpia
Sao Paulo, Brazil 04551060
Phone: 551121668800
Website: www.stratusbr.com

Management and Staff
Alberto Camoes, Partner
Eduardo Oliveira, Principal
Jesus Russo, Chief Financial Officer
Luiz Recchia, Managing Director

Type of Firm
Private Equity Firm

Association Membership
Brazilian Venture Capital Association (ABCR)
Emerging Markets Private Equity Association

Project Preferences

Type of Financing Preferred:
Leveraged Buyout
Early Stage
Expansion
Mezzanine
Generalist PE
Balanced
Later Stage
Acquisition

Geographical Preferences

International Preferences:
Latin America
Brazil

Industry Preferences

In Communications prefer:
Commercial Communications
Data Communications
Other Communication Prod.

In Industrial/Energy prefer:
Alternative Energy
Energy Conservation Relat
Environmental Related

Additional Information
Year Founded: 1999
Capital Under Management: $6,800,000
Current Activity Level : Actively seeking new investments

STRAY DOG CAPITAL LLC

8880 Ward Parkway, Suite 568
Kansas City, MO USA 64102
Website: straydogcapital.com

Management and Staff
Jennifer Laue, Co-Founder
Lisa Feria, Chief Executive Officer

Type of Firm
Private Equity Firm

Project Preferences

Type of Financing Preferred:
Early Stage

Additional Information
Year Founded: 2015
Current Activity Level : Actively seeking new investments

STREAMLINED VENTURES

1825 Emerson Street
Palo Alto, CA USA 94301
Phone: 6504555270
Website: www.streamlinedventures.com

Management and Staff
Ullas Naik, Founder

Type of Firm
Private Equity Firm

Project Preferences

Type of Financing Preferred:
Seed
Startup

Industry Preferences

In Communications prefer:
Wireless Communications
Data Communications

In Internet Specific prefer:
Internet

Additional Information
Year Founded: 2013
Capital Under Management: $33,400,000
Current Activity Level : Actively seeking new investments

STRENGTH CAPITAL PARTNERS LLC

350 North Old Woodward Avenue, Suite 100
Birmingham, MI USA 48009
Phone: 2485935800
Fax: 2485936875
E-mail: info@strengthcapital.com
Website: www.strengthcapital.com

Other Offices
2035 Madison Road
CINCINNATI, OH USA 45208
Phone: 5133211666

Management and Staff
David Boesler, Chief Financial Officer
David Hiemstra, Principal
Mark McCammon, Managing Partner
Michael Bergeron, Managing Partner
Steven Labarre, Vice President

Type of Firm
Private Equity Firm

Project Preferences

Type of Financing Preferred:
Leveraged Buyout
Acquisition

Geographical Preferences

United States Preferences:
Midwest

Industry Focus

(% based on actual investment)
Other Products 83.4%
Industrial/Energy 16.6%

Additional Information

Name of Most Recent Fund: Strength Capital Partners II, LP
Most Recent Fund Was Raised: 06/30/2005
Year Founded: 2000
Capital Under Management: $265,000,000
Current Activity Level : Actively seeking new investments

STRIKER PARTNERS

224 County Line Road
Wayne, PA USA 19087
Phone: 6107220500
Fax: 6107220800
Website: www.strikerpartners.com

Management and Staff

Charles French, Principal
Gregory Okupniarek, Chief Financial Officer

Type of Firm

Private Equity Firm

Project Preferences

Type of Financing Preferred:
Leveraged Buyout
Later Stage
Management Buyouts
Acquisition
Recapitalizations

Geographical Preferences

United States Preferences:
North America

Canadian Preferences:
All Canada

Industry Preferences

In Communications prefer:
Wireless Communications

In Computer Software prefer:
Software

In Biotechnology prefer:
Agricultural/Animal Bio.

In Business Serv. prefer:
Consulting Services

In Manufact. prefer:
Manufacturing

Additional Information

Year Founded: 1998
Current Activity Level : Actively seeking new investments

STRING VENTURES

96 Toledo Way
106
San Francisco, CA USA 94123
Website: www.stringventures.com

Type of Firm

Private Equity Firm

Project Preferences

Type of Financing Preferred:
Early Stage

Geographical Preferences

United States Preferences:

International Preferences:
Turkey

Industry Preferences

In Communications prefer:
Communications and Media

In Computer Software prefer:
Software

In Internet Specific prefer:
Internet

In Consumer Related prefer:
Consumer Services

Additional Information

Year Founded: 2013
Current Activity Level : Actively seeking new investments

STRIPES GROUP LLC

402 West 13th Street
New York, NY USA 10014
Phone: 2128230720
Fax: 2128230721
E-mail: info@stripesgroup.com
Website: www.stripesgroup.com

Other Offices

70 East 55th Street
11th Floor
NEW YORK, NY USA 10022

Management and Staff

Dan Marriott, Managing Partner
Karen Kenworthy, Vice President
Kenneth Fox, Managing Partner
Ron Shah, Vice President

Type of Firm

Private Equity Firm

Association Membership

National Venture Capital Association - USA (NVCA)

Project Preferences

Type of Financing Preferred:
Leveraged Buyout
Early Stage
Expansion
Balanced
Later Stage
Acquisition

Geographical Preferences

United States Preferences:

Canadian Preferences:
All Canada

International Preferences:
Europe

Industry Preferences

In Computer Software prefer:
Software

In Internet Specific prefer:
Internet

In Medical/Health prefer:
Medical/Health
Health Services

In Consumer Related prefer:
Consumer Products

In Financial Services prefer:
Financial Services

In Business Serv. prefer:
Services
Media

Additional Information

Year Founded: 2003
Capital Under Management: $555,000,000
Current Activity Level : Actively seeking new investments

STRONG VENTURES LLC

3435 Wilshire Boulevard, Suite 2700
Los Angeles, CA USA 90010
Phone: 3104016487
Fax: 3109432376
E-mail: info@strongvc.com
Website: www.strongvc.com

Management and Staff

John Nahm, Managing Director
Kihong Bae, Managing Director

Type of Firm
Private Equity Firm

Project Preferences

Type of Financing Preferred:
Seed
Startup

Geographical Preferences

United States Preferences:

International Preferences:
Kiribati
Asia
Korea, South

Additional Information
Name of Most Recent Fund: Strong Seed Fund I, L.P.
Most Recent Fund Was Raised: 09/06/2012
Year Founded: 2012
Capital Under Management: $1,500,000
Current Activity Level : Actively seeking new investments

STRUCK CAPITAL

6070 W. Studio Court
Los Angeles, CA USA 90038
Website: www.struckcapital.com

Type of Firm
Private Equity Firm

Project Preferences

Type of Financing Preferred:
Early Stage
Later Stage

Additional Information
Year Founded: 2014
Current Activity Level : Actively seeking new investments

STRUCTURAL CAPITAL GP LLC

3555 Alameda de Las Pulgas, Suite 208
Menlo Park, CA USA 94025
Phone: 6264372771
Website: structuralcapital.com

Management and Staff
Bill Elkus, Venture Partner
Kai Tse, Co-Founder
Larry Gross, Co-Founder

Type of Firm
Private Equity Firm

Project Preferences

Type of Financing Preferred:
Early Stage
Balanced
Start-up Financing
Seed

Geographical Preferences

United States Preferences:
All U.S.

Additional Information
Year Founded: 2014
Capital Under Management: $18,350,000
Current Activity Level : Actively seeking new investments

STRUCTURE CAPITAL LP

720 California Street
San Francisco, CA USA 94108
Phone: 4156027060
Website: www.structure.vc

Other Offices
156 Second Street
San Francisco, CA USA 94105

Management and Staff
Michael Walsh, Managing Director

Type of Firm
Private Equity Firm

Project Preferences

Type of Financing Preferred:
Early Stage
Seed

Size of Investments Considered:
Min Size of Investment Considered (000s): $100
Max Size of Investment Considered (000s): $200

Additional Information
Year Founded: 2013
Current Activity Level : Actively seeking new investments

STRUCTURE PARTNERS

510 Leslie Lane
Beverly Hills, CA USA 90210
Phone: 3102482438
E-mail: contact@structurepartners.com
Website: www.structurepartners.com

Type of Firm
Incubator/Development Program

Project Preferences

Type of Financing Preferred:
Early Stage
Seed
Startup

Industry Preferences

In Financial Services prefer:
Real Estate

In Business Serv. prefer:
Media

Additional Information
Year Founded: 2013
Capital Under Management: $700,000
Current Activity Level : Actively seeking new investments

STS VENTURES GMBH

Vogelsanger Strasse 68a
Cologne, Germany 50823
E-mail: niklas@sts-ventures.de
Website: www.sts-ventures.de

Type of Firm
Private Equity Firm

Project Preferences

Type of Financing Preferred:
Early Stage
Expansion
Later Stage
Seed

Geographical Preferences

International Preferences:
Europe
Germany

Additional Information
Year Founded: 2015
Current Activity Level : Actively seeking new investments

STUART MILL CAPITAL, INC.

252 North Washington Street
Falls Church, VA USA 22046
Phone: 7035332461
E-mail: contact@stuartmillcap.com
Website: www.stuartmillvp.com

Management and Staff
Chip Lubsen, Principal
Jeff Salinger, Principal

Type of Firm
Private Equity Firm

Project Preferences

Type of Financing Preferred:
Expansion

Geographical Preferences

United States Preferences:
All U.S.

Industry Preferences

In Consumer Related prefer:
Hotels and Resorts

In Business Serv. prefer:
Services

Additional Information

Name of Most Recent Fund: Stuart Mill Venture Partners, L.P.
Most Recent Fund Was Raised: 06/27/2007
Year Founded: 1997
Current Activity Level : Actively seeking new investments

STYRBJORN GROWTH AS

Jattavagveien 7
Postboks 130
Stavanger, Norway 4065
Phone: 47-51-577-900
Fax: 47-51-577-901
Website: www.styrbjorn.no

Management and Staff

Runar Holthe, Chief Financial Officer
Tore Gjedebo, Managing Director

Type of Firm

Private Equity Firm

Project Preferences

Type of Financing Preferred:
Balanced

Geographical Preferences

International Preferences:
Norway

Additional Information

Year Founded: 2000
Current Activity Level : Actively seeking new investments

SUANFARMA BIOTECH SGECR SA

C/ Einstein 8, 3planta
28108 Alcobendas
Madrid, Spain
Phone: 915671556
Fax: 915671557
E-mail: suanfarmabiotech@suanfarma.com
Website: www.suanfarmabiotech.com

Management and Staff

Gonzalo Marin Zirotti, Managing Partner
Ion Arocena Veez, Partner
Sofia De la Maza Arroyo, Partner
Teodoro Leon Cillero, Partner

Type of Firm

Incubator/Development Program

Association Membership

Spanish Venture Capital Association (ASCRI)

Project Preferences

Type of Financing Preferred:
Seed
Startup

Geographical Preferences

International Preferences:
Spain

Industry Preferences

In Biotechnology prefer:
Biotechnology

In Medical/Health prefer:
Pharmaceuticals

Additional Information

Year Founded: 2007
Capital Under Management: $12,426,000
Current Activity Level : Actively seeking new investments

SUBTRACTION CAPITAL

2100 Park Avenue, Suite 680967
Park City, UT USA 84068
Phone: 4352003252
Website: subtractioncapital.com

Management and Staff

Jason Portnoy, Founder
Paul Willard, Partner

Type of Firm

Private Equity Firm

Project Preferences

Type of Financing Preferred:
Early Stage
Balanced
Later Stage

Additional Information

Year Founded: 2013
Current Activity Level : Actively seeking new investments

SUCSY FISCHER & CO., INC.

799 Central Avenue, Suite 350
Highland Park, IL USA 60035
Phone: 312-554-7575
Fax: 312-554-7501
E-mail: sfco@sfco.com
Website: www.sfco.com

Type of Firm

Bank Affiliated

Project Preferences

Role in Financing:
Prefer role as deal originator

Type of Financing Preferred:
Leveraged Buyout
Mezzanine
Generalist PE
Management Buyouts
Special Situation

Size of Investments Considered:
Min Size of Investment Considered (000s): $50,000
Max Size of Investment Considered: No Limit

Geographical Preferences

United States Preferences:

Additional Information

Year Founded: 1972
Current Activity Level : Actively seeking new investments
Method of Compensation: Function primarily in service area, receive contingent fee in cash or equity

SUD SICAR

Rue 8366, Res. Omar
Bloc A 1073
Tunis, Tunisia 1002
Phone: 21671846387
Fax: 21671845800

Type of Firm

Private Equity Firm

Association Membership

Tunisian Venture Capital Association

Project Preferences

Type of Financing Preferred:
Early Stage

Geographical Preferences

International Preferences:
Tunisia

Additional Information
Year Founded: 1997
Current Activity Level : Actively seeking new investments

SUDINNOVA SA

2, rue President Carnot
Espace Cordeliers
Lyon, France 69293
Phone: 33472569100
Fax: 33472775855
Website: www.bpifrance.fr

Type of Firm
Private Equity Firm

Project Preferences

Type of Financing Preferred:
Early Stage
Later Stage
Startup

Size of Investments Considered:
Min Size of Investment Considered (000s): $130
Max Size of Investment Considered (000s): $1,300

Geographical Preferences

International Preferences:
Europe
France

Industry Preferences

In Industrial/Energy prefer:
Energy
Environmental Related

In Other prefer:
Environment Responsible

Additional Information
Name of Most Recent Fund: Sudinnova II
Most Recent Fund Was Raised: 09/04/2000
Year Founded: 1983
Current Activity Level : Actively seeking new investments

SUFFOLK EQUITY PARTNERS LLC

Cambridge Innovation Center
One Broadway, Fourth Floor
Cambridge, MA USA 02142
Phone: 6174013076
Website: www.suffolkequity.com

Type of Firm
Private Equity Firm

Project Preferences

Type of Financing Preferred:
Balanced
Startup

Additional Information
Year Founded: 2011
Current Activity Level : Actively seeking new investments

SUMA CAPITAL SGECR SA

Avda. Diagonal 477
Barcelona, Spain 08006
Phone: 34933680203
Fax: 34933687257
E-mail: lcampins@sumacapital.com
Website: www.sumacapital.com

Management and Staff
Enrique Tombas, Chief Executive Officer

Type of Firm
Private Equity Firm

Association Membership
Spanish Venture Capital Association (ASCRI)

Project Preferences

Type of Financing Preferred:
Expansion
Generalist PE
Balanced
Later Stage
Management Buyouts
Acquisition
Startup

Size of Investments Considered:
Min Size of Investment Considered (000s): $3,925
Max Size of Investment Considered (000s): $15,699

Geographical Preferences

International Preferences:
Spain

Industry Preferences

In Industrial/Energy prefer:
Energy
Alternative Energy
Energy Conservation Relat
Environmental Related

Additional Information
Year Founded: 2006
Capital Under Management: $101,721,000
Current Activity Level : Actively seeking new investments

SUMA VERWALTUNGS GMBH

Hamburger Allee 4
Frankfurt, Germany 60486
Phone: 49697950000
Fax: 496979500060
E-mail: contact@quadriga-capital.de
Website: www.quadriga-capital.de

Other Offices
20, Daev pereulok
suite 430
Moscow, Russia 107045
Phone: 7-495-604-8262
Fax: 7-495-604-8417

Management and Staff
Andreas Fendel, Managing Director
Birkhardt Bonsels, Managing Director
Max W. Roemer, Managing Director
Peter Besthof, Managing Director
Philipp Jacobi, Managing Director
Roland Egerer, Managing Director

Type of Firm
Private Equity Firm

Association Membership
German Venture Capital Association (BVK)
Russian Venture Capital Association (RVCA)
European Private Equity and Venture Capital Assoc.

Project Preferences

Role in Financing:
Prefer role as deal originator

Type of Financing Preferred:
Leveraged Buyout
Later Stage
Management Buyouts

Geographical Preferences

International Preferences:
Liechtenstein
Luxembourg
Europe
Czech Republic
Netherlands
Switzerland
Western Europe
Poland
Austria
Eastern Europe
Belgium
Germany
Russia
France

Industry Focus
(% based on actual investment)

Industry	%
Industrial/Energy	37.3%
Other Products	32.5%
Consumer Related	19.9%
Medical/Health	7.6%
Communications and Media	2.7%

Additional Information
Name of Most Recent Fund: Quadriga Capital Private Equity Fund IV
Most Recent Fund Was Raised: 02/26/2013
Year Founded: 1994
Capital Under Management: $910,000,000
Current Activity Level : Actively seeking new investments
Method of Compensation: Return on invest. most important, but chg. closing fees, service fees, etc.

SUMERU EQUITY PARTNERS, L.P.

950 Tower Lane, Suite 1788
San Mateo, CA USA 94404
Phone: 16504791080
Fax: 16507532417
E-mail: contact@sumeruequity.com
Website: www.sumeruequity.com

Management and Staff
George Kadifa, Managing Director
Jason Babcoke, Co-Founder
John Brennan, Co-Founder
Kyle Ryland, Managing Partner
Mark Haller, Vice President
Paul Mercadante, Co-Founder
Sanjeet Mitra, Co-Founder
Sean Kendra, Vice President

Type of Firm
Private Equity Firm

Project Preferences

Type of Financing Preferred:
Leveraged Buyout

Industry Preferences

In Computer Software prefer:
Software

In Business Serv. prefer:
Services

Additional Information
Year Founded: 2014
Capital Under Management: $363,020,000
Current Activity Level : Actively seeking new investments

SUMITOMO MITSUI TRUST INVESTMENT CO LTD

No. 13, No. 4-chome, Kyobashi,
Chuo-ku,
Tokyo, Japan
Phone: 81-3-6214-0260
Fax: 81-3-6214-0261
E-mail: info@stb-ifund.co.jp
Website: www.smtic.jp

Management and Staff
Atsuhiko Mizukawa, Chief Executive Officer
David Seu, Managing Director
Hiroki Kawakami, Principal
Mizukawa Atsuhiko, Chief Executive Officer
Toshihiko Tsuji, Managing Director

Type of Firm
Private Equity Firm

Project Preferences

Type of Financing Preferred:
Leveraged Buyout
Early Stage
Expansion
Generalist PE
Turnaround
Later Stage
Seed
Management Buyouts
Recapitalizations

Geographical Preferences

International Preferences:
Asia
Japan

Industry Preferences

In Business Serv. prefer:
Consulting Services

Additional Information
Year Founded: 2000
Capital Under Management: $400,000
Current Activity Level : Actively seeking new investments

SUMMA EQUITY AB

Vastra Tradgardsgatan 15
Stockholm, Sweden 111 53
Website: summaequity.com

Type of Firm
Private Equity Firm

Project Preferences

Type of Financing Preferred:
Leveraged Buyout
Management Buyouts
Acquisition

Geographical Preferences

International Preferences:
Scandanavia/Nordic Region

Industry Preferences

In Computer Software prefer:
Software

In Internet Specific prefer:
Internet
Ecommerce

In Medical/Health prefer:
Medical/Health
Medical Products

In Consumer Related prefer:
Education Related

In Industrial/Energy prefer:
Energy
Environmental Related

In Agr/Forestr/Fish prefer:
Agriculture related

In Other prefer:
Environment Responsible

Additional Information
Year Founded: 2016
Capital Under Management: $505,110,000
Current Activity Level : Actively seeking new investments

SUMMATION HEALTH VENTURES LP

320 Golden Shore Avenue, Suite 120
Long Beach, CA USA 90802
Phone: 5624320051
Website: shv.io

Management and Staff
Brant Heise, Senior Managing Director

Type of Firm
Private Equity Firm

Project Preferences

Type of Financing Preferred:
Early Stage
Startup

Industry Preferences

In Medical/Health prefer:
Medical/Health
Medical Products
Health Services

Additional Information
Year Founded: 2014
Capital Under Management: $80,000,000
Current Activity Level : Actively seeking new investments

SUMMER STREET CAPITAL PARTNERS LLC

70 West Chippewa Street, Suite 500
Buffalo, NY USA 14202
Phone: 7165662900
Fax: 7165662910
Website: www.summerstreetcapital.com

Management and Staff
Amy Standing, Chief Financial Officer
Andrew Fors, Partner
Baris Civelek, Partner
Brian D Amico, Co-Founder
Garth Troxell, Partner
Gary Hull, Co-Founder
Jennifer Balbach, Co-Founder
John Collins, Vice President
Michael Petri, Partner
Michael McQueeney, Co-Founder
Randy Bianchi, Partner
Ryan Martin, Vice President

Type of Firm
Private Equity Firm

Association Membership
Natl Assoc of Small Bus. Inv. Co (NASBIC)
Canadian Venture Capital Association

Project Preferences

Role in Financing:
Prefer role as deal originator but will also invest in deals created by others

Type of Financing Preferred:
Leveraged Buyout
Expansion
Management Buyouts
Acquisition
Recapitalizations

Geographical Preferences

United States Preferences:

Canadian Preferences:
All Canada

Industry Focus
(% based on actual investment)

Medical/Health	44.6%
Consumer Related	17.9%
Other Products	13.2%
Communications and Media	11.2%
Computer Hardware	9.0%
Computer Software and Services	2.3%
Semiconductors/Other Elect.	1.8%

Additional Information
Name of Most Recent Fund: Summer Street Capital III, L.P.
Most Recent Fund Was Raised: 08/09/2011
Year Founded: 1999
Capital Under Management: $300,000,000
Current Activity Level: Actively seeking new investments
Method of Compensation: Return on invest. most important, but chg. closing fees, service fees, etc.

SUMMERHILL VENTURE PARTNERS MANAGEMENT INC

1 St Clair Avenue West, Suite 403
Toronto, Canada M4V 1K6
Phone: 4164080700
Fax: 4165859749
Website: www.summerhillvp.com

Other Offices
53 State Street
Sixth Floor
Boston, MA USA 02109

Management and Staff
Brian Kobus, Vice President
Gary Rubinoff, Managing Partner
Joe Catalfamo, Managing Partner
Ommer Chohan, Chief Financial Officer
William Kohler, General Partner

Type of Firm
Private Equity Firm

Association Membership
Canadian Venture Capital Association

Project Preferences

Role in Financing:
Prefer role as deal originator but will also invest in deals created by others

Type of Financing Preferred:
Early Stage
Balanced
Seed

Size of Investments Considered:
Min Size of Investment Considered (000s): $500
Max Size of Investment Considered (000s): $4,000

Geographical Preferences

United States Preferences:
Northeast
Massachusetts
Washington
New York
All U.S.
East Coast

Canadian Preferences:
All Canada

Industry Focus
(% based on actual investment)

Computer Software and Services	32.3%
Communications and Media	31.0%
Internet Specific	25.1%
Computer Hardware	7.0%
Semiconductors/Other Elect.	4.6%

Additional Information
Year Founded: 1993
Capital Under Management: $175,000,000
Current Activity Level: Actively seeking new investments
Method of Compensation: Return on investment is of primary concern, do not charge fees

SUMMIT EQUITY GROUP LLC

801 Grand Avenue, Suite 3560
Des Moines, IA USA 50309
Website: www.summitequity.com

Type of Firm
Private Equity Firm

Additional Information
Year Founded: 2016
Current Activity Level: Actively seeking new investments

SUMMIT PARK LLC

1111 Metropolitan Avenue, Suite 1025
Charlotte, NC USA 28204
Phone: 7046543400
Fax: 7049274376
Website: www.summitparkllc.com

Management and Staff
Matt Magan, Principal
Robert Calton, Founder

Type of Firm
Private Equity Firm

Project Preferences

Type of Financing Preferred:
Leveraged Buyout
Generalist PE
Opportunistic
Management Buyouts
Acquisition
Recapitalizations

Size of Investments Considered:
Min Size of Investment Considered (000s): $10,000
Max Size of Investment Considered (000s): $40,000

Geographical Preferences

United States Preferences:

Industry Preferences

In Semiconductor/Electr prefer:
Controllers and Sensors
Component Testing Equipmt
Analytic/Scientific

In Medical/Health prefer:
Drug/Equipmt Delivery
Disposable Med. Products

In Consumer Related prefer:
Consumer Products
Consumer Services

In Industrial/Energy prefer:
Environmental Related

In Transportation prefer:
Transportation

In Business Serv. prefer:
Services
Distribution

In Manufact. prefer:
Manufacturing

Additional Information
Year Founded: 2006
Capital Under Management: $130,000,000
Current Activity Level : Actively seeking new investments

SUMMIT PARTNERS LP

222 Berkeley Street
18th Floor
Boston, MA USA 02116
Phone: 6178241000
Fax: 6178241100
Website: www.summitpartners.com

Other Offices

Three North Avenue, Maker Maxity
Bandra-Kurla Complex, Bandra (East), #25
Mumbai, India 400 051
Phone: 912266808000
Fax: 912266808050

200 Middlefield Road, Suite 200
Menlo Park, CA USA
Phone: 6503211166
Fax: 6503211188

Management and Staff

Adam Britt, Principal
Adam Britt, Managing Director
Alexander Whittemore, Managing Director
Alexander Whittemore, Managing Director
Andrew Collins, Managing Director
Andrew Collins, Vice President
Antony Clavel, Principal
Brenda Franciose, Vice President
Bruce Evans, Managing Director
Bruce Evans, Managing Director
Charles Fitzgerald, Managing Director
Christian Strain, Managing Director
Christopher Dean, Managing Director
Craig Frances, Managing Director
Darren Black, Managing Director
David Averett, Managing Director
David Averett, Principal
David Klein, Vice President
Dennis Kim, Vice President
Devin O Malley, Vice President
E. Roe Stamps, Managing Director
Gabriel Carreiro, Vice President
Greg Goldfarb, Managing Director
Gregg Nardone, Managing Director
Gregg Nardone, Managing Director
Gregory Avis, Managing Director
Gus Phelps, Vice President
Han Sikkens, Managing Director
Harrison Miller, Managing Director
Jack Roy, Principal
Jack Le Roy, Principal
James Freeland, Managing Director
James Freeland, Managing Director
Jason Kreuziger, Vice President
Jason Glass, Principal
Jay Pauley, Vice President
Jay Pauley, Managing Director
Jesse Lane, Principal
John Doran, Vice President
John Carroll, Managing Director
John Carroll, Managing Director
Joseph Kardwell, Managing Director
Justin Craigie, Vice President
Leonard Ferrington, Principal
Leslie Noonan, Vice President
Mark Nordstrom, Vice President
Mark deLaar, Managing Director
Mark deLaar, Managing Director
Martin Mannion, Managing Director
Matthew Hamilton, Principal
Matthew Hamilton, Vice President
Matthias Allgaier, Managing Director
Michael Medici, Managing Director
Michael Medici, Principal
Michael Anderson, Principal
Peter Francis, Principal
Peter Rottier, Principal
Peter Connolly, Principal
Peter Chung, Managing Director
Robert Hassel, Principal
Robert Hassell, Managing Director
Ross Stern, Vice President
Scott Collins, Managing Director
Stephen Woodsum, Managing Director
Thomas Roberts, Managing Director
Thomas Jennings, Managing Director
Thomas Roberts, Managing Director
Thomas Tarnowski, Managing Director
Thomas Jennings, Managing Director
Todd Hearle, Managing Director
Vincent Lambert, Principal
Zachary Gut, Vice President

Type of Firm
Private Equity Firm

Association Membership
New England Venture Capital Association
National Venture Capital Association - USA (NVCA)
European Private Equity and Venture Capital Assoc.

Project Preferences

Role in Financing:
Prefer role as deal originator but will also invest in deals created by others

Type of Financing Preferred:
Leveraged Buyout
Early Stage
Expansion
Mezzanine
Generalist PE
Balanced
Turnaround
Later Stage
Management Buyouts
Recapitalizations

Size of Investments Considered:
Min Size of Investment Considered (000s): $5,000
Max Size of Investment Considered (000s): $500,000

Geographical Preferences

United States Preferences:
North America

International Preferences:
India
Europe
Asia

Industry Focus
(% based on actual investment)

Industry	%
Internet Specific	38.5%
Computer Software and Services	20.0%
Other Products	17.8%
Communications and Media	5.8%
Medical/Health	5.1%
Computer Hardware	3.9%
Semiconductors/Other Elect.	3.7%
Consumer Related	2.9%
Industrial/Energy	1.5%
Biotechnology	0.7%

Additional Information
Name of Most Recent Fund: Summit Partners Credit Fund II, L.P.
Most Recent Fund Was Raised: 12/31/2013
Year Founded: 1984
Capital Under Management: $15,000,000,000
Current Activity Level : Actively seeking new investments
Method of Compensation: Return on investment is of primary concern, do not charge fees

SUMMIT PRIVATE CAPITAL GROUP

240 Cedar Knolls Road, Suite 306
Cedar Knolls, NJ USA 07927
Phone: 9087812545
Fax: 9087812646
Website: www.summitpcg.com

Management and Staff
Lawrence Katz, Chief Executive Officer

Type of Firm
Bank Affiliated

Project Preferences

Role in Financing:
Prefer role as deal originator but will also invest in deals created by others

Type of Financing Preferred:
Leveraged Buyout
Control-block Purchases
Mezzanine
Special Situation

Size of Investments Considered:
Min Size of Investment Considered (000s): $400
Max Size of Investment Considered: No Limit

Geographical Preferences

United States Preferences:
Northeast

Industry Preferences

In Semiconductor/Electr prefer:
Sensors
Component Testing Equipmt
Analytic/Scientific

In Medical/Health prefer:
Diagnostic Test Products
Medical Products

In Consumer Related prefer:
Entertainment and Leisure
Retail
Franchises(NEC)
Food/Beverage
Consumer Products
Education Related

In Industrial/Energy prefer:
Industrial Products
Materials
Factory Automation
Machinery
Environmental Related

In Financial Services prefer:
Financial Services

In Agr/Forestr/Fish prefer:
Agriculture related

Additional Information
Year Founded: 1994
Capital Under Management: $7,000,000
Current Activity Level : Actively seeking new investments

SUMMITVIEW CAPITAL

No. 18 Dongfang Road
Room 1101, Block E, Poly Plaza
Shanghai, China 200120
Phone: 862150801725
Fax: 862168816012
E-mail: bp@summitviewcapital.com
Website: www.summitviewcapital.com

Management and Staff
Bernard Xavier, Partner
Feng Li, Founder
Liang Xu, Partner
Ping Wu, Founder

Type of Firm
Private Equity Firm

Project Preferences

Type of Financing Preferred:
Leveraged Buyout
Generalist PE
Balanced

Industry Preferences

In Internet Specific prefer:
Internet

In Semiconductor/Electr prefer:
Semiconductor

In Medical/Health prefer:
Medical/Health

In Industrial/Energy prefer:
Environmental Related

Additional Information
Year Founded: 2011
Current Activity Level : Actively seeking new investments

SUN CAPITAL MANAGEMENT CORP

2-3-15, Kawaramachi, Chuo-ku
Kawaramachi Building
Osaka, Japan 541-0048
Phone: 81662055611
Fax: 81662055711
Website: www.sun-capitalmanagement.co.jp

Type of Firm
Private Equity Firm

Project Preferences

Type of Financing Preferred:
Turnaround

Geographical Preferences

International Preferences:
Asia

Additional Information
Year Founded: 1997
Capital Under Management: $4,800,000
Current Activity Level : Actively seeking new investments

SUN CAPITAL PARTNERS INC

5200 Town Center Circle, Suite 600
Boca Raton, FL USA 33486
Phone: 5613940550
Website: www.suncappart.com

Other Offices

2 Park Street
1st Floor
London, United Kingdom W1K 2HX
Phone: 44-207-318-1100

Unit A & G & H, 42nd Floor, Block A
4003 Shennan East Road, Luohu District
Shenzhen, China 518001
Phone: 86-755-2598-1628
Fax: 86-755-2598-1638

Aerogolf Center
1B, rue Heienhaff
Senningerberg, Luxembourg L-1736
Phone: 352-26-340-321

11111 Santa Monica Boulevard, Suite 1050
Los Angeles, CA USA 90025
Phone: 310-473-1116

100 Park Avenue
33rd Floor
New York, NY USA 10017
Phone: 212-588-9156

29 Rue de Bassano
Paris, France 75008
Phone: 33-1-7225-6578
Fax: 33-1-7225-6579

Mainzer Landstr. 27-31
Frankfurt, Germany 60329
Phone: 4969-7401-5575
Fax: 49-69-7401-5805

580 Nanjing West Road
Rm 2508, Nanzheng Building
Shanghai, China 200041
Phone: 86-21-5228-5511

Management and Staff

Aaron Wolfe, Managing Director
Andreas Bosenberg, Managing Director
Anthony Polazzi, Managing Director
Bob Steelhammer, Vice President
Brian Urbanek, Managing Director
Clarence Terry, Senior Managing Director
Daniel Florian, Managing Director
David Lippin, Principal
David Mezzanotte, Managing Director
David Finnigan, Managing Director
Jared Wien, Managing Director
Jeremy Stone, Managing Director
Jerome Nomme, Managing Director
Jonathan Borell, Managing Director
Jordan Wadsworth, Principal
Lionel de Posson, Principal
Lynn Skillen, Managing Director
M. Kurt Lentz, Principal
Mark Brody, Managing Director
Matthew Garff, Managing Director
Michael Palm, Managing Director
Michael Kalb, Senior Managing Director
Paul Daccus, Managing Director
Richard Brown, Managing Director
Ryan Esko, Principal
Scott Edwards, Managing Director
Steven Liff, Senior Managing Director
Timothy Stubbs, Senior Managing Director
Todd Plosker, Managing Director
William James, Vice President

Type of Firm
Private Equity Firm

Project Preferences

Role in Financing:
Prefer role as deal originator

Type of Financing Preferred:
Leveraged Buyout
Mezzanine
Turnaround
Acquisition
Special Situation
Recapitalizations

Geographical Preferences

International Preferences:
Europe

Industry Focus

(% based on actual investment)
Consumer Related	61.1%
Industrial/Energy	31.8%
Other Products	6.2%
Communications and Media	0.5%
Semiconductors/Other Elect.	0.2%
Computer Software and Services	0.1%

Additional Information

Name of Most Recent Fund: Sun Capital Partners VI, L.P.
Most Recent Fund Was Raised: 02/05/2013
Year Founded: 1995
Capital Under Management: $8,000,000,000
Current Activity Level : Actively seeking new investments
Method of Compensation: Other

SUN MOUNTAIN CAPITAL ADVISORS LLC

301 Griffin Street
Santa Fe, NM USA 87501
Phone: 5059545474
Fax: 5059545497
E-mail: info@sunmountaincapital.com
Website: sunmountaincapital.com

Other Offices

527 DON GASPAR AVE.
SANTA FE, NM USA 87505

Management and Staff

Brian Birk, Co-Founder
Eddy Markman, Chief Financial Officer
Lee Rand, Partner
Mark Hollis, Principal
Sally Corning, Partner

Type of Firm
Investment Management Firm

Project Preferences

Type of Financing Preferred:
Fund of Funds
Balanced

Additional Information

Year Founded: 2006
Capital Under Management: $750,000,000
Current Activity Level : Actively seeking new investments

SUN PRIVATE EQUITIES LLC

340 Poinciana Way, Suite 317-111
Palm Beach, FL USA 33480
Phone: 8886732180
Website: www.spequities.com

Type of Firm
Private Equity Firm

Project Preferences

Type of Financing Preferred:
Leveraged Buyout
Acquisition

Additional Information

Year Founded: 2012
Current Activity Level : Actively seeking new investments

SUN-EIGHT TRADING CO LTD

1-15-7 Toranomon Minato-ku
7F TG115 Building
Tokyo, Japan
Phone: 81335970345
Fax: 81335970522
E-mail: info@sun-8.jp

Type of Firm
Private Equity Firm

Project Preferences

Type of Financing Preferred:
Generalist PE
Balanced
Management Buyouts

Geographical Preferences

International Preferences:
Asia

Additional Information

Year Founded: 2004
Current Activity Level : Actively seeking new investments

SUNBRIDGE CAPITAL MANAGEMENT LLC

5425 Wisconsin Avenue, Suite 701
Chevy Chase, MD USA 20815
Phone: 3016341900
Fax: 3016341243
E-mail: information@sunbridgecap.com
Website: www.sunbridgecap.com

Management and Staff
Timothy Peterson, Managing Director

Type of Firm
Private Equity Firm

Project Preferences

Type of Financing Preferred:
Acquisition

Industry Preferences

In Medical/Health prefer:
Health Services

In Consumer Related prefer:
Education Related

In Industrial/Energy prefer:
Machinery

In Financial Services prefer:
Real Estate

Pratt's Guide to Private Equity & Venture Capital Sources

In Business Serv. prefer:
Distribution

Additional Information
Year Founded: 1969
Current Activity Level : Actively seeking new investments

SUNBRIDGE GLOBAL VENTURES INC

8-5-26 Akasaka, Minato-ku
3F Akasaka DS Building
Tokyo, Japan 107-0052
Phone: 81368042686
Fax: 81357721565
Website: www.sunbridge-gv.jp

Type of Firm
Incubator/Development Program

Association Membership
Japan Venture Capital Association

Project Preferences

Type of Financing Preferred:
Seed
Startup

Geographical Preferences

International Preferences:
Japan

Industry Preferences

In Communications prefer:
Wireless Communications

In Internet Specific prefer:
Internet

Additional Information
Year Founded: 2011
Current Activity Level : Actively seeking new investments

SUNBRIDGE INVESTMENT MANAGEMENT CO LTD

Yitian Road, Futian District
A2903 Jiangsu Building
Shenzhen, China 518026
Phone: 8675582852990
Fax: 8675582852991
E-mail: sunbridge@sunbridge-partners.com
Website: www.sunbridge-partners.com

Management and Staff
Chengguo Qu, Partner
Haixiao Ma, Partner
Shiming Pan, Partner
Xiaochuan Zhou, Partner

Type of Firm
Private Equity Firm

Project Preferences

Type of Financing Preferred:
Later Stage

Geographical Preferences

International Preferences:
China

Industry Preferences

In Consumer Related prefer:
Consumer Products

In Business Serv. prefer:
Services

In Manufact. prefer:
Manufacturing

Additional Information
Year Founded: 2006
Current Activity Level : Actively seeking new investments

SUNBRIDGE PARTNERS INC

3659 Green Road, Suite 118
Beachwood, OH USA 44122
Phone: 2163600151
Website: www.sunbridgepartners.com

Other Offices
1-5-5 Minami, Ebisu
11F, JR Ebisu Building
Tokyo, Japan 150-0022

6135 Park South Drive, Suite 510
CHARLOTTE, NC USA 28210
Phone: 7049457174

440 North Wolfe Road, Suite 118
SUNNYVALE, CA USA 94085
Phone: 6503535401

Management and Staff
Varouzhan Ebrahimian, Venture Partner

Type of Firm
Private Equity Firm

Association Membership
National Venture Capital Association - USA (NVCA)

Project Preferences

Role in Financing:
Prefer role as deal originator but will also invest in deals created by others

Type of Financing Preferred:
Early Stage
Seed
Startup

Geographical Preferences

United States Preferences:

Canadian Preferences:
All Canada

International Preferences:
Europe
Japan

Industry Preferences

In Communications prefer:
Wireless Communications

In Computer Software prefer:
Software
Systems Software

In Internet Specific prefer:
Ecommerce

In Computer Other prefer:
Computer Related

In Semiconductor/Electr prefer:
Electronics
Semiconductor

In Business Serv. prefer:
Services
Media

In Other prefer:
Environment Responsible

Additional Information
Name of Most Recent Fund: SunBridge Partners Technology Fund EF, L.P.
Most Recent Fund Was Raised: 09/20/2005
Year Founded: 1999
Capital Under Management: $100,000,000
Current Activity Level : Actively seeking new investments

SUNRISE STRATEGIC PARTNERS LLC

6106 Sunrise Ranch Drive
Longmont, CO USA 80503
Website: www.sunrisestrategicpartners.com

Management and Staff
Vincent Love, Co-Founder

Type of Firm
Private Equity Firm

Project Preferences

Type of Financing Preferred:
Early Stage
Expansion
Balanced
Later Stage

Industry Preferences

In Medical/Health prefer:
Health Services

In Consumer Related prefer:
Sports
Food/Beverage

Additional Information

Year Founded: 2016
Current Activity Level : Actively seeking new investments

SUNROCK VENTURES MANAGEMENT LLC

201 East Kennedy Boulevard, Suite 950
Tampa, FL USA 33602
Phone: 813-990-0361
Fax: 813-936-4764

Other Offices

1205 Lincoln Road, Suite 216
Miami Beach, FL USA 33139
Phone: 305-432-4684
Fax: 305-503-8566

Management and Staff

Jeffrey Wolf, Managing Director
Matthew Shaw, Managing Director
Tate Garrett, Managing Director

Type of Firm

Private Equity Firm

Project Preferences

Type of Financing Preferred:
Early Stage
Balanced
Later Stage

Size of Investments Considered:
Min Size of Investment Considered (000s): $4,000
Max Size of Investment Considered (000s): $7,000

Geographical Preferences

United States Preferences:
Southeast
Florida
All U.S.

Additional Information

Year Founded: 2007
Current Activity Level : Actively seeking new investments

SUNSHINE RONGHUI CAPITAL INVESTMENT MANAGEMENT CO LTD

No. 1 East 3rd Ring Middle Roa
22F, East Building, Global Fin
Beijing, China
Phone: 861058111666
Fax: 861058111555
Website: www.riverheadcapital.cn

Type of Firm

Insurance Firm Affiliate

Project Preferences

Type of Financing Preferred:
Balanced

Geographical Preferences

International Preferences:
China

Industry Preferences

In Communications prefer:
Commercial Communications

In Medical/Health prefer:
Medical/Health

In Consumer Related prefer:
Consumer
Retail

In Industrial/Energy prefer:
Energy
Materials

In Financial Services prefer:
Financial Services

In Manufact. prefer:
Manufacturing

Additional Information

Year Founded: 2015
Capital Under Management: $35,000,000,000
Current Activity Level : Actively seeking new investments

SUNSTONE CAPITAL A/S

Lautrupsgade 7
Fifth Floor
Copenhagen, Denmark 2100
Phone: 4520126000
Fax: 4539209898
E-mail: reception@sunstonecapital.com
Website: www.sunstonecapital.com

Other Offices

1370 Willow Road
2nd floor, Silicon Valley Office
MENLO PARK, CA USA 94025
Phone: 6505871518

Angelholmsvagen 28
Bastad, Sweden 269 31
Phone: 46431311740

Management and Staff

Andreas Seggerros, Venture Partner
Christer Fahraeus, Venture Partner
Christian Lindergard Jepsen, Partner
Eric-Alan Rapp, Partner
Jeppe Fur Hoier, Founder
Jimmy Nielsen, Managing Partner
Joergen Smidt, Partner
Juha Christensen, Venture Partner
Max Niederhofer, Partner
Nikolaj Nyholm, Partner
Pekka Vartiainen, Venture Partner
Peter Benson, Managing Partner
Soeren Lemonius, Partner
Sten Verland, Partner
Yvonne Martensson, Venture Partner

Type of Firm

Private Equity Firm

Association Membership

Danish Venture Capital Association (DVCA)
European Private Equity and Venture Capital Assoc.

Project Preferences

Type of Financing Preferred:
Early Stage
Seed
Startup

Geographical Preferences

International Preferences:
United Kingdom
Central Europe
Europe
Netherlands
Switzerland
Eastern Europe
Scandanavia/Nordic Region
Denmark

Industry Preferences

In Communications prefer:
Wireless Communications
Entertainment

In Computer Software prefer:
Software
Applications Software

In Internet Specific prefer:
E-Commerce Technology
Internet
Ecommerce

In Semiconductor/Electr prefer:
Semiconductor

In Biotechnology prefer:
Biotechnology

In Medical/Health prefer:
Medical/Health
Medical Diagnostics
Diagnostic Services
Pharmaceuticals

In Business Serv. prefer:
Media

Additional Information
Name of Most Recent Fund: Sunstone Life Science Ventures Fund III K/S
Most Recent Fund Was Raised: 12/16/2011
Year Founded: 2007
Capital Under Management: $1,187,900,000
Current Activity Level : Actively seeking new investments

SUNSTONE PARTNERS

505 Hamilton Ave., Suite 200
Palo Alto, CA USA 94301
Phone: 6502894400
Fax: 6502894444
E-mail: info@sunstonepartners.com
Website: www.sunstonepartners.com

Type of Firm
Private Equity Firm

Geographical Preferences

United States Preferences:
North America

Industry Preferences

In Internet Specific prefer:
Internet

Additional Information
Year Founded: 2015
Capital Under Management: $300,000,000
Current Activity Level : Actively seeking new investments

SUNTRUST BANKS INC

303 Peachtree Street, N.E.
Atlanta, GA USA 30308
Phone: 4045887711
Website: www.suntrust.com

Management and Staff
Phillip Humann, Chief Executive Officer

Type of Firm
Investment Management Firm

Project Preferences

Type of Financing Preferred:
Later Stage

Additional Information
Year Founded: 1984
Current Activity Level : Actively seeking new investments

SUNTX CAPITAL PARTNERS LP

5420 LBJ Freeway
Two Lincoln Center, Suite 1000
Dallas, TX USA 75240
Phone: 9726638900
Fax: 9726619977
E-mail: info@suntx.com
Website: www.suntx.com

Management and Staff
David Webb, Principal
Jason Jelen, Principal
Mark Matteson, Partner
Michael Ilagan, Principal

Type of Firm
Private Equity Firm

Project Preferences

Type of Financing Preferred:
Leveraged Buyout
Balanced
Management Buyouts
Acquisition
Recapitalizations

Geographical Preferences

United States Preferences:
New Mexico
Oklahoma
Tennessee
Arizona
Mississippi
Southeast
Alabama
North Carolina
South Carolina
Virginia
Florida
Louisiana
Georgia
Arkansas
Kentucky
Texas

Industry Focus
(% based on actual investment)
Semiconductors/Other Elect. 68.9%
Other Products 31.1%

Additional Information
Year Founded: 2001

Capital Under Management: $600,000,000
Current Activity Level : Actively seeking new investments

SUNU VENTURES BV

Johannes Vermeer Plein 9
Amsterdam, Netherlands

Type of Firm
Private Equity Firm

Project Preferences

Type of Financing Preferred:
Early Stage

Geographical Preferences

United States Preferences:

International Preferences:
Europe

Industry Preferences

In Medical/Health prefer:
Medical/Health

Additional Information
Year Founded: 2014
Current Activity Level : Actively seeking new investments

SUNUP VENTURE CAPITAL

No.229, Mid North 4th Ring Rd
Rm1725, Haitai Bldg, Haidian
Beijing, China 100083
Phone: 861052776866
Fax: 861052776866
E-mail: contact@sunupcapital.com
Website: sunupcapital.com

Type of Firm
Private Equity Firm

Project Preferences

Type of Financing Preferred:
Expansion
Balanced
Later Stage
Seed

Geographical Preferences

International Preferences:
China

Additional Information
Year Founded: 2007
Current Activity Level : Actively seeking new investments

SUOMEN ITSENAISYYDEN JUHLARAHASTO

Itamerentori 2
P.O. Box 160
Helsinki, Finland 00181
Phone: 3589618991
Fax: 3589645072
E-mail: sitra@sitra.fi
Website: www.sitra.fi

Management and Staff

Jari Pasanen, Vice President
Mikko Kosonen, President

Type of Firm

Endowment, Foundation or Pension Fund

Association Membership

Finnish Venture Capital Association (FVCA)

Project Preferences

Role in Financing:
Will function either as deal originator or investor in deals created by others

Type of Financing Preferred:
Early Stage
Seed
Startup

Size of Investments Considered:
Min Size of Investment Considered (000s): $500
Max Size of Investment Considered (000s): $3,000

Geographical Preferences

United States Preferences:

International Preferences:
Europe
Finland

Industry Focus

(% based on actual investment)
Medical/Health	30.5%
Other Products	23.8%
Internet Specific	10.5%
Industrial/Energy	10.2%
Biotechnology	9.9%
Semiconductors/Other Elect.	5.2%
Computer Hardware	4.7%
Computer Software and Services	3.0%
Communications and Media	1.2%
Consumer Related	1.0%

Additional Information

Year Founded: 1967
Capital Under Management: $1,131,100,000
Current Activity Level : Actively seeking new investments
Method of Compensation: Return on investment is of primary concern, do not charge fees

SUOMEN TEOLLI-SUUSSIJOITUS OY

Mannerheimintie 14 A
P.O. Box 685
Helsinki, Finland 00101
Phone: 35896803680
Fax: 35896121680
E-mail: tesi@teollisuussijoitus.fi
Website: www.teollisuussijoitus.fi

Management and Staff

Marko Haikio, Chief Financial Officer

Type of Firm

Government Affiliated Program

Association Membership

Finnish Venture Capital Association (FVCA)

Project Preferences

Role in Financing:
Will function either as deal originator or investor in deals created by others

Type of Financing Preferred:
Fund of Funds
Early Stage
Mezzanine
Generalist PE
Balanced
Turnaround
Later Stage
Seed

Size of Investments Considered:
Min Size of Investment Considered (000s): $69
Max Size of Investment Considered (000s): $13,797

Geographical Preferences

International Preferences:
Finland

Industry Focus

(% based on actual investment)
Other Products	82.9%
Industrial/Energy	6.1%
Computer Software and Services	4.2%
Semiconductors/Other Elect.	3.0%
Medical/Health	1.8%
Internet Specific	0.7%
Communications and Media	0.5%
Consumer Related	0.4%
Biotechnology	0.3%
Computer Hardware	0.0%

Additional Information

Name of Most Recent Fund: FoF Growth II
Most Recent Fund Was Raised: 02/07/2014
Year Founded: 1995
Capital Under Management: $587,100,000
Current Activity Level : Actively seeking new investments
Method of Compensation: Return on invest. most important, but chg. closing fees, service fees, etc.

SUPER VENTURES

1355 Market Street
#488
San Francisco, CA USA 94103
Website: www.superventures.com

Type of Firm

Incubator/Development Program

Additional Information

Year Founded: 2016
Capital Under Management: $10,000,000
Current Activity Level : Actively seeking new investments

SUPERIOR CAPITAL PARTNERS LLC

500 Griswold Street, Suite 2320
Detroit, MI USA 48226
Phone: 3155969600
Fax: 3135969610
Website: www.superiorfund.com

Management and Staff

Andrew Wiegand, Vice President
Brian Demkowicz, Partner
Mark Carroll, Managing Partner
Scott Hauncher, Managing Director
Scott Reilly, Partner

Type of Firm

Private Equity Firm

Project Preferences

Type of Financing Preferred:
Leveraged Buyout
Management Buyouts
Acquisition
Recapitalizations

Size of Investments Considered:
Min Size of Investment Considered (000s): $3,000
Max Size of Investment Considered (000s): $15,000

Geographical Preferences

United States Preferences:
All U.S.

Industry Preferences

In Industrial/Energy prefer:
Industrial Products

In Business Serv. prefer:
Services
Distribution

In Manufact. prefer:
Manufacturing

SUPERIOR STREET PARTNERS LLC

19010 Shaker Boulevard
Shaker Heights
Cleveland, OH USA 44122
Fax: 2169219018
Website: www.sstreetpartners.com

Type of Firm
Private Equity Firm

Project Preferences

Type of Financing Preferred:
Leveraged Buyout
Mezzanine
Management Buyouts
Acquisition

Geographical Preferences

United States Preferences:
Mid Atlantic
Midwest
Mississippi

Industry Preferences

In Semiconductor/Electr prefer:
Electronics

In Consumer Related prefer:
Food/Beverage
Consumer Products
Other Restaurants

In Industrial/Energy prefer:
Alternative Energy
Energy Conservation Relat

In Transportation prefer:
Aerospace

In Business Serv. prefer:
Services
Distribution

In Manufact. prefer:
Manufacturing

In Agr/Forestr/Fish prefer:
Agriculture related

Additional Information
Year Founded: 1969
Current Activity Level : Actively seeking new investments

SUPERNOVA INVEST SAS

25, Rue Leblanc
Paris, France 75015
Website: www.supernovainvest.com

Type of Firm
Government Affiliated Program

Project Preferences

Type of Financing Preferred:
Early Stage
Expansion
Later Stage
Seed

Geographical Preferences

International Preferences:
France

Additional Information
Name of Most Recent Fund: Amorcage Technologique Investissement Fund
Most Recent Fund Was Raised: 04/03/2013
Year Founded: 2017
Capital Under Management: $134,140,000
Current Activity Level : Actively seeking new investments

SUPPLY CHAIN EQUITY PARTNERS

1300 East Ninth Street, Suite 600
Cleveland, OH USA 44114
Phone: 2169254184
Fax: 2163630135
E-mail: info@SupplyChainEquity.com
Website: www.supplychainequity.com

Management and Staff
Jay Greyson, Principal
Jim Miller, Principal
Nir Gabriely, Principal

Type of Firm
Private Equity Firm

Project Preferences

Type of Financing Preferred:
Leveraged Buyout
Expansion
Acquisition

Size of Investments Considered:
Min Size of Investment Considered (000s): $2,000
Max Size of Investment Considered (000s): $20,000

Geographical Preferences

United States Preferences:

Industry Preferences

In Business Serv. prefer:
Distribution

Additional Information
Name of Most Recent Fund: Supply Chain Equity Partners II LLC
Most Recent Fund Was Raised: 01/24/2014
Year Founded: 2007
Capital Under Management: $25,000,000
Current Activity Level : Actively seeking new investments

SUPPLY CHAIN VENTURES LLC

148 Hills Beach Road, Suite 200
Biddeford, ME USA 04005
Phone: 2079674691
Website: supplychainventure.com

Management and Staff
David Anderson, Managing Director

Type of Firm
Private Equity Firm

Project Preferences

Type of Financing Preferred:
Early Stage
Balanced
Seed

Industry Preferences

In Computer Software prefer:
Software

In Biotechnology prefer:
Biotechnology

In Business Serv. prefer:
Distribution

Additional Information
Year Founded: 2009
Current Activity Level : Actively seeking new investments

SURE VENTURES GP LLC

650 Castro Street, Suite 120-411
Mountain View, CA USA 94041
Phone: 4154804674

Type of Firm
Private Equity Firm

Additional Information
Year Founded: 2007
Current Activity Level : Actively seeking new investments

Project Preferences

Type of Financing Preferred:
Early Stage

Industry Preferences

In Financial Services prefer:
Insurance

Additional Information

Year Founded: 2017
Current Activity Level : Actively seeking new investments

SURGE PRIVATE EQUITY LLC

100 Crescent Court
Seventh Floor
Dallas, TX USA 75201
Website: www.surgepe.com

Type of Firm

Private Equity Firm

Project Preferences

Type of Financing Preferred:
Leveraged Buyout
Management Buyouts
Recapitalizations

Industry Preferences

In Medical/Health prefer:
Health Services

Additional Information

Year Founded: 2017
Current Activity Level : Actively seeking new investments

SURYA CAPITAL MANAGEMENT LLP

6th Floor, Tower A
1 Cybercity
Ebene, Mauritius
Website: www.suryacapital.com

Other Offices

19 Sokoine Drive
PoBox 409
Dar es Salaam, Tanzania

Yewubdar Building 5th Floor Bole
Addis Ababa, Ethiopia

14 Cork Street
London , United Kingdom W1S 3NS
Phone: 442031417050

Type of Firm

Private Equity Firm

Project Preferences

Type of Financing Preferred:
Generalist PE

Geographical Preferences

International Preferences:
Ethiopia
Angola
Rwanda
Tunisia
Mauritius
Nigeria
Uganda
Tanzania
Egypt
Algeria
Ghana
Kenya
Congo
Morocco
Mozambique
South Africa
Libya
Sudan

Industry Preferences

In Medical/Health prefer:
Health Services

In Consumer Related prefer:
Consumer
Education Related

In Industrial/Energy prefer:
Energy

In Transportation prefer:
Transportation

In Financial Services prefer:
Financial Services
Real Estate

Additional Information

Year Founded: 2005
Current Activity Level : Actively seeking new investments

SUSA VENTURES LP

540 North Sweetzer Avenue
Los Angeles, CA USA 90069
Phone: 3104137398
E-mail: partners@susaventures.com
Website: www.susaventures.com

Management and Staff

Chad Byers, General Partner
Eva Ho, General Partner
Leo Polovets, General Partner
Seth Berman, General Partner

Type of Firm

Private Equity Firm

Project Preferences

Type of Financing Preferred:
Early Stage
Seed

Additional Information

Year Founded: 2013
Capital Under Management: $75,000,000
Current Activity Level : Actively seeking new investments

SUSQUEHANNA CAPITAL

325 Hellam Street
Wrightsville, PA USA 17368
Phone: 7177640032
Fax: 7177642682
Website: www.susquehannacapital.com

Management and Staff

Lucy Kniseley, President

Type of Firm

Private Equity Firm

Project Preferences

Type of Financing Preferred:
Leveraged Buyout
Recapitalizations

Geographical Preferences

United States Preferences:
Mid Atlantic
Ohio

Industry Preferences

In Business Serv. prefer:
Distribution

In Manufact. prefer:
Manufacturing

Additional Information

Year Founded: 1993
Current Activity Level : Actively seeking new investments

SUSQUEHANNA GROWTH EQUITY LLC

401 City Avenue, Suite 526
Bala Cynwyd, PA USA 19004
Phone: 6106172600
Fax: 6106172689
E-mail: info@sgep.com
Website: www.sgep.com

Other Offices

401 City Avenue, Suite 526
BELMONT HILLS, PA USA 19004
Phone: 6106172600
Fax: 6106172689

Management and Staff
Shamit Mehta, Vice President

Type of Firm
Bank Affiliated

Project Preferences

Type of Financing Preferred:
Leveraged Buyout
Generalist PE
Balanced
Public Companies
Acquisition
Recapitalizations

Size of Investments Considered:
Min Size of Investment Considered (000s): $5,000
Max Size of Investment Considered (000s): $50,000

Geographical Preferences

United States Preferences:
North America

International Preferences:
Europe
Israel

Industry Preferences

In Computer Software prefer:
Software

In Internet Specific prefer:
Internet

In Financial Services prefer:
Financial Services

In Business Serv. prefer:
Services

Additional Information
Year Founded: 2006
Current Activity Level : Actively seeking new investments

SUSQUEHANNA PRIVATE CAPITAL LLC

401 City Avenue
Bala Cynwyd, PA USA 19004

Management and Staff
Andrew Peix, Principal
Daniel Gedney, Vice President
Drew Johnson, Co-Founder
James Jackson, Principal
John Vedro, Chief Financial Officer
Sam Banon, Vice President
Tom Mckelvey, Co-Founder
Whitney Bowman, Partner

Type of Firm
Bank Affiliated

Project Preferences

Type of Financing Preferred:
Leveraged Buyout
Generalist PE
Acquisition

Industry Preferences

In Medical/Health prefer:
Health Services

In Consumer Related prefer:
Consumer

In Industrial/Energy prefer:
Industrial Products

In Transportation prefer:
Aerospace

Additional Information
Year Founded: 2016
Current Activity Level : Actively seeking new investments

SUSSEX PLACE VENTURES LTD

18-20 Huntsworth Mews
London, United Kingdom NW1 6DD
Phone: 442070000022
Fax: 442070000001
E-mail: info@spventures.co.uk

Management and Staff
John Brimacombe, Venture Partner
Richard Gourlay, Managing Director

Type of Firm
University Program

Association Membership
British Venture Capital Association (BVCA)

Project Preferences

Type of Financing Preferred:
Early Stage
Balanced
Seed
Startup

Size of Investments Considered:
Min Size of Investment Considered (000s): $100
Max Size of Investment Considered (000s): $100,000

Geographical Preferences

International Preferences:
United Kingdom

Industry Preferences

In Semiconductor/Electr prefer:
Analytic/Scientific

In Business Serv. prefer:
Services
Media

Additional Information
Name of Most Recent Fund: Sussex Place Partners II
Most Recent Fund Was Raised: 07/25/2000
Year Founded: 1998
Capital Under Management: $23,000,000
Current Activity Level : Actively seeking new investments

SUSTAINABLE DEVELOPMENT TECHNOLOGY CANADA

45 O'Connor Street, Suite 1850
Ottawa, Canada K1P 1A4
Phone: 6132346313
Fax: 6132340303
E-mail: info@sdtc.ca
Website: www.sdtc.ca

Management and Staff
David Kolada, Vice President
Sailesh Thaker, Vice President

Type of Firm
Government Affiliated Program

Association Membership
Canadian Venture Capital Association

Project Preferences

Type of Financing Preferred:
Early Stage
Later Stage

Geographical Preferences

Canadian Preferences:
All Canada

Industry Preferences

In Industrial/Energy prefer:
Oil & Gas Drilling,Explor
Alternative Energy
Energy Conservation Relat
Environmental Related

In Agr/Forestr/Fish prefer:
Agriculture related

In Other prefer:
Environment Responsible

Additional Information
Year Founded: 2001
Current Activity Level : Actively seeking new investments

SUSTAINABLE RESOURCE VENTURES

Damon Mill Square, Suite 6C
Concord, MA USA 01742
Website: www.sustainvc.com

Other Offices

200 North Magnum Street, Suite 203
DURHAM, NC USA 27701
Phone: 9195301177

Type of Firm

Private Equity Firm

Project Preferences

Type of Financing Preferred:
Early Stage
Expansion

Industry Preferences

In Medical/Health prefer:
Medical/Health

In Consumer Related prefer:
Food/Beverage
Education Related

In Industrial/Energy prefer:
Energy
Environmental Related

In Other prefer:
Socially Responsible

Additional Information

Name of Most Recent Fund: Patient Capital Collaborative '13, L.P.
Most Recent Fund Was Raised: 02/05/2014
Year Founded: 2006
Capital Under Management: $4,100,000
Current Activity Level : Actively seeking new investments

SUSTAINVC LLC

1150 Main Street
Unit 9
Concord, MA USA 01742
Website: www.sustainvc.com

Type of Firm

Private Equity Firm

Project Preferences

Type of Financing Preferred:
Early Stage

Additional Information

Year Founded: 2016
Current Activity Level : Actively seeking new investments

SUTTER HILL VENTURES

755 Page Mill Road, Suite A-200
Palo Alto, CA USA 94304
Phone: 6504935600
Fax: 6508581854
Website: www.shv.com

Management and Staff

Andrew Sheehan, Partner
David Anderson, Partner
Doug Mohr, Managing Director
James Gaither, Partner
James White, Managing Director
Jeffrey Bird, Managing Director
Len Baker, Partner
Mike Speiser, Managing Director
Sam Pullara, Managing Director
Stefan Dyckerhoff, Managing Director
Tench Coxe, Managing Director
William Younger, Partner

Type of Firm

Private Equity Firm

Association Membership

Western Association of Venture Capitalists (WAVC)
National Venture Capital Association - USA (NVCA)

Project Preferences

Role in Financing:
Prefer role as deal originator but will also invest in deals created by others

Type of Financing Preferred:
Early Stage
Startup

Geographical Preferences

United States Preferences:

Industry Focus

(% based on actual investment)

Internet Specific	26.7%
Computer Software and Services	25.2%
Biotechnology	11.8%
Medical/Health	10.4%
Computer Hardware	9.9%
Communications and Media	8.0%
Other Products	2.9%
Consumer Related	2.4%
Semiconductors/Other Elect.	2.3%
Industrial/Energy	0.4%

Additional Information

Year Founded: 1962
Capital Under Management: $1,100,000,000
Current Activity Level : Actively seeking new investments
Method of Compensation: Return on invest. most important, but chg. closing fees, service fees, etc.

SUZHOU COWIN ZHENGDE INVESTMENT MANAGEMENT CO LTD

No. 345, Fengli St, Ind Park
Bldg 1, Shahu VC Center
Suzhou, China
Phone: 8651266969517
Fax: 8651266969533
E-mail: wuxm@cowinvc.com
Website: www.cowinvc.com

Type of Firm

Private Equity Firm

Project Preferences

Type of Financing Preferred:
Early Stage
Expansion

Geographical Preferences

International Preferences:
China

Industry Preferences

In Communications prefer:
Telecommunications
Entertainment

In Computer Software prefer:
Software

In Internet Specific prefer:
Internet
Ecommerce

In Semiconductor/Electr prefer:
Circuit Boards

In Biotechnology prefer:
Biotechnology

In Medical/Health prefer:
Medical/Health
Pharmaceuticals

In Industrial/Energy prefer:
Energy
Materials

Additional Information

Year Founded: 2006
Current Activity Level : Actively seeking new investments

SUZHOU DATAI VENTURE CAPITAL INVESTMENT MANAGEMENT CO LTD

345 Fengli St. Suzhou Ind. Pk.
Block 1, San Lake Square
Jiangsu, Suzhou, China 215026
Phone: 8651266969676
Fax: 8651265969677
E-mail: admin@delta-capital.cn
Website: www.delta-capital.cn

Other Offices

Keyuan South Road, Hi-tech District
Rm 1701, Oversea Students Venture Plaza
Shenzhen, China 518057
Phone: 8675533659221

No. 188, Wuyi Road
Shanghai, China 200050
Phone: 862132181261
Fax: 862132181262

C/O Maples Corporate Services, Ltd.
Ugland House,
, Cayman Islands KY1-1104
Phone: 345 949-8066

Management and Staff

Greg Ye, Managing Partner
James Ju Zhang, Managing Partner
Jason Quansheng Li, Managing Partner

Type of Firm

Private Equity Firm

Project Preferences

Type of Financing Preferred:
Early Stage
Expansion
Balanced

Later Stage
Seed

Size of Investments Considered:

Min Size of Investment Considered (000s): $3,164
Max Size of Investment Considered (000s): $15,821

Geographical Preferences

International Preferences:
Asia Pacific
Europe
China
Cayman Islands
Asia
All International

Industry Preferences

In Communications prefer:
Telecommunications

In Consumer Related prefer:
Consumer Products
Consumer Services

In Industrial/Energy prefer:
Energy Conservation Relat
Environmental Related

In Business Serv. prefer:
Media

In Manufact. prefer:
Manufacturing

In Other prefer:
Environment Responsible

Additional Information

Year Founded: 2008
Capital Under Management: $157,406,000
Current Activity Level : Actively seeking new investments

SUZHOU EMERGING INDUSTRIES VENTURE CAPITAL GUIDANCE FUND

No.129, Huizhan Road
4F, Qihuo Building
Dalian, China
Phone: 8641186768566
Fax: 8641186768576
E-mail: info@chnpsf.com
Website: www.chn-psf.com

Type of Firm

Government Affiliated Program

Project Preferences

Type of Financing Preferred:
Balanced

Geographical Preferences

International Preferences:
China

Additional Information

Year Founded: 2011
Capital Under Management: $16,100,000
Current Activity Level : Actively seeking new investments

SUZHOU HAIRONGTIAN INVESTMENT CO LTD

No. 777,Yangchenghu West Road
Suzhou, China

Type of Firm

Private Equity Firm

Project Preferences

Type of Financing Preferred:
Leveraged Buyout

Geographical Preferences

International Preferences:
China

Additional Information

Year Founded: 2014
Current Activity Level : Actively seeking new investments

SUZHOU HI-TECH VC GROUP RONGLIAN MANAGEMENT CO., LTD.

c/o, No. 35 Shishan Road
Suzhou, Jiangsu, China 215011
Phone: 8651268072571
Fax: 8651268099281

Type of Firm

Private Equity Firm

Project Preferences

Type of Financing Preferred:
Early Stage
Expansion
Balanced

Geographical Preferences

International Preferences:
China

Additional Information

Year Founded: 2011
Capital Under Management: $59,544,000
Current Activity Level : Actively seeking new investments

SUZHOU HIGH TECH VENTURE CAPITAL GROUP CO LTD

Suzhou High-tech Zone
No.37 Keliang Road
Suzhou, China 215163
Phone: 8651268310566
Fax: 8651268311200
Website: www.sndvc.com

Type of Firm

Government Affiliated Program

Project Preferences

Type of Financing Preferred:
Balanced

Geographical Preferences

International Preferences:
China

Additional Information

Year Founded: 2008
Current Activity Level : Actively seeking new investments

SUZHOU HONGYU EQUITY INVESTMENT MANAGE-MENT ENTRP CO LTD

Huaqiao
Kunshan, Jiangsu, China

Type of Firm
Private Equity Firm

Project Preferences

Type of Financing Preferred:
Balanced

Geographical Preferences

International Preferences:
China

Industry Preferences

In Medical/Health prefer:
Medical/Health

In Industrial/Energy prefer:
Energy

In Agr/Forestr/Fish prefer:
Agriculture related

In Other prefer:
Environment Responsible

Additional Information

Year Founded: 2011
Capital Under Management: $78,339,000
Current Activity Level : Actively seeking new investments

SUZHOU INDUSTRIAL PARK SUNGENT BIOVENTURE MANAGEMENT CO LTD

BioBAY, Suzhou Ind. Park
F2, Building A1 North
Suzhou, China

Type of Firm
Private Equity Firm

Project Preferences

Type of Financing Preferred:
Early Stage
Expansion
Seed
Startup

Geographical Preferences

International Preferences:
China

Industry Preferences

In Biotechnology prefer:
Biotechnology

In Medical/Health prefer:
Medical/Health

Additional Information

Year Founded: 2013
Current Activity Level : Actively seeking new investments

SUZHOU LANHAI FANG-ZHOU EQUITY INVESTMENT MANGEMENT CO LTD

Xinghai St., Suzhou Indl Prk
Room 1203, Hengyu Plaza, 188,
Suzhou, China 215000
Phone: 8651267061888

Type of Firm
Private Equity Firm

Project Preferences

Type of Financing Preferred:
Balanced

Geographical Preferences

International Preferences:
China

Industry Preferences

In Computer Software prefer:
Applications Software

In Computer Other prefer:
Computer Related

Additional Information

Year Founded: 2011
Capital Under Management: $100,000,000
Current Activity Level : Actively seeking new investments

SUZHOU ORIZA HOLDINGS CO LTD

183 Suhong Dong Road
BLK19,Sandlake VC/PE Communit
Suzhou, China 215000
Phone: 8651266969999
Fax: 8651266969998
E-mail: orizaholdings@oriza.com.cn
Website: www.oriza.com.cn

Management and Staff

Gang Sheng, Vice President
Ying Li, Chief Financial Officer

Type of Firm
Private Equity Firm

Project Preferences

Type of Financing Preferred:
Leveraged Buyout
Early Stage
Balanced
Later Stage
Seed
Startup

Geographical Preferences

International Preferences:
China

Industry Preferences

In Communications prefer:
Commercial Communications
Telecommunications

In Internet Specific prefer:
Internet
Ecommerce

In Biotechnology prefer:
Human Biotechnology

In Medical/Health prefer:
Medical/Health
Pharmaceuticals

In Consumer Related prefer:
Consumer Services

In Industrial/Energy prefer:
Energy
Alternative Energy

In Financial Services prefer:
Financial Services

In Business Serv. prefer:
Consulting Services
Media

In Agr/Forestr/Fish prefer:
Mining and Minerals

Additional Information
Year Founded: 2001
Capital Under Management: $400,000,000
Current Activity Level : Actively seeking new investments

SUZHOU QIAOJING ORIENTAL INVESTMENT MANAGEMENT CONSULTING

No.300 Renmin Road
Jiangsu, China
Website: www.qjcap.com

Type of Firm
Private Equity Firm

Project Preferences

Type of Financing Preferred:
Balanced
Seed
Startup

Geographical Preferences

International Preferences:
China

Industry Preferences

In Communications prefer:
Telecommunications

In Medical/Health prefer:
Medical/Health

In Industrial/Energy prefer:
Materials

In Business Serv. prefer:
Media

In Manufact. prefer:
Manufacturing

In Other prefer:
Environment Responsible

Additional Information
Year Founded: 2013
Current Activity Level : Actively seeking new investments

SUZHOU SHENGSHANG UNITED INVESTMENT CENTER PARTNERSHIP LTD

Shengze Town
Wujiang, China 215226

Management and Staff
Tao Wu, Vice President

Type of Firm
Bank Affiliated

Additional Information
Year Founded: 2007
Current Activity Level : Actively seeking new investments

SUZHOU SHUIMU QINGHUA CAPITAL MANAGEMENT CO LTD

National Level Hi-tech Park
No. 8, Yunhe Road
Suzhou, China 215011

Type of Firm
Private Equity Firm

Project Preferences

Type of Financing Preferred:
Balanced

Geographical Preferences

International Preferences:
China

Additional Information
Year Founded: 2011
Capital Under Management: $15,174,000
Current Activity Level : Actively seeking new investments

SUZHOU TAIHAO VENTURE CAPITAL MANAGEMENT PARTNER ENTERPRISE

Tongyuan Road, Industrial Park
Building No.23
Suzhou, China
Website: www.tahoevc.com

Type of Firm
Private Equity Firm

Project Preferences

Type of Financing Preferred:
Early Stage

Geographical Preferences

International Preferences:
China

Industry Preferences

In Internet Specific prefer:
Internet

In Manufact. prefer:
Manufacturing

Additional Information
Year Founded: 2014
Current Activity Level : Actively seeking new investments

SUZHOU XIERUI VENTURE CAPITAL MANAGEMENT CO LTD

No. 181, Cuiyuan Road, Ind Pk
Rm 1105, Bldg 6, Shanglv Plaza
Suzhou, China

Type of Firm
Private Equity Firm

Project Preferences

Type of Financing Preferred:
Balanced

Geographical Preferences

International Preferences:
China

Additional Information
Year Founded: 2012
Capital Under Management: $34,876,000
Current Activity Level : Actively seeking new investments

SUZHOU YIPU EQUITY INVESTMENT FUND MANAGEMENT CO LTD

No. 118 Suzhou St. West
Room 801, North Building, Suyu
Suzhou, China 215123
Phone: 8651267990578

Type of Firm
Investment Management Firm

Project Preferences

Type of Financing Preferred:
Balanced

Geographical Preferences

International Preferences:
China

Additional Information
Year Founded: 2016
Current Activity Level : Actively seeking new investments

SV ANGEL

588 Sutter Street, Suite 299
San Francisco, CA USA 94102
Phone: 6508544500
Website: www.svangel.com

Other Offices
770 Chimalus Drive
PALO ALTO, CA USA 94306

Management and Staff
Brian Pokorny i, Managing Partner
Kevin Carter, Partner
Robert Pollak, Partner
Topher Conway, Partner

Type of Firm
Private Equity Firm

Project Preferences

Type of Financing Preferred:
Early Stage
Balanced
Later Stage

Industry Preferences

In Internet Specific prefer:
Internet

Additional Information
Name of Most Recent Fund: SV Angel III, L.P.
Most Recent Fund Was Raised: 05/04/2011
Year Founded: 2009
Capital Under Management: $64,795,000
Current Activity Level : Actively seeking new investments

SV HEALTH INVESTORS LLP

201 Washington Street, Suite 3900, One Boston Place
Boston, MA USA 02108
Phone: 6173678100
Fax: 6173671590
E-mail: info@svlsa.com
Website: svhealthinvestors.com

Other Offices
71 Kingsway
London, United Kingdom WC2B 6ST
Phone: 442074217070
Fax: 442074217077

Management and Staff
Ashish Khanna, Principal
Bob Palmisano, Venture Partner
Bruce Cerullo, Venture Partner
Bruce Peacock, Venture Partner
Catherine Bingham, Managing Partner
Daniel Burgess, Venture Partner
Darren Black, Managing Partner
David Milne, Managing Partner
David Guyer, Venture Partner
Dev Mishra, Venture Partner
Ed Mascioli, Venture Partner
Elizabeth Campbell, Principal
George Wallace, Venture Partner
Graham Boulnois, Partner
Hamish Cameron, Venture Partner
Heinrich Dreismann, Venture Partner
James Garvey, Venture Partner
Jim Wachtman, Venture Partner
Joshua Resnick, Partner
Kelly DeKeyser, Venture Partner
Lutz Giebel, Managing Partner
Mark Cherney, Venture Partner
Michael Ross, Managing Partner
Michael Balmuth, Partner
Michael Carter, Venture Partner
Michael Mendelsohn, Venture Partner
Nicholas Coleman, Partner
Nick Coleman, Partner
Patrick Ryan, Venture Partner
Paul LaViolette, Partner
Robert Palmisano, Venture Partner
Stephen Kahane, Venture Partner
Tillman Gerngross, Venture Partner
Tom Flynn, Managing Partner

Type of Firm
Private Equity Firm

Association Membership
British Venture Capital Association (BVCA)
New England Venture Capital Association
National Venture Capital Association - USA (NVCA)

Project Preferences

Role in Financing:
Prefer role as deal originator but will also invest in deals created by others

Type of Financing Preferred:
Leveraged Buyout
Expansion
Public Companies
Seed
Startup

Size of Investments Considered:
Min Size of Investment Considered (000s): $1,000
Max Size of Investment Considered (000s): $40,000

Geographical Preferences

United States Preferences:

International Preferences:
India
Ireland
Sweden
United Kingdom
East Germany
Luxembourg
Europe
Switzerland
All International
France

Industry Focus
(% based on actual investment)
Medical/Health	41.4%
Biotechnology	35.4%
Computer Software and Services	9.6%
Industrial/Energy	5.7%
Other Products	4.5%
Internet Specific	1.8%
Computer Hardware	1.5%
Consumer Related	0.1%
Semiconductors/Other Elect.	0.1%

Additional Information
Name of Most Recent Fund: SV Life Sciences Fund V, L.P.
Most Recent Fund Was Raised: 06/29/2010
Year Founded: 1993
Capital Under Management: $3,500,000,000
Current Activity Level : Actively seeking new investments
Method of Compensation: Return on invest. most important, but chg. closing fees, service fees, etc.

SV INVESTMENT CORP

27-2 Yeoidodong, Yeungdeungpogu
11/F, Sahagyeongeum Bldg
Seoul, South Korea
Phone: 822-3775-1020
Fax: 822-3775-1021
E-mail: svvc@svvc.co.kr
Website: svinvestment.co.kr

Management and Staff
Sungho Park, President

Type of Firm
Private Equity Firm

Association Membership
Korean Venture Capital Association (KVCA)

Project Preferences

Type of Financing Preferred:
Leveraged Buyout
Balanced

Geographical Preferences

International Preferences:
Korea, South

Additional Information
Year Founded: 2006
Capital Under Management: $20,300,000
Current Activity Level : Actively seeking new investments

SV TECH VENTURES

545 Bryant Street
Palo Alto, CA USA 94301
Website: svtechventures.com

Type of Firm
Private Equity Firm

Project Preferences

Type of Financing Preferred:
Balanced

Additional Information
Year Founded: 2015
Capital Under Management: $11,520,000
Current Activity Level : Actively seeking new investments

SVAROG CAPITAL ADVISORS LTD

Bolshaya Ordynka Street
40 Buliding Four
Moscow, Russia 119017
Phone: 74957455757
Fax: 74959812921
E-mail: office@svarogcapital.com
Website: www.svarogcapital.com

Management and Staff
Alexei Perekhojev, Chief Financial Officer
Andrey Daleky, Vice President
Evgeny Rudakov, Partner
Mikhail Stukalo, Partner
Oleg Tsarkov, Managing Partner

Type of Firm
Private Equity Firm

Project Preferences

Role in Financing:
Prefer role as deal originator but will also invest in deals created by others

Type of Financing Preferred:
Leveraged Buyout
Early Stage
Expansion
Later Stage

Size of Investments Considered:
Min Size of Investment Considered (000s): $30,000
Max Size of Investment Considered (000s): $50,000

Geographical Preferences

International Preferences:
Kazakhstan
Ukraine
Russia

Industry Preferences

In Internet Specific prefer:
Ecommerce

In Consumer Related prefer:
Retail
Food/Beverage

In Industrial/Energy prefer:
Machinery

In Business Serv. prefer:
Services
Distribution

Additional Information
Name of Most Recent Fund: Earlier Stage Alternative Fund L.P.
Most Recent Fund Was Raised: 04/17/2008
Year Founded: 2003
Capital Under Management: $290,000,000
Current Activity Level : Actively seeking new investments

SVC-AG FUER KMU RISIKOKAPITAL

Tessinerplatz 7
Zurich, Switzerland 8070
Phone: 41443331063
E-mail: info@svc-riskcapital.ch
Website: www.svc-risikokapital.ch

Management and Staff
Johannes Suter, Chief Executive Officer

Type of Firm
Bank Affiliated

Association Membership
Swiss Venture Capital Association (SECA)

Project Preferences

Type of Financing Preferred:
Early Stage
Later Stage
Startup

Size of Investments Considered:
Min Size of Investment Considered (000s): $173
Max Size of Investment Considered (000s): $1,730

Geographical Preferences

International Preferences:
Switzerland

Industry Preferences

In Communications prefer:
Publishing

In Consumer Related prefer:
Food/Beverage

In Industrial/Energy prefer:
Industrial Products

Additional Information
Year Founded: 2010
Capital Under Management: $86,500,000
Current Activity Level : Actively seeking new investments

SVERICA INTERNATIONAL BOSTON LLC

800 Boylston Street, Suite 3325, Prudential Tower
Boston, MA USA 02199
Phone: 6176950221
Fax: 6172360110
Website: www.sverica.com

Other Offices
44 Montgomery Street, Suite 3000
San Francisco, CA USA 94104
Phone: 415-249-4900
Fax: 415-249-4901

Management and Staff
Alessandro Mina, Co-Founder
Christopher Wolf, Chief Financial Officer
David Finley, Managing Director
Frank Young, Managing Director
Jordan Richards, Managing Director
K. Gunnar Bjorklund, Co-Founder

Type of Firm
Private Equity Firm

Project Preferences

Type of Financing Preferred:
Leveraged Buyout
Management Buyouts
Acquisition

Geographical Preferences

United States Preferences:

Canadian Preferences:
All Canada

Industry Preferences

In Computer Software prefer:
Software

In Medical/Health prefer:
Health Services

In Industrial/Energy prefer:
Advanced Materials

In Financial Services prefer:
Financial Services

In Business Serv. prefer:
Services
Distribution
Consulting Services

In Manufact. prefer:
Manufacturing

Additional Information
Year Founded: 1993
Capital Under Management: $430,000,000
Current Activity Level : Actively seeking new investments

SVILUPPO IMPRESE CENTRO ITALIA SGR SPA

Viale Giuseppe Mazzini, 46
Firenze, Italy 50132
Phone: 39055200751
Fax: 390552007597
E-mail: info@fondisici.it
Website: www.fondisici.it

Management and Staff
Fabrizio Buzzatti, Chief Executive Officer

Type of Firm
Private Equity Firm

Association Membership
Italian Venture Capital Association (AIFI)

Project Preferences

Type of Financing Preferred:
Early Stage
Expansion
Later Stage
Startup

Geographical Preferences

International Preferences:
Italy

Industry Preferences

In Consumer Related prefer:
Food/Beverage

In Industrial/Energy prefer:
Alternative Energy
Energy Conservation Relat

In Other prefer:
Environment Responsible

Additional Information
Year Founded: 1998
Current Activity Level : Actively seeking new investments

SVILUPPO ITALIA SPA

46, Via Calabria
Rome, Italy 00187
Phone: 39-06-421-601
Fax: 39-06-421-60975
E-mail: info@sviluppoitalia.it
Website: www.svit.it

Type of Firm
Government Affiliated Program

Project Preferences

Type of Financing Preferred:
Second Stage Financing
Expansion
Startup

Geographical Preferences

International Preferences:
Italy

Industry Preferences

In Consumer Related prefer:
Entertainment and Leisure

In Business Serv. prefer:
Services

In Manufact. prefer:
Manufacturing

In Agr/Forestr/Fish prefer:
Agribusiness
Agriculture related

Additional Information
Year Founded: 2000
Current Activity Level : Actively seeking new investments

SVOBODA CAPITAL PARTNERS LLC

One North Franklin Street, Suite 1500
Chicago, IL USA 60606
Phone: 3122678750
Fax: 3122676025
E-mail: info@svoco.com
Website: www.svoco.com

Management and Staff
Andrew Albert, Managing Director
David Schumacher, Vice President
Jeffrey Piper, Principal
John Svoboda, Co-Founder
Joseph Thomas, Vice President
Peter Gotsch, Managing Director
Richard Harpster, Principal

Type of Firm
Private Equity Firm

Association Membership
Illinois Venture Capital Association

Project Preferences

Role in Financing:
Prefer role as deal originator but will also invest in deals created by others

Type of Financing Preferred:
Leveraged Buyout
Acquisition
Recapitalizations

Industry Focus
(% based on actual investment)
Internet Specific	30.2%
Consumer Related	22.8%
Other Products	20.3%
Computer Software and Services	17.6%
Industrial/Energy	9.1%

Additional Information
Year Founded: 1998
Capital Under Management: $250,000,000
Current Activity Level : Actively seeking new investments
Method of Compensation: Return on invest. most important, but chg. closing fees, service fees, etc.

SW CAPITAL PARTNERS

Scotia Centre 700 - 2nd Street, Suite 1800
Calgary, Canada T2P 2W1
Phone: 4032658077
Fax: 4032186797

Type of Firm
Private Equity Firm

Project Preferences

Type of Financing Preferred:
Leveraged Buyout
Acquisition

Geographical Preferences

United States Preferences:
North America

Industry Preferences

In Industrial/Energy prefer:
Energy
Oil and Gas Exploration
Oil & Gas Drilling,Explor

Additional Information
Year Founded: 2011
Current Activity Level : Actively seeking new investments

SWAN & LEGEND VENTURE PARTNERS

109 North King Street, Suite B
Leesburg, VA USA 20176
Phone: 7037716301
Website: www.swanandlegend.com

Type of Firm
Private Equity Firm

Project Preferences

Type of Financing Preferred:
Later Stage

Industry Preferences

In Communications prefer:
Communications and Media

In Internet Specific prefer:
E-Commerce Technology

In Consumer Related prefer:
Consumer
Entertainment and Leisure
Sports
Retail
Food/Beverage
Education Related

Additional Information

Name of Most Recent Fund: Swan & Legend Fund 2, L.P.
Most Recent Fund Was Raised: 06/30/2013
Year Founded: 2012
Capital Under Management: $70,000,000
Current Activity Level : Actively seeking new investments

SWANCAP INVESTMENT MANAGEMENT SA

5, Rue Heienhaff
Senningerberg, Luxembourg 1736
Website: www.swancap.eu

Type of Firm
Investment Management Firm

Project Preferences

Type of Financing Preferred:
Leveraged Buyout
Management Buyouts
Acquisition

Additional Information

Name of Most Recent Fund: SwanCap Opportunities Fund SCS - SIF
Most Recent Fund Was Raised: 01/30/2014
Year Founded: 2013
Capital Under Management: $1,946,826,000
Current Activity Level : Actively seeking new investments

SWANDER PACE CAPITAL LLC

101 Mission Street, Suite 1900
San Francisco, CA USA 94105
Phone: 4154778500
Fax: 4154778510
E-mail: info@spcap.com
Website: www.spcap.com

Other Offices

550 Hills Drive, Suite 106
BEDMINSTER, NJ USA 07921
Phone: 908-719-2322
Fax: 908-719-9311

81273 North Service Road East
Oakville, Canada L6H 1A7

Management and Staff

Alex Litt, Vice President
Andrew Richards, Chief Executive Officer
Ann Kim, Vice President
C. Morris Stout, Managing Director
Corby Reese, Managing Director
Heather Thorne, Managing Director
Heather Fraser, Chief Financial Officer
Mark Poff, Managing Director
Robert DesMarais, Managing Director
Robert Vassel, Principal
Valerie Scott, Principal

Type of Firm
Private Equity Firm

Association Membership
Canadian Venture Capital Association

Project Preferences

Role in Financing:
Prefer role as deal originator but will also invest in deals created by others

Type of Financing Preferred:
Leveraged Buyout
Management Buyouts
Acquisition
Recapitalizations

Geographical Preferences

United States Preferences:
North America

Industry Focus

(% based on actual investment)

Consumer Related	56.7%
Other Products	16.5%
Medical/Health	14.1%
Internet Specific	10.9%
Computer Software and Services	1.6%
Communications and Media	0.2%

Additional Information

Name of Most Recent Fund: Swander Pace Capital V, L.P.
Most Recent Fund Was Raised: 05/01/2013
Year Founded: 1996
Capital Under Management: $85,000,000
Current Activity Level : Actively seeking new investments
Method of Compensation: Return on invest. most important, but chg. closing fees, service fees, etc.

SWANLAAB VENTURE FACTORY SGEIC SA

Arbea Campus Empresarial
Bulding 2
Alcobendas, Spain 28108
Phone: 34913346004
E-mail: info@swanlaab.com

Type of Firm
Private Equity Firm

Project Preferences

Type of Financing Preferred:
Balanced

Geographical Preferences

International Preferences:
Spain

Additional Information

Year Founded: 2016
Capital Under Management: $44,550,000
Current Activity Level : Actively seeking new investments

SWARRATON PARTNERS LTD

79 Knightsbridge
London, United Kingdom SW1X 7RB
Phone: 442077520860
Fax: 442077520590
E-mail: info@swarraton.com

Management and Staff

Christophe Jungels-Winkler, Co-Founder
Stephen Henry Ralph Brooke, Co-Founder

Type of Firm
Private Equity Firm

Project Preferences

Type of Financing Preferred:
Early Stage
Later Stage
Seed

Geographical Preferences

United States Preferences:
All U.S.

International Preferences:
United Kingdom
Europe
Switzerland
Germany

Additional Information

Year Founded: 2007
Current Activity Level : Actively seeking new investments

SWAT EQUITY PARTNERS LP

299 Broadway, Suite 920
New York, NY USA 10007
E-mail: info@swatequitypartners.com
Website: www.swatequitypartners.com

Type of Firm
Private Equity Firm

Project Preferences
Type of Financing Preferred:
Early Stage

Industry Preferences

In Medical/Health prefer:
Health Services

In Consumer Related prefer:
Consumer
Sports
Retail
Food/Beverage

In Transportation prefer:
Transportation

Additional Information
Year Founded: 2016
Current Activity Level : Actively seeking new investments

SWEAT EQUITY PARTNERS LP

3131 Turtle Creek Boulevard
Dallas, TX USA 75219
Phone: 6508237090
Website: www.seplp.com

Type of Firm
Private Equity Firm

Project Preferences
Type of Financing Preferred:
Balanced

Additional Information
Year Founded: 2017
Current Activity Level : Actively seeking new investments

SWEDFUND INTERNATIONAL AB

Sveavagen 24-26
Stockholm, Sweden 103 65
Phone: 4687259400
Fax: 468203093
E-mail: info@swedfund.se
Website: www.swedfund.se

Other Offices
Eden Square
PO Box 630, 3rd floor, Block A
Nairobi, Kenya 00621
Phone: 254203748624

Management and Staff
Anders Craft, Managing Director

Type of Firm
Government Affiliated Program

Association Membership
Emerging Markets Private Equity Association
Swedish Venture Capital Association (SVCA)
African Venture Capital Association (AVCA)

Project Preferences
Type of Financing Preferred:
Balanced

Size of Investments Considered:
Min Size of Investment Considered (000s): $4,701
Max Size of Investment Considered (000s): $15,671

Geographical Preferences
International Preferences:
Latin America
Central Europe
Eastern Europe
Asia
Africa

Industry Focus
(% based on actual investment)
Other Products	62.3%
Internet Specific	23.8%
Semiconductors/Other Elect.	7.0%
Medical/Health	5.2%
Consumer Related	1.7%

Additional Information
Year Founded: 1979
Current Activity Level : Actively seeking new investments

SWEETWATER CAPITAL PARTNERS LP

662 Encinitas Blvd, Suite 230
Encinitas, CA USA 92024
Phone: 7606526353
E-mail: info@Sweetwater.Capital
Website: www.sweetwatercapitalpartners.com

Management and Staff
Joseph Siletto, Venture Partner
Ronald Heinz, Principal

Type of Firm
Private Equity Firm

Geographical Preferences
United States Preferences:
All U.S.

Additional Information
Year Founded: 1969
Current Activity Level : Actively seeking new investments

SWICORP CAPITAL PARTNERS SA

King Fahd Road,
Kingdom Tower, 49th Floor
Riyadh, Saudi Arabia 11451
Phone: 96612110737
Fax: 96612110733
E-mail: info@swicorp.com
Website: www.swicorp.com

Other Offices
8, Quai Gustave-Ador
Geneva 6, Switzerland 1211
Phone: 41-22-737-3737
Fax: 41-22-737-3700

Emaar Square, Building 1, Office 503
Burj Dubai District
Dubai, Utd. Arab Em.
Phone: 971-4-314-2300
Fax: 971-4-314-2301

13 rue Mohamed Semani, Hydra BP #539
World Trade Center Association Algeria
Algiers, Algeria

Madinah Road, Saudi Business Center
10th Floor, Office No.1
Jeddah, Saudi Arabia 21456
Phone: 966-2-657-4160
Fax: 966-2-652-6541

Rue du Lac Ontario, Les Berges du Lac
Immeuble Sun
Tunis, Tunisia 1053
Phone: 216-71-960-137
Fax: 216-71-960-237

Management and Staff
David Rey, Managing Director
Mehdi Sethom, Managing Director
Nabil Triki, Managing Director
Simon Rowe, Managing Director

Type of Firm
Bank Affiliated

Association Membership
Gulf Venture Capital Association
Emerging Markets Private Equity Association
European Private Equity and Venture Capital Assoc.
African Venture Capital Association (AVCA)

Project Preferences

Type of Financing Preferred:
Leveraged Buyout
Early Stage
Expansion
Mezzanine
Generalist PE
Public Companies
Later Stage
Management Buyouts
Private Placement
Recapitalizations

Size of Investments Considered:
Min Size of Investment Considered (000s): $15,000
Max Size of Investment Considered (000s): $150,000

Geographical Preferences

International Preferences:
Pakistan
Bahrain
Oman
Tunisia
Jordan
Turkey
Europe
Qatar
Iran
Lebanon
Egypt
Utd. Arab Em.
Algeria
Middle East
Saudi Arabia
Israel
Morocco
Syria
Asia
South Africa
Kuwait
Libya
Africa
Iraq
Sudan

Industry Preferences

In Communications prefer:
Communications and Media
Commercial Communications
Radio & TV Broadcasting
Media and Entertainment

In Medical/Health prefer:
Medical/Health

In Consumer Related prefer:
Consumer
Retail
Food/Beverage
Consumer Products

In Industrial/Energy prefer:
Energy
Oil and Gas Exploration
Oil & Gas Drilling,Explor
Alternative Energy
Coal Related
Energy Conservation Relat
Industrial Products
Materials

In Transportation prefer:
Transportation

In Financial Services prefer:
Financial Services
Real Estate
Financial Services

In Business Serv. prefer:
Media

Additional Information

Year Founded: 1987
Capital Under Management: $1,000,000
Current Activity Level : Actively seeking new investments

SWIFT CAPITAL PARTNERS GMBH

Hopfenmarkt 31
Hamburg, Germany 20457
Phone: 49403060500
Fax: 494030605050
E-mail: contact@scpartners.de
Website: www.scpartners.de

Management and Staff

Hendrik Nitschke, Managing Director

Type of Firm

Private Equity Advisor or Fund of Funds

Association Membership

European Private Equity and Venture Capital Assoc.

Project Preferences

Type of Financing Preferred:
Fund of Funds

Geographical Preferences

International Preferences:
Europe

Additional Information

Year Founded: 1999
Current Activity Level : Actively seeking new investments

SWIFTSURE CAPITAL LLC

1201 Third Avenue, Suite 1601
Seattle, WA USA 98101
E-mail: info@swiftsurecap.com

Management and Staff

Gordon Gardiner, Chief Financial Officer
Scott Wilson, Managing Partner

Type of Firm

Private Equity Firm

Project Preferences

Type of Financing Preferred:
Expansion
Later Stage

Geographical Preferences

United States Preferences:
Northwest

Industry Preferences

In Computer Software prefer:
Software

Additional Information

Year Founded: 2004
Current Activity Level : Actively seeking new investments

SWISS FOUNDERS FUND AG

Kirchlistrasse 50A
St. Gallen, Switzerland
Website: www.sff.vc

Type of Firm

Private Equity Firm

Project Preferences

Type of Financing Preferred:
Early Stage
Seed

Additional Information

Year Founded: 2013
Current Activity Level : Actively seeking new investments

SWISSCOM AG

Alte Tiefenaustrasse 6
Worblaufen, Switzerland 3048
E-mail: media@swisscom.com
Website: www.swisscom.ch

Management and Staff

Dominique Megret, Chief Executive Officer
Mario Rossi, Chief Financial Officer
Urs Schaeppi, Chief Executive Officer

Type of Firm

Corporate PE/Venture

Pratt's Guide to Private Equity & Venture Capital Sources

Association Membership
Swiss Venture Capital Association (SECA)
European Private Equity and Venture Capital Assoc.

Project Preferences

Type of Financing Preferred:
Leveraged Buyout
Early Stage
Later Stage
Seed
Startup

Geographical Preferences

United States Preferences:
All U.S.

International Preferences:
Europe
Switzerland

Industry Preferences

In Communications prefer:
Communications and Media
Telecommunications
Wireless Communications
Media and Entertainment

In Internet Specific prefer:
Internet

In Industrial/Energy prefer:
Environmental Related

In Business Serv. prefer:
Media

Additional Information
Name of Most Recent Fund: Early Stage Fund
Most Recent Fund Was Raised: 05/28/2013
Year Founded: 1998
Capital Under Management: $20,232,000
Current Activity Level : Actively seeking new investments

SWITCH VENTURES LP

2433 Fillmore Street, Suite 380-9447
San Francisco, CA USA 94115
Phone: 6503872027
Website: www.switch.vc

Type of Firm
Private Equity Firm

Project Preferences

Type of Financing Preferred:
Startup

Additional Information
Year Founded: 2015
Current Activity Level : Actively seeking new investments

SWMF LIFE SCIENCE VENTURE FUND, L.P.

241 East Michigan Avenue
Kalamazoo, MI USA 49007
Phone: 2695539588
Fax: 2695536897
Website: www.southwestmichiganfirst.com

Management and Staff
Heather Baker, Vice President
Jennifer Owens, Vice President
Kevin McLeod, Vice President
Tim Terrentine, Vice President

Type of Firm
Government Affiliated Program

Project Preferences

Type of Financing Preferred:
Early Stage
Expansion
Seed

Geographical Preferences

United States Preferences:
Michigan

Industry Preferences

In Manufact. prefer:
Manufacturing

Additional Information
Year Founded: 2006
Capital Under Management: $50,000,000
Current Activity Level : Actively seeking new investments

SYCAMORE PARTNERS LP

9 West 57th Street
31st Floor
New York, NY USA 10019
Phone: 2127968500
E-mail: info@sycamorepartners.com
Website: www.sycamorepartners.com

Management and Staff
Paul Fossati, Managing Director

Type of Firm
Private Equity Firm

Association Membership
Natl Assoc of Investment Cos. (NAIC)

Project Preferences

Type of Financing Preferred:
Leveraged Buyout
Management Buyouts
Acquisition

Industry Preferences

In Consumer Related prefer:
Consumer
Retail

Additional Information
Year Founded: 2011
Capital Under Management: $3,500,000,000
Current Activity Level : Actively seeking new investments

SYCAMORE VENTURES INC

One North Bridge Road, Suite 13-03 High Street Center
Singapore, Singapore 179094
Phone: 6565350112
Fax: 6565325870

Other Offices
3 Columbus Circle, Suite 1402
New York, NY USA 10019
Phone: 212-247-4590
Fax: 212-247-4801

845 Alexander Road
Princeton, NJ USA 08540
Phone: 609-759-8888
Fax: 609-759-8900

19925 Stevens Creek Boulevard
Cupertino, CA USA 95014
Phone: 408-973-7861
Fax: 408-973-7261

Management and Staff
David Lichtenstein, Chief Financial Officer
John Whitman, Managing Partner
Jonas Wang, Partner
Kilin To, Managing Partner
Peter Gerry, Managing Partner
Ravi Singh, Partner
Seth Pierrepont, Partner
Stephen Sun Chiao, Managing Partner

Type of Firm
Private Equity Firm

Project Preferences

Role in Financing:
Prefer role as deal originator but will also invest in deals created by others

Type of Financing Preferred:
Expansion
Later Stage

Size of Investments Considered:
Min Size of Investment Considered (000s): $5,000
Max Size of Investment Considered (000s): $25,000

Pratt's Guide to Private Equity & Venture Capital Sources

Geographical Preferences

United States Preferences:

International Preferences:
India
China

Industry Focus

(% based on actual investment)
Internet Specific	19.7%
Semiconductors/Other Elect.	19.7%
Medical/Health	19.5%
Computer Software and Services	14.0%
Communications and Media	13.1%
Biotechnology	5.9%
Computer Hardware	4.4%
Other Products	2.4%
Consumer Related	1.2%

Additional Information

Year Founded: 1995
Capital Under Management: $550,000,000
Current Activity Level : Actively seeking new investments
Method of Compensation: Return on investment is of primary concern, do not charge fees

SYDNEY SEED FUND MANAGEMENT PTY LTD

60 Clarence Street
Level Two
Sydney, Australia NSW 2000
E-mail: info@sydneyseedfund.com.au
Website: www.sydneyseedfund.com.au

Management and Staff

Ari Klinger, General Partner
Benjamin Chong, General Partner
Garry Visontay, General Partner

Type of Firm

Private Equity Firm

Project Preferences

Type of Financing Preferred:
Early Stage

Geographical Preferences

International Preferences:
Australia

Industry Preferences

In Internet Specific prefer:
Internet

Additional Information

Year Founded: 2013
Capital Under Management: $1,805,950,000
Current Activity Level : Actively seeking new investments

SYDSVENSK ENTREPRENORFOND AB

Scheelevagen 15
Lund, Sweden 223 63
Phone: 46462868757
E-mail: info@ssefond.se
Website: www.ssefond.se

Type of Firm

Incubator/Development Program

Association Membership

Swedish Venture Capital Association (SVCA)

Project Preferences

Type of Financing Preferred:
Early Stage
Seed
Startup

Size of Investments Considered:
Min Size of Investment Considered (000s): $298
Max Size of Investment Considered (000s): $2,983

Geographical Preferences

International Preferences:
Sweden

Industry Preferences

In Biotechnology prefer:
Biotechnology
Industrial Biotechnology
Biosensors

In Medical/Health prefer:
Medical/Health
Medical Diagnostics
Medical Therapeutics

In Industrial/Energy prefer:
Alternative Energy
Energy Conservation Relat

In Other prefer:
Environment Responsible

Additional Information

Year Founded: 2009
Capital Under Management: $21,500,000
Current Activity Level : Actively seeking new investments

SYFREX GMBH

Donaustrasse 19
Hannover, Germany 30519
Phone: 49511165975610
Fax: 49511165975619
E-mail: info@syfrex.de
Website: www.syfrex.de

Management and Staff

Joerg Paulmann, Chief Executive Officer

Type of Firm

Private Equity Firm

Project Preferences

Type of Financing Preferred:
Early Stage
Later Stage
Startup

Geographical Preferences

International Preferences:
Germany

Industry Preferences

In Internet Specific prefer:
Internet
Ecommerce

In Consumer Related prefer:
Retail
Franchises(NEC)

In Financial Services prefer:
Financial Services

In Manufact. prefer:
Manufacturing

Additional Information

Year Founded: 2007
Current Activity Level : Actively seeking new investments

SYMBION CAPITAL I A/S

Symbion Science Park
Fruebjergvej 3
Copenhagen, Denmark 2100
Phone: 4539179999
Fax: 4539179900
E-mail: info@symbion.dk
Website: www.symbion.dk

Other Offices

Ole Maaloes Vej 3
Copenhagen, Denmark 2200
Phone: 4670702980

Njalsgade 106
Copenhagen, Denmark 2300
Phone: 4639179999

Rued Langgaards Vej 7
Copenhagen, Denmark 2300
Phone: 4639179999

Management and Staff

Jakob Nielsen, Chief Financial Officer

Type of Firm

Incubator/Development Program

Project Preferences

Type of Financing Preferred:
Seed

Size of Investments Considered:
Min Size of Investment Considered (000s): $120
Max Size of Investment Considered (000s): $2,400

Geographical Preferences

International Preferences:
Denmark

Industry Preferences

In Communications prefer:
Telecommunications

In Computer Software prefer:
Software

In Internet Specific prefer:
Internet

In Biotechnology prefer:
Biotechnology

In Medical/Health prefer:
Medical/Health

In Financial Services prefer:
Financial Services

Additional Information

Year Founded: 2001
Capital Under Management: $36,700,000
Current Activity Level : Actively seeking new investments

SYMMETRY INVESTMENT ADVISORS INC

374 South Avenue
Glencoe, IL USA 60022
Fax: 847-835-2510
Website: symmetryinvestmentadvisors.com

Other Offices

3460 Garland Street
Wheat Ridge, CO USA 80033
Fax: 303-756-0274

Management and Staff

Larry Wonnacott, Principal
Marshall Greenwald, Principal

Type of Firm

Private Equity Advisor or Fund of Funds

Project Preferences

Type of Financing Preferred:
Fund of Funds of Second

Geographical Preferences

United States Preferences:
Midwest

Industry Preferences

In Financial Services prefer:
Financial Services

Additional Information

Year Founded: 2003
Current Activity Level : Actively seeking new investments

SYMPHONY ALPHA VENTURES LLC

22 East Mifflin Street, Suite 400
Madison, WI USA 53703
Phone: 6082944090
Fax: 6082949321
E-mail: info@symphonycorp.com
Website: www.symphonyalpha.com

Type of Firm

Private Equity Firm

Project Preferences

Type of Financing Preferred:
Early Stage
Startup

Geographical Preferences

United States Preferences:
Midwest

Additional Information

Year Founded: 2014
Current Activity Level : Actively seeking new investments

SYMPHONY ASIA HOLDINGS PTE LTD

Nine Raffles Place,Suite 52-02
Republic Plaza Tower One
Singapore, Singapore 048619
Phone: 6565366177
Fax: 6565366077

Other Offices

Suite 1408, Two Exchange Square
8 Connaught Place
Central, Hong Kong
Phone: 852-2801-6199
Fax: 852-2801-7979

Management and Staff

David LaRue, Partner
Jagdish Parmanand, Vice President
Raj Rajkumar, Partner
Ramon Lo, Partner
Sunil Chandiramani, Partner

Type of Firm

Private Equity Firm

Association Membership

Hong Kong Venture Capital Association (HKVCA)
Singapore Venture Capital Association (SVCA)

Project Preferences

Role in Financing:
Prefer role as deal originator

Type of Financing Preferred:
Core
Leveraged Buyout
Early Stage
Expansion
Generalist PE
Later Stage
Management Buyouts
Acquisition
Special Situation

Geographical Preferences

International Preferences:
Asia Pacific
Vietnam
Indonesia
India
Taiwan
Hong Kong
China
Thailand
Australia
Sri Lanka
Singapore
Malaysia

Industry Preferences

In Medical/Health prefer:
Medical/Health
Health Services
Hospitals/Clinics/Primary
Hospital/Other Instit.

In Consumer Related prefer:
Consumer
Food/Beverage
Consumer Products
Other Restaurants
Hotels and Resorts

In Financial Services prefer:
Real Estate

In Business Serv. prefer:
Media

Additional Information

Year Founded: 1981
Capital Under Management: $870,000,000
Current Activity Level : Actively seeking new investments

SYMPHONY TECHNOLOGY GROUP LLC

2475 Hanover Street
Palo Alto, CA USA 94304
Phone: 6509359500
Fax: 6509359501
Website: www.symphonytg.com

Management and Staff

Bradley MacMillin, Chief Financial Officer
Doug Smith, Principal
J.T. Treadwell, Managing Director
John Treadwell, Managing Director
John Fors, Principal
Mahinder Mathrani, Managing Director
Marshall Haines, Managing Director
Mattias Derynck, Vice President
Pallab Chatterjee, Managing Director
R. Andrew Eckert, Managing Director
Salil Pitroda, Principal
Sarah Mears Kim, Vice President
William Chisholm, Managing Director

Type of Firm
Private Equity Firm

Project Preferences

Type of Financing Preferred:
Leveraged Buyout
Turnaround
Later Stage
Acquisition

Geographical Preferences

United States Preferences:

Industry Preferences

In Computer Software prefer:
Software

In Internet Specific prefer:
Internet

In Business Serv. prefer:
Services

Additional Information

Name of Most Recent Fund: Symphony Technology IV, L.P.
Most Recent Fund Was Raised: 03/27/2012
Year Founded: 2002
Capital Under Management: $870,000,000
Current Activity Level : Actively seeking new investments

SYNCOM MANAGEMENT CO INC

8515 Georgia Avenue, Suite 725
Silver Spring, MD USA 20910
Phone: 3016083203
Fax: 3016083307
E-mail: info@syncom.com
Website: www.syncomfunds.com

Management and Staff

Herb Wilkins, General Partner
Milford Thomas, Partner
Robert Greene, Principal
Stanley Smith, Principal
Terry Jones, Managing Partner

Type of Firm
Private Equity Firm

Association Membership
Natl Assoc of Investment Cos. (NAIC)

Project Preferences

Type of Financing Preferred:
Expansion
Balanced

Size of Investments Considered:
Min Size of Investment Considered (000s): $5,000
Max Size of Investment Considered (000s): $15,000

Geographical Preferences

United States Preferences:

Industry Preferences

In Communications prefer:
Communications and Media
Telecommunications

In Internet Specific prefer:
Internet

In Business Serv. prefer:
Services
Media

Additional Information

Name of Most Recent Fund: Syndicated Communications Venture Partners V, L.P.
Most Recent Fund Was Raised: 10/18/2007
Year Founded: 1977
Current Activity Level : Actively seeking new investments

SYNERGETIC INNOVATION FUND MANAGEMENT CO LTD

Haide Three Road Nanshan Dist
3306-3309 A Block Tianli Centr
Shenzhen, China 518054
Phone: 8675586332495
Fax: 8675586639552
Website: syncapital.com

Type of Firm
Investment Management Firm

Project Preferences

Type of Financing Preferred:
Generalist PE

Geographical Preferences

International Preferences:
China

Additional Information

Year Founded: 2013
Capital Under Management: $156,900,000
Current Activity Level : Actively seeking new investments

SYNERGIA CAPITAL PARTNERS BV

Plesmanstraat 62
Veenendaal, Netherlands 3905 KZ
Phone: 31318553675
Fax: 31318554084
E-mail: office@synergia.nl
Website: www.synergia.nl

Management and Staff

Leo Schenk, Managing Director

Type of Firm
Private Equity Firm

Association Membership
Dutch Venture Capital Associaton (NVP)

Project Preferences

Type of Financing Preferred:
Leveraged Buyout
Expansion
Later Stage
Management Buyouts
Acquisition

Size of Investments Considered:
Min Size of Investment Considered (000s): $2,678
Max Size of Investment Considered (000s): $26,784

Geographical Preferences

International Preferences:
Europe
Netherlands

Industry Preferences

In Computer Hardware prefer:
Computers

In Computer Software prefer:
Software

In Internet Specific prefer:
Internet

In Computer Other prefer:
Computer Related

In Industrial/Energy prefer:
Industrial Products

In Business Serv. prefer:
Services

In Agr/Forestr/Fish prefer:
Agribusiness
Agriculture related

Additional Information
Year Founded: 1999
Capital Under Management: $65,700,000
Current Activity Level : Actively seeking new investments

SYNERGO SGR SPA

Via Campo Lodigiano, 3
Milan, Italy 20122
Phone: 392859111
Fax: 39272094122
E-mail: welcome@synergosgr.it
Website: www.synergosgr.it

Management and Staff
Alessandra Gavirati, Partner
Federica Bacci, Chief Financial Officer
Gianfilippo Cuneo, Principal
Paolo Zapparoli, Chief Executive Officer
Rossano Rufini, Partner

Type of Firm
Private Equity Firm

Project Preferences

Type of Financing Preferred:
Leveraged Buyout

Size of Investments Considered:
Min Size of Investment Considered (000s): $20,297
Max Size of Investment Considered (000s): $67,655

Geographical Preferences

International Preferences:
Italy

Industry Preferences

In Computer Other prefer:
Computer Related

In Medical/Health prefer:
Medical/Health

In Consumer Related prefer:
Consumer Products

In Industrial/Energy prefer:
Energy

Additional Information
Name of Most Recent Fund: Sinergia con Imprenditori
Most Recent Fund Was Raised: 04/13/2005
Year Founded: 2004
Capital Under Management: $426,200,000
Current Activity Level : Actively seeking new investments

SYNERGY CAPITAL MANAGERS

Levl 3, Alexander House,
3 Cybercity
Ebene, Mauritius
E-mail: info@synergycapitalmanagers.com
Website: www.synergycapitalmanagers.com

Other Offices
Levl 3, Alexander House,
3 Cybercity
Ebene, Mauritius

Type of Firm
Private Equity Firm

Project Preferences

Type of Financing Preferred:
Leveraged Buyout
Expansion
Generalist PE
Management Buyouts

Geographical Preferences

International Preferences:
Nigeria
Ghana
Africa

Industry Preferences

In Communications prefer:
Telecommunications

In Consumer Related prefer:
Consumer

In Industrial/Energy prefer:
Energy
Oil & Gas Drilling,Explor

In Financial Services prefer:
Investment Groups

In Business Serv. prefer:
Services

Additional Information
Year Founded: 2010
Capital Under Management: $100,000,000
Current Activity Level : Actively seeking new investments

SYNERGY LIFE SCIENCE PARTNERS LP

Postoffice. Box 22489
San Francisco, CA USA 94122
Phone: 6508547155
Fax: 6503321581
Website: www.synergylsp.com

Management and Staff
Mudit Jain, Managing Director
Richard Stack, Co-Founder
Tracy Pappas, Chief Financial Officer
William Starling, Co-Founder

Type of Firm
Private Equity Firm

Project Preferences

Role in Financing:
Prefer role as deal originator but will also invest in deals created by others

Type of Financing Preferred:
Early Stage

Size of Investments Considered:
Min Size of Investment Considered (000s): $1,000
Max Size of Investment Considered (000s): $15,000

Geographical Preferences

United States Preferences:

Industry Preferences

In Medical/Health prefer:
Medical/Health
Medical Therapeutics
Medical Products

Additional Information
Name of Most Recent Fund: Synergy Life Science Partners, L.P.
Most Recent Fund Was Raised: 12/08/2006
Year Founded: 2006
Capital Under Management: $143,300,000
Current Activity Level : Actively seeking new investments

SYNERGY PARTNERS INTERNATIONAL

545 Middlefield Road, Suite 205
Menlo Park, CA USA 94025
Phone: 6503223475
Fax: 6503263735

Management and Staff
Allan Johnston, Managing Director
Robert Okun, Managing Director

Type of Firm
Private Equity Firm

Project Preferences

Role in Financing:
Will function either as deal originator or investor in deals created by others

Type of Financing Preferred:
Early Stage
Balanced
Later Stage
Seed
Startup

Size of Investments Considered:
Min Size of Investment Considered (000s): $250
Max Size of Investment Considered (000s): $1,000

Geographical Preferences

United States Preferences:

Industry Focus

(% based on actual investment)
Medical/Health   86.5%
Biotechnology   11.8%
Internet Specific   1.5%
Other Products   0.3%

Additional Information

Name of Most Recent Fund: Synergy Ventures II, L.P.
Most Recent Fund Was Raised: 03/10/2006
Year Founded: 1985
Capital Under Management: $15,000,000
Current Activity Level : Actively seeking new investments
Method of Compensation: Return on investment is of primary concern, do not charge fees

SYNETRO GROUP LLC

810 West Washington Boulevard
Chicago, IL USA 60607
Phone: 3123722600
Fax: 3128032035
Website: www.synetro.com

Management and Staff

Russell Faulk, Principal
Simo Kamppari, Principal

Type of Firm

Private Equity Firm

Project Preferences

Role in Financing:
Prefer role as deal originator but will also invest in deals created by others

Type of Financing Preferred:
Leveraged Buyout
Early Stage
Balanced
Seed
Startup
Special Situation

Size of Investments Considered:
Min Size of Investment Considered (000s): $100
Max Size of Investment Considered (000s): $4,000

Geographical Preferences

United States Preferences:
Midwest
Michigan

Industry Preferences

In Computer Software prefer:
Software

In Internet Specific prefer:
Internet
Ecommerce

In Medical/Health prefer:
Medical Products
Health Services

In Consumer Related prefer:
Consumer Products

In Industrial/Energy prefer:
Industrial Products

In Business Serv. prefer:
Services
Distribution
Consulting Services

In Manufact. prefer:
Manufacturing

Additional Information

Year Founded: 2000
Capital Under Management: $75,000,000
Current Activity Level : Actively seeking new investments
Method of Compensation: Return on investment is of primary concern, do not charge fees

SYNO CAPITAL LLC

122 East 42nd Street, Suite 825
New York, NY USA 10168
Website: www.synocapital.com

Management and Staff

Joseph Weilgus, Co-Founder
Justin Xiang, Co-Founder

Type of Firm

Private Equity Firm

Project Preferences

Type of Financing Preferred:
Balanced

Geographical Preferences

United States Preferences:

International Preferences:
Europe
China

Industry Preferences

In Medical/Health prefer:
Health Services

Additional Information

Year Founded: 2015
Current Activity Level : Actively seeking new investments

SYNOVA CAPITAL LLP

Five Welbeck Street
London, United Kingdom W1G 9YQ
Phone: 442034757660
Fax: 442034757661
E-mail: info@synova-capital.com
Website: www.synova-capital.com

Management and Staff

Alex Bowden, Partner
David Menton, Co-Founder
Philip Shapiro, Co-Founder
Shirley Palmer, Chief Financial Officer

Type of Firm

Private Equity Firm

Association Membership

British Venture Capital Association (BVCA)

Project Preferences

Type of Financing Preferred:
Leveraged Buyout
Expansion
Balanced
Management Buyouts

Size of Investments Considered:
Min Size of Investment Considered (000s): $4,684
Max Size of Investment Considered (000s): $31,232

Geographical Preferences

International Preferences:
United Kingdom

Industry Preferences

In Medical/Health prefer:
Medical/Health
Health Services

In Consumer Related prefer:
Consumer
Entertainment and Leisure

In Financial Services prefer:
Financial Services
Financial Services

Additional Information

Name of Most Recent Fund: Synova Capital Fund II
Most Recent Fund Was Raised: 08/22/2013
Year Founded: 2007
Capital Under Management: $324,895,000
Current Activity Level : Actively seeking new investments

SYNTAXIS CAPITAL UNTERNEHMENS UND FINANZIERUNGSBERATUNG GMBH

Wipplingerstrasse 31/1
Vienna, Austria 1010
Phone: 4315134469
Fax: 431513446920
E-mail: office@syntaxis-capital.com
Website: www.syntaxis-capital.com

Other Offices

Wipplingerstrasse 31/1
Vienna, Austria 1010
Phone: 43-1-513-4469
Fax: 43-1-513-4581

Management and Staff

Ben Edwards, Managing Partner
Gabriela Dostal, Founder
Przemek Szczepanski, Partner
Thomas Spring, Partner

Type of Firm

Private Equity Firm

Association Membership

Polish Venture Capital Association (PSIC/PPEA)
African Venture Capital Association (AVCA)

Project Preferences

Type of Financing Preferred:
Leveraged Buyout
Mezzanine
Management Buyouts
Acquisition
Recapitalizations

Geographical Preferences

International Preferences:
Central Europe
Eastern Europe

Industry Preferences

In Communications prefer:
Communications and Media
Radio & TV Broadcasting

In Medical/Health prefer:
Pharmaceuticals

In Transportation prefer:
Transportation

In Financial Services prefer:
Financial Services

In Business Serv. prefer:
Services

Additional Information

Year Founded: 2006
Current Activity Level : Actively seeking new investments

SYNTEGRA CAPITAL INVESTORS LTD

17 Hanover Square, Suite 2.09, Hanover House
London, United Kingdom W1S 1HU
Phone: 442073550840
Fax: 442073550841
E-mail: info@syntegracapital.com
Website: www.syntegracapital.com

Other Offices

2, Via T. Grossi
Milan, Italy 20123
Phone: 39028550151

153 Boulevard Haussmann
Paris, France 75008
Phone: 33612164574

Management and Staff

Marco Ariello, Partner
Michael Hoy, Chief Financial Officer
Patrick Bergot, Partner
Philip Percival, Partner
Philippe Sevin, Partner
Theo Bot, Partner

Type of Firm

Private Equity Firm

Association Membership

French Venture Capital Association (AFIC)
European Private Equity and Venture Capital Assoc.

Project Preferences

Role in Financing:
Will function either as deal originator or investor in deals created by others

Type of Financing Preferred:
Management Buyouts
Acquisition

Geographical Preferences

International Preferences:
Italy
Luxembourg
Switzerland
Belgium
Germany
France

Additional Information

Year Founded: 1997
Capital Under Management: $658,100,000
Current Activity Level : Actively seeking new investments
Method of Compensation: Return on investment is of primary concern, do not charge fees

SZECHENYI TOKEALAP-KEZELO ZRT

Wesselenyi u 28
Budapest, Hungary
Website: www.szta.hu

Type of Firm

Government Affiliated Program

Association Membership

Hungarian Venture Capital Association (HVCA)

Project Preferences

Type of Financing Preferred:
Early Stage
Expansion
Later Stage
Seed
Startup
Special Situation

Geographical Preferences

International Preferences:
Hungary
Europe

Additional Information

Year Founded: 2012
Current Activity Level : Actively seeking new investments

- T -

20 SCOOPS VENTURE CAPITAL GMBH & CO KG

Friedensallee 7-9
Hamburg, Germany 22765
Phone: 4940607711460
E-mail: mail@20scoops.com
Website: www.20scoops.com

Type of Firm
Private Equity Firm

Additional Information
Year Founded: 2016
Current Activity Level : Actively seeking new investments

21 CENTRALE PARTNERS SA

9 avenue Hoche
Paris, France 75008
Phone: 33156883300
Fax: 33156883320
E-mail: info@21centralepartners.com
Website: www.21partners.com

Other Offices

Via G. Felissent, 90
Treviso, Italy 31100
Phone: 39-04-2231-6611
Fax: 39-04-2231-6600

Via Monte Napoleone, 8
Milano, Italy 20121
Phone: 39-2771-213-11
Fax: 39-2771-213-33

Management and Staff
Alain Rougon, Founder
Alessandro Benetton, Managing Partner
Andrea Mazzucato, Principal
Cedric Abitbol, Managing Partner
Cristina David, Principal
Dino Furlan, Managing Partner
Eustache Besancon, Principal
Francois Barbier, Managing Partner
Francois Tranie, Principal
Gerard Pluvinet, Managing Partner
Giovanni Bonandini, Principal
Henry Huyghues Despointes, Managing Partner
Jacques Rossignol, Partner
Marco Monis, Managing Partner
Matteo Chieregato, Principal
Stefano Tanzi, Managing Partner
Stephane Perriquet, Managing Partner

Type of Firm
Bank Affiliated

Association Membership
French Venture Capital Association (AFIC)

Project Preferences

Type of Financing Preferred:
Leveraged Buyout
Management Buyouts
Acquisition

Geographical Preferences

International Preferences:
Italy
Europe
France

Additional Information
Name of Most Recent Fund: 21 Centrale Partners IV
Most Recent Fund Was Raised: 07/17/2009
Year Founded: 1909
Capital Under Management: $668,200,000
Current Activity Level : Actively seeking new investments

21 INVESTIMENTI SGR SPA

Via G. Felissent, 90
Treviso, Italy 31100
Phone: 390422316611
Fax: 390422316600
E-mail: info@21investimenti.it
Website: www.21investimenti.it

Other Offices

22 Grenville Street
St Helier
Jersey - Channel Islands, United Kingdom JE4 8PX
Phone: 44-1534-609-000

Aleje Jerozolimskie 65/79
Warsaw, Poland 00697
Phone: 48226307575
Fax: 48226307576

Via Monte Napoleone 8
Milan, Italy 20121
Phone: 39-2-7712-1311
Fax: 39-2-7712-1333

9 avenue Hoche
Paris, France 75008
Phone: 33156883300
Fax: 33156883320

Management and Staff
Dino Furlan, Managing Partner

Type of Firm
Investment Management Firm

Project Preferences

Role in Financing:
Prefer role as deal originator

Type of Financing Preferred:
Leveraged Buyout
Generalist PE
Public Companies
Later Stage
Recapitalizations

Size of Investments Considered:
Min Size of Investment Considered (000s): $14,601
Max Size of Investment Considered (000s): $43,802

Geographical Preferences

International Preferences:
Italy
Poland
France

Industry Preferences

In Medical/Health prefer:
Health Services

Additional Information
Year Founded: 1992
Capital Under Management: $584,000,000
Current Activity Level : Actively seeking new investments

21ST CENTURY VC INVEST CO LTD

11/A Shennan Road, C
Shenzhen, China 518031
Phone: 86-755-83295527
Fax: 86-755-83295534

Type of Firm
Private Equity Firm

Project Preferences

Type of Financing Preferred:
Balanced

Geographical Preferences

International Preferences:
China

Industry Preferences

In Medical/Health prefer:
Medical/Health

In Industrial/Energy prefer:
Energy Conservation Relat
Materials
Environmental Related

Additional Information
Year Founded: 2000
Current Activity Level : Actively seeking new investments

24HAYMARKET LTD

One-Two Panton Street
London, United Kingdom SW1Y 4DG
E-mail: contact@24haymarket.com
Website: www.24haymarket.com

Management and Staff

Gilbert Chalk, Principal
Paul Tselentis, Chief Executive Officer
Richard Tudor, Principal

Type of Firm
Private Equity Firm

Project Preferences

Type of Financing Preferred:
Early Stage
Seed

Geographical Preferences

International Preferences:
United Kingdom

Industry Preferences

In Biotechnology prefer:
Industrial Biotechnology

In Medical/Health prefer:
Health Services

In Consumer Related prefer:
Consumer

In Business Serv. prefer:
Media

Additional Information
Year Founded: 2017
Current Activity Level : Actively seeking new investments

280 CAPITAL PARTNERS LLC

14573 Big Basin Way
Saratoga, CA USA 95070
Phone: 4088287818
E-mail: info@280capitalpartners.com
Website: www.280capitalpartners.com

Other Offices
Former HQ: 1560 Sunnyvale Saratoga Road, Suite 200
Sunnyvale, CA USA 94087
Phone: 4087189027

Management and Staff
David Martin, Managing Director
David Peterschmidt, Managing Director
Greg Back, Managing Director

Type of Firm
Private Equity Firm

Project Preferences

Type of Financing Preferred:
Leveraged Buyout
Acquisition
Recapitalizations

Additional Information
Year Founded: 2008
Current Activity Level : Actively seeking new investments

2B ANGELS LTD

Medinat Hayehudim 60
Herzelia
Pituach, Israel
Website: www.2b-angels.com

Other Offices
175 Varick Street
New York, NY USA 10013

Type of Firm
Incubator/Development Program

Project Preferences

Type of Financing Preferred:
Early Stage
Seed
Startup

Geographical Preferences

United States Preferences:

International Preferences:
Israel

Industry Preferences

In Communications prefer:
Communications and Media
Wireless Communications

In Internet Specific prefer:
Internet

Additional Information
Year Founded: 2009
Current Activity Level : Actively seeking new investments

2BCAPITAL SA

Aveneda Brigadeiro Faria Lima
3729 Cj. 1 andar
Sao Paulo, Brazil 04542000
Phone: 55 11 3073-62
E-mail: contacto@2b-capital.com
Website: www.2bcapital.com.br

Management and Staff
Manuel De Sousa, Chief Executive Officer

Type of Firm
Private Equity Firm

Association Membership
Brazilian Venture Capital Association (ABCR)

Project Preferences

Type of Financing Preferred:
Leveraged Buyout
Management Buyouts
Acquisition

Industry Preferences

In Consumer Related prefer:
Retail
Education Related

In Financial Services prefer:
Real Estate

Additional Information
Year Founded: 2004
Current Activity Level : Actively seeking new investments

2BPARTNER SOCIEDADE DE CAPITAL DE RISCO SA

Rua de Pitancinhos
apartado 208 - Palmeira
Braga, Portugal 4711-911
Phone: 351253307200
Fax: 351253307210
E-mail: geral@2bpartner.pt
Website: www.2bpartner.com

Type of Firm
Private Equity Firm

Association Membership
Portuguese Venture Capital Association (APCRI)

Project Preferences

Type of Financing Preferred:
Early Stage
Seed
Startup

Geographical Preferences

International Preferences:
Portugal

Industry Preferences

In Consumer Related prefer:
Retail
Hotels and Resorts

Pratt's Guide to Private Equity & Venture Capital Sources

In Industrial/Energy prefer:
Energy
Industrial Products

In Transportation prefer:
Transportation

In Business Serv. prefer:
Services

Additional Information
Year Founded: 2007
Current Activity Level : Actively seeking new investments

2C INVEST SA

236, boulevard Marechal
Leclerc
Toulon, France 83107
Phone: 33494228994
Fax: 33494228994
Website: www.2cinvest.fr

Type of Firm
Private Equity Firm

Project Preferences

Type of Financing Preferred:
Early Stage
Later Stage

Size of Investments Considered:
Min Size of Investment Considered (000s): $65
Max Size of Investment Considered (000s): $195

Geographical Preferences

International Preferences:
Europe
France

Additional Information
Year Founded: 2010
Current Activity Level : Actively seeking new investments

2I CAPITAL ASSET MANAGEMENT CO LTD

IFS Court
28 Cybercity
Ebene, Mauritius
Phone: 2304046000
Fax: 2304681600
E-mail: info@2icapital.com
Website: www.2icapital.com

Other Offices
E-14/19,
1st Floor, Vasant Vihar
New Delhi, India 110057
Phone: 91-11-6565-7267

613 Oxford Towers
139 Airport Road,
Bangalore, India 560 008
Phone: 91-80-4115-1990
Fax: 91-80-4115-1994

Management and Staff
Shailesh Singh, Vice President
Sudhir Kamath, Managing Director

Type of Firm
Private Equity Firm

Project Preferences

Type of Financing Preferred:
Early Stage
Expansion
Mezzanine
Balanced
Later Stage
Seed
Startup

Size of Investments Considered:
Min Size of Investment Considered (000s): $1,000
Max Size of Investment Considered (000s): $20,000

Geographical Preferences

United States Preferences:

International Preferences:
India
Europe
Asia

Industry Preferences

In Communications prefer:
Communications and Media
Telecommunications

In Computer Software prefer:
Software

In Computer Other prefer:
Computer Related

In Semiconductor/Electr prefer:
Electronics

In Biotechnology prefer:
Biotechnology

In Medical/Health prefer:
Medical/Health
Health Services
Pharmaceuticals

In Consumer Related prefer:
Retail

In Business Serv. prefer:
Distribution

In Agr/Forestr/Fish prefer:
Agribusiness

Additional Information
Year Founded: 2000
Current Activity Level : Actively seeking new investments

2SV CAPITAL LLC

400 TradeCenter
100 Sylvan Road, Suite 5900
Woburn, MA USA 01801
Phone: 6174449430
E-mail: info@2svcapital.com
Website: www.2svcapital.com

Type of Firm
Private Equity Firm

Project Preferences

Type of Financing Preferred:
Leveraged Buyout
Acquisition
Recapitalizations

Additional Information
Year Founded: 2008
Current Activity Level : Actively seeking new investments

2X CONSUMER PRODUCTS GROWTH PARTNERS L P

205 West Randolph Street, Suite 1830
Chicago, IL USA 60606
Phone: 312-357-1800
Fax: 312-873-4509
E-mail: info@2xpartners.com

Management and Staff
Andrew Whitman, Managing Partner
David Bauserman, Partner
Gary Sebek, Managing Partner
Sharon Kieffer, Managing Partner

Type of Firm
Private Equity Firm

Project Preferences

Type of Financing Preferred:
Later Stage

Geographical Preferences

United States Preferences:
All U.S.

Industry Preferences

In Consumer Related prefer:
Food/Beverage
Consumer Products
Consumer Services

Additional Information

Name of Most Recent Fund: 2x Consumer Products Growth Partners II, L.P.
Most Recent Fund Was Raised: 09/11/2013
Year Founded: 2007
Capital Under Management: $33,050,000
Current Activity Level : Actively seeking new investments

3 DEGREES ASSET MANAGEMENT PTE LTD

600 North Bridge Road 08-08
Parkview Square
Singapore, Singapore 188778
Phone: 65-6750-2260
Fax: 65-6534-5157
E-mail: info@3degrees.com.sg
Website: www.theasiandebtfund.com

Management and Staff

Akanksha Sagar, Principal
Jeffrey Tolk, Principal

Type of Firm

Private Equity Firm

Project Preferences

Type of Financing Preferred:
Turnaround
Special Situation
Distressed Debt
Recapitalizations

Geographical Preferences

International Preferences:
India
Asia

Additional Information

Year Founded: 2002
Current Activity Level : Actively seeking new investments

3 RIVERS CAPITAL

437 Grant Street, Suite 500
Pittsburgh, PA USA 15219
Phone: 4127652491
E-mail: info@3riverscap.com
Website: 3riverscap.com

Type of Firm

Private Equity Firm

Project Preferences

Type of Financing Preferred:
Leveraged Buyout
Acquisition
Recapitalizations

Geographical Preferences

United States Preferences:
Mid Atlantic
Midwest

Industry Preferences

In Business Serv. prefer:
Services

In Manufact. prefer:
Manufacturing

Additional Information

Year Founded: 2005
Current Activity Level : Actively seeking new investments

32 DEGREES CAPITAL

635 8th Avenue Southwest, Suite 650
Calgary, Canada T2P 3M3
Phone: 4036951069
Fax: 4032338040
E-mail: info@32degrees.ca
Website: www.32degrees.ca

Management and Staff

Art Robinson, Partner
Larry Evans, Managing Partner
Mitch Putnam, Managing Partner
Trent Baker, Managing Partner

Type of Firm

Private Equity Firm

Association Membership

Canadian Venture Capital Association

Project Preferences

Type of Financing Preferred:
Leveraged Buyout
Early Stage
Balanced
Management Buyouts
Acquisition

Geographical Preferences

United States Preferences:
All U.S.

Canadian Preferences:
Alberta
All Canada

International Preferences:
Rest of World

Industry Preferences

In Industrial/Energy prefer:
Energy
Oil and Gas Exploration
Oil & Gas Drilling,Explor
Alternative Energy

In Manufact. prefer:
Manufacturing

Additional Information

Name of Most Recent Fund: 32 Degrees Diversified Energy Fund II LP
Most Recent Fund Was Raised: 09/23/2013
Year Founded: 2004
Capital Under Management: $246,022,000
Current Activity Level : Actively seeking new investments

3311 VENTURES LLC

6255 Sunset Boulevard
Hollywood, CA USA 90028
Website: www.3311ventures.com

Type of Firm

Private Equity Firm

Project Preferences

Type of Financing Preferred:
Early Stage

Industry Preferences

In Internet Specific prefer:
Ecommerce

In Business Serv. prefer:
Media

Additional Information

Year Founded: 2016
Current Activity Level : Actively seeking new investments

354 PARTNERS LLC

1133 Broadway
New York, NY USA 10010
Phone: 6467067210
Fax: 6467067560
Website: www.354partners.com

Management and Staff

Emmanuel Tesone, Managing Partner
Matthew Holmes, Managing Partner

Type of Firm

Private Equity Firm

Project Preferences

Type of Financing Preferred:
Leveraged Buyout
Acquisition

Geographical Preferences

United States Preferences:
North America

Pratt's Guide to Private Equity & Venture Capital Sources

Industry Preferences

In Internet Specific prefer:
Internet
Ecommerce
Web Aggregation/Portals

Additional Information
Name of Most Recent Fund: 354 Online Holdings, L.P.
Most Recent Fund Was Raised: 03/05/2012
Year Founded: 2012
Capital Under Management: $9,300,000
Current Activity Level : Actively seeking new investments

360 CAPITAL MANAGEMENT SA

38, Avenue de la Faiencerie
Luxembourg, Luxembourg 1510
Phone: 352621294505
E-mail: info@360capitalpartners.com

Other Offices
Via Brisa 3
Milan, Italy 20123
Phone: 39-02-3656-0950

68 Boulevard De Sebastopol
Paris, France 75003
Phone: 33-1-7118-2912

Management and Staff
Diana Saraceni, General Partner
Emanuele Levi, General Partner
Fausto Boni, General Partner
Francois Tison, General Partner
Laurent Laffy, Venture Partner
Nicolas Carbonari, Venture Partner

Type of Firm
Private Equity Firm

Association Membership
French Venture Capital Association (AFIC)
European Private Equity and Venture Capital Assoc.

Project Preferences

Type of Financing Preferred:
Early Stage
Public Companies
Later Stage
Seed
Strategic Alliances
Startup

Size of Investments Considered:
Min Size of Investment Considered (000s): $1,200
Max Size of Investment Considered (000s): $5,998

Geographical Preferences

International Preferences:
Italy
Europe
France

Industry Preferences

In Communications prefer:
Wireless Communications

In Medical/Health prefer:
Medical/Health
Medical Diagnostics
Diagnostic Services

In Consumer Related prefer:
Retail

In Industrial/Energy prefer:
Energy

In Financial Services prefer:
Financial Services

In Other prefer:
Environment Responsible

Additional Information
Year Founded: 1997
Capital Under Management: $38,160,000
Current Activity Level : Actively seeking new investments

360 VENTURES INC

890 West Pender Street, Suite 440
Vancouver , Canada V6C 1J9
Phone: 7788883892
Website: 360capital.ca

Type of Firm
Private Equity Firm

Industry Preferences

In Communications prefer:
Communications and Media

In Industrial/Energy prefer:
Environmental Related

In Business Serv. prefer:
Media

In Manufact. prefer:
Manufacturing

Additional Information
Year Founded: 2016
Current Activity Level : Actively seeking new investments

3A VENTURE SAS

8, Rue Worth
Suresnes, France 92150
Phone: 33142046539

Type of Firm
Government Affiliated Program

Project Preferences

Type of Financing Preferred:
Early Stage
Expansion
Later Stage
Seed

Size of Investments Considered:
Min Size of Investment Considered (000s): $33
Max Size of Investment Considered (000s): $108

Geographical Preferences

International Preferences:
France

Additional Information
Year Founded: 2005
Current Activity Level : Actively seeking new investments

3G CAPITAL INC

600 Third Avenue
37 Floor
New York, NY USA 10016
Phone: 2128936727
E-mail: ir@3g-capital.com
Website: www.3g-capital.com

Other Offices
Rua Humaita
275/9 andar
Rio de Janeiro, Brazil 22261-001
Phone: 552135156227

Management and Staff
Alexandre Behring, Co-Founder
Anuroop Duggal, Partner
Bernardo Piquet, Partner
Bernardo Hees, Partner
Carlos Sicupira, Co-Founder
Claudio Chonchol Bahbout, Partner
Daniel Dreyfus, Partner
Daniel Schwartz, Partner
Jorge Lemann, Co-Founder
Joshua Klivan, Partner
Marcel Telles, Co-Founder
Marcos Romaneiro, Partner
Munir Javeri, Partner
Paulo Basilio, Partner
Pedro Drevon, Partner
Roberto Moses Thompson Motta, Co-Founder

Type of Firm
Private Equity Firm

Project Preferences

Type of Financing Preferred:
Leveraged Buyout
Acquisition
Special Situation

Industry Preferences

In Consumer Related prefer:
Consumer
Retail

Additional Information

Year Founded: 2004
Capital Under Management: $36,990,000
Current Activity Level : Actively seeking new investments

3I

375 Park Avenue
Seagram Building, Suite 3001
New York, NY USA 10152
Phone: 2128481400
Fax: 2128481401
E-mail: eastcoast@3i.com
Website: www.3i.com

Other Offices

16 Palace Street
London, United Kingdom SW1E5JD
Phone: 442079753131
Fax: 442079753232

Management and Staff

Andrew Olinick, Principal
Andrew Bellis, Managing Director
Crevan O Grady, Partner
Donald McDonough, Principal
Jim Rutherfurd, Partner
Kenneth Hanau, Managing Partner
Richard Relyea, Principal
Sundip Murthy, Principal

Type of Firm

Private Equity Firm

Association Membership

Singapore Venture Capital Association (SVCA)

Project Preferences

Role in Financing:
Will function either as deal originator or investor in deals created by others

Type of Financing Preferred:
Leveraged Buyout
Early Stage
Expansion
Balanced
Later Stage
Acquisition

Geographical Preferences

United States Preferences:

International Preferences:
Europe
Asia

Industry Focus

(% based on actual investment)
Other Products	22.7%
Internet Specific	17.5%
Industrial/Energy	14.4%
Computer Software and Services	13.8%
Semiconductors/Other Elect.	9.1%
Communications and Media	9.0%
Medical/Health	7.6%
Computer Hardware	2.2%
Consumer Related	2.1%
Biotechnology	1.5%

Additional Information

Year Founded: 1965
Capital Under Management: $601,000,000
Current Activity Level : Actively seeking new investments
Method of Compensation: Return on investment is of primary concern, do not charge fees

3I GROUP PLC

16 Palace Street
London, United Kingdom SW1E 5JD
Phone: 442079753456
Fax: 442079280058
Website: www.3i.com

Other Offices

Engelbrektsplan One
T-House
Stockholm, Sweden 11434
Phone: 46850610100
Fax: 46850621130

Calle Ruiz de Alarcon
n 12 - 2 - B
Madrid, Spain 28014
Phone: 34-91-521-4419
Fax: 34-91-521-9819

400 Madison Avenue
9th floor
NEW YORK, NY USA 10017
Phone: 212-848-1400
Fax: 212-848-1401

Landstrasse 2-4
Bockenheimer
Frankfurt, Germany 60306
Phone: 49-69-710-0000
Fax: 49-69-710-000113

3 rue Paul Cezanne
Paris, France 75008
Phone: 33-1-7315-1100

3/F, Nicholas Piramal Twr, Peninsula Prk
Ganpatrao Kadam Marg, Lower Parel (West)
Mumbai, India 400013
Phone: 91-22-6652-3131
Fax: 91-22-6652-3141

Diplomatic Enclave, Suite 1751, ITC Maurya
New Delhi, India 110021
Phone: 91-11-4166-8830
Fax: 91-11-4166-8831

No.79 Jianguo Road, Chaoyang District
Unit 01, 25 F, Tower 2, China Central Pl
Beijing, China 100025
Phone: 86-10-6598-1288
Fax: 86-10-8588-8980

Cornelis Schuytstraat 72
Amsterdam, Netherlands 1071 JL
Phone: 31-20-3057-444
Fax: 31-20-3057-455

Rua Iguatemi Street 151
28th Floor Spazio Faria Lima Itaim Bibi
Sao Paolo, Brazil 01451-011
Phone: 551120505656
Fax: 551120505657

Management and Staff

Agustin Pla, Partner
Albert Xu, Partner
Andrew Olinick, Principal
Anil Kohli, Partner
Anna Cheung, Partner
Crevan O Grady, Partner
David Whileman, Partner
Deepak Bagla, Partner
Denis Ribon, Partner
Fredrik Karlsson, Partner
Girish Baliga, Partner
Ian Lobley, Partner
Jenny Dunstan, Partner
Jim Rutherfurd, Partner
Ken Beaty, Partner
Ken Hanau, Managing Partner
Maite Ballester, Partner
Marcelo di Lorenzo, Partner
Mattias Eklund, Partner
Neil King, Partner
Neil Johnson, Partner
Olivier Le Gall, Partner
Paul Su, Managing Director
Peter Wirtz, Managing Director
Peter Goody, Partner
Pieter De Jong, Managing Director
Remi Carnimolla, Partner
Richard Relyea, Principal
Robert Van Goethem, Partner
Samir Palod, Partner
Saurabh Shah, Partner
Simon Borrows, Chief Executive Officer
Stephen Halliwell, Chief Financial Officer
Stuart McMinnies, Partner
Sundip Murthy, Principal
Tomas Ekman, Partner

Ulf Von Haacke, Managing Director

Type of Firm
Private Equity Firm

Association Membership
Finnish Venture Capital Association (FVCA)
Hong Kong Venture Capital Association (HKVCA)
China Venture Capital Association
British Venture Capital Association (BVCA)
French Venture Capital Association (AFIC)
Hungarian Venture Capital Association (HVCA)
Belgium Venturing Association
Danish Venture Capital Association (DVCA)
German Venture Capital Association (BVK)
Norwegian Venture Capital Association
Swedish Venture Capital Association (SVCA)
Dutch Venture Capital Associaton (NVP)
European Private Equity and Venture Capital Assoc.
Spanish Venture Capital Association (ASCRI)

Project Preferences

Role in Financing:
Prefer role as deal originator but will also invest in deals created by others

Type of Financing Preferred:
Leveraged Buyout
Mezzanine
Later Stage
Other
Management Buyouts
Acquisition

Geographical Preferences

United States Preferences:
North America

International Preferences:
Asia Pacific
India
Sweden
United Kingdom
Europe
Netherlands
China
Brazil
Spain
Asia
Finland
Singapore
Germany
Denmark
France

Industry Focus
(% based on actual investment)

Other Products	23.2%
Industrial/Energy	14.9%
Consumer Related	13.7%
Medical/Health	12.4%
Communications and Media	11.7%
Internet Specific	8.6%
Computer Software and Services	7.3%
Semiconductors/Other Elect.	3.8%
Biotechnology	3.4%
Computer Hardware	1.1%

Additional Information
Name of Most Recent Fund: 3i Growth Fund
Most Recent Fund Was Raised: 03/25/2010
Year Founded: 1945
Capital Under Management: $21,667,100,000
Current Activity Level : Actively seeking new investments
Method of Compensation: Return on invest. most important, but chg. closing fees, service fees, etc.

3I INFRASTRUCTURE PLC

22 Grenville Street
St. Helier
Jersey, Channel Islands JE4 8PX
Phone: 44-1534711444
Fax: 44-1534609333
Website: www.3i-infrastructure.com

Management and Staff
Cressida Hogg, Managing Partner
Deepak Bagla, Partner
Girish Baliga, Partner
Neil King, Partner
Phil White, Partner
Samir Palod, Partner
Stephen Halliwell, Chief Financial Officer

Type of Firm
Private Equity Firm

Project Preferences

Type of Financing Preferred:
Balanced

Geographical Preferences

United States Preferences:
All U.S.

International Preferences:
Europe
Asia

Additional Information
Year Founded: 2007
Current Activity Level : Actively seeking new investments

3ONE4 CAPITAL.

70 Millers Road
Third Floor, Grace Towers
Bengaluru, India
E-mail: hello@3one4capital.com
Website: www.3one4capital.com

Type of Firm
Private Equity Firm

Project Preferences

Type of Financing Preferred:
Early Stage
Seed

Geographical Preferences

International Preferences:
India

Additional Information
Year Founded: 2016
Current Activity Level : Actively seeking new investments

3TS CAPITAL PARTNERS, LTD.

Americka 23
Prague, Czech Republic 120 00
Phone: 420225990487
Fax: 420225990857
E-mail: info@3tscapital.com
Website: www.3tscapital.com

Other Offices
ul. Sienna 72/6
Warsaw, Poland 00-833
Phone: 48-22-890-2215
Fax: 48-22-890-2215

Rotenturmstrasse 12
Vienna, Austria 1010
Phone: 43-1-229-7296

Brassai Samuel u. 16
Budapest, Hungary H-1126
Phone: 36-1-393-5060
Fax: 36-1-393-5069

50-52 Putul lui Zamfir St, Et. 2, Ap. 5
Bucharest, Romania RO-011367
Phone: 40-3-1100-0259
Fax: 40-3-1100-0260

Management and Staff
Daniel Lynch, Managing Partner
Pekka Santeri Maki, Managing Director

Type of Firm
Bank Affiliated

Association Membership
Austrian PE and Venture Capital Association (AVCO)
Hungarian Venture Capital Association (HVCA)
Czech Venture Capital Association (CVCA)
Polish Venture Capital Association (PSIC/PPEA)
European Private Equity and Venture Capital Assoc.

Project Preferences

Type of Financing Preferred:
Leveraged Buyout
Early Stage
Expansion
Generalist PE
Balanced
Later Stage
Seed
Acquisition
Startup

Size of Investments Considered:
Min Size of Investment Considered (000s): $500
Max Size of Investment Considered (000s): $5,000

Geographical Preferences

International Preferences:
Slovenia
Hungary
Slovak Repub.
Turkey
Central Europe
Europe
Czech Republic
Poland
Austria
Eastern Europe
Croatia
Ukraine
Bulgaria
Estonia
Romania
Latvia
Lithuania

Industry Preferences

In Communications prefer:
Communications and Media
Telecommunications
Media and Entertainment

In Computer Software prefer:
Software

In Internet Specific prefer:
Internet

In Computer Other prefer:
Computer Related

In Semiconductor/Electr prefer:
Electronics

In Medical/Health prefer:
Health Services

In Industrial/Energy prefer:
Energy
Environmental Related

In Financial Services prefer:
Financial Services

In Business Serv. prefer:
Media

Additional Information
Name of Most Recent Fund: 3TS Central European Fund II
Most Recent Fund Was Raised: 05/17/2005
Year Founded: 2000
Capital Under Management: $224,300,000
Current Activity Level : Actively seeking new investments

3W PARTNERS
1 Connaught Place Central, Hon
Jardine House, 1 Connaught Pla
Hong Kong, Hong Kong
Website: www.3wpcap.com

Type of Firm
Private Equity Firm

Project Preferences

Type of Financing Preferred:
Balanced

Geographical Preferences

International Preferences:
China

Industry Preferences

In Medical/Health prefer:
Medical/Health

In Consumer Related prefer:
Consumer Services

In Financial Services prefer:
Financial Services

In Manufact. prefer:
Manufacturing

Additional Information
Year Founded: 2013
Current Activity Level : Actively seeking new investments

T & M MANAGEMENT SERVICES LTD
5500 Parkwood Way
Richmond, Canada V6V 2M4
Phone: 6042701108
Fax: 6042704168
E-mail: info@tandmcompanies.com
Website: www.tandmcompanies.com

Management and Staff
George Melville, Co-Founder
Jim Treliving, Co-Founder
Jordan Melville, President
Jordan Holm, Vice President

Type of Firm
Private Equity Firm

Project Preferences

Type of Financing Preferred:
Leveraged Buyout
Acquisition

Additional Information
Year Founded: 1973
Current Activity Level : Actively seeking new investments

T S P P SA
32 Avenue Hedi Karray
Centre Urbain Nord
Tunis, Tunisia 1082
Phone: 21671716550
Fax: 21671719233
E-mail: stusid@gnet.tn

Type of Firm
Private Equity Firm

Project Preferences

Type of Financing Preferred:
Early Stage
Later Stage

Geographical Preferences

International Preferences:
Tunisia
Africa

Additional Information
Year Founded: 2004
Current Activity Level : Actively seeking new investments

T SQUARED CAPITAL LLC
1325 Sixth Avenue
Floor 27
New York, NY USA 10019
Phone: 212-763-8615
Fax: 212-671-1403
E-mail: investor@tsquaredpartners.com
Website: www.tsquaredpartners.com

Management and Staff
Mark Jensen, Co-Founder
Thomas Sauve, Co-Founder

Type of Firm
Private Equity Firm

2081

Project Preferences

Type of Financing Preferred:
Early Stage
Balanced
Public Companies

Size of Investments Considered:
Min Size of Investment Considered (000s): $2,500
Max Size of Investment Considered (000s): $4,000

Industry Preferences

In Biotechnology prefer:
Biotechnology

Additional Information

Year Founded: 2009
Current Activity Level : Actively seeking new investments

T. ROWE PRICE THRESHOLD PARTNERSHIPS

100 East Pratt Street
Baltimore, MD USA 21202
Phone: 410-345-2000
Fax: 410-345-2800
Website: https://www3.troweprice.com/usis/corporate/en/home

Other Offices

Yamato Seimei Building, 12th Floor
1-7, Uchisaiwai-cho 1-chome
Chiyoda-ku, Tokyo , Japan 100-0011
Phone: 81-3-3504-1863

4515 Painters Mill Road
Owings Mills, MD USA

1 Connaught Place
8/F, Rm. 802-809, Jardine House
Central, Hong Kong

333 Bush Street, Suite 2550
San Francisco, CA USA

4211 West Boy Scout Boulevard
TAMPA, FL USA 33607
Phone: 800-225-5132

Strawinskylaan 3051
Atrium Gebouw
Amsterdam, Netherlands 1077 ZX
Phone: 31-20-301-2114

ATEAC Paris Champs Elysees
90, avenue de Champs Elysees
Paris, France 75008

Lautrupsgade 7
1st Floor
Copenhagen, Denmark 2100
Phone: 45-33-360-500

60 Queen Victoria Street
London, United Kingdom EC4N 4TZ
Phone: 44-20-7651-8200

No. 290 Orchard Road
#14-04 Paragon
Singapore, Singapore 238859

2260 Briargate Parkway
COLORADO SPRINGS, CO USA 80920
Phone: 800-225-5132

Stureplan 4c
4th Floor
Stockholm, Sweden 114 35
Phone: 46-8-463-3212

Type of Firm

Investment Management Firm

Project Preferences

Role in Financing:
Prefer role as deal originator but will also invest in deals created by others

Type of Financing Preferred:
Leveraged Buyout
Expansion
Mezzanine
Turnaround
Later Stage
Special Situation
Distressed Debt

Size of Investments Considered:
Min Size of Investment Considered (000s): $3,000
Max Size of Investment Considered (000s): $5,000

Geographical Preferences

United States Preferences:
All U.S.

Industry Focus

(% based on actual investment)
Internet Specific	42.8%
Computer Software and Services	25.6%
Biotechnology	7.6%
Other Products	6.8%
Computer Hardware	4.8%
Consumer Related	4.3%
Medical/Health	4.0%
Semiconductors/Other Elect.	1.9%
Communications and Media	1.2%
Industrial/Energy	0.9%

Additional Information

Name of Most Recent Fund: T. Rowe Price Recovery Fund II
Most Recent Fund Was Raised: 05/31/1997
Year Founded: 1983
Capital Under Management: $245,000,000
Current Activity Level : Actively seeking new investments
Method of Compensation: Return on investment is of primary concern, do not charge fees

TA ASSOCIATES MANAGEMENT LP

200 Clarendon Street
John Hancock Tower, 56/F
Boston, MA USA 02116
Phone: 6175746700
Fax: 6175746728
E-mail: info@ta.com
Website: www.ta.com

Other Offices

64 Willow Place, Suite 100
Menlo Park, CA USA 94025
Phone: 6504732200
Fax: 6504732235

One Exchange Square, 16th Floor
8 Connaught Place
Central, Hong Kong
Phone: 85236566300
Fax: 85236566301

25 Knightsbridge
2nd Floor
London, United Kingdom SW1X 7RZ
Phone: 442078230200
Fax: 442078230201

Dr. Annie Besant Road, Avantha House
Crompton Greaves Bldg, 12/F, Worli
Mumbai, India 400 030
Phone: 912261443100
Fax: 912261443101

Management and Staff

A. Bruce Johnston, Managing Director
Ajit Nedungadi, Managing Director
Brian Conway, Managing Director
Clara Jackson, Vice President
J. Morgan Seigler, Principal
Jeffrey Chambers, Managing Director
Jeffrey Barber, Managing Director
Jennifer Mulloy, Managing Director
Jonathan Goldstein, Managing Director
Jonathan Meeks, Managing Director
Kenneth Schiciano, Managing Director
Kurt Jaggers, Managing Director
Lisa Harris Millhauser, Vice President
Michael Wilson, Managing Director
Michael Berk, Managing Director
Richard Tadler, Managing Director
Roger Kafker, Managing Director
Todd Crockett, Managing Director

Type of Firm

Private Equity Firm

Association Membership

New England Venture Capital Association
Private Equity Council (PEC)

Project Preferences

Role in Financing:
Prefer role as deal originator but will also invest in deals created by others

Type of Financing Preferred:
Leveraged Buyout
Mezzanine
Generalist PE
Later Stage
Management Buyouts
Acquisition
Recapitalizations

Geographical Preferences

United States Preferences:
North America

International Preferences:
India
Europe
Australia
Asia

Industry Focus

(% based on actual investment)

Computer Software and Services	23.7%
Communications and Media	21.3%
Medical/Health	13.2%
Other Products	12.7%
Internet Specific	11.6%
Consumer Related	6.0%
Semiconductors/Other Elect.	4.1%
Industrial/Energy	2.7%
Computer Hardware	2.4%
Biotechnology	2.2%

Additional Information

Name of Most Recent Fund: TA Strategic Partners Fund III, L.P.
Most Recent Fund Was Raised: 04/03/2012
Year Founded: 1968
Capital Under Management: $10,792,000,000
Current Activity Level : Actively seeking new investments
Method of Compensation: Return on investment is of primary concern, do not charge fees

TA VENTURE

72, Velyka Vasylkivska Street
Olimpiysky Bus. Ctr,Ofc. 1,9F
Kyiv, Ukraine 03150
Phone: 38445937777
Fax: 38445937280
E-mail: info@taventure.com
Website: www.taventure.com

Management and Staff

Denis Dovgopoly, Founder
Igor Semenov, Venture Partner
Teodoro D Ambrosio, Venture Partner
Viktoriya Tigipko, Managing Director

Type of Firm
Private Equity Firm

Project Preferences

Type of Financing Preferred:
Early Stage
Seed
Startup

Geographical Preferences

United States Preferences:
All U.S.

International Preferences:
Europe
Ukraine
Russia

Industry Preferences

In Computer Software prefer:
Software
Applications Software

Additional Information

Year Founded: 2010
Current Activity Level : Actively seeking new investments

TACTIC CAPITAL (PTY) LTD

416 West Avenue
Unit D, West On Oxford
Ferndale, South Africa 2160
Phone: 27861822842
Fax: 27117931225
E-mail: info@tactic.co.za
Website: www.tactic.co.za

Management and Staff

Gerbrand Bothma, Chief Executive Officer

Type of Firm
Private Equity Firm

Project Preferences

Type of Financing Preferred:
Leveraged Buyout
Early Stage
Expansion
Generalist PE
Balanced
Later Stage
Acquisition

Geographical Preferences

International Preferences:
South Africa

Additional Information

Year Founded: 2003
Current Activity Level : Actively seeking new investments

TACTICO, INC.

481 Viger West, Suite 200
Montreal, Canada H2Z 1G6
E-mail: info@tactico.com
Website: www.tactico.com

Other Offices

31681 Camino Capistrano, Suite 102
San Juan Capistrano, CA USA 92675

Type of Firm
Investment Management Firm

Project Preferences

Type of Financing Preferred:
Early Stage
Seed
Startup

Geographical Preferences

Canadian Preferences:
All Canada
Quebec

Additional Information

Year Founded: 2013
Current Activity Level : Actively seeking new investments

TAG ENERGY SOLUTIONS LTD

1155 Dairy Ashford Street, Suite 806
Houston, TX USA 77079
Phone: 7136212693

Management and Staff

Brenda Heartfield, President
Neil Adamson, Chief Financial Officer

Type of Firm
Private Equity Firm

Additional Information

Year Founded: 2009
Current Activity Level : Actively seeking new investments

TAGLICH PRIVATE EQUITY LLC

275 Madison Avenue, Suite 1618
New York, NY USA 10016
Phone: 2126610936
Website: www.taglichpe.com

Type of Firm
Investment Management Firm

Pratt's Guide to Private Equity & Venture Capital Sources

Project Preferences

Type of Financing Preferred:
Leveraged Buyout
Expansion
Management Buyouts
Acquisition
Recapitalizations

Geographical Preferences

United States Preferences:

Industry Preferences

In Business Serv. prefer:
Services
Distribution

In Manufact. prefer:
Manufacturing

Additional Information
Year Founded: 2001
Current Activity Level : Actively seeking new investments

TAGUA CAPITAL

Calle Velazquez 16
3 Derecha
Madrid, Spain 28001
Phone: 34915750075
E-mail: info@taguacapital.com
Website: www.taguacapital.com

Management and Staff
Pau Bermudez-Canete, Managing Partner

Type of Firm
Private Equity Firm

Project Preferences

Type of Financing Preferred:
Early Stage
Later Stage
Seed
Startup

Geographical Preferences

International Preferences:
Latin America
Mexico
Brazil
Spain

Industry Preferences

In Communications prefer:
Commercial Communications

In Biotechnology prefer:
Biotechnology

In Medical/Health prefer:
Medical/Health

In Industrial/Energy prefer:
Environmental Related

Additional Information
Year Founded: 2011
Current Activity Level : Actively seeking new investments

TAHOMA ADVISORS INC

2130 Mesa Drive
Boulder, CO USA 80304
Phone: 3038090787

Management and Staff
John Ives, Founder

Type of Firm
Private Equity Firm

Project Preferences

Type of Financing Preferred:
Seed
Startup

Geographical Preferences

United States Preferences:
All U.S.

Additional Information
Year Founded: 2013
Current Activity Level : Actively seeking new investments

TAILWIND CAPITAL PARTNERS LP

485 Lexington Avenue
New York, NY USA 10017
Phone: 2122713800
Fax: 2122714911
Website: www.tailwind.com

Management and Staff
Adam Stulberger, Partner
Andrew Mayer, Vice President
David Bauman, Managing Director
Frank Sica, Partner
Geoffrey Raker, Partner
James Hoch, Partner
Jeffrey Calhoun, Partner
Jonathan Levy, Vice President
Lawrence Sorrel, Co-Founder
Melanie Harris, Vice President

Type of Firm
Private Equity Firm

Project Preferences

Role in Financing:
Prefer role as deal originator but will also invest in deals created by others

Type of Financing Preferred:
Leveraged Buyout

Industry Preferences

In Communications prefer:
Communications and Media

In Medical/Health prefer:
Medical/Health

In Business Serv. prefer:
Services

Additional Information
Year Founded: 2003
Capital Under Management: $1,200,000,000
Current Activity Level : Actively seeking new investments
Method of Compensation: Return on invest. most important, but chg. closing fees, service fees, etc.

TAISHAN INVEST AG

Dufourstrasse 121
Saint Gallen, Switzerland 9001
Phone: 41447838034
Fax: 41447838040
E-mail: contact@taishanangel.com
Website: www.taishan-invest.com

Other Offices
Chaowai Avenue A 6
Room 1805, C Building
Beijing, China 10020
Phone: 86-10-59071909
Fax: 86-10-59073119

Management and Staff
Jackie Liang Chen, Partner
Raymond Lei Yang, Partner
Sebastian Kuebler, Partner

Type of Firm
Angel Group

Project Preferences

Type of Financing Preferred:
Early Stage
Balanced
Seed
Startup

Size of Investments Considered:
Min Size of Investment Considered (000s): $50
Max Size of Investment Considered (000s): $500

Geographical Preferences

International Preferences:
Europe
China

Industry Preferences

In Communications prefer:
Communications and Media
Telecommunications
Wireless Communications
Data Communications
Entertainment

In Internet Specific prefer:
E-Commerce Technology
Ecommerce
Web Aggregration/Portals

In Semiconductor/Electr prefer:
Electronics
Micro-Processing

In Consumer Related prefer:
Consumer

In Business Serv. prefer:
Media

Additional Information
Year Founded: 2008
Current Activity Level : Actively seeking new investments

TAITO CAPITAL PARTNERS OY

Linnoitustie 4 A
Espoo, Finland 02600
E-mail: info@tcp.fi
Website: www.tcp.fi

Management and Staff
Arno Pelkonen, Partner
Atte Kekkonen, Partner

Type of Firm
Private Equity Firm

Project Preferences

Type of Financing Preferred:
Balanced

Geographical Preferences

International Preferences:
Scandanavia/Nordic Region
Finland

Industry Preferences

In Industrial/Energy prefer:
Energy
Alternative Energy
Energy Conservation Relat
Industrial Products
Machinery

In Manufact. prefer:
Manufacturing

Additional Information
Year Founded: 2010

Current Activity Level : Actively seeking new investments

TAKEDA VENTURES INC

435 Tasso Street, Suite 300
Palo Alto, CA USA 94301
Phone: 6503282900
Fax: 6503282922
E-mail: contact@tri-takeda.com

Other Offices
435 Tasso Street, Suite 300
PALO ALTO, CA USA 94301
Phone: 6503282900
Fax: 6503282922

Type of Firm
Corporate PE/Venture

Project Preferences

Role in Financing:
Will function either as deal originator or investor in deals created by others

Type of Financing Preferred:
Second Stage Financing
Early Stage
Start-up Financing
Later Stage
Seed

Size of Investments Considered:
Min Size of Investment Considered (000s): $250
Max Size of Investment Considered (000s): $3,000

Geographical Preferences

United States Preferences:

Canadian Preferences:
All Canada

International Preferences:
Europe

Industry Preferences

In Biotechnology prefer:
Biotechnology
Human Biotechnology

In Medical/Health prefer:
Medical/Health

Additional Information
Year Founded: 2001
Capital Under Management: $80,300,000
Current Activity Level : Actively seeking new investments

TAKEOFF VC MANAGEMENT GMBH

Bleichstrasse 10
Muelheim an der Ruhr, Germany 45468
Phone: 492083000340
Fax: 492083000345
E-mail: info@takeoff-vc.de
Website: www.takeoff-vc.de

Management and Staff
Hans-Peter Dietz, Chief Executive Officer

Type of Firm
Private Equity Firm

Association Membership
German Venture Capital Association (BVK)

Project Preferences

Role in Financing:
Prefer role as deal originator but will also invest in deals created by others

Type of Financing Preferred:
Early Stage
Seed
Startup

Geographical Preferences

International Preferences:
Europe
Germany

Industry Preferences

In Communications prefer:
Communications and Media

In Computer Software prefer:
Software

In Internet Specific prefer:
Internet

In Computer Other prefer:
Computer Related

In Semiconductor/Electr prefer:
Electronics

Additional Information
Year Founded: 1999
Current Activity Level : Actively seeking new investments

TAKURA CAPITAL

153 Josiah Chinamano Avenue
Harare, Zimbabwe
Phone: 2634794940
Fax: 2634707393
Website: www.takuracapital.com

Management and Staff
G. Tafadzwa Nyamayi, Chief Financial Officer

Type of Firm
Private Equity Firm

Project Preferences

Type of Financing Preferred:
Leveraged Buyout
Early Stage
Expansion
Generalist PE
Balanced
Management Buyouts
Acquisition
Recapitalizations

Geographical Preferences

International Preferences:
Zimbabwe
Africa

Additional Information
Year Founded: 1997
Current Activity Level : Actively seeking new investments

TALLWAVE LLC

6263 N. Scottsdale Rd, Suite 180
Scottsdale, AZ USA 85250
Phone: 6028400400
Website: tallwave.com

Management and Staff
Jeffrey Pruitt, Chief Executive Officer
Robert Hobbs, Co-Founder
Robert Wallace, Partner

Type of Firm
Private Equity Firm

Project Preferences

Type of Financing Preferred:
Early Stage

Geographical Preferences

United States Preferences:
North America

Industry Preferences

In Communications prefer:
Communications and Media
Telecommunications

In Computer Software prefer:
Software

In Internet Specific prefer:
Ecommerce

Additional Information
Year Founded: 2013

Capital Under Management: $13,150,000
Current Activity Level : Actively seeking new investments

TALLWOOD VENTURE CAPITAL

3000 Sand Hill Road
Building Three, Suite 240
Menlo Park, CA USA 94025
Phone: 6504736750
Fax: 6504736755
E-mail: information@tallwoodvc.com
Website: www.tallwoodvc.com

Other Offices
Suite 21-1 Chang Jiang Road, Suite 1002, WuXi New District
JiangSu Province, China 214028
Phone: 86051081816335
Fax: 86051081814997

Management and Staff
George Pavlov, General Partner
Luis Arzubi, General Partner
Natasha Skok, Chief Financial Officer

Type of Firm
Private Equity Firm

Project Preferences

Type of Financing Preferred:
Early Stage
Later Stage

Size of Investments Considered:
Min Size of Investment Considered (000s): $50
Max Size of Investment Considered (000s): $15,000

Geographical Preferences

International Preferences:
All International

Industry Preferences

In Semiconductor/Electr prefer:
Semiconductor

Additional Information
Name of Most Recent Fund: Tallwood III, L.P
Most Recent Fund Was Raised: 12/13/2005
Year Founded: 2000
Capital Under Management: $600,000,000
Current Activity Level : Actively seeking new investments

TALU VENTURES PTY LTD

379 Queen Street
Level Eight
Brisbane, Australia 4000
Phone: 61738382888
Fax: 61738311256
E-mail: t.kirchner@taluventures.com

Website: www.taluventures.com

Management and Staff
Andrew Jane, Managing Director
Carrie Hillyard, Co-Founder
Jonathan Whitehouse, Chief Financial Officer
Mark Gill, Managing Director
Michael Begun, Co-Founder

Type of Firm
Private Equity Firm

Project Preferences

Role in Financing:
Will function either as deal originator or investor in deals created by others

Type of Financing Preferred:
Early Stage
Expansion
Balanced
Seed
Startup

Size of Investments Considered:
Min Size of Investment Considered (000s): $517
Max Size of Investment Considered (000s): $23,795

Geographical Preferences

International Preferences:
Pacific
Australia
New Zealand

Industry Preferences

In Communications prefer:
Telecommunications

In Biotechnology prefer:
Biotechnology

In Medical/Health prefer:
Medical Products

In Industrial/Energy prefer:
Energy
Alternative Energy

Additional Information
Name of Most Recent Fund: CM - IIFF Trust
Most Recent Fund Was Raised: 09/17/2009
Year Founded: 1998
Capital Under Management: $268,700,000
Current Activity Level : Actively seeking new investments
Method of Compensation: Return on investment is of primary concern, do not charge fees

TAMARACE CAPITAL

Mintian Road, Futian District
Room 415, Huarong Building
Shenzhen, China
Phone: 8675582824272
Fax: 8675582824272
E-mail: Janus@tamarace.com
Website: www.tamarace.com

Type of Firm
Private Equity Firm

Project Preferences

Type of Financing Preferred:
Generalist PE

Geographical Preferences

International Preferences:
China

Industry Preferences

In Communications prefer:
Telecommunications

In Medical/Health prefer:
Medical/Health

In Consumer Related prefer:
Consumer Products
Education Related

In Industrial/Energy prefer:
Alternative Energy
Materials

In Agr/Forestr/Fish prefer:
Agriculture related

Additional Information
Year Founded: 2015
Current Activity Level : Actively seeking new investments

TAMARIND HILL

411 Montgomery Ave
Ann Arbor, MI USA 48103
Phone: 4193457688
Website: www.tamarind-hill.com

Type of Firm
Private Equity Firm

Project Preferences

Type of Financing Preferred:
Early Stage

Industry Preferences

In Computer Software prefer:
Software

In Medical/Health prefer:
Health Services

Additional Information
Year Founded: 2015
Current Activity Level : Actively seeking new investments

TAMARISC LLC

111 Pacifica, Suite 130
Irvine, CA USA 92618
E-mail: info@tamarisc.com
Website: www.tamarisc.com

Type of Firm
Private Equity Firm

Project Preferences

Type of Financing Preferred:
Early Stage
Expansion
Balanced

Industry Preferences

In Medical/Health prefer:
Medical/Health

In Financial Services prefer:
Real Estate

Additional Information
Year Founded: 2014
Current Activity Level : Actively seeking new investments

TAMARIX CAPITAL CORP

515 Madison Avenue
41st Floor
New York, NY USA 10022
Phone: 2123080623
Website: www.tamarixcapital.com

Management and Staff
Mark Hauser, Managing Director
Peter Fidler, Principal
Peter Rothschild, Principal

Type of Firm
Private Equity Firm

Association Membership
Natl Assoc of Small Bus. Inv. Co (NASBIC)

Project Preferences

Type of Financing Preferred:
Leveraged Buyout
Management Buyouts
Acquisition
Recapitalizations

Geographical Preferences

United States Preferences:

International Preferences:
All International

Industry Preferences

In Consumer Related prefer:
Consumer

In Industrial/Energy prefer:
Industrial Products

In Financial Services prefer:
Financial Services

In Business Serv. prefer:
Services
Distribution

In Manufact. prefer:
Manufacturing

Additional Information
Name of Most Recent Fund: Tamarix Capital Partners, L.P.
Most Recent Fund Was Raised: 04/25/2012
Year Founded: 1994
Capital Under Management: $37,000,000
Current Activity Level : Actively seeking new investments

TAMBURI INVESTMENT PARTNERS SPA

Via Pontaccio 10
20121
Milan, Italy 20121
Phone: 39028858801
Fax: 39028900421
Website: www.tipspa.it

Type of Firm
Private Equity Firm

Project Preferences

Type of Financing Preferred:
Expansion
Later Stage

Geographical Preferences

International Preferences:
Italy
Europe

Industry Preferences

In Computer Other prefer:
Computer Related

In Consumer Related prefer:
Consumer

In Industrial/Energy prefer:
Industrial Products

Additional Information
Year Founded: 2000
Capital Under Management: $2,700,000
Current Activity Level : Actively seeking new investments

TANDEM CAPITAL GESTION

Dr. Romagosa, 1-2 planta
Valencia, Spain 46002
Phone: 34902106974
Fax: 34963942400
E-mail: info@tandemcapital.es
Website: www.tandemcapital.es

Management and Staff
Eduardo Navarro, Chief Executive Officer

Type of Firm
Private Equity Firm

Project Preferences

Type of Financing Preferred:
Leveraged Buyout
Management Buyouts
Acquisition
Special Situation

Geographical Preferences

International Preferences:
Latin America
Gibraltar
Portugal
Andorra
China
Ghana
Spain
France

Industry Preferences

In Computer Software prefer:
Software

In Consumer Related prefer:
Retail
Food/Beverage
Consumer Products
Consumer Services

Additional Information
Year Founded: 2007
Current Activity Level : Actively seeking new investments

TANDEM ENTREPRENEURS LLC

1450 Chapin Avenue
Burlingame, CA USA 94010
Phone: 6502403190

E-mail: info@tandeme.com
Website: www.tandemcap.com

Management and Staff
Doug Renert, Principal
Joyo Wijaya, Principal
Sunil Bhargava, Principal

Type of Firm
Incubator/Development Program

Project Preferences

Type of Financing Preferred:
Early Stage
Expansion
Seed
Startup

Geographical Preferences

United States Preferences:

International Preferences:
India

Industry Preferences

In Communications prefer:
Communications and Media
Commercial Communications
Wireless Communications

In Computer Software prefer:
Software

Additional Information
Year Founded: 2007
Capital Under Management: $132,000,000
Current Activity Level : Actively seeking new investments

TANDEM EXPANSION FUND I LP

225 King Street West
MetroCentre, Suite 905
Toronto, Canada M5V 3M2
Phone: 4166454885
E-mail: info@tandemexpansion.com
Website: www.tandemexpansion.com

Other Offices
666 Burrard Street, Suite 600
Vancouver, Canada V6C 3P6
Phone: 6046393191

150 Rene Levesque Boulevard West
38th Floor
Montreal, Canada H3B 4W8
Phone: 5145108900

Management and Staff
Alex Moorhead, Managing Partner
Andre Gauthier, Managing Partner
Antoine Michaud, Principal
Brent Belzberg, Partner

Charles Sirois, Partner
Christopher Legg, Managing Partner
David Bookbinder, Managing Partner
Marc Weiner, Vice President
Sandy Scott, Principal

Type of Firm
Private Equity Firm

Association Membership
Canadian Venture Capital Association

Project Preferences

Type of Financing Preferred:
Leveraged Buyout
Expansion
Generalist PE
Balanced
Later Stage
Acquisition

Size of Investments Considered:
Min Size of Investment Considered (000s): $10,322
Max Size of Investment Considered (000s): $30,966

Geographical Preferences

Canadian Preferences:
All Canada

Industry Preferences

In Computer Software prefer:
Software

In Industrial/Energy prefer:
Energy
Energy Conservation Relat
Advanced Materials

In Business Serv. prefer:
Services

Additional Information
Name of Most Recent Fund: Tandem Expansion Fund I, L.P.
Most Recent Fund Was Raised: 12/08/2009
Year Founded: 2009
Capital Under Management: $282,273,000
Current Activity Level : Actively seeking new investments

TANDEM PARTNERS

PO Box 65010, Office 909
Grosvenor Business Tower
Dubai, Utd. Arab Em.
Phone: 97144471587
Website: www.tandem.ae

Type of Firm
Private Equity Firm

Project Preferences

Type of Financing Preferred:
Early Stage
Expansion
Start-up Financing

Industry Preferences

In Communications prefer:
Media and Entertainment

In Industrial/Energy prefer:
Materials

Additional Information
Year Founded: 2009
Current Activity Level : Actively seeking new investments

TANDEMLAUNCH TECH-NOLOGIES INC

245 Victoria Avenue, Suite 200 Westmount
Quebec, Canada H3Z 2M6
Phone: 4383805435
E-mail: info@tandemlaunch.com
Website: www.tandemlaunchtech.com

Type of Firm
Incubator/Development Program

Association Membership
Canadian Venture Capital Association

Project Preferences

Type of Financing Preferred:
Early Stage
Seed
Startup

Industry Preferences

In Consumer Related prefer:
Consumer Products

Additional Information
Name of Most Recent Fund: TandemLaunch Technologies
Most Recent Fund Was Raised: 08/08/2013
Year Founded: 2010
Capital Under Management: $20,837,000
Current Activity Level : Actively seeking new investments

TANGRONG INVESTMENT CO LTD

Huaqiao City
No.1003 Hantang Mansion
Shenzhen, China
Phone: 8675526742691
Website: www.tangrongcapital.com

Type of Firm
Private Equity Firm

Project Preferences

Type of Financing Preferred:
Balanced

Geographical Preferences

International Preferences:
China

Industry Preferences

In Communications prefer:
Telecommunications
Media and Entertainment

In Medical/Health prefer:
Medical/Health

In Consumer Related prefer:
Consumer Services

Additional Information
Year Founded: 2001
Capital Under Management: $3,000,000,000
Current Activity Level : Actively seeking new investments

TANGSHAN HIGHTECH VENTURE CAPITAL CO LTD

Block B, 2nd Floor, South
Xichang Road
Tangshan, China 063020
Phone: 86-315-3858
Fax: 86-315-3858
E-mail: tsvc@tsdz.net

Type of Firm
Private Equity Firm

Project Preferences

Type of Financing Preferred:
Balanced

Geographical Preferences

International Preferences:
China

Additional Information
Year Founded: 2007
Current Activity Level : Actively seeking new investments

TANK HILL VENTURES

125 Edgewood Avenue
San Francisco, CA USA 94117
Website: www.th-vp.com

Type of Firm
Private Equity Firm

Project Preferences

Type of Financing Preferred:
Early Stage
Expansion

Additional Information
Year Founded: 2015
Capital Under Management: $12,000,000
Current Activity Level : Actively seeking new investments

TANO CAPITAL LLC

One Franklin Parkway
Building 970, Second Floor
San Mateo, CA USA 94403
Phone: 6502120330
Fax: 6502120006
E-mail: information@tanocapital.com
Website: www.tanocapital.com

Other Offices
c/o International Financial Services
IFS Court TwentyEight, Cybercity
Ebene, Mauritius
Phone: 230-467-3000
Fax: 230-467-4000

10F, No.87, Section 4
Chung Hsiao East Road
Taipei, Taiwan
Phone: 886-2-2771-7663
Fax: 886-2-8773-3987

6 Temasek Boulevar
#35-03, Suntec Tower 4
Tianjin, Singapore 038986
Phone: 65-6235-5000
Fax: 65-6643-5369

No.94, Lane 468, Urumqi Road North
Shanghai, China 200040
Phone: 86-21-6248-8877
Fax: 86-21-6249-5659

9 Nirlon House, Ground Floor
254-B Dr. Annie Besant Rd.
Mumbai, India 400025
Phone: 91-22-6746-8000
Fax: 91-22-6746-8002

Management and Staff
Carlton Pereira, Managing Director
Charles Johnson, Founder
Frank Liu, Managing Director
Hetal Gandhi, Managing Director
Peter Dabrowski, Managing Director
Pyari Menon, Managing Director
Timothy Chatard, Managing Director

Type of Firm
Private Equity Firm

Association Membership
Indian Venture Capital Association (IVCA)

Geographical Preferences

International Preferences:
China
Asia

Industry Preferences

In Medical/Health prefer:
Health Services

In Consumer Related prefer:
Consumer

In Manufact. prefer:
Manufacturing

Additional Information
Year Founded: 2004
Current Activity Level : Actively seeking new investments

TAO CAPITAL PARTNERS

One Letterman Drive
San Francisco, CA USA 94101
Phone: 4155494984
Website: www.taocap.com

Type of Firm
Private Equity Firm

Project Preferences

Type of Financing Preferred:
Generalist PE

Industry Preferences

In Medical/Health prefer:
Medical/Health

In Consumer Related prefer:
Consumer

In Industrial/Energy prefer:
Alternative Energy

In Financial Services prefer:
Financial Services
Real Estate

Additional Information
Year Founded: 2014
Current Activity Level : Actively seeking new investments

TAPPAN HILL VENTURES

425 N Main Street
Ann Arbor, MI USA 48104
E-mail: contact@tappanhillventures.com
Website: www.tappanhillventures.com

Type of Firm
Private Equity Firm

Project Preferences

Type of Financing Preferred:
Early Stage
Seed

Industry Preferences

In Computer Software prefer:
Software

Additional Information
Year Founded: 2016
Current Activity Level : Actively seeking new investments

TAPPAN ZEE CAPITAL CORP

201 Lower Notch Road
Little Falls, NJ USA 07424
Phone: 9732568280
Fax: 9732562841

Management and Staff
Jeffrey Birnberg, President

Type of Firm
SBIC

Project Preferences

Role in Financing:
Prefer role as deal originator but will also invest in deals created by others

Type of Financing Preferred:
Mezzanine

Industry Preferences

In Communications prefer:
Other Communication Prod.

In Semiconductor/Electr prefer:
Electronics

In Consumer Related prefer:
Franchises(NEC)
Food/Beverage
Consumer Products
Other Restaurants

In Industrial/Energy prefer:
Industrial Products

Additional Information
Year Founded: 1962
Capital Under Management: $4,000,000
Current Activity Level : Actively seeking new investments
Method of Compensation: Return on invest. most important, but chg. closing fees, service fees, etc.

TAR HEEL CAPITAL SP Z O O

Ostroroga 24c
Warsaw, Poland 01-163
Website: www.tarheelcap.com

Management and Staff
Grzegorz Bielowicki, Partner
Tomasz Firczyk, Partner

Type of Firm
Private Equity Firm

Project Preferences

Type of Financing Preferred:
Leveraged Buyout
Management Buyouts

Geographical Preferences

International Preferences:
Poland

Industry Preferences

In Communications prefer:
Communications and Media
Telecommunications

In Transportation prefer:
Transportation

In Manufact. prefer:
Manufacturing

Additional Information
Name of Most Recent Fund: Tar Heel Capital II FIZAN
Most Recent Fund Was Raised: 09/25/2012
Year Founded: 1998
Capital Under Management: $64,666,000
Current Activity Level : Actively seeking new investments

TARGE CAPITAL

Black River Park, Fir Street
2nd Floor, Old Warehouse Bldg.
Cape Town, South Africa 7925
Phone: 27214476793
Fax: 27865570068

Type of Firm
Private Equity Firm

Project Preferences

Type of Financing Preferred:
Leveraged Buyout
Expansion
Generalist PE
Management Buyouts
Acquisition

Geographical Preferences

International Preferences:
Africa

Additional Information
Year Founded: 2010
Current Activity Level : Actively seeking new investments

TARGET PARTNERS GMBH

Kardinal-Faulhaber-Strasse 10
Munich, Germany 80333
Phone: 49892070490
Fax: 498920704999
E-mail: info@targetpartners.de
Website: www.targetpartners.de

Management and Staff
Berthold von Freyberg, Partner
Jan Wolter, Venture Partner
Kurt Mueller, Partner
Michael Birkel, Venture Partner
Michael Kowalzik, Venture Partner
Michael Brehm, Venture Partner
Olaf Jacobi, Partner
Tim Stracke, Venture Partner
Waldemar Jantz, Partner

Type of Firm
Private Equity Firm

Association Membership
German Venture Capital Association (BVK)
European Private Equity and Venture Capital Assoc.

Project Preferences

Type of Financing Preferred:
Early Stage
Later Stage
Seed
Startup

Geographical Preferences

United States Preferences:
All U.S.

International Preferences:
Europe
Switzerland
Austria
Germany

Industry Preferences

In Communications prefer:
Communications and Media
Telecommunications
Wireless Communications

In Computer Software prefer:
Software

In Internet Specific prefer:
Internet

In Semiconductor/Electr prefer:
Electronic Components
Semiconductor
Fiber Optics

In Medical/Health prefer:
Medical/Health

In Industrial/Energy prefer:
Alternative Energy
Environmental Related

Additional Information
Name of Most Recent Fund: Target Partners Fund II
Most Recent Fund Was Raised: 02/26/2008
Year Founded: 1999
Capital Under Management: $309,300,000
Current Activity Level : Actively seeking new investments

TARGET VENTURES IF

2 Gorbunova, 204
Grand Setun Plaza BC
Moscow, Russia 121596
E-mail: info@targetventures.ru
Website: targetventures.ru

Type of Firm
Private Equity Firm

Project Preferences

Type of Financing Preferred:
Early Stage
Expansion
Balanced
Later Stage
Seed
Startup

Geographical Preferences

International Preferences:
Russia

Industry Preferences

In Internet Specific prefer:
Ecommerce

In Consumer Related prefer:
Consumer

In Business Serv. prefer:
Services

Additional Information
Year Founded: 2013
Current Activity Level : Actively seeking new investments

TARNAGULLA VENTURES PTY LTD

360 Collins Street
Level 33
Melbourne, Australia 3000
Website: tarnagullaventures.com

Type of Firm
Private Equity Firm

Additional Information
Year Founded: 2017
Current Activity Level : Actively seeking new investments

TARSADIA INVESTMENTS LLC

620 Newport Center Drive
Fourteenth Floor
Newport Beach, CA USA 92660
Phone: 9496108100
E-mail: contact@tarsadia.com
Website: www.tarsadiainvestments.com

Type of Firm
Private Equity Firm

Project Preferences

Type of Financing Preferred:
Leveraged Buyout
Early Stage
Expansion
Generalist PE
Public Companies
Turnaround
Acquisition

Size of Investments Considered:
Min Size of Investment Considered (000s): $5,000
Max Size of Investment Considered (000s): $200,000

Industry Preferences

In Biotechnology prefer:
Biotechnology

In Medical/Health prefer:
Medical/Health
Medical Products
Health Services
Pharmaceuticals

In Industrial/Energy prefer:
Alternative Energy
Environmental Related

In Financial Services prefer:
Financial Services
Real Estate

Additional Information
Year Founded: 2011

Current Activity Level : Actively seeking new investments

TASK FORCE X CAPITAL LLC

1750 Highway 160, Suite 101-266
Fort Mill, SC USA 29708
Website: www.tfxcap.com

Type of Firm
Private Equity Firm

Project Preferences

Type of Financing Preferred:
Balanced

Industry Preferences

In Computer Software prefer:
Software

In Business Serv. prefer:
Services

Additional Information
Year Founded: 1969
Current Activity Level : Actively seeking new investments

TASMAN CAPITAL INVESTMENTS AUSTRALIA PTY LTD

50 Pitt Street
Level Ten
Sydney, Australia 2000
Phone: 61282262200
Fax: 61292528449
E-mail: info@tasmancapital.com.au

Management and Staff
Gene Lorenz, Co-Founder
Janine Middleton, Co-Founder
Rob Nichols, Co-Founder

Type of Firm
Private Equity Firm

Project Preferences

Type of Financing Preferred:
Leveraged Buyout
Expansion
Turnaround
Later Stage
Management Buyouts
Private Placement
Industry Rollups

Geographical Preferences

International Preferences:
Australia

Industry Preferences

In Medical/Health prefer:
Health Services

In Consumer Related prefer:
Retail

In Financial Services prefer:
Financial Services

In Business Serv. prefer:
Services
Distribution
Consulting Services

Additional Information
Name of Most Recent Fund: Tasman Capital Partners Fund
Most Recent Fund Was Raised: 12/20/2011
Year Founded: 2008
Capital Under Management: $15,400,000
Current Activity Level : Actively seeking new investments

TATA CAPITAL GENERAL PARTNERS LLP

8 Cross Street No.11-00
PwC Building
Singapore, Singapore 048424

Type of Firm
Private Equity Firm

Association Membership
Singapore Venture Capital Association (SVCA)

Project Preferences

Type of Financing Preferred:
Early Stage
Expansion
Balanced
Seed

Geographical Preferences

International Preferences:
India

Additional Information
Year Founded: 2010
Capital Under Management: $195,714,000
Current Activity Level : Actively seeking new investments

TATE & LYLE PLC

One Kingsway
London, United Kingdom WC2B 6AT
Phone: 442072572100
Fax: 442072572200
Website: www.tateandlyle.com

Management and Staff
Anthony Hampton, Chief Financial Officer
Javed Ahmed, Chief Executive Officer

Type of Firm
Corporate PE/Venture

Association Membership
European Private Equity and Venture Capital Assoc.

Project Preferences

Type of Financing Preferred:
Early Stage
Expansion
Startup

Geographical Preferences

United States Preferences:
All U.S.

Canadian Preferences:
All Canada

International Preferences:
United Kingdom
Western Europe

Industry Preferences

In Biotechnology prefer:
Biotechnology
Industrial Biotechnology

In Consumer Related prefer:
Food/Beverage

In Industrial/Energy prefer:
Materials

Additional Information
Year Founded: 1903
Current Activity Level : Actively seeking new investments

TAU CAPITAL LTD

Hope Street
IOMA House
Douglas, United Kingdom IM1 1AP
Phone: 441624681250
Fax: 441624681392
E-mail: info@iomagroup.co.im
Website: www.taucapitalplc.com

Type of Firm
Investment Management Firm

Project Preferences

Type of Financing Preferred:
Leveraged Buyout
Expansion
Balanced
Acquisition

Geographical Preferences

International Preferences:
Mongolia
Kazakhstan
Kyrgyzstan
Tajikistan
Turkmenistan
Uzbekistan
Russia

Industry Preferences

In Communications prefer:
Wireless Communications

In Consumer Related prefer:
Consumer

In Industrial/Energy prefer:
Oil and Gas Exploration
Advanced Materials

In Transportation prefer:
Transportation

In Financial Services prefer:
Financial Services

In Business Serv. prefer:
Distribution

Additional Information
Year Founded: 2007
Current Activity Level : Actively seeking new investments

TAURUS VENTURES GP LLC

385 RIVER OAKS PKWY APT 5117
San Jose, CA USA 95134
Website: www.taurus.vc

Management and Staff
Saniya Gandhi, Partner
Vivek Mahapatra, Partner
Win Thanapisitkul, Partner

Type of Firm
Private Equity Firm

Project Preferences

Type of Financing Preferred:
Early Stage

Geographical Preferences

United States Preferences:
Southeast

International Preferences:
Asia

Additional Information
Year Founded: 2016
Current Activity Level : Actively seeking new investments

TAUTONA GROUP LP

4040 Campbell Avenue, Suite 110
Menlo Park, CA USA 94025
Phone: 650-331-2450
Fax: 650-331-2451
E-mail: info@tautonagroup.com
Website: www.tautonagroup.com

Management and Staff
Douglas Koo, Partner
Duke Rohlen, Partner
Geoffrey Gurtner, Partner
Matthew Pollman, Partner
Michael Longaker, Partner

Type of Firm
Private Equity Firm

Project Preferences

Type of Financing Preferred:
Early Stage

Geographical Preferences

United States Preferences:
All U.S.

Industry Preferences

In Medical/Health prefer:
Medical Products
Disposable Med. Products

Additional Information
Name of Most Recent Fund: TauTona Group Fund
Most Recent Fund Was Raised: 10/07/2010
Year Founded: 2010
Capital Under Management: $50,000,000
Current Activity Level : Actively seeking new investments

TAVEEKAN CAPITAL

9118 Potomac Ridge Road
Great Falls, VA USA 22066
Phone: 2027405664
Website: www.taveekancapital.com

Management and Staff
Clift Briscoe, Partner
Laurence Chang, Partner

Type of Firm
Private Equity Firm

Project Preferences

Type of Financing Preferred:
Early Stage
Startup

Industry Preferences

In Computer Software prefer:
Software
Systems Software

Additional Information
Year Founded: 2014
Capital Under Management: $400,000
Current Activity Level : Actively seeking new investments

TAVISTOCK GROUP INC

9350 Conroy Windermere Road
Tavistock House
Windermere, FL USA 34786
E-mail: info@tavistock.com

Management and Staff
Joe Lewis, Founder
Karen Turpin, Vice President

Type of Firm
Private Equity Firm

Project Preferences

Type of Financing Preferred:
Generalist PE

Geographical Preferences

United States Preferences:

International Preferences:
Europe
Argentina
Bahamas
China
Mexico

Industry Preferences

In Biotechnology prefer:
Biotechnology

In Consumer Related prefer:
Other Restaurants
Hotels and Resorts

In Industrial/Energy prefer:
Energy

In Financial Services prefer:
Financial Services
Real Estate

In Business Serv. prefer:
Distribution

In Manufact. prefer:
Manufacturing

Additional Information
Year Founded: 1969
Current Activity Level : Actively seeking new investments

Pratt's Guide to Private Equity & Venture Capital Sources

TAXIM CAPITAL PRIVATE EQUITY

Harbiye Mah
Istanbul, Turkey 34367
Phone: 902122604170
Fax: 902122604178
Website: www.taximcapital.com

Type of Firm
Private Equity Firm

Project Preferences

Type of Financing Preferred:
Leveraged Buyout
Early Stage
Expansion
Later Stage
Management Buyouts
Acquisition

Size of Investments Considered:
Min Size of Investment Considered (000s): $5,349
Max Size of Investment Considered (000s): $32,096

Industry Preferences

In Computer Software prefer:
Software

In Medical/Health prefer:
Medical/Health

In Consumer Related prefer:
Retail
Food/Beverage
Consumer Products

In Financial Services prefer:
Financial Services

In Manufact. prefer:
Manufacturing

Additional Information
Year Founded: 2015
Capital Under Management: $123,330,000
Current Activity Level : Actively seeking new investments

TBL CAPITAL LP

One Embarcadero Center, Suite 3810
San Francisco, CA USA 94111
Phone: 4157058008
Fax: 4157055279
E-mail: info@tblcapital.com

Other Offices
Former HQ
1505 Bridgeway, Suite 128
Sausalito, CA USA 94965
Phone: 4153313200
Fax: 4153310707

Management and Staff
Brent Knudsen, Managing Partner
Susie Lee, Principal

Type of Firm
Private Equity Firm

Project Preferences

Type of Financing Preferred:
Expansion
Balanced

Industry Preferences

In Computer Software prefer:
Software

In Medical/Health prefer:
Medical/Health

In Consumer Related prefer:
Consumer
Retail
Consumer Products

In Industrial/Energy prefer:
Alternative Energy
Energy Conservation Relat

In Business Serv. prefer:
Services

Additional Information
Year Founded: 2007
Capital Under Management: $35,000,000
Current Activity Level : Actively seeking new investments

TC CAPITAL PTE LTD

4 Shenton Way
#13-06 SGX Center 2
Singapore, Singapore 068807
Phone: 65-6511-0688
E-mail: info@tccapital.com
Website: www.tccapital.com

Other Offices
16/F Cheung Kong Center
2 Queen's Road
Central, Hong Kong
Phone: 852-2297-2386

Management and Staff
Ravi Chidambaram, President, Founder
Tommy Tan, Co-Founder

Type of Firm
Private Equity Firm

Project Preferences

Type of Financing Preferred:
Balanced

Additional Information
Year Founded: 2006
Current Activity Level : Actively seeking new investments

TC GROWTH PARTNERS

505 Hamilton Avenue, Suite 200
Palo Alto, CA USA 94301
Phone: 6502894400
Fax: 6502894444
Website: tcgrowth.com

Type of Firm
Private Equity Firm

Project Preferences

Type of Financing Preferred:
Expansion
Balanced
Later Stage

Industry Preferences

In Internet Specific prefer:
Internet

In Medical/Health prefer:
Health Services

Additional Information
Year Founded: 2015
Capital Under Management: $300,000,000
Current Activity Level : Actively seeking new investments

TCR CAPITAL SAS

5, Rue Paul Cezanne
Paris, France 75008
Phone: 33153817781
Fax: 33153817799
E-mail: info@tcrcapital.com
Website: www.tcrcapital.com

Management and Staff
David Robin, Partner
Marc Demicheli, Managing Partner
Roberta Nataf, Partner

Type of Firm
Private Equity Firm

Association Membership
French Venture Capital Association (AFIC)

Project Preferences

Role in Financing:
Prefer role as deal originator

Type of Financing Preferred:
Leveraged Buyout

Size of Investments Considered:
Min Size of Investment Considered (000s): $10,000
Max Size of Investment Considered: No Limit

Geographical Preferences

International Preferences:
Italy
Spain
France

Industry Focus
(% based on actual investment)
Consumer Related	61.0%
Medical/Health	37.6%
Other Products	1.4%

Additional Information
Year Founded: 1988
Capital Under Management: $100,000,000
Current Activity Level : Actively seeking new investments
Method of Compensation: Return on invest. most important, but chg. closing fees, service fees, etc.

TD CAPITAL GROUP LTD

111 Huntington Ave, Suite 1400
Boston, MA USA 02199
Phone: 6174250800
Fax: 6174250801

Other Offices
79 Wellington Street West
6th Floor
Toronto, Canada M5K 1A2
Phone: 866-831-2343
Fax: 416-983-9763

909 Fannin, Suite 1700
Houston, TX USA 77010
Phone: 713-653-8200
Fax: 713-652-2647

Management and Staff
Ian Kidson, Managing Director
John Greenwood, Managing Director
Mel Gabel, Chief Financial Officer
Richard Greene, Managing Director
Robert MacLellan, President
Stuart Waugh, Managing Director
Tom Rashotte, Managing Director

Type of Firm
Bank Affiliated

Project Preferences

Role in Financing:
Will function either as deal originator or investor in deals created by others

Type of Financing Preferred:
Fund of Funds
Leveraged Buyout
Early Stage
Expansion
Mezzanine
Generalist PE
Balanced
Management Buyouts
Recapitalizations

Size of Investments Considered:
Min Size of Investment Considered (000s): $500
Max Size of Investment Considered: No Limit

Geographical Preferences

United States Preferences:

Canadian Preferences:
All Canada

International Preferences:
Europe

Industry Focus
(% based on actual investment)
Other Products	39.8%
Communications and Media	24.8%
Internet Specific	14.0%
Medical/Health	8.1%
Industrial/Energy	6.7%
Computer Software and Services	3.3%
Consumer Related	1.9%
Semiconductors/Other Elect.	0.8%
Computer Hardware	0.6%
Biotechnology	0.0%

Additional Information
Name of Most Recent Fund: TD Capital Mezzanine Partners CDN
Most Recent Fund Was Raised: 03/31/2004
Year Founded: 1995
Capital Under Management: $120,000,000
Current Activity Level : Actively seeking new investments
Method of Compensation: Return on invest. most important, but chg. closing fees, service fees, etc.

TDJ SA

Armii Krajowej 51
Katowice, Poland 40-698
Phone: 48 32 359 63 01
Fax: 48 32 359 63 51
Website: www.tdj.pl

Other Offices
Grzybowska 2/29
Warsaw, Poland 00-131

Management and Staff
Jacek Leonkiewicz, Managing Partner
Maciej Wojcik, Managing Partner
Magdalena Zajaczkowska-Ejsymont, Managing Partner
Oliwia Kwiatkowska, Managing Partner
Tomasz Czajor, Chief Financial Officer
Wojciech Fedorowicz, Managing Partner

Type of Firm
Private Equity Firm

Project Preferences

Type of Financing Preferred:
Leveraged Buyout
Opportunistic
Later Stage

Geographical Preferences

International Preferences:
Poland
All International

Industry Preferences

In Industrial/Energy prefer:
Energy
Industrial Products

Additional Information
Year Founded: 2010
Capital Under Management: $55,000,000
Current Activity Level : Actively seeking new investments

TDR CAPITAL LLP

One Stanhope Gate
London, United Kingdom W1K 1AF
Phone: 442073994200
Fax: 442073994242
E-mail: info@tdrcapital.com
Website: www.tdrcapital.com

Management and Staff
Blair Thompson, Partner
David Melvin, Partner
Jonathan Rosen, Partner
Manjit Dale, Partner
Stephen Robertson, Partner
Tom Mitchell, Founder

Type of Firm
Private Equity Firm

Association Membership
British Venture Capital Association (BVCA)
European Private Equity and Venture Capital Assoc.

Project Preferences

Type of Financing Preferred:
Leveraged Buyout
Management Buyouts
Acquisition

Geographical Preferences

United States Preferences:

Canadian Preferences:
All Canada

International Preferences:
United Kingdom
Europe
Western Europe

Industry Preferences

In Consumer Related prefer:
Consumer
Entertainment and Leisure

In Financial Services prefer:
Financial Services

In Business Serv. prefer:
Services

Additional Information

Year Founded: 2002
Capital Under Management: $3,433,700,000
Current Activity Level : Actively seeking new investments

TEACHERS INSURANCE AND ANNUITY ASSOCIATION OF AMERICA

730 Third Avenue
New York, NY USA 10017
Phone: 2124909000
Website: www.tiaa-cref.org

Type of Firm
Endowment, Foundation or Pension Fund

Project Preferences

Role in Financing:
Prefer role in deals created by others

Type of Financing Preferred:
Core
Leveraged Buyout
Generalist PE
Balanced
Other

Geographical Preferences

United States Preferences:
North America

International Preferences:
Europe
Brazil
Australia

Industry Preferences

In Communications prefer:
Telecommunications

In Medical/Health prefer:
Pharmaceuticals

In Consumer Related prefer:
Consumer Products
Consumer Services

In Industrial/Energy prefer:
Energy

In Financial Services prefer:
Financial Services
Insurance
Real Estate

In Manufact. prefer:
Manufacturing

In Agr/Forestr/Fish prefer:
Agribusiness
Agriculture related

Additional Information

Year Founded: 1918
Capital Under Management: $6,000,000,000
Current Activity Level : Actively seeking new investments
Method of Compensation: Return on investment is of primary concern, do not charge fees

---

TEAK CAPITAL SDN BHD

27 Jalan Sultan Ismail, Suite 22-01 Menara Dion
Kuala Lumpur, Malaysia 50250
Phone: 60320312202
Fax: 60320312205
E-mail: info@teakcapital.com.my

Management and Staff

Eliza Noordin, Vice President
Kwee Bee Chok, Managing Director

Type of Firm
Private Equity Firm

Association Membership
Malaysian Venture Capital Association

Project Preferences

Type of Financing Preferred:
Early Stage
Expansion
Balanced
Later Stage

Industry Preferences

In Communications prefer:
Commercial Communications
Wireless Communications

In Computer Software prefer:
Software

In Internet Specific prefer:
Internet

In Semiconductor/Electr prefer:
Electronics
Semiconductor

In Industrial/Energy prefer:
Environmental Related

In Business Serv. prefer:
Media

Additional Information

Year Founded: 2008
Current Activity Level : Actively seeking new investments

TEAK VENTURES DO BRAZIL SA

Joao Americo de Oliveira 177
Curitiba, Brazil 80035
Phone: 554133432005
E-mail: info@teakventures.com
Website: www.teakventures.com

Type of Firm
Private Equity Firm

Association Membership
Brazilian Venture Capital Association (ABCR)

Project Preferences

Type of Financing Preferred:
Balanced

Geographical Preferences

International Preferences:
Brazil

Additional Information

Year Founded: 2014
Current Activity Level : Actively seeking new investments

TEAKWOOD CAPITAL LP

8226 Douglas Avenue
Douglas Plaza, Suite 355
Dallas, TX USA 75225
Phone: 2147501590
Fax: 2147501468
E-mail: contact@teakwoodcapital.com
Website: teakwoodcapital.com

Management and Staff

Bharti Subramanian, Managing Director
Daniel Shimer, Managing Director
Edward Olkkola, Managing Director
Jonathan Hustis, Managing Director
Mike Taylor, Managing Director
Shawn Kelly, Managing Director
Stu Bell, Managing Director

Type of Firm
Private Equity Firm

Project Preferences

Type of Financing Preferred:
Leveraged Buyout
Management Buyouts
Acquisition
Recapitalizations

Geographical Preferences

United States Preferences:
New Mexico
Tennessee
Arizona
Colorado
Louisiana
Missouri
Texas

Industry Preferences

In Computer Software prefer:
Software

In Consumer Related prefer:
Consumer Products
Consumer Services

Additional Information

Name of Most Recent Fund: Teakwood Capital III, L.P.
Most Recent Fund Was Raised: 03/03/2014
Year Founded: 2005
Capital Under Management: $125,531,000
Current Activity Level : Actively seeking new investments

TEALL INVESTMENTS LLC

PO Box 21528
Winston-Salem, NC USA 27120
E-mail: contactus@teallinvestments.com
Website: teallinvestments.com

Type of Firm
Private Equity Firm

Project Preferences

Type of Financing Preferred:
Generalist PE

Additional Information
Year Founded: 2017
Current Activity Level : Actively seeking new investments

TEAM DCL LTD

20 Galgaley Haplada Street
PO Box 2031
Herzlia, Israel 46120
Phone: 972-9-9555-215
Fax: 972-9-9555-316
E-mail: contact@teamdcl.com
Website: www.xagoon.com/teamdcl

Management and Staff
Benny Davidson, Chief Executive Officer

Type of Firm
Bank Affiliated

Project Preferences

Type of Financing Preferred:
Seed
Startup

Geographical Preferences

International Preferences:
Israel

Industry Preferences

In Communications prefer:
Commercial Communications

In Internet Specific prefer:
Internet

Additional Information
Year Founded: 2000
Capital Under Management: $8,500,000
Current Activity Level : Actively seeking new investments

TEAM EUROPE MANAGEMENT GMBH

Mohrenstrasse 60
Berlin, Germany 10117
Phone: 493060981050
Fax: 4930609810590
E-mail: info@teameurope.net
Website: www.teameurope.net

Management and Staff
Daniel Offermann, Venture Partner
Kolja Hebenstreit, Founder
Lukasz Gadowski, Founder
Markus Fuhrmann, Partner
Sebastian Bielski, Partner
Steffen Hoellinger, Partner

Type of Firm
Private Equity Firm

Project Preferences

Type of Financing Preferred:
Early Stage
Seed
Startup

Size of Investments Considered:
Min Size of Investment Considered (000s): $34
Max Size of Investment Considered (000s): $6,830

Geographical Preferences

United States Preferences:
All U.S.

International Preferences:
Europe
Poland
Germany

Industry Preferences

In Communications prefer:
Entertainment

In Internet Specific prefer:
E-Commerce Technology
Internet

In Consumer Related prefer:
Consumer Services

Additional Information
Year Founded: 2008
Capital Under Management: $8,108,000
Current Activity Level : Actively seeking new investments

TEAM PARTNERS LLC

6701 Joyce Way
Dallas, TX USA 75225
Phone: 2146210192
E-mail: david@teampartnersllc.com
Website: teampartnersllc.com

Type of Firm
Private Equity Firm

Project Preferences

Type of Financing Preferred:
Leveraged Buyout

Geographical Preferences

United States Preferences:
Texas

Industry Preferences

In Communications prefer:
Commercial Communications

In Consumer Related prefer:
Consumer

In Industrial/Energy prefer:
Industrial Products

In Business Serv. prefer:
Services

Additional Information
Year Founded: 2002
Current Activity Level : Actively seeking new investments

TEC VENTURES LP

555 Bryant Street, Suite 392
Palo Alto, CA USA 94301
Phone: 6502780431
E-mail: info@tec.vc

Type of Firm
Private Equity Firm

Project Preferences

Type of Financing Preferred:
Seed
Startup

Industry Preferences

In Computer Software prefer:
Software

In Internet Specific prefer:
Internet

Additional Information
Year Founded: 2016
Current Activity Level : Actively seeking new investments

TECH COAST ANGELS INC

3720 Hughes Avenue, Suite Five
Los Angeles, CA USA 90034
Phone: 3108412345
Fax: 3108412346

Type of Firm
Angel Group

Project Preferences

Type of Financing Preferred:
Early Stage
Seed

Size of Investments Considered:
Min Size of Investment Considered (000s): $50
Max Size of Investment Considered (000s): $1,000

Geographical Preferences

United States Preferences:
Southern California

Industry Preferences

In Computer Software prefer:
Software

In Consumer Related prefer:
Consumer Products
Consumer Services

In Industrial/Energy prefer:
Industrial Products
Environmental Related

In Financial Services prefer:
Financial Services

Additional Information
Year Founded: 1997
Capital Under Management: $1,000,000
Current Activity Level : Actively seeking new investments

TECH SQUARE LABS LLC

859 Spring Street Northwest
Atlanta, GA USA 30308
E-mail: info@techsquare.co
Website: techsquare.co

Management and Staff
Allen Nance, Partner
Paul Judge, Partner
Rodney Sampson, Partner

Type of Firm
Incubator/Development Program

Project Preferences

Type of Financing Preferred:
Seed

Industry Preferences

In Computer Software prefer:
Software

Additional Information
Year Founded: 2016
Capital Under Management: $4,050,000
Current Activity Level : Actively seeking new investments

TECH SQUARE VENTURES

75 Fifth Street NW, Suite 427
Atlanta, GA USA 30308
Phone: 4042062653
E-mail: info@techsquareventures.com
Website: www.techsquareventures.com

Management and Staff
Thiago Olson, Managing Director

Type of Firm
Private Equity Firm

Project Preferences

Type of Financing Preferred:
Early Stage
Seed
Startup

Geographical Preferences

United States Preferences:
Southeast
Georgia

Industry Preferences

In Computer Software prefer:
Data Processing
Software
Applications Software

In Internet Specific prefer:
E-Commerce Technology
Internet
Ecommerce

In Semiconductor/Electr prefer:
Sensors

In Medical/Health prefer:
Medical Products

Additional Information
Name of Most Recent Fund: Tech Square Ventures
Most Recent Fund Was Raised: 02/20/2014
Year Founded: 2014
Capital Under Management: $25,000,000
Current Activity Level : Actively seeking new investments

TECH WILDCATTERS II LLC

2700 Fairmount
Dallas, TX USA 75201
E-mail: info@techwildcatters.com
Website: www.techwildcatters.com

Management and Staff
Gabriella Draney, Managing Partner

Type of Firm
Incubator/Development Program

Project Preferences

Type of Financing Preferred:
Seed
Startup

Size of Investments Considered:
Min Size of Investment Considered (000s): $20
Max Size of Investment Considered (000s): $25

Geographical Preferences

United States Preferences:
Texas

Industry Preferences

In Communications prefer:
Entertainment

In Computer Software prefer:
Data Processing
Systems Software
Applications Software

In Computer Other prefer:
Computer Related

Additional Information
Name of Most Recent Fund: Tech Wildcatters II LLC
Most Recent Fund Was Raised: 09/02/2011
Year Founded: 2011
Current Activity Level : Actively seeking new investments

TECHACCEL LLC

6811 Shawnee Mission Parkway, Suite 215
Mission, KS USA 66202
Phone: 9135494124
Fax: 9134169509
Website: www.techaccel.net

Management and Staff
Brett Morris, Principal
Michael Helmstetter, President
Mike DeMaio, Chief Financial Officer

Type of Firm
Private Equity Firm

Project Preferences

Type of Financing Preferred:
Early Stage
Balanced

Industry Preferences

In Biotechnology prefer:
Agricultural/Animal Bio.

In Consumer Related prefer:
Food/Beverage

In Agr/Forestr/Fish prefer:
Agriculture related

Additional Information
Year Founded: 2014
Current Activity Level : Actively seeking new investments

TECHBANC INC

181 University Avenue, Suite 1206
Toronto, Canada M5H 3M7
Phone: 416-947-1492
Fax: 416-947-9673

Type of Firm
Private Equity Advisor or Fund of Funds

Additional Information
Year Founded: 2000
Current Activity Level : Actively seeking new investments

TECHCOLUMBUS

1275 Kinnear Road
Columbus, OH USA 43212
Phone: 6144873700
Fax: 6144873704
E-mail: info@techcolumbus.org
Website: www.rev1ventures.com

Management and Staff
David Dillman, Chief Financial Officer
Kristy Campbell, Chief Operating Officer
Mike McCann, Vice President
Ron Landthorn, Vice President

Type of Firm
Private Equity Firm

Project Preferences

Role in Financing:
Prefer role as deal originator but will also invest in deals created by others

Type of Financing Preferred:
Early Stage
Expansion
Seed
Startup

Size of Investments Considered:
Min Size of Investment Considered (000s): $200
Max Size of Investment Considered (000s): $2,000

Geographical Preferences

United States Preferences:
Midwest
Ohio

Industry Preferences

In Computer Hardware prefer:
Computer Graphics and Dig

In Computer Software prefer:
Software

In Internet Specific prefer:
Ecommerce

In Semiconductor/Electr prefer:
Semiconductor

In Biotechnology prefer:
Biotechnology
Human Biotechnology
Industrial Biotechnology
Biosensors

In Medical/Health prefer:
Medical/Health
Medical Diagnostics
Medical Therapeutics
Medical Products

In Consumer Related prefer:
Retail

In Industrial/Energy prefer:
Energy
Industrial Products
Materials

In Business Serv. prefer:
Distribution

In Agr/Forestr/Fish prefer:
Agriculture related

Additional Information
Year Founded: 2007
Capital Under Management: $67,000,000
Current Activity Level : Actively seeking new investments

TECHFUND CAPITAL EUROPE

233 Rue De La Croix Nivert, Suite 13
Paris, France 75015
Phone: 33140430020
Fax: 33140430111
Website: www.techfundcapitaleurope.com

Other Offices
14510 Big Basin Way, 150
Saratoga, CA USA 95070
Phone: 1-408-872-0300
Fax: 1-408-872-0333

Management and Staff
Alain Bravo, Venture Partner
Francoise Lohezic, Partner
Jim Whims, Venture Partner
Kurt Keilhacker, Co-Founder
Mike Kaul, Venture Partner
Roger Chevrel, Venture Partner

Type of Firm
Private Equity Firm

Association Membership
French Venture Capital Association (AFIC)

Project Preferences

Type of Financing Preferred:
Early Stage
Seed
Startup

Geographical Preferences

United States Preferences:

International Preferences:
Europe
Germany
France

Industry Preferences

In Communications prefer:
Telecommunications
Wireless Communications

In Computer Software prefer:
Software

In Business Serv. prefer:
Media

Pratt's Guide to Private Equity & Venture Capital Sources

Additional Information
Year Founded: 1990
Capital Under Management: $22,600,000
Current Activity Level : Actively seeking new investments

TECHINA INVESTMENT MANAGEMENT LTD

Rm 2614, China Merchant Tower
161 Eastern Lu Jia Zui Road
Shanghai, China
Phone: 86-21-5882-8186
Fax: 86-21-5054-1122

Management and Staff
Li Qi, Managing Partner

Type of Firm
Private Equity Firm

Project Preferences

Type of Financing Preferred:
Mezzanine
Balanced
Seed

Geographical Preferences

International Preferences:
China

Industry Preferences

In Communications prefer:
Commercial Communications
Wireless Communications

In Medical/Health prefer:
Medical Products

Additional Information
Year Founded: 2001
Current Activity Level : Actively seeking new investments

TECHNOLOGIE UND GRU-ENDERZENTRUM WALL-DORF STIFTUNG GMBH

Robert-Bosch-Strasse 49
Walldorf, Germany 69190
Phone: 496227899340
Fax: 4962278993499
E-mail: kontakt@innowerft.com
Website: www.innowerft.com

Management and Staff
Hans-Heinrich Siemers, Managing Director

Type of Firm
Incubator/Development Program

Project Preferences

Type of Financing Preferred:
Seed
Startup

Geographical Preferences

International Preferences:
Germany

Additional Information
Year Founded: 2011
Current Activity Level : Actively seeking new investments

TECHNOLOGY CROSSOVER VENTURES LP

528 Ramona Street
Palo Alto, CA USA 94301
Phone: 6506148200
Fax: 6506148222
Website: www.tcv.com

Other Offices
83 Pall Mall
London, United Kingdom SW1Y 5ES
Phone: 440-20-7930-9236

280 Park Avenue
East Building 26th Floor
MANHATTAN, NY USA 10017
Phone: 212--808-0200
Fax: 212-808-0259

Management and Staff
Bob Burke, Venture Partner
Christopher Marshall, General Partner
Chuck Davis, Venture Partner
David Yuan, General Partner
Douglas Gilstrap, Venture Partner
Erik Blachford, Venture Partner
Jake Reynolds, General Partner
Jay Hoag, Co-Founder
John Drew, General Partner
John Doran, General Partner
John Rosenberg, General Partner
Kapil Venkatachalam, General Partner
Michelle Peluso, Venture Partner
Nari Ansari, Principal
Nathan Sanders, General Partner
Ric Fenton, General Partner
Richard Kimball, Co-Founder
Robert Trudeau, General Partner
Sean Giese, Principal
Simon Breakwell, Venture Partner
Ted Coons, General Partner
Timothy McAdam, General Partner

Type of Firm
Private Equity Firm

Association Membership
Western Association of Venture Capitalists (WAVC)
National Venture Capital Association - USA (NVCA)

Project Preferences

Role in Financing:
Prefer role as deal originator but will also invest in deals created by others

Type of Financing Preferred:
Early Stage
Expansion
Balanced
Later Stage
Recapitalizations

Size of Investments Considered:
Min Size of Investment Considered (000s): $20,000
Max Size of Investment Considered (000s): $200,000

Geographical Preferences

United States Preferences:
North America

International Preferences:
Europe
All International

Industry Focus
(% based on actual investment)
Internet Specific   42.2%
Computer Software and Services   36.5%
Communications and Media   9.5%
Other Products   6.9%
Consumer Related   3.0%
Computer Hardware   1.0%
Semiconductors/Other Elect.   0.7%

Additional Information
Year Founded: 1995
Capital Under Management: $10,000,000,000
Current Activity Level : Actively seeking new investments
Method of Compensation: Return on investment is of primary concern, do not charge fees

TECHNOLOGY PARTNERS

550 University Avenue
Palo Alto, CA USA 94301
Phone: 6502899000
Fax: 6502899001
E-mail: admin@technologypartners.com
Website: www.technologypartners.com

Other Offices
100 Shoreline Highway, Suite 282, Building B
Mill Valley, CA USA 94941
Phone: 415-332-9999
Fax: 415-332-9998

Management and Staff
Ira Ehrenpreis, General Partner
James Glasheen, General Partner
Roger Quy, General Partner
Ted Ardell, Partner

Type of Firm
Private Equity Firm

Association Membership
Western Association of Venture Capitalists (WAVC)

Project Preferences

Role in Financing:
Prefer role as deal originator but will also invest in deals created by others

Type of Financing Preferred:
Early Stage
Balanced
Seed

Size of Investments Considered:
Min Size of Investment Considered (000s): $1,000
Max Size of Investment Considered (000s): $30,000

Industry Focus
(% based on actual investment)

Industrial/Energy	22.8%
Medical/Health	18.7%
Biotechnology	15.0%
Computer Software and Services	10.0%
Other Products	8.4%
Semiconductors/Other Elect.	7.0%
Internet Specific	6.2%
Communications and Media	5.1%
Consumer Related	4.4%
Computer Hardware	2.4%

Additional Information
Name of Most Recent Fund: Technology Partners Fund VIII, LP
Most Recent Fund Was Raised: 08/03/2007
Year Founded: 1984
Capital Under Management: $700,000,000
Current Activity Level : Actively seeking new investments
Method of Compensation: Return on investment is of primary concern, do not charge fees

---

TECHNOLOGY STRATEGY BOARD

North Star Avenue
North Star House
Swindon, United Kingdom SN2 1UE
Phone: 441793442700
Website: www.gov.uk

Management and Staff
Iain Gray, Chief Executive Officer

Type of Firm
Government Affiliated Program

Project Preferences

Type of Financing Preferred:
Early Stage
Seed
Startup

Geographical Preferences

International Preferences:
United Kingdom

Industry Preferences

In Communications prefer:
Communications and Media

In Semiconductor/Electr prefer:
Electronics
Sensors

In Biotechnology prefer:
Biotechnology

In Medical/Health prefer:
Medical/Health

In Consumer Related prefer:
Food/Beverage

In Industrial/Energy prefer:
Energy
Advanced Materials
Environmental Related

In Transportation prefer:
Transportation
Aerospace

In Financial Services prefer:
Financial Services

In Manufact. prefer:
Manufacturing

Additional Information
Year Founded: 2007
Current Activity Level : Actively seeking new investments

TECHNOLOGY VENTURE PARTNERS

8500 Normandale Lake Boulevard, Suite 2170
Minneapolis, MN USA 55437
Phone: 9526463000
Fax: 9526463010
E-mail: email@tvp.com
Website: www.tvp.com

Management and Staff
Donald Bossi, Venture Partner
Ryan DiBrito, Partner

Type of Firm
Private Equity Firm

Project Preferences

Role in Financing:
Will function either as deal originator or investor in deals created by others

Type of Financing Preferred:
Early Stage
Balanced
Later Stage

Additional Information
Name of Most Recent Fund: Technology Venture Partners, L.P.
Most Recent Fund Was Raised: 04/01/2000
Year Founded: 2000
Capital Under Management: $85,000,000
Current Activity Level : Actively seeking new investments
Method of Compensation: Return on investment is of primary concern, do not charge fees

---

TECHNOLOGY VENTURE PARTNERS PTY., LTD.

55 Miller Street, Suite 2.14
Pyrmont, Australia 2009
Phone: 61295629000
Fax: 61295629001
E-mail: enquiries@tvp.com.au
Website: www.tvp.com.au

Other Offices
555 Bryant Street, Suite 556
Palo Alto, CA USA 94301
Phone: 415-516-0618
Fax: 61295629001

Management and Staff
Allan Aaron, Co-Founder
John Murray, Co-Founder

Type of Firm
Private Equity Firm

Project Preferences

Role in Financing:
Prefer role as deal originator

Type of Financing Preferred:
Early Stage
Expansion
Balanced
Later Stage
Seed
Management Buyouts
Startup

Size of Investments Considered:
Min Size of Investment Considered (000s): $500
Max Size of Investment Considered (000s): $15,000

Geographical Preferences

International Preferences:
Australia
New Zealand

Industry Focus

(% based on actual investment)
Internet Specific	46.7%
Computer Software and Services	29.0%
Semiconductors/Other Elect.	8.5%
Computer Hardware	6.3%
Industrial/Energy	4.6%
Other Products	2.3%
Biotechnology	1.6%
Medical/Health	0.8%
Communications and Media	0.3%

Additional Information

Name of Most Recent Fund: TVP No.3 Fund
Most Recent Fund Was Raised: 02/07/2001
Year Founded: 1997
Capital Under Management: $155,400,000
Current Activity Level : Actively seeking new investments
Method of Compensation: Return on investment is of primary concern, do not charge fees

TECHNOLOGY VENTURES FUND I GP LLC

2005 Research Park Circle, Suite 119
Manhattan, KS USA 66502
Phone: 7853414434

Type of Firm
Private Equity Firm

Project Preferences

Type of Financing Preferred:
Balanced

Additional Information

Name of Most Recent Fund: Technology Ventures Fund I, L.P.
Most Recent Fund Was Raised: 12/21/2011
Year Founded: 2010
Capital Under Management: $101,000
Current Activity Level : Actively seeking new investments

TECHOPERATORS LLC

3060 Peachtree Road, NorthWest, Suite 720, One Buckhead Plaza
Atlanta, GA USA 30305
Phone: 4045372525
E-mail: info@techoperators.com
Website: www.techoperators.com

Management and Staff

Glenn McGonnigle, General Partner
Said Mohammadioun, Managing Partner

Type of Firm
Private Equity Firm

Project Preferences

Role in Financing:
Prefer role as deal originator but will also invest in deals created by others

Type of Financing Preferred:
Early Stage
Balanced
Later Stage
Startup

Size of Investments Considered:
Min Size of Investment Considered (000s): $200
Max Size of Investment Considered (000s): $4,000

Geographical Preferences

United States Preferences:

Industry Preferences

In Computer Software prefer:
Software

In Internet Specific prefer:
Internet

Additional Information

Name of Most Recent Fund: Technology Operators Fund II, L.P.
Most Recent Fund Was Raised: 03/27/2013
Year Founded: 2008
Capital Under Management: $30,000,000
Current Activity Level : Actively seeking new investments

TECHSTARS CENTRAL LLC

1375 Walnut Street, Suite 010
Boulder, CO USA 80302
Phone: 4254672272
Website: www.techstars.com

Other Offices

222 W. Merchandise Mart Plaza, Suite 1212
CHICAGO, IL USA 60654

727 Massachusetts Avenue
Third Floor
CAMBRIDGE, MA USA 02139
Phone: 303-957-0226

Management and Staff

David Tisch, Managing Director
Jason Seats, Managing Director
Katie Rae, Managing Director
Nicole Glaros, Managing Director

Type of Firm
Incubator/Development Program

Project Preferences

Type of Financing Preferred:
Early Stage
Seed
Strategic Alliances
Startup

Geographical Preferences

United States Preferences:
Illinois
Oregon
Massachusetts
Indiana
Texas
All U.S.

Industry Preferences

In Computer Software prefer:
Software

In Internet Specific prefer:
Internet
Web Aggregation/Portals

Additional Information

Name of Most Recent Fund: Bullet Time Ventures II, L.P.
Most Recent Fund Was Raised: 03/19/2012
Year Founded: 2006
Capital Under Management: $185,720,000
Current Activity Level : Actively seeking new investments

TECHU VENTURES LP

Three Crampton Avenue
Great Neck, NY USA 11023

Type of Firm
Private Equity Firm

Project Preferences

Type of Financing Preferred:
Balanced

Additional Information

Year Founded: 2017
Current Activity Level : Actively seeking new investments

TECNET EQUITY NOE TECHNOLOGIEBETEILIGU-NGS INVEST GMBH

Niederoesterreichring 2
Haus B
Sankt Poelten, Austria 3100
Phone: 432742900019300
Fax: 432742900019319
E-mail: office@tecnet.co.at
Website: www.tecnet.co.at

Other Offices
Seidengasse 9-11
Vienna, Austria 1070

Management and Staff
Doris Agneter, Chief Executive Officer

Type of Firm
Government Affiliated Program

Association Membership
Austrian PE and Venture Capital Association (AVCO)
European Private Equity and Venture Capital Assoc.

Project Preferences

Type of Financing Preferred:
Early Stage
Later Stage
Seed
Startup

Size of Investments Considered:
Min Size of Investment Considered (000s): $436
Max Size of Investment Considered (000s): $4,364

Geographical Preferences

International Preferences:
Europe
Austria

Industry Preferences

In Communications prefer:
Telecommunications

In Computer Other prefer:
Computer Related

In Semiconductor/Electr prefer:
Electronics

In Biotechnology prefer:
Biotechnology

In Medical/Health prefer:
Medical/Health

In Industrial/Energy prefer:
Energy
Industrial Products
Materials
Factory Automation
Environmental Related

Additional Information
Year Founded: 2002
Capital Under Management: $24,500,000
Current Activity Level : Actively seeking new investments

TECTONIC VENTURES LP
19 Street
Newton Highlands, MA USA 02461
Website: tectonicventures.com

Management and Staff
Matthew Rhodes-Kropf, Managing Partner
Morris Miller, Managing Partner

Type of Firm
Private Equity Firm

Project Preferences

Type of Financing Preferred:
Seed
Startup

Additional Information
Year Founded: 2016
Current Activity Level : Actively seeking new investments

TECUM CAPITAL PARTNERS
8000 Brooktree Road, Suite 310
Wexford, PA USA 15090
Phone: 7246024399
Website: tecum.com

Management and Staff
Daniel Wingard, Vice President
Joel Pokorney, Vice President
Matt Steve, Vice President
Matt Harnett, Vice President
Stephen Gurgovits, Managing Partner

Type of Firm
SBIC

Association Membership
Natl Assoc of Small Bus. Inv. Co (NASBIC)

Project Preferences

Type of Financing Preferred:
Early Stage
Mezzanine
Later Stage
Acquisition

Size of Investments Considered:
Min Size of Investment Considered (000s): $2,000
Max Size of Investment Considered (000s): $9,000

Industry Preferences

In Industrial/Energy prefer:
Advanced Materials

In Business Serv. prefer:
Distribution

Additional Information
Name of Most Recent Fund: F.N.B. Capital Partners, L.P.
Most Recent Fund Was Raised: 05/01/2013
Year Founded: 2013
Capital Under Management: $191,000,000
Current Activity Level : Actively seeking new investments

TEDA VENTURE CAPITAL CORP LTD
3/F North Area, Software Bldg.
No. 80, Fourth Avenue, TEDA
Tianjin, China 300457
Phone: 862266299990
Fax: 862266297288
E-mail: public@tedavc.com.cn
Website: www.tedavc.com.cn

Type of Firm
Private Equity Firm

Project Preferences

Type of Financing Preferred:
Balanced

Geographical Preferences

International Preferences:
China

Industry Preferences

In Biotechnology prefer:
Biotechnology

In Medical/Health prefer:
Pharmaceuticals

In Industrial/Energy prefer:
Materials
Environmental Related

Additional Information
Year Founded: 2000
Capital Under Management: $80,000,000
Current Activity Level : Actively seeking new investments

TEGNA INC
7950 Jones Branch Drive
McLean, VA USA 22107
Phone: 7038546000
Website: www.tegna.com

Management and Staff
Anne Bentley, Vice President

Type of Firm
Corporate PE/Venture

Project Preferences

Type of Financing Preferred:
Balanced

Additional Information
Year Founded: 1972
Current Activity Level : Actively seeking new investments

TEKA CAPITAL SAS

Carrera Seven No. 77-07
Of. 503
Bogota, Colombia
Phone: 5713215200
Fax: 5713215207
Website: www.tekacapital.com

Other Offices
Av. Brig. Faria Lima, 1485
19 Andar Brasilinvest Plaza
Sao Paulo, Brazil 01480-900
Phone: 5713215200
Fax: 5713215207

Management and Staff
Diego Cordoba, Managing Partner
Juan Antonio Pungiluppi, Managing Director

Type of Firm
Private Equity Firm

Project Preferences

Type of Financing Preferred:
Leveraged Buyout
Acquisition

Geographical Preferences

International Preferences:
Latin America
Brazil
Colombia

Industry Preferences

In Communications prefer:
Entertainment

In Medical/Health prefer:
Medical/Health

In Consumer Related prefer:
Retail

In Industrial/Energy prefer:
Energy
Alternative Energy
Industrial Products

In Transportation prefer:
Transportation

In Financial Services prefer:
Financial Services

In Agr/Forestr/Fish prefer:
Agribusiness
Agriculture related

Additional Information
Year Founded: 2009
Capital Under Management: $104,000,000
Current Activity Level : Actively seeking new investments

TEKES PAAOMASIJOITUS OY

Kayntiosoite 2
Lansi-Pasila
Helsinki, Finland 00240
E-mail: info@tekes.vc
Website: www.tekes.vc

Type of Firm
Private Equity Firm

Project Preferences

Type of Financing Preferred:
Early Stage
Seed
Startup

Geographical Preferences

International Preferences:
Europe
Finland

Additional Information
Year Founded: 2014
Current Activity Level : Actively seeking new investments

TEKLA CAPITAL MANAGEMENT LLC

Two Liberty Square, Ninth Floor
Boston, MA USA 02109
Phone: 6177728500
Fax: 6177728577
Website: www.teklacap.com

Other Offices
30 Rowes Wharf
Fourth Floor
Boston, MA USA 02110
Phone: 617-772-8500

Management and Staff
Laura Woodward, Vice President

Type of Firm
Private Equity Firm

Additional Information
Year Founded: 2002
Current Activity Level : Actively seeking new investments

TEKNOINVEST AS

Stranden 1A
Oslo, Norway 0250
Phone: 4722979000
Fax: 4722979001
E-mail: teknoinvest@teknoinvest.com
Website: www.teknoinvest.no

Management and Staff
Rune Dybesland, Chief Financial Officer
Steinar Engelsen, Partner
Steven Morrell, Partner

Type of Firm
Private Equity Advisor or Fund of Funds

Association Membership
Norwegian Venture Capital Association

Project Preferences

Role in Financing:
Will function either as deal originator or investor in deals created by others

Type of Financing Preferred:
Early Stage
Seed
Startup

Size of Investments Considered:
Min Size of Investment Considered (000s): $900
Max Size of Investment Considered (000s): $9,000

Geographical Preferences

United States Preferences:

International Preferences:
Europe
Scandanavia/Nordic Region

Industry Preferences

In Communications prefer:
Communications and Media
Commercial Communications
Telecommunications
Wireless Communications

In Computer Hardware prefer:
Terminals

In Computer Software prefer:
Software

In Biotechnology prefer:
Biotechnology

In Medical/Health prefer:
Medical/Health
Medical Diagnostics
Medical Therapeutics
Medical Products

In Industrial/Energy prefer:
Energy
Alternative Energy
Energy Conservation Relat

In Other prefer:
Environment Responsible

Additional Information
Name of Most Recent Fund: Teknoinvest VIII
Most Recent Fund Was Raised: 07/02/2002
Year Founded: 1984
Capital Under Management: $105,900,000
Current Activity Level : Actively seeking new investments
Method of Compensation: Return on investment is of primary concern, do not charge fees

TEKTON VENTURES

50 California Street, Suite 3200
San Francisco, CA USA 94111
Website: www.tektonventures.com

Type of Firm
Private Equity Firm

Project Preferences

Type of Financing Preferred:
Seed

Additional Information
Year Founded: 2008
Current Activity Level : Actively seeking new investments

TEL VENTURE CAPITAL INC

3100 West Warren Avenue
Fremont, CA USA 94538
Phone: 5106243450
Fax: 5106243451
Website: www.tel.com/about/telvc.htm

Other Offices
Akasaka Biz Tower
3-1 Akasaka 5-chome, Minato-ku
Tokyo, Japan 107-6325
Phone: 81355617270
Fax: 81355617066

Management and Staff
Kay Enjoji, President
Ruben Serrato, Venture Partner
Scott Sechovec, Co-Founder
Tsutomu Awaji, Venture Partner
Tsuyoshi Mihara, Venture Partner

Type of Firm
Corporate PE/Venture

Association Membership
Japan Venture Capital Association
New England Venture Capital Association

Project Preferences

Type of Financing Preferred:
Early Stage
Expansion
Balanced
Later Stage

Industry Preferences

In Semiconductor/Electr prefer:
Electronics
Semiconductor

In Medical/Health prefer:
Medical/Health

In Industrial/Energy prefer:
Energy

In Manufact. prefer:
Manufacturing

Additional Information
Year Founded: 2006
Capital Under Management: $10,000,000
Current Activity Level : Actively seeking new investments

TELECOM TECHNOLOGIES TRANSFERT 3T SAS

46, Rue Barrault
Paris, France 75634
E-mail: contact@3tcapital.com
Website: fr.3tcapital.com

Management and Staff
Daniel Caclin, Managing Partner
Gilles Debuchy, Managing Partner
Nicholas Tcherdakoff, Venture Partner

Type of Firm
Private Equity Firm

Project Preferences

Type of Financing Preferred:
Early Stage
Seed
Startup

Size of Investments Considered:
Min Size of Investment Considered (000s): $395
Max Size of Investment Considered (000s): $1,974

Geographical Preferences

International Preferences:
Europe
France

Industry Preferences

In Communications prefer:
Telecommunications
Wireless Communications
Media and Entertainment

In Internet Specific prefer:
E-Commerce Technology

Additional Information
Year Founded: 2010
Current Activity Level : Actively seeking new investments

TELECOMMUNICATIONS DEVELOPMENT FUND

Two Wisconsin Circle, Suite 920
Chevy Chase, MD USA 20815
Phone: 2404834286
Fax: 3019078850
Website: www.tdfventures.com

Management and Staff
James Pastoriza, Managing Partner
Joseph Harar, Principal
Neal Douglas, Venture Partner

Type of Firm
Private Equity Firm

Association Membership
Mid-Atlantic Venture Association
National Venture Capital Association – USA (NVCA)

Project Preferences

Role in Financing:
Will function either as deal originator or investor in deals created by others

Type of Financing Preferred:
Early Stage
Balanced
Later Stage

Geographical Preferences

United States Preferences:

Industry Focus
(% based on actual investment)

Industry	%
Computer Software and Services	36.8%
Communications and Media	19.1%
Internet Specific	18.7%
Other Products	7.5%
Medical/Health	7.3%
Semiconductors/Other Elect.	5.8%
Computer Hardware	4.9%

Additional Information
Name of Most Recent Fund: Telecommunications Development Fund II
Most Recent Fund Was Raised: 08/04/2004
Year Founded: 1996
Capital Under Management: $50,000,000
Current Activity Level : Actively seeking new investments
Method of Compensation: Return on investment is of primary concern, do not charge fees

TELEGRAPH HILL GROUP LLC

582 Market Street, Suite 1700
San Francisco, CA USA 94104
E-mail: contact@thcap.com
Website: www.thcap.com

Pratt's Guide to Private Equity & Venture Capital Sources

Other Offices
Paseo de Gracia 63
Barcelona, Spain 08008

Management and Staff
Luis Roy, Managing Partner
Pili Cora, Venture Partner

Type of Firm
Investment Management Firm

Project Preferences

Type of Financing Preferred:
Expansion
Later Stage

Geographical Preferences

United States Preferences:
North America

International Preferences:
India
Europe
Israel

Industry Preferences

In Communications prefer:
Telecommunications
Wireless Communications
Media and Entertainment

In Computer Software prefer:
Software

In Internet Specific prefer:
Internet

In Consumer Related prefer:
Consumer Services

Additional Information
Name of Most Recent Fund: Telegraph Hill Capital Fund I LLC
Most Recent Fund Was Raised: 10/10/2008
Year Founded: 2008
Current Activity Level : Actively seeking new investments

TELEGRAPH HILL PARTNERS

360 Post Street, Suite 601
San Francisco, CA USA 94108
Phone: 4157656980
Fax: 4157656983
E-mail: info@thpartners.net
Website: www.thpartners.net

Management and Staff
Deval Lashkari, Partner
Rob Hart, Principal
Robert Shepler, Managing Director
Thomas Raffin, Partner

Type of Firm
Private Equity Firm

Project Preferences

Type of Financing Preferred:
Early Stage
Expansion
Management Buyouts
Acquisition

Size of Investments Considered:
Min Size of Investment Considered (000s): $2,000
Max Size of Investment Considered (000s): $8,000

Geographical Preferences

United States Preferences:

International Preferences:
Europe
Pacific Rim

Industry Preferences

In Communications prefer:
Communications and Media
Telecommunications

In Biotechnology prefer:
Agricultural/Animal Bio.

In Medical/Health prefer:
Medical/Health
Medical Products
Health Services

Additional Information
Name of Most Recent Fund: Telegraph Hill Partners III, L.P.
Most Recent Fund Was Raised: 07/26/2013
Year Founded: 2001
Capital Under Management: $42,000,000
Current Activity Level : Actively seeking new investments

TELENOR MOBIL AS AVD BARDU BEDRIFTS-IDRETTSLAG

Snaroyveien 30
Fornebu, Norway 1331
Phone: 4781077000

Type of Firm
Corporate PE/Venture

Project Preferences

Type of Financing Preferred:
Balanced

Geographical Preferences

International Preferences:
Europe

Additional Information
Year Founded: 2004
Current Activity Level : Actively seeking new investments

TELESCOPE PARTNERS

1161 Mission Street, Suite 526
San Francisco, CA USA 94103
Website: www.telescopepartners.com

Type of Firm
Private Equity Firm

Project Preferences

Type of Financing Preferred:
Early Stage

Additional Information
Year Founded: 2016
Current Activity Level : Actively seeking new investments

TELESOFT PARTNERS

One California Street
28th Floor
San Francisco, CA USA 94111
Phone: 4157657240
Fax: 4157657265
E-mail: investors@telesoftvc.com
Website: www.telesoftvc.com

Management and Staff
Al Howard, Chief Financial Officer
Alan Foster, Managing Director
Arjun Gupta, Managing Partner
George Schmitt, Managing Director
Marcia Burkey, Managing Director
Paul Unruh, Managing Director
William Magill, Managing Director

Type of Firm
Private Equity Firm

Association Membership
Natl Assoc of Small Bus. Inv. Co (NASBIC)

Project Preferences

Role in Financing:
Will function either as deal originator or investor in deals created by others

Type of Financing Preferred:
Early Stage
Expansion
Balanced
Later Stage

Size of Investments Considered:
Min Size of Investment Considered (000s): $1,000
Max Size of Investment Considered (000s): $15,000

Geographical Preferences

United States Preferences:

International Preferences:
India
Europe
Israel

Industry Focus

(% based on actual investment)
Communications and Media	35.6%
Semiconductors/Other Elect.	26.5%
Internet Specific	18.0%
Computer Software and Services	13.5%
Computer Hardware	2.9%
Other Products	1.7%
Consumer Related	1.7%

Additional Information

Year Founded: 1996
Capital Under Management: $462,600,000
Current Activity Level : Actively seeking new investments
Method of Compensation: Return on investment is of primary concern, do not charge fees

TELEVENTURE MANAGEMENT AS

Tollbugaten 24
Sixth Floor
Oslo, Norway 0157
Phone: 4722779910
Fax: 4722779921
E-mail: post@televenture.no
Website: www.telenorventure.no

Management and Staff

Dag Terje Rian, Partner
Jorgen Andre Nilsen, Partner
Rune Rinnan, Managing Partner
Rune Sorum, Partner
Yngve Dahle, Partner

Type of Firm

Corporate PE/Venture

Association Membership

Norwegian Venture Capital Association

Project Preferences

Type of Financing Preferred:
Early Stage
Balanced

Geographical Preferences

United States Preferences:
All U.S.

International Preferences:
Europe
Scandanavia/Nordic Region
Norway

Industry Preferences

In Communications prefer:
Communications and Media
Commercial Communications
Telecommunications
Wireless Communications
Media and Entertainment

In Computer Software prefer:
Software

In Internet Specific prefer:
Internet

In Biotechnology prefer:
Biotechnology

In Industrial/Energy prefer:
Energy
Oil and Gas Exploration
Alternative Energy
Energy Conservation Relat
Environmental Related

In Business Serv. prefer:
Media

In Other prefer:
Environment Responsible

Additional Information

Year Founded: 1993
Capital Under Management: $7,400,000
Current Activity Level : Actively seeking new investments

TELLURIDE VENTURE ACCELERATOR

101 Skunk Creek Road
Telluride, CO USA 81435
E-mail: info@tellurideva.com
Website: www.tellurideva.com

Type of Firm

Incubator/Development Program

Project Preferences

Type of Financing Preferred:
Startup

Geographical Preferences

United States Preferences:
Colorado

Additional Information

Year Founded: 2015
Current Activity Level : Actively seeking new investments

TELLUS PARTNERS I LLC

400 Marina Circle
Lehi, UT USA 84045
Website: tellus.partners

Type of Firm

Private Equity Firm

Project Preferences

Type of Financing Preferred:
Generalist PE

Industry Preferences

In Agr/Forestr/Fish prefer:
Agribusiness

Additional Information

Year Founded: 2017
Current Activity Level : Actively seeking new investments

TELOPEA CAPITAL PARTNERS PTY LTD

Seven Macquarie Place
Level 12
Sydney, Australia 2000
Phone: 612-8241-1700
Fax: 612-9252-9597
E-mail: info@telopeacapital.com
Website: www.telopeacapital.com

Other Offices

One Alfred Street
Level Ten, Gold Fields House
Sydney, Australia 2000

No. 2 Dong San Huan Bei Lu
603 Silver Tower
Beijing, China 100027
Phone: 86-10-6410-7388
Fax: 86-10-6410-7389

Management and Staff

Andrew Kerr, Managing Director
Craig Carracher, Managing Director
David Mackenzie, Managing Director
Desmond Lee, Vice President
Stephen Gaitanos, Vice President

Type of Firm

Investment Management Firm

Project Preferences

Type of Financing Preferred:
Leveraged Buyout
Expansion
Special Situation

Geographical Preferences

International Preferences:
Australia
Asia

Additional Information

Year Founded: 2009
Current Activity Level : Actively seeking new investments

TELUS VENTURES

6-3777 Kingsway
12th Floor
Vancouver, Canada V5H 3Z7
Phone: 6044322150
Fax: 6044380325
E-mail: ventureinfo@telus.com

Management and Staff

Mathew George, Vice President

Type of Firm

Corporate PE/Venture

Association Membership

Canadian Venture Capital Association

Project Preferences

Type of Financing Preferred:
Later Stage

Size of Investments Considered:
Min Size of Investment Considered (000s): $1,000
Max Size of Investment Considered (000s): $5,000

Geographical Preferences

United States Preferences:

Canadian Preferences:
All Canada

Industry Preferences

In Communications prefer:
Telecommunications
Wireless Communications
Data Communications

In Business Serv. prefer:
Media

Additional Information

Year Founded: 2001
Capital Under Management: $100,000,000
Current Activity Level : Actively seeking new investments

TEMASEK HOLDINGS (PRIVATE) LTD

60B Orchard Road, Suite 06-18, Tower Two
Singapore, Singapore 238891
Phone: 6568286828
Fax: 6568211188
E-mail: enquiry@temasek.com.sg
Website: www.temasek.com.sg

Other Offices

Suite 1806, Two Pacific Place
88 Queensway
Central, Hong Kong
Phone: 852-3589-3200
Fax: 852-2156-1180

Unit 2201, Plaza 66
1266 Nan Jing Xi Road
Shanghai, China 200040
Phone: 86-21-6133-1900
Fax: 86-21-6133-1901

F705 Winland Int'l Finance Center
No. 7 Financial Street, Xicheng District
Beijing, China 100033
Phone: 86-10-5930-4900
Fax: 86-10-5930-4901

Unit 406, Level 4, Hanoi Towers
49 Hai Ba Trung Street
Hanoi, Vietnam
Phone: 84-4-3936-9069
Fax: 84-4-3936-9066

Ruben Dario 281-1301
Bosque de Chapultepec
Mexico D.F, Mexico 11580
Phone: 525543353050
Fax: 525543353099

New No. 75 (Old No.39) TTK Road
2/F, Century Centre, Alwarpet
Chennai, India 600 018
Phone: 91-44-4225-5000
Fax: 91-44-4225-5099

Rua Jeronimo da Veiga, 384/5 andar
Itaim Bibi
Sao Paulo, Brazil 04536
Phone: 55-11-3636-7575
Fax: 55-11-3636-7599

Express Towers, 12th Floor
Nariman Point
Mumbai, India 400 021
Phone: 91-22-6654-5500
Fax: 91-22-6654-5599

101 California Street, Suite 3700
SAN FRANCISCO, CA USA 94111
Phone: 6282203800
Fax: 6282203801

65 Le Loi Boulevard, Saigon Centre
5th Floor, Unit 2, District 1
Ho Chi Minh, Vietnam
Phone: 84838212789
Fax: 84838212767

F707 Winland Int'l Finance Center
No. 7 Financial Street, Xicheng District
Beijing, China 100033
Phone: 861059304900
Fax: 861059304901

Unit 2212, Plaza 66
1266 Nan Jing Xi Road
Shanghai, China 200040
Phone: 862161331900
Fax: 862161331901

Management and Staff

Ching Ho, Chief Executive Officer
David Heng, Senior Managing Director
Hock Kuan Cheo, Senior Managing Director
Nagi Hamiyeh, Senior Managing Director
Wai Leng Leong, Chief Financial Officer

Type of Firm

Government Affiliated Program

Association Membership

Indian Venture Capital Association (IVCA)

Project Preferences

Type of Financing Preferred:
Fund of Funds
Leveraged Buyout
Generalist PE
Later Stage
Management Buyouts
Acquisition
Recapitalizations

Geographical Preferences

International Preferences:
Asia Pacific
Armenia
Belarus
Kazakhstan
Taiwan
Hong Kong
China
Kyrgyzstan
Tajikistan
Turkmenistan
Azerbaijan
Moldova
Ukraine
Uzbekistan
Asia
Singapore
Russia
Africa

Industry Preferences

In Communications prefer:
Telecommunications
Media and Entertainment

In Consumer Related prefer:
Consumer
Consumer Products
Consumer Services
Education Related

In Industrial/Energy prefer:
Energy
Industrial Products
Environmental Related

In Transportation prefer:
Transportation

In Financial Services prefer:
Real Estate
Financial Services

In Business Serv. prefer:
Media

In Agr/Forestr/Fish prefer:
Agriculture related

Additional Information
Year Founded: 1974
Current Activity Level : Actively seeking new investments

TEMBO CAPITAL LLP

180 Piccadilly
London, United Kingdom W1J 9ER
Website: www.tembocapital.com

Management and Staff
David Street, Co-Founder
John Hodder, Co-Founder
Paul Siveyer, Chief Financial Officer
Peter Ruxton, Co-Founder

Type of Firm
Investment Management Firm

Project Preferences

Type of Financing Preferred:
Leveraged Buyout

Industry Preferences

In Agr/Forestr/Fish prefer:
Mining and Minerals

Additional Information
Year Founded: 2009
Current Activity Level : Actively seeking new investments

TEMBUSU PARTNERS PTE LTD

10 Collyer Quay, #03-10
Ocean Financial Centre
Singapore, Singapore 049315
Phone: 6531525500
Fax: 6531520730
E-mail: enquiry@tembusupartners.com
Website: www.tembusupartners.com

Other Offices
268 Zhongshan Road
23rd Floor, Huijie Plaza
Nanjing, China 210008
Phone: 862583191520
Fax: 862583192351

283 Huaihai Road Central
Office 1001 Hong Kong Plaza
Shanghai, China 200021
Phone: 862163906123
Fax: 862163907306

155 Queen Street
Auckland, New Zealand
Phone: 64212828988

20 Cecil Street, #14-05
Equity Plaza
Singapore , Singapore 048693

Falkenstrasse 12
Zurich, Switzerland 80008
Phone: 41443836710
Fax: 41443836720

Management and Staff
Kim Seng Tan, Co-Founder
Mahim Chellappa, Principal
Peter Lai Hock Meng, Managing Director

Type of Firm
Private Equity Firm

Association Membership
Singapore Venture Capital Association (SVCA)

Project Preferences

Type of Financing Preferred:
Leveraged Buyout
Mezzanine
Later Stage
Acquisition
Private Placement
Recapitalizations

Geographical Preferences

United States Preferences:
Southeast

International Preferences:
India
China
Asia
Singapore

Industry Preferences

In Medical/Health prefer:
Medical/Health
Health Services

In Consumer Related prefer:
Education Related

In Industrial/Energy prefer:
Oil and Gas Exploration
Oil & Gas Drilling,Explor
Energy Conservation Relat
Industrial Products

In Manufact. prefer:
Manufacturing

In Other prefer:
Environment Responsible

Additional Information
Year Founded: 2007
Capital Under Management: $57,000,000
Current Activity Level : Actively seeking new investments

TEMBUSU VENTURES PTE LTD

80 Raffles Place
UOB Plaza 1 #51-02
Singapore, Singapore 048624
Phone: 6565383345
Fax: 6565368129
Website: www.tembusugroup.com

Management and Staff
Nicholas Chua Hwee Song, Managing Director
Wong Yek Meng, Venture Partner

Type of Firm
Private Equity Firm

Project Preferences

Type of Financing Preferred:
Early Stage
Seed
Startup

Geographical Preferences

International Preferences:
Singapore

Additional Information
Year Founded: 2004
Current Activity Level : Actively seeking new investments

TEMERITY CAPITAL PARTNERS LLC

1255 23rd St Northwest, Suite 550
Washington, DC USA 20037
Website: www.temeritycap.com

Type of Firm
Private Equity Firm

2109

Project Preferences

Type of Financing Preferred:
Core
Generalist PE
Balanced

Industry Preferences

In Financial Services prefer:
Real Estate

Additional Information

Year Founded: 1969
Current Activity Level : Actively seeking new investments

TEMPLETON ASSET MANAGEMENT LTD

Seven Temasek Boulevard, Suite 38-03 Suntec Tower One
Singapore, Singapore 038987
Phone: 6562412662
Fax: 6563322295
E-mail: query@franklintempleton.com.sg

Other Offices

P.O. Box 2258
Rancho Cordova, CA USA 95741

1st Floor, Empire Tower
26-28 Ham Nghi Boulevard, District 1
Ho Chi Minh City, Vietnam
Phone: 84-8-915-1800
Fax: 84-8-915-1787

2701 Shui On Centre
6-8 Harbour Rd.
Hong Kong, Hong Kong
Phone: 852-2829-0600
Fax: 852-2519-9482

360 Collins Street
Level 25
Melbourne, Australia 3000
Fax: 61-3-9603-1299

Management and Staff

Donna Ikeda, Vice President
Holly Gibson, Vice President
Penelope Alexander, Vice President

Type of Firm

Investment Management Firm

Association Membership

Singapore Venture Capital Association (SVCA)

Project Preferences

Type of Financing Preferred:
Expansion
Balanced

Geographical Preferences

International Preferences:
Asia Pacific
India
Central Europe
China
Eastern Europe
Singapore
All International

Additional Information

Year Founded: 1994
Capital Under Management: $220,000,000
Current Activity Level : Actively seeking new investments

TEMPRANO TECHVESTORS

2105 Northwest Blvd
Newton, NC USA 28658
E-mail: info@temprano.com
Website: www.temprano.com

Type of Firm

Private Equity Firm

Project Preferences

Type of Financing Preferred:
Early Stage

Industry Preferences

In Computer Software prefer:
Software

Additional Information

Year Founded: 2016
Current Activity Level : Actively seeking new investments

TEN ELEVEN VENTURES LP

250 Northern Avenue, Suite 300
Boston, MA USA 02108
Phone: 6179865040
E-mail: info@1011vc.com
Website: www.1011vc.com

Type of Firm

Private Equity Firm

Project Preferences

Type of Financing Preferred:
Early Stage
Balanced

Geographical Preferences

United States Preferences:

Industry Preferences

In Computer Software prefer:
Software
Systems Software
Applications Software

In Internet Specific prefer:
Internet

Additional Information

Year Founded: 2014
Capital Under Management: $103,730,000
Current Activity Level : Actively seeking new investments

TENAYA CAPITAL, INC.

3280 Alpine Road
Portola Valley, CA USA 94028
Phone: 6506876500
E-mail: info@tenayacapital.com
Website: www.tenayacapital.com

Other Offices

Former: 2965 Woodside Road, Suite A
Woodside, CA USA 94062

572 Washington Street, Suite Eight
Wellesley, MA USA 02482
Phone: 7816630220

Management and Staff

Benjamin Boyer, Managing Director
Brian Paul, Managing Director
Brian Melton, Managing Director
Stewart Gollmer, Managing Director
Thomas Banahan, Managing Director

Type of Firm

Private Equity Firm

Association Membership

National Venture Capital Association - USA (NVCA)

Project Preferences

Role in Financing:
Prefer role as deal originator

Type of Financing Preferred:
Early Stage

Size of Investments Considered:
Min Size of Investment Considered (000s): $5,000
Max Size of Investment Considered (000s): $15,000

Geographical Preferences

United States Preferences:
All U.S.

Industry Preferences

In Communications prefer:
Communications and Media

In Computer Software prefer:
Software

In Semiconductor/Electr prefer:
Electronics

In Consumer Related prefer:
Consumer

Additional Information
Name of Most Recent Fund: Tenaya Capital VI, L.P.
Most Recent Fund Was Raised: 07/24/2012
Year Founded: 1995
Capital Under Management: $1,000,000,000
Current Activity Level : Actively seeking new investments

TENDENCE CAPITAL

Science Faculty South Rd. No.2
Rongke Information Center
Beijing, China
Website: www.tendencevc.com

Type of Firm
Private Equity Firm

Industry Preferences

In Internet Specific prefer:
Internet

In Medical/Health prefer:
Medical/Health

In Financial Services prefer:
Financial Services

In Business Serv. prefer:
Services

Additional Information
Year Founded: 2014
Current Activity Level : Actively seeking new investments

TENDERLOIN VENTURES AG

Gotthardstrasse 20
Zug, Switzerland 6304
Phone: 41 55 220 03 19
E-mail: info@tenderloin.ch
Website: www.tenderloin.ch

Type of Firm
Private Equity Firm

Association Membership
Swiss Venture Capital Association (SECA)

Project Preferences

Type of Financing Preferred:
Early Stage
Seed
Startup

Geographical Preferences

International Preferences:
United Kingdom
Switzerland
Austria
Germany

Industry Preferences

In Computer Software prefer:
Software

In Internet Specific prefer:
E-Commerce Technology

Additional Information
Year Founded: 2014
Current Activity Level : Actively seeking new investments

TENE KIBBUTZ INVESTMENT MANAGEMENT LTD

Four Berkovich Street
Tel Aviv, Israel 64238
Phone: 97236093525
Fax: 97236093530
E-mail: info@tenecapital.com
Website: www.tenecapital.com

Management and Staff
Ariel Halperin, Managing Partner
Avraham Levin, Vice President
Avshalom Horan, Venture Partner
Dana Preminger, Chief Financial Officer
Dori Brown, Managing Partner
Eyal Attia, Managing Partner
Ran Ben-Or, Managing Partner

Type of Firm
Private Equity Firm

Project Preferences

Type of Financing Preferred:
Leveraged Buyout
Balanced
Management Buyouts
Acquisition

Geographical Preferences

International Preferences:
Asia Pacific
Israel

Additional Information
Year Founded: 2004
Current Activity Level : Actively seeking new investments

TENEX CAPITAL MANAGEMENT LP

60 East 42nd Street, Suite 4510
New York, NY USA 10165
Phone: 212-457-1138
Website: www.tenexcm.com

Management and Staff
J.P. Bretl, Principal
Joe Cottone, Principal
Michael Green, CEO & Managing Director
Michael Williams, Managing Director
Scott Galletti, Managing Director
Varun Bedi, Principal

Type of Firm
Private Equity Firm

Project Preferences

Type of Financing Preferred:
Leveraged Buyout
Turnaround
Acquisition
Special Situation
Recapitalizations

Geographical Preferences

United States Preferences:

Canadian Preferences:
All Canada

Industry Preferences

In Communications prefer:
Telecommunications

In Medical/Health prefer:
Medical/Health

In Industrial/Energy prefer:
Industrial Products

In Transportation prefer:
Transportation

In Business Serv. prefer:
Services

In Manufact. prefer:
Manufacturing

Additional Information
Name of Most Recent Fund: Tenex Capital Partners, L.P.
Most Recent Fund Was Raised: 12/02/2010
Year Founded: 2009
Capital Under Management: $814,000,000
Current Activity Level : Actively seeking new investments

TENGELMANN SOCIAL VENTURES GMBH

Wissollstrasse 5-43
Mulheim an der Ruhr, Germany 45478
Phone: 492085830
Fax: 492085832148
E-mail: social@e-tengelmann.de
Website: www.tev-social.de

Type of Firm
Private Equity Firm

Project Preferences

Type of Financing Preferred:
Early Stage
Seed
Startup

Industry Preferences

In Other prefer:
Socially Responsible

Additional Information
Year Founded: 2011
Current Activity Level: Actively seeking new investments

TENGELMANN VENTURES GMBH

Wissollstr. 5-43
Muelheim an der Ruhr, Germany 45478
Phone: 492085830
Fax: 492085832148
E-mail: info@vastervikinvest.se
Website: www.tev.de

Type of Firm
Private Equity Firm

Project Preferences

Type of Financing Preferred:
Early Stage
Seed
Startup

Geographical Preferences

International Preferences:
Sweden

Industry Preferences

In Manufact. prefer:
Manufacturing

Additional Information
Year Founded: 2006
Current Activity Level: Actively seeking new investments

TENGRAM CAPITAL PARTNERS LLC

15 Riverside Avenue
Westport, CT USA 06880
Phone: 2034546999
Fax: 2034546998
E-mail: info@tengramcapital.com
Website: www.tengramcapital.com

Management and Staff
Brian Cooper, Principal
Kris Parks, Principal
Matthew Eby, Managing Partner
Richard Gersten, Partner
William Sweedler, Managing Partner

Type of Firm
Private Equity Firm

Project Preferences

Type of Financing Preferred:
Leveraged Buyout
Acquisition

Industry Preferences

In Semiconductor/Electr prefer:
Electronics

In Medical/Health prefer:
Medical/Health

In Consumer Related prefer:
Consumer
Sports
Retail
Food/Beverage
Consumer Products

Additional Information
Name of Most Recent Fund: Tengram Capital Partners GEN2 Fund
Most Recent Fund Was Raised: 04/16/2013
Year Founded: 2010
Capital Under Management: $511,400,000
Current Activity Level: Actively seeking new investments

TENNANT CAPITAL PARTNERS L L C

79 Ledyard Road
West Hartford, CT USA 06117
Phone: 8602802140
E-mail: info@tennantcapital.com
Website: www.tennantcapital.com

Other Offices
Former HQ: 99 Pratt Street, Suite 200
Hartford, CT USA 06103

Management and Staff
Joseph Sargent, Managing Partner
Robert Sargent, Managing Partner
Thomas Sargent, Managing Partner

Type of Firm
Private Equity Firm

Project Preferences

Type of Financing Preferred:
Balanced

Industry Preferences

In Financial Services prefer:
Insurance

In Business Serv. prefer:
Services
Distribution

Additional Information
Year Founded: 2007
Current Activity Level: Actively seeking new investments

TENNENBAUM CAPITAL PARTNERS LLC

2951 28th Street, Suite 1000
Santa Monica, CA USA 90405
Phone: 3105661000
Fax: 3108994950
Website: www.tennenbaumcapital.com

Other Offices
Two Embarcadero Center, Suite 1670
San Francisco, CA USA 94111

320 Park Avenue
28th Floor
New York, NY USA 10022

Management and Staff
Christian Donohue, Managing Director
David Hollander, Managing Partner
David Whitehouse, Managing Director
David Adler, Senior Managing Director
Gabriel Goldstein, Principal
Howard Levkowitz, Managing Partner
Kenneth Chan, Principal
Lee Landrum, Managing Director
Michael Leitner, Managing Partner
Paul Davis, Chief Financial Officer
Philip Tseng, Partner
Rajneesh Vig, Managing Partner
Sean Berry, Principal
Timothy Gravely, Principal
Todd Gerch, Managing Director
Winifred Webb, Managing Director

Type of Firm
Private Equity Firm

Association Membership
Natl Assoc of Small Bus. Inv. Co (NASBIC)

Project Preferences

Type of Financing Preferred:
Mezzanine
Turnaround
Special Situation
Distressed Debt

Size of Investments Considered:
Min Size of Investment Considered (000s): $10,000
Max Size of Investment Considered (000s): $125,000

Geographical Preferences

United States Preferences:
North America

Industry Preferences

In Communications prefer:
Telecommunications

In Medical/Health prefer:
Medical/Health

In Consumer Related prefer:
Consumer
Entertainment and Leisure
Retail

In Industrial/Energy prefer:
Energy
Advanced Materials

In Transportation prefer:
Transportation
Aerospace

In Financial Services prefer:
Financial Services

In Business Serv. prefer:
Services
Media

In Manufact. prefer:
Manufacturing

In Agr/Forestr/Fish prefer:
Mining and Minerals

In Utilities prefer:
Utilities

Additional Information
Name of Most Recent Fund: Tennenbaum Waterman Fund, L.P.
Most Recent Fund Was Raised: 01/11/2013
Year Founded: 1996
Capital Under Management: $7,000,000,000
Current Activity Level : Actively seeking new investments

TENNESSEE COMMUNITY VENTURES FUND LLC

3841 Green Hills Village Drive, Suite 400
Nashville, TN USA 37215
E-mail: bizplan@tncvfund.com
Website: www.tncvfund.com

Type of Firm
Private Equity Firm

Project Preferences

Type of Financing Preferred:
Early Stage
Expansion
Generalist PE
Later Stage
Seed
Startup
Special Situation

Size of Investments Considered:
Min Size of Investment Considered (000s): $50
Max Size of Investment Considered (000s): $2,000

Geographical Preferences

United States Preferences:
Tennessee

Industry Preferences

In Internet Specific prefer:
Ecommerce

In Consumer Related prefer:
Retail
Food/Beverage
Consumer Products
Consumer Services

In Industrial/Energy prefer:
Advanced Materials

In Business Serv. prefer:
Services
Media

In Manufact. prefer:
Manufacturing

In Other prefer:
Women/Minority-Owned Bus.

Additional Information
Name of Most Recent Fund: Tennessee Community Ventures Fund LLC
Most Recent Fund Was Raised: 01/18/2010
Year Founded: 1969
Capital Under Management: $14,500,000
Current Activity Level : Actively seeking new investments

TENONETEN VENTURES LP

1999 Avenue of the Stars
Floor 35
Los Angeles, CA USA 90067
Phone: 5104211887
Website: tenoneten.net

Management and Staff
David Waxman, Managing Partner
Gil Elbaz, Founder

Type of Firm
Private Equity Firm

Project Preferences

Type of Financing Preferred:
Startup

Geographical Preferences

United States Preferences:
Southern California

Additional Information
Year Founded: 2013
Capital Under Management: $13,180,000
Current Activity Level : Actively seeking new investments

TENSILITY VENTURE PARTNERS LLC

225 West Washington, Suite 1550
Chicago, IL USA 60606
Website: www.tensilityvc.com

Other Offices
440 North Wells Street, Suite 420
CHICAGO, IL USA 60654
Phone: 3129521654

Type of Firm
Private Equity Firm

Project Preferences

Type of Financing Preferred:
Early Stage

Industry Preferences

In Computer Software prefer:
Artificial Intelligence

In Medical/Health prefer:
Health Services

Additional Information
Year Founded: 2017
Current Activity Level : Actively seeking new investments

TENTH AVENUE HOLDINGS LLC

483 Tenth Avenue
6th Floor
New York, NY USA 10018
Phone: 2122734920
Website: www.tenave.com

Management and Staff
Constance D Aurizio, Chief Financial Officer
Daniel Denihan, Managing Director
Donald Denihan, Managing Director
John Ferrari, Managing Director

Type of Firm
Investment Management Firm

Project Preferences

Type of Financing Preferred:
Leveraged Buyout
Generalist PE
Opportunistic
Acquisition

Geographical Preferences

United States Preferences:
East Coast

Canadian Preferences:
All Canada

International Preferences:
All International

Industry Preferences

In Financial Services prefer:
Real Estate

Additional Information
Year Founded: 2008
Current Activity Level : Actively seeking new investments

TENTH STREET CAPITAL PARTNERS LLC

Two Union Square
901 Tallan Building
Chattanooga, TN USA 37402
Phone: 4232667723
Fax: 4232667590
Website: www.tenthstreetcapital.com

Other Offices
20 Burton Hills Boulevard, Suite 430
Nashville, TN USA 37215
Phone: 6156653636

Management and Staff
Caroline Ducas, Principal
Casey Hammontree, Partner
Meredith Duke, Principal
Mike Rouse, Vice President
R. Alton Duke, Partner
William Nutter, Partner

Type of Firm
Private Equity Firm

Association Membership
Natl Assoc of Small Bus. Inv. Co (NASBIC)

Project Preferences

Type of Financing Preferred:
Mezzanine

Geographical Preferences

United States Preferences:

Additional Information
Name of Most Recent Fund: Tenth Street Fund I, L.P.
Most Recent Fund Was Raised: 06/09/2005
Year Founded: 2005
Capital Under Management: $26,900,000
Current Activity Level : Actively seeking new investments

TENZING PE LTD

Two Riding House Street
Henry Wood House
London, United Kingdom W1W 7FA
Phone: 2032827560
Fax: 2032827135
E-mail: hello@tenzing.pe

Type of Firm
Private Equity Firm

Project Preferences

Type of Financing Preferred:
Leveraged Buyout

Geographical Preferences

International Preferences:
Ireland
United Kingdom

Additional Information
Year Founded: 2015
Capital Under Management: $245,220,000
Current Activity Level : Actively seeking new investments

TEOLLISEN YHTEISTYON RAHASTO OY

Uudenmaankatu 16 B
4th floor
Helsinki, Finland 00120
Phone: 3589348434
Fax: 358934843346
E-mail: finnfund@finnfund.fi
Website: www.finnfund.fi

Management and Staff
Jaakko Kangasniemi, CEO & Managing Director

Type of Firm
Private Equity Firm

Project Preferences

Role in Financing:
Prefer role as deal originator but will also invest in deals created by others

Type of Financing Preferred:
Fund of Funds
Early Stage
Mezzanine
Seed
Startup

Geographical Preferences

International Preferences:
Vietnam
Latin America
India
China
Eastern Europe
Middle East
Afghanistan
Asia
Russia
Africa

Industry Preferences

In Communications prefer:
Communications and Media

In Computer Other prefer:
Computer Related

In Semiconductor/Electr prefer:
Electronic Components

In Biotechnology prefer:
Biotechnology

In Medical/Health prefer:
Medical/Health

In Consumer Related prefer:
Consumer

In Industrial/Energy prefer:
Energy
Industrial Products

In Business Serv. prefer:
Services
Distribution

In Agr/Forestr/Fish prefer:
Agriculture related

TERALYS CAPITAL INC

999 boulevard de Maisonnevue O, Suite 1700
Montreal, Canada H3A 3L4
Phone: 514-509-2080
Fax: 514-509-2080
E-mail: info@teralyscapital.com
Website: www.teralyscapital.com

Management and Staff
Cedric Bisson, Partner
Eric Legault, Co-Founder
Jacques Bernier, Co-Founder
Julien Guimond, Principal
Luc Couture, Partner

Type of Firm
Private Equity Advisor or Fund of Funds

Association Membership
Canadian Venture Capital Association

Project Preferences

Type of Financing Preferred:
Fund of Funds
Leveraged Buyout
Acquisition

Additional Information
Year Founded: 1999
Capital Under Management: $1,689,000,000
Current Activity Level : Actively seeking new investments

TERANET ENTERPRISES INC

123 Front Street West, Suite 700
Toronto, Canada M5J 2M2
Phone: 416-360-5263
E-mail: info@teranet.ca

Management and Staff
Elgin Farewell, Vice President
Lawrence Franco, Vice President

Type of Firm
Investment Management Firm

Additional Information
Year Founded: 1991
Current Activity Level : Actively seeking new investments

Additional Information
Year Founded: 1980
Capital Under Management: $101,900,000
Current Activity Level : Actively seeking new investments
Method of Compensation: Return on investment is of primary concern, do not charge fees

TERAWATT VENTURES LLC

Four Cambridge Center
Cambridge, MA USA 02142
Phone: 6172526900
Fax: 6172626910
E-mail: info@terawattventures.com
Website: www.terawattventures.com

Management and Staff
Mark Goodman, Founder
Prapti Mittal, Principal

Type of Firm
Private Equity Firm

Project Preferences

Type of Financing Preferred:
Balanced

Industry Preferences

In Consumer Related prefer:
Consumer

In Industrial/Energy prefer:
Energy
Alternative Energy
Energy Conservation Relat
Environmental Related

In Agr/Forestr/Fish prefer:
Agriculture related

In Other prefer:
Environment Responsible

Additional Information
Year Founded: 2009
Current Activity Level : Actively seeking new investments

TERES CAPITAL OOD SOFIA

1 Kuzman Shapkarev Street
Sofia, Bulgaria 1000
Phone: 35924452220
E-mail: info@teres-capital.com
Website: www.teres-capital.com

Management and Staff
Dimitar Botaev, Chief Operating Officer
Ivan Genadiev, Chief Executive Officer
Maxim Gurvits, Partner

Type of Firm
Private Equity Firm

Project Preferences

Type of Financing Preferred:
Early Stage
Seed
Startup

Geographical Preferences

International Preferences:
Eastern Europe

Industry Preferences

In Computer Software prefer:
Software

In Consumer Related prefer:
Education Related

In Industrial/Energy prefer:
Energy

Additional Information
Year Founded: 2012
Current Activity Level : Actively seeking new investments

TERRA FIRMA CAPITAL PARTNERS LTD

Two More London Riverside
London, United Kingdom SE1 2AP
Phone: 442070159500
E-mail: info@terrafirma.com
Website: www.terrafirma.com

Other Offices

Garden Towers
Neue Mainzer - Strasse 46-50
Frankfurt am Main, Germany 60311
Phone: 49-69-380-756-000
Fax: 49-69-380-756-001

Unit 11, 9th Floor
Tower W1, Oriental Plaza
Beijing, China
Phone: 861085199700

Fourth Floor, Royal Chambers
St. Julians Avenue, St. Peter Port
Guernsey, United Kingdom GY1 3RE
Phone: 44-1481-754-690

Old Bank Chambers
La Grande Rue
Guernsey, United Kingdom GY4 6RT
Phone: 44-1481-715-601

An der Welle Four
Frankfurt, Germany 60322
Phone: 496975937611

Management and Staff
Alex Williams, Managing Director
Dominic Spiri, Chief Financial Officer
Fred Hervouet, General Partner
Iain Stokes, General Partner
John Stares, General Partner
Julie Williamson, Managing Director
Jyrki Korhonen, Managing Director
Michele Russo, Managing Director
Peter Miholich, Managing Director

Robbie Barr, Managing Director
Tim Pryce, Managing Director
Trudy Cooke, Chief Operating Officer

Type of Firm
Private Equity Firm

Association Membership
British Venture Capital Association (BVCA)
European Private Equity and Venture Capital Assoc.

Project Preferences

Role in Financing:
Prefer role as deal originator

Type of Financing Preferred:
Leveraged Buyout
Other
Acquisition

Geographical Preferences

United States Preferences:

International Preferences:
Italy
France

Industry Focus
(% based on actual investment)
Consumer Related	80.6%
Industrial/Energy	10.5%
Other Products	8.8%
Medical/Health	0.1%

Additional Information
Year Founded: 1994
Capital Under Management: $16,711,300,000
Current Activity Level : Actively seeking new investments

TERRA ROSSA CAPITAL PTY LTD

33 King William Street
Level 15
Adelaide, Australia 5000
Phone: 61882176450
Fax: 61882176451
E-mail: info@terrarossacapital.com
Website: www.terrarossacapital.com

Management and Staff
Jurgen Michaelis, Founder

Type of Firm
Private Equity Firm

Association Membership
Australian Venture Capital Association (AVCAL)

Project Preferences

Type of Financing Preferred:
Early Stage
Seed

Size of Investments Considered:
Min Size of Investment Considered (000s): $210
Max Size of Investment Considered (000s): $2,101

Geographical Preferences

International Preferences:
Australia

Industry Preferences

In Biotechnology prefer:
Agricultural/Animal Bio.
Industrial Biotechnology

In Medical/Health prefer:
Medical/Health
Medical Products
Health Services

Additional Information
Year Founded: 2006
Capital Under Management: $29,400,000
Current Activity Level : Actively seeking new investments

TERRA VENTURE PARTNERS

41 Harlap Street
Jerusalem, Israel 92341
Phone: 97225670126
Fax: 97225670103
E-mail: info@terravp.com
Website: www.terravp.com

Management and Staff
Astorre Modena, General Partner
Barak Goldstein, Venture Partner
Harold Wiener, General Partner
Larry Gross, Venture Partner

Type of Firm
Private Equity Firm

Project Preferences

Type of Financing Preferred:
Early Stage
Balanced
Later Stage
Seed
Startup

Geographical Preferences

International Preferences:
Israel
Asia

Industry Preferences

In Communications prefer:
Telecommunications
Wireless Communications

In Computer Software prefer:
Software

In Internet Specific prefer:
Internet

In Industrial/Energy prefer:
Energy
Alternative Energy
Environmental Related

In Other prefer:
Environment Responsible

Additional Information
Year Founded: 2006
Capital Under Management: $20,000,000
Current Activity Level : Actively seeking new investments

TERRAPIN PARTNERS LLC

590 Madison Avenue
35th Floor
New York, NY USA 10022
Phone: 2127104117
Fax: 2127104105
E-mail: info@terrapinpartners.com
Website: www.terrapinpartners.com

Other Offices
1001 Rivas Canyon Road
Pacific Palisades, CA USA 90272
Phone: 310-459-5132
Fax: 310-459-5822

Management and Staff
Darren Rabenou, Managing Director
Dean Rubino, President
Nathalie Cunningham, Partner
Nathan Leight, Co-Founder
Stuart Gallin, Chief Financial Officer

Type of Firm
Private Equity Firm

Project Preferences

Type of Financing Preferred:
Generalist PE
Seed

Geographical Preferences

United States Preferences:
All U.S.

Industry Preferences

In Medical/Health prefer:
Medical Products
Health Services

In Consumer Related prefer:
Retail
Food/Beverage

In Industrial/Energy prefer:
Energy

In Financial Services prefer:
Real Estate

In Business Serv. prefer:
Media

Additional Information
Year Founded: 1998
Current Activity Level : Actively seeking new investments

TERTIAIRE DEVELOPPE-MENT SERVICE SARL

47 rue de Chaillot
Paris, France 75016
Phone: 33156622100
Fax: 33147202858
E-mail: terdev@club-internet.fr

Management and Staff
Herve Debache, President

Type of Firm
Private Equity Firm

Association Membership
French Venture Capital Association (AFIC)

Project Preferences

Type of Financing Preferred:
Early Stage
Later Stage

Geographical Preferences

International Preferences:
France

Additional Information
Year Founded: 2007
Current Activity Level : Actively seeking new investments

TERTIUM SAS

22 bd Charles Moretti
Marseille, France 13014
Phone: 33491787785
E-mail: contact@tertium-invest.com
Website: www.tertium-invest.com

Management and Staff
Florence Canonge, Partner
Pierre Grand-Dufay, Partner
Stephane Assuied, Partner

Type of Firm
Private Equity Firm

Project Preferences

Type of Financing Preferred:
Leveraged Buyout
Early Stage
Generalist PE
Later Stage
Acquisition

Geographical Preferences

International Preferences:
Europe
France

Additional Information
Year Founded: 2012
Current Activity Level : Actively seeking new investments

TETON CAPITAL GROUP LLC

19300 Shaker Boulevard
Shaker Heights
Cleveland, OH USA 44122
Website: www.tetoncapitalgroup.com

Type of Firm
Private Equity Firm

Project Preferences

Type of Financing Preferred:
Leveraged Buyout
Management Buyouts

Geographical Preferences

United States Preferences:

Industry Preferences

In Business Serv. prefer:
Services
Distribution

In Manufact. prefer:
Manufacturing

Additional Information
Year Founded: 2003
Capital Under Management: $1,450,000
Current Activity Level : Actively seeking new investments

TEUZA A FAIRCHILD TECHNOLOGY VENTURE LTD

P.O. Box 25266
Haifa, Israel 31250
Phone: 97248728788
Fax: 97248729393
E-mail: teuza@teuzafund.com
Website: www.teuzafund.com

Management and Staff
Moshe Zimmerman, Chief Financial Officer

Type of Firm
Private Equity Advisor or Fund of Funds

Association Membership
Israel Venture Association

Project Preferences

Type of Financing Preferred:
Early Stage
Seed
Startup

Size of Investments Considered:
Min Size of Investment Considered (000s): $500
Max Size of Investment Considered (000s): $4,000

Geographical Preferences

International Preferences:
Israel

Industry Preferences

In Communications prefer:
Telecommunications

In Computer Software prefer:
Software

In Semiconductor/Electr prefer:
Electronic Components
Semiconductor

In Biotechnology prefer:
Biotechnology

In Medical/Health prefer:
Medical/Health
Medical Products

Additional Information
Year Founded: 1991
Capital Under Management: $23,000,000
Current Activity Level : Actively seeking new investments

TEXAS ATLANTIC CAPITAL

4141 Southwest Freeway, Suite 340
Houston, TX USA 77027
Phone: 7133415326
Website: www.atlantic.vc

Type of Firm
Private Equity Firm

Project Preferences

Type of Financing Preferred:
Startup

Geographical Preferences

United States Preferences:

International Preferences:
Europe
Israel

Additional Information
Year Founded: 2010
Current Activity Level : Actively seeking new investments

TEXAS INTREPID VENTURES LLC

24370 Blanco Road, Suite 101
San Antonio, TX USA 78260
Phone: 210-340-0116
Fax: 210-558-1860
Website: www.txintrepid.com

Management and Staff
David Spencer, President, Founder

Type of Firm
Private Equity Firm

Project Preferences

Type of Financing Preferred:
Balanced

Geographical Preferences

United States Preferences:
Texas

Industry Preferences

In Medical/Health prefer:
Medical/Health
Medical Therapeutics
Health Services

Additional Information
Year Founded: 2008
Current Activity Level : Actively seeking new investments

TEXAS NEXT CAPITAL LP

250 W. Nottingham, Suite 120
San Antonio, TX USA 78209
Phone: 2108262250
Fax: 2108262252
Website: texasnextcapital.com

Management and Staff
Chris Edelen, Chief Executive Officer
John Kerr, Co-Founder
Matt Murphy, Co-Founder
Steve Hassmann, Co-Founder

Type of Firm
Private Equity Firm

Project Preferences

Type of Financing Preferred:
Leveraged Buyout
Management Buyouts
Acquisition
Recapitalizations

Geographical Preferences

United States Preferences:
Texas

Industry Preferences

In Medical/Health prefer:
Health Services

In Consumer Related prefer:
Consumer

In Industrial/Energy prefer:
Energy
Materials

In Financial Services prefer:
Financial Services

Additional Information
Year Founded: 1969
Current Activity Level : Actively seeking new investments

TEXAS TECHNOLOGY DEVELOPMENT CENTER

12500 Network Boulevard, Suite 105
San Antonio, TX USA 78249
Phone: 2105584696
Fax: 2105589485
Website: t3dc.org

Type of Firm
Private Equity Firm

Project Preferences

Type of Financing Preferred:
Early Stage
Seed
Startup

Geographical Preferences

United States Preferences:
Texas

Industry Preferences

In Biotechnology prefer:
Biotechnology

In Medical/Health prefer:
Medical/Health
Medical Products
Health Services

Additional Information
Year Founded: 2012
Current Activity Level : Actively seeking new investments

TEXO VENTURES

6034 West Courtyard Drive, Suite 100
Austin, TX USA 78730
Phone: 8774888396
Website: www.texoventures.com

Management and Staff
Jerry DeVries, Co-Founder
Philip Sanger, Co-Founder
Randall Crowder, Co-Founder

Type of Firm
Private Equity Firm

Project Preferences

Type of Financing Preferred:
Early Stage
Seed

Geographical Preferences

United States Preferences:

Industry Preferences

In Communications prefer:
Commercial Communications

In Medical/Health prefer:
Medical/Health
Diagnostic Services
Diagnostic Test Products
Medical Products
Health Services

Additional Information
Name of Most Recent Fund: TEXO Ventures I, L.P.
Most Recent Fund Was Raised: 02/08/2012
Year Founded: 2010
Capital Under Management: $15,410,000
Current Activity Level : Actively seeking new investments

TGAP VENTURES LLC

7171 Stadium Drive
Kalamazoo, MI USA 49009
Website: www.tgapventures.com

Management and Staff
Jack Ahrens, General Partner
Peter Farner, General Partner

Type of Firm
Private Equity Firm

Project Preferences

Type of Financing Preferred:
Early Stage
Seed

Size of Investments Considered:
Min Size of Investment Considered (000s): $500
Max Size of Investment Considered (000s): $1,000

Geographical Preferences

United States Preferences:
Midwest

Industry Preferences

In Communications prefer:
Telecommunications

In Computer Software prefer:
Software

In Internet Specific prefer:
Internet

In Medical/Health prefer:
Medical Products
Health Services

In Manufact. prefer:
Manufacturing

Additional Information

Name of Most Recent Fund: TGap Venture Capital Fund II, L.P.
Most Recent Fund Was Raised: 06/12/2009
Year Founded: 2002
Capital Under Management: $20,300,000
Current Activity Level : Actively seeking new investments

TGP INVESTMENTS LLC

4900 Main Street, Suite 900
Kansas City, MO USA 64112
Phone: 816-994-8600
Fax: 816-994-8610
Website: www.tgpinvestments.com

Management and Staff

Eric Graham, Managing Director
Shane Parr, Managing Director
Timothy Leland, Managing Director
William Thomas, Senior Managing Director

Type of Firm

Private Equity Firm

Project Preferences

Type of Financing Preferred:
Acquisition

Geographical Preferences

United States Preferences:
Midwest

Industry Preferences

In Business Serv. prefer:
Services
Distribution

In Manufact. prefer:
Manufacturing

Additional Information

Year Founded: 2005
Capital Under Management: $31,500,000
Current Activity Level : Actively seeking new investments

THAI DEVELOPMENT CAPITAL FUND LTD (THE)

3/F 36c Bermuda Tower
Dr. Roy's Drive, George Town
Grand Cayman, Cayman Islands
Website: www.tdcf.com

Type of Firm

Private Equity Firm

Project Preferences

Role in Financing:
Will function either as deal originator or investor in deals created by others

Type of Financing Preferred:
Balanced

Geographical Preferences

International Preferences:
Thailand

Additional Information

Year Founded: 2000
Current Activity Level : Actively seeking new investments
Method of Compensation: Return on investment is of primary concern, do not charge fees

THAI INCUBATOR DOT COM CO LTD

159/21 Sukhumvit 21 Road
14th Floor, Serm-Mit Tower
Bangkok, Thailand 10110
Phone: 6626617898
Fax: 6626617899
E-mail: idea@thaiincubator.com
Website: www.thaiincubator.com

Other Offices

90/25 North Sathorn Road
, Thailand 10500
Phone: 662-636-8282
Fax: 662-268-1483

Type of Firm

Incubator/Development Program

Project Preferences

Type of Financing Preferred:
Startup

Geographical Preferences

International Preferences:
Thailand

Industry Preferences

In Computer Software prefer:
Software

In Internet Specific prefer:
Internet

In Semiconductor/Electr prefer:
Electronics

In Consumer Related prefer:
Food/Beverage
Education Related

In Transportation prefer:
Transportation

Additional Information

Year Founded: 2000
Current Activity Level : Actively seeking new investments

THALES CORPORATE VENTURES SAS

45, Rue De Villiers
Neuilly-sur-Seine, France 92200
Phone: 33157778000
Fax: 33153778733
Website: www.thalesgroup.com

Other Offices

c/o Cetia, Inc.
350 Cambridge Avenue
Palo Alto, CA USA 94306
Phone: 415-325-5349
Fax: 415-325-6226

Type of Firm

Corporate PE/Venture

Project Preferences

Role in Financing:
Will function either as deal originator or investor in deals created by others

Type of Financing Preferred:
Early Stage
Later Stage
First Stage Financing
Startup
Distressed Debt

Size of Investments Considered:
Min Size of Investment Considered (000s): $283
Max Size of Investment Considered (000s): $2,825

Geographical Preferences

United States Preferences:
All U.S.

International Preferences:
Europe
Asia

Industry Preferences

In Communications prefer:
Telecommunications

In Computer Software prefer:
Software

In Computer Other prefer:
Computer Related

In Semiconductor/Electr prefer:
Electronics

In Business Serv. prefer:
Media

Additional Information
Year Founded: 1986
Capital Under Management: $66,900,000
Current Activity Level : Actively seeking new investments

THARAWAT INVESTMENT HOUSE BSCC

Bahrain World Trade Centre
East Tower, 13th floor
Manama, Bahrain
Phone: 97317560777
Fax: 97317560778
E-mail: info@tharawat.net
Website: www.tharawat.net

Type of Firm
Private Equity Firm

Project Preferences

Type of Financing Preferred:
Leveraged Buyout
Early Stage
Generalist PE
Balanced
Later Stage
Acquisition
Startup

Geographical Preferences

International Preferences:
Europe
Middle East
Yemen

Industry Preferences

In Biotechnology prefer:
Agricultural/Animal Bio.

In Medical/Health prefer:
Medical/Health
Health Services

In Consumer Related prefer:
Food/Beverage
Education Related

In Industrial/Energy prefer:
Energy

In Transportation prefer:
Transportation

In Financial Services prefer:
Real Estate

In Business Serv. prefer:
Services

In Agr/Forestr/Fish prefer:
Agriculture related

Additional Information
Year Founded: 2008
Current Activity Level : Actively seeking new investments

THAYER VENTURES

400 Pacific Avenue
Second Floor West
San Francisco, CA USA 94133
Phone: 4157821414
Website: www.thayerventures.com

Management and Staff
Christopher Hemmeter, Managing Director
Jeff Jackson, Venture Partner
Leland Pillsbury, Managing Director
Lucien Ruby, Managing Director
Mark Farrell, Managing Director
R. Stephen Doyle, Venture Partner
Stephen Moore, Venture Partner

Type of Firm
Private Equity Firm

Project Preferences

Type of Financing Preferred:
Balanced

Industry Preferences

In Consumer Related prefer:
Casino/Gambling
Food/Beverage
Other Restaurants

In Transportation prefer:
Transportation
Aerospace

Additional Information
Name of Most Recent Fund: Quest Hospitality Ventures I, L.P.
Most Recent Fund Was Raised: 02/09/2011

Year Founded: 2009
Capital Under Management: $5,000,000
Current Activity Level : Actively seeking new investments

THE HATCH FIRM BV

95, Zaaiersweg
Amsterdam, Netherlands 1097SR
Phone: 205771234
Website: www.thehatchfirm.com

Type of Firm
Private Equity Firm

Project Preferences

Type of Financing Preferred:
Early Stage
Expansion
Later Stage
Seed

Size of Investments Considered:
Min Size of Investment Considered (000s): $329
Max Size of Investment Considered (000s): $1,095

Geographical Preferences

International Preferences:
Europe
Netherlands

Industry Preferences

In Communications prefer:
Data Communications

In Computer Software prefer:
Software

In Internet Specific prefer:
Internet
Ecommerce

Additional Information
Year Founded: 2014
Current Activity Level : Actively seeking new investments

THEFAMILY SAS

9 rue Villehardouin
Paris, France 75003
Website: www.thefamily.co

Management and Staff
Jean De La Roche-Brochard, Partner
Nicolas Colin, Co-Founder
Nicolas Saillant, Chief Executive Officer
Oussama Ammar, Co-Founder

Type of Firm
Private Equity Firm

Project Preferences

Type of Financing Preferred:
Early Stage
Seed
Startup

Geographical Preferences

International Preferences:
Europe
France

Industry Preferences

In Communications prefer:
Commercial Communications
Data Communications

In Computer Software prefer:
Applications Software

Additional Information

Year Founded: 2013
Current Activity Level : Actively seeking new investments

THEODORUS SCA

40, Avenue Joseph Wybran
Anderlecht, Belgium 1070
Phone: 3225295934
Website: www.theodorus.be

Type of Firm
University Program

Project Preferences

Type of Financing Preferred:
Early Stage
Seed

Geographical Preferences

International Preferences:
Belgium

Additional Information

Year Founded: 2003
Current Activity Level : Actively seeking new investments

THERMI VENTURES SA

9 km Thessaloniki-Thermi
Thessaloniki, Greece 57001
Phone: 302311999999
Fax: 302311999997
E-mail: info@thermi-ventures.com
Website: www.thermi-ventures.gr

Type of Firm
Private Equity Firm

Project Preferences

Type of Financing Preferred:
Early Stage
Startup

Geographical Preferences

International Preferences:
Greece

Industry Preferences

In Communications prefer:
Wireless Communications

In Biotechnology prefer:
Biotechnology

In Medical/Health prefer:
Medical/Health

In Consumer Related prefer:
Consumer

In Industrial/Energy prefer:
Energy
Alternative Energy
Environmental Related

In Financial Services prefer:
Real Estate

Additional Information

Year Founded: 2008
Current Activity Level : Actively seeking new investments

THERMO CAPITAL PARTNERS LLC

1735 19th Street, Suite 200
Denver, CO USA 80202
Phone: 504-585-1390
Fax: 504-585-1393
Website: www.thermoco.com

Other Offices
PO Box 746
Pelham, NY USA 10803
Phone: 914-576-7357
Fax: 914-206-4237

Management and Staff
James Lynch, Managing Partner

Type of Firm
Private Equity Firm

Project Preferences

Type of Financing Preferred:
Balanced

Size of Investments Considered:
Min Size of Investment Considered (000s): $5,000
Max Size of Investment Considered (000s): $50,000

Geographical Preferences

United States Preferences:
All U.S.

Industry Preferences

In Communications prefer:
Telecommunications

In Industrial/Energy prefer:
Industrial Products

In Business Serv. prefer:
Services

Additional Information

Year Founded: 2001
Current Activity Level : Actively seeking new investments

THEVENTURECITY

1111 Lincoln Road, Suite 801
Miami Beach, FL USA 33139
Website: theventure.city

Type of Firm
Incubator/Development Program

Project Preferences

Type of Financing Preferred:
Startup

Additional Information

Year Founded: 2017
Current Activity Level : Actively seeking new investments

THINK HEALTH GMBH

Veit-Stoss-Strasse 8
Fuerstenfeldbruck, Germany 82256
E-mail: info@think-health.de
Website: www.think-health.de

Type of Firm
Private Equity Firm

Project Preferences

Type of Financing Preferred:
Early Stage

Additional Information

Year Founded: 2004
Current Activity Level : Actively seeking new investments

THINK VENTURES LP

235 Alma Street
Palo Alto, CA USA 94301
Phone: 6509064128

Management and Staff
Safa Rashtchy, Managing Director

Type of Firm
Private Equity Firm

Project Preferences

Type of Financing Preferred:
Balanced

Additional Information
Year Founded: 2014
Current Activity Level : Actively seeking new investments

THIRD KIND VENTURE CAPITAL LLC

555 W. 18th Street
New York, NY USA 10011
Phone: 2123147431

Type of Firm
Private Equity Firm

Project Preferences

Type of Financing Preferred:
Early Stage

Industry Preferences

In Financial Services prefer:
Financial Services

Additional Information
Year Founded: 2017
Capital Under Management: $44,320,000
Current Activity Level : Actively seeking new investments

THIRD POINT VENTURES LP

390 Park Avenue
New York, NY USA 10022
Phone: 2122247400

Type of Firm
Corporate PE/Venture

Project Preferences

Type of Financing Preferred:
Balanced

Additional Information
Year Founded: 2005
Current Activity Level : Actively seeking new investments

THIRD PRIME CAPITAL MANAGEMENT LLC

18 East 50th Street, Sixth Floor
New York, NY USA 10022

Type of Firm
Private Equity Firm

Project Preferences

Type of Financing Preferred:
Early Stage

Industry Preferences

In Financial Services prefer:
Real Estate

Additional Information
Year Founded: 2014
Current Activity Level : Actively seeking new investments

THIRD ROCK VENTURES LLC

29 Newbury Street
Third Floor
Boston, MA USA 02116
Phone: 6175852000
Fax: 6178592891
E-mail: info@thirdrockventures.com
Website: www.thirdrockventures.com

Other Offices
455 Mission Bay Boulevard South, Suite 575
SAN FRANCISCO, CA USA 94158
Phone: 4157663600
Fax: 4157663699

Management and Staff
Alexis Borisy, Partner
Barbara Weber, Venture Partner
Brian Albrecht, Principal
Cary Pfeffer, Partner
Charles Homcy, Partner
Christoph Lengauer, Venture Partner
Craig Muir, Partner
Frank Gentile, Venture Partner
Jeffrey Tong, Venture Partner
Kevin Starr, Co-Founder
Mark Levin, Co-Founder
Mark Goldsmith, Venture Partner
Neil Exter, Partner
Perry Karsen, Venture Partner
Philip Reilly, Venture Partner
Robert Tepper, Co-Founder
Sarah Larson, Partner
Stephen Sherwin, Venture Partner

Type of Firm
Private Equity Firm

Association Membership
New England Venture Capital Association
National Venture Capital Association - USA (NVCA)

Project Preferences

Role in Financing:
Will function either as deal originator or investor in deals created by others

Type of Financing Preferred:
Early Stage
Seed

Geographical Preferences

United States Preferences:
Massachusetts
West Coast
East Coast

Industry Preferences

In Computer Software prefer:
Data Processing

In Biotechnology prefer:
Biotechnology

In Medical/Health prefer:
Medical/Health
Medical Diagnostics
Medical Therapeutics
Pharmaceuticals

Additional Information
Name of Most Recent Fund: Third Rock Ventures III, L.P.
Most Recent Fund Was Raised: 03/15/2013
Year Founded: 2007
Capital Under Management: $2,222,000,000
Current Activity Level : Actively seeking new investments
Method of Compensation: Return on investment is of primary concern, do not charge fees

THIRD ROME

Kosmonavta Volkova 5
Building 1
Moscow, Russia 127299
Website: www.third-rome.com

Other Offices
3bis Cours des Bastions
Geneva, Switzerland 1205

Type of Firm
Private Equity Firm

Project Preferences

Type of Financing Preferred:
Early Stage
Expansion
Later Stage
Seed

Geographical Preferences

International Preferences:
Armenia
Belarus
Kazakhstan
Kyrgyzstan
Tajikistan
Turkmenistan
Azerbaijan
Moldova
Ukraine
Uzbekistan
Russia

Industry Preferences

In Communications prefer:
Media and Entertainment

In Computer Other prefer:
Computer Related

Additional Information
Year Founded: 900
Current Activity Level : Actively seeking new investments

THIRD SECURITY LLC

1881 Grove Avenue
The Governor Tyler
Radford, VA USA 24141
Phone: 5406337900
Fax: 5406337939
Website: www.thirdsecurity.com

Other Offices

2875 South Ocean Boulevard, Suite 214
Palm Beach, FL USA 33480
Phone: 5618557831
Fax: 5613550627

735 Market Street
Third Floor
San Francisco, CA USA 94103
Phone: 415-644-5365
Fax: 415-344-0677

Management and Staff
Clifton Herndon, Managing Director
Doit Koppler, Managing Director
Jason Gabriel, Vice President
Jeffrey Perez, Managing Director
Julian Kirk, Managing Director
Lisa Moose, Managing Director
Marcus Smith, Senior Managing Director
Randal Kirk, CEO & Managing Director
Sanjeev Balhara, Vice President
Scott Horner, Managing Director
Theodore Fisher, Managing Director

Type of Firm
Private Equity Firm

Project Preferences

Type of Financing Preferred:
Expansion
Balanced
Later Stage
Seed
Startup

Geographical Preferences

United States Preferences:
Southeast
Virginia
Southwest
West Virginia

Industry Preferences

In Communications prefer:
Communications and Media

In Business Serv. prefer:
Services

Additional Information
Name of Most Recent Fund: Valleys' Ventures, L.P.
Most Recent Fund Was Raised: 05/06/2013
Year Founded: 1999
Capital Under Management: $800,000,000
Current Activity Level : Actively seeking new investments

THIRD WAVE VENTURES

410 South Barrington Avenue
Los Angeles, CA USA 90049
Phone: 3104726148
Fax: 3104729869
E-mail: info@thirdwaveventures.com

Management and Staff
Babak Cyrus Razi, Founder
Faryan Andrew Afifi, Co-Founder

Type of Firm
Private Equity Firm

Additional Information
Year Founded: 2004
Current Activity Level : Actively seeking new investments

THIRDSTREAM PARTNERS LLC

650 California Street
31st Floor
San Francisco, CA USA 94108
E-mail: info@thirdstreampartners.com
Website: www.thirdstreampartners.com

Type of Firm
Private Equity Firm

Project Preferences

Type of Financing Preferred:
Early Stage
Later Stage

Industry Preferences

In Financial Services prefer:
Financial Services

Additional Information
Year Founded: 1969
Current Activity Level : Actively seeking new investments

THOLONS CAPITAL

5 Penn Plaza
23rd Floor
New York, NY USA 10001
Phone: 6463782296
Fax: 6463493546
E-mail: info@tholonscapital.com
Website: www.tholonscapital.com

Other Offices

21 San Miguel Avenue, Ortigas Center
Unit 803 Richmonde Plaza
Pasig City, Philippines 1600
Phone: 6326359236

Av. Italia 6201
Latu Los Sauces Of. 104
Montevideo, Uruguay 11500
Phone: 59898485225

22 Marsh Wall
2505, The Landmark West Tower
London, United Kingdom E14 9AL
Phone: 441628566140

345, R A De Mel Mawatha
1st Floor, Regent Building
Colombo 3, Sri Lanka
Phone: 94112574083

346, 17th Cross
HIG Colony, Dollars Colony
Bangalore, India 560 094
Phone: 918023519760

Management and Staff
Ankita Vashistha, Principal
B. Paul Santos, Managing Partner
Debneel Mukherjee, Partner

Type of Firm
Investment Management Firm

Project Preferences

Type of Financing Preferred:
Value-Add
Early Stage

Geographical Preferences

United States Preferences:
North America

International Preferences:
India
Asia

Industry Preferences

In Financial Services prefer:
Real Estate

Additional Information

Year Founded: 2006
Current Activity Level : Actively seeking new investments

THOMA BRAVO LLC

300 North La Salle Street, Suite 4350
Chicago, IL USA 60654
Phone: 3122543300
Fax: 3122543301
Website: thomabravo.com

Other Offices

600 Montgomery Street
32nd Floor
San Francisco, CA USA 94111
Phone: 415-263-3660
Fax: 415-392-6480

Management and Staff

A.J. Rohde, Vice President
AJ Jangalapalli, Vice President
Amy Coleman Redenbaugh, Chief Financial Officer
Arvindh Kumar, Principal
Carl Thoma, Managing Partner
Chip Virnig, Principal
Corey Whisner, Principal
Holden Spaht, Partner
Hudson Smith, Partner
Jeffrey Del Papa, Vice President
Lee Mitchell, Managing Partner
Matt Gilbert, Vice President
Orlando Bravo, Managing Partner
Robert Sayle, Partner
Scott Crabill, Managing Partner
Seth Boro, Partner

Type of Firm

Private Equity Firm

Association Membership

Illinois Venture Capital Association
Private Equity Council (PEC)

Project Preferences

Role in Financing:
Prefer role as deal originator but will also invest in deals created by others

Type of Financing Preferred:
Expansion
Acquisition

Industry Preferences

In Computer Software prefer:
Applications Software

In Consumer Related prefer:
Education Related

In Financial Services prefer:
Financial Services

In Business Serv. prefer:
Media

Additional Information

Name of Most Recent Fund: Thoma Bravo Fund X, L.P.
Most Recent Fund Was Raised: 02/28/2012
Year Founded: 2008
Capital Under Management: $4,000,000,000
Current Activity Level : Actively seeking new investments

THOMA CRESSEY BRAVO INC

300 North LaSalle Street, Suite 4350
Chicago, IL USA 60654
Phone: 3122543300
Fax: 3122543301
Website: www.tcb.com

Other Offices

155 North Wacker Drive, Suite 4500
Chicago, IL USA 60606
Phone: 3129455700
Fax: 3129455701

Management and Staff

Katherine Brennan, Chief Financial Officer

Type of Firm

Private Equity Firm

Project Preferences

Role in Financing:
Prefer role as deal originator

Type of Financing Preferred:
Leveraged Buyout
Later Stage
Recapitalizations

Geographical Preferences

United States Preferences:

Canadian Preferences:
All Canada

Industry Focus

(% based on actual investment)
Other Products	31.8%
Medical/Health	27.2%
Computer Software and Services	18.4%
Computer Hardware	13.5%
Internet Specific	4.4%
Consumer Related	3.2%
Biotechnology	1.5%

Additional Information

Name of Most Recent Fund: Thoma Cressey Fund VIII, L.P.
Most Recent Fund Was Raised: 10/27/2005
Year Founded: 1998
Capital Under Management: $1,017,400,000
Current Activity Level : Actively seeking new investments
Method of Compensation: Return on invest. most important, but chg. closing fees, service fees, etc.

THOMAS H LEE PARTNERS LP

100 Federal Street
35th Floor
Boston, MA USA 02110
Phone: 6172271050
Fax: 6172273514
Website: www.thl.com

Management and Staff

Beverly Berman, Managing Director
Daniel Jones, Managing Director
David Jackson, Vice President
David Wachsman, Vice President
Douglas Haber, Principal
Erik Zimmer, Managing Director
Ganesh Rao, Managing Director
Gregory White, Managing Director
Gregory Maxon, Managing Director
Hobart Cook, Vice President
James Martin, Principal
James Carlisle, Managing Director
Jay Bhatt, Managing Director
Jeff Swenson, Managing Director
Joshua Bresler, Managing Director
Joshua Nelson, Managing Director
Julia Donnelly, Principal
Justin Roberts, Vice President
Kent Weldon, Managing Director
Mark Garcia, Vice President
Mark Benaquista, Managing Director
Megan Preiner, Vice President
Michael Borom, Managing Director
Robert Spies, Vice President
Santiago Delgado, Vice President
Seth Lawry, Managing Director
Soren Oberg, Managing Director
Thomas Hagerty, Managing Director
Todd Abbrecht, Managing Director
Tyler Griffith, Vice President
Uttam Jain, Principal
Vicente Piedrahita, Principal

Type of Firm
Private Equity Firm

Project Preferences

Type of Financing Preferred:
Leveraged Buyout
Mezzanine

Geographical Preferences

United States Preferences:
North America

Industry Preferences

In Medical/Health prefer:
Medical/Health

In Consumer Related prefer:
Consumer

In Financial Services prefer:
Financial Services

In Business Serv. prefer:
Services
Media

Additional Information
Name of Most Recent Fund: Thomas H. Lee Equity Partners VI, L.P.
Most Recent Fund Was Raised: 07/14/2006
Year Founded: 1974
Capital Under Management: $20,000,000,000
Current Activity Level : Actively seeking new investments

THOMAS MCNERNEY AND PARTNERS LLC

One Landmark Square, Suite 1920
Stamford, CT USA 06901
Phone: 203978200
Fax: 2039782005
Website: www.tm-partners.com

Other Offices

One Landmark Square, Suite 1920
STAMFORD, CT USA 06901
Phone: 2039782000
Fax: 2039782005

3366 North Torrey Pines Court, Suite 220
LA JOLLA, CA USA 92037
Phone: 8583735800
Fax: 8582285751

Management and Staff
Alex Zisson, Partner
Eric Aguiar, Partner
James Thomas, Co-Founder
Jason Brown, Principal
Kathleen Tune, Partner
Peter McNerney, Co-Founder
Pratik Shah, Partner

Susan Haedt, Chief Financial Officer

Type of Firm
Private Equity Firm

Association Membership
National Venture Capital Association - USA (NVCA)

Project Preferences

Type of Financing Preferred:
Early Stage
Expansion
Balanced
Later Stage
Seed

Size of Investments Considered:
Min Size of Investment Considered (000s): $5,000
Max Size of Investment Considered (000s): $50,000

Geographical Preferences

United States Preferences:
Midwest
West Coast
East Coast

Industry Preferences

In Biotechnology prefer:
Biotechnology

In Medical/Health prefer:
Medical Diagnostics
Medical Products
Pharmaceuticals

Additional Information
Name of Most Recent Fund: Thomas, McNerney & Partners II, L.P.
Most Recent Fund Was Raised: 09/30/2006
Year Founded: 2002
Capital Under Management: $600,000,000
Current Activity Level : Actively seeking new investments

THOMAS WEISEL PARTNERS GROUP INC

One Montgomery Street
San Francisco, CA USA 94104
Phone: 4153642500
Fax: 4153642695

Management and Staff
Adam Stulberger, Principal
Andrew Sessions, General Partner
Bowman Wingard, Partner
Caley Castelein, General Partner
Chris Hurst, Vice President
Christian Munafo, Principal
Christy Richardson, Principal
Clifford Meijer, Managing Partner
Curt Futch, Vice President
David Crowder, General Partner
David Bauman, Principal

Derek Lemke-von Ammon, Partner
Dorian Faust, Vice President
Douglas Karp, Managing Partner
Eric Fitzgerald, Partner
Geoffrey Raker, Principal
Gregory White, Partner
James Streator, Partner
James Hoch, Partner
James Shapiro, Founder
Jeffrey Calhoun, Vice President
Kimberly Ng, Vice President
Lawrence Sorrel, Partner
Mark Lieberman, Partner
Richard Spalding, General Partner
Rob Steele, Managing Director
Rob Born, Vice President
Ryan Stroub, Chief Financial Officer
William Bunting, Partner

Type of Firm
Bank Affiliated

Project Preferences

Type of Financing Preferred:
Generalist PE

Industry Focus
(% based on actual investment)
Computer Software and Services	50.1%
Communications and Media	12.0%
Computer Hardware	11.7%
Semiconductors/Other Elect.	7.9%
Medical/Health	6.9%
Consumer Related	5.5%
Internet Specific	3.7%
Biotechnology	2.2%

Additional Information
Name of Most Recent Fund: Thomas Weisel Strategic Opportunities Partners, L.P.
Most Recent Fund Was Raised: 07/01/2001
Year Founded: 1999
Capital Under Management: $2,000,000,000
Current Activity Level : Actively seeking new investments

THOMPSON STREET CAPITAL PARTNERS LP

120 South Central Avenue, Suite 600
Saint Louis, MO USA 63105
Phone: 3147272112
Fax: 3147272118
E-mail: info@tscp.com
Website: www.tscp.com

Other Offices

Five Cascades Terrace
Branchburg, NJ USA 08876
Phone: 908-707-8587

2200 Renaissance Boulevard
King of Prussia, PA USA 19406
Phone: 610-275-7382

Pratt's Guide to Private Equity & Venture Capital Sources

120 Grenville
Southampton, PA USA 18966

Management and Staff

Anthony Chambers, Vice President
Brian Kornmann, Vice President
Elizabeth Borow, Managing Director
Harry Holiday, Chief Operating Officer
James Cooper, Managing Partner
Jennifer Ehlen, Vice President
Kellie Cramer, Chief Financial Officer
Kelly Wittenbrink, Vice President
Neal Berman, Managing Director
Peter Villhard, Managing Director
Robert Dunn, Managing Director
Vincent Warrick, Managing Director
William Willhite, Managing Partner

Type of Firm

Private Equity Firm

Project Preferences

Role in Financing:
Prefer role as deal originator but will also invest in deals created by others

Type of Financing Preferred:
Leveraged Buyout
Turnaround
Management Buyouts
Acquisition
Recapitalizations

Size of Investments Considered:
Min Size of Investment Considered (000s): $3,000
Max Size of Investment Considered (000s): $75,000

Geographical Preferences

United States Preferences:
North America

Industry Preferences

In Medical/Health prefer:
Medical Diagnostics
Drug/Equipmt Delivery
Medical Products
Disposable Med. Products

In Consumer Related prefer:
Food/Beverage

In Industrial/Energy prefer:
Industrial Products
Factory Automation
Process Control
Machinery

In Transportation prefer:
Transportation
Aerospace

In Business Serv. prefer:
Services
Distribution

In Manufact. prefer:
Manufacturing

Additional Information

Name of Most Recent Fund: Thompson Street Capital Partners III, L.P.
Most Recent Fund Was Raised: 02/03/2012
Year Founded: 2000
Capital Under Management: $140,000,000
Current Activity Level : Actively seeking new investments
Method of Compensation: Return on invest. most important, but chg. closing fees, service fees, etc.

THOMVEST VENTURES INC

203 Redwood Shores Parkway, Suite 680
Redwood City, CA USA 94065
Phone: 6509654700
Fax: 6506181509
E-mail: info@thomvest.com
Website: www.thomvest.com

Other Offices

222 Pine Street
Philadelphia, PA USA 19106
Phone: 242-356-9336
Fax: 650-618-1509

65 Queen Street West, Suite 2400
Toronto, Canada M5H 2M8
Phone: 416-364-8700
Fax: 416-361-9129

Management and Staff

Donald Butler, Managing Director
Jonathan Barker, Venture Partner
Kip Knight, Venture Partner
Stefan Clulow, Managing Director
William Dodds, Managing Director

Type of Firm

Private Equity Firm

Association Membership

Western Association of Venture Capitalists (WAVC)

Project Preferences

Type of Financing Preferred:
Early Stage
Balanced
Later Stage

Geographical Preferences

United States Preferences:
West Coast

Canadian Preferences:
All Canada

Industry Preferences

In Communications prefer:
Telecommunications
Wireless Communications

In Computer Software prefer:
Software

In Internet Specific prefer:
E-Commerce Technology
Internet

In Financial Services prefer:
Financial Services

Additional Information

Year Founded: 1996
Capital Under Management: $150,000,000
Current Activity Level : Actively seeking new investments

THOROUGHBRED SPIRITS PARTNERS

1201 Elm Street, Suite 4920
Dallas, TX USA 75270
E-mail: info@tbspiritspartners.com
Website: www.tbspiritspartners.com

Type of Firm

Private Equity Firm

Industry Preferences

In Consumer Related prefer:
Food/Beverage

Additional Information

Year Founded: 2016
Current Activity Level : Actively seeking new investments

THREE ARCH PARTNERS LP

3200 Alpine Road
Portola Valley, CA USA 94028
Phone: 6505298000
Fax: 6505298039
E-mail: info@threearchpartners.com
Website: www.threearchpartners.com

Management and Staff

Mark Wan, Partner
Stephen Bonelli, Chief Financial Officer
Wilfred Jaeger, Co-Founder

Type of Firm

Private Equity Firm

Project Preferences

Role in Financing:
Prefer role as deal originator but will also invest in deals created by others

Size of Investments Considered:
Min Size of Investment Considered (000s): $100
Max Size of Investment Considered (000s): $15,000

Geographical Preferences

United States Preferences:

Industry Focus

(% based on actual investment)
Medical/Health	83.2%
Biotechnology	9.7%
Internet Specific	3.7%
Computer Software and Services	1.8%
Computer Hardware	1.3%
Other Products	0.1%

Additional Information

Year Founded: 1993
Capital Under Management: $1,000,000,000
Current Activity Level : Actively seeking new investments
Method of Compensation: Return on investment is of primary concern, do not charge fees

---

THREE BRIDGES VENTURES

One Tunnel Road
Berkeley, CA USA 94705
E-mail: info@tbv.vc
Website: www.tbv.vc

Type of Firm

Private Equity Firm

Project Preferences

Type of Financing Preferred:
Early Stage

Industry Preferences

In Computer Software prefer:
Data Processing
Software

Additional Information

Year Founded: 2014
Current Activity Level : Actively seeking new investments

THREE HILLS CAPITAL PARTNERS LLP

170 Piccadilly
London, United Kingdom W1J 9EJ
Phone: 442030569
E-mail: nfo@thcp.eu
Website: www.thcp.eu

Management and Staff

Lance Contento, Principal
Leks Boer, Partner
Michele Prencipe, Partner

Type of Firm

Private Equity Firm

Project Preferences

Type of Financing Preferred:
Leveraged Buyout
Acquisition
Recapitalizations

Geographical Preferences

International Preferences:
United Kingdom
Luxembourg
Europe

Additional Information

Year Founded: 2013
Capital Under Management: $346,133,000
Current Activity Level : Actively seeking new investments

THREE LEAF VENTURES LLC

252 Clayton Street
4th Floor
Denver, CO USA 80206
Website: threeleafventures.com

Type of Firm

Private Equity Firm

Project Preferences

Type of Financing Preferred:
Balanced

Industry Preferences

In Medical/Health prefer:
Medical/Health

Additional Information

Year Founded: 2014
Current Activity Level : Actively seeking new investments

THRIVE CAPITAL PARTNERS LLC

295 Lafayette Street
New York, NY USA 10012
Phone: 2125277058
E-mail: info@thrivecap.com
Website: www.thrivecap.com

Management and Staff

Jared Kushner, General Partner
Joshua Kushner, Managing Partner

Type of Firm

Private Equity Firm

Project Preferences

Type of Financing Preferred:
Early Stage
Startup

Industry Preferences

In Communications prefer:
Media and Entertainment

In Internet Specific prefer:
Internet

Additional Information

Name of Most Recent Fund: Thrive Capital Partners III, L.P.
Most Recent Fund Was Raised: 09/06/2012
Year Founded: 2009
Capital Under Management: $1,137,000,000
Current Activity Level : Actively seeking new investments

THUJA CAPITAL BV

Yalelaan 40
Alexander Numan Building G/F
Utrecht, Netherlands 3584 CM
Phone: 31302539898
Fax: 31302539969
E-mail: info@thujacapital.com

Management and Staff

Harrold van Barlingen, Managing Partner
Michel Briejer, Partner

Type of Firm

Private Equity Firm

Association Membership

Dutch Venture Capital Associaton (NVP)

Project Preferences

Type of Financing Preferred:
Early Stage
Seed
Startup

Geographical Preferences

International Preferences:
Luxembourg
Europe
Netherlands
Belgium

Industry Preferences

In Biotechnology prefer:
Human Biotechnology

In Medical/Health prefer:
Medical Products
Health Services
Pharmaceuticals

Additional Information

Year Founded: 2007
Capital Under Management: $38,470,000

Current Activity Level : Actively seeking new investments

TI CAPITAL

Post Office Box 49976
Los Angeles, CA USA 90049
Phone: 310-470-0520
Fax: 310-556-4636
E-mail: info@ticapital.com
Website: www.ticapital.com

Management and Staff
Aref Mikati, Chief Operating Officer
Ziad Ghandour, President, Founder

Type of Firm
Private Equity Firm

Project Preferences

Role in Financing:
Will function either as deal originator or investor in deals created by others

Type of Financing Preferred:
Early Stage
Balanced
Later Stage

Geographical Preferences

United States Preferences:
West Coast

Industry Preferences

In Industrial/Energy prefer:
Energy
Alternative Energy

In Financial Services prefer:
Real Estate

Additional Information
Year Founded: 1997
Current Activity Level : Actively seeking new investments

TIANGUIS LTD

Five Edwardes Place
London, United Kingdom W8 6LR
Phone: 44-20-7603-7788
Fax: 44-20-7603-7667
E-mail: info@tianguis-ltd.com
Website: www.tianguis-ltd.com

Other Offices
The Tailors House
Great Budworth
Cheshire, United Kingdom CW9 6HF
Phone: 44-16-0689-2313
Fax: 44-16-0689-2314

Type of Firm
Private Equity Firm

Project Preferences

Role in Financing:
Prefer role as deal originator but will also invest in deals created by others

Type of Financing Preferred:
Leveraged Buyout
Acquisition

Size of Investments Considered:
Min Size of Investment Considered (000s): $500
Max Size of Investment Considered (000s): $10,000

Industry Preferences

In Biotechnology prefer:
Agricultural/Animal Bio.

In Industrial/Energy prefer:
Industrial Products

Additional Information
Year Founded: 1985
Capital Under Management: $10,100,000
Current Activity Level : Actively seeking new investments
Method of Compensation: Return on invest. most important, but chg. closing fees, service fees, etc.

TIANIJN YUFENG EQUITY INVESTMENT MANAGEMENT CO LTD

10B Middle Rd of East 3rd Ring
Room 05B, 12A/F, AVIC Bldg
Beijing, China 100022
Phone: 861065675211
Fax: 861065675201
E-mail: office@avicfund.com
Website: www.avicfund.com

Type of Firm
Bank Affiliated

Project Preferences

Type of Financing Preferred:
Later Stage

Geographical Preferences

International Preferences:
China

Industry Preferences

In Transportation prefer:
Transportation
Aerospace

Additional Information
Year Founded: 2010
Capital Under Management: $177,516,000
Current Activity Level : Actively seeking new investments

TIANJI VENTURE CAPITAL (BEIJING) INVESTMENT FUND MGMT CO LTD

No. 1750, Jianghong
Tower A, Xindaya International
Beijing, China
Phone: 8657185395797
Website: www.tianjivc.com

Type of Firm
Private Equity Firm

Project Preferences

Type of Financing Preferred:
Balanced

Geographical Preferences

International Preferences:
China

Industry Preferences

In Communications prefer:
Telecommunications

In Medical/Health prefer:
Medical/Health

In Industrial/Energy prefer:
Energy
Advanced Materials

In Business Serv. prefer:
Media

In Manufact. prefer:
Manufacturing

Additional Information
Year Founded: 2015
Current Activity Level : Actively seeking new investments

TIANJIN BINHAI HAISHENG EQUITY INVESTMENT FUND MGMT CO.

No. 53 Weiti Avenue
26/F Lijing Building
Tianjin, China
Phone: 86-22-2830-1122
Fax: 86-22-2830-1133
E-mail: binhaihaisheng@163.com
Website: www.haishengpe.com

Other Offices
Guangcheng Street, Xicheng District
#2, Room 808
Beijing, China
Phone: 86-10-6621-2366

Management and Staff
Rui Yang, Vice President
Songliang Ding, Vice President
Weiwei Gao, Vice President
Zhenzhong Wang, President

Type of Firm
Private Equity Firm

Project Preferences

Type of Financing Preferred:
Balanced

Geographical Preferences

International Preferences:
China

Industry Preferences

In Biotechnology prefer:
Biotechnology

In Medical/Health prefer:
Medical/Health

In Industrial/Energy prefer:
Energy
Materials
Environmental Related

In Business Serv. prefer:
Services

In Manufact. prefer:
Manufacturing

Additional Information
Year Founded: 2009
Capital Under Management: $63,013,000
Current Activity Level : Actively seeking new investments

TIANJIN DEHOU FUND MANAGEMENT CO LTD

No. 360 Pudong South Road
21B New Shanghai Int'l Bldg.
Shanghai, China
Phone: 86-21-5528-0598
Fax: 86-21-6886-3501

Type of Firm
Private Equity Firm

Project Preferences

Type of Financing Preferred:
Public Companies
Later Stage

Industry Preferences

In Industrial/Energy prefer:
Energy
Materials
Environmental Related

Additional Information
Year Founded: 2008
Capital Under Management: $146,800,000
Current Activity Level : Actively seeking new investments

TIANJIN GOBI-HITECH INVESTMENT MANAGEMENT CO LTD

No. 8, Huatian Avenue
B-906 Haitai Information Plaza
Tianjin, China 300384
Phone: 862223708556
Fax: 862223708556
Website: www.htgvc.com

Management and Staff
Xuemei Wang, Vice President

Type of Firm
Private Equity Firm

Project Preferences

Type of Financing Preferred:
Early Stage
Balanced
Later Stage

Geographical Preferences

International Preferences:
China

Industry Preferences

In Communications prefer:
Telecommunications

In Biotechnology prefer:
Biotechnology

In Medical/Health prefer:
Pharmaceuticals

In Industrial/Energy prefer:
Energy
Alternative Energy
Materials

In Transportation prefer:
Aerospace

In Business Serv. prefer:
Media

Additional Information
Year Founded: 2002
Current Activity Level : Actively seeking new investments

TIANJIN HAITAI RED INNOVATIVE INVESTMENT CO LTD

Tianjin New Tech Ind. Park
67, Kexin Villa, Huayuan Park
Tianjin, China 300384
Phone: 862283713640
Fax: 862283715773

Type of Firm
Private Equity Firm

Project Preferences

Type of Financing Preferred:
Balanced

Geographical Preferences

International Preferences:
China

Industry Preferences

In Computer Software prefer:
Software

In Medical/Health prefer:
Health Services

In Industrial/Energy prefer:
Alternative Energy
Advanced Materials

In Business Serv. prefer:
Services

In Other prefer:
Environment Responsible

Additional Information
Year Founded: 1997
Current Activity Level : Actively seeking new investments

TIANJIN HIDEA VENTURE CAPITAL CO LTD

No. 79 First Avenue, TEDA
23F, TEDA MSD Tower C1
Tianjin, China 300457
Phone: 862259852166
Fax: 862259852168
E-mail: tjhd@hideavc.com
Website: www.hideavc.com

Type of Firm
Private Equity Firm

Project Preferences

Type of Financing Preferred:
Early Stage
Expansion
Balanced
Later Stage

Geographical Preferences

International Preferences:
China

Industry Preferences

In Communications prefer:
Communications and Media
Wireless Communications

In Internet Specific prefer:
Internet

In Medical/Health prefer:
Medical/Health

In Consumer Related prefer:
Consumer
Food/Beverage

In Industrial/Energy prefer:
Energy Conservation Relat

In Financial Services prefer:
Investment Groups
Financial Services

In Business Serv. prefer:
Media

In Manufact. prefer:
Manufacturing

In Agr/Forestr/Fish prefer:
Agriculture related

Additional Information
Year Founded: 2009
Capital Under Management: $47,400,000
Current Activity Level : Actively seeking new investments

TIANJIN HUIXIN CHUANG-FU EQUITY INVEST FUND MANAGEMENT LTD

No.432, Dongman Middle Road
Room 203, Chuangzhi Mansion
Tianjin, China

Type of Firm
Private Equity Firm

Project Preferences

Type of Financing Preferred:
Leveraged Buyout

Geographical Preferences

International Preferences:
China

Additional Information
Year Founded: 2014
Capital Under Management: $24,403,000
Current Activity Level : Actively seeking new investments

TIANJIN HUIZHI LIANHE PRIVATE EQUITY

Binhai New District
Hangu District
Tianjin, China

Type of Firm
Private Equity Firm

Project Preferences

Type of Financing Preferred:
Balanced

Geographical Preferences

International Preferences:
China

Additional Information
Year Founded: 2010
Capital Under Management: $2,900,000
Current Activity Level : Actively seeking new investments

TIANJIN SHIAN HAITAI ENERGY S&T VC INVESTMENT ENTERPRISE

New Binhai Zone
Tianjin, China

Type of Firm
Private Equity Firm

Project Preferences

Type of Financing Preferred:
Balanced

Geographical Preferences

International Preferences:
China

Industry Preferences

In Medical/Health prefer:
Medical/Health

In Consumer Related prefer:
Education Related

In Industrial/Energy prefer:
Energy
Environmental Related

Additional Information
Year Founded: 2010
Capital Under Management: $18,800,000
Current Activity Level : Actively seeking new investments

TIANJIN YINGXIN EQUITY INVESTMENT FUND MANAGEMENT CO LTD

No.2759, Tanggu XinBei Road
Binghai New District
Tianjin, China
Phone: 862266221802
Fax: 862266223687
Website: www.yxtzjj.com

Type of Firm
Private Equity Firm

Project Preferences

Type of Financing Preferred:
Early Stage
Expansion
Balanced
Later Stage

Geographical Preferences

International Preferences:
China

Industry Preferences

In Biotechnology prefer:
Biotechnology

In Medical/Health prefer:
Pharmaceuticals

In Industrial/Energy prefer:
Environmental Related

In Transportation prefer:
Transportation

In Business Serv. prefer:
Services

In Agr/Forestr/Fish prefer:
Agriculture related

Additional Information
Year Founded: 2012
Current Activity Level : Actively seeking new investments

TIANJIN YUANXIANG INVESTMENT MANAGEMENT PARTNER ENTERPRISE

No.6 Huafeng Road
Huaming Industry Park
Tianjin, China

Type of Firm
Private Equity Firm

Project Preferences

Type of Financing Preferred:
Balanced

Geographical Preferences

International Preferences:
China

Additional Information
Year Founded: 2010
Current Activity Level : Actively seeking new investments

TIANJING SCIENCE & TECHNOLOGY INVESTMENT CO LTD

23-25, Room 801
Tianjin Science & Tech. Bldg.
Tianjin, China 300201
Phone: 86-22-28455-801
E-mail: sticoffice@126.com
Website: www.stic.com.cn

Type of Firm
Private Equity Firm

Project Preferences

Type of Financing Preferred:
Early Stage
Balanced
Later Stage
Startup

Geographical Preferences

International Preferences:
China

Additional Information
Year Founded: 2010
Current Activity Level : Actively seeking new investments

TIANYU VENTURE CAPITAL INVESTMENT CO LTD

Fortune Building, No,28
Room 703, Tower A
Beijing, China 100031
Phone: 861088092061
Fax: 861088092065
E-mail: tycthr@tyct.cc
Website: www.tyvc.com.cn

Type of Firm
Private Equity Firm

Association Membership
Venture Capital Association of Beijing (VCAB)

Project Preferences

Type of Financing Preferred:
Expansion
Later Stage

Geographical Preferences

International Preferences:
China

Industry Preferences

In Industrial/Energy prefer:
Energy
Materials

In Business Serv. prefer:
Services

In Manufact. prefer:
Manufacturing

In Agr/Forestr/Fish prefer:
Agriculture related
Mining and Minerals

Additional Information
Year Founded: 2010
Current Activity Level : Actively seeking new investments

TIANYUN RUIHAI VENTURE CAPITAL INC

Guodingzhi Road, Yangpu
Room 2005, No 26
Shanghai, China

Management and Staff
Suning Tian, Founder

Type of Firm
Private Equity Firm

Project Preferences

Type of Financing Preferred:
Balanced

Geographical Preferences

International Preferences:
China

Additional Information
Year Founded: 2012
Current Activity Level : Actively seeking new investments

TIBET HUAYING INVESTMENT MANAGEMENT CO LTD

Liuwu New District, Lasa
Room 1205, Liuwu Building
Lhasa, China

Type of Firm
Investment Management Firm

Project Preferences

Type of Financing Preferred:
Balanced

Geographical Preferences

International Preferences:
China

Additional Information
Year Founded: 2016
Current Activity Level : Actively seeking new investments

TIBURON PARTNERS AG

Theresienstrasse 40
Munich, Germany 80333
Phone: 4989200046449
E-mail: info@tiburon.de
Website: www.tiburon.de

Type of Firm
Corporate PE/Venture

Project Preferences

Type of Financing Preferred:
Early Stage
Seed
Startup

Geographical Preferences

International Preferences:
Germany

Industry Preferences

In Internet Specific prefer:
Internet
Ecommerce

Additional Information
Year Founded: 2001
Current Activity Level : Actively seeking new investments

TIE LAUNCHPAD

2903 Bunker Hill Lane, Suite 150
Santa Clara, CA USA 95054
Phone: 4085670700
Website: www.tielaunchpad.com

Management and Staff
Prashant Shah, Managing Director

Type of Firm
Incubator/Development Program

Project Preferences

Type of Financing Preferred:
Seed
Startup

Geographical Preferences

United States Preferences:
California

Industry Preferences

In Computer Software prefer:
Software

Additional Information
Year Founded: 2014
Capital Under Management: $4,900,000
Current Activity Level : Actively seeking new investments

TIG HOLDING LTD

Av Brigadeiro Faria Lima 3355
23rd Floor, Itaim Bibi
Sao Paulo, Brazil 04538133
Phone: 551130745800
Fax: 551130745801
E-mail: contato@tarponinvest.com.br
Website: www.tig.bm

Management and Staff
Jose Carlos Reis De Magalhaes, Partner

Type of Firm
Private Equity Firm

Association Membership
Brazilian Venture Capital Association (ABCR)

Project Preferences

Type of Financing Preferred:
Leveraged Buyout
Early Stage
Generalist PE
Balanced
Later Stage
Management Buyouts
Acquisition

Geographical Preferences

International Preferences:
Brazil

Additional Information
Year Founded: 2002
Current Activity Level : Actively seeking new investments

TIGER GLOBAL MANAGEMENT LLC

101 Park Avenue
48th Floor
New York, NY USA 10178
Phone: 2129842562

Management and Staff
Charles Coleman, Founder

Type of Firm
Investment Management Firm

Project Preferences

Type of Financing Preferred:
Leveraged Buyout
Early Stage
Generalist PE
Balanced
Later Stage
Management Buyouts

Geographical Preferences

United States Preferences:

International Preferences:
Laos
Vietnam
Indonesia
Latin America
India
Brunei
China
Thailand
Cambodia
Philippines
Singapore
Malaysia
All International
Burma

Industry Preferences

In Communications prefer:
Telecommunications

In Industrial/Energy prefer:
Energy

In Financial Services prefer:
Real Estate

In Business Serv. prefer:
Media

Additional Information
Name of Most Recent Fund: Tiger Global Private Investment Partners VII, L.P.
Most Recent Fund Was Raised: 03/05/2012
Year Founded: 2001
Capital Under Management: $7,985,000,000
Current Activity Level : Actively seeking new investments

TIGER GROUP INVESTMENTS

1 Connaught Place
1401 Jardine House
Hongkong, Hong Kong
Website: www.tigergroup.hk

Type of Firm
Private Equity Firm

Project Preferences

Type of Financing Preferred:
Leveraged Buyout
Mezzanine
Generalist PE

Geographical Preferences

International Preferences:
Asia Pacific

Industry Preferences

In Transportation prefer:
Transportation

Additional Information
Year Founded: 1969
Current Activity Level : Actively seeking new investments

TIGER MANAGEMENT CORP

101 Park Avenue
48th Floor
New York, NY USA 10178
Phone: 2129163300

Management and Staff
John Townsend, Managing Partner
Julian Robertson, Founder

Type of Firm
Private Equity Firm

Additional Information
Year Founded: 1980
Current Activity Level : Actively seeking new investments

TIGRIS CAPITAL

1 North Bridge Road
Collision8, High St Ctr Rd
Singapore, Singapore 179094
Website: www.tigriscapital.com.sg

Type of Firm
Private Equity Firm

Project Preferences

Type of Financing Preferred:
Balanced
Seed

Geographical Preferences

International Preferences:
Asia

Additional Information
Year Founded: 2004
Current Activity Level : Actively seeking new investments

TIKEHAU INVESTMENT MANAGEMENT SAS

32 Rue de Monceau
Paris, France 75008
Phone: 3340062626
Fax: 33153590520
Website: www.tikehauim.com

Management and Staff
Mathieu Chabran, Managing Director

Type of Firm
Investment Management Firm

Association Membership
French Venture Capital Association (AFIC)

Project Preferences

Type of Financing Preferred:
Leveraged Buyout
Early Stage
Mezzanine
Generalist PE
Later Stage
Acquisition

Size of Investments Considered:
Min Size of Investment Considered (000s): $2,630
Max Size of Investment Considered (000s): $32,873

Geographical Preferences

International Preferences:
Europe
France

Additional Information
Year Founded: 2007
Capital Under Management: $2,900,000,000
Current Activity Level : Actively seeking new investments

TILENIUS INVESTMENTS

1900 South Norfolk Street, Suite 350
San Mateo, CA USA 94403
Phone: 650-577-2344
Fax: 650-745-7372

Management and Staff
Eric Tilenius, Partner

Type of Firm
Private Equity Firm

Project Preferences

Type of Financing Preferred:
Early Stage
Seed

Geographical Preferences

United States Preferences:
All U.S.

Industry Preferences

In Computer Software prefer:
Software

In Internet Specific prefer:
Internet

In Consumer Related prefer:
Entertainment and Leisure
Consumer Products

In Business Serv. prefer:
Media

Additional Information
Year Founded: 2005
Current Activity Level : Actively seeking new investments

TILLERY CAPITAL LLC

7013 Willow Trace Lane
Charlotte, NC USA 28212
Phone: 7042589885
Website: www.tillerycapital.com

Management and Staff
Chris Weidenhammer, Co-Founder
James Buck, Co-Founder
Richard Fetter, Partner

Type of Firm
Private Equity Firm

Project Preferences

Type of Financing Preferred:
Leveraged Buyout
Management Buyouts
Recapitalizations

Geographical Preferences

United States Preferences:
Midwest

Industry Preferences

In Medical/Health prefer:
Health Services

In Manufact. prefer:
Manufacturing

In Other prefer:
Environment Responsible

Additional Information
Year Founded: 2006
Current Activity Level : Actively seeking new investments

TILLRIDGE GLOBAL AGRI-BUSINESS PARTNERS

5221 N. OConnor Blvd., Suite 1100
Irving, TX USA 75039
Phone: 9724321440
Fax: 9724321441
E-mail: inquiries@ngpgap.com
Website: www.tillridge.com

Other Offices
1 Berkeley Street, Suite 315
London, United Kingdom W1J 8DJ
Phone: 442070169896
Fax: 442070169783

Management and Staff
A. Judson Hill, Managing Director
Mark Zenuk, Managing Director
Murray Starkel, Managing Director
Robert Edwards, Managing Director

Type of Firm
Private Equity Firm

Project Preferences

Type of Financing Preferred:
Leveraged Buyout
Later Stage
Management Buyouts

Geographical Preferences

United States Preferences:
North America

Canadian Preferences:
All Canada

International Preferences:
Pacific
Australia

Industry Preferences

In Consumer Related prefer:
Food/Beverage

In Industrial/Energy prefer:
Environmental Related

In Business Serv. prefer:
Services

In Agr/Forestr/Fish prefer:
Agriculture related

Additional Information

Year Founded: 2010
Capital Under Management: $375,200,000
Current Activity Level : Actively seeking new investments

TIMBERLINE VENTURE PARTNERS

800 Fifth Avenue, Suite 4100
Seattle, WA USA 98104
Phone: 206-224-0131
Fax: 206-224-0132
E-mail: Partners@timberlinevc.com
Website: www.timberlinevc.com

Other Offices

400 Seaport Court, Suite 250
Redwood City, CA USA 94063
Phone: 650-599-9000
Fax: 650-599-9726

800 Fifth Aveune, Suite 4100
Seattle, WA USA 98104
Phone: 206-224-0131
Fax: 206-224-0132

3655 Torrance Boulevard, Suite 345
Torrance, CA USA 90503

Management and Staff

Gayle Kovacs, Chief Financial Officer
Jeffrey Tung, Managing Partner
Timothy Draper, General Partner
William Kallman, Managing Partner

Type of Firm
Private Equity Firm

Project Preferences

Role in Financing:
Will function either as deal originator or investor in deals created by others

Type of Financing Preferred:
Second Stage Financing
Early Stage
Seed
First Stage Financing
Startup

Size of Investments Considered:
Min Size of Investment Considered (000s): $500
Max Size of Investment Considered (000s): $5,000

Geographical Preferences

United States Preferences:
Northwest
Oregon
California
Washington

Industry Preferences

In Communications prefer:
Commercial Communications
Wireless Communications

In Computer Software prefer:
Computer Services
Software
Systems Software
Applications Software

In Internet Specific prefer:
Internet
Ecommerce
Web Aggregration/Portals

In Semiconductor/Electr prefer:
Semiconductor
Laser Related
Fiber Optics

Additional Information

Name of Most Recent Fund: Timberline Venture Partners
Most Recent Fund Was Raised: 07/01/1999
Year Founded: 1999
Current Activity Level : Actively seeking new investments
Method of Compensation: Return on investment is of primary concern, do not charge fees

TIME FOR GROWTH SA

18, Rue Bayard
Paris, France 75008
Phone: 33140738730
Fax: 33140737800
E-mail: contact@time-ep.com
Website: www.time-4g.com

Management and Staff

Henri de Bodinat, President
Jean-Luc Cyrot, Partner
Jean-Stephane Bonneton, Partner

Type of Firm
Private Equity Firm

Association Membership
French Venture Capital Association (AFIC)

Project Preferences

Type of Financing Preferred:
Leveraged Buyout
Later Stage
Acquisition

Size of Investments Considered:
Min Size of Investment Considered (000s): $3,894
Max Size of Investment Considered (000s): $19,470

Geographical Preferences

International Preferences:
Europe
France

Industry Preferences

In Communications prefer:
Telecommunications

In Internet Specific prefer:
Internet
Ecommerce

In Consumer Related prefer:
Entertainment and Leisure

In Business Serv. prefer:
Media

Additional Information

Year Founded: 2009
Current Activity Level : Actively seeking new investments

TIME INNOVATION VENTURES (SHANGHAI) CO LTD

563 SongTao Road
4th floor, Hi-Tech Park
Shanghai, China 201203
Phone: 862150803282
Fax: 86-21-50803
E-mail: time@time-iv.com
Website: www.time-iv.com/

Type of Firm
Private Equity Firm

Project Preferences

Type of Financing Preferred:
Balanced

Industry Preferences

In Semiconductor/Electr prefer:
Semiconductor

In Medical/Health prefer:
Medical/Health

In Financial Services prefer:
Financial Services

Additional Information
Year Founded: 2012
Current Activity Level : Actively seeking new investments

TIME WARNER INVESTMENTS

One Time Warner Center
New York, NY USA 10019
Phone: 2124848000
E-mail: ir@timewarner.com
Website: www.timewarner.com

Management and Staff
Ron Peele, Vice President

Type of Firm
Corporate PE/Venture

Project Preferences

Role in Financing:
Prefer role as deal originator

Type of Financing Preferred:
Early Stage
Expansion

Additional Information
Year Founded: 1996
Capital Under Management: $250,000,000
Current Activity Level : Actively seeking new investments

TIMELESS GROUP, THE

520 MADISON AVENUE
New York, NY USA 10022
Website: www.timelesscapital.com

Type of Firm
Private Equity Firm

Industry Preferences

In Medical/Health prefer:
Medical/Health
Health Services

In Business Serv. prefer:
Media

Additional Information
Year Founded: 2015
Current Activity Level : Actively seeking new investments

TINICUM CAPITAL PARTNERS

800 Third Avenue, 40th Floor
New York, NY USA 10022
Phone: 2124469300
E-mail: info@tinicum.com
Website: www.tinicum.com

Management and Staff
Eric Ruttenberg, General Partner
Seth Hedon, Partner

Type of Firm
Private Equity Firm

Project Preferences

Type of Financing Preferred:
Leveraged Buyout
Turnaround
Management Buyouts
Acquisition
Recapitalizations

Industry Preferences

In Medical/Health prefer:
Medical Products

In Consumer Related prefer:
Franchises(NEC)

In Industrial/Energy prefer:
Industrial Products
Advanced Materials
Process Control
Machinery

In Transportation prefer:
Aerospace

In Financial Services prefer:
Financial Services

In Business Serv. prefer:
Media

In Manufact. prefer:
Manufacturing

Additional Information
Name of Most Recent Fund: Tinicum, L.P.
Most Recent Fund Was Raised: 02/21/2012
Year Founded: 1998
Capital Under Management: $1,325,000,000
Current Activity Level : Actively seeking new investments

TINKBIG VENTURE SDN BHD

Third Floor,Bangunan Cheong
Wing Chan, Jalan Maharajalela
Kuala Lumpur, Malaysia 50150
Website: www.tinkbig.vc

Type of Firm
Private Equity Firm

Project Preferences

Type of Financing Preferred:
Early Stage
Seed

Additional Information
Year Founded: 2016
Current Activity Level : Actively seeking new investments

TISIWI VENTURE CAPITAL

90 Wensan Road, West Lake Dist
1102, Bldg1,East Software Park
Hangzhou, Zhejiang, China 310012
E-mail: admin@tisiwi.com
Website: tisiwi.com

Type of Firm
Private Equity Firm

Project Preferences

Type of Financing Preferred:
Seed

Size of Investments Considered:
Min Size of Investment Considered (000s): $31
Max Size of Investment Considered (000s): $943

Geographical Preferences

International Preferences:
China

Industry Preferences

In Internet Specific prefer:
Internet
Ecommerce

Additional Information
Year Founded: 2011
Current Activity Level : Actively seeking new investments

TITLECARD CAPITAL GROUP LLC

210 University Boulevard, Suite 650
Denver, CO USA 80206
E-mail: contact@titlecardcapital.com
Website: www.titelcardcapital.com

Type of Firm
Private Equity Firm

Project Preferences

Type of Financing Preferred:
Balanced

Industry Preferences

In Medical/Health prefer:
Medical/Health

In Consumer Related prefer:
Consumer Products
Consumer Services

In Financial Services prefer:
Financial Services

In Business Serv. prefer:
Media

Additional Information
Year Founded: 1969
Capital Under Management: $12,910,000
Current Activity Level : Actively seeking new investments

TL VENTURES INC

435 Devon Park Drive
700 Building
Wayne, PA USA 19087
Phone: 6109711515
Fax: 6109759330
E-mail: info@tlventures.com
Website: www.tlventures.com

Other Offices
1001 Bayhill Drive, Suite 200
SAN BRUNO, CA USA 94066

Management and Staff
Janet Stott, Chief Financial Officer
Mark DeNino, Managing Director
Robert Keith, Co-Founder
Robert McParland, Partner

Type of Firm
Private Equity Firm

Project Preferences

Role in Financing:
Prefer role as deal originator but will also invest in deals created by others

Type of Financing Preferred:
Early Stage
Balanced
Later Stage

Geographical Preferences

United States Preferences:
Oregon
Northern California
Northeast

Industry Focus
(% based on actual investment)

Internet Specific	25.2%
Computer Software and Services	21.9%
Semiconductors/Other Elect.	14.7%
Communications and Media	10.9%
Biotechnology	8.5%
Medical/Health	7.3%
Other Products	4.6%
Computer Hardware	3.7%
Consumer Related	1.7%
Industrial/Energy	1.5%

Additional Information
Name of Most Recent Fund: TL Ventures VII
Most Recent Fund Was Raised: 11/20/2008
Year Founded: 1988
Capital Under Management: $14,368,000,000
Current Activity Level : Actively seeking new investments
Method of Compensation: Return on investment is of primary concern, do not charge fees

TLCOM CAPITAL LLP

188 Hammersmith Road
London, United Kingdom W6 7DJ
Phone: 4420823770
Fax: 4420823770
E-mail: info@tlcom.co.uk
Website: www.tlcom.co.uk

Management and Staff
Mark McDonald, Founder
Maurizio Caio, Managing Partner
Mauro Pretolani, General Partner

Type of Firm
Private Equity Firm

Association Membership
African Venture Capital Association (AVCA)

Project Preferences

Role in Financing:
Will function either as deal originator or investor in deals created by others

Type of Financing Preferred:
Early Stage
Expansion
Balanced
Later Stage
Seed
Fund of Funds of Second

Size of Investments Considered:
Min Size of Investment Considered (000s): $1,000
Max Size of Investment Considered (000s): $15,000

Geographical Preferences

United States Preferences:

International Preferences:
Europe
Israel

Industry Preferences

In Communications prefer:
Communications and Media
Telecommunications
Wireless Communications

In Computer Software prefer:
Applications Software

In Internet Specific prefer:
Internet

In Semiconductor/Electr prefer:
Semiconductor

In Industrial/Energy prefer:
Materials

In Business Serv. prefer:
Services
Media

Additional Information
Year Founded: 1999
Capital Under Management: $282,200,000
Current Activity Level : Actively seeking new investments

TMFOX VENTURE PARTNERS CO LTD

C-1, General Service Building
Room 315, 3F, Chuangtou Plaza
Shenzhen, China 518000
Phone: 8675586366421
E-mail: information@tmfox.com
Website: www.tmfox.com

Management and Staff
Donnie Horton, Partner
Sally Liu, Partner
Wilson Sieg, Partner

Type of Firm
Private Equity Firm

Association Membership
Venture Capital Association of Beijing (VCAB)

Project Preferences

Type of Financing Preferred:
Early Stage
Seed
Startup

Size of Investments Considered:
Min Size of Investment Considered (000s): $500
Max Size of Investment Considered (000s): $1,500

Geographical Preferences

International Preferences:
Vietnam
China

Industry Preferences

In Consumer Related prefer:
Consumer
Retail

In Industrial/Energy prefer:
Energy

Additional Information

Year Founded: 2000
Current Activity Level : Actively seeking new investments

TMG PARTNERS LLC

Rua Joaquim Floriano
72, CJ 93, Itaim Bibi
Sao Paulo, Brazil 04534
Phone: 551140645050
Fax: 551140645056
E-mail: tmg_capital@tmg.com.br
Website: www.tmg.com.br

Management and Staff

Eduardo Buarque De Almeida, Partner
Pedro Paulo Teixeira, Partner

Type of Firm

Private Equity Firm

Association Membership

Brazilian Venture Capital Association (ABCR)

Project Preferences

Type of Financing Preferred:
Leveraged Buyout
Early Stage
Generalist PE
Balanced
Later Stage
Acquisition

Geographical Preferences

International Preferences:
Brazil

Industry Preferences

In Communications prefer:
Communications and Media

In Medical/Health prefer:
Medical/Health

In Consumer Related prefer:
Retail

In Business Serv. prefer:
Services

Additional Information

Year Founded: 1997
Capital Under Management: $100,000,000
Current Activity Level : Actively seeking new investments

TMG VENTURE CAPITAL CO.

18530 Mack Avenue, Suite 301
Grosse Pointe Woods, MI USA 48236
Phone: 8853628
Fax: 2842266
E-mail: info@tmgvventure.com
Website: www.tmgventures.com

Type of Firm

Private Equity Firm

Project Preferences

Type of Financing Preferred:
Early Stage
Later Stage

Industry Preferences

In Communications prefer:
Wireless Communications

Additional Information

Year Founded: 2015
Current Activity Level : Actively seeking new investments

TMT INVESTMENTS PLC

Hilgrove Street, Saint Helier
Queensway House
Jersey, United Kingdom JE1 1ES
Phone: 441534281890
Fax: 448451258623
E-mail: info@tmtinvestments.com
Website: www.tmtinvestments.com

Type of Firm

Private Equity Firm

Project Preferences

Type of Financing Preferred:
Early Stage
Expansion
Balanced
Later Stage

Size of Investments Considered:
Min Size of Investment Considered (000s): $250
Max Size of Investment Considered (000s): $10,000

Geographical Preferences

International Preferences:
United Kingdom
Europe

Industry Preferences

In Communications prefer:
Telecommunications

In Computer Software prefer:
Applications Software

In Internet Specific prefer:
Ecommerce

In Consumer Related prefer:
Consumer Services

In Business Serv. prefer:
Media

Additional Information

Year Founded: 2010
Current Activity Level : Actively seeking new investments

TNF VENTURES PTE LTD

71, Ayer Rajah Crescent
#06-01/02 and #04-23/24/25/26
Singapore, Singapore 139951
E-mail: info@tnfventures.com
Website: www.tnfventures.com

Management and Staff

Shirley Wong, Managing Partner

Type of Firm

Private Equity Firm

Project Preferences

Type of Financing Preferred:
Early Stage
Expansion
Seed

Geographical Preferences

International Preferences:
Asia
Singapore

Industry Preferences

In Communications prefer:
Communications and Media

In Medical/Health prefer:
Medical/Health

In Business Serv. prefer:
Media

Additional Information

Year Founded: 2012
Current Activity Level : Actively seeking new investments

TNP PARTNERS CORP

8F Shinyokohama SR Bldg
3-6-1 Shinyokohama, Kohoku-ku
Yokohama, Japan 222-0033
Phone: 81-45-470-8088
Fax: 81-45-470-8090
E-mail: info@tsunami2000.co.jp
Website: www.tnp-g.jp

Type of Firm
Government Affiliated Program

Association Membership
Japan Venture Capital Association

Project Preferences

Type of Financing Preferred:
Balanced

Additional Information
Year Founded: 2000
Capital Under Management: $2,300,000
Current Activity Level : Actively seeking new investments

TOBAGO HOUSE OF ASSEMBLY VENTURE CAPITAL CO

Tam Building
Glen Road
Tobago, Trinidad/Tob.
Phone: 868-639-2570
Fax: 868-639-1746

Type of Firm
Government Affiliated Program

Project Preferences

Type of Financing Preferred:
Early Stage
Expansion
Balanced
Later Stage

Geographical Preferences

International Preferences:
Europe
Trinidad/Tob.

Industry Preferences

In Industrial/Energy prefer:
Environmental Related

Additional Information
Year Founded: 2011
Capital Under Management: $3,943,000
Current Activity Level : Actively seeking new investments

TOCQUEVILLE FINANCE SA

34 Rue De La Federation
Paris, France 75015
Phone: 33153772020
Fax: 33145610506
E-mail: info@tocquevillefinance.fr
Website: www.tocquevillefinance.fr

Other Offices
40 West 57 Street
19th Floor
New York, NY USA 10019
Phone: 1-212-698-0800

1 Rue de la Rotisserie
Geneve, Switzerland CH12004
Phone: 41-2-2716-2700
Fax: 41-2-2716-2701

Management and Staff
Bruno Julien, Chief Executive Officer
Frederic Cirier, Chief Financial Officer
Marc Tournier, Chief Operating Officer

Type of Firm
Investment Management Firm

Association Membership
Francophone Venture Capital Association
French Venture Capital Association (AFIC)

Project Preferences

Type of Financing Preferred:
Leveraged Buyout
Acquisition

Geographical Preferences

United States Preferences:
All U.S.

International Preferences:
Europe
France

Additional Information
Year Founded: 1991
Current Activity Level : Actively seeking new investments

TOHO BANK LTD

1-8-1 Marunouchi, Chiyoda-Ku
14F, Marunouchi Trust Tower
Tokyo, Japan 100-0005
Phone: 81362122510
Website: www.tohobank.co.jp

Management and Staff
Kenichi Kogure, Managing Director
Masayuki Sakaji, Managing Director
Mitsuo Moriya, Managing Director
Satoshi Aji, Managing Director
Seiji Takeuchi, Managing Director
Shinsuke Tanno, Senior Managing Director
Takahiro Kato, Senior Managing Director

Type of Firm
Investment Management Firm

Project Preferences

Type of Financing Preferred:
Early Stage
Startup

Geographical Preferences

International Preferences:
Japan

Additional Information
Year Founded: 1941
Capital Under Management: $10,004,000
Current Activity Level : Actively seeking new investments

TOKALON

44 Wall Street
New York, NY USA 10005
Phone: 2123441000
E-mail: info@tokalon.com
Website: www.tokalon.com

Type of Firm
Private Equity Firm

Project Preferences

Type of Financing Preferred:
Early Stage
Expansion

Geographical Preferences

International Preferences:
Abu Dhabi

Additional Information
Year Founded: 2016
Current Activity Level : Actively seeking new investments

TOKIO MARINE CAPITAL CO LTD

1-2-1, Marunouchi, TMN Bldg
Shinkan 6F, Chiyodaku
Tokyo, Japan 100-0005
Phone: 81352233516
E-mail: tmcinfo@tmcap.co.jp
Website: www.tmcap.co.jp

Management and Staff

Hideaki Fukazawa, President
Hirokazu Nagaoka, Vice President
Kazutaka Komori, Partner
Koji Sasaki, General Partner
Masayuki Kuruma, Vice President
Shigeru Matsumoto, Partner
Shunichiro Nakagawa, Partner
Takayuki Ohgishi, Principal
Yoshihiro Osako, Vice President
Yuji Komiya, Managing Partner
Yuji Kimoto, General Partner

Type of Firm

Private Equity Firm

Association Membership

Hong Kong Venture Capital Association (HKVCA)

Project Preferences

Type of Financing Preferred:
Leveraged Buyout
Early Stage
Generalist PE
Balanced
Later Stage
Seed
Management Buyouts
Startup

Geographical Preferences

International Preferences:
Asia
Japan

Additional Information

Year Founded: 1991
Capital Under Management: $638,071,000
Current Activity Level : Actively seeking new investments

TOKYO SMALL & MEDIUM BUSINESS INVESTMENT & CONSULTATION CO.

3-29-22 Shibuya
Shibuya-ku
Tokyo, Japan 150-0002
Phone: 81354691811
Fax: 81354695875
E-mail: iida@sbic.co.jp
Website: www.sbic.co.jp

Management and Staff

Katsutoshi Fukami, Managing Director

Type of Firm

Private Equity Firm

Project Preferences

Role in Financing:
Prefer role as deal originator

Type of Financing Preferred:
Early Stage
Balanced

Geographical Preferences

International Preferences:
Japan

Industry Focus

(% based on actual investment)
Industrial/Energy	28.6%
Other Products	27.8%
Consumer Related	11.6%
Semiconductors/Other Elect.	7.8%
Internet Specific	5.6%
Computer Software and Services	5.4%
Medical/Health	4.1%
Computer Hardware	3.3%
Biotechnology	3.2%
Communications and Media	2.6%

Additional Information

Year Founded: 1963
Capital Under Management: $350,000,000
Current Activity Level : Actively seeking new investments
Method of Compensation: Return on investment is of primary concern, do not charge fees

---

TOLA CAPITAL LLC

520 East Denny Way
Seattle, WA USA 98122
Phone: 2062258465
E-mail: info@tolacapital.com
Website: www.tolacapital.com

Management and Staff

Sheila Gulati, Managing Director
Stacey Giard, Chief Operating Officer
Tashi Schmidt, Chief Financial Officer

Type of Firm

Private Equity Firm

Project Preferences

Type of Financing Preferred:
Early Stage
Balanced
Later Stage

Geographical Preferences

United States Preferences:

International Preferences:
United Kingdom
Europe

Industry Preferences

In Computer Software prefer:
Software
Applications Software

Additional Information

Year Founded: 2010
Capital Under Management: $329,185,000
Current Activity Level : Actively seeking new investments

TOLERO VENTURES LLC

11999 San Vicente Blvd, Suite 220
Los Angeles, CA USA 90049
Website: www.toleroventures.com

Management and Staff

Aaron Enz, Venture Partner
Justin Lemmon, Partner
Konrad Jarausch, Venture Partner
Mark Huang, Partner

Type of Firm

Private Equity Firm

Industry Preferences

In Consumer Related prefer:
Food/Beverage

In Industrial/Energy prefer:
Energy

In Financial Services prefer:
Real Estate

In Agr/Forestr/Fish prefer:
Agriculture related

Additional Information

Year Founded: 1969
Current Activity Level : Actively seeking new investments

TOLOMEI PARTICIPATIONS SAS

89 Rue Reaumur
Paris, France 75002
Phone: 33145081125
Fax: 33140390363

Management and Staff

Eric Dailey, President

Type of Firm

Private Equity Firm

Association Membership

French Venture Capital Association (AFIC)

Project Preferences

Type of Financing Preferred:
Balanced

Geographical Preferences

International Preferences:
Europe

Additional Information
Year Founded: 2004
Current Activity Level : Actively seeking new investments

TOM CAPITAL ASSOCIATES INC

1210 - 11th Avenue SW, Suite 200
Calgary, Canada T3C 0M4
Phone: 4035714440
Fax: 4035714444
Website: www.tomcapital.com

Management and Staff
Bevan May, Vice President
Candice Selby, Vice President
Craig Bell, Managing Director
Glen Swail, Managing Director
Jim Grenon, Managing Director
Tom Pointer, Vice President
Tony Grenon, Managing Director

Type of Firm
Private Equity Firm

Project Preferences

Type of Financing Preferred:
Leveraged Buyout
Generalist PE
Turnaround
Acquisition
Special Situation

Geographical Preferences

Canadian Preferences:
All Canada
Western Canada

Industry Preferences

In Industrial/Energy prefer:
Oil and Gas Exploration
Oil & Gas Drilling,Explor

In Financial Services prefer:
Real Estate

In Agr/Forestr/Fish prefer:
Agriculture related
Mining and Minerals

Additional Information
Year Founded: 1995
Current Activity Level : Actively seeking new investments

TOMA CAPITAL MANAGEMENT LLC

3103 Nelson Way, Suite A
Santa Monica, CA USA 90405
Phone: 2133733363
Website: www.tomacapital.com

Management and Staff
Ned Tomasevic, Founder

Type of Firm
Private Equity Firm

Project Preferences

Type of Financing Preferred:
Leveraged Buyout
Acquisition

Geographical Preferences

United States Preferences:

Additional Information
Year Founded: 1969
Current Activity Level : Actively seeking new investments

TOMORROWVENTURES LLC

555 Bryant Street, Suite 555
San Francisco, CA USA 94103
Phone: 6508157087
E-mail: info@tomorrowvc.com
Website: www.tomorrowvc.com

Other Offices
700 North Colorado Boulevard, Suite 121
Denver, CO USA 80206

Management and Staff
Court Coursey, Managing Partner

Type of Firm
Private Equity Firm

Project Preferences

Type of Financing Preferred:
Early Stage
Seed

Additional Information
Year Founded: 2009
Current Activity Level : Actively seeking new investments

TONGXI BEIJING CAPITAL MANAGEMENT CO LTD

No.1 Jianguomenwai Street
13F,Tower 1, GuomaoOfficeBuldg
Beijing, China
Phone: 861059471157
Fax: 861059471156
Website: www.tongxicapital.com

Type of Firm
Private Equity Firm

Project Preferences

Type of Financing Preferred:
Balanced

Geographical Preferences

International Preferences:
China

Industry Preferences

In Internet Specific prefer:
Internet

In Biotechnology prefer:
Industrial Biotechnology

Additional Information
Year Founded: 2015
Capital Under Management: $62,900,000
Current Activity Level : Actively seeking new investments

TONIC VENTURE CAPITAL LTD

10B, Summit Building
30 Man Yue St., Hunghom, Kl
Hong Kong, Hong Kong
Phone: 852-2364-9365
Fax: 852-2303-0471

Management and Staff
Gary Liu, Chief Executive Officer

Type of Firm
Corporate PE/Venture

Association Membership
Hong Kong Venture Capital Association (HKVCA)

Project Preferences

Type of Financing Preferred:
Turnaround
Recapitalizations

Geographical Preferences

International Preferences:
China

Industry Preferences

In Semiconductor/Electr prefer:
Electronics

Additional Information
Year Founded: 2006
Capital Under Management: $10,000,000
Current Activity Level : Actively seeking new investments

TONKA BAY EQUITY PARTNERS LLC

301 Carlson Parkway, Suite 325
Minnetonka, MN USA 55305
Phone: 9523452030
Fax: 9523452001
E-mail: info@tonkabayequity.com
Website: tonkabayequity.com

Management and Staff
Cary Musech, Partner
Peter Kooman, Partner
Shane Slominski, Partner
Steve Soderling, Partner

Type of Firm
Private Equity Firm

Association Membership
Natl Assoc of Small Bus. Inv. Co (NASBIC)

Project Preferences

Role in Financing:
Prefer role as deal originator but will also invest in deals created by others

Type of Financing Preferred:
Leveraged Buyout
Acquisition
Recapitalizations

Industry Preferences

In Business Serv. prefer:
Services
Distribution

In Manufact. prefer:
Manufacturing

Additional Information
Name of Most Recent Fund: Bayview Capital Partners III, L.P.
Most Recent Fund Was Raised: 10/31/2011
Year Founded: 1998
Capital Under Management: $350,000,000
Current Activity Level : Actively seeking new investments
Method of Compensation: Return on invest. most important, but chg. closing fees, service fees, etc.

TOP RENERGY INC

3995 Dunbar Street
Vancouver, Canada
Website: www.toprenergy.com

Type of Firm
Private Equity Firm

Association Membership
Canadian Venture Capital Association

Project Preferences

Type of Financing Preferred:
Early Stage
Seed

Geographical Preferences

Canadian Preferences:
All Canada

International Preferences:
Asia

Industry Preferences

In Industrial/Energy prefer:
Energy

In Other prefer:
Environment Responsible

Additional Information
Year Founded: 2010
Current Activity Level : Actively seeking new investments

TOP TECHNOLOGY VENTURES LTD

24 Cornhill
London, United Kingdom EC3V 3ND
Phone: 442074440050
Fax: 442079296415

Management and Staff
Harry Fitzgibbons, Managing Director

Type of Firm
Bank Affiliated

Association Membership
British Venture Capital Association (BVCA)

Project Preferences

Type of Financing Preferred:
Early Stage
Balanced
Later Stage
Startup

Size of Investments Considered:
Min Size of Investment Considered (000s): $619
Max Size of Investment Considered (000s): $1,548

Geographical Preferences

International Preferences:
United Kingdom
Europe

Industry Focus
(% based on actual investment)
Semiconductors/Other Elect.	36.2%
Computer Software and Services	28.2%
Biotechnology	14.8%
Internet Specific	11.1%
Other Products	4.1%
Computer Hardware	2.2%
Communications and Media	1.5%
Industrial/Energy	1.2%
Consumer Related	0.6%

Additional Information
Name of Most Recent Fund: IP Venture Fund II
Most Recent Fund Was Raised: 05/23/2013
Year Founded: 1986
Capital Under Management: $64,700,000
Current Activity Level : Actively seeking new investments

TOP TIER CAPITAL PARTNERS LLC

600 Montgomery Street, Suite 480
San Francisco, CA USA 94111
Phone: 4158357500
Fax: 4158357501
Website: www.ttcp.com

Management and Staff
Dan Townsend, Managing Director
David York, CEO & Managing Director
Garth Timoll, Principal
Jessica Archibald, Principal
Lisa Edgar, Managing Director

Type of Firm
Private Equity Firm

Association Membership
Australian Venture Capital Association (AVCAL)
National Venture Capital Association - USA (NVCA)

Project Preferences

Type of Financing Preferred:
Early Stage
Expansion
Generalist PE
Balanced
Turnaround
Later Stage
Acquisition
Recapitalizations

Geographical Preferences

United States Preferences:

Additional Information
Name of Most Recent Fund: Top Tier Venture Capital VI, L.P.
Most Recent Fund Was Raised: 06/25/2013
Year Founded: 2002
Capital Under Management: $3,300,000,000
Current Activity Level : Actively seeking new investments

TOPANGA PARTNERS LP

285 KAPPA DRIVE
Pittsburgh, PA USA 15238
Website: topangafund.com

Management and Staff
Christopher Hartman, Vice President
John Hathaway, Managing Director
Laurie Barkman, Managing Partner
Tara Ronel, Managing Director

Type of Firm
Private Equity Firm

Project Preferences

Type of Financing Preferred:
Early Stage

Industry Preferences

In Computer Software prefer:
Software

Additional Information
Year Founded: 2016
Current Activity Level : Actively seeking new investments

TOPINA CAPITAL

Central Area
2806, Morden International Bld
Futian, Shenzhen, China
Phone: 8675533352211
Fax: 8675583734079
Website: www.topina.com.cn

Type of Firm
Private Equity Firm

Project Preferences

Type of Financing Preferred:
Early Stage
Expansion
Mezzanine
Balanced
Opportunistic
Later Stage

Geographical Preferences

International Preferences:
China

Industry Preferences

In Medical/Health prefer:
Medical/Health

In Consumer Related prefer:
Consumer
Education Related

In Industrial/Energy prefer:
Alternative Energy
Energy Conservation Relat
Environmental Related

In Financial Services prefer:
Real Estate

In Business Serv. prefer:
Services

In Manufact. prefer:
Manufacturing

Additional Information
Year Founded: 2000
Capital Under Management: $826,328,000
Current Activity Level : Actively seeking new investments

TOPSPIN PARTNERS LP

Three Expressway Plaza, Suite 100
Roslyn Heights, NY USA 11577
Phone: 5166259400
Fax: 5166259499
E-mail: info@topspinpartners.com
Website: www.topspinpartners.com

Management and Staff
Leigh Randall, Co-Founder
Leo Guthart, Co-Founder
Ojas Vahia, Vice President
Stephen Lebowitz, Co-Founder
Stephen Parks, Vice President

Type of Firm
Private Equity Firm

Project Preferences

Type of Financing Preferred:
Leveraged Buyout
Early Stage
Expansion
Generalist PE
Balanced
Turnaround
Later Stage
Management Buyouts
Acquisition
Recapitalizations

Size of Investments Considered:
Min Size of Investment Considered (000s): $1,000
Max Size of Investment Considered (000s): $15,000

Geographical Preferences

United States Preferences:

International Preferences:
No Preference

Industry Preferences

In Communications prefer:
Media and Entertainment
Publishing

In Computer Software prefer:
Software

In Computer Other prefer:
Computer Related

In Consumer Related prefer:
Consumer
Food/Beverage
Consumer Products
Other Restaurants

In Business Serv. prefer:
Services
Distribution
Media

In Manufact. prefer:
Manufacturing

Additional Information
Year Founded: 2000
Capital Under Management: $213,000,000
Current Activity Level : Actively seeking new investments

TORCH HILL INVESTMENT PARTNERS LLC

2000 Pennsylvania Avenue NW, Suite 5100
Washington, DC USA 20006
Phone: 2025361200
Website: www.torchhill.com

Management and Staff
Art Brown, Partner
Brent Scowcroft, Partner
Bruce Albrecht, Partner
Chuck Jones, Partner
David Miller, Partner
Gabriel Patricio, Partner
Gregory Newbold, Partner
James Richardson, Partner
Jeremy Mackenzie, Partner
Jerry Durrant, Partner
Jesse Walcott, Principal
Jim Feigley, Partner
Joe Ratzloff, Partner
John Abizaid, Partner
Matt Broderick, Partner
Michael Fallon, Partner
Norm Carley, Partner
Roy Carter, Partner
Stephen Minor, Vice President
William Parrish, Partner
William Sullivan, Partner

Type of Firm
Private Equity Firm

Project Preferences

Type of Financing Preferred:
Leveraged Buyout
Management Buyouts
Acquisition

Geographical Preferences

United States Preferences:

International Preferences:
All International

Industry Preferences

In Computer Software prefer:
Systems Software

In Business Serv. prefer:
Services

Additional Information
Name of Most Recent Fund: Torch Hill Fund, L.P.
Most Recent Fund Was Raised: 10/13/2005
Year Founded: 2005
Current Activity Level : Actively seeking new investments

TORQUE CAPITAL GROUP LLC

437 Madison Avenue
33rd Floor, Suite 33A
New York, NY USA 10022
Phone: 2127050164
Fax: 2127050196
E-mail: contact@torquecap.com
Website: www.torquecap.com

Management and Staff
Jonathan Saltzman, Co-Founder
Joseph Parzick, Co-Founder

Type of Firm
Private Equity Firm

Project Preferences

Type of Financing Preferred:
Leveraged Buyout
Turnaround
Special Situation

Industry Preferences

In Consumer Related prefer:
Consumer
Retail

In Industrial/Energy prefer:
Industrial Products

In Transportation prefer:
Aerospace

In Manufact. prefer:
Manufacturing

Additional Information
Year Founded: 2011
Current Activity Level : Actively seeking new investments

TORQUEST PARTNERS INC

161 Bay St. Brookfield Place
Ste.4240 TD Canada Trust Tower
Toronto, Canada M5J 2S1
Phone: 4169567022
Fax: 4169567000
E-mail: info@torquest.com
Website: www.torquest.com

Management and Staff
Alan Lever, Partner
Brent Belzberg, Managing Partner
Daniel Sonshine, Partner
Eric Berke, Managing Partner
Kimberly Davis, Chief Financial Officer
Marc Lipton, Partner
Mathew Chapman, Partner
Michael Hollend, Partner
Wayne Pommen, Vice President

Type of Firm
Private Equity Firm

Association Membership
Canadian Venture Capital Association

Project Preferences

Type of Financing Preferred:
Leveraged Buyout
Expansion
Management Buyouts
Acquisition
Recapitalizations

Geographical Preferences

United States Preferences:

Canadian Preferences:
All Canada

Industry Preferences

In Consumer Related prefer:
Food/Beverage
Consumer Products
Consumer Services

In Industrial/Energy prefer:
Materials

In Financial Services prefer:
Financial Services

In Business Serv. prefer:
Services

In Manufact. prefer:
Manufacturing

Additional Information
Name of Most Recent Fund: TorQuest Partners Fund III, L.P.
Most Recent Fund Was Raised: 07/16/2012
Year Founded: 2002
Capital Under Management: $1,227,480,000
Current Activity Level : Actively seeking new investments
Method of Compensation: Return on invest. most important, but chg. closing fees, service fees, etc.

TORREAL SA

Fortuny 1
Madrid, Spain 28010
Phone: 34915756622
Fax: 34915780397
E-mail: info@torreal.com
Website: www.torreal.com

Management and Staff
Alvaro Garteiz Castellanos, Founder
Jose Diaz-Rato Revuelta, Managing Director
Pedro Lomas, Managing Director

Type of Firm
Private Equity Firm

Project Preferences

Type of Financing Preferred:
Leveraged Buyout
Early Stage
Expansion
Generalist PE
Balanced
Turnaround
Later Stage
Management Buyouts
Acquisition
Startup

Size of Investments Considered:
Min Size of Investment Considered (000s): $38,790
Max Size of Investment Considered (000s): $258,598

Geographical Preferences

International Preferences:
Spain
All International

Additional Information
Year Founded: 1990
Current Activity Level : Actively seeking new investments

TORRENS CAPITAL MANAGEMENT

246 Glen Osmond Road
Fullarton, Australia 5063
Phone: 61882129600
Fax: 612345671098
E-mail: info@torrenscapital.com.au
Website: www.torrenscapital.com.au

Other Offices
GPO Box 11040
Adelaide, Australia 5001
Phone: 61882129600
Fax: 12345671098

Management and Staff
Joel Hepburn-Brown, Managing Director

Type of Firm
Private Equity Firm

Association Membership
Australian Venture Capital Association (AVCAL)

Project Preferences

Type of Financing Preferred:
Acquisition

Geographical Preferences

International Preferences:
Australia

Industry Preferences

In Medical/Health prefer:
Health Services

In Consumer Related prefer:
Retail
Food/Beverage
Education Related

In Financial Services prefer:
Financial Services

In Business Serv. prefer:
Services

In Manufact. prefer:
Manufacturing

In Agr/Forestr/Fish prefer:
Mining and Minerals

Additional Information
Year Founded: 2009
Current Activity Level : Actively seeking new investments

TORREY PINES INVESTMENT, INC.

6605 Nancy Ridge Drive, Suite 207
San Diego, CA USA 92121
Phone: 8587240581
Fax: 8583453761
E-mail: deals@torreypinesinv.com
Website: www.torreypinesinv.com

Management and Staff
Ronald Demuth, President

Type of Firm
Incubator/Development Program

Project Preferences

Role in Financing:
Will function either as deal originator or investor in deals created by others

Type of Financing Preferred:
Early Stage

Geographical Preferences

United States Preferences:
All U.S.

International Preferences:
Russia

Additional Information
Year Founded: 2002
Capital Under Management: $60,000,000
Current Activity Level : Actively seeking new investments

TORSA CAPITAL SGECR SA

Avenida De La Constitucion 88
1 D
Gijon, Spain 33207
Phone: 34985174029
E-mail: info@torsacapital.es

Management and Staff
Beatriz Alvarez, Founder
Jesus Garcia, Chief Executive Officer

Type of Firm
Private Equity Firm

Association Membership
Spanish Venture Capital Association (ASCRI)

Project Preferences

Type of Financing Preferred:
Early Stage
Expansion
Generalist PE
Balanced
Seed
Management Buyouts
Acquisition
Startup

Size of Investments Considered:
Min Size of Investment Considered (000s): $1,326
Max Size of Investment Considered (000s): $26,525

Geographical Preferences

International Preferences:
Spain

Industry Preferences

In Biotechnology prefer:
Biotechnology

In Medical/Health prefer:
Medical/Health
Health Services
Pharmaceuticals

In Industrial/Energy prefer:
Alternative Energy

In Business Serv. prefer:
Services

Additional Information
Year Founded: 2006
Capital Under Management: $8,035,000
Current Activity Level : Actively seeking new investments

TORYS LLP

79 Wellington Street West
Toronto, Canada M5K 1N2
Phone: 416-865-7500
Fax: 416-865-7380
Website: www.torys.com

Other Offices
4600 Eighth Avenue Place East
525 - 8th Avenue S.W.
Calgary, Canada
Phone: 4037763700
Fax: 4037763800

1114 Avenue of the Americas
23rd Floor
NEW YORK, NY USA 10036
Phone: 2128806000
Fax: 2126820200

Management and Staff
Cindy Bordin, Chief Operating Officer
Les Viner, Partner
Michael Pickersgill, President
Michael Amm, Partner
Michael Akkawi, Partner
Sylvie Rodrigue, Partner

Type of Firm
Private Equity Firm

Additional Information
Year Founded: 2009
Current Activity Level : Actively seeking new investments

TOSCAFUND ASSET MANAGEMENT LLP

90 Long Acre
Seventh Floor
London, United Kingdom
Phone: 4402078456100
Fax: 4402078456101
E-mail: ir@toscafund.com
Website: www.toscafund.com

Type of Firm
Investment Management Firm

Project Preferences

Type of Financing Preferred:
Leveraged Buyout
Acquisition

Additional Information
Year Founded: 2000
Capital Under Management: $356,720,000
Current Activity Level : Actively seeking new investments

TOTTORI CAPITAL CO LTD

9-2 Oogi-cho
2F Torigin Plaza Building
Tottori, Japan 680-0846
Phone: 81857202733
Fax: 81857256193
E-mail: info@tottoricap.com
Website: www.tottoricap.com

Type of Firm
Bank Affiliated

Association Membership
Japan Venture Capital Association

Project Preferences

Type of Financing Preferred:
Balanced

Geographical Preferences

International Preferences:
Japan

Additional Information
Year Founded: 1997
Capital Under Management: $6,704,000
Current Activity Level : Actively seeking new investments

TOUCHSTONE CAPITAL PARTNERS LTD

c/o Armillary Private Capital
58 Victoria St. Ballinger Bldg
Wellington, New Zealand 6140
Phone: 6449749269
Fax: 6449749282
Website: www.touchstonecapital.co.nz

Type of Firm
Private Equity Firm

Project Preferences

Type of Financing Preferred:
Turnaround
Distressed Debt
Recapitalizations

Additional Information
Year Founded: 2005
Current Activity Level : Actively seeking new investments

TOUCHSTONE INNOVATIONS PLC

52 Princes Gate, Exhibition Rd
South Kensington
London, United Kingdom SW7 2PG
Phone: 442075814949
Fax: 442075946584
E-mail: info@imperialinnovations.co.uk
Website: www.touchstoneinnovations.com

Management and Staff
Anthony Hickson, Managing Director
Russell Cummings, Chief Executive Officer

Type of Firm
University Program

Association Membership
British Venture Capital Association (BVCA)

Project Preferences

Type of Financing Preferred:
Early Stage
Seed
Startup

Geographical Preferences

International Preferences:
United Kingdom

Industry Preferences

In Biotechnology prefer:
Biotechnology

In Medical/Health prefer:
Medical/Health

In Industrial/Energy prefer:
Alternative Energy

Additional Information
Year Founded: 1986
Current Activity Level : Actively seeking new investments

TOWARZYSTWO FUNDUSZY INWESTYCYJNYCH CAPITAL PARTNERS SA

ul. Franciszka Nullo 2
Biurowiec Nullo
Warsaw, Poland 00-486
Phone: 48-2-2502-5550
Fax: 48-2-2502-5551
E-mail: biuro@akjtfi.pl
Website: www.tficp.pl

Type of Firm
Private Equity Firm

Project Preferences

Type of Financing Preferred:
Early Stage
Balanced
Seed

Geographical Preferences

International Preferences:
Europe
No Preference
Poland

Industry Preferences

In Communications prefer:
Telecommunications

In Medical/Health prefer:
Medical/Health
Medical Products

In Consumer Related prefer:
Consumer

In Industrial/Energy prefer:
Materials
Machinery

In Financial Services prefer:
Real Estate
Financial Services

Additional Information
Year Founded: 2005
Current Activity Level : Actively seeking new investments

TOWER ARCH CAPITAL LLC

13961 South Minuteman Drive, Suite 375
Draper, UT USA 84020
Phone: 8019975808
E-mail: info@towerarch.com
Website: www.towerarch.com

Management and Staff
David Parkin, Partner
David Topham, Partner
Rhett Neuenschwander, Partner
Ryan Stratton, Partner

Type of Firm
Private Equity Firm

Project Preferences

Type of Financing Preferred:
Leveraged Buyout
Management Buyouts
Recapitalizations

Geographical Preferences

United States Preferences:
All U.S.

Additional Information

Year Founded: 2013
Capital Under Management: $272,000,000
Current Activity Level : Actively seeking new investments

TOWER THREE PARTNERS LLC

Two Sound View Drive
Greenwich, CT USA 06830
Phone: 2034855800
Fax: 2034855885
Website: www.tower3partners.com

Management and Staff

Christopher Jacobs, Chief Financial Officer
Peter Fitzsimmons, Managing Director
William Forrest, Founder

Type of Firm

Private Equity Firm

Project Preferences

Type of Financing Preferred:
Turnaround
Distressed Debt

Geographical Preferences

United States Preferences:

Additional Information

Name of Most Recent Fund: Tower Three Partners Fund I, L.P.
Most Recent Fund Was Raised: 08/21/2008
Year Founded: 2007
Current Activity Level : Actively seeking new investments

TOWERBROOK CAPITAL PARTNERS LP

65 East 55th Street
Park Avenue Tower
New York, NY USA 10022
Phone: 2126992200
Fax: 9175919851
E-mail: contact@towerbrook.com
Website: www.towerbrook.com

Other Offices

One Market, Steuart Tower, Suite 1475
San Francisco, CA USA 94105
Phone: 415-259-5001

Kinnaird House
One Pall Mall East
London, United Kingdom SW1Y 5AU

Phone: 44-20-7451-2020
Fax: 44-20-7451-2022

Management and Staff

Alessandro Luongo, Principal
Andrew Rolfe, Managing Director
Axel Meyersiek, Managing Director
Brian Jacobsen, Managing Director
David De Laureal, Principal
Elisabetta Ricci, Principal
Filippo Cardini, Managing Partner
Glenn Miller, Managing Director
Gordon Holmes, Managing Director
Hugh Harper, Managing Director
Ian Sacks, Managing Director
Jeroen Bischops, Principal
Jonathan Bilzin, Senior Managing Director
Jose Arellano, Principal
Karim Saddi, Managing Director
Michael Karangelen, Managing Director
Nicholas Callias, Principal
Niclas Gabran, Managing Director
Patrick Smulders, Managing Director
Robin Esterson, Managing Director
Travis Nelson, Managing Director
Winston Ginsberg, Managing Director

Type of Firm

Private Equity Firm

Association Membership

British Venture Capital Association (BVCA)
European Private Equity and Venture Capital Assoc.

Project Preferences

Type of Financing Preferred:
Leveraged Buyout
Acquisition

Geographical Preferences

United States Preferences:
North America

International Preferences:
Europe

Industry Focus

(% based on actual investment)
Other Products	24.9%
Internet Specific	21.2%
Communications and Media	15.0%
Computer Software and Services	14.4%
Consumer Related	8.6%
Medical/Health	6.9%
Industrial/Energy	4.0%
Semiconductors/Other Elect.	2.1%
Biotechnology	1.7%
Computer Hardware	1.1%

Additional Information

Year Founded: 1995
Capital Under Management: $3,500,000,000
Current Activity Level : Actively seeking new investments

TOWNSGATE MEDIA

2629 Townsgate Road, Suite 205
Westlake Village, CA USA 91361
E-mail: info@townsgatemedia.com
Website: www.townsgatemedia.com

Type of Firm

Private Equity Firm

Project Preferences

Type of Financing Preferred:
Early Stage
Seed

Geographical Preferences

United States Preferences:
California

Industry Preferences

In Internet Specific prefer:
Internet

In Consumer Related prefer:
Consumer Services

In Business Serv. prefer:
Media

Additional Information

Year Founded: 2012
Current Activity Level : Actively seeking new investments

TPG CAPITAL MANAGEMENT LP

301 Commerce Street, Suite 3300
Fort Worth, TX USA 76102
Phone: 8178714000
Fax: 8178714001
E-mail: info@tpg.com
Website: tpg.com

Other Offices

156, Maker Chamber VI
15th floor, Nariman Point
Mumbai, India 400 021
Phone: 91-22-4039-1000
Fax: 91-22-4039-1002

Atago Green Hills MORI Tower
36F, 2-5-1, Atago, Minato-ku
Tokyo, Japan 105-6236
Phone: 81-3-5408-6900
Fax: 81-3-5408-0691

Rua Iguatemi, 151
8th Floor - Suite 81
Sao Paulo, Brazil 01451-011
Phone: 55-11-3192-2300

4600 Wells Fargo Center
90 South Seventh Sreet
MINNEAPOLIS, MN USA 55402

6, Rue Christophe Colomb
Paris, France 75008
Phone: 33-1-5357-2700
Fax: 33-1-5357-2701

Regus, Smolensky Passage
Smolenskaya Square 3
Moscow, Russia 121099
Phone: 7-495-660-8600
Fax: 7-495-660-8601

345 California Street, Suite 3300
SAN FRANCISCO, CA USA 94104
Phone: 4157431550

888 Seventh Avenue
38th Floor
NEW YORK, NY USA 10019
Phone: 212-601-4700
Fax: 212-601-4701

Two International Place, Suite 2230
BOSTON, MA USA 02110
Phone: 6177932000

, Suite 3801, Jianguomenwai Avenue
China World Trade Center
Beijing, China 100004
Phone: 86-10-5965-3888
Fax: 86-10-5965-3999

No. 2 Fortune Avenue
20/F, Fortune Tower A
Chongqing, China 401121
Phone: 86-23-6342-3388
Fax: 86-23-6342-3399

401 Congress Avenue, Suite 2750
AUSTIN, TX USA 78701
Phone: 512-533-6600
Fax: 512-533-6601

The Goldbell Centre
5 rue Eugene Ruppert
Luxembourg, Luxembourg L-2453
Phone: 352-2700-41251
Fax: 352-2700-412599

Level 31
101 Collins Street
Melbourne, Australia 3000
Phone: 61-3-9664-4444
Fax: 61-3-9663-7005

One George Street
#14-01
Singapore, Singapore 049145
Phone: 65-6390-5000
Fax: 65-6390-5001

8 Century Avenue
4501 Shanghai IFC Tower II
Shanghai, China 200120
Phone: 86-21-2035-3588
Fax: 86-21-2035-3599

8 Finance Street
57/F Two Int'l Finance Ctr
Central, Hong Kong
Phone: 852-3515-8888
Fax: 852-3515-8999

Management and Staff
Andrew Tirbeni, Vice President
Asiff Hirji, Partner
Carrie Wheeler, Partner
Christopher Ortega, Principal
David Trujill, Principal
David Bonderman, Founder
Jack Daly, Partner
James Coulter, Partner
Kevin Burns, Partner
Matthias Calice, Partner
Michael MacDougall, Partner
Sanghoon Lee, Partner
Stephen Peel, Managing Partner
Steve Ellis, Managing Partner
Zubin Irani, Managing Director

Type of Firm
Private Equity Firm

Association Membership
British Venture Capital Association (BVCA)
China Venture Capital Association
French Venture Capital Association (AFIC)
German Venture Capital Association (BVK)
European Private Equity and Venture Capital Assoc.
Private Equity Council (PEC)

Project Preferences

Type of Financing Preferred:
Core
Leveraged Buyout
Value-Add
Expansion
Turnaround
Distressed Debt
Recapitalizations

Size of Investments Considered:
Min Size of Investment Considered (000s): $10,000
Max Size of Investment Considered: No Limit

Geographical Preferences

United States Preferences:
All U.S.

International Preferences:
Asia Pacific
Australia

Industry Focus
(% based on actual investment)
Industrial/Energy	24.4%
Other Products	21.0%
Consumer Related	15.7%
Computer Software and Services	12.4%
Medical/Health	8.4%
Internet Specific	8.2%
Computer Hardware	4.7%
Semiconductors/Other Elect.	2.6%
Communications and Media	1.9%
Biotechnology	0.8%

Additional Information
Name of Most Recent Fund: TSL Equity Partners, L.P.
Most Recent Fund Was Raised: 07/05/2011
Year Founded: 1992
Capital Under Management: $57,600,000,000
Current Activity Level : Actively seeking new investments

TPG GROWTH LLC
345 California Street, Suite 3300
San Francisco, CA USA 94104
Phone: 4157431500
Fax: 4157431601
E-mail: growthinfo@tpg.com
Website: www.tpggrowth.com

Other Offices
704, Platina Plot No. C-59
G-Block Bandra Kurla Complex
Mumbai, India 400 051
Phone: 91-22-4039-1000
Fax: 91-22-4039-1024

One George Street, Suite 14-01
Singapore, Singapore 049145
Phone: 656390-5000
Fax: 656390-5001

888 Seventh Avenue
38th Floor
NEW YORK, NY USA 10019
Phone: 212-601-4700
Fax: 212-601-4701

China World Trade Center, Suite 1520, Tower One
Beijing, China 100004
Phone: 86-10-5965-3888
Fax: 86-10-5965-3999

8 Finance Street, 57th Floor
Two International Finance Center
Central, Hong Kong
Phone: 852-3515-8888
Fax: 852-3515-8999

301 Commerce Street, Suite 3300
FORT WORTH, TX USA 76102
Phone: 817-871-4000
Fax: 817-871-4010

Management and Staff
Akshay Tanna, Vice President
Andrew Tirbeni, Vice President
David Bonderman, Co-Founder
David Gowdey, Vice President
Jim Coulter, Co-Founder
Jing Huang, Partner
John Bailey, Principal
Keith Nilsson, Partner
Leung Hung, Principal
Manas Tandon, Principal
Matt Hobart, Partner
Michael Fu, Principal
Ransom Langford, Partner
Sanjay Banker, Principal
Scott Gilbertson, Partner
Shamik Patel, Vice President
Sing Wang, Partner
Steve Wong, Vice President
Vish Narain, Principal
William McGlashan, Co-Founder
Zachary Ferguson, Vice President

Type of Firm
Private Equity Firm

Project Preferences

Role in Financing:
Will function either as deal originator or investor in deals created by others

Type of Financing Preferred:
Leveraged Buyout
Early Stage
Expansion
Generalist PE
Balanced
Later Stage

Geographical Preferences

United States Preferences:
North America

International Preferences:
Vietnam
India
Europe
China
Brazil
Australia
Asia

Industry Preferences

In Internet Specific prefer:
Internet

In Biotechnology prefer:
Biotechnology
Industrial Biotechnology

In Medical/Health prefer:
Medical/Health
Pharmaceuticals

In Consumer Related prefer:
Consumer
Retail

In Industrial/Energy prefer:
Energy
Alternative Energy
Industrial Products
Environmental Related

In Transportation prefer:
Transportation

In Business Serv. prefer:
Services

Additional Information
Year Founded: 2000
Capital Under Management: $4,000,000,000
Current Activity Level : Actively seeking new investments
Method of Compensation: Return on investment is of primary concern, do not charge fees

TPH PARTNERS LLC

1111 Bagby, Heritage Plaza, Suite 4950
Houston, TX USA 77002
Phone: 7133337100
Fax: 7133375354
E-mail: info@tphpartners.com
Website: tphpartners.com:8080

Management and Staff
Claire Harvey, Vice President
Curt Schaefer, Managing Director
George McCormick, Managing Partner

Type of Firm
Bank Affiliated

Project Preferences

Type of Financing Preferred:
Leveraged Buyout
Other
Acquisition

Size of Investments Considered:
Min Size of Investment Considered (000s): $10,000
Max Size of Investment Considered (000s): $25,000

Industry Preferences

In Industrial/Energy prefer:
Energy
Oil and Gas Exploration

Additional Information
Name of Most Recent Fund: TPH Partners II, L.P.
Most Recent Fund Was Raised: 05/24/2012
Year Founded: 2009
Capital Under Management: $88,100,000
Current Activity Level : Actively seeking new investments

TR ADVISORS LTD

Unit C, 7/F, On Hing Building
On Hing Terrace
Central, Hong Kong
Phone: 852-2526-7080
Fax: 852-2526-9112
E-mail: Info@tr-capital.com
Website: www.tr-capital.com

Management and Staff
Antoine Flamarion, Founding Partner
Mathieu Chabran, Founding Partner
Paul Robine, Founder

Type of Firm
Private Equity Advisor or Fund of Funds

Association Membership
Hong Kong Venture Capital Association (HKVCA)

Project Preferences

Type of Financing Preferred:
Fund of Funds
Expansion
Balanced
Special Situation
Fund of Funds of Second

Geographical Preferences

International Preferences:
Pakistan
India
China
Asia

Industry Preferences

In Medical/Health prefer:
Medical/Health

In Consumer Related prefer:
Consumer
Consumer Services

In Industrial/Energy prefer:
Energy

In Business Serv. prefer:
Services

Additional Information
Year Founded: 2007
Current Activity Level : Actively seeking new investments

TRACKER CAPITAL MANAGEMENT LLC

875 Third Avenue
New York, NY USA 10022
E-mail: info@trackercap.com
Website: www.trackercap.com

Type of Firm
Private Equity Firm

Project Preferences

Type of Financing Preferred:
Early Stage

Additional Information
Year Founded: 2017
Current Activity Level : Actively seeking new investments

TRAIL MIX VENTURES FUND LP

250 East 65th Street
11th Floor
New York, NY USA 10065
Phone: 2037225087
E-mail: hi@trailmix.vc
Website: www.trailmix.vc

Type of Firm
Private Equity Firm

Project Preferences

Type of Financing Preferred:
Early Stage

Additional Information
Year Founded: 2017
Capital Under Management: $5,300,000
Current Activity Level : Actively seeking new investments

TRAILBLAZER CAPITAL LP

2708 Fairmount Street, Suite 202
Dallas, TX USA 75201
Phone: 2148718050
E-mail: info@trailblazercapital.com

Other Offices
700 West Sheridan Ave
OKLAHOMA CITY, OK USA 73102
Phone: 4053670897

Management and Staff
David Matthews, Managing Partner
Joel Fontenot, Managing Partner

Type of Firm
Private Equity Firm

Project Preferences

Type of Financing Preferred:
Early Stage
Later Stage

Size of Investments Considered:
Min Size of Investment Considered (000s): $500
Max Size of Investment Considered (000s): $5,000

Geographical Preferences

United States Preferences:
Oklahoma
Texas

Industry Preferences

In Communications prefer:
Communications and Media
Telecommunications
Wireless Communications

In Computer Hardware prefer:
Disk Relat. Memory Device

In Computer Software prefer:
Data Processing
Applications Software

In Internet Specific prefer:
Ecommerce

In Computer Other prefer:
Computer Related

Additional Information
Name of Most Recent Fund: Trailblazer Capital Fund II
Most Recent Fund Was Raised: 03/15/2011
Year Founded: 2006
Capital Under Management: $30,000,000
Current Activity Level : Actively seeking new investments

TRAILCREEK CAPITAL GROUP LLC

1550 Wewatta Street
Second Floor
Denver, CO USA 80202
Phone: 9177569368
E-mail: contactus@trailcreekcapitalgroup.com
Website: www.trailcreekcapitalgroup.com

Management and Staff
Andrew Pozatek, Founder

Type of Firm
Private Equity Firm

Project Preferences

Type of Financing Preferred:
Generalist PE

Industry Preferences

In Communications prefer:
Telecommunications

In Consumer Related prefer:
Consumer Services

In Financial Services prefer:
Financial Services

In Business Serv. prefer:
Services
Media

Additional Information
Year Founded: 1969
Current Activity Level : Actively seeking new investments

TRANCE-SCIENCE INC

1-1-1 Uchisaiwaicho
Eighth Floor, Imperial Hotel
Tokyo, Japan 100-0011
Phone: 81-3-3500-3588
Fax: 81-3-3500-3589

Type of Firm
Incubator/Development Program

Project Preferences

Type of Financing Preferred:
Seed
Startup

Geographical Preferences

International Preferences:
Japan

Industry Preferences

In Biotechnology prefer:
Biotechnology

In Medical/Health prefer:
Medical/Health

In Industrial/Energy prefer:
Energy
Materials
Environmental Related

Additional Information
Year Founded: 2001
Current Activity Level : Actively seeking new investments

TRANSEQUITY NETWORK BV

Julianaplein 8
's-Hertogenbosch, Netherlands 5211 BC
Phone: 31736145937
Fax: 31877846895
E-mail: info@transequity.nl
Website: www.transequity.nl

Management and Staff
Albert Bos, Chief Financial Officer
Jurgen Van Olphen, Co-Founder

Type of Firm
Private Equity Firm

Association Membership
Dutch Venture Capital Associaton (NVP)

Project Preferences

Type of Financing Preferred:
Leveraged Buyout
Generalist PE
Balanced
Turnaround
Later Stage
Recapitalizations

Geographical Preferences

International Preferences:
Netherlands

Additional Information
Year Founded: 2002
Current Activity Level : Actively seeking new investments

TRANSFERATOR AB (PUBL)

Skeppsbron 6
Box 607
Stockholm, Sweden 111 30
E-mail: info@transferator.com
Website: www.transferator.se

Type of Firm
Private Equity Firm

Association Membership
Swedish Venture Capital Association (SVCA)

Project Preferences

Type of Financing Preferred:
Balanced

Size of Investments Considered:
Min Size of Investment Considered (000s): $158
Max Size of Investment Considered (000s): $1,265

Geographical Preferences

International Preferences:
Sweden

Industry Preferences

In Communications prefer:
Communications and Media
Commercial Communications
Telecommunications
Wireless Communications

In Internet Specific prefer:
Internet

Additional Information
Year Founded: 2005
Capital Under Management: $18,500,000
Current Activity Level : Actively seeking new investments

TRANSITION CAPITAL PARTNERS

2100 McKinney Avenue, Suite 1501
Dallas, TX USA 75201
Phone: 2149783800
Fax: 2149783899
Website: www.transitioncapitalpartners.com

Management and Staff
Andy Foskey, Managing Director
Forrest Williams, Principal
Kevyn DeMartino, Managing Director
Paul Thompson, Partner
Rick Baldwin, Managing Director

Type of Firm
Private Equity Firm

Project Preferences

Role in Financing:
Prefer role as deal originator but will also invest in deals created by others

Type of Financing Preferred:
Leveraged Buyout
Management Buyouts
Recapitalizations

Geographical Preferences

United States Preferences:

Industry Preferences

In Communications prefer:
Telecommunications

In Computer Software prefer:
Software

In Medical/Health prefer:
Medical/Health
Health Services
Hospitals/Clinics/Primary

In Consumer Related prefer:
Retail
Food/Beverage
Education Related

In Industrial/Energy prefer:
Oil & Gas Drilling,Explor
Alternative Energy

In Business Serv. prefer:
Services

Additional Information
Year Founded: 1993
Current Activity Level : Actively seeking new investments

TRANSLINK CAPITAL LLC

228 Hamilton Avenue, Suite 210
Palo Alto, CA USA 94301
Phone: 6503307353
Fax: 6503307351
E-mail: info@translinkcapital.com
Website: translinkcapital.com

Management and Staff
Duen-Chian Cheng, Venture Partner
Eric Hsia, Venture Partner
Gwong-Yih Lee, Senior Managing Director
Hong Chen, Venture Partner
Jackie Yang, Co-Founder
Jay Eum, Managing Director
Jay Eum, Co-Founder
Kazunori Ozaki, Venture Partner
Manabu Ando, Partner
Nobuyuki Akimoto, Managing Partner
Shirley Chen, Chief Financial Officer
Sung Park, Venture Partner
Sung Park, Co-Founder
Toshi Otani, Co-Founder

Type of Firm
Private Equity Firm

Association Membership
National Venture Capital Association - USA (NVCA)

Project Preferences

Role in Financing:
Will function either as deal originator or investor in deals created by others

Type of Financing Preferred:
Early Stage
Expansion
Later Stage

Geographical Preferences

United States Preferences:

International Preferences:
China
Korea, South
Japan

Industry Preferences

In Communications prefer:
Telecommunications
Wireless Communications
Data Communications

In Computer Software prefer:
Applications Software

Pratt's Guide to Private Equity & Venture Capital Sources

Additional Information
Name of Most Recent Fund: TransLink Capital Partners II, L.P.
Most Recent Fund Was Raised: 09/09/2011
Year Founded: 2007
Capital Under Management: $350,000,000
Current Activity Level : Actively seeking new investments
Method of Compensation: Return on investment is of primary concern, do not charge fees

TRANSMEDIA CAPITAL LLC
717 Market Street, Suite 100
San Francisco, CA USA 94103
E-mail: info@transmediacapital.com

Management and Staff
Chris Redlitz, General Partner
Peter Boboff, General Partner

Type of Firm
Private Equity Firm

Project Preferences

Type of Financing Preferred:
Early Stage
Seed
Startup

Size of Investments Considered:
Min Size of Investment Considered (000s): $250
Max Size of Investment Considered (000s): $2,000

Industry Preferences

In Communications prefer:
Wireless Communications
Media and Entertainment

In Internet Specific prefer:
Internet

In Financial Services prefer:
Financial Services

In Business Serv. prefer:
Distribution
Media

Additional Information
Year Founded: 2008
Capital Under Management: $18,350,000
Current Activity Level : Actively seeking new investments

TRANSOM CAPITAL GROUP LLC
12300 Wilshire Boulevard, Suite 405
West Los Angeles, CA USA 90025
Phone: 3104070935
Website: transomcap.com

Other Offices
10990 Wilshire Boulevard, Suite 440
Los Angeles, CA USA 90024
Phone: 3104070940

Management and Staff
Adam Fraser, Principal
David Ascher, Managing Director
James Oh, Partner
Ken Firtel, Managing Director
Russ Roenick, Managing Director

Type of Firm
Private Equity Firm

Project Preferences

Type of Financing Preferred:
Leveraged Buyout

Size of Investments Considered:
Min Size of Investment Considered (000s): $5,000
Max Size of Investment Considered (000s): $25,000

Geographical Preferences

United States Preferences:
All U.S.

Industry Preferences

In Consumer Related prefer:
Consumer
Entertainment and Leisure
Retail

In Industrial/Energy prefer:
Industrial Products

In Transportation prefer:
Aerospace

In Business Serv. prefer:
Media

In Manufact. prefer:
Manufacturing

Additional Information
Year Founded: 2008
Capital Under Management: $433,000,000
Current Activity Level : Actively seeking new investments

TRANSPACIFIC VENTURE PARTNERS
Zhouzi Street, Neihu District
3Floor, No.80
Taipei, Taiwan
Phone: 886226271778
Fax: 886226272317
Website: www.tpv-ventures.com

Type of Firm
Private Equity Firm

Project Preferences

Type of Financing Preferred:
Balanced

Size of Investments Considered:
Min Size of Investment Considered (000s): $100
Max Size of Investment Considered (000s): $300

Geographical Preferences

United States Preferences:

International Preferences:
India
Europe
Taiwan
China

Industry Preferences

In Biotechnology prefer:
Industrial Biotechnology

In Medical/Health prefer:
Medical/Health

In Consumer Related prefer:
Consumer

Additional Information
Year Founded: 2014
Current Activity Level : Actively seeking new investments

TRANSPORTATION RESOURCE PARTNERS LP
2555 Telegraph Road
Bloomfield Hills, MI USA 48302
Phone: 2486482101
Fax: 2486482105
Website: www.trpfund.com

Other Offices
200 Connell Drive, Suite 1100
Berkeley Heights, NJ USA 07922
Phone: 9083636000
Fax: 9083636010

Management and Staff
David Mitchell, Managing Director
James Hislop, Managing Director
Jeffery Bullard, Principal
Michael DiRienzo, Vice President
Richard Peters, Managing Director
Roger Penske, Managing Director
Steven Carrel, Principal

Type of Firm
Private Equity Firm

Project Preferences

Pratt's Guide to Private Equity & Venture Capital Sources

Type of Financing Preferred:
Leveraged Buyout
Acquisition
Recapitalizations

Geographical Preferences

United States Preferences:

Industry Focus

(% based on actual investment)
Internet Specific	47.2%
Consumer Related	22.9%
Other Products	21.5%
Industrial/Energy	5.1%
Semiconductors/Other Elect.	3.3%

Additional Information

Name of Most Recent Fund: Penske Capital Partners
Most Recent Fund Was Raised: 06/30/1997
Year Founded: 2003
Capital Under Management: $109,820,000
Current Activity Level : Actively seeking new investments

TRAVEL STARTUPS INCUBATOR LLC

4201 Village Court
Lake Wales, FL USA 33898
Phone: 2074600740
Website: www.travelstartups.co

Management and Staff

Matt Zito, Managing Partner

Type of Firm

Incubator/Development Program

Project Preferences

Type of Financing Preferred:
Early Stage
Seed

Industry Preferences

In Computer Software prefer:
Applications Software

In Consumer Related prefer:
Entertainment and Leisure

Additional Information

Year Founded: 2014
Current Activity Level : Actively seeking new investments

TREA CAPITAL PARTNERS, S.V. SA

Avda. Diagonal 640, 3rd E
Barcelona, Spain 08017
Phone: 34934675510
Fax: 34934675389
E-mail: treainfo@treacapital.com
Website: www.treacapital.com

Type of Firm

Investment Management Firm

Project Preferences

Type of Financing Preferred:
Fund of Funds
Leveraged Buyout
Mezzanine
Generalist PE
Later Stage
Other
Distressed Debt

Geographical Preferences

United States Preferences:

International Preferences:
Europe
Asia

Additional Information

Year Founded: 2006
Current Activity Level : Actively seeking new investments

TREACLE VENTURE PARTNERS

52 Grosvenor Road
Fairway Office Park, Suite 5
Bryanston, South Africa
Phone: 27114637476
Fax: 27114631213
Website: www.treacle.co.za

Management and Staff

Christoff Botha, Partner
Pieter Pretorius, Partner

Type of Firm

Private Equity Firm

Association Membership

South African Venture Capital Association (SAVCA)

Project Preferences

Type of Financing Preferred:
Early Stage
Expansion
Balanced
Turnaround
Later Stage
Management Buyouts
Startup
Special Situation
Recapitalizations

Size of Investments Considered:
Min Size of Investment Considered (000s): $1,245
Max Size of Investment Considered (000s): $5,603

Geographical Preferences

International Preferences:
South Africa

Industry Preferences

In Communications prefer:
Telecommunications
Wireless Communications

In Semiconductor/Electr prefer:
Electronics

In Business Serv. prefer:
Media

Additional Information

Year Founded: 2001
Capital Under Management: $30,500,000
Current Activity Level : Actively seeking new investments

TREEHOUSE HEALTH LLC

1635 Hennepin Avenue, Suite 200
Minneapolis, MN USA 55403
Phone: 6124865932
Website: treehouse-health.com

Management and Staff

David Dickey, Partner
Jeffrey Blank, Managing Director
Joseph Whitney, Partner

Type of Firm

Private Equity Firm

Project Preferences

Type of Financing Preferred:
Early Stage
Seed
Startup

Industry Preferences

In Medical/Health prefer:
Health Services

In Financial Services prefer:
Investment Groups

Additional Information

Year Founded: 2016
Current Activity Level : Actively seeking new investments

TREEHOUSE INVESTMENTS LLC

Casa Bonita Business Center, Suite 101
Dorado, PR USA 00646
Phone: 787-796-4487
Fax: 787-796-4409
E-mail: info@treehouseinvestments.com

Type of Firm
Private Equity Firm

Project Preferences

Type of Financing Preferred:
Balanced

Industry Preferences

In Industrial/Energy prefer:
Alternative Energy
Environmental Related

In Other prefer:
Socially Responsible

Additional Information
Year Founded: 2013
Current Activity Level : Actively seeking new investments

TREETOP VENTURES INC

11837 Miracle Hills Drive, Suite 101
Omaha, NE USA 68154
Phone: 4025057195
Fax: 4025041779
Website: www.treetopventures.com

Management and Staff
Dwight Hanson, Partner
Mary Stigge, Principal
Pam Knutson, Principal
Thomas Boje, Partner
William Fisher, Partner

Type of Firm
Investment Management Firm

Project Preferences

Type of Financing Preferred:
Startup

Geographical Preferences

United States Preferences:
Nebraska

Additional Information
Year Founded: 2013
Current Activity Level : Actively seeking new investments

TREGARON CAPITAL CO LLC

540 University Avenue, Suite 250
Palo Alto, CA USA 94301
Phone: 6504032080
Fax: 6506182550
E-mail: info@tregaroncapital.com
Website: www.tregaroncapital.com

Management and Staff
JR Matthews, Managing Director
John Thornton, Managing Director
Todd Collins, Managing Director

Type of Firm
Private Equity Firm

Association Membership
Natl Assoc of Small Bus. Inv. Co (NASBIC)

Project Preferences

Role in Financing:
Prefer role as deal originator but will also invest in deals created by others

Type of Financing Preferred:
Leveraged Buyout
Control-block Purchases
Expansion
Mezzanine
Public Companies
Management Buyouts
Acquisition
Recapitalizations

Geographical Preferences

United States Preferences:
West Coast

Industry Preferences

In Communications prefer:
Publishing

In Medical/Health prefer:
Medical/Health

In Financial Services prefer:
Financial Services

In Business Serv. prefer:
Services

In Manufact. prefer:
Publishing

Additional Information
Name of Most Recent Fund: Tregaron Opportunity Fund I, L.P.
Most Recent Fund Was Raised: 02/19/2010
Year Founded: 2001
Capital Under Management: $57,846,000
Current Activity Level : Actively seeking new investments

TRELLIS CAPITAL CORP

330 Bay Street, Suite 1302
Toronto, Canada M5H 2S8
Phone: 4163982299
Fax: 4163981799
E-mail: info@trelliscapital.com
Website: trelliscapital.com

Management and Staff
Dominic Talalla, Managing Partner
Sunil Selby, Managing Partner

Type of Firm
Private Equity Firm

Association Membership
Canadian Venture Capital Association

Project Preferences

Role in Financing:
Will function either as deal originator or investor in deals created by others

Type of Financing Preferred:
Expansion
Balanced

Size of Investments Considered:
Min Size of Investment Considered (000s): $500
Max Size of Investment Considered (000s): $2,000

Geographical Preferences

Canadian Preferences:
All Canada

Industry Preferences

In Industrial/Energy prefer:
Alternative Energy
Industrial Products

In Manufact. prefer:
Manufacturing

Additional Information
Name of Most Recent Fund: Trellis Capital Corporation
Most Recent Fund Was Raised: 05/01/2000
Year Founded: 2000
Capital Under Management: $6,700,000
Current Activity Level : Actively seeking new investments
Method of Compensation: Return on invest. most important, but chg. closing fees, service fees, etc.

TRELLIS PARTNERS

138 Trinity Street
Cedar Creek, TX USA 78612
Phone: 5123309200
Website: www.trellis.com

Management and Staff
Alexander Broeker, General Partner
John Long, Co-Founder
Sonja Eagle, Partner

Type of Firm
Private Equity Firm

Project Preferences

Role in Financing:
Will function either as deal originator or investor in deals created by others

Type of Financing Preferred:
Balanced

Geographical Preferences

United States Preferences:

Industry Focus

(% based on actual investment)
Internet Specific	39.3%
Computer Software and Services	38.2%
Communications and Media	15.4%
Other Products	3.8%
Semiconductors/Other Elect.	3.2%

Additional Information

Name of Most Recent Fund: Trellis Partners II, L.P.
Most Recent Fund Was Raised: 02/02/2000
Year Founded: 1997
Capital Under Management: $67,000,000
Current Activity Level : Actively seeking new investments
Method of Compensation: Return on investment is of primary concern, do not charge fees

TREND FORWARD CAPITAL MANAGEMENT LLC

560 South Winchester Boulevard, Suite 400
San Jose, CA USA 95128
Website: www.trendforward.com

Type of Firm
Private Equity Firm

Project Preferences

Type of Financing Preferred:
Early Stage

Additional Information
Year Founded: 2017
Current Activity Level : Actively seeking new investments

TRENDLINES GROUP LTD

Misgav Business Park
The Trendlines Building
D.N. Misgav, Israel 20174
Phone: 972722607000
Fax: 972722607200
E-mail: info@trendlines.com
Website: www.trendlines.com

Other Offices

Asternweg 2
Friedrichsdorf, Germany D-61381
Phone: 49-6172-77150
Fax: 49-6172-737940

4 Bezalel Street
Second Floor
, Israel 52521

2940 West 123rd Terrace
Shawnee Mission, KS USA 66209
Phone: 913-317-8788
Fax: 913-317-8787

Migdal Shalom
26th floor
Tel Aviv, Israel 65251
Phone: 972-4-958-3323
Fax: 972-4-958-3325

Management and Staff

Moshe Katzenelson, Vice President
Yosef Ron, Chief Operating Officer

Type of Firm
Private Equity Firm

Association Membership
Israel Venture Association

Project Preferences

Type of Financing Preferred:
Early Stage
Balanced
Seed

Geographical Preferences

International Preferences:
Israel

Industry Preferences

In Biotechnology prefer:
Biotechnology

In Medical/Health prefer:
Medical/Health
Medical Products
Pharmaceuticals

In Industrial/Energy prefer:
Environmental Related

Additional Information
Year Founded: 2007
Capital Under Management: $10,000,000
Current Activity Level : Actively seeking new investments

TRESTLE VENTURES

760 Constitution Drive, Suite 106
Exton, PA USA 19341
Phone: 6108519950
Website: www.trestleventures.com

Management and Staff

Frank Lordi, Co-Founder
Jeff White, Managing Partner
Vincent Menichelli, Co-Founder

Type of Firm
Private Equity Firm

Project Preferences

Type of Financing Preferred:
Early Stage

Additional Information
Name of Most Recent Fund: Trestle Ventures, L.P.
Most Recent Fund Was Raised: 06/10/2008
Year Founded: 2008
Current Activity Level : Actively seeking new investments

TREVI HEALTH VENTURES LP

110 East 59th Street
33rd Floor
New York, NY USA 10022
Phone: 2128139201
E-mail: info@trevihealth.com
Website: www.trevihealth.com

Other Offices

52 Conduit Street
Third Floor
London, United Kingdom W1S 2YX
Phone: 442072922570

Management and Staff

Andrew Fink, Co-Founder
David Robbins, Co-Founder
Guy Shapira, Principal
James Cha, Principal
Scott Cragg, Partner
Warren Roiter, Managing Director

Type of Firm
Private Equity Firm

Project Preferences

Role in Financing:
Will function either as deal originator or investor in deals created by others

Type of Financing Preferred:
Leveraged Buyout
Early Stage
Expansion
Generalist PE
Balanced
Later Stage
Seed
Startup
Special Situation
Recapitalizations

Geographical Preferences

United States Preferences:
All U.S.

International Preferences:
United Kingdom

Industry Preferences

In Medical/Health prefer:
Medical/Health
Medical Diagnostics
Medical Therapeutics
Medical Products
Health Services
Pharmaceuticals

Additional Information

Name of Most Recent Fund: Trevi Health Ventures, L.P.
Most Recent Fund Was Raised: 03/20/2013
Year Founded: 2005
Capital Under Management: $33,412,000
Current Activity Level : Actively seeking new investments

TRG MANAGEMENT LP

280 Park Avenue
27th Floor West
New York, NY USA 10017
Phone: 2129842900
E-mail: TRG@rohatyngroup.com
Website: www.rohatyngroup.com

Other Offices

136 Sejong-daero
2nd floor, Seoul Finance Center
Seoul, South Korea

8 Connaught Road
Room 3007-08, One Exchange Square
Hong Kong, Hong Kong
Phone: 852 2912 1400
Fax: 852 2869 8400

Management and Staff

Bernard Steinberg, Partner
Bob Khanna, Partner
Christopher Seaver, Partner
Ernest Stern, Partner
Goetz Eggelhoefer, Partner
Guido Mosca, Partner
Jay Cohen, Partner
Jon Marom, Chief Financial Officer
Marc Desaedeleer, Partner
Michael DeAngelo, Managing Director
Nicholas Rohatyn, Chief Executive Officer
Philippe I Equilbec, Managing Director
Vincent Low, Partner
Vladimir Krin, Partner

Type of Firm

Investment Management Firm

Association Membership

Emerging Markets Private Equity Association

Project Preferences

Type of Financing Preferred:
Leveraged Buyout
Mezzanine
Generalist PE
Other

Geographical Preferences

International Preferences:
Latin America
Hong Kong
China
Mexico

Industry Preferences

In Communications prefer:
Telecommunications

In Medical/Health prefer:
Pharmaceuticals

In Consumer Related prefer:
Consumer

In Industrial/Energy prefer:
Energy
Alternative Energy

In Financial Services prefer:
Financial Services

In Business Serv. prefer:
Services
Media

In Agr/Forestr/Fish prefer:
Mining and Minerals

Additional Information

Year Founded: 2002
Capital Under Management: $160,000,000
Current Activity Level : Actively seeking new investments

TRI ARTISAN CAPITAL PARTNERS LLC

600 Fifth Avenue
14th Floor
New York, NY USA 10022
Phone: 2122183700
Fax: 2122183719
E-mail: contact@mjtagroup.com
Website: mjtagroup.com

Management and Staff

Gerald Cromack, President
Rohit Manocha, President

Type of Firm

Investment Management Firm

Project Preferences

Type of Financing Preferred:
Leveraged Buyout

Additional Information

Year Founded: 2002
Current Activity Level : Actively seeking new investments

TRIAGE VENTURES LLC

188 Minna Street, Suite 24F
San Francisco, CA USA 94105
Phone: 4154885270
Website: www.triageventures.com

Management and Staff

Doug Derwin, Managing Director

Type of Firm

Private Equity Firm

Project Preferences

Type of Financing Preferred:
Early Stage
Startup

Additional Information

Year Founded: 2011
Current Activity Level : Actively seeking new investments

TRIANGLE CAPITAL PARTNERS L L C

3700 Glenwood Avenue, Suite 530
Raleigh, NC USA 27612
Phone: 9197194770
E-mail: scolquitt@tcap.com

Management and Staff

C. Robert Knox, Vice President
Cary Nordan, Managing Director
Douglas Vaughn, Managing Director
Garland Tucker, Chief Executive Officer
James Burke, Vice President
Jeffrey Dombcik, Managing Director
Matthew Young, Vice President
Sheri Colquitt, Vice President

Type of Firm

SBIC

Association Membership

Natl Assoc of Small Bus. Inv. Co (NASBIC)

Project Preferences

Role in Financing:
Will function either as deal originator or investor in deals created by others

Type of Financing Preferred:
Leveraged Buyout
Expansion
Mezzanine
Management Buyouts
Acquisition
Recapitalizations

Size of Investments Considered:
Min Size of Investment Considered (000s): $5,000
Max Size of Investment Considered (000s): $20,000

Geographical Preferences

United States Preferences:
Mid Atlantic
Southeast
All U.S.

Industry Preferences

In Communications prefer:
Telecommunications

In Medical/Health prefer:
Medical Diagnostics
Diagnostic Services
Diagnostic Test Products
Medical Therapeutics
Drug/Equipmt Delivery
Health Services
Hospitals/Clinics/Primary
Hospital/Other Instit.

In Consumer Related prefer:
Consumer
Retail
Franchises(NEC)
Food/Beverage
Education Related

In Industrial/Energy prefer:
Industrial Products

In Business Serv. prefer:
Services
Distribution
Media

In Manufact. prefer:
Manufacturing

Additional Information
Year Founded: 2006
Current Activity Level : Actively seeking new investments
Method of Compensation: Return on invest. most important, but chg. closing fees, service fees, etc.

TRIANGLE PEAK PARTNERS LP

505 Hamilton Avenue, Suite 300
Palo Alto, CA USA 94301
Phone: 8319989540
E-mail: info@trianglepeakpartners.com
Website: www.trianglepeakpartners.com

Other Offices
11 Greenway Plaza, Suite 2000
Houston, TX USA 77046

Management and Staff
Dain DeGroff, Partner
David Pesikoff, Partner

Type of Firm
Investment Management Firm

Project Preferences

Type of Financing Preferred:
Early Stage
Expansion
Balanced
Public Companies
Later Stage

Size of Investments Considered:
Min Size of Investment Considered (000s): $2,000
Max Size of Investment Considered (000s): $10,000

Industry Preferences

In Industrial/Energy prefer:
Energy
Alternative Energy

Additional Information
Name of Most Recent Fund: Triangle Peak Partners II, L.P.
Most Recent Fund Was Raised: 08/14/2012
Year Founded: 2008
Capital Under Management: $160,034,000
Current Activity Level : Actively seeking new investments

TRIANGLE VENTURE CAPITAL GROUP

Marktstrasse 65
St. Leon-Rot, Germany 68789
Phone: 496251800830
Fax: 496251800839
E-mail: info@triangle-venture.com
Website: www.triangle-venture.com

Management and Staff
Anthony Park, Venture Partner
Bernd Geiger, Managing Partner
Gabriele Egger, Chief Financial Officer
Joachim Redmer, Venture Partner
Joerg Kreisel, Venture Partner
John Rosati, Venture Partner
Michael Rossbach, Venture Partner
Uli Fricke, Managing Partner

Type of Firm
Private Equity Firm

Association Membership
German Venture Capital Association (BVK)
European Private Equity and Venture Capital Assoc.

Project Preferences

Type of Financing Preferred:
Early Stage
Seed
Startup

Size of Investments Considered:
Min Size of Investment Considered (000s): $220
Max Size of Investment Considered (000s): $880

Geographical Preferences

International Preferences:
Europe
Switzerland
Austria
Germany

Industry Preferences

In Communications prefer:
Communications and Media
Telecommunications

In Computer Software prefer:
Software

In Computer Other prefer:
Computer Related

In Semiconductor/Electr prefer:
Electronics

In Biotechnology prefer:
Biotechnology

In Medical/Health prefer:
Medical/Health

In Industrial/Energy prefer:
Energy
Industrial Products
Environmental Related

Additional Information
Name of Most Recent Fund: Open Sky Technologies Fund
Most Recent Fund Was Raised: 03/04/2010
Year Founded: 1997
Capital Under Management: $144,800,000
Current Activity Level : Actively seeking new investments

TRIATHLON MEDICAL VENTURES LLC

300 East Business Way, Suite 200
Sharonville, OH USA 45241
Phone: 5137232600
E-mail: info@tmvp.com
Website: www.tmvp.com

Other Offices

201 North Illinois Street
16th Floor
Indianapolis, IN USA 46204
Phone: 317-280-8233
Fax: 317-328-9743

231 South Bemiston, Suite 800
Saint Louis, MO USA 63105
Phone: 314-854-1332
Fax: 314-854-9118

222 South First Street, Suite 200
Louisville, KY USA 40202
Phone: 5024101652
Fax: 5025846335

Management and Staff

Carrie Bates, Managing Partner
Dennis Costello, Co-Founder
George Emont, Managing Partner
John Rice, Co-Founder
Mark Collar, Venture Partner
Randy Weiss, Partner
Suzette Dutch, Managing Partner

Type of Firm
Private Equity Firm

Project Preferences

Type of Financing Preferred:
Early Stage
Balanced
Later Stage

Size of Investments Considered:
Min Size of Investment Considered (000s): $500
Max Size of Investment Considered (000s): $7,000

Geographical Preferences

United States Preferences:
Midwest

Industry Preferences

In Biotechnology prefer:
Biotechnology

In Medical/Health prefer:
Medical/Health

Additional Information
Year Founded: 2004
Capital Under Management: $103,900,000
Current Activity Level : Actively seeking new investments

TRIBAL VENTURES LLC

195 Harbour Drive
Chicago, IL USA 60601
Phone: 3129383803
E-mail: info@tribalventuresllc.com
Website: www.tribalventuresllc.com

Management and Staff
Alan Mattew, CEO & Managing Director
Ann Murphy, Managing Partner

Type of Firm
Private Equity Firm

Project Preferences

Type of Financing Preferred:
Early Stage
Seed
Strategic Alliances
Startup

Geographical Preferences

United States Preferences:
Illinois

Industry Preferences

In Computer Hardware prefer:
Integrated Turnkey System

In Computer Software prefer:
Software

In Internet Specific prefer:
Internet

Additional Information
Year Founded: 2012
Capital Under Management: $248,000
Current Activity Level : Actively seeking new investments

TRIBECA VENTURE PARTNERS LLC

99 Hudson Street
15th Floor
New York, NY USA 10013
Phone: 2129669333
E-mail: admin@tribecavp.com

Management and Staff
BRIAN HIRSCH, Co-Founder
CHIP MEAKEM, General Partner
Chip Meakem, Managing Partner
Zander Farkas, Principal

Type of Firm
Private Equity Firm

Project Preferences

Role in Financing:
Will function either as deal originator or investor in deals created by others

Type of Financing Preferred:
Early Stage
Seed

Size of Investments Considered:
Min Size of Investment Considered (000s): $100
Max Size of Investment Considered (000s): $4,000

Geographical Preferences

United States Preferences:
New York

Industry Preferences

In Communications prefer:
Wireless Communications

In Computer Software prefer:
Software
Applications Software

In Internet Specific prefer:
Ecommerce

In Consumer Related prefer:
Education Related

In Financial Services prefer:
Financial Services

In Business Serv. prefer:
Services
Media

Additional Information
Name of Most Recent Fund: Tribeca Venture Fund II, L.P.
Most Recent Fund Was Raised: 09/28/2012
Year Founded: 1998
Capital Under Management: $115,000,000
Current Activity Level : Actively seeking new investments
Method of Compensation: Return on investment is of primary concern, do not charge fees

---

TRICENT CAPITAL

1000 Texan Trail, Suite 212
Grapevine, TX USA 76051
Phone: 8173286158
Website: www.tricentcapital.com

Type of Firm
Private Equity Firm

Project Preferences

Type of Financing Preferred:
Early Stage

Geographical Preferences

United States Preferences:
All U.S.

Industry Preferences

In Computer Software prefer:
Software

Additional Information
Year Founded: 2014
Current Activity Level : Actively seeking new investments

TRICOR PACIFIC FOUNDERS CAPITAL INC

1111 West Hastings St, Suite 200
Vancouver, Canada V6E 2J3
Website: www.tricorfounders.com

Management and Staff
Brian Pettipas, Co-Founder
Christian Maas, Co-Founder
Derek Senft, Co-Founder
Mark Townsend, Co-Founder
Richard Harris, Co-Founder
Roderick Senft, Co-Founder
Trevor Johnstone, Co-Founder

Type of Firm
Private Equity Firm

Association Membership
Canadian Venture Capital Association

Geographical Preferences

United States Preferences:
West Coast

Canadian Preferences:
All Canada

Industry Preferences

In Consumer Related prefer:
Food/Beverage
Consumer Products
Consumer Services

In Financial Services prefer:
Real Estate

Additional Information
Year Founded: 2014
Current Activity Level : Actively seeking new investments

TRIDENT CAPITAL

505 Hamilton Avenue, Suite 200
Palo Alto, CA USA 94301
Phone: 6502894400
Fax: 6502894444
Website: www.tridentcap.com

Management and Staff
Arneek Multani, Managing Director
Donald Dixon, Co-Founder
Eric Jeck, Managing Director
Gustavo Alberelli, Managing Director
J. Alberto Yepez, Managing Director
John Reardon, Managing Director
John Moragne, Co-Founder
Michael Derrick, Chief Financial Officer
Michael Biggee, Managing Director

Type of Firm
Private Equity Firm

Association Membership
Western Association of Venture Capitalists (WAVC)
National Venture Capital Association - USA (NVCA)

Project Preferences

Role in Financing:
Prefer role as deal originator but will also invest in deals created by others

Type of Financing Preferred:
Early Stage
Expansion
Balanced
Later Stage
Seed
Acquisition
Startup

Geographical Preferences

United States Preferences:
North America

Industry Focus
(% based on actual investment)

Computer Software and Services	37.9%
Internet Specific	28.0%
Other Products	9.6%
Communications and Media	8.6%
Medical/Health	6.4%
Computer Hardware	4.1%
Industrial/Energy	3.4%
Semiconductors/Other Elect.	1.2%
Consumer Related	0.7%

Additional Information
Name of Most Recent Fund: Trident Capital Fund - VII, L.P.
Most Recent Fund Was Raised: 01/15/2010
Year Founded: 1993
Capital Under Management: $1,400,000,000
Current Activity Level : Actively seeking new investments
Method of Compensation: Return on invest. most important, but chg. closing fees, service fees, etc.

TRIDENT CAPITAL CYBERSECURITY FUND I LP

400 S El Camino Real, Suite 300
San Mateo, CA USA 94402
Website: www.tridentcybersecurity.com

Management and Staff
Donald Dixon, Co-Founder
Howard Zeprun, Chief Operating Officer
J. Alberto Yepez, Co-Founder
Ken Gonzalez, Managing Director
Michael Michael, Chief Financial Officer
Sean Cunningham, Managing Director
Will Lin, Vice President

Type of Firm
Private Equity Firm

Project Preferences

Type of Financing Preferred:
Later Stage

Industry Preferences

In Computer Software prefer:
Software

Additional Information
Year Founded: 2015
Capital Under Management: $300,000,000
Current Activity Level : Actively seeking new investments

TRILANTIC CAPITAL MANAGEMENT LP

375 Park Avenue
30th Floor
New York, NY USA 10152
Phone: 2126078450
E-mail: Investor.Relations@trilantic.com
Website: www.trilanticpartners.com

Other Offices

3414 Peachtree Road, Suite 200
ATLANTA, GA USA 30326
Phone: 404-262-4800

200 Crescent Court, Suite 400
DALLAS, TX USA 75201
Phone: 214-720-9470

155 Linfield Drive
MENLO PARK, CA USA 94025
Phone: 650-289-6000

11, Via Santa Radegonda
Milan, Italy 20121
Phone: 39-02-9434-0086

301 Congress Avenue, Suite 2050
AUSTIN, TX USA 78701
Phone: 5123626260

Brandywine Building
1000 West Street, Suite 200
WILMINGTON, DE USA 19801
Phone: 800-372-8464

270 Munoz Rivera, Suite 501
SAN JUAN, PR USA 00918
Phone: 787-296-6831

35 Portman Square
London, United Kingdom W1H 6LR
Phone: 44-20-3326-8600

Pratt's Guide to Private Equity & Venture Capital Sources

101 Hudson Street
JERSEY CITY, NJ USA 07302
Phone: 2015242000

1111 Brickell Avenue
MIAMI, FL USA 33131
Phone: 305-789-8700

555 California Street
30th Floor
SAN FRANCISCO, CA USA 94104
Phone: 415-263-3300

450 Royal Palm Way
3rd Floor
PALM BEACH, FL USA 33480
Phone: 561-671-1250

26 Boulevard Royal
Luxembourg, Luxembourg L-2449

25 Bank Street
30th Floor
, United Kingdom
Phone: 442071021000
Fax: 442072602722

Former HQ: 399 Park Avenue
15th Floor
NEW YORK, NY USA 10022

600 Travis Street, Suite 7200
HOUSTON, TX USA 77002
Phone: 713-236-3950

2001 K Street Northwest, Suite 1125
WASHINGTON, DC USA 20006
Phone: 202-452-4700

Rincon 477
Montevideo, Uruguay
Phone: 598-2-402-5716

Le Marchant Street
Heritage Hall, St. Peter Port
Guernsey, United Kingdom GY1 4HY

Roppongi Hills Mori Tower
31st Floor, 6-10-1 Roppongi
Minato-ku, Tokyo, Japan 106-6131
Phone: 81364403000

Torre Alem Plaza
Av. Leandro N. Alem 855
Buenos Aires, Argentina
Phone: 54-11-4319-2700

10250 Constellation Boulevard
25th Floor
LOS ANGELES, CA USA 90067
Phone: 800-582-4904

Bank of America Tower
701 Fifth Avenue, Suite 7101
SEATTLE, WA USA 98104
Phone: 206-344-5870

125 High Street
BOSTON, MA USA 02110
Phone: 617-330-5800

190 South LaSalle Street
26th Floor
CHICAGO, IL USA 60603
Phone: 312-609-7200

2600 Corporate Exchange Drive, Suite 110
COLUMBUS, OH USA 43231
Phone: 614-840-9080

Management and Staff

Charles Moore, Partner
Christopher Manning, Partner
Daniel James, Partner
E. Daniel James, Partner
Elliot Attie, Partner
Fernando Tome, Principal
Giacinto D Onofrio, Principal
Gina Chon, Vice President
Glenn Jacobson, Principal
Glenn Jacobson, Partner
Grant Palmer, Principal
Grant Palmer, Vice President
Henrik Bodenstab, Partner
James Manges, Principal
James Manges, Partner
Javier Banon, Managing Partner
Javier Olascoaga, Principal
Jeremy Lynch, Partner
Jeremy Lynch, Principal
Joe Cohen, Partner
Jon Mattson, Partner
Joseph Cohen, Managing Partner
Li Zhang, Principal
Li Zhang, Partner
Michael Khutorsky, Vice President
Michael Madar, Partner
Ronald Mackey, Vice President
Sanjay Nandi, Principal
Vittorio Pignatti-Morano, Managing Partner

Type of Firm
Bank Affiliated

Project Preferences

Type of Financing Preferred:
Expansion
Balanced
Later Stage
Management Buyouts
Acquisition

Size of Investments Considered:
Min Size of Investment Considered (000s): $75,000
Max Size of Investment Considered (000s): $200,000

Geographical Preferences

United States Preferences:

International Preferences:
Europe

Industry Preferences

In Medical/Health prefer:
Medical/Health

In Consumer Related prefer:
Consumer

In Industrial/Energy prefer:
Energy
Oil & Gas Drilling,Explor
Alternative Energy
Coal Related
Industrial Products

In Financial Services prefer:
Financial Services

In Business Serv. prefer:
Services

Additional Information

Name of Most Recent Fund: Trilantic Capital Partners V (North America), L.P.
Most Recent Fund Was Raised: 08/08/2012
Year Founded: 2009
Capital Under Management: $3,938,133,000
Current Activity Level : Actively seeking new investments

TRILLIUM GROUP LLC

1221 Pittsford-Victor Road
Pittsford, NY USA 14534
Phone: 5853835680
Fax: 5853830042
E-mail: info@trillium-group.com
Website: www.trillium-group.com

Management and Staff

Christopher O Donnell, General Partner
Dennis DeLeo, General Partner
Frank Strong, General Partner
Jose Coronas, General Partner
Joseph Harris, Venture Partner
Kevin Phelps, General Partner
Robert Frame, General Partner

Type of Firm
Private Equity Firm

Association Membership
National Venture Capital Association - USA (NVCA)

Project Preferences

Role in Financing:
Prefer role as deal originator but will also invest in deals created by others

Pratt's Guide to Private Equity & Venture Capital Sources

Type of Financing Preferred:
Leveraged Buyout
Early Stage
Expansion
Start-up Financing
Seed
Recapitalizations

Size of Investments Considered:
Min Size of Investment Considered (000s): $500
Max Size of Investment Considered (000s): $5,000

Geographical Preferences

United States Preferences:
New York

Industry Preferences

In Communications prefer:
Telecommunications
Wireless Communications

In Computer Software prefer:
Software
Systems Software

In Internet Specific prefer:
Internet

In Medical/Health prefer:
Medical/Health
Medical Diagnostics
Diagnostic Services
Medical Therapeutics

In Consumer Related prefer:
Consumer

In Business Serv. prefer:
Services
Distribution
Consulting Services

In Manufact. prefer:
Manufacturing

Additional Information

Name of Most Recent Fund: Trillium Lakefront Partners III, L.P.
Most Recent Fund Was Raised: 06/03/2004
Year Founded: 1997
Capital Under Management: $61,800,000
Current Activity Level : Actively seeking new investments
Method of Compensation: Return on investment is of primary concern, do not charge fees

TRILOGY EQUITY PARTNERS LLC

155 108th Avenue North East, Suite 400
Bellevue, WA USA 98015
Phone: 4254585900
E-mail: info@trilogypartnership.com
Website: www.trilogypartnership.com

Management and Staff

Alan Bender, Partner
Amy McCullough, Partner
Bradley Horwitz, Partner
Charles Stonecipher, Partner
Cole Brodman, Partner
Cregg Baumbaugh, Partner
Donald Guthrie, Partner
John Stanton, Partner
Mikal Thomsen, Partner
Peter Van Oppen, Partner
Scott Alderman, Partner
Theresa Gillespie, Partner
Timothy Wong, Partner
Todd Heiner, Partner
Yuval Neeman, Partner

Type of Firm

Private Equity Firm

Project Preferences

Type of Financing Preferred:
Balanced

Geographical Preferences

United States Preferences:
All U.S.

Industry Preferences

In Communications prefer:
Wireless Communications

Additional Information

Year Founded: 2005
Current Activity Level : Actively seeking new investments

TRILOGY GROWTH LP

161 Bay Street
47th Floor
Toronto, Canada M5J 2T3
Phone: 4167262922
E-mail: info@trilogygrowth.com
Website: www.trilogygrowth.com

Management and Staff

Joel Silver, Managing Director

Type of Firm

Private Equity Firm

Association Membership

Canadian Venture Capital Association

Project Preferences

Type of Financing Preferred:
Acquisition

Industry Preferences

In Internet Specific prefer:
E-Commerce Technology

Additional Information

Year Founded: 2011
Capital Under Management: $20,481,000
Current Activity Level : Actively seeking new investments

TRIMARAN CAPITAL LLC

1325 Avenue of the Americas
34th Floor
New York, NY USA 10019
Phone: 2126163700
Fax: 2126163701
E-mail: info@trimarancapital.com
Website: www.trimarancapital.com

Management and Staff

Alberto Robaina, Managing Director
Alvaro Ramirez, Managing Director
Andrea Kellett, Managing Director
Cheryl Root, Vice President
David Lakoff, Managing Director
Dominick Mazzitelli, Managing Director
Hetal Patel, Vice President
James Tierney, Chief Financial Officer
Jay Bloom, Managing Partner
Jay Levine, Managing Director
Michael Kim, Vice President
Michael Maselli, Managing Director
Wesley Barton, Vice President

Type of Firm

Private Equity Firm

Project Preferences

Role in Financing:
Prefer role as deal originator but will also invest in deals created by others

Type of Financing Preferred:
Leveraged Buyout
Expansion
Later Stage
Management Buyouts
Acquisition
Recapitalizations

Size of Investments Considered:
Min Size of Investment Considered (000s): $5,000
Max Size of Investment Considered (000s): $150,000

Geographical Preferences

United States Preferences:

International Preferences:
Italy
United Kingdom
Luxembourg
Europe
Netherlands
Belgium
Germany
France

Industry Focus
(% based on actual investment)

Other Products	57.4%
Consumer Related	15.8%
Communications and Media	9.1%
Medical/Health	7.9%
Internet Specific	5.4%
Computer Software and Services	2.5%
Semiconductors/Other Elect.	1.7%
Biotechnology	0.2%

Additional Information
Name of Most Recent Fund: Trimaran Pollo Partners LLC
Most Recent Fund Was Raised: 07/27/2011
Year Founded: 1990
Capital Under Management: $3,900,000,000
Current Activity Level : Actively seeking new investments
Method of Compensation: Return on investment is of primary concern, do not charge fees

---

TRINDADE CONSULTORIA E INVESTIMENTOS LTDA

Avenida Nove de Julho, 4939
12 andar
Sao Paulo, Brazil
Phone: 551130787573
E-mail: contato@trindadeinvestimentos.com.br
Website: www.trindadeinvestimentos.com.br

Type of Firm
Private Equity Firm

Association Membership
Brazilian Venture Capital Association (ABCR)

Project Preferences

Type of Financing Preferred:
Startup

Geographical Preferences

International Preferences:
Brazil

Additional Information
Year Founded: 2013
Current Activity Level : Actively seeking new investments

TRINITAS PRIVATE EQUITY (PTY) LTD

29 Scott Street
Waverley, South Africa 2090
Phone: 27-11-809-7529
Fax: 27-86-638-3077
E-mail: info@trinitaspe.co.za
Website: www.trinitaspe.co.za

Type of Firm
Private Equity Firm

Association Membership
South African Venture Capital Association (SAVCA)

Project Preferences

Type of Financing Preferred:
Leveraged Buyout
Expansion
Management Buyouts
Acquisition

Geographical Preferences

International Preferences:
South Africa

Additional Information
Year Founded: 2010
Capital Under Management: $57,024,000
Current Activity Level : Actively seeking new investments

TRINITY CAPITAL INVESTMENT

2121 West Chandler Boulevard, Suite 103
Chandler, AZ USA 85224
Phone: 4803745350
Fax: 4802475099
Website: www.trincapinvestment.com

Type of Firm
Private Equity Firm

Association Membership
National Venture Capital Association - USA (NVCA)

Project Preferences

Type of Financing Preferred:
Mezzanine

Geographical Preferences

United States Preferences:

Industry Preferences

In Communications prefer:
Telecommunications

In Semiconductor/Electr prefer:
Semiconductor

In Medical/Health prefer:
Health Services
Pharmaceuticals

In Consumer Related prefer:
Consumer Services

In Industrial/Energy prefer:
Energy

In Financial Services prefer:
Financial Services

Additional Information
Year Founded: 2012
Capital Under Management: $99,848,000
Current Activity Level : Actively seeking new investments

TRINITY HUNT PARTNERS

2001 Ross Avenue, Suite 4800
Dallas, TX USA 75201
Phone: 2147776600
Fax: 2145455248
Website: www.trinityhunt.com

Management and Staff
Blake Apel, Principal
Daniel Dross, Managing Partner
Hunter Peterson, Partner
James Holland, Partner
Michael Steindorf, Vice President
Peter Stein, Managing Partner
Scott Colvert, Partner
William Bixby, Partner

Type of Firm
Private Equity Firm

Project Preferences

Role in Financing:
Prefer role as deal originator

Type of Financing Preferred:
Leveraged Buyout
Later Stage
Management Buyouts
Acquisition
Recapitalizations

Geographical Preferences

United States Preferences:
Midwest
Southeast
Southwest
Texas

Industry Preferences

In Medical/Health prefer:
Health Services

In Consumer Related prefer:
Entertainment and Leisure

In Industrial/Energy prefer:
Industrial Products

In Business Serv. prefer:
Services

Additional Information
Name of Most Recent Fund: Trinity Hunt Partners IV, L.P.
Most Recent Fund Was Raised: 11/23/2011
Year Founded: 2004
Capital Under Management: $215,000,000

Current Activity Level : Actively seeking new investments

TRINITY INVESTIMENTOS LTDA

Av. Brigadeiro Faria Lima
3729, 5 andares
Sao Paulo, Brazil 04538-905
Phone: 551134437300
E-mail: contato@trinityinvestimentos.com.br
Website: www.trinityinvestimentos.com.br

Type of Firm
Private Equity Firm

Project Preferences

Type of Financing Preferred:
Leveraged Buyout
Early Stage
Generalist PE
Balanced
Later Stage
Management Buyouts
Acquisition

Industry Preferences

In Financial Services prefer:
Real Estate

Additional Information
Year Founded: 2011
Current Activity Level : Actively seeking new investments

TRINITY VENTURES LLP

2480 Sand Hill Road, Suite 200
Menlo Park, CA USA 94025
Phone: 6508549500
Fax: 6508549501
E-mail: info@trinityventures.com
Website: www.trinityventures.com

Management and Staff
Ajay Chopra, General Partner
Anjula Acharia-Bath, Partner
Augustus Tai, General Partner
Daniel Scholnick, General Partner
Fred Wang, General Partner
Karan Mehandru, General Partner
Lawrence Orr, General Partner
Matthew Goldstein, Principal
Noel Fenton, Co-Founder
Patricia Nakache, General Partner
Schwark Satyavolu, General Partner

Type of Firm
Private Equity Firm

Association Membership
Western Association of Venture Capitalists (WAVC)
National Venture Capital Association - USA (NVCA)

Project Preferences

Role in Financing:
Will function either as deal originator or investor in deals created by others

Type of Financing Preferred:
Early Stage
Seed

Industry Focus
(% based on actual investment)
Computer Software and Services   41.6%
Internet Specific   32.8%
Communications and Media   8.9%
Other Products   6.1%
Consumer Related   4.4%
Computer Hardware   3.8%
Semiconductors/Other Elect.   1.8%
Medical/Health   0.6%
Industrial/Energy   0.1%

Additional Information
Name of Most Recent Fund: Trinity Ventures XI, L.P.
Most Recent Fund Was Raised: 10/10/2012
Year Founded: 1986
Capital Under Management: $1,236,000,000
Current Activity Level : Actively seeking new investments
Method of Compensation: Return on invest. most important, but chg. closing fees, service fees, etc.

TRINNOVATE VENTURES INC

2444 W Las Palmaritas
Phoenix, AZ USA 85021
Website: www.trinnovateventures.com

Type of Firm
Private Equity Firm

Project Preferences

Type of Financing Preferred:
Balanced

Additional Information
Year Founded: 2016
Current Activity Level : Actively seeking new investments

TRIODOS INTERNATIONAL FUND MANAGEMENT BV

60 Utrechtseweg
P.O. Box 55
Zeist, Netherlands 3700 AB
Phone: 31306936500
Fax: 31306936555
E-mail: triodos@triodos.nl
Website: www.triodos.com

Other Offices
Brunel House
11 The Promenade Clifton
Bristol, United Kingdom BS8 3NN
Phone: 44 117 973 9339
Fax: 44 117 973 9303

Rue Haute 139/3
Bruxelles, Belgium 1000

Avda. Diagonal, 418
Barcelona, Spain 08037

Management and Staff
Glen Saunders, Managing Director
Hans Schut, Partner
Marilou van Golstein Brouwers, Partner
Peter Blom, Chief Executive Officer

Type of Firm
Bank Affiliated

Project Preferences

Type of Financing Preferred:
Balanced
Later Stage

Size of Investments Considered:
Min Size of Investment Considered (000s): $141
Max Size of Investment Considered (000s): $942

Geographical Preferences

International Preferences:
Latin America
United Kingdom
Europe
Netherlands
Egypt
Belgium
Asia
Germany
Africa

Industry Preferences

In Medical/Health prefer:
Medical/Health

In Consumer Related prefer:
Food/Beverage

In Industrial/Energy prefer:
Energy
Alternative Energy
Energy Conservation Relat
Advanced Materials
Environmental Related

In Transportation prefer:
Transportation

In Financial Services prefer:
Real Estate

In Business Serv. prefer:
Services

In Other prefer:
Socially Responsible
Environment Responsible

Additional Information
Year Founded: 1990
Capital Under Management: $84,700,000
Current Activity Level : Actively seeking new investments

TRIPLEPOINT CAPITAL LLC
2755 Sand Hill Road
Menlo Park, CA USA 94025
Phone: 6508542090
Fax: 6508542094
E-mail: info@triplepointcapital.com

Management and Staff
Erez Levy, Managing Director
Harold Zagunis, Chief Financial Officer
Hutch Corbett, Managing Director
Jon Baird, Managing Director
Kai Tse, Managing Director
Sajal Srivastava, Co-Founder

Type of Firm
Private Equity Firm

Project Preferences

Role in Financing:
Will function either as deal originator or investor in deals created by others

Type of Financing Preferred:
Mezzanine
Balanced

Size of Investments Considered:
Min Size of Investment Considered (000s): $25
Max Size of Investment Considered (000s): $5,000

Industry Preferences

In Industrial/Energy prefer:
Energy
Alternative Energy
Environmental Related

In Agr/Forestr/Fish prefer:
Agriculture related

Additional Information
Name of Most Recent Fund: TriplePoint Capital LLC
Most Recent Fund Was Raised: 07/13/2005
Year Founded: 1987
Capital Under Management: $52,800,000
Current Activity Level : Actively seeking new investments

TRIPOD CAPITAL INTERNATIONAL LTD
No. 1518 Min Sheng Road
Tower A, Golden Eagle Mansion
Shanghai, China 200135
Phone: 862161042968
Fax: 862161042969
E-mail: contact@tripodcapital.com
Website: www.tripodcapital.com

Type of Firm
Private Equity Firm

Project Preferences

Type of Financing Preferred:
Leveraged Buyout

Geographical Preferences

International Preferences:
China
Asia

Industry Preferences

In Industrial/Energy prefer:
Alternative Energy
Environmental Related

In Financial Services prefer:
Financial Services

In Manufact. prefer:
Manufacturing

Additional Information
Year Founded: 2006
Capital Under Management: $350,000,000
Current Activity Level : Actively seeking new investments

TRIRIVER CAPITAL CORP
No.161 Lujiazui East Road
Room2106, Zhaoshangju Building
Shanghai, China 200120
Phone: 862150159388
Fax: 862150159355
E-mail: info@tririvercapital.com
Website: www.tririvercapital.com

Management and Staff
Charles Yang, President
Weizheng Xu, Partner

Type of Firm
Bank Affiliated

Project Preferences

Type of Financing Preferred:
Early Stage
Seed

Geographical Preferences

International Preferences:
China

Industry Preferences

In Biotechnology prefer:
Biotechnology

In Medical/Health prefer:
Medical Products
Health Services
Pharmaceuticals

Additional Information
Year Founded: 2008
Capital Under Management: $16,323,000
Current Activity Level : Actively seeking new investments

TRISCORP INVESTIMENTOS LTDA
Rua Rainha Guilhermina, 75, 2
Rio de Janeiro, Brazil 22441-120
Phone: 552132025000
Fax: 552122598104
E-mail: contato@triscorpinvest.com
Website: www.triscorpinvest.com

Management and Staff
Mauricio Bicalho, Co-Founder
Ronaldo Tristao, Co-Founder

Type of Firm
Private Equity Firm

Project Preferences

Type of Financing Preferred:
Leveraged Buyout
Acquisition

Geographical Preferences

International Preferences:
Brazil

Industry Preferences

In Industrial/Energy prefer:
Energy

In Financial Services prefer:
Real Estate

In Agr/Forestr/Fish prefer:
Agribusiness
Agriculture related

Additional Information
Year Founded: 2003
Current Activity Level : Actively seeking new investments

TRISTAR TECHNOLOGY VENTURES LLC

3322 West End Avenue, Suite 1100
Nashville, TN USA 37203
Phone: 6155159880
Fax: 6155159891

Management and Staff
Brian Laden, Co-Founder
Christopher Rand, Co-Founder
Harry Jacobson, Co-Founder

Type of Firm
Private Equity Firm

Project Preferences

Role in Financing:
Will function either as deal originator or investor in deals created by others

Type of Financing Preferred:
Early Stage
Startup

Size of Investments Considered:
Min Size of Investment Considered (000s): $100
Max Size of Investment Considered (000s): $1,500

Geographical Preferences

United States Preferences:

Industry Preferences

In Biotechnology prefer:
Biotechnology
Human Biotechnology

In Medical/Health prefer:
Medical/Health
Medical Diagnostics
Medical Therapeutics
Medical Products
Health Services
Pharmaceuticals

Additional Information
Year Founded: 2009
Capital Under Management: $37,000,000
Current Activity Level : Actively seeking new investments

TRITIUM PARTNERS LLC

221 West Sixth Street, Suite 700
Austin, TX USA 78701
Phone: 5124934100
E-mail: info@tritiumpartners.com
Website: tritiumpartners.com

Management and Staff
Brett Shobe, Principal
David Lack, Co-Founder
Matt Bowman, Partner
Philip Siegel, Co-Founder
Terry Browne, Chief Operating Officer

Type of Firm
Private Equity Firm

Project Preferences

Type of Financing Preferred:
Leveraged Buyout
Management Buyouts
Acquisition
Recapitalizations

Industry Preferences

In Internet Specific prefer:
Internet

In Transportation prefer:
Transportation

In Financial Services prefer:
Financial Services

In Business Serv. prefer:
Services
Media

Additional Information
Year Founded: 2014
Capital Under Management: $309,000,000
Current Activity Level : Actively seeking new investments

TRITON BETEILIGUNGS-BERATUNG GMBH

Schillerstrasse 20
Frankfurt, Germany 60313
Phone: 4969921020
Fax: 496992102100
E-mail: info@triton-partners.com
Website: www.triton-partners.com

Other Offices
26 - 28 rue Edward Steichen
Luxembourg, Luxembourg 2540
Phone: 352267530
Fax: 35226753100

Kungstradgardsgatan 20, 7th floor
Stockholm, Sweden 111 47
Phone: 46850559600
Fax: 46850559699

Charter Place (1st Floor)
23-27 Seaton Place
St Helier, United Kingdom JE2 3QL
Phone: 441534709400
Fax: 441534709450

9 South Street, 3rd Floor
London, United Kingdom W1K 2XA
Phone: 442072976150
Fax: 442072976189

Management and Staff
Lars Frankfelt, Managing Partner
Mats Eklund, Chief Financial Officer
Peder Prahl, Managing Partner

Type of Firm
Private Equity Firm

Association Membership
Finnish Venture Capital Association (FVCA)
Danish Venture Capital Association (DVCA)
German Venture Capital Association (BVK)
Swedish Venture Capital Association (SVCA)
European Private Equity and Venture Capital Assoc.

Project Preferences

Type of Financing Preferred:
Leveraged Buyout
Acquisition
Distressed Debt

Geographical Preferences

International Preferences:
Sweden
Europe
Scandanavia/Nordic Region
Finland
Norway
Germany
Denmark

Additional Information
Name of Most Recent Fund: Triton Debt Opportunities Fund I, L.P.
Most Recent Fund Was Raised: 11/12/2013
Year Founded: 1997
Capital Under Management: $607,000,000
Current Activity Level : Actively seeking new investments

TRITON PACIFIC CAPITAL LLC

10877 Wilshire Boulevard
12th Floor
Los Angeles, CA USA 90024
Phone: 3109434990
Fax: 3109434995
E-mail: info@tritonpacific.com
Website: www.tritonpacific.com

Management and Staff
Brian Buehler, Partner
Ivan Faggen, Managing Partner
Joseph Davis, Managing Partner
Kirk Michie, Partner
Sean Gjos, Partner
Thomas Scott, Partner

Type of Firm
Private Equity Firm

Project Preferences

Role in Financing:
Prefer role as deal originator but will also invest in deals created by others

Type of Financing Preferred:
Leveraged Buyout
Expansion
Management Buyouts
Acquisition
Recapitalizations

Size of Investments Considered:
Min Size of Investment Considered (000s): $2,000
Max Size of Investment Considered (000s): $10,000

Geographical Preferences

United States Preferences:

Industry Preferences

In Computer Software prefer:
Software

In Medical/Health prefer:
Health Services

In Consumer Related prefer:
Consumer Products

In Business Serv. prefer:
Services
Distribution

In Manufact. prefer:
Manufacturing

Additional Information

Name of Most Recent Fund: Triton Pacific Platinum Fund IV, L.P.
Most Recent Fund Was Raised: 01/10/2012
Year Founded: 2001
Capital Under Management: $150,000,000
Current Activity Level : Actively seeking new investments

TRIVE CAPITAL MANAGEMENT LLC

2021 McKinney Avenue, Suite 1200
Dallas, TX USA 75201
Phone: 2144999715
Fax: 4693109961
E-mail: info@trivecapital.com
Website: www.trivecapital.com

Type of Firm
Private Equity Firm

Project Preferences

Type of Financing Preferred:
Leveraged Buyout
Public Companies
Acquisition
Special Situation

Geographical Preferences

United States Preferences:
North America
All U.S.

Canadian Preferences:
All Canada

Industry Preferences

In Communications prefer:
Communications and Media
Commercial Communications

In Medical/Health prefer:
Medical/Health
Health Services

In Consumer Related prefer:
Consumer Products

In Industrial/Energy prefer:
Energy
Industrial Products

In Transportation prefer:
Transportation
Aerospace

In Business Serv. prefer:
Services
Distribution

In Manufact. prefer:
Manufacturing

Additional Information

Name of Most Recent Fund: Trive Capital Fund I, L.P.
Most Recent Fund Was Raised: 07/18/2013
Year Founded: 2012
Capital Under Management: $1,800,000,000
Current Activity Level : Actively seeking new investments

TRIVENTURES MANAGEMENT LTD

Six Hahoshlim Street
P.O. Box 12006
Herzliya, Israel 46722
Phone: 97299721080
Website: www.triventures.net

Other Offices

Six Hahoshlim Street
P.O. Box 12006
Herzliya, Israel
Phone: 97299721080

Management and Staff

Michal Geva, Founder

Type of Firm
Private Equity Firm

Project Preferences

Type of Financing Preferred:
Early Stage
Later Stage
Seed

Size of Investments Considered:
Min Size of Investment Considered (000s): $100
Max Size of Investment Considered (000s): $3,000

Geographical Preferences

International Preferences:
Israel

Industry Preferences

In Medical/Health prefer:
Medical/Health
Medical Products

Additional Information

Name of Most Recent Fund: TriVentures
Most Recent Fund Was Raised: 01/13/2009
Year Founded: 2007
Current Activity Level : Actively seeking new investments

TRIVEST PARTNERS LP

550 South Dixie Highway, Suite 300
Coral Gables, FL USA 33146
Phone: 3058582200
Fax: 3052850102
E-mail: info@trivest.com
Website: www.trivest.com

Management and Staff

Amir Mirheydar, Principal
Brian Connell, Principal
Chip Vandenberg, Partner
Earl Powell, Partner
Forest Wester, Partner
Jamie Elias, Partner
Jorge Gross, Principal
Richard Moran, Chief Financial Officer
Russ Wilson, Partner
Todd Jerles, Chief Operating Officer
Troy Templeton, Managing Partner

Type of Firm
Private Equity Firm

Project Preferences

Role in Financing:
Prefer role as deal originator but will also invest in deals created by others

Type of Financing Preferred:
Leveraged Buyout
Acquisition

Geographical Preferences

United States Preferences:

Canadian Preferences:
All Canada

Industry Focus
(% based on actual investment)

Consumer Related	45.2%
Industrial/Energy	29.0%
Medical/Health	15.3%
Other Products	8.6%
Internet Specific	1.3%
Communications and Media	0.5%

Additional Information
Year Founded: 1981
Capital Under Management: $600,000,000
Current Activity Level : Actively seeking new investments
Method of Compensation: Return on invest. most important, but chg. closing fees, service fees, etc.

TRIVEST TRIUM INVESTMENTS (PTY) LTD

244 Jean Avenue
Unit 18, Norma Jean Square
Centurion, South Africa 0157
Phone: 27861874742
Fax: 27126642452
E-mail: info@trivest.co.za
Website: www.trivest.co.za

Management and Staff
Andre Sturmer, Managing Director
Niels Von Hase, Founder

Type of Firm
Private Equity Firm

Association Membership
South African Venture Capital Association (SAVCA)

Project Preferences

Type of Financing Preferred:
Early Stage
Expansion
Generalist PE
Acquisition
Startup
Recapitalizations

Geographical Preferences

International Preferences:
South Africa

Industry Preferences

In Semiconductor/Electr prefer:
Electronic Components

In Biotechnology prefer:
Biotech Related Research

In Medical/Health prefer:
Health Services

In Industrial/Energy prefer:
Energy
Energy Conservation Relat

Additional Information
Year Founded: 2011
Current Activity Level : Actively seeking new investments

TRIWEST CAPITAL MGMT CORP

400 3rd Avenue Southwest, Suite 4600
Calgary, Canada T2P 4H2
Phone: 4032251144
Fax: 4032253547
E-mail: info@triwest.ca
Website: www.triwest.ca

Other Offices
525-Eighth Avenue Southwest, Suite 4050
Calgary, Canada T2P 1G1
Phone: 4032251144
Fax: 4032253547

Management and Staff
Chad Danard, Managing Director
Cody Church, Senior Managing Director
Jeff Belford, Senior Managing Director
Lorne Jacobson, Senior Managing Director
Mick MacBean, Senior Managing Director
Norm Rokosh, Senior Managing Director
Ron Jackson, Co-Founder
Ryan Giles, Managing Director

Type of Firm
Private Equity Firm

Association Membership
Canadian Venture Capital Association

Project Preferences

Type of Financing Preferred:
Leveraged Buyout
Expansion
Later Stage
Management Buyouts
Acquisition

Geographical Preferences

Canadian Preferences:
All Canada
Western Canada

Industry Focus
(% based on actual investment)

Other Products	96.2%
Industrial/Energy	2.6%
Medical/Health	1.2%

Additional Information
Name of Most Recent Fund: TriWest Capital Partners IV, L.P.
Most Recent Fund Was Raised: 06/30/2011
Year Founded: 1998
Capital Under Management: $132,900,000
Current Activity Level : Actively seeking new investments

TROIKA CAPITAL PARTNERS LTD

4 Romanov Pereulok
Moscow, Russia 125009
Phone: 74952580500
Fax: 74952580547
Website: www.troika.ru

Other Offices
3/01, Prospekt Mira, Novyj Gorod
Naberezhnye Chelny, Russia 423810
Phone: 78552395100
Fax: 78552395103

11, Mira Str.
Volgograd, Russia 400131
Phone: 78442968211
Fax: 78442968212

101, Tole Bi Str., 5th floor, Blok B
Business Center "Hermes"
Almaty, Kazakhstan
Phone: 7273553355
Fax: 7273553356

204, Molodogvardeyskaya Str.
Samara, Russia 443001
Phone: 78463780000
Fax: 78462733328

6, Mordovtseva Str.
Vladivostok, Russia 690091
Phone: 74232499925
Fax: 74232499926

22, Trefoleva Str.
Yaroslavl, Russia 15000
Phone: 74852670407
Fax: 74852670406

85 Fleet Street, 4th Floor
London, United Kingdom EC4Y 1AE
Phone: 442075833257
Fax: 442078220779

206, Krasnoarmeyskaya Str.
Rostov-on-Don, Russia
Phone: 78632688899
Fax: 78632688389

57 Digeni Akrita Ave
Zachariades Building, Office 301
Nicosia, Cyprus 1070
Phone: 35722875380
Fax: 35722875393

26, Prospekt Mira
Krasnoyarsk, Russia 660049
Phone: 73912918100
Fax: 73912918102

10/16, Alekseyevskaya str.
Business Center "Lobachevskiy Plaza"
Nizhni Novgorod, Russia 603006
Phone: 78312201949

1, Dimitrova Prospekt
Novosibirsk, Russia 630004
Phone: 73832105502
Fax: 73832105503

4, let. A, Finlyandski pr.
"Petrovski Fort" Business Center
Saint Petersburg, Russia 194153
Phone: 78123323300
Fax: 78123326657

100/1, Dostoyevskogo Str.
Ufa, Russia 450077
Phone: 73472798880
Fax: 73472798881

19, Lenina Str.
Irkutsk, Russia 664003
Phone: 73952563636
Fax: 73952203156

58, Lenina Str.
Perm, Russia 614000
Phone: 73422186146
Fax: 73422186149

43, Plekhanovskaya Str.
Voronezh, Russia 394000
Phone: 74732616961
Fax: 74732355634

6, Spartakovskaya Str.
Suvar Plaza
Kazan, Russia 420107
Phone: 78435265522
Fax: 78435265307

2/9A, March 8 Str.
Tyumen, Russia 625000
Phone: 73452395450
Fax: 73452395451

152 W. 57th Street, 44 floor
Carnegie Tower
New York, NY USA 10019
Phone: 12123009600
Fax: 12123009601

38, Karla Marksa Str.
Business Center "Arkaim Plaza"
Chelyabinsk, Russia 454091
Phone: 73517786120
Fax: 73517786121

10, Khokhryakova Str.
Business Center "Palladium", 5th Floor
Ekaterinburg, Russia 620014
Phone: 73433107000
Fax: 73433792164

6, Rylskyi Pereulok, 6 floor
Kiev, Ukraine 01025
Phone: 380442073780
Fax: 380442073784

22A, Postysheva Str.
Business Center "Khabarovsk-City"
Khabarovsk, Russia 680030
Phone: 74212415162
Fax: 74212415163

41, Krasnaya Str.
Krasnodar, Russia 350000
Phone: 7-861-210-6061
Fax: 7-861-279-6099

Management and Staff
Evgeny Gavrilenkov, Managing Director
Gor Nakhapetyan, Managing Director
Rob Leith, Managing Director
Serguei Skvortsov, Managing Director
Todd Berman, Managing Director

Type of Firm
Bank Affiliated

Association Membership
Russian Venture Capital Association (RVCA)

Project Preferences

Role in Financing:
Prefer role as deal originator

Type of Financing Preferred:
Leveraged Buyout
Generalist PE
Balanced

Geographical Preferences

International Preferences:
Kazakhstan
Europe
Eastern Europe
Ukraine
Russia

Industry Preferences

In Communications prefer:
Communications and Media
Media and Entertainment

In Medical/Health prefer:
Medical/Health
Medical Diagnostics
Diagnostic Services
Health Services

In Consumer Related prefer:
Consumer
Retail

In Financial Services prefer:
Financial Services

In Business Serv. prefer:
Media

In Manufact. prefer:
Manufacturing

Additional Information
Name of Most Recent Fund: Russia New Growth Fund, L.P.
Most Recent Fund Was Raised: 01/27/2006
Year Founded: 1991
Capital Under Management: $509,600,000
Current Activity Level: Actively seeking new investments

TROPHAS MANAGEMENT BV

Eemnesserweg 27A
Baarn, Netherlands 3743AD
Phone: 31613117128
Website: www.trophas.nl

Management and Staff
Dick Eijmeren, Partner
Hennie Gijsbers, Partner
Jeroen Meeuwissen, Partner
Ronald Kiel, Partner

Type of Firm
Private Equity Firm

Project Preferences

Type of Financing Preferred:
Early Stage
Expansion
Later Stage
Seed

Geographical Preferences

International Preferences:
Europe
Netherlands

Industry Preferences

In Consumer Related prefer:
Food/Beverage

Additional Information
Year Founded: 2016
Current Activity Level: Actively seeking new investments

Pratt's Guide to Private Equity & Venture Capital Sources

TROUT CREEK VENTURES LP

6864 Maplecrest Drive SE
Grand Rapids, MI USA 49546
Phone: 6168360386
Website: www.troutcreekventures.com

Management and Staff
Paul D Amato, General Partner

Type of Firm
Private Equity Firm

Project Preferences

Type of Financing Preferred:
Early Stage

Geographical Preferences

United States Preferences:
Michigan

Industry Preferences

In Computer Software prefer:
Software

In Industrial/Energy prefer:
Acvanced Materials

In Manufact. prefer:
Manufacturing

Additional Information
Year Founded: 2012
Current Activity Level : Actively seeking new investments

TROY VENTURES LLC

22990 Mallard Avenue
Angora, MN USA 55703
Phone: 248-802-6867
E-mail: info@troyventures.com

Other Offices
22990 West Seventh Street
Minneapolis, MN USA

Management and Staff
E. Boyan Josic, Managing Partner

Type of Firm
Private Equity Firm

Project Preferences

Type of Financing Preferred:
Leveraged Buyout
Early Stage
Seed
Startup

Industry Preferences

In Internet Specific prefer:
Internet

Additional Information
Year Founded: 2009
Current Activity Level : Actively seeking new investments

TRUCKS VENTURE CAPITAL

500 Third Street
San Francisco, CA USA 94107
Website: www.trucks.vc

Other Offices
500 Third Street
San Francisco, CA USA

Type of Firm
Private Equity Firm

Project Preferences

Type of Financing Preferred:
Early Stage

Industry Preferences

In Transportation prefer:
Transportation

Additional Information
Year Founded: 2016
Capital Under Management: $9,880,000
Current Activity Level : Actively seeking new investments

TRUE CAPITAL PARTNERS LLP

11 Francis Street
Francis House
London, United Kingdom SW1P 1DE
Phone: 442037406940
E-mail: investors@truecapital.co.uk
Website: www.truecapital.co.uk

Management and Staff
Christopher Spira, Partner
Matthew Truman, Chief Executive Officer
Paul Cocker, Co-Founder

Type of Firm
Incubator/Development Program

Project Preferences

Type of Financing Preferred:
Early Stage
Seed
Startup

Geographical Preferences

International Preferences:
United Kingdom

Industry Preferences

In Consumer Related prefer:
Consumer
Retail

Additional Information
Year Founded: 2012
Capital Under Management: $55,180,000
Current Activity Level : Actively seeking new investments

TRUE GLOBAL PARTNERS

159-6 Samsung-dong,Gangnam-gu
5 Korea City Air Terminal Bldg
Seoul, South Korea 135728
Phone: 8225389821
Fax: 8225389885
Website: www.trueglobalpartners.com

Management and Staff
Jae Wu Yim, Chief Executive Officer

Type of Firm
Private Equity Firm

Project Preferences

Type of Financing Preferred:
Balanced

Additional Information
Year Founded: 2009
Current Activity Level : Actively seeking new investments

TRUE NORTH

Santacruz (East), Suite F9C, Grand Hyatt Plaza
Mumbai, India 400 055
E-mail: contactus@ivfa.com
Website: www.ivfa.com

Other Offices
Rocklines House, Ground Floor
9/2, Museum Road
Bangalore, India 560 001
Phone: 91-80-4132-1845
Fax: 91-80-2559-0800

18, Marshall Street, Suite 112
SOUTH NORWALK, CT USA 06854
Phone: 203-956-6565
Fax: 203-956-6546

Management and Staff
Haresh Chawla, Partner
Mahesh Krishnamurthy, Partner
Michael Borom, Partner
Murry Stegelmann, Partner

Paul Street, Partner
Peter Keenoy, Partner
Pramod Kabra, Partner
Sanjay Arte, Partner
Sunil Vasudevan, Partner
Vikram Nirula, Partner
Vishal Nevatia, Managing Partner

Type of Firm
Private Equity Firm

Association Membership
Indian Venture Capital Association (IVCA)

Project Preferences

Type of Financing Preferred:
Leveraged Buyout
Management Buyouts
Acquisition

Geographical Preferences

International Preferences:
India

Industry Preferences

In Communications prefer:
Media and Entertainment

In Medical/Health prefer:
Medical/Health
Health Services

In Consumer Related prefer:
Consumer
Retail
Food/Beverage
Education Related

In Industrial/Energy prefer:
Environmental Related

In Financial Services prefer:
Financial Services

In Business Serv. prefer:
Distribution

Additional Information
Year Founded: 1999
Capital Under Management: $600,000,000
Current Activity Level : Actively seeking new investments

TRUE NORTH EQUITY LLC

300 Park Street, Suite 210
Birmingham, MI USA 48009
Phone: 2482204216
Fax: 2487866847
Website: www.truenorthequity.com

Management and Staff
Jim Wigginton, Managing Partner

Type of Firm
Private Equity Firm

Project Preferences

Type of Financing Preferred:
Leveraged Buyout
Acquisition

Geographical Preferences

United States Preferences:

Canadian Preferences:
All Canada

Industry Preferences

In Industrial/Energy prefer:
Oil and Gas Exploration

In Business Serv. prefer:
Services

Additional Information
Year Founded: 1969
Current Activity Level : Actively seeking new investments

TRUE NORTH VENTURE PARTNERS LP

2390 East Camelback Road, Suite 203
Phoenix, AZ USA 85016
Phone: 6024765800

Other Offices
205 North Michigan Avenue, Suite 2930
Chicago, IL USA 60601
Phone: 3125741700

Management and Staff
Michael Ahearn, Founder

Type of Firm
Private Equity Firm

Project Preferences

Role in Financing:
Prefer role as deal originator

Type of Financing Preferred:
Early Stage
Balanced
Later Stage
Seed
Startup

Size of Investments Considered:
Min Size of Investment Considered (000s): $100
Max Size of Investment Considered (000s): $25,000

Industry Preferences

In Industrial/Energy prefer:
Energy
Environmental Related

In Agr/Forestr/Fish prefer:
Agribusiness
Agriculture related

Additional Information
Name of Most Recent Fund: TNVP Harvest Power Fund I, L.P.
Most Recent Fund Was Raised: 04/13/2012
Year Founded: 2010
Capital Under Management: $242,000,000
Current Activity Level : Actively seeking new investments

TRUE VENTURES LLC

575 High Street, Suite 400
Palo Alto, CA USA 94301
Phone: 6503192150
Fax: 6503307330
E-mail: hello@trueventures.com
Website: www.trueventures.com

Other Offices
766-B Walker Road
GREAT FALLS, VA USA 22066

27 South Park Avenue
SAN FRANCISCO, CA USA 94107

Management and Staff
James Stewart, Chief Financial Officer
John Burke, Founder
Jonathan Callaghan, Founder
Om Malik, Venture Partner
Philip Black, Founder
Puneet Agarwal, General Partner
Rohit Sharma, Venture Partner
Toni Schneider, Venture Partner
Tony Conrad, Venture Partner

Type of Firm
Private Equity Firm

Association Membership
National Venture Capital Association - USA (NVCA)

Project Preferences

Role in Financing:
Prefer role as deal originator

Type of Financing Preferred:
Early Stage
Balanced
Seed
Startup

Geographical Preferences

United States Preferences:

Industry Preferences

In Communications prefer:
Wireless Communications

In Computer Software prefer:
Software

In Internet Specific prefer:
Internet
Ecommerce

In Consumer Related prefer:
Consumer Products

In Business Serv. prefer:
Services
Media

Additional Information
Year Founded: 2006
Capital Under Management: $850,000,000
Current Activity Level : Actively seeking new investments

TRUE WEALTH VENTURES

500 E. 4th Street
PMB Suite 471
Austin, TX USA 78701
Phone: 5125379315
Website: truewealthinnovations.com

Type of Firm
Private Equity Firm

Project Preferences

Type of Financing Preferred:
Early Stage

Geographical Preferences

United States Preferences:
Texas

Industry Preferences

In Consumer Related prefer:
Consumer

Additional Information
Year Founded: 2016
Capital Under Management: $4,700,000
Current Activity Level : Actively seeking new investments

TRUE WIND CAPITAL MANAGEMENT LLC

480 Pacific Avenue, Suite 200
San Francisco, CA USA 94133
Phone: 4157809975
Fax: 4157809976
Website: www.truewindcapital.com

Management and Staff
Aaron Matto, Principal
Matthew Wilson, Principal
Sean Giese, Principal

Type of Firm
Private Equity Firm

Project Preferences

Type of Financing Preferred:
Leveraged Buyout
Management Buyouts
Acquisition

Industry Preferences

In Computer Software prefer:
Software

In Internet Specific prefer:
Internet

In Semiconductor/Electr prefer:
Semiconductor

In Industrial/Energy prefer:
Industrial Products

Additional Information
Year Founded: 2013
Capital Under Management: $558,020,000
Current Activity Level : Actively seeking new investments

TRUEBRIDGE CAPITAL PARTNERS LLC

1350 Environ Way
Bldg 1000 3F Suite 1350
Chapel Hill, NC USA 27517
Phone: 9194425201
Fax: 9198691444
E-mail: info@truebridgecapital.com
Website: www.truebridgecapital.com

Management and Staff
Dominic Hong, Chief Financial Officer
Kate Simpson, Vice President
Mike Whitticom, Principal
Robert Mazzoni, Principal

Type of Firm
Private Equity Advisor or Fund of Funds

Geographical Preferences

United States Preferences:

International Preferences:
India
China

Additional Information
Year Founded: 2007
Capital Under Management: $1,033,390,000
Current Activity Level : Actively seeking new investments

TRUFFLE CAPITAL SAS

5 Rue de la Baume
Paris, France 75008
Phone: 33147202220
Fax: 33147201209
E-mail: contact@truffle.com
Website: www.truffle.com

Management and Staff
Bernard-Louis Roques, General Partner
Gwen Chapman, Chief Financial Officer
Jean-Francois Fourt, General Partner
Jean-Jacques Bertrand, Venture Partner
Miguel Sieler, Venture Partner
Philippe Pouletty, General Partner
Ron Belt, Venture Partner
Ruud Bakker, Venture Partner

Type of Firm
Private Equity Firm

Association Membership
European Private Equity and Venture Capital Assoc.

Project Preferences

Type of Financing Preferred:
Fund of Funds
Leveraged Buyout
Early Stage
Generalist PE
Public Companies
Later Stage
Seed
Acquisition
Startup

Size of Investments Considered:
Min Size of Investment Considered (000s): $5,033
Max Size of Investment Considered (000s): $15,098

Geographical Preferences

International Preferences:
Luxembourg
Europe
Netherlands
Switzerland
Belgium
Germany
France

Industry Preferences

In Computer Software prefer:
Software

In Biotechnology prefer:
Biotechnology

In Medical/Health prefer:
Medical/Health

In Industrial/Energy prefer:
Energy
Alternative Energy

Additional Information
Year Founded: 2001
Capital Under Management: $905,900,000
Current Activity Level : Actively seeking new investments

TRUST AND INVESTMENT BANK

4/4 Kolpachny per.
Moscow, Russia 101990
Phone: 7952472583
Fax: 7952472581
E-mail: office@tibank.ru

Type of Firm
Bank Affiliated

Project Preferences

Type of Financing Preferred:
Early Stage
Expansion

Geographical Preferences

International Preferences:
Europe
Russia

Industry Preferences

In Communications prefer:
Telecommunications

In Consumer Related prefer:
Food/Beverage

In Industrial/Energy prefer:
Energy

In Transportation prefer:
Transportation

Additional Information
Year Founded: 2001
Current Activity Level : Actively seeking new investments

TRUST COMPANY OF THE WEST

865 South Figueroa Street, Suite 1800
Los Angeles, CA USA 90017
Phone: 2132440000
Fax: 2132440489
E-mail: contact@tcw.com
Website: www.tcw.com

Other Offices
88 Queensway
One Pacific Place
Hong Kong, Hong Kong
Phone: 85229181880

11100 Santa Monica Boulevard, Suite 2000
West Los Angeles, CA USA 90025
Phone: 3102355900

54-56 avenue Hoche
Paris, France 75008
Phone: 33140641101

1251 Avenue of the Americas, Suite 4700
New York, NY USA 10020
Phone: 2127714000

200 Clarendon Street,
John Hancock Tower, 51st Floor
Boston, MA USA 02116
Phone: 6179362275

Management and Staff
Anthony Valencia, Managing Director
Barr Segal, Managing Director
Blaise Antin, Managing Director
Brandon Bond, Managing Director
Bret Barker, Managing Director
Brian Cone, Managing Director
Brian McNamara, Managing Director
Bryan Whalen, Managing Director
Chang Lee, Managing Director
Charles Baldiswieler, Managing Director
Cheryl Marzano, Managing Director
Christopher Scibelli, Managing Director
Clare Polidore, Managing Director
Craig Blum, Managing Director
Daniel Kale, Managing Director
David Robbins, Managing Director
David Loevinger, Managing Director
Diane Jaffee, Managing Director
Eric Arensten, Managing Director
Gino Nucci, Managing Director
Heinrich Riehl, Managing Director
James Lewis, Vice President
Jamie Farnham, Managing Director
Javier Segovia, Managing Director
Jeffrey Anderson, Managing Director
Jerry Cudzil, Managing Director
Jess Ravich, Managing Director
John Snider, Managing Director
Joseph Magpayo, Managing Director
Laird Landmann, Managing Director
Michael Reilly, Managing Director
Mike Olson, Managing Director
Mitchell Flack, Managing Director
Patrick Moore, Managing Director
Patrick Doyle, Managing Director
Penelope Foley, Managing Director
Peter Viles, Managing Director
Pierre de Bonneville, Managing Director
Rohit Sah, Managing Director
Scott Thornton, Managing Director
Stacy Hsu, Managing Director

Stephen Kane, Managing Director
Tad Rivelle, Managing Director
Thomas Lyon, Managing Director
Tom McKissick, Managing Director

Type of Firm
Private Equity Firm

Project Preferences

Type of Financing Preferred:
Leveraged Buyout
Mezzanine
Generalist PE
Turnaround
Management Buyouts
Distressed Debt

Geographical Preferences

United States Preferences:

Canadian Preferences:
All Canada

International Preferences:
Latin America

Industry Focus
(% based on actual investment)
Internet Specific	27.3%
Medical/Health	24.2%
Industrial/Energy	19.7%
Other Products	15.4%
Consumer Related	6.5%
Computer Software and Services	3.4%
Communications and Media	1.8%
Semiconductors/Other Elect.	1.6%

Additional Information
Name of Most Recent Fund: TCW/Crescent Mezzanine Partners V, L.P.
Most Recent Fund Was Raised: 12/26/2007
Year Founded: 1971
Capital Under Management: $335,300,000
Current Activity Level : Actively seeking new investments

TRUSTCAPITAL PARTNERS NV

Kapel ter Bede 84
Ter Bede Business Center
Kortrijk, Belgium 8500
Phone: 3256249605
Fax: 3256228699
E-mail: info@koramic.be

Type of Firm
Private Equity Firm

Association Membership
Belgium Venturing Association

Project Preferences

Type of Financing Preferred:
Early Stage
Balanced
Later Stage
Seed

Geographical Preferences

International Preferences:
Belgium

Industry Focus

(% based on actual investment)
Internet Specific	30.1%
Computer Software and Services	24.0%
Medical/Health	22.4%
Biotechnology	8.8%
Consumer Related	8.6%
Other Products	3.7%
Computer Hardware	1.0%
Semiconductors/Other Elect.	0.7%
Industrial/Energy	0.6%

Additional Information

Year Founded: 1998
Capital Under Management: $142,700,000
Current Activity Level : Actively seeking new investments

TRUVENTURO GMBH

Grosse Reichenstrasse 27
Hamburg, Germany 20457
Website: www.truventuro.de

Type of Firm
Private Equity Firm

Project Preferences

Type of Financing Preferred:
Early Stage
Expansion
Start-up Financing
Later Stage
Seed

Industry Preferences

In Computer Software prefer:
Software

In Internet Specific prefer:
E-Commerce Technology
Ecommerce

Additional Information

Year Founded: 2009
Current Activity Level : Actively seeking new investments

TSC VENTURE MANAGEMENT INC

No. 50, Sec. 1, Xinsheng S Rd.
Fifth Floor, Room 500
Taipei, Taiwan 10059
Phone: 886223582556
Fax: 886223582280
Website: www.tscventures.com

Other Offices

No. 130 SZU Wei Road
2F-2
Hsinchu, Taiwan
Phone: 88635257928
Fax: 88635257930

Management and Staff

Tony Lin, Vice President

Type of Firm
Private Equity Firm

Association Membership
Taiwan Venture Capital Association(TVCA)

Project Preferences

Type of Financing Preferred:
Balanced

Geographical Preferences

United States Preferences:
All U.S.

International Preferences:
Asia Pacific
Taiwan

Additional Information

Year Founded: 1997
Current Activity Level : Actively seeking new investments

TSG CONSUMER PARTNERS, L.P.

600 Montgomery Street, Suite 2900
San Francisco, CA USA 94111
Phone: 4152172300
Fax: 4152172350
Website: www.tsgconsumer.com

Other Offices

712 Fifth Avenue
31st Floor
New York, NY USA 10019
Phone: 212-265-4111
Fax: 212-265-4845

Management and Staff

Alexander Panos, Managing Director
Blythe Jack, Managing Director
Brian Krumrei, Managing Director
Charles Esserman, Chief Executive Officer
Chase Brogan, Principal
Colin Welch, Partner
Daniel Costello, Managing Director
Edward Wong, Principal
Irena Blind, Principal
James O Hara, President
Jennifer Baxter, Principal
Jessica Duran, Chief Financial Officer
John Kenney, Managing Director
Karen Hart, Vice President
Kim Savul, Vice President
M. Hadley Mullin, Managing Director
Mary Miller, Principal
Melis Kahya, Vice President
Michael Layman, Managing Director
Pierre LeComte, Managing Director
Robyn Lawrie Rutledge, Managing Director

Type of Firm
Private Equity Firm

Project Preferences

Type of Financing Preferred:
Leveraged Buyout
Management Buyouts
Acquisition

Geographical Preferences

United States Preferences:

Industry Focus

(% based on actual investment)
Consumer Related	85.5%
Internet Specific	9.3%
Medical/Health	5.2%

Additional Information

Name of Most Recent Fund: TSG6, L.P.
Most Recent Fund Was Raised: 11/30/2011
Year Founded: 1987
Capital Under Management: $3,800,000,000
Current Activity Level : Actively seeking new investments

TSING CAPITAL

No. 1, East Qinghua Road
SP Tower Tsinghua Science Park
Beijing, China 100084
Phone: 861082151160
Fax: 861082151150
E-mail: info@tsingcapital.com
Website: www.tsingcapital.com

Other Offices

500 Hongbaoshi Road
B2102, Dawning Center
Shanghai, China 201103
Phone: 862160907180
Fax: 862160907181

1 Austin Road West, Kowloon
1212, International Commerce Center
Hong Kong, Hong Kong
Phone: 85236698367
Fax: 85236698300

Management and Staff
Michael Li, Partner
Shelby Chen, Managing Partner

Type of Firm
Private Equity Firm

Association Membership
Venture Capital Association of Beijing (VCAB)

Project Preferences

Type of Financing Preferred:
Early Stage
Expansion
Balanced
Seed
Startup

Geographical Preferences

International Preferences:
China

Industry Preferences

In Communications prefer:
Telecommunications

In Computer Software prefer:
Software

In Semiconductor/Electr prefer:
Electronics
Semiconductor

In Biotechnology prefer:
Biotechnology

In Medical/Health prefer:
Medical/Health

In Industrial/Energy prefer:
Energy
Alternative Energy
Energy Conservation Relat
Materials
Environmental Related

In Transportation prefer:
Transportation

In Agr/Forestr/Fish prefer:
Agriculture related

In Other prefer:
Environment Responsible

Additional Information
Year Founded: 2001
Capital Under Management: $24,100,000
Current Activity Level : Actively seeking new investments

TSING VENTURES TECHNOLOGY SERVICE BEIJING CO LTD

Haidian District
C Tower, Science Building
Beijing, China

Type of Firm
Private Equity Firm

Project Preferences

Type of Financing Preferred:
Early Stage
Expansion
Seed
Startup

Size of Investments Considered:
Min Size of Investment Considered (000s): $152
Max Size of Investment Considered (000s): $1,524

Geographical Preferences

International Preferences:
China

Industry Preferences

In Internet Specific prefer:
Internet

In Industrial/Energy prefer:
Industrial Products

Additional Information
Year Founded: 2016
Capital Under Management: $1,000,000,000
Current Activity Level : Actively seeking new investments

TSING-TECH INNOVATIONS CO LTD

44 - 46 Hung To Road
Eighth Floor, Century Centre
Kowloon, Hong Kong
Phone: 85223576191
Fax: 85227236362
E-mail: info@tsing-tech.com.hk
Website: www.tsing-tech.com.hk

Other Offices
Room 806, Block B, Xue Yan Building
Tsinghua Science Park, Haidian District
Beijing, China 100084
Phone: 86-10-6279-7157
Fax: 86-10-6277-1053

Type of Firm
Private Equity Firm

Project Preferences

Type of Financing Preferred:
Balanced

Geographical Preferences

International Preferences:
China

Industry Preferences

In Communications prefer:
Wireless Communications

In Medical/Health prefer:
Health Services

In Industrial/Energy prefer:
Environmental Related

Additional Information
Year Founded: 2003
Current Activity Level : Actively seeking new investments

TSINGHUA HOLDING CO LTD

Tsinghua Science Park
25/F, Block A
Beijing, China 100084
Phone: 861082150088
E-mail: thholding@thholding.com.cn
Website: www.thholding.com.cn

Type of Firm
Corporate PE/Venture

Project Preferences

Type of Financing Preferred:
Fund of Funds
Generalist PE

Geographical Preferences

International Preferences:
China

Industry Preferences

In Medical/Health prefer:
Medical/Health

In Manufact. prefer:
Manufacturing

In Other prefer:
Environment Responsible

Additional Information
Year Founded: 2010
Capital Under Management: $1,952,201,000
Current Activity Level : Actively seeking new investments

TSINGHUA UNISPLENDOUR HI-TECH VENTURE CAPITAL INC

1 Zhong Guangcun South Street, Suite 62528, Yiyuan Apartment
Beijing, China 100086
Phone: 86-10-6894-9919
Fax: 86-10-6894-7226
E-mail: thuvc@163.com
Website: www.thuvc.com

Type of Firm
Private Equity Firm

Association Membership
Venture Capital Association of Beijing (VCAB)

Project Preferences

Type of Financing Preferred:
Balanced

Geographical Preferences

International Preferences:
China

Industry Preferences

In Biotechnology prefer:
Biotechnology

In Medical/Health prefer:
Medical/Health

In Industrial/Energy prefer:
Energy

Additional Information
Year Founded: 2000
Current Activity Level : Actively seeking new investments

TT CAPITAL PARTNERS LLC

3600 Minnesota Drive, Suite 250
Edina, MN USA 55435
Phone: 9525404500
E-mail: info@ttcapitalpartners.com
Website: www.ttcapitalpartners.com

Management and Staff
Charles Boorady, Managing Partner
Conor Green, Vice President
Dave Henderson, Co-Founder
Kevin Green, Co-Founder
Mike Healy, Principal
Thomas O Donnell, Partner

Type of Firm
Bank Affiliated

Project Preferences

Type of Financing Preferred:
Expansion
Later Stage

Industry Preferences

In Medical/Health prefer:
Health Services

Additional Information
Name of Most Recent Fund: TTCP Fund I, L.P.
Most Recent Fund Was Raised: 12/18/2013
Year Founded: 2013
Capital Under Management: $131,960,000
Current Activity Level : Actively seeking new investments

TTP VENTURE MANAGERS LTD

Melbourn Science Park
Hertfordshire
Melbourn, United Kingdom SG8 6EE
Phone: 441763262626
Fax: 441763262265
E-mail: mailventures@ttpventures.com
Website: www.ttpventures.com

Management and Staff
David Gee, Chief Executive Officer

Type of Firm
Corporate PE/Venture

Association Membership
British Venture Capital Association (BVCA)

Project Preferences

Type of Financing Preferred:
Early Stage
Balanced

Size of Investments Considered:
Min Size of Investment Considered (000s): $400
Max Size of Investment Considered (000s): $23,975

Geographical Preferences

International Preferences:
United Kingdom
Europe

Industry Preferences

In Communications prefer:
Telecommunications
Wireless Communications
Data Communications

In Semiconductor/Electr prefer:
Electronics
Electronic Components
Semiconductor

In Medical/Health prefer:
Medical/Health
Medical Products

In Industrial/Energy prefer:
Alternative Energy
Energy Conservation Relat
Materials
Environmental Related

Additional Information
Year Founded: 1998
Capital Under Management: $53,100,000
Current Activity Level : Actively seeking new investments

TTV CAPITAL LLC

1230 Peachtree Street, Suite 1150, Promenade II
Atlanta, GA USA 30309
Phone: 4043478400
Fax: 4043478420
Website: www.ttvcapital.com

Management and Staff
Gardiner Garrard, Co-Founder
Mark Johnson, Partner
Sean Banks, Chief Financial Officer
W. Thomas Smith, Co-Founder

Type of Firm
Private Equity Firm

Project Preferences

Role in Financing:
Will function either as deal originator or investor in deals created by others

Type of Financing Preferred:
Early Stage
Expansion
Balanced
Later Stage

Geographical Preferences

United States Preferences:
Southeast

Industry Preferences

In Communications prefer:
Communications and Media

In Internet Specific prefer:
E-Commerce Technology
Ecommerce

In Financial Services prefer:
Financial Services

Additional Information
Name of Most Recent Fund: TTV Fund III, L.P.
Most Recent Fund Was Raised: 06/09/2011
Year Founded: 2000
Capital Under Management: $147,000,000
Current Activity Level : Actively seeking new investments

Method of Compensation: Return on invest. most important, but chg. closing fees, service fees, etc.

TUATARA CAPITAL LP

12 East 44th Street
8th Floor
New York, NY USA 10017
Website: www.tuataracapital.com

Management and Staff
Al Foreman, Partner
Robert Hunt, Partner

Type of Firm
Investment Management Firm

Project Preferences

Type of Financing Preferred:
Balanced

Geographical Preferences

United States Preferences:

Industry Preferences

In Biotechnology prefer:
Biotech Related Research

In Medical/Health prefer:
Medical/Health

In Consumer Related prefer:
Consumer
Retail

In Financial Services prefer:
Real Estate

Additional Information
Year Founded: 2015
Capital Under Management: $37,080,000
Current Activity Level : Actively seeking new investments

TUCKERBROOK ALTERNATIVE INVESTMENTS LP

30 Doaks Lane
Marblehead, MA USA 01945
Website: www.tuckerbrook.com

Type of Firm
Private Equity Advisor or Fund of Funds

Project Preferences

Type of Financing Preferred:
Fund of Funds

Additional Information
Year Founded: 2006
Current Activity Level : Actively seeking new investments

TUCKERMAN CAPITAL

80 South Main Street
Hanover, NH USA 03755
Phone: 6036402291
Fax: 6036402239
Website: www.tuckermancapital.com

Management and Staff
Nicholas Russell, Partner
Peter Milliken, Co-Founder
Timothy Briglin, Co-Founder

Type of Firm
Private Equity Firm

Project Preferences

Type of Financing Preferred:
Leveraged Buyout
Acquisition

Geographical Preferences

United States Preferences:

Industry Preferences

In Business Serv. prefer:
Services
Distribution

In Manufact. prefer:
Manufacturing

Additional Information
Name of Most Recent Fund: Tuckerman Capital IV, L.P.
Most Recent Fund Was Raised: 06/14/2012
Year Founded: 2001
Capital Under Management: $33,909,000
Current Activity Level : Actively seeking new investments

TUDOR VENTURES

50 Rowes Wharf, Fifth Floor
Boston, MA USA 02110
Phone: 6173916300
Fax: 6173916390
E-mail: info@springlep.com
Website: www.springlakeequitypartners.com

Other Offices
1275 King Street
Greenwich, CT USA 06831
Phone: 2038638677
Fax: 2038631868

Management and Staff
Carmen Scarpa, Co-Founder
Dan MacKeigan, Co-Founder
Jeffrey Williams, Co-Founder
Jon Danielson, Co-Founder
Richard Ganong, Partner
Robert Forlenza, Co-Founder

Type of Firm
Private Equity Firm

Project Preferences

Type of Financing Preferred:
Expansion
Later Stage
Acquisition
Recapitalizations

Size of Investments Considered:
Min Size of Investment Considered (000s): $7,000
Max Size of Investment Considered (000s): $15,000

Geographical Preferences

United States Preferences:
North America

Canadian Preferences:
All Canada

Industry Focus
(% based on actual investment)
Computer Software and Services	23.4%
Internet Specific	19.2%
Communications and Media	15.3%
Other Products	14.4%
Semiconductors/Other Elect.	6.5%
Medical/Health	5.5%
Computer Hardware	5.3%
Consumer Related	5.2%
Industrial/Energy	4.6%
Biotechnology	0.6%

Additional Information
Name of Most Recent Fund: Spring Lake Equity Partners LLC
Most Recent Fund Was Raised: 07/12/2013
Year Founded: 1994
Capital Under Management: $500,000,000
Current Activity Level : Actively seeking new investments

TUFAN VENTURE PARTNERS, INC.

146 West Beaver Creek Road, Suite Three
Toronto, Canada L4B 1C2
Phone: 905-762-8770
Fax: 905-762-8799

Other Offices
146 West Beaver Creek Road, Suite Three
Toronto, Canada L4B 1C2
Phone: 905-762-8770
Fax: 905-762-8799

Management and Staff
Hardev Arora, Managing Partner
Roy Pathak, Managing Partner
Zool Kassum, Managing Partner

Type of Firm
Private Equity Firm

Project Preferences

Type of Financing Preferred:
Seed

Additional Information
Year Founded: 2000
Current Activity Level : Actively seeking new investments

TUGBOAT VENTURES LP

306 Cambridge Avenue
Palo Alto, CA USA 94306
Phone: 6504701400

Management and Staff
Christopher Alden, Venture Partner
David Whorton, Founder
David Whorton, Founder

Type of Firm
Private Equity Firm

Project Preferences

Role in Financing:
Prefer role as deal originator but will also invest in deals created by others

Type of Financing Preferred:
Early Stage
Balanced
Seed
Startup

Geographical Preferences

United States Preferences:

Industry Preferences

In Computer Software prefer:
Software
Systems Software

In Internet Specific prefer:
Internet
Ecommerce
Web Aggregation/Portals

In Business Serv. prefer:
Services
Media

Additional Information
Name of Most Recent Fund: Tugboat Strategic Limited Partners II, L.P.
Most Recent Fund Was Raised: 02/25/2009
Year Founded: 2006
Capital Under Management: $125,000,000
Current Activity Level : Actively seeking new investments

TUHUA

117-125 St Georges Bay Road
Level Four, The Textile Centre
Auckland, New Zealand 1052
Phone: 093086222
E-mail: funding@tuhua.vc
Website: www.tuhuaventures.co.nz

Type of Firm
Private Equity Firm

Project Preferences

Type of Financing Preferred:
Early Stage
Startup

Geographical Preferences

International Preferences:
New Zealand

Additional Information
Year Founded: 2016
Current Activity Level : Actively seeking new investments

TULCAN

2001 Kirby Drive, Suite 1314
Houston, TX USA 77019
Phone: 7135268500
Fax: 8774718160
E-mail: inquiries@TULCAN.com
Website: www.tulcan.com

Type of Firm
Private Equity Firm

Project Preferences

Type of Financing Preferred:
Leveraged Buyout
Acquisition

Additional Information
Year Founded: 1969
Current Activity Level : Actively seeking new investments

TULLIS HEALTH INVESTORS

11770 U.S. Highway One, Suite 503
North Palm Beach, FL USA 33408
Phone: 2039008577
Fax: 2036299293
Website: www.tullisfunds.com

Other Offices
263 Tresser Boulevard
One Stamford Plaza, 12 F
STAMFORD, CT USA 06901
Phone: 2033234200

Management and Staff
Barbara Bierer, Venture Partner
David Leffell, Venture Partner
James Tullis, Founder
John Tullis, Principal
Neil Ryan, Principal
Nora Mende, Chief Financial Officer

Type of Firm
Private Equity Firm

Project Preferences

Role in Financing:
Prefer role as deal originator but will also invest in deals created by others

Type of Financing Preferred:
Early Stage
Balanced
Later Stage

Geographical Preferences

United States Preferences:

Industry Preferences

In Biotechnology prefer:
Biotechnology

In Medical/Health prefer:
Medical/Health
Medical Products
Health Services
Pharmaceuticals

Additional Information
Name of Most Recent Fund: Tullis Opportunity Fund II, L.P.
Most Recent Fund Was Raised: 08/23/2010
Year Founded: 1986
Capital Under Management: $350,000,000
Current Activity Level : Actively seeking new investments
Method of Compensation: Return on investment is of primary concern, do not charge fees

TULLY AND HOLLAND INC

20 William Street, Suite 135
Wellesley, MA USA 02481
Phone: 781-239-2900
Fax: 781-239-2901
E-mail: info@tullyandholland.com
Website: www.tullyandholland.com

Management and Staff
Alfred Rossow, Managing Director
Andrew Crain, Managing Director
Christopher Kampe, Managing Director
Donald O Connor, Managing Director
Russell Robb, Managing Director
Stuart Rose, Managing Director
Timothy Tully, President

Type of Firm
Bank Affiliated

Project Preferences

Role in Financing:
Other

Type of Financing Preferred:
Second Stage Financing
Leveraged Buyout
Mezzanine
Recapitalizations

Size of Investments Considered:
Min Size of Investment Considered (000s): $5,000
Max Size of Investment Considered: No Limit

Geographical Preferences

United States Preferences:
Midwest
Southeast
Northeast

Industry Preferences

In Medical/Health prefer:
Diagnostic Services
Diagnostic Test Products
Other Therapeutic
Medical Products
Disposable Med. Products

In Consumer Related prefer:
Retail
Computer Stores
Food/Beverage
Consumer Products
Consumer Services
Other Restaurants

Additional Information
Year Founded: 1992
Current Activity Level : Actively seeking new investments
Method of Compensation: Other

TUNISIE VALEUR SA

Immeuble INTEGRA Centre Urbain
Tunis Mahrajene, Tunisia 1082
Phone: 21671189600
Fax: 21671189630
Website: www.tunisievaleurs.com

Type of Firm
Investment Management Firm

Project Preferences

Type of Financing Preferred:
Early Stage
Expansion

Geographical Preferences

International Preferences:
Tunisia

Industry Preferences

In Business Serv. prefer:
Services

Additional Information
Year Founded: 2009
Current Activity Level : Actively seeking new investments

TURENNE CAPITAL PARTENAIRES SASU

29-31 rue Saint Augustin
Paris, France 75002
Phone: 33153430303
Fax: 33153430304
E-mail: turenne@turennecapital.com
Website: www.turennecapital.com

Other Offices
31, rue Montgrand
BP 303
Marseille, France 13177
Phone: 33491143135
Fax: 33491556259

Management and Staff
Beatrice Vernet, Chief Operating Officer
Francois Lombard, President
Yves Guez, Partner

Type of Firm
Private Equity Firm

Association Membership
French Venture Capital Association (AFIC)

Project Preferences

Type of Financing Preferred:
Core
Leveraged Buyout
Early Stage
Generalist PE
Public Companies
Later Stage
Management Buyouts
Acquisition
Startup

Geographical Preferences

International Preferences:
Europe
Western Europe
France

Industry Preferences

In Communications prefer:
Telecommunications

In Internet Specific prefer:
E-Commerce Technology
Internet

In Computer Other prefer:
Computer Related

In Semiconductor/Electr prefer:
Electronics

In Medical/Health prefer:
Medical/Health
Medical Diagnostics
Diagnostic Services
Diagnostic Test Products
Medical Therapeutics
Other Therapeutic
Disposable Med. Products
Health Services
Hospital/Other Instit.

In Consumer Related prefer:
Consumer
Consumer Services
Hotels and Resorts

In Industrial/Energy prefer:
Industrial Products
Environmental Related

In Financial Services prefer:
Real Estate

In Business Serv. prefer:
Services
Distribution

In Other prefer:
Environment Responsible

Additional Information
Name of Most Recent Fund: Capital Sante 1 FCPR
Most Recent Fund Was Raised: 12/31/2013
Year Founded: 1999
Capital Under Management: $269,800,000
Current Activity Level : Actively seeking new investments

TURK VENTURE PARTNERS LTD

Muallim Naci Caddesi No 40
Ortakoy
Istanbul, Turkey 34347
Phone: 902123268400
Fax: 902123268484
E-mail: info@turkven.com
Website: www.turkven.com

Type of Firm
Bank Affiliated

Project Preferences

Type of Financing Preferred:
Leveraged Buyout
Expansion
Generalist PE
Balanced
Later Stage
Management Buyouts
Acquisition
Special Situation
Recapitalizations

Geographical Preferences

International Preferences:
Turkey
Europe
Rest of World

Industry Preferences

In Communications prefer:
Commercial Communications
Media and Entertainment

In Computer Hardware prefer:
Integrated Turnkey System

In Semiconductor/Electr prefer:
Electronics

In Medical/Health prefer:
Health Services
Hospitals/Clinics/Primary

In Consumer Related prefer:
Food/Beverage
Consumer Services

In Financial Services prefer:
Financial Services

In Business Serv. prefer:
Services

Additional Information
Year Founded: 2000
Capital Under Management: $41,000,000
Current Activity Level : Actively seeking new investments

TURKI ALMADHI VENTURES INC.

14 Curzon Street
Mayfair
London, United Kingdom W1J5HN
Phone: 4402032891440
E-mail: hello@turkialmadhi.com
Website: www.turkialmadhi.com

Type of Firm
Incubator/Development Program

Project Preferences

Type of Financing Preferred:
Seed
Startup

Additional Information
Year Founded: 2005
Current Activity Level : Actively seeking new investments

TURN/RIVER CAPITAL LP

8 Bernice Street
Unit 102
San Francisco, CA USA 94103
Phone: 4156378142
E-mail: contact@turnrivercapital.com
Website: www.turnrivercapital.com

Management and Staff
Evan Ginsburg, Managing Director

Type of Firm
Private Equity Firm

Additional Information
Year Founded: 2015
Current Activity Level : Actively seeking new investments

TURN8

Office 1705, Fortune Tower
Cluster C, JLT,
Dubai, Utd. Arab Em.
Phone: 97143197645
E-mail: contact@turn8.co
Website: turn8.co

Other Offices
Office 1705, Fortune Tower Cluster C, JL
Dubai, Utd. Arab Em.
Phone: 97143197645

Type of Firm
Private Equity Firm

Project Preferences

Type of Financing Preferred:
Early Stage
Seed

Geographical Preferences

United States Preferences:
All U.S.

Canadian Preferences:
All Canada

International Preferences:
Europe
Middle East
Asia
Africa

Industry Preferences

In Communications prefer:
Data Communications

In Computer Software prefer:
Software
Systems Software
Applications Software

In Internet Specific prefer:
Internet

In Computer Other prefer:
Computer Related

In Consumer Related prefer:
Education Related

In Financial Services prefer:
Financial Services

Additional Information
Year Founded: 2013
Capital Under Management: $60,000,000
Current Activity Level : Actively seeking new investments

TURNING ROCK PARTNERS GP LLC

400 Park Avenue, Suite 610
New York, NY USA 10022
Phone: 2122072394
Website: www.turningrockpartners.com

Management and Staff
David Markus, Partner
Louis Mayer, Vice President
Maggie Arvedlund, Founder

Type of Firm
Private Equity Firm

Project Preferences

Type of Financing Preferred:
Balanced

Geographical Preferences

United States Preferences:
North America

Additional Information
Year Founded: 2017
Capital Under Management: $4,200,000
Current Activity Level : Actively seeking new investments

TURNSPIRE CAPITAL PARTNERS LLC

1290 Avenue of the Americas, Suite 914
New York, NY USA 10104
Website: turnspirecap.com

Management and Staff
Abel Osorio, Principal
Ilya Koffman, Co-Founder
Michael Khutorsky, Co-Founder
Peter Nortrup, Principal

Type of Firm
Private Equity Firm

Project Preferences

Type of Financing Preferred:
Leveraged Buyout
Turnaround
Acquisition
Special Situation
Recapitalizations

Geographical Preferences

United States Preferences:

Canadian Preferences:
All Canada

Industry Preferences

In Consumer Related prefer:
Consumer

In Industrial/Energy prefer:
Materials
Advanced Materials
Machinery

In Transportation prefer:
Transportation
Aerospace

In Manufact. prefer:
Manufacturing
Publishing

Additional Information
Year Founded: 2014
Current Activity Level : Actively seeking new investments

TURNSTONE CAPITAL MANAGEMENT LLC

15 Riverside Avenue
Westport, CT USA 06880
Phone: 2034166581
Fax: 6465140314
E-mail: info@turnstonecapital.com
Website: www.turnstonecapital.com

Management and Staff
Craig Samuel, Partner
Marc La Magna, Managing Partner
Ronald Wooldridge, Partner

Type of Firm
Private Equity Firm

Project Preferences

Type of Financing Preferred:
Balanced

Industry Preferences

In Communications prefer:
Communications and Media

In Industrial/Energy prefer:
Alternative Energy
Energy Conservation Relat

Additional Information
Year Founded: 2004
Current Activity Level : Actively seeking new investments

TUSK STRATEGIES INC

251 Park Ave South
Eighth Floor
New York, NY USA 10010
E-mail: info@tuskventures.com
Website: tuskventures.com

Type of Firm
Private Equity Firm

Project Preferences

Type of Financing Preferred:
Early Stage

Industry Preferences

In Business Serv. prefer:
Media

Additional Information
Year Founded: 2015
Current Activity Level : Actively seeking new investments

TVC CAPITAL LLC

11260 El Camino Real, Suite 220
San Diego, CA USA 92130
Phone: 8587043261
Fax: 8585239560
Website: www.tvccapital.com

Management and Staff
Christopher Noser, Principal
Jeb Spencer, Co-Founder
Steven Hamerslag, Co-Founder
Tighe Reardon, Chief Financial Officer

Type of Firm
Private Equity Firm

Project Preferences

Type of Financing Preferred:
Leveraged Buyout
Expansion
Generalist PE
Later Stage
Acquisition
Recapitalizations

Geographical Preferences

United States Preferences:

Industry Preferences

In Communications prefer:
Wireless Communications

In Computer Hardware prefer:
Computer Graphics and Dig

In Computer Software prefer:
Software
Systems Software
Applications Software

In Internet Specific prefer:
Internet

In Financial Services prefer:
Financial Services

Additional Information
Name of Most Recent Fund: TVC Capital II, L.P.
Most Recent Fund Was Raised: 09/12/2012
Year Founded: 2002
Capital Under Management: $60,000,000
Current Activity Level : Actively seeking new investments

TVM CAPITAL GMBH

Ottostrasse 4
Munich, Germany 80333
Phone: 49899989920
Fax: 498999899255
E-mail: info@tvm-capital.com
Website: www.tvm-capital.com

Other Offices
2 Place Alexis Nihon, Suite 902
3500 Blvd De Maisonneuve West
Westmount, Canada H3Z3C1
Phone: 15149314111

DIFC Gate Village, Building 4
Dubai, Utd. Arab Em. 113355
Phone: 97144390220

Management and Staff
Alexandra Goll, General Partner
Axel Polack, General Partner
Cynthia Lavoie, General Partner
Friedrich Bornikoel, Managing Partner
Hans Schreck, General Partner
Hoda Abou-Jamra, Partner
Hubert Birner, Managing Partner
Josef Moosholzer, Partner

Luc Marengere, Managing Partner
Mark Cipriano, General Partner
Peter Neubeck, Venture Partner
Stefan Fischer, General Partner
Youssef Haidar, Partner

Type of Firm
Private Equity Firm

Association Membership
Gulf Venture Capital Association
German Venture Capital Association (BVK)
Canadian Venture Capital Association
European Private Equity and Venture Capital Assoc.

Project Preferences

Role in Financing:
Prefer role as deal originator but will also invest in deals created by others

Type of Financing Preferred:
Second Stage Financing
Early Stage
Balanced
Later Stage
Seed
First Stage Financing
Startup

Size of Investments Considered:
Min Size of Investment Considered (000s): $5,000
Max Size of Investment Considered (000s): $20,000

Geographical Preferences

United States Preferences:
All U.S.

Canadian Preferences:
All Canada
Quebec

International Preferences:
Europe
Middle East
Africa

Industry Focus
(% based on actual investment)

Biotechnology	45.3%
Medical/Health	24.5%
Computer Software and Services	10.8%
Communications and Media	6.7%
Semiconductors/Other Elect.	6.4%
Internet Specific	3.3%
Other Products	1.4%
Computer Hardware	1.2%
Consumer Related	0.2%
Industrial/Energy	0.2%

Additional Information
Name of Most Recent Fund: TVM Life Science Ventures VII
Most Recent Fund Was Raised: 05/28/2012
Year Founded: 1983
Capital Under Management: $1,542,900,000

Current Activity Level : Actively seeking new investments
Method of Compensation: Return on investment is of primary concern, do not charge fees

TWELVE19 VENTURES LLC

801 Grand Avenue
Des Moines, IA USA 50309
E-mail: info@twelve19ventures.com
Website: www.welve19ventures.com

Type of Firm
Private Equity Firm

Project Preferences

Type of Financing Preferred:
Early Stage
Expansion
Balanced
Seed

Additional Information
Year Founded: 1969
Current Activity Level : Actively seeking new investments

TWILIGHT VENTURE PARTNERS

One American Square, Suite 2900
Indianapolis, IN USA 46282
Phone: 3174233240
Fax: 3174233242

Management and Staff
August Watanabe, Partner
Harry Gonso, Partner
James Cornelius, Senior Managing Director
James Baumgardt, Partner
P. Kent Hawryluk, Partner
Richard DiMarchi, Partner
Ronald Henriksen, Partner

Type of Firm
Private Equity Firm

Project Preferences

Size of Investments Considered:
Min Size of Investment Considered (000s): $100
Max Size of Investment Considered (000s): $1,000

Geographical Preferences

United States Preferences:
Midwest

Additional Information
Year Founded: 2002
Capital Under Management: $15,000,000
Current Activity Level : Actively seeking new investments

TWIN HAVEN CAPITAL PARTNERS LLC

11111 Santa Monica Boulevard, Suite 525
West Los Angeles, CA USA 90025
Phone: 2032931810
Website: www.twinhavencap.com

Management and Staff
Arthur Samberg, Managing Director
Kevin O Brien, Managing Director
Paul Mellinger, Principal
Peter Dartley, Managing Director
Robert Webster, Principal
Sheila Clancy, Managing Director

Type of Firm
Private Equity Firm

Project Preferences

Type of Financing Preferred:
Turnaround
Special Situation
Distressed Debt

Additional Information
Name of Most Recent Fund: Twin Haven Special Opportunities Fund IV, L.P.
Most Recent Fund Was Raised: 03/29/2011
Year Founded: 2002
Capital Under Management: $100,000,000
Current Activity Level : Actively seeking new investments

TWJ CAPITAL LLC

Six Landmark Square, Suite 404
Stamford, CT USA 06901
Phone: 2033595610
Fax: 2033595810
Website: www.twjcapital.com

Other Offices
7272 Wisconsin Avenue, Suite 300
Bethesda, MD USA 20814
Phone: 3019411959
Fax: 30194112656

Management and Staff
Nigel Jones, Partner
Thomas Jones, Founder

Type of Firm
Private Equity Firm

Project Preferences

Type of Financing Preferred:
Early Stage
Expansion

Size of Investments Considered:
Min Size of Investment Considered (000s): $500
Max Size of Investment Considered (000s): $25,000

Industry Preferences

In Communications prefer:
Telecommunications
Wireless Communications

In Internet Specific prefer:
Internet

In Consumer Related prefer:
Retail

In Business Serv. prefer:
Services

Additional Information

Name of Most Recent Fund: TWJ Capital Opportunity Fund I, L.P.
Most Recent Fund Was Raised: 05/05/2005
Year Founded: 2005
Current Activity Level : Actively seeking new investments

TWO ROADS GROUP LLC

205 North Fremont Street
Chicago, IL USA 60614
Website: tworoadsgroup.com

Type of Firm
Investment Management Firm

Project Preferences

Type of Financing Preferred:
Leveraged Buyout
Acquisition

Industry Preferences

In Computer Software prefer:
Software

In Industrial/Energy prefer:
Robotics

Additional Information
Year Founded: 2015
Current Activity Level : Actively seeking new investments

TWO SIGMA INVESTMENTS LP

100 Avenue of the Americas
23rd Floor
New York, NY USA 10013
Phone: 2126255700
Fax: 2126255800
E-mail: investor-relations@twosigma.com
Website: www.twosigma.com

Other Offices

Two Exchange Square, Suite 1504
, Hong Kong
Phone: 85258043900
Fax: 85221109460

73 Watling Street
London, United Kingdom EC4M 9BJ
Phone: 4402071539820
Fax: 4402071521101

708 Main Street
Tenth Floor
HOUSTON, TX USA 77002
Phone: 18325486700
Fax: 19172373400

Type of Firm
Investment Management Firm

Project Preferences

Type of Financing Preferred:
Core
Leveraged Buyout
Expansion
Generalist PE
Balanced
Later Stage

Industry Preferences

In Computer Software prefer:
Data Processing

In Computer Other prefer:
Computer Related

In Medical/Health prefer:
Medical/Health

In Consumer Related prefer:
Education Related

In Financial Services prefer:
Real Estate

Additional Information
Year Founded: 2001
Current Activity Level : Actively seeking new investments

TWV CAPITAL MANAGEMENT LLC

3625 N. Hall Street, Suite 615
Dallas, TX USA 75219
Phone: 2144447890
E-mail: info@twvcapital.com
Website: www.twvcapital.com

Management and Staff
Carol Nichols, Co-Founder
Cynthia Pharr-Lee, Co-Founder
Greg O Shea, Managing Director
Valerie Freeman, Co-Founder
Whitney Johns-Martin, Managing Director

Type of Firm
Private Equity Firm

Association Membership
Natl Assoc of Small Bus. Inv. Co (NASBIC)

Project Preferences

Type of Financing Preferred:
Leveraged Buyout
Expansion
Generalist PE
Balanced
Later Stage
Management Buyouts
Acquisition
Recapitalizations

Geographical Preferences

United States Preferences:
Southwest
Texas

Industry Preferences

In Medical/Health prefer:
Health Services

In Business Serv. prefer:
Services
Distribution

In Manufact. prefer:
Manufacturing

In Other prefer:
Women/Minority-Owned Bus.

Additional Information
Year Founded: 2002
Capital Under Management: $3,000,000
Current Activity Level : Actively seeking new investments

TYCHE PARTNERS LP

1735 North First Street, Suite 303
San Jose, CA USA 95112
Website: tyche-partners.com

Management and Staff
Fang Li, Partner
Michael Wishart, Venture Partner
Wejie Yun, Managing Partner

Type of Firm
Private Equity Firm

Project Preferences

Type of Financing Preferred:
Early Stage
Expansion

Geographical Preferences

United States Preferences:
California

International Preferences:
China

Industry Preferences

In Internet Specific prefer:
Internet

In Semiconductor/Electr prefer:
Electronics
Semiconductor

In Industrial/Energy prefer:
Robotics

Additional Information

Year Founded: 2015
Capital Under Management: $1,000,000
Current Activity Level : Actively seeking new investments

TYLT LAB

1158 26th Street, Suite 325
Santa Monica, CA USA 90403
Phone: 3103318797
Fax: 3108707039
Website: www.tyltlab.com

Other Offices

604 Arizona Avenue
Santa Monica, CA USA 90401

Type of Firm

Investment Management Firm

Project Preferences

Type of Financing Preferred:
Early Stage
Seed
Startup

Geographical Preferences

United States Preferences:
Southern California

Industry Preferences

In Communications prefer:
Telecommunications

In Semiconductor/Electr prefer:
Electronics

In Medical/Health prefer:
Medical/Health

In Consumer Related prefer:
Entertainment and Leisure
Consumer Products

In Other prefer:
Environment Responsible

Additional Information

Name of Most Recent Fund: TYLT Lab Partners I, L.P.
Most Recent Fund Was Raised: 03/10/2014
Year Founded: 2013
Capital Under Management: $20,000,000

Current Activity Level : Actively seeking new investments

TYREE & D ANGELO PARTNERS LLC

233 North Michigan Avenue, Suite 2420
Chicago, IL USA 60601
Phone: 3124895050
Fax: 3124895043
E-mail: info@tdpfund.com
Website: www.tdpfund.com

Type of Firm

Private Equity Firm

Project Preferences

Type of Financing Preferred:
Leveraged Buyout
Expansion
Acquisition

Geographical Preferences

United States Preferences:
Midwest

Canadian Preferences:
All Canada

Industry Preferences

In Medical/Health prefer:
Medical/Health

In Consumer Related prefer:
Consumer

In Financial Services prefer:
Financial Services

In Agr/Forestr/Fish prefer:
Agriculture related

Additional Information

Year Founded: 2013
Current Activity Level : Actively seeking new investments

TYROL EQUITY AG

Kaiserjaegerstrasse 30
Innsbruck, Austria 6020
Phone: 435125801580
Fax: 4351258015845
E-mail: office@tyrolequity.com
Website: www.tyrolequity.com

Type of Firm

Private Equity Firm

Project Preferences

Type of Financing Preferred:
Leveraged Buyout
Turnaround
Management Buyouts
Acquisition

Geographical Preferences

International Preferences:
Italy
Switzerland
Austria
Germany

Industry Preferences

In Consumer Related prefer:
Consumer Products

In Industrial/Energy prefer:
Industrial Products

Additional Information

Year Founded: 2007
Current Activity Level : Actively seeking new investments

TZP GROUP LLC

Seven Times Square, Suite 4307
New York, NY USA 10036
Phone: 2123980300
Fax: 2123981909
E-mail: info@tzpgroup.com
Website: www.tzpgroup.com

Management and Staff

Daniel Galpern, Partner
Daniel Gaspar, Partner
Harris Newman, Managing Director
Nathan Chandrasekaran, Principal
Paul Davis, Principal
Samuel Katz, Managing Partner
Sheera Michael, Chief Financial Officer
Vladimir Gutin, Partner

Type of Firm

Private Equity Firm

Project Preferences

Type of Financing Preferred:
Acquisition

Size of Investments Considered:
Min Size of Investment Considered (000s): $20,000
Max Size of Investment Considered (000s): $50,000

Industry Preferences

In Medical/Health prefer:
Health Services

In Consumer Related prefer:
Consumer Services

In Financial Services prefer:
Financial Services
Real Estate

In Business Serv. prefer:
Services
Distribution
Media

Additional Information
Name of Most Recent Fund: TZP Capital Partners II, L.P.
Most Recent Fund Was Raised: 05/13/2013
Year Founded: 2007
Capital Under Management: $1,112,000,000
Current Activity Level : Actively seeking new investments

- U -

U I GESTION SA

22 Avenue Franklin Roosevelt
Paris, France 75008
Phone: 33142566600
Fax: 33142566600
E-mail: contact@uigestionsa.fr
Website: www.uigestion.fr

Management and Staff
Jean-Jacques Vaury, Partner
Michel Deprez, Partner
Olivier Jarousse, Partner

Type of Firm
Bank Affiliated

Association Membership
French Venture Capital Association (AFIC)
European Private Equity and Venture Capital Assoc.

Project Preferences

Type of Financing Preferred:
Leveraged Buyout
Early Stage
Generalist PE
Later Stage
Management Buyouts
Acquisition

Size of Investments Considered:
Min Size of Investment Considered (000s): $2,666
Max Size of Investment Considered (000s): $13,331

Geographical Preferences

International Preferences:
Europe
France

Industry Focus
(% based on actual investment)
Other Products	53.4%
Consumer Related	19.0%
Medical/Health	17.0%
Industrial/Energy	7.7%
Computer Software and Services	2.9%

Additional Information
Year Founded: 1998
Capital Under Management: $910,100,000
Current Activity Level : Actively seeking new investments

U.S. VENTURE PARTNERS

1460 El Camino Real, Suite 100
Menlo Park, CA USA 94025
Phone: 6508549080
Fax: 6508543018
E-mail: contact@usvp.com
Website: www.usvp.com

Other Offices
Unit 1605B, 16th Floor Shui On Plaza
No. 333 Huaihai Central Road
Shanghai, China 200020

2735 Sand Hill Road
MENLO PARK, CA USA 94025
Phone: 6508549080

Management and Staff
Alan Kaganov, Partner
Casey Tansey, General Partner
Dafina Toncheva, Partner
David Liddle, Venture Partner
Geoffrey Baehr, Venture Partner
Irwin Federman, General Partner
Jacques Benkoski, Partner
John Hadl, Venture Partner
Jonathan Root, General Partner
Larry Lasky, Partner
Michael Maher, Chief Financial Officer
Philip Young, Venture Partner
Philip Schlein, Venture Partner
Rick Lewis, General Partner
Steve Krausz, General Partner
William Bowes, Partner

Type of Firm
Private Equity Firm

Association Membership
Israel Venture Association
Western Association of Venture Capitalists (WAVC)
National Venture Capital Association - USA (NVCA)

Project Preferences

Role in Financing:
Prefer role as deal originator but will also invest in deals created by others

Type of Financing Preferred:
Early Stage
Balanced

Industry Focus
(% based on actual investment)
Computer Software and Services	20.1%
Internet Specific	18.5%
Semiconductors/Other Elect.	17.0%
Medical/Health	11.5%
Communications and Media	11.5%
Biotechnology	8.6%
Computer Hardware	5.1%
Consumer Related	3.8%
Industrial/Energy	3.3%
Other Products	0.5%

Additional Information
Name of Most Recent Fund: U.S. Venture Partners X, L.P.
Most Recent Fund Was Raised: 07/07/2008
Year Founded: 1981
Capital Under Management: $3,250,000,000
Current Activity Level : Actively seeking new investments

Method of Compensation: Return on investment is of primary concern, do not charge fees

UA VENTURE CAPITAL LLC

607 North Sixth Avenue
Tucson, AZ USA 85705
Phone: 5205008282
Website: www.uaventurecap.com

Type of Firm
University Program

Project Preferences

Type of Financing Preferred:
Balanced

Geographical Preferences

United States Preferences:
Arizona

Industry Preferences

In Business Serv. prefer:
Services

Additional Information
Year Founded: 2017
Current Activity Level : Actively seeking new investments

UAMCO LTD

58-7 Seosomoondong, Junggu
13F Dongwha Building
Seoul, South Korea
Phone: 82221792400
Fax: 82221792401
Website: www.uamco.co.kr

Type of Firm
Investment Management Firm

Project Preferences

Type of Financing Preferred:
Leveraged Buyout
Turnaround
Distressed Debt
Recapitalizations

Geographical Preferences

International Preferences:
Korea, South

Additional Information
Year Founded: 2009
Capital Under Management: $188,854,000
Current Activity Level : Actively seeking new investments

UBEQUITY CAPITAL PARTNERS INC

36 Lombard Street, Suite 700
Toronto, Canada M5C 2X3
Phone: 4169419069
Fax: 4163610130
E-mail: info@ubequitycapital.com
Website: www.ubequitycapital.com

Other Offices
36 Lombard Street, Suite 700
Toronto, Canada M5C 2X3
Phone: 4169419069
Fax: 4163610130

131 Rue De la Faisanderie
Paris, France 75116
Phone: 33017193556

150 East 52nd Street
21st Floor
New York, NY USA 10022
Phone: 2125745454
Fax: 2125745453

1030 West Georgia Street, Suite 1218
Vancouver, Canada V6E 2Y3
Phone: 6044845761
Fax: 6064845760

Management and Staff
Bill Calsbeck, Managing Director
Howard Margulis, Chief Operating Officer
Kia Besharat, Managing Director
Martin Doane, CEO & Managing Director
Paul Amsellem, Managing Director
Richard Meloff, Managing Director

Type of Firm
Private Equity Firm

Project Preferences

Type of Financing Preferred:
Generalist PE

Industry Preferences

In Computer Other prefer:
Computer Related

In Industrial/Energy prefer:
Oil and Gas Exploration
Alternative Energy
Energy Conservation Relat
Environmental Related

In Financial Services prefer:
Financial Services

In Business Serv. prefer:
Media

In Agr/Forestr/Fish prefer:
Mining and Minerals

In Other prefer:
Environment Responsible

Additional Information
Year Founded: 2005
Current Activity Level : Actively seeking new investments

UBS CAPITAL MARKETS LP

111 Pavonia Avenue East
Newport Financial Center
Jersey City, NJ USA 07310
Phone: 212-713-3090

Other Offices
111 Pavonia Avenue East
Newport Financial Center
Jersey City, NJ USA 07310
Phone: 212-713-3090

Management and Staff
Joseph Mecane, Managing Director
Ron Schwartz, Managing Director

Type of Firm
Bank Affiliated

Additional Information
Year Founded: 2000
Current Activity Level : Actively seeking new investments

UBS GLOBAL ASSET MANAGEMENT (CHINA) LTD

#7 Financial Street, Unit 306
Winland International Center
Beijing, China 100033
Phone: 861058369362
Website: www.ubs.com

Type of Firm
Investment Management Firm

Project Preferences

Type of Financing Preferred:
Balanced

Geographical Preferences

International Preferences:
China

Additional Information
Year Founded: 2011
Current Activity Level : Actively seeking new investments

UC CAPITAL

Avenida Diagonal 535
4th flr 1a
Barcelona, Spain 08029
Phone: 34931890009
Website: www.uc-cap.com

Type of Firm
Private Equity Firm

Geographical Preferences

International Preferences:
Europe

Industry Preferences

In Medical/Health prefer:
Health Services

In Industrial/Energy prefer:
Advanced Materials
Machinery

In Transportation prefer:
Transportation

Additional Information
Year Founded: 2016
Current Activity Level : Actively seeking new investments

UFENAU CAPITAL PARTNERS AG

Huobstrasse 3
Pfaeffikon Schwyz, Switzerland 8808
Phone: 41444826666
Fax: 41444826663
E-mail: info@ucp.ch
Website: www.ucp.ch

Other Offices
2-8 Avenue Charles de Gaulle
Luxembourg, Luxembourg 1653

Type of Firm
Private Equity Firm

Additional Information
Year Founded: 2015
Capital Under Management: $254,480,000
Current Activity Level : Actively seeking new investments

UK INFRASTRUKTURNYE INVESTITSII AO

Shabolovka 23
Office 39
Moscow, Russia 119049
Phone: 74956484708
Fax: 74956484708
E-mail: Info@infra-invest.ru
Website: www.infra-invest.ru

Type of Firm
Investment Management Firm

Association Membership
Russian Venture Capital Association (RVCA)

Project Preferences

Type of Financing Preferred:
Early Stage
Expansion

Geographical Preferences

International Preferences:
Russia

Industry Preferences

In Biotechnology prefer:
Industrial Biotechnology

Additional Information
Year Founded: 2004
Current Activity Level : Actively seeking new investments

UK RFPI OOO

Presnenskaia Naberezhnaia, 8/1
MFK Iuzhnaia stolitsa, Fl. 7-8
Moscow, Russia 123112
Phone: 74956443414
Fax: 74956443413

Management and Staff
Kirill Dmitriev, Chief Executive Officer

Type of Firm
Bank Affiliated

Project Preferences

Type of Financing Preferred:
Generalist PE

Size of Investments Considered:
Min Size of Investment Considered (000s): $50,000
Max Size of Investment Considered (000s): $500,000

Geographical Preferences

International Preferences:
Europe
China
Asia
Russia

Industry Preferences

In Communications prefer:
Telecommunications

In Medical/Health prefer:
Medical/Health

In Consumer Related prefer:
Food/Beverage

In Industrial/Energy prefer:
Energy
Alternative Energy
Industrial Products
Materials

In Transportation prefer:
Transportation

In Agr/Forestr/Fish prefer:
Agribusiness
Mining and Minerals

Additional Information
Name of Most Recent Fund: RDIF - Mubadala co-investment Fund
Most Recent Fund Was Raised: 06/20/2013
Year Founded: 2011
Capital Under Management: $12,000,000,000
Current Activity Level : Actively seeking new investments

UK RWM KAPITAL ZAO

Zamlyanoy Val 9
Moscow, Russia 105064
Phone: 74956607030
Fax: 74956607032
E-mail: info@rwmcapital.ru
Website: www.rwmcapital.ru

Type of Firm
Private Equity Firm

Association Membership
European Private Equity and Venture Capital Assoc.

Project Preferences

Type of Financing Preferred:
Fund of Funds
Leveraged Buyout
Early Stage
Seed
Acquisition

Geographical Preferences

International Preferences:
Russia

Industry Preferences

In Transportation prefer:
Transportation

In Financial Services prefer:
Financial Services
Insurance

In Agr/Forestr/Fish prefer:
Mining and Minerals

Additional Information
Year Founded: 2005
Current Activity Level : Actively seeking new investments

UK SGKM OOO

B. Savvinsky Per., 11
Moscow, Russia 119435
Phone: 74956627020
Fax: 74957835627
E-mail: info@sgcm.ru
Website: www.sgcm.ru

Management and Staff
Aidar Gabidoullin, Partner
Maxim Shemetov, Vice President
Vladimir Yakushev, Managing Partner

Type of Firm
Private Equity Firm

Project Preferences

Type of Financing Preferred:
Early Stage
Generalist PE
Seed
Startup

Geographical Preferences

International Preferences:
Russia

Industry Preferences

In Semiconductor/Electr prefer:
Laser Related

In Biotechnology prefer:
Biotechnology

In Consumer Related prefer:
Entertainment and Leisure
Consumer Products

In Industrial/Energy prefer:
Alternative Energy
Advanced Materials
Environmental Related

In Financial Services prefer:
Financial Services

Additional Information
Year Founded: 2007
Current Activity Level : Actively seeking new investments

ULTIMATE SPORTS GROUP PLC

Seven Paddington Street, Suite Three
London, United Kingdom W1U 5QQ
Phone: 442079350823
Fax: 442079350843
E-mail: info@westsideacquisitions.com
Website: www.ultimatesportsgroup.me

Type of Firm
Private Equity Firm

Project Preferences

Type of Financing Preferred:
Leveraged Buyout
Acquisition

Industry Preferences

In Consumer Related prefer:
Sports

Additional Information
Year Founded: 1999
Current Activity Level : Actively seeking new investments

ULU VENTURES

600 Hansen Way
Palo Alto, CA USA 94304
Phone: 6508438766
E-mail: info@uluventures.com

Management and Staff
Clinton Korver, Co-Founder
Miriam Rivera, Managing Partner

Type of Firm
Corporate PE/Venture

Project Preferences

Type of Financing Preferred:
Early Stage

Size of Investments Considered:
Min Size of Investment Considered (000s): $500
Max Size of Investment Considered (000s): $1,000

Geographical Preferences

United States Preferences:

Industry Preferences

In Communications prefer:
Communications and Media

In Internet Specific prefer:
Internet

In Consumer Related prefer:
Consumer Services

In Business Serv. prefer:
Media

Additional Information
Year Founded: 2010
Capital Under Management: $22,000,000
Current Activity Level : Actively seeking new investments

ULYSSES MANAGEMENT LLC

One Rockefeller Plaza
20th Floor
New York, NY USA 10020
Phone: 2124556237
Fax: 2124556281
E-mail: info@ulyss.com
Website: www.ulyssesmgmt.com

Type of Firm
Private Equity Firm

Project Preferences

Type of Financing Preferred:
Leveraged Buyout
Management Buyouts
Acquisition
Distressed Debt
Recapitalizations

Geographical Preferences

United States Preferences:

International Preferences:
Europe

Additional Information
Year Founded: 1969
Current Activity Level : Actively seeking new investments

UM ACCELMED LP

6 Hachoshlim Street
6 Floor
Herzliya Pituach, Israel 46120
Phone: 97297885599
Fax: 97299588594
Website: www.accelmed.co.il

Management and Staff
Uri Geiger, Managing Partner

Type of Firm
Private Equity Firm

Project Preferences

Type of Financing Preferred:
Early Stage
Balanced

Geographical Preferences

International Preferences:
Israel
Asia

Industry Preferences

In Medical/Health prefer:
Medical/Health
Drug/Equipmt Delivery
Medical Products

Additional Information
Year Founded: 2012
Capital Under Management: $115,400,000
Current Activity Level : Actively seeking new investments

UMC CAPITAL CORP

P.O. Box 1034GT
Grand Cayman, Cayman Islands

Other Offices
No. 338, West, Nanjing Road, Suite 2604, Tian An Center
Shanghai, China 200003
Phone: 862163580505
Fax: 862163586798

Type of Firm
Corporate PE/Venture

Project Preferences

Type of Financing Preferred:
Balanced
Later Stage

Geographical Preferences

International Preferences:
All International

Additional Information
Year Founded: 2001
Current Activity Level : Actively seeking new investments

UNC KENAN-FLAGLER PRIVATE EQUITY FUND

The Kenan Center
Campus Box 3440
Chapel Hill, NC USA 27599
Phone: 9198435482
Fax: 9198439178
E-mail: contact@kfpefund.com
Website: www.kfpefund.com

Management and Staff
Geordy Johnson, Managing Director
George Vincent, Managing Director
Jeff Bicksler, CEO & Managing Director
Sagar Rathie, Managing Director

Type of Firm
University Program

Project Preferences

Type of Financing Preferred:
Leveraged Buyout
Early Stage
Expansion
Mezzanine
Generalist PE
Later Stage

Geographical Preferences

United States Preferences:

Industry Preferences

In Consumer Related prefer:
Education Related

Additional Information
Year Founded: 2007
Capital Under Management: $5,000,000
Current Activity Level : Actively seeking new investments

UNCORK CAPITAL

4 Palo Alto Square
Second Floor
Palo Alto, CA USA 94306
Phone: 6506881801
Fax: 6504753937
Website: uncorkcapital.com

Management and Staff
Andy McLoughlin, Partner
Charles Hudson, Venture Partner
Stephanie Palmeri, Partner

Type of Firm
Private Equity Firm

Association Membership
National Venture Capital Association - USA (NVCA)

Project Preferences

Role in Financing:
Will function either as deal originator or investor in deals created by others

Type of Financing Preferred:
Early Stage
Seed
Startup

Size of Investments Considered:
Min Size of Investment Considered (000s): $250
Max Size of Investment Considered (000s): $750

Geographical Preferences

United States Preferences:
California
New York

Canadian Preferences:
Ontario

Industry Preferences

In Computer Software prefer:
Applications Software

In Internet Specific prefer:
Internet
Ecommerce
Web Aggregration/Portals

Additional Information
Name of Most Recent Fund: SoftTech VC III, L.P.
Most Recent Fund Was Raised: 01/05/2011
Year Founded: 2004
Capital Under Management: $302,000,000
Current Activity Level : Actively seeking new investments

UNDERDOG VENTURES LLC

23 Route 105
East Brighton Road
Island Pond, VT USA 05846
Phone: 8027239909
Fax: 8027239933
E-mail: info@underdogventures.com
Website: www.underdogventures.com

Management and Staff
David Berge, President

Type of Firm
Private Equity Firm

Project Preferences

Type of Financing Preferred:
Early Stage
Expansion
Balanced
Later Stage

Size of Investments Considered:
Min Size of Investment Considered (000s): $500
Max Size of Investment Considered (000s): $1,000

Geographical Preferences

United States Preferences:

Canadian Preferences:
All Canada

Industry Preferences

In Consumer Related prefer:
Food/Beverage
Consumer Products

In Industrial/Energy prefer:
Environmental Related

In Other prefer:
Women/Minority-Owned Bus.

Additional Information
Year Founded: 2001
Capital Under Management: $5,500,000
Current Activity Level : Actively seeking new investments

UNDERSCORE.VC

53 State Street
Tenth Floor
Boston, MA USA 02109
Phone: 6173030064
Website: underscore.vc

Type of Firm
Private Equity Firm

Project Preferences

Type of Financing Preferred:
Early Stage
Expansion
Later Stage
Seed

Additional Information
Year Founded: 2015
Capital Under Management: $95,000,000
Current Activity Level : Actively seeking new investments

UNEXO SAS

7 bis bd de la Tour d'Auvergne
C.S. 86505
Rennes Cedex, France 35065
Phone: 33299672014
Fax: 33299670226
E-mail: contact@ueo.fr
Website: www.unexo.fr

Type of Firm
Private Equity Firm

Association Membership
French Venture Capital Association (AFIC)

Project Preferences

Type of Financing Preferred:
Leveraged Buyout
Generalist PE
Later Stage
Management Buyouts
Acquisition

Size of Investments Considered:
Min Size of Investment Considered (000s): $193
Max Size of Investment Considered (000s): $7,731

Geographical Preferences

International Preferences:
France

Additional Information
Year Founded: 1993
Current Activity Level : Actively seeking new investments

UNI VENTURE CAPITAL CO LTD

832-21,Yeoksam-dong,Gangnam-gu
10/F, Taeyang 21 Building
Seoul, South Korea 135080
Phone: 8225670369
Fax: 8225672346
E-mail: info@univc.co.kr
Website: www.univc.co.kr

Management and Staff
Dong Hwan Cho, Chief Executive Officer
Won Bae Lee, Managing Director

Type of Firm
Private Equity Firm

Association Membership
Korean Venture Capital Association (KVCA)

Project Preferences

Type of Financing Preferred:
Balanced
Startup

Geographical Preferences

International Preferences:
Korea, South

Industry Preferences

In Agr/Forestr/Fish prefer:
Agribusiness

Additional Information
Year Founded: 2010
Capital Under Management: $20,486,000
Current Activity Level : Actively seeking new investments

UNI-QUANTUM FUND MANAGEMENT CO LTD

No.77, Jianguo Avenue Chaoyang
Rm906 Twr3 China Central Place
Beijing, China 100025
Phone: 861059696069
Fax: 861059696068
Website: uniquantum.com

Management and Staff
Ercel Baker, Managing Director
Fan Chen, Chairman & CEO
Mingchen Zhou, Managing Director
Xiaoming Lai, Chief Operating Officer

Type of Firm
Private Equity Firm

Project Preferences

Type of Financing Preferred:
Expansion

Geographical Preferences

International Preferences:
China

Industry Preferences

In Medical/Health prefer:
Medical/Health

In Consumer Related prefer:
Consumer Products
Consumer Services
Education Related

In Industrial/Energy prefer:
Energy
Energy Conservation Relat
Materials
Environmental Related

In Financial Services prefer:
Financial Services

Additional Information
Year Founded: 2011
Capital Under Management: $151,745,000
Current Activity Level : Actively seeking new investments

UNICORN CAPITAL ADVISERS GMBH

Schottengasse 1
Wien, Austria 1010
Phone: 4315229476
Website: www.unicorncapital.at

Type of Firm
Private Equity Firm

Project Preferences

Type of Financing Preferred:
Leveraged Buyout
Turnaround
Recapitalizations

Geographical Preferences

International Preferences:
Armenia
Belarus
Kazakhstan
Europe
Kyrgyzstan
Tajikistan
Azerbaijan
Moldova
Uzbekistan
Russia

Industry Preferences

In Industrial/Energy prefer:
Energy
Oil and Gas Exploration
Industrial Products
Materials
Machinery

In Business Serv. prefer:
Distribution

In Utilities prefer:
Utilities

Additional Information
Name of Most Recent Fund: Unicorn Capital Partners
Most Recent Fund Was Raised: 05/20/2013
Year Founded: 2013
Capital Under Management: $100,000,000
Current Activity Level : Actively seeking new investments

UNICORN INDIA VENTURES ADVISORS LLP

302. Jhalawar Service Premise
Patanwala Estate
Mumbai, India
E-mail: info@unicornvc.com
Website: www.unicornvc.com

Management and Staff
Aayush Jain, Co-Founder
Anil Joshi, Co-Founder
Bhaskar Majumdar, Co-Founder
Manoj Laddha, Partner
Mitesh Majithia, Venture Partner
Vinay Ambardekar, Chief Financial Officer

Type of Firm
Private Equity Firm

Project Preferences

Type of Financing Preferred:
Early Stage

Industry Preferences

In Communications prefer:
Telecommunications
Media and Entertainment

In Computer Software prefer:
Software

Additional Information
Year Founded: 2015
Capital Under Management: $98,170,000
Current Activity Level : Actively seeking new investments

UNICREDIT SPA

Via Specchi 16
Rome, Italy 00186
Phone: 39-45-808-1140
Fax: 39-45-867-9769
Website: www.unicreditgroup.eu

Management and Staff
Ranieri de Marchis, Chief Operating Officer

Type of Firm
Bank Affiliated

Additional Information
Year Founded: 2004
Current Activity Level : Actively seeking new investments

UNICREDIT START LAB

Piazza Gae Aulenti 3
Tower A
Milan, Italy 20154
E-mail: unicreditstartlab@unicredit.eu
Website: www.unicreditstartlab.eu

Type of Firm
Incubator/Development Program

Project Preferences

Type of Financing Preferred:
Seed
Startup

Geographical Preferences

International Preferences:
Italy

Industry Preferences

In Biotechnology prefer:
Biotechnology

In Medical/Health prefer:
Medical/Health
Health Services

In Consumer Related prefer:
Consumer Products

In Industrial/Energy prefer:
Alternative Energy
Energy Conservation Relat

Additional Information
Year Founded: 2009

Current Activity Level : Actively seeking new investments

UNIFIED GROWTH PARTNERS L P

Two Greenwich Office Park
Greenwich, CT USA 06831
Phone: 203-422-0650
Fax: 203-422-0650
E-mail: info@unifiedgrowth.com
Website: www.unifiedgrowth.com

Type of Firm
Private Equity Firm

Geographical Preferences

United States Preferences:

Canadian Preferences:
All Canada

Industry Preferences

In Consumer Related prefer:
Consumer Services

In Business Serv. prefer:
Services

Additional Information
Name of Most Recent Fund: Unified Growth Partners, L.P.
Most Recent Fund Was Raised: 01/05/2007
Year Founded: 2005
Current Activity Level : Actively seeking new investments

UNIGESTION HOLDING SA

Avenue de Champel 8C
Geneva, Switzerland 1206
Phone: 41227044111
Fax: 41227044211
E-mail: info@unigestion.com
Website: www.unigestion.com

Other Offices
105 Piccadilly
London, United Kingdom W1J 7NJ
Phone: 44-207-529-4150

Plaza 10 Harborside Financial Center, Suite 203
Jersey City, NJ USA 07311
Phone: 201-714-2400

12 Avenue Matignon
Paris, France 75008
Phone: 33-14-359-7373

152 Beach Road, Suite #23-05/06
The Gateway East
Singapore, Singapore 189721
Phone: 65-64-96-0200

2189

Farnley House, La Charroterie
St. Peter Port
Guernsey, Channel Islands GY1 1EJ
Phone: 44-1481-812-600

Management and Staff
Annette Voss, Chief Operating Officer
Anthony Payot, Vice President
Fiona Frick, Managing Director
Hanspeter Bader, Managing Director
Jean-Francois Hirschel, Managing Director
Patrick Fenal, Chief Executive Officer
Philippe Gougenheim, Managing Director
Regis Martin, Chief Financial Officer
Robbin Maggi, Chief Operating Officer

Type of Firm
Private Equity Advisor or Fund of Funds

Association Membership
Swiss Venture Capital Association (SECA)
European Private Equity and Venture Capital Assoc.

Project Preferences

Type of Financing Preferred:
Fund of Funds
Fund of Funds of Second

Geographical Preferences

United States Preferences:
All U.S.

International Preferences:
Latin America
Europe
Switzerland
Western Europe
Asia
Japan

Industry Preferences

In Industrial/Energy prefer:
Alternative Energy
Environmental Related

In Other prefer:
Environment Responsible

Additional Information
Year Founded: 1971
Capital Under Management: $11,732,200,000
Current Activity Level : Actively seeking new investments

UNIGRAINS DIVERSIFICATION SA

23 avenue de Neuilly
Paris, France 75116
Phone: 33144311000
Fax: 33144311087
E-mail: contact@unigrains.fr
Website: www.unigrains.fr

Type of Firm
Private Equity Firm

Association Membership
French Venture Capital Association (AFIC)

Project Preferences

Type of Financing Preferred:
Leveraged Buyout
Mezzanine
Generalist PE
Turnaround
Later Stage
Acquisition

Size of Investments Considered:
Min Size of Investment Considered (000s): $644
Max Size of Investment Considered (000s): $64,433

Geographical Preferences

International Preferences:
Europe
France

Industry Preferences

In Biotechnology prefer:
Agricultural/Animal Bio.
Industrial Biotechnology
Biotech Related Research

In Agr/Forestr/Fish prefer:
Agriculture related

Additional Information
Year Founded: 1964
Current Activity Level : Actively seeking new investments

UNILAZER VENTURES PVT LTD

Solitaire Corporate Park, 7F
Bldg 5, Andheri Kurla Road
Andheri (East), Mumbai, India 400093
Phone: 912240983730
Fax: 912240983722
E-mail: investments@unilazer.com

Management and Staff
Amit Banka, Managing Director
Chetan Juthani, Chief Financial Officer
Ronnie Screwvala, Founder

Type of Firm
Private Equity Firm

Project Preferences

Type of Financing Preferred:
Early Stage
Expansion
Balanced
Later Stage
Seed

Geographical Preferences

International Preferences:
India

Industry Preferences

In Biotechnology prefer:
Biotechnology

In Medical/Health prefer:
Medical/Health
Health Services

In Consumer Related prefer:
Consumer Services
Education Related

In Financial Services prefer:
Financial Services

In Agr/Forestr/Fish prefer:
Agriculture related

Additional Information
Year Founded: 1991
Current Activity Level : Actively seeking new investments

UNILEVER VENTURES LTD

16 Charles Two Street
First Floor
London, United Kingdom SW1Y 4QU
Phone: 442073216199
Fax: 442073216198
Website: www.unileverventures.com

Other Offices
Unilever Technology Ventures Advisory Co
812 Anacapa Street, Suite A
Santa Barbara, CA USA 93101
Phone: 805-963-0250
Fax: 805-963-0270

Management and Staff
John Coombs, Managing Director
Stephen Willson, Principal

Type of Firm
Corporate PE/Venture

Project Preferences

Type of Financing Preferred:
Fund of Funds
Leveraged Buyout
Early Stage
Expansion
Seed
Management Buyouts
Startup

Size of Investments Considered:
Min Size of Investment Considered (000s): $698
Max Size of Investment Considered (000s): $13,955

Geographical Preferences

United States Preferences:

International Preferences:
India
Europe

Industry Preferences

In Biotechnology prefer:
Biotechnology
Genetic Engineering

In Medical/Health prefer:
Health Services

In Consumer Related prefer:
Entertainment and Leisure
Consumer Products
Consumer Services

In Industrial/Energy prefer:
Materials

In Business Serv. prefer:
Media

Additional Information
Year Founded: 2002
Current Activity Level : Actively seeking new investments

UNION BANCAIRE PRIVEE PRIVATE EQUITY

26 St. James's Square
London, United Kingdom SW1Y 4JH
Phone: 44-20-7663-1525
Fax: 44-20-7369-0461
Website: www.ubp.ch

Other Offices

30 Rockefeller Center, Suite 2800
New York, NY USA 10112
Phone: 212-218-6750
Fax: 212-218-6755

Emarut Atrium, Office 252
Sheikh Zayed Road
Dubai, Utd. Arab Em.
Phone: 97-14-343-2277
Fax: 97-14-343-9164

96-98, rue du Rhone
Switzerland, Switzerland CH-1204
Phone: 41-22-819-2111
Fax: 41-22-819-2200

Management and Staff
Kathleen Cira, Partner
Morten Thorsen, Partner
Vincenzo Narciso, Chief Executive Officer

Type of Firm
Bank Affiliated

Project Preferences

Type of Financing Preferred:
Fund of Funds

Geographical Preferences

International Preferences:
Europe

Additional Information
Year Founded: 2007
Current Activity Level : Actively seeking new investments

UNION BAY CAPITAL

1910 Fairview Avenue East, Suite 500
Seattle, WA USA 98102
Phone: 2067289063
E-mail: info@unionbaycapital.com
Website: www.unionbaycapital.com

Type of Firm
Private Equity Firm

Project Preferences

Type of Financing Preferred:
Later Stage

Additional Information
Name of Most Recent Fund: Union Bay Capital Partners I LLC
Most Recent Fund Was Raised: 12/19/2012
Year Founded: 2012
Capital Under Management: $88,500,000
Current Activity Level : Actively seeking new investments

UNION GROUP (UK) LLP

15 Berkeley Street
London, United Kingdom W1J 8DY
Phone: 442036030530
Website: www.uniongrp.com

Other Offices

Plaza Independencia 737
Montevideo
, Uruguay 11000
Phone: 59829000000

Avenue Del Pinar 180
Chacarilla
Surco, Lima, Peru 033
Phone: 5112002650

Management and Staff
Francisco Roque De Pinho, Chief Executive Officer

Type of Firm
Investment Management Firm

Project Preferences

Type of Financing Preferred:
Balanced

Geographical Preferences

International Preferences:
Uruguay
Latin America
Peru
Colombia
Africa

Industry Preferences

In Industrial/Energy prefer:
Energy
Oil and Gas Exploration
Environmental Related

In Financial Services prefer:
Real Estate

In Agr/Forestr/Fish prefer:
Agribusiness
Agriculture related

In Other prefer:
Environment Responsible

Additional Information
Year Founded: 2011
Capital Under Management: $25,000,000
Current Activity Level : Actively seeking new investments

UNION GROVE VENTURE PARTNERS 2014 LLC

301 West Barbee Chapel Road, Suite 200
Chapel Hill, NC USA 27517
Phone: 9198698080
Fax: 8664805880

Management and Staff
Greg Bohlen, Co-Founder
John Spilman, Co-Founder

Type of Firm
Private Equity Firm

Project Preferences

Type of Financing Preferred:
Fund of Funds
Expansion
Later Stage

Additional Information
Year Founded: 2014
Capital Under Management: $153,500,000
Current Activity Level : Actively seeking new investments

UNION INVESTMENT PARTNERS

23-3, Yeouido-Dong, Yeongdeung
Hana Securities Bldg. 10/F
Seoul, South Korea 137-069
Phone: 822-594-8470
Fax: 822-594-8471

Management and Staff
Hyung Tae Park, President

Type of Firm
Investment Management Firm

Project Preferences

Type of Financing Preferred:
Balanced

Geographical Preferences

International Preferences:
Korea, South

Industry Preferences

In Communications prefer:
Media and Entertainment
Entertainment

Additional Information
Year Founded: 2000
Capital Under Management: $79,300,000
Current Activity Level : Actively seeking new investments

UNION PARK CAPITAL

200 Newbury Street
Boston, MA USA 02116
Website: www.union-park.com

Type of Firm
Private Equity Firm

Project Preferences

Type of Financing Preferred:
Leveraged Buyout
Expansion
Management Buyouts
Acquisition
Recapitalizations

Geographical Preferences

United States Preferences:
North America

International Preferences:
Europe

Industry Preferences

In Communications prefer:
Communications and Media

In Industrial/Energy prefer:
Energy
Oil and Gas Exploration
Industrial Products
Materials
Environmental Related

In Transportation prefer:
Aerospace

In Manufact. prefer:
Manufacturing

In Utilities prefer:
Utilities

Additional Information
Year Founded: 2013
Capital Under Management: $102,000,000
Current Activity Level : Actively seeking new investments

UNION SQUARE VENTURES LLC

915 Broadway
19th Floor
New York, NY USA 10010
Phone: 2129947880
Fax: 2129947399
E-mail: info@unionsquareventures.com
Website: www.usv.com

Management and Staff
Albert Wenger, Partner
Andrew Weissman, Partner
Fred Wilson, Managing Partner
John Buttrick, Partner
R. Bradford Burnham, Managing Partner
Rebecca Kade, General Partner

Type of Firm
Private Equity Firm

Project Preferences

Role in Financing:
Prefer role as deal originator

Type of Financing Preferred:
Early Stage
Expansion
Balanced
Later Stage

Size of Investments Considered:
Min Size of Investment Considered (000s): $250
Max Size of Investment Considered (000s): $25,000

Geographical Preferences

United States Preferences:
California
New York

International Preferences:
United Kingdom
Europe

Industry Preferences

In Internet Specific prefer:
Internet

In Computer Other prefer:
Computer Related

Additional Information
Name of Most Recent Fund: USV 2014, L.P.
Most Recent Fund Was Raised: 01/24/2014
Year Founded: 2003
Capital Under Management: $450,000,000
Current Activity Level : Actively seeking new investments

UNION TECH VENTURES LTD

67 Yigal Alon
Tel Aviv, Israel 67443
Phone: 972747155544
E-mail: info@uniontech.co.il
Website: uniontech.co.il

Type of Firm
Private Equity Firm

Project Preferences

Type of Financing Preferred:
Early Stage
Expansion
Later Stage
Seed
Startup

Geographical Preferences

International Preferences:
Israel

Industry Preferences

In Communications prefer:
Telecommunications

In Computer Software prefer:
Software

Additional Information
Year Founded: 2017
Current Activity Level : Actively seeking new investments

UNIPOL MERCHANT BANCA PER LE IMPRESE SPA

Piazza della Costituzione 2, 2
Bologna, Italy 40128
Phone: 39516318211
Fax: 39516318229
E-mail: info@unipolmerchant.it
Website: www.unipolmerchant.it

Management and Staff
Ivan Soncini, Vice President
Luciano Colombini, Vice President
Sergio Tiscali, President

Type of Firm
Investment Management Firm

Association Membership
Italian Venture Capital Association (AIFI)

Project Preferences

Type of Financing Preferred:
Leveraged Buyout
Later Stage
Management Buyouts

Geographical Preferences

International Preferences:
Italy
Europe

Industry Preferences

In Industrial/Energy prefer:
Industrial Products

In Financial Services prefer:
Financial Services

In Business Serv. prefer:
Services

Additional Information
Year Founded: 2003
Current Activity Level : Actively seeking new investments

UNIQUE CAPITAL GROUP AG

Blegistrasse 5
Baar, Switzerland 6340
Phone: 4113502811
Fax: 4113502813
E-mail: info@ucg-ag.ch
Website: www.ucg-ag.ch

Management and Staff
Claudio Luchetti, Managing Partner

Type of Firm
Private Equity Firm

Project Preferences

Type of Financing Preferred:
Early Stage
Expansion
Later Stage

Size of Investments Considered:
Min Size of Investment Considered (000s): $133
Max Size of Investment Considered (000s): $26,529

Geographical Preferences

United States Preferences:

International Preferences:
Europe

Industry Preferences

In Communications prefer:
Communications and Media
Wireless Communications

In Internet Specific prefer:
Internet
Ecommerce

In Medical/Health prefer:
Health Services

Additional Information
Year Founded: 2001
Current Activity Level : Actively seeking new investments

UNIQUE VENTURE CAPITAL MANAGEMENT COMPANY LTD

40 Marina
5th Floor, Old Union Bank Bldg
Lagos, Nigeria
Phone: 23418912071
E-mail: info@uvcmc.com
Website: www.uvcmc.com

Management and Staff
Anthony Oboh, CEO & Managing Director

Type of Firm
Private Equity Firm

Association Membership
African Venture Capital Association (AVCA)

Project Preferences

Type of Financing Preferred:
Early Stage
Expansion
Seed

Size of Investments Considered:
Min Size of Investment Considered (000s): $100
Max Size of Investment Considered (000s): $500

Geographical Preferences

International Preferences:
Liberia
Nigeria
Sierra Leone
Africa

Industry Preferences

In Consumer Related prefer:
Food/Beverage
Consumer Services

In Business Serv. prefer:
Services

Additional Information
Year Founded: 2004
Current Activity Level : Actively seeking new investments

UNISEED MANAGEMENT PTY LTD

Staff House Road
Level Seven, GP South Building
St Lucia, Australia 4072
Phone: 61733656937
Fax: 61733654433
E-mail: enquiries@uniseed.com
Website: www.uniseed.com

Other Offices
New South Innovations
Rupert Myers Building, UNSW
Sydney, Australia 2052
Phone: 612-9385-6525
Fax: 612-9385-6600

205-211 Grattan Street
Parkville, Australia 3053
Phone: 613-8344-3193
Fax: 613-9347-5888

Management and Staff
Peter Devine, Chief Executive Officer
Richard Symons, Chief Financial Officer

Type of Firm
University Program

Project Preferences

Type of Financing Preferred:
Early Stage
Seed

Size of Investments Considered:
Min Size of Investment Considered (000s): $50
Max Size of Investment Considered (000s): $500

Geographical Preferences

International Preferences:
Pacific

Pratt's Guide to Private Equity & Venture Capital Sources

Industry Preferences

In Biotechnology prefer:
Biotechnology
Biotech Related Research

In Medical/Health prefer:
Medical/Health

In Manufact. prefer:
Manufacturing

Additional Information
Year Founded: 2000
Capital Under Management: $61,000,000
Current Activity Level: Actively seeking new investments

UNISON CAPITAL, INC.

4-1, Kioicho, Chiyoda-ku
9F, The New Otani Garden Court
Tokyo, Japan 102-0094
Phone: 81335113901
Fax: 81335113981
Website: www.unisoncap.com

Management and Staff
Hitoshi Yamaguchi, Partner
Kiyoto Matsuda, Partner
Koichi Tateno, Partner
Nobuyoshi Ehara, Co-Founder
Osamu Yamamoto, Partner
Soomin Kim, Partner
Tatsuo Kawasaki, Co-Founder
Tatsuya Hayashi, Co-Founder
Teppei Kono, Partner

Type of Firm
Private Equity Firm

Project Preferences

Type of Financing Preferred:
Leveraged Buyout
Management Buyouts
Acquisition

Geographical Preferences

International Preferences:
Japan

Industry Focus
(% based on actual investment)
Other Products	42.9%
Consumer Related	41.9%
Semiconductors/Other Elect.	15.2%

Additional Information
Year Founded: 1998
Capital Under Management: $2,761,000,000
Current Activity Level: Actively seeking new investments

UNISUN BEIJING INVESTMENT CO LTD

30th Floor Nexus Center, #19A
East 3rd Ring Road North
Beijing, China 100020
Phone: 86-10-5933-0010
Fax: 86-10-5933-0917
E-mail: unisun@unisun.com.cn
Website: www.unisun.com.cn

Management and Staff
Amy Liang, Co-Founder
Brian Yuan, Co-Founder
Hailin Jiang, Co-Founder
James Liao, Chief Executive Officer

Type of Firm
Private Equity Firm

Project Preferences

Type of Financing Preferred:
Leveraged Buyout
Acquisition

Geographical Preferences

International Preferences:
All International

Additional Information
Year Founded: 2002
Current Activity Level: Actively seeking new investments

UNITED CAPITAL PARTNERS ADVISORY OOO

Two Paveletskaya Square
Building 2, Paveletskaya Plaza
Moscow, Russia 115054
Phone: 74956431100
Fax: 74956431300
E-mail: info@ucpfund.com
Website: ucpfund.com

Management and Staff
Alexander Shmelev, Partner
Mikhail Trofimov, Partner
Victoria Lazareva, Managing Partner
Yuri Kachuro, Partner

Type of Firm
Investment Management Firm

Project Preferences

Type of Financing Preferred:
Leveraged Buyout
Generalist PE
Public Companies

Geographical Preferences

International Preferences:
Europe
Russia

Industry Preferences

In Communications prefer:
Telecommunications
Entertainment

In Biotechnology prefer:
Agricultural/Animal Bio.

In Consumer Related prefer:
Retail
Consumer Products

In Industrial/Energy prefer:
Oil and Gas Exploration

In Financial Services prefer:
Financial Services
Real Estate

In Business Serv. prefer:
Services

In Manufact. prefer:
Manufacturing

In Agr/Forestr/Fish prefer:
Agriculture related

Additional Information
Year Founded: 2006
Capital Under Management: $297,297,000
Current Activity Level: Actively seeking new investments

UNITED FINANCIAL GROUP ASSET MANAGEMENT

Tsvetnoi blvd, 2
Moscow, Russia 107031
Phone: 7-4956623030
Fax: 7-4957211210
E-mail: ufgam@ufgam.com
Website: www.ufgam.com

Other Offices
55 Market Street, Suite 209
Ipswich, MA USA 01938
Phone: 19783562256
Fax: 19783562251

Management and Staff
Dimitri Elkin, Managing Director
Dmitry Khilov, Managing Director
Dominic Reed, Managing Director
Florian Fenner, Managing Partner
Mikhail Tarasov, Managing Director

Type of Firm
Bank Affiliated

Geographical Preferences

International Preferences:
Belarus

Industry Preferences

In Communications prefer:
Communications and Media
Telecommunications

In Consumer Related prefer:
Retail

In Industrial/Energy prefer:
Energy
Materials

In Transportation prefer:
Transportation

In Financial Services prefer:
Financial Services
Insurance
Financial Services

In Business Serv. prefer:
Services
Media

In Agr/Forestr/Fish prefer:
Mining and Minerals

Additional Information

Year Founded: 1996
Capital Under Management: $2,300,000,000
Current Activity Level : Actively seeking new investments

UNITED GULF BANK SECURITIES CO. B.S.C

P.O. Box 5964, Diplomatic Area
UGB Tower
Manama, Bahrain
Phone: 97317533233
Fax: 97317533137
E-mail: info@ugbbah.com
Website: www.ugbbh.com

Management and Staff

Hussain Lalani, Chief Financial Officer
Rabih Soukarieh, Chief Executive Officer

Type of Firm

Private Equity Firm

Project Preferences

Type of Financing Preferred:
Leveraged Buyout
Early Stage
Generalist PE
Later Stage

Industry Preferences

In Communications prefer:
Telecommunications

In Industrial/Energy prefer:
Energy

In Business Serv. prefer:
Media

Additional Information

Year Founded: 1980
Current Activity Level : Actively seeking new investments

UNITED INC

3-3-11 Kitaaoyama, Minatoku
RENAI AOYAMA Bldg 6F
Tokyo, Japan 107-0061
Phone: 81368210000
Fax: 81357700557
E-mail: int-member@motionbeat.com
Website: united.jp

Type of Firm

Corporate PE/Venture

Project Preferences

Type of Financing Preferred:
Balanced

Geographical Preferences

International Preferences:
Asia

Industry Preferences

In Internet Specific prefer:
Internet

Additional Information

Year Founded: 1998
Current Activity Level : Actively seeking new investments

UNITED STATES GROWTH FUNDS

201 Main Street
1310 City Center
Fort Worth, TX USA 76102
Phone: 8173381310
Fax: 8173381318
Website: www.usgf.com

Management and Staff

Robert McGee, Managing Partner

Type of Firm

Private Equity Firm

Project Preferences

Role in Financing:
Prefer role as deal originator but will also invest in deals created by others

Type of Financing Preferred:
Leveraged Buyout
Management Buyouts
Acquisition
Special Situation
Distressed Debt
Recapitalizations

Geographical Preferences

United States Preferences:
All U.S.

Industry Preferences

In Consumer Related prefer:
Entertainment and Leisure
Food/Beverage
Consumer Products

In Financial Services prefer:
Financial Services

In Business Serv. prefer:
Services

Additional Information

Year Founded: 1992
Capital Under Management: $150,000,000
Current Activity Level : Actively seeking new investments
Method of Compensation: Return on invest. most important, but chg. closing fees, service fees, etc.

UNITED TALENT AGENCY LLC

9336 Civic Center Drive
Beverly Hills, CA USA 90210
Phone: 13102736700
Fax: 13102471111
E-mail: ventures@unitedtalent.com
Website: unitedtalent.com

Type of Firm

Private Equity Firm

Project Preferences

Type of Financing Preferred:
Early Stage
Startup

Additional Information

Year Founded: 2017
Current Activity Level : Actively seeking new investments

UNITED VENTURES SRL

Via Chiossetto 7
Milan, Italy 20122
Phone: 390287284050
Fax: 390287284050
Website: www.unitedventures.it

Type of Firm
Private Equity Firm

Association Membership
Italian Venture Capital Association (AIFI)

Project Preferences

Type of Financing Preferred:
Early Stage
Expansion
Later Stage
Seed
Startup

Geographical Preferences

International Preferences:
Italy

Industry Preferences

In Communications prefer:
Wireless Communications

In Computer Software prefer:
Software

Additional Information
Year Founded: 2009
Current Activity Level : Actively seeking new investments

UNITEK CAPITAL CORP

No. 25 Jen-Ai Road
Section 4, 9th Floor
Taipei, Taiwan
Phone: 886-2-8773-0501
Fax: 8862--8773-0502

Type of Firm
Private Equity Firm

Association Membership
Taiwan Venture Capital Association(TVCA)

Additional Information
Year Founded: 1998
Capital Under Management: $9,300,000
Current Activity Level : Actively seeking new investments

UNITUS IMPACT PARTNERS LLC

254 Ritch Street
San Francisco, CA USA 94107
Phone: 4158292473
E-mail: info@unitusimpact.com
Website: unitusimpact.com

Management and Staff
Beau Seil, Managing Partner
Joseph Grenny, Co-Founder
Joseph Du Bey, Vice President
Lee FitzGerald, Managing Partner
Mike Murray, Co-Founder
Robert Gay, Co-Founder
Shalaka Joshi, Managing Director
Tim Stay, Co-Founder

Type of Firm
Private Equity Firm

Project Preferences

Type of Financing Preferred:
Early Stage
Expansion

Geographical Preferences

International Preferences:
Vietnam
Indonesia
Pakistan
India
China
Nepal
Thailand
Philippines
Asia
Singapore
Korea, South
Japan
Malaysia
Africa
Burma

Industry Preferences

In Financial Services prefer:
Financial Services

In Agr/Forestr/Fish prefer:
Agribusiness

Additional Information
Year Founded: 2011
Capital Under Management: $20,925,000
Current Activity Level : Actively seeking new investments

UNIVEN CAPITAL SCR SA

Fuentebravia Road, 0.8 Km
Hindustan Building
Cadiz, Spain 11500
Phone: 34956871799
Fax: 34956859471
E-mail: info@univencapital.es
Website: www.univencapital.es

Type of Firm
Private Equity Firm

Project Preferences

Type of Financing Preferred:
Seed
Startup

Geographical Preferences

International Preferences:
Spain

Industry Preferences

In Business Serv. prefer:
Media

Additional Information
Year Founded: 2007
Current Activity Level : Actively seeking new investments

UNIVERSE INVEST SICAR SA

4 Rue Greece The Palmarium
Center 3rd Floor Office A04
Tunis, Tunisia 100
Phone: 21671331788
Fax: 21671247342
Website: www.universinvest-sicar.com

Type of Firm
Bank Affiliated

Project Preferences

Type of Financing Preferred:
Early Stage
Later Stage

Geographical Preferences

International Preferences:
Tunisia
Africa

Industry Preferences

In Communications prefer:
Telecommunications

In Semiconductor/Electr prefer:
Electronics

In Medical/Health prefer:
Medical Products
Pharmaceuticals

In Consumer Related prefer:
Food/Beverage

In Industrial/Energy prefer:
Industrial Products

Additional Information
Year Founded: 2001
Capital Under Management: $3,600,000
Current Activity Level : Actively seeking new investments

UNIVERSITY OF CAMBRIDGE CHALLENGE FUND (AKA UCF)

10 Trumpington Street
Cambridge, United Kingdom CB2 1QA
Phone: 44-1223-763-723
Fax: 44-1223-764-888
Website: www.challengefund.cam.ac.uk

Type of Firm
University Program

Project Preferences

Type of Financing Preferred:
Seed
Startup

Geographical Preferences

International Preferences:
United Kingdom

Additional Information
Year Founded: 1999
Capital Under Management: $6,500,000
Current Activity Level : Actively seeking new investments

UNIVERSITY OF EDINBURGH

Old College
South Bridge
Edinburgh, United Kingdom EH8 9YL
Phone: 441316501000
Fax: 441316502147
E-mail: communications.office@ed.ac.uk
Website: www.ed.ac.uk

Type of Firm
University Program

Project Preferences

Type of Financing Preferred:
Expansion
Start-up Financing
Later Stage

Geographical Preferences

International Preferences:
United Kingdom

Additional Information
Year Founded: 1583
Current Activity Level : Actively seeking new investments

UNIVERSITY OF MICHIGAN

701 Tappan Street
R3200
Ann Arbor, MI USA 48109
Phone: 7346154419
E-mail: zlicontact@umich.edu
Website: umich.edu

Management and Staff
Timothy Faley, Managing Director

Type of Firm
University Program

Project Preferences

Type of Financing Preferred:
Early Stage
Start-up Financing
Seed
Startup

Geographical Preferences

United States Preferences:
Michigan

Industry Preferences

In Medical/Health prefer:
Medical/Health
Health Services

In Consumer Related prefer:
Consumer
Food/Beverage
Consumer Products
Education Related

In Industrial/Energy prefer:
Environmental Related

In Financial Services prefer:
Financial Services

In Other prefer:
Environment Responsible

Additional Information
Year Founded: 1999
Capital Under Management: $24,600,000
Current Activity Level : Actively seeking new investments

UNIVERSITY OF TEXAS SYSTEM

601 Colorado Street
Austin, TX USA 78701
Phone: 5124994200
Fax: 5124994215
Website: www.utsystem.edu

Management and Staff
Amy Shaw-Thomas, Vice President
Barry McBee, Vice President
Francisco Cigarroa, Chief Executive Officer
Patricia Hurn, Vice President
Randa Safady, Vice President
Stephanie Huie, Vice President
William Shute, Vice President

Type of Firm
University Program

Project Preferences

Type of Financing Preferred:
Balanced
Seed
Startup

Geographical Preferences

United States Preferences:
Texas

Additional Information
Year Founded: 1876
Capital Under Management: $10,000,000
Current Activity Level : Actively seeking new investments

UNIVERSITY OF TOKYO EDGE CAPITAL CO LTD

7-3-1 Hongo, Bunkyo-ku
4F UCR Plaza
Tokyo, Japan 113-0033
Phone: 81358446671
Fax: 81358446672
E-mail: info@ut-ec.co.jp
Website: www.ut-ec.co.jp

Management and Staff
Hideki Tsuji, General Partner
Maiko Katadae, Principal
Miki Hirai, Principal
Naonori Kurokawa, Principal
Tetsuya Yamamoto, General Partner
Tomotaka Goji, Managing Partner
Yumiko Nagatsuma, Partner

Type of Firm
University Program

Association Membership
Japan Venture Capital Association

Project Preferences

Type of Financing Preferred:
Early Stage
Seed
Startup

Geographical Preferences

International Preferences:
Japan

Industry Preferences

In Biotechnology prefer:
Biotechnology

In Medical/Health prefer:
Medical/Health

In Industrial/Energy prefer:
Environmental Related

Additional Information
Year Founded: 2004
Current Activity Level : Actively seeking new investments

UNIVERSITY OF VIRGINIA LICENSING & VENTURES GROUP

722 Preston Avenue, Suite 107
Charlottesville, VA USA 22903
Phone: 4349241275
E-mail: lvg@virginia.edu
Website: lvg.virginia.edu

Type of Firm
University Program

Project Preferences

Type of Financing Preferred:
Balanced

Geographical Preferences

United States Preferences:
Virginia

Additional Information
Year Founded: 1977
Capital Under Management: $10,000,000
Current Activity Level : Actively seeking new investments

UNIVERSITY VENTURE FUND

299 South Main Street, Suite 310
Salt Lake City, UT USA 84111
Phone: 8013263590
Fax: 8013263598
E-mail: info@uventurefund.com

Management and Staff
Peter Harris, Principal
Ryan Davis, Chief Executive Officer
Tom Stringham, Managing Director

Type of Firm
University Program

Project Preferences

Type of Financing Preferred:
Leveraged Buyout
Early Stage
Expansion
Balanced
Seed

Geographical Preferences

United States Preferences:
Utah

Industry Preferences

In Medical/Health prefer:
Health Services

In Industrial/Energy prefer:
Energy

In Financial Services prefer:
Financial Services

Additional Information
Name of Most Recent Fund: University Growth Fund I, L.P.
Most Recent Fund Was Raised: 01/14/2015
Year Founded: 2001
Capital Under Management: $5,000,000
Current Activity Level : Actively seeking new investments

UNIVERSITY VENTURES

1745 Broadway
19th Floor
New York, NY USA 10019
Phone: 3473913440
E-mail: info@universityventuresfund.com
Website: www.universityventuresfund.com

Other Offices
1745 Broadway
19th Floor
New York, NY USA 10019
Phone: 3473913440

Management and Staff
Daniel Pianko, Partner
David Figuli, Partner
Gregg Rosenthal, Partner
Ryan Craig, Partner

Type of Firm
Private Equity Firm

Project Preferences

Type of Financing Preferred:
Balanced
Later Stage

Industry Preferences

In Consumer Related prefer:
Education Related

Additional Information
Name of Most Recent Fund: University Ventures Fund II, L.P.
Most Recent Fund Was Raised: 10/01/2013
Year Founded: 2011
Capital Under Management: $300,000,000
Current Activity Level : Actively seeking new investments

UNIVEST CAPITAL

719-8, Yeoksam-Dong, Kangnam-G
2/F,Floor, Yong Bldg
Seoul, South Korea 135-080
Phone: 82-2-564-1881
Fax: 82-2-565-1454

Management and Staff
Taeksu Kang, President

Type of Firm
Bank Affiliated

Project Preferences

Type of Financing Preferred:
Balanced

Geographical Preferences

International Preferences:
Korea, South

Additional Information
Year Founded: 2006
Current Activity Level : Actively seeking new investments

UNTERNEHMENS INVEST AG

Am Hof 4
Wien, Austria 1010
Phone: 43140597710
Fax: 43140597719
E-mail: office@uiag.at
Website: www.uiag.at

Management and Staff
Rudolf Knuenz, Chief Executive Officer

Type of Firm
Private Equity Firm

Project Preferences

Type of Financing Preferred:
Leveraged Buyout
Later Stage
Management Buyouts

Geographical Preferences

International Preferences:
Austria

Industry Focus

(% based on actual investment)
Other Products	82.5%
Consumer Related	5.7%
Medical/Health	4.8%
Semiconductors/Other Elect.	4.3%
Industrial/Energy	2.6%
Computer Software and Services	0.0%
Communications and Media	0.0%

Additional Information

Year Founded: 1990
Capital Under Management: $60,400,000
Current Activity Level : Actively seeking new investments

UNTERNEHMERTUM GMBH

Lichtenbergstrasse 8
Garching, Germany 85748
Phone: 49891894690
Fax: 49891894691199
E-mail: info@unternehmertum.de
Website: www.unternehmertum.de

Management and Staff

Helmut Schonenberger, Managing Director
Ingo Potthof, Managing Partner
Timo Komulainen, Managing Director

Type of Firm

University Program

Association Membership

German Venture Capital Association (BVK)

Project Preferences

Type of Financing Preferred:
Early Stage
Seed
Startup

Size of Investments Considered:
Min Size of Investment Considered (000s): $727
Max Size of Investment Considered (000s): $4,364

Geographical Preferences

International Preferences:
Germany

Industry Preferences

In Communications prefer:
Communications and Media

In Medical/Health prefer:
Medical/Health

In Industrial/Energy prefer:
Alternative Energy
Environmental Related

Additional Information

Year Founded: 2002
Capital Under Management: $25,000,000
Current Activity Level : Actively seeking new investments

UNTITLED, THE

Varshavskoe shosse, 25 A
Stroenie 6, Office 201E
Moscow, Russia
E-mail: info@theuntitled.net
Website: www.theuntitled.net

Type of Firm

Private Equity Firm

Project Preferences

Type of Financing Preferred:
Early Stage
Seed
Startup

Size of Investments Considered:
Min Size of Investment Considered (000s): $85
Max Size of Investment Considered (000s): $254

Geographical Preferences

United States Preferences:
All U.S.

International Preferences:
Russia

Industry Preferences

In Internet Specific prefer:
E-Commerce Technology

In Business Serv. prefer:
Services

Additional Information

Year Founded: 2011
Current Activity Level : Actively seeking new investments

UOB BIOVENTURES MANAGEMENT PTE LTD

80 Raffles Place, Suite 30-20, UOB Plaza Two
Singapore, Singapore 048624
Phone: 6565393044
Fax: 6565382569
E-mail: info@uobvm.com.sg
Website: www.uobvm.com.sg

Management and Staff

Kian Wee Seah, Managing Director
Seah Kian-Wee, Managing Director

Type of Firm

Bank Affiliated

Project Preferences

Type of Financing Preferred:
Early Stage
Balanced
Later Stage

Geographical Preferences

United States Preferences:

International Preferences:
Taiwan
Hong Kong
China
Asia
Singapore
Japan

Industry Preferences

In Biotechnology prefer:
Biotechnology

In Medical/Health prefer:
Medical/Health

In Consumer Related prefer:
Consumer Products
Consumer Services

In Industrial/Energy prefer:
Energy
Industrial Products
Materials
Environmental Related

Additional Information

Year Founded: 2001
Current Activity Level : Actively seeking new investments

UOB VENTURE MANAGEMENT PTE LTD

80 Raffles Place, Suite 30-20 UOB Plaza Two
Singapore, Singapore 048624
Phone: 6565393044
Fax: 6565382569
E-mail: info@uobvm.com.sg
Website: www.uobvm.com.sg

Other Offices

11/F Investment Building No. 4009
Shennan Road, Futian Centre District
Shenzhen, China 518026
Phone: 86-755-8291-2888
Fax: 86-755-8290-4093

Room 3307, United Plaza
1468 Nanjing Road West
Shanghai, China 200040
Phone: 86-21-6247-6228
Fax: 86-21-6289-8817

Eighth Floor, Taiji Building
No.211 Bei Si Huan Middle Road
Beijing, China 100083
Phone: 86-10-5161-6671
Fax: 86-10-5161-6700

Management and Staff

Kian Wee Seah, Managing Director

Type of Firm

Bank Affiliated

Association Membership

Singapore Venture Capital Association (SVCA)

Project Preferences

Role in Financing:
Prefer role in deals created by others

Type of Financing Preferred:
Early Stage
Balanced
Later Stage

Geographical Preferences

United States Preferences:
All U.S.

International Preferences:
Asia Pacific
China
Asia

Industry Preferences

In Communications prefer:
Telecommunications

In Semiconductor/Electr prefer:
Electronics
Semiconductor

In Medical/Health prefer:
Medical/Health
Medical Products
Health Services

In Consumer Related prefer:
Retail
Food/Beverage
Consumer Products
Consumer Services
Education Related

In Industrial/Energy prefer:
Energy
Oil and Gas Exploration
Oil & Gas Drilling, Explor
Alternative Energy
Industrial Products
Advanced Materials
Environmental Related

In Transportation prefer:
Transportation
Aerospace

In Business Serv. prefer:
Distribution
Media

In Manufact. prefer:
Manufacturing

In Agr/Forestr/Fish prefer:
Mining and Minerals

In Other prefer:
Environment Responsible

Additional Information

Year Founded: 1991
Capital Under Management: $489,900,000
Current Activity Level: Actively seeking new investments
Method of Compensation: Return on investment is of primary concern, do not charge fees

UP INVEST OU

Ravala puiestee 4
Tallinn, Estonia 10143
Phone: 3726663450
Fax: 3726663472
E-mail: info@upi.ee
Website: www.upi.ee

Management and Staff

Kristjan Vilosius, Managing Director

Type of Firm

Private Equity Firm

Project Preferences

Type of Financing Preferred:
Core
Leveraged Buyout
Value-Add
Early Stage
Opportunistic
Later Stage
Seed
Management Buyouts
Acquisition
Startup

Geographical Preferences

International Preferences:
Estonia
Germany
Latvia
Lithuania

Industry Preferences

In Communications prefer:
Media and Entertainment

In Medical/Health prefer:
Medical/Health

In Consumer Related prefer:
Retail

In Industrial/Energy prefer:
Energy

In Financial Services prefer:
Real Estate

In Other prefer:
Environment Responsible

Additional Information

Year Founded: 2012
Current Activity Level: Actively seeking new investments

UP2398 LLC

1991 Broadway, Suite 140
Redwood City, CA USA 94063
Website: www.up2398.com

Type of Firm

Private Equity Firm

Project Preferences

Type of Financing Preferred:
Start-up Financing
Seed

Additional Information

Year Founded: 2015
Current Activity Level: Actively seeking new investments

UPAYA SOCIAL VENTURES

P.O. Box 9603
Seattle, WA USA 98109
Website: www.upayasv.org

Type of Firm
Incubator/Development Program

Project Preferences

Type of Financing Preferred:
Startup

Geographical Preferences

International Preferences:
India

Industry Preferences

In Biotechnology prefer:
Agricultural/Animal Bio.

In Business Serv. prefer:
Services

In Manufact. prefer:
Manufacturing

In Agr/Forestr/Fish prefer:
Agriculture related

Additional Information
Year Founded: 2011
Current Activity Level : Actively seeking new investments

UPDATA PARTNERS

2099 Pennsylvania Ave NW
Eighth Floor
Washington, DC USA 20006
Phone: 2026188750
Fax: 2023152668
E-mail: info@updata.com

Other Offices
Former HQ: 11955 Freedom Drive, Suite 7000
RESTON, VA USA 20190
Phone: 7037360020
Fax: 7037360022

Management and Staff
Barry Goldsmith, Co-Founder
Carter Griffin, General Partner
Dan Moss, Vice President
Greg Olear, Chief Financial Officer
Jon Seeber, General Partner

Type of Firm
Private Equity Firm

Association Membership
Mid-Atlantic Venture Association

Project Preferences

Role in Financing:
Will function either as deal originator or investor in deals created by others

Type of Financing Preferred:
Leveraged Buyout
Early Stage
Expansion
Generalist PE
Balanced
Later Stage
Acquisition
Recapitalizations

Size of Investments Considered:
Min Size of Investment Considered (000s): $5,000
Max Size of Investment Considered (000s): $20,000

Geographical Preferences

United States Preferences:
North America

International Preferences:
Western Europe
Asia

Industry Preferences

In Communications prefer:
Communications and Media
Data Communications

In Computer Software prefer:
Computer Services
Software
Systems Software
Applications Software

In Internet Specific prefer:
E-Commerce Technology
Internet
Ecommerce
Web Aggregation/Portals

In Business Serv. prefer:
Services
Media

Additional Information
Name of Most Recent Fund: Updata Partners IV, L.P.
Most Recent Fund Was Raised: 03/13/2007
Year Founded: 1998
Capital Under Management: $750,000,000
Current Activity Level : Actively seeking new investments
Method of Compensation: Return on investment is of primary concern, do not charge fees

---

UPFRONT VENTURES

2121 Avenue of the Stars, Suite 1630
Los Angeles, CA USA 90067
Phone: 3107855100
Website: upfront.com

Management and Staff
Dana Kibler, Chief Financial Officer
Gregory Bettinelli, Partner
Hamet Watt, Venture Partner
Jordan Hudson, Principal
Kara Nortman, Partner
Kevin Zhang, Principal
Kobie Fuller, Partner
Mark Suster, Managing Partner
Steven Dietz, Partner
Stuart Lander, Partner
Yves Sisteron, Managing Partner

Type of Firm
Private Equity Firm

Association Membership
National Venture Capital Association - USA (NVCA)

Project Preferences

Role in Financing:
Prefer role as deal originator but will also invest in deals created by others

Type of Financing Preferred:
Early Stage
Balanced
Seed

Geographical Preferences

United States Preferences:
Southern California

Industry Focus
(% based on actual investment)
Internet Specific	52.8%
Computer Software and Services	24.8%
Consumer Related	8.8%
Other Products	7.6%
Computer Hardware	1.9%
Communications and Media	1.7%
Semiconductors/Other Elect.	1.3%
Industrial/Energy	1.0%
Biotechnology	0.0%

Additional Information
Name of Most Recent Fund: Upfront IV, L.P.
Most Recent Fund Was Raised: 10/31/2012
Year Founded: 1996
Capital Under Management: $1,000,000,000
Current Activity Level : Actively seeking new investments
Method of Compensation: Return on investment is of primary concern, do not charge fees

UPS STRATEGIC ENTERPRISE FUND

55 Glenlake Parkway, Northeast
Bldg One, Fourth Floor
Atlanta, GA USA 30328
Phone: 4048284905
Fax: 4048288088
E-mail: sef@ups.com

Management and Staff
Bob Burman, Principal

Type of Firm
Corporate PE/Venture

Association Membership
National Venture Capital Association - USA (NVCA)

Project Preferences

Role in Financing:
Prefer role in deals created by others

Size of Investments Considered:
Min Size of Investment Considered (000s): $250
Max Size of Investment Considered (000s): $1,500

Industry Focus
(% based on actual investment)
Internet Specific	46.9%
Communications and Media	24.7%
Computer Software and Services	14.9%
Other Products	7.5%
Computer Hardware	3.7%
Semiconductors/Other Elect.	2.3%

Additional Information
Year Founded: 1997
Capital Under Management: $50,000,000
Current Activity Level : Actively seeking new investments
Method of Compensation: Return on investment is of primary concern, do not charge fees

---

UPSTART LABS LLC

1104 NW 15th Avenue
Portland, OR USA 97209
Phone: 5034779907
E-mail: info@upstartlabs.com

Type of Firm
Incubator/Development Program

Project Preferences

Type of Financing Preferred:
Early Stage
Seed
Startup

Geographical Preferences

United States Preferences:
Oregon

Industry Preferences

In Communications prefer:
Wireless Communications

In Internet Specific prefer:
Internet
Ecommerce
Web Aggregation/Portals

Additional Information
Name of Most Recent Fund: Upstart Labs Fund I LLC
Most Recent Fund Was Raised: 01/18/2013
Year Founded: 2011
Capital Under Management: $200,000
Current Activity Level : Actively seeking new investments

UPSTART VENTURES MANAGEMENT LLC

417 Wakara Way, Suite 3510
Salt Lake City, UT USA 84108
Phone: 8015050630
Fax: 8015050631
E-mail: info@upstartvc.com
Website: www.upstartvc.com

Management and Staff
Dennis Farrar, Managing Director
Steven Borst, Managing Director
Theodore Stanley, Managing Director

Type of Firm
Private Equity Firm

Project Preferences

Type of Financing Preferred:
Early Stage
Seed

Geographical Preferences

United States Preferences:
Utah

Industry Preferences

In Biotechnology prefer:
Biotechnology

In Medical/Health prefer:
Medical/Health
Medical Diagnostics
Medical Products
Health Services
Pharmaceuticals

Additional Information
Name of Most Recent Fund: UpStart Life Sciences Capital, L.P.
Most Recent Fund Was Raised: 07/14/2009
Year Founded: 2009
Capital Under Management: $9,880,000
Current Activity Level : Actively seeking new investments

UPTECH LLC

300 Dave Cowens Drive
Newport, KY USA 41071
Website: www.uptechideas.org

Management and Staff
Adam Caswell, Founder

Type of Firm
Incubator/Development Program

Project Preferences

Type of Financing Preferred:
Early Stage
Startup

Geographical Preferences

United States Preferences:
Ohio
Indiana
Kentucky

Additional Information
Year Founded: 2012
Current Activity Level : Actively seeking new investments

UPWEST LABS

460 Everett Avenue
Apartment Two
Palo Alto, CA USA 94301
Phone: 6505614303
E-mail: info@upwestlabs.com
Website: www.upwestlabs.com

Type of Firm
Incubator/Development Program

Project Preferences

Type of Financing Preferred:
Seed
Startup

Geographical Preferences

International Preferences:
Israel

Industry Preferences

In Communications prefer:
Wireless Communications

In Computer Software prefer:
Software
Applications Software

In Internet Specific prefer:
Ecommerce
Web Aggregration/Portals

In Consumer Related prefer:
Entertainment and Leisure

Additional Information
Year Founded: 2012
Capital Under Management: $4,100,000
Current Activity Level : Actively seeking new investments

URBAN INNOVATION FUND

645 Harrison Street, Suite 200
San Francisco, CA USA 94107

Type of Firm
Private Equity Firm

Project Preferences

Type of Financing Preferred:
Seed

Additional Information
Year Founded: 2016
Current Activity Level : Actively seeking new investments

URBAN SELECT CAPITAL CORP

1055 West Hastings Street, Suite 300
Vancouver, Canada V6E 2E9
Phone: 6046890618
Fax: 6046890628
Website: www.urbanselect.com

Other Offices
77 Jianguo Road, Tower 3
Level 24, China Central Place
Beijing, China 100025

Type of Firm
Investment Management Firm

Project Preferences

Type of Financing Preferred:
Balanced

Industry Preferences

In Consumer Related prefer:
Consumer
Retail

In Industrial/Energy prefer:
Energy
Industrial Products

In Agr/Forestr/Fish prefer:
Agriculture related

Additional Information
Year Founded: 2007
Current Activity Level : Actively seeking new investments

URBAN US PUBLIC BENEFIT CORP

400 NW 26th Street
Miami, FL USA 33127
Website: urban.us

Management and Staff
Shaun Abrahamson, Co-Founder
Stonly Baptiste, Co-Founder

Type of Firm
Private Equity Firm

Project Preferences

Type of Financing Preferred:
Early Stage
Seed

Additional Information
Year Founded: 2014
Capital Under Management: $280,000
Current Activity Level : Actively seeking new investments

US CHINA GREEN INVESTMENT MANAGEMENT CO LTD

No. 1 Jianguomen Outer Street
4908, Building B, Guomao Mansi
Beijing, China
Phone: 861085406200
Fax: 861085206262
Website: www.uschinagreenfund.com

Type of Firm
Government Affiliated Program

Project Preferences

Type of Financing Preferred:
Balanced

Geographical Preferences

International Preferences:
China

Industry Preferences

In Industrial/Energy prefer:
Energy
Energy Conservation Relat
Environmental Related

In Transportation prefer:
Transportation

Additional Information
Year Founded: 2016
Current Activity Level : Actively seeking new investments

US ISRAEL GEFEN CAPITAL MANAGEMENT LTD

85 Medinat Hayehudim
Hertzlia Pituach, Israel
Phone: 97299508690
E-mail: info@gefencapital.com
Website: www.gefencapital.com

Type of Firm
Private Equity Firm

Project Preferences

Type of Financing Preferred:
Early Stage
Expansion
Later Stage

Geographical Preferences

International Preferences:
Israel

Industry Preferences

In Medical/Health prefer:
Medical/Health

Additional Information
Year Founded: 2016
Current Activity Level : Actively seeking new investments

UTAH FUND OF FUNDS LLC

170 South Main Street, Suite 1130
Salt Lake City, UT USA 84101
Phone: 8015213078
Fax: 8015213079
E-mail: info@utahfof.com
Website: www.utahfundoffunds.com

Management and Staff
Matthew Peterson, Vice President
Ryan Davis, Chief Financial Officer
Timothy Bridgewater, Managing Director

Type of Firm
Private Equity Advisor or Fund of Funds

Project Preferences

Type of Financing Preferred:
Fund of Funds

Geographical Preferences

United States Preferences:
Utah

Pratt's Guide to Private Equity & Venture Capital Sources

Additional Information
Year Founded: 2006
Capital Under Management: $300,000,000
Current Activity Level : Actively seeking new investments

UTC INVESTMENT CO LTD (AKA UTC VENTURE CO LTD)

10-2 Youido-dong
Youngdeungpo-gu
Seoul, South Korea 150-868
Phone: 822-783-3347
Fax: 822-783-3551
Website: www.utc.co.kr

Management and Staff
Hoon Shik Kim, President

Type of Firm
Private Equity Firm

Association Membership
Korean Venture Capital Association (KVCA)

Project Preferences

Type of Financing Preferred:
Leveraged Buyout
Generalist PE
Balanced
Turnaround
Recapitalizations

Geographical Preferences

International Preferences:
No Preference
Asia
Korea, South

Industry Preferences

In Biotechnology prefer:
Biotech Related Research

Additional Information
Year Founded: 1988
Capital Under Management: $10,000,000
Current Activity Level : Actively seeking new investments

UTTHISHTA MANAGEMENT ADVISORS LLP

82334/40/C, Road
No.3, Banjara Hills
Hyderabad, India 500 034
Phone: 914023306677
Website: www.utthishta.com

Management and Staff
P. Ramakrishna, General Partner

Type of Firm
Private Equity Firm

Association Membership
Indian Venture Capital Association (IVCA)

Project Preferences

Type of Financing Preferred:
Early Stage
Expansion
Seed

Geographical Preferences

International Preferences:
India

Industry Preferences

In Communications prefer:
Wireless Communications
Data Communications

In Computer Software prefer:
Software

In Internet Specific prefer:
Internet

Additional Information
Year Founded: 2012
Current Activity Level : Actively seeking new investments

V FUND MANAGEMENT CO LTD

No.89 Jinbao Street, Dongcheng
609A-610B, 6 Floor, Jinbao
Beijing, China
Phone: 861085893080
Fax: 861085183610
Website: www.cvfund.cn

Type of Firm
Private Equity Firm

Project Preferences

Type of Financing Preferred:
Generalist PE

Geographical Preferences

International Preferences:
China

Industry Preferences

In Communications prefer:
Telecommunications

In Consumer Related prefer:
Consumer

In Transportation prefer:
Transportation

In Business Serv. prefer:
Services
Media

In Manufact. prefer:
Manufacturing

Additional Information
Year Founded: 2015
Current Activity Level : Actively seeking new investments

V&A CAPITAL

1271 Avenue of the Americas, Suite 4300
New York, NY USA 10020
Phone: 2122923790
E-mail: info@vandacapital.com
Website: vandacapital.com

Management and Staff
Galeazzo Scarampi, Principal
Joel Kress, Vice President
Pier Andrea Comoglio, Vice President

Type of Firm
Bank Affiliated

Project Preferences

Type of Financing Preferred:
Leveraged Buyout
Management Buyouts
Acquisition
Recapitalizations

Geographical Preferences

United States Preferences:

International Preferences:
Europe

Additional Information
Year Founded: 1969
Current Activity Level : Actively seeking new investments

V+BETEILIGUNGS 2 GMBH

Kapuzinerweg 8
Landshut, Germany 01309
Phone: 498714306080
Fax: 4987143060849
E-mail: info@venture-plus.de
Website: www.venture-plus.de

Management and Staff
Anke Schiller, Managing Director
Michael Vogel, Chief Executive Officer
Werner Schaar, Managing Director

Type of Firm
Private Equity Firm

Project Preferences

Role in Financing:
Prefer role in deals created by others

Type of Financing Preferred:
Early Stage
Later Stage
Seed
Startup

Geographical Preferences

International Preferences:
Liechtenstein
Switzerland
Austria
Germany

Industry Preferences

In Communications prefer:
Communications and Media

In Biotechnology prefer:
Biotechnology

In Medical/Health prefer:
Medical/Health
Medical Products

Additional Information
Year Founded: 2005
Current Activity Level : Actively seeking new investments

V-BIO VENTURES

Rijvisschestraat 126
3rd floor
Gent, Belgium 9052
Website: www.v-bio.ventures.com

Type of Firm
Private Equity Firm

Project Preferences

Type of Financing Preferred:
Early Stage

Additional Information
Year Founded: 2015
Capital Under Management: $67,630,000
Current Activity Level : Actively seeking new investments

V-TEN CAPITAL PARTNERS LLC

9020 Stony Point Parkway, Suite 180
Richmond, VA USA 23235
Phone: 8043270710
Fax: 8043270739
E-mail: info@vtencp.com
Website: www.vtencp.com

Management and Staff
James Karides, Partner
Richard Sharp, Managing Director

Type of Firm
Private Equity Firm

Project Preferences

Type of Financing Preferred:
Early Stage
Balanced
Later Stage
Seed

Industry Preferences

In Medical/Health prefer:
Medical/Health

In Consumer Related prefer:
Consumer
Retail

In Transportation prefer:
Transportation

In Financial Services prefer:
Financial Services
Insurance
Real Estate

Additional Information
Year Founded: 2008
Current Activity Level : Actively seeking new investments

VAAKA PARTNERS OY

Kasarmikatu 36
Helsinki, Finland 00130
Phone: 358505148401
Fax: 358103212901
E-mail: vaakapartners@vaakapartners.fi
Website: www.vaakapartners.fi

Management and Staff
Ilkka Pentikainen, Partner
Illkka Hietala, Partner
Juha Peltola, Partner
Mikko Kumpulainen, Partner
Panu Vuorela, Partner
Reijo Gronholm, Partner

Type of Firm
Private Equity Firm

Association Membership
Finnish Venture Capital Association (FVCA)
European Private Equity and Venture Capital Assoc.

Project Preferences

Type of Financing Preferred:
Leveraged Buyout
Mezzanine
Later Stage
Management Buyouts
Fund of Funds of Second

Size of Investments Considered:
Min Size of Investment Considered (000s): $300
Max Size of Investment Considered (000s): $300,000

Geographical Preferences

International Preferences:
Scandanavia/Nordic Region
Finland

Industry Preferences

In Communications prefer:
Communications and Media
Commercial Communications
Telecommunications
Wireless Communications

In Computer Other prefer:
Computer Related

In Semiconductor/Electr prefer:
Electronics

In Biotechnology prefer:
Biotechnology

In Consumer Related prefer:
Consumer
Food/Beverage

In Industrial/Energy prefer:
Industrial Products

In Transportation prefer:
Transportation

In Business Serv. prefer:
Services

In Manufact. prefer:
Manufacturing

Additional Information
Year Founded: 1989
Capital Under Management: $317,600,000
Current Activity Level : Actively seeking new investments

VAEKSTFONDEN

Strandvejen 104 A
Hellerup, Denmark 2900
Phone: 4535298600
Fax: 4535298635
E-mail: vf@vf.dk
Website: www.vf.dk

Management and Staff
Bjarne Jensen, Partner
Christian Motzfeldt, Chief Executive Officer
Jame Elleholm, Partner
Martin Vang Hansen, Chief Financial Officer
Soeren Steen Rasmussen, Partner
Stig Poulsen, Partner
Tonni Bulow-Nielsen, Partner

Type of Firm
Government Affiliated Program

Association Membership
Danish Venture Capital Association (DVCA)
European Private Equity and Venture Capital Assoc.

Project Preferences

Type of Financing Preferred:
Fund of Funds
Early Stage
Mezzanine
Later Stage
Seed
Startup

Geographical Preferences

International Preferences:
Denmark

Industry Preferences

In Biotechnology prefer:
Biotechnology

In Medical/Health prefer:
Medical/Health

In Industrial/Energy prefer:
Alternative Energy
Energy Conservation Relat

In Other prefer:
Environment Responsible

Additional Information
Year Founded: 1992
Capital Under Management: $631,100,000
Current Activity Level : Actively seeking new investments

VAEKSTPARTNER KAPITAL APS

Rugaards Skovvej 36
Ry, Denmark 8680
Website: vpkapital.dk

Type of Firm
Private Equity Firm

Project Preferences

Type of Financing Preferred:
Expansion
Generalist PE
Later Stage
Management Buyouts
Acquisition

Geographical Preferences

International Preferences:
Denmark

Industry Preferences

In Industrial/Energy prefer:
Industrial Products

Additional Information
Year Founded: 2016
Current Activity Level : Actively seeking new investments

VALAR VENTURES MANAGEMENT LLC

One Letterman Drive
Building C, Suite 400
San Francisco, CA USA 94129
Phone: 4152484653

Management and Staff
Andrew McCormack, Partner
Bryce Steeg, Principal
James Fitzgerald, Partner
John Selby, Principal
Nathan Linn, Chief Financial Officer
Peter Thiel, Partner

Type of Firm
Private Equity Firm

Project Preferences

Type of Financing Preferred:
Early Stage
Expansion
Seed

Geographical Preferences

International Preferences:
Taiwan
Rest of World
New Zealand

Industry Preferences

In Computer Software prefer:
Software

In Internet Specific prefer:
Internet

Additional Information
Name of Most Recent Fund: Valar Ventures Fund
Most Recent Fund Was Raised: 03/22/2012
Year Founded: 2012
Capital Under Management: $40,000,000
Current Activity Level : Actively seeking new investments

VALCAPITAL GESTION SGECR S A

C/Salva 10, Puerta 6
Valencia, Spain 46002
Phone: 34963427240
Fax: 34963427241
E-mail: valcapital@valcapital.com
Website: www.valcapital.com

Management and Staff
Arturo Llopis, Chief Executive Officer
Xavier Alfonso, Founder

Type of Firm
Private Equity Firm

Project Preferences

Type of Financing Preferred:
Leveraged Buyout
Early Stage
Expansion
Generalist PE
Turnaround
Later Stage
Seed
Management Buyouts
Recapitalizations

Geographical Preferences

International Preferences:
Spain

Industry Preferences

In Consumer Related prefer:
Consumer Products

In Financial Services prefer:
Real Estate

Additional Information
Year Founded: 2003
Capital Under Management: $2,722,000
Current Activity Level : Actively seeking new investments

VALCO CAPITAL PARTNERS PARTNERSHIP LTD

80 Bond Street
London, United Kingdom W1S 1SB
Phone: 442070547888
Fax: 442073172051

Management and Staff
Andrew Pepper, Principal
Howard Gunn, Chief Financial Officer
Igor de la Sota, Managing Director
Paul McGowan, Principal

Type of Firm
Private Equity Firm

Project Preferences

Type of Financing Preferred:
Leveraged Buyout
Management Buyouts

Geographical Preferences

International Preferences:
United Kingdom

Additional Information
Year Founded: 2012
Current Activity Level : Actively seeking new investments

VALDE CAPITAL INVESTMENT CO

100 North 18th Street, Suite 300
Philadelphia, PA USA 19103
Phone: 2672073542
Website: valdecapital.com

Management and Staff
Felix Odigie, Principal

Type of Firm
Private Equity Firm

Project Preferences

Type of Financing Preferred:
Leveraged Buyout

Additional Information
Year Founded: 2014
Capital Under Management: $16,759,000
Current Activity Level : Actively seeking new investments

VALEDO PARTNERS FUND I AB

Kungsbron 1
Seventh Floor
Stockholm, Sweden 111 22
Phone: 4686780850
Fax: 4686780851
E-mail: info@valedopartners.com
Website: www.valedopartners.com

Type of Firm
Private Equity Firm

Project Preferences

Type of Financing Preferred:
Leveraged Buyout
Management Buyouts

Geographical Preferences

International Preferences:
Sweden
Scandanavia/Nordic Region

Industry Preferences

In Communications prefer:
Media and Entertainment

In Medical/Health prefer:
Health Services

In Consumer Related prefer:
Consumer Products

In Business Serv. prefer:
Services

In Manufact. prefer:
Manufacturing

Additional Information
Name of Most Recent Fund: Valedo Partners Fund II AB
Most Recent Fund Was Raised: 07/27/2011
Year Founded: 2006
Capital Under Management: $146,000,000
Current Activity Level : Actively seeking new investments

VALENCE LIFE SCIENCES LLC

500 Park Avenue
New York, NY USA 10022
Phone: 2128911100
E-mail: info@valencefund.com

Other Offices
12481 High Bluff Drive, Suite 150
San Diego, CA USA 92130
Phone: 8584802410

Management and Staff
Eric Roberts, Managing Director
James Cecil, Managing Director
Rachel Leheny, Founder
Scott Morenstein, Managing Director

Type of Firm
Investment Management Firm

Project Preferences

Type of Financing Preferred:
Later Stage

Geographical Preferences

United States Preferences:

Additional Information
Year Founded: 2012
Current Activity Level : Actively seeking new investments

VALENCIA CAPITAL LLC

PO Box 14-1369
Miami, FL USA 33114
Phone: 8557016056
Fax: 8557016056
E-mail: info@valenciacapitalllc.com
Website: www.valenciacapitalllc.com

Management and Staff
Jessica Brack, Partner
Kim Rose, Partner
William Rose, Partner

Type of Firm
Private Equity Firm

Project Preferences

Type of Financing Preferred:
Leveraged Buyout
Acquisition

Industry Preferences

In Medical/Health prefer:
Health Services

Additional Information
Year Founded: 2008
Current Activity Level : Actively seeking new investments

2207

VALENTIS CAPITAL LLC

7921 Jones Branch Drive
#222
McLean, VA USA 22102
Phone: 8669361036
Fax: 7033882858
E-mail: info@velentiscapital.com

Management and Staff
Enzo Ugolini, Co-Founder
Frank Knesh, Co-Founder
Mehmet Ogden, President

Type of Firm
Private Equity Firm

Project Preferences

Type of Financing Preferred:
Startup

Geographical Preferences

United States Preferences:
All U.S.

Industry Preferences

In Consumer Related prefer:
Food/Beverage

In Industrial/Energy prefer:
Energy

In Financial Services prefer:
Real Estate

Additional Information
Year Founded: 2015
Current Activity Level : Actively seeking new investments

VALESCO INDUSTRIES INC

325 N. St. Paul Street, Suite 3200
Dallas, TX USA 75201
Phone: 2148808690
Fax: 2148808646
Website: www.valescoind.com

Management and Staff
Bud Moore, Founder
Jack Sadden, Co-Founder

Type of Firm
Private Equity Firm

Association Membership
Natl Assoc of Small Bus. Inv. Co (NASBIC)

Project Preferences

Type of Financing Preferred:
Leveraged Buyout
Expansion
Management Buyouts
Acquisition
Recapitalizations

Geographical Preferences

United States Preferences:
All U.S.

International Preferences:
All International

Industry Preferences

In Consumer Related prefer:
Consumer Products

In Business Serv. prefer:
Services
Distribution

In Manufact. prefer:
Manufacturing

Additional Information
Year Founded: 1993
Capital Under Management: $59,000,000
Current Activity Level : Actively seeking new investments

VALHALLA INVESTMENTS INC

Orchard Cottage La Marette
Alderney
Guernsey, United Kingdom

Type of Firm
Private Equity Firm

Project Preferences

Type of Financing Preferred:
Balanced

Industry Preferences

In Consumer Related prefer:
Entertainment and Leisure

Additional Information
Year Founded: 2008
Current Activity Level : Actively seeking new investments

VALHALLA PARTNERS LP

8000 Towers Crescent Drive, Suite 1050
Vienna, VA USA 22182
Phone: 7034481400
Fax: 7034481441
E-mail: info@valhallapartners.com
Website: www.valhallapartners.com

Management and Staff
Arthur Marks, Managing Partner
Charles Curran, General Partner
Farah Giga, Principal
Harry D Andrea, Chief Financial Officer
Hooks Johnston, General Partner
Kevin Greene, Partner
Kiran Hebbar, General Partner
Randy Jacops, Venture Partner
Scott Frederick, General Partner

Type of Firm
Private Equity Firm

Project Preferences

Role in Financing:
Prefer role as deal originator but will also invest in deals created by others

Type of Financing Preferred:
Early Stage
Balanced
Seed

Geographical Preferences

United States Preferences:
Mid Atlantic

Industry Preferences

In Communications prefer:
Communications and Media

In Computer Software prefer:
Software
Systems Software
Applications Software

In Internet Specific prefer:
Internet

In Computer Other prefer:
Computer Related

In Semiconductor/Electr prefer:
Electronics
Semiconductor

In Consumer Related prefer:
Entertainment and Leisure

Additional Information
Name of Most Recent Fund: Valhalla Partners II, L.P.
Most Recent Fund Was Raised: 10/31/2006
Year Founded: 2002
Capital Under Management: $440,900,000
Current Activity Level : Actively seeking new investments
Method of Compensation: Return on investment is of primary concern, do not charge fees

VALIDOR CAPITAL LLC

4755 Technology Way, Suite 109
Boca Raton, FL USA 33431
Phone: 5619622351
E-mail: contact@validorcap.com
Website: www.validorcap.com

Type of Firm
Private Equity Firm

Project Preferences

Type of Financing Preferred:
Leveraged Buyout
Management Buyouts

Additional Information
Year Founded: 2012
Current Activity Level : Actively seeking new investments

VALLEY VENTURES

1275 West Washington Street, Suite 101
Tempe, AZ USA 85281
Phone: 4806616600
Fax: 6022865284
Website: www.valleyventures.com

Management and Staff
Jock Holliman, General Partner
Terence Winters, Partner

Type of Firm
Private Equity Firm

Project Preferences

Role in Financing:
Prefer role as deal originator but will also invest in deals created by others

Type of Financing Preferred:
Early Stage
Balanced
Later Stage

Geographical Preferences

United States Preferences:
New Mexico
Arizona
California
Colorado
Utah
Southwest

Industry Preferences

In Medical/Health prefer:
Medical/Health
Medical Diagnostics
Medical Products
Pharmaceuticals

Additional Information
Name of Most Recent Fund: Valley Ventures III, L.P.
Most Recent Fund Was Raised: 09/17/2002
Year Founded: 1985
Capital Under Management: $95,000,000
Current Activity Level : Actively seeking new investments
Method of Compensation: Return on investment is of primary concern, do not charge fees

VALLIS CAPITAL PARTNERS SGPS SA

Avenida Da Boavista 36
1st Floor
Porto, Portugal 4050112
Phone: 351220164444
Website: www.vallis.pt

Other Offices
Avenue de la Liberte 13-15
Luxembourg, Luxembourg 1931

Rue Guillaume Kroll 5
Luxembourg, Luxembourg 1882

Management and Staff
Luis Ferreira Carvalho, Chief Financial Officer

Type of Firm
Private Equity Firm

Association Membership
Portuguese Venture Capital Association (APCRI)

Project Preferences

Type of Financing Preferred:
Leveraged Buyout
Later Stage
Management Buyouts
Acquisition

Geographical Preferences

International Preferences:
Portugal
Spain

Industry Preferences

In Medical/Health prefer:
Medical/Health
Hospital/Other Instit.

In Consumer Related prefer:
Food/Beverage

In Industrial/Energy prefer:
Alternative Energy
Environmental Related

In Business Serv. prefer:
Services

In Agr/Forestr/Fish prefer:
Agribusiness

Additional Information
Year Founded: 2010
Current Activity Level : Actively seeking new investments

VALOR CAPITAL GROUP LLC

Ten East 53rd Street
25th Floor
New York, NY USA 10022
Phone: 2128037170
E-mail: info@valorcapitalgroup.com
Website: www.valorcapitalgroup.com

Management and Staff
Antoine Colaco, Partner
Everson Lopes, Venture Partner
Michael Nicklas, Partner
Scott Sobel, Co-Founder

Type of Firm
Private Equity Firm

Project Preferences

Type of Financing Preferred:
Early Stage
Expansion

Geographical Preferences

United States Preferences:
California
New York

International Preferences:
Brazil

Additional Information
Year Founded: 2011
Current Activity Level : Actively seeking new investments

VALOR EQUITY PARTERS L P

200 South Michigan Avenue, Suite 1020
Chicago, IL USA 60604
Phone: 3126831900
Fax: 3126831881
E-mail: info@valorep.comc
Website: www.valorep.com

Management and Staff
Antonio Gracias, Chief Executive Officer
Bradley Sheftel, Principal
Christopher Murphy, Vice President
David Heskett, Vice President
Douglas Fumagalli, Managing Director
Juan Sabater, Managing Director
Timothy Watkins, Managing Director

Type of Firm
Private Equity Firm

Project Preferences

Type of Financing Preferred:
Leveraged Buyout
Acquisition

Industry Preferences

In Medical/Health prefer:
Health Services

In Consumer Related prefer:
Consumer
Consumer Products
Consumer Services

In Industrial/Energy prefer:
Energy
Industrial Products

In Financial Services prefer:
Financial Services

In Business Serv. prefer:
Services
Distribution
Consulting Services

In Manufact. prefer:
Manufacturing

Additional Information
Year Founded: 2002
Capital Under Management: $565,000,000
Current Activity Level : Actively seeking new investments

VALORA GESTAO DE INVESTIMENTOS LTDA

Rua Iguatemi 448
Cj 1301, Itaim Bibi
Sao Paulo, Brazil 01451010
Phone: 551130160900
E-mail: valorainvest@valorainvest.com.br
Website: www.valorainvest.com.br

Other Offices

SHIS QI 9 Conjunto 17 Casa 16
Lago Sul
Brasilia, Brazil 71625-170
Phone: 55-61-248-3731
Fax: 55-61-248-0162

Rua Lauro Muller, 116/ Conjunto 1803
Torre de Rio Sul
Rio de Janeiro, Brazil
Phone: 55-21-2541-1550
Fax: 55-21-2275-3389

Type of Firm
Private Equity Advisor or Fund of Funds

Association Membership
Brazilian Venture Capital Association (ABCR)

Project Preferences

Type of Financing Preferred:
Fund of Funds
Early Stage
Balanced
Later Stage

Geographical Preferences

International Preferences:
Brazil

Industry Preferences

In Industrial/Energy prefer:
Energy
Oil and Gas Exploration
Oil & Gas Drilling, Explor
Alternative Energy

In Financial Services prefer:
Real Estate

Additional Information
Year Founded: 2002
Current Activity Level : Actively seeking new investments

VALSTONE PARTNERS LLC

260 East Brown Street, Suite 250
Birmingham, MI USA 48009
Phone: 2486469200
Fax: 2486463322
E-mail: inquiries@valstonepartners.com
Website: www.valstonepartners.com

Other Offices

300 East Lombard Street, Suite 1111
Baltimore, MD USA 21202
Phone: 410-244-0000
Fax: 410-244-0703

Management and Staff
Eric Abel, Co-Founder
Gerald Timmis, Co-Founder
Hee-Jin Yi, Vice President
Larry Jennings, Co-Founder
Richard Huddleston, Vice President

Type of Firm
Private Equity Firm

Project Preferences

Role in Financing:
Will function either as deal originator or investor in deals created by others

Type of Financing Preferred:
Leveraged Buyout
Turnaround
Opportunistic
Special Situation
Distressed Debt

Size of Investments Considered:
Min Size of Investment Considered (000s): $2,000
Max Size of Investment Considered (000s): $40,000

Geographical Preferences

United States Preferences:

Canadian Preferences:
All Canada

Industry Preferences

In Financial Services prefer:
Financial Services
Real Estate

Additional Information
Name of Most Recent Fund: ValStone Opportunity Fund V LLC
Most Recent Fund Was Raised: 12/11/2012
Year Founded: 1998
Capital Under Management: $494,000,000
Current Activity Level : Actively seeking new investments
Method of Compensation: Other

VALUE CAPITAL ASSET MANAGEMENT PTE LTD

5 Shenton Way
#10-10, Uic Building
Singapore, Singapore 208628
Phone: 6562235478

Type of Firm
Private Equity Firm

Project Preferences

Type of Financing Preferred:
Balanced

Geographical Preferences

International Preferences:
Asia

Additional Information
Year Founded: 2006
Capital Under Management: $545,000,000
Current Activity Level : Actively seeking new investments

VALUE CREATION CAPITAL BV

260, Soestdijkseweg Zuid
Bilthoven, Netherlands 3721 AK
Phone: 31302253506
Fax: 31302253507
Website: www.vcxc.com

Management and Staff
Aldebert Wiersinga, Managing Partner
Jos Bourgonje, Managing Partner
Ronald Wissink, Managing Partner
Willem Van den Berg, Managing Partner

Type of Firm
Private Equity Firm

Project Preferences

Type of Financing Preferred:
Early Stage
Expansion
Later Stage
Seed

Geographical Preferences

International Preferences:
Netherlands

Industry Preferences

In Computer Software prefer:
Software

In Internet Specific prefer:
Internet

In Industrial/Energy prefer:
Robotics

Additional Information
Year Founded: 2005
Capital Under Management: $9,690,000
Current Activity Level : Actively seeking new investments

VALUE DIMENSIONS MANAGEMENT SERVICES GMBH

Garnisongasse 4/10
Vienna, Austria 1090
Phone: 4315120555
Fax: 43151205555
E-mail: info@valuemanagement.at
Website: www.valuemanagement.at

Type of Firm
Private Equity Firm

Association Membership
Austrian PE and Venture Capital Association (AVCO)

Project Preferences

Type of Financing Preferred:
Leveraged Buyout
Turnaround
Management Buyouts
Special Situation

Geographical Preferences

International Preferences:
Italy
Switzerland
Austria
Germany

Industry Preferences

In Consumer Related prefer:
Consumer
Retail

In Industrial/Energy prefer:
Industrial Products

In Business Serv. prefer:
Services

In Manufact. prefer:
Manufacturing

Additional Information
Name of Most Recent Fund: REB II Restrukturierungs- und Beteiligungs GmbH & Co KG
Most Recent Fund Was Raised: 01/18/2006
Year Founded: 1999
Current Activity Level : Actively seeking new investments

VALUE INVESTMENT KOREA CO LTD

231-1, Nonhyeon-dong
4/5F, PAX TOWER
Seoul, South Korea
Phone: 8225386208
Fax: 8225386211
Website: www.vikorea.co.kr

Type of Firm
Private Equity Firm

Project Preferences

Type of Financing Preferred:
Balanced
Later Stage
Startup

Additional Information
Year Founded: 2007
Current Activity Level : Actively seeking new investments

VALUE INVESTMENTS PERU SAFI

Manuel Olguin 571 Piso 5
Santiago de Surco
Lima, Peru 33
Phone: 5116105600
Fax: 5116105610
Website: www.valinvest.net

Management and Staff
Aaron Slater, Principal

Type of Firm
Private Equity Firm

Project Preferences

Type of Financing Preferred:
Balanced

Geographical Preferences

International Preferences:
Peru

Additional Information
Year Founded: 2007
Current Activity Level : Actively seeking new investments

VALUE PLUS VENTURES LLC

5755 North Point Parkway, Suite 41
Alpharetta, GA USA 30022
Phone: 7706642774
Fax: 7706642775
Website: www.v-pventures.com

Management and Staff
Christopher Demetree, Co-Founder
Steve Nussrallah, Co-Founder
Travis Lee Provow, Partner

Type of Firm
Private Equity Firm

Project Preferences

Type of Financing Preferred:
Early Stage

Size of Investments Considered:
Min Size of Investment Considered (000s): $200
Max Size of Investment Considered (000s): $5,000

Industry Preferences

In Communications prefer:
Commercial Communications
CATV & Pay TV Systems
Telecommunications
Wireless Communications

In Computer Software prefer:
Software
Systems Software
Applications Software

In Internet Specific prefer:
Internet
Ecommerce
Web Aggregation/Portals

In Consumer Related prefer:
Consumer

In Business Serv. prefer:
Services

Additional Information
Name of Most Recent Fund: Value Plus Ventures
Most Recent Fund Was Raised: 09/25/2008
Year Founded: 2008
Current Activity Level : Actively seeking new investments

VALUEACT CAPITAL MANAGEMENT LP

One Letterman Drive
Building D, 4th floor
San Francisco, CA USA 94129
Phone: 4153623700
Fax: 4153625727
E-mail: info@valueact.com
Website: www.valueact.com

Type of Firm
Private Equity Firm

Project Preferences

Type of Financing Preferred:
Leveraged Buyout
Acquisition

Additional Information
Year Founded: 1969
Current Activity Level : Actively seeking new investments

VALUESTREAM LABS SYNDICATE II LLC

1460 Broadway
Fourth Floor
New York, NY USA 10036
E-mail: info@valuestreamlabs.com
Website: www.valuestreamlabs.com

Management and Staff
Josh Elwell, Managing Partner
Karl Antle, Managing Partner

Type of Firm
Incubator/Development Program

Project Preferences

Type of Financing Preferred:
Early Stage
Seed

Industry Preferences

In Biotechnology prefer:
Biosensors

Additional Information
Year Founded: 2015
Current Activity Level : Actively seeking new investments

VAM INVESTMENTS SPA

Viale Luigi Majno 31
Milano, Italy 20122
Phone: 390285582224
E-mail: info@vaminvestments.com
Website: vaminvestments.com

Management and Staff
Ennio Boccardi, Co-Founder
Marco Piana, Co-Founder

Type of Firm
Private Equity Firm

Project Preferences

Type of Financing Preferred:
Leveraged Buyout
Later Stage
Management Buyouts
Acquisition

Geographical Preferences

International Preferences:
Italy
Switzerland

Industry Preferences

In Consumer Related prefer:
Retail

In Industrial/Energy prefer:
Industrial Products

Additional Information
Year Founded: 2011
Current Activity Level : Actively seeking new investments

VAN DEN ENDE & DEITMERS BV

Johannes Vermeerstraat 23
Amsterdam, Netherlands 1071 DK
Phone: 31207947777
Fax: 31207947700
E-mail: info@endeit.nl
Website: www.endeit.nl

Management and Staff
Hubert Deitmers, Managing Partner
Martijn Hamann, Partner
Robert Wilhelm, Partner

Type of Firm
Private Equity Firm

Project Preferences

Type of Financing Preferred:
Early Stage
Later Stage
Management Buyouts
Recapitalizations

Size of Investments Considered:
Min Size of Investment Considered (000s): $657
Max Size of Investment Considered (000s): $26,278

Geographical Preferences

International Preferences:
Western Europe

Industry Preferences

In Communications prefer:
Telecommunications

In Computer Software prefer:
Software
Systems Software

In Internet Specific prefer:
E-Commerce Technology
Internet

In Business Serv. prefer:
Media

In Manufact. prefer:
Publishing

Additional Information
Year Founded: 2006
Capital Under Management: $150,000,000
Current Activity Level : Actively seeking new investments

VAN HERK MANAGEMENT SERVICES BV

Lichtenauerlaan 30
Rotterdam, Netherlands 3062 ME
Phone: 31102411555
Fax: 31104362453
E-mail: info@vanherkgroep.nl
Website: www.vanherkgroep.nl

Management and Staff
Erik Esveld, Founder

Type of Firm
Private Equity Firm

Project Preferences

Type of Financing Preferred:
Balanced

Geographical Preferences

International Preferences:
Europe

Industry Preferences

In Biotechnology prefer:
Biotechnology

In Industrial/Energy prefer:
Energy
Alternative Energy

In Financial Services prefer:
Financial Services
Real Estate

In Other prefer:
Environment Responsible

Additional Information

Year Founded: 1951
Current Activity Level : Actively seeking new investments

VAN LANSCHOT PARTICI-PATIES BV

Beethovenstraat 300
Amsterdam, Netherlands 1077 WZ
Phone: 31205705000
Fax: 31205705101
Website: corporate.vanlanschot.nl

Management and Staff

Arjan Huisman, Managing Director
Ieko Sevinga, Managing Director

Type of Firm

Bank Affiliated

Association Membership

Dutch Venture Capital Associaton (NVP)

Project Preferences

Type of Financing Preferred:
Leveraged Buyout
Management Buyouts

Geographical Preferences

International Preferences:
Netherlands

Industry Preferences

In Communications prefer:
Communications and Media
Telecommunications

In Internet Specific prefer:
Internet

In Computer Other prefer:
Computer Related

In Consumer Related prefer:
Consumer
Consumer Products

In Industrial/Energy prefer:
Energy

In Business Serv. prefer:
Services

Additional Information

Year Founded: 2005
Capital Under Management: $184,800,000
Current Activity Level : Actively seeking new investments

VAN LEER XENIA GP

High-Tech Village
Givat Ram Campus
Jerusalem, Israel 91391
Phone: 97226553333
Fax: 97225661881
E-mail: admin@vlx.co.il
Website: vlx.co.il

Type of Firm

Incubator/Development Program

Project Preferences

Type of Financing Preferred:
Early Stage
Seed

Size of Investments Considered:
Min Size of Investment Considered (000s): $550
Max Size of Investment Considered (000s): $650

Geographical Preferences

International Preferences:
Israel

Industry Preferences

In Computer Software prefer:
Software

In Internet Specific prefer:
Internet

In Medical/Health prefer:
Medical/Health

Additional Information

Year Founded: 2013
Current Activity Level : Actively seeking new investments

VANCE STREET CAPITAL LLC

11150 Santa Monica Boulevard, Suite 750
Los Angeles, CA USA 90025
Phone: 3102317100
E-mail: contact@vancestreetcapital.com
Website: www.vancestreetcapital.com

Management and Staff

Brian Martin, Principal
Jake Blumenthal, Principal
John Lerosen, Vice President
Richard Crowell, Founder
Richard Roeder, Partner

Type of Firm

Private Equity Firm

Project Preferences

Type of Financing Preferred:
Leveraged Buyout
Expansion
Recapitalizations

Size of Investments Considered:
Min Size of Investment Considered (000s): $50,000
Max Size of Investment Considered (000s): $200,000

Geographical Preferences

United States Preferences:
All U.S.

Additional Information

Year Founded: 2007
Current Activity Level : Actively seeking new investments

VANCITY CAPITAL CORP

530-815 Hastings Street West
Vancouver, Canada V6C 1B4
Phone: 6048776582
Fax: 6048515409
Website: www.vancity.com

Type of Firm

Corporate PE/Venture

Project Preferences

Type of Financing Preferred:
Mezzanine

Geographical Preferences

Canadian Preferences:
All Canada

Additional Information

Year Founded: 1998
Current Activity Level : Actively seeking new investments

VANCOUVER FOUNDER FUND

520 Alexander Street
Vancouver, Canada
E-mail: info@vanfounder.com
Website: www.vanfounder.com

Management and Staff
Dan Eisenhardt, Partner
Fraser Hall, Partner

Type of Firm
Private Equity Firm

Project Preferences

Type of Financing Preferred:
Early Stage
Seed

Geographical Preferences

Canadian Preferences:
Western Canada

Additional Information
Year Founded: 2015
Current Activity Level : Actively seeking new investments

VANDAI INVESTMENTS LTD

4-3-1 Toranomon, Minato-ku
36F Shiroyama Trust Tower
Tokyo, Japan 105-6036
Phone: 81-3-5776-6870
Fax: 81-3-5402-1280

Type of Firm
Private Equity Firm

Project Preferences

Type of Financing Preferred:
Balanced

Additional Information
Year Founded: 2005
Current Activity Level : Actively seeking new investments

VANEDGE CAPITAL INC

1333 West Broadway, Suite 750
Vancouver, Canada V6H 4C1
Phone: 6045693883
Fax: 6045693813
E-mail: info@vanedgecapital.com
Website: www.vanedgecapital.com

Management and Staff
Amy Rae, Principal
Divesh Sisodraker, Partner
Glenn Entis, Co-Founder
Howard Donaldson, Chief Financial Officer
Moe Kermani, Partner
Tony Lam, Principal
V. Paul Lee, Managing Partner

Type of Firm
Private Equity Firm

Association Membership
Canadian Venture Capital Association

Project Preferences

Type of Financing Preferred:
Early Stage
Expansion
Later Stage

Geographical Preferences

United States Preferences:

Canadian Preferences:
All Canada

International Preferences:
Asia

Industry Preferences

In Communications prefer:
Media and Entertainment

In Computer Software prefer:
Applications Software

Additional Information
Name of Most Recent Fund: Vanedge Capital I L.P.
Most Recent Fund Was Raised: 05/24/2010
Year Founded: 2009
Capital Under Management: $297,000,000
Current Activity Level : Actively seeking new investments

VANGOO CAPITAL LTD CO LTD

No. 1 Jianguomenwai Street
36F Tower 3 Inter'l Trade Ctr
Beijing, China
Phone: 861085187708201
E-mail: info@vangoocapital.com
Website: www.vangoocapital.com

Other Offices
1-15-1 Otemachi, Chiyoda
4/F, Otemachi First Square East Tower
Tokyo, Japan
Phone: 81352191362
Fax: 81352191201

Management and Staff
Kazunori Ozaki, Founder

Type of Firm
Private Equity Firm

Project Preferences

Type of Financing Preferred:
Expansion
Balanced
Later Stage

Geographical Preferences

International Preferences:
China

Industry Preferences

In Industrial/Energy prefer:
Energy

Additional Information
Year Founded: 2007
Current Activity Level : Actively seeking new investments

VANGUARD ATLANTIC LTD

P.O. Box 1199
Saranac Lake, NY USA 12983
Phone: 5182616608
Fax: 2082757423
E-mail: Partner@VanguardAtlantic.com
Website: www.vanguardatlantic.com

Management and Staff
Ernest Keet, Chief Executive Officer

Type of Firm
Private Equity Firm

Project Preferences

Type of Financing Preferred:
Leveraged Buyout
Early Stage
Seed
Startup

Size of Investments Considered:
Min Size of Investment Considered (000s): $150
Max Size of Investment Considered (000s): $6,000

Geographical Preferences

United States Preferences:

International Preferences:
Europe

Industry Preferences

In Computer Software prefer:
Software

In Internet Specific prefer:
E-Commerce Technology

Additional Information
Name of Most Recent Fund: Vanguard Atlantic, L.P.
Most Recent Fund Was Raised: 12/31/1989
Year Founded: 1984
Current Activity Level : Actively seeking new investments

VANTAGE VENTURE PARTNERS

Three Melrose Boulevard
Unit 9B, First Floor
Johannesburg, South Africa 2121
Phone: 27115309100
Fax: 27115309101
E-mail: info@vantagecapital.co.za
Website: www.vantagecapital.co.za

Management and Staff
Ashley Benatar, Managing Director
Colin Rezek, Managing Partner
Luc Albinski, Managing Partner
Mokgome Mogoba, Partner
Warren Van der Merwe, Chief Financial Officer
Zaheer Cassim, Partner

Type of Firm
Private Equity Firm

Association Membership
South African Venture Capital Association (SAVCA)

Project Preferences

Type of Financing Preferred:
Early Stage
Expansion
Mezzanine
Later Stage

Geographical Preferences

International Preferences:
Europe
Africa

Industry Preferences

In Communications prefer:
Telecommunications

In Computer Software prefer:
Software

In Biotechnology prefer:
Biotechnology

In Business Serv. prefer:
Services
Distribution

Additional Information
Year Founded: 2000
Capital Under Management: $25,000,000
Current Activity Level : Actively seeking new investments

VANTAGEPOINT MANAGEMENT INC

1001 Bayhill Drive, Suite 300
San Bruno, CA USA 94066
Phone: 6508663100
Fax: 6508696078
E-mail: IR@vpcp.com
Website: www.vpcp.com

Other Offices
77 Jan Guo Road
Unit 601, Tower 3, China Central Place
Beijing, China 100025
Phone: 86-10-6598-9650
Fax: 86-10-6598-9884

Eight Connaught Place
Level 8, Unit 39, Two Exchange Square
Central, Hong Kong
Phone: 852-2297-2325

Management and Staff
Annette Bianchi, Managing Director
Bernard Bulkin, Venture Partner
Boris Lipkin, Venture Partner
David Fries, Managing Director
Doug Kirkpatrick, Managing Director
E. Richard Prostko, Vice President
Eve Kurtin, Venture Partner
Feng Li, Venture Partner
Gene Gable, Vice President
Geraldine Chan, Vice President
Harold Friedman, Chief Financial Officer
J. Stephan Dolezalek, Managing Director
James Marver, Managing Director
Jason Whitt, Principal
Jim Mills, Managing Director
John Leggate, Venture Partner
Kal Patel, Partner
Lee Burrows, Managing Director
Marc van den Berg, Managing Director
Melissa Guzy, Managing Director
Neil Wolf, Managing Director
Pat Splinter, Managing Director
Patrick Gallagher, Principal
R. James Woolsey, Venture Partner
Rafael Simon, Venture Partner
Richard Harroch, Managing Director
Robert Kennedy, Venture Partner
Stephen Gray, Partner
Terry Chen, Venture Partner
Thomas Bevilacqua, Managing Director
Thomas Huot, Partner
Thomas Ley, Managing Director
William Harding, Managing Director
William McDonough, Venture Partner
William Harding, Managing Director
Yanyan Gong, Principal

Type of Firm
Private Equity Firm

Association Membership
Western Association of Venture Capitalists (WAVC)
National Venture Capital Association - USA (NVCA)

Project Preferences

Role in Financing:
Prefer role as deal originator

Type of Financing Preferred:
Early Stage
Expansion
Balanced
Later Stage

Industry Focus
(% based on actual investment)
Semiconductors/Other Elect.	23.6%
Internet Specific	18.1%
Computer Software and Services	16.1%
Industrial/Energy	11.2%
Communications and Media	8.9%
Biotechnology	7.1%
Other Products	6.1%
Computer Hardware	4.3%
Medical/Health	2.5%
Consumer Related	2.0%

Additional Information
Name of Most Recent Fund: VantagePoint CleanTech Partners II, L.P.
Most Recent Fund Was Raised: 11/21/2008
Year Founded: 1996
Capital Under Management: $4,500,000,000
Current Activity Level : Actively seeking new investments
Method of Compensation: Other

VANTERRA CAPITAL LTD

320 Park Avenue at 51st Street
18th Floor
New York, NY USA 10022
Phone: 2122313930
Fax: 2122313939
E-mail: info@vanterra.com
Website: www.vanterra.com

Management and Staff
Alan Quasha, Partner
Jason Young, Partner
Shad Azimi, Partner

Type of Firm
Private Equity Firm

Project Preferences

Type of Financing Preferred:
Fund of Funds
Balanced

Size of Investments Considered:
Min Size of Investment Considered (000s): $20,000
Max Size of Investment Considered (000s): $300,000

Geographical Preferences

United States Preferences:

International Preferences:
India
Brazil

Industry Preferences

In Medical/Health prefer:
Medical/Health

In Industrial/Energy prefer:
Alternative Energy
Materials

In Financial Services prefer:
Real Estate

Additional Information
Name of Most Recent Fund: Vanterra C Change Transformative Energy & Materials Fund I
Most Recent Fund Was Raised: 08/23/2010
Year Founded: 2008
Capital Under Management: $100,000,000
Current Activity Level : Actively seeking new investments

VARAGON CAPITAL PARTNERS LP

488 Madison Avenue
22nd Floor
New York, NY USA 10022
Phone: 2122352600
E-mail: info@varagon.com
Website: www.varagon.com

Management and Staff
Arcinee Hermiston, Partner
Brett Shapiro, Partner
Inoki Suarez, Managing Director
Ren Plastina, Partner
Steven Warden, Partner

Type of Firm
Private Equity Firm

Project Preferences

Type of Financing Preferred:
Mezzanine

Industry Preferences

In Medical/Health prefer:
Medical/Health

In Industrial/Energy prefer:
Energy
Industrial Products

Additional Information
Year Founded: 2013
Current Activity Level : Actively seeking new investments

VARDE PARTNERS INC

901 Marquette Avenue South, Suite 3300
Minneapolis, MN USA 55402
Phone: 9528931554
Fax: 9528939613
Website: varde.com

Other Offices
50 New Bond Street
Level 2
London, United Kingdom W1S 1BJ
Phone: 44-20-7808-3370
Fax: 44-20-7808-3371

6 Battery Road
#15-05
Singapore, Singapore 049909
Phone: 65-6579-0800
Fax: 65-6579-0801

Management and Staff
Ali Haroon, Partner
Andy Lenk, Partner
Brian Schmidt, Partner
George Hicks, Managing Partner
Jason Spaeth, Managing Partner
Jon Fox, Partner
Marcia Page, Managing Partner
Rick Noel, Partner

Type of Firm
Private Equity Firm

Project Preferences

Type of Financing Preferred:
Leveraged Buyout
Turnaround

Geographical Preferences

United States Preferences:

International Preferences:
Europe

Industry Focus
(% based on actual investment)
Other Products   100.0%

Additional Information
Name of Most Recent Fund: Varde Fund X
Most Recent Fund Was Raised: 02/19/2010
Year Founded: 1993
Capital Under Management: $3,740,000,000
Current Activity Level : Actively seeking new investments

VARDY PROPERTY GROUP

Venture House
Aykley Heads
Durham, United Kingdom DH1 5TS
Phone: 4407850494949

Website: www.vardygroup.com

Management and Staff
Peter Vardy, Founder

Type of Firm
Private Equity Firm

Project Preferences

Type of Financing Preferred:
Generalist PE
Balanced

Size of Investments Considered:
Min Size of Investment Considered (000s): $768
Max Size of Investment Considered (000s): $3,071

Geographical Preferences

International Preferences:
United Kingdom

Industry Preferences

In Consumer Related prefer:
Consumer

In Financial Services prefer:
Real Estate

Additional Information
Year Founded: 2006
Capital Under Management: $95,000,000
Current Activity Level : Actively seeking new investments

VARENNE CAPITAL PARTNERS SAS

50, avenue Montaigne
Paris, France 75008
Phone: 33170388122
Fax: 3370388120
E-mail: contact@varennecapital.com
Website: www.varennecapital.fr

Management and Staff
David Mellul, Chief Operating Officer
Marco Sormani, Managing Partner

Type of Firm
Private Equity Firm

Project Preferences

Type of Financing Preferred:
Leveraged Buyout

Geographical Preferences

International Preferences:
Europe

Additional Information
Year Founded: 2003
Current Activity Level : Actively seeking new investments

VARIV CAPITAL

Baha Santa Barbara 145
Mexico City, Mexico CDMX
E-mail: info@variv.com
Website: www.variv.com

Type of Firm
Private Equity Firm

Project Preferences

Type of Financing Preferred:
Early Stage
Seed

Geographical Preferences

United States Preferences:

International Preferences:
Mexico

Additional Information
Year Founded: 2013
Current Activity Level : Actively seeking new investments

VAROVA BV

Maliebaan 27-1
Utrecht, Netherlands 3581 CC
Phone: 31302305930
Fax: 31302305939
Website: varova.nl

Other Offices
Wibautstraat 129
Parooltoren 6e etage
, Netherlands 1091 GL

Management and Staff
Jan Stroeve, Partner
Joris Kaak, Partner
Maarten Vaessen, Co-Founder
Patrick Van Rossum, Co-Founder

Type of Firm
Private Equity Firm

Project Preferences

Type of Financing Preferred:
Leveraged Buyout
Management Buyouts
Acquisition

Geographical Preferences

International Preferences:
Europe

Additional Information
Year Founded: 2004
Current Activity Level : Actively seeking new investments

VARSHNEY CAPITAL CORP

1055 West Georgia Street, Suite 2050, Royal Centre
Vancouver, Canada V6E 3P3
Phone: 6046842181
Fax: 6046824768
Website: www.varshneycapital.com

Management and Staff
Hari Varshney, Partner
Peeyush Varshney, Partner
Praveen Varshney, Partner

Type of Firm
Private Equity Firm

Project Preferences

Type of Financing Preferred:
Generalist PE

Industry Preferences

In Financial Services prefer:
Real Estate

In Agr/Forestr/Fish prefer:
Mining and Minerals

Additional Information
Year Founded: 1985
Current Activity Level : Actively seeking new investments

VARSITY HEALTHCARE PARTNERS

1875 Century Park East, Suite 1980
Los Angeles, CA USA 90067
Phone: 3103074930
Website: varsityhealthcarepartners.com

Management and Staff
David Alpern, Co-Founder
Kenton Rosenberry, Co-Founder
Michael Jablon, Principal
Steven Bressler, Principal

Type of Firm
Private Equity Firm

Project Preferences

Type of Financing Preferred:
Leveraged Buyout
Acquisition

Industry Preferences

In Medical/Health prefer:
Medical/Health

Additional Information
Year Founded: 2014
Capital Under Management: $540,000,000
Current Activity Level : Actively seeking new investments

VASDAQ INVESTMENT LTD

9F Aiosu Meguroekimae Bldg.
2-15-19 Kami-Osaki,Shinagawaku
Tokyo, Japan 141-0021
Phone: 81-3-5772-8568
Fax: 81-3-5772-9581
E-mail: info@v-investment.jp
Website: www.v-investment.jp

Other Offices
IP Innovation Ltd Innovatioon House
139 Hillcrest, Weybridge
Surrey, United Kingdom KT13 8AS

Type of Firm
Private Equity Firm

Additional Information
Year Founded: 2003
Current Activity Level : Actively seeking new investments

VAST VENTURES

331 West 57th Street, Suite 197
New York, NY USA 10019
Phone: 9172155214
Website: www.vastvc.wordpress.com

Management and Staff
Doug Chertok, Founder

Type of Firm
Private Equity Firm

Project Preferences

Type of Financing Preferred:
Fund of Funds
Early Stage
Balanced

Geographical Preferences

United States Preferences:
New York

Industry Preferences

In Computer Software prefer:
Software

In Business Serv. prefer:
Media

In Manufact. prefer:
Publishing

Additional Information
Year Founded: 2004
Current Activity Level : Actively seeking new investments

VATEL CAPITAL SAS

12 rue Sainte-Anne
Paris, France 75001
Phone: 33140156177
Fax: 33177729801
E-mail: contact@vatelcapital.com
Website: www.vatelcapital.com

Management and Staff
Antoine Herbinet, Co-Founder
Francois Gerber, President, Founder
Marc Meneau, Co-Founder

Type of Firm
Private Equity Firm

Association Membership
French Venture Capital Association (AFIC)

Project Preferences

Type of Financing Preferred:
Leveraged Buyout
Early Stage
Expansion
Generalist PE
Later Stage
Management Buyouts
Acquisition

Size of Investments Considered:
Min Size of Investment Considered (000s): $340
Max Size of Investment Considered (000s): $2,267

Geographical Preferences

Canadian Preferences:
All Canada

International Preferences:
Europe
France

Industry Preferences

In Computer Hardware prefer:
Computers

In Computer Software prefer:
Software

In Internet Specific prefer:
Internet

In Medical/Health prefer:
Medical/Health
Health Services

In Consumer Related prefer:
Entertainment and Leisure
Hotels and Resorts

In Industrial/Energy prefer:
Energy
Alternative Energy
Industrial Products

In Business Serv. prefer:
Services

In Agr/Forestr/Fish prefer:
Agribusiness
Agriculture related

Additional Information
Year Founded: 2008
Capital Under Management: $13,225,000
Current Activity Level: Actively seeking new investments

VATERA HEALTHCARE PARTNERS LLC

499 Park Avenue
23rd Floor
New York, NY USA 10022
Phone: 2125902950
Fax: 2125902951
Website: www.vaterahealthcare.com

Management and Staff
Michael Jaharis, Founder

Type of Firm
Private Equity Firm

Project Preferences

Type of Financing Preferred:
Early Stage

Industry Preferences

In Biotechnology prefer:
Human Biotechnology

In Medical/Health prefer:
Pharmaceuticals

Additional Information
Year Founded: 2007
Current Activity Level: Actively seeking new investments

VAUBAN PARTENAIRES SA

15, Avenue Victor Hugo
Paris, France 75116
Phone: 33149240707
Fax: 33149240808
E-mail: courrier@vauban-sa.fr
Website: vauban-sa.fr

Other Offices
1, rue Esquermoise - BP 112
Lille Cedex, France 59027
Phone: 33320219380
Fax: 33320219389

Management and Staff
Laurence Leonardi, Chief Financial Officer
Robert Mazaud, Chief Executive Officer

Type of Firm
Private Equity Firm

Association Membership
French Venture Capital Association (AFIC)

Project Preferences

Type of Financing Preferred:
Early Stage
Balanced
Later Stage

Size of Investments Considered:
Min Size of Investment Considered (000s): $370
Max Size of Investment Considered (000s): $12,333

Geographical Preferences

International Preferences:
Europe
France

Industry Preferences

In Consumer Related prefer:
Consumer

In Business Serv. prefer:
Services
Distribution

In Manufact. prefer:
Manufacturing

Additional Information
Year Founded: 1992
Capital Under Management: $30,200,000
Current Activity Level: Actively seeking new investments

VBS INVESTMENT BANK LTD

Suourlandsbraut 22
Reykjavik, Iceland 108
Phone: 3545701200
Fax: 3545701209
Website: www.vbs.is

Type of Firm
Private Equity Firm

Project Preferences

Type of Financing Preferred:
Later Stage

Geographical Preferences

International Preferences:
Europe

Additional Information
Year Founded: 2004
Current Activity Level: Actively seeking new investments

VC PARTICIPACOES LTDA

Avenida Ataulfo de Paiva 1251
Rio de Janeiro, Brazil 22440-031
Phone: 552122941876
Fax: 552125113721
E-mail: info@vogacapital.com.br
Website: www.voga.com.br

Type of Firm
Private Equity Firm

Project Preferences

Type of Financing Preferred:
Balanced

Geographical Preferences

International Preferences:
Brazil

Industry Preferences

In Financial Services prefer:
Real Estate

Additional Information
Year Founded: 2002
Current Activity Level : Actively seeking new investments

VCAPITAL MANAGEMENT CO LLC

1420 N Lake Shore Drive
11B
Chicago, IL USA 60610
Website: www.vcapital.com

Type of Firm
Private Equity Firm

Project Preferences

Type of Financing Preferred:
Early Stage
Seed

Industry Preferences

In Communications prefer:
Telecommunications

In Biotechnology prefer:
Biotechnology

In Medical/Health prefer:
Medical Products

In Consumer Related prefer:
Education Related

In Business Serv. prefer:
Media

In Other prefer:
Environment Responsible

Additional Information
Year Founded: 2016
Current Activity Level : Actively seeking new investments

VCCHINA LTD

Kuntai International Plaza
No. 12 Chaowai Street
Beijing, China 100028
Phone: 86-10-5879-7706
Fax: 86-10-5879-7705
E-mail: questions@vcchina.com

Other Offices

31/F, Room 3105 Panglin Square
2001 Jiabin Road, Luohu District
Shenzhen, China 518005
Phone: 86-755-5185-223
Fax: 86-755-5185-232

Management and Staff
Wayne Zhao, President
Wolfgang Yang, Vice President

Type of Firm
Private Equity Firm

Association Membership
Venture Capital Association of Beijing (VCAB)

Project Preferences

Type of Financing Preferred:
Seed
Startup

Geographical Preferences

International Preferences:
No Preference
China

Industry Preferences

In Communications prefer:
Telecommunications

In Computer Software prefer:
Software

In Biotechnology prefer:
Biotechnology

In Medical/Health prefer:
Medical/Health

In Industrial/Energy prefer:
Energy
Materials

Additional Information
Year Founded: 1999
Current Activity Level : Actively seeking new investments

VCWILL CAPITAL

9,East 3rd Ring Road, Chaoyang
1705,17F,W Tower, Wangzuo Ctr.
Beijing, China 100020
Phone: 861065020345
Fax: 861065020345
E-mail: info@vcwill.cn
Website: www.vcwill.cn

Other Offices

No. 2, Guangyaqian Street
Rm 308, Xiwan Road, Liwan District
Guangzhou, China 510160
Phone: 862081341874
Fax: 862081341874

No. 108, West 2nd Ring, West Section
Rm 1202, Zizhu Plaza, Building A
Xi'an, China 710065
Phone: 862985733356
Fax: 862985733356

Management and Staff
Guangjie Liu, Vice President
Jinshang Xu, Vice President
Xuguang Long, Vice President

Type of Firm
Bank Affiliated

Project Preferences

Type of Financing Preferred:
Early Stage
Expansion

Geographical Preferences

International Preferences:
China

Industry Preferences

In Medical/Health prefer:
Medical/Health

In Consumer Related prefer:
Consumer Products

In Industrial/Energy prefer:
Energy Conservation Relat
Environmental Related

In Business Serv. prefer:
Services

In Agr/Forestr/Fish prefer:
Agriculture related

Additional Information
Year Founded: 2010
Current Activity Level : Actively seeking new investments

VEB INNOVATIONS

Chistoprudnyi Bul'var 11/1
Moscow, Russia 101000
Phone: 849578461
Website: www.innoveb.ru

Type of Firm
Government Affiliated Program

Project Preferences

Type of Financing Preferred:
Early Stage
Start-up Financing
Seed
Startup

Geographical Preferences

International Preferences:
Russia

Industry Preferences

In Computer Software prefer:
Software

In Semiconductor/Electr prefer:
Electronic Components
Semiconductor

In Biotechnology prefer:
Biotechnology

In Industrial/Energy prefer:
Energy
Energy Conservation Relat
Advanced Materials

In Transportation prefer:
Aerospace

Additional Information
Year Founded: 2011
Current Activity Level : Actively seeking new investments

VECTIS PARTICIPATIES NV

Stratem 11 bus 2
Aalter, Belgium 9880
Phone: 3293756900
Fax: 3293746900
E-mail: vectis@vectisparticipaties.be
Website: www.vectisparticipaties.be

Management and Staff
Stefaan Vanquaethem, Co-Founder
Walter Beyen, Co-Founder

Type of Firm
Private Equity Firm

Project Preferences

Type of Financing Preferred:
Leveraged Buyout
Early Stage
Generalist PE
Balanced
Later Stage
Management Buyouts
Acquisition
Startup

Size of Investments Considered:
Min Size of Investment Considered (000s): $144
Max Size of Investment Considered (000s): $2,157

Geographical Preferences

International Preferences:
Europe
Belgium

Industry Preferences

In Industrial/Energy prefer:
Industrial Products

In Business Serv. prefer:
Services

Additional Information
Year Founded: 1997
Current Activity Level : Actively seeking new investments

VECTOR CAPITAL MANAGEMENT LP

One Market Street
Steuart Tower, 23rd Floor
San Francisco, CA USA 94105
Phone: 4152935000
Fax: 4152935100
Website: www.vectorcapital.com

Management and Staff
Aalok Jain, Vice President
Alex Beregovsky, Managing Director
Alexander Slusky, Managing Partner
Alok Pandey, Vice President
Amish Mehta, Partner
Andy Fishman, Managing Director
David Fishman, Partner
Ilya Voytov, Vice President
Jim Murray, Chief Financial Officer
John Beauclair, Principal
Nick Lukens, Vice President
Nick Ghoussaini, Vice President
Robert Amen, Principal
Robert Hansen, Principal
Rock Meng, Vice President
Stephen Wolfe, Vice President
Tom Walsh, Vice President

Type of Firm
Private Equity Firm

Association Membership
Western Association of Venture Capitalists (WAVC)
Natl Assoc of Small Bus. Inv. Co (NASBIC)
Private Equity Council (PEC)

Project Preferences

Role in Financing:
Prefer role as deal originator

Type of Financing Preferred:
Leveraged Buyout
Turnaround
Management Buyouts
Acquisition
Recapitalizations

Geographical Preferences

United States Preferences:

Industry Focus
(% based on actual investment)
Computer Software and Services   75.8%
Computer Hardware   16.5%
Internet Specific   7.2%
Other Products   0.5%

Additional Information
Name of Most Recent Fund: Vector Capital IV, L.P.
Most Recent Fund Was Raised: 06/13/2007
Year Founded: 1997
Capital Under Management: $2,000,000,000
Current Activity Level : Actively seeking new investments
Method of Compensation: Return on invest. most important, but chg. closing fees, service fees, etc.

VECTORPOINT VENTURES

9786 Southwest Nimbus Avenue
Beaverton, OR USA 97008
Phone: 5032223693
E-mail: info@vpointv.com
Website: www.vpointv.com

Management and Staff
Dennis Powers, Co-Founder
Donald Megrath, Co-Founder
Rick Nagle, Co-Founder

Type of Firm
Private Equity Firm

Project Preferences

Type of Financing Preferred:
Leveraged Buyout
Expansion
Acquisition

Geographical Preferences

United States Preferences:
Northwest

Industry Preferences

In Computer Software prefer:
Software

In Medical/Health prefer:
Medical/Health
Medical Products

In Consumer Related prefer:
Food/Beverage
Consumer Products

In Manufact. prefer:
Manufacturing

Additional Information

Year Founded: 2012
Current Activity Level : Actively seeking new investments

VEDANTA CAPITAL LP

540 Madison Avenue
30th Floor
New York, NY USA 10022
Phone: 2127105220
Fax: 2127105221
E-mail: info@vedacap.com
Website: www.vedacap.com

Management and Staff

Alessandro Piol, Co-Founder
Andrew Dworkin, Partner
Gonzalo Cordova, Partner
Howard Goldstein, Co-Founder
Margaret Riley, Partner
Michael Patterson, General Partner
Parag Saxena, Co-Founder
Shrikant Sathe, General Partner

Type of Firm

Private Equity Advisor or Fund of Funds

Project Preferences

Type of Financing Preferred:
Fund of Funds
Balanced

Industry Preferences

In Communications prefer:
Communications and Media

In Internet Specific prefer:
Ecommerce

Additional Information

Year Founded: 2006
Capital Under Management: $110,000,000
Current Activity Level : Actively seeking new investments

VEDDIS VENTURES

Europort, Suite 931
Gibraltar, Gibraltar
Phone: 35020047703
Website: www.veddis.com

Management and Staff

Vikrant Bhargava, Founder

Type of Firm

Private Equity Firm

Project Preferences

Type of Financing Preferred:
Early Stage
Later Stage
Startup

Geographical Preferences

International Preferences:
India
Europe

Industry Preferences

In Communications prefer:
Telecommunications
Media and Entertainment

In Internet Specific prefer:
Internet

Additional Information

Year Founded: 2006
Current Activity Level : Actively seeking new investments

VEGAGEST AZIONARI ASIA A

Largo Donegani 2 angolo
Via Moscova 3
Milano, Italy 20121
Phone: 39-02-3046-8301
Fax: 39-02-3046-8318
E-mail: info@vegagest.it

Management and Staff

Alessandro Betti, Partner
Alessandro Cameroni, Partner
Francesco Conforti, Partner
Mario Roncaglia, Partner
Riccardo Alaimo, Partner
Stefano Costagli, Partner

Type of Firm

Corporate PE/Venture

Association Membership

Italian Venture Capital Association (AIFI)

Project Preferences

Type of Financing Preferred:
Expansion
Balanced

Geographical Preferences

International Preferences:
Italy

Additional Information

Year Founded: 2007
Current Activity Level : Actively seeking new investments

VEGASTECHFUND

3540 West Sahara Avenue
Las Vegas, NV USA 89102
Phone: 4158940081
Website: vegastechfund.com

Management and Staff

Andy White, Partner
Fred Mossler, Partner
Tony Hsieh, Partner
Will Young, Partner
Zach Ware, Partner

Type of Firm

Incubator/Development Program

Project Preferences

Type of Financing Preferred:
Seed
Startup

Geographical Preferences

United States Preferences:
Nevada
Texas

Additional Information

Year Founded: 2012
Current Activity Level : Actively seeking new investments

VELA CAPITAL SRL

Via Santa Marta 19
Milano, Italy 20123
Phone: 39272093833
Fax: 39272015230
E-mail: info@velacapital.it
Website: www.velacapital.it

Type of Firm

Private Equity Firm

Association Membership

Italian Venture Capital Association (AIFI)

Project Preferences

Type of Financing Preferred:
Expansion

Geographical Preferences

International Preferences:
Italy

Industry Preferences

In Medical/Health prefer:
Medical Products
Pharmaceuticals

In Industrial/Energy prefer:
Alternative Energy

In Financial Services prefer:
Financial Services

Additional Information

Year Founded: 2000
Current Activity Level : Actively seeking new investments

VELA IMPRESE SRL

Via Ponte Vetero 22
Milan, Italy 20121
Phone: 390292889360
Fax: 390289690970
E-mail: info@velaimprese.it
Website: www.velaimprese.it

Type of Firm
Private Equity Firm

Project Preferences

Type of Financing Preferred:
Start-up Financing

Geographical Preferences

International Preferences:
Italy

Additional Information

Year Founded: 2013
Current Activity Level : Actively seeking new investments

VELOCITAS PARTNERS LLC

2113 Duck Hunter Pointe
Florence, SC USA 29501
Phone: 1646244179
Fax: 19172103518
E-mail: office@velocitaspartners.com
Website: www.velocitaspartners.com

Type of Firm
Private Equity Firm

Project Preferences

Type of Financing Preferred:
Generalist PE
Joint Ventures

Geographical Preferences

United States Preferences:

International Preferences:
Austria

Additional Information

Year Founded: 2017
Capital Under Management: $5,000,000
Current Activity Level : Actively seeking new investments

VELOCITY

200 University Avenue West
Waterloo, Canada N2L 3G1
Website: velocity.uwaterloo.ca

Type of Firm
University Program

Project Preferences

Type of Financing Preferred:
Early Stage
Balanced
Later Stage
Seed
Startup

Geographical Preferences

Canadian Preferences:
All Canada

Industry Preferences

In Computer Software prefer:
Software

Additional Information

Year Founded: 2008
Current Activity Level : Actively seeking new investments

VELOCITY CAPITAL BV

Hoofdstraat 178
Driebergen-Rijsenburg, Netherlands 3972 LG
Phone: 31343523850
E-mail: contact@velocitycapital-pe.com
Website: www.velocitycapital.nl

Management and Staff
Rogier Gasseling, Chief Financial Officer
Willem Willemstein, Chief Executive Officer

Type of Firm
Private Equity Firm

Project Preferences

Type of Financing Preferred:
Early Stage
Seed
Startup

Geographical Preferences

United States Preferences:
All U.S.

International Preferences:
Europe
Netherlands
Asia
Africa

Industry Preferences

In Computer Software prefer:
Systems Software

In Internet Specific prefer:
E-Commerce Technology

In Financial Services prefer:
Financial Services

Additional Information

Year Founded: 2014
Current Activity Level : Actively seeking new investments

VELOCITY VENTURE CAPITAL INC

181 Blue Ravine Road, Suite 120
Folsom, CA USA 95630
Phone: 8882924748
Fax: 9164045098
E-mail: info@velocityvc.com
Website: impactvc.com

Management and Staff
Christian Hendricks, Vice President
Dan Becker, Venture Partner
Dan Wadhwani, Venture Partner
Gary Simon, Venture Partner
Gary Hooper, Venture Partner
Gayathri Radhakrishnan, Venture Partner
Jack Crawford, General Partner
Jeff Harbach, Venture Partner
Ken Bossung, Managing Director
Monique Brown, Venture Partner
Shawn Gillogly, Venture Partner

Type of Firm
Private Equity Firm

Association Membership
National Venture Capital Association - USA (NVCA)

Project Preferences

Type of Financing Preferred:
Early Stage
Seed

Geographical Preferences

United States Preferences:
California

Industry Preferences

In Communications prefer:
Wireless Communications
Data Communications

In Computer Software prefer:
Software

In Internet Specific prefer:
Internet

In Semiconductor/Electr prefer:
Semiconductor

In Medical/Health prefer:
Medical Products

In Consumer Related prefer:
Education Related

In Industrial/Energy prefer:
Energy

Additional Information

Name of Most Recent Fund: Velocity VC Partners III
Most Recent Fund Was Raised: 06/30/2008
Year Founded: 2005
Capital Under Management: $28,000,000
Current Activity Level : Actively seeking new investments

VELOS PARTNERS

10960 Wilshire Boulevard, Suite 1420
Los Angeles, CA USA 90024
E-mail: info@velospartners.com
Website: www.velospartners.com

Type of Firm
Private Equity Firm

Project Preferences

Type of Financing Preferred:
Balanced

Industry Preferences

In Consumer Related prefer:
Consumer

Additional Information
Year Founded: 2012
Capital Under Management: $39,525,000
Current Activity Level : Actively seeking new investments

VELTI CENTER FOR INNOVATION SA

Kifissias Avenue 42
Marousi
Athens, Greece 15125
Phone: 302106378900
Fax: 302106378999
E-mail: vci@vci.gr
Website: www.vci.gr

Type of Firm
Incubator/Development Program

Association Membership
Hellenic Venture Capital Association

Project Preferences

Type of Financing Preferred:
Early Stage
Expansion
Balanced
Seed
Startup

Geographical Preferences

International Preferences:
Greece
Europe

Industry Preferences

In Communications prefer:
Telecommunications
Media and Entertainment

In Consumer Related prefer:
Consumer Services

Additional Information
Year Founded: 2012
Current Activity Level : Actively seeking new investments

VELUM VENTURES SAS

Calle 10 A No. 34 - 11
Medellin, Colombia 4014
Phone: 5742669243
Website: www.velumventures.com

Type of Firm
Private Equity Firm

Project Preferences

Type of Financing Preferred:
Seed
Startup

Size of Investments Considered:
Min Size of Investment Considered (000s): $100
Max Size of Investment Considered (000s): $500

Geographical Preferences

International Preferences:
Colombia

Industry Preferences

In Communications prefer:
Wireless Communications

In Medical/Health prefer:
Medical/Health

In Other prefer:
Environment Responsible

Additional Information
Year Founded: 2012
Capital Under Management: $5,000,000
Current Activity Level : Actively seeking new investments

VENBIO PARTNERS LLC

1700 Owens Street, Suite 595
San Francisco, CA USA 94158
Phone: 4158000800
E-mail: info@venbio.com
Website: www.venbio.com

Management and Staff
Corey Goodman, Managing Director
Kurt von Emster, Managing Director
Paul Brooke, Managing Director
Robert Adelman, Managing Director

Type of Firm
Private Equity Firm

Project Preferences

Type of Financing Preferred:
Balanced

Industry Preferences

In Medical/Health prefer:
Medical/Health
Other Therapeutic

Additional Information
Name of Most Recent Fund: venBio Global Strategic Fund, L.P.
Most Recent Fund Was Raised: 11/12/2010
Year Founded: 2010
Capital Under Management: $315,000,000
Current Activity Level : Actively seeking new investments

VENCAP INTERNATIONAL PLC

King Charles House
Park End Street
Oxford, United Kingdom OX1 1JD
Phone: 441865799300
Fax: 441865799301
Website: www.vencapintl.com

Management and Staff
Ann Cooke, Founder

Type of Firm
Private Equity Firm

Association Membership
European Private Equity and Venture Capital Assoc.

Project Preferences

Type of Financing Preferred:
Fund of Funds

Geographical Preferences

United States Preferences:

International Preferences:
India
Europe
China

Additional Information
Year Founded: 1987
Capital Under Management: $1,900,000,000
Current Activity Level : Actively seeking new investments

VENCON MANAGEMENT, INC.

65 West 55th Street
New York, NY USA 10019
Phone: 212-581-8787
Fax: 212-397-4126
E-mail: vencon@att.net
Website: www.venconinc.com

Type of Firm
Private Equity Firm

Project Preferences

Role in Financing:
Prefer role as deal originator but will also invest in deals created by others

Type of Financing Preferred:
Second Stage Financing
Leveraged Buyout
Early Stage
Expansion
Balanced
Start-up Financing
Later Stage
Seed
Management Buyouts
First Stage Financing
Acquisition
Special Situation

Size of Investments Considered:
Min Size of Investment Considered (000s): $500
Max Size of Investment Considered (000s): $3,000

Geographical Preferences

United States Preferences:

Canadian Preferences:
All Canada

International Preferences:
Hong Kong
China
Middle East

Industry Preferences

In Communications prefer:
Satellite Microwave Comm.
Other Communication Prod.

In Computer Software prefer:
Artificial Intelligence

In Internet Specific prefer:
Internet

In Semiconductor/Electr prefer:
Electronic Components
Sensors
Fiber Optics

In Biotechnology prefer:
Industrial Biotechnology
Biosensors
Biotech Related Research

In Medical/Health prefer:
Diagnostic Services
Diagnostic Test Products
Medical Therapeutics
Drug/Equipmt Delivery
Disposable Med. Products

In Industrial/Energy prefer:
Alternative Energy
Coal Related
Energy Conservation Relat
Industrial Products
Environmental Related

Additional Information
Year Founded: 1973
Current Activity Level : Actively seeking new investments
Method of Compensation: Return on invest. most important, but chg. closing fees, service fees, etc.

VENDEP CAPITAL OY

Tammasaarenkatu 1
Helsinki, Finland 00180
Phone: 358207571490
E-mail: info@vendep.com
Website: www.vendep.com

Management and Staff
Juha Litola, Partner
Sakari Pihlava, Chief Executive Officer

Type of Firm
Private Equity Firm

Project Preferences

Type of Financing Preferred:
Seed

Industry Preferences

In Communications prefer:
Wireless Communications

Additional Information
Year Founded: 1969
Capital Under Management: $39,445,000
Current Activity Level : Actively seeking new investments

VENDIS CAPITAL NV

Pontbeekstraat 2
Groot-Bijgaarden, Belgium 1702
Phone: 3224676080
Fax: 3224658480
E-mail: info@vendiscapital.com

Management and Staff
Cedric Olbrechts, Partner
Jean Cailliau, Partner
Luc Geuten, Partner
Michiel Deturck, Partner
Willem Van Aelten, Partner

Type of Firm
Private Equity Firm

Association Membership
Belgium Venturing Association
French Venture Capital Association (AFIC)
Dutch Venture Capital Associaton (NVP)

Project Preferences

Type of Financing Preferred:
Leveraged Buyout
Management Buyouts
Acquisition

Size of Investments Considered:
Min Size of Investment Considered (000s): $7,502
Max Size of Investment Considered (000s): $60,015

Geographical Preferences

International Preferences:
Sweden
Europe
Netherlands
Belgium
Norway
Germany
Denmark
France

Industry Preferences

In Consumer Related prefer:
Retail
Consumer Products
Consumer Services

In Business Serv. prefer:
Consulting Services

Additional Information
Year Founded: 2009
Capital Under Management: $200,530,000
Current Activity Level : Actively seeking new investments

VENETO SVILUPPO SPA

Via delle Industrie 19/D
Parco Scientifico Tecnologico
Venezia, Italy 30175
Phone: 39 -41-396-7211
Fax: 39 -41-538-3605
E-mail: info@venetosviluppo.it
Website: www.venetosviluppo.it

Management and Staff
N. Polato, Managing Director

Type of Firm
Incubator/Development Program

Association Membership
Italian Venture Capital Association (AIFI)

Project Preferences

Type of Financing Preferred:
Second Stage Financing
Expansion

Geographical Preferences

International Preferences:
Italy

Additional Information
Year Founded: 1999
Current Activity Level : Actively seeking new investments

VENICE EUROPEAN INVESTMENT CAPITAL SPA

11 , Via Fiori Oscuri
Milan, Italy 20121
Phone: 39272730700
Fax: 39272730730
Website: www.aifi.it

Type of Firm
Investment Management Firm

Association Membership
Italian Venture Capital Association (AIFI)

Project Preferences

Type of Financing Preferred:
Leveraged Buyout
Generalist PE
Startup

Geographical Preferences

International Preferences:
Italy

Industry Preferences

In Financial Services prefer:
Real Estate

Additional Information
Year Founded: 2010
Capital Under Management: $675,600,000
Current Activity Level : Actively seeking new investments

VENIONAIRE CAPITAL GMBH

Aspernbrueckengasse 2
Vienna, Austria 1020
Phone: 4313480338
E-mail: office@venionaire.com
Website: www.venionaire.com

Type of Firm
Private Equity Firm

Association Membership
Austrian PE and Venture Capital Association (AVCO)

Project Preferences

Type of Financing Preferred:
Early Stage
Seed
Startup

Geographical Preferences

International Preferences:
Switzerland
Western Europe
Austria
Germany

Additional Information
Year Founded: 2012
Current Activity Level : Actively seeking new investments

VENISTA VENTURES GMBH & CO KG

Spichernstrasse 6b
Cologne, Germany 50672
Phone: 49221933167700
Fax: 49221933167170
E-mail: contact@venista.com
Website: venista-ventures.com

Management and Staff
Christian Teichert, Managing Director
Oliver Wimmeroth, Managing Director

Type of Firm
Private Equity Firm

Project Preferences

Type of Financing Preferred:
Early Stage
Startup

Geographical Preferences

International Preferences:
Europe
Germany

Industry Preferences

In Communications prefer:
Wireless Communications

Additional Information
Year Founded: 2004
Current Activity Level : Actively seeking new investments

VENREX INVESTMENT MANAGEMENT LLP

105 Ladbroke Grove
London, United Kingdom W8 5EP
Phone: 44020891261

Type of Firm
Private Equity Firm

Project Preferences

Type of Financing Preferred:
Early Stage
Expansion
Startup

Geographical Preferences

International Preferences:
United Kingdom

Industry Preferences

In Consumer Related prefer:
Consumer
Retail

Additional Information

Year Founded: 2002
Capital Under Management: $290,000
Current Activity Level : Actively seeking new investments

VENROCK INC

3340 Hillview Avenue
Palo Alto, CA USA 94304
Phone: 6505619580
Fax: 6505619180
Website: www.venrock.com

Other Offices

530 Fifth Avenue
22nd Floor
NEW YORK, NY USA 10036
Phone: 212-444-4100
Fax: 212-444-4101

Management and Staff

Anders Hove, Partner
Bong Koh, Partner
Brian Ascher, Partner
Bryan Roberts, Partner
Camille Samuels, Partner
Colin Cahill, Vice President
David Pakman, Partner
Mike Tyrrell, Partner
Nick Beim, Partner
Nicole Pack, Vice President
Nimish Shah, Vice President
Richard Kerby, Vice President
Robert Kocher, Partner

Type of Firm

Private Equity Firm

Association Membership

New England Venture Capital Association
Western Association of Venture Capitalists (WAVC)
National Venture Capital Association – USA (NVCA)

Project Preferences

Role in Financing:
Prefer role as deal originator but will also invest in deals created by others

Type of Financing Preferred:
Early Stage
Balanced
Later Stage

Geographical Preferences

United States Preferences:

Industry Focus

(% based on actual investment)
Biotechnology	22.3%
Computer Software and Services	21.2%
Internet Specific	14.2%
Medical/Health	13.1%
Communications and Media	12.1%
Semiconductors/Other Elect.	7.5%
Industrial/Energy	4.1%
Computer Hardware	2.9%
Consumer Related	1.5%
Other Products	1.0%

Additional Information

Name of Most Recent Fund: Venrock Associates VI, L.P.
Most Recent Fund Was Raised: 06/25/2010
Year Founded: 1969
Capital Under Management: $2,300,000,000
Current Activity Level : Actively seeking new investments
Method of Compensation: Return on investment is of primary concern, do not charge fees

VENSTAR CAPITAL MANAGEMENT PTE LTD

61, Robinson Road
13-03, Robinson Centre
Singapore, Singapore 068893
Phone: 6562226221
Fax: 6562221721
Website: www.venstar-capital.com

Management and Staff

Beng Chua, Co-Founder
Eng Hong Koh, Co-Founder
Jeffrey Ng Ah Bah, Co-Founder
Kian Heng Ang, Co-Founder

Type of Firm

Private Equity Firm

Project Preferences

Type of Financing Preferred:
Leveraged Buyout
Early Stage
Expansion
Generalist PE
Balanced
Later Stage
Management Buyouts
Acquisition

Size of Investments Considered:
Min Size of Investment Considered (000s): $1,154
Max Size of Investment Considered (000s): $8,654

Geographical Preferences

International Preferences:
China
Asia
Singapore

Industry Preferences

In Biotechnology prefer:
Agricultural/Animal Bio.

In Medical/Health prefer:
Medical/Health
Health Services

In Consumer Related prefer:
Consumer

In Industrial/Energy prefer:
Energy
Environmental Related

In Manufact. prefer:
Manufacturing

Additional Information

Year Founded: 2010
Capital Under Management: $72,303,000
Current Activity Level : Actively seeking new investments

VENTANA CAPITAL MANAGEMENT LP

22431 Antonio Parkway, Suite B160-1002
Rancho Santa Margarita, CA USA 92688
Phone: 9494814200
Fax: 9497664487
Website: www.ventanavc.com

Other Offices

Avenida Loma de la Palma 275, Suite Two
Mexico City, Mexico 05100
Phone: 52-5-259-4660
Fax: 52-5-259-5099

Rio Vista Towers
8880 Rio San Diego Drive
San Diego, CA USA 92108
Phone: 619-291-2757
Fax: 619-295-0189

Management and Staff

Allen Bah, Venture Partner
Barry Toyonaga, Managing Director
Brantley Haigh, Principal
C. Ian Sym-Smith, Venture Partner
Cyndi Abee, Chief Financial Officer
Ed Berkey, Managing Director
Fred Thiel, Venture Partner
Paul DeRidder, Managing Director
Robert Tufts, Venture Partner
Thomas Papa, Managing Director
Wayne Huang, Managing Director
Xin Li, Managing Director

Type of Firm
Private Equity Firm

Project Preferences

Role in Financing:
Will function either as deal originator or investor in deals created by others

Type of Financing Preferred:
Early Stage

Size of Investments Considered:
Min Size of Investment Considered (000s): $1,000
Max Size of Investment Considered: No Limit

Geographical Preferences

United States Preferences:
Southern California

Industry Preferences

In Communications prefer:
Telecommunications
Wireless Communications

In Semiconductor/Electr prefer:
Semiconductor
Micro-Processing
Controllers and Sensors
Sensors

In Biotechnology prefer:
Human Biotechnology
Biosensors

In Medical/Health prefer:
Pharmaceuticals

Additional Information
Year Founded: 1984
Capital Under Management: $15,000,000
Current Activity Level : Actively seeking new investments
Method of Compensation: Return on investment is of primary concern, do not charge fees

---

VENTECH SA

47 Avenue de l'Opera
Paris, France 75002
Phone: 33158192150
Fax: 33158192160
E-mail: contact@ventech.fr
Website: www.ventechvc.com

Other Offices
9th Floor, China Central Place
Tower II 79 Jianguo Road
Beijing, China 100025
Phone: 86-10-5920-4215
Fax: 85-10-5920-7652

Management and Staff
Alain Caffi, Founder
Cindy Guo, General Partner
Claire Houry, General Partner
Emmanuelle De Roux, Chief Financial Officer
Eric Huet, General Partner
Jean Bourcereau, General Partner
Joe Tang, Principal
Mounia Chaoui, General Partner

Type of Firm
Bank Affiliated

Association Membership
French Venture Capital Association (AFIC)
European Private Equity and Venture Capital Assoc.

Project Preferences

Role in Financing:
Prefer role as deal originator but will also invest in deals created by others

Type of Financing Preferred:
Fund of Funds
Early Stage
Expansion
Balanced
Seed
Startup

Geographical Preferences

United States Preferences:
All U.S.

International Preferences:
Europe
Switzerland
China
Scandanavia/Nordic Region
Israel
Asia
Germany
France

Industry Preferences

In Communications prefer:
Communications and Media
Telecommunications
Media and Entertainment
Entertainment
Other Communication Prod.

In Computer Software prefer:
Software

In Internet Specific prefer:
E-Commerce Technology
Internet

In Computer Other prefer:
Computer Related

In Semiconductor/Electr prefer:
Electronics
Electronic Components

In Biotechnology prefer:
Biotechnology

In Medical/Health prefer:
Medical Products

In Business Serv. prefer:
Services
Media

Additional Information
Name of Most Recent Fund: Ventech Capital III
Most Recent Fund Was Raised: 09/10/2007
Year Founded: 1998
Capital Under Management: $471,100,000
Current Activity Level : Actively seeking new investments

VENTEGIS CAPITAL AG

Kurfuerstendamm 119
Berlin, Germany 10711
Phone: 493089021180
Fax: 493089021189
E-mail: info@ventegis-capital.de
Website: www.ventegis-capital.de

Type of Firm
Private Equity Firm

Association Membership
German Venture Capital Association (BVK)

Project Preferences

Type of Financing Preferred:
Early Stage
Seed
Startup

Size of Investments Considered:
Min Size of Investment Considered (000s): $656
Max Size of Investment Considered (000s): $1,967

Geographical Preferences

International Preferences:
Germany

Industry Preferences

In Communications prefer:
Communications and Media

In Computer Software prefer:
Software

In Biotechnology prefer:
Biotechnology

In Medical/Health prefer:
Medical/Health

In Industrial/Energy prefer:
Energy
Industrial Products
Environmental Related

Additional Information
Year Founded: 1996
Capital Under Management: $28,700,000
Current Activity Level : Actively seeking new investments

VENTIZZ CAPITAL PARTNERS ADVISORY AG

Graf-Adolf-Strasse 18
Duesseldorf, Germany 40212
Phone: 492118628690
Fax: 4921186286977
E-mail: info@ventizz.de
Website: www.ventizz.de

Other Offices
Vadianstrasse 59
St. Gallen, Switzerland 9000
Phone: 41-71-226-8800
Fax: 41-71-226-8801

Management and Staff
Andreas Marty, Chief Financial Officer
Bjoern Soendgerath, General Partner
Daniel Saxena, Managing Director
Willi Mannheims, General Partner

Type of Firm
Private Equity Firm

Association Membership
German Venture Capital Association (BVK)
European Private Equity and Venture Capital Assoc.

Project Preferences

Type of Financing Preferred:
Leveraged Buyout
Later Stage
Acquisition

Geographical Preferences

United States Preferences:
All U.S.

International Preferences:
Europe
Switzerland
Austria
Germany
Denmark

Industry Preferences

In Communications prefer:
Communications and Media
Telecommunications

In Computer Software prefer:
Software

In Internet Specific prefer:
Internet

In Semiconductor/Electr prefer:
Electronics
Semiconductor
Fiber Optics

In Biotechnology prefer:
Biotechnology

In Medical/Health prefer:
Medical/Health

In Industrial/Energy prefer:
Energy
Alternative Energy
Industrial Products

Additional Information
Year Founded: 2000
Capital Under Management: $943,700,000
Current Activity Level : Actively seeking new investments

VENTURCAP SCR DE REGIMEN COMUN SA

Diagonal, 427-429
Barcelona, Spain 08036
Phone: 933662727
Fax: 935504775
E-mail: venturcap@gvcgaesco.es
Website: www.venturcap.es

Type of Firm
Private Equity Firm

Project Preferences

Type of Financing Preferred:
Early Stage
Expansion
Balanced

Geographical Preferences

International Preferences:
Europe

Industry Preferences

In Computer Software prefer:
Software

In Internet Specific prefer:
Ecommerce

In Medical/Health prefer:
Medical/Health

In Industrial/Energy prefer:
Industrial Products

In Financial Services prefer:
Financial Services

In Business Serv. prefer:
Distribution

Additional Information
Year Founded: 2000
Current Activity Level : Actively seeking new investments

VENTURE ASSOCIATES LTD

4950 East Evans Street, Suite 105
Denver, CO USA 80222
Phone: 303-758-8710
Fax: 303-758-8747
Website: www.venturea.com

Other Offices
4811 Trailwood Way
Springfield, MO USA 65804
Phone: 417-882-9218

Management and Staff
James Arkebauer, President

Type of Firm
Private Equity Firm

Project Preferences

Role in Financing:
Prefer role as deal originator but will also invest in deals created by others

Type of Financing Preferred:
Second Stage Financing
Leveraged Buyout
Early Stage
Expansion
Generalist PE
Turnaround
Seed
First Stage Financing
Acquisition
Private Placement
Startup
Recapitalizations

Size of Investments Considered:
Min Size of Investment Considered (000s): $100
Max Size of Investment Considered (000s): $10,000

Geographical Preferences

United States Preferences:

Additional Information
Year Founded: 1982
Capital Under Management: $20,000,000
Current Activity Level : Actively seeking new investments
Method of Compensation: Return on invest. most important, but chg. closing fees, service fees, etc.

Pratt's Guide to Private Equity & Venture Capital Sources

VENTURE ASSOCIATES PARTNERS LLC

355 Sweetbriar Road
Memphis, TN USA 38120
Phone: 9017631434
Fax: 9017631428
E-mail: email@venture-associates.com
Website: www.venture-associates.com

Management and Staff
Burton Weil, Chief Executive Officer

Type of Firm
Private Equity Firm

Project Preferences

Role in Financing:
Prefer role as deal originator

Type of Financing Preferred:
Leveraged Buyout
Control-block Purchases
Generalist PE
Turnaround
Management Buyouts
Acquisition
Industry Rollups
Recapitalizations

Size of Investments Considered:
Min Size of Investment Considered (000s): $20,000
Max Size of Investment Considered (000s): $200,000

Geographical Preferences

United States Preferences:

International Preferences:
Mexico

Industry Preferences

In Semiconductor/Electr prefer:
Electronic Components

In Transportation prefer:
Aerospace

In Manufact. prefer:
Manufacturing

Additional Information
Year Founded: 1985
Current Activity Level : Actively seeking new investments
Method of Compensation: Return on investment is of primary concern, do not charge fees

VENTURE CAPITAL BANK BSCC

Road 1704, Block 317
Building 247
Manama, Bahrain
Phone: 97317518888
Fax: 97317518880
E-mail: info@VC-Bank.com
Website: www.vc-bank.com

Management and Staff
Abdulla Nooruddin, Principal
Adel Rasheed, Principal
Hassan Murad, Chief Operating Officer
Khalid Ateeq, Chief Executive Officer
Mahmood Zainal, Principal

Type of Firm
Bank Affiliated

Project Preferences

Type of Financing Preferred:
Early Stage
Balanced
Later Stage
Startup

Geographical Preferences

International Preferences:
Bahrain
Oman
Qatar
Middle East
Saudi Arabia
Africa

Industry Preferences

In Financial Services prefer:
Financial Services
Real Estate

In Business Serv. prefer:
Consulting Services

Additional Information
Year Founded: 2005
Current Activity Level : Actively seeking new investments

VENTURE CAPITAL FUND OF NEW ENGLAND

30 Washington Street
Wellesley, MA USA 02481
Phone: 7814318400
Fax: 7812376578
E-mail: inquiries@vcfne.com
Website: www.vcfne.com

Management and Staff
Carl Novotny, Managing Director
E. Jack Stewart, Managing Director
George Aggouras, Chief Financial Officer
Gordon Penman, Managing Director

Type of Firm
Private Equity Firm

Project Preferences

Role in Financing:
Prefer role as deal originator

Type of Financing Preferred:
Early Stage
Seed
Startup

Size of Investments Considered:
Min Size of Investment Considered (000s): $1,000
Max Size of Investment Considered (000s): $1,500

Geographical Preferences

United States Preferences:
Northeast

Industry Focus
(% based on actual investment)
Computer Software and Services	16.8%
Internet Specific	16.8%
Medical/Health	11.6%
Communications and Media	11.2%
Semiconductors/Other Elect.	10.9%
Industrial/Energy	10.2%
Consumer Related	7.2%
Other Products	6.9%
Computer Hardware	6.0%
Biotechnology	2.3%

Additional Information
Name of Most Recent Fund: Venture Capital Fund of New England IV, L.P.
Most Recent Fund Was Raised: 07/31/2001
Year Founded: 1981
Capital Under Management: $81,000,000
Current Activity Level : Actively seeking new investments
Method of Compensation: Return on investment is of primary concern, do not charge fees

VENTURE CATALYST INC

591 Camino de la Reina, Suite 418
San Diego, CA USA 92108
Phone: 858-385-1000
Fax: 858-385-1001
E-mail: info@vcat.com

Other Offices
3420 Ocean Park Boulevard, Suite 3020
Santa Monica, CA USA 90405
Phone: 310-399-4059
Fax: 310-399-3431

315 Queen Street
Alexandria, VA USA 22314
Phone: 703-684-1306
Fax: 703-684-1481

Type of Firm
Incubator/Development Program

2229

Project Preferences

Type of Financing Preferred:
Early Stage

Industry Preferences

In Internet Specific prefer:
Internet

Additional Information

Year Founded: 2000
Current Activity Level : Making few, if any, new investments

VENTURE CORPORATION OF AUSTRALIA PTY LTD

Unit 2, 92 Pacific Highway
Roseville, Australia 2069
Phone: 612-9413-1944
Fax: 612-9413-9618

Management and Staff

John Paterson, Managing Director

Type of Firm

Private Equity Firm

Project Preferences

Role in Financing:
Prefer role as deal originator

Type of Financing Preferred:
Balanced
Startup

Geographical Preferences

International Preferences:
Pacific Rim

Industry Preferences

In Computer Software prefer:
Computer Services
Software

In Manufact. prefer:
Manufacturing

Additional Information

Year Founded: 1984
Capital Under Management: $3,900,000
Current Activity Level : Actively seeking new investments

VENTURE FUND ROTTERDAM BV

Westerkade 3
Rotterdam, Netherlands 3016 CL
Phone: 31104143444
Fax: 31104332879

Type of Firm

Private Equity Firm

Association Membership

European Private Equity and Venture Capital Assoc.

Project Preferences

Type of Financing Preferred:
Leveraged Buyout
Generalist PE
Turnaround
Later Stage
Management Buyouts
Acquisition

Size of Investments Considered:
Min Size of Investment Considered (000s): $6,553
Max Size of Investment Considered (000s): $26,212

Geographical Preferences

United States Preferences:
All U.S.

International Preferences:
Europe

Additional Information

Year Founded: 1978
Capital Under Management: $235,400,000
Current Activity Level : Actively seeking new investments

VENTURE INVESTORS LLC

505 South Rosa Road
University Research Park #201
Madison, WI USA 53719
Phone: 6084412700
Fax: 6084412727
E-mail: venture@ventureinvestors.com
Website: ventureinvestors.com

Management and Staff

James Adox, Managing Director
John Neis, Managing Director
Paul Weiss, Managing Director
Scott Button, Managing Director

Type of Firm

Private Equity Firm

Association Membership

National Venture Capital Association - USA (NVCA)

Project Preferences

Role in Financing:
Will function either as deal originator or investor in deals created by others

Type of Financing Preferred:
Early Stage
Seed
Startup

Size of Investments Considered:
Min Size of Investment Considered (000s): $50
Max Size of Investment Considered (000s): $8,000

Geographical Preferences

United States Preferences:
Midwest

Industry Focus

(% based on actual investment)
Biotechnology	47.6%
Medical/Health	35.8%
Other Products	6.6%
Computer Software and Services	3.2%
Semiconductors/Other Elect.	2.8%
Consumer Related	1.2%
Internet Specific	0.9%
Communications and Media	0.8%
Computer Hardware	0.5%
Industrial/Energy	0.5%

Additional Information

Year Founded: 1982
Capital Under Management: $201,000,000
Current Activity Level : Actively seeking new investments
Method of Compensation: Return on investment is of primary concern, do not charge fees

VENTURE LABO CO LTD

6-17-4, Tsukiji, Chuo-ku
4F, Tsukiji Park Bldg.
Tokyo, Japan 104-0045
Phone: 81362641861
Fax: 81362651862
Website: www.venturelabo.co.jp

Type of Firm

Private Equity Firm

Project Preferences

Type of Financing Preferred:
Balanced

Industry Preferences

In Computer Software prefer:
Software

In Biotechnology prefer:
Biotech Related Research

In Industrial/Energy prefer:
Robotics

In Manufact. prefer:
Manufacturing

Additional Information

Year Founded: 1999
Current Activity Level : Actively seeking new investments

VENTURE MANAGEMENT LLC

401 Charmany Drive, Suite 320
Madison, WI USA 53719
Phone: 6088198888
Fax: 6088198811
E-mail: inquiries@vmllc.com
Website: www.venturellc.com

Management and Staff
Richard Raabe, Founder

Type of Firm
Private Equity Firm

Project Preferences

Type of Financing Preferred:
Balanced

Geographical Preferences

United States Preferences:
Wisconsin

Industry Preferences

In Internet Specific prefer:
Internet
Ecommerce

In Biotechnology prefer:
Biotechnology

In Medical/Health prefer:
Medical Products
Pharmaceuticals

In Industrial/Energy prefer:
Alternative Energy
Environmental Related

Additional Information
Year Founded: 1994
Current Activity Level : Actively seeking new investments

VENTURE SPUR

700 1/2 West Sheridan Avenue
Oklahoma City, OK USA 73102
Phone: 4053670897
E-mail: Info@VentureSpur.com
Website: www.venturespur.com

Management and Staff
Kraettli Lawrence Epperson, Managing Director

Type of Firm
Incubator/Development Program

Project Preferences

Type of Financing Preferred:
Early Stage
Seed

Geographical Preferences

United States Preferences:
Oklahoma

Additional Information
Year Founded: 2011
Capital Under Management: $540,000
Current Activity Level : Actively seeking new investments

VENTURE STARS GMBH

Bayerstrasse 14
Munich, Germany 80336
E-mail: info@venture-stars.com
Website: www.venture-stars.com

Management and Staff
Florian Calmbach, Partner
Martin Junker, Partner
Stefan Pfannmoller, Managing Director

Type of Firm
Incubator/Development Program

Project Preferences

Type of Financing Preferred:
Early Stage
Startup

Industry Preferences

In Computer Software prefer:
Software

Additional Information
Year Founded: 2011
Capital Under Management: $16,358,000
Current Activity Level : Actively seeking new investments

VENTURE TDF PTE LTD

19 A, Ann Siang Road
Singapore, Singapore 069699
Phone: 6562366920
Fax: 6568870535

Other Offices
Unit 2505, K.WAH Center
1010 Huaihai Zhong Road
Shanghai, China 200031
Phone: 86-21-5467-0500
Fax: 86-21-5404-7557

Management and Staff
Forrest Zhong, Partner

Type of Firm
Private Equity Firm

Project Preferences

Type of Financing Preferred:
Early Stage
Expansion
Balanced
Seed
Startup

Size of Investments Considered:
Min Size of Investment Considered (000s): $500
Max Size of Investment Considered (000s): $3,000

Geographical Preferences

United States Preferences:
North America

International Preferences:
Europe
Asia

Industry Preferences

In Communications prefer:
Telecommunications

In Internet Specific prefer:
Internet

In Computer Other prefer:
Computer Related

In Semiconductor/Electr prefer:
Electronics
Semiconductor

In Medical/Health prefer:
Medical/Health

In Financial Services prefer:
Investment Groups
Financial Services

Additional Information
Year Founded: 1995
Capital Under Management: $350,000,000
Current Activity Level : Actively seeking new investments

VENTURE UNITED INC

Shibuya 1-2-5 Shibuya-ku
9F, Alive Mitake
Tokyo, Japan 150-0002
Website: ventureunited.jp

Type of Firm
Private Equity Firm

Project Preferences

Type of Financing Preferred:
Early Stage
Startup

Geographical Preferences

International Preferences:
Asia
Japan

Industry Preferences

In Internet Specific prefer:
Internet

Additional Information

Year Founded: 2011
Capital Under Management: $12,081,000
Current Activity Level : Actively seeking new investments

VENTURE51 CAPITAL FUND LLP

315 South Coast Highway 101, Suite U-294
Encinitas, CA USA 92024
Phone: 4804193857
Website: www.venture51.com

Other Offices

20343 North Hayden Road
SCOTTSDALE, AZ USA 85255
Phone: 4804193857

Management and Staff

Brandon Zeuner, Managing Partner
Greg Kero, Partner
Ryan Swagar, Managing Partner

Type of Firm

Private Equity Firm

Project Preferences

Type of Financing Preferred:
Early Stage
Seed
Startup

Size of Investments Considered:

Min Size of Investment Considered (000s): $51
Max Size of Investment Considered (000s): $500

Geographical Preferences

United States Preferences:
South Carolina
Northern California
Massachusetts
Colorado
New York

Additional Information

Name of Most Recent Fund: Venture51 Capital Partners III, L.P.
Most Recent Fund Was Raised: 02/14/2017
Year Founded: 2010
Capital Under Management: $12,115,000
Current Activity Level : Actively seeking new investments

VENTUREAST

Sheesh Mahal, Road No. 7
8-2-546, Plot No.140
Hyderabad, India 500 034
Phone: 914023351044
Fax: 914023351047
E-mail: info@ventureast.net
Website: www.ventureast.net

Other Offices

5B, Ramachandra Avenue
Seethammal Colony, First Main Road
Chennai , India 600 018
Phone: 91-44-2432-9864
Fax: 91-44-2432-9865

Management and Staff

A. Ramesh, General Partner
Bobba Venkatadari, General Partner
C. Shekhar Kundur, General Partner
K. A. Srinivasan, Chief Financial Officer
M. Krishna Meka, Principal
Raghu Mendu, General Partner
Ramesh Alur, General Partner
Sarath Naru, Managing Partner
Sateesh Andra, Managing Partner
Siddhartha Das, General Partner
Vishesh Rajaram, Principal

Type of Firm

Corporate PE/Venture

Association Membership

Indian Venture Capital Association (IVCA)

Project Preferences

Role in Financing:
Prefer role as deal originator but will also invest in deals created by others

Type of Financing Preferred:
Early Stage
Expansion
Balanced
Seed
Startup

Geographical Preferences

International Preferences:
India

Industry Preferences

In Medical/Health prefer:
Medical/Health

In Consumer Related prefer:
Education Related

In Industrial/Energy prefer:
Energy
Energy Conservation Relat
Environmental Related

Additional Information

Year Founded: 1990
Capital Under Management: $300,000,000
Current Activity Level : Actively seeking new investments
Method of Compensation: Return on invest. most important, but chg. closing fees, service fees, etc.

VENTUREBAYCOM

Verdunstraat 742
Haren, Belgium 1130
Phone: 322473700
Fax: 322473701
E-mail: info@venturebay.com

Management and Staff

Danny Lein, Managing Partner
Paul Janssens, Managing Partner

Type of Firm

Incubator/Development Program

Project Preferences

Type of Financing Preferred:
Early Stage
Seed
Startup

Geographical Preferences

International Preferences:
Europe
Belgium

Industry Preferences

In Communications prefer:
Other Communication Prod.

In Internet Specific prefer:
Internet

Additional Information

Year Founded: 1999
Capital Under Management: $1,200,000
Current Activity Level : Actively seeking new investments

VENTURELABOUR.COM INC

52 Royal Road
Unit A
Guelph, Canada N1H 1G3
Phone: 8882484893
E-mail: info@vlinteractive.com
Website: www.venturelabour.com

Other Offices

1790 Dundas Street
London, United Kingdom N5W 3E5
Phone: 8774385729

Management and Staff
Graham Dyer, Chief Operating Officer

Type of Firm
Private Equity Firm

Additional Information
Year Founded: 1998
Current Activity Level : Actively seeking new investments

VENTURELINK FUNDS

3 Church Street, Suite 602
Toronto, Canada M5E 1M2
Phone: 4166816676
Fax: 4166816661
E-mail: info@venturelinkfunds.com
Website: www.venturelinkfunds.com

Management and Staff
Geoffrey Horton, Managing Partner
Jim Whitaker, Managing Partner

Type of Firm
Private Equity Firm

Association Membership
Canadian Venture Capital Association

Project Preferences

Type of Financing Preferred:
Balanced
Later Stage

Geographical Preferences

Canadian Preferences:
All Canada

Industry Preferences

In Communications prefer:
Telecommunications
Wireless Communications

In Computer Software prefer:
Software

In Semiconductor/Electr prefer:
Fiber Optics

In Biotechnology prefer:
Biotechnology

Additional Information
Year Founded: 2000
Capital Under Management: $7,431,000
Current Activity Level : Actively seeking new investments

VENTUREPARTNER INVESTMENTBERATUNGS GMBH

Rudolphstrasse 28
Nuernberg, Germany 90489
Phone: 499115390610
Fax: 499115390620
E-mail: dialog@venture-investment.de
Website: www.venture-investment.de

Management and Staff
Adolf Bloss, Managing Director

Type of Firm
Private Equity Firm

Project Preferences

Type of Financing Preferred:
Seed
Startup

Geographical Preferences

International Preferences:
Germany

Industry Preferences

In Communications prefer:
Communications and Media

In Biotechnology prefer:
Biotechnology

In Medical/Health prefer:
Medical/Health
Pharmaceuticals

In Industrial/Energy prefer:
Alternative Energy
Environmental Related

Additional Information
Year Founded: 2002
Current Activity Level : Actively seeking new investments

VENTURETECH ALLIANCE HOLDINGS LLC

2585 Junction Avenue
San Jose, CA USA 95134
Website: www.vtalliance.com

Other Offices
Number 10, Li-Hsin 6th Road
Hsin-Chu Science-Based Industrial Park
Hsin-Chu, Taiwan 300
Phone: 88636669980
Fax: 88636669970

Type of Firm
Private Equity Firm

Project Preferences

Role in Financing:
Prefer role in deals created by others

Type of Financing Preferred:
Early Stage
Expansion
Balanced
Later Stage

Size of Investments Considered:
Min Size of Investment Considered (000s): $1,000
Max Size of Investment Considered (000s): $3,000

Industry Preferences

In Semiconductor/Electr prefer:
Semiconductor

Additional Information
Name of Most Recent Fund: VentureTech Alliance Fund III, L.P.
Most Recent Fund Was Raised: 09/30/2006
Year Founded: 2001
Capital Under Management: $230,000,000
Current Activity Level : Actively seeking new investments
Method of Compensation: Return on investment is of primary concern, do not charge fees

VERAVENTURE OY

PO Box 1127
Kallanranta 11
Kuopio, Finland FI-70111
Phone: 358294602582
Website: www.finnvera.fi

Other Offices
Hameenkatu 9
PL 559
Tampere, Finland 33101

Asemakatu 37
Oulu, Finland 90100

Etelaesplanadi 8
PL 1010
Helsinki, Finland 00101

Management and Staff
Leo Houtsonen, Managing Director

Type of Firm
Private Equity Advisor or Fund of Funds

Association Membership
Finnish Venture Capital Association (FVCA)

Project Preferences

Type of Financing Preferred:
Fund of Funds
Early Stage
Later Stage
Seed
Startup

Industry Preferences

In Communications prefer:
Wireless Communications
Data Communications
Entertainment

In Computer Software prefer:
Computer Services

In Computer Other prefer:
Computer Related

In Semiconductor/Electr prefer:
Laser Related

In Medical/Health prefer:
Medical/Health
Medical Diagnostics
Medical Products
Health Services

In Consumer Related prefer:
Sports
Consumer Products
Consumer Services
Education Related

In Industrial/Energy prefer:
Energy
Robotics
Environmental Related

In Business Serv. prefer:
Consulting Services

Additional Information
Year Founded: 2003
Capital Under Management: $162,300,000
Current Activity Level : Actively seeking new investments

VERDANE CAPITAL ADVISORS AS

P.O. Box 1216 Vika
Oslo, Norway NO-0110
Phone: 4724137000
Fax: 4724137001
E-mail: office@verdanecapital.com
Website: www.verdanecapital.com

Other Offices

Birger Jarlsgatan 32 B
Stockholm, Sweden 114 29
Phone: 4684074200
Fax: 4684074210

Rikhardinkatu 4 B
Helsinki, Finland 00130
Phone: 35896980334

Management and Staff
Anders Thuve, Partner
Arne Handeland, Partner
Atle Sovik, Partner
Bjarne Lie, Managing Partner
Goran Strandberg, Partner
Henrik Aspen, Partner
Lars Thoresen, Managing Partner
Pal Malmros, Partner
Per Nordlander, Partner
Staffan Morndal, Partner

Type of Firm
Private Equity Firm

Association Membership
Finnish Venture Capital Association (FVCA)
Danish Venture Capital Association (DVCA)
Norwegian Venture Capital Association
Swedish Venture Capital Association (SVCA)
European Private Equity and Venture Capital Assoc.

Project Preferences

Role in Financing:
Prefer role as deal originator but will also invest in deals created by others

Type of Financing Preferred:
Leveraged Buyout
Early Stage
Balanced
Turnaround
Later Stage
Seed
Startup

Size of Investments Considered:
Min Size of Investment Considered (000s): $1,200
Max Size of Investment Considered (000s): $7,500

Geographical Preferences

International Preferences:
Europe
Scandanavia/Nordic Region

Industry Preferences

In Communications prefer:
Telecommunications
Data Communications

In Computer Software prefer:
Software

In Internet Specific prefer:
E-Commerce Technology
Internet
Ecommerce

In Computer Other prefer:
Computer Related

In Semiconductor/Electr prefer:
Electronics
Electronic Components

In Biotechnology prefer:
Biotechnology

In Medical/Health prefer:
Medical/Health
Diagnostic Test Products
Pharmaceuticals

In Consumer Related prefer:
Retail

In Industrial/Energy prefer:
Energy
Industrial Products
Factory Automation

In Business Serv. prefer:
Services
Media

Additional Information
Year Founded: 1985
Capital Under Management: $942,600,000
Current Activity Level : Actively seeking new investments

VERDEXUS

55 King Street West, Suite 700, Kitchener
Waterloo, Canada N2G 4W1
Phone: 5199572230
Fax: 5199572239
E-mail: canada@verdexus.com
Website: www.verdexus.com

Other Offices

Artur-Kutscher-Platz 2A
Toronto, Germany 80802
Phone: 442071009770
Fax: 442071009780

Management and Staff
Randall Howard, General Partner
Ray Simonson, General Partner

Type of Firm
Private Equity Firm

Project Preferences

Type of Financing Preferred:
Leveraged Buyout
Management Buyouts
Acquisition

Geographical Preferences

Canadian Preferences:
All Canada

International Preferences:
Europe

Industry Preferences

In Communications prefer:
Commercial Communications
Telecommunications
Wireless Communications
Media and Entertainment

In Computer Software prefer:
Software

In Internet Specific prefer:
Internet

Additional Information
Year Founded: 2001
Current Activity Level : Actively seeking new investments

VERGE FUND

317 Commercial St. Northeast
Albuquerque, NM USA 87102
Phone: 5052471038
Fax: 5052448040
E-mail: information@vergefund.com
Website: www.vergefund.com

Management and Staff
H.Raymond Radosevich, Founder
James Higdon, Partner
Ron McPhee, Partner
Thomas Stephenson, Co-Founder
William Bice, Founder

Type of Firm
Private Equity Firm

Association Membership
National Venture Capital Association - USA (NVCA)

Project Preferences

Type of Financing Preferred:
Balanced
Later Stage
Seed

Geographical Preferences

United States Preferences:
New Mexico
Southwest

Industry Preferences

In Communications prefer:
Commercial Communications
Telecommunications
Wireless Communications
Data Communications
Other Communication Prod.

In Computer Hardware prefer:
Computer Graphics and Dig

In Computer Software prefer:
Computer Services
Software
Systems Software
Applications Software

In Internet Specific prefer:
E-Commerce Technology
Internet
Ecommerce
Web Aggregation/Portals

In Semiconductor/Electr prefer:
Electronic Components
Semiconductor
Controllers and Sensors
Laser Related
Fiber Optics
Optoelectronics

In Medical/Health prefer:
Medical Diagnostics
Medical Products

In Consumer Related prefer:
Entertainment and Leisure
Sports

In Industrial/Energy prefer:
Energy

In Other prefer:
Environment Responsible

Additional Information
Name of Most Recent Fund: Verge I.5, L.P.
Most Recent Fund Was Raised: 10/28/2006
Year Founded: 2003
Capital Under Management: $21,000,000
Current Activity Level : Actively seeking new investments

VERIDIAN CREDIT UNION

1827 Ansborough Ave
Waterloo, IA USA 50702
Phone: 8002353228
E-mail: MSREmail@VeridianCU.org
Website: www.veridiancu.org

Type of Firm
Bank Affiliated

Geographical Preferences

United States Preferences:
Iowa

Additional Information
Year Founded: 1934
Current Activity Level : Actively seeking new investments

VERITAS CAPITAL FUND MANAGEMENT LLC

Nine West 57th Street
29th Floor
New York, NY USA 10019
Phone: 2124156700
Fax: 2126889411
E-mail: info@veritascapital.com
Website: www.veritascapital.com

Management and Staff
Aneal Krishnan, Principal
Benjamin Polk, Partner
Brian Gorczynski, Partner
Daniel Sugar, Principal
Hugh Evans, Managing Partner
James Dimitri, Partner
Jason Donner, Chief Financial Officer
Jay Longosz, Vice President
Joe Benavides, Partner
Rick Cosgrove, Vice President
Shane Tiemann, Principal
William Shanahan, Vice President

Type of Firm
Private Equity Firm

Project Preferences

Type of Financing Preferred:
Leveraged Buyout
Acquisition
Recapitalizations

Geographical Preferences

United States Preferences:
All U.S.

Industry Focus
(% based on actual investment)
Other Products	44.8%
Semiconductors/Other Elect.	36.5%
Communications and Media	17.3%
Industrial/Energy	1.1%
Internet Specific	0.3%

Additional Information
Name of Most Recent Fund: Veritas Capital Fund IV, L.P.
Most Recent Fund Was Raised: 12/09/2009
Year Founded: 1992
Capital Under Management: $5,425,000,000
Current Activity Level : Actively seeking new investments

VERIZON MEDIA TECH VENTURE STUDIO

119 West
24th Street
New York, NY USA 10011
Website: www.verizonventurestudio.com

Type of Firm
Incubator/Development Program

Project Preferences

Type of Financing Preferred:
Early Stage
Seed
Startup

Additional Information
Year Founded: 2017
Current Activity Level: Actively seeking new investments

VERLINVEST SA

Place Eugene Flagey 18
Brussels, Belgium 1050
Phone: 3226269870
Fax: 3226269878
E-mail: bp@verlinvest.com
Website: verlinvest.be

Management and Staff
Frederic de Mevius, Managing Director

Type of Firm
Private Equity Firm

Association Membership
Belgium Venturing Association

Project Preferences

Type of Financing Preferred:
Leveraged Buyout
Early Stage
Mezzanine
Generalist PE
Later Stage
Acquisition
Distressed Debt

Size of Investments Considered:
Min Size of Investment Considered (000s): $6,849
Max Size of Investment Considered (000s): $102,739

Geographical Preferences

United States Preferences:
All U.S.

International Preferences:
Europe

Industry Preferences

In Medical/Health prefer:
Health Services

In Consumer Related prefer:
Food/Beverage
Consumer Products
Consumer Services

Additional Information
Year Founded: 1995
Current Activity Level: Actively seeking new investments

VERMEER CAPITAL PARTNERS SAS

120 Avenue des Champs Elysees
Paris, France 75008
Phone: 33144200202
Fax: 33145625909
E-mail: info@vermeercapital.fr
Website: www.vermeercapital.fr

Management and Staff
Jean-Louis Detry, President

Type of Firm
Private Equity Firm

Association Membership
French Venture Capital Association (AFIC)

Project Preferences

Type of Financing Preferred:
Leveraged Buyout
Turnaround

Size of Investments Considered:
Min Size of Investment Considered (000s): $3,927
Max Size of Investment Considered (000s): $39,277

Geographical Preferences

International Preferences:
Europe
France

Industry Preferences

In Consumer Related prefer:
Consumer Products

In Business Serv. prefer:
Services

Additional Information
Year Founded: 2008
Capital Under Management: $117,261,000
Current Activity Level: Actively seeking new investments

VERMONT CENTER FOR EMERGING TECHNOLOGIES

210 Colchester Avenue
Burlington, VT USA 05401
Phone: 8026563880
Website: www.vermonttechnologies.com

Management and Staff
Andrew Stickney, Vice President
David Bradbury, President

Type of Firm
Incubator/Development Program

Association Membership
New England Venture Capital Association

Project Preferences

Role in Financing:
Will function either as deal originator or investor in deals created by others

Type of Financing Preferred:
Early Stage
Seed
Startup

Geographical Preferences

United States Preferences:
Vermont

Industry Preferences

In Computer Software prefer:
Software

In Medical/Health prefer:
Medical Therapeutics
Medical Products

In Business Serv. prefer:
Media

Additional Information
Year Founded: 2005
Capital Under Management: $5,000,000
Current Activity Level: Actively seeking new investments

VERNAL INTERNATIONAL CAPITAL EQUITY INVEST MGMT CO LTD

No. 7,East Third Ring Road
30/F,Tower A, Fortune Plaza
Beijing, China 100020
Phone: 861065330656
Fax: 861080115555
E-mail: master@vi-capital.com
Website: www.vi-capital.com

Type of Firm
Investment Management Firm

Project Preferences

Type of Financing Preferred:
Later Stage

Size of Investments Considered:
Min Size of Investment Considered (000s): $7,872
Max Size of Investment Considered (000s): $31,490

Geographical Preferences

International Preferences:
China

Industry Preferences

In Consumer Related prefer:
Consumer Products

In Financial Services prefer:
Financial Services
Real Estate

Additional Information

Year Founded: 2010
Current Activity Level : Actively seeking new investments

VERNON & PARK CAPITAL LP

One North LaSalle, Suite 2475
Chicago, IL USA 60602
Phone: 3122626211
E-mail: contact@vernonpark.com
Website: www.vernonpark.com

Management and Staff

James Ginsburg, Managing Partner
Linda Ginsburg, Managing Director

Type of Firm

Private Equity Firm

Additional Information

Year Founded: 2001
Current Activity Level : Actively seeking new investments

VERNYI KAPITAL AO

77 Kunayev str
Almaty, Kazakhstan 050000
Website: www.verny.kz

Type of Firm

Investment Management Firm

Project Preferences

Type of Financing Preferred:
Leveraged Buyout
Management Buyouts
Acquisition

Geographical Preferences

International Preferences:
Kazakhstan
Asia

Industry Preferences

In Communications prefer:
Communications and Media
Telecommunications

In Consumer Related prefer:
Consumer
Consumer Products
Consumer Services

In Industrial/Energy prefer:
Oil and Gas Exploration
Oil & Gas Drilling,Explor

In Financial Services prefer:
Financial Services

In Agr/Forestr/Fish prefer:
Mining and Minerals

Additional Information

Year Founded: 2006
Current Activity Level : Actively seeking new investments

VEROD CAPITAL MANAGEMENT LTD

235 Muri Okunola Street
2nd Floor, Rio Plaza
Victoria Island, Lagos, Nigeria
Phone: 2344628646
Fax: 2344628648
E-mail: info@verodcapital.com
Website: verodgroup.com

Management and Staff

Danladi Verheijen, CEO & Managing Director
Eric Idiahi, Managing Director

Type of Firm

Private Equity Firm

Association Membership

African Venture Capital Association (AVCA)

Project Preferences

Type of Financing Preferred:
Leveraged Buyout
Acquisition

Geographical Preferences

International Preferences:
Nigeria

Industry Preferences

In Consumer Related prefer:
Consumer Products
Consumer Services

In Industrial/Energy prefer:
Energy

In Financial Services prefer:
Financial Services

In Business Serv. prefer:
Media

In Manufact. prefer:
Manufacturing

In Agr/Forestr/Fish prefer:
Agribusiness

Additional Information

Year Founded: 2008
Capital Under Management: $85,000,000
Current Activity Level : Actively seeking new investments

VERONIS SUHLER STEVENSON LLC

55 East 52nd Street
33rd Floor, Park Avenue Plaza
New York, NY USA 10055
Phone: 2129354990
Fax: 2123818168
Website: www.vss.com

Management and Staff

Andrew Goscinski, Chief Financial Officer
Christopher Russell, Managing Director
David Bainbridge, Managing Director
Jeffrey Stevenson, Managing Partner
Lacey Mehran, Vice President
Patrick Turner, Managing Director
Trent Hickman, Managing Director

Type of Firm

Private Equity Firm

Association Membership

British Venture Capital Association (BVCA)
Natl Assoc of Small Bus. Inv. Co (NASBIC)

Project Preferences

Type of Financing Preferred:
Leveraged Buyout
Expansion
Mezzanine
Management Buyouts
Acquisition
Recapitalizations

Industry Focus

(% based on actual investment)
Other Products	47.4%
Internet Specific	27.0%
Communications and Media	23.6%
Consumer Related	2.0%
Computer Software and Services	0.0%

Additional Information

Name of Most Recent Fund: VSS Structured Capital II, L.P.
Most Recent Fund Was Raised: 06/25/2008
Year Founded: 1981
Capital Under Management: $3,000,000,000
Current Activity Level : Actively seeking new investments

VERSA CAPITAL MANAGEMENT INC

2929 Arch Street
Cira Centre, Suite 1800
Philadelphia, PA USA 19104
Phone: 2156093400
Fax: 2156093499
E-mail: info@versa.com
Website: www.versa.com

Management and Staff

Aaron Headley, Vice President
Alexander Popovich, Vice President
David Lorry, Principal
Jeffrey Armbrister, Principal
Joel Biran, Principal
John Buck, Principal
Jonathan Tyburski, Vice President
Keith Polak, Principal
Lewis Aronson, Principal
Mark Walsh, Principal
Matthew Levitties, Principal
Randall Schultz, Chief Financial Officer
Raymond French, Chief Operating Officer
Stephen Dorman, Principal
Suzanne Yoon, Principal
William Quinn, Principal

Type of Firm
Private Equity Firm

Project Preferences

Type of Financing Preferred:
Leveraged Buyout
Turnaround
Management Buyouts
Special Situation
Distressed Debt
Recapitalizations

Size of Investments Considered:
Min Size of Investment Considered (000s): $5,000
Max Size of Investment Considered (000s): $30,000

Geographical Preferences

United States Preferences:
North America

Additional Information
Year Founded: 2005
Capital Under Management: $52,800,000
Current Activity Level : Actively seeking new investments

VERSANT VENTURE MANAGEMENT, LLC

One Sansome, Suite 3630
San Francisco, CA USA 94104
Phone: 4158018100
Fax: 4158018101
E-mail: investorrelations@versantventures.com
Website: www.versantventures.com

Other Offices
887 Great Northern Way, Suite 210
Vancouver, Canada V5T 4T5
Phone: 6044249913

1700 Owens Street, Suite 541
SAN FRANCISCO, CA USA 94158
Phone: 650-233-7877
Fax: 650-854-9513

Aeschenvorstadt 36
Basel, Switzerland CH-4051

Management and Staff

Alex Mayweg, Venture Partner
Barbara Lubash, Co-Founder
Bradley Bolzon, Managing Director
Brian Atwood, Co-Founder
Carlo Rizzuto, Partner
Clare Ozawa, Managing Director
Donald Milder, Co-Founder
Gianni Gromo, Partner
Guido Magni, Partner
Jerel Davis, Managing Director
Kirk Nielsen, Managing Director
Mary Haak-Frendscho, Venture Partner
Rebecca Robertson, Co-Founder
Ross Jaffe, Co-Founder
Samuel Colella, Co-Founder
Thomas Woiwode, Managing Director
William Link, Co-Founder

Type of Firm
Private Equity Firm

Association Membership
Western Association of Venture Capitalists (WAVC)
National Venture Capital Association - USA (NVCA)

Project Preferences

Role in Financing:
Prefer role as deal originator but will also invest in deals created by others

Type of Financing Preferred:
Early Stage
Later Stage
Seed
Startup

Size of Investments Considered:
Min Size of Investment Considered (000s): $250
Max Size of Investment Considered (000s): $30,000

Geographical Preferences

United States Preferences:

Canadian Preferences:
All Canada

International Preferences:
Western Europe

Industry Focus
(% based on actual investment)
Medical/Health	54.9%
Biotechnology	38.0%
Other Products	2.8%
Internet Specific	2.1%
Computer Software and Services	1.3%
Computer Hardware	0.6%
Consumer Related	0.2%
Semiconductors/Other Elect.	0.1%

Additional Information
Name of Most Recent Fund: Versant Venture Capital IV, L.P.
Most Recent Fund Was Raised: 07/31/2008
Year Founded: 1999
Capital Under Management: $1,900,000,000
Current Activity Level : Actively seeking new investments
Method of Compensation: Return on investment is of primary concern, do not charge fees

VERSION ONE VENTURES

1250 Homer Street, Suite 407
Vancouver, Canada V6B 1C6
Website: www.versionone.vc

Type of Firm
Private Equity Firm

Association Membership
Canadian Venture Capital Association

Project Preferences

Type of Financing Preferred:
Early Stage
Later Stage
Seed
Startup

Geographical Preferences

United States Preferences:
North America

Industry Preferences

In Communications prefer:
Wireless Communications

In Computer Software prefer:
Software

In Internet Specific prefer:
Internet
Ecommerce

Additional Information
Name of Most Recent Fund: Version One Ventures
Most Recent Fund Was Raised: 07/24/2012
Year Founded: 2012
Capital Under Management: $50,339,000
Current Activity Level : Actively seeking new investments

VERSO CAPITAL PARTNERS

4015 Hillsborough Pike, Suite 214
Nashville, TN USA 37215
Phone: 6156901050
E-mail: info@versocap.com
Website: versocapitalmanagement.com

Other Offices
West Hill Road
36 Tollard Court
Bournemouth, United Kingdom BH2 5EH
Phone: 441202551203

Management and Staff
Peter Jeyes, Chief Financial Officer

Type of Firm
Investment Management Firm

Project Preferences

Type of Financing Preferred:
Leveraged Buyout
Expansion
Generalist PE
Balanced
Later Stage
Management Buyouts
Acquisition

Size of Investments Considered:
Min Size of Investment Considered (000s): $100
Max Size of Investment Considered (000s): $5,000

Additional Information
Year Founded: 2012
Current Activity Level : Actively seeking new investments

VERTEX & CO INC

800 Place Victoria, Suite 3700
Montreal, Canada H4Z 1E9

Type of Firm
Private Equity Firm

Additional Information
Year Founded: 2013
Current Activity Level : Actively seeking new investments

VERTEX CAPITAL LLC

335 Madison Avenue
10th Floor
New York, NY USA 10017
Phone: 2126925800
Fax: 2126824398
E-mail: info@vertex-capital.com
Website: www.vertex-capital.com

Management and Staff
Larry Nusbaum, Chief Operating Officer

Type of Firm
Private Equity Firm

Project Preferences

Type of Financing Preferred:
Leveraged Buyout
Turnaround
Distressed Debt
Recapitalizations

Additional Information
Year Founded: 2008
Capital Under Management: $4,000,000,000
Current Activity Level : Actively seeking new investments

VERTEX ISRAEL II MANAGEMENT LTD

One HaShikma Street
Savyon, Israel 56530
Phone: 97237378888
Fax: 97237378889
E-mail: contact@VertexVC.com
Website: www.vertexvc.com

Other Offices
250 North Bridge Road, Suite 05-01 Raffles City Tower
Singapore, Singapore 179101
Phone: 6568288088
Fax: 6568288090

Management and Staff
David Heller, Managing Partner
Ehud Levy, Managing Partner
Elisheva Yakobovich, Venture Partner
Emanuel Timor, Managing Partner
Moty Ben-Arie, Managing Partner
Remy de Tonnac, Venture Partner
Robert Genieser, Venture Partner
Steven Katz, Principal
Yifat Oron, Managing Partner

Type of Firm
Private Equity Firm

Association Membership
Israel Venture Association

Project Preferences

Type of Financing Preferred:
Early Stage
Balanced
Seed
Startup

Size of Investments Considered:
Min Size of Investment Considered (000s): $1,000
Max Size of Investment Considered (000s): $10,000

Geographical Preferences

United States Preferences:
All U.S.

International Preferences:
Europe
Israel
Asia

Industry Preferences

In Communications prefer:
Communications and Media
CATV & Pay TV Systems
Wireless Communications

In Computer Software prefer:
Software
Applications Software

In Internet Specific prefer:
Internet

In Semiconductor/Electr prefer:
Electronics
Semiconductor
Component Testing Equipmt

In Business Serv. prefer:
Media

In Other prefer:
Environment Responsible

Additional Information
Year Founded: 1997
Capital Under Management: $600,000,000
Current Activity Level : Actively seeking new investments

VERTEX VENTURE HOLDINGS LTD.

250 North Bridge Road, Suite 05-01 Raffles City Tower
Singapore, Singapore 179101
Phone: 6568288088
Fax: 6568288090
E-mail: contact@vertexmgt.com
Website: www.vertexmgt.com

Other Offices
1 HaShikma St.
P.O. Box 89
Savyon, Israel 56530
Phone: 972-3737-8888
Fax: 972-3737-8889

UB City, 1 Vittal Mallya Road
14 and 15th Floor, Concord Tower
Bangalore, India 560001
Phone: 91-80-40300555
Fax: 91-80-40300400

Pratt's Guide to Private Equity & Venture Capital Sources

No. 1 Jian Guo Men Wai Ave
2113-2116 China World Tower 1
Beijing, China 100004
Phone: 86-10-650-59555
Fax: 86-10-650-52555

ZhongXiao East Road, Daan District
11/F No. 293 Sec. 4
Taipei, Taiwan
Phone: 886-2-87735799
Fax: 886-2-87735166

New 46, Rangachari Road
Flat no. 1, Ground Floor, Old 102
Chennai, India 600004
Phone: 91-98-40074616

210A Twin Dolphin Drive
Redwood City, CA USA 94065
Phone: 650-508-2400

1468 Nanjing West Road, JingAn District
Room 4202, United Plaza
Shanghai, China 200040
Phone: 86-21-62711688
Fax: 86-21-62710019

Management and Staff
Choon Chong Tay, Managing Director

Type of Firm
Private Equity Firm

Association Membership
Hong Kong Venture Capital Association (HKVCA)

Project Preferences

Role in Financing:
Prefer role as deal originator but will also invest in deals created by others

Type of Financing Preferred:
Fund of Funds
Early Stage
Mezzanine
Generalist PE
Balanced
Later Stage
Seed
Acquisition
Startup

Size of Investments Considered:
Min Size of Investment Considered (000s): $1,000
Max Size of Investment Considered (000s): $20,000

Geographical Preferences

United States Preferences:

International Preferences:
Europe
Taiwan
Hong Kong
China
Israel
Asia
Singapore

Industry Focus

(% based on actual investment)
Internet Specific	34.3%
Computer Software and Services	25.3%
Other Products	13.2%
Communications and Media	9.0%
Semiconductors/Other Elect.	5.7%
Medical/Health	5.6%
Biotechnology	4.3%
Computer Hardware	1.4%
Industrial/Energy	1.3%

Additional Information
Year Founded: 1988
Capital Under Management: $1,000,000,000
Current Activity Level: Actively seeking new investments
Method of Compensation: Return on investment is of primary concern, do not charge fees

VERTEX VENTURES

345 South California Avenue
Palo Alto, CA USA 94306
Website: www.vertexventures.com

Other Offices
405 El Camino Real, Suite 429
MENLO PARK, CA USA 94025

250 North Bridge Road
#05-01 Raffles City Tower
Singapore, Singapore 179101
Phone: 68288088
Fax: 68288090

Unit 802, 8/F, Tower B, The Millenia
No. 1&2, Murphy Road, Ulsoor
Bangalore, India 560 008
Phone: 67034800

Type of Firm
Private Equity Firm

Project Preferences

Type of Financing Preferred:
Balanced

Geographical Preferences

United States Preferences:

International Preferences:
China
Israel
Asia

Additional Information
Year Founded: 2015
Capital Under Management: $150,950,000
Current Activity Level: Actively seeking new investments

VERTICAL GROUP INC

106 Allen Road, Suite 207
Basking Ridge, NJ USA 07920
Phone: 9082773737
Fax: 9082739434
E-mail: info@vertical-group.com
Website: www.vertical-group.com

Other Offices
160 Bovet Road, Suite 400
San Mateo, CA USA 94402
Phone: 6505669060
Fax: 6505669061

25 DeForest Avenue
Summit, NJ USA 07901
Phone: 9082773737
Fax: 9082739434

Management and Staff
Jack Lasersohn, General Partner
John Runnells, General Partner
Richard Emmitt, General Partner
Tony Chou, General Partner

Type of Firm
Private Equity Firm

Association Membership
National Venture Capital Association - USA (NVCA)

Project Preferences

Role in Financing:
Prefer role as deal originator but will also invest in deals created by others

Type of Financing Preferred:
Early Stage
Balanced
Later Stage
Special Situation

Size of Investments Considered:
Min Size of Investment Considered (000s): $250
Max Size of Investment Considered (000s): $5,000

Industry Focus
(% based on actual investment)
Medical/Health	74.5%
Biotechnology	20.9%
Internet Specific	3.2%
Other Products	0.6%
Semiconductors/Other Elect.	0.5%
Communications and Media	0.2%
Computer Software and Services	0.1%

Additional Information
Year Founded: 1988
Capital Under Management: $200,000,000
Current Activity Level : Actively seeking new investments
Method of Compensation: Return on investment is of primary concern, do not charge fees

VERTICAL VENTURE PARTNERS

3945 Freedom Circle, Suite 360
Santa Clara, CA USA 95054
Phone: 6507044072
E-mail: info@verticalventurepartners.com

Type of Firm
Private Equity Firm

Project Preferences

Type of Financing Preferred:
Balanced

Industry Preferences

In Communications prefer:
Telecommunications

In Computer Software prefer:
Software

In Internet Specific prefer:
Internet

In Medical/Health prefer:
Medical/Health

In Transportation prefer:
Transportation

In Financial Services prefer:
Financial Services

Additional Information
Year Founded: 2015
Capital Under Management: $51,300,000
Current Activity Level : Actively seeking new investments

VERTICALS CAPITAL ADMINISTRACAO DE RECURSOS LTDA

Avenida Paulista 2300
2nd Floor
Sao Paulo, Brazil 01310300
Phone: 551132620447
E-mail: info@verticals.com.br
Website: www.verticals.com.br

Type of Firm
Private Equity Firm

Project Preferences

Type of Financing Preferred:
Leveraged Buyout
Early Stage
Generalist PE
Balanced
Turnaround
Later Stage
Seed
Management Buyouts

Geographical Preferences

International Preferences:
Brazil

Industry Preferences

In Communications prefer:
Telecommunications

In Biotechnology prefer:
Biotechnology

Additional Information
Year Founded: 1998
Current Activity Level : Actively seeking new investments

VERTIS SGR SPA

Via Francesco Caracciolo 18
Naples, Italy 80122
Phone: 39-081-2404-096
Fax: 39-081-660-643
E-mail: vertis@vertissgr.it
Website: www.vertissgr.it

Management and Staff
Claudio Porzio, President
Marco Agostini, Vice President

Type of Firm
Private Equity Firm

Project Preferences

Type of Financing Preferred:
Leveraged Buyout
Early Stage
Management Buyouts
Acquisition

Geographical Preferences

International Preferences:
Italy

Additional Information
Year Founded: 2001
Capital Under Management: $35,822,000
Current Activity Level : Actively seeking new investments

VERTO CAPITAL EUROPE SASU

25, Rue des Fontaines
Paris, France 75003

Type of Firm
Private Equity Firm

Project Preferences

Type of Financing Preferred:
Leveraged Buyout
Management Buyouts
Acquisition

Geographical Preferences

International Preferences:
Europe

Additional Information
Year Founded: 2016
Current Activity Level : Actively seeking new investments

VERUS INVESTMENT PARTNERS

52 Vanderbilt Avenue, Suite 401
New York, NY USA 10017
Phone: 2126129170
Fax: 2129520950
E-mail: info@uniworldcapital.com
Website: www.uniworldcapital.com

Management and Staff
Christopher Fuller, Managing Partner
Christopher Snyder, Vice President
Erik Miller, Partner
Mark Deutsch, Partner
Richard Moreau, Partner

Type of Firm
Private Equity Firm

Project Preferences

Type of Financing Preferred:
Leveraged Buyout
Management Buyouts

Geographical Preferences

United States Preferences:
All U.S.

Industry Preferences

In Consumer Related prefer:
Food/Beverage
Consumer Products

In Financial Services prefer:
Financial Services

In Business Serv. prefer:
Services

In Manufact. prefer:
Manufacturing

Additional Information
Name of Most Recent Fund: Uni-World Capital, L.P.
Most Recent Fund Was Raised: 10/25/2007
Year Founded: 2007
Current Activity Level : Actively seeking new investments

VERUSA HOLDING AS

Eski Buyukdere Caddesi Ayazaga
Yolu Iz Plaza Giz No 9
Istanbul, Turkey 34398
Phone: 902122907490
Fax: 902122907490
E-mail: info@verusaholding.com.tr
Website: www.verusa.com.tr

Type of Firm
Private Equity Firm

Project Preferences

Type of Financing Preferred:
Leveraged Buyout
Early Stage
Expansion
Generalist PE
Management Buyouts
Acquisition

Geographical Preferences

International Preferences:
Turkey
Europe

Industry Preferences

In Communications prefer:
Telecommunications

In Medical/Health prefer:
Medical/Health

In Transportation prefer:
Transportation

In Financial Services prefer:
Real Estate

Additional Information
Year Founded: 2006
Current Activity Level : Actively seeking new investments

VERUSATURK GIRISIM SERMAYESI YATIRIM ORTAKLIGI AS

Buyukdere Cad. Ayazaga Yolu Iz
Plaza No:9 Kat:14
Istanbul, Turkey 34398
Phone: 902122907478
Fax: 902122907493
E-mail: info@verusaturk.com.tr
Website: www.verusaturk.com

Type of Firm
Private Equity Firm

Project Preferences

Type of Financing Preferred:
Early Stage
Generalist PE
Balanced
Seed
Startup

Geographical Preferences

International Preferences:
Turkey
Europe

Industry Preferences

In Communications prefer:
Telecommunications

In Semiconductor/Electr prefer:
Electronics
Fiber Optics

In Medical/Health prefer:
Medical/Health
Medical Products

In Industrial/Energy prefer:
Energy
Oil and Gas Exploration

In Transportation prefer:
Transportation
Aerospace

In Financial Services prefer:
Real Estate

Additional Information
Year Founded: 2012
Current Activity Level : Actively seeking new investments

VESALIUS BIOCAPITAL PARTNERS SARL

1B rue Thomas Edison
Strassen, Luxembourg 1445
Phone: 35226845682
E-mail: info@vesaliusbiocapital.com
Website: www.vesaliusbiocapital.com

Management and Staff
Alain Parthoens, Managing Partner
Christian Schneider, Managing Partner
Gaston Matthyssens, Managing Partner
Guy Geldhof, Partner
Jean-Yves Nothias, Partner
Stephane Verdood, Managing Partner

Type of Firm
Private Equity Firm

Association Membership
Belgium Venturing Association
European Private Equity and Venture Capital Assoc.

Project Preferences

Type of Financing Preferred:
Early Stage
Expansion
Balanced
Later Stage
Seed
Startup

Size of Investments Considered:
Min Size of Investment Considered (000s): $1,312
Max Size of Investment Considered (000s): $3,936

Geographical Preferences

International Preferences:
Sweden
United Kingdom
Luxembourg
Europe
Netherlands
Belgium
Finland
Norway
Germany
Denmark
France

Industry Preferences

In Medical/Health prefer:
Medical/Health
Medical Diagnostics
Diagnostic Test Products
Medical Therapeutics
Medical Products
Pharmaceuticals

Additional Information
Year Founded: 2007
Capital Under Management: $38,020,000
Current Activity Level : Actively seeking new investments

VESEY STREET CAPITAL PARTNERS LLC

101 Avenue of the Americas
New York, NY USA 10013
Phone: 2122134156
Website: www.vscpllc.com

Type of Firm
Private Equity Firm

Project Preferences

Type of Financing Preferred:
Leveraged Buyout
Acquisition
Recapitalizations

Industry Preferences

In Medical/Health prefer:
Medical/Health
Medical Diagnostics
Medical Therapeutics
Medical Products
Health Services

Additional Information
Year Founded: 2014
Current Activity Level : Actively seeking new investments

VESNA INVESTMENT

19 Leninskaya Sloboda Street
Moscow, Russia
E-mail: info@vesnainvestment.com
Website: www.vesnainvestment.com

Type of Firm
Private Equity Firm

Project Preferences

Type of Financing Preferred:
Start-up Financing
Seed

Size of Investments Considered:
Min Size of Investment Considered (000s): $100
Max Size of Investment Considered (000s): $500

Geographical Preferences

International Preferences:
Armenia
Belarus
Kazakhstan
Kyrgyzstan
Tajikistan
Turkmenistan
Azerbaijan
Moldova
Estonia
Uzbekistan
Latvia
Lithuania
Russia

Industry Preferences

In Communications prefer:
Telecommunications

Additional Information
Year Founded: 2011
Current Activity Level : Actively seeking new investments

VESPA CAPITAL LLP

27b Floral Street
Amadeus House
London, United Kingdom WC2E 9DP
Phone: 442078127145
Fax: 442078126495
E-mail: info@vespacapital.com
Website: www.vespacapital.com

Other Offices

12F, rue Guillaume Kroll,
Luxembourg, Luxembourg L-1882
Phone: 352-2712-5053
Fax: 352-2712-5054

25 rue Marbeuf
Paris, France 75008
Phone: 33-1-7997-2430
Fax: 33-1-7997-2439

Management and Staff
Denis Leroy, Co-Founder
Matthew Lyons, Partner
Megan Lester, Partner
Nathalie Leroutier, Founder
Nigel Hammond, Co-Founder

Type of Firm
Private Equity Firm

Association Membership
French Venture Capital Association (AFIC)

Project Preferences

Type of Financing Preferred:
Leveraged Buyout
Management Buyouts

Geographical Preferences

International Preferences:
United Kingdom
France

Additional Information
Year Founded: 2008
Current Activity Level : Actively seeking new investments

VESTAR CAPITAL PARTNERS INC

245 Park Avenue
41st Floor
New York, NY USA 10167
Phone: 2123511600
E-mail: info@vestarcapital.com
Website: www.vestarcapital.com

Other Offices

1555 Blake Street, Suite 200
Denver, CO USA 80202
Phone: 3032261717

Seventeenth Street Plaza
1225 17th Street, Suite 1660
Denver, CO USA 80202
Phone: 303-292-6300

500 Boylston Street
17th Floor
Boston, MA USA 02116
Phone: 617-247-1200

Management and Staff
Alexander Kerr, Vice President
Andrew Cavanna, Managing Director
Arthur Nagle, Partner
Benjamin Funk, Vice President
Brian O Connor, Managing Director
Brian Schwartz, Managing Director
Erin Russell, Principal
James Elrod, Managing Director
James Kelley, Founder
Kevin Mundt, Managing Director
Matthew Dubbioso, Vice President
Nikhil Bhat, Vice President
Roger Holstein, Managing Director
Winston Song, Principal

Type of Firm
Private Equity Firm

Association Membership
Private Equity Council (PEC)

Project Preferences

Type of Financing Preferred:
Leveraged Buyout
Early Stage
Later Stage
Management Buyouts
Acquisition
Recapitalizations

Geographical Preferences

United States Preferences:
North America
Colorado

Industry Focus
(% based on actual investment)
Consumer Related	62.3%
Other Products	15.1%
Industrial/Energy	10.7%
Medical/Health	6.3%
Communications and Media	2.8%
Internet Specific	2.2%
Computer Software and Services	0.5%
Semiconductors/Other Elect.	0.1%

Additional Information
Name of Most Recent Fund: Vestar Capital Partners VI, L.P.
Most Recent Fund Was Raised: 07/27/2012
Year Founded: 1988
Capital Under Management: $4,318,000,000
Current Activity Level : Actively seeking new investments

VESTECH PARTNERS LLC

3110 SouthEast 17th Court
Ocala, FL USA 34471
Phone: 3522070123
Website: www.vestechpartners.com

Management and Staff
Manal Fakhoury, Managing Director
Riadh Fakhoury, Partner

Type of Firm
Private Equity Firm

Project Preferences

Type of Financing Preferred:
Early Stage

Additional Information
Year Founded: 1969
Current Activity Level : Actively seeking new investments

VESTIGO VENTURES LLC

One Kendall Square
Building 200, Suite B2106
Cambridge, MA USA 02139
Website: www.vestigoventures.com

Management and Staff
David Blundin, General Partner
Ian Sheridan, Co-Founder
Mike Nugent, Managing Director

Type of Firm
Private Equity Firm

Project Preferences

Type of Financing Preferred:
Early Stage

Industry Preferences

In Financial Services prefer:
Financial Services

Additional Information
Year Founded: 2016
Current Activity Level : Actively seeking new investments

VESTOR DOM MAKLERSKI SA

ul. Mokotowska One
Zebra Tower
Warsaw, Poland 00 640
Phone: 48223789190
Fax: 482237489191
E-mail: di@investors.pl
Website: www.vestor.pl

Management and Staff
Jakub Bartikiewicz, CEO & Managing Director

Type of Firm
Private Equity Advisor or Fund of Funds

Association Membership
Polish Venture Capital Association (PSIC/PPEA)

Project Preferences

Type of Financing Preferred:
Leveraged Buyout
Turnaround

Geographical Preferences

International Preferences:
Poland

Industry Preferences

In Semiconductor/Electr prefer:
Electronics

In Consumer Related prefer:
Entertainment and Leisure
Food/Beverage
Consumer Products
Consumer Services

In Manufact. prefer:
Manufacturing

Additional Information
Year Founded: 2007
Current Activity Level : Actively seeking new investments

VESTOR.IN

Nikolskaia, 10
Moscow, Russia 109012
Phone: 74957770051
E-mail: info@vestor.in
Website: www.vestor.in

Type of Firm
Private Equity Firm

Project Preferences

Type of Financing Preferred:
Early Stage
Expansion
Seed
Startup

Geographical Preferences

International Preferences:
Russia

Industry Preferences

In Communications prefer:
Communications and Media

In Computer Software prefer:
Applications Software

Additional Information
Year Founded: 2013
Current Activity Level : Actively seeking new investments

VETURI GROWTH PARTNERS OY

Betonimiehenkuja 3
Espoo, Finland 02150
Website: www.veturi.ac

Management and Staff
Jussi Harvela, Partner
Marja-Reetta Paaso, Partner
Mikael Honkavaara, Partner
Moaffak Ahmed, Partner

Type of Firm
Incubator/Development Program

Project Preferences

Type of Financing Preferred:
Seed
Startup

Geographical Preferences

International Preferences:
Finland

Industry Preferences

In Communications prefer:
Wireless Communications
Data Communications
Media and Entertainment

In Computer Software prefer:
Software
Applications Software

In Internet Specific prefer:
E-Commerce Technology
Internet

Additional Information
Year Founded: 2008
Current Activity Level : Actively seeking new investments

VEXIOM EQUITY PARTNERS, L.P.

4355 Cobb Parkway, Suite 440, Building J
Atlanta, GA USA 30339
Phone: 404-671-8060
Fax: 770-459-8525
E-mail: mail@vexiom.com
Website: www.vexiom.com

Other Offices
2002 Summit Boulevard
Third Floor
Atlanta, GA USA 30319
Phone: 404-566-4779

Management and Staff
Brian Caprioli, Senior Managing Director
James Hill, Senior Managing Director
John Smith, Chief Operating Officer
Kenneth Newman, Senior Managing Director
Michael Greenberg, Chief Financial Officer
Nicholas Sampson, Managing Director
Scott Fisher, Senior Managing Director
William Geiss, Senior Managing Director

Type of Firm
Investment Management Firm

Project Preferences

Type of Financing Preferred:
Leveraged Buyout
Balanced
Public Companies
Seed

Industry Preferences

In Computer Hardware prefer:
Mini and Personal/Desktop

In Computer Software prefer:
Applications Software

In Consumer Related prefer:
Consumer
Entertainment and Leisure

In Industrial/Energy prefer:
Energy

In Transportation prefer:
Transportation

In Financial Services prefer:
Financial Services

In Business Serv. prefer:
Services

In Manufact. prefer:
Manufacturing

In Utilities prefer:
Utilities

Additional Information
Year Founded: 1992
Current Activity Level : Actively seeking new investments

VEZIRIS VENTURES LLC

225 East 46th Street, Suite 3J
New York, NY USA 10017
Phone: 6466494391
E-mail: info@veziris.com
Website: www.veziris.com

Management and Staff
Andreas Argyrides, Managing Director
Anthony Argyrides, Managing Director

Type of Firm
Private Equity Firm

Project Preferences

Type of Financing Preferred:
Expansion

Industry Preferences

In Biotechnology prefer:
Biotechnology

Additional Information
Year Founded: 2011
Current Activity Level : Actively seeking new investments

VF CAPITAL SDN BHD

Sublot 1187 & 1188, Lot 901
Block 9, MCLD, Miri Waterfront
Sarawak, Malaysia 98000
Phone: 603-8542-6000
Fax: 603-8542-0029
E-mail: enquiry@vfcapital.com.my
Website: www.vfcapital.com.my

Management and Staff
Chia Pheng, Chief Executive Officer

Type of Firm
Private Equity Firm

Project Preferences

Type of Financing Preferred:
Early Stage
Balanced
Later Stage
Startup

Geographical Preferences

International Preferences:
Malaysia

Industry Preferences

In Communications prefer:
Communications and Media

In Biotechnology prefer:
Biotechnology

Additional Information
Year Founded: 2004
Current Activity Level : Actively seeking new investments

VI (VIETNAM INVESTMENTS) GROUP LLC

63 Pham Ngoc Thach Street
8/F, Ward 6, District 3
Ho Chi Minh, Vietnam
Phone: 84838208664
Fax: 84838208665
E-mail: contact@vigroup.com
Website: www.vigroup.com

Type of Firm
Private Equity Firm

Project Preferences

Type of Financing Preferred:
Early Stage
Expansion
Balanced

Geographical Preferences

International Preferences:
Vietnam
Asia

Industry Preferences

In Communications prefer:
Communications and Media

In Consumer Related prefer:
Retail
Consumer Products
Hotels and Resorts
Education Related

In Industrial/Energy prefer:
Industrial Products

In Transportation prefer:
Transportation

In Business Serv. prefer:
Services
Media

In Manufact. prefer:
Manufacturing

In Agr/Forestr/Fish prefer:
Agriculture related

In Other prefer:
Environment Responsible

Additional Information
Year Founded: 2008
Capital Under Management: $172,400,000
Current Activity Level : Actively seeking new investments

VI PARTNERS

Kjopmannsgata 37
Postboks 1734 Sentrum
Trondheim, Norway 7011
Phone: 47-73600290
Fax: 47-73600291

Management and Staff
Kjell Hagan, Partner

Type of Firm
Private Equity Firm

Project Preferences

Type of Financing Preferred:
Balanced

Additional Information
Year Founded: 2001
Current Activity Level : Actively seeking new investments

VI PARTNERS AG

Baarerstrasse 86
Zug, Switzerland 6302
Phone: 41417290000
Fax: 41417290001
E-mail: info@vipartners.ch
Website: www.vipartners.ch

Management and Staff
Alain Nicod, Managing Partner
Arnd Kaltofen, General Partner
Daniel Gutenberg, General Partner
Diego Braguglia, General Partner

Type of Firm
Private Equity Firm

Association Membership
Swiss Venture Capital Association (SECA)

Project Preferences

Type of Financing Preferred:
Early Stage
Startup

Size of Investments Considered:
Min Size of Investment Considered (000s): $602
Max Size of Investment Considered (000s): $1,805

Geographical Preferences

International Preferences:
Italy
Switzerland
Austria
Germany
France

Industry Preferences

In Communications prefer:
Communications and Media

In Computer Software prefer:
Software

In Semiconductor/Electr prefer:
Sensors

In Biotechnology prefer:
Biotechnology

In Medical/Health prefer:
Medical/Health

In Industrial/Energy prefer:
Industrial Products
Materials
Factory Automation

Additional Information
Year Founded: 2001
Current Activity Level : Actively seeking new investments

VIA EQUITY A/S

Strandvejen 58
Hellerup, Denmark 2900
Phone: 4539775060
Fax: 4539435330
E-mail: info@viaventurepartners.com
Website: viaequity.com

Other Offices
Floragatan 13
Stockholm, Sweden 11475

Management and Staff
Jesper Horsholt, Chief Financial Officer
John Helmsoe-Zinck, Founder
Peter Thorlund Haahr, Partner

Type of Firm
Private Equity Firm

Association Membership
Danish Venture Capital Association (DVCA)
Swedish Venture Capital Association (SVCA)

Project Preferences

Type of Financing Preferred:
Leveraged Buyout
Balanced
Later Stage
Seed
Acquisition
Startup

Industry Preferences

In Communications prefer:
Communications and Media
Telecommunications
Wireless Communications

In Computer Software prefer:
Software

In Internet Specific prefer:
Internet

In Semiconductor/Electr prefer:
Electronics
Electronic Components

In Medical/Health prefer:
Medical/Health

In Consumer Related prefer:
Entertainment and Leisure

In Industrial/Energy prefer:
Industrial Products

Additional Information
Name of Most Recent Fund: Via Venture Partners Fund II K/S
Most Recent Fund Was Raised: 11/30/2010
Year Founded: 2006
Capital Under Management: $328,600,000
Current Activity Level : Actively seeking new investments

VIANOVA CAPITAL LLP

100 Pall Mall
London, United Kingdom SW1Y 5HP
Phone: 44-20-7664-8695
Fax: 44-20-7664-8697
E-mail: info@vianova-capital.com
Website: www.vianova-capital.com

Other Offices
Waldmannstrasse 4
Zurich, Switzerland CH-8001
Phone: 41-43-243-6700
Fax: 41-43-243-6701

Management and Staff
Andrew Evans, Managing Partner
Martin Dreher, Managing Partner
Thomas Bischoff, Managing Partner

Type of Firm
Private Equity Advisor or Fund of Funds

Project Preferences

Type of Financing Preferred:
Fund of Funds

Geographical Preferences

International Preferences:
Europe

Additional Information

Year Founded: 2003
Current Activity Level : Actively seeking new investments
Method of Compensation: Other

VIAVIGO

Porto do Molle
Nigran, Spain
E-mail: viavigo@zonafrancavigo.com
Website: www.zfv.es/viavigo/

Type of Firm
Incubator/Development Program

Project Preferences

Type of Financing Preferred:
Early Stage
Seed

Industry Preferences

In Business Serv. prefer:
Services

Additional Information

Year Founded: 2013
Current Activity Level : Actively seeking new investments

VIC TECHNOLOGY VENTURE DEVELOPMENT LLC

535 West Research Center Blvd., Suite 135
Fayetteville, AR USA 72701
Phone: 4795712592
Website: www.victvd.com

Type of Firm
Incubator/Development Program

Project Preferences

Type of Financing Preferred:
Early Stage
Seed
Startup

Geographical Preferences

United States Preferences:

Industry Preferences

In Computer Other prefer:
Computer Related

In Biotechnology prefer:
Biotechnology

In Medical/Health prefer:
Medical Diagnostics
Medical Products
Pharmaceuticals

In Consumer Related prefer:
Food/Beverage

In Industrial/Energy prefer:
Materials
Environmental Related

In Manufact. prefer:
Manufacturing

Additional Information

Year Founded: 2000
Current Activity Level : Actively seeking new investments

VICENTE CAPITAL PARTNERS LLC

11726 San Vicente Boulevard, Suite 300
Los Angeles, CA USA 90049
Phone: 3108262255
Fax: 3108262299
E-mail: info@vicentecapital.com
Website: www.vicentecapital.com

Management and Staff
David Casares, Partner
Greg Arsenault, Chief Financial Officer
Jason Beck, Vice President
Klaus Koch, Managing Partner
Nicholas Memmo, Managing Partner

Type of Firm
Private Equity Firm

Association Membership
Natl Assoc of Investment Cos. (NAIC)

Project Preferences

Role in Financing:
Will function either as deal originator or investor in deals created by others

Type of Financing Preferred:
Leveraged Buyout
Expansion
Later Stage
Management Buyouts
Acquisition
Recapitalizations

Geographical Preferences

United States Preferences:
North America

Canadian Preferences:
All Canada

Industry Preferences

In Communications prefer:
Telecommunications
Wireless Communications

In Medical/Health prefer:
Health Services

In Consumer Related prefer:
Consumer
Education Related

In Industrial/Energy prefer:
Environmental Related

In Business Serv. prefer:
Services

In Manufact. prefer:
Manufacturing

Additional Information

Name of Most Recent Fund: Vicente Capital Partners Growth Equity Fund, L.P.
Most Recent Fund Was Raised: 02/23/2007
Year Founded: 2007
Capital Under Management: $164,300,000
Current Activity Level : Actively seeking new investments
Method of Compensation: Return on invest. most important, but chg. closing fees, service fees, etc.

VICI PRIVATE EQUITY FUND II LTD

381 Ontdekkers Road
Roodepoort
Gauteng, South Africa 1709
Phone: 27105931000
Fax: 27865387129
E-mail: info@vicifund.co.za
Website: www.vicifund.co.za

Type of Firm
Private Equity Firm

Association Membership
South African Venture Capital Association (SAVCA)

Project Preferences

Type of Financing Preferred:
Leveraged Buyout
Expansion
Generalist PE
Balanced
Later Stage
Acquisition

Geographical Preferences

International Preferences:
South Africa

Industry Preferences

In Communications prefer:
Commercial Communications

In Consumer Related prefer:
Consumer

In Industrial/Energy prefer:
Energy

In Transportation prefer:
Transportation

In Financial Services prefer:
Financial Services

In Manufact. prefer:
Manufacturing

In Agr/Forestr/Fish prefer:
Mining and Minerals

Additional Information
Year Founded: 2012
Current Activity Level : Actively seeking new investments

VICKERS VENTURE PARTNERS

7 Temasek Boulevard
#26-01, Suntec Tower One
Singapore, Singapore 038987
Phone: 6563390338
Fax: 6563393380
E-mail: info@vickersventure.com
Website: www.vickersventure.com

Other Offices
1266 Nanjing West Road
Plaza 66, Suite 1202
Shanghai, China 200040
Phone: 86-21-6288-2626
Fax: 86-21-6288-2825

Management and Staff
Raymond Kong, Managing Director

Type of Firm
Private Equity Firm

Association Membership
Singapore Venture Capital Association (SVCA)

Project Preferences

Type of Financing Preferred:
Early Stage
Expansion
Mezzanine
Balanced
Later Stage
Startup

Geographical Preferences

International Preferences:
China
Asia

Industry Preferences

In Medical/Health prefer:
Medical/Health
Pharmaceuticals

In Consumer Related prefer:
Education Related

In Industrial/Energy prefer:
Energy

In Financial Services prefer:
Real Estate

In Business Serv. prefer:
Media

Additional Information
Year Founded: 2004
Capital Under Management: $230,000,000
Current Activity Level : Actively seeking new investments

VICTOR CAPITAL PARTNERS

444 Madison Avenue
35th Floor
New York, NY USA 10022
Phone: 2122023340
Website: www.victorcapitalpartners.com

Type of Firm
Private Equity Firm

Project Preferences

Type of Financing Preferred:
Leveraged Buyout
Acquisition

Industry Preferences

In Consumer Related prefer:
Consumer

In Industrial/Energy prefer:
Industrial Products

In Manufact. prefer:
Manufacturing

Additional Information
Year Founded: 2017
Current Activity Level : Actively seeking new investments

VICTORIA CAPITAL PTY LTD

28 Claremont Street
Level One
Victoria, Australia
Phone: 61398635000
E-mail: info@viccap.com
Website: www.viccap.com

Type of Firm
Private Equity Firm

Project Preferences

Type of Financing Preferred:
Expansion
Later Stage

Geographical Preferences

International Preferences:
Australia
New Zealand
All International

Industry Preferences

In Internet Specific prefer:
Internet

In Business Serv. prefer:
Media

Additional Information
Year Founded: 2013
Current Activity Level : Actively seeking new investments

VICTORIA VENTURE CAPITAL SOCIEDAD DE CAPITAL RIESGO PYME SA

Calle del Bisbe Casadevall 1
4th floor
Barcelona, Spain 08500
E-mail: info@victoriascr.com
Website: www.victoriascr.com

Type of Firm
Private Equity Firm

Project Preferences

Type of Financing Preferred:
Early Stage

Geographical Preferences

International Preferences:
Spain

Additional Information
Year Founded: 2015
Current Activity Level : Actively seeking new investments

VICTORY PARK CAPITAL ADVISORS LLC

227 West Monroe, Suite 3900
Chicago, IL USA 60606
Phone: 3127011777
Fax: 3127010794

Other Offices
699 Boylston Street
Tenth Floor, One Exeter Plaza
Boston, MA USA 02116
Phone: 6175980440

Management and Staff
Brendan Carroll, Co-Founder
Chad Peterson, Vice President
Charles Asfour, Principal
Derek Ferguson, Vice President
Gordon Watson, Principal
Jeffrey Schneider, Chief Financial Officer
Matthew Ray, Co-Founder
Robert Goldstein, Vice President
Thomas Affolter, Principal
Thomas Welch, Vice President

Type of Firm
Investment Management Firm

Association Membership
Natl Assoc of Small Bus. Inv. Co (NASBIC)
Illinois Venture Capital Association

Project Preferences

Type of Financing Preferred:
Leveraged Buyout
Mezzanine
Turnaround
Acquisition
Special Situation
Distressed Debt
Recapitalizations

Geographical Preferences

United States Preferences:

Additional Information
Name of Most Recent Fund: VPC SBIC I, L.P.
Most Recent Fund Was Raised: 08/22/2012
Year Founded: 2007
Capital Under Management: $518,870,000
Current Activity Level : Actively seeking new investments

VIDA VENTURES GMBH

Invalidenstrasse 112
Berlin, Germany 10115
Phone: 493057703944
E-mail: contact@makers.do
Website: www.makers.do

Type of Firm
Private Equity Firm

Project Preferences

Type of Financing Preferred:
Early Stage
Seed
Startup

Additional Information
Year Founded: 2013
Current Activity Level : Actively seeking new investments

VIDA VENTURES LLC

40 Broad Street, Suite 201
Boston, MA USA 02109

Type of Firm
Private Equity Firm

Project Preferences

Type of Financing Preferred:
Early Stage

Additional Information
Year Founded: 2017
Capital Under Management: $254,800,000
Current Activity Level : Actively seeking new investments

VIETCOMBANK FUND MANAGEMENT CO

198 Tran Quang Khai Street
15 Floor Vietcombank Tower
Ha Noi, Vietnam
Phone: 84439364540
Fax: 8443936454
E-mail: info@vcbf.com
Website: www.vcbf.com

Type of Firm
Investment Management Firm

Project Preferences

Type of Financing Preferred:
Early Stage
Expansion
Balanced
Later Stage

Geographical Preferences

International Preferences:
Asia Pacific
Vietnam

Industry Preferences

In Financial Services prefer:
Financial Services

Additional Information
Year Founded: 2005
Current Activity Level : Actively seeking new investments

VIETNAM PIONEER PARTNERS

Loyal Office Bldg., 9th Floor
151 Vo Thi Sau Street, Dist. 3
Ho Chi Minh, Vietnam
Phone: 84-8-820-8975
Fax: 84-8-820-8871
E-mail: info@vnpioneers.com
Website: www.vnpioneers.com

Other Offices
DMC Bldg., 5th Floor
535 Kim Ma Street, Ba Dinh District
Hanoi, Vietnam
Phone: 84-4-220-3127
Fax: 84-4-220-3128

Management and Staff
Hoa Thi Dinh, Co-Founder
Trung Ha Nguyen, Co-Founder
Viet Hung Do, Co-Founder

Type of Firm
Private Equity Firm

Project Preferences

Type of Financing Preferred:
Leveraged Buyout
Expansion
Generalist PE
Recapitalizations

Geographical Preferences

International Preferences:
Vietnam

Industry Preferences

In Communications prefer:
Media and Entertainment

In Medical/Health prefer:
Health Services

In Consumer Related prefer:
Retail
Consumer Products

In Industrial/Energy prefer:
Energy

In Financial Services prefer:
Financial Services

Additional Information
Year Founded: 2009
Capital Under Management: $20,000,000
Current Activity Level : Actively seeking new investments

VIKING VENTURE AS

Nedre Bakklandet 77
Trondheim, Norway 7014
Phone: 4773600190
Fax: 4773600195
E-mail: post@vikingventure.no
Website: vikingventure.com

Management and Staff
Eivind Bergsmyr, Partner
Erik Hagen, Managing Partner
Hege Kristine Kvistsand, Chief Financial Officer
Joar Welde, Partner
Jostein Vik, Partner

Type of Firm
Private Equity Firm

Association Membership
Norwegian Venture Capital Association

Project Preferences

Type of Financing Preferred:
Early Stage
Balanced
Later Stage
Seed
First Stage Financing
Startup

Geographical Preferences

International Preferences:
United Kingdom
Scandanavia/Nordic Region
Norway

Industry Preferences

In Communications prefer:
Commercial Communications

In Computer Software prefer:
Software

In Semiconductor/Electr prefer:
Electronics

In Biotechnology prefer:
Biotechnology

In Medical/Health prefer:
Medical/Health

In Industrial/Energy prefer:
Energy
Oil and Gas Exploration
Oil & Gas Drilling,Explor
Materials
Environmental Related

Additional Information
Year Founded: 2001
Capital Under Management: $193,900,000
Current Activity Level : Actively seeking new investments

VILA RICA CAPITAL GESTORA DE RECURSOS LTDA

Rua Olimpiadas, 194/200
6 andar
Sao Paulo, Brazil 04551
Phone: 1123444853
E-mail: ri@vilaricacapital.com.br
Website: vilaricacapital.com.br

Management and Staff
Alan Rigoni, Managing Partner
Flavio Souto, Partner

Type of Firm
Investment Management Firm

Association Membership
Brazilian Venture Capital Association (ABCR)

Project Preferences

Type of Financing Preferred:
Leveraged Buyout
Acquisition
Special Situation
Distressed Debt

Geographical Preferences

International Preferences:
Brazil

Additional Information
Year Founded: 1969
Current Activity Level : Actively seeking new investments

VILICUS VENTURES LLC

10 South 5th Street, Suite 888
Minneapolis, MN USA 55402
Phone: 6126435060
Website: www.vilicusventures.com

Management and Staff
Dan Madson, General Partner
Jonathan Otterstatter, Managing Partner
Matt Otterstatter, General Partner

Type of Firm
Private Equity Firm

Association Membership
National Venture Capital Association - USA (NVCA)

Project Preferences

Type of Financing Preferred:
Balanced

Industry Preferences

In Medical/Health prefer:
Medical/Health

Additional Information
Year Founded: 2014
Current Activity Level : Actively seeking new investments

VILING VENTURE PARTNERS INC

6-15-1 Nishishinjuku
La Tour Shinjuku 605
Tokyo, Japan 160-0023
Website: www.vilingvp.com

Type of Firm
Private Equity Firm

Project Preferences

Type of Financing Preferred:
Early Stage
Seed
Startup

Geographical Preferences

International Preferences:
Japan

Industry Preferences

In Consumer Related prefer:
Education Related

Additional Information
Year Founded: 1969
Current Activity Level : Actively seeking new investments

VILLAGE CAPITAL

419 7th Street, Suite 200
Washington, DC USA 20004
Website: www.vilcap.com

Type of Firm
Private Equity Firm

Project Preferences

Type of Financing Preferred:
Early Stage
Balanced
Later Stage
Seed
Startup

Industry Preferences

In Industrial/Energy prefer:
Environmental Related

Additional Information
Year Founded: 2010
Capital Under Management: $13,200,000
Current Activity Level : Actively seeking new investments

VILLAGE GLOBAL MANAGEMENT LLC

340 South Lemon Ave
#3976
Walnut, CA USA 91789

Type of Firm
Private Equity Firm

Project Preferences

Type of Financing Preferred:
Early Stage

Industry Preferences

In Computer Software prefer:
Software

Additional Information
Year Founded: 2017
Current Activity Level : Actively seeking new investments

VILLGRO

Kanagam Road
3rd Floor, IIT Madras Research
Chennai, India 600113
Phone: 914466630400
E-mail: info@villgro.org
Website: www.villgro.org

Type of Firm
Incubator/Development Program

Project Preferences

Type of Financing Preferred:
Seed
Startup

Industry Preferences

In Other prefer:
Socially Responsible

Additional Information
Year Founded: 2001
Current Activity Level : Actively seeking new investments

VINACAPITAL INVESTMENT MANAGEMENT LTD

115 Nguyen Hue, District 1
17th Floor Sun Wah Tower
Ho Chi Minh City, Vietnam
Phone: 84838219930
Fax: 84838219931
E-mail: info@vinacapital.com
Website: www.vinacapital.com

Other Offices
13 Hai Ba Trung, Hoan Kiem District
5th Floor, Sun City Building
Hanoi, Vietnam
Phone: 84-4-3936-4630
Fax: 84-4-3936-4629

Son Tra, Dien Ngoc
Hoa Hai, Ngu Hanh Son
Danang, Vietnam
Phone: 84-511-3961-800
Fax: 84-511-3961-801

26-28 Tran Phu Street
5/F, Sheraton Nha Trang Hotel & Spa
Nha Trang, Vietnam
Phone: 84-58-3523-555
Fax: 84-58-3523-144

No. 315, Ang Duong Street
20/F Candia Tower
Phnom-Penh, Cambodia
Phone: 855-023-99-66-88
Fax: 855-023-99-60-50

6 Temasek Boulevard, Suite 42-01, Suntec Tower 4
Singapore, Singapore 038986
Phone: 65-6332-9081
Fax: 65-6333-9081

Management and Staff
Andy Ho, Managing Director
Anthony House, Managing Director
Brook Taylor, Chief Operating Officer
Cuong Nguyen, Managing Director
David Blackhall, Managing Director
David Henry, Managing Director
Loan Dang Pham, Managing Director
Tony Hsun, Managing Director

Type of Firm
Investment Management Firm

Association Membership
Singapore Venture Capital Association (SVCA)

Project Preferences

Type of Financing Preferred:
Leveraged Buyout
Early Stage
Expansion
Generalist PE
Balanced
Turnaround
Opportunistic
Other
Startup

Geographical Preferences

International Preferences:
Laos
Vietnam
China
Cambodia

Industry Preferences

In Communications prefer:
Telecommunications

In Internet Specific prefer:
Internet

In Consumer Related prefer:
Consumer

In Industrial/Energy prefer:
Energy
Alternative Energy
Environmental Related

In Transportation prefer:
Transportation

In Financial Services prefer:
Real Estate

In Business Serv. prefer:
Services
Media

In Other prefer:
Environment Responsible

Additional Information
Year Founded: 2003
Capital Under Management: $1,663,000,000
Current Activity Level : Actively seeking new investments

VINCI CAPITAL SWITZERLAND SA

Parc Scientifique PSE
Batiment C
Lausanne, Switzerland 1015
Phone: 41216939234
Fax: 41216939230
E-mail: info@vincicapital.ch
Website: www.vincicapital.ch

Management and Staff
Christian Waldvogel, Managing Partner
Luc Otten, Principal
Xavier Paternot, Managing Partner

Type of Firm
Private Equity Firm

Association Membership
Swiss Venture Capital Association (SECA)

Project Preferences

Type of Financing Preferred:
Leveraged Buyout
Early Stage
Turnaround
Later Stage
Management Buyouts
Acquisition

Industry Preferences

In Medical/Health prefer:
Pharmaceuticals

Additional Information
Name of Most Recent Fund: Renaissance Technologies 4
Most Recent Fund Was Raised: 10/15/2013
Year Founded: 2003
Capital Under Management: $150,800,000
Current Activity Level : Actively seeking new investments

VINCI EQUITIES GESTORA DE RECURSOS LTDA

Avenida Ataulfo de Paiva 153
5th floor, Leblon
Rio de Janeiro, Brazil 22440032
Phone: 552121596000

Other Offices
Av. Brigadeiro Faria Lima
2.277 14th floor - Jardim Paulistano
Sao Paulo, Brazil 01452-000
Phone: 551135723700

Av. Presidente Vargas
2.121 8th floor - Jardim America
Ribeirao Preto, Brazil 14020-260
Phone: 551632389400

Management and Staff
Aldo Santos Laureano, Partner
Alexandre Lindenbojm, Partner
Ana Marta Pitta de Gouveia Bodra, Partner
Bruno Zaremba, Partner
Fabio Rodriguez Pegas, Partner
Felipe Sousa Bittencourt, Partner
Fernando Lovisotto, Partner
Fernando Marcondes Monteiro Chibante, Partner
Gabriel Felzenswalb, Partner
Gilberto Sayao de Silva, Chief Executive Officer

Guy Perelmuter, Partner
Jose Luis Pano, Partner
Jose Guilherme Cruz Souza, Partner
Luiz Otavio Bianchini Laydner, Partner
Marcello Almeida, Partner
Marcelo Rabbat, Partner
Mariano Ceppas Figueiredo, Partner
Nelson Rocha, Partner
Olavo Vieira Tortelli, Partner
Pedro Quintella, Partner
Pedro Dreux, Partner
Renato Moritz Cavalcanti, Partner
Ricardo Kobayashi, Partner
Ronaldo Boruchovitch, Partner
Sergio Passos, Partner

Type of Firm
Investment Management Firm

Association Membership
Brazilian Venture Capital Association (ABCR)

Project Preferences

Type of Financing Preferred:
Leveraged Buyout
Early Stage

Geographical Preferences

International Preferences:
Brazil

Additional Information
Year Founded: 2009
Capital Under Management: $1,400,000,000
Current Activity Level : Actively seeking new investments

VINE STREET VENTURES LLC

425 Walnut Street, Suite 1800
Cincinnati, OH USA 45202
Phone: 5133579626
E-mail: info@vinestventures.com
Website: www.vinestventures.com

Type of Firm
Private Equity Firm

Project Preferences

Type of Financing Preferred:
Balanced

Industry Preferences

In Communications prefer:
Wireless Communications

In Internet Specific prefer:
Internet

Additional Information
Name of Most Recent Fund: Vine Street Ventures Fund I LLC

Most Recent Fund Was Raised: 08/23/2012
Year Founded: 2012
Capital Under Management: $3,465,000
Current Activity Level : Actively seeking new investments

VINEYARD VENTURES

P.O. Box 1268
Edgartown, MA USA 02539
Phone: 508-292-1612
Fax: 508-627-9694
Website: www.vineyardventures.co.za

Other Offices
Level 40, Tower 2
Petronas Twin Towers
Kuala Lumpur, Malaysia
Phone: 603-2168-4311
Fax: 603-2168-4657

Management and Staff
Robb Fipp, Managing Partner
Warren Adams, Managing Partner

Type of Firm
Private Equity Firm

Project Preferences

Type of Financing Preferred:
Early Stage

Additional Information
Year Founded: 2000
Current Activity Level : Actively seeking new investments

VINTAGE CAPITAL PARTNERS, L.P.

11611 San Vicente Boulevard, Tenth Floor
Los Angeles, CA USA 90049
Phone: 3109799090
Fax: 3102070035
Website: www.vintage-vfm.com

Management and Staff
Chris Pace, Principal
Mark Sampson, Co-Founder
Thomas Webster, Principal

Type of Firm
Private Equity Firm

Project Preferences

Role in Financing:
Prefer role as deal originator

Type of Financing Preferred:
Leveraged Buyout
Expansion
Management Buyouts
Acquisition
Recapitalizations

Geographical Preferences

United States Preferences:

Additional Information
Year Founded: 2004
Capital Under Management: $162,500,000
Current Activity Level : Actively seeking new investments

VINTAGE VENTURE PARTNERS IV (CAYMAN) LP

12 Abba Eban Avenue
10F, Ackerstein Towers Bldg. D
Herzilyah Pituach, Israel 46120
Phone: 972-9-954-8464
Fax: 972-9-954-1012
E-mail: info@vintageventures.com
Website: www.vintageventures.com

Management and Staff
Abe Finkelstein, Principal
Alan Feld, Managing Partner
Amit Frenkel, Venture Partner
Hagai Goldhirsch, Chief Financial Officer

Type of Firm
Private Equity Advisor or Fund of Funds

Association Membership
Israel Venture Association

Project Preferences

Type of Financing Preferred:
Fund of Funds
Fund of Funds of Second

Size of Investments Considered:
Min Size of Investment Considered (000s): $3,000
Max Size of Investment Considered (000s): $10,000

Geographical Preferences

United States Preferences:

International Preferences:
Israel

Industry Preferences

In Communications prefer:
Communications and Media

In Internet Specific prefer:
Internet

In Semiconductor/Electr prefer:
Semiconductor

In Medical/Health prefer:
Medical Products

Additional Information
Name of Most Recent Fund: Vintage VI
Most Recent Fund Was Raised: 06/05/2013
Year Founded: 2003
Capital Under Management: $500,000,000
Current Activity Level : Actively seeking new investments

VIOLA PRIVATE EQUITY I LP

12 Abba Eban Avenue
Ackerstein Towers, Building D
Herzeliya, Israel 46725
Phone: 97299720500
Fax: 97299720515
E-mail: gality@violape.com
Website: www.violape.com

Management and Staff
Harel Beit-On, General Partner
Jonathan Kolber, General Partner
Osnat Ronen, General Partner
Sami Totah, General Partner

Type of Firm
Private Equity Firm

Association Membership
Israel Venture Association

Project Preferences

Type of Financing Preferred:
Expansion

Geographical Preferences

International Preferences:
Netherlands

Industry Preferences

In Internet Specific prefer:
Ecommerce

Additional Information
Year Founded: 2008
Capital Under Management: $250,000,000
Current Activity Level : Actively seeking new investments

VIRGIN GREEN FUND

65 Bleecker Street
New York, NY USA 10012
Phone: 2124979061
E-mail: info@virgingreenfund.com
Website: www.virgingreenfund.com

Other Offices
6 Kean Street
6th Floor, Kean House
London, United Kingdom WC2B 4AS
Phone: 442073391500

Management and Staff
Anup Jacob, Co-Founder
Evan Lovell, Partner
Michael Willis, Principal
Shai Weiss, Partner
Toby Coppel, Partner

Type of Firm
Private Equity Firm

Project Preferences

Type of Financing Preferred:
Leveraged Buyout
Early Stage
Expansion
Generalist PE
Balanced
Later Stage
Acquisition

Geographical Preferences

United States Preferences:
North America

International Preferences:
Turkey
Central Europe
Europe
Eastern Europe
Russia

Industry Preferences

In Industrial/Energy prefer:
Energy
Alternative Energy
Energy Conservation Relat
Environmental Related

In Other prefer:
Environment Responsible

Additional Information
Name of Most Recent Fund: VGF Emerging Market Growth I, L.P.
Most Recent Fund Was Raised: 10/31/2012
Year Founded: 2007
Capital Under Management: $200,000,000
Current Activity Level : Actively seeking new investments

VIRGO CAPITAL

815A Brazos Street, Suite 501
Austin, TX USA 78704
Phone: 5126929857
Fax: 5125191656
Website: www.virgocapital.com

Management and Staff
Arun Prakash, Partner
Guhan Swaminathan, Co-Founder
Hemanth Parasuram, Co-Founder
Nathaniel Robinson, Partner

Type of Firm
Private Equity Firm

Project Preferences

Role in Financing:
Prefer role as deal originator but will also invest in deals created by others

Type of Financing Preferred:
Leveraged Buyout
Management Buyouts
Acquisition
Recapitalizations

Industry Preferences

In Computer Software prefer:
Software

In Business Serv. prefer:
Services

Additional Information
Name of Most Recent Fund: Virgo Capital Fund II, L.P.
Most Recent Fund Was Raised: 12/06/2012
Year Founded: 2005
Capital Under Management: $80,000,000
Current Activity Level : Actively seeking new investments
Method of Compensation: Return on investment is of primary concern, do not charge fees

VIRGO INVESTMENT GROUP LLC

555 Twin Dolphin Drive, Suite 615
Redwood City, CA USA 94065
Phone: 6504533627
E-mail: vig@virgo-llc.com
Website: www.virgo-llc.com

Management and Staff
Chris MacDonald, Partner
Jesse Watson, Managing Partner
Mack McNair, Partner
Mark Perez, Partner
Robert Racusin, Partner

Type of Firm
Private Equity Firm

Project Preferences

Type of Financing Preferred:
Leveraged Buyout
Turnaround
Acquisition
Special Situation
Distressed Debt

Additional Information
Year Founded: 2014
Current Activity Level : Actively seeking new investments

VIRTUS CAPITAL PARTNERS SRL

Via Bruno Buozzi 10
Torino, Italy 10123
Phone: 39011542384
Fax: 390115069407

Management and Staff
Emanuele di Gresy, President
Silvia Rovere, Partner
Walter Ricciotti, Partner

Type of Firm
Private Equity Advisor or Fund of Funds

Project Preferences

Type of Financing Preferred:
Second Stage Financing
Leveraged Buyout
Expansion
Later Stage

Geographical Preferences

International Preferences:
Italy
United Kingdom
Switzerland

Industry Preferences

In Internet Specific prefer:
Internet

In Computer Other prefer:
Computer Related

In Medical/Health prefer:
Medical/Health

In Industrial/Energy prefer:
Energy
Industrial Products

In Business Serv. prefer:
Services

In Manufact. prefer:
Manufacturing

Additional Information
Year Founded: 2000
Capital Under Management: $26,400,000
Current Activity Level : Actively seeking new investments

VIS MUNDI LTD

JLT Mazaya Business Avenue
Tower AA1, Level 16
Dubai, Utd. Arab Em. 54058
Phone: 9714458107584
Fax: 97144581149
E-mail: info@vis-mundi.com
Website: www.vis-mundi.com

Type of Firm
Investment Management Firm

Additional Information
Year Founded: 2014
Current Activity Level : Actively seeking new investments

VISA INC

P.O. Box 8999
San Francisco, CA USA 94128
Phone: 4159322213
Fax: 6504325788
E-mail: ir@visa.com
Website: usa.visa.com

Management and Staff
Ryan McInerney, President

Type of Firm
Corporate PE/Venture

Project Preferences

Role in Financing:
Prefer role in deals created by others

Type of Financing Preferred:
Later Stage

Geographical Preferences

United States Preferences:

International Preferences:
All International

Industry Preferences

In Communications prefer:
Wireless Communications

In Computer Software prefer:
Data Processing
Software
Applications Software
Artificial Intelligence

In Internet Specific prefer:
E-Commerce Technology
Internet
Ecommerce
Web Aggregation/Portals

In Financial Services prefer:
Financial Services

Additional Information
Year Founded: 1995
Capital Under Management: $10,000,000
Current Activity Level : Actively seeking new investments
Method of Compensation: Return on investment is of primary concern, do not charge fees

VISCOGLIOSI BROTHERS LLC

505 Park Avenue
14th Floor
New York, NY USA 10022
Phone: 2125839700
Fax: 2128269509
Website: www.vbllc.com

Management and Staff
Anthony Viscogliosi, Co-Founder
David Lown, Partner
John Viscogliosi, Co-Founder
Marc Viscogliosi, Co-Founder

Type of Firm
Bank Affiliated

Project Preferences

Type of Financing Preferred:
Balanced

Geographical Preferences

United States Preferences:
All U.S.

International Preferences:
Europe

Industry Preferences

In Medical/Health prefer:
Medical/Health
Medical Products

Additional Information
Name of Most Recent Fund: Viscogliosi Brothers LLC
Most Recent Fund Was Raised: 05/09/2005
Year Founded: 1999
Capital Under Management: $120,000
Current Activity Level : Actively seeking new investments

VISION CAPITAL ADVISORS LLC

20 West 55th Street
Fifth Floor
New York, NY USA 10019
Phone: 2128498225
Fax: 2128671416
E-mail: investorrelations@visicap.com
Website: www.visicap.com

Management and Staff
Adam Benowitz, Co-Founder
Carl Kleidman, Managing Director
Randolph Cohen, President

Type of Firm
Investment Management Firm

Project Preferences

Type of Financing Preferred:
Later Stage

Size of Investments Considered:
Min Size of Investment Considered (000s): $3,000
Max Size of Investment Considered (000s): $20,000

Geographical Preferences

United States Preferences:
North America

International Preferences:
China

Industry Preferences

In Communications prefer:
Telecommunications

In Biotechnology prefer:
Biotechnology

In Medical/Health prefer:
Medical Products
Pharmaceuticals

In Consumer Related prefer:
Consumer Products

In Industrial/Energy prefer:
Industrial Products

In Business Serv. prefer:
Media

Additional Information
Year Founded: 2005
Current Activity Level : Actively seeking new investments

VISION CAPITAL LLP

55 St. James's Street
London, United Kingdom SW1A 1LA
Phone: 4402073896410
Fax: 442073896411
E-mail: info@visioncapital.com
Website: www.visioncapital.com

Other Offices
681 Fifth Avenue
Between 53rd and 54th
MANHATTAN, NY USA 10022
Phone: 2123036200

Management and Staff
Andrew Schweibold, Principal
Christophe Browne, Principal
David Lamb, Partner
Emil Fajersson, Principal
Giulio Piccinini, Principal
Iva Anguelov, Principal
Jonathan Guest, Principal
Matt Shafer, Partner
Michael Adams, Chief Financial Officer
Samer Cortas, Partner

Type of Firm
Private Equity Firm

Project Preferences

Type of Financing Preferred:
Leveraged Buyout
Management Buyouts
Acquisition

Geographical Preferences

United States Preferences:
All U.S.

International Preferences:
Europe

Additional Information
Year Founded: 1997
Capital Under Management: $2,332,500,000
Current Activity Level : Actively seeking new investments

VISION INVESTMENT CORP

No. 32 Zhongguancun Street
20/F Hengsheng Tower, Haidian
Beijing, China 100086
Phone: 86152926696
Fax: 861052926613
E-mail: biz@vision-investment.com
Website: www.vision-investment.com

Type of Firm
Private Equity Firm

Project Preferences

Type of Financing Preferred:
Later Stage

Geographical Preferences

International Preferences:
Macau
Taiwan
Hong Kong
China

Industry Preferences

In Consumer Related prefer:
Consumer
Retail
Consumer Services

In Industrial/Energy prefer:
Energy
Materials

Additional Information
Year Founded: 2006
Current Activity Level : Actively seeking new investments

2255

VISION KNIGHT CAPITAL

No. 1155, Fangdian Road
33/F, Kerry Parkside Office
Shanghai, China 201204
Phone: 862120281659
Fax: 862120281678
Website: www.vkc-partners.com

Management and Staff
Hailong Zhu, Venture Partner
Huating Wu, Partner
Xu Huang, Partner

Type of Firm
Private Equity Firm

Association Membership
Hong Kong Venture Capital Association (HKVCA)

Project Preferences

Type of Financing Preferred:
Balanced

Geographical Preferences

International Preferences:
China

Industry Preferences

In Internet Specific prefer:
Internet
Ecommerce

In Consumer Related prefer:
Consumer
Retail
Consumer Services

Additional Information
Year Founded: 1969
Capital Under Management: $575,000,000
Current Activity Level : Actively seeking new investments

VISION VENTURE PARTNERS

335 North Maple Drive, Suite 353
Beverly Hills, CA USA 90210
Phone: 4243892260
E-mail: info@vvpllc.com
Website: www.vvpllc.com

Type of Firm
Private Equity Firm

Project Preferences

Type of Financing Preferred:
Leveraged Buyout
Expansion
Later Stage
Acquisition

Geographical Preferences

United States Preferences:

Industry Preferences

In Computer Software prefer:
Applications Software

In Internet Specific prefer:
E-Commerce Technology

In Consumer Related prefer:
Food/Beverage

Additional Information
Year Founded: 2017
Current Activity Level : Actively seeking new investments

VISIONARY VENTURE FUND LP

65 Enterprise
Laguna Niguel, CA USA 92656

Type of Firm
Incubator/Development Program

Project Preferences

Type of Financing Preferred:
Balanced

Industry Preferences

In Medical/Health prefer:
Medical/Health

Additional Information
Year Founded: 2016
Capital Under Management: $30,000,000
Current Activity Level : Actively seeking new investments

VISIONNAIRE VENTURES LLC

One Circle Star Way
San Carlos, CA USA 94070
Phone: 6505758816
E-mail: contact@visionnaireventures.com
Website: visionnaireventures.com

Type of Firm
Private Equity Firm

Project Preferences

Type of Financing Preferred:
Early Stage
Seed

Industry Preferences

In Consumer Related prefer:
Entertainment and Leisure

Additional Information
Name of Most Recent Fund: Visionnaire Ventures Fund I, L.P.
Most Recent Fund Was Raised: 03/31/2014
Year Founded: 2014
Capital Under Management: $80,000,000
Current Activity Level : Actively seeking new investments

VISIONPLUS OYJ

Kampinkuja 2
Helsinki, Finland 00100
E-mail: info@visionplus.fi
Website: www.visionplus.fi

Management and Staff
Jari Tuovinen, Co-Founder
Marko Tulonen, Co-Founder
Tanu-Matti Tuominen, Co-Founder
Tero Ojanpera, Co-Founder

Type of Firm
Private Equity Firm

Project Preferences

Type of Financing Preferred:
Early Stage

Additional Information
Year Founded: 2012
Current Activity Level : Actively seeking new investments

VISIUM ASSET MANAGEMENT LP

888 Seventh Avenue
22nd Floor
New York, NY USA 10019
Phone: 2124748800
E-mail: info@visiumfunds.com

Management and Staff
Jacob Gottlieb, Founder
Mark Yacos, Chief Financial Officer
Steven Ku, Chief Operating Officer

Type of Firm
Investment Management Firm

Project Preferences

Type of Financing Preferred:
Mezzanine

Geographical Preferences

United States Preferences:
New York

International Preferences:
United Kingdom

Additional Information
Year Founded: 2005
Capital Under Management: $275,000,000
Current Activity Level : Actively seeking new investments

VISTA EQUITY PARTNERS LLC

4 Embarcadero Center
20th Floor
San Francisco, CA USA 94111
Phone: 4157656500
Fax: 4157656666
E-mail: contact@vistaequitypartners.com
Website: www.vistaequitypartners.com

Other Offices
401 Congress Avenue, Suite 3100
Austin, TX USA 78701
Phone: 5127302400
Fax: 5127302453

180 North Stetson Avenue, Suite 4000, Two Prudential Plaza
Chicago, IL USA 60601
Phone: 3122299500
Fax: 3122299599

Management and Staff
Alan Cline, Principal
Anand Anbalagan, Vice President
Christian Sowul, Principal
James Hickey, Principal
Jamie Ford, Chief Operating Officer
John Warnken-Brill, Chief Financial Officer
Justin Cho, Vice President
Jyoti Gupta, Vice President
Marc Teillon, Vice President
Martin Taylor, Principal
Michael Fosnaugh, Principal
Rachel Arnold, Vice President
Regan Garrett, Vice President
Rene Yang, Vice President
Robert Rogers, Principal
Vincent Burkett, Principal

Type of Firm
Private Equity Firm

Association Membership
Natl Assoc of Investment Cos. (NAIC)

Project Preferences

Role in Financing:
Prefer role as deal originator but will also invest in deals created by others

Type of Financing Preferred:
Leveraged Buyout
Management Buyouts
Acquisition
Recapitalizations

Geographical Preferences

United States Preferences:

Industry Focus
(% based on actual investment)
Computer Software and Services   75.8%
Internet Specific   24.2%

Additional Information
Year Founded: 2000
Capital Under Management: $11,500,000,000
Current Activity Level : Actively seeking new investments
Method of Compensation: Return on invest. most important, but chg. closing fees, service fees, etc.

VISTA RIDGE CAPITAL PARTNERS LLC

12655 SW Center Street, Suite 3000
Beaverton, OR USA 97005
Phone: 5036415170
E-mail: info@vistaridgecapital.com
Website: vistaridgecapital.com

Management and Staff
Dilip Ratnam, Co-Founder
Don Vollum, Co-Founder

Type of Firm
Private Equity Advisor or Fund of Funds

Project Preferences

Type of Financing Preferred:
Fund of Funds
Leveraged Buyout
Expansion
Generalist PE
Balanced
Management Buyouts
Acquisition
Special Situation

Geographical Preferences

United States Preferences:
North America

International Preferences:
Latin America
Europe
Asia
All International

Additional Information
Name of Most Recent Fund: Vista Ridge Diversified Fund II, L.P.
Most Recent Fund Was Raised: 02/26/2013
Year Founded: 2010
Capital Under Management: $44,296,000
Current Activity Level : Actively seeking new investments

VISTA VENTURES

1011 Walnut Street
4th Floor
Boulder, CO USA 80302
Phone: 3035435716
Fax: 3033625570
E-mail: info@vistavc.com
Website: www.vistavc.com

Management and Staff
Catharine Merigold, General Partner
Kirk Holland, General Partner
Lisa Reeves, General Partner
Molly Nasky, Chief Financial Officer

Type of Firm
Private Equity Firm

Project Preferences

Role in Financing:
Prefer role as deal originator but will also invest in deals created by others

Type of Financing Preferred:
Early Stage

Geographical Preferences

United States Preferences:

Rocky Mountain
Southwest

Industry Preferences

In Communications prefer:
Wireless Communications

In Computer Software prefer:
Software

In Business Serv. prefer:
Media

Additional Information
Name of Most Recent Fund: Vista Ventures I
Most Recent Fund Was Raised: 04/15/2000
Year Founded: 2000
Capital Under Management: $75,000,000
Current Activity Level : Actively seeking new investments
Method of Compensation: Return on investment is of primary concern, do not charge fees

VISTARA CAPITAL PARTNERS

400 Burrard Street, Suite 1910
Vancouver, Canada V6C 3A6
Website: vistaracapital.com

Type of Firm
Private Equity Firm

Project Preferences

Type of Financing Preferred:
Leveraged Buyout
Generalist PE
Later Stage
Recapitalizations

Geographical Preferences

United States Preferences:
North America
West Coast

Canadian Preferences:
All Canada

Additional Information

Year Founded: 2015
Capital Under Management: $80,872,000
Current Activity Level : Actively seeking new investments

VISTECH CORP

P.O. Box 510
Westport, CT USA 06881
Phone: 203-454-0300
Fax: 203-454-1054
E-mail: admin@vistechcorp.com
Website: www.vistechcorp.com

Management and Staff

E. Per Sorensen, Managing Director
Lincoln Rathman, Managing Director
William Melvin, Managing Director

Type of Firm

Private Equity Advisor or Fund of Funds

Project Preferences

Role in Financing:
Prefer role as deal originator

Type of Financing Preferred:
Joint Ventures
Private Placement

Geographical Preferences

United States Preferences:

International Preferences:
Latin America
Mexico

Industry Preferences

In Biotechnology prefer:
Human Biotechnology
Industrial Biotechnology
Biosensors

In Medical/Health prefer:
Drug/Equipmt Delivery

In Consumer Related prefer:
Food/Beverage
Hotels and Resorts

In Industrial/Energy prefer:
Energy
Industrial Products
Process Control

In Financial Services prefer:
Financial Services

In Business Serv. prefer:
Consulting Services

In Utilities prefer:
Utilities

Additional Information

Year Founded: 1980
Current Activity Level : Actively seeking new investments
Method of Compensation: Professional fee required whether or not deal closes

VISTRIA GROUP, L.P., THE

300 East Randolph Street, Suite 4030
Chicago, IL USA 60601
Phone: 3126261101
Website: www.vistria.com

Type of Firm

Private Equity Firm

Project Preferences

Type of Financing Preferred:
Leveraged Buyout

Industry Preferences

In Medical/Health prefer:
Medical/Health

In Financial Services prefer:
Financial Services

Additional Information

Year Founded: 2013
Capital Under Management: $1,202,595,000
Current Activity Level : Actively seeking new investments

VITAL VENTURE CAPITAL LLC

7101 Wisconsin Avenue, Suite 1210
Bethesda, MD USA 20814
Phone: 4152976451
Website: www.vitalvc.com

Management and Staff

A. Craig Asher, Principal
Nathaniel Brinn, Principal
Norman Norris, Principal

Type of Firm

Private Equity Firm

Association Membership

Mid-Atlantic Venture Association

Project Preferences

Type of Financing Preferred:
Early Stage
Balanced
Later Stage
Startup

Size of Investments Considered:
Min Size of Investment Considered (000s): $1,000
Max Size of Investment Considered (000s): $3,000

Industry Preferences

In Computer Software prefer:
Software

In Medical/Health prefer:
Medical Diagnostics
Medical Products

Additional Information

Year Founded: 2007
Current Activity Level : Actively seeking new investments

VITAMINA K

Principe de Vergara 38, 5 Left
Madrid, Spain 28001
Phone: 915613719
E-mail: hola@vitaminak.com
Website: www.vitaminak.com

Management and Staff

Inaki Arrola, Co-Founder

Type of Firm

Private Equity Firm

Project Preferences

Type of Financing Preferred:
Early Stage
Seed

Size of Investments Considered:
Min Size of Investment Considered (000s): $143
Max Size of Investment Considered (000s): $430

Geographical Preferences

International Preferences:
Spain

Industry Preferences

In Communications prefer:
Media and Entertainment
Entertainment

In Computer Hardware prefer:
Computer Graphics and Dig

In Internet Specific prefer:
Internet
Ecommerce

In Consumer Related prefer:
Consumer
Retail
Education Related

Additional Information
Year Founded: 2011
Current Activity Level : Actively seeking new investments

VITO VENTURES MANAGEMENT GMBH

Bavariaring 26
Munich, Germany 80336
Phone: 498959991653
E-mail: info@vito.vc
Website: www.vito.vc

Type of Firm
Private Equity Firm

Additional Information
Year Founded: 2015
Current Activity Level : Actively seeking new investments

VITRUVIAN PARTNERS LLP

105 Wigmore Street
London, United Kingdom W1U 1QY
Phone: 442075182800
Fax: 442075182801
Website: www.vitruvianpartners.com

Other Offices
Strandvagen 7A
Stockholm, Sweden 114 56
Phone: 4684596660

Maximilianstrasse 13
Munich, Germany 80539
Phone: 4989203006310

Management and Staff
Ben Johnson, Partner
David Nahama, Co-Founder
Erik Larsson, Partner
Ian Riley, Co-Founder
Joseph O Mara, Principal
Jussi Wuoristo, Principal
Mark Harford, Co-Founder
Michael Risman, Co-Founder
Norman Bremer, Vice President
Oscar Severin, Principal
Philip Russmeyer, Partner
Sophie Bower-Straziota, Vice President
Stephen Byrne, Partner
Thomas Studd, Principal

Toby Wyles, Co-Founder
Torsten Winkler, Partner

Type of Firm
Private Equity Firm

Association Membership
British Venture Capital Association (BVCA)

Project Preferences

Type of Financing Preferred:
Leveraged Buyout
Balanced
Later Stage
Management Buyouts
Acquisition
Private Placement
Recapitalizations

Geographical Preferences

International Preferences:
Ireland
Netherlands
Scandanavia/Nordic Region

Industry Preferences

In Medical/Health prefer:
Medical/Health

In Consumer Related prefer:
Entertainment and Leisure

In Business Serv. prefer:
Services
Media

Additional Information
Name of Most Recent Fund: Vitruvian Investment Partnership II
Most Recent Fund Was Raised: 12/05/2013
Year Founded: 2006
Capital Under Management: $4,830,640,000
Current Activity Level : Actively seeking new investments

VITULUM VENTURES BV

Mediarena 7
Amsterdam, Netherlands 1099
E-mail: info@vitulumventures.com
Website: vitulumventures.com

Management and Staff
Ian Zein, Founder

Type of Firm
Private Equity Firm

Project Preferences

Type of Financing Preferred:
Seed
Startup

Size of Investments Considered:
Min Size of Investment Considered (000s): $67
Max Size of Investment Considered (000s): $134

Geographical Preferences

International Preferences:
Europe
Netherlands

Industry Preferences

In Computer Software prefer:
Software

In Internet Specific prefer:
Internet

Additional Information
Year Founded: 2013
Current Activity Level : Actively seeking new investments

VIVANT VENTURES PTY LTD

Two Market Street
Level 21
Sydney, Australia 2000
Phone: 61292607300
Website: www.vivant.com.au

Management and Staff
Anthony Farah, Chief Executive Officer

Type of Firm
Incubator/Development Program

Project Preferences

Type of Financing Preferred:
Seed
Startup

Geographical Preferences

International Preferences:
Australia

Additional Information
Year Founded: 2013
Capital Under Management: $41,556,000
Current Activity Level : Actively seeking new investments

VIVARIS CAPITAL LLC

Palmeras Street #53
Caribe Plaza Sixth Floor
San Juan, PR USA 00901
Phone: 8585255141
E-mail: info@vivariscapital.com
Website: vivariscapital.com

Type of Firm
Private Equity Firm

2259

Project Preferences

Type of Financing Preferred:
Core
Value-Add
Generalist PE
Later Stage

Geographical Preferences

United States Preferences:
Puerto Rico

Industry Preferences

In Financial Services prefer:
Real Estate

Additional Information
Year Founded: 2017
Current Activity Level : Actively seeking new investments

VIVERGI SOCIAL IMPACT FUND

Calle Serrano, 57
Madrid, Spain 28006
E-mail: info@vivergi.com
Website: vivergi.com

Type of Firm
Incubator/Development Program

Project Preferences

Type of Financing Preferred:
Early Stage

Geographical Preferences

International Preferences:
Europe
Spain

Industry Preferences

In Medical/Health prefer:
Medical/Health

In Consumer Related prefer:
Food/Beverage
Education Related

In Industrial/Energy prefer:
Environmental Related

In Agr/Forestr/Fish prefer:
Agriculture related

In Other prefer:
Socially Responsible

Additional Information
Year Founded: 2013
Capital Under Management: $66,094,000
Current Activity Level : Actively seeking new investments

VIVO CAPITAL LLC

505 Hamilton Ave, Suite 207
Palo Alto, CA USA 94301
Phone: 6506880818
Fax: 6506880815
E-mail: info@vivoventures.com
Website: www.vivoventures.com

Other Offices

100 Century Avenue
63F, Shanghai World Financial Center
Shanghai, China 200120
Phone: 862168880037
Fax: 862168880095

1480 Tianfu Boulevard North Section
La Defense Building #405
Chengdu, China 610041
Phone: 862885315718

B-12 Jiangoumenwai Avenue, Suite 1105, West Tower, Twin Towers
Beijing, China 100022
Phone: 861058793590
Fax: 861058793591

Management and Staff

Albert Cha, Managing Partner
Chen Yu, Managing Partner
Edgar Engleman, Managing Partner
Frank Kung, Managing Partner
James Zhao, Managing Partner
Mahendra Shah, Venture Partner

Type of Firm
Private Equity Firm

Project Preferences

Role in Financing:
Prefer role as deal originator

Type of Financing Preferred:
Early Stage
Expansion
Balanced
Public Companies
Later Stage

Geographical Preferences

United States Preferences:

International Preferences:
China

Industry Focus
(% based on actual investment)

Biotechnology	53.8%
Medical/Health	40.1%
Consumer Related	2.8%
Computer Software and Services	1.0%
Internet Specific	0.8%
Industrial/Energy	0.8%
Communications and Media	0.6%

Additional Information
Name of Most Recent Fund: Vivo Ventures Fund VII, L.P.
Most Recent Fund Was Raised: 01/03/2012
Year Founded: 1996
Capital Under Management: $1,022,000,000
Current Activity Level : Actively seeking new investments
Method of Compensation: Return on invest. most important, but chg. closing fees, service fees, etc.

VKRM

27500A La Vida Real
Los Altos, CA USA 94022
Phone: 6509414768
Fax: 6509412617
E-mail: info@vkrm.com
Website: www.vkrm.com

Type of Firm
Private Equity Firm

Project Preferences

Type of Financing Preferred:
Early Stage

Industry Preferences

In Computer Software prefer:
Software

In Internet Specific prefer:
Internet

In Consumer Related prefer:
Education Related

In Business Serv. prefer:
Services

Additional Information
Year Founded: 2007
Current Activity Level : Actively seeking new investments

VMG PARTNERS, L.P.

39 Mesa Street, Suite 201
San Francisco, CA USA 94129
Phone: 4156324200
Fax: 4156324222
Website: www.vmgequity.com

Other Offices

200 Avenue of the Stars, Suite 300 North
Los Angeles, CA USA 90067
Phone: 3107758603
Fax: 3103193986

Management and Staff
David Baram, Managing Director
Kara Cissell-Roell, Managing Director
Mary Kayser, Chief Financial Officer
Michael Mauze, Managing Director
Robert Schult, Managing Director
Robin Tsai, Managing Director
Scott Elaine Case, Managing Director
Wayne Wu, Managing Director

Type of Firm
Private Equity Firm

Project Preferences

Type of Financing Preferred:
Leveraged Buyout
Expansion
Acquisition

Geographical Preferences

United States Preferences:

Industry Preferences

In Consumer Related prefer:
Consumer
Entertainment and Leisure
Food/Beverage
Consumer Products
Consumer Services

Additional Information
Name of Most Recent Fund: VMG Partners II, L.P.
Most Recent Fund Was Raised: 06/21/2011
Year Founded: 2005
Capital Under Management: $1,425,000,000
Current Activity Level : Actively seeking new investments

VNT MANAGEMENT OY

Alatori 1B
Vaasa, Finland 65100
Fax: 35863120260
Website: www.vntm.com

Other Offices
Sepankatu 20
Oulu, Finland 90100

Hameenkatu 5A
Tampere, Finland 33100

Ayritie 12 C
Vantaa, Finland 01510
Fax: 358925178480

Arnulfstrasse 25
Munich, Germany 80335
Phone: 498951563628
Fax: 498951463697

Management and Staff
Harri Ollila, Partner
Jussi Palmroth, Managing Partner
Torsten Wipiejewski, Partner
Veijo Karppinen, Founder
Vesa Sadeharju, Partner

Type of Firm
Private Equity Firm

Association Membership
Finnish Venture Capital Association (FVCA)
German Venture Capital Association (BVK)

Project Preferences

Role in Financing:
Will function either as deal originator or investor in deals created by others

Type of Financing Preferred:
Early Stage
Balanced

Size of Investments Considered:
Min Size of Investment Considered (000s): $700
Max Size of Investment Considered (000s): $7,000

Geographical Preferences

United States Preferences:

International Preferences:
Europe
Finland
Germany

Industry Preferences

In Semiconductor/Electr prefer:
Electronics

In Industrial/Energy prefer:
Energy
Alternative Energy
Energy Conservation Relat
Environmental Related

In Other prefer:
Environment Responsible

Additional Information
Name of Most Recent Fund: Power Fund III Ky
Most Recent Fund Was Raised: 11/01/2011
Year Founded: 2002
Capital Under Management: $156,000,000
Current Activity Level : Actively seeking new investments

VOC CAPITAL PARTNERS BV

Wilhelminakade 312
Rotterdam, Netherlands 3072AR
Phone: 31102827468
Fax: 31102827469
Website: www.voccp.com

Management and Staff
Han de Groot, Partner
Jan Willem Gerritsen, Managing Partner
Nico Schuurbiers, Partner
Pieter Schoen, Partner

Type of Firm
Private Equity Firm

Association Membership
Dutch Venture Capital Associaton (NVP)

Project Preferences

Type of Financing Preferred:
Early Stage

Size of Investments Considered:
Min Size of Investment Considered (000s): $129
Max Size of Investment Considered (000s): $1,294

Geographical Preferences

International Preferences:
Europe
Netherlands

Industry Preferences

In Communications prefer:
Radio & TV Broadcasting
Wireless Communications
Other Communication Prod.

In Internet Specific prefer:
Internet

In Business Serv. prefer:
Services
Media

In Other prefer:
Environment Responsible

Additional Information
Year Founded: 2009
Current Activity Level : Actively seeking new investments

VOCAP INVESTMENT PARTNERS LLC

2770 Indian River Blvd, Suite 500
Vero Beach, FL USA 32960
Website: vocappartners.com

Management and Staff
Mike Becker, Managing Director
Patrick Welsh, Partner
Vinny Olmstead, Founder
Wendy Coya, Vice President

Type of Firm
Private Equity Firm

Project Preferences

Type of Financing Preferred:
Expansion
Balanced
Later Stage

Size of Investments Considered:
Min Size of Investment Considered (000s): $1,000
Max Size of Investment Considered (000s): $15,000

Industry Preferences

In Communications prefer:
Communications and Media

In Computer Software prefer:
Software

In Medical/Health prefer:
Health Services

In Business Serv. prefer:
Media

Additional Information
Year Founded: 2014
Current Activity Level : Actively seeking new investments

VODIA VENTURES LLC

97 Lowell Road
Second Floor
Concord, MA USA 01742
Phone: 9783180900
Website: vodiaventures.com

Management and Staff
David Matias, Managing Director

Type of Firm
Private Equity Firm

Project Preferences

Type of Financing Preferred:
Seed
Startup

Geographical Preferences

United States Preferences:
Massachusetts

Additional Information
Name of Most Recent Fund: Vodia Ventures Fund I, L.P.
Most Recent Fund Was Raised: 02/19/2013
Year Founded: 2013
Capital Under Management: $2,600,000
Current Activity Level : Actively seeking new investments

VOGO FUND ASSET MANAGEMENT

16F, AIA Tower
16, Tongil-ro 2-Gil, Jung-gu
Seoul, South Korea 04511
Phone: 82237880700
Fax: 82237880730
E-mail: contact@vogo-fund.com
Website: www.vogo-investment.com

Management and Staff
Byung Moo Park, Managing Partner
Changhoon Shin, Vice President
Jae Ha Shin, Managing Partner
Jae Wu Lee, Managing Partner
Yang Ho Byun, Managing Partner

Type of Firm
Private Equity Firm

Project Preferences

Type of Financing Preferred:
Leveraged Buyout
Expansion
Acquisition

Geographical Preferences

International Preferences:
Korea, South

Additional Information
Year Founded: 2005
Capital Under Management: $600,000,000
Current Activity Level : Actively seeking new investments

VOIVODA VENTURES

1868 Greenwich Street
San Francisco, CA USA 94123
Phone: 4157428636
E-mail: contact@voivoda.com
Website: www.voivoda.com

Other Offices
11 Magnaurska shkola Street
Office 407
Sofia, United Kingdom 1784

3501 Ocean View Boulevard
Glendale, CA USA 91208
Phone: 4157428636

Management and Staff
Emil Babajov, Managing Director
Henrique Gomes, Principal

Type of Firm
Incubator/Development Program

Project Preferences

Role in Financing:
Prefer role as deal originator

Type of Financing Preferred:
Early Stage
Seed
Startup

Size of Investments Considered:
Min Size of Investment Considered (000s): $500
Max Size of Investment Considered (000s): $1,500

Geographical Preferences

United States Preferences:

International Preferences:
Latin America
Europe
Israel
Asia
All International

Industry Preferences

In Communications prefer:
Wireless Communications

In Computer Software prefer:
Software
Applications Software

Additional Information
Year Founded: 2007
Current Activity Level : Actively seeking new investments

VOLATI AB

Engelbrektsplan 1
Stockholm, Sweden 114 34
Phone: 468216840
Fax: 468216918
E-mail: info@volati.se
Website: www.volati.se

Management and Staff
Marten Andersson, Chief Executive Officer
Mattias Bjork, Chief Financial Officer

Type of Firm
Private Equity Firm

Project Preferences

Type of Financing Preferred:
Leveraged Buyout
Acquisition

Geographical Preferences

International Preferences:
Sweden
Scandanavia/Nordic Region

Industry Preferences

In Medical/Health prefer:
Medical Products

In Industrial/Energy prefer:
Industrial Products

In Agr/Forestr/Fish prefer:
Agriculture related

Additional Information

Year Founded: 2003
Capital Under Management: $60,600,000
Current Activity Level : Actively seeking new investments

VOLCANO CAPITAL LLC

1270 Avenue of the Americas, Suite 302
New York, NY USA 10020
Phone: 6468333700
Website: www.volcanocap.com

Management and Staff

Doug Wall, Managing Partner

Type of Firm

Private Equity Firm

Project Preferences

Type of Financing Preferred:
Leveraged Buyout
Early Stage
Expansion
Generalist PE
Later Stage
Seed

Geographical Preferences

United States Preferences:
All U.S.

Industry Preferences

In Medical/Health prefer:
Medical/Health
Medical Products
Health Services

Additional Information

Year Founded: 2009
Current Activity Level : Actively seeking new investments

VOLIO CAPITAL SA

Parque Empresarial Forum
Torre G, Piso 7
Santa Ana, Costa Rica
Phone: 506-204-7080
Fax: 506-204-7667
E-mail: info@voliocapital.com
Website: www.voliocapital.com

Other Offices

Bosques de Duraznos
No.61 Piso 1
Bosques de Las Lomas, Mexico 11 700
Phone: 5255-5245-8676
Fax: 5255-5245-1693

Edificio CAR, Piso 3
4 km Carretera a Masaya
Managua, Nicaragua
Phone: 505-270-2112
Fax: 505-270-5225

World Trade Center Building 89 North Ave
El Mirador Street, Tower 1, Level 2
San Salvador, El Salvador
Phone: 503-2500-0895
Fax: 503-2500-0851

Management and Staff

Jorge Volio, Founding Partner

Type of Firm

Bank Affiliated

Project Preferences

Type of Financing Preferred:
Balanced

Geographical Preferences

International Preferences:
Mexico
El Salvador
Costa Rica
Nicaragua

Additional Information

Year Founded: 2007
Capital Under Management: $150,000,000
Current Activity Level : Actively seeking new investments

VOLITION CAPITAL LLC

177Huntington Avenue
16th Floor
Boston, MA USA 02115
Phone: 6178302100
E-mail: info@volitioncapital.com
Website: www.volitioncapital.com

Management and Staff

Andrew Flaster, Managing Partner
Andy Flaster, Co-Founder
Jake Colognesi, Vice President
Larry Cheng, Co-Founder
Robert Ketterson, Co-Founder
Roger Hurwitz, Co-Founder
Sean Cantwell, Co-Founder

Type of Firm

Private Equity Firm

Association Membership

New England Venture Capital Association

Project Preferences

Type of Financing Preferred:
Early Stage
Balanced
Later Stage

Size of Investments Considered:
Min Size of Investment Considered (000s): $5,000
Max Size of Investment Considered (000s): $20,000

Industry Preferences

In Communications prefer:
Communications and Media

In Computer Software prefer:
Software
Applications Software

In Internet Specific prefer:
Internet

In Medical/Health prefer:
Medical/Health

In Consumer Related prefer:
Consumer

In Business Serv. prefer:
Services

Additional Information

Name of Most Recent Fund: Volition Capital Fund II, L.P.
Most Recent Fund Was Raised: 07/09/2013
Year Founded: 2010
Capital Under Management: $400,000,000
Current Activity Level : Actively seeking new investments

VOLPI CAPITAL LLP

64 Sloane Street
London, United Kingdom SW1X 9SH
Website: www.volpicapital.com

Type of Firm

Private Equity Firm

Project Preferences

Type of Financing Preferred:
Generalist PE

Geographical Preferences

International Preferences:
Europe

Industry Preferences

In Computer Software prefer:
Software

Additional Information
Year Founded: 2015
Capital Under Management: $479,350,000
Current Activity Level: Actively seeking new investments

VOLTA GLOBAL LLC
2601 South Bayshore Drive, Suite 1700
Miami, FL USA 33133
Website: voltaglobal.com

Type of Firm
Private Equity Firm

Project Preferences

Type of Financing Preferred:
Leveraged Buyout
Generalist PE
Balanced
Later Stage
Other
Acquisition

Industry Preferences

In Computer Software prefer:
Software

In Consumer Related prefer:
Consumer

In Financial Services prefer:
Real Estate

Additional Information
Year Founded: 2016
Current Activity Level: Actively seeking new investments

VOLTA LABS INC
1505 Barrington Street
Sevent & Sixth floor
Halifax, Canada B3J 3K5
Phone: 9027020194
Website: voltaeffect.com

Type of Firm
Incubator/Development Program

Project Preferences

Type of Financing Preferred:
Startup

Geographical Preferences

Canadian Preferences:
All Canada

Additional Information
Year Founded: 2017
Current Activity Level: Actively seeking new investments

VOLVO GROUP VENTURE CAPITAL CORP
Gotaverksgatan 2
Gothenburg, Sweden 40508
Website: www.volvogroup.com

Management and Staff
Charlotta Modig, Chief Financial Officer

Type of Firm
Corporate PE/Venture

Association Membership
Swedish Venture Capital Association (SVCA)
European Private Equity and Venture Capital Assoc.

Project Preferences

Type of Financing Preferred:
Early Stage
Seed
Startup

Geographical Preferences

International Preferences:
Europe
Scandanavia/Nordic Region

Industry Preferences

In Communications prefer:
Wireless Communications

In Industrial/Energy prefer:
Energy
Industrial Products

Additional Information
Year Founded: 1997
Capital Under Management: $65,900,000
Current Activity Level: Actively seeking new investments

VOODOO VENTURES LLC
643 Magazine, Suite 102
New Orleans, LA USA 70130
Phone: 5042988884
Website: www.voodooventures.com

Type of Firm
Incubator/Development Program

Project Preferences

Type of Financing Preferred:
Seed
Startup

Industry Preferences

In Computer Software prefer:
Software

In Internet Specific prefer:
Internet

Additional Information
Year Founded: 2003
Current Activity Level: Actively seeking new investments

VOPNE CAPITAL LLC
One Maritime Plaza, Suite 1650
San Francisco, CA USA 94111
Phone: 4155628468
E-mail: info@vopne.com

Type of Firm
Private Equity Firm

Project Preferences

Type of Financing Preferred:
Leveraged Buyout
Turnaround
Acquisition
Recapitalizations

Geographical Preferences

United States Preferences:
North America

Industry Preferences

In Medical/Health prefer:
Medical/Health
Health Services

In Industrial/Energy prefer:
Industrial Products

In Transportation prefer:
Aerospace

In Business Serv. prefer:
Services

In Manufact. prefer:
Manufacturing

Additional Information
Name of Most Recent Fund: Vopne Capital Fund I
Most Recent Fund Was Raised: 05/21/2014
Year Founded: 2012
Capital Under Management: $20,000,000
Current Activity Level: Actively seeking new investments

VORTEX CAPITAL PARTNERS BV
Barbara Strozzilaan 101
Spaces Zuidas
Amsterdam, Netherlands 1083HN
Phone: 31651504925
Website: www.vortexcp.com

Type of Firm
Private Equity Firm

Project Preferences

Type of Financing Preferred:
Leveraged Buyout
Early Stage
Expansion
Later Stage
Management Buyouts
Acquisition

Size of Investments Considered:
Min Size of Investment Considered (000s): $543
Max Size of Investment Considered (000s): $6,518

Geographical Preferences

International Preferences:
Europe
Netherlands

Industry Preferences

In Computer Software prefer:
Software

In Internet Specific prefer:
Internet

Additional Information
Year Founded: 2012
Current Activity Level : Actively seeking new investments

VOSTOK EMERGING FINANCE LTD

2 Church Street
Clarendon House
Hamilton, Bermuda HM 11
Website: www.vostokemergingfinance.com

Management and Staff
David Nangle, Managing Director
Henrik Stenlund, Chief Financial Officer

Type of Firm
Private Equity Firm

Project Preferences

Type of Financing Preferred:
Early Stage
Expansion
Later Stage

Industry Preferences

In Internet Specific prefer:
E-Commerce Technology

In Financial Services prefer:
Financial Services

Additional Information
Year Founded: 2015
Current Activity Level : Actively seeking new investments

VOYAGER CAPITAL LLC

719 Second Avenue, Suite 1400
Seattle, WA USA 98104
Phone: 2064381800
Fax: 2064381900
Website: www.voyagercapital.com

Other Offices
1044 North West 9th Avenue
PORTLAND, OR USA 97209
Phone: 5036216668

Management and Staff
Bill Hughlett, Chief Financial Officer
Bill McAleer, Co-Founder
Bruce Chizen, Venture Partner
Chrismon Nofsinger, Venture Partner
Curtis Feeny, Managing Director
Diane Fraiman, Partner
Enrique Godreau, Managing Director
Erik Benson, Managing Director
Geoffrey Entress, Venture Partner
James Newell, Partner
Tom Kippola, Venture Partner
William McAleer, Managing Director

Type of Firm
Private Equity Firm

Association Membership
Western Association of Venture Capitalists (WAVC)

Project Preferences

Role in Financing:
Prefer role as deal originator but will also invest in deals created by others

Type of Financing Preferred:
Early Stage
Later Stage

Geographical Preferences

United States Preferences:
Northwest
Oregon
California
West Coast
Washington

Industry Focus
(% based on actual investment)
Computer Software and Services	53.1%
Internet Specific	27.8%
Other Products	6.7%
Communications and Media	5.1%
Computer Hardware	4.6%
Semiconductors/Other Elect.	2.1%
Industrial/Energy	0.5%

Additional Information
Name of Most Recent Fund: Voyager Capital Fund III, L.P.
Most Recent Fund Was Raised: 03/31/2006
Year Founded: 1997
Capital Under Management: $420,000,000
Current Activity Level : Actively seeking new investments
Method of Compensation: Return on investment is of primary concern, do not charge fees

VR EQUITYPARTNER GMBH

Platz der Republik
Frankfurt am Main, Germany 60265
Phone: 496974477209
Fax: 496974471632
E-mail: mail@vrep.de
Website: www.vrep.de

Other Offices
Graben 14-15
Vienna, Austria 1010
Phone: 43-1-5322-0140
Fax: 43-1-532201499

Management and Staff
Martin Voelker, Chief Executive Officer
Peter Sachse, Chief Executive Officer

Type of Firm
Bank Affiliated

Association Membership
German Venture Capital Association (BVK)

Project Preferences

Type of Financing Preferred:
Leveraged Buyout
Early Stage
Mezzanine
Later Stage
Management Buyouts
Recapitalizations

Geographical Preferences

International Preferences:
Switzerland
Austria
Germany

Industry Focus
(% based on actual investment)
Computer Software and Services	42.1%
Biotechnology	18.8%
Other Products	14.7%
Internet Specific	11.3%
Communications and Media	7.3%
Industrial/Energy	5.7%

Additional Information
Year Founded: 1992
Capital Under Management: $698,000,000
Current Activity Level : Actively seeking new investments

VRG CAPITAL CORP

70 University Avenue, Suite 1200
Toronto, Canada M5J 2M4
E-mail: info@vrgcapital.com
Website: www.vrgcapital.com

Type of Firm
Private Equity Firm

Industry Preferences

In Medical/Health prefer:
Health Services

In Financial Services prefer:
Financial Services
Insurance

Additional Information
Year Founded: 1982
Current Activity Level : Actively seeking new investments

VSJF FLEXIBLE CAPITAL FUND, THE

Three Pitkin Court, Suite 301E
Montpelier, VT USA 05602
Phone: 8028281260
E-mail: info@vsjf.org
Website: www.vsjf.org

Type of Firm
Government Affiliated Program

Project Preferences

Type of Financing Preferred:
Early Stage
Mezzanine
Later Stage

Geographical Preferences

United States Preferences:
Vermont

Industry Preferences

In Industrial/Energy prefer:
Energy
Environmental Related

In Agr/Forestr/Fish prefer:
Agriculture related

Additional Information
Name of Most Recent Fund: VSJF Flexible Capital Fund L3C
Most Recent Fund Was Raised: 01/03/2013
Year Founded: 2013
Capital Under Management: $3,300,000
Current Activity Level : Actively seeking new investments

VSTONE YANGTZE INVESTMENT MANAGAMENT CO LTD

No. 1, Yanan East Road
F4, Kaishi Building, Huangpu
Shanghai, China 200002
Phone: 862163336966
Fax: 862163336908
Website: www.vstoneyangtze.com

Management and Staff
Jiwu Chen, President

Type of Firm
Investment Management Firm

Project Preferences

Type of Financing Preferred:
Balanced
Later Stage

Geographical Preferences

International Preferences:
China

Industry Preferences

In Communications prefer:
Media and Entertainment

In Internet Specific prefer:
Internet

In Biotechnology prefer:
Biotechnology

In Medical/Health prefer:
Medical/Health
Pharmaceuticals

In Industrial/Energy prefer:
Energy
Energy Conservation Relat
Materials
Environmental Related

In Business Serv. prefer:
Services

In Manufact. prefer:
Manufacturing

Additional Information
Year Founded: 2007
Capital Under Management: $783,700,000
Current Activity Level : Actively seeking new investments

VTB KAPITAL AO

Presnenskaia Naberezhnaia, 12
Federation Tower
Moscow, Russia 123100
Phone: 74959609999
Fax: 74956634700
E-mail: info@vtbcapital.com
Website: www.vtbcapital.ru

Other Offices

Bubai International Financial
Centre, Currency House Tower 2
Dubai, Utd. Arab Em. 482088
Phone: 97143770777
Fax: 97143770888

4 Kniaz Alexander I
Sofia, Bulgaria 1000
Phone: 35928052885
Fax: 35928052881

9 Battery Road
Singapore, Singapore 068882
Phone: 6562209422
Fax: 6562250140

2 Queen's Road Central, 23/F
Cheung Kong Center
Hong Kong, Hong Kong 2301
Phone: 85231953630
Fax: 85231953699

452 Fifth Avenue
23rd Floor
MIDTOWN, NY USA 10018
Phone: 16465276300
Fax: 16465276301

14 Cornhill
London, United Kingdom EC3V 3ND
Phone: 442033348000
Fax: 442033348900

Bular. T. Shevchenko/Pushkinskaia 8/26
Kiev, Ukraine
Phone: 380442393526

Parkring 6
Wien, Austria 1010

79, Boulevard Haussmann
Paris, France 75008
Phone: 33140064321
Fax: 33140064848

Varshavskoe shosse, 28A
office 416-420
Moscow, Russia 117105
Phone: 74957809277

Type of Firm
Bank Affiliated

Association Membership
Emerging Markets Private Equity Association
Russian Venture Capital Association (RVCA)

Project Preferences

Type of Financing Preferred:
Leveraged Buyout
Generalist PE
Later Stage
Seed
Acquisition

Geographical Preferences

United States Preferences:
Georgia

International Preferences:
Armenia
Belarus
Kazakhstan
Kyrgyzstan
Eastern Europe
Tajikistan
Turkmenistan
Azerbaijan
Moldova
Ukraine
Uzbekistan
Asia
Russia

Industry Preferences

In Computer Software prefer:
Artificial Intelligence

In Internet Specific prefer:
Ecommerce

In Industrial/Energy prefer:
Oil and Gas Exploration

Additional Information

Name of Most Recent Fund: VTB Venture Fund
Most Recent Fund Was Raised: 09/21/2007
Year Founded: 2008
Current Activity Level : Actively seeking new investments

VULCAN INC

505 Fifth Avenue South, Suite 900
Seattle, WA USA 98104
Phone: 2063422000
Fax: 2063423000
Website: capital.vulcan.com

Management and Staff

Abhishek Agrawal, Managing Director
Geoff McKay, Managing Director
Steven Hall, Managing Director

Type of Firm

Private Equity Firm

Project Preferences

Type of Financing Preferred:
Leveraged Buyout
Early Stage
Generalist PE
Balanced
Turnaround
Later Stage
Acquisition
Distressed Debt

Size of Investments Considered:
Min Size of Investment Considered (000s): $10,000
Max Size of Investment Considered (000s): $100,000

Geographical Preferences

United States Preferences:

Industry Focus

(% based on actual investment)
Communications and Media	66.9%
Internet Specific	10.9%
Consumer Related	10.0%
Biotechnology	4.2%
Computer Software and Services	2.5%
Computer Hardware	1.7%
Industrial/Energy	1.6%
Semiconductors/Other Elect.	1.2%
Other Products	0.8%
Medical/Health	0.3%

Additional Information

Year Founded: 2003
Capital Under Management: $2,533,400,000
Current Activity Level : Actively seeking new investments

VUNANI PRIVATE EQUITY PARTNERS PTY. LTD.

Vunani House, Block C
151 Katherine Street, Sandown
Sandton, South Africa 2196
Phone: 27112639500
Fax: 27117843095
Website: www.vunanilimited.co.za

Other Offices

33 Church Street
Cape Town, South Africa 8001
Phone: 27214816200
Fax: 27214222823

Type of Firm

Corporate PE/Venture

Project Preferences

Type of Financing Preferred:
Fund of Funds

Geographical Preferences

International Preferences:
Africa

Additional Information

Year Founded: 2004
Capital Under Management: $164,500,000
Current Activity Level : Actively seeking new investments

VY CAPITAL MANAGEMENT CO LTD

901, 902,Level 9
Emirates Financial Towers DIFC
Dubai, Utd. Arab Em. 506950
Phone: 971042701400
Website: www.vycapital.com

Other Offices

901, 902Level 9, Emirates
Dubai International Financial
Dubai, Utd. Arab Em.

Type of Firm

Private Equity Firm

Project Preferences

Type of Financing Preferred:
Early Stage

Geographical Preferences

United States Preferences:
All U.S.

Industry Preferences

In Computer Software prefer:
Software

In Internet Specific prefer:
Internet

Additional Information

Year Founded: 2013
Current Activity Level : Actively seeking new investments

- W -

W CAPITAL MANAGEMENT LLC

One East 52nd Street
Fifth Floor
New York, NY USA 10022
Phone: 2125615240
Fax: 2125615241
Website: www.wcapgroup.com

Management and Staff

Alison Killilea, Managing Director
Blake Heston, Principal
David Wachter, Co-Founder
John Lambrech, Chief Financial Officer
Katie Stitch, Principal
Kyle Morgan, Vice President
Robert Migliorino, Co-Founder
Simon Harris, Vice President
Stephen Wertheimer, Co-Founder
Todd Miller, Managing Director

Type of Firm

Private Equity Advisor or Fund of Funds

Project Preferences

Role in Financing:
Prefer role as deal originator

Type of Financing Preferred:
Fund of Funds
Fund of Funds of Second

Size of Investments Considered:
Min Size of Investment Considered (000s): $5,000
Max Size of Investment Considered (000s): $50,000

Geographical Preferences

United States Preferences:

International Preferences:
Europe
Asia

Industry Focus

(% based on actual investment)
Internet Specific	46.8%
Computer Software and Services	26.6%
Other Products	13.2%
Communications and Media	4.4%
Medical/Health	2.6%
Consumer Related	2.4%
Computer Hardware	2.2%
Semiconductors/Other Elect.	1.8%

Additional Information

Name of Most Recent Fund: W Capital Partners III, L.P.
Most Recent Fund Was Raised: 12/14/2012
Year Founded: 2001
Capital Under Management: $1,500,000,000
Current Activity Level : Actively seeking new investments

W FUND LP

P.O. Box 95259
Seattle, WA USA 98145
Phone: 8777537997
Fax: 2065430586
E-mail: admin@thewfund.com
Website: www.thewfund.com

Type of Firm

University Program

Project Preferences

Type of Financing Preferred:
Early Stage
Seed
Startup

Geographical Preferences

United States Preferences:
Washington

Industry Preferences

In Communications prefer:
Wireless Communications

In Computer Software prefer:
Software

In Industrial/Energy prefer:
Environmental Related

In Other prefer:
Environment Responsible

Additional Information

Name of Most Recent Fund: W Fund, L.P., The
Most Recent Fund Was Raised: 06/14/2012
Year Founded: 2012
Capital Under Management: $10,584,000
Current Activity Level : Actively seeking new investments

W R HAMBRECHT & CO L L C

Pier One
Bay Three
San Francisco, CA USA 94111
Phone: 4155518600
Fax: 4155518686
E-mail: info@wrhambrecht.com
Website: www.wrhambrecht.com

Other Offices

555 Lancaster Avenue, Suite 200
Berwyn, PA USA 19312
Phone: 610-725-1150
Fax: 610-725-1167

One East 52nd Street
Third Floor
New York, NY USA 10022
Phone: 2123135900
Fax: 2123135959

Management and Staff

Barrie Graham, Chief Operating Officer
Creighton Reed, Vice President
Ian Zwicker, Partner
Michael Black, Vice President
Peter Morrissey, Managing Director

Type of Firm

Investment Management Firm

Project Preferences

Type of Financing Preferred:
Leveraged Buyout
Early Stage
Balanced
Later Stage

Industry Preferences

In Computer Software prefer:
Software

In Internet Specific prefer:
Internet

In Consumer Related prefer:
Consumer Products

Additional Information

Name of Most Recent Fund: WR Hambrecht Ventures II, L.P.
Most Recent Fund Was Raised: 06/14/2007
Year Founded: 1998
Capital Under Management: $5,005,000
Current Activity Level : Actively seeking new investments
Method of Compensation: Return on invest. most important, but chg. closing fees, service fees, etc.

WA DE VIGIER STIFTUNG

Untere Steingrubenstrasse 25
Solothurn, Switzerland 4500
Website: www.devigier.ch

Management and Staff

Beat Graf, Vice President
Regula Buob, Managing Director

Type of Firm

Endowment, Foundation or Pension Fund

Project Preferences

Type of Financing Preferred:
Early Stage
Seed

Geographical Preferences

International Preferences:
Europe

Industry Preferences

In Biotechnology prefer:
Biotechnology
Biotech Related Research

Additional Information

Year Founded: 1987
Current Activity Level : Actively seeking new investments

WADI VENTURES SCA

10 Hanechoshet Street
Tel Aviv, Israel 69719
Phone: 97237712585
Fax: 97237712584
E-mail: info@wadiventures.com
Website: wadiventures.com

Management and Staff

Jonathan Pacifici, General Partner
Marco Norberto Bernabe, General Partner
Reuven Ulmansky, Partner

Type of Firm

Private Equity Firm

Project Preferences

Type of Financing Preferred:
Early Stage
Seed
Startup

Geographical Preferences

International Preferences:
Israel

Industry Preferences

In Communications prefer:
Media and Entertainment

In Computer Software prefer:
Applications Software

In Internet Specific prefer:
Internet

Additional Information

Year Founded: 2012
Current Activity Level : Actively seeking new investments

WADINKO NV

Zeven Alleetjes 1
Postbus 445
Zwolle, Netherlands 8000 AK
Phone: 31384259360
Fax: 31384259369
E-mail: info@wadinko.nl
Website: www.wadinko.nl

Type of Firm

Private Equity Firm

Association Membership

Dutch Venture Capital Associaton (NVP)

Project Preferences

Type of Financing Preferred:
Early Stage
Turnaround
Later Stage
Startup

Geographical Preferences

International Preferences:
Netherlands

Industry Preferences

In Communications prefer:
Telecommunications

In Computer Software prefer:
Software

In Semiconductor/Electr prefer:
Electronic Components

In Medical/Health prefer:
Medical/Health
Medical Products

In Consumer Related prefer:
Consumer
Publishing-Retail

In Industrial/Energy prefer:
Industrial Products

In Manufact. prefer:
Manufacturing

Additional Information

Year Founded: 1992
Capital Under Management: $47,600,000
Current Activity Level : Actively seeking new investments

WAFRA PARTNERS LLC

345 Park Avenue, 41st Floor
New York, NY USA 10154
Phone: 2127593700
Fax: 2124862678
Website: www.wafrapartners.com

Management and Staff

Andrew Thompson, Managing Director
Eric Norfleet, Managing Director
Jeffrey Gerson, Managing Director
Michael Goodman, Managing Director
Peter Petrillo, Senior Managing Director
Ryan Wierck, Managing Director

Type of Firm

Private Equity Firm

Project Preferences

Role in Financing:
Prefer role as deal originator but will also invest in deals created by others

Type of Financing Preferred:
Leveraged Buyout
Management Buyouts
Acquisition
Recapitalizations

Industry Focus

(% based on actual investment)
Other Products	63.3%
Communications and Media	24.1%
Internet Specific	10.0%
Computer Hardware	2.0%
Computer Software and Services	0.6%

Additional Information

Name of Most Recent Fund: Wafra Private Equity Fund V, L.P.
Most Recent Fund Was Raised: 03/27/2014
Year Founded: 1994
Capital Under Management: $250,000,000
Current Activity Level : Actively seeking new investments
Method of Compensation: Return on invest. most important, but chg. closing fees, service fees, etc.

WAHA CAPITAL PJSC

Etihad Towers 42nd 43rd Floor
Ras Al Akhdar Area
Abu Dhabi, Utd. Arab Em.
Phone: 97126677343
Fax: 97126677383
E-mail: info@wahacapital.ae
Website: www.wahacapital.ae

Management and Staff

Chakib Aabouche, Managing Director
Fahad Al Qassim, Managing Director
Michael Raynes, Chief Operating Officer
Salem Al Noaimi, Chief Executive Officer
Sana Khater, Chief Financial Officer

Type of Firm

Private Equity Firm

Project Preferences

Type of Financing Preferred:
Generalist PE
Acquisition

Geographical Preferences

International Preferences:
Middle East
Africa

Pratt's Guide to Private Equity & Venture Capital Sources

Industry Preferences

In Medical/Health prefer:
Health Services

In Industrial/Energy prefer:
Energy
Industrial Products

In Transportation prefer:
Transportation

In Financial Services prefer:
Financial Services
Real Estate
Investment Groups

Additional Information
Year Founded: 1997
Current Activity Level : Actively seeking new investments

WAITT CO

1125 South 103rd Street, Suite 425
Omaha, NE USA 68124
Phone: 4026978000
Website: www.waittcompany.com

Management and Staff
Dana Bradford, Chief Executive Officer
John Schuele, President

Type of Firm
Private Equity Firm

Project Preferences

Type of Financing Preferred:
Leveraged Buyout
Later Stage
Acquisition
Recapitalizations

Additional Information
Year Founded: 1969
Current Activity Level : Actively seeking new investments

WAKABAYASHI FUND LLC

4-13-20 Mita
Minato-Ku
Tokyo, Japan 108-0073
Phone: 810366578339
Fax: 810366578340
Website: www.wakabayashifund.com

Other Offices
110 Wall Street
Eleventh Floor
New York, NY USA 10005
Phone: 19146133002
Fax: 16465141601

Management and Staff
Jeffery Stone, Co-Founder

Type of Firm
Private Equity Firm

Project Preferences

Type of Financing Preferred:
Early Stage
Expansion
Generalist PE
Management Buyouts
Recapitalizations

Additional Information
Year Founded: 1969
Current Activity Level : Actively seeking new investments

WAKEFIELD GROUP

1110 East Morehead Street
Charlotte, NC USA 28204
Phone: 7043720355
Fax: 7043728216

Other Offices
5915 Farrington Road, Suite 201
Chapel Hill, NC USA 27517
Phone: 919-442-2160
Fax: 919-442-2162

Management and Staff
Anna Spangler Nelson, Partner
Steve Nelson, Managing Director
Tom Nelson, Co-Founder

Type of Firm
Private Equity Firm

Project Preferences

Role in Financing:
Prefer role as deal originator but will also invest in deals created by others

Type of Financing Preferred:
Early Stage

Size of Investments Considered:
Min Size of Investment Considered (000s): $1,000
Max Size of Investment Considered (000s): $5,000

Geographical Preferences

United States Preferences:
Southeast

Industry Focus
(% based on actual investment)
Computer Software and Services 26.3%
Communications and Media 22.7%
Medical/Health 15.7%
Internet Specific 13.4%
Computer Hardware 7.2%
Biotechnology 5.9%
Consumer Related 5.1%
Other Products 3.7%

Additional Information
Year Founded: 1988
Capital Under Management: $100,000,000
Current Activity Level : Actively seeking new investments
Method of Compensation: Return on investment is of primary concern, do not charge fees

---

WALDEN INTERNATIONAL

One California Street, Suite 2800
San Francisco, CA USA 94111
Phone: 4157657100
Fax: 4157657200
E-mail: usa@waldenintl.com
Website: www.waldenintl.com

Other Offices
18th Floor-2 Ruentex Banking Tower
No. 76, Tun Hua South Road, Section 2
Taipei, Taiwan
Phone: 8862-2704-8018
Fax: 8862-2704-2787

2806A, Central Plaza
18 Harbour Road, Wanchai
Hong Kong, Hong Kong
Phone: 852-2523-0615
Fax: 852-2521-5778

, Suite 320, Shanghai Centre
1376 Nanjing Xi Lu
Shanghai, China 200040
Phone: 86-21-6279-8200
Fax: 86-21-6279-8203

Unit 1416 Tower One and Exchange Plaza
Ayala Triangle, Ayala Avenue
Makati, Philippines 1226
Phone: 632-759-4170
Fax: 632-812-3996

#22-01, Menara Dion, No. 27
Jalan Sultan Ismail
Kuala Lumpur, Malaysia 50250
Phone: 60-3-2031-2202
Fax: 60-3-2031-2205

361 Lytton Avenue
Second Floor
Palo Alto, CA USA
Phone: 650-330-3500
Fax: 650-330-3535

104 EPIP Zone, Whitefield
Prestige Omega, Regus – 2F
Bangalore, India 560 066
Phone: 91-80-4060-0719
Fax: 91-80-4060-0700

71 Ayer Rajah Crescent
#05-05
Singapore, Singapore 139951

2270

222 Yan An Road East, Suite 2501, Bund Center
Shanghai, China 200002
Phone: 86-21-3135-2488
Fax: 86-21-3135-2499

36 Hashacham Street
Building D, Fifth floor
Petach-Tikva, Israel
Phone: 972-37-585-585
Fax: 972-3-535-0999

, Suite 1806, Beijing China Resources Bldg
No. 8 Jiangoumenbei Ave., Dongcheng
Beijing, China 100005
Phone: 86-10-8519-2519
Fax: 86-10-8519-2520

Management and Staff
Andrew Kau, Managing Director
Bill Li, Managing Director
Brian Chiang, Managing Director
Carson Chen, Venture Partner
Clifford Higgerson, Venture Partner
Esther Liu, Vice President
Hing Wong, Managing Director
Hock Loo, Managing Director
Joana Tieu, Vice President
Kris Leong Seok Wan, Vice President
Roni Hefetz, Venture Partner
Soo Yong, Vice President
Steve Ahn, Venture Partner
Teresa Smith, Chief Financial Officer
Yimin Zimmerer, Managing Director

Type of Firm
Private Equity Firm

Association Membership
Hong Kong Venture Capital Association (HKVCA)
Israel Venture Association
Taiwan Venture Capital Association (TVCA)
National Venture Capital Association - USA (NVCA)
Indian Venture Capital Association (IVCA)

Project Preferences

Role in Financing:
Will function either as deal originator or investor in deals created by others

Type of Financing Preferred:
Early Stage
Expansion
Balanced
Later Stage
Seed
Startup

Geographical Preferences

United States Preferences:
Southeast

International Preferences:
India
Taiwan
China
Israel
Asia
Korea, South

Industry Focus
(% based on actual investment)
Semiconductors/Other Elect.	26.3%
Internet Specific	18.6%
Computer Software and Services	14.8%
Communications and Media	14.0%
Other Products	10.5%
Computer Hardware	6.1%
Medical/Health	4.4%
Industrial/Energy	2.3%
Biotechnology	2.0%
Consumer Related	0.9%

Additional Information
Year Founded: 1987
Capital Under Management: $2,200,000,000
Current Activity Level: Actively seeking new investments
Method of Compensation: Other

WALDEN VENTURE CAPITAL

750 Battery Street, Suite 700
San Francisco, CA USA 94111
Phone: 4153917225
Fax: 4153917262
E-mail: info@waldenvc.com
Website: www.waldenvc.com

Other Offices
2105 Woodside Road
Redwood City, CA USA 94062

Management and Staff
Arthur Berliner, Co-Founder
George Sarlo, Co-Founder
Larry Marcus, Managing Director
Matthew Miller, Managing Director
Robert Raynard, Chief Financial Officer
William McDonagh, Venture Partner

Type of Firm
Private Equity Firm

Project Preferences

Role in Financing:
Prefer role as deal originator but will also invest in deals created by others

Type of Financing Preferred:
Early Stage
Balanced
Later Stage
Seed
Startup

Size of Investments Considered:
Min Size of Investment Considered (000s): $1,000
Max Size of Investment Considered (000s): $4,000

Industry Focus
(% based on actual investment)
Internet Specific	34.0%
Computer Software and Services	18.4%
Communications and Media	16.5%
Semiconductors/Other Elect.	10.3%
Computer Hardware	8.5%
Other Products	3.7%
Consumer Related	3.4%
Medical/Health	2.2%
Biotechnology	1.8%
Industrial/Energy	1.3%

Additional Information
Year Founded: 1974
Capital Under Management: $400,000,000
Current Activity Level: Actively seeking new investments
Method of Compensation: Return on investment is of primary concern, do not charge fees

WALL STREET VENTURE CAPITAL LTD

110 Wall Street
Eleventh Floor
New York, NY USA 10005
Phone: 877-748-4468
Fax: 860-599-3799
E-mail: wallstreetventurecapital@yahoo.com
Website: www.wallstreetventurecapital.net

Other Offices
28 East Jackson Building
Tenth Floor
Chicago, IL USA 60604
Phone: 877-748-4468

75 State Street
Boston, MA USA 02109
Phone: 877-748-4468

23 Nanjing East Road
Shanghai, China 200002
Phone: 8621-6329-5787
Fax: 8621-6329-5787

Management and Staff
Frank O Connell, Partner
John Adair, Partner
John Meyer, Partner
Jonathan Morrone, Partner
Joseph Gill, Partner
Joseph McAndrew, Chief Executive Officer
Joseph DeMarco, Partner
Leo Nolan, Partner
Nico Eboma, Partner
T. Claycomb, Partner
William Nielson, Partner

Type of Firm
Private Equity Firm

Project Preferences

Type of Financing Preferred:
Expansion
Mezzanine
Generalist PE
Turnaround
Acquisition
Distressed Debt
Recapitalizations

Size of Investments Considered:
Min Size of Investment Considered (000s): $3,000
Max Size of Investment Considered (000s): $100,000

Industry Preferences

In Communications prefer:
Communications and Media

In Medical/Health prefer:
Medical Products
Health Services
Pharmaceuticals

In Consumer Related prefer:
Retail
Food/Beverage
Consumer Products

In Industrial/Energy prefer:
Energy

Additional Information
Year Founded: 2008
Current Activity Level : Actively seeking new investments

WALLER CAPITAL PARTNERS LLC

One Rockefeller Plaza
23rd Floor
New York, NY USA 10020
Phone: 2126323600
Fax: 2126323607
E-mail: info@wallercapital.com
Website: www.wallercc.com

Management and Staff
Brian Stengel, Managing Director
Christine Frank, Managing Director
Garrett Baker, President
Jeffrey Brandon, Managing Director
John Woodruff, Managing Partner
Michael McHugh, Managing Director
Rajive Kumar, Vice President
Steven Soraparu, Managing Director
William Bradley, Managing Director

Type of Firm
Investment Management Firm

Project Preferences

Type of Financing Preferred:
Leveraged Buyout
Acquisition

Industry Preferences

In Communications prefer:
Telecommunications
Wireless Communications
Media and Entertainment

Additional Information
Year Founded: 1982
Current Activity Level : Actively seeking new investments

WALNUT GROUP

312 Walnut Street, Suite 1151
Cincinnati, OH USA 45202
Phone: 5136513300
Fax: 5136511084
Website: www.thewalnutgroup.com

Management and Staff
Daniel Staton, Managing Partner
Frederic Mayerson, Managing Partner
R. Scott Barnes, Chief Financial Officer

Type of Firm
Private Equity Firm

Project Preferences

Role in Financing:
Will function either as deal originator or investor in deals created by others

Type of Financing Preferred:
Expansion
Generalist PE
Balanced
Later Stage
Acquisition
Special Situation
Recapitalizations

Geographical Preferences

United States Preferences:
North America

Industry Preferences

In Communications prefer:
Communications and Media

In Consumer Related prefer:
Consumer
Entertainment and Leisure
Retail
Consumer Products
Other Restaurants

In Financial Services prefer:
Real Estate

In Business Serv. prefer:
Services

In Manufact. prefer:
Manufacturing

Additional Information
Name of Most Recent Fund: Walnut Private Equity Fund, L.P.
Most Recent Fund Was Raised: 09/30/2004
Year Founded: 2002
Capital Under Management: $400,000,000
Current Activity Level : Actively seeking new investments
Method of Compensation: Return on investment is of primary concern, do not charge fees

---

WAMDA LTD

Mecca Street 33,11196
Amman, Jordan 960913
Phone: 96264814487
Fax: 96265812413
E-mail: connect@wamda.com
Website: www.wamda.com

Other Offices
2304 Business Central Towers
Tower A
Media, Utd. Arab Em.
Phone: 97142118308

Type of Firm
Incubator/Development Program

Project Preferences

Type of Financing Preferred:
Early Stage
Startup

Geographical Preferences

International Preferences:
Jordan
Egypt
Africa

Industry Preferences

In Internet Specific prefer:
E-Commerce Technology

Additional Information
Year Founded: 2011
Capital Under Management: $60,700,000
Current Activity Level : Actively seeking new investments

WAMEX PRIVATE EQUITY MANAGEMENT

Ruben Dario 281-1901
Bosques de Chapultepec
Mexico DF, Mexico 11580
Phone: 525553955222
Fax: 525550835084
E-mail: wamex@wamex.mx
Website: www.wamex.mx

Other Offices
Sudetenstrasse 79
Ottobrunn, Germany D-85521
Phone: 49-89-6659-3943
Fax: 49-89-6659-3944

Knappenweg 107
Stuttgart, Germany D-70569
Phone: 49-711-687-6412
Fax: 49-711-687-6410

Management and Staff
Christian Warnholtz, Partner
Jose Antonio Contreras, Partner
Kurt Lipp, Partner
Sergio Del Valle, Partner

Type of Firm
Private Equity Firm

Project Preferences

Type of Financing Preferred:
Leveraged Buyout
Expansion
Mezzanine
Acquisition

Size of Investments Considered:
Min Size of Investment Considered (000s): $3,000
Max Size of Investment Considered (000s): $10,000

Geographical Preferences

International Preferences:
Europe
Mexico
All International

Industry Preferences

In Semiconductor/Electr prefer:
Electronics

In Medical/Health prefer:
Health Services

In Consumer Related prefer:
Entertainment and Leisure

In Industrial/Energy prefer:
Environmental Related

In Transportation prefer:
Transportation

In Financial Services prefer:
Financial Services

In Business Serv. prefer:
Services

In Manufact. prefer:
Manufacturing

Additional Information
Year Founded: 2000
Current Activity Level : Actively seeking new investments

WANGZHUO INVESTMENT MANAGEMENT SHANGHAI CO LTD

369 Fuxing Middle Road
Shanghai, China
Website: www.zzgroup.co

Type of Firm
Private Equity Firm

Project Preferences

Type of Financing Preferred:
Acquisition

Geographical Preferences

International Preferences:
China

Industry Preferences

In Internet Specific prefer:
Internet

In Medical/Health prefer:
Health Services

In Consumer Related prefer:
Consumer Services

Additional Information
Year Founded: 2015
Current Activity Level : Actively seeking new investments

WANNABIZ

22 Rybalska Street
Kyiv, Ukraine
Website: www.wannabiz.com.ua

Type of Firm
Incubator/Development Program

Project Preferences

Type of Financing Preferred:
Early Stage
Seed
Startup

Geographical Preferences

International Preferences:
Ukraine
Russia

Industry Preferences

In Computer Software prefer:
Systems Software

Additional Information
Year Founded: 2012
Current Activity Level : Actively seeking new investments

WANXIANG AMERICA CAPITAL LLC

123 North Wacker Drive, Suite 820
Chicago, IL USA 60606
Phone: 3125258500
Fax: 3125258509
E-mail: info@genevaglencapital.com
Website: www.genevaglencapital.com

Management and Staff
Adam Schecter, Managing Director
Jeffrey Gonyo, Managing Director
Tom Wuellner, Vice President

Type of Firm
Private Equity Firm

Project Preferences

Type of Financing Preferred:
Leveraged Buyout
Acquisition

Geographical Preferences

United States Preferences:

Canadian Preferences:
All Canada

Industry Preferences

In Medical/Health prefer:
Medical/Health

In Consumer Related prefer:
Food/Beverage
Consumer Products
Consumer Services
Education Related

In Industrial/Energy prefer:
Advanced Materials
Environmental Related

In Financial Services prefer:
Insurance

In Business Serv. prefer:
Services
Distribution
Media

In Manufact. prefer:
Manufacturing
Publishing

Additional Information
Year Founded: 2010
Current Activity Level : Actively seeking new investments

WARBURG PINCUS LLC

450 Lexington Avenue
New York, NY USA 10017
Phone: 2128780600
Fax: 2128789351
E-mail: info@warburgpincus.com
Website: www.warburgpincus.com

Other Offices

Av. Brig. Faria Lima 2277 - 9 andar
Jd.Paulistano
Sao Paulo, Brazil 01451-001
Phone: 551130343086
Fax: 551130343145

28 King Street, St. James's
Almack House
London, United Kingdom SW1Y 6QW
Phone: 442073060306
Fax: 442073210881

One Market Plaza
Spear Tower, Suite 1700
SAN FRANCISCO, CA USA 94105
Phone: 4157965200
Fax: 4157961922

Seventh Floor, Express Towers
Nariman Point
Mumbai, India 400 021
Phone: 912266500000
Fax: 912266500001

Liebigstr. 51- 53
Frankfurt, Germany D-60323
Phone: 496977035500
Fax: 496977035555

9th Floor, China World Tower 1
1 Jianguomenwai Avenue
Beijing, China 100004
Phone: 861059232533
Fax: 861065056683

1 Jianguomenwai Avenue
9th Floor, China World Tower 1
Shanghai, China 200002
Phone: 861059232533
Fax: 861065056683

Management and Staff

Adarsh Sarma, Managing Director
Alain Belda, Managing Director
Alex Berzofsky, Managing Director
Amit Sobti, Principal
Anish Saraf, Principal
Arjun Thimmaya, Principal
Ashutosh Somani, Principal
Bert Janssens, Principal
Bing Li, Principal
Blake Holden, Managing Director
Bo Bai, Principal
Brian Spillane, Vice President
Cary Davis, Managing Director
Cecilia Gonzalo, Managing Director
Cezary Pietrasik, Principal
Chandler Reedy, Principal
Chanho Park, Principal
Charles Carmel, Managing Director
Dai Feng, Managing Director
Daniel Zilberman, Managing Director
Daniel Zamlong, Managing Director
David Li, Managing Director
David Krieger, Managing Director
Doug Madden, Vice President
E. Davisson Hardman, Managing Director
Ellen Ng, Principal
Eric Liu, Principal
Frank Wei, Managing Director
Fred Hassan, Managing Director
Gordon Ding, Principal
Gregory Baecher, Principal
Hauke Lubben, Principal
Henry Kressel, Managing Director
Henry Schacht, Managing Director
Ian Chiu, Principal
In Seon Hwang, Managing Director
James Levy, Principal
James Neary, Managing Director
Jeffrey Goldfaden, Managing Director
Jeffrey Perlman, Principal
Jeremy Young, Managing Director
John Vogelstein, Managing Director
John Rowan, Principal
John Shearburn, Managing Director
Jonathan Cosgrave, Principal
Jonathan Leff, Managing Director
Joseph Gagnon, Managing Director
Julian Cheng, Managing Director
Jun Liu, Vice President
Justin Sadrian, Managing Director
Kenneth Juster, Managing Director
Konrad Stoebe, Principal
Lars Singbartl, Managing Director
Luca Molinari, Managing Director
Mark Colodny, Managing Director
Martin Dunnett, Managing Director
Max Fowinkel, Principal
Mazin Al Khatib, Managing Director
Miao Chi, Managing Director
Michael Martin, Managing Director
Michael Graff, Managing Director
Min Fang, Principal
Narendra Ostawal, Principal
Niten Malhan, Managing Director
Nitin Nayar, Managing Director
Noah Knauf, Principal
Patrick Hackett, Managing Director
Patrick Severson, Managing Director
Paul Best, Managing Director
Peder Bratt, Principal
Peter Kagan, Managing Director
Peter Wilson, Managing Director
Philipp Bruchmann, Principal
Prashant Kumar, Principal
Qian Wang, Principal
Qiang Chang Sun, Managing Director
Robert Buonanno, Principal
Robert Feuer, Managing Director
Rosanne Zimmerman, Managing Director
Sean Carney, Managing Director
Simon Begg, Managing Director
Simon Eyers, Managing Director
Somit Varma, Managing Director
Steve Coates, Managing Director
Tara O Neill, Vice President
Timothy Geithner, President
Uzair Dossani, Principal
Viraj Sawhney, Principal
Vishal Mahadevia, Managing Director
Vishnu Menon, Managing Director
Wei Cao, Principal
William Janeway, Managing Director
William Peng, Principal
Zhiming Yue, Managing Director

Type of Firm
Private Equity Firm

Association Membership
Hong Kong Venture Capital Association (HKVCA)
British Venture Capital Association (BVCA)
China Venture Capital Association
Emerging Markets Private Equity Association
Hungarian Venture Capital Association (HVCA)
National Venture Capital Association - USA (NVCA)
Polish Venture Capital Association (PSIC/PPEA)
European Private Equity and Venture Capital Assoc.
Indian Venture Capital Association (IVCA)

Project Preferences

Role in Financing:
Prefer role as deal originator but will also invest in deals created by others

Type of Financing Preferred:
Leveraged Buyout
Early Stage
Expansion
Generalist PE
Balanced
Turnaround
Later Stage
Other
Management Buyouts
Acquisition
Startup

Geographical Preferences

United States Preferences:

International Preferences:
India
Europe
China
Brazil
Asia

Industry Focus

(% based on actual investment)
Other Products	24.7%
Consumer Related	22.5%
Industrial/Energy	20.8%
Computer Software and Services	8.3%
Medical/Health	7.8%
Internet Specific	7.5%
Communications and Media	4.6%
Biotechnology	1.6%
Computer Hardware	1.4%
Semiconductors/Other Elect.	0.9%

Additional Information

Name of Most Recent Fund: Warburg Pincus XI Partners, L.P.
Most Recent Fund Was Raised: 05/23/2012
Year Founded: 1971
Capital Under Management: $14,000,000,000
Current Activity Level : Actively seeking new investments
Method of Compensation: Return on investment is of primary concern, do not charge fees

---

WARD VENTURES LLC

3963 Maple Avenue, Suite 300
Dallas, TX USA 75219
E-mail: david@ward.ventures
Website: www.ward.ventures

Type of Firm

Private Equity Firm

Additional Information

Year Founded: 2015
Current Activity Level : Actively seeking new investments

WARREN EQUITY PARTNERS LLC

320 1st Street N,, Suite 608
Jacksonville Beach, FL USA 32250
Website: www.warrenequity.com

Management and Staff

Scott Bruckmann, Partner
Steven Wacaster, Partner

Type of Firm

Private Equity Firm

Project Preferences

Type of Financing Preferred:
Leveraged Buyout
Acquisition
Recapitalizations

Geographical Preferences

United States Preferences:
North America

Industry Preferences

In Industrial/Energy prefer:
Industrial Products

In Business Serv. prefer:
Services

Additional Information

Year Founded: 2014
Current Activity Level : Actively seeking new investments

WARSAW EQUITY MANAGEMENT SP Z O O

ul. Piekna 18
Warsaw, Poland 00-549
Phone: 48224407350
Fax: 48224407351
E-mail: office@warsawequity.com

Management and Staff

Jacek Giedrojc, Partner
Mariusz Banaszuk, Managing Partner
Piotr Kuffel, Partner
Witold Grzesiak, Partner

Type of Firm

Private Equity Firm

Association Membership

Polish Venture Capital Association (PSIC/PPEA)

Geographical Preferences

International Preferences:
Central Europe
Eastern Europe

Industry Preferences

In Communications prefer:
Wireless Communications
Media and Entertainment

In Biotechnology prefer:
Biotechnology

In Medical/Health prefer:
Medical/Health
Pharmaceuticals

In Consumer Related prefer:
Consumer
Retail

In Industrial/Energy prefer:
Industrial Products

In Financial Services prefer:
Real Estate

In Business Serv. prefer:
Distribution

In Manufact. prefer:
Manufacturing

Additional Information

Year Founded: 1993
Current Activity Level : Actively seeking new investments

WASABI VENTURES LLC

1067 Amarillo Avenue
Palo Alto, CA USA 94303
Website: www.wasabiventures.com

Management and Staff

Alex Hollis, Venture Partner
Bobby Touran, Venture Partner
Chris Yeh, Managing Partner
Nick Daley, Venture Partner
Ray Thek, Venture Partner
Tom Kuegler, Managing Partner

Type of Firm

Incubator/Development Program

Project Preferences

Type of Financing Preferred:
Early Stage
Startup

Geographical Preferences

United States Preferences:
Illinois
Arizona
Northeast
Maryland
California
Connecticut
Florida
Georgia

Industry Preferences

In Communications prefer:
Wireless Communications
Media and Entertainment

In Computer Software prefer:
Software

In Internet Specific prefer:
Ecommerce

In Semiconductor/Electr prefer:
Electronics

In Industrial/Energy prefer:
Energy

Additional Information
Name of Most Recent Fund: Wasabi Angel Fund LLC
Most Recent Fund Was Raised: 12/19/2011
Year Founded: 2011
Capital Under Management: $250,000
Current Activity Level : Actively seeking new investments

WASHINGTON EQUITY PARTNERS LLC

1420 Spring Hill Road,, Suite 600
McLean, VA USA 22102
Phone: 2028393410
Website: www.w-equity.com

Management and Staff
B. Hagen Saville, Co-Founder
Jesse Liu, Co-Founder
Robert Knibb, Co-Founder

Type of Firm
Private Equity Firm

Project Preferences

Type of Financing Preferred:
Acquisition

Geographical Preferences

United States Preferences:
North America

Industry Preferences

In Computer Software prefer:
Software

In Industrial/Energy prefer:
Advanced Materials

In Transportation prefer:
Aerospace

Additional Information
Year Founded: 2016
Current Activity Level : Actively seeking new investments

WATER STREET HEALTHCARE PARTNERS LLC

333 West Wacker Drive, Suite 2800
Chicago, IL USA 60606
Phone: 3125062900
E-mail: info@waterstreet.com
Website: waterstreet.com

Management and Staff
Christopher Sweeney, Partner
James Connelly, Partner
Jeffrey Holway, Chief Financial Officer
Kevin Swan, Partner
Maxwell Mishkin, Vice President
Mike Brennan, Vice President
Ned Villers, Partner
Nicklaus Daley, Vice President
Peter Strothman, Partner
Robert Womsley, Partner
Timothy Dugan, Managing Partner

Type of Firm
Private Equity Firm

Association Membership
Illinois Venture Capital Association

Project Preferences

Type of Financing Preferred:
Leveraged Buyout
Management Buyouts
Acquisition
Recapitalizations

Geographical Preferences

United States Preferences:

Industry Preferences

In Medical/Health prefer:
Diagnostic Test Products
Medical Products
Health Services
Pharmaceuticals

In Business Serv. prefer:
Services
Distribution

Additional Information
Name of Most Recent Fund: Water Street Healthcare Partners III, L.P.
Most Recent Fund Was Raised: 07/31/2012
Year Founded: 2005
Capital Under Management: $1,610,000,000
Current Activity Level : Actively seeking new investments

WATER TOWER CAPITAL LLC

218 North Jefferson Street, Suite 100
Chicago, IL USA 60661
Phone: 312-373-8000
Fax: 312-373-8025

Management and Staff
F. John Stark, Chief Executive Officer
Lewis Rieck, Principal
Melissa Stark, Vice President
Rob Woseth, Vice President
Terry Coleman, Vice President
Timothy Shanahan, Vice President

Type of Firm
Private Equity Firm

Project Preferences

Type of Financing Preferred:
Distressed Debt

Geographical Preferences

United States Preferences:

Additional Information
Year Founded: 2001
Current Activity Level : Actively seeking new investments

WATERLAND PRIVATE EQUITY INVESTMENTS BV

Nieuwe 's-Gravelandseweg 17
Bussum, Netherlands 1405 HK
Phone: 31356941680
Fax: 31356970972
E-mail: info@waterland.nu
Website: waterland.de

Other Offices
Neuer Zollhof 1
Dusseldorf, Germany 40221
Phone: 492116878400
Fax: 4921168784029

Uitbreidingstraat 10-16
, Belgium
Phone: 3232929660
Fax: 3232929661

Plac Trzech Krzyzy 18
Warsaw, Poland 00-499
Phone: 48224178530
Fax: 48224178531

Theatinerstrasse 14
, Germany
Phone: 498924443040
Fax: 4989244430420

Management and Staff
Bart Elema, Chief Financial Officer
Maciej Szymanski, Principal

Type of Firm
Private Equity Firm

Association Membership
Belgium Venturing Association
Swiss Venture Capital Association (SECA)
German Venture Capital Association (BVK)
Polish Venture Capital Association (PSIC/PPEA)
Dutch Venture Capital Associaton (NVP)
European Private Equity and Venture Capital Assoc.

Project Preferences

Role in Financing:
Prefer role in deals created by others

Type of Financing Preferred:
Leveraged Buyout
Management Buyouts

Size of Investments Considered:
Min Size of Investment Considered (000s): $13,980
Max Size of Investment Considered (000s): $139,802

Geographical Preferences

International Preferences:
Netherlands
Belgium
Germany

Industry Preferences

In Communications prefer:
Communications and Media

In Biotechnology prefer:
Biotechnology

In Medical/Health prefer:
Medical/Health

In Consumer Related prefer:
Consumer

In Industrial/Energy prefer:
Industrial Products

In Business Serv. prefer:
Services

Additional Information

Name of Most Recent Fund: Waterland Private Equity Fund V CV
Most Recent Fund Was Raised: 07/28/2011
Year Founded: 1999
Capital Under Management: $7,073,300,000
Current Activity Level : Actively seeking new investments

WATERLINE VENTURES LLC

44 Brattle Street
Cambridge, MA USA 02138
E-mail: info@waterlineventures.com
Website: www.waterlineventures.com

Type of Firm
Private Equity Firm

Project Preferences

Type of Financing Preferred:
Balanced

Additional Information

Year Founded: 2015
Current Activity Level : Actively seeking new investments

WATERMAN CAPITAL LTD

Level 1, Shortland Street
Chambers, 70 Shortland St
Auckland, New Zealand
Phone: 64-9-362-0522
Fax: 64-9-362-0533
Website: www.waterman.co.nz

Management and Staff
Amanda Smith, Chief Financial Officer

Type of Firm
Private Equity Firm

Association Membership
New Zealand Venture Capital Association

Project Preferences

Type of Financing Preferred:
Leveraged Buyout
Expansion
Later Stage
Acquisition

Geographical Preferences

International Preferences:
New Zealand

Additional Information

Name of Most Recent Fund: Waterman Fund 2, L.P.
Most Recent Fund Was Raised: 08/30/2010
Year Founded: 2004
Capital Under Management: $58,507,000
Current Activity Level : Actively seeking new investments

WATERMARK VENTURE CAPITAL INC

620 Newport Center Drive, Suite 1100
Costa Mesa, CA USA 92626
Website: watermarkvc.com

Type of Firm
Private Equity Firm

Project Preferences

Type of Financing Preferred:
Early Stage
Seed

Geographical Preferences

United States Preferences:
California

Industry Preferences

In Computer Software prefer:
Software

Additional Information

Year Founded: 1969
Current Activity Level : Actively seeking new investments

WATERMILL GROUP LLC

750 Marrett Road, Suite 401, One Cranberry Hill
Lexington, MA USA 02421
Phone: 7818916660
Fax: 7818919712
Website: www.watermill.com

Management and Staff
Benjamin Procter, Partner
Dale Okonow, Partner
Julia Karol, President & COO
Matthias Bergin, Principal
Michael Choukas, Partner
Michael Fuller, Chief Financial Officer
Robert Ackerman, Partner
Steve Kotler, Chief Financial Officer
Timothy Eburne, Partner

Type of Firm
Bank Affiliated

Project Preferences

Type of Financing Preferred:
Leveraged Buyout
Turnaround
Special Situation
Distressed Debt
Recapitalizations

Geographical Preferences

United States Preferences:
All U.S.

Additional Information

Name of Most Recent Fund: Watermill-Tubes Partners, L.P.
Most Recent Fund Was Raised: 09/24/2012
Year Founded: 2000
Capital Under Management: $13,967,000
Current Activity Level : Actively seeking new investments

WATEROUS ENERGY FUND CANADIAN LP

301 - 8th Avenue SW, Suite 600
Calgary, Canada T2P 1C5

Type of Firm
Private Equity Firm

Project Preferences

Type of Financing Preferred:
Balanced

Geographical Preferences

United States Preferences:
North America

Industry Preferences

In Industrial/Energy prefer:
Oil and Gas Exploration
Oil & Gas Drilling,Explor

Additional Information

Year Founded: 1969
Current Activity Level : Actively seeking new investments

WATERSTONE CAPITAL MANAGEMENT SHANGHAI LP

2108 Air China Plaza
No. 36 Xiao Yun Rd., Chaoyang
Beijing, China 100027
Phone: 861084475682
Fax: 861084475853
Website: www.waterstonecapitalltd.com

Type of Firm

Private Equity Firm

Project Preferences

Type of Financing Preferred:
Early Stage

Additional Information

Year Founded: 1969
Current Activity Level : Actively seeking new investments

WATERVALE EQUITY PARTNERS, LLC

22039 McCauley Road
Shaker Heights, OH USA 44122
E-mail: grow@watervalepartners.com
Website: www.watervalepartners.com

Type of Firm

Private Equity Firm

Project Preferences

Type of Financing Preferred:
Leveraged Buyout
Acquisition
Distressed Debt

Geographical Preferences

United States Preferences:
North America

Industry Preferences

In Consumer Related prefer:
Food/Beverage

In Transportation prefer:
Aerospace

Additional Information

Year Founded: 2017
Current Activity Level : Actively seeking new investments

WATERVEIN PARTNERS KK

2-8-9 Sangenjaya
Setagaya-ku
Tokyo, Japan 154-0024
Phone: 0354335030
Fax: 0354335031
E-mail: info@watervein.jp
Website: www.watervein.jp

Management and Staff

Masanori Ishikiwa, Partner
Tatsuzo Ishigami, Partner
Tetsuya Mishima, Partner

Type of Firm

Private Equity Firm

Project Preferences

Type of Financing Preferred:
Balanced
Seed

Industry Preferences

In Biotechnology prefer:
Biotechnology

Additional Information

Year Founded: 2004
Current Activity Level : Actively seeking new investments

WATERWOOD INVESTMENT MANAGEMENT LTD

43/F China Resources Bldg., Suite 4305
Wanchai, Hong Kong

Type of Firm

Private Equity Firm

Project Preferences

Type of Financing Preferred:
Later Stage
Acquisition

Industry Preferences

In Medical/Health prefer:
Health Services

In Financial Services prefer:
Financial Services

Additional Information

Year Founded: 2014
Current Activity Level : Actively seeking new investments

WATTLE HILL RHC MANAGEMENT PTY LTD

Level 11, 179 Elizabeth Street
Sydney, Australia 2000

Type of Firm

Private Equity Firm

Project Preferences

Type of Financing Preferred:
Balanced

Geographical Preferences

International Preferences:
China
Australia
New Zealand
Asia

Industry Preferences

In Consumer Related prefer:
Consumer
Retail

In Manufact. prefer:
Manufacturing

Additional Information

Year Founded: 2016
Capital Under Management: $200,000,000
Current Activity Level : Actively seeking new investments

WAUD CAPITAL PARTNERS LLC

300 North LaSalle Street, Suite 4900
Chicago, IL USA 60654
Phone: 3126768400
Fax: 3126768444
E-mail: info@waudcapital.com
Website: www.waudcapital.com

Other Offices

321 North Clark Street, Suite 1465
Chicago, IL USA 60610
Phone: 312-676-8400
Fax: 312-676-8444

Management and Staff

Christopher Graber, Principal
David Neighbours, Partner
Justin DuPere, Principal
Kyle Lattner, Vice President
Mark Flower, Chief Financial Officer
Matthew Clary, Partner
Matthew London, Principal
Paul Sutphin, Vice President
Philip Kemp, Principal
Tim Lawler, Principal
Timothy Cremieux, Vice President

Type of Firm
Private Equity Firm

Project Preferences

Role in Financing:
Will function either as deal originator or investor in deals created by others

Type of Financing Preferred:
Leveraged Buyout
Management Buyouts
Acquisition
Recapitalizations

Industry Focus
(% based on actual investment)

Medical/Health	86.1%
Computer Software and Services	10.6%
Other Products	2.4%
Internet Specific	0.9%

Additional Information

Name of Most Recent Fund: Waud Capital Partners III, L.P.
Most Recent Fund Was Raised: 04/13/2011
Year Founded: 1993
Capital Under Management: $115,000,000
Current Activity Level : Actively seeking new investments
Method of Compensation: Return on invest. most important, but chg. closing fees, service fees, etc.

WAVE EQUITY PARTNERS LLC

177 Milk Street
Boston, MA USA 02109
Phone: 6173509808
Fax: 6173509899
E-mail: info@waveep.com
Website: waveep.com

Management and Staff

Charles Bridge, Chief Financial Officer
Mark Robinson, Managing Director
Praveen Sahay, Managing Director
Robert Roeper, Managing Director

Type of Firm
Private Equity Firm

Project Preferences

Type of Financing Preferred:
Early Stage
Expansion
Seed
Startup
Distressed Debt

Size of Investments Considered:
Min Size of Investment Considered (000s): $2,000
Max Size of Investment Considered (000s): $15,000

Geographical Preferences

United States Preferences:
All U.S.

Canadian Preferences:
All Canada

International Preferences:
All International

Industry Preferences

In Industrial/Energy prefer:
Energy
Alternative Energy

In Other prefer:
Environment Responsible

Additional Information

Name of Most Recent Fund: WAVE Equity Fund, L.P.
Most Recent Fund Was Raised: 01/25/2013
Year Founded: 2008
Capital Under Management: $27,950,000
Current Activity Level : Actively seeking new investments

WAVECREST GROWTH PARTNERS

53 State Street, Suite 500
Boston, MA USA 02109
Website: www.wavecrestgrowth.com

Type of Firm
Private Equity Firm

Project Preferences

Type of Financing Preferred:
Generalist PE

Industry Preferences

In Computer Software prefer:
Software

Additional Information

Year Founded: 1969
Current Activity Level : Actively seeking new investments

WAVELAND CAPITAL GROUP LLC

19800 MacArthur Boulevard, Suite 650
Irvine, CA USA 92612
Phone: 9497065000
Fax: 9497065001
E-mail: info@wavelandgroup.com
Website: www.wavelandgroup.com

Management and Staff

Aman Singha, Vice President
R. Thomas Fetters, Managing Director
Sam Irvani, Managing Director
Steven Sunstein, President
Vickie Greer, Chief Operating Officer
Wayne Ross, Chief Financial Officer

Type of Firm
Investment Management Firm

Project Preferences

Type of Financing Preferred:
Other

Industry Preferences

In Industrial/Energy prefer:
Energy
Oil and Gas Exploration
Alternative Energy

In Utilities prefer:
Utilities

Additional Information

Name of Most Recent Fund: Waveland Resource Partners II, L.P.
Most Recent Fund Was Raised: 09/27/2012
Year Founded: 2000
Capital Under Management: $130,377,000
Current Activity Level : Actively seeking new investments

WAVELAND INVESTMENTS LLC

1850 Second Street, Suite 201
Highland Park, IL USA 60035
Phone: 3125066450
Fax: 3125066455
Website: www.wavelandinvestments.com

Management and Staff

Cristina Lasko, Chief Financial Officer
Dennis Zaslavsky, Principal
Greg Maletsky, Vice President
Meghan Otis, Principal
Taryn Goldstein, Chief Financial Officer

Type of Firm
Private Equity Firm

Project Preferences

Type of Financing Preferred:
Leveraged Buyout
Turnaround
Acquisition
Industry Rollups

Geographical Preferences

United States Preferences:
All U.S.

Industry Preferences

In Financial Services prefer:
Financial Services

In Business Serv. prefer:
Services
Distribution
Consulting Services

In Manufact. prefer:
Manufacturing

Additional Information
Year Founded: 2000
Current Activity Level : Actively seeking new investments

WAVEMAKER LABS PTE LTD

Ayer Rajah Crescent, Suite 05-01, Block 71
Singapore, Singapore 139951
Website: www.wavemakerlabs.com

Management and Staff
David Siemer, Partner
Debneel Mukherjee, Managing Partner
Paul Santos, Managing Partner

Type of Firm
Incubator/Development Program

Association Membership
Singapore Venture Capital Association (SVCA)

Project Preferences

Type of Financing Preferred:
Early Stage
Expansion
Seed

Geographical Preferences

International Preferences:
India
China
Asia

Additional Information
Year Founded: 2012
Current Activity Level : Actively seeking new investments

WAVEMAKER PARTNERS

1333 Second Street, Suite 600
Santa Monica, CA USA 90401
Phone: 3108612100
Fax: 8008750757
Website: wavemaker.vc

Other Offices
Suite 05-01, Block 71,
Ayer Raja Crescent
Singapore, Singapore 139951

Management and Staff
Adrian Vanzyl, Venture Partner
Ari Klinger, Venture Partner
B. Paul Santos, Managing Partner
David Siemer, Managing Partner
Dennis Goh, Partner
Eric Manlunas, Co-Founder
Gavin Lee, Principal
Lisa Riedmiller, Chief Financial Officer
Victor Alvarez, Venture Partner

Type of Firm
Private Equity Firm

Project Preferences

Type of Financing Preferred:
Early Stage
Seed

Size of Investments Considered:
Min Size of Investment Considered (000s): $250
Max Size of Investment Considered (000s): $500

Geographical Preferences

United States Preferences:

International Preferences:
Asia

Industry Preferences

In Consumer Related prefer:
Consumer

Additional Information
Year Founded: 2011
Capital Under Management: $38,000,000
Current Activity Level : Actively seeking new investments

WAVEPOINT VENTURES LLC

1107 Investment Boulevard, Suite 180
El Dorado Hills, CA USA 95762
Phone: 9169411400
Fax: 9169417551
Website: www.capitalvalleyventures.com

Other Offices
535 Middlefield Road, Suite 280
Menlo Park, CA USA 94025
Phone: 6503317393
Fax: 6503317393

Management and Staff
Daniel Lankford, Managing Director
Pete Bernardoni, Managing Director
Peter Gardner, Managing Director

Type of Firm
Private Equity Firm

Project Preferences

Role in Financing:
Will function either as deal originator or investor in deals created by others

Type of Financing Preferred:
Early Stage

Size of Investments Considered:
Min Size of Investment Considered (000s): $100
Max Size of Investment Considered (000s): $250

Geographical Preferences

United States Preferences:
California

Industry Preferences

In Communications prefer:
Telecommunications
Wireless Communications
Data Communications

In Computer Software prefer:
Software

In Internet Specific prefer:
E-Commerce Technology
Internet

In Semiconductor/Electr prefer:
Electronic Components
Micro-Processing

In Biotechnology prefer:
Biosensors

In Medical/Health prefer:
Medical Diagnostics
Diagnostic Services
Diagnostic Test Products
Pharmaceuticals

In Industrial/Energy prefer:
Energy

In Other prefer:
Environment Responsible

Additional Information
Name of Most Recent Fund: Wavepoint Partners II, L.P.
Most Recent Fund Was Raised: 07/01/2010
Year Founded: 2003
Capital Under Management: $6,300,000
Current Activity Level : Actively seeking new investments

WAYFOUNDER
2524 Barry Avenue
Los Angeles, CA USA 90064
Website: www.wayfounder.com

Type of Firm
Private Equity Firm

Project Preferences

Type of Financing Preferred:
Startup

Geographical Preferences

United States Preferences:

Additional Information
Year Founded: 2013
Current Activity Level : Actively seeking new investments

WAYGATE CAPITAL INDIA PVT LTD
201 A, Gagangiri
10 Carter Road, Khar
Mumbai, India 400 052
Phone: 91-22-2600-8606
Fax: 91-22-2600-8608

Management and Staff
Rajesh Jog, Managing Director

Type of Firm
Private Equity Firm

Project Preferences

Type of Financing Preferred:
Mezzanine
Management Buyouts

Size of Investments Considered:
Min Size of Investment Considered (000s): $100
Max Size of Investment Considered (000s): $200

Geographical Preferences

International Preferences:
India

Industry Preferences

In Communications prefer:
Media and Entertainment

In Computer Software prefer:
Computer Services
Systems Software

In Computer Other prefer:
Computer Related

Additional Information
Year Founded: 1994
Current Activity Level : Actively seeking new investments

WAYRA
Ronda de la Communicacion
Madrid , Spain
Website: www.wayra.co

Type of Firm
Incubator/Development Program

Project Preferences

Type of Financing Preferred:
Seed

Additional Information
Year Founded: 2011
Current Activity Level : Actively seeking new investments

WAYZATA INVESTMENT PARTNERS LLC
701 East Lake Street, Suite 300
Wayzata, MN USA 55391
Phone: 9523450700
Fax: 9523458901
Website: wayzatainvestmentpartners.com

Other Offices
500 Boylton Street, Suite 1850
Boston, MA USA 02116
Phone: 617-375-5835
Fax: 617-375-1033

Management and Staff
Blake Carlson, Partner
Christopher Keenan, Principal
Daniel Kubes, Principal
Jay Kanive, Principal
John McEvoy, Partner
John Foley, Partner
Joseph Deignan, Partner
Kelly Aubrey, Chief Financial Officer
Mary Burns, Partner
Patrick Halloran, Partner
Ray Wallander, Principal
Tyler Duncan, Principal
William Murnane, Principal

Type of Firm
Private Equity Firm

Project Preferences

Type of Financing Preferred:
Leveraged Buyout
Turnaround
Acquisition
Distressed Debt

Geographical Preferences

United States Preferences:
All U.S.

Industry Preferences

In Industrial/Energy prefer:
Energy
Industrial Products

In Transportation prefer:
Aerospace

In Manufact. prefer:
Manufacturing

Additional Information
Name of Most Recent Fund: Wayzata Opportunities Fund III, L.P.
Most Recent Fund Was Raised: 07/13/2012
Year Founded: 2004
Capital Under Management: $5,000,000,000
Current Activity Level : Actively seeking new investments

WCW VENTURE HLDG GMBH
Hohe Warte 25/3
Vienna, Austria 1190
Website: wcwventure.com

Type of Firm
Private Equity Firm

Project Preferences

Type of Financing Preferred:
Early Stage
Seed
Startup

Geographical Preferences

International Preferences:
Russia

Additional Information
Year Founded: 2015
Current Activity Level : Actively seeking new investments

WEALTHCAP INITIATOREN GMBH

Am Eisbach 3
Munich, Germany 80538
Phone: 4989678205500
Fax: 498967820555550
E-mail: vertrieb@wealthcap.com
Website: www.wealthcap.com

Management and Staff
Christian Kuehni, Managing Director
Gabriele Volz, Managing Director
Rainer Kruetten, Managing Director

Type of Firm
Private Equity Advisor or Fund of Funds

Association Membership
German Venture Capital Association (BVK)
European Private Equity and Venture Capital Assoc.

Project Preferences

Type of Financing Preferred:
Fund of Funds
Fund of Funds of Second

Geographical Preferences

United States Preferences:
All U.S.

International Preferences:
Europe

Industry Preferences

In Communications prefer:
Communications and Media

In Computer Software prefer:
Software

In Internet Specific prefer:
Internet

In Industrial/Energy prefer:
Industrial Products

In Business Serv. prefer:
Services

Additional Information
Year Founded: 1994
Capital Under Management: $40,202,000
Current Activity Level : Actively seeking new investments

WEARABLE WORLD INC

2513 Van Ness Ave
San Francisco, CA USA 94109
Website: wearableworld.co

Management and Staff
Kyle Ellicott, Co-Founder
Mike Morrisett, Chief Financial Officer
S.Neil Vineberg, Managing Director

Type of Firm
Incubator/Development Program

Additional Information
Year Founded: 2013
Current Activity Level : Actively seeking new investments

WEATHERFORD PARTNERS

100 North Tampa Street, Suite 2320
Tampa, FL USA 33602
E-mail: info@weatherfordpartners.com
Website: www.weatherfordpartners.com

Type of Firm
Private Equity Advisor or Fund of Funds

Additional Information
Year Founded: 2016
Current Activity Level : Actively seeking new investments

WEBFOLIO MANAGEMENT INC

507 Casazza Drive, Suite A
Reno, NV USA 89502
Phone: 7758253234
Website: webfoliomanagement.com

Type of Firm
Private Equity Firm

Project Preferences

Type of Financing Preferred:
Leveraged Buyout
Acquisition

Industry Preferences

In Computer Software prefer:
Software

Additional Information
Year Founded: 2013
Current Activity Level : Actively seeking new investments

WEBSTER CAPITAL MANAGEMENT LLC

950 Winter Street, Suite 4200
Waltham, MA USA 02451
Phone: 7814191515
Fax: 7814191516
E-mail: info@webstercapital.com
Website: www.webstercapital.com

Management and Staff
Andrew McKee, Co-Founder
Charles Larkin, General Partner
David Malm, General Partner
Mark Greene, Chief Financial Officer
Robert Long, General Partner

Type of Firm
Private Equity Firm

Project Preferences

Type of Financing Preferred:
Leveraged Buyout
Later Stage
Management Buyouts
Acquisition

Geographical Preferences

United States Preferences:
All U.S.

Industry Preferences

In Medical/Health prefer:
Medical/Health

In Consumer Related prefer:
Consumer

In Business Serv. prefer:
Services

In Manufact. prefer:
Manufacturing

Additional Information
Year Founded: 2002
Capital Under Management: $1,200,000
Current Activity Level : Actively seeking new investments

WEDBUSH CAPITAL PARTNERS LP

1000 Wilshire Boulevard, Suite 830
Los Angeles, CA USA 90017
Phone: 2136888018
Fax: 2136888095
E-mail: info@wedbushcapital.com
Website: www.wedbushcapital.com

Management and Staff
Daniel Simon, Chief Financial Officer
Eric Wedbush, Managing Director
Geoff Bland, Managing Director
Kevin Tom, Vice President
Peter Shoemaker, Managing Director

Type of Firm
Private Equity Firm

Project Preferences

Role in Financing:
Prefer role as deal originator

Type of Financing Preferred:
Leveraged Buyout
Expansion
Management Buyouts
Acquisition
Recapitalizations

Geographical Preferences

United States Preferences:
Midwest
West Coast

Industry Preferences

In Consumer Related prefer:
Consumer

In Industrial/Energy prefer:
Industrial Products

In Financial Services prefer:
Financial Services

In Business Serv. prefer:
Services

In Manufact. prefer:
Manufacturing

Additional Information

Name of Most Recent Fund: Wedbush Capital Partners
Most Recent Fund Was Raised: 06/30/2005
Year Founded: 2005
Capital Under Management: $120,000,000
Current Activity Level : Actively seeking new investments
Method of Compensation: Return on invest. most important, but chg. closing fees, service fees, etc.

WEFORGE SAS

25, rue Lenepveu
Angers, France 49100
Website: www.weforge.fr

Type of Firm
Incubator/Development Program

Project Preferences

Type of Financing Preferred:
Early Stage
Seed

Geographical Preferences

International Preferences:
France

Industry Preferences

In Computer Hardware prefer:
Computers

In Computer Software prefer:
Software

In Internet Specific prefer:
Internet

In Medical/Health prefer:
Medical/Health

In Consumer Related prefer:
Education Related

Additional Information
Year Founded: 2015
Capital Under Management: $7,264,000
Current Activity Level : Actively seeking new investments

WEIFANG FINANCIAL HOLDING GROUP CO LTD

86 Siping Rd., Kuiwen district
13F, intl financial bldg
Weifang, China 261041
Phone: 05365166889
Fax: 05365166710
Website: www.wfjkjt.com

Type of Firm
Investment Management Firm

Project Preferences

Type of Financing Preferred:
Generalist PE
Balanced

Geographical Preferences

International Preferences:
China

Industry Preferences

In Internet Specific prefer:
Internet

Additional Information
Year Founded: 2015
Capital Under Management: $16,439,000
Current Activity Level : Actively seeking new investments

WEINAN ZHONGSHI DINGC-HENG INVESTMENT MAN-AGEMENT CO LTD

Chaoyang RoadXi Hi-tech Weinan
Venture Incubation Base
Shanxi, China

Type of Firm
Private Equity Firm

Project Preferences

Type of Financing Preferred:
Balanced

Geographical Preferences

International Preferences:
China

Additional Information
Year Founded: 2014
Current Activity Level : Actively seeking new investments

WEINBERG & BELL GROUP

5005 Rockside Road, Suite 1140
Cleveland, OH USA 44131
Fax: 2165038313
E-mail: inquiries@weinbergbell.com
Website: www.weinbergbell.com

Management and Staff
Daniel Bell, Managing Director

Type of Firm
Private Equity Firm

Project Preferences

Type of Financing Preferred:
Leveraged Buyout
Acquisition

Geographical Preferences

United States Preferences:
North America

Industry Preferences

In Medical/Health prefer:
Medical/Health
Health Services

In Consumer Related prefer:
Retail

In Financial Services prefer:
Financial Services

In Business Serv. prefer:
Services
Distribution

In Manufact. prefer:
Manufacturing

Additional Information
Name of Most Recent Fund: WBG Partners V LLC
Most Recent Fund Was Raised: 09/04/2008
Year Founded: 2003
Current Activity Level : Actively seeking new investments

WEINBERG CAPITAL GROUP

5005 Rockside Road, Suite 1140
Cleveland, OH USA 44131
Website: www.weinbergcap.com

Management and Staff
John Herman, Principal
Ronald Weinberg, Principal

Type of Firm
Private Equity Firm

Project Preferences

Type of Financing Preferred:
Leveraged Buyout
Acquisition

Geographical Preferences

United States Preferences:
North America

Industry Preferences

In Medical/Health prefer:
Medical/Health

In Consumer Related prefer:
Consumer Products

In Transportation prefer:
Aerospace

In Business Serv. prefer:
Services
Distribution

In Manufact. prefer:
Manufacturing

Additional Information
Year Founded: 2003
Current Activity Level: Actively seeking new investments

WEINBERG CAPITAL PARTNERS SAS

20 rue Quentin Bauchart
Paris, France 75008
Phone: 33153535500
Fax: 33153535519
E-mail: contact@weinbergcapital.com
Website: www.weinbergcapital.com

Management and Staff
Aymeric Plassard, Chief Operating Officer
Jerome Louvet, Partner
Laurent Halimi, Partner
Nicholas Truelle, Partner
Nicolas Teboul, Partner
Philippe Klocanas, Partner
Wandrille Ract-Madoux, Vice President
Yann Ballan, Vice President

Type of Firm
Private Equity Firm

Association Membership
French Venture Capital Association (AFIC)

Project Preferences

Type of Financing Preferred:
Leveraged Buyout
Value-Add
Expansion
Public Companies
Opportunistic
Later Stage
Acquisition

Size of Investments Considered:
Min Size of Investment Considered (000s): $10,682
Max Size of Investment Considered (000s): $82,091

Geographical Preferences

International Preferences:
Europe
Western Europe
France

Industry Preferences

In Medical/Health prefer:
Health Services

In Consumer Related prefer:
Retail

In Financial Services prefer:
Real Estate

In Business Serv. prefer:
Services
Distribution

In Manufact. prefer:
Manufacturing

Additional Information
Name of Most Recent Fund: Weinberg Real Estate Partners 2
Most Recent Fund Was Raised: 08/01/2013
Year Founded: 2005
Capital Under Management: $732,081,000
Current Activity Level: Actively seeking new investments

WELLBORN VENTURES

Aba Hille 16
Ramat Gan, Israel
Phone: 542557780
Website: www.wellbornvc.com

Type of Firm
Private Equity Firm

Project Preferences

Type of Financing Preferred:
Early Stage
Seed

Industry Preferences

In Communications prefer:
Wireless Communications

In Computer Software prefer:
Software

In Internet Specific prefer:
Internet

In Business Serv. prefer:
Media

Additional Information
Year Founded: 2016
Current Activity Level: Actively seeking new investments

WELLER EQUITY PARTNERS

333 East Main Street, Suite 310
Louisville, KY USA 40202
E-mail: info@wellerequity.com
Website: www.wellerequity.com

Type of Firm
Private Equity Firm

Project Preferences

Type of Financing Preferred:
Leveraged Buyout

Additional Information
Year Founded: 2015
Current Activity Level: Actively seeking new investments

WELLINGTON FINANCIAL LP

Scotia Plaza, 40 King St. West, Suite 5001
Toronto, Canada M5H 3Y2
Phone: 4166826007
E-mail: info@wellingtonfund.com
Website: www.wellingtonfund.com

Management and Staff
Amit Rajput, Chief Financial Officer
Ash Vaidya, Partner
Eric Speer, Vice President
Jason Nardari, Vice President
Jeff Chapman, Partner
Kul Mani, Partner
Mark Usher, Partner
Paul McKinlay, Vice President
Robin Gill, Partner

Type of Firm
Private Equity Firm

Association Membership
Mid-Atlantic Venture Association
Canadian Venture Capital Association
National Venture Capital Association - USA (NVCA)

Project Preferences

Type of Financing Preferred:
Expansion
Mezzanine
Public Companies
Later Stage
Other

Size of Investments Considered:
Min Size of Investment Considered (000s): $1,967
Max Size of Investment Considered (000s): $39,347

Geographical Preferences

United States Preferences:
North America
All U.S.

Canadian Preferences:
All Canada

Industry Preferences

In Communications prefer:
Telecommunications
Wireless Communications

In Internet Specific prefer:
Internet

In Biotechnology prefer:
Biotechnology

In Medical/Health prefer:
Medical/Health
Medical Products
Health Services

In Industrial/Energy prefer:
Oil and Gas Exploration
Oil & Gas Drilling,Explor
Alternative Energy
Factory Automation
Environmental Related

In Transportation prefer:
Aerospace

In Business Serv. prefer:
Services
Consulting Services

In Manufact. prefer:
Manufacturing
Office Automation Equipmt

Additional Information
Name of Most Recent Fund: Wellington Financial Fund IV
Most Recent Fund Was Raised: 09/05/2012
Year Founded: 2000
Capital Under Management: $300,000,000
Current Activity Level : Actively seeking new investments

WELLINGTON MANAGEMENT COMPANY LLP

280 Congress Street
Boston, MA USA 02210
Phone: 6179515000
E-mail: info@wellington.com
Website: www.wellington.com

Type of Firm
Private Equity Firm

Project Preferences

Type of Financing Preferred:
Balanced

Additional Information
Year Founded: 1969
Current Activity Level : Actively seeking new investments

WELLINGTON PARTNERS GMBH

Theresienstrasse 6
Munich, Germany 80333
Phone: 49892199410
E-mail: munich@wellington-partners.com
Website: www.wellington-partners.com

Other Offices

11 Berkeley Street
London, United Kingdom W1J8DS
Phone: 44-20-3006-4190

855 El Camino Real Building 4, Suite 272
Silicon Valley BusinessDevelopmentOffice
Palo Alto, CA USA 94301

Seidengasse 16
Zurich, Switzerland 8001
Phone: 41-44-567-2700

Management and Staff
Alexandre Gonthier, Venture Partner
Arun Jayadev, Principal
Bart Markus, General Partner
Christian Thaler-Wolski, Principal
Christian Reitberger, General Partner
Daniel Waterhouse, General Partner
Eberhard Plattfaut, Venture Partner
Eric Ly, Venture Partner
Eric Archambeau, General Partner
Erich Schlick, General Partner
Ernst Mannheimer, General Partner
Frank Boehnke, General Partner
Jeanne-Marie Gescher, Venture Partner
Jigar Shah, Venture Partner
Loic Le Meur, Venture Partner
Lukas Guenther, Principal
Mark Woodall, Venture Partner
Melvin Spigelman, Venture Partner
Mossadiq Umedaly, Venture Partner
Neal Margulis, Venture Partner
Neil Richardson, Venture Partner
Niklas Eklund, Venture Partner
Rainer Strohmenger, General Partner
Ram Srinivasan, Venture Partner
Regina Hodits, General Partner
Rolf Dienst, General Partner
Royston Hoggarth, Venture Partner
Spencer Hyman, Venture Partner
Thomas Widmann, General Partner
Ulrich Granzer, Venture Partner
Victor Christou, Venture Partner

Type of Firm
Private Equity Firm

Association Membership
German Venture Capital Association (BVK)
European Private Equity and Venture Capital Assoc.

Project Preferences

Role in Financing:
Prefer role as deal originator but will also invest in deals created by others

Type of Financing Preferred:
Early Stage
Expansion
Later Stage
Seed
Startup

Size of Investments Considered:
Min Size of Investment Considered (000s): $679
Max Size of Investment Considered (000s): $40,744

Geographical Preferences

International Preferences:
United Kingdom
Europe
Netherlands
Switzerland
Austria
Germany
France

Industry Focus
(% based on actual investment)
Internet Specific	27.0%
Biotechnology	17.9%
Computer Software and Services	17.3%
Medical/Health	8.9%
Consumer Related	8.7%
Communications and Media	6.9%
Industrial/Energy	5.6%
Semiconductors/Other Elect.	4.8%
Other Products	1.7%
Computer Hardware	1.0%

Additional Information
Name of Most Recent Fund: Wellington Partners IV Life Science Fund
Most Recent Fund Was Raised: 09/19/2012
Year Founded: 1991
Capital Under Management: $1,099,800,000

Current Activity Level : Actively seeking new investments

WELLROCK CAPITAL PARTNERS LLC

129 Patrick Street, Suite 21
Frederick, MD USA 21701
Website: www.wellrockcp.com

Management and Staff
Paul Tinney, Managing Director

Type of Firm
Private Equity Firm

Project Preferences

Type of Financing Preferred:
Leveraged Buyout
Management Buyouts
Acquisition
Recapitalizations

Industry Preferences

In Consumer Related prefer:
Food/Beverage
Other Restaurants

Additional Information
Year Founded: 2014
Current Activity Level : Actively seeking new investments

WELLS FARGO STARTUP ACCELERATOR

333 Market Street
23rd Floor
San Francisco, CA USA 94105
E-mail: wfsa@wellsfargo.com
Website: accelerator.wellsfargo.com

Type of Firm
Incubator/Development Program

Project Preferences

Type of Financing Preferred:
Early Stage
Seed
Startup

Size of Investments Considered:
Min Size of Investment Considered (000s): $50
Max Size of Investment Considered (000s): $500

Industry Preferences

In Financial Services prefer:
Financial Services

Additional Information
Year Founded: 2014
Current Activity Level : Actively seeking new investments

WELLSPRING CAPITAL MANAGEMENT LLC

390 Park Avenue
Lever House
New York, NY USA 10022
Phone: 2123189800
E-mail: info@wellspringcapital.com
Website: www.wellspringcapital.com

Management and Staff
Alexander Carles, Partner
Carl Stanton, Managing Partner
Daniel Han, Principal
Greg Feldman, Managing Partner
John Morningstar, Partner
Joshua Cascade, Partner
Matthew Harrison, Partner
Paul Kaminski, Chief Financial Officer
Seth Pearson, Partner
William Dawson, Managing Partner

Type of Firm
Private Equity Firm

Project Preferences

Type of Financing Preferred:
Leveraged Buyout
Public Companies
Turnaround
Acquisition
Private Placement
Recapitalizations

Size of Investments Considered:
Min Size of Investment Considered (000s): $50,000
Max Size of Investment Considered: No Limit

Industry Focus
(% based on actual investment)
Consumer Related	63.9%
Other Products	30.2%
Internet Specific	5.3%
Medical/Health	0.6%

Additional Information
Name of Most Recent Fund: Wellspring Capital Partners V, L.P.
Most Recent Fund Was Raised: 04/20/2009
Year Founded: 1995
Capital Under Management: $350,000,000
Current Activity Level : Actively seeking new investments

WELLSTREET PARTNERS AB

Kungsgatan 8
Stockholm, Sweden 111 43
Website: www.wellstreet.se

Type of Firm
Private Equity Firm

Project Preferences

Type of Financing Preferred:
Generalist PE

Geographical Preferences

International Preferences:
Scandanavia/Nordic Region

Industry Preferences

In Computer Software prefer:
Software

In Internet Specific prefer:
Internet
Ecommerce

In Consumer Related prefer:
Consumer

Additional Information
Year Founded: 2016
Current Activity Level : Actively seeking new investments

WELSH CARSON ANDERSON & STOWE

320 Park Avenue, Suite 2500
New York, NY USA 10022
Phone: 2128939500
Fax: 2128939575
Website: www.welshcarson.com

Management and Staff
Brian Regan, General Partner
Bruce Anderson, Co-Founder
Christopher Hooper, General Partner
Christopher Solomon, General Partner
Conner Mulvee, Vice President
D. Scott Mackesy, General Partner
Darren Battistoni, Principal
David Caluori, Principal
Edward Sobol, Principal
Eric Lee, General Partner
Gregory Lau, General Partner
Jonathan Rather, Chief Financial Officer
Michael Donovan, General Partner
Patrick Welsh, Co-Founder
Russell Carson, Co-Founder
Ryan Harper, Principal
Sanjay Swani, General Partner
Sean Traynor, General Partner
Thomas Scully, General Partner
Tony Ecock, General Partner

Type of Firm
Private Equity Firm

Association Membership
Private Equity Council (PEC)

Project Preferences

Role in Financing:
Prefer role as deal originator

Type of Financing Preferred:
Leveraged Buyout
Expansion
Mezzanine
Management Buyouts
Acquisition
Recapitalizations

Industry Focus

(% based on actual investment)

Medical/Health	29.9%
Other Products	27.1%
Computer Software and Services	13.7%
Communications and Media	13.2%
Internet Specific	12.1%
Computer Hardware	2.4%
Consumer Related	1.5%
Semiconductors/Other Elect.	0.2%
Industrial/Energy	0.1%
Biotechnology	0.1%

Additional Information

Name of Most Recent Fund: Welsh Carson Anderson & Stowe XI, L.P.
Most Recent Fund Was Raised: 06/13/2008
Year Founded: 1979
Capital Under Management: $12,000,000,000
Current Activity Level : Actively seeking new investments
Method of Compensation: Return on invest. most important, but chg. closing fees, service fees, etc.

WENDEL SE

89, rue Taitbout
Paris, France 75312
Phone: 33142853000
Fax: 33142806867
E-mail: communication@wendelgroup.com
Website: www.wendelgroup.com

Management and Staff

Benoit Drillaud, Chief Financial Officer
Dirk J. Van Ommeren, Managing Director
Patrick Tanguy, Managing Director

Type of Firm

Private Equity Firm

Association Membership

Emerging Markets Private Equity Association
French Venture Capital Association (AFIC)

Project Preferences

Type of Financing Preferred:
Leveraged Buyout
Acquisition

Geographical Preferences

International Preferences:
Luxembourg
Europe
Netherlands
Belgium
Germany
France

Industry Preferences

In Industrial/Energy prefer:
Industrial Products
Materials
Advanced Materials

In Business Serv. prefer:
Services
Distribution

Additional Information

Year Founded: 2002
Current Activity Level : Actively seeking new investments

WENGUO (XIAMEN) EQUITY FOUNDATION CO., LTD.

Jimei District
R403, No.8, Xinchengji Square
Xiamen, China
Website: www.wgvc.com.cn

Type of Firm

Private Equity Firm

Project Preferences

Type of Financing Preferred:
Balanced

Geographical Preferences

International Preferences:
China

Additional Information

Year Founded: 2015
Current Activity Level : Actively seeking new investments

WENZHOU WEIDU WEIYI INVESTMENT CENTER LP

Lucheng District
2/F, No.262 Xueyuan Middle Rd.
Wenzhou, China

Type of Firm

Private Equity Firm

Project Preferences

Type of Financing Preferred:
Early Stage
Seed
Startup

Geographical Preferences

International Preferences:
China

Additional Information

Year Founded: 2015
Current Activity Level : Actively seeking new investments

WERKLUND CAPITAL CORP

3rd Avenue Southwest
400 - 4500 Devon Tower
Calgary, Canada T2P 4H2
Phone: 4032316545
Fax: 4032316549
Website: werklundgroup.com

Management and Staff

Barbara Atkinson, Vice President
Peter Huff, Chief Financial Officer
Stefan Erasmus, President

Type of Firm

Private Equity Firm

Project Preferences

Type of Financing Preferred:
Generalist PE

Industry Preferences

In Financial Services prefer:
Real Estate

Additional Information

Year Founded: 2002
Current Activity Level : Actively seeking new investments

WERU INVESTMENT CO LTD

65 Kikuicho, Shinjuku-ku
3F, Kasuya Building
Tokyo, Japan 162-0044
Phone: 81352720471
Fax: 81352720472
Website: www.weruinvest.com

Type of Firm

Private Equity Firm

Association Membership

Japan Venture Capital Association

Project Preferences

Type of Financing Preferred:
Early Stage
Balanced

Geographical Preferences

International Preferences:
Japan

Additional Information
Year Founded: 1998
Capital Under Management: $8,400,000
Current Activity Level : Actively seeking new investments

WESLEY CLOVER INTERNATIONAL CORPORATION

390 March Road, Suite 110
Ottawa, Canada K2K 0G7
Phone: 6132716305
Fax: 6132719810
E-mail: info@wesleyclover.com
Website: www.wesleyclover.com

Other Offices

326, Udyog Vihar
Phase II Gurgaon
Haryana, India 122061
Phone: 911244198900
Fax: 911244198901

390 March Road, Suite 110
Ottawa, Canada K2K 0G7
Phone: 6132716305
Fax: 6132719810

The Manor House
South Wales
Newport, United Kingdom NP18 1HQ
Phone: 441633410383
Fax: 441633410384

3800 Concorde Parkway, Suite 1500
CHANTILLY, VA USA 20151
Phone: 7033184355

Management and Staff
Ben Morris, Vice President
David Black, Vice President
Debbie Pinard, Vice President
Michael Turner, Vice President
Paul Chiarelli, President & COO
Simon Gibson, Chief Executive Officer
Simon Gwatkin, Vice President

Type of Firm
Private Equity Firm

Association Membership
Canadian Venture Capital Association

Project Preferences

Type of Financing Preferred:
Early Stage
Seed
Startup

Geographical Preferences

International Preferences:
United Kingdom

Industry Preferences

In Communications prefer:
Telecommunications

In Computer Other prefer:
Computer Related

In Business Serv. prefer:
Media

Additional Information
Year Founded: 2000
Capital Under Management: $250,000,000
Current Activity Level : Actively seeking new investments

WEST BENGAL ASSET MANAGEMENT CO LTD

Webel Bhavan
Block EP & GP, Sector-V
Kolkata, India 700 091
Phone: 91-33-2357-1704
Fax: 91-33-2357-1708
E-mail: contact@webel-india.com
Website: www.webel-india.com

Type of Firm
Government Affiliated Program

Project Preferences

Type of Financing Preferred:
Early Stage
Expansion

Size of Investments Considered:
Min Size of Investment Considered (000s): $1,000
Max Size of Investment Considered (000s): $5,000

Geographical Preferences

International Preferences:
India

Industry Preferences

In Communications prefer:
Communications and Media
Telecommunications

In Computer Software prefer:
Software

In Semiconductor/Electr prefer:
Electronics

Additional Information
Year Founded: 2000
Capital Under Management: $1,100,000
Current Activity Level : Actively seeking new investments

WEST CAPITAL ADVISORS LLC

7755 Montgomery Road, Suite 155
Cincinnati, OH USA 45236
Phone: 5139847980
Website: www.westcapadv.com

Management and Staff
Mark Richey, Managing Director
Michelle Murcia, Venture Partner

Type of Firm
Private Equity Firm

Project Preferences

Type of Financing Preferred:
Early Stage

Geographical Preferences

United States Preferences:

Additional Information
Year Founded: 2011
Capital Under Management: $855,500,000
Current Activity Level : Actively seeking new investments

WEST CIRQUE RESOURCES LTD

95 Water Street, Second Floor
P.O. Box 5383, Stn C
St. John's, Canada A1C 5W2
Phone: 7097385513
Fax: 7097385578
E-mail: inquiries@killickcapital.com
Website: www.westcirqueresources.com

Management and Staff
Nigel Luckman, Chief Operating Officer
Tom Williams, Vice President

Type of Firm
Private Equity Firm

Project Preferences

Type of Financing Preferred:
Balanced
Later Stage

Geographical Preferences

Canadian Preferences:
All Canada

Additional Information
Year Founded: 2007
Current Activity Level : Actively seeking new investments

WEST COAST CAPITAL

Olympic Business Park
Dundonald
Kilmarnock, United Kingdom KA2 9AE
Phone: 441563852200
Fax: 441563850091
E-mail: info@westcoastcapital.co.uk
Website: www.westcoastcapital.co.uk

Management and Staff

Jim McMahon, Founding Partner
Paul Davidson, Partner
Tom Hunter, Founding Partner

Type of Firm

Private Equity Firm

Project Preferences

Role in Financing:
Will function either as deal originator or investor in deals created by others

Type of Financing Preferred:
Balanced

Geographical Preferences

International Preferences:
United Kingdom
Europe

Industry Preferences

In Internet Specific prefer:
E-Commerce Technology
Ecommerce

In Consumer Related prefer:
Retail

In Financial Services prefer:
Real Estate

Additional Information

Year Founded: 2001
Capital Under Management: $293,700,000
Current Activity Level : Actively seeking new investments

WEST END HOLDINGS LLC

3102 West End Avenue, Suite 150, Two American Center
Nashville, TN USA 37203
Phone: 6159532165
E-mail: info@westendholdings.com
Website: www.westendholdings.com

Type of Firm

Private Equity Firm

Project Preferences

Type of Financing Preferred:
Leveraged Buyout
Management Buyouts
Recapitalizations

Industry Preferences

In Medical/Health prefer:
Health Services

In Business Serv. prefer:
Services

Additional Information

Year Founded: 2011
Current Activity Level : Actively seeking new investments

WEST FACE CAPITAL INC

2 Bloor Street East, Suite 810
Toronto, Canada M4W 1A8
Phone: 6477248900
Website: www.westfacecapital.com

Type of Firm

Corporate PE/Venture

Project Preferences

Type of Financing Preferred:
Leveraged Buyout
Mezzanine

Additional Information

Year Founded: 2007
Current Activity Level : Actively seeking new investments

WEST LOOP VENTURES LLC

60 East Monroe Street
Chicago, IL USA 60654
Website: www.westloopventures.com

Management and Staff

Jeff Carter, Partner
Kenny Estes, Partner

Type of Firm

Private Equity Firm

Project Preferences

Type of Financing Preferred:
Early Stage

Geographical Preferences

United States Preferences:
Midwest

Industry Preferences

In Computer Software prefer:
Software

In Financial Services prefer:
Financial Services

Additional Information

Year Founded: 2017
Current Activity Level : Actively seeking new investments

WEST MIDLANDS ENTERPRISE LTD

17 High Street
Forward House
Henley-in-Arden, United Kingdom B95 5AA
Phone: 4403302231430
E-mail: info@merciafund.co.uk
Website: www.merciafund.co.uk

Other Offices

Former: 31-34 Waterloo Street
Wellington House
Birmingham, United Kingdom B2 5TJ
Phone: 441216630940

2nd Floor Orbital House
85-87 Croydon Road
Caterham, United Kingdom CR3 6PD
Phone: 44-1883-337-111
Fax: 44-1883-337-112

Management and Staff

Martyn Booth, Chief Executive Officer

Type of Firm

Private Equity Firm

Association Membership

British Venture Capital Association (BVCA)

Project Preferences

Role in Financing:
Prefer role as deal originator but will also invest in deals created by others

Type of Financing Preferred:
Early Stage
Expansion
Balanced
Later Stage
Seed

Size of Investments Considered:
Min Size of Investment Considered (000s): $81
Max Size of Investment Considered (000s): $1,623

Geographical Preferences

International Preferences:
United Kingdom

Industry Preferences

In Medical/Health prefer:
Medical Diagnostics

In Industrial/Energy prefer:
Environmental Related

In Transportation prefer:
Transportation

In Business Serv. prefer:
Services

In Manufact. prefer:
Manufacturing

Additional Information
Name of Most Recent Fund: South East Growth Fund
Most Recent Fund Was Raised: 06/03/2003
Year Founded: 1982
Capital Under Management: $140,500,000
Current Activity Level : Actively seeking new investments
Method of Compensation: Return on invest. most important, but chg. closing fees, service fees, etc.

WEST OAK CAPITAL LLC

25 Highland Park Village, Suite 100-567
Dallas, TX USA 75205
Phone: 214-762-9106
Fax: 972-490-2345
Website: www.westoakcap.com

Management and Staff
Harbert Mulherin, Managing Partner

Type of Firm
Private Equity Firm

Project Preferences

Type of Financing Preferred:
Fund of Funds of Second

Size of Investments Considered:
Min Size of Investment Considered (000s): $5,000
Max Size of Investment Considered (000s): $20,000

Geographical Preferences

International Preferences:
Albania

Additional Information
Name of Most Recent Fund: Live Oak Investment Furd I LLC
Most Recent Fund Was Raised: 09/26/2011
Year Founded: 2004
Capital Under Management: $100,000,000
Current Activity Level : Actively seeking new investments

WEST PARTNERS LLC

5796 Armada Drive, Suite 300
Carlsbad, CA USA 92008
Phone: 7606025783
Website: www.westpartners.com

Management and Staff
Dennis O Brien, Co-Founder
Gary West, Co-Founder
Marc Harper, Chief Financial Officer

Type of Firm
Private Equity Firm

Project Preferences

Type of Financing Preferred:
Leveraged Buyout
Value-Add
Generalist PE
Management Buyouts

Geographical Preferences

United States Preferences:

Industry Preferences

In Communications prefer:
Media and Entertainment

In Financial Services prefer:
Real Estate

In Business Serv. prefer:
Services

Additional Information
Year Founded: 2007
Current Activity Level : Actively seeking new investments

WEST SECURITY EQUITY INVESTMENT CO LTD

2 Linjiangzhi Road, Yuzhong
22/F, Hejing Building
Chongqing, China

Type of Firm
Bank Affiliated

Project Preferences

Type of Financing Preferred:
Balanced

Geographical Preferences

International Preferences:
China

Additional Information
Year Founded: 2010
Capital Under Management: $29,300,000
Current Activity Level : Actively seeking new investments

WEST VIRGINIA STATE JOBS INVESTMENT TRUST BOARD

1012 Kanawha Boulevard
Fifth Floor
Charleston, WV USA 25301
Phone: 3043456200
Fax: 3043456262
Website: www.wvjit.org

Type of Firm
Government Affiliated Program

Association Membership
Community Development Venture Capital Alliance

Project Preferences

Type of Financing Preferred:
Early Stage
Expansion
Balanced
Later Stage

Geographical Preferences

United States Preferences:
Virginia

Additional Information
Year Founded: 1992
Current Activity Level : Actively seeking new investments

WEST WEB VALLEY SAS

90, rue Charles Nungesser
Guipavas, France 29490
Phone: 330272881747
Website: west-web-valley.fr

Type of Firm
Incubator/Development Program

Project Preferences

Type of Financing Preferred:
Early Stage
Seed
Startup

Geographical Preferences

International Preferences:
France

Industry Preferences

In Computer Software prefer:
Software

In Biotechnology prefer:
Industrial Biotechnology

In Medical/Health prefer:
Health Services

In Industrial/Energy prefer:
Energy

Additional Information

Year Founded: 2012
Current Activity Level : Actively seeking new investments

WESTBOURNE CAPITAL PARTNERS LLC

30 North LaSalle Street, Suite 2250
Chicago, IL USA 60602
E-mail: sberchem@westbournecp.com
Website: www.westbournecp.com

Type of Firm

Private Equity Firm

Project Preferences

Type of Financing Preferred:
Acquisition

Industry Preferences

In Consumer Related prefer:
Food/Beverage

In Manufact. prefer:
Manufacturing

Additional Information

Year Founded: 2018
Current Activity Level : Actively seeking new investments

WESTBRIDGE CAPITAL ADVISORS (INDIA) PVT LTD

24, Vittal Mallya Road
Level 11, East Wing, UB City
Bangalore, India 560001
Phone: 918049070900
Fax: 918049070901
Website: www.westbridgecap.com

Management and Staff

K.P Balaraj, Co-Founder
SK Jain, Co-Founder
Sandeep Singhal, Co-Founder
Sumir Chadha, Co-Founder

Type of Firm

Investment Management Firm

Association Membership

Indian Venture Capital Association (IVCA)

Project Preferences

Type of Financing Preferred:
Generalist PE
Public Companies
Later Stage
Acquisition

Size of Investments Considered:
Min Size of Investment Considered (000s): $10,000
Max Size of Investment Considered (000s): $50,000

Geographical Preferences

International Preferences:
India

Industry Preferences

In Communications prefer:
Communications and Media
CATV & Pay TV Systems
Telecommunications
Wireless Communications

In Medical/Health prefer:
Hospital/Other Instit.

In Consumer Related prefer:
Franchises(NEC)
Consumer Services

Additional Information

Year Founded: 2000
Capital Under Management: $39,800,000
Current Activity Level : Actively seeking new investments

WESTBRIDGE FUND MANAGERS LTD

1, Mayfair Place
Deevnoshire House
London, United Kingdom W1J 8AJ
Phone: 443332406500
Fax: 442920546251
E-mail: info@westbridgecapital.co.uk
Website: www.wfml.co.uk

Other Offices

Cypress Drive
The Gatehouse, Melrose Hall
Cardiff, United Kingdom CF3 0EG

Management and Staff

Alexander Smart, Partner
Guy Davies, Partner
Valerie Kendall, Partner

Type of Firm

Private Equity Firm

Association Membership

British Venture Capital Association (BVCA)

Project Preferences

Type of Financing Preferred:
Leveraged Buyout
Expansion
Management Buyouts
Acquisition
Private Placement
Recapitalizations

Size of Investments Considered:
Min Size of Investment Considered (000s): $199
Max Size of Investment Considered (000s): $1,987

Geographical Preferences

International Preferences:
United Kingdom
Europe

Industry Focus

(% based on actual investment)
Computer Software and Services	45.1%
Semiconductors/Other Elect.	25.6%
Computer Hardware	17.3%
Consumer Related	6.1%
Other Products	3.4%
Internet Specific	2.0%
Industrial/Energy	0.6%

Additional Information

Name of Most Recent Fund: WestBridge SME Fund
Most Recent Fund Was Raised: 06/30/2010
Year Founded: 2008
Capital Under Management: $21,900,000
Current Activity Level : Actively seeking new investments

WESTBRIDGE VENTURES LLC

One Maritime Plaza, Suite 1545
San Francisco, CA USA 94111
Phone: 4152771000
Fax: 4152771077

Management and Staff

Jason Breaux, Vice President
Steven Strandberg, Founder

Type of Firm

Private Equity Firm

Project Preferences

Type of Financing Preferred:
Later Stage

Size of Investments Considered:
Min Size of Investment Considered (000s): $3,000
Max Size of Investment Considered (000s): $10,000

Geographical Preferences

United States Preferences:

Canadian Preferences:
All Canada

International Preferences:
United Kingdom

Industry Preferences

In Communications prefer:
Radio & TV Broadcasting
Telecommunications
Wireless Communications
Data Communications
Satellite Microwave Comm.

In Computer Software prefer:
Computer Services
Software
Systems Software
Applications Software

In Internet Specific prefer:
Internet
Ecommerce

In Semiconductor/Electr prefer:
Semiconductor

Additional Information
Year Founded: 1999
Capital Under Management: $100,000,000
Current Activity Level : Actively seeking new investments

WESTBURY PARTNERS

100 Motor Parkway, Suite 165
Hauppauge, NY USA 11788
Phone: 6312314121
Fax: 6312318121
Website: www.westburypartners.com

Management and Staff
James Schubauer, President & COO
Richard Sicoli, Co-Founder

Type of Firm
Private Equity Firm

Project Preferences

Role in Financing:
Prefer role as deal originator but will also invest in deals created by others

Type of Financing Preferred:
Balanced

Size of Investments Considered:
Min Size of Investment Considered (000s): $3,000
Max Size of Investment Considered (000s): $9,000

Geographical Preferences

United States Preferences:

Canadian Preferences:
All Canada

Industry Focus
(% based on actual investment)

Computer Software and Services	42.0%
Communications and Media	26.1%
Internet Specific	15.8%
Computer Hardware	7.0%
Other Products	6.5%
Medical/Health	2.6%
Consumer Related	0.0%

Additional Information
Year Founded: 1995
Capital Under Management: $150,000,000
Current Activity Level : Actively seeking new investments
Method of Compensation: Return on investment is of primary concern, do not charge fees

WESTCAP MANAGEMENT LTD

410 22nd Street East, Suite 830
Saskatoon, Canada S7K 5T6
Phone: 3066525557
Fax: 3066528186
Website: www.goldenopportunities.ca

Management and Staff
Douglas Banzet, Chief Operating Officer
Jamie Schwitzer, Vice President
Robert Connoly, Chief Financial Officer
Wanda Hunchak, Vice President

Type of Firm
Private Equity Firm

Association Membership
Canadian Venture Capital Association

Project Preferences

Type of Financing Preferred:
Leveraged Buyout
Generalist PE
Balanced
Management Buyouts

Geographical Preferences

Canadian Preferences:
All Canada
Western Canada

Additional Information
Year Founded: 1991
Capital Under Management: $500,000,000
Current Activity Level : Actively seeking new investments

WESTERKIRK CAPITAL INC

95 Wellington Street West, Suite 1410
Toronto, Canada M5J 2N7
Phone: 4169272231
Fax: 4169232132
Website: www.westerkirk.ca

Management and Staff
Douglas Bradley, Managing Director
Joanne Ranger, Managing Director
Mairi MacGillivray, Managing Director
William Stevens, Managing Director
Zachary McIsaac, Managing Director

Type of Firm
Private Equity Firm

Additional Information
Year Founded: 2003
Current Activity Level : Actively seeking new investments

WESTERN DEVELOPMENT COMMISSION

Dillon House
Ballaghaderreen, Ireland
Phone: 353949861441
Fax: 353949861443
E-mail: info@wdc.ie
Website: www.wdc.ie

Management and Staff
Ian Brannigan, Chief Executive Officer

Type of Firm
Government Affiliated Program

Association Membership
Irish Venture Capital Association
European Private Equity and Venture Capital Assoc.

Project Preferences

Type of Financing Preferred:
Balanced

Geographical Preferences

International Preferences:
Ireland

Industry Preferences

In Medical/Health prefer:
Medical Products

In Consumer Related prefer:
Food/Beverage

In Industrial/Energy prefer:
Energy

In Manufact. prefer:
Manufacturing

In Agr/Forestr/Fish prefer:
Agribusiness

Additional Information
Year Founded: 2003
Current Activity Level : Actively seeking new investments

WESTERN HERITAGE CAPITAL LLC

299 South Main
13th Floor
Salt Lake City, UT USA 84111
Website: www.westernheritagecap.com

Management and Staff
David Glenn, Founder

Type of Firm
Private Equity Firm

Geographical Preferences

United States Preferences:
Rocky Mountain

Industry Preferences

In Agr/Forestr/Fish prefer:
Agribusiness
Agriculture related

Additional Information
Year Founded: 2015
Current Activity Level : Actively seeking new investments

WESTERN STATES INVESTMENT GROUP

6335 Ferris Square, Suite A
San Diego, CA USA 92121
Phone: 858-678-0800
Fax: 858-678-0900
Website: www.wsig.com

Management and Staff
William Patch, Vice President

Type of Firm
Private Equity Firm

Project Preferences

Role in Financing:
Prefer role as deal originator but will also invest in deals created by others

Type of Financing Preferred:
Leveraged Buyout
Research and Development
Start-up Financing
Seed
First Stage Financing

Size of Investments Considered:
Min Size of Investment Considered (000s): $1,000
Max Size of Investment Considered: No Limit

Geographical Preferences

United States Preferences:
West Coast
Southwest

Industry Focus
(% based on actual investment)
Computer Software and Services	26.3%
Medical/Health	24.0%
Industrial/Energy	18.1%
Communications and Media	12.1%
Semiconductors/Other Elect.	10.4%
Biotechnology	9.2%

Additional Information
Year Founded: 1976
Capital Under Management: $35,000,000
Current Activity Level : Making few, if any, new investments
Method of Compensation: Return on investment is of primary concern, do not charge fees

WESTERN TECHNOLOGY INVESTMENT

104 La Mesa Drive, Suite 102
Portola Valley, CA USA 94028
Phone: 6502344300
Fax: 6502344343
E-mail: info@westerntech.com
Website: www.westerntech.com

Management and Staff
Andrew Baldwin, Principal
David Wanek, Partner
David Gravano, Partner
Hagi Schwartz, Venture Partner
Jay Cohan, Partner
Jonathan Beizer, Venture Partner
Josh Brody, Venture Partner
Martin Eng, Chief Financial Officer
Maurice Werdegar, President
Patrick Lee, Partner
Ron Swenson, Partner
Ross Glasser, Principal
Rudy Ruano, Partner
Salvador Gutierrez, Partner

Type of Firm
Private Equity Firm

Association Membership
Western Association of Venture Capitalists (WAVC)
National Venture Capital Association - USA (NVCA)

Project Preferences

Role in Financing:
Prefer role as deal originator

Type of Financing Preferred:
Early Stage
Expansion
Balanced
Public Companies
Later Stage

Size of Investments Considered:
Min Size of Investment Considered (000s): $250
Max Size of Investment Considered (000s): $30,000

Geographical Preferences

United States Preferences:

Industry Preferences

In Communications prefer:
Communications and Media
Wireless Communications

In Computer Hardware prefer:
Computers

In Computer Software prefer:
Software

In Internet Specific prefer:
Internet

In Semiconductor/Electr prefer:
Semiconductor

In Biotechnology prefer:
Biotechnology

In Medical/Health prefer:
Medical Products
Health Services

In Manufact. prefer:
Manufacturing

Additional Information
Name of Most Recent Fund: Venture Lending & Leasing VII LLC
Most Recent Fund Was Raised: 12/28/2012
Year Founded: 1980
Capital Under Management: $767,000,000
Current Activity Level : Actively seeking new investments
Method of Compensation: Return on investment is of primary concern, do not charge fees

WESTERNONE EQUITY INCOME FUND

925 West Georgia Street, Suite 910
Vancouver, Canada V6C 3L2
Phone: 6046784042
Fax: 6046815969
Website: www.weq.ca

Type of Firm
Private Equity Firm

Project Preferences

Type of Financing Preferred:
Leveraged Buyout
Acquisition

Geographical Preferences

Canadian Preferences:
Western Canada

Industry Preferences

In Industrial/Energy prefer:
Alternative Energy
Industrial Products

In Transportation prefer:
Transportation

In Financial Services prefer:
Financial Services

In Business Serv. prefer:
Services

Additional Information
Year Founded: 2006
Current Activity Level : Actively seeking new investments

WESTFIELD CAPITAL MANAGEMENT COMPANY LP

One Financial Center
24th Floor
Boston, MA USA 02110
Phone: 6174287100
Fax: 6174287190
Website: www.westfieldcapital.com

Management and Staff
Bruce Jacobs, Managing Partner
Dee Silveira, Vice President
Ethan Meyers, Partner
Hamlen Thompson, Managing Partner
John Montgomery, Managing Partner
Justin Moscardelli, Vice President
Kathryn Kearney, Chief Financial Officer
Kimberly D Agostino, Vice President
Matthew Coll, Vice President
Morton Fearey, Managing Partner
Richard Lee, Partner
Robert Flores, Managing Partner
Scott Emerman, Partner
Steven Wilner, Vice President
William Muggia, President

Type of Firm
Private Equity Firm

Project Preferences

Type of Financing Preferred:
Balanced
Public Companies

Additional Information
Year Founded: 2001
Current Activity Level : Actively seeking new investments

WESTLY GROUP LLC

2200 Sand Hill Road, Suite 250
Menlo Park, CA USA 94025
Phone: 6502757420
Fax: 6503622338
E-mail: wg@westlygroup.com
Website: westlygroup.com

Management and Staff
Gary Dillabough, Managing Partner
Isaac Applbaum, Venture Partner
Ken Goldman, Venture Partner
Michael Dorsey, Managing Partner
Mike Jackson, Principal
Steven Westly, Managing Partner
Tony Luh, General Partner

Type of Firm
Private Equity Firm

Project Preferences

Role in Financing:
Prefer role as deal originator but will also invest in deals created by others

Type of Financing Preferred:
Early Stage
Expansion
Balanced
Later Stage
Seed

Geographical Preferences

United States Preferences:
North America

Industry Preferences

In Industrial/Energy prefer:
Energy
Alternative Energy
Environmental Related

Additional Information
Year Founded: 2007
Capital Under Management: $287,000,000
Current Activity Level : Actively seeking new investments
Method of Compensation: Return on invest. most important, but chg. closing fees, service fees, etc.

WESTON PRESIDIO CAPITAL

200 Clarendon Street
50th Floor, John Hancock Tower
Boston, MA USA 02116
Phone: 6179882500
Fax: 6179882515
Website: www.westonpresidio.com

Management and Staff
Jeffrey Mills, Partner
John McKee, Partner
Josh McDowell, Partner
Kevin Hayes, Partner
Kirk Syme, Principal
Mark Bono, Partner
Michael Cronin, Founder
R. Sean Honey, Managing Partner
Scott Bell, Partner
Therese Mrozek, Partner

Type of Firm
Private Equity Firm

Association Membership
New England Venture Capital Association
Western Association of Venture Capitalists (WAVC)
National Venture Capital Association - USA (NVCA)

Project Preferences

Role in Financing:
Will function either as deal originator or investor in deals created by others

Type of Financing Preferred:
Leveraged Buyout
Early Stage
Balanced
Later Stage
Management Buyouts

Size of Investments Considered:
Min Size of Investment Considered (000s): $10,000
Max Size of Investment Considered (000s): $50,000

Geographical Preferences

United States Preferences:
North America

Industry Focus
(% based on actual investment)
Consumer Related	36.4%
Other Products	21.1%
Internet Specific	13.7%
Communications and Media	7.8%
Industrial/Energy	7.4%
Computer Software and Services	5.4%
Semiconductors/Other Elect.	3.8%
Medical/Health	3.1%
Biotechnology	0.9%
Computer Hardware	0.3%

Additional Information
Name of Most Recent Fund: Weston Presidio Capital V, L.P.
Most Recent Fund Was Raised: 03/31/2005
Year Founded: 1991
Capital Under Management: $3,991,000,000
Current Activity Level : Actively seeking new investments
Method of Compensation: Return on investment is of primary concern, do not charge fees

WESTRIVER CAPITAL

450 Park Avenue, Suite 1203
New York, NY USA 10022
Phone: 2122475333
Fax: 2122477118

Management and Staff
Erik Anderson, President

Type of Firm
Private Equity Firm

Project Preferences

Type of Financing Preferred:
Generalist PE
Balanced

Additional Information
Year Founded: 2002
Capital Under Management: $249,800,000
Current Activity Level : Actively seeking new investments

WESTRIVER GROUP INC

3720 Carillon Point
Kirkland, WA USA 98033
Website: www.wrg.vc

Type of Firm
Private Equity Firm

Project Preferences

Type of Financing Preferred:
Early Stage

Additional Information
Year Founded: 2002
Current Activity Level : Actively seeking new investments

WESTSHORE CAPITAL PARTNERS LP

400 North Ashley Drive
Rivergate Tower, Suite 2610
Tampa, FL USA 33602
Phone: 8132233600
Fax: 8132233699
Website: www.westshorecapitalpartners.com

Management and Staff
David Malizia, Managing Partner
Earl Powell, Principal
Michael Sullivan, Vice President
P. Craig Sanford, Vice President
Ryan Cortner, Vice President
W. Andrew Krusen, Principal

Type of Firm
Private Equity Firm

Project Preferences

Role in Financing:
Prefer role as deal originator but will also invest in deals created by others

Type of Financing Preferred:
Leveraged Buyout
Management Buyouts
Recapitalizations

Geographical Preferences

United States Preferences:
All U.S.

Canadian Preferences:
All Canada

Industry Preferences

In Medical/Health prefer:
Medical/Health

In Consumer Related prefer:
Consumer
Food/Beverage
Education Related

In Industrial/Energy prefer:
Industrial Products

In Business Serv. prefer:
Services
Distribution

In Manufact. prefer:
Manufacturing

Additional Information
Year Founded: 2006
Capital Under Management: $20,000,000
Current Activity Level : Actively seeking new investments
Method of Compensation: Return on invest. most important, but chg. closing fees, service fees, etc.

WESTSUMMIT CAPITAL MANAGEMENT LTD

No. A6 Changyangmenwai Street
B-901, Vantone Center
Beijing, China 100020
Phone: 861059797669
Fax: 861058043607
Website: www.westsummitcap.com

Other Offices
720 University Avenue, Suite 100
Palo Alto, CA USA 94301
Phone: 16508471886
Fax: 16508871789

8/F, Two Exchange Square
8 Connaught Place
Hongkong, Hong Kong
Phone: 85221680893
Fax: 85222970066

Management and Staff
Datong Chen, Co-Founder
David Lam, Managing Director
Elise Huang, Partner
Jie Deng, Co-Founder
John Yu, Co-Founder
Lei Yang, Co-Founder
Mingyu Liu, Vice President
Yilun Lin, Vice President

Type of Firm
Private Equity Firm

Project Preferences

Type of Financing Preferred:
Expansion
Balanced

Size of Investments Considered:
Min Size of Investment Considered (000s): $10,000
Max Size of Investment Considered (000s): $30,000

Geographical Preferences

United States Preferences:
All U.S.

International Preferences:
Ireland
Europe
China

Industry Preferences

In Communications prefer:
Telecommunications

In Computer Software prefer:
Software

In Internet Specific prefer:
Internet

In Semiconductor/Electr prefer:
Semiconductor

In Medical/Health prefer:
Health Services

In Consumer Related prefer:
Food/Beverage

In Industrial/Energy prefer:
Energy
Environmental Related

In Financial Services prefer:
Financial Services

In Business Serv. prefer:
Media

In Agr/Forestr/Fish prefer:
Agriculture related

Additional Information
Year Founded: 2011
Capital Under Management: $325,000,000
Current Activity Level: Actively seeking new investments

WESTVIEW CAPITAL PARTNERS LP

125 High Street
High Street Tower, 26th Floor
Boston, MA USA 02110
Phone: 6172612050
Fax: 6172612060
Website: www.wvcapital.com

Management and Staff
Carlo von Schroeter, Managing Partner
Greg Thomas, Vice President
John Turner, General Partner
Jonathan Hunnicutt, General Partner
Matthew Carroll, General Partner
Richard Williams, Managing Partner
Thomas Reardon, Principal

Type of Firm
Private Equity Firm

Association Membership
New England Venture Capital Association

Project Preferences

Role in Financing:
Prefer role as deal originator but will also invest in deals created by others

Type of Financing Preferred:
Leveraged Buyout
Expansion
Acquisition
Recapitalizations

Geographical Preferences

United States Preferences:
North America

Industry Preferences

In Computer Software prefer:
Software

In Medical/Health prefer:
Medical/Health
Health Services

In Consumer Related prefer:
Retail
Consumer Products

In Industrial/Energy prefer:
Industrial Products

In Business Serv. prefer:
Services
Distribution
Media

In Manufact. prefer:
Manufacturing
Publishing

Additional Information
Year Founded: 1990
Capital Under Management: $195,000,000
Current Activity Level: Actively seeking new investments

WESTWARD PARTNERS LLC

3131 Western Avenue, Suite 318
Seattle, WA USA 98121
Fax: 2062993054
E-mail: info@westwardpartnersllc.com
Website: www.westwardpartnersllc.com

Management and Staff
Andy Baldridge, Partner
Blake Araki, Partner
Erik Tolzmann, Partner

Type of Firm
Private Equity Firm

Project Preferences

Type of Financing Preferred:
Generalist PE

Geographical Preferences

United States Preferences:
Northwest

Industry Preferences

In Consumer Related prefer:
Consumer Products

In Industrial/Energy prefer:
Energy
Oil & Gas Drilling, Explor

In Transportation prefer:
Transportation

In Manufact. prefer:
Manufacturing

In Agr/Forestr/Fish prefer:
Agribusiness

Additional Information
Year Founded: 2010
Current Activity Level: Actively seeking new investments

WESTWAVE CAPITAL I LP

3175 Hanover Street
Palo Alto, CA USA 94304
Phone: 4156408911

Type of Firm
Private Equity Firm

Additional Information
Year Founded: 2017
Current Activity Level: Actively seeking new investments

WEXFORD CAPITAL LP

411 West Putnam Avenue
Greenwich, CT USA 06830
Phone: 2038627300
E-mail: ir@wexford.com
Website: www.wexford.com

Management and Staff
James Rubin, Partner
John Sites, Partner
John Doyle, Partner
Joseph Jacobs, President, Founder
Kenneth Rubin, Partner
Mark Zand, Partner
Paul Jacobi, Vice President
Robert Holtz, Partner
Steven West, Partner

Type of Firm
Private Equity Firm

Project Preferences

Type of Financing Preferred:
Leveraged Buyout
Turnaround
Distressed Debt

Industry Focus
(% based on actual investment)

Medical/Health	54.7%
Semiconductors/Other Elect.	12.6%
Internet Specific	12.0%
Biotechnology	7.9%
Industrial/Energy	7.4%
Other Products	4.3%
Computer Software and Services	1.1%

Additional Information
Name of Most Recent Fund: Wexford Partners 10, L.P.
Most Recent Fund Was Raised: 08/08/2006
Year Founded: 1994
Current Activity Level: Actively seeking new investments

WFD VENTURES LLC

1500 Broadway
29th Floor
New York, NY USA 10036
Phone: 2127677500
Fax: 2127677575
E-mail: info@wfdventures.com
Website: www.wfdventures.com

Management and Staff

Tim Langloss, Managing Director
William Doyle, Managing Director

Type of Firm

Private Equity Firm

Project Preferences

Type of Financing Preferred:
Early Stage
Expansion
Balanced
Later Stage
Seed
Startup

Size of Investments Considered:
Min Size of Investment Considered (000s): $2,000
Max Size of Investment Considered (000s): $15,000

Geographical Preferences

United States Preferences:

International Preferences:
All International

Industry Preferences

In Medical/Health prefer:
Medical/Health
Medical Diagnostics
Medical Therapeutics
Drug/Equipmt Delivery
Medical Products
Health Services

Additional Information

Name of Most Recent Fund: WFD Ventures Fund II, L.P.
Most Recent Fund Was Raised: 03/02/2010
Year Founded: 2002
Capital Under Management: $116,100,000
Current Activity Level : Actively seeking new investments

WGL HOLDINGS INC

6801 Industrial Road
Springfield, VA USA 22151
Phone: 703-750-1000
Fax: 703-750-5922
Website: www.wglholdings.com

Management and Staff

Adrian Chapman, President & COO
Anthony Nee, Vice President
Douglas Bonawitz, Vice President
Louis Hutchinson, Vice President
Marcellous Frye, Vice President
Mark Lowe, Vice President
Richard Moore, Vice President
Tracy Townsend, Vice President

Type of Firm

Corporate PE/Venture

Project Preferences

Type of Financing Preferred:
Balanced

Size of Investments Considered:
Min Size of Investment Considered (000s): $1,000
Max Size of Investment Considered (000s): $20,000

Geographical Preferences

United States Preferences:

Industry Preferences

In Industrial/Energy prefer:
Energy
Oil and Gas Exploration
Oil & Gas Drilling,Explor

Additional Information

Year Founded: 2000
Current Activity Level : Actively seeking new investments

WHARTON EQUITY PARTNERS LLC

505 Park Avenue, 18th Floor
New York, NY USA 10022
Phone: 212-570-5959
Fax: 212-570-0777
Website: www.whartonequity.com

Management and Staff

David Eisenberg, Chief Executive Officer
John Baxter, Managing Director
Paul Stern, Managing Director
Paul LeBlanc, Managing Director
Peter Lewis, President
Richard Serko, Chief Operating Officer
Richard Kulick, Vice President

Type of Firm

Private Equity Firm

Project Preferences

Type of Financing Preferred:
Early Stage
Generalist PE
Balanced
Opportunistic

Geographical Preferences

United States Preferences:
All U.S.

Industry Preferences

In Computer Software prefer:
Software

In Semiconductor/Electr prefer:
Electronics

In Biotechnology prefer:
Biotechnology

In Medical/Health prefer:
Medical/Health

In Financial Services prefer:
Real Estate

In Manufact. prefer:
Manufacturing

Additional Information

Year Founded: 1987
Current Activity Level : Actively seeking new investments

WHEATLEY PARTNERS

80 Cuttermill Road, Suite 302
Great Neck, NY USA 11021
Phone: 5167731024
Fax: 5167730996
E-mail: info@wheatleypartners.com
Website: www.wheatleypartners.com

Other Offices

747 Third Avenue
24th Floor
New York, NY USA 10017

Management and Staff

Barry Fingerhut, General Partner
Barry Rubenstein, General Partner
David Dantzker, General Partner
Irwin Lieber, General Partner
Jonathan Lieber, General Partner
Lawrence Wagenberg, General Partner
Nancy Casey, General Partner
Seth Lieber, General Partner

Type of Firm

Private Equity Firm

Project Preferences

Role in Financing:
Will function either as deal originator or investor in deals created by others

Type of Financing Preferred:
Balanced

Industry Focus
(% based on actual investment)
Computer Software and Services	38.8%
Internet Specific	23.4%
Communications and Media	11.8%
Biotechnology	7.7%
Medical/Health	7.2%
Semiconductors/Other Elect.	5.5%
Other Products	5.4%
Industrial/Energy	0.1%

Additional Information
Year Founded: 1992
Capital Under Management: $200,000,000
Current Activity Level : Actively seeking new investments
Method of Compensation: Return on investment is of primary concern, do not charge fees

WHEELHOUSE CAPITAL PARTNERS LLC

131 Third Avenue North
Franklin, TN USA 37064
Phone: 6155674200
Website: wheelhousecapitalpartners.com

Management and Staff
Mark Graham, Managing Partner
Merle Glasgow, Principal
Michael LaChance, Principal
Steven Simpson, Managing Partner

Type of Firm
Private Equity Firm

Project Preferences
Type of Financing Preferred:
Leveraged Buyout
Acquisition

Industry Preferences
In Biotechnology prefer:
Industrial Biotechnology

In Medical/Health prefer:
Medical/Health
Health Services

In Industrial/Energy prefer:
Industrial Products

Additional Information
Year Founded: 2009
Current Activity Level : Actively seeking new investments

WHITE CLOUD CAPITAL ADVISORS LTD

66 Seymour Street
Marble Arch House
London, United Kingdom W1H 5BT
Website: www.whcloud.com

Other Offices
Raffles Tower
12th Floor
Cybercity, Mauritius

Type of Firm
Private Equity Firm

Project Preferences
Type of Financing Preferred:
Leveraged Buyout
Opportunistic
Acquisition

Geographical Preferences
International Preferences:
Asia Pacific
Europe

Industry Preferences
In Medical/Health prefer:
Medical/Health

In Consumer Related prefer:
Consumer
Education Related

In Industrial/Energy prefer:
Energy
Industrial Products

In Agr/Forestr/Fish prefer:
Agribusiness

Additional Information
Year Founded: 2010
Current Activity Level : Actively seeking new investments

WHITE DEER ENERGY LP

700 Louisiana Street, Suite 4770
Houston, TX USA 77002
Phone: 7135816900
Fax: 7135816901
Website: www.whitedeerenergy.com

Other Offices
667 Madison Avenue
Fourth Floor
NEW YORK, NY USA 10065
Phone: 2123711117
Fax: 2128886877

Management and Staff
Benjamin Guill, Managing Partner
James Saxton, Managing Director
Jim Meneely, Managing Director
Joseph Edwards, Managing Director
Thomas Edelman, Managing Partner

Type of Firm
Private Equity Firm

Project Preferences
Type of Financing Preferred:
Leveraged Buyout
Other
Acquisition

Size of Investments Considered:
Min Size of Investment Considered (000s): $50,000
Max Size of Investment Considered (000s): $100,000

Industry Preferences
In Industrial/Energy prefer:
Energy
Oil and Gas Exploration
Oil & Gas Drilling,Explor

Additional Information
Name of Most Recent Fund: White Deer Energy II, L.P.
Most Recent Fund Was Raised: 03/01/2013
Year Founded: 2008
Capital Under Management: $1,717,200,000
Current Activity Level : Actively seeking new investments

WHITE FIELD CAPITAL LLC

2525 15th Street
Denver, CO USA 80211
Phone: 3038958254
Website: www.whitefieldcapital.com

Type of Firm
Private Equity Firm

Project Preferences
Type of Financing Preferred:
Leveraged Buyout
Management Buyouts
Acquisition

Industry Preferences
In Medical/Health prefer:
Medical/Health

In Business Serv. prefer:
Services
Distribution

Additional Information
Year Founded: 2015
Capital Under Management: $13,730,000
Current Activity Level : Actively seeking new investments

WHITE OAK EQUITY PARTNERS LLC

250 Park Avenue
Seventh Floor
New York, NY USA 10177
Phone: 6467661445
E-mail: info@whiteoakequity.com
Website: whiteoakequity.com

Management and Staff
Kurt Overley, Partner
Robert Stockton, Partner

Type of Firm
Private Equity Firm

Project Preferences

Type of Financing Preferred:
Acquisition

Additional Information
Year Founded: 2017
Current Activity Level : Actively seeking new investments

WHITE OAK GLOBAL ADVISORS LLC

3 Embarcadero Center, Suite 550
San Francisco, CA USA 94111
Phone: 4156444100
Fax: 4156444199
Website: www.whiteoaksf.com

Type of Firm
Private Equity Firm

Project Preferences

Type of Financing Preferred:
Acquisition
Recapitalizations

Geographical Preferences

United States Preferences:

Additional Information
Year Founded: 2015
Capital Under Management: $50,000,000
Current Activity Level : Actively seeking new investments

WHITE OAK INVESTMENTS LLC

5665 New Northside Drive, Suite 500
Atlanta, GA USA 30328
Phone: 4048759994
Fax: 4048759545
E-mail: info@thewhiteoakgroup.com
Website: www.thewhiteoakgroup.com

Type of Firm
Private Equity Firm

Association Membership
Natl Assoc of Small Bus. Inv. Co (NASBIC)

Project Preferences

Type of Financing Preferred:
Leveraged Buyout
Expansion
Management Buyouts
Acquisition
Recapitalizations

Geographical Preferences

United States Preferences:
Mid Atlantic
Southeast

Industry Preferences

In Communications prefer:
Data Communications

In Medical/Health prefer:
Medical/Health
Health Services

In Industrial/Energy prefer:
Environmental Related

In Transportation prefer:
Aerospace

Additional Information
Year Founded: 1969
Current Activity Level : Actively seeking new investments

WHITE OAK PARTNERS INC

5150 E. Dublin Granville Road, Suite One
Westerville, OH USA 43081
Phone: 6148551155
E-mail: info@whiteoakpartners.com
Website: www.whiteoakpartners.com

Management and Staff
Michael Menzer, Founder

Type of Firm
Private Equity Firm

Project Preferences

Type of Financing Preferred:
Core
Generalist PE
Opportunistic

Size of Investments Considered:
Min Size of Investment Considered (000s): $5,000
Max Size of Investment Considered (000s): $100,000

Industry Preferences

In Industrial/Energy prefer:
Energy

In Financial Services prefer:
Financial Services
Real Estate

In Business Serv. prefer:
Distribution

Additional Information
Year Founded: 1969
Capital Under Management: $68,490,000
Current Activity Level : Actively seeking new investments

WHITE ROAD INVESTMENTS LLC

1451 66th Street
Emeryville, CA USA 94608
E-mail: info@whiteroadinvestments.com
Website: www.whiteroadinvestments.com

Management and Staff
Deven Clemens, Managing Partner

Type of Firm
Private Equity Firm

Project Preferences

Type of Financing Preferred:
Balanced

Size of Investments Considered:
Min Size of Investment Considered (000s): $750
Max Size of Investment Considered (000s): $2,000

Industry Preferences

In Consumer Related prefer:
Consumer Products

Additional Information
Year Founded: 2008
Current Activity Level : Actively seeking new investments

WHITE WOLF CAPITAL LLC

600 Third Avenue
Second Floor
New York, NY USA 10016
Phone: 6465712347
Fax: 2129373467
E-mail: info@whitewolfcapital.com
Website: whitewolfcapital.com

Type of Firm
Private Equity Firm

Project Preferences

Type of Financing Preferred:
Leveraged Buyout
Management Buyouts
Recapitalizations

Industry Preferences

In Business Serv. prefer:
Services

In Manufact. prefer:
Manufacturing

Additional Information
Name of Most Recent Fund: White Wolf Capital Investment Partners II LLC
Most Recent Fund Was Raised: 11/11/2013
Year Founded: 2011
Capital Under Management: $3,175,000
Current Activity Level : Actively seeking new investments

WHITECASTLE INVESTMENTS LTD

22 St. Clair Avenue East, Suite 1010
Toronto, Canada M4T 2S3
Phone: 4169615355
Fax: 4169613232
Website: www.whitecapvp.com

Management and Staff
A. Ephraim Diamond, Founder
David Strom, Chief Financial Officer

Type of Firm
Bank Affiliated

Association Membership
Canadian Venture Capital Association

Project Preferences

Role in Financing:
Prefer role in deals created by others

Type of Financing Preferred:
Leveraged Buyout
Early Stage
Management Buyouts
Acquisition

Geographical Preferences

Canadian Preferences:
All Canada

Industry Preferences

In Communications prefer:
Telecommunications

In Computer Software prefer:
Software

In Internet Specific prefer:
Internet

In Medical/Health prefer:
Medical/Health

In Consumer Related prefer:
Food/Beverage

In Financial Services prefer:
Financial Services

In Manufact. prefer:
Manufacturing

In Other prefer:
Environment Responsible

Additional Information
Year Founded: 1959
Capital Under Management: $81,222,000
Current Activity Level : Actively seeking new investments

WHITEHORSE LIQUIDITY PARTNERS INC

80 Richmond Street West, Suite 903
Toronto, Canada M5H 2A4
Website: www.whitehorseliquidity.com

Management and Staff
Michael Gubbels, Partner
Rob Gavin, Principal
Sean Connor, Chief Financial Officer
Yann Robard, Managing Partner

Type of Firm
Private Equity Firm

Project Preferences

Type of Financing Preferred:
Fund of Funds
Generalist PE
Acquisition

Additional Information
Year Founded: 2016
Capital Under Management: $393,410,000
Current Activity Level : Actively seeking new investments

WHITESTAR CAPITAL LTD

St Peter Port
Guernsey, United Kingdom
E-mail: info@whitestarvc.com
Website: www.whitestarvc.com

Management and Staff
Christian Hernandez, Co-Founder
David Szekely, Principal
Eric Martineau-Fortin, Co-Founder
John Henderson, Principal

Type of Firm
Private Equity Firm

Project Preferences

Type of Financing Preferred:
Early Stage
Expansion
Later Stage
Seed

Geographical Preferences

International Preferences:
Guernsey

Industry Preferences

In Communications prefer:
Telecommunications

In Internet Specific prefer:
Ecommerce

In Business Serv. prefer:
Media

Additional Information
Year Founded: 2007
Capital Under Management: $67,000,000
Current Activity Level : Actively seeking new investments

WHIZ PARTNERS INC

2-5-1, Atago, Minato-ku
36th Floor, Atago Green Hills
Tokyo, Japan 105-6236
Phone: 81364306778
Fax: 81364306774
E-mail: info@whizp.com
Website: www.whizp.com

Management and Staff
Atsushi Matsumura, Chief Operating Officer
Kazunari Kono, Senior Managing Director
Satoru Iino, Senior Managing Director
Tomoyuki Fujisawa, Managing Director
Yujiro Goto, Senior Managing Director

Type of Firm
Investment Management Firm

Project Preferences

Role in Financing:
Prefer role in deals created by others

Type of Financing Preferred:
Leveraged Buyout
Early Stage
Balanced
Later Stage
Seed

Geographical Preferences

United States Preferences:

International Preferences:
Europe
Asia
Japan

Industry Focus

(% based on actual investment)
Medical/Health	22.9%
Internet Specific	19.1%
Consumer Related	12.2%
Communications and Media	10.3%
Computer Software and Services	9.6%
Biotechnology	8.3%
Other Products	7.9%
Semiconductors/Other Elect.	7.0%
Industrial/Energy	2.1%
Computer Hardware	0.6%

Additional Information

Year Founded: 1988
Capital Under Management: $300,000,000
Current Activity Level : Actively seeking new investments
Method of Compensation: Return on investment is of primary concern, do not charge fees

---

WI HARPER GROUP INC

50 California Street, Suite 2920
San Francisco, CA USA 94111
Phone: 4153976200
Fax: 4153976280
E-mail: info@wiharper.com
Website: www.wiharper.com

Other Offices

806 Tower A
Pacific Century Place
Beijing, China 100027
Phone: 86-10-6539-1366
Fax: 86-10-6539-1367

Management and Staff

Charles Wu, Managing Director
Chen Yvonne, Partner
Derrick Hsiang, Vice President
Edward Liu, Partner
Forest Xu, Partner
Jeffrey Chu, Partner
Jimmy Lu, Managing Director
Paul Chau, Managing Director
Sean Peng, Managing Director
Shahi Ghanem, Managing Director
Winnie Hsu, Vice President
Yigong Wang, Chief Operating Officer
Yk Chu, Managing Director

Type of Firm

Private Equity Firm

Association Membership

Venture Capital Association of Beijing (VCAB)
Taiwan Venture Capital Association(TVCA)

Project Preferences

Role in Financing:
Prefer role as deal originator but will also invest in deals created by others

Type of Financing Preferred:
Early Stage
Expansion
Balanced

Size of Investments Considered:
Min Size of Investment Considered (000s): $5,000
Max Size of Investment Considered (000s): $15,000

Geographical Preferences

United States Preferences:

International Preferences:
Taiwan
China

Industry Focus

(% based on actual investment)
Internet Specific	35.4%
Computer Software and Services	15.4%
Industrial/Energy	14.1%
Medical/Health	9.2%
Semiconductors/Other Elect.	7.4%
Consumer Related	7.1%
Computer Hardware	3.9%
Communications and Media	2.9%
Biotechnology	2.4%
Other Products	2.1%

Additional Information

Name of Most Recent Fund: WI Harper Inc. Fund VI, Ltd.
Most Recent Fund Was Raised: 05/31/2005
Year Founded: 1993
Capital Under Management: $750,000,000
Current Activity Level : Actively seeking new investments
Method of Compensation: Return on invest. most important, but chg. closing fees, service fees, etc.

WICKLOW CAPITAL INC

53 W. Jackson, Suite 1204
Chicago, IL USA 60604

Type of Firm

Private Equity Firm

Additional Information

Year Founded: 2004
Current Activity Level : Actively seeking new investments

WICKS GROUP OF COMPANIES LLC

400 Park Avenue
New York, NY USA 10022
Phone: 2128382100
Fax: 2122232109
E-mail: info@wicksgroup.com
Website: www.wicksgroup.com

Other Offices

Former HQ: 405 Park Avenue, Suite 702
New York, NY USA 10022

Management and Staff

Craig Klosk, Co-Founder
Daniel Kortick, Managing Partner
Daniel Black, Managing Partner
E.J. Sloboda, Principal
Matthew Gormly, Managing Partner
Max Von Zuben, Principal
Thomas Kearney, Vice President

Type of Firm

Private Equity Firm

Association Membership

Natl Assoc of Investment Cos. (NAIC)

Project Preferences

Role in Financing:
Prefer role as deal originator

Type of Financing Preferred:
Leveraged Buyout
Management Buyouts
Acquisition

Geographical Preferences

United States Preferences:

Canadian Preferences:
All Canada

Industry Focus

(% based on actual investment)
Other Products	47.1%
Communications and Media	25.1%
Consumer Related	17.5%
Computer Software and Services	10.3%

Additional Information

Name of Most Recent Fund: Wicks Capital Partners IV, L.P.
Most Recent Fund Was Raised: 05/12/2011
Year Founded: 1989
Capital Under Management: $450,000,000
Current Activity Level : Actively seeking new investments
Method of Compensation: Return on invest. most important, but chg. closing fees, service fees, etc.

WIFLEUR, INC.

30 Saint Clair Avenue West, Suite 900
Toronto, Canada M4V 3A1
Phone: 4169272000
Fax: 4169272013

Management and Staff
David Posluns, Managing Director

Type of Firm
Corporate PE/Venture

Additional Information
Year Founded: 1995
Current Activity Level : Actively seeking new investments

WIL INC

102 University Avenue, Suite 1A
Palo Alto, CA USA 94301
E-mail: contact@wilab.co
Website: www.wilab.co

Management and Staff
Saijo Shinichi, Co-Founder
ShinSho Matsumoto, Co-Founder
Yuan Isayama, Co-Founder

Type of Firm
Private Equity Firm

Project Preferences

Type of Financing Preferred:
Startup

Geographical Preferences

United States Preferences:
Northern California

International Preferences:
Japan

Industry Preferences

In Communications prefer:
Telecommunications

In Internet Specific prefer:
Ecommerce

In Semiconductor/Electr prefer:
Electronics

In Business Serv. prefer:
Media

Additional Information
Name of Most Recent Fund: WiL Fund I, L.P.
Most Recent Fund Was Raised: 01/17/2014
Year Founded: 2013
Capital Under Management: $589,500,000
Current Activity Level : Actively seeking new investments

WILBOW GROUP PTY LTD

32-36 Camberwell Road, Suite Eight
Victoria, Australia 3123
Phone: 0398052000
Fax: 0398052020
E-mail: office@wilbow.com.au
Website: www.wilbow.com.au

Management and Staff
Michael Herskope, Chief Executive Officer

Type of Firm
Private Equity Firm

Project Preferences

Type of Financing Preferred:
Balanced

Additional Information
Year Founded: 2013
Current Activity Level : Actively seeking new investments

WILDCAT VENTURE PARTNERS LLC

3000 Sand Hill Road, Suite 3-290
Menlo Park, CA USA 94025
Phone: 6508547236
Fax: 6508547365
E-mail: Founders@wildcat.vc
Website: wildcat.vc

Management and Staff
Abhas Gupta, Principal
Brett Teele, Chief Financial Officer
Elizabeth Burstein, Principal
Geoffrey Moore, Venture Partner

Type of Firm
Private Equity Firm

Project Preferences

Type of Financing Preferred:
Early Stage

Additional Information
Year Founded: 2015
Capital Under Management: $56,500,000
Current Activity Level : Actively seeking new investments

WILL CAPITAL

Fuhua 3 Road, Futian District
1602 Int'l Shanghui Center
Shenzhen, China 518034
Phone: 8675526712071
Fax: 8675526712072
Website: www.willcapital.cn

Other Offices
No. 9 Hong Kong Middle Road
2306 Shangrila Center
Qingdao, China 266071
Phone: 8653268995888
Fax: 8653285025218

Management and Staff
Changgui Zhao, Partner
Dong Wang, Partner
Haiqing Wu, President
Yuedong Xu, Managing Director

Type of Firm
Private Equity Firm

Project Preferences

Type of Financing Preferred:
Balanced

Geographical Preferences

International Preferences:
China

Additional Information
Year Founded: 2006
Capital Under Management: $6,405,000
Current Activity Level : Actively seeking new investments

WILLCREST PARTNERS LLC

100 Spear Street, Suite 1500
San Francisco, CA USA 94105
Website: willcrest.com

Management and Staff
Benjamin Krick, Co-Founder
Bret Forster, Co-Founder

Type of Firm
Private Equity Firm

Project Preferences

Type of Financing Preferred:
Leveraged Buyout

Industry Preferences

In Medical/Health prefer:
Health Services

In Financial Services prefer:
Financial Services

In Business Serv. prefer:
Services

In Manufact. prefer:
Manufacturing

Additional Information
Year Founded: 2011
Current Activity Level : Actively seeking new investments

WILLFLY VENTURE CAPITAL

New Link Road, Andheri (West)
530, Laxmi Plaza
Mumbai, India 400053
E-mail: seed@willfly.in
Website: www.willfly.in

Type of Firm
Incubator/Development Program

Project Preferences

Type of Financing Preferred:
Early Stage
Startup

Industry Preferences

In Communications prefer:
Media and Entertainment

In Internet Specific prefer:
Internet
Ecommerce

In Consumer Related prefer:
Consumer
Education Related

Additional Information
Year Founded: 2015
Current Activity Level : Actively seeking new investments

WILLIS STEIN & PARTNERS LP

One North Wacker Drive, Suite 4800
Chicago, IL USA 60606
Phone: 3124222400
Website: www.willisstein.com

Other Offices
12 East 49th Street
27th Floor
New York, NY USA 10017
Phone: 212-994-7300
Fax: 212-994-7301

Management and Staff
Christopher Boehm, Managing Director
Jeffrey Beyer, Managing Director
Paul Mayfield, Managing Director
Philip Pool, Managing Director
R. Jason Weller, Managing Director
Robert Froetscher, Managing Director
Todd Smith, Chief Financial Officer

Type of Firm
Private Equity Firm

Project Preferences

Role in Financing:
Prefer role as deal originator

Type of Financing Preferred:
Leveraged Buyout
Acquisition

Geographical Preferences

United States Preferences:
Midwest

Industry Focus
(% based on actual investment)
Internet Specific	36.4%
Consumer Related	28.4%
Communications and Media	15.5%
Other Products	12.1%
Computer Software and Services	2.8%
Medical/Health	2.5%
Industrial/Energy	2.4%

Additional Information
Name of Most Recent Fund: Willis Stein & Partners III, L.P.
Most Recent Fund Was Raised: 07/05/2000
Year Founded: 1989
Capital Under Management: $2,983,000,000
Current Activity Level : Actively seeking new investments
Method of Compensation: Return on investment is of primary concern, do not charge fees

---

WILLOW IMPACT

Sheikh Zayed Road
The Fairmont
Dubai, Utd. Arab Em. 2504
Phone: 97143587450
Fax: 97143587460
E-mail: info@willowimpact.com
Website: www.willowimpact.com

Management and Staff
Gabriel Rabinovici, Managing Partner
Joe Kawkabani, Managing Partner
Nadine Kettaneh, Managing Partner
Nicolas Farah, Managing Partner
Pasha Bakhtiar, Managing Partner

Type of Firm
Private Equity Firm

Project Preferences

Type of Financing Preferred:
Early Stage
Expansion
Balanced
Later Stage
Seed

Geographical Preferences

International Preferences:
Middle East
Africa

Industry Preferences

In Medical/Health prefer:
Medical/Health
Health Services

In Consumer Related prefer:
Food/Beverage
Education Related

In Agr/Forestr/Fish prefer:
Agriculture related

In Other prefer:
Socially Responsible
Environment Responsible

Additional Information
Year Founded: 2010
Current Activity Level : Actively seeking new investments

WILSHIRE PRIVATE MARKETS

210 Sixth Avenue, Suite 3720
Pittsburgh, PA USA 15222
Phone: 4124341580
Fax: 4124341584

Other Offices
4th flr. East Tower, Otemachi 1st Square
1-5-1 Otemachi, Chiyoda-ku
Tokyo, Japan 100-0004
Phone: 81-3-5219-1376
Fax: 81-3-5219-1201

3 Pickering Street
#02-39, Nankin Row, China Square Central
Singapore, Singapore 048660
Phone: 65-6435-2169
Fax: 65-6538-1633

525 Washington Boulevard, Suite 2205
Jersey City, NJ USA 07310
Phone: 201-984-4899
Fax: 201-653-4102

23 Austin Friars
London, United Kingdom EC2N 2NB
Phone: 44-20-7920-3100
Fax: 44-20-7920-3101

101 East 52nd Street
20th Floor
New York, NY USA 10022
Phone: 212-308-9500
Fax: 212-308-3930

370 Interlocken Boulevard, Suite 620
Broomfield, CO USA 80021
Phone: 310-451-3051
Fax: 303-466-1537

World Trade Center
Tower H, 25th floor, Zuidplein 204
Amsterdam, Netherlands 1077 XV
Phone: 31-20-305-7530
Fax: 31-20305-7539

Level 6, AMP
1 Hobart Place
Canberra, Australia 2601
Phone: 612-6279-6000
Fax: 612-6230-5144

222 West Adams Street, Suite 1725
Chicago, IL USA 60606
Phone: 312-762-5500
Fax: 312-762-5501

1299 Ocean Avenue, Suite 700
Santa Monica, CA USA 90401
Phone: 310-451-3051
Fax: 310-

Management and Staff
Alexa Zhang, Managing Director
Alexandra Ramirez, Vice President
David Chiang, Managing Director
Grant Harrison, Managing Director
Ilona Brom, Managing Director
Kevin Nee, President
Marc Friedberg, Managing Director
Paul Rodgers, Vice President
Robyn Weiss, Vice President
Steve Choi, Vice President
William Van Eesteren, Managing Director

Type of Firm
Investment Management Firm

Association Membership
Australian Venture Capital Association (AVCAL)
Hong Kong Venture Capital Association (HKVCA)

Project Preferences

Type of Financing Preferred:
Fund of Funds
Leveraged Buyout
Generalist PE

Additional Information
Name of Most Recent Fund: Wilshire Global Private Markets Fund IX, L.P.
Most Recent Fund Was Raised: 03/05/2014
Year Founded: 1972
Capital Under Management: $6,242,200,000
Current Activity Level : Actively seeking new investments

WILSQUARE CAPITAL LLC
Three CityPlace Drive, Suite 1090
Saint Louis, MO USA 63141
Phone: 3149257650
Website: www.wilsquare.com

Management and Staff
James Wilmsen, Co-Founder
William Willhite, Co-Founder

Type of Firm
Private Equity Firm

Project Preferences

Type of Financing Preferred:
Generalist PE

Geographical Preferences

United States Preferences:
Midwest
Southeast
Southwest

Industry Preferences

In Internet Specific prefer:
Internet

In Consumer Related prefer:
Retail

In Business Serv. prefer:
Services

Additional Information
Year Founded: 2015
Capital Under Management: $37,000,000
Current Activity Level : Actively seeking new investments

WINCHESTER CAPITAL PARTNERS LLC
Winchester House
445 Orange Street
New Haven, CT USA 06511
Phone: 203-787-5029
Fax: 203-785-0018
E-mail: info@winchestercapital.com
Website: www.winchestercapital.com

Other Offices
33 St. James' Square
, United Kingdom SW1Y 4JS
Phone: 44 (0) 20 7661 93
Fax: 44 (0) 20 7661 979

Type of Firm
Bank Affiliated

Project Preferences

Type of Financing Preferred:
Early Stage
Generalist PE
Acquisition

Geographical Preferences

United States Preferences:

Canadian Preferences:
All Canada

International Preferences:
Europe

Industry Preferences

In Medical/Health prefer:
Health Services

Additional Information
Year Founded: 1986
Current Activity Level : Actively seeking new investments

WINCOVE CAPITAL
1501 Broadway
12th Floor
New York, NY USA 10036
Phone: 6465712143
Website: www.wincovecapital.com

Other Offices
708 Third Avenue
31st Floor
New York, NY USA 10017
Phone: 2123703500

Management and Staff
John Lenahan, Partner
Michael McGovern, Partner

Type of Firm
Private Equity Firm

Project Preferences

Type of Financing Preferred:
Leveraged Buyout
Management Buyouts
Acquisition
Recapitalizations

Geographical Preferences

United States Preferences:
All U.S.

Canadian Preferences:
All Canada

Industry Preferences

In Business Serv. prefer:
Services
Distribution

In Manufact. prefer:
Manufacturing

Additional Information
Year Founded: 2008
Current Activity Level : Actively seeking new investments

WIND POINT ADVISORS LLC

676 North Michigan Avenue, Suite 3700
Chicago, IL USA 60611
Phone: 3122554800
Fax: 3122554820
Website: www.windpointpartners.com

Management and Staff

Alex Washington, Managing Director
Bob Cummings, Managing Director
David Stott, Managing Director
James Tenbroek, Managing Director
Joe Lawler, Principal
Konrad Salaber, Managing Director
LeAnn Kilarski, Chief Financial Officer
Mark Burgett, Managing Director
Matt Moran, Vice President
Nathaniel Brown, Managing Director
Paul Peterson, Principal
Richard Kracum, Managing Director

Type of Firm

Private Equity Firm

Association Membership

Illinois Venture Capital Association

Project Preferences

Role in Financing:
Prefer role as deal originator but will also invest in deals created by others

Type of Financing Preferred:
Leveraged Buyout
Acquisition

Size of Investments Considered:
Min Size of Investment Considered (000s): $30,000
Max Size of Investment Considered (000s): $100,000

Geographical Preferences

United States Preferences:

Industry Focus

(% based on actual investment)
Other Products	35.4%
Consumer Related	33.2%
Medical/Health	7.5%
Internet Specific	7.5%
Communications and Media	7.1%
Industrial/Energy	6.3%
Biotechnology	1.1%
Semiconductors/Other Elect.	0.8%
Computer Hardware	0.8%
Computer Software and Services	0.4%

Additional Information
Year Founded: 1984
Capital Under Management: $2,500,000,000
Current Activity Level : Actively seeking new investments
Method of Compensation: Return on invest. most important, but chg. closing fees, service fees, etc.

WINDFORCE VENTURES LLC

317 Madison Avenue, Suite 1500
New York, NY USA 10017
Website: windforceventures.com

Management and Staff

Jason Stein, Co-Founder
Mario Montoya, President
Michoel Ogince, Co-Founder

Type of Firm

Private Equity Firm

Project Preferences

Type of Financing Preferred:
Early Stage

Industry Preferences

In Communications prefer:
Wireless Communications

In Business Serv. prefer:
Media

Additional Information
Year Founded: 2012
Current Activity Level : Actively seeking new investments

WINDHAM CAPITAL ADVISORY GROUP INC

5065 Westheimer Road
Houston, TX USA 77098
Phone: 713-622-1866
Fax: 713-993-9678
E-mail: info@windhamsecurities.com

Type of Firm

Investment Management Firm

Project Preferences

Role in Financing:
Prefer role in deals created by others

Type of Financing Preferred:
Second Stage Financing
Leveraged Buyout
Control-block Purchases

Size of Investments Considered:
Min Size of Investment Considered (000s): $1,000
Max Size of Investment Considered: No Limit

Geographical Preferences

United States Preferences:
All U.S.

Additional Information
Year Founded: 1987
Current Activity Level : Actively seeking new investments
Method of Compensation: Other

WINDHAM VENTURE PARTNERS

1325 Avenue of the Americas
27th Floor
New York, NY USA 10019
Phone: 2127638525
Fax: 9175917274
E-mail: adam@windhamventures.com
Website: www.windhamvp.com

Management and Staff

Joseph Proto, Co-Founder
Roger Fine, Co-Founder

Type of Firm

Private Equity Firm

Project Preferences

Type of Financing Preferred:
Early Stage
Balanced
Later Stage

Additional Information
Year Founded: 2010
Current Activity Level : Actively seeking new investments

WINDJAMMER CAPITAL INVESTORS LLC

610 Newport Center Drive, Suite 1100
Newport Beach, CA USA 92660
Phone: 9497219944
Fax: 9497204222
E-mail: info@windjammercapital.com
Website: www.windjammercapital.com

Other Offices

890 Winter Street, Suite 130
Waltham, MA USA 02451
Phone: 781-530-9100
Fax: 7815309200

Management and Staff
Caleb Clark, Vice President
Craig Majernik, Principal
Daniel Lee, Vice President
Gregory Bondick, Managing Director
J. Derek Watson, Managing Director
Jeff Miehe, Managing Director
Jeffery Dunnigan, Chief Financial Officer
John Donahue, Principal
Matt Anderson, Vice President

Type of Firm
Private Equity Firm

Project Preferences

Role in Financing:
Prefer role as deal originator but will also invest in deals created by others

Type of Financing Preferred:
Leveraged Buyout
Mezzanine
Management Buyouts
Acquisition
Distressed Debt
Recapitalizations

Geographical Preferences

United States Preferences:

Canadian Preferences:
All Canada

Industry Preferences

In Business Serv. prefer:
Services
Distribution

In Manufact. prefer:
Manufacturing

Additional Information
Year Founded: 1990
Capital Under Management: $2,000,000,000
Current Activity Level : Actively seeking new investments
Method of Compensation: Return on invest. most important, but chg. closing fees, service fees, etc.

WINDQUEST GROUP INC
201 Monroe Ave NorthWest
Number 500
Grand Rapids, MI USA 49503
Phone: 16164594500
E-mail: contact@windquest.com
Website: windquest.com

Type of Firm
Investment Management Firm

Project Preferences

Type of Financing Preferred:
Early Stage
Balanced
Later Stage

Industry Preferences

In Industrial/Energy prefer:
Alternative Energy
Environmental Related

In Manufact. prefer:
Manufacturing

Additional Information
Year Founded: 1988
Current Activity Level : Actively seeking new investments

WINDSAIL CAPITAL GROUP LLC
133 Federal Street, Suite 1201
Boston, MA USA 02110
Phone: 6173787971
E-mail: info@windsailcapital.com
Website: www.windsailcapital.com

Other Offices
Four Liberty Square
Second Floor
BOSTON, MA USA 02109
Phone: 6173787971
Fax: 6174236064

Type of Firm
Private Equity Firm

Project Preferences

Type of Financing Preferred:
Later Stage

Industry Preferences

In Industrial/Energy prefer:
Energy
Alternative Energy

Additional Information
Name of Most Recent Fund: WindSail Capital III LLC
Most Recent Fund Was Raised: 03/12/2013
Year Founded: 2009
Capital Under Management: $89,900,000
Current Activity Level : Actively seeking new investments

WINDSOR PRIVATE CAPITAL
28 Hazelton Avenue, Suite 200
Toronto, Canada M5R 2E2
Phone: 5152318
Fax: 5152315
Website: www.windsorgp.com

Other Offices
Five Hazelton Avenue, Suite 300
Toronto, Canada M5R 2E1
Phone: 4169726574

Management and Staff
John Cundari, Managing Director
Ron Schmeichel, Managing Director

Type of Firm
Investment Management Firm

Association Membership
Canadian Venture Capital Association

Project Preferences

Type of Financing Preferred:
Leveraged Buyout
Expansion
Management Buyouts
Acquisition
Special Situation
Recapitalizations

Industry Preferences

In Communications prefer:
Telecommunications

In Medical/Health prefer:
Health Services

In Consumer Related prefer:
Retail

In Industrial/Energy prefer:
Environmental Related

In Financial Services prefer:
Financial Services
Real Estate

In Business Serv. prefer:
Services

In Manufact. prefer:
Manufacturing

Additional Information
Year Founded: 2006
Current Activity Level : Actively seeking new investments

WINDSPEED VENTURES
52 Waltham Street
Lexington, MA USA 02421
Phone: 7818608888
Fax: 7818600493
E-mail: info@wsventures.com
Website: www.wsventures.com

Management and Staff
Bernard Haan, Partner
Daniel Bathon, General Partner
David Safaii, Principal
John Bullock, Managing Partner
Steven Karlson, General Partner

Type of Firm
Private Equity Firm

Project Preferences

Role in Financing:
Prefer role as deal originator but will also invest in deals created by others

Type of Financing Preferred:
Early Stage

Size of Investments Considered:
Min Size of Investment Considered (000s): $1,000
Max Size of Investment Considered (000s): $5,000

Geographical Preferences

United States Preferences:
Northeast

Industry Preferences

In Communications prefer:
Communications and Media

In Computer Software prefer:
Software
Systems Software

In Internet Specific prefer:
Internet

In Business Serv. prefer:
Services
Media

Additional Information
Year Founded: 1999
Capital Under Management: $176,000,000
Current Activity Level : Actively seeking new investments
Method of Compensation: Return on investment is of primary concern, do not charge fees

WINDWARD VENTURES

530 B Street, Suite 700
San Diego, CA USA 92101
Phone: 6194355600
E-mail: mailbox@windwardventures.com

Management and Staff
James Cole, Managing Director
M. David Titus, Managing Director
Renee Masi, Partner

Type of Firm
Private Equity Firm

Project Preferences

Role in Financing:
Will function either as deal originator or investor in deals created by others

Type of Financing Preferred:
Early Stage

Geographical Preferences

United States Preferences:
Southern California

Industry Focus
(% based on actual investment)
Medical/Health	45.2%
Computer Software and Services	22.5%
Internet Specific	11.1%
Computer Hardware	9.4%
Communications and Media	9.4%
Semiconductors/Other Elect.	1.9%
Other Products	0.5%

Additional Information
Name of Most Recent Fund: Windward Ventures 2000, L.P.
Most Recent Fund Was Raised: 04/20/2000
Year Founded: 1997
Capital Under Management: $100,000,000
Current Activity Level : Actively seeking new investments
Method of Compensation: Return on investment is of primary concern, do not charge fees

WING CAPITAL GROUP LLC

780 North Water Street
Milwaukee, WI USA 53202
Phone: 2623756401
Website: www.wingcapitalgroup.com

Type of Firm
Private Equity Firm

Project Preferences

Type of Financing Preferred:
Leveraged Buyout
Management Buyouts

Geographical Preferences

United States Preferences:
Midwest

Industry Preferences

In Business Serv. prefer:
Services
Distribution

In Manufact. prefer:
Manufacturing

Additional Information
Year Founded: 2008
Current Activity Level : Actively seeking new investments

WING EQUITY MANAGEMENT

Thomas-Klestil-Platz 3
TownTown
Vienna, Austria 1030
Phone: 43171690
Fax: 4317169020
E-mail: office@soravia.at
Website: www.soravia.at

Management and Staff
Erwin Soravia, Co-Founder
Hanno Soravia, Co-Founder

Type of Firm
Private Equity Firm

Project Preferences

Type of Financing Preferred:
Core
Leveraged Buyout
Early Stage
Balanced
Later Stage
Acquisition

Geographical Preferences

International Preferences:
Slovak Repub.
Europe
Macedonia
Austria
Bulgaria
Romania
Latvia

Industry Preferences

In Communications prefer:
Entertainment

In Medical/Health prefer:
Medical/Health
Health Services
Pharmaceuticals

In Consumer Related prefer:
Consumer
Retail
Food/Beverage

In Industrial/Energy prefer:
Industrial Products
Materials
Machinery
Environmental Related

In Financial Services prefer:
Real Estate
Financial Services

In Business Serv. prefer:
Services

In Manufact. prefer:
Manufacturing

Additional Information
Year Founded: 1989
Current Activity Level : Actively seeking new investments

WING VENTURE CAPITAL

2061 Avy Avenue
Second Floor
Menlo Park, CA USA 94025
Phone: 6503168300
E-mail: info@wing.vc
Website: www.wing.vc

Management and Staff
Hilary Strain, Chief Financial Officer
Jay Kidd, Partner
Jeff Schneble, Partner
Martin Giles, Partner

Type of Firm
Private Equity Firm

Association Membership
National Venture Capital Association - USA (NVCA)

Project Preferences

Type of Financing Preferred:
Early Stage

Size of Investments Considered:
Min Size of Investment Considered (000s): $8,000
Max Size of Investment Considered (000s): $10,000

Industry Preferences

In Communications prefer:
Wireless Communications

In Computer Software prefer:
Data Processing

In Internet Specific prefer:
Internet

Additional Information
Name of Most Recent Fund: Wing Venture Partners, L.P.
Most Recent Fund Was Raised: 07/03/2013
Year Founded: 2013
Capital Under Management: $361,000,000
Current Activity Level : Actively seeking new investments

WINGATE PARTNERS LP

750 North St. Paul Street, Suite 1200
Dallas, TX USA 75201
Phone: 2147201313
Fax: 2148718799

Website: www.wingatepartners.com

Other Offices
950 Echo Lane, Suite 335
Houston, TX USA 77024
Phone: 7139737722
Fax: 7139738237

750 North St. Paul, Suite 1200
Dallas, TX USA

Management and Staff
Bradley Brenneman, Principal
Brian Steinbrueck, Vice President
James Johnson, Principal
Jason Reed, Principal
Jay Applebaum, Principal
Michael Decker, Principal

Type of Firm
Private Equity Firm

Project Preferences

Role in Financing:
Prefer role as deal originator but will also invest in deals created by others

Type of Financing Preferred:
Leveraged Buyout
Turnaround
Management Buyouts
Acquisition
Recapitalizations

Geographical Preferences

United States Preferences:

Industry Preferences

In Business Serv. prefer:
Services
Distribution

In Manufact. prefer:
Manufacturing

Additional Information
Name of Most Recent Fund: Wingate Partners V, L.P.
Most Recent Fund Was Raised: 07/31/2013
Year Founded: 1987
Capital Under Management: $500,000,000
Current Activity Level : Actively seeking new investments
Method of Compensation: Return on invest. most important, but chg. closing fees, service fees, etc.

WINGEFORS INVEST AB

Alvgatan 1
Karlstad, Sweden 652 25
Phone: 46702299073
E-mail: info@wingeforsinvest.se
Website: www.wingeforsinvest.se

Management and Staff
Per Fredriksson, Managing Director

Type of Firm
Private Equity Firm

Association Membership
Swedish Venture Capital Association (SVCA)

Project Preferences

Type of Financing Preferred:
Leveraged Buyout
Generalist PE
Later Stage
Acquisition
Startup

Geographical Preferences

International Preferences:
Sweden

Industry Preferences

In Computer Software prefer:
Software

In Internet Specific prefer:
Ecommerce

In Biotechnology prefer:
Biotechnology

In Consumer Related prefer:
Consumer Services

In Business Serv. prefer:
Services

In Manufact. prefer:
Publishing

Additional Information
Year Founded: 2009
Capital Under Management: $4,200,000
Current Activity Level : Actively seeking new investments

WINNEBAGO CAPITAL PARTNERS

124 West Wisconsin Avenue, Suite 240F
Neenah, WI USA 54956
Website: www.winnebagoseedfund.com

Type of Firm
Private Equity Firm

Project Preferences

Type of Financing Preferred:
Seed

Additional Information
Year Founded: 2017
Capital Under Management: $11,000,000
Current Activity Level : Actively seeking new investments

WINONA CAPITAL MANAGEMENT LLC

980 North Michigan Avenue, Suite 1950
Chicago, IL USA 60611
Phone: 3123348800
Fax: 3122239484
E-mail: info@winonacapital.com
Website: www.winonacapital.com

Other Offices

801 Second Avenue, Suite 1300
Seattle, WA USA 98104
Phone: 206-464-3855
Fax: 206-464-5250

Management and Staff

Dan Kipp, Managing Director
Jason Sowers, Partner
Jason Starr, Vice President
John McBlain, Chief Financial Officer
Laird Koldyke, Managing Director
Luke Reese, Managing Director

Type of Firm

Private Equity Firm

Association Membership

Illinois Venture Capital Association

Project Preferences

Type of Financing Preferred:
Management Buyouts

Size of Investments Considered:
Min Size of Investment Considered (000s): $5,000
Max Size of Investment Considered (000s): $15,000

Industry Preferences

In Consumer Related prefer:
Entertainment and Leisure
Sports
Consumer Products
Consumer Services
Education Related

In Business Serv. prefer:
Distribution

In Manufact. prefer:
Manufacturing

Additional Information

Name of Most Recent Fund: Winona Capital Partners II, L.P.
Most Recent Fund Was Raised: 04/19/2013
Year Founded: 2005
Capital Under Management: $165,285,000
Current Activity Level : Actively seeking new investments

WINTHROP VENTURES

74 Trinity Place, Suite 600
New York, NY USA 10023
Phone: 212-422-0100

Management and Staff

Cyrus Brown, President

Type of Firm

Bank Affiliated

Project Preferences

Role in Financing:
Prefer role as deal originator

Type of Financing Preferred:
Second Stage Financing
Leveraged Buyout
Start-up Financing
First Stage Financing

Size of Investments Considered:
Min Size of Investment Considered (000s): $1,000
Max Size of Investment Considered: No Limit

Industry Preferences

In Communications prefer:
Commercial Communications
CATV & Pay TV Systems
Telecommunications
Data Communications
Satellite Microwave Comm.
Other Communication Prod.

In Computer Hardware prefer:
Computers
Computer Graphics and Dig
Integrated Turnkey System
Terminals
Disk Relat. Memory Device

In Computer Software prefer:
Computer Services
Systems Software
Applications Software

In Semiconductor/Electr prefer:
Electronics
Electronic Components
Semiconductor
Laser Related
Analytic/Scientific

In Biotechnology prefer:
Industrial Biotechnology
Biosensors
Biotech Related Research

In Medical/Health prefer:
Medical Diagnostics
Diagnostic Test Products
Drug/Equipmt Delivery
Other Therapeutic
Medical Products
Disposable Med. Products
Hospitals/Clinics/Primary
Hospital/Other Instit.
Pharmaceuticals

In Consumer Related prefer:
Entertainment and Leisure
Retail
Computer Stores
Food/Beverage
Consumer Products
Consumer Services
Education Related

In Industrial/Energy prefer:
Alternative Energy
Energy Conservation Relat
Industrial Products

In Transportation prefer:
Transportation

In Financial Services prefer:
Financial Services

In Manufact. prefer:
Office Automation Equipmt
Publishing

Additional Information

Year Founded: 1972
Current Activity Level : Actively seeking new investments
Method of Compensation: Return on invest. most important, but chg. closing fees, service fees, etc.

WINTON VENTURES LTD

27 Hammersmith Grove
Grove House
London, United Kingdom W6 0NE
Phone: 4402085765
Website: www.wintoncapital.com/winton-ventures/

Management and Staff

Raj Patel, Chief Operating Officer

Type of Firm

Incubator/Development Program

Project Preferences

Type of Financing Preferred:
Early Stage

Industry Preferences

In Computer Software prefer:
Data Processing
Software

WINVEST CAPITAL FOR DEVELOPMENT AND INVESTMENT SAE

5 Pharmacists buildings
Smouha
Alexandria, Egypt
Phone: 2034243007
Fax: 2034282642
E-mail: contact@winvest-capital.com
Website: winvest-capital.com

Type of Firm
Private Equity Firm

Project Preferences

Type of Financing Preferred:
Early Stage
Expansion
Balanced
Later Stage
Seed

Additional Information
Year Founded: 2012
Current Activity Level: Actively seeking new investments

WINVEST VENTURE PARTNERS INC

7F, Yoongjeon Building
154-10 Samsung-Dong Gangnam-Gu
Seoul, South Korea
Phone: 8225653626
Fax: 8225653484

Management and Staff
Taeksu Lee, President

Type of Firm
Private Equity Firm

Association Membership
Korean Venture Capital Association (KVCA)

Project Preferences

Type of Financing Preferred:
Balanced

Geographical Preferences

International Preferences:
Korea, South

Additional Information
Year Founded: 2000
Capital Under Management: $7,000,000
Current Activity Level: Actively seeking new investments

WIREFRAME VENTURES

35 Miller Avenue, Suite 308
Mill Valley, CA USA 94941
Website: www.wireframevc.com

Type of Firm
Private Equity Firm

Project Preferences

Type of Financing Preferred:
Early Stage

Additional Information
Year Founded: 2016
Capital Under Management: $27,500,000
Current Activity Level: Actively seeking new investments

WISC PARTNERS LP

1714 McCarthy Boulevard
Milpitas, CA USA 95035
Website: wiscpartners.com

Other Offices
401 Charmany Drive, Suite 310
Madison, WI USA 53719

Management and Staff
David Guinther, General Partner
Michael Splinter, General Partner
Sanjeev Chitre, General Partner

Type of Firm
Private Equity Firm

Project Preferences

Type of Financing Preferred:
Early Stage

Geographical Preferences

United States Preferences:
Wisconsin

Additional Information
Year Founded: 2014
Capital Under Management: $1,000,000
Current Activity Level: Actively seeking new investments

WISDOM CAPITAL GROUP

47th Floor, The Center
99 Queen's Road
Central, Hong Kong
Phone: 852-2312-7696
Fax: 852-2312-1515
E-mail: info@wisdomcapital.net
Website: www.wisdomcapital.com

Type of Firm
Private Equity Firm

Project Preferences

Type of Financing Preferred:
Balanced

Geographical Preferences

International Preferences:
China

Industry Preferences

In Computer Software prefer:
Data Processing

In Biotechnology prefer:
Biotechnology

In Consumer Related prefer:
Education Related

In Industrial/Energy prefer:
Energy

In Financial Services prefer:
Real Estate

Additional Information
Year Founded: 2005
Current Activity Level: Actively seeking new investments

WISE VENTURE SGR SPA

Foro Buonaparte 76
Milan, Italy 20121
Phone: 39028545691
Fax: 390280509485
E-mail: info@wisesgr.it
Website: www.wisesgr.it

Management and Staff
Fabrizio Medea, Partner
Michele Semenzato, Partner
Paolo Gambarini, Partner
Roberto Saviane, Partner
Stefano Ghetti, Partner
Valentina Franceschini, Partner

Type of Firm
Private Equity Firm

Association Membership
European Private Equity and Venture Capital Assoc.

Project Preferences

Type of Financing Preferred:
Leveraged Buyout
Generalist PE
Later Stage

Geographical Preferences

United States Preferences:

International Preferences:
Italy
Europe

Industry Preferences

In Communications prefer:
Telecommunications
Wireless Communications

In Computer Software prefer:
Software

In Internet Specific prefer:
Internet

In Industrial/Energy prefer:
Industrial Products
Machinery

In Business Serv. prefer:
Media

Additional Information
Year Founded: 2000
Capital Under Management: $393,500,000
Current Activity Level : Actively seeking new investments

WISEMONT CAPITAL

11639 91st Lane NE
#12
Kirkland, WA USA 98034
Phone: 8666507561
E-mail: info@wisemontcapital.com
Website: www.wisemontcapital.com

Type of Firm
Private Equity Firm

Project Preferences

Type of Financing Preferred:
Early Stage

Industry Preferences

In Communications prefer:
Wireless Communications

In Computer Software prefer:
Software

Additional Information
Year Founded: 2015
Capital Under Management: $750,000
Current Activity Level : Actively seeking new investments

WIT INVESTMENT PARTNERS LTD

No.169 Jen-Ai Road
16th Floor, Section 4
Taipei, Taiwan
Phone: 886-2-2711-3401
Fax: 886-2-2711-3403
E-mail: witip@mail.sysnet.net.tw

Management and Staff
C. H. Hsiao, President

Type of Firm
Private Equity Firm

Association Membership
Taiwan Venture Capital Association(TVCA)

Project Preferences

Type of Financing Preferred:
Expansion
Mezzanine
Balanced
Seed
Startup

Geographical Preferences

International Preferences:
Taiwan

Industry Preferences

In Communications prefer:
Telecommunications

In Semiconductor/Electr prefer:
Electronics
Semiconductor

Additional Information
Year Founded: 1997
Capital Under Management: $15,600,000
Current Activity Level : Actively seeking new investments

WITHFOUNDERS SRL

Via del Bosco Renovated
Assago - Milanofiori Nord
Milan, Italy
E-mail: amministrazione@italiaonline.it
Website: www.withfounders.it

Type of Firm
Private Equity Firm

Additional Information
Year Founded: 2014
Current Activity Level : Actively seeking new investments

WKBG WIENER KREDIT-BUERGSCHAFTS UND BETEILIGUNGSBANK AG

Ungargasse 64-66
Top 501
Vienna, Austria 1030
Phone: 43-1-712-5259
Fax: 43-1-712-525928
Website: wkbg.at

Management and Staff
Christoph Schneider, CEO & Managing Director
Johann Szalony, CEO & Managing Director

Type of Firm
Incubator/Development Program

Project Preferences

Type of Financing Preferred:
Early Stage
Balanced
Later Stage

Size of Investments Considered:
Min Size of Investment Considered (000s): $135
Max Size of Investment Considered (000s): $675

Geographical Preferences

International Preferences:
Austria

Industry Preferences

In Communications prefer:
Telecommunications
Entertainment

In Consumer Related prefer:
Retail
Consumer Services

In Industrial/Energy prefer:
Energy
Industrial Products

In Transportation prefer:
Transportation

Additional Information
Year Founded: 1997
Capital Under Management: $11,700,000
Current Activity Level : Actively seeking new investments

WL ROSS & CO LLC

1166 Avenue of the Americas
27th Floor
New York, NY USA 10036
Phone: 2128261100
Fax: 2124033578

Management and Staff
David Shirreffs, Managing Director
David Wax, Managing Director
Denny Kim, Vice President
Greg Stoeckle, Senior Managing Director
Harvey Tepner, Principal
Israel Wallach, Managing Director
Jie Zheng, Vice President
Josh Seegopaul, Principal
Michael Gibbons, Chief Financial Officer
Pamela Wilson, Managing Director
Shaia Hosseinzadeh, Principal
Stephen Toy, Senior Managing Director
Wendy Teramoto, Managing Director
William Morton, Vice President

Type of Firm
Private Equity Firm

Project Preferences
Type of Financing Preferred:
Leveraged Buyout
Turnaround
Acquisition
Special Situation
Distressed Debt

Geographical Preferences
United States Preferences:
North America

International Preferences:
Latin America
India
Europe
China
Thailand
Asia
Korea, South
Japan

Industry Focus
(% based on actual investment)
Other Products   75.9%
Industrial/Energy   24.1%

Additional Information
Name of Most Recent Fund: WLR Recovery Fund V, L.P.
Most Recent Fund Was Raised: 08/12/2011
Year Founded: 1976
Capital Under Management: $2,657,675,000
Current Activity Level : Actively seeking new investments

WM PARTNERS LP
1815 Griffin Road, Suite 404
Dania, FL USA 33004
Phone: 7542606500
Fax: 7542606505
E-mail: info@wmplp.com
Website: wmplp.com

Type of Firm
Private Equity Firm

Project Preferences
Type of Financing Preferred:
Leveraged Buyout
Acquisition

Geographical Preferences
United States Preferences:
North America

International Preferences:
Europe

Industry Preferences
In Medical/Health prefer:
Health Services

Additional Information
Year Founded: 2016
Capital Under Management: $307,000,000
Current Activity Level : Actively seeking new investments

WMAS MANAGEMENT GROUP
2061 Avy Avenue
First Floor
Menlo Park, CA USA 94025
Website: www.wmasgroup.com

Type of Firm
Private Equity Firm

Project Preferences
Type of Financing Preferred:
Early Stage
Expansion
Startup

Industry Preferences
In Communications prefer:
Media and Entertainment

In Medical/Health prefer:
Medical/Health

In Consumer Related prefer:
Education Related

In Industrial/Energy prefer:
Environmental Related

In Financial Services prefer:
Real Estate

In Agr/Forestr/Fish prefer:
Agribusiness

Additional Information
Year Founded: 2000
Current Activity Level : Actively seeking new investments

WOLF CAPITAL VENTURES
2108 Sand Hill Road
Menlo Park, CA USA 94025
Website: www.wolfcapitalventures.com

Type of Firm
Private Equity Firm

Project Preferences
Type of Financing Preferred:
Startup

Additional Information
Year Founded: 2016
Current Activity Level : Actively seeking new investments

WOLFENSOHN & COMPANY LLC
1350 Avenue of the Americas
29th Floor
New York, NY USA 10019
Phone: 2129740111
E-mail: info@wolfensohn.com
Website: www.wolfensohn.com

Other Offices
One Mansingh Road, Suite 1001, The Taj Mahal Hotel
New Delhi, India 110011
Phone: 911166135501

Four Saint James's Place
London, United Kingdom SWIA INP
Phone: 442076599601

Management and Staff
Adam Wolfensohn, Managing Director
Ameya Bijoor, Principal
Asad Naqvi, Principal
Beverly Roberts, Chief Financial Officer
Cesare Calari, Managing Director
Diana Taylor, Managing Director
Jonathan Morris, Managing Director
Naomi Wolfensohn, Managing Director
Sanjiv Kapur, Managing Director
Tony Lent, Senior Managing Director

Type of Firm
Private Equity Firm

Association Membership
Emerging Markets Private Equity Association

Pratt's Guide to Private Equity & Venture Capital Sources

Project Preferences

Type of Financing Preferred:
Leveraged Buyout
Later Stage
Other
Acquisition

Geographical Preferences

United States Preferences:

International Preferences:
India
Poland
Brazil

Industry Preferences

In Industrial/Energy prefer:
Energy

In Financial Services prefer:
Financial Services

In Business Serv. prefer:
Consulting Services

Additional Information
Year Founded: 2005
Current Activity Level : Actively seeking new investments

WOLSELEY PRIVATE EQUITY

2 Bulletin Place
Level 4
Sydney, Australia 2000
Phone: 61288154200
Fax: 61288154201
E-mail: info@wolseley.com.au
Website: www.wolseley.com.au

Management and Staff
Alan Lee, Chief Financial Officer
Andrew Petering, Managing Director
James Todd, Co-Founder
Mark Richardson, Co-Founder

Type of Firm
Private Equity Firm

Association Membership
Australian Venture Capital Association (AVCAL)

Project Preferences

Role in Financing:
Prefer role as deal originator but will also invest in deals created by others

Type of Financing Preferred:
Leveraged Buyout
Expansion
Generalist PE
Management Buyouts
Acquisition

Geographical Preferences

International Preferences:
Australia
New Zealand

Industry Preferences

In Business Serv. prefer:
Services
Distribution

In Manufact. prefer:
Manufacturing

Additional Information
Name of Most Recent Fund: Wolseley Partners Fund II, L.P.
Most Recent Fund Was Raised: 12/17/2007
Year Founded: 1999
Capital Under Management: $357,600,000
Current Activity Level : Actively seeking new investments
Method of Compensation: Return on investment is of primary concern, do not charge fees

WOMEN'S VENTURE CAPITAL FUND

311 NW 12th Avenue, Suite 1003
Portland, OR USA 97209
Phone: 5032275748
Website: www.womensvcfund.com

Other Offices
1030 University Avenue
PALO ALTO, CA USA 94301
Phone: 6503296884

Management and Staff
Marie Jorajuria, Chief Financial Officer

Type of Firm
Private Equity Firm

Project Preferences

Type of Financing Preferred:
Early Stage

Industry Preferences

In Communications prefer:
Telecommunications
Media and Entertainment

In Computer Software prefer:
Software

In Consumer Related prefer:
Entertainment and Leisure
Consumer Products

In Business Serv. prefer:
Services

Additional Information
Year Founded: 2011
Current Activity Level : Actively seeking new investments

WONDER ANGELS

Daechi-dong Gangnam-ku
6F 996-17
Seoul, South Korea
Phone: 82234521300
Fax: 82234526900

Management and Staff
Hur Min, Chief Executive Officer

Type of Firm
Private Equity Firm

Project Preferences

Type of Financing Preferred:
Balanced

Industry Preferences

In Internet Specific prefer:
Internet

In Consumer Related prefer:
Entertainment and Leisure

Additional Information
Year Founded: 2011
Capital Under Management: $6,690,000
Current Activity Level : Actively seeking new investments

WONDER VENTURES

5th & Santa Monica Blvd
Santa Monica, CA USA 90401
Website: www.wondervc.com

Type of Firm
Private Equity Firm

Project Preferences

Type of Financing Preferred:
Early Stage

Additional Information
Year Founded: 2014
Current Activity Level : Actively seeking new investments

WONIK INVESTMENT PARTNERS

1329-7 Seocho-dong, Seocho-gu
4F Shindeok Bldg
Seoul, South Korea 137070
Phone: 82264467125
Fax: 82264467199
Website: www.wiipco.com

Pratt's Guide to Private Equity & Venture Capital Sources

Management and Staff
Dong Su Kim, Managing Director
Gi Jin Lee, Partner
Hyeong Wu Lee, Partner
Jun Min Kim, Partner
Seong Il Choi, Partner
Su Beom Lee, Vice President
Yong Sung Lee, Chief Executive Officer

Type of Firm
Corporate PE/Venture

Association Membership
Korean Venture Capital Association (KVCA)

Project Preferences

Type of Financing Preferred:
Fund of Funds
Early Stage
Expansion
Balanced

Geographical Preferences

International Preferences:
Asia
Korea, South

Industry Preferences

In Semiconductor/Electr prefer:
Electronics

In Biotechnology prefer:
Biotechnology
Agricultural/Animal Bio.

In Business Serv. prefer:
Services

In Manufact. prefer:
Manufacturing

Additional Information
Year Founded: 1997
Capital Under Management: $39,800,000
Current Activity Level : Actively seeking new investments

WOODBOURNE CANADA PARTNERS ADVISORS LLC

1919 14th Street, Suite 300
Boulder, CO USA 80302

Type of Firm
Private Equity Firm

Project Preferences

Type of Financing Preferred:
Balanced

Additional Information
Year Founded: 2007
Capital Under Management: $41,600,000
Current Activity Level : Actively seeking new investments

WOODBROOK CAPITAL INC

501 Fairmount Avenue, Suite 300
Towson, MD USA 21286
Phone: 4107696131
Fax: 4103214468
Website: www.woodbrookcapital.com

Management and Staff
Earl Linehan, President

Type of Firm
Private Equity Advisor or Fund of Funds

Project Preferences

Role in Financing:
Prefer role as deal originator but will also invest in deals created by others

Type of Financing Preferred:
Expansion
Generalist PE
Management Buyouts
Acquisition
Recapitalizations

Geographical Preferences

United States Preferences:
Mid Atlantic

Industry Preferences

In Medical/Health prefer:
Health Services

In Industrial/Energy prefer:
Materials

In Financial Services prefer:
Real Estate

Additional Information
Year Founded: 1988
Current Activity Level : Actively seeking new investments
Method of Compensation: Return on invest. most important, but chg. closing fees, service fees, etc.

WOODSIDE FUND

303 Twin Dolphin Drive, Suite 600
Redwood City, CA USA 94065
Phone: 6506108050
Fax: 6506108051
E-mail: info@woodsidefund.com
Website: www.woodsidefund.com

Management and Staff
Gary Tyrrell, Chief Financial Officer
John Occhipinti, Managing Director
Mark Hoover, Venture Partner
Rick Shriner, Venture Partner
Robert Larson, Co-Founder
Vincent Occhipinti, Co-Founder

Type of Firm
Private Equity Firm

Project Preferences

Role in Financing:
Prefer role as deal originator but will also invest in deals created by others

Type of Financing Preferred:
Early Stage
Later Stage
Seed
Startup

Size of Investments Considered:
Min Size of Investment Considered (000s): $5,000
Max Size of Investment Considered (000s): $10,000

Geographical Preferences

United States Preferences:
West Coast

Industry Focus
(% based on actual investment)

Semiconductors/Other Elect.	21.1%
Communications and Media	21.0%
Computer Software and Services	18.8%
Biotechnology	14.9%
Computer Hardware	10.9%
Internet Specific	9.2%
Industrial/Energy	1.5%
Other Products	1.4%
Consumer Related	1.0%
Medical/Health	0.3%

Additional Information
Year Founded: 1983
Capital Under Management: $209,200,000
Current Activity Level : Actively seeking new investments
Method of Compensation: Return on investment is of primary concern, do not charge fees

WOODSIDE O BRIEN LLC

819 Seventh Street North West
Washington, DC USA 20001
E-mail: info@woodsideobrien.com
Website: www.woodsideobrien.com

Type of Firm
Private Equity Firm

Project Preferences

Type of Financing Preferred:
Balanced

Additional Information
Year Founded: 1969
Current Activity Level : Actively seeking new investments

WOORI BANK
606-1 Daechi-dong Kangnam
4/F Daehung Bldg.
Seoul, South Korea 135 280
Phone: 822-768-8000
Fax: 822-768-8059
Website: www.wooribank.com

Management and Staff
Kim Jong-wook, Vice President
Lee Duk-hoon, President
Min Jong-ku, Managing Director

Type of Firm
Bank Affiliated

Project Preferences
Type of Financing Preferred:
Leveraged Buyout
Turnaround
Management Buyouts
Recapitalizations

Geographical Preferences
International Preferences:
Asia
Korea, South

Additional Information
Year Founded: 1899
Current Activity Level : Actively seeking new investments

WOORI TECHNOLOGY INVESTMENT CO LTD
14F, Hongwoo Building
945-1 Daechi-dong Gangnam-ku
Seoul, South Korea 305348
Phone: 822-2008-3100
Fax: 822-2008-3123
Website: www.wooricapital.com

Other Offices
59-4 Hwaam-dong
Yusung-gu
Taejeon, South Korea
Phone: 8242-861-1540

Type of Firm
Corporate PE/Venture

Association Membership
Korean Venture Capital Association (KVCA)

Project Preferences
Type of Financing Preferred:
Early Stage
Expansion
Balanced
Later Stage

Geographical Preferences
International Preferences:
Korea, South

Industry Preferences
In Communications prefer:
Telecommunications

In Computer Software prefer:
Software

In Internet Specific prefer:
Internet

In Semiconductor/Electr prefer:
Electronics
Semiconductor

In Biotechnology prefer:
Biotechnology

In Medical/Health prefer:
Medical/Health

Additional Information
Year Founded: 1996
Capital Under Management: $12,000,000
Current Activity Level : Actively seeking new investments

WOOSHIN VENTURE INVESTMENT CORP
726 Yeoksam-dong
15/F Asia Tower, Kangnam-ku
Seoul, South Korea 135080
Phone: 8225385906
Fax: 8225673184
Website: www.wooshinvc.com

Type of Firm
Corporate PE/Venture

Association Membership
Korean Venture Capital Association (KVCA)

Project Preferences
Role in Financing:
Prefer role as deal originator

Type of Financing Preferred:
Early Stage
Expansion
Balanced

Size of Investments Considered:
Min Size of Investment Considered (000s): $500
Max Size of Investment Considered (000s): $5,000

Geographical Preferences
International Preferences:
Korea, South

Industry Preferences
In Communications prefer:
CATV & Pay TV Systems
Data Communications
Satellite Microwave Comm.

In Computer Other prefer:
Computer Related

In Semiconductor/Electr prefer:
Electronic Components

In Biotechnology prefer:
Biotechnology

In Medical/Health prefer:
Medical/Health

In Consumer Related prefer:
Consumer Products

In Industrial/Energy prefer:
Industrial Products

Additional Information
Year Founded: 1986
Capital Under Management: $1,200,000
Current Activity Level : Making few, if any, new investments
Method of Compensation: Return on investment is of primary concern, do not charge fees

WORK-BENCH
110 Fifth Avenue
Fifth Floor
New York, NY USA 10011
Phone: 646494-6231
Website: www.work-bench.com

Type of Firm
Incubator/Development Program

Project Preferences
Type of Financing Preferred:
Early Stage
Startup

Geographical Preferences
United States Preferences:
North America

Additional Information
Year Founded: 2012
Capital Under Management: $10,000,000
Current Activity Level : Actively seeking new investments

WORKS CAPITAL INC

1-9-1 Marunouchi, Chiyoda-ku
10F TokyoMarunouchi Chuo Bldg.
Tokyo, Japan 100-0005
Phone: 81-3-3538-4310

Management and Staff

Hiroshi Ikegaya, Partner
Kenji Suzuki, Partner

Type of Firm

Private Equity Firm

Project Preferences

Type of Financing Preferred:
Balanced

Geographical Preferences

International Preferences:
Japan

Industry Preferences

In Computer Other prefer:
Computer Related

In Semiconductor/Electr prefer:
Semiconductor

Additional Information

Year Founded: 2000
Current Activity Level : Actively seeking new investments

WORLD INVESTMENTS INC

World Herald Square
Omaha, NE USA 68102
Phone: 402-444-1480
Fax: 402-444-1355

Management and Staff

Duane Polodna, President

Type of Firm

Bank Affiliated

Project Preferences

Role in Financing:
Prefer role as deal originator but will also invest in deals created by others

Type of Financing Preferred:
Early Stage
Expansion
Balanced

Geographical Preferences

United States Preferences:
Midwest

Industry Preferences

In Communications prefer:
Communications and Media
Other Communication Prod.

In Computer Hardware prefer:
Computers

In Computer Other prefer:
Computer Related

In Semiconductor/Electr prefer:
Semiconductor
Component Testing Equipmt
Laser Related
Fiber Optics

In Medical/Health prefer:
Diagnostic Services

In Industrial/Energy prefer:
Robotics

In Manufact. prefer:
Publishing

Additional Information

Year Founded: 1987
Capital Under Management: $2,500,000
Current Activity Level : Actively seeking new investments
Method of Compensation: Return on investment is of primary concern, do not charge fees

WORLDQUANT VENTURES LLC

1700 East Putnam Avenue
Third Floor
Old Greenwich, CT USA 06870
Phone: 2033446350
Fax: 2033446850
E-mail: info@worldquantventures.com
Website: worldquantventures.com

Management and Staff

Jonathan Marom, Chief Financial Officer
Mark Danchak, Managing Director
Michael Deaddio, Chief Operating Officer

Type of Firm

Private Equity Firm

Project Preferences

Type of Financing Preferred:
Early Stage

Additional Information

Year Founded: 2016
Current Activity Level : Actively seeking new investments

WORLDVIEW TECHNOLOGY PARTNERS, INC.

101 South Ellsworth Avenue, Suite 401
San Mateo, CA USA 94401
Phone: 6503223800
Fax: 6503223880
Website: www.worldview.com

Other Offices

1-51-1, Hatsidai, Shibuya-ku
6F, Hatsudai Center Building
Tokyo, Japan 151-0061
Phone: 81353507888
Fax: 81353507889

Former HQ: 2207 Bridgepointe Parkway, Suite 100
Foster City, CA USA 94404

Management and Staff

James Strawbridge, Chief Operating Officer
James Wei, General Partner
Michael Orsak, General Partner
Peter Goettner, General Partner
Susumu Tanaka, General Partner
Yasuharu Watanabe, Partner

Type of Firm

Private Equity Firm

Association Membership

Western Association of Venture Capitalists (WAVC)

Project Preferences

Role in Financing:
Prefer role as deal originator but will also invest in deals created by others

Type of Financing Preferred:
Early Stage
Expansion
Balanced
Later Stage
Seed
Startup

Geographical Preferences

United States Preferences:

Industry Focus

(% based on actual investment)

Communications and Media	33.3%
Internet Specific	25.3%
Semiconductors/Other Elect.	21.2%
Computer Software and Services	12.3%
Computer Hardware	3.8%
Other Products	3.1%
Industrial/Energy	1.0%

Additional Information

Name of Most Recent Fund: Worldview Strategic Partners IV, L.P.
Most Recent Fund Was Raised: 06/20/2001
Year Founded: 1996
Capital Under Management: $1,400,000,000
Current Activity Level : Actively seeking new investments
Method of Compensation: Return on investment is of primary concern, do not charge fees

WP GLOBAL PARTNERS INC

155 North Wacker Drive, Suite 4400
Chicago, IL USA 60606
Phone: 3122771300
Fax: 3122772011
Website: www.wpglobalpartners.com

Other Offices

Bilker Strasse 29
Dusseldorf, Germany 40213
Phone: 4921187594701
Fax: 4921187594705

350 West Colorado Boulevard, Suite 215
Pasadena, CA USA 91105
Phone: 310-918-3346
Fax: 626-578-5710

590 Madison Avenue
Eighth Floor
New York, NY USA 10022
Phone: 212-558-2300
Fax: 212-558-2098

Management and Staff

Brady Hyde, Vice President
Carsten Schmeding, Managing Director
Celia Chapman, Senior Managing Director
Gregory Oberholtzer, Senior Managing Director
Gregory Jania, Managing Director
Kumber Husain, Vice President
Ryan Phillips, Vice President
Sharon Murphy, Chief Financial Officer
Tom Boudakian, Partner
Tom Thompson, Senior Managing Director
 Berry, Managing Director

Type of Firm

Private Equity Advisor or Fund of Funds

Association Membership

Illinois Venture Capital Association

Project Preferences

Type of Financing Preferred:
Fund of Funds
Leveraged Buyout
Balanced
Acquisition
Special Situation

Geographical Preferences

United States Preferences:
All U.S.

Additional Information

Name of Most Recent Fund: COREalpha Private Equity Partners Partnership Fund IV, L.P.
Most Recent Fund Was Raised: 07/27/2013
Year Founded: 2005
Capital Under Management: $254,100,000
Current Activity Level : Actively seeking new investments

WREN CAPITAL LLP

60 Goswel Road
Devonshire House
London, United Kingdom EC1M 7AD
Phone: 442033973390
E-mail: contact@wrencapfooital.co.uk
Website: www.wrencapital.co.uk

Type of Firm

Private Equity Firm

Project Preferences

Type of Financing Preferred:
Early Stage
Seed

Geographical Preferences

International Preferences:
United Kingdom
Europe

Industry Preferences

In Medical/Health prefer:
Health Services

In Consumer Related prefer:
Food/Beverage

In Industrial/Energy prefer:
Energy

Additional Information

Year Founded: 2010
Current Activity Level : Actively seeking new investments

WRF CAPITAL

2815 Eastlake Avenue East, Suite 300
Seattle, WA USA 98102
Phone: 2063365600
Fax: 2063365615
E-mail: info@wrfcapital.com
Website: www.wrfseattle.org

Management and Staff

Jeff Eby, Chief Financial Officer
John Reagh, Managing Director
Loretta Little, Managing Director
Lortetta Little, Managing Director
Ronald Howell, Chief Executive Officer
Thong Le, Managing Director

Type of Firm

Government Affiliated Program

Project Preferences

Type of Financing Preferred:
Seed

Size of Investments Considered:
Min Size of Investment Considered (000s): $1
Max Size of Investment Considered (000s): $2,000

Geographical Preferences

United States Preferences:
Washington

Industry Preferences

In Other prefer:
Socially Responsible

Additional Information

Year Founded: 1997
Current Activity Level : Actively seeking new investments

WUHAN EAST-LAKE VENTURE CAPITAL CO LTD

Road No. 32 state-owned bldgs
Block B, 027-85
Wuhan, Hubei, China
Fax: 02785613636
E-mail: whsamc@sina.com
Website: www.whdhct.com

Type of Firm

Private Equity Firm

Project Preferences

Type of Financing Preferred:
Early Stage
Expansion
Balanced
Later Stage

Geographical Preferences

International Preferences:
China

Industry Preferences

In Computer Software prefer:
Software

In Internet Specific prefer:
Ecommerce

In Biotechnology prefer:
Biotechnology
Biotech Related Research

In Industrial/Energy prefer:
Alternative Energy
Energy Conservation Relat
Environmental Related

Additional Information
Year Founded: 1999
Capital Under Management: $28,642,000
Current Activity Level : Actively seeking new investments

WUHAN HUAGONG TECHNOLOGY BUSINESS INCUBATOR CO LTD

No. 243 Luoyu Road
Hongshan District
Wuhan, China 430074
Phone: 86-27-8752-2618
Fax: 86-27-8752-2800
E-mail: info@whbi.com.cn

Management and Staff
Wei Fang, Vice President
Xin Li, Vice President

Type of Firm
Incubator/Development Program

Project Preferences

Type of Financing Preferred:
Early Stage
Seed

Geographical Preferences

International Preferences:
China

Industry Preferences

In Biotechnology prefer:
Biotechnology

In Industrial/Energy prefer:
Materials

Additional Information
Year Founded: 1993
Current Activity Level : Actively seeking new investments

WUHAN JIANMIN VENTURE CAPITAL CO LTD

No.484 Yingwu Avenue
Hanyang District
Wuhan, China 430052
Phone: 862784533250

Type of Firm
Private Equity Firm

Project Preferences

Type of Financing Preferred:
Balanced

Geographical Preferences

International Preferences:
China

Additional Information
Year Founded: 2008
Capital Under Management: $4,800,000
Current Activity Level : Actively seeking new investments

WUHAN KEYWIN VENTURE CAPITAL CO LTD

15F, Tower A, Wuhan Int'l Bldg
Dandong Crossing
Wuhan, China 430022
Phone: 86-27-8542-3662
Fax: 86-27-8541-7459
E-mail: Info@keywin.com.cn
Website: www.keywin.com.cn

Type of Firm
Private Equity Firm

Project Preferences

Type of Financing Preferred:
Balanced

Geographical Preferences

International Preferences:
China

Additional Information
Year Founded: 2000
Current Activity Level : Actively seeking new investments

WUHAN OPTICAL VALLEY VC FUND MANAGEMENT CO LTD

No. 2 Guandongyuan Road
3/F Hi-Tech Building
Wuhan, China
Phone: 862787618838
Fax: 862787618808
Website: chinaovvc.com

Type of Firm
Private Equity Firm

Project Preferences

Type of Financing Preferred:
Balanced

Industry Preferences

In Communications prefer:
Communications and Media

In Computer Software prefer:
Software

In Semiconductor/Electr prefer:
Electronic Components

In Biotechnology prefer:
Biotechnology

In Medical/Health prefer:
Medical/Health

In Industrial/Energy prefer:
Energy
Materials
Machinery
Environmental Related

In Business Serv. prefer:
Services

In Manufact. prefer:
Manufacturing

In Agr/Forestr/Fish prefer:
Agriculture related

Additional Information
Year Founded: 2008
Capital Under Management: $16,339,000
Current Activity Level : Actively seeking new investments

WUHAN OPTICAL VALLEY VENTURE CAPITAL CO LTD

23F, Tower B, Yamao Plz
628 Wuluo Rd,Wuchang
Wuhan, China 430070
Phone: 86-027-8766
Fax: 86-027-8764

Type of Firm
Private Equity Firm

Project Preferences

Type of Financing Preferred:
Balanced

Geographical Preferences

International Preferences:
China

Additional Information
Year Founded: 2007
Current Activity Level : Actively seeking new investments

WUHAN PROTON VENTURE CAPITAL FUND MANAGEMENT CO LTD

Wuhan Eco & Dev'l Zone
Wuhan, Hubei, China

Management and Staff
Haitao Zhang, President

Type of Firm
Private Equity Firm

Project Preferences

Type of Financing Preferred:
Later Stage

Geographical Preferences

International Preferences:
China

Additional Information
Year Founded: 2010
Capital Under Management: $15,100,000
Current Activity Level : Actively seeking new investments

WUHAN UNIVERSITY ASSET INVESTMENT MANAGEMENT CO LTD

Wuchang Dist
Luojiasha
Wuhan, China 430072
Website: cyb.whu.edu.cn

Type of Firm
University Program

Project Preferences

Type of Financing Preferred:
Balanced

Geographical Preferences

International Preferences:
China

Additional Information
Year Founded: 2015
Capital Under Management: $16,120,000
Current Activity Level : Actively seeking new investments

WUHAN ZHONGTOU JIANHUA VENTURE CAPITAL MANAGEMENT CO LTD

No.250, Jianghan Road
Wuhan, China

Type of Firm
Private Equity Firm

Project Preferences

Type of Financing Preferred:
Balanced

Geographical Preferences

International Preferences:
China

Industry Preferences

In Industrial/Energy prefer:
Materials

In Business Serv. prefer:
Services

In Manufact. prefer:
Manufacturing

In Other prefer:
Environment Responsible

Additional Information
Year Founded: 2014
Current Activity Level : Actively seeking new investments

WUHU YUANDA VENTURE CAPITAL CO., LTD.

Jiangbei Industrial Zone
Room315-B, Building B
Wuhu, China

Type of Firm
Government Affiliated Program

Project Preferences

Type of Financing Preferred:
Balanced

Geographical Preferences

International Preferences:
China

Additional Information
Year Founded: 2009
Current Activity Level : Actively seeking new investments

WUXI GUOLIAN ASSETS MANAGEMENT CO LTD

No.8 Jinrong 1st Street
10F, Guolian Finance Building
Wuxi, China

Type of Firm
Corporate PE/Venture

Project Preferences

Type of Financing Preferred:
Balanced

Geographical Preferences

International Preferences:
China

Industry Preferences

In Communications prefer:
Telecommunications
Media and Entertainment

In Biotechnology prefer:
Biotechnology

In Medical/Health prefer:
Medical/Health
Pharmaceuticals

In Industrial/Energy prefer:
Materials

Additional Information
Year Founded: 2011
Current Activity Level : Actively seeking new investments

WUXI HEALTHCARE VENTURES

22 3rd Street, Suite 100
Cambridge, MA USA 02142
Website: www.wuxiventures.com

Type of Firm
Private Equity Firm

Project Preferences

Type of Financing Preferred:
Early Stage

Geographical Preferences

United States Preferences:

International Preferences:
China

Additional Information
Year Founded: 2015
Capital Under Management: $290,000,000
Current Activity Level : Actively seeking new investments

WUXI NUTS EQUITY INVESTMENT PARTNER ENTERPRISE LP

No.10, Xinli Road
Photoelectric Industrial Park
Wuxi, China
Website: www.nutsinvest.com

Type of Firm
Private Equity Firm

Project Preferences

Type of Financing Preferred:
Balanced

Geographical Preferences

International Preferences:
China

Industry Preferences

In Internet Specific prefer:
Internet

In Medical/Health prefer:
Medical/Health

In Consumer Related prefer:
Education Related

In Industrial/Energy prefer:
Energy Conservation Relat

In Financial Services prefer:
Financial Services

Additional Information
Year Founded: 2014
Current Activity Level : Actively seeking new investments

WWB ASSET MANAGEMENT LLC

Eight West 40th Street
Ninth Floor
New York, NY USA 10018
Phone: 2127688513
Fax: 2127688519
E-mail: communications@womensworldbanking.org
Website: www.womensworldbanking.org

Type of Firm
Bank Affiliated

Project Preferences

Type of Financing Preferred:
Generalist PE

Industry Preferences

In Financial Services prefer:
Financial Services

In Other prefer:
Women/Minority-Owned Bus.

Additional Information
Year Founded: 2012
Capital Under Management: $43,775,000
Current Activity Level : Actively seeking new investments

WWC CAPITAL FUND L P

11911 Freedom Drive, Suite 1010
Reston, VA USA 20190
Phone: 7032251500
Fax: 7032251515
Website: www.wwcfirm.com

Other Offices
80 William Street, Suite 250
Wellesley, MA USA 02481
Phone: 7032251500
Fax: 7032251515

Management and Staff
Arnie Freedman, Managing Director
Braun Jones, Managing Director
Jonathan Wallace, Managing Director
Michael Cromwell, Managing Director
Oded Ben-Joseph, Managing Director
Paul Klick, Managing Director

Type of Firm
Bank Affiliated

Project Preferences

Type of Financing Preferred:
Expansion
Balanced
Later Stage

Industry Preferences

In Communications prefer:
Communications and Media

In Computer Software prefer:
Software

In Internet Specific prefer:
Internet

In Financial Services prefer:
Financial Services

In Business Serv. prefer:
Services
Media

Additional Information
Name of Most Recent Fund: WWC Capital Fund II, L.P.
Most Recent Fund Was Raised: 01/20/2005
Year Founded: 1998
Current Activity Level : Actively seeking new investments

WYNNCHURCH CAPITAL LTD

6250 North River Road, Suite 10-100
Rosemont, IL USA 60018
Phone: 8476046100
Fax: 8476046105
Website: www.wynnchurch.com

Other Offices
39400 Woodward Avenue, Suite 185
Bloomfield, MI USA 48304
Phone: 2485933800
Fax: 2485935728

110 Yonge Street, Suite 1100
Toronto, Canada M5C 1T4
Phone: 4163631423
Fax: 4163633905

200 Crescent Court, Suite 1450
Dallas, TX USA 75201
Phone: 2147209200
Fax: 2147209205

Management and Staff
Alison Miller, Partner
Brian Long, Managing Director
Brian Crumbaugh, Managing Director
Brian Riordan, Vice President
Carl Howe, Vice President
Christopher O Brien, Partner
David Matthews, Vice President
Dominic LaValle, Managing Director
Duncan Bourne, Managing Director
Erin Murphy, Managing Director
Frank Hayes, Managing Partner
Greg Gleason, Managing Director
Ian Kirson, Partner
John Newman, Managing Director
Michael Teplitsky, Managing Director
Morty White, Managing Director
Neel Mayenkar, Managing Director
Roy Sroka, Chief Financial Officer
Scott Fitch, Managing Director
Stephen Welborn, Managing Director
Terry Theodore, Partner

Type of Firm
Private Equity Firm

Association Membership
Illinois Venture Capital Association
Canadian Venture Capital Association

Project Preferences

Role in Financing:
Prefer role as deal originator but will also invest in deals created by others

Pratt's Guide to Private Equity & Venture Capital Sources

Type of Financing Preferred:
Leveraged Buyout
Turnaround
Later Stage
Management Buyouts
Acquisition
Special Situation
Distressed Debt
Recapitalizations

Geographical Preferences

United States Preferences:
North America

Canadian Preferences:
All Canada

Industry Focus

(% based on actual investment)
Other Products	48.5%
Industrial/Energy	42.1%
Computer Software and Services	4.0%
Communications and Media	3.2%
Consumer Related	2.3%

Additional Information

Name of Most Recent Fund: Wynnchurch Capital Partners II, L.P.
Most Recent Fund Was Raised: 12/30/2005
Year Founded: 1999
Capital Under Management: $1,073,000,000
Current Activity Level : Actively seeking new investments
Method of Compensation: Return on invest. most important, but chg. closing fees, service fees, etc.

WYSE CAPITAL GROUP

101 East Park Boulevard, Suite 715
Plano, TX USA 75074
Phone: 4699108444
Fax: 4698148655
Website: www.wysecapital.com

Management and Staff
Milton Arch, Chief Executive Officer

Type of Firm
Private Equity Firm

Project Preferences

Type of Financing Preferred:
Early Stage

Additional Information
Year Founded: 1969
Current Activity Level : Actively seeking new investments

- X -

X/SEED CAPITAL MANAGEMENT

3130 Alpine Road, Suite 200
Portola Valley, CA USA 94028
Phone: 6503311230
Fax: 6508541583
E-mail: info@xseedcap.com
Website: www.xseedcap.com

Management and Staff
Alan Chiu, Partner
Damon Cronkey, Partner
David Hanzel, Partner
Jeff Thermond, Venture Partner
Jonathan Feiber, Venture Partner
Lev Mass, Venture Partner
Michael Borrus, General Partner
Michael Borrus, Partner
Robert Siegel, Partner
Robert Siegel, General Partner

Type of Firm
Private Equity Firm

Project Preferences

Type of Financing Preferred:
Early Stage
Seed
Startup

Industry Preferences

In Computer Software prefer:
Artificial Intelligence

In Medical/Health prefer:
Health Services

In Industrial/Energy prefer:
Robotics

Additional Information
Year Founded: 2006
Current Activity Level : Actively seeking new investments

XANGE PRIVATE EQUITY SA

12 Rue Tronchet
Paris, France 75008
Phone: 33153430530
Fax: 33153300225
E-mail: contact@xange.fr
Website: www.xange.fr

Other Offices
44 place de la Republique
Lyon, France 69002
Phone: 33437262530

Maximilianstrase 45
Munich, Germany D-80538
Phone: 49-89-381-699-730
Fax: 49-89-381-699-730

Management and Staff
Bernhard Schmid, Partner
Cyril Bertrand, Partner
Dominique Agrech, Partner
Etienne Renoux, Chief Financial Officer
Francois Cavalie, Managing Director
Herve Schricke, Chief Executive Officer
Ines Sen, Partner
Nicolas Rose, Partner

Type of Firm
Private Equity Firm

Association Membership
French Venture Capital Association (AFIC)
German Venture Capital Association (BVK)

Project Preferences

Type of Financing Preferred:
Leveraged Buyout
Early Stage
Generalist PE
Balanced
Later Stage
Acquisition
Startup

Size of Investments Considered:
Min Size of Investment Considered (000s): $659
Max Size of Investment Considered (000s): $6,590

Geographical Preferences

United States Preferences:

International Preferences:
Europe
Israel
Germany
France

Industry Preferences

In Communications prefer:
Communications and Media
Telecommunications
Data Communications

In Computer Software prefer:
Software

In Internet Specific prefer:
Internet
Ecommerce

In Computer Other prefer:
Computer Related

In Semiconductor/Electr prefer:
Electronics

In Biotechnology prefer:
Biotechnology

In Medical/Health prefer:
Medical/Health

In Consumer Related prefer:
Retail
Consumer Services

In Industrial/Energy prefer:
Energy
Industrial Products
Materials
Environmental Related

In Financial Services prefer:
Financial Services

In Business Serv. prefer:
Services
Distribution

Additional Information
Name of Most Recent Fund: XPansion 2 FCPR
Most Recent Fund Was Raised: 02/11/2013
Year Founded: 2004
Capital Under Management: $455,400,000
Current Activity Level : Actively seeking new investments

XBE CAPITAL LTD

188 Lockhart Road
12th Floor Siu On Centre
Wanchai, Hong Kong
Website: www.xbecapital.com

Type of Firm
Private Equity Firm

Association Membership
Hong Kong Venture Capital Association (HKVCA)

Project Preferences

Type of Financing Preferred:
Early Stage

Geographical Preferences

International Preferences:
Hong Kong
China
Australia

Industry Preferences

In Communications prefer:
Communications and Media

In Industrial/Energy prefer:
Energy

In Financial Services prefer:
Financial Services

In Business Serv. prefer:
Media

In Manufact. prefer:
Manufacturing

Additional Information
Year Founded: 2013
Current Activity Level : Actively seeking new investments

XENIA VENTURE CAPITAL LTD

1 Leshem Street
Kiryat Gat, Israel 82000
Phone: 97286811761
Fax: 97286811763
E-mail: info@xenia.co.il
Website: www.xenia.co.il

Management and Staff
Eli Sorzon, Chief Executive Officer

Type of Firm
Private Equity Firm

Association Membership
Israel Venture Association

Project Preferences

Type of Financing Preferred:
Early Stage
Seed
Startup

Geographical Preferences

International Preferences:
Israel

Industry Preferences

In Medical/Health prefer:
Medical Products

Additional Information
Year Founded: 2003
Current Activity Level : Actively seeking new investments

XERAYA CAPITAL SDN BHD

199 Jalan Tun Razak
Kuala Lumpur, Malaysia 50400
E-mail: xeraya@xeraya.com
Website: www.xeraya.com

Type of Firm
Private Equity Firm

Project Preferences

Type of Financing Preferred:
Early Stage
Expansion
Balanced
Later Stage

Geographical Preferences

International Preferences:
Malaysia

Industry Preferences

In Biotechnology prefer:
Biotechnology
Agricultural/Animal Bio.
Industrial Biotechnology

In Medical/Health prefer:
Medical/Health

In Industrial/Energy prefer:
Environmental Related

Additional Information
Year Founded: 1969
Capital Under Management: $150,000,000
Current Activity Level : Actively seeking new investments

XERYS GESTION SAS

7 rue dAguesseau
Paris, France 75008
E-mail: contact@xerys.com
Website: www.xerys.com

Type of Firm
Private Equity Firm

Project Preferences

Type of Financing Preferred:
Early Stage
Later Stage
Seed
Startup

Geographical Preferences

International Preferences:
Europe
Western Europe
France

Additional Information
Year Founded: 2013
Capital Under Management: $69,110,000
Current Activity Level : Actively seeking new investments

XESGALICIA SGECR SA

Barrio de San Lazero s/n
Santiago de Compostela, Spain 15703
Phone: 34981541621
Fax: 34981580658
E-mail: xesgalicia@xesgalicia.org
Website: www.xesgalicia.org

Type of Firm
Private Equity Firm

Association Membership
Spanish Venture Capital Association (ASCRI)

Project Preferences

Type of Financing Preferred:
Early Stage
Expansion
Balanced
Later Stage

Geographical Preferences

International Preferences:
Europe
Spain

Industry Preferences

In Communications prefer:
Telecommunications

In Biotechnology prefer:
Biotechnology

In Industrial/Energy prefer:
Alternative Energy
Environmental Related

Additional Information
Year Founded: 1969
Current Activity Level : Actively seeking new investments

XEVIN INVESTMENTS SP Z O O

Ul. Jelinka 32
Warsaw, Poland 01-646
Phone: 48222112166
Fax: 48226160950
E-mail: contact@xevin.eu
Website: www.xevin.eu

Management and Staff
Radoslaw Czyrko, Partner

Type of Firm
Private Equity Firm

Project Preferences

Type of Financing Preferred:
Early Stage
Seed

Geographical Preferences

International Preferences:
Central Europe
Eastern Europe

Industry Preferences

In Internet Specific prefer:
Internet

In Business Serv. prefer:
Media

Additional Information
Year Founded: 2008
Current Activity Level : Actively seeking new investments

XIAMEN A&Z INVESTMENT MANAGEMENT CO LTD

China (Fujian) Pilot Free Tra
B-6, Unit 03, 8F, Block D
Xiamen, China 361000

Type of Firm
Private Equity Firm

Project Preferences

Type of Financing Preferred:
Early Stage
Seed
Startup

Geographical Preferences

International Preferences:
China

Industry Preferences

In Communications prefer:
Telecommunications
Media and Entertainment

Additional Information
Year Founded: 2015
Current Activity Level : Actively seeking new investments

XIAMEN ACEON VENTURE INVESTMENT CO LTD

Kangli Financial Building
Unit 1901
Xiamen, China
Phone: 865922953195
Fax: 865922953199
Website: www.ansisheng.com

Management and Staff
Jingjing Weng, Managing Director

Type of Firm
Private Equity Firm

Project Preferences

Type of Financing Preferred:
Early Stage
Seed
Startup

Geographical Preferences

International Preferences:
China

Industry Preferences

In Communications prefer:
Telecommunications
Media and Entertainment

In Consumer Related prefer:
Education Related

Additional Information
Year Founded: 2012
Current Activity Level : Actively seeking new investments

XIAMEN DEYI CAPITAL EQUITY INVESTMENT MANAGEMENT CO LTD

No. 3999 Huandao South Rd., Si
Unit V7, Haiyue Villa, Haiyue
Xiamen, China
Phone: 865922518818
Website: www.dyeecapital.com

Type of Firm
Investment Management Firm

Project Preferences

Type of Financing Preferred:
Balanced

Geographical Preferences

International Preferences:
China

Additional Information
Year Founded: 2016
Capital Under Management: $184,840,000
Current Activity Level : Actively seeking new investments

XIAMEN HAICANG INVESTMENT GROUP CO LTD

No. 8 Zhonglin Road
Haicang District
Xiamen, China 361026
Phone: 865926892545
Fax: 865926892052
Website: www.haitou.cn

Type of Firm
Investment Management Firm

Project Preferences

Type of Financing Preferred:
Balanced

Geographical Preferences

International Preferences:
China

Industry Preferences

In Biotechnology prefer:
Biotechnology

Additional Information

Year Founded: 2011
Capital Under Management: $12,201,000
Current Activity Level : Actively seeking new investments

XIAMEN HENGYI VENTURE CAPITAL MANAGEMENT CO LTD

No.388, Hubing South Road
43F, Guomao Bldg
Xiamen, China 361004
Phone: 865925892257
Fax: 865925892252
Website: www.itgholding.com.cn

Type of Firm
Private Equity Firm

Project Preferences

Type of Financing Preferred:
Early Stage
Expansion

Geographical Preferences

International Preferences:
China

Industry Preferences

In Communications prefer:
Telecommunications

In Computer Hardware prefer:
Computers

In Computer Software prefer:
Data Processing
Software

In Internet Specific prefer:
Internet

In Semiconductor/Electr prefer:
Electronic Components
Semiconductor
Circuit Boards

Additional Information

Year Founded: 2012
Capital Under Management: $39,548,000
Current Activity Level : Actively seeking new investments

XIAMEN HONGSOFT VENTURE CAPITAL MANAGEMENT CO LTD

No. 55, Wanghai Road, Siming
Room704, Building B
Xiamen, Fujian, China
Phone: 865926308096
Fax: 865926308081
Website: www.hongsoft.cn

Management and Staff
Longrun Hu, Partner
Xichu Guo, Partner

Type of Firm
Private Equity Firm

Project Preferences

Type of Financing Preferred:
Early Stage
Expansion
Balanced
Later Stage

Geographical Preferences

International Preferences:
China

Additional Information

Year Founded: 2010
Current Activity Level : Actively seeking new investments

XIAMEN QIANSHAN INVESTMENT MANAGEMENT CO LTD

No. 80 Jinshang Road, Xiamen
Peking University Biological P
Xiamen, China
Website: www.qianshanvc.com

Type of Firm
Private Equity Firm

Project Preferences

Type of Financing Preferred:
Balanced

Geographical Preferences

International Preferences:
China

Industry Preferences

In Biotechnology prefer:
Biotechnology

In Medical/Health prefer:
Medical/Health

In Consumer Related prefer:
Consumer

Additional Information

Year Founded: 2017
Capital Under Management: $14,590,000
Current Activity Level : Actively seeking new investments

XIAMEN XINBAIYI INVESTMENT GROUP CO LTD

No. 1507 North Fanghu 2nd Road
Room 902, Huli District
Xiamen, China

Type of Firm
Private Equity Firm

Project Preferences

Type of Financing Preferred:
Balanced

Geographical Preferences

International Preferences:
China

Additional Information

Year Founded: 2009
Current Activity Level : Actively seeking new investments

XIAN PRUTENTION INVESTMENT & DEVELOPMENT CO LTD

Tower A, No. 1 High-tech Fourt
Room 1602 1603
Xi'an, China 710075
Phone: 2988365302
Fax: 2988365638
E-mail: bdx@prutention.com
Website: www.prutention.com

Other Offices
Former HQ: 13F, B Section, Century Plaza
93, Heping road
Xi'an, China 710001
Phone: 86-29-875-1407
Fax: 86-29-8742-7310

Management and Staff
Xiang Jun Qu, President

Type of Firm
Private Equity Firm

Project Preferences

Type of Financing Preferred:
Balanced

Geographical Preferences

International Preferences:
China

Industry Preferences

In Semiconductor/Electr prefer:
Electronics

In Medical/Health prefer:
Medical/Health

In Consumer Related prefer:
Education Related

In Transportation prefer:
Transportation

In Financial Services prefer:
Real Estate
Financial Services

In Agr/Forestr/Fish prefer:
Agriculture related

In Other prefer:
Environment Responsible

Additional Information

Year Founded: 1998
Current Activity Level : Actively seeking new investments

XIAN SCIENCE TECHNOLOGY INVESTMENT CO LTD

Gaoxin Second Road
2A, Xietong Building
Xi'an, China
Phone: 86-29-83860
Fax: 86-29-83864

Type of Firm

Government Affiliated Program

Additional Information

Year Founded: 1998
Current Activity Level : Actively seeking new investments

XIAN ZHONGKE CHUANGXING TECHNOLOGY INCUBATOR CO LTD

Chang An District
17 Xinxi Avenue
Xian, China
Website: www.casstar.com.cn

Type of Firm

Incubator/Development Program

Project Preferences

Type of Financing Preferred:
Seed
Startup

Geographical Preferences

International Preferences:
China

Additional Information

Year Founded: 2013
Current Activity Level : Actively seeking new investments

XIANFENG HUAXING VENTURE CAPITAL LTD

No.6, Jianwai Road
C, Central World Trade Center
Beijing, China
Phone: 86
Fax: 86
Website: www.k2vc.com

Other Offices

Po Box 10008 Willow House
Grand Cayman, Cayman Islands
Phone: 3457492000

Management and Staff

Fan Bao, Co-Founder
Keyi Chen, Co-Founder

Type of Firm

Private Equity Firm

Project Preferences

Type of Financing Preferred:
Early Stage
Balanced

Geographical Preferences

International Preferences:
China
Cayman Islands

Additional Information

Year Founded: 2010
Capital Under Management: $150,770,000
Current Activity Level : Actively seeking new investments

XIANG HE CAPITAL

Haidian District
21F, Building C, Tsinghua Tech
Beijing, China
Website: www.xianghecap.com

Type of Firm

Private Equity Firm

Project Preferences

Type of Financing Preferred:
Early Stage
Expansion

Geographical Preferences

International Preferences:
China

Industry Preferences

In Communications prefer:
Telecommunications
Media and Entertainment

Additional Information

Year Founded: 2016
Current Activity Level : Actively seeking new investments

XIANGCAI SECURITIES CO LTD

18/F Huaneng Union Tower
139 Yincheng Road East
Pudong, China 200120
Phone: 86-21-6863-4518
Fax: 86-21-5054-3470
E-mail: ibd@xcsc.com
Website: www.xcsc.com

Type of Firm

Investment Management Firm

Association Membership

Venture Capital Association of Beijing (VCAB)

Project Preferences

Type of Financing Preferred:
Expansion

Geographical Preferences

International Preferences:
China

Industry Preferences

In Communications prefer:
Telecommunications

In Computer Software prefer:
Software

In Semiconductor/Electr prefer:
Semiconductor

In Biotechnology prefer:
Biotechnology

In Medical/Health prefer:
Medical/Health

In Industrial/Energy prefer:
Energy
Materials

In Manufact. prefer:
Manufacturing

In Other prefer:
Environment Responsible

Additional Information
Year Founded: 1993
Current Activity Level : Actively seeking new investments

XIANGJIANG INDUSTRIAL INVESTMENT CO LTD

17/F,Tianqi, Gold Source Hotel
No.279 Furong Middle Rd Sec 2
Changsha, China 410007
Phone: 8673185952988
Fax: 8673188711088

Other Offices

No. 9 Zhanqian Street, Beijing Station
Rm 647-649, Hunan Building
Beijing, China 100005
Phone: 861085079956
Fax: 861085079955

Fuhua 3rd Road, Futian Dist
Rm 1512 Bldg 3 Zhuoyue Shiji Center
Shenzhen, China 518000
Phone: 8675583478409
Fax: 8675588300485

No. 577 Pudian Road, Pudong Dist
HKU 2/F, Gezhouba Bldg West
Shanghai, China 200122
Phone: 862151785164
Fax: 862151785165

Type of Firm
Private Equity Firm

Project Preferences

Type of Financing Preferred:
Later Stage

Geographical Preferences

International Preferences:
China

Industry Preferences

In Semiconductor/Electr prefer:
Electronics

In Biotechnology prefer:
Biotechnology

In Medical/Health prefer:
Medical/Health
Pharmaceuticals

In Consumer Related prefer:
Entertainment and Leisure

In Industrial/Energy prefer:
Energy
Alternative Energy
Industrial Products
Materials
Advanced Materials
Machinery

In Transportation prefer:
Transportation

In Financial Services prefer:
Financial Services

In Business Serv. prefer:
Services

In Manufact. prefer:
Manufacturing

In Agr/Forestr/Fish prefer:
Agriculture related
Mining and Minerals

Additional Information
Year Founded: 2008
Capital Under Management: $179,466,000
Current Activity Level : Actively seeking new investments

XILINX INC

2100 Logic Drive
San Jose, CA USA 95124
Phone: 408-559-7778
Fax: 408-559-7114
Website: www.xilinx.com

Other Offices

3 Changi Business Park Vista
Singapore, Singapore 486040
Phone: 65-6407-3000
Fax: 65-6789-8886

Management and Staff
Stacy Fender, Managing Director

Type of Firm
Corporate PE/Venture

Project Preferences

Type of Financing Preferred:
Balanced

Geographical Preferences

International Preferences:
India
Taiwan
China
Asia
Singapore
Korea, South

Industry Preferences

In Communications prefer:
Communications and Media
Wireless Communications

In Semiconductor/Electr prefer:
Electronics
Controllers and Sensors

Additional Information
Year Founded: 1984
Current Activity Level : Actively seeking new investments

XINDAFENG INVESTMENT MANAGEMENT CO LTD

No. 2 Guangningbo Street, Fina
8F, East Building, Jinze Mansi
Beijing, China 100033
Phone: 861052601167
Fax: 861052601190
Website: www.cindafund.com

Type of Firm
Investment Management Firm

Project Preferences

Type of Financing Preferred:
Generalist PE

Geographical Preferences

International Preferences:
China

Additional Information
Year Founded: 2013
Current Activity Level : Actively seeking new investments

XINGFU INVESTMENT MANAGEMENT CO LTD

No. 1518 Minsheng Road, Pudong
Room 903, Building A, Golden E
Shanghai, China 200135
Phone: 862160756658
Website: xffunds.com

Type of Firm
Private Equity Firm

Project Preferences

Type of Financing Preferred:
Balanced

Geographical Preferences

International Preferences:
China

Industry Preferences

In Communications prefer:
Telecommunications

In Industrial/Energy prefer:
Environmental Related

In Business Serv. prefer:
Media

Additional Information

Year Founded: 2015
Current Activity Level : Actively seeking new investments

XINJIANG PRODUCTION & CONSTRUCTION CORPS LIANCHUANG EQUITY

56 Community, Dongcheng Street
3-1, No. 37, Beisi East Road
Shihezi , China

Type of Firm
Private Equity Firm

Project Preferences

Type of Financing Preferred:
Balanced

Geographical Preferences

International Preferences:
China

Additional Information

Year Founded: 2011
Current Activity Level : Actively seeking new investments

XINYU HESI INVESTMENT MANAGEMENT CENTER LP

Xiannv Lake District
Yuxiushan Office
Xinyu, China

Type of Firm
Private Equity Firm

Project Preferences

Type of Financing Preferred:
Leveraged Buyout
Balanced

Geographical Preferences

International Preferences:
China

Industry Preferences

In Communications prefer:
Entertainment

In Internet Specific prefer:
Internet

Additional Information

Year Founded: 2014
Current Activity Level : Actively seeking new investments

XIO (UK) LLP

32 London Bridge Street
The Shard Suite 1502
London, United Kingdom SE1 9SG
E-mail: info@xiogroup.com

Type of Firm
Private Equity Firm

Project Preferences

Type of Financing Preferred:
Leveraged Buyout
Acquisition

Additional Information

Year Founded: 1969
Current Activity Level : Actively seeking new investments

XL HEALTH AG

Oberwallstrasse 10
Berlin, Germany 10117
Phone: 493022605270
E-mail: info@xlhealth.de
Website: www.xlhealth.de

Type of Firm
Incubator/Development Program

Project Preferences

Type of Financing Preferred:
Early Stage
Seed
Startup

Geographical Preferences

International Preferences:
Germany

Industry Preferences

In Medical/Health prefer:
Medical/Health

Additional Information

Year Founded: 2013
Current Activity Level : Actively seeking new investments

XLR CAPITAL SAS

55 Avenue Marceau
Paris, France 75116
Website: xlr.fr

Type of Firm
Incubator/Development Program

Project Preferences

Type of Financing Preferred:
Early Stage
Expansion
Seed
Startup

Geographical Preferences

International Preferences:
France

Additional Information

Year Founded: 2015
Current Activity Level : Actively seeking new investments

XPLORER CAPITAL

1260 San Mateo Drive
Sunnyvale, CA USA 94089
Website: www.xplorercapital.com

Type of Firm
Private Equity Firm

Project Preferences

Type of Financing Preferred:
Expansion
Balanced

Geographical Preferences

International Preferences:
Asia Pacific
Latin America
India
Europe
Middle East

Industry Preferences

In Internet Specific prefer:
Internet

In Business Serv. prefer:
Media

Additional Information

Year Founded: 2011
Capital Under Management: $25,950,000
Current Activity Level : Actively seeking new investments

XPND CAPITAL

355 Saint-Catherine West Street
Fifth floor
Montreal, Canada H3B 1A5
Website: www.xpnd.com

Management and Staff
Alexandre Taillefer, Managing Director
Dominic Becotte, Partner
Eric Albert, Vice President

Type of Firm
Private Equity Firm

Project Preferences

Type of Financing Preferred:
Generalist PE

Industry Preferences

In Communications prefer:
Media and Entertainment

Additional Information
Year Founded: 2011
Capital Under Management: $55,870,000
Current Activity Level : Actively seeking new investments

XPV CAPITAL CORP

266 King Street West, Suite 403
Toronto, Canada M5V 1H8
Fax: 4168640514

Management and Staff
David Henderson, Managing Director
Debra Coy, Partner
John Coburn, Managing Director
Khalil Maalouf, Managing Director
Spencer Timm, Partner

Type of Firm
Private Equity Firm

Association Membership
Canadian Venture Capital Association

Project Preferences

Type of Financing Preferred:
Early Stage
Balanced
Later Stage

Geographical Preferences

United States Preferences:

Canadian Preferences:
All Canada

International Preferences:
All International

Industry Preferences

In Industrial/Energy prefer:
Alternative Energy
Energy Conservation Relat
Environmental Related

Additional Information
Name of Most Recent Fund: XPV Water Fund II, L.P.
Most Recent Fund Was Raised: 12/17/2013
Year Founded: 2006
Capital Under Management: $363,088,000
Current Activity Level : Actively seeking new investments

XSEED CAPITAL

3130 Alpine Road, Suite 200
Portola Valley, CA USA 94028
Phone: 6503311230
Website: www.xseedcap.com

Type of Firm
Private Equity Firm

Project Preferences

Type of Financing Preferred:
Early Stage

Additional Information
Year Founded: 2006
Current Activity Level : Actively seeking new investments

XSML MANAGEMENT BV

Science Park 400
Amsterdam, Netherlands 1098 XH
Phone: 31208884379
Website: xsmlcapital.com

Management and Staff
Barthout van Slingelandt, Principal
Jarl Heijstee, Co-Founder
Marcel Posthuma, Co-Founder

Type of Firm
Investment Management Firm

Project Preferences

Type of Financing Preferred:
Early Stage
Later Stage

Geographical Preferences

International Preferences:
Congo
Congo, Dem Rep
C. African Rep

Industry Preferences

In Communications prefer:
Telecommunications

In Medical/Health prefer:
Medical/Health
Pharmaceuticals

Additional Information
Name of Most Recent Fund: Central Africa SME Fund
Most Recent Fund Was Raised: 04/25/2013
Year Founded: 2008
Capital Under Management: $64,000,000
Current Activity Level : Actively seeking new investments

XYZ VENTURE CAPITAL LLC

257 Collingwood Street
San Francisco, CA USA 94114

Type of Firm
Private Equity Firm

Project Preferences

Type of Financing Preferred:
Seed

Industry Preferences

In Financial Services prefer:
Financial Services

Additional Information
Year Founded: 2017
Current Activity Level : Actively seeking new investments

- Y -

Y COMBINATOR INC

320 Pioneer Way
Mountain View, CA USA 94041
Phone: 6175760695
E-mail: info@ycombinator.com
Website: www.ycombinator.com

Other Offices

135 Garden Street
Cambridge, MA USA 02138

Management and Staff

Geoff Ralston, Partner
Harj Taggar, Partner
Jessica Livingston, Partner
Paul Graham, Founding Partner
Paul Buchheit, Partner
Robert Morris, Partner
Trevor Blackwell, Partner

Type of Firm

Private Equity Firm

Project Preferences

Type of Financing Preferred:
Seed
Startup

Industry Preferences

In Computer Software prefer:
Software
Applications Software

In Internet Specific prefer:
Internet
Web Aggregration/Portals

Additional Information

Year Founded: 2005
Current Activity Level : Actively seeking new investments

YA GLOBAL INVESTMENTS LP

101 Hudson Street, Suite.3700
Jersey City, NJ USA 07302
Phone: 2019858300
Fax: 2019858266
Website: www.cornellcapital.com

Type of Firm

Private Equity Firm

Project Preferences

Type of Financing Preferred:
Balanced

Geographical Preferences

International Preferences:
All International

Industry Preferences

In Industrial/Energy prefer:
Alternative Energy

Additional Information

Year Founded: 2001
Current Activity Level : Actively seeking new investments

YABEO CAPITAL GMBH

Bergham 19
Bad Endorf, Germany 83093
Phone: 498924245722
Fax: 498924245724
E-mail: info@yabeo.de
Website: www.yabeo.de

Type of Firm

Private Equity Firm

Project Preferences

Type of Financing Preferred:
Early Stage
Balanced
Later Stage
Seed
Startup

Geographical Preferences

International Preferences:
Germany

Additional Information

Year Founded: 2013
Current Activity Level : Actively seeking new investments

YALETOWN VENTURE PARTNERS

1122 Mainland Street, Suite 510
Vancouver, Canada V6B 5L1
Phone: 6046887807
E-mail: info@yaletown.com
Website: www.yaletown.com

Other Offices

601 Union Street, Suite 4200
SEATTLE, WA USA 98101
Phone: (206) 826-1987

805-Tenth Avenue Southwest, Suite 300
Alberta, Canada T2R 0B4
Phone: 4034448300

Management and Staff

Brad Johns, Partner
David Kolada, Venture Partner
Glenn Bindley, Partner
Greg Peet, Partner
Haig Farris, Partner
John Seminerio, Partner
Kirk Washington, Partner
Laurie Wallace, Partner
Martin Tobias, Partner
Mike Satterfield, Partner
Ralph Turfus, Partner
Salil Munjal, Partner
Shyam Gupta, Principal

Type of Firm

Private Equity Firm

Association Membership

Canadian Venture Capital Association

Project Preferences

Role in Financing:
Prefer role as deal originator

Type of Financing Preferred:
Early Stage

Geographical Preferences

United States Preferences:
Northwest
Washington

Canadian Preferences:
Alberta
All Canada
British Columbia
Western Canada

International Preferences:
Pacific

Industry Preferences

In Computer Software prefer:
Software

In Industrial/Energy prefer:
Energy
Alternative Energy

In Other prefer:
Environment Responsible

Additional Information

Year Founded: 2001
Capital Under Management: $95,400,000
Current Activity Level : Actively seeking new investments
Method of Compensation: Return on investment is of primary concern, do not charge fees

YAMAGUCHI CAPITAL CO LTD

1-10 Nakaichi-machi
Yamaguchi-shi, Japan 753-0077
Phone: 0839229088
Fax: 0839229093
E-mail: info@yamaguchi-capital.co.jp
Website: www.yamaguchi-capital.co.jp

Management and Staff
Seiji Shibuya, President

Type of Firm
SBIC

Association Membership
Japan Venture Capital Association

Project Preferences

Type of Financing Preferred:
Early Stage

Additional Information
Year Founded: 1996
Current Activity Level : Actively seeking new investments

YAMANASHI CHUGIN MANAGEMENT CONSULTING CO LTD

20-8 Marunouchi 1-chome
Kofu-shi, Japan 400-0031
Phone: 81-55-224-1032
Website: www.yamanashiconsul.co.jp

Type of Firm
Bank Affiliated

Additional Information
Year Founded: 1996
Current Activity Level : Actively seeking new investments

YANGTZE CHINA INVESTMENT LTD

One Capital Place
Grand Cayman, Cayman Islands KY1-1103
Phone: 0207-398-7712
Fax: 0207-398-7799
E-mail: enquiry@yangtzecn.com
Website: www.yangtzecn.com

Other Offices
125 Old Broad Street
London, United Kingdom EC2N 1AR
Phone: 0207-398-7712
Fax: 0207-398-7799

Type of Firm
Private Equity Firm

Project Preferences

Type of Financing Preferred:
Early Stage

Geographical Preferences

International Preferences:
China

Additional Information
Year Founded: 2007
Current Activity Level : Actively seeking new investments

YANGZHOU YINGFEI MAYA VENTURE CAPITAL CENTER LP

Yangzhou Info Industry Base
4/F, Bldg 8, Phase 1
Yangzhou, China 225000
Phone: 8651487785512

Type of Firm
Private Equity Firm

Project Preferences

Type of Financing Preferred:
Balanced

Geographical Preferences

International Preferences:
China

Additional Information
Year Founded: 2013
Capital Under Management: $4,640,000
Current Activity Level : Actively seeking new investments

YANKEE EQUITY SOLUTION

P.O. Box 630
Cotuit, MA USA 02635
Website: www.yankeeequitysolution.com

Management and Staff
John Williams, Managing Director

Type of Firm
Private Equity Firm

Project Preferences

Type of Financing Preferred:
Expansion
Balanced

Geographical Preferences

United States Preferences:
Massachusetts

Industry Preferences

In Medical/Health prefer:
Medical/Health

Additional Information
Year Founded: 2008
Capital Under Management: $50,000,000
Current Activity Level : Actively seeking new investments

YANYUAN INNOVATION (BEIJING) INVESTMENT MANAGEMENT CO., LTD.

No.1 Zhichun Road Haidian
Xueyuan Internation Building
Beijing, China 100083
Phone: 861082333060
Fax: 861082332499
E-mail: yype@yype.com.cn

Type of Firm
Investment Management Firm

Project Preferences

Type of Financing Preferred:
Balanced

Geographical Preferences

International Preferences:
China

Industry Preferences

In Medical/Health prefer:
Medical/Health

In Consumer Related prefer:
Consumer

In Manufact. prefer:
Manufacturing

Additional Information
Year Founded: 2015
Current Activity Level : Actively seeking new investments

YAO CAPITAL

Zhongshan Nan Road 28
Jiushi Plaza A
Shanghai, China 200010
Website: www.yaoweicapital.com

Type of Firm
Private Equity Firm

Project Preferences

Type of Financing Preferred:
Leveraged Buyout
Balanced

Industry Preferences

In Consumer Related prefer:
Sports

Additional Information

Year Founded: 2016
Capital Under Management: $2,000,000,000
Current Activity Level: Actively seeking new investments

YARPA INVESTIMENTI SGR SPA

Via Roma 3
Genova (GE), Italy 16121
Phone: 39010581061
Fax: 39010581400

Type of Firm

Private Equity Firm

Project Preferences

Type of Financing Preferred:
Leveraged Buyout
Expansion

Geographical Preferences

International Preferences:
Europe

Additional Information

Year Founded: 2008
Capital Under Management: $88,700,000
Current Activity Level: Actively seeking new investments

YASUDA ENTERPRISE DEVELOPMENT CO LTD

3-3-8 Kojimachi, Chiyoda-ku
8F Marumasu Kojimachi Bldg
Tokyo, Japan 102-0083
Phone: 81368117100
Fax: 81352133405
E-mail: info@yedvc.co.jp
Website: www.yedvc.co.jp

Other Offices

525 Middlefield Road, Suite 100
Menlo Park, CA USA 94025
Phone: 6502899733
Fax: 6502899145

Management and Staff

Masaki Ando, Senior Managing Director

Type of Firm

Insurance Firm Affiliate

Association Membership

Japan Venture Capital Association

Project Preferences

Role in Financing:
Will function either as deal originator or investor in deals created by others

Type of Financing Preferred:
Early Stage
Expansion
Balanced
Startup

Geographical Preferences

United States Preferences:

International Preferences:
Japan

Industry Focus

(% based on actual investment)
Biotechnology	33.3%
Semiconductors/Other Elect.	19.3%
Industrial/Energy	13.3%
Computer Hardware	8.4%
Medical/Health	8.4%
Communications and Media	6.8%
Computer Software and Services	6.3%
Internet Specific	4.3%

Additional Information

Year Founded: 1996
Capital Under Management: $10,000,000
Current Activity Level: Actively seeking new investments
Method of Compensation: Return on investment is of primary concern, do not charge fees

YB PARTNERS CO LTD

32F, Asem Tower
159-1 Samsung-dong Kangnam-ku
Seoul, South Korea
Phone: 82260015610
Fax: 82260015611
E-mail: ccb@ybpartners.net
Website: www.ybpartners.net

Management and Staff

Youngbu Kim, President

Type of Firm

Private Equity Firm

Project Preferences

Type of Financing Preferred:
Balanced

Geographical Preferences

International Preferences:
Korea, South

Additional Information

Year Founded: 2000
Capital Under Management: $7,300,000
Current Activity Level: Actively seeking new investments

YEARLING MANAGEMENT LLC

600 East Main Street
Louisville, KY USA 40202

Management and Staff

William Lomicka, General Partner

Type of Firm

Private Equity Firm

Project Preferences

Type of Financing Preferred:
Early Stage
Balanced
Startup

Geographical Preferences

United States Preferences:
Kentucky

Additional Information

Year Founded: 2005
Capital Under Management: $7,000,000
Current Activity Level: Actively seeking new investments

YELLOW BRICK CAPITAL ADVISERS (UK) LTD

13 Abernale Street
London, United Kingdom W1S 4HJ
Phone: 442031376699
Fax: 442030041799
E-mail: info@ybcap.com
Website: ybcap.com

Management and Staff

Adam Blass, Partner

Type of Firm

Investment Management Firm

Project Preferences

Type of Financing Preferred:
Value-Add
Expansion
Generalist PE
Balanced
Opportunistic
Later Stage

Industry Preferences

In Computer Software prefer:
Software

In Semiconductor/Electr prefer:
Electronics
Micro-Processing
Sensors

In Consumer Related prefer:
Education Related

In Financial Services prefer:
Real Estate

Additional Information

Year Founded: 2009
Current Activity Level: Actively seeking new investments

YELLOW POINT EQUITY PARTNERS LP

1235 West Pender Street, Suite 1000
Vancouver, Canada V6E 4B1
Phone: 6046591850
Fax: 6046591899

Other Offices

1285 West Pender, Suite 1000
Vancouver, Canada

Management and Staff

Brian Begert, Co-Founder
David Phillips, Partner
David Chapman, Co-Founder
Tyler Smyrski, Partner

Type of Firm

Private Equity Firm

Project Preferences

Type of Financing Preferred:
Leveraged Buyout
Expansion
Management Buyouts
Acquisition
Recapitalizations

Size of Investments Considered:
Min Size of Investment Considered (000s): $5,000
Max Size of Investment Considered (000s): $25,000

Geographical Preferences

United States Preferences:
Northwest

Canadian Preferences:
All Canada
Western Canada

Industry Preferences

In Communications prefer:
Communications and Media

In Medical/Health prefer:
Medical/Health

In Industrial/Energy prefer:
Energy

In Financial Services prefer:
Financial Services

In Business Serv. prefer:
Services

In Manufact. prefer:
Manufacturing

Additional Information

Year Founded: 2004
Capital Under Management: $300,000,000
Current Activity Level: Actively seeking new investments
Method of Compensation: Return on invest. most important, but chg. closing fees, service fees, etc.

YELLOW WOOD PARTNERS LLC

20 Custom House Street, Suite 920
Boston, MA USA 02110
Phone: 6175006340
Website: yellowwoodpartners.com

Other Offices

One Bridge Street, Suite 50
Irvington, NY USA 10533

Management and Staff

Dana Schmaltz, Partner
Kevin McCafferty, Principal
Peter Mann, Partner
Tad Yanagi, Principal

Type of Firm

Endowment, Foundation or Pension Fund

Project Preferences

Type of Financing Preferred:
Leveraged Buyout
Acquisition

Industry Preferences

In Consumer Related prefer:
Consumer
Consumer Products

Additional Information

Name of Most Recent Fund: Yellow Wood Partners Fund
Most Recent Fund Was Raised: 01/11/2012
Year Founded: 2009
Capital Under Management: $370,000,000
Current Activity Level: Actively seeking new investments

YELLOW&BLUE INVESTMENT MANAGEMENT BV

Kernkade 10
Energy Building
Utrecht, Netherlands 3542 CH
Phone: 31880102400
E-mail: yandb@yellowandblue.nl
Website: www.yellowandblue.nl

Management and Staff

Albert Fischer, Managing Director
Alexander van Os, Principal
Dudley Hawes, Principal

Type of Firm

Private Equity Firm

Association Membership

Dutch Venture Capital Associaton (NVP)

Project Preferences

Type of Financing Preferred:
Later Stage
Seed
Startup

Size of Investments Considered:
Min Size of Investment Considered (000s): $668
Max Size of Investment Considered (000s): $5,344

Geographical Preferences

International Preferences:
Europe

Industry Preferences

In Industrial/Energy prefer:
Energy
Alternative Energy
Energy Conservation Relat
Environmental Related

In Other prefer:
Environment Responsible

Additional Information

Year Founded: 2008
Capital Under Management: $43,000,000
Current Activity Level: Actively seeking new investments

YELLOWSTONE CAPITAL, INC.

1177 West Loop South, Suite 1425
Houston, TX USA 77027
Phone: 7136500065
Fax: 7136500055
E-mail: info@yellowstonecapital.com
Website: www.yellowstonecapital.com

Management and Staff
Anthony Nguyen, Principal
Omar Sawaf, Chairman & CEO
Vreij Arthur Kolandjian, Partner
William Brewer, Partner

Type of Firm
Private Equity Firm

Project Preferences

Role in Financing:
Prefer role as deal originator but will also invest in deals created by others

Type of Financing Preferred:
Leveraged Buyout
Early Stage
Expansion
Mezzanine
Generalist PE
Other
Acquisition

Geographical Preferences

United States Preferences:
Southwest
All U.S.

Industry Focus
(% based on actual investment)

Industrial/Energy	84.5%
Medical/Health	8.1%
Semiconductors/Other Elect.	5.3%
Biotechnology	2.0%

Additional Information
Name of Most Recent Fund: Yellowstone Energy Ventures II, L.P.
Most Recent Fund Was Raised: 09/10/2008
Year Founded: 1993
Current Activity Level : Actively seeking new investments

YENNI CAPITAL

1271 Avenue of the Americas, Suite 4300
New York, NY USA 10020
E-mail: info@yennicapital.com
Website: www.yennicapital.com

Type of Firm
Private Equity Firm

Geographical Preferences

United States Preferences:

Industry Preferences

In Business Serv. prefer:
Services

In Manufact. prefer:
Manufacturing

Additional Information
Year Founded: 2015
Capital Under Management: $7,400,000
Current Activity Level : Actively seeking new investments

YES BANK LTD

Nehru Centre, Ninth Floor
Discovery of India, Dr. AB Rd
Mumbai, India 400 018
Phone: 91-22-6669-9000
Fax: 91-22-2490-0314
E-mail: yestouch@yesbank.in
Website: www.yesbank.in

Other Offices
48, Nyaya Marg
Chanakya Puri,
New Delhi, India 110 021
Phone: 91-11-6656-9000
Fax: 91-11-5168-0144

Management and Staff
Rajat Monga, Chief Financial Officer
Rana Kapoor, Chief Executive Officer
Shivanand Shettigar, President
Vivek Ganguly, Vice President

Type of Firm
Bank Affiliated

Project Preferences

Type of Financing Preferred:
Expansion
Balanced

Size of Investments Considered:
Min Size of Investment Considered (000s): $5,000
Max Size of Investment Considered (000s): $7,500

Geographical Preferences

International Preferences:
India
Asia

Industry Preferences

In Consumer Related prefer:
Food/Beverage

In Industrial/Energy prefer:
Environmental Related

In Agr/Forestr/Fish prefer:
Agribusiness

Additional Information
Year Founded: 2007
Current Activity Level : Actively seeking new investments

YI CAPITAL INC.

Ping An International
Xinyuan South Road
Beijing, China
Phone: 861084442268
Website: zhiyivc.com

Type of Firm
Private Equity Firm

Project Preferences

Type of Financing Preferred:
Early Stage
Expansion
Seed
Startup

Geographical Preferences

International Preferences:
China

Industry Preferences

In Communications prefer:
Telecommunications

In Medical/Health prefer:
Medical/Health

In Consumer Related prefer:
Education Related

In Financial Services prefer:
Financial Services
Real Estate

In Business Serv. prefer:
Media

Additional Information
Year Founded: 2013
Capital Under Management: $200,000,000
Current Activity Level : Actively seeking new investments

YICHANG YUEHE EQUITY INVESTMENT FUND MANAGEMENT CO LTD

High-tech Zone
No.62, Development AVENUE
Yichang, China 443005

Type of Firm
Investment Management Firm

Project Preferences

Type of Financing Preferred:
Balanced

Geographical Preferences

International Preferences:
China

Industry Preferences

In Industrial/Energy prefer:
Materials

Additional Information

Year Founded: 2016
Capital Under Management: $30,810,000
Current Activity Level : Actively seeking new investments

YIELD LAB LLC

911 Washington Avenue, Suite 801
Saint Louis, MO USA 63101
Website: www.theyieldlab.com

Type of Firm

Incubator/Development Program

Project Preferences

Type of Financing Preferred:
Early Stage
Seed

Industry Preferences

In Agr/Forestr/Fish prefer:
Agriculture related

Additional Information

Year Founded: 2014
Capital Under Management: $820,000
Current Activity Level : Actively seeking new investments

YILIAN EQUITY INVESTMENT FUND

Suzhou Industrial Park
Suzhou, China

Type of Firm

Private Equity Firm

Project Preferences

Type of Financing Preferred:
Later Stage

Geographical Preferences

International Preferences:
China

Industry Preferences

In Consumer Related prefer:
Consumer

In Industrial/Energy prefer:
Energy

In Business Serv. prefer:
Services

Additional Information

Year Founded: 2010
Current Activity Level : Actively seeking new investments

YIMEI CAPITAL MANAGEMENT

1468 West Nanjing Road
Room 1105, United Plaza
Shanghai, China
Phone: 862162890399201
Fax: 862162890399210
E-mail: info@yimeicapital.com
Website: www.yimeicapital.com

Management and Staff

Judy Qing Ye, Managing Partner
Zhenghong Fan, Managing Partner

Type of Firm

Private Equity Advisor or Fund of Funds

Project Preferences

Type of Financing Preferred:
Fund of Funds
Balanced

Geographical Preferences

International Preferences:
China

Additional Information

Name of Most Recent Fund: YiMei Capital Management RMB Fund of Funds
Most Recent Fund Was Raised: 11/19/2010
Year Founded: 2010
Capital Under Management: $75,304,000
Current Activity Level : Actively seeking new investments

YING CAPITAL

No.79 Jianguo Road
Rm 1502 China Central Place II
Beijing, China 100025
Phone: 861085887568
Fax: 861085887569
E-mail: info@aqlcapital.com
Website: www.yingcapital.com

Other Offices

No.213 East Queen's Road
22nd Floor Wu Chung House
Hong Kong, Hong Kong
Phone: 85227828706
Fax: 85230117160

Management and Staff

Hui Chen, Vice President
Jiwen Luo, Vice President
Zhaoding Ding, Partner

Type of Firm

Bank Affiliated

Project Preferences

Type of Financing Preferred:
Leveraged Buyout
Later Stage

Geographical Preferences

International Preferences:
China

Industry Preferences

In Biotechnology prefer:
Biotechnology

In Medical/Health prefer:
Pharmaceuticals

In Industrial/Energy prefer:
Energy
Machinery

In Manufact. prefer:
Manufacturing

In Agr/Forestr/Fish prefer:
Agribusiness

In Other prefer:
Environment Responsible

Additional Information

Year Founded: 2011
Capital Under Management: $46,414,000
Current Activity Level : Actively seeking new investments

YINGCAIYUAN INVESTMENT MANAGEMENT CO LTD

No. 373-381, South Suzhou Road
Room 408G05
Shanghai , China

Type of Firm

Private Equity Firm

Project Preferences

Type of Financing Preferred:
Balanced

Geographical Preferences

International Preferences:
China

Additional Information
Year Founded: 2015
Current Activity Level : Actively seeking new investments

YINGKE INNOVATION ASSETS MANAGEMENT CO LTD

#388 Tongpan Rd Gulou District
Fujian, China
Website: www.yingkepe.com

Management and Staff
Ruihua Chen, President
Zhenguang Huang, Vice President

Type of Firm
Private Equity Firm

Project Preferences

Type of Financing Preferred:
Balanced

Geographical Preferences

International Preferences:
China

Industry Preferences

In Manufact. prefer:
Manufacturing

Additional Information
Year Founded: 2010
Current Activity Level : Actively seeking new investments

YINGTAI GERUI INVESTMENT CO LTD

East Third Ring, Chaoyang
7F, Donghuan Intl Mansion
Beijing, China 100022
Phone: 861067748799
Fax: 861067748977
Website: www.ytgrtrusts.com

Type of Firm
Private Equity Firm

Project Preferences

Type of Financing Preferred:
Balanced

Geographical Preferences

International Preferences:
China

Industry Preferences

In Financial Services prefer:
Real Estate

Additional Information
Year Founded: 2013
Current Activity Level : Actively seeking new investments

YL VENTURES GP LTD

42 Miller Ave
Mill Valley, CA USA 94941
Phone: 4156921000
E-mail: info@ylventures.com

Management and Staff
John Quigley, Partner
Robert Goldberg, Venture Partner
Yoav Leitersdorf, Managing Partner

Type of Firm
Private Equity Firm

Project Preferences

Type of Financing Preferred:
Early Stage
Mezzanine
Seed
Startup

Geographical Preferences

International Preferences:
Europe
Israel

Industry Preferences

In Communications prefer:
Communications and Media
Telecommunications
Wireless Communications
Data Communications
Media and Entertainment

In Computer Software prefer:
Data Processing
Software

In Internet Specific prefer:
E-Commerce Technology
Internet
Ecommerce

In Business Serv. prefer:
Services

Additional Information
Name of Most Recent Fund: YLV II, L.P.
Most Recent Fund Was Raised: 07/30/2013
Year Founded: 2007
Capital Under Management: $102,500,000
Current Activity Level : Actively seeking new investments

YONG WAN CAPITAL ASSET MANAGEMENT GROUP CO LTD

10/F, 7 Qingdao Software Park
288 Ningxia Road
Qingdao, China 266071
Phone: 86-532-85710050
Fax: 86-532-85739676
E-mail: info@uonemanagement.com
Website: www.yongwanchina.com

Type of Firm
Private Equity Firm

Project Preferences

Type of Financing Preferred:
Early Stage
Expansion
Balanced
Later Stage

Geographical Preferences

International Preferences:
China
Asia

Industry Preferences

In Communications prefer:
Telecommunications

In Biotechnology prefer:
Biotechnology
Agricultural/Animal Bio.

In Medical/Health prefer:
Pharmaceuticals

In Industrial/Energy prefer:
Alternative Energy
Materials

In Business Serv. prefer:
Services
Media

Additional Information
Year Founded: 2009
Capital Under Management: $14,600,000
Current Activity Level : Actively seeking new investments

YONGCHUN INVESTMENT ADVISOR SHANGHAI CO LTD

No.868 Yinghua Road Pudong
Shanghai, China
Website: www.yccapital.com.cn

Type of Firm
Investment Management Firm

Project Preferences

Type of Financing Preferred:
Balanced

Geographical Preferences

International Preferences:
China

Industry Preferences

In Communications prefer:
Telecommunications
Media and Entertainment

In Medical/Health prefer:
Medical/Health

In Other prefer:
Environment Responsible

Additional Information

Year Founded: 2006
Current Activity Level : Actively seeking new investments

YORK ANGEL INVESTORS INC

11 Cidermill Avenue, Suite 204
Vaughn, Canada L4K 4B6
Phone: 9055320617
Fax: 9055320092
Website: www.yorkangels.com

Other Offices

11 Cidermill Avenue, Suite 204
Vaughn, Canada L4K 4B6
Phone: 9055320617
Fax: 9055320092

Type of Firm

Angel Group

Project Preferences

Type of Financing Preferred:
Early Stage

Geographical Preferences

Canadian Preferences:
Ontario

Industry Preferences

In Communications prefer:
Telecommunications

In Computer Software prefer:
Applications Software

In Internet Specific prefer:
Internet

In Medical/Health prefer:
Pharmaceuticals

In Consumer Related prefer:
Retail

Additional Information

Year Founded: 2005
Current Activity Level : Actively seeking new investments

YORK CAPITAL MANAGEMENT LP

767 Fifth Avenure
17th Floor
New York, NY USA 10153
Phone: 2123001300
Fax: 2123001301
E-mail: info@yorkcapital.com

Other Offices

1150 Connecticut Avenue North West, Suite 701
Washington, DC USA 20036
Phone: 202-785-8021
Fax: 202-785-8022

10 Brook Street
5th Floor
London, United Kingdom W1S 1BG
Phone: 44-0207-907-5600
Fax: 44-0207-907-5601

Two International Finance Centre
21st Floor, 8 Finance Street
Hong Kong, Hong Kong
Phone: 852-3718-5800
Fax: 852-3718-5801

Type of Firm

Private Equity Firm

Project Preferences

Type of Financing Preferred:
Leveraged Buyout
Acquisition
Distressed Debt

Geographical Preferences

United States Preferences:
All U.S.

International Preferences:
United Kingdom
Hong Kong
China

Additional Information

Year Founded: 1991
Current Activity Level : Actively seeking new investments

YORK PLAINS INVESTMENT CORP

25 Sheppard Avenue West, Suite 1600
Toronto, Canada M2M 6S6
Phone: 4162211511
Website: www.yorkplains.com

Management and Staff

Jason Drummond, Managing Director
Mark Silver, Partner
Shawn Dym, Managing Director

Type of Firm

Private Equity Firm

Project Preferences

Type of Financing Preferred:
Leveraged Buyout
Acquisition

Industry Preferences

In Industrial/Energy prefer:
Energy
Alternative Energy
Energy Conservation Relat
Environmental Related

Additional Information

Year Founded: 2012
Current Activity Level : Actively seeking new investments

YORKTOWN PARTNERS LLC

410 Park Avenue
19th Floor
New York, NY USA 10022
Phone: 2125152100
Fax: 2125152105

Management and Staff

Bryan Lawrence, Founder
Peter Leidel, President

Type of Firm

Private Equity Firm

Project Preferences

Type of Financing Preferred:
Leveraged Buyout
Generalist PE
Other
Acquisition
Recapitalizations

Geographical Preferences

United States Preferences:
All U.S.

Industry Focus
(% based on actual investment)
Industrial/Energy	94.2%
Other Products	5.2%
Communications and Media	0.6%

Additional Information
Name of Most Recent Fund: Yorktown Energy Partners X, L.P.
Most Recent Fund Was Raised: 05/28/2013
Year Founded: 1983
Capital Under Management: $1,229,100,000
Current Activity Level : Actively seeking new investments

YORKVILLE ADVISORS MANAGEMENT LLC

101 Hudson Street, Suite 3700
Jersey City, NJ USA 07302
Phone: 2019858300
Fax: 2019858266
E-mail: info@yorkvilleadvisors.com

Other Offices
150 US Highway One, Suite 505
Jupiter, FL USA 33477
Phone: 561-427-6200
Fax: 561-427-6204

1125 17th Street, Suite 2300
Denver, CO USA 80202
Phone: 303-308-0650
Fax: 303-308-1590

Golden Bear Plaza, East Tower
Fourth Floor, Suite 406
North Palm Beach, FL USA 33408
Phone: 561 427 6200
Fax: 561 427 6204

Management and Staff
Brian Kinane, Managing Partner
James Carr, Vice President
Jerry Eicke, Partner
Lester Garrett, Senior Managing Director
Mark Angelo, President
Matthew Beckman, Partner
Michael Rosselli, Managing Director
Saad Gilani, Vice President
Troy Rillo, Senior Managing Director
Viral Mehta, Vice President

Type of Firm
Investment Management Firm

Project Preferences

Type of Financing Preferred:
Fund of Funds
Leveraged Buyout
Acquisition

Geographical Preferences

United States Preferences:
All U.S.

Canadian Preferences:
All Canada

International Preferences:
Italy
Greece
United Kingdom
Europe
Hong Kong
Iran
Israel
France

Industry Preferences

In Communications prefer:
Telecommunications

In Medical/Health prefer:
Health Services

In Industrial/Energy prefer:
Energy

In Financial Services prefer:
Financial Services

In Business Serv. prefer:
Media

In Agr/Forestr/Fish prefer:
Mining and Minerals

Additional Information
Year Founded: 2001
Capital Under Management: $965,000,000
Current Activity Level : Actively seeking new investments

YOUNG ASSOCIATES LTD

19 Cavendish Square
Harcourt House
London, United Kingdom W1G 0PL
Phone: 442074478800
Fax: 442074478849
E-mail: info@youngassoc.com
Website: www.yaec.co.uk

Type of Firm
Private Equity Firm

Association Membership
British Venture Capital Association (BVCA)

Project Preferences

Type of Financing Preferred:
Early Stage

Geographical Preferences

International Preferences:
United Kingdom
Europe
Israel

Industry Preferences

In Communications prefer:
Communications and Media

Additional Information
Year Founded: 1996
Current Activity Level : Actively seeking new investments

YOUNGOR INVESTMENT CO LTD

Yinzhou District
No.2 West Section Yinxian Road
Ningbo, China 315153
Phone: 862168866135
Fax: 862168866139
E-mail: office@youngor.com
Website: www.youngor.com

Type of Firm
Investment Management Firm

Project Preferences

Type of Financing Preferred:
Leveraged Buyout
Expansion
Balanced

Geographical Preferences

International Preferences:
China

Industry Preferences

In Biotechnology prefer:
Biotech Related Research

In Medical/Health prefer:
Medical/Health

Additional Information
Year Founded: 2007
Current Activity Level : Actively seeking new investments

YOUNGSHIN VENTURE CAPITAL

1480-3 Yeonhang-dong
Sooncheon-si Jeollanamdo
Jeollanamdo, South Korea 540-951
Phone: 822-3424-1977
Fax: 822-3436-9127

2337

Other Offices
2512 Technomart Building
546-4 Kooeui-dong Kwangjin-ku
Seoul, South Korea

Management and Staff
Mink Chang, Chief Executive Officer

Type of Firm
Private Equity Firm

Project Preferences

Type of Financing Preferred:
Balanced

Geographical Preferences

International Preferences:
Korea, South

Additional Information
Year Founded: 1999
Capital Under Management: $1,600,000
Current Activity Level : Actively seeking new investments

YOURNEST CAPITAL ADVISORS PVT LTD
Opposite Unitech Cyber Park
101, 1st Flr, Greenwood Plaza
Sector 45, Gurgaon, India 122 001
Phone: 911244284310
E-mail: yournest@yournest.in
Website: yournest.in

Management and Staff
Girish Shivani, Founder
Sunil Goyal, Chief Executive Officer

Type of Firm
Private Equity Firm

Project Preferences

Type of Financing Preferred:
Early Stage
Seed
Startup

Geographical Preferences

International Preferences:
India
Asia

Additional Information
Year Founded: 2012
Current Activity Level : Actively seeking new investments

YSIOS CAPITAL PARTNERS SGECR SAU
Travessera de Gracia, 11
Parc Cientific de Barcelona
Barcelona, Spain 08021
Phone: 34935173545
E-mail: ysios@ysioscapital.com
Website: www.ysioscapital.com

Other Offices
Mikeletegi, 56 1a planta
Parque Tecnologico De San Sebastian
Donostia-San Sebastian , Spain 20009
Phone: 34935173545

Management and Staff
Cristina Garmendia, Partner
Joel Jean-Mairet, Partner
Josep Sanfeliu, Partner
Julia Salaverria, Partner
Karen Wagner, Venture Partner
Marc Casellas, Chief Financial Officer

Type of Firm
Private Equity Firm

Association Membership
European Private Equity and Venture Capital Assoc.
Spanish Venture Capital Association (ASCRI)

Project Preferences

Type of Financing Preferred:
Early Stage
Expansion
Balanced
Later Stage
Seed

Size of Investments Considered:
Min Size of Investment Considered (000s): $1,250
Max Size of Investment Considered (000s): $7,499

Geographical Preferences

United States Preferences:
North America

Canadian Preferences:
All Canada

International Preferences:
Europe
Spain

Industry Preferences

In Biotechnology prefer:
Biotechnology

In Medical/Health prefer:
Medical/Health
Medical Diagnostics
Diagnostic Services
Diagnostic Test Products
Pharmaceuticals

Additional Information
Year Founded: 2007
Capital Under Management: $139,070,000
Current Activity Level : Actively seeking new investments

YUANANGEL
No.238 North 4th Middle Road
No.603 Room, Boyan Building
Beijing, China
Phone: 861082311910
Fax: 861082311910
Website: www.yuanhecapital.com

Type of Firm
Private Equity Advisor or Fund of Funds

Project Preferences

Type of Financing Preferred:
Fund of Funds

Geographical Preferences

International Preferences:
China

Additional Information
Year Founded: 2016
Current Activity Level : Actively seeking new investments

YUANJING WANFANG (TIANJIN) EQUITY INVEST MGMT ENTRP, L.P.
20, Plaza E Rd, Dvl'p District
4052, E2-ABC-4, Binhai Finl St
Tianjin, China
Phone: 861085221230

Type of Firm
Private Equity Firm

Project Preferences

Type of Financing Preferred:
Balanced

Geographical Preferences

International Preferences:
China

Additional Information
Year Founded: 2008
Capital Under Management: $362,215,000
Current Activity Level : Actively seeking new investments

YUANTA VENTURE CAPITAL CO LTD

No. 66 Sec.1 Dunhua South Rd.
11F
Taipei, Taiwan, Taiwan 10557
Phone: 886221736633
Fax: 886227720248
Website: www.yuanta.com

Type of Firm
Investment Management Firm

Project Preferences

Type of Financing Preferred:
Balanced

Geographical Preferences

International Preferences:
Taiwan
Asia

Industry Preferences

In Communications prefer:
Telecommunications

In Semiconductor/Electr prefer:
Electronics
Semiconductor
Sensors

In Biotechnology prefer:
Biotechnology

In Medical/Health prefer:
Medical/Health
Health Services
Pharmaceuticals

In Consumer Related prefer:
Entertainment and Leisure

In Industrial/Energy prefer:
Energy
Advanced Materials
Machinery

In Transportation prefer:
Transportation
Aerospace

In Financial Services prefer:
Financial Services

In Business Serv. prefer:
Services
Consulting Services

In Agr/Forestr/Fish prefer:
Mining and Minerals

In Other prefer:
Environment Responsible

Additional Information
Year Founded: 2002
Current Activity Level : Actively seeking new investments

YUCAIPA COS

9130 West Sunset Boulevard
Los Angeles, CA USA 90069
Phone: 3107897200
Fax: 3107897201
E-mail: investorrelations@yucaipaco.com
Website: www.yucaipaco.com

Type of Firm
Private Equity Firm

Project Preferences

Type of Financing Preferred:
Leveraged Buyout
Management Buyouts
Acquisition
Recapitalizations

Geographical Preferences

United States Preferences:
All U.S.

Industry Focus
(% based on actual investment)
Other Products	57.6%
Consumer Related	39.5%
Communications and Media	2.4%
Computer Software and Services	0.5%

Additional Information
Year Founded: 1986
Capital Under Management: $196,250,000
Current Activity Level : Actively seeking new investments

YUKON NV

Maria-Theresiastraat 38
Leuven, Belgium 3000
Phone: 3227126940
Fax: 3227126943
E-mail: info@yukon.be
Website: www.yukon.be

Management and Staff
Filip Legein, Managing Partner
Steven Vander Meeren, Managing Partner

Type of Firm
Private Equity Firm

Association Membership
Belgium Venturing Association

Project Preferences

Type of Financing Preferred:
Leveraged Buyout
Turnaround
Management Buyouts
Acquisition

Geographical Preferences

International Preferences:
Europe
Belgium

Industry Preferences

In Medical/Health prefer:
Medical/Health

In Consumer Related prefer:
Publishing-Retail

In Business Serv. prefer:
Services
Distribution
Media

In Utilities prefer:
Utilities

Additional Information
Year Founded: 1999
Capital Under Management: $4,400,000
Current Activity Level : Actively seeking new investments

YUKON PARTNERS MANAGEMENT LLC

8500 Normandale Lake Boulevard, Suite 1160
Minneapolis, MN USA 55437
Phone: 6124357800
Fax: 6124357801
E-mail: info@yukonpartners.com
Website: yukonpartners.com

Management and Staff
Aaron Arnett, Principal
Corey Peters, Chief Financial Officer
Michael Hall, Managing Partner
Michael Furey, Partner
William Dietz, Managing Partner

Type of Firm
Private Equity Firm

Project Preferences

Type of Financing Preferred:
Leveraged Buyout
Mezzanine
Acquisition
Recapitalizations

Geographical Preferences

United States Preferences:

Canadian Preferences:
All Canada

Industry Preferences

In Medical/Health prefer:
Medical/Health

In Consumer Related prefer:
Consumer Products

In Transportation prefer:
Transportation

In Business Serv. prefer:
Distribution

In Manufact. prefer:
Manufacturing

Additional Information
Name of Most Recent Fund: Yukon Capital Partners II, L.P.
Most Recent Fund Was Raised: 12/11/2013
Year Founded: 2008
Capital Under Management: $958,740,000
Current Activity Level : Actively seeking new investments

YUKON VENTURE GROUP

409 Black Street
Whitehorse, Canada Y1A 2N2
Phone: 867-668-6925
Fax: 867-668-3127
E-mail: dnv@dananaye.com
Website: www.dananaye.yk.net

Type of Firm
Private Equity Firm

Geographical Preferences

Canadian Preferences:
Yukon
British Columbia

Additional Information
Year Founded: 2002
Current Activity Level : Actively seeking new investments

YUNNAN AGRICULTURE VENTURE CAPITAL CO LTD

Beijing Road
Yanchangxian Jinsenianhua Bldg
Kunshan, Yunnan, China 650224
Phone: 86-871-5749-925

Type of Firm
Private Equity Firm

Project Preferences

Type of Financing Preferred:
Expansion
Later Stage

Geographical Preferences

International Preferences:
China

Industry Preferences

In Business Serv. prefer:
Services

In Agr/Forestr/Fish prefer:
Agriculture related

Additional Information
Year Founded: 2008
Current Activity Level : Actively seeking new investments

YUNNAN INDUSTRIAL INVESTMENT HOLDING GROUP CO LTD

Export Processing Zone
No. 50 Shuntong Street
Kunming, China 650217
Phone: 8687163959600
Website: www.ygtgp.com

Type of Firm
Government Affiliated Program

Project Preferences

Type of Financing Preferred:
Balanced

Geographical Preferences

International Preferences:
China

Industry Preferences

In Biotechnology prefer:
Biotechnology

Additional Information
Year Founded: 2008
Current Activity Level : Actively seeking new investments

YUNYI INVESTMENT MANAGEMENT SHANGHAI CO LTD

No.161, Lujiazui East Road
China Merchants Building
Shanghai, China
Phone: 862150188785
Website: www.yunyiinvestment.com

Type of Firm
Private Equity Firm

Project Preferences

Type of Financing Preferred:
Leveraged Buyout

Geographical Preferences

International Preferences:
China

Industry Preferences

In Communications prefer:
Telecommunications

In Business Serv. prefer:
Media

Additional Information
Year Founded: 2014
Current Activity Level : Actively seeking new investments

YUUWA CAPITAL LP

9 De Laeter Way
Enterprise Unit 3, Suite 4
Bentley, Australia 6102
Phone: 61861424778
Fax: 61893555694
E-mail: enquiries@yuuwa.com.au
Website: www.yuuwa.com.au

Management and Staff
James Williams, Co-Founder
Matthew Macfarlane, Co-Founder

Type of Firm
Private Equity Firm

Project Preferences

Role in Financing:
Prefer role as deal originator but will also invest in deals created by others

Type of Financing Preferred:
Early Stage
Seed

Size of Investments Considered:
Min Size of Investment Considered (000s): $361
Max Size of Investment Considered (000s): $5,772

Geographical Preferences

International Preferences:
Australia

Industry Preferences

In Communications prefer:
Communications and Media

In Computer Software prefer:
Software

In Biotechnology prefer:
Biotechnology

In Industrial/Energy prefer:
Alternative Energy

Additional Information
Name of Most Recent Fund: Yuuwa Capital IIF Fund
Most Recent Fund Was Raised: 11/09/2009
Year Founded: 2009
Capital Under Management: $40,000,000
Current Activity Level : Actively seeking new investments

- Z -

01 VENTURES LLP
Chalk Farm Rd
3F, Triangle Bldg Stables Mkt
London, United Kingdom NW1 8AB
Website: www.01ventures.com

Management and Staff
Chris Haley, Co-Founder
Correy Voo, Partner
Eeswaran Navaratnam, Co-Founder

Type of Firm
Private Equity Firm

Project Preferences

Type of Financing Preferred:
Early Stage

Additional Information
Year Founded: 2017
Current Activity Level : Actively seeking new investments

Z CAPITAL HF ADVISER LLC
150 Field Drive, 2 Conway Park, Suite 300
Lake Forest, IL USA 60045
Phone: 8472358100
Fax: 8472358111

Management and Staff
Andrei Scrivens, Managing Director
Ashwini Sawhney, Managing Director
Catherine Chiavetta, Managing Director
Christopher Kipley, Senior Managing Director
Claire Kendrick, Managing Director
David DeMilt, Managing Director
Gianni Russello, Managing Director
Irene Hong, Managing Director
Rahul Sawhney, Senior Managing Director
Sean Maddock, Managing Director
Steve Parsons, Managing Director
William Monagle, Managing Director

Type of Firm
Private Equity Firm

Project Preferences

Type of Financing Preferred:
Leveraged Buyout
Turnaround
Special Situation
Distressed Debt
Recapitalizations

Industry Preferences

In Communications prefer:
Entertainment

In Consumer Related prefer:
Consumer Products

In Industrial/Energy prefer:
Industrial Products

In Transportation prefer:
Transportation

In Financial Services prefer:
Financial Services
Real Estate

In Business Serv. prefer:
Services

In Manufact. prefer:
Manufacturing

In Agr/Forestr/Fish prefer:
Agriculture related

Additional Information
Year Founded: 2006
Capital Under Management: $1,036,500,000
Current Activity Level : Actively seeking new investments

Z INVESTMENTS LLP
Two Downshire Hill
Studio Two
London, United Kingdom
Website: www.zipartners.com

Type of Firm
Private Equity Firm

Additional Information
Year Founded: 2012
Capital Under Management: $650,000,000
Current Activity Level : Actively seeking new investments

Z-ACQUISITION GROUP
19009 Preston Road, Suite 215232
Dallas, TX USA 75252
Phone: 2143474239
Website: www.z-acquisitiongroup.com

Type of Firm
Private Equity Firm

Project Preferences

Type of Financing Preferred:
Generalist PE
Balanced
Turnaround
Acquisition
Distressed Debt

Geographical Preferences

United States Preferences:
California
Maine

Additional Information
Year Founded: 2008
Current Activity Level : Actively seeking new investments

Z9 CAPITAL LLC

999 Yamato Rd, Suite 101
Boca Raton, FL USA 33431
Phone: 5619239554
E-mail: Info@z9Capital.com
Website: z9capital.com

Type of Firm
Private Equity Firm

Project Preferences

Type of Financing Preferred:
Early Stage

Industry Preferences

In Internet Specific prefer:
Ecommerce

In Consumer Related prefer:
Retail

Additional Information
Year Founded: 2014
Current Activity Level : Actively seeking new investments

ZACHARY SCOTT & CO

1200 Fifth Avenue, Suite 1500
Seattle, WA USA 98101
Phone: 206-224-7380
Fax: 206-224-7384
E-mail: info@zacharyscott.com
Website: www.zacharyscott.com

Management and Staff
Frank Buhler, Principal
Mark Working, Principal
Michael Newsome, Vice President
Ray Rezab, Vice President
William Hanneman, Principal

Type of Firm
Bank Affiliated

Project Preferences

Type of Financing Preferred:
Leveraged Buyout
Expansion
Mezzanine
Turnaround
Management Buyouts
Acquisition
Recapitalizations

Geographical Preferences

United States Preferences:
Northwest
Rocky Mountain
West Coast
All U.S.

Additional Information
Year Founded: 1991
Current Activity Level : Actively seeking new investments

ZAD INVESTMENT CO

P.O. Box 41888
10, Jabal Al-Rabaabah
Jeddah, Saudi Arabia 21531
Phone: 966505621331
Fax: 966504327924
Website: zad.com.sa

Type of Firm
Private Equity Firm

Project Preferences

Type of Financing Preferred:
Value-Add
Generalist PE
Balanced
Acquisition
Special Situation

Additional Information
Year Founded: 2014
Current Activity Level : Actively seeking new investments

ZAFFRE INVESTMENTS LLC

401 Park Drive
M/S 01-08
Boston, MA USA 02215
Website: www.zaffreinvestments.com

Type of Firm
Private Equity Firm

Project Preferences

Type of Financing Preferred:
Early Stage
Expansion
Balanced
Later Stage
Seed
Startup

Industry Preferences

In Medical/Health prefer:
Medical/Health
Medical Products
Health Services

Additional Information
Year Founded: 2014
Current Activity Level : Actively seeking new investments

ZAMBIA DEVELOPMENT AGENCY

Privatization House
Nasser Road
Lusaka, Zambia
Phone: 260-211-222858
Fax: 260-211-225270
E-mail: info@zda.org.zm
Website: www.zda.org.zm

Other Offices
Kwacha House Annex
Cairo Road
Lusaka, Zambia
Phone: 260-211-228107
Fax: 260-211-222509

Type of Firm
Government Affiliated Program

Project Preferences

Type of Financing Preferred:
Early Stage
Expansion
Later Stage

Geographical Preferences

International Preferences:
Zambia
Africa

Additional Information
Year Founded: 2006
Capital Under Management: $4,000,000
Current Activity Level : Actively seeking new investments

ZANA CAPITAL PTE LTD

Unit 2005, United Plaza
No. 146B, West Nanjing Road
Shanghai, China 200040
Phone: 86-21-61415788
Fax: 86-21-61415700
E-mail: zana@zanacapital.com
Website: www.zanacapital.com

Other Offices
Guanyinqiao Road, Jiangbei District
Unit 20-8 Future International Building
Chongqing, China 401121
Phone: 862367701878
Fax: 862367702378

3 Phillip Street
#09-02 Commerce Point
Singapore, Singapore
Phone: 6563091100
Fax: 6563091116

Management and Staff
Dahong Xie, Partner
Edmund Tan, Partner
Hock Eng Chan, Managing Partner
Kok Peng Leow, Partner
Koon Siong Ng, Managing Partner

Type of Firm
Private Equity Firm

Association Membership
China Venture Capital Association
Singapore Venture Capital Association (SVCA)

Project Preferences

Type of Financing Preferred:
Expansion
Later Stage

Geographical Preferences

International Preferences:
China

Industry Preferences

In Medical/Health prefer:
Pharmaceuticals

In Consumer Related prefer:
Consumer

In Industrial/Energy prefer:
Environmental Related

In Transportation prefer:
Transportation

In Business Serv. prefer:
Services

In Manufact. prefer:
Manufacturing

In Agr/Forestr/Fish prefer:
Mining and Minerals

Additional Information
Year Founded: 2011
Current Activity Level : Actively seeking new investments

ZANITE VENTURES LLC

100 Public Square, Suite 2300
Cleveland, OH USA 44114

Type of Firm
Private Equity Firm

Project Preferences

Type of Financing Preferred:
Early Stage

Industry Preferences

In Computer Software prefer:
Artificial Intelligence

In Medical/Health prefer:
Health Services

In Industrial/Energy prefer:
Robotics

Additional Information
Year Founded: 2017
Current Activity Level : Actively seeking new investments

ZARPAMOS ACELERADORA DE EMPRESAS TIC SL

Calle Del Hospital, 21
La Coruna, Spain 15002
Phone: 34649686119
Website: zarpamos.com

Type of Firm
Incubator/Development Program

Project Preferences

Type of Financing Preferred:
Seed
Startup

Industry Preferences

In Communications prefer:
Communications and Media
Wireless Communications

In Computer Software prefer:
Applications Software

In Internet Specific prefer:
Internet
Ecommerce
Web Aggregration/Portals

In Medical/Health prefer:
Medical/Health

In Consumer Related prefer:
Education Related

In Business Serv. prefer:
Services

Additional Information
Year Founded: 2012
Current Activity Level : Actively seeking new investments

ZEEUWS INVESTERINGS-FONDS BV

Edisonweg 41 A7
Vlissingen, Netherlands 4382NV
Phone: 31624810367
Website: www.zeeuwsinvesteringsfonds.com

Type of Firm
Private Equity Firm

Project Preferences

Type of Financing Preferred:
Early Stage
Seed

Size of Investments Considered:
Min Size of Investment Considered (000s): $441
Max Size of Investment Considered (000s): $1,102

Geographical Preferences

International Preferences:
Netherlands

Additional Information
Year Founded: 2012
Current Activity Level : Actively seeking new investments

ZEEV VENTURES MANAGEMENT LLC

555 Bryant Street, Suite 811
Palo Alto, CA USA 94301
Phone: 6503889883

Type of Firm
Private Equity Firm

Additional Information
Year Founded: 2015
Capital Under Management: $52,000,000
Current Activity Level : Actively seeking new investments

ZELKOVA VENTURES

667 Madison Avenue
New York, NY USA 10065

Management and Staff
Jay Levy, Founding Partner
Larry Scheinfeld, Founding Partner

Type of Firm
Private Equity Firm

Project Preferences

Type of Financing Preferred:
Early Stage
Balanced
Seed

Additional Information

Year Founded: 2008
Current Activity Level : Actively seeking new investments

ZEN CAPITAL ONE SP Z O O SKA

Kielecka 41A/2
Warsaw, Poland 02-530
Phone: 48224041269
Website: www.zencapital.pl

Type of Firm
Private Equity Firm

Project Preferences

Type of Financing Preferred:
Early Stage
Seed
Startup

Geographical Preferences

International Preferences:
Poland

Additional Information

Year Founded: 2013
Current Activity Level : Actively seeking new investments

ZENITH VENTURE CAPITAL AB

Norrlandsgatan 15
Stockholm, Sweden 111 43
Phone: 46 85550962
Website: www.zenith.vc

Type of Firm
Private Equity Firm

Project Preferences

Type of Financing Preferred:
Early Stage

Geographical Preferences

International Preferences:
Scandanavia/Nordic Region

Industry Preferences

In Communications prefer:
Entertainment

In Consumer Related prefer:
Retail

Additional Information

Year Founded: 2015
Current Activity Level : Actively seeking new investments

ZENO VENTURES

255 California Street, Suite 800
San Francisco, CA USA 94111
Phone: 14156517154
Fax: 14156519297
Website: www.zenoventures.com

Type of Firm
Private Equity Firm

Project Preferences

Type of Financing Preferred:
Leveraged Buyout
Early Stage
Later Stage
Seed
Acquisition

Geographical Preferences

United States Preferences:

International Preferences:
Switzerland

Industry Preferences

In Consumer Related prefer:
Consumer

Additional Information

Year Founded: 2016
Current Activity Level : Actively seeking new investments

ZENSHIN CAPITAL MANAGEMENT

535 Middlefield Road, Suite 280
Menlo Park, CA USA 94025
Phone: 6502402734
Fax: 6503249101
E-mail: db@zenshincapital.com
Website: www.zenshincp.com

Management and Staff

Clancey Stahr, Managing Partner
Phil Brady, Principal
Takeshi Mori, Co-Founder

Type of Firm
Private Equity Firm

Association Membership
National Venture Capital Association - USA (NVCA)

Project Preferences

Role in Financing:
Will function either as deal originator or investor in deals created by others

Type of Financing Preferred:
Early Stage
Expansion
Balanced
Later Stage

Geographical Preferences

United States Preferences:

International Preferences:
Japan

Additional Information

Name of Most Recent Fund: ADS-ZenShin I-Investment L.P.
Most Recent Fund Was Raised: 04/29/2006
Year Founded: 2005
Capital Under Management: $40,000,000
Current Activity Level : Actively seeking new investments

ZEPHYR MANAGEMENT LP

320 Park Avenue
New York, NY USA 10022
Phone: 2125089400
Fax: 2125089494
E-mail: zephyr@zmlp.com
Website: www.zmlp.com

Other Offices

22 Hurlingham Road
Unihold House, 1st floor
Johannesburg, South Africa 2196
Phone: 27112686911
Fax: 27112686917

11 Vittal Mallya Road, Suite 201 Embassy Classic
Bangalore, India 560001
Phone: 918042613300
Fax: 918042613400

Chiromo Road
M2, Mirage Towers
Nairobi, Kenya 10964

25 Hill Street
London, United Kingdom W1J 5LW
Phone: 44-207-907-2400
Fax: 44-207-907-2420

Management and Staff

Bruce Lueck, Managing Director
Cesar Urrea, Managing Director
J.Kofi Bucknor, Managing Partner
Jim Awad, Managing Director
John Cerminaro, Chief Financial Officer
Lekan Odugbesan, Vice President
Mark Ransford, Partner
Mukul Gulati, Managing Director
Peter Sheft, Managing Director
Robert Horton, Partner
Seyi Owudunni, Partner
Stephen Canter, Chief Operating Officer

Type of Firm
Investment Management Firm

Association Membership
Emerging Markets Private Equity Association
Indian Venture Capital Association (IVCA)

Project Preferences

Type of Financing Preferred:
Leveraged Buyout
Early Stage
Expansion
Generalist PE
Balanced
Later Stage
Seed
Management Buyouts
Acquisition
Startup
Recapitalizations

Geographical Preferences

United States Preferences:
North America

International Preferences:
India
Mexico
Sri Lanka
Asia
South Africa
Korea, South
Africa
All International

Industry Preferences

In Communications prefer:
Communications and Media
Telecommunications

In Computer Software prefer:
Applications Software

In Internet Specific prefer:
Internet

In Computer Other prefer:
Computer Related

In Medical/Health prefer:
Medical/Health
Health Services

In Consumer Related prefer:
Consumer
Entertainment and Leisure
Food/Beverage
Consumer Products
Consumer Services
Education Related

In Industrial/Energy prefer:
Environmental Related

In Transportation prefer:
Transportation

In Financial Services prefer:
Financial Services

In Business Serv. prefer:
Distribution
Consulting Services
Media

In Manufact. prefer:
Manufacturing

In Agr/Forestr/Fish prefer:
Agriculture related

Additional Information
Year Founded: 1994
Capital Under Management: $1,300,000,000
Current Activity Level: Actively seeking new investments

ZERNIKE META VENTURES SPA

Viake Tuoini Umberto 116
Rome, Italy 00144
E-mail: info@zernikemetaventures.com
Website: www.zernikemetaventures.com

Type of Firm
Private Equity Firm

Project Preferences

Type of Financing Preferred:
Early Stage
Expansion
Balanced
Later Stage
Seed
Startup

Geographical Preferences

United States Preferences:

International Preferences:
Italy
Slovenia
United Kingdom
Argentina
Spain

Industry Preferences

In Computer Software prefer:
Software

Additional Information
Year Founded: 2010
Capital Under Management: $20,060,000
Current Activity Level: Actively seeking new investments

ZERO2IPO VENTURES

No. 26 Xiaoyun Road, Suite 1203, Eagle Run Plaza
Beijing, China 100125
Phone: 861084580476
Fax: 861084580480
Website: www.zero2ipovc.com

Other Offices
No. 567 Weihai Rd, Jing An Dist
Rm. 5E, Crystal Century Tower
Shanghai, China 200041
Phone: 86-21-6288-9090
Fax: 86-21-6288-6716

100 Hamilton Avenue, Suite 100
Palo Alto, CA USA 94301
Phone: 650-461-8100
Fax: 650-461-8101

20 Westlands Road, Quarry Bay
2101, 21/F, Westland Center
Central, Hong Kong
Phone: 852-2960-4611
Fax: 852-2960-0185

No. 3038 Jiantian Road
Rm 703 Modern International Building
Shenzhen, China 518048
Phone: 86-755-8831-5318
Fax: 86-755-8831-5328

Management and Staff
Bin Ye, Managing Director
Runbing Yuan, Managing Director
Weidong Qu, Managing Director
Zhonghui Wang, Venture Partner

Type of Firm
Corporate PE/Venture

Project Preferences

Type of Financing Preferred:
Fund of Funds
Early Stage
Expansion
Balanced
Later Stage
Seed
Startup

Geographical Preferences

International Preferences:
China

Industry Preferences

In Communications prefer:
Telecommunications
Wireless Communications

In Internet Specific prefer:
Internet

In Consumer Related prefer:
Consumer
Consumer Products

In Industrial/Energy prefer:
Energy

In Business Serv. prefer:
Media

In Agr/Forestr/Fish prefer:
Mining and Minerals

Additional Information
Year Founded: 2006
Capital Under Management: $345,798,000
Current Activity Level : Actively seeking new investments

ZESIGER CAPITAL GROUP LLC

460 Park Avenue
22nd Floor
New York, NY USA 10022
Phone: 2125086300
Fax: 2125086399
E-mail: info@zesigercapital.com
Website: www.zcgllc.com

Management and Staff
Albert Zesiger, Managing Director
Barrie Zesiger, Managing Director
Colleen Behan, Principal
Donald DeVivo, Managing Director
James Cleary, Managing Director
John Kayola, Managing Director
Mary Estabil, Principal
Robert Winters, Managing Director

Type of Firm
Private Equity Firm

Project Preferences

Type of Financing Preferred:
Balanced

Geographical Preferences

United States Preferences:
All U.S.

Additional Information
Year Founded: 1996
Current Activity Level : Actively seeking new investments

ZETTA VENTURE PARTNERS

140 Geary Street, Suite 1000
San Francisco, CA USA 94103
Phone: 4158280852
Website: www.zettavp.com

Other Offices
1160 Battery Street East, Suite 40
SAN FRANCISCO, CA USA 94111
Phone: 4158280852

Management and Staff
Ash Fontana, Managing Director
Jeff Kearl, Venture Partner
Jocelyn Goldfein, Partner
Josh James, Venture Partner
Mark Gorenberg, Managing Director

Type of Firm
Private Equity Firm

Association Membership
National Venture Capital Association - USA (NVCA)

Project Preferences

Type of Financing Preferred:
Early Stage
Seed

Industry Preferences

In Computer Software prefer:
Software

In Semiconductor/Electr prefer:
Analytic/Scientific

Additional Information
Year Founded: 2013
Capital Under Management: $185,000,000
Current Activity Level : Actively seeking new investments

ZEVC MANAGEMENT CO LTD

Shennan Road, Futian District
10/F, Aerospace Bldg, Block A
Shenzen, China 518048
Phone: 8675588265920
Fax: 8675588265923
E-mail: bp@zevc.cn
Website: www.zevc.cn

Management and Staff
Jianfeng Wu, Vice President
Jun Han, Vice President
Weiguo Liu, President
Xiaoju Wang, Vice President
Xiaoli Wang, Vice President
Yuzhi Shen, Vice President

Type of Firm
Investment Management Firm

Project Preferences

Type of Financing Preferred:
Expansion
Balanced
Later Stage

Geographical Preferences

International Preferences:
China

Industry Preferences

In Communications prefer:
Telecommunications
Media and Entertainment

In Consumer Related prefer:
Consumer Products

In Industrial/Energy prefer:
Energy
Materials

Additional Information
Year Founded: 2010
Capital Under Management: $121,396,000
Current Activity Level : Actively seeking new investments

ZFHN ZUKUNFTSFONDS HEILBRONN GMBH & CO KG

Edisonstrasse 19
Heilbronn, Germany 74076
Phone: 49-713-18731830
Fax: 49-713187318320
E-mail: info@zf-hn.de
Website: www.zukunftsfonds-hn.com

Management and Staff
Gunter Steffen, Managing Director
Thomas Villinger, Managing Director

Type of Firm
Private Equity Firm

Association Membership
German Venture Capital Association (BVK)

Project Preferences

Type of Financing Preferred:
Early Stage
Later Stage
Seed
Startup

Size of Investments Considered:
Min Size of Investment Considered (000s): $653
Max Size of Investment Considered (000s): $10,440

Geographical Preferences

International Preferences:
Germany

Industry Preferences

In Computer Software prefer:
Software

In Biotechnology prefer:
Biotechnology

In Medical/Health prefer:
Medical/Health

In Industrial/Energy prefer:
Energy
Environmental Related

Additional Information
Year Founded: 2007
Current Activity Level : Actively seeking new investments

ZHAOQING HUAXIN INVEST CO LTD

No. 13, Duanzhousi Road
11/F, Seattle Commercial Plaza
Zhaoqing, China 526040
Phone: 867582229839
Website: www.0758vc.com

Type of Firm
Private Equity Firm

Project Preferences

Type of Financing Preferred:
Early Stage
Expansion
Balanced
Later Stage

Geographical Preferences

International Preferences:
China

Industry Preferences

In Internet Specific prefer:
Internet

In Consumer Related prefer:
Entertainment and Leisure

Additional Information
Year Founded: 2008
Current Activity Level : Actively seeking new investments

ZHEJIANG CHENGXIANG INVESTMENT MANAGEMENT CO LTD

1088 Jiangnan Ave. Binjiang
20/F, Zhongnan Intl' Bldg.
Hangzhou, China
Phone: 8657187700322
Fax: 8657187700169
Website: www.chengxiangtz.com

Type of Firm
Private Equity Firm

Project Preferences

Type of Financing Preferred:
Leveraged Buyout
Balanced

Geographical Preferences

International Preferences:
China

Industry Preferences

In Internet Specific prefer:
Ecommerce

In Business Serv. prefer:
Services
Media

Additional Information
Year Founded: 2015
Current Activity Level : Actively seeking new investments

ZHEJIANG CHENGZE JINKAI INVESTMENT MANAGEMENT CO LTD

No.118, Zhoushan East Road
Zhejiang, China 310007
Website: www.gold-finance.com

Type of Firm
Investment Management Firm

Project Preferences

Type of Financing Preferred:
Leveraged Buyout

Geographical Preferences

International Preferences:
China

Industry Preferences

In Communications prefer:
Entertainment

Additional Information
Year Founded: 2008
Capital Under Management: $82,594,000
Current Activity Level : Actively seeking new investments

ZHEJIANG FUJU INVESTMENT MANAGEMENT CO LTD

Huanglong Times Plaza, Wantang
Room 1505, Block A
Hangzhou, China 310000
Phone: 8657187203404
Website: www.fjvc.cn

Type of Firm
Private Equity Firm

Project Preferences

Type of Financing Preferred:
Balanced

Geographical Preferences

International Preferences:
China

Industry Preferences

In Medical/Health prefer:
Medical/Health
Drug/Equipmt Delivery

In Consumer Related prefer:
Consumer

In Industrial/Energy prefer:
Energy Conservation Relat

In Business Serv. prefer:
Services

In Manufact. prefer:
Manufacturing

Additional Information
Year Founded: 2012
Current Activity Level : Actively seeking new investments

ZHEJIANG FUXIN VENTURE CAPITAL CO LTD

Room304, No.2, Taohua Nong
West Lake District
Hangzhou, Zhejiang, China

Type of Firm
Private Equity Firm

Project Preferences

Type of Financing Preferred:
Balanced

Geographical Preferences

International Preferences:
China

Additional Information
Year Founded: 2008
Current Activity Level : Actively seeking new investments

ZHEJIANG HAODE JIAHUI INVESTMENT MANAGEMENT CO LTD

Jingbian Mansion
Room B-371, 3F, Building 2
Haining, China

Management and Staff
Jing Li, Partner

Type of Firm
Private Equity Firm

Project Preferences

Type of Financing Preferred:
Balanced

Geographical Preferences

International Preferences:
China

Industry Preferences

In Manufact. prefer:
Manufacturing

Additional Information
Year Founded: 2013
Current Activity Level : Actively seeking new investments

ZHEJIANG HUAOU VENTURE CAPITAL CO LTD

No. 8, Lingyin Road
Hangzhou, China 310013
Phone: 8657188301885
Fax: 8657187988858
E-mail: ho@hovc.cn
Website: www.hovc.cn

Other Offices
Former HQ: No. 658 North Jianguo Road
14/F Haihua Plaza C
, China 310004
Phone: 86-571-88301885
Fax: 86-571-88301882

Type of Firm
Private Equity Firm

Project Preferences

Type of Financing Preferred:
Later Stage

Industry Preferences

In Industrial/Energy prefer:
Materials
Environmental Related

ZHEJIANG JUREN CAPITAL MANAGEMENT CO LTD

76 Yuhuangshan Rd.,Shangcheng
Honglou, Haiqin Sanatorium
Hangzhou, China 310002
Website: www.jurencapital.com

Type of Firm
Private Equity Firm

Project Preferences

Type of Financing Preferred:
Leveraged Buyout

Geographical Preferences

International Preferences:
China

Additional Information
Year Founded: 2013
Current Activity Level : Actively seeking new investments

ZHEJIANG LANGUI ASSET MANAGEMENT CO LTD

No. 33, Xiangyuan Road
Room 322, Building No. 3
Hangzhou, China

Type of Firm
Private Equity Firm

Project Preferences

Type of Financing Preferred:
Balanced

Geographical Preferences

International Preferences:
China

Additional Information
Year Founded: 2010
Current Activity Level : Actively seeking new investments

ZHEJIANG LONGZHOU INVESTMENT GROUP CO LTD

419 Tingqiao Road
Jiashan
Jiaxing, China

In Business Serv. prefer:
Media

Additional Information
Year Founded: 2006
Capital Under Management: $34,702,000
Current Activity Level : Actively seeking new investments

Phone: 86-573-8423
Fax: 86-573-8423

Type of Firm
Private Equity Firm

Additional Information
Year Founded: 2005
Current Activity Level : Actively seeking new investments

ZHEJIANG PUHUA TIANQIN EQUITY INVESTMENT MANAGEMENT CO LTD

No. 173, Guyu Road
Floor 16, Zhongtian Building
Hangzhou, China
Phone: 8657187759107
Fax: 8657185460681
Website: www.puhuacapital.com

Type of Firm
Private Equity Firm

Project Preferences

Type of Financing Preferred:
Balanced

Geographical Preferences

International Preferences:
China

Industry Preferences

In Communications prefer:
Telecommunications

In Medical/Health prefer:
Medical Therapeutics
Drug/Equipmt Delivery

In Consumer Related prefer:
Consumer

In Industrial/Energy prefer:
Energy
Energy Conservation Relat

In Business Serv. prefer:
Media

In Manufact. prefer:
Manufacturing

In Agr/Forestr/Fish prefer:
Agriculture related

Additional Information
Year Founded: 2011
Current Activity Level : Actively seeking new investments

ZHEJIANG SHENGGANG INVESTMENT MANAGEMENT CO LTD

Changhe Subdistrict, Binjiang
Room 156, Building 7
Hangzhou, China
Phone: 8657156707084

Type of Firm
Investment Management Firm

Project Preferences

Type of Financing Preferred:
Early Stage
Seed

Geographical Preferences

International Preferences:
China

Industry Preferences

In Internet Specific prefer:
Internet

Additional Information
Year Founded: 2016
Current Activity Level : Actively seeking new investments

ZHEJIANG SINOWISDOM CAPITAL CO LTD

No. 2, Zijinhua Road
Tower A, Lianhe Building, Xihu
Hangzhou, China
Phone: 8657187181219
Fax: 8657188163180
Website: www.sinowisdom.cn

Management and Staff
Baiqi Xu, Venture Partner
Haizhong Jin, Venture Partner
Wei Kang, Venture Partner
Xuwei Zhang, Managing Partner

Type of Firm
Investment Management Firm

Project Preferences

Type of Financing Preferred:
Leveraged Buyout
Balanced
Later Stage

Geographical Preferences

International Preferences:
China

Industry Preferences

In Semiconductor/Electr prefer:
Optoelectronics

In Consumer Related prefer:
Consumer

Additional Information
Year Founded: 2002
Capital Under Management: $125,469,000
Current Activity Level : Actively seeking new investments

ZHEJIANG STARTVC INVESTMENT MANAGEMENT CO LTD

Wenyi West Rd, Xihu District
No.522, Xixi Kechuang Park
Hangzhou, China
Website: www.startvc.net

Type of Firm
Incubator/Development Program

Project Preferences

Type of Financing Preferred:
Early Stage
Seed
Startup

Geographical Preferences

International Preferences:
China

Industry Preferences

In Communications prefer:
Telecommunications

In Internet Specific prefer:
Internet

In Business Serv. prefer:
Media

Additional Information
Year Founded: 2015
Current Activity Level : Actively seeking new investments

ZHEJIANG UNIVERSITY VENTURE CAPITAL CO LTD

No. 116 Yugu Road
Room 309 Fangyuan Building
Hangzhou, Zhejiang, China 310011
Phone: 8657187996206
Fax: 8657187961070

Management and Staff
Guoying Zhu, President, Founder

Type of Firm
University Program

Project Preferences

Type of Financing Preferred:
Balanced

Geographical Preferences

International Preferences:
China

Industry Preferences

In Computer Software prefer:
Software

In Biotechnology prefer:
Biotechnology

In Industrial/Energy prefer:
Environmental Related

Additional Information
Year Founded: 2001
Current Activity Level : Actively seeking new investments

ZHEJIANG VENTURE CAPITAL GROUP CO LTD

1 Hua Zhe Plaza, Miduqiao Road
Level 28, Building A
Hangzhou, China
Phone: 8657185270524
Website: www.zjvc.cn

Type of Firm
Government Affiliated Program

Project Preferences

Type of Financing Preferred:
Fund of Funds
Early Stage
Expansion
Seed

Geographical Preferences

International Preferences:
China

Additional Information
Year Founded: 2009
Capital Under Management: $79,300,000
Current Activity Level : Actively seeking new investments

ZHEJIANG VENTURE CAPITAL GROUP CO., LTD.

No207, Wen'er Road
15F, Wenxin Building
Hangzhou, Zhejiang, China 310012
Phone: 8657188259218
Fax: 8657188259222
E-mail: zjvc@zjvc.cn
Website: www.zjvc.cn

Type of Firm
Private Equity Firm

Project Preferences

Type of Financing Preferred:
Balanced

Geographical Preferences

International Preferences:
China

Industry Preferences

In Biotechnology prefer:
Biotechnology

In Medical/Health prefer:
Medical/Health

In Industrial/Energy prefer:
Energy
Materials

Additional Information
Year Founded: 2000
Current Activity Level : Actively seeking new investments

ZHEJIANG YINTAI RUIQI VENTURE INVESTMENT CO LTD

Fuqiang Road 501
Ningbo, China

Type of Firm
Private Equity Firm

Project Preferences

Type of Financing Preferred:
Balanced

Geographical Preferences

International Preferences:
China

Additional Information
Year Founded: 2009
Current Activity Level : Actively seeking new investments

ZHEJIANG YINXINGGU INVESTMENT CO LTD

289, Wengjiashan
Xihu
Hangzhou, China 310007
Phone: 86571-87382716
Fax: 86571-87382720
Website: www.yxgzb.com

Type of Firm
Private Equity Firm

Project Preferences

Type of Financing Preferred:
Early Stage

Geographical Preferences

International Preferences:
China

Industry Preferences

In Internet Specific prefer:
Internet

Additional Information
Year Founded: 2014
Current Activity Level : Actively seeking new investments

ZHEJIANG YONGXIN ASSETS MANAGEMENT LTD

Cicheng Town, Jiangbei Distric
Room 210, No. 332 Cihu Renjia
Ningbo, China

Type of Firm
Private Equity Firm

Project Preferences

Type of Financing Preferred:
Balanced

Geographical Preferences

International Preferences:
China

Additional Information
Year Founded: 2015
Current Activity Level : Actively seeking new investments

ZHEJIANG YOUCHUANG VENTURE CAPITAL CO LTD

No.2, Huanzhen North Rd.
Shaoxing, China

Type of Firm
Private Equity Firm

Project Preferences

Type of Financing Preferred:
Balanced

Geographical Preferences

International Preferences:
China

Additional Information
Year Founded: 2011
Current Activity Level : Actively seeking new investments

ZHESHANG VENTURE CAPITAL CO LTD

No. 8 Qiushi Rd. Xihu District
10F North Tower Gongyuan Bldg.
Hangzhou, China 310013
Phone: 8657189922222
Fax: 8657189922221
E-mail: info@zsvc.com.cn
Website: www.zsvc.com.cn

Other Offices
Shennan Avenue
Jinyun Century Building
Shenzhen, China

Management and Staff
Dongqiu Liu, Partner
Hanjie Xu, Venture Partner
Ruping Chen, Partner
Su Zhao, Partner
Xianwen Li, Partner
Xun Chen, Partner
Yeyu Hua, Venture Partner
Yuemeng Chen, President
Zhilong Yang, Partner

Type of Firm
Private Equity Firm

Project Preferences

Type of Financing Preferred:
Early Stage
Expansion
Mezzanine
Balanced
Later Stage
Seed
Startup

Geographical Preferences

International Preferences:
China

Industry Preferences

In Communications prefer:
Media and Entertainment

In Computer Software prefer:
Software

In Internet Specific prefer:
Web Aggregation/Portals

In Biotechnology prefer:
Biotechnology
Agricultural/Animal Bio.
Biotech Related Research

In Medical/Health prefer:
Medical/Health
Drug/Equipmt Delivery
Pharmaceuticals

In Consumer Related prefer:
Consumer
Entertainment and Leisure
Education Related

In Industrial/Energy prefer:
Energy
Materials
Advanced Materials
Environmental Related

In Transportation prefer:
Transportation

In Financial Services prefer:
Financial Services

In Business Serv. prefer:
Services

In Manufact. prefer:
Manufacturing

In Agr/Forestr/Fish prefer:
Agriculture related

Additional Information

Year Founded: 2007
Capital Under Management: $29,252,000
Current Activity Level : Actively seeking new investments

ZHIYING CAPITAL

Haidian North 2 Rd, Haidian
702, 6F, No 8
Beijing, China 100080
Phone: 861085903016
Website: www.xiangtou.la

Type of Firm
Private Equity Firm

Project Preferences

Type of Financing Preferred:
Balanced

Geographical Preferences

International Preferences:
China

Industry Preferences

In Internet Specific prefer:
Internet

In Medical/Health prefer:
Medical/Health

In Consumer Related prefer:
Consumer

In Business Serv. prefer:
Media

Additional Information

Year Founded: 2014
Capital Under Management: $2,000,000,000
Current Activity Level : Actively seeking new investments

ZHONGCHUAN SHENGTANG INVESTMENT HOLDINGS CO LTD

Yuanyangguanghua International
1702, Tower AB
Beijing, China 100000

Type of Firm
Private Equity Firm

Project Preferences

Type of Financing Preferred:
Balanced

Geographical Preferences

International Preferences:
China

Industry Preferences

In Communications prefer:
Media and Entertainment

In Medical/Health prefer:
Medical/Health

In Industrial/Energy prefer:
Energy

In Agr/Forestr/Fish prefer:
Agriculture related

Additional Information

Year Founded: 2015
Current Activity Level : Actively seeking new investments

ZHONGDING KAIYUAN VENTURE CAPITAL MANAGEMENT CO LTD

3F, 10 Business Waihuan Road
Zhengdong New Zone
Zhengzhou, China 450018
Phone: 8637169177108
Fax: 8637169177108
E-mail: zt@ccnew.com
Website: www.ccnew.com

Type of Firm
Bank Affiliated

Project Preferences

Type of Financing Preferred:
Balanced

Geographical Preferences

International Preferences:
China

Additional Information

Year Founded: 2012
Capital Under Management: $80,590,000
Current Activity Level : Actively seeking new investments

ZHONGGUANCUN VC DEVELOPMENT CO

North 4th Ring West Road 66
1218, China Tech, Jiaoyi Tower
Beijing, China 100080
Phone: 861082483087
Fax: 861082483075
Website: www.zgcvc.com

Type of Firm
Private Equity Advisor or Fund of Funds

Project Preferences

Type of Financing Preferred:
Fund of Funds
Balanced

Geographical Preferences

International Preferences:
China

Industry Preferences

In Communications prefer:
Telecommunications

In Biotechnology prefer:
Biotechnology

In Medical/Health prefer:
Pharmaceuticals

In Industrial/Energy prefer:
Energy
Materials
Environmental Related

In Business Serv. prefer:
Media

Additional Information
Year Founded: 1998
Capital Under Management: $793,900,000
Current Activity Level: Actively seeking new investments

ZHONGGUANG GREAT WALL INVESTMENT MANAGEMENT BEIJING CO LTD

Chaoyang District, Beijing
Block AB-1, Advertising Indust
Beijing, China

Type of Firm
Private Equity Firm

Project Preferences

Type of Financing Preferred:
Generalist PE

Geographical Preferences

International Preferences:
China

Industry Preferences

In Internet Specific prefer:
Internet

In Business Serv. prefer:
Media

Additional Information
Year Founded: 2016
Current Activity Level: Actively seeking new investments

ZHONGHAI RUANYIN INVESTMENT MANAGEMENT CO LTD

No.1 ChangAn St., Dongcheng
1106, C1 Office, Dongfang Plaza
Beijing, China
Phone: 861085180608
Fax: 861085180609
Website: www.zhsoftbank.com

Type of Firm
Investment Management Firm

Project Preferences

Type of Financing Preferred:
Leveraged Buyout

Geographical Preferences

International Preferences:
China

Additional Information
Year Founded: 2013
Current Activity Level: Actively seeking new investments

ZHONGJI INVESTMENT CO LTD

Yuhua District, Shijiazhuang
22F, Block A, Fangbei Building
Shijiazhuang, China
Phone: 8631187099959
Website: www.zj-inv.cn

Type of Firm
Private Equity Firm

Project Preferences

Type of Financing Preferred:
Balanced

Geographical Preferences

International Preferences:
China

Industry Preferences

In Medical/Health prefer:
Medical/Health

In Consumer Related prefer:
Entertainment and Leisure
Education Related

In Industrial/Energy prefer:
Energy Conservation Relat

In Other prefer:
Environment Responsible

Additional Information
Year Founded: 2016
Current Activity Level: Actively seeking new investments

ZHONGJUN TIANBAO CAPITAL MANAGEMENT BEIJING CO LTD

No.8 Beichen Road, Chaoyang
Beichen Time Buildin
Beijing, China 100101
Phone: 861084872813
Fax: 861084872813
Website: www.zj-capital.com.cn

Type of Firm
Private Equity Firm

Project Preferences

Type of Financing Preferred:
Leveraged Buyout
Balanced

Geographical Preferences

International Preferences:
China

Industry Preferences

In Communications prefer:
Entertainment

In Medical/Health prefer:
Medical/Health

In Consumer Related prefer:
Sports

In Industrial/Energy prefer:
Energy
Robotics

In Transportation prefer:
Transportation

In Financial Services prefer:
Financial Services

Additional Information
Year Founded: 2014
Capital Under Management: $164,710,000
Current Activity Level: Actively seeking new investments

ZHONGRONG INTERNATIONAL TRUST CO LTD

No. 2, Wudinghou Street
9F, Taikang Guoji Mansion
Beijing, China
Phone: 864006508666
E-mail: zritc@zritc.com
Website: www.zritc.com

Management and Staff
Dong Zhang, Vice President
Hai Wang, Vice President
Jinhua Lian, Chief Financial Officer
Qiaofeng Wu, Vice President
Wei Yang, Vice President
Wei Liu, Vice President
Zhiqiang He, Vice President

Type of Firm
Private Equity Firm

Project Preferences

Type of Financing Preferred:
Generalist PE

Geographical Preferences

International Preferences:
China

Industry Preferences

In Financial Services prefer:
Real Estate
Financial Services

Additional Information

Year Founded: 1993
Current Activity Level : Actively seeking new investments

ZHONGSHAN TECHNOLOGY INNOVATION INVESTMENT MANAGEMENT CO LTD

No. 13 Xingwen Road
Zhonghuan Commerce Street
Zhongshan, China

Management and Staff

Gangzheng Lv, Managing Director
Jian Liu, Managing Director

Type of Firm

Private Equity Firm

Project Preferences

Type of Financing Preferred:
Early Stage
Balanced
Later Stage
Seed

Geographical Preferences

International Preferences:
China

Additional Information

Year Founded: 2010
Capital Under Management: $14,648,000
Current Activity Level : Actively seeking new investments

ZHONGSHAN TIANYU EQUITY INVESTMENT CO LTD

Room A, 15F, No. 118
Xinhua Middle Road, Xiaolan
Zhongshan, China
Phone: 8676022112911
Website: www.skyfame.cn

Type of Firm

Private Equity Firm

Project Preferences

Type of Financing Preferred:
Balanced

Geographical Preferences

International Preferences:
China

Industry Preferences

In Communications prefer:
Entertainment

In Medical/Health prefer:
Medical/Health

In Consumer Related prefer:
Education Related

In Industrial/Energy prefer:
Energy

In Business Serv. prefer:
Media

Additional Information

Year Founded: 2014
Current Activity Level : Actively seeking new investments

ZHUHAI BOYUAN INVESTMENT CO LTD

Xingfa Nan Road, No.1 Xisi Str
6th Ecno Dev Zone
Wushali Wu, Chang'an Town, China 523860
Phone: 8676989998656
Fax: 8676989999656
Website: www.600656.net

Management and Staff

Fei Huang, Chief Financial Officer

Type of Firm

Investment Management Firm

Project Preferences

Type of Financing Preferred:
Balanced

Geographical Preferences

International Preferences:
China

Additional Information

Year Founded: 2001
Current Activity Level : Actively seeking new investments

ZHUHAI QIANHENG INVESTMENT MANAGEMENT CO LTD

Linhexi Road 9
1816B, Building B
Guangzhou, China 510610

Type of Firm

Private Equity Firm

Project Preferences

Type of Financing Preferred:
Balanced

Geographical Preferences

International Preferences:
China

Additional Information

Year Founded: 2015
Current Activity Level : Actively seeking new investments

ZIBO HIGH-TECH VENTURE CAPITAL CO LTD

Hi-tech Pioneering Park No.135
Zhengtong Road
Zibo, Shandong, China 255086
Phone: 86-0533-3585656
Fax: 86-0533-3586969
E-mail: sdzbvc@sina.com
Website: www.zbvc.net

Type of Firm

Private Equity Firm

Project Preferences

Type of Financing Preferred:
Early Stage

Geographical Preferences

International Preferences:
China

Additional Information

Year Founded: 2003
Current Activity Level : Actively seeking new investments

ZICO CAPITAL

2 Cullinan Close, Morningside
1/F,Block B,Cullinan Place
Sandton, South Africa 2057
Phone: 27112173300
Fax: 27118831799
E-mail: info@zico.co.za
Website: www.zico.co.za

Management and Staff
Tshegofatso Sefolo, Managing Director

Type of Firm
Private Equity Firm

Association Membership
South African Venture Capital Association (SAVCA)

Project Preferences

Type of Financing Preferred:
Leveraged Buyout
Expansion
Later Stage
Management Buyouts
Acquisition

Geographical Preferences

International Preferences:
South Africa

Industry Preferences

In Financial Services prefer:
Financial Services

In Business Serv. prefer:
Services
Consulting Services

In Manufact. prefer:
Manufacturing
Office Automation Equipmt

In Agr/Forestr/Fish prefer:
Mining and Minerals

Additional Information
Year Founded: 2000
Current Activity Level : Actively seeking new investments

ZIEGLER ALTERNATIVE INVESTMENTS

200 South Wacker Drive, Suite 2000
Chicago, IL USA 60606
Phone: 3122630110
Fax: 3122635217
E-mail: info@ziegler.com
Website: www.ziegler.com/alternative-investments

Management and Staff
S. Charles O Meara, Senior Managing Director

Type of Firm
Private Equity Firm

Project Preferences

Type of Financing Preferred:
Value-Add
Early Stage
Generalist PE
Later Stage
Startup

Geographical Preferences

United States Preferences:
All U.S.

International Preferences:
Israel

Industry Preferences

In Medical/Health prefer:
Medical/Health
Medical Products
Health Services

In Financial Services prefer:
Real Estate

Additional Information
Name of Most Recent Fund: Ziegler HealthVest Partners, L.P.
Most Recent Fund Was Raised: 05/06/2008
Year Founded: 2005
Capital Under Management: $70,000,000
Current Activity Level : Actively seeking new investments

ZIEGLER LINK-AGE MANAGEMENT LLC

735 North Water Street, Suite 1000
Milwaukee, WI USA 53202
Phone: 4149786400

Type of Firm
Private Equity Firm

Project Preferences

Type of Financing Preferred:
Balanced
Later Stage

Industry Preferences

In Medical/Health prefer:
Medical Products

In Consumer Related prefer:
Consumer Products

In Other prefer:
Socially Responsible

Additional Information
Year Founded: 2014
Capital Under Management: $26,600,000
Current Activity Level : Actively seeking new investments

ZIFF BROTHERS INVESTMENTS LLC

350 Park Avenue
#1100
New York, NY USA 10022
Phone: 12122926000

Management and Staff
Alexander Crawford, Managing Director
Timothy Mitchell, Chief Financial Officer

Type of Firm
Private Equity Firm

Project Preferences

Type of Financing Preferred:
Expansion
Balanced

Additional Information
Year Founded: 1992
Current Activity Level : Actively seeking new investments

ZIG CAPITAL

152 West 57th Street
Floor 26, Carnegie Hall Tower
New York, NY USA 10019
Phone: 2125860100
Website: www.zigcapital.com

Management and Staff
Andrew Mitchell, Managing Partner
Frank Fazzinga, Managing Partner

Type of Firm
Private Equity Firm

Project Preferences

Type of Financing Preferred:
Early Stage

Additional Information
Year Founded: 2008
Current Activity Level : Actively seeking new investments

ZIPDRAGON VENTURES

600 Montgomery Street
44th Floor
San Francisco, CA USA 94111
E-mail: sheeraz@zipdragon.com
Website: zipdragon.com

Type of Firm
Private Equity Firm

Project Preferences

Type of Financing Preferred:
Early Stage
Seed

Geographical Preferences

United States Preferences:

Industry Preferences

In Computer Software prefer:
Software

Additional Information

Year Founded: 2016
Current Activity Level : Actively seeking new investments

ZMC

19 West 44th Street
18th Floor
New York, NY USA 10036
Phone: 2122231383
Fax: 2122231384
Website: www.zmclp.com

Management and Staff

Andrew Vogel, Partner
Brian Motechin, Chief Financial Officer
Jordan Turkewilz, Partner
Karl Slatoff, Partner
Seymour Sammell, Partner
Strauss Zelnick, Co-Founder

Type of Firm

Private Equity Firm

Project Preferences

Type of Financing Preferred:
Leveraged Buyout
Acquisition

Geographical Preferences

United States Preferences:
All U.S.

International Preferences:
Europe
Australia
Asia

Industry Preferences

In Communications prefer:
Media and Entertainment

In Computer Software prefer:
Software

Additional Information

Year Founded: 2001
Capital Under Management: $360,720,000
Current Activity Level : Actively seeking new investments

ZONE VENTURES

2882 Sand Hill Road, Suite 150
Menlo Park, CA USA 94025
Phone: 6502339000
E-mail: more.info@zonevc.com
Website: www.zonevc.com

Management and Staff

Frank Creer, Founder
Frank Creer, Co-Founder
N Darius Sankey, Partner
Timothy Draper, Co-Founder
William Lewis, Partner

Type of Firm

Private Equity Firm

Project Preferences

Role in Financing:
Prefer role as deal originator

Type of Financing Preferred:
Early Stage
Seed
Startup

Size of Investments Considered:
Min Size of Investment Considered (000s): $500
Max Size of Investment Considered (000s): $3,000

Industry Focus

(% based on actual investment)
    Internet Specific   72.4%
    Computer Software and Services   15.7%
    Semiconductors/Other Elect.   9.7%
    Other Products   2.2%

Additional Information

Year Founded: 1998
Capital Under Management: $135,000,000
Current Activity Level : Actively seeking new investments
Method of Compensation: Return on investment is of primary concern, do not charge fees

ZOUK CAPITAL LLP

140 Brompton Road
London, United Kingdom SW3 1HY
Phone: 442079473400
Fax: 442079473449
E-mail: contact@zouk.com
Website: www.zouk.com

Management and Staff

Alois Flatz, Partner
Anthony Fox, Partner
Christopher Hoffmann, Principal
Colin Campbell, Partner
Erich Becker, Partner
Felix von Schubert, Founding Partner
Lee Moscovitch, Principal
Massimo Resta, Principal
Samer Salty, Chief Executive Officer
Sven Hansen, Venture Partner
Tom Singh, Venture Partner

Type of Firm

Private Equity Firm

Association Membership

European Private Equity and Venture Capital Assoc.

Project Preferences

Type of Financing Preferred:
Expansion
Balanced
Later Stage
Other
Seed
Startup

Geographical Preferences

International Preferences:
Europe
Western Europe
All International

Industry Preferences

In Communications prefer:
Telecommunications

In Internet Specific prefer:
Internet

In Computer Other prefer:
Computer Related

In Industrial/Energy prefer:
Energy
Alternative Energy
Coal Related
Energy Conservation Relat
Environmental Related

In Transportation prefer:
Transportation

Additional Information

Year Founded: 1999
Capital Under Management: $79,700,000
Current Activity Level : Actively seeking new investments

ZS FUND LP

1133 Avenue of the Americas
New York, NY USA 10036
Phone: 2123986200
Fax: 2123981808
E-mail: contact@zsfundlp.com
Website: www.zsfundlp.com

Management and Staff
Adam Lehrhoff, Partner
David Affinito, Partner
Jeff Obligen, Partner
Ned Sherwood, Partner
Nick Burger, Partner
Robert Horne, Partner

Type of Firm
Private Equity Firm

Project Preferences

Role in Financing:
Prefer role as deal originator but will also invest in deals created by others

Type of Financing Preferred:
Leveraged Buyout
Recapitalizations

Size of Investments Considered:
Min Size of Investment Considered (000s): $90,000
Max Size of Investment Considered: No Limit

Geographical Preferences

United States Preferences:
All U.S.

Canadian Preferences:
All Canada

International Preferences:
United Kingdom
China
Bermuda
France

Industry Preferences

In Communications prefer:
Communications and Media

In Semiconductor/Electr prefer:
Electronics
Electronic Components
Sensors

In Medical/Health prefer:
Disposable Med. Products

In Consumer Related prefer:
Entertainment and Leisure
Retail
Food/Beverage
Consumer Products
Consumer Services
Other Restaurants
Education Related

In Industrial/Energy prefer:
Industrial Products
Materials
Factory Automation
Machinery

In Manufact. prefer:
Office Automation Equipmt
Publishing

Additional Information
Name of Most Recent Fund: ZS Fund, L.P. V
Most Recent Fund Was Raised: 01/01/2004
Year Founded: 1985
Capital Under Management: $150,000,000
Current Activity Level: Actively seeking new investments
Method of Compensation: Return on invest. most important, but chg. closing fees, service fees, etc.

ZUERCHER KANTONAL-BANK

Geroldstrasse 20
Zurich, Switzerland 8005
Phone: 41844843823
Website: www.zkb.ch

Other Offices
Bahnhofstrasse 50
Dietlikon, Switzerland 8305
Phone: 41-844-843-823

Bahnhofstrasse 9
Zuerich, Switzerland 8001
Phone: 41-844-843-823

Zuerichstrasse 10
Adliswil, Switzerland 8134
Phone: 41-844-843-823

Landstrasse 42
Andelfingen, Switzerland 8450
Phone: 41-844-843-823

Bahnhofstrasse 3
Buelach, Switzerland 8180
Phone: 41-844-843-823

Watterstrasse 57
Regensdorf, Switzerland 8105
Phone: 41-844-843-823

Zentralstrasse 19
Dietlikon, Switzerland 8953
Phone: 41-844-843-823

Forchstrasse 138
Egg, Switzerland 8123
Phone: 41-844-843-823

Obere Bahnhofstrasse 25
Affoltern, Switzerland 8910
Phone: 41-844-843-823

Turmstrasse
Pfaeffikon, Switzerland 8330
Phone: 41-844-843-823

Untertor 30
Wintherthur, Switzerland 8401
Phone: 41-844-843-823

Management and Staff
Bruno Meier, Chief Executive Officer
Martin Scholl, Chief Executive Officer
Rudolf Sigg, Chief Financial Officer

Type of Firm
Bank Affiliated

Association Membership
Swiss Venture Capital Association (SECA)

Project Preferences

Type of Financing Preferred:
Early Stage
Mezzanine
Later Stage
Startup

Geographical Preferences

International Preferences:
Switzerland

Industry Preferences

In Computer Software prefer:
Software

Additional Information
Year Founded: 1870
Current Activity Level: Actively seeking new investments

ZURMONT MADISON MANAGEMENT AG

Talacker 50
Zurich, Switzerland 8001
Phone: 41 58 787 00 00
Fax: 41 58 787 00 01
E-mail: sekretariat@zurmontmadison.ch
Website: www.zurmontmadison.ch

Other Offices
Ground Floor Liberation House Castle
Street St Helier
Jersey, Channel Islands JE2 3AT

Management and Staff
Christoph Syz, Chief Executive Officer
Daniel Heine, Managing Director
Werner Schnorf, Managing Director

Type of Firm
Private Equity Firm

Association Membership
Swiss Venture Capital Association (SECA)
German Venture Capital Association (BVK)
European Private Equity and Venture Capital Assoc.

Project Preferences

Type of Financing Preferred:
Turnaround
Management Buyouts
Recapitalizations

Geographical Preferences

International Preferences:
Germany

Industry Preferences

In Computer Software prefer:
Software

In Semiconductor/Electr prefer:
Electronics

In Biotechnology prefer:
Biotechnology

In Medical/Health prefer:
Health Services

In Consumer Related prefer:
Consumer
Consumer Products
Consumer Services
Education Related

In Industrial/Energy prefer:
Industrial Products
Machinery

In Transportation prefer:
Transportation

Additional Information

Year Founded: 1987
Capital Under Management: $112,000,000
Current Activity Level : Actively seeking new investments

Type of Financing Preferred:
Leveraged Buyout
Generalist PE
Turnaround
Seed
Startup
Special Situation
Recapitalizations

Industry Preferences

In Medical/Health prefer:
Medical/Health

In Financial Services prefer:
Financial Services

In Business Serv. prefer:
Services

In Manufact. prefer:
Manufacturing

Additional Information

Year Founded: 1983
Current Activity Level : Actively seeking new investment

ZYNIK CAPITAL CORP

1040 West Georgia Street, Suite 950, Grosvenor Building
Vancouver, Canada V6E 4H1
Phone: 6046542555
Fax: 6048997995
Website: www.zynik.com

Management and Staff

Nabil Kassam, Managing Director

Type of Firm

Private Equity Firm

Project Preferences

Pratt's Guide to Private Equity & Venture Capital Sources

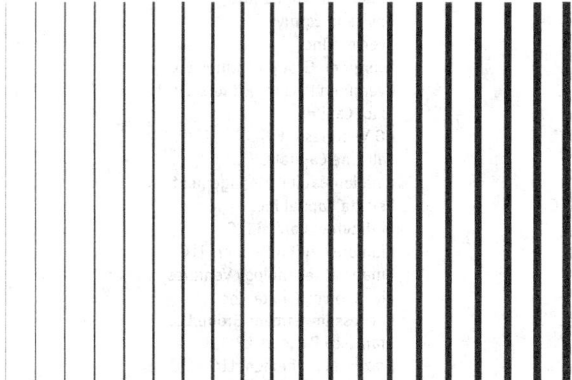

U.S. Firm Cross Reference by State

For more comprehensive querying, searching and referencing, Buyouts Insider supplies Pratt's Guide online at www.prattsguide.com.

Annual subscriptions are available for USD $1,995 per user. For more information, please contact Robert Raidt at (646)-356-4502 or email rraidt@buyoutsinsider.com.

Pratt's Guide to Private Equity & Venture Capital Sources

Buyout Firms—Alabama
Fenwick Brands Inc
Fidelis Capital LLC
Harbert Management Corp
Lazarus Capital Partners
Milost Global Inc
Stonehenge Growth Capital LLC

Buyout Firms—Alaska
Lindsay Goldberg & Bessemer LP

Buyout Firms—Arizona
Beechtree Capital Ltd
C3 Capital LLC
Canal Partners LLC
Capital International Inc
Cave Creek Capital Management
Dev Equity LLC
Eberhart Capital LLC
Estancia Capital Management LLC
Grayhawk Capital
Montage Partners Inc
Piper Jaffray Ventures Inc
Pivotal Group Inc
7Bridge Capital Partners Ltd
Serene Capital Management LLC

Buyout Firms—Arkansas
Diamond State Ventures, L.P.
SF Holding Corp

Buyout Firms—California
ABP Capital LLC
ACP Inc
AG BD LLC
AKN Holdings LLC
AP Capital Investments LP
Accel-KKR
Adams Street Partners LLC
Admiralty Partners Inc
Aequitas Capital Management Inc
Agile Capital Partners
Alpine Investors LP
Alta Communications Inc
Altos Capital Partners LLC
American Discovery Capital LLC
Anacapa Partners, L.P.
Angeles Equity Partners LLC
Anholt (USA) LLC
Antares Capital Corp
Anthos Capital LP
Apollo Global Management LLC
Archytas Ventures LLC
Ares Capital Corp
Ares Management LLC
Atar Capital LLC
Atlantic-Pacific Capital Inc
Audax Group, Inc.
Aurora Capital Group Ltd
Aurora Resurgence Management Partners LLC
BBVA Ventures
Bacchus Capital Management LLC
Bain Capital Inc
Balmoral Advisors LLC
Banneker Partners
Barings LLC

Bay Grove Capital LLC
Behrman Capital
BelHealth Investment Partners LLC
Bertram Capital Management LLC
Bison Capital Asset Management LLC
Black River Asset Management LLC
Blackford Capital LLC
Blackstone Group LP
Blue Coast Securities Inc
Blue Horizon Equity LLC
Blum Capital Partners LP
Brentwood Associates, L.P.
Breyer Capital
Bridgescale Partners LP
Britt Private Capital LLC
Broadstream Capital Partners, LLC
Builders Fund L.P, The
CDK Ventures LLC
CRESCENDO CAPITAL PARTNERS LLC
CVC Capital Partners Ltd
Calera Capital Management Inc
Caltius Equity Partners
Cambridge Companies Spg LLC
Canyon Bridge Capital Partners Inc
Capital Dynamics Sdn Bhd
Capital International Inc
CapitalAsia Group
Cappello Capital Corp
Carlyle Group LP
Carpenter and Co Inc
Castle Creek Capital LLC
Celerity Partners LP
Centerview Partners LLC
Centre Partners Management LLC
Century Park Capital Partners LLC
Champlain Capital Partners LP
Chicago Growth Partners LLC
China Resources Investment Management Co Ltd
ChinaRock Capital Management, Ltd.
ChrysCapital Management Co
Cipio Partners GmbH
Claritas Capital LLC
ClearVision Equity Partners LLC
Clearlake Capital Group LP
Clearlight Partners LLC
Clearpoint Investment Partners LLC
Clearview Capital LLC
CloudBreak Capital LLC
CoVestia Capital Partners
Continuum Capital LLC
Corbel Structured Equity Partners
Cornerstone Capital Holdings LLC
Corporate Finance Associates Worldwide Inc
Corridor Capital LLC
Coughlin Capital LLC
CounterPoint Capital Partners LLC
Courtney Group Inc
Cowen Capital Partners LLC
Crane Street Capital LLC
Crimson Investments Ltd
Crocker Capital, Inc.
Csfb Private Equity Advisers
Cypress Capital Corp
D E Shaw & Co LP
DCA Capital Partners LP

Darling Ventures LLC
Denovo Health Partners LLC
Dick Israel & Partners
Diversis Capital LLC
Duff Ackerman & Goodrich LLC
819 Capital LLC
EagleTree Capital, LP
Elevation Partners LP
Encore Consumer Capital Fund L P
Endeavour Capital Inc
Envisage Equity
Evercore Inc
Evergreen Group Ventures LLC
Evergreen Pacific Partners GP LLC
Extol Capital
4G Ventures LLC
Fall Line Capital GP LLC
Farallon Capital Management LLC
Fertitta Capital Inc
Fifth Street Capital LLC
Fillmore Capital Partners LLC
Financial Technology Ventures
Five Crowns Capital Inc
Fortress Investment Group LLC
Francisco Partners LP
Frazier Management LLC
Freeman Spogli & Co LLC
Friedman Fleischer & Lowe Cap Ptnrs L P
Fulcrum Venture Capital Corp
Fundamental Capital Management LLC
G8 Capital LLC
GC Capital Inc
GI Partners
Garnett & Helfrich Capital LP
Garnett Theis Capital
Gemini Partners, Inc.
General Atlantic LLC
Generation Partners LP
Geneva Venture Group Inc
Genstar Capital LLC
Gerken Capital Associates
Gic Special Investments Pte Ltd
Golden Gate Capital Inc
Goldman Sachs & Co LLC
Goode Partners LLC
Gores Group LLC
Grayson & Associates Inc
Green Tree Capital
Greenfield Capital Group, Inc.
Greenoaks Capital Partners LLC
Griffin Holdings LLC
Gryphon Investors Inc
H&Q Asia Pacific, Ltd.
HGGC LLC
HIG Capital LLC
Hancock Park Associates A California LP
HandsOn3 LLC
Harbert Management Corp
Harvest Partners LP
Hauser Private Equity
Headwaters BD LLC
Hellman & Friedman LLC
Hemp Deposit And Distribution Corp
Hercules Capital Inc
Highview Capital LLC

2360

Pratt's Guide to Private Equity & Venture Capital Sources

Himel Capital
Hispania Capital Partners LLC
Horizon Holdings LLC
Houlihan Lokey Inc
Housatonic Partners Management Co Inc
Industrial Growth Partners
Insignia Capital Group LP
Integral Capital Partners
Invesco Private Capital Inc
Investor Growth Capital AB
Invision Capital Management LLC
Iris Capital Management SAS
JAM Equity Partners LLC
JMI Management Inc
JPMorgan Chase & Co
Jabodon PT Co
Japan Asia Investment Co Ltd
Jasper Ridge Partners LP
Jefferies Group LLC
Jh Partners LLC
Jupiter Holdings LLC
K1 Capital Advisors LLC
K2 Capital Partners LLC
KCB Management LLC
KKR & Co LP
Karmel Capital LLC
Kayne Anderson Capital Advisors LP
Kennet Partners Ltd
Kingfish Group Inc
Kingswood Capital Management
Kodiak Capital Group LLC
Kohlberg & Co LLC
Lateral Investment Management LLC
Leonard Green & Partners LP
Levine Leichtman Capital Partners Inc
Li & Fung Investments
Liberty Capital Management Corp
LightBay Capital LLC
Lincolnshire Management Inc
Lombard Investments Inc
Lovell Minnick Partners LLC
Luminate Capital Partners
M/C Venture Partners LLC
MSD Capital LP
MTS Health Partners LP
Madison Parker Capital LLC
Main Post Partners
Mainsail Partners LP
Marlin Equity Partners LLC
Marwit Capital Corp
Mccall Springer LLC
Mentor Capital Inc
Meridian General Capital LLC
Milbank Tweed Hadley & Mccloy LLP
Monogram Capital Partners
Morgenthaler Ventures
Morrison & Foerster LLP
Mosaic Capital LLC
Next Point Capital Corp
Northleaf Capital Partners Ltd
Norwest Venture Partners
Oak Hill Capital Management Inc
Oaktree Capital Management LP
Ocean Avenue Capital Partners LP
Odyssey Investment Partners LLC

Olympic Valley Capital LLC
Omidyar Network Commons LLC
One Equity Partners LLC
OrbiMed Advisors LLC
Orix Venture Finance
Oval Partners
P4G Capital Management LLC
Pacific Community Ventures LLC
Pacific Growth Investors LLC
Pacific Road Capital Management Pty Ltd
Paine Schwartz Partners LLC
Palisade Capital Management LLC
Palisades Ventures
Parallax Capital Partners LLC
Parthenon Capital LLC
Partners Group Holding AG
Partners for Growth Inc
Pegasus Capital Group Inc
Pelican Point Investment Group LLC
Peninsula Pacific Strategic Partners LLC
Perella Weinberg Partners LP
Permira Advisers LLP
Piedmont Partners Group Ventures LLC
PineBridge Investments LLC
Piper Jaffray Ventures Inc
Platinum Equity LLC
Prelude Partners
Presidio Investors LLC
Pylon Capital LLC
Quad Ventures LLC
Queensland BioCapital Funds Ld Pty
RUBICON Technology Partners LLC
Rbc Capital Partners
Regent LP
Revolution Capital Group LLC
Riordan Lewis & Haden
Riverside Co
Riverwood Capital Group LLC
Rizvi Traverse Management LLC
Rosewood Capital LLC
Rossiiskaia Korporatsiia Nanotekhnologii GK
6 Pacific Group
SPK Capital LLC
STIC Investment Inc
Saban Capital Group Inc
Sageview Capital LP
Saints Ventures
Salt Creek Capital Management LLC
San Francisco Equity Partners LP
Saybrook Capital LLC
Seidler Equity Partners
Serent Capital LLC
Shamrock Capital Advisors LLC
SierraConstellation Partners LLC
Silver Lake Partners LP
Silver Sail Capital LLC
SilverStream Capital LLC
Siparex Group
SkyLake Investment & Co
Skyview Capital LLC
Socius Capital Group LLC
Solace Capital Partners LLC
Solis Capital Partners LLC
Source Capital LLC
Spanos Barber Jesse & Co LLC

Spectrum Equity Investors LP
Spectrum Healthcare Fund LLC
St Cloud Capital LLC
Steelpoint Capital Partners LP
StepStone Group LP
Stone Canyon Industries LLC
StoneCalibre LLC
StoneCreek Capital
Stratim Capital LLC
Sumeru Equity Partners, L.P.
Summit Partners LP
Sun Capital Partners Inc
Sunstone Partners
Sverica International Boston LLC
Swander Pace Capital LLC
Sweetwater Capital Partners LP
Symphony Technology Group LLC
280 Capital Partners LLC
TA Associates Management LP
TPG Capital Management LP
TSG Consumer Partners, L.P.
TVC Capital LLC
Tao Capital Partners
Tarsadia Investments LLC
Temasek Holdings (Private) Ltd
Terrapin Partners LLC
Thoma Bravo LLC
Thomas Weisel Partners Group Inc
Toma Capital Management LLC
Top Tier Capital Partners LLC
Towerbrook Capital Partners LP
Tpg Growth LLC
Transom Capital Group LLC
Tregaron Capital Co LLC
Trilantic Capital Management LP
Triton Pacific Capital LLC
True Wind Management LLC
Trust Company of the West
Turn/River Capital LP
Twin Haven Capital Partners LLC
VERDEXUS
VMG Partners, L.P.
VOPNE Capital LLC
Valueact Capital Management LP
Vance Street Capital LLC
Varsity Healthcare Partners
Vector Capital Management LP
Vertex Venture Holdings Ltd.
Vicente Capital Partners LLC
Vintage Capital Partners, L.P.
Virgo Investment Group LLC
Vision Venture Partners
Vista Equity Partners LLC
W R Hambrecht & Co L L C
Warburg Pincus LLC
Wedbush Capital Partners LP
West Partners LLC
White Oak Global Advisors LLC
Willcrest Partners LLC
Wilshire Private Markets
Windjammer Capital Investors LLC
Yucaipa Cos
Zeno Ventures

Pratt's Guide to Private Equity & Venture Capital Sources

Buyout Firms—Colorado
AMG Private Capital Group
ASI Capital LLC
Asia Investment Partners Inc
Black Diamond Financial Group LLC
Bow River Capital Partners LLC
Brown Brothers Harriman & Co
Carlyle Group LP
Consolidated Investment Group Inc
Corporate Finance Associates Worldwide Inc
Cowen Capital Partners LLC
Crescent Point Energy Corp
Endeavour Capital Inc
Excellere Capital Management LLC
FrontRange Capital Partners LLC
Gores Group LLC
Grayson & Associates Inc
Green Manning & Bunch Ltd
Grey Mountain Partners LLC
Headwaters BD LLC
Hercules Capital Inc
Highline Equity Partners LLC
Impact Opportunities Fund LP
Iron Gate Capital LLC
KRG Capital Management LP
KSL Capital Partners LLC
Lariat Partners LP
Lion Equity Partners LLC
MGI Holdings Inc
Mantucket Capital LLC
Meritage Funds
Montis Capital LLC
Morgenthaler Ventures
Morrison & Foerster LLP
Mountain Ridge Capital LLC
Mountaingate Capital Management LP
Ogdon Ventures
Perella Weinberg Partners LP
Piper Jaffray Ventures Inc
Platte River Ventures LLC
Progress Equity Partners Ltd
Rcf Management LLC
Renovo Capital LLC
Revelry Brands LLC
Revelstoke Capital Partners LLC
Socius Capital Group LLC
Stage Fund, The
Stonehenge Growth Capital LLC
Sunrise Strategic Partners LLC
Thermo Capital Partners LLC
Trailcreek Capital Group LLC
Venture Associates Ltd
Vestar Capital Partners Inc
White Field Capital LLC
Wilshire Private Markets
Yorkville Advisors Management LLC

Buyout Firms—Connecticut
A&M Capital Advisors LLC
AEA Investors LLC
Activant Capital Group LLC
AeroEquity Partners LLC
Algonquin Advisors LLC
Altus Capital Partners Inc
American Industrial Acquisition Corp
Amulet Capital Partners LLC
Anholt (USA) LLC
Annapurna Capital Management LLC
Antares Capital Corp
Atlantic Street Capital Management LLC
Atlantic-Pacific Capital Inc
Atlas Holdings FRM LLC
Balance Point Capital Partners, L.P.
Bayou Steel Corp
Beacon Partners Inc
Bluff Point Associates Corp
Broadhaven Capital Partners LLC
Brookside International
Brynwood Partners L.P.
Capital Partners, Inc.
Capricorn Holdings LLC
Catterton Partners Corp
Centripetal Capital Partners LLC
Charter Oak Equity, L.P.
Clearview Capital LLC
Cohen Private Ventures LLC
Craig Capital Corp
Developing World Markets Inc
Dolphin Capital Group LLC
Dowling Capital Partners I LP
Education Growth Partners LLC
Ferrer Freeman & Co LLC
Fifth Street Capital LLC
Five Peaks Capital Management
Fortress Investment Group LLC
GI Partners
Gainline Capital Partners, L.P.
Gallatin Point Capital LLC
Gemspring Capital LLC
General Atlantic LLC
Generation Partners LP
Gilbert Global Equity Capital LLC
Glade Brook Capital LLC
Gramercy Inc
Great Point Partners LLC
GreenView Associates LLC
Gridiron Capital LLC
Hamilton Robinson LLC
Headwaters BD LLC
Henderson Global Investors Ltd
Inverness Management LLC
J.H. Whitney & Co LLC
JHP Enterprises LLC
JM GALEF & CO
Jefferies Group LLC
Karpreilly LLC
Kidd & Company LLC
LJ2 & Co LLC
Lakewood Capital LLC
Long Road Investment Counsel LLC
Lumis Partners
MILLENNIUM EQUITY TRADING L L C
MML Capital Partners LLP
Maidstone Capital Corp
Med Opportunity Partners LLC
Mill Road Capital Management LLC
MissionPoint Capital Partners LLC
Monhegan Partners LLC
North Castle Partners LLC
Oak Hill Capital Management Inc
Oaktree Capital Management LP
Olympus Partners
Orix Venture Finance
Pegasus Capital Advisors LP
Peloton Equity LLC
Petros Partners
Pilgrim Capital Partners LLC
Pillsman Partners LLC
Piper Jaffray Ventures Inc
Portfolio Advisors, LLC
Propel Equity Partners LLC
Proprium Capital Partners LP
Prostar Investments Pte Ltd
RFE Investment Partners
RUBICON Technology Partners LLC
Rbc Capital Partners
Rizvi Traverse Management LLC
Rosser Capital Partners
SCP III LP
SF Holding Corp
Sageview Capital LP
Saugatuck Capital Co
Seven Point Equity Partners LLC
Silver Point Capital LLC
Silverhawk Capital Partners LLC
Southern Cross Capital Management SA
Southfield Capital Advisors LLC
Squadron Capital LLC
Starboard Capital Partners LLC
Sterling Investment Partners II LP
Stone Point Capital LLC
Stonegate Capital Group LLC
Strategic Value Partners LLC
Tengram Capital Partners LLC
Tower Three Partners LLC
True North
Wexford Capital LP
Winchester Capital Partners LLC

Buyout Firms—D. of Columbia
Abraaj Capital Ltd
Advanced Finance and Investment Group LLC
Ares Capital Corp
Ares Management LLC
Artemis Holdings Group LLC
Astra Capital Management
Bancroft Group Ltd
Capital International Inc
Carlyle Group LP
Darby Overseas Investments, Ltd.
Dfw Capital Partners LP
Emerging Capital Partners
Evercore Inc
Friedman Capital
Goldman Sachs & Co LLC
Greenhall Capital Partners LLC
HCI Equity LLC
Halifax Group LLC
Hauser Private Equity
Headwaters BD LLC
Hovde Private Equity Advisors LLC
Inter-American Investment Corp
International Finance Corp
KKR & Co LP
McLarty Capital Partners

Minority Broadcast Investment Corporation
Morgan Noble LLC
Morrison & Foerster LLP
Newspring Capital
Oakcrest Capital Partners LLC
Omidyar Network Commons LLC
Pan African Capital Group LLC
Perseus LLC
Potomac Equity Partners LLC
SF Holding Corp
Southern Africa Enterprise Development Fund
Stagwell Group LLC
Temerity Capital Partners LLC
Torch Hill Investment Partners LLC
Trilantic Capital Management LP
Updata Partners
York Capital Management LP

Buyout Firms—Delaware
Brown Brothers Harriman & Co
Cape Kauri Partners LLC
Kodiak Capital Group LLC
Southport Lane Management LLC
Trilantic Capital Management LP

Buyout Firms—Florida
Addison Capital Partners LLC
AeroEquity Partners LLC
Ambina Partners LLC
Amzak Capital Management LLC
Andlinger & Co Inc
Ark Applications LLC
BIG Capital LLC
Baldwin Beach Capital LLC
Bayside Capital Inc
Bespoke Capital Partners LLC
Blue Sea Capital LLC
Boyne Capital Partners LLC
Brinkmere Capital Partners LLC
Brockway Moran & Partners Inc
Brown Brothers Harriman & Co
CXO Collective International LLC
Cambridge Capital LLC
Capital International Inc
Comvest Partners
Craig Capital Corp
Darby Overseas Investments, Ltd.
Delany Capital Management Corp
Delavaco Holdings Inc
Empire Investment Holdings LLC
4C Capital LLC
Fireman Capital Partners LLC
Florescence Capital Co Ltd
Florida Capital Partners Inc
Ganot Capital LLC
Gmp Securities Ltd
Goldman Sachs & Co LLC
HGGC LLC
HIG Capital LLC
Harbor Beach Capital LLC
Harren Equity Partners
Headwaters BD LLC
HealthEdge Investment Partners LLC
Hidden Harbor Capital Partners LLC
Hispania Capital Partners LLC
Horizon Partners, Ltd.

Hyde Park Holdings Inc
JPB Partners LLC
KJM Capital LLC
KLH Capital LP
Kawa Capital Management Inc
Lindsay Goldberg & Bessemer LP
Lucor Holdings LLC
MBF Healthcare Partners LP
MGM Innova Capital LLC
Maplewood Partners LP
Mercapital SL
Millpond Equity Partners LLC
Minella Capital Management LLC
New Water Capital LP
NewGate Capital Partners LLC
Osceola Capital Management LLC
Palisade Capital Management LLC
Palm Beach Capital Management LLC
Pine Tree Equity Management LP
Piper Jaffray Ventures Inc
RHV Capital LLC
777 Partners
SF Holding Corp
Sk Capital Partners LP
Southern Cross Capital Management SA
Spring Bay Companies
Stage1Funding LLC
Stenton Leigh Group, Inc.
Sterling Partners GP LLC
Stonehenge Growth Capital LLC
Sun Capital Partners Inc
Sun Private Equities LLC
Tavistock Group Inc
Trilantic Capital Management LP
Trivest Partners LP
Valencia Capital LLC
Validor Capital LLC
Volta Global LLC
WM Partners LP
Warren Equity Partners LLC
Westshore Capital Partners LP
Yorkville Advisors Management LLC

Buyout Firms—Georgia
Accel-KKR
AeroEquity Partners LLC
All-American Holdings LLC
Arbor Private Investment Co LLC
Arcapita Inc
Ares Capital Corp
Ares Management LLC
Argonne Capital Group LLC
Atlanta Capital Partners LLC
Atlanta Equity Investors LLC
Birch Equity Partners LLC
Blackstone Group LP
Blue Ridge Capital LLC
Brighton Partners LLC
Buckhead Investment Partners LLC
Capital International Inc
Caymus Equity Partners
Cgw Southeast Partners
Constellation Capital AG
Corporate Finance Associates Worldwide Inc
Croft & Bender LLC

EDG Partners LLC
Eagle Merchant Partners
Ethos Capital Partners
Fulcrum Equity Partners
Georgia Oak Partners LLC
Goldman Sachs & Co LLC
Gray & Co
HIG Capital LLC
Harbert Management Corp
Houlihan Lokey Inc
Invesco Private Capital Inc
JAM Capital Partners
Jefferies Group LLC
KT Capital Management LLC
Kurt Salmon Capital Advisors Inc
Lincolnshire Management Inc
Lindsay Goldberg & Bessemer LP
Linx Partners LLC
Littlejohn Capital LLC
MSouth Equity Partners LLC
NRD Capital Management LLC
Navigation Capital Partners Inc
Rbc Capital Partners
Resurgens Technology Partners LLC
Riverside Co
Roark Capital Group Inc
SF Holding Corp
Seek Capital LLC
Source Capital LLC
SouthPointe Ventures LLC
Trilantic Capital Management LP
Vexiom Equity Partners, L.P.
White Oak Investments LLC

Buyout Firms—Hawaii
Koa Capital Partners LLC

Buyout Firms—Idaho
Corporate Finance Associates Worldwide Inc
Headwaters BD LLC
Montlake Capital LLC
Partner One Capital

Buyout Firms—Illinois
AG BD LLC
Acas LLC
Adams Street Partners LLC
Akoya Capital Partners LLC
Albion Investors LLC
Allstate Private Equity
Alpha Capital Partners, Ltd.
Annison Capital Partners LLC
Antares Capital Corp
Arbor Private Investment Co LLC
Ares Capital Corp
Ares Management LLC
Armory Capital LLC
Ashland Capital Partners
Asset Allocation & Management Company LLC
Atlantic-Pacific Capital Inc
BDT Capital Partners LLC
Baird Capital
Baker & McKenzie LLP
Bayou Steel Corp
Beecken Petty O'Keefe & Company LLC
Benford Capital Partners LLC

2363

Pratt's Guide to Private Equity & Venture Capital Sources

Beverly Capital LLC
Bolder Capital LLC
Bounds Equity Partners, LLC
Bridge Investments LLC
Broadhaven Capital Partners LLC
Brown Brothers Harriman & Co
Brown Gibbons Lang & Company LLC
CHS Capital LLC
CID Capital Inc
CIVC Partners LP
CORE Industrial Partners
Capital International Inc
Caretta Partners LLC
Castleray LLC
Cedar Hill Associates LLC
Cerberus Capital Management LP
Chicago Growth Partners LLC
Chicago Pacific Founders Fund LP
City Capital Ventures LLC
Clearview Capital LLC
Cognitive Capital Partners LLC
Concentric Equity Partners, L.P.
Continental Investors Life Inc
Corinthian Capital Group LLC
Corporate Finance Associates Worldwide Inc
Cowen Capital Partners LLC
Creation Investments Capital Management LLC
Credit Agricole Corporate and Investment Bank SA
Cressey and Company LP
DN Partners LLC
DNS Capital LLC
Dresner Capital Resources Inc
Driehaus Private Equity LLC
Echelon Capital LLC
Edgewater Funds
Edwards Capital LLC
Ellipse Capital LLC
Equity Group Investments
Evercore Inc
Evolution Capital Partners LLC
Expedition Capital Partners LLC
Ficus Capital LLC
Fifth Street Capital LLC
Focus Healthcare Partners LLC
Forest Hill Partners LLC
Forstmann Little & Co
Fortress Investment Group LLC
Freeport Financial Partners LLC
Frontenac Company LLC
Fulton Capital LLC
GI Partners
GLL Investors (Two) Inc
GTCR Golder Rauner LLC
Generation Growth Capital Inc
Glencoe Capital LLC
Goldman Sachs & Co LLC
Granite Creek Partners LLC
Graue Mill Partners LLC
Grosvenor Capital Management LP
Growth Catalyst Partners LLC
Gryffindor Capital Partners LLC
HCI Equity LLC
HIG Capital LLC
Hadley Capital
Hall Capital LLC

Headwaters BD LLC
Henderson Global Investors Ltd
Hercules Capital Inc
High Street Capital
Hilco Consumer Capital Corp
Hilco Equity Management LLC
Hispania Capital Partners LLC
Horizon Capital Management
Houlihan Lokey Inc
Industrial Opportunity Partners LLC
Inoca Capital Partners LLC
Invision Capital Management LLC
Iron Range Capital Partners LLC
Jabodon PT Co
Jefferies Group LLC
Jordan Company LP
Jump Capital LLC
Keystone Capital Inc
Kingsman Capital LLC
Kinzie Capital Partners LLC
L Squared Capital Partners
LaSalle Capital
Lake Capital
Levine Leichtman Capital Partners Inc
Lincoln Hills Holding Company LLC
Lincoln Park Capital
Lincolnshire Management Inc
Linden LLC
Lindsay Goldberg & Bessemer LP
Lion Equity Partners LLC
Madison Capital Funding LLC
Madison Capital Partners Corp
Madison Dearborn Partners LLC
Masi Ltd
Matthew Pritzker Company LLC
Maxim Partners LLC
May River Capital LLC
Mesirow Financial Private Equity Inc
Monroe Capital LLC
NB Distressed Debt Investment Fund Ltd
New Harbor Capital Management LLC
Nextgen Growth Partners LLC
Nicolet Capital Partners LLC
North Branch Capital LP
Nova Capital Management, Ltd.
One Equity Partners LLC
Origami Capital Partners, LLC
PPM America Capital Partners LLC
PSP Capital Partners LLC
Paine Schwartz Partners LLC
Parallel49 Equity
ParkerGale LP
Periscope Equity LLC
Pfingsten Partners LLC
Piper Jaffray Ventures Inc
Prairie Capital, L.P.
Pricoa Capital Group Ltd
Promus Equity Partners
Prospect Partners LLC
Redshift Capital LLC
Resource Financial Corp
Riverside Co
Roundtable Healthcare Partners LP
Roynat Capital Inc
Rural American Fund LP

SE Capital LLC
SF Holding Corp
SOLIC Capital Partners LLC
Sangamon Industries LLC
Sheridan Capital Partners
Shore Capital Partners LLC
Shorehill Capital LLC
Siguler Guff & Company LP
Silkroad Equity LLC
Silver Oak Services Partners
Sterling Partners GP LLC
Stone Pointe LLC
Storehill Capital LLC
Sucsy Fischer & Co., Inc.
Svoboda Capital Partners LLC
Thoma Bravo LLC
Thoma Cressey Bravo Inc
Trilantic Capital Management LP
Two Roads Group LLC
Tyree & D Angelo Partners LLC
Valor Equity Parters L P
Vernon & Park Capital LP
Victory Park Capital Advisors LLC
Vista Equity Partners LLC
Vistria Group, L.P., The
Wall Street Venture Capital Ltd
Wanxiang America Capital LLC
Water Street Healthcare Partners LLC
Water Tower Capital LLC
Waud Capital Partners LLC
Waveland Investments LLC
Westbourne Capital Partners LLC
Willis Stein & Partners LP
Wilshire Private Markets
Wind Point Advisors LLC
WinoNA Capital Management LLC
Wynnchurch Capital Ltd
Z Capital HF Adviser LLC
Ziegler Alternative Investments

Buyout Firms—Indiana
AlpInvest Partners BV
CID Capital Inc
Capital International Inc
Cardinal Equity Partners LLC
Corporate Finance Associates Worldwide Inc
Hammond Kennedy Whitney & Company Inc
Heron Capital Equity Partners
Norris Equity Partners
North River Capital LLC
Piper Jaffray Ventures Inc
Tillery Capital LLC

Buyout Firms—Iowa
Aavin Equity Advisors LLC
Bridgepoint Investment Partners I LLLP
Piper Jaffray Ventures Inc
St. Martin Land Co
Summit Equity Group LLC

Buyout Firms—Kansas
Arcady Capital Company
Catalyst Equity Group LLC
Corporate Finance Associates Worldwide Inc
D E Shaw & Co LP
Great Range Capital

KT Equity Partners LLC
Kansas Venture Capital Inc
MidStates Capital LP
Piper Jaffray Ventures Inc
Silverhawk Capital Partners LLC
Stewart Capital Management LLC

Buyout Firms—Kentucky
Blue Equity LLC
Corporate Finance Associates Worldwide Inc
KKR & Co LP
Millstone Capital Partners LLC
Southfield Capital Advisors LLC
Weller Equity Partners

Buyout Firms—Louisiana
Jefferies Group LLC
Longuevue Capital
SF Holding Corp
Stonehenge Growth Capital LLC

Buyout Firms—Maine
Anania & Associates Investment Company LLC
Corporate Finance Associates Worldwide Inc

Buyout Firms—Maryland
Acas LLC
Access Holdings Management Company LLC
Aldrich Capital Partners
Antson Capital Partners LLC
Arlington Capital Partners
Bilgola Capital LLC
Blackstreet Capital Management LLC
Broadoak Capital Partners LLC
Calvert Street Capital Partners Inc
Camden Partners Holdings LLC
Columbia Partners Private Capital
Cordish Private Ventures LLC
Corstone Corp
England Capital Partners LLC
Farragut Capital Partners
GEF Management Corp
Integral Capital Partners
JMI Management Inc
JPB Partners LLC
Juggernaut Partners LP
Leading Ridge Capital Partners LLC
MJH Group LLC
Merida Capital Partners LLC
Newspring Capital
Northlane Capital Partners LLC
Orix Venture Finance
Pharos Capital Group LLC
RLJ Equity Partners LLC
Redwood Capital Investments LLC
Rotunda Capital Partners LLC
Sachs Capital LLC
Slate Capital Group LLC
Stellus Capital Management LLC
Sterling Partners GP LLC
Sunbridge Capital Management LLC
Valstone Partners LLC
Wellrock Capital Partners LLC
Woodbrook Capital Inc

Buyout Firms—Massachusetts
ABRY Partners LLC
AMX Capital Ltd
Able Capital Management LLC
Acas LLC
Advent International Corp
Alta Communications Inc
Ampersand Capital Partners
Antares Capital Corp
Anvil Capital LLC
Argonaut Partners LLC
Artemis Capital Partners
Audax Group, Inc.
Avalt LLC
Bain Capital Inc
Bank of America Capital Advisors (BACA)
Barings LLC
Bayside Capital Inc
Beamonte Capital Partners LLC
Beechwood Capital
Berkshire Partners LLC
Berwind Private Equity
Bio Equity Risk Management LLC
Blackstone Group LP
Boston Harbor Capital Partners LLC
Boston Ventures
Boulder Brook Partners LLC
Brook Venture Partners LLC
Brown Brothers Harriman & Co
Building Industry Partners LLC
Bunker Hill Capital LP
Calera Capital Management Inc
Candescent Partners LLC
Cannon Capital Gp Inc
Capital Resource Partners
Castanea Partners Inc
Castle Island Partners LLC
Century Capital Management / Massachusetts Inc
Champlain Capital Partners LP
Charlesbank Capital Partners LLC
Chestnut Street Partners Inc
Copley Equity Partners LLC
Corinthian Capital Group LLC
Corporate Finance Associates Worldwide Inc
Cove Hill Partners LLC
Cowen Capital Partners LLC
Crofton Capital LLC
Crossharbor Capital Partners
D E Shaw & Co LP
Digital Fuel Capital LLC
Easterly Capital LLC
Evercore Inc
Falcon Investment Advisors LLC
Fireman Capital Partners LLC
Fulham & Co Inc
GB Credit Partners LLC
Gemini Investors Inc
Gennx360 Capital Partners LP
Gilde Healthcare Partners BV
Goldman Sachs & Co LLC
Great Hill Equity Partners LLC
Gurnet Point Capital LLC
HGGC LLC
HarbourVest Partners LLC
Hawthorn Equity Partners

Headwaters BD LLC
Hercules Capital Inc
Housatonic Partners Management Co Inc
Invus Group LLC
Islington Capital Partners LLC
J.W.Childs Associates LP
JMC Capital Partners LP
Jefferies Group LLC
Kamylon Capital LLC
Longmeadow Capital Partners LLC
M/C Venture Partners LLC
M33 Growth LLC
MGI Holdings Inc
Monitor Clipper Partners LLC
Morgenthaler Ventures
Mustang Group LLC
New England Capital Partners
New Heritage Capital LLC
Newbury Piret & Co Inc
Omega Fund Management LLC
Overall Capital Partners
PAR Capital Management Inc
Palladin Capital Group Inc
Parthenon Capital LLC
Partners Capital Investment Group Holdings LLC
Piper Jaffray Ventures Inc
Pleasant Bay Capital Partners LLC
Provident Healthcare Partners
Quabbin Capital Inc
Riverside Partners LLC
SF Holding Corp
Siguler Guff & Company LP
Solamere Group LLC
Spectrum Equity Investors LP
Spring Lane Capital Fund I LP
Staley Capital Management LLC
Stone-Goff Partners LLC
Summit Partners LP
Sverica International Boston LLC
2SV Capital LLC
TA Associates Management LP
TD Capital Group Ltd
TPG Capital Management LP
Thomas H Lee Partners LP
Trilantic Capital Management LP
Trust Company of the West
Tully and Holland Inc
UNITED FINANCIAL GROUP ASSET MANAGEMENT
Union Park Capital
Vestar Capital Partners Inc
Victory Park Capital Advisors LLC
Wall Street Venture Capital Ltd
Watermill Group LLC
Wavecrest Growth Partners
Wayzata Investment Partners LLC
Webster Capital Management LLC
Weston Presidio Capital
Westview Capital Partners LP
Windjammer Capital Investors LLC
Yellow Wood Partners LLC

Buyout Firms—Michigan
Alpha Capital Partners, Ltd.
Anderson Group LLC, The
Annox Capital

Pratt's Guide to Private Equity & Venture Capital Sources

Beringea LLC
Blackeagle Partners Fund L P
Blackford Capital LLC
Corporate Finance Associates Worldwide Inc
Dempsey Ventures Inc
Forest Hill Partners LLC
Glencoe Capital LLC
Huron Capital Partners LLC
Intellisys Capital LLC
Long Lake Partners
Long Point Capital
O2 Investment Partners LLC
Oakland Standard Co
Pulte Capital Partners LLC
Questor Partners Holdings Inc
Relativity Capital LLC
Rizvi Traverse Management LLC
Rockbridge Growth Equity LLC
SEAS Capital Partners LLC
Soaring Pine Capital Management
Strength Capital Partners LLC
Superior Capital Partners LLC
Transportation Resource Partners LP
True North Equity LLC
Valstone Partners LLC
Wynnchurch Capital Ltd

Buyout Firms—Minnesota
Arctic Capital LLC
Black River Asset Management LLC
CarVal Investors LLC
Castlelake LP
Churchill Equity Inc
CoVestia Capital Partners
Convergent Capital Partners
EXMARQ Capital Partners Inc
Evercore Inc
Gemini Investors Inc
Goldner Hawn Johnson & Morrison Inc
Granite Equity Partners LLC
GrowthFire LLC
HCI Equity LLC
Hillcrest Capital Partners LP
Houlihan Lokey Inc
LFE Capital LLC
Lindsay Goldberg & Bessemer LP
Mill City Capital LP
North Sky Capital LLC
Northern Pacific Group LLC
Norwest Equity Partners
Norwest Venture Partners
PCM Companies LLC
Piper Jaffray Ventures Inc
Proterra Investment Partners LP
RAIN Source Capital, Inc.
Shoreview Industries
Spell Capital Partners LLC
Stone Arch Capital LLC
TPG Capital Management LP
Tonka Bay Equity Partners LLC
Varde Partners Inc
Wayzata Investment Partners LLC

Buyout Firms—Mississippi
SF Holding Corp
Stonehenge Growth Capital LLC

Buyout Firms—Missouri
B12 Capital Partners LLC
C3 Capital LLC
Capital for Business Inc
Curran Companies
DTI Capital LLC
Eagle Private Capital LLC
FTL Capital LLC
Forsyth Capital Investors LLC
HBM Holdings Co
Harbour Group Ltd
Millstone Capital Advisors LLC
O'Brien Capital LLC
Piper Jaffray Ventures Inc
Stonehenge Growth Capital LLC
TGP Investments LLC
Thompson Street Capital Partners LP
Venture Associates Ltd
WILsquare Capital LLC

Buyout Firms—Montana
Montlake Capital LLC

Buyout Firms—Nebraska
Corporate Finance Associates Worldwide Inc
Everest Investment Management LLC
First Capital Partners LLC
MGI Holdings Inc
Panorama Point Partners LLC
Waitt Co

Buyout Firms—Nevada
Capital International Inc
Elmcore Group Inc
ProEquita Fund LLC
Skytree Capital Partners LP
Webfolio Management Inc

Buyout Firms—New Hampshire
Focus Acquisition Partners
Liberty Lane Partners LLC
Tuckerman Capital

Buyout Firms—New Jersey
Atlantic-Pacific Capital Inc
Aztec Equity Partners LLC
BASF New Business GmbH
Bedminster Capital Management
Black Opal Equity LLC
BlackRock Inc
Brown Brothers Harriman & Co
CIT Group Inc
Charterhouse Group Inc
Corporate Finance Associates Worldwide Inc
Darr Global Holdings Inc
Dfw Capital Partners LP
Edison Partners
FFR Capital Partners
Friend Skoler & Co. LLC
GVC Holdings Inc
Goldman Sachs & Co LLC
Indigo Group LLC
Jefferies Group LLC
Leo Group LLC
Lightview Capital
Megale LLC

Midmark Capital LP
Navigator Equity Partners LLC
Newspring Capital
Palisade Capital Management LLC
Prettybrook Partners LLC
Princeton University Investment Co
Princeton Ventures Management LLC
Sidereal Capital Group LLC
Summit Private Capital Group
Swander Pace Capital LLC
Thompson Street Capital Partners LP
Transportation Resource Partners LP
Trilantic Capital Management LP
Wilshire Private Markets
Yorkville Advisors Management LLC

Buyout Firms—New Mexico
Southwestern Growth Partners LLC

Buyout Firms—New York
AEA Investors LLC
AG BD LLC
AIG Capital Partners Inc
ATL Partners
AUA Private Equity Partners LLC
Abatis Capital LLC
Abraaj Capital Ltd
Acas LLC
Accretive Solutions Inc
Actis LLP
Admiral Capital Group
Advent International Corp
Aequitas Capital Management Inc
African Capital Alliance
Akayi Capital Partners LLC
Alara Capital Partners LLC
Albion Investors LLC
Allen & Company Inc
AllianceBernstein LP
Alothon Group LLC
AlpInvest Partners BV
Alston Capital Partners LLC
Altaris Capital Partners LLC
Alumina Partners LLC
Alumni Capital Network Management Co LLC
American Industrial Partners
Andlinger & Co Inc
Angler Capital Management LLC
Annex Capital Management LLC
Antarctica Capital LLC
Antares Capital Corp
Apax Partners LLP
Apollo Global Management LLC
Aquiline Capital Partners LLC
Ardian France SA
Arenal Capital Management
Ares Capital Corp
Ares Management LLC
Argand Partners LLC
Argentum Group LLC
Arias Resource Capital Management LP
Arlon Group LLC
Arrow Venture Gp LLC
Arsenal Capital Partners LP
Ascend Global Investments LLC
Ascribe Capital, LLC

Pratt's Guide to Private Equity & Venture Capital Sources

Aterian Investment Management LP
Athyrium Capital Management LLC
Atlantic-Pacific Capital Inc
Audax Group, Inc.
Australis Partners
Auven Therapeutics Management LLLP
Avenue Capital Group LLC
Avista Capital Holdings LP
Axxess Capital Partners SA
BASF New Business GmbH
BC Partners LLP
BDS Capital Management LLC
BHMS Investments, L.P.
Bacchus Capital Management LLC
Backcast Partners LLC
Bain Capital Inc
Banco BTG Pactual SA
Bank of New York Mellon Corp
Bankcap Partners Fund I LP
Barings LLC
Bayside Capital Inc
Bedford Funding Capital Management LLC
Beechtree Capital Ltd
Beekman Group LLC
Behrman Capital
BelHealth Investment Partners LLC
Bendigo Partners LLC
Berenson & Company LLC
Bergen Asset Management LLC
Berggruen Holdings Inc
Bison Capital Asset Management LLC
Black Granite Capital
Black River Asset Management LLC
BlackRock Inc
Blackbern Partners LLC
Blackeagle Partners Fund L P
Blackstone Group LP
Blue Road Capital
Blue Sky Private Equity
Blue Wolf Capital Partners LLC
Blum Capital Partners LP
Bolshoi Management
Bookend Capital LLC
Boston Ventures
Bradford Equities Management LLC
Branford Castle Partners
Bravia Capital Partners Inc
Bregal Investments LLP
Bridge Growth Partners LLC
Brightstar Capital Partners GRS LP
Brightwood Capital Advisors LLC
Broad Sky Partners LLC
Brookfield Asset Management Inc
Brooklyn Equity
Brookstone Partners LLP
Brown Brothers Harriman & Co
Bruckmann Rosser Sherrill & Co LP
Bruin Sports Capital LLC
CCMP Capital Advisors LP
CI Capital Partners LLC
CIP Capital
CIT Group Inc
CITIC Capital Partners Ltd
CM Equity Partners LP
CN Private Equity Partners

COGR Inc
CSFC Management Co, LLC
CVC Asia Pacific Ltd
CVC Capital Partners Ltd
Cai Capital Management Co
Capgen Financial Group LP
Capital Dynamics Sdn Bhd
Capital International Inc
Capital Z Partners Ltd
Cappello Capital Corp
CarVal Investors LLC
Caravel Management LLC
Carlyle Group LP
Cartesian Capital Group LLC
Castle Harlan Aus Mezzanine
Castle Harlan Inc
Catalyst Investors LLC
Cavalry Investments LLC
Caymus Equity Partners
Centenium-Pinetree China Private Equity
Centerbridge Partners LP
Centerview Partners LLC
Central Park Group LLC
Centre Lane Partners LLC
Centre Partners Management LLC
Cerberus Capital Management LP
Channel Group LLC, The
Charlesbank Capital Partners LLC
Chartwell Investments, Inc.
Checketts Partners Investment GP LLC
China International Capital Corp Ltd
Cimb Private Equity Sdn Bhd
Circle Peak Capital LLC
Citigroup Private Equity LP
Clarion Capital Partners LLC
Clayton Dubilier & Rice LLC
Clb Partners LLC
Clearlake Capital Group LP
Clearwater Capital Partners Cyprus Ltd
Cloud Equity Group LLC
Cloverleaf Group
CoBe Equities LLC
CoVestia Capital Partners
Coastline Capital LLC
Cohesive Capital Partners
Commonview Capital LLC
Compass Partners International LLC
Comvest Partners
Consonance Capital Partners LP
Conversion Venture Capital LLC
Cooper Investment Partners
Corigin Private Equity Group
Corinthian Capital Group LLC
Corsair Capital LLC
Corvm Capital Partners SAS
Court Square Capital Partners LP
CoveView Capital Partners LLC
Cowen Capital Partners LLC
CranRidge Capital LP
Crest Group LLC
Crestview Advisors, LLC
Csfb Private Equity Advisers
Current Capital LLC
Cypress Advisors, L.P.
Cyrus Capital Partners LLC

D E Shaw & Co LP
DTI Capital LLC
Deerfield Management Company LP
Defoe Partners & Co
DeltaPoint Capital Management LLC
Diamond Castle Holdings LLC
Diamond State Ventures LP
Dlj Merchant Banking Partners
Dominus Capital LP
Dubai Investment Group
Dunes Point Capital
EQT Funds Management Ltd
EagleTree Capital, LP
Eaglehill Advisors LLC
Edwards Capital LLC
Eg Capital Group LLC
Egis Capital Partners
Egyptian-American Enterprise Fund
Elevation Partners LP
Elm Equity Partners LLC
Emigrant Capital
Empeiria Capital Partners LLC
Enhanced Equity Fund, L.P.
Enlightened Hospitality Investments LP
Envoy Capital Management LLC
Eos Partners LP
Equifin Capital Partners
Ergo Media Capital LLC
Evercore Inc
Evolvence Capital Ltd
Exigent Capital Management LLC
Exium Partners LLC
Falcon Investment Advisors LLC
Falconhead Capital LLC
Farol Asset Management LP
Fenway Partners LLC
Fidus Capital LLC
Financial Technology Ventures
First Atlantic Capital, Ltd.
Flatworld Capital LLC
Flexis Capital LLC
Florescence Capital Co Ltd
Forstmann Little & Co
Forte Capital Advisors LLC
Fortress Investment Group LLC
Founders Equity, Inc.
Fredrick D Scott LLC
Freeman Spogli & Co LLC
Fulcrum Management Inc
Fundamental Advisors LP
GB Credit Partners LLC
GCP Capital Partners Holdings LLC
GF Capital Management & Advisors LLC
GPI Capital
Gainline Capital Partners, L.P.
Gamut Capital Management LP
Garrison Investment Group LP
Gatewood Capital Partners LLC
General Atlantic LLC
Gennx360 Capital Partners LP
Gic Special Investments Pte Ltd
Gilbert Global Equity Capital LLC
Glenwood Capital LLC
Global Capital Finance
Global Emerging Markets

2367

Pratt's Guide to Private Equity & Venture Capital Sources

Gmp Securities Ltd
Go Capital LLC
GoldPoint Partners LLC
Goldman Sachs & Co LLC
Goldman Sachs Specialty Lending Group LP
Good Energies AG
Goode Partners LLC
Gotham Private Equity Partners LP
Graycliff Partners LP
Grayson & Associates Inc
Greenbriar Equity Group LLC
Greenfield Capital Partners BV
Greenhall Capital Partners LLC
Grey Mountain Partners LLC
Gruss Asset Management LP
Gustafson & Co Inc
HIG Capital LLC
HPS Investment Partners LLC
Hale Fund Management, L.P.
Halyard Capital
Hammond Kennedy Whitney & Company Inc
Harbert Management Corp
Harbinger Capital Partners
Harbour Point Capital
Harkness Capital Partners LLC
Harvest Partners LP
Hastings Private Equity Fund IIA Pty Ltd
Hawthorn Equity Partners
HeadHaul Capital Partners LLC
Headwaters BD LLC
HealthpointCapital LLC
Hellman & Friedman LLC
Hercules Capital Inc
High Road Capital Partners LLC
Highland Capital Management LP
Highstar Capital LP
Hildred Capital Partners LLC
Hill Path Capital LP
Hilltop Private Capital LLC
Houlihan Lokey Inc
Ht Capital Advisors LLC
Hudson Ferry Capital LLC
Hudson River Capital
Hypatia Capital Group LLC
ICV Partners LLC
IEP Fund Advisors Pvt Ltd
IMB Development Corp
Impetus Capital LLC
Incyte Capital Holdings LLC
Indigo Group LLC
Ingleside Investors LLC
Insight Equity Holdings LLC
Insight Venture Partners LLC
Invesco Private Capital Inc
Investcorp Bank BSC
Investcorp Technology Investments Group
Investindustrial Services Ltd
Investor Growth Capital AB
Invus Group LLC
Ironwood Partners LLC
Irving Place Capital LLC
iEurope Capital LLC
JAM Equity Partners LLC
JC Flowers & Co LLC
JFLehman & Co

JLL Partners Inc
JP Morgan Investment Management Inc
JPMorgan Chase & Co
JZ Capital Partners Ltd
Jacobson Partners
Jefferies Group LLC
Jmk Consumer Growth Partners LLC
Jordan Company LP
Juna Equity Partners LP
KBW Capital Partners I L P
KKR & Co LP
KPS Capital Partners LP
KSL Capital Partners LLC
Kain Capital LLC
Kayne Anderson Capital Advisors LP
Kelso & Company LP
Kinderhook Industries LLC
Kodiak Capital Group LLC
Kohlberg & Co LLC
Kranos Capital
Kuramo Capital Management LLC
LJH Linley Capital LLC
LNK Partners LLC
Leading Ridge Capital Partners LLC
Lee Equity Partners LLC
Leeds Equity Advisors Inc
Leeward Ventures Management SA
Levine Leichtman Capital Partners Inc
Liberty Hall Capital Partners LP
Liberty Partners Ltd
Light Beam Capital LLC
Lightyear Capital LLC
Lincolnshire Management Inc
Lindsay Goldberg & Bessemer LP
Linx Partners LLC
Lion Capital LLP
Long Point Capital
Long Ridge Equity Partners LLC
Longuevue Capital
Lorraine Capital LLC
MFG Partners LLC
MSD Capital LP
MTS Health Partners LP
MVC Capital Inc
Macoma Capital Group
Marvin TRAUB LLC
Maverick Capital Ltd
Mcc Capital Partners LLC
Meridian Development Partners LLC
Metalmark Capital Holdings LLC
Metropolitan Equity Partners LLC
Mid-Ocean Partners LP
MidCap Equity Partners
Middlemarch Partners LLC
Milbank Tweed Hadley & Mccloy LLP
Millstein & Co LP
Mistral Equity Partners LP
Moelis Capital Partners LLC
Monarch Alternative Capital LP
Monomoy Capital Partners LLC
Morgan Stanley Energy Partners
Morgan Stanley Private Equity
Morpheus Capital Advisors LLC
Morrison & Foerster LLP
Mtn Capital Partners LLC

NIBC Principal Investments BV
NRDC Equity Partners
Napier Park Global Capital (US) LP
Natixis Private Equity SA
Neuberger Berman LLC
New 2Nd Capital Advisors LP
New Legacy Capital LLC
New MainStream Capital
New Mountain Capital I LLC
New Silk Route Partners, LLC
New State Capital Partners LLC
NexPhase Capital LLC
Noble Four Partners LLC
Northwood Ventures
Norwest Equity Partners
Noson Lawen Partners LLC
1847 Holdings LLC
O3 Capital Advisors Pvt Ltd
OMERS Private Equity Inc
Oak Hill Advisors LP
Oak Hill Capital Management Inc
Oaktree Capital Management LP
Oasis Capital Partners LLC
Oceanbridge Partners LLC
Och-Ziff Capital Management Group LLC
Odyssey Investment Partners LLC
One Equity Partners LLC
One Line Partners LLC
One Rock Capital Partners LLC
One Stone Energy Partners
Onex Corp
Ontario Teachers' Pension Plan
Orangewood Partners LLC
OrbiMed Advisors LLC
Orix Venture Finance

Buyout Firms—New York
P Schoenfeld Asset Management LP
PPM America Capital Partners LLC
Paine Schwartz Partners LLC
Palladian Capital Partners LLC
Palladium Equity Partners LLC
Pamplona Capital Management LLP
Partners Group Holding AG
Pegasus Capital Advisors LP
Perella Weinberg Partners LP
Permira Advisers LLP
Pershing Square Capital Management LP
Petrichor Healthcare Capital Management LP
Pierpoint Capital LLC
Pine Brook Road Partners LLC
PineBridge Investments LLC
Piper Jaffray Ventures Inc
Platinum Equity LLC
Poplar Capital Partners LLC
Post Capital Partners LLC
Potenza Capital, LLC
Pouschine Cook Capital Management LLC
Praesidian Capital
Princeton Growth Ventures LLC
Prospect Street Ventures
Providence Equity Partners LLC
Public Pension Capital LLC
Pulse Equity Partners LLC
Quad Ventures LLC

Pratt's Guide to Private Equity & Venture Capital Sources

Quadrangle Group LLC
Quadrivio SGR SpA
Quilvest Private Equity SCA SICAR
Rcf Management LLC
Red Diamond Capital
Relativity Capital LLC
Reservoir Capital Group LLC
Resonetics LLC
Reverence Capital Partners LLC
Revolution Capital Group LLC
Rhone Capital LLC
Rift Valley Equity Partners LLC
Ripplewood Holdings LLC
River Hollow Partners LLC
Riveria Investment Group
Riverside Co
Riverwood Capital Group LLC
Rizk Ventures LLC
RobeCo Private Equity
Rockwood Equity Partners LLC
SAM Private Equity AG
SF Holding Corp
SFW Capital Partners LLC
SJ Partners LLC
Safanad Inc
Sagamore Capital Group LLC
Sand Oak Capital Partners LLC
Sandbridge Capital LLC
Sandler Capital Management
Sandton Capital LP
Saratoga Partners LP
Saw Mill Capital LLC
Schroders PLC
Scorpion Capital Partners LP
Seal Rock Partners
Seaport Capital LLC
Searchlight Capital Partners LLC
Sentinel Capital Partners LLC
Seven Mile Capital Partners LP
Shore Points Capital Management LLC
Signet Healthcare Partners
Siguler Guff & Company LP
Silver Lake Partners LP
Silverfern Group Inc
Siris Capital Group LLC
Sixpoint Partners LLC
Sk Capital Partners LP
Snow Phipps Group LLC
Solace Capital Partners LLC
Soros Strategic Partners LP
Soundcore Capital Partners LLC
Southport Lane Management LLC
Spectrum Healthcare Fund LLC
Spire Capital Partners LP
Spring Mountain Capital LP
Stairway Capital Management
Staple Street Capital LLC
Star Avenue Capital LLC
Star Mountain Capital LLC
Starr International Company Inc
Steel Pier Capital Advisors LLC
Steelpoint Capital Partners LP
Stella Point Capital LLC
Stellex Capital Management LP
Stellus Capital Management LLC

StepStone Group LP
Stone-Goff Partners LLC
Stonebridge Partners LP
Stonehenge Growth Capital LLC
Strategic Investments, L.P.
Summer Street Capital Partners LLC
Sun Capital Partners Inc
Sycamore Partners LP
354 Partners LLC
3G Capital Inc
3i
3i Group PLC
TPG Capital Management LP
TRG Management LP
TSG Consumer Partners, L.P.
TZP Group LLC
Taglich Private Equity LLC
Tailwind Capital Partners LP
Tamarix Capital Corp
Teachers Insurance and Annuity Association of America
Tenex Capital Management LP
Tenth Avenue Holdings LLC
Terrapin Partners LLC
Thermo Capital Partners LLC
Tiger Global Management LLC
Tinicum Capital Partners
Tocqueville Finance SA
Topspin Partners LP
Torque Capital Group LLC
Towerbrook Capital Partners LP
Tpg Growth LLC
Trevi Health Ventures LP
Tri Artisan Capital Partners LLC
Trilantic Capital Management LP
Trimaran Capital LLC
Troika Capital Partners Ltd
Trust Company of the West
Turning Rock Partners Gp LLC
Turnspire Capital Partners LLC
Two Sigma Investments LP
Ubequity Capital Partners Inc
Ulysses Management LLC
V&A Capital
VTB Kapital AO
Vanguard Atlantic Ltd
Veritas Capital Fund Management LLC
Veronis Suhler Stevenson LLC
Vertex Capital LLC
Verus Investment Partners
Vesey Street Capital Partners LLC
Vestar Capital Partners Inc
Victor Capital Partners
Vision Capital LLP
Volcano Capital LLC
W R Hambrecht & Co L L C
WL Ross & Co LLC
WWB Asset Management LLC
Wafra Partners LLC
Wakabayashi Fund LLC
Wall Street Venture Capital Ltd
Waller Capital Partners LLC
Warburg Pincus LLC
Wellspring Capital Management LLC
Welsh Carson Anderson & Stowe

Wharton Equity Partners LLC
White Oak Equity Partners LLC
White Wolf Capital LLC
Wicks Group of Companies LLC
Willis Stein & Partners LP
Wilshire Private Markets
Wincove Capital
Wolfensohn & Company LLC
Yellow Wood Partners LLC
Yenni Capital
York Capital Management LP
ZMC
ZS Fund LP
Zephyr Management LP

Buyout Firms—North Carolina

Axum Capital Partners LLC
Barings LLC
Bb&T Capital Partners LLC
Bison Capital Asset Management LLC
BlackRock Inc
Blue Point Capital Partners LP
Brown Brothers Harriman & Co
Capitala Investment Advisors LLC
Carlyle Group LP
Carousel Capital Partners
Colville Capital LLC
Copeley Capital Partners I LP
Corporate Finance Associates Worldwide Inc
Falfurrias Capital Partners LP
Ferro Management Group Inc
Fidus Capital LLC
Frontier Capital LLC
Guidon Capital Partners
Halifax Group LLC
Hargett Hunter Capital Partners
HealthView Capital Partners LLC
Investors Management Corp
Jefferies Group LLC
Kendall Capital Associates LLC
Lookout Capital LLC
Metroview Capital LLC
Mosaic Capital Partners LLC
Nations Funds Inc
Pamlico Capital Management LP
Piper Jaffray Ventures Inc
Plexus Capital LLC
Presidio Investors LLC
Ridgemont Partners Management LLC
Roynat Capital Inc
SF Holding Corp
Sconce and Associates LLC
Silverhawk Capital Partners LLC
Summit Park LLC
Teall Investments LLC
Tillery Capital LLC
UNC Kenan-Flagler Private Equity Fund
Union Grove Venture Partners 2014 LLC

Buyout Firms—North Dakota

Gen7 Investment LLC

Buyout Firms—Ohio

Alpha Capital Partners, Ltd.
Blue Loop Capital LLC
Blue Point Capital Partners LP

2369

Pratt's Guide to Private Equity & Venture Capital Sources

Brantley Venture Partners L P
Bratenahl Capital Partners Ltd
Brixey & Meyer Capital LLC
Brown Gibbons Lang & Company LLC
CID Capital Inc
CapitalWorks LLC
Cleveland Health-Tech Corridor, The
Corporate Finance Associates Worldwide Inc
Cowen Capital Partners LLC
Directional Aviation Capital
Edgewater Capital Group, Inc.
Edison Partners
Evolution Capital Partners LLC
Fillmore Capital Partners LLC
Gates Group Capital Partners LLC
Hauser Private Equity
Jwi Capital LLC
Linsalata Capital Partners Inc
MRM Capital Inc
Main Market Partners LLC
MavenHill Capital
Mcm Capital Partners L P
Mifsud Group LLC
Morgenthaler Ventures
Natcity Investments Inc
National City Equity Partners Inc
Ninth Street Capital Partners LLC
Orchard Holdings Group LLC
Paragon Advisors Inc
Peppertree Capital Management Inc
Piper Jaffray Ventures Inc
Portal Capital LLC
Primus Capital
Resilience Capital Partners LLC
Rockwood Equity Partners LLC
SFW Capital Partners LLC
Solomon Global Holdings Inc
Stonehenge Growth Capital LLC
Stonehenge Partners Inc
Strength Capital Partners LLC
Superior Street Partners LLC
Supply Chain Equity Partners
Teton Capital Group LLC
Trilantic Capital Management LP
Walnut Group
Watervale Equity Partners, LLC
Weinberg & Bell Group
Weinberg Capital Group
White Oak Partners Inc

Buyout Firms—Oklahoma
Acorn Growth Companies
Argonaut Private Equity LLC
Corporate Finance Associates Worldwide Inc
Hall Capital Inc
Omega Capital Management LLC
SF Holding Corp

Buyout Firms—Oregon
Aequitas Capital Management Inc
Endeavour Capital Inc
Gorge Holdings LLC
Montlake Capital LLC
Piper Jaffray Ventures Inc
Riverlake Partners LLC
VectorPoint Ventures

Buyout Firms—Pennsylvania
Accretia Capital LLC
Acrewood Holdings LLC
Actua Corp
Alara Capital Partners LLC
Aldus Equity
Allied Growth Strategies & Management LLC
Argosy Capital Group Inc
Atairos Management LP
Berwind Corp
Brant Point Partners LLC
Brown Brothers Harriman & Co
CMS Mezzanine Fund
Cimarron Healthcare Capital
Clearwater Capital Management
Cloverlay
Drayton Park Capital LP
Enertech Capital
Entrepreneur Partners LP
Eureka Growth Capital
Evergreen Industries LLC
Fortress Investment Group LLC
GMH Ventures
Goldin Ventures Co
Goldman Sachs & Co LLC
Graham Partners Inc
Guardian Capital Partners
H Katz Capital Group Inc
Hawk Capital Partners LP
Hawthorne Group
Incline Management Corp
Inverness Graham Investments
Joshua Partners LLC
Julip Run Capital LLC
L2 Capital Partners
LLR Partners Inc
Landis and Gyr AG
Larsen Maccoll Partners LP
Laurel Capital Partners
Lindsay Goldberg & Bessemer LP
Lovell Minnick Partners LLC
MSI Capital Partners LLC
Main Line Equity Partners LLC
Main Street Capital Holdings LLC
Meidlinger Partners LLC
Meridian Venture Partners
Metro Global Ventures LLC
Milestone Partners LP
Mill Creek Capital Advisors LLC
Miller Investment Management LP
Newlin Investment Company LP
Newspring Capital
Noson Lawen Partners LLC
PNC Equity Management Corp
Patriot Financial Partners LP
PeakEquity Partners
Penn Venture Partners, L.P.
Piper Jaffray Ventures Inc
ProvCo Group
RAF Industries, Inc.
Renovus Capital Partners LP
Roch Capital Inc
Rosemont Investment Partners LLC
Safeguard Scientifics Inc
Schroders PLC

Speyside Equity LLC
Spire Capital Partners LP
Stonewood Capital Management Inc
Striker Partners
SusquehanNA Capital
Susquehanna Growth Equity LLC
Susquehanna Private Capital LLC
3 Rivers Capital
Thompson Street Capital Partners LP
Valde Capital Investment Co
Versa Capital Management Inc
W R Hambrecht & Co L L C
Wilshire Private Markets

Buyout Firms—Puerto Rico
MoonSail Partners LP
Trilantic Capital Management LP
Vivaris Capital LLC

Buyout Firms—Rhode Island
Nautic Partners LLC
Phoenix Strategy Investments LLC
Providence Equity Partners LLC

Buyout Firms—South Carolina
Azalea Capital LLC
Capstone Financial Group
SF Holding Corp
Velocitas Partners LLC

Buyout Firms—Tennessee
All-American Holdings LLC
Andrew W Byrd & Co LLC
BC General Partners LLC
Brentwood Capital Advisors LLC
Castle Venture Group LLC
Claritas Capital LLC
Corporate Finance Associates Worldwide Inc
Council Capital
Cressey and Company LP
Gen Cap America Inc
Harbert Management Corp
Harpeth Ventures LLC
Hermitage Equity Partners
Jefferies Group LLC
LFM Capital LLC
Lindsay Goldberg & Bessemer LP
Morris Capital Management LLC
Nova Capital Management, Ltd.
Petra Capital Partners LLC
Pharos Capital Group LLC
Piper Jaffray Ventures Inc
River Associates LLC
SF Holding Corp
SSM Partners LP
Shannon Capital Management LLC
Tennessee Community Ventures Fund LLC
Venture Associates Partners LLC
West End Holdings LLC
Wheelhouse Capital Partners LLC

Buyout Firms—Texas
AV Capital Holdings, LLC
Acacia Partners LLC
Acas LLC
Admiral Capital Group

Pratt's Guide to Private Equity & Venture Capital Sources

Aequitos Capital Management LLC
Alara Capital Partners LLC
Align Capital Partners LP
Amvensys Capital Group LLC
Ancor Capital Partners
Apollo Global Management LLC
Ares Capital Corp
Ares Management LLC
Argenta Partners, L.P.
Ascent Equity Group LLC
Atlantic-Pacific Capital Inc
Austin Ventures
Avista Capital Holdings LP
B-29 Investments, L.P.
B4 Ventures LLC
Bankcap Partners Fund I LP
Bayou City Energy LP
Blue Sage Capital LP
Brazos Private Equity Partners LLC
Brown Brothers Harriman & Co
Building Industry Partners LLC
C3 Capital LLC
CCMP Capital Advisors LP
CIC Partners, L.P.
Calidant Capital LLC
Camwood Capital Group LLC
Capital International Inc
Capital Southwest Corp
Cappello Capital Corp
Capstar Partners LLC
Capstreet Group LLC
Caruth Capital Partners LLC
Castleray LLC
Castletop Capital
Cedar Springs Capital LLC
CenterGate Capital LP
CenterOak Partners LLC
Cielo Management LLC
Cimbria Capital
Clarion Offshore Partners LLC
Colt Ventures
Comerica Inc
Congruent Investment Partners LLC
Corporate Finance Associates Worldwide Inc
Corporate Strategies LLC
Cotton Creek Capital Management LLC
Cowen Capital Partners LLC
Craftsman Capital Partners
Credit Agricole Corporate and Investment Bank SA
District 5 Investments LP
Dos Rios Partners LP
ESW Capital LLC
Elm Creek Partners
Evercore Inc
Evolve Capital Ltd
Exhilway Global
First Capital Group Management Company LLC
FishHawk Advisors LLC
Fortress Investment Group LLC
Framework Capital Partners LLC
Freeman Group LLC
Freestone Partners LLC
FundCorp Inc
Gauge Capital LLC
Gemini Investors Inc
Generation Partners LP
Genesis Park, L.P.
Gmp Securities Ltd
Goldman Sachs & Co LLC
Greenridge Investment Partners
glendonTodd Capital LLC
HBC Investments
HIG Capital LLC
Halifax Group LLC
Hall Capital LLC
Hancock Park Associates A California LP
HealthCap Partners LLC
Herrera Partners
Hicks Equity Partners LLC
Highland Capital Management LP
Highlander Partners LP
Highstar Capital LP
Houlihan Lokey Inc
Incyte Capital Holdings LLC
Insight Equity Holdings LLC
Invesco Real Estate, Ltd.
J B Poindexter & Co Inc
Jasper Ridge Partners LP
Jefferies Group LLC
Juniper Capital Management
KKR & Co LP
Kahala Investments Inc
Kainos Capital LLC
Kayne Anderson Capital Advisors LP
LKCM Headwater Investments
Lantern Asset Management LP
Latticework Capital Management LLC
Levine Leichtman Capital Partners Inc
Lindsay Goldberg & Bessemer LP
Lone Rock Technology Group LLC
Long Lake Partners
Long Road Investment Counsel LLC
Longwater Opportunities LLC
MPK Equity Partners LLC
Magellan Capital Partners Ltd
Main Street Capital Corp
Marginxl Capital Partners LLC
Matador Capital Partners LLC
Maverick Capital Ltd
NCK Capital LLC
New MainStream Capital
North Sky Capital LLC
ORIX Mezzanine & Private Equity
Oak Hill Advisors LP
Orix Venture Finance
Owner Resource Group LLC
Pangea S Edge Holdings Ltd
Partners Group Holding AG
Pavonis Group LLC
Peak Rock Capital LLC
Pepperwood Partners LLC
Perella Weinberg Partners LP
Petros Partners
Pharos Capital Group LLC
Phoenix Strategy Investments LLC
Pine Brook Road Partners LLC
PineBridge Investments LLC
Piper Jaffray Ventures Inc
Platform Partners Investment Company LLC
Presidio Investors LLC
Progress Equity Partners Ltd
Prophet Equity LLC
Pummerin Investments LLC
Renegade Capital LP
Renovo Capital LLC
Riverside Co
Rock Hill Capital Group LLC
SF Holding Corp
Satori Capital LLC
Scaleworks Inc
Sendero Capital Partners Inc
Signet Healthcare Partners
Small Ventures Usa LP
Solaris Energy Capital LLC
Southlake Equity Group
Spanos Barber Jesse & Co LLC
Steelhead Capital Management
Stellus Capital Management LLC
Sterling Group LP
Stonehenge Growth Capital LLC
Strait Lane Capital Partners LLC
Strattam Capital LLC
SunTx Capital Partners LP
Surge Private Equity LLC
TAG Energy Solutions Ltd
TD Capital Group Ltd
TPG Capital Management LP
TPH Partners LLC
TULCAN
TWV Capital Management LLC
Teakwood Capital LP
Team Partners LLC
Texas Next Capital LP
Tillridge Global Agribusiness Partners
Tpg Growth LLC
Transition Capital Partners
Trilantic Capital Management LP
Trinity Hunt Partners
Tritium Partners LLC
Trive Capital Management LLC
Two Sigma Investments LP
United States Growth Funds
Valesco Industries Inc
Virgo Capital
Vista Equity Partners LLC
WINDHAM CAPITAL ADVISORY GROUP INC
Ward Ventures LLC
Wingate Partners LP
Wynnchurch Capital Ltd
Yellowstone Capital, Inc.
Z-Acquisition Group

Buyout Firms—Utah
Altalink Capital LLC
Aries Capital Partners LLC
Bestige Holdings LLC
Brown Gibbons Lang & Company LLC
Cross Creek Capital LP
Decathlon Capital Partners LLC
Dolphin Capital Group LLC
Dw Healthcare Partners
Goldman Sachs & Co LLC
HGGC LLC
Huntsman Family Investments LLC
Leavitt Equity Partners LLC

Pratt's Guide to Private Equity & Venture Capital Sources

Longuevue Capital
New Value Capital
Nexo Capital Partners
Peterson Partners LP
RLG Capital LLC
Sorenson Capital Partners LP
Springwater Capital LLC
Tellus Partners I LLC
Tower Arch Capital LLC
Western Heritage Capital LLC

Buyout Firms—Vermont
Craig Capital Corp
Headwaters BD LLC
Private Equity Partners SpA

Buyout Firms—Virginia
Blazar Ventures LLC
Boxwood Capital Partners LLC
Capital International Inc
DC Capital Partners LLC
EDG Partners LLC
Envest Ventures
Fairfax Africa Fund LLC
Fox Three Partners LLC
Gladstone Investment Corp
Harbert Management Corp
Harren Equity Partners
Hercules Capital Inc
Houlihan Lokey Inc
JFLehman & Co
Jefferson Capital Partners Ltd
Kiddar Capital
LLR Partners Inc
LNC Partners
Lindsay Goldberg & Bessemer LP
Militello Capital LLC
Morrison & Foerster LLP
P3M Capital Group LLC
Perpetual Capital Partners LLC
Quad-C Management Inc
Relativity Capital LLC
Rezon8 Capital & Advisory Group LLC
Ridge Capital Partners LLC
SF Holding Corp
Updata Partners
Washington Equity Partners LLC

Buyout Firms—Washington
Aequitas Capital Management Inc
Banyan Capital Partners LP
Blue Point Capital Partners LP
Brown Gibbons Lang & Company LLC
CMBIgroup
Columbia Pacific Advisors LLC
Endeavour Capital Inc
Evergreen Pacific Partners GP LLC
Frazier Management LLC
Gennx360 Capital Partners LP
Goldman Sachs & Co LLC
Jesup & Lamont Securities Corp
Joshua Green Corp
LIGHTHOUSE VENTURES L L C
LRI Vision Partners Fund I LP
Milbank Tweed Hadley & Mccloy LLP
Montlake Capital LLC

NCA Partners Inc
Oneaccord Capital LLC
Overlake Capital LLC
Piper Jaffray Ventures Inc
Point B Capital LLC
Ranch Creek Partners LLC
Southport Lane Management LLC
Swiftsure Capital LLC
Trilantic Capital Management LP
Vulcan Inc
Westward Partners LLC
WinoNA Capital Management LLC
Zachary Scott & Co

Buyout Firms—Wisconsin
Baird Capital
Blackthorne Partners, Ltd.
Cedar Creek Partners
Generation Growth Capital Inc
Lakeview Equity Partners LLC
Mason Wells Inc
Northwestern Mutual Capital LLC
Piper Jaffray Ventures Inc
Resource Financial Corp
Stonehenge Growth Capital LLC
Wing Capital Group LLC

Buyout Firms—Wyoming
Petros Partners

Fund of Funds—Alaska
Alaska Permanent Fund Corp

Fund of Funds—California
Akkadian Ventures LLC
Altegris Investments LLC
Asia Alternatives Management LLC
Bay Hills Capital Partners II LP
California University of Law & Business
Cendana Capital GP LLC
Centinela Capital Partners LLC
Commonfund Capital Inc
57 Stars LLC
FRANK RUSSELL CAPITAL CO
Firestarter Partners LLC
GKM Newport Generation Funds
Golding Capital Partners GmbH
Greenspring Associates Inc
Hall Capital Partners LLC
Hamilton Lane Advisors LLC
Headlands Capital Management LLC
Horsley Bridge Partners LLC
Industry Ventures LLC
Institutional Global Investors LLC
Jacobs Capital Group LLC
Keystone National Group LLC
Liquid Realty Partners
Medley Partners Management LLC
Montauk TriGuard Management Inc
Morgan Stanley Alternative Investment Partners LP
Northgate Capital LLC
O'Melveny & Myers LLP
Park Street Capital LLC
Progress Investment Management Co
RCP Advisors LLC
Roth Capital Partners LLC

Silicon Valley Bancventures LP
Single Oak Ventures LP
Square 1 Ventures
WP Global Partners Inc

Fund of Funds—Colorado
Aether Investment Partners LLC
Crestone Capital LLC
Emerald Hill Capital Partners Ltd
Mount Yale Asset Management LLC
Square 1 Ventures
Symmetry Investment Advisors Inc

Fund of Funds—Connecticut
AXA Investment Managers Inc
Commonfund Capital Inc
FLAG Capital Management LLC
Kline Hill Partners LLC
Landmark Partners Inc
Newbury Partners LLC
Northern Trust Corp
Performance Equity Management LLC

Fund of Funds—D. of Columbia
Accolade Capital Management LLC
EMAlternatives LLC
57 Stars LLC
Morgan Stanley Alternative Investment Partners LP
O'Melveny & Myers LLP
Overseas Private Investment Corp
PCGI LLC

Fund of Funds—Delaware
DCM Private Equity

Fund of Funds—Florida
FRANK RUSSELL CAPITAL CO
Florida First Partners
Genspring Holdings Inc
Hamilton Lane Advisors LLC
Morgan Stanley Alternative Investment Partners LP
Weatherford Partners

Fund of Funds—Georgia
Invest Georgia LLC
Morgan Stanley Alternative Investment Partners LP

Fund of Funds—Illinois
Baml Capital Access Funds Management LLC
CAMBRIDGE CAPITAL PARTNERS L L C
Capvent AG
DORAZIO CAPITAL PARTNERS, LLC
50 South Capital Advisors LLC
FRANK RUSSELL CAPITAL CO
Frye-Louis Capital Advisors LLC
Granite Hall Partners Inc
Morgan Stanley Alternative Investment Partners LP
Muller & Monroe Asset Management LLC
Northern Trust Corp
RCP Advisors LLC
Stonetree Capital Management LLC
Symmetry Investment Advisors Inc
WP Global Partners Inc

Fund of Funds—Iowa
Great River Capital LLC

Pratt's Guide to Private Equity & Venture Capital Sources

Fund of Funds—Maryland
Avanz Capital Partners Ltd
Greenspring Associates Inc

Fund of Funds—Massachusetts
Brooke Private Equity Associates Management LLC
Constitution Capital Partners LLC
F&C Asset Management PLC
FLAG Capital Management LLC
Glouston Capital Partners LLC
Hermes Gpe Llp
Landmark Partners Inc
Lexington Partners Inc
Mercer LLC
Method Advisors LLC
Morgan Stanley Alternative Investment Partners LP
Park Street Capital LLC
Rossiyskaya venchurnaya kompaniya OAO
Silicon Valley Bancventures LP
Sl Capital Partners Llp
Square 1 Ventures
Tuckerbrook Alternative Investments LP

Fund of Funds—Michigan
Detroit Renaissance

Fund of Funds—Minnesota
Advantus Capital Management Inc
Mount Yale Asset Management LLC

Fund of Funds—Nevada
Akkadian Ventures LLC
Hamilton Lane Advisors LLC

Fund of Funds—New Hampshire
Stafford Timberland Ltd

Fund of Funds—New Jersey
Prodigy Capital Management LLC
Rumson Capital Advisors
Unigestion Holding SA

Fund of Funds—New Mexico
Fort Washington Capital

Fund of Funds—New York
ATP Private Equity Partners
Abbott Capital Management LLC
Adveq Management AG
Allen Capital Group LLC
Arcis Finance SA
Auldbrass Partners LP
Bessemer Trust Co
BlackRock Private Equity Partners AG
Bowside Capital LLC
CAMBRIDGE CAPITAL PARTNERS L L C
CZR Capital LLC
Capital E Group
Centinela Capital Partners LLC
Coller Capital Ltd
DB Private Equity GmbH
FRANK RUSSELL CAPITAL CO
Florida First Partners
Hall Capital Partners LLC
Hamilton Lane Advisors LLC
IFM Investors Pty Ltd
Landmark Partners Inc

Lexington Partners Inc
Mercer LLC
Metropolitan Real Estate Equity Management LLC
Millennium TVP Management Co LLC
Morgan Creek Capital Management LLC
Morgan Stanley Alternative Investment Partners LP
NEWBROOK CAPITAL MANAGEMENT INC
Newglobe Capital Partners LLP
O'Melveny & Myers LLP
PEI Funds LLC
Pantheon Ventures (UK) LLP
Precision Capital Advisors LLC
Private Advisors LLC
747 Capital LLC
Second Alpha Partners LLC
Square 1 Ventures
Union Bancaire Privee Private Equity
Vanterra Capital Ltd
Vedanta Capital LP
W Capital Management LLC
WP Global Partners Inc

Fund of Funds—North Carolina
Morgan Creek Capital Management LLC
Square 1 Ventures
Truebridge Capital Partners LLC

Fund of Funds—Ohio
Cintrifuse
Fort Washington Capital
Fund Evaluation Group LLC
Private Advisors LLC

Fund of Funds—Oregon
Vista Ridge Capital Partners LLC

Fund of Funds—Pennsylvania
Archean Capital Partners I LP
Griffon Venture Partners
Hamilton Lane Advisors LLC
Hirtle Callaghan & Co LLC
Morgan Stanley Alternative Investment Partners LP
Penn Square Real Estate Group LLC

Fund of Funds—South Carolina
Bowside Capital LLC

Fund of Funds—Tennessee
Diversified Trust Company Inc

Fund of Funds—Texas
American Beacon Advisors Inc
Morgan Stanley Alternative Investment Partners LP
NB Private Equity Partners Ltd
Square 1 Ventures
West Oak Capital LLC

Fund of Funds—Utah
Fort Washington Capital
Utah Fund of Funds LLC

Fund of Funds—Virginia
Industry Ventures LLC
Investure LLC
Pavilion Alternatives Group Ltd
Private Advisors LLC
Signature Financial Management Inc
Square 1 Ventures

Fund of Funds—Washington
FRANK RUSSELL CAPITAL CO
Roth Capital Partners LLC
Square 1 Ventures

Fund of Funds—Wisconsin
FRANK RUSSELL CAPITAL CO

Mezzanine Firms—Arizona
Trinity Capital Investment

Mezzanine Firms—California
Avante Mezzanine Inc
Breakaway Capital Partners LLC
Breakwater Investment Management LLC
CAPX PARTNERS III L L C
CVF Capital Partners LLC
Caltius Mezzanine
Crescent Capital Group LP
GLC Merchant Banking
Greyrock Capital Group
Huntington Capital I
Leader Ventures LLC
Medley Capital LLC
Multiplier Capital LP
Newstone Capital Partners LLC
OCEAN TOMO CAPITAL L L C
Permira Debt Managers Ltd
Prudential Capital Group LP
Rw Capital Partners LLC
Seacoast Capital
Tennenbaum Capital Partners LLC

Mezzanine Firms—Colorado
Coulton Creek Capital LLC
Foundation Specialty Financing Fund LLC
Genesis Financial Services Fund LLC

Mezzanine Firms—Connecticut
Arrowhead Mezzanine LLC
Greyrock Capital Group
New Canaan Funding
OCEAN TOMO CAPITAL L L C
Southwest Middle Market M&A

Mezzanine Firms—D. of Columbia
Latin American Partners LLC

Mezzanine Firms—Florida
Asssurance Mezzanine Fund
Banyan Capital Advisors LLC
CapitalSouth Partners LLC
OCEAN TOMO CAPITAL L L C
Penta Mezzanine Fund

Mezzanine Firms—Georgia
CapitalSouth Partners LLC
Capstone Financial Partners LLC
Certus Capital Partners
Chatham Capital
Golub Capital Master Funding LLC
Kian Capital Partners LLC
Nancy Creek Capital
Prudential Capital Group LP
Salem Capital Partners, LP (FKA: Venture Capital Solutions)

2373

Pratt's Guide to Private Equity & Venture Capital Sources

Mezzanine Firms—Illinois
Aldine Capital Partners Inc
BMO Capital Corp
CAPX PARTNERS III L L C
Golub Capital Master Funding LLC
Greyrock Capital Group
LBC Credit Partners Inc
MMF Capital Management LLC
Maranon Capital LP
Marquette Capital Partners Inc
McNally Capital LLC
Merit Capital Partners IV LLC
New Canaan Funding
OCEAN TOMO CAPITAL L L C
Orchard First Source Inc
Patriot Capital Funding Inc
Prudential Capital Group LP

Mezzanine Firms—Indiana
Centerfield Capital Partners LP
Maranon Capital LP

Mezzanine Firms—Iowa
Veridian Credit Union

Mezzanine Firms—Kentucky
CapitalSouth Partners LLC

Mezzanine Firms—Maine
Endurance Capital Holdings LLC

Mezzanine Firms—Maryland
Enlightenment Capital
Multiplier Capital LP
OCEAN TOMO CAPITAL L L C
Patriot Capital Funding Inc
Spring Capital Partners

Mezzanine Firms—Massachusetts
Avante Mezzanine Inc
Barings (UK) Ltd
CAPX PARTNERS III L L C
Capstone Financial Partners LLC
Eastward Capital Partners LLC
Endurance Capital Holdings LLC
Fresh Source Capital LLC
Hancock Capital Management LLC
Ironwood Investment Management LLC
Massachusetts Capital Resource
OCEAN TOMO CAPITAL L L C
Pine Street Capital Partners LP
Prides Crossing Capital LP
Seacoast Capital

Mezzanine Firms—Michigan
Grow Michigan LLC
MMF Capital Management LLC
Maranon Capital LP
Peninsula Capital Partners LLC

Mezzanine Firms—Minnesota
Lakeside Capital Management LLC
Marquette Capital Partners Inc
Medallion Capital Inc
Northstar Capital LLC
Norwest Mezzanine Partners
Prudential Capital Group LP

Yukon Partners Management LLC

Mezzanine Firms—New Jersey
Prudential Capital Group LP
Tappan Zee Capital Corp

Mezzanine Firms—New York
Amerra Capital Management LLC
Atalaya Capital Management LP
BMO Capital Corp
Barclays Capital Inc
Barings (UK) Ltd
Benefit Street Partners LLC
CAPX PARTNERS III L L C
CT Investment Management Co LLC
Capital Trust Ltd
Cyprium Investment Partners LLC
Deerpath Capital Management LP
Freedom 3 Capital
GLC Merchant Banking
Golub Capital Master Funding LLC
Hancock Capital Management LLC
Intermediate Capital Group PLC
LBC Credit Partners Inc
Medley Capital LLC
Morgan Stanley Credit Partners LP
Multiplier Capital LP
PennantPark Investment Corporation
Permira Debt Managers Ltd
Pine Street Capital Partners LP
Prudential Capital Group LP
Tennenbaum Capital Partners LLC
Varagon Capital Partners LP
Visium Asset Management LP

Mezzanine Firms—North Carolina
Barings (UK) Ltd
CapitalSouth Partners LLC
Kian Capital Partners LLC
Salem Capital Partners, LP (FKA: Venture Capital Solutions)
Triangle Capital Partners L L C

Mezzanine Firms—Ohio
Canal Holdings LLC
Cyprium Investment Partners LLC
Laux Capital Partners
Northcreek Mezzanine
Oxer Capital Inc

Mezzanine Firms—Pennsylvania
Boathouse Capital
LBC Credit Partners Inc
Merion Investment Partners LP
Spring Capital Partners
Tecum Capital Partners

Mezzanine Firms—Rhode Island
Bay Capital Investment Partners LLC
Chatham Capital

Mezzanine Firms—South Carolina
Certus Capital Partners

Mezzanine Firms—Tennessee
Resolute Capital Partners Fund IV LP
Tenth Street Capital Partners LLC

Mezzanine Firms—Texas
Capital Point Partners LLC
Capital Royalty LP
CapitalSouth Partners LLC
Chatham Capital
ESCALATE CAPITAL I L P
Independent Bankers Capital Funds
Newstone Capital Partners LLC
Patriot Capital Funding Inc
Prudential Capital Group LP
Quadrant Mezzanine Partners LLC
Simmons & Company International
Southwest Middle Market M&A

Mezzanine Firms—Vermont
VSJF Flexible Capital Fund, The

Mezzanine Firms—Virginia
Capital Trust Ltd
Enlightenment Capital
Snowbird Capital Inc

OPE—California
Cavalry Management Group LLC
G3W Ventures LLC
Mathematica Capital Management LLC
654 Advisors LLC
Waveland Capital Group LLC

OPE—Colorado
Cirrus Investment Partners LLC

OPE—Connecticut
Addison Clark Management LLC
Atlantic Asset Management LLC
First Reserve Corp
Global Infrastructure Holdings
Lime Rock Partners LLC
Natural Gas Partners

OPE—Illinois
OCV Investors LLC

OPE—Kansas
Atlantic Asset Management LLC

OPE—Maryland
Calvert Fund

OPE—Massachusetts
ArcLight Capital Holdings LLC
Braemar Energy Ventures LP
Hammerman Capital LLC
Hastings Equity Partners LLC
Intervale Capital LLC

OPE—New Jersey
Eagle Trading Systems Inc
Hudson Clean Energy Partners

OPE—New York
ArcLight Capital Holdings LLC
Braemar Energy Ventures LP
Brahman Management LLC
Echo Street Capital Advisors LLC
Global Infrastructure Holdings
Healy Circle Capital LLC
Hull Capital Management LLC

I Squared Capital Advisors (US) LLC
Riverstone Holdings LLC
Special Situations Fund Advisors, Inc.
White Deer Energy LP
Yorktown Partners LLC

OPE—Pennsylvania
Henry Investment Trust LP
Mid Atlantic Financial Management Inc

OPE—Texas
Best Patterson Crothers & Yeoham Ltd
EIV Capital Management Company LLC
Energy Ventures AS
First Reserve Corp
Haddington Ventures LLC
Hastings Equity Partners LLC
Hitecvision AS
Intervale Capital LLC
Lime Rock Partners LLC
Natural Gas Partners
Riverstone Holdings LLC
SCF Partners LP
Sage Road Capital
White Deer Energy LP

REAL—Arizona
Desert Cedars LLC

REAL—California
Colony Capital LLC
Shorenstein Co LLC
Starwood Capital Group I LP

REAL—Connecticut
Commonfund Realty
Starwood Capital Group I LP

REAL—D. of Columbia
Starwood Capital Group I LP

REAL—Georgia
Starwood Capital Group I LP

REAL—Massachusetts
Colony Capital LLC

REAL—New York
Colony Capital LLC
Lone Star Fund Ltd
Shorenstein Co LLC

REAL—Texas
Lone Star Fund Ltd

Venture Firms—Alabama
Advantage Capital Partners
Bonaventure Capital LLC
Camp One Ventures LLC
Eastside Partners
Greer Capital Advisors LLC
Jemison Investment Co Inc
Murphree Venture Partners
New Capital Partners
Redmont Venture Partners

Venture Firms—Alaska
Launch:Alaska
Pt Capital LLC

Venture Firms—Arizona
AZ Digital Farm LLC
Alliance Healthcare Partners
Arizona Founders Fund LLC
Arris Ventures LLC
Coplex Ventures Fund I LP
Cornerstone Advisors Inc
DWP Investments LLC
E & I Ventures LLC
GBT Capital LLC
Indigo Partners LLC
Initium Capital LLC
Mayo Medical Ventures
Nest Ventures LLC
Research Corporation Technologies
Social Leverage LLC
Tallwave LLC
Trinnovate Ventures Inc
True North Venture Partners LP
UA Venture Capital LLC
Valley Ventures
venture51 Capital Fund LLP

Venture Firms—Arkansas
Cadron Creek Capital LLC
Newroad Capital Partners LLC
S2G Ventures LLC
VIC Technology Venture Development LLC

Venture Firms—California
AI8 Ventures, L.P.
AL Capital Holdings 2016 Ltd
AME Cloud Ventures LLC
ANGEL CAPITAL NETWORK INC
ATEL Ventures Inc
Aavishkaar Venture Management Services Pvt Ltd
Aberdare Ventures
Abingworth Management Ltd
Accel Partners & Co Inc
Acceleprise LLC
Accelerate-IT Ventures Management LLC
Accelerator Ventures
Acer Technology Ventures Asia Pacific
Acero Capital, L.P.
Acorn Campus Ventures
Acorn Pacific Ventures
Acorn Ventures, Inc.
Act One Ventures LP
Adams Capital Management, Inc.
Adaptive Healthcare LLC
Advance Venture Partners LLC
Advanced Technology Ventures
Advantage Capital Partners
Afore Capital LP
Agile Venture Capital LLC
Airbus Ventures
Alacon Ventures LLC
Alafi Capital Co LLC
Alexandria Real Estate Equities, LLC
Aligned Partners LLC
All Mobile Fund
AllegisCyber
Alloy Ventures Inc
Almaz Capital Partners
Almond Tree Capital Management Co LLC
Alpha Edison Partners LLC
Alsop Louie Partners
Alta Partners
Altos Ventures
Amadeus Capital Partners Ltd
American World Trade Fund Inc
Amgen Inc
Amicus Capital LLC
Amidzad Partners, Co.
Amino Capital Management Company LLC
Amkey Ventures LLC
Amplify Partners LP
Amplify.LA
Analytics Ventures
Andreessen Horowitz LLC
Angel Investors, LP
Angeleno Group Investors LLC
Angels' Forum & the Halo Fund
Anorak Ventures Inc.
Anthem Venture Partners
Aphelion Capital LLC
Applied Ventures LLC
Aquillian Investments LLC
Arafura Ventures Inc
Arch Venture Partners LLC
Archer Venture Capital LLC
Arena Ventures GP LLC
Argon Venture Partners
Array Ventures LP
Arrowpath Venture Capital
Arrowroot Capital LP
Arsenal
Artiman Management LLC
Artis Ventures
Asia Pacific Ventures
Asiatech Management LLC
Aspect Ventures LP
Asset Management Co
Astellas Venture Management LLC
Ata Ventures
Athena Capital Partners LLC
Atlas Peak Capital
Atomic Management LLC
August Capital Management LLC
Austral Capital
Authentic Ventures, L.P.
Autochrome Ventures LLC
Autotech Management LLC
Avalon Ventures, LLC
Avenue Ventures LLC
Azure Capital Partners, L.P.
B Capital Group
B37 Ventures LLC
BASF Venture Capital GmbH
BSD Venture Capital LLC
Bain Capital Venture Partners LLC
Baker & Eastlack Ventures
Bam Ventures GP LLC
Band of Angels Venture Fund LP
Baroda Ventures LLC
Base Ventures
Base10 Partners
Baseline Ventures LLC
Basis Set Ventures LLC
Battery Ventures LP

Pratt's Guide to Private Equity & Venture Capital Sources

Bay City Capital LLC
Bay Partners
Be Great Partners LLC
Beanstalk Ventures LP
Bee Partners, LLC
Benchmark Capital Management Gesellschaft MBH In Liqu
Benhamou Global Ventures LLC
Better Ventures LLC
Big Sky Partners
Binary Capital
Binary Capital Management LLC
Bioveda Capital Pte Ltd
Birchmere Ventures
Bisk Ventures Inc
Black Diamond Ventures Inc
Blade Partners
Block 26 LLC
Blockchain Capital
Blue Bear Capital LLC
Blue Consumer Capital
Blue Swell Capital
Blueberry Ventures
Bluepointe Ventures LLC
Bluerun Ventures LP
Blumberg International Partners LLC
Bold Capital Partners LP
BootUP World
Boost VC
Bootstrap Incubation LLC
BootstrapLabs LLC
Bow Capital Management LLC
Bow Ventures L.P.
Brain Trust Accelerator Fund LP
Brandon Capital Partners Pty Ltd
Breakout Ventures Inc
Brentwood Venture Capital
Brick & Mortar Ventures
Brightpath Capital Partners LP
Bryant Stibel & Company LLC
Builders VC Fund I LP
Bullpen Capital LP
Burrill & Company
CDIB BioScience Venture Management
CHP Management Inc
CLI Ventures
CLUB AUTO SPORT SILICON VALLEY L L C
CMEA Development Company LLC
COLLABORATIVE CAPITAL L L C
CRCM Venture Capital
Caffeinated Capital LLC
Calibrate Ventures LP
California Technology Ventures LLC
Cambrian Ventures Inc
CampVentures
Canaan Partners
Canaccord Genuity Group Inc
Canter Capital Management LLC
Canvas Venture Fund
Canyon Capital Advisors LLC
Canyon Healthcare Partners LLC
Capricorn Investment Group LLC
Cardinal Venture Capital
Carrick Capital Management Company LLC
Casa Verde Capital LLC

Catamount Ventures LP
Cerium Technology LLC
CerraCap Ventures LLC
Cervin Ventures
Charter Life Sciences II L P
Chengwei Ventures
Chilango Ventures LLC
CircleUp Network Inc
Cisco Investments Inc
Cisco Systems Inc
City Hill Ventures LLC
Civilization Ventures
Claremont Creek Ventures LP
Clean Pacific Ventures Management LLC
Clear Venture Management LLC
Clearstone Venture Management Services LLC
Clocktower Technology Ventures LLC
Cloud Apps Management LLC
Cognite Ventures LLC
Columbus Nova Technology Partner
Column Group
Combine VC
Comcast Ventures
Comerica Venture Capital Group
Comet Labs Inc
Commerce Ventures Management LLC
Commercial Drone Fund
Community Investment Management LLC
Congruent Ventures LLC
Connexus Equity Management Partners LLC
Cooley LLP
Core Innovation Capital I LP
Corporate Finance Partners CFP Beratungs GmbH
Correlation Ventures LP
Costanoa Venture Capital, L.P.
Cota Capital Inc
Cowboy Capital
Craton Equity Partners LLC
Crescendo Venture Management LLC
Crescent Ridge Partners Inc
Crestlight Venture Productions LLC
Cross Culture Ventures
CrossCut Ventures Management LLC
Crosslink Capital Inc
Crosspoint Venture Partners 2001 LP
CrunchFund
Curious Minds
Cycad Group LLC
crowdfunder Inc
DBL Investors
DFJ Athena
DN Capital Global Venture Capital Ii LP
DOCOMO Innovations Inc
DT Capital Partners
Danhua Capital LP
Data Collective LLC
De Novo Ventures LLC
Deep Fork Capital
DeepBlue Ventures LLC
Defta Partners
Defy Partners Management LLC
Delphi Ventures
Designer Fund
Deutsche Telekom Strategic Investments
Diamond TechVentures

Digitx Partners LLC
Dolby Family Ventures LP
Doll Capital Management Inc
Domain Associates LLC
Double M Partners LP
DoubleRock LLC
DragonVenture, Inc.
Draper Associates Inc
Draper Fisher Jurvetson
Draper Nexus Venture Partners LLC
Draper Richards Kaplan Foundation
Duke Equity Partners Inc
8VC
EDB Investments Pte Ltd
EW Healthcare Partners
Eastlink Capital
EchoVC Partners LLC
Eclipse Ventures
EcoR1 Capital LLC
Ecosystem Ventures LLC
Eileses Capital LLC
El Dorado Ventures
Embark Ventures LP
Emergence Capital Partners
Emergence Venture Partners LLC
Emergent Medical Partners LP
Endeavour Ventures Ltd
Endure Capital
Enerdigm Ventures LLC
Engineering Capital LLC
Entangled Ventures LLC
Enterprise Partners Management LLC
Entrepreneurs Fund LP
Equip Ventures LLC
Europlay Capital Advisors LLC
Evolution Media Partners
Expa Capital LLC
Explorer Group, The
Extreme Venture Partners Inc
e.ventures
ePlanet Capital
eVenture Capital Partners GmbH
4.0 Partners
500 Mexico City
500 Startups, L.P.
5AM Ventures LLC
FINISTERE VENTURES L L C
Felicis Ventures
Fenox Venture Capital Inc
Fifth Wall Ventures
Fika Ventures LP
Finaventures
Firelake Capital Management LLC
First Round Capital
Firsthand Technology Value Fund Inc
Fjord Ventures LLC
Floodgate Fund, L.P.
Florence Venture Partners
Fluxus Ventures LLP
Focus Ventures Ltd
Forentis Partners LLC
Forerunner Ventures LLC
Foresite Capital Management LLC
Formation 8 Partners LP
Formation Group Inc

Formative Ventures
Forte Ventures
Fortex Capital Inc
Forward Ventures
Foundation Capital LLC
Founders Capital Partners
Founders Circle Capital
Founders Club LP
Founders Fund, The
Four Rivers Partners LP
Freestyle Capital
Fremont Group LLC
Frontier Tech Ventures
Frontier Venture Capital
Frost Data Capital
FundersClub Inc
Fuse Capital
FusionX Ventures
Fyrfly Venture Partners LLC
G2VP LLC
GARON FINANCIAL GROUP
GC&H Partners
GGV Capital
GSV Acceleration Fund I LP
Garage Technology Ventures LLC
Gateway Incubator LLC
General Catalyst Partners LLC
Geodesic Capital
Gideon Hixon Fund LP
Gigafund
Global Catalyst Partners
Glynn Capital Management LLC
Gold Hill Capital Management LLC
Govtech Fund
Gramercy Private Equity LLC
Granite Hill Capital Partners LLC
Granite Ventures LLC
Graph Ventures LLC
Graphene Ventures
Green Bay Advisors LLC
Green Visor Capital
Greener Capital Partners LP
Greenhouse Capital Partners
Greycroft Partners LLC
Greylock Partners LLC
Greywolf
GroundWork Equity LLC
Growth Street Management LLC
GrowthX
Gsr Ventures Management Llc
Gva Capital LLC
H Barton Asset Management LLC
HALO FUND L P
HIMALAYA CAPITAL PARTNERS L P
HLM Management Co LLC
Halley Venture Partners LP
Halogen Ventures Partners LLC
Harbinger Venture Management
Harbor Pacific Capital LLC
Harmony Partners
Harrison Metal Capital
Hattery
Haystack
Health Velocity Capital
HealthQuest Capital

Healthy Ventures Management LLC
HeathQuest Capital
Heavybit
Heda Ventures
Heide Probstel Trust
Heidrick & Struggles International Inc
Helix Ventures
Hemi Ventures Fund I LP
Heuristic Capital Partners Management Co LLC
HighBAR Ventures
Hillcrest Venture Partners
Hina Capital Partners
Hive LLC
Homebrew LLC
Horizon Technology Finance Management LLC
Horizon Ventures
Hotung International Co Ltd
House Fund LP
Hub Ventures
Hummer Winblad Venture Partner
Hustle Fund
IDG Ventures USA
IECP Fund Management LLC
IMI.VC
Idealab
Ideo Ventures
Ignite Farm LLC
Ignition Ventures Management LLC
Illumina Accelerator Program
Illumina Ventures
Illuminate Ventures
Imagine K12 LLC
Immersive Capital LP
Impact America Fund LP
Impact Venture Capital
InCube Ventures LLC
Incubic Managment LLC
Index Ventures
Industrial Technology Investment Corp
Infinity Capital LLC
Infocomm Investments Pte Ltd
Infotech Ventures Co Ltd
Initialized Capital
InnerProduct Partners LLC
InnoSpring Inc
Innovacom Gestion SAS
Innovate Partners LLC
Innovation Endeavors LLC
Innovation Global Capital LLC
Inspiration Ventures LLC
Institutional Venture Partners
Intel Capital Corp
InterWest Partners LLC
Interuniversitair Micro-Electronica Centrum
Invent Ventures Inc
Inventus Capital Partners Fund I L P
Investor Group, The
Ironfire Capital LLC
Istuary Venture Capital Inc
Itochu Technology Inc
i/o ventures
iFly.vc
iGlobe Partners Ltd
iNovia Capital Inc
iSeed Ventures

J. F. Shea Co Inc
JAZZ Venture Partners LP
Jackson Square Ventures
Jafco Co Ltd
Jafco Ventures
Javelin Venture Partners LP
Jumpstartup Fund Advisors Pvt Ltd
Juniper Networks Inc
K2 Global
K5 Ventures
K9 Ventures LP
KPG Ventures
KTB Investment & Securities Co Ltd
KTB Ventures, Inc.
Kairos Venture Investments LLC
Kaiser Permanente Ventures LLC
Kalaari Capital Partners LLC
Kapor Capital
Karlin Ventures
Kearny Venture Partners LP
Keiretsu Forum
Keiretsu Ventures Inc
Kenson Ventures LLC
Kern Whelan Capital LLC
Keshif Ventures LLC
Khosla Ventures LLC
Kinzon Capital
Kleiner Perkins Caufield & Byers LLC
KohFounders Management LLC
Kohlberg Ventures LLC
LA Dodgers Sports & Entertainment Accelerator with R/GA
LAUNCH Fund
LDV Partners
LEAP Global Partners
LINCOLN FUNDS INTERNATIONAL INC
LUX CAPITAL GROUP L L C
Labrador Ventures
Latterell Venture Partners LP
Lauder Partners LLC
LaunchCapital LLC
Launchpad Digital Health LLC
Launchpad LA Inc
Leapfrog Ventures L P
Learn Capital Venture Partners LP
Leerink Capital Partners LLC
Lemnos Labs
Lighthouse Capital Partners LP
Lightspeed Management Company LLC
Lightstone Ventures LP
Linse Capital CP LLC
Liquid 2 Ventures LP
Longevity Fund, The
Longitude Capital Management Co LLC
Lotus Innovations LLC
Lucas Venture Group
Lumia Capital LLC
Luminari Capital LP
M13 Co
M34 Capital Inc
MHS Capital Management LLC
MK Capital
MVP Capital LLC
Mach Ventures LP
Madrone Capital Partners

Pratt's Guide to Private Equity & Venture Capital Sources

Maiden Lane Ventures
Manifest Investment Partners LLC
Manos Accelerator LLC
March Capital Partners GP LLC
Marsman-Drysdale Corp
Matrix Partners, L.P.
Matter Ventures
Maven Venture Partners
Maven Ventures Growth Labs
Maveron LLC
Mayfield Fund
MedFocus Fund LLC
Medical Technology Venture Partners LLC
Medventure Associates
Menlo Ventures
MergerTech Advisors
Meritech Capital Partners
Merus Capital Investment
Mesa Verde Venture Partners LP
Metrix Capital Group LLC
Middle East Venture Partners
Mighty Capital Management LLC
Milliways Ventures
Mindset Ventures
Mingly Capital
Mirador Capital
Miramar Venture Partners L P
Mission Bay Capital LLC
Mission Ventures Inc
Mithril Capital Management LLC
Mitsui & Co Global Investment Ltd
Mitsui & Co. Global Investment, Ltd.
Mohr Davidow Ventures
Moment Ventures LLC
Moneta Ventures LP
Monitor Venture Associates LLC
Monta Vista Capital LP
Montage Ventures
Monterey Venture Partners LLC
Montgomery & Co LLC
Montreux Equity Partners
Morado Venture Management LLC
Mosaik Partners LLC
Motus Ventures
MuckerLab LLC
mc3 ventures (FKA: McKenna Venture Accelerator (MVA))
NALA Investments LLC
NETCIRQ
NGEN Partners LLC
NGP Capital
NMS Capital Partners
NXT Capital Venture Finance
NanoDimension Management Ltd
National Healthcare Services
Navitas Capital

Venture Firms—California

Naxuri Capital
NeoTribe Management Company, LLC
New Cycle Capital LLC
New Enterprise Associates Inc
New Leaf Venture Partners LLC
NewGen Capital II LP
NewGen Venture Partners

NewSchools Venture Fund
Newbury Ventures
Newcap Partners Inc
Nex Cubed LLC
Nexos Capital Partners
Next World Capital LLC
NextEquity Partners LLC
Nexus Venture Partners
Nomo Ventures Management LLC
Noname Ventures LLC
Northern Light Venture Capital Development Ltd
Novo Holdings A/S
Nth Power LLC
137 Ventures LP
1517 Fund
180 Degree Capital Corp
1984 Ventures LP
1confirmation
O'Reilly Alphatech Ventures LLC
OC Cove Fund I LLC
OMRON ADVANCED SYSTEMS INC
ONSET Ventures
OVO Fund LLC
Oak Investment Partners
Oakhouse Partners LLC
Oakstone Venture Partners LLC
Obvious Ventures Management LLC
Oceanic Partners Inc
Okapi Venture Capital LLC
Omidyar Technology Ventures LLC
One Earth Capital LLC
Onramp
Operative Capital GP LLC
Opus Capital
Oriza Ventures
Otter Capital LLC
Outlook Ventures
Outpost Capital LLC
Owl Ventures LP
Oxford Bioscience Partners
P39 Capital LP
PAC-LINK Management Corp
PHI Capital Holdings Inc
PS SEED II L L C
PTI Ventures
Pacific Enterprise Capital LLC
Pacific General Ventures LLC
Pacific Partners
Pacific View Asset Management LLC
Paladin Capital Management LLC
Palapa Ventures
Palm Ventures LLC
Palo Alto Investors LLC
Palo Alto Venture Partners
Palo Alto Venture Science LLC
Palomar Ventures
Panasonic Venture Group
Pantera Capital Management LP
Parakletos@Ventures Millenium Fund LP
Partech International
Partnership Capital Growth LLC
Pasadena Angels, Inc.
Passport Capital LLC
Pathbreaker Ventures
PeakSpan Capital LLC

Pear Ventures
Peate Ventures LLC
Peninsula Ventures
People Fund LLC
Persistence Partners, L.P.
Phoenix Venture Partners LLC
Physic Ventures LLC
Pilot Growth Equity Partners
Pinnacle Ventures
Pipeline Capital Partners
Pitango Venture Capital Management Israel, Ltd.
PivotNorth Capital
Pivotal BioVenture Partners LLC
Pivotal Capital Partners LLC
Playground Global LLC
Playground Ventures GP LLC
Plug and Play Tech Center
Point Guard Ventures LLC
Polaris Venture Partners
Pond Venture Partners Ltd
Ponoi Capital LP
Pontifax Management Company Ltd
Poseidon Asset Management LLC
Powerplant LLC
Precursor Ventures
Prelude Ventures LLC
Presidio Partners
Presidio Ventures Inc
Princeville Global Partners Ltd
Pritzker Group Venture Capital
ProQuest Investments
Probitas Partners Inc
Proof Ventures LLC
Propel Venture Partners
Prospect Venture Partners
Provenance Ventures
Psilos Group Managers LLC
PurpleTalk, Inc.
Qualcomm Ventures
Queensbridge Venture Partners LLC
Quest Venture Partners LLC
Questa Capital Management LLC
Quicksilver Ventures
RB Webber and Comapny Inc
RETRO VENTURE PARTNERS L P
RINCON VENTURE PARTNERS L P
RUSNANO USA Inc
Radar Partners LLC
Radicle Accelerator
Radicle Impact
Rady School of Management
Raine Group LLC, The
Rally Ventures
Reach Capital
Recruit Strategic Partners Inc
Red Rock Ventures
Redpoint Ventures
Redwood Capital, Inc.
Redwood Venture Partners
Reed Elsevier Inc
Refactor Capital LP
Regard Venture Solutions
Relay Ventures
Rembrandt Venture Management LLC
Revolution Ventures LLC

Pratt's Guide to Private Equity & Venture Capital Sources

RezVen Partners LLC
Rho Capital Partners Inc
Ribbit Capital LP
Richmond Global
Ridgelift Ventures
Right Side Capital Management LLC
Rise Capital Management LLC
Rivet Ventures Management LLC
Rock Health
Rocket Ventures
Rocketship.vc
Rockpoint Capital Ltd
Rockport Capital Partners
Roda Group, The
Root Ventures
Rosemont Seneca Technology Partners
Runa Capital
Rustic Partners LP
Rutberg and Co LLC
79 Ventures
S Cubed Capital LLC
SAIL Capital Partners LLC
SBI Investment Korea Co Ltd
SG VC, L.P.
SIG Asia Investments LLLP
SJF Ventures
SRI International
SV Angel
SV Tech Ventures
Saastr Fund
Salem Partners LLC
Samsara BioCapital LP
Samsung Venture Investment Corp
San Joaquin Capital LLC
Sand Hill Group LLC
Sanderling Ventures
Sandwith Ventures LLC
Sapphire Ventures LLC
Saratoga Ventures, L.P.
Scale Up Venture Capital
Scale Venture Partners
SciFi VC
Scopus Ventures LLC
Scrum Ventures LLC
Sdl Ventures LLC
Sea Change Management LLC
Seabury Venture Partners LLC
Seafront Capital LLC
Sears Capital Management, Inc.
Section 32 LLC
Sequoia Capital Operations LLC
Seraph Group
Seven Seas Partners
Sevin Rosen Funds
SharesPost Financial Corp
Shasta Ventures LP
Shatter Fund
Shepherd Ventures LP
Sherpa Capital
Sherpalo Ventures
Shoreline Venture Management, LLC
Sibling Capital LLC
Siemens Venture Capital GmbH
Sierra Ventures
Sierra Wasatch Capital

Sigma Partners
Signalfire LLC
Signature Capital LLC
Silcon Valley Data Capital Management LLC
Silicon Valley Future Capital
Silicon Valley Growth Syndicate
Simon Equity Partners LLC
Simplepitch Ventures
Sippl Macdonald Ventures
Sirius Venture Consulting Pte Ltd
Skyline Ventures Inc
Skywood Ventures LLC
Slow Ventures LLC
SoGal Ventures
Social+Capital Partnership
Sofinnova Ventures Inc
Softbank Capital Partners L P
Soma Capital Management LLC
Sonoma Brands
Southern Cross Venture Partners Pty Ltd
Sozo Ventures LLC
Spark Capital
Sparkland Capital
Spectrum 28
Spinnaker Ventures
Spruce Capital Partners LLC
Sr One Ltd
Stage 1 Ventures LLC
Stage Venture Partners LLC
Starburst Accelerator SARL
Start Smart Labs
StartX
Startcaps Ventures
Startup Capital Ventures LP
Steamboat Ventures
Steelhead Ventures LLC
Stereo Capital
Sterling Johnston Capital Management LP
Stone Canyon Venture Partners
Storm Ventures Inc
Strathspey Crown LLC
Streamlined Ventures
String Ventures
Strong Ventures LLC
Struck Capital
Structural Capital GP LLC
Structure Capital LP
Structure Partners
Summation Health Ventures LP
Sunbridge Partners Inc
Sunstone Capital A/S
Super Ventures
Sure Ventures GP LLC
Susa Ventures LP
Sutter Hill Ventures
Switch Ventures LP
Sycamore Ventures Inc
Synergy Life Science Partners LP
Synergy Partners International
3311 Ventures LLC
T. Rowe Price Threshold Partnerships
TBL Capital LP
TC Growth Partners
TEC Ventures LP
TEL Venture Capital Inc

TI Capital
TL Ventures Inc
TYLT Lab
Tactico, Inc.
Takeda Ventures Inc
Tallwood Venture Capital
Tamarisc LLC
Tandem Entrepreneurs LLC
Tank Hill Ventures
Tano Capital LLC
Taurus Ventures GP LLC
Tautona Group Lp
Tech Coast Angels Inc
Techfund Capital Europe
Technology Crossover Ventures LP
Technology Partners
Technology Venture Partners Pty., Ltd.
Tekton Ventures
TeleSoft Partners
Telegraph Hill Group LLC
Telegraph Hill Partners
Telescope Partners
Templeton Asset Management Ltd
TenOneTen Ventures LP
Tenaya Capital, Inc.
Thales Corporate Ventures SAS
Thayer Ventures
Think Ventures LP
Third Rock Ventures LLC
Third Security LLC
Third Wave Ventures
Thirdstream Partners LLC
Thomas Mcnerney and Partners LLC
Thomvest Ventures Inc
Three Arch Partners LP
Three Bridges Ventures
TiE LaunchPad
Tilenius Investments
Timberline Venture Partners
Tolero Ventures LLC
TomorrowVentures LLC
Torrey Pines Investment, Inc.
Townsgate Media
Translink Capital LLC
Transmedia Capital Llc
Trend Forward Capital Management LLC
Triage Ventures LLC
Triangle Peak Partners LP
Trident Capital
Trident Capital Cybersecurity Fund I LP
Trinity Ventures LLP
TriplePoint Capital LLC
Trucks Venture Capital
True Ventures LLC
Tugboat Ventures LP
Tyche Partners LP
U.S. Venture Partners
Ulu Ventures
Uncork Capital
Undisclosed Firm
Unilever Ventures Ltd
United Talent Agency LLC
Unitus Impact Partners LLC
Up2398 LLC
UpWest Labs

2379

Pratt's Guide to Private Equity & Venture Capital Sources

Upfront Ventures
Urban Innovation Fund
VKRM
Valar Ventures Management LLC
Valence Life Sciences LLC
Vantagepoint Management Inc
Velocity Venture Capital Inc
Velos Partners
Venbio Partners LLC
Venrock Inc
Ventana Capital Management LP
Venture Catalyst Inc
VentureTech Alliance Holdings LLC
Versant Venture Management, LLC
Vertex Ventures
Vertical Group Inc
Vertical Venture Partners
Village Global Management LLC
Visa Inc
Visionary Venture Fund LP
Visionnaire Ventures LLC
Vivo Capital LLC
VoiVoda Ventures
venture51 Capital Fund LLP
WI Harper Group Inc
WISC Partners LP
WMAS Management Group
Walden International
Walden Venture Capital
Wasabi Ventures LLC
Watermark Venture Capital Inc
Wavemaker Partners
Wavepoint Ventures LLC
Wayfounder
Wearable World Inc
Wellington Partners GmbH
Wells Fargo Startup Accelerator
WestSummit Capital Management Ltd
Westbridge Ventures LLC
Western States Investment Group
Western Technology Investment
Westly Group LLC
Westwave Capital I LP
White Road Investments LLC
WiL Inc
Wildcat Venture Partners LLC
Windward Ventures
Wing Venture Capital
Wireframe Ventures
Wolf Capital Ventures
Women's Venture Capital Fund
Wonder Ventures
Woodside Fund
Worldview Technology Partners, Inc.
X/Seed Capital Management
XSeed Capital
Xilinx Inc
Xplorer Capital
Xyz Venture Capital LLC
Y Combinator Inc
YL Ventures GP Ltd
Yasuda Enterprise Development Co Ltd
Zeev Ventures Management LLC
Zenshin Capital Management
Zero2IPO Ventures

Zetta Venture Partners
Zipdragon Ventures
Zone Ventures

Venture Firms—Colorado
Access Venture Partners
Advantage Capital Partners
Altira Group LLC
Altitude Funds LLC
Appian Ventures, Inc.
Aravaipa Ventures LLC
ArrowMark Partners
Aweida Venture Partners
Blackhorn Ventures Capital Management LLC
Blue Note Ventures
Boulder Food Group LLC
Boulder Investment Group Reprise
Boulder Ventures Ltd
CanopyCentral LLC
Capital for Founders LLC
Centennial Ventures Vii L P
Cooley LLP
Crossroads Liquidating Trust
Delta-V Capital LLC
Dove Capital Partners LLC
Econergy International Corp
Enhanced Capital Partners LLC
enVision Capital
eonCapital, LLC
First Capital Ventures LLC
FirstTracks Ventures LLC
Fisher Capital Partners Ltd
Foundry Group LLC
Fraser McCombs Capital
GC&H Partners
Galvanize Ventures
Ganesh Capital LLC
Goff Capital Partners, L.P.
Gore Range Capital LLC
Green Lion Partners LLC
Greenline Ventures LLC
Greenmont Capital Partners
Grotech Ventures
Harbinger Ventures LLC
Hexagon Investments LLC
High Country Venture LLC
Highland Ventures Group LLC
Infield Capital LLC
iSherpa Capital
Lacuna LLC
Lightstone Ventures LP
Lonetree Capital Management LLC
MVP Capital LLC
Marker Hill Capital LLC
MergeLane LLC
Murphree Venture Partners
9th Street Investments
Northern Lights Capital Group LLC
Oakstone Venture Partners LLC
Partisan Management Group Inc
Pearl Street Capital Group
Primera Capital
Pv Ventures LLC
Range Light LLC
Rocky Mountain Innovation Initiative Inc

Sequel Venture Partners
Service Provider Capital LLC
T. Rowe Price Threshold Partnerships
Tahoma Advisors Inc
Techstars Central LLC
Telluride Venture Accelerator
Three Leaf Ventures LLC
TitleCard Capital Group LLC
TomorrowVentures LLC
Vista Ventures
Woodbourne Canada Partners Advisors LLC

Venture Firms—Connecticut
AEGIS LLC
ASML Ventures
Alerion Partners LLC
Axiom Venture Partners LP
BEV Capital
Balyasny Asset Management LP
Bio-Investigations Ltd
Biomark Capital
Bulldog Innovation Group LLC
CHL Medical Partners LP
Capital Resource Company of Connecticut
Cava Capital
Connecticut Innovations Inc
dmg :: information
Elm Street Ventures LP
Emerge Venture Capital
Emerging Energy & Environment LLC
Energy Technology Ventures
Enhanced Capital Partners LLC
Expansion Capital Partners LLC
FE Clean Energy Group Inc
FirstMark Capital LLC
Foundation Medical Partners LP
GE Energy Financial Services Inc
Galen Associates Inc
Goff Capital Partners, L.P.
Greenwoods Capital Partners
Horizon Technology Finance Management LLC
IT Matrix Ventures
LaunchCapital LLC
Longitude Capital Management Co LLC
Mirador Capital
Moonrise Venture Partners, L.P.
NGN Capital LLC
New China Capital Management LP
New Ground Ventures
Next Wave Funds
Oak HC/FT Partners LP
Oak Investment Partners
Oxford Bioscience Partners
PRC Venture Partners LLC
STRATEGIC ADVISORY GROUP INC
Signal Lake Management LLC
Skandia Innovation AB
Skyline Ventures Inc
Spencer Trask Ventures Inc
TENNANT CAPITAL PARTNERS L L C
TWJ Capital LLC
Thomas Mcnerney and Partners LLC
Tudor Ventures
Tullis Health Investors
Turnstone Capital Management LLC

UNIFIED GROWTH PARTNERS L P
Vistech Corp
Worldquant Ventures LLC

Venture Firms—D. of Columbia
AKT IP Ventures
Acceleprise LLC
Accion International
Advantage Capital Partners
Africa Group LLC
Anzu Partners
Carmichael Partners LLC
Cooley LLP
Core Capital Partners Ii L P
Cultivate Ventures LLC
Econergy International Corp
Efromovich/Silva Capital Partners
Energy Ventures Group LLC
Enhanced Capital Partners LLC
Fortify Ventures LLC
Gilfus Venture Partners LLC
Kiwi Venture Partners LLC
Lazard Technology Partners
Leaf Clean Energy USA LLC
Middle Bridge Partners LLC
Middleland Capital
Modern Africa Fund Managers, LLC
National Corn Growers Association
NaviMed Capital Advisors LLC
New Horizons Venture Capital LLC
New Magellan Venture Partners LLC
NewSchools Venture Fund
NextGen Venture Partners LLC
1776
Paladin Capital Management LLC
Paras Ventures LLC
Quona Capital Management Ltd
Revolution
Revolution Ventures LLC
Sawari Ventures LLC
Small Enterprise Assistance Funds
Springboard Venture Fund LLC
Strategic Cyber Ventures LLC
Village Capital
Woodside O Brien LLC

Venture Firms—Delaware
Chartline Capital Partners
DuPont Ventures
Fairbridge Venture Partners
Innovation Capital Advisors LLC
Leading Edge Ventures LLC

Venture Firms—Florida
ACA Ventures LLC
Advantage Capital Partners
Allen & Company of Florida, Inc.
Allure Capital Inc
Antares Capital Corporation
Arsenal
Athenian Fund Management Inc
Avery Business Development Services
Axioma Ventures LLC
Axon Partners Group Investment
Azoic Ventures Inc
Backlog Capital LLC

Ballast Point Venture Partners LLC
Boston Capital Ventures LP
Caerus Ventures LLC
ClearSky Power & Technology Fund I LLC
CoreCo Holdings LLC
Corporate Finance Partners CFP Beratungs GmbH
Cross Valley Capital
Cybersec 3 LLC
Easton Hunt Capital Partners LP
Enhanced Capital Partners LLC
F1 BioVentures LLC
Florida Institute for Commercialization of Public Research
Fundamental Management Corp
Gordon River Capital
Healthbox LLC
I-4 Capital Partners LLC
Inflexion Partners
John S. and James L. Knight Foundation
Keen Growth Capital Advisors LLC
Lane Five Ventures LLC
Las Olas Venture Capital
Littlebanc Merchant
Ljh Global Investments L L C
Looking Glass Partners LLC
MPM Capital LLC
MTH Ventures
MaverixLab Inc
Mayo Medical Ventures
Medina Capital Partners Inc
New Brand Ventures LLC
New World Angels, Inc.
North Bay Equity Partners
OnPoint Technologies
Orlando Venture Capital Inc
PS 27 Ventures LLC
Partisan Management Group Inc
Phyto Partners
Prax Capital Management Co
ProQuest Investments
Proton Enterprises LLC
Quark Ventures LLC
Responder Ventures LLC
Richmond Global
Rock Creek Capital LLC
SK Ventures LLC
Smart Ventures Inc
South Ventures
Stanmore Medical Investments
Star Capital Management Inc
Sunrock Ventures Management LLC
T. Rowe Price Threshold Partnerships
TheVentureCity
Third Security LLC
Travel Startups Incubator LLC
Tullis Health Investors
URBAN US PUBLIC BENEFIT Corp
Vestech Partners LLC
Vocap Investment Partners LLC
Z9 Capital LLC

Venture Firms—Georgia
Accelerant Equity LLC
Accuitive Medical Ventures LLC
Acquisition Search Corp

Aflac Corporate Ventures
Atlanta Technology Angels
Atlanta Ventures
BIP Capital
BLH Venture Partners LLC
CEO Ventures
Cassius Family Management LLC
Ellis Capital
FII Capital Partners LLC
Forte Ventures
GRA Venture Fund LLC
Genesis Capital Advisors LLC
Gray Ghost Ventures
Gray Matters Capital Inc
Hamilton Ventures LLC
HealthQuest Capital
ITC Holdings Corp
Imlay Investments
Jerusalem Global Ventures
Kinetic Ventures LLC
Knoll Ventures Ecp Llc
Lira VC
Mosley Ventures
NMP Management Corp
Native American Venture Fund LLC
Seraph Group
Spirits Capital Partners LLC
SunTrust Banks Inc
TTV Capital LLC
Tech Square Labs LLC
Tech Square Ventures
TechOperators LLC
UPS Strategic Enterprise Fund
Value Plus Ventures LLC

Venture Firms—Hawaii
Dragonbridge Capital L L C
Enerdigm Ventures LLC
Mbloom LLC
Reef Capital Ventures LLC
Startup Capital Ventures LP

Venture Firms—Idaho
Epic Ventures Inc
Highway 12 Ventures

Venture Firms—Illinois
Abundant Venture Partners LLC
Advantage Capital Partners
Amiti Ventures LLC
Ansley Equity Partners
Apex Venture Partners LLC
Arch Development Partners LLC
Arch Venture Partners LLC
Balyasny Asset Management LP
Batterson Venture Capital
Breakout Capital LLC
Bridge Street Capital Partners LLC
Bulgarian-American Enterprise Fund
Caldera Venture Partners LLC
Canaccord Genuity Group Inc
Cane Investment Partners LLC
Capital Strategy Management Co
Chicago Innovation Exchange
Chicago Ventures
Cleveland Avenue LLC

Pratt's Guide to Private Equity & Venture Capital Sources

Corazon Capital LLC
Cultivian Sandbox Venture Partners LLC
Duchossois Technology Partners LLC
DunRobin Ventures LLC
Equator Capital Partners LLC
FII Capital Partners LLC
FireStarter Fund LLC
First Analysis Corp
Focal Point Ventures LLC
Founder Equity LLC
Fraser McCombs Capital
G2T3V LLC
GREATPOINT VENTURES
Gentry Venture Partners
Grand Crossing Capital LLC
Guild Capital LLC
Hard 8 Venture Capital
Healthbox LLC
Heidrick & Struggles International Inc
Hopewell Ventures
Hyde Park Venture Partners
Illinois Partners LLC
Illinois Ventures LLC
Impact Engine LLC
InDecatur Ventures LLC
Independence Equity Management LLC
Invenergy Future Fund Manager LLC
JK&B Capital LLC
JVC Investment Partners LLC
K8 Ventures LLC
KB Partners LLC
Lakewest Venture Partners
Laveer Growth Capital LLC
Lightbank
Listen LLC
MK Capital
Mab Capital Management LLC
Math Venture Partners LP
Merrick Ventures LLC
Method Capital
Mitsubishi Corp
Moderne Ventures Fund I LP
Mosaix Ventures LLC
Motorola Solutions Venture Capital
NXT Capital Venture Finance
Network Ventures
New Coast Ventures LLC
Next Frontier Capital LLC
Northport Investments
OCA Ventures
ORGONE CAPITAL I L L C
Open Prairie Ventures
Origin Ventures LLC
Pritzker Group Venture Capital
Promus Ventures
Red Arts Capital LLC
Ringleader Ventures LLC
7wire Ventures
Salveo Capital
Sandbox Industries LLC
Schultz Investment Co
Second Century Ventures LLC
Seneca Partners Inc
Serra Ventures LLC
Seyen Capital LLC

Shorebank Capital Corp
Sigvion Capital
Spencer Trask Ventures Inc
Spiral Sun Ventures LLC
Strand Equity Partners LLC
Synetro Group LLC
2X CONSUMER PRODUCTS GROWTH PARTNERS L P
Techstars Central LLC
Tensility Venture Partners LLC
Tribal Ventures LLC
True North Venture Partners LP
VCapital Management Co LLC
West Loop Ventures LLC
Wicklow Capital Inc

Venture Firms—Indiana
Allos Ventures LLC
Apex One Equity LLC
Arch Development Partners LLC
Barnard Associates, Inc.
Biocrossroads
Blue Chip Venture Co
CHV Capital Inc
Charmides Capital
Chatham Venture Partners
Collina Ventures LLC
Cultivian Ventures LLC
Elevate Ventures Inc
Eli Lilly and Co
Heron Capital LLC
High Alpha Co-Investment LLC
Indiana University
Lilly Ventures Management Company LLC
M25 Group LLC
Meridian Street Capital
Spring Mill Venture Partners
Triathlon Medical Ventures LLC
Twilight Venture Partners

Venture Firms—Iowa
Ag Ventures Alliance
CMA Ventures Inc
InvestAmerica Venture Group, Inc.
Iowa Corn Opportunities LLC
Iowa Seed Fund II LLC
Iowa Startup Accelerator Management Inc
Manchester Story Group
Next Level Ventures LLC
North Iowa Venture Capital Fund II LLC
Prairie Crest Capital LLC
Prairie Oak Capital LLC
Renew Rural Iowa
River Glen Private Capital LLC
Rock River Capital LLC
Twelve19 Ventures LLC

Venture Firms—Kansas
Firebrand Management LLC
Five Elms Capital LLC
KC Venture Group LLC
Koch Genesis LLC
Leawood Ventures
MPM Capital LLC
Midwest Venture Alliance
Nueterra Capital
Open Prairie Ventures

Techaccel LLC
Technology Ventures Fund I GP LLC
Trendlines Group Ltd

Venture Firms—Kentucky
Access Ventures
AshHill Pharmaceutical Investments LLC
Awesome Inc
Bluegrass Angels
Chrysalis Ventures Inc
Commonwealth Seed Capital LLC
Kentucky Seed Capital Fund
Marshall Ventures
Meritus Ventures LP
Poplar Ventures LLC
Triathlon Medical Ventures LLC
UpTech LLC
Yearling Management LLC

Venture Firms—Louisiana
Adams and Reese LLP
Advantage Capital Partners
BVM Capital LLC
CenturyLink Inc
Enhanced Capital Partners LLC
SAIL Capital Partners LLC
Sibling Capital LLC
Voodoo Ventures LLC

Venture Firms—Maine
CEI Ventures Inc
Cei Community Ventures Inc
Clear Venture Partners Inc
Masthead Venture Partners
North Atlantic Capital
Signature Capital LLC
Supply Chain Ventures LLC

Venture Firms—Maryland
ABS Capital Partners, Inc.
Abell Venture Fund
Anthem Capital Management Inc
Ashby Point Capital
CNF Investments LLC
DataTribe
Epidarex Capital
Fenway Summer Ventures LP
Grotech Ventures
Highcape Partners LP
India Venture Partners
Inflection Point Ventures
Internet Ventures Scandinavia
jVen Capital LLC
Kinetic Ventures LLC
Maryland Department of Business and Economic Development
Maryland Technology Development Corp
Medimmune LLC
Microvest Capital Management LLC
New Enterprise Associates Inc
New Markets Venture Partners
Novak Biddle Venture Partners LP
Panacea Capital Advisors Inc
Potomac Energy Fund LP
Questmark Partners LP
Redshift Ventures Management Inc

Rock Springs Capital Management LP
SFP Capital LLC
Sinclair Ventures Inc
Syncom Management Co Inc
T. Rowe Price Threshold Partnerships
TWJ Capital LLC
Telecommunications Development Fund
Vital Venture Capital LLC

Venture Firms—Massachusetts

@Ventures
ABS Ventures
AH Ventures
Abingworth Management Ltd
Accion International
Accomplice LLC
Adams Capital Management, Inc.
Advancit Capital LLC
Agent Capital LLC
Allied Minds LLC
Altimeter Capital Management LP
Amplify Partners LP
Anterra Capital BV
Ascent Venture Management Inc
AssembleVC Fund I LP
Atlas Venture Advisors Inc
Avalon Ventures, LLC
BT Venture Fund Management LLC
Bain Capital Venture Partners LLC
Barings Corporate Investors
Battery Ventures LP
Bayboston Managers LLC
Bessemer Venture Partners
BioVentures Investors
Biotechonomy Ventures LLC
Black Coral Capital LLC
Blade LLC
Bolt Innovation Group LLC
Boston Capital Ventures LP
Boston Community Capital Inc
Boston Global Ventures LLC
Boston Millennia Partners LP
Boston Seed Capital LLC
Brain Robotics Capital LLC
Breakaway
Broadview Ventures Inc
Brookline Venture Partners
COSIMO Ventures
Canaccord Genuity Group Inc
Castile Ventures
Catalyst Health And Technology Partners LLC
Causeway Media Partners LP
Centerman Capital
Charles River Ventures LLC
Chestnut Hill Ventures LLC
Chiesi Ventures
Clarus Ventures LLC
Clean Energy Venture Group
Collaborative Seed and Growth Partners LLC
Columbia Capital LP
Commonwealth Capital Ventures
Converge
Cooley LLP
Cue Ball Group LLC
Cypresstree Investment Management Company Inc

Dace Ventures
Data Point Capital I LP
Drydock Ventures LP
E14 GP LLC
EDB Investments Pte Ltd
Echelon Ventures LLC
Egan Managed Capital LP
Elephant Partners LP
Engine, The
Excel Venture Management
Excelestar Ventures
Expansion Capital Partners LLC
406 Ventures LLC
5AM Ventures LLC
F-Prime Capital Partners
Fa Technology Ventures Corp
Fairhaven Capital Partners, L.P.
Fidelity Investment Funds II
Flagship Pioneering
Flare Capital Partners
Fletcher Spaght Ventures LP
Flybridge Capital Partners
Fontinalis Partners LLC
Foundation Medical Partners LP
Founder Collective LP
G20 Associates LLC
GEN3 Partners, Inc.
GREATPOINT VENTURES
Garvin Hill Capital Partners LLC
General Catalyst Partners LLC
Glasswing Ventures LLC
Globespan Capital Partners
Gold Hill Capital Management LLC
Grandbanks Capital
Greybird Ventures LLC
Guidepost Growth Equity
HLM Management Co LLC
Harvard Management Company Inc
Harvard School of Engineering and Applied Sciences
Healthcare Ventures LLC
Highland Capital Partners LLC
Hyperplane Venture Capital
IncTANK Ventures
Indicator Ventures
Inflection Point Ventures
Innosight Ventures
Jarvinian LLC
Kepha Partners
Key Venture Partners
Kodiak Venture Partners LP
Kormeli LLC
Kraft Group LLC
LCC Legacy Holdings Inc
LaunchCapital LLC
LearnLaunchX
Leerink Capital Partners LLC
Liberty Mutual Innovation
Life Sciences Partners BV
Lighthouse Capital Partners LP
Link Ventures LLLP
Long River Ventures, Inc.
Longwood Founders Management LLC
Longworth Venture Partners, L.P.
MIT Sandbox Innovation Fund Program

MP Healthcare Venture Management Inc
MPM Capital LLC
MVM Partners LLP
MVP Capital LLC
Mansa Capital Management LLC
Mass Ventures
MassMutual Ventures LLC
Massachusetts Clean Energy Center
Massachusetts Mutual Life Insurance Co
Masthead Venture Partners
Material Impact Fund I LP
Matrix Partners, L.P.
Medscience Ventures LLC
Momentum Equity Partners LLC
Mti Partners Ltd
NAV.VC
NXT Capital Venture Finance
NXT Ventures Fund 1 LLC
Nauta Capital SL
New Hill Management LLC
NewSchools Venture Fund
NextView Ventures LP
Nexus Medical Partners
North Hill Ventures LP
Norwich Ventures
Novartis Venture Funds
One Way Ventures Management PBC Inc
Openview Venture Partners LP
Orion Healthcare Equity Partners
Oxford Bioscience Partners
Partners Innovation Fund LLC
Pearl Street Capital Group
Phoenix Venture Partners LLC
Pillar Companies Management LLC
Pilot House Ventures Group, LLC
Point Judith Capital
Polaris Venture Partners
Prism Ventureworks
Procyon Ventures
Progress Ventures Inc
Project 11 Ventures, L.P.
Provident Healthcare Ventures LLC
Puretech Ventures
Quest Capital Inc
RA Capital Management LLC
Raptor Capital Management LP
Resolute.VC
Rexiter Capital Management Ltd
Rockport Capital Partners
Romulus Capital LLC
Rose Park Advisors LLC
Rudyard Partners
Rutberg and Co LLC
SV Health Investors LLP
Sanofi-Sunrise
Saturn Management LLC
Schooner Capital LLC
Scivantage FinTech Incubator Program
Seed Capital Partners
Sherbrooke Capital
Shiprock Capital LLC
Siemens Venture Capital GmbH
Sigma Prime Ventures LLC
Silversmith Capital Partners LLC
Sky Ventures International LLC

Pratt's Guide to Private Equity & Venture Capital Sources

Skyline Ventures Inc
Softbank Capital Partners L P
Solstice Capital
Spark Capital
Spray Venture Partners
Sr One Ltd
Stage 1 Ventures LLC
Stata Venture Partners
Suffolk Equity Partners LLC
Summerhill Venture Partners Management Inc
Sustainable Resource Ventures
Sustainvc LLC
Techstars Central LLC
Tectonic Ventures LP
Tekla Capital Management LLC
Ten Eleven Ventures LP
Tenaya Capital, Inc.
Terawatt Ventures LLC
Third Rock Ventures LLC
Tudor Ventures
Underscore.VC
Venture Capital Fund of New England
Vestigo Ventures LLC
Vida Ventures LLC
Vineyard Ventures
Vodia Ventures LLC
Volition Capital LLC
Waterline Ventures LLC
Wave Equity Partners LLC
Wellington Management Company LLP
Westfield Capital Management Company LP
WindSail Capital Group LLC
Windspeed Ventures
Wuxi Healthcare Ventures
Wwc Capital Fund L P
Y Combinator Inc
Yankee Equity Solution
Zaffre Investments LLC

Venture Firms—Michigan
Amherst Fund LLC
Ann Arbor Spark Foundation
Apjohn Ventures LLC
Arboretum Ventures Inc
Arch Development Partners LLC
Arsenal
Augment Ventures Fund I LP
Belle Michigan Fund LP
Biostar Ventures II LLC
Boomerang Catapult LLC
Bridge Street Capital Partners LLC
CIG Securities Inc
Capital Bidco Inc
Chrysalis Ventures Inc
Coolhouse Labs LLC
Detroit Venture Partners LLC
Donnelly Penman & Partners Inc
Early Stage Partners LP
Edf Ventures
eLab Ventures
Flagship Pioneering
Fontinalis Partners LLC
Grand Ventures
Hopen Life Science Ventures
Huron River Venture Partners LLC

IncWell LLC
Invest Michigan
MK Capital
Michigan Accelerator Fund I Management LLC
Michigan Economic Development Corp
North Coast Technology Investors, L.P.
Novus Biotechnology Fund
Oakland Energy & Water Ventures
Oracle Capital Partners LLC
Plymouth Venture Partners
RPM Ventures Management LLC
RSVP Capital
Red Cedar Ventures LLC
Resonant Venture Partners
SWMF Life Science Venture Fund, L.P.
Seneca Partners Inc
Skypoint Ventures LLC
TMG Venture Capital Co.
Tamarind Hill
Tappan Hill Ventures
Tgap Ventures LLC
Trout Creek Ventures LP
University of Michigan
Windquest Group Inc

Venture Firms—Minnesota
Affinity Capital Management Co
BlueFire Partners Capital Markets Group
Brightstone Venture Capital
Canaccord Genuity Group Inc
Come Up Capital
Coral Ventures Inc
Crawford Capital Corp
Crimson Ventures LLC
El Dorado Ventures
Invenshure LLC
Lemhi Ventures, Inc.
Loup Ventures
MatchStick Ventures
Mayo Medical Ventures
New Asia Partners LLC
Omphalos Venture Partners LLC
Rally Ventures
Sherpa Partners LLC
Sightline Partners LLC
Split Rock Partners LLC
St Paul Venture Capital Inc
Stonehammer Capital LLC
TT Capital Partners LLC
Technology Venture Partners
Treehouse Health LLC
Troy Ventures LLC
Vilicus Ventures LLC

Venture Firms—Mississippi
Serpent Venture Capital LP

Venture Firms—Missouri
Ahv Holding Company LLC
Arsenal Capital Management LLC
Augury Capital Partners
BioGenerator
Capital Innovators LLC
Cultivation Capital
Former Charter Communications Parent Inc
Helix Center Biotech Incubator

InvestAmerica Venture Group, Inc.
iSelect Fund LLC
KC Venture Group LLC
KCRise Fund LLC
Lewis & Clark Venture Capital LLC
MVP Capital LLC
National Corn Growers Association
OPENAIR Equity Partners
Oakwood Medical Investors
Pilgrim Baxter
Prolog Ventures
Prosper Capital LLC
RiverVest Venture Partners LLC
Savvis Inc
Six Thirty
SparkLabKC
Stadia Ventures LLC
Stray Dog Capital LLC
Triathlon Medical Ventures LLC
Yield Lab LLC

Venture Firms—Montana
Good Works Ventures LLC
Next Frontier Capital

Venture Firms—Nebraska
Aksarben Innovation Initiative
Dundee Venture Capital
Invest Nebraska Corp
Nebraska Global
Prairie Ventures LLC
Router Ventures LP
Treetop Ventures Inc
World Investments Inc

Venture Firms—Nevada
Cypress Growth Capital LLC
Global Asia Partners
Novus Via LLC
Redhills Ventures LLC
SAIC Venture Capital Corporation
Skywood Ventures LLC
VegasTechFund

Venture Firms—New Hampshire
Arete Corp
Borealis Ventures
Harbor Light Capital Partners LLC
New Energy Capital Corp
10X Venture Partners LLC

Venture Firms—New Jersey
Alcatel-Lucent Ventures
Arrowpath Venture Capital
Auster Capital Partners LLC
Battelle Ventures LP
Beta Bridge Capital
CHP Management Inc
Care Capital LLC
Celgene Corp
Chaac Ventures
Channel Mark Ventures
Chart Venture Partners LP
Condor Capital Management Corp
Conexus Capital Management, Inc.
Coniston Capital Corp

Pratt's Guide to Private Equity & Venture Capital Sources

DeSimone Group Investments LLC
Domain Associates LLC
Dynamk Capital LLC
Foundation Venture Capital Group LLC
ff Venture Capital
HU Investments LLC
Innovation Garden LLC
Johnson & Johnson Innovation-JJDC Inc
Johnston Associates Inc
KEC Holdings LLC
Merck Capital Ventures LLC
NJTC Venture Fund
New Jersey Economic Development Authority
New Venture Partners LLC
Northern Capital Management Group
Novitas Capital LP
Omni Capital Group LLC
Osage Venture Partners
Peesh Venture Capital
Pharma Capital Ventures
Princeton Biopharma Capital Partners LLC
Ridgewood Capital Management LLC
Rowan University Foundation Inc
SCP Private Equity Partners
Scivantage FinTech Incubator Program
Selway Partners L L C
Sycamore Ventures Inc
UBS Capital Markets LP
Vertical Group Inc
YA Global Investments LP

Venture Firms—New Mexico
Camino Real Capital Partners LLC
Cottonwood Capital Partners LLC
Epic Ventures Inc
Flywheel Ventures
Jerome Capital LLC
New Mexico Community Capital
Psilos Group Managers LLC
Sun Mountain Capital Advisors LLC
Verge Fund

Venture Firms—New York
AVANTALION LLC
Abundance Partners LLC
Accel Partners & Co Inc
Accelerate Long Island Inc
Accelfoods LLC
Accretive LLC
Actinic Ventures LLC
Activate Venture Partners
Acumen Fund Inc
Advantage Capital Partners
Aisling Capital LLC
Alliance Consumer Growth LLC
Alpha Venture Partners
AlphaPrime Ventures
Alpine Meridian Inc
Altpoint Capital Partners LLC
Altpoint Ventures LP
Ankar Capital Management LLC
Aperture Venture Partners LLC
Apple Tree Partners
Archimedes Health Investors
Archipel Capital LLC
Arcus Ventures

Armory Square Ventures Manager LLC
Arrowpath Venture Capital
Artesian Capital Management Australia Pty Ltd
Ascend Capital Partners
Ascent Biomedical Ventures
Asia Pacific Investment Partners
Asia West LLC
Asimov Ventures Management LLC
Atw Partners LLC
BOC International Holdings Ltd
BOLDstart Ventures II LP
BR Ventures
BRM Capital LLC
BVM Capital LLC
Bain Capital Venture Partners LLC
Baker Bros Advisors LP
Balyasny Asset Management LP
Basset Investment Group LLC
Beanstalk Ventures LP
Bessemer Venture Partners
Betaworks Studio LLC
BiotechVest LP
Black Coral Capital LLC
Bleu Capital LLC
Blue Cloud Ventures
Blue Scorpion Investments LP
Blue Seed Capital LLC
Bowery Capital
Brand Foundry Ventures
Brave Ventures
Broadline Capital LLC
Brooklyn Bridge Ventures
Bseed Investments LLC
Burch Creative Capital LLC
CAVU Venture Partners, LLC
CB Alliance Inc
CLS Capital Ltd
COLLABORATIVE CAPITAL L L C
CREATION CAPITAL L L C
CRITICAL CAPITAL GROWTH FUND L P
CVF Technologies Corp
Calgary Enterprises Inc
Campus Evolution Incubator LLC
Canaan Partners
Canaccord Genuity Group Inc
Cantor Ventures
Canyon Capital Advisors LLC
Capstone Partners LLC
Casdin Capital LLC
Cava Capital
Cavendish Impact Capital
Cayuga Venture Fund
Centana Growth Partners
Chart Venture Partners LP
Chazen Capital Partners
China US Strategy Capital Group, Ltd.
Chobani Food Incubator
City Light Capital
Closed Loop Partners LLC
Coatue Management L L C
Coburn Ventures LLC
Collaborative Fund
Colle Capital
Columbus Nova Technology Partner
Comcast Ventures

Communitas Capital Partners LLC
Compound Ventures
ConnectedVC
Consigliere Brand Capital LLC
Contour Venture Partners
Conversion Capital LLC
Cooley LLP
Core Innovation Capital I LP
Corigin Ventures
Corporate Finance Partners CFP Beratungs GmbH
Cortlandt Private Capital LLC
Courtside Venture Partners RG LLC
Coventure LLC
Cranberry Capital LLC
Credit Suisse Asset Management LLC
Cross Atlantic Partners
Culbro LLC
DGNL Ventures LP
Dace Ventures
Danone Manifesto Ventures Inc
Davies Ward Phillips & Vineber
Delta Capital Management LLC
Digital Entertainment Ventures LLC
Digitalis Ventures LLC
Dolik Ventures LLC
Double C Capital
Downing Partners LLC
EW Healthcare Partners
EarlyStage.NYC
Easton Hunt Capital Partners LP
Edelweiss Financial Services Ltd
Elephant Ventures LLC
Elevate Innovation Partners LLC
Emerald Development Managers LP
Energy Impact Partners LLC
Enhanced Capital Partners LLC
Eniac Ventures LP
Enso Ventures Ltd
Equip Ventures LLC
Ernst & Young LLP
Evolution Corporate Advisors LLC
Excell Partners Inc
Expansion Capital Partners LLC
eValue Ventures AG
FJ Labs
Finaves I SA
Fintech Collective Inc
First Round Capital
FirstMark Capital LLC
Flybridge Capital Partners
Foresite Capital Management LLC
Fortex Capital Inc
Forum Capital Partner
Fos Capital Partners LLC
Founder Collective LP
Frontier Equities VC LLC
FundersGuild
Fundrx Inc
Future Perfect Ventures LLC
ff Venture Capital
Galtere Ltd
Gaspar Global Ventures LLC
Gefinor Ventures
Generation Investment Management LLP
Genesis Angels

2385

Pratt's Guide to Private Equity & Venture Capital Sources

Glenmont Partners, LLC
Global Technology Investment
Gmg Capital Partners LP
Gotham Ventures LLC
Great Oaks Venture Capital LLC
Greycroft Partners LLC
Grishin Robotics
HOF Capital Inc
Hamilton Investments Inc
Harmony Partners
Hattery
Haystack Partners
Health Catalyst Capital Management LLC
Health Enterprise Partners LP
HealthCor Partners Management LP
Healthsharestm Inc
Hilltop Capital Partners LLC
Homeland Defense Ventures
Huntsman-Lion Capital LLC
I2Bf Global Ventures
IA Capital Group Inc
IA Ventures
Ibero American Investors Corp
Icealab
Imaginary Ventures LLC
Impact Capital Inc
Impax Asset Management Ltd
Inherent Group LLC
Initialized Capital
International Business Machines Corp
Intuitive Venture Partners LLC
Investor Growth Capital Inc
Israel Infinity Venture Capital Fund Israel LP
Iterative Instinct Management LP
Itochu Technology Inc
JDRF International
JVP Jerusalem Venture Partners Israel Management, Ltd.
Jobi Capital
KBL HEALTHCARE VENTURES L P
KCP&L Greater Missouri Operations Co
KEC Ventures Inc
Kiwi Venture Partners LLC
Klingenstein Fields Venture Fund LP
L Capital Partners, L.P.
LUMA Captial Partners
LUX CAPITAL GROUP L L C
Laconia Ventures LLC
Lakehouse Venture Partners LP
Lambda Fund Management Inc
Lateral Capital LLC
Lattice Ventures LLC
Laughing Angels Foundation
LaunchCapital LLC
Lazard Technology Partners
Lead Edge Capital
Learnstart LLC
Ledra Capital LLC
Lerer Ventures II LP
Level Equity Management LLC
Lightbank
Lighthouse Fund LLC
Loeb Enterprises LLC
LunaCap Ventures Partners LLC
MI Ventures LLC

MR Investment Partners
Mac6 LLC
Macandrews & Forbes Inc
Madison Bay Capital Partners
Manhattan Venture Partners
Marker Financial Advisors LLC
MathCapital Management LP
Matrix Partners, L.P.
Maxim Merchant Capital
Mccune Capital Management LLC
Media Development Investment Fund Inc
Merlin Nexus
Mesa+
Meyer Ventures LLC
Mitsubishi International Corp
Morgan Stanley Expansion Capital
Morgan Stanley Multicultural Innovation Lab
Motive Partners GP LLC
NCH Capital Inc
NGEN Partners LLC
NGN Capital LLC
NMS Capital Partners
NYC Seed LLC
Nbt Capital Corp
New Amsterdam Growth Capital LLC
New Enterprise Associates Inc
New Leaf Venture Partners LLC
New Science Ventures LLC
New York Business Development Corp
New York City Economic Development Corp
New York Digital Health Accelerator
New York Times Co
NewWorld Capital Group LLC
Nexos Capital Partners
Nomura Co Ltd
Northzone Ventures
Novartis Venture Funds
Nyca Partners
Nystar
180 Degree Capital Corp
OXEON Partners
Odeon Capital Partners LP
Olympus Capital Holdings Asia Hong Kong Ltd
Onondaga Venture Capital Fund LLC
Open Field Capital LLC
Orchestra Medical Ventures LLC
Ore Ventures LLC
Orkila Capital LLC
Outbound Ventures LLC
Paladin Capital Management LLC
Palm Drive Ventures LLC
Partnership Fund for New York City
Perceptive Advisors LLC
Pereg Ventures LLC
Pfizer Venture Investments
Phoenix Venture Fund LLC
Pilot Group LP
Pivot Investment Partners LLC
Plus Eight Capital Management LLC
Primary Venture Partners
Probitas Partners Inc
Progress Ventures Inc
Psilos Group Managers LLC
Pura Vida Investments LLC
Purvi Capital LLC

QB1 Ventures LLC
Quilvest USA Inc
R/GA Ventures
RRE Ventures LLC
RSE Ventures
RTW Investments
Radiant Capital LLC
Radius Ventures LLC
Raine Group LLC, The
Rand Capital Corp
Raptor Capital Management LP
Rationalwave Capital Partners LLC
Reciprocal Venture Management LLC
RedBird Capital Partners Platform LP
Remiges BioPharma Fund LP
Research Partners Ltd
Rethink Education LP
Rethink Impact Management LLC
Revel Partners LLC
Reynolds & Company Venture Partners LLC
Rho Capital Partners Inc
Richmond Global
Rose Tech Ventures LLC
Rosecliff Venture Partners LP
Rosepaul Investments LLC
Round Hill Music Royalty Fund LP
ru-Net Ventures
645 Ventures
SAIL Capital Partners LLC
SC Capital Management LLC
SCS Capital Sdn Bhd
SENTINEL ADVISORS L L C
SJF Ventures
STG Capital LLC
STRATEGIC ADVISORY GROUP INC
SWAT Equity Partners LP
Salmon River Capital LLC
Scout Ventures LLC
Seavest Capital Partners LLC
Security Growth Partners
SeedInvest Technology LLC
Selway Partners L L C
SenaHill Investment Group LLC
Silas Capital LLC
Sindicatum Carbon Capital Ltd
Sipadan Capital
Social Discovery Ventures
Social Internet Fund, The
Softbank Capital Partners L P
Spark Capital
Spencer Trask Ventures Inc
StarVest Partners LP
Story Ventures LLC
Stripes Group LLC
Sycamore Ventures Inc
Syno Capital LLC
2B Angels Ltd
T Squared Capital LLC
TOKALON
TechU Ventures LP
Technology Crossover Ventures LP
Third Kind Venture Capital LLC
Third Point Ventures LP
Third Prime Capital Management LLC
Tholons Capital

Thrive Capital Partners LLC
Tiger Management Corp
Time Warner Investments
Timeless Group, The
Torys LLP
Tracker Capital Management LLC
Trail Mix Ventures Fund LP
Tribeca Venture Partners LLC
Trillium Group LLC
Tuatara Capital LP
Tusk Strategies Inc
Undisclosed Firm
Union Square Ventures LLC
University Ventures
Valence Life Sciences LLC
Valor Capital Group LLC
ValueStream Labs Syndicate II LLC
Vast Ventures
Vatera Healthcare Partners LLC
Vencon Management, Inc.
Venrock Inc
Verizon Media Tech Venture Studio
Veziris Ventures LLC
Virgin Green Fund
Viscogliosi Brothers LLC
Vision Capital Advisors LLC
WFD Ventures LLC
WINTHROP VENTURES
WestRiver Capital
Westbury Partners
Wheatley Partners
Windforce Ventures LLC
Windham Venture Partners
Work-Bench
ZIG Capital
Zelkova Ventures
Zesiger Capital Group LLC
Ziff Brothers Investments LLC

Venture Firms—North Carolina
Acorn Innovestments LLC
AgTech Accelerator Corp
Aurora Funds Inc
Black Wall Street Investments LLC
Bull City Venture Partners LLC
Carmichael Partners LLC
Center for Innovation and Entrepreneurship
Charlotte Angel Partners
Cofounders Capital Management LLC
Dioko Health Ventures GP LLC
Excelerate Health Ventures LLC
Gaston Capital Partners LP
Hatteras Venture Partners
Idea Fund Partners LLC
Intersouth Partners
Julz Co LLC
KdT GP LLC
Next Sector Capital
Novaquest Infosystems Inc
Packard Place Properties LLC
Pappas Ventures
RevTech Labs
SJF Ventures
Southern Capitol Ventures LLC
Sovereign's Capital LP

Sunbridge Partners Inc
Sustainable Resource Ventures
Temprano Techvestors
Wakefield Group

Venture Firms—North Dakota
Arthur Ventures LLC
Dakota Venture Group Inc
InvestAmerica Venture Group, Inc.
Linn Grove Ventures LLC

Venture Firms—Ohio
Accelerant Fund I LP
Adena Ventures
Allos Ventures LLC
Arsenal
Athenian Fund Management Inc
Blue Chip Venture Co
Bridge Investment Fund LP
Charter Life Sciences II L P
Chrysalis Ventures Inc
CincyTech
Draper Triangle Ventures LP
Drive Capital LLC
Drummond Road Capital Inc
EVC Ventures
Early Stage Partners LP
FlashStarts Inc
Glengary LLC
IECP Fund Management LLC
Ikove Venture Partners LLC
Innovation Forward LLC
Jumpstart Inc
LEGEND PARTNERS I L P
LaunchHouse
Loud Capital LLC
Luxemburg Capital LLC
Maywic Select Investments
Mutual Capital Partners
NCT Ventures LLC
Nationwide Mutual Capital LLC
Nationwide Ventures LLC
North Coast Angel Fund L L C
Ocean Accelerator Inc
Ohio Innovation Fund
Ohio Tech Angels
Plymouth Venture Partners
Reservoir Venture Partners 2 LP
River Cities Capital Fund LP
RiverVest Venture Partners LLC
Rocket Ventures LLC
Sapling Fund LP
Societatea de Investitii Financiare Banat Crisana SA
Sunbridge Partners Inc
TechColumbus
Triathlon Medical Ventures LLC
Vine Street Ventures LLC
West Capital Advisors LLC
Zanite Ventures LLC

Venture Firms—Oklahoma
Accele BioPharma Inc
Altus Ventures LLC
Bounty Equity Fund LLC
Cowboy Technologies LLC
First United Venture Capital Corp

i2E, Inc
JANVEST Technologies LLC
Oklahoma Equity Partners LLC
Oklahoma Life Science Fund LLC
Trailblazer Capital LP
Venture Spur

Venture Firms—Oregon
Allegory Ventures Management LLC
Altien Ventures LLC
Bridge City Management LLC
Cheever Capital Management LLC
Frontier Venture Capital
Marquam Hill Capital LLC
Northwest Technology Ventures
Peninsula Ventures
Pivotal Investments LLC
Seven Peaks Ventures
Shaw Venture Partners
SmartForest Ventures
Upstart Labs LLC
Voyager Capital LLC
Women's Venture Capital Fund

Venture Firms—Pennsylvania
Adams Capital Management, Inc.
Anthem Capital Management Inc
Ben Franklin Technology Partners Of Central And Northern PA
Ben Franklin Technology Partners Of Northeastern PA
Ben Franklin Technology Partners Southeastern PA
BioAdvance
Birchmere Ventures
Blue Hill Partners LLC
CHP Management Inc
Chrysalis Ventures Inc
Closed Loop Capital
Comcast Ventures
Cross Atlantic Capital Partners LLC
Devon Park Bioventures LP
Draper Triangle Ventures LP
DreamIt Ventures
Dublin Capital Partners LP
Emerald Stage2 Capital Ventures LP
FTFD Fund Distributor Inc
First Round Capital
Future Fund
INE Ventures
INETWORKS LLC
Innovation Capital Advisors LLC
Innovation Philadelphia
Innovation Transfer Center - Carnegie Mellon University
Innovation Works Inc
Launchcyte L L C
Leading Edge Ventures LLC
Liberty Ventures Inc
Life Sciences Greenhouse of Central Pennsylvania
Meakem Becker Venture Capital LLC
MentorTech Ventures LLC
Mission Engine LLC
Murex Investments, Inc.
Nextstage Capital LP
Nittany Lion Venture Capital
Novitas Capital LP

2387

Pratt's Guide to Private Equity & Venture Capital Sources

1315 Capital LLC
Originate Ventures
Osage University Partners
Osage Venture Partners
Pittsburgh Equity Partners LP
Pittsburgh Life Sciences Greenhouse
Primary Care Innovation Fund
Quaker Partners Management LP
Red & Blue Ventures LLC
Robin Hood Ventures
Robotics Hub SPV 1 LLC
SCP Private Equity Partners
Sama Fund LLC
Sandwith Ventures LLC
Select Capital Ventures
Seventy Six Capital
Sr One Ltd
TL Ventures Inc
Thomvest Ventures Inc
Topanga Partners LP
Trestle Ventures

Venture Firms—Puerto Rico
Acvent Morro Equity Partners Inc
Treehouse Investments LLC

Venture Firms—Rhode Island
China Capital Management Ltd
East Hill Management Co LLC
Firsthand Capital Management Inc
Slater Technology Fund Inc

Venture Firms—South Carolina
Alerion Ventures LLC
CCM Investment Advisers LLC
CF Investment, Co.
Columbia Capital Group, Inc.
Gold Ridge Asset Management LLC
Nexus Medical Partners
Task Force X Capital LLC

Venture Firms—South Dakota
Bluestem Capital Partners
Prairiegold Venture Partners

Venture Firms—Tennessee
a>m ventures
Capital Services & Resources Inc
Clayton Associates LLC
Dynamo Accelerator
Enhanced Capital Partners LLC
FINTOP Capital LLC
First Avenue Partners, L.P.
Genera Capital LLC
Healthbox LLC
Heritage Group LLC
Innova Memphis Inc
Jumpstart Foundry
Launch Tennessee
MB VENTURE PARTNERS L L C
Martin Companies LLC
Medcare Investment Fund Ltd
Meritus Ventures LP
Mountain Group Capital LLC
Nest-TN LLC
Pinnacle Financial Partners Inc

Relevance Capital Inc
River Street Management LLC
SENTINEL ADVISORS L L C
Salix Ventures LP
Solas BioVentures (Aegea) LLC
Solidus Company, L.P.
TriStar Technology Ventures LLC
Verso Capital Partners

Venture Firms—Texas
ATP Management Company LLC
ATX Seed Ventures
Actinver Securities Inc
Active Capital LLC
Active Venture Partners LLC
Advantage Capital Partners
Align Capital LLC
Allegory Ventures Management LLC
Altpoint Capital Partners LLC
Arch Venture Partners LLC
Aristos Ventures
Asia Capital Management Ltd
Athlone International Ltd
Bandgap Ventures LLC
Bios Partners
Blossom Street Ventures
Buildgroup Management LLC
Canaccord Genuity Group Inc
Capital Factory Properties LLC
Centennial Ventures Vii L P
Centerpoint Venture Partners LP
Cerium Technology LLC
Chevron Technology Ventures L L C
Clavis Capital Partners LLC
Comerica Venture Capital Group
Corsa Ventures
Cottonwood Capital Partners LLC
Cottonwood Venture Partners LLC
Covera Ventures LP
Cypress Growth Capital LLC
Dallas Venture Partners LP
Digitech Venture Capital Fund Inc
Duchossois Technology Partners LLC
EDCO Ventures
EES Ventures
EW Healthcare Partners
Ect Merchant Investments Corp
Elsewhere Partners
Enhanced Capital Partners LLC
Exigent Ventures Inc
Fitzrandolph Gateway Management LLC
G 51 Capital Management LLC
Geekdom LC
Gideon Hixon Fund LP
Goff Capital Partners, L.P.
Goldcrest Investments LP
Green Park & Golf Ventures LLC
Hangar Ventures LLC
Haynes and Boone LLC
Health Wildcatters
Heartland Ventures LLC
Houston Health Ventures LLC
Houston Ventures
Incyte Venture Partners LLC
Infrastructure Fund The

International Accelerator Inc
KC Venture Group LLC
Kenda Capital BV
Learn Capital Venture Partners LP
Learnstart LLC
LiveOak Venture Partners
M Seven 8 LLC
MDB Capital Group LLC
MPower Ventures, L.P.
MagnaSci Ventures
Maverick Capital Ventures LLC
Mavor Lane LLC
Mercury Fund
Mercury Ventures Ltd
Microangel Capital Partners
Mobility Ventures LLC
Moonshots Capital
Murphree Venture Partners
Naya Ventures LLC
New Capital Partners
Next Coast Ventures LLC
OpenIncubate
PTV Healthcare Capital
Pilot Wall Group LLC
Remeditex Ventures LLC
Ridgewood Capital Management LLC
S3 Ventures LLC
START Group LLC
Sandleigh Ventures LLC
Sante Ventures
Scientific Health Development
Seed Capital Partners
Serve Capital Partners LLC
Sevin Rosen Funds
Sid R Bass Associates LP
Silver Creek Ventures Corp
Silverton Partners
Singularity Investments LLC
Spindletop Capital Management LLC
Startuprunner Capital LLC
Sweat Equity Partners LP
TEXO Ventures
Tech Wildcatters Ii LLC
Texas Atlantic Capital
Texas Intrepid Ventures LLC
Texas Technology Development Center
Thoroughbred Spirits Partners
Trailblazer Capital LP
Trellis Partners
Triangle Peak Partners LP
Tricent Capital
True Wealth Ventures
Undisclosed Firm
University of Texas System
WYSE Capital Group

Venture Firms—Utah
Aster Capital Partners SAS
Cougar Capital LLC
Cynosure Group, The
Epic Ventures Inc
Gmg Capital Partners LP
HealthRight Partners
Innoventures Capital Partners
Kickstart Seed Fund LP

Mercato Management LLC
Pelion Venture Partners
Peterson Ventures LLC
Royal Street Investment and Innovation Center LLC
Seed Equity Capital Partners LLC
Signal Peak Ventures
Stoneway Capital LC
Subtraction Capital
University Venture Fund
UpStart Ventures Management LLC

Venture Firms—Vermont
Freshtracks Capital LP
Underdog Ventures LLC
Vermont Center for Emerging Technologies

Venture Firms—Virginia
Accelerated Growth Partners
Amplifier Management LLC
Annex, The
Arab Angel Fund
Blu Venture Investors LLC
Blue Delta Capital Partners LLC
Blue Heron Capital LLC
Blue Water Capital LLC
Calvert Social Venture Partners, L.P.
Center For Innovative Technology
Columbia Capital LP
Comerica Venture Capital Group
Comspace Development LLC
Cooley LLP
Court Square Ventures LLC
Csi
Disruption Corporation
Disruptor Inc
Dominion Investment Group
Dynamis Advisors LLC
Foxhaven Asset Management LP
Gilfus Venture Partners LLC
In-Q-Tel Inc
Inova Personalized Health Accelerator
Jefferson Education Accelerator LLC
Lavrock Ventures LLC
MCG Capital Corp
Meloy Fund I LP
Middleburg Capital Development Ltd
NAV.VC
NeuroVentures Capital LLC
New Richmond Ventures
New Vantage Group
New Ventures LLC
NextGen Venture Partners LLC
1717 Partners
Papillon Capital LLC
Redshift Ventures Management Inc
Renaissance Ventures L L C
Route 66 Ventures LLC
SRI International
SWaN & Legend Venture Partners
Sands Capital Management LLC
Select Venture Partners LLC
Sequoia Apps LLC
Stuart Mill Capital, Inc.
Taveekan Capital
Tegna Inc
Third Security LLC

True Ventures LLC
Undisclosed Firm
University of Virginia Licensing & Ventures Group
V-Ten Capital Partners LLC
Valentis Capital LLC
Valhalla Partners LP
Venture Catalyst Inc
WGL Holdings Inc
Wesley Clover International Corporation
Wwc Capital Fund L P

Venture Firms—Washington
Accelerator Corp
Alpine BioVentures GP LLC
Altitude Funds LLC
Arch Venture Partners LLC
Attractor Investment Management Inc
angelMD Inc
Benaroya Capital Company
Bezos Expeditions
Big Basin Partners LP
Bioeconomy Capital GP LLC
Biomatics Capital Partners LP
Breakthrough Energy Ventures LLC
Capria Ventures LLC
Compass Capital Services Inc
Cooley LLP
Cronus Ventures
Curious Capital
Divergent Venture Partners Affiliates I LP
Echo Health Ventures LLC
Energy Innovation Capital
Fledge LLC
Fluke Venture Partners II LP
Flying Fish Management LLC
Founders Co op
Global Partnerships
H-Farm SpA
Ignition Capital Partners
Ignition Ventures Management LLC
Inception Capital Management LLC
InvestAmerica Venture Group, Inc.
MW Capital Inc
MadroNA Venture Group
Maveron LLC
9Mile Labs LLC
Naya Ventures LLC
New Enterprise East Investments
Northern Lights Capital Group LLC
Pacific Horizon Ventures LLC
Pacific Wirless Ventures LLC
Pioneer Venture Partners LLC
Providence Ventures LLC
Qiming Venture Partners Ii LP
Rally Capital LLC
Seapoint Ventures
Second Avenue Partners
SpringRock Ventures LLC
Timberline Venture Partners
Tola Capital LLC
Trilogy Equity Partners Llc
Union Bay Capital
Upaya Social Ventures
Voyager Capital LLC
W Fund LP

WRF Capital
Westriver Group Inc
Wisemont Capital
Yaletown Venture Partners

Venture Firms—West Virginia
INETWORKS LLC
Mountaineer Capital, L.P.
Novitas Capital LP
West Virginia State Jobs Investment Trust Board

Venture Firms—Wisconsin
Advantage Capital Partners
American Family Ventures
CSA Partners LLC
Calumet Venture Fund
Capital Midwest Fund LP
DaneVest Tech Fund Advisors
Diamond Capital Management LLC
FISK VENTURES INC
FUTURE VALUE VENTURES INC
GreenPoint Investment Counsel
gener8tor
HealthX Management LLC
InvestAmerica Venture Group, Inc.
Keane D Souza Venture Capital LLC
Kegonsa Capital Partners LLC
Magma Partners
New Capital Management Inc
Phenomenelle Angels Management LLC
Rock River Capital Partners
State of Wisconsin Investment Board
Symphony Alpha Ventures LLC
Venture Investors LLC
Venture Management LLC
WISC Partners LP
Winnebago Capital Partners
Ziegler Link-Age Management LLC

Venture Firms—Wyoming
Enhanced Capital Partners LLC
Sapient Capital Management LLC

Pratt's Guide to Private Equity & Venture Capital Sources

Non-U.S. Firm Cross Reference by Nation

For more comprehensive querying, searching and referencing, Buyouts Insider supplies Pratt's Guide online at www.prattsguide.com.

Annual subscriptions are available for USD $1,995 per user. For more information, please contact Robert Raidt at (646)-356-4502 or email rraidt@buyoutsinsider.com.

Pratt's Guide to Private Equity & Venture Capital Sources

Buyout Firms—Algeria
Africinvest Tunisia SARL
Credit Agricole Corporate and Investment Bank SA
European Bank for Reconstruction and Development
Qalaa Holdings SAE
Swicorp Capital Partners SA

Buyout Firms—Angola
Angola Capital Partners

Buyout Firms—Argentina
Advent International Corp
Axxon Group Servicos De Consultoria E Assessoria Ltda
Black River Asset Management LLC
Credit Agricole Corporate and Investment Bank SA
Goldman Sachs & Co LLC
JPMorgan Chase & Co
Linzor Capital Partners LP
Neuberger Berman LLC
Patagonia Capital Partners, LLC
Schroders PLC
Southern Cross Capital Management SA
Trilantic Capital Management LP

Buyout Firms—Armenia
European Bank for Reconstruction and Development

Buyout Firms—Australia
AG BD LLC
AMP Capital Investors Ltd
Advent Private Capital Pty Ltd
Affinity Equity Partners HK Ltd
Alium Capital Management Pty Ltd
Allegro Funds Pty Ltd
Anacacia Capital Pty Ltd
Anchorage Capital Partners Ltd
Archer Capital Pty Ltd
Ares Management LLC
Aura Capital Group
Banksia Capital
Barings LLC
Black Sheep Capital
Blackstone Group LP
Blue Sky Private Equity
Bobcock & Brown
CLSA Capital Partners HK Ltd
CVC Asia Pacific Ltd
CVC Capital Partners Ltd
CVC Managers Pty Ltd
Capital International Inc
Carlyle Group LP
Castle Harlan Aus Mezzanine
Catalyst Investment Managers Pty, Ltd.
Catapult Partners Pty Ltd
Champ Ventures Pty Ltd
Crescendo Partners Capital Pty Ltd
Crescent Capital Partners Ltd
Csfb Private Equity Advisers
Dorado Capital Pty Ltd
EMR Capital Group
Fortress Investment Group LLC
Global Capital Finance
Growth Fund, The
Harbert Management Corp
Hastings Private Equity Fund IIA Pty Ltd
Hawkesbridge Capital
Helmsman Funds Management, Ltd.
Impact Investment Group Pty Ltd
InGlobo Private Equity
Investec Wentworth Private Equity Pty Ltd
Ironbridge Capital Pty Ltd
JPMorgan Chase & Co
KKR & Co LP
Kestrel Capital Pty Limited
Lazard Australia Private Equity
Maam Gp Pty Ltd
Macquarie Group Ltd
Macquarie Investment Management Ltd
Mercury Capital Investments
Monash Private Capital Pty Ltd
NBC Capital Pty Ltd
Navis Management Sdn Bhd
Neuberger Berman LLC
New South Capital Pty Ltd
Next Capital Pty Ltd
Oak Hill Advisors LP
Oceania Capital Partners Ltd
Pacific Equity Partners Pty Ltd
Pacific Road Capital Management Pty Ltd
Partners Group Holding AG
PineBridge Investments LLC
Pitt Capital Partners Ltd
Prostar Investments Pte Ltd
Quadrant Private Equity
Queensland BioCapital Funds Ld Pty
RMB Investment Advisory Pty Ltd
Rcf Management LLC
Riverside Co
Schroders PLC
Silverfern Group Inc
TPG Capital Management LP
Tasman Capital Investments Australia Pty Ltd
Telopea Capital Partners Pty Ltd
Torrens Capital Management
Wilshire Private Markets
Wolseley Private Equity

Buyout Firms—Austria
Afinum Management GmbH
Andlinger & Co Inc
Ardian France SA
Asp Consulting Gesellschaft Mbh
BA Private Equity GmbH
ConValue Investment GmbH
Csfb Private Equity Advisers
Cudos Advisors GmbH
Darby Overseas Investments, Ltd.
EMR Capital Group
Gain Capital Participations GmbH
Global Capital Finance
Hannover Finanz GmbH
Henderson Global Investors Ltd
IPO Wachstumsfonds Beteiligungs Management GmbH
Invest Unternehmensbeteiligungs AG
LPC Capital Partners GmbH
Lead Equities GmbH
Noe Beteiligungsfinanzierungen GmbH
One Equity Partners LLC
Raiffeisenlandesbank Oberoesterreich AG
3TS Capital Partners, Ltd.
Tyrol Equity AG
Unicorn Capital Advisers GmbH
Unternehmens Invest AG
VR Equitypartner GmbH
VTB Kapital AO
Value Dimensions Management Services GmbH
Wing Equity Management

Buyout Firms—Azerbaijan
European Bank for Reconstruction and Development

Buyout Firms—Bahamas
BG Capital Group Ltd
Csfb Private Equity Advisers

Buyout Firms—Bahrain
Arcapita Inc
Awal Bank BSCC
Cimb Private Equity Sdn Bhd
Esterad Investment Co BSC
First Equity Partners WLL
GFH Financial Group BSC
Global Banking Corporation BSCC
Global Investment House KSCC
Investcorp Bank BSC
PineBridge Investments LLC
Pinebridge Investments Middle East BSCC
Tharawat Investment House BSCC
United Gulf Bank Securities Co. B.S.C

Buyout Firms—Bangladesh
Asian Tiger Capital Partners Ltd
IPS Industrial Promotion Services Ltd

Buyout Firms—Belarus
European Bank for Reconstruction and Development

Buyout Firms—Belgium
A Capital Asia Ltd
Alpha Group
Andlinger & Co Inc
BNP Paribas Fortis Private Equity Growth NV
Baltisse NV
Belfius Private Equity
Belgian Invest NV
Bencis Capital Partners BV
Business Angels Netwerk Vlaanderen VZW
Buysse & Partners BVBA
CVC Asia Pacific Ltd
CVC Capital Partners Ltd
Catella AB
Clean Energy Invest CVBA
Compagnie Benelux Participations SA
Credit Agricole Corporate and Investment Bank SA
Down2Earth Capital NV
E Capital Management Scrl
Ekkofund SA
Fortino Capital Arkiv Comm.VA
Gilde Buy Out Partners BV
Gimv Investeringsmaatschappij Voor Vlanderen NV
Groep Brussel Lambert NV
Group MC NV
Indufin SA
Ing Belgique SA
KeBeK Management NV
LRM NV

Merifin Capital
Meusinvest SA
Morrison & Foerster LLP
NIBC Principal Investments BV
NPM Capital NV
ParticipatieMaatschappij Vlaanderen NV
Pentahold NV
QAT Investments SA
Rabo Participaties BV
Riverside Co
RobeCo Private Equity
Robur Capital NV
Saffelberg Investments SA
Sofina SA
Sofindev Management NV
Sofinim NV
Vectis Participaties NV
Vendis Capital NV
Verlinvest SA
Waterland Private Equity Investments BV
Yukon NV

Buyout Firms—Bermuda
Brookfield Asset Management Inc
D E Shaw & Co LP
GP Investimentos Ltda
Oakley Capital Investments Ltd
Schroders PLC
Starr International Company Inc

Buyout Firms—Bosnia/Herz.
European Bank for Reconstruction and Development

Buyout Firms—Botswana
African Alliance Private Equity
Ariya Capital Group Ltd

Buyout Firms—Br. Virgin I.
IC Africa Private Equity Ltd
Richwise International Investment Hldg Ltd

Buyout Firms—Brazil
Actis LLP
Advent International Corp
Alothon Group LLC
Apax Partners LLP
Aqua Capital Consultoria Ltda
Axxon Group Servicos De Consultoria E Assessoria Ltda
Banco BTG Pactual SA
Banco Nacional de Desenvolvimento Economico e Social BNDES
Banco Santander Brasil SA
Black River Asset Management LLC
Bozano Agente Autonomo de Investimentos Ltda
Bravia Capital Investimentos Ltda
CRP Companhia de Participacoes
Capital Criativo SCR SA
Capital Dynamics Sdn Bhd
Carlyle Group LP
Cartesian Capital Group LLC
Casaforte Investimentos SA
Credit Agricole Corporate and Investment Bank SA
Csfb Private Equity Advisers
Darby Overseas Investments, Ltd.
Dlj Merchant Banking Partners

Evercore Inc
FAMA Private Equity
GP Investimentos Ltda
Gavea Investimentos Ltda
General Atlantic LLC
Gic Special Investments Pte Ltd
Global Equity Administradora de Recursos SA
Goldman Sachs & Co LLC
Graycliff Partners LP
HAL Investments BV
HIG Capital LLC
Haitong Capital SCR SA
Highland Capital Management LP
Inflexion PLC
JPMorgan Chase & Co
KKR & Co LP
Kinea Investimentos Ltda
Leblon Equities Gestao de Recursos Ltda
MHFT Investimentos SA
Mantiq Investimentos Ltda
Mare Investimentos Ltda
Mercapital SL
Milbank Tweed Hadley & Mccloy LLP
Nova Gestao de Recursos Ltda
Olimpia Partners Gestao de Recursos SA
PII Investimentos Imobiliarios Ltda
Partners Group Holding AG
Riviera Gestora de Recursos Ltda
Schroders PLC
Siguler Guff & Company LP
Southern Cross Capital Management SA
Stratus Investimentos Ltda
2Bcapital SA
3G Capital Inc
3i Group PLC
TIG Holding Ltd
TMG Partners LLC
TPG Capital Management LP
Teka Capital SAS
Temasek Holdings (Private) Ltd
Trinity Investimentos Ltda
Triscorp Investimentos Ltda
Verticals Capital Administracao de Recursos Ltda
Vila Rica Capital Gestora de Recursos Ltda
Vinci Equities Gestora de Recursos Ltda
Warburg Pincus LLC

Buyout Firms—Brunei
Cimb Private Equity Sdn Bhd

Buyout Firms—Bulgaria
Axxess Capital Partners SA
Bancroft Group Ltd
European Bank for Reconstruction and Development
Fiera Capital (UK) Ltd
Ged Group
Oriens IM Hungary Szolgaltato Kft
P&S Capital doo
Rosslyn Capital Partners OOD Sofia
Southeast Europe Equity Fund
VTB Kapital AO

Buyout Firms—Burma
Anthem Asia
Bagan Capital Ltd
Cimb Private Equity Sdn Bhd

Buyout Firms—Cambodia
Asia Frontier Investments Ltd
City Star Private Equity Sas
Vinacapital Investment Management Ltd

Buyout Firms—Cameroon
Emerging Capital Partners

Buyout Firms—Canada
A5 Capital
ACE Management SA
AIP Private Capital
AXIAL Group of Companies
Abacus Private Equity Ltd
Aberdeen Gould Capital Markets Ltd
Acces Capital Quebec
Alaris Royalty Corp
Alberta Investment Management Corp
Alignvest Capital Management Inc
Alpine Growth Partners
Altas Partners LP
Andover Capital Corp
Ardenton Capital Corp
Artemis Investment Management Ltd
Associes Magnum Capital Partners
Auxo Management LP
Banque Pictet & Cie SA
Banyan Capital Partners LP
Beedie Capital Partners
Bennett Jones Verchere
Beringer Capital Inc
Birch Hill Equity Partners Management Inc
Bluesky Equities Ltd
Bond Capital Partners, Ltd.
Brookfield Asset Management Inc
CDP Capital Private Equity
CPS Capital
Cai Capital Management Co
Cairn Merchant Partners LP
Canada Pension Plan Investment Board
Capital International Inc
CapitalAsia Group
Carpedia Capital Ltd
Catalyst Capital Group Inc
Chrysalis Capital Advisors Inc
Clairvest Group Inc
Claridge Inc
Clarke Inc
Clearspring Capital Partners
Cordiant Capital Inc
Corporate Finance Associates Worldwide Inc
Corporate Growth Assistance Ltd
Corporation Financiere Champlain Canada Inc
Cowen Capital Partners LLC
Credit Agricole Corporate and Investment Bank SA
Crescent Point Energy Corp
Cronos Group Inc
Crosbie & Co Inc
Crosswinds Holdings Inc
Csfb Private Equity Advisers
Cypress Hills Partners Inc
DGC Capital Inc
Dane Creek Capital Corp
Delavaco Holdings Inc
Desjardins Capital

Dundee Sarea LP
Dw Healthcare Partners
ELGNER GROUP INVESTMENTS LTD
Enertech Capital
Entrepreneur Capital Inc
Equicapita Income LP
Eventi Capital Partners Inc
Everest Investment Management LLC
FDC Capital Partners Inc
Fairfax Africa Fund LLC
Fairfax Financial Holdings Ltd
Fairfax India Holdings Corp
Fondaction Csn
Fonds Manufacturier Quebecois SEC
Fortress Investment Group LLC
Front Street Capital
Fulcrum Capital Partners Inc
Gestalt Equity Partners
Global Mining Capital Corp
Gmp Securities Ltd
Goldenmount Capital International Inc
Goldman Sachs & Co LLC
Granite Partners
Grano Retail Investments Inc
GreenBank Capital Inc
Greenfield Capital Group, Inc.
Groupe Aliston Inc
HarbourVest Partners LLC
Hardy Capital Partners
Hawthorn Equity Partners
Headwater Equity Partners Inc
Hedgewood Inc
High Park Capital Partners
Highland West Capital Ltd
Horizonone Asset Management Inc
Huron Capital Partners LLC
Hypoid Partners
IPS Industrial Promotion Services Ltd
Imperial Capital Corp
Integrated Partners
InvesteCo Capital Corp
Investel Capital Corp
Investissement Quebec
Investissements Novacap Inc
Invico Capital Corp
Iris Capital Management SAS
Ironbridge Equity Partners Management Ltd
iGan Partners Inc
Jog Capital Inc
KKR & Co LP
KV Private Equity Inc
Kensington Capital Partners Ltd
Kilmer Capital Partners Ltd
Knight s Bridge Capital Corp
Krystal Financial Corp
LIGHTHOUSE EQUITY PARTNERS
Lindsay Goldberg & Bessemer LP
Litera Investments Inc
Long Road Investment Counsel LLC
Longview Asset Management Ltd
Lynx Equity Ltd
MacKinnon Bennett & Company Inc
Macluan Capital Corp
Macquarie Group Ltd
Market Square Equity Partners

Mill Street & Co
Monitor Clipper Partners LLC
Monteco Ltd
Mosaic Capital Corp
Nesta Brand Co Inc
Next Equities
Northbridge Capital Partners
Northern Plains Capital Ltd
Northleaf Capital Partners Ltd
Northrock Capital Partners
Nova Capital Management, Ltd.
Noverra Consulting and Capital Partners
OMERS Private Equity Inc
ONCAP INVESTMENT PARTNERS L P
OPTrust Private Markets Group
Oak Bridge Holding, Inc.
Obelysk Inc
Onex Corp
Ontario Teachers' Pension Plan
PFM Capital Inc
PRIVEQ Capital Funds
Parallel49 Equity
Parkview Capital Pratners
Partner One Capital
Peerage Capital Inc
Pender West Capital Partners, Inc.
Persistence Capital Partners Lp
Phoenix Partners
Polar Capital Investments
Portland Holdings Inc
Portland Private Equity LP
Public Sector Pension Investment Board
Quantum Capital
Rbc Capital Partners
Rcf Management LLC
Regimen Capital Partners
Richardson Capital Ltd
Riverside Co
Robson Capital Partners Corp
Rouge River Capital
Roynat Capital Inc
Russell Square Partners Inc
6 Pacific Group
7Bridge Capital Partners Ltd
SIDEX LP
SW Capital Partners
SeaFort Capital Inc
Seacliff Private Equity
Searchlight Capital Partners LLC
Second City Capital Partners
Sectoral Asset Management Inc
Signal Hill Equity Partners
Skidmore Group
Solidarity Fund QFL
SouthPac Partners Inc
Southbridge Capital Inc
Sprott Resource Corp
Stern Partners Inc
Stornoway Portfolio Management Inc
Swander Pace Capital LLC
32 Degrees Capital
T & M Management Services Ltd
TD Capital Group Ltd
TOM Capital Associates Inc
TorQuest Partners Inc

Tricor Pacific Founders Capital Inc
Trilogy Growth LP
Triwest Capital Mgmt Corp
Ubequity Capital Partners Inc
VERDEXUS
VRG Capital Corp
Varshney Capital Corp
Vertex & Co Inc
Vistara Capital Partners
Waterous Energy Fund Canadian LP
Werklund Capital Corp
West Face Capital Inc
Westcap Management Ltd
Westerkirk Capital Inc
Westernone Equity Income Fund
Whitehorse Liquidity Partners Inc
Wifleur, Inc.
Windsor Private Capital
Wynnchurch Capital Ltd
XPND Capital
Yellow Point Equity Partners LP
York Plains Investment Corp
Zynik Capital Corp

Buyout Firms—Cayman Islands
AL Masah Paper Industries LLC
Brown Brothers Harriman & Co
CDH China Management Co., Ltd.
CITIC Capital Partners Ltd
Carlyle Group LP
Csfb Private Equity Advisers
EMR Capital Group
Emergevest Ltd
Everstone Capital Management, Ltd.
Farallon Capital Management LLC
Goldman Sachs & Co LLC
Horizon21 AG
Schroders PLC
Southport Lane Management LLC

Buyout Firms—Channel Islands
Alpha Group
Apax Partners LLP
Ariya Capital Group Ltd
Cross Equity Partners AG
IK Investment Partners Ltd
Invision AG
Nordic Capital
PPF Partners as
Stirling Square Capital Partners Lp
Zurmont Madison Management AG

Buyout Firms—Chile
Ecus Administradora General de Fondos SA
Linzor Capital Partners LP
PineBridge Investments LLC
Southern Cross Capital Management SA

Buyout Firms—China
A Capital Asia Ltd
AEA Investors LLC
AID Partners Capital Ltd
AMP Capital Investors Ltd
Abraaj Capital Ltd
Actis LLP
Adams Street Partners LLC

2393

Pratt's Guide to Private Equity & Venture Capital Sources

Adm Capital
Advent International Corp
Aeternam Stella Financial Holdings Co Ltd
Affinity Equity Partners HK Ltd
Agricultural Bank of China Ltd
Aif Capital Asia Iii LP
Aktis Capital Group
Anhui Guofu Property Investment Fund Management Ltd
Ants Assets Management Co Ltd
Apax Partners LLP
Ardian France SA
Ares Management LLC
Arsenal Capital Partners LP
Ascribe Capital, LLC
Asia Bridge Capital Ltd
Avantage Ventures Capital LLC
Bain Capital Inc
Baird Capital
Baolong Kangde Investment Management Co Ltd
Baring Private Equity Asia Ltd
Beijing Beida Medical Industrial Fund Management Co Ltd
Beijing Bosi Chenguang Asset Management Co Ltd
Beijing Capital Dynamics Investment Management Co Ltd
Beijing Capital Equity Investment Fund Management Co Ltd
Beijing Capital Science and Technology Group Co Ltd
Beijing China Bridge Investment Management Co Ltd
Beijing Dongfang Youlian Investment Consulting Co Ltd
Beijing E-Town International Investment & Development Co Ltd
Beijing Fundturn Investment Co Ltd
Beijing Gold Fount Venture Capital Co Ltd
Beijing Guangneng Investment Fund Management Co Ltd
Beijing Haoxiang Capital Management Co Ltd
Beijing Holch Investment Management, Ltd.
Beijing Honden Capital Co Ltd
Beijing Jianguang Asset Management Co Ltd
Beijing Jilei Venture Capital Investment Co Ltd
Beijing Jinhuifeng Investment Management Co Ltd
Beijing Junhui Venture Capital Center
Beijing Rock Capital Management Co Ltd
Beijing Said Wise Fund Co Ltd
Beijing Shengshijing Investment Co Ltd
Beijing Shixin Rongze Investment Management Co Ltd
Beijing Shouyen Junli Investment Management Co Ltd
Beijing Success Great Capital Management Co Ltd
Beijing Tongchuang Jinding Investment Management Co Ltd
Beijing Wanrong Times Capital Management Co Ltd
Beijing Wu Investment Management Co Ltd
Beijing Zenith Taifu Investment Management Co Ltd
Beijing Zhongshi Rongchuan Equity Investment Mgmt Co Ltd
Beijing Zuoyu Investment Management Co Ltd
Black River Asset Management LLC
Blackstone Group LP
Blue Point Capital Partners LP
Bohai Harvest RST (Shanghai) Equity Investment Fund Mgmt
Boxin Capital
Bridgepoint Advisers II Ltd
Bridgepoint Advisers Ltd
Broadhaven Capital Partners LLC
Brown Brothers Harriman & Co
CAS Capital Inc
CDBI Partners
CDH China Management Co., Ltd.
CEC Capital Group
CITIC Capital Partners Ltd
CITICS Property Fund Management Co Ltd
CLSA Capital Partners HK Ltd
CRP-Fanya Investment Consultants Beijing Co Ltd
CVC Asia Pacific Ltd
CVC Capital Partners Ltd
Capital International Inc
CapitalAsia Group
Cappello Capital Corp
Capvis Equity Partners AG
CarVal Investors LLC
Carlyle Group LP
Cartesian Capital Group LLC
Cathay Capital Private Equity SAS
Cathay Fortune Corp
Centenium-Pinetree China Private Equity
Centurion Investment Management Pte Ltd
Chengdao Tianhua Investment Management Co Ltd
China Culture Industrial Investment Fund Management Co Ltd
China Development Finance Co., Ltd.
China Ecapital Corp
China Everbright Ltd
China Highrun Capital Ltd
China International Capital Corp Ltd
China Investment Corp
China Life Investment Holding Co Ltd
China Media Capital Co Ltd
China Merchants Capital Co Ltd
China Merchants Kunlun Equity Invest Management Co Ltd
China OperVestors Inc
China Orient Asset Management International Holding Ltd
China Resources Investment Management Co Ltd
China United Fortune Intl. Invest. Fund Mgmt (Beijing)
China Western Economic Development Co Ltd
China-Africa Development Fund
ChinaRock Capital Management, Ltd.
Chongqing Chungshui Equity Investment Co Ltd
Chunshan Pujiang Shanghai Investment Management Co Ltd
Citic Private Equity Funds Management Co Ltd
Climate Change Capital Ltd
Cmia Capital Partners Pte Ltd
Core Capital Management Co Ltd
Corstone Corp
Crescent Point Group
Crimson Capital China
Crimson Investments Ltd
D E Shaw & Co LP
D&F Equity Investment Fund Management Co Ltd
Daiwa Corporate Investment Co Ltd
Daoyuan Capital Management Beijing Co Ltd
Defu Fund Management Co Ltd
EQT Funds Management Ltd
East Capital Private Equity AB
Edmond de Rothschild Investment Partners SAS
Everbright Jinkong Shanghai Investment Management Co Ltd
Everpine Capital Ltd
F & H Fund Management Pte Ltd
Fengli Fortune (Beijing) International Capital Management Co
Florescence Capital Co Ltd
Fortress Investment Group LLC
FountainVest Partners Asia Ltd
General Atlantic LLC
Gic Special Investments Pte Ltd
Gimpo Ind Invest Fund Mgmt Co
Global Mining Capital Corp
Gold Innovation (Beijing) International Investment Mgmt.
Golden Sunflower Capital Management Co Ltd
Goldman Sachs & Co LLC
Granite Creek Partners LLC
Greenfield Capital Group, Inc.
Guangdong Huiyu Yihao Investment Management Co Ltd
Guangdong Pacific Technology Venture Co Ltd
Guangdong RC Equity Investment Fund Management Co Ltd
Guangdong Technology Venture Investment Co Ltd
Guangzhou Anjianxin Investment Management Co Ltd
Guangzhou Black Hole Investment Co Ltd
Guangzhou Industrial Investment Fund Management Co Ltd
Guangzhou Sinvo Spring Investment Management Co Ltd
Guangzhou Zhuoshi Investment Management Co Ltd
Guiyin Zhongke Industrial Investment Fund Management Ltd
H&Q Asia Pacific, Ltd.
HPEF Capital Partners Ltd
Haitong Buyout Capital Management Shanghai Co Ltd
Haitong Jihe Private Equity Investment Fund Management Co
Hangzhou Zheke Youye Investment Management Co Ltd
HarbourVest Partners LLC
Hebei Yanhai Industrial Investment Fund Management Co Ltd
Hefei Hi-tech Venture Capital Co Ltd
Hejun Capital Co Ltd
Henderson Global Investors Ltd
Hollyhigh Intl Capital Co Ltd
Hony Capital Beijing Co Ltd
Hope Investments Management Co Ltd
Houlihan Lokey Inc
Huatai Ruitong Investment Management Co Ltd
Hubei Jindingsheng Equity Investment Fund Co Ltd
Huili Beijing Investment Fund Management Co Ltd
Hunan Everassion Equity Investment Management Co Ltd
Hunan Haijie Investment Co Ltd

Pratt's Guide to Private Equity & Venture Capital Sources

Investindustrial Services Ltd
Investor Growth Capital AB
Iris Capital Management SAS
JC Asia Alpha Private Equity
Japan Asia Investment Co Ltd
Jefferies Group LLC
Jiangsu Addor Equity Investment Fund Management Co Ltd
Jiaxing Yinrui Investment Management Partner Enterprise
Jinyingfeng Equity Investment Fund Shenzhen Co Ltd
Jordan Company LP
KKR & Co LP
Khazanah Nasional Bhd
L Catterton Asia
Leon Capital
Lianke Chuangying Capital Management Co Ltd
Longreach Group Ltd
MBK Partners Inc
Macquarie Infrastructure and Real Assets (Europe) Ltd
Mandarin Capital Partners SCA SICAR
Mercuria Investment Co Ltd
Milbank Tweed Hadley & Mccloy LLP
Milestone Capital Management Ltd
Morgan Stanley Private Equity
Morrison & Foerster LLP
Nanjing Sharelink Investment Management Co Ltd
Navis Management Sdn Bhd
Neo Capital Management Group Co Ltd
Neuberger Berman LLC
New Enterprise Investment Co Ltd
Ningbo Jiaming Haochun Investment Management Co Ltd
Noble (Beijing) Fund Management Inc
Nomura China Asset Management Co Ltd
OCBC CAPITAL MANAGEMENT
Oaktree Capital Management LP
Och-Ziff Capital Management Group LLC
On Capital Ltd
Onegate Capital
OrbiMed Advisors LLC
Origo Partners PLC
Pacific Alliance Group Ltd
Pagoda Investment Advisors S PTE Ltd
Partners Group Holding AG
Perella Weinberg Partners LP
Pfingsten Partners LLC
PinPoint Fund
Pioneer Beijing Investment Fund Co Ltd
Poalim Asia Direct Ltd
Primavera Capital
Principle Capital Ltd
Private Equity Partners SpA
Providence Equity Partners LLC
Qianhai Industry University Research Fund Management Co Ltd
Qingdao Huayao Capital Management Center LP
Richlink International Capital Co Ltd
Rockstead Capital Pte., Ltd.
Rongxin Capital Fund Management Ltd
Rongzhong Capital Investment Group Co Ltd
SDIC Innovation Investment Management Ltd
SEAVI Advent Corporation Ltd

SIG Capital Partners Ltd
STIC Investment Inc
Schroders PLC
Shanghai Alliance Investment Ltd
Shanghai Ample Harvest Financial Services Co Ltd
Shanghai Broadview Capital Management Co Ltd
Shanghai Dongzhen Investment Co Ltd
Shanghai GMALL Venture Capital Management Co Ltd
Shanghai Haiji Investment Development Co Ltd
Shanghai Hongzhang Investment Management Co Ltd
Shanghai Mefund Assets Management Co Ltd
Shanghai Milestone Asset Management Co Ltd
Shanghai NSR Wealth Investment Management Co Ltd
Shanghai Panasia Strategy Investment Co Ltd
Shanghai Shangqi Investment Mgmt Partnership Enterprise
Shanghai Triumph Investment Management Co Ltd
Shanghai Vstone Capital Co., Ltd
Shanghai Yinlai Investment Group Co Ltd
Shanghai Zhonglu (Group) Co Ltd
Shanghai Zongquan Investment Management Co Ltd
Shanghai Zuhe Investment Management Co Ltd
Shenjin Investment Management Co Ltd
Shenzhen Capital Fortune Investment Co Ltd
Shenzhen Changrun Lianhe Asset Management Co Ltd
Shenzhen DG Capital Management Co Ltd
Shenzhen Gold Match Silver Fund Management Co Ltd
Shenzhen HengTaiHuaSheng Asset Management Co Ltd
Shenzhen Jiaqiao Investment Co Ltd
Shenzhen Jiupai Capital Management Co Ltd
Shenzhen Maliang Equity Invesment Management Co Ltd
Shenzhen Puhe Assets Management Co Ltd
Shenzhen Qianhai Anxing Assets Management Co Ltd
Shenzhen Qianhai Bainuo International Buyout Invest Mgmt Ltd
Shenzhen Qianhai Harsun Capital Management Co Ltd
Shenzhen Qianhai Qinzhi International Capital Mngmt Co Ltd
Shenzhen Qianhai Sequoia Guangjing Investment Management
Shenzhen Qianhai Shourun Investment Management Co Ltd
Shenzhen Qianhai Yuntai Equity Invt Fund Mgmt Co., Ltd.
Shenzhen Qiushi Asset Management Co Ltd
Shenzhen Readysun Investment Group Co Ltd
Shenzhen Shengtai Investment Management Co Ltd
Shenzhen Tempus Wutong Investment Co Ltd
Shenzhen Waranty Asset Management Co Ltd
Shenzhen Weilida Fund Management Co Ltd
Shenzhen Yuanzhi Investment Co Ltd
Shenzhen Yueshangzhifu Asset Management Co Ltd
Shoutai Jinxin Equity Investment Fund Management Co Ltd
Sichuan Dingxiang Equity Investment Fund Co Ltd
Sichuan Shuxiang Investment Co Ltd

Sichuan Yuehua Investment Management Co Ltd
Siguler Guff & Company LP
Silicon Valley Paradise Venture Investment Co., Ltd.
Silver Lake Partners LP
SinoLatin Capital
Southern Raytai Fund Management Co Ltd
Spring Capital Asia Ltd
Standard Chartered Private Equity Ltd
StepStone Group LP
SummitView Capital
Sun Capital Partners Inc
Suzhou Hairongtian Investment Co Ltd
Synergetic Innovation Fund Management Co Ltd
3i Group PLC
TPG Capital Management LP
Tamarace Capital
Telopea Capital Partners Pty Ltd
Temasek Holdings (Private) Ltd
Tembusu Partners Pte Ltd
Terra Firma Capital Partners Ltd
Tianjin Huixin Chuangfu Equity Invest Fund Management Ltd
Topina Capital
Tpg Growth LLC
Tripod Capital International Ltd
Tsinghua Holding Co Ltd
Unisun Beijing Investment Co Ltd
V Fund Management Co Ltd
Vertex Venture Holdings Ltd.
Wall Street Venture Capital Ltd
Wangzhuo Investment Management Shanghai Co Ltd
Warburg Pincus LLC
Weifang Financial Holding Group Co Ltd
Wuhan Jianmin Venture Capital Co Ltd
Xindafeng Investment Management Co Ltd
Yao Capital
Ying Capital
Youngor Investment Co Ltd
Yunyi Investment Management Shanghai Co Ltd
Zhejiang Chengze Jinkai Investment Management Co Ltd
Zhejiang Juren Capital Management Co Ltd
Zhongguang Great Wall Investment Management Beijing Co Ltd
Zhonghai Ruanyin Investment Management Co Ltd
Zhongjun Tianbao Capital Management Beijing Co Ltd
Zhongrong International Trust Co Ltd

Buyout Firms—Colombia
Abraaj Capital Ltd
Advent International Corp
Altra Investments
Ashmore Investment Management Ltd
Black River Asset Management LLC
Darby Overseas Investments, Ltd.
Delavaco Holdings Inc
Diana Capital SGECR SA
Evolvere Capital SAS
HarbourVest Partners LLC
Linzor Capital Partners LP
Southern Cross Capital Management SA
Teka Capital SAS

2395

Buyout Firms—Congo
IPS Industrial Promotion Services Ltd

Buyout Firms—Costa Rica
Norfund

Buyout Firms—Croatia
European Bank for Reconstruction and Development
Quaestus Private Equity doo

Buyout Firms—Cyprus
CEE Equity Partners Ltd
Elements Capital Partners Ltd
Penta Investments Ltd
Troika Capital Partners Ltd

Buyout Firms—Czech Republic
Advent International Corp
Argus Capital Ltd
Bancroft Group Ltd
Benson Oak Capital Ltd
Enercap Capital Partners
Genesis Capital sro
Hartenberg Capital sro
Invesco Real Estate, Ltd.
PPF Partners as
Penta Investments Ltd
Riverside Co
Rockaway Capital SE
Royalton Partners
3TS Capital Partners, Ltd.

Buyout Firms—Denmark
Altor Equity Partners AB
Axcel Industriinvestor A/S
Bjert Invest A/S
CVC Asia Pacific Ltd
CVC Capital Partners Ltd
Capidea Management ApS
Catacap Management A/S
Catella AB
Dansk Generationsskifte
Erhvervsinvest Management A/S
FSN Capital Partners AS
Finance Zealand Management ApS
Gro Capital A/S
Industri Udvikling A/S
Ld Equity
Nordic Capital
Odin Equity Partners K/S
PAI Partners SAS
Polaris Management A/S
SE Blue Holding A/S
SMV Management A/S
Schroders PLC
Solstra Capital Partners A/S
VIA equity A/S
VaekstPartner Kapital ApS

Buyout Firms—Egypt
Abraaj Capital Ltd
Actis LLP
BPE Partners
Carlyle Group LP
Compass Capital for Financial Investments
EFG Hermes Holdings SAE
FEP Capital

Global Investment House KSCC
NBK Capital Partners Ltd
Qalaa Holdings SAE
Silk Invest Ltd

Buyout Firms—Estonia
BaltCap Management Estonia OU
East Capital Private Equity AB
UP Invest OU

Buyout Firms—Ethiopia
China-Africa Development Fund
Surya Capital Management LLP

Buyout Firms—Finland
Ahlstrom Capital Oy
Ajanta Oy
Altor Equity Partners AB
Bridgepoint Advisers II Ltd
CapMan Oyj
Catella AB
Credit Agricole Corporate and Investment Bank SA
Dasos Capital Oy
EQT Funds Management Ltd
Essedel Oy
Evolver Investment Group Ltd
Fenno Management Oy
Intera Equity Partners Oy
JSH Capital Oy
Juuri Partners Oy
Korona Invest Oy
MB Rahastot Oy
Midinvest Management Oy
Mvi Support SA
Nordic Mezzanine Ltd
Panostaja Oyj
Sentica Partners Oy
Sponsor Capital Oy
Suomen Teollisuussijoitus Oy
Vaaka Partners Oy

Buyout Firms—France
A Plus Finance SASU
ACE Management SA
ACG Capital SA
ACG Management SA
AKN Holdings LLC
AUTONOMIE & SOLIDARITE
Ab2 SAS
Abenex Capital SAS
Acofi Gestion SA
Activa Capital SAS
Adaxtra Capital
Advent International Corp
Africinvest Tunisia SARL
Agence Francaise de Developpement EPIC
Agro Invest SAS
Alantra
Alliance Entreprendre SAS
Alp Capital SAS
Alpes Developpement Durable Investissement SAS
Alpha Group
Alter Equity SAS
Altur Investissement SCA
Amethis Advisory SAS
Amundi Private Equity Funds SA

Apax Partners Development SA
Apax Partners SA
Apicap SAS
Aquasourca France SAS
Aquitaine Creation Investissement SAS
Archimed SA
Ardens & Associes SAS
Ardian France SA
Ares Management LLC
Arkea Capital Investissement SA
Arkeon Gestion SAS
Astorg Partners SAS
Atalante SAS
Aurinvest Sas
Axio Capital SAS
Azulis Capital SA
BNP Paribas Capital Partners SAS
BNP Paribas Developpement SA
BNP Paribas Fortis Private Equity Growth NV
BPCE Immobilier Exploitation SAS
BTP Capital Investissement SA
Banque Pictet & Cie SA
Blackfin Capital Partners SAS
Blackstone Group LP
Bpifrance EPIC
Bpifrance Investissement Regions SAS
Bpifrance Investissement SASU
Bridgepoint Advisers II Ltd
Bridgepoint Advisers Ltd
Bridgepoint Portfolio Services SAS
Bruere &Associes SARL
Butler Capital Partners SA
CDC International Capital SA
CITA Gestion SA
CM CIC Investissement SA
CM-CIC Capital Prive SA
CVC Asia Pacific Ltd
CVC Capital Partners Ltd
Calao Finance SAS
Calcium Capital Partners SAS
Candover Investments PLC
Capatria SASU
Capelia SAS
Capital Croissance SAS
Capital Et Dirigeants Partenaires SARL
Capital Export SAS
Capital Grand Est SAS
Capitem Partenaires SAS
CarVal Investors LLC
Carlyle Group LP
Carvest Credit Agricole Regions Invertis SAS
Catella AB
Cathay Capital Private Equity SAS
Cavipar SASU
Centre Capital Developpement
Cerea Partenaire SAS
Charente Perigord Expansion SASU
Charterhouse Capital Partners LLP
Chequers Capital Partners SA
Ciclad Participations SAS
Citizen Capital Partenaires SAS
City Star Private Equity Sas
Conseil Plus Gestion SAS
Constellation Capital AG
Corvm Capital Partners SAS

Pratt's Guide to Private Equity & Venture Capital Sources

Cowen Capital Partners LLC
Creadev SAS
Credit Agricole Alpes Developpement SNC
Credit Agricole Aquitaine Expansion SAS
Credit Agricole Corporate and Investment Bank SA
Credit Agricole des Savoie Capital SAS
Credit Industriel et Commercial SA
Croissance Nord Pas de Calais SAS
Csfb Private Equity Advisers
Demeter SAS
Developpement et Partenariat PME SAS
Doughty Hanson and Co.
Duke Street Capital Ltd
Dzeta Conseil SAS
EME Capital LLP
East Capital Private Equity AB
Edmond de Rothschild Investment Partners SAS
Efeso Consulting Group SA
Elais Capital SAS
Emerging Capital Partners
Esfin Gestion SA
Etoile D Aquitaine
Eurazeo Pme Capital SAS
Eurazeo SA
Eurefi SA
Euro Capital SAS
European Capital
European Capital Financial Services Ltd
Evolem 2 Sas
Expansinvest SASU
Experienced Capital Management SAS
Extendam SA
FFP SA
FINAPERE Capital SAS
Federal Finance Gestion SA
Finadvance SA
Financiere Meeschaert SA
Finorpa PP SAS
Florac SAS
Fondations Capital France SAS
Fondations Capital SA
Fonds de Reserve Pour Les Retraites
Food and Beverage Private Equity SASU
Galia Gestion SAS
Galiena Capital SAS
Galileo Partners
Garibaldi Participations SAS
Gemmes Venture SA
Gilde Buy Out Partners BV
Gilde Investment Management BV
Gimv Investeringsmaatschappij Voor Vlanderen NV
Global Emerging Markets
Goldman Sachs & Co LLC
Grand Sud Ouest Capital SA
Groupe Arnault SE
Groupe IRD SA
HIG Capital LLC
HLD SCA
Harbert Management Corp
Henderson Global Investors Ltd
Herrikoa SCA
Hivest Capital Partners SASU
Houlihan Lokey Inc
IDI Asset Management SA
IK Investment Partners Ltd

IRDI Midi Pyrenees SA
IRPAC Developpement SA
Idinvest Partners SA
Ile de France Capital SA
Industries et Finances Partenaires SAS
Initiative & Finance Investissement SA
Innovafonds SAS
Institut Lorrain de Participation SA
Institut de Developpement Economique de la Bourgogne SA
Intuitis Investisseurs Prives
Invesco Real Estate, Ltd.
Invest PME SA
Investir & + SAS
Investors In Private Equity
Invus Group LLC
Irdi Soridec Gestion SAS
Iris Capital Management SAS
Isatis Capital SA
Ixen Partners SA
Ixo Private Equity SASU
Jacana Invest SAS
Jefferies Group LLC
Jolt Capital SAS
K Ariege S.C.
KKR & Co LP
Keensight Capital SAS
L Catterton Asia
L Catterton Europe SAS
LBO France Gestion SAS
La Financiere Patrimoniale d'Investissement SAS
Latour Capital Management Sas
M Capital Partners SAS
MML Capital Partners LLP
Massena Partners SA
Mbo Partenaires SAS
Michel Fraisse Gestion et Investissement SARL
Midi Pyrenees Croissance SA
Milestone Capital Partners Ltd
Montefiore Investment SAS
Motion Equity Partners LLP
Multicroissance SAS
NBGI Private Equity Ltd
NCI SAS
Natixis Private Equity SA
Naxicap Partners SA
Newfund Management SA
Nord Capital Partenaires SAS
Nord Europe Partenariat SA
Nord France Amorcage SASU
123 Investment Managers SA
Oaktree Capital Management LP
Ocean Participations SAS
Odyssee Venture SAS
Omnes Capital SAS
Orium SAS
Orkos Capital SAS
Oryx Partner SARL
Ouest Croissance SAS
PAI Partners SAS
Paluel Marmont Capital SASU
Participex Gestion SAS
Partners Group Holding AG
Parvilla SASU
Pechel Industries SAS

Perceva SAS
Perfectis Private Equity SA
Permira Advisers LLP
Phillimore Investissement SAS
Picardie Investissements SA
Platina Finance, Ltd.
Poincare Gestion SAS
Poitou Charentes Expansion SAS
Pragma Capital SA
Pricoa Capital Group Ltd
Private Equity Investments II BV
Proparco SA
Pyrenees Gascogne Developpement SASU
Quadrille Capital SAS
Qualium Investissement SAS
Quilvest Private Equity SCA SICAR
Rb Capital SASU
Re Sources Capital SAS
Rhone Alpes PME Gestion SA
Rhone Capital LLC
Rhone Dauphine Developpement SA
RiverRock European Capital Partners LLP
RobeCo Private Equity
Rothschild & Co SCA
SGH Capital SA
Sagard SAS
Schroders PLC
Seventure Partners SA
Silverfleet Capital Partners LLP
Siparex Group
Siparex Proximite Innovation SAS
Socadif
Societe Antilles Guyane d Investissement et Participations
Societe Financiere Lorient Developpement SA
Societe Generale Capital Partenaires SAS
Sodero Participations SAS
Sodica SASU
Sofilaro Gestion SAS
Sofimac Partners SA
Sopromec Participations SA
Soridec Ingenierie SARL
Sun Capital Partners Inc
Syntegra Capital Investors Ltd
21 Centrale Partners SA
21 Investimenti SGR SpA
3i Group PLC
TCR Capital SAS
TPG Capital Management LP
Tertium SAS
Tikehau Investment Management SAS
Time for Growth SA
Tocqueville Finance SA
Truffle Capital SAS
Trust Company of the West
Turenne Capital Partenaires SASU
U I Gestion SA
Ubequity Capital Partners Inc
Undisclosed Firm
Unexo SAS
Unigrains Diversification SA
VTB Kapital AO
Varenne Capital Partners SAS
Vatel Capital SAS
Vermeer Capital Partners SAS

2397

Pratt's Guide to Private Equity & Venture Capital Sources

Verto Capital Europe SASU
Vespa Capital LLP
Weinberg Capital Partners SAS
Wendel SE
Xange Private Equity SA

Buyout Firms—Gambia
Databank Private Equity Ltd

Buyout Firms—Georgia
European Bank for Reconstruction and Development Private Equity Investments II BV

Buyout Firms—Germany
ADCURAM Group AG
AEA Investors LLC
AGIC Partners GmbH
Adiuva Capital GmbH
Advent International Corp
Afinum Management GmbH
Aheim Capital GmbH
Alantra
Allegra Capital GmbH
Allianz Capital Partners GmbH
Alpina Capital Partners LLP
Alternative Strategic Investment GmbH
Amundi Private Equity Funds SA
Apax Partners LLP
Apollo Global Management LLC
Apriori Beteiligungen GmbH
Arcaris Management GmbH
Arcus Capital AG
Ardian France SA
Ares Management LLC
Auctus Capital Partners AG
Aurelius AG
Avedon Capital Partners BV
abacus alpha GmbH
BASF New Business GmbH
BID Equity Advisory GmbH
BKK Investitionsfonds GmbH
BTH Berlin Technologie Holding GmbH
BWK GmbH Unternehmensbeteiligungsgesellschaft
Bain Capital Inc
Bankhaus Lampe KG
Banque Pictet & Cie SA
BayBG Bayerische Beteiligungsgesellschaft mbH
Bayernlb Private Equity Management GmbH
Beaufort Capital GmbH
Berggruen Holdings Inc
Beyond Capital Partners GmbH
Blackstone Group LP
Bm H Beteiligungs Managementgesellschaft Hessen mbH
Bm T Beteiligungsmanagement
Bpe Unternehmensbeteiligungen GmbH
Bregal Unternehmerkapital GmbH
Bridgepoint Advisers II Ltd
Bridgepoint Advisers Ltd
Brockhaus Private Equity GmbH
CEE Management GmbH
CFH Beteiligungsgesellschaft mbH
CMP Capital Management Partners GmbH
COREST GmbH Corporate Restructuring
CVC Asia Pacific Ltd
CVC Capital Partners Ltd

Callista Holdings GmbH & Co KG
Capcellence Mittelstandspartner GmbH
Capital Dynamics Sdn Bhd
Capital Stage AG
Capiton AG
Capvis Equity Partners AG
Carlyle Group LP
Castik Capital Sarl
Cbr Management GmbH
Chequers Capital Partners SA
Cinven Group Ltd
Cipio Partners GmbH
CoBe Equities LLC
CornerstoneCapital Verwaltungs AG
Corvus Capital GmbH
DB1 Ventures GmbH
DEG Deutsche Investitions- und Entwicklungsgesellschaft mbH
DMB Deutsche Mittelstandsbeteiligungs GmbH
DPE Deutsche Private Equity GmbH
DUBAG Deutsche Unternehmensbeteiligungen AG
Demeter SAS
Deutsche Beteiligungs AG
Deutsche Effecten und Wechsel Beteiligungsgesellschaft AG
Deutsche Mittelstandsholding GmbH
Dievini Hopp Biotech Holding GmbH & Co KG
Doughty Hanson and Co.
Dr Engelhardt Kaupp Kiefer Beteiligungsberatung GmbH
ECM Equity Capital Management GmbH
EQT Funds Management Ltd
Econa AG
Elvaston Capital Management GmbH
Emeram Capital Partners GmbH
Equistone Partners Europe Ltd
4K Invest International Ltd
Finatem Fonds Management Verwaltungs GmbH
Findos Investor GmbH
Finlab AG
Fischer Buchschacher Gruppe AG
Fonterelli GmbH & Co KGaA
Fortress Investment Group LLC
Franger Investment KGaA
Fronteris Consulting AG
GI Partners
GMF Capital GmbH
GMPVC German Media Pool GmbH
Gebruder Heller Dinklage
General Atlantic LLC
German Startups Group Berlin GmbH & Co KGaA
Gilde Buy Out Partners BV
Gimv Investeringsmaatschappij Voor Vlanderen NV
Goldman Sachs & Co LLC
Gores Group LLC
Gramax Capital AG
Gruenwald Equity Management GmbH
H Siedentopf GmbH & Co KG
H2 Equity Partners BV
HIG Capital LLC
HQ Equita GmbH
Hannover Finanz GmbH
Hanseatische VC GmbH
Haspa Beteiligungsgesellschaft fuer den Mittelstand mbH

Heidelbergcapital Asset Management GmbH
Heliad Equity Partners GmbH & Co KGaA
Henderson Global Investors Ltd
Houlihan Lokey Inc
ICS Partners GmbH
ILP III SARL
INVICTO Holding GmbH
Indus Holding AG
Invesco Real Estate, Ltd.
Iris Capital Management SAS
iVentureCapital GmbH
independent capital AG
JPMorgan Chase & Co
Jefferies Group LLC
K5 Advisors GmbH & Co KG
KGAL Investment Management & GmbH Co KG
KPS Capital Partners LP
Kapitalbeteiligungsgesellschaft NRW GmbH
Kreissparkasse Reutlingen
L Eigenkapitalagentur
Lindsay Goldberg & Bessemer LP
MBG Schleswig-Holstein mbH
Max 21 AG
Maxburg Capital Partners
Media Ventures GmbH
Milbank Tweed Hadley & Mccloy LLP
Mittelstaendische Beteiligungsgesellschaft
Mittelstaendische Beteiligungsgesellschaft Sachsen mbH
Montagu Private Equity LLP
Motus Mittelstandskapital GmbH
Mpool Beteiligungen GmbH
Mutares AG
Myonic Holding GmbH
NIBC Principal Investments BV
NORD Holding Unternehmensbeteiligungsgesellschaft mbH
NRW Bank
Neuberger Berman LLC
Nordic Capital
nwk nordwest Kapitalbeteiligungsgesellschaft der Sparkasse
Oaktree Capital Management LP
Odewald & Compagnie fuer Beteiligungen GmbH
Omos Equitypartners GmbH
One Equity Partners LLC
Onics GmbH
Orlando Management AG
PAI Partners SAS
Palladion Partners Gesellschaft fuer Private Equity mbH
Paragon Partners GmbH
Partners Group Holding AG
Pecuniano GmbH
Perseus LLC
Perusa GmbH
Pinova Capital GmbH
Premium Equity Partners GmbH
Pricoa Capital Group Ltd
palero capital GmbH
Quantum Capital Partners AG
Radial Capital Partners GmbH & Co KG
Riverside Co
RobeCo Private Equity
Rocket Internet AG

S Partner Kapital AG
S Refit AG
S Ubg AG
SBG Saechsische Beteiligungsgesellschaft mbH
SHS Gesellschaft fuer Beteiligungsmanagement mbH
SLEEPZ AG
Schroders PLC
Seafort Advisors GmbH
Serafin Unternehmensgruppe GmbH
Seventure Partners SA
Silver Investment Partners GmbH & Co KG
Silverfern Group Inc
Silverfleet Capital Partners LLP
Sparkassenbeteiligungs Heilbronn Franken GmbH & Co KG
Steadfast Capital GmbH
Strategic Value Capital Partners Management GmbH
Strategic Value Partners LLC
Suma Verwaltungs GmbH
Sun Capital Partners Inc
3i Group PLC
Terra Firma Capital Partners Ltd
Triton Beteiligungsberatung GmbH
VERDEXUS
VR Equitypartner GmbH
Ventizz Capital Partners Advisory AG
Vitruvian Partners LLP
Wamex Private Equity Management
Warburg Pincus LLC
Waterland Private Equity Investments BV
Xange Private Equity SA

Buyout Firms—Ghana
Abraaj Capital Ltd
African Alliance Private Equity
Databank Private Equity Ltd

Buyout Firms—Haiti
Asia Frontier Investments Ltd

Buyout Firms—Hong Kong
A Capital Asia Ltd
AEA Investors LLC
AG BD LLC
AID Partners Capital Ltd
AMP Capital Investors Ltd
Adam Smith Capital Ltd
Adm Capital
Advanced Capital Ltd
Advantage Partners LLP
Affinity Equity Partners HK Ltd
Afinum Management GmbH
Aif Capital Asia Iii LP
Aktis Capital Group
AlpInvest Partners BV
Apax Partners LLP
Apollo Global Management LLC
Ares Management LLC
Ascendent Capital Partners Asia Ltd
Asia Frontier Investments Ltd
Asia Pacific Capital (HK) Ltd
Atlantic-Pacific Capital Inc
Atlantis Investment Management Hong Kong Ltd
Avantage Ventures Capital LLC
BASF New Business GmbH

Bagan Capital Ltd
Bain Capital Inc
Banque Pictet & Cie SA
Baring Private Equity Asia Ltd
Blackstone Group LP
Boxin Capital
Bravia Capital Partners Inc
Broadhaven Capital Partners LLC
Brown Brothers Harriman & Co
CDH China Management Co., Ltd.
CDIB Capital International Corp
CITIC Capital Partners Ltd
CITIC SECURITIES INTERNATIONAL PRTNS LTD
CLSA Capital Partners HK Ltd
CVC Asia Pacific Ltd
CVC Capital Partners Ltd
Canada Pension Plan Investment Board
Candover Investments PLC
Capital Dynamics Sdn Bhd
Capital International Inc
Capital VC Ltd
CapitalAsia Group
Catcha Group Pte Ltd
Centurion Investment Management Pte Ltd
China Everbright Ltd
China International Capital Corp Ltd
China Merchants China Direct Investments Ltd
China OperVestors Inc
ChinaRock Capital Management, Ltd.
Cimb Private Equity Sdn Bhd
Cinven Group Ltd
Clearwater Capital Partners Cyprus Ltd
Cmia Capital Partners Pte Ltd
Credit Agricole Corporate and Investment Bank SA
Csfb Private Equity Advisers
D E Shaw & Co LP
DB Capital Partners Ltd
Daiwa Corporate Investment Co Ltd
Darby Overseas Investments, Ltd.
Dlj Merchant Banking Partners
Dubai Investment Group
Dymon Asia Equity Pte Ltd
EQT Funds Management Ltd
Evercore Inc
First Eastern Investment Group
Fortress Investment Group LLC
FountainVest Partners Asia Ltd
General Atlantic LLC
Global Emerging Markets
Goldman Sachs & Co LLC
Gramercy Inc
Gruss Asset Management LP
Guosen Securities HK Asset Management Co Ltd
H&Q Asia Pacific, Inc.
HPEF Capital Partners Ltd
Henderson Global Investors Ltd
Hilco Equity Management LLC
Hony Capital Beijing Co Ltd
Hsbc Private Equity Investments (Uk) Ltd
IBID Holdings Ltd
Interleader Capital Ltd
International Finance Corp
Investor Growth Capital AB
Invus Group LLC
JP Morgan Investment Management Inc

JPMorgan Chase & Co
Japan Asia Investment Co Ltd
Jynwel Capital Ltd
K5 Advisors GmbH & Co KG
KKR & Co LP
Leeward Ventures Management SA
Leon Capital
Li & Fung Investments
Lloyds Development Capital (Holdings) Ltd
Lombard Investments Inc
Longreach Group Ltd
MBK Partners Inc
MEC Advisory Ltd
Mercer Private Markets AG
Milbank Tweed Hadley & Mccloy LLP
Morgan Stanley Private Equity
Morrison & Foerster LLP
Mount Kellett Capital Hong Kong Ltd
Myo Capital Advisers Ltd
Navis Management Sdn Bhd
Neuberger Berman LLC
OCP Asia Hong Kong Ltd
Oaktree Capital Management LP
Och-Ziff Capital Management Group LLC
On Capital Ltd
One Equity Partners LLC
Pacific Advantage Capital Ltd
Pacific Alliance Group Ltd
Pacific Capital SARL
Partners Capital Investment Group Holdings LLC
Permira Advisers LLP
PineBridge Investments LLC
Piper Jaffray Ventures Inc
Portfolio Advisors, LLC
Primavera Capital
Providence Equity Partners LLC
Quadrangle Group LLC
Quadrivio SGR SpA
Quam Asset Management Ltd
Quilvest Private Equity SCA SICAR
RRJ Capital Fund
Richlink International Capital Co Ltd
Riverside Co
RobeCo Private Equity
Rongxin Capital Fund Management Ltd
7Bridge Capital Partners Ltd
SEAVI Advent Corporation Ltd
SSG Capital Management Hong Kong Ltd
STIC Investment Inc
Saban Capital Group Inc
Samena Capital Management LLP
Saphir Capital Partners SA
Schroders PLC
Shaw Kwei & Partners
Silver Lake Partners LP
Spring Capital Asia Ltd
Standard Chartered Private Equity Ltd
Starr International Company Inc
Symphony Asia Holdings Pte Ltd
TA Associates Management LP
TPG Capital Management LP
TRG Management LP
Temasek Holdings (Private) Ltd
Tiger Group Investments
Tonic Venture Capital Ltd

2399

Pratt's Guide to Private Equity & Venture Capital Sources

Tpg Growth LLC
Trust Company of the West
Two Sigma Investments LP
VTB Kapital AO
Waterwood Investment Management Ltd
Ying Capital
York Capital Management LP

Buyout Firms—Hungary
Argus Capital Ltd
Bancroft Group Ltd
COVENT Toke Befekteto Zartkoruen Mukodo Rt
Darby Overseas Investments, Ltd.
European Bank for Reconstruction and Development
Global Capital Finance
InvestLife Europai es Tengerentuli Tokebefekteto Zrt
iEurope Capital LLC
Mid Europa Partners LLP
Oriens IM Hungary Szolgaltato Kft
Riverside Co
3TS Capital Partners, Ltd.

Buyout Firms—Iceland
Aftvinnuprounarsjoour Suourlands

Buyout Firms—India
AMP Capital Investors Ltd
Abraaj Capital Ltd
Actis LLP
Aditya Birla Capital Advisors Pvt Ltd
Adm Capital
Advent International Corp
Aif Capital Asia Iii LP
Amvensys Capital Group LLC
Ananta Capital
Apax Partners LLP
Apollo Global Management LLC
Asia Pacific Capital (HK) Ltd
Asia Pacific Healthcare Advisors Pvt Ltd
Ask Pravi Capital Advisors Pvt Ltd
Bain Capital Inc
Baring Private Equity Asia Ltd
Black River Asset Management LLC
Blackstone Group LP
Bravia Capital Partners Inc
CDP Capital Private Equity
CLSA Capital Partners HK Ltd
CX Partners
Canada Pension Plan Investment Board
Candover Investments PLC
Capital International Inc
Carlyle Group LP
Caspian Advisors Pvt Ltd
Centrum Capital Ltd
ChrysCapital Management Co
Cimb Private Equity Sdn Bhd
Citigroup Private Equity LP
Clearwater Capital Partners Cyprus Ltd
Creador Capital Group
Csfb Private Equity Advisers
D E Shaw & Co LP
Darby Overseas Investments, Ltd.
EQ India Advisors
Everstone Capital Management, Ltd.
Evolvence Capital Ltd
Exhilway Global

Flatworld Capital LLC
Fulcrum Venture India
GEF Management Corp
Gaja Capital Partners
General Atlantic LLC
Gennx360 Capital Partners LP

Buyout Firms—India
Gic Special Investments Pte Ltd
Global Investment House KSCC
Goldman Sachs & Co LLC
HPEF Capital Partners Ltd
Henderson Global Investors Ltd
ICICI Venture Funds Management Company Ltd
IDFC Alternatives Ltd
IEP Fund Advisors Pvt Ltd
IL & FS Investment Managers Ltd
Ic2 Capital
India Alternatives Investment Advisors Pvt Ltd
International Finance Corp
JP Morgan Investment Management Inc
Jefferies Group LLC
KKR & Co LP
Kaizen Private Equity
Kotak Investment Advisors Ltd
L Catterton Asia
Lazard India Advisors Pvt Ltd
LotusPool Capital Advisors Pvt Ltd
Lumis Partners
Mape Advisory Group Private Ltd
Morgan Stanley Private Equity
Motilal Oswal Pvt Equity Advisors Pvt Ltd
Mount Kellett Capital Hong Kong Ltd
Multiples Alternate Asset Management Pvt Ltd
Navis Management Sdn Bhd
New Silk Route Partners, LLC
Norwest Venture Partners
O3 Capital Advisors Pvt Ltd
Och-Ziff Capital Management Group LLC
Oman India Joint Investment Fund
Omidyar Network Commons LLC
OrbiMed Advisors LLC
Pacific Alliance Group Ltd
Partners Group Holding AG
Pfingsten Partners LLC
PineBridge Investments LLC
Private Equity Partners SpA
Providence Equity Partners LLC
Quadria Capital Investment Advisors Pvt Ltd
Redclays Capital Pvt Ltd
Reliance Capital Ventures Ltd
Samara Capital Management Ltd
Sealink Capital Partners
Siguler Guff & Company LP
Sonoma Management Partners Pvt Ltd
Standard Chartered Private Equity Ltd
Summit Partners LP
3i Group PLC
TA Associates Management LP
TPG Capital Management LP
Temasek Holdings (Private) Ltd
Tpg Growth LLC
True North
Vertex Venture Holdings Ltd.
Warburg Pincus LLC

Westbridge Capital Advisors (India) Pvt Ltd
Wolfensohn & Company LLC
Zephyr Management LP

Buyout Firms—Indonesia
Abraaj Capital Ltd
Affinity Equity Partners HK Ltd
Catcha Group Pte Ltd
Creador Capital Group
Garuda Capital Partners
Japan Asia Investment Co Ltd
KV Asia Capital Pte Ltd
Saratoga Investama Sedaya Tbk PT
Schroders PLC
Standard Chartered Private Equity Ltd

Buyout Firms—Iran
Griffon Capital

Buyout Firms—Ireland
Atlantic Bridge
Beltrae Partners Ltd
Better Capital LLP
Broadlake Capital Ltd
Brown Brothers Harriman & Co
Carlyle Group LP
Causeway Capital Partners I LP
Goldman Sachs & Co LLC
IBRC Capital Partners Ltd
Investec Ventures Ireland Ltd
Ireland Strategic Investment Fund
KKR & Co LP
Lioncourt Investments Ltd
MML Capital Partners LLP
Ronoc

Buyout Firms—Israel
Agate Medical Investments LP
Berggruen Holdings Inc
China Everbright Ltd
Claridge Inc
Exigent Capital Management LLC
First Israel Mezzanine Investors Ltd
Fortissimo Captial Fund Israel LP
Goldman Sachs & Co LLC
Goldrock Capital
Israel Discount Capital Markets & Investments, Ltd.
Maoz Everest Funds Management Ltd
Norwest Venture Partners
Omnes Capital SAS
OrbiMed Advisors LLC
Poalim Asia Direct Ltd
Poalim Cap Mark Tech, Ltd.
Siraj Fund Management Co
Tene Kibbutz Investment Management Ltd
Vertex Venture Holdings Ltd.
Viola Private Equity I LP

Buyout Firms—Italy
Advent International Corp
Aksia Group SpA
Alantra
Alcedo Societa di Gestione del Risparmio SpA
Aliante Partners Srl
Allianz Global Investors Italia SGR SpA
Alpha Group

Alto Partners SRL
Amber Capital Italia SGR SpA
Ambienta SGR SpA
Anthilia Capital Partners SGR SpA
Arcadia SGR SpA
Ardian France SA
Argan Capital
Atlantis Capital Markets NA LLC
BC Partners LLP
Banque Pictet & Cie SA
Bridgepoint Advisers II Ltd
Bridgepoint Advisers Ltd
CDP Equity SpA
CVC Asia Pacific Ltd
CVC Capital Partners Ltd
Candover Investments PLC
Carlyle Group LP
Charme Capital Partners SGR SpA
Chequers Capital Partners SA
Cinven Group Ltd
Clessidra Societa di Gestione del Risparmio SpA
Consilium SGR pA
Csfb Private Equity Advisers
DVR Capital SpA
Doughty Hanson and Co.
Equistone Partners Europe Ltd
FIRA Finanziaria Regionale Abruzzese SpA
Finanziaria Regionale Friuli Venezia Giulia SpA
Finint Partners Srl
Fondo Italiano d'Investimento SGR SpA
Foresight Group LLP
Fortress Investment Group LLC
Goldman Sachs & Co LLC
Gradiente SGR SpA
HIG Capital LLC
Henderson Global Investors Ltd
ILP III SARL
Idea Capital Funds Societa di Gestione del Risparmio SpA
Imi Fondi Chiusi SGR SpA
Industrial Assets SpA
Iniziativa Gestione Investimenti SGR SpA
L Catterton Europe SAS
LBO Italia Investimenti Srl
La Finanziaria Trentina SpA
M&C SpA
MVI Italia Srl
Mandarin Capital Partners SCA SICAR
Mediolanum State Street Sgr
Motion Equity Partners LLP
Neuberger Berman LLC
NextEnergy Capital Ltd
Omnes Capital SAS
Orizzonte SGR SpA
PAI Partners SAS
PM & Partners SpA
Platina Finance, Ltd.
Private Equity Partners SpA
Progressio SGR SpA
Quadrivio SGR SpA
R&D Advisory Srl
R72 PARTNERS
RiverRock European Capital Partners LLP
S+R Investimenti e Gestioni SGR SpA
Sator SpA

Schroders PLC
Siparex Group
Star Capital SGR SpA
Synergo SGR SpA
Syntegra Capital Investors Ltd
21 Centrale Partners SA
21 Investimenti SGR SpA
Trilantic Capital Management LP
UniCredit SpA
Unipol Merchant Banca per le Imprese SpA
VAM Investments SpA
Vela Capital Srl
Vela Imprese Srl
Venice European Investment Capital SpA
Wise Venture SGR SpA
Yarpa Investimenti SGR SpA

Buyout Firms–Ivory Coast
Africinvest Tunisia SARL
Cauris Management
Emerging Capital Partners

Buyout Firms–Jamaica
Caribbean Equity Partners Ltd

Buyout Firms–Japan
AG BD LLC
AMP Capital Investors Ltd
Active Investment Partners
Adams Street Partners LLC
Advantage Partners LLP
Amundi Private Equity Funds SA
Ant Capital Partners Co Ltd
Asia Investment Partners Inc
Bain Capital Inc
Banque Pictet & Cie SA
Baring Private Equity Asia Ltd
Blackstone Group LP
Brown Brothers Harriman & Co
CAS Capital Inc
CITIC Capital Partners Ltd
CLSA Capital Partners HK Ltd
CVC Asia Pacific Ltd
CVC Capital Partners Ltd
Capital Dynamics Sdn Bhd
Capital International Inc
CarVal Investors LLC
Carlyle Group LP
Csfb Private Equity Advisers
D E Shaw & Co LP
Daiwa Corporate Investment Co Ltd
Dlj Merchant Banking Partners
Fortress Investment Group LLC
Gic Special Investments Pte Ltd
Goldman Sachs & Co LLC
H&Q Asia Pacific, Ltd.
HarbourVest Partners LLC
Henderson Global Investors Ltd
Hiroshima Innovation Network Inc
Innovation Network Corporation of Japan
Integral Corp
Iris Capital Management SAS
J Will Partners Co Ltd
J-STAR Co Ltd
JPMorgan Chase & Co
Japan Asia Investment Co Ltd

Japan Industrial Partners Inc
Japan Private Equity Co Ltd
Jefferies Group LLC
KK Kagawagin Capital
KKR & Co LP
Kyushu Jigyo Keizoku Bridge Investment LPS
Longreach Group Ltd
MBK Partners Inc
Mercuria Investment Co Ltd
Milbank Tweed Hadley & Mccloy LLP
Milestone Turnaround Management Co Ltd
Mizuho Capital Partners Co Ltd
Morgan Stanley Private Equity
Morrison & Foerster LLP
Neuberger Berman LLC
New Frontier Partners Co Ltd
New Horizon Capital Co Ltd
Nippon Sangyo Suishin Kiko Ltd
Oak Capital Corp
Oaktree Capital Management LP
Pacific Alliance Group Ltd
Partners Group Holding AG
Permira Advisers LLP
Phoenix Capital Co Ltd
PineBridge Investments LLC
Polaris Capital Group Co Ltd
Rising Japan Equity Inc
Riverside Co
Schroders PLC
Shinsei Bank Ltd
Shizuoka Capital Co Ltd
Silver Lake Partners LP
Strategic Value Partners LLC
Sumitomo Mitsui Trust Investment Co Ltd
Sun Capital Management Corp
Sun-Eight Trading Co Ltd
TPG Capital Management LP
Tokio Marine Capital Co Ltd
Trilantic Capital Management LP
Unison Capital, Inc.
Wakabayashi Fund LLC
Wilshire Private Markets

Buyout Firms–Jordan
Abraaj Capital Ltd
Foursan Group
Global Investment House KSCC

Buyout Firms–Kazakhstan
Abraaj Capital Ltd
Adm Capital
Centras Capital Partners
Da Vinci Capital Management Ltd
European Bank for Reconstruction and Development
Kazyna Kapital Management AO
Troika Capital Partners Ltd
Vernyi Kapital AO

Buyout Firms–Kenya
Abraaj Capital Ltd
Actis LLP
African Alliance Private Equity
Africinvest Tunisia SARL
Bamboo Finance SA
Catalyst Principal Partners LLC
Centum Investment Company Plc

Pratt's Guide to Private Equity & Venture Capital Sources

Emerging Capital Partners
Helios Investment Partners LLP
IPS Industrial Promotion Services Ltd
Norfund
Progression Capital Africa Ltd.
Silk Invest Ltd
Zephyr Management LP

Buyout Firms—Kuwait
Action Group Holdings KSCC
Al Aman Investment Company KPSC
Al Fawares Holding Co KSCC
Al Rouyah Investment and Leasing Company
Amwal International Investment Company KSCP
Asiya Capital Investments Company KSCP
Boubyan Bank KSCP
Coast Investment and Development Co KSCP
GCC Private Equity
Global Investment House KSCC
Gulf Investment Corporation SAG
KFH Capital Investment Co KSCC
Khatif Holding Company KSC
Kuwait Finance and Investment Company KSCP
Markab Capital
NBK Capital Partners Ltd
National Investments Co KSCP

Buyout Firms—Kyrgyzstan
European Bank for Reconstruction and Development

Buyout Firms—Latvia
BaltCap Management Estonia OU
Catella AB
European Bank for Reconstruction and Development
LR Capital SIA
Livonia Partners

Buyout Firms—Lebanon
Abraaj Capital Ltd
BLC Invest SAL
Carlyle Group LP
Daher Capital
Emerging Investment Partners Co
Fransabank SAL
MENA Capital S A L
Middle East Capital Group SAL

Buyout Firms—Lesotho
African Alliance Private Equity

Buyout Firms—Lithuania
BaltCap Management Estonia OU
European Bank for Reconstruction and Development
LANDMARK CAPITAL UAB

Buyout Firms—Luxembourg
AMP Capital Investors Ltd
Abac Capital SL
Alpha Group
Apollo Global Management LLC
Aquasourca France SAS
Ardian France SA
Ares Management LLC
Armat Group SA
BIP Investment Partners SA
BV Capital Partners Luxemburg SA
Bain Capital Inc

Bamboo Finance SA
Banque Lombard Odier & Cie SA
Bridgepoint Advisers II Ltd
Bridgepoint Advisers Ltd
Brown Brothers Harriman & Co
CEE Equity Partners Ltd
CVC Asia Pacific Ltd
CVC Capital Partners Ltd
CapMan Oyj
Capital Dynamics SCA
CarVal Investors LLC
Carlyle Group LP
Castik Capital Sarl
Cinven Group
Cohen & Company Financial Ltd
Credit Agricole Corporate and Investment Bank SA
Darby Overseas Investments, Ltd.
Doughty Hanson and Co.
Equi Sicav Sif Sca
Eurefi SA
4K Invest International Ltd
Fondations Capital SA
Henderson Global Investors Ltd
IK Investment Partners Ltd
ILP III SARL
Iberian Capital III SICAR
Invesco Real Estate, Ltd.
Investindustrial Services Ltd
L-Gam Advisers LLP
La Financiere Patrimoniale d'Investissement SAS
Leeward Ventures Management SA
Mandarin Capital Partners SCA SICAR
Massena Partners SA
Mercer Private Markets AG
Monitor Clipper Partners LLC
Oaktree Capital Management LP
Oraxys SA
P&S Capital doo
PAI Partners SAS
Pacific Capital SARL
Partners Group Holding AG
Permira Advisers LLP
Quilvest Private Equity SCA SICAR
Riverside Co
RobeCo Private Equity
Rothschild & Co SCA
Royalton Partners
SGH Capital SA
Saphir Capital Partners SA
Schroders PLC
Strategic Value Partners LLC
Sun Capital Partners Inc
SwanCap Investment Management SA
TPG Capital Management LP
Trilantic Capital Management LP
Triton Beteiligungsberatung GmbH
Ufenau Capital Partners AG
Vallis Capital Partners SGPS SA
Vespa Capital LLP

Buyout Firms—Macedonia
European Bank for Reconstruction and Development

Buyout Firms—Madagascar
Undisclosed Firm

Buyout Firms—Malawi
African Alliance Private Equity

Buyout Firms—Malaysia
Abraaj Capital Ltd
Azka Capital Sdn Bhd
Catcha Group Pte Ltd
Cimb Private Equity Sdn Bhd
Creador Capital Group
Dubai Investment Group
Ekuiti Nasional Bhd
Goldis Bhd
Ingenious Haus Group
Khazanah Nasional Bhd
Mayban-Jaic Capital Management Sdn Bhd
Musharaka Venture Management Sdn Bhd
Navis Management Sdn Bhd

Buyout Firms—Malta
Blackstar Group PLC
Pamplona Capital Management LLP

Buyout Firms—Mauritius
Adenia Partners Ltd
Advanced Finance and Investment Group LLC
African Alliance Private Equity
ChrysCapital Management Co
Creador Capital Group
Everstone Capital Management, Ltd.
IEP Fund Advisors Pvt Ltd
Kibo Capital Partners Ltd
LotusPool Capital Advisors Pvt Ltd
Mcb Equity Fund Ltd
Phatisa Group Ltd
Samara Capital Management Ltd
Surya Capital Management LLP
Synergy Capital Managers
White Cloud Capital Advisors Ltd

Buyout Firms—Mexico
Adobe Capital
Advent International Corp
Alta Growth Capital SC
Axis Capital Management
Carlyle Group LP
Credit Agricole Corporate and Investment Bank SA
Csfb Private Equity Advisers
Darby Overseas Investments, Ltd.
EMX Capital Partners LP
Evercore Inc
Goldman Sachs & Co LLC
Gramercy Inc
Linzor Capital Partners LP
Monterrey Capital Partners
Newgrowth Fund
Nexxus Capital SA de CV
PineBridge Investments LLC
Promecap SA de CV
Schroders PLC
Southern Cross Capital Management SA
Temasek Holdings (Private) Ltd
Wamex Private Equity Management

Buyout Firms—Moldova
European Bank for Reconstruction and Development

Buyout Firms—Monaco
Alpha Group
Cloverleaf Group
Goldman Sachs & Co LLC

Buyout Firms—Mongolia
European Bank for Reconstruction and Development
Silk Road Management

Buyout Firms—Morocco
Africinvest Tunisia SARL
Almamed
Brookstone Partners LLP
Capital Invest
Emerging Capital Partners
Ithmar Al Mawarid SA
MarocInvest Finance Group
Riva y Garcia Private Equity
Silk Invest Ltd
Ste Holding Financiere De Participation Et d'investissements

Buyout Firms—Namibia
African Alliance Private Equity
PointBreak Private Equity

Buyout Firms—Neth. Antilles
Curacao Growth Fund CV
Greenfield Capital Partners BV
Oresa Ventures Sp z oo

Buyout Firms—Netherlands
AAC CAPITAL PARTNERS
ABN AMRO Participaties BV
ACE Partners BV
AG BD LLC
Active Capital Co BV
Advent International Corp
AlpInvest Partners BV
Alpha Group
Antea Participaties Management BV
Astor Participaties BV
Atlantic Capital BV
Avedon Capital Partners BV
Axivate Capital BV
BB Capital BV
BNP Paribas Fortis Private Equity Growth NV
BXR Group BV
Bencis Capital Partners BV
Berggruen Holdings Inc
Bitterfontein BV
Breedinvest BV
CVC Asia Pacific Ltd
CVC Capital Partners Ltd
Craic BV
Dasym Investment Strategies BV
Egeria BV
European Hotel Capital BV
5Square BV
Fields Group BV
Finles NV
Gebruder Heller Dinklage
General Atlantic LLC
Gilde Buy Out Partners BV
Gilde Equity Management GEM Benelux Partners BV
Gilde Healthcare Partners BV
Gilde Investment Management BV
Gimv Investeringsmaatschappij Voor Vlanderen NV
Greenfield Capital Partners BV
H2 Equity Partners BV
HAL Investments BV
Henderson Global Investors Ltd
Holland Food Ventures BV
Holland Venture BV
IK Investment Partners Ltd
Informal Capital Network BV
Intersaction Ventures BV
Investor Growth Capital AB
KRC Capital BV
Karmijn Kapitaal Management BV
Main Capital Partners BV
Matcorp Holding BV
Mentha Capital BV
NIBC Principal Investments BV
NPM Capital NV
Navitas Management BV
Nedvest Capital Beheer BV
Neuberger Berman LLC
Newion Investments BV
Nordian Capital BV
Oaktree Capital Management LP
Penta Investments Ltd
Private Equity Investments II BV
QAT Investments SA
Rabo Participaties BV
Ramphastos Investments Management BV
Riverside Co
RobeCo Private Equity
Schroders PLC
Silverfern Group Inc
Standard Investment BV
Stichting Bewaarder Amsterdams Klimaat & Energiefonds
Synergia Capital Partners BV
3i Group PLC
Transequity Network BV
Van Lanschot Participaties BV
Varova BV
Venture Fund Rotterdam BV
Vortex Capital Partners BV
Waterland Private Equity Investments BV
Wilshire Private Markets

Buyout Firms—New Zealand
AMP Capital Investors Ltd
Direct Capital Private Equity
Ironbridge Capital Pty Ltd
Lincoln Capital Partners Ltd
Maui Capital Ltd
Murray Capital Ltd
Oriens Capital
Pencarrow Private Equity Ltd
Perpetual Capital Management Ltd
Rangatira Ltd
Tembusu Partners Pte Ltd
Touchstone Capital Partners Ltd
Waterman Capital Ltd

Buyout Firms—Niger
Helios Investment Partners LLP

Buyout Firms—Nigeria
ARM Capital Partners
Actis LLP
African Capital Alliance
Africinvest Tunisia SARL
Avante Capital Partners Ltd
Carlyle Group LP
First Funds Ltd
Verod Capital Management Ltd

Buyout Firms—Norway
Altor Equity Partners AB
CapMan Oyj
EQT Funds Management Ltd
East Capital Private Equity AB
FSN Capital Partners AS
Ferd Capital Partners AS
Herkules Capital AS
Investinor AS
JP Anderson (SL) Ltd
Kistefos Venture Capital As
Klaveness Marine Holding AS
Lindsay Goldberg & Bessemer LP
Nord Kapitalforvaltning AS
Nordic Capital
Norfund
Norvestor Equity AS
Oderc AS
Progressus Management As
Reiten & Co AS
Smedvig Capital Ltd

Buyout Firms—Pakistan
Abraaj Capital Ltd
IPS Industrial Promotion Services Ltd

Buyout Firms—Panama
Ecoforest

Buyout Firms—Peru
Altra Investments
Carlyle Group LP
Nexuss Group SAC
Salkantay Partners SAC

Buyout Firms—Philippines
Bonifacio Capital
CAS Capital Inc
Macquarie Infrastructure and Real Assets (Europe) Ltd
Sierra Madre Managers

Buyout Firms—Poland
Abris Capital Partners Sp zoo
Advantum Investments Sp z o o
Advent International Corp
Amundi Private Equity Funds SA
Argan Capital
Arx Equity Partners Sp z o o
Avallon Sp z o o
Bachleda Grupa Inwestycyjna Sp z o o
Bridgepoint Advisers II Ltd
Bridgepoint Advisers Ltd
CORNERSTONE PARTNERS sp. z o.o.
Darby Overseas Investments, Ltd.
EQT Funds Management Ltd
Enterprise Investors Sp z o o

Pratt's Guide to Private Equity & Venture Capital Sources

European Bank for Reconstruction and Development
Hedgehog Sp z o o
Highlander Partners LP
Icentis Capital Sp z o o
Investors Towarzystwo Funduszy Inwestycyjnych SA
Luma Investment SA
Mid Europa Partners LLP
Midven SA
Montagu Private Equity LLP
Oresa Ventures Sp z oo
Penta Investments Ltd
Private Equity Partners SpA
Resource Partners Sp z o o
Riverside Co
RobeCo Private Equity
Royalton Partners
21 Investimenti SGR SpA
3TS Capital Partners, Ltd.
TDJ SA
Tar Heel Capital Sp z o o
Tcwarzystwo Funduszy Inwestycyjnych Capital Partners SA
Vestor Dom Maklerski SA
Warsaw Equity Management Sp z o o
Waterland Private Equity Investments BV

Buyout Firms—Portugal
Caixa Capital BV
Capital Criativo SCR SA
Change Partners
Ecs Capital SA
Explorer Investments Sociedade de Capital de Risco SA
Ged Group
Haitong Capital SCR SA
Inter Risco Sociedade de Capital de Risco SA
Magnum Industrial Partners
Oxy Capital Sociedade de Capital de Risco SA
Vallis Capital Partners SGPS SA

Buyout Firms—Qatar
Global Investment House KSCC
Goldman Sachs & Co LLC
QInvest Ltd
Qatar First Bank LLC
Qatar Holding LLC
Qatar Investment Authority

Buyout Firms—Romania
Abris Capital Partners Sp zoo
Advent International Corp
Amundi Private Equity Funds SA
Argus Capital Ltd
Arx Equity Partners Sp z o o
Axxess Capital Partners SA
Enterprise Investors Sp z o o
European Bank for Reconstruction and Development
Fondul Roman pentru Eficienta Energiei
Ged Group
Oresa Ventures Sp z oo
Oriens IM Hungary Szolgaltato Kft
P&S Capital doo
Pactinvest SA
Post-Privatization Foundation
3TS Capital Partners, Ltd.

Buyout Firms—Russia
Astor Capital Group, Inc
Bank Sankt-Peterburg PAO
Baring Vostok Capital Partners Ltd
Black River Asset Management LLC
Bolshoi Management
CapMan Oyj
Csfb Private Equity Advisers
Da Vinci Capital Management Ltd
East Capital Private Equity AB
Elbrus Kapital OOO
European Bank for Reconstruction and Development
FINAM Global
Finstar Financial Group
Goldman Sachs & Co LLC
InVenture Partners
Indigo Capital Partners
International Finance Corp
iTechCapital
KhK Interros ZAO
Korporatsiya razvitiya Severnogo Kavkaza AO
Leta Group ZAO
Penta Investments Ltd
Private Equity Partners SpA
RT-Invest OOO
Rossiiskaia Korporatsiia Nanotekhnologii GK
Siguler Guff & Company LP
Suma Verwaltungs GmbH
Svarog Capital Advisors LTD
TPG Capital Management LP
Troika Capital Partners Ltd
UK RFPI OOO
UK RWM Kapital ZAO
UNITED FINANCIAL GROUP ASSET MANAGEMENT
United Capital Partners Advisory OOO
VTB Kapital AO

Buyout Firms—Saudi Arabia
Abraaj Capital Ltd
Al Khabeer Capital Co
AlTouq Group
Anfaal Capital Co CJSC
Crescent Point Group
Global Derayah
Global Investment House KSCC
Goldman Sachs & Co LLC
Iris Capital Management SAS
Itqan Capital Co
Jadwa Investment Co SJSC
KKR & Co LP
Kingdom Holding Co
Malaz Capital Company
Mohammed Ibrahim Alsubeaei and Sons Investment Co
ReAya Holding
Riyadh Valley Co
SEDCO Capital Co
Saudi Arabian Investment Co
Swicorp Capital Partners SA
ZAD Investment Co

Buyout Firms—Senegal
Advanced Finance and Investment Group LLC

Buyout Firms—Sierra Leone
JP Anderson (SL) Ltd

Buyout Firms—Singapore
AMP Capital Investors Ltd
Actis LLP
Adams Street Partners LLC
Affinity Equity Partners HK Ltd
Aif Capital Asia Iii LP
Aktis Capital Group
Allianz Capital Partners GmbH
Apollo Global Management LLC
Arcapita Inc
Ardian France SA
Asia Growth Capital Advisors, Ltd.
Aura Capital Group
Aventures Capital Management Pte Ltd
Baring Private Equity Asia Ltd
Black River Asset Management LLC
Blackstone Group LP
CVC Asia Pacific Ltd
CVC Capital Partners Ltd
Capital Square Partners Pte Ltd
CarVal Investors LLC
Carlyle Group LP
Castle Harlan Aus Mezzanine
Catcha Group Pte Ltd
Centurion Investment Management Pte Ltd
China International Capital Corp Ltd
Cimb Private Equity Sdn Bhd
City Star Private Equity Sas
Clearwater Capital Partners Cyprus Ltd
Clermont Group
Cmia Capital Partners Pte Ltd
Corstone Corp
Credence Partners Pte Ltd
Crescent Point Group
Csfb Private Equity Advisers
Dlj Merchant Banking Partners
Dymon Asia Equity Pte Ltd
EQT Funds Management Ltd
ESW Manage Pte Ltd
Everstone Capital Management, Ltd.
F & H Fund Management Pte Ltd
First Alverstone Partners Pte Ltd
Fortress Investment Group LLC
Galena Asset Management Ltd
General Atlantic LLC
Gic Special Investments Pte Ltd
Goldman Sachs & Co LLC
Gramercy Inc
HPEF Capital Partners Ltd
Heliconia Capital Management Pte Ltd
Henderson Global Investors Ltd
Highland Capital Management LP
Ingenious Haus Group
Japan Asia Investment Co Ltd
Jefferies Group LLC
KKR & Co LP
KV Asia Capital Pte Ltd
Kestrel Capital Pty Limited
Kingsbridge Capital Pte Ltd
L Catterton Asia
Makara Capital
Milbank Tweed Hadley & Mccloy LLP
Morrison & Foerster LLP
NIBC Principal Investments BV
Navis Management Sdn Bhd

Neuberger Berman LLC
Novo Tellus Capital Partners Pte Ltd
OCBC CAPITAL MANAGEMENT
OCP Asia Hong Kong Ltd
Oaktree Capital Management LP
Partners Group Holding AG
PineBridge Investments LLC
Prostar Investments Pte Ltd
Providence Equity Partners LLC
Quadria Capital Investment Advisors Pvt Ltd
Quilvest Private Equity SCA SICAR
Rockstead Capital Pte., Ltd.
SEAVI Advent Corporation Ltd
Saban Capital Group Inc
Schroders PLC
Sebrina Holdings Ltd
Southern Capital Group Pte Ltd
Standard Chartered Private Equity Ltd
Symphony Asia Holdings Pte Ltd
3 Degrees Asset Management Pte Ltd
TPG Capital Management LP
Temasek Holdings (Private) Ltd
Tembusu Partners Pte Ltd
Tpg Growth LLC
VTB Kapital AO
Varde Partners Inc
Venstar Capital Management Pte Ltd
Vertex Venture Holdings Ltd.
Vinacapital Investment Management Ltd
Wilshire Private Markets

Buyout Firms—Slovakia
Across Wealth Management OCP As
European Bank for Reconstruction and Development
Penta Investments Ltd

Buyout Firms—Slovenia
KD dd
P&S Capital doo
Slovenski Podjetniski Sklad

Buyout Firms—South Africa
Abraaj Capital Ltd
Actis LLP
Advanced Finance and Investment Group LLC
African Alliance Private Equity
Amb Private Equity Partners Ltd
Blackstar Group PLC
Boe Bank Ltd
Bopa Moruo
Botenya Advisors (Pty) Ltd
Capitalworks Investment Partners (Pty) Ltd
Capitau Advisory Ltd
Carlyle Group LP
China-Africa Development Fund
Coast2Coast Investments Pty Ltd
Collins Private Equity Holdings Pty Ltd
Convergence Partners Investments (Pty) Ltd
Credit Agricole Corporate and Investment Bank SA
Delta Partners FZ LLC
EVI Capital Partners LLP
Emerging Capital Partners
Ethos Private Equity (Proprietary) Ltd
Export Venture Capital Corporation (Pty) Ltd
Freetel Capital (Pty) Ltd
Goldman Sachs & Co LLC

Harith General Partners (Pty) Ltd
Horizon Equity Partners Pty Ltd
Identity Capital Partners (Pty) Ltd
International Finance Corp
Investec Private Equity
Kleoss Capital (Pty) Ltd
LeapFrog Investments
Lereko Investment Holdings Pty Ltd
Medu Capital(Pty)Ltd
Mineworkers Investment Co
Molash Group
Motseng Investment Holdings (Pty) Ltd
Norfund
Old Mutual PLC
Ontario Private Equity Ltd
Paean Advisors Pty Ltd
PointBreak Private Equity
RMB Corvest (Pty) Limited
Richmond Capital (Pty) Ltd
SP Aktif
Sanlam Private Equity
Sasfin Private Equity Fund Managers Pty Ltd
Silk Invest Ltd
Southern Africa Enterprise Development Fund
Spinnaker Growth Partners (Pty) Ltd
Spirit Capital (Pty) Ltd
Standard Chartered Private Equity Ltd
Tactic Capital (Pty) Ltd
Targe Capital
Trinitas Private Equity (Pty) Ltd
Trivest Trium Investments (Pty) Ltd
VICI Private Equity Fund II Ltd
Zephyr Management LP
zico capital

Buyout Firms—South Korea
AG BD LLC
AIP Private Capital
Affinity Equity Partners HK Ltd
CVC Asia Pacific Ltd
CVC Capital Partners Ltd
Cappello Capital Corp
Carlyle Group LP
Centurion Technology Investment Corp
Clearwater Capital Partners Cyprus Ltd
Consus Asset Management Co Ltd
Corstone Corp
cornerstone equity partners
Darby Overseas Investments, Ltd.
East Bridge Partners
Gic Special Investments Pte Ltd
Global & Associates Inc
Global Capital Finance
Goldman Sachs & Co LLC
H&Q Asia Pacific, Ltd.
Hahn & Company Eye Holdings Co Ltd
Hanwha Investment Corp
HarbourVest Partners LLC
Hi Investment & Securities Co Ltd
Highland Capital Management LP
IMM Investment Corp
IMM Private Equity Inc
JKL Partners, Inc.
Japan Asia Investment Co Ltd
KKR & Co LP

KTB Private Equity Co Ltd
Kb Investment Co Ltd
Korea Development Bank
MBK Partners Inc
Mercer Private Markets AG
Mirae Asset Venture Investment Co Ltd
Moorim Capital Co Ltd
Morgan Stanley Private Equity
Neuberger Berman LLC
Oaktree Capital Management LP
Pacific Alliance Group Ltd
Partners Group Holding AG
PineBridge Investments LLC
Praxis Capital Partners Co Ltd
Q Capital Partners Co Ltd
Richmond Asset Management
Riverside Co
STIC Investment Inc
Schroders PLC
Shinhan Private Equity Inc
SkyLake Investment & Co
Standard Chartered Private Equity Ltd
Stonebridge Capital Inc
TRG Management LP
UAMCO Ltd
Utc Investment Co Ltd (Aka Utc Venture Co Ltd)
VOGO Fund Asset Management
Woori Bank

Buyout Firms—Spain
Abac Capital SL
Advent International Corp
Alantra
Alta Capital
Apax Partners LLP
Axis Participaciones Empresariales SGEIC SAU
BNP Paribas Fortis Private Equity Growth NV
Bankinter Capital Riesgo SGECR SA
Banque Pictet & Cie SA
Belmert Capital SA
Black Toro Capital LLP
Bridgepoint Advisers II Ltd
Bridgepoint Advisers Ltd
CVC Asia Pacific Ltd
Caixa Capital BV
Caixa Capital Desarrollo Scr
Caja de Seguros Reunidos Compania de Seguros y Reaseguros SA
Candover Investments PLC
Carlyle Group LP
Corpfin Capital Asesores SA SGEIC
Csfb Private Equity Advisers
Demeter SAS
Diana Capital SGECR SA
Doughty Hanson and Co.
Eneas Alternative Investments SL
Eneas Capital SL
Espiga Capital Gestion SGCR SA
Evercore Inc
Fordahl Capital SA
Foresight Group LLP
Gala Capital Partners SL
Ged Group
Gestion De Capital Riesgo Del
Goldman Sachs & Co LLC

2405

Pratt's Guide to Private Equity & Venture Capital Sources

HIG Capital LLC
Haitong Capital SCR SA
Harbert Management Corp
Henderson Global Investors Ltd
Hiperion Capital Management SGECR SA
Impala Capital Partners SA
Inversiones Grupo Zriser SL
Inversiones Ibersuizas SA
Invesco Real Estate, Ltd.
Investindustrial Services Ltd
KKR & Co LP
L Catterton Europe SAS
Landon Investments Scr SA
MCH Private Equity Asesores SL
Magnum Industrial Partners
Magnum Industrial Partners SL
Mccall Springer LLC
Mercapital SL
Meridia Capital Partners SL
Miura Private Equity SGEIC SA
Nazca Capital SGEIC SA
Next Capital Partners SGECR SA
One Equity Partners LLC
PAI Partners SAS
Permira Advisers LLP
Phi Industrial Acquisitions SL
Plenium Partners SL
Portobello Capital Advisors SL
Praedium Management Co SL
PrcA Capital de Inversiones SGEIC SA
Qualitas Equity Partners Sgecr SA
Realza Capital SGECR SA
Riva y Garcia Private Equity
Riverside Co
RobeCo Private Equity
Sabadell Capital
Sherpa Capital Gestion
Siparex Group
Suma Capital SGECR SA
3i Group PLC
TREA Capital Partners, S.V. SA
Tandem Capital Gestion
Torreal SA
Torsa Capital SGECR SA
UC Capital
Valcapital Gestion Sgecr S A

Buyout Firms—Sri Lanka
Asia Frontier Investments Ltd
JP Anderson (SL) Ltd
Lanka Ventures PLC

Buyout Firms—Sudan
Global Investment House KSCC

Buyout Firms—Swaziland
African Alliance Private Equity

Buyout Firms—Sweden
AAC CAPITAL PARTNERS
Accent Equity Partners AB
Ackra Invest AB
Adelis Equity Partners AB
Alder
Altor Equity Partners AB
Ares Management LLC

Axcel Industriinvestor A/S
Bridgepoint Advisers II Ltd
Bridgepoint Advisers Ltd
Bure Equity AB
CVC Asia Pacific Ltd
CVC Capital Partners Ltd
CapMan Oyj
Capital International Inc
Carlyle Group LP
Catella AB
Cevian Capital AB
Connecting Capital Sweden AB
EQT Funds Management Ltd
East Capital Private Equity AB
FSN Capital Partners AS
Fianchetto Capital AB
Goldman Sachs & Co LLC
ICA Gruppen AB
IK Investment Partners Ltd
Inlandsinnovation AB
Investment Latour AB
Investor Growth Capital AB
K III Sweden AB
Litorina Capital Advisors AB
MedCap AB (publ)
Monterro Investment AB
Motala Verkstad Group AB
Mvi Support SA
New Equity Venture International AB
Nordic Capital
Nordstjernan AB
Odlander Fredrikson & Co AB
Orlando Nordics AB
Permira Advisers LLP
Priveq Partners AB
Procuritas Partners Kb
Profura AB
Ratos AB
Riverside Co
Schroders PLC
Segulah Advisor AB
Small Cap Partners Management i Malmo AB
Summa Equity AB
3i Group PLC
Triton Beteiligungsberatung GmbH
VIA equity A/S
Valedo Partners Fund I AB
Vitruvian Partners LLP
Volati AB
Wellstreet Partners AB
Wingefors Invest AB

Buyout Firms—Switzerland
Ace & Company SA
Affentranger Associates SA
Afinum Management GmbH
Alpha Group
Ambrian Resources AG
Aralon AG
Ardian France SA
Argos Soditic SA
aventic partners AG
BASF New Business GmbH
BC Partners LLP
BNP Paribas Capital Partners SAS

BV Holding AG
Banque Lombard Odier & Cie SA
Banque Pictet & Cie SA
Black River Asset Management LLC
Brown Brothers Harriman & Co
b to v Partners AG
CVC Asia Pacific Ltd
CVC Capital Partners Ltd
Calibrium Ltd
Capital Dynamics Sdn Bhd
Capital Transmission SA
Capvis Equity Partners AG
Cevian Capital AB
Constellation Capital AG
Cowen Capital Partners LLC
Credit Agricole Corporate and Investment Bank SA
Cross Equity Partners AG
Csfb Private Equity Advisers
Defi gestion SA
Dlj Merchant Banking Partners
ENR Russia Invest SA
EQT Funds Management Ltd
Equistone Partners Europe Ltd
Euro Private Equity SA
FIDES Business Partner AG
Fischer Buchschacher Gruppe AG
Fortress Investment Group LLC
Galena Asset Management Ltd
Gilde Buy Out Partners BV
Gilde Investment Management BV
Good Energies AG
Henderson Global Investors Ltd
Herculis Partners SA
Horizon21 AG
ICS Partners GmbH
IPS Industrial Promotion Services Ltd
Investindustrial Services Ltd
Invision AG
Jefferies Group LLC
Kharis Capital Advisory AG
LYRIQUE Srrl
La Financiere Patrimoniale d'Investissement SAS
Lydian Capital Advisors SA
Massena Partners SA
Mercer Private Markets AG
Merifin Capital
Monitor Clipper Partners LLC
Mountain Cleantech AG
Mountain Partners AG
Mueller Moehl Group
Napier Park Global Capital (US) LP
Neuberger Berman LLC
Occident Group AG
Odlander Fredrikson & Co AB
Orlando Management AG
Pala Investments
Partners Group Holding AG
PineBridge Investments LLC
Piper Jaffray Ventures Inc
Portfolio Advisors, LLC
Private Equity Invest AG
Procuritas Partners Kb
Quadia SA
Quilvest Private Equity SCA SICAR
Rive Private Investment Switzerland SA

2406

RobeCo Private Equity
SAM Private Equity AG
Schroders PLC
Sectoral Asset Management Inc
Springwater Capital LLC
Swicorp Capital Partners SA
Tembusu Partners Pte Ltd
Tocqueville Finance SA
Ufenau Capital Partners AG
Ventizz Capital Partners Advisory AG
Vinci Capital Switzerland SA
Zurmont Madison Management AG

Buyout Firms—Taiwan
Alliance Mangement Consulting Co Ltd (Taiwan Branch)
CAS Capital Inc
Cappello Capital Corp
Crimson Investments Ltd
Csfb Private Equity Advisers
Goldman Sachs & Co LLC
H&Q Asia Pacific, Ltd.
Japan Asia Investment Co Ltd
Leon Capital
PineBridge Investments LLC
STIC Investment Inc
Schroders PLC
Vertex Venture Holdings Ltd.

Buyout Firms—Tajikistan
European Bank for Reconstruction and Development

Buyout Firms—Tanzania
Surya Capital Management LLP

Buyout Firms—Thailand
CVC Capital Partners Ltd
Cimb Private Equity Sdn Bhd
Goldman Sachs & Co LLC
Japan Asia Investment Co Ltd
Lakeshore Capital Partners Co Ltd
Lombard Investments Inc
Mekong Capital Ltd

Buyout Firms—Togo
Cauris Management

Buyout Firms—Tunisia
ACG Management SA
Africinvest Tunisia SARL
Credit Agricole Corporate and Investment Bank SA
Emerging Capital Partners
Fidelium Finance
Societe d Investissement A Capital Risque du Groupe STB
Swicorp Capital Partners SA

Buyout Firms—Turkey
Abraaj Capital Ltd
Adm Capital
Advent International Corp
Alantra
Alter Danismanlik Hizmetleri Ticaret AS
Berggruen Holdings Inc
Black River Asset Management LLC
Bosphera Advisory, Ltd.
Bravia Capital Partners Inc

Bridgepoint Advisers II Ltd
Bridgepoint Advisers Ltd
Carlyle Group LP
Darby Overseas Investments, Ltd.
Egeli & Co Tarim Girisim Sermayesi Yatirim Ortakligi AS
Esas Holding AS
European Bank for Reconstruction and Development
Gedik Girisim Sermayesi Yatirim Ortakligi AS
International Finance Corp
Is Girisim Sermayesi Yatirim Ortakligi AS
Istanbul Investment Group
Mediterra Capital Management Ltd
Mid Europa Partners LLP
NBGI Private Equity Ltd
NBK Capital Partners Ltd
Pera Capital Partners Advisory Ltd
Rhea Girisim Sermayesi Yatirim Ortakligi AS
Stratejik Yonetim Hizmetleri AS
Taxim Capital Private Equity
Turk Venture Partners Ltd
Verusa Holding AS
Verusaturk Girisim Sermayesi Yatirim Ortakligi AS

Buyout Firms—Turkmenistan
European Bank for Reconstruction and Development

Buyout Firms—Uganda
African Alliance Private Equity

Buyout Firms—Ukraine
Adm Capital
Advent International Corp
Concorde Capital TOV
Csfb Private Equity Advisers
East Capital Private Equity AB
Horizon Capital Management
IK Ineko PAT
P&S Capital doo
Troika Capital Partners Ltd
VTB Kapital AO

Buyout Firms—United Kingdom
AAC CAPITAL PARTNERS
AEA Investors LLC
AG BD LLC
AGDEVCO UK
AMP Capital Investors Ltd
Abbey Road Venture Ltd
Abraaj Capital Ltd
Accel-KKR
Actis LLP
Active Private Equity
Adfisco
Adm Capital
Advantage Capital
Advent International Corp
African Frontier Capital Partners LLP
Agilitas Partners LLP
Alantra
Alberta Investment Management Corp
Alchemy Partners LLP
Alcuin Capital Partners LLP
Aleph Capital Partners LLP
Aletheia Partners Ltd
Alliance Fund Managers Ltd

Allstate Private Equity
Alpina Capital Partners LLP
Altitude Partners LLP
Amery Capital
Amundi Private Equity Funds SA
Amvensys Capital Group LLC
AnaCap Financial Partners Llp
Apax Partners LLP
Apis Partners LLP
Apollo Global Management LLC
Apposite Capital LLP
Arcapita Inc
Archangel Informal Investment Ltd
Ardian France SA
Ares Management LLC
Argan Capital
Argus Capital Ltd
Arix Bioscience PLC
Ariya Capital Group Ltd
Arle Heritage LLP
Ashmore Investment Management Ltd
Atami Capital
Atlantic-Pacific Capital Inc
August Equity Llp
Avista Capital Holdings LP
Azini Capital Partners LLP
BC Partners LLP
Bain Capital Inc
Banco Nacional de Desenvolvimento Economico e Social BNDES
Bancroft Group Ltd
Banque Pictet & Cie SA
Barclays Ventures Ltd
Bayou Steel Corp
Beaubridge Ltd
Beechbrook Capital LLP
Better Capital LLP
Black River Asset Management LLC
Black Toro Capital LLP
Bluegem Capital Partners LLP
Bowmark Capital LLP
Bregal Capital LLP
Bregal Investments LLP
Bridgepoint Advisers II Ltd
Bridgepoint Advisers Ltd
Bridges Fund Management Ltd
Broadlake Capital Ltd
Brown Brothers Harriman & Co
Business Growth Fund PLC
CAMCO Private Equity Group
CBPE Capital LLP
CCMP Capital Advisors LP
CVC Asia Pacific Ltd
CVC Capital Partners Ltd
Cabot Square Capital Advisors Ltd
Cairngorm Capital Ltd
Canada Pension Plan Investment Board
Candover Investments PLC
CapMan Oyj
Capital Dynamics Sdn Bhd
Capital International Inc
Capvest Ltd
Capvis Equity Partners AG
CarVal Investors LLC
Carlyle Group LP

2407

Pratt's Guide to Private Equity & Venture Capital Sources

Catapult Venture Managers Ltd
Centerbridge Partners LP
Centerview Partners LLC
Cevian Capital AB
Change Capital Partners LLP
Charterhouse Capital Partners LLP
Chiltern Capital LLP
China International Capital Corp Ltd
Cimb Private Equity Sdn Bhd
Cinven Group Ltd
Circularity Capital LLP
Citigroup Private Equity LP
Clearbrook Capital Partners LLP
Climate Change Capital Ltd
Cohen & Company Financial Ltd
Columna Capital LLP
Committed Capital, Ltd.
Compass Investment Management Ltd
Compass Partners International LLC
Compass Partners International Llp
Connection Capital LLP
Consensus Capital Private Equity Ltd
Consilla Partners Ltd
Continental Capital Markets Ltd
Core Capital Partners LLP
Corpacq Ltd
Corstone Corp
Cowen Capital Partners LLC
Credit Agricole Corporate and Investment Bank SA
Crescent Capital NI Ltd
Csfb Private Equity Advisers
D E Shaw & Co LP
Da Vinci Capital Management Ltd
Darwin Private Equity LLP
Defoe Partners & Co
Development Bank of Wales Public Ltd Co
Development Partners International LLP
Dlj Merchant Banking Partners
Doughty Hanson and Co.
Dubai International Capital LLC
Dubai Investment Group
Duet Capital Ltd
Duke Street Capital Ltd
Dunedin Capital Partners Ltd
8 Miles LLP
E I Capital LLP
ECI Partners LLP
EME Capital LLP
EMF Capital Partners Ltd
EMK Capital Partners LP
EQT Funds Management Ltd
EVI Capital Partners LLP
Earth Capital Partners LLP
Elaghmore Partners Ltd
Electra Private Equity Plc
Elysian Capital LLP
Emerisque Brands UK Ltd
Endless LLP
Ennismore Capital
Epi-V LLP
Epiris LLP
Equistone Partners Europe Ltd
Esas Holding AS
European Bank for Reconstruction and Development
European Capital

European Capital Financial Services Ltd
Evercore Inc
Exponent Private Equity LLP
4BIO Ventures Management Ltd
54 Capital Ltd
F&C Equity Partners PLC
Fiera Capital (UK) Ltd
Finance Yorkshire Ltd
Foresight Group LLP
Fortress Investment Group LLC
Foursan Group
Fpe Capital LLP
Francisco Partners LP
Future Capital Partners Ltd
G Square Healthcare Private Equity Fund LLP
GCP Member Ltd
GHO Capital Partners LLP
GI Partners
GMT Communications Partners LLP
Galena Asset Management Ltd
Gic Special Investments Pte Ltd
Gimv Investeringsmaatschappij Voor Vlanderen NV
Global Capital Finance
Global Emerging Markets
Global Private Equity PLC
Goldman Sachs & Co LLC
Good Energies AG
Gores Group LLC
Gramercy Inc
Graphite Capital Management LLP
Greenhill Capital Partners LP
Gresham Llp
Grovepoint Capital LLP
Gruss Asset Management LP
H2 Equity Partners BV
HIG Capital LLC
Harbert Management Corp
HarbourVest Partners LLC
Harwood Capital LLP
Hastings Private Equity Fund IIA Pty Ltd
Hattington Investment Partners LLP
Havenvest Private Equity Middle East Ltd
Headway Capital Partners LLP
Helios Investment Partners LLP
Hellman & Friedman LLC
Henderson Global Investors Ltd
Hermes Growth Partners Ltd
HgCapital Trust PLC
Highland Capital Management LP
Highland Capital Partners (UK), LLP
Houlihan Lokey Inc
Hsbc Private Equity Investments (Uk) Ltd
IBID Holdings Ltd
IK Investment Partners Ltd
IPS Industrial Promotion Services Ltd
Ic2 Capital
InVenture Partners
Inflexion PLC
Invesco Private Capital Inc
Invesco Real Estate, Ltd.
Investcorp Technology Investments Group
Investec Private Equity
Investec Ventures Ireland Ltd
Investindustrial Services Ltd
Invex Capital Llp

Invus Group LLC
JC Flowers & Co LLC
JFLehman & Co
JPMorgan Chase & Co
JRJ Ventures LLP
JZ Capital Partners Ltd
JZ International Ltd
Jefferies Group LLC
KARTESIA ADVISOR LLP
Kennet Partners Ltd
Key Capital Partners
Kings Park Capital LLP
Kingsley Capital Partners LLP
Kingsway Capital LLP
L-Gam Advisers LLP
LGV Capital Ltd
Langholm Capital LLP
Levine Leichtman Capital Partners Inc
Li & Fung Investments
Limerston Capital LLP
Lion Capital LLP
Lion's Head Global Partners LLP
Lloyds Development Capital (Holdings) Ltd
Lonsdale Capital Partners LLP
Lyceum Capital
M/C Venture Partners LLC
MML Capital Partners LLP
MSD Capital LP
Macquarie Infrastructure and Real Assets (Europe) Ltd
Manzanita Capital Ltd
Marlin Equity Partners LLC
Marwyn Investment Management LLP
Maven Capital Partners UK LLP
Mayfair Equity Partners LLP
Mediterra Capital Management Ltd
Mercia Fund Managers
Merseyside Special Investment Fund Ltd
Metric Capital Partners LLP
Mid Europa Partners LLP
Mid-Ocean Partners LP
Milbank Tweed Hadley & Mccloy LLP
Milestone Capital Partners Ltd
Millhouse Inc PLC
Miroma Ventures Ltd
Mobeus Equity Partners LLP
Monarch Alternative Capital LP
Montagu Private Equity LLP
Morgan Stanley Private Equity
Morrison & Foerster LLP
Motion Equity Partners LLP
Mount Kellett Capital Hong Kong Ltd
Mvi Support SA
NBGI Private Equity Ltd
NIBC Principal Investments BV
NVM Pe Ltd
NVM Private Equity LLP
Naxos Capital Partners
Neo Capital LLP
Neo Investment Partners LLP
Neuberger Berman LLC
New World Private Equity Partners LLP
Newable Investments Ltd
Next Wave Partners LLP
NextEnergy Capital Ltd

2408

Nordic Capital
NorthEdge Capital LLP
Northill Capital LLP
Northleaf Capital Partners Ltd
Northwestern Mutual Capital LLC
Nova Capital Management, Ltd.
Novator Partners LLP
17 Capital LLP
OMERS Private Equity Inc
Oak Hill Advisors LP
Oakfield Capital Partners LLP
Oakley Capital Ltd
Oaktree Capital Management LP
Oceanbridge Partners LLC
Och-Ziff Capital Management Group LLC
Octopus Ventures Ltd
Old Mutual PLC
Ombu Ltd
Omidyar Network Commons LLC
One Peak Partners LLP
Onex Corp
Ontario Teachers' Pension Plan
OpCapita LLP
Origami Capital Partners, LLC
P Schoenfeld Asset Management LP
P&S Capital doo
PAI Partners SAS
PHD Equity Partners LLP
Pacific Investments Management Ltd
Palamon Capital Partners LP
Palatine Private Equity LLP
Pamplona Capital Management LLP
Panoramic Growth Equity (Fund Management) LLP
Partners Capital Investment Group Holdings LLC
Partners Group Holding AG
Pembroke VCT PLC
Peninsula Capital Advisors LLP
Penta Capital Llp
Perella Weinberg Partners LP
Permira Advisers LLP
Perwyn LLLP
Phoenix Equity Partners Ltd
PineBridge Investments LLC
Pioneer Point Partners LLP
Piper Jaffray Ventures Inc
Piper PE LLP
Platina Finance, Ltd.
Platinum Equity LLC
Portchester Equity Ltd
Praesidian Capital
Pricoa Capital Group Ltd
Primary Capital Ltd
Privet Capital LLP
Providence Equity Partners LLC
Queensland BioCapital Funds Ld Pty
Quilvest Private Equity SCA SICAR
RJD Partners Ltd
Rcapital Ltd
Rcf Management LLC
Redcliffe Capital
Revolution Capital Group LLC
Rhone Capital LLC
Richmond Park Partners LLP
Risk Capital Partners Ltd
RiverRock European Capital Partners LLP

RobeCo Private Equity
Rockpool Investments LLP
RooGreen Ventures LLP
Root Capital LLP
Rutland Partners LLP
SB Capital Partners Ltd
SF Holding Corp
Saints Ventures
Samena Capital Management LLP
Samos Investments Advisory Ltd
Sandbox & Co Ltd
Saphir Capital Partners SA
Schroders PLC
Sea Equity Ltd
Searchlight Capital Partners LLC
Seneca Partners Ltd
Silk Invest Ltd
Silver Lake Partners LP
Silverfleet Capital Partners LLP
Smedvig Capital Ltd
Solstra Capital Partners A/S
Southport Lane Management LLC
Sovereign Capital Ltd
Spire Ventures, Ltd.
Spirit Capital Partners Llp
Stage Capital LLP
Stanhope Capital LLP
Star Capital Partners Ltd
Starr International Company Inc
StepStone Group LP
Stirling Square Capital Partners Lp
Strategic Value Partners LLC
Sun Capital Partners Inc
Surya Capital Management LLP
Synova Capital LLP
Syntegra Capital Investors Ltd
21 Investimenti SGR SpA
3i
3i Group PLC
TA Associates Management LP
TDR Capital LLP
TIANGUIS LTD
Tau Capital Ltd
Tembo Capital LLP
Tenzing Pe Ltd
Terra Firma Capital Partners Ltd
Three Hills Capital Partners LLP
Tillridge Global Agribusiness Partners
Toscafund Asset Management LLP
Towerbrook Capital Partners LP
Trevi Health Ventures LP
Trilantic Capital Management LP
Triton Beteiligungsberatung GmbH
Troika Capital Partners Ltd

Buyout Firms—United Kingdom
Two Sigma Investments LP
Ultimate Sports Group PLC
Undisclosed Firm
VTB Kapital AO
Valco Capital Partners Partnership Ltd
Varde Partners Inc
Vardy Property Group
Vespa Capital LLP
Vision Capital LLP

Vitruvian Partners LLP
Volpi Capital LLP
Warburg Pincus LLC
WestBridge Fund Managers Ltd
White Cloud Capital Advisors Ltd
Wilshire Private Markets
Winchester Capital Partners LLC
Wolfensohn & Company LLC
Xio (UK) LLP
Yellow Brick Capital Advisers (UK) Ltd
York Capital Management LP
Z Investments LLP
Zephyr Management LP

Buyout Firms—Uruguay
Banco Nacional de Desenvolvimento Economico e Social BNDES
Credit Agricole Corporate and Investment Bank SA
Quilvest Private Equity SCA SICAR
Trilantic Capital Management LP

Buyout Firms—Utd. Arab Em.
AIP Private Capital
Abraaj Capital Ltd
Abu Dhabi Financial Group LLC
Abu Dhabi Investment Authority
Algebra Capital Ltd
Auvest Markets FZ LLC
Banque Pictet & Cie SA
Capital Investment LLC
Carlyle Group LP
Crescent Enterprises
Csfb Private Equity Advisers
DP World Ltd
Delta Partners FZ LLC
Dubai International Capital LLC
Dubai Investment Group
EFG Hermes Holdings SAE
EME Capital LLP
Evolvence Capital Ltd
First Abu Dhabi Bank PJSC
GFH Capital Ltd
Global Investment House KSCC
Goldman Sachs & Co LLC
Gulf Capital Pvt JSC
Gulf Islamic Investments LLC
Havenvest Private Equity Middle East Ltd
Infra Capital Investments PJSC
Iris Capital Management SAS
Jefferies Group LLC
KKR & Co LP
Levant Investment Management Ltd
Mizuho Gulf Capital Partners Ltd
Mobeus Equity Partners LLP
Mubadala Infrastructure Partners Ltd
Myrisoph Capital
NBK Capital Partners Ltd
NCB Capital DIFC Ltd
Napier Park Global Capital (US) LP
Nbd Sana Capital Ltd
New Silk Route Partners, LLC
Partners Group Holding AG
Perella Weinberg Partners LP
Quilvest Private Equity SCA SICAR
SEDCO Holding
Samena Capital Management LLP

Schroders PLC
Silk Invest Ltd
Starling International Management Ltd (Dubai Branch)
Swicorp Capital Partners SA
VTB Kapital AO
Vis Mundi Ltd
Waha Capital PJSC

Buyout Firms—Uzbekistan
European Bank for Reconstruction and Development

Buyout Firms—Venezuela
Credit Agricole Corporate and Investment Bank SA

Buyout Firms—Vietnam
Daiwa Corporate Investment Co Ltd
Japan Asia Investment Co Ltd
Mekong Capital Ltd
STIC Investment Inc
Temasek Holdings (Private) Ltd
Vietnam Pioneer Partners
Vinacapital Investment Management Ltd

Buyout Firms—Yemen
Global Investment House KSCC

Buyout Firms—Zambia
African Alliance Private Equity
China-Africa Development Fund

Buyout Firms—Zimbabwe
Batanai Capital Finance Pvt Ltd
Takura Capital

Fund of Funds—Argentina
Morgan Stanley Alternative Investment Partners LP

Fund of Funds—Australia
AXA Investment Managers Inc
Committed Advisors SAS
Continuity Capital
FRANK RUSSELL CAPITAL CO
IFM Investors Pty Ltd
Jolimont Capital Pty Ltd
Morgan Stanley Alternative Investment Partners LP
ROC Capital Pty Ltd
Stafford Timberland Ltd

Fund of Funds—Austria
AXA Investment Managers Inc

Fund of Funds—Belgium
AXA Investment Managers Inc
Access Capital Partners SA
Arkimedes Management NV
European Investment Fund
O'Melveny & Myers LLP

Fund of Funds—Brazil
57 Stars LLC
Hamilton Lane Advisors LLC
Morgan Stanley Alternative Investment Partners LP
Ocroma Investimentos E Gestao Ltda

Fund of Funds—Canada
Alberta Enterprise Corp
Balmoral Wood Litigation Finance
FIER Partners LP

FRANK RUSSELL CAPITAL CO
Kirchner Private Capital Group
Morgan Stanley Alternative Investment Partners LP
Ontario Venture Capital Fund Inc
Sarona Asset Management Inc
Teralys Capital Inc

Fund of Funds—Channel Islands
NB Private Equity Partners Ltd
Unigestion Holding SA

Fund of Funds—Chile
Altamar Private Equity SGIIC SAU
Lexington Partners Inc

Fund of Funds—China
AXA Investment Managers Inc
Adveq Management AG
Asia Alternatives Management LLC
Beijing Flourish Libra Venture Capital Co Ltd
Beijing Kaifu Shengshi Investment Management Co Ltd
Beijing Shengshi Hongming Investment Fund Management Co Ltd
Beijing Tengye Venture Capital Management Co Ltd
CDC Group PLC
CNSTONE
Capvent AG
China Venture Capital Research Institute Ltd
EMAlternatives LLC
Gopher Asset Management Co Ltd
Hanking International Co Ltd
Horsley Bridge Partners LLC
hanghai SmallVille Financial Advisor Co Ltd
Jade Investment Consulting (Shanghai) Co Ltd
Jilin Venture Capital Fund of Funds Management Co Ltd
Magic Stone Alternative Investment Co Ltd
Morgan Creek Capital Management LLC
Morgan Stanley Alternative Investment Partners LP
O'Melveny & Myers LLP
Purple Horse Fund
Qianhai Fund of Funds Equity Investment Shenzhen Co Ltd
Shenzhen Jin sheng Shuo Industry Asset Management Co., Ltd.
Stone Drum Capital Ltd
YiMei Capital Management
YuanAngel
Zhejiang Venture Capital Group Co Ltd
Zhongguancun VC Development Co

Fund of Funds—Denmark
ATP Private Equity Partners
Danske Private Equity A/S

Fund of Funds—Egypt
Amundi Private Equity Funds SA

Fund of Funds—Finland
eQ Oyj
Veraventure Oy

Fund of Funds—France
AXA Investment Managers Inc
Access Capital Partners SA
Acg Private Equity SA

Amundi Private Equity Funds SA
Arcis Finance SA
Bex Capital SAS
Committed Advisors SAS
FRANK RUSSELL CAPITAL CO
Gimar Capital Investissement SCA
Morgan Stanley Alternative Investment Partners LP
Unigestion Holding SA

Fund of Funds—Germany
AXA Investment Managers Inc
Access Capital Partners SA
Acg Private Equity SA
Adveq Management AG
Astorius Capital GmbH
Bvt Holding GmbH & Co KG
DB Private Equity GmbH
equitrust AG
57 Stars LLC
F&C Asset Management PLC
Generali Private Equity Investments GmbH
Golding Capital Partners GmbH
HCI Private Equity GmbH
IFM Investors Pty Ltd
Morgan Stanley Alternative Investment Partners LP
Sobera Capital GmbH
Sonanz GmbH
Swift Capital Partners GmbH
WP Global Partners Inc
Wealthcap Initiatoren GmbH

Fund of Funds—Greece
Acg Private Equity SA
New Economy Development Fund SA

Fund of Funds—Hong Kong
AXA Investment Managers Inc
Asia Alternatives Management LLC
China Venture Capital Research Institute Ltd
Coller Capital Ltd
Continuity Capital
Emerald Hill Capital Partners Ltd
F&C Asset Management PLC
FGF Management Ltd
FLAG Capital Management LLC
Hamilton Lane Advisors LLC
Ichigo Inc
Lexington Partners Inc
Morgan Stanley Alternative Investment Partners LP
NewQuest Capital Advisors HK Ltd
Northgate Capital LLC
O'Melveny & Myers LLP
Pantheon Ventures (UK) LLP
TR Advisors Ltd

Fund of Funds—Hungary
Morgan Stanley Alternative Investment Partners LP

Fund of Funds—India
AXA Investment Managers Inc
Capvent AG
Morgan Stanley Alternative Investment Partners LP
Northgate Capital LLC

Fund of Funds—Indonesia
Morgan Stanley Alternative Investment Partners LP
O'Melveny & Myers LLP

Fund of Funds—Ireland
F&C Asset Management PLC
Morgan Stanley Alternative Investment Partners LP

Fund of Funds—Israel
Hamilton Lane Advisors LLC
Israel Secondary Ltd
Morgan Stanley Alternative Investment Partners LP
Vintage Venture Partners Iv (Cayman) LP

Fund of Funds—Italy
AXA Investment Managers Inc
Acg Private Equity SA
Advanced Capital SGR SpA
Morgan Stanley Alternative Investment Partners LP

Fund of Funds—Japan
AXA Investment Managers Inc
Alternative Investment Capital Ltd
FRANK RUSSELL CAPITAL CO
Hamilton Lane Advisors LLC
IFM Investors Pty Ltd
Ichigo Inc
Morgan Stanley Alternative Investment Partners LP
O'Melveny & Myers LLP

Fund of Funds—Luxembourg
AXA Investment Managers Inc
Advanced Capital SGR SpA
European Investment Bank
European Investment Fund
Generali Private Equity Investments GmbH
Golding Capital Partners GmbH

Fund of Funds—Malaysia
Morgan Stanley Alternative Investment Partners LP

Fund of Funds—Mauritius
South Suez Capital Ltd

Fund of Funds—Mexico
Fondo de Fondos
Morgan Stanley Alternative Investment Partners LP
Northgate Capital LLC

Fund of Funds—Morocco
Amundi Private Equity Funds SA

Fund of Funds—Netherlands
AXA Investment Managers Inc
EMAlternatives LLC
Morgan Stanley Alternative Investment Partners LP

Fund of Funds—New Zealand
FRANK RUSSELL CAPITAL CO
New Zealand Venture Investment Fund, Ltd.

Fund of Funds—Norway
Anchor Capital Management Ltd

Fund of Funds—Philippines
Morgan Stanley Alternative Investment Partners LP

Fund of Funds—Poland
Amundi Private Equity Funds SA

Fund of Funds—Portugal
AXA Investment Managers Inc
F&C Asset Management PLC

Fund of Funds—Qatar
AXA Investment Managers Inc

Fund of Funds—Romania
Amundi Private Equity Funds SA

Fund of Funds—Russia
Morgan Stanley Alternative Investment Partners LP
Rossiyskaya venchurnaya kompaniya OAO

Fund of Funds—Saudi Arabia
Morgan Stanley Alternative Investment Partners LP

Fund of Funds—Singapore
Axiom Asia Private Capital Pte Ltd
CDC Group PLC
DB Private Equity GmbH
57 Stars LLC
FRANK RUSSELL CAPITAL CO
Hermes Gpe Llp
IDFC Capital (Singapore) Pte Ltd
Morgan Creek Capital Management LLC
Morgan Stanley Alternative Investment Partners LP
O'Melveny & Myers LLP
Pavilion Alternatives Group Ltd
Unigestion Holding SA

Fund of Funds—South Africa
Morgan Stanley Alternative Investment Partners LP
Sango Capital Management
Vunani Private Equity Partners Pty. Ltd.

Fund of Funds—South Korea
CAMBRIDGE CAPITAL PARTNERS L L C
K2 Investment Partners LLC
Morgan Stanley Alternative Investment Partners LP

Fund of Funds—Spain
AXA Investment Managers Inc
Acg Private Equity SA
Altamar Private Equity SGIIC SAU
European Investment Fund
Galdana Ventures
Morgan Stanley Alternative Investment Partners LP

Fund of Funds—Sweden
Anchor Capital Management Ltd
Coeli Private Equity Management AB
Morgan Stanley Alternative Investment Partners LP
Seb Invest GmbH
Sixth Swedish National Pension

Fund of Funds—Switzerland
AXA Investment Managers Inc
Acg Private Equity SA
Advanced Capital SGR SpA
Adveq Management AG
BlackRock Private Equity Partners AG
Capvent AG
Clearsight Investments AG
Matador Private Equity AG
Montana Capital Partners AG
Morgan Stanley Alternative Investment Partners LP
Rising Star AG
SIFEM AG
Shape Capital Ag In Liquidation
Spice Private Equity AG
Unigestion Holding SA

Union Bancaire Privee Private Equity
Vianova Capital LLP

Fund of Funds—Taiwan
Morgan Stanley Alternative Investment Partners LP

Fund of Funds—Thailand
Morgan Stanley Alternative Investment Partners LP

Fund of Funds—Tunisia
Amundi Private Equity Funds SA

Fund of Funds—United Kingdom
AXA Investment Managers Inc
Abbott Capital Management LLC
Access Capital Partners SA
Acg Private Equity SA
Advanced Capital SGR SpA
Adveq Management AG
Anchor Capital Management Ltd
Arcis Finance SA
Bramdean Asset Management LLP
CDC Group PLC
Capital for Enterprise Ltd
Coller Capital Ltd
Commonfund Capital Inc
Crystal Partners & Company LLP
DB Private Equity GmbH
Draper Esprit Secondaries LLP
F&C Asset Management PLC
FGF Management Ltd
FRANK RUSSELL CAPITAL CO
Hermes Gpe Llp
Hollyport Capital Capital LLP
IFM Investors Pty Ltd
Innisfree Group Ltd
Isomer Capital LLP
Keyhaven Capital Partners Ltd
Landmark Partners Inc
Lexington Partners Inc
Mbuyu Capital Partners Ltd
Mithras Capital Partners LLP
Morgan Stanley Alternative Investment Partners LP
Newglobe Capital Partners LLP
Northgate Capital LLC
O'Melveny & Myers LLP
Orthogonal Partners LLP
Pantheon Ventures (UK) LLP
Pavilion Alternatives Group Ltd
Private Advisors LLC
Seligman Private Equity Select LLP
Sl Capital Partners Llp
Stafford Timberland Ltd
Unigestion Holding SA
Union Bancaire Privee Private Equity
Vencap International PLC
Vianova Capital LLP

Fund of Funds—Utd. Arab Em.
Abu Dhabi Capital Management LLC
Jade Investment Consulting (Shanghai) Co Ltd
Morgan Stanley Alternative Investment Partners LP
Union Bancaire Privee Private Equity

Fund of Funds—Vietnam
Morgan Stanley Alternative Investment Partners LP

2411

Pratt's Guide to Private Equity & Venture Capital Sources

Mezzanine Firms—Australia
Intermediate Capital Group PLC

Mezzanine Firms—Austria
IKIB Mittelstandsfinanzierungs GmbH
Mezzanine Management Finanz und Unternehmensberatung gmbH
Syntaxis Capital Unternehmens und Finanzierungsberatung GmbH

Mezzanine Firms—Belgium
SBI - BMI

Mezzanine Firms—Canada
BMO Capital Corp
Crown Capital Partners Inc
FirePower Capital Corp
First West Capital
Global Capital Partners
Mckenna Gale Capital Inc
Penfund Partners Inc
Vancity Capital Corp
Wellington Financial Lp

Mezzanine Firms—Denmark
Kirk & Thorsen Invest A/S

Mezzanine Firms—Estonia
BPM Capital OU
Hanseatic Capital As

Mezzanine Firms—France
Cm Cic Mezzanine Sas
Euromezzanine Gestion SaS
Garibaldi Mezzo SAS
Ife Mezzanine SARL
Indigo Capital LLP
Indigo Capital SAS
Intermediate Capital Group PLC

Mezzanine Firms—Germany
BE Beteiligungen GmbH & Co KG
CBG Commerz Beteiligungskapital GmbH & Co KG
Intermediate Capital Group PLC
Mittelstaendische Beteiligungsgesellschaft Niedersachsen mbH
Rartum Capital Management GmbH

Mezzanine Firms—Honduras
Latin American Partners LLC

Mezzanine Firms—Hong Kong
Asia Mezzanine Capital Advisers Ltd
Barclays Capital Inc
Intermediate Capital Group PLC

Mezzanine Firms—Hungary
Mezzanine Management Finanz und Unternehmensberatungsgmbh

Mezzanine Firms—India
Banyantree Finance Pvt Ltd
Waygate Capital India Pvt Ltd

Mezzanine Firms—Italy
Mezzanove Capital I
Prudential Capital Group LP

Mezzanine Firms—Japan
Mezzanine Corp

Mezzanine Firms—Lebanon
Capital Trust Ltd

Mezzanine Firms—Luxembourg
Park Square Capital LLP

Mezzanine Firms—Mexico
Capital Indigo
Latin American Partners LLC

Mezzanine Firms—Netherlands
Intermediate Capital Group PLC

Mezzanine Firms—Philippines
Argosy Partners, Inc.

Mezzanine Firms—Poland
Hanseatic Capital As
Mezzanine Management Finanz und Unternehmensberatungsgmbh

Mezzanine Firms—Qatar
Qatari Fortis Investment Management

Mezzanine Firms—Romania
Mezzanine Management Finanz und Unternehmensberatungsgmbh

Mezzanine Firms—South Africa
Makalani Holdings Ltd
Mezzanine Partners (Pty) Ltd

Mezzanine Firms—South Korea
Dream Venture Investment Co Ltd

Mezzanine Firms—Spain
Intermediate Capital Group PLC
Oquendo Capital SL

Mezzanine Firms—Sweden
Intermediate Capital Group PLC

Mezzanine Firms—Switzerland
KMU Capital AG

Mezzanine Firms—Ukraine
Mezzanine Management Finanz und Unternehmensberatungsgmbh

Mezzanine Firms—United Kingdom
Barings (UK) Ltd
Capital Trust Ltd
Gemcorp Capital LLP
Hutton Collins Partners LLP
Indigo Capital LLP
Intermediate Capital Group PLC
Palio Capital Partners LLP
Park Square Capital LLP
Permira Debt Managers Ltd
Simmons & Company International

OPE—Australia
Equity Partners
Sentient Group Ltd

OPE—Canada
ACM Ltd
Arc Financial Corp.
FirstEnergy Capital Corp
Lex Capital Management Inc
OMERS Infrastructure
SCF Partners LP
Sentient Group Ltd

OPE—Cayman Islands
Sentient Group Ltd

OPE—China
Hudson Clean Energy Partners

OPE—France
4D Global Energy Advisors SAS

OPE—Hong Kong
First Reserve Corp

OPE—India
Power Finance Corporation Ltd

OPE—Luxembourg
ArcLight Capital Holdings LLC

OPE—Mexico
Riverstone Holdings LLC

OPE—Norway
Energy Ventures AS
Hitecvision AS

OPE—Spain
ArcLight Capital Holdings LLC

OPE—United Kingdom
Braemar Energy Ventures LP
Energy Ventures AS
First Reserve Corp
Global Infrastructure Holdings
Hudson Clean Energy Partners
Lime Rock Partners LLC
Riverstone Holdings LLC
SCF Partners LP

OPE—Utd. Arab Em.
Lime Rock Partners LLC

REAL—Belgium
Lone Star Fund Ltd

REAL—Bermuda
Lone Star Fund Ltd

REAL—Brazil
Starwood Capital Group I LP

REAL—Canada
Lone Star Fund Ltd

REAL—China
Colony Capital LLC

REAL—France
Colony Capital LLC
Lone Star Fund Ltd

REAL—Germany
Lone Star Fund Ltd

REAL—India
ArthVeda Fund Management Pvt Ltd
Ask Property Investment Advisors Pvt Ltd
HDFC Venture Capital Ltd
Starwood Capital Group I LP

REAL—Ireland
Lone Star Fund Ltd

REAL—Italy
Colony Capital LLC
Patron Capital Advisers LLP

REAL—Japan
Lone Star Fund Ltd
Prologis Inc
Starwood Capital Group I LP

REAL—Lebanon
Colony Capital LLC

REAL—Luxembourg
Lone Star Fund Ltd
Patron Capital Advisers LLP
Starwood Capital Group I LP

REAL—South Korea
Colony Capital LLC

REAL—Spain
Colony Capital LLC
Patron Capital Advisers LLP

REAL—Taiwan
Colony Capital LLC

REAL—United Kingdom
ArthVeda Fund Management Pvt Ltd
Colony Capital LLC
Moorfield Group Ltd
Patron Capital Advisers LLP
Starwood Capital Group I LP

REAL—Utd. Arab Em.
ArthVeda Fund Management Pvt Ltd
Ask Property Investment Advisors Pvt Ltd

Venture Firms—Albania
NCH Capital Inc

Venture Firms—Argentina
Aconcagua Ventures
Bisa
Litexco Mediterranea SURL
NXTP Labs SRL
Nazca Ventures
Quasar Builders

Venture Firms—Armenia
Granatus Ventures CJSC

Venture Firms—Australia
AI Investments & Resources Ltd
ANU Connect Ventures Pty Ltd
Accord Capital Investors Pty Ltd
African Lion Management Ltd
AirTree Ventures
Altezza Ventures
Amwin Management Pty Ltd

Artesian Capital Management Australia Pty Ltd
Bailador Investment Management Pty Ltd
Beacon New Ventures
BioScience Managers Pty Ltd
Blackbird Ventures
Brandon Capital Partners Pty Ltd
CMB Advisory Pty Ltd
Capital Technologies Pty Ltd
Carthona Capital FS Pty Ltd
Colonial First State Private Equity Pty, Ltd.
CtechBA Pty Ltd
Disruptive Capital Pty Ltd
Dominet Digital Corporation Pty Ltd
88 Green Ventures
Elcano Capital LP
Eli Lilly and Co
Ellerston Capital Ltd
Equity Venture Partners Pty Ltd
Exto Partners Pty Ltd
Falconer Bellomo & Co Ltd
First Quay Capital Pty Ltd
Follow Seed Australia Pty Ltd
GBS Venture Partners
Generation Investment Management LLP
Gledden Ventures
Grokventures Pty Ltd
H2 Ventures Pty Ltd
Imprimatur Capital Hldg Ltd
Innovation Capital Associates Pty, Ltd.
Investment Capital Partners Pty Ltd
incite Capital Management Pty Ltd
Kaz Capital Pty Ltd
Latitude Investments Pty Ltd
MH Carnegie & Co Pty Ltd
Macquarie Capital Alliance Management Pty Ltd
Mirin Capital Pty, Ltd.
muru-D
Nab Ventures
Oneventures Pty Ltd
Oxygen Ventures Ltd
Perle Ventures Pty Ltd
Proto Investment Partners Pty Ltd
Quartet Ventures
Rampersand
Raven Capital Pty Ltd
RedFire Investments Pty Ltd
Right Click Capital
River Capital Pty Ltd
SapienVentures LLP
Skandia Innovation AB
Southern Cross Venture Partners Pty Ltd
Southmore Capital Pty Ltd
Springstar GmbH
Sproutx Pty Ltd
St Baker Energy Innovation Fund
St George Bank Venture Capital
Starfish Ventures Pty Ltd
Sydney Seed Fund Management Pty Ltd
Talu Ventures Pty Ltd
Tarnagulla Ventures Pty Ltd
Technology Venture Partners Pty., Ltd.
Templeton Asset Management Ltd
Terra Rossa Capital Pty Ltd
Uniseed Management Pty Ltd
Venture Corporation of Australia Pty Ltd

Victoria Capital Pty Ltd
Vivant Ventures Pty Ltd
Wattle Hill Rhc Management Pty Ltd
Wilbow Group Pty Ltd
Yuuwa Capital LP

Venture Firms—Austria
ARAX Capital Partners GmbH
Advengys Advanced Energy Systems AG
Alps Venture Capital GmbH
Altair Capital Management GmbH
Austria Wirtschaftsservice GmbH
Corporate Finance Partners CFP Beratungs GmbH
Eli Lilly and Co
Eqventure GmbH
Fiedler Capital GmbH
GUB Unternehmensbeteiligungen GmbH & Co KGaA
Gcp Gamma Capital Partners Beratungs & Beteiligungs AG
Gruenderfonds GmbH Co KeG
INEO Beteiligungs GmbH
Initial Factor Speed Invest GmbH & Co KG
i5invest Beratungs GmbH
MINAS Beteiligungs- u. Management GmbH
OOE Hightechfonds GmbH
Oberoesterreichische Unternehmensbeteiligungs GmbH
Proregio Mittelstandsfinanzierungs AG
Salzburger Unternehmensbeteiligungs-gesellschaft mbH in Liqu
Schilling Unternehmensbeteiligung GmbH
Skandia Innovation AB
Tecnet Equity NOE Technologiebeteiligungs Invest GmbH
Venionaire Capital GmbH
WCW Venture Hldg GmbH
WKBG Wiener Kreditbuergschafts und Beteiligungsbank AG

Venture Firms—Bahamas
inventages venture capital GmbH

Venture Firms—Bahrain
Bahrain Development Bank BSCC
Islamic Development Bank
Stratum WLL
Venture Capital Bank BSCC

Venture Firms—Bangladesh
BD Venture Ltd
Catalyst Microfinance Investors

Venture Firms—Belgium
Airtek Capital Group SA
Allegro Investment Fund NV
Aqua Alta SA
Axe Investments NV
Banque Degroof Petercam SA
Big Bang Ventures CVA
Capital-E NV
Capricorn Venture Partners NV
Creafund Management NV
Droia NV
E Merge SA
EntwicklungsUnd Beteiligungsgesellschaft Ostbelgiens AG

2413

Pratt's Guide to Private Equity & Venture Capital Sources

Fund + NV
Gemma Frisius Fonds K.U.Leuven SA
Gevaert SA
Gogreen Capital SA
Igeo SPRL
Internet Attitude SCRL
Interuniversitair Micro-Electronica Centrum
Investsud SA
KfW
Korys Management NV
Lean Fund SA
NIVELINVEST SA
Namur Invest SA
Nausicaa Ventures SCA
Next World Capital LLC
Pamica NV
QiFund Partners NV
Sambrinvest SA
Seeder Fund SA
Si2 Fund CVBA
Smartfin Capital NV
Sniper Investments NV
Societe Regionale D'Investissement de Wallonie SA
Sopartec SA
Srib
Theodorus SCA
Triodos International Fund Management BV
Trustcapital Partners NV
V-Bio Ventures
Venturebaycom

Venture Firms—Bermuda
DreamLab Finance Ltd
Radiant Capital
Vostok Emerging Finance Ltd

Venture Firms—Bolivia
Small Enterprise Assistance Funds

Venture Firms—Brazil
A5 Internet Investments Ltd
Accion International
Ascet Investimentos Ltda
Astella Investimentos
Atomico Ventures
Austro Gestao de Recursos Ltda
BPE Investimentos
BTG Pactual Gestora De Investimentos Alternativos Ltda
Bessemer Venture Partners
Brasil Plural Gestao de Recursos Ltda
CVentures Participacoes S.A.
Confrapar Administracao e Gestao de Recursos SA
Copacabana House Ventures
DLM Invista Gestao de Recursos Ltda
Darien Business Development Corp
Dgf Investimentos Gestao De Fundos Ltda
Econergy International Corp
Evolution Partners Participacoes SA
e.ventures
eBricks Digital
FIR Capital Partners Gestao de Investimentos SA
Financiadora de Estudos e Projetos FINEP
Finaves I SA
Franklin Templeton Investimentos Brasil Ltda
Gera Venture Capital

Go4it Esportes e Entretenimento SA
HFPX Holding Ltda
I5 Empresas Consultoria e Participacoes Ltda
Imprimatur Capital Hldg Ltd
Inseed Investimentos Ltda
Invest Tech Participacoes E Investimentos Ltda
Investidor Profissional Gestao de Recursos Ltda
Itamby Participacao e Desenvolvimento Ltda
Itau Unibanco Holding SA
Monashees Gestao de Investimentos Ltda
Mountain do Brasil Participacoes Ltda
MultiCapital do Brasil Consultoria e Participacoes
Novabase Capital Sociedade de Capital de Risco SA
Novo Horizonte Investimentos e Consultoria Ltda
Orbe Investimentos e Participacoes Ltda
Performa Investimentos Ltda
Plataforma Capital Partners Gestao de Investimentos Ltda
Portbank Capital Gestora de Recursos SA
Porto Capital Gestora de Recursos SA
Promon Ventures(Promon)
Qualcomm Ventures
Redpoint Eventures Consultoria Empresarial Ltda
SP Ventures Gestora de Recursos SA
Sindicatum Carbon Capital Ltd
Spinnaker Capital Group
Springstar GmbH
Teak Ventures do Brazil SA
Trindade Consultoria e Investimentos Ltda
VC Participacoes Ltda
Valora Gestao de Investimentos Ltda

Venture Firms—Bulgaria
Bulgarian-American Enterprise Fund
ECM-Bulgarian Post-Privatisation Fund
Eleven Accelerator Venture Fund
Litexco Mediterranea SURL
NCH Capital Inc
New Europe Venture Equity
Small Enterprise Assistance Funds
Teres Capital OOD Sofia

Venture Firms—Burma
Delta Capital Myanmar

Venture Firms—Cambodia
Frontier Investment & Capital Advisors Pte Ltd

Venture Firms—Canada
Accelerator Centre
Alberta Rev Ppty Corp
Aligo Innovation Societe en Commandite
Allon Therapeutics Inc
Alphanorth Asset Management
Altura Mgmt Inc
Ansera Ventures Ltd
ArcTern Ventures
Argon Venture Partners
Athlone International Ltd
Atlantic Canada Opportunities Agency
Avrio Capital Management Corp
Axis Capital Corp
Azure Capital Partners, L.P.
BC Advantage Funds Ltd
Balmoral Partners Ltd
Bioenterprise Corp

Black Coral Capital LLC
BlackPoynt Brand Ventures
Block One Capital Inc
Blue Sky Capital Corp
Blueline Bioscience
Brightspark Ventures
British Columbia Investment Management Corp
British Columbia Ministry of Economic Development
Business Arts, Ltd.
Business Development Bank of Canada
Business Instincts Group
CDP Capital Inc
CORE Partners LLC
Camelot Capital Corp
Campbell Resources Inc
Campfire Capital
Canaccord Genuity Group Inc
Cannabis Growth Fund I LP
Cansbridge Capital Corp
Capital Benoit Inc
Cassels Brock & Blackwell LLP
Cedarpoint Investments Inc
Celtic House Venture Partners Inc
Cfi Capital
China Canada Angels Alliance Ltd
Chrysalix Energy
Cisco Systems Inc
Clarica Life Insurance Co
Communitech Ltd
Coradin Inc
CorpoSana Capital Inc
Covington Capital Corp
CrossPacific Capital Partners
Cti Capital Securities Inc
Cycle Capital Management (CCM) Inc
DIATEM Networks Inc
Dana Naye Ventures
Davies Ward Phillips & Vineber
Difference Capital Financial Inc
Discovery Capital Corp
District Ventures
Dynamic Venture Opportunities Fund Ltd
ENHANCED PERFORMANCE INDEXED CREDIT TR
East Valley Ventures Inc
Echo Capital
Eli Lilly and Co
Emedici Capital Inc
Emerald Technology Ventures AG
Emerillon Capital, Inc.
Entreprises Interaction SEC
Epic Capital Management Inc
Espresso Capital Partners
Evok Innovations
Export Development Canada
Extreme Startups
Extreme Venture Partners Inc
500 Startups, L.P.
F.J. Stork Holdings, Ltd.
FairVentures
Fairwater Growth Resources, Inc.
Fashion Zone at Ryerson University
Federal Economic Development Agency for Southern Ontario
Ferst Capital Partners Inc
Fier Succes

2414

Pratt's Guide to Private Equity & Venture Capital Sources

Fight Against Cancer Innovation Trust
First Canadian Title Company Ltd
First Nations Equity Inc
First Stone Venture Partners Inc
Fonds Innovexport
Foragen Technologies Management Inc
Forbes Alliance Partners Inc
FounderFuel
Frontier Capital Partners
Full Stack Foundry GP
GTI Capital, Inc.
GeneChem Financial Corp
Genesys Capital Partners Inc
Genome Canada
Georgian Partners Growth Fund Founders International I LP
Gibraltar & Company
Golden Venture Partners Inc
Green Acre Capital
Green Century Investment
GreenSky Capital Inc
Greensoil Investments Management Ltd
GrowLab Ventures Inc
Growth Works Capital Ltd
Hacking Health Accelerator Inc
Highgate Venture Capital Fund
Huff Capital Inc
ID Capital
INKEF Capital BV
Imagination Catalyst
Impression Ventures
Induran Ventures Inc
Inerjys Ventures Inc
Information Venture Partners
Innovacorp
Innovatech Sud du Quebec
Innovation Support
Inwest Investments Ltd
Istuary Venture Capital Inc
iNovia Capital Inc
JC Simmons & Associates
Jolt
KPMG Corporate Finance Inc
Kaofu Venture and Investment Corp
Kinetic Capital Partners
Kingsway Capital of Canada Inc
Klass Capital Corp
L-Spark Corp
LBC Capital Inc
LCC Legacy Holdings Inc
LE Groupe Forces SENC
Laprade Champlin Inc
Laurentian Bank of Canada
Leaders Funds
MMI Group Inc
MaRS Investment Accelerator Fund Inc
Macquarie Capital Markets Canada Ltd
Macquarie Private Wealth Inc
Manitoba Capital Fund
Manitoba Metis Federation Inc
Mantella Venture Partners
Maple Partners Finanl Group
Mars Discovery District
McRock Capital Corp
Mercator Investments Ltd

Meridius Capital
Miralta Capital Inc
Mistral Venture Partners
Moneta Capital Partners Ltd
Mosaic Venture Partners
NEXT Canada
NFQ Ventures
NSBI Venture Capital
National Research Council Canada
Native Venture Capital Co., Ltd.
Neotech Capital
New Brunswick Innovation Foundation
New Media Innovation Centre
Newbury Ventures
Nibiru Capital Management Ltd
Northwater Capital Management Inc
OMERS Ventures
OnWave Ventures
Ontario Capital Growth Corp
Ontario Centres of Excellence
Opportunities NB
Optimum Technology Fund LP
Overture Capital Partners (AKA: Overture)
Pact Research Fund
Pangaea Ventures Ltd
Pelorus Venture Capital Ltd
Pinetree Capital Ltd
Pinnacle Capital
Pinnacle Group
Plaza Ventures Ltd
Portag3 Ventures Inc GP
PowerOne Capital Markets Ltd
ProQuest Investments
Propulsion Ventures Inc
Pymble Holdings Inc
QUEBEC EQUITY & CAPITAL CO
Quantum Valley Investments
Quark Venture
Quebecor Fund
Quest Investment Corp
Radar Capital Inc
Real Ventures
Relay Ventures
Renewal Partners
Rho Capital Partners Inc
Roadmap Capital Inc
Rogers Ventures Ltd
Round13 Capital
Ryerson Futures Inc
7 Gate Ventures
SAIL Capital Partners LLC
Sanderling Ventures
Saskatchewan Opportunities Corp
Scotiabank Pvt Equity
Shanghai Amara Equity Investment Management Co Ltd
Six Squared Capital
Socit d investissement Tremplin 2000, Inc.
Sportsnet 360 Media Inc
Springstar GmbH
Startup Canada Women Founders Fund
Summerhill Venture Partners Management Inc
Sustainable Development Technology Canada
360 Ventures Inc
TELUS Ventures

TUFAN Venture Partners, Inc.
TVM Capital GmbH
Tactico, Inc.
Tandem Expansion Fund I LP
TandemLaunch Technologies Inc
Techbanc Inc
Techstars Central LLC
Teranet Enterprises Inc
Thomvest Ventures Inc
Top Renergy Inc
Torys LLP
Trellis Capital Corp
Urban Select Capital Corp
Vancouver Founder Fund
Vanedge Capital Inc
VeloCity
VentureLink Funds
Venturelabour.Com Inc
Versant Venture Management, LLC
Version One Ventures
Volta Labs Inc
Wesley Clover International Corporation
West Cirque Resources Ltd
Whitecastle Investments Ltd
XPV Capital Corp
Yaletown Venture Partners
York Angel Investors Inc
Yukon Venture Group

Venture Firms—Cayman Islands
Argonautic Ventures Spc
Beijing N5 Capital Consulting Co Ltd
Bull Capital Partners Ltd
Generation Investment Management LLP
Globis Capital Partners & Co
HBM Healthcare Investments AG
Harwell Capital SPC
Lightspeed Venture Partners China Co Ltd
NanoDimension Management Ltd
Pride Investments Group Ltd
6 Dimensions Capital LLC
Suzhou Datai Venture Capital Investment Management Co Ltd
Thai Development Capital Fund Ltd (The)
UMC Capital Corp
Xianfeng Huaxing Venture Capital Ltd
Yangtze China Investment Ltd

Venture Firms—Channel Islands
Emerald Technology Ventures AG
Neomed Management As
3i Infrastructure PLC

Venture Firms—Chile
Aurus Gestion de Inversiones SPA
Austral Capital
Corporacion Santiago Innova
InverSur Capital SA
Skandia Innovation AB

Venture Firms—China
ABC Capital Management Co Ltd
Accel Partners & Co Inc
Accion International
Acer Technology Ventures Asia Pacific
Aigle Private Equity Fund Management Co Ltd

2415

Pratt's Guide to Private Equity & Venture Capital Sources

Allshare Capital
Ample Luck International Capital Group Ltd
Anhui Hongtu Venture Capital Management Co Ltd
Anhui Province Venture Investment Ltd
Ants Capital
Artesian Capital Management Australia Pty Ltd
Ascend Capital Partners
Asia Capital Management Ltd
Asiatech Management LLC
Aster Capital Partners SAS
Atomico Ventures
Aviation Investment Management Co Ltd
BOC International Holdings Ltd
BOCGI Zheshang Investment Fund Management Zhejiang Co Ltd
BOCOM Int l (Shanghai) Equity Invest Management Co., Ltd.
BOCOM International Holdings Co Ltd
Bank of China Finance Equity Investment Fund Management
Banyan Capital
Beihang Investment Co Ltd
Beijig Dongdong Investment Co Ltd
Beijing Angel Around Investment Management Co Ltd
Beijing Angel Growth Technology Incubator Co Ltd
Beijing Angelcrunch Venture Financial Information Services
Beijing Apple Funds investment LP
Beijing Bigger Venture Technology Incubator Co Ltd
Beijing Bo Le Zong Heng Investment Management Center LP
Beijing Bo Wei Zhi Hong Investment Co Ltd
Beijing Bopai Qingtian Management Consulting Co Ltd
Beijing Capital Investment Co Ltd
Beijing Century Wantong Science & Technology Investment Co.
Beijing Chuangkebang Technology Incubator Co Ltd
Beijing Chun Xin Capital Management Corp Ltd
Beijing Chunfeng Shili Investment Center LP
Beijing Chuxin Yuanjing Investment Management Co Ltd
Beijing Clutural Center Construction Dvlpmt Fund Mgmt Co Ltd
Beijing College Venture Capital Company, Ltd.
Beijing Comprehensive Investment Inc
Beijing Cornerstone Capital Management Co Ltd
Beijing Dingxin Capital Co Ltd
Beijing Dongfang Hongdao Asset Management Co Ltd
Beijing Dream Link Technology Co Ltd
Beijing Electricity Investment Company, Ltd.
Beijing Extensive and Profound Information Technology Co Ltd
Beijing Faith Capital Co Ltd
Beijing Fellow Partners Investment Management Ltd
Beijing Fengbo Huifu Investment Management Co Ltd
Beijing Forise Assets Management Co Ltd
Beijing Golden Growth Investment & Management Co Ltd
Beijing Grit Investment Management Co Ltd
Beijing Guan Hui Century Equity Investment Fund Co Ltd
Beijing Guige Angel Investment Management Co Ltd
Beijing Guoheng Technology Group Co Ltd
Beijing Guoju Venture Capital Co Ltd
Beijing Guotai Venture Capital Fund Management Co Ltd
Beijing Hepu Yunzhou Investment Management Co Ltd
Beijing Hexin Dongli Investment Management Co Ltd
Beijing Hosen Capital Management Center LP
Beijing Huachuang Property Investment Co Ltd
Beijing Hualin Hechuang Investment Management Co Ltd
Beijing Huinong Capital Management Co Ltd
Beijing Industrial Development Investment Management Co Ltd
Beijing Jike Menggongchang Venture Capital Center (L.P.)
Beijing Jin Guan Investment Co Ltd
Beijing JinGang Venture Capital Adviser Co Ltd
Beijing Jinchang Investment & Consultation Co Ltd
Beijing Jinke Hightech & Innovation Ventures Co Ltd
Beijing Juxin Taihe Energy Investment Fund Management Co
Beijing Kaixing Capital Management Co Ltd
Beijing LF Capital Management Ltd
Beijing Lan Xue Technology Venture Capital Co Ltd
Beijing Langmafeng Venture Capital Management Co Ltd
Beijing Lapamcapital Management Consulting Center
Beijing Lebang Lecheng Venture Investment Managemet Co Ltd
Beijing Leyo Capital Management Co Ltd
Beijing Liando Investment Group Co Ltd
Beijing Macro Vision Venture Capital Management Consultancy
Beijing Maoxin Investment Management Co Ltd
Beijing Millennium Capital Services Co Ltd
Beijing Mingjia Investment Management Co Ltd
Beijing N5 Capital Consulting Co Ltd
Beijing Oriental-Focus Investment Management Co Ltd
Beijing Pacific Union Technology Venture Fund Co Ltd
Beijing Pangu Venture Capital Ltd
Beijing Peakvalley Capital Management Co Ltd
Beijing Phoenix Capital Investment Management Co Ltd
Beijing Prophet Capital Investment Management Co Ltd
Beijing Qianshan Capital Management Co Ltd
Beijing Qingshan Tongchuang Investment Co Ltd
Beijing Rich Land Capital Management Center LP
Beijing River Investment Ltd
Beijing Ruifu Times Investment Co Ltd
Beijing SEEC Investment Management Co Ltd
Beijing Sanxing Capital Management Co Ltd
Beijing Shangshi Investment Management Co Ltd
Beijing Shengjing Wanglian Technology Co Ltd
Beijing Shitela Venture Capital Management Co Ltd
Beijing Shulian Capital Investment Management Co Ltd
Beijing Silicon Industry Investment Co Ltd
Beijing Star Angel Equity Investment Fund LP
Beijing THE CAPITAL Management Co Ltd
Beijing Taikang Investment Management Co Ltd
Beijing Taiyou Investment Management Co Ltd
Beijing Technology Yuan Portfolio Valuation Co., Ltd.
Beijing Tianxing Chuanglian Investment Management Co., Ltd.
Beijing Torch Chengxin Investment & Consultation Co Ltd
Beijing Union Fortune Investment Management Co Ltd
Beijing Wanze Investment Management Co Ltd
Beijing Xiaomafeng Investment Consulting Co Ltd
Beijing Xinding Ronghui Capital Management Co Ltd
Beijing Xinghan Legend Capital Management Co Ltd
Beijing Xinhe Taidao Investment Management Co Ltd
Beijing Yingfei Hailin Venture Capital Co Ltd
Beijing Yingshan Investment Co Ltd
Beijing Yirun Venture Capital Co Ltd
Beijing Yuanxingtu Venture Capital Investment Co Ltd
Beijing Zhengyuan Strategic Investment Co Ltd
Beijing Zhenru Investment Management Co Ltd
Beijing Zhongcheng Yongdao Investment Management Center LP
Beijing Zhongguancun Gazella Fund Management Co Ltd Co Ltd
Beijing Zhongjin Huicai Investment Management Co Ltd
Beijing Zhonglian Guoxin Investment Fund Management Co., Ltd
Beijing Zhongrong Dingxin Investment Management Co Ltd
Bioveda China Fund
Bizovo Capital (Beijing) Co Ltd
Bluerun Ventures LP
Bohai Sea Region Venture Capital Management Co Ltd
Bonanza Investment Co Ltd
Boquan Investment Consultation Shanghai Co Ltd
Bright Stone Investment Management (Hong Kong) Ltd
Broadline Capital LLC
Bscope Partners Inc
Bull Capital Partners Ltd
CAC Capital Management Co Ltd
CAPI VENTURE
CAS Investment Management Co Ltd
CAS Jiahe Fund Management Co
CASH Capital
CBC Capital
CCBT Private Equity Fund
CDIB Capital Group
CEL Venture Capital (Shenzhen) Ltd
CID Group
Cambrian Venture Capital
Canton Venture Capital Co Ltd
Capital Nuts
Capital Today China Growth HK Ltd
Capitech Venture Capital Co Ltd
Central Investment Group
Ceyuan Ventures Management LLC
ChangAn Blue Oak Venture Capital Co Ltd

Changan Capital
Changchun S&T Venture Capital Co Ltd
Changsha Science & Technology Venture Capital Co Ltd
Changzhou Aoyang Venture Capital Co Ltd
Changzhou Hejia Capital Management Co Ltd
Changzhou Henuo Capital Management Co Ltd
Changzhou High-Tech Venture Capital Co Ltd
Cheers Capital Partners Co., Ltd.
Chengdu China Railway Hidea Equity Investment Fund Managemen
Chengdu Dinxing Investment Management Co Ltd
Chengdu Gaotou Venture Capital Co Ltd
Chengdu Hi-tech Innovation Investment Co Ltd
Chengdu Merchants Yinke Venture Capital Management Co Ltd
Chengdu Qidian Chuangke Enterprise Management Consulting Co
Chengdu Tianzhuan Jiawa Technology Co Ltd
Chengdu Yingchuang Xingke Equity Invest. Fund Mgmt Co., Ltd.
Chengwei Ventures
Chenjun Beijing Asset Management Co Ltd
Chifufund Investment Consulting Shanghai Co Ltd
China Capital Management Ltd
China Century Venture Capital
China Development Bank
China Export & Credit Insurance Corp
China Financial International Investments Ltd
China Galaxy Investment Management Co Ltd
China Internet Investment Fund Mnagement Co Ltd
China Investment Fortune Capital Management (Tianjin) Co Ltd
China King Link Corp
China Materialia LLC
China Merchants Securities Co Ltd
China Peace(Beijing)Invest Co
China Prosper Investment & Management Tianjin Co Ltd
China Reform Fund Management Co Ltd
China Renaissance Capital Investment Ltd
China SDIC Hi-tech Industrial Investment Co
China Science & Merchants Investment Management Group Co Ltd
China US Strategy Capital Group, Ltd.
China Venture Capital Co Ltd
China Venture Labs Ltd
China Zheshang Bank Longwan Branch
ChinaEquity Group Inc
ChinaRun Capital Partners Chongqing Ltd
Chinalliance Venture Partners Ltd
Chongqing Gaotejia Equity Investment Fund Management Co Ltd
Chongqing Hi-Tech Venture Capital Co Ltd
Chongqing Hi-tech Venture Capial Red Horse Management Co Ltd
Chongqing Liangzi Coal Fund Partner Enterprise
Chongqing Warp Venture Capital Management Co Ltd
Chongqing Zhengyin Guanghui Equity Investment Mgmt Co., Ltd.
Cinda Capital Management Co Ltd
Citic Asset Management Corp Ltd
ClearVue Partners, L.P.
Cnstar Capital Pte Ltd

Coco Space Investment (Shanghai) Co Ltd
Conduit Ventures Ltd
Conseco Global Investments
Conventional Wisdom Capital Ltd
Cooley LLP
CreditEase Venture
Crescent HydePark Investment Consulting Shanghai Co Ltd
Crest Capital Partners
Cybernaut (China) Venture Capital Management Co Ltd
Cypress & Kingwin Capital Group Ltd
DALIAN CHENGDA TECH INVEST
DT Capital Partners
Dalian Innovation Investment Management Co Ltd
Dalian Kaida Venture Capital Co Ltd
Daosheng Fujian Investment Co Ltd
Decheng Capital LLC
Deshi Zhongyuan Investment Management Co Ltd
Diamond TechVentures
Dianlian Venture Capital Co Ltd
Dianliang Investment Management Shanghai Co Ltd
Discovery Angel Investment Management Beijing Co Ltd
Dojane Capital
Doll Capital Management Inc
Dongguan Huichuang Zhicheng Venture Capital Enterprise LP
Dongguan Lake Venture Capital Management Inc
Dongguan Rongke Investment Consulting Co Ltd
Dongguan Rongyi Innovation Investment Co., Ltd.
DragonVenture, Inc.
Draper Fisher Jurvetson
EW Healthcare Partners
Eastern Bell Venture Capital Co Ltd
Ecolutions Management GmbH
Elevation China Capital
Elite Capital
Empower Investment
Enlightenment Capital
Envision Capital
Everyoung Capital Management Co Ltd
e.ventures
ePlanet Capital
Fair Value Capital
Fang Group Co Ltd
Feima Fund
Fenbushi Capital
Fenghou Capital
Fengyang Capital
Fidelity Growth Partners Asia
Finergy Capital
First Eastern Shanghai Equity Investment Management Ltd
Fitch Crown Venture Capital Management (Shenzhen) Co Ltd
Florescence Huamao Equity Capital Management Co Ltd
Formation 8 Partners LP
Fortex Capital Inc
Fortune Venture Capital Co Ltd
Foshan Ji Cheng Venture Capital Co., Ltd.
Foshan Kehai Venture Capital Co Ltd
Foshan Shunde Dexin Venture Capital Co Ltd
Frontline BioVenture Co Ltd

Fudan Quantum Venture Capital Management Co Ltd
Fujian Investment and Development Company Ltd
Fujian Red Bridge Capital Management Co Ltd
Fujian Venture Capital Co Ltd
Fuzhou Investment Management Co
GAXQ Emerging Industry Development Fund Management Co Ltd
GF Xinde Investment Management Co Ltd
GGV Capital
GTJA Innovation Investment Co Ltd
GUOSEN H&S Investment Co Ltd
GUSM Capital Management Co Ltd
Galaxy Internet Holding Beijing Co Ltd
Gateway International Investment Co Ltd
Genesis Capital Consulting & Management Ltd
Ginkgo Group Co Ltd
Ginkgo Venture Capital Management Beijing Co Ltd
Glory Ventures
Gobi Partners
Gold Stone Investment Ltd
GoldTel Venture Capital Fund
Golden Bridge Venture Capital, L.P.
Grace Assets Management LLP
Grand Group Investment PLC
Great Wall Securities Co Ltd
Green Harbor Management Shenzhen Co Ltd
Greenwoods Asset Management Ltd
Greylock Partners LLC
Growth Enterprise Market
Gsr Ventures Management Llc
Guangdong 100 Capital Co Ltd
Guangdong Deyi Capital Management Co Ltd
Guangdong Finance Investment Holdings Co Ltd
Guangdong Guangken Hejin Modern Agriculture Investment Mgmt
Guangdong Infore Capital Management Co Ltd
Guangdong Jinhai Asset Management Co Ltd
Guangdong Jinri Investment Ltd
Guangdong Xiyu Investment Management Co Ltd
Guanghua 898 Capital Management Co Ltd
Guangxi Guidong Haida Investment Management Co Ltd
Guangxin Investment Management Beijing Co Ltd
Guangzhou Angel Investment Co Ltd
Guangzhou Get Capital Co Ltd
Guangzhou Hengzhaoyuan Investment Management Center LP
Guangzhou Huiyin Aofeng Equity Investment Fund Management
Guangzhou InnoHub Acceleration Technology Co Ltd
Guangzhou Innovation Valley Incubator Accelerator
Guangzhou Suiyong Original Capital Co Ltd
Guangzhou Venture Capital Co Ltd
Guangzhou Zhishang Equity Investment Center LP
Guangzhou Zhongda Venture Capital Management Co Ltd
Guigu Tiantang Venture Capital Co Ltd
Guojin Dingxing Co., Ltd.
Guosen Bole Equity Investment Management Co Ltd
Guyin International Investment Fund Mgmt Beijing Co Ltd
HAO Capital
HGI Finaves China Fund
HNA Tourism Group Co Ltd

2417

Pratt's Guide to Private Equity & Venture Capital Sources

Haishi Equity Investment Fund Management Co., Ltd.
Haitong Capital Co Ltd
Haixiang Tianjin Venture Capital Management Co Ltd
Haiyin Capital
Hanfor (Beijing) Investment Co Ltd
Hangzhou Ali Venture Capital Co Ltd
Hangzhou Bangshi Investment Management Co Ltd
Hangzhou Beijia Investment Management Co Ltd
Hangzhou Chongdong Investment Management Co Ltd
Hangzhou Datou Investment Management Co Ltd
Hangzhou Deneng Equity Investment Partnership LP
Hangzhou Dingju Investment Management Co Ltd
Hangzhou Haibang Investment Management Co Ltd
Hangzhou Hi-Tech Venture Capital Co Ltd
Hangzhou Incapital Management Co., Ltd.
Hangzhou Jinying Investment Management Co Ltd
Hangzhou Jisu Investment Partners Enterprise LP
Hangzhou Junshang Investment Management Co Ltd
Hangzhou Kedi Capital Group Co Ltd
Hangzhou Qiyi Investment Management Co Ltd
Hangzhou River Hill Fund Capital Management Co Ltd
Hangzhou Taiheng Investment Management Co Ltd
Hangzhou Tobon Venture Capital Investment Co Ltd
Hangzhou Toutou Shidao Investment Partnership Enterprise LP
Hangzhou Yuanzhi Investment Management Co Ltd
Harbin Israel Venture Capital Management Co Ltd
Harbin S&T Venture Capital Investment Center
Harbin Venture Capital Management Co Ltd
Harbinger Venture Management
Harlyn Capital
Heaven-Sent Capital Management Group Co Ltd
Hebei Technology Venture Capital Co Ltd
Hebei Xingshi Venture Capital Co Ltd
Hebei Xuanyuan Private Equity Investment Fund Management Co.
Hefei State-Owned Assets Holding Co Ltd
Henan Agriculture Investment Fund Management Co Ltd
Henan Huaxia Haina Venture Capital Co Ltd
Henan Jin en Investment Co Ltd
Henan Zhongcai Venture Capital Management Co Ltd
Hengji Puye Asset Management Co Ltd
Hermed Capital Co Ltd
Hi-fortune Capital Management Ltd
HighLight Capital
Highland Capital Partners LLC
Hina Capital Partners
Hofan Venture Capital
Honghua Capital Management Shenzhen Co Ltd
Hongjin Jiye (Beijing) Investment Management Co Ltd
Hongqiao Capital
Hongta Hotland Asset Management Co Ltd
Hua Capital Management Co Ltd
Huarong Rongde Asset Management Co Ltd
Huarong Tianze Investment Co Ltd
Huaxin Investment Management Co Ltd
Huaxing Venture
Hubei Aoxin Venture Capital Co Ltd
Hubei Provincial High Technology Industry Investment Co Ltd
Huiding Capital Management Co Ltd
Huizhou Zhongkai Hi-tech Zone Technology Park Co Ltd
Hunan High-Tech Venture Capital Fortune Management Co Ltd
Hunan High-tech Venture Capital Co Ltd
Hunan Xiangtou High-Tech Venture Capital Co Ltd
Hunan Xiangtou Holdings Group Co Ltd
IDG Capital Partners Inc
Ier Venture Capital Co Ltd
Industrial Innovation Capital Management Co Ltd
Industrial and Commercial Bank of China Ltd
Infocomm Investments Pte Ltd
Infotech Ventures Co Ltd
Innovation Camp Investment Consulting (Shanghai) Co Ltd
Innovation Works Weishen (Shanghai) Invest. Mgmt. Consulting
Integral Investment Management Advisory Shanghai Co Ltd
Intel Capital Corp
Interuniversitair Micro-Electronica Centrum
Investor Growth Capital Inc
Invimed Europejskie Centrum Macierzynstwa Sp z o o
Israel Infinity Venture Capital Fund Israel LP
Ivy Capital Ltd
J.P. Morgan (China) Venture Capital Investment Co Ltd
JAFCO Investment (Asia Pacific) Ltd
Jafco Co Ltd
James & Hina Capital Management Co Ltd
Jiangsu Gaotou Zijin Culture Investment Management Co Ltd
Jiangsu High-tech Investment Group Co Ltd
Jiangsu Jinmao Venture Capital Management Co Ltd
Jiangsu Jiuzhou Capital Co Ltd
Jiangsu Kaiteng Venture Capital Co Ltd
Jiangsu Rongzhuo Investment Co Ltd
Jiangsu Suda Tiangong Venture Capital Management Co Ltd
Jiangsu Xincheng Capital Co Ltd
Jiangsu Xingke Venture Capital Co Ltd
Jiangxi Copper Beijing International Investment Co Ltd
Jiangxi High-Tech Industry Investment Co Ltd
Jiaxing Lvmintou Equity Investment Fund Management Co Ltd
Jiaxing Xinghe Venture Capital Investment Management Co Ltd
Jilin Huizheng Investment Co Ltd
Jilin Province Equity Fund Investment Co Ltd
Jinan Huayue Investment Mangement Co Ltd
Jinan Sci-Tech Venture Capital Co Ltd
Jinhua Hi-tech Investment Co Ltd
Jinxiu Zhonghe Beijing Capital Management Co Ltd
Jublon Investment & Consultancy Co Ltd
Junion Capital Management Co Ltd
Junsan Capital
KTB Investment & Securities Co Ltd
KTB Ventures, Inc.
Kaiwu Capital Co Ltd
Keytone Ventures
Kiwi Space
Kleiner Perkins Caufield & Byers LLC
Korea Investment Partners Co Ltd
Kunshan Across Straits Investment Enterprise, L.P.
Kunwu Jiuding Capital Holdings Co Ltd
Kymco Hangzhou Venture Capital Management Co Ltd
LB Investment Inc
La China Capital Co Ltd
Lantu Innovation Investment Management Beijing Co Ltd
Learn Capital Venture Partners LP
Legend Capital Co Ltd
Legend Star Venture Incubator
Liaoning Neusoft Venture Capital Co Ltd
Liaoning Technology Venture Capital Liability Ltd Co Ltd
Lightspeed Management Company LLC
Lightspeed Venture Partners China Co Ltd
Lilly Asian Ventures
Linear Venture
Lingfeng Capital Management Co Ltd
Lingyi Venture Capital Co Ltd
Liuhe Capital LLC
Liwick Investment Management Ltd
Liyang Hongtu New Economic Venture Capital Fund LP
Long Hill Capital
Longling Capital Co Ltd
Luminor Capital Pte Ltd
Lunar Capital Management Ltd
Luxin Venture Capital Group Co Ltd
MW Capital Inc
Mahon China Investment Management Ltd
Maple Valley Investments Co Ltd
Matrix Partners, L.P.
Media Dream Works
Meridian Growth Fund Management Co Ltd
Milestone Investment Management Co Ltd
Millennium Ark Investment Co Ltd
Mingly Capital
Minsheng Shanglian Capital Management Co Ltd
Mitsui & Co Global Investment Ltd
Mitsui & Co. Global Investment, Ltd.
Morningside Venture Capital
NGP Capital
Nanjing Heding Venture Capital Management Co Ltd
Nanjing Jushi Venture Capital Co Ltd
Nanjing Tongren Boda Investment Management Co Ltd
Nanjing Weizhongxiang Equity Investment Fund Management Co
Nanjing Zijin Science & Technology Venture Investment Group
Nantong Woofoo Jinxin Investment Management Co Ltd
Neowing Capital
New Access Capital
New Asia Partners LLC
New China Capital Management LP
New Enterprise Associates Inc
New Horizon Capital
Newcap Partners Inc
Newsion Venture Capital Co., Ltd.
Ningbo Angel Capital Guiding Fund Co Ltd

Ningbo Chenhai Lingbi Equity Investment Parner Enterprise
Ningbo Gaoxin District Jiaxin Equity Invt Mgmt Co Ltd
Ningbo Junrun Equity Investment Management Co Ltd
Ningbo Junrun Venture Capital Investment Mgmt Co Ltd
Ningbo Rongyin Equity Investment Partnership LP
Noah Private Wealth Management Centre Co Ltd
Nonggu Investment Co Ltd
Northern Capital Management Group
Northern Light Venture Capital Development Ltd
OWW Capital Partners Pte Ltd
Olympus Capital Holdings Asia Hong Kong Ltd
Optics Valley Creative Industry Base Construction Invest Co.
Orchid Asia Group Management Ltd
Orica Capital Co Ltd
PAC-LINK Management Corp
PEF (Beijing) Investment Consultation Ltd
PRC Venture Partners LLC
Pacific Enterprise Capital LLC
Pacific Venture Partners Co Ltd
Panda Capital Asia Ltd
Panthera Capital Group
Phoenix Asset Management Co Ltd
Ping An Bright Fortune Investment Management Co
Ping An Life Insurance Co of China Ltd
Ping An Ventures
Ppf Investments Ltd
Prax Capital Management Co
PreIPO Capital Partners Ltd
Pride Investments Group Ltd
Prime Mont Venture Capital Co Ltd
Prime Value Capital Management Ltd
Probing Shanghai Venture Capital Partnership Enterprise LP
Prometheus Capital Co Ltd
Puji Holding Inc
Qianhai Great Wall Fund Management Shenzhen Co Ltd
Qianhe Venture Management Ltd
Qiming Venture Partners Ii LP
Qingdao Haili Fangzhou Equity Investment Management Co Ltd
Qingdao Haiyinda Venture Capital Co Ltd
Qingdao Huatong Jianli Venture Capital Co Ltd
Qingdao Morning Capital Management Co Ltd
Qingsong Fund
Qinhuangdao Science Technology Investment Co Ltd
Qualcomm Ventures
Raine Group LLC, The
Red Banyan Capital Management Co Ltd
Redpoint Ventures
Redrock Capital Venture Ltd
Redstone Capital Investment Management Co Ltd
Redwood Capital, Inc.
Reiter Capital Co Ltd
Renfei Investment Management Shanghai Co Ltd
Richmond Global
Rico Harvest (Shanghai) Private Equity Management Ltd.
Robeco Teda Tianjin Investment Management Co Ltd
Rockley Group
Rongyin Capital Investment Management Co Ltd
Runze Yunneng (Beijing) Investment Management Co., Ltd.
SAIF Partners
SIG Asia Investments LLLP
SMS Private Equity Fund Management Co Ltd
SSC Fund Co Ltd
Sbcvc Fund Ii L P
SeaBright Asset Management Ltd
Sealand Innovation Capital Investment Management Co Ltd
Sequoia Capital Operations LLC
Shaanxi Cultural Industry Investment Management Co Ltd
Shaanxi Guantian Xixian Equity Investment Management Co Ltd
Shaanxi Haishi Venture Investment Co Ltd
Shaanxi Harlyn Investment Management Co Ltd
Shaanxi High-Tech Investment Co Ltd
Shaanxi Technology Venture Capital Management Co Ltd
Shaanxi Zenisun Venture Capital Co Ltd
Shandong Jiahua Shengyu Venture Capital Co Ltd
Shandong Kexin Venture Capital Co Ltd
Shanghai Aiyun Venture Capital Management Co Ltd
Shanghai Amara Equity Investment Management Co Ltd
Shanghai Atlas Capital Ltd
Shanghai Bangming Investment Management Co Ltd
Shanghai Beyond Binghong Equity Investment Management Co Ltd
Shanghai Bojiang Investment Management Co Ltd
Shanghai Broad Resources Investment Management Co Ltd
Shanghai Buttonwood Capital Co Ltd
Shanghai CCI Investment Co Ltd
Shanghai Cenova Ventures Management Co Ltd
Shanghai Cheng Feng Investment Co Ltd
Shanghai Chessboard Investment Management Co Ltd
Shanghai China Summit Capital Co., Ltd.
Shanghai Corun Venture Capital Co Ltd
Shanghai Cura Investment & Management Co Ltd
Shanghai Decent Investment Group Co Ltd
Shanghai Dinghui Investment Management Co Ltd
Shanghai Dingjia Ventures Co Ltd
Shanghai Divine Investment Management Co Ltd
Shanghai Donfcesheng Asset Management Co Ltd
Shanghai Dong Xi Investment Development Co Ltd
Shanghai Dongkai Jingxu Venture Capital Management Co Ltd
Shanghai Ever Bright Investment Management Co Ltd
Shanghai Fengshang Investment Management Co Ltd
Shanghai Fenyi Investment Management Consulting Co Ltd
Shanghai Forte Auspicious Investment Management Partners Ent
Shanghai Fortune United Investment Group Co Ltd
Shanghai Forward Technology Venture Co Ltd
Shanghai Fosun Capital Investment Management Co Ltd
Shanghai Fuhai Wansheng Investment Management Co Ltd
Shanghai Fuyuan Yinkong Investment Management Co Ltd
Shanghai Grand Yangtze Capital Investment Management Co Ltd
Shanghai Guangzhiyuan Investment Management Co Ltd
Shanghai Guohe Capital
Shanghai Guosheng Group Co Ltd
Shanghai Hantan Investment Management Co Ltd
Shanghai Heduo Investment Management Co Ltd
Shanghai Hejing Leyi Investment Advisory Co Ltd
Shanghai Huaqiang Equity Investment Management Co Ltd
Shanghai Huitong Tianxia Equity Investment Co Ltd
Shanghai INESA Venture Capital Co Ltd
Shanghai Incufortune Venture Capital Management Co Ltd
Shanghai Jiahao Capital Co Ltd
Shanghai Jianming Asset Management Co Ltd
Shanghai Langcheng Investment Management Co Ltd
Shanghai Leading Capital Co Ltd
Shanghai Lianxin Equity Investment Management Center LP
Shanghai Lianxin Investment Management Co Ltd
Shanghai Linnai Industrial Investment Center LP
Shanghai Liyi Investment Management Partnership LP
Shanghai Lonyer Holding Co Ltd
Shanghai Maiteng Yonglian Venture Investment Management
Shanghai Multimedia Park Venture Capital Co Ltd
Shanghai NCE Venture Capital Management Co Ltd
Shanghai NewMargin Ventures Co Ltd
Shanghai Newgen Venture Capital Center LP
Shanghai Peeli Investment Management Co Ltd
Shanghai Plinth Capital Management Co Ltd
Shanghai Providence Equity Invest. Mgmt. Patner Enterprise
Shanghai Pudong Science and Technology Investment Co Ltd
Shanghai Pudong Venture Capital Co Ltd
Shanghai Qianlong Yuhan Investment Management Co Ltd
Shanghai Qingcong Asset Management Co Ltd
Shanghai Qingke Huagai Investment Management Co Ltd
Shanghai Realeader Investment Fund Management Co Ltd
Shanghai Reliance Capital Management Co Ltd
Shanghai Rongxi Venture Capital Investment Management Co Ltd
Shanghai Ruiqi Science & Technology Development Co Ltd
Shanghai SMC Capital Co Ltd
Shanghai Saitian Investment Management Co Ltd
Shanghai Science & Technology Investment Holding Co Ltd
Shanghai Seasonal Capital Co Ltd
Shanghai Seeinfront Network Technology Ltd
Shanghai Shangchuang Junqiang Investment Management Co Ltd
Shanghai Shanlan Investment Management Co Ltd Co Ltd

Shanghai Shengdian Yinghua Investment Co Ltd
Shanghai Shenghu Investment Management Co Ltd
Shanghai Shibei Technology Venture Capital Co Ltd
Shanghai Sinohead Capital Co Ltd
Shanghai Sova Capital Co Ltd
Shanghai Stone Capital Co Ltd
Shanghai Sun Terra Capital Management Co Ltd
Shanghai Taoshi Investment Management Partner Enterprise LP
Shanghai Technology Venture Capital Group Co Ltd
Shanghai Tiancheng Investment Centre LP
Shanghai Tiandi Renhe Venture Capital Co
Shanghai Tianyi Industrial Holding Group Co Ltd
Shanghai Tongjiang Investment Management Co Ltd
Shanghai Tronfund Management Co Ltd
Shanghai Visino Investment Management Co Ltd
Shanghai Volcanics Investment Management Co Ltd
Shanghai Win Capital Pte Ltd
Shanghai Wuqiong Venture Capital Management Co Ltd
Shanghai Xiangcai String Investment Management Co Ltd
Shanghai Xinxin Investment Co Ltd
Shanghai Xinyou Investment Management Co Ltd
Shanghai Xiyu Asset Management Co Ltd
Shanghai Xuhui Venture Capital Ltd
Shanghai Yabao Fanghe Investment Management Center LP
Shanghai Yangpu High-Tech Venture Center Co Ltd
Shanghai Yidezeng Equity Investment Management Center GP
Shanghai Yifan Investment Management Co Ltd
Shanghai Yijin Investment Management Co Ltd
Shanghai Yonghua Capital Management Co Ltd
Shanghai Yuanhe Venture Capital Investment Centre LP
Shanghai Zhangjiang Biomedical Industry Fund
Shanghai Zhangjiang Technolgy Venture Investment Co Ltd
Shanghai Zhangjiang Torch Venture Park Investment Dvlp.
Shanghai Zhengsailian Venture Capital Management Co Ltd
Shanghai Zhiyi Chengxi Asset Management Co Ltd
Shanghai ZhongBo Capital Co Ltd
Shanghai ZhongZhi Venture Capital Co Ltd
Shanghai Zhongmi Investment Management Co Ltd
Shanghai Zhongxin Technology Investment Co Ltd
Shanghai Zhongyi Zhijiao Equity Investment Co., Ltd.
Shanghai Zhulu Investment Management Co Ltd
Shanghai Zhuopu Investment Management Center LP
Shanghai Zhuozhong Investment Management Co Ltd Co Ltd
Shanghai Zijiang Venture Capital Co Ltd
Share Capital Partners LP
Sharewin Equity Fund Management Co Ltd
ShenZhen CDF-Capital Co Ltd
ShenZhen GTJA Investment Group Co Ltd
ShenZhen GuoCheng Venture Capital Ltd
ShenZhen Scinfo Venture Capital Management Co Ltd

Venture Firms—China
Shengshang Capital Management Co Ltd
Shengyang Investment and Financing Management Center
Shenzhen Aerospace Hi-Tech Investment Management Co Ltd
Shenzhen Anzhuoxin Venture Capital Investment Co Ltd
Shenzhen Bori Venture Capital Co Ltd
Shenzhen Capital Group Co Ltd
Shenzhen Centergate Vc Mgmt Co
Shenzhen China Merchants Qihang Intnt Invstmt Mngmt Co Ltd
Shenzhen Chuangtong Jiali Investment Partnership LP
Shenzhen Classics Venture Capital Co Ltd
Shenzhen Co-Power Venture Capital Co Ltd
Shenzhen Co-Win Venture Capital Investments Ltd
Shenzhen Cornerstone of Entrepreneurial Cci Capital Ltd
Shenzhen Cuican Innovation Capital Co Ltd
Shenzhen Darwin Capital Management Co Ltd
Shenzhen Dezheng Jiacheng Investment Fund Partnership LP
Shenzhen Dingxin Capital Management Co Ltd
Shenzhen Dinova Capital Investment Management Partner LP
Shenzhen Dongfang Shengfu Venture Capital Management Co Ltd
Shenzhen Dongsheng Venture Capital Co Ltd
Shenzhen Efung Venture Capital Co Ltd
Shenzhen Fortune Caizhi Venture Capital Management Co Ltd
Shenzhen Fortune Link Venture Capital Management Co Ltd
Shenzhen Fu Si Er Wan Investment Partnership LP
Shenzhen Fuhai Yintao Venture Capital Co Ltd
Shenzhen G Street Capital Co Ltd
Shenzhen Gaozhang Capital Investment Co Ltd
Shenzhen Goldport Capital Management Co Ltd
Shenzhen Green Pine Capital Partners Co Ltd
Shenzhen Guangliang Cailve Investment Management Co Ltd
Shenzhen Guozhong Venture Capital Management Co Ltd
Shenzhen Hehui Xinda Investment Co Ltd
Shenzhen High Tech Investment Group Co Ltd
Shenzhen Hongchou Investment Co Ltd
Shenzhen Hongshisan Capital Co Ltd
Shenzhen Hongxiu Capital Management Co Ltd
Shenzhen Huaxin Venture Capital Co Ltd
Shenzhen Huitou Capital Co Ltd
Shenzhen Huocheng Accelerator Co Ltd
Shenzhen Innovation Center Co. Ltd.
Shenzhen Jiahe Asset Management Co Ltd
Shenzhen Jidi Xintian Venture Investment Co Ltd
Shenzhen Jieao Fund Management Co Ltd
Shenzhen Jieshibo Capital Management Co Ltd
Shenzhen Jizhi Equity Investment Co Ltd
Shenzhen Leaguer Venture Capital Co Ltd
Shenzhen Lepro Entertainment Technology Co Ltd
Shenzhen Liangke Venture Capital Co Ltd
Shenzhen Lihe Qingyuan Venture Capital Management Co., Ltd.
Shenzhen Litong Industry Investment Fund Co Ltd

Shenzhen Maison Capital Management Co Ltd
Shenzhen Maixing Investment Co Ltd
Shenzhen Merchants Bureau Technology Investment Co Ltd
Shenzhen Nalanda Investment Fund Management CoLtd
Shenzhen Oriental Fortune Capital Co Ltd
Shenzhen Ping An New Capital Investment Co Ltd
Shenzhen Pinqing Capital Management Co Ltd
Shenzhen QF Capital Management Co Ltd
Shenzhen Qianhai Creation Venture Partners Management
Shenzhen Qianhai Dayi Investment Fund Management Co Ltd
Shenzhen Qianhai Guotai Fund Management Co Ltd
Shenzhen Qianhai Hengxing Asset Management Co Ltd
Shenzhen Qianhai Huineng Financial Holdings Group Co Ltd
Shenzhen Qianhai Huizhong Donglu Invst Mgmt Partnership LP
Shenzhen Qianhai Huxing Asset Management Co Ltd
Shenzhen Qianhai Joint Win Investment Management Co Ltd
Shenzhen Qianhai Mass Eagle Venture Capital Investment Ltd
Shenzhen Qianhai Midday Capital Management Co Ltd
Shenzhen Qianhai Qianyuankunyi Equity Invst Fund Mgmt Co Ltd
Shenzhen Qianhai Xingwang Investment Management Co Ltd
Shenzhen Richland Investment Co Ltd
Shenzhen Rongchuang Venture Capital Co Ltd
Shenzhen Ruiying Zhuoyue Capital Management Partnership (LP)
Shenzhen SUVC Guiguxing Fund Management Enterprise LP
Shenzhen Sangel Venture Capital Co Ltd
Shenzhen Silver Star Investment Group Co Ltd
Shenzhen Sino Pacific Capital Management Co Ltd
Shenzhen Team-top Investment Management Co Ltd
Shenzhen Tiantu Capital Management Center LP
Shenzhen Timesbole Venture Capital Investment Mgmt. Co., Ltd
Shenzhen Wanhai Investment Management Co Ltd
Shenzhen Weiguang Qiming Investment Management Co Ltd
Shenzhen Weixi Investment Partnership Co Ltd
Shenzhen Winking Venture Capital Management Co Ltd
Shenzhen Xinheng Lida Capital Management Co Ltd
Shenzhen Yuanzheng Investment Development Co Ltd
Shenzhen Yunchuang Capital Investment Management Co Ltd
Shenzhen Zhengxuan Investment Ltd
Shenzhen Zhongjiaxing Investment Co Ltd
Shenzhen Zhongjinfu Venture Capital Management Co Ltd
Shenzhen Zhongshi Fund Management Co Ltd
Shenzhen Zhongyi Assets Management Co Ltd
Shihezi Haoyu PE Investment Management Co Ltd
Shiyu Capital

Sias Amidi US-China Startups Incubation Center
Sichuan Yinzheng Jiahua Equity Invest Fund Mgmt Co., Ltd.
Sichuan Yunkun Investment Management Co Ltd
Siemens Venture Capital GmbH
Sindicatum Carbon Capital Ltd
Sino H & B Private Equity Fund Co Ltd
Sino IC Capital Co Ltd
Sino Resources Investment Co Ltd
Sino-Can Harvest Capital Co Ltd
Sinovation Ventures Ltd
Skandia Innovation AB
Sky 9 Capital
Small Enterprise Assistance Funds
SoftBank China & India Holdings Ltd
Solid Wood Shanghai Investment Management Co Ltd
Soochow Venture Capital Co Ltd
Spark Venture Capital Co Ltd
Startup Capital Ventures LP
State Development & Investment Corp Ltd
Steamboat Ventures
Sunbridge Investment Management Co Ltd
Sunshine Ronghui Capital Investment Management Co Ltd
Sunup Venture Capital
Suzhou Cowin Zhengde Investment Management Co Ltd
Suzhou Datai Venture Capital Investment Management Co Ltd
Suzhou Emerging Industries Venture Capital Guidance Fund
Suzhou Hi-tech VC Group Ronglian Management Co., Ltd.
Suzhou High Tech Venture Capital Group Co Ltd
Suzhou Hongyu Equity Investment Management Entrp Co Ltd
Suzhou Industrial Park Sungent BioVenture Management Co Ltd
Suzhou Lanhai Fangzhou Equity Investment Mangement Co Ltd
Suzhou Oriza Holdings Co Ltd
Suzhou Qiaojing Oriental Investment Management Consulting
Suzhou Shengshang United Investment Center Partnership Ltd
Suzhou Shuimu Qinghua Capital Management Co Ltd
Suzhou Taihao Venture Capital Management Partner Enterprise
Suzhou Xierui Venture Capital Management Co Ltd
Suzhou Yipu Equity Investment Fund Management Co Ltd
21st Century Vc Invest Co Ltd
TVM Capital GmbH
Taishan Invest AG
Tallwood Venture Capital
Tangrong Investment Co Ltd
Tangshan Hightech Venture Capital Co Ltd
Tano Capital LLC
TeChina Investment Management Ltd
Teda Venture Capital Corp Ltd
Tendence Capital
Tianijn Yufeng Equity Investment Management Co Ltd
Tianji Venture Capital (Beijing) Investment Fund Mgmt Co Ltd
Tianjin Binhai Haisheng Equity Investment Fund Mgmt Co.
Tianjin Dehou Fund Management Co Ltd
Tianjin Gobi-Hitech Investment Management Co Ltd
Tianjin Haitai Red Innovative Investment Co Ltd
Tianjin Hidea Venture Capital Co Ltd
Tianjin Huizhi Lianhe Private Equity
Tianjin Shian Haitai Energy S&T VC Investment Enterprise
Tianjin Yingxin Equity Investment Fund Management Co Ltd
Tianjin Yuanxiang Investment Management Partner Enterprise
Tianjing Science & Technology Investment Co Ltd
Tianyu Venture Capital Investment Co Ltd
Tianyun Ruihai Venture Capital Inc
Tibet Huaying Investment Management Co Ltd
Time Innovation Ventures (Shanghai) Co Ltd
Tisiwi Venture Capital
Tmfox Venture Partners Co Ltd
Tongxi Beijing Capital Management Co Ltd
Tririver Capital Corp
Tsing Capital
Tsing Ventures Technology Service Beijing Co Ltd
Tsing-Tech Innovations Co Ltd
Tsinghua Unisplendour Hi-tech Venture Capital Inc
U.S. Venture Partners
UBS Global Asset Management (China) Ltd
UMC Capital Corp
UOB Venture Management Pte Ltd
US China Green Investment Management Co Ltd
Uni-Quantum Fund Management Co Ltd
Urban Select Capital Corp
Vangoo Capital Ltd Co Ltd
Vantagepoint Management Inc
VcWiLL Capital
Vcchina Ltd
Ventech SA
Venture TDF Pte Ltd
Vernal International Capital Equity Invest Mgmt Co Ltd
Vickers Venture Partners
Vision Investment Corp
Vision Knight Capital
Vivo Capital LLC
Vstone Yangtze Investment Managament Co Ltd
WI Harper Group Inc
Walden International
Waterstone Capital Management Shanghai LP
Weinan Zhongshi Dingcheng Investment Management Co Ltd
Wenguo (Xiamen) Equity Foundation Co., Ltd.
Wenzhou Weidu Weiyi Investment Center LP
West Security Equity Investment Co Ltd
WestSummit Capital Management Ltd
Will Capital
Wuhan East-Lake Venture Capital Co Ltd
Wuhan Huagong Technology Business Incubator Co Ltd
Wuhan KeyWin Venture Capital Co Ltd
Wuhan Optical Valley VC Fund Management Co Ltd
Wuhan Optical Valley Venture Capital Co Ltd
Wuhan Proton Venture Capital Fund Management Co Ltd
Wuhan University Asset Investment Management Co Ltd
Wuhan Zhongtou Jianhua Venture Capital Management Co Ltd
Wuhu Yuanda Venture Capital Co., Ltd.
Wuxi Guolian Assets Management Co Ltd
Wuxi Nuts Equity Investment Partner Enterprise LP
XiAn Prutention Investment & Development Co Ltd
XiAn Science Technology Investment Co Ltd
XiAn Zhongke Chuangxing Technology Incubator Co Ltd
Xiamen A&Z Investment Management Co Ltd
Xiamen Aceon Venture Investment Co Ltd
Xiamen Deyi Capital Equity Investment Management Co Ltd
Xiamen Haicang Investment Group Co Ltd
Xiamen Hengyi Venture Capital Management Co Ltd
Xiamen Hongsoft Venture Capital Management Co Ltd
Xiamen Qianshan Investment Management Co Ltd
Xiamen Xinbaiyi Investment Group Co Ltd
Xianfeng Huaxing Venture Capital Ltd
Xiang He Capital
Xiangcai Securities Co Ltd
Xiangjiang Industrial Investment Co Ltd
Xingfu Investment Management Co Ltd
Xinjiang Production & Construction Corps Lianchuang Equity
Xinyu Hesi Investment Management Center LP
Yangzhou Yingfei Maya Venture Capital Center LP
Yanyuan Innovation (Beijing) Investment Management Co., Ltd.
Yi Capital Inc.
Yichang Yuehe Equity Investment Fund Management Co Ltd
Yilian Equity Investment Fund
Yingcaiyuan Investment Management Co Ltd
Yingke Innovation Assets Management Co Ltd
Yingtai Gerui Investment Co Ltd
Yong Wan Capital Asset Management Group Co Ltd
Yongchun Investment Advisor Shanghai Co Ltd
Yuanjing Wanfang (Tianjin) Equity Invest Mgmt Entrp, L.P.
Yunnan Agriculture Venture Capital Co Ltd
Yunnan Industrial Investment Holding Group Co Ltd
ZEVC Management Co Ltd
Zana Capital Pte Ltd
Zero2IPO Ventures
Zhaoqing Huaxin Invest Co Ltd
ZheShang Venture Capital Co Ltd
Zhejiang Chengxiang Investment Management Co Ltd
Zhejiang Fuju Investment Management Co Ltd
Zhejiang Fuxin Venture Capital Co Ltd
Zhejiang Haode Jiahui Investment Management Co Ltd
Zhejiang Huaou Venture Capital Co Ltd
Zhejiang Langui Asset Management Co Ltd
Zhejiang Longzhou Investment Group Co Ltd
Zhejiang Puhua Tianqin Equity Investment Management Co Ltd
Zhejiang Shenggang Investment Management Co Ltd
Zhejiang Sinowisdom Capital Co Ltd

Pratt's Guide to Private Equity & Venture Capital Sources

Zhejiang Startvc Investment Management Co Ltd
Zhejiang University Venture Capital Co Ltd
Zhejiang Venture Capital Group Co., Ltd.
Zhejiang Yintai Ruiqi Venture Investment Co Ltd
Zhejiang Yinxinggu Investment Co Ltd
Zhejiang Yongxin Assets Management Ltd
Zhejiang Youchuang Venture Capital Co Ltd
Zhiying Capital
Zhongchuan Shengtang Investment Holdings Co Ltd
Zhongding Kaiyuan Venture Capital Management Co Ltd
Zhongji Investment Co Ltd
Zhongshan Technology Innovation Investment Management Co Ltd
Zhongshan Tianyu Equity Investment Co Ltd
ZhuHai BoYuan Investment Co Ltd
Zhuhai Qianheng Investment Management Co Ltd
Zibo High-tech Venture Capital Co Ltd

Venture Firms—Colombia
Accion International
Axon Partners Group Investment
CORPORACION INVERSIONES ABONO SUPER SA
Efromovich/Silva Capital Partners
JVax Investment Group LLC
Promotora de Proyectos SA
Skandia Innovation AB
Small Enterprise Assistance Funds
Velum Ventures SAS

Venture Firms—Costa Rica
CoreCo Holdings LLC
EcoEnterprises Fund
Econergy International Corp
Volio Capital SA

Venture Firms—Croatia
Small Enterprise Assistance Funds

Venture Firms—Cyprus
Diogenes Business Incubator University of Cyprus
Emergo Ventures
Skandia Innovation AB

Venture Firms—Czech Republic
Credo Ventures as
Media Development Investment Fund Inc
Prague Startup Centre
Reflex Capital SE
Startup Yard Ltd

Venture Firms—Denmark
Accelerace Invest K/S
BOREAN Innovation
Energi Invest Fyn A/S
Founders A/S
Internet Ventures Scandinavia
Magne Larsen Investments ApS
Nes Partner Holding ApS
Nordic Eye K/S
Nordic Makers IVS
Nordic Venture Partners Aps
Northcap Partners ApS
Northzone Ventures
Novo Holdings A/S
Oestjysk Innovation A/S
Pre-Seed Innovation A/S

SEED Capital Management I/S
Scale Capital ApS
Scandinavian Life Science Venture
Skandia Innovation AB
Sunstone Capital A/S
Symbion Capital I A/S
T. Rowe Price Threshold Partnerships
VAEKSTFONDEN

Venture Firms—Dominica
Athlone International Ltd

Venture Firms—Egypt
Algebra Ventures
Ezdehar Management
Flat6Labs
Sawari Ventures LLC
Sindicatum Carbon Capital Ltd
Winvest Capital for Development and Investment SAE

Venture Firms—El Salvador
Volio Capital SA

Venture Firms—Estonia
Eesti Arengufond
Karma Ventures OU
Small Enterprise Assistance Funds
SmartCap AS

Venture Firms—Ethiopia
Ascent Capital Africa Ltd

Venture Firms—Finland
Butterfly Ventures Oy
C & M Capital Ab Oy
Conor Venture Partners Oy
Green Campus Innovations Oy
Guida Invest Oy
IPR.VC Management Oy
Innovestor Oy
Inveni Capital Oy
Inventure Oy
KoppiCatch Oy
Lifeline Ventures GP II Oy
Loudspring Oyj
Metsola Ventures Oy
Miraimon Oy
NGP Capital
Nexit Ventures Oy
Nordic Option Oy
Nordic Venture Partners Aps
Norvestia Oyj
Open Ocean Capital Oy
PC-Capital Oy
Reaktor Ventures Ltd
Skandia Innovation AB
Straightforward Capital Management Oy
Suomen itsenaisyyden juhlarahasto
Taito Capital Partners Oy
Tekes Paaomasijoitus Oy
Teollisen yhteistyon rahasto Oy
Vendep Capital Oy
Verdane Capital Advisors AS
Veturi Growth Partners Oy
Visionplus Oyj
Vnt Management Oy

Venture Firms—France
Alliansys SAS
Alpes Capital Innovation SASU
Alto Invest SA
Alven Capital Partners SA
Apicil Gestion
Aqua Asset Management SAS
Arkea Capital Partenaire SAS
Aster Capital Partners SA
Audacia SAS
Auriga Partners SA
Auxitex SA
Axa Strategic Ventures Us LLC
Axeleo SAS
Bamboo SAS
Banexi Ventures Partners SA
Bizmedtech SASU
Boost&Co SAS
Braintime SAS
Breega Capital SARL
Breizh Up SASU
Bretagne De Nestadio Capital
Bretagne Participations SA
Brighteye Advisors SAS
Btwinz SAS
CDC Climat SA
CDC Infra Management SAS
CDI Investissement SASU
Caisse Regionale de Credit Agricole Mutuel Sud Rhone Alpes
Caisse d'Epargne Nord France Investissement SAS
Cap Creation SARL
Cap Decisif Management SAS
Capagro SAS
Caphorn Invest SAS
Capital Provence Business Angels SAS
Cea Investissement SA
Cedres Participations SARL
Cic Vizille Capital Innovation
Courtin Investment SAS
Credit Agricole Creation SAS
Creinvest Champagne Bourgogne SAS
Daphni SAS
Ecomobility Ventures
Elaia Partners SAS
Emergences SARL
Emertec
Energy Access Ventures SAS
Engie New Ventures SA
Entrepreneur Venture Gestion SA
Entrepreneurs Factory SAS
Entrepreneurs Fund Management LLP
Equitis Gestion SAS
Esperante BV
Essec Ventures 1 SAS
Euratechnologies
Eurekap SAS
Expanso Capital SAS
Extens SASU
5 M Ventures SAS
50 Partners SAS
Fa Diese 2 SAS
Fashion Capital Partners SAS
Femui Qui SA SA
Financiere Fonds Prives SAS

Finovam SAS
Frenchfood Capital SAS
GO Capital SAS
Generis Capital Partners SAS
Hemera SAS
Hi Inov SAS
I&P SARL
IMPACT Partenaires SAS
IT-Translation SA
Incubateur Paca-Est
Innovacom Gestion SAS
Innovation Capital SAS
Inocap Gestion SAS
Inserm Transfert Initiative SAS
Intellagri SA
Inter Invest Capital SAS
Ipsa SAS
Isai Gestion SAS
iBionext SASU
Jaina Capital SASU
Kapinno SAS
Kerala Ventures
Korelya Capital SAS
Kurma Partners SA
L'Accelerateur SAS
L'Express Ventures SAS
Litto Invest SAS
Loire Centre Capital SAS
Maif Avenir SAS
Matignon Investissement et Gestion SAS
Medevice Accelerator SAS
Merieux Developpement SAS
Mirabaud Asset Management France SAS
Nef Investissement SA
Network Finances SAS
Neuflize Obc Cinema SCA SICAR
New Alpha Asset Management SAS
Newbury Ventures
Next World Capital LLC
Nfactory Invest SAS
Normandie Participations SASU
OCTALFA SAS
Oddo Bhf Asset Management SAS
Open Cnp SASU
Otium Capital SARL
Ouest Angels Developpement SAS
P Factory SAS
Paris Business Angels
Pentalabbs SAS
Petit Poucet SAS
Phitrust Impact Investors SA
Pleiade Investissement SAS
Poitou-Charentes Innovation SAS
Pole Capital SAS
RAC I SA
Red River West SASU
Republic Alley SA
SIDE Capital
SMG Group SA
Sagacity Ventures SAS
Scientipole Ile de France Capital SAS
Sem Genopole SAEM
Serena Capital SAS
Sigma Gestion SA
Sindicatum Carbon Capital Ltd

Skandia Innovation AB
Soc Capital Risque Provencale et Corse SAS
Sofimac Innovation SAS
Sofinnova Partners SAS
Sofipaca SA
Sparkling Partners SAS
Starburst Accelerator SARL
Starquest ISF SAS
Startup Avenue SAS
Sudinnova SA
Supernova Invest SAS
2C Invest SAS
360 Capital Management SA
3A Venture SAS
T. Rowe Price Threshold Partnerships
Techfund Capital Europe
Telecom Technologies Transfert 3T SAS
Tertiaire Developpement Service SARL
Thales Corporate Ventures SAS
Thefamily SAS
Tolomei Participations SAS
Undisclosed Firm
Vauban Partenaires SA
Ventech SA
Weforge SAS
West Web Valley SAS
XLR Capital SAS
Xerys Gestion SAS

Venture Firms—Georgia
Small Enterprise Assistance Funds

Venture Firms—Germany
AM Ventures Holding GmbH
Acton Capital Partners GmbH
Advantec Unternehmensbeteil
Advisum GmbH
Alfred Wieder AG
Ananda Ventures GmbH
Asgard Capital Verwaltung GmbH
Astutia Ventures GmbH
Atlantic Capital Partners GmbH
Atlantic Internet GmbH
Auden AG
Aumenta GmbH
Aura Capital Management GmbH
Aurelia Private Equity GmbH
BASF Venture Capital GmbH
BC Brandenburg Capital GmbH
BERENBERG-BALKAN-BALTIKUM-UNIVER-SAL-FONDS
BITKRAFT Esports Ventures GmbH & Co I Gr KG
BLS Venture Capital GmbH
BLSW Management GmbH & Co KG
BTV Beteiligungsverwaltung GmbH & Co. KG
BVP Berlin Venture Partners GmbH
BY Capital Management GmbH
Bayern Kapital GmbH
Baytech Venture Capital GmbH & Co KG
Berlin Ventures BG GmbH
Beteiligungsfonds Wirtschaftsfoerderung Mannheim GmbH
Biom AG
Born2Grow & GmbH Co KG
Brandenburg Ventures GmbH
Burda Digital Ventures GmbH

CD Venture GmbH
COMMERZBANK AG
Catagonia Capital GmbH
Cavalry Ventures Management GmbH
Chancenkapitalfonds Der Kreissparkasse Biberach GmbH
Cherry Ventures GmbH
Clover Venture GmbH
Comvest Holding GmbH
Coparion Gmbh & Co KG
Corporate Finance Partners CFP Beratungs GmbH
Creathor Venture Management GmbH
DHV Management GmbH
DLD Ventures GmbH
Deutsche Telekom AG
Deutsche Telekom Strategic Investments
Digitalplus GmbH
Dipl.-Kfm. Wunderlich & Partner
Discovery Ventures GmbH & Co KG
EMBL Ventures GmbH
Earlybird Venture Capital GmbH & Co KG
Ecapital Entrepreneurial Partners AG
Eckert Wagniskapital und Fruehphasenfinanzierung GmbH
Ecolutions Management GmbH
Edelweiss & Berge UG haftungsbeschraenkt & Co KG
EnBW New Ventures GmbH
Extorel GmbH
e.ventures
eValue Ventures AG
eVenture Capital Partners GmbH
enjoyventure Management GmbH
FS Vencube GmbH
Familie Graef Holding GmbH
Fastlane Ventures GmbH
Fidura Capital Consult GmbH
Fifth Force GmbH
Finaves I SA
Finleap GmbH
Floor 13 GmbH
Fly Ventures Management GmbH
Forbion Capital Partners
Foundcenter Investment GmbH
Freudenberg Venture Capital GmbH
GLG Green Lifestyle GmbH
GSM Industries GmbH
GUB Unternehmensbeteiligungen GmbH & Co KGaA
Genius Venture Capital GmbH
Genui GmbH
Global Founders Capital Management GmbH
Global Life Science Ventures GmbH
Goodvent Beteiligungsmanagement GmbH & Co KG
Grazia Equity GmbH
Greencoat Capital LLP
GxP German Properties AG
H2 Properties GmbH
HCM Handwerk Consult Mittelstandsberatung eK
HCS Beteiligungsgesellschaft mbH
HW Capital GmbH
HackFwd GmbH & Co KG
Hanse Ventures BSJ GmbH
Hasso Plattner Ventures Management GmbH
Henkel AG & Co KgaA
High Tech Grunderfonds Management GmbH
Unspecified Fund

2423

Pratt's Guide to Private Equity & Venture Capital Sources

Holland Private Equity BV
Holtzbrinck Ventures GmbH
IBB Beteiligungs GmbH
IFB Innovationsstarter GmbH
Ibg Beteiligungsgesellschaft
Inovis Capital GmbH
Inveni Capital Oy
Investitions Strukturbk Rhein Pfalz GmbH
Investitions und Strukturbank Rheinland Pfalz ISB
Iris Capnamic Management GmbH
J C M B Beteiligungs GmbH
Join Capital GmbH
KfW
Kizoo Technology Capital GmbH
LBBW Venture Capital GmbH
LITTLEROCK GmbH
La Famiglia GmbH
Leonardo Venture GmbH & Co KGaA
Life Sciences Partners BV
M Cube Incubator GmbH
M Invest GmbH
MAIRDUMONT VENTURES GmbH
MBG Baden-Wuerttemberg GmbH
MIDAS Management AG
MIG Verwaltungs AG
MPM Capital LLC
MVP Management GmbH
Mail.Ru Group Ltd
Medicis Capital GmbH
Menden Ventures Consulting GmbH
Mic AG
MicroMountains Venture AG
Milestone Venture Capital GmbH
Mittelstaendische Beteiligungsgesellschaft MV mbH
Mittelstaendische Beteiligungsgesellschaft Sachsen-Anhalt
Mittelstaendische Beteiligungsgesellschaft Thueringen mbH
Moeller Ventures GmbH
Motu Ventures Management GmbH
NGN Capital LLC
Neuhaus Partners GmbH
Next Wave Funds
newten Ventures GmbH
Online Solutions Ventures GmbH
Partech International
Paua Ventures GmbH
Peppermint VenturePartners GmbH
Phoenix Contact Innovation Ventures GmbH
Picus Capital GmbH
Project A Ventures GmbH & Co KG
Protektus AG
QVentures Management GmbH
Rainmaker Investments GmbH
Rheingau Founders GmbH
Richmond View Ventures GmbH
Risikokapital Fonds Allgaeu GmbH & Co KG
Runa Capital
S Kap Unternehmensbeteiligungs GmbH & Co KG
S-Beteiligungsgesellschaft der Sparkasse Freiburg
S-Unternehmensbeteiligungsgesellschaft der Sparkasse Leipzig
SIB Innovations und Beteiligungsgesellschaft mbH
STS Ventures GmbH
Saarlandische Wagnisfinanzierungsgesellschaft
Mbh (Aka Swg)
Seed & Speed GmbH
SeedCapital Dortmund & GmbH Co KG
Senovo GmbH
Siemens Technology Accelerator GmbH
Siemens Venture Capital GmbH
Sirius Venture Partners GmbH
Skandia Innovation AB
Springstar GmbH
Startkapital Fonds Augsburg GmbH
Statkraft Ventures GmbH
Steelhouse Ventures Ltd
Syfrex GmbH
20 Scoops Venture Capital GmbH & Co KG
TVM Capital GmbH
TakeOff VC Management GmbH
Target Partners GmbH
Team Europe Management GmbH
Technologie und Gruenderzentrum Walldorf Stiftung GmbH
Tengelmann Social Ventures GmbH
Tengelmann Ventures GmbH
Think Health GmbH
Tiburon Partners AG
Trendlines Group Ltd
Triangle Venture Capital Group
Truventuro GmbH
Unternehmertum GmbH
V+Beteiligungs 2 GmbH
Venista Ventures GmbH & Co KG
Ventegis Capital AG
Venture Stars GmbH
VenturePartner InvestmentBeratungs GmbH
Vida Ventures GmbH
Vito Ventures Management GmbH
Vnt Management Oy
Wellington Partners GmbH
XL Health AG
Yabeo Capital GmbH
ZFHN Zukunftsfonds Heilbronn GmbH & Co KG

Venture Firms—Ghana
Accion International
GroFin Capital (Pty) Ltd
Jacana Partners
Oasis Capital Ghana Ltd

Venture Firms—Gibraltar
Veddis Ventures

Venture Firms—Greece
AVC SA
Capital Connect Venture Partners AKES
Dianko Holdings SA
European Finance Associates SA
Incubation for Growth SA
Incubator Laboratory Holding Company SA
Innovative Ventures SA
Logo Ventures SA
Marathon Venture Capital
Odyssey Venture Partners Single Member Private Company
Parthenon Trust SA
Thermi Ventures SA
Velti Center for Innovation SA

Venture Firms—Greenland
Greenland Venture A/S
SRI International

Venture Firms—Guatemala
CoreCo Holdings LLC

Venture Firms—Hong Kong
AID Partners Technology Holdings Ltd
Ally Bridge Group Capital Partners II LP
Aquitaine Investment Advisors Ltd
Ascend Capital Partners
Asia Capital Management Ltd
Asia Pacific Investment Partners
Asia Ventures Corp
Avanta Investment Management Ltd
BASF Venture Capital GmbH
BOC International Holdings Ltd
BOCOM International Holdings Co Ltd
Balyasny Asset Management LP
Beijing Golden Growth Investment & Management Co Ltd
Beijing Millennium Capital Services Co Ltd
Bigcolors
Bizovo Capital (Beijing) Co Ltd
Boyer Allan Investment Management, LLP.
Bright Stone Investment Management (Hong Kong) Ltd
Brinc
Broadline Capital LLC
Bull Capital Partners Ltd
CBC Capital
CCB International Group Holdings Ltd
CLOVE CAPITAL PARTNERS LTD
Capital Today China Growth HK Ltd
Cassia Investments Ltd
Ceyuan Ventures Management LLC
Chengwei Ventures
China Capital Management Ltd
China Financial International Investments Ltd
China King Link Corp
China Merchants Securities Co Ltd
China Renaissance Capital Investment Ltd
China SDIC Hi-tech Industrial Investment Co
Clearbridge Partners Ltd
DSE Investment Services Ltd
DT Capital Partners
Egarden Ventures Hong Kong Ltd
Entrepreneur Venture Gestion SA
ePlanet Capital
Fidelity Growth Partners Asia
Genesis Capital Consulting & Management Ltd
Gobi Partners
Grace Assets Management LLP
Greenwoods Asset Management Ltd
Gsr Ventures Management Llc
Guangdong Investment Ltd
HAO Capital
HGI Finaves China Fund
Heliant Investment Management, Ltd.
Horizons Ventures Ltd
Hua Yu Investment Management Ltd
Huamei Capital Co Inc
IDG Capital Partners Inc
Imprimatur Capital Hldg Ltd

Intel Capital Corp
Israel Infinity Venture Capital Fund Israel LP
iTM Ventures Inc
JAFCO Investment (Asia Pacific) Ltd
Jafco Co Ltd
Jiangsu Jiuzhou Capital Co Ltd
Junyuan Capital Investment Management Ltd
Kinled Holdings Ltd
LionRock Capital Ltd
Lunar Capital Management Ltd
Mandra Capital Ltd
MindWorks Venture
Mingly Capital
NMS Capital Partners
Nest
New Asia Partners LLC
New China Capital Management LP
New Horizon Capital
Northern Capital Management Group
Northern Light Venture Capital Development Ltd
Nova Founders Capital
Olympus Capital Holdings Asia Hong Kong Ltd
Orchid Asia Group Management Ltd
Oxford Capital Partners Holdings Ltd
Pacific Alliance Capital Group Ltd
Panda Capital Asia Ltd
Prax Capital Management Co
Pride Investments Group Ltd
Probitas Partners Inc
Qed Global
Qiming Venture Partners Ii LP
Qleap Accelerators Ltd
Redwood Capital, Inc.
SAIF Partners
SI TECHNOLOGY VENTURE CAPITAL
San Shan Capital Partners Ltd
Sequoia Capital Operations LLC
Shanghai Amara Equity Investment Management Co Ltd
Shanghai SMC Capital Co Ltd
Shanghai Trustbridge Partners Investment Management Co Ltd
Shenzhen Richland Investment Co Ltd
Shk Fund Management Ltd
Sirius Venture Consulting Pte Ltd
SoftBank Group Corp
Spinnaker Capital Group
Startup Capital Ventures LP
Steamboat Ventures
3W Partners
T. Rowe Price Threshold Partnerships
Tc Capital Pte Ltd
Templeton Asset Management Ltd
Tsing Capital
Tsing-Tech Innovations Co Ltd
Vantagepoint Management Inc
Walden International
WestSummit Capital Management Ltd
Wisdom Capital Group
Xbe Capital Ltd
Zero2IPO Ventures

Venture Firms—Hungary
Corporate Finance Partners CFP Beratungs GmbH
DBH Investment Zrt
Day One Capital Kockazati Tokealap Kezelo Zrt
Eclipse Rt
Euroventures Capital Tanacsado Kft
Finext Startup Kockazati Tokealap-kezelo Zrt
Gran Private Equity Zrt
Hiventures Kockazati Tokealap-kezelo Zrt
Litexco Mediterranea SURL
Perion Kockazati Tokealap Kezelo Zrt
PortfoLion Kockazati Tokealap kezelo Zrt
Primus Capital Partners Llc
Szechenyi Tokealap-kezelo Zrt

Venture Firms—Iceland
Frumkvodull ehf
Nyskopunarsjodur
SA Framtak GP ehf
Stefnir Asset Management Company hf
VBS Investment Bank Ltd

Venture Firms—India
Aarin Asset Advisors LLP
Aavishkaar Venture Management Services Pvt Ltd
Accel India Venture Fund
Accel Partners & Co Inc
Access Asset Managers Pvt Ltd
Accion International
Acumen Fund Inc
Agnus Capital LLP
Ambit Pragma Ventures Pvt Ltd
Americorp Ventures Ltd
Ankur Capital Advisors
Artiman Management LLC
Ascent Capital Advisors India Pvt Ltd
Aspada Advisors
August Capital Partners
Axilor Venture Capital
Axon Partners Group Investment
Balyasny Asset Management LP
Bessemer Venture Partners
BitKemy Ventures
Blume Venture Advisors
Canaan Partners
Canbank Venture Capital Fund Ltd
CapAleph Advisors India Pvt Ltd
Capria Ventures LLC
Contrarian Capital India Partners Pvt Ltd
Crossover Advisors Pvt Ltd
Dalit Indian Chamber of Commerce & Industry
Draper Fisher Jurvetson
Duke Equity Partners Inc
EFG Wealth Management India Pvt Ltd
Ecolutions Management GmbH
Edelweiss Financial Services Ltd
Elevar Equity Advisors Pvt Ltd
Endiya Partners
Exfinity Venture Partners LLP
Exponentia Capital Partners LLP
eHealth Technology Business Incubator
ePlanet Capital
FIL Capital Advisors (India) Pvt Ltd
Footprint Ventures
Fortex Capital Inc
Forum Synergies India Pe Fund Managers P Ltd
Gemini New Media Ventures LLP
GenNext Innovation Hub
Global Asia Partners
Global Technology Investment
Gray Ghost Ventures
Greylock Partners LLC
Gvfl Ltd
H-Farm SpA
HealthQuad Advisors Pvt Ltd
Helion Venture Partners LLC
Hyderabad Information Technology Venture Enterprises Ltd
IDG Ventures India Advisors Pvt Ltd
IIFL Holdings Ltd
IXORA Ventures Pvt Ltd
Ideaspring Capital
Idein Ventures
Impanix Capital
India Innovation Fund
Indian Steps and Business Incubators Association
Infocomm Investments Pte Ltd
Innosight Ventures
Innoven Capital India Pvt Ltd
Intel Capital Corp
Inventus Capital Partners Fund I L P
Ip Venture Advisors Pvt Ltd
IvyCap Ventures Advisors Pvt Ltd
JGI Ventures India Pvt Ltd
Jacob Ballas Capital India Pvt Ltd
Jm Finl Invest Managers Ltd
Jumpstartup Fund Advisors Pvt Ltd
KCP&L Greater Missouri Operations Co
Kae Capital
Kalaari Capital Partners LLC
Karnataka Information Technology Venture Capital Fund
Kerala Venture Capital Fund Pvt Ltd
Lighthouse Fund LLC
Lightspeed Management Company LLC
Lodha Group
Lok Capital
Mantra Ventures
Matrix Partners, L.P.
Menterra Venture Advisors Pvt Ltd
Milestone Religare Investment Advisors Pvt Ltd
Mitsui & Co Global Investment Ltd
Mitsui & Co. Global Investment, Ltd.
Morpheus
NGP Capital
Nadathur Estates Pvt Ltd
National Innovation Council
Navam Capital Ltd
Naya Ventures LLC
Ndusage Partners
Nereus Capital
New Enterprise Associates Inc
Next Orbit Ventures Pvt Ltd
Nexus Venture Partners
Nirvana Venture Advisors Pvt Ltd
Ojas Venture Partners
Olympus Capital Holdings Asia Hong Kong Ltd
Omnivore Capital Management Advisors Pvt Ltd
PATHFINDER INVESTMENT CO
Palaash Ventures Pvt Ltd
Paragon Partners
Parampara Capital & Management Consultants LLP
Peepul Capital Llc
Peesh Venture Capital

Pragati India Fund Pvt Ltd
Punjab Venture Capital Ltd
PurpleTalk, Inc.
Qualcomm Ventures
Rabo India Finance Ltd
Radiant Capital
Rainmatter
Rajasthan Asset Management Co Pvt Ltd
SAIF Partners
SBI Capital Ventures
SIDBI Venture Capital Ltd
SRI Capital
Sabre Partners India Advisors Pvt Ltd
Saha Fund
Scale Ventures Pvt Ltd
Seedfund
Sequoia Capital India
Sequoia Capital Operations LLC
Siemens Venture Capital GmbH
Small Enterprise Assistance Funds
Solitaire Capital Advisors Pvt Ltd
Spinnaker Capital Group
Springstar GmbH
StartupXseed Ventures LLP
Stellaris Venture Partners
2I Capital Asset Management Co Ltd
3One4 Capital
Tandem Entrepreneurs LLC
Tano Capital LLC
Tholons Capital
Unicorn India Ventures Advisors LLP
Unilazer Ventures Pvt Ltd
Utthishta Management Advisors LLP
VKRM
Ventureast
Vertex Ventures
Villgro
Walden International
Wesley Clover International Corporation
West Bengal Asset Management Co Ltd
WillFly Venture Capital
Yes Bank Ltd
YourNest Capital Advisors Pvt Ltd

Venture Firms—Indonesia
AID Partners Technology Holdings Ltd
Convergence Accel
Convergence Ventures
Crest Capital Partners
Fatfish Medialab Pte Ltd
Global Digital Prima PT
Grupara, Inc.
Ideabox Ventures
Ideosource Asia PT
Mountain Kejora Ventures
PT Celebes Artha Ventura
Pama Ventura Indonesia PT
Sindicatum Carbon Capital Ltd
Skystar Ventures
Sovereign's Capital LP
Spinnaker Capital Group

Venture Firms—Iraq
GroFin Capital (Pty) Ltd

Venture Firms—Ireland
Act Venture Capital Ltd
Amicus Partners
Business Venture Partners
Cantor Ventures
Cross Atlantic Capital Partners LLC
Delta Partners Ltd
Dublin Business Innovation Centre
EBT Venture Fund Ltd
Enterprise Equity Venture Capital Group
Enterprise Ireland
4Th Level Ventures
FINISTERE VENTURES L L C
First Step Ltd
Frontline Ventures (GP) Ltd
Greencoat Capital LLP
Growcorp Group Ltd
Icc Venture Capital
International Investment and Underwriting
Kernel Capital Partners
Leaf Investments Ltd
Nucleus Venture Partners Ltd
OLMA Capital Management Ltd
Oyster Capital Partners
Polaris Venture Partners
Pulsar Ecosystem LLC
Seroba Kernel Life Sciences Ltd
Sofinnova Ventures Inc
Undisclosed Firm
Western Development Commission

Venture Firms—Israel
A Heifetz Technologies Ltd
AL Capital Holdings 2016 Ltd
Aleph Venture Capital
Aurum Ventures MKI
Aviv Venture Capital, Ltd.
al bawader
BRM Capital LLC
Battery Ventures LP
Benchmark Capital Management Gesellschaft MBH In Liqu
Benhamou Global Ventures LLC
Bessemer Venture Partners
Bridge Investment Fund LP
CIRTech Fund
Canaan Partners
Capital Point Ltd
Carmel Ventures IV Principals Fund LP
Catalyst Investments LP
Clal Venture Capital Fund Management, Ltd.
Copia Agro and Food Ltd
Cyhawk Ventures Ltd
Darien Business Development Corp
Defta Partners
Disruptive Technologies LP
Docor International BV
Ehealth Ventures Israel Ltd
Elah Fund I LP
Elron Electronic Industries Ltd
Emerge Ventures Capital Ltd
Eshbol Investment in Vital LP
Evergreen Venture Partners
Evolution Venture Capital Fund I Israel LP
Foodlab Capital Ltd
Fortex Capital Inc
GEMINI CAPITAL FUND MGMT LTD
Genesis Angels
Genesis Partners Ltd
Giza Venture Capital
Glilot Capital Investments GP Ltd
Greensoil Investments Management Ltd
Greylock Israel Global Management Ltd
Greylock Partners LLC
Impact First Investmants Ltd
Incentive II Management Ltd
Investments in ATI Ltd
Israel Biotech Fund I LP
Israel Cleantech Ventures
Israel Infinity Venture Capital Fund Israel LP
JVP Jerusalem Venture Partners Israel Management, Ltd.
Jal Ventures Fund LP
Jerusalem Global Ventures
KDC Media Fund
Kaedan Capital Ltd
Kinrot Technology Ventures
Kreos Capital Managers Ltd
L Capital Partners, L.P.
Landa Ventures Ltd
Lightspeed Management Company LLC
Lionbird Ventures Ltd
MAGNUM COMMUNICATIONS FUND L P
Maayan Ventures Ltd
Mail.Ru Group Ltd
Marker Financial Advisors LLC
Maverick Ventures Israel LP
Medica Venture Partners, Ltd.
Mofet B-Yehuda Technological and Business Incubator
Ofer Hi Tech Ltd
Ourcrowd Investment in Shopial LP
Phenomen Ventures
Pitango Venture Capital Management Israel, Ltd.
Pond Venture Partners Ltd
Pontifax Management Company Ltd
Previz Ventures Ltd
ProSeed Venture Capital Fund, Ltd.
Qualcomm Ventures
Qumra Capital Israel I Ltd
Rhodium Ltd
7 Health Ventures
SIDER ISRA'EL IYE`UTS KALKALI BE`AM
Shaked Global Group
Siemens Venture Capital GmbH
Singulariteam Ltd
Spectro Investor Group LLC
StageOne Ventures
State Of Mind Ventures
2B Angels Ltd
TEAM DCL LTD
Terra Venture Partners
Teuza a Fairchild Technology Venture Ltd
Trendlines Group Ltd
Triventures Management Ltd
UM Accelmed LP
US Israel Gefen Capital Management Ltd
Union Tech Ventures Ltd
Van Leer Xenia GP
Vertex Israel II Management Ltd

Pratt's Guide to Private Equity & Venture Capital Sources

Wadi Ventures SCA
Walden International
Wellborn Ventures
Xenia Venture Capital Ltd
YL Ventures GP Ltd

Venture Firms—Italy

Abruzzocapital SpA
Ame Ventures Srl
Argy Venture Capital Srl
Banca Profilo SpA
Club Digitale Srl
Cofiri SpA
Como Venture Srl
Coopfond SpA
Digital Magics SpA
Embed Capital Srl
Fidi Toscana SpA
Fincalabra SpA
Finpiemonte Partecipazioni SpA
Friulia Veneto Sviluppo SGR SpA
Garanzia Partecipazioni e Finanziamenti SpA
H-Farm SpA
HAT Holding All Together SpA
Holding Di Iniziativa Industriale SpA
Hospital Holding SpA
Idooo Srl
Innogest Sgr SpA
Intesa Sanpaolo SpA
Invitalia Ventures SGR SpA
LVenture Group SpA
Leonardoweb Group Srl
Ligurcapital SpA
Litexco Mediterranea SURL
M.P.S. Merchant SpA- Ducato Gestioni SGR P.A.
New Venture Development SpA
Nordest Merchant SpA
Palladio Holding SpA
Panakes Partners SGR SpA
Programma 101 Srl
Quantica Sgr SpA
R204 Partners SpA
R301 Capital
Redseed Srl
Shark Bites SpA
Sigefi Italia Private Equity SpA
Sistema Investimenti SpA
Skandia Innovation AB
Societa Finanziaria Laziale di Sviluppo FILAS SpA
Societa Finanziaria Regione Sardegna SpA
Startupbootcamp Iot Ltd
Sviluppo Imprese Centro Italia SGR SpA
Sviluppo Italia SpA
360 Capital Management SA
Tamburi Investment Partners SpA
UniCredit Start Lab
United Ventures Srl
Vegagest Azionari Asia A
Veneto Sviluppo SpA
Vertis SGR SpA
Virtus Capital Partners Srl
Withfounders Srl
Zernike Meta Ventures SpA

Venture Firms—Japan

Accord Ventures Inc
Advanced Science and Technology Enterprise Corp
Agribusiness Investment & Consultation Ltd
Angel Capital Co Ltd
Aquitaine Investment Advisors Ltd
Archetype Corp
Asahi Gin Jigyou Toushi
Aster Capital Partners SAS
Atomico Ventures
B Dash Ventures Inc
BASF Venture Capital GmbH
Beenos Inc
Beyond Next Ventures KK
Bizovo Capital (Beijing) Co Ltd
Bugin Capital Co Ltd
Challenge Japan Invest Co Ltd
Chartline Capital Partners
Chibagin Capital Co Ltd
Chugin Lease Co Ltd
Cool Japan Fund Inc
Corporate Finance Partners CFP Beratungs GmbH
DBJ Capital Co., Ltd
Daiwa Securities SMBC Principal Investments Co., Ltd.
Defta Partners
DentsuCom
Digital Garage Inc
Doll Capital Management Inc
Draper Nexus Venture Partners LLC
Dream Incubator Inc
Eli Lilly and Co
Energy & Environment Investment Inc
Epidarex Capital
Euglena SMBC Nikko Leave-a-Nest Capital LLC
e.ventures
ePlanet Capital
500 Startups, L.P.
FGI Capital Partners Inc
Femto Startup LLP
Fidea Venture Capital Ltd
Funai Capital CO LTD
Future International Ltd
Future Venture Capital Co Ltd
GMO VenturePartners Inc
Genuine Startups KK
Gifushin Sogo Finance KK
Global Brain Corp
Global Catalyst Partners
Global Venture Capital Inc
Globis Capital Partners & Co
Gogin Capital Co Ltd
HOKURIKU CAPITAL
Hachijuni Capital Co Ltd
Hirogin Capital Co Ltd
Hiroshima Venture Capital Co Ltd
Hoya Corp
Hurray Inc
ICP Inc
IDA Capital KK
IncTANK Ventures
Incubate Fund No1 Investment LPS
Innovation Engine Inc
Innovations and Future Creation Inc
Inspire Corp
Intel Capital Corp
Interuniversitair Micro-Electronica Centrum

Israel Infinity Venture Capital Fund Israel LP
It-Farm Corp
Itochu Corp
Iyogin Capital Co Ltd
J-Seed Ventures Inc
JVIC Venture Capital Co Ltd
Jafco Co Ltd
Juroku Capital Co Ltd
KK ABBALab
KK DG Daiwa Ventures
KK Miyazaki Taiyo Capital
KK SK Ventures
KK Shigin Chiiki Economic Research Institute
KTB Investment & Securities Co Ltd
KTB Ventures, Inc.
Kanagawa Science Park Inc
kk bhp
Lead Capital Management Co Ltd
MBL Venture Capital Co Ltd
MOVIDA JAPAN Inc
Marubeni Corp
Minato Capital Co Ltd
Mistletoe Inc
Mitsubishi Corp
Mitsubishi Tanabe Pharma Corp
Mitsubishi UFJ Capital Co Ltd
Mitsui & Co Global Investment Ltd
Mitsui & Co. Global Investment, Ltd.
Mitsui Sumitomo Insurance Venture Capital Co Ltd
Miyako Capital KK
Mizuho Capital Co Ltd
Mobile Internet Capital Inc
NTT Finance Corp
Nagoya Small & Medium Business Investment & Consultation Co.
Navasota Group
Niigata Venture Capital Co Ltd
Nippon Angels Investment Co Ltd
Nippon Technology Venture Partners Ltd
Nippon Venture Capital Co Ltd
Nissay Capital Co Ltd
OGI Venture Capital Co Ltd
OPT Ventures Inc
Oita Venture Capital Co Ltd
Okasan Venture Capital Co Ltd
Okinawa Human Capital Inc
Olympus Capital Holdings Asia Hong Kong Ltd
Omron Ventures Co Ltd
Open Network Lab Inc
Osaka Small & Medium Business Investment & Consultation Co.
Primal Capital
Rebright Partners Inc
SBI Investment Co Ltd
SCS Capital Sdn Bhd
SMBC Venture Capital Co Ltd
SRI International
STRATEGIC CAPITAL PARTNERS
Sagin Capital & Consulting Co Ltd
Samurai Incubate Inc
Sansei Capital Investment Co Ltd
Sapporo Hokuyo Lease Co Ltd
Senshu Ikeda Capital Co Ltd
Shanghai SMC Capital Co Ltd
Shikata Venture Fund

2427

Pratt's Guide to Private Equity & Venture Capital Sources

Shinkin Capital Co Ltd
Shinwa Venture Capital Co Ltd
Sirius Venture Consulting Pte Ltd
Skyland Ventures
SoftBank Group Corp
Sparx Capital Partners Co Ltd
SunBridge Global Ventures Inc
Sunbridge Partners Inc
T. Rowe Price Threshold Partnerships
TEL Venture Capital Inc
TNP Partners Corp
Toho Bank Ltd
Tokyo Small & Medium Business Investment & Consultation Co.
Tottori Capital Co Ltd
Trance-Science Inc
United Inc
University of Tokyo Edge Capital Co Ltd
Vandai Investments Ltd
Vangoo Capital Ltd Co Ltd
Vasdaq Investment Ltd
Venture Labo Co Ltd
Venture United Inc
Viling Venture Partners Inc
Watervein Partners KK
Weru Investment Co Ltd
Whiz Partners Inc
Works Capital Inc
Worldview Technology Partners, Inc.
Yamaguchi Capital Co Ltd
Yamanashi Chugin Management Consulting Co Ltd
Yasuda Enterprise Development Co Ltd

Venture Firms—Jordan
Amwal Invest Company PSC
DASH Ventures Ltd
GroFin Capital (Pty) Ltd
Silicon Badia
Wamda Ltd

Venture Firms—Kazakhstan
Athlone International Ltd
Genesis Angels
Small Enterprise Assistance Funds

Venture Firms—Kenya
Acumen Fund Inc
Ascent Capital Africa Ltd
88mph Garage
East Africa Capital Partners
Fanisi Capital, Ltd.
Fusion Capital
GroFin Capital (Pty) Ltd
InReturn Capital (K) Ltd
Jacana Partners
Kenya Capital Partners Ltd
Novastar Ventures
Swedfund International AB

Venture Firms—Kuwait
Al Jawhara Invest Holding Group Co KSCC
Arzan Venture Capital
Faith Capital Holding KSCC
Impulse International for Telecommunications KSCC
KAMCO Investment Co KSCP
Khazaen Venture Capital

Kuwait Financial Centre KPSC
Sima Capital Holding Company KSCC

Venture Firms—Latvia
FlyCap AIFP SIA
Imprimatur Capital Hldg Ltd
NCH Capital Inc
Small Enterprise Assistance Funds
StartupHighway

Venture Firms—Lebanon
B&Y Venture Partners
Bader Young Entrepreneurs Program
Berytech SCAL
Flat6Labs
Leap Ventures
Middle East Venture Partners
Phoenician Funds
Saned Equity Partners Ltd
SpEED@BDD SAL

Venture Firms—Liechtenstein
Litexco Mediterranea SURL

Venture Firms—Lithuania
Litcapital Asset Management UAB
Practica Capital UAB
Siauliu Bankas AB
Sindicatum Carbon Capital Ltd
Skandinaviska Enskilda Banken AB

Venture Firms—Luxembourg
Advans SA
Anthemis Group SA
Brait Capital Partners
Careventures SA
Chameleon Invest SCA
Digital Space Ventures SCSp
Expon Capital SARL
Fanisi Capital, Ltd.
Karma Ventures OU
Mangrove Capital Partners SA
Nexus Medical Partners
Paladin Capital Management LLC
Silverstreet Capital Llp
360 Capital Management SA
Vesalius Biocapital Partners SARL

Venture Firms—Macedonia
Small Enterprise Assistance Funds

Venture Firms—Malaysia
Abundance Venture Capital Sdn Bhd
Banyan Ventures Sdn Bhd
BootstrapLabs LLC
CMS Opus Private Equity Sdn Bhd
Crest Capital Partners
Fatfish Medialab Pte Ltd
FirstFloor Capital Sdn Bhd
Gobi Partners
iCapital M Sdn Bhd
iSpring Capital Sdn Bhd
Kumpulan Modal Perdana Sdn Bhd
Malaysia Venture Capital Management Bhd
Malaysian Technology Development Corporation Sdn Bhd
Maybank Venture Capital Company Sdn Bhd

1337 Ventures Sdn Bhd
OSK Ventures International Bhd
Pembangunan Ekuiti Sdn Bhd
SCS Capital Sdn Bhd
Teak Capital Sdn Bhd
TinkBig Venture Sdn Bhd
VF Capital Sdn Bhd
Vineyard Ventures
Walden International
Xeraya Capital Sdn Bhd

Venture Firms—Malta
essDOCS Ventures

Venture Firms—Mauritius
Brait Capital Partners
FIRE CAPITAL FUND MAURITIUS PRIVATE LTD
FW Asset Management Ltd
GroFin Capital (Pty) Ltd
Helion Venture Partners LLC
IDG Ventures India Advisors Pvt Ltd
Inventus Capital Partners Fund I L P
Jacob Ballas Capital India Pvt Ltd
Madison India Capital Management Co
Mayfield Fund
Peepul Capital Llc
Saama Capital LLC
2I Capital Asset Management Co Ltd
Tano Capital LLC

Venture Firms—Mexico
Alta Ventures Mexico
Antoni & Lelo de Larrea Venture Partners
DILA Capital
500 Mexico City
500 Startups, L.P.
Gerbera Capital Asesores SC
Greener Capital Partners LP
IGNIA Partners LLC
Invent Capital MX
Latin Idea Ventures LLC
NALA Investments LLC
ORGONE CAPITAL I L L C
Omnimedia Live SA de CV
PC Capital SAPI de CV
Sindicatum Carbon Capital Ltd
Skandia Innovation AB
Springstar GmbH
Stella Maris Partners
VARIV Capital
Ventana Capital Management LP
Volio Capital SA

Venture Firms—Moldova
NCH Capital Inc

Venture Firms—Monaco
Helsinn Investment Fund SA

Venture Firms—Mongolia
Asia Pacific Investment Partners

Venture Firms—Morocco
Maroc Numeric Fund SAS

Venture Firms—Neth. Antilles
DBH Investment Zrt

Pratt's Guide to Private Equity & Venture Capital Sources

Venture Firms—Netherlands
Aboss BV
Aescap Venture I BV
Airbus Group SE
Anterra Capital BV
Apex Ventures BV
Aqua Spark BV
Biogeneration Ventures BV
Brabantse Ontwikkelings Maatschappij NV
BrightVentures
Brooklyn Ventures BV
CE Tech Invest BV
Capital Mills Invest BV
Carduso Capital BV
Catalyst Microfinance Investors
Chemelot Ventures Management BV
Cottonwood Capital Partners LLC
DSM Venturing BV
Doen Participaties BV
EVO Venture Partners
Ecart Invest 1 BV
Esperante BV
eVentures Europe BV
Filsa BV
Finch Capital Partners BV
Forbion Capital Partners
ForestEffect Fund
Global Cleantech Capital BV
Go Capital Asset Management BV
Goodwell Investments BV
Greensoil Investments Management Ltd
Health Innovations BV
Henq Invest BV
Holland Private Equity BV
Holland Startup BV
Hydra Ventures BV
ICOS Capital Management BV
ING Ventures
INKEF Capital BV
InReturn Capital (K) Ltd
Investinfuture BV
Javest Investment Fund BV
KPN Ventures BV
Keadyn
Kenda Capital BV
Kickstart Venlo BV
Life Sciences Partners BV
Management Technostars BV
Merapar Advisory BV
Movipart BV
NBI Investors BV
NV Industriebank Liof
NV NOM
Nascent Ventures BV
Navus Ventures BV
Netherlands Development Finance Company NV
1&12 Ventures BV
Ondernemend Twente Participaties BV
Optima Investments BV
Participatiemaatschappij InnovationQuarter BV
Participatiemaatschappij Oost Nederland NV
Peak Capital BV
Prime Technology Ventures NV
Quest for Growth NV
Residex BV
Revo Capital Management BV
Royal Dutch Shell PLC
SET Venture Partners BV
SUNU Ventures BV
Silver Point Ventures BV
Slingshot Management BV
Small Enterprise Assistance Funds
Solid Ventures BV
Start Green Fund BV
Startup Factory
T. Rowe Price Threshold Partnerships
The Hatch Firm BV
Thuja Capital BV
Triodos International Fund Management BV
Trophas Management BV
VOC Capital Partners BV
Value Creation Capital BV
Van Den Ende & Deitmers BV
Van Herk Management Services BV
Velocity Capital BV
Vitulum Ventures BV
Wadinko NV
XSML Management BV
Yellow&Blue Investment Management BV
Zeeuws Investeringsfonds BV

Venture Firms—New Zealand
FAR PACIFIC CAPITAL LTD
Iglobe Treasury Management Ltd
Imprimatur Capital Hldg Ltd
iGlobe Partners Ltd
inventages venture capital GmbH
Kiwi Growth Partners Ltd
Pioneer Capital Partners AS
Punakaiki Fund Ltd
powerHouse
Tuhua

Venture Firms—Nicaragua
Volio Capital SA

Venture Firms—Nigeria
GroFin Capital (Pty) Ltd
HEIRS Capital Ltd
Unique Venture Capital Management Company Ltd

Venture Firms—Norway
Alliance Venture AS
Birk Venture AS
Cardo Partners As
Energy Capital Management AS
Energy Future Invest As
Incitia Ventures AS
Indo-nordic Private Equity AS
Koksa 2 AS
Kongsberg Innovasjon AS
Mallin AS
Midvestor Management AS
Neomed Management As
Nordika Asset Management AS
Norinnova Forvaltning AS
Northzone Ventures
PRE Management AS
Proventure Management AS
Redalpine Venture Partners AG
Sakorninvest Nord AS
Sarsia Seed Management AS
Selvaag Invest AS
Sintef Mrb
Skagerak Venture Capital AS
Skandia Innovation AB
Springfondet Management AS
Styrbjorn Growth AS
Teknoinvest AS
Telenor Mobil AS Avd Bardu Bedriftsidrettslag
Televenture Management As
VI Partners
Verdane Capital Advisors AS
Viking Venture As

Venture Firms—Oman
Financial Corporation Co SAOG
GroFin Capital (Pty) Ltd
Kitara Capital
Pak Oman Investment Company Ltd
Public Authority for Investment Promotion&Export Development

Venture Firms—Pakistan
AID Partners Technology Holdings Ltd
Acumen Fund Inc
Jahangir Siddiqui Group Associates
Kasb Techventures
National ICT R&D Fund
Pak Oman Investment Company Ltd

Venture Firms—Peru
Macrocapitales SAFI SA
Small Enterprise Assistance Funds
Union Group (UK) LLP
Value Investments Peru SAFI

Venture Firms—Philippines
AB Capital and Investment Corp
Advent Capital and Finance Corp
Asia Capital Management Ltd
Asian Development Bank
First Asia Venture Capital Inc
Hatchd Inc
ICCP Venture Partners Inc
IdeaSpace Foundation Inc
Kickstart Ventures Inc
Marsman-Drysdale Corp
Narra Venture Capital
Small Business Guarantee and Finance Corporation
Tholons Capital
Walden International

Venture Firms—Poland
Arkley Venture Capital Sp z o o
Baltic Bridge SA
Black Pearls VC SA
Capital Partners SA
Erne Ventures SA
Giza Venture Capital
Hardgamma Ventures Sp z o o
IQ Partners SA
Innova Capital Sp z o o
Innovation Nest Sp z o o
Inovo Sp z o o
Intel Capital Corp
Joint Polish Investment Fund

Knowledge Hub Sp z o o
Litexco Mediterranea SURL
MBF Group SA
MCI Capital SA
Pekao Investment Banking SA
Protos Venture Capital Sp z o o
Rtaventures VC Sp z o o Sk
SECUS ASSET MANAGEMENT SA
Skandia Innovation AB
Small Enterprise Assistance Funds
SpeedUp Iqbator Sp z o o
Xevin Investments Sp z o o
Zen Capital One Sp z o o SKA

Venture Firms—Portugal
Aitec SGPS SA
Armilar Venture Partners Sociedade de Capital de Risco SA
Empresario Digital
Novabase Capital Sociedade de Capital de Risco SA
Pathena SA
Portugal Capital Ventures SGPS SA
Rising Ventures SA
Skandia Innovation AB
Sonae Investment Management Software and Technology SGPS SA
2bpartner Sociedade de Capital de Risco SA
Undisclosed Firm

Venture Firms—Qatar
Amwal QSCC

Venture Firms—Romania
DBH Investment Zrt
Fond Sodeystviya Razvitiyu MFP v Nauch-Tekh sfere
Litexco Mediterranea SURL
Mackenzie Capital, Srl.
NCH Capital Inc
Small Enterprise Assistance Funds
Societatea de Investitii Financiare Banat Crisana SA
Societatea de Investitii Financiare Transilvania SA

Venture Firms—Russia
A3RT Venchurnyi fond
AktivFinansMenedzhment OOO
Almaz Capital Partners
Binomial Ventures
Bright Capital OOO
Buran Venture Capital
Burrill & Company
Edison.VC
e-Trust Investment Group
404 group
Fast Lane Ventures OOO
Finematika OOO
Fond Razvitiya Internet-Initsiativ
Frontier Ventures
GVA LaunchGurus
Genesis Angels
Gruppa Sputnik OOO
I2Bf Global Ventures
IMI.VC
IPT Ideya ZAO
ImpulseVC
Inbio Ventures DC Ltd
Innovestor Oy

iDealMachine
Life.SREDA VC
Lythgoe Enterprises Ltd
Mail.Ru Group Ltd
NCH Capital Inc
NIKOIL INVESTMENT BANK
Nikorrinvest Co Ltd
Pangaea Ventures Ltd
Phenomen Ventures
Prostor Capital
Pulsar Ecosystem LLC
QIWI AO
RBV Capital
RosnanoMedInvest OOO
RuStars Ventures
Run Capital
Runa Capital
Russkiye Fondy ZAO
ru-Net Ventures
7Vizhn OOO
Simakh Invest ZAO
Simile Venture Partners
SmartHub OOO
Springstar GmbH
Starta Capital
Target Ventures IF
Third Rome
Trust And Investment Bank
UK Infrastrukturnye Investitsii AO
UK SGKM OOO
Untitled, The
VEB Innovations
Vesna Investment
Vestor.in

Venture Firms—Rwanda
GroFin Capital (Pty) Ltd

Venture Firms—Saudi Arabia
Anan Holding
Flat6Labs
Islamic Development Bank
King Abdullah University of Science and Technology
National Net Ventures
Raed Ventures
Riyad Capital LLC
Saad Investments
Saudi Technology Development and Investment Co

Venture Firms—Senegal
Partech International

Venture Firms—Singapore
AID Partners Technology Holdings Ltd
Aavishkaar Venture Management Services Pvt Ltd
Aetius Capital Pte Ltd
Al Salam Asia-Pacific Pte Ltd
Arb Investments Pte Ltd
Artesian Capital Management Australia Pty Ltd
BOC International Holdings Ltd
Beacon New Ventures
Bio*One Capital Pte Ltd
Bioveda Capital Pte Ltd
Clearbridge Partners Ltd
Cnstar Capital Pte Ltd
Cocoon Capital Pte Ltd

Coent Venture Partners Pte. Ltd.
Crest Capital Partners
Crossover Advisors Pvt Ltd
Digital Media Partners Pte Ltd
Disruptive Capital Pty Ltd
DragonVenture, Inc.
EDB Investments Pte Ltd
East West Capital Partners Pte Ltd
Enspire Capital Pte Ltd
Evia Capital Partners Pte Ltd
Expara Pte Ltd
ePlanet Capital
Fatfish Medialab Pte Ltd
Feo Ventures Pte Ltd
Formation 8 Partners LP
Frontier Investment & Capital Advisors Pte Ltd
GIMV Asia Management Pte Ltd
Genesis Angels
Golden Equator Capital Pte Ltd
Golden Gate Ventures Pte Ltd
Govin Capital Pte Ltd
Hatcher Pte Ltd
Hera Capital Partners Pte Ltd
Hupomone Capital Partners Pte, Ltd.
Iglobe Treasury Management Ltd
Imprimatur Capital Hldg Ltd
Incuvest Pte Ltd
Inflexion Point Capital Pte. Ltd
Infocomm Investments Pte Ltd
Innosight Ventures
Insignia Ventures Partners Pte Ltd
Intervest Co Ltd
iGlobe Partners Ltd
JAFCO Investment (Asia Pacific) Ltd
Jafco Co Ltd
Jubilee Capital Management Pte Ltd
Jungle Ventures Pte Ltd
KK Fund Pte Ltd
KTB Ventures, Inc.
Life.SREDA VC
Luminor Capital Pte Ltd
Macquarie Capital Alliance Management Pty Ltd
Majuven, Pte. Ltd.
Middle East & Asia Capital Partners Pte Ltd
Monk's Hill Ventures Pte Ltd
NMS Capital Partners
NSI Ventures
Nadathur Estates Pvt Ltd
Nalanda Capital Pte Ltd
Neoteny Labs Pte Ltd
New Protein Capital Pte Ltd
OWW Capital Partners Pte Ltd
Pacific Agri Capital Ltd
Peepul Capital Llc
Phillip Private Equity Pte Ltd
Phoenix Venture Partners LLC
Pix Vine Capital Pte Ltd
Raging Bull Pte Ltd
Rexiter Capital Management Ltd
Ruvento Ventures Pte Ltd
SPH Plug and Play
SPRING SEEDS Capital Pte, Ltd.
Sbi Ven Capital Pte Ltd
Sembawang Capital Pte Ltd
Shk Fund Management Ltd

Singapore Power Group
Singapore Technologies Kinetics Ltd
Singapore Technologies Telemedia Pte Ltd
Sirius Venture Consulting Pte Ltd
Skyven Asset Management Pte Ltd
Sl Investment Co Ltd
Small World Group Incubator Pte Ltd
Solitaire Capital Advisors Pvt Ltd
Spinnaker Capital Group
Starburst Accelerator SARL
Sycamore Ventures Inc
T. Rowe Price Threshold Partnerships
TNF Ventures Pte Ltd
Tano Capital LLC
Tata Capital General Partners LLP
Tc Capital Pte Ltd
Tembusu Ventures Pte Ltd
Templeton Asset Management Ltd
Tigris Capital
UOB Bioventures Management Pte Ltd
UOB Venture Management Pte Ltd
Value Capital Asset Management Pte Ltd
Venture TDF Pte Ltd
Vertex Israel II Management Ltd
Vertex Ventures
Vickers Venture Partners
Walden International
WaveMaker Labs Pte Ltd
Wavemaker Partners
Xilinx Inc
Zana Capital Pte Ltd

Venture Firms–Slovakia
DBH Investment Zrt
Gcp Gamma Capital Partners Beratungs & Beteiligungs AG
janom sro
Narodny Holdingovy Fond sro
Rozvojovy Fond pre male a stredne podnikanie as

Venture Firms–Slovenia
Prophetes dd

Venture Firms–South Africa
Acorn Private Equity
Alphacode Pty Ltd
Argil Venture Capital PTY Ltd
Aurik Investment Holdings (Pty) Ltd
Brait Capital Partners
Business Partners Ltd
Capricorn Capital Partners
Decorum Capital Partners Pty Ltd
88mph Garage
ECo
EXEO Capital
Enablis Financial Corporation SA (Pty) Ltd
Enko Capital Management LLP
edge Pty Ltd
First South Investment Managers (Pty) Ltd
Glenhove Fund Managers (Pty) Ltd
Global Capital Private Equity
Greenfields Venture Capital (Pty) Ltd
GroFin Capital (Pty) Ltd
Grovest Venture Capital Co (Pty) Ltd
Hasso Plattner Ventures Management GmbH
Ingenious Ventures Lp
Intrepid Venture Capital (Pty) Ltd
Investec Asset Management (Pty) Ltd
Kagiso Ventures
Khula Enterprise
Lireas Hldg
Median Fund PTY Ltd
Modern Africa Fund Managers, LLC
RAPS Finance (Pty) Ltd
Sabvest Ltd
Satya Capital Ltd
Treacle Venture Partners
Undisclosed Firm
Vantage Venture Partners

Venture Firms–South Korea
AK Gangwon Investment Co Ltd
AKG Investment
APL Partners Co., Ltd.
Aju IB Investment Co Ltd
Albatross Inverstment Co Ltd
Alpine Technology Investment Co Ltd
Altos Ventures
Asia Culture Technology Investment
Atinum Investment Co Ltd
BK Investment Co Ltd
Bokwang Investment Corp
Buepoint Partners
CDIB & MBS Venture Capital Co Ltd
Capital One Co Ltd
Capstone Partners LLC
Choongnam Venture Capital
Coolidge Corner Investment
Crest Capital Partners
DFJ Athena
DSC Investment Inc
Daedeok Investment
Daekyo Co Ltd
Daesung Private Equity Inc
Darwin Venture Capital Co Ltd
E Trust Venture Capital
ESang Technology Investment
East Gate Partners LLC
Epidarex Capital
ePlanet Capital
Formation 8 Partners LP
Frontier Investment Corp
Gemini Investment Corp
Geo Investment Co Ltd
Globon Co Ltd
Grren Busan Investment Co Ltd
Hana Daetoo Securities Co Ltd
Hanju Investment Co Ltd
Hyundai Venture Investment Corp
IBK Capital Corp
ISU Venture Capital Co Ltd
Ilshin Investment Co Ltd
Industrial Bank Of Korea
Intellectual Discovery Ventures
Intervest Co Ltd
JAFCO Investment (Asia Pacific) Ltd
JNT Investment Co Ltd
Jafco Co Ltd
K Cube Ventures Co Ltd
K-Net Investment Partners LLC
KDB Capital Corp
KTB Investment & Securities Co Ltd
KTB Ventures, Inc.
Kiwoom Investment Co Ltd
Korea Finance Corp
Korea Investment & Securities Co Ltd
Korea Investment Partners Co Ltd
Korean Venture Fund Management Co
Kunyoung Investment Co Ltd
L&S VentureCapital Corp
LB Investment Inc
LTI Investment Co Ltd
Lee&Co Investments Co
Lindeman Asia Investment Corp
MICHIGAN VENTURE CAPITAL CO LTD
MK Venture Capital
Magilink Investment Corp
Medici Investment Co Ltd
Medivate Partners LLC
MegaInvestment Co Ltd
Munhwa Investment
NHN Investment Co Ltd
Neoplux Co Ltd
Next Venture Investment Corp
Olympus Capital Holdings Asia Hong Kong Ltd
Partners Venture Capital Co Ltd
Poibos Venture Capital
Premier Partners LLC
Qualcomm Ventures
Rexiter Capital Management Ltd
Royal Bridge Investment Co Ltd
SBI Investment Korea Co Ltd
SHIN POONG VENTURE CAPITAL
SK Telecom Co Ltd
SRI International
SV Investment Corp
Samsung Venture Investment Corp
Seir Venture Capital
Sejin TS Co Ltd
Shinhan Venture Capital Co Ltd
Shinwon Venture Capital Co Ltd
Sky Investment
Sl Investment Co Ltd
Smilegate Investment Inc
Softbank Ventures Korea Inc
Solborn Venture Investment Co Ltd
Solidus Investment Co Ltd
SparkLabs
True Global Partners
Undisclosed Firm
Uni Venture Capital Co Ltd
Union Investment Partners
Univest Capital
Value Investment Korea Co Ltd
Winvest Venture Partners Inc
Wonder Angels
Wonik Investment Partners
Woori Technology Investment Co Ltd
Wooshin Venture Investment Corp
YB Partners Co Ltd
Youngshin Venture Capital

Venture Firms–Spain
ALEPH CAPITAL SA
Active Capital Partners SA
Adara Venture Partners

Pratt's Guide to Private Equity & Venture Capital Sources

Addquity Growth Capital SA
Alma Mundi Ventures SGEIC SA
Alta Partners Capital
Amidzad Partners, Co.
Arta Capital SGEIC SA
Aser Capital SCR SA
Atitlan SA
Avindia SGECR Capital SA
Axon Partners Group Investment
Banco Santander SA
Barcelona NUMA
Basque, Autonomous Community of
Big Sur Ventures
Bihoop Ventures SL
Bonsai Venture Capital SCR de Regimen Comun SA
Bullnet Capital Sc R SA
COMPAS PRIVATE EQUITY
Caixa Capital RISC SGEIC SA
Cajastur Capital Scr De Regimen Simplificado SA
Capital Stock SCR SA
Centro para el Desarrollo Tecnologico Industrial
Cia Espanola de Financiacion del Desarrollo
COFIDES SA SME
Civeta Investment SA
Clave Mayor SA SGECR
Conector SL
Cross Road Biotech SCR de Regimen Comun SA
Daruan Venture Capital SCR de Regimen Simplificado SA
Digital Assets Deployment SL
Efromovich/Silva Capital Partners
Empresa Nacional de Innovacion SA
Extremadura Avante SL
Fides Capital SL
Finaves I SA
Flint Capital OOO
Fundaci Catalana per a la Recerca i la Innovaci
Fundacion Creas
GPF Capital
Game BCN
ICF Capital SGEIC SAU
IG Expansion Business Development SL
Idea
Inception Capital
Instituto Aragones de Fomento
Inveready Seed Capital SCR SA
Inversion y Gestion de Capital de Riesgo de Andalucia SAU
Isis Venture Capital SL
JME Venture Capital SGEIC SA
Jose Manuel Entrecanales Foundation
K Fund
Kibo Ventures SL
Lanzame Capital
Litexco Mediterranea SURL
Modara Technologies SL
Mola Factory SL
Murcia Emprende SCR de Regimen Simplificado SA
Nauta Capital SL
Nordkapp Gestion SGIIC SA
Novabase Capital Sociedade de Capital de Risco SA
101 Seeds
Ona Capital Privat, SCR de R.S., S.A.
Onza Capital
Parkwalk Advisors Ltd

Piumoc Inversions SCR de Regimen Simplificado SA
Plataforma Capital Partners Gestao de Investimentos Ltda
Prax Capital Management Co
Samaipata Ventures
Seaya Capital Gestion SGECR SA
Seed Capital de Bizkaia SGEIC SA
Seed Syndicates SL
Skandia Innovation AB
Sociedad de Desarrollo de Navarra SL
Sociedad para el Desarrollo de las Comarcas Mineras SA
Sodical Scr
Sodicaman Castilla La Mancha
Sodiex SA
Sonar Ventures SL
Sprita Startups
Suanfarma Biotech SGECR SA
Swanlaab Venture Factory Sgeic SA
Tagua Capital
Telegraph Hill Group LLC
Triodos International Fund Management BV
Univen Capital SCR SA
Venturcap SCR de Regimen Comun SA
Viavigo
Victoria Venture Capital Sociedad de Capital Riesgo Pyme SA
Vitamina K
Vivergi Social Impact Fund
Wayra
XesgaliCia Sgecr SA
Ysios Capital Partners SGECR SAU
Zarpamos Aceleradora de empresas TIC SL

Venture Firms—Sri Lanka
Blue Ocean Ventures
Ironwood Capital Partners
Jupiter Capital Partners (Private) Ltd
Litexco Mediterranea SURL
N D B Capital Holdings PLC
Tholons Capital

Venture Firms—Sweden
Aggregate Stockholm AB
Almi Invest AB
Backstage Invest AB
Boforsstiftelsen
Carlson Invest AB
Chalmers Innovation
Coach & Capital Nordic 1 AB
Creandum AB
Department of Ventures
Djakne SS II AB
Eig Venture Capital Ltd
eEquity AB
Firm Factory Network AB
Fore C Investment AB
Fouriertransform AB
GLD Invest AB
Gkl Growth Capital AB
Imog Investment AB
Industrifonden
Innovacom Gestion SAS
Innovationskapital Nordic Advisors AB
Innoventus Project AB
Investor Growth Capital Inc

itKapital AB
KTH-Chalmers Capital KB
Karolinska Development AB
Kichi Invest AB
Kinnevik AB
Kreos Capital Managers Ltd
Lund University
Moor&Moor AB
NFT Ventures AB
NORRLANDS
Newcap Partners Inc
Nexit Ventures Oy
Nischer Properties AB
Nordic Venture Partners Aps
Northzone Ventures
NovAx AB
Novartis Venture Funds
Partnerinvest Ovre Norrland AB
Port-Monnaie Venture AB
Prosper Capital Corp
Sagri Development AB
Scandinavian Life Science Venture
Scope Capital Advisory AB
Serendipity Ixora AB (publ)
Skandia Innovation AB
Skandinaviska Enskilda Banken AB
Spiltan Investment AB
Spintop Private Partners AB
Starbright Invest AB
Startkapital i Norr AB
Startup Factory
Stockholm Innovation & Growth AB
Sunstone Capital A/S
Swedfund International AB
Sydsvensk Entreprenorfond AB
T. Rowe Price Threshold Partnerships
Transferator AB (publ)
Verdane Capital Advisors AS
Volvo Group Venture Capital Corp
Zenith Venture Capital AB

Venture Firms—Switzerland
AO Invest AG
Adinvest AG
Agire Invest SA
Alta Berkeley Venture Partners
Aravis SA
Armada Investment AG
Athlone International Ltd
Atlantic Ventures GmbH
BT&T Asset Management AG
Bellevue Asset Management AG
BioMedPartners AG
BlueOcean Ventures SA
Business Creation Investments AG
Co Investor AG
Commission for Technology and Innovation CTI
Creathor Venture Management GmbH
Credit Suisse Asset Management LLC
Digital Capital AG
EVA Basel Life Sciences Agency
Eclosion2 SA
Ecosystem Ventures LLC
Emerald Technology Ventures AG
Endeavour Vision SA

Pratt's Guide to Private Equity & Venture Capital Sources

Evolution Equity Partners GmbH
F Hoffmann La Roche AG
Finoris AG
Fongit Seed Invest SA
GUB Unternehmensbeteiligungen GmbH & Co KGaA
Ginko Ventures Sarl
Global Life Science Ventures GmbH
HBM Healthcare Investments AG
HTG Ventures AG
Highland Capital Partners LLC
Incuray AG
Index Ventures
Innovationskapital Nordic Advisors AB
Internet Ventures Scandinavia
Ippon Capital SA
inventages venture capital GmbH
LGT Venture Philanthropy Foundation Switzerland
Lakestar Advisors GmbH
Medholdings SA
NGP Capital
NMS Capital Partners
NanoDimension Management Ltd
Neomed Management As
Next Generation Finance Invest AG
Nextech Invest Ltd
Onelife Advisors SA
Oxford Capital Partners Holdings Ltd
Polytech Ventures & Cie SCPC
Qino Flagship AG
Quan Ventures LP
Redalpine Venture Partners AG
Remora Partners SA
SVC-AG fuer KMU Risikokapital
Saentis Capital Investment AG
Sandpiper Digital Payments AG
Scope Capital Advisory AB
Springstar GmbH
Swiss Founders Fund AG
Swisscom AG
Taishan Invest AG
Tenderloin Ventures AG
Third Rome
Unique Capital Group AG
VI Partners AG
Versant Venture Management, LLC
WA de Vigier Stiftung
Wellington Partners GmbH
Zuercher Kantonalbank

Venture Firms—Taiwan
AAA Capital Management Co Ltd
Acer Technology Ventures Asia Pacific
Asiatech Management LLC
Beijing Millennium Capital Services Co Ltd
Bio World Venture Capital Corp
Birch Venture Capital Inc
CDIB BioScience Venture Management
CDIB Capital Group
CDIB Venture Capital Corp
CID Group
Cathay Financial Holding Co Ltd
China Export & Credit Insurance Corp
ChinaRun Capital Partners Chongqing Ltd
Cnstar Capital Pte Ltd
Eminent Venture Capital Corp

Fortune Venture Capital Corp
Fubon Financial Holding Venture Co Ltd
Harbinger Venture Management
Hotung International Co Ltd
Huanan Venture Capital Co Ltd
Hyield Consulting Group
Industrial Technology Investment Corp
Interuniversitair Micro-Electronica Centrum
JAFCO Investment (Asia Pacific) Ltd
Jafco Co Ltd
Joint Choice Venture Capital Corp
Kuo-Chun Financial Management Inc
Mesh Ventures Inc
National Development Fund Executive Yuan
PAC-LINK Management Corp
PTI Ventures
Pacific Venture Partners Co Ltd
Panda Capital Asia Ltd
Stage 1 Ventures LLC
TSC Venture Management Inc
Tano Capital LLC
TransPacific Venture Partners
Unitek Capital Corp
VentureTech Alliance Holdings LLC
WIT Investment Partners Ltd
Walden International
Yuanta Venture Capital Co Ltd

Venture Firms—Tanzania
GroFin Capital (Pty) Ltd
InReturn Capital (K) Ltd
Mkoba Private Equity Fund

Venture Firms—Thailand
Alpha Founders
Ardent Capital Ltd
500 Startups, L.P.
Food Capitals PCL
K2 Venture Capital Co Ltd
Office of Small and Medium Enterprises Promotion
Thai Incubator Dot Com Co Ltd

Venture Firms—Trinidad/Tob.
Caribbean Development Capital Ltd
Tobago House of Assembly Venture Capital Co

Venture Firms—Tunisia
Avenir SICAR
Cdc Gestion SA
DELTA PROJET SICAR
FRDCM SICAR
Flat6Labs
Gabes Invest SICAR PLC
Global Invest Sicar
INTERNATIONAL MAGHREB MERCHANT
INVEST DEVELOPMENT SICAR
Maghrebia Financiere
Sidco SICAR
Societe d'Assistance Et De Gestion Des Fonds d'Essaimage
Societe d'Investissements et de Participations SICAR
Societe de Developpement et d'Investissement du Nord-Ouest
Societe de l'Investissement Moderne
Sodis Sicar SA
Ste Amen Investissement SA

Ste Inves Part SICAR
Ste de Developpement Economique Kasserine SA
Sud SICAR
T S P P SA
Tunisie Valeur SA
Undisclosed Firm
Universe Invest SICAR SA

Venture Firms—Turkey
Alesta Girisim Sermayesi Yatirim Ortakligi AS
Aslanoba Capital
Atomico Ventures
Big Bang Ventures CVA
500 Startups, L.P.
Fiba Kapital Holding AS
Ilab Holding AS
Intel Capital Corp
MV Holding AS
Springstar GmbH

Venture Firms—Uganda
African Agricultural Capital Ltd
Ascent Capital Africa Ltd
GroFin Capital (Pty) Ltd

Venture Firms—Ukraine
AVentures Capital TOV
Digital Future
eVenture Capital Partners GmbH
Growth Up Group
Happy Farm LLP
Imprimatur Capital Hldg Ltd
Krypton Capital
NCH Capital Inc
TA Venture
WannaBiz

Venture Firms—United Kingdom
AI Seed
AID Partners Technology Holdings Ltd
Aberdeen Asset Management PLC
Abingworth Management Ltd
Accel Partners & Co Inc
Accelerator Academy
Advent Venture Partners LLP
Albion Capital Group LLP
Allele Fund
Alta Berkeley Venture Partners
Amadeus Capital Partners Ltd
Amicus Partners
Andromeda Capital
Andurance Ventures LLP
Anglo Scientific Ltd
Anthemis Group SA
Apsara Capital LLP
Ariadne Capital Ltd
Arie Capital Ltd
Artemis Investment Management LLP
Artesian Capital Management Australia Pty Ltd
Arts Alliance Advisors
Ascension Ventures Ltd
Asclepios Bioresearch (UK) Ltd
Asia Pacific Investment Partners
Athlone International Ltd
Atomico Ventures
Audere Capital Ltd

Pratt's Guide to Private Equity & Venture Capital Sources

Augmentum Capital LLP
Auster Capital Partners LLC
Axm Venture Capital Ltd
B.P. Marsh & Partners PLC
BOC International Holdings Ltd
Backed VC
Balderton Capital LLP
Balyasny Asset Management LP
Banco Santander SA
Big Bang Ventures CVA
BioScience Managers Pty Ltd
Bloc Ventures Ltd
Blue Wire Capital Ltd
Breed Reply Ltd
Brightbridge Ventures
C4 Ventures
CLS Capital Ltd
CT Investment Partners LLP
Cadmus Organisation Ltd
Calibrate Management Ltd
Cambridge Innovation Capital
Canbank Venture Capital Fund Ltd
Canyon Capital Advisors LLC
Capricorn Capital Partners
Castrol InnoVentures
Catalyst Fund Management and Research Ltd
Celtic House Venture Partners Inc
Centrica Innovations UK Ltd
ChangAn Blue Oak Venture Capital Co Ltd
Charmex Ventures Ltd
Chimera Partners Ltd
Clarendon Fund Managers Ltd
Clearbridge Partners Ltd
Clydesdale Bank PLC
Columbia Lake Partners Growth Lending (Holdings Sub) Ltd
Compound Semiconductor Technologies Global Ltd
Conduit Ventures Ltd
Connect Ventures LLP
Crane Venture Partners LLP
Crowdcube Ltd
Curzon Park Capital Ltd
D5 Capital (UK) Ltd
DBW FM Ltd
DN Capital Global Venture Capital Ii LP
Dawn Capital LLP
Dawnay Day Group
Deepbridge Capital LLP
Defta Partners
Delin Capital Uk Ltd
Delta Partners Ltd
Derwent London PLC
Draper Esprit PLC
E3 Media Ltd
EC1 Capital Ltd
ETF Partners LLP
EW Healthcare Partners
Earlsfield Capital
Earlymarket LLP
East Africa Capital Partners
East Hill Management Co LLC
Ecomachines Ventures Ltd
Econergy International Corp
Eden Ventures Ltd
Edge Investments Ltd
Eight Roads Ventures Europe
Elderstreet Investments Ltd
Eli Lilly and Co
Empresaria Group PLC
Endeavour Ventures Ltd
Enko Capital Management LLP
Enso Ventures Ltd
Enterprise Private Equity Ltd
Entrepreneur First Investment Manager LLP
Entrepreneurs Fund Management LLP
Envestors Ltd
Epidarex Capital
Episode 1 Ventures LLP
Equinox Securities Ltd
Eternity Capital Advisors Ltd
Euclid Opportunities Ltd
Eurovestech PLC
ePlanet Capital
500 Startups, L.P.
FSE CIC
FW Capital Ltd
Fajr Capital Ltd
Felix Capital Partners LLP
Find Invest Grow Ltd
Firstminute Capital I LP
Fort Rock Capital Ltd
Fortex Capital Inc
Forward Investment Partners
Forward Partners Ltd
Founders Club LP
Founders Factory Ltd
Framestore Ventures
Freelands Ventures LLP
Frog Capital Ltd
Frontline Ventures (GP) Ltd
Future Planet Capital
GSTC Health Innovations Ltd
Gatcombe Park Ventures Ltd
Gateway Global (Fka Nw Brown Capital Partners)
Gatx European Technology Ventures
Generation Investment Management LLP
Genesis Angels
Georgetown Venture Partners
Global Impact Investors
Global Innovation Fund
Global Leisure Partners Llc
Goeast Ventures Ltd
Grafton Capital Ltd
Greencoat Capital LLP
Gresham House Strategic PLC
H-Farm SpA
H2o Venture Partners Pe Ltd
Haatch Ltd
Hambro Perks Ltd
Hamilton Portfolio Ltd
Healthbox LLC
Hemisphere Capital LLC
Highland Capital Partners LLC
Highland Venture Capital
Hill Capital Partners LLP
Hotspur Capital Development Ltd
I2Bf Global Ventures
IP Group PLC
IQ Capital Partners LLP
IW Capital Ltd
Idealab
Ignite 100 Ltd
Illuminate Financial Management LLP
Impax Asset Management Ltd
Imprimatur Capital Hldg Ltd
InReach Ventures LLP
InReturn Capital (K) Ltd
Index Ventures
Industrial Investors Group
Ingenious Ventures Lp
Inkopo Ltd
Innervation Capital Partners Ltd
Innvotec Ltd
Intel Capital Corp
Internet Ventures Scandinavia
Investec Asset Management (Pty) Ltd
Invoke Capital
Iron Capital Ltd
Israel Infinity Venture Capital Fund Israel LP
inventages venture capital GmbH
JXC Ventures Ltd
Jacana Partners
Jahangir Siddiqui Group Associates
JamJar Investments LLP
Javelin Ventures Ltd
KI Capital Ltd
Keen Venture Partners LLP
Kelvin Capital Ltd
Kindred Capital
Kinetik UK Ltd
Kohli Ventures Ltd
Kreos Capital Managers Ltd
Lakestar Advisors GmbH
Leopard Rock Capital Partners Ltd
Lepe Partners LLP
LocalGlobe LLP
Longwall Venture Partners LLP
Low Carbon Accelerator Ltd
Loxbridge Research Llp
Ludgate Investments Ltd
MMC Ventures Ltd
MTM Capital Partners Ltd
MVM Partners LLP
Medicxi Ventures (UK) LLP
Mercia Technologies PLC
Midven Ltd
Milamber Ventures PLC
Mitsui & Co Global Investment Ltd
Mosaic Private Equity Ltd
Mosaic Ventures Ltd
Mti Partners Ltd
Mustard Seed Impact Ltd
m8 Capital
NF Holdings Ltd
NMS Capital Partners
National Endowment for Science Technology and the Arts
New Anglia Capital Ltd
New Hill Management LLC
Newable Private Investing
Northzone Ventures
Notion Capital Partners LLP
Nova Technology Management Ltd
Novotech Investment Ltd
Origin Capital Ltd

2434

Osprey Capital Ltd
Outlier Ventures Ltd
Oxford Capital Partners Holdings Ltd
Oxford Early Investments
Oxford Technology Management Ltd
Oxx Ltd
PCP Capital Partners LLP
PROfounders Capital Ltd
Palace Ventures Ltd
Par Equity Llp
Parkwalk Advisors Ltd
Partnerships Uk PLC
Passion Capital Investments LLP
Pentech Ventures LLP
Percipient Capital
Phase4 Ventures Ltd
Pi Labs Ltd
Piton Capital LLP
Pond Venture Partners Ltd
Ppf Investments Ltd
Prime Technology Ventures NV
Probitas Partners Inc
Promethean Investments Fund LP
Proxy Ventures UK Ltd
Qualcomm Ventures
RIT Capital Partners PLC
Radiant Capital
Redbus Investments
Reed Elsevier Inc
Rev Venture Partners Ltd
Rexiter Capital Management Ltd
Rivers Capital Partners Ltd
Rockley Group
Rockspring
Rosetta Capital Ltd
Ruffena Capital Ltd
SBT Venture Capital
SCS Capital Sdn Bhd
SILK Ventures Ltd
SPARK Impact Ltd
SV Health Investors LLP
Sapphire Capital Partners LLP
Satya Capital Ltd
Scale Up Venture Capital
Scottish Enterprise Glasgow
Scottish Equity Partners LLP
Scottish Microelectronics Centre
Seedcamp Investments LLP
Seraphim Capital (General Partner) LLP
Seroba Kernel Life Sciences Ltd
Shackleton Ventures Ltd
Shanghai Amara Equity Investment Management Co Ltd
Shanghai SMC Capital Co Ltd
Shard Capital Partners LLP
Silverstreet Capital Llp
Simfonec Co
Sindicatum Carbon Capital Ltd
Skandinaviska Enskilda Banken AB
SoftBank Group Corp
Spinnaker Capital Group
Sr One Ltd
Startup Yard Ltd
Startupbootcamp Iot Ltd
Steelhouse Ventures Ltd
Strand Ventures Ltd
Sussex Place Ventures Ltd
Swarraton Partners Ltd
24Haymarket Ltd
T. Rowe Price Threshold Partnerships
TLcom Capital LLP
TMT Investments PLC
TTP Venture Managers Ltd
Tate & Lyle PLC
Technology Crossover Ventures LP
Technology Strategy Board
Tholons Capital
Top Technology Ventures Ltd
Touchstone Innovations PLC
Triodos International Fund Management BV
True Capital Partners LLP
Turki Almadhi Ventures Inc.
Undisclosed Firm
Unilever Ventures Ltd
Union Group (UK) LLP
University Of Cambridge Challenge Fund (Aka Ucf)
University of Edinburgh
Valhalla Investments Inc
Vasdaq Investment Ltd
Venrex Investment Management LLP
Venturelabour.Com Inc
Verso Capital Partners
Virgin Green Fund
VoiVoda Ventures
Wellington Partners GmbH
Wesley Clover International Corporation
West Coast Capital
West Midlands Enterprise Ltd
Whitestar Capital Ltd
Winton Ventures Ltd
Wren Capital LLP
Yangtze China Investment Ltd
Young Associates Ltd
01 Ventures LLP
Zouk Capital LLP

Venture Firms—Uruguay
ACPE Advisors SA
Kaszek Ventures I LP
Tholons Capital
Union Group (UK) LLP

Venture Firms—Utd. Arab Em.
Active-M
Arabian Gulf Fund
Arzan Venture Capital
Athlone International Ltd
BECO Capital Investment LLC
Cupola Group
Dunamis Ventures
Emirates Investment and Development PSC
Envestors Ltd
Fajr Capital Ltd
Flat6Labs
Genero Capital LLC
GroFin Capital (Pty) Ltd
I2Bf Global Ventures
Iliad Partners
Jabbar Internet Group
Jahangir Siddiqui Group Associates
KCP Capital Ltd
Macquarie Capital Alliance Management Pty Ltd
Mail.Ru Group Ltd
Masdar Capital
Middle East Venture Partners
Millennial Partners & Co LLC
Mulverhill Associates
NM Investments Ltd
NMS Capital Partners
New Enterprise East Investments
Paladin Capital Management LLC
Prime Venture Partners
Pulsar Ecosystem LLC
Rio Technology Partners
SeedStartup
Shanghai Amara Equity Investment Management Co Ltd
Silicon Oasis Founders FZCO
Spinnaker Capital Group
Springstar GmbH
TVM Capital GmbH
Tandem Partners
Turn8
Vy Capital Management Co Ltd
Wamda Ltd
Willow Impact

Venture Firms—Uzbekistan
Small Enterprise Assistance Funds

Venture Firms—Vietnam
Saigon Fund Management JSC
Templeton Asset Management Ltd
VI (Vietnam Investments) Group LLC
Vietcombank Fund Management Co

Venture Firms—Zambia
Zambia Development Agency

Pratt's Guide to Private Equity & Venture Capital Sources

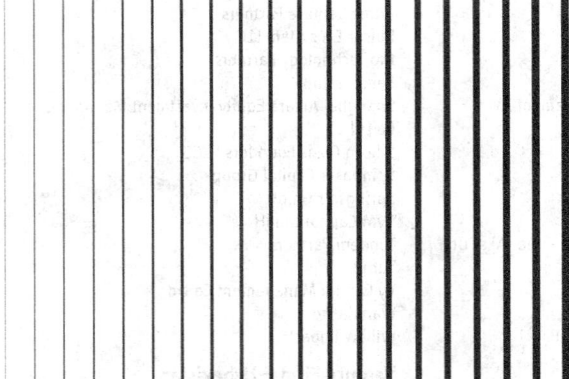

Executive Cross Reference by Firm Name

For more comprehensive querying, searching and referencing, Buyouts Insider supplies Pratt's Guide online at www.prattsguide.com.

Annual subscriptions are available for USD $1,995 per user. For more information, please contact Robert Raidt at (646)-223-6246 or email rraidt@buyoutsinsider.com.

Pratt's Guide to Private Equity & Venture Capital Sources

Aabouche, Chakib–Waha Capital PJSC
Aagaard, Peter–Internet Ventures Scandinavia
Aaker, Ian–StepStone Group LP
Aannestad, Anders–Morrison & Foerster LLP
Aaron, Allan–Technology Venture Partners Pty., Ltd.
Aaron, Wayne–Milbank Tweed Hadley & Mccloy LLP
Aarts, Hubert–Impax Asset Management Ltd
Aasmyr, Arild–Midvestor Management AS
Aba, Shay–Apax Partners LLP
Abad, Javier–Arle Heritage LLP
Abad, Javier–Candover Investments PLC
Abadi, Benjamin–Calera Capital Management Inc
Abadi, Michelle–Maverick Ventures Israel LP
Abadi, Miguel–Maverick Ventures Israel LP
Abanto, Melvin–Small Business Guarantee and Finance Corporation
Abaziou, Jean-Luc–Highland Capital Partners LLC
Abbas, Jasmani–Pembangunan Ekuiti Sdn Bhd
Abbasi, Faraz–Centerfield Capital Partners LP
Abbie, Pauline–Gresham Llp
Abbott, Chris–NCH Capital Inc
Abbott, Justin–Satya Capital Ltd
Abbott, Michael–Kleiner Perkins Caufield & Byers LLC
Abbott, Robert–Norwest Venture Partners
Abbott, Shawn–iNovia Capital Inc
Abbott, Steve–Sapphire Ventures LLC
Abbott, Steven–Sapphire Ventures LLC
Abbouchi, Samer–Global Investment House KSCC
Abboud, Sam–Pioneer Point Partners LLP
Abbrecht, Todd–Thomas H Lee Partners LP
Abdel Hakim, Nehal–Onex Corp
Abdel Khabir, Mohamed–EFG Hermes Holdings SAE
Abdel-Meguid, Tarek–Perella Weinberg Partners LP
AbdelJaber, Ramzi–Investcorp Bank BSC
AbdelJaber, Ramzi–Investcorp Technology Investments Group
Abdi, A. Jabbar–Sidereal Capital Group LLC
Abdi-Dezfuli, Farzad–Sarsia Seed Management AS
Abdo, Ashley–Gores Group LLC
Abdrazakov, Eldar–Centras Capital Partners
Abdul Rahim, Abdullah–First Abu Dhabi Bank PJSC
Abdul Rahim, Tamer–Al Khabeer Capital Co
Abdul Wahid, Ahamed–Auvest Markets FZ LLC
Abdul, Oluwakemi–Mubadala Infrastructure Partners Ltd
AbdulRaheem, Abdulla–First Abu Dhabi Bank PJSC
Abduljalil Al-Gharabally, Hanan–KAMCO Investment Co KSCP
Abdullah Al-Nafisi, Talal–KAMCO Investment Co KSCP
Abdullah, Aamer–MI Ventures LLC
Abdullah, Mohammed–Qalaa Holdings SAE
Abe, Shuhei–Sparx Capital Partners Co Ltd
Abecassis, Arie–Research Partners Ltd
Abee, Cyndi–Ventana Capital Management LP
Abel, Eric–Valstone Partners LLC
Abel, Ric–Prudential Capital Group LP
Abgaryan, Vagan–Baring Vostok Capital Partners Ltd
Abida, Riadh–Sidco SICAR
Abitbol, Cedric–21 Centrale Partners SA
Abizaid, John–Torch Hill Investment Partners LLC
Ableitinger, Markus–Capital Dynamics Sdn Bhd
Ablon, Brooke–Able Capital Management LLC

Abony, Lorne–Sandleigh Ventures LLC
Abou Sahyoun, Ziad–Algebra Capital Ltd
Abou-Jamra, Hoda–TVM Capital GmbH
Abouchalache, F. Michel–Quilvest Private Equity SCA SICAR
Abraham, Chad–Piper Jaffray Ventures Inc
Abraham, Derrick–Imperial Capital Corp
Abraham, Joel–gener8tor
Abraham, William–Lakeview Equity Partners LLC
Abrahams, Gary–Excelerate Health Ventures LLC
Abrahamson, Darren–Bain Capital Inc
Abrahamson, Shaun–URBAN US PUBLIC BENEFIT Corp
Abramov, Sergey–Baring Vostok Capital Partners Ltd
Abramovitz, Debra–Morgan Stanley Credit Partners LP
Abramowitz, Kenneth–NGN Capital LLC
Abrams, David–Cerberus Capital Management LP
Abrams, Elizabeth–Millstein & Co LP
Abrams, Zachary–Stratim Capital LLC
Abramson, Adam–Audax Group, Inc.
Abramson, Josh–FirstMark Capital LLC
Abramson, Leigh–Metalmark Capital Holdings LLC
Abreu, Alex–Clb Partners LLC
Abromavicius, Aivaras–East Capital Private Equity AB
Abu Manneh, Rola–First Abu Dhabi Bank PJSC
Acampora, Dave–Barings LLC
Acconcia, Angelo–Blackstone Group LP
Acevedo, Diego–Southern Cross Capital Management SA
Acevedo, Joseph–Pharos Capital Group LLC
Achadjian, Nina–Cota Capital Inc
Acharia-Bath, Anjula–Trinity Ventures LLP
Acharya, David–Ascend Global Investments LLC
Acher, Eric–Monashees Gestao de Investimentos Ltda
Acheson, Darren–Mill City Capital LP
Acheson, Michael–Blue Water Capital LLC
Achler, Mark–Math Venture Partners LP
Ackah-Yensu, Denis–Axum Capital Partners LLC
Acker, Eric–Morrison & Foerster LLP
Acker, John–Spring Capital Partners
Ackerman, Andrew–DreamIt Ventures
Ackerman, Arnold–Duff Ackerman & Goodrich LLC
Ackerman, Christopher–Edwards Capital LLC
Ackerman, John–Cardinal Equity Partners LLC
Ackerman, Robert–AllegisCyber
Ackerman, Robert–Watermill Group LLC
Ackerman, Tomas–Natural Gas Partners
Ackman, William–Pershing Square Capital Management LP
Ackourey, Fredrick–GroundWork Equity LLC
Acland, Michael–MTM Capital Partners Ltd
Acquaviva, John–Plus Eight Capital Management LLC
Acuna, Pablo–Oaktree Capital Management LP
Acworth, Ted–Drydock Ventures LP
Adachi, Tamotsu–Carlyle Group LP
Adair, John–Wall Street Venture Capital Ltd
Adamek, Peter–Scotiabank Pvt Equity
Adamo, Carlos–Aconcagua Ventures
Adams, Andrew–Oak HC/FT Partners LP
Adams, Andrew–Oak Investment Partners
Adams, Ben–CenterOak Partners LLC

Adams, Ben–Lindsay Goldberg & Bessemer LP
Adams, Byron–Anthos Capital LP
Adams, Byron–Rosewood Capital LLC
Adams, Charles–Adams and Reese LLP
Adams, Chris–Emergent Medical Partners LP
Adams, Chris–Focus Ventures Ltd
Adams, Chris–Francisco Partners LP
Adams, David–Rocket Ventures
Adams, Drew–StoneCreek Capital
Adams, George–Piper PE LLP
Adams, James–MTM Capital Partners Ltd
Adams, Jan–EMBL Ventures GmbH
Adams, Jeffrey–Brown Brothers Harriman & Co
Adams, Joseph–Fortress Investment Group LLC
Adams, Mark–Medicis Capital GmbH
Adams, Michael–Vision Capital LLP
Adams, Nick–AME Cloud Ventures LLC
Adams, Rob–Nextstage Capital LP
Adams, Samantha–Berkshire Partners LLC
Adams, Susan–ABS Ventures
Adams, Warren–Vineyard Ventures
Adams, Will–Alpine Investors LP
Adamson, Jonathan–Hall Capital LLC
Adamson, Neil–TAG Energy Solutions Ltd
Adamson, Stephen–Avante Mezzanine Inc
Adderley, David–Celtic House Venture Partners Inc
Addiego, Joe–Alsop Louie Partners
Addison, Rob–Castlelake LP
Addleman, Kit–Haynes and Boone LLC
Adell, Jorge–Baker & McKenzie LLP
Adelman, Robert–Venbio Partners LLC
Adelson, Marc–Monroe Capital LLC
Adelson, Robert–Osage Venture Partners
Adeosun, Wale–Kuramo Capital Management LLC
Adeoye, Bunmi–African Capital Alliance
Adeoye, Mobolaji–Kuramo Capital Management LLC
Adereth, Jonathan–Jerusalem Global Ventures
Ades, Daniel–Kawa Capital Management Inc
Adetoro, Gbenga–African Capital Alliance
Adin, Lara–CSFC Management Co, LLC
Adjoubel, Eric–Advent International Corp
Adkin, Steve–Apposite Capital LLP
Adkins, Michael–Gores Group LLC
Adkins, Paul–Highland Capital Management LP
Adkins, Wilford–Oasis Capital Partners LLC
Adlam, Tom–African Agricultural Capital Ltd
Adler, Alan–Oaktree Capital Management LP
Adler, Daniel–Lyceum Capital
Adler, David–Tennenbaum Capital Partners LLC
Adler, Eric–Blu Venture Investors LLC
Adler, Gerald–Paine Schwartz Partners LLC
Adler, John–Silver Creek Ventures Corp
Adler, Kevin–Southport Lane Management LLC
Adler, Mati–Oaktree Capital Management LP
Adler, Robert–Strategic Value Partners LLC
Adler, Vanessa–Metalmark Capital Holdings LLC
Adoni, Uri–JVP Jerusalem Venture Partners Israel Management, Ltd.
Adox, James–Venture Investors LLC
Adrien, Nicole–Oaktree Capital Management LP
Advani, Deepak–Hellman & Friedman LLC
Advani, Kamal–Actua Corp
Advani, Mark–F&C Equity Partners PLC
Afeyan, Noubar–Flagship Pioneering
Affinito, David–ZS Fund LP

2437

Pratt's Guide to Private Equity & Venture Capital Sources

Affleck, Andrew–Low Carbon Accelerator Ltd
Affolter, Thomas–Victory Park Capital Advisors LLC
Afifi, Faryan Andrew–Third Wave Ventures
Agamirzyan, Igor–Rossiyskaya venchurnaya kompaniya OAO
Agarwal, A.J.–Blackstone Group LP
Agarwal, Ajay–Bain Capital Inc
Agarwal, Ajay–Bain Capital Venture Partners LLC
Agarwal, Anika–Insight Venture Partners LLC
Agarwal, Ashish–India Alternatives Investment Advisors Pvt Ltd
Agarwal, Kris–Lime Rock Partners LLC
Agarwal, Kunal–HGGC LLC
Agarwal, Prabodh–IIFL Holdings Ltd
Agarwal, Puneet–True Ventures LLC
Agarwal, Sandeep–Beechbrook Capital LLP
Agarwal, Sanjay–NCB Capital DIFC Ltd
Agarwal, Sunil–Sofinnova Ventures Inc
Agarwala, Sandip–Longitude Capital Management Co LLC
Agble, Doug–8 Miles LLP
Agboti, Ijeoma–JP Morgan Investment Management Inc
Agesand, Jonas–Blackstone Group LP
Aggarwal, Anil–Oak HC/FT Partners LP
Aggarwal, Rahul–Brentwood Associates, L.P.
Aggarwal, Rahul–Brentwood Venture Capital
Aggarwal, Sanjay–F-Prime Capital Partners
Aggarwal, Sanjay–Global Technology Investment
Aggarwal, Sanjeev–Helion Venture Partners LLC
Aggarwal, Sanjiv–Actis LLP
Aggarwal, Vijay–Channel Group LLC, The
Agge, Ameya–Apax Partners LLP
Aggouras, George–Palladin Capital Group Inc
Aggouras, George–Venture Capital Fund of New England
Agneter, Doris–Tecnet Equity NOE Technologiebeteiligungs Invest GmbH
Agnew, James–Harwood Capital LLP
Agnew, Timothy–Masthead Venture Partners
Agoglia, Michael–Morrison & Foerster LLP
Agostinelli, Robert–Rhone Capital LLC
Agostini, Marco–Vertis SGR SpA
Agrawal, Abhishek–Vulcan Inc
Agrawal, Ajay–NEXT Canada
Agrawal, Andy–Kirchner Private Capital Group
Agrawal, Awadh–ICICI Venture Funds Management Company Ltd
Agrawal, Deepak–Global Infrastructure Holdings
Agrawal, Krishna–Lindsay Goldberg & Bessemer LP
Agrawal, Neeraj–Battery Ventures LP
Agrawal, Neeraj–Battery Ventures LP
Agrawal, Rahul–Global Technology Investment
Agrech, Dominique–Xange Private Equity SA
Agroskin, Daniel–JLL Partners Inc
Aguiar, Eric–Thomas Mcnerney and Partners LLC
Aguiar, Newton–Avista Capital Holdings LP
Aguiar, Steven–Provident Healthcare Partners
Aguilar, Gerardo–MGM Innova Capital LLC
Aguirre Peman, Claudio–Altamar Private Equity SGIIC SAU
Aguirre, Jaime–Austin Ventures
Aguirre, Javier–Farragut Capital Partners
Agular, Stephen–Mansa Capital Management LLC
Aharonovitch, Shelly–Ofer Hi Tech Ltd

Ahearn, Chris–FirstMark Capital LLC
Ahearn, Michael–Greylock Partners LLC
Ahearn, Michael–True North Venture Partners LP
Ahlgren, Peter–Firm Factory Network AB
Ahlgren, Ross–Kreos Capital Managers Ltd
Ahlstrom, Lars–Mainsail Partners LP
Ahlstrom, Mikael–Procuritas Partners Kb
Ahlstrom, Paul–Alta Ventures Mexico
Ahluwalia, Siddartha–Carlyle Group LP
Ahmad, Imran–OCA Ventures
Ahmad, Javed–Fajr Capital Ltd
Ahmadi, Anmar–Amwal International Investment Company KSCP
Ahmed, Affan–Investcorp Bank BSC
Ahmed, Fahim–BC Partners LLP
Ahmed, Iftikar–Oak Investment Partners
Ahmed, Javed–Tate & Lyle PLC
Ahmed, Moaffak–Veturi Growth Partners Oy
Ahmed, Zia–Small Enterprise Assistance Funds
Ahn, Garrick–Caltius Equity Partners
Ahn, Geun Yeong–LB Investment Inc
Ahn, James–Clayton Dubilier & Rice LLC
Ahn, Min Soo–Q Capital Partners Co Ltd
Ahn, Min Su–Q Capital Partners Co Ltd
Ahn, Steve–Walden International
Ahopelto, Timo–Lifeline Ventures GP II Oy
Ahrens, Brenton–Canaan Partners
Ahrens, Jack–Tgap Ventures LLC
Ahsan, Shameem–Fenox Venture Capital Inc
Ahuja, Ashim–HandsOn3 LLC
Ahuja, Gautam–Blue Scorpion Investments LP
Ahuja, Sanjiv–Solitaire Capital Advisors Pvt Ltd
Ahuja, Sudhir–Alcatel-Lucent Ventures
Ahvenniemi, Sami–Conor Venture Partners Oy
Ai, Di–Shanghai NewMargin Ventures Co Ltd
Aiello, John–Lindsay Goldberg & Bessemer LP
Aiguabella, Julio Cazorla–Landon Investments Scr SA
Aikman, Robert–Odyssey Investment Partners LLC
Aime, Alex-Handrah–Emerging Capital Partners
Aipel, Ulf–itKapital AB
Aitcheson, Susan–Center For Innovative Technology
Aitchison, Nigel–Foresight Group LLP
Aitelli, Peter–Morrison & Foerster LLP
Aitken, Melanie–Bennett Jones Verchere
Aitken-Davies, George–Altaris Capital Partners LLC
Aizenberg, Salo–RLJ Equity Partners LLC
Aji, Satoshi–Toho Bank Ltd
Ajila, Rohan–Capvent AG
Ajouz, Michael–New Mountain Capital I LLC
Akaiwa, Sumiyuki–Daiwa Corporate Investment Co Ltd
Akansu, Ali–Aztec Equity Partners LLC
Akaogi, Takao–Ant Capital Partners Co Ltd
Akasaka, Naoko–JP Morgan Investment Management Inc
Akaura, Tohru–Incubate Fund No1 Investment LPS
Akelman, Chris–Fireman Capital Partners LLC
Akers, Jeffrey–Adams Street Partners LLC
Akerson, Daniel–Forstmann Little & Co
Akesson, Jan–Adelis Equity Partners AB
Akhrass, Jameel–Perella Weinberg Partners LP
Akhtar, Kareem–Monomoy Capital Partners LLC
Akhurst, Neil–MVM Partners LLP
Akiba, Kaori–Global Brain Corp

Akimoto, Nobuyuki–Translink Capital LLC
Akiyama, Satoshi–Mizuho Capital Co Ltd
Akkaraju, Srinivas–New Leaf Venture Partners LLC
Akkaraju, Srinivas–Samsara BioCapital LP
Akkawi, Michael–Torys LLP
Akmal, Haider–Rho Capital Partners Inc
Akram, Imran–DN Capital Global Venture Capital Ii LP
Aksenov, Andrey–Elbrus Kapital OOO
Aktihanoglu, Murat–Mac6 LLC
Al Abdul Jaleel, Fahad–Kuwait Financial Centre KPSC
Al Ali, Fadhel–Dubai Investment Group
Al Amine, Firas–Investcorp Bank BSC
Al Aradi, Mahmood–First Abu Dhabi Bank PJSC
Al Aujan, Nedhal Saleh–Bahrain Development Bank BSCC
Al Ballaa, Rashid–National Net Ventures
Al Bin Mohammed, Hassan–Bahrain Development Bank BSCC
Al Hajeri, Manaf–Kuwait Financial Centre KPSC
Al Hamad, Ahmad–Asiya Capital Investments Company KSCP
Al Haram, Osama–Arcapita Inc
Al Hellow, Mishal–Arcapita Inc
Al Hosni, Nasr–Financial Corporation Co SAOG
Al Ismaily, Salim Ben Nasser–Public Authority for Investment Promotion&Export Development
Al Issa, Mohammed Ibrahim–Jadwa Investment Co SJSC
Al Jazzar, Abdul Karim–Mubadala Infrastructure Partners Ltd
Al Khatib, Mazin–Warburg Pincus LLC
Al Khazendar, Hisham–Qalaa Holdings SAE
Al Khouri, Saeed–First Abu Dhabi Bank PJSC
Al Maiman, Talal–Kingdom Holding Co
Al Mansoori, Ali–Capital Investment LLC
Al Mukhaizim, Fahad–National Investments Co KSCP
Al Najem, Hafedh–Arcapita Inc
Al Nehayan, Hamed–Abu Dhabi Investment Authority
Al Noaimi, Salem–SeedStartup
Al Noaimi, Salem–Waha Capital PJSC
Al Qadhi, Ibrahim–Gulf Investment Corporation SAG
Al Qassim, Fahad–Waha Capital PJSC
Al Qattan, Tawfeeq–Bahrain Development Bank BSCC
Al Raee, Hisham–Arcapita Inc
Al Rayes, Hisham–GFH Financial Group BSC
Al Shehhi, Saif–First Abu Dhabi Bank PJSC
Al Shroogi, Mohammed–Investcorp Bank BSC
Al Sonbaty, Hany–Sawari Ventures LLC
Al Tamimi, Osama–Arcapita Inc
Al Thani, Hamad–Qatar Investment Authority
Al Umran, Ahmad–Stratum WLL
Al Usaimi, Khalid–Coast Investment and Development Co KSCP
Al Zayani, Ahmed–Arcapita Inc
Al-Arrayed, Ayman–Investcorp Technology Investments Group
Al-Bader, Fatma–Khatif Holding Company KSC
Al-Ghunaim, Maha–Global Investment House KSCC
Al-Khuzam, Mansour–Khazaen Venture Capital
Al-Majed, Adel–Boubyan Bank KSCP
Al-Qaimi, Zaid–Calibrate Management Ltd

Al-Rawi, Ghazi—NCB Capital DIFC Ltd
Al-Rubaie, Sulaiman—Global Investment House KSCC
Al-Sager, Isam—NBK Capital Partners Ltd
Al-Saleh, Abdul-Salam—Boubyan Bank KSCP
Al-Sayed, Ahmad—Qatar Holding LLC
Al-Tuwaijri, Abdulla—Boubyan Bank KSCP
AlTouq, AbdulMohsen—AlTouq Group
Alafi, Christopher—Alafi Capital Co LLC
Alaimo, Riccardo—Vegagest Azionari Asia A
Alaluf, Eliav—Follow Seed Australia Pty Ltd
Alanen, Scott—KV Private Equity Inc
Alarcon, Stephen—Peninsula Pacific Strategic Partners LLC
Alba, Glenn—Blackstone Group LP
Alberdingk Thijm, Christiaan—Peak Capital BV
Alberelli, Gustavo—Trident Capital
Alberg, Tom—MadroNA Venture Group
Albergotti, Robert—Haynes and Boone LLC
Alberici, Gilles—OCTALFA SAS
Albert, Alex—Friedman Fleischer & Lowe Cap Ptnrs L P
Albert, Andrew—Svoboda Capital Partners LLC
Albert, Christian—Bowside Capital LLC
Albert, David—Carlyle Group LP
Albert, Eric—XPND Capital
Albert, Kevin—Pantheon Ventures (UK) LLP
Albert, M. Mark—Crescent Capital Group LP
Albert, Scott—Aurora Funds Inc
Albertsen, Henrik—Nordic Venture Partners Aps
Albeseder, Werner—Sixpoint Partners LLC
Albinski, Luc—Vantage Venture Partners
Alborghetti, Dario—Atlantic Internet GmbH
Albrecht, Brian—Third Rock Ventures LLC
Albrecht, Bruce—Torch Hill Investment Partners LLC
Albrecht, Hans—Pecuniano GmbH
Albrecht, Laura—Maranon Capital LP
Albright, Bear—Bain Capital Inc
Albright, John—Relay Ventures
Albro, Jon—Penn Square Real Estate Group LLC
Alcalay, Eduardo—GP Investimentos Ltda
Alcock, Gary—Revolution Capital Group LLC
Alden, Christopher—Tugboat Ventures LP
Alder, Ronnie—Shard Capital Partners LLP
Alderman, Scott—Trilogy Equity Partners Llc
Aldred, Duncan—Charterhouse Capital Partners LLP
Aldrich, Rich—Longwood Founders Management LLC
Aldridge, Andrew—Deepbridge Capital LLP
Aldridge, Claire—Remeditex Ventures LLC
Ale, John—NMP Management Corp
Alejandro, Billy—Amzak Capital Management LLC
Alemu, Yonatan—Leaf Clean Energy USA LLC
Aleotti, Filippo—Investindustrial Services Ltd
Aleti, Sasank—LLR Partners Inc
Alexander, Douglas—Actua Corp
Alexander, Patrick—Garuda Capital Partners
Alexander, Penelope—Templeton Asset Management Ltd
Alexander, Ralph—Riverstone Holdings LLC
Alexander, Ted—Mission Ventures Inc
Alexander, Tyler—RedBird Capital Partners Platform LP
Alexander, William—Investec Asset Management (Pty) Ltd
Alexanderson, Marcus—Cevian Capital AB

Alexandre, Yves—L-Gam Advisers LLP
Alexandrov, Daniel—Rosslyn Capital Partners OOD Sofia
Alexopoulos, Spyro—Golub Capital Master Funding LLC
Alexos, Nicholas—Madison Dearborn Partners LLC
Alfano, Michael—Coller Capital Ltd
Alfaro, Alfredo—Advent International Corp
Alfaro, Alfredo—Northgate Capital LLC
Alfeld, Chad—Landmark Partners Inc
Alfonso, Xavier—Valcapital Gestion Sgecr S A
Alhadeff, Tara—Permira Advisers LLP
Ali Redha, Huda—Abraaj Capital Ltd
Ali, Ahmad—Auldbrass Partners LP
Ali, Alisher—Silk Road Management
Ali, Mansoor—Global Emerging Markets
Ali, Mohd Nizar—FirstFloor Capital Sdn Bhd
Aliberti, Giancarlo—Apax Partners LLP
Alim, Zubier—Carlyle Group LP
Alimov, Dmitry—Frontier Ventures
Alipbayev, Dauren—Centras Capital Partners
Alipour, Navid—Analytics Ventures
Alix, Jay—Questor Partners Holdings Inc
Alkassar, Eyad—Rocket Internet AG
Allamby, Paula—Cross Atlantic Partners
Allegra, Joe—Edison Partners
Allegra, Joseph—Edison Partners
Allegre, Herve—CDC Climat SA
Allen, Andrew—Dakota Venture Group Inc
Allen, Brad—Keystone National Group LLC
Allen, Chris—Gennx360 Capital Partners LP
Allen, Chris—Palladium Equity Partners LLC
Allen, Christopher—CVC Capital Partners Ltd
Allen, Christopher—Evercore Inc
Allen, Dave—Freeport Financial Partners LLC
Allen, Gertrude—inventages venture capital GmbH
Allen, Kirk—Rose Park Advisors LLC
Allen, Len—Lone Star Fund Ltd
Allen, Mark—Agile Capital Partners
Allen, Nancy—Clayton Associates LLC
Allen, Peter—Mercator Investments Ltd
Allen, Steve—Digitalis Ventures LLC
Allen, William—Carlyle Group LP
Alley, J—Houlihan Lokey Inc
Allgaier, Matthias—Summit Partners LP
Alli, Deji—ARM Capital Partners
Allietta, Michael—Sheridan Capital Partners
Allison, David—5AM Ventures LLC
Allison, Harvey—Attractor Investment Management Inc
Allison, Robert—Innovate Partners LLC
Allison, Steve—Haynes and Boone LLC
Allon, Aaron—MI Ventures LLC
Allorto, Richard—Medley Capital LLC
Allsopp, Craig—Focus Acquisition Partners
Allsteadt, Mark—Capital Partners, Inc.
Allums, Mark—P4G Capital Management LLC
Allweiss, Allan—LBC Credit Partners Inc
Almagor, Jacob—Pacific Venture Partners Co Ltd
Almany, Steven—Biostar Ventures II LLC
Almeida, Antonio—Haitong Capital SCR SA
Almeida, Aymar—Kinea Investimentos Ltda
Almeida, John—Five Peaks Capital Management
Almeida, Marcello—Vinci Equities Gestora de Recursos Ltda

Almeida, Robert—Portland Private Equity LP
Almeling, Florian—KPS Capital Partners LP
Almond, James—Duke Street Capital Ltd
Alon, Ruti—Pitango Venture Capital Management Israel, Ltd.
Alon, Zohar—Evolution Venture Capital Fund I Israel LP
Alonso, Manuel—Phi Industrial Acquisitions SL
Alparslan, Artun—Gramercy Inc
Alpern, David—Varsity Healthcare Partners
Alperwitch, Fabio—FAMA Private Equity
Alpeyrie, Jean-Louis—Heidrick & Struggles International Inc
Alrahma, Ali—Investcorp Bank BSC
Alsenz, Evert—ABP Capital LLC
Alsikafi, Zaid—Madison Dearborn Partners LLC
Alsop, Joe—Alsop Louie Partners
Alsop, Stewart—Alsop Louie Partners
Alsowaidi, Nasser—Gulf Capital Pvt JSC
Alt, Eric—Hall Capital Partners LLC
Alt, Jonathan—Cornerstone Capital Holdings LLC
Altberger, Brad—GI Partners
Alter, Doron—Innovation Endeavors LLC
Altman, David—Gorge Holdings LLC
Altman, Jonathan—ACP Inc
Altman, Matthew—Arlington Capital Partners
Altman, Matthew—Arlington Capital Partners
Altman, Rodney—Spindletop Capital Management LLC
Altman, Samuel—Signet Healthcare Partners
Altman, Stephen—New World Private Equity Partners LLP
Altschul, Esteban—Accion International
Altszul, Jonatan—Aconcagua Ventures
Alun-Jones, Jeremy—Adm Capital
Alur, Ramesh—Ventureast
Alva, Juan—Fifth Street Capital LLC
Alva, Reshma—Asia Frontier Investments Ltd
Alva, Sandeep—Falcon Investment Advisors LLC
Alvarado, Oscar—Northgate Capital LLC
Alvarez Alvarez, Jose—Banco Santander SA
Alvarez, Antonio—Acero Capital, L.P.
Alvarez, Beatriz—Torsa Capital SGECR SA
Alvarez, James—10X Venture Partners LLC
Alvarez, Victor—Wavemaker Partners
Alvarez-Demalde, Francisco—Riverwood Capital Group LLC
Alverson, Harry—Carlyle Group LP
Alves, Alexandre—Inseed Investimentos Ltda
Alves, Melissa—Jackson Square Ventures
Alves, Melissa—Sigma Partners
Alves, Melissa—Sigma Prime Ventures LLC
Alvi, Farzad—Dev Equity LLC
Alvino, John—Actinic Ventures LLC
Alvord, Seth—Balance Point Capital Partners, L.P.
Amadeo, Eduardo—Nazca Ventures
Amann, Matthew—Lariat Partners LP
Amar, Maor—Impression Ventures
Amara, Rajeev—Golden Gate Capital Inc
Amato, Bert—Golden Venture Partners Inc
Ambardekar, Vinay—Unicorn India Ventures Advisors LLP
Ambrosi, Christophe—Perceva SAS
Amen, Robert—Vector Capital Management LP
Ament, David—Parthenon Capital LLC

Pratt's Guide to Private Equity & Venture Capital Sources

Amereller, Philipp–Silver Investment Partners GmbH & Co KG
Amero, Adam–Charles River Ventures LLC
Amiaz, Ronit–Carmel Ventures IV Principals Fund LP
Amidi, Rahim–Amidzad Partners, Co.
Amidi, Saeed–Amidzad Partners, Co.
Amiel, Paul–Haynes and Boone LLC
Amin, Vipul–Carlyle Group LP
Amine, Firas Ei–Investcorp Technology Investments Group
Amirana, Omar–Allied Minds LLC
Amirault, Dennis–Clarke Inc
Amis, Robert–Pantheon Ventures (UK) LLP
Amm, Michael–Torys LLP
Ammann, Stefan–Capital Dynamics Sdn Bhd
Ammar, George–Resilience Capital Partners LLC
Ammar, Oussama–Thefamily SAS
Ammerman, Robert–Capital Resource Partners
Ammirati, Sean–Birchmere Ventures
Amos, John–Bioveda China Fund
Amour, Peter–Aif Capital Asia Iii LP
Amouyal, Philippe–Invus Group LLC
Ampleford, Glen–Carpedia Capital Ltd
Amsellem, Paul–Ubequity Capital Partners Inc
Amundson, Paul–Gen7 Investment LLC
An, Michael–Perle Ventures Pty Ltd
An, Sungji–Hamilton Lane Advisors LLC
An, Xin–Boxin Capital
Anacreonte, Nick–Chatham Capital
Anand, Abheek–Sequoia Capital India
Anand, Amit–Jungle Ventures Pte Ltd
Anandaram, Sanjay–Jumpstartup Fund Advisors Pvt Ltd
Anandaram, Sanjay–Seedfund
Anatriello, Marco–Bluegem Capital Partners LLP
Anbalagan, Anand–Vista Equity Partners LLC
Anchia, Rafael–Haynes and Boone LLC
Andelman, Jim–RINCON VENTURE PARTNERS L P
Anders, Adam–Anterra Capital BV
Anders, Adam–Rabo Participaties BV
Anders, Bob–Plexus Capital LLC
Anders, Will–Plexus Capital LLC
Andersen, Claus–Nordic Venture Partners Aps
Andersen, Lars–SEED Capital Management I/S
Andersen, Ric–Milestone Partners LP
Andersen, Soren–ATP Private Equity Partners
Anderson, Brendan–Evolution Capital Partners LLC
Anderson, Brian–Arlon Group LLC
Anderson, Brian–HealthEdge Investment Partners LLC
Anderson, Brian–Nationwide Ventures LLC
Anderson, Bruce–Welsh Carson Anderson & Stowe
Anderson, Carl–Glynn Capital Management LLC
Anderson, Carl–Social+Capital Partnership
Anderson, Christopher–Kohlberg & Co LLC
Anderson, Cory–Accuitive Medical Ventures LLC
Anderson, Craig–Pentech Ventures LLP
Anderson, David–Ampersand Capital Partners
Anderson, David–Supply Chain Ventures LLC
Anderson, David–Sutter Hill Ventures
Anderson, Dean–Inverness Management LLC
Anderson, Debra–Blackstone Group LP
Anderson, Eddie–Pentech Ventures LLP
Anderson, Emma–Capital Dynamics Sdn Bhd
Anderson, Eric–Scale Venture Partners
Anderson, Erik–WestRiver Capital
Anderson, Frederick–Elevation Partners LP
Anderson, Greg–Green Manning & Bunch Ltd
Anderson, Jared–Skywood Ventures LLC
Anderson, Jeffrey–Trust Company of the West
Anderson, Jeremy–Carlyle Group LP
Anderson, Jerome–High Road Capital Partners LLC
Anderson, Jerry–Skywood Ventures LLC
Anderson, Joe–Abingworth Management Ltd
Anderson, John–Kayne Anderson Capital Advisors LP
Anderson, Jon–Ignition Capital Partners
Anderson, Joseph–Arix Bioscience PLC
Anderson, Kyle–Rosewood Capital LLC
Anderson, Leah–Pencarrow Private Equity Ltd
Anderson, Mark–GTCR Golder Rauner LLC
Anderson, Matt–Windjammer Capital Investors LLC
Anderson, Michael–Bregal Investments LLP
Anderson, Michael–Kohlberg & Co LLC
Anderson, Michael–Mainsail Partners LP
Anderson, Michael–Summit Partners LP
Anderson, Richard–Massachusetts Capital Resource
Anderson, Rick–PTV Healthcare Capital
Anderson, Robert–Financial Technology Ventures
Anderson, Roland–Battery Ventures LP
Anderson, Ryan–CCMP Capital Advisors LP
Anderson, Steve–Baseline Ventures LLC
Anderson, Sumner–Deerfield Management Company LP
Anderson, Yeatts–Ridgemont Partners Management LLC
Andersson, Joakim–Kinnevik AB
Andersson, Marten–Volati AB
Andersson, Matts–BaltCap Management Estonia OU
Andersson, Thomas–Lund University
Andjelic, Milorad–Abris Capital Partners Sp zoo
Andlinger, Merrick–Andlinger & Co Inc
Ando, Manabu–Translink Capital LLC
Ando, Masaki–Yasuda Enterprise Development Co Ltd
Ando, Tomoko–J-STAR Co Ltd
Ando, Yasushi–New Horizon Capital Co Ltd
Andonian, David–Dace Ventures
Andra, Sateesh–Endiya Partners
Andra, Sateesh–Ventureast
Andrade, Ines–Altamar Private Equity SGIIC SAU
Andrade, Manuel Noronha–Ecs Capital SA
Andrasco, Frank–Egan Managed Capital LP
Andrasco, Frank–Egan Managed Capital LP
Andre, Lukas–Affentranger Associates SA
Andreassen, Alf–Paladin Capital Management LLC
Andreen, Robert–Nordic Capital
Andreessen, Marc–Andreessen Horowitz LLC
Andreev, Alexei–Autotech Management LLC
Andreu, Celia–MCH Private Equity Asesores SL
Andrew, Mark–Lexington Partners Inc
Andrew, Russ–Roynat Capital Inc
Andrews, Brooks–EW Healthcare Partners
Andrews, David–Lioncourt Investments Ltd
Andrews, R. David–Gryphon Investors Inc
Andrey, Prokofiev–GEN3 Partners, Inc.
Andrich, Will–Astor Capital Group, Inc
Andrienko, Vladimir–Siguler Guff & Company LP
Andryc, Joel–Saban Capital Group Inc
Andy, Andy–Henderson Global Investors Ltd
Aneed, Roy–Natural Gas Partners
Aneja, Sandeep–Kaizen Private Equity
Ang, Jonathan–Brentwood Associates, L.P.
Ang, Jonathan–Brentwood Venture Capital
Ang, Kian Heng–Venstar Capital Management Pte Ltd
Angel, Joseph–Antares Capital Corp
Angel, Nick–Milbank Tweed Hadley & Mccloy LLP
Angeldorff, Simon–AAC CAPITAL PARTNERS
Angelini-Hurll, Rogan–PROfounders Capital Ltd
Angelis, Kevin–BHMS Investments, L.P.
Angelo, Mark–Yorkville Advisors Management LLC
Angelo, Virgilio–Small Business Guarantee and Finance Corporation
Angoitia, Juan–Ardian France SA
Angrist, Gregory–Cohesive Capital Partners
Angue, Louis-Michel–Galileo Partners
Anguelov, Iva–Vision Capital LLP
Anguelova, Irina–Hypatia Capital Group LLC
Anigian, Richard–Haynes and Boone LLC
Anjarwala, Mohammed–Advent International Corp
Ankerbrandt, Kristen–Carlyle Group LP
Ankerst, Peter–Polaris Management A/S
Annese, Brian–Commonwealth Capital Ventures
Annunziato, A. Anthony–EIV Capital Management Company LLC
Annuscheit, Frank–COMMERZBANK AG
Ansanelli, Joseph–Greylock Partners LLC
Ansari, Kamran–Greycroft Partners LLC
Ansari, Nari–Technology Crossover Ventures LP
Anson, George–Baml Capital Access Funds Management LLC
Anson, George–HarbourVest Partners LLC
Antaya, Matthew–Industrial Growth Partners
Anthony, Richard–Evercore Inc
Anthony, Ryan–LaSalle Capital
Anthony, Scott–Innosight Ventures
Antika, Isak–Stratejik Yonetim Hizmetleri AS
Antill, Egan–Evercore Inc
Antin, Blaise–Trust Company of the West
Antle, Karl–ValueStream Labs Syndicate II LLC
Antoine, Nicholas–Red Arts Capital LLC
Anton, Angelica–SILK Ventures Ltd
Anton, Richard–Amadeus Capital Partners Ltd
Antonen, Brian–Celtic House Venture Partners Inc
Antoniades, Alain–Algebra Capital Ltd
Antoniades, Robert–Rbc Capital Partners
Antonio, Susan–Saturn Management LLC
Anttila, Kaisa–Dasos Capital Oy
Anttila, Olli–Sponsor Capital Oy
Antwi-Asimeng, Stephen–Jacana Partners
Anzalone, Thomas–Cantor Ventures
Anzanello, Luciano–Atlantis Capital Markets NA LLC
Aoaeh, Brian–KEC Ventures Inc
Aoki, Hidetaka–Global Brain Corp
Aomatsu, Hideo–Active Investment Partners
Aouad, Saad–54 Capital Ltd
Aoyama, Toshihiko–Sapporo Hokuyo Lease Co Ltd
Apel, Blake–Trinity Hunt Partners
Apel, Stephan–Outlier Ventures Ltd
Aplin, John–CID Capital Inc
Aportela, Fernando–Evercore Inc
Appel, Lloyd–Aisling Capital LLC
Appel, Majory–O'Melveny & Myers LLP
Applbaum, Isaac–Westly Group LLC

Applebaum, Jay–Wingate Partners LP
Appleby, R. Dale–Pepperwood Partners LLC
Appleby, Robert–Adm Capital
Applegate, Brion–Spectrum Equity Investors LP
Appleton, Alyson–Advantage Capital Partners
Appleton, Jim–Akoya Capital Partners LLC
Appleton, Matt–Doughty Hanson and Co.
Appleton, Michael–Palisade Capital Management LLC
Apprendi, Joseph–Revel Partners LLC
April, Timothy–Business Development Bank of Canada
Apte, Shailendra–Centrum Capital Ltd
Apter, Jonathan–Evercore Inc
Aquilano, Don–Allos Ventures LLC
Arafat, Tawfiq–Relay Ventures
Aragona, Joseph–Austin Ventures
Arai, Akiyo–New Horizon Capital Co Ltd
Arakaki, Fernando–Siguler Guff & Company LP
Arakaki, Lisa–Oaktree Capital Management LP
Arakawa, Satoru–J-STAR Co Ltd
Araki, Blake–Westward Partners LLC
Araki, Dale–Morrison & Foerster LLP
Araki, Hideki–Daiwa Securities SMBC Principal Investments Co., Ltd.
Araki, Motonori–Morrison & Foerster LLP
Arangala, Sumith–Lanka Ventures PLC
Arango, Paula–Elevar Equity Advisors Pvt Ltd
Arango, Sebastian–Blackstone Group LP
Arastu, Naeem–Oaktree Capital Management LP
Araujo, Gabriel–PC Capital SAPI de CV
Aravind, MJ–Artiman Management Ltd
Arbess, Daniel–Perella Weinberg Partners LP
Arbeter, Eitan–Oak Hill Advisors LP
Arboleda, Francisco–HarbourVest Partners LLC
Arboli, Guillermo–Alantra
Arbour, Philippe–Palamon Capital Partners LP
Arbuzov, Vitaliy–Fenox Venture Capital Inc
Arch, Milton–WYSE Capital Group
Archambeau, Eric–Wellington Partners GmbH
Archer, Nick–CVC Capital Partners Ltd
Archibald, Bruce–Federal Economic Development Agency for Southern Ontario
Archibald, Jessica–Top Tier Capital Partners LLC
Archibald, Nick–Cybernaut (China) Venture Capital Management Co Ltd
Arcioni, Filippo–Como Venture Srl
Ardell, Ted–Technology Partners
Arditi, Robert–Norwest Venture Partners
Arekat, Ayman–Abraaj Capital Ltd
Arellano, Jose–Towerbrook Capital Partners LP
Arena, Thomas–Milbank Tweed Hadley & Mccloy LLP
Arendt, Jeremy–Cottonwood Venture Partners LLC
Arensten, Eric–Trust Company of the West
Arenz, Thomas–Harvest Partners LP
Arguelles, Michael–Stonehenge Partners Inc
Argyrides, Andreas–Veziris Ventures LLC
Argyrides, Anthony–Veziris Ventures LLC
Argyriou, Kerensa–Brandon Capital Partners Pty Ltd
Argyriou, Kerensa–Helmsman Funds Management, Ltd.
Argyros, Tasso–FirstMark Capital LLC
Arie, Renato–Ecs Capital SA
Ariel, Aviad–Bessemer Venture Partners

Ariello, Marco–Syntegra Capital Investors Ltd
Ariello, Marco–Syntegra Capital Investors Ltd
Arietta, Ignacio–Investindustrial Services Ltd
Arik, Yasemin–Apax Partners LLP
Arippol, Patrick–Dgf Investimentos Gestao De Fundos Ltda
Arjomand, Mehran–Morrison & Foerster LLP
Arkebauer, James–Venture Associates Ltd
Armbrister, Jeffrey–Versa Capital Management Inc
Armbrust, Dan–gener8tor
Armburst, Ryan–ff Venture Capital
Armenta, Carrie–Oaktree Capital Management LP
Armenter, Marcelino–Caixa Capital RISC SGEIC SA
Armitage, Leslie–Relativity Capital LLC
Armitage, Peter–Key Capital Partners
Armony, Izhar–Charles River Ventures LLC
Armstrong, Alan–Rockpool Investments LLP
Armstrong, Andrew–Spire Capital Partners LP
Armstrong, Brian–Point B Capital LLC
Armstrong, Curtis–Lex Capital Management Inc
Armstrong, James–Clearstone Venture Management Services LLC
Armstrong, Jim–Canal Partners LLC
Armstrong, Jim–March Capital Partners GP LLC
Armstrong, Paul–Permira Advisers LLP
Armstrong, Thomas–Cartesian Capital Group LLC
Armstrong, Timothy–Roark Capital Group Inc
Armstrong, W. Bradford–Lovell Minnick Partners LLC
Arnaboldi, Simone–Arcadia SGR SpA
Arnaud, Frederic–Phillimore Investissement SAS
Arnett, Aaron–Yukon Partners Management LLC
Arney, Johnathan–Arle Heritage LLP
Arney, Johnathan–Candover Investments PLC
Arnold, Bill–Neuberger Berman LLC
Arnold, Jeff–Oaktree Capital Management LP
Arnold, John–HBM Healthcare Investments AG
Arnold, Mark–Albion Investors LLC
Arnold, Peter–Research Partners Ltd
Arnold, Rachel–Vista Equity Partners LLC
Arnold, Scott–Accelerate-IT Ventures Management LLC
Arnold, Stephen–Polaris Venture Partners
Arnoldy, Jason–Intervale Capital LLC
Arnone, Miles–Acas LLC
Arnone, Steven–Atlantic Asset Management LLC
Arnson, Eric–Originate Ventures
Arnstein, Peter–Maplewood Partners LP
Arocena Veez, Ion–Suanfarma Biotech SGECR SA
Aroesty, Dave–Platinum Equity LLC
Aron, Michael–iGan Partners Inc
Aronoff, David–Flybridge Capital Partners
Arons, Ian–Jordan Company LP
Aronson, Jeffrey–Centerbridge Partners LP
Aronson, Lewis–Versa Capital Management Inc
Aronson, Michael–MentorTech Ventures LLC
Aronson, Neal–Roark Capital Group Inc
Aronson, Thomas–Monroe Capital LLC
Aronstein, Marc–Odeon Capital Partners LP
Aronzon, Paul–Milbank Tweed Hadley & Mccloy LLP
Arora, Arjun–500 Startups, L.P.
Arora, Hardev–TUFAN Venture Partners, Inc.
Arora, Manik–IDG Ventures India Advisors Pvt Ltd
Arp, Frederik–Arle Heritage LLP
Arpajian, Ralph–Haynes and Boone LLC
Arpe, Matteo–Sator SpA

Arra, Phillip–Monomoy Capital Partners LLC
Arras, Joanna–Baird Capital
Arrate, Norberto–Apax Partners LLP
Arrese, Miguel–Eneas Capital SL
Arrieta, Ariel–NXTP Labs SRL
Arrington, Lloyd–Columbia Capital Group, Inc.
Arrington, Michael–CrunchFund
Arrola, Inaki–Vitamina K
Arrowsmith, Peter–JMI Management Inc
Arsenault, Chris–iNovia Capital Inc
Arsenault, Greg–Vicente Capital Partners LLC
Artale, Frank–Ignition Ventures Management LLC
Artale, Frank–Ignition Ventures Management LLC
Arte, Sanjay–True North
Arthur, Douglas–Evercore Inc
Artinian, Christopher–Beekman Group LLC
Artunkal, Ali–Argus Capital Ltd
Arul, Alain–Incuvest Pte Ltd
Arulanandam, Ed–Riverstone Holdings LLC
Arunachalam, Abhi–Battery Ventures LP
Arunachalam, Ramu–Andreessen Horowitz LLC
Arvedlund, Maggie–Turning Rock Partners Gp LLC
Arya, Abhi–Sandbox & Co Ltd
Arya, Ved–Milestone Religare Investment Advisors Pvt Ltd
Arzubi, Luis–Tallwood Venture Capital
Asakura, Haruyasu–Innovation Network Corporation of Japan
Asarnoj, Samuel–Firm Factory Network AB
Asarnow, David–Craton Equity Partners LLC
Ascher, Brian–Venrock Inc
Ascher, David–Transom Capital Group LLC
Ascione, Michael–Berkshire Partners LLC
Asciutto, Steven–Perella Weinberg Partners LP
Aseff, Jorge–Brown Brothers Harriman & Co
Asel, Paul–NGP Capital
Asen, Scott–Accretia Capital LLC
Asfour, Charles–Victory Park Capital Advisors LLC
Ashai, Zaid–Point Judith Capital
Ashe, Prescott–Golden Gate Capital Inc
Asher, A. Craig–Vital Venture Capital LLC
Asher, Gideon–Evercore Inc
Asher, Kyle–Monroe Capital LLC
Ashiya, Mona–OrbiMed Advisors LLC
Ashley, Bradley–PRIVEQ Capital Funds
Ashley, Jonathan–Fortress Investment Group LLC
Ashley, Trevor–Rosewood Capital LLC
Ashman, Eric–Lerer Ventures II LP
Ashmore, Bill–Ethos Private Equity (Proprietary) Ltd
Ashton, James–Newspring Capital
Ashton, Kay–Silverfleet Capital Partners LLP
Ashton, Michael–ABRY Partners LLC
Ashton, Steve–Lyceum Capital
Askew, Anthony–Reed Elsevier Inc
Askew, Glenn–Brazos Private Equity Partners LLC
Askew, Tony–Rev Venture Partners Ltd
Aslam, Kashif–Blackstone Group LP
Aspback, Lasse–Evolver Investment Group Ltd
Aspen, Henrik–Verdane Capital Advisors AS
Aspergren, Lindsay–North Coast Technology Investors, L.P.
Aspillaga, Martin–Salkantay Partners SAC
Asquith, Alex–Abingworth Management Ltd
Assaad, Hany–Avanz Capital Partners Ltd
Assam, Saif–Blackstone Group LP

Pratt's Guide to Private Equity & Venture Capital Sources

Assante, Linda—Jasper Ridge Partners LP
Assiak, Emmanuel—African Capital Alliance
Assuied, Stephane—Tertium SAS
Astashkina, Tetyana—b to v Partners AG
Astley-Sparke, Philip—Forbion Capital Partners
Astolfi, Lorenzo—Alantra
Aston-Duff, Victoria—AG BD LLC
Astor, Jake—Cassia Investments Ltd
Astor, Sam—Atlas Holdings FRM LLC
Astruc, Gilles—Equitis Gestion SAS
Astruc, Rafael—Private Advisors LLC
Ateeq, Khalid—Venture Capital Bank BSCC
Athas, Robert—Hudson Ferry Capital LLC
Atinsky, Lawrence—Deerfield Management Company LP
Atkins, Colin—Carlyle Group LP
Atkins, Dean—British Columbia Investment Management Corp
Atkins, Lee—Econergy International Corp
Atkinson, Barbara—Werklund Capital Corp
Atkinson, Dennis—ePlanet Capital
Atkinson, Paul—Par Equity Llp
Atogami, Kenichi—Daiwa Corporate Investment Co Ltd
Atsuhiko, Mizukawa—Sumitomo Mitsui Trust Investment Co Ltd
Attanasio, Antonio—HAT Holding All Together SpA
Attanasio, Mark—Crescent Capital Group LP
Attanasio, Michael—Cooley LLP
Atterbury, David—Baml Capital Access Funds Management LLC
Atterbury, David—HarbourVest Partners LLC
Atteya, Tariq—Qalaa Holdings SAE
Attia, Eyal—Tene Kibbutz Investment Management Ltd
Attie, Elliot—Trilantic Capital Management LP
Attieh, Walid—Saned Equity Partners Ltd
Attolini, Marco—Paragon Partners GmbH
Attwood, James—Carlyle Group LP
Atwood, Allie—Halifax Group LLC
Atwood, Brian—Versant Venture Management, LLC
Aube, Richard—Pine Brook Road Partners LLC
Aubell, Tomas—EQT Funds Management Ltd
Auber, Nathalie—HeathQuest Capital
Auberger, Marc—Qualium Investissement SAS
Aubin, Guillaume—Alven Capital Partners SA
Aubrey, Alan—IP Group PLC
Aubrey, Kelly—Wayzata Investment Partners LLC
Aubry, Marion—Seventure Partners SA
Aubry, Stephane—Blackstone Group LP
Auclair, Elisabeth—Eurazeo Pme Capital SAS
Auclair, Pascale—Siparex Proximite Innovation SAS
Audouin, Philippe—Eurazeo SA
Auerbach, Daniel—Fidelity Growth Partners Asia
Auerbach, Jon—Charles River Ventures LLC
Auerbach, Josh—Betaworks Studio LLC
Auerbach, Neil—Hudson Clean Energy Partners
Auerbach, Stuart—Ampersand Capital Partners
Augustin, Larry—Azure Capital Partners, L.P.
Augustyn, Richard—Accretia Capital LLC
Ault, Ben—Grey Mountain Partners LLC
Aumenier, Pierre—Seventure Partners SA
Aurelio, Louis—Kinderhook Industries LLC
Auritt, Robert—Brant Point Partners LLC
Auspitz, Ben—F-Prime Capital Partners

Austen, Christopher—Brooke Private Equity Associates Management LLC
Auster, Charles—Auster Capital Partners LLC
Austin, B.—Irving Place Capital LLC
Austin, M. Leigh—Saybrook Capital LLC
Austin, Mark—North Sky Capital LLC
Austin, Philip—Anterra Capital BV
Avari, Zubin—Charter Oak Equity, L.P.
Avellaneda Vila, Javier—Inveready Seed Capital SCR SA
Avendano, Pablo—Macrocapitales SAFI SA
Averett, David—Summit Partners LP
Averett, David—Summit Partners LP
Averitt, B. Marc—Okapi Venture Capital LLC
Avery, Henry—Avery Business Development Services
Avery, Stuart—E3 Media Ltd
Avida, Dan—Opus Capital
Avila, Joaquin—EMX Capital Partners LP
Avirett, John—Greenspring Associates Inc
Avis, Gregory—Summit Partners LP
Avner, Alon—Bain Capital Inc
Avni, Micah—Jerusalem Global Ventures
Avni, Yuval—Giza Venture Capital
Avon, Michael—ABS Capital Partners, Inc.
Avrutin, Brandon—Rethink Education LP
Awad, Dewey—Bain Capital Inc
Awad, Jim—Zephyr Management LP
Awad, Karim—EFG Hermes Holdings SAE
Awaji, Tsutomu—TEL Venture Capital Inc
Awbery, Richard—Atlantic-Pacific Capital Inc
Aweida, Daniel—Aweida Venture Partners
Aweida, Jesse—Aweida Venture Partners
Axel, Andrew—Great River Capital LLC
Axel, Merrick—Cressey and Company LP
Axel, Steven—Calvert Street Capital Partners Inc
Axel, Steven—Southfield Capital Advisors LLC
Axelrod, Jonathan—Mac6 LLC
Axon, Robin—Mantella Venture Partners
Aydinoglu, Levent—Bancroft Group Ltd
Aye, Christopher—Skyview Capital LLC
Aynechi, Tiba—Novo Holdings A/S
Ayoub, Faris—Cassia Investments Ltd
Azad, David—Galen Associates Inc
Azarmehr, Mehron—Cielo Management LLC
Azeke, Robert—Farol Asset Management LP
Azema, David—Perella Weinberg Partners LP
Azim, Khanzada—KAMCO Investment Co KSCP
Azimi, Shad—Vanterra Capital Ltd
Aziz, Noor Azman—Fajr Capital Ltd
Azulay-Oz, Eliav—Previz Ventures Ltd
Azzam, Fouad—Life Sciences Partners BV
B. Wang, Charles—AVANTALION LLC
BLUME, CATHERINE—Enhanced Capital Partners LLC
Ba, Allen—Canyon Capital Advisors LLC
Baal, Daniel—Credit Industriel et Commercial SA
Babajov, Emil—VoiVoda Ventures
Babani, Solomon—Auven Therapeutics Management LLLP
Babb, Harold—Osceola Capital Management LLC
Babb, Melissa—Harbert Management Corp
Babb, Michael—Osceola Capital Management LLC
Babcock, John—Rustic Partners LP
Babcoke, Jason—Sumeru Equity Partners, L.P.
Babecki, Julio—L Catterton Europe SAS
Baber, Tyson—Georgian Partners Growth Fund

Founders International I LP
Babiarz, Michael—Clayton Dubilier & Rice LLC
Babikian, Shant—Oaktree Capital Management LP
Babitt, Cindy—Cyprium Investment Partners LLC
Babson, Stephen—Endeavour Capital Inc
Babu, Arvin—Greylock Partners LLC
Babu, Vijay—Start Smart Labs
Bacci, Federica—Synergo SGR SpA
Bacdayan, Wangdali—Incline Management Corp
Bacdayan, Wangdali—PNC Equity Management Corp
Bach, Anne-Valerie—Alter Equity SAS
Bachand, Raymond—Solidarity Fund QFL
Bachik, Aaron—Green Manning & Bunch Ltd
Bachireddy, Ashvin—Andreessen Horowitz LLC
Bachle, Christian M.—NIBC Principal Investments BV
Bachleda, Simon—Eos Partners LP
Bachleda, Simon—Revelstoke Capital Partners LLC
Bachleda-Curus, Adam—Bachleda Grupa Inwestycyjna Sp z o o
Bachleda-Curus, Adam—Bachleda Grupa Inwestycyjna Sp z o o
Bachleda-Curus, Bernadetta—Bachleda Grupa Inwestycyjna Sp z o o
Bachleda-Curus, Malgorzata—Bachleda Grupa Inwestycyjna Sp z o o
Bachmeier, Dean—PCM Companies LLC
Bacica, Stephen—MCG Capital Corp
Back, Greg—280 Capital Partners LLC
Backer, Patrice—Advanced Finance and Investment Group LLC
Backman, Patrik—Open Ocean Capital Oy
Backman, Philip—Bennett Jones Verchere
Backus, John—NAV.VC
Bacon, Kathleen—Baml Capital Access Funds Management LLC
Bacon, Kathleen—HarbourVest Partners LLC
Bacot, Maximilien—Breega Capital SARL
Badami, Vinay—BR Ventures
Bader, Daniel—gener8tor
Bader, Hanspeter—Unigestion Holding SA
Bader, Lisa—In-Q-Tel Inc
Badine, Leila—Kuwait Financial Centre KPSC
Badr, Karim—Qalaa Holdings SAE
Bae, Ji Sung—IMM Investment Corp
Bae, Kihong—Strong Ventures LLC
Bae, Seon—STIC Investment Inc
Bae, Sung-Il—Lee&Co Investments Co
Baecher, Gregory—Warburg Pincus LLC
Baehr, Geoffrey—U.S. Venture Partners
Baek, Seung Heon—Hana Daetoo Securities Co Ltd
Baenziger, Hugo—Banque Lombard Odier & Cie SA
Baerheim, Mariann—Hitecvision AS
Baerst, Benedict—Middlemarch Partners LLC
Baeten, Sofie—Capital-E NV
Baez, Cesar—Centinela Capital Partners LLC
Bagga, Kavita—Lion Capital LLP
Bagini, Martino—Astella Investimentos
Bagla, Deepak—3i Group PLC
Bagla, Deepak—3i Infrastructure PLC
Bagla, Prakash—Motilal Oswal Pvt Equity Advisors Pvt Ltd
Bagley, Thomas—Pfingsten Partners LLC
Bagot, Drew—Calidant Capital LLC
Bagusch, Thomas—NORD Holding Unternehmensbeteiligungsgesellschaft mbH

Bah, Allen—Ventana Capital Management LP
Bahl, Anish—Deerpath Capital Management LP
Bahounoui, Aurore—Emerging Capital Partners
Bahram, Bobby—Excelerate Health Ventures LLC
Bai, Bo—Warburg Pincus LLC
Bai, Guoguang—SDIC Innovation Investment Management Ltd
Bai, Hongjun—Golden Bridge Venture Capital, L.P.
Bai, Liguo—Beijing Tianxing Chuanglian Investment Management Co., Ltd.
Bai, Qiang—Ample Luck International Capital Group Ltd
Bai, Ru Guang—Harbinger Venture Management
Bai, Xiao-Bing—Carlyle Group LP
Baiardo, Stefano—DVR Capital SpA
Baier, Jerome—Northwestern Mutual Capital LLC
Baig, Gawir—O3 Capital Advisors Pvt Ltd
Baijal, Shishir—Everstone Capital Management, Ltd.
Bailey, Brian—Carmichael Partners LLC
Bailey, Christian—IncTANK Ventures
Bailey, Irving—Chrysalis Ventures Inc
Bailey, Jason—GrowLab Ventures Inc
Bailey, John—Tpg Growth LLC
Bailey, Mark—Draper Fisher Jurvetson
Bailey, Michael—Argosy Capital Group Inc
Bailey, Michael—Progress Equity Partners Ltd
Bailey, Robert—Akkadian Ventures LLC
Bailey, Robin—Pantheon Ventures (UK) LLP
Bailey, Stephen—Carlyle Group LP
Bailey, Steve—Frazier Management LLC
Bain, Adam—Accelerate-IT Ventures Management LLC
Bain, Thomas—Columbia Partners Private Capital
Bainbridge, David—Veronis Suhler Stevenson LLC
Baines, Peter—Advent Venture Partners LLP
Bair, Andy—Accelerate-IT Ventures Management LLC
Baird, Charles—North Castle Partners LLC
Baird, Chip—Perella Weinberg Partners LP
Baird, Darran—Stone Point Capital LLC
Baird, Dayne—Carlyle Group LP
Baird, Drew—Star Avenue Capital LLC
Baird, Jamie—Blackstone Group LP
Baird, Jon—TriplePoint Capital LLC
Baird, Laura—Private Advisors LLC
Baird, Tripp—Partnership Capital Growth LLC
Bajaj, Aman—Revolution Capital Group LLC
Bajsair, Yaser—Investcorp Bank BSC
Bak, Sander—Milbank Tweed Hadley & Mccloy LLP
Bakatin, Dmitriy—Gruppa Sputnik OOO
Baker, Alex—Relay Ventures
Baker, Ercel—Uni-Quantum Fund Management Co Ltd
Baker, Erik—GF Capital Management & Advisors LLC
Baker, Felix—Baker Bros Advisors LP
Baker, Frank—Siris Capital Group LLC
Baker, Garrett—Waller Capital Partners LLC
Baker, Griffith—Chengwei Ventures
Baker, Heather—SWMF Life Science Venture Fund, L.P.
Baker, Hugh—Evercore Inc
Baker, James—River Associates LLC
Baker, Julian—Baker Bros Advisors LP
Baker, Lance—Nations Funds Inc
Baker, Len—Sutter Hill Ventures
Baker, Matthew—Private Advisors LLC
Baker, Ryan—Ignition Ventures Management LLC
Baker, Ryan—KPS Capital Partners LP
Baker, Scott—Oak Hill Capital Management Inc
Baker, Skardon—Carlyle Group LP
Baker, Trent—32 Degrees Capital
Baker, W. Craig—River Associates LLC
Bakhshandehpour, Sam—Fertitta Capital Inc
Bakhshi, Bharat—Jacob Ballas Capital India Pvt Ltd
Bakhtiar, Pasha—Willow Impact
Bakken, Terje—Reiten & Co AS
Bakker, Juliet—Longitude Capital Management Co LLC
Bakker, Juliet—Longitude Capital Management Co LLC
Bakker, Maurice—Holland Startup BV
Bakker, Ruud—Truffle Capital SAS
Bakr, Walid—Abraaj Capital Ltd
Bala, Rajiv—S3 Ventures LLC
Balachandran, Mahendran—Accel India Venture Fund
Balagopal, C.—Hyderabad Information Technology Venture Enterprises Ltd
Balaji, Anita—Carlyle Group LP
Balaraj, K.P—Westbridge Capital Advisors (India) Pvt Ltd
Balaratnam, Gana—Arcapita Inc
Balbach, Jennifer—Summer Street Capital Partners LLC
Balch, Robert—Cycad Group LLC
Baldassarre, Carl—National City Equity Partners Inc
Baldassarre, Mark—Silverfern Group Inc
Baldassarro, Mallindi—Argus Capital Ltd
Balderston, Monty—Mosaic Capital Corp
Balderston, Thomas—Rosemont Investment Partners LLC
Baldim, Cristina—Kawa Capital Management Inc
Baldinger, Michael—SAM Private Equity AG
Baldini, Andrea—Earlybird Venture Capital GmbH & Co KG
Baldiswieler, Charles—Trust Company of the West
Baldridge, Andy—Westward Partners LLC
Baldwin, Andrew—Western Technology Investment
Baldwin, Brian C.—Barings LLC
Baldwin, David—SCF Partners LP
Baldwin, John—Parallax Capital Partners LLC
Baldwin, Kerry—IQ Capital Partners LLP
Baldwin, Rick—Transition Capital Partners
Baldwin, Thomas—Bruckmann Rosser Sherrill & Co LP
Baldwin, Travis—Congruent Investment Partners LLC
Balen, John—Canaan Partners
Bales, Kevin—Focus Ventures Ltd
Balfour, Carter—Norwest Mezzanine Partners
Balhara, Sanjeev—Third Security LLC
Bali, Mudit—Samena Capital Management LLP
Baliga, Girish—3i Group PLC
Baliga, Girish—3i Infrastructure PLC
Baliga, Subhash—EQ India Advisors
Balijepalli, Gautam—Ojas Venture Partners
Baliotti, Marc—Blackstone Group LP
Balis, Janet—Betaworks Studio LLC
Balistreri, Steve—Blackthorne Partners, Ltd.
Balkanski, Alex—Benchmark Capital Management Gesellschaft MBH In Liqu
Ball, Antony Charles—Brait Capital Partners
Ball, Bradley—Evercore Inc
Ball, C. Thomas—Austin Ventures
Ball, Charles—Andlinger & Co Inc
Ball, Damon—AEA Investors LLC
Ball, David—Madison Capital Partners Corp
Ball, James—Milbank Tweed Hadley & Mccloy LLP
Ball, Michael—Brandon Capital Partners Pty Ltd
Ball, Patrick—Developing World Markets Inc
Ball, Thomas—Next Coast Ventures LLC
Ballan, Yann—Weinberg Capital Partners SAS
Ballard, C. Andrew—Hellman & Friedman LLC
Ballard, Perry—Edwards Capital LLC
Ballart, Antonio Gallardo—Landon Investments Scr SA
Ballein, Valarie—Peterson Ventures LLC
Ballen, Dan—Pine Brook Road Partners LLC
Ballen, Maxine—NJTC Venture Fund
Ballester, Maite—3i Group PLC
Ballew, Lee—Claritas Capital LLC
Balloch, Hugh—Goff Capital Partners, L.P.
Ballta, Andi—NCH Capital Inc
Bally, Jean-Marc—Aster Capital Partners SAS
Balmuth, Michael—SV Health Investors LLP
Baloff, Steven—Advanced Technology Ventures
Balogh, Ed—Ridgemont Partners Management LLC
Balser, Paul—Ironwood Partners LLC
Balsiger, Peter—aventic partners AG
Balson, Andrew—Cove Hill Partners LLC
Balsys, Vytautas—Eight Roads Ventures Europe
Baltimore, David—Column Group
Baltzell, Joshua—Split Rock Partners LLC
Baly, Elena—Capital Dynamics Sdn Bhd
Bamas, Patrick—Auriga Partners SA
Bamelis, Tom—Sofinim NV
Banahan, Thomas—Tenaya Capital, Inc.
Banas, Christopher—Incyte Venture Partners LLC
Banaszuk, Mariusz—Warsaw Equity Management Sp z o o
Bancroft, Charles—Capital Services & Resources Inc
Bancroft, Townsend—Snow Phipps Group LLC
Band, Alex—Bain Capital Inc
Bandini, Matthew—Antares Capital Corp
Baneat, Didier—Alto Invest SA
Banerjee, Jayanta—Ask Pravi Capital Advisors Pvt Ltd
Banerjee, Samonnoi—Bain Capital Inc
Banerjee, Supratim—IEP Fund Advisors Pvt Ltd
Banerji, Ajitabh—Ask Pravi Capital Advisors Pvt Ltd
Banga, Franceska—New Zealand Venture Investment Fund, Ltd.
Banga, Manvinder Singh—Clayton Dubilier & Rice LLC
Bangash, Alex—Rumson Capital Advisors
Banglani, Ritesh—Stellaris Venture Partners
Bank, Keith—KB Partners LLC
Banka, Amit—Unilazer Ventures Pvt Ltd
Banka, Bharat—Aditya Birla Capital Advisors Pvt Ltd
Banka, Roshan—Samena Capital Management LLP
Banker, Sanjay—Bain Capital Inc
Banker, Sanjay—Tpg Growth LLC
Banks, Andrew—ABRY Partners LLC
Banks, Edward—Evercore Inc
Banks, Peter—Bennett Jones Verchere
Banks, Sean—TTV Capital LLC
Banks, Stephen—S3 Ventures LLC
Banks, Stuart—Hellman & Friedman LLC

Pratt's Guide to Private Equity & Venture Capital Sources

Bannick, Matthew–Omidyar Network Commons LLC
Bannister, Janet–Real Ventures
Bannister-Parker, William–Capital International Inc
Bannon, Anne–Icc Venture Capital
Bannwart, Ana Paula–Alothon Group LLC
Banon, Javier–Trilantic Capital Management LP
Banon, Javier–Trilantic Capital Management LP
Banon, Sam–Susquehanna Private Capital LLC
Bansal, Amit–Digitalis Ventures LLC
Bansal, Rohit–Jefferies Group LLC
Banse, Amy–Comcast Ventures
Banta, Derria–Platte River Ventures LLC
Banta, John–Illinois Ventures LLC
Bantin, Lewis–ECI Partners LLP
Banu, Michael–Castanea Partners Inc
Banz, Alexander–LYRIQUE Srrl
Banzet, Douglas–Westcap Management Ltd
Bao, Fan–Xianfeng Huaxing Venture Capital Ltd
Bao, Xiaobin–Hony Capital Beijing Co Ltd
Bao, Yue–Guigu Tiantang Venture Capital Co Ltd
Baptiste, Stonly–URBAN US PUBLIC BENEFIT Corp
Baquero-Cifuentes, Alejandro–New York City Economic Development Corp
Baquiran, Les–Blackstone Group LP
Bar, Moshe–Atlantic Capital Partners GmbH
Bar-Kat, Roi–Genesis Partners Ltd
Barach, Michael–Inflexion Partners
Barak, Tuvia–LUX CAPITAL GROUP L L C
Barakat, Nadim–AlpInvest Partners BV
Barallobre, Carlos–Mercapital SL
Barallobre, Carlos–Mercapital SL
Baram, David–VMG Partners, L.P.
Barancik, Gary–Perella Weinberg Partners LP
Barandiaran, Walter–Argentum Group LLC
Baranov, Eugene–IK Ineko PAT
Baranowski, Stephen–Adams Street Partners LLC
Barashi, Shmoulik–Fortissimo Captial Fund Israel LP
Barasz, Zach–Kleiner Perkins Caufield & Byers LLC
Baratam, Srinivas–Milestone Religare Investment Advisors Pvt Ltd
Barbarosh, Milton–Stenton Leigh Group, Inc.
Barbashev, Sergey–KhK Interros ZAO
Barbeau, J. Paul–Bennett Jones Verchere
Barbeau, Mark–Renovo Capital LLC
Barben, Michael–Partners Group Holding AG
Barber, Ann–Hall Capital Partners LLC
Barber, Darryl–Bennett Jones Verchere
Barber, Jeffrey–TA Associates Management LP
Barber, John–Bridgepoint Advisers Ltd
Barber, John–Cohesive Capital Partners
Barber, Kevin–Columbia Pacific Advisors LLC
Barber, Paul–JMI Management Inc
Barber, Rick–Refactor Capital LP
Barber, Stephen–Banque Pictet & Cie SA
Barber, Tom–Spanos Barber Jesse & Co LLC
Barberio, Caroline–Mission Ventures Inc
Barbier, Christopher–Siguler Guff & Company LP
Barbier, Francois–21 Centrale Partners SA
Barbieri, Leonard–Stata Venture Partners
Barbour, David–Fpe Capital LLP
Barbour, Dominic–Hutton Collins Partners LLP
Barbour, Nathan–Croft & Bender LLC
Barcelo, Pedro–Patron Capital Advisers LLP
Barchilon, Julie–Alven Capital Partners SA
Barcoma, Carl–Graycliff Partners LP

Bard, Alex–Redpoint Ventures
Bard, David–Ascribe Capital, LLC
Bard, Gustav–Adelis Equity Partners AB
Bard, Jonathan–Carlyle Group LP
Bard, Lawrence–Morrison & Foerster LLP
Bardt, Sylvius–Catagonia Capital GmbH
Barefield, Timothy–Pershing Square Capital Management LP
Barennes, Pierre-Olivier–Citizen Capital Partenaires SAS
Baret, Matthieu–Idinvest Partners SA
Barfield, O. Scott–Nancy Creek Capital
Bargach, Saad–Lime Rock Partners LLC
Barger, Gregory–Newsprong Capital
Barichello, Enzo–Bennett Jones Verchere
Baris, Brett–IA Capital Group Inc
Baris, Jay–Morrison & Foerster LLP
Barishaw, Scott–Evercore Inc
Barkat, Eran–BRM Capital LLC
Barker, Alexander–HarbourVest Partners LLC
Barker, Bret–Trust Company of the West
Barker, David–Cinven Group Ltd
Barker, Frank–Kinetic Capital Partners
Barker, Jonathan–Thomvest Ventures Inc
Barker, Karey–Cross Creek Capital LP
Barker, Nicholas–Huron Capital Partners LLC
Barker, Richard–Homeland Defense Ventures
Barker, Wade–glendonTodd Capital LLC
Barkman, Laurie–Topanga Partners LP
Barkman, Sean–Ballast Point Venture Partners LLC
Barkwell, David–Parallel49 Equity
Barlow, Daniel–May River Capital LLC
Barlow, Heather–Harbert Management Corp
Barlow, Jared–Kline Hill Partners LLC
Barlow, Todd–Pitt Capital Partners Ltd
Barman, Jeffrey–Performance Equity Management LLC
Barna, Hayley–First Round Capital
Barnard, Brian–Haynes and Boone LLC
Barnard, Douglas–Cantor Ventures
Barnard, Douglas–Cantor Ventures
Barnard, John–Barnard Associates, Inc.
Barnds, Thomas–Accel-KKR
Barnea, Assaf–Kinrot Technology Ventures
Barnes, Cristy–Lighthouse Capital Partners LP
Barnes, Donna–Oaktree Capital Management LP
Barnes, Greg–Hyde Park Venture Partners
Barnes, Jeff–Clean Pacific Ventures Management LLC
Barnes, Jeffrey–BioVentures Investors
Barnes, Jeremy–OLMA Capital Management Ltd
Barnes, Jonathan–Halyard Capital
Barnes, Phin–First Round Capital
Barnes, R. Scott–LEGEND PARTNERS I L P
Barnes, R. Scott–Walnut Group
Barnes, Robert–Alchemy Partners LLP
Barnes, Steven–Bain Capital Inc
Barnett, Troy–Adams Street Partners LLC
Barnhill, Mark–Platinum Equity LLC
Barns, Tim–Bain Capital Inc
Barnum, Michaela–Algonquin Advisors LLC
Barnum, William–Brentwood Associates, L.P.
Barnum, William–Brentwood Venture Capital
Baron, Claudia–PPM America Capital Partners LLC
Baron, Harold–Blackstone Group LP

Baroni, Alessandro–Doughty Hanson and Co.
Baronsky, Kenneth–Milbank Tweed Hadley & Mccloy LLP
Baroyan, Eric–American Industrial Partners
Barozzi, Mario–Idea Capital Funds Societa di Gestione del Risparmio SpA
Barquist, Charles–Morrison & Foerster LLP
Barr, Gregory–Silver Oak Services Partners
Barr, Katherine–Mohr Davidow Ventures
Barr, Matthew–Milbank Tweed Hadley & Mccloy LLP
Barr, Michael–Sterling Investment Partners II LP
Barr, Rob–Pantheon Ventures (UK) LLP
Barr, Robbie–Terra Firma Capital Partners Ltd
Barra, James–Ironwood Investment Management LLC
Barrack, Thomas–Halifax Group LLC
Barrage, Khalil–Invus Group LLC
Barras, Claude–SIFEM AG
Barras, David–Northwestern Mutual Capital LLC
Barras, Emmanuel–Caisse Regionale de Credit Agricole Mutuel Sud Rhone Alpes
Barratt, Henry–Blue Water Capital LLC
Barreda, Jorge–SinoLatin Capital
Barrelet, Blaise–Analytics Ventures
Barrett, David–Polaris Venture Partners
Barrett, Jamie–Acrewood Holdings LLC
Barrett, Kerry–Accretive Solutions Inc
Barrett, Paul–BelHealth Investment Partners LLC
Barrett, Peter–Atlas Venture Advisors Inc
Barrett, Randal–Pioneer Capital Partners AS
Barrett, Ross–BVM Capital LLC
Barrette, Sean–Chicago Growth Partners LLC
Barrica, Andrea–500 Startups, L.P.
Barrigh, Jorge–Emerging Energy & Environment LLC
Barrile, Parker–Norwest Venture Partners
Barringer, Charles–Farol Asset Management LP
Barrington, Patrick–Optimum Technology Fund LP
Barrington, Scott–North Sky Capital LLC
Barrios, Kathryn–Developing World Markets Inc
Barrios, Raymond–Crescent Capital Group LP
Barris, Peter–New Enterprise Associates Inc
Barron, Adam–Bregal Capital LLP
Barron, Adam–Bregal Investments LLP
Barron, Bruce–Origin Ventures LLC
Barron, Ronald–Bennett Jones Verchere
Barrows, Timothy–Matrix Partners, L.P.
Barry, Brendan–Kenda Capital BV
Barry, Daniel–Antares Capital Corp
Barry, David–Blackstone Group LP
Barry, Deanna–Incline Management Corp
Barry, Jeff–Plymouth Venture Partners
Barry, Jeffery–Plymouth Venture Partners
Barry, John–First Reserve Corp
Barry, John–Prospect Street Ventures
Barry, Melissa–New Heritage Capital LLC
Barry, Michael–Castle Island Partners LLC
Barry, Scott–EW Healthcare Partners
Barry-Reed, Jessica–Alta Communications Inc
Barsony, Les–Hypoid Partners
Bartee, William–Southern Cross Venture Partners Pty Ltd
Bartelt, Jonathan–Fluxus Ventures LLP
Bartfeld, Daniel–Milbank Tweed Hadley & Mccloy LLP
Barthelemy, Brennan–Sterling Partners GP LLC

Pratt's Guide to Private Equity & Venture Capital Sources

Bartholomew, David–Cambridge Companies Spg LLC
Bartkiewicz, Jakub–Vestor Dom Maklerski SA
Bartkowsk, William–BlueFire Partners Capital Markets Group
Bartlett, Blake–Battery Ventures LP
Bartlett, Blake–Openview Venture Partners LP
Bartlett, Jason–Morrison & Foerster LLP
Bartlett, Paul–Rho Capital Partners Inc
Bartlett, Samuel–Charlesbank Capital Partners LLC
Bartok, Jared–Ampersand Capital Partners
Bartoli, Jeffrey–Centre Partners Management LLC
Bartolini, Charles–Nautic Partners LLC
Barton, Alicia–Massachusetts Clean Energy Center
Barton, Melanie–Progress Equity Partners Ltd
Barton, Michael–Pala Investments
Barton, Richard–Benchmark Capital Management Gesellschaft MBH In Liqu
Barton, Todd–Compass Capital Services Inc
Barton, Wesley–Trimaran Capital LLC
Bartos, Andrzej–Innova Capital Sp z o o
Bartos, Ondrej–Credo Ventures as
Barua, Rajat–Lime Rock Partners LLC
Baruch, Thomas–CMEA Development Company LLC
Baruch, Thomas–M34 Capital Inc
Baruchi, Dan–Previz Ventures Ltd
Baruchowitz, Mitch–Merida Capital Partners LLC
Barzyk, Michael–Jabodon PT Co
Basak, Amit–Staley Capital Management LLC
Basak, Selim–Gemcorp Capital LLP
Bashir, Imran–Extreme Venture Partners Inc
Bashour, Fouad–CIC Partners, L.P.
Basil, Paul–Menterra Venture Advisors Pvt Ltd
Basilio, Paulo–3G Capital Inc
Baskett, Forest–New Enterprise Associates Inc
Baskin, Bo–Dos Rios Partners LP
Basra, Harinder–Bennett Jones Verchere
Bass, Daniel–Fortress Investment Group LLC
Bass, Sarah–Adams Street Partners LLC
Bassett, Jon–NextGen Venture Partners LLC
Bassford, Stephen–Diamond Castle Holdings LLC
Bassi, Benoit–Bridgepoint Advisers Ltd
Bassi, Luca–Bain Capital Inc
Bassi, Rohit–Corridor Capital LLC
Bassichis, Daniel–Admiral Capital Group
Bassil, Jeremy–Northill Capital LLP
Basta, Steve–Spindletop Capital Management LLC
Bastable, Jordan–Longwater Opportunities LLC
Bastaki, Abdul Monaim–Global Banking Corporation BSCC
Bastin, Charles–Capital E Group
Bastlein, Sonke–Nordic Capital
Basto, David–Broad Sky Partners LLC
Basu, Jayanta–CX Partners
Basu, Upal–NGP Capital
Bataille de Longprey, Gautier–Banque Degroof Petercam SA
Batalha, Goncalo–Ecs Capital SA
Batcheller, Paul–Prairiegold Venture Partners
Batchelor, Nicholas–RMB Investment Advisory Pty Ltd
Batekhin, Sergey–KhK Interros ZAO
Bateman, Justin–BC Partners LLP
Bates, Brian–Morrison & Foerster LLP
Bates, Carrie–Triathlon Medical Ventures LLC

Bates, Gavin–Caltius Mezzanine
Bates, John–Potomac Equity Partners LLC
Bateson, Marcia–SAIL Capital Partners LLC
Bathon, Daniel–Windspeed Ventures
Bator, Rafal–Enterprise Investors Sp z o o
Batra, Rajeev–Mayfield Fund
Batra, Rohit–Evolvence Capital Ltd
Batta, Raghu–Ojas Venture Partners
Battaglia, Blake–ABRY Partners LLC
Battcock, Humphrey–Advent International Corp
Battenfeld, Marc–Capvis Equity Partners AG
Batterson, Leonard–Batterson Venture Capital
Battey, Rik–Sagard SAS
Battista, Jacqueline–Siguler Guff & Company LP
Battistoni, Darren–Welsh Carson Anderson & Stowe
Battle, David–Metalmark Capital Holdings LLC
Baty, Daniel–Columbia Pacific Advisors LLC
Baty, Greg–Hamilton Lane Advisors LLC
Baty, Stanley–Columbia Pacific Advisors LLC
Batzel, John–Bennett Jones Verchere
Bauchet, Pierrick–Inocap Gestion SAS
Baud, Jan–NPM Capital NV
Baudon, Thierry–Mid Europa Partners LLP
Bauer, Axel–MIDAS Management AG
Bauer, Bruce–Newbury Ventures
Bauer, Stacey–Galen Associates Inc
Bauerly, Richard–Granite Equity Partners LLC
Baum, Andrew–H2o Venture Partners Pe Ltd
Baum, Daniel–Russell Square Partners Inc
Baum, David–Stage 1 Ventures LLC
Baum, James–Openview Venture Partners LP
Baum, Michael–Rembrandt Venture Management LLC
Baum, Woody–One Line Partners LLC
Bauman, Dan–North Branch Capital LP
Bauman, David–Tailwind Capital Partners LP
Bauman, David–Thomas Weisel Partners Group Inc
Bauman, J.P.–Altira Group LLC
Bauman, Janet–Hamilton Lane Advisors LLC
Baumann, Julie–Avenue Capital Group LLC
Baumbaugh, Cregg–Trilogy Equity Partners Llc
Baumberger, Roger–Spencer Trask Ventures Inc
Baumeister, Ralf–Motus Mittelstandskapital GmbH
Baumer, John–Leonard Green & Partners LP
Baumgardt, James–Twilight Venture Partners
Baumgarten, Joshua–AG BD LLC
Baumgarten, Joshua–Blackstone Group LP
Baumli, Greg–Roundtable Healthcare Partners LP
Baumstark, John–Resurgens Technology Partners LLC
Baus, Stephen–Jh Partners LLC
Bauserman, David–2X CONSUMER PRODUCTS GROWTH PARTNERS L P
Bautin, Max–IQ Capital Partners LLP
Bawa, Ramesh–IL & FS Investment Managers Ltd
Baxter, Bob–Craton Equity Partners LLC
Baxter, Jennifer–TSG Consumer Partners, L.P.
Baxter, John–Wharton Equity Partners LLC
Baxter, Stuart–Riverside Co
Bayazid, Wael–Carlyle Group LP
Bayerl, Thomas–inventages venture capital GmbH
Bayko, Nathaniel–Blackstone Group LP
Bayless, Jon–Sevin Rosen Funds
Baylin, Gregory–ONCAP INVESTMENT PARTNERS L P
Bayliss, Kane–Graphite Capital Management LLP

Bayliss, Scott–Saybrook Capital LLC
Baynes, Brian–Flagship Pioneering
Baynes, David–IP Group PLC
Baynes-Reid, Charlie–River Hollow Partners LLC
Bayol, Guillaume–Oaktree Capital Management LP
Bazin, Sebastien–Colony Capital LLC
Bazos, Frank–Century Capital Management / Massachusetts Inc
Bazzi, Rami–GFH Capital Ltd
Beach, Kristin–Playground Global LLC
Beach, Kristin–Playground Ventures GP LLC
Beach, Tim–MVP Capital LLC
Beakey, Jim–Nautic Partners LLC
Beale, James–Oriens Capital
Beamish, Victor–Leopard Rock Capital Partners Ltd
Bean, Alex–Plexus Capital LLC
Bean, William Bao–SoftBank China & India Holdings Ltd
Bear, Alan–Probitas Partners Inc
Beard, Brooks–Morrison & Foerster LLP
Beard, Dennis–Serra Ventures LLC
Beard, Donald–Harbert Management Corp
Beard, F.Russell–Brazos Private Equity Partners LLC
Bearden, Robert–Benchmark Capital Management Gesellschaft MBH In Liqu
Beasley, Allen–Redpoint Ventures
Beasley, Kathleen–Haynes and Boone LLC
Beaton, Andrew–Capital Dynamics Sdn Bhd
Beaton, Kirk–Lexington Partners Inc
Beaty, Derek–GEF Management Corp
Beaty, Ken–3i Group PLC
Beau, Emmanuel–Energy Access Ventures SAS
Beauclair, John–Vector Capital Management LP
Beaudette, Edna–NCH Capital Inc
Beaudoin, Rene–Mercer LLC
Beaulieu, Nathalie–Acas LLC
Beaulieu, Nathalie–European Capital
Beaumont, Michael–Industrial Growth Partners
Beaumont, Renee–Providence Equity Partners LLC
Beaupain, Taylor–K1 Capital Advisors LLC
Beaurivage, Jacqueline–Ontario Teachers' Pension Plan
Bebb, Sheri–Proterra Investment Partners LP
Bechara, Nemer–Duet Capital Ltd
Becher, Gabriel–Dw Healthcare Partners
Bechtel, Karen–Carlyle Group LP
Bechtel, Mike–Ringleader Ventures LLC
Becirovic, Dino–Kleiner Perkins Caufield & Byers LLC
Beck, Brian–Oaktree Capital Management LP
Beck, Carsten–Peak Rock Capital LLC
Beck, James–Mayfield Fund
Beck, Jason–Vicente Capital Partners LLC
Beck, Katie–Darwin Private Equity LLP
Beck, Martin–Baird Capital
Beck, Martin–Pecuniano GmbH
Beck, Ronald–Oaktree Capital Management LP
Beck, Tom–Oaktree Capital Management LP
Becker, Claus–Perella Weinberg Partners LP
Becker, Dan–Velocity Venture Capital Inc
Becker, David–Meakem Becker Venture Capital LLC
Becker, Eric–Caretta Partners LLC
Becker, Eric–Sterling Partners GP LLC
Becker, Erich–Zouk Capital LLP
Becker, Jeffrey–Haynes and Boone LLC

2445

Becker, John–American Industrial Partners
Becker, Josh–Akkadian Ventures LLC
Becker, Josh–New Cycle Capital LLC
Becker, Lars–DPE Deutsche Private Equity GmbH
Becker, Mark–Hammond Kennedy Whitney & Company Inc
Becker, Mark–New Water Capital LP
Becker, Michael–Plexus Capital LLC
Becker, Mike–Vocap Investment Partners LLC
Becker, Noah–LLR Partners Inc
Becker, Paul–ABP Capital LLC
Becker, Randi–Oaktree Capital Management LP
Becker, Sandra–NewSchools Venture Fund
Becker, Scott–Northstar Capital LLC
Becker, Wiley–Alerion Ventures LLC
Becker, Wiley–Square 1 Ventures
Beckers, Frank–First Abu Dhabi Bank PJSC
Beckers, Jan–Finleap GmbH
Beckett, Steven–Peninsula Capital Partners LLC
Beckett, William–FUTURE VALUE VENTURES INC
Beckett, William–Gefinor Ventures
Beckham, Charles–Haynes and Boone LLC
Beckloff, Bruce–Bloc Ventures Ltd
Beckman, Jay–CIT Group Inc
Beckman, Matthew–Yorkville Advisors Management LLC
Beckner, James–BC General Partners LLC
Becks, Bas–CVC Capital Partners Ltd
Becotte, Dominic–XPND Capital
Beczak, John–Carlyle Group LP
Beddows, John–Amicus Partners
Bedegi, Mary–NGP Capital
Bedi, Varun–Tenex Capital Management LP
Bednar, Andrew–Perella Weinberg Partners LP
Bednarski, Eric–MVM Partners LLP
Beebe, Andrew–Obvious Ventures Management LLC
Beecken, David–Beecken Petty O'Keefe & Company LLC
Beecroft, Thomas–Navis Management Sdn Bhd
Beecroft, Tom–New South Capital Pty Ltd
Beedie, Ryan–Beedie Capital Partners
Beegle, Ron–Goode Partners LLC
Beekman, Gavin–COLLABORATIVE CAPITAL L L C
Beeler, Charles–El Dorado Ventures
Beeney, Marisa–Blackstone Group LP
Beer, Joshua–Charlesbank Capital Partners LLC
Beerekamp, Rikkert–Avedon Capital Partners BV
Beerle, Tom–Bertram Capital Management LLC
Beers, Seth–Revelry Brands LLC
Beetz, Michael–Palamon Capital Partners LP
Beg, Murad–Linsalata Capital Partners Inc
Begert, Brian–Yellow Point Equity Partners LP
Begg, Simon–Warburg Pincus LLC
Beggerow, Chason–Pavilion Alternatives Group Ltd
Beggs, Austin–Saskatchewan Opportunities Corp
Beghin, Jean-Michel–Keensight Capital SAS
Begley, Lawrence–406 Ventures LLC
Begnal, Dorr–Park Street Capital LLC
Bego, Michael–Kline Hill Partners LLC
Begun, Michael–Talu Ventures Pty Ltd
Behan, Colleen–Zesiger Capital Group LLC
Behan, Rosemary–American Beacon Advisors Inc
Behar, Howard–Anthos Capital LP
Behbahani, Ali–New Enterprise Associates Inc
Behm, Dennis–OnPoint Technologies

Behm, Denny–Arsenal
Behnke, Linda–Golding Capital Partners GmbH
Behr, Jonathan–JDRF International
Behrens, Christopher–CCMP Capital Advisors LP
Behrens, Thad–Haynes and Boone LLC
Behrens-Ramberg, Wolfgang–Cbr Management GmbH
Behring, Alexandre–3G Capital Inc
Behrman, Grant–Behrman Capital
Beier, David–Bay City Capital LLC
Beil, Stefan–Sobera Capital GmbH
Beim, Nick–Venrock Inc
Beinart, Eldon–Molash Group
Beinecke, Walter–Brook Venture Partners LLC
Beirit, Konstantin A.–Russkiye Fondy ZAO
Beisel, David–NextView Ventures LP
Beit-On, Harel–Viola Private Equity I LP
Beith, Mark–Silver Lake Partners LP
Beizer, Jonathan–Western Technology Investment
Bek, Eitan–Pitango Venture Capital Management Israel, Ltd.
Bekemeyer, Colin–Oaktree Capital Management LP
Bekenstein, Joshua–Bain Capital Inc
Beker, Limor–Hamilton Lane Advisors LLC
Bekiroglu, Murat–Quantum Capital Partners AG
Bekkali, Zin–Silk Invest Ltd
Bekx, Paul A.–Gilde Buy Out Partners BV
Bekx, Paul A.–Gilde Investment Management BV
Belaman, Cecile–Bain Capital Inc
Belanger, Alain–Investissements Novacap Inc
Belard, Andre–Azulis Capital SA
Belcastro, Vincent–CIT Group Inc
Belcher, Paul–Impact Investment Group Pty Ltd
Belda, Alain–Warburg Pincus LLC
Belden, Nathan–Partnership Capital Growth LLC
Belding, Katie–Norwest Venture Partners
Belen, Saturnino–First Asia Venture Capital Inc
Beletic, John–Oak Investment Partners
Belfer, Todd–Canal Partners LLC
Belford, David–Colony Capital LLC
Belford, Jeff–Triwest Capital Mgmt Corp
Belhassen, David–Neo Capital LLP
Belinfanti, Greg–One Equity Partners LLC
Belingheri, Massimiliano–Apax Partners LLP
Belitsos, John–Bain Capital Inc
Belke, Robert–Lovell Minnick Partners LLC
Belkin, Jeffrey–Curzon Park Capital Ltd
Bell, Craig–TOM Capital Associates Inc
Bell, Daniel–Weinberg & Bell Group
Bell, David–Cfi Capital
Bell, David–Haynes and Boone LLC
Bell, David–Oriens Capital
Bell, Doug–Macquarie Capital Markets Canada Ltd
Bell, George–General Catalyst Partners LLC
Bell, Jeffrey–Morrison & Foerster LLP
Bell, Jory–Playground Global LLC
Bell, Josh–Dawn Capital LLP
Bell, Julie–San Francisco Equity Partners LP
Bell, Maury–DN Partners LLC
Bell, Michael–Monitor Clipper Partners LLC
Bell, Peter–Highland Capital Partners LLC
Bell, Peter–Highland Capital Partners LLC
Bell, Richard–East Africa Capital Partners
Bell, Ron–Actis LLP
Bell, Scott–Weston Presidio Capital

Bell, Stu–Teakwood Capital LP
Bell, Thatcher–Gotham Ventures LLC
Bell, Thatcher–Gotham Ventures LLC
Bell-Jones, Robin–Permira Advisers LLP
Bell-Jones, Robin–Permira Debt Managers Ltd
Bellas, Robin–Lightstone Ventures LP
Belle, Juanita–Consolidated Investment Group Inc
Bellingham, Susan–Canada Pension Plan Investment Board
Bellis, Andrew–3i
Bellissimo, Barbara–Monterey Venture Partners LLC
Bello, Jerry–Keen Growth Capital Advisors LLC
Bello, John–Quest Capital Inc
Bello, John–Sherbrooke Capital
Bellucci, Michael–Milbank Tweed Hadley & Mccloy LLP
Belluck, David–Riverside Partners LLC
Belniak, John–Propel Equity Partners LLC
Beloe, Seb–Alpina Capital Partners LLP
Beloussov, Serguei–Almaz Capital Partners
Belt, Donald–Allied Growth Strategies & Management LLC
Belt, Ron–Truffle Capital SAS
Beltnick, Luke–Castlelake LP
Beltramini, Enrico–Naxuri Capital
Beltramino, Danilo–Idea Capital Funds Societa di Gestione del Risparmio SpA
Beltz, Scott–Oaktree Capital Management LP
Belur, Harish–Riverwood Capital Group LLC
Belusko, Vincent–Morrison & Foerster LLP
Belyakov, Alexey–I2Bf Global Ventures
Belzberg, Brent–Tandem Expansion Fund I LP
Belzberg, Brent–TorQuest Partners Inc
Belzberg, Samuel–Second City Capital Partners
Belzer, David–Prospect Street Ventures
Bemis, Rob–Highland Capital Partners LLC
Ben-Ami, Assaf–Carmel Ventures IV Principals Fund LP
Ben-Arie, Moty–Vertex Israel II Management Ltd
Ben-Avinoam, Barak–Benhamou Global Ventures LLC
Ben-Dror, Yoav–Impact First Investmants Ltd
Ben-Haim, Ron–First Israel Mezzanine Investors Ltd
Ben-Joseph, Oded–Wwc Capital Fund L P
Ben-Or, Ran–Tene Kibbutz Investment Management Ltd
Ben-Zvi, Gideon–Aviv Venture Capital, Ltd.
Benacerraf, Ari–Diamond Castle Holdings LLC
Benaissa, Nasr-Eddine–NCB Capital DIFC Ltd
Benaquista, Mark–Thomas H Lee Partners LP
Benard, Laurent–Atalante SAS
Benaroya, Philippe–Blackstone Group LP
Benatar, Ashley–Vantage Venture Partners
Benati, Walter–Arcadia SGR SpA
Benavides, Joe–Veritas Capital Fund Management LLC
Benazech, Victor–Lion Capital LLP
Benbenek, Marcin–Royalton Partners
Benbouzid, Reyda Ferid–INTERNATIONAL MAGHREB MERCHANT
Bender, Alan–Trilogy Equity Partners Llc
Bender, Michael–Churchill Equity Inc
Bender, Theodore–Croft & Bender LLC
Bendikson, Aaron–Oaktree Capital Management LP
Bendisch, Roger–IBB Beteiligungs GmbH

Bendori, Ori—Carmel Ventures IV Principals Fund LP
Bendori, Ronit—Evergreen Venture Partners
Benear, Jay—Dw Healthcare Partners
Benedetti, Riccardo—Perella Weinberg Partners LP
Benedetti, Tom—Blue Heron Capital LLC
Benedict, James—Kidd & Company LLC
Benedict, James—Milbank Tweed Hadley & Mccloy LLP
Benedicto, Jose—Shard Capital Partners LLP
Benefield, John—Argenta Partners, L.P.
Benetton, Alessandro—21 Centrale Partners SA
Benfield, James—Baird Capital
Benford, Edward—Benford Capital Partners LLC
Beng, Aw Soon—Kingsbridge Capital Partners Pte Ltd
Beng, Choo Chee—OSK Ventures International Bhd
Bengolea, Santiago—Nazca Ventures
Benham, Mark—Celerity Partners LP
Benik, Alexander—Battery Ventures LP
Benik, Alexander—Battery Ventures LP
Benjamin, Gerald—Atlanta Equity Investors LLC
Benjamin, Reni—Burrill & Company
Benjelloun, Yassine—54 Capital Ltd
Benkoski, Jacques—U.S. Venture Partners
Benkoski, Jacques—U.S. Venture Partners
Bennett, Andrew—Nordic Capital
Bennett, Bradley—Siguler Guff & Company LP
Bennett, Dougal—Dunedin Capital Partners Ltd
Bennett, James—Glengary LLC
Bennett, James—Morrison & Foerster LLP
Bennett, Kent—Bessemer Venture Partners
Bennett, Mike—E3 Media Ltd
Bennett, Peter—OLMA Capital Management Ltd
Bennett, Piers—Ardent Capital Ltd
Bennett, Scott—Mobility Ventures LLC
Bennett, Stephen—Stonehenge Growth Capital LLC
Bennett, W. J.—MacKinnon Bennett & Company Inc
Bennett, W. Russell—Metalmark Capital Holdings LLC
Bennion, John—Sorenson Capital Partners LP
Benowitz, Adam—Vision Capital Advisors LLC
Bensimon, Stephanie—Ardian France SA
Benson, Buzz—Sightline Partners LLC
Benson, Erik—Voyager Capital LLC
Benson, Gregory—HGGC LLC
Benson, Liza—StarVest Partners LP
Benson, Peter—Sunstone Capital A/S
Benson, Seth—Green Manning & Bunch Ltd
Benson, Steven—Prism Ventureworks
Benson, Woody—LaunchCapital LLC
Benster, Tyler—Asimov Ventures Management LLC
Bentinck, Alice—Entrepreneur First Investment Manager LLP
Bentkover, Adam—Comvest Partners
Bentley, Anne—Tegna Inc
Benton, Caroline—CVC Capital Partners Ltd
Benton, Dave—Austin Ventures
Bentz, Brad—ATX Seed Ventures
Benudiz, Peter—Milbank Tweed Hadley & Mccloy LLP
Benvenuti, Raynard—Greenbriar Equity Group LLC
Benyaminy, David—AUA Private Equity Partners LLC
Benzie, Patrick—Lunar Capital Management Ltd
Beovich, Anthony—Blackstone Group LP
Beracha, Rami—Pitango Venture Capital Management Israel, Ltd.
Beraha, Stuart—Morrison & Foerster LLP

Berardino, Thomas—Saugatuck Capital Co
Berbon, Patrick—China Materialia LLC
Berden, H.J.M.—Antea Participates Management BV
Beregovsky, Alex—Vector Capital Management LP
Berendes, Birger—Greenhill Capital Partners LP
Berendes, Robert—Flagship Pioneering
Berendsen, Caspar—Cinven Group Ltd
Berengian, Anderee—RezVen Partners LLC
Berenstein, Jason—Kilmer Capital Partners Ltd
Berg, Hakon—Midvestor Management AS
Berg, Jon—Sarsia Seed Management AS
Berg, Kevin—Deerfield Management Company LP
Berg, Nicolas—Redalpine Venture Partners AG
Berg, Steven—Castanea Partners Inc
Berg, Thomas—Anchor Capital Management Ltd
Berg, Thomas—Anchor Capital Management Ltd
Berg-Utby, Terje—Skagerak Venture Capital AS
Berge, David—Underdog Ventures LLC
Berge, Jean-Lin—Capital Grand Est SAS
Bergel, Jaime—HIG Capital LLC
Bergenholtz, Jacob—Odin Equity Partners K/S
Berger, Gene—Ruvento Ventures Pte Ltd
Berger, Gideon—Blackstone Group LP
Berger, Lawrence—Blackstreet Capital Management LLC
Berger, Mark—Incuray AG
Berger, Nigel—New World Private Equity Partners LLP
Berger, Peter—Siris Capital Group LLC
Berger, Scott—Siguler Guff & Company LP
Berger, Stefan—Alto Invest SA
Bergeron, Alain—Canada Pension Plan Investment Board
Bergeron, Michael—Strength Capital Partners LLC
Berges, Baldwin—Silk Invest Ltd
Berges, James—Clayton Dubilier & Rice LLC
Berggren, Marie—California University of Law & Business
Bergheim, Olav—Fjord Ventures LLC
Bergin, James—Morrison & Foerster LLP
Bergin, Matthias—Watermill Group LLC
Berglund, James—Enterprise Partners Management LLC
Berglund, Thomas—First Atlantic Capital, Ltd.
Bergmann, Daniel—PROfounders Capital Ltd
Bergmann, Kristina—Ignition Ventures Management LLC
Bergmann, Kristina—Ignition Ventures Management LLC
Bergmann, Michael—AMG Private Capital Group
Bergmann, Robert—Bregal Investments LLP
Bergot, Patrick—Syntegra Capital Investors Ltd
Bergot, Patrick—Syntegra Capital Investors Ltd
Bergsmyr, Eivind—Viking Venture As
Bergstresser, Gretchen—CVC Capital Partners Ltd
Bergstrom, Jeanine—Connecting Capital Sweden AB
Bergstrom, Nils—Connecting Capital Sweden AB
Beringsmith, Alan—Altos Ventures
Berk, Elijah—KBL HEALTHCARE VENTURES L P
Berk, Howard—MSD Capital LP
Berk, Michael—TA Associates Management LP
Berk, Seth—DreamIt Ventures
Berk, Ted—Bain Capital Inc
Berke, Carl—Partners Innovation Fund LLC
Berke, Eric—TorQuest Partners Inc

Berkeley, Richard—Camden Partners Holdings LLC
Berkery, Dermot—Delta Partners Ltd
Berkey, Ed—Ventana Capital Management LP
Berkley, Kent—Frazier Management LLC
Berkner, Chris—One Earth Capital LLC
Berknov, Kim—Enso Ventures Ltd
Berkowitz, Mortimer—HealthpointCapital LLC
Berkson, Michael—Fulcrum Capital Partners Inc
Berlin, Eli—Parthenon Capital LLC
Berlin, Lawrence—First Analysis Corp
Berlin, Scott—Brown Gibbons Lang & Company LLC
Berliner, Arthur—Walden Venture Capital
Berman, Beverly—Thomas H Lee Partners LP
Berman, Douglas—HIG Capital LLC
Berman, Dror—Innovation Endeavors LLC
Berman, Neal—Thompson Street Capital Partners LP
Berman, Seth—Susa Ventures LP
Berman, Todd—Troika Capital Partners Ltd
Bermejo, Alberto—Magnum Industrial Partners SL
Bermudez-Canete, Pau—Tagua Capital
Bernabe, Marco Norberto—Wadi Ventures SCA
Bernal, Ronald—New Enterprise Associates Inc
Bernard, Michael—Linden LLC
Bernard, Olivia—Massena Partners SA
Bernard, William—Quad Ventures LLC
Bernardez, Stephen—ONSET Ventures
Bernardez, Timothy—Evergreen Pacific Partners GP LLC
Bernardi, David—ID Capital
Bernardini, Jean-Paul—Ixen Partners SA
Bernardo, Allen—SIDER ISRA'EL IYE`UTS KALKALI BE`AM
Bernardon, Roland—Capital Z Partners Ltd
Bernardoni, Pete—Wavepoint Ventures LLC
Bernards, James—Brightstone Venture Capital
Bernasek, Brian—Carlyle Group LP
Bernbach, Allison—CCMP Capital Advisors LP
Bernecker, Marco—Steadfast Capital GmbH
Berner, Robert—Ripplewood Holdings LLC
Berney, Philip—Kelso & Company LP
Bernier, Jacques—Teralys Capital Inc
Bernier, Mark—Antares Capital Corp
Bernier, Stephen—Stellus Capital Management LLC
Bernloehr, John—LEGEND PARTNERS I L P
Bernstein, Adam—New Energy Capital Corp
Bernstein, Alexander—Arlon Group LLC
Bernstein, Beth—Eos Partners LP
Bernstein, Brad—Financial Technology Ventures
Bernstein, Jay—KPS Capital Partners LP
Bernstein, John—General Atlantic LLC
Bernstein, Jon—Blackbern Partners LLC
Bernstein, Michael—Baird Capital
Bernstein, Richard—Eurovestech PLC
Bernstein, Robert—Leeds Equity Advisors Inc
Bernstein, Scott—Lewis & Clark Venture Capital LLC
Bernstein, Tim—Fairbridge Venture Partners
Bero, Bret—Acas LLC
Bero, G. Lawrence—JMC Capital Partners LP
Berry,—WP Global Partners Inc
Berry, David—Flagship Pioneering
Berry, Grant—NorthEdge Capital LLP
Berry, Sean—Tennenbaum Capital Partners LLC
Berry, Timothy—Private Advisors LLC
Bersoff, Edward—Amplifier Management LLC
Berson, Brett—First Round Capital

Bersot, Ross—Bay City Capital LLC
Bertiaux, Patrick—Capatria SASU
Bertin, Philippe—Equitis Gestion SAS
Bertisen, Jasper—Rcf Management LLC
Bertke, Mary Kate—Great Hill Equity Partners LLC
Bertke, Mary Kate—Providence Equity Partners LLC
Bertke, Mary—Providence Equity Partners LLC
Bertocci, Louis—Boston Ventures
Bertoch, Tim—Consolidated Investment Group Inc
Bertolini, Andrea—Cinven Group Ltd
Berton, John—Georgian Partners Growth Fund Founders International I LP
Bertram, Dan—Alaris Royalty Corp
Bertram, Justin—Incline Management Corp
Bertram, Justin—PNC Equity Management Corp
Bertrand, Cyril—Xange Private Equity SA
Bertrand, Jean-Jacques—Orkos Capital SAS
Bertrand, Jean-Jacques—Truffle Capital SAS
Bertrand, Jerome—Bain Capital Inc
Bertrand, Jerome—L-Gam Advisers LLP
Bertrand, Marc—Siparex Proximite Innovation SAS
Berty, Zoltan—D E Shaw & Co LP
Berzofsky, Alex—Warburg Pincus LLC
Besancon, Eustache—21 Centrale Partners SA
Beschinsky, Jorge—Phi Industrial Acquisitions SL
Besharat, Kia—Ubequity Capital Partners Inc
Bess, Stephanie—Investcorp Technology Investments Group
Besset, Yves—Sofipaca SA
Bessette, Guy—Entrepreneur Capital Inc
Best, Brian—Leader Ventures LLC
Best, David—Newable Investments Ltd
Best, Paul—Warburg Pincus LLC
Best, Thomas—Investcorp Bank BSC
Best, Tony—Oaktree Capital Management LP
Besthof, Peter—Suma Verwaltungs GmbH
Besthoff, Skip—Castile Ventures
Betanabhatla, Ganesh—Pine Brook Road Partners LLC
Bethea, Brandon—Aterian Investment Management LP
Bethel, Erik—SinoLatin Capital
Bethell, Melissa—Bain Capital Inc
Bethlen, Nikolaus—Mid Europa Partners LLP
Bettegowda, Manu—Olympus Partners
Better, James—Capricorn Holdings LLC
Betti, Alessandro—Vegagest Azionari Asia A
Bettinelli, Gregory—Upfront Ventures
Betts, John—Climate Change Capital Ltd
Bettum, Ole—Undisclosed Firm
Beukema, Rene—Aescap Venture I BV
Bevacqua, Michael—Bain Capital Inc
Bevan, Oliver—Dunedin Capital Partners Ltd
Beverina, Alessio—Sofinnova Partners SAS
Bevierre, Jerome—Edmond de Rothschild Investment Partners SAS
Bevilacqua, Thomas—Arrowpath Venture Capital
Bevilacqua, Thomas—Vantagepoint Management Inc
Bevitt, Ann—Morrison & Foerster LLP
Beyda, Gil—Comcast Ventures
Beyen, Walter—Vectis Participaties NV
Beyer, Andreas—Fonterelli GmbH & Co KGaA
Beyer, David—Amplify Partners LP
Beyer, Jeffrey—Willis Stein & Partners LP
Beyer, Karen—Blackstone Group LP

Bezancon, Damien—Boost&Co SAS
Bezozo, Kenneth—Haynes and Boone LLC
Bezza, Pietro—Connect Ventures LLP
Bhabal, Amol—O3 Capital Advisors Pvt Ltd
Bhadkamkar, Neal—Monitor Venture Associates LLC
Bhalakia, Sujal—Nexo Capital Partners
Bhalla, Tajinder—Asclepios Bioresearch (UK) Ltd
Bhalla, Uniti—Star Capital Partners Ltd
Bhalwani, Arif—Pinnacle Capital
Bhaman, Maina—Sofinnova Partners SAS
Bhandari, R.K.—Punjab Venture Capital Ltd
Bhansali, Ameet—Intel Capital Corp
Bhappu, Ross—Rcf Management LLC
Bharadia, Vijay—Blackstone Group LP
Bharadwaj, Neeraj—Accel India Venture Fund
Bharadwaj, Neeraj—Accel Partners & Co Inc
Bharadwaj, V.T.—Sequoia Capital India
Bharadwaj, VT—Sequoia Capital India
Bhardwaj, Achin—Aditya Birla Capital Advisors Pvt Ltd
Bhargava, Anurag—IEP Fund Advisors Pvt Ltd
Bhargava, Sameer—Carlyle Group LP
Bhargava, Sanjay—Samara Capital Management Ltd
Bhargava, Sunil—Tandem Entrepreneurs LLC
Bhargava, Vikrant—Veddis Ventures
Bhartiya, Sachin—Lighthouse Fund LLC
Bhat, Jayaram—Shasta Ventures LP
Bhat, Nethra—Elevar Equity Advisors Pvt Ltd
Bhat, Nikhil—Vestar Capital Partners Inc
Bhat, Rohit—Sequoia Capital India
Bhat, Sandeep—Aditya Birla Capital Advisors Pvt Ltd
Bhatacharjee, Jishnu—Nexus Venture Partners
Bhatia, Sunny—Global Investment House KSCC
Bhatiani, Amit—CX Partners
Bhatnagar, Mohit—Sequoia Capital India
Bhatt, Jay—Breakout Capital LLC
Bhatt, Jay—Thomas H Lee Partners LP
Bhatt, Kevin—Long Ridge Equity Partners LLC
Bhatt, Paresh—Morgan Stanley Alternative Investment Partners LP
Bhattacharya, Promit—Hall Capital Partners LLC
Bhattacharyya, Ambar—Bessemer Venture Partners
Bhattacharyya, Joydeep—Canaan Partners
Bhavnani, Sanjeet—SB Capital Partners Ltd
Bhavsar, Umang—Oaktree Capital Management LP
Bhayana, Rohit—Lumis Partners
Bhayani, Anwar—NRD Capital Management LLC
Bhise, Bharat—Bravia Capital Partners Inc
Bhuiyan, Jainal—Fundrx Inc
Bhuniya, Aloke—Everstone Capital Management, Ltd.
Bhusri, Aneel—Greylock Partners LLC
Bhutani, Gurdane—Fundrx Inc
Bi, Mingjian—China International Capital Corp Ltd
Biale, Enrico—Stirling Square Capital Partners Lp
Biamonti, Jean-Luc—Calcium Capital Partners SAS
Bian, Danyang—Shanghai Divine Investment Management Co Ltd
Bian, Jin—Shanghai Divine Investment Management Co Ltd
Bianchi, Annette—Vantagepoint Management Inc
Bianchi, Randy—Summer Street Capital Partners LLC
Bianchini Laydner, Luiz Otavio—Vinci Equities Gestora de Recursos Ltda
Bianco, Maurizio—Motion Equity Partners LLP

Bianco, William—Sandler Capital Management
Bicalho, Mauricio—Triscorp Investimentos Ltda
Bicanic, Nick—Mbloom LLC
Bice, William—Milbank Tweed Hadley & Mccloy LLP
Bice, William—Verge Fund
Bicer, Murat—Charles River Ventures LLC
Bichara, Axel—Bolt Innovation Group LLC
Bickerton, Steve—Prostar Investments Pte Ltd
Bickford, John—819 Capital LLC
Bickham, John—Former Charter Communications Parent Inc
Bickle, Justin—Oaktree Capital Management LP
Bickley, Anna—Morgan Creek Capital Management LLC
Bicknell, Gene—Midwest Venture Alliance
Bicksler, Jeff—UNC Kenan-Flagler Private Equity Fund
Biddelman, Paul—Undisclosed Firm
Biddle, A.G.W.—Novak Biddle Venture Partners LP
Biddle, Brendon—HCI Equity LLC
Biddulph, Michael—Promethean Investments Fund LP
Bidinger, Eric—Pamplona Capital Management LLP
Biederman, Carson—Mustang Group LLC
Biedermann, Wolfgang—HIG Capital LLC
Bielicki, Przemyslaw—Royalton Partners
Bieligk, Wesley—Carlyle Group LP
Bielinski, Robert—CIT Group Inc
Bielowicki, Grzegorz—Tar Heel Capital Sp z o o
Bielski, Sebastian—Team Europe Management GmbH
Bienfait, Fabrice—ETF Partners LLP
Bienstock, Anthony—Cohesive Capital Partners
Bierer, Barbara—Tullis Health Investors
Bieri, Josef—Partners Group Holding AG
Bierman, Ben—Business Partners Ltd
Biermann, Jens—Capcellence Mittelstandspartner GmbH
Biezychudek, Piotr—KRG Capital Management LP
Biezychudek, Piotr—Mountaingate Capital Management LP
Bigby, Wayne—Hedgewood Inc
Bigelow, Rick—Revolution Capital Group LLC
Bigge, Matt—Crosslink Capital Inc
Bigge, Matt—Paladin Capital Management LLC
Biggee, Michael—Trident Capital
Biggerstaff, J. Finley—Herrera Partners
Biggs, Jonathan—Accel Partners & Co Inc
Bigham, Michael—Abingworth Management Ltd
Biglieri, Susan—Kleiner Perkins Caufield & Byers LLC
Bigolin, Rodolfo—NextEnergy Capital Ltd
Bihler, Susan—Catalyst Investors LLC
Bijnens, Stijn—LRM NV
Bijoor, Ameya—Wolfensohn & Company LLC
Biko, Hlumelo—Spinnaker Growth Partners (Pty) Ltd
Bildtsen, Pelle—Energy Ventures AS
Bilenker, Josh—Aisling Capital LLC
Bilimer, Evren—Invus Group LLC
Bilimoria, Zal—Refactor Capital LP
Billan, Jeremy—Parallel49 Equity
Billawala, Omar—Firsthand Technology Value Fund Inc
Biller, Joe—Sightline Partners LLC
Billing, Tomas—Nordstjernan AB
Billings, Timothy—Quad-C Management Inc

Billyard, Paul—Evercore Inc
Bilzin, Jonathan—Towerbrook Capital Partners LP
Bin Hj Mokhtar, Azman—Khazanah Nasional Bhd
Bin Mohammed, Ahmad—Anfaal Capital Co CJSC
Bin Rasheed, Rashid—Gulf Investment Corporation SAG
Binas, Peter—Schooner Capital LLC
Binch, James—Lincolnshire Management Inc
Binderow, Alex—Crestview Advisors, LLC
Bindley, Glenn—Yaletown Venture Partners
Binford, Joy—Novak Biddle Venture Partners LP
Bingham, Catherine—SV Health Investors LLP
Bingle, Mike—Silver Lake Partners LP
Biniak, Bryan—Provenance Ventures
Binning, Gary—Dominus Capital LP
Binur, Yuval—Orchestra Medical Ventures LLC
Biondi, Roberto—Permira Advisers LLP
Biotti, Jon—Charlesbank Capital Partners LLC
Biran, Joel—Versa Capital Management Inc
Birch, Michael—PROfounders Capital Ltd
Birch, Thomas—ID Capital
Bird, Catherine—Boston Ventures
Bird, Jeffrey—Sutter Hill Ventures
Bird, Steve—Focus Ventures Ltd
Bird, Walter—Mass Ventures
Birk, Brian—Sun Mountain Capital Advisors LLC
Birkel, Michael—Target Partners GmbH
Birkeland, Peter—RAIN Source Capital, Inc.
Birkett, Mark—Antares Capital Corp
Birkill, Anne-Marie—Oneventures Pty Ltd
Birle, Jim—Evercore Inc
Birnbaum, Michel—iGlobe Partners Ltd
Birnberg, Jeffrey—Tappan Zee Capital Corp
Birner, Hubert—TVM Capital GmbH
Biro, Timothy—Ohio Innovation Fund
Bischoff, Thomas—Vianova Capital LLP
Bischops, Jeroen—Towerbrook Capital Partners LP
Bisconti, Ben—Accel-KKR
Bisgaard, Peter—Novo Holdings A/S
Bisgaard-Frantzen, Jens—Private Advisors LLC
Bishko, Christopher—Omidyar Technology Ventures LLC
Bishop, Anthony Paul—Iglobe Treasury Management Ltd
Bishop, Janice—Barings Corporate Investors
Bishop, Keith—Stonehenge Partners Inc
Bishop, Nathan—Baml Capital Access Funds Management LLC
Bishop, Nathan—HarbourVest Partners LLC
Bishop, Stacey—Scale Venture Partners
Bishop, William—Odyssey Investment Partners LLC
Bismuth, Didier—Duke Street Capital Ltd
Bismuth, Fabien—La Financiere Patrimoniale d'Investissement SAS
Bisnow, Elliott—Learn Capital Venture Partners LP
Bissig, Josef—BioMedPartners AG
Bisso, Mark—ArcLight Capital Holdings LLC
Bisson, Cedric—Teralys Capital Inc
Bisson, Donald—Century Capital Management / Massachusetts Inc
Bitar, Nawaf—AllegisCyber
Bitterman, Kevin—Atlas Venture Advisors Inc
Bitterman, Kevin—Polaris Venture Partners
Bitting, Thomas—Advantage Capital Partners
Bittman, Christopher—Perella Weinberg Partners LP

Bittner, Ashley—Owl Ventures LP
Bixby, William—Trinity Hunt Partners
Bixel, Kim—Greenmont Capital Partners
Bizer, David—Jasper Ridge Partners LP
Bizot, Jacques—HealthpointCapital LLC
Bizoza, Brian—Deerfield Management Company LP
Bjaarstad, Cathrine—Hitecvision AS
Bjerkan, John—Reiten & Co AS
Bjork, Mattias—Volati AB
Bjorklund, K. Gunnar—Sverica International Boston LLC
Bjornson, John—Point B Capital LLC
Bjursten, Oskar—Firm Factory Network AB
Bjurstrom, Johan—AAC CAPITAL PARTNERS
Blabey, Robert—LJH Linley Capital LLC
Blacher, Perry—Amadeus Capital Partners Ltd
Blacher, Perry—Episode 1 Ventures LLP
Blachford, Erik—Technology Crossover Ventures LP
Blachman, Josh—Atlas Peak Capital
Black, Adam—Doughty Hanson and Co.
Black, Benjamin—New Cycle Capital LLC
Black, Daniel—Wicks Group of Companies LLC
Black, Darren—SV Health Investors LLP
Black, Darren—Summit Partners LP
Black, David—Oak HC/FT Partners LP
Black, David—Wesley Clover International Corporation
Black, Ian—Blackbern Partners LLC
Black, Jason—Fundamental Advisors LP
Black, Michael—Bridgepoint Advisers Ltd
Black, Michael—W R Hambrecht & Co L L C
Black, Philip—True Ventures LLC
Black, Robert—IECP Fund Management LLC
Black, Robin—Catalyst Fund Management and Research Ltd
Blackburn, Tara—Hamilton Lane Advisors LLC
Blackburn, Thomas—Kansas Venture Capital Inc
Blackburn, William—Kilmer Capital Partners Ltd
Blackhall, David—Vinacapital Investment Management Ltd
Blacklow, Peter—Boston Seed Capital LLC
Blackwell, Graham—Bain Capital Inc
Blackwell, Len—Sorenson Capital Partners LP
Blackwell, Trevor—Y Combinator Inc
Blaeser, John—Ascent Venture Management Inc
Blaesius, Michael—Kreissparkasse Reutlingen
Blain, David—Moneta Capital Partners Ltd
Blair, Cherie—Allele Fund
Blair, Jack—MB VENTURE PARTNERS L L C
Blair, James—Domain Associates LLC
Blair, Joe—Chrysalix Energy
Blair, Trace Ryan—Haynes and Boone LLC
Blais, Alain—Campbell Resources Inc
Blaisdell, Thomas—Doll Capital Management Inc
Blake, Claire—Queensland BioCapital Funds Ld Pty
Blake, James—GCP Member Ltd
Blakely, Timothy—Morrison & Foerster LLP
Blakey-Hart, Pamela—Hall Capital Partners LLC
Blanc, Jose-Maria—Intel Capital Corp
Blanchard, Jeffrey—First Capital Group Management Company LLC
Blanchard, Victor—CVC Capital Partners Ltd
Blanchet, Stephane—Investissements Novacap Inc
Blanco, Cynthia—Link Ventures LLLP
Blanco, Jonathan—Bb&T Capital Partners LLC

Blanco, Jose—CVF Capital Partners LLC
Bland, Geoff—Wedbush Capital Partners LP
Blank Tremblay, Jennifer—Fifth Street Capital LLC
Blank, Debra—Stellus Capital Management LLC
Blank, Esana—CCMP Capital Advisors LP
Blank, Greg—Blackstone Group LP
Blank, Jeffrey—Treehouse Health LLC
Blank, Paul—Kayne Anderson Capital Advisors LP
Blank, Richard—SF Holding Corp
Blank, Robert—Chicago Growth Partners LLC
Blank, Rudiger—Park Square Capital LLP
Blank, Stefan—BASF New Business GmbH
Blank, Steven—M34 Capital Inc
Blanks, Cameron—Pacific Equity Partners Pty Ltd
Blasco, Ian—Riverside Partners LLC
Blasel, Doris—Siemens Venture Capital GmbH
Blass, Adam—Yellow Brick Capital Advisers (UK) Ltd
Blasselle, Patric—Siparex Group
Blaszczynsk, Kristian—Raven Capital Pty Ltd
Blatherwick, Nell—RCP Advisors LLC
Blatt, Eli—Fortissimo Captial Fund Israel LP
Blaustein, Michael—DuPont Ventures
Blavnsfeldt, Lars—Industri Udvikling A/S
Blaylock, Ronald—Gennx360 Capital Partners LP
Blazensky, Derek—Cardinal Venture Capital
Blecher, Lennart—EQT Funds Management Ltd
Blechman, David—New State Capital Partners LLC
Blehle, Christine—Ambina Partners LLC
Blevin, Andrew—Abatis Capital LLC
Blevins, Matthew—Clearview Capital LLC
Blewitt, Stephen—Hancock Capital Management LLC
Blilious, Cecile—Impact First Investmants Ltd
Blind, Irena—TSG Consumer Partners, L.P.
Bliska, Thomas—Crosslink Capital Inc
Bliss, Caroline—Crestview Advisors, LLC
Bliss, Simon—Nova Capital Management, Ltd.
Blitz, Leon—Grovepoint Capital LLP
Blitzer, David—Blackstone Group LP
Blix, Ellen—Commonfund Capital Inc
Bliznyuk, Andre—Runa Capital
Bloch, Jonathan—GKM Newport Generation Funds
Bloch, Stephen—Canaan Partners
Blocho, Neda—Pear Ventures
Block, David—Hidden Harbor Capital Partners LLC
Bloemen, Peter-Paul—OMERS Infrastructure
Bloise, Christopher—Court Square Capital Partners LP
Blom, Peter—Triodos International Fund Management BV
Blomme, William—Groep Brussel Lambert NV
Blomquist, Daniel—Creandum AB
Blomqvist, Roger—Nischer Properties AB
Blood, David—Generation Investment Management LLP
Bloom, Bradley—Berkshire Partners LLC
Bloom, Jay—Trimaran Capital LLC
Bloomberg, Ken—AlpInvest Partners BV
Bloomfield, Olivia—Curzon Park Capital Ltd
Bloomstein, Joshua—Ares Capital Corp
Bloss, Adolf—VenturePartner InvestmentBeratungs GmbH
Blott, Andrew—Quantum Capital
Blount, Byron—Blackstone Group LP
Bloy, Nicholas—Navis Management Sdn Bhd
Blue, Harold—BelHealth Investment Partners LLC

Pratt's Guide to Private Equity & Venture Capital Sources

Bluestein, Jared–Berggruen Holdings Inc
Bluff, David–Carlyle Group LP
Blum, Craig–Trust Company of the West
Blum, Tripp–Brown Brothers Harriman & Co
Blumberger, Nir–Accel Partners & Co Inc
Blume, Frederick–Excel Venture Management
Blumenthal, Adam–Blue Wolf Capital Partners LLC
Blumenthal, Jake–Vance Street Capital LLC
Blumenwitz, Peter–Aheim Capital GmbH
Blumerw, David–BlackRock Inc
Blundin, David–Vestigo Ventures LLC
Bluth, Timothy–Shamrock Capital Advisors LLC
Blutt, Mitchell–Consonance Capital Partners LP
Blyth, Stephen–Harvard Management Company Inc
Blythe, Christopher–Potomac Equity Partners LLC
Boal, David–Siguler Guff & Company LP
Bobo, Cedric–Carlyle Group LP
Boboff, Peter–Transmedia Capital Llc
Bobrow, Nick–Hypoid Partners
Boccanera, Gianluca–NextEnergy Capital Ltd
Boccardi, Ennio–VAM Investments SpA
Boccasam, Prashanth–Novak Biddle Venture Partners LP
Boccia, Cristiano–Graycliff Partners LP
Boches, Bryan–Medley Capital LLC
Bochnowski, James–Delphi Ventures
Bock, Lawrence–LUX CAPITAL GROUP L L C
Bockman, Jonathan–Morrison & Foerster LLP
Bocskov, Jordan–Fiedler Capital GmbH
Bode, Bob–Irving Place Capital LLC
Bodenham, Martin–Advantage Capital
Bodenstab, Henrik–Trilantic Capital Management LP
Bodie, Charles–Drayton Park Capital LP
Bodie, J. Scott–Bennett Jones Verchere
Bodine, Chris–Newspring Capital
Bodine, Peter–AllegisCyber
Bodman, John–Elevate Ventures Inc
Bodnar, Kevin–Resonetics LLC
Boecking, Joerg–Freudenberg Venture Capital GmbH
Boehm, Ami–First Israel Mezzanine Investors Ltd
Boehm, Christopher–Willis Stein & Partners LP
Boehm, Hans-Joachim–Aravis SA
Boehnke, Frank–Wellington Partners GmbH
Boehringer, Chris–Oaktree Capital Management LP
Boehringer, Christoph–CD Venture GmbH
Boel, Harold–Sofina SA
Boer, Leks–Three Hills Capital Partners LLP
Boeren, Leni–RobeCo Private Equity
Boersch, Cornelius–Sandpiper Digital Payments AG
Boesler, David–Strength Capital Partners LLC
Boettcher, James–Focus Ventures Ltd
Boey, Wylinn–Aravis SA
Bogan, Thomas–Greylock Partners LLC
Bogdan, Michael–Atalaya Capital Management LP
Bogdanov, Pavel–Almaz Capital Partners
Boger, Owen–Blackstone Group LP
Boget, Franck–Azulis Capital SA
Boggett, Mark–Seraphim Capital (General Partner) LLP
Boggs, Mike–Saints Ventures
Bogue, Zachary–Data Collective LLC
Bogusz, Jim–Beedie Capital Partners
Bohart, Stuart–Fortress Investment Group LLC

Bohl, Jeff–HIG Capital LLC
Bohlen, Greg–Union Grove Venture Partners 2014 LLC
Bohm, Gregor–Carlyle Group LP
Bohn, Lawrence–General Catalyst Partners LLC
Bohnert, Shawn–Ignition Capital Partners
Bohnett, David–Baroda Ventures LLC
Bohnsack, William–Oak Hill Advisors LP
Bohorquez, Eduardo–Nexos Capital Partners
Bohr, Ryan–Hilco Equity Management LLC
Bohren, Philipp–Adams Street Partners LLC
Bohrmann, Braden–Masthead Venture Partners
Bohrmann, Brady–Avalon Ventures, LLC
Boian, Adriana–Societatea de Investitii Financiare Transilvania SA
Boich, Mike–Formative Ventures
Boige, Jean-Philippe–Idinvest Partners SA
Boisseau, Andrew–Insight Equity Holdings LLC
Boisvert, Marie-Claude–Kilmer Capital Partners Ltd
Bojc, Janez–KD dd
Boje, Thomas–Treetop Ventures Inc
Bok, Gaye–Excel Venture Management
Boksa, Pawel–Abris Capital Partners Sp zoo
Bolduc, John–Bayside Capital Inc
Bolebruch, John–Resonetics LLC
Boleski, Joseph–Brown Gibbons Lang & Company LLC
Bolger, Paul–Massachusetts Capital Resource
Bolin, Kurt–Stone Point Capital LLC
Bolland, Anthony–Boston Ventures
Bolland, Martin–Alchemy Partners LLP
Bollini, Richard–Farallon Capital Management LLC
Bologna, Michael–Novaquest Infosystems Inc
Bologna, Mike–Green Lion Partners LLC
Bolten, Charlie–BioGenerator
Bolton, Michael–Novitas Capital LP
Bolyky, Janos–COVENT Toke Befekteto Zartkoruen Mukodo Rt
Bolzan, Denio–Pfingsten Partners LLC
Bolzon, Bradley–Versant Venture Management, LLC
Bomela, Mary–Mineworkers Investment Co
Bomer, Jesse–Natural Gas Partners
Bomholt, Jan–b to v Partners AG
Bommart, Karen–Battery Ventures LP
Bommer, Eric–Sentinel Capital Partners LLC
Boms, Elon–LaunchCapital LLC
Bon, Olivier–Neo Investment Partners LLP
Bona, Tony–Autotech Management LLC
Bonandini, Giovanni–21 Centrale Partners SA
Bonanno, Andrew–Kohlberg & Co LLC
Bonanzinga, Roberto–InReach Ventures LLP
Bonatsos, Niko–General Catalyst Partners LLC
Bonawitz, Douglas–WGL Holdings Inc
Bond, Brandon–Trust Company of the West
Bond, Jonathon–Actis LLP
Bond, Joseph–NCH Capital Inc
Bonde, Thomas–SE Blue Holding A/S
Bonderman, David–Halifax Group LLC
Bonderman, David–TPG Capital Management LP
Bonderman, David–Tpg Growth LLC
Bondick, Gregory–Windjammer Capital Investors LLC
Bondy, Craig–GTCR Golder Rauner LLC
Bone, Ryan–Silver Lake Partners LP
Bonee, Pete–Innosight Ventures

Bonelli, Stephen–Three Arch Partners LP
Boner, Frank–Global Capital Private Equity
Bonfiglio, Stefano–Stirling Square Capital Partners Lp
Bonham, Scott–GGV Capital
Bonham, Warren–Insight Equity Holdings LLC
Boni, Fausto–360 Capital Management SA
Boniface, Barry–MSouth Equity Partners LLC
Bonisch, Michael–Afinum Management GmbH
Bonita, David–OrbiMed Advisors LLC
Bonnar, Mark–Southern Cross Venture Partners Pty Ltd
Bonnavion, Jean–Palamon Capital Partners LP
Bonnecuelle, Alexandre–Montefiore Investment SAS
Bonnet, Yue–Palladium Equity Partners LLC
Bonneton, Jean-Stephane–Time for Growth SA
Bono, Mark–Weston Presidio Capital
Bonoff, Daniel–Goode Partners LLC
Bonomi, Carlo–Investindustrial Services Ltd
Bonsal, Frank–New Markets Venture Partners
Bonsal, Frank–New Markets Venture Partners
Bonsels, Birkhardt–Suma Verwaltungs GmbH
Bonte-Friedheim, Michael–NextEnergy Capital Ltd
Bookbinder, David–Tandem Expansion Fund I LP
Booker, Charles–Advantage Capital Partners
Booker, Niall–Havenvest Private Equity Middle East Ltd
Bookout, John–KKR & Co LP
Booma, Jason–Columbia Capital LP
Boomsma, Maurits–Gilde Buy Out Partners BV
Boon, Tan Keng–SEAVI Advent Corporation Ltd
Boone, Brigitte–BNP Paribas Fortis Private Equity Growth NV
Boone, Michael–Haynes and Boone LLC
Boone, Ray–Multiplier Capital LP
Boone, Rod–Dw Healthcare Partners
Boorady, Charles–Health Catalyst Capital Management LLC
Boorady, Charles–TT Capital Partners LLC
Boorman, Andy–Henderson Global Investors Ltd
Boorsma, Marco–Forbion Capital Partners
Boorsma, Michiel–Beechbrook Capital LLP
Boorstein, Brian–Granite Creek Partners LLC
Boos, Richard–Arbor Private Investment Co LLC
Boot, Hank–Palm Ventures LLC
Booth, Bruce–Atlas Venture Advisors Inc
Booth, Kay–Cappello Capital Corp
Booth, Martyn–West Midlands Enterprise Ltd
Booth, Michael–Calvert Street Capital Partners Inc
Booth, Ralph–Fontinalis Partners LLC
Booth, Robert–Bennett Jones Verchere
Boothby, James–Palisade Capital Management LLC
Bootsma, Jan–Bellevue Asset Management AG
Borah, David–Century Capital Management / Massachusetts Inc
Boralli, Dario–Dgf Investimentos Gestao De Fundos Ltda
Borch, Fredrik–Nord Kapitalforvaltning AS
Borchardt, Gregory–Caerus Ventures LLC
Borcher, Christian–Cardinal Venture Capital
Borcherding, Craig–Oaktree Capital Management LP
Borchers, John–Crescendo Venture Management LLC
Bordeau, David–Berkshire Partners LLC
Bordeaux Montrieux, Pierre–Siparex Group
Bordelon, Don–Roth Capital Partners LLC

2450

Pratt's Guide to Private Equity & Venture Capital Sources

Borden, Paul–Morrison & Foerster LLP
Borden, Philip–Riverside Partners LLC
Bordin, Cindy–Torys LLP
Borell, Jonathan–Sun Capital Partners Inc
Borelli, Ralph–CLUB AUTO SPORT SILICON VALLEY LLC
Borenstein, Ruth–Morrison & Foerster LLP
Borg, Alex–NBGI Private Equity Ltd
Borges Lemos, Mauricio–Banco Nacional de Desenvolvimento Economico e Social BNDES
Borges, Fernando–Carlyle Group LP
Borges, Peter–Levine Leichtman Capital Partners Inc
Borggard, Bradley–Crescent Point Energy Corp
Borho, Sven–OrbiMed Advisors LLC
Borie, Christian–Orkos Capital SAS
Borisy, Alexis–Third Rock Ventures LLC
Borjesson, Hans–Starbright Invest AB
Bork, Michael–Equistone Partners Europe Ltd
Borkowski, Patricia–Invision Capital Management LLC
Borlo, David–Crestlight Venture Productions LLC
Bormann, Rainer–newten Ventures GmbH
Born, Rob–Thomas Weisel Partners Group Inc
Bornhoeft, David–Silver Oak Services Partners
Bornikoel, Friedrich–TVM Capital GmbH
Bornmann, Michael–DEG Deutsche Investitions- und Entwicklungsgesellschaft mbH
Bornstein, Josh–Footprint Ventures
Boro, Seth–Thoma Bravo LLC
Boroian, Patrick–LNK Partners LLC
Borok, Daniel–Millennium TVP Management Co LLC
Borom, Michael–Thomas H Lee Partners LP
Borom, Michael–True North
Borow, Elizabeth–Thompson Street Capital Partners LP
Borrastero, Raul–Rcf Management LLC
Borrows, Simon–3i Group PLC
Borrus, Michael–X/Seed Capital Management
Borrus, Michael–X/Seed Capital Management
Borst, Steven–UpStart Ventures Management LLC
Bort, Randy–CoVestia Capital Partners
Borton, Kenneth–HIG Capital LLC
Boruchovitch, Ronaldo–Vinci Equities Gestora de Recursos Ltda
Bos, Albert–Transequity Network BV
Bosa, Colin–Second City Capital Partners
Bosatta, Luca–Catalyst Fund Management and Research Ltd
Bosch, Sake–Prime Technology Ventures NV
Bosch, Willem–Business Partners Ltd
Bose, Anik–Benhamou Global Ventures LLC
Bose, Simita–Novak Biddle Venture Partners LP
Bose, Supratim–New Silk Route Partners, LLC
Bosenberg, Andreas–Sun Capital Partners Inc
Boshkoff, Katharine–RB Webber and Comapny Inc
Bosio, Edoardo–Embed Capital Srl
Bosio, Emanuele–Embed Capital Srl
Boskie, Shawn–Arris Ventures LLC
Bosma, Paul–Pala Investments
Bosman, Erin–Morrison & Foerster LLP
Bosmans, Hugo–Belgian Invest NV
Bossart, Charles–High Street Capital
Bossi, Donald–Technology Venture Partners
Bossung, Ken–Velocity Venture Capital Inc
Bostandjiev, Atanas–Gemcorp Capital LLP

Boszhardt, Andrew–Great Oaks Venture Capital LLC
Bot, Theo–Syntegra Capital Investors Ltd
Bot, Theo–Syntegra Capital Investors Ltd
Botaev, Dimitar–Teres Capital OOD Sofia
Botein, Matthew–Gallatin Point Capital LLC
Botha, Christoff–Treacle Venture Partners
Bothma, Gerbrand–Tactic Capital (Pty) Ltd
Botin, Alfonso–ALEPH CAPITAL SA
Botman, Frank–Dasym Investment Strategies BV
Botman, Gijs–Mentha Capital BV
Botsman, Rachel–Collaborative Fund
Bott, Charlie–BC Partners LLP
Botta, Nicholas–Pershing Square Capital Management LP
Bottcher, Jeff–Antares Capital Corp
Bottger, Craig–Investcorp Technology Investments Group
Bottinelli, Maurizio–Clessidra Societa di Gestione del Risparmio SpA
Bottne, Patric–Starbright Invest AB
Bottorff, Dennis–Council Capital
Bottorff, Leslie–ONSET Ventures
Botwood, Deborah–Investcorp Technology Investments Group
Bouaziz, Charles–PAI Partners SAS
Boublik, Miroslav–Craig Capital Corp
Boucher, Jonathan–Jordan Company LP
Boudakian, Tom–WP Global Partners Inc
Boudo, David–Metalmark Capital Holdings LLC
Bouffard, Lauren–Advent International Corp
Boufis, Eli–Driehaus Private Equity LLC
Boughton, Marc–CVC Capital Partners Ltd
Bougie, Jean-Marc–Abacus Private Equity Ltd
Bougrov, Andrei–KhK Interros ZAO
Boulais, Wayne–Apex Venture Partners LLC
Boulay, Nicolas–Sofimac Innovation SAS
Bould, Stanley–Highlander Partners LP
Boulnois, Graham–SV Health Investors LLP
Bouman, Tom–Fordahl Capital SA
Bounds, Mark–Bounds Equity Partners, LLC
Bounous, Edoardo–Amber Capital Italia SGR SpA
Bourcereau, Jean–Ventech SA
Bourdelas, Olivier–Inocap Gestion SAS
Bourderye, Pierre–Blackstone Group LP
Bourdie, Mathieu–Acg Private Equity SA
Bourgeois, Anne-Marie–Enertech Capital
Bourgeois, Mark–Abraaj Capital Ltd
Bourgett, Eric–Goodvent Beteiligungsmanagement GmbH & Co KG
Bourgonje, Jos–Value Creation Capital BV
Bourn, Jonathan–AAC CAPITAL PARTNERS
Bourn, Jonathan–Lyceum Capital
Bourne, Duncan–Wynnchurch Capital Ltd
Bourque, Janice–Hercules Capital Inc
Bourquin, Robert–Harbert Management Corp
Bousnina, Kacem–INTERNATIONAL MAGHREB MERCHANT
Bouten, Jan–Aurora Funds Inc
Bouten, Jan–Innova Memphis Inc
Boutros-Ghali, Teymour–Monitor Venture Associates LLC
Bouvier, Pascal–Route 66 Ventures LLC
Bouwmeester, Bart–ICOS Capital Management BV
Bouyea, Lee–Freshtracks Capital LP
Bouyer, Marc-Antonio–Blackstone Group LP

Bouyoux, Laurent–Aquiline Capital Partners LLC
Bovellan, Aapo–Proxy Ventures UK Ltd
Bovellan, Miia–Proxy Ventures UK Ltd
Bowden, Alex–Synova Capital LLP
Bowden, Laurel–Greylock Israel Global Management Ltd
Bowden, Roger–Mount Yale Asset Management LLC
Bowen, Louis–Asia Capital Management Ltd
Bower, Scott–Bennett Jones Verchere
Bower-Straziota, Sophie–Vitruvian Partners LLP
Bowerman, Bret–Harbour Point Capital
Bowerman, Bret–Irving Place Capital LLC
Bowers, Jonathan–CVC Capital Partners Ltd
Bowes, William–U.S. Venture Partners
Bowker, Neil–CORE Partners LLC
Bowles, Erskine–Carousel Capital Partners
Bowley, Richard–Stafford Timberland Ltd
Bowman, Alan–Global Infrastructure Holdings
Bowman, Matt–Austin Ventures
Bowman, Matt–Jabodon PT Co
Bowman, Matt–Tritium Partners LLC
Bowman, Michael–Northleaf Capital Partners Ltd
Bowman, Stephen–Bennett Jones Verchere
Bowman, Whitney–Gauge Capital LLC
Bowman, Whitney–Susquehanna Private Capital LLC
Bowsher, Steve–In-Q-Tel Inc
Boyacigiller, Ziya–Formative Ventures
Boyce, Craig–Bain Capital Inc
Boyce, Patrick–Highland Capital Management LP
Boychenko, Lisa Ann–Morrison & Foerster LLP
Boyd, Andrew–ABS Capital Partners, Inc.
Boyd, Garry–Ethos Private Equity (Proprietary) Ltd
Boyd, Liza–HPS Investment Partners LLC
Boyd, Liza–StarVest Partners LP
Boyd, Sara–Graham Partners Inc
Boyd, Stephen–Richardson Capital Ltd
Boyd, Suzanne–Noverra Consulting and Capital Partners
Boyden, Adam–RPM Ventures Management LLC
Boyer, Andrea–Sigma Prime Ventures LLC
Boyer, Benjamin–Tenaya Capital, Inc.
Boyer, Rebecca–Adams Street Partners LLC
Boylan, Bernie–Mithras Capital Partners LLP
Boylan, Gerry–Long Point Capital
Boylan, Pete–Orchard Holdings Group LLC
Boyle, Brendan–Blackstone Group LP
Boyle, Chris–CLSA Capital Partners HK Ltd
Boyle, David–Morgan Stanley Alternative Investment Partners LP
Boyle, Jim–Inflexion Partners
Boyle, Richard–Canaan Partners
Boynton, John–Shorenstein Co LLC
Boyter, Erik–Odin Equity Partners K/S
Bozeman, Keith–Blu Venture Investors LLC
Bozeman, Robert–Angel Investors, LP
Bozic, Aleksandra–Investcorp Bank BSC
Brabers, Alex–Gimv Investeringsmaatschappij Voor Vlanderen NV
Brack, Jessica–Valencia Capital LLC
Brackett, David–Antares Capital Corp
Brackett, Gregory–Caltius Equity Partners
Brackett, Gregory–Caltius Mezzanine
Bradbury, David–Vermont Center for Emerging Technologies
Braddock, Tony–Stellex Capital Management LP

2451

Brade, Jeremy–Harwood Capital LLP
Braden, James–Cotton Creek Capital Management LLC
Bradford, Dana–Waitt Co
Bradford, Jay–CIC Partners, L.P.
Bradford, Kyle–Acas LLC
Bradkin, Brandon–CVC Capital Partners Ltd
Bradkin, Brandon–Park Square Capital LLP
Bradley, Christopher–Mistral Equity Partners LP
Bradley, Douglas–Westerkirk Capital Inc
Bradley, Ken–Arch Venture Partners LLC
Bradley, Sarah–Kainos Capital LLC
Bradley, Tim–Gryphon Investors Inc
Bradley, Tom–DN Capital Global Venture Capital Ii LP
Bradley, Tom–StepStone Group LP
Bradley, William–Allen & Company of Florida, Inc.
Bradley, William–Waller Capital Partners LLC
Bradlow, John–Penfund Partners Inc
Bradlow, Richard–Penfund Partners Inc
Bradshaw, Larry–ESCALATE CAPITAL I L P
Brady, Christopher–Chart Venture Partners LP
Brady, John–Oaktree Capital Management LP
Brady, Laura–Royal Street Investment and Innovation Center LLC
Brady, Matt–Militello Capital LLC
Brady, Pat–Growth Works Capital Ltd
Brady, Paul–Carlyle Group LP
Brady, Phil–Zenshin Capital Management
Brady, Robert–Stonetree Capital Management LLC
Brady, Tim–Imagine K12 LLC
Braeuer, Uwe–Genius Venture Capital GmbH
Braeunig, Guenther–KfW
Braffman, Peter–Grosvenor Capital Management LP
Bragiel, Dan–i/o ventures
Bragiel, Paul–i/o ventures
Braguglia, Diego–VI Partners AG
Braguglia, Federico–Advanced Capital SGR SpA
Brahin, Olivier–Lone Star Fund Ltd
Brahm, Bert–Aldine Capital Partners Inc
Brailer, David–Spectrum Healthcare Fund LLC
Brainin, Stacy–Haynes and Boone LLC
Brajovic, Milos–Lantern Asset Management LP
Bram, Jonathan–Global Infrastructure Holdings
Bramblett, George–Haynes and Boone LLC
Brambring, Dominik–Blackstone Group LP
Bramley, Donald–Audax Group, Inc.
Branca, George–Acas LLC
Brancaccio, John–Orchestra Medical Ventures LLC
Branch, Barrington–Nancy Creek Capital
Brand, Christopher–Evercore Inc
Brand, David–Sagamore Capital Group LLC
Brand, Martin–Blackstone Group LP
Brand, Monica–Saama Capital LLC
Brandels, Ulf–Startup Factory
Brandes, David–Bay Grove Capital LLC
Brandes, Kai–CMP Capital Management Partners GmbH
Brandewie, Richard–Ballast Point Venture Partners LLC
Brandin, Jacqueline–Glynn Capital Management LLC
Brandis, Dirk–Lead Equities GmbH
Brandkamp, Michael–High Tech Grunderfonds Management GmbH Unspecified Fund
Brandolini, Nuno–Scorpion Capital Partners LP

Brandon, George–MDB Capital Group LLC
Brandon, Henry–Oracle Capital Partners LLC
Brandon, Jeffrey–Waller Capital Partners LLC
Brandt, Chuck–Innovation Works Inc
Braner, Philip–Highland Capital Management LP
Branitzky, Rami–Sapphire Ventures LLC
Branitzky, Rami–Sapphire Ventures LLC
Branman, Jheff–Hilco Consumer Capital Corp
Brannan, Stan–Midwest Venture Alliance
Brannigan, Ian–Western Development Commission
Brannon, Jeff–Metrix Capital Group LLC
Brannon, Schad–NMS Capital Partners
Brannon, Steven–Nancy Creek Capital
Brant, BC–Founders Club LP
Braquehais, Enrique–Blue Swell Capital
Brasch, Dennin–Point B Capital LLC
Brasch, Sam–Kaiser Permanente Ventures LLC
Braslavsky, Roman–GI Partners
Brass, Jason–Goldner Hawn Johnson & Morrison Inc
Brass, Jason–Goldner Hawn Johnson & Morrison Inc
Brassard, David–Investissements Novacap Inc
Brasted, Patricia–Midwest Venture Alliance
Brath Ingero, Bard–Reiten & Co AS
Brathwaite, Nicholas–Riverwood Capital Group LLC
Bratt, Peder–Warburg Pincus LLC
Braud, K. Colton–Main Street Capital Corp
Braude, Paul–Blackstone Group LP
Brauer, A. Jason–Kamylon Capital LLC
Braun, Christoph–Acton Capital Partners GmbH
Braun, Christoph–Burda Digital Ventures GmbH
Braun, Hugo–North Coast Technology Investors, L.P.
Braun, Joachim–Silverfleet Capital Partners LLP
Braun, Michael–Morrison & Foerster LLP
Braun, Nadav–Oak Hill Advisors LP
Braunfeld, Roger–Laurel Capital Partners
Brauns, Ryan–Acas LLC
Bravo Garcia, Gregorio–Blackstone Group LP
Bravo, Alain–Techfund Capital Europe
Bravo, Orlando–Thoma Bravo LLC
Bray, Gregory–Milbank Tweed Hadley & Mccloy LLP
Brazelton, Frederick–Platform Partners Investment Company LLC
Breakley, Tia–Blackstone Group LP
Breakwell, Simon–Technology Crossover Ventures LP
Breaux, Jason–Westbridge Ventures LLC
Breaux, Ronald–Haynes and Boone LLC
Breck, Peter–Rosewood Capital LLC
Breckenridge, James–Med Opportunity Partners LLC
Brecker, John–Hamilton Lane Advisors LLC
Breckheimer, Mark–Akoya Capital Partners LLC
Breeden, Todd–Kiwi Venture Partners LLC
Breeman, Jason–Everstone Capital Management, Ltd.
Breen, Kerri–Arsenal
Breen, Michael–Cfi Capital
Breen, Sean–Consonance Capital Partners LP
Brehm, Michael–Target Partners GmbH
Brein, Jason–Francisco Partners LP
Breitman, Alan–Resonetics LLC
Breitner, Cameron–CVC Capital Partners Ltd
Brekka, Richard–Second Alpha Partners LLC
Brem, Monte–StepStone Group LP
Bremer, Norman–Vitruvian Partners LLP
Bremner, Thomas–Adams Street Partners LLC

Brenan, Coley–KSL Capital Partners LLC
Brenes, Chris–Evergreen Pacific Partners GP LLC
Brennan, Anthony–Praesidian Capital
Brennan, David–Glengary LLC
Brennan, Jessica Hoffman–Carlyle Group LP
Brennan, John–Sumeru Equity Partners, L.P.
Brennan, Katherine–Thoma Cressey Bravo Inc
Brennan, Kelly–Ridgemont Partners Management LLC
Brennan, Mike–Water Street Healthcare Partners LLC
Brennan, Phillip–Go Capital LLC
Brennan, Phillip–Prospect Partners LLC
Brennan, Ryan–Advantage Capital Partners
Brennan, Stephen–Hamilton Lane Advisors LLC
Brennan, T.–Arch Venture Partners LLC
Brennan, William–Brown Brothers Harriman & Co
Brenneman, Bradley–Wingate Partners LP
Brenner, Hans–East West Capital Partners Pte Ltd
Brenner, Johan–Creandum AB
Brenner, Johan–PROfounders Capital Ltd
Brenninkmeijer, Dennis–Entrepreneurs Fund Management LLP
Brenninkmeijer, Marcel–Good Energies AG
Brenninkmeijer, Wolter–Bregal Investments LLP
Brenninkmeyer, Frank–Performance Equity Management LLC
Brereton, Richard–Harbert Management Corp
Brero, Emanuela–CVC Capital Partners Ltd
Breslauer, Keith–Patron Capital Advisers LLP
Bresler, Joshua–Thomas H Lee Partners LP
Breslin, Adam–Penfund Partners Inc
Bresnahan, John–Southwest Middle Market M&A
Bressler, Leon–Perella Weinberg Partners LP
Bressler, Steven–Varsity Healthcare Partners
Bressner, Glen–Originate Ventures
Bretl, J.P.–Tenex Capital Management LP
Brett, Brian–American Beacon Advisors Inc
Brett, Edward–Elysian Capital LLP
Brettman, Ari–Clarus Ventures LLC
Breuer, Juergen–Astorius Capital GmbH
Breukelman, W. David–Business Arts, Ltd.
Brevard, Mary-Belle Michigan Fund LP
Brew, Thomas–AeroEquity Partners LLC
Brewer, Brett–CrossCut Ventures Management LLC
Brewer, Clete–Newroad Capital Partners LLC
Brewer, Elizabeth–Mid-Ocean Partners LP
Brewer, Matthew–Siguler Guff & Company LP
Brewer, Samuel–Merion Investment Partners LP
Brewer, William–Yellowstone Capital, Inc.
Brewington, Jim–Omni Capital Group LLC
Brewster, Stephen–Grosvenor Capital Management LP
Breyer, James–Accel Partners & Co Inc
Briant, Penelope–Capvest Ltd
Bricault, Paul–Amplify.LA
Bricault, Paul–Greycroft Partners LLC
Brice, John–CarVal Investors LLC
Brice, Preston–Apple Tree Partners
Bricio, Jordi–Phi Industrial Acquisitions SL
Brickell, David–Oakley Capital Ltd
Bricker, Debra–Harvest Partners LP
Bricker, Ross–Optimum Technology Fund LP
Brickman, C. Andrew–Baird Capital
Bridge, Charles–Wave Equity Partners LLC

Bridge, Jeffrey—Hyde Park Holdings Inc
Bridge, Michael—Lee Equity Partners LLC
Bridgeland, Charles—Lexington Partners Inc
Bridges, Iain—ACP Inc
Bridgewater, Timothy—Utah Fund of Funds LLC
Bridwell, Paul—Platinum Equity LLC
Briejer, Michel—Thuja Capital BV
Briere, Marc—Arkea Capital Investissement SA
Briggs, Frank—Croft & Bender LLC
Briggs, Jim—Freestone Partners LLC
Briggs, Michael—Anchorage Capital Partners Ltd
Bright Blomquist, Erika—Haynes and Boone LLC
Bright, Aaron—Glouston Capital Partners LLC
Briglin, Timothy—Tuckerman Capital
Brignola, John—LBC Credit Partners Inc
Brilando, Joseph—RB Webber and Comapny Inc
Brill, Kendra—DeSimone Group Investments LLC
Brilliant, William—Global Infrastructure Holdings
Brillon, Timothy—Evergreen Pacific Partners GP LLC
Brimacomb, Richard—Sherpa Partners LLC
Brimacombe, John—Sussex Place Ventures Ltd
Brimmage, Marty—Haynes and Boone LLC
Brin, Slava—Evercore Inc
Brind, Ira—Pulse Equity Partners LLC
Briner, Bradford—Morgan Creek Capital Management LLC
Brink, Stephen—Bridge City Management LLC
Brinkenhoff, Daniel—Centre Partners Management LLC
Brinkhaus, Bert—enjoyventure Management GmbH
Brinkman, Roland—SI Capital Partners Llp
Brinn, Nathaniel—Vital Venture Capital LLC
Brisbourne, Nicholas—Forward Investment Partners
Brisbourne, Nicholas—Forward Partners Ltd
Briscoe, Clift—Taveekan Capital
Briscoe, Zuri—Post Capital Partners LLC
Britain, Lane—Highland Capital Management LP
Britt, Adam—Summit Partners LP
Britt, Adam—Summit Partners LP
Britt, Ben—Route 66 Ventures LLC
Britt, Chris—Britt Private Capital LLC
Britt, Chris—Marwit Capital Corp
Brittain, Keith—Hamilton Lane Advisors LLC
Brittain, Rob—Mobeus Equity Partners LLP
Britton, Stuart—Evercore Inc
Britts, David—Fuse Capital
Britts, David—Gramercy Inc
Brixey, David—Brixey & Meyer Capital LLC
Broadhead, Neale—CVC Capital Partners Ltd
Broby, Daniel—Silk Invest Ltd
Brock, Clay—Hadley Capital
Brock, Justin—Newspring Capital
Brock-Wilson, Jane—Berkshire Partners LLC
Brockenhuus-Schack, Ulla—Pre-Seed Innovation A/S
Brockenhuus-Schack, Ulla—SEED Capital Management I/S
Brockhaus, Marco—Brockhaus Private Equity GmbH
Brocklebank, James—Advent International Corp
Brockman, Ivan—Blackstone Group LP
Brockway, Peter—Brockway Moran & Partners Inc
Brockwell, Christine—Global Capital Finance
Brod, Jonathan—Next Wave Partners LLP
Broda, Tal—Entrepreneurs Fund LP
Brodbeck, Christina—Rivet Ventures Management LLC

Brodbeck, Rolf—BE Beteiligungen GmbH & Co KG
Broderick, Dan—BioGenerator
Broderick, Daniel—Prolog Ventures
Broderick, Jim—Lightstone Ventures LP
Broderick, Matt—Torch Hill Investment Partners LLC
Broderick, Phillip—ABP Capital LLC
Brodlieb, Jeffrey—Centripetal Capital Partners LLC
Brodman, Cole—Trilogy Equity Partners Llc
Brodsky, Bert—BelHealth Investment Partners LLC
Brody, Jeffrey—Redpoint Eventures Consultoria Empresarial Ltda
Brody, Jeffrey—Redpoint Ventures
Brody, Josh—Western Technology Investment
Brody, Leonard—GrowLab Ventures Inc
Brody, Mark—Sun Capital Partners Inc
Brody, Matthew—AG BD LLC
Brody, Seth—Apax Partners LLP
Broe-Andersen, Thomas—FSN Capital Partners AS
Broekelmann, Katrin—Pinova Capital GmbH
Broeker, Alexander—Trellis Partners
Brogan, Chase—TSG Consumer Partners, L.P.
Broglio, Geoff—Gemspring Capital LLC
Broglio, Geoff—Hudson Clean Energy Partners
Brokaw, Clifford—Corsair Capital LLC
Brokaw, George—HPS Investment Partners LLC
Brom, Ilona—Wilshire Private Markets
Broman, Dag—Alder
Bron, Guillermo—Pine Brook Road Partners LLC
Bronckers, Maurice—AAC CAPITAL PARTNERS
Brondum, Jeppe—Blackstone Group LP
Bronfman, Edgar—Accretive LLC
Bronfman, Samuel—Bacchus Capital Management LLC
Bronk, Brian—Sanofi-Sunrise
Bronner, Beth—Mistral Equity Partners LP
Bronner, Philip—Novak Biddle Venture Partners LP
Bronshtein, Ari—Elron Electronic Industries Ltd
Bronsteatter, Phillip—Pfingsten Partners LLC
Brook, Clare—Alpina Capital Partners LLP
Brooke, Geoffrey—GBS Venture Partners
Brooke, Graham—CVC Asia Pacific Ltd
Brooke, Graham—CVC Capital Partners Ltd
Brooke, John—Brooke Private Equity Associates Management LLC
Brooke, Paul—Venbio Partners LLC
Brooke, Stephen Henry Ralph—Swarraton Partners Ltd
Brooke, William—Harbert Management Corp
Brookfield, Chris—Elevar Equity Advisors Pvt Ltd
Brookman, David—Oaktree Capital Management LP
Brooks, Ben—Southern Capitol Ventures LLC
Brooks, David—Fortress Investment Group LLC
Brooks, Erik—ABRY Partners LLC
Brooks, Graham—406 Ventures LLC
Brooks, Greg—Evercore Inc
Brooks, James—First Reserve Corp
Brooks, Jason—Invico Capital Corp
Brooks, John—Pittsburgh Life Sciences Greenhouse
Brooks, John—Prism Ventureworks
Brooks, Mark—Scale Venture Partners
Brooks, Michael—Quad-C Management Inc
Brooks, Rory—MML Capital Partners LLP
Brooks, Sam—Highland Capital Partners LLC
Brooks, Stephen—JFLehman & Co
Brooks, Steve—Newroad Capital Partners LLC

Brooks, Wendell—Intel Capital Corp
Broomberg, Ashley—Mobeus Equity Partners LLP
Broomberg, Barry—Oaktree Capital Management LP
Broos, Kenneth—Atlantic Capital BV
Brophy, Kevin—Meidlinger Partners LLC
Brophy, Ruth—HIG Capital LLC
Brosnan, Denis—Lydian Capital Advisors SA
Bross, Jason—Argon Venture Partners
Brost, Gary—Strategic Investments, L.P.
Brothag, Arthur—Apax Partners LLP
Brothers, Christopher—Solace Capital Partners LLC
Brotherton, Paige—Coller Capital Ltd
Brothman, Daniel—Plaza Ventures Ltd
Brotman, Eric—Carlyle Group LP
Brotzge, Lawrence—Robin Hood Ventures
Brougham, Robert—Newstone Capital Partners LLC
Broughton, Kenneth—Haynes and Boone LLC
Broun, Stephen—Capital for Business Inc
Brous, Michael—Jerusalem Global Ventures
Brouwer, Rist—Silverfern Group Inc
Brown, Alastair—Shard Capital Partners LLP
Brown, Alec—Pantheon Ventures (UK) LLP
Brown, Alec—Seven Mile Capital Partners LP
Brown, Alex—Asssurance Mezzanine Fund
Brown, Andrew—Beekman Group LLC
Brown, Art—Torch Hill Investment Partners LLC
Brown, C.J.—Blackstone Group LP
Brown, Cyrus—WINTHROP VENTURES
Brown, Daniel—Arrowpath Venture Capital
Brown, David—Pacific Equity Partners Pty Ltd
Brown, David—Richardson Capital Ltd
Brown, Dori—Tene Kibbutz Investment Management Ltd
Brown, Edward—Grafton Capital Ltd
Brown, Eric—Audax Group, Inc.
Brown, Garrick—Harren Equity Partners
Brown, Gillian—Mithras Capital Partners LLP
Brown, Gillian—Ontario Teachers' Pension Plan
Brown, Graham—Rockpool Investments LLP
Brown, Grant—Covington Capital Corp
Brown, Greg—Elevate Innovation Partners LLC
Brown, J. David—Jemison Investment Co Inc
Brown, James—Long Ridge Equity Partners LLC
Brown, Jamie—Difference Capital Financial Inc
Brown, Jason—Thomas Mcnerney and Partners LLC
Brown, John—Eagle Private Capital LLC
Brown, Josh—McNally Capital LLC
Brown, Kevin—Court Square Capital Partners LP
Brown, Kevin—Reed Elsevier Inc
Brown, Kevin—Rev Venture Partners Ltd
Brown, Mark—Blackstone Group LP
Brown, Mark—Platte River Ventures LLC
Brown, Mark—Round Hill Music Royalty Fund LP
Brown, Matthew—HandsOn3 LLC
Brown, Maud—Investcorp Bank BSC
Brown, Michael—Battery Ventures LP
Brown, Michael—Battery Ventures LP
Brown, Michael—Column Group
Brown, Mike—Bowery Capital
Brown, Monique—Velocity Venture Capital Inc
Brown, Nancy—Oak HC/FT Partners LP
Brown, Nathaniel—Wind Point Advisors LLC
Brown, Ned—Spectrum Healthcare Fund LLC
Brown, Paul—Sandbox Industries LLC
Brown, Payne—HPS Investment Partners LLC

Brown, Randall—Haynes and Boone LLC
Brown, Randolph—Brentwood Associates, L.P.
Brown, Randolph—Brentwood Venture Capital
Brown, Richard—Sun Capital Partners Inc
Brown, Robert—Advent International Corp
Brown, Robert—Encore Consumer Capital Fund L P
Brown, Robert—Meridian Venture Partners
Brown, Ross—Align Capital LLC
Brown, Scott—New Energy Capital Corp
Brown, Scott—New Energy Capital Corp
Brown, Simon—Equistone Partners Europe Ltd
Brown, Sonya—Norwest Venture Partners
Brown, Steven—Promus Equity Partners
Brown, Timothy—England Capital Partners LLC
Brown, W. Quincy—Fund Evaluation Group LLC
Brown, William—First Reserve Corp
Brown, Winthrop—Milbank Tweed Hadley & Mccloy LLP
Browne, Alfred—Cooley LLP
Browne, Christophe—Newglobe Capital Partners LLP
Browne, Christophe—Vision Capital LLP
Browne, David—Marwit Capital Corp
Browne, Gregory—Fifth Street Capital LLC
Browne, Hugh—P4G Capital Management LLC
Browne, Hugh—Rho Capital Partners Inc
Browne, Lord—Riverstone Holdings LLC
Browne, Terry—Tritium Partners LLC
Brownell, Robert—Emergent Medical Partners LP
Brownhill, Alison—Balderton Capital LLP
Browning, Jeff—Austin Ventures
Brownlie, Smith—Cotton Creek Capital Management LLC
Brownlie, Steve—ACP Inc
Brownstein, Linda—Footprint Ventures
Brownstein, Neill—Footprint Ventures
Broyhill, Hunt—CapitalSouth Partners LLC
Brucato, C. J.—ABRY Partners LLC
Bruce, Adam—Advanced Technology Ventures
Bruce, Adam—Lightstone Ventures LP
Bruchmann, Philipp—Warburg Pincus LLC
Bruckmann, Bruce—Bruckmann Rosser Sherrill & Co LP
Bruckmann, Scott—Warren Equity Partners LLC
Bruckner, Scott—Perella Weinberg Partners LP
Bruckner, Zoltan—Primus Capital Partners Llc
Brueggen, Lauren—Spring Mountain Capital LP
Bruehl, Alexander—Atlantic Capital Partners GmbH
Bruggioni, Fabio—eBricks Digital
Bruin, Dennis—EVO Venture Partners
Bruix, Cedric—Argos Soditic SA
Brujis, Leon—Palladium Equity Partners LLC
Bruls, Nathalie—General Atlantic LLC
Brumfield, Bruce—FINISTERE VENTURES L L C
Brumme, Kurt—Parthenon Capital LLC
Brun, Leslie—CCMP Capital Advisors LP
Brune, Richard—Oneaccord Capital LLC
Brune, Steve—Deerpath Capital Management LP
Brunett, Brian—Ancor Capital Partners
Bruning, Timothy—Carlyle Group LP
Brunk, Gerry—LCC Legacy Holdings Inc
Bruno, Frank—Cerberus Capital Management LP
Bruno, Michael—Stonebridge Partners LP
Brusco, Lynn Banaszak—Pittsburgh Life Sciences Greenhouse
Brush, Jed—Shorenstein Co LLC

Brutocao, Brad—Freeman Spogli & Co LLC
Bruun, Eric—CID Capital Inc
Bruyn, Terence—Silverfern Group Inc
Bruzzese, Kayla—Small Ventures Usa LP
Bruzzichesi, Leonardo—Private Equity Partners SpA
Bryan, Daniel—Craig Capital Corp
Bryan, Larry—Diversified Trust Company Inc
Bryan, Lee—Comvest Partners
Bryan, Lee—Comvest Partners
Bryant, Colin—Paladin Capital Management LLC
Bryant, Jay—CVC Capital Partners Ltd
Bryant, Kathy—SF Holding Corp
Bryant, Peter—Steelhouse Ventures Ltd
Bryant, R. Kenneth—Sidereal Capital Group LLC
Bryant, Robert—Roark Capital Group Inc
Bryant, Vernon—Austin Ventures
Bryant, William—Draper Fisher Jurvetson
Bryers, Jonathan—CT Investment Partners LLP
Bryson, Matthew—Copley Equity Partners LLC
Bryson, Nancy—Evercore Inc
Brzobohaty, Tomas—PPF Partners as
Bu, Jay—MBK Partners Inc
Buarque, Fernando—Casaforte Investimentos SA
Buatois, Eric—Benhamou Global Ventures LLC
Bubnack, Tim—Huntington Capital I
Bubnack, Tim—Huntington Capital I
Bubnov, Sergey—RT-Invest OOO
Buch, Wally—Medventure Associates
Buchanan, Brandon—Iterative Instinct Management LP
Buchanan, Cameron—Castle Harlan Aus Mezzanine
Buchanan, Doug—Granite Partners
Buchanan, H. Lee—Paladin Capital Management LLC
Buchanan, Stephen—Mosaic Capital Partners LLC
Buchenau, Christian—Paua Ventures GmbH
Bucher, Philippe—Adveq Management AG
Bucher, Rudiger—Investitions Strukturbk Rhein Pfalz GmbH
Buchheit, Paul—Y Combinator Inc
Buchwald, Adam—Carlyle Group LP
Buck, James—Tillery Capital LLC
Buck, John—Versa Capital Management Inc
Buckenauer, Karsten—Bayernlb Private Equity Management GmbH
Buckerfield, Lee—Digital Media Partners Pte Ltd
Buckeridge, David—Paine Schwartz Partners LLC
Buckland, Michael—Mobility Ventures LLC
Buckle, Chris—Mezzanine Management Finanz und UnternehmensberatungsgmbH
Buckley, Chris—Castlelake LP
Buckley, Colin—CDC Group PLC
Buckley, Colin—CDC Group PLC
Buckley, Jennifer—Private Advisors LLC
Buckley, Kelly—Edison Partners
Buckley, Matthew—Arlington Capital Partners
Buckley, Mike—Intel Capital Corp
Buckley, Russell—Kindred Capital
Buckley, Steven—Innova Capital Sp z o o
Buckley, William—Haynes and Boone LLC
Bucklin, Christine—Gryphon Investors Inc
Buckman, Chris—Enertech Capital
Buckman, Rebecca—Battery Ventures LP
Bucknor, J.Kofi—Zephyr Management LP
Bucolo, Andrew—Madison Capital Funding LLC
Budde, Daniel—Hancock Capital Management LLC

Buddensiek, Dirk—MBG Baden-Wuerttemberg GmbH
Budenberg, Robin—Centerview Partners LLC
Budesa, Mari—Media Development Investment Fund Inc
Budnick, Victor—Ironwood Investment Management LLC
Budoff, Scott—Saw Mill Capital LLC
Budzynski, Jim—Open Prairie Ventures
Buehl-Reichard, Jaime—Lindsay Goldberg & Bessemer LP
Buehler, Alan—Naya Ventures LLC
Buehler, Alan—Sevin Rosen Funds
Buehler, Brian—Triton Pacific Capital LLC
Buehler, Stephen—Blackstone Group LP
Buenneke, Brian—Pantheon Ventures (UK) LLP
Buergel, Ulf—Resilience Capital Partners LLC
Buesing, Melanie—ECM Equity Capital Management GmbH
Buesser, Vanessa—Capital Dynamics Sdn Bhd
Bueth, Christoph—Kapitalbeteiligungsgesellschaft NRW GmbH
Buettner, Jan Henric—eVenture Capital Partners GmbH
Buettner, Jan—e.ventures
Buff, Eugene—Chartline Capital Partners
Buffenbarger, David—AshHill Pharmaceutical Investments LLC
Buffington, Mark—Buckhead Investment Partners LLC
Bugas, J. Andrew—Radar Partners LLC
Bugden, Lisa—NSBI Venture Capital
Bugwadia, Shiraz—O3 Capital Advisors Pvt Ltd
Buhindi, Muhannad—Arcapita Inc
Buhl, W. Peter—Bluerun Ventures LP
Buhler, Frank—Zachary Scott & Co
Buhler, Thomas—Afinum Management GmbH
Bui, Luan—Oaktree Capital Management LP
Buisson, Catherine—Seventure Partners SA
Bujnowski, Dave—Coburn Ventures LLC
Bulkin, Bernard—Vantagepoint Management Inc
Bull, David—Archer Capital Pty Ltd
Bullard, Jeffery—Transportation Resource Partners LP
Bullard, Matt—Novaquest Infosystems Inc
Buller, Jordan—Ringleader Ventures LLC
Bullitt, Christian—LLR Partners Inc
Bullock, D. Fraser—Sorenson Capital Partners LP
Bullock, John—Windspeed Ventures
Bulman, Francis—RJD Partners Ltd
Bulmer, Patrick—AAC CAPITAL PARTNERS
Bulock, Eric—Darr Global Holdings Inc
Bulow-Nielsen, Tonni—VAEKSTFONDEN
Bultynck, Hector—Peninsula Capital Partners LLC
Bultynck, Hector—Peninsula Capital Partners LLC
Bund, Ian—Innovation Capital Associates Pty, Ltd.
Bunker, Brian—Riverside Co
Bunker, Mike—Early Stage Partners LP
Bunting, Martin—CORE Partners LLC
Bunting, Tim—Balderton Capital LLP
Bunting, William—Thomas Weisel Partners Group Inc
Buob, Regula—WA de Vigier Stiftung
Buonanno, Bernie—Nautic Partners LLC
Buonanno, Robert—Warburg Pincus LLC

Buonanno, Sergio–Idea Capital Funds Societa di Gestione del Risparmio SpA
Buoymaster, John–Hall Capital Partners LLC
Burak, Jacob–Evergreen Venture Partners
Burba, Andre–Pine Brook Road Partners LLC
Burbidge, Eileen–Passion Capital Investments LLP
Burch, John–Clayton Associates LLC
Burch, Mark–Arcis Finance SA
Burcham, David–LightBay Capital LLC
Burcham, Michael–Galen Associates Inc
Burchardt, Michael–Mittelstaendische Beteiligungsgesellschaft Thueringen mbH
Burchill, Thomas–Seven Point Equity Partners LLC
Burckhardt, Peter–EVA Basel Life Sciences Agency
Burckmyer, Charlie–JMC Capital Partners LP
Burdel, Sebastien–Coller Capital Ltd
Burden, Justin–Industry Ventures LLC
Burdett, James–First Abu Dhabi Bank PJSC
Burdick, Jim–ClearVision Equity Partners LLC
Burgel, Oliver–Barings (UK) Ltd
Burger, Bill–Formative Ventures
Burger, Nick–ZS Fund LP
Burger, Thomas–Gridiron Capital LLC
Burgermeister, Patrick–BioMedPartners AG
Burgers, Gerard–Avedon Capital Partners BV
Burgers, Gerard–NIBC Principal Investments BV
Burgess, Andrew–Carlyle Group LP
Burgess, Andy–Russell Square Partners Inc
Burgess, Bill–ABS Ventures
Burgess, Dale–Ontario Teachers' Pension Plan
Burgess, Daniel–SV Health Investors LLP
Burgess, Elizabeth–Altus Capital Partners Inc
Burgess, Eve–Starfish Ventures Pty Ltd
Burgess, Kay–Intersouth Partners
Burgess, Mark–Steel Pier Capital Advisors LLC
Burgess, Trevor–Lime Rock Partners LLC
Burgess, Vince–OrbiMed Advisors LLC
Burgett, Mark–Wind Point Advisors LLC
Burgett, Paul–Undisclosed Firm
Burgis, Jeffrey–Adams Street Partners LLC
Burgoon, Adam–Karpreilly LLC
Burgstahler, David–Avista Capital Holdings LP
Burgum, Brooks–Longwater Opportunities LLC
Burgum, James–Arthur Ventures LLC
Burke, Bob–Technology Crossover Ventures LP
Burke, Christopher–Founders Club LP
Burke, Edwin–Pillsman Partners LLC
Burke, James–Formative Ventures
Burke, James–Triangle Capital Partners L L C
Burke, John–True Ventures LLC
Burke, Rugger–Satori Capital LLC
Burke, T. Robert–Metropolitan Real Estate Equity Management LLC
Burke, Timothy–Castanea Partners Inc
Burke, Timothy–Rosewood Capital LLC
Burkett, Vincent–Vista Equity Partners LLC
Burkey, Marcia–TeleSoft Partners
Burkhardt, C.A.–Ht Capital Advisors LLC
Burkhardt, Daniel–Oakwood Medical Investors
Burkhart, Charles–Rosemont Investment Partners LLC
Burks, Russell–Ansley Equity Partners
Burley, Sharon–Blackstone Group LP
Burman, Bob–UPS Strategic Enterprise Fund
Burmeister, Sebastian–Ahlstrom Capital Oy

Burnes, Christopher–MTS Health Partners LP
Burnett, Grady–Bow Capital Management LLC
Burnett, Kevin–Oaktree Capital Management LP
Burnett, Will–Owner Resource Group LLC
Burnham, Ciara–Evercore Inc
Burnham, R. Bradford–Union Square Ventures LLC
Burns, Allyson–Revolution
Burns, Brian–Grayhawk Capital
Burns, David–Phoenix Equity Partners Ltd
Burns, Jim–KKR & Co LP
Burns, John–Derwent London PLC
Burns, John–Raptor Capital Management LP
Burns, Kate–Hambro Perks Ltd
Burns, Kenneth–Siguler Guff & Company LP
Burns, Kevin–TPG Capital Management LP
Burns, Luke–Ascent Venture Management Inc
Burns, Luke–Ascent Venture Management Inc
Burns, Mary–Wayzata Investment Partners LLC
Burns, Matthew–Hall Capital Partners LLC
Burns, Michael–Axia Capital Partners LLC
Burns, Steve–Quad-C Management Inc
Burow, Kristina–Arch Venture Partners LLC
Burr, James–Carlyle Group LP
Burrows, David–Macquarie Private Wealth Inc
Burrows, Lee–Vantagepoint Management Inc
Burstein, Daniel–Millennium TVP Management Co LLC
Burstein, Elizabeth–Wildcat Venture Partners LLC
Burt, Michael–Promethean Investments Fund LP
Burt, William–Blackstone Group LP
Burtin, Jerome–Siparex Group
Burton, Andrew–Inkopo LLC
Burton, Diane–Antares Capital Corp
Burton, Donald–Ballast Point Venture Partners LLC
Burton, Steve–Shackleton Ventures Ltd
Busby, Christopher–Bridgepoint Advisers Ltd
Busby, Christopher–Great Hill Equity Partners LLC
Busby, Loren–NGN Capital LLC
Busch, Clemens–Steadfast Capital GmbH
Busch, Sarah–Argosy Capital Group Inc
Buschmann, Kay–Steadfast Capital GmbH
Buschmann, Mark–Blackstone Group LP
Buschmann, Scott–Kian Capital Partners LLC
Buser, Curtis–Carlyle Group LP
Buser, John–Neuberger Berman LLC
Busey, Andrew–Austin Ventures
Busey, G. Brian–Morrison & Foerster LLP
Bush, A. Peyton–Longuevue Capital
Bushell, Andrew–Cornerstone Capital Holdings LLC
Bushery, Glen–Falconhead Capital LLC
Bushner, Erica–GKM Newport Generation Funds
Bussgang, Jeffrey–Flybridge Capital Partners
Busslinger, Philippe–OMERS Infrastructure
Bussman, David–Asia Mezzanine Capital Advisers Ltd
Butalid, Modesto–Small Business Guarantee and Finance Corporation
Butcher, Keith–Mosaic Capital Partners LLC
Buten, Marion-Sophie–Blackstone Group LP
Buthman, Julia–Prudential Capital Group LP
Butler, Donald–Thomvest Ventures Inc
Butler, Duncan–Centennial Ventures Vii L P
Butler, Michael–NCT Ventures LLC
Butler, Ryan–Portfolio Advisors, LLC
Butler, Tara–Ahv Holding Company LLC

Butt, Rizwan–Kasb Techventures
Butterworth, Scott–Clydesdale Bank PLC
Buttiaux, Remi–IK Investment Partners Ltd
Button, Scott–Venture Investors LLC
Buttrick, John–Union Square Ventures LLC
Buxbaum, Steven–Haynes and Boone LLC
Buyse, Steven–CVC Capital Partners Ltd
Buzik, Alexander–MTS Health Partners LP
Buzzatti, Fabrizio–Sviluppo Imprese Centro Italia SGR SpA
Bybee, Clinton–Arch Venture Partners LLC
Bye, Mark–Morgan Stanley Private Equity
Byers, Brook–Kleiner Perkins Caufield & Byers LLC
Byers, Chad–Susa Ventures LP
Byers, Jackie–Centerfield Capital Partners LP
Bylin, Jonathan–Carlyle Group LP
Bynum, Frank–Kelso & Company LP
Bynum, Scott–CVC Capital Partners Ltd
Byrapaneni, Ramesh–Endiya Partners
Byrd, Andrew–Andrew W Byrd & Co LLC
Byrne, Brian–Pamplona Capital Management LLP
Byrne, Ed–Scaleworks Inc
Byrne, Jani–International Business Machines Corp
Byrne, Stephen–Vitruvian Partners LLP
Byrne, Tom–Antares Capital Corp
Byrnes, Craig–Great Hill Equity Partners LLC
Byrnes, James–Evercore Inc
Byron, Goodloe–Potomac Energy Fund LP
Byun, Hyun-Sup–Carlyle Group LP
Byun, Jimmy–Acas LLC
Byun, Yang Ho–VOGO Fund Asset Management
Byunn, Eric–Financial Technology Ventures
Cabala, Jake–Blackstone Group LP
Caballero, Lou–Bison Capital Asset Management LLC
Cabes, Robert–Avista Capital Holdings LP
Cabessa, Sydney–CM CIC Investissement SA
Cabo, Daniel–Care Capital LLC
Cabral, Antonio–Riverside Co
Cabrera, Marcio–MBF Healthcare Partners LP
Caclin, Daniel–Telecom Technologies Transfert 3T SAS
Caddy, Neil–Milbank Tweed Hadley & Mccloy LLP
Cadeddu, John–Duff Ackerman & Goodrich LLC
Caden, Dermot–Blackstone Group LP
Cadigan, Mike–CMBIgroup
Cadigan, Shane–CMBIgroup
Caesar, Torbjorn–Actis LLP
Cafasso, John–Avista Capital Holdings LP
Caffi, Alain–Ventech SA
Cagnassola, Phillip–Hamilton Robinson LLC
Cahill, Colin–Venrock Inc
Cahill, Dan–Constitution Capital Partners LLC
Cahill, Edward–Cohen & Company Financial Ltd
Cahill, Edward–HLM Management Co LLC
Cahill, Edward–HLM Management Co LLC
Cahill, Jason–Mccune Capital Management LLC
Cahill, Jennifer–Investcorp Bank BSC
Cahoon, Arthur–Rock Creek Capital LLC
Cai, Irene–ClearVue Partners, L.P.
Cai, Lei–Kunwu Jiuding Capital Holdings Co Ltd
Cai, Lei–Shanghai Lianxin Investment Management Co Ltd
Cai, Mingpo–Cathay Capital Private Equity SAS
Cai, Scott–SAIF Partners

2455

Pratt's Guide to Private Equity & Venture Capital Sources

Cai, Yutian–SI TECHNOLOGY VENTURE CAPITAL
Caillaux, Gabriel–General Atlantic LLC
Cailliau, Jean–Vendis Capital NV
Cain, Daniel–Health Enterprise Partners LP
Cain, Elizabeth–Openview Venture Partners LP
Cain, Thomas–Greener Capital Partners LP
Caine, Shlomo–Jerusalem Global Ventures
Caio, Maurizio–TLcom Capital LLP
Cairney, Lesley–Artemis Investment Management LLP
Cairns, Alistair–Smedvig Capital Ltd
Cairns, Andy–First Abu Dhabi Bank PJSC
Cairns, Niall–Kestrel Capital Pty Limited
Calabrese, Anthony–Shorenstein Co LLC
Calabrese, Christopher–LBC Credit Partners Inc
Calabrese, Madelyn–Haynes and Boone LLC
Calamari, Peter–Platte River Ventures LLC
Calari, Cesare–Wolfensohn & Company LLC
Calcano, Lawrence–Foundation Medical Partners LP
Caldas, Filipe–Hamilton Lane Advisors LLC
Caldas, Miguel–Rising Ventures SA
Calder, David–Halifax Group LLC
Calder, David–Penta Capital Llp
Calder, Lynn–Lime Rock Partners LLC
Calderini, Mario–Finpiemonte Partecipazioni SpA
Calderon, Cindy–Small World Group Incubator Pte Ltd
Caldwell, Dale–Morrison & Foerster LLP
Calenda, Valerie–Merieux Developpement SAS
Calhoun, Hal–Menlo Ventures
Calhoun, Jeffrey–Tailwind Capital Partners LP
Calhoun, Jeffrey–Thomas Weisel Partners Group Inc
Calice, Clemens–Lion's Head Global Partners LLP
Calice, Matthias–TPG Capital Management LP
Caliento, Paul–Clearview Capital LLC
Calissendorff, Percy–Segulah Advisor AB
Callaghan, Jonathan–True Ventures LLC
Callaghan, Kevin–Berkshire Partners LLC
Callaghan, Mark–Andlinger & Co Inc
Callaghan, Mike–Saints Ventures
Callahan, Jerry–Hopen Life Science Ventures
Callahan, Kevin–Century Capital Management / Massachusetts Inc
Callahan, Neil–Rosemont Seneca Technology Partners
Callahan, Robert–Global Infrastructure Holdings
Callahan, Shannon–Andreessen Horowitz LLC
Callahan, Thomas–Lincolnshire Management Inc
Callanan, Joe–Blu Venture Investors LLC
Callanan, William–Fortress Investment Group LLC
Callaway, Thomas–Cross Valley Capital
Callaway, Thomas–HealthQuest Capital
Callaway, Thomas–HeathQuest Capital
Calleja Merino, Fernando–Sodical Scr
Callerstrom, Caspar–EQT Funds Management Ltd
Callet, Fabrice–Abraaj Capital Ltd
Callias, Nicholas–Towerbrook Capital Partners LP
Callister, Todd–Medcare Investment Fund Ltd
Callow, A. Dana–Boston Millennia Partners LP
Callow, Bradford–Boston Millennia Partners LP
Calmbach, Florian–Venture Stars GmbH
Calmels, Didier–Developpement et Partenariat PME SAS
Calsbeck, Bill–Ubequity Capital Partners Inc
Calton, Robert–Summit Park LLC

Caluori, David–General Atlantic LLC
Caluori, David–Welsh Carson Anderson & Stowe
Camaggi, Alberto–R&D Advisory Srl
Camargo, Mauricio–Altra Investments
Camenzind, Pia–Illuminate Ventures
Camenzind, Pia–Startup Capital Ventures LP
Cameron, Dennis–Eastward Capital Partners LLC
Cameron, Duncan–Catapult Venture Managers Ltd
Cameron, Hamish–SV Health Investors LLP
Cameron, Ian–Capital International Inc
Cameron, James–Milbank Tweed Hadley & Mccloy LLP
Cameroni, Alessandro–Vegagest Azionari Asia A
Camilleri, Luis–Advent International Corp
Camoes, Alberto–Stratus Investimentos Ltda
Camp, Jerome–CampVentures
Camp, John–Arbor Private Investment Co LLC
Camp, John–Lincolnshire Management Inc
Camp, Steven–Orchestra Medical Ventures LLC
Company, Nicholas–Fundamental Advisors LP
Campbell, Andrew–DC Capital Partners LLC
Campbell, Carolyn–Emerging Capital Partners
Campbell, Christopher–Capvest Ltd
Campbell, Colin–Zouk Capital LLP
Campbell, David–Capital for Enterprise Ltd
Campbell, Elizabeth–SV Health Investors LLP
Campbell, Gregory–Julip Run Capital LLC
Campbell, John–Morrison & Foerster LLP
Campbell, Kristy–TechColumbus
Campbell, Mary–Edf Ventures
Campbell, Richard–Parallax Capital Partners LLC
Campbell, Ruaraidh–Blackstone Group LP
Campbell, Stephen–Panoramic Growth Equity (Fund Management) LLP
Campbell, Stewart–Norwest Venture Partners
Campbell, Tom–Blackstone Group LP
Campbell, Troy–Oaktree Capital Management LP
Campbell-White, Annette–Medventure Associates
Campe, Stephen–Investor Growth Capital AB
Campe, Stephen–Investor Growth Capital Inc
Campelli, Andrew–Sageview Capital LP
Campin, Richard–Exponent Private Equity LLP
Campion, Jay–Access Venture Partners
Campion, Jim–Enercap Capital Partners
Campion, Thomas–Merit Capital Partners IV LLC
Campolo, Giovanni–Private Equity Partners SpA
Campolo, Joseph–Arbor Private Investment Co LLC
Campos, Eric–Caisse Regionale de Credit Agricole Mutuel Sud Rhone Alpes
Camposano, Felipe–Austral Capital
Canali, Guy–Iris Capital Management SAS
Canann, Brian–NaviMed Capital Advisors LLC
Canarick, Jonathan–North Castle Partners LLC
Candeli, Fabio–Banca Profilo SpA
Candelier, Thierry–Siparex Group
Canedo, Jose Antonio–Axis Capital Management
Canete, Jose–Ecus Administradora General de Fondos SA
Canfield, Philip–GTCR Golder Rauner LLC
Caniglia, Kyle–Guidon Capital Partners
Cannaday, James–HeadHaul Capital Partners LLC
Cannaliato, Doug–Antares Capital Corp
Canning, Tom–Milbank Tweed Hadley & Mccloy LLP
Cannon, A. Martin–GreenView Associates LLC
Cannon, Louis–Biostar Ventures II LLC

Cannon, Mike–Capital Royalty LP
Cano, Adriana–Longview Asset Management Ltd
Cano, Alejandro–Oaktree Capital Management LP
Canonge, Florence–Tertium SAS
Canova, Chris–Axioma Ventures LLC
Cantell, Aaro–Fenno Management Oy
Canter, Stephen–Zephyr Management LP
Canto, Roberto–Pine Tree Equity Management LP
Cantrell, Kevin–Riordan Lewis & Haden
Cantu, James–GTCR Golder Rauner LLC
Cantwell, Andrew–Norwest Equity Partners
Cantwell, Sean–Volition Capital LLC
Cantwell, Wayne–Crescendo Venture Management LLC
Canty, Ed–Band of Angels Venture Fund LP
Cao, Amanda–Mingly Capital
Cao, Jian–Origo Partners PLC
Cao, Ron–Lightspeed Venture Partners China Co Ltd
Cao, Sheng–Beijing Huinong Capital Management Co Ltd
Cao, Wei–Warburg Pincus LLC
Capaldo, Trudy–CCMP Capital Advisors LP
Capart, Vivian–Sopartec SA
Capasso, Michael–Clearwater Capital Partners Cyprus Ltd
Capell, Ben–Peterson Partners LP
Capello, Luigi–LVenture Group SpA
Capello, Marco–Bluegem Capital Partners LLP
Caplain, Jason–Bull City Venture Partners LLC
Caplain, Jason–Southern Capitol Ventures LLC
Caplan, Kenneth–Blackstone Group LP
Caple, John–Comvest Partners
Caple, John–Hidden Harbor Capital Partners LLC
Caporrino, Jason–Corinthian Capital Group LLC
Cappel, Jeffery–Dowling Capital Partners I LP
Cappelletti, Samuele–Oaktree Capital Management LP
Cappello, Alexander–Cappello Capital Corp
Cappello, Gerard–Cappello Capital Corp
Capps, Jacob–Lion Capital LLP
Cappuccini, Bruno–Richmond Park Partners LLP
Caprio, Frank–Chatham Capital
Caprioli, Brian–Vexiom Equity Partners, L.P.
Capuano, Luigi–Patron Capital Advisers LLP
Caputo, A. Richard–Jordan Company LP
Caputo, Paulo Sergio–DLM Invista Gestao de Recursos Ltda
Carano, Bandel–Oak Investment Partners
Carassai, Amedeo–Apax Partners LLP
Carballo, Juan-Antonio–Argon Venture Partners
Carbery, Paul–Frontenac Company LLC
Carbo, Carlos–Nazca Capital SGEIC SA
Carbonari, Nicolas–360 Capital Management SA
Carbone, Paul–Jabodon PT Co
Carbonell, John–Snowbird Capital Inc
Cardenas, L. David–Olympus Partners
Cardew-Hall, Michael–ANU Connect Ventures Pty Ltd
Cardinale, Gerry–RedBird Capital Partners Platform LP
Cardini, Filippo–Towerbrook Capital Partners LP
Cardona, Anthony–Cinven Group Ltd
Cardone, Scott–Intuitive Venture Partners LLC
Cardwell, Jack–Greenridge Investment Partners
Cardy, Tom–New World Angels, Inc.

Carelli, Chuck–Flagship Pioneering
Carew, David–Sindicatum Carbon Capital Ltd
Carey, Ray–Azure Capital Partners, L.P.
Carey, Richard–Permira Advisers LLP
Carey, Ryan–Sixpoint Partners LLC
Carey, Thomas–Proprium Capital Partners LP
Carey, Vincent–Gryphon Investors Inc
Cargill, Virginia–Alerion Partners LLC
Caringi, Anthony–Merion Investment Partners LP
Carlberg, Erik–Alta Growth Capital SC
Carlborg, W. Eric–August Capital Management LLC
Carle, Sylvain–Real Ventures
Carles, Alexander–Wellspring Capital Management LLC
Carley, Norm–Torch Hill Investment Partners LLC
Carlick, David–Rho Capital Partners Inc
Carlin, Robert–EDG Partners LLC
Carlino, Andrew–Bain Capital Inc
Carlisle, Douglas–Menlo Ventures
Carlisle, Douglas–Menlo Ventures
Carlisle, Greg–Gefinor Ventures
Carlisle, James–Thomas H Lee Partners LP
Carlisle, Mel–Oaktree Capital Management LP
Carlsen, Soren–Novo Holdings A/S
Carlson, Baron–AEA Investors LLC
Carlson, Blake–Wayzata Investment Partners LLC
Carlson, Dave–eonCapital, LLC
Carlson, Goran–Carlson Invest AB
Carlson, Keith–CapitalSouth Partners LLC
Carlson, Stephen–Harvest Partners LP
Carlson, Tim–Evercore Inc
Carlsson, Magnus–Skandinaviska Enskilda Banken AB
Carlyle, Matthew–Allon Therapeutics Inc
Carmel, Charles–Warburg Pincus LLC
Carmichael, Tanya–Ontario Teachers' Pension Plan
Carmona, Guillermo–Northgate Capital LLC
Carmona, Jacob–Inverness Management LLC
Carnahan, Ellen–Seyen Capital LLC
Carne, Ramon–Mercapital SL
Carne, Ramon–Mercapital SL
Carneiro Da Cunha, Daniel–Darien Business Development Corp
Carney, Brian–Harbert Management Corp
Carney, Erin–Blackstone Group LP
Carney, Sean–Warburg Pincus LLC
Carni, Yaron–Maverick Ventures Israel LP
Carnimolla, Remi–3i Group PLC
Carnot, Lionel–Bay City Capital LLC
Carnot, Lionel–Earlybird Venture Capital GmbH & Co KG
Caro, Francisco–MCH Private Equity Asesores SL
Caroe, Mark–Eden Ventures Ltd
Carolan, Jennifer–NewSchools Venture Fund
Carolan, Shawn–Menlo Ventures
Carolan, Shawn–Menlo Ventures
Carolin, Roger–SCP Private Equity Partners
Carp, Barry–River Capital Pty Ltd
Carpenter, Charles–State of Wisconsin Investment Board
Carpenter, Harold–Pinnacle Financial Partners Inc
Carpenter, Hunter–RedBird Capital Partners Platform LP
Carpenter, Matthew–Genesis Financial Services Fund LLC

Carpenter, Mike–Burrill & Company
Carpenter, Philip–Irving Place Capital LLC
Carr, Chris–Morrison & Foerster LLP
Carr, Francis–Sterling Group LP
Carr, James–Yorkville Advisors Management LLC
Carr, Karen–Imperial Capital Corp
Carrabino, Joseph–AEA Investors LLC
Carracher, Craig–Telopea Capital Partners Pty Ltd
Carrano, Michael–Landmark Partners Inc
Carrarini, Kilian–Ambrian Resources AG
Carratt, David–Kennet Partners Ltd
Carratu, Richard–Prospect Street Ventures
Carraway, Rob–Acas LLC
Carre, Francois–Euromezzanine Gestion SaS
Carreiro, Gabriel–Summit Partners LP
Carrel, Steven–Transportation Resource Partners LP
Carrel-Billiard, Dominique–AXA Investment Managers Inc
Carreras, Julian–Palamon Capital Partners LP
Carretta, John–Forest Hill Partners LLC
Carretti, Fabrizio–Permira Advisers LLP
Carrier, Alain–Canada Pension Plan Investment Board
Carrihill, Gordon–GEF Management Corp
Carroll, Ashley–Social+Capital Partnership
Carroll, Brendan–Victory Park Capital Advisors LLC
Carroll, Frank–Oaktree Capital Management LP
Carroll, J. Ryan–Charlesbank Capital Partners LLC
Carroll, John–Summit Partners LP
Carroll, John–Summit Partners LP
Carroll, Mark–Superior Capital Partners LLC
Carroll, Matthew–Westview Capital Partners LP
Carroll, Rob–Catapult Venture Managers Ltd
Carroll, Ted–Noson Lawen Partners LLC
Carruthers, Andrew–SPARK Impact Ltd
Carruthers, Corwynne–Kinderhook Industries LLC
Carruthers, Evan–Castlelake LP
Carryer, Babs–Launchcyte L L C
Carsello, John–Hammond Kennedy Whitney & Company Inc
Carson, Donald–Ansley Equity Partners
Carson, Jarett–Enertech Capital
Carson, Lee–Carlyle Group LP
Carson, Russell–Welsh Carson Anderson & Stowe
Carsten, Jack–Horizon Ventures
Carteaux, Nick–Brentwood Capital Advisors LLC
Carter, Andrew–OCEAN TOMO CAPITAL L L C
Carter, Arthur–Haynes and Boone LLC
Carter, Christopher–Jarvinian LLC
Carter, Christopher–Natural Gas Partners
Carter, Christy–CCMP Capital Advisors LP
Carter, Cynthia–Blackstone Group LP
Carter, David–Capital Royalty LP
Carter, Jeff–West Loop Ventures LLC
Carter, Julian–ECI Capital Ltd
Carter, Kellan–Ignition Ventures Management LLC
Carter, Kevin–SV Angel
Carter, Larry–Diamond State Ventures, L.P.
Carter, Michael–SV Health Investors LLP
Carter, Phillip–Kestrel Capital Pty Limited
Carter, Roy–Torch Hill Investment Partners LLC
Carter, Stephanie–ABS Capital Partners, Inc.
Carter, Susan–Commonfund Capital Inc
Carter, Tyson–Continuum Capital LLC
Carthy, Roi–Darien Business Development Corp

Cartner, Craig–Archer Capital Pty Ltd
Carton, Gerald–Coller Capital Ltd
Cartwright, Paul–Rutland Partners LLP
Cartwright, Peter–AnaCap Financial Partners Llp
Carusi, Michael–Advanced Technology Ventures
Carusi, Mike–Lightstone Ventures LP
Caruso, P. Jelf–Nibiru Capital Management Ltd
Caruso, Richard–ProvCo Group
Caruso, Victor–Blue Wolf Capital Partners LLC
Carvajal Arguelles, Juan–Espiga Capital Gestion SGCR SA
Carvajal Urquijo, Jaime–Advent International Corp
Carvajal, Juan–Espiga Capital Gestion SGCR SA
Carvalho, Luis Ferreira–Vallis Capital Partners SGPS SA
Carver, Dave–Accretia Capital LLC
Carver, Timothy–Northern Lights Capital Group LLC
Cary, Lucius–Oxford Technology Management Ltd
Casagrande, Humberto–Dgf Investimentos Gestao De Fundos Ltda
Casale, Alexander–Audax Group, Inc.
Casale, Francis–NRDC Equity Partners
Casale, John–AIG Capital Partners Inc
Casarella, Thomas–Oaktree Capital Management LP
Casares, David–Vicente Capital Partners LLC
Cascade, Joshua–Wellspring Capital Management LLC
Casciato, Chris–Lightyear Capital LLC
Casdagli, Thomas–MVM Partners LLP
Case, Gregory–PeakEquity Partners
Case, Jeff–Advent International Corp
Case, Roy–Magellan Capital Partners Ltd
Case, Scott Elaine–VMG Partners, L.P.
Case, Stephen–Emerald Development Managers LP
Case, William–Clearview Capital LLC
Casella, Kyle–J.W.Childs Associates LP
Casella-Esposito, Julie–CCMP Capital Advisors LP
Casellas, Marc–Ysios Capital Partners SGECR SAU
Casey, Colleen–AG BD LLC
Casey, Mike–Blackstone Group LP
Casey, Nancy–Wheatley Partners
Casey, Patrick–GEN3 Partners, Inc.
Casey, Richard–Carlyle Group LP
Casey, Richard–Square 1 Ventures
Casgar, Christopher–Catterton Partners Corp
Cash, Ian–Alchemy Partners LLP
Cashell, Lee–Asia Pacific Investment Partners
Cashin, Richard–JPMorgan Chase & Co
Cashin, Richard–One Equity Partners LLC
Cashin, Stephen–Modern Africa Fund Managers, LLC
Cashion, Matthew–GoldPoint Partners LLC
Cashman, Gillis–M/C Venture Partners LLC
Cashman, Gregory–Golub Capital Master Funding LLC
Cashwell, John–Blackstone Group LP
Casilli, Gerald–Rembrandt Venture Management LLC
Caskey, C. Thomas–EW Healthcare Partners
Caslin, Melissa–JMI Management Inc
Caso, Michael–Rosecliff Venture Partners LP
Casperson, Bill–Oaktree Capital Management LP
Caspi, Sophie–Aviv Venture Capital, Ltd.
Cass, A. Baron–C3 Capital LLC
Cass, Edwin–Canada Pension Plan Investment Board

Cass, Nancy—Looking Glass Partners LLC
Cassano, Anthony—Spire Capital Partners LP
Cassel, Fredrik—Creandum AB
Cassell, Dennis—Haynes and Boone LLC
Casserlov, Goran—Cevian Capital AB
Cassetta, Michael—GB Credit Partners LLC
Cassidy, Brian—Crestview Advisors, LLC
Cassidy, Chris—Mainsail Partners LP
Cassidy, Karen—Partisan Management Group Inc
Cassidy, Paul—Penta Capital Llp
Cassidy, Shauna—Northwater Capital Management Inc
Cassim, Zaheer—Vantage Venture Partners
Cassin, Carolyn—Belle Michigan Fund LP
Cassis, John—Cross Atlantic Partners
Cassutt, Tom—Accretia Capital LLC
Cast, Carter—Pritzker Group Venture Capital
Castaldi, Alexander—JLL Partners Inc
Castanino, James—GEF Management Corp
Castelein, Caley—Kearny Venture Partners LP
Castelein, Caley—Thomas Weisel Partners Group Inc
Castell, Andrew—Par Equity Llp
Castella, Paul—Incyte Venture Partners LLC
Castellanos, Alvaro Garteiz—Torreal SA
Castello, Fabien—Platina Finance, Ltd.
Castellon, Enrique—Cross Road Biotech SCR de Regimen Comun SA
Castillo Badia, Enrique—Nexxus Capital SA de CV
Castillo, Eduardo—Marsman-Drysdale Corp
Castillo, Robert—Invision Capital Management LLC
Castillo, Santiago—Advent International Corp
Castine, Charles—Gennx360 Capital Partners LP
Castleberry, Brian—Blue Point Capital Partners LP
Castleman, Randy—Court Square Ventures LLC
Castner, Clarey—Panorama Point Partners LLC
Caston, Richard—RJD Partners Ltd
Castor, Anthony—Kidd & Company LLC
Castro, Jan—Pala Investments
Caswell, Adam—UpTech LLC
Catalano, Manuel—Clessidra Societa di Gestione del Risparmio SpA
Cataldo, Mike—Long River Ventures, Inc.
Catalfamo, Joe—Summerhill Venture Partners Management Inc
Catanzaro, Sarah—Amplify Partners LP
Catapano, Angelo—Progressio SGR SpA
Catapano, Salvatore—Investindustrial Services Ltd
Catarozoli, Taylor—Liberty Hall Capital Partners LP
Cater, Todd—GEF Management Corp
Cateriano, Hector—Small Enterprise Assistance Funds
Cathcart, Chris—Halifax Group LLC
Catherman, Gary—Kurt Salmon Capital Advisors Inc
Catoire, Stephan—Equitis Gestion SAS
Catt, Ben—Evercore Inc
Catt, Simon—Gmp Securities Ltd
Cattaneo, Valerio—Finpiemonte Partecipazioni SpA
Catterall, Peter—Cinven Group Ltd
Catunda, Rodrigo—General Atlantic LLC
Caukin, Craig—Pearl Street Capital Group
Caulder, Jerry—FINISTERE VENTURES L L C
Cauley, Lauren—MPM Capital LLC
Caulfield, Brian—Draper Esprit PLC
Caulier, Guillaume—Lexington Partners Inc
Caulkin, Chris—General Atlantic LLC

Caupers, Ricardo—Palamon Capital Partners LP
Cavalcanti, Renato Moritz—Vinci Equities Gestora de Recursos Ltda
Cavalie, Francois—Xange Private Equity SA
Cavalier, John—Hudson Clean Energy Partners
Cavanagh, Christopher—Great Hill Equity Partners LLC
Cavanaugh, James—Healthcare Ventures LLC
Cavanaugh, Michael—Resilience Capital Partners LLC
Cavaney, Pat—Morrison & Foerster LLP
Cavanna, Andrew—Vestar Capital Partners Inc
Cave, Phillip—Anchorage Capital Partners Ltd
Cavoli, James—Milbank Tweed Hadley & Mccloy LLP
Cavusoglu, Murat—Stratejik Yonetim Hizmetleri AS
Cayce, Brian—Gray Ghost Ventures
Cayer, Nicholas—Great Hill Equity Partners LLC
Cayrol Darnaudet, Veronique—Perceva SAS
Cazabon, Charles—Business Development Bank of Canada
Cebula, Vincent—Solace Capital Partners LLC
Cecchetto, Marcelo—HIG Capital LLC
Cecchini, J.T—Montgomery & Co LLC
Cecil, James—Valence Life Sciences LLC
Cekin, Yagiz—Stratejik Yonetim Hizmetleri AS
Celaya, Jorge—Avanz Capital Partners Ltd
Celentano, Daniel—Evercore Inc
Celier, Nicolas—Alven Capital Partners SA
Cellini, Paolo—Innogest Sgr SpA
Celniker, Craig—Morrison & Foerster LLP
Cels, Hadewych—Karmijn Kapitaal Management BV
Cenanovic, Bogdan—Ontario Teachers' Pension Plan
Centeno, Roberto—Atitlan SA
Centerman, Jorgen—Segulah Advisor AB
Centner, Oliver—Klass Capital Corp
Cerda-Lecaros, Raimundo—Aurus Gestion de Inversiones SPA
Cerdeiras, Ramon—Portobello Capital Advisors SL
Cereghino, Christopher—Oak Hill Advisors LP
Cerina, Ivica—NGN Capital LLC
Cerminaro, John—Zephyr Management LP
Cerny, Edward—Kayne Anderson Capital Advisors LP
Cerra, John—Clearview Capital LLC
Cerrina Feroni, Marco—Imi Fondi Chiusi SGR SpA
Cerritelli, Jose—Gramercy Inc
Cerullo, Bruce—SV Health Investors LLP
Cerullo, Michael—Acas LLC
Cervantes, Luis—General Atlantic LLC
Cervantes, Pablo—PC Capital SAPI de CV
Cervone, Margarita—MTS Health Partners LP
Cesafsky, Robert—JMI Management Inc
Cesarek, Tim—Koch Genesis LLC
Cesario, Fabrizio—AnaCap Financial Partners Llp
Cesarz, John—Perella Weinberg Partners LP
Cesarz, Joseph—Lakeview Equity Partners LLC
Cesky, Daniel—ARAX Capital Partners GmbH
Cetin, Benan—Esas Holding AS
Ceva, Valerie—Homeland Defense Ventures
Cha, Albert—Vivo Capital LLC
Cha, James—Trevi Health Ventures LP
Cha, Joseph—Carlyle Group LP
Chabanel, Michel—Cerea Partenaire SAS
Chaboche, Didier—Ouest Croissance SAS
Chabran, Mathieu—TR Advisors Ltd
Chabran, Mathieu—Tikehau Investment Management SAS

Chacartegui, Igor—Gores Group LLC
Chadakhtzian, Mark—Cti Capital Securities Inc
Chaddha, Navin—Mayfield Fund
Chadehumbe, Wellington—Undisclosed Firm
Chadha, Jito—HandsOn3 LLC
Chadha, Kanwar—HandsOn3 LLC
Chadha, Kapil—August Capital Partners
Chadha, Rattan—KRC Capital BV
Chadha, Sumir—Westbridge Capital Advisors (India) Pvt Ltd
Chadha, Surya—Madison India Capital Management Co
Chadha, Yogesh—Akayi Capital Partners LLC
Chadwick, Bethany—LNK Partners LLC
Chadwick, Gavin—Capricorn Capital Partners
Chadwick, John—Claritas Capital LLC
Chae, DooSeok—LB Investment Inc
Chae, Michael—Blackstone Group LP
Chae, Tim—500 Startups, L.P.
Chae, Yoon—ISU Venture Capital Co Ltd
Chafets, Shmuel—Giza Venture Capital
Chaffee, Darren McKenzie—CoBe Equities LLC
Chaffee, Todd—Institutional Venture Partners
Chaffin, Tracey—Pamlico Capital Management LP
Chagnon, Alain—FFP SA
Chai, Carina—EQT Funds Management Ltd
Chai, Du—Horsley Bridge Partners LLC
Chai, William—Grace Assets Management LLP
Chaikin, Chip—Blue Point Capital Partners LP
Chait, Jonathan—Dace Ventures
Chak, Ranjan—Oak Investment Partners
Chakrabarti, Suma—European Bank for Reconstruction and Development
Chakrabarty, Sanjay—Capital Square Partners Pte Ltd
Chalfen, Michael—Advent Venture Partners LLP
Chalian, Patricia—First Avenue Partners, L.P.
Chalk, Gilbert—24Haymarket Ltd
Chalk, Gilbert—Baring Private Equity Asia Ltd
Chalmers, Rachel—Ignition Ventures Management LLC
Chalmers, Rachel—Ignition Ventures Management LLC
Chaloult, Pamela—Renewal Partners
Chalsen, Christopher—Milbank Tweed Hadley & Mccloy LLP
Chalupec, Igor—Icentis Capital Sp z o o
Chamberlain, Alex—InvesteCo Capital Corp
Chambers, Anthony—Thompson Street Capital Partners LP
Chambers, Dewey—Clean Pacific Ventures Management LLC
Chambers, Eleanor—PAI Partners SAS
Chambers, Jeffrey—TA Associates Management LP
Chambers, Joe—Evercore Inc
Chambers, Robert—Roark Capital Group Inc
Chambon, Philippe—New Leaf Venture Partners LLC
Chameh, Sidney—Dgf Investimentos Gestao De Fundos Ltda
Champagne, Michel—SIDEX LP
Champenois, Denis—Innovacom Gestion SAS
Champion, Richard—New York Business Development Corp
Champsi, Aly—Clairvest Group Inc
Champsi, Aly—Dw Healthcare Partners
Champsi, Farah—Alta Partners

2458

Champsi, Farah—InterWest Partners LLC
Chan, Alan—7Bridge Capital Partners Ltd
Chan, Alfa—Silverfleet Capital Partners LLP
Chan, Edward—1315 Capital LLC
Chan, Eric—Altpoint Capital Partners LLC
Chan, Eric—CITIC Capital Partners Ltd
Chan, Eric—Disruptive Capital Pty Ltd
Chan, Frankie—Catterton Partners Corp
Chan, Geraldine—Vantagepoint Management Inc
Chan, Hock Eng—Zana Capital Pte Ltd
Chan, Jacqueline—Milbank Tweed Hadley & Mccloy LLP
Chan, James—Neoteny Labs Pte Ltd
Chan, Janice—Clarion Capital Partners LLC
Chan, Kathy—137 Ventures LP
Chan, Kenneth—Tennenbaum Capital Partners LLC
Chan, Kevin—SEAVI Advent Corporation Ltd
Chan, Pearl—Omidyar Technology Ventures LLC
Chan, Perry—Oaktree Capital Management LP
Chan, Peter—Baring Private Equity Asia Ltd
Chan, Peter—Crest Capital Partners
Chan, Raymond—Adams Street Partners LLC
Chan, Raymond—Atalaya Capital Management LP
Chan, Raymond—Keystone National Group LLC
Chan, Ryan—Second City Capital Partners
Chan, Sonny—HPEF Capital Partners Ltd
Chan, Timothy—Phillip Private Equity Pte Ltd
Chan, Wesley—Felicis Ventures
Chan-Lee, Polai—Carlyle Group LP
Chanana, Ravdeep—Gemspring Capital LLC
Chand, Sohil—Norwest Venture Partners
Chander, Amit—Baring Private Equity Asia Ltd
Chandiramani, Sunil—Symphony Asia Holdings Pte Ltd
Chandler, David—Chicago Growth Partners LLC
Chandler, Dennis—Akoya Capital Partners LLC
Chandler, Edward—PAI Partners SAS
Chandler, Stephen—Notion Capital Partners LLP
Chandna, Asheem—Greylock Partners LLC
Chandna, Rishi—Golden Gate Capital Inc
Chandra, Amit—57 Stars LLC
Chandra, Amit—Bain Capital Inc
Chandra, Anurag—NXT Capital Venture Finance
Chandra, Rahul—Helion Venture Partners LLC
Chandra, Samarth—Enhanced Equity Fund, L.P.
Chandran, Renee Marcia—Malaysia Venture Capital Management Bhd
Chandrasekaran, Nathan—TZP Group LLC
Chandrasekaran, S—Crossover Advisors Pvt Ltd
Chandrasekhar, Akshay—Elevar Equity Advisors Pvt Ltd
Chandratillake, Suranga—Balderton Capital LLP
Chang, Alan—Capricorn Investment Group LLC
Chang, Andy—STIC Investment Inc
Chang, Charles—CID Group
Chang, Chia-Juch—CDIB Capital Group
Chang, Dale—Scale Venture Partners
Chang, Daniel—Blackstone Group LP
Chang, Daniel—DFJ Athena
Chang, Dongshik—L&S VentureCapital Corp
Chang, Erin—General Atlantic LLC
Chang, Herman—Carlyle Group LP
Chang, Hyun—Golub Capital Master Funding LLC
Chang, Jason—Ontario Teachers' Pension Plan
Chang, Jeffrey—Performance Equity Management LLC
Chang, Jennifer Tai—Blackstone Group LP
Chang, Joe—Eight Roads Ventures Europe
Chang, Joel—AID Partners Capital Ltd
Chang, Julia—KPG Ventures
Chang, Justin—Colony Capital LLC
Chang, Kristen—LLR Partners LLC
Chang, Laurence—Taveekan Capital
Chang, Milton—Incubic Managment LLC
Chang, Mink—Youngshin Venture Capital
Chang, Paul—JMI Management Inc
Chang, Raymond—NXT Ventures Fund 1 LLC
Chang, Richard—Carlyle Group LP
Chang, Sheldon—Pantheon Ventures (UK) LLP
Chang, Stephen—Acrewood Holdings LLC
Chang, Steve—Sterling Partners GP LLC
Chang, Steven—Clearlake Capital Group LP
Chang, Timothy—IMM Private Equity Inc
Chang, Timothy—Mayfield Fund
Chang, Yong Taek—SHIN POONG VENTURE CAPITAL
Chang, Yongbing—CAC Capital Management Co Ltd
Chao, Cedric—Morrison & Foerster LLP
Chao, Clint—Formative Ventures
Chao, David—Doll Capital Management Inc
Chao, K. Bobby—DragonVenture, Inc.
Chao, Lesley—Oaktree Capital Management LP
Chao, Pierre—Enlightenment Capital
Chao, Rachel—Oaktree Capital Management LP
Chaoui, Mounia—Ventech SA
Chapin II, Aldus—Blackstreet Capital Management LLC
Chapin, Allan—Compass Partners International LLC
Chapin, Ben—Antares Capital Corp
Chaplinsky, Robert—Bridgescale Partners LP
Chapman, Adrian—WGL Holdings Inc
Chapman, Celia—WP Global Partners Inc
Chapman, David—Yellow Point Equity Partners LP
Chapman, Duncan—Lexington Partners Inc
Chapman, Gwen—Truffle Capital SAS
Chapman, Jeff—Wellington Financial Lp
Chapman, Kyle—Forsyth Capital Investors LLC
Chapman, Mathew—TorQuest Partners Inc
Chapman, Michael—Altimeter Capital Management LP
Chapman, Nick—Evercore Inc
Chapman, Richard—ECI Partners LLP
Chapman, Stuart—Draper Esprit PLC
Chapman, Tannaz—GTCR Golder Rauner LLC
Chappell, Jonathan—Evercore Inc
Chapus, Jean-Marc—Crescent Capital Group LP
Charalambous, Michael—KI Capital Ltd
Charbonneau, Magaly—iNovia Capital Inc
Charest, Mark—New Leaf Venture Partners LLC
Charest, Raymond—Oxford Bioscience Partners
Charko, Rod—Alberta Enterprise Corp
Charlebois, Richard—Growth Works Capital Ltd
Charles, Ian—Landmark Partners Inc
Charlton, Harry—Millhouse Inc PLC
Charlton, Kevin—River Hollow Partners LLC
Charlton, William—Pavilion Alternatives Group Ltd
Charlwood, Christopher—SouthPac Partners Inc
Charnock, David—Kingsway Capital of Canada Inc
Charon, Jean-Louis—City Star Private Equity Sas
Charquet, Philippe—Generis Capital Partners SAS
Charrington, N.J.—BlackRock Inc
Charto, Timur—Korporatsiya razvitiya Severnogo Kavkaza AO
Chartoff, Beth—Blackstone Group LP
Chartove, Alex—Morrison & Foerster LLP
Chary, Sasank—Sageview Capital LP
Chase, Jayne—Mti Partners Ltd
Chase, John—Atlantic-Pacific Capital Inc
Chasin, Scott—Blue Cloud Ventures
Chasser, Eric—Metropolitan Equity Partners LLC
Chasty, Billie—Cabot Square Capital Advisors Ltd
Chatain, Jacques—Auriga Partners SA
Chatard, Timothy—Tano Capital LLC
Chateau, Cedric—Advent International Corp
Chatillon, Jean—Silverfleet Capital Partners LLP
Chatterjee, Pallab—Symphony Technology Group LLC
Chatterjee, Sanjoy—Everstone Capital Management, Ltd.
Chatterjee, Somnath—Morrison & Foerster LLP
Chattopadhyay, Sanjoy—HIG Capital LLC
Chaturvedi, Anantshree—Romulus Capital LLC
Chau, Charles—Morrison & Foerster LLP
Chau, Paul—WI Harper Group Inc
Chau, Solina—Horizons Ventures Ltd
Chau, Wilton—Qleap Accelerators Ltd
Chaucer, Gary—Hony Capital Beijing Co Ltd
Chaudhary, Adam—Pelican Point Investment Group LLC
Chaudhary, Kapil—Chicago Ventures
Chaudhary, Shiv—Norwest Venture Partners
Chaudhry, Atif—Oaktree Capital Management LP
Chaudhry, Om—FIRE CAPITAL FUND MAURITIUS PRIVATE LTD
Chaudron, Nicolas—Idinvest Partners SA
Chauhan, Kulwant—Abacus Private Equity Ltd
Chaurette, Francois—Investissements Novacap Inc
Chaus, Natalie—Horizon Capital Management
Chauvet, Jean-Marie—Phitrust Impact Investors SA
Chavanon, Claude-Henri—First Abu Dhabi Bank PJSC
Chaveles, Spyros—Capcellence Mittelstandspartner GmbH
Chavez, Lawrence—Flywheel Ventures
Chavez, Martin—New MainStream Capital
Chavez, Tom—Entrepreneurs Fund LP
Chawla, Haresh—True North
Chawla, Maneesh—Prospect Partners LLC
Chawla, Nish—Madison India Capital Management Co
Chawla, Sunil—Jacob Ballas Capital India Pvt Ltd
Chaya, Dina—Neomed Management As
Cheah, Jin—Stone Canyon Industries LLC
Cheah, Teik Seng—Aktis Capital Group
Chebotareva, Polina—Cambridge Companies Spg LLC
Chechelnitsky, Michael—ArcLight Capital Holdings LLC
Chee, Brian—Polaris Venture Partners
Chee, Max—Millennium TVP Management Co LLC
Chee, Menes—Blackstone Group LP
Cheek, Giles—European Capital Financial Services Ltd
Cheek, John—Fidus Capital LLC
Cheek, Jon—Serent Capital LLC
Cheever, Chris—Fontinalis Partners LLC
Cheever, Edward—Cheever Capital Management LLC
Cheever, Milton—Cheever Capital Management LLC
Chefitz, Robert—Egis Capital Partners
Chefitz, Robert—NJTC Venture Fund

Chehade, Christina–Middle East Venture Partners
Chehime, Hasan–Investcorp Technology Investments Group
Cheifetz, Yoni–Lightspeed Management Company LLC
Chell, Cameron–Business Instincts Group
Chellapa, Shrinivas–ICICI Venture Funds Management Company Ltd
Chellappa, Mahim–Tembusu Partners Pte Ltd
Chelouche, Yoav–Aviv Venture Capital, Ltd.
Chen Nobles, Kimberley–Haynes and Boone LLC
Chen, Andrew–Bluerun Ventures LP
Chen, Baohua–Shenzhen Hongshisan Capital Co Ltd
Chen, Bill–Asiatech Management LLC
Chen, Bing–HighLight Capital
Chen, Bonnie–Baird Capital
Chen, Carson–Walden International
Chen, Cory–CID Group
Chen, Dar–Baring Private Equity Asia Ltd
Chen, Datong–WestSummit Capital Management Ltd
Chen, David–Lightspeed Management Company LLC
Chen, Dechun–State Development & Investment Corp Ltd
Chen, Drew–Bain Capital Inc
Chen, Ethel–Norwest Venture Partners
Chen, Fan–Uni-Quantum Fund Management Co Ltd
Chen, Fei–Noble (Beijing) Fund Management Inc
Chen, Frank–Andreessen Horowitz LLC
Chen, Frank–Shanghai Atlas Capital Ltd
Chen, Gongmen–China Venture Capital Research Institute Ltd
Chen, Grace–Cathay Financial Holding Co Ltd
Chen, Guowei–Prax Capital Management Co
Chen, Han–Carlyle Group LP
Chen, Hao–Legend Capital Co Ltd
Chen, Hong–Translink Capital LLC
Chen, Hong–Translink Capital LLC
Chen, Hui–Principle Capital Ltd
Chen, Hui–Ying Capital
Chen, Jenny–Jasper Ridge Partners LP
Chen, Jerry–Greylock Partners LLC
Chen, Jialu–Asset Management Co
Chen, Jihao–Shanghai Tronfund Management Co Ltd
Chen, Jiwu–Vstone Yangtze Investment Management Co Ltd
Chen, Joanne–Foundation Capital LLC
Chen, Jun–Baring Private Equity Asia Ltd
Chen, Justin–Comvest Partners
Chen, Kent–Neuberger Berman LLC
Chen, Keyi–Xianfeng Huaxing Venture Capital Ltd
Chen, Leon–Fidelity Growth Partners Asia
Chen, Liling–Industrial Technology Investment Corp
Chen, Nick–Capital International Inc
Chen, Norman–Fidelity Growth Partners Asia
Chen, Peng–Guosen Bole Equity Investment Management Co Ltd
Chen, Peng–Morrison & Foerster LLP
Chen, Ping–Morgan Stanley Alternative Investment Partners LP
Chen, Qiudong–Hangzhou Incapital Management Co., Ltd.
Chen, Qiwei–ABC Capital Management Co Ltd
Chen, Qiwei–Shanghai NCE Venture Capital Management Co Ltd
Chen, Roland–ChinaRun Capital Partners Chongqing Ltd
Chen, Ruihua–Yingke Innovation Assets Management Co Ltd
Chen, Ruping–ZheShang Venture Capital Co Ltd
Chen, Shelby–Tsing Capital
Chen, Sherwin–Elevation Partners LP
Chen, Shijun–Shenzhen Green Pine Capital Partners Co Ltd
Chen, Shirley–Translink Capital LLC
Chen, Shuai–Hony Capital Beijing Co Ltd
Chen, Shuang–China Everbright Ltd
Chen, Shuonan–Agile Venture Capital LLC
Chen, Sichao–Sparkland Capital
Chen, Steven–Blu Venture Investors LLC
Chen, Tao–Shenzhen Cornerstone of Entrepreneurial Cci Capital Ltd
Chen, Terry–Vantagepoint Management Inc
Chen, Thomas–Cybernaut (China) Venture Capital Management Co Ltd
Chen, Tinghe–Beijing Flourish Libra Venture Capital Co Ltd
Chen, Tom–Haynes and Boone LLC
Chen, Wen–Hony Capital Beijing Co Ltd
Chen, Wenzheng–Shenzhen Capital Group Co Ltd
Chen, William–Apax Partners LLP
Chen, Xiangdong–Shenzhen Tiantu Capital Management Center LP
Chen, Xiaodong–Greenwoods Asset Management Ltd
Chen, Xing–Milestone Capital Management Ltd
Chen, Xun–ZheShang Venture Capital Co Ltd
Chen, Yanli–Shenzhen Cornerstone of Entrepreneurial Cci Capital Ltd
Chen, Yansong–Prime Value Capital Management Ltd
Chen, Yibiao–Kaiwu Capital Co Ltd
Chen, Yilu–Shanghai NCE Venture Capital Management Co Ltd
Chen, Yonghua–Anhui Province Venture Investment Ltd
Chen, Yuanyuan–Shenzhen QF Capital Management Co Ltd
Chen, Yuemeng–ZheShang Venture Capital Co Ltd
Chen, Yuliang–Shanghai Broad Resources Investment Management Co Ltd
Chen, Yunshan–Shenzhen Jiupai Capital Management Co Ltd
Chen, Zach–CID Group
Chen, Zhonghua–Feima Fund
Cheney, Dale–Annex Capital Management LLC
Cheng, Albert–Fidelity Growth Partners Asia
Cheng, Andrew–Blackstone Group LP
Cheng, Bryan–iSeed Ventures
Cheng, CK–Asiatech Management LLC
Cheng, Chih-Kai–Harbinger Venture Management
Cheng, Chuange–BOCOM International Holdings Co Ltd
Cheng, Daniel–Clairvest Group Inc
Cheng, Duen-Chian–Translink Capital LLC
Cheng, Houbo–Shenzhen Oriental Fortune Capital Co Ltd
Cheng, Jose–Li & Fung Investments
Cheng, Julian–Warburg Pincus LLC
Cheng, Larry–Volition Capital LLC
Cheng, Selena–First Alverstone Partners Pte Ltd
Cheng, Shao-Shao–HandsOn3 LLC
Cheng, Tan Lei–Goldis Bhd
Cheng, Xin–HandsOn3 LLC
Cheng, Xin–Hunan Xiangtou Holdings Group Co Ltd
Chenoweth, Adam–Adams Street Partners LLC
Cheo, Hock Kuan–Temasek Holdings (Private) Ltd
Cheon, Seung-Wook–Premier Partners LLC
Cherian, Brinda–First Atlantic Capital, Ltd.
Cherington, Charles–Intervale Capital LLC
Chermont, Pedro–Leblon Equities Gestao de Recursos Ltda
Cherney, Mark–SV Health Investors LLP
Chernock, Jerry–DC Capital Partners LLC
Cherry, Brian–J.H. Whitney & Co LLC
Cherry, JB–One Equity Partners LLC
Cherry, Zachary–Caerus Ventures LLC
Cherry-Seto, Joshua–Blue Wolf Capital Partners LLC
Chertok, Doug–Dace Ventures
Chertok, Doug–Vast Ventures
Cherun, Robert–Auxo Management LP
Chesler, Mark–G3W Ventures LLC
Chesler, Mark–Oaktree Capital Management LP
Chesnais, Fabrice–Lion Capital LLP
Chesney, Kelly–Detroit Renaissance
Chesnoff, Adam–Saban Capital Group Inc
Chesonis, Algimantas–Cranberry Capital LLC
Chesonis, Arunas–Cranberry Capital LLC
Chess, Mark–Israel Infinity Venture Capital Fund Israel LP
Chesson, Shane–NSI Ventures
Chester, Marquette–Invesco Private Capital Inc
Cheung, Anna–3i Group PLC
Cheung, Cindy–Crestview Advisors, LLC
Cheung, Cliff–Interleader Capital Ltd
Cheung, David–CLSA Capital Partners HK Ltd
Cheung, Emil–CITIC Capital Partners Ltd
Cheung, Patrick–Qed Global
Cheung, Ryan–Robson Capital Partners Corp
Cheung, Savio–Ichigo Inc
Cheung, Tiffany–Morrison & Foerster LLP
Cheung, Vincent–Pivotal BioVenture Partners LLC
Chevalier, Jerome–Quadrille Capital SAS
Chevrel, Roger–Techfund Capital Europe
Chevrier, Stephane–Equifin Capital Partners
Chew, Mok Lee–SPRING SEEDS Capital Pte, Ltd.
Chew, Yen Li–Oaktree Capital Management LP
Chewens, Michael–Nbt Capital Corp
Chhabra, Kate–Catamount Ventures LP
Chhabria, Mahesh–Actis LLP
Chhachhi, Vivek–CX Partners
Chheda, Neil–Romulus Capital LLC
Chi, Jianxin–China-Africa Development Fund
Chi, Miao–Warburg Pincus LLC
Chi, Stephanie–Oaktree Capital Management LP
Chia, Brenda–Paladin Capital Management LLC
Chiang, Albert–Bay Hills Capital Partners II LP
Chiang, Brian–Walden International
Chiang, David–Wilshire Private Markets
Chiang, H. Eric–Invus Group LLC
Chiang, Helen–Ascribe Capital, LLC
Chiang, Richard–Redwood Capital, Inc.
Chiang, Rick–H&Q Asia Pacific, Ltd.
Chiang, Robin–AEA Investors LLC

Chiang, Yao-Chye—Clearwater Capital Partners Cyprus Ltd
Chiao, Stephen Sun—Sycamore Ventures Inc
Chiarelli, Paul—Wesley Clover International Corporation
Chiasson, Sabrina—Battery Ventures LP
Chiate, Greg—GC Capital Inc
Chiavacci, Ingrid—Hummer Winblad Venture Partner
Chiaverini, Anthony—50 South Capital Advisors LLC
Chiavetta, Catherine—Z Capital HF Adviser LLC
Chicoski, Robert—Saturn Management LLC
Chidambaram, Ravi—Tc Capital Pte Ltd
Chidambaram, Srinivas—Jacob Ballas Capital India Pvt Ltd
Chien, Chi-Hua—Kleiner Perkins Caufield & Byers LLC
Chieregato, Matteo—21 Centrale Partners SA
Chigwende, Marlon—Carlyle Group LP
Chihi, Kyce—AUA Private Equity Partners LLC
Chikhachev, Dmitry—Runa Capital
Child, Iain—Penta Investments Ltd
Childers, Al—Southern Capitol Ventures LLC
Childres, Chris—Edgewater Capital Group, Inc.
Childres, Nathaniel—Castle Harlan Aus Mezzanine
Childress, Stacey—NewSchools Venture Fund
Childress, Tod—Private Advisors LLC
Chill, Michael—HBM Holdings Co
Chimovits, Erez—OrbiMed Advisors LLC
Chin, David—Palladin Capital Group Inc
Chin, Eric—Crosslink Capital Inc
Chin, Tae-joon—Neoplux Co Ltd
Chinai, Raj—Kalaari Capital Partners LLC
Chinchurreta, Fernando—Portobello Capital Advisors SL
Ching, Stanley—CITIC Capital Partners Ltd
Ching, Wei Hong—OCBC CAPITAL MANAGEMENT
Chingwende, Marlon—Standard Chartered Private Equity Ltd
Chinn, Adam—Centerview Partners LLC
Chinoy, Tariq—India Alternatives Investment Advisors Pvt Ltd
Chiodo, Tim—Anholt (USA) LLC
Chiok, Ivonne—Southwest Middle Market M&A
Chirillo, Michael—Antares Capital Corp
Chisholm, William—Symphony Technology Group LLC
Chitnis, Sach—Jump Capital LLC
Chitre, Sanjeev—WISC Partners LP
Chityala, Shreyas—Elevate Innovation Partners LLC
Chiu, Alan—X/Seed Capital Management
Chiu, Emily—500 Startups, L.P.
Chiu, Ian—Warburg Pincus LLC
Chiu, Linda—New Mountain Capital I LLC
Chizen, Bruce—Voyager Capital LLC
Chizmar, Michael—Palisade Capital Management LLC
Chmelar, Philippe—Blackstone Group LP
Cho, Alex—Partners Group Holding AG
Cho, Byung Sik—Magilink Investment Corp
Cho, Dong Hwan—Uni Venture Capital Co Ltd
Cho, E. Sue—KRG Capital Management LP
Cho, Hoon—GI Partners
Cho, Hyeon Jun—Hana Daetoo Securities Co Ltd
Cho, Hyoung Jun—Q Capital Partners Co Ltd
Cho, Il Hyung—MICHIGAN VENTURE CAPITAL CO LTD
Cho, Ilhyun—ePlanet Capital

Cho, Joonyoun—Premier Partners LLC
Cho, Justin—Vista Equity Partners LLC
Cho, Kyung Hoon—LB Investment Inc
Cho, Serena—Bio*One Capital Pte Ltd
Cho, Su Hyeon—BK Investment Co Ltd
Cho, Sue—Mountaingate Capital Management LP
Cho, Sungjoon—Formation Group Inc
Cho, Thomas—Corstone Corp
Chock, Carty—Arsenal Capital Partners LP
Chock, Carty—Clearpoint Investment Partners LLC
Choe, Anthony—Brentwood Associates, L.P.
Choe, Anthony—Brentwood Venture Capital
Choe, Michael—Charlesbank Capital Partners LLC
Choe, William—Morrison & Foerster LLP
Chohan, Ommer—Atlas Venture Advisors Inc
Chohan, Ommer—Summerhill Venture Partners Management Inc
Choi, Ben—Maveron LLC
Choi, Chris—Serent Capital LLC
Choi, Hui Yong—KTB Investment & Securities Co Ltd
Choi, Hwa Jin—Capstone Partners LLC
Choi, Hyun Joo—Seir Venture Capital
Choi, Jai—Partech International
Choi, Jayna—LB Investment Inc
Choi, Jean—Lindeman Asia Investment Corp
Choi, Jeong Ho—Hana Daetoo Securities Co Ltd
Choi, Jung—Peak Rock Capital LLC
Choi, Justin—Seaport Capital LLC
Choi, Justin—Seaport Capital LLC
Choi, Ken—Alphanorth Asset Management
Choi, Seong Il—Wonik Investment Partners
Choi, Seung Wu—SkyLake Investment & Co
Choi, Steve—Oaktree Capital Management LP
Choi, Steve—Wilshire Private Markets
Choi, Sung Yong—Carlyle Group LP
Choi, Yonsog—MBK Partners Inc
Choi, Yumin—Bain Capital Venture Partners LLC
Choi, Yumin—HLM Management Co LLC
Choi, Yumin—HLM Management Co LLC
Choix, Didier—Massena Partners SA
Chojnacka, Miki—Sandbox & Co Ltd
Chok, Kwee Bee—Teak Capital Sdn Bhd
Choksi, Homyar—LBC Credit Partners Inc
Cholet, Phillippe—Sigma Gestion SA
Chon, Gina—Trilantic Capital Management LP
Chonchol Bahbout, Claudio—3G Capital Inc
Chong, Benjamin—Right Click Capital
Chong, Benjamin—Sydney Seed Fund Management Pty Ltd
Chong, Davis—City Star Private Equity Sas
Chong, Pearlyn—Oaktree Capital Management LP
Chong, Simon—Georgian Partners Growth Fund Founders International I LP
Choo, Yong—Hana Daetoo Securities Co Ltd
Chopack, John—HealthpointCapital LLC
Chopova, Tatiana—AlpInvest Partners BV
Chopra, Ajay—Trinity Ventures LLP
Chopra, Harish—KAMCO Investment Co KSCP
Chopra, Nitin—Shasta Ventures LP
Chopra, Tejpreet Singh—Global Technology Investment
Chorazy, Ryan—Liberty Partners Ltd
Chorengel, Maya—Elevar Equity Advisors Pvt Ltd
Chorpash, Michael—CAMBRIDGE CAPITAL PARTNERS L L C

Chotai, Beena—ICICI Venture Funds Management Company Ltd
Chou, Allan—Northgate Capital LLC
Chou, Art—Stadia Ventures LLC
Chou, Calvin—Marvin TRAUB LLC
Chou, Elizabeth—New Markets Venture Partners
Chou, Fang Soong—Pix Vine Capital Pte Ltd
Chou, Jonathan—Eureka Growth Capital
Chou, Michael—Harmony Partners
Chou, Polong—CDIB BioScience Venture Management
Chou, T.C.—Harbinger Venture Management
Chou, Thomas—Morrison & Foerster LLP
Chou, Tony—Vertical Group Inc
Choudhury, Abhijit—First Abu Dhabi Bank PJSC
Choudhury, Partha—Small Enterprise Assistance Funds
Chough, HS Richard—LTI Investment Co Ltd
Choukas, Michael—Watermill Group LLC
Choung, S. Eugene—Emerald Hill Capital Partners Ltd
Chow, Kelly—Broadline Capital LLC
Chow, Lon—Apex Venture Partners LLC
Chow, Timothy—Capital Dynamics Sdn Bhd
Chowdhri, Rahul—Stellaris Venture Partners
Chowdhury, Shakawat—Rethink Impact Management LLC
Choy, Chris—Quam Asset Management Ltd
Chrastecka, Hana—Bancroft Group Ltd
Chrisney, Craig—Idealab
Christ, Matthew—Gramercy Inc
Christanto, Bryant—General Atlantic LLC
Christensen, Bjorn—Alliance Venture AS
Christensen, Clayton—Rose Park Advisors LLC
Christensen, Gavin—Kickstart Seed Fund LP
Christensen, Gustavus—Evercore Inc
Christensen, Juha—Catagonia Capital GmbH
Christensen, Juha—Sunstone Capital A/S
Christensen, Matthew—Rose Park Advisors LLC
Christensen, Per—Axcel Industriinvestor A/S
Christensen, Richard—Madison Capital Funding LLC
Christensen, Sara—Raptor Capital Management LP
Christensen, Soeren—Cinven Group Ltd
Christensen, Thorkil—Novo Holdings A/S
Christenson, Johan—Odlander Fredrikson & Co AB
Christhilf, Stuart—Pamlico Capital Management LP
Christiaens, Frank—CrossPacific Capital Partners
Christian, Michael—Analytics Ventures
Christian, Phil—DreamIt Ventures
Christians, Andrew—Donnelly Penman & Partners Inc
Christiansen, Robert—Southern Cross Venture Partners Pty Ltd
Christie, Robert—Potomac Equity Partners LLC
Christman, Jeffrey—Rock Hill Capital Group LLC
Christner, Michael—JC Flowers & Co LLC
Christodoulo, Peter—Francisco Partners LP
Christoffersen, Chris—Lightstone Ventures LP
Christopher, Clayton—CAVU Venture Partners, LLC
Christopher, David—Star Mountain Capital LLC
Christopher, James—Blackstone Group LP
Christopher, Mark—Carlyle Group LP
Christopher, Michael—ArcLight Capital Holdings LLC
Christopher, Nicholas—LaSalle Capital
Christou, Victor—Wellington Partners GmbH

Chrust, Steven—Centripetal Capital Partners LLC
Chrysanthou, Chrys—Notion Capital Partners LLP
Chrystall, Paul—Maui Capital Ltd
Chu, Chinh—Blackstone Group LP
Chu, Gang—China International Capital Corp Ltd
Chu, Janie—Carlyle Group LP
Chu, Jeffrey—WI Harper Group Inc
Chu, Mabel—Horizons Ventures Ltd
Chu, Michael—IGNIA Partners LLC
Chu, Nelson—Kinetic Ventures LLC
Chu, Quentin—Crestview Advisors, LLC
Chu, Seok-Don—Carlyle Group LP
Chu, Shelley—Abingworth Management Ltd
Chu, Sherman—Grayhawk Capital
Chu, Swee-Yeok—Bio*One Capital Pte Ltd
Chu, Wei-Kan—PTV Healthcare Capital
Chu, Yee-Ping—Bison Capital Asset Management LLC
Chu, Yk—WI Harper Group Inc
Chua Hwee Song, Nicholas—Tembusu Ventures Pte Ltd
Chua, Beng—Venstar Capital Management Pte Ltd
Chua, Boon Ping—Bio*One Capital Pte Ltd
Chua, Ted—Fidelity Growth Partners Asia
Chuang, George—FountainVest Partners Asia Ltd
Chuchkevich, Mikhail—Bright Capital OOO
Chueri, Paulo—BPE Investimentos
Chuet, Jean-Pierre—Ipsa SAS
Chugg, Brett—Koch Genesis LLC
Chui, Perry—Steamboat Ventures
Chui-Miller, Grace—Correlation Ventures LP
Chuisano, Michael—Johnson & Johnson Innovation—JJDC Inc
Chun, Vincent—Allied Minds LLC
Chung, Andrew—Carlyle Group LP
Chung, Andrew—Khosla Ventures LLC
Chung, Brian—Keystone Capital Inc
Chung, Christopher—Blackstone Group LP
Chung, David—Blum Capital Partners LP
Chung, Henry—DFJ Athena
Chung, Hong-Jen—Hyield Consulting Group
Chung, Hwa-mok—Korea Investment Partners Co Ltd
Chung, Joyce—Garage Technology Ventures LLC
Chung, Katherine—Crestview Advisors, LLC
Chung, Patrick—Naxuri Capital
Chung, Peter—Morgan Stanley Expansion Capital
Chung, Peter—Summit Partners LP
Chung, Theresa—Aif Capital Asia Iii LP
Chung, Young—Duff Ackerman & Goodrich LLC
Chuphi, Ngalaah—Ethos Private Equity (Proprietary) Ltd
Chura, Niles—Capital Royalty LP
Churbanov, Igor—Centras Capital Partners
Churbuck, Thomas—AeroEquity Partners LLC
Church, Cody—Triwest Capital Mgmt Corp
Churchwell, Thomas—Arch Development Partners LLC
Cialino, Andrew—SFW Capital Partners LLC
Cianciolo, Paul—FirstMark Capital LLC
Ciardi, Robert—Provident Healthcare Ventures LLC
Ciaverelli, Gregory—Private Advisors LLC
Cibinic, John—Papillon Capital LLC
Ciborowski, Tomasz—Enterprise Investors Sp z o o
Cicco, Marty—Evercore Inc
Cicco, Susan—Massachusetts Mutual Life Insurance Co

Cichos, Troy—MadroNA Venture Group
Ciesielski, Gregory—HarbourVest Partners LLC
Cifelli, Paul—Kinderhook Industries LLC
Cigarroa, Francisco—University of Texas System
Cihra, Rob—Evercore Inc
Cimino, Thomas—DeltaPoint Capital Management LLC
Cimino, Thomas—DeltaPoint Capital Management LLC
Cimmet, Peter—Olympus Capital Holdings Asia Hong Kong Ltd
Cinquegrana, Pietro—Aleph Capital Partners LLP
Ciofalo, Mario—New Venture Development SpA
Cioffi, Robert—Alerion Partners LLC
Ciporin, Daniel—Canaan Partners
Cipparrone, Gabriele—Apax Partners LLP
Cipriani, Andrea—Monomoy Capital Partners LLC
Cipriano, Mark—TVM Capital GmbH
Cira, Kathleen—Union Bancaire Privee Private Equity
Cirella, Blinn—Saw Mill Capital LLC
Ciriello, Paul—Fairhaven Capital Partners, L.P.
Cirier, Frederic—Tocqueville Finance SA
Cirilli, Mark—MissionPoint Capital Partners LLC
Cirillo, Riccardo—Platina Finance, Ltd.
Cirino, Maria—406 Ventures LLC
Cirla, Giorgio—Iniziativa Gestione Investimenti SGR SpA
Cirla, Matteo—Iniziativa Gestione Investimenti SGR SpA
Cirne, Lew—Four Rivers Partners LP
Cissell-Roell, Kara—VMG Partners, L.P.
Citrino, Mary—Blackstone Group LP
Citron, Emanuel—Stone Point Capital LLC
Citron, Jeffrey—KEC Ventures Inc
Ciuffo, Philip—New York Times Co
Civantos, John—Court Square Capital Partners LP
Civelek, Baris—Summer Street Capital Partners LLC
Civins, Jeff—Haynes and Boone LLC
Claassen, Robert—Camp One Ventures LLC
Clackson, Patrick—Barclays Capital Inc
Claeys, Frank—BNP Paribas Fortis Private Equity Growth NV
Clair, Kuldip—Ic2 Capital
Clancy, Sheila—Twin Haven Capital Partners LLC
Clapham, Jesse—Oaktree Capital Management LP
Clapp, Todd—Catalyst Investors LLC
Clapper, David—CMS Mezzanine Fund
Clare, Daniel—Constitution Capital Partners LLC
Clark, Alistair—European Bank for Reconstruction and Development
Clark, B. Jefferson—Aurora Funds Inc
Clark, Bernard—Haynes and Boone LLC
Clark, Brad—Bb&T Capital Partners LLC
Clark, Brad—Parallax Capital Partners LLC
Clark, Brian—M/C Venture Partners LLC
Clark, Caleb—Palladium Equity Partners LLC
Clark, Caleb—Windjammer Capital Investors LLC
Clark, Colby—Farallon Capital Management LLC
Clark, David—Elevate Ventures Inc
Clark, Drew—International Business Machines Corp
Clark, Dwight—New Asia Partners LLC
Clark, George—Freestone Partners LLC
Clark, Greg—Horizon Technology Finance Management LLC
Clark, Guy—Oaktree Capital Management LP

Clark, J. Ryan—Genstar Capital LLC
Clark, James—Cabot Square Capital Advisors Ltd
Clark, James—Granite Creek Partners LLC
Clark, Jeff—Ontario Teachers' Pension Plan
Clark, John—CVC Capital Partners Ltd
Clark, John—New World Angels, Inc.
Clark, John—Performance Equity Management LLC
Clark, Lisa—SFP Capital LLC
Clark, Matthew—European Capital Financial Services Ltd
Clark, Peter—Carousel Capital Partners
Clark, Peter—Growth Works Capital Ltd
Clark, Rena—Gennx360 Capital Partners LP
Clark, Robert—Bunker Hill Capital LP
Clark, Roddy—Enhanced Capital Partners LLC
Clark, Roddy—Redmont Venture Partners
Clark, Sarah—Commonfund Capital Inc
Clark, Scott—Covington Capital Corp
Clark, Scott—Market Square Equity Partners
Clark, Simon—Eight Roads Ventures Europe
Clark, Thomas—Apax Partners LLP
Clark, Timothy—Gridiron Capital LLC
Clark, Tom—Comvest Partners
Clark, Tom—Comvest Partners
Clark, Trevor—AG BD LLC
Clark, Trevor—Madison Capital Funding LLC
Clarke Adamson, Martha—Sierra Ventures
Clarke, Adrian—Meridia Capital Partners SL
Clarke, Anthony—Seraphim Capital (General Partner) LLP
Clarke, Jason—Strategic Value Partners LLC
Clarke, John—CHP Management Inc
Clarke, Lisa—Kinderhook Industries LLC
Clarke, Martin—Oceanbridge Partners LLC
Clarke, Nigel—Caribbean Equity Partners Ltd
Clarke, Pete—F&C Equity Partners PLC
Clarke, Richard—7Bridge Capital Partners Ltd
Clarke, Timothy—August Equity Llp
Clarkson, Elizabeth—Sapphire Ventures LLC
Clarkson, Macon—Private Advisors LLC
Clarkson, Thomas—Morgan Stanley Alternative Investment Partners LP
Clarry, Nicholas—CVC Capital Partners Ltd
Clary, Matthew—Waud Capital Partners LLC
Claudino, Felipe—Leblon Equities Gestao de Recursos Ltda
Claus, Thorsten—Next World Capital LLC
Claus, Thorsten—Northgate Capital LLC
Claussen, Lisa—Bain Capital Inc
Claussen, Maximilian—Earlybird Venture Capital GmbH & Co KG
Clavel, Antony—Summit Partners LP
Clawson, Spencer—Peterson Partners LP
Clay, C. Kenneth—Corinthian Capital Group LLC
Claycomb, T.—Wall Street Venture Capital Ltd
Clayton, Jim—Antares Capital Corp
Clayton, Kevin—Oaktree Capital Management LP
Clayton, Ollie—Evercore Inc
Cleary, James—Zesiger Capital Group LLC
Clegg, Christopher—Endless LLP
Clegg, Todd—Onex Corp
Cleghorn, Grant—Crosslink Capital Inc
Cleland, Andrew—Comcast Ventures
Cleland, Mark—Donnelly Penman & Partners Inc
Clemens, Adam—Portfolio Advisors, LLC

Clemens, Deven–White Road Investments LLC
Clement, John–GeneChem Financial Corp
Clements, Charlie–Consensus Capital Private Equity Ltd
Clements, Kendra–Acorn Growth Companies
Clemins, Archie–Highway 12 Ventures
Cleveland, Bruce–InterWest Partners LLC
Clevenger, Wayne–Midmark Capital LP
Clevers, Hans–Life Sciences Partners BV
Clevinger, Brian–Prolog Ventures
Clevy, W. Michael–BC General Partners LLC
Clifford, Robert–MDB Capital Group LLC
Cline, Alan–Vista Equity Partners LLC
Cline, J. Michael–Accretive LLC
Cline, Roland–European Capital
Clingan, John–Proprium Capital Partners LP
Clisdell, Robert–Bergen Asset Management LLC
Cloghessy, Mark–Allstate Private Equity
Close, Ronald–Portag3 Ventures Inc GP
Clott, Darlene–Navigation Capital Partners Inc
Cloud, Sanford–Ironwood Investment Management LLC
Clough, Max–Oneaccord Capital LLC
Clouston, Harry–Gainline Capital Partners, L.P.
Cloutier, Jean–Fairfax Financial Holdings Ltd
Cloutier, Richard–Solidarity Fund QFL
Clow, Eric–Hina Capital Partners
Clowe, Kevin–AIG Capital Partners Inc
Clulow, Stefan–Thomvest Ventures Inc
Clunies-Ross, Matthew–Artesian Capital Management Australia Pty Ltd
Clymer, Beth–Bain Capital Inc
Co, Eugene–Compass Partners International LLC
Coady, James–Sentinel Capital Partners LLC
Coakley, Khadijah–IECP Fund Management LLC
Coates, Steve–Warburg Pincus LLC
Coats, David–Correlation Ventures LP
Coballasi, Pablo–PC Capital SAPI de CV
Cobanera, Aitor–Gestion De Capital Riesgo Del
Cobb, Brodie–Presidio Investors LLC
Cobb, Douglas–Chrysalis Ventures Inc
Cobo Bachiller, Inaki–CVC Capital Partners Ltd
Coburn, Brooke–Carlyle Group LP
Coburn, John–XPV Capital Corp
Coburn, Pip–Coburn Ventures LLC
Cochran, Hope–MadroNA Venture Group
Cochran, John–Lovell Minnick Partners LLC
Cochran, Mark–NeuroVentures Capital LLC
Cocke, Charles–Investure LLC
Cocker, James–Lion Capital LLP
Cocker, Paul–True Capital Partners LLP
Cockerell, Clay–PTV Healthcare Capital
Cockrell, Ross–ESCALATE CAPITAL I L P
Cocuzza, Charles–GoldPoint Partners LLC
Code, Adam–Creation Investments Capital Management LLC
Code, Andrew–Promus Equity Partners
Coelho Borges, Joao–Magnum Industrial Partners
Coelho Borges, Joao–Magnum Industrial Partners SL
Coelho, George–PROfounders Capital Ltd
Coelho, John–StepStone Group LP
Coelho, Tony–Potomac Equity Partners LLC
Coes, Ben–Mustang Group LLC
Coffey, Mark–Global Partnerships

Coffey, Steve–Covera Ventures LP
Coffill, Eric–Morrison & Foerster LLP
Cofino, Rafael–Great Hill Equity Partners LLC
Cogan, Gill–Opus Capital
Cogburn, Ronald–HandsOn3 LLC
Cohan, Jay–Western Technology Investment
Cohen, Aaron–GTCR Golder Rauner LLC
Cohen, Arthur–Haynes and Boone LLC
Cohen, Arthur–HealthCor Partners Management LP
Cohen, Cody–Double C Capital
Cohen, Dalia–JLL Partners Inc
Cohen, Dalia–Oak Hill Advisors LP
Cohen, Dan–Poalim Cap Mark Tech, Ltd.
Cohen, Daniel–GEMINI CAPITAL FUND MGMT LTD
Cohen, David–Centerview Partners LLC
Cohen, David–GEMINI CAPITAL FUND MGMT LTD
Cohen, David–Highview Capital LLC
Cohen, David–Milbank Tweed Hadley & Mccloy LLP
Cohen, Ethan–Early Stage Partners LP
Cohen, Frank–Blackstone Group LP
Cohen, Harvey–Nystar
Cohen, Jay–TRG Management LP
Cohen, Jennifer Schultz–Oak Hill Advisors LP
Cohen, Joe–Trilantic Capital Management LP
Cohen, Joseph–Trilantic Capital Management LP
Cohen, Josh–City Light Capital
Cohen, Josh–Golden Gate Capital Inc
Cohen, Marshall–Pilot Group LP
Cohen, Matt–City Light Capital
Cohen, Matthew–Osage Venture Partners
Cohen, Michael–Morrison & Foerster LLP
Cohen, Mitchell–Athenian Fund Management Inc
Cohen, Nathaniel–LBC Credit Partners Inc
Cohen, Neal–CoBe Equities LLC
Cohen, Peter–Blackstone Group LP
Cohen, Randolph–Vision Capital Advisors LLC
Cohen, Robert–Benson Oak Capital Ltd
Cohen, Robert–Blackstone Group LP
Cohen, Robert–Iron Gate Capital LLC
Cohen, Rodney–Carlyle Group LP
Cohen, Sheldon–ECo
Cohen, Trevor–Prophet Equity LLC
Cohen, Wayne–Och-Ziff Capital Management Group LLC
Cohen, Yuval–StageOne Ventures
Cohen, Zehavit–Apax Partners LLP
Cohler, Matthew–Benchmark Capital Management Gesellschaft MBH In Liqu
Cohn, Billy–Sante Ventures
Cohn, Gary–Goldman Sachs & Co LLC
Cohn, Greg–Source Capital LLC
Cohn, Hillel–Morrison & Foerster LLP
Cohn, Paul–Fort Washington Capital
Cohn, William–PTV Healthcare Capital
Cohn-Rupp, Stephanie–Omidyar Network Commons LLC
Cohn-Sfetcu, Dan–Acas LLC
Coit, David–North Atlantic Capital
Coit, Rennie–Ignition Capital Partners
Coker, Jonathan–MMC Ventures Ltd
Colaco, Antoine–Valor Capital Group LLC
Colaianne, John–Industrial Opportunity Partners LLC
Colangelo, Stephen–Morrison & Foerster LLP
Colas, Benoit–Carlyle Group LP
Colasson, Pierre–Bridgepoint Advisers II Ltd

Colasson, Pierre–Bridgepoint Advisers Ltd
Colavita, Jason–Evercore Inc
Colavito, Nicola–Peninsula Capital Advisors LLP
Colayco, Aloysius–Argosy Partners, Inc.
Colayco, Rufo–Argosy Partners, Inc.
Colby, Jonathan–Carlyle Group LP
Colciago, Luca–Kreos Capital Managers Ltd
Coldwell, Deborah–Haynes and Boone LLC
Cole, Alan–Cedar Hill Associates LLC
Cole, Alliott–Octopus Ventures Ltd
Cole, Allison–CCMP Capital Advisors LP
Cole, C. Taylor–Charterhouse Group Inc
Cole, Cali–Citigroup Private Equity LP
Cole, Charles–Morrison & Foerster LLP
Cole, Dan–Oxford Bioscience Partners
Cole, Darrick–Skytree Capital Partners LP
Cole, Douglas–Flagship Pioneering
Cole, J. Daniel–Spray Venture Partners
Cole, James–Windward Ventures
Cole, John–Global Infrastructure Holdings
Cole, Jonathan–New World Angels, Inc.
Cole, Matt–Spanos Barber Jesse & Co LLC
Cole, Matthew–North Bay Equity Partners
Cole, Michael–Madison Dearborn Partners LLC
Colella, Samuel–Versant Venture Management, LLC
Coleman Redenbaugh, Amy–Thoma Bravo LLC
Coleman, Alexander–Annex Capital Management LLC
Coleman, Bill–Alsop Louie Partners
Coleman, Charles–Tiger Global Management LLC
Coleman, Debi–SmartForest Ventures
Coleman, Nicholas–SV Health Investors LLP
Coleman, Nick–SV Health Investors LLP
Coleman, Paul–H2o Venture Partners Pe Ltd
Coleman, Sean–Golub Capital Master Funding LLC
Coleman, Terry–Water Tower Capital LLC
Coleman, Timothy–Blackstone Group LP
Coleman-Chen, Elizabeth–Blackstone Group LP
Coles, Chris–Actis LLP
Colette, Monique–Atlantic Canada Opportunities Agency
Colin, Nicolas–Thefamily SAS
Colin, Patrick–Picardie Investissements SA
Colins, Morton–Battelle Ventures LP
Coll, Matthew–Westfield Capital Management Company LP
Collar, Mark–Triathlon Medical Ventures LLC
Collas, Philippe–Amundi Private Equity Funds SA
Collatos, William–Spectrum Equity Investors LP
Colleran, Kevin–General Catalyst Partners LLC
Colless, Jeremy–Proto Investment Partners Pty Ltd
Collier, Cesar–Siguler Guff & Company LP
Collier, David–CMEA Development Company LLC
Colligan, Bud–Accel Partners & Co Inc
Collignon, Yann–Azulis Capital SA
Collin, Andre–Lone Star Fund Ltd
Collin, Daniel–Monomoy Capital Partners LLC
Collings, Gregory–Fulcrum Capital Partners Inc
Collins, Alexander–Oakley Capital Ltd
Collins, Andrew–Summit Partners LP
Collins, Andrew–Summit Partners LP
Collins, Charles–Emerald Development Managers LP
Collins, Christopher–Kelso & Company LP
Collins, Emma–Platina Finance, Ltd.
Collins, John–Haynes and Boone LLC

Pratt's Guide to Private Equity & Venture Capital Sources

Collins, John–Summer Street Capital Partners LLC
Collins, Kenneth–Audax Group, Inc.
Collins, Matthew–Hutton Collins Partners LLP
Collins, Patrick–Grand Crossing Capital LLC
Collins, Patrick–Jh Partners LLC
Collins, Phil–Orchard Holdings Group LLC
Collins, Richard–Indigo Capital LLP
Collins, Robert–Osceola Capital Management LLC
Collins, Robert–Partners Group Holding AG
Collins, Robert–Stellus Capital Management LLC
Collins, Scott–Summit Partners LP
Collins, Stephen–Oaktree Capital Management LP
Collins, Steven–Advent International Corp
Collins, Terence–Columbia Partners Private Capital
Collins, Timothy–Northwestern Mutual Capital LLC
Collins, Timothy–Ripplewood Holdings LLC
Collins, Todd–Tregaron Capital Co LLC
Collinson, Jeffrey–CHL Medical Partners LP
Collinson, Stuart–Forward Ventures
Collis, James–Seaport Capital LLC
Collis, Jim–Seaport Capital LLC
Collombel, Philippe–Partech International
Colloton, J. Edmund–Bessemer Venture Partners
Collum, Peter–MTS Health Partners LP
Collyer, Skye–Alphanorth Asset Management
Colmone, Andy–Sterling Partners GP LLC
Colodny, Mark–Warburg Pincus LLC
Colognesi, Jake–Volition Capital LLC
Colombini, Luciano–Unipol Merchant Banca per le Imprese SpA
Colombo, Dina–CCMP Capital Advisors LP
Colon, Daniel–CM Equity Partners LP
Colosimo, Louis–Comvest Partners
Colpitts, Christopher–CVC Capital Partners Ltd
Colpitts, Susan–Signature Financial Management Inc
Colquitt, Sheri–Triangle Capital Partners L L C
Colson, Randall–Haynes and Boone LLC
Colton, Brian–Brooklyn Equity
Colvert, Scott–Trinity Hunt Partners
Coly, Jean- Marc–Siparex Proximite Innovation SAS
Com, Monica–Macrocapitales SAFI SA
Comeau, David–Keen Growth Capital Advisors LLC
Comer, B. Bragg–Fidus Capital LLC
Comer, Steven–Morrison & Foerster LLP
Comerford, Jay–Lightyear Capital LLC
Comey, Charles–Morrison & Foerster LLP
Comfort, Stuyvie–Stirling Square Capital Partners Lp
Comfort, William–Court Square Capital Partners LP
Comis, James–Inverness Management LLC
Comizio, Robert–Medley Capital LLC
Comoglio, Pier Andrea–V&A Capital
Comolli, Kevin–Accel Partners & Co Inc
Compall, John–CIVC Partners LP
Compton, Bob–MB VENTURE PARTNERS L L C
Compton, Kevin–Radar Partners LLC
Comstock, Cory–Sherbrooke Capital
Conaton, Michael–Cyprium Investment Partners LLC
Conboy, Philip–Milestone Capital Partners Ltd
Conchillo, Federico–PAI Partners SAS
Conder, Simon–Asclepios Bioresearch (UK) Ltd
Condron, Brett–Blackstone Group LP
Cone, Brian–Trust Company of the West
Conese, Eugene–Gridiron Capital LLC
Coneway, Peter–Riverstone Holdings LLC

Coneybeer, Robert–Shasta Ventures LP
Conforti, Francesco–Vegagest Azionari Asia A
Conjeevaram, Srini–SC Capital Management LLC
Conklin, Richard–First Analysis Corp
Conley, Paul–Paladin Capital Management LLC
Conlon, James–Bullpen Capital LP
Conn, Alastair–NVM Pe Ltd
Conn, Michele–Moderne Ventures Fund I LP
Conn, Richard–Innovate Partners LLC
Conn, Robert–Innova Capital Sp z o o
Connaughton, John–Bain Capital Inc
Connell, Brian–Trivest Partners LP
Connell, Mark–Evercore Inc
Connell, Patrick–Riverstone Holdings LLC
Connell, William–High Road Capital Partners LLC
Connelly, James–Water Street Healthcare Partners LLC
Connelly, Patrick–Intervale Capital LLC
Connelly, Robert–Flagship Pioneering
Connelly, W. Patrick–SCF Partners LP
Conner, Charles–Arlon Group LLC
Conner, David–OCBC CAPITAL MANAGEMENT
Conner, Jeff–Innovate Partners LLC
Conner, Terry–Haynes and Boone LLC
Conners, Timothy–PivotNorth Capital
Connolly, John–Bain Capital Inc
Connolly, Nicole–Northgate Capital LLC
Connolly, Peter–Summit Partners LP
Connoly, Robert–Westcap Management Ltd
Connor, John–ABRY Partners LLC
Connor, Sean–Whitehorse Liquidity Partners Inc
Connor, Tim–Sequel Venture Partners
Connors, Brian–Formative Ventures
Connors, John–Ignition Ventures Management LLC
Connors, John–Ignition Ventures Management LLC
Connors, Kevin–Spray Venture Partners
Connors, Robert–HGGC LLC
Connors, Travis–Egan Managed Capital LP
Connors, Travis–Egan Managed Capital LP
Connors, William–Stonebridge Partners LP
Conrad, Barry–Independent Bankers Capital Funds
Conrad, Jean-Pierre–Ambrian Resources AG
Conrad, Jeremy–Lemnos Labs
Conrad, Tony–True Ventures LLC
Conrades, George–Polaris Venture Partners
Conroy, Charles–Milbank Tweed Hadley & Mccloy LLP
Conroy, James–Gramercy Inc
Conroy, James–Olympus Partners
Conroy, Joe–Cooley LLP
Conroy, Patrick–Intervale Capital LLC
Consoli, Victor–Perella Weinberg Partners LP
Contant, Brendan–Pacific View Asset Management LLC
Conte, Kathy–Hercules Capital Inc
Contento, Lance–Three Hills Capital Partners LLP
Conti, Carlos–Inveready Seed Capital SCR SA
Conti, Vincent–Radius Ventures LLC
Contrella, Larry–JMI Management Inc
Contreras, Jose Antonio–Wamex Private Equity Management
Conway, Arnold–Navasota Group
Conway, Brian–TA Associates Management LP
Conway, Damon–Altas Partners LP

Conway, David–Front Street Capital
Conway, Kevin–Clayton Dubilier & Rice LLC
Conway, Mark–Steelhouse Ventures Ltd
Conway, Paul–Spark Capital
Conway, Ronald–Angel Investors, LP
Conway, Ronald–Baseline Ventures LLC
Conway, Ronway–Andreessen Horowitz LLC
Conway, Shawn–Questa Capital Management LLC
Conway, Topher–SV Angel
Cook, Alexander–Fortress Investment Group LLC
Cook, Andrew–Southfield Capital Advisors LLC
Cook, Cory–HarbourVest Partners LLC
Cook, David–Morgan Stanley Private Equity
Cook, Everett–Pouschine Cook Capital Management LLC
Cook, Hobart–Thomas H Lee Partners LP
Cook, James–Silverhawk Capital Partners LLC
Cook, Jason–Gramercy Inc
Cook, John–InvesteCo Capital Corp
Cook, John–Landmark Partners Inc
Cook, Joseph–Mountain Group Capital LLC
Cook, Joseph–Mountain Group Capital LLC
Cook, Michael–Macquarie Capital Alliance Management Pty Ltd
Cook, Patrick–SilverStream Capital LLC
Cook, Robert–Cedar Creek Partners
Cook, Simon–Draper Esprit PLC
Cook, Stephen–Andrew W Byrd & Co LLC
Cook, Steve–LFM Capital LLC
Cook, Tim–General Atlantic LLC
Cook, Timothy–General Atlantic LLC
Cook, Todd–Bain Capital Inc
Cook-Stevenson, Craig–Lexington Partners Inc
Cooke, Ann–Vencap International PLC
Cooke, Ian–Ecomachines Ventures Ltd
Cooke, Kim–Blue Water Capital LLC
Cooke, Trudy–Terra Firma Capital Partners Ltd
Cookler, Hillary–Oaktree Capital Management LP
Coombs, John–Unilever Ventures Ltd
Cooney, David–Beecken Petty O'Keefe & Company LLC
Coons, Ted–Technology Crossover Ventures LP
Cooper, Adam–Platinum Equity LLC
Cooper, Andrew–Pegasus Capital Advisors LP
Cooper, Brian–GB Credit Partners LLC
Cooper, Brian–Tengram Capital Partners LLC
Cooper, Charles–LYRIQUE Srrl
Cooper, Chris–Pelion Venture Partners
Cooper, Douglas–Acas LLC
Cooper, James–Merck Capital Ventures LLC
Cooper, James–Thompson Street Capital Partners LP
Cooper, Jordan–Lerer Ventures II LP
Cooper, Ken–Capital for Enterprise Ltd
Cooper, Kendall–AllegisCyber
Cooper, Kendall–Ridgelift Ventures
Cooper, Michael–Shore Capital Partners LLC
Cooper, Nancy–Rhone Capital LLC
Cooper, Piers–mc3 ventures (FKA: McKenna Venture Accelerator (MVA))
Cooper, Russell–Shorenstein Co LLC
Cooper, Vaishali–Jungle Ventures Pte Ltd
Cooper-Evans, Alexander–Electra Private Equity Plc
Coopersmith, Warren–Leading Ridge Capital Partners LLC
Coopersmith, Zach–Building Industry Partners LLC

Coopersmith, Zach—Leading Ridge Capital Partners LLC
Cooray, Joseph—N D B Capital Holdings PLC
Cooreman, Andre—Sofinim NV
Coors, Andrew—9th Street Investments
Coors, Doug—9th Street Investments
Cope, Brandon—Accretia Capital LLC
Cope, Brandon—Peterson Partners LP
Cope, Brandon—Peterson Ventures LLC
Copeland, Clare—European Capital Financial Services Ltd
Copeland, David—Onex Corp
Copeland, Martin—Evercore Inc
Copland, Lindsay—Lyceum Capital
Coppedge, Rob—Echo Health Ventures LLC
Coppedge, Roy—Boston Ventures
Coppel, Toby—Virgin Green Fund
Coppens, Brad—One Equity Partners LLC
Coppens, Steven—Gimv Investeringsmaatschappij Voor Vlanderen NV
Coppola, Michael—Dallas Venture Partners LP
Coquema, Christophe—AXA Investment Managers Inc
Coquillette, David—New Mountain Capital I LLC
Coquis, Laura—BC Partners LLP
Cora, Pili—Telegraph Hill Group LLC
Corash, Michele—Morrison & Foerster LLP
Corbacho, Alexander—Paine Schwartz Partners LLC
Corbacioglu, Bulend—AP Capital Investments LP
Corbett, Adam—Phoenix Equity Partners Ltd
Corbett, Bryan—Carlyle Group LP
Corbett, Chris—Rcf Management LLC
Corbett, Hutch—TriplePoint Capital LLC
Corbin, Alicia—Blackstone Group LP
Corcione, Rosario—First Reserve Corp
Corcodel, Claudiu—Mezzanine Management Finanz und UnternehmensberatungsgmbH
Corcoran, Brendan—Partners Capital Investment Group Holdings LLC
Corcoran, Daniel—Massachusetts Capital Resource
Corcoran, Rick—Slate Capital Group LLC
Corcostegui, Angel—Magnum Industrial Partners
Corcostegui, Angel—Magnum Industrial Partners SL
Cordeau, Michel—Propulsion Ventures Inc
Cordeiro, Hugo Fabiano—HFPX Holding Ltda
Cordell, Thomas—Haynes and Boone LLC
Cordes, Eckhard—Emeram Capital Partners GmbH
Cordes, John—DeltaPoint Capital Management LLC
Cordey, Martin—Lyceum Capital
Cordoba, Diego—Teka Capital SAS
Cordova, Gonzalo—Vedanta Capital LP
Corey, Chris—Nautic Partners LLC
Corkran, Greg—ACP Inc
Corl, James—Siguler Guff & Company LP
Corley, Evan—Pantheon Ventures (UK) LLP
Cormier, Lionel—Demeter SAS
Cornelis, Kelly—LaSalle Capital
Cornelius, Craig—Hudson Clean Energy Partners
Cornelius, James—Twilight Venture Partners
Cornelius, Ronn—Montauk TriGuard Management Inc
Cornelius, Wolf—Mutares AG
Cornell, Brad—Excellere Capital Management LLC
Cornell, Chad—Goldner Hawn Johnson & Morrison Inc
Cornell, John—Global Asia Partners
Cornell, Michael—Mcc Capital Partners LLC
Cornell, Michael—Propel Equity Partners LLC
Cornell, Peter—Metric Capital Partners LLP
Cornella, Guido—Spice Private Equity AG
Cornieti, Mathieu—IMPACT Partenaires SAS
Corning, Sally—Sun Mountain Capital Advisors LLC
Coronas, Jose—Trillium Group LLC
Corr, Peter—Auven Therapeutics Management LLLP
Corrales, Rafael—Charles River Ventures LLC
Correa, Maria Claudia—Efromovich/Silva Capital Partners
Corrie, Nancy—Apex Venture Partners LLC
Corrie, Nancy—Hyde Park Venture Partners
Corrie, Nancy—Hyde Park Venture Partners
Corriero, Timothy—Anthos Capital LP
Corrigan, Jay—Bain Capital Inc
Corrigan, Maura—Glengary LLC
Corriggio, Anthony—Siguler Guff & Company LP
Corrin, Matthew—Klass Capital Corp
Corscadden, Jay—AH Ventures
Corsellis, James—Marwyn Investment Management LLP
Corsini, Araceli—Blackstone Group LP
Cortas, Samer—Vision Capital LLP
Cortas, Usama—Leonard Green & Partners LP
Cortell, Nina—Haynes and Boone LLC
Cortinovis, Stephen—Current Capital LLC
Cortner, Ryan—Westshore Capital Partners LP
Cosan, Roy—Fjord Ventures LLC
Cosentino, John—Ironwood Partners LLC
Coseriff, Robert—Allen & Company of Florida, Inc.
Cosgrave, Jonathan—Warburg Pincus LLC
Cosgrove, Rick—Veritas Capital Fund Management LLC
Cosson, Nicolas—Azulis Capital SA
Costa de Beauregard, Paul—Qualium Investissement SAS
Costa, Dulio—Macrocapitales SAFI SA
Costa, Patricia—Change Partners
Costa, Saverio—Hancock Capital Management LLC
Costagli, Stefano—Vegagest Azionari Asia A
Costantino, John—NGN Capital LLC
Costello, Daniel—TSG Consumer Partners, L.P.
Costello, Dennis—Braemar Energy Ventures LP
Costello, Dennis—Triathlon Medical Ventures LLC
Costello, Jonathan—Morgan Stanley Alternative Investment Partners LP
Costello, Neal—AlpInvest Partners BV
Costello, Timothy—Newstone Capital Partners LLC
Costello, Tom—Baird Capital
Costes, Pierre—Butler Capital Partners SA
Costi Ruiz, Pablo—CVC Capital Partners Ltd
Costin, Tom—Owl Ventures LP
Cote, Arhtur—Backlog Capital LLC
Cote, Cathleen—Resonetics LLC
Cote, Jeffrey—Pfingsten Partners LLC
Cote, Michel—Investissements Novacap Inc
Cottam, David—Park Square Capital LLP
Cotter, Kevin—MDB Capital Group LLC
Cotton, Newell—Novo Tellus Capital Partners Pte Ltd
Cotton, Ryan—Bain Capital Inc
Cotton, Tanguy—Atlantic-Pacific Capital Inc
Cottone, Joe—Tenex Capital Management LP
Cottrill, Bruce—CtechBA Pty Ltd
Cottrill, Lance—Horsley Bridge Partners LLC
Coudreau, Frederic—Credit Agricole Corporate and Investment Bank SA
Couet, Catherine—Astorg Partners SAS
Coufal, Sandra—Sibling Capital LLC
Coughlan, Elaine—Atlantic Bridge
Coughlin, Carl—Coughlin Capital LLC
Coughlin, Francis—Coughlin Capital LLC
Coughlin, Kevin—Coughlin Capital LLC
Coughlin, William—Delta Capital Management LLC
Coughlon, Jay—Lariat Partners LP
Coughran, William—Sequoia Capital Operations LLC
Couillard, Philippe—Persistence Capital Partners Lp
Coulombe, Lorie—Oak Hill Capital Management Inc
Coulson, Fred—Five Elms Capital LLC
Coulter, Chris—Morrison & Foerster LLP
Coulter, James—TPG Capital Management LP
Coulter, Jim—Tpg Growth LLC
Counihan, Jim—Prism Ventureworks
Cournoyer, Jean-Sebastien—Real Ventures
Coursey, Court—TomorrowVentures LLC
Court, Frederic—Advent Venture Partners LLP
Court, Frederic—Felix Capital Partners LLP
Courtney, Jeff—Fight Against Cancer Innovation Trust
Courtney, Wyatt—Brown Brothers Harriman & Co
Cousin, Robert—JP Morgan Investment Management Inc
Coutinho, Claudio—Mare Investimentos Ltda
Couture, Luc—Teralys Capital Inc
Couturier, Christian—Astorg Partners SAS
Couwenberg, Corneille—Go Capital Asset Management BV
Covati, Giovanni—ILP III SARL
Covello, Alexandre—Bex Capital SAS
Covey, Paul—O'Melveny & Myers LLP
Covington, Richard—Natural Gas Partners
Cowan, David—Bessemer Venture Partners
Cowan, Matthew—Bridgescale Partners LP
Cowan, Steve—PCGI LLC
Cowan, Steven—57 Stars LLC
Coward, Iain—Rivers Capital Partners Ltd
Cowart, Greta—Haynes and Boone LLC
Cowen, William—Long River Ventures, Inc.
Cowett, Jason—Odyssey Investment Partners LLC
Cowie, James—Frontenac Company LLC
Cowin, Jack—Quantum Capital
Cox, Christopher—Carlyle Group LP
Cox, Everett—Emergence Capital Partners
Cox, Howard—Greylock Partners LLC
Cox, Jonathan—JC Flowers & Co LLC
Coxe, Tench—Sutter Hill Ventures
Coy, Debra—XPV Capital Corp
Coy, Robert—CincyTech
Coya, Wendy—Vocap Investment Partners LLC
Coyle, John—Permira Advisers LLP
Coyle, Roger—Blackstone Group LP
Coyne, Chris—Corazon Capital LLC
Coyne, J. Peter—Saw Mill Capital LLC
Coyne, Kevin—Canal Holdings LLC
Coyne, Patrick—Lincolnshire Management Inc
Cozean, Ron—Resilience Capital Partners LLC
Cozewith, Andrew—Monroe Capital LLC
Cozzens, Todd—Sequoia Capital Operations LLC
Cozzi, John—AEA Investors LLC
Crabill, Scott—Thoma Bravo LLC

Pratt's Guide to Private Equity & Venture Capital Sources

Cracco, Adelaide—Finaves I SA
Craddock, Peter—Shoreline Venture Management, LLC
Craft, Anders—Swedfund International AB
Crager, Bruce—Impact Capital Inc
Cragg, Scott—Trevi Health Ventures LP
Craig, Andrew—Maven Capital Partners UK LLP
Craig, Andrew—Maven Capital Partners UK LLP
Craig, Brett—Hidden Harbor Capital Partners LLC
Craig, Bruce—England Capital Partners LLC
Craig, Jackson—Bayside Capital Inc
Craig, Ryan—Bertram Capital Management LLC
Craig, Ryan—University Ventures
Craigie, Justin—Summit Partners LP
Crail, Emily—Fund Evaluation Group LLC
Crain, Andrew—Antares Capital Corp
Crain, Andrew—Tully and Holland Inc
Crain, Eberhard—Cbr Management GmbH
Cramer, Kellie—Thompson Street Capital Partners LP
Crandall, Duke—Nbt Capital Corp
Crandall, J. Taylor—Oak Hill Capital Management Inc
Crandall, Rick—NewSchools Venture Fund
Crandell, Keith—Arch Venture Partners LLC
Crane, Alan—Polaris Venture Partners
Crane, Bruce—OMERS Infrastructure
Crane, Ronald—DCA Capital Partners LP
Cranford, Adam—New Capital Partners
Crankshaw, Andrew—Atomico Ventures
Cranney, Mark—Andreessen Horowitz LLC
Cranswick, Russ—Rcf Management LLC
Crants, D. Robert—Pharos Capital Group LLC
Crary, Robert—Fulcrum Management Inc
Craven, Hannah—Stone-Goff Partners LLC
Craven, Mackey—Openview Venture Partners LP
Craver, Jeffrey—Advantage Capital Partners
Craves, Frederick—Bay City Capital LLC
Cravey, Richard—Cgw Southeast Partners
Cravey, Rick—Kian Capital Partners LLC
Crawford, Alexander—Ziff Brothers Investments LLC
Crawford, Andrew—Advent International Corp
Crawford, Andrew—General Atlantic LLC
Crawford, Douglas—Mission Bay Capital LLC
Crawford, Gilbert—Microvest Capital Management LLC
Crawford, Jack—Impact Venture Capital
Crawford, Jack—Velocity Venture Capital Inc
Crawford, Matthew—PTV Healthcare Capital
Crawford, Reginald—Gemcorp Capital LLP
Crawford, Ryan—Jog Capital Inc
Crawford, Thomas—Berggruen Holdings Inc
Crawley, Derek—Investec Ventures Ireland Ltd
Crayford, Ian—Formative Ventures
Creamer, Glenn—Providence Equity Partners LLC
Creange, Jean-Pierre—Pragma Capital SA
Creecy, John—Remeditex Ventures LLC
Creed, Tim—Adveq Management AG
Creedon, Lindsay—StepStone Group LP
Creel, George—DTI Capital LLC
Creemers, Edgard—Investinfuture BV
Creer, Frank—Zone Ventures
Creer, Frank—Zone Ventures
Cremer, Johannes—MIDAS Management AG
Cremieux, Timothy—Waud Capital Partners LLC
Cremin, David—Frontier Venture Capital
Crenshaw, Scott—Private Advisors LLC

Crepaldi, Joseph—Crescendo Partners Capital Pty Ltd
Crequit, Jean-Claude—BPCE Immobilier Exploitation SAS
Cressall, Justin—Acas LLC
Cressey, Bryan—Cressey and Company LP
Cresswell, Neil—Savvis Inc
Creswell, Bradford—NCA Partners Inc
Crevello, Derek—Stellus Capital Management LLC
Crewe, Maxim—Cinven Group Ltd
Crhonek, Jakub—Clearsight Investments AG
Crihfield, Owen—Hamilton Robinson LLC
Crisan, Jeffrey—Bain Capital Inc
Crisan, Jeffrey—Silversmith Capital Partners LLC
Criss, Kenneth—Rock Creek Capital LLC
Crist, Jason—Columbia Partners Private Capital
Cristeto, Begona—Empresa Nacional de Innovacion SA
Croasdale, Sherry—Rcf Management LLC
Croce, Robert—New Enterprise Associates Inc
Crocker, Bruce—Pitango Venture Capital Management Israel, Ltd.
Crocker, Curtis—Reservoir Venture Partners 2 LP
Crockett, Todd—TA Associates Management LP
Croft, E. Stockton—Eagle Merchant Partners
Croft, Edward—Croft & Bender LLC
Crohn, Oscar—Solstra Capital Partners A/S
Croll, David—Chestnut Street Partners Inc
Croll, David—M/C Venture Partners LLC
Cromack, Gerald—Tri Artisan Capital Partners LLC
Cromie, Daniel—Atlas Holdings FRM LLC
Cromwell, Michael—Wwc Capital Fund L P
Cromwell, Ridgely—Starboard Capital Partners LLC
Cronholm, Ola—Profura AB
Cronin, Jerry—Arbor Private Investment Co LLC
Cronin, Michael—Weston Presidio Capital
Cronkey, Damon—X/Seed Capital Management
Crooke, Graham—Helix Ventures
Crookes, Zoe—Loxbridge Research Llp
Cros, Pierre-Charles—Neo Investment Partners LLP
Crosbie-Walsh, Gordon—RedFire Investments Pty Ltd
Crosby, Brian—Falconhead Capital LLC
Crosby, Chris—Nautic Partners LLC
Crosby, Kevin—ArcLight Capital Holdings LLC
Croset, Jean-Claude—Mercer Private Markets AG
Crosland, David—Atlanta Equity Investors LLC
Cross, Cairn—Freshtracks Capital LP
Cross, Richard—Alston Capital Partners LLC
Crossan, William—GCP Member Ltd
Crothers, Mike—Evolve Capital Ltd
Crotty, Jason—Morrison & Foerster LLP
Crotty, Paul—Portfolio Advisors, LLC
Crotty, Thomas—Battery Ventures LP
Crow, Carol—Growth Works Capital Ltd
Crowder, David—Thomas Weisel Partners Group Inc
Crowder, Randall—TEXO Ventures
Crowe, Dean—Medley Capital LLC
Crowe, Jeffrey—Norwest Venture Partners
Crowell, Richard—Vance Street Capital LLC
Crowell, William—Alsop Louie Partners
Crowley, Bob—Mustang Group LLC
Crowley, Jack—Hall Capital Partners LLC
Crowley, Peter—MTS Health Partners LP
Croxon, Bruce—Round13 Capital
Cruickshank, Paula—Business Development Bank of Canada

Cruise, Kevin—Grace Assets Management LLP
Crumbaugh, Brian—Wynnchurch Capital Ltd
Crumpler, John—Hatteras Venture Partners
Crutchfield, Robert—Harbert Management Corp
Cruz Souza, Jose Guilherme—Vinci Equities Gestora de Recursos Ltda
Cruz, Antonio—Aurus Gestion de Inversiones SPA
Cruz, Ines—Gemcorp Capital LLP
Cruz, Reidan—Probitas Partners Inc
CuUnjieng, Stephen—Evercore Inc
Cubeisy, Emile—Silicon Badia
Cuccioli, Leandro—Capital International Inc
Cudd, Robert—Morrison & Foerster LLP
Cudzil, Jerry—Trust Company of the West
Cuesta, Lisa—NextGen Venture Partners LLC
Cuff, Michael—JFLehman & Co
Cui, Chengyu—Shenzhen Fuhai Yintao Venture Capital Co Ltd
Cui, Min—Bay City Capital LLC
Cui, Min—Decheng Capital LLC
Cui, Tracy—Hony Capital Beijing Co Ltd
Cukier, Ben—Centana Growth Partners
Cukier, Ben—Financial Technology Ventures
Cukierman, Edouard—Catalyst Investments LP
Cukierman, Francis—Invus Group LLC
Culas, Rahul—Carlyle Group LP
Culhane, Robert—Allied Growth Strategies & Management LLC
Cullinane, John—Islington Capital Partners LLC
Culman, Anne La—Abell Venture Fund
Cummings, Benton—Prospect Street Ventures
Cummings, Bob—Wind Point Advisors LLC
Cummings, Craig—Moonshots Capital
Cummings, David—Draper Esprit PLC
Cummings, Russell—Touchstone Innovations PLC
Cummings, Stephen—LCC Legacy Holdings Inc
Cundari, John—Windsor Private Capital
Cundy, Tim—CVC Capital Partners Ltd
Cuneo, Gianfilippo—Synergo SGR SpA
Cunha, Guilherme—Graycliff Partners LP
Cunicelli, Jeanne—Bay City Capital LLC
Cunjak, Robert—Bain Capital Inc
Cunningham, David—Blackstone Group LP
Cunningham, Emmett—Clarus Ventures LLC
Cunningham, Jason—Eaglehill Advisors LLC
Cunningham, Joe—Sante Ventures
Cunningham, Kevin—Canada Pension Plan Investment Board
Cunningham, Kevin—LNC Partners
Cunningham, Nathalie—Terrapin Partners LLC
Cunningham, Sean—GTCR Golder Rauner LLC
Cunningham, Sean—Trident Capital Cybersecurity Fund I LP
Cupers, Benjamin—Investsud SA
Cupido, Frank—Medley Capital LLC
Cupples, Jeffrey—Monroe Capital LLC
Cupta, Mark—Prelude Ventures LLC
Curatolo, Giuseppe—Pioneer Point Partners LLP
Cureton, Peter—Odyssey Investment Partners LLC
Curis, Duran—Ocean Avenue Capital Partners LP
Curley, Bruce—KPS Capital Partners LP
Curnock Cook, Jeremy—BioScience Managers Pty Ltd
Curran, Charles—Valhalla Partners LP
Curran, D. Patrick—C3 Capital LLC
Curran, Garrett—GCP Member Ltd

Pratt's Guide to Private Equity & Venture Capital Sources

Curran, John—Proprium Capital Partners LP
Curran, Stephen—Seacliff Private Equity
Currie, James—EW Healthcare Partners
Currie, Michael—Foresight Group LLP
Currie, Rigdon—Pacific Venture Partners Co Ltd
Currie, Steve—Communitech Ltd
Curry, Andrew—Carlyle Group LP
Curry, Bob—Latterell Venture Partners LP
Curry, Christopher—Piper PE LLP
Curry, Michael—InvesteCo Capital Corp
Curtin, Adam—Milestone Partners LP
Cusano, Anthony—Siguler Guff & Company LP
Cushing, Sara—Adams Street Partners LLC
Cushman, Chip—Golub Capital Master Funding LLC
Cushman, Chip—Oaktree Capital Management LP
Cusick, John—Georgetown Venture Partners
Cusimano, David—Accel-KKR
Custar, Kristin—Jordan Company LP
Custar, Kristin—Jordan Company LP
Cusumano, Dino—American Industrial Partners
Cutler, Joel—General Catalyst Partners LLC
Cutler, Lucas—Brazos Private Equity Partners LLC
Cutler, Lucas—CenterOak Partners LLC
Cuyegkeng, Eduardo—Argosy Partners, Inc.
Cyman, Robert—Marker Hill Capital LLC
Cyr, Daniel—ID Capital
Cyriac, Matthew—Blackstone Group LP
Cyrot, Jean-Luc—Time for Growth SA
Czajor, Tomasz—TDJ SA
Czapski, Piotr—EQT Funds Management Ltd
Czarny, Samuel—Berggruen Holdings Inc
Czirjak, Laszlo—iEurope Capital LLC
Czyrko, Radoslaw—Xevin Investments Sp z o o
D Addario, Paul—Palisades Ventures
D Agostino, Kimberly—Westfield Capital Management Company LP
D Agostino, Michael—Glouston Capital Partners LLC
D Alessandro, Hank—Morgan Stanley Credit Partners LP
D Amato, Paul—Trout Creek Ventures LP
D Ambrosio, Teodoro—TA Venture
D Amelio, Michael—Ascent Venture Management Inc
D Amelio, Michael—JMC Capital Partners LP
D Amico, Brian—Summer Street Capital Partners LLC
D Amore, Matthew—Morrison & Foerster LLP
D Amore, Richard—Guidepost Growth Equity
D Andrea, Harry—Valhalla Partners LP
D Angelo, Dean—Stellus Capital Management LLC
D Aquila, Jim—CoVestia Capital Partners
D Aurizio, Constance—Tenth Avenue Holdings LLC
D Epinay, Maya Lalive—Redalpine Venture Partners AG
D Herouville, Baudouin—Ardian France SA
D Ippolito, Marco Nicola—PII Investimentos Imobiliarios Ltda
D Onofrio, David—PowerOne Capital Markets Ltd
D Onofrio, Edward—Hamilton Lane Advisors LLC
D Onofrio, Giacinto—Trilantic Capital Management LP
D Onofrio, Giacinto—Trilantic Capital Management LP
D Ovidio, Thomas—Shoreview Industries
D Souza, Darryl—Investcorp Bank BSC
D Souza, Darryl—Investcorp Technology Investments Group
D Souza, Russ—DreamIt Ventures
D Souza, Tony—Evercore Inc
D Souza, Trevor—Keane D Souza Venture Capital LLC
D agostino, Stephane—ACG Capital SA
DINKLER, CARLING—Enhanced Capital Partners LLC
Da Silva, Duarte—First South Investment Managers (Pty) Ltd
Da Veiga Cardozo Monteiro, Paulo Roberto—Bozano Agente Autonomo de Investimentos Ltda
DaCosta, John—Abatis Capital LLC
DaValle, Albert—JK&B Capital LLC
Daar, Evan—Francisco Partners LP
Dabrowski, Peter—Tano Capital LLC
Daccus, Paul—Sun Capital Partners Inc
Dadoo, Rajeev—Sr One Ltd
Dady, T. Gail—DC Capital Partners LLC
Daftary, Krish—New Mountain Capital I LLC
Dagi, Teo Forcht—Capstone Financial Partners LLC
Dagi, Teo Forcht—HLM Management Co LLC
Dagres, Todd—Spark Capital
Daguere, Tania—Blackstone Group LP
Daguet, Gilles—ACE Management SA
Dahan, Sivan—Qumra Capital Israel I Ltd
Daher, Oussama—Carlyle Group LP
Dahl, Alan—EDG Partners LLC
Dahl, Benjamin—Pelion Venture Partners
Dahl, Bob—Accretia Capital LLC
Dahl, Erik—PRE Management AS
Dahl, Henrik—Sixth Swedish National Pension
Dahl, James—Rock Creek Capital LLC
Dahlawi, Adil—Itqan Capital Co
Dahle, Yngve—Televenture Management As
Dahlfors, Johan—Bridgepoint Advisers II Ltd
Dahlfors, Johan—Bridgepoint Advisers Ltd
Dahlquist, Karen—Antares Capital Corp
Dahlqvist, Jan—Polaris Management A/S
Dahmani, Pierre—Mtn Capital Partners LLC
Dahms, Peter—Acas LLC
Dai, Jim—Illuminate Ventures
Dai, Stephen—Olympus Capital Holdings Asia Hong Kong Ltd
Dai, Xiaoping—Shenzhen Rongchuang Venture Capital Co Ltd
Daileader, John—Greenbriar Equity Group LLC
Dailey, Ed—Colony Capital LLC
Dailey, Eric—Tolomei Participations SAS
Dailey, Kristine—Park Street Capital LLC
Dailey, Peter—Richmond Park Partners LLP
Dailey, Shamus—P4G Capital Management LLC
Dajani, Adel—INTERNATIONAL MAGHREB MERCHANT
Dakin-Grimm, Linda—Milbank Tweed Hadley & Mccloy LLP
Dakolias, Constantine—Fortress Investment Group LLC
Dal Bello, Michael—Jabodon PT Co
Dalal, Anupam—Kearny Venture Partners LP
Dalal, Rajesh—OrbiMed Advisors LLC
Dalala, Rafik—Abraaj Capital Ltd
Dale, Andrew—Montlake Capital LLC
Dale, Bernard—Connection Capital LLP
Dale, Manjit—TDR Capital LLP
Dale, Peter—Compass Investment Management Ltd
Dale, Richard—Sigma Partners
Daleky, Andrey—Svarog Capital Advisors LTD
Daley, Christopher—Pilgrim Capital Partners LLC
Daley, George—MPM Capital LLC
Daley, Nick—Wasabi Ventures LLC
Daley, Nicklaus—Water Street Healthcare Partners LLC
Dalfonso, Thomas—Empire Investment Holdings LLC
Dalgaard, Lars—Andreessen Horowitz LLC
Dalibot, Denis—Groupe Arnault SE
Dalle, Bernard—Index Ventures
Dalli, Dominic—Sovereign Capital Ltd
Dalmasso, Jean-Michel—PAI Partners SAS
Dalmia, Gaurav—Global Technology Investment
Dalsgaard, Carl-Johan—Odlander Fredrikson & Co AB
Dalton, Angela—Evercore Inc
Dalton, Barbara—Pfizer Venture Investments
Dalton, Frank—Fulcrum Equity Partners
Dalton, Sean—Highland Capital Partners LLC
Dalton, Sean—Highland Capital Partners LLC
Dalvey, David—Brightstone Venture Capital
Dalvie, Shivanandan—AEA Investors LLC
Daly, Jack—TPG Capital Management LP
Daly, Jeremiah—Highland Capital Partners LLC
Daly, Paige—Harvest Partners LP
Daly, Patrick—Blackstone Group LP
Daly, Tracey—Pacific View Asset Management LLC
Dambach, Hermann—Oaktree Capital Management LP
Dame, David—Sorenson Capital Partners LP
Dameris, Ted—Highland Capital Management LP
Dames, Greg—Marquette Capital Partners Inc
Damico, Joseph—Roundtable Healthcare Partners LP
Damjakob, Christian—Bm T Beteiligungsmanagement
Damsgaard, Jens—Energi Invest Fyn A/S
Danard, Chad—Triwest Capital Mgmt Corp
Dancausa Trevino, Maria Dolores—Bankinter Capital Riesgo SGECR SA
Dancer, Jacques—Eurekap SAS
Dancewicz, John—DN Partners LLC
Danchak, Mark—Worldquant Ventures LLC
Dando, Gareth—Southern Cross Venture Partners Pty Ltd
Dane, Kevin—Fortex Capital Inc
Danel Cendoya, Carlos Antonio—IGNIA Partners LLC
Daneshzadeh, Neda—Catterton Partners Corp
Danford, Timothy—Storm Ventures Inc
Dang Pham, Loan—Vinacapital Investment Management Ltd
DangVu, Huy—Clearlight Partners LLC
Danhakl, John—Leonard Green & Partners LP
Dani, Nick—DoubleRock LLC
Daniel, Anand—Accel India Venture Fund
Daniel, Anand—Accel Partners & Co Inc
Daniel, David—Carlyle Group LP
Daniele, Greg—Maranon Capital LP
Daniels, Amanda—RA Capital Management LLC
Daniels, Brian—5AM Ventures LLC
Daniels, Bryan—Prairie Capital, L.P.
Danielsen, John—Danske Private Equity A/S
Danielson, Jon—Tudor Ventures
Danielsson, Hans—PineBridge Investments LLC
Danilov, Nikolay—CLS Capital Ltd
Danilov, Nikolay—Enso Ventures Ltd
Danis, Mark—Morrison & Foerster LLP

2467

Pratt's Guide to Private Equity & Venture Capital Sources

Danis, Timothy–Sheridan Capital Partners
Dann, Mitchell–Sapient Capital Management LLC
Dann, Thomas–Maryland Department of Business and Economic Development
Dannaoui, Ziad–Safanad Inc
Dannen, Chris–Iterative Instinct Management LP
Dannenfeldt, Thomas–Deutsche Telekom AG
Danson, Mike–PROfounders Capital Ltd
Dantas Leite, Joao Marcello–Banco BTG Pactual SA
Dantchik, Arthur–SIG Asia Investments LLLP
Dantinne, Stephane–Investsud SA
Dantzker, David–Wheatley Partners
Dapice, Joshua–Farallon Capital Management LLC
Dapuzzo, Carlo–Monashees Gestao de Investimentos Ltda
Darbon, Guillaume–Advent International Corp
Darby, Nicholas–Rho Capital Partners Inc
Darchiville, Pam–Alpina Capital Partners LLP
Dardani, Ted–Harkness Capital Partners LLC
Dardani, Ted–Oak Hill Capital Management Inc
Dardis, Lance–Evercore Inc
Dargan, Alan–Lonsdale Capital Partners LLP
Darkins, James–Henderson Global Investors Ltd
Darko, Rexford–Crossroads Liquidating Trust
Darling, Mark–Hawkesbridge Capital
Darman, William–Carlyle Group LP
Darmon, Fiona–JVP Jerusalem Venture Partners Israel Management, Ltd.
Darnell, James–KLH Capital LP
Darnell, Ryan–Basset Investment Group LLC
Darre, Bruno–Bow River Capital Partners LLC
Darsy, Julien–European Capital Financial Services Ltd
Dartley, Peter–Twin Haven Capital Partners LLC
Darville, Marcus–Quadrant Private Equity
Darvish, Nissim–OrbiMed Advisors LLC
Darwent, Robert–Lion Capital LLP
Darwish, Issam–Singularity Investments LLC
Darwish, Mohamad–Singularity Investments LLC
Daryanani, Jay–Oaktree Capital Management LP
Das, Jai–Sapphire Ventures LLC
Das, Jai–Sapphire Ventures LLC
Das, Samayita–Pantheon Ventures (UK) LLP
Das, Siddhartha–Ventureast
Dascoli, James–Abundance Partners LLC
Dasgupta, Sanjeev–ICICI Venture Funds Management Company Ltd
Dash, Somesh–Institutional Venture Partners
Dashiell, Alex–Ares Management LLC
Dassios, Angelos–Paine Schwartz Partners LLC
Dassler, Marc–Alpha Founders
Dassy, Arnaud–Perella Weinberg Partners LP
Daswani, Mohit–JMI Management Inc
Date, Rajeev–Fenway Summer Ventures LP
Daubar, Michelle–General Catalyst Partners LLC
Daubar, Michelle–Oak HC/FT Partners LP
Dauber, Mike–Amplify Partners LP
Dauber, Mike–Battery Ventures LP
Dauchy, Craig–Cooley LLP
Dauchy, Jill–Millstein & Co LP
Daughdrill, J. Hal–Diversified Trust Company Inc
Daugherty, F. Joseph–Grayson & Associates Inc
Daugherty, Kevin–Speyside Equity LLC
Daulon du Laurens, Charles–Idinvest Partners SA
Daum, Falk–Serafin Unternehmensgruppe GmbH

Daum, Scott–Parallel49 Equity
Daumann, Christian–palero capital GmbH
Daumet, Jean–Amundi Private Equity Funds SA
Daun, Malte–Online Solutions Ventures GmbH
Dauphin, Steven–Bonaventure Capital LLC
Dauphin, Steven–Fidelis Capital LLC
Dauphin, Steven–Murphree Venture Partners
Dauphinais, Bill–Crosslink Capital Inc
Dauphinais, Todd–Aster Capital Partners SAS
Dauphinais, Todd–Clavis Capital Partners LLC
Daussun, Robert–LBO France Gestion SAS
Dauten, Kent–Keystone Capital Inc
Dauvillaire, Pierre–Gimar Capital Investissement SCA
Davamanirajan, Prabu–Carlyle Group LP
Dave, Ashish–Abraaj Capital Ltd
Davenport, Aaron–Sk Capital Partners LP
Davenport, Becky–Augment Ventures Fund I LP
Davenport, Bill–Roth Capital Partners LLC
Davenport, Jim–Castlelake LP
Davenport, John–Private Advisors LLC
Davenport, Peter–Bisa
Davenport, Robert–Brightpath Capital Partners LP
Davenport, Robert–Cerberus Capital Management LP
Daverman, Benjamin–GTCR Golder Rauner LLC
Davey, Brian–First Nations Equity Inc
Davey, Tim–Entrepreneur First Investment Manager LLP
David, Cristina–21 Centrale Partners SA
David, Fitzgerald–Petra Capital Partners LLC
David, John–Palamon Capital Partners LP
David, Michael–Orix Venture Finance
David, Nathaniel–Arch Venture Partners LLC
David, Peter–Amicus Partners
David, Roy–Poalim Cap Mark Tech, Ltd.
David, Tang–NGP Capital
Davidoff, Rony–Agate Medical Investments LP
Davidson, Benny–TEAM DCL LTD
Davidson, Brian–RooGreen Ventures LLP
Davidson, Carey–Carlyle Group LP
Davidson, Daniel–Insight Equity Holdings LLC
Davidson, Duncan–Bullpen Capital LP
Davidson, Graham–Perella Weinberg Partners LP
Davidson, James–Banyan Capital Advisors LLC
Davidson, James–Silver Lake Partners LP
Davidson, Jamie–Redpoint Ventures
Davidson, Mel–NAV.VC
Davidson, Mitchell–Post Capital Partners LLC
Davidson, Paul–West Coast Capital
Davidson, Scott–E3 Media Ltd
Davidson, Scott–Great Point Partners LLC
Davidson, Simon–Exponent Private Equity LLP
Davidson, Stephen–Morgan Stanley Alternative Investment Partners LP
Davidson, Stuart–Labrador Ventures
Davidson, Stuart–Labrador Ventures
Daviee, David–i2E, Inc
Davies, Andrew–CVC Capital Partners Ltd
Davies, G. Huw–Harbert Management Corp
Davies, Gavyn–Active Private Equity
Davies, Gavyn–Anthos Capital LP
Davies, George–Hambro Perks Ltd
Davies, Godfrey–CDC Group PLC
Davies, Godfrey–CDC Group PLC

Davies, Guy–WestBridge Fund Managers Ltd
Davies, Lew–Accretia Capital LLC
Davies, Michael–PCM Companies LLC
Davies, Peter–Stonehenge Partners Inc
Davies, Robert–Brown Brothers Harriman & Co
Davies, Ron–Chicago Growth Partners LLC
Davies, Stuart–Bain Capital Inc
Davila, Miguel Angel–Latin Idea Ventures LLC
Davis, Andrea–Investcorp Bank BSC
Davis, Andrew–Boston Ventures
Davis, Andrew–Lindsay Goldberg & Bessemer LP
Davis, Bob–Highland Capital Partners LLC
Davis, Brian–Golub Capital Master Funding LLC
Davis, Bruce–Asian Development Bank
Davis, Bruce–InGlobo Private Equity
Davis, Bryn–Palomar Ventures
Davis, C. Larry–Chartwell Investments, Inc.
Davis, Cary–Warburg Pincus LLC
Davis, Charles–Houston Ventures
Davis, Charles–Stone Point Capital LLC
Davis, Chris–Forstmann Little & Co
Davis, Chris–Gefinor Ventures
Davis, Christopher–Larsen Maccoll Partners LP
Davis, Chuck–Technology Crossover Ventures LP
Davis, Clark F.–Ridge Capital Partners LLC
Davis, Donn–Revolution
Davis, Eli–Cane Investment Partners LLC
Davis, Elliott–Next Wave Funds
Davis, Grant–Abatis Capital LLC
Davis, J. Bradley–Ridge Capital Partners LLC
Davis, Jay–Diversified Trust Company Inc
Davis, Jeff–Acorn Growth Companies
Davis, Jeffrey–Fund Evaluation Group LLC
Davis, Jerel–Versant Venture Management, LLC
Davis, Jessamyn–Corridor Capital LLC
Davis, John–CLUB AUTO SPORT SILICON VALLEY L L C
Davis, John–Council Capital
Davis, John–Stone Canyon Venture Partners
Davis, Jordan–Radius Ventures LLC
Davis, Joseph–Triton Pacific Capital LLC
Davis, Joshua–Stellus Capital Management LLC
Davis, K.Rodger–Northcreek Mezzanine
Davis, Kim–Charlesbank Capital Partners LLC
Davis, Kimberly–TorQuest Partners Inc
Davis, Lorn–Hancock Capital Management LLC
Davis, Mark–Primary Venture Partners
Davis, Matthew–First Stone Venture Partners Inc
Davis, Owen–NYC Seed LLC
Davis, Parker–Frontenac Company LLC
Davis, Parker–Slate Capital Group LLC
Davis, Paul–TZP Group LLC
Davis, Paul–Tennenbaum Capital Partners LLC
Davis, Ralph–Cressey and Company LP
Davis, Robert–Highland Capital Partners LLC
Davis, Robert–LJ2 & Co LLC
Davis, Ryan–Epic Ventures Inc
Davis, Ryan–University Venture Fund
Davis, Ryan–Utah Fund of Funds LLC
Davis, Sam–Allstate Private Equity
Davis, Timothy–Freshtracks Capital LP
Davis, Tom–General Atlantic LLC
Davis, Tony–Brightspark Ventures
Davis, Trayton–Milbank Tweed Hadley & Mccloy LLP
Davis, W. Ryan–Main Street Capital Holdings LLC

Davis, Wade–Learn Capital Venture Partners LP
Davison, Andrew–Scottish Equity Partners LLP
Davison, Chris–Permira Advisers LLP
Davison, Guy–Cinven Group Ltd
Davison, Jeffrey–Inflection Point Ventures
Davison, Jerry–Crowdcube Ltd
Davison, Kristina–iEurope Capital LLC
Davison, Todd–Centerview Partners LLC
Davisson, Ross–CircleUp Network Inc
Davoli, Robert–Sigma Partners
Davoli, Robert–Sigma Prime Ventures LLC
Davy, Michael–Bridgepoint Advisers Ltd
Daw, Richard–Phoenix Equity Partners Ltd
Dawes, James–LGV Capital Ltd
Dawson, Andrew–Standard Chartered Private Equity Ltd
Dawson, Jim–AMP Capital Investors Ltd
Dawson, William–Wellspring Capital Management LLC
Day, Andrew–Hastings Private Equity Fund IIA Pty Ltd
Day, Jeffrey–Madison Capital Funding LLC
Day, Martin–OMERS Private Equity Inc
Day, Matthew–Black Opal Capital LLC
Day, Matthew–Peterson Partners LP
Day, Robert–Black Coral Capital LLC
Day, Tyler–Creation Investments Capital Management LLC
Daya, Moez–Satya Capital Ltd
Dayan, Jean-Marc–Duke Street Capital Ltd
Daych, Diane–Apple Tree Partners
Daza, Felipe–Efromovich/Silva Capital Partners
De Abreu Filho, Jose Carlos Franco–MHFT Investimentos SA
De Almeida, Eduardo Buarque–TMG Partners LLC
De Almeida, Fernando–Mercapital SL
De Almeida, Fernando–Mercapital SL
De Andrea Costantini, Laura Mello–Astella Investimentos
De Back, Hans–Finch Capital Partners BV
De Baubigny, Andre–Deep Fork Capital
De Beer, Anthonie–Ethos Private Equity (Proprietary) Ltd
De Benedetti, Marco–Carlyle Group LP
De Boeck, Robert–Antea Participates Management BV
De Boer, Mark–Index Ventures
De Borja, Alex–Oaktree Capital Management LP
De Boucaud, Cedriane Marie–Curzon Park Capital Ltd
De Breda, Hans–Undisclosed Firm
De Callatay, Etienne–Banque Degroof Petercam SA
De Castro, Olympia–Community Investment Management LLC
De Clercq, Casper–Norwest Venture Partners
De Corainville, Robert–17 Capital LLP
De Courten, Raffaele–Alto Partners SRL
De Datta, Raj–Founder Collective LP
De Esteban, Pedro–Carlyle Group LP
De Geus, Willem–Proprium Capital Partners LP
De Giglio, Francesco–Advent International Corp
De Groot, Jay–Morrison & Foerster LLP
De Hoop, Roel–Prime Technology Ventures NV
De Jong, Jelmar–Oaktree Capital Management LP
De Jong, Pieter–3i Group PLC

De Kersauson, Florent–Bretagne De Nestadio Capital
De Ketelaere, Serge–Investsud SA
De La Riviere, Erik–Iris Capital Management SAS
De La Roche-Brochard, Jean–Thefamily SAS
De Laureal, David–Towerbrook Capital Partners LP
De Leeuw, Mike–Sentient Group Ltd
De Liedekerke, Humbert–One Peak Partners LLP
De Lisi, Paul–Capstreet Group LLC
De Luca, Martina–NextEnergy Capital Ltd
De Magalhaes, Jose Carlos Reis–TIG Holding Ltd
De Marignan, Olivier–Garibaldi Mezzo SAS
De Marzio, Alfredo–Cofiri SpA
De Metz, Jerome–Mbo Partenaires SAS
De Mojana, Francesco–Permira Advisers LLP
De Montgolfier, Eric–Bridgepoint Portfolio Services SAS
De Palma, Giorgio–CVC Capital Partners Ltd
De Paola, Lauren–First Reserve Corp
De Pinho, Francisco Roque–Union Group (UK) LLP
De Rooij, Hans–Peak Capital BV
De Rooij, Marco–ICOS Capital Management BV
De Rose, Umberto–Fincalabra SpA
De Rossi, Roberto–Consilium SGR pA
De Roux, Emmanuelle–Ventech SA
De Roux, Thibaut–Generis Capital Partners SAS
De Rycker, Sonali–Accel Partners & Co Inc
De Saint-Malo, Roberto–Adara Venture Partners
De Santis, Robert–Ontario Teachers' Pension Plan
De Schrevel, Pierre-Paul–Banque Degroof Petercam SA
De Selancy, Pierre-Antoine–17 Capital LLP
De Silva, Patrick–Pix Vine Capital Pte Ltd
De Silva, Richard–Highland Capital Partners LLC
De Simone, Fabrizio–DVR Capital SpA
De Smet, Fitz–Bscope Partners Inc
De Sousa, Manuel–2Bcapital SA
De St. Quentin, Annabelle–Draper Esprit Secondaries LLP
De Taurines, Christophe–Colony Capital LLC
De Vecchi, Filippo–Advent International Corp
De Vitry, Benoit–Barclays Capital Inc
De Vivo, Guido–Progressio SGR SpA
De Vries, Coenraad–Start Green Fund BV
De Vries, Yann–Redpoint Eventures Consultoria Empresarial Ltda
De Vries, Yann–e.ventures
De Vries, Yann–eVenture Capital Partners GmbH
De Waen, Thomas–Bain Capital Inc
De Warenghien, Amaury–AXA Investment Managers Inc
De Watteville, Emmanuel–BlueOcean Ventures SA
De Weck, Anne-Marie–Banque Lombard Odier & Cie SA
De Windt, E.–Gates Group Capital Partners LLC
De la Calle Negro, Julia–Fides Capital SL
De la Maza Arroyo, Sofia–Suanfarma Biotech SGECR SA
De la Pena, Alberto–Haynes and Boone LLC
De los Santos, Rogelio–Alta Ventures Mexico
DeAngelis, Kenneth–Austin Ventures
DeAngelis, Laura Spence–Antares Capital Corp
DeAngelis, Pasquale–ProQuest Investments
DeAngelo, Michael–TRG Management LP
DeBacco, Stephen–Leaders Funds

DeBaun, Denise–inventages venture capital GmbH
DeBenedetto, Robert–Clarus Ventures LLC
DeBiasi, Gerard–Kidd & Company LLC
DeBlois, Mark–Bunker Hill Capital LP
DeBolt, Robert–Mesirow Financial Private Equity Inc
DeBruin, Robert–New Capital Management Inc
DeCola, Michael–HBM Holdings Co
DeCorte, Evan–Columbia Capital LP
DeFalco, Joseph–Blackstone Group LP
DeFlorio, Michael–Harvest Partners LP
DeGrado, Emily–Providence Equity Partners LLC
DeGroff, Dain–Triangle Peak Partners LP
DeGroot, Will–Boston Millennia Partners LLC
DeHart, John–Meridius Capital
DeHoff, Owen–Jasper Ridge Partners LP
DeKeyser, Kelly–SV Health Investors LLP
DeKnikker, Gretchen–Saastr Fund
DeLatte, Herman–Solid Ventures BV
DeLeo, Dennis–Trillium Group LLC
DeLoche, John–Rosemont Seneca Technology Partners
DeLong, Matthew–JZ Capital Partners Ltd
DeMaio, Mike–Techaccel LLC
DeMarco, Joseph–Wall Street Venture Capital Ltd
DeMarco, Nick–Altus Capital Partners Inc
DeMartini, Richard–Crestview Advisors, LLC
DeMartini, Stephen–Prudential Capital Group LP
DeMartino, Kevyn–Transition Capital Partners
DeMilt, David–Oaktree Capital Management LP
DeMilt, David–Z Capital HF Adviser LLC
DeMontrond, George–First Reserve Corp
DeMott, Harry–Raptor Capital Management LP
DeMott, Tom–Encore Consumer Capital Fund L P
DeMuth, Donald–Dfw Capital Partners LP
DeNey, Richard–Roth Capital Partners LLC
DeNino, Mark–TL Ventures Inc
DeParle, Nancy-Ann–Consonance Capital Partners LP
DePasquale, Scott–Braemar Energy Ventures LP
DePietro, Douglas–Evercore Inc
DePlatchett, Kristin–StepStone Group LP
DePonte, Kelly–Probitas Partners Inc
DeRidder, Paul–Ventana Capital Management LP
DeRosa, Ben–American Industrial Partners
DeRosa-Farag, Sameh–Morgan Creek Capital Management LLC
DeSantis, Daniel–Linsalata Capital Partners Inc
DeSantis, David–Medley Capital LLC
DeShazer, Ronelle–CHS Capital LLC
DeShazer, Ronelle–Shorehill Capital LLC
DeSimone, Jonathan–Bain Capital Inc
DeVito, Jerry–Blackstone Group LP
DeVivo, Donald–Zesiger Capital Group LLC
DeVore, Chris–Founders Co op
DeVries, Jerry–TEXO Ventures
DeVries, Lawson–Grotech Ventures
DeVries, Michael–Edf Ventures
DeVries, Timothy–Norwest Equity Partners
DeVries, Timothy–Norwest Mezzanine Partners
DeWalt, David–AllegisCyber
DeYonker, Greg–Forte Capital Advisors LLC
DeZara, Max–Akoya Capital Partners LLC
Dea, Michelle–Carlyle Group LP
Deaddio, Michael–Worldquant Ventures LLC
Deaker, Michelle–Oneventures Pty Ltd

Dealy, Ty—Monroe Capital LLC
Dean, Allan—Greer Capital Advisors LLC
Dean, Allan—Incyte Venture Partners LLC
Dean, Christopher—Summit Partners LP
Dean, John—Startup Capital Ventures LP
Deane, H. William—Exto Partners Pty Ltd
Dearborn, John—Jumpstart Inc
Dearing, Stephen—SF Holding Corp
Deas, Gordon—Future Capital Partners Ltd
Deaton, Laurie—Hall Capital Partners LLC
Deb, Dipanjan—Francisco Partners LP
Debache, Herve—Tertiaire Developpement Service SARL
Debbas, Christopher—Julip Run Capital LLC
Debevec, Cynthia—Peppertree Capital Management Inc
Debock, Nicolas—Balderton Capital LLP
Debow, Kenneth—Stellus Capital Management LLC
Debuchy, Gilles—Telecom Technologies Transfert 3T SAS
Deceuninck, Dirk—QiFund Partners NV
Decker, Brian—Francisco Partners LP
Decker, Michael—Wingate Partners LP
Decker, Robert—Global Leisure Partners Llc
Deckoff, Stephen—Bayou Steel Corp
Dee, Phillips—Guidon Capital Partners
Deel, Chris—Boxwood Capital Partners LLC
Deely, Mike—Guidon Capital Partners
Dees, Michael—Lindsay Goldberg & Bessemer LP
Deeter, Byron—Bessemer Venture Partners
Deffebach, Matthew Thomas—Haynes and Boone LLC
Defforey, Christophe—Paua Ventures GmbH
Defforey-Crepet, Sophie—Aquasourca France SAS
Defieux, Rick—SJF Ventures
Deftos, Kristen—Bain Capital Venture Partners LLC
Degn, Doug—Newroad Capital Partners LLC
Degnan, Nicole—Blackstone Group LP
Degryse, Laurent—American Discovery Capital LLC
Dehejia, Adi—Sandler Capital Management
Deignan, Joseph—Wayzata Investment Partners LLC
Deitch, Billy—Francisco Partners LP
Deitch, Paul—Oaktree Capital Management LP
Deitelzweig, Brian—Palisade Capital Management LLC
Deitmers, Hubert—Van Den Ende & Deitmers BV
Dejoie, Eric—Mbo Partenaires SAS
Dejonckheere, Koen—Gimv Investeringsmaatschappij Voor Vlaanderen NV
Dekleer, Rolf—Growth Works Capital Ltd
Del Guercio, Joe—CNF Investments LLC
Del Papa, David—Riverside Partners LLC
Del Papa, Jeffrey—Thoma Bravo LLC
Del Punta, Stefano—Intesa Sanpaolo SpA
Del Rio, Manuel Gomez—Next Capital Partners SGECR SA
Del Valle, Martin—Investindustrial Services Ltd
Del Valle, Sergio—Wamex Private Equity Management
DelMuto, Kristy—LLR Partners Inc
Delach, Robert—Allied Growth Strategies & Management LLC
Delagardelle, Jeani—New Leaf Venture Partners LLC
Delagaye, Luc—Gevaert SA
Delaney, Daniel—Industrial Growth Partners

Delaney, Donal—Pinnacle Ventures
Delaney, John—Morrison & Foerster LLP
Delaney, Michael—Court Square Capital Partners LP
Delano-Valenzuela, Juan Carlos—Aurus Gestion de Inversiones SPA
Delany, Logan—Delany Capital Management Corp
Delatte, Stephane—CLSA Capital Partners HK Ltd
Delaveau, Emmanuel—Partech International
Delcomminette, Rene—Eurefi SA
Deldag, Can—Carlyle Group LP
Deleglise, Pierre-Michel—ACG Capital SA
Deleray, Michael—Broadhaven Capital Partners LLC
Delgado, Alberto Joe—CCMP Capital Advisors LP
Delgado, Bruno—Mercapital SL
Delgado, Bruno—Mercapital SL
Delgado, Lister—Idea Fund Partners LLC
Delgado, Santiago—Thomas H Lee Partners LP
Delgado-Moreira, Juan—Hamilton Lane Advisors LLC
Deliso, John—Longmeadow Capital Partners LLC
Delistathis, Thanasis—NAV.VC
Delivanis, Constantin—Sand Hill Group LLC
Dell, Adam—Austin Ventures
Dell, Michael—MSD Capital LP
Dellenbach, Hans—Emerald Technology Ventures AG
Delmarre, Raphael—Apax Partners Development SA
Delmore, David—Highland Capital Partners LLC
Delos, Alexandre—Access Capital Partners SA
Delson, Christopher—Morrison & Foerster LLP
Deltrieu, Vincent—Innovacom Gestion SAS
Demes, Justin—Grand Crossing Capital LLC
Demetree, Christopher—Value Plus Ventures LLC
Demetree, Mark—Silverhawk Capital Partners LLC
Demetriou, Konstantin—Rossiiskaia Korporatsiia Nanotekhnologii GK
Demicheli, Marc—TCR Capital SAS
Demko, Steve—Rockwood Equity Partners LLC
Demkowicz, Brian—Huron Capital Partners LLC
Demkowicz, Brian—Superior Capital Partners LLC
Demmer, Daniel—Openview Venture Partners LP
Demmler, Frank—Innovation Works Inc
Demont, Michel—Aurinvest Sas
Demonteverde, Joyce—Castle Harlan Inc
Demontis, Claudio—ATP Private Equity Partners
Demos, George—O'Melveny & Myers LLP
Demos, Steven—Greenmont Capital Partners
Dempsey, Andrew—Fortress Investment Group LLC
Dempsey, Michael—Compound Ventures
Dempsey, Neal—Bay Partners
Dempsey, Sean—Merus Capital Investment
Dempsey, Steve—Greyrock Capital Group
Dempster, Mark—Sequoia Capital Operations LLC
Demuth, Ronald—Torrey Pines Investment, Inc.
Demuynck, Pieter—BNP Paribas Fortis Private Equity Growth NV
Den Bosch, Fred Van—Atlantic Capital Partners GmbH
Den Hartog, Gijs—Capital Mills Invest BV
Den Ouden, Daan—ICOS Capital Management BV
Denaro, Paul—Milbank Tweed Hadley & Mccloy LLP
Denatale, Mark—CVC Capital Partners Ltd
Denbeau, Michael—American Discovery Capital LLC
Denenberg, Byron—KB Partners LLC
Denesuk, Matthew—International Business Machines Corp
Deng, Feng—Northern Light Venture Capital Development Ltd
Deng, Huajin—Feima Fund
Deng, Jie—WestSummit Capital Management Ltd
Deng, Ke—Milestone Capital Management Ltd
Deng, Kui—Liuhe Capital LLC
Deng, Xiangxiong—Shenzhen Centergate Vc Mgmt Co
Deng, Xihong—Hony Capital Beijing Co Ltd
Denham, Michael—Business Development Bank of Canada
Deni, Zaini Hj.—Maybank Venture Capital Company Sdn Bhd
Denihan, Daniel—Tenth Avenue Holdings LLC
Denihan, Donald—Tenth Avenue Holdings LLC
Denious, Peter—FLAG Capital Management LLC
Denious, Robert—Questor Partners Holdings Inc
Denis, Bruno—Naxicap Partners SA
Denis, Pascal—Audax Group, Inc.
Denis, Pascal—Potomac Equity Partners LLC
Denkmann, Andreas—Capiton AG
Denman, Ken—Accelerate-IT Ventures Management LLC
Dennedy, Tom—Artiman Management LLC
Dennert, Roland—Cipio Partners GmbH
Denney, Karen—Haynes and Boone LLC
Denning, Neal—Blackstone Group LP
Dennis, Alda Leu—137 Ventures LP
Dennis, Jeffrey—Northstar Capital LLC
Dennis, Josh—Nextgen Growth Partners LLC
Dennison, Piers—Providence Equity Partners LLC
Denny, David—Longwall Venture Partners LLP
Denomme, Mark—Siguler Guff & Company LP
Dent, Andrew—Aries Capital Partners LLC
Dent, Stephen—Birch Hill Equity Partners Management Inc
Denten, Mary—Scale Venture Partners
Denton, James—Broadhaven Capital Partners LLC
Deprez, Michel—U I Gestion SA
Der Kinderen, Marc—747 Capital LLC
Der Megreditchian, Philippe—OLMA Capital Management Ltd
Der Wielen, Hein Van—First Abu Dhabi Bank PJSC
Deres, Karl—BioMedPartners AG
Derksen, Chris—Investec Asset Management (Pty) Ltd
Derrick, Michael—Trident Capital
Derrick, Robert—Prudential Capital Group LP
Derry, Giles—Dunedin Capital Partners Ltd
Derungs, Bruno—Climate Change Capital Ltd
Derwin, Doug—Triage Ventures LLC
Derynck, Mattias—Symphony Technology Group LLC
DesMarais, Robert—Swander Pace Capital LLC
DesRosiers, Caleb—Mansa Capital Management LLC
Desaedeleer, Marc—TRG Management LP
Desai, Ankur—MDB Capital Group LLC
Desai, Dinesh—Darr Global Holdings Inc
Desai, Jatin—Parampara Capital & Management Consultants LLP
Desai, Keval—InterWest Partners LLC
Desai, V.—Ecapital Entrepreneurial Partners AG
Desautel, Eric—Harbert Management Corp
Desbard, Michel—Innovation Capital SAS
Descamps, Olivier—European Bank for Reconstruction and Development
Descarpentries, Sebastien—Auriga Partners SA

Deschamps, Bernard—Capital Benoit Inc
Deschamps, Marc—Breega Capital SARL
Deschner, Peter—Oaktree Capital Management LP
Deshpande, Amol—Kleiner Perkins Caufield & Byers LLC
Deshpande, Salil—Bain Capital Venture Partners LLC
Deshpande, Salil—Bay Partners
Desio, Marcelo—Crosslink Capital Inc
Deslandes, Maire—Silverfleet Capital Partners LLP
Desmond, Dermot—International Investment and Underwriting
Desouza, Joanna—Everstone Capital Management, Ltd.
Dessenante, Arthur—Corvm Capital Partners SAS
Dessertenne, Renaud—G Square Healthcare Private Equity Fund LLP
Detrixhe, Pierre—Investsud SA
Detry, Jean-Louis—Vermeer Capital Partners SAS
Deturck, Michiel—Vendis Capital NV
Deusch, Kai—Medicis Capital GmbH
Deutsch, Adam—River Hollow Partners LLC
Deutsch, Mark—Hudson Ferry Capital LLC
Deutsch, Mark—Verus Investment Partners
Deutsch, Robert—Cappello Capital Corp
Deutsch, Robert—Greenhill Capital Partners LP
Deutschmann, Robert—OMERS Infrastructure
Devaney, Thomas—Morrison & Foerster LLP
Devani, Neil—HOF Capital Inc
Devenny, John—Invision Capital Management LLC
Devine, Michael—Algonquin Advisors LLC
Devine, Peter—Uniseed Management Pty Ltd
Devitte, Jesse—Borealis Ventures
Devlin, Michael—Pharos Capital Group LLC
Devloo, Steven—Prospect Street Ventures
Devor, Ross—Insight Venture Partners LLC
Devore, Cary—SilverStream Capital LLC
Devries, Garrett—Haynes and Boone LLC
Dewan, Amant—Annex Capital Management LLC
Dewar, John—Milbank Tweed Hadley & Mccloy LLP
Dewitt, Gregory—Crossharbor Capital Partners
Dexheimer, Ulrich—Investitions Strukturbk Rhein Pfalz GmbH
Dey, Partha—ICICI Venture Funds Management Company Ltd
Dey, Sudip—Investcorp Bank BSC
Dey, Sudip—Investcorp Technology Investments Group
Dhaduk, Waleed—Stratum WLL
Dhaduk, Walid—Stratum WLL
Dhaliwal, Sunil—Battery Ventures LP
Dhalla, Omar—Real Ventures
Dham, Rajeev—Sapphire Ventures LLC
Dham, Vinod—Kalaari Capital Partners LLC
Dhamija, Deepshikha—Kotak Investment Advisors Ltd
Dhar, Ash—Horizon Ventures
Dhar, Madhav—Global Technology Investment
Dharmaraj, Satish—Redpoint Ventures
Dhawan, Ashish—ChrysCapital Management Co
Dhawan, Prateek—Accel India Venture Fund
Dhawan, Rajeev—Equity Partners
Dhillon, Romi—Arizona Founders Fund LLC
Dhinsa, Jojar Singh—Athlone International Ltd
Dhir, Rahul—Global Technology Investment
Dhol, Parag—Inventus Capital Partners Fund I L P

Dhonte, Sebastien—Clairvest Group Inc
Dhoot, Prakash—Motilal Oswal Pvt Equity Advisors Pvt Ltd
Di Geronimo, Robert—Glouston Capital Partners LLC
Di Montezemolo, Matteo—Charme Capital Partners SGR SpA
Di Sciullo, Gino—Charter Life Sciences II L P
Di Spiezio Sardo, Emilio—Bluegem Capital Partners LLP
Di Valmarana, Francesco—Pantheon Ventures (UK) LLP
Di, Kai—Shanghai Lianxin Investment Management Co Ltd
DiBrito, Ryan—Technology Venture Partners
DiCapo, Pasquale—PowerOne Capital Markets Ltd
DiCarlo, Peter—Brook Venture Partners LLC
DiCenzo, Aaron—Avante Mezzanine Inc
DiGesualdo, Antonio—Cotton Creek Capital Management LLC
DiGiandomenico, Anthony—MDB Capital Group LLC
DiGiovanni, John—Baird Capital
DiLaura, Brian—Atlas Peak Capital
DiLella, Gary—ProvCo Group
DiMaggio, Vincenzo—New York Times Co
DiMarchi, Richard—Twilight Venture Partners
DiMartino, Peter—Oaktree Capital Management LP
DiMarzio, Gregory—Century Capital Management / Massachusetts Inc
DiPaolo, David—Star Mountain Capital LLC
DiPaolo, Edward—Southwest Middle Market M&A
DiPiano, Michael—Newspring Capital
DiRienzo, Michael—Transportation Resource Partners LP
DiSanto, James—Motus Ventures
DiSibio, Carmine—Ernst & Young LLP
DiSimone, Anthony—Peak Rock Capital LLC
Diab, Mohammed—Defi gestion SA
Diamond, A. Ephraim—Whitecastle Investments Ltd
Diamond, Richard—Strait Lane Capital Partners LLC
Diao, Juanhuan—Shenzhen Oriental Fortune Capital Co Ltd
Diao, Yang—CRP-Fanya Investment Consultants Beijing Co Ltd
Dias, Chris—Alta Communications Inc
Diaz Etienne, Alonso B.—Gerbera Capital Asesores SC
Diaz Plata, Martin—Capital International Inc
Diaz, Omar—Dresner Capital Resources Inc
Diaz, Reinaldo—Auven Therapeutics Management LLLP
Diaz, Reinaldo—Longitude Capital Management Co LLC
Diaz-Laviada, Juan—Advent International Corp
Diaz-Reganon, Joaquin—Altamar Private Equity SGIIC SAU
Dibner, Gil—Index Ventures
Dick, Christopher—Ascent Venture Management Inc
Dick, Christopher—Ascent Venture Management Inc
Dick, Jonathan—Primus Capital
Dick, Timothy—Startup Capital Ventures LP
Dicker, Thomas—Ipsa SAS
Dickerson, Paul—Haynes and Boone LLC
Dickes, Scott—Hadley Capital
Dickey, David—Treehouse Health LLC
Dickie, John—FLAG Capital Management LLC

Dickin, Tony—Palatine Private Equity LLP
Dickinson, Brendan—Canaan Partners
Dickinson, Daniel—HCI Equity LLC
Dickinson, George—Ibero American Investors Corp
Dickinson, Mark—Arle Heritage LLP
Dickinson, Mark—Candover Investments PLC
Dickman, Michael—Perella Weinberg Partners LP
Dickson, Benjamin—Ascribe Capital, LLC
Dickson, Frank—Maryland Department of Business and Economic Development
Dickson, Jeffrey—Prudential Capital Group LP
Dickson, Paul—Milestone Capital Partners Ltd
Didden, James—Blackstone Group LP
Didier, Jean-Marie—AUTONOMIE & SOLIDARITE
Dieber, Gary—Behrman Capital
Diedrichs, Anja—Spiltan Investment AB
Diegruber, Juergen—Partners Group Holding AG
Diehl, Bowen—Acas LLC
Diehl, Charles—Activa Capital SAS
Diehl, Michael—Activa Capital SAS
Diekmann, Marc—Dipl.-Kfm. Wunderlich & Partner
Diekroeger, Ken—Golden Gate Capital Inc
Diem, Gregory—Pine Tree Equity Management LP
Dienst, Rolf—Wellington Partners GmbH
Dienstag, Josh—Carlyle Group LP
Diep, Michael—Maxim Partners LLC
Dieppe, Timothy—Alpina Capital Partners LLP
Dierckx, Filip—BNP Paribas Fortis Private Equity Growth NV
Diesbach, Benjamin—Oak Hill Capital Management Inc
Diesler, Erwin—Strategic Value Capital Partners Management GmbH
Diessner, Alison—Jasper Ridge Partners LP
Diestal, Kevin—Sapphire Ventures LLC
Diestel, Kevin—Sapphire Ventures LLC
Dietrich, Marc—Mountain Cleantech AG
Dietrich, Orlo—Ansley Equity Partners
Dietrick, Greg—Montgomery & Co LLC
Dietz, Hans-Peter—TakeOff VC Management GmbH
Dietz, Steven—Upfront Ventures
Dietz, William—Yukon Partners Management LLC
Diez de Bonilla Martinez, Antonio—Haynes and Boone LLC
Diforio, Richard—Gorge Holdings LLC
Diggines, Jonathan—Mercia Fund Managers
Diggins, Jeffrey—Endurance Capital Holdings LLC
Dighton, Simon—Catalyst Investment Managers Pty, Ltd.
Dijkstra, Gerben—Investec Asset Management (Pty) Ltd
Dilda, Mirco—Argos Soditic SA
Dill, Matthias—Statkraft Ventures GmbH
Dillabough, Gary—Westly Group LLC
Dillard, Lauren—Carlyle Group LP
Diller, Christian—Montana Capital Partners AG
Dillman, David—TechColumbus
Dillon, Cris—Coast2Coast Investments Pty Ltd
Dillon, John—RJD Partners Ltd
Dillon, Kevin—Atlantic Bridge
Dillon, Sara—General Atlantic LLC
Dillon, Tim—Ridgemont Partners Management LLC
Dimaculangan, Alfredo—Small Business Guarantee and Finance Corporation
Dimitri, James—Veritas Capital Fund Management

2471

LLC
Dimitroff, Sashe–Haynes and Boone LLC
Dimitrov, Ivelin–Fifth Street Capital LLC
Diner, Fahri–Sigma Partners
Dinerman, David–Probitas Partners Inc
Dinerstein, Jeff–Haynes and Boone LLC
Ding, Baoyu–Shenzhen Co-Win Venture Capital Investments Ltd
Ding, Cheng–ABC Capital Management Co Ltd
Ding, Gordon–Warburg Pincus LLC
Ding, James–Gsr Ventures Management Llc
Ding, Ran–Norwest Venture Partners
Ding, Rui–Guangxin Investment Management Beijing Co Ltd
Ding, Shiguo–Beijing Zenith Taifu Investment Management Co Ltd
Ding, Songliang–Tianjin Binhai Haisheng Equity Investment Fund Mgmt Co.
Ding, Yameng–Legend Star Venture Incubator
Ding, Zhaoding–Ying Capital
Dingle, Phillip–HealthEdge Investment Partners LLC
Dingreville, Sophie–Iris Capital Management SAS
Dinh, Hoa Thi–Vietnam Pioneer Partners
Dinnen, Sean–CBPE Capital LLP
Dinnie, Kevin–Blackstone Group LP
Dinning, Anne–D E Shaw & Co LP
Dinning, Peter–Saigon Fund Management JSC
Dinsel, Detlef–IK Investment Partners Ltd
Dinte, Boaz–Evergreen Venture Partners
Dinte, Boaz–Qumra Capital Israel I Ltd
Dinur, Arnon–Greylock Israel Global Management Ltd
Dionne, John–Blackstone Group LP
Dipp, Michelle–General Atlantic LLC
Dipp, Michelle–Longwood Founders Management LLC
Dircks, Thomas–Charterhouse Group Inc
Dirk, Posner–Baring Private Equity Asia Ltd
Dirks, Dave–EVO Venture Partners
Disa, John–New Water Capital LP
Dittmer, Janke–Gilde Healthcare Partners BV
Dittmers, Hermann–S-Beteiligungsgesellschaft der Sparkasse Freiburg
Dixit, Amit–Blackstone Group LP
Dixon, Brian–Elm Street Ventures LP
Dixon, Brian–Kapor Capital
Dixon, Donald–Trident Capital
Dixon, Donald–Trident Capital Cybersecurity Fund I LP
Dixon, Rocky–Endeavour Capital Inc
Dixon, Tom–Neo Investment Partners LLP
Dizengremel, Bruno–Innovacom Gestion SAS
Dizon, Kirk–Institutional Global Investors LLC
Dmitriev, Kirill–UK RFPI OOO
Do, Frank–Riverside Partners LLC
Do, Viet Hung–Vietnam Pioneer Partners
Doane, Harvey–NSBI Venture Capital
Doane, Martin–Ubequity Capital Partners Inc
Dobbs-Higginson, Justine–Aleph Capital Partners LLP
Dobeck, Michael–Beekman Group LLC
Doberstein, Damian–e.ventures
Doberstein, Damian–eVenture Capital Partners GmbH
Dobrenski, Joe–Sequoia Capital Operations LLC

Dobres, Jonathan–Flexis Capital LLC
Dobron, Albert–Providence Equity Partners LLC
Dockery, J. Stephen–Fidus Capital LLC
Doctor, Jonathan–Denovo Health Partners LLC
Doctoroff, Adam–Monitor Clipper Partners LLC
Dodd, Andy–PHD Equity Partners LLP
Dodd, Jason–HealthCap Partners LLC
Dodd, Michael–Austin Ventures
Dodds, William–Thomvest Ventures Inc
Dodge, Gary–Small Enterprise Assistance Funds
Dodhia, Khilan–E I Capital LLP
Dodson, Andrew–Parthenon Capital LLC
Dodson, David–Headwaters BD LLC
Doering, Ralph–Fund Evaluation Group LLC
Doernte, Walther–Outlier Ventures Ltd
Doersam, Ryan–OMERS Infrastructure
Dogmeh Saz, Omid–FS Vencube GmbH
Dohadwala, Tasneem–Excelestar Ventures
Doherty, Bryan–Fireman Capital Partners LLC
Doherty, Christopher–Columbia Partners Private Capital
Doherty, Kyle–General Catalyst Partners LLC
Doherty, Michael–Morrison & Foerster LLP
Doherty, Phyllis–Matrix Partners, L.P.
Doherty, Sean–Bain Capital Inc
Doi, Yasuhito–FGI Capital Partners Inc
Doig, Michelle–Abingworth Management Ltd
Dokas, Elias–Mid-Ocean Partners LP
Dolan, Brian–Rcf Management LLC
Dolan, David–Signal Hill Equity Partners
Dolan, Geoffrey–StepStone Group LP
Dolan, Isabel–Albion Capital Group LLP
Dolan, John–Investec Ventures Ireland Ltd
Doldan, Kevin–Lightyear Capital LLC
Dolder, Adam–Great Point Partners LLC
Dolezalek, J. Stephan–Vantagepoint Management Inc
Dolfato, Mark–OMERS Private Equity Inc
Dolginow, Dustin–Accomplice LLC
Doll, Dixon–Doll Capital Management Inc
Doll, Norbert–Lead Equities GmbH
Dolle, Bruce–BSD Venture Capital LLC
Dollhopf, Thomas–Marwit Capital Corp
Domach, Jim–Mason Wells Inc
Domanig, Gina–Emerald Technology Ventures AG
Dombalagian, Vahe–Madison Dearborn Partners LLC
Dombcik, Jeffrey–Triangle Capital Partners L L C
Dombi, Robert–Landmark Partners Inc
Dombkowski, Ashley–Bay City Capital LLC
Domdey, Horst–Biom AG
Domenik, Stephen–Sevin Rosen Funds
Domin, Alexander–Alpina Capital Partners LLP
Domingos, Andre–Carlyle Group LP
Dominguez, John–Institutional Global Investors LLC
Dominguez, Michael–Providence Equity Partners LLC
Dominik, David–Golden Gate Capital Inc
Domonkos, Joseph–Ascribe Capital, LLC
Donahue, John–Windjammer Capital Investors LLC
Donahue, Thomas–Alumni Capital Network Management Co LLC
Donaldson, Christine–Onex Corp
Donaldson, Howard–Vanedge Capital Inc
Donaldson, Scott–Austin Ventures

Donchev, Angel–Blackstreet Capital Management LLC
Dondero, James–Highland Capital Management LP
Donelan, James–Seacoast Capital
Doner, Michael–Abacus Private Equity Ltd
Dong, Guixin–Beijing Huinong Capital Management Co Ltd
Dong, Liang–Jiangsu Addor Equity Investment Fund Management Co Ltd
Dong, Yeshun–IDG Capital Partners Inc
Dong, Zheng–Hina Capital Partners
Donkor, Edward–Pine Brook Road Partners LLC
Donkor, Edward–Sk Capital Partners LP
Donlan, Joseph–Brown Brothers Harriman & Co
Donne, Theo–LRM NV
Donnelly, Eugene–Apollo Global Management LLC
Donnelly, John–Donnelly Penman & Partners Inc
Donnelly, Julia–Thomas H Lee Partners LP
Donnelly, Martin–Blackstone Group LP
Donnelly, Stephen–Darr Global Holdings Inc
Donner, Andy–Physic Ventures LLC
Donner, Jason–Veritas Capital Fund Management LLC
Donnini, David–GTCR Golder Rauner LLC
Donnon, Jeffrey–First Round Capital
Donofrio, Anthony–Hamilton Lane Advisors LLC
Donoghue, Michael–Spring Capital Partners
Donoghue, Michael–Spring Capital Partners
Donohoe, Kevin–Liberty Capital Management Corp
Donohue, Christian–Tennenbaum Capital Partners LLC
Donohue, Liam–406 Ventures LLC
Donohue, Lilly–Fortress Investment Group LLC
Donovan, Alvin–Kiwi Growth Partners Ltd
Donovan, Andrew–Evercore Inc
Donovan, Michael–Welsh Carson Anderson & Stowe
Donvito, Giuseppe–Programma 101 Srl
Doody, Christopher–Stone Point Capital LLC
Doogan, Kevin–LBC Credit Partners Inc
Dooley, John–Jarvinian LLC
Dooley, Patrick–Canyon Capital Advisors LLC
Dooling, Patrick–Bain Capital Inc
Dooling, Patrick–Riverside Partners LLC
Doolittle, Harold–Clearview Capital LLC
Doomany, George–Andlinger & Co Inc
Doose, Jeff–Adena Ventures
Doppelt, Michael–Lightyear Capital LLC
Doppelt, Yoav–Ofer Hi Tech Ltd
Doppler, Clemens–Heidelbergcapital Asset Management GmbH
Dopsch, Peter–Morrison & Foerster LLP
Dorairaj, Anand–New Silk Route Partners, LLC
Doramus, Mark–SF Holding Corp
Doran, John–Summit Partners LP
Doran, John–Technology Crossover Ventures LP
Dore, Chantal–Solidarity Fund QFL
Doremus, Teresa–O'Melveny & Myers LLP
Dorhout Mees, Evert–Greenfield Capital Partners BV
Dorman, D. Mark–Endeavour Capital Inc
Dorman, Stephen–Versa Capital Management Inc
Dormer, Esther–Future Fund
Dorofeeva, Olga–SmartHub OOO
Dorr, Thomas–Morgan Stanley Alternative Investment Partners LP
Dorrell, Dean–Redbus Investments

Dorrian, James–Crosspoint Venture Partners 2001 LP
Dorrill, Jeff–Haynes and Boone LLC
Dorsey, Michael–Westly Group LLC
Dorsey, Patrick–Atlantic Canada Opportunities Agency
Dorsey, Sean–Natcity Investments Inc
Dortch, Elyn–CapitalSouth Partners LLC
Dorton, Stephen–Invision Capital Management LLC
Doshi, Amy–Arcapita Inc
Doshi, Hemir–IDG Ventures India Advisors Pvt Ltd
Doshi, Rutvik–Inventus Capital Partners Fund I L P
Dospiva, Marek–Penta Investments Ltd
Dossani, Uzair–Warburg Pincus LLC
Dossett, Corey–Chicago Growth Partners LLC
Dossey, Douglas–Blum Capital Partners LP
Dostal, Gabriela–Syntaxis Capital Unternehmens und Finanzierungsberatung GmbH
Dotzler, Frederick–De Novo Ventures LLC
Doub, Robb–New Markets Venture Partners
Douchet, Matthieu–Initiative & Finance Investissement SA
Dougan, Brady–Csfb Private Equity Advisers
Dougery, John–Inventus Capital Partners Fund I L P
Dougherty, Dennis–Intersouth Partners
Dougherty, James–Arcus Ventures
Dougherty, James–Cross Atlantic Partners
Dougherty, Marcus–Milbank Tweed Hadley & Mccloy LLP
Doughty, Dennis–Blade LLC
Douglas, David–Fiedler Capital GmbH
Douglas, Neal–Telecommunications Development Fund
Douglass, David–Delphi Ventures
Douglass, James–Fulcrum Equity Partners
Douglass, Mathew–Prudential Capital Group LP
Douglass, Robert–Madison Capital Funding LLC
Doumani, Roy–Fulcrum Venture Capital Corp
Doumar, Robin–Park Square Capital LLP
Dounis, Demetrios–Anholt (USA) LLC
Douville, Elizabeth–GeneChem Financial Corp
Dove, David–Dove Capital Partners LLC
Dove, Robert–Carlyle Group LP
Dovey, Brian–Domain Associates LLC
Dovgopoly, Denis–TA Venture
Dovrat, Shlomo–Carmel Ventures IV Principals Fund LP
Dow, James–PHD Equity Partners LLP
Dow, Stephen–Sevin Rosen Funds
Dowden, William–KLH Capital LP
Dowdle, Robin–Affinity Capital Management Co
Dowds, Allan–Solamere Group LLC
Dowlin, Kristopher–Casaforte Investimentos SA
Dowling, Sean–Osage Venture Partners
Dowling, Vincent–Dowling Capital Partners I LP
Dowman, Philip–IFM Investors Pty Ltd
Downer, Tony–Oak Investment Partners
Downey, Bruce–Newspring Capital
Downey, Lisa–Dw Healthcare Partners
Downey, Maureen–Pantheon Ventures (UK) LLP
Downey, Sarah–Accomplice LLC
Downing, Barry–Dundee Sarea LP
Downs, Doug–Avalon Ventures, LLC
Downs, Mark–Navigation Capital Partners Inc
Downs, Matthew–Sandbox Industries LLC
Doyle, Brett–SilverStream Capital LLC

Doyle, Brian–Hellman & Friedman LLC
Doyle, David–Morrison & Foerster LLP
Doyle, John–Wexford Capital LP
Doyle, Kenneth–Halifax Group LLC
Doyle, Maurice–Advantage Capital Partners
Doyle, Michael–Goldin Ventures Co
Doyle, Noah–Javelin Venture Partners LP
Doyle, Patrick–Trust Company of the West
Doyle, R. Stephen–Thayer Ventures
Doyle, William–WFD Ventures LLC
Doyon, Eric–Entrepreneur Capital Inc
Dozie, Pascal–African Capital Alliance
Drablos, Scott–Haynes and Boone LLC
Dracon, Greg–406 Ventures LLC
Dracos, F–Investcorp Bank BSC
Dracs, Matthieu–Extendam SA
Drago, Giorgio–Palladio Holding SpA
Drago, Giorgio–Star Capital SGR SpA
Drago, Stefano–PAI Partners SAS
Drai, Michael–Sterling Partners GP LLC
Drake, John–Quantum Capital
Drake, Josh–Fulcrum Venture Capital Corp
Drake, Nicholas–SCF Partners LP
Drakeman, Donald–Advent Venture Partners LLP
Draney, Gabriella–Health Wildcatters
Draney, Gabriella–Tech Wildcatters Ii LLC
Dranikoff, Lee–Ascribe Capital, LLC
Drant, Ryan–Questa Capital Management LLC
Draper, Joseph–Pacific Advantage Capital Ltd
Draper, Martin–Lloyds Development Capital (Holdings) Ltd
Draper, Timothy–Draper Fisher Jurvetson
Draper, Timothy–Gotham Ventures LLC
Draper, Timothy–Timberline Venture Partners
Draper, Timothy–Zone Ventures
Dratch, Dana–Acas LLC
Drattell, Jason–Praesidian Capital
Draycott, Jonathan–Ironbridge Equity Partners Management Ltd
Drazan, Jeffrey–Bertram Capital Management LLC
Drazan, Kenneth–Bertram Capital Management LLC
Dreher, Martin–Vianova Capital LLP
Dreher, Peter–Aralon AG
Drehkoff, William–Linden LLC
Dreier, Robert–Bunker Hill Capital LP
Dreimanis, Dagnis–BaltCap Management Estonia OU
Dreismann, Heinrich–SV Health Investors LLP
Dresdale, Richard–Fenway Partners LLC
Dresner, Edward–Eastward Capital Partners LLC
Dresner, Steven–Dresner Capital Resources Inc
Dresser, Gregory–Morrison & Foerster LLP
Dressler, Ryan–Advantage Capital Partners
Dreux, Pedro–Vinci Equities Gestora de Recursos Ltda
Drevon, Pedro–3G Capital Inc
Drew, John–Technology Crossover Ventures LP
Drewlo, Norm–Stern Partners Inc
Drews, Thomas–Mittelstaendische Beteiligungsgesellschaft MV mbH
Dreyfous, James–Pelion Venture Partners
Dreyfus, Daniel–3G Capital Inc
Driehaus, Richard–Driehaus Private Equity LLC
Driessen, C.–Siguler Guff & Company LP
Drillaud, Benoit–Wendel SE

Drilling, John–Rock Creek Capital LLC
Driscoll, Craig–Highland Capital Partners LLC
Driscoll, Darren–Alaris Royalty Corp
Driscoll, Jude–Fortress Investment Group LLC
Drislane, Dennis–BelHealth Investment Partners LLC
Dritz, Russell–Quad Ventures LLC
Driver, Cyrus–Partners Group Holding AG
Drobny, Jeffrey–Black River Asset Management LLC
Droga, Ari–Global Infrastructure Holdings
Droller, Remi–Kurma Partners SA
Dross, Daniel–Trinity Hunt Partners
Drouin, Francois–Bpifrance EPIC
Drouin, Pascal–Cycle Capital Management (CCM) Inc
Druce, Phillip–Atlantic Street Capital Management LLC
Drucker, Geoff–RedFire Investments Pty Ltd
Drugan, Mark–Capital Dynamics Sdn Bhd
Druilhe, Celine–Healthbox LLC
Drummond, Jason–York Plains Investment Corp
Drury, Ian–OCA Ventures
Drury, Paul–Levine Leichtman Capital Partners Inc
Drury, Robert–Laurel Capital Partners
Drury, Simon–Climate Change Capital Ltd
Drvota, Viktor–Karolinska Development AB
Drysdale, George–Marsman-Drysdale Corp
Du Bey, Jesse–Orkila Capital LLC
Du Bey, Joseph–Unitus Impact Partners LLC
Du Pelloux, Dominique–Chequers Capital Partners SA
Du Roy, Corentin–Baml Capital Access Funds Management LLC
Du, Longquan–Fair Value Capital
Du, Steven–Mingly Capital
Du, Yongbo–CRP-Fanya Investment Consultants Beijing Co Ltd
Du, Yongzhong–Fitch Crown Venture Capital Management (Shenzhen) Co Ltd
DuFour, Justin–Acas LLC
DuPere, Justin–GTCR Golder Rauner LLC
DuPere, Justin–Waud Capital Partners LLC
DuPont, Benjamin–Fairbridge Venture Partners
Duan, Haiqing–Legend Star Venture Incubator
Duan, Lei–Shanghai Leading Capital Co Ltd
Duan, Song–CtechBA Pty Ltd
Duan, Yi–Guangdong Infore Capital Management Co Ltd
Duarte Casimiro, Alfredo–Capital Criativo SCR SA
Duault, Blaise–PAI Partners SAS
Dubbioso, Matthew–Vestar Capital Partners Inc
Dubens, Peter–Oakley Capital Ltd
Dubens, Peter–PROfounders Capital Ltd
Dubi, Shay–Ofer Hi Tech Ltd
Dubick, David–Lightspeed Management Company LLC
Dubiel, Christian–Kingfish Group Inc
Dubois, Enrique–Mola Factory SL
Dubourdieu, Cedric–BC Partners LLP
Dubrova, Aleksandra–Colony Capital LLC
Dubuisson, Olivier–Cap Decisif Management SAS
Dubuque, Louis–Advantage Capital Partners
Dubus, Geoffroy–Gimv Investeringsmaatschappij Voor Vlanderen NV
Duca, Ken–Blackstone Group LP
Ducarre, Nicolas–Oaktree Capital Management LP
Ducas, Caroline–Tenth Street Capital Partners LLC

Duckworth, Claire–Signal Hill Equity Partners
Duda, Cynthia–Capital Dynamics Sdn Bhd
Duda, Jim–Dallas Venture Partners LP
Duda, Mike–Consigliere Brand Capital LLC
Dudley-Cave, Richard–Castlelake LP
Dudzinski, Anthony–Healthsharestm Inc
Due, Christopher–Iglobe Treasury Management Ltd
Dueholm, Kim–Novo Holdings A/S
Duerr, Christian–Bvt Holding GmbH & Co KG
Duesterhoeft, Andreas–BT&T Asset Management AG
Duff, Declan–GFH Capital Ltd
Duff, John–Duff Ackerman & Goodrich LLC
Duff, Ramsay–Maven Capital Partners UK LLP
Duffy, Patrick–MGI Holdings Inc
Dugal, Sig–Origo Partners PLC
Dugan, Ian–Bridgepoint Advisers Ltd
Dugan, James–OCA Ventures
Dugan, John–OCA Ventures
Dugan, Michael–Oceanbridge Partners LLC
Dugan, Timothy–Water Street Healthcare Partners LLC
Dugar, Raj–FIL Capital Advisors (India) Pvt Ltd
Duggal, Anuroop–3G Capital Inc
Duggal, Rajat–Friedman Fleischer & Lowe Cap Ptnrs L P
Duggan, Chris–Go Capital LLC
Duggan, Kevin–Ontario Teachers' Pension Plan
Duggan, Robin–Riverstone Holdings LLC
Dugoni, Patrick–HGGC LLC
Duguay, Bruno-Etienne–Investissements Novacap Inc
Duguid, Rob–PFM Capital Inc
Duhamel, Augustin–17 Capital LLP
Duhamel, Franck–Park Square Capital LLP
Duhnkrack, Thomas–Premium Equity Partners GmbH
Duignan, Andrew–Seroba Kernel Life Sciences Ltd
Duimich, David–Asia Pacific Ventures
Duing, Jens–Frog Capital Ltd
Duk-hoon, Lee–Woori Bank
Duke, Meredith–Tenth Street Capital Partners LLC
Duke, R. Alton–Tenth Street Capital Partners LLC
Duke, Sergio–Orizzonte SGR SpA
Dukic, Vesna–Hamilton Lane Advisors LLC
Dulanto, Gonzalo–Southern Cross Capital Management SA
Dulberg, Ronit–JVP Jerusalem Venture Partners Israel Management, Ltd.
Dulger, Prumiys–KBW Capital Partners I L P
Dulude, Richard–AssembleVC Fund I LP
Dumanian, Peter–Red Rock Ventures
Dumanis, Alon–Docor International BV
Dumas, Laurent–Idinvest Partners SA
Dumay, Harry–Harvard School of Engineering and Applied Sciences
Dumler, Richard–Activate Venture Partners
Dunbar, John–Strategic Investments, L.P.
Dunbar, William–Core Capital Partners Ii L P
Duncan, Alan–Draper Esprit PLC
Duncan, Cori–Jasper Ridge Partners LP
Duncan, David–FINISTERE VENTURES L L C
Duncan, Erica–American Beacon Advisors Inc
Duncan, Patrick–Azalea Capital LLC
Duncan, Patrick–Birch Hill Equity Partners Management Inc

Duncan, R. Foster–SAIL Capital Partners LLC
Duncan, Tyler–Wayzata Investment Partners LLC
Duncanson, Timothy A.–Onex Corp
Dundonald, Douglas–Anglo Scientific Ltd
Dunfield, Ryan–Second City Capital Partners
Dunham, Jim–Next Coast Ventures LLC
Dunlap, David–Impact Capital Inc
Dunlea, Lisa–Signal Peak Ventures
Dunlevie, Bruce–Benchmark Capital Management Gesellschaft MBH In Liqu
Dunlop, Sinclair–Epidarex Capital
Dunn, Andrew–One Equity Partners LLC
Dunn, Barry–GTCR Golder Rauner LLC
Dunn, Brian–Sorenson Capital Partners LP
Dunn, Leonard–Saybrook Capital LLC
Dunn, Mark–Cedar Springs Capital LLC
Dunn, Martin–Bridgepoint Advisers Ltd
Dunn, Martin–Gramercy Inc
Dunn, Melinda–Sequoia Capital Operations LLC
Dunn, Robert–Thompson Street Capital Partners LP
Dunn, Timothy–Phoenix Equity Partners Ltd
Dunne, Dennis–Milbank Tweed Hadley & Mccloy LLP
Dunne, Richard–AlpInvest Partners BV
Dunne, Stephen–AMP Capital Investors Ltd
Dunnett, Martin–Warburg Pincus LLC
Dunnigan, Jeffery–Windjammer Capital Investors LLC
Dunnigan, Patrick–River Cities Capital Fund LP
Dunstan, Jenny–3i Group PLC
Dunster, Ashley–Capital International Inc
Dunwoodie, Kevin–Pantheon Ventures (UK) LLP
Dunwoody, W.–Inverness Management LLC
Duong, Victor–Difference Capital Financial Inc
Dupont, Daniel–Northleaf Capital Partners Ltd
Dupper, Craig–Solis Capital Partners LLC
Dupree, David–Halifax Group LLC
Dupree, Robert–Oaktree Capital Management LP
Dupuis, Aaron–Serent Capital LLC
Dupuis, Sylvain–Desjardins Capital
Dupuy, Benjamin–BC Partners LLP
Dur, Philip–Investor Growth Capital AB
Dur, Philip–Investor Growth Capital Inc
Dur, Philip–PeakSpan Capital LLC
Duran, Dario–Altra Investments
Duran, Jessica–TSG Consumer Partners, L.P.
Durand, Remy–Frazier Management LLC
Durban, Egon–Silver Lake Partners LP
Durgun, Cankut–Romulus Capital LLC
Durieux, Philippe–Sopartec SA
Durkee, Mal–Perella Weinberg Partners LP
Durkes, Richard–Bayboston Managers LLC
Durkin, David–Avista Capital Holdings LP
Durkin, Timothy–JMC Capital Partners LP
Durrant, Dick–Shard Capital Partners LLP
Durrant, Jerry–Torch Hill Investment Partners LLC
Durrett, Park–Accel-KKR
Durteste, Benoit–Intermediate Capital Group PLC
Durvasula, Sriram–Loud Capital LLC
Duster, Luke–Capital Royalty LP
Dutch, Suzette–Triathlon Medical Ventures LLC
Duthie, Tony–Pacific Equity Partners Pty Ltd
Dutnall, Bob–Amicus Partners
Dutt, Indroneel–Sonoma Management Partners Pvt Ltd

Dutta, Barundeb–Alta Berkeley Venture Partners
Dutta, Subhashree–Clearwater Capital Partners Cyprus Ltd
Dutton, Mike–Dolphin Capital Group LLC
Dutton, Stephen–Kelso & Company LP
Duval, David–Castile Ventures
Duval, Don–Ontario Centres of Excellence
Duvvuru, Sakya–Social+Capital Partnership
Duyck, Geert–CVC Capital Partners Ltd
Duzan, Jason–Glencoe Capital LLC
Dvergsten, Dag–Burrill & Company
Dwan, Thomas–Carlyle Group LP
Dwin, Damien–Brightwood Capital Advisors LLC
Dwin, Dasha–Grosvenor Capital Management LP
Dworkin, Andrew–Vedanta Capital LP
Dworkin, James–GB Credit Partners LLC
Dwyer, Clement–Beekman Group LLC
Dwyer, John–Cooley LLP
Dwyer, Suzanne–Massachusetts Capital Resource
Dyal, Tom–Redpoint Ventures
Dybbs, Michael–New Leaf Venture Partners LLC
Dybesland, Rune–Teknoinvest AS
Dybkjaer, Lars–Gro Capital A/S
Dychiao, Harvey–Bonifacio Capital
Dyckerhoff, Stefan–Sutter Hill Ventures
Dyer, Campbell–Carlyle Group LP
Dyer, Graham–Venturelabour.Com Inc
Dyer, Michael–Morgan Stanley Alternative Investment Partners LP
Dyer, William–Boathouse Capital
Dyett, John–Salem Partners LLC
Dym, Andrew–Perella Weinberg Partners LP
Dym, Shawn–York Plains Investment Corp
Dyrud, Trygve–Klaveness Marine Holding AS
Dyson, John–Starfish Ventures Pty Ltd
Dyson, Steven–Apax Partners LLP
Dziadek, Piotr–Investors Towarzystwo Funduszy Inwestycyjnych SA
Dzialga, Mark–General Atlantic LLC
Dziarski, Stefan–Permira Advisers LLP
Dzielnicki, Adrian–Quark Ventures LLC
Dziurzynski, Richard–Blackstone Group LP
Dzulko, Jan–M Cube Incubator GmbH
E Oliveira, Joao Arantes–Haitong Capital SCR SA
Eade, Mark–Crescent Point Energy Corp
Eadie, Graeme–Canada Pension Plan Investment Board
Eadie, James–Sante Ventures
Eady, Alex–Quadrant Private Equity
Eagle, Sean–Acas LLC
Eagle, Sonja–Trellis Partners
Eakes, Ben–Prophet Equity LLC
Eakin, Rory–CircleUp Network Inc
Eales, Darryl–Lloyds Development Capital (Holdings) Ltd
Eames, Matthew–PROfounders Capital Ltd
Eapen, Paulo–Blackstone Group LP
Earl, Joshua–GTCR Golder Rauner LLC
Earle, Ralph–Clean Energy Venture Group
Earley, Rory–Capital for Enterprise Ltd
Earls, Alex–Gryphon Investors Inc
Earls, Alexander–Gryphon Investors Inc
Earner, Bill–Connect Ventures LLP
Earnhardt, Jonathan–Harren Equity Partners
Earp, George–Leblon Equities Gestao de Recursos

Pratt's Guide to Private Equity & Venture Capital Sources

Ltda
Eason, Evan–Olympus Partners
Eason, Randall–ACP Inc
East, Daniel–Carlyle Group LP
Easter, Jeff–Evercore Inc
Eastland, Christopher–Seidler Equity Partners
Eastman, Ronald–EW Healthcare Partners
Easton, Jamie–Evercore Inc
Easton, Loren–Ascribe Capital, LLC
Easton, Robert–Carlyle Group LP
Eastwood, Michael–Jefferies Group LLC
Eaton, Gregory–Harmony Partners
Eaton, J. Stephen–EDG Partners LLC
Eaton, James–Longview Asset Management Ltd
Eaton, Theresa–SCF Partners LP
Eaton, Winston–ArcLight Capital Holdings LLC
Eatroff, Bruce–Halyard Capital
Eaves, Cory–General Atlantic LLC
Ebersole, John–Sterling Partners GP LLC
Ebert, Christian–Partners Group Holding AG
Ebert, Sean–Altira Group LLC
Ebinger, Jonathan–Bluerun Ventures LP
Eblin, Michael–Gores Group LLC
Ebner, Phil–North Sky Capital LLC
Eboma, Nico–Wall Street Venture Capital Ltd
Ebrahim, Ebrahim Hussain–Investcorp Technology Investments Group
Ebrahim, Ebrahim–Investcorp Bank BSC
Ebrahimian, Varouzhan–Sunbridge Partners Inc
Eburne, Timothy–Watermill Group LLC
Eby, Douglas–Omni Capital Group LLC
Eby, Jeff–WRF Capital
Eby, Matthew–Tengram Capital Partners LLC
Echarri i Torres, Josep Maria–Inveready Seed Capital SCR SA
Echenique, Miguel–Altamar Private Equity SGIIC SAU
Echeverria, Enrique Centelles–Ged Group
Eckermann, Henning–Partners Group Holding AG
Eckerstrom, Hans–Nordic Capital
Eckert, John–Round13 Capital
Eckert, Kevin–SF Holding Corp
Eckert, R. Andrew–Symphony Technology Group LLC
Eckhardt, Jon–gener8tor
Eckhardt, Ueli–Capvis Equity Partners AG
Eckloff-Boehme, Maren–e.ventures
Eckloff-Boehme, Maren–eVenture Capital Partners GmbH
Eckman, John–Lone Rock Technology Group LLC
Eckstein, Jens–Sr One Ltd
Ecock, Tony–Welsh Carson Anderson & Stowe
Edant, Francois–Ecus Administradora General de Fondos SA
Edds, Teall–OCP Asia Hong Kong Ltd
Eddy, Thomas–Jarvinian LLC
Edeburn, Patrick–Granite Equity Partners LLC
Edelen, Chris–Texas Next Capital LP
Edell, Michael–GroundWork Equity LLC
Edelman, Daniel–Edwards Capital LLC
Edelman, Joseph–Perceptive Advisors LLC
Edelman, Scott–Milbank Tweed Hadley & Mccloy LLP
Edelman, Thomas–White Deer Energy LP
Edelson, Jonathan–Ascent Biomedical Ventures
Edelstein, Mark–Morrison & Foerster LLP

Ederwall, Barbro–Inlandsinnovation AB
Edgar, Benjamin–CVC Capital Partners Ltd
Edgar, Lisa–Top Tier Capital Partners LLC
Edgerley, Paul–Bain Capital Inc
Edgerton, Matthew–Kelso & Company LP
Edmands, Benjamin–Consonance Capital Partners LP
Edmonds, Brendan–Atlantic-Pacific Capital Inc
Edmondson, Charlie–Kian Capital Partners LLC
Edmunds, Jim–Accretia Capital LLC
Edvardsen, Andre–Skagerak Venture Capital AS
Edwards, Ben–Syntaxis Capital Unternehmens und Finanzierungsberatung GmbH
Edwards, Doug–Haynes and Boone LLC
Edwards, Gary–Haynes and Boone LLC
Edwards, Irene–Lovell Minnick Partners LLC
Edwards, Joe–Lyceum Capital
Edwards, John–Oaktree Capital Management LP
Edwards, Joseph–White Deer Energy LP
Edwards, Mark–Five Peaks Capital Management
Edwards, Rob–Ridgemont Partners Management LLC
Edwards, Robert–Natural Gas Partners
Edwards, Robert–Tillridge Global Agribusiness Partners
Edwards, S. Whitfield–Bb&T Capital Partners LLC
Edwards, Scott–Sun Capital Partners Inc
Edwards, Stephen–Core Capital Partners LLP
Edwards, Warren–Strait Lane Capital Partners LLC
Edwards, William–Palo Alto Investors LLC
Effinger, Rainer–NORD Holding Unternehmensbeteiligungsgesellschaft mbH
Effron, Blair–Centerview Partners LLC
Efrusy, Kevin–Accel Partners & Co Inc
Efstratis, Nicholaus–Epic Ventures Inc
Egan, Ash–Converge
Egan, Christopher–Advent International Corp
Egan, Glenn–Business Development Bank of Canada
Egan, John–Egan Managed Capital LP
Egan, John–Egan Managed Capital LP
Egan, Michelle–O'Melveny & Myers LLP
Egan, Robert–Alston Capital Partners LLC
Egan, Tom–LaunchCapital LLC
Egan, William–Accretia Capital LLC
Egan, William–Alta Communications Inc
Egbuna, Tony–African Capital Alliance
Ege, John–KSL Capital Partners LLC
Egeland, Patrik–Herkules Capital AS
Egerer, Roland–Suma Verwaltungs GmbH
Egerton-Warburton, Christopher–Lion's Head Global Partners LLP
Eggelhoefer, Goetz–TRG Management LP
Eggemeyer, John–Castle Creek Capital LLC
Eggenberg, Andreas–Ecoforest
Egger, Gabriele–Triangle Venture Capital Group
Eggers, Barry–Lightspeed Management Company LLC
Eggerss, Candice–Firelake Capital Management LLC
Eghbali, Behdad–Clearlake Capital Group LP
Ehara, Nobuyoshi–Unison Capital, Inc.
Ehlen, Jennifer–Thompson Street Capital Partners LP
Ehmer, Frank–Apax Partners LLP
Ehmke, Andrew–Haynes and Boone LLC

Ehrenberg, Roger–IA Ventures
Ehrenpreis, Ira–Technology Partners
Ehrenreich, Michael–BiotechVest LP
Ehrhart, Matt–Casdin Capital LLC
Ehrhart, Robert–Bain Capital Inc
Ehrich, Peter–Cressey and Company LP
Ehrig, Charles–Corstone Corp
Ehrlich, Jason–Lightyear Capital LLC
Ehrlich, Jonathan–Foundation Capital LLC
Ehrlich, Shuki–Giza Venture Capital
Ehrnrooth, Rebeca–Pantheon Ventures (UK) LLP
Ehrnrooth, Sebastian–Segulah Advisor AB
Ehses, Willibrord–Mangrove Capital Partners SA
Eibl, Carl–Enterprise Partners Management LLC
Eichelberger, Harry–Oak Hill Capital Management Inc
Eichenbaum, Linda–AG BD LLC
Eichenberger, Marc–Allied Minds LLC
Eichler, Gabriel–Benson Oak Capital Ltd
Eichmann, Chris–Pillsman Partners LLC
Eichmann, Ken–GHO Capital Partners LLP
Eichmeyer, Axel–ECM Equity Capital Management GmbH
Eicke, Jerry–Yorkville Advisors Management LLC
Eide, Christopher–Morrison & Foerster LLP
Eidem, Karl–Doughty Hanson and Co.
Eidinger, John–Blum Capital Partners LP
Eidson, Michelle–Platte River Ventures LLC
Eidson, Michelle–Shorehill Capital LLC
Eierhoff, Klaus–Odewald & Compagnie fuer Beteiligungen GmbH
Eijgenhuijsen, Martin–INKEF Capital BV
Eijmeren, Dick–Trophas Management BV
Eilers, Patrick–Madison Dearborn Partners LLC
Einav, Guy–Brynwood Partners L.P.
Einav, Shmuel–Channel Group LLC, The
Einhorn, Dalton–Johnson & Johnson Innovation–JJ-DC Inc
Einhorn, Daniel–Capital Midwest Fund LP
Einhorn, Stephen–Capital Midwest Fund LP
Einhorn, Theresa–Haynes and Boone LLC
Einset, Erik–Global Infrastructure Holdings
Einstein, Ben–Bolt Innovation Group LLC
Eisel, Amanda–Bain Capital Inc
Eiseler, Sebastian–Oaktree Capital Management LP
Eisenberg, David–Wharton Equity Partners LLC
Eisenberg, Scott–Blackstone Group LP
Eisenberger, Elliot–Blackstone Group LP
Eisenchteter, Patrick–Motion Equity Partners LLP
Eisenhardt, Dan–Vancouver Founder Fund
Eisenlohr, Verena–Beteiligungsfonds Wirtschaftsfoerderung Mannheim GmbH
Eisenman, Randy–Satori Capital LLC
Eisenstein, Stephen–Harvest Partners LP
Eisinger, Gernot–Afinum Management GmbH
Eisler, David–Banyan Capital Partners LP
Eitan, Yaron–SCP Private Equity Partners
Ekberg, Jorgen–Litorina Capital Advisors AB
Ekeland, Marie–Elaia Partners SAS
Ekenvi, David–Firm Factory Network AB
Eklo, Noel–Cauris Management
Eklund, Mats–Triton Beteiligungsberatung GmbH
Eklund, Mattias–3i Group PLC
Eklund, Niklas–Wellington Partners GmbH
Eklund, Thomas–Investor Growth Capital AB

Eklund, Thomas—Investor Growth Capital Inc
Ekman, Tomas—3i Group PLC
Ekstrand, Helena—Priveq Partners AB
Ekstrom, Claes—Altor Equity Partners AB
El Alami, Ghislaine—Emerging Capital Partners
El Amine, Firas—Investcorp Bank BSC
El Baze, Nicholas—Partech International
El Ebiary, Abdullah—Qalaa Holdings SAE
El Hachem, Nizar—I2Bf Global Ventures
El Haddad, Hisham—HOF Capital Inc
El Hariri, Nader—Bader Young Entrepreneurs Program
El Houssieny, Ahmed—Qalaa Holdings SAE
El Khazindar, Hisham—Qalaa Holdings SAE
El Mallawany, Yasser—EFG Hermes Holdings SAE
El Shamy, Ahmed—Qalaa Holdings SAE
El Sharkawy, Ahmed—Qalaa Holdings SAE
El Wakeel, Mohamed—EFG Hermes Holdings SAE
El-Afifi, Alaa—Qalaa Holdings SAE
El-Araj, Ezaldeen—Evolvence Capital Ltd
El-Asmar, Marwan—Corsair Capital LLC
El-Ayat, Omar—Crosslink Capital Inc
El-Nashar, Rony—SeedStartup
ElBardissi, Andrew—Longitude Capital Management Co LLC
ElHalabi, Jamil—First Abu Dhabi Bank PJSC
Elalouf, Daniel—Montefiore Investment SAS
Eland, James—Capstone Financial Partners LLC
Elaraby, Marwan—Qalaa Holdings SAE
Elbaz, Gil—TenOneTen Ventures LP
Elborn, Mark—Silver Investment Partners GmbH & Co KG
Elburn, Jeffrey—Sterling Partners GP LLC
Elchahal, Roni—General Atlantic LLC
Elden, Thomas—Origami Capital Partners, LLC
Elder, Andrew—Albion Capital Group LLP
Eldridge, John—Haynes and Boone LLC
Eldridge, Paul—Fulcrum Capital Partners Inc
Elefant, Ken—Intel Capital Corp
Elema, Bart—Waterland Private Equity Investments BV
Elenko, Eric—Puretech Ventures
Elfers, Moritz—BC Partners LLP
Elfers, William—Greylock Partners LLC
Elfman, Rick—Sterling Partners GP LLC
Elghandour, Rami—Johnson & Johnson Innovation-JJDC Inc
Elgood, Leslie—New Mexico Community Capital
Elhafed, Morad—Battery Ventures LP
Elhafed, Morad—Battery Ventures LP
Elia, Stephen—AEA Investors LLC
Eliadis, Karen—Bluerun Ventures LP
Eliadis, Karen—LUX CAPITAL GROUP L L C
Elias, Dominic—Investcorp Bank BSC
Elias, Jamie—Trivest Partners LP
Elias, Mercedes—Morgan Stanley Alternative Investment Partners LP
Elias, Michael—Kennet Partners Ltd
Eliasek, M.Grier—Prospect Street Ventures
Eliasson, Jesper—Altor Equity Partners AB
Eliot, Philip—Paladin Capital Management LLC
Eliot, Philip—Paladin Capital Management LLC
Elkhatib, Rami—Acero Capital, L.P.
Elkin, Dimitri—UNITED FINANCIAL GROUP ASSET MANAGEMENT

Elkin, Judith—Haynes and Boone LLC
Elkington, Charles—Electra Private Equity Plc
Elkins, Kimberly—Capstone Financial Group
Elkins, Linda—Colonial First State Private Equity Pty, Ltd.
Elkus, Bill—Structural Capital GP LLC
Elleholm, Jarne—VAEKSTFONDEN
Ellenrieder, Dominik—Endeavour Vision SA
Ellens, Daan—Life Sciences Partners BV
Ellicott, Kyle—Wearable World Inc
Elliot, Sean—Investcorp Bank BSC
Elliott, Derek—Darwin Private Equity LLP
Elliott, Gregory—Sterling Group LP
Elliott, Kevin—Kainos Capital LLC
Elliott, Michael—NMP Management Corp
Elliott, Nathan—Balance Point Capital Partners, L.P.
Elliott, Sean—Investcorp Bank BSC
Elliott, Sean—Investcorp Technology Investments Group
Elliott, Shane—Beringea LLC
Ellis, Alexander—Rockport Capital Partners
Ellis, David—Asssurance Mezzanine Fund
Ellis, Jason—Audax Group, Inc.
Ellis, Jim—Accretia Capital LLC
Ellis, Jim—CSFC Management Co, LLC
Ellis, Seth—CapitalSouth Partners LLC
Ellis, Steve—TPG Capital Management LP
Ellis, Van—Morrison & Foerster LLP
Ellison, David—Altaris Capital Partners LLC
Ellison, James—Compass Capital Services Inc
Ellman, Stuart—RRE Ventures LLC
Ellsworth, Cathleen—First Reserve Corp
Elman, Josh—Greylock Partners LLC
Elman, Sheldon—Persistence Capital Partners Lp
Elman, Stuart—Persistence Capital Partners Lp
Elmer, Donald—Pacific Horizon Ventures LLC
Elmore, Qian—ICV Partners LLC
Elmore, William—Foundation Capital LLC
Elmore-Jones, Katherine—Carlyle Group LP
Elms, Steven—Aisling Capital LLC
Elrod, James—Vestar Capital Partners Inc
Elsner, Jim—Delany Capital Management Corp
Elson, Craig—Star Avenue Capital LLC
Elson, Louis—Palamon Capital Partners LP
Elsser, Stefan—Draper Esprit Secondaries LLP
Elstrott, John—SAIL Capital Partners LLC
Elton, John—Greycroft Partners LLC
Eltrich, Martin—AEA Investors LLC
Elvey, Malcolm—COLLABORATIVE CAPITAL L L C
Elvey, Matthew—COLLABORATIVE CAPITAL L L C
Elving, Peter—Segulah Advisor AB
Elwell, Josh—ValueStream Labs Syndicate II LLC
Emanuel, Ezekiel—Oak HC/FT Partners LP
Emara, Ahmad—ReAya Holding
Emberger, Markus—Adveq Management AG
Embleton, David—Eden Ventures Ltd
Emborg, Esben—Small Enterprise Assistance Funds
Embree, Wayne—i2E, Inc
Embry, Robert—Abell Venture Fund
Emerman, Scott—Westfield Capital Management Company LP
Emerson, Mike—New Mexico Community Capital
Emerson, Russell—Haynes and Boone LLC
Emery, Matt—JMI Management Inc
Emineth, Austin—Dakota Venture Group Inc

Emmert, Robert—MGI Holdings Inc
Emmet, Rustey—Acas LLC
Emmitt, Richard—Vertical Group Inc
Emmons, Eric—MassMutual Ventures LLC
Emmons, Eric—Siemens Venture Capital GmbH
Emont, George—Kentucky Seed Capital Fund
Emont, George—Triathlon Medical Ventures LLC
Emrich, Adam—Coburn Ventures LLC
Emrich, Eric—Quaker Partners Management LP
Ender, Rainer—Adveq Management AG
Enderle, Paul—Hercules Capital Inc
Endicott, Dominic—Nauta Capital SL
Enelamah, Okechukwu—African Capital Alliance
Eng, Elaine—Rhone Capital LLC
Eng, Martin—Western Technology Investment
Eng, Pinda—Blackstone Group LP
Eng, Richard—Investure LLC
Eng, San—Panthera Capital Group
Eng, San—Shanghai SMC Capital Co Ltd
Engel, Jerome—Monitor Venture Associates LLC
Engel, Jerry—Monitor Venture Associates LLC
Engel, John—57 Stars LLC
Engel, Larry—Morrison & Foerster LLP
Engel, Markus—Investitions Strukturbk Rhein Pfalz GmbH
Engel, Monica—Quona Capital Management Ltd
Engelberg, Steve—Sandbox Industries LLC
Engelbrecht, Carien—Aurik Investment Holdings (Pty) Ltd
Engelhard, Teresa—Jolimont Capital Pty Ltd
Engelhardt, Stefan—Morrison & Foerster LLP
Engelhardt, Tobias—Dr Engelhardt Kaupp Kiefer Beteiligungsberatung GmbH
Engelking, William—Prudential Capital Group LP
Engelman, Christopher—Cedar Hill Associates LLC
Engelman, Peter—KC Venture Group LLC
Engels, Stephen—COMMERZBANK AG
Engelsen, Steinar—Teknoinvest AS
Engelsma, Rogier—Gilde Buy Out Partners BV
Enger, Oivind—Sarsia Seed Management AS
England, Craig—England Capital Partners LLC
England, David—Lyceum Capital
Engleman, Edgar—Vivo Capital LLC
Engler, Edward—Pittsburgh Equity Partners LP
Englert, Marcus—Atlantic Capital Partners GmbH
English, Peter—Foresight Group LLP
Enjoji, Kay—TEL Venture Capital Inc
Ennis, Gregory—Peninsula Ventures
Ennis, Jeff—Ocean Avenue Capital Partners LP
Ennis, Yehoshua—JVP Jerusalem Venture Partners Israel Management, Ltd.
Enright, Erin—Prettybrook Partners LLC
Enright, Patrick—Longitude Capital Management Co LLC
Enright, Patrick—Longitude Capital Management Co LLC
Enriquez, Juan—Excel Venture Management
Enriquez, Raymundo—Baker & McKenzie LLP
Entis, Glenn—Vanedge Capital Inc
Entrecanales, Bruno—Bullnet Capital Sc R SA
Entress, Geoffrey—Voyager Capital LLC
Enz, Aaron—Tolero Ventures LLC
Epperson, Kraettli Lawrence—Venture Spur
Epperson, Lanny—Bayou Steel Corp
Epps, Sean—Snow Phipps Group LLC

Epstein, Bart–Jefferson Education Accelerator LLC
Epstein, Jason–CN Private Equity Partners
Epstein, Jason–Oak Hill Advisors LP
Epstein, Kenneth–Newcap Partners Inc
Epstein, Mark–MTS Health Partners LP
Erasmus, Stefan–Werklund Capital Corp
Eraso, Javier Echarri–Ged Group
Erb, Eric–Bain Capital Inc
Erber, Florian–Ananda Ventures GmbH
Erbmann, Clement–First Analysis Corp
Erdei, Sandor–DBH Investment Zrt
Erdle, Joachim–Myonic Holding GmbH
Ergul, Emmanuel–Accent Equity Partners AB
Erhard, John–ArcLight Capital Holdings LLC
Erhardt, Martin–Milbank Tweed Hadley & Mccloy LLP
Erickson, Elaine–Longitude Capital Management Co LLC
Erickson, Elaine–Nth Power LLC
Erickson, Mark–Haynes and Boone LLC
Erickson, Richard–Lightview Capital
Erickson, Trent–Northern Lights Capital Group LLC
Ericson, Bill–Mohr Davidow Ventures
Ericsson, Per–ETF Partners LLP
Eriksen, Jon–Investinor AS
Eriksson, Lars–Riverside Co
Ermolin, Vyacheslav–Bank Sankt-Peterburg PAO
Ernest, Jamison–Blue Scorpion Investments LP
Erni, Marcel–Partners Group Holding AG
Ernoult-Dairaine, Antoine–Sagard SAS
Ernst, Jer-Joost–Bencis Capital Partners BV
Erony, Joyce–Signet Healthcare Partners
Erony, Joyce–Signet Healthcare Partners
Errett, Amy–Maveron LLC
Ertvaag, Ole–Hitecvision AS
Es Sabar, Karimah–Quark Ventures LLC
Esber, Ed–HALO FUND L P
Eschmann, Roland–BE Beteiligungen GmbH & Co KG
Escklilsen, Christine–Piper Jaffray Ventures Inc
Escobar, Rafael–ORGONE CAPITAL I L L C
Escobari, Martin–General Atlantic LLC
Escolano Olivares, Roman–European Investment Bank
Eshak, Kristen–Blackstone Group LP
Eshelman, Rodney–Alston Capital Partners LLC
Esko, Ryan–Sun Capital Partners Inc
Eslambolchi, Hossein–AllegisCyber
Esmeraldo, Fernando–Ecs Capital SA
Espalioux, Jean-Marc–Montefiore Investment SAS
Esparrago, Peter–Cultivation Capital
Espe, Michal–Klaveness Marine Holding AS
Espinal, Carlos–Seedcamp Investments LLP
Espinal, Carolina–Baml Capital Access Funds Management LLC
Espinosa, Stephen–Single Oak Ventures LP
Espitallier, David–Finaventures
Esposito, Gerry–Newbury Partners LLC
Esposito, Grant–Morrison & Foerster LLP
Esposito, Massimo–HAT Holding All Together SpA
Essaid, Ihsan–Perella Weinberg Partners LP
Essas, Joseph–FirstMark Capital LLC
Esserman, Charles–TSG Consumer Partners, L.P.
Essig, Mark–Sangamon Industries LLC
Essinger, Jacques–Aravis SA

Esson, Brad–Inverness Management LLC
Estabil, Mary–Zesiger Capital Group LLC
Estanislao, Arnold–Oaktree Capital Management LP
Estefanell, David–Mercapital SL
Estefanell, David–Mercapital SL
Esteireiro, John–Canaccord Genuity Group Inc
Estela, Juan Miguel–Acas LLC
Estense, Umberto Selvatico–Industrial Assets SpA
Esterson, Robin–Towerbrook Capital Partners LP
Estes, Dan–Frazier Management LLC
Estes, Derrick–Corsair Capital LLC
Estes, John–Blackstone Group LP
Estes, Kenny–West Loop Ventures LLC
Estes, Phillip–Horizon Holdings LLC
Esteves de Carvalho, Pedro–Capital Criativo SCR SA
Esteves, Rodrigo–Confrapar Administracao e Gestao de Recursos SA
Estey, George–Evercore Inc
Estie Venart, Corinne–NIVELINVEST SA
Esveld, Erik–Van Herk Management Services BV
Etemad, Alireza–IK Investment Partners Ltd
Eth, Jordan–Morrison & Foerster LLP
Etinberg, Inna–One Equity Partners LLC
Etlin, Craig–Morrison & Foerster LLP
Etlin, Patrice–Advent International Corp
Etrillard, Gilles–La Financiere Patrimoniale d'Investissement SAS
Etter, Stephen–Greyrock Capital Group
Etzioni, Oren–MadroNA Venture Group
Etzkorn, Kevin–Heron Capital Equity Partners
Etzkorn, Kevin–Heron Capital LLC
Eubank, Frederick–Pamlico Capital Management LP
Eubanks, Mary Lynn–Blackstone Group LP
Eugeni, Ray–Deepbridge Capital LLP
Eum, Jay–Translink Capital LLC
Eum, Jay–Translink Capital LLC
Evan, Dana–Jafco Ventures
Evangelista, James–Ponoi Capital LP
Evangelista, Tenio–OMERS Infrastructure
Evans, Alexander–Atairos Management LP
Evans, Alexander–Providence Equity Partners LLC
Evans, Andrew–Vianova Capital LLP
Evans, Bruce–Summit Partners LP
Evans, Bruce–Summit Partners LP
Evans, Colin–Sandwith Ventures LLC
Evans, Emily–Morrison & Foerster LLP
Evans, Geoff–Friedman Fleischer & Lowe Cap Ptnrs L P
Evans, Greg–Avista Capital Holdings LP
Evans, Hugh–Veritas Capital Fund Management LLC
Evans, Jim–SCP Private Equity Partners
Evans, Kate–Investcorp Bank BSC
Evans, Kate–Investcorp Technology Investments Group
Evans, Larry–32 Degrees Capital
Evans, Michael–Ancor Capital Partners
Evans, Michael–Barclays Capital Inc
Evans, Nick–Active Private Equity
Evans, Paul–Ironbridge Capital Pty Ltd
Evans, Roger–Greylock Partners LLC
Evans, Scott–Guardian Capital Partners
Evans, Stephen–Silver Lake Partners LP
Evans, Thomas–Acas LLC
Evans, Timothy–ArcLight Capital Holdings LLC
Evans-Freke, Stephen–Auven Therapeutics Management LLLP
Evdemon, Chris–Eastern Bell Venture Capital Co Ltd
Evdemon, Chris–Sinovation Ventures Ltd
Eve, Derek–Endeavour Capital Inc
Eveloff, Adam–Castanea Partners Inc
Even, Hans–BTH Berlin Technologie Holding GmbH
Even, Nicholas–Haynes and Boone LLC
Ever, Dennis–Catterton Partners Corp
Everaert, Geert–Allegro Investment Fund NV
Everett, Scott–Haynes and Boone LLC
Evers, Elliot–MVP Capital LLC
Eversfield, Andrew–Antares Capital Corp
Eversole, Robert–Stonehenge Partners Inc
Every, Nathan–Frazier Management LLC
Evison, Roderick–CDC Group PLC
Evnin, Luke–MPM Capital LLC
Ewald, Frank–Internet Ventures Scandinavia
Ewald, Michael–Bain Capital Inc
Ewald, Oliver–Audax Group, Inc.
Ewart, Donna–International Business Machines Corp
Ewell, Jason–Insight Venture Partners LLC
Ewen, Zakary–Battery Ventures LP
Ewing, R. Stewart–CenturyLink Inc
Exter, Neil–Third Rock Ventures LLC
Eyers, Simon–4D Global Energy Advisors SAS
Eyers, Simon–Warburg Pincus LLC
Ezekiev, Pavel–New Europe Venture Equity
Ezra, Menashe–GEMINI CAPITAL FUND MGMT LTD
Ezzeddine, Samer–Monitor Clipper Partners LLC
FLYNN, JAMES–Deerfield Management Company LP
Faber, Jan–Bregal Investments LLP
Faber, Michael–ff Venture Capital
Faber, Robert–Ballast Point Venture Partners LLC
Fabian, Michael–Sentinel Capital Partners LLC
Fabiani, Vincent–HLM Management Co LLC
Fabiani, Vincent–HLM Management Co LLC
Fabiano, Michael–Blackstone Group LP
Fabich, Simon–Atlantic Ventures GmbH
Fabre, Denis–Blackstone Group LP
Fabre, Jean-Marie–Parvilla SASU
Fabry, Mark–Lexington Partners Inc
Fabuss, Leslie–Evercore Inc
Facca, Horacio–Headwaters BD LLC
Fachetti, David–Globespan Capital Partners
Facioni, Richard–Silverfern Group Inc
Fade, Richard–Ignition Ventures Management LLC
Fade, Richard–Ignition Ventures Management LLC
Fadel, Robert–Bader Young Entrepreneurs Program
Faes, Stefan–BioMedPartners AG
Fagan, Erik–Jordan Company LP
Fagan, Ryan–Gryphon Investors Inc
Fagerlund, Markku–Inveni Capital Oy
Fagg, Graham–Kernel Capital Partners
Fagg, Graham–Rosetta Capital Ltd
Faggen, Ivan–Triton Pacific Capital LLC
Fagnan, Jeff–Accomplice LLC
Fahey, Kevin–Bluff Point Associates Corp
Fahoury, Douglas–Iron Gate Capital LLC
Fahraeus, Christer–Sunstone Capital A/S
Fahrman, Kenneth–Carlyle Group LP
Failing, Bruce–Alerion Partners LLC
Fair, Peter–NXT Capital Venture Finance
Fair-Tis, Carolyn–Oaktree Capital Management LP
Fairbairn, Robert–BlackRock Inc

Fairbank, Josh–Sigvion Capital
Fairfax, Cydonii–Acas LLC
Fairman, Francis–Piper Jaffray Ventures Inc
Faison, Lane–Copeley Capital Partners I LP
Fajersson, Emil–Vision Capital LLP
Fajgenbaum, Jonas–Invus Group LLC
Fake, Caterina–Founder Collective LP
Fakhoury, Manal–Vestech Partners LLC
Fakhoury, Riadh–Vestech Partners LLC
Fakhry, Walid–Core Capital Partners LLP
Falch, Henrik–Klaveness Marine Holding AS
Falck, Jens–Incitia Ventures AS
Falcon, Michael–Alara Capital Partners LLC
Falcon, Michael–Bandgap Ventures LLC
Falcone, Valeria–Carlyle Group LP
Faley, Timothy–University of Michigan
Falezan, Franck–Carlyle Group LP
Falk, Joakim–Port-Monnaie Venture AB
Falk, Karl-Anders–Coeli Private Equity Management AB
Falk, Michael–Comvest Partners
Falk, Robert–Morrison & Foerster LLP
Falk, Thomas–Revel Partners LLC
Falkenstein, Joseph–NJTC Venture Fund
Fallen, Malcolm–Candover Investments PLC
Fallon, Julie–Celtic House Venture Partners Inc
Fallon, Michael–Torch Hill Investment Partners LLC
Famaey, Hilde–NIBC Principal Investments BV
Fambrough, Douglas–Oxford Bioscience Partners
Fan, Chunlin–Ningbo Junrun Venture Capital Investment Mgmt Co Ltd
Fan, George–Blackstone Group LP
Fan, Liping–Jiangsu Addor Equity Investment Fund Management Co Ltd
Fan, Min–Feima Fund
Fan, Rong–Rico Harvest (Shanghai) Private Equity Management Ltd.
Fan, Waisum–Shanghai SMC Capital Co Ltd
Fan, Xingcha–CBC Capital
Fan, Zhenghong–YiMei Capital Management
Fanch, Suzanne–Marker Hill Capital LLC
Fancher, Justin–Benson Oak Capital Ltd
Fandozzi, Vincent–Seven Mile Capital Partners LP
Fang, Leo–AEA Investors LLC
Fang, Min–Warburg Pincus LLC
Fang, Pamela–General Atlantic LLC
Fang, Penny–China Capital Management Ltd
Fang, Wei–Wuhan Huagong Technology Business Incubator Co Ltd
Fang, Xiangming–Aif Capital Asia Iii LP
Fanini, Robert–Inspiration Ventures LLC
Fann, Emerson–Eastside Partners
Fanning, Bill–MVP Capital LLC
Fantin, Piergiorgio–Finint Partners Srl
Fantozzi, John–Park Street Capital LLC
Farah, Anthony–Vivant Ventures Pty Ltd
Farah, Michael–Linden LLC
Farah, N. Michael–Metalmark Capital Holdings LLC
Farah, Nicolas–Willow Impact
Faraone, Steve–Ontario Teachers' Pension Plan
Farazmand, Tim–Lloyds Development Capital (Holdings) Ltd
Farber, Jonathan–Lime Rock Partners LLC
Farcas, Alan–Nazca Ventures
Farden, R. Scott–Providence Equity Partners LLC

Farello, Michael–Catterton Partners Corp
Faremouth, Michael–Linsalata Capital Partners Inc
Farewell, Elgin–Teranet Enterprises Inc
Farias, Sandeep–Elevar Equity Advisors Pvt Ltd
Farid, Ahmed–Safanad Inc
Farina, Bobby–Sixpoint Partners LLC
Farina, Lara–Gradiente SGR SpA
Farinholt, Robert–Propel Equity Partners LLC
Farkas, Zander–Tribeca Venture Partners LLC
Farley, Claire–KKR & Co LP
Farley, Louise–Deepbridge Capital LLP
Farley, Pat–CSA Partners LLC
Farman, Charles–Morrison & Foerster LLP
Farmer, Chris–General Catalyst Partners LLC
Farmer, Mark–Eden Ventures Ltd
Farner, Peter–Tgap Ventures LLC
Farnham, Jamie–Trust Company of the West
Farnsworth, Craig–Citigroup Private Equity LP
Farooqui, Omar–Algebra Capital Ltd
Farquharson, Andrew–InCube Ventures LLC
Farr, Paul–Anthos Capital LP
Farrar, Dennis–UpStart Ventures Management LLC
Farrar, James–Second City Capital Partners
Farrell, Carol–Marwit Capital Corp
Farrell, James–Calera Capital Management Inc
Farrell, Lauren–Apple Tree Partners
Farrell, Mark–Thayer Ventures
Farrell, Michael–Spectrum Equity Investors LP
Farrell, Todd–Growth Works Capital Ltd
Farrero, Jeffery–Chicago Growth Partners LLC
Farrington, Christopher–Centinela Capital Partners LLC
Farrington, Deborah–StarVest Partners LP
Farris, Haig–Yaletown Venture Partners
Farron, Matt–Gryphon Investors Inc
Farscht, Russell–Carlyle Group LP
Farshchi, Shahin–LUX CAPITAL GROUP L L C
Farsht, Steven–Corazon Capital LLC
Farzad, Navid–Morgan Noble LLC
Fasano, Jim–Canada Pension Plan Investment Board
Fass, Jarret–Pierpoint Capital LLC
Fassbender, David–Icc Venture Capital
Fassler, Sally–Bain Capital Inc
Fastrich, Henrik–Orlando Management AG
Fates, Matt–Ascent Venture Management Inc
Fates, Matt–Ascent Venture Management Inc
Faubion, J. Patrick–Comerica Venture Capital Group
Faucher, Cornel–Battery Ventures LP
Faughnan, R. Thomas–New York Business Development Corp
Faughnan, Stephen–Siguler Guff & Company LP
Faulk, Russell–Synetro Group LLC
Faulkingham, Ryan–Anholt (USA) LLC
Faulkner, Carl–Cornerstone Advisors Inc
Faulstich, Blair–Providence Equity Partners LLC
Faure Beaulieu, Nathalie–European Capital Financial Services Ltd
Fauser, Tobias–Afinum Management GmbH
Faust, Dorian–Gryphon Investors Inc
Faust, Dorian–Gryphon Investors Inc
Faust, Dorian–Thomas Weisel Partners Group Inc
Faust, Halley–Jerome Capital LLC
Faust, Heather–Castle Harlan Inc
Faust, Matthew–CoveView Capital Partners LLC
Faux, Geoffrey–Caymus Equity Partners

Fay, Timothy–Seacoast Capital
Faye, Cheikh–Global Emerging Markets
Fazackerley, Adam–Fortify Ventures LLC
Fazakerley, Ed–Palatine Private Equity LLP
Fazal, Qazi–Evercore Inc
Fazekas, Michael–Edwards Capital LLC
Fazio, Timothy–Atlas Holdings FRM LLC
Fazzinga, Frank–ZIG Capital
Fazzino, Maryellen–Morgan Stanley Alternative Investment Partners LP
Fealy, Robert–Duchossois Technology Partners LLC
Fearey, Morton–Westfield Capital Management Company LP
Fearnow, Brian–Calera Capital Management Inc
Fechtmeyer, G. Kevin–Cave Creek Capital Management
Fecker, Betina–Dr Engelhardt Kaupp Kiefer Beteiligungsberatung GmbH
Feder, Dan–Princeton University Investment Co
Feder, Jordan–Impact First Investmants Ltd
Federico, Charlie–MB VENTURE PARTNERS L L C
Federman, Irwin–U.S. Venture Partners
Fedorin, Vasily–4BIO Ventures Management Ltd
Fedorowicz, Wojciech–TDJ SA
Fedors, Matthew–Leaf Clean Energy USA LLC
Fedronich, Ryan–Mesirow Financial Private Equity Inc
Feeley, Edmund–LJ2 & Co LLC
Feeley, Sean–Barings Corporate Investors
Feeney, Jonathan–Investcorp Bank BSC
Feeney, Shane–Canada Pension Plan Investment Board
Feeny, Curtis–Voyager Capital LLC
Fehrman, David–Morrison & Foerster LLP
Fei, Bin–Beijing Tianxing Chuanglian Investment Management Co., Ltd.
Feiber, Jon–Mohr Davidow Ventures
Feiber, Jonathan–X/Seed Capital Management
Feidler, Mark–MSouth Equity Partners LLC
Feiff, Mattias–Procuritas Partners Kb
Feig, Greg–CCMP Capital Advisors LP
Feigley, Jim–Torch Hill Investment Partners LLC
Feiler, Michael–Palisade Capital Management LLC
Fein, Iris–Oaktree Capital Management LP
Fein, John–Firebrand Management LLC
Fein, Russ–Resonetics LLC
Feinblum, Barney–Greenmont Capital Partners
Feinblum, Kevin–Advent International Corp
Feiner, Michael–Irving Place Capital LLC
Feinglass, Michael–RCP Advisors LLC
Feinstein, Brian–Bessemer Venture Partners
Feinstein, Peter–BioVentures Investors
Feistel, Matthias–Capcellence Mittelstandspartner GmbH
Fekete, John–Crescent Capital Group LP
Feld, Alan–Vintage Venture Partners Iv (Cayman) LP
Feld, Bradley–Foundry Group LLC
Feld, Stacy–Physic Ventures LLC
Feldberg, Warren–Champlain Capital Partners LP
Feldbusch, Jean-Paul–Namur Invest SA
Feldman, Greg–Wellspring Capital Management LLC
Feldman, Jesse–Battery Ventures LP
Feldman, Jesse–Battery Ventures LP
Feldman, Jill–Morrison & Foerster LLP
Feldman, Matthew–Clarion Capital Partners LLC

Feldman, Michael–Lightspeed Management Company LLC
Feldman, Stephen–Morrison & Foerster LLP
Felger, Jason–Chicago Ventures
Feliciano, Jose–Clearlake Capital Group LP
Felisiak, Nick–Pentech Ventures LLP
Felix, Juan Carlos–Carlyle Group LP
Fell, Michael–Key Capital Partners
Fellars, Dan–Cross Creek Capital LP
Feller, Andrew–Metalmark Capital Holdings LLC
Felsenthal, Martin–HLM Management Co LLC
Felser, Josh–Freestyle Capital
Felsher, Jon–LNC Partners
Felsman, Loren–JC Flowers & Co LLC
Felzenswalb, Gabriel–Vinci Equities Gestora de Recursos Ltda
Fenal, Patrick–Unigestion Holding SA
Fencik, Gary–Adams Street Partners LLC
Fencl, Thomas–Green Manning & Bunch Ltd
Fendel, Andreas–Suma Verwaltungs GmbH
Fender, Stacy–Xilinx Inc
Feng, Ben–PAC-LINK Management Corp
Feng, Bo–Ceyuan Ventures Management LLC
Feng, Dai–Warburg Pincus LLC
Feng, Eric–Kleiner Perkins Caufield & Byers LLC
Feng, Hongtao–China Merchants Kunlun Equity Invest Management Co Ltd
Feng, Janine–Carlyle Group LP
Feng, Michael–Innovation Camp Investment Consulting (Shanghai) Co Ltd
Feng, Pengcheng–Hanfor (Beijing) Investment Co Ltd
Feng, Tao–Ceyuan Ventures Management LLC
Feng, Tao–Shanghai NewMargin Ventures Co Ltd
Feng, Xin–Beijing Jike Menggongchang Venture Capital Center (L.P.)
Feng, Xin–Guigu Tiantang Venture Capital Co Ltd
Feng, Zhiwei–Shenzhen Green Pine Capital Partners Co Ltd
Fenn, Nick–Beechbrook Capital LLP
Fennelly, Kathleen–Gramercy Inc
Fenner, Florian–UNITED FINANCIAL GROUP ASSET MANAGEMENT
Fenner, Helmut–BioMedPartners AG
Fenton, Benjamin–Boulder Food Group LLC
Fenton, Greg–Axioma Ventures LLC
Fenton, Jenny–Pavilion Alternatives Group Ltd
Fenton, Lance–Serent Capital LLC
Fenton, Noel–Trinity Ventures LLP
Fenton, Peter–Benchmark Capital Management Gesellschaft MBH In Liqu
Fenton, Ric–Technology Crossover Ventures LP
Fentress, Andrew–Medley Capital LLC
Fenty, Brian–Hamilton Investments Inc
Fenwick-Smith, Robert–Aravaipa Ventures LLC
Fergus, Joe–Oaktree Capital Management LP
Ferguson, Andrew–Baird Capital
Ferguson, Andrew–Maven Capital Partners UK LLP
Ferguson, Andrew–Maven Capital Partners UK LLP
Ferguson, David–Perella Weinberg Partners LP
Ferguson, Dennis–Juniper Networks Inc
Ferguson, Derek–Victory Park Capital Advisors LLC
Ferguson, Diana–Cleveland Avenue LLC
Ferguson, T. Craig–Mckenna Gale Capital Inc
Ferguson, Thomas–FFR Capital Partners

Ferguson, Zachary–Tpg Growth LLC
Feria, Lisa–Stray Dog Capital LLC
Feriod, Colleen–Canaan Partners
Ferland, Louis-Simon–Blackstone Group LP
Fern, Brian–Palisade Capital Management LLC
Fernandes, Denise–Longview Asset Management Ltd
Fernandes, Lou–Hall Capital Partners LLC
Fernandes, Mark–Sierra Ventures
Fernandes, Norbert–IvyCap Ventures Advisors Pvt Ltd
Fernandez, Dorothy–Morrison & Foerster LLP
Fernandez, Edward–Mobility Ventures LLC
Fernandez, Jesus–Galena Asset Management Ltd
Fernandez, Jose–StepStone Group LP
Fernandez, Phil–Shasta Ventures LP
Fernandez, Rene–Newgrowth Fund
Fernandez, Ricardo–Hamilton Lane Advisors LLC
Fernandez, Rocio–Altamar Private Equity SGIIC SAU
Ferneau, Phil–Borealis Ventures
Ferran, Javier–Lion Capital LLP
Ferrara, Alex–Bessemer Venture Partners
Ferrara, Giovanni–Novartis Venture Funds
Ferrara, James–Anholt (USA) LLC
Ferraresi, Roberto–PAI Partners SAS
Ferrari, Ben–Imprimatur Capital Hldg Ltd
Ferrari, John–Tenth Avenue Holdings LLC
Ferrari, Paul–Advent International Corp
Ferrari, Richard–De Novo Ventures LLC
Ferrari, Richard–Saratoga Ventures, L.P.
Ferraro, Gustavo–Gramercy Inc
Ferraro, Paul–Carlyle Group LP
Ferraro, Saran–Five Elms Capital LLC
Ferraz, Joao Carlos–Banco Nacional de Desenvolvimento Economico e Social BNDES
Ferreira, Beth–FirstMark Capital LLC
Ferreira, Frederico–General Atlantic LLC
Ferreira, Jose–Goode Partners LLC
Ferrell, Eric–Midwest Venture Alliance
Ferrer, Andrew–General Atlantic LLC
Ferrer, Carles–Nauta Capital SL
Ferrer, Carlos–Ferrer Freeman & Co LLC
Ferrer, Carlos–Peloton Equity LLC
Ferrero, Sara–Neo Investment Partners LLP
Ferri, Paul–Matrix Partners, L.P.
Ferrigno, Joseph–Asia Mezzanine Capital Advisers Ltd
Ferrington, Leonard–Summit Partners LP
Ferris, George–Bilgola Capital LLC
Ferris, Paul–Azure Capital Partners, L.P.
Ferry, Dennis–SCP Private Equity Partners
Ferry, Jack–Columbia Pacific Advisors LLC
Ferry, Jack–Ignition Ventures Management LLC
Festa, Anthony–Fund Evaluation Group LLC
Festa, Deborah–Milbank Tweed Hadley & Mccloy LLP
Fester, Ben–HOF Capital Inc
Fetisov, Evgeny–Da Vinci Capital Management Ltd
Fetter, Richard–Tillery Capital LLC
Fetters, R. Thomas–Waveland Capital Group LLC
Fetting, Andreas–Odewald & Compagnie fuer Beteiligungen GmbH
Feuer, Hannah–Poalim Cap Mark Tech, Ltd.
Feuer, Jonathan–CVC Capital Partners Ltd
Feuer, Robert–Warburg Pincus LLC

Feuersenger, Uwe–Calibrium Ltd
Feuille, James–Crosslink Capital Inc
Feurstein, Burkhard–Gcp Gamma Capital Partners Beratungs & Beteiligungs AG
Fey, Lawrence–GTCR Golder Rauner LLC
Feygenson, Oleg–GEN3 Partners, Inc.
Ffrench, Kathleen–Northleaf Capital Partners Ltd
Fiaccadori, Ugo–RiverRock European Capital Partners LLP
Fialkow, David–General Catalyst Partners LLC
Fiascaris, Alessandro–Blackstone Group LP
Ficken, Jason–Headwaters BD LLC
Fidelman, Barry–Accomplice LLC
Fidler, Eduard–First Reserve Corp
Fidler, Peter–Tamarix Capital Corp
Fiehler, Dennis–Bulgarian-American Enterprise Fund
Field, Ezra–Roark Capital Group Inc
Fielding, Christopher–Doughty Hanson and Co.
Fielding, Kevin–Alta Berkeley Venture Partners
Fields, Craig–Morrison & Foerster LLP
Fields, David–Haynes and Boone LLC
Fields, Henry–Morrison & Foerster LLP
Fields, J. Michael–Nations Funds Inc
Fieldstone, Michael–Aterian Investment Management LP
Fiers, Thomas–Arkimedes Management NV
Fiessinger, Emmanuel–Seventure Partners SA
Fife, David–Sandbridge Capital LLC
Figge, Christian–General Atlantic LLC
Figueira, Tomas–Ecs Capital SA
Figueiredo, Mariano Ceppas–Vinci Equities Gestora de Recursos Ltda
Figuli, David–University Ventures
Figur, David–Blackstone Group LP
Fihlani, Zola–EVI Capital Partners LLP
Fijolek, Richard–Haynes and Boone LLC
Filer, Bella–CAVU Venture Partners, LLC
Fileti, Thomas–Morrison & Foerster LLP
Filipek, Andrew–Quark Ventures LLC
Filipek, Eric–Kennet Partners Ltd
Filipovic, Adi–Resurgens Technology Partners LLC
Filippelis, Phillip–AG BD LLC
Filzmoser, Friedrich–Oberoesterreichische Unternehmensbeteiligungs GmbH
Finch, Lawrence–Sigma Partners
Finch, Tamara–Ontario Teachers' Pension Plan
Findlay, John–Periscope Equity LLC
Fine, Drew–Milbank Tweed Hadley & Mccloy LLP
Fine, Leonard–Glenhove Fund Managers (Pty) Ltd
Fine, Roger–Windham Venture Partners
Fineberg, Andrew–MTS Health Partners LP
Finegan, Ross–Lonsdale Capital Partners LLP
Finegan, Scott–Pfingsten Partners LLC
Finelli, Francis–Carlyle Group LP
Finger, Rick–AG BD LLC
Fingerhut, Barry–Wheatley Partners
Fingersh, Paul–KC Venture Group LLC
Fink, Andrew–Trevi Health Ventures LP
Fink, Bernhard–Access Capital Partners SA
Fink, Jesse–MissionPoint Capital Partners LLC
Fink, Peter–Private Advisors LLC
Fink, Rick–Miramar Venture Partners L P
Fink, Todd–O2 Investment Partners LLC
Finke, Thomas–Barings LLC

Finkelstein, A. Mark—Evercore Inc
Finkelstein, Abe—Vintage Venture Partners Iv (Cayman) LP
Finkelstein, Alexander—Spark Capital
Finkelstein, Brian—Fifth Street Capital LLC
Finkelstein, Ohad—Marker Financial Advisors LLC
Finkelston, Karin—International Finance Corp
Finkle, Jeffrey—Odeon Capital Partners LP
Finkton, Darryl—Fundrx Inc
Finlay, Euan—Partners Capital Investment Group Holdings LLC
Finlay, Matthew—Midmark Capital LP
Finley, David—Sverica International Boston LLC
Finley, Michael—Court Square Capital Partners LP
Finn, Christopher—Carlyle Group LP
Finn, Nicholas—Fillmore Capital Partners LLC
Finne, Carl Petter—Klaveness Marine Holding AS
Finnegan, Ed—Crescent Capital NI Ltd
Finnegan, Kelli—HarbourVest Partners LLC
Finnegan, Michael—New Magellan Venture Partners LLC
Finneran, Sarah—Adams Street Partners LLC
Finnie, Charles—Greener Capital Partners LP
Finnie, Shaun—Evercore Inc
Finnigan, David—Sun Capital Partners Inc
Finocchio, Robert—Advanced Technology Ventures
Fiocca, Demian—Mare Investimentos Ltda
Fioccola, David—Morrison & Foerster LLP
Fioramonti, Marie—Prudential Capital Group LP
Fiore, Andrew—Spring Mountain Capital LP
Fiore, Fernando—CIT Group Inc
Fiore, Frederic—Capitem Partenaires SAS
Fiore, Matthew—Signal Hill Equity Partners
Fiore, Norman—Dawn Capital LLP
Fiorentino, David—J.W.Childs Associates LP
Fioretti, Robert—Falconhead Capital Group LLC
Fioretti, Robert—Mistral Equity Partners LP
Fipp, Robb—Vineyard Ventures
Firczyk, Tomasz—Tar Heel Capital Sp z o o
Fireman, Daniel—Fireman Capital Partners LLC
Firlik, Andrew—Foundation Medical Partners LP
Firouz, Fereydoun—Gurnet Point Capital LLC
First, Mark—Eos Partners LP
Firtel, Ken—Transom Capital Group LLC
Fisch, Andrew—Investcorp Bank BSC
Fischer, Albert—Yellow&Blue Investment Management BV
Fischer, Carrie—Sk Capital Partners LP
Fischer, David—Gold Hill Capital Management LLC
Fischer, Donald—Greylock Partners LLC
Fischer, Niccolo—Aliante Partners Srl
Fischer, Rick—Morrison & Foerster LLP
Fischer, Scot—Amzak Capital Management LLC
Fischer, Stefan—TVM Capital GmbH
Fischerstrom, Rickard—Private Advisors LLC
Fish, Guy—Fletcher Spaght Ventures LP
Fish, Jonathan—Ombu Ltd
Fishbin, Paul—Hancock Capital Management LLC
Fisher, Adam—Bessemer Venture Partners
Fisher, Ambrose—Oaktree Capital Management LP
Fisher, David—Brandon Capital Partners Pty Ltd
Fisher, Don—Fisher Capital Partners Ltd
Fisher, Douglas—InterWest Partners LLC
Fisher, John—Balmoral Wood Litigation Finance
Fisher, John—Draper Fisher Jurvetson

Fisher, Julie—Providence Equity Partners LLC
Fisher, Patrick—Creation Investments Capital Management LLC
Fisher, Peter—BlackRock Inc
Fisher, R. Neale—Croft & Bender LLC
Fisher, Robert—Claritas Capital LLC
Fisher, Ronald—Softbank Capital Partners L P
Fisher, Scott—Pleasant Bay Capital Partners LLC
Fisher, Scott—Vexiom Equity Partners, L.P.
Fisher, Stephen—Hudson Ferry Capital LLC
Fisher, Stewart—KRG Capital Management LP
Fisher, Stewart—Mountaingate Capital Management LP
Fisher, Theodore—Third Security LLC
Fisher, William—Fisher Capital Partners Ltd
Fisher, William—Treetop Ventures Inc
Fisher-Wolfson, Justin—137 Ventures LP
Fishman, Andy—Vector Capital Management LP
Fishman, David—Vector Capital Management LP
Fishman, Lee—Blum Capital Partners LP
Fitch, Scott—Wynnchurch Capital Ltd
Fitting, Philip—Brookside International
Fitts, Stuart—Scientific Health Development
FitzGerald, Lee—Unitus Impact Partners LLC
Fitzgerald, Brian—Capital Partners, Inc.
Fitzgerald, Charles—Summit Partners LP
Fitzgerald, David—Petra Capital Partners LLC
Fitzgerald, Eric—Thomas Weisel Partners Group Inc
Fitzgerald, James—Valar Ventures Management LLC
Fitzgerald, Michael—Commonwealth Capital Ventures
Fitzgerald, Patrick—Catamount Ventures LP
Fitzgerald, Peter—Latterell Venture Partners LP
Fitzgerald, William—General Catalyst Partners LLC
Fitzgibbons, Harry—Top Technology Ventures Ltd
Fitzner, Adam—Corinthian Capital Group LLC
Fitzpatrick, Joseph—HealthpointCapital LLC
Fitzpatrick, Michael—Seabury Venture Partners LLC
Fitzpatrick, Patricia—Seabury Venture Partners LLC
Fitzpatrick, Sharon—New Canaan Funding
Fitzpatrick, Todd—J.W.Childs Associates LP
Fitzsimmons, Peter—Tower Three Partners LLC
Fitzsimmons, Robert—High Road Capital Partners LLC
Five, Thor Egil—Proventure Management AS
Fiyod, John—Charlesbank Capital Partners LLC
Fizzell, Michael—Atlas Venture Advisors Inc
Fjeldsoe-Nielsen, Lars—Balderton Capital LLP
Flach, James—Accel Partners & Co Inc
Flack, Mitchell—Trust Company of the West
Flaherty, John—Carlyle Group LP
Flaig, Daniel—Capvis Equity Partners AG
Flais, Jean-Pierre—Societe Generale Capital Partenaires SAS
Flamarion, Antoine—TR Advisors Ltd
Flamenbaum, Walter—Channel Group LLC, The
Flanagan, Damien—Global Infrastructure Holdings
Flanagan, David—Intel Capital Corp
Flanagan, Lauren—Phenomenelle Angels Management LLC
Flanagan, Michael—Blackstone Group LP
Flanagan, Paul—British Columbia Investment Management Corp
Flanagan, Paul—Sigma Partners
Flanagan, Paul—Sigma Prime Ventures LLC

Flanagan, Robert—CNF Investments LLC
Flanigan, Drew—Riverside Co
Flanigan, James—Granite Hall Partners Inc
Flanigan, Robert—Brown Gibbons Lang & Company LLC
Flanigan, Robert—Hamilton Lane Advisors LLC
Flaningan, Daniel—Carlyle Group LP
Flannery, Timothy—Glencoe Capital LLC
Flaskjer, Sverre—Herkules Capital AS
Flaster, Andrew—Volition Capital LLC
Flaster, Andy—Volition Capital LLC
Flater, Graham—Fulcrum Capital Partners Inc
Flatley, Daniel—Masthead Venture Partners
Flatley, Tim—Robin Hood Ventures
Flatz, Alois—Zouk Capital LLP
Fleck, Evan—Milbank Tweed Hadley & Mccloy LLP
Fleck, Roman—Index Ventures
Fleischer, David—Haynes and Boone LLC
Fleischer, Hilary—Strattam Capital LLC
Fleischer, Russell—Battery Ventures LP
Fleischer, Spencer—Friedman Fleischer & Lowe Cap Ptnrs L P
Fleischhacker, Jean—Bayou Steel Corp
Fleisher, Randy—Quadrant Mezzanine Partners LLC
Fleiss, Andrew—Liberty Partners Ltd
Fleming, Daniel—River Cities Capital Fund LP
Fleming, Jim—Columbia Capital LP
Fleming, Jonathan—Oxford Bioscience Partners
Fleming, Robert—Nexus Medical Partners
Fleming, Robert—Prism Ventureworks
Fleming, Standish—Forward Ventures
Flemming, John—Carpenter and Co Inc
Flemons, Wade—Pender West Capital Partners, Inc.
Flesch, Andrew—Acas LLC
Fleshman, Skip—Asset Management Co
Fless, Adam—Paine Schwartz Partners LLC
Flessner, Mark J.—Barings LLC
Fletcher, Edward—Atlas Holdings FRM LLC
Fletcher, Phillip—Milbank Tweed Hadley & Mccloy LLP
Flett, Richard—Horizon Equity Partners Pty Ltd
Flichy, Joel—Galileo Partners
Fliegler, Brett—Enhanced Equity Fund, L.P.
Fliesler, Jared—Matrix Partners, L.P.
Flinn, Sean—Southwest Middle Market M&A
Flint, Jonathan—Polaris Venture Partners
Flint, Peter—Polaris Venture Partners
Flodin, Erik—Evolver Investment Group Ltd
Floering, Brad—Montgomery & Co LLC
Flood, James—Harbert Management Corp
Flood, Justin—Anderson Group LLC, The
Flood, Michael—Northleaf Capital Partners Ltd
Florance, Stephen—Hall Capital Partners LLC
Flore, Ralf—Constellation Capital AG
Florence, Anthony—New Enterprise Associates Inc
Florence, Walter—Frontenac Company LLC
Flores, Henry—Haynes and Boone LLC
Flores, Javier—iGan Partners Inc
Flores, Robert—Westfield Capital Management Company LP
Florian, Daniel—Sun Capital Partners Inc
Florian, Mark—First Reserve Corp
Flory, Marc-Eric—Butler Capital Partners SA
Floss, Craig—Iowa Corn Opportunities LLC
Flower, Mark—Waud Capital Partners LLC

Flower, Tim—Baml Capital Access Funds Management LLC
Flowers, J. Christopher—JC Flowers & Co LLC
Flowers, Robert—Atalaya Capital Management LP
Floyd, Joe—Emergence Capital Partners
Floyd, Nancy—Nth Power LLC
Floyd, Ryan—Storm Ventures Inc
Flucht, Brian—Blade Partners
Flum, Paul—Morrison & Foerster LLP
Flyer, Steven—AUA Private Equity Partners LLC
Flygar, Henrik—Alder
Flynn, Beth-Anne—Metropolitan Real Estate Equity Management LLC
Flynn, Chuck—Bregal Investments LLP
Flynn, John—Act Venture Capital Ltd
Flynn, Michael—AG BD LLC
Flynn, Patrick—NB Distressed Debt Investment Fund Ltd
Flynn, Sean—Shasta Ventures LP
Flynn, Susan—Coller Capital Ltd
Flynn, Timothy—Leonard Green & Partners LP
Flynn, Tom—SV Health Investors LLP
Flynn, Tony—Altura Mgmt Inc
Foata, Laurent—Ardian France SA
Fock, Wai Hoong—CVC Capital Partners Ltd
Fogarty, Thomas—Emergent Medical Partners LP
Fogel, Rafael—Falcon Investment Advisors LLC
Fogelson, Robert—EagleTree Capital, LP
Fogelsong, John—Glynn Capital Management LLC
Fogelsong, Norman—Institutional Venture Partners
Foglio, Alfred—GI Partners
Fogtdal, Soren—Internet Ventures Scandinavia
Fohrer, Andre—Aurora Capital Group Ltd
Foist, Brian—GEF Management Corp
Foisy, Michael—Hammond Kennedy Whitney & Company Inc
Fojtasek, Randall—CenterOak Partners LLC
Foldi, Antal—Research Partners Ltd
Foley, David—Blackstone Group LP
Foley, Heather—Park Street Capital LLC
Foley, Ian—SILK Ventures Ltd
Foley, John—Wayzata Investment Partners LLC
Foley, Paul—Cypresstree Investment Management Company Inc
Foley, Penelope—Trust Company of the West
Foley, Pete—Antares Capital Corp
Foley, Thomas—Indigo Group LLC
Foley, Todd—MPM Capital LLC
Folge, Endre—Hitecvision AS
Folino, Anthony—Graham Partners Inc
Folkmann, Camila—Mindset Ventures
Follens, Albert—Gevaert SA
Foltz, Rachel—Endeavour Capital Inc
Fomicevs, Armands—Small Enterprise Assistance Funds
Fones, Roger—Morrison & Foerster LLP
Fong, Bryant—Biomark Capital
Fong, Bryant—Burrill & Company
Fong, Feco—Brain Robotics Capital LLC
Fong, Felix—Baring Private Equity Asia Ltd
Fong, Joseph—Empeiria Capital Partners LLC
Fons, Randall—Morrison & Foerster LLP
Fonseca, Nelson—Medina Capital Partners Inc
Fonseca, Rodrigo—Carlyle Group LP
Fonstad, Jennifer—Aspect Ventures LP

Font, Victor—Delta Partners FZ LLC
Fonta, Herve—Bridgepoint Portfolio Services SAS
Fontaine, Alain—On Capital Ltd
Fontana, Ash—Zetta Venture Partners
Fontana, Pedro—Isis Venture Capital SL
Fontenot, Joel—Trailblazer Capital LP
Fonts Cavestany, Ignacio—Inveready Seed Capital SCR SA
Foo, Fatt Kah—Aravis SA
Foo, Jixun—GGV Capital
Foo, Jixun—GGV Capital
Foo, Peng Mun—Global Mining Capital Corp
Foong, Natasha—Incuvest Pte Ltd
Foote, Sean—Labrador Ventures
Foran, Derek—Morrison & Foerster LLP
Foran, Michael—Eureka Growth Capital
Forberg, Lars—Cevian Capital AB
Forchielli, Alberto—Mandarin Capital Partners SCA SICAR
Ford, Chris—Morrison & Foerster LLP
Ford, Jamie—Vista Equity Partners LLC
Ford, Jeremy—Metropolitan Real Estate Equity Management LLC
Ford, Jim—Oaktree Capital Management LP
Ford, Kelly—Edison Partners
Ford, Matthew—Bregal Investments LLP
Ford, Scott—OPENAIR Equity Partners
Ford, William—Fontinalis Partners LLC
Ford, William—General Atlantic LLC
Forde, Tara—Global Partnerships
Fordyce, James—J.H. Whitney & Co LLC
Foreman, Al—Tuatara Capital LP
Forer, Michael—Auven Therapeutics Management LLLP
Forer, Michael—Rosetta Capital Ltd
Forese, James—HCI Equity LLC
Forest, Sophie—Brightspark Ventures
Forgacs, Andras—Richmond Global
Forgeron, Lynn—Communitech Ltd
Forlano, Lori—Lightyear Capital LLC
Forlenza, Michael—Lincolnshire Management Inc
Forlenza, Robert—Tudor Ventures
Forman, Michael—Murex Investments, Inc.
Formandl, George—Enercap Capital Partners
Formela, Jean-Francois—Atlas Venture Advisors Inc
Formica, Andrew—Henderson Global Investors Ltd
Formolo, Thomas—CHS Capital LLC
Forrest, Todd—Jh Partners LLC
Forrest, William—Tower Three Partners LLC
Forrester, Christopher—Morrison & Foerster LLP
Fors, Andrew—Summer Street Capital Partners LLC
Fors, John—Symphony Technology Group LLC
Forsberg, Anki—Odlander Fredrikson & Co AB
Forsberg, Per-Ola—Lund University
Forschner, Jakob—Stirling Square Capital Partners Lp
Forshaw, Darren—Endless LLP
Forsingdal, Susanne—ATP Private Equity Partners
Forste, Adam—Bay Grove Capital LLC
Forster, Bret—Willcrest Partners LLC
Forster, Lou—Cerberus Capital Management LP
Forster, R. Patrick—Industrial Growth Partners
Forster, Ralph—Nova Capital Management, Ltd.
Forstmann, J. Anthony—Forstmann Little & Co
Fort, Bryce—Emerging Capital Partners
Fort, Sam—Draper Fisher Jurvetson

Fortescue, Alexander—Electra Private Equity Plc
Forth, Bradford—Oaktree Capital Management LP
Fortier, Andrew—Birch Hill Equity Partners Management Inc
Fortino, Adrian—Mercury Fund
Fortunato, Chris—KEC Ventures Inc
Fortunato, Robert—Anvil Capital LLC
Fortune, Patrick—Boston Millennia Partners LP
Foskey, Andy—Transition Capital Partners
Fosnaugh, Michael—Vista Equity Partners LLC
Fossati, Paul—Sycamore Partners LP
Fossorier, Gabriel—Perfectis Private Equity SA
Foster, Alan—TeleSoft Partners
Foster, C. Michael—MMF Capital Management LLC
Foster, Douglas—Longitude Capital Management Co LLC
Foster, Faye—Harwood Capital LLP
Foster, Frank—Frontier Venture Capital
Foster, Frank—Gideon Hixon Fund LP
Foster, Franklin—Audax Group, Inc.
Foster, J. David—Arbor Private Investment Co LLC
Foster, John—Natural Gas Partners
Foster, Jon—Spindletop Capital Management LLC
Foster, Jonathan—Current Capital LLC
Foster, Kent—Arc Financial Corp.
Foster, Mark—Morrison & Foerster LLP
Foster, Michael—RFE Investment Partners
Foster, Michael—Sdl Ventures LLC
Foster, Richard—LUX CAPITAL GROUP L L C
Foster, Richard—Mansa Capital Management LLC
Foster, Wilbur—Milbank Tweed Hadley & Mccloy LLP
Fotakidis, Alexander—CVC Capital Partners Ltd
Fougner, Erik—Procuritas Partners Kb
Fouletier, Fabrice—PAI Partners SAS
Foulon, Koenraad—Capital International Inc
Fountain, Adam—Jesup & Lamont Securities Corp
Fountas, Christopher—Arsenal
Fouque, Erick—Bridgepoint Portfolio Services SAS
Fournier, Marc—Serena Capital SAS
Fournier, Marcel—Castle Harlan Inc
Fourt, Jean-Francois—Truffle Capital SAS
Fourticq, Michael—Hancock Park Associates A California LP
Fourticq, Michael—Hancock Park Associates A California LP
Fourticq, Ted—Hancock Park Associates A California LP
Foushee, Scott—AIG Capital Partners Inc
Fousse, Thomas—Carlyle Group LP
Fowinkel, Max—Warburg Pincus LLC
Fowler, Amber—EchoVC Partners LLC
Fowler, Felicity—Haynes and Boone LLC
Fowler, Lan M.—Barings LLC
Fowler, Neil—Siguler Guff & Company LP
Fowler, Robert—Annex Capital Management LLC
Fowler, Ulysses—G3W Ventures LLC
Fowler, Ulysses—Oaktree Capital Management LP
Fowler, Wendell—Consonance Capital Partners LP
Fowlkes, Dana—Hatteras Venture Partners
Fowlkes, Ryan—Oaktree Capital Management LP
Fox, Ann—SCF Partners LP
Fox, Anthony—Loxbridge Research Llp
Fox, Anthony—Zouk Capital LLP
Fox, Benjamin—Morrison & Foerster LLP
Fox, Brett—Brookfield Asset Management Inc

Pratt's Guide to Private Equity & Venture Capital Sources

Fox, Gregory–Harbour Group Ltd
Fox, John–Perseus LLC
Fox, Jon–Varde Partners Inc
Fox, Kenneth–Stripes Group LLC
Fox, Natasha–Avante Mezzanine Inc
Fox, Patrick–Bridgepoint Advisers Ltd
Fox, Patrick–New Energy Capital Corp
Fox, Richard–Cross Atlantic Capital Partners LLC
Fox, Richard–Idea Fund Partners LLC
Fox, Steven–Harbour Group Ltd
Fox, Susan–Pinetree Capital Ltd
Fox, Thomas–Alumni Capital Network Management Co LLC
Foy, Lorna–Scottish Equity Partners LLP
Foy, Matthew–Sr One Ltd
Foyston, Richard–Navis Management Sdn Bhd
Fradin, Alain–Credit Industriel et Commercial SA
Fradin, Russell–Four Rivers Partners LP
Fradin, William–JLL Partners Inc
Fraga, Luiz Henrique–Gavea Investimentos Ltda
Fraga, Raphael–Nova Gestao de Recursos Ltda
Fragodt, Jonathan–Castlelake LP
Fraiman, Cheri–AEA Investors LLC
Fraiman, Diane–Voyager Capital LLC
Fraimow, David–LBC Credit Partners Inc
Fralic, Christopher–First Round Capital
Fram, Michael–Liberty Partners Ltd
Fram-Schwartz, Max–500 Startups, L.P.
Frame, Ian–Rangatira Ltd
Frame, Robert–Trillium Group LLC
Franca e Leite Eboli, Joao Marcelo–CRP Companhia de Participacoes
France, Michael–First Reserve Corp
France, Robert–High Street Capital
Frances, Craig–Summit Partners LP
Franceschini, Valentina–Wise Venture SGR SpA
Franchini, John–Milbank Tweed Hadley & Mccloy LLP
Franciose, Brenda–Summit Partners LP
Francis, Carl–Amicus Partners
Francis, Melissa–ACP Inc
Francis, Peter–Summit Partners LP
Francis, Tod–Shasta Ventures LP
Franck, Antonio–Haynes and Boone LLC
Franco Frazao, Emilia–Haitong Capital SCR SA
Franco, Lawrence–Teranet Enterprises Inc
Franco, Ryan–Maxim Partners LLC
Franco, Thomas–Clayton Dubilier & Rice LLC
Franger, Bernhard–Franger Investment KGaA
Franger, Helmut–Franger Investment KGaA
Franger, Stefan–Franger Investment KGaA
Frangione, Tom–Greylock Partners LLC
Frank, Alexander–Fifth Street Capital LLC
Frank, Andrew–Cerberus Capital Management LP
Frank, Brian–MSD Capital LP
Frank, Christine–Waller Capital Partners LLC
Frank, Edward–Advanced Technology Ventures
Frank, Lincoln–Quad Ventures LLC
Frank, Marshall–Monterey Venture Partners LLC
Frank, Michael–Morrison & Foerster LLP
Frank, Peter–Meridian General Capital LLC
Frank, Sean–Cloud Equity Group LLC
Franke, William–Indigo Partners LLC
Frankel, David–Founder Collective LP
Frankel, John–ff Venture Capital

Frankel, Matthew–Levine Leichtman Capital Partners Inc
Frankel, Zachary–Fundrx Inc
Franken, Arthur–Gilde Healthcare Partners BV
Frankfelt, Lars–Triton Beteiligungsberatung GmbH
Franklin, Cody–Leonard Green & Partners LP
Franklin, David–Houston Health Ventures LLC
Franklin, John–Investcorp Bank BSC
Franklin, Will–Lime Rock Partners LLC
Franks, Paul–Gresham Llp
Franks, Ted–Alpina Capital Partners LLP
Franks, Timothy–Advent International Corp
Franky, Alex–Monroe Capital LLC
Frantz, Jerry–Jumpstart Inc
Frantz, Mark–Blue Delta Capital Partners LLC
Frantz, Mark–Redshift Ventures Management Inc
Franz, Ingo–Creathor Venture Management GmbH
Franz, Peter–Florida Capital Partners Inc
Fraser, Adam–Transom Capital Group LLC
Fraser, Alexander–GI Partners
Fraser, Chase–Fraser McCombs Capital
Fraser, Gary–Foresight Group LLP
Fraser, Heather–Swander Pace Capital LLC
Fraser, James–Permira Advisers LLP
Fraser, John–JP Morgan Investment Management Inc
Fraser, Nicol–Dunedin Capital Partners Ltd
Fraser, Robert–Aurora Capital Group Ltd
Fraser-Allen, William–Albion Capital Group LLP
Frausin, Alberto–Arcadia SGR SpA
Frawley, Damien–Queensland BioCapital Funds Ld Pty
Frazer, Amanda–Alaris Royalty Corp
Frazier, A.–Georgia Oak Partners LLC
Frazier, A.D.–Georgia Oak Partners LLC
Frazier, Alan–Frazier Management LLC
Frazier, Diana–FLAG Capital Management LLC
Frazier, Kimberly–Crescent Capital Group LP
Freccero, Stephen–Morrison & Foerster LLP
Frech, Andreas–Cudos Advisors GmbH
Frecon, Laurent–LFE Capital LLC
Freda, Adam–50 South Capital Advisors LLC
Frederick, Alisa–Caltius Mezzanine
Frederick, Scott–Valhalla Partners LP
Fredrick, Stephen–Grotech Ventures
Fredriksen, Hakon–Midvestor Management AS
Fredrikson, Peder–Odlander Fredrikson & Co AB
Fredriksson, Per–Wingefors Invest AB
Fredston, David–Gores Group LLC
Freebern, Todd–JC Flowers & Co LLC
Freed, Jeffrey–Arlington Capital Partners
Freedland, Cory–Sofinnova Ventures Inc
Freedman, Andrew–Gores Group LLC
Freedman, Arnie–Wwc Capital Fund L P
Freedman, Constance–Second Century Ventures LLC
Freedman, Daniel–iNovia Capital Inc
Freedman, Natasha–Calibrate Management Ltd
Freeland, James–Summit Partners LP
Freeland, James–Summit Partners LP
Freeland, Pete–Buildgroup Management LLC
Freeland, Peter–General Catalyst Partners LLC
Freely, Dominic–Evercore Inc
Freeman,–Ferrer Freeman & Co LLC
Freeman, Andrew–HIG Capital LLC
Freeman, Andrew–Paine Schwartz Partners LLC

Freeman, Ben–Aleph Capital Partners LLP
Freeman, Bradford–Freeman Spogli & Co LLC
Freeman, Brandon–Freeman Group LLC
Freeman, Brian–GREATPOINT VENTURES
Freeman, D. Reed–Morrison & Foerster LLP
Freeman, Jonathan–Coller Capital Ltd
Freeman, Josh–Horsley Bridge Partners LLC
Freeman, Keith–Hilco Equity Management LLC
Freeman, Kenneth–Harbert Management Corp
Freeman, Louis–SAIL Capital Partners LLC
Freeman, Marcus–Canaccord Genuity Group Inc
Freeman, Mason–5AM Ventures LLC
Freeman, Mike–Rocky Mountain Innovation Initiative Inc
Freeman, Roger–SFW Capital Partners LLC
Freeman, Terry–Northern Plains Capital Ltd
Freeman, Tracy–Oaktree Capital Management LP
Freeman, Valerie–TWV Capital Management LLC
Freeman, Varel–European Bank for Reconstruction and Development
Freeze, Christopher–Carlyle Group LP
Freger, Ashley–Siguler Guff & Company LP
Fregin, Douglas–Quantum Valley Investments
Frei, Alan–aventic partners AG
Freidheim, Stephen–Cyrus Capital Partners LLC
Freiman, Paul–Burrill & Company
Freishtat, Scott–Altaris Capital Partners LLC
Freitag, Chris–Great Range Capital
Fremd, Thomas–Montreux Equity Partners
Fremuth, Gunnar–PEI Funds LLC
Fremuth, Gunnar–PEI Funds LLC
French, Andrew–FGF Management Ltd
French, Charles–Striker Partners
French, Douglas–Sante Ventures
French, Heather–Acas LLC
French, Mark–Greyrock Capital Group
French, Raymond–Versa Capital Management Inc
Frend, Tim–HCI Equity LLC
Frenkel, Amit–Vintage Venture Partners Iv (Cayman) LP
Frenkel, Lila–Israel Cleantech Ventures
Frenkiel, Steve–Clairvest Group Inc
Frenzel, Debbiann–Cedar Hill Associates LLC
Frere, Baron Albert–Groep Brussel Lambert NV
Freuchet-Sibilia, Jonathan–Draper Esprit PLC
Freudenberg, Hans–Findos Investor GmbH
Freund, Chris–Mekong Capital Ltd
Freund, Jay–National City Equity Partners Inc
Freund, John–Skyline Ventures Inc
Frew, Paul–Elderstreet Investments Ltd
Frewin, Ben–Archer Capital Pty Ltd
Frey, John–Kayne Anderson Capital Advisors LP
Frey, Oliver–AEA Investors LLC
Freyberg, Rich–Shoreline Venture Management, LLC
Freyman, Daniel–Lightyear Capital LLC
Freysz, Antoine–Kerala Ventures
Freysz, Antoine–Otium Capital SARL
Freytag, Rudolf–Siemens Technology Accelerator GmbH
Frezza, William–Adams Capital Management, Inc.
Friant, Todd–Acas LLC
Friar, Scott–Excellere Capital Management LLC
Frias, Justo–Nexos Capital Partners
Frick, Christopher–Plymouth Venture Partners
Frick, Fiona–Unigestion Holding SA

Frick, Jonas–Alder
Frick, Kevin–Serent Capital LLC
Fricke, Uli–Triangle Venture Capital Group
Fridlyand, Alex–Soros Strategic Partners LP
Fried, Bradley–Grovepoint Capital LLP
Friedberg, Ezra–Multiplier Capital LP
Friedberg, Marc–Wilshire Private Markets
Friedberg, Victor–S2G Ventures LLC
Frieder, Samuel–Kohlberg & Co LLC
Friedland, JD–Pulse Equity Partners LLC
Friedli, Rolf–Capvis Equity Partners AG
Friedman, Andrew–Shorenstein Co LLC
Friedman, Ashley–Investor Growth Capital AB
Friedman, Brian–First Analysis Corp
Friedman, Chaim–Lionbird Ventures Ltd
Friedman, Clifford–HPS Investment Partners LLC
Friedman, Darren–Citigroup Private Equity LP
Friedman, Darren–StepStone Group LP
Friedman, Dusty–Bridgepoint Investment Partners I LLLP
Friedman, Harold–Vantagepoint Management Inc
Friedman, Itschak–Lionbird Ventures Ltd
Friedman, J. Kent–Haynes and Boone LLC
Friedman, Jeremy–Palm Ventures LLC
Friedman, Jonathan–Lionbird Ventures Ltd
Friedman, Josef–Storm Ventures Inc
Friedman, Joshua–Canyon Capital Advisors LLC
Friedman, Kenneth–Haynes and Boone LLC
Friedman, Louis–P Schoenfeld Asset Management LP
Friedman, Mark–Evercore Inc
Friedman, Paul–Morrison & Foerster LLP
Friedman, Seth–RLJ Equity Partners LLC
Friedman, Steven–Eos Partners LP
Friedrich, Alexander–Gilde Buy Out Partners BV
Friedrich, Mark–Mutares AG
Frieman, Adam–Probitas Partners Inc
Friend, Alexander–Friend Skoler & Co. LLC
Friend, David–Bain Capital Venture Partners LLC
Friend, Marc–Saints Ventures
Friend, Scott–Bain Capital Inc
Friend, Scott–Bain Capital Venture Partners LLC
Frient, Jeffrey–Edgewater Funds
Fries, Alexander–Ecosystem Ventures LLC
Fries, David–Vantagepoint Management Inc
Friese, Stefan–Beaufort Capital GmbH
Friese-Dormann, Ulrike–Milbank Tweed Hadley & Mccloy LLP
Friesel, Jonathan–Oak Hill Capital Management Inc
Frietch, Mark–Fort Washington Capital
Frigiani, Jason–HarbourVest Partners LLC
Friis, Klaus–Danske Private Equity A/S
Friis, Soren–Odin Equity Partners K/S
Friley, Joel–Morrison & Foerster LLP
Frimodig, Joakim–CapMan Oyj
Frisbee, Selden–Diversified Trust Company Inc
Frist, William–Cressey and Company LP
Fritz, Ben–GEF Management Corp
Fritzinger, Timothy–FLAG Capital Management LLC
Frodigh, Judy–HGGC LLC
Froehlich, Rainer–Constellation Capital AG
Froetscher, Robert–Willis Stein & Partners LP
Frohn, Matthew–Longwall Venture Partners LLP
Frohn, Paul–Gebruder Heller Dinklage
Frohn-Bernau, Felix–palero capital GmbH

Froideval, Bruno–Euromezzanine Gestion SaS
Froland, Charles–Performance Equity Management LLC
Fromager, Cyril–Rhone Alpes PME Gestion SA
Froning, Paul–Focus Healthcare Partners LLC
Fronizer, Greg–Ann Arbor Spark Foundation
Fronte, Michael–Blackstone Group LP
Frontini, Elisabetta–Permira Advisers LLP
Fronzaglia, Gil–Revelry Brands LLC
Frost, Andrew–SIG Asia Investments LLLP
Frost, David–New Mountain Capital I LLC
Frouin, Marc–GO Capital SAS
Fruchterman, Todd–Spindletop Capital Management LLC
Fruehan, Mark–Mobility Ventures LLC
Fruehwirth, John–Rotunda Capital Partners LLC
Fry, Bill–Ascribe Capital, LLC
Fry, Dietz–Endeavour Capital Inc
Fry, Eric–Lindsay Goldberg & Bessemer LP
Fry, Eric–Morgan Stanley Private Equity
Fry, Peter–Burrill & Company
Frye, Marcellous–WGL Holdings Inc
Fu, Ben–Next World Capital LLC
Fu, Benson–Scale Venture Partners
Fu, Dekun–Shenzhen Hongshisan Capital Co Ltd
Fu, Juanita–Bioveda Capital Pte Ltd
Fu, Lei–Ivy Capital Ltd
Fu, Linxuan–Boxin Capital
Fu, Michael–Tpg Growth LLC
Fu, Shan–Blackstone Group LP
Fu, Zhonghong–Fortune Venture Capital Co Ltd
Fu, Zhonghong–Fortune Venture Capital Corp
Fuchikami, Kinji–Mitsui & Co Global Investment Ltd
Fuchs, Harald–LBBW Venture Capital GmbH
Fuchs, Stuart–Gryffindor Capital Partners LLC
Fuger, Rolf–Milbank Tweed Hadley & Mccloy LLP
Fuglede Nielsen, Jakob–Pre-Seed Innovation A/S
Fuhrman, Glenn–MSD Capital LP
Fuhrman, Paul–Colony Capital LLC
Fuhrmann, Lutz–Lexington Partners Inc
Fuhrmann, Markus–Team Europe Management GmbH
Fujihira, Katsuhiko–Morrison & Foerster LLP
Fujii, Daniel–Blackstone Group LP
Fujii, Hideyuki–Chartline Capital Partners
Fujisawa, Tomoyuki–Whiz Partners Inc
Fujiyama, Ian–Carlyle Group LP
Fukami, Katsutoshi–Tokyo Small & Medium Business Investment & Consultation Co.
Fukazawa, Hideaki–Tokio Marine Capital Co Ltd
Fukuoka, Hirotaka–Archetype Corp
Fulham, John–Fulham & Co Inc
Fulham, Timothy–Fulham & Co Inc
Fulkerson, Davis–Century Capital Management / Massachusetts Inc
Fuller, Adam–Bregal Investments LLP
Fuller, Christopher–Verus Investment Partners
Fuller, Kate–Brown Brothers Harriman & Co
Fuller, Kobie–Upfront Ventures
Fuller, Mark–Paine Schwartz Partners LLC
Fuller, Michael–Private Advisors LLC
Fuller, Michael–Watermill Group LLC
Fuller, Thomas–AG BD LLC
Fuller, Walker–River Cities Capital Fund LP
Fuller, Wesley–Falcon Investment Advisors LLC

Fulpius, Nicolas–Affentranger Associates SA
Fulton, Bill–Macquarie Capital Markets Canada Ltd
Fulton, J. Michael–Comerica Venture Capital Group
Fulton, Jason–Riverside Co
Fumagalli, Douglas–Valor Equity Partners L P
Fung, Annie–CITIC Capital Partners Ltd
Fung, Gary–CDIB Capital International Corp
Fung, Pamela–Morgan Stanley Alternative Investment Partners LP
Funk, Benjamin–Vestar Capital Partners Inc
Funk, Jonathan–AllegisCyber
Funk, R. Clayton–MVP Capital LLC
Fuqua, Christian–Colony Capital LLC
Fur Hoier, Jeppe–Sunstone Capital A/S
Furest, Howie–Deerfield Management Company LP
Furey, Daniel–Craton Equity Partners LLC
Furey, Michael–Yukon Partners Management LLC
Furlan, Dino–21 Centrale Partners SA
Furlan, Dino–21 Investimenti SGR SpA
Furlong, Tom–Granite Ventures LLC
Furman, Alejandro–Aurus Gestion de Inversiones SPA
Furman, Sergio–Aurus Gestion de Inversiones SPA
Furness, Aimee Minick–Haynes and Boone LLC
Furquharson, Natasha–Hudson Clean Energy Partners
Furstein, Marc–Fortress Investment Group LLC
Furuhjelm, Robert–Nordic Capital
Furukawa, Daisuke–Global Brain Corp
Furuta, Oharu–SMBC Venture Capital Co Ltd
Fusaris, Dana–Fundamental Advisors LP
Futch, Curt–Thomas Weisel Partners Group Inc
Futrell, Kimberly–Pharos Capital Group LLC
Fyrwarld, Erik–Eli Lilly and Co
Gabay, Henry–Duet Capital Ltd
Gabb, Les–Advent Venture Partners LLP
Gabb, Les–Felix Capital Partners LLP
Gabbani, Nadim El–Blackstone Group LP
Gabbard, O. Gene–Ballast Point Venture Partners LLC
Gabbart, Aaron–Peterson Partners LP
Gabel, Mel–TD Capital Group Ltd
Gabelein, Kevin–Fluke Venture Partners II LP
Gabidoullin, Aidar–UK SGKM OOO
Gable, Gene–Vantagepoint Management Inc
Gable, Ryan–Forsyth Capital Investors LLC
Gabran, Niclas–Towerbrook Capital Partners LP
Gabriel, Jason–Third Security LLC
Gabriel, Manfred–Advisum GmbH
Gabriele, Neil–Bluff Point Associates Corp
Gabriele, Sergio–Kinea Investimentos Ltda
Gabrieli, Christopher–Bessemer Venture Partners
Gabrieli, Christopher–Ironwood Investment Management LLC
Gabriels, Sofie–Korys Management NV
Gabriely, Nir–Supply Chain Equity Partners
Gaby, Max–Linden LLC
Gacek, Hildegard–European Bank for Reconstruction and Development
Gachui, James–East Africa Capital Partners
Gackle, Jeremy–Arc Financial Corp.
Gadhia, Jitesh–Blackstone Group LP
Gadicke, Ansbert–MPM Capital LLC
Gadowski, Lukasz–Team Europe Management GmbH

Pratt's Guide to Private Equity & Venture Capital Sources

Gadre, Rudy—Founders Co op
Gaeddert, Gregory—B12 Capital Partners LLC
Gaede, Jason—Impact Opportunities Fund LP
Gaenzle, Richard—Gilbert Global Equity Capital LLC
Gaertner, Claus—Bvt Holding GmbH & Co KG
Gaertner, Daniel—ConValue Investment GmbH
Gaffey, Jacob—Bay Capital Investment Partners LLC
Gaffney, Christopher—Great Hill Equity Partners LLC
Gaffney, Cory—Anderson Group LLC, The
Gaffney, Edmund—Jacobson Partners
Gaffney, Michael—EDG Partners LLC
Gaffney, Thomas—Anderson Group LLC, The
Gagandeep, Chhina—ICICI Venture Funds Management Company Ltd
Gage, Scott—Shoreview Industries
Gaggini, Filippo—Progressio SGR SpA
Gagna, Pascal—Pragma Capital SA
Gagnard, James—Hyde Park Venture Partners
Gagnon, Janet—Atlantic Canada Opportunities Agency
Gagnon, Joseph—Warburg Pincus LLC
Gahan, Thomas—Providence Equity Partners LLC
Gai, Xiaoxia—China Materialia LLC
Gailar, Steve—Kentucky Seed Capital Fund
Gaillard, Jacqueline—Axioma Ventures LLC
Gaitanos, Stephen—Telopea Capital Partners Pty Ltd
Gaither, James—Sutter Hill Ventures
Gaither, Steve—Spiral Sun Ventures LLC
Gajdos, Peter—Presidio Ventures Inc
Galakatos, Nicholas—Clarus Ventures LLC
Galambos, Nicholas—Industrial Opportunity Partners LLC
Galan, Art—Oaktree Capital Management LP
Galant, Aline—MHFT Investimentos SA
Galante, Jacques—Leeds Equity Advisors Inc
Galantini, Eugene—Second Alpha Partners LLC
Galantini, Eugene—Second Alpha Partners LLC
Galashan, J. Kristofer—Leonard Green & Partners LP
Galbreath, Michael—Portfolio Advisors, LLC
Gale, James—Signet Healthcare Partners
Gale, Michael—Gramercy Private Equity LLC
Gale, Robert—Mckenna Gale Capital Inc
Galef, James—JM GALEF & CO
Galiette, Carolyn—Ironwood Investment Management LLC
Galioto, Frank—McNally Capital LLC
Gallagher, Barry—Blackstone Group LP
Gallagher, Brian—Sr One Ltd
Gallagher, Carol—New Enterprise Associates Inc
Gallagher, Evan—IDFC Capital (Singapore) Pte Ltd
Gallagher, Gerald—Oak Investment Partners
Gallagher, Patrick—CrunchFund
Gallagher, Patrick—Vantagepoint Management Inc
Gallagher, Shannon—Blackstone Group LP
Gallagher, Wendy—Mtn Capital Partners LLC
Gallatin, W.Michael—Frazier Management LLC
Gallazzi, Fausto—Aksia Group SpA
Gallegos, Hector—Morrison & Foerster LLP
Galleher, Patrick—Boxwood Capital Partners LLC
Gallenberger, Robert—Gimv Investeringsmaatschappij Voor Vlanderen NV
Galles, Daniel—HLM Management Co LLC
Galletti, Marc-Henri—Longitude Capital Management Co LLC
Galletti, Marc-Henri—Longitude Capital Management Co LLC
Galletti, Scott—Tenex Capital Management LP
Gallin, Stuart—Terrapin Partners LLC
Gallinson, Evan—Merit Capital Partners IV LLC
Gallix, Pierre—IK Investment Partners Ltd
Gallo, Michele—Alcedo Societa di Gestione del Risparmio SpA
Gallo, Thomas—Emerald Development Managers LP
Gallogly, Mark—Centerbridge Partners LP
Galloro, Michael—Delavaco Holdings Inc
Galloro, Thomas—Ile de France Capital SA
Galloway, Jil—Mitsubishi International Corp
Galluzzo, Jay—North Castle Partners LLC
Galpern, Daniel—TZP Group LLC
Galtung, Hege—Kistefos Venture Capital As
Galuhn, Thomas—Mesirow Financial Private Equity Inc
Galvao, Miguel—Leblon Equities Gestao de Recursos Ltda
Galvin, Denise—North Sky Capital LLC
Galyon, L.A.—Brentwood Capital Advisors LLC
Gamali, Yaser—Qalaa Holdings SAE
Gambarini, Paolo—Wise Venture SGR SpA
Gambill, Katie—Council Capital
Gambino, James—Ben Franklin Technology Partners Southeastern PA
Gambino, Joseph—Freeport Financial Partners LLC
Gamble, J.S.—Blu Venture Investors LLC
Gamboa, Danilo—GP Investimentos Ltda
Gamett, James—StepStone Group LP
Gamman, Einar—Energy Ventures AS
Gammans, Richard—Accele BioPharma Inc
Gammill, F. Kneeland—Diversified Trust Company Inc
Gammill, Keri—Blackstone Group LP
Gan, Adi—Evergreen Venture Partners
Gan, Harold—Sebrina Holdings Ltd
Gan, Jianping—Qiming Venture Partners Ii LP
Gan, Ker Ann—Jynwel Capital Ltd
Gan, Meilan—CDH China Management Co., Ltd.
Gan, Meilan—Prax Capital Management Co
Ganapathy, PR—Menterra Venture Advisors Pvt Ltd
Gandarias, Patrick—Corpfin Capital Asesores SA SGEIC
Gandesha, Parag—MML Capital Partners LLP
Gandhi, Hetal—Tano Capital LLC
Gandhi, Meena—JP Morgan Investment Management Inc
Gandhi, Parth—ICICI Venture Funds Management Company Ltd
Gandhi, Pravin—Seedfund
Gandhi, Rahul—Primary Venture Partners
Gandhi, Sameer—Accel Partners & Co Inc
Gandhi, Saniya—Taurus Ventures GP LLC
Gandhi, Shirin—E I Capital LLP
Gandhi, Shruti—Array Ventures LP
Gandhi, Tapan—Ask Pravi Capital Advisors Pvt Ltd
Gandhi, Vishal—MTS Health Partners LP
Ganem, Laurent—G Square Healthcare Private Equity Fund LLP
Ganesan, Krishnan—ICICI Venture Funds Management Company Ltd
Ganesan, N.—Iglobe Treasury Management Ltd
Ganev, Georgi—Kinnevik AB
Ganguly, Vivek—Yes Bank Ltd
Ganis, Frank—Gilfus Venture Partners LLC
Gannalo, Richard—Blackstone Group LP
Gannes, Stuart—Defta Partners
Gannett, Allen—Acceleprise LLC
Gannon, John—Polaris Venture Partners
Gannot, Gary—Genesis Partners Ltd
Ganong, Richard—Tudor Ventures
Gao, Dong—Shanghai Yonghua Capital Management Co Ltd
Gao, Fengyong—Shanghai Leading Capital Co Ltd
Gao, Guohua—SDIC Innovation Investment Management Ltd
Gao, Meng—Blackstone Group LP
Gao, Peng—Bright Stone Investment Management (Hong Kong) Ltd
Gao, Weiwei—Tianjin Binhai Haisheng Equity Investment Fund Mgmt Co.
Gao, Xiqing—China Investment Corp
Gao, Yanyan—Blackstone Group LP
Gao, Yi—Beijing Tianxing Chuanglian Investment Management Co., Ltd.
Gao, Zhen—Mandarin Capital Partners SCA SICAR
Gaona Sanchez, Alejandra—Gerbera Capital Asesores SC
Garber, Lee—Newspring Capital
Garbers, Grant—Headwaters BD LLC
Garbers, Wendy—Morrison & Foerster LLP
Garbus, Joseph—New York Times Co
Garcia Cantera, Jose—Banco Santander SA
Garcia Espada, Carlos—Bayboston Managers LLC
Garcia Ortiz, Antonio—Caja de Seguros Reunidos Compania de Seguros y Reaseguros SA
Garcia, Alex—Aztec Equity Partners LLC
Garcia, Christopher—Enhanced Equity Fund, L.P.
Garcia, David—Geekdom LC
Garcia, Francisco—Easton Hunt Capital Partners LP
Garcia, JR—Green Park & Golf Ventures LLC
Garcia, Jesus—Torsa Capital SGECR SA
Garcia, Marcos—Eaglehill Advisors LLC
Garcia, Mark—Thomas H Lee Partners LP
Garcia, Oscar—Alantra
Garcia, Quin—Autotech Management LLC
Garcia, Rommel—Maranon Capital LP
Garcia, Victoria—Stellus Capital Management LLC
Garcia-Moreno, Ricardo—Haynes and Boone LLC
Garcia-Norena, Javier Rivero—Bankinter Capital Riesgo SGECR SA
Garcia-Teruel, Javier—Alta Growth Capital SC
Gard, Jon—Satori Capital LLC
Gardell, Christer—Cevian Capital AB
Gardell, Rickard—Pacific Equity Partners Pty Ltd
Gardella, Lee—Adveq Management AG
Garden, Mary—British Columbia Investment Management Corp
Gardhouse, Mark—Mosaic Capital Corp
Gardi, Paul—Liberty Capital Management Corp
Gardiner, Alexandra—EMAlternatives LLC
Gardiner, Gordon—Swiftsure Capital LLC
Gardiner, Jock—Maven Capital Partners UK LLP
Gardiner, Jock—Maven Capital Partners UK LLP
Gardner, Alston—Fulcrum Equity Partners
Gardner, John—ICOS Capital Management BV
Gardner, John—NGP Capital
Gardner, Kenneth—Entrepreneurs Fund LP
Gardner, Lee—One Equity Partners LLC
Gardner, Peter—Wavepoint Ventures LLC

Gardner, Sonia–Avenue Capital Group LLC
Gardner, Ted–Silverhawk Capital Partners LLC
Gardner, Tim–Akoya Capital Partners LLC
Garel, John–Envest Ventures
Garff, Matthew–Sun Capital Partners Inc
Garfield, Scott–Hancock Capital Management LLC
Garfinkel, Pablo–Aconcagua Ventures
Garfinkle, Jan–Arboretum Ventures Inc
Garfunkle, Matt–Pantheon Ventures (UK) LLP
Garg, Ashu–Foundation Capital LLC
Garg, Deepesh–O3 Capital Advisors Pvt Ltd
Garg, Gaurav–Sequoia Capital Operations LLC
Garg, Nikhil–Black Coral Capital LLC
Garg, Praneet–Asia Alternatives Management LLC
Garg, Randy–Beedie Capital Partners
Gargasz, John–10X Venture Partners LLC
Garland, C. Kevin–Sterling Group LP
Garland, Wil–Acas LLC
Garlinghouse, Scott–Antares Capital Corp
Garlock, Grant–Quadrant Mezzanine Partners LLC
Garman, Andrew–New Venture Partners LLC
Garman, Richard–Financial Technology Ventures
Garmendia, Cristina–Ysios Capital Partners SGECR SAU
Garner, Kathryn–Haynes and Boone LLC
Garner, Richard–Pivotal Group Inc
Garnett, Terence–Garnett & Helfrich Capital LP
Garnett, Terry–Garnett & Helfrich Capital LP
Garofalo, Art–10X Venture Partners LLC
Garran, Peter–Great Hill Equity Partners LLC
Garrard, Gardiner–TTV Capital LLC
Garratt, Matthew–Battery Ventures LP
Garrett, Brian–CrossCut Ventures Management LLC
Garrett, Gregory–Portfolio Advisors, LLC
Garrett, Laurence–Highland Capital Partners LLC
Garrett, Lester–Yorkville Advisors Management LLC
Garrett, Regan–Vista Equity Partners LLC
Garrett, Tate–Sunrock Ventures Management LLC
Garrett, Wayne–AeroEquity Partners LLP
Garrigues, Antoine–Iris Capital Management SAS
Garrisson, Nina–Signature Capital LLC
Garrood, Shirley–Henderson Global Investors Ltd
Garrou, Blair–Mercury Fund
Garrow, Michael–Blackstone Group LP
Garside, Andrew–F&C Equity Partners PLC
Garson, Palmer–Jefferson Capital Partners Ltd
Garsson, Brian–Align Capital LLC
Gartland, Robert–NexPhase Capital LLC
Gartner, Mark–Clearlight Partners LLC
Garton, Anthony–Lexington Partners Inc
Garulli, Michele–Investindustrial Services Ltd
Garvey, Eileen–Anderson Group LLC, The
Garvey, James–SV Health Investors LLP
Garvey, Jeff–Austin Ventures
Garza, Hugo–Evercore Inc
Garza, Rudy–G 51 Capital Management LLC
Garza, Theresa–G 51 Capital Management LLC
Gaspar, Andrew–Gaspar Global Ventures LLC
Gaspar, Christopher–Milbank Tweed & McCloy LLP
Gaspar, Daniel–Gotham Private Equity Partners LP
Gaspar, Daniel–High Road Capital Partners LLC
Gaspar, Daniel–TZP Group LLC
Gaspar, Jordan–Accelfoods LLC
Gasparro, David–Lonsdale Capital Partners LLP

Gasperoni, Jim–FLAG Capital Management LLC
Gasse, Ulrich–Permira Advisers LLP
Gassee, Jean-Louis–AllegisCyber
Gasseling, Rogier–Velocity Capital BV
Gatenby, Jason–Montagu Private Equity LLP
Gates, Jay–Charterhouse Group Inc
Gates, Jerome–Hamilton Lane Advisors LLC
Gates, Sean–Morrison & Foerster LLP
Gatison Hatter, Debra–Haynes and Boone LLC
Gatto, Matt–Insight Venture Partners LLC
Gatto, Vic–Jumpstart Foundry
Gatto, Vic–Solidus Company, L.P.
Gaudin, Damien–Riverside Co
Gaudio, Julius–D E Shaw & Co LP
Gauer, Jim–Palomar Ventures
Gault, Bernard–Perella Weinberg Partners LP
Gault, Joseph–Sterling Investment Partners II LP
Gault, Josh–Gridiron Capital LLC
Gaur, Alok–Carlyle Group LP
Gaur, Manish–Carlyle Group LP
Gauri, Vishal–IvyCap Ventures Advisors Pvt Ltd
Gaus, Wesley–CM Equity Partners LP
Gausling, Mike–Originate Ventures
Gauthier, Andre–Tandem Expansion Fund I LP
Gauthier, David–Foragen Technologies Management Inc
Gautier, Bertrand–Greencoat Capital LLP
Gavagan, David–Business Venture Partners
Gavin, Brenda–Quaker Partners Management LP
Gavin, Brenda–Quaker Partners Management LP
Gavin, Brian–Blackstone Group LP
Gavin, Rob–Whitehorse Liquidity Partners Inc
Gavirati, Alessandra–Synergo SGR SpA
Gavish, Yael–CircleUp Network Inc
Gavito, Juan Carlos–Nexxus Capital SA de CV
Gavrilenkov, Evgeny–Troika Capital Partners Ltd
Gavrilov, Roman–Life.SREDA VC
Gawne, Martin–Adams Street Partners LLC
Gay, Jonathon–HGGC LLC
Gay, Mary–Arrowhead Mezzanine LLC
Gay, Robert–HGGC LLC
Gay, Robert–Unitus Impact Partners LLC
Gaydos, Lawrence–Haynes and Boone LLC
Gaynor, Sam–ACP Inc
Gaywood, Carl–Forward Investment Partners
Gazor, Max–Charles River Ventures LLC
Ge, Alma–SAIF Partners
Ge, Song–SAIF Partners
Ge, Yajun–Harlyn Capital
Gebreyes, Tsega–Satya Capital Ltd
Gedalin, Martin–Lumia Capital LLC
Geddes, John–SCF Partners LP
Gedney, Daniel–Susquehanna Private Capital LLC
Gee, David–TTP Venture Managers Ltd
Geerts, Harmen–H2 Equity Partners BV
Geesaman, Bard–MPM Capital LLC
Geeslin, Keith–Francisco Partners LP
Gefaell, Robert–Plexus Capital LLC
Geidt, Elliot–Redpoint Ventures
Geiger, Adam–New Legacy Capital LLC
Geiger, Bernd–Triangle Venture Capital Group
Geiger, Charley–Blue Point Capital Partners LP
Geiger, Debra–Gideon Hixon Fund LP
Geiger, Markus–Steadfast Capital GmbH
Geiger, Uri–UM Accelmed LP

Geiling, Greg–Blackstone Group LP
Geisler, John–Golub Capital Master Funding LLC
Geisler, John–Gryphon Investors Inc
Geismar, Xavier–Cinven Group Ltd
Geiss, William–Vexiom Equity Partners, L.P.
Geithner, Timothy–Warburg Pincus LLC
Gekiere, Barry–MaRS Investment Accelerator Fund Inc
Gekiere, Barry–Ontario Centres of Excellence
Gelb, Sean–GoldPoint Partners LLC
Gelberd, Jason–Comvest Partners
Geldart, Michael–Excellere Capital Management LLC
Geldhof, Guy–Vesalius Biocapital Partners SARL
Gelenbe, Pamir–Big Bang Ventures CVA
Gelfand, David–Milbank Tweed Hadley & Mccloy LLP
Gelfand, Jeffrey–Centerbridge Partners LP
Geller, Ehud–Medica Venture Partners, Ltd.
Geller, Marshall–St Cloud Capital LLC
Geller, Rachel–Insight Venture Partners LLC
Gellermann, Lynn–Adena Ventures
Gelles, Jeffrey–American Discovery Capital LLC
Gelsomini, Jesse–Haynes and Boone LLC
Gemmell, John–Doughty Hanson and Co.
Gen, Ozgur–Bravia Capital Partners Inc
Genadiev, Ivan–Teres Capital OOD Sofia
Genda, Kevin–Cerberus Capital Management LP
Genereux, Michael–Blackstone Group LP
Geneser, Christopher–CIVC Partners LP
Geng, Bin–Shanghai Lianxin Investment Management Co Ltd
Genieser, Robert–ETF Partners LLP
Genieser, Robert–Vertex Israel II Management Ltd
Geninazza, Marco–Find Invest Grow Ltd
Gennaro, Michael–Leonard Green & Partners LP
Genova, Joseph Steven–Milbank Tweed Hadley & Mccloy LLP
Gent, Stuart–Bain Capital Inc
Gentile, Frank–Third Rock Ventures LLC
Gentry, Evan–G8 Capital LLC
Gentry, Hal–Capital Innovators LLC
Gentsch, Jeffrey–Advantage Capital Partners
Georgacacos, Aki–Avrio Capital Management Corp
George, David–General Atlantic LLC
George, Harry–Solstice Capital
George, Jean–Advanced Technology Ventures
George, Jean–Lightstone Ventures LP
George, Marcus–CHS Capital LLC
George, Mathew–TELUS Ventures
George, Patrick–Gordon River Capital
George, Ross–Direct Capital Private Equity
George, Simeon–Sr One Ltd
Georges, Edouard–Golding Capital Partners GmbH
Gera, Michael–Energy Access Ventures SAS
Geraghty, Clem–Pantheon Ventures (UK) LLP
Gerard, Rene Xavier–SpeedUp Iqbator Sp z o o
Gerbaldi, Alain–Siparex Proximite Innovation SAS
Gerber, Francois–Vatel Capital SAS
Gerber, Laurie–Great Hill Equity Partners LLC
Gerber, Phillip–Fulton Capital LLC
Gerber, William–Bay City Capital LLC
Gerbet, Valerie–Siparex Group
Gerch, Todd–Tennenbaum Capital Partners LLC
Gerdes, Matt–Freeport Financial Partners LLC
Gereghty, James–Siguler Guff & Company LP
Gergaud, Gilles–Ouest Angels Developpement SAS

Pratt's Guide to Private Equity & Venture Capital Sources

Gerlinger, Christoph—German Startups Group Berlin GmbH & Co KGaA
Germani, Jean-Christophe—CVC Capital Partners Ltd
Gerne, Donald—Metalmark Capital Holdings LLC
Gerngross, Tillman—SV Health Investors LLP
Gerrard, Michael—Partnerships Uk PLC
Gerrish, Steve—Apex One Equity LLC
Gerrits, Rony—Morrison & Foerster LLP
Gerritsen, Jan Willem—VOC Capital Partners BV
Gerry, Peter—Sycamore Ventures Inc
Gerschwer, Lawrence—Morrison & Foerster LLP
Gersh, Lewis—Compound Ventures
Gershenberg, Aaron—Silicon Valley Bancventures LP
Gershenfeld, Kenneth—Fortress Investment Group LLC
Gershenson, Michael—Carlyle Group LP
Gersht, Eran—Poalim Cap Mark Tech, Ltd.
Gerson, Jeffrey—Wafra Partners LLC
Gersten, Richard—Tengram Capital Partners LLC
Gerstner, William—Saw Mill Capital LLC
Gertsell, Glenn—Milbank Tweed Hadley & Mccloy LLP
Gertz, Barry—Clarus Ventures LLC
Gervais, Bernard—Ardens & Associes SAS
Gervase, David—Concentric Equity Partners, L.P.
Gervasio, Michael—Rizk Ventures LLC
Gerzof, David—GREATPOINT VENTURES
Gescher, Jeanne-Marie—Wellington Partners GmbH
Gessner, Christopher—Peninsula Capital Partners LLC
Gester, David—Catterton Partners Corp
Gestrelius, Staffan—Port-Monnaie Venture AB
Geszti, Andras—Euroventures Capital Tanacsado Kft
Geuten, Luc—Vendis Capital NV
Geva, Michal—Triventures Management Ltd
Geveda, Eric—Leeds Equity Advisors Inc
Geyser, Russell—Sandleigh Ventures LLC
Gezon, David—MMF Capital Management LLC
Gfoeller, Joachim—Gmg Capital Partners LP
Ghadiali, Shraddha—Granite Hill Capital Partners LLC
Ghai, Pankaj—Olympus Capital Holdings Asia Hong Kong Ltd
Ghammachi, Dan—K1 Capital Advisors LLC
Ghandour, Ziad—TI Capital
Ghanem, Shahi—WI Harper Group Inc
Ghani, Izani—Khazanah Nasional Bhd
Gharavi, Navid—Riordan Lewis & Haden
Ghareeb, Basma—Kuwait Financial Centre KPSC
Gharegozlou, Roham—Newbury Ventures
Ghazi Kheriba, Mustafa—Abu Dhabi Capital Management LLC
Ghegan, Thomas—Founders Equity, Inc.
Ghei, Aman—Finch Capital Partners BV
Ghelani, Naina—Oaktree Capital Management LP
Ghelberg, Alan—Berkshire Partners LLC
Ghelberg, Alan—General Atlantic LLC
Gherghina, Leo—Baring Private Equity Asia Ltd
Ghetti, Stefano—Wise Venture SGR SpA
Ghidirim, Patrick—NCH Capital Inc
Ghosal, Amitava—AL Masah Paper Industries LLC
Ghose, Shomit—ONSET Ventures
Ghose, Shomit—ONSET Ventures
Ghosh, Deepak—Silverfern Group Inc
Ghoussaini, Nick—Vector Capital Management LP
Ghouth, Ahmad—Al Khabeer Capital Co
Giacalone, Francoise—Oaktree Capital Management LP
Giacomelli, Ed—Crosbie & Co Inc
Giacomotto, Lionel—Charterhouse Capital Partners LLP
Giambanco, Sal—Omidyar Network Commons LLC
Giammarco, Jacqueline—Stone Point Capital LLC
Giammittorio, Greg—Morrison & Foerster LLP
Giampetroni, John—Rizvi Traverse Management LLC
Giannamore, Joe—AnaCap Financial Partners Llp
Giannandrea, Federico—Foresight Group LLP
Giannini, Mario—Hamilton Lane Advisors LLC
Giannini, Valerio—Newcap Partners Inc
Giannuzzi, John—Sherbrooke Capital
Gianos, Flip—InterWest Partners LLC
Giard, Stacey—Tola Capital LLC
Giarraputo, Barry—Antares Capital Corp
Gibaratz, Scott—HCI Equity LLC
Gibb, Ewan—Enercap Capital Partners
Gibbins, Brooks—Fintech Collective Inc
Gibbons, Alastair—Bridgepoint Advisers Ltd
Gibbons, Judy—Accel Partners & Co Inc
Gibbons, Michael—Brown Gibbons Lang & Company LLC
Gibbons, Michael—WL Ross & Co LLC
Gibbons, Paul—Castanea Partners Inc
Gibbs, Kevin—Merida Capital Partners LLC
Gibbs, Matthew—Oxford Bioscience Partners
Gibbs, Peter—Permira Advisers LLP
Gibson McGinnis, Ellen—Haynes and Boone LLC
Gibson, Brett—NextGen Venture Partners LLC
Gibson, Darren—Palio Capital Partners LLP
Gibson, David—Carlyle Group LP
Gibson, Greg—Aldine Capital Partners Inc
Gibson, Holly—Templeton Asset Management Ltd
Gibson, Jim—CORE Partners LLC
Gibson, Libby—Piper PE LLP
Gibson, Paul—Horizon Technology Finance Management LLC
Gibson, Simon—Wesley Clover International Corporation
Gibson, Steven—Genesis Park, L.P.
Gichini, Anthony—InReturn Capital (K) Ltd
Gichini, Anthony—Jacana Partners
Giddens, Michele—Bridges Fund Management Ltd
Giebel, Lutz—SV Health Investors LLP
Giedrojc, Jacek—Warsaw Equity Management Sp z oo
Giese, Sean—Technology Crossover Ventures LP
Giese, Sean—True Wind Capital Management LLC
Gieselman, Scott—Natural Gas Partners
Gieselman, Thomas—e.ventures
Gieselmann, Thomas—eVenture Capital Partners GmbH
Giess, Benjamin—Anvil Capital LLC
Gifford, Charles—New Heritage Capital LLC
Giga, Farah—Valhalla Partners LP
Gigliani, Marcelo—Apax Partners LLP
Gigov, Emil—Albion Capital Group LLP
Gijsbers, Hennie—Trophas Management BV
Gil, Gonzalo—Axis Capital Management
Gil, Joseph—Morgan Creek Capital Management LLC
Giladi, Ran—AL Capital Holdings 2016 Ltd
Gilani, Atif—Renovus Capital Partners LP
Gilani, Aziz Ahmed—Mercury Fund
Gilani, Saad—Yorkville Advisors Management LLC
Gilbard, Marc—Moorfield Group Ltd
Gilbert, Andrew—Mid-Ocean Partners LP
Gilbert, Avrom—Jerusalem Global Ventures
Gilbert, Dan—Detroit Venture Partners LLC
Gilbert, Daniel—Rockbridge Growth Equity LLC
Gilbert, Douglas—Dfw Capital Partners LP
Gilbert, Jan—Haynes and Boone LLC
Gilbert, Jon—JZ Capital Partners Ltd
Gilbert, Karen—Financial Technology Ventures
Gilbert, Kristin—Pine Brook Road Partners LLC
Gilbert, Martin—Aberdeen Asset Management PLC
Gilbert, Matt—Thoma Bravo LLC
Gilbert, Simon—H2 Equity Partners BV
Gilbert, Trish—Edgewater Funds
Gilbert, Walter—BioVentures Investors
Gilbertson, Scott—Pfingsten Partners LLC
Gilbertson, Scott—Tpg Growth LLC
Gilchrest, Eric—Ancor Capital Partners
Gilchrist, Ralph—Enko Capital Management LLP
Gildea, Brian—Hamilton Lane Advisors LLC
Giles, Eerik—Navigation Capital Partners Inc
Giles, Jeff—Bertram Capital Management LLC
Giles, Martin—Wing Venture Capital
Giles, Ryan—Triwest Capital Mgmt Corp
Gilfix, Jeffrey—Gmg Capital Partners LP
Gilfus, Stephen—Gilfus Venture Partners LLC
Gilhuly, Edward—Sageview Capital LP
Gili, Roberto—Alta Partners Capital
Gilis, Konstantin—Onex Corp
Gilis, Kosty—Onex Corp
Gilkes, Martin—Bain Capital Inc
Gill, Daniel—Silver Oak Services Partners
Gill, Joseph—Wall Street Venture Capital Ltd
Gill, Mark—Southern Cross Venture Partners Pty Ltd
Gill, Mark—Talu Ventures Pty Ltd
Gill, Robin—Wellington Financial Lp
Gill-Roberts, Jennifer—Maven Venture Partners
Gillan, Steve—Azure Capital Partners, L.P.
Gillard, Keith—Pangaea Ventures Ltd
Gillen, Michael—Gryphon Investors Inc
Gillespie, Brad—IA Ventures
Gillespie, Murdoch—Impact Capital Inc
Gillespie, Theresa—Trilogy Equity Partners Llc
Gillespie-Smith, Andrew—Global Infrastructure Holdings
Gilliam, John—Bluff Point Associates Corp
Gillies, Charles—Jolimont Capital Pty Ltd
Gilligan, Colin—Global Infrastructure Holdings
Gilligan, Patrick—Blackstone Group LP
Gilligan, Patrick—Clearlake Capital Group LP
Gilliland, Brett—G8 Capital LLC
Gillinov, A. Marc—Foundation Medical Partners LP
Gillion, Frencel—Kagiso Ventures
Gillis, Michael—Jabodon PT Co
Gillis, Neil—Round Hill Music Royalty Fund LP
Gillis, Steven—Arch Venture Partners LLC
Gillis, Tom—AllegisCyber
Gillogly, Shawn—Velocity Venture Capital Inc
Gillot, Olivier—Finadvance SA
Gills, Duncan—Battery Ventures LP
Gillum, Winston—Harbert Management Corp
Gilman, Jeremy—McRock Capital Corp
Gilmer, Barrett—Mid-Ocean Partners LP
Gilmore, Cass—ABS Capital Partners, Inc.
Gilmore, Martin—Bb&T Capital Partners LLC

Gilpin, Winston—Mercury Fund
Gilroy, Michael—Canaan Partners
Gilstrap, Douglas—Technology Crossover Ventures LP
Gimbel, Jonathan—Gores Group LLC
Gimbert, Christopher—Star Mountain Capital LLC
Gimelshtein, Igor—Birch Hill Equity Partners Management Inc
Gimena, Francisco—Mola Factory SL
Giner Hernandez, Emilio—Avindia SGECR Capital SA
Giner, Olivier—iGan Partners Inc
Gingrich, James—AllianceBernstein LP
Ginsberg, Alex—One Line Partners LLC
Ginsberg, Andrew—Gen Cap America Inc
Ginsberg, Erik—Slate Capital Group LLC
Ginsberg, Jeffrey—Mistral Equity Partners LP
Ginsberg, Winston—Towerbrook Capital Partners LP
Ginsburg, Evan—Turn/River Capital LP
Ginsburg, James—Vernon & Park Capital LP
Ginsburg, Linda—Vernon & Park Capital LP
Gionfriddo, Julie—Apple Tree Partners
Gionfriddo, Julie—Landmark Partners Inc
Giordano, Gary—Berkshire Partners LLC
Giordano, Jason—Blackstone Group LP
Giorgini, Giuseppe—Innogest Sgr SpA
Giovacchini, Paul—Landmark Partners Inc
Gips, Donald—Columbia Capital LP
Giralt, Luis—Looking Glass Partners LLC
Girard, Cliff—Acorn Ventures, Inc.
Girardi, Robert—Avista Capital Holdings LP
Giraud, Lionel—Neo Investment Partners LLP
Giraudon, Gerard—Incubateur Paca-Est
Gire, Philippe—Elaia Partners SAS
Girgenti, Christopher—Jabodon PT Co
Girgenti, Christopher—Pritzker Group Venture Capital
Girgis, Daniel—Kaz Capital Pty Ltd
Giroti, Tony—10X Venture Partners LLC
Girotra, Anuj—Capital International Inc
Giroux, Jean-Francois—Cycle Capital Management (CCM) Inc
Girsault, Herve—inventages venture capital GmbH
Girshovich, Stephanie—Morgan Stanley Alternative Investment Partners LP
Girszyn, Jerome—Platina Finance, Ltd.
Girvan, Brian—Ascent Venture Management Inc
Girvan, Brian—Ascent Venture Management Inc
Gissel, Peter—CBPE Capital LLP
Gitig, Liron—Financial Technology Ventures
Gitlin, Ruth—AG BD LLC
Gitsels, Mark—5Square BV
Gitter, David—New Capital Management Inc
Giuffrida, Alfred—Horsley Bridge Partners LLC
Giugliano, Anthony—Partnership Fund for New York City
Giugliano, Anthony—Partnership Fund for New York City
Giuliani, Francesco—First Reserve Corp
Giuliani, Germano—Mosaix Ventures LLC
Giuliano, Claudio—Innogest Sgr SpA
Giulini, Christoph—One Equity Partners LLC
Giuriceo, Kenneth—Clayton Dubilier & Rice LLC
Giuseppetti, Fabio Massimo—Palamon Capital Partners LP
Giusti, Margot—Blumberg International Partners LLC
Given, David—Blue Point Capital Partners LP

Given, Douglass—Bay City Capital LLC
Gjedebo, Tore—Styrbjorn Growth AS
Gjelsvik, Einar—Hitecvision AS
Gjesdahl, Johan—Springfondet Management AS
Gjos, Sean—Triton Pacific Capital LLC
Gladden, Robert—Pfingsten Partners LLC
Gladitz, Rupert—Harwell Capital SPC
Gladstone, Jane—Evercore Inc
Gladstone, Michael—Atlas Venture Advisors Inc
Glaenzer, Stefan—Passion Capital Investments LLP
Glaeser, Carl—Palladian Capital Partners LLC
Glantz, Alexander—Centerview Partners LLC
Glanville, Robert—Pine Brook Road Partners LLC
Glarner, Gregory—Affinity Capital Management Co
Glaros, Nicole—Techstars Central LLC
Glas, Johannes—Investcorp Bank BSC
Glaser, Herbert—Haynes and Boone LLC
Glaser, Rob—Accel Partners & Co Inc
Glaser, Robert—Maplewood Partners LP
Glasgow, Merle—Wheelhouse Capital Partners LLC
Glasheen, James—Technology Partners
Glass, Charlie—Act Venture Capital Ltd
Glass, Jason—Summit Partners LP
Glass, Jeffrey—Bain Capital Inc
Glass, Jonathan—Millennium TVP Management Co LLC
Glass, Sean—Acceleprise LLC
Glass, Sean—Novak Biddle Venture Partners LP
Glass, Steven—STG Capital LLC
Glasser, Ross—Western Technology Investment
Glastris, William—Prospect Partners LLC
Glaws, Ryan—Excellere Capital Management LLC
Glaza, Patricia—Arsenal
Glazier, Bill—Redwood Venture Partners
Gleason, Greg—Wynnchurch Capital Ltd
Gleason, Gregory—Corigin Private Equity Group
Glebocki, Przemyslaw—Mezzanine Management Finanz und UnternehmensberatungsgmbH
Gledhil, Neal—Optimum Technology Fund LP
Glein, Randall—Draper Fisher Jurvetson
Glen, Alicia—Goldman Sachs & Co LLC
Glenister, Russel—PROfounders Capital Ltd
Glenn, David—Western Heritage Capital LLC
Glennon, Andrew—Spirit Capital Partners Llp
Glerum, Peter—Castlelake LP
Gleser, Theodore—Carlyle Group LP
Gleven, Stefan—EQT Funds Management Ltd
Glick, Craig—Natural Gas Partners
Glickman, Daniel—Antares Capital Corp
Glickman, David—Resilience Capital Partners LLC
Glickman, Donald—JFLehman & Co
Glimmerveen, Geert—Egeria BV
Glisson, Wade—Silver Oak Services Partners
Glorioso, Antonio—Consilium SGR pA
Glouchevitch, Michel—Riordan Lewis & Haden
Glover, John—Incline Management Corp
Glover, John—PNC Equity Management Corp
Glucksman, Adam—Carlyle Group LP
Glushik, John—Intersouth Partners
Glynn, David—Glynn Capital Management LLC
Glynn, John—Glynn Capital Management LLC
Go, Robert—NextView Ventures LP
Go, Yvette—SET Venture Partners BV
Gobbo, Mario—Asia Pacific Healthcare Advisors Pvt Ltd

Goc, Wojciech—Argan Capital
Goch, Jaap—EVO Venture Partners
Gochnour, Jeffrey—Cottonwood Capital Partners LLC
Godbersen, Fabian—Blackstone Group LP
Godbout, Martin—Burrill & Company
Goddard, Stephen—Kamylon Capital LLC
Goddu, Roger—Brentwood Associates, L.P.
Gode, Gautam—Samara Capital Management Ltd
Godfrey, Kent—Pond Venture Partners Ltd
Godfrey, Neil—Barings (UK) Ltd
Godner, Michael—Cavalry Investments LLC
Godreau, Enrique—Voyager Capital LLC
Godron, Louis—Argos Soditic SA
Godsey, R—Birch Equity Partners LLC
Godwin, Michael—Resonant Venture Partners
Goebel, Markus—Novartis Venture Funds
Goebel, Stefan-Joerg—Statkraft Ventures GmbH
Goebel, Thomas—Neomed Management As
Goeddel, David—Column Group
Goeke, Peter—MIDAS Management AG
Goel, Aakash—Bessemer Venture Partners
Goel, Anita—Akayi Capital Partners LLC
Goel, Nipun—IIFL Holdings Ltd
Goel, Vab—Norwest Venture Partners
Goelzer, Daniel—Baker & McKenzie LLP
Goerig, Steffen—Quantum Capital Partners AG
Goesch, Torsten—Rosetta Capital Ltd
Goette, Gerd—Siemens Venture Capital GmbH
Goettemoeller, Michael—Brown Gibbons Lang & Company LLC
Goettner, Peter—Worldview Technology Partners, Inc.
Goetz, Stefan—Hellman & Friedman LLC
Goetz, Tim—San Joaquin Capital LLC
Goetze, Holger—Capital Stage AG
Goff, Charlie—New Capital Management Inc
Goff, John—Goff Capital Partners, L.P.
Goff, Laurens—Stone-Goff Partners LLC
Gogel, Donald—Clayton Dubilier & Rice LLC
Goh, Andress—Allianz Capital Partners GmbH
Goh, Dennis—Wavemaker Partners
Goh, Eugene—Aetius Capital Pte Ltd
Goh, Hian—NSI Ventures
Goh, Jun Yong—Moorim Capital Co Ltd
Goh, Yewhong—Axiom Asia Private Capital Pte Ltd
Goheen, Kevin—Axis Capital Corp
Gohman, Susan—Lakeside Capital Management LLC
Goik, Sven—Capcellence Mittelstandspartner GmbH
Goila, Thomas—Aequitas Capital Management Inc
Goila, Tom—Comvest Partners
Goji, Tomotaka—University of Tokyo Edge Capital Co Ltd
Goker, Hakan—Aescap Venture I BV
Gola, Bartlomiej—SpeedUp Iqbator Sp z o o
Gold, Aaron—Carlyle Group LP
Gold, Daniel—Haynes and Boone LLC
Gold, Darren—Gryphon Investors Inc
Gold, David—Access Venture Partners
Gold, David—Morrison & Foerster LLP
Gold, Peter—Archer Capital Pty Ltd
Goldberg, Alan—Lindsay Goldberg & Bessemer LP
Goldberg, Allan—Channel Group LLC, The
Goldberg, Avi—GREATPOINT VENTURES
Goldberg, David—Endeavour Capital Inc
Goldberg, Garrett—Blackstone Group LP

2487

Goldberg, Gary—Saugatuck Capital Co
Goldberg, Jason—Agile Capital Partners
Goldberg, Joel—Pharos Capital Group LLC
Goldberg, Marc—BioVentures Investors
Goldberg, Michael—Bridge Investment Fund LP
Goldberg, Michael—Kelso & Company LP
Goldberg, Michelle—Ignition Ventures Management LLC
Goldberg, Michelle—Ignition Ventures Management LLC
Goldberg, Morey—CMS Mezzanine Fund
Goldberg, Robert—Bridge Investments LLC
Goldberg, Robert—Ridgelift Ventures
Goldberg, Robert—YL Ventures GP Ltd
Goldberg, Sandra—MergerTech Advisors
Goldberg, Ze ev—Compass Partners International LLC
Goldblatt, Brett—Milbank Tweed Hadley & Mccloy LLP
Golde, David—Genstar Capital LLC
Golden, Andrew—Princeton University Investment Co
Golden, Bruce—Accel Partners & Co Inc
Golden, David—Revolution Ventures LLC
Golden, Leslie—Ridgewood Capital Management LLC
Golden, Matt—Golden Venture Partners Inc
Golden, Richard—Alumni Capital Network Management Co LLC
Goldenberg, Adam—CrossCut Ventures Management LLC
Goldenberg, Edward—Bennett Jones Verchere
Goldenberg, Irena—Highland Capital Partners LLC
Goldenberg, Ryan—LLR Partners Inc
Goldenstein, Jonathan—Kingfish Group Inc
Goldfaden, Jeffrey—Warburg Pincus LLC
Goldfarb, Andrew—Globespan Capital Partners
Goldfarb, Andrew—JLL Partners Inc
Goldfarb, Andrew—NexPhase Capital LLC
Goldfarb, Arnon—Israel Cleantech Ventures
Goldfarb, Greg—Summit Partners LP
Goldfein, Jocelyn—Zetta Venture Partners
Goldfeld, Malvina—Battery Ventures LP
Goldfischer, Carl—Bay City Capital LLC
Goldhaber, Nat—Claremont Creek Ventures LP
Goldhirsch, Hagai—Vintage Venture Partners Iv (Cayman) LP
Goldin, Adi—Docor International BV
Goldin, Josh—Alliance Consumer Growth LLC
Golding, Eric—Fundrx Inc
Golding, Gary—Edison Partners
Golding, Gary—Edison Partners
Golding, Jeremy—Golding Capital Partners GmbH
Golding, Jeremy—HCI Private Equity GmbH
Golding, Robert—Star Mountain Capital LLC
Goldinger, James—Fairhaven Capital Partners, L.P.
Goldman, Charles—Mill Road Capital Management LLC
Goldman, Dan—GREATPOINT VENTURES
Goldman, Daniel—Clean Energy Venture Group
Goldman, Jon—Greycroft Partners LLC
Goldman, Josh—Norwest Venture Partners
Goldman, Ken—Westly Group LLC
Goldman, Ronald—Croft & Bender LLC
Goldsmith, Barry—Updata Partners
Goldsmith, Benjamin—Alpina Capital Partners LLP
Goldsmith, Brian—Bain Capital Venture Partners LLC
Goldsmith, Mark—Third Rock Ventures LLC

Goldstein, Aaron—Goldner Hawn Johnson & Morrison Inc
Goldstein, Aaron—Goldner Hawn Johnson & Morrison Inc
Goldstein, Asha—Cedar Hill Associates LLC
Goldstein, Barak—Terra Venture Partners
Goldstein, Bruce—Middlemarch Partners LLC
Goldstein, Dennis—Bain Capital Inc
Goldstein, Dov—Aisling Capital LLC
Goldstein, Edward—Coller Capital Ltd
Goldstein, Gabriel—Tennenbaum Capital Partners LLC
Goldstein, George—SilverStream Capital LLC
Goldstein, Heidi—Altus Capital Partners Inc
Goldstein, Howard—Cortlandt Private Capital LLC
Goldstein, Howard—Vedanta Capital LP
Goldstein, Jeffrey—Hellman & Friedman LLC
Goldstein, Jonathan—Advantage Capital Partners
Goldstein, Jonathan—Southfield Capital Advisors LLC
Goldstein, Jonathan—TA Associates Management LP
Goldstein, Joseph—Column Group
Goldstein, Matthew—Trinity Ventures LLP
Goldstein, Oliver—Pine Brook Road Partners LLC
Goldstein, Richard—Oaktree Capital Management LP
Goldstein, Robert—BlackRock Inc
Goldstein, Robert—Capgen Financial Group LP
Goldstein, Robert—Victory Park Capital Advisors LLC
Goldstein, Ross—Gotham Ventures LLC
Goldstein, Ross—Gotham Ventures LLC
Goldstein, Sandy—Fundamental Advisors LP
Goldstein, Stephen—Evercore Inc
Goldstein, Taryn—Waveland Investments LLC
Goldstein, Wendy—Cooley LLP
Goldwater, Fred—Hatteras Venture Partners
Golenberg, Glenn—Denovo Health Partners LLC
Golinowski, Craig—Jog Capital Inc
Goll, Alexandra—TVM Capital GmbH
Gollenberg, Keith—Oaktree Capital Management LP
Gollmer, Stewart—Tenaya Capital, Inc.
Golson, Brian—Parthenon Capital LLC
Golub, David—Golub Capital Master Funding LLC
Golubieski, James—Foundation Venture Capital Group LLC
Golubovich, Ilya—I2Bf Global Ventures
Golynskaya, Anna—General Atlantic LLC
Gombert, Peter—Neuhaus Partners GmbH
Gomes, Gene—Abacus Private Equity Ltd
Gomes, Henrique—VoiVoda Ventures
Gomez Cobo, Luis—SinoLatin Capital
Gomez Garcia, Daniel—Aser Capital SCR SA
Gomez, Alberto—Adara Venture Partners
Gomez, Carlos—Linzor Capital Partners LP
Gomez, Gabriel—Advent International Corp
Gomez, Gabriel—Defi gestion SA
Gomez, Juan Pablo—Altra Investments
Gomez, Lorenzo—Geekdom LC
Gomez, Santiago—ProA Capital de Inversiones SGEIC SA
Gomez-Zubeldia, Francisco—Diana Capital SGECR SA
Gomm, Read—Evercore Inc
Gona, Pithambar—Blackstone Group LP
Goncalves, Patrician—Empresario Digital
Gondel, Xavier-Jacques—SMG Group SA
Gonen, David—Curious Minds
Gong, Fengtao—Hebei Yanhai Industrial Investment Fund Management Co Ltd

Gong, Jianzhong—BOC International Holdings Ltd
Gong, Lin—Hollyhigh Intl Capital Co Ltd
Gong, Nina—Carlyle Group LP
Gong, Raymond—Oaktree Capital Management LP
Gong, Shumin—HarbourVest Partners LLC
Gong, Yanyan—Vantagepoint Management Inc
Gong, Yuan—Richlink International Capital Co Ltd
Goni, Fernando—Gores Group LLC
Gonsenheim, Eric—Crosslink Capital Inc
Gonso, Harry—Twilight Venture Partners
Gonthier, Alexandre—Wellington Partners GmbH
Gonyo, Jeffrey—Wanxiang America Capital LLC
Gonzales, Daniel—Small Business Guarantee and Finance Corporation
Gonzales, Richard—CIG Securities Inc
Gonzalez del Valle, Martin—Realza Capital SGECR SA
Gonzalez, Alvaro—Altamar Private Equity SGIIC SAU
Gonzalez, Arturo—Morrison & Foerster LLP
Gonzalez, Charles—Albion Investors LLC
Gonzalez, Ken—Trident Capital Cybersecurity Fund I LP
Gonzalez, Luis—MBF Healthcare Partners LP
Gonzalez, Pablo—Sodiex SA
Gonzalez, Rodolfo—Foundation Capital LLC
Gonzalez, William—Sterling Partners GP LLC
Gonzalez-Heres, Jose—Morgan Stanley Alternative Investment Partners LP
Gonzalo, Cecilia—Warburg Pincus LLC
Good, Chris—Cinven Group Ltd
Good, Nathan—Prairie Capital, L.P.
Goodacre, Glenn—Accord Capital Investors Pty Ltd
Goode, Peter—Arle Heritage LLP
Goodell, Bill—Maverick Capital Ltd
Goodhart, Kathleen—Cooley LLP
Goodlett, Clarissa—Black Wall Street Investments LLC
Goodman, Andrew—Colony Capital LLC
Goodman, Bob—Bessemer Venture Partners
Goodman, Corey—Venbio Partners LLC
Goodman, Daniel—Natural Gas Partners
Goodman, Douglas—Equifin Capital Partners
Goodman, Edwin—Activate Venture Partners
Goodman, James—Gemini Investors Inc
Goodman, Jonathan—Bain Capital Inc
Goodman, Mark—Brookline Venture Partners
Goodman, Mark—MassMutual Ventures LLC
Goodman, Mark—Terawatt Ventures LLC
Goodman, Melissa—Haynes and Boone LLC
Goodman, Michael—Wafra Partners LLC
Goodman, Rob—Precision Capital Advisors LLC
Goodman, Saul—Evercore Inc
Goodrich, Jeffrey—High Road Capital Partners LLC
Goodrich, Paul—MadroNA Venture Group
Goodrich, R. Thomas—Duff Ackerman & Goodrich LLC
Goodrich, Sean—Aether Investment Partners LLC
Goodrich, Tom—Stafford Timberland Ltd
Goodsell, Sally—FSE CIC
Goodstein, Marcia—Idealab
Goodwin, Don—Mercury Ventures Ltd
Goodwin, Dustin—Blackstone Group LP
Goodwin, John—Antares Capital Corp
Goodwin, John—DeSimone Group Investments LLC
Goodwin, Jonathan—PROfounders Capital Ltd

Goody, Peter—3i Group PLC
Goolsby, Michelle—Greenmont Capital Partners
Goos, Craig—Biomark Capital
Goossens, Maarten—Anterra Capital BV
Gootee, Ting—Elevate Ventures Inc
Gopal, Ayesha—Elevar Equity Advisors Pvt Ltd
Gopal, Patwardhan—Duke Equity Partners Inc
Goran, Andrea—Phoenix Venture Fund LLC
Gorbach, Eugene—Arsenal Capital Management LLC
Gorbach, Eugene—Arsenal Capital Partners LP
Gorbacheva, Alina—Duet Capital Ltd
Gorchow, Bruce—PPM America Capital Partners LLC
Gorczynski, Brian—Veritas Capital Fund Management LLC
Gord, Steven—Boathouse Capital
Gordan, Patrick—Leader Ventures LLC
Gordijn, Stefan—SAM Private Equity AG
Gordon, Arthur—Canaccord Genuity Group Inc
Gordon, Benjamin—Cambridge Capital LLC
Gordon, Bing—Kleiner Perkins Caufield & Byers LLC
Gordon, Brett—Baml Capital Access Funds Management LLC
Gordon, Chris—Bain Capital Inc
Gordon, David—Catalyst Investors LLC
Gordon, Eric—Skyline Ventures Inc
Gordon, James—Edgewater Funds
Gordon, John—Palladian Capital Partners LLC
Gordon, Jonathan—Stage 1 Ventures LLC
Gordon, M.—AG BD LLC
Gordon, Mark—ONCAP INVESTMENT PARTNERS L P
Gordon, Misha—Bonaventure Capital LLC
Gordon, Mitchell—Morpheus Capital Advisors LLC
Gore, Daniel—Orthogonal Partners LLP
Gore, Jean—Pechel Industries SAS
Gore, Theresa—Clayton Dubilier & Rice LLC
Gorelick, Kenneth—NGN Capital LLC
Goren, Todd—Morrison & Foerster LLP
Gorenberg, Mark—Zetta Venture Partners
Gorenstein, Michael—Cronos Group Inc
Gorevic, Brittany—Lattice Ventures LLC
Gorgi, Habib—Nautic Partners LLC
Gorham, Eric—Farallon Capital Management LLC
Goriainoff, Romee—Neo Investment Partners LLP
Gorin, Matthew—Contour Venture Partners
Gorkov, Evgeney—Bolshoi Management
Gorkov, Evgeniy—Siguler Guff & Company LP
Gorkova, Vita—StepStone Group LP
Gorman, Michael—Split Rock Partners LLC
Gorman, Thomas—Seacoast Capital
Gormin, Jonathan—Owner Resource Group LLC
Gormley, Dave—Beedie Capital Partners
Gormley, Mark—Lee Equity Partners LLC
Gormly, Matthew—Wicks Group of Companies LLC
Goros, Mark—Equip Ventures LLC
Gorski, David—Brown Brothers Harriman & Co
Gorton, David—JFLehman & Co
Goryacheva, Irina—Almaz Capital Partners
Goschin, Jorg—Alternative Strategic Investment GmbH
Goscinski, Andrew—Veronis Suhler Stevenson LLC
Gosline, Tim—Riverside Co
Goss, Horst—BTV Beteiligungsverwaltung GmbH & Co. KG
Goss, Michael—Bain Capital Inc
Goswami, Bobby—ABS Capital Partners, Inc.

Goth, Jay—Forentis Partners LLC
Goto, Yujiro—Whiz Partners Inc
Gotsch, Peter—Ellipse Capital LLC
Gotsch, Peter—Svoboda Capital Partners LLC
Gottdiener, Charles—Providence Equity Partners LLC
Gottesman, Blake—Berkshire Partners LLC
Gottesman, Greg—MadroNA Venture Group
Gottlieb, Adam—Industrial Opportunity Partners LLC
Gottlieb, Jacob—Visium Asset Management LP
Gottschalk, Chris—Blumberg International Partners LLC
Gottschalk, Jennifer—EIV Capital Management Company LLC
Gottwald, Hans—Orlando Management AG
Goucha, Adel—Abraaj Capital Ltd
Gougenheim, Philippe—Unigestion Holding SA
Gough, Jeremy—Graphite Capital Management LLP
Gough, Paul—Star Capital Partners Ltd
Gougne, Arnaud—Republic Alley SA
Gould, Alan—Evercore Inc
Gould, James—LEGEND PARTNERS I L P
Gould, Kevin—CAMCO Private Equity Group
Gould, Paul—Allen & Company of Florida, Inc.
Gould, Terry—Adams Street Partners LLC
Gouled, Mohamed—International Finance Corp
Goulet, Nicolas—Adara Venture Partners
Goundrey, Thomas—Clarion Capital Partners LLC
Gourgey, Bill—Omni Capital Group LLC
Gourlay, Richard—Sussex Place Ventures Ltd
Gouw, Theresia—Aspect Ventures LP
Goux, Ben—Pioneer Venture Partners LLC
Govan, Christopher—Onex Corp
Gowda, Anand—SilverStream Capital LLC
Gowdey, David—Jungle Ventures Pte Ltd
Gowdey, David—Tpg Growth LLC
Gowdy, Jonathan—Morrison & Foerster LLP
Goyal, Alok—Stellaris Venture Partners
Goyal, Anil—Next Orbit Ventures Pvt Ltd
Goyal, Neal—Caldera Venture Partners LLC
Goyal, Prashant—Axon Partners Group Investment
Goyal, Prashant—Forum Synergies India Pe Fund Managers P Ltd
Goyal, Rahul—AEA Investors LLC
Goyal, Sandeep—Jacob Ballas Capital India Pvt Ltd
Goyal, Sunil—YourNest Capital Advisors Pvt Ltd
Goyal, Udayan—Anthemis Group SA
Goyal, Vikas—Sr One Ltd
Gozycki, Michael—Carlyle Group LP
Graber, Christopher—Waud Capital Partners LLC
Graber, Lee—Pacific Road Capital Management Pty Ltd
Graber, Shani—Norwest Mezzanine Partners
Grabherr, Oliver—Gcp Gamma Capital Partners Beratungs & Beteiligungs AG
Grabowsky, Bryan—Juniper Capital Management
Grabowsky, Lou—Juniper Capital Management
Grace, Charles—May River Capital LLC
Grace, Michael—Milbank Tweed Hadley & Mccloy LLP
Gracias, Antonio—Valor Equity Parters L P
Grad, Patricia—Arsenal Capital Partners LP
Gradel, Christopher—Pacific Alliance Group Ltd
Grady, Michael—Spire Capital Partners LP
Grady, Prisca—Icc Venture Capital
Grady, Robert—Gryphon Investors Inc

Graeser, Suzanne—Morrison & Foerster LLP
Graf, A. Jay—New Enterprise Associates Inc
Graf, Beat—WA de Vigier Stiftung
Graff, Michael—Warburg Pincus LLC
Graffagna, Michael—Morrison & Foerster LLP
Graffe, Viviane—BIP Investment Partners SA
Graffner Nordberg, Malin—Innoventus Project AB
Grafstrom, Beth—New Mountain Capital I LLC
Gragg, Joel—Huntington Capital I
Graham Ford, Nancy—Friedman Fleischer & Lowe Cap Ptnrs L P
Graham, Barrie—W R Hambrecht & Co L L C
Graham, Bruce—Infinity Capital LLC
Graham, Chris—Exponent Private Equity LLP
Graham, Drew—Ballast Point Venture Partners LLC
Graham, Eric—TGP Investments LLC
Graham, Hatch—Ata Ventures
Graham, Jim—Sante Ventures
Graham, Kenneth—Inverness Graham Investments
Graham, Mark—Wheelhouse Capital Partners LLC
Graham, Martin—Oaktree Capital Management LP
Graham, Michael—OMERS Private Equity Inc
Graham, Paul—Y Combinator Inc
Graham, Robert—Penn Venture Partners, L.P.
Graham, Rod—Northern Plains Capital Ltd
Graham, Ty—Ignition Capital Partners
Grainger, David—Index Ventures
Gramat, Gilles—Pragma Capital SA
Granatino, Nicolas—Andurance Ventures LLP
Grand, Paul—Research Corporation Technologies
Grand, Ryan—Hammond Kennedy Whitney & Company Inc
Grand-Dufay, Pierre—Tertium SAS
Granger, Philippe—Auriga Partners SA
Granick, Lisa—Fletcher Spaght Ventures LP
Granovsky, Stephen—Grano Retail Investments Inc
Granski, Miki—Coral Ventures Inc
Grant Lang, Laurie—Haynes and Boone LLC
Grant, Charles—Lexington Partners Inc
Grant, Christopher—Salix Ventures LP
Grant, Hamish—Bridgepoint Advisers Ltd
Grant, Ian—August Equity Llp
Grant, Jason—HeadHaul Capital Partners LLC
Grant, Joseph—Bankcap Partners Fund I LP
Grant, Kimberly—Crescent Capital Group LP
Grant, Murray—Actis LLP
Grant, Peter—Stone Arch Capital LLC

Grant, Stuart—Blackstone Group LP
Granville-Smith, Elizabeth—Boston Ventures
Granzer, Ulrich—Wellington Partners GmbH
Grapengiesser, Jacob—East Capital Private Equity AB
Grapkowski, Andrew—Altpoint Ventures LP
Gras, Karine—Sodica SASU
Gras, Karine—Sodica SASU
Grassby, Kevin—Bowmark Capital LLP
Grasselli, Massimo—PM & Partners SpA
Grassgreen, Randi—Crestone Capital LLC
Grasshoff, Sven—Falcon Investment Advisors LLC
Grassl, Walter—MVP Management GmbH
Grauel, Richard—Capital Dynamics Sdn Bhd
Graulich, Benoit—Bencis Capital Partners BV
Gravano, David—Western Technology Investment
Gravely, Timothy—Tennenbaum Capital Partners LLC
Graver, Matthew—Morgan Stanley Alternative Invest-

2489

Pratt's Guide to Private Equity & Venture Capital Sources

ment Partners LP
Graves, James—Bankcap Partners Fund I LP
Graves, Scott—Oaktree Capital Management LP
Gray, Amy—Private Advisors LLC
Gray, Andrew—Archer Capital Pty Ltd
Gray, Brian—Fund Evaluation Group LLC
Gray, Cameron—MDB Capital Group LLC
Gray, Daniel—KPS Capital Partners LP
Gray, Derek—Pentech Ventures LLP
Gray, Gregory—Archipel Capital LLC
Gray, Iain—Technology Strategy Board
Gray, Ian—Candover Investments PLC
Gray, Jacob—Murex Investments, Inc.
Gray, Jeff—Revolution Capital Group LLC
Gray, Laurence—Gray & Co
Gray, Mark—Richardson Capital Ltd
Gray, Richard—Milbank Tweed Hadley & Mccloy LLP
Gray, Samuel—Apposite Capital LLP
Gray, Stephen—Vantagepoint Management Inc
Gray, Timothy—Medimmune LLC
Grayce, David—Pacific Equity Partners Pty Ltd
Grayken, John—Lone Star Fund Ltd
Grayson, Bruns—ABS Ventures
Grayson, Dayna—New Enterprise Associates Inc
Grayson, Gerald—Grayson & Associates Inc
Grayson, Matthew—Aquiline Capital Partners LLC
Grayson, McComma—HarbourVest Partners LLC
Grayver, Leonard—Pulsar Ecosystem LLC
Grayzel, David—Atlas Venture Advisors Inc
Graziano, Chane—Ascent Venture Management Inc
Grazioli, Glenda—Programma 101 Srl
Greathouse, John—RINCON VENTURE PARTNERS L P
Greaves, Karen—Industrial Growth Partners
Grec, Alain—Siparex Proximite Innovation SAS
Greck, Scott—Archer Capital Pty Ltd
Greco, Daniel—Ark Applications LLC
Gredenhoff, Anna—Capital Dynamics Sdn Bhd
Greeley, Michael—Flybridge Capital Partners
Green, Anthony—Ben Franklin Technology Partners Southeastern PA
Green, Charlie—Candover Investments PLC
Green, Conor—TT Capital Partners LLC
Green, Holcombe—Birch Equity Partners LLC
Green, Jason—Emergence Capital Partners
Green, Jeff—Blum Capital Partners LP
Green, Jonathan—Brook Venture Partners LLC
Green, Jonathan—Milbank Tweed Hadley & Mccloy LLP
Green, Joshua—Mohr Davidow Ventures
Green, Justin—Palladium Equity Partners LLC
Green, Ken—Spring Mill Venture Partners
Green, Kevin—TT Capital Partners LLC
Green, Kirsten—Forerunner Ventures LLC
Green, Laurence—Paean Advisors Pty Ltd
Green, Martin—NVM Pe Ltd
Green, Michael—Oak Hill Capital Management Inc
Green, Michael—Tenex Capital Management LP
Green, Mitchell—Ancor Capital Partners
Green, Peter—Morrison & Foerster LLP
Green, Richard—August Equity Llp
Green, Thomas—Ardenton Capital Corp
Green, Timothy—GMT Communications Partners LLP
Greenbarg, Todd—Avenue Capital Group LLC
Greenbaum, Gabe—Pritzker Group Venture Capital
Greenberg, Bart—Haynes and Boone LLC

Greenberg, David—JMI Management Inc
Greenberg, Gregory—Altus Capital Partners Inc
Greenberg, Jeffrey—Aquiline Capital Partners LLC
Greenberg, Martin—Iglobe Treasury Management Ltd
Greenberg, Michael—Acumen Fund Inc
Greenberg, Michael—Vexiom Equity Partners, L.P.
Greenberg, Myles—CHL Medical Partners LP
Greenberg, Russell—Altus Capital Partners Inc
Greendale, Corey—First Analysis Corp
Greene, Adam—Deerfield Management Company LP
Greene, I. Robert—Contour Venture Partners
Greene, Jonathan—Bain Capital Inc
Greene, Kevin—Valhalla Partners LP
Greene, Mark—JDRF International
Greene, Mark—Webster Capital Management LLC
Greene, Michael—AeroEquity Partners LLC
Greene, Richard—TD Capital Group Ltd
Greene, Robert—Syncom Management Co Inc
Greene, Ryan—Stagwell Group LLC
Greene, Sean—Siguler Guff & Company LP
Greene, Stephen—Silverfern Group Inc
Greene, William—MPM Capital LLC
Greenfield, Matt—Rethink Education LP
Greenhalgh, Jeremy—Innervation Capital Partners Ltd
Greenhalgh, Lisa—Merseyside Special Investment Fund Ltd
Greenleaf, Peter—Medimmune LLC
Greenman, Simon—DN Capital Global Venture Capital Ii LP
Greenough, Mark—Monta Vista Capital LP
Greensmith, Anthony—Lyceum Capital
Greenstein, Joe—Four Rivers Partners LP
Greenstein, Julia—JDRF International
Greenwald, Marshall—Symmetry Investment Advisors Inc
Greenwood, Drew—LJ2 & Co LLC
Greenwood, John—TD Capital Group Ltd
Greenwood, Paul—Northern Lights Capital Group LLC
Greer, Billy—Prudential Capital Group LP
Greer, Christopher—Rutberg and Co LLC
Greer, David—Keystone Capital Inc
Greer, Lawrence—Greer Capital Advisors LLC
Greer, Philip—Opus Capital
Greer, Thomas—Fulcrum Equity Partners
Greer, Vickie—Waveland Capital Group LLC
Greff, John—Sequel Venture Partners
Grefsrud, Brian—Oaktree Capital Management LP
Gregg, Terry—Galen Associates Inc
Grego, Gregory—New Asia Partners LLC
Gregor, Alex—Pfingsten Partners LLC
Gregorich, Michael—Stone Point Capital LLC
Gregory, Daniel—Greylock Partners LLC
Gregory, Gordon—Mosaic Capital LLC
Gregory, Jason—Blackstone Group LP
Gregory, Jim—Acas LLC
Gregory, Jonathan—Mobeus Equity Partners LLP
Gregory, Michael—Highland Capital Management LP
Gregory, Tom—Maranon Capital LP
Greif, Michael—Empire Investment Holdings LLC
Greig, Thomas—Liberty Partners Ltd
Grein, Timothy—Platte River Partners LLC
Greitl, Robert—Afinum Management GmbH
Grenny, Joseph—Unitus Impact Partners LLC

Grenon, Jim—TOM Capital Associates Inc
Grenon, Tony—TOM Capital Associates Inc
Gres, Stephane—Capitem Partenaires SAS
Gresham, Zane—Morrison & Foerster LLP
Gretsch, Gregory—Sigma Partners
Greulich, Geoff—Oaktree Capital Management LP
Greve, Frederico—Dgf Investimentos Gestao De Fundos Ltda
Greve, Moritz—Maxburg Capital Partners
Greves, Philip—Elysian Capital LLP
Grevet, Jean-Louis—Perceva SAS
Greville, Roger—Henderson Global Investors Ltd
Grewal, Gurinder—Advent International Corp
Grewal, Mandhir—East Africa Capital Partners
Grewal, Nick—Ascent Venture Management Inc
Grey, Michael—Pappas Ventures
Greyson, Jay—Supply Chain Equity Partners
Griarte, Ghia—Saints Ventures
Gribetz, Eric—Pegasus Capital Advisors LP
Grichnik, Kaj—Gebruder Heller Dinklage
Gridley, Michael—Industry Ventures LLC
Gridley, Mike—Akkadian Ventures LLC
Gridley, Mike—Industry Ventures LLC
Grier, Ross—NextEnergy Capital Ltd
Griest, David—SJF Ventures
Griffin, Carter—Updata Partners
Griffin, Elliott—Business Venture Partners
Griffin, James—Acas LLC
Griffin, Kelly—Gramercy Inc
Griffin, Kevin—Michigan Accelerator Fund I Management LLC
Griffin, Marshall—Comvest Partners
Griffin, Marshall—Comvest Partners
Griffin, Michael—Golub Capital Master Funding LLC
Griffin, Richard—Jabodon PT Co
Griffin, Robert—Open Field Capital LLC
Griffith, Tyler—Thomas H Lee Partners LP
Griffiths, Barry—Landmark Partners Inc
Griffiths, James—Julip Run Capital LLC
Griffor, Jeff—Lighthouse Capital Partners LP
Grigg, Charles—Carousel Capital Partners
Grigg, Jared—Comvest Partners
Grigg, Jared—Comvest Partners
Grigg, John—Fidus Capital LLC
Grigorenko, Irina—Capital International Inc
Grigsby, Brian—Corsa Ventures
Grill, Bennet—Gemspring Capital LLC
Grills, Jeffrey—Gramercy Inc
Grimaldi, Brendyn—Halyard Capital
Grimaldi, Ferdinando—L-Gam Advisers LLP
Grimaldi, Laurent—Breega Capital SARL
Grimes, John—Southwest Middle Market M&A
Grimm, Lutz—newten Ventures GmbH
Grimonprez, Eric—Alliansys SAS
Grimoux, Jean-Pierre—Namur Invest SA
Grimsdale, Charles—Eden Ventures Ltd
Grinker, Sandra—Montgomery & Co LLC
Grinnell, Richard—Fairhaven Capital Partners, L.P.
Grinnell, Rick—Fairhaven Capital Partners, L.P.
Grinstein, Keith—Second Avenue Partners
Grippi, James—Carlyle Group LP
Gripton, John—Capital Dynamics Sdn Bhd
Grishin, Dmitry—Grishin Robotics
Grison, Violaine—PAI Partners SAS
Grissom, Douglas—Madison Dearborn Partners LLC

Griswold, E. Bulkeley–Centripetal Capital Partners LLC
Griswold, Kirk–Argosy Capital Group Inc
Griswold, Kyle–Financial Technology Ventures
Gritsch, Richard–ECM Equity Capital Management GmbH
Gritzfeldt, Ryan–Crescent Point Energy Corp
Grizzelle, Mark–CVC Capital Partners Ltd
Grobbink, Guido–Standard Investment BV
Grobman, Ranan–Jerusalem Global Ventures
Groce, David–Aequitos Capital Management LLC
Grogan, Dale–Michigan Accelerator Fund I Management LLC
Grogan, Linda–Diamond Castle Holdings LLC
Gromada, Grzegorz–MCI Capital SA
Gromo, Gianni–Versant Venture Management, LLC
Gronholm, Reijo–Vaaka Partners Oy
Gronlund, Lasse–Sentica Partners Oy
Groome, Kelsey–Marvin TRAUB LLC
Groos, Ferdinand–Rhone Capital LLC
Groos, Tom–City Light Capital
Gros, Florent–Novartis Venture Funds
Groschopp, Maria–Firm Factory Network AB
Grose, Austin–Shasta Ventures LP
Grosfield, Stephen–Lynx Equity Ltd
Grosman, Doron–Court Square Capital Partners LP
Gross, Arnie–Kilmer Capital Partners Ltd
Gross, Dana–Carmel Ventures IV Principals Fund LP
Gross, Daniel–Pegasus Capital Advisors LP
Gross, David–Persistence Partners, L.P.
Gross, Jorge–Trivest Partners LP
Gross, Larry–Structural Capital GP LLC
Gross, Larry–Terra Venture Partners
Gross, Lauren–Founders Fund, The
Gross, Michael–Beringea LLC
Gross, Stewart–Lightyear Capital LLC
Gross, William–Idealab
Gross-Loh, David–Bain Capital Inc
Grossberg, Erik–Jerusalem Global Ventures
Grosshandler, Richard–Harren Equity Partners
Grosskopf, Peter–Sprott Resource Corp
Grossman, Aron–Gemspring Capital LLC
Grossman, Kevin–Hercules Capital Inc
Grossman, Nathan–Growth Street Management LLC
Grossmann, Benoist–Idinvest Partners SA
Grosz, Andrea–Marquette Capital Partners Inc
Grotenfelt, Martin–Intera Equity Partners Oy
Groth, Ole–JZ Capital Partners Ltd
Groth, Raymond–Axum Capital Partners LLC
Grousbeck, H. Irving–Housatonic Partners Management Co Inc
Grover, Anthony–Indigo Capital LLP
Grover, Anthony–RPM Ventures Management LLC
Grover, Gavin–Morrison & Foerster LLP
Grover, Tony–RPM Ventures Management LLC
Groves, Thomas–AEA Investors LLC
Grovic, Mark–New Markets Venture Partners
Growney, Robert–Edgewater Funds
Groya, Steven–Prairie Capital, L.P.
Grua, Peter–HLM Management Co LLC
Grua, Peter–HLM Management Co LLC
Grub, Werner–Richmond Park Partners LLP
Gruber, Adam–Eos Partners LP
Gruber, Desiree–DGNL Ventures LP
Gruber, Michael–Independence Equity Management LLC
Gruber, Steven–Oak Hill Capital Management Inc
Grubstein, Peter–NGEN Partners LLC
Grudniewicz, Krys–Coller Capital Ltd
Gruenfelder, Klaus–Siemens Venture Capital GmbH
Grumer, Joshua–Crescent Capital Group LP
Grunberg, Gregory–Longitude Capital Management Co LLC
Grunberg, Gregory–Longitude Capital Management Co LLC
Grunberg, Lee–PRIVEQ Capital Funds
Grunditz, Beata–IK Investment Partners Ltd
Grundy, Tony–Morrison & Foerster LLP
Gruner, Harry–JMI Management Inc
Gruninger, Christoph–Awal Bank BSCC
Grunow, Kenneth–Scale Capital ApS
Grunow, Paul–Ecapital Entrepreneurial Partners AG
Gruschka, Martin–Springwater Capital LLC
Grushkin, Jay–Milbank Tweed Hadley & Mccloy LLP
Grutman, Sasha–Middlemarch Partners LLC
Gruzen, Alexander–Corsa Ventures
Grychta, Matthias–Neuhaus Partners GmbH
Grylls, David–Actis LLP
Grytz, Eduardo–Performa Investimentos Ltda
Grzesiak, Witold–Warsaw Equity Management Sp z o o
Gu, Bon Yong–KTB Investment & Securities Co Ltd
Gu, Huaming–Baird Capital
Gu, Jerry–HPEF Capital Partners Ltd
Gu, Jin–Asia Alternatives Management LLC
Gu, John–Spring Mountain Capital LP
Gu, Kai–Shenzhen QF Capital Management Co Ltd
Gu, Kang–Shanghai Dingjia Ventures Co Ltd
Gu, Rongliang–Prime Value Capital Management Ltd
Gu, Yan–Cybernaut (China) Venture Capital Management Co Ltd
Gu, Yeong Gwon–Smilegate Investment Inc
Guagliano, Anthony–Gores Group LLC
Gualmini, Nicola–DVR Capital SpA
Guan, Huaming–Shenzhen Green Pine Capital Partners Co Ltd
Guan, Manjia–Capital Dynamics Sdn Bhd
Guan, Xin–SIG Capital Partners Ltd
Guardiola, Jose–Ecoforest
Gubbay, David–Falconhead Capital LLC
Gubbels, Michael–Whitehorse Liquidity Partners Inc
Guber, Vladimir–4BIO Ventures Management Ltd
Guccione, John–OMERS Infrastructure
Gudaszewski, Wojciech–Quark Ventures LLC
Guddy, James–Linsalata Capital Partners Inc
Gudgeon, Martin–Blackstone Group LP
Gudgin, David–Albion Capital Group LLP
Gueikian, Cesar–Monroe Capital LLC
Guennoun, Anas–Abraaj Capital Ltd
Guenther, Lukas–Wellington Partners GmbH
Guenther, Matthew–Gennx360 Capital Partners LP
Guenther, Ralph–Pantheon Ventures (UK) LLP
Gueorguiev, Stephan–Advent Venture Partners LLP
Guerette, Jacques–Genome Canada
Guericke, Konstantin–Earlybird Venture Capital GmbH & Co KG
Guerin, Brian–Calvert Street Capital Partners Inc
Guerra, Adrian–Capstreet Group LLC
Guerra, Javier–Alpina Capital Partners LLP
Guerreiro de Sousa, Jose–Armilar Venture Partners Sociedade de Capital de Risco SA
Guest, Jonathan–Vision Capital LLP
Gueth, Anton–Burrill & Company
Guez, Yves–Turenne Capital Partenaires SASU
Guff, Andrew–Siguler Guff & Company LP
Guffey, Jeffrey–Enlightenment Capital
Guffey, Lawrence–Blackstone Group LP
Gugl, Johannes–FIDES Business Partner AG
Guha, Indranil–Bain Capital Venture Partners LLC
Guichard, Justin–Oaktree Capital Management LP
Guidolin, Marco–Alcedo Societa di Gestione del Risparmio SpA
Guiley, Shelley–Carlyle Group LP
Guilfoile, Thomas–Highland Capital Partners LLC
Guilford, Mark–Headwaters BD LLC
Guill, Benjamin–White Deer Energy LP
Guillaud, Sebastien–Hera Capital Partners Pte Ltd
Guillaume, Carlos Eduardo–Confrapar Administracao e Gestao de Recursos SA
Guillaumot, Vincent–Archimed SA
Guillemin, Mathieu–Oaktree Capital Management LP
Guillet, Louis-Marie–Bamboo SAS
Guillette, Stephen–Carlyle Group LP
Guimaraes, Aflalo–Invus Group LLC
Guimaraes, Rodrigo–Explorer Investments Sociedade de Capital de Risco SA
Guimond, Julien–Teralys Capital Inc
Guinand, Phil–Permira Advisers LLP
Guinee, John–Constitution Capital Partners LLC
Guinther, David–WISC Partners LP
Guirgis, Sherif–Lion Capital LLP
Guitti, Nelson–Mare Investimentos Ltda
Guiva, Alex–Highlander Partners LP
Gujral, Sanjay–L Catterton Asia
Gul, F. Banu–Is Girisim Sermayesi Yatirim Ortakligi AS
Gul, Fatma–Is Girisim Sermayesi Yatirim Ortakligi AS
Gula, Kurt–Century Park Capital Partners LLC
Gulati, Daniel–Comcast Ventures
Gulati, Maninder–Lightspeed Management Company LLC
Gulati, Mukul–Zephyr Management LP
Gulati, Puneet–Quadrangle Group LLC
Gulati, Richa–Oaktree Capital Management LP
Gulati, Sheila–Tola Capital LLC
Gulati, Sumeet–EQT Funds Management Ltd
Gulati, Vishal–Draper Esprit PLC
Gulati, Vishal–Radiant Capital
Guld, Benny–Internet Ventures Scandinavia
Guldstrand, Lars–Gkl Growth Capital AB
Gulec, Karani–Fiba Kapital Holding AS
Guler, Alp–Carlyle Group LP
Guleri, Tim–Sierra Ventures
Gullans, Steven–Excel Venture Management
Gullen, Matt–Comvest Partners
Gulley, Marc–Altira Group LLC
Gulliver, Kate–Bain Capital Inc
Gulve, Eric–BioGenerator
Gumina, Buddy–Apax Partners LLP
Gummert, Stephan–Bpe Unternehmensbeteiligungen GmbH
Gunawan, Glory–HPEF Capital Partners Ltd

Pratt's Guide to Private Equity & Venture Capital Sources

Gunderson, Maurice–CMEA Development Company LLC
Gunn, Graeme–Sl Capital Partners Llp
Gunn, Howard–Valco Capital Partners Partnership Ltd
Gunn, Patrick–Cooley LLP
Gunner, Paul–Bridgepoint Advisers Ltd
Gunnlaugsson, Gordon–Lakeview Equity Partners LLC
Gunsenheimer, Curt–Iris Capital Management SAS
Gunst, Jeff–Avista Capital Holdings LP
Gunter, Roy–Mobility Ventures LLC
Gunter, Scott–Keystone National Group LLC
Gunterberg, Jacob–Odlander Fredrikson & Co AB
Gunther, Craig–Blade Partners
Gunther, Ryan–HarbourVest Partners LLC
Gunton, James–NJTC Venture Fund
Gunty, Murry–Blackstreet Capital Management LLC
Guo, Bob–Goldenmount Capital International Inc
Guo, Cindy–Ventech SA
Guo, Dong–Sparkland Capital
Guo, Jack–Blue Point Capital Partners LP
Guo, Jian–China Merchants Kunlun Equity Invest Management Co Ltd
Guo, Jiehui–ShenZhen GTJA Investment Group Co Ltd
Guo, Jinrong–Industrial Technology Investment Corp
Guo, Li–CDH China Management Co., Ltd.
Guo, Minglei–Hony Capital Beijing Co Ltd
Guo, Owen–Hony Capital Beijing Co Ltd
Guo, Rong–Fang Group Co Ltd
Guo, Rong–Shanghai Cheng Feng Investment Co Ltd
Guo, Xichu–Xiamen Hongsoft Venture Capital Management Co Ltd
Guo, Young–IDG Capital Partners Inc
Guo, Zhijun–Shanghai Lianxin Investment Management Co Ltd
Gupta, Abhas–Mohr Davidow Ventures
Gupta, Abhas–Wildcat Venture Partners LLC
Gupta, Akhilesh–Blackstone Group LP
Gupta, Alok–HPEF Capital Partners Ltd
Gupta, Amit–Clearwater Capital Partners Cyprus Ltd
Gupta, Amit–NewQuest Capital Advisors HK Ltd
Gupta, Andy–ArcLight Capital Holdings LLC
Gupta, Anju–IvyCap Ventures Advisors Pvt Ltd
Gupta, Ankur–Antares Capital Corp
Gupta, Anupam–StepStone Group LP
Gupta, Arjun–TeleSoft Partners
Gupta, Arun–Accretive LLC
Gupta, Arun–Columbia Capital LP
Gupta, Asheesh–Audax Group, Inc.
Gupta, Ashish–Helion Venture Partners LLC
Gupta, Chandan–GFH Financial Group BSC
Gupta, Girish–Rajasthan Asset Management Co Pvt Ltd
Gupta, Jyoti–Vista Equity Partners LLC
Gupta, Krishna–Romulus Capital LLC
Gupta, Manu–Springstar GmbH
Gupta, Narendra–Nexus Venture Partners
Gupta, Neal–Kiwi Venture Partners LLC
Gupta, Neeraj–Cervin Ventures
Gupta, Pankaj–Acas LLC
Gupta, Rahul–Sonoma Management Partners Pvt Ltd
Gupta, Raj–Flatworld Capital LLC
Gupta, Rakesh–Kiwi Venture Partners LLC
Gupta, Rishi–OrbiMed Advisors LLC
Gupta, Sanjay–Adveq Management AG
Gupta, Shyam–Yaletown Venture Partners
Gupta, Siddhartha–Blackstone Group LP
Gupta, Sonia–IvyCap Ventures Advisors Pvt Ltd
Gupta, TJ–Riveria Investment Group
Gupta, Vikram–IvyCap Ventures Advisors Pvt Ltd
Gupta, Vinod–Everest Investment Management LLC
Gupta, Vishal–Bessemer Venture Partners
Gupta, Vishal–Motilal Oswal Pvt Equity Advisors Pvt Ltd
Gur, Saar–Charles River Ventures LLC
Gurau, Michael–Cei Community Ventures Inc
Gurau, Michael–Clear Venture Partners Inc
Gurevich, Alex–Javelin Venture Partners LP
Gurewitz, Aaron–Roth Capital Partners LLC
Gurgovits, Stephen–Tecum Capital Partners
Gurgovits, Stephen–Tecum Capital Partners
Gurka, Rene–newten Ventures GmbH
Gurley, Bill–Benchmark Capital Management Gesellschaft MBH In Liqu
Gurney, Ryan–Cottonwood Venture Partners LLC
Gurtler, Henrik–Novo Holdings A/S
Gurtner, Geoffrey–Tautona Group Lp
Gurvits, Maxim–Teres Capital OOD Sofia
Gurwitz, Sam–Intervale Capital LLC
Gussarsky, David–Lightspeed Management Company LLC
Gust, Ben–GBS Venture Partners
Gustafson, Mark–Gustafson & Co Inc
Gustainis, Simonas–BaltCap Management Estonia OU
Gustin, Andrew–Platte River Ventures LLC
Gut, Zachary–Summit Partners LP
Gutenberg, Daniel–VI Partners AG
Guthart, Leo–Topspin Partners LP
Guthrie, Brian–Riverside Partners LLC
Guthrie, Donald–Trilogy Equity Partners Llc
Guthrie, George–OLMA Capital Management Ltd
Gutierrez Chapa, Juan Jose–IGNIA Partners LLC
Gutierrez, Alfredo–North Bay Equity Partners
Gutierrez, Eduardo–Development Partners International LLP
Gutierrez, Marcela–Omnimedia Live SA de CV
Gutierrez, Matias–Linzor Capital Partners LP
Gutierrez, Salvador–RETRO VENTURE PARTNERS L P
Gutierrez, Salvador–Western Technology Investment
Gutierrez, Xavier–Clearlake Capital Group LP
Gutin, Boris–Greenhill Capital Partners LP
Gutin, Vladimir–TZP Group LLC
Gutman, Collin–Acceleprise LLC
Gutrich, Peter–Morgan Creek Capital Management LLC
Gutry, Phil–MPM Capital LLC
Guttman, Amir–Aviv Venture Capital, Ltd.
Guttman, Josh–Softbank Capital Partners L P
Guttman, William–Saturn Management LLC
Gutwein, Victor–M25 Group LLC
Guy, Henry–Basset Investment Group LLC
Guyer, David–SV Health Investors LLP
Guzik, Thomas Joseph–All-American Holdings LLC
Guzy, Melissa–Vantagepoint Management Inc
Gwagwa, Lulu–Lereko Investment Holdings Pty Ltd
Gwatkin, Simon–Wesley Clover International Corporation
Gwilliam, Scott–Keystone Capital Inc
Gwilliam, Vincent–Bridgepoint Advisers Ltd
Gwin, Howard–Leaders Funds
Gwin, Howard–OMERS Ventures
Gwirtsman, Charles–KRG Capital Management LP
Gwosden, Laura–Maven Venture Partners
Gwosden, Laura–Red Rock Ventures
Gyani, Mohanbir–Primera Capital
Gygax, Rudolf–Nextech Invest Ltd
HENSHAW, LESLIE–Deerfield Management Company LP
HIRSCH, BRIAN–Tribeca Venture Partners LLC
Ha, Perry–DFJ Athena
Ha, Ryun–Undisclosed Firm
Ha, Tae Hun–DSC Investment Inc
Haab, Larry–InDecatur Ventures LLC
Haabestad, Peter–Guardian Capital Partners
Haag, John–CMEA Development Company LLC
Haak-Frendscho, Mary–Versant Venture Management, LLC
Haan, Bernard–Windspeed Ventures
Haan, Thomas–Michigan Accelerator Fund I Management LLC
Haar, Jacob–Community Investment Management LLC
Haarmann, Oliver–Searchlight Capital Partners LLC
Haas, Alesia–Och-Ziff Capital Management Group LLC
Haas, Clifford–Sigma Partners
Haas, Jan–NXT Capital Venture Finance
Haas, Jonathan–Clarion Capital Partners LLC
Haas, Ken–Abingworth Management Ltd
Haas, Sarah–Level Equity Management LLC
Haas, Tracy–Roark Capital Group Inc
Haavisto, Niko–CapMan Oyj
Haaxman, Remco–Coller Capital Ltd
Haaz, Jennifer–Carlyle Group LP
Haber, Douglas–Thomas H Lee Partners LP
Haber, Warren–Founders Equity, Inc.
Haberkorn, Charles–Stonehenge Growth Capital LLC
Habermann, Jan–Credo Ventures as
Habib, Elie–Abraaj Capital Ltd
Habib, Michel–Agate Medical Investments LP
Habibi, Ramzi–Oaktree Capital Management LP
Habichler, Juergen–Mountain Cleantech AG
Habicht, F. Henry–SAIL Capital Partners LLC
Habicht, F. Henry–SAIL Capital Partners LLC
Habiger, David–Pritzker Group Venture Capital
Habstritt, Brett–Shoreview Industries
Hachimura, Tsuyoshi–Itochu Corp
Hackett, James–Riverstone Holdings LLC
Hackett, Patrick–Warburg Pincus LLC
Hackett, Shane–Looking Glass Partners LLC
Hackler, Kevin–Castlelake LP
Hacohen, Yochai–Fortissimo Captial Fund Israel LP
Hadani, David–Crossroads Liquidating Trust
Hadass, Leon–Pantheon Ventures (UK) LLP
Haddad, David–Olympus Partners
Haddad, Philip–Mubadala Infrastructure Partners Ltd
Haddock, John–Castle Harlan Aus Mezzanine
Hadibhai, Aly–Clearspring Capital Partners
Hadjis, Alexander–Morrison & Foerster LLP

Hadjnaceur, Abderrahmen—INTERNATIONAL MAGHREB MERCHANT
Hadl, John—U.S. Venture Partners
Hadley, Charles—CHP Management Inc
Hadley, Chris—Berkshire Partners LLC
Hadley, Michael—Carlyle Group LP
Hadzic, Edin—Paragon Partners GmbH
Haedt, Susan—Thomas Mcnerney and Partners LLC
Haeger, Kent—High Street Capital
Haegg, Lars—CVC Capital Partners Ltd
Hafeez, Qayyum—Odeon Capital Partners LP
Haffar, Sam—Real Ventures
Haffner, Bill—Antares Capital Corp
Haft, Jay—CN Private Equity Partners
Haft, Robert—Morgan Noble LLC
Hagan, Andrea—Flexis Capital LLC
Hagan, Kjell—VI Partners
Hagan, Michael—Hawk Capital Partners LP
Hagberg, Karen—Morrison & Foerster LLP
Hagedorn, John—Formative Ventures
Hagen, Erik—Viking Venture As
Hagenah, Pamela—Integral Capital Partners
Hagenbuche, Carsten—Investcorp Bank BSC
Hager, Henry—KKR & Co LP
Hagerman, Jocelyn—Skypoint Ventures LLC
Hagerman, Philip—Skypoint Ventures LLC
Hagerty, John—Anthos Capital LP
Hagerty, Laurence—Boston Millennia Partners LP
Hagerty, Thomas—Thomas H Lee Partners LP
Haggenmuller, Bernd—Ardian France SA
Haggerty, William—Natcity Investments Inc
Haggis, Iain—Innova Capital Sp z o o
Hagglund, Kaj—Sponsor Capital Oy
Haghgooie, Anna—Sandbox Industries LLC
Hagopian, Joanne—Hall Capital Partners LLC
Hahn, Elana—Morrison & Foerster LLP
Hahn, Eugene—JLL Partners Inc
Hahn, James—JC Asia Alpha Private Equity
Hahn, John—Providence Equity Partners LLC
Hahn, Maria—Liberty Ventures Inc
Hahn-Petersen, Jens—Catacap Management A/S
Hahn-Petersen, Vilhelm—Catacap Management A/S
Hai, Yusuf—CIG Securities Inc
Haiching, Zhao—Corstone Corp
Haidar, Youssef—TVM Capital GmbH
Haigh, Brantley—Ventana Capital Management LP
Haigh, Byron—DOCOMO Innovations Inc
Haikio, Marko—Suomen Teollisuussijoitus Oy
Haims, Joel—Morrison & Foerster LLP
Hain, J. Travis—Ridgemont Partners Management LLC
Haindl, Philipp—Serafin Unternehmensgruppe GmbH
Haines, Jake—Pacific Equity Partners Pty Ltd
Haines, Marshall—Symphony Technology Group LLC
Haines, Timothy—Abingworth Management Ltd
Hainguerlot, Bertrand—Pechel Industries SAS
Haisch, Robert—Charterhouse Group Inc
Haivas, Irina—GHO Capital Partners LLP
Hajarnavis, Heramb—Sealink Capital Partners
Haji-Touma, Raja—Corsair Capital LLC
Hajjaji, Haykel—Global Emerging Markets
Hajostek, John—Gen7 Investment LLC
Hakes, Luke—Octopus Ventures Ltd
Hakim, Ben—Blackstone Group LP

Halak, Brian—Domain Associates LLC
Halbout, Jerome—4D Global Energy Advisors SAS
Halbye, Steen—Pre-Seed Innovation A/S
Haldea, Rohan—Apax Partners LLP
Hale, James—Argentum Group LLC
Hale, James—Financial Technology Ventures
Hale, James—Parallax Capital Partners LLC
Hale, John—Perella Weinberg Partners LP
Hale, Lisa—Parallax Capital Partners LLC
Hale, Martin—Hale Fund Management, L.P.
Hale, Mike—Parallax Capital Partners LLC
Hale, Randall—Rock Hill Capital Group LLC
Hale, Robert—Copley Equity Partners LLC
Haleva, Selmi—Stratejik Yonetim Hizmetleri AS
Haley, Chris—01 Ventures LLP
Haley, Eric—OMERS Private Equity Inc
Haley, Eric—Resonetics LLC
Haley, Timothy—Redpoint Ventures
Halimi, Laurent—Weinberg Capital Partners SAS
Hall, Alan—Mercato Management LLC
Hall, Carl—Alder
Hall, Colin—Rhone Capital LLC
Hall, David—Newable Investments Ltd
Hall, David—Revolution
Hall, Eric—mc3 ventures (FKA: McKenna Venture Accelerator (MVA))
Hall, Fraser—Vancouver Founder Fund
Hall, Garrett—JLL Partners Inc
Hall, Geoff—Antares Capital Corp
Hall, Gregory—Blackstone Group LP
Hall, James—Key Capital Partners
Hall, Jason—DeltaPoint Capital Management LLC
Hall, Jeffrey—Caribbean Equity Partners Ltd
Hall, John—Horizon Ventures
Hall, Jonathan—Mulverhill Associates
Hall, Joshua—Calvert Street Capital Partners Inc
Hall, Justin—Golden Gate Ventures Pte Ltd
Hall, Mark—Graphite Capital Management LLP
Hall, Matthew—Biocrossroads
Hall, Matthew—Market Square Equity Partners
Hall, Michael—Yukon Partners Management LLC
Hall, Milo—FII Capital Partners LLC
Hall, Samuel—Apple Tree Partners
Hall, Steve—Lilly Ventures Management Company LLC
Hall, Steven—Vulcan Inc
Hall, Timothy—CI Capital Partners LLC
Hall, Tom—Apax Partners LLP
Hall, W. Bradley—Headwaters BD LLC
Hall, W. Tompie—HandsOn3 LLC
Hall, William—Align Capital LLC
Hall, William—Lincolnshire Management Inc
Hallahane, Dennis—Compass Investment Management Ltd
Halldorsson, Floki—Stefnir Asset Management Company hf
Haller, Mark—Sumeru Equity Partners, L.P.
Hallert, Asa—EQT Funds Management Ltd
Hallett, Bruce—Miramar Venture Partners L P
Hallett, Cheryl—North Atlantic Capital
Halliday, Sarah—New York Business Development Corp
Hallisey, William—NewWorld Capital Group LLC
Halliwell, Stephen—3i Group PLC
Halliwell, Stephen—3i Infrastructure PLC

Hallman, Jonathan—Haynes and Boone LLC
Hallock, Bradley—Compass Capital Services Inc
Halloran, Patrick—Wayzata Investment Partners LLC
Hallweger, Matthias—Alfred Wieder AG
Halow, James—Calera Capital Management Inc
Halperin, Ariel—Tene Kibbutz Investment Management Ltd
Halpin, Christopher—Providence Equity Partners LLC
Halpin, Kevin—DeltaPoint Capital Management LLC
Halsall, Andrew—Palace Ventures Ltd
Halsted, John—Pamplona Capital Management LLP
Halsted, Scott—Saints Ventures
Halstedt, Steven—Centennial Ventures Vii L P
Halstenberg, Dominik—Lion Capital LLP
Haltia, Olli—Dasos Capital Oy
Halverson, Eric—Augment Ventures Fund I LP
Halverson, Eric—Qualitas Equity Partners Sgecr SA
Halvey, Mary—Bay Capital Investment Partners LLC
Ham, Ji—CN Private Equity Partners
Hamade, Sami—Aberdare Ventures
Hamade, Sami—Apple Tree Partners
Hamadouche, Alexandre—Abraaj Capital Ltd
Hamamoto, Hidetsugu—Mitsubishi UFJ Capital Co Ltd
Hamann, Martijn—Van Den Ende & Deitmers BV
Hamberg, Britney—River Cities Capital Fund LP
Hambrett, Bruce—Baker & McKenzie LLP
Hambro, Rupert—Hambro Perks Ltd
Hamdani, Ahmed—Bayside Capital Inc
Hamdouni, Brahim—Republic Alley SA
Hamed, Ali—Coventure LLC
Hamel, John—Cue Ball Group LLC
Hamelsky, Lawrence—Berkshire Partners LLC
Hamerslag, Steven—TVC Capital LLC
Hamid, David—OpCapita LLP
Hamid, Mamoon—Kleiner Perkins Caufield & Byers LLC
Hamid, Mamoon—Social+Capital Partnership
Hamill, Leo—Investec Ventures Ireland Ltd
Hamilton, Alistair—Inflexion PLC
Hamilton, Charles—KRG Capital Management LP
Hamilton, Douglas—Hamilton Investments Inc
Hamilton, Fred—Cirrus Investment Partners LLC
Hamilton, Jacki—BC Partners LLP
Hamilton, Jennifer—Phase4 Ventures Ltd
Hamilton, Julie—Alaska Permanent Fund Corp
Hamilton, Mark—RB Webber and Comapny Inc
Hamilton, Matthew—Summit Partners LP
Hamilton, Matthew—Summit Partners LP
Hamilton, Philip—Gemcorp Capital LLP
Hamilton, Thomas—Cirrus Investment Partners LLC
Hamilton, Todd—Bolder Capital LLC
Hamiyeh, Nagi—Temasek Holdings (Private) Ltd
Hamlin, Geoffrey—Cartesian Capital Group LLC
Hamlin, Lauren—Merit Capital Partners IV LLC
Hammad, Saad—Gores Group LLC
Hamman, John—PointBreak Private Equity
Hammarskjold, Philip—Hellman & Friedman LLC
Hammarskjold, Philip—Hellman & Friedman LLC
Hammer, Jan—Index Ventures
Hammermann, Peter—Equistone Partners Europe Ltd
Hammerschlag, Nick—General Atlantic LLC
Hammond, Alastair—Enercap Capital Partners
Hammond, Chris—Green Manning & Bunch Ltd
Hammond, Kevin—JLL Partners Inc

Hammond, Matthew–Mail.Ru Group Ltd
Hammond, Nigel–Vespa Capital LLP
Hammond, Peter–Exto Partners Pty Ltd
Hammons, Michael–SAIL Capital Partners LLC
Hammons, Michael–SAIL Capital Partners LLC
Hammontree, Casey–Tenth Street Capital Partners LLC
Hamner, Brad–Antares Capital Corp
Hamner, Patrick–Patriot Capital Funding Inc
Hamner, Scott–AlpInvest Partners BV
Hampp, Wes–First Capital Partners LLC
Hampton, Anthony–Tate & Lyle PLC
Hampton, Philip–Haynes and Boone LLC
Hamrick, L. Watts–Pamlico Capital Management LP
Hamwee, Robert–New Mountain Capital I LLC
Han, Allen–CVC Asia Pacific Ltd
Han, Allen–CVC Capital Partners Ltd
Han, Christina–Morgan Stanley Alternative Investment Partners LP
Han, Daniel–Wellspring Capital Management LLC
Han, David–One Equity Partners LLC
Han, Edward–Bain Capital Inc
Han, Herry–Lightspeed Management Company LLC
Han, Jun–ZEVC Management Co Ltd
Han, Ronald–Harbinger Venture Management
Han, Yuze–Shanghai NewMargin Ventures Co Ltd
Han, Zaiwu–Shenzhen Cornerstone of Entrepreneurial Cci Capital Ltd
Hanafi, Ammar–Alloy Ventures Inc
Hanan, Lars–Broadoak Capital Partners LLC
Hanau, Ken–3i Group PLC
Hanau, Kenneth–3i
Hanauer, Nicolas–Second Avenue Partners
Hance, Carol–Longuevue Capital
Hance, Carol–STRATEGIC ADVISORY GROUP INC
Hance, Pierce–STRATEGIC ADVISORY GROUP INC
Hancock, Robert–Sands Capital Management LLC
Hancock, Thomas–Nexus Medical Partners
Hand, Jeremy–Lyceum Capital
Hand, Justin–Provident Healthcare Partners
Handeland, Arne–Verdane Capital Advisors AS
Handelsman, Karl–CMEA Development Company LLC
Handle, Manfred–FIDES Business Partner AG
Handler, Aaron–Elm Creek Partners
Handler, David–Centerview Partners LLC
Handy, Alice–Investure LLC
Hane, Werner–Aralon AG
Hanetho, Ellen–Oderc AS
Haney, Joel–Pegasus Capital Advisors LP
Hanford, Timothy–JC Flowers & Co LLC
Hangen, Jack–Blu Venture Investors LLC
Hanham, Ann–Burrill & Company
Hanhausen, Ernesto–Emerging Energy & Environment LLC
Hanington, Mark–Find Invest Grow Ltd
Hanke, Thomas–Heliad Equity Partners GmbH & Co KGaA
Hankins, Matt–Sterling Partners GP LLC
Hanks, Christopher–Coulton Creek Capital LLC
Hanna, Christopher–Electra Private Equity Plc
Hanna, Nej–Morgan Stanley Alternative Investment Partners LP
Hanna, Stephen–Stonebridge Partners LP
Hanna, Walid–Middle East Venture Partners

Hanna, William–California Technology Ventures LLC
Hanna, William–Jacobs Capital Group LLC
Hannah, Josh–Matrix Partners, L.P.
Hannah, Lynn–British Columbia Investment Management Corp
Hannan, Stephen–Evercore Inc
Hanneman, William–Zachary Scott & Co
Hannon, Robert–Quabbin Capital Inc
Hanrahan, Lauren–Milbank Tweed Hadley & Mccloy LLP
Hanrahan, Marc–Milbank Tweed Hadley & Mccloy LLP
Hansch, Neal–Rustic Partners LP
Hansch, Neal–Saints Ventures
Hansen, Al–Signet Healthcare Partners
Hansen, Andrew–137 Ventures LP
Hansen, Carl–CVC Capital Partners Ltd
Hansen, Casper Tind–Novo Holdings A/S
Hansen, Eric–Antares Capital Corp
Hansen, Glenn–Oneaccord Capital LLC
Hansen, Jeffrey–Jh Partners LLC
Hansen, Jens Thoger–Capidea Management ApS
Hansen, John–Jh Partners LLC
Hansen, Kai–Rheingau Founders GmbH
Hansen, Nico–Apax Partners LLP
Hansen, Robert–Vector Capital Management LP
Hansen, Sven–Zouk Capital LLP
Hansing, Axel–Coller Capital Ltd
Hanson, Chris–Battery Ventures LP
Hanson, Craig–Next World Capital LLC
Hanson, Dwight–Treetop Ventures Inc
Hanson, Eric–Berggruen Holdings Inc
Hanson, Eric–San Joaquin Capital LLC
Hanson, Jeff–Ohio Innovation Fund
Hanson, Karen–Moneta Capital Partners Ltd
Hanson, Mark–Genstar Capital LLC
Hanson, Matt–Blu Venture Investors LLC
Hanson, Vivian–Morrison & Foerster LLP
Hanssens, Christopher–Eureka Growth Capital
Hansson, Peter–Nordic Capital
Hanton, Karen–PROfounders Capital Ltd
Hanzel, David–X/Seed Capital Management
Hanzl, Radan–Genesis Capital sro
Hao, Fan–Shaanxi Zenisun Venture Capital Co Ltd
Hao, Kenneth–Silver Lake Partners LP
Hao, Qing–Shenzhen Lihe Qingyuan Venture Capital Management Co., Ltd.
Hao, Wei–Lightspeed Management Company LLC
Hapgood, Kallie–Gridiron Capital LLC
Haque, Adil–Apax Partners LLP
Haque, Promod–Norwest Venture Partners
Hara, Benjamin–BC Partners LLP
Hara, Steve–New World Angels, Inc.
Harada, Kenichi–J-STAR Co Ltd
Harar, Joseph–Telecommunications Development Fund
Harbach, Jeff–Velocity Venture Capital Inc
Harbin, Katherine–Source Capital LLC
Harbin, Thomas–Source Capital LLC
Hardeman, Kelly–Insight Venture Partners LLC
Harder, Tom–Pecuniano GmbH
Hardes, Bernd–Econa AG
Hardie, Donald–Kidd & Company LLC
Hardin, Elizabeth–Milbank Tweed Hadley & Mccloy LLP

Harding, Edward–JPB Partners LLC
Harding, Mikel–CapitalWorks LLC
Harding, William–Vantagepoint Management Inc
Harding, William–Vantagepoint Management Inc
Hardman, E. Davisson–Warburg Pincus LLC
Hardt, Ulrich–Headway Capital Partners LLP
Hardy, Marc–Gray & Co
Hardymon, G. Felda–Bessemer Venture Partners
Hare, Matthew–Huron Capital Partners LLC
Hare, Steve–Apax Partners LLP
Hareid, Jan-Erik–Alliance Venture AS
Harel, Boaz–Catalyst Investments LP
Harel, Ittai–Pitango Venture Capital Management Israel, Ltd.
Harford, Mark–Vitruvian Partners LLP
Harford, Simon–Actis LLP
Hargest, Brittany–Greenspring Associates Inc
Hargreaves, Richard–Endeavour Ventures Ltd
Hariharan, Anand–NBK Capital Partners Ltd
Harinarayan, Venky–Cambrian Ventures Inc
Hariri, Amin–GI Partners
Haritakis, Nikolaos–New Economy Development Fund SA
Haritos, Dean–Small World Group Incubator Pte Ltd
Harkness, Jason–Piper Jaffray Ventures Inc
Harknett, Daniel–J.H. Whitney & Co LLC
Harland, Bonnie–Pouschine Cook Capital Management LLC
Harland, Deborah–Sr One Ltd
Harleaux, Antoine–Finorpa PP SAS
Harman, C. Alexander–JFLehman & Co
Harman, Frederic–Oak Investment Partners
Harman, Jeri–Avante Mezzanine Inc
Harmetz, Lloyd–Morrison & Foerster LLP
Harmon, Michael–G3W Ventures LLC
Harmon, Michael–Oaktree Capital Management LP
Harms, W.B.–Global Leisure Partners Llc
Harmsel, Willem–EVO Venture Partners
Harmsen, A.Th.–Antea Participaties Management BV
Harmsen, Josh–Solis Capital Partners LLC
Harmsen, Sven–BASF Venture Capital GmbH
Harned, Carter–Leeds Equity Advisors Inc
Harned, Christopher–Arbor Private Investment Co LLC
Harned, Christopher–Cypress Advisors, L.P.
Harnett, Matt–Tecum Capital Partners
Harnish, Eric–Gores Group LLC
Haroon, Ali–Varde Partners Inc
Harper, Christopher–Baird Capital
Harper, David–Haynes and Boone LLC
Harper, Hugh–Towerbrook Capital Partners LP
Harper, John–Duke Street Capital Ltd
Harper, John–Morrison & Foerster LLP
Harper, Jonathan–Proprium Capital Partners LP
Harper, Marc–West Partners LLC
Harper, Neil–Morgan Stanley Alternative Investment Partners LP
Harper, Robert–Blackstone Group LP
Harper, Ryan–Welsh Carson Anderson & Stowe
Harper, Scott–Primus Capital
Harpster, Richard–Svoboda Capital Partners LLC
Harray, Stuart–Milbank Tweed Hadley & Mccloy LLP
Harrel, Nathan–Monroe Capital LLC
Harrell, Douglas–Fund Evaluation Group LLC

Harrell, Erin—Spectrum Healthcare Fund LLC
Harrick, Stephen—Institutional Venture Partners
Harrigan, Todd—Intuitive Venture Partners LLC
Harriman, Gregory—BioAdvance
Harring, Carl—HIG Capital LLC
Harrington, Jack—Brentwood Capital Advisors LLC
Harrington, Jon—Omni Capital Group LLC
Harrington, Rupert—Advent Private Capital Pty Ltd
Harrington, Todd—CIT Group Inc
Harrington, Tony—Oaktree Capital Management LP
Harrington, William—Osage Venture Partners
Harris Millhauser, Lisa—TA Associates Management LP
Harris, Andrew—Forum Capital Partner
Harris, Anne-Marie—Bridges Fund Management Ltd
Harris, Arlan—Mobility Ventures LLC
Harris, Bill—Buckhead Investment Partners LLC
Harris, Calvin—IECP Fund Management LLC
Harris, Christopher—Imperial Capital Corp
Harris, Daniel—Carlyle Group LP
Harris, Duane—LFE Capital LLC
Harris, Duane—Next Level Ventures LLC
Harris, Elaine—Gramercy Private Equity LLC
Harris, George—Morrison & Foerster LLP
Harris, Ian—Sl Capital Partners Llp
Harris, Jane—Probitas Partners Inc
Harris, Joseph—Trillium Group LLC
Harris, Joshua—Apollo Global Management LLC
Harris, Keith—Bain Capital Inc
Harris, Lauren—Northleaf Capital Partners Ltd
Harris, Lisa—Align Capital LLC
Harris, Mark—Avenue Capital Group LLC
Harris, Mark—Carlyle Group LP
Harris, Mark—Northgate Capital LLC
Harris, Matt—Borealis Ventures
Harris, Matt—Dove Capital Partners LLC
Harris, Matthew—Bain Capital Venture Partners LLC
Harris, Matthew—Global Infrastructure Holdings
Harris, Melanie—Tailwind Capital Partners LP
Harris, Michael—Core Innovation Capital I LP
Harris, Michael—Rutland Partners LLP
Harris, Nick—Lexington Partners Inc
Harris, Peter—Generation Investment Management LLP
Harris, Peter—University Venture Fund
Harris, Richard—Tricor Pacific Founders Capital Inc
Harris, Ryan—Norwest Venture Partners
Harris, Simon—W Capital Management LLC
Harris, Steven—Committed Capital, Ltd.
Harris, Steven—Frontier Capital LLC
Harris, Timothy—Morrison & Foerster LLP
Harris, Tom—Haynes and Boone LLP
Harris, Walter—Mill Creek Capital Advisors LLC
Harris-Koizumi, Satoshi—Battery Ventures LP
Harrison, Alexander—Princeton Ventures Management LLC
Harrison, Bradley—Scout Ventures LLC
Harrison, Donny—Ridgemont Partners Management LLC
Harrison, Grant—Wilshire Private Markets
Harrison, John—Harbert Management Corp
Harrison, Justin—Boston Ventures
Harrison, Matthew—Wellspring Capital Management LLC
Harrison, Michael—First Analysis Corp

Harrison, Peter—Schroders PLC
Harrison, Seth—Apple Tree Partners
Harrison, Thomas—Colony Capital LLC
Harrison, Thomas—Invision Capital Management LLC
Harroch, Richard—Vantagepoint Management Inc
Harrod, Hugo—MVM Partners LLP
Harrop, Bradley—C3 Capital LLC
Hart, Christopher—KLH Capital LP
Hart, James—50 South Capital Advisors LLC
Hart, Jason—Carlyle Group LP
Hart, Jay—Crossharbor Capital Partners
Hart, Jeff—Ringleader Ventures LLC
Hart, Karen—TSG Consumer Partners, L.P.
Hart, Rob—Telegraph Hill Partners
Hart, Scott—StepStone Group LP
Hartch, Timothy—Brown Brothers Harriman & Co
Harth, Oliver—BERENBERG-BALKAN-BALTIKUM-UNIVERSAL-FONDS
Hartley, Neil—First Reserve Corp
Hartman, Christopher—Topanga Partners LP
Hartman, David—Blackstreet Capital Management LLC
Hartman, Steven—Levine Leichtman Capital Partners Inc
Hartmann, Philipp—Rheingau Founders GmbH
Hartnett, Kevin—Brynwood Partners L.P.
Hartong, Hendrik—Brynwood Partners L.P.
Hartstone, Joel—Stonegate Capital Group LLC
Hartung, Steffen—Mittelstaendische Beteiligungsgesellschaft MV mbH
Hartwig, David—Sapphire Ventures LLC
Harvela, Jussi—Veturi Growth Partners Oy
Harvey MacKissack, Luis Alberto—Nexxus Capital SA de CV
Harvey, Alex—Macquarie Group Ltd
Harvey, Claire—TPH Partners LLC
Harvey, Colin—Iglobe Treasury Management Ltd
Harvey, David—Coburn Ventures LLC
Harvey, Kevin—Benchmark Capital Management Gesellschaft MBH In Liqu
Harvey, Michael—Ontario Centres of Excellence
Harvey, Nicholas—Shiprock Capital LLC
Harvey, Paul—Abbey Road Venture Ltd
Harvey, R. Burton—Claritas Capital LLC
Harvey, Warren—Gramercy Inc
Harward, Seth—Frontier Capital LLC
Harward, Seth—Frontier Capital LLC
Hasan, Kamil—Granite Hill Capital Partners LLC
Hasan, Ramiz—Samena Capital Management LLP
Hasan, Talat—Granite Hill Capital Partners LLC
Hasan, Tas—Deerpath Capital Management LP
Hascak, Jaroslav—Penta Investments Ltd
Hascoet, Gerard—Sofinnova Partners SAS
Hase, Peter—Auster Capital Partners LLC
Hasebroock, Mark—Dundee Venture Capital
Hasegawa, Hirokazu—Global Venture Capital Inc
Hasegawa, Tomohiko—Global Venture Capital Inc
Hasegawa, Tsuneo—Daiwa Corporate Investment Co Ltd
Haselsteiner, Robert—HW Capital GmbH
Hashkes, Yoni—Jerusalem Global Ventures
Hass, Anthony—KKR & Co LP
Hass, John—RRE Ventures LLC
Hassan, Aatif—August Equity Llp
Hassan, Fred—Warburg Pincus LLC

Hassan, Hass—Greenmont Capital Partners
Hassan, Huwaida—Siguler Guff & Company LP
Hassanally, Amyn—Coller Capital Ltd
Hassanein, Ossama—Newbury Ventures
Hassanein, Ryan—Morrison & Foerster LLP
Hassanein, Tamer—Newbury Ventures
Hasse, Joseph—Calvert Street Capital Partners Inc
Hassel, Robert—Summit Partners LP
Hassel, Shawn—Bestige Holdings LLC
Hassell, Robert—Summit Partners LP
Hassmann, Steve—Texas Next Capital LP
Hasson, Neil—Investcorp Bank BSC
Hastings, Mark—Garvin Hill Capital Partners LLC
Haswell, Robert—Dominus Capital LP
Hatakeyama, Naoko—New Horizon Capital Co Ltd
Hatch, Aris—Baml Capital Access Funds Management LLC
Hatch, Aris—Grosvenor Capital Management LP
Hatch, Aris—HarbourVest Partners LLC
Hatch, Robert—Constitution Capital Partners LLC
Hatcher, Krista—Chicago Pacific Founders Fund LP
Hatcher, Mary—glendonTodd Capital LLC
Hatfield, Mark—Fairhaven Capital Partners, L.P.
Hathaway, John—Topanga Partners LP
Hathi, Nirav—Richmond Park Partners LLP
Hattangdi, Ajay—Innoven Capital India Pvt Ltd
Hau, Bosun—MVM Partners LLP
Hau, Sandor—Charlesbank Capital Partners LLC
Haubenstricker, Thomas—GoldPoint Partners LLC
Haubold, Etienne—European Capital Financial Services Ltd
Haug, Andreas—e.ventures
Haug, Andreas—eVenture Capital Partners GmbH
Hauge, Martin—Creandum AB
Haughian, Andrew—Pangaea Ventures Ltd
Haugland, Olav—Kistefos Venture Capital As
Hauncher, Scott—Superior Capital Partners LLC
Hausberg, William—Gridiron Capital LLC
Hauser, Felix—Bain Capital Inc
Hauser, Hermann—Amadeus Capital Partners Ltd
Hauser, Mark—LEGEND PARTNERS I L P
Hauser, Mark—Tamarix Capital Corp
Hausler, Greg—Probitas Partners Inc
Hausman, Joel—Crosslink Capital Inc
Hausman, Jonathan—Ontario Teachers' Pension Plan
Hausman, Joshua—Onex Corp
Hausman, Ken—Mirador Capital
Haussler, Jakki—Adena Ventures
Hautin, Herve—Alpha Group
Havas, Krisztina—Bancroft Group Ltd
Haw, Dustin—Clarke Inc
Hawes, Dudley—Anterra Capital BV
Hawes, Dudley—Yellow&Blue Investment Management BV
Hawes, Tom—Sandbox Industries LLC
Hawkins, Anne—Great Hill Equity Partners LLC
Hawkins, David—CHS Capital LLC
Hawkins, David—Shorehill Capital LLC
Hawkins, John—Sterling Group LP
Hawkins, Michele—Fort Washington Capital
Hawkins, Peter—Oakstone Venture Partners LLC
Hawkins, Richard—Spindletop Capital Management LLC
Hawkins, Tom—Forte Ventures
Hawks, Donald—Brookside International

Pratt's Guide to Private Equity & Venture Capital Sources

Hawks, Randy–Claremont Creek Ventures LP
Hawley, Frank–Saugatuck Capital Co
Hawley, Stuart–Saugatuck Capital Co
Hawley, Wallace–Anthos Capital LP
Hawman, Chris–Canada Pension Plan Investment Board
Hawn, Van–Goldner Hawn Johnson & Morrison Inc
Hawn, Van–Goldner Hawn Johnson & Morrison Inc
Hawryluk, P. Kent–Twilight Venture Partners
Hay, Alexander–RJD Partners Ltd
Hay, Stewart–SL Capital Partners Llp
Hayakawa, Masato–Morrison & Foerster LLP
Hayama, Paul–Avante Mezzanine Inc
Hayase, Jun–Rising Japan Equity Inc
Hayase, Makiko–Integral Corp
Hayashi, Satoru–Carlyle Group LP
Hayashi, Shunsa–Ant Capital Partners Co Ltd
Hayashi, Tatsuya–Unison Capital, Inc.
Hayashi, Tetsujiro–Innovation Engine Inc
Hayat, Philippe–Serena Capital SAS
Haydel, Marcia–Performance Equity Management LLC
Hayden, Gideon–Leaders Funds
Hayden, Parker–Carlyle Group LP
Hayden, Tim–Stadia Ventures LLC
Hayes, Anne–Riverside Co
Hayes, Brendan–Millstein & Co LP
Hayes, Brooke–Milestone Partners LP
Hayes, Dan–Saybrook Capital LLC
Hayes, David–Natural Gas Partners
Hayes, Frank–Wynnchurch Capital Ltd
Hayes, John–Great Hill Equity Partners LLC
Hayes, Kevin–Mcm Capital Partners L P
Hayes, Kevin–Weston Presidio Capital
Hayes, Luke–Craton Equity Partners LLC
Hayes, Michael–Lake Capital
Hayes, Patrick–Golub Capital Master Funding LLC
Hayes, Peter–Blu Venture Investors LLC
Hayes, Richard–Jasper Ridge Partners LP
Hayes, Robert–First Round Capital
Hayes, William–Mosaic Capital Partners LLC
Haygood, David–Ideo Ventures
Hayhurst, Brian–Carlyle Group LP
Haykin, Randy–Outlook Ventures
Haymoz, Sacha–BlueOcean Ventures SA
Haynes, David–Greenmont Capital Partners
Haynes, Stephen–Glengary LLC
Hayon, Ellan–Lightyear Capital LLC
Hayoun, Eric–CDC Infra Management SAS
Hays, James–St Cloud Capital LLC
Hays, Joe–Diamond State Ventures, L.P.
Hays, Robert–Levine Leichtman Capital Partners Inc
Hayward, Hal–Bravia Capital Partners Inc
Hayward, Kenyon–Alara Capital Partners LLC
Hayward, Laurence–Independence Equity Management LLC
Haywood, Jeffrey–Spectrum Equity Investors LP
Haza, Christopher–Fidus Capital LLC
Hazard, Charles–Flybridge Capital Partners
Hazen, Ned–Lighthouse Capital Partners LP
Hazenberg, Wil–Biogeneration Ventures BV
Hazum, Eli–Medica Venture Partners, Ltd.
Hazzan, Habib–al bawader
He, Boquan–Feima Fund
He, John–Granite Creek Partners LLC

He, Junqi–Shanghai NewMargin Ventures Co Ltd
He, Mingyan–Industrial Technology Investment Corp
He, Molly–Foresite Capital Management LLC
He, Peizhao–Beijing Tianxing Chuanglian Investment Management Co., Ltd.
He, Rachel–Mingly Capital
He, Xiaoqiu–Shanghai Sova Capital Co Ltd
He, Zhiqiang–Zhongrong International Trust Co Ltd
He-Chen, Melody–Morrison & Foerster LLP
Headley, Aaron–Versa Capital Management Inc
Headley, Robert–Ignition Ventures Management LLC
Headley, Robert–Qiming Venture Partners Ii LP
Headrick, Mark–Coral Ventures Inc
Heady, Christopher–Blackstone Group LP
Healey, Joseph–HealthCor Partners Management LP
Healey, Martin–Canada Pension Plan Investment Board
Healey, Russell–Foresight Group LLP
Healey, Thomas–Anthos Capital LP
Healy, JJ–Grandbanks Capital
Healy, James–Sofinnova Ventures Inc
Healy, Mike–TT Capital Partners LLC
Healy, Patrick–C3 Capital LLC
Healy, Patrick–Hellman & Friedman LLC
Healy, Robert–Chicago Growth Partners LLC
Healy, Seth–Crescent Capital Group LP
Healy, Susan–Global Infrastructure Holdings
Heard, Sue–Connection Capital LLP
Hearle, Todd–Summit Partners LP
Hearne, Thomas–Sportsnet 360 Media Inc
Hearns, Graham–Riverside Co
Heartfield, Brenda–TAG Energy Solutions Ltd
Heasley, Tim–Artesian Capital Management Australia Pty Ltd
Heath, Chad–Endeavour Capital Inc
Heath, Janusz–Capital Dynamics Sdn Bhd
Heath, Stephen–Farallon Capital Management LLC
Heath, Stratton–Oak Hill Capital Management Inc
Heath, Travis–Signal Peak Ventures
Hebbar, Kiran–Valhalla Partners LP
Hebel, Davor–Eight Roads Ventures Europe
Hebenstreit, Kolja–Team Europe Management GmbH
Heberle, Sarah–Mill Road Capital Management LLC
Hebert, Peter–LUX CAPITAL GROUP L L C
Hecht, Beth–Auven Therapeutics Management LLLP
Hedberg, Par–Stockholm Innovation & Growth AB
Hedges, Robert–OMERS Private Equity Inc
Hedon, Seth–Tinicum Capital Partners
Hee, Andrew–MSD Capital LP
Heersink, Ewout–Onex Corp
Hees, Bernardo–3G Capital Inc
Hefetz, Roni–Walden International
Heffernan, Peter–Cfi Capital
Heffler, Dale–Foundation Venture Capital Group LLC
Heflin, William–Kinetic Ventures LLC
Hegab, Moataz–Kuwait Finance and Investment Company KSCP
Hegazy, Mia–Catalyst Investors LLC
Hegedus, Robert–Fiedler Capital GmbH
Hegenbart, Joseph–Harvest Partners LP
Heggelund, Richard–Stonebridge Partners LP
Heh, Jeffrey–GTCR Golder Rauner LLC
Heidecorn, David–Catterton Partners Corp
Heidemann, Harald–S Ubg AG

Heiden, Thomas–Dr Engelhardt Kaupp Kiefer Beteiligungsberatung GmbH
Heidenreich, Daniel–Hauser Private Equity
Heidl, Christian–Praesidian Capital
Heighten, Clay–Health Wildcatters
Heijstee, Jarl–XSML Management BV
Heikkila, Sami–Sponsor Capital Oy
Heiland, Gunter–Gramercy Inc
Heilbronn, Michael–Ontario Centres of Excellence
Heilbronner, Rob–Headwaters BD LLC
Heilbrunn, David–Carlyle Group LP
Heimann, Robert–River Cities Capital Fund LP
Heine, Chris–Canyon Capital Advisors LLC
Heine, Daniel–Zurmont Madison Management AG
Heine, Guido–Goodvent Beteiligungsmanagement GmbH & Co KG
Heinen, Joseph–Goldner Hawn Johnson & Morrison Inc
Heinen, Joseph–Goldner Hawn Johnson & Morrison Inc
Heinen, Steven–Marquette Capital Partners Inc
Heiner, Todd–Trilogy Equity Partners Llc
Heining, Matthias–BWK GmbH Unternehmensbeteiligungsgesellschaft
Heinmiller, Joseph–Graham Partners Inc
Heinrich, George–Foundation Venture Capital Group LLC
Heinrich, Luc–Bpifrance Investissement SASU
Heintschel, Eric–Carousel Capital Partners
Heinz, Ronald–Signal Peak Ventures
Heinz, Ronald–Sweetwater Capital Partners LP
Heinze, Hendrik–Allegra Capital GmbH
Heinze, Kristina–Chicago Growth Partners LLC
Heischuber, Sam–Angeles Equity Partners LLC
Heise, Brant–National Healthcare Services
Heise, Brant–Summation Health Ventures LP
Heitzmann, Rick–FirstMark Capital LLC
Hejazi, Shahram–BioAdvance
Hejka, Marcin–Intel Capital Corp
Hektor, Tjarko–AlpInvest Partners BV
Held, Laura–Shamrock Capital Advisors LLC
Held, Raymond–Abbott Capital Management LLC
Helfrich, David–Garnett & Helfrich Capital LP
Helgerson, David–Hamilton Lane Advisors LLC
Helgesson, Staffan–Creandum AB
Helgesson, Staffan–Startup Factory
Helle, Daniel–CIVC Partners LP
Hellenius, Ragnar–PAI Partners SAS
Heller, David–Vertex Israel II Management Ltd
Heller, Ephraim–7 Health Ventures
Heller, Jake–Spectrum Equity Investors LP
Heller, Michael–Oak HC/FT Partners LP
Heller, Paul–Blackstone Group LP
Hellerstein, Rebecca–Investcorp Bank BSC
Hellier, David–Bertram Capital Management LLC
Hellman, F. Warren–Hellman & Friedman LLC
Hellman, Todd–Headwaters BD LLC
Hellyer, Debra–Select Capital Ventures
Helm, John–DN Capital Global Venture Capital Ii LP
Helm, Rob–Gold Hill Capital Management LLC
Helman, William–Greylock Partners LLC
Helmers, Leo–Carlyle Group LP
Helmersen, Tor–Investinor AS
Helms, Carolyn–Longitude Capital Management Co LLC

Helms, Joseph–Goldner Hawn Johnson & Morrison Inc
Helmsoe-Zinck, John–VIA equity A/S
Helmstaedter, Stephan–CornerstoneCapital Verwaltungs AG
Helmstetter, Michael–Techaccel LLC
Helmy, Youssri–Newbury Ventures
Helon, Ryan–Nationwide Mutual Capital LLC
Heltzer, Jason–Origin Ventures LLC
Heltzer, Jason–Origin Ventures LLC
Helzberg, Bush–Expedition Capital Partners LLC
Hemaraj, Yashwanth–Benhamou Global Ventures LLC
Hemaraj, Yashwanth–Benhamou Global Ventures LLC
Hemiadan, Daniel–Lakeside Capital Management LLC
Hemley, Simon–Gresham Llp
Hemmerle, Christophe–Finatem Fonds Management Verwaltungs GmbH
Hemmers, Irina–Apax Partners LLP
Hemmeter, Christopher–Thayer Ventures
Hemmi, Yoshihiro–Integral Corp
Hemphill, Jonathan–Old Mutual PLC
Hempill, John–Morrison & Foerster LLP
Henagan, Barbara–Linx Partners LLC
Henahan, Pat–Antares Capital Corp
Henault, Damien–Andurance Ventures LLP
Henckels, Lutz–Alara Capital Partners LLC
Henderson, Austin–Ancor Capital Partners
Henderson, Dave–TT Capital Partners LLC
Henderson, David–XPV Capital Corp
Henderson, Doug–Oak Hill Advisors LP
Henderson, John–Whitestar Capital Ltd
Henderson, Richard–Mti Partners Ltd
Henderson, Robert–Greylock Partners LLC
Henderson, Ted–Schooner Capital LLC
Henderson, Will–Graycliff Partners LP
Henderson-Londono, Ian–Alcuin Capital Partners LLP
Hendren, Jeffrey–Siris Capital Group LLC
Hendricks, Christian–Velocity Venture Capital Inc
Hendricks, Douglas–Morrison & Foerster LLP
Hendrickson, Doug–MidCap Equity Partners
Hendrie, Gardner–Sigma Partners
Hendriks, Harry–KPN Ventures BV
Hendrix, Blair–Bain Capital Inc
Hendry, Bever–Aberdeen Asset Management PLC
Hendy, Patrick–Columbia Capital LP
Heneghan, Megan–Adams Street Partners LLC
Heng, David–Temasek Holdings (Private) Ltd
Henikoff, Troy–Math Venture Partners LP
Henke, Bernd–Advantec Unternehmensbeteil
Henkelmann, Frank–Aheim Capital GmbH
Henkin, Douglas–Milbank Tweed Hadley & Mccloy LLP
Henkin, Julian–Impact Capital Inc
Henley, J. Rudy–Mountaineer Capital, L.P.
Henley, Jerry–Sorenson Capital Partners LP
Henneberg, Janis–Oaktree Capital Management LP
Hennegan, John–Shore Capital Partners LLC
Henner, Dennis–Clarus Ventures LLC
Hennes, Pierre–Granatus Ventures CJSC
Hennessy, Daniel–CHS Capital LLC
Hennessy, Mark–Evercore Inc

Hennessy, Michael–Morgan Creek Capital Management LLC
Hennigan, Thomas–Carlyle Group LP
Henning, Jason–Global Partnerships
Hennings-Huep, Patrick–Seafort Advisors GmbH
Henningsen, Michael–Blackstone Group LP
Henrich, Craig–KSL Capital Partners LLC
Henrich, Guenther–BayBG Bayerische Beteiligungsgesellschaft mbH
Henriksen, Ronald–Twilight Venture Partners
Henriksson, Tom–Open Ocean Capital Oy
Henrion, Denis–Equitis Gestion SAS
Henritze, Tyler–Blackstone Group LP
Henry, Bob–Mobeus Equity Partners LLP
Henry, Brian–Sterling Group LP
Henry, David–Vinacapital Investment Management Ltd
Henry, Gareth–AG BD LLC
Henry, George–Lincolnshire Management Inc
Henry, Jeanne–Excel Venture Management
Henry, Joanne–BlueFire Partners Capital Markets Group
Henry, Kimberly–Bennett Jones Verchere
Henry, Larry–Hudson Clean Energy Partners
Henry, Meng–Seven Seas Partners
Henry, Paul–Birch Hill Equity Partners Management Inc
Henry, Richard–Sandbridge Capital LLC
Henshaw, Nathaniel–CEI Ventures Inc
Henske, Robert–Hellman & Friedman LLC
Hensley, Carolina–Progress Equity Partners Ltd
Henson, Michael–MedFocus Fund LLC
Henson, Warren–Green Manning & Bunch Ltd
Hentsch, Christophe–Banque Lombard Odier & Cie SA
Hentze, Adam–Beecken Petty O'Keefe & Company LLC
Hentze, G. Adam–Roundtable Healthcare Partners LP
Hepburn, Claudia–NEXT Canada
Hepburn-Brown, Joel–Torrens Capital Management
Hepper, Richard–Capital for Enterprise Ltd
Hepple, Jonathan–Rosetta Capital Ltd
Heravi, Amanda–Avista Capital Holdings LP
Heravi, Kayvan–LNK Partners LLC
Herb, Robert–Scale Venture Partners
Herberg, Axel–Blackstone Group LP
Herberg, Erica–Carlyle Group LP
Herbert, Gary–LeapFrog Investments
Herbert, James–Find Invest Grow Ltd
Herbert, Jon–Beechbrook Capital LLP
Herbert, Philippe–Banexi Ventures Partners SA
Herbinet, Antoine–Vatel Capital SAS
Herbst, Marco–Clayton Dubilier & Rice LLC
Herchel, Marek–AlpInvest Partners BV
Herdegen, Richard–Bison Capital Asset Management LLC
Herger, Ivan–Capital Dynamics Sdn Bhd
Hergert, Ken–Moneta Capital Partners Ltd
Hering, Michael–Industrial Opportunity Partners LLC
Herman, John–Weinberg Capital Group
Herman, Jonathan–KV Private Equity Inc
Herman, Joseph–Blackstone Group LP
Hermann, Klaus–AIG Capital Partners Inc
Hermann, Matthew–Ahv Holding Company LLC

Hermelin, Brian–Rockbridge Growth Equity LLC
Hermiston, Arcinee–Varagon Capital Partners LP
Hernand, David–Cooley LLP
Hernandez, Bruce–Spire Capital Partners LP
Hernandez, Christian–Whitestar Capital Ltd
Hernandez, Eddie–Small Ventures Usa LP
Hernandez, Maurice–Accel-KKR
Herndon, Clifton–Third Security LLC
Hernon, Martin–Boston Millennia Partners LP
Heron, Patrick–Frazier Management LLC
Herr, Eric–Carlyle Group LP
Herr, John–Francisco Partners LP
Herr, Stefan–EMBL Ventures GmbH
Herrera, Gilbert–Herrera Partners
Herrera, Greg–Energy Ventures AS
Herrera, Julio–Oaktree Capital Management LP
Herrera, Miguel–Quona Capital Management Ltd
Herrera, William–Blue Equity LLC
Herrero, Gustavo–Aconcagua Ventures
Herrero, Javier–MCH Private Equity Asesores SL
Herrero, Jose Miguel–Big Sur Ventures
Herring, John–Corstone Corp
Herrmann, Timothy–Intuitive Venture Partners LLC
Herrmann, Xavier–ACE Management SA
Herrod, Stephen–General Catalyst Partners LLC
Herron, Craig–iSelect Fund LLC
Herron, Dave–Clean Pacific Ventures Management LLC
Hersch, Lisa–Bain Capital Inc
Herschman, Jerome–Blackstone Group LP
Hersh, Kenneth–Natural Gas Partners
Hershenson, Mar–Pear Ventures
Hershenson, Matt–Playground Global LLC
Herskope, Michael–Wilbow Group Pty Ltd
Hersman, Brian–JMI Management Inc
Herstatt, Johann–Beaufort Capital GmbH
Herstatt, Johann–Seafort Advisors GmbH
Hertweck, Manuel–Capiton AG
Hertzmark, Andrew–Generation Partners LP
Hertzmark, Andrew–Generation Partners LP
Herubin, Terri–AG BD LLC
Hervouet, Fred–Terra Firma Capital Partners Ltd
Herz, Kenneth–Haynes and Boone LLC
Herzberg, David–Gramercy Inc
Hesketh, Roberto–MultiCapital do Brasil Consultoria e Participacoes
Heskett, David–Valor Equity Partners L P
Hess, Alexandra–Cinven Group Ltd
Hess, David–First Analysis Corp
Hess, Ronald–Primus Capital
Hesselbarth, Reik–S-Unternehmensbeteiligungsgesellschaft der Sparkasse Leipzig
Hessevick, Ken–Pfingsten Partners LLC
Hessing, Michael–Cbr Management GmbH
Hessing, Shawn–Oak Hill Capital Management Inc
Hester, Robert–Novaquest Infosystems Inc
Hesthamar, Bjorn–Nord Kapitalforvaltning AS
Heston, Blake–W Capital Management LLC
Heston, Tim–Bertram Capital Management LLC
Hett, Thorben–Silicon Valley Bancventures LP
Hettich, Christof–Dievini Hopp Biotech Holding GmbH & Co KG
Hetu, Daniel–LCC Legacy Holdings Inc
Heuer, Kenneth–Kidd & Company LLC
Hevrdejs, Frank–Sterling Group LP

2497

Pratt's Guide to Private Equity & Venture Capital Sources

Hewat, Mary-Jo–OMERS Infrastructure
Hewett, Greg–Blackstone Group LP
Hewitt, Nicholas–Oceanbridge Partners LLC
Hewson, Doug–Axis Capital Corp
Hewson, Doug–Portland Private Equity LP
Hewson, Paul–Elevation Partners LP
Hexter, James–Catterton Partners Corp
Heyat, Afsaneh–LYRIQUE Srrl
Heyer, Andrew–Mistral Equity Partners LP
Heyes, Jim–GEF Management Corp
Heyman, Justin–GEF Management Corp
Heymann, Maia–Converge
Heywood, Ivan–LGV Capital Ltd
Hiatt, David–Anania & Associates Investment Company LLC
Hiatt, Thomas–Centerfield Capital Partners LP
Hichert, Volker–DPE Deutsche Private Equity GmbH
Hickey, Brett–Star Mountain Capital LLC
Hickey, James–Renegade Capital LP
Hickey, James–Vista Equity Partners LLC
Hickey, Tom–Quad-C Management Inc
Hickman, Trent–Veronis Suhler Stevenson LLC
Hicks, Carolyn–Diversified Trust Company Inc
Hicks, Creighton–Kleiner Perkins Caufield & Byers LLC
Hicks, George–Varde Partners Inc
Hicks, Lee–Farallon Capital Management LLC
Hicks, Matthew–Excellere Capital Management LLC
Hicks, Peter–Linx Partners LLC
Hicks, R–Capstar Partners LLC
Hicks, Terrence–Ben Franklin Technology Partners Southeastern PA
Hickson, Anthony–Touchstone Innovations PLC
Hidaka, Hideyuki–MBK Partners Inc
Hiemstra, David–Strength Capital Partners LLC
Hietala, Illkka–Vaaka Partners Oy
Higbee, Scott–Partners Group Holding AG
Higdon, James–Verge Fund
Higgerson, Clifford–Walden International
Higgins, Dan–LNC Partners
Higgins, Doug–Sapphire Ventures LLC
Higgins, Doug–Sapphire Ventures LLC
Higgins, Frank–Second Avenue Partners
Higgins, Gerry–Lyceum Capital
Higgins, Kevin–Montgomery & Co LLC
Higgins, Robert–Highland Capital Partners LLC
Higginson, Jon–Doughty Hanson and Co.
Higginson, Robert–Par Equity Llp
Highberger, Greg–Lime Rock Partners LLC
Highet, Ian–Court Square Capital Partners LP
Higuchi, Osamu–Archetype Corp
Hilal, Paul–Pershing Square Capital Management LP
Hild, Robert–Compass Capital Services Inc
Hildebrand, Andreas–Bison Capital Asset Management LLC
Hildebrandt, James–Bain Capital Inc
Hildebrandt, Joseph–DaneVest Tech Fund Advisors
Hildebrandt, Joseph–Phenomenelle Angels Management LLC
Hilderbrand, Mark–Accretia Capital LLC
Hilderbrand, Mark–Housatonic Partners Management Co Inc
Hildisch, Michael–Afinum Management GmbH
Hildreth, Jaime–Blackstone Group LP

Hilhorst, Remko–IK Investment Partners Ltd
Hilinski, Scott–Nautic Partners LLC
Hilkene, Amber–AnaCap Financial Partners Llp
Hill, A. Judson–Tillridge Global Agribusiness Partners
Hill, Alexandra–Blackstone Group LP
Hill, Belinda–Gramercy Inc
Hill, Brent–Origin Ventures LLC
Hill, Cory–Perella Weinberg Partners LP
Hill, Douglas–Nautic Partners LLC
Hill, Duncan–Mantella Venture Partners
Hill, Erin–One Equity Partners LLC
Hill, Geoff–Roark Capital Group Inc
Hill, James–Vexiom Equity Partners, L.P.
Hill, Jason–MVP Capital LLC
Hill, John–Hyde Park Holdings Inc
Hill, Juan–Castanea Partners Inc
Hill, Karen A.–Collina Ventures LLC
Hill, Lowell–Oaktree Capital Management LP
Hill, Mark E.–Collina Ventures LLC
Hill, Michael–Ironbridge Capital Pty Ltd
Hill, Neal–Business Development Bank of Canada
Hill, S–Brown Brothers Harriman & Co
Hill, Shaun–Investcorp Technology Investments Group
Hill, Simon–Find Invest Grow Ltd
Hill, Stephen–Socius Capital Group LLC
Hille, Craig–Juggernaut Partners LP
Hillel, Isaac–Pitango Venture Capital Management Israel, Ltd.
Hillenbrand, Justin–Monomoy Capital Partners LLC
Hiller, Jeffrey–Pearl Street Capital Group
Hillman, David Mcl.–PNC Equity Management Corp
Hillman, Thomas–Lewis & Clark Venture Capital LLC
Hillmann, Ron–BVP Berlin Venture Partners GmbH
Hills, Mason–Rcf Management LLC
Hillstrom, Klas–ETF Partners LLP
Hillyard, Carrie–Talu Ventures Pty Ltd
Hilson, William–Cronos Group Inc
Hilverkus, Gregor–CVC Capital Partners Ltd
Hilzinger, Kurt–Court Square Capital Partners LP
Himawan, Jeffrey–EW Healthcare Partners
Himbury, Brett–IFM Investors Pty Ltd
Himelfarb, Matt–Dallas Venture Partners LP
Himes, Gary–Naya Ventures LLC
Himmel, Kenneth–Gulf Capital Pvt JSC
Hin, Ong Guan–Southern Capital Group Pte Ltd
Hinaman, Robert–Acorn Growth Companies
Hinchman, Brook–Oaktree Capital Management LP
Hinck, Jeff–El Dorado Ventures
Hinderling, Julian–Ascribe Capital, LLC
Hindmarch, Stephen–Graycliff Partners LP
Hindo, Ziad–Ontario Teachers' Pension Plan
Hineman, Yoav–Fortissimo Capital Fund Israel LP
Hingorani, Archana–IL & FS Investment Managers Ltd
Hiniker, Kevin–Castlelake LP
Hinman, Brian–Oak Investment Partners
Hinrichs, Lars–HackFwd GmbH & Co KG
Hinrichs, Steve–Monroe Capital LLC
Hinteregger, Hannes–Avedon Capital Partners BV
Hintz, John–Haynes and Boone LLC
Hintzen, Herman–Henq Invest BV
Hippe, Alan–F Hoffmann La Roche AG
Hippeau, Eric–Lerer Ventures II LP

Hippeau, Eric–Softbank Capital Partners L P
Hirai, Daigo–Blackstone Group LP
Hirai, Miki–University of Tokyo Edge Capital Co Ltd
Hird, Melanie–Seneca Partners Ltd
Hirji, Asiff–TPG Capital Management LP
Hirman, Brian–eVentures Europe BV
Hirn, Karine–East Capital Private Equity AB
Hirooka, Ryo–Hoya Corp
Hirsch, David–Compound Ventures
Hirsch, David–Longitude Capital Management Co LLC
Hirsch, David–Longitude Capital Management Co LLC
Hirsch, David–Onex Corp
Hirsch, Leonard–NGN Capital LLC
Hirsch, Russell–Prospect Venture Partners
Hirschbiel, Paul–Envest Ventures
Hirschel, Jean-Francois–Unigestion Holding SA
Hirschfeld, David–Fertitta Capital Inc
Hirschfield, Marc–Resonetics LLC
Hirschhorn, Joshua–New Mountain Capital I LLC
Hirschmann, David–Barings (UK) Ltd
Hirsekorn, Andrew–Eagle Merchant Partners
Hirsh, David–Blackstone Group LP
Hirshfeld, Michael–Milbank Tweed Hadley & Mccloy LLP
Hirshland, Michael–Resolute.VC
Hirt, Dietmar–Conexus Capital Management, Inc.
Hirt, Lance–Lindsay Goldberg & Bessemer LP
Hirzebruch, Walter–Mezzanine Partners (Pty) Ltd
Hiscock, Toby–Henderson Global Investors Ltd
Hisham Jaafar, Badrul–Kumpulan Modal Perdana Sdn Bhd
Hislop, James–Transportation Resource Partners LP
Hislop, Joanna–Park Square Capital LLP
Hitch, Jordan–Bain Capital Inc
Hitchan, Gregory–Blum Capital Partners LP
Hitchcock, Simon–Lyceum Capital
Hite, Darren–Aberdare Ventures
Hite, David–B37 Ventures LLC
Hixon, Dylan–Gideon Hixon Fund LP
Hixon, Eric–Gideon Hixon Fund LP
Hixon, F.Perkins–Evercore Inc
Hixon, Todd–NAV.VC
Hjerpe, Eric–Kepha Partners
Hlawaty, Roland–Milbank Tweed Hadley & Mccloy LLP
Ho, Andy–Vinacapital Investment Management Ltd
Ho, Bernard–Shanghai Atlas Capital Ltd
Ho, Brian–Spring Capital Asia Ltd
Ho, Ching–Temasek Holdings (Private) Ltd
Ho, Clara–HPEF Capital Partners Ltd
Ho, Derrick–Covington Capital Corp
Ho, Derrick–Market Square Equity Partners
Ho, Eva–Susa Ventures LP
Ho, Gregory–Spring Mountain Capital LP
Ho, James–AEA Investors LLC
Ho, James–Capital International Inc
Ho, Katherine–Oaktree Capital Management LP
Ho, Kyung-sik–Korea Investment Partners Co Ltd
Ho, Paul–Hudson Clean Energy Partners
Ho, Sam–Aberdeen Gould Capital Markets Ltd
Ho, Sarah–Bio*One Capital Pte Ltd
Ho, Simmy–Global Private Equity PLC
Ho, Simon–IDG Capital Partners Inc

Ho, Stella–LightBay Capital LLC
Ho, Thierry–Lightyear Capital LLC
Ho, William–CVC Asia Pacific Ltd
Ho, William–CVC Capital Partners Ltd
Hoag, Jay–Technology Crossover Ventures LP
Hoang, Nam–Probitas Partners Inc
Hobart, Matt–Tpg Growth LLC
Hobart, Ted–Chart Venture Partners LP
Hobbs, Jason–NF Holdings Ltd
Hobbs, Robert–Tallwave LLC
Hobbs, William–Blackstone Group LP
Hobbs, William–Carousel Capital Partners
Hobbs, William–High Road Capital Partners LLC
Hoberg, Wenzel–Canada Pension Plan Investment Board
Hoberman, Brent–PROfounders Capital Ltd
Hobman, Steven–Newspring Capital
Hobson, Jared–Century Capital Management / Massachusetts Inc
Hoch, James–Tailwind Capital Partners LP
Hoch, James–Thomas Weisel Partners Group Inc
Hoch, Scott–Frontier Capital LLC
Hoch, Scott–Frontier Capital LLC
Hoch, Thomas–Co Investor AG
Hochberg, Benjamin–Lee Equity Partners LLC
Hochberg, Steve–Ascent Biomedical Ventures
Hocher, Jean-Yves–Credit Agricole Corporate and Investment Bank SA
Hochfelder, Peter–Brahman Management LLC
Hochholzer, Michael–Baytech Venture Capital GmbH & Co KG
Hochman, Andrew–Roundtable Healthcare Partners LP
Hochman, David–Orchestra Medical Ventures LLC
Hodan, Matthew–Lexington Partners Inc
Hodara, Jeremy–Rocket Internet AG
Hodder, John–Tembo Capital LLP
Hodge, Bruce–Pender West Capital Partners, Inc.
Hodges, Michael–Ata Ventures
Hodges, Philip–Enhanced Capital Partners LLC
Hodges, Philip–Redmont Venture Partners
Hodges, Robert–Carlyle Group LP
Hodgkinson, Jessica–AEA Investors LLC
Hodgkinson, Kerry–Business Partners Ltd
Hodgkinson, Matthew–Satya Capital Ltd
Hodgman, Jacob–HGGC LLC
Hodgson, David–General Atlantic LLC
Hodgson, Ryan–American Industrial Partners
Hodgson, Tim–NEXT Canada
Hodits, Regina–Wellington Partners GmbH
Hodson, Ryan–Kodiak Capital Group LLC
Hodson, Stephen–Fund Evaluation Group LLC
Hoe, Janey–Cisco Investments Inc
Hoehn-Saric, Chris–Sterling Partners GP LLC
Hoeing, Mark–Commonfund Capital Inc
Hoekman, Scott–Next Level Ventures LLC
Hoellinger, Steffen–Team Europe Management GmbH
Hoerr, Tim–Serra Ventures LLC
Hoesterey, Brian–AEA Investors LLC
Hofeditz, Robert–Probitas Partners Inc
Hofer, Andrew–Brown Brothers Harriman & Co
Hoff, Bob–Crosspoint Venture Partners 2001 LP
Hoffinger, Adam–Morrison & Foerster LLP
Hoffman, A. Michael–Palamon Capital Partners LP

Hoffman, Alexander–AEA Investors LLC
Hoffman, Dan–Invest Nebraska Corp
Hoffman, David–Charterhouse Group Inc
Hoffman, Elizabeth–Berkshire Partners LLC
Hoffman, G.–Northwest Technology Ventures
Hoffman, Michael–Metalmark Capital Holdings LLC
Hoffman, Michael–Riverstone Holdings LLC
Hoffman, Reid–Greylock Partners LLC
Hoffman, Spencer–Lovell Minnick Partners LLC
Hoffmann, Andrew–Capricorn Investment Group LLC
Hoffmann, Anne–CBPE Capital LLP
Hoffmann, Christopher–Zouk Capital LLP
Hoffmann, Jackie–Siemens Venture Capital GmbH
Hoffmann, Michael–Probitas Partners Inc
Hoffmann, Sebastian–Permira Advisers LLP
Hoffmann, Trevor–Haynes and Boone LLC
Hoffmeister, Marc–Capital Export SAS
Hoffmeister, Mark–Prudential Capital Group LP
Hoffmeister, Stephen–Advent International Corp
Hofmann, Donald–Alston Capital Partners LLC
Hofmann, Philip–Oaktree Capital Management LP
Hofmeister, Helge–BID Equity Advisory GmbH
Hofmeister, Ron–O'Melveny & Myers LLP
Hogan, John–Norwest Mezzanine Partners
Hogan, Kathleen–Blackstone Group LP
Hogan, Kevin–Altpoint Capital Partners LLC
Hogan, Peter–Atlantic Canada Opportunities Agency
Hogan, Rob–Storehill Capital LLC
Hogan, Robert–CHS Capital LLC
Hogan, Robert–Shorehill Capital LLC
Hogan, Tracy–Elevation Partners LP
Hogan, Tracy–Institutional Venture Partners
Hogeg, Moshe–Genesis Angels
Hogerty, Reagan–JZ Capital Partners Ltd
Hogg, Cressida–3i Infrastructure PLC
Hogg, Sam–Open Prairie Ventures
Hoggarth, Royston–Wellington Partners GmbH
Hoh, Jennifer–Bain Capital Inc
Hojlo, Christopher–CVC Capital Partners Ltd
Hokenson, Michael–Community Investment Management LLC
Holbrook, David–Mti Partners Ltd
Holbrooke, David–Medventure Associates
Holcomb, Brett–Prospect Partners LLC
Holcomb, Richard–Aurora Funds Inc
Holden, Blake–Warburg Pincus LLC
Holden, Bradley–Heidrick & Struggles International Inc
Holden, Christopher–Court Square Ventures LLC
Holden, Gregory–Adams Street Partners LLC
Holder, David–Neo Investment Partners LLP
Holder, Francis–Neo Investment Partners LLP
Holdsberg, Jeffrey–Caltius Equity Partners
Hole, Sveinung–Sarsia Seed Management AS
Holec, Monica–Levine Leichtman Capital Partners Inc
Holekamp, Cliff–Cultivation Capital
Holiday, Harry–Thompson Street Capital Partners LP
Holland, George–Hull Capital Management LLC
Holland, James–Trinity Hunt Partners
Holland, Jeffrey–Seacoast Capital
Holland, Kirk–Access Venture Partners
Holland, Kirk–Vista Ventures
Holland, Michael–OMERS Infrastructure
Holland, Paul–Foundation Capital LLC

Holland, Thomas–Patriot Capital Funding Inc
Holland, Thomas–Patriot Capital Funding Inc
Hollander, Age–H2 Equity Partners BV
Hollander, David–Tennenbaum Capital Partners LLC
Hollander, Michael–GTCR Golder Rauner LLC
Hollander, Seth–Kohlberg & Co LLC
Hollars, Kiersten–Andreessen Horowitz LLC
Holldack, Johanna–Aravis SA
Holleman, Joost–Prime Technology Ventures NV
Hollenbeck, Chris–Granite Ventures LLC
Hollenbeck, Christopher–Granite Ventures LLC
Hollend, Michael–TorQuest Partners Inc
Holleran, Matt–Cloud Apps Management LLC
Holley, Matt–Haynes and Boone LLC
Holliman, Jock–Valley Ventures
Hollin, Mitchell–LLR Partners Inc
Hollings, Michael–Shard Capital Partners LLP
Hollingshead, Robert–Morrison & Foerster LLP
Hollington, Richard–CapitalWorks LLC
Hollins, Kevin–Blu Venture Investors LLC
Hollis, Alex–Wasabi Ventures LLC
Hollis, Mark–Centerfield Capital Partners LP
Hollis, Mark–Sun Mountain Capital Advisors LLC
Hollmen, Harri–Intera Equity Partners Oy
Holloway, Adam–F&C Equity Partners PLC
Holloway, Jim–Baker & McKenzie LLP
Holm, Jordan–T & M Management Services Ltd
Holm, Magnus–Peppermint VenturePartners GmbH
Holman, Kelly–Genesys Capital Partners Inc
Holman, Kelly–Genesys Capital Partners Inc
Holmberg, Michael–NB Distressed Debt Investment Fund Ltd
Holmen, Bob–Miramar Venture Partners L P
Holmes, Andrew–Calera Capital Management Inc
Holmes, Benjamin–Index Ventures
Holmes, Clive–Silvertern Group Inc
Holmes, Gordon–Towerbrook Capital Partners LP
Holmes, James–Caerus Ventures LLC
Holmes, Matthew–354 Partners LLC
Holmes, Reeta–Silverfern Group Inc
Holmes, Roger–Change Capital Partners LLP
Holmes, Stephen–InterWest Partners LLC
Holmes, Whitney–Morrison & Foerster LLP
Holmquist, Mark–Beecken Petty O'Keefe & Company LLC
Holmsen, Cato–FSN Capital Partners AS
Holmstrand, Marcus–Catella AB
Holson, Laura–New Mountain Capital I LLC
Holsted, David–Hall Capital LLC
Holstein, Kurt–Azoic Ventures Inc
Holstein, Roger–Vestar Capital Partners Inc
Holt, Allan–Carlyle Group LP
Holt, Charles–InvesteCo Capital Corp
Holt, Matthew–New Mountain Capital I LLC
Holt, Thomas–Shorenstein Co LLC
Holthe, Runar–Styrbjorn Growth AS
Holthuis, Joost–Biogeneration Ventures BV
Holton, Rick–Cultivation Capital
Holtrup, Axel–AEA Investors LLC
Holtschneider, Andreas–Silverfleet Capital Partners LLP
Holtz, Jerry–ProvCo Group
Holtz, Robert–Wexford Capital LP
Holtze, David–Ernst & Young LLP
Holtzer, Peter–Oriens IM Hungary Szolgaltato Kft

2499

Pratt's Guide to Private Equity & Venture Capital Sources

Holway, Jeffrey—Water Street Healthcare Partners LLC
Holyoak, Chris—European Bank for Reconstruction and Development
Holzbaur, Ines—GeneChem Financial Corp
Holzman Graziano, Glori—Carlyle Group LP
Holzman, Ben—Bain Capital Inc
Holzman, Ben—Bain Capital Venture Partners LLC
Holzman, Nicolas—PAI Partners SAS
Hom, Benjamin—St Cloud Capital LLC
Homan, Yuen—NewGen Capital II LP
Homcy, Charles—Third Rock Ventures LLC
Homer, James—Steadfast Capital GmbH
Homer, Paul—Northwood Ventures
Homme, Matthew—Aurora Resurgence Management Partners LLC
Homme, Matthew—Peninsula Pacific Strategic Partners LLC
Hommels, Klaus—Springstar GmbH
Hommeyer, John—Blue Horizon Equity LLC
Hompe, John—KBW Capital Partners I L P
Homsany, Nadim—Serent Capital LLC
Hon, Johnny—Global Private Equity PLC
Honda, Osuke—Doll Capital Management Inc
Honeker, Daniel—Crescent Capital Group LP
Honey, Charles—Private Advisors LLC
Honey, R. Sean—Weston Presidio Capital
Honeybourne, Will—First Reserve Corp
Hong, Augustin—Riverwood Capital Group LLC
Hong, Brian—CVC Asia Pacific Ltd
Hong, Brian—CVC Capital Partners Ltd
Hong, Dominic—Truebridge Capital Partners LLC
Hong, Irene—Z Capital HF Adviser LLC
Hong, Karen—ProQuest Investments
Hong, Lance—HPEF Capital Partners Ltd
Hong, Nancy—RiverVest Venture Partners LLC
Hong, Qinghua—Feima Fund
Hong, Youn—AlpInvest Partners BV
Honig, Michael—HQ Equita GmbH
Honis, John—Highland Capital Management LP
Honkavaara, Mikael—Veturi Growth Partners Oy
Honma, Masahiko—Incubate Fund No1 Investment LPS
Honohan, James—Alumni Capital Network Management Co LLC
Honore, Olin—Hamilton Lane Advisors LLC
Honts, John—Evercore Inc
Hood, Aaron—Perella Weinberg Partners LP
Hood, J. Kyle—Industrial Opportunity Partners LLC
Hood, Michael—Haynes and Boone LLC
Hoogendijk, Patrick—Capital E Group
Hook, Daniel—Blackstone Group LP
Hook, Matthew—Centerfield Capital Partners LP
Hooke, Rob—eonCapital, LLC
Hoon, Douglas—GEN3 Partners, Inc.
Hooper, Chris—ACM Ltd
Hooper, Christopher—Welsh Carson Anderson & Stowe
Hooper, Gary—Velocity Venture Capital Inc
Hooper, Herbert—Ampersand Capital Partners
Hooper, Pev—CVC Capital Partners Ltd
Hooper, Steve—Ignition Ventures Management LLC
Hoornaert, Kris—Gevaert SA
Hooten, Kenneth—Concentric Equity Partners, L.P.
Hootnick, Mark—Millstein & Co LP
Hoover, Mark—Woodside Fund
Hopcraft, Brian—Lewis & Clark Venture Capital LLC
Hope, Richard—Hamilton Lane Advisors LLC
Hopfner, Rob—Bay City Capital LLC
Hopkin, Andrew—Audax Group, Inc.
Hopkin, Daniel—Kainos Capital LLC
Hopkins, Adam—Elevation Partners LP
Hopkins, Mark—CRESCENDO CAPITAL PARTNERS LLC
Hopkins, Robert—CM Equity Partners LP
Hopkins, Ross—Raven Capital Pty Ltd
Hopkins, Thomas—Cooley LLP
Hopkinson, R. Ronald—Cooley LLP
Hoppenot, David—Atalante SAS
Hoppner, Dorte—Riverside Co
Hopson, Anthony—HAO Capital
Horan, Avshalom—Tene Kibbutz Investment Management Ltd
Horan, Harrison—Jacobson Partners
Horan, Richard—Slater Technology Fund Inc
Horbach, Sandra—Carlyle Group LP
Horck, Bas—Apex Ventures BV
Horesh, Asaf—Greylock Israel Global Management Ltd
Horgan, Anna-Marie—Blackstone Group LP
Horgan, Mark—Atlantic Bridge
Horgan, Michael—Olympus Partners
Hori, Yoshito—Globis Capital Partners & Co
Horie, Toshiyasu—Rising Japan Equity Inc
Horikawa, Masakazu—Mitsubishi International Corp
Horing, David—Ascribe Capital, LLC
Horing, Jeffrey—Insight Venture Partners LLC
Horlick, Nicola—Bramdean Asset Management LLP
Hormazdi, Cyrus—Greenhill Capital Partners LP
Horn, Charles—Morrison & Foerster LLP
Horn, Claudia—Stonegate Capital Group LLC
Horn, Mark—Comerica Venture Capital Group
Horn, Robert—Blackstone Group LP
Hornberger, Kusi—Global Partnerships
Hornby, Mary—Abbott Capital Management LLC
Horne, Martin—Barings (UK) Ltd
Horne, Robert—ZS Fund LP
Horner, Kelly—Stone Arch Capital LLC
Horner, Pat—G 51 Capital Management LLC
Horner, Scott—Third Security LLC
Hornig, George—PineBridge Investments LLC
Hornthal, Jim—CMEA Development Company LLC
Horowitz, Benjamin—Andreessen Horowitz LLC
Horowitz, Joseph—Jafco Ventures
Horowitz, Joshua—Palm Ventures LLC
Horowitz, Richard—RAF Industries, Inc.
Horsburgh, Peter—ETF Partners LLP
Horsholt, Jesper—VIA equity A/S
Horsley, Erich—Intervale Capital LLC
Horst, Volker—Dr Engelhardt Kaupp Kiefer Beteiligungsberatung GmbH
Horstmann, Jens—Crestlight Venture Productions LLC
Horstmann, Uwe—Project A Ventures GmbH & Co KG
Horton, Donnie—Tmfox Venture Partners Co Ltd
Horton, Geoffrey—VentureLink Funds
Horton, Lynette—Harbert Management Corp
Horton, Paul—Arrowhead Mezzanine LLC
Horton, R. Evan—Pine Tree Equity Management LP
Horton, Robert—Zephyr Management LP
Horvilleur, Camilo—HIG Capital LLC
Horvitz, H. Robert—MPM Capital LLC
Horwitz, Bradley—Trilogy Equity Partners Llc
Horwitz, Lawrence—Maywic Select Investments
Hosang, Markus—BioMedPartners AG
Hoscalek, Marek—Genesis Capital sro
Hosler, Daniel—Sterling Partners GP LLC
Hosoya, Jun—Innovation Network Corporation of Japan
Hosseinzadeh, Shaia—WL Ross & Co LLC
Hostetter, Davis—Halifax Group LLC
Hotard, Ed—China Materialia LLC
Hotard, Edgar—Arch Venture Partners LLC
Hotchkiss, Michael—Sands Capital Management LLC
Hothum, Mathias—Dievini Hopp Biotech Holding GmbH & Co KG
Hou, Chi-Chien—Star Avenue Capital LLC
Hou, Faye—Coburn Ventures LLC
Hou, Hong—Arch Venture Partners LLC
Hou, Jessica—Montreux Equity Partners
Hou, Kenny—IDG Capital Partners Inc
Hou, Vincent—CID Group
Hough, James—Morrison & Foerster LLP
Houlot, Vincent—Ixen Partners SA
Hourigan, Stephen—Elevate Ventures Inc
Houry, Claire—Ventech SA
House, Anthony—Vinacapital Investment Management Ltd
House, Dawn—Innovacorp
House, Macie—Baird Capital
House, Roger—Platinum Equity LLC
Houthan, Nahar—Carlyle Group LP
Houtman, Matthew—Pioneer Capital Partners AS
Houtsonen, Leo—Veraventure Oy
Hove, Anders—Venrock Inc
Howard, Al—TeleSoft Partners
Howard, Alex—MergerTech Advisors
Howard, Andrew—Shamrock Capital Advisors LLC
Howard, Arthur—Haynes and Boone LLC
Howard, Chris—Ignition Ventures Management LLC
Howard, Chris—Ignition Ventures Management LLC
Howard, Grant—Emedici Capital Inc
Howard, Jeffrey—Peppertree Capital Management Inc
Howard, John—Irving Place Capital LLC
Howard, Matthew—Norwest Venture Partners
Howard, Nigel—RLJ Equity Partners LLC
Howard, Randall—VERDEXUS
Howard, Robert—ArcLight Capital Holdings LLC
Howard, Russell—Primary Venture Partners
Howard-Johnston, Xenia—Impact Capital Inc
Howcroft, Anthony—Frost Data Capital
Howe, Carl—Wynnchurch Capital Ltd
Howe, Christopher—Indigo Capital LLP
Howe, Darcy—KCRise Fund LLC
Howe, David—AeroEquity Partners LLC
Howe, Dennis—Keystone Capital Inc
Howe, Kevin—Mercury Ventures Ltd
Howe, Niloofar—Paladin Capital Management LLC
Howe, Robert—AIG Capital Partners Inc
Howe, Stephen—Ernst & Young LLP
Howe, Timothy—CHL Medical Partners LP
Howell, Daniel—Mesirow Financial Private Equity Inc
Howell, Richard—PAI Partners SAS
Howell, Ronald—WRF Capital
Howell, Sheldon—ICV Partners LLC
Howells, Thomas—Euroventures Capital Tanacsado

Kft
Hower, Lee–NextView Ventures LP
Hower, Robert–Advanced Technology Ventures
Hower, Robert–G20 Associates LLC
Howery, Ken–Founders Fund, The
Howie, Josh–Freeport Financial Partners LLC
Howley, Michael–Bratenahl Capital Partners Ltd
Howorth, Greg–Caltius Mezzanine
Hoy, Michael–Syntegra Capital Investors Ltd
Hoy, Michael–Syntegra Capital Investors Ltd
Hromadko, Gary–Crosslink Capital Inc
Hsia, Alan–Parakletos@Ventures Millenium Fund LP
Hsia, Eric–Translink Capital LLC
Hsiang, Derrick–WI Harper Group Inc
Hsiang, Yong Ho–Cmia Capital Partners Pte Ltd
Hsiao, C. H.–WIT Investment Partners Ltd
Hsiao, Paul–Canvas Venture Fund
Hsiao, Peter–Morrison & Foerster LLP
Hsieh, Jason–CID Group
Hsieh, Steven–Israel Infinity Venture Capital Fund Israel LP
Hsieh, Tony–VegasTechFund
Hsin, Jennifer–CNF Investments LLC
Hsing, Peter–Merus Capital Investment
Hsu, Allen–PAC-LINK Management Corp
Hsu, Arfen–Panda Capital Asia Ltd
Hsu, Eric–Lee Equity Partners LLC
Hsu, Geoffrey–OrbiMed Advisors LLC
Hsu, Henry–Blackstone Group LP
Hsu, Jimmy–Natixis Private Equity SA
Hsu, Junlee–HPEF Capital Partners Ltd
Hsu, Mark–H&Q Asia Pacific, Ltd.
Hsu, Ming–PAC-LINK Management Corp
Hsu, Stacy–Trust Company of the West
Hsu, Vincent–StepStone Group LP
Hsu, William–MuckerLab LLC
Hsu, Winnie–WI Harper Group Inc
Hsun, Tony–Vinacapital Investment Management Ltd
Hu, Bin–Qiming Venture Partners Ii LP
Hu, Dehua–Fortune Venture Capital Co Ltd
Hu, Dehua–Fortune Venture Capital Corp
Hu, Fan–Shenzhen Green Pine Capital Partners Co Ltd
Hu, Haibo–Guangzhou Zhongda Venture Capital Management Co Ltd
Hu, Haichen–Gsr Ventures Management Llc
Hu, Haiping–Ivy Capital Ltd
Hu, Hanliang–Beijing Hexin Dongli Investment Management Co Ltd
Hu, Jiawu–Shenzhen Richland Investment Co Ltd
Hu, Jiwei–Shanghai Dingjia Ventures Co Ltd
Hu, Li–HighLight Capital
Hu, Longrun–Xiamen Hongsoft Venture Capital Management Co Ltd
Hu, Matt–F & H Fund Management Pte Ltd
Hu, Ning–CDH China Management Co., Ltd.
Hu, Qiu–Guosen Bole Equity Investment Management Co Ltd
Hu, Robert–Israel Infinity Venture Capital Fund Israel LP
Hu, Terry Yongmin–FountainVest Partners Asia Ltd
Hu, Thomas–CDIB Capital International Corp
Hu, William–Qiming Venture Partners Ii LP

Hu, Xiaobo–Guangzhou Sinvo Spring Investment Management Co Ltd
Hu, Xiaoling–CDH China Management Co., Ltd.
Hu, Yongmin–HGI Finaves China Fund
Hu, Yu–Milestone Capital Management Ltd
Hu, Zhenni–Guangxin Investment Management Beijing Co Ltd
Hua, Jingdong–International Finance Corp
Hua, Peter–Sbcvc Fund Ii L P
Hua, Sean–Mingly Capital
Hua, Xinyi–Shanghai Broad Resources Investment Management Co Ltd
Hua, Yeyu–ZheShang Venture Capital Co Ltd
Hua, Zhengjin–Hollyhigh Intl Capital Co Ltd
Huang, Andrew–Neoteny Labs Pte Ltd
Huang, Chengxian–Beijing Tianxing Chuanglian Investment Management Co., Ltd.
Huang, Chunsheng–China Venture Capital Co Ltd
Huang, Crystal–GGV Capital
Huang, Edward–Blackstone Group LP
Huang, Elise–Asiatech Management LLC
Huang, Elise–WestSummit Capital Management Ltd
Huang, Fei–ZhuHai BoYuan Investment Co Ltd
Huang, Filippo–Gobi Partners
Huang, Haixia–Guangzhou Sinvo Spring Investment Management Co Ltd
Huang, Haiying–Shenzhen Hongshisan Capital Co Ltd
Huang, Hanji–L Catterton Asia
Huang, He–Northern Light Venture Capital Development Ltd
Huang, Hui–GUOSEN H&S Investment Co Ltd
Huang, Ivy–Beijing Macro Vision Venture Capital Management Consultancy
Huang, Jessica–PAC-LINK Management Corp
Huang, Jessica–Providence Equity Partners LLC
Huang, Jing–Tpg Growth LP
Huang, Joseph–Kenson Ventures LLC
Huang, Li–Shenzhen Co-Win Venture Capital Investments Ltd
Huang, Ligao–Principle Capital Ltd
Huang, Mark–Tolero Ventures LLC
Huang, Nathan–Loud Capital LLC
Huang, Qing–Mingly Capital
Huang, Shaobing–Fujian Venture Capital Co Ltd
Huang, Sibing–Pantheon Ventures (UK) LLP
Huang, Silin–Ceyuan Ventures Management LLC
Huang, Stanley–Atar Capital LLC
Huang, Tao–Jiangsu Addor Equity Investment Fund Management Co Ltd
Huang, Tao–Shenzhen Team-top Investment Management Co Ltd
Huang, Terry–Birch Venture Capital Inc
Huang, Thomas–EagleTree Capital, LP
Huang, Tianyi–Shenzhen Weixi Investment Partnership Co Ltd
Huang, Timothy–Lexington Partners Inc
Huang, Tony–CID Group
Huang, Wayne–Ventana Capital Management LP
Huang, Wensheng–Guangdong 100 Capital Co Ltd
Huang, Xiaohong–Legend Capital Co Ltd
Huang, Xiaojie–Kunwu Jiuding Capital Holdings Co Ltd
Huang, Xu–Vision Knight Capital
Huang, Yan–CDH China Management Co., Ltd.

Huang, Yi–Shanghai Cenova Ventures Management Co Ltd
Huang, Yu–ShenZhen GTJA Investment Group Co Ltd
Huang, Zhen–Kunwu Jiuding Capital Holdings Co Ltd
Huang, Zhenguang–Yingke Innovation Assets Management Co Ltd
Huban, Tim–Antares Capital Corp
Hubbard, George–Algonquin Advisors LLC
Hubbell, Robert–Morrison & Foerster LLP
Huber, Andreas–EQT Funds Management Ltd
Huber, Andreas–IKIB Mittelstandsfinanzierungs GmbH
Huber, Bill–North Branch Capital LP
Huber, Debra–Oaktree Capital Management LP
Huber, Gabriella–Royalton Partners
Huber, Paul–Clearlake Capital Group LP
Huber, Roman–Bayern Kapital GmbH
Huberman, Jonathan–Gores Group LLC
Huberman, Ron–Chicago Growth Partners LLC
Huberman, Ron–Prairie Capital, L.P.
Hubers, Gert Jan–Gebruder Heller Dinklage
Hubert, Nicolas–Blackstone Group LP
Hubertz, Heiko–H2 Properties GmbH
Hubler, Jodi–Lemhi Ventures, Inc.
Huckfield, David–Baring Private Equity Asia Ltd
Huddleston, Richard–Valstone Partners LLC
Hudecek, Lukas–Startup Yard Ltd
Hudson, Charles–Uncork Capital
Hudson, David–Darby Overseas Investments, Ltd.
Hudson, Deborah–Shackleton Ventures Ltd
Hudson, Jacob–Atlas Holdings FRM LLC
Hudson, Joe–One Earth Capital LLC
Hudson, Jordan–Upfront Ventures
Hudson, M. Ashton–Rock Creek Capital LLC
Hudson, Paul–Blackstone Group LP
Hudson, Peter–Alta Partners
Hudson, Ricardo–eBricks Digital
Huebner, Matt–Headwaters BD LLC
Huerta, Nick–MPK Equity Partners LLC
Huet, Eric–Ventech SA
Huey, Henry–Arsenal
Huey, Henry–OnPoint Technologies
Huff, Carrie–Haynes and Boone LLC
Huff, Craig–Reservoir Capital Group LLC
Huff, Henry–Cambrian Ventures Inc
Huff, James–ClearSky Power & Technology Fund I LLC
Huff, Jesse–Carlyle Group LP
Huff, Peter–Blue Sage Capital LP
Huff, Peter–Werklund Capital Corp
Huffsmith, Joseph–One Equity Partners LLC
Hug, Joachim–Myonic Holding GmbH
Hugenholtz, Paul–AAC CAPITAL PARTNERS
Hugger, Thomas–Asia Frontier Investments Ltd
Hughes, Andrew–Deepbridge Capital LLP
Hughes, Charles–Easton Hunt Capital Partners LP
Hughes, David–Foresight Group LLP
Hughes, Donald–Camden Partners Holdings LLC
Hughes, Emma–Chartline Capital Partners
Hughes, Gayle–Merion Investment Partners LP
Hughes, Larry–Morris Capital Management LLC
Hughes, Mark–Comvest Partners
Hughes, Patrick–Haynes and Boone LLC
Hughes, Todd–Portfolio Advisors, LLC

Pratt's Guide to Private Equity & Venture Capital Sources

Hughes, William–Providence Equity Partners LLC
Hughlett, Bill–Voyager Capital LLC
Huh, Charles–Standard Chartered Private Equity Ltd
Huh, Dae Young–Centurion Technology Investment Corp
Hui, Daniel–Aif Capital Asia Iii LP
Hui, Kenin–Redrock Capital Venture Ltd
Hui, Kersten–Israel Infinity Venture Capital Fund Israel LP
Hui, Richard–Panthera Capital Group
Huie, Allen–Shaw Kwei & Partners
Huie, Stephanie–University of Texas System
Huisken, Christopher–Oaktree Capital Management LP
Huisman, Arjan–Van Lanschot Participaties BV
Huitink, Jon–Comvest Partners
Hukari, Scott–Anderson Group LLC, The
Hulecki, Gregory–Fa Technology Ventures Corp
Hulileh, Samir–Siraj Fund Management Co
Hull, Brandon–CHP Management Inc
Hull, David–Centennial Ventures Vii L P
Hull, Gary–Summer Street Capital Partners LLC
Hull, Hewes–Lazarus Capital Partners
Hull, James Mitchell–Hull Capital Management LLC
Hull, John–Marquam Hill Capital LLC
Hull, Mark–Prospect Street Ventures
Hull, Robert–Providence Equity Partners LLC
Hullett, J.–Lacuna LLC
Hullinger, Michael–Endurance Capital Holdings LLC
Hultguist, Gary–Newcap Partners Inc
Hultin, Anders–Nordic Capital
Humann, Phillip–SunTrust Banks Inc
Humbaugh, Matthew–Carlyle Group LP
Humber, Michael–Redmont Venture Partners
Humber, Scott–Landmark Partners Inc
Humbert, Frederic–Innovacom Gestion SAS
Hume, Jo–Southern Cross Venture Partners Pty Ltd
Hume, Kathryn–ff Venture Capital
Humenansky, Michael–City Capital Ventures LLC
Humer, Franz–Pappas Ventures
Humes, Robert–JK&B Capital LLC
Hummelmose, Morten–EQT Funds Management Ltd
Hummer, James–Luxemburg Capital LLC
Hummer, John–Hummer Winblad Venture Partner
Humphrey, David–Bain Capital Inc
Humphrey, David–Oklahoma Equity Partners LLC
Humphrey, David–Oklahoma Equity Partners LLC
Humphreys, Thomas–Morrison & Foerster LLP
Humphries, Nic–HgCapital Trust PLC
Hunchak, Wanda–Westcap Management Ltd
Hung, Leung–Tpg Growth LLC
Hung, Richard–Morrison & Foerster LLP
Hunkapiller, Michael–Alloy Ventures Inc
Hunnicutt, Jonathan–Westview Capital Partners LP
Hunt, Christopher–Riverstone Holdings LLC
Hunt, Elaine–Atlantic Asset Management LLC
Hunt, James–Blu Venture Investors LLC
Hunt, Jeremy–Morrison & Foerster LLP
Hunt, John–ABRY Partners LLC
Hunt, Marshall–All-American Holdings LLC
Hunt, Martin–H2o Venture Partners Pe Ltd
Hunt, Peter–J B Poindexter & Co Inc
Hunt, Randall–Satori Capital LLC
Hunt, Robert–Tuatara Capital LP
Hunt, Ronald–New Leaf Venture Partners LLC

Hunter, Brian–Northbridge Capital Partners
Hunter, Matthew–Carlyle Group LP
Hunter, Michael–Heidrick & Struggles International Inc
Hunter, Peter–Artemis Capital Partners
Hunter, Sue–Frog Capital Ltd
Hunter, Tom–West Coast Capital
Hunter, Wally–Enertech Capital
Hunter, Wayne–Harbert Management Corp
Hunwick, Terese–Belle Michigan Fund LP
Huo, Richard–Lincolnshire Management Inc
Huo, Xiaohu–Beijing Tianxing Chuanglian Investment Management Co., Ltd.
Huot, Jacques–Cfi Capital
Huot, Thomas–Vantagepoint Management Inc
Huot, Valery–Innovation Capital SAS
Hur, Justin–IMM Private Equity Inc
Hurd, Jason–Bunker Hill Capital LP
Huret, Robert–Financial Technology Ventures
Huriez, Alain–Advent Venture Partners LLP
Hurley, Chris–Lloyds Development Capital (Holdings) Ltd
Hurn, Patricia–University of Texas System
Hursever, Evis–EW Healthcare Partners
Hursever, Umur–Capital International Inc
Hurst, Bob–Crestview Advisors, LLC
Hurst, Chris–Thomas Weisel Partners Group Inc
Hurst, Jeffrey–Commonwealth Capital Ventures
Hurth, Kevin–Insight Venture Partners LLC
Hurwitz, Cary–MDB Capital Group LLC
Hurwitz, Kenneth–Haynes and Boone LLC
Hurwitz, Richard–Larsen Maccoll Partners LP
Hurwitz, Roger–Volition Capital LLC
Husain, Fazle–CVC Capital Partners Ltd
Husain, Kumber–WP Global Partners Inc
Husain, M. Fazle–Metalmark Capital Holdings LLC
Huse, Del–Oakley Capital Ltd
Huseby, Thomas–Covera Ventures LP
Huseby, Thomas–Oak Investment Partners
Huskinson, Todd–Stellus Capital Management LLC
Husmann, Christoph–Capital Stage AG
Hussein, Abdul Aziz Feisal–Malaysia Venture Capital Management Bhd
Hussein, Farouk–HGGC LLC
Husseini, Fayez–Abraaj Capital Ltd
Hustis, Jonathan–Teakwood Capital LP
Huston, James–Morrison & Foerster LLP
Huston, Jim–Bridge City Management LLC
Hutcheson, Edward–Platte River Ventures LLC
Hutchins, Glenn–Silver Lake Partners LP
Hutchinson, Geoff–Pacific Equity Partners Pty Ltd
Hutchinson, Louis–WGL Holdings Inc
Hutchinson, Mathew–CBPE Capital LLP
Hutchison, William–HealthCap Partners LLC
Huth, Florian–Adm Capital
Hutt, Joseph–Formative Ventures
Hutter, Michael–Bellevue Asset Management AG
Hutter, Robert–Learn Capital Venture Partners LP
Hutton, Graham–Hutton Collins Partners LLP
Hutton, Peter–Coller Capital Ltd
Hutton, Wende–Canaan Partners
Huwendiek, Carsten–Pantheon Ventures (UK) LLP
Huyghues Despointes, Henry–21 Centrale Partners SA
Huygues-Despointes, Pierre–Remora Partners SA

Hwang, Chang Seok–Atinum Investment Co Ltd
Hwang, In Seon–Warburg Pincus LLC
Hwang, John–Crescent Capital Group LP
Hwang, Natalie–Blackstone Group LP
Hwang, Rebeca–Rivet Ventures Management LLC
Hwang, Tien-Lai–Acorn Campus Ventures
Hwang, Victor–Industry Ventures LLC
Hwang, Victor–Industry Ventures LLC
Hway, Gerry–Cfi Capital
Hyans, Hollis–Morrison & Foerster LLP
Hyatt, Jared–Norwest Venture Partners
Hyatt, Nabeel–Spark Capital
Hyatt, W. Michael–Jasper Ridge Partners LP
Hyde, Brady–WP Global Partners Inc
Hyde-Thomson, Henry–Anglo Scientific Ltd
Hyman, Frank–Root Capital LLP
Hyman, John–Algonquin Advisors LLC
Hyman, Matthew–Brown Brothers Harriman & Co
Hyman, Spencer–Wellington Partners GmbH
Hyndman, Stephen–GGV Capital
Hyndman, Stephen–GGV Capital
Hynes, Alanna–Ascribe Capital, LLC
Hynes, Rory–Enterprise Equity Venture Capital Group
Hyslop, Ian–Scottish Microelectronics Centre
Hyun, Seung Hui–KTB Investment & Securities Co Ltd
Hyzak, Dwayne–Main Street Capital Corp
I Equilbec, Philippe–TRG Management LP
Iaffaldano, Paul–Accelerant Equity LLC
Iamiceli, Daniel–FLAG Capital Management LLC
Iamoni, Stefano–Consilium SGR pA
Ianello, Peter–OCA Ventures
Ianiro, Thomas–First Analysis Corp
Iannariello, Maria Pia–MGM Innova Capital LLC
Iannazzo, Claudia–Pereg Ventures LLC
Ibrahim, Ameenah–Mcb Equity Fund Ltd
Ibrahim, Lila–Kleiner Perkins Caufield & Byers LLC
Ibrahim, Maha–Canaan Partners
Ibrahim, Munaf–Jahangir Siddiqui Group Associates
Ibri, Daniel–Mindset Ventures
Icaza, Alexandre–I5 Empresas Consultoria e Participacoes Ltda
Icaza, Gabriella–I5 Empresas Consultoria e Participacoes Ltda
Ichinose, Stephanie–Accel Partners & Co Inc
Ide, Keisuke–Globis Capital Partners & Co
Ideguchi, Akihiro–Globis Capital Partners & Co
Idemoto, Derek–Cisco Investments Inc
Idiahi, Eric–Verod Capital Management Ltd
Idriss, Talal–Saned Equity Partners Ltd
Iga, Kanami–Mitsui & Co Global Investment Ltd
Igea, Felix Guerrero–Ged Group
Igel, Fabio–Monashees Gestao de Investimentos Ltda
Iglehart, Judith–Keiretsu Forum
Ignaczak, Anthony–Quad-C Management Inc
Iijima, Christine–Metropolitan Real Estate Equity Management LLC
Iijima, Hisao–Carlyle Group LP
Iino, Satoru–Whiz Partners Inc
Iinuma, Ryosuke–Ant Capital Partners Co Ltd
Ikebuchi, Shohei–Gogin Capital Co Ltd
Ikeda, Donna–Templeton Asset Management Ltd
Ikeda, Eiichiro–Hoya Corp

Ikegami, Hayato—Samurai Incubate Inc
Ikegami, Manabu—Novaquest Infosystems Inc
Ikegaya, Hiroshi—Works Capital Inc
Ilagan, Michael—SunTx Capital Partners LP
Ilchuk, Vlad—OnWave Ventures
Iliev, Ilian—Ecomachines Ventures Ltd
Illat, Florent—Quadrille Capital SAS
Illig, Randy—Selway Partners L L C
Illikman, James—Peninsula Capital Partners LLC
Illovsky, Eugene—Morrison & Foerster LLP
Ilsoe, Bo—NGP Capital
Ilundain, Daniel—Palladium Equity Partners LLC
Ilzarbe, Miguel—Flagship Pioneering
Imaizumi, Tomoyuki—Ant Capital Partners Co Ltd
Imano, Minoru—Globis Capital Partners & Co
Imbrogno, Edward—Fidus Capital LLC
Imershein, Robert—Loeb Enterprises LLC
Imeson, Patrick—Black Diamond Financial Group LLC
Imhoff, Kevin—Atlantic-Pacific Capital Inc
Imhoff, W. Joseph—Navigator Equity Partners LLC
Immergut, Mel—Milbank Tweed Hadley & Mccloy LLP
Imran, Mir—InCube Ventures LLC
In, Young—Oaktree Capital Management LP
Inamdar, Samir—Axon Partners Group Investment
Inamdar, Samir—Forum Synergies India Pe Fund Managers P Ltd
Inan, Altug—Ilab Holding AS
Inbar, Doron—Carmel Ventures IV Principals Fund LP
Inchley, Simon—Gresham Llp
Ind, Charles—Bowmark Capital LLP
Indahl, Reynir—Altor Equity Partners AB
Indelicato, William—Portfolio Advisors, LLC
Indest, Will—Draper Triangle Ventures LP
Ines, Henry—DragonVenture, Inc.
Infurchia, Chris—Dolphin Capital Group LLC
Ingeborn, Staffan—Innovationskapital Nordic Advisors AB
Ingebrigtsen, Kristin—Sakorninvest Nord AS
Ingenhoven, Thomas—Milbank Tweed Hadley & Mccloy LLP
Ingersoll, W. Brett—Cerberus Capital Management LP
Ingestrom, Anders—Coach & Capital Nordic 1 AB
Ingham, Carlos—Linzor Capital Partners LP
Ingle, Jason—Closed Loop Capital
Inglis, Chris—Paladin Capital Management LLC
Ingraham, David—M/C Venture Partners LLC
Ingram, Robert—Hatteras Venture Partners
Ingster, Mike—Formative Ventures
Inkinen, Sami—Obvious Ventures Management LLC
Inman, Bobby—Gefinor Ventures
Inman, Thomas—Gefinor Ventures
Inorio, Kathi—Orchard First Source Inc
Inose, Sotaro—Polaris Capital Group Co Ltd
Inoue, Kanako—Genuine Startups KK
Inouye Tarter, Susan—Perseus LLC
Insalaco, Steven—Calgary Enterprises Inc
Insull, Jonathan—Crescent Capital Group LP
Intlekofer, Paul—SFP Capital LLC
Ioannou, John—Metropolitan Equity Partners LLC
Iorillo, Christopher—CounterPoint Capital Partners LLC
Iorio, Scott—GoldPoint Partners LLC
Ip, Dennis—On Capital Ltd

Ippolito, John—Headwaters BD LLC
Ippolito, Roberto—RiverRock European Capital Partners LLP
Irani, Martin—Hancock Park Associates A California LP
Irani, Zubin—TPG Capital Management LP
Ireland, David—Navis Management Sdn Bhd
Ireland, Oliver—Morrison & Foerster LLP
Irigoin, Alfredo—Linzor Capital Partners LP
Ironside, Adrian—Guardian Capital Partners
Irvani, Sam—Waveland Capital Group LLC
Irving, Charles—Pond Venture Partners Ltd
Irving, Richard—Pond Venture Partners Ltd
Irwin, Alex—Growth Works Capital Ltd
Irwin, John—Brookside International
Irwin, Michael—El Dorado Ventures
Irwin, Scott—Rembrandt Venture Management LLC
Isaacs, Jeremy—JRJ Ventures LLP
Isaacs, Mark—First Avenue Partners, L.P.
Isaacson, Jon—Acas LLC
Isacoff, Oren—Longitude Capital Management Co LLC
Isaji, Masataka—NTT Finance Corp
Isaly, Samuel—OrbiMed Advisors LLC
Isayama, Yuan—WiL Inc
Isenrich, Markus—Ferro Management Group Inc
Isern, Brian—Sibling Capital LLC
Ishbia, Justin—Shore Capital Partners LLC
Ishigami, Tatsuzo—Watervein Partners KK
Ishihara, Minoru—Ichigo Inc
Ishikawa, Junya—Bain Capital Inc
Ishikawa, Naomi—Milbank Tweed Hadley & Mccloy LLP
Ishikiwa, Masanori—Watervein Partners KK
Ishikure, Tomoaki—Global Brain Corp
Isikoff, Andrew—Silverfern Group Inc
Islam, Ifty—Asian Tiger Capital Partners Ltd
Ismael, Ahmet—Orthogonal Partners LLP
Ismail, Mohamed—Boubyan Bank KSCP
Isnard, Arnaud—Arcis Finance SA
Isnard, Henri—Arcis Finance SA
Isoda, Jun—Siguler Guff & Company LP
Isono, Masa—Defta Partners
Isozaki, Eiichi—Southern Capital Group Pte Ltd
Israel, James—Ingleside Investors LLC
Israel, Michael—Mill City Capital LP
Israeli, David—Pitango Venture Capital Management Israel, Ltd.
Israely, Gal—SIDER ISRA'EL IYE`UTS KALKALI BE`AM
Issott, David—Apax Partners LLP
Italahti, Kari—Nordic Option Oy
Ito, Joichi—Neoteny Labs Pte Ltd
Ito, Katsuhiro—Mitsubishi International Corp
Ito, Kengo—Genuine Startups KK
Ittycheria, Dev—Greylock Partners
Itwaru, M. Glen—Metalmark Capital Holdings LLC
Ivanov, Mikhail—Baring Vostok Capital Partners Ltd
Iven, Arend—BVP Berlin Venture Partners GmbH
Ivers, Joel—Accelerant Fund I LP
Iversen, Brian—Blue Bear Capital LLC
Iversen, Brian—Riverstone Holdings LLC
Iversen, Jens—Kirk & Thorsen Invest A/S
Iverson, Carol—British Columbia Investment Management Corp
Ives, Christopher—Advent International Corp
Ives, John—Tahoma Advisors Inc

Ivey, Grahame—Investcorp Bank BSC
Ivey, Grahame—Investcorp Technology Investments Group
Ivey, Phil—Crofton Capital LLC
Ivy, Li—Seven Seas Partners
Iwaki, Yuichi—kk bhp
Iwamura, Kimihiko—OMRON ADVANCED SYSTEMS INC
Iwasa, Mitsukazu—Shinwa Venture Capital Co Ltd
Iyer, Krishnan—IEP Fund Advisors Pvt Ltd
Iyer, Prakash—Reliance Capital Ventures Ltd
Iz, Ali—NewWorld Capital Group LLC
Izard, Charles—Brown Brothers Harriman & Co
Izumida, Ryugo—Mitsubishi International Corp
J.L. Duarte, Antonio—Dgf Investimentos Gestao De Fundos Ltda
Jaber, Ronnie—Carlyle Group LP
Jablon, Michael—Varsity Healthcare Partners
Jablonski, Lisa—Antares Capital Corp
Jacimovic, Vladimir—Continuum Capital LLC
Jack, Blythe—TSG Consumer Partners, L.P.
Jacks, Joel—CM Equity Partners LP
Jackson, Angela—Bridge City Management LLC
Jackson, Brodi—Caerus Ventures LLC
Jackson, Chad—IncTANK Ventures
Jackson, Chrisman—HealthCap Partners LLC
Jackson, Clara—TA Associates Management LP
Jackson, David—Thomas H Lee Partners LP
Jackson, Donald—Haynes and Boone LLC
Jackson, Dustin—KRG Capital Management LP
Jackson, Grant—Council Capital
Jackson, Herbert—Renaissance Ventures L L C
Jackson, James—Insight Equity Holdings LLC
Jackson, James—Susquehanna Private Capital LLC
Jackson, Jeff—Thayer Ventures
Jackson, Jerry—Polar Capital Investments
Jackson, Kevin—Gridiron Capital LLC
Jackson, Michael—Housatonic Partners Management Co Inc
Jackson, Michael—Ironwood Partners LLC
Jackson, Michael—Mangrove Capital Partners SA
Jackson, Mike—Westly Group LLC
Jackson, Peg—Cava Capital
Jackson, Robert—Deerfield Management Company LP
Jackson, Ron—Triwest Capital Mgmt Corp
Jackson, Thomas—Easton Hunt Capital Partners LP
Jackson, William—Bridgepoint Advisers Ltd
Jacob, Anup—Virgin Green Fund
Jacob, Bharati—Seedfund
Jacob, David—Henderson Global Investors Ltd
Jacob, Josh—Hamilton Lane Advisors LLC
Jacobi, Olaf—Target Partners GmbH
Jacobi, Paul—Wexford Capital LP
Jacobi, Philipp—Suma Verwaltungs GmbH
Jacobi, Tal—StageOne Ventures
Jacobs van Merlen, Christophe—Bain Capital Inc
Jacobs, Andrew—Metropolitan Real Estate Equity Management LLC
Jacobs, Brian—Emergence Capital Partners
Jacobs, Bruce—Westfield Capital Management Company LP
Jacobs, Christopher—Tower Three Partners LLC
Jacobs, David—Nova Capital Management, Ltd.
Jacobs, John—NCA Partners Inc

Jacobs, Joseph–Wexford Capital LP
Jacobs, Justin–Mill Road Capital Management LLC
Jacobs, Laurence–Milbank Tweed Hadley & Mccloy LLP
Jacobs, Mark–Oaktree Capital Management LP
Jacobs, Michael–Morrison & Foerster LLP
Jacobs, Russell–Milbank Tweed Hadley & Mccloy LLP
Jacobsen, Brad–Irving Place Capital LLC
Jacobsen, Brian–Grand Crossing Capital LLC
Jacobsen, Brian–Towerbrook Capital Partners LP
Jacobsen, Kjell–Energy Ventures AS
Jacobsen, Mark–O'Reilly Alphatech Ventures LLC
Jacobsen, Robert–Fundamental Advisors LP
Jacobsohn, Sean–Norwest Venture Partners
Jacobson, Aaron–New Enterprise Associates Inc
Jacobson, Benjamin–Jacobson Partners
Jacobson, Daniel–Crossharbor Capital Partners
Jacobson, Darryl–Antares Capital Corp
Jacobson, David–Monroe Capital LLC
Jacobson, Dean–Accel-KKR
Jacobson, Glenn–Trilantic Capital Management LP
Jacobson, Glenn–Trilantic Capital Management LP
Jacobson, Harry–TriStar Technology Ventures LLC
Jacobson, Lorne–Triwest Capital Mgmt Corp
Jacobson, Matthew–Battery Ventures LP
Jacobson, Matthew–Charlesbank Capital Partners LLC
Jacobson, Perry–Brookstone Partners LLP
Jacobson, S. Alexander–137 Ventures LP
Jacobson, Scott–MadroNA Venture Group
Jacops, Randy–Valhalla Partners LP
Jacqueau, Guillaume–Equistone Partners Europe Ltd
Jacquin, Ken–Dolphin Capital Group LLC
Jacquinet, Dominique Michel Ren–Ocean Participations SAS
Jadot, Bryan–Hercules Capital Inc
Jaeckel, Jeff–Morrison & Foerster LLP
Jaeger, Karl–Argonne Capital Group LLC
Jaeger, Ralph–Siguler Guff & Company LP
Jaeger, Wilfred–Three Arch Partners LP
Jafar, Badr–Crescent Enterprises
Jafar, Imran–Gaja Capital Partners
Jaffe, Danny–Angeleno Group Investors LLC
Jaffe, David–Centre Partners Management LLC
Jaffe, Ross–Versant Venture Management, LLC
Jaffe, Steven–Jacobson Partners
Jaffee, Diane–Trust Company of the West
Jaffee, Steven–Reservoir Venture Partners 2 LP
Jagannath, Ram–Carlyle Group LP
Jagdale, Rajendra–Indian Steps and Business Incubators Association
Jager, Remko A.–Gilde Investment Management BV
Jager, Remko–Gilde Equity Management GEM Benelux Partners BV
Jaggers, John–Sevin Rosen Funds
Jaggers, Kurt–TA Associates Management LP
Jaggers, Tom–Oaktree Capital Management LP
Jaggi, Gautam–O3 Capital Advisors Pvt Ltd
Jagla, Daniel–Cedar Creek Partners
Jaharis, Michael–Vatera Healthcare Partners LLC
Jahic, Jodi–Aligned Partners LLC
Jahn, Paul–Morrison & Foerster LLP
Jahnke, James–Palisade Capital Management LLC
Jahns, David–Galen Associates Inc

Jaidi, Fouad–BC Partners LLP
Jaime, Londono–Pantheon Ventures (UK) LLP
Jain, Aalok–Vector Capital Management LP
Jain, Aayush–Unicorn India Ventures Advisors LLP
Jain, Ankur–Blumberg International Partners LLC
Jain, Arvind–Banyantree Finance Pvt Ltd
Jain, Aviral–Siguler Guff & Company LP
Jain, Gaurav–Founder Collective LP
Jain, Gopal–Gaja Capital Partners
Jain, Hetal–EQ India Advisors
Jain, Mitin–Banyantree Finance Pvt Ltd
Jain, Mudit–Synergy Life Science Partners LP
Jain, Neha–Chilango Ventures LLC
Jain, Pankaj–500 Startups, L.P.
Jain, Prashant–O3 Capital Advisors Pvt Ltd
Jain, Pravin–Sonoma Management Partners Pvt Ltd
Jain, Rakesh–Star Mountain Capital LLC
Jain, Rohit–HandsOn3 LLC
Jain, SK–Westbridge Capital Advisors (India) Pvt Ltd
Jain, Sumit–Kalaari Capital Partners LLC
Jain, Sunil–Aditya Birla Capital Advisors Pvt Ltd
Jain, Uttam–Thomas H Lee Partners LP
Jain, Vishal–Nadathur Estates Pvt Ltd
Jakobovits, Aya–OrbiMed Advisors LLC
Jakola, Karl-Johan–Norinnova Forvaltning AS
Jalan, Sonu–Kotak Investment Advisors Ltd
Jalil, Effendi Abdul–Malaysia Venture Capital Management Bhd
Jalkanen, Markku–Inveni Capital Oy
Jama, Mustafa–Morgan Stanley Alternative Investment Partners LP
James, Anthony–Awal Bank BSCC
James, Christopher–Blackstone Group LP
James, Daniel–Trilantic Capital Management LP
James, E. Daniel–Trilantic Capital Management LP
James, Heb–Southfield Capital Advisors LLC
James, Janet–Rockport Capital Partners
James, Joanna–Advent International Corp
James, Josh–Zetta Venture Partners
James, Mathew–Motion Equity Partners LLP
James, Ransom–Eagle Merchant Partners
James, Stephanie–Atlantic Street Capital Management LLC
James, Trevor–Morrison & Foerster LLP
James, William–Rockport Capital Partners
James, William–Sun Capital Partners Inc
Jameson, Jonathan–Probitas Partners Inc
Jamieson, Don–Caltius Mezzanine
Jamison, Jay–Bluerun Ventures LP
Jamison, Kevin–Diversified Trust Company Inc
Jammayrac, Louis–Inserm Transfert Initiative SAS
Jamp, Ray–Acorn Campus Ventures
Jamp, Rueiming–Acorn Campus Ventures
Jamsen, Risto–Midinvest Management Oy
Jamsheer, Abdulrahman–Esterad Investment Co BSC
Janacek, Anina–LYRIQUE Srrl
Janahi, Faisal–Esterad Investment Co BSC
Janahi, Rashad–Infra Capital Investments PJSC
Janchar, Matthew–Berkshire Partners LLC
Jander, Richard–Maranon Capital LP
Jane, Andrew–Talu Ventures Pty Ltd
Janes, Robert–SF Holding Corp
Janetschek, William–KKR & Co LP
Janeway, William–Warburg Pincus LLC
Jang, Daniel–Monitor Clipper Partners LLC

Jang, Lae–Formation Group Inc
Jang, Sang-hyuk–Korea Investment Partners Co Ltd
Jang, Seok Hwan–Intellectual Discovery Ventures
JangJan, Lynn–Acas LLC
Jangalapalli, AJ–Thoma Bravo LLC
Jani, Ajay–Gramercy Inc
Jani, Amish–FirstMark Capital LLC
Jania, Gregory–WP Global Partners Inc
Janiak Earthy, Carolyn–Avista Capital Holdings LP
Janiak, Danny–Mercury Fund
Jankura, Richard–Jumpstart Inc
Janmohamed, Arif–Lightspeed Management Company LLC
Jannetta, David–Alara Capital Partners LLC
Janney, Daniel–Alta Partners
Janning, Jim–Harbour Group Ltd
Janower, Andrew–Charlesbank Capital Partners LLC
Jansa, Michael–Emerging Capital Partners
Jansen, Axel–BID Equity Advisory GmbH
Jansen, Corne–Holland Private Equity BV
Jansen, Richard–CCMP Capital Advisors LP
Jansen, Siem–NV NOM
Jansen, Yvan–E Capital Management Scrl
Janson, Paul–Headwaters BD LLC
Janson, Thomas–Milbank Tweed Hadley & Mccloy LLP
Janssens, Bert–Warburg Pincus LLC
Janssens, Paul–Greenfield Capital Partners BV
Janssens, Paul–Venturebaycom
Jansson, Marcus–Segulah Advisor AB
Janszky, Andrew–Milbank Tweed Hadley & Mccloy LLP
Jantz, Waldemar–Target Partners GmbH
Jantzen, Mark–Jwi Capital LLC
Jantzen, Tammi–Battelle Ventures LP
January, Ernest–Medu Capital(Pty)Ltd
January, Mikala–C3 Capital LLC
Janus, Minou–Nordian Capital BV
Jaquette, George–Clayton Dubilier & Rice LLC
Jarausch, Konrad–Tolero Ventures LLC
Jarchow, Craig–Pine Brook Road Partners LLC
Jardim, Francisco–SP Ventures Gestora de Recursos SA
Jaresko, Natalie–Horizon Capital Management
Jargiello, David–Flywheel Ventures
Jarjour, Michael–Mansa Capital Management LLC
Jarmak, Antoine–CM CIC Investissement SA
Jarmel, Steve–Periscope Equity LLC
Jarockis, Marijus–LANDMARK CAPITAL UAB
Jarosz, William–Cartesian Capital Group LLC
Jarousse, Olivier–U I Gestion SA
Jarrard, Michelle–GRA Venture Fund LLC
Jarrett, Gary–Black River Asset Management LLC
Jarrett, Lauranne–G 51 Capital Management LLC
Jarrsten, Fredrik–Karolinska Development AB
Jarve, John–Menlo Ventures
Jarve, John–Menlo Ventures
Jarvenas, Ulf–Fouriertransform AB
Jarvis, Bill–Blue Loop Capital LLC
Jarvis, Garth–Horizon Equity Partners Pty Ltd
Jarvis, Kenneth–Portfolio Advisors, LLC
Jarvis, Scot–Oak Investment Partners
Jasek, Radim–Genesis Capital sro
Jauhari, Anadi–Emerging Energy & Environment LLC
Jaunich, Robert–Calera Capital Management Inc

Javeri, Hamchandra—Axon Partners Group Investment
Javeri, Hemchandra—Forum Synergies India Pe Fund Managers P Ltd
Javeri, Munir—3G Capital Inc
Javier, Carlos—NextEnergy Capital Ltd
Javier, Joey—Alphanorth Asset Management
Jawa, Ahmed—Starling International Management Ltd (Dubai Branch)
Jawad, Amin—Arcapita Inc
Jawahar, R. M. P.—Indian Steps and Business Incubators Association
Jay, Andrew—Siemens Venture Capital GmbH
Jay, Jeffrey—Great Point Partners LLC
Jay, Quinton—Bacchus Capital Management LLC
Jayachander, AJV—Financial Corporation Co SAOG
Jayadev, Arun—Wellington Partners GmbH
Jayakumar, A.R.—Karnataka Information Technology Venture Capital Fund
Jayakumar, Vinoth—Draper Esprit PLC
Jayanti, D.T.—Corsair Capital LLC
Jayaraman, Karthic—Carlyle Group LP
Jayaratnam, Ajit—Euromezzanine Gestion SaS
Jayawardana, Kusal—N D B Capital Holdings PLC
Jaysane-Darr, Evan—Invesco Private Capital Inc
Jazbec, Daniel—Bellevue Asset Management AG
Jean-Baptiste, Nick—Peterson Partners LP
Jean-Mairet, Joel—Ysios Capital Partners SGECR SAU
Jeandron, Raymond—Longuevue Capital
Jeblonski, Wolfgang—Premium Equity Partners GmbH
Jeck, Eric—Trident Capital
Jeevarathnam, Brijesh—Commonfund Capital Inc
Jeffe, Dean—Antares Capital Corp
Jefferies, Shirley—Sterling Group LP
Jefferson, Lamont—Haynes and Boone LLC
Jeffrey, David—StepStone Group LP
Jeffs, James—Kairos Venture Investments LLC
Jegen, David—F-Prime Capital Partners
Jelen, Jason—SunTx Capital Partners LP
Jelezko, Oleg—Da Vinci Capital Management Ltd
Jellema, Albert—Go Capital Asset Management BV
Jelley, Keith—Harwood Capital LLP
Jelski, Robert—Capital-E NV
Jen, Katherine—Asiatech Management LLC
Jenkins, D. Scott—Carlyle Group LP
Jenkins, Donald—Main Street Capital Holdings LLC
Jenkins, James—Global Infrastructure Holdings
Jenkins, Paula—Indiana University
Jenkins, Robert—Pouschine Cook Capital Management LLC
Jenkins, Steven—Haynes and Boone LLC
Jenks, Stephen—Candescent Partners LLC
Jenkyn-Jones, Bruce—Impax Asset Management Ltd
Jenney, Frederick—Morrison & Foerster LLP
Jennings, Dennis—4Th Level Ventures
Jennings, J. Webb—Hancock Park Associates A California LP
Jennings, Ken—Homeland Defense Ventures
Jennings, Larry—Valstone Partners LLC
Jennings, Robert—Lazarus Capital Partners
Jennings, Simon—HarbourVest Partners LLC
Jennings, Thomas—Summit Partners LP
Jennings, Thomas—Summit Partners LP
Jennings-Mares, Jeremy—Morrison & Foerster LLP

Jensen, Andrew—Kearny Venture Partners LP
Jensen, Bjarne—VAEKSTFONDEN
Jensen, Charles—Greenline Ventures LLC
Jensen, Eric—Abundant Venture Partners LLC
Jensen, Eric—Beedie Capital Partners
Jensen, Eric—Newspring Capital
Jensen, Erik Balleby—Capidea Management ApS
Jensen, Henning—Kistefos Venture Capital As
Jensen, Kurt Jan—Nord Kapitalforvaltning AS
Jensen, Lars—Scale Capital ApS
Jensen, Mark—T Squared Capital LLC
Jensen, Per—Progressus Management As
Jensen, Peter—Spectrum Equity Investors LP
Jensen, Rune—Progressus Management As
Jensen, Stefan—Riordan Lewis & Haden
Jensen, Timothy—Oaktree Capital Management LP
Jentzsch, Stefan—Perella Weinberg Partners LP
Jenuth, Jacki—LCC Legacy Holdings Inc
Jeon, Yeong Bae—Hana Daetoo Securities Co Ltd
Jeong, David—STIC Investment Inc
Jerles, Todd—Trivest Partners LP
Jernigan, Clark—Austin Ventures
Jerstad, Michael—Prairiegold Venture Partners
Jerusalmi, Raffaele—Atlantic Capital Partners GmbH
Jeschke, Arnt—Rocket Internet AG
Jeschke, Stephen—GTCR Golder Rauner LLC
Jesse, Bill—Spanos Barber Jesse & Co LLC
Jessee, Daniel—CVF Capital Partners LLC
Jessup, Kevin—Salem Capital Partners, LP (FKA: Venture Capital Solutions)
Jester, Jay—Audax Group, Inc.
Jethwa, Sapna—Consonance Capital Partners LP
Jetley, Dinkar—Pivot Investment Partners LLC
Jetley, Rahul—Jacob Ballas Capital India Pvt Ltd
Jett, Lydia—M/C Venture Partners LLC
Jevon, Robert—Boston Millennia Partners LP
Jeyes, Peter—Verso Capital Partners
Jez, Vladislav—Credo Ventures as
Jezierski, Wojciech—Abris Capital Partners Sp zoo
Ji, Qinan—Feima Fund
Ji, Sungbae—IMM Investment Corp
Ji, Wei—Meridian Growth Fund Management Co Ltd
Jia, Ke—Prax Capital Management Co
Jia, Liangyi—Beijing Holch Investment Management, Ltd.
Jia, Wenzhong—Spring Capital Asia Ltd
Jiang, Bo—Shenzhen Fuhai Yintao Venture Capital Co Ltd
Jiang, Ce—Changsha Science & Technology Venture Capital Co Ltd
Jiang, David—PineBridge Investments LLC
Jiang, Don—Gobi Partners
Jiang, Elton—Northern Light Venture Capital Development II
Jiang, Gao Ming—Shanghai CCI Investment Co Ltd
Jiang, Guoliang—BOCGI Zheshang Investment Fund Management Zhejiang Co Ltd
Jiang, Hailin—Unisun Beijing Investment Co Ltd
Jiang, Hua—Gsr Ventures Management Llc
Jiang, Huichang—Ningbo Junrun Equity Investment Management Co Ltd
Jiang, Jian—CBC Capital
Jiang, Lin—Shenzhen Richland Investment Co Ltd
Jiang, Nanchun—Feima Fund
Jiang, Pengcheng—China King Link Corp

Jiang, Qunyi—Shenzhen Richland Investment Co Ltd
Jiang, Tao—Beijing Jike Menggongchang Venture Capital Center (L.P.)
Jiang, Tony—Carlyle Group LP
Jiang, Yongxiang—Shanghai Dingjia Ventures Co Ltd
Jiang, Yujie—Shenzhen Jidi Xintian Venture Investment Co Ltd
Jiang, Zhenglin—Beijing Hexin Dongli Investment Management Co Ltd
Jiao, Zhen—CDH China Management Co., Ltd.
Jikovski, George—Canyon Capital Advisors LLC
Jimenez-Ugarte, Nicolas—Mercapital SL
Jimenez-Ugarte, Nicolas—Mercapital SL
Jin, Angsheng—ShenZhen CDF-Capital Co Ltd
Jin, Chaoran—Keystone Capital Inc
Jin, Chris—SAIF Partners
Jin, Haizhong—Zhejiang Sinowisdom Capital Co Ltd
Jin, Jessie—GGV Capital
Jin, Jessie—GGV Capital
Jin, Jiong—SIG Capital Partners Ltd
Jin, Ming—Providence Equity Partners LLC
Jin, Xi—Keytone Ventures
Jin, Ying—Southern Raytai Fund Management Co Ltd
Jin, Yudan—SAIF Partners
Jin, Zhongren—Principle Capital Ltd
Jin-Hwee, Choo—Investor Growth Capital AB
Jiraskova, Katerina—PPF Partners as
Jirovec, Jan—Rockaway Capital SE
Jivanji, Shabbir—Cupola Group
Jivraj, Kabir—Noverra Consulting and Capital Partners
Jo, Michael—KSL Capital Partners LLC
Joannou, Bob—Gramercy Inc
Joaquin, James—Catamount Ventures LP
Joaquin, James—Obvious Ventures Management LLC
Jobson, Simon—GCP Member Ltd
Joednapa, Pattama—Food Capitals PCL
Joerger, Scott—Oaktree Capital Management LP
Joffe, Sean—Sixpoint Partners LLC
Jog, Rajesh—Waygate Capital India Pvt Ltd
Johal, Balbinder—MML Capital Partners LLP
Johan, Paul—Ballast Point Venture Partners LLC
Johann, Peter—NGN Capital LLC
Johansen, Ashley—AlpInvest Partners BV
Johansen, Ashley—Coller Capital Ltd
Johansen, Ashley—Monomoy Capital Partners LLC
Johansen, Jesper—Gro Capital A/S
Johansen, Neil—Fulcrum Capital Partners Inc
Johansen, Soren—Altor Equity Partners AB
Johansson, Curtis—Cai Capital Management Co
Johansson, Hakan—Bridgepoint Advisers Ltd
Johansson, Lars—New Mountain Capital I LLC
Johansson, Mats—Spintop Private Partners AB
Johansson, Tomas—Procuritas Partners Kb
John, Deepu—iSherpa Capital
John, Llewellyn—Fpe Capital LLP
John, Michael—Jh Partners LLC
John, Rebecca—Lexington Partners Inc
John, Veronica—IDFC Capital (Singapore) Pte Ltd
Johns, Brad—Yaletown Venture Partners
Johns-Martin, Whitney—TWV Capital Management LLC
Johnson, Abigail—Fidelity Investment Funds II
Johnson, Anne—Haynes and Boone LLC
Johnson, B. Kristine—Affinity Capital Management

2505

Cc
Johnson, Ben–Vitruvian Partners LLP
Johnson, Brett–Pantheon Ventures (UK) LLP
Johnson, Charles–Private Advisors LLC
Johnson, Charles–Tano Capital LLC
Johnson, Christian–AEA Investors LLC
Johnson, Cort–Accomplice LLC
Johnson, David–Carlyle Group LP
Johnson, Debbie–ABRY Partners LLC
Johnson, Don–Matthew Pritzker Company LLC
Johnson, Drew–CIC Partners, L.P.
Johnson, Drew–Gauge Capital LLC
Johnson, Drew–Susquehanna Private Capital LLC
Johnson, Dustin–Haynes and Boone LLC
Johnson, Edward–DLJ Merchant Banking Partners
Johnson, Edward–Gores Group LLC
Johnson, Emily–Hellman & Friedman LLC
Johnson, Geordy–UNC Kenan-Flagler Private Equity Fund
Johnson, Glenn–Global Infrastructure Holdings
Johnson, Grant–Newstone Capital Partners LLC
Johnson, Gregory–Prolog Ventures
Johnson, H.–FISK VENTURES INC
Johnson, Ian–Helmsman Funds Management, Ltd.
Johnson, James–Apex Venture Partners LLC
Johnson, James–Signal Hill Equity Partners
Johnson, James–Wingate Partners LP
Johnson, Jason–Brown Brothers Harriman & Co
Johnson, Jeffrey–Blackford Capital LLC
Johnson, Jerry–RLJ Equity Partners LLC
Johnson, Joseph–Starr International Company Inc
Johnson, Joshua–Berkshire Partners LLC
Johnson, Kenneth–Kegonsa Capital Partners LLC
Johnson, Kevin–Index Ventures
Johnson, Kimberly–Oaktree Capital Management LP
Johnson, Kinney–Sequel Venture Partners
Johnson, Kristin–ACP Inc
Johnson, L. Robert–Founders Capital Partners
Johnson, Lon–Andrew W Byrd & Co LLC
Johnson, Luke–Platinum Equity LLC
Johnson, Luke–Risk Capital Partners Ltd
Johnson, Mark–Carlyle Group LP
Johnson, Mark–TTV Capital LLC
Johnson, Matthew–Gemini Partners, Inc.
Johnson, Monica–NGP Capital
Johnson, Nathan–Gemini Partners, Inc.
Johnson, Neil–3i Group PLC
Johnson, Patrik–Bregal Capital LLP
Johnson, Patrik–Bregal Investments LLP
Johnson, Peter–Developing World Markets Inc
Johnson, Rob–Delta Partners Ltd
Johnson, Robert–Founders Capital Partners
Johnson, Scott–NAV.VC
Johnson, Stephen–Integrated Partners
Johnson, Steve–Marlin Equity Partners LLC
Johnson, Susan–Front Street Capital
Johnson, Timothy–Blackstone Group LP
Johnson, Timothy–England Capital Partners LLC
Johnson, Timothy–Goldner Hawn Johnson & Morrison Inc
Johnson, Timothy–Goldner Hawn Johnson & Morrison Inc
Johnson, Wendy–ProQuest Investments
Johnson, William–Perella Weinberg Partners LP
Johnson-Miller, Joyce–Relativity Capital LLC

Johnsson, Mikael–Amadeus Capital Partners Ltd
Johnston, A. Bruce–TA Associates Management LP
Johnston, Alan–Morrison & Foerster LLP
Johnston, Allan–Synergy Partners International
Johnston, Ben–Battery Ventures LP
Johnston, Benjamin–Pine Brook Road Partners LLC
Johnston, David–Oaktree Capital Management LP
Johnston, David–Pfingsten Partners LLC
Johnston, Hooks–Valhalla Partners LP
Johnston, James–Moelis Capital Partners LLC
Johnston, Jim–NexPhase Capital LLC
Johnston, John–August Capital Management LLC
Johnston, Kelvin–Jog Capital Inc
Johnston, Lynn–Johnston Associates Inc
Johnston, Robert–Johnston Associates Inc
Johnstone, J. Trevor–Parallel49 Equity
Johnstone, Kathryn–Morrison & Foerster LLP
Johnstone, Trevor–Tricor Pacific Founders Capital Inc
Jokelainen, Ari–Sponsor Capital Oy
Jol, Arg–Brooklyn Ventures BV
Joliet, John–American Discovery Capital LLC
Joll, Toby–Partners Capital Investment Group Holdings LLC
Jolly, Anjali–Perseus LLC
Jolly, David–Coller Capital Ltd
Joly, Francois–Headlands Capital Management LLC
Jones, Aled–L-Gam Advisers LLP
Jones, Andrew–RIT Capital Partners PLC
Jones, Andy–Maryland Technology Development Corp
Jones, Brandon–Haynes and Boone LLC
Jones, Braun–Wwc Capital Fund L P
Jones, Brent–Northgate Capital LLC
Jones, Brian–Bankcap Partners Fund I LP
Jones, Brian–Iowa Corn Opportunities LLC
Jones, Cathy–Northill Capital LLP
Jones, Charles–Bedford Funding Capital Management LLC
Jones, Christopher–Bb&T Capital Partners LLC
Jones, Chuck–Torch Hill Investment Partners LLC
Jones, D. Thompson–Draper Triangle Ventures LP
Jones, Daniel–Cedar Hill Associates LLC
Jones, Daniel–Thomas H Lee Partners LP
Jones, Daryl–British Columbia Investment Management Corp
Jones, David–Bull City Venture Partners LLC
Jones, David–Chrysalis Ventures Inc
Jones, David–Crossharbor Capital Partners
Jones, David–Merit Capital Partners IV LLC
Jones, David–Southern Capitol Ventures LLC
Jones, E. Bartow–Riverstone Holdings LLC
Jones, Elaine–Pfizer Venture Investments
Jones, Elliott–Arrowhead Mezzanine LLC
Jones, Gareth–Fintech Collective Inc
Jones, Gregory–Edgewater Funds
Jones, Ian–Apax Partners LLP
Jones, J–Bluff Point Associates Corp
Jones, J. Chris–Haddington Ventures LLC
Jones, J. Mark–River Associates LLC
Jones, Jim–Industry Ventures LLC
Jones, Jonathan–Phase4 Ventures Ltd
Jones, Kathryn–Nova Capital Management, Ltd.
Jones, Kenneth–Boathouse Capital
Jones, Kevin–Alumni Capital Network Management Co LLC
Jones, Leland–Endeavour Capital Inc
Jones, Liz–F&C Equity Partners PLC
Jones, Luke–MML Capital Partners LLP
Jones, M. Scott–Haddington Ventures LLC
Jones, Madelaine–Oaktree Capital Management LP
Jones, Matt–Nth Power LLC
Jones, Matthew–Pantheon Ventures (UK) LLP
Jones, Michael–Seraphim Capital (General Partner) LLP
Jones, Mike–Rustic Partners LP
Jones, Nigel–TWJ Capital LLC
Jones, Oliver–Rutland Partners LLP
Jones, Paul–Pantheon Ventures (UK) LLP
Jones, Peter–Eden Ventures Ltd
Jones, Quentin–Equity Partners
Jones, Richard–Copeley Capital Partners I LP
Jones, Ross–Berkshire Partners LLC
Jones, Ryan–HarbourVest Partners LLC
Jones, Stephan–Spell Capital Partners LLC
Jones, Terrell–General Catalyst Partners LLC
Jones, Terry–Syncom Management Co Inc
Jones, Thad–Quad-C Management Inc
Jones, Thomas–TWJ Capital LLC
Jones, Timothy–Coller Capital Ltd
Jones, Tom–Single Oak Ventures LP
Jones, Trevor–Advantage Capital
Jones, Wink–Lacuna LLC
Jong, Brent–Castlelake LP
Jong-ku, Min–Woori Bank
Jong-wook, Kim–Woori Bank
Jonge Poerink, John–LJH Linley Capital LLC
Jonk, Rense–Navitas Management BV
Jonk, Wouter–SET Venture Partners BV
Jonke, Gert Reinhard–Gain Capital Participations GmbH
Jonovic, Andrej–HandsOn3 LLC
Jonovic, Sarah–HandsOn3 LLC
Jonquet, Philippe–La Financiere Patrimoniale d'Investissement SAS
Jonson, John–Capricorn Investment Group LLC
Jonson, Max–Bure Equity AB
Jonsson, Ingemar–Boforsstiftelsen
Joo, Kho Choon–Bioveda Capital Pte Ltd
Joo, Yik Su–Hana Daetoo Securities Co Ltd
Joost, Peter–Orchid Asia Group Management Ltd
Jorajuria, Marie–Women's Venture Capital Fund
Jordaan, Daniel–Carlyle Group LP
Jordaan, Hendrick–Morrison & Foerster LLP
Jordan, Darren–Silverfleet Capital Partners LLP
Jordan, Darren–Solomon Global Holdings Inc
Jordan, Gregory–Harbert Management Corp
Jordan, Jeff–Andreessen Horowitz LLC
Jordan, John–JZ Capital Partners Ltd
Jordan, John–Jordan Company LP
Jordan, Kevin–New MainStream Capital
Jordan, Len–MadroNA Venture Group
Jordan, Michael–Mill Creek Capital Advisors LLC
Jordan, Robert–Blackstone Group LP
Jordan, Ryan–Morgan Stanley Private Equity
Jordan, Stephen–RB Webber and Comapny Inc
Jordan, Todd–Harbert Management Corp
Jordon, Scott–Glynn Capital Management LLC
Jorgensen, Esben Bay–Odin Equity Partners K/S
Jorn, Todd–Medicis Capital GmbH

Joseph, Jeffrey—Oaktree Capital Management LP
Joseph, K.A.—Kerala Venture Capital Fund Pvt Ltd
Joseph, Mark—Oakley Capital Ltd
Joseph, Shaw—General Atlantic LLC
Josephson, John—Allen & Company of Florida, Inc.
Josephson, Marge—Bay City Capital LLC
Joshi, Anil—Unicorn India Ventures Advisors LLP
Joshi, Mihir—Gvfl Ltd
Joshi, Shalaka—Unitus Impact Partners LLC
Joshi, Shirish—Blackstone Group LP
Josic, E. Boyan—Troy Ventures LLC
Josse, Yannis—PAI Partners SAS
Joubert, Christian—Galia Gestion SAS
Joung, Richard—JAFCO Investment (Asia Pacific) Ltd
Jourdain, Pierre—Azulis Capital SA
Joy, Andrew—Hidden Harbor Capital Partners LLC
Joy, Bill—Kleiner Perkins Caufield & Byers LLC
Joyce, Kasey—Six Thirty
Jrolf, Mark—New Heritage Capital LLC
Ju, Sunglin—L&S VentureCapital Corp
Juban, Christopher—Evercore Inc
Judge, Geoffrey—iNovia Capital Inc
Judge, Paul—Tech Square Labs LLC
Judson, K. Leonard—Cycad Group LLC
Jugi, Frederic—City Star Private Equity Sas
Juliano, Richard—FTFD Fund Distributor Inc
Julianto, Awy—SparkLabs
Julich, Chris—ESCALATE CAPITAL I L P
Julien, Bruno—Tocqueville Finance SA
Julis, Mitchell—Canyon Capital Advisors LLC
Jullien, Thierry—Developpement et Partenariat PME SAS
Jump, Leslie—Sawari Ventures LLC
Jun, Richard—Bam Ventures GP LLC
Jun, Wooseok—Providence Equity Partners LLC
Junco, Pilar—Blackstone Group LP
Juneja, Bob—Harbour Point Capital
Juneja, Robert—Irving Place Capital LLC
Jung, Alexandra—Oak Hill Advisors LP
Jung, Hans—STIC Investment Inc
Jung, Jae Wuk—Hana Daetoo Securities Co Ltd
Jung, Oliver—Springstar GmbH
Jung, Stefan—Monk's Hill Ventures Pte Ltd
Jungblut, Eric—Finatem Fonds Management Verwaltungs GmbH
Jungels-Winkler, Christophe—Swarraton Partners Ltd
Jungerhans, Marius—Carlyle Group LP
Jungerman, Don—Renovo Capital LLC
Jungersen, Nicolai—Capidea Management ApS
Junker, Martin—Venture Stars GmbH
Junoy, Sebastian—Headway Capital Partners LLP
Junqueira, Gustavo—Inseed Investimentos Ltda
Jupiter, Lauren—Accelfoods LLC
Juracek, Tom—Marker Hill Capital LLC
Jurczak, Lubomir—Rtaventures VC Sp z o o Sk
Jurvetson, Steve—Draper Fisher Jurvetson
Juster, Kenneth—Warburg Pincus LLC
Justin, Tsang—Seven Seas Partners
Juthani, Chetan—Unilazer Ventures Pvt Ltd
Jyrkas, Tarja—Nexit Ventures Oy
KAPLAN, JEFF—Deerfield Management Company LP
KHANNA, SUNIL—Enhanced Capital Partners LLC
KIM, JEAN—Deerfield Management Company LP
Kaak, Joris—Varova BV
Kabakoff, David—Cross Valley Capital

Kabakoff, David—HealthQuest Capital
Kabakoff, David—HeathQuest Capital
Kabile, David—4D Global Energy Advisors SAS
Kabra, Pramod—True North
Kabrit, Tarek—Abraaj Capital Ltd
Kacer, Peter—KT Capital Management LLC
Kacergis, Joseph—Dresner Capital Resources Inc
Kachalia, Nirav—Morgan Creek Capital Management LLC
Kachmer, Carol—Kairos Venture Investments LLC
Kachuro, Yuri—United Capital Partners Advisory OOO
Kacprzyk, Aleksander—Resource Partners Sp z o o
Kaczynski, William—Bridge Street Capital Partners LLC
Kadaba, Neena—Mission Bay Capital LLC
Kadavy, Annie—Charles River Ventures LLC
Kaddaras, James—Developing World Markets Inc
Kade, Rebecca—Union Square Ventures LLC
Kaden, Douglas—Oak Hill Capital Management Inc
Kadeyan, Danielle—A Plus Finance SASU
Kadhiresan, V. Kadir—Johnson & Johnson Innovation-JJDC Inc
Kadifa, George—Arch Venture Partners LLC
Kadifa, George—Sumeru Equity Partners, L.P.
Kadlic, Jeffrey—Evolution Capital Partners LLC
Kaelin, Matthew—Roark Capital Group Inc
Kafka, Miles—Elephant Ventures LLC
Kafker, Roger—TA Associates Management LP
Kagan, Peter—Warburg Pincus LLC
Kaganov, Alan—U.S. Venture Partners
Kagle, Robert—Benchmark Capital Management Gesellschaft MBH In Liqu
Kagunye, Peter—Capital Resource Partners
Kahane, Stephen—SV Health Investors LLP
Kahane, William—GF Capital Management & Advisors LLC
Kahmann, Mike—CIT Group Inc
Kahn, Joshua—Hamilton Lane Advisors LLC
Kahn, Matthew—GB Credit Partners LLC
Kahr, Julia—Blackstone Group LP
Kahvejian, Avak—Flagship Pioneering
Kahya, Melis—General Atlantic LLC
Kahya, Melis—TSG Consumer Partners, L.P.
Kai, Gang—Beijing Wanze Investment Management Co Ltd
Kailian, Vaughn—MPM Capital LLC
Kaimal, Nithin—New Silk Route Partners, LLC
Kairouz, Habib—Rho Capital Partners Inc
Kaiser, Harold—Litorina Capital Advisors AB
Kaiser, Nick—Marlin Equity Partners LLC
Kaiser, William—Greylock Partners LLC
Kaiserswerth, Matthias—Commission for Technology and Innovation CTI
Kaji, Himanshu—Edelweiss Financial Services Ltd
Kak, Susheel—Adm Capital
Kakar, Sandip—Siguler Guff & Company LP
Kakaulin, Gene—Hudson Clean Energy Partners
Kakihira, Hiroshi—Mitsui & Co. Global Investment, Ltd.
Kakiriwaragodage, Senaka—N D B Capital Holdings PLC
Kalaman, Piotr—Small Enterprise Assistance Funds
Kalamea, Kulli—BPM Capital OU
Kalandar, Boris—MentorTech Ventures LLC
Kalawski, Eva—Platinum Equity LLC

Kalb, Michael—Sun Capital Partners Inc
Kale, Daniel—Trust Company of the West
Kalen, Lennart—Segulah Advisor AB
Kalik, Robert—Blackstone Group LP
Kalinske, Tom—Alsop Louie Partners
Kalish, Adam—LUX CAPITAL GROUP L L C
Kalish, Geoffrey—Aquiline Capital Partners LLC
Kalish, Rami—Pitango Venture Capital Management Israel, Ltd.
Kalish, Shlomo—Jerusalem Global Ventures
Kalisky-Bannett, Tilli—Greylock Israel Global Management Ltd
Kalkanis, Peter—Rho Capital Partners Inc
Kalker, Johannes—Patron Capital Advisers LLP
Kall, David—Glengary LLC
Kall, Pia—CapMan Oyj
Kallen, Christian—Hamilton Lane Advisors LLC
Kallen, Paul-Bernhard—Acton Capital Partners GmbH
Kallinis, Dimitri—Axon Partners Group Investment
Kallioniemi, Kimmo—Nordic Mezzanine Ltd
Kalliovaara, Juhani—Sponsor Capital Oy
Kallman, Rhonda—Impact Capital Inc
Kallman, William—Timberline Venture Partners
Kallmeyer, M. Neil—Capstreet Group LLC
Kalnow, Andrew—Alpha Capital Partners, Ltd.
Kalra, Tarun—Next World Capital LLC
Kalteis, Stefan—i5invest Beratungs GmbH
Kalter, Steven—LJ2 & Co LLC
Kaltofen, Arnd—VI Partners AG
Kalverboer, Patrick—H2 Equity Partners BV
Kam, Boaz—Capital Point Ltd
Kamal, Samir—EQT Funds Management Ltd
Kamar-Vardi, Ahuva—International Business Machines Corp
Kamat, Ajay—Pear Ventures
Kamath, Sudhir—2I Capital Asset Management Co Ltd
Kamdar, Kim—Domain Associates LLC
Kamieniecky, Gilbert—Investcorp Bank BSC
Kamimaeda, Naoki—Global Brain Corp
Kaminski, John—Oneaccord Capital LLC
Kaminski, Paul—Wellspring Capital Management LLC
Kaminski, Peter—Oakstone Venture Partners LLC
Kaminski, Tek—Carlyle Group LP
Kaminsky, Jennifer—Blackstone Group LP
Kammert, Mark—Seven Point Equity Partners LLC
Kamp, W. Taylor—CIT Group Inc
Kampe, Christopher—Tully and Holland Inc
Kamperman, Gustav—Fianchetto Capital AB
Kamppari, Simo—Synetro Group LLC
Kampwerth, Herr—SIB Innovations und Beteiligungsgesellschaft mbH
Kamra, Deepak—Canaan Partners
Kamran, Faraaz—Madison Capital Funding LLC
Kamras, Mikael—Scope Capital Advisory AB
Kan, Elizabeth—First Eastern Investment Group
Kan, Laurie—On Capital Ltd
Kan, Zhidong—Orica Capital Co Ltd
Kan, Zhidong—Shenzhen Fortune Link Venture Capital Management Co Ltd
Kanaley, Chris—Parallax Capital Partners LLC
Kanayev, Alex—AIP Private Capital
Kanazeh, Lama—Blackstone Group LP
Kandanuru, Rahim—Investcorp Bank BSC

Kandel, Andrew—Cerberus Capital Management LP
Kandrac, Martin—Blackstone Group LP
Kane, Matthew—Antares Capital Corp
Kane, Michael—Caltius Mezzanine
Kane, Neil—Illinois Partners LLC
Kane, Stephen—Trust Company of the West
Kane, Wendy—Mantucket Capital LLC
Kane, William—Antares Capital Corp
Kanehann, Garrett—Blackeagle Partners Fund L P
Kaneko, Yasunori—Skyline Ventures Inc
Kaneshiro, Masaru—Global Brain Corp
Kaneshiro, Wako—Okinawa Human Capital Inc
Kang, Daniel—Estancia Capital Management LLC
Kang, Pei—Chengwei Ventures
Kang, Taeksu—Univest Capital
Kang, Takyoung—Gemini Investment Corp
Kang, Thomas Chan-Soo—Fortress Investment Group LLC
Kang, Wei—Zhejiang Sinowisdom Capital Co Ltd
Kangasniemi, Jaakko—Teollisen yhteistyon rahasto Oy
Kania, Ed—Flagship Pioneering
Kanitz, Ricardo—Ocroma Investimentos E Gestao Ltda
Kanive, Jay—Wayzata Investment Partners LLC
Kanji, Azra—ABRY Partners LLC
Kanji, Shafin—KV Private Equity Inc
Kanji, Shamez—North Hill Ventures LP
Kannry, Brian—Court Square Ventures LLC
Kanodia, Prashant—Blackstone Group LP
Kanodia, Raj—Ascribe Capital, LLC
Kant, Avinash—Phoenix Venture Partners LLC
Kantarian, Kathryn—Siguler Guff & Company LP
Kanter, Eric—Morgan Stanley Private Equity
Kantesaria, Devang—Devon Park Bioventures LP
Kantoff, Aaron—Apple Tree Partners
Kantonen, Marja—Midinvest Management Oy
Kantor, Bernard—Investec Private Equity
Kantor, Steven—Cantor Ventures
Kao, Joseph—Millennium TVP Management Co LLC
Kao, Peter—A1 Investments & Resources Ltd
Kapadia, Sandeep—Prime Technology Ventures NV
Kapelin, Aleksandr—Life.SREDA VC
Kapetanis, Brian—Newbury Partners LLC
Kapito, Robert—BlackRock Inc
Kaplan, Andrew—Quad Ventures LLC
Kaplan, Benjamin—Lovell Minnick Partners LLC
Kaplan, Daniel—Firm Factory Network AB
Kaplan, Effram—Brown Gibbons Lang & Company LLC
Kaplan, Jesse—Plaza Ventures Ltd
Kaplan, Justin—Balance Point Capital Partners, L.P.
Kaplan, Michael—Albion Capital Group LLP
Kaplan, Michael—LJ2 & Co LLC
Kaplan, Michael—Spiral Sun Ventures LLC
Kaplan, Ronnie—Levine Leichtman Capital Partners Inc
Kaplan, Steve—G3W Ventures LLC
Kaplan, Steve—Oaktree Capital Management LP
Kaplan, Steve—Riverside Partners LLC
Kaplan, Teddy—AG BD LLC
Kaplan, Teddy—New Mountain Capital I LLC
Kaplan, Zach—Corazon Capital LLC
Kaplan, Zachary—General Atlantic LLC
Kapler, A. William—Alumni Capital Network Management Co LLC
Kapoor, Arrun—SJF Ventures
Kapoor, Rana—Yes Bank Ltd
Kapoor, Rishi—Investcorp Technology Investments Group
Kapor Klein, Freada—Kapor Capital
Kapor, Mitchell—Kapor Capital
Kapp, Andrew—Arclight Capital Holdings LLC
Kappeler, Marc—aventic partners AG
Kapturkiewicz, Marek—Innovation Nest Sp z o o
Kapur, Gagan—Argonaut Private Equity LLC
Kapur, Sanjiv—Wolfensohn & Company LLC
Kapur, Varun—HOF Capital Inc
Karabelas, Argeris—Care Capital LLC
Karadogan, Yalin—Cinven Group Ltd
Karaivanova, Maria—MadroNA Venture Group
Karandikar, Ashish—Apax Partners LLP
Karangelen, Michael—Towerbrook Capital Partners LP
Karbenk, Christoph—Capiton AG
Kardwell, Joseph—Summit Partners LP
Kares, Gregory—Carlyle Group LP
Kargieman, Emiliano—Aconcagua Ventures
Karides, James—V-Ten Capital Partners LLC
Karim, Farhad—Blackstone Group LP
Karimov, Albert—IPT Ideya ZAO
Karimov, Maxim—e-Trust Investment Group
Kariuki, Shaka—Kuramo Capital Management LLC
Kariv, Tomer—Pontifax Management Company Ltd
Kariyazono, Shoichi—Globis Capital Partners & Co
Karkaletsos, Zoe—Headway Capital Partners LLP
Karkkainen, Pentti—ACM Ltd
Karlander, Hans—K III Sweden AB
Karlen, John—Flybridge Capital Partners
Karlson, Steven—Windspeed Ventures
Karlson, Thomas—Rural American Fund LP
Karlsson, Fredrik—3i Group PLC
Karlsson, Joakim—Nordic Capital
Karlsson, Karl—Accelerate-IT Ventures Management LLC
Karlsson, Karl-Magnus—Gkl Growth Capital AB
Karlsson, Mikael—Actis LLP
Karnal, Alex—Deerfield Management Company LP
Karnani, Nitin—Blackstone Group LP
Karnes, Carl—B4 Ventures LLC
Karnitschnig, Peter—Capcellence Mittelstandspartner GmbH
Karol, Julia—Watermill Group LLC
Karp, Allan—Karpreilly LLC
Karp, Douglas—Thomas Weisel Partners Group Inc
Karpavicius, Gintas—SB Capital Partners Ltd
Karppinen, Veijo—Vnt Management Oy
Karsen, Perry—Third Rock Ventures LLC
Karter, Elizabeth—Enhanced Capital Partners LLC
Kartje, Daniel—Finatem Fonds Management Verwaltungs GmbH
Karvelis, Christophe—Atalante SAS
Karvelis, Christophe—Atalante SAS
Kary, Rex—Moneta Capital Partners Ltd
Karyakin, Anatoliy—Baring Vostok Capital Partners Ltd
Kasanen, Juha—Norvestia Oyj
Kasdin, Rakefet—Battelle Ventures LP
Kase, George—Marlin Equity Partners LLC
Kase, James—Baml Capital Access Funds Management LLC
Kase, James—HarbourVest Partners LLC
Kashdin, Jeffrey—Hovde Private Equity Advisors LLC
Kasher, Marc—AIG Capital Partners Inc
Kashiyama, Yuki—J-STAR Co Ltd
Kashyap, Vinay—Mainsail Partners LP
Kask, Carl Johan—Oaktree Capital Management LP
Kasper, Paul—Enhanced Capital Partners LLC
Kasraian, Pouyan—Port-Monnaie Venture AB
Kass, Lawrence—Milbank Tweed Hadley & Mccloy LLP
Kassam, Nabil—Zynik Capital Corp
Kasser, Susan—Carlyle Group LP
Kasser, Susan—Neuberger Berman LLC
Kassin, Philip—Evercore Inc
Kassinis, George—Diogenes Business Incubator University of Cyprus
Kassum, Zool—TUFAN Venture Partners, Inc.
Kastka, Maximilian—BC Partners LLP
Kaswan, Michael—KBL HEALTHCARE VENTURES L P
Katadae, Maiko—University of Tokyo Edge Capital Co Ltd
Katakura, Yasunari—Integral Corp
Katarincic, Jay—Draper Triangle Ventures LP
Katcha, Joseph—High Street Capital
Katira, Tarang—Hamilton Lane Advisors LLC
Katkoria, Vishal—O3 Capital Advisors Pvt Ltd
Katmo, Ingvar—Proventure Management AS
Kato, Dean—Oneaccord Capital LLC
Kato, Takahiro—Toho Bank Ltd
Kato, Takashi—Global Brain Corp
Katona, David—Abundance Partners LLC
Katra, Hani—Qatar First Bank LLC
Kats, Victor—Ahv Holding Company LLC
Katsnelson, Boris—Mountain Ridge Capital LLC
Katsuya, Hisashi—International Business Machines Corp
Kattner, Kenric—Haynes and Boone LLC
Katz, Brandon—Clarion Capital Partners LLC
Katz, Charles—Morrison & Foerster LLP
Katz, Danielle—Antares Capital Corp
Katz, Jason—Kings Park Capital LLP
Katz, Jed—Javelin Venture Partners LP
Katz, Jennifer—Abatis Capital LLC
Katz, Jeremy—Grosvenor Capital Management LP
Katz, Jerry—Marlin Equity Partners LLC
Katz, Jordan—Angeles Equity Partners LLC
Katz, Jordan—Gores Group LLC
Katz, Lawrence—Summit Private Capital Group
Katz, Michael—Greener Capital Partners LP
Katz, Mike—Battery Ventures LP
Katz, Rami—Excell Partners Inc
Katz, Samuel—TZP Group LLC
Katz, Shraga—MAGNUM COMMUNICATIONS FUND L P
Katz, Steven—Vertex Israel II Management Ltd
Katzenberg, John—Socius Capital Group LLC
Katzenelson, Moshe—Trendlines Group Ltd
Katzman, Elliot—Commonwealth Capital Ventures
Katzovicz, Roy—Pershing Square Capital Management LP
Katzwer, Norman—Reservoir Capital Group LLC
Kau, Andrew—Walden International
Kauffman, Rodd—Gramercy Inc
Kauffman, Scott—Acas LLC

Kauffman, Scott–Oak Hill Capital Management Inc
Kaufman, David–Envest Ventures
Kaufman, David–Morrison & Foerster LLP
Kaufman, Jamie–NexPhase Capital LLC
Kaufman, Jonathan–Blackstone Group LP
Kaufman, Kathryn–New Magellan Venture Partners LLC
Kaufman, Peter–Bacchus Capital Management LLC
Kaufman, Rebekah–Morrison & Foerster LLP
Kaufman, Robert–Financial Technology Ventures
Kaufman, Sy–Crosslink Capital Inc
Kaul, Harsh–SIDBI Venture Capital Ltd
Kaul, Mike–Techfund Capital Europe
Kaul, Pradeep–Blu Venture Investors LLC
Kaul, Samir–Khosla Ventures LLC
Kaul, Sunil–Carlyle Group LP
Kaull, Kurtis–A&M Capital Advisors LLC
Kaup, Eric–Hilco Consumer Capital Corp
Kaupinen, Wesley–Quaker Partners Management LP
Kaupp, Karl-Friedrich–Dr Engelhardt Kaupp Kiefer Beteiligungsberatung GmbH
Kaushal, Mohit–Aberdare Ventures
Kauter, Christoph–FS Vencube GmbH
Kaveney, Emily–Quadrant Private Equity
Kavuma, Paul–Catalyst Principal Partners LLC
Kawaguchi, Tetsushi–Globis Capital Partners & Co
Kawahara, Hiroshi–Carlyle Group LP
Kawakami, Hiroki–Sumitomo Mitsui Trust Investment Co Ltd
Kawamura, Haruo–CAS Capital Inc
Kawasaki, Guy–Garage Technology Ventures LLC
Kawasaki, Kenichi–Daiwa Securities SMBC Principal Investments Co., Ltd.
Kawasaki, Tatsuo–Unison Capital, Inc.
Kawkabani, Joe–Algebra Capital Ltd
Kawkabani, Joe–Willow Impact
Kawkabani, Remy–Siguler Guff & Company LP
Kay, Henry–Medica Venture Partners, Ltd.
Kay, Matthew–Hypoid Partners
Kay, Max–Pacific Partners
Kaya, Kemal–Blackstone Group LP
Kayden, Joelle–Accolade Capital Management LLC
Kayden, Joelle–Accolade Capital Management LLC
Kaye, Alexander–Milbank Tweed Hadley & Mccloy LLP
Kayle, Bruce–Milbank Tweed Hadley & Mccloy LLP
Kayler, J. Allan–MMF Capital Management LLC
Kayola, John–Zesiger Capital Group LLC
Kayser, Mary–VMG Partners, L.P.
Kayukov, Edward–Milbank Tweed Hadley & Mccloy LLP
Kazah, Hernan–Kaszek Ventures I LP
Kazandjian, Raffy–Equitis Gestion SAS
Kazem, Mustafa–Small Enterprise Assistance Funds
Kazhimuratov, Gabbas–Baring Vostok Capital Partners Ltd
Kaziewicz, Philip–GI Partners
Kazim, Abid–NextEnergy Capital Ltd
Kazimi, Mak–Axum Capital Partners LLC
Ke, Gang–Beijing Capital Equity Investment Fund Management Co Ltd
Ke, Hong–Centenium-Pinetree China Private Equity
Ke, Yan–Northern Light Venture Capital Development Ltd
Keach, Dawn–Cedar Hill Associates LLC

Kealey, Harris–New Mountain Capital I LLC
Kealey, Tom–Montlake Capital LLC
Kean, Thomas–Quad Ventures LLC
Keane, David–SilverStream Capital LLC
Keane, John–SCP Private Equity Partners
Keane, Tim–Keane D Souza Venture Capital LLC
Kearl, Jeff–Zetta Venture Partners
Kearney, Douglas–Glencoe Capital LLC
Kearney, Kathryn–Westfield Capital Management Company LP
Kearney, Thomas–Wicks Group of Companies LLC
Kearns, Bonnie–Centana Growth Partners
Keating, Andrew–Karpreilly LLC
Keating, Kevin–Mill Creek Capital Advisors LLC
Keating, Patrick–Haynes and Boone LLC
Keating, Stephen–Privet Capital LLP
Keating, Tony–NBC Capital Pty Ltd
Keaton, Sean–Milbank Tweed Hadley & Mccloy LLP
Keaveney, Michael–Capstone Financial Partners LLC
Keay, Jeffrey–Baml Capital Access Funds Management LLC
Kebet-Koulibaly, Saran–International Finance Corp
Keck, Kevin–Phoenix Equity Partners Ltd
Keck, Tom–StepStone Group LP
Kedar, Sharon–Sands Capital Management LLC
Kedrosky, Paul–SK Ventures LLC
Kedzia, Michal–Enterprise Investors Sp z o o
Keefe, Edward–M/C Venture Partners LLC
Keefe, Kevin–PPM America Capital Partners LLC
Keefe, Patrick–Innovacorp
Keeffe, Emmett–Insight Venture Partners LLC
Keele, Lawrence–Oaktree Capital Management LP
Keeley, Sabrina–Detroit Renaissance
Keen, Eric–Council Capital
Keenan, Christopher–Wayzata Investment Partners LLC
Keenan, Jeffrey–Roark Capital Group Inc
Keenan, Joseph–Crescent Capital Group LP
Keenan, Sam–Kinderhook Industries LLC
Keene, J. Randall–Ancor Capital Partners
Keene, Sean–Blackstone Group LP
Keenley, Kevin–Fundamental Capital Management LLC
Keenoy, Peter–True North
Keers, Richard–Schroders PLC
Keese, Jack–Pacific Alliance Group Ltd
Keesey, Michael–CHS Capital LLC
Keesler, William–Paine Schwartz Partners LLC
Keet, Ernest–Vanguard Atlantic Ltd
Kefeli, Abdullah–Rhea Girisim Sermayesi Yatirim Ortakligi AS
Kehoe, Scott–Inverness Graham Investments
Keil, Brian–Antares Capital Corp
Keilhacker, Kurt–Techfund Capital Europe
Keilin, Eugene–KPS Capital Partners LP
Keilp, Judith–Palisade Capital Management LLC
Keis, Matthew–Gemini Investors Inc
Keith, Brett–Rockwood Equity Partners LLC
Keith, Robert–TL Ventures Inc
Kekkonen, Atte–Taito Capital Partners Oy
Keleher, Todd–RB Webber and Comapny Inc
Kelif, Franck–Perceva SAS
Kellam, Joelle–Origami Capital Partners, LLC
Keller, Chris–NextGen Venture Partners LLC
Keller, Derek–Highway 12 Ventures

Keller, Hubert–Banque Lombard Odier & Cie SA
Keller, Jason–Oaktree Capital Management LP
Keller, Michael–Brown Brothers Harriman & Co
Keller, Philip–Intermediate Capital Group PLC
Keller, Walter–Partners Group Holding AG
Kellett, Andrea–Trimaran Capital LLC
Kelley, Alan–SJF Ventures
Kelley, Brian–Investcorp Bank BSC
Kelley, Brian–Lindsay Goldberg & Bessemer LP
Kelley, Douglas–Acas LLC
Kelley, James–Vestar Capital Partners Inc
Kelley, Mary–Invesco Private Capital Inc
Kelley, Neil–Genesis Park, L.P.
Kelley, Rich–Accretia Capital LLC
Kelley, Ryan–Shore Capital Partners LLC
Kelley, Sean–Gridiron Capital LLC
Kelliher, James–Ironwood Partners LLC
Kellman, Joel–GGV Capital
Kelln, Bryan–Platinum Equity LLC
Kellner, Ted–Lakeview Equity Partners LLC
Kellogg, James–Bain Capital Inc
Kelly, Alison–Brown Brothers Harriman & Co
Kelly, Bob–Ignition Ventures Management LLC
Kelly, Bobby–CIP Capital
Kelly, Braden–Spectrum Healthcare Fund LLC
Kelly, Brian–RINCON VENTURE PARTNERS L P
Kelly, Bryan–Anthos Capital LP
Kelly, Denis–Alumni Capital Network Management Co LLC
Kelly, Douglas–Alloy Ventures Inc
Kelly, Edward–Strategic Value Partners LLC
Kelly, Hugh–Ascent Venture Management Inc
Kelly, J. Ryan–Founders Equity, Inc.
Kelly, Joe–Columbia Pacific Advisors LLC
Kelly, John–MVC Capital Inc
Kelly, Jonathan–Capital Z Partners Ltd
Kelly, Martin–Apollo Global Management LLC
Kelly, Martin–International Business Machines Corp
Kelly, Michael–Hamilton Lane Advisors LLC
Kelly, Michael–Nova Capital Management, Ltd.
Kelly, Paul–Oneventures Pty Ltd
Kelly, Regis–Mission Bay Capital LLC
Kelly, Robert–Carlyle Group LP
Kelly, Robert–StarVest Partners LP
Kelly, Sean–Cappello Capital Corp
Kelly, Shawn–Teakwood Capital LP
Kelly, Thomas–Blackstone Group LP
Kelty, Matt–LNC Partners
Kelvin, Roy–GI Partners
Kemp, Andrew–First Capital Partners LLC
Kemp, Patricia–Oak HC/FT Partners LP
Kemp, Philip–Waud Capital Partners LLC
Kemp, Renee–Oaktree Capital Management LP
Kemp-Welch, Peter–Piper PE LLP
Kemper, Charles–Mac6 LLC
Kemper, Charlie–Revel Partners LLC
Kempner, Brian–FirstMark Capital LLC
Kemppinen, Kristian–IK Investment Partners Ltd
Kemps, Pieter–Sequoia Capital India
Kencel, Kenneth–Carlyle Group LP
Kendal-Ward, Nancy–Ridge Capital Partners LLC
Kendall, Enmi–Healthy Ventures Management LLC
Kendall, Valerie–WestBridge Fund Managers Ltd
Kendig, Jeffrey–Caltius Equity Partners
Kendra, Sean–Sumeru Equity Partners, L.P.

Kendrick, Claire—Mill Creek Capital Advisors LLC
Kendrick, Claire—Z Capital HF Adviser LLC
Kene, Yayati—Kotak Investment Advisors Ltd
Kenealey, Kevin—Mason Wells Inc
Kenealy, Patrick—IDG Ventures USA
Kenefick, James—Antares Capital Corp
Kengelbach, Jan—BC Partners LLP
Kenna, Christine—IGNIA Partners LLC
Kennealey, Douglas—Brazos Private Equity Partners LLC
Kennealey, Douglas—MPK Equity Partners LLC
Kennealy, Michael—Spectrum Equity Investors LP
Kennedy, Bill—Maven Capital Partners UK LLP
Kennedy, Bill—Maven Capital Partners UK LLP
Kennedy, Bob—NewWorld Capital Group LLC
Kennedy, David—Serent Capital LLC
Kennedy, Giles—Milbank Tweed Hadley & Mccloy LLP
Kennedy, Iain—Duke Street Capital Ltd
Kennedy, Joe—Arafura Ventures Inc
Kennedy, Melissa—ACP Inc
Kennedy, Neil—Harbert Management Corp
Kennedy, Peter—CLSA Capital Partners HK Ltd
Kennedy, Robert—Ascend Global Investments LLC
Kennedy, Robert—Business Instincts Group
Kennedy, Robert—Vantagepoint Management Inc
Kennedy, Thomas—Kensington Capital Partners Ltd
Kennedy, William—Falcon Investment Advisors LLC
Kennell, Geraldine—Silverfleet Capital Partners LLP
Kenney, George—Shepherd Ventures LP
Kenney, George—Shepherd Ventures LP
Kenney, John—Jmk Consumer Growth Partners LLC
Kenney, John—TSG Consumer Partners, L.P.
Kenney, Philip—Crescent Capital Group LP
Kenny, Frank—Delta Partners Ltd
Kenny, J. Kevin—Carlyle Group LP
Kenny, Laurel—Green Manning & Bunch Ltd
Kensy, Olaf—Findos Investor GmbH
Kent, Richard—Intersouth Partners
Kenter, Louis—Prospect Partners LLC
Kenter, Menno—Peak Capital BV
Kenworthy, Hugh—Guardian Capital Partners
Kenworthy, Karen—Stripes Group LLC
Keough, Kevin—Arcapita Inc
Keppler, Heiko—Oaktree Capital Management LP
Keppler, Robert—Saints Ventures
Kerby, Richard—Venrock Inc
Kerdman, Bryan—Impression Ventures
Kereiakes, David—River Cities Capital Fund LP
Kerins, William—Oaktree Capital Management LP
Kerlin, Eliot—Insight Equity Holdings LLC
Kermani, Moe—Vanedge Capital Inc
Kermode, Bill—inventages venture capital GmbH
Kermorgant, Thomas—CoBe Equities LLC
Kern, Justin—Paine Schwartz Partners LLC
Kern, Rene—General Atlantic LLC
Kernodle, Jeremy—Haynes and Boone LLC
Kero, Greg—venture51 Capital Fund LLP
Kerr, Alastair—Leopard Rock Capital Partners Ltd
Kerr, Alexander—Vestar Capital Partners Inc
Kerr, Andrew—Telopea Capital Partners Pty Ltd
Kerr, Brian—Scottish Equity Partners LLP
Kerr, Charles—Morrison & Foerster LLP
Kerr, Derek—Innovation Capital Associates Pty, Ltd.
Kerr, Ian—Beltrae Partners LLC
Kerr, John—Texas Next Capital LP
Kerr, Thomas—Hamilton Lane Advisors LLC
Kerschen, John—Michigan Accelerator Fund I Management LLC
Kersey, Christopher—Camden Partners Holdings LLC
Kersten, Dirk—Gilde Healthcare Partners BV
Kersten, Dirk—Gilde Investment Management BV
Kersting, Kevin—Fund Evaluation Group LLC
Kertzman, Mitchell—Hummer Winblad Venture Partner
Kertzner, Adam—Oak Hill Advisors LP
Keshian, Daniel—Fairhaven Capital Partners, L.P.
Kesrouani, Remy—Calibrate Management Ltd
Kessel, Alex—Adams Street Partners LLC
Kessel, Alex—Baird Capital
Kesselheim, Jared—Bain Capital Inc
Kesselheim, Jared—Bain Capital Venture Partners LLC
Kesselman, Todd—Precision Capital Advisors LLC
Kesselring, Bill—Gmg Capital Partners LP
Kessenich, David—Excellere Capital Management LLC
Kessinger, William—Parthenon Capital LLC
Kessler, Alex—PAI Partners SAS
Kessler, Daniel—Cyprium Investment Partners LLC
Kessler, Randall—Blackstone Group LP
Kesten, Raffi—JVP Jerusalem Venture Partners Israel Management, Ltd.
Kestenbaum, Russell—Milbank Tweed Hadley & Mccloy LLP
Kester, Kevin—Siguler Guff & Company LP
Keta, Andile—Kleoss Capital (Pty) Ltd
Kettaneh, Nadine—Willow Impact
Kettering, Charlie—Mantucket Capital LLC
Ketterson, Robert—Volition Capital LLC
Kettnich, John—StepStone Group LP
Keul, Thomas—Elvaston Capital Management GmbH
Keusters, Patrick—Banque Degroof Petercam SA
Kewalramani, Kabir—Berggruen Holdings Inc
Keyes, Jared—Brown Brothers Harriman & Co
Keynejad, Jamshid—Sk Capital Partners LP
Keyoung, Michael—Burrill & Company
Khairallah, Karim—Oaktree Capital Management LP
Khajeh-Hosseiny, Hosein—Northgate Capital LLC
Khajey-Hosseiny, Hosein—Northgate Capital LLC
Khalaf, Delzar—Krypton Capital
Khalaf, Shawki—Gulf Investment Corporation SAG
Khalifa, Mahmoud—FEP Capital
Khalil, Ali—Kuwait Financial Centre KPSC
Khalili, Ahmad—Itqan Capital Co
Khan, Agha—Stone Point Capital LLC
Khan, Altaf—Kasb Techventures
Khan, Farah—Catterton Partners Corp
Khan, Farah—Sandler Capital Management
Khan, Mudassir—Graphite Capital Management LLP
Khan, Nayeem—Qatar First Bank LLC
Khan, Saad—CMEA Development Company LLC
Khan, Shahbaz—Investcorp Technology Investments Group
Khan, Sherjeel—Cohen & Company Financial Ltd
Khan, Syeed—Asian Tiger Capital Partners Ltd
Khan, Umair—Entrepreneurs Fund LP
Khan, Waseem—Silk Invest Ltd
Khandelwal, Gaurav—START Group LLC
Khandelwal, Rahul—Lumis Partners
Khandelwal, Sukesh—Sabre Partners India Advisors Pvt Ltd
Khanjenkova, Natasha—European Bank for Reconstruction and Development
Khanna, Ashish—SV Health Investors LLP
Khanna, Bob—TRG Management LP
Khanna, Karan—MergerTech Advisors
Khanna, Nitin—MergerTech Advisors
Khanna, Pankaj—Artesian Capital Management Australia Pty Ltd
Khanna, Raghav—Oaktree Capital Management LP
Khanna, Raman—ONSET Ventures
Khanna, Tarun—CX Partners
Kharchyshyn, Alex—Digital Future
Khare, Dev—Lightspeed Management Company LLC
Khater, Sana—Waha Capital PJSC
Khatod, Anil—Argonaut Private Equity LLC
Khatod, Sumit—Lee Equity Partners LLC
Khatoun, Nael—Oaktree Capital Management LP
Khatri, Ethan—Fulcrum Venture India
Khatwani, Hemant—ePlanet Capital
Khaydarova, Aliya—Inverness Graham Investments
Khayrullin, Robert—Global Mining Capital Corp
Kheng, Jennifer—Lexington Partners Inc
Khera, Anil—Blackstone Group LP
Khilov, Dmitry—UNITED FINANCIAL GROUP ASSET MANAGEMENT
Khizver, Alexandr—Grey Mountain Partners LLC
Khoele, Nthime—Bopa Moruo
Khor, Chieh Suang—Digital Media Partners Pte Ltd
Khorana, Sunny—Fifth Street Capital LLC
Khosla, Vinod—Khosla Ventures LLC
Khouri, Andrew—Quaker Partners Management LP
Khouri, Rabih—Investcorp Bank BSC
Khouri-Haddad, Najib—Accelerate-IT Ventures Management LLC
Khungar, Gaurav—O3 Capital Advisors Pvt Ltd
Khuong, Chau—OrbiMed Advisors LLC
Khurana, Shivani—MVC Capital Inc
Khutorsky, Michael—Trilantic Capital Management LP
Khutorsky, Michael—Turnspire Capital Partners LLC
Kian-Wee, Seah—UOB Bioventures Management Pte Ltd
Kibayashi, Yasuji—CAS Capital Inc
Kibble, Robert—Mission Ventures Inc
Kibler, Dana—Upfront Ventures
Kicillof, Nico—Axioma Ventures LLC
Kid, Laurent—Abenex Capital SAS
Kidd, Jay—Wing Venture Capital
Kidd, William—Kidd & Company LLC
Kidle, Dan—Arboretum Ventures Inc
Kido, Masahisa—Genuine Startups KK
Kidson, Ian—TD Capital Group Ltd
Kiefer, Georg—Dr Engelhardt Kaupp Kiefer Beteiligungsberatung GmbH
Kiefer-Goldenberg, Maureen—Fund Evaluation Group LLC
Kieffer, Andy—Moelis Capital Partners LLC
Kieffer, Andy—NexPhase Capital LLC
Kieffer, Sharon—2X CONSUMER PRODUCTS GROWTH PARTNERS L P
Kiehn, Tony—Blackford Capital LLC
Kiel, Jan—CEE Management GmbH
Kiel, Ronald—Trophas Management BV
Kienzle, Trevor—Correlation Ventures LP
Kieras, Eric—JZ Capital Partners Ltd
Kiernan, John—Altimeter Capital Management LP

Kiggen, James–Blackstone Group LP
Kight, Peter–Comvest Partners
Kikas, Kalmer–BPM Capital OU
Kikas, Kalmer–Hanseatic Capital As
Kikta, Roman–Mobility Ventures LLC
Kikuchi, Isao–Epidarex Capital
Kilarski, LeAnn–Wind Point Advisors LLC
Kilburn, E. Miles–Mosaik Partners LLC
Kile, Kimberly–ABS Capital Partners, Inc.
Kilgallon, John–Bain Capital Inc
Kilicaslan, Erkan–Iris Capital Management SAS
Killackey, Christopher–Prairie Capital, L.P.
Killen, Heather–Hemisphere Capital LLC
Killick, Lucy–Framestore Ventures
Killilea, Alison–W Capital Management LLC
Killion, Joel–Moelis Capital Partners LLC
Killion, Joel–NexPhase Capital LLC
Kilpatrick, Daniel–Crestview Advisors, LLC
Kilroy, Kenneth–Stone Canyon Venture Partners
Kilroy, William–Portal Capital LLC
Kim, Albert–Investor Growth Capital AB
Kim, Ann–Swander Pace Capital LLC
Kim, Anne–Quadria Capital Investment Advisors Pvt Ltd
Kim, Anthony–Centerview Partners LLC
Kim, B. Christopher–Oxford Bioscience Partners
Kim, Brian–Blackstone Group LP
Kim, Brian–Newspring Capital
Kim, Carol–Blackstone Group LP
Kim, Chang Suk–STIC Investment Inc
Kim, Dal-je–Sejin TS Co Ltd
Kim, Daniel–Bregal Investments LLP
Kim, David–Apax Partners LLP
Kim, David–Blackstone Group LP
Kim, David–Farallon Capital Management LLC
Kim, David–Morgan Creek Capital Management LLC
Kim, Dennis–Summit Partners LP
Kim, Denny–WL Ross & Co LLC
Kim, Dong Su–Wonik Investment Partners
Kim, Edmund–M/C Venture Partners LLC
Kim, Eugene–Compass Partners International Llp
Kim, Eung Suk–Mirae Asset Venture Investment Co Ltd
Kim, Evgeyny–Kazyna Kapital Management AO
Kim, Grace–Arsenal Capital Management LLC
Kim, Grace–Arsenal Capital Partners LP
Kim, Grace–Pine Brook Road Partners LLC
Kim, Gyu Tae–KTB Investment & Securities Co Ltd
Kim, Hallie–Lion Capital LLP
Kim, Han Ok–Kb Investment Co Ltd
Kim, Han–Altos Ventures
Kim, Harry–SkyLake Investment & Co
Kim, Ho Min–SparkLabs
Kim, Hoon Shik–Utc Investment Co Ltd (Aka Utc Venture Co Ltd)
Kim, Hyukjin–MBK Partners Inc
Kim, Hyung-Kie–Lee&Co Investments Co
Kim, Il-Chun–Neoplux Co Ltd
Kim, James–Carlyle Group LP
Kim, Jay–IMM Private Equity Inc
Kim, Jeonghwan–MBK Partners Inc
Kim, Ji-Won–Aju IB Investment Co Ltd
Kim, Ji-whan–Hana Daetoo Securities Co Ltd
Kim, Jihun–IMM Investment Corp
Kim, Jim–Formation 8 Partners LP
Kim, Jin Yeong–KTB Investment & Securities Co Ltd
Kim, Jin–Stone-Goff Partners LLC
Kim, John–CVC Asia Pacific Ltd
Kim, John–CVC Capital Partners Ltd
Kim, John–HighBAR Ventures
Kim, Jong Pil–ESang Technology Investment
Kim, Jong-pil–Korea Investment Partners Co Ltd
Kim, Joseph–m8 Capital
Kim, Jun Min–Wonik Investment Partners
Kim, Jung Yong–Global Brain Corp
Kim, Jung-hyun–Neoplux Co Ltd
Kim, Kenny–Cimb Private Equity Sdn Bhd
Kim, Kun-ho–Korea Investment Partners Co Ltd
Kim, Kwang Il–MBK Partners Inc
Kim, Leonard–Capital International Inc
Kim, Michael–Brown Brothers Harriman & Co
Kim, Michael–Cendana Capital GP LLC
Kim, Michael–MBK Partners Inc
Kim, Michael–Trimaran Capital LLC
Kim, Min-Yong–Blackstone Group LP
Kim, Moon–Harbor Pacific Capital LLC
Kim, Myeng Ki–Intervest Co Ltd
Kim, Oh Jin–Hanju Investment Co Ltd
Kim, Peter–5AM Ventures LLC
Kim, Peter–Clearlight Partners LLC
Kim, Peter–Coller Capital Ltd
Kim, Rich–Morrison & Foerster LLP
Kim, Rita–Partners for Growth Inc
Kim, Rudy–Morrison & Foerster LLP
Kim, Ryan–Castle Island Partners LLC
Kim, Samuel–Bandgap Ventures LLC
Kim, SangWook–IMM Investment Corp
Kim, Sarah–Clayton Dubilier & Rice LLC
Kim, Sarah–Halyard Capital
Kim, Seok Jin–Korea Investment & Securities Co Ltd
Kim, Seong Soo–Baker & McKenzie LLP
Kim, Seong–Premier Partners LLC
Kim, Shin–StepStone Group LP
Kim, Shincheon–L&S VentureCapital Corp
Kim, Soomin–Unison Capital, Inc.
Kim, Su-jin–Korea Investment Partners Co Ltd
Kim, Suyi–Canada Pension Plan Investment Board
Kim, Taejo–Oaktree Capital Management LP
Kim, Un Tae–Munhwa Investment
Kim, Yeong Chan–ESang Technology Investment
Kim, Yeong Gi–KDB Capital Corp
Kim, Yoo Jin–Lee Equity Partners LLC
Kim, Young Ho–IMM Private Equity Inc
Kim, Young Joon–Milbank Tweed Hadley & Mccloy LLP
Kim, Young-min–SkyLake Investment & Co
Kim, Youngbu–YB Partners Co Ltd
Kim, Yun Gwon–LB Investment Inc
Kim-Suk, Sandra–Catterton Partners Corp
Kimball, Kyle–New York City Economic Development Corp
Kimball, Richard–Technology Crossover Ventures LP
Kimber, Kevin–Eight Roads Ventures Europe
Kimberly, Adam–Montis Capital LLC
Kimm, John–Evercore Inc
Kimmel, Noel–Cantor Ventures
Kimmel, Orit–JVP Jerusalem Venture Partners Israel Management, Ltd.
Kimoto, Yuji–Tokio Marine Capital Co Ltd
Kimpel, Stephen–Stonehenge Partners Inc
Kimsa, Kevin–OMERS Ventures
Kimura, Taiou–Grace Assets Management LLP
Kimzey, Jackie–Sevin Rosen Funds
Kinane, Brian–Yorkville Advisors Management LLC
Kincaid, Stacy–Probitas Partners Inc
Kindle, Fred–Clayton Dubilier & Rice LLC
Kindler, Jeffrey–LUX CAPITAL GROUP L L C
King, Aidan–Undisclosed Firm
King, Callum–Comcast Ventures
King, Charles–Prudential Capital Group LP
King, Christopher–Gridiron Capital LLC
King, Colton–KRG Capital Management LP
King, Colton–Mountaingate Capital Management LP
King, David–Quaker Partners Management LP
King, Edward–Barclays Capital Inc
King, Gil–JDRF International
King, James–Find Invest Grow Ltd
King, John–New York Business Development Corp
King, Linda–Southbridge Capital Inc
King, Madding–Camp One Ventures LLC
King, Mark–Revelstoke Capital Partners LLC
King, Matthew–Clayton Associates LLC
King, Neil–3i Group PLC
King, Neil–3i Infrastructure PLC
King, Richard–Rockpool Investments LLP
King, Stephen–Omidyar Network Commons LLC
King, Stephen–Prairie Capital, L.P.
King, Suzanne–New Enterprise Associates Inc
King, Walter–Blue Hill Partners LLC
King-Shaw, Ruben–Mansa Capital Management LLC
Kingery, David–Carlyle Group LP
Kingsbury, Raymond–Ancor Capital Partners
Kingsbury, Robert–Mcm Capital Partners L P
Kingsbury, Shaun–Hudson Clean Energy Partners
Kingsland, Samuel–Granite Ventures LLC
Kingsley, Anthony–Proprium Capital Partners LP
Kingsley, William–Enertech Capital
Kingston, Mark–Pavonis Group LLC
Kinnaird, John–G 51 Capital Management LLC
Kinney, Jonathan–Riverside Co
Kinoshita, Yoshihiko–Skyland Ventures
Kinsbourg, Roger–Impact Capital Inc
Kinsella, Kevin–Avalon Ventures, LLC
Kinsey, Matthew–Boston Ventures
Kinsman, Brian–Bunker Hill Capital LP
Kipley, Christopher–Z Capital HF Adviser LLC
Kipp, Dan–WinoNA Capital Management LLC
Kippola, Tom–Voyager Capital LLC
Kirani, Shekhar–Accel India Venture Fund
Kirby, James–Deerpath Capital Management LP
Kirby, John–Blue Point Capital Partners LP
Kirby, Miles–Qualcomm Ventures
Kirby, Steve–Bluestem Capital Partners
Kirchen, Christopher–BEV Capital
Kircher, Demian–Maranon Capital LP
Kirchheimer, David–Oaktree Capital Management LP
Kireker, Charles–Freshtracks Capital LP
Kirgues, Joe–gener8tor
Kirk Johansen, Casper–Kirk & Thorsen Invest A/S
Kirk, David–Bailador Investment Management Pty Ltd
Kirk, James–Corsair Capital LLC
Kirk, Julian–Third Security LLC
Kirk, Randal–Third Security LLC
Kirkpatrick, David–SJF Ventures

Kirkpatrick, Doug—Vantagepoint Management Inc
Kirkpatrick, Justin—Questa Capital Management LLC
Kirkpatrick, Norm—Nibiru Capital Management Ltd
Kirkston, Joel—Johnson & Johnson Innovation-JJDC Irc
Kirsch, Peter—Merida Capital Partners LLC
Kirschbaum, Brian—Relativity Capital LLC
Kirschner, Jason—Carlyle Group LP
Kirshner, Ori—Giza Venture Capital
Kirson, Ian—Wynnchurch Capital Ltd
Kirt, Jeffrey—Oak Hill Advisors LP
Kirtley, John—KLH Capital LP
Kirton, Michael—Leonard Green & Partners LP
Kirwan, Tom—Icc Venture Capital
Kirwin, John Paul—Argosy Capital Group Inc
Kiser, David—Bridge City Management LLC
Kishi, Steven—Hummer Winblad Venture Partner
Kishler, Mark—Northwestern Mutual Capital LLC
Kishon, Eyal—Genesis Partners Ltd
Kishore, Ganesh—Spruce Capital Partners LLC
Kisic, Drago—Macrocapitales SAFI SA
Kispert, John—Black Diamond Ventures Inc
Kiss, Brandon—Snow Phipps Group LLC
Kita, Masakazu—Mizuho Capital Co Ltd
Kitamura, Mitch—Draper Nexus Venture Partners LLC
Kitani, Douglas—CAMBRIDGE CAPITAL PARTNERS L L C
Kitao, Tomoko—Hamilton Lane Advisors LLC
Kitao, Yoshitaka—SBI Investment Co Ltd
Kitsuka, Kenta—Global Brain Corp
Kitta, Daisuke—Blackstone Group LP
Kitterman, Roger—Partners Innovation Fund LLC
Kittler, Fred—Firelake Capital Management LLC
Kitzinger, Dino—Serafin Unternehmensgruppe GmbH
Kivinen, Jaakko—Altor Equity Partners AB
Kivinen, Juuso—Sponsor Capital Oy
Kivisto, Marko—Avalt LLC
Kivisto, Marko—Bain Capital Inc
Kiyozuka, Megumi—CLSA Capital Partners HK Ltd
Kjaergaard, Kent—ATP Private Equity Partners
Kjellson, Nina—Canaan Partners
Kjerulf, Dan—Danske Private Equity A/S
Kjesbu, Geir—Investinor AS
Klaassen, Eldon—Cerium Technology LLC
Klaassen, Merijn—Life Sciences Partners BV
Klab, Andreas—BC Partners LLP
Klaff, Julie—Origami Capital Partners, LLC
Klaff, Larry—GB Credit Partners LLC
Klaffky, Richard—Balance Point Capital Partners, L.P.
Klammer, Ronald—IT Matrix Ventures
Klap, Robert—Platinum Equity LLC
Klarnet, Renato—Evercore Inc
Klass, Daniel—Klass Capital Corp
Klatik, Kelly—Cypress Hills Partners Inc
Klausner, Richard—Column Group
Klebe, Evan—Lindsay Goldberg & Bessemer LP
Kleber, Klee—Buildgroup Management LLC
Kleer, Patrick—Undisclosed Firm
Kleidman, Carl—Vision Capital Advisors LLC
Kleijwegt, Martijn—Life Sciences Partners BV
Klein, Adam—Crestview Advisors, LLC
Klein, Adam—Palm Beach Capital Management LLC
Klein, Charles—Ascribe Capital, LLC
Klein, David—One Peak Partners LLP

Klein, David—Summit Partners LP
Klein, Dietmar—COREST GmbH Corporate Restructuring
Klein, Eric—Lemnos Labs
Klein, Gentry—LJ2 & Co LLC
Klein, Jason—Accel-KKR
Klein, Jay—Klass Capital Corp
Klein, Jens-Philipp—Atlantic Internet GmbH
Klein, Jens-Philipp—Atlantic Ventures GmbH
Klein, Mary—Berggruen Holdings Inc
Klein, Michael—LJ2 & Co LLC
Klein, Nathaniel—Hale Fund Management, L.P.
Klein, Robert—Acas LLC
Klein, Robin—Index Ventures
Klein, Spencer—Morrison & Foerster LLP
Klein, Todd—Revolution
Klein, Zach—Founder Collective LP
Kleinhandler, Mitchell—Scout Ventures LLC
Kleinheisterkamp, Thomas—Milbank Tweed Hadley & Mccloy LLP
Kleinhenz, Peter—CID Capital Inc
Kleinhenz, Peter—Fletcher Spaght Ventures LP
Kleinman, Bill—Haynes and Boone LLC
Kleinman, Blake—Hellman & Friedman LLC
Kleinman, Ira—Harvest Partners LP
Kleiterp, Nanno—Netherlands Development Finance Company NV
Klemens, Jeffrey—Sageview Capital LP
Klement, Amy—Omidyar Network Commons LLC
Klemm, Richard—OrbiMed Advisors LLC
Klemmer, Jochen—Afinum Management GmbH
Klessel, Lew—Bain Capital Inc
Klevens, Joshua—Charlesbank Capital Partners LLC
Klick, Paul—Wwc Capital Fund L P
Klier, Stephan—CBG Commerz Beteiligungskapital GmbH & Co KG
Klima, Daniel—Lexington Partners Inc
Kliman, Gilbert—InterWest Partners LLC
Klimczak, Sean—Blackstone Group LP
Klimley, Brooks—Silverfern Group Inc
Klimmeck, K. Thomas—Madison Capital Funding LLC
Kline, Charles—Century Capital Management / Massachusetts Inc
Kline, Dean—Penn Venture Partners, L.P.
Kline, John—New Mountain Capital I LLC
Klinefelter, Jeffrey—Piper Jaffray Ventures Inc
Klinefelter, Josh—Aurora Capital Group Ltd
Klingbeil, Brian—Savvis Inc
Klinge, John—Levine Leichtman Capital Partners Inc
Klingensmith, David—European Bank for Reconstruction and Development
Klinger, Ari—Right Click Capital
Klinger, Ari—Sydney Seed Fund Management Pty Ltd
Klinger, Ari—Wavemaker Partners
Klinger, Matt—Potomac Energy Fund LP
Klitbo, Thomas—IK Investment Partners Ltd
Klivan, Joshua—3G Capital Inc
Klocanas, Philippe—Weinberg Capital Partners SAS
Klopf, Marie-Belle Michigan Fund LP
Klopp, John—CT Investment Management Co LLC
Kloppenborg, Paul—Global Cleantech Capital BV
Kloppsteck, Lars—BID Equity Advisory GmbH
Klosk, Craig—Wicks Group of Companies LLC
Klotz, Radford—Brown Brothers Harriman & Co
Klueger, Randy—Core Capital Partners Ii L P

Klueppel, Jochen—Grazia Equity GmbH
Kluger, David—Sands Capital Management LLC
Kluger, Michael—Altaris Capital Partners LLC
Klump, Michael—Argonne Capital Group LLC
Kluyskens, Jean—Namur Invest SA
Kluzik, Janet—Gryphon Investors Inc
Klyce, Harvey—New Enterprise East Investments
Knapp, Michael—Arch Venture Partners LLC
Knauer, Scott—Pivotal Group Inc
Knauf, Noah—Warburg Pincus LLC
Knecht, Andreas—Partners Group Holding AG
Knechtli, Patrick—Sl Capital Partners Llp
Knee, Jonathan—Evercore Inc
Kneen, John—Beecken Petty O'Keefe & Company LLC
Kneis, Henry—Difference Capital Financial Inc
Knell, Harvey—KCB Management LLC
Knepley, Katie—Silicon Valley Bancventures LP
Knesh, Frank—Valentis Capital LLC
Knez, Brian—Castanea Partners Inc
Knibb, Robert—Arlington Capital Partners
Knibb, Robert—Washington Equity Partners LLC
Knickel, David—Kainos Capital LLC
Knight, Kip—Thomvest Ventures Inc
Knight, Lester—Roundtable Healthcare Partners LP
Knights, Julian—Ironbridge Capital Pty Ltd
Kniseley, Lucy—SusquehanNA Capital
Knisely, Matthew—Shorenstein Co LLC
Knoblach, Korbinian—Emeram Capital Partners GmbH
Knobler, Mary—Oaktree Capital Management LP
Knoch, David—Irving Place Capital LLC
Knoch, Doug—CHS Capital LLC
Knoch, Doug—Shorehill Capital LLC
Knoch, Doug—Storehill Capital LLC
Knoll, John—Golden Gate Capital Inc
Knoll, John—Oval Partners
Knoll, Scott—Anania & Associates Investment Company LLC
Knorr, Robert—Mid Europa Partners LLP
Knott, F. Stuart—Spring Capital Partners
Knottenbelt, Daan—Palamon Capital Partners LP
Knowles, Todd—Rizvi Traverse Management LLC
Knox, Adam—KSL Capital Partners LLC
Knox, C. Robert—Triangle Capital Partners L L C
Knox, Jason—SB Capital Partners Ltd
Knox, Joy—Mohr Davidow Ventures
Knox, Thomas—Morrison & Foerster LLP
Knuckey, Stuart—Barclays Ventures Ltd
Knudsen, Brent—Partnership Capital Growth LLC
Knudsen, Brent—TBL Capital LP
Knudsen, Thomas—Northcap Partners ApS
Knuenz, Rudolf—Unternehmens Invest AG
Knutsen, John—Madison Dearborn Partners LLC
Knutson, Pam—Treetop Ventures Inc
Ko, Elizabeth—Crescent Capital Group LP
Ko, James—Providence Equity Partners LLC
Ko, Peter—Shaw Kwei & Partners
Kob, Randall—Prudential Capital Group LP
Kobayashi, Kazushige—Capital Dynamics Sdn Bhd
Kobayashi, Masashi—e.ventures
Kobayashi, Masashi—eVenture Capital Partners GmbH
Kobayashi, Ricardo—Vinci Equities Gestora de Recursos Ltda
Kobel, Olivier—Atlantic Ventures GmbH

Koblents, Pavel Yu—GEN3 Partners, Inc.
Kobus, Brian—Summerhill Venture Partners Management Inc
Koby, Michael—1315 Capital LLC
Koby, Michael—Palm Ventures LLC
Kobza, John—Hall Capital LLC
Kocen, Ari—Stonehenge Growth Capital LLC
Koch, Edward—CranRidge Capital LP
Koch, Fred—Greenline Ventures LLC
Koch, Klaus—Vicente Capital Partners LLC
Koch, Mia—Rural American Fund LP
Koch, Robert—Milbank Tweed Hadley & Mccloy LLP
Koch, Steven—Haynes and Boone LLC
Kocher, Robert—Venrock Inc
Kodde, Pieter—Lincolnshire Management Inc
Koeber, Scott—Performance Equity Management LLC
Koebler, Jeffrey—Seek Capital LLC
Koehl, Patrick—Antares Capital Corp
Koehler, Cedric—Creathor Venture Management GmbH
Koehler, Eva—Mittelstaendische Beteiligungsgesellschaft Sachsen mbH
Koehler, Gert—Creathor Venture Management GmbH
Koehler, Thomas—AM Ventures Holding GmbH
Koeller, Brian—Pearl Street Capital Group
Koeneman, Keith—Kingsman Capital LLC
Koenig, Anja—Novartis Venture Funds
Koenig, Jason—Hale Fund Management, L.P.
Koenig, Michael—Hamilton Lane Advisors LLC
Koenig, Raimund—Gruenwald Equity Management GmbH
Koenig, Simon—Armada Investment AG
Koenigsberger, Robert—Gramercy Inc
Koeppel, Christian—Mittelstaendische Beteiligungsgesellschaft Sachsen mbH
Koeppel, Christian—Mittelstaendische Beteiligungsgesellschaft Sachsen-Anhalt
Koestel, Gilles—Investsud SA
Koffel, Paul—Coller Capital Ltd
Koffler, Peter—Blackstone Group LP
Koffman, Ilya—Turnspire Capital Partners LLC
Kogan, Eric—Clarion Capital Partners LLC
Kogler, Jeremy—Blue Wolf Capital Partners LLC
Kogure, Kenichi—Toho Bank Ltd
Koh, Bong—Venrock Inc
Koh, Eng Hong—Aventures Capital Management Pte Ltd
Koh, Eng Hong—Venstar Capital Management Pte Ltd
Koh, Jay—Siguler Guff & Company LP
Koh, Judy—Bay City Capital LLC
Koh, Melody—NextView Ventures LP
Koh, Soo Boon—iGlobe Partners Ltd
Koh, Sung-Que—STIC Investment Inc
Kohlberg, Jerome—Kohlberg & Co LLC
Kohlenberger, G.L.—Blu Venture Investors LLC
Kohler, Bertram—Deutsche Effecten und Wechsel Beteiligungsgesellschaft AG
Kohler, William—Lightspeed Management Company LLC
Kohler, William—Summerhill Venture Partners Management Inc
Kohli, Anil—3i Group PLC
Kohlmeyer, Thomas—Access Capital Partners SA
Kohn, Ben—Rizvi Traverse Management LLC

Koifman, Roberto—Aurus Gestion de Inversiones SPA
Kok, Frits—Carduso Capital BV
Kokkinen, Antti—Bluerun Ventures LP
Kokoricha, Paul—African Capital Alliance
Kokorotsikos, Paris—Incubation for Growth SA
Kokron, Carlos—Qualcomm Ventures
Kokubo, Takashi—Integral Corp
Kola, Vani—Kalaari Capital Partners LLC
Kolada, David—Sustainable Development Technology Canada
Kolada, David—Yaletown Venture Partners
Kolade, Wol—F&C Equity Partners PLC
Kolandjian, Vreij Arthur—Yellowstone Capital, Inc.
Kolb, Uwe—Bridgepoint Advisers Ltd
Kolbe, Jim—Dev Equity LLC
Kolbe, Natalie—Actis LLP
Kolbe, Oliver—Silver Investment Partners GmbH & Co KG
Kolber, Jonathan—Viola Private Equity I LP
Kolchinsky, Peter—RA Capital Management LLC
Koldyke, Laird—WinoNA Capital Management LLC
Koldyke, Martin—Frontenac Company LLC
Kole, John—Long River Ventures, Inc.
Kolke, Jeffrey—Monroe Capital LLC
Kollender, Richard—Quaker Partners Management LP
Kolln, Thies—Aavin Equity Advisors LLC
Kolluri, Krishna—New Enterprise Associates Inc
Kolodny, Lauren—Aspect Ventures LP
Kolodyuk, Andrey—AVentures Capital TOV
Kolodziejcyk, Richard—EW Healthcare Partners
Kolpachev, Georgiy—Rossiiskaia Korporatsiia Nanotekhnologii GK
Kolster, Christian—C & M Capital Ab Oy
Koltun, Gregory—Morrison & Foerster LLP
Komada, Tim—Deep Fork Capital
Komarappagari, Sruti—Endiya Partners
Kometz, Avi—Ascent Biomedical Ventures
Kometz, Avi—Deerfield Management Company LP
Komisar, Randy—Kleiner Perkins Caufield & Byers LLC
Komiya, Kazuyoshi—CAS Capital Inc
Komiya, Yuji—Tokio Marine Capital Co Ltd
Komori, Kazutaka—Tokio Marine Capital Co Ltd
Kompernass, Hans—BTH Berlin Technologie Holding GmbH
Komulainen, Timo—Unternehmertum GmbH
Konda, Chisato—Blackstone Group LP
Kondrashov, Alexander—Rossiiskaia Korporatsiia Nanotekhnologii GK
Konduru, Mahesh—Potomac Energy Fund LP
Konev, Oleg—Da Vinci Capital Management Ltd
Konfong, Victoria—Enhanced Equity Fund, L.P.
Kong, Chu—Actis LLP
Kong, Gang—Shanghai Broadview Capital Management Co Ltd
Kong, Garheng—Cross Valley Capital
Kong, Garheng—HeathQuest Capital
Kong, Jianhe—Shenzhen Hongshisan Capital Co Ltd
Kong, Qiang—Shanghai Beyond Binghong Equity Investment Management Co Ltd
Kong, Raymond—Vickers Venture Partners
Kong, Teck Chien—MBK Partners Inc
Kong, Yanwen—Shenzhen Hongshisan Capital Co Ltd

Konig, Olav—Baml Capital Access Funds Management LLC
Konigsberg, Robert—Carlyle Group LP
Kono, Kazunari—Whiz Partners Inc
Kono, Teppei—Unison Capital, Inc.
Konrad, Robert—KT Capital Management LLC
Konrath, Daniela—Pantheon Ventures (UK) LLP
Konuk, Murat—Castle Harlan Inc
Koo, Bo-Hoi—Lee&Co Investments Co
Koo, Douglas—Tautona Group Lp
Koo, Jason—LB Investment Inc
Koo, Kyeong-Cheol—STIC Investment Inc
Koo, Timothy—Olympus Capital Holdings Asia Hong Kong Ltd
Kook, Kyungoh—Siguler Guff & Company LP
Kooman, Kevin—Patriot Financial Partners LP
Kooman, Peter—Tonka Bay Equity Partners LLC
Koontz, Paul—Foundation Capital LLC
Koop, Fritz—Rantum Capital Management GmbH
Koopersmith, Adam—Jabodon PT Co
Koopersmith, Adam—Pritzker Group Venture Capital
Koopman, Edward—Motion Equity Partners LLP
Koops, Koos—Carduso Capital BV
Kopans, Haim—JVP Jerusalem Venture Partners Israel Management, Ltd.
Kopchinsky, Gregory—New Canaan Funding
Kopel, Shelly—Granite Equity Partners LLC
Kopelman, Josh—First Round Capital
Kopelman, Michael—Edison Partners
Kopelman, Michael—Edison Partners
Kopera, Robert—CI Capital Partners LLC
Koplovitz, Jonathan—Blackstone Group LP
Koplovitz, Kay—Springboard Venture Fund LLC
Koplow-McAdams, Hilarie—New Enterprise Associates Inc
Koponen, Petteri—Lifeline Ventures GP II Oy
Kopp, Darby—Harbor Light Capital Partners LLC
Kopp, Timothy—Hyde Park Venture Partners
Koppel, Adam—Bain Capital Inc
Koppelkamm, Daniel—Mountain Cleantech AG
Koppen, Kai—Emeram Capital Partners GmbH
Kopple, Elizabeth—Bounty Equity Fund LLC
Koppler, Doit—Third Security LLC
Kopplin, Stacia—NXT Capital Venture Finance
Kopra, Timothy—Blue Bear Capital LLC
Kopyleva, Anya—Gemcorp Capital LLP
Kopylov, Denis—IK Ineko PAT
Koray, Cem—Perella Weinberg Partners LP
Korczak, James—Adams Street Partners LLC
Kordes, Olaf—Alpha Group
Kordyback, Frances—Northwater Capital Management Inc
Korff, Campbell—Avenue Capital Group LLC
Korhonen, Jyrki—Terra Firma Capital Partners Ltd
Korloev, Pavel—Pulsar Ecosystem LLC
Korn, Andrew—Sageview Capital LP
Korn, Douglas—Irving Place Capital LLC
Korngold, Jonathan—General Atlantic LLC
Kornman, Grant—NCK Capital LLC
Kornman, Michael—NCK Capital LLC
Kornmann, Brian—Thompson Street Capital Partners LP
Korolev, Nikolay—Rossiyskaya venchurnaya kompaniya OAO
Korpala, Jacek—Arx Equity Partners Sp z o o

2513

Pratt's Guide to Private Equity & Venture Capital Sources

Kersten, Eric–Branford Castle Partners
Kert, Rachel–Hall Capital Partners LLC
Korterud, Fredrik–Norvestor Equity AS
Kortick, Daniel–Wicks Group of Companies LLC
Kortlang, Ben–Kleiner Perkins Caufield & Byers LLC
Korver, Clinton–Ulu Ventures
Korver, Michael–Global Venture Capital Inc
Korzinstone, Michael–Silver Lake Partners LP
Kos, John–GTCR Golder Rauner LLC
Kosacz, Barbara–Cooley LLP
Kosch, Jurgen–MIG Verwaltungs AG
Kosch, Tiffany–CenterGate Capital LP
Kosch, Tiffany–Peak Rock Capital LLC
Kosciusko-Morizet, Pierre–Isai Gestion SAS
Koseff, Stephen–Investec Private Equity
Kosel, Howard–Abatis Capital LLC
Kosematoglu, Mehmet–Berggruen Holdings Inc
Koslow, Michael–Desert Cedars LLC
Koslow, Patricia–Desert Cedars LLC
Kosofsky, Kristen–Horizon Technology Finance Management LLC
Kosonen, Mikko–Suomen itsenaisyyden juhlararahasto
Kosonen, Tuomas–Inventure Oy
Kosoy, Daniel–Athenian Fund Management Inc
Kosoy, Stewart–Digital Capital AG
Koss, Stan–Balmoral Advisors LLC
Kossow, Jon–Norwest Venture Partners
Kostenko, Bill–Beringer Capital Inc
Koster, Linda–Cohen & Company Financial Ltd
Kostoff, Mike–Blu Venture Investors LLC
Kostuchenko, Malcolm–Enhanced Equity Fund, L.P.
Kosturanov, Oliver–Small Enterprise Assistance Funds
Kosty, Michael–Bregal Investments LLP
Kosugi, Akira–Blackstone Group LP
Kothari, Ashok–Asia Pacific Capital (HK) Ltd
Kothari, Manish–SRI International
Kothari, Rajesh–Seneca Partners Inc
Kotler, Steve–Watermill Group LLC
Kott, Laurent–IT-Translation SA
Kotting, Michiel–Northzone Ventures
Kottkamp, Eckart–Premium Equity Partners GmbH
Kotzubei, Jacok–Platinum Equity LLC
Koulogeorge, Mark–MK Capital
Kourakos, William–Perella Weinberg Partners LP
Kouwenhoven, Vincent–eVentures Europe BV
Kovach, Jeffrey–Arsenal Capital Management LLC
Kovach, Jeffrey–Arsenal Capital Partners LP
Kovach, Jeffrey–Arsenal Capital Partners LP
Kovacs, Gayle–Shaw Venture Partners
Kovacs, Gayle–Timberline Venture Partners
Kovalkova, Anna–Pharos Capital Group LLC
Kovatchis, Michele–Antares Capital Corp
Koven, James–One Equity Partners LLC
Kovick, Jeff–Gemini Partners, Inc.
Kowal, Andrew–Francisco Partners LP
Kowalczyk, Krzysztof–Hardgamma Ventures Sp z o o
Kowalik, Marcin–Black Pearls VC SA
Kowalski, Andrea–Boost&Co SAS
Kowalzik, Michael–Target Partners GmbH
Koyfman, Mo–Spark Capital
Kozlov, Andrey–4BIO Ventures Management Ltd
Kozlov, Andrey–CLS Capital Ltd
Kozlov, Andrey–Enso Ventures Ltd

Kpedekpo, Malcolm–Panoramic Growth Equity (Fund Management) LLP
Kra, Gabriel–Prelude Ventures LLC
Kracum, Richard–Wind Point Advisors LLC
Kraeutler, Lisa–Domain Associates LLC
Kraft, Jonathan–Kraft Group LLC
Kraig, Leon–IGNIA Partners LLC
Krall, Phillip–Arrowhead Mezzanine LLC
Kramer, Andrea–Hamilton Lane Advisors LLC
Kramer, Brian–Morrison & Foerster LLP
Kramer, Caleb–Oaktree Capital Management LP
Kramer, Eric–Crestone Capital LLC
Kramer, Karl–Morrison & Foerster LLP
Kramer, Michael–Perella Weinberg Partners LP
Kramer, Michael–Safanad Inc
Kramer, Richard–Investcorp Bank BSC
Kramer, Richard–Investcorp Technology Investments Group
Kramer, Roxane–KJM Capital LLC
Kramer, Ted–Hammond Kennedy Whitney & Company Inc
Krancki, Joseph–Frog Capital Ltd
Kranenburg, Mike–Go Capital Asset Management BV
Kranjac, Daniella–Dynamk Capital LLC
Kranjac, Mario–Dynamk Capital LLC
Krapf, Joshua–Blackstone Group LP
Krasner, Dan–Platinum Equity LLC
Krasnov, Joel–Milbank Tweed Hadley & Mccloy LLP
Krattinger, Marc–Aravis SA
Kraus, Elizabeth–MergeLane LLC
Kraus, Larry–Ingleside Investors LLC
Kraus, Laura–Monroe Capital LLC
Kraus, Matthew–Celerity Partners LP
Kraus, Stephen–Bessemer Venture Partners
Krause, Richard–Kamylon Capital LLC
Krauskopf, David–Blu Venture Investors LLC
Krauss, Marlene–KBL HEALTHCARE VENTURES L P
Krausz, Steve–U.S. Venture Partners
Krausz, Steve–U.S. Venture Partners
Kravit, Ronald–Cerberus Capital Management LP
Krawczyk, Krzysztof–Innova Capital Sp z o o
Krawinkel, Hendrik–Finleap GmbH
Kray, Scott–Chatham Capital
Kreager, JT–NCT Ventures LLC
Krebs, Amy–Antares Capital Corp
Krebs, Stephanie–Antares Capital Corp
Krediet, Rudolph–Anholt (USA) LLC
Kreeger, Matthew–Morrison & Foerster LLP
Kreger, Michael–Madison Dearborn Partners LLC
Kreidler, Robert–Carousel Capital Partners
Kreidler, Robert–Fidus Capital LLC
Kreie, Paul–MMF Capital Management LLC
Kreimer, Thomas–Lakeside Capital Management LLC
Kreindl, Torsten–Grazia Equity GmbH
Kreisel, Joerg–Triangle Venture Capital Group
Krejci, David–Blackstone Group LP
Krekel, Tig–Galileo Partners
Krekel, Tig–JFlehman & Co
Kreller, Thomas–Milbank Tweed Hadley & Mccloy LLP
Kremer, William–Crossharbor Capital Partners
Krenteras, Nicholaos–Pine Brook Road Partners LLC
Krentz, Jeff–CRITICAL CAPITAL GROWTH FUND L P
Kresnicka, Kevin–50 South Capital Advisors LLC

Kress, Joel–V&A Capital
Kressel, Henry–Warburg Pincus LLC
Kreter, David–GI Partners
Kretz, Nikolaus–Proregio Mittelstandsfinanzierungs AG
Kreulen, Joost–Empresaria Group PLC
Kreutz, Philipp–DEG Deutsche Investitions- und Entwicklungsgesellschaft mbH
Kreuziger, Jason–Summit Partners LP
Krevans, Rachel–Morrison & Foerster LLP
Krichevsky, Eugene–Acas LLC
Krick, Benjamin–Willcrest Partners LLC
Kriebel, Brian–Blackstone Group LP
Krieger, David–Warburg Pincus LLC
Krikorian, Jason–Doll Capital Management Inc
Krin, Vladimir–TRG Management LP
Krinsky, Simon–Hall Capital Partners LLC
Kripalani, Nitin–Evolvence Capital Ltd
Kriscunas, Suzanne–Riverside Co
Kriser, Daniel–Cedar Hill Associates LLC
Krish, Nanda–Start Smart Labs
Krishna, Vikram–GMT Communications Partners LLP
Krishnamurthy, Balaji–QInvest Ltd
Krishnamurthy, Jill–Dolphin Capital Group LLC
Krishnamurthy, K. G.–HDFC Venture Capital Ltd
Krishnamurthy, Mahesh–True North
Krishnamurthy, Pavan–Ojas Venture Partners
Krishnan, Anand–Dubai International Capital LLC
Krishnan, Aneal–Veritas Capital Fund Management LLC
Krishnan, Jyotsna–Elevar Equity Advisors Pvt Ltd
Krishnan, Rajeev–SBI Capital Ventures
Krishnan, Rohit–Eight Roads Ventures Europe
Krishnan, Sanjeev–S2G Ventures LLC
Krishnaswami, Mukund–Lighthouse Fund LLC
Kristoffersen, January–Norinnova Forvaltning AS
Kritsberg, Valerie–Blackstone Group LP
Krna, Matt–Softbank Capital Partners L P
Kro, Lisa–Mill City Capital LP
Krocke, Ingo–Auctus Capital Partners AG
Kroeger, Christopher–Aurora Funds Inc
Kroener, Martin–MVP Management GmbH
Kroeze, Peter–H2 Equity Partners BV
Krogstad, Nils–Investinor AS
Krohn, Max–Corazon Capital LLC
Kroin, David–Great Point Partners LLC
Kroizer, Israel–Israel Cleantech Ventures
Krol, Patrick–Aescap Venture I BV
Krol, Sebastian–Enterprise Investors Sp z o o
Kroloff, Noah–NGN Capital LLC
Kromayer, Matthias–MIG Verwaltungs AG
Kromwijk Smits, Jelto–Prime Technology Ventures NV
Kroner, Ken–BlackRock Inc
Kronfol, Mohieddine–Algebra Capital Ltd
Kronforst, Nathan–BelHealth Investment Partners LLC
Krongard, Timothy–Questmark Partners LP
Krotee, Chip–Perella Weinberg Partners LP
Kroupa, Karel–Argos Soditic SA
Krueger, Travis–GTCR Golder Rauner LLC
Kruetten, Rainer–Wealthcap Initiatoren GmbH
Krug, Antonie–Siparex Group
Krug, Reiner–MIDAS Management AG
Kruizenga, Ryan–Arthur Ventures LLC

Kruizenga, Ryan—Mainsail Partners LP
Krukov, Dmitri—Elbrus Kapital OOO
Krukrubo, Ibi—Ernst & Young LLP
Krulick, Jarrad—Siguler Guff & Company LP
Krumm, Torsten—Odewald & Compagnie fuer Beteiligungen GmbH
Krumpfes, Austin—PPM America Capital Partners LLC
Krumrei, Brian—TSG Consumer Partners, L.P.
Krunnies, Manfred—Premium Equity Partners GmbH
Krupa, Stephen—Psilos Group Managers LLC
Krupka, Michael—Bain Capital Inc
Krupka, Michael—Bain Capital Venture Partners LLC
Krupp, Richard—Pierpoint Capital LLC
Kruse, Jordon—Oaktree Capital Management LP
Kruse, Kevin—Seven Mile Capital Partners LP
Krusen, W. Andrew—Westshore Capital Partners LP
Kryeziu, Arben—Mbloom LLC
Ksenak, Brian—Morgan Stanley Alternative Investment Partners LP
Ku, Ja-deug—Neoplux Co Ltd
Ku, Mark—CVC Capital Partners Ltd
Ku, Steven—Visium Asset Management LP
Kuan, Roy—CVC Asia Pacific Ltd
Kuan, Roy—CVC Capital Partners Ltd
Kuang, Yi—Legend Star Venture Incubator
Kuatov, Orinbasar—Adm Capital
Kubal, Lawrence—Labrador Ventures
Kubes, Daniel—Wayzata Investment Partners LLC
Kubin, Karen—Morrison & Foerster LLP
Kubitz, Ralf—nwk nordwest Kapitalbeteiligungsgesellschaft der Sparkasse
Kubo, Tatsuya—Baml Capital Access Funds Management LLC
Kubota, Glenn—Morrison & Foerster LLP
Kudsi, Yusef—Oaktree Capital Management LP
Kuebler, Sebastian—Taishan Invest AG
Kuegler, Tom—Wasabi Ventures LLC
Kuehl, Ronald—Frontenac Company LLC
Kuehl, Timothy—Norwest Equity Partners
Kuehn, Christian—DMB Deutsche Mittelstandsbeteiligungs GmbH
Kuehni, Christian—Wealthcap Initiatoren GmbH
Kuepper, Hans—Global Life Science Ventures GmbH
Kues, Matthias—NORD Holding Unternehmensbeteiligungsgesellschaft mbH
Kuffel, Piotr—Warsaw Equity Management Sp z o o
Kuflik, Mitchell—Brahman Management LLC
Kugelman, David—Atlanta Capital Partners LLC
Kuhl, Jan—Polaris Management A/S
Kuhling, Robert—ONSET Ventures
Kuhlmann, Frederic—Nord Capital Partenaires SAS
Kuijten, Rene—Life Sciences Partners BV
Kukushkin, Yury—4BIO Ventures Management Ltd
Kukutai, Arama—FINISTERE VENTURES L L C
Kulesza, Piotr—Rtaventures VC Sp z o o Sk
Kulick, Richard—Wharton Equity Partners LLC
Kulig, Krzysztof—Innova Capital Sp z o o
Kulikov, Vadim—Bright Capital OOO
Kulkarni, Anant—Milestone Religare Investment Advisors Pvt Ltd
Kulkarni, Manoj—Samena Capital Management LLP
Kulkarni, Nicholas—Long Lake Partners
Kulmala, Pentti—Evolver Investment Group Ltd
Kulperger, Robert—Blackstone Group LP
Kumakura, Jiro—Global Brain Corp

Kumar, Ajit—Evolvence Capital Ltd
Kumar, Ankit—Gryphon Investors Inc
Kumar, Ankur—Providence Equity Partners LLC
Kumar, Arvindh—Thoma Bravo LLC
Kumar, Deepak—General Catalyst Partners LLC
Kumar, Manu—K9 Ventures LP
Kumar, Nalin—Rabo India Finance Ltd
Kumar, Nisha—Greenbriar Equity Group LLC
Kumar, Prashant—Warburg Pincus LLC
Kumar, R.V. Dilip—SIDBI Venture Capital Ltd
Kumar, Rajive—Waller Capital Partners LLC
Kumar, Sajit—SIDBI Venture Capital Ltd
Kumar, Samir—Inventus Capital Partners Fund I L P
Kumar, Suketu—ICICI Venture Funds Management Company Ltd
Kumar, Vinay—AEA Investors LLC
Kumaramangalam, Kartik—Papillon Capital LLC
Kumin, Michael—Great Hill Equity Partners LLC
Kummerer, Kenneth—Milestone Partners LP
Kump, Eric—Carlyle Group LP
Kumpulainen, Mikko—Vaaka Partners Oy
Kundra, Monish—Columbia Capital LP
Kundrun, Bernd—Hanse Ventures BSJ GmbH
Kundur, C. Shekhar—Ventureast
Kunec, Nathan—ACM Ltd
Kung, Frank—Vivo Capital LLC
Kung, Hsing—Acorn Campus Ventures
Kung, Kuo Chuan—MBK Partners Inc
Kunica, Matthew—Birch Hill Equity Partners Management Inc
Kunkle, Gary—Evolution Capital Partners LLC
Kunse, Jim—El Dorado Ventures
Kuntz, Kevin—Juggernaut Partners LP
Kuntz, Norma—Carlyle Group LP
Kuntz, Richard—Shepherd Ventures LP
Kuntz, William—Housatonic Partners Management Co Inc
Kuntz, William—Peak Rock Capital LLC
Kuntze, Joern-Carlos—BTH Berlin Technologie Holding GmbH
Kunz, Christopher—Lexington Partners Inc
Kunz, Kevin—Austin Ventures
Kuo, Andrew—Blackstone Group LP
Kuo, Daniel—Entangled Ventures LLC
Kuo, David—Newcap Partners Inc
Kuo, Jeff—Grey Mountain Partners LLC
Kuo, Julia—Spectrum Equity Investors LP
Kuo, Steve—Hercules Capital Inc
Kuo, Tom—Berkshire Partners LLC
Kuper, Andrew—LeapFrog Investments
Kuplic, David—Advantus Capital Management Inc
Kupor, Scott—Andreessen Horowitz LLC
Kurabayashi, Akira—Draper Nexus Venture Partners LLC
Kurian, Jacob—New Silk Route Partners, LLC
Kuriyan, Vikram—Ananta Capital
Kuroda, Keigo—Blackstone Group LP
Kuroda, Toshi—Oaktree Capital Management LP
Kurokawa, Naonori—University of Tokyo Edge Capital Co Ltd
Kurosaki, Morimine—It-Farm Corp
Kurosawa, Yoichiro—New Horizon Capital Co Ltd
Kurrik, Ilomai—Siguler Guff & Company LP
Kurtenbach, Jim—Prairie Oak Capital LLC
Kurteson, George—Carlyle Group LP

Kurth, Thomas—Haynes and Boone LLC
Kurtin, Eve—Vantagepoint Management Inc
Kurtz, Evan—Acas LLC
Kurtz, Tom—Patriot Capital Funding Inc
Kuruma, Masayuki—Tokio Marine Capital Co Ltd
Kurz, Charles—Hall Capital Partners LLC
Kurz, Karl—CCMP Capital Advisors LP
Kurzweil, Ethan—Bessemer Venture Partners
Kusaka, Kazuki—MTS Health Partners LP
Kushel, J Richard—BlackRock Inc
Kushman, Lauren—NewSchools Venture Fund
Kushner, Jared—Thrive Capital Partners LLC
Kushner, Joshua—Thrive Capital Partners LLC
Kusik, Martin—Penta Investments Ltd
Kusurin, Ante—One Equity Partners LLC
Kutrieh, Tarek—Gores Group LLC
Kutsenda, Eric—Seidler Equity Partners
Kutzkey, Tim—Column Group
Kuwayti, Kenneth—Morrison & Foerster LLP
Kuykendall, Kevin—Acas LLC
Kuzmin, Dmitry—4BIO Ventures Management Ltd
Kuznetsov, Yev—Crescent Capital Group LP
Kvamme, Mark—Drive Capital LLC
Kvamme, Mark—Sequoia Capital Operations LLC
Kvammen, Morten—GFH Capital Ltd
Kvistsand, Hege Kristine—Viking Venture As
Kw, Yeung—Cassia Investments Ltd
Kwag, Dae Hwan—STIC Investment Inc
Kwan, Allan—Oak Investment Partners
Kwan, David—Charlesbank Capital Partners LLC
Kwan, Dick—Baring Private Equity Asia Ltd
Kwatinetz, Michael—Azure Capital Partners, L.P.
Kwee, Hoe Boon—SEAVI Advent Corporation Ltd
Kwiatkowska, Oliwia—TDJ SA
Kwiecien, Tomasz—Mezzanine Management Finanz und UnternehmensberatungsgmbH
Kwok, Amy—HPEF Capital Partners Ltd
Kwok, Celine—Great Oaks Venture Capital LLC
Kwok, Edward—Haynes and Boone LLC
Kwok, Ivan—Cinven Group Ltd
Kwok, Steven—Orchid Asia Group Management Ltd
Kwon, Charles—China Materialia LLC
Kwon, Don—MICHIGAN VENTURE CAPITAL CO LTD
Kwon, Jennifer—Gores Group LLC
Kwon, OhSang—Avista Capital Holdings LP
Kwon, Samuel—Carlyle Group LP
Kwon, Sooin—MTS Health Partners LP
Kyte, Darren—NIBC Principal Investments BV
L Eplattenier, Francois—Aravis SA
L Heureux, Alexandre—Auven Therapeutics Management LLLP
LANGE, ALAN—Enhanced Capital Partners LLC
La Forge, Andre—Entrepreneur Capital Inc
La Magna, Marc—Turnstone Capital Management LLC
La Runa, Angelo Piero—Progressio SGR SpA
La Salle, Bradford—Archipel Capital LLC
La Voun, Veronica—Hamilton Investments Inc
LaChance, Michael—Wheelhouse Capital Partners LLC
LaCroix, Robert—Cti Capital Securities Inc
LaFayette, Justin—Georgian Partners Growth Fund Founders International I LP
LaFayette, William—Asia Alternatives Management LLC

Pratt's Guide to Private Equity & Venture Capital Sources

LaHatte, Kevin–Comvest Partners
LaLonde, Timothy–Evercore Inc
LaMarque, Dack–Spanos Barber Jesse & Co LLC
LaMascolo, Angelo–PBM Capital Group LLC
LaPeer, Karl–Peninsula Capital Partners LLC
LaPorte, Kathleen–New Leaf Venture Partners LLC
LaPorte, Steve–ONSET Ventures
LaRue, David–Symphony Asia Holdings Pte Ltd
LaRue, Scott–Piper Jaffray Ventures Inc
LaRussa, Benny–Azalea Capital LLC
LaSalle, Michael–Shamrock Capital Advisors LLC
LaValle, Dominic–Wynnchurch Capital Ltd
LaVersa, Gina–Precision Capital Advisors LLC
LaVersa, Stephen–Gramercy Inc
LaViolette, Paul–SV Health Investors LLP
Laanemaa, Kristjan–Karma Ventures OU
Labarre, Steven–Strength Capital Partners LLC
Labarthe Costas, Carlos–IGNIA Partners LLC
Labastida, Jorge–Haynes and Boone LLC
Laber, Ilias–Cevian Capital AB
Labib, Taimoor–Standard Chartered Private Equity Ltd
Labossiere, Gilles–Republic Alley SA
Labouret, Alexandre–Platina Finance, Ltd.
Labrum, Brandon–Sterling Partners GP LLC
Lacasse, Louis–GeneChem Financial Corp
Lace, Tom–Longview Asset Management Ltd
Lacenere, Anthony–INETWORKS LLC
Lacey, Doug–LeapFrog Investments
Lachman, Charles–Resonetics LLC
Lack, David–Austin Ventures
Lack, David–Tritium Partners LLC
Lack, Jeremy–COGR Inc
Lacob, Joseph–Kleiner Perkins Caufield & Byers LLC
Lacoste, Francois–Idinvest Partners SA
Lacourte, Joel–Astorg Partners SAS
Lacovara, Christopher–Kohlberg & Co LLC
Lacroix, Martial–GeneChem Financial Corp
Lacy, Craig–Madison Capital Funding LLC
Ladak, Omar–Noverra Consulting and Capital Partners
Ladak, Zuher–Falconhead Capital LLC
Ladd, Robert–Haynes and Boone LLC
Ladda, A. Todd–Fortress Investment Group LLC
Laddha, Manoj–Unicorn India Ventures Advisors LLP
Laden, Brian–TriStar Technology Ventures LLC
Ladha, Farouk–Four Rivers Partners LP
Ladner, Mark–Morrison & Foerster LLP
Lafer, Peter–EW Healthcare Partners
Laffer, Shaun–Molash Group
Lafferty, Edward–Saturn Management LLC
Laffitte, Michel–CDC Climat SA
Laffont, Philippe–Coatue Management L L C
Laffy, Laurent–360 Capital Management SA
Lafortune, Francois–Portag3 Ventures Inc GP
Lagace, Etienne–Hacking Health Accelerator Inc
Lagarde, Michel–JLL Partners Inc
Lagarde, Pascal–Bpifrance Investissement SASU
Lagod, Martin–Firelake Capital Management LLC
Lagoudas, Dimitris–PTV Healthcare Capital
Lagreze, Julien–AKN Holdings LLC
Laher, Zain–Emerging Capital Partners
Laher, Zain–Kleoss Capital (Pty) Ltd
Laheurte, Jean-Pierre–Incubateur Paca-Est
Lahham, Nabil–Perella Weinberg Partners LP
Lahmar, Sofiane–Development Partners International LLP
Lahnstein, Florian–Siguler Guff & Company LP
Lai, David–Calidant Capital LLC
Lai, Eugene–Southern Capital Group Pte Ltd
Lai, Gregory–Clayton Dubilier & Rice LLC
Lai, Jing Dong–Carlyle Group LP
Lai, Sin Jat–Iglobe Treasury Management Ltd
Lai, Xiaoming–Uni-Quantum Fund Management Co Ltd
Lai, Zhigang–Prax Capital Management Co
Lai-Goldman, Myla–Hatteras Venture Partners
Laibow, Brian–Oaktree Capital Management LP
Laing, Andrew–Aberdeen Asset Management PLC
Laino, Peter–Monitor Clipper Partners LLC
Laird, Douglas–Formative Ventures
Lajchter, Marcelo Andre–Evercore Inc
Lajous, Rene–Accretia Capital LLC
Lake, Douglas–DC Capital Partners LLC
Lake, Fred–New Media Innovation Centre
Lake, Marianne–JPMorgan Chase & Co
Lakhaney, Aman–Abraaj Capital Ltd
Lakhani, Shailesh–Sequoia Capital India
Lakhmichand, Bikesh–1337 Ventures Sdn Bhd
Lakoff, David–Trimaran Capital LLC
Lal, Ajay–Aif Capital Asia Iii LP
Lal, Nityen–ICOS Capital Management BV
Lalande, Kevin–Sante Ventures
Lalani, Hussain–United Gulf Bank Securities Co. B.S.C
Laliberte, Benoit–Investel Capital Corp
Lall, Rajiv–Lok Capital
Lally, Brenda Lee–Pfingsten Partners LLC
Lalonde, Chris–Century Capital Management / Massachusetts Inc
Lam, Alfred–Chrysalix Energy
Lam, Alvin–CVC Asia Pacific Ltd
Lam, Alvin–CVC Capital Partners Ltd
Lam, Charles–Baring Private Equity Asia Ltd
Lam, Chihtsung–Axiom Asia Private Capital Pte Ltd
Lam, Chivas–Qiming Venture Partners Ii LP
Lam, David–WestSummit Capital Management Ltd
Lam, Kevin–Incuvest Pte Ltd
Lam, Lily–Covington Capital Corp
Lam, Rachel–Undisclosed Firm
Lam, Rony–Mcb Equity Fund Ltd
Lam, Tony–Vanedge Capital Inc
Lam, Van–Merit Capital Partners IV LLC
Lama, Mariel–Advent Morro Equity Partners Inc
Lamarche, Normand–Front Street Capital
Lamarche, Regis–Capital Croissance SAS
Lamb, Damian–Genesys Capital Partners Inc
Lamb, Damian–Genesys Capital Partners Inc
Lamb, David–Milbank Tweed Hadley & Mccloy LLP
Lamb, David–Vision Capital LLP
Lamb, Jeffrey–Socius Capital Group LLC
Lamb, Priscilla–HFPX Holding Ltda
Lamb, Steve–CoveView Capital Partners LLC
Lamba, Jagmeet–Sonoma Management Partners Pvt Ltd
Lambers, Ernest–NIBC Principal Investments BV
Lambert, Jean-Francois–Sofina SA
Lambert, Joel–First Reserve Corp
Lambert, Lionel–Ciclad Participations SAS
Lambert, Matt–Montreux Equity Partners
Lambert, Michel–Cycle Capital Management (CCM) Inc
Lambert, Miguel–Oakcrest Capital Partners LLC
Lambert, Vince–MTS Health Partners LP
Lambert, Vincent–Summit Partners LP
Lambert, Virginie–Naxicap Partners SA
Lambie, Mensah–Beechbrook Capital LLP
Lambrech, John–W Capital Management LLC
Lameloise, Christian–Eurekap SAS
Lamensdorf, Jonathan–Highland Capital Management LP
Lamfalussy, Jerome–E Capital Management Scrl
Lamm, Charlie–Hall Capital Partners LLC
Lamm, Peter–Fenway Partners LLC
Lammers, Eric–ArcLight Capital Holdings LLC
Lammerts, Dirk–Burrill & Company
Lammoglia, Julien–Cinven Group Ltd
Lamond, Pierre–Khosla Ventures LLC
Lamont, Annie–Oak HC/FT Partners LP
Lamont, Annie–Oak Investment Partners
Lamont, Kenneth–Crescent Point Energy Corp
Lamoureux, Pierre-Olivier–Golub Capital Master Funding LLC
Lampe, Jeffrey–Hopewell Ventures
Lamphere, Gilbert–Flatworld Capital LLC
Lampinen, Sami–Inventure Oy
Lamport, Anthony–Lambda Fund Management Inc
Lamstein, Josh–KEC Ventures Inc
Lan, Shujun–Richlink International Capital Co Ltd
Lanava, Robert–Gramercy Inc
Lancaster, N. John–Riverstone Holdings LLC
Lancaster, Richard–DPE Deutsche Private Equity GmbH
Land, Elderd–Gimv Investeringsmaatschappij Voor Vlanderen NV
Land, Peter–Harbert Management Corp
Landa, Debbie–GrowLab Ventures Inc
Landau, David–LNK Partners LLC
Landau, Yair–MK Capital
Lander, Jonathan–Dawnay Day Group
Lander, Stuart–Upfront Ventures
Landherr, Thomas–Corigin Private Equity Group
Landim, Rodolfo–Mare Investimentos Ltda
Landis, Daniel–Antares Capital Corp
Landis, Kel–Plexus Capital LLC
Landman, David–Perella Weinberg Partners LP
Landman, Sam–Comcast Ventures
Landman, William–CMS Mezzanine Fund
Landman, William–Renovus Capital Partners LP
Landmann, Laird–Trust Company of the West
Landmann, Ran–CVC Capital Partners Ltd
Lando, Anthony–Accuitive Medical Ventures LLC
Landrin, Nicolas–Sofimac Innovation SAS
Landrum, Lee–Tennenbaum Capital Partners LLC
Landry, Carl–Arc Financial Corp.
Landry, Dan–MDB Capital Group LLC
Landry, Danielle–Business Development Bank of Canada
Landsberg, Ken–ECI Partners LLP
Landsberger, Frank–INKEF Capital BV
Landskowsky, David–Intuitive Venture Partners LLC
Landthorn, Ron–TechColumbus
Landuyt, William–Charterhouse Group Inc
Lane, Christopher–Columbia Partners Private Capital
Lane, Christopher–KRG Capital Management LP

2516

Lane, Curtis—MTS Health Partners LP
Lane, Damien—Episode 1 Ventures LLP
Lane, Daniel—Harmony Partners
Lane, David—ONSET Ventures
Lane, Holly—Prairie Capital, L.P.
Lane, Ian—Baml Capital Access Funds Management LLC
Lane, Jesse—Summit Partners LP
Lane, Joseph—Ben Franklin Technology Partners Of Northeastern PA
Lane, Joseph—Napier Park Global Capital (US) LP
Lane, Linda—Morrison & Foerster LLP
Lane, Ray—Kleiner Perkins Caufield & Byers LLC
Lane, Thao—GO Capital SAS
Lane, Tripp—Apax Partners LLP
Lanfranchi, Vanina—A Plus Finance SASU
Lang, Christine—Sinovation Ventures Ltd
Lang, David—Pamplona Capital Management LLP
Lang, Tuomas—Intera Equity Partners Oy
Langdale, Richard—NCT Ventures LLC
Langdon, Michael—Frontenac Company LLC
Langdon, Stewart—LeapFrog Investments
Lange, Louis—Asset Management Co
Lange, Ulf—ADCURAM Group AG
Langemar Olsson, Angela—Nordstjernan AB
Langensand, Leif—Angels' Forum & the Halo Fund
Langensand, Leif—HALO FUND L P
Langer, Bradley—Brown Brothers Harriman & Co
Langer, Mark—Anholt (USA) LLC
Langer, Michael—Diamond Castle Holdings LLC
Langer, Robert—Puretech Ventures
Langer, Uli—AM Ventures Holding GmbH
Langezaal, Rob—KPN Ventures BV
Langford, Margo—First Stone Venture Partners Inc
Langford, Ransom—Tpg Growth LLC
Langille, Kim—Clarke Inc
Langley, Paul—CenterGate Capital LP
Langloss, Tim—WFD Ventures LLC
Langman, M. Steven—Rhone Capital LLC
Langshur, Eric—Abundant Venture Partners LLC
Lanier, Campbell—ITC Holdings Corp
Lanier, John—Excellere Capital Management LLC
Lanik, Joel—Frontier Capital LLC
Lank, Michael—OMERS Private Equity Inc
Lankenau, Steven—Cotton Creek Capital Management LLC
Lankes, Hans Peter—European Bank for Reconstruction and Development
Lankes, Hans—International Finance Corp
Lankford, Daniel—Wavepoint Ventures LLC
Lanna, Paul—Coller Capital Ltd
Lannin, Charlie—Stone Arch Capital LLC
Lanning, Chris—General Atlantic LLC
Lanphere, Scott—Aletheia Partners Ltd
Lanscioni, Todd—JZ Capital Partners Ltd
Lantz, Jennifer—Haynes and Boone LLC
Lapeyre, Pierre—Riverstone Holdings LLC
Lapham, Andrew—Onex Corp
Lapides, Matthew—ABRY Partners LLC
Lapierre, Lise—Acces Capital Quebec
Lapique, Carlos—Peninsula Capital Advisors LLP
Laporte, Sandrine—Archimed SA
Laporte, Steven—ONSET Ventures
Lapping, Andrew—Hamilton Portfolio Ltd
Laranjeiro, Tiago—Angola Capital Partners

Laraway, Roberta—Headwaters BD LLC
Larcen, Dell—Gryphon Investors Inc
Larco, Vanessa—New Enterprise Associates Inc
Lardieg, Frederic—Octopus Ventures Ltd
Lardin, Cliff—Cayuga Venture Fund
Lardo, Nicholas—Long Lake Partners
Larkey, Adam—O3 Capital Advisors Pvt Ltd
Larkin, Charles—Webster Capital Management LLC
Larkin, Ian—Maranon Capital LP
Larkin, John—Avenue Capital Group LLC
Larkin, Thomas—Avenue Capital Group LLC
Larkins, Stuart—Chicago Ventures
Larma, Janne—eQ Oyj
Larocque, Jim—Carlyle Group LP
Laroque, Thomas—Blackstone Group LP
Larrea, Joan—GEF Management Corp
Larrick, Jim—CMEA Development Company LLC
Larsen, Charles—Accuitive Medical Ventures LLC
Larsen, Jeff—Larsen Maccoll Partners LP
Larsen, Jess—Highland Capital Management LP
Larsen, Kurt—Moelis Capital Partners LLC
Larsen, Kurt—NexPhase Capital LLC
Larsen, Mads—IK Investment Partners Ltd
Larsen, Michael—Harbert Management Corp
Larsen, Peter—Atlantic-Pacific Capital Inc
Larsen, Peter—Hamilton Lane Advisors LLC
Larsen, Sten—Internet Ventures Scandinavia
Larson, Christopher—Adams Street Partners LLC
Larson, Eric—Black River Asset Management LLC
Larson, Keith—Intel Capital Corp
Larson, Robert—Woodside Fund
Larson, Sarah—Third Rock Ventures LLC
Larsson, Erik—Vitruvian Partners LLP
Larsson, Nils-Gunnar—Ackra Invest AB
Larsson, Urban—Nischer Properties AB
Lascelles, Edward—Albion Capital Group LLP
Lasch, Michael—Pine Street Capital Partners LP
Laschinger, Beth—Cyprium Investment Partners LLC
Lasersohn, Jack—Vertical Group Inc
Lashina, Maria—Elbrus Kapital OOO
Lashkari, Deval—Telegraph Hill Partners
Laska, Esther—Cmia Capital Partners Pte Ltd
Lasko, Cristina—Waveland Investments LLC
Lasky, Larry—U.S. Venture Partners
Lasky, Mitch—Benchmark Capital Management Gesellschaft MBH In Liqu
Lasocki, Vladimir—Carlyle Group LP
Lasota, Stephen—Cowen Capital Partners LLC
Lassalle, Paul—Adams and Reese LLP
Lassey, Elom—Satya Capital Ltd
Lassonde, Christian—Impression Ventures
Laszlo, Andrew—137 Ventures LP
Laszlo, Andy—Hercules Capital Inc
Lateef, Z. Ed—Amvensys Capital Group LLC
Latham, George—Alpina Capital Partners LLP
Latham, Philip—Navis Management Sdn Bhd
Lathi, Vijay—New Leaf Venture Partners LLC
Latorre, Philippe—Activa Capital SAS
Lattanzio, Paul—Star Avenue Capital LLC
Latterell, Patrick—Latterell Venture Partners LP
Lattner, Kyle—Waud Capital Partners LLC
Latto, Richard—Long Road Investment Counsel LLC
Lau, Allen—Colony Capital LLC
Lau, Alvin—Longview Asset Management Ltd
Lau, Edwin—ICCP Venture Partners Inc

Lau, Gregory—Welsh Carson Anderson & Stowe
Lau, Jessica—HPEF Capital Partners Ltd
Lau, Kin Wai—Fatfish Medialab Pte Ltd
Lau, Lynda—SAIF Partners
Lau, Michael—Round Hill Music Royalty Fund LP
Lau, Wai Kit—Gobi Partners
Laub, Eric—Burrill & Company
Laubscher, Pieter—PointBreak Private Equity
Lauck, Andrew—RedBird Capital Partners Platform LP
Laudato, Janna—Hauser Private Equity
Lauder, Gary—Lauder Partners LLC
Laue, Carsten—Remora Partners SA
Laue, Jennifer—Stray Dog Capital LLC
Lauer, Robert—Haynes and Boone LLC
Lauer, Stephan—Capvis Equity Partners AG
Lauer, Tom—Advent International Corp
Laufer, Michael—Mach Ventures LP
Laufer, Michael—Medventure Associates
Laufik, Theodore—Resilience Capital Partners LLC
Laugel, Thierry—Kurma Partners SA
Laughland, Barclay—Mosaic Capital Corp
Laughlin, Jeffrey—Boston Harbor Capital Partners LLC
Laul, Varun—Providence Equity Partners LLC
Laura, Fina—Finpiemonte Partecipazioni SpA
Laurain, Jean-Francois—Cerea Partenaire SAS
Laurant, Lionel—Bayside Capital Inc
Laurel, Romeo—Beechtree Capital Ltd
Laurence, Fabrice—Startup Avenue SAS
Laurencin, Thierry—Undisclosed Firm
Laurent Josi, Jean-Marie—Compagnie Benelux Participations SA
Laurent, Marc—Kerala Ventures
Lauretti, Cristiano Gioia—Kinea Investimentos Ltda
Lauridsen, Robert—RB Webber and Comapny Inc
Laurimaa, Jussi—Catalyst Fund Management and Research Ltd
Laurinaitis, Peter—Blackstone Group LP
Lautenberg, Luciano—Kawa Capital Management Inc
Lautman, Martin—Liberty Capital Management Corp
Lautour, Guillaume—Idinvest Partners SA
Lautz, Robert—St Cloud Capital LLC
Lauwers, Bernard—International Finance Corp
Laux, William—Laux Capital Partners
Lauzet, Florent—Siparex Group
Lavakare, Ashutosh—Everstone Capital Management, Ltd.
Lavallee, Pierre—Canada Pension Plan Investment Board
Laveu, Jean-Michel—Initiative & Finance Investissement SA
Lavie, Scott—Renovo Capital LLC
Lavilla, Carlos—Corpfin Capital Asesores SA SGEIC
Lavin, Thomas—New Science Ventures LLC
Lavine, Jonathan—Bain Capital Inc
Lavinia, Scott—Serene Capital Management LLC
Lavins, David—Ridgemont Partners Management LLC
Lavirotte, Jean-Marie—Perfectis Private Equity SA
Lavoie, Armand—Foragen Technologies Management Inc
Lavoie, Cynthia—TVM Capital GmbH
Lavoie, Louis—Crescent Capital Group LP
Lavolle, Bruno—Azulis Capital SA
Lavrysen, Michael—CVC Capital Partners Ltd

2517

Law, Andy–CLOVE CAPITAL PARTNERS LTD
Law, Janson–SAIF Partners
Law, Shane–Patron Capital Advisers LLP
Law, Warren–China OperVestors Inc
Lawani, Tope–Helios Investment Partners LLP
Lawford, Jason–Duke Street Capital Ltd
Lawler, Joe–Wind Point Advisors LLC
Lawler, Kenneth–Battery Ventures LP
Lawler, Tim–Waud Capital Partners LLC
Lawless, Richard–New Magellan Venture Partners LLC
Lawlor, Augustine–Healthcare Ventures LLC
Lawrence, Brett–Carpenter and Co Inc
Lawrence, Bryan–Yorktown Partners LLC
Lawrence, Frederick–Shepherd Ventures LP
Lawrence, J. Alexander–Morrison & Foerster LLP
Lawrence, Justin–Adams Street Partners LLC
Lawrence, Margaret–Pilot House Ventures Group, LLC
Lawrence, Peter–FLAG Capital Management LLC
Lawrence, Scott–Canada Pension Plan Investment Board
Lawrence, Shane–NBC Capital Pty Ltd
Lawry, Seth–Thomas H Lee Partners LP
Lawson, Brian–Brookfield Asset Management Inc
Lawson, Richard–HGGC LLC
Lawton, Greg–Antares Capital Corp
Lax, Andrew–Blackstone Group LP
Lax, Charles–Grandbanks Capital
Lax, Larry–O2 Investment Partners LLC
Lax, Leo–L-Spark Corp
Laxer, Randy Steven–Morrison & Foerster LLP
Lay, Michael–ONCAP INVESTMENT PARTNERS L P
Layden, Christopher–Star Mountain Capital LLC
Laylock, Matthew–Aurora Capital Group Ltd
Layman, Michael–TSG Consumer Partners, L.P.
Layton, Casey–DCA Capital Partners LP
Layton, Tim–Sorenson Capital Partners LP
Layton, Wade–CIT Group Inc
Lazar, Spencer–General Catalyst Partners LLC
Lazareva, Victoria–United Capital Partners Advisory OOO
Lazaridis, Michael–Quantum Valley Investments
Lazarus, Edmund–Bregal Capital LLP
Lazarus, Edmund–Bregal Investments LLP
Lazarus, Jared–Oaktree Capital Management LP
Lazarus, Steven–Arch Venture Partners LLC
Lazarus, Xavier–Elaia Partners SAS
Lazier, Dave–Accretia Capital LLC
Le Blanc, Robert–Onex Corp
Le Bourdiec, Mariane–Sagard SAS
Le Chang, Jan–Centinela Capital Partners LLC
Le Chevallier, Denis–Undisclosed Firm
Le Doussal, Jean-Marc–Remora Partners SA
Le Gal, Jocelyne–ACE Management SA
Le Gall, Olivier–3i Group PLC
Le Gallais, Marc–Naxicap Partners SA
Le Houerou, Philippe–International Finance Corp
Le Huray, Martin–OMERS Private Equity Inc
Le Jossec, Bruno–Societe Financiere Lorient Developpement SA
Le Ligne, Erwann–Eurazeo Pme Capital SAS
Le Meur, Loic–Wellington Partners GmbH
Le Roux, Mathieu–Idinvest Partners SA
Le Roy, Jack–Summit Partners LP

Le Sueur, Gary–Scottish Equity Partners LLP
Le, Huan–Houston Health Ventures LLC
Le, Thong–WRF Capital
Le, Truong–Mekong Capital Ltd
LeBaron, Matthew–Ascribe Capital, LLC
LeBlanc, Matthew–ArcLight Capital Holdings LLC
LeBlanc, Paul–Atlantic Canada Opportunities Agency
LeBlanc, Paul–Wharton Equity Partners LLC
LeClercq, Ray–Gores Group LLC
LeComte, Pierre–TSG Consumer Partners, L.P.
LeMay, John–Blue Point Capital Partners LP
LeMay, Lance–OPENAIR Equity Partners
LeMay, Ronald–OPENAIR Equity Partners
LeMoine, Daniel–Brooke Private Equity Associates Management LLC
LePera, Gabe–Anholt (USA) LLC
LeSieur, Jean-Marc–HBM Healthcare Investments AG
LeSieur, Stephen–Spectrum Equity Investors LP
LeVert-Chiasson, Serge–Sarona Asset Management Inc
Lea, Lyndon–Lion Capital LLP
Leach, Jason–Platinum Equity LLC
Leach, Raymond–Jumpstart Inc
Leader, Tom–Nova Capital Management, Ltd.
Leaf Wilmes, Kathryn–Pantheon Ventures (UK) LLP
Leaf, Ron–RAIN Source Capital, Inc.
Leafstedt, Jon–Iowa Corn Opportunities LLC
Leak, Bruce–Playground Global LLC
Leake, Nan–Partners Group Holding AG
Leakos, Steven–Avrio Capital Management Corp
Leaman, John–Devon Park Bioventures LP
Learner, James–HGGC LLC
Leary, Dennis–Champlain Capital Partners LP
Leathers, David–Abingworth Management Ltd
Lebel, Felix-Etienne–Birch Hill Equity Partners Management Inc
Leblanc, Andrew–Milbank Tweed Hadley & Mccloy LLP
Lebowitz, Stephen–Topspin Partners LP
Lebre, Marco–Explorer Investments Sociedade de Capital de Risco SA
Lebus, Andrew–Pantheon Ventures (UK) LLP
Lecce, Domenico–Fincalabra SpA
Leck, Derek–American Industrial Partners
Leck, P. Jeffrey–KLH Capital LP
Leckie, Lars–Hummer Winblad Venture Partner
Leclerc, Olivier–Amundi Private Equity Funds SA
Lecoeur, Jerome–Innovacom Gestion SAS
Lecumberri, Javier–Proprium Capital Partners LP
Ledbetter, Carl–Pelion Venture Partners
Ledbetter, Dale–BC Partners LLP
Lederer, Klaus–Rizk Ventures LLC
Lederhausen, Mats–Cue Ball Group LLC
Lederle, Achim–Cipio Partners GmbH
Lederman, Marc–Newspring Capital
Lederman, Mike–Horizon Technology Finance Management LLC
Ledesma-Arocena, Javier–Graycliff Partners LP
Ledford, Gregory–Carlyle Group LP
Ledoux, Patrick–Actis LLP
Lee, A. Scott–HealthEdge Investment Partners LLC
Lee, Aileen–Cowboy Capital
Lee, Aileen–Kleiner Perkins Caufield & Byers LLC

Lee, Alan–Wolseley Private Equity
Lee, Amy–Blackstone Group LP
Lee, Anthony–Altos Ventures
Lee, Benjamin–Evolvence Capital Ltd
Lee, Brian–Bam Ventures GP LLC
Lee, Brian–Colony Capital LLC
Lee, Brian–Relativity Capital LLC
Lee, C–Hana Daetoo Securities Co Ltd
Lee, Chang Geun–KTB Investment & Securities Co Ltd
Lee, Chang–Trust Company of the West
Lee, Cheol Hee–Prodigy Capital Management LLC
Lee, Chong Min–Cmia Capital Partners Pte Ltd
Lee, Christina–Kleiner Perkins Caufield & Byers LLC
Lee, Christina–Oaktree Capital Management LP
Lee, Christophe–Shk Fund Management Ltd
Lee, Christopher–Highstar Capital LP
Lee, Chul-Joo–Affinity Equity Partners HK Ltd
Lee, D.C.–SAIF Partners
Lee, Daniel–Comvest Partners
Lee, Daniel–STIC Investment Inc
Lee, Daniel–Windjammer Capital Investors LLC
Lee, Danny–Bain Capital Inc
Lee, David–Refactor Capital LP
Lee, David–Roark Capital Group Inc
Lee, Desmond–Telopea Capital Partners Pty Ltd
Lee, Dong-yeong–Korea Investment Partners Co Ltd
Lee, Doug–Metropolitan Real Estate Equity Management LLC
Lee, Edan–Olympus Capital Holdings Asia Hong Kong Ltd
Lee, Edgar–Oaktree Capital Management LP
Lee, Eojin–High Road Capital Partners LLC
Lee, Eric–Welsh Carson Anderson & Stowe
Lee, Euiyong–Centurion Technology Investment Corp
Lee, Gary–Morrison & Foerster LLP
Lee, Gavin–Wavemaker Partners
Lee, George–Amkey Ventures LLC
Lee, Gi Jin–Wonik Investment Partners
Lee, Gloria–NewSchools Venture Fund
Lee, Gwong-Yih–Translink Capital LLC
Lee, Han Ju–SparkLabs
Lee, Ho Chan–KTB Ventures, Inc.
Lee, Hong Wei–GGV Capital
Lee, Howard–CID Group
Lee, Hwachie–Blackstone Group LP
Lee, Hyeong Wu–Wonik Investment Partners
Lee, In Kyung–MBK Partners Inc
Lee, Jae Ho–Hana Daetoo Securities Co Ltd
Lee, Jae Wu–VOGO Fund Asset Management
Lee, James–Blackstone Group LP
Lee, James–G3W Ventures LLC
Lee, James–Oaktree Capital Management LP
Lee, Jane–Blackstone Group LP
Lee, Janet–Invus Group LLC
Lee, Jason–Carlyle Group LP
Lee, Jason–Friedman Fleischer & Lowe Cap Ptnrs L P
Lee, Jeffrey–Northern Light Venture Capital Development LP
Lee, Jeffrey–Spring Mountain Capital LP
Lee, Jenny–GGV Capital
Lee, Jess–Sequoia Capital Operations LLC
Lee, Jessica–Carlyle Group LP
Lee, Jin Yong–Shinhan Private Equity Inc

Lee, Jin–Formation Group Inc
Lee, John–Kamylon Capital LLC
Lee, John–Lexington Partners Inc
Lee, John–Osage Venture Partners
Lee, Jonathan–DunRobin Ventures LLC
Lee, Jong Chan–STIC Investment Inc
Lee, Jong Gap–Neoplux Co Ltd
Lee, Jong Ho–Premier Partners LLC
Lee, Jong Won–H&Q Asia Pacific, Ltd.
Lee, JooWon–LB Investment Inc
Lee, Jung Jin–H&Q Asia Pacific, Ltd.
Lee, Jung Yup–HPEF Capital Partners Ltd
Lee, Kang Seok–SkyLake Investment & Co
Lee, Kenneth–Hatteras Venture Partners
Lee, Kenneth–Oaktree Capital Management LP
Lee, Kenneth–SAIF Partners
Lee, Kheng Nam–GGV Capital
Lee, Kristin–MMF Capital Management LLC
Lee, Kristin–Newspring Capital
Lee, Kwan–IMM Private Equity Inc
Lee, Lay Hong–Natixis Private Equity SA
Lee, Leonard–Seidler Equity Partners
Lee, Linda–Beijing Macro Vision Venture Capital Management Consultancy
Lee, Lisa–CVC Capital Partners Ltd
Lee, Lisa–Firelake Capital Management LLC
Lee, Luke–Asset Management Co
Lee, Meow Chan–SEAVI Advent Corporation Ltd
Lee, Michael–Roark Capital Group Inc
Lee, Michael–Shanghai ZhongZhi Venture Capital Co Ltd
Lee, Mike–Rogers Ventures Ltd
Lee, Nancy–Alsop Louie Partners
Lee, Patrick–Western Technology Investment
Lee, Peter–Baroda Ventures LLC
Lee, Peter–Bessemer Venture Partners
Lee, Richard–Westfield Capital Management Company LP
Lee, Robert–JFlehman & Co
Lee, Robert–Morgan Stanley Private Equity
Lee, Roger–Battery Ventures LP
Lee, Roger–Battery Ventures LP
Lee, Sam–Finaventures
Lee, Sam–Infinity Capital LLC
Lee, Sam–STIC Investment Inc
Lee, Samuel–Epidarex Capital
Lee, Sandra–Carlyle Group LP
Lee, Sang-jin–Korea Investment Partners Co Ltd
Lee, Sanghoon–TPG Capital Management LP
Lee, Sanghyun–Carlyle Group LP
Lee, Scott–BelHealth Investment Partners LLC
Lee, Seongkyu–STIC Investment Inc
Lee, Seung Yong–Atinum Investment Co Ltd
Lee, Seung-Woo–Lee&Co Investments Co
Lee, Shuxian–Qiming Venture Partners Ii LP
Lee, Stephen–Aif Capital Asia Iii LP
Lee, Steve–Softbank Ventures Korea Inc
Lee, Steven–DFJ Athena
Lee, Steven–H&Q Asia Pacific, Ltd.
Lee, Su Beom–Wonik Investment Partners
Lee, Susie–Northleaf Capital Partners Ltd
Lee, Susie–TBL Capital LP
Lee, Taeksu–Winvest Venture Partners Inc
Lee, Tee Wee–Burrill & Company
Lee, Thomas–Lee Equity Partners LLC

Lee, Tokyou–Asiya Capital Investments Company KSCP
Lee, Tony–One Rock Capital Partners LLC
Lee, V. Paul–Vanedge Capital Inc
Lee, Warren–Canaan Partners
Lee, Wende–Oaktree Capital Management LP
Lee, William–Carlyle Group LP
Lee, Won Bae–Uni Venture Capital Co Ltd
Lee, Yong Cheol–Hana Daetoo Securities Co Ltd
Lee, Yong Sung–Wonik Investment Partners
Lee, Youn–Audax Group, Inc.
Lee, Young Min–Albatross Inverstment Co Ltd
Lee, Yun Hui–IBK Capital Corp
Lee, Yun Hui–Industrial Bank Of Korea
Leeb, Alexander–LGT Venture Philanthropy Foundation Switzerland
Leeds, Jeffrey–Leeds Equity Advisors Inc
Leedy, Kurt–Ridgemont Partners Management LLC
Leefe, Simon–Candover Investments PLC
Leeming, Lex–Moelis Capital Partners LLC
Leeming, Lex–NexPhase Capital LLC
Leeney, David–LightBay Capital LLC
Lees, Andy–Palatine Private Equity LLP
Leese, Steven–Quabbin Capital Inc
Leeson, Cathy–Genesis Park, L.P.
Lefanowicz, Mark–Fenway Summer Ventures LP
Lefcourt, Jennifer–Freestyle Capital
Lefebvre, Alexandre–Silverfleet Capital Partners LLP
Lefebvre, Jocelyn–Sagard SAS
Lefebvre, Leslie–Ontario Teachers' Pension Plan
Lefebvre, Michel–CDP Capital Inc
Lefevre, Didier–Acas LLC
Lefevre, Didier–European Capital
Lefevre, Didier–European Capital Financial Services Ltd
Leff, Daniel–Luminari Capital LP
Leff, Jonathan–Deerfield Management Company LP
Leff, Jonathan–Warburg Pincus LLC
Leffell, David–Tullis Health Investors
Lefkowitz, Barry–Rizk Ventures LLC
Lefkowitz, Steven–CI Capital Partners LLC
Lefranc, Laura–Headway Capital Partners LLP
Leftley, David–Bloc Ventures Ltd
Legault, Eric–Teralys Capital Inc
Legault, Richard–Cycle Capital Management (CCM) Inc
Legein, Filip–Yukon NV
Legg, Christopher–Tandem Expansion Fund I LP
Legg, Dexter–Liberty Mutual Innovation
Leggate, John–Vantagepoint Management Inc
Leggett, Mark–Blue Bear Capital LLC
Legnani, Raffaele–Atlantis Capital Markets NA LLC
Legoupil, Herve–Finadvance SA
Legrand, Stephane–European Capital Financial Services Ltd
Leguet, Benoit–CDC Climat SA
Leheny, Chris–Stairway Capital Management
Leheny, Rachel–Valence Life Sciences LLC
Lehman, Katherine–Hilltop Private Capital LLC
Lehman, Katherine–Lincolnshire Management Inc
Lehman, Matt–Sorenson Capital Partners LP
Lehman, Peter–Granite Creek Partners LLC
Lehman, Rachel–P4G Capital Management LLC
Lehman, Robyn–ABS Capital Partners, Inc.
Lehman, Stephen–Monitor Clipper Partners LLC

Lehmann, Michal–SpeedUp Iqbator Sp z o o
Lehner, Bernhard–i5invest Beratungs GmbH
Lehot, Louis–Cooley LLP
Lehr, Seth–LLR Partners Inc
Lehrhoff, Adam–ZS Fund LP
Lehrman, Michael–Cantor Ventures
Lehtinen, Pasi–Korona Invest Oy
Lehtomaki, Vesa–Korona Invest Oy
Lehtonen, Oskari–KoppiCatch Oy
Lei Ortiz, Ana–Hamilton Lane Advisors LLC
Lei Yang, Raymond–Taishan Invest AG
Lei, Joanna–Baring Private Equity Asia Ltd
Lei, Wei–Beijing Tianxing Chuanglian Investment Management Co., Ltd.
Leiba, Rebecca–Provident Healthcare Partners
Leibman, Howard–Equity Venture Partners Pty Ltd
Leibman, Peter–Peak Rock Capital LLC
Leibovici, Pierre-Eric–Orkos Capital SAS
Leibowitz, Matthew–Plaza Ventures Ltd
Leicester, Alex–Alchemy Partners LLP
Leidel, Peter–Yorktown Partners LLC
Leigh, Jamie–Cooley LLP
Leight, Nathan–Terrapin Partners LLC
Leightell, Steve–Georgian Partners Growth Fund
Founders International I LP
Leiman, Jonathan–North Branch Capital LP
Leiman, Jonathan–Pfingsten Partners LLC
Lein, Danny–Venturebaycom
Leininger, James–Medcare Investment Fund Ltd
Leinss, Edward–Linx Partners LLC
Leistner, Steven–HGGC LLC
Leisure, Lawrence–Chicago Pacific Founders Fund LP
Leitch, Paul–Queensland BioCapital Funds Ld Pty
Leitersdorf, Jonathan–L Capital Partners, L.P.
Leitersdorf, Yoav–YL Ventures GP Ltd
Leith, Rob–Troika Capital Partners Ltd
Leitner, Michael–Tennenbaum Capital Partners LLC
Leiva, George–Oaktree Capital Management LP
Leland, Timothy–TGP Investments LLC
Lele, Abhijeet–Investor Growth Capital AB
Lele, Abhijeet–Investor Growth Capital Inc
Lelliott, Darren–Elcano Capital LP
Lelliott, Shonna–Elcano Capital LP
Lelogeais, Jean-Louise–Strategic Value Partners LLC
Lemaire, Alain–BPCE Immobilier Exploitation SAS
Lemann, Jorge–3G Capital Inc
Lemelman, Jon–Riverside Partners LLC
Lemke-von Ammon, Derek–Thomas Weisel Partners Group Inc
Lemkin, Todd–Canyon Capital Advisors LLC
Lemmer, Johan–Fulcrum Capital Partners Inc
Lemmon, Justin–Tolero Ventures LLC
Lemonius, Soeren–Sunstone Capital A/S
Lemonnier, Xavier–BC Partners LLP
Lemos, Felipe–Kawa Capital Management Inc
Lenahan, Dan–Insight Equity Holdings LLC
Lenahan, John–Wincove Capital
Lenain, Angelique–Jaina Capital SASU
Lencz, Scott–Parallax Capital Partners LLC
Lendvai-Lintner, Bela–Arx Equity Partners Sp z o o
Lenet, Scott–Frontier Venture Capital
Leng Smith, Chris–New York City Economic Development Corp
Lengaigne, Gilles–Blackstone Group LP

2519

Pratt's Guide to Private Equity & Venture Capital Sources

Lengauer, Christoph–Third Rock Ventures LLC
Lenihan, Lawrence–FirstMark Capital LLC
Lenk, Andy–Varde Partners Inc
Lenssen, Jeroen–Riverside Co
Lent, Tony–Wolfensohn & Company LLC
Lentz, M. Kurt–Atlantic Street Capital Management LLC
Lentz, M. Kurt–Sun Capital Partners Inc
Lenz, Andre–CRP Companhia de Participacoes
Leon Cillero, Teodoro–Suanfarma Biotech SGECR SA
Leon, Alfonso–Axon Partners Group Investment
Leon, Roberto–Alantra
Leonard, Alex–Blackstone Group LP
Leonard, Colin–Clearlake Capital Group LP
Leonard, Damien–Pinetree Capital Ltd
Leonard, H. Jeffrey–GEF Management Corp
Leonard, Richard–AG BD LLC
Leonard, Walter–Seacoast Capital
Leonardi, Laurence–Vauban Partenaires SA
Leone, Nicholas–Blackstone Group LP
Leone, Sibani–Imi Fondi Chiusi SGR SpA
Leone, Tony–Abacus Private Equity Ltd
Leong Seok Wan, Kris–Walden International
Leong, Chris–Argentum Group LLC
Leong, Gregory–Blackstone Group LP
Leong, Wai Leng–Temasek Holdings (Private) Ltd
Leong, Wendy–Chrysalix Energy
Leonhardt, Hubertus–SHS Gesellschaft fuer Beteiligungsmanagement mbH
Leoni, Lorenzo–Agire Invest SA
Leonkiewicz, Jacek–TDJ SA
Leow, Kok Peng–Zana Capital Pte Ltd
Lepage, Guy–Siparex Proximite Innovation SAS
Lepene, Ryan–Peppertree Capital Management Inc
Lepinard, Sebastien–Next World Capital LLC
Lepine, Xavier–Perceva SAS
Leppin, Jonny–AKN Holdings LLC
Lerer, Benjamin–Lerer Ventures II LP
Lerer, Kenneth–Lerer Ventures II LP
Lerner, Adam–McNally Capital LLC
Lerner, Andrew–IA Capital Group Inc
Lerner, Jonathan–Smedvig Capital Ltd
Lerner, Joseph–819 Capital LLC
Lerner, Robert–Princeton Ventures Management LLC
Lerohl, Mark–Radar Capital Inc
Lerosen, John–Vance Street Capital LLC
Leroutier, Nathalie–Vespa Capital LLP
Leroux, James–Ashby Point Capital
Leroy, Denis–Vespa Capital LLP
Leschke, Juergen–Aurelia Private Equity GmbH
Leschly, Mark–Rho Capital Partners Inc
Lescure, Franck–Auriga Partners SA
Lese, William–Braemar Energy Ventures LP
Leshnock, Bradley–Granite Hall Partners LLC
Leshuk, Dave–First Analysis Corp
Leskinen, Eero–Sentica Partners Oy
Lesley, Lee–JMI Management Inc
Lesniak, Beth–Grey Mountain Partners LLC
Lesnick, Marc–Fortissimo Captial Fund Israel LP
Lessem, Joel–Klass Capital Corp
Lessig, Brian–Southport Lane Management LLC
Lessner, Daniel–General Atlantic LLC
Lester, Brook–Diversified Trust Company Inc
Lester, Cameron–Azure Capital Partners, L.P.
Lester, Laura–CHS Capital LLC

Lester, Megan–Vespa Capital LLP
Lester, Tami–Round Hill Music Royalty Fund LP
Letinic, Kresimir–Easton Hunt Capital Partners LP
Letoublon, Herve–Aqua Asset Management SAS
Letoublon, Herve–Capitem Partenaires SAS
Letourneur, Charles–Alven Capital Partners SA
Lettmann, Jason–Lightstone Ventures LP
Leue-Bahns, Petra–Ecolutions Management GmbH
Leung, Anthony–Blackstone Group LP
Leung, Nate–Industry Ventures LLC
Leung, Titus–Perella Weinberg Partners LP
Leung, Wilson–AG BD LLC
Leuschen, David–Riverstone Holdings LLC
Leuw, Martin–Lyceum Capital
Lev, Arthur–Morgan Stanley Alternative Investment Partners LP
Lev, Eric–Ampersand Capital Partners
Levande, Robert–MDB Capital Group LLC
Levandov, Richard–Avalon Ventures, LLC
Levandov, Richard–Masthead Venture Partners
Levanson, David–Sands Capital Management LLC
Levenberg, Michael–LLR Partners Inc
Levene, David–HandsOn3 LLC
Levene, Simon–Index Ventures
Levene, Tim–Augmentum Capital LLP
Levenson, Matt–Kian Capital Partners LLC
Levental, Alex–Ironwood Investment Management LLC
Leventhal, Daniel–Morrison & Foerster LLP
Leveque, Jean-Claude–Phitrust Impact Investors SA
Lever, Alan–TorQuest Partners Inc
Lever, Nancy–Arc Financial Corp.
Leverich, Robert–Brown Brothers Harriman & Co
Levet, Marie-Christine–Jaina Capital SASU
Leveton, Jay–Stagwell Group LLC
Levett, Stuart–CVC Capital Partners Ltd
Levey, Stephen–Stone Point Capital LLC
Levi, Andre–Doll Capital Management Inc
Levi, Cecile–Ardian France SA
Levi, Debbie–Carmel Ventures IV Principals Fund LP
Levi, Emanuele–360 Capital Management SA
Levi, Enrico–Leonardoweb Group Srl
Levi-Gardes, Nick–Satya Capital Ltd

Levi-Minzi, Raffaele–Saphir Capital Partners SA
Levin, Andrew–RA Capital Management LLC
Levin, Avraham–Tene Kibbutz Investment Management Ltd
Levin, Becca–Radicle Impact
Levin, Benjamin–Level Equity Management LLC
Levin, Jeff–Morgan Stanley Credit Partners LP
Levin, Jonathan–Grosvenor Capital Management LP
Levin, Mark–Third Rock Ventures LLC
Levin, Matthew–Bain Capital Inc
Levin, Micah–Odyssey Investment Partners LLC
Levin, Moshe–AL Capital Holdings 2016 Ltd
Levin, Shira Nadich–Cooley LLP
Levine, Alan–Cooley LLP
Levine, Arthur–Levine Leichtman Capital Partners Inc
Levine, Brian–Blackstone Group LP
Levine, Dan–Oaktree Capital Management LP
Levine, Daniel–Burrill & Company
Levine, Ezra–Morrison & Foerster LLP
Levine, Jay–Trimaran Capital LLC

Levine, Jeremy–Bessemer Venture Partners
Levine, Ken–Brookline Venture Partners
Levine, Mark–Core Capital Partners Ii L P
Levine, Peter–Andreessen Horowitz LLC
Levine, Samuel–Eos Partners LP
Levine, Seth–Foundry Group LLC
Levinson, Adam–Fortress Investment Group LLC
Levinson, Barry–Princeton Biopharma Capital Partners LP
Levinson, Frank–Phoenix Venture Partners LLC
Levinson, Ilene–Hamilton Lane Advisors LLC
Levinson, Jennifer–Ellipse Capital LLC
Levinson, Marina–Benhamou Global Ventures LLC
Levinson, Naomi–Grano Retail Investments Inc
Levison, A. Andrew–Southfield Capital Advisors LLC
Levison, Daniel–Morrison & Foerster LLP
Levit, Dmitry–Digital Media Partners Pte Ltd
Levitan, Dan–Maveron LLC
Levitan, Steve–Haynes and Boone LLC
Levitas, E. James–Lion Equity Partners LLC
Levitt, Art–JVP Jerusalem Venture Partners Israel Management, Ltd.
Levitt, Jamie–Morrison & Foerster LLP
Levitt, Jeffrey–Liberty Capital Management Corp
Levitt, Mark–Global Infrastructure Holdings
Levitt, Michael–Kayne Anderson Capital Advisors LP
Levitt, Raymond–Blackhorn Ventures Capital Management LLC
Levitties, Matthew–Versa Capital Management Inc
Levkowitz, Howard–Tennenbaum Capital Partners LLC
Levy, Alan–Frazier Management LLC
Levy, Andrew–Newbury Partners LLC
Levy, Anton–General Atlantic LLC
Levy, Benjamin–Berkshire Partners LLC
Levy, Benjamin–Sportsnet 360 Media Inc
Levy, Douglas–Sentinel Capital Partners LLC
Levy, Ehud–Vertex Israel II Management Ltd
Levy, Erez–TriplePoint Capital LLC
Levy, Eytan–Israel Cleantech Ventures
Levy, Harold–Palm Ventures LLC
Levy, Jack–Israel Cleantech Ventures
Levy, James–Warburg Pincus LLC
Levy, Jamie–Pinetree Capital Ltd
Levy, Jay–Zelkova Ventures
Levy, Jimmy–al bawader
Levy, Joe–AllegisCyber
Levy, Jonathan–Tailwind Capital Partners LP
Levy, Jordan–Softbank Capital Partners L P
Levy, Olivier–Cic Vizille Capital Innovation
Levy, Paul–JLL Partners Inc
Levy, Scott–Oaktree Capital Management LP
Levy, Tim–Future Capital Partners Ltd
Levy, Tom–Carlyle Group LP
Levy-Rueff, Didier–ACG Capital SA
Levyn, Adam–Leonard Green & Partners LP
Lewin, Timothy–I2Bf Global Ventures
Lewis, Bonnie–Openview Venture Partners LP
Lewis, C. McKenzie–Sherpa Partners LLC
Lewis, Charlie–Arris Ventures LLC
Lewis, Charlie–Berwind Corp
Lewis, Charlie–Greener Capital Partners LP
Lewis, Clayton–Maveron LLC
Lewis, Elizabeth–GEF Management Corp
Lewis, Geoff–Founders Fund, The

Lewis, Jack—Morrison & Foerster LLP
Lewis, James—Trust Company of the West
Lewis, Joe—Tavistock Group Inc
Lewis, John—Donnelly Penman & Partners Inc
Lewis, Jonathan—Dev Equity LLC
Lewis, Jonathan—Sheridan Capital Partners
Lewis, Joshua—Salmon River Capital LLC
Lewis, LeGrand—Sorenson Capital Partners LP
Lewis, Leland—Cyprium Investment Partners LLC
Lewis, Mark—Hawksbridge Capital
Lewis, Peter—Wharton Equity Partners LLC
Lewis, Philip—Fulcrum Equity Partners
Lewis, Rand—Centennial Ventures Vii L P
Lewis, Rick—U.S. Venture Partners
Lewis, Rick—U.S. Venture Partners
Lewis, Timothy—Atlantic Street Capital Management LLC
Lewis, William—Brightpath Capital Partners LP
Lewis, William—Zone Ventures
Lewis, john—Riordan Lewis & Haden
Ley, Jean-Pascal—Ife Mezzanine SARL
Ley, Thomas—Seacoast Capital
Ley, Thomas—Vantagepoint Management Inc
Leybold, Christian—e.ventures
Leybold, Christian—eVenture Capital Partners GmbH
Leyerle, Mark—Freestone Partners LLC
Leykikh, Alexander—Atlantic-Pacific Capital Inc
Lezec, Robert—AKN Holdings LLC
Lezec, Robert—Atar Capital LLC
Lhee, Edward—CHS Capital LLC
Lhila, Mrinalini—StepStone Group LP
Li, Aimin—China Venture Capital Co Ltd
Li, Alvin—CCB International Group Holdings Ltd
Li, Anjie—Beijing Wanze Investment Management Co Ltd
Li, Annie—SAIF Partners
Li, Bill—Walden International
Li, Bing—State Development & Investment Corp Ltd
Li, Bing—Warburg Pincus LLC
Li, Changcai—Ample Luck International Capital Group Ltd
Li, Changgao—Beijing Tianxing Chuanglian Investment Management Co., Ltd.
Li, Christine—HPEF Capital Partners Ltd
Li, Chun—Hina Capital Partners
Li, Chunyi—Shanghai Grand Yangtze Capital Investment Management Co Ltd
Li, David—Warburg Pincus LLC
Li, Fang Roger—Infotech Ventures Co Ltd
Li, Fang—Tyche Partners LP
Li, Fei—Shanghai Lianxin Investment Management Co Ltd
Li, Feng—IDG Capital Partners Inc
Li, Feng—SummitView Capital
Li, Feng—Vantagepoint Management Inc
Li, Gabriel—Orchid Asia Group Management Ltd
Li, Haojun—GGV Capital
Li, Jason Quansheng—Suzhou Datai Venture Capital Investment Management Co Ltd
Li, Jian—Beijing Capital Science and Technology Group Co Ltd
Li, Jian—CITIC Capital Partners Ltd
Li, Jianguang—IDG Capital Partners Inc
Li, Jiaqing—Legend Capital Co Ltd
Li, Jiaxing—Beijing Holch Investment Management, Ltd.
Li, Jing—Shanghai Lianxin Investment Management Co Ltd
Li, Jing—Zhejiang Haode Jiahui Investment Management Co Ltd
Li, Jinxia—Golden Bridge Venture Capital, L.P.
Li, Jinyi—Hina Capital Partners
Li, Joanna—SAIF Partners
Li, Jun—Innovation Camp Investment Consulting (Shanghai) Co Ltd
Li, Junbin—Centenium-Pinetree China Private Equity
Li, Karen—CITIC Capital Partners Ltd
Li, Ken—Mingly Capital
Li, Kevin—DT Capital Partners
Li, Leenong—Commonfund Capital Inc
Li, Lidong—Shenzhen Rongchuang Venture Capital Co Ltd
Li, Lixin—Northern Light Venture Capital Development Ltd
Li, Man—Elevation China Capital
Li, Mei—Adm Capital
Li, Mengling—Shenzhen Green Pine Capital Partners Co Ltd
Li, Michael—Tsing Capital
Li, Nan—Obvious Ventures Management LLC
Li, Puyu—Partech International
Li, Quinn—Qualcomm Ventures
Li, Renjie—Prax Capital Management Co
Li, Ron—Adveq Management AG
Li, Roy—Bull Capital Partners Ltd
Li, Ruigang—Shanghai Ruiqi Science & Technology Development Co Ltd
Li, Ruizhu—Industrial Technology Investment Corp
Li, Scott—Capital Royalty LP
Li, Shoujing—China Media Capital Co Ltd
Li, Shujun—Shanghai Trustbridge Partners Investment Management Co Ltd
Li, Wanshou—Shenzhen Capital Group Co Ltd
Li, Wei—Ample Luck International Capital Group Ltd
Li, Wei—Shenzhen Green Pine Capital Partners Co Ltd
Li, Winnie—Beijing Golden Growth Investment & Management Co Ltd
Li, Xianwen—ZheShang Venture Capital Co Ltd
Li, Xiaojun—IDG Capital Partners Inc
Li, Xiaoyi—Shenzhen Tiantu Capital Management Center LP
Li, Xin—Ventana Capital Management LP
Li, Xin—Wuhan Huagong Technology Business Incubator Co Ltd
Li, Yan—Eastern Bell Venture Capital Co Ltd
Li, Yang—Shanghai Yonghua Capital Management Co Ltd
Li, Yi—Bioveda China Fund
Li, Yinan—Gsr Ventures Management Llc
Li, Ying—BOCOM International Holdings Co Ltd
Li, Ying—IDG Capital Partners Inc
Li, Ying—Suzhou Oriza Holdings Co Ltd
Li, Yingqi—Silver Lake Partners LP
Li, Yiran—Avantage Ventures Capital LLC
Li, Yishan—Kenson Ventures LLC
Li, Yong—Carlyle Group LP
Li, Yuhui—Shanghai Fortune United Investment Group Co Ltd
Li, Zane—HAO Capital
Li, Zhen—Shanghai Divine Investment Management Co Ltd
Li, Zhengqing—Shanghai Tronfund Management Co Ltd
Li, Zhenhe—Shanghai Beyond Binghong Equity Investment Management Co Ltd
Li, Zhi—Shenzhen Hongshisan Capital Co Ltd
Li, Zongjun—China Merchants Securities Co Ltd
Li, Zongzhi—Hina Capital Partners
Liamos, Charles—Medventure Associates
Lian, Jie—Primavera Capital
Lian, Jinhua—Zhongrong International Trust Co Ltd
Lian, Meng—IDG Capital Partners Inc
Liang Chen, Jackie—Taishan Invest AG
Liang, Amy—Unisun Beijing Investment Co Ltd
Liang, Dong—Shenzhen Richland Investment Co Ltd
Liang, Ernie—Rizk Ventures LLC
Liang, Gang—Hangzhou Haibang Investment Management Co Ltd
Liang, Guozhi—Fortune Venture Capital Co Ltd
Liang, Guozhi—Fortune Venture Capital Corp
Liang, James—CID Group
Liang, Jennifer—Mingly Capital
Liang, Juyuan—Junyuan Capital Investment Management Ltd
Liang, Kenneth—Oaktree Capital Management LP
Liang, Leo—AAA Capital Management Co Ltd
Liang, Michael—Baird Capital
Liang, Qing—Legend Star Venture Incubator
Liang, Sophie—Centinela Capital Partners LLC
Liang, Tong—Shenzhen Richland Investment Co Ltd
Liang, Victoria—Cota Capital Inc
Liang, Xianhong—Beijing Langmafeng Venture Capital Management Co Ltd
Liang, Yingyu—Qiming Venture Partners Ii LP
Liang, Youchuan—China Media Capital Co Ltd
Liang, Zhixin—James & Hina Capital Management Co Ltd
Liao, Arthur—Blackstone Group LP
Liao, Bing—Ample Luck International Capital Group Ltd
Liao, Changhong—ABC Capital Management Co Ltd
Liao, James—Unisun Beijing Investment Co Ltd
Liao, Jon—500 Startups, L.P.
Liao, Marvin—500 Startups, L.P.
Liautaud, Bernard—Balderton Capital LLP
Liaw, Eric—Institutional Venture Partners
Liber, Dominic—LeapFrog Investments
Liberato, Lynne—Haynes and Boone LLC
Liberboim, Nir—DGNL Ventures LP
Libes, Michael—Fledge LLC
Libin, Phil—General Catalyst Partners LLC
Lich, Miles—Northern Plains Capital Ltd
Lichstein, Henry—Palisades Ventures
Lichtenstein, Adam—Allianz Capital Partners GmbH
Lichtenstein, David—Sycamore Ventures Inc
Lichter, Jay—Avalon Ventures, LLC
Lichter, Richard—Newbury Partners LLC
Liddle, David—U.S. Venture Partners
Liddy, Edward—Clayton Dubilier & Rice LLC
Lidgren, Alexander—Loudspring Oyj
Lie, Bjarne—Verdane Capital Advisors AS
Lie, Robert—CITIC Capital Partners Ltd
Lieber, Brian—Battery Ventures LP
Lieber, Brian—Battery Ventures LP

Pratt's Guide to Private Equity & Venture Capital Sources

Lieber, Irwin–Wheatley Partners
Lieber, Jonathan–Wheatley Partners
Lieber, Seth–Wheatley Partners
Lieberman, Cheri–Charterhouse Group Inc
Lieberman, Cheri–Charterhouse Group Inc
Lieberman, Cheri–Dfw Capital Partners LP
Lieberman, Jeffrey–Insight Venture Partners LLC
Lieberman, Jonathan–AG BD LLC
Lieberman, Mark–Thomas Weisel Partners Group Inc
Liebert, Debra–Domain Associates LLC
Lieberthal, Geoffrey–Lee Equity Partners LLC
Liebler, Hans–Maxburg Capital Partners
Liebmann, Diana–Haynes and Boone LLC
Liebowitz, Jay–Blackstone Group LP
Liechtenstein, Constantin–Gruenwald Equity Management GmbH
Lien, Catherine–McNally Capital LLC
Liencres, Bjorn–Juniper Networks Inc
Liepert, Matt–Antares Capital Corp
Liepins, Janis–FlyCap AIFP SIA
Liesching, Karen–Housatonic Partners Management Co Inc
Lietz, Nori–Partners Group Holding AG
Lieu, Norm–CranRidge Capital LP
Liew, Jeremy–Lightspeed Management Company LLC
Liff, Steven–Sun Capital Partners Inc
Lifshitz, Alon–Blumberg International Partners LLC
Ligertwood, Mark–Dunedin Capital Partners Ltd
Lightcap, Jeffrey–HealthCor Partners Management LP
Liker, Todd–Oaktree Capital Management LP
Likuev, Alexey–Altpoint Ventures LP
Lilani, Ash–Saama Capital LLC
Lilienfeldt, Sigurd–Axcel Industriinvestor A/S
Lillis, Charles–Lonetree Capital Management LLC
Lilly, John–Greylock Partners LLC
Lim Hock, Tay–Gic Special Investments Pte Ltd
Lim, Brian–Pantheon Ventures (UK) LLP
Lim, Cherry–7Bridge Capital Partners Ltd
Lim, Christine–iCapital M Sdn Bhd
Lim, Chung Hae–Dream Venture Investment Co Ltd
Lim, Damien–Bioveda Capital Pte Ltd
Lim, Damien–Stone Canyon Industries LLC
Lim, Ho Kee–Majuven, Pte. Ltd.
Lim, James–Greenspring Associates Inc
Lim, Jon-F–Prime Capital Partners
Lim, Kuo-Yi–Infocomm Investments Pte Ltd
Lim, Kuo-Yi–Monk's Hill Ventures Pte Ltd
Lim, Meng Ann–Actis LLP
Lim, Richard–Gsr Ventures Management Llc
Lim, Richard–Omega Fund Management LLC
Lim, Siong Guan S.–Gic Special Investments Pte Ltd
Lim, Terry–Maybank Venture Capital Company Sdn Bhd
Lim, Yong-kee–Korea Investment Partners Co Ltd
Limeri, Philip–KEC Ventures Inc
Limoges, Bertrand–Innovation Capital SAS
Limon, Zvi–MAGNUM COMMUNICATIONS FUND L P
Lin, Adam–iSeed Ventures
Lin, Anthony–Intel Capital Corp
Lin, Artis–Carlyle Group LP
Lin, Axin–Shanghai Sinohead Capital Co Ltd
Lin, Ben–Great Oaks Venture Capital LLC
Lin, Bo–Elevation China Capital

Lin, Brandon–SAIF Partners
Lin, Bryan–Carlyle Group LP
Lin, Chris–LFM Capital LLC
Lin, Dongliang–IDG Capital Partners Inc
Lin, Han-Fei–CID Group
Lin, Henry–Point B Capital LLC
Lin, Heyuan–Industrial Technology Investment Corp
Lin, Hurst–Doll Capital Management Inc
Lin, Jiachang–CRP-Fanya Investment Consultants Beijing Co Ltd
Lin, Jiang–Shanghai Divine Investment Management Co Ltd
Lin, Leon–Onegate Capital
Lin, Ling–Shenzhen Cornerstone of Entrepreneurial Cci Capital Ltd
Lin, Min–NewQuest Capital Advisors HK Ltd
Lin, Moun-Rong–Harbinger Venture Management
Lin, Mushun–Shanghai Divine Investment Management Co Ltd
Lin, Real–Crimson Capital China
Lin, Rebecca–Fidelity Growth Partners Asia
Lin, Richard–Cross Valley Capital
Lin, Richard–HeathQuest Capital
Lin, Sheng–Hony Capital Beijing Co Ltd
Lin, Sibil–Oaktree Capital Management LP
Lin, Stephen–Mobility Ventures LLC
Lin, Sucheng–Shanghai Tronfund Management Co Ltd
Lin, Susan Shui-Shien–AEA Investors LLC
Lin, Tony–GI Partners
Lin, Tony–TSC Venture Management Inc
Lin, Will–Trident Capital Cybersecurity Fund I LP
Lin, Xi–Shanghai Fortune United Investment Group Co Ltd
Lin, Xuefei–Shenzhen Rongchuang Venture Capital Co Ltd
Lin, Yihong–Industrial Technology Investment Corp
Lin, Yilun–WestSummit Capital Management Ltd
Lin, Yunfeng–ShenZhen CDF-Capital Co Ltd
Lin, Zhiliang–Shenzhen Green Pine Capital Partners Co Ltd
Lind, Douglas–Biomark Capital
Lind, Douglas–Burrill & Company
Lind, Eric–Oneaccord Capital LLC
Lind, N. Colin–Blum Capital Partners LP
Lindahl, John–Norwest Equity Partners
Lindback, Leif–Blackstone Group LP
Lindberg, Bjorn–Procuritas Partners Kb
Lindberg, Brooks–Partners Group Holding AG
Lindberg, Eric–Lion Capital LLP
Lindberg, Jakob–Investor Growth Capital AB
Lindberg, Jon–Acas LLC
Lindberg, Marcus–Golub Capital Master Funding LLC
Lindberg, Soren–Axcel Industriinvestor A/S
Lindblad, Jonas–Jade Investment Consulting (Shanghai) Co Ltd
Lindblad, Tyler–Antares Capital Corp
Linde, Yoseph–Jerusalem Global Ventures
Linden, Dean–Cypress Hills Partners Inc
Linden, Steve–Rockbridge Growth Equity LLC
Lindenauer, Alice–Hamilton Lane Advisors LLC
Lindenbojm, Alexandre–Vinci Equities Gestora de Recursos Ltda
Lindencrona, Asa–Creandum AB

Lindenfield, Susannah–Blackstone Group LP
Linder, Stefan–Altor Equity Partners AB
Lindergard Jepsen, Christian–Sunstone Capital A/S
Lindermeir, Mathias–Extorel GmbH
Lindguist, Halbert–Blackstone Group LP
Lindh, Peter–Gkl Growth Capital AB
Lindhorst, Britta–Generali Private Equity Investments GmbH
Lindner, Andrew–Frontier Capital LLC
Lindner, Andrew–Frontier Capital LLC
Lindquist, Barry–Lakeside Capital Management LLC
Lindroos, Johanna–Dasos Capital Oy
Lindsay, Ken–ECI Partners LLP
Lindsay, Robert–Lindsay Goldberg & Bessemer LP
Lindsey-Clark, Matthew–Evercore Inc
Lindskog, Sven–ICA Gruppen AB
Lindstrand, Staffan–Odlander Fredrikson & Co AB
Lindstrom, Peter–Evolver Investment Group Ltd
Lindstrom, Thomas–Carlyle Group LP
Lindtvedt, Jorn–Skagerak Venture Capital AS
Linehan, Chip–GC Capital Inc
Linehan, Earl–Liberty Capital Management Corp
Linehan, Earl–Woodbrook Capital Inc
Linfield, James–Cooley LLP
Ling, Benjamin–Khosla Ventures LLC
Ling, Christopher–Brown Brothers Harriman & Co
Ling, Gabe–General Catalyst Partners LLC
Ling, Richard–Rembrandt Venture Management LLC
Ling, Yong Wah–SEAVI Advent Corporation Ltd
Lingam, Bharath–PurpleTalk, Inc.
Linge, Penelope–Montgomery & Co LLC
Lingjaerde, Sven–Endeavour Vision SA
Link, Ulrich–Investitions Strukturbk Rhein Pfalz GmbH
Link, William–Versant Venture Management, LLC
Linkens, Nicolas–Gilde Buy Out Partners BV
Linklater, William–Baker & McKenzie LLP
Linn, Nathan–Valar Ventures Management LLC
Lins, Guilherme–Capital International Inc
Linse, Michael–Kleiner Perkins Caufield & Byers LLC
Lintag, Ronald–Blackstone Group LP
Linthwaite, Peter–CT Investment Partners LLP
Lints, Michael–Golden Gate Ventures Pte Ltd
Lion, Paul–Morrison & Foerster LLP
Lioon, Jason–Diversified Trust Company Inc
Lipari, Paul–CN Private Equity Partners
Lipchin, Steven–Horizon Equity Partners Pty Ltd
Lipfeld, Joanna–Lynx Equity Ltd
Lipian, Bruce–StoneCreek Capital
Lipke, D.J.–Prairie Capital, L.P.
Lipkin, Boris–Vantagepoint Management Inc
Lipkin, David–Morrison & Foerster LLP
Lipman, Matthew–Brookstone Partners LLP
Lipp, Ernst-Moritz–Odewald & Compagnie fuer Beteiligungen GmbH
Lipp, Kurt–Wamex Private Equity Management
Lippe, Stefan–BlackRock Private Equity Partners AG
Lippera, Daniel–Access Capital Partners SA
Lippin, David–One Equity Partners LLC
Lippin, David–Sun Capital Partners Inc
Lippman, Christopher–Carlyle Group LP
Lipsitz, Jeffrey–COGR Inc
Lipson, Dan–Rotunda Capital Partners LLC
Lipson, Paul–Able Capital Management LLC
Lipson, Peter–Baml Capital Access Funds Manage-

ment LLC
Lipson, Ross–Fenway Partners LLC
Liptak, Robert–Clarus Ventures LLC
Lipton, Justin–CIP Capital
Lipton, Marc–TorQuest Partners Inc
Lires Rial, Sergio Agapito–Banco Santander Brasil SA
Lisac, Jamie–Dresner Capital Resources Inc
Lisaeth, Henrik–FSN Capital Partners AS
Lisenkov, Dmitriy–Rossiiskaia Korporatsiia Nanotekhnologii GK
Lisher, Erik–Blackstone Group LP
Lisiak, Paul–Metropolitan Equity Partners LLC
Liska, Paul–Ripplewood Holdings LLC
Lisker, Marc–MSD Capital LP
Lisonbee, Mark–RLG Capital LLC
Liss, Joe–Bridgepoint Investment Partners I LLLP
Lissot, Gerard–NCI SAS
List, Robert–Bvt Holding GmbH & Co KG
Listen, Kevin–Hancock Park Associates A California LP
Lister, Stephen–Imperial Capital Corp
Lisyansky, Andrei–I2Bf Global Ventures
Litola, Juha–Vendep Capital Oy
Litt, Alex–Swander Pace Capital LLC
Litten, H. Randall–Brockway Moran & Partners Inc
Little, Gary–Canvas Venture Fund
Little, Gary–Morgenthaler Ventures
Little, Jim–New Capital Partners
Little, Jonathan–Northill Capital LLP
Little, Loretta–WRF Capital
Little, Lortetta–WRF Capital
Little, Malcolm–Avista Capital Holdings LP
Little, Rob–Golden Gate Capital Inc
Littlechild, John–Healthcare Ventures LLC
Littlefield, Otis–Morrison & Foerster LLP
Littlejohn, Robert Duncan–BPE Investimentos
Litvin, Peter–Samena Capital Management LLP
Litvin, Simon–GEN3 Partners, Inc.
Liu, Baojie–Shenzhen Richland Investment Co Ltd
Liu, Bo–CVC Capital Partners Ltd
Liu, Bo–Shenzhen Capital Group Co Ltd
Liu, Bo–Shenzhen Richland Investment Co Ltd
Liu, Charlotte–Oaktree Capital Management LP
Liu, Christopher–AIG Capital Partners Inc
Liu, Chuanzhi–Legend Capital Co Ltd
Liu, Chunfang–Core Capital Management Co Ltd
Liu, DS–Jublon Investment & Consultancy Co Ltd
Liu, Dan–Beijing THE CAPITAL Management Co Ltd
Liu, Daniel–Asiatech Management LLC
Liu, Danping–Beijing THE CAPITAL Management Co Ltd
Liu, Diana–Cansbridge Capital Corp
Liu, Dongqiu–ZheShang Venture Capital Co Ltd
Liu, Edward–WI Harper Group Inc
Liu, Erhai–Legend Capital Co Ltd
Liu, Eric–Fitch Crown Venture Capital Management (Shenzhen) Co Ltd
Liu, Eric–Warburg Pincus LLC
Liu, Esther–Walden International
Liu, Fang–ePlanet Capital
Liu, Frank–Tano Capital LLC
Liu, Gary–Tonic Venture Capital Ltd
Liu, Guangjie–VcWiLL Capital
Liu, Hai–Gsr Ventures Management Llc
Liu, Hao–Shenzhen Green Pine Capital Partners Co Ltd
Liu, Hongqiang–Noble (Beijing) Fund Management Inc
Liu, Huatao–Shanghai Cenova Ventures Management Co Ltd
Liu, Irene–Apax Partners LLP
Liu, Jackie–Morrison & Foerster LLP
Liu, Jesse–Arlington Capital Partners
Liu, Jesse–Washington Equity Partners LLC
Liu, Jian–Zhongshan Technology Innovation Investment Management Co Ltd
Liu, Jianyun–Shenzhen Lihe Qingyuan Venture Capital Management Co., Ltd.
Liu, Jun–Warburg Pincus LLC
Liu, Ke–Korea Investment Partners Co Ltd
Liu, Kyle–Redpoint Ventures
Liu, Lefei–Citic Private Equity Funds Management Co Ltd
Liu, Ling–New China Capital Management LP
Liu, Longjiu–Orica Capital Co Ltd
Liu, Louie–Asiatech Management LLC
Liu, Mingyu–WestSummit Capital Management Ltd
Liu, Peter–Pritzker Group Venture Capital
Liu, Qianye–Kaiwu Capital Co Ltd
Liu, Qing–Shenzhen Oriental Fortune Capital Co Ltd
Liu, Roy–Hercules Capital Inc
Liu, Sally–Tmfox Venture Partners Co Ltd
Liu, Shaojun–Hunan High-tech Venture Capital Co Ltd
Liu, Shijun–CRP-Fanya Investment Consultants Beijing Co Ltd
Liu, Shoa-Kai–Mobility Ventures LLC
Liu, Susan–Scale Venture Partners
Liu, Taihe–Industrial Technology Investment Corp
Liu, Tim–Sbcvc Fund Ii L P
Liu, Timothy–CenterGate Capital LP
Liu, Tingru–Infotech Ventures Co Ltd
Liu, Wei–CBC Capital
Liu, Wei–Legend Star Venture Incubator
Liu, Wei–Shanghai Lianxin Investment Management Co Ltd
Liu, Wei–Zhongrong International Trust Co Ltd
Liu, Weiguo–ZEVC Management Co Ltd
Liu, Weijin–Infotech Ventures Co Ltd
Liu, Wendy–Arc Financial Corp.
Liu, Xiang–Beijing Chun Xin Capital Management Corp Ltd
Liu, Xiaobing–China Venture Capital Co Ltd
Liu, Xiaopin–CITIC Capital Partners Ltd
Liu, Xiaoqin–Beijing Tianxing Chuanglian Investment Management Co., Ltd.
Liu, Xiaoyong–Guosen Bole Equity Investment Management Co Ltd
Liu, Xin–Beijing Tianxing Chuanglian Investment Management Co., Ltd.
Liu, Xinyu–Blackstone Group LP
Liu, Xiuping–Sinovation Ventures Ltd
Liu, Xufeng–Fortune Venture Capital Co Ltd
Liu, Xufeng–Fortune Venture Capital Corp
Liu, Yang Sheng–HAO Capital
Liu, Yefei–Dalian Kaida Venture Capital Co Ltd
Liu, Yidong–Shanghai Divine Investment Management Co Ltd
Liu, Yingna–China Canada Angels Alliance Ltd
Liu, Yiru–Carlyle Group LP
Liu, Yu–CAC Capital Management Co Ltd
Liu, Yuheng–Shanghai Fortune United Investment Group Co Ltd
Liu, Zehui–Legend Capital Co Ltd
Liu, Zhanbin–Hollyhigh Intl Capital Co Ltd
Liu, Zhaochen–ChinaEquity Group Inc
Liu, Zhishuo–China Canada Angels Alliance Ltd
Liu, Zhongqing–Elevation China Capital
Liu, Zhou–Fortune Venture Capital Corp
Liubicic, Robert–Milbank Tweed Hadley & Mccloy LLP
Lium, Gretchen–Headwaters BD LLC
Livanos, Basil–Albion Investors LLC
Livingston, Jessica–Y Combinator Inc
Livingstone, Elly–Pantheon Ventures (UK) LLP
Livingstone, Eric–Oaktree Capital Management LP
Livingstone, James–Ardenton Capital Corp
Livingstone, James–Regimen Capital Partners
Lixandru, Luciana–Accel Partners & Co Inc
Lizarraga, Patricia–Hypatia Capital Group LLC
Lizotte, Pierre–Coradin Inc
Lizura, Timothy–New Jersey Economic Development Authority
Ljungman, Mattias–Atomico Ventures
Llanos, Claudia–Anthem Venture Partners
Llewellyn, Scott–Morrison & Foerster LLP
Llewelyn, Jeremy–Black River Asset Management LLC
Llopis, Arturo–Valcapital Gestion Sgecr S A
Llovera, Bernardo–Expansion Capital Partners LLC
Lloyd, Adrian–Episode 1 Ventures LLP
Lloyd, L. John–Skywood Ventures LLC
Lloyd-Harris, Genghis–Abingworth Management Ltd
Lo, Anna–SoftBank China & India Holdings Ltd
Lo, Bonnie–NewQuest Capital Advisors HK Ltd
Lo, Felix–Golden Gate Capital Inc
Lo, Lisa–CID Group
Lo, Philip–Siris Capital Group LLC
Lo, Ramon–Symphony Asia Holdings Pte Ltd
LoParco, Jack–Culbro LLC
LoRusso, Matthew–Carlyle Group LP
Loader, Adrian–Allegro Funds Pty Ltd
Lobdell, Judson–Morrison & Foerster LLP
Lobel, David–Sentinel Capital Partners LLC
Lobley, Ian–3i Group PLC
Lobmeyr, Stephan–Change Capital Partners LLP
Lobo, Richard–CHS Capital LLC
Lobo, Vernon–Mosaic Venture Partners
Lobstein, Romain–Massena Partners SA
Loch, Mark–Highland Ventures Group LLC
Lock, Chris–Impact Investment Group Pty Ltd
Lock, James–Blackstone Group LP
Lockhart, H. Eugene–Oak Investment Partners
Lockledge, Scott–Fairbridge Venture Partners
Loden, Kevin–Redwood Capital Investments LLC
Lodesani, Eliano Omar–Intesa Sanpaolo SpA
Lodge, Andrew–Relativity Capital LLC
Loe, Bente–Springfondet Management AS
Loehr, Judy–Cloud Apps Management LLC
Loevinger, David–Trust Company of the West
Loew, Jennifer–Oaktree Capital Management LP
Loewenson, Carl–Morrison & Foerster LLP
Lofberg, Per–Pharma Capital Ventures
Loftus, John–Actua Corp

Loftus, Sydney–Cedarpoint Investments Inc
Logan, Billy–Karpreilly LLC
Logan, David–F&C Asset Management PLC
Logan, David–Mill Creek Capital Advisors LLC
Logigian, Douglas–Blackstone Group LP
Loginova, Vera–7Vizhn OOO
Logue, Genie–Rosemont Investment Partners LLC
Loh Nahmias, Vivian–Glynn Capital Management LLC
Loh, Jeremy–EDB Investments Pte Ltd
Loh, John–Birch Hill Equity Partners Management Inc
Lohani, Bindu–Asian Development Bank
Lohezic, Francoise–Techfund Capital Europe
Lohrer, Joseph–Blackstone Group LP
Loiacono, John–Ata Ventures
Lok, Joseph–Diversis Capital LLC
Loke, Wai San–Baring Private Equity Asia Ltd
Loke, Wai San–Novo Tellus Capital Partners Pte Ltd
Loken, Jacqueline–CAVU Venture Partners, LLC
Lolli, Francis–Carlyle Group LP
Lollo, Mauro–First Stone Venture Partners Inc
Lomako, Sergei–Haynes and Boone LLC
Lomas, Eric–Ht Capital Advisors LLC
Lomas, Greg–Shard Capital Partners LLP
Lomas, Pedro–Torreal SA
Lomazow, Tyson–Milbank Tweed Hadley & Mccloy LLP
Lombard, Francois–Altur Investissement SCA
Lombard, Francois–Turenne Capital Partenaires SASU
Lombard, Sophie–PAI Partners SAS
Lombardi, Gregory–Landmark Partners Inc
Lombardi, Regina–Brown Brothers Harriman & Co
Lombardi, Ricardo–Newglobe Capital Partners LLP
Lomicka, William–Yearling Management LLC
Lomtadze, Michael–Baring Vostok Capital Partners Ltd
Londal, Douglas–MSD Capital LP
Londal, Douglas–New Mountain Capital I LLC
Londeix, Laurent–Incubateur Paca-Est
Londen, Jack–Morrison & Foerster LLP
London, Matthew–Waud Capital Partners LLC
Londono, Jaime–Pantheon Ventures (UK) LLP
Londono, Laura–Altra Investments
Lonergan, Michael–Georgia Oak Partners LLC
Lonergan, Sara–Pantheon Ventures (UK) LLP
Lonergan, Simon–Behrman Capital
Long, Ashley–GMT Communications Partners LLP
Long, Ben–Duke Street Capital Ltd
Long, Brian–Atlantic Bridge
Long, Brian–Wynnchurch Capital Ltd
Long, Elizabeth–Arch Development Partners LLC
Long, Frederick–Olympus Capital Holdings Asia Hong Kong Ltd
Long, Greg–Maranon Capital LP
Long, Jeffrey–Commonfund Capital Inc
Long, John–Trellis Partners
Long, Michael–Cgw Southeast Partners
Long, Michael–MSouth Equity Partners LLC
Long, Robert–Star Mountain Capital LLC
Long, Robert–Webster Capital Management LLC
Long, Xuguang–VcWiLL Capital
Long, Yunxia–Shenzhen QF Capital Management Co Ltd

Longaker, Michael–Tautona Group Lp
Longbottom, Wayne–Kestrel Capital Pty Limited
Longe, Kikelomo–African Capital Alliance
Longeval, Jan–Banque Degroof Petercam SA
Longo, Nicholas–Geekdom LC
Longobardi, Colleen–Blackstone Group LP
Longosz, Jay–Veritas Capital Fund Management LLC
Longosz, Joseph–Golub Capital Master Funding LLC
Lonnqvist, Markku–Pamplona Capital Management LLP
Lonsdale, David–August Equity Llp
Lonsdale, Jon–Accelerate-IT Ventures Management LLC
Loo, Hock–Walden International
Looke, Joseph–Natural Gas Partners
Loop, Floyd–Radius Ventures LLC
Loose, Wolf-Dietrich–Premium Equity Partners GmbH
Lopes da Silva, Alvaro–GP Investimentos Ltda
Lopes, Everson–Valor Capital Group LLC
Lopes, Joaquim Hierro–Ged Group
Lopez, Fred–Allen & Company Inc
Lopez, Gerard–Mangrove Capital Partners SA
Lopez, Johnny–Platinum Equity LLC
Lopez, Nicolas–Huntington Capital I
Lopez, Pedro–Permira Advisers LLP
Lopez, Sonia–Hamilton Lane Advisors LLC
Lopez-Cruz, Daniel–Investcorp Bank BSC
Lopez-Figueroa, Manuel–Bay City Capital LLC
Lorang, Gilles–Argos Soditic SA
Lorang, Gilles–Efeso Consulting Group SA
Lordi, Frank–Trestle Ventures
Lorentzen, Johan Ewald–Solstra Capital Partners A/S
Lorenz, Gene–Tasman Capital Investments Australia Pty Ltd
Lorenzet, Sonia–Alcedo Societa di Gestione del Risparmio SpA
Lorenzini, Phillip–Edgewater Funds
Lori, Mathew–New Mountain Capital I LLC
Lorimer, Adrian–Oaktree Capital Management LP
Lorimer, Scott–Antares Capital Corp
Loring, Ian–Bain Capital Inc
Lorphelin, Xavier–Serena Capital SAS
Lorry, David–Versa Capital Management Inc
Lorusso, Mike–CIT Group Inc
Losito, David–Cappello Capital Corp
Losorelli, Lou–Freeman Spogli & Co LLC
Lotane, Nancy–Bain Capital Inc
Lotke, Mark–Harmony Partners
Lou, Donglai–Arie Capital Ltd
Lou, Samuel–China Capital Management Ltd
Lou, Yunli–Milestone Capital Management Ltd
Loucks, Drew–Great Hill Equity Partners LLC
Loughrey, Gavin–Alchemy Partners LLP
Louie, Alan–Imagine K12 LLC
Louie, Gilman–Alsop Louie Partners
Louie, Mark–Mingly Capital
Louisy, Myron–Impact Capital Inc
Louvet, Jerome–Weinberg Capital Partners SAS
Louziotis, Demetrios–Pavonis Group LLC
Love, Colleen–Castanea Partners Inc
Love, Vincent–Sunrise Strategic Partners LLC
Lovejoy, Jaime–Scale Venture Partners
Loveland, Douglas–Siguler Guff & Company LP
Loveless, Ken–Silicon Valley Bancventures LP

Lovell, Evan–Virgin Green Fund
Lovell, Joseph–Asia Frontier Investments Ltd
Lovell, Joseph–Perella Weinberg Partners LP
Loverro, Frank–Kelso & Company LP
Loverro, John–Lexington Partners Inc
Loverro, Thomas–Institutional Venture Partners
Loverro, Thomas–RRE Ventures LLC
Lovett, Aly–Financial Technology Ventures
Lovett, Joseph–Adams and Reese LLP
Lovett, Mark–Ascribe Capital, LLC
Lovgren, Mikael–Bridgepoint Advisers Ltd
Loving, James–Blue Water Capital LLC
Lovisotto, Fernando–Vinci Equities Gestora de Recursos Ltda
Low, Kiam Cheow–Evia Capital Partners Pte Ltd
Low, Lisa–Covington Capital Corp
Low, Michael–Shackleton Ventures Ltd
Low, Peter–Axis Capital Corp
Low, Szen–Jynwel Capital Ltd
Low, Teck Seng–Majuven, Pte. Ltd.
Low, Vincent–TRG Management LP
Lowder, Maya–Hall Capital LLC
Lowe, Mark–WGL Holdings Inc
Lowery, Stephen–Frog Capital Ltd
Lowes, J. Andrew–Haynes and Boone LLC
Lown, David–Viscogliosi Brothers LLC
Lowndes, Rodrigo–Southern Cross Capital Management SA
Lowry, Brad–Haynes and Boone LLC
Lozowick, Pini–Alta Berkeley Venture Partners
Lu, Allen–Fudan Quantum Venture Capital Management Co Ltd
Lu, Andy–New Access Capital
Lu, Dan–Guangdong Infore Capital Management Co Ltd
Lu, Dazhong–SDIC Innovation Investment Management Ltd
Lu, Feng–Bioveda China Fund
Lu, Gavin–Carlyle Group LP
Lu, Guo–NGP Capital
Lu, Hao–SAIF Partners
Lu, Jeffrey–Battery Ventures LP
Lu, Jimmy–WI Harper Group Inc
Lu, Kai–LYRIQUE Srrl
Lu, Mei–SinoLatin Capital
Lu, Po-Yen–CID Group
Lu, Sean–Carlyle Group LP
Lu, Vincent–Blackstone Group LP
Lu, Wei–Cybernaut (China) Venture Capital Management Co Ltd
Lu, Wei–Guangxin Investment Management Beijing Co Ltd
Lu, Weiming–Boxin Capital
Lu, Wenyi–Beijing Capital Investment Co Ltd
Lu, Xueyong–Shenzhen Green Pine Capital Partners Co Ltd
Lu, Yi–CRP-Fanya Investment Consultants Beijing Co Ltd
Lu, Yi–Hina Capital Partners
Lu, Yoh Chie–Majuven, Pte. Ltd.
Lu, Yu–Prime Mont Venture Capital Co Ltd
Lu, Yuzhe–Shenzhen Lihe Qingyuan Venture Capital Management Co., Ltd.
Lu, Zuqiang–Bright Stone Investment Management (Hong Kong) Ltd

Lubanski, Alexander–Black Pearls VC SA
Lubash, Barbara–Versant Venture Management, LLC
Lubben, Hauke–Warburg Pincus LLC
Lubben, Marcel–DSM Venturing BV
Lubeck, Dan–Solis Capital Partners LLC
Lubert, Ira–LBC Credit Partners Inc
Lubert, Ira–LLR Partners Inc
Lubert, Ira–Patriot Financial Partners LP
Lubert, Ira–Quaker Partners Management LP
Lubert, Ira–Quaker Partners Management LP
Lubert, Wolfgang–enjoyventure Management GmbH
Lubin, Daniel–Radius Ventures LLC
Lubin, Gary–Pharma Capital Ventures
Lubin, Richard–Berkshire Partners LLC
Lubov, Josh–Softbank Capital Partners L P
Lubreski, Donald–Small Enterprise Assistance Funds
Lubsen, Chip–Stuart Mill Capital, Inc.
Luby, William–Seaport Capital LLC
Luby, William–Seaport Capital LLC
Lucas Mendes, Goncalo–Ecs Capital SA
Lucas, Christian–Silver Lake Partners LP
Lucas, Christopher–Black Diamond Ventures Inc
Lucas, Donald–Lucas Venture Group
Lucas, Kees–inventages venture capital GmbH
Lucas, Robert–CVC Capital Partners Ltd
Lucas, Wes–Gryphon Investors Inc
Lucchese, Joseph–Oasis Capital Partners LLC
Luce, Michael–Harbert Management Corp
Luce, Michael–Montlake Capital LLC
Luce, Zachary–Ironwood Investment Management LLC
Lucey, Kevin–Hamilton Lane Advisors LLC
Luchansky, Elliot–Elm Equity Partners LLC
Luchetti, Claudio–Unique Capital Group AG
Lucia, Rebecca–5AM Ventures LLC
Lucia, Rebecca–Prospect Venture Partners
Luck, Pascal–Core Capital Partners Ii L P
Lucke, Marc-Olivier–Atlantic Internet GmbH
Luckman, Nigel–West Cirque Resources Ltd
Luckock, Nick–Actis LLP
Ludwig, Eugene–Capgen Financial Group LP
Ludwig, Harald–Macluan Capital Corp
Ludwig, John–Ignition Ventures Management LLC
Ludwig, Mark–Sorenson Capital Partners LP
Ludwig, Thomas–Francisco Partners LP
Ludwig, Tim–Accretia Capital LLC
Ludwin, Adam–RRE Ventures LLC
Luebbenhusen, Michael–Ecapital Entrepreneurial Partners AG
Lueck, Bruce–Zephyr Management LP
Lueck, Chris–Pylon Capital LLC
Luedemann, Olaf–CEE Management GmbH
Luehrs, Bruce–Emerald Stage2 Capital Ventures LP
Lueken, Bastian–Platinum Equity LLC
Lueken, Jeffrey–Northwestern Mutual Capital LLC
Luersen, Morten E.–Cardo Partners As
Luh, Tony–DragonVenture, Inc.
Luh, Tony–Westly Group LLC
Lui, Alex–Olympus Capital Holdings Asia Hong Kong Ltd
Lui, Bradley–Morrison & Foerster LLP
Lui, Danny–Startup Capital Ventures LP
Lui, Norman–Shanghai SMC Capital Co Ltd
Luina, Miguel–Hamilton Lane Advisors LLC
Luis Pano, Jose–Vinci Equities Gestora de Recursos Ltda
Lukac, Zeljko–Quaestus Private Equity doo
Lukacs, Monika–Bancroft Group Ltd
Lukaitis, Shauna–British Columbia Investment Management Corp
Lukander, Arve–Inventure Oy
Lukatch, Heath–Novo Holdings A/S
Lukawski, Wojciech–Abris Capital Partners Sp zoo
Luke, Keith–Commonfund Capital Inc
Luke, Robert–Ged Group
Luke, Suraj–Fortex Capital Inc
Lukens, Nick–Vector Capital Management LP
Lukins, Edward–Morrison & Foerster LLP
Lukkariniemi, Ilkka–Nordic Option Oy
Lum, Philip–Iglobe Treasury Management Ltd
Lumbard, Jeff–Pantheon Ventures (UK) LLP
Lump, William–Prospect Partners LLC
Lund, Christian–Hamilton Robinson LLC
Lund, David–Hercules Capital Inc
Lund, Richard–Doughty Hanson and Co.
Lund, Simon–HarbourVest Partners LLC
Lundberg, Theodore–Ferrer Freeman & Co LLC
Lundberg, Theodore–Peloton Equity LLC
Lundby, Liv–Hitecvision AS
Lundh, Erik–Spindletop Capital Management LLC
Lundquist, Lars–Seb Invest GmbH
Lundstrom, Bill–Eagle Merchant Partners
Lung, Friedrich–Bull Capital Partners Ltd
Lung, Wendy–International Business Machines Corp
Lunsford, Richard–Mill Creek Capital Advisors LLC
Luo, Angela–Centenium-Pinetree China Private Equity
Luo, Bin–HGI Finaves China Fund
Luo, Fei–Shenzhen Green Pine Capital Partners Co Ltd
Luo, Hanjie–Industrial Technology Investment Corp
Luo, Jiwen–Ying Capital
Luo, Lina–Hunan Xiangtou Holdings Group Co Ltd
Luongo, Alessandro–Towerbrook Capital Partners LP
Lupu, Dan–Earlybird Venture Capital GmbH & Co KG
Lurie, Geoffrey–Marvin TRAUB LLC
Lurvey, Jonathan–Blackstone Group LP
Luscombe, Roger C.–Continental Capital Markets Ltd
Lustbader, Michael–Arlington Capital Partners
Lustbader, Michael–Arlington Capital Partners
Lustig, Ivan–Mtn Capital Partners LLC
Luth, Torben–JZ Capital Partners Ltd
Luthria, Avinash–Gaja Capital Partners
Lutken Frigast, Povl–Axcel Industriinvestor A/S
Lutz, Claude–Massena Partners SA
Lutzke, Scott–Centerfield Capital Partners LP
Lutzker, Joshua–Berkshire Partners LLC
Lux, Steve–Noverra Consulting and Capital Partners
Luxenberg-Grant, Mindy–HeadHaul Capital Partners LLC
Lv, Gangzheng–Zhongshan Technology Innovation Investment Management Co Ltd
Lv, Houjun–Gimpo Ind Invest Fund Mgmt Co
Ly, Eric–Wellington Partners GmbH
Ly, Eva–Oaktree Capital Management LP
Ly, Hoang Duy–STIC Investment Inc
Lyall, Les–Growth Works Capital Ltd
Lyall, Les–Kirchner Private Capital Group
Lycheva, Alisa–HealthRight Partners
Lyden, Jack–Rizk Ventures LLC
Lydon, Kevin–Strategic Value Partners LLC
Lydon, Mark–Intel Capital Corp
Lye, Meng Yiau–OWW Capital Partners Pte Ltd
Lykke Pedersen, Casper–Axcel Industriinvestor A/S
Lyles, Sheryl–All-American Holdings LLC
Lyles, Thomas–Medcare Investment Fund Ltd
Lyman, Art–Masi Ltd
Lynch, Casey–ACP Inc
Lynch, Christopher–Accomplice LLC
Lynch, Christopher–Ascent Venture Management Inc
Lynch, Christopher–Evercore Inc
Lynch, Daniel–3TS Capital Partners, Ltd.
Lynch, Desmond–Canyon Capital Advisors LLC
Lynch, Gerard–Galena Asset Management Ltd
Lynch, Harry–Argenta Partners, L.P.
Lynch, James–MVC Capital Inc
Lynch, James–Patriot Financial Partners LP
Lynch, James–Thermo Capital Partners LLC
Lynch, Jeremy–Trilantic Capital Management LP
Lynch, Jeremy–Trilantic Capital Management LP
Lynch, Jonathan–CCMP Capital Advisors LP
Lynch, Justin–Undisclosed Firm
Lynch, Kevin–Cava Capital
Lynch, Kevin–Cava Capital
Lynch, Kirstin–Farallon Capital Management LLC
Lynch, Liz–Evercore Inc
Lynch, M. Katherine–Patriot Financial Partners LP
Lynch, Peter–Argenta Partners, L.P.
Lynch, Susan–Bain Capital Inc
Lynch, Thomas–Mill Road Capital Management LLC
Lynden, Sean–Gold Hill Capital Management LLC
Lyne, Timothy–Antares Capital Corp
Lynett, Patricia–Blackstone Group LP
Lynn, Barry–Shoreline Venture Management, LLC
Lynn, Brody–Arbor Private Investment Co LLC
Lynn, David–Morrison & Foerster LLP
Lynn, Rebecca–Canvas Venture Fund
Lynn, Rebecca–Morgenthaler Ventures
Lynn, Williard–Gryphon Investors Inc
Lyon, Christine–Morrison & Foerster LLP
Lyon, Clifford–Avante Mezzanine Inc
Lyon, Thomas–Trust Company of the West
Lyon-Mercado, Peter–Crescent Capital Partners Ltd
Lyons, Bill–City Light Capital
Lyons, Matthew–Vespa Capital LLP
Lyons, Michael–Lincolnshire Management Inc
Lyons, Richard–Capital Dynamics Sdn Bhd
Lyren, Melanie–Argosy Capital Group Inc
Lyritzis, Sotiris–Innervation Capital Partners Ltd
Lysne, Alan–Ryerson Futures Inc
Lyubomirskiy, Alex–GEN3 Partners, Inc.
Lyudkevych, Stanislav–IK Ineko PAT
Lyytikainen, Antti–eQ Oyj
MAJOR, BRITTANY–Enhanced Capital Partners LLC
MEAKEM, CHIP–Tribeca Venture Partners LLC
MELLET, VINCE–Deerfield Management Company LP
Ma, Dongbing–Fair Value Capital
Ma, Fangjun–Hunan Xiangtou Holdings Group Co Ltd
Ma, Haixiao–Sunbridge Investment Management Co Ltd
Ma, Huan–Shanghai NewMargin Ventures Co Ltd
Ma, Jiong–Braemar Energy Ventures LP
Ma, John–Roth Capital Partners LLC
Ma, Jun–Hony Capital Beijing Co Ltd

Ma, Kevin–Diversis Capital LLC
Ma, Larry–Jade Investment Consulting (Shanghai) Co Ltd
Ma, Melissa–Asia Alternatives Management LLC
Ma, Michael–Liquid 2 Ventures LP
Ma, Michelle–IDG Capital Partners Inc
Ma, Philip–MergerTech Advisors
Ma, Qun–Rongxin Capital Fund Management Ltd
Ma, Rui–500 Startups, L.P.
Ma, Xiaofeng–Elevation China Capital
Ma, Xiaohu–Morrison & Foerster LLP
Maa, Ted–Pine Brook Road Partners LLC
Maalouf, Khalil–XPV Capital Corp
Maartman-Moe, Erling–Alliance Venture AS
Maas, Christian–Tricor Pacific Founders Capital Inc
Maass, Jochen–Hanse Ventures BSJ GmbH
Mabbs, Kenneth–Fa Technology Ventures Corp
Mac Cormac, Susan–Morrison & Foerster LLP
MacAskill, Peter–NSBI Venture Capital
MacBean, Mick–Triwest Capital Mgmt Corp
MacColl, Tim–Larsen Maccoll Partners LP
MacCormack, Justin–Imperial Capital Corp
MacCormack, Suzanne–Ampersand Capital Partners
MacDonald, Caitlyn–Lee Equity Partners LLC
MacDonald, Chris–Virgo Investment Group LLC
MacDonald, Gregory–Carlyle Group LP
MacDonald, James–First Analysis Corp
MacDonald, Robert–Craton Equity Partners LLC
MacDonald, Scott–McRock Capital Corp
MacDonald, Sean–Siguler Guff & Company LP
MacDougall, Michael–TPG Capital Management LP
MacDougall, Neil–Silverfleet Capital Partners LLP
MacDowell, Jeffrey–Acas LLC
MacFarlane, Bruce–Aquiline Capital Partners LLC
MacGillivray, Mairi–Westerkirk Capital Inc
MacInnis, Robert–ABRY Partners LLC
MacIntosh, Alan–Real Ventures
MacIntyre, John–Birch Hill Equity Partners Management Inc
MacKay, Alan–Hermes Gpe Llp
MacKeigan, Dan–Tudor Ventures
MacKellar, Richard–Chrysalix Energy
MacKelvey, Kristin–Bayou City Energy LP
MacKenzie, David–Silverfleet Capital Partners LLP
MacKenzie, Robert–Oceanbridge Partners LLC
MacKenzie, Timothy–Merit Capital Partners IV LLC
MacKinnon, Alastair–Phase4 Ventures Ltd
MacLaren, Blair–Active Capital Partners SA
MacLean, Ken–CORE Partners LLC
MacLean, Todd–Silversmith Capital Partners LLC
MacLellan, Robert–TD Capital Group Ltd
MacLennan, Bruce–Global Infrastructure Holdings
MacLeod, Scott–GEF Management Corp
MacManus, Nichol–Brown Brothers Harriman & Co
MacMillan, Charles–Early Stage Partners LP
MacMillin, Bradley–Symphony Technology Group LLC
MacNaughton, Torquil–Penta Capital Llp
MacQuitty, Jonathan–Abingworth Management Ltd
MacRae, Bruce–Hastings Equity Partners LLC
MacTaggart, Ian–Brynwood Partners L.P.
MacTavish, Mark–ONCAP INVESTMENT PARTNERS LP
Macdonald, Jacqueline–Sippl Macdonald Ventures
Macdonald, Jonathan–First Abu Dhabi Bank PJSC
Macdonald, Peter–Bison Capital Asset Management LLC
Macdonald, Tommy–Sorenson Capital Partners LP
Macey, M. William–Sterling Investment Partners II LP
Macfarlane, Bruce–MMC Ventures Ltd
Macfarlane, Matthew–Yuuwa Capital LP
Mach, Bernard–Aravis SA
Machado, Roberto–Banco Nacional de Desenvolvimento Economico e Social BNDES
Machida, Jenny–IMB Development Corp
Machiels, Alec–Pegasus Capital Advisors LP
Maciariello, Patrick–Anholt (USA) LLC
Maciel Ramundo, Julio Cesar–Banco Nacional de Desenvolvimento Economico e Social BNDES
Macinnis, Robert–Blue Bear Capital LLC
Mack, Andrew–Pt Capital LLC
Mack, Christian–Lotus Innovations LLC
Mack, Frank–Accretive Solutions Inc
Mack, John–Egis Capital Partners
Mack, Joshua–Clearlight Partners LLC
Mack, Timothy–Audax Group, Inc.
Mackay, Alan–GHO Capital Partners LLP
Mackay, Christopher–Private Advisors LLC
Mackenzie, David–Telopea Capital Partners Pty Ltd
Mackenzie, Douglas–Radar Partners LLC
Mackenzie, Jeremy–Torch Hill Investment Partners LLC
Mackenzie, Roy–Apax Partners LLP
Mackenzie, Stuart–Ethos Private Equity (Proprietary) Ltd
Mackesy, D. Scott–Welsh Carson Anderson & Stowe
Mackey, Ronald–Trilantic Capital Management LP
Mackhoul, Lawrence–Asia Frontier Investments Ltd
Mackinnon, Simon–Shanghai SMC Capital Co Ltd
Macksey, Alan–Sterling Partners GP LLC
Mackworth, Hugh–SmartForest Ventures
Maclaughlan, Kevin–Century Capital Management / Massachusetts Inc
Maclean, Colin–Sentient Group Ltd
Maclean, Richard–Frontier Capital LLC
Maclean, Richard–Frontier Capital LLC
Maclean, Robert–Francisco Partners LP
Maclennan, Donald–Foresight Group LLP
Macleod, Alistair–Awal Bank BSCC
Macmillan, Rory–Carlyle Group LP
Macnay, Nick–CBPE Capital LLP
Macomber, Earl–Noson Lawen Partners LLC
Macon, James–Closed Loop Capital
Maconell, Ian–Crosbie & Co Inc
Macquin, Nicolas–Alpha Group
Mactaggart, Terry–Fairwater Growth Resources, Inc.
Madan, Kyle–American Discovery Capital LLC
Madan, Rashmi–Blackstone Group LP
Madar, Michael–Trilantic Capital Management LP
Madar, Michael–Trilantic Capital Management LP
Madasamy, Karthee–Qualcomm Ventures
Madbouly, Ahmed–BPE Partners
Madden, Claire–Connection Capital LLP
Madden, Doug–Warburg Pincus LLC
Madden, James–Carrick Capital Management Company LLC
Madden, Kevin–KPS Capital Partners LP
Madden, Kyle–KLH Capital LP
Madden, Michael–Blackeagle Partners Fund L P
Madden, Richard–Future Fund
Maddin, Keith–Cabot Square Capital Advisors Ltd
Maddock, Mike–Ringleader Ventures LLC
Maddock, Sean–Z Capital HF Adviser LLC
Maddox, Carolyn–Next Wave Partners LLP
Maddox, Clara–Fireman Capital Partners LLC
Maddox, Joe–Anderson Group LLC, The
Madeline, Charles–Republic Alley SA
Madenyika, Rachel–HealthRight Partners
Madersbacher, Georg–Orlando Management AG
Madhavan, Rajeev–Clear Venture Management LLC
Madison, Rhett–JZ Capital Partners Ltd
Madnani, Sean–Blackstone Group LP
Madni, Asad–Crocker Capital, Inc.
Madorsky, Jon–RCP Advisors LLC
Madra, Sundeep–Extreme Venture Partners Inc
Madriz, Yasser–Haynes and Boone LLC
Madry, Eric–Stellus Capital Management LLC
Madsen, Dion–Physic Ventures LLC
Madsen, Jay–Accretia Capital LLC
Madsen, Kent–Epic Ventures Inc
Madson, Dan–Vilicus Ventures LLC
Maduras, Mark–AG BD LLC
Maechling, Michael–AEA Investors LLC
Maeda, Hironobu–Draper Nexus Venture Partners LLC
Maeda, Hironori–Beenos Inc
Maeda, John–Kleiner Perkins Caufield & Byers LLC
Maeder, Gary–Morrison & Foerster LLP
Maeder, Paul–Highland Capital Partners LLC
Maene, Frank–Big Bang Ventures CVA
Maeng, Aaron–Ascribe Capital, LLC
Maestroni, Roberto–Investindustrial Services Ltd
Maeter, Pascal–Richmond Park Partners LLP
Maffeo, Alex–IA Capital Group Inc
Magaletskyi, Konstantin–Horizon Capital Management
Magalhaes, Pedro–Casaforte Investimentos SA
Magan, Matt–Summit Park LLC
Magana, Daryl–Cybernaut (China) Venture Capital Management Co Ltd
Magas, Peter–Beecken Petty O'Keefe & Company LLC
Mager, Zach–Aurora Capital Group Ltd
Maggard, John–Caymus Equity Partners
Maggi, Robbin–Unigestion Holding SA
Maggs, Roger–Celtic House Venture Partners Inc
Magid, Deborah–International Business Machines Corp
Magida, Stephen–Andlinger & Co Inc
Magill, William–TeleSoft Partners
Magliacano, Marc–Catterton Partners Corp
Magliano, John–Blackstone Group LP
Magnani, Enrico–Associes Magnum Capital Partners
Magnano, Ben–Frazier Management LLC
Magnay, Charles–Pavilion Alternatives Group Ltd
Magnette, Jean-Marie–European Investment Fund
Magni, Guido–Versant Venture Management, LLC
Magnuson, Richard–GI Partners
Mago, Gautam–Sequoia Capital India
Mago, Hope–Huntington Capital I
Magold, Rainer–Milbank Tweed Hadley & Mccloy LLP
Magowan, Peter–Alta Berkeley Venture Partners
Magpayo, Joseph–Trust Company of the West

Magro, Tony—Evercore Inc
Maguire, Alan—Leaf Investments Ltd
Maguire, Gerry—Atlantic Bridge
Maguire, Juan—Alothon Group LLC
Maguire, Robert—Perella Weinberg Partners LP
Maguy, Billy—Alpine Investors LP
Mah, Nicholas—Oak Hill Advisors LP
Mahadevia, Vishal—Warburg Pincus LLC
Mahajan, Rahul—Gennx360 Capital Partners LP
Mahapatra, Vivek—Taurus Ventures GP LLC
Mahedy, Stephen—Providence Equity Partners LLC
Maher, Fintan—Growcorp Group Ltd
Maher, Killian—Blackstone Group LP
Maher, Michael—U.S. Venture Partners
Maheshwaran, Kanthimany—Lanka Ventures PLC
Mahmood, Kaasim—Advent Venture Partners LLP
Mahn, Tammy—Hamilton Lane Advisors LLC
Mahon, David—Antares Capital Corp
Mahon, Elizabeth—Passport Capital LLC
Mahon, Joseph—Coller Capital Ltd
Mahoney, Brian—Calvert Street Capital Partners Inc
Mahoney, Dennis—Empire Investment Holdings LLC
Mahoney, Gerald—Argosy Capital Group Inc
Mahoney, James—CVC Capital Partners Ltd
Mahoney, James—Horizonone Asset Management Inc
Mahoney, James—Huron Capital Partners LLC
Mahoney, James—Investcorp Bank BSC
Mahoney, Michael—Medallion Capital Inc
Mahoney, William—Milbank Tweed Hadley & Mccloy LLP
Mahony, TJ—Accomplice LLC
Mai, Gang—DragonVenture, Inc.
Maidenberg, Ted—Social+Capital Partnership
Maier, Dominic—Adams Street Partners LLC
Maier, Oliver—Speyside Equity LLC
Maier, Thomas—European Bank for Reconstruction and Development
Maigaard, Michael—Danske Private Equity A/S
Mailender, Kevin—Oak Hill Capital Management Inc
Maillebiau, Eric—Da Vinci Capital Management Ltd
Mailman, Elisa—New Legacy Capital LLC
Main, Jennifer—Millstein & Co LP
Main, Tim—Evercore Inc
Maine, Douglas—Brown Brothers Harriman & Co
Maiore, Alain—Kurma Partners SA
Maire, Christophe—Atlantic Ventures GmbH
Mairs, Chris—Entrepreneur First Investment Manager LLP
Maisonrouge, Francois—Evercore Inc
Maizel, Jonathan—Milbank Tweed Hadley & Mccloy LLP
Majeed, Ibrahim—Landmark Partners Inc
Majernik, Craig—Windjammer Capital Investors LLC
Majgaard, Torben—PROfounders Capital Ltd
Majid, Tamim—OCA Ventures
Majithia, Mitesh—Unicorn India Ventures Advisors LLP
Major, James—Arc Financial Corp.
Majoros, George—EagleTree Capital, LP
Majors, Michael—Data Point Capital I LP
Majors, Mike—Siemens Venture Capital GmbH
Majotra, Allan—Axon Partners Group Investment
Majteles, Robert—Oak Investment Partners
Majumdar, Bhaskar—Unicorn India Ventures

Advisors LLP
Mak, Cecilia—Pacific Alliance Capital Group Ltd
Mak, Tak—Aravis SA
Mak, Wouter—Blackstone Group LP
Makadia, Jay—Berkshire Partners LLC
Makam, Raj—Oaktree Capital Management LP
Makela, Manu—Conor Venture Partners Oy
Makhzoumi, Mohamad—New Enterprise Associates Inc
Maki, Pekka Santeri—3TS Capital Partners, Ltd.
Maki, Shun—Oaktree Capital Management LP
Makino, Daisuke—Novaquest Infosystems Inc
Makkawi, Ziad—Qatar First Bank LLC
Makower, Joshua—New Enterprise Associates Inc
Malangoni, Joseph—Blackstone Group LP
Malayery, Amir—Industry Ventures LLC
Malcarney, David—Acas LLC
Maldonado, John—Advent International Corp
Maldonado, Jose Maria—Bridgepoint Advisers Ltd
Malekzadeh, Reza—Partech International
Maletsky, Greg—Waveland Investments LLC
Malfettone, John—Clayton Dubilier & Rice LLC
Malhan, Arvind—New Silk Route Partners, LLC
Malhan, Niten—Warburg Pincus LLC
Malherbe, Paul—Business Partners Ltd
Malhotra, Arwind—Firm Factory Network AB
Malhotra, Deep—Gemini New Media Ventures LLP
Malhotra, Heavent—Rocket Internet AG
Malhotra, Ramesh—Gemini New Media Ventures LLP
Malhotra, Rohit—StepStone Group LP
Malhotra, Satyan—Natixis Private Equity SA
Malick, Joseph—NB Private Equity Partners Ltd
Malik, Gaurav—Olympus Capital Holdings Asia Hong Kong Ltd
Malik, Nisreen—ePlanet Capital
Malik, Om—True Ventures LLC
Malik, R. Neil—K1 Capital Advisors LLC
Malik, Shahzad—Advent Venture Partners LLP
Malik, Vikram—Strathspey Crown LLC
Malinger, Eyal—Oaktree Capital Management LP
Maliwal, Rajiv—Standard Chartered Private Equity Ltd
Malizia, David—Westshore Capital Partners LP
Malka, Ben—F-Prime Capital Partners
Malka, Ben—North Hill Ventures LP
Malka, Meyer—Ribbit Capital LP
Malkani, Abhijit—Everstone Capital Management, Ltd.
Malkov, Mihail—Essedel Oy
Mallement, Harvey—Harvest Partners LP
Mallik, Ajoy—Follow Seed Australia Pty Ltd
Mallin, Tony—Star Capital Partners Ltd
Mallion, Mikael—RiverRock European Capital Partners LLP
Mallo, Carlos—Permira Advisers LLP
Malloy, Bill—Accelerate-IT Ventures Management LLC
Malloy, John—Bluerun Ventures LP
Malloy, John—Edgewater Funds
Malm, David—Webster Capital Management LLC
Malmros, Pal—Verdane Capital Advisors AS
Malone, James—Boyne Capital Partners LLC
Malone, Nancy—Eastward Capital Partners LLC
Maloney, Mark—Paladin Capital Management LLC
Maloney, T.J.—Lincolnshire Management Inc

Maloney, Timothy—Abbott Capital Management LLC
Maltz, Jules—Institutional Venture Partners
Maluth, Elliot—HIG Capital LLC
Maly, John—People Fund LLC
Mamba, Gloria—GEF Management Corp
Mamdani, Sulu—Silicon Valley Bancventures LP
Mammola, Carlo—Argan Capital
Mampuru, Cedrick—Lereko Investment Holdings Pty Ltd
Man, Bernard—HPEF Capital Partners Ltd
Manaktala, Neha—HOF Capital Inc
Manastersky, Tony—Rbc Capital Partners
Manby, William—Monterey Venture Partners LLC
Mancarella, Giorgio—Arcadia SGR SpA
Mancera, Eileen—Morgan Creek Capital Management LLC
Manchanda, Suneet—Alpha Founders
Mancini, Domenic—Investissements Novacap Inc
Mancinskis, Maris—Bank Sankt-Peterburg PAO
Manda, Horia—Axxess Capital Partners SA
Mandahl, Michael—Nexit Ventures Oy
Mandal, Sumant—Clearstone Venture Management Services LLC
Mandal, Sumant—Hive LLC
Mandal, Sumant—March Capital Partners GP LLC
Mandan, Nakul—Battery Ventures LP
Mandan, Nakul—Lightspeed Management Company LLC
Mandato, Joseph—De Novo Ventures LLC
Mandel, F. Howard—Peppertree Capital Management Inc
Mandel, Harlan—Media Development Investment Fund Inc
Mandel, Mark—Milbank Tweed Hadley & Mccloy LLP
Mandelbaum, Fern—Monitor Venture Associates LLC
Mandell, Aaron—GREATPOINT VENTURES
Mandhana, Satish—IDFC Alternatives Ltd
Mandile, John—Sigma Partners
Mandile, John—Sigma Prime Ventures LLC
Mandl, Eric—Evercore Inc
Mandon, Thierry—Sem Genopole SAEM
Manek, Rahul—Reliance Capital Ventures Ltd
Maner, Skip—Newspring Capital
Manger, Roland—Earlybird Venture Capital GmbH & Co KG
Manges, James—Trilantic Capital Management LP
Manges, James—Trilantic Capital Management LP
Manglano, Sonsoles—Realza Capital SGECR SA
Mani, Kul—Wellington Financial Lp
Mani, Roy—Star Capital Partners Ltd
Manias, Paul—OMERS Infrastructure
Maniatis, Tom—Column Group
Manjarres, David—Natixis Private Equity SA
Mankad, Vipul—SIDBI Venture Capital Ltd
Mankodi, Hiren—Audax Group, Inc.
Mankovski, Aaron—Pitango Venture Capital Management Israel, Ltd.
Mankowski, Michael—Echo Health Ventures LLC
Mankwitz, Brian—Mantucket Capital LLC
Manley, Graham—Antares Capital Corp
Manlunas, Eric—Wavemaker Partners
Mann, David—Spring Mill Venture Partners
Mann, Jeffrey—Silver Oak Services Partners
Mann, Laura—Glenmont Partners, LLC
Mann, Peter—Yellow Wood Partners LLC

2527

Mannaioni, Duilio-Fidi Toscana SpA
Mannetti, Peter-iSherpa Capital
Mannheimer, Ernst-Wellington Partners GmbH
Mannheims, Willi-Ventizz Capital Partners Advisory AG
Manning, Christopher-Trilantic Capital Management LP
Manning, Christopher-Trilantic Capital Management LP
Manning, Damian-Digital Entertainment Ventures LLC
Manning, Joe-Riverside Co
Manning, Ralph-Progress Equity Partners Ltd
Mannion, Martin-Summit Partners LP
Mannix, David-San Francisco Equity Partners LP
Mannix, Hank-Kelso & Company LP
Manocha, Rohit-Tri Artisan Capital Partners LLC
Manos, Peter-Arlington Capital Partners
Manos, Peter-Arlington Capital Partners
Manrique, Jose-Magnum Industrial Partners
Manrique, Jose-Magnum Industrial Partners SL
Manry, Charlie-Blackstreet Capital Management LLC
Mansbridge, Lance-Bay Hills Capital Partners II LP
Mansell, David-Onex Corp
Mansfield, Melainie-Milbank Tweed Hadley & Mccloy LLP
Mansour, Bassem-Resilience Capital Partners LLC
Mansour, Jana-Morrison & Foerster LLP
Mansour, Mark-Mcm Capital Partners L P
Mansour, Mohsen-Qalaa Holdings SAE
Mantel, Alan-Snow Phipps Group LLC
Manuel, Victor-Atlantic-Pacific Capital Inc
Manz, Robert-Enterprise Investors Sp z o o
Manzano, A. David-AEA Investors LLC
Mao, Benjamin-Kohlberg & Co LLC
Mao, Chenglin-Shenzhen Fuhai Yintao Venture Capital Co Ltd
Mao, Duanyi-China Merchants Kunlun Equity Invest Management Co Ltd
Mao, Michael-IDG Capital Partners Inc
Mao, Yongzhi-Fair Value Capital
Maor, Alon-BRM Capital LLC
Maoz, Elchanan-Maoz Everest Funds Management Ltd
Mapes, Eduardo-Northgate Capital LLC
Mapes, John-Aurora Capital Group Ltd
Maples, Michael-Floodgate Fund, L.P.
Mar-Yohana, Marc-Pfingsten Partners LLC
Marakovic, Nino-Sapphire Ventures LLC
Marakovic, Nino-Sapphire Ventures LLC
Maranhao, Fabio-Axxon Group Servicos De Consultoria E Assessoria Ltda
Marasigan, Glenn-Gold Hill Capital Management LLC
Marazzi, Marco-Baker & McKenzie LLP
Marcal, Mauricio-GEF Management Corp
Marchetti, Kevin-Bay Grove Capital LLC
Marchington, Allan-Apposite Capital LLP
Marcks, Grant-Atlantic Street Capital Management LLC
Marco, Jose Antonio-Magnum Industrial Partners SL
Marcolini, Pierre-Neo Investment Partners LLP
Marcondes Rodrigues, Mauro-Financiadora de Estudos e Projetos FINEP
Marcos, Jorge-Evercore Inc

Marcovitz, Neil-Northleaf Capital Partners Ltd
Marcum, Fran-Nest-TN LLC
Marcum, Fran-Relevance Capital Inc
Marcus, Adam-Openview Venture Partners LP
Marcus, G. Robert-Conexus Capital Management, Inc.
Marcus, Ian-New Energy Capital Corp
Marcus, Jeffrey-Crestview Advisors, LLC
Marcus, Joy-Gotham Ventures LLC
Marcus, Joy-Gotham Ventures LLC
Marcus, Larry-Walden Venture Capital
Marcus, Lenard-Edison Partners
Marcus, Lenard-Edison Partners
Marcus, Maged-Oaktree Capital Management LP
Marden, James-Sk Capital Partners LP
Marden, Scott-CIP Capital
Marderosian, Mike-50 South Capital Advisors LLC
Marengere, Luc-TVM Capital GmbH
Marengi, Joseph-Austin Ventures
Mareschal, Helen-CM-CIC Capital Prive SA
Margalit, Erel-JVP Jerusalem Venture Partners Israel Management, Ltd.
Margetts, Jill-Centerfield Capital Partners LP
Margolese, Mel-Crosbie & Co Inc
Margolin, Adam-Spectrum Equity Investors LP
Margolin, Roman-Genstar Capital LLC
Margoline, Alexandre-Permira Advisers LLP
Margolis, Amy-Riverside Co
Margolis, Paul-Longworth Venture Partners, L.P.
Margulis, Howard-Ubequity Capital Partners Inc
Margulis, Neal-Wellington Partners GmbH
Margve, Dario-Brynwood Partners L.P.
Mariani, Paul-ABS Capital Partners, Inc.
Mariategui, Alvaro-Nazca Capital SGEIC SA
Mariette, Christine-Azulis Capital SA
Marimow, Scott-Providence Equity Partners LLC
Marin Zirotti, Gonzalo-Suanfarma Biotech SGECR SA
Marin, Jose-IG Expansion Business Development SL
Marin, Lucia-Acas LLC
Marin, Marino-Silverfern Group Inc
Marin, Miguel-Eneas Capital SL
Marinaccio, Louis-North Castle Partners LLC
Marinas, Maria-Indigo Capital LLP
Marinelli, Joseph-Spencer Trask Ventures Inc
Marino, Andrew-Carlyle Group LP
Marino, Benjamin-Glouston Capital Partners LLC
Marino, Gene-Evolution Capital Partners LLC
Marino, Maura-NewSchools Venture Fund
Marino, Michael-Aurora Capital Group Ltd
Marinuzzi, Lorenzo-Morrison & Foerster LLP
Mario, Ernest-Pappas Ventures
Marion, Jessica-One Equity Partners LLC
Maris, Bill-Section 32 LLC
Marjomaa, Tuulikki-Nordic Option Oy
Mark, Douglas-Brown Brothers Harriman & Co
Mark, Douglas-Northstar Capital LLC
Markey, Ann-Greencoat Capital LLP
Markey, Bernard-Navigator Equity Partners LLC
Markham, James-Graphite Capital Management LLP
Markham, Richard-Care Capital LLC
Markman, Eddy-Sun Mountain Capital Advisors LLC
Markman, Michael-Siguler Guff & Company LP
Markova, Sonja-Keiretsu Forum
Markowitz, Jeff-Greylock Partners LLC

Markowitz, Jeff-Heidrick & Struggles International Inc
Markowitz, Marcia-Muller & Monroe Asset Management LLC
Markowitz, Steven-Goldin Ventures Co
Marks, Allan-Milbank Tweed Hadley & Mccloy LLP
Marks, Arthur-Valhalla Partners LP
Marks, George-Robin Hood Ventures
Marks, Jerry-Milbank Tweed Hadley & Mccloy LLP
Marks, Joseph-Capital Dynamics Sdn Bhd
Marks, Michael-Riverwood Capital Group LLC
Marks, Neil-CranRidge Capital LP
Marks, Tricia-Madison Capital Funding LLC
Markus, Bart-Wellington Partners GmbH
Markus, David-Turning Rock Partners Gp LLC
Markus, Richard-Omos Equitypartners GmbH
Marley, James-Graycliff Partners LP
Marley, Julianne-Blue Point Capital Partners LP
Marlot, Michel-Sambrinvest SA
Marlow, Jonathan-Mid-Ocean Partners LP
Marlowe, Christopher-Silverfern Group Inc
Marmalefsky, Dan-Morrison & Foerster LLP
Marmer, Craig-Probitas Partners Inc
Marocco, Michael-Sandler Capital Management
Marolda, Andrew-Beekman Group LLC
Marom, Jon-TRG Management LP
Marom, Jonathan-Worldquant Ventures LLC
Maroo, Mehul-Aditya Birla Capital Advisors Pvt Ltd
Marquardt, Andrew-Evercore Inc
Marquardt, David-August Capital Management LLC
Marquardt, Stephen-Century Capital Management / Massachusetts Inc
Marquardt, Stephen-Coller Capital Ltd
Marquardt, Stephen-Doughty Hanson and Co.
Marques dos Santos, Fernando-Banco Nacional de Desenvolvimento Economico e Social BNDES
Marquez, Angel-Isis Venture Capital SL
Marquez, Michael-Morado Venture Management LLC
Marquis, Joelle-Arsenal Capital Management LLC
Marquis, Joelle-Arsenal Capital Partners LP
Marquis, Joelle-Arsenal Capital Partners LP
Marraccino, Anthony-Compass Partners International Llp
Marrachine, Eduardo-Kinea Investimentos Ltda
Marrel, Benoit-Breega Capital SARL
Marrero, Roger-Comvest Partners
Marrero, Roger-Comvest Partners
Marriott, Christiian-Equistone Partners Europe Ltd
Marriott, Dan-Stripes Group LLC
Marrone, James-Palisade Capital Management LLC
Marsh, Andy-Gresham Llp
Marsh, Cathy-Milbank Tweed Hadley & Mccloy LLP
Marsh, Nick-FirstMark Capital LLC
Marsh, Richard-Draper Esprit PLC
Marsh, Rupert-B.P. Marsh & Partners PLC
Marsh, Sean-Point Judith Capital
Marshall, Benjamin-Genstar Capital LLC
Marshall, Brad-Blackstone Group LP
Marshall, Christopher-Technology Crossover Ventures LP
Marshall, Frank-Big Basin Partners LP
Marshall, Marcy-Arboretum Ventures Inc
Marshall, Michael-Halifax Group LLC
Marshall, Robin-Bain Capital Inc

Marshall, Seton—New Capital Partners
Marshbanks, Tracy—First Analysis Corp
Marsiello, Lawrence—Pine Brook Road Partners LLC
Marsteller, Todd—Larsen Maccoll Partners LP
Marstrand, Thomas—Erhvervsinvest Management A/S
Marta, Jessica—Mesirow Financial Private Equity Inc
Martel, Vincent—Inerjys Ventures Inc
Martelli, Marco—Invision AG
Martens, Herbert—Natcity Investments Inc
Martensson, Yvonne—Sunstone Capital A/S
Marthinson, Matt—J B Poindexter & Co Inc
Marti, Alfredo—Riverstone Holdings LLC
Marti, Jean-Christophe—Navis Management Sdn Bhd
Martin, Aaron—Providence Ventures LLC
Martin, Bradley—Fairfax Financial Holdings Ltd
Martin, Brian—Vance Street Capital LLC
Martin, Christopher—Research Corporation Technologies
Martin, Craig—Morrison & Foerster LLP
Martin, David—280 Capital Partners LLC
Martin, David—CIG Securities Inc
Martin, David—Corpacq Ltd
Martin, Douglas—SF Holding Corp
Martin, Edward—Clarion Capital Partners LLC
Martin, Eff—Anthos Capital LP
Martin, Ernest—Haynes and Boone LLC
Martin, Graham—Blackstone Group LP
Martin, Greg—Archer Venture Capital LLC
Martin, Helen—Crosswinds Holdings Inc
Martin, J. Landis—Platte River Ventures LLC
Martin, James—Thomas H Lee Partners LP
Martin, Jane—Spring Mill Venture Partners
Martin, Jason—Argonaut Private Equity LLC
Martin, Jason—Omega Capital Management LLC
Martin, John—Delavaco Holdings Inc
Martin, Kevin—Carmichael Partners LLC
Martin, Michael—Banyan Capital Partners LP
Martin, Michael—Warburg Pincus LLC
Martin, Neil—Compound Semiconductor Technologies Global Ltd
Martin, Pamela—Audax Group, Inc.
Martin, Phillip—Salem Capital Partners, LP (FKA: Venture Capital Solutions)
Martin, Regis—Unigestion Holding SA
Martin, Richard—Haynes and Boone LLC
Martin, Robert—Excellere Capital Management LLC
Martin, Ryan—Summer Street Capital Partners LLC
Martin, Steven—Current Capital LLC
Martin, Stuart—EagleTree Capital, LP
Martin, Tony—Proprium Capital Partners LP
Martin, W. Todd—CapitalWorks LLC
Martin, Warren—Cooley LLP
Martin, William—Princeton Ventures Management LLC
Martin-Odette, Vicki—Haynes and Boone LLC
Martineau, Alexis—CVC Capital Partners Ltd
Martineau-Fortin, Eric—Whitestar Capital Ltd
Martinez, Borja—Apax Partners LLP
Martinez, Ignacio—Flagship Pioneering
Martinez, Jean-Claude—Sofinnova Partners SAS
Martinez, Steven—Peak Rock Capital LLC
Martino, Nicholas—High Road Capital Partners LLC
Martino, Paul—Bullpen Capital LP
Martino, Rocco—LaSalle Capital
Martins, Carlos—Kinea Investimentos Ltda
Martinson, John—Edison Partners
Martiny, Manuel—Partners Group Holding AG
Martirano, David—Point Judith Capital
Martone, Patricia—Morrison & Foerster LLP
Marty, Andreas—Ventizz Capital Partners Advisory AG
Maruenda, Luc—Idinvest Partners SA
Maruri, Victor—Hispania Capital Partners LLC
Maruszewski, Mark—StepStone Group LP
Maruyama, Tetsuo—Rising Japan Equity Inc
Marver, James—Vantagepoint Management Inc
Marvin, Kim—American Industrial Partners
Marzano, Cheryl—Trust Company of the West
Marzouk, Ben—Monroe Capital LLC
Masalin, Walter—NGP Capital
Masanotti, Peter—Potomac Equity Partners LLC
Masarof, Jonathan—Palisade Capital Management LLC
Masaya, Victor—Presidio Investors LLC
Mascellaro, Nino—Progressio SGR SpA
Maschek, Marko—Pinova Capital GmbH
Maschmeyer, Jonathan—Jabodon PT Co
Mascioli, Ed—SV Health Investors LLP
Masciopinto, Elizabeth—Acas LLC
Masek, Christopher—IK Investment Partners Ltd
Maselli, Michael—Trimaran Capital LLC
Masetti, Maurizio—Alcedo Societa di Gestione del Risparmio SpA
Mashaal, Michael—HealthCor Partners Management LP
Masi, Renee—Biostar Ventures II LLC
Masi, Renee—Windward Ventures
Masiello, Mark—Providence Equity Partners LLC
Maskalunas, Scott—Cressey and Company LP
Mason, Alexander—Carrick Capital Management Company LLC
Mason, Etsuko—Alexandria Real Estate Equities, LLC
Mason, Kevin—ACP Inc
Mason, Neil—Harvard Management Company Inc
Mason, Ryan—Siguler Guff & Company LP
Mason, Susan—Aligned Partners LLC
Masri, Bashar—Siraj Fund Management Co
Masri, Nashat—Foursan Group
Mass, Lev—X/Seed Capital Management
Mass, Stuart—Haynes and Boone LLC
Massara, Darren—NewQuest Capital Advisors HK Ltd
Massard, Nicolas—ABRY Partners LLC
Massey, Jennifer—Cooley LLP
Massey, Lauren—Abbott Capital Management LLC
Massey, Preston—Congruent Investment Partners LLC
Massey, Tim—Band of Angels Venture Fund LP
Massonnat, Ivan—PAI Partners SAS
Massot, Martin—Qualium Investissement SAS
Massoud, I. Joseph—Anholt (USA) LLC
Master, Nico—Evercore Inc
Masto, Christopher—Friedman Fleischer & Lowe Cap Ptnrs L P
Masu, Kazuyuki—Mitsubishi Corp
Masucci, Peter—New Mountain Capital I LLC
Masuda, Takeshi—Nomura Co Ltd
Masur, Mark—Silver Creek Ventures Corp
Masur, Mark—Silver Creek Ventures Corp
Matak, Eduard—Penta Investments Ltd
Matar, Marie-Cecile—Euromezzanine Gestion SaS
Matelich, George—Kelso & Company LP
Materne, Stewart Kirk—Evercore Inc
Maters, Jeffrey—Jabodon PT Co
Maters, Jeffrey—Pritzker Group Venture Capital
Mathe, Tomas—Northgate Capital LLC
Mathers, David—Csfb Private Equity Advisers
Mathers, Edward—New Enterprise Associates Inc
Mathes, Marie-France—Emerging Capital Partners
Matheu, Jorge—Linzor Capital Partners LP
Mathew, Jacob—Mape Advisory Group Private Ltd
Mathew, Vivek—Antares Capital Corp
Mathews, Devin—Chicago Growth Partners LLC
Mathewson, David—Bedminster Capital Management
Mathias, Franco Ottavio—HCM Handwerk Consult Mittelstandsberatung eK
Mathies, Rolf—Earlybird Venture Capital GmbH & Co KG
Mathieson, Stuart—Barings (UK) Ltd
Mathieu, Didier—Grand Sud Ouest Capital SA
Mathieu, Romen—Capital Trust Ltd
Mathrani, Mahinder—Symphony Technology Group LLC
Mathur, Gaurav—IEP Fund Advisors Pvt Ltd
Mathur, Hemendra—Small Enterprise Assistance Funds
Mathur, Shantanu—Springstar GmbH
Mathure, Sunay—Ask Pravi Capital Advisors Pvt Ltd
Matias, David—Vodia Ventures LLC
Matic, Tomislav—Quaestus Private Equity doo
Matise, John—Stone Canyon Venture Partners
Matly, Michael—Montreux Equity Partners
Matsanyuk, Igor—IMI.VC
Matson, Scott—Partech International
Matsubara, Yoshitaka—Global Venture Capital Inc
Matsuda, Humberto—Performa Investimentos Ltda
Matsuda, Kiyoto—Unison Capital, Inc.
Matsui, Brian—Morrison & Foerster LLP
Matsukawa, Rikizo—CITIC Capital Partners Ltd
Matsumoto, Glen—EQT Funds Management Ltd
Matsumoto, Shigeru—Tokio Marine Capital Co Ltd
Matsumoto, ShinSho—WiL Inc
Matsumoto, Takashi—Innovation Engine Inc
Matsumoto, Takeo—kk bhp
Matsumura, Atsushi—Whiz Partners Inc
Matsumura, Shin—MOVIDA JAPAN Inc
Matsuoka, Etsuko—Olympus Capital Holdings Asia Hong Kong Ltd
Mattar, Wael—Infra Capital Investments PJSC
Matte, Bernard—Jacobson Partners
Matteson, Mark—SunTx Capital Partners LP
Mattessich, Claude—CIT Group Inc
Mattew, Alan—Tribal Ventures LLC
Mattheopoulou, Evi—Incubation for Growth SA
Matthes, William—Behrman Capital
Matthews, Alan—Origo Partners PLC
Matthews, Brian—Cultivation Capital
Matthews, Brian—Questmark Partners LP
Matthews, Clint—Growth Works Capital Ltd
Matthews, David—Trailblazer Capital LP
Matthews, David—Wynnchurch Capital Ltd
Matthews, Gary—Morgan Stanley Private Equity
Matthews, JR—Tregaron Capital Co LLC
Matthews, James—Stone Point Capital LLC

Matthews, Ray—BC Advantage Funds Ltd
Matthews, Richard—Augmentum Capital LLP
Matthews, Sharon—Linzor Capital Partners LP
Matthews, Will—New Capital Partners
Matthyssens, Gaston—Vesalius Biocapital Partners SARL
Mattiussi, Alexandre—Neo Investment Partners LLP
Matto, Aaron—True Wind Capital Management LLC
Mattson, Eric—Excellere Capital Management LLC
Mattson, Jon—Trilantic Capital Management LP
Mattson, Jon—Trilantic Capital Management LP
Mattson, Robert—Morrison & Foerster LLP
Mattsson, Magnus—Apax Partners LLP
Matus, Geoff—iGan Partners Inc
Matusich, Anthony—Felicis Ventures
Matusich, Anthony—Sapphire Ventures LLC
Mauceri, Mark—Lee Equity Partners LLC
Mauchel, Phil—OMERS Private Equity Inc
Maughan, Alistair—Morrison & Foerster LLP
Maulucci, Ludovic—OLMA Capital Management Ltd
Maunder, Andrew—Alara Capital Partners LLC
Maunder, Trevor—Artemis Investment Management Ltd
Maunsbach, Bengt—Altor Equity Partners AB
Maurer, Erik—Prospect Partners LLC
Maurer, Greg—Heron Capital Equity Partners
Maurer, Greg—Heron Capital LLC
Maurer, Klaus—Silverfleet Capital Partners LLP
Mauro, Greg—Learn Capital Venture Partners LP
Maurstad, Hugo—Altor Equity Partners AB
Mauze, Michael—VMG Partners, L.P.
Mavroyannis, Irene—First Reserve Corp
Mawhinney, Thomas—Jafco Ventures
Mawson, Alan—Innvotec Ltd
Max, Adam—Jordan Company LP
Maxon, Gregory—Thomas H Lee Partners LP
Maxwell, Bret—MK Capital
Maxwell, Brian—Mill Creek Capital Advisors LLC
Maxwell, Paul—Great Range Capital
Maxwell, Ray—Invesco Private Capital Inc
Maxwell, Scott—Openview Venture Partners LP
May, Allan—Emergent Medical Partners LP
May, Bevan—TOM Capital Associates Inc
May, Graham—Conexus Capital Management, Inc.
May, Guido—Silverfleet Capital Partners LLP
May, Jeremy—St Cloud Capital LLC
May, John—Calvert Social Venture Partners, L.P.
May, John—New Vantage Group
May, Kevin—Horizon Technology Finance Management LLC
May, Robert—Industry Ventures LLC
May, Robert—Industry Ventures LLC
May, Robert—Pillar Companies Management LLC
Maybaum, Richard—LJ2 & Co LLC
Mayenkar, Neel—Wynnchurch Capital Ltd
Mayer, Alan—Green Manning & Bunch Ltd
Mayer, Andrew—Tailwind Capital Partners LP
Mayer, Ashley—Social+Capital Partnership
Mayer, Christoph—One Peak Partners LLP
Mayer, David—Abingworth Management Ltd
Mayer, Ernst—Sirius Venture Partners GmbH
Mayer, Kelly—Lion Capital LLP
Mayer, Louis—Turning Rock Partners Gp LLC
Mayer, Mika—Morrison & Foerster LLP
Mayer, Peter—Blackstone Group LP

Mayer, Steven—Cerberus Capital Management LP
Mayerson, Frederic—Maywic Select Investments
Mayerson, Frederic—Walnut Group
Mayert, Christian—Allianz Capital Partners GmbH
Mayfield, John—Prairie Capital, L.P.
Mayfield, Paul—Willis Stein & Partners LP
Mayfield, R. Glen—River Cities Capital Fund LP
Mayhew, Nicholas—DSE Investment Services Ltd
Mayn, Robert—Leading Ridge Capital Partners LLC
Maynard, Alan—Darwin Private Equity LLP
Maynard, Deanne—Morrison & Foerster LLP
Maynard, James—Investors Management Corp
Maynard, Jason—Mount Kellett Capital Hong Kong Ltd
Mayne, Kathryn—Horsley Bridge Partners LLC
Mayo, Charles—Mayo Medical Ventures
Mayo, Christopher—Probitas Partners Inc
Mayo, Jordan—Smedvig Capital Ltd
Mayor, Hedley—Baring Private Equity Asia Ltd
Mayrhofer, Thomas—Carlyle Group LP
Mays, Carol—O'Melveny & Myers LLP
Mayweg, Alex—Versant Venture Management, LLC
Mazahreh, Ashraf—First Abu Dhabi Bank PJSC
Mazan, Michael—Birch Hill Equity Partners Management Inc
Mazard, Laurent—Grand Sud Ouest Capital SA
Mazaud, Robert—Vauban Partenaires SA
Mazero, Joyce—Haynes and Boone LLC
Mazul, Ingrid—Clearpoint Investment Partners LLC
Mazza, Giampiero—CVC Capital Partners Ltd
Mazza, Mia—Morrison & Foerster LLP
Mazzalovo, Gerald—Aravis SA
Mazzarella, Robert—Ascent Venture Management Inc
Mazzeo, Michael—Elm Equity Partners LLC
Mazzitelli, Dominick—Trimaran Capital LLC
Mazzoli, Stefano—Oaktree Capital Management LP
Mazzone, Michael—Haynes and Boone LLC
Mazzoni, Robert—Truebridge Capital Partners LLC
Mazzucato, Andrea—21 Centrale Partners SA
Mbaru, Jimnah—East Africa Capital Partners
McAdam, Timothy—Technology Crossover Ventures LP
McAfee, Shelley—Greenridge Investment Partners
McAffee, W. Gage—Asia Pacific Capital (HK) Ltd
McAleer, Bill—Voyager Capital LLC
McAleer, William—Voyager Capital LLC
McAllister, Kevin—Sterling Partners GP LLC
McAlpine, Eric—Blackstone Group LP
McAlpine, Stuart Anderson—Cinven Group Ltd
McAndrew, Joseph—Wall Street Venture Capital Ltd
McAndrew, Marie-Helene—Perella Weinberg Partners LP
McAndrews, Susan—Pantheon Ventures (UK) LLP
McArthur, Lex—Jolimont Capital Pty Ltd
McArthur, Sean—Riverwood Capital Group LLC
McAulay, Mac—Medley Capital LLC
McBee, Barry—University of Texas System
McBlain, John—WinoNA Capital Management LLC
McBride, Jim—Blue Sage Capital LP
McBride, Jim—Duff Ackerman & Goodrich LLC
McBride, Patrick—LEGEND PARTNERS I L P
McCabe, Jim—Morrison & Foerster LLP
McCabe, Joan—Brynwood Partners L.P.
McCabe, Michael—StepStone Group LP

McCabe, Patrick—Morrison & Foerster LLP
McCafferty, Kevin—Catalyst Health And Technology Partners LLC
McCafferty, Kevin—Yellow Wood Partners LLC
McCaffrey, T.—Atar Capital LLC
McCaig, Murray—ArcTern Ventures
McCaleb, William—Atlanta Equity Investors LLC
McCall, Bill—Lyceum Capital
McCall, Edward—Brentwood Associates, L.P.
McCall, Matthew—Jabodon PT Co
McCall, Matthew—Pritzker Group Venture Capital
McCallum, James—Richardson Capital Ltd
McCammon, Mark—Strength Capital Partners LLC
McCammon, Mark—Strength Capital Partners LLC
McCann, Corey—MPM Capital LLC
McCann, Mike—TechColumbus
McCants, Amber—IMB Development Corp
McCarron, Neil—Birch Hill Equity Partners Management Inc
McCarter, Patrick—Carlyle Group LP
McCarthy, Alison—Edge Investments Ltd
McCarthy, Brian—Carlyle Group LP
McCarthy, Courtney—Pamlico Capital Management LP
McCarthy, David—Bain Capital Inc
McCarthy, Edward—River Cities Capital Fund LP
McCarthy, Elizabeth—Alaris Royalty Corp
McCarthy, Jack—A&M Capital Advisors LLC
McCarthy, Jay—SparkLabs
McCarthy, Jeffrey—Guidepost Growth Equity
McCarthy, John—Morrison & Foerster LLP
McCarthy, Kathleen—Blackstone Group LP
McCarthy, Kevin—Kayne Anderson Capital Advisors LP
McCarthy, Kevin—Kian Capital Partners LLC
McCarthy, Kevin—Scorpion Capital Partners LP
McCarthy, Mark—Shorenstein Co LLC
McCarthy, Michael—MGI Holdings Inc
McCarthy, Ryan—Aurora Capital Group Ltd
McCarthy, Ryan—Aurora Resurgence Management Partners LLC
McCarthy, Ryan—Highview Capital LLC
McCarthy, Scott—Alacon Ventures LLC
McCarthy, Scott—Platinum Equity LLC
McCarthy, Shane—Enhanced Capital Partners LLC
McCartney, John—Artesian Capital Management Australia Pty Ltd
McCartney, Terry—Amicus Partners
McCarty, Chris—People Fund LLC
McCarty, John—Star Mountain Capital LLC
McCaw, Brennan—Cyrus Capital Partners LLC
McClain, Richard—High Street Capital
McClean, Rosemarie—Ontario Teachers' Pension Plan
McClellan, David—Heritage Group LLC
McClelland, Spence—NMP Management Corp
McClements, James—Rcf Management LLC
McClintock, Carolyn—Fund Evaluation Group LLC
McClure, David—500 Startups, L.P.
McComas, Debbie—Haynes and Boone LLC
McCombe, Mark—BlackRock Inc
McCombs, David—Haynes and Boone LLC
McComiskey, Niall—Greenbriar Equity Group LLC
McConahey, Steve—Iron Gate Capital LLC
McConnell, Eamonn—Kensington Capital Partners

Ltd
McConnell, Holly–General Catalyst Partners LLC
McConnell, James–Landmark Partners Inc
McConnell, Joe–Castlelake LP
McConnell, Nigel–Motion Equity Partners LLP
McCooe, Matthew–Chart Venture Partners LP
McCooe, Matthew–Connecticut Innovations Inc
McCord, Tony–Antares Capital Corp
McCormack, Andrew–Valar Ventures Management LLC
McCormack, Chris–Acas LLC
McCormack, John–Sentinel Capital Partners LLC
McCormack, R. Stephen–Commonwealth Capital Ventures
McCormack, Scott–Seaport Capital LLC
McCormack, Scott–Seaport Capital LLC
McCormick, Douglas–HCI Equity LLC
McCormick, Douglas–Rho Capital Partners Inc
McCormick, George–TPH Partners LLC
McCormick, Jen–Nystar
McCormick, John–Blackstone Group LP
McCormick, John–HealthpointCapital LLC
McCormick, Mark–Brown Brothers Harriman & Co
McCormick, Pete–Maveron LLC
McCormick, Sarah–Blackstone Group LP
McCormick, Susan–Crosswinds Holdings Inc
McCown, Ben–KRG Capital Management LP
McCown, Ben–Mountaingate Capital Management LP
McCoy, David–RCP Advisors LLC
McCrary, Dennis–Pantheon Ventures (UK) LLP
McCrath, Eric–Morrison & Foerster LLP
McCreadie, Paul–Arboretum Ventures Inc
McCreary, Trace–Barclays Capital Inc
McCrimmon, Daniel–Avrio Capital Management Corp
McCrory, Christopher–50 South Capital Advisors LLC
McCroskey, Nancy–Ata Ventures
McCrossan, Neil–Castlelake LP
McCrystal, Amanda–Pantheon Ventures (UK) LLP
McCue, Matthew–Hopewell Ventures
McCullagh, Paul–Pacific Equity Partners Pty Ltd
McCulloch, A. Donald–Liberty Capital Management Corp
McCulloch, George–Level Equity Management LLC
McCullough, Amy–Trilogy Equity Partners Llc
McCullough, Conor–Beltrae Partners Ltd
McCullough, Michael–Independence Equity Management LLC
McCusker, Charles–Patriot Capital Funding Inc
McCutcheon, Doug–Longview Asset Management Ltd
McDaid, Brian–Spring Capital Partners
McDaniel, Brenda–Meritus Ventures LP
McDaniel, Teresa–Arrowpath Venture Capital
McDermott, Charles–Rockport Capital Partners
McDermott, Chris–OpCapita LLP
McDermott, Christopher–Coller Capital Ltd
McDermott, Dirk–Altira Group LLC
McDermott, James–Bennett Jones Verchere
McDermott, Peter–KSL Capital Partners LLC
McDonagh, Dennis–Blackstone Group LP
McDonagh, William–Walden Venture Capital
McDonald, Devon–Openview Venture Partners LP
McDonald, Diane–Endurance Capital Holdings LLC

McDonald, John–Hyde Park Holdings Inc
McDonald, Lawson–Amicus Partners
McDonald, Mark–Morrison & Foerster LLP
McDonald, Mark–TLcom Capital LLP
McDonald, Robert–Spindletop Capital Management LLC
McDonald, Todd–Horizon Technology Finance Management LLC
McDonald, Warwick–Capital Dynamics Sdn Bhd
McDonnell, Conor–Patriot Financial Partners LP
McDonnell, David–mc3 ventures (FKA: McKenna Venture Accelerator (MVA))
McDonnell, Joseph–Morgan Stanley Alternative Investment Partners LP
McDonnell, Mark–Arch Venture Partners LLC
McDonough, Donald–3i
McDonough, James–Irving Place Capital LLC
McDonough, John–Endurance Capital Holdings LLC
McDonough, Mattia–Blackstone Group LP
McDonough, Scott–Alta Growth Capital SC
McDonough, Tim–Hercules Capital Inc
McDonough, William–Vantagepoint Management Inc
McDowell, David–Morrison & Foerster LLP
McDowell, Derek–Boyne Capital Partners LLC
McDowell, Josh–Weston Presidio Capital
McElhattan, Matt–Chevron Technology Ventures L L C
McElhone, Christopher–Altas Partners LP
McElroy, Megan–North Sky Capital LLC
McEvoy, Bruce–Blackstone Group LP
McEvoy, John–Wayzata Investment Partners LLC
McEwen, Max–Bunker Hill Capital LP
McEwen, Sandra–Ontario Teachers' Pension Plan
McFadden, Christopher–Spectrum Healthcare Fund LLC
McFadden, Mark–CCMP Capital Advisors LP
McFadden, Teri–Norwest Venture Partners
McFarland, Bill–Cornerstone Advisors Inc
McFarland, Josh–Greylock Partners LLC
McFarland, Matt–Broadoak Capital Partners LLC
McFarlane, Anita–First Analysis Corp
McFerran, Michael–Ares Capital Corp
McFetridge, Scott–Hancock Capital Management LLC
McGarry, James–Parallax Capital Partners LLC
McGaughey, Robert–ArcLight Capital Holdings LLC
McGee, Brian–New Water Capital LP
McGee, Jim–Advent International Corp
McGee, Michael–Avrio Capital Management Corp
McGee, Patrick–Brazos Private Equity Partners LLC
McGee, Patrick–MPK Equity Partners LLC
McGee, Robert–United States Growth Funds
McGhee, Michael–Global Infrastructure Holdings
McGibbon, Jason–Bridgepoint Advisers Ltd
McGill, Nathan–Stonehenge Partners Inc
McGill, Paul–Bregal Investments LLP
McGill, Sue–Jolt
McGill, Thomas–Evergreen Pacific Partners GP LLC
McGinley, Jack–Roundtable Healthcare Partners LP
McGinn, Richard–MR Investment Partners
McGinnis, Patrick–AIG Capital Partners Inc
McGinty, Kevin–Peppertree Capital Management Inc
McGlade, Alan–Digital Entertainment Ventures LLC
McGlashan, William–Tpg Growth LLC
McGlinn, Jack–CapitalSouth Partners LLC

McGlynn, Casey–Angel Investors, LP
McGoldrick, Mark–Mount Kellett Capital Hong Kong Ltd
McGonnigle, Glenn–TechOperators LLC
McGovern, David–Marlin Equity Partners LLC
McGovern, Michael–MGI Holdings Inc
McGovern, Michael–Wincove Capital
McGovern, Ryan–Star Mountain Capital LLC
McGovern, Thomas–Morrison & Foerster LLP
McGowan, John–Haynes and Boone LLC
McGowan, Paul–Center For Innovative Technology
McGowan, Paul–Valco Capital Partners Partnership Ltd
McGrady, Colin–Cedar Springs Capital LLC
McGrath, Alexander–Candescent Partners LLC
McGrath, Steve–mc3 ventures (FKA: McKenna Venture Accelerator (MVA))
McGreenery, Mark–Perella Weinberg Partners LP
McGrew, Frank–McNally Capital LLC
McGriff, Deborah–NewSchools Venture Fund
McGrory, Clare–Atairos Management LP
McGruder, Shaun–Palm Beach Capital Management LLC
McGuigan, James–Capital International Inc
McGuinness, Liam–Oaktree Capital Management LP
McGuinness, Steve–Strategic Value Partners LLC
McGuire, Bernard–PCGI LLC
McGuire, James–Morrison & Foerster LLP
McGuire, Meghan–Camden Partners Holdings LLC
McGuire, Terrance–Polaris Venture Partners
McHenry, Maurice–Icc Venture Capital
McHugh, Michael–Lakeside Capital Management LLC
McHugh, Michael–Waller Capital Partners LLC
McIlwain, Matthew–MadroNA Venture Group
McIlwraith, John–Allos Ventures LLC
McInerney, John–Bluff Point Associates Corp
McInerney, Paula–Bluff Point Associates Corp
McInerney, Ryan–Visa Inc
McIntire, John–Nexos Capital Partners
McIntosh, Mark–Portland Private Equity LP
McIntyre, Daniel–Flagship Pioneering
McIntyre, David–Apple Tree Partners
McIntyre, Ryan–Foundry Group LLC
McIntyre, Stephen–Frontline Ventures (GP) Ltd
McIsaac, Zachary–Westerkirk Capital Inc
McJannet, Melissa–Northleaf Capital Partners Ltd
McKay, Chris–Granite Ventures LLC
McKay, Chris–Granite Ventures LLC
McKay, Geoff–Vulcan Inc
McKay, Jaquie–Pelion Venture Partners
McKay, Samuel–Axiom Venture Partners LP
McKean, Joshua–Ironbridge Capital Pty Ltd
McKearn, John–RiverVest Venture Partners LLC
McKee, Andrew–Webster Capital Management LLC
McKee, Elena–Metalmark Capital Holdings LLC
McKee, John–Weston Presidio Capital
McKee, Rhodes–MavenHill Capital
McKee, T. David–Monroe Capital LLC
McKee, William–Graham Partners Inc
McKellar, Peter–Sl Capital Partners Llp
McKelvey, Jim–Cultivation Capital
McKelvey, Jim–Six Thirty
McKelvey, Tom–Gauge Capital LLC
McKelvie, Ian–Sk Capital Partners LP

Pratt's Guide to Private Equity & Venture Capital Sources

McKenna, David—Advent International Corp
McKenna, Kevin—Mckenna Gale Capital Inc
McKenna, Patrick—Ingenious Ventures Lp
McKenna, Stephen—Consonance Capital Partners LP
McKenzie, Paul—Morrison & Foerster LLP
McKenzie, Ryan—Arbor Private Investment Co LLC
McKenzie, Sharon—Norwest Venture Partners
McKeon, Patrick—Blackstone Group LP
McKeone, Brett—Oaktree Capital Management LP
McKibben, Timothy—Ancor Capital Partners
McKiernan, John—Greencoat Capital LLP
McKinlay, Paul—Wellington Financial Lp
McKinlay, Timothy—Navis Management Sdn Bhd
McKinley, Taylor—Mainsail Partners LP
McKinley, Thomas—CHP Management Inc
McKinley, William—Huron Capital Partners LLC
McKinney, Daniel—Nextstage Capital LP
McKinney, Ryan—EXMARQ Capital Partners Inc
McKinney, Terri—American Beacon Advisors Inc
McKinnon, Hull—Altira Group LLC
McKinnon, Sandy—Pentech Ventures LLP
McKissick, Tom—Trust Company of the West
McKittrick, Stacey—Appian Ventures, Inc.
McKnight, Andrew—Fortress Investment Group LLC
McKnight, Margaret—Metropolitan Real Estate Equity Management LLC
McKnight, Steven—PTV Healthcare Capital
McLane, J.—Lime Rock Partners LLC
McLarty, Robb—NGEN Partners LLC
McLaughlin, Christopher—CIVC Partners LP
McLaughlin, James—Lincolnshire Management Inc
McLean, Bart—Cgw Southeast Partners
McLean, Bart—MSouth Equity Partners LLC
McLean, Brian—Mount Yale Asset Management LLC
McLean, David—Sevin Rosen Funds
McLean, Stephen—Arsenal Capital Management LLC
McLean, Stephen—Arsenal Capital Partners LP
McLean, Stephen—Arsenal Capital Partners LP
McLeese, David—First Capital Partners LLC
McLemore, J. Donald—Claritas Capital LLC
McLeod, Christopher—Elm Street Ventures LP
McLeod, Kevin—SWMF Life Science Venture Fund, L.P.
McLoone, Brian—PineBridge Investments LLC
McLoughlin, Andy—Uncork Capital
McLravy, R. Charles—Masi Ltd
McMahan, W. Edwin—Falfurrias Capital Partners LP
McMahon, Frank—American Discovery Capital LLC
McMahon, Jim—West Coast Capital
McMahon, Michael—Jump Capital LLC
McMahon, Michael—Pine Brook Road Partners LLC
McManigal, Mark—Claritas Capital LLC
McManus, Marc—CIVC Partners LP
McManus, Ryan—Colony Capital LLC
McMaster, Pierre—Investissements Novacap Inc
McMinnies, Stuart—3i Group PLC
McMinnies, Stuart—Duke Street Capital Ltd
McMorris, Marc—Carrick Capital Management Company LLC
McMullan, Robert—Blackstone Group LP
McMullan, William—Carlyle Group LP
McMullen, Daniel—Blackstone Group LP
McMurchy, Kevin—Dresner Capital Resources Inc
McNabb, J. Carter—River Cities Capital Fund LP
McNair, James—Corinthian Capital Group LLC

McNair, Mack—Virgo Investment Group LLC
McNally, Nannette—AEA Investors LLC
McNally, Rich—Fundamental Capital Management LLC
McNally, Ryan—Catalyst Investors LLC
McNally, Sean—Prairie Capital, L.P.
McNally, Ward—McNally Capital LLC
McNamara, Brian—Trust Company of the West
McNamara, Bruce—Haynes and Boone LLC
McNamara, David—Innovacorp
McNamee, George—Fa Technology Ventures Corp
McNamee, Roger—Elevation Partners LP
McNaught-Davis, James—Alpina Capital Partners LLP
McNeil, Barry—Haynes and Boone LLC
McNeil, Robert—Sanderling Ventures
McNeill, Philip—Farragut Capital Partners
McNerney, Peter—Thomas Mcnerney and Partners LLC
McNichol, Paul—Pilot Group LP
McNicholas, Kerri—Gainline Capital Partners, L.P.
McNulty, Edward—CVF Capital Partners LLC
McNulty, Martin—Metalmark Capital Holdings LLC
McOran-Campbell, Alexandra—Impact Capital Inc
McParland, Robert—TL Ventures Inc
McPhee, Amie—Sarona Asset Management Inc
McPhee, Ron—Verge Fund
McPhee, Scott—Morrison & Foerster LLP
McPherron, Matthew—Bain Capital Inc
McPherson, George—GEF Management Corp
McPherson, George—GEF Management Corp
McPherson, Mark David—Morrison & Foerster LLP
McPherson, Megan—Resilience Capital Partners LLC
McQuade, Jim—Avalt LLC
McQuail, Tom—Morrison & Foerster LLP
McQueeney, Michael—Summer Street Capital Partners LLC
McQuilkin, David—Asia Pacific Ventures
McQuillan, Kevin—Focus Ventures Ltd
McQuillan, William—Frontline Ventures (GP) Ltd
McReynolds, David—Five Crowns Capital Inc
McTeague, Peter—Fortress Investment Group LLC
McVay, Brent—Northstar Capital LLC
McVey, George—Dynamis Advisors LLC
McVey, Henry—KKR & Co LP
McVicar, Tracey—Cai Capital Management Co
McWhirter, Alex—Finance Yorkshire Ltd
McWilliams, Patrick—Natural Gas Partners
McWilliams, Peter—Sanderling Ventures
McWilliams, Thomas—Court Square Capital Partners LP
McWhinny, Harold—Morrison & Foerster LLP
Mcfall, Samuel—Mill Creek Capital Advisors LLC
Mckelvey, Tom—Susquehanna Private Capital LLC
Mead, Dana—Kleiner Perkins Caufield & Byers LLC
Mead, James—Radius Ventures LLC
Mead, Matthew—National Endowment for Science Technology and the Arts
Mead, Scott—Richmond Park Partners LLP
Mead, Winter—Sapphire Ventures LLC
Meade, Daniel—Farallon Capital Management LLC
Meadow, Scott—Edgewater Funds
Meads, Chris—Pantheon Ventures (UK) LLP
Meagher, Michael—Golub Capital Master Funding LLC
Meakem, Chip—Kodiak Venture Partners LP

Meakem, Chip—Tribeca Venture Partners LLC
Meakem, Glen—Meakem Becker Venture Capital LLC
Meals, Randall—Quicksilver Ventures
Mealy, Mark—Colville Capital LLC
Means, Ron—GroundWork Equity LLC
Means, William—Merion Investment Partners LP
Meany, Ryan—Edgewater Capital Group, Inc.
Mears Kim, Sarah—Symphony Technology Group LLC
Mecane, Joseph—UBS Capital Markets LP
Mecca, John—Morgan Stanley Alternative Investment Partners LP
Mecklenburg, John—Rutberg and Co LLC
Meckler, Alan—Asimov Ventures Management LLC
Medea, Fabrizio—Wise Venture SGR SpA
Medhekar, Ajit—Arch Venture Partners LLC
Medici, Michael—Summit Partners LP
Medici, Michael—Summit Partners LP
Medina, Alejandro—Northgate Capital LLC
Medio, Ashley—Antares Capital Corp
Medlien, Arne—Mallin AS
Meduna, Cyril—Advent Morro Equity Partners Inc
Medved, Joe—Softbank Capital Partners L P
Meehan, Bryan—Greenmont Capital Partners
Meek, Jason—CIT Group Inc
Meek, Jeffrey—Fort Washington Capital
Meeker, Jeffrey—Hamilton Lane Advisors LLC
Meeker, Mary—Kleiner Perkins Caufield & Byers LLC
Meeks, Jonathan—TA Associates Management LP
Meenakshisundaram, T.C.—IDG Ventures India Advisors Pvt Ltd
Meerschman, Pierre-Yves—Orkos Capital SAS
Meeting, Liu Wen—Shaanxi Zenisun Venture Capital Co Ltd
Meeusen, Ron—Cultivian Sandbox Venture Partners LLC
Meeusen, Ronald—Cultivian Ventures LLC
Meeuwissen, Jeroen—Trophas Management BV
Meghji, Nadeem—Blackstone Group LP
Megiddo, Dalia—7 Health Ventures
Megiddo, Dalia—Jerusalem Global Ventures
Megrath, Donald—VectorPoint Ventures
Megret, Dominique—Swisscom AG
Megrue, John—Apax Partners LLP
Mehaignerie, Laurence—Citizen Capital Partenaires SAS
Mehandru, Karan—Trinity Ventures LLP
Mehanna, Omar—First Abu Dhabi Bank PJSC
Mehenny, David—Blackstone Group LP
Mehfar, Alex—AEA Investors LLC
Mehlman, Paul—Landmark Partners Inc
Mehmi, Rajesh—Pavilion Alternatives Group Ltd
Mehra, Anand—Sofinnova Ventures Inc
Mehra, Nipun—Sequoia Capital India
Mehra, Pawan—mc3 ventures (FKA: McKenna Venture Accelerator (MVA))
Mehra, Rajan—Clearstone Venture Management Services LLC
Mehra, Rajan—Nirvana Venture Advisors Pvt Ltd
Mehra, Sarah—Hamilton Lane Advisors LLC
Mehraein, Shadi—EchoVC Partners LLC
Mehraein, Shadi—Rivet Ventures Management LLC
Mehran, Lacey—Veronis Suhler Stevenson LLC
Mehrberg, Peter—Pacific Community Ventures LLC
Mehrgardt, Soenke—MVP Management GmbH
Mehrotra, Rajat—Investcorp Bank BSC

Mehta, Amish–Vector Capital Management LP
Mehta, Anu–Lime Rock Partners LLC
Mehta, Mit–CCMP Capital Advisors LP
Mehta, Nihal–Eniac Ventures LP
Mehta, Nimish–Monta Vista Capital LP
Mehta, Ravi–Starling International Management Ltd (Dubai Branch)
Mehta, Sameet–Granite Hill Capital Partners LLC
Mehta, Shailesh–Granite Hill Capital Partners LLC
Mehta, Shamit–Susquehanna Growth Equity LLC
Mehta, Suhrud–Milbank Tweed Hadley & Mccloy LLP
Mehta, Viral–Yorkville Advisors Management LLC
Mehta, Vishal–Lok Capital
Mei, Jian–Shenzhen Oriental Fortune Capital Co Ltd
Meicler, Philip–Hellman & Friedman LLC
Meidlinger, Karen–Meidlinger Partners LLC
Meier, Bruno–Zuercher Kantonalbank
Meier, Olaf–Callista Holdings GmbH & Co KG
Meier, Seth–Antares Capital Corp
Meier-Ewert, Sebastian–MPM Capital LLC
Meignen, Pierre–Eurazeo Pme Capital SAS
Meijer, Clifford–Thomas Weisel Partners Group Inc
Meijs, Bart–Jacana Partners
Meiler, Martin–Aravis SA
Meilner, John–Bridge Street Capital Partners LLC
Meinel, Wulf–Carlyle Group LP
Meinhardt, Rob–RB Webber and Comapny Inc
Meiring, Paul–Prudential Capital Group LP
Meisberger, Patrick–Deutsche Telekom Strategic Investments
Meise, Florian–ADCURAM Group AG
Meise, Matthias–ADCURAM Group AG
Meisel, Micah–J.H. Whitney & Co LLC
Meisel, Seth–Bain Capital Inc
Meissner, Thomas–Capcellence Mittelstandspartner GmbH
Meister, Gabriel–Morrison & Foerster LLP
Meister, Kenneth–KJM Capital LLC
Meister, Max–Incuray AG
Mejer, Preben–Internet Ventures Scandinavia
Mejia, Alexander–Atlantic-Pacific Capital Inc
Mejia, Franklin–Gramercy Inc
Mejias, Nate–Clearlake Capital Group LP
Meka, M. Krishna–Ventureast
Melanson, Peter–Constitution Capital Partners LLC
Melanson, William–Oaktree Capital Management LP
Melberg, Ole–Energy Ventures AS
Melby, Christian–Reiten & Co AS
Melcher, Patricia–EIV Capital Management Company LLC
Mele, Francesco–ACM Ltd
Melia, Kevin–Boulder Brook Partners LLC
Melia, Kevin–Storm Ventures Inc
Melin de Carvalho e Silva, Luiz Eduardo–Banco Nacional de Desenvolvimento Economico e Social BNDES
Melinder, Kristoffer–Nordic Capital
Melka, Eric–Forbes Alliance Partners Inc
Mellinger, Douglas–Clarion Capital Partners LLC
Mellinger, Paul–Twin Haven Capital Partners LLC
Mellinger, Pierre–AIG Capital Partners Inc
Mello, Glen–Hercules Capital Inc
Mello, Kevin–Bridgescale Partners LP
Mello, Kevin–Four Rivers Partners LP

Mello, Kirsten–Menlo Ventures
Mello, Kirsten–Menlo Ventures
Mellor, Christopher–NVM Pe Ltd
Mellul, David–Varenne Capital Partners SAS
Melmed, Jonathan–Morrison & Foerster LLP
Melmon, Richard–Bullpen Capital LP
Melnick, Michael–CMEA Development Company LLC
Melnik, Jared–KSL Capital Partners LLC
Melnikova, Irena–Burrill & Company
Melo, Roberto–Casaforte Investimentos SA
Meloff, Richard–Ubequity Capital Partners Inc
Melrose, Evan–PTV Healthcare Capital
Melrose, Evan–Spindletop Capital Management LLC
Melton, Brian–Tenaya Capital, Inc.
Melton, Emily–Draper Fisher Jurvetson
Melville, George–T & M Management Services Ltd
Melville, Jordan–T & M Management Services Ltd
Melvin, David–TDR Capital LLP
Melvin, William–Vistech Corp
Melvin-Joswick, Lisa–Novitas Capital LP
Melwani, Prakash–Blackstone Group LP
Melymuka, Matt–PeakSpan Capital LLC
Melzer, Thomas–RiverVest Venture Partners LLC
Memminger, Peter–Milbank Tweed Hadley & Mccloy LLP
Memmo, Nicholas–Vicente Capital Partners LLC
Menachem, Avraham–Jerusalem Global Ventures
Menard, Luc–Desjardins Capital
Menashy, Simon–MMC Ventures Ltd
Mende, Georg–Northgate Capital LLC
Mende, Nora–SFW Capital Partners LLC
Mende, Nora–Tullis Health Investors
Mendel, Steve–Alsop Louie Partners
Mendelow, Daniel–Evercore Inc
Mendelsohn, Arnaud–Initiative & Finance Investissement SA
Mendelsohn, Michael–SV Health Investors LLP
Mendelson, Alan–Axiom Venture Partners LP
Mendelson, Barbara–Morrison & Foerster LLP
Mendelson, Jason–Foundry Group LLC
Menden, Stefan–Menden Ventures Consulting GmbH
Mendez, Alex–Storm Ventures Inc
Mendez, Jesus–Belmert Capital SA
Mendez, Michael–Estancia Capital Management LLC
Mendicino, V. Frank–Access Venture Partners
Mendoza, Carolina–Kapor Capital
Mendoza, Elias–Siris Capital Group LLC
Mendoza, Felipe–Aristos Ventures
Mendu, Raghu–Ventureast
Meneau, Marc–Vatel Capital SAS
Meneely, Jim–White Deer Energy LP
Menell, Mark–Maveron LLC
Meng, Lee Li–Cmia Capital Partners Pte Ltd
Meng, Peter Lai Hock–Tembusu Partners Pte Ltd
Meng, Rock–Vector Capital Management LP
Meng, Tongyi–Beijing Tianxing Chuanglian Investment Management Co., Ltd.
Meng, Viktor–Bscope Partners Inc
Meng, Yubin–Artesian Capital Management Australia Pty Ltd
Menichelli, Vincent–Actua Corp
Menichelli, Vincent–Trestle Ventures
Menietti, Matt–Six Thirty
Menn, Robert–Gemini Investors Inc

Menon, P. K. B.–Indian Steps and Business Incubators Association
Menon, Pyari–Tano Capital LLC
Menon, Ranjith–IDG Ventures India Advisors Pvt Ltd
Menon, Vishnu–Warburg Pincus LLC
Mensink, Ronald–State of Wisconsin Investment Board
Ment, Jason–StepStone Group LP
Menton, David–Synova Capital LLP
Menzer, Michael–White Oak Partners Inc
Meran, Johannes–GxP German Properties AG
Mercadante, Paul–Sumeru Equity Partners, L.P.
Mercader, Luis–Corinthian Capital Group LLC
Merchant, Stephen–Noble Four Partners LLC
Mercier, Charles–Euromezzanine Gestion SaS
Mercke, Andrew–Kentucky Seed Capital Fund
Mere, Philippe–Banexi Ventures Partners SA
Meredith, Debby–Jafco Ventures
Meredith, Ryan–Morgan Stanley Alternative Investment Partners LP
Meretta, Michael–Acas LLC
Mergelkamp, Howard–Mosaik Partners LLC
Merhai, Fazia–Coburn Ventures LLC
Merieux, Alexandre–Merieux Developpement SAS
Merieux, Henry-Louis–MML Capital Partners LLP
Merigold, Catharine–Vista Ventures
Merkel, Stephen–Cantor Ventures
Merlano, Paolo–Iniziativa Gestione Investimenti SGR SpA
Merlino, Robert–Capgen Financial Group LP
Merlo, Gretell–Developing World Markets Inc
Merlo, Mark–Castle Creek Capital LLC
Meron, Frederic–Credit Agricole Corporate and Investment Bank SA
Meron, Gil–FINISTERE VENTURES L L C
Merricks, Ian–Accelerator Academy
Merrifield, Ben–Causeway Capital Partners I LP
Merrifield, Bruce–Mountaineer Capital, L.P.
Merrill, Eliot–Carlyle Group LP
Merrill, H. Josef–Rockwood Equity Partners LLC
Merriman, Michael–Glengary LLC
Merritt, Roy–Oakfield Capital Partners LLP
Merry del Val, Felipe–Bain Capital Inc
Merry del Val, Felipe–L-Gam Advisers LLP
Merry, David–KI Capital Ltd
Mersky, Seth–Onex Corp
Mersten, Robert–EagleTree Capital, LP
Merth, Mike–PFM Capital Inc
Mertsola, Matti–MB Rahastot Oy
Merwin, Bruce–Haynes and Boone LLC
Mesbah, Bardia–Brookstone Partners LLP
Mesches, Ben–Haynes and Boone LLC
Meserve, Nicholas–Main Street Capital Corp
Mesic, Brian–Anthem Venture Partners
Meskin, Jeffrey–Brown Brothers Harriman & Co
Mesnier, Patrice–Cap Decisif Management SAS
Mesquita, Marcelo–Leblon Equities Gestao de Recursos Ltda
Mesrie, John–InReach Ventures LLP
Messa, Anibal–Plataforma Capital Partners Gestao de Investimentos Ltda
Messerly, Trevor–Hamilton Lane Advisors LLC
Messersmith, Michael–Acas LLC
Messick, Diane–Inflection Point Ventures
Messina, Carlo–Intesa Sanpaolo SpA

Messina, Philip–ArcLight Capital Holdings LLC
Mestchersky, Pierre–Industries et Finances Partenaires SAS
Mestiri, Fethi–Africinvest Tunisia SARL
Mestres, Jose–Blackstone Group LP
Metaj, Dee–Indiana University
Metcalf, Mervyn–Global Leisure Partners Llc
Metcalfe, Robert–Polaris Venture Partners
Methot, Andree-Lise–Cycle Capital Management (CCM) Inc
Metter, David–Innisfree Group Ltd
Metz, Forrest–Dev Equity LLC
Metz, Lloyd–ICV Partners LLC
Metz, Travis–Monitor Clipper Partners LLC
Metzer, Einat–GEMINI CAPITAL FUND MGMT LTD
Metzger, Denis–Chequers Capital Partners SA
Metzger, Denis–Chequers Capital Partners SA
Meulle, Guillaume–Iris Capital Management SAS
Meunier, Bertrand–CVC Capital Partners Ltd
Meunier, Pierre-Andre–Celtic House Venture Partners Inc
Meurer, William–BEV Capital
Meurisse, Jean-Bernard–Initiative & Finance Investissement SA
Mew, David–Carlyle Group LP
Meyer Stutz, Myriam–Commission for Technology and Innovation CTI
Meyer, Benjamin–Spire Capital Partners LP
Meyer, Carter–Scientific Health Development
Meyer, Dale–Probitas Partners Inc
Meyer, Dale–Revelstoke Capital Partners LLC
Meyer, David–Morrison & Foerster LLP
Meyer, Edward–Blackstone Group LP
Meyer, Felipe–Nazca Ventures
Meyer, John–Wall Street Venture Capital Ltd
Meyer, Leopold–Florac SAS
Meyer, Marcus–Antares Capital Corp
Meyer, Marcus–Madison Capital Funding LLC
Meyer, Marie-Jeanne–Florac SAS
Meyer, Michael–Route 66 Ventures LLC
Meyer, Philipp–AEA Investors LLC
Meyer, Robert–Paine Schwartz Partners LLC
Meyer, Timothy–Angeles Equity Partners LLC
Meyer, Timothy–Gores Group LLC
Meyer-Schoenherr, Mirko–PAI Partners SAS
Meyering, Paul–Medallion Capital Inc
Meyerrose, Todd–P4G Capital Management LLC
Meyers, Drew–Gryphon Investors Inc
Meyers, Ethan–Westfield Capital Management Company LP
Meyersiek, Axel–Towerbrook Capital Partners LP
Meyohas, Olivier–Blackstone Group LP
Mezzanotte, David–Sun Capital Partners Inc
Mhatre, Nagesh–HALO FUND L P
Mhatre, Ravi–Lightspeed Management Company LLC
Mi, James–Lightspeed Venture Partners China Co Ltd
Mialdea, Elena–Phi Industrial Acquisitions SL
Miao, Lawrence–Olympus Capital Holdings Asia Hong Kong Ltd
Miao, Xingdong–Noble (Beijing) Fund Management Inc
Miao, Yu–Bright Stone Investment Management (Hong Kong) Ltd
Michael, Douglas–OPTrust Private Markets Group

Michael, Joseph–Fort Washington Capital
Michael, Michael–Trident Capital Cybersecurity Fund I LP
Michael, Sheera–TZP Group LLC
Michaeli, Tomer–Carmel Ventures IV Principals Fund LP
Michaelis, Jurgen–Terra Rossa Capital Pty Ltd
Michalchuk, Daniel–Milbank Tweed Hadley & Mccloy LLP
Michalik, Christian–Kinderhook Industries LLC
Michalik, Robert–Kinderhook Industries LLC
Michalow, Markus–Mittelstaendische Beteiligungsgesellschaft Sachsen mbH
Michat, Gilles–Acg Private Equity SA
Michaud, Antoine–Tandem Expansion Fund I LP
Michaud, Brian–LJ2 & Co LLC
Michaud, Jerry–Horizon Technology Finance Management LLC
Michel, Marc–Compound Ventures
Michel, Stephane–Ouest Croissance SAS
Michelman, Jennifer–Graphite Capital Management LLP
Michelson, Greg–Haynes and Boone LLC
Michie, Kirk–Triton Pacific Capital LLC
Michienzi, Steven–Edwards Capital LLC
Michlitsch, Kenneth–Morgan Stanley Alternative Investment Partners LP
Michotey, Nadine–Naxicap Partners SA
Mickelson, Mark–Next Point Capital Corp
Middlemas, George–Apex Venture Partners LLC
Middleton, Fred–Sanderling Ventures
Middleton, Janine–Tasman Capital Investments Australia Pty Ltd
Middleton, Shaun–Dunedin Capital Partners Ltd
Middleton, Thomas–Blackstone Group LP
Midle, Mark–Bain Capital Inc
Miege, Jean-Pierre–FINAPERE Capital SAS
Miehe, Jeff–Windjammer Capital Investors LLC
Miele, Giovanni–Metric Capital Partners LLP
Mielle, Dominique–Canyon Capital Advisors LLC
Mieskonen, Jari–Conor Venture Partners Oy
Migliorino, Robert–W Capital Management LLC
Mihaescu, Mircea–SBT Venture Capital
Mihara, Ryuichi–Mitsui & Co. Global Investment, Ltd.
Mihara, Tsuyoshi–TEL Venture Capital Inc
Mihas, Constantine–GTCR Golder Rauner LLC
Miholich, Peter–Terra Firma Capital Partners Ltd
Mika, Ronald–Sorenson Capital Partners LP
Mikati, Aref–TI Capital
Mikkelsen, Erik–Auxo Management LP
Mikli, Alain–Neo Investment Partners LLP
Mikolic, Dean–P&S Capital doo
Mikuta, Julie–NewSchools Venture Fund
Milakofsky, Adam–Jabodon PT Co
Milanese, Stefano–Finanziaria Regionale Friuli Venezia Giulia SpA
Milbourn, Ian–Notion Capital Partners LLP
Milde, Heiko–IFB Innovationsstarter GmbH
Milder, Don–Crosspoint Venture Partners 2001 LP
Milder, Donald–Versant Venture Management, LLC
Milenthal, Rick–NCT Ventures LLC
Miles, Michael–Forstmann Little & Co
Miles, Vincent–Abingworth Management Ltd
Milgravis, Girts–FlyCap AIFP SIA

Milius, Craig–Brentwood Associates, L.P.
Milius, Jeffrey–Peppertree Capital Management Inc
Milken, Gregory–March Capital Partners GP LLC
Millan, Adrian–Blackstone Group LP
Milledge, Eric–Endeavour Vision SA
Miller, Alex–Athlone International Ltd
Miller, Alison–Wynnchurch Capital Ltd
Miller, Andrew–Copley Equity Partners LLC
Miller, Andrew–Highland Capital Partners LLC
Miller, Anna–Capital E Group
Miller, Anthony–Pacific Alliance Group Ltd
Miller, Arden–Pulse Equity Partners LLC
Miller, Atara–Milbank Tweed Hadley & Mccloy LLP
Miller, Brett–Morrison & Foerster LLP
Miller, Brian–Addison Capital Partners LLC
Miller, Brian–Linden LLC
Miller, Bruce–Investure LLC
Miller, Caroline–Blackstreet Capital Management LLC
Miller, Charles–Blue Wolf Capital Partners LLC
Miller, Christian–Eureka Growth Capital
Miller, Daniel–Roda Group, The
Miller, David–CIVC Partners LP
Miller, David–Relativity Capital LLC
Miller, David–Torch Hill Investment Partners LLC
Miller, Dayton–Boulder Food Group LLC
Miller, Donald–HGGC LLC
Miller, Dorin–SIDER ISRA'EL IYE`UTS KALKALI BE`AM
Miller, Eric–Cerberus Capital Management LP
Miller, Erik–Verus Investment Partners
Miller, Ethan–Antares Capital Corp
Miller, F. Clayton–Stone Arch Capital LLC
Miller, Glenn–Towerbrook Capital Partners LP
Miller, Greg–Magellan Capital Partners Ltd
Miller, Gregg–Haynes and Boone LLC
Miller, Harley–Insight Venture Partners LLC
Miller, Harrison–Summit Partners LP
Miller, J. Sanford–Institutional Venture Partners
Miller, Jack–Focus Acquisition Partners
Miller, James–Allon Therapeutics Inc
Miller, James–NMS Capital Partners
Miller, Jason–Olympus Partners
Miller, Jeb–Jafco Ventures
Miller, Jeff–Pantheon Ventures (UK) LLP
Miller, Jeffrey–Alumni Capital Network Management Co LLC
Miller, Jeffrey–Jordan Company LP
Miller, Jim–Supply Chain Equity Partners
Miller, John–Banyan Capital Advisors LLC
Miller, John-Paul–Blackstone Group LP
Miller, Joseph–Europlay Capital Advisors LLC
Miller, Keith–Goode Partners LLC
Miller, Mark–Blackstone Group LP
Miller, Mark–Huron Capital Partners LLC
Miller, Marlin–Norwich Ventures
Miller, Mary–TSG Consumer Partners, L.P.
Miller, Matthew–Crescent Capital Group LP
Miller, Matthew–Origami Capital Partners, LLC
Miller, Matthew–Spring Bay Companies
Miller, Matthew–Walden Venture Capital
Miller, Michael–Centerfield Capital Partners LP
Miller, Michael–Comspace Development LLC
Miller, Michael–Morrison & Foerster LLP
Miller, Michael–Perseus LLC

Miller, Mike−Liquid 2 Ventures LP
Miller, Morgan−Huntington Capital I
Miller, Morris−Tectonic Ventures LP
Miller, Patricia−Neuberger Berman LLC
Miller, Paul−Empire Investment Holdings LLC
Miller, Piotr−Avallon Sp z o o
Miller, Rainer−SHS Gesellschaft fuer Beteiligungsmanagement mbH
Miller, Randy−Endeavour Capital Inc
Miller, Rich−Shoreline Venture Management, LLC
Miller, Rod−Milbank Tweed Hadley & Mccloy LLP
Miller, Ryan−Lindsay Goldberg & Bessemer LP
Miller, Scott−Bolt Innovation Group LLC
Miller, Steven−Origin Ventures LLC
Miller, Todd−Sterling Partners GP LLC
Miller, Todd−W Capital Management LLC
Miller, Tony−Lemhi Ventures, Inc.
Miller, William−Angeleno Group Investors LLC
Millerchip, Simon−OpCapita LLP
Millet, David−Gemini Investors Inc
Millet, Jean-Pierre−Carlyle Group LP
Millhauser, Greg−Palm Ventures LLC
Millhauser, Lisa−Eureka Growth Capital
Millhouse, David−Millhouse Inc PLC
Milliet, Philippe−Belmert Capital SA
Milligan, David−Bay City Capital LLC
Milligan, Ryan−Chicago Growth Partners LLC
Milligan, Todd−Private Advisors LLC
Milliken, Peter−Tuckerman Capital
Millman, Robert−MPM Capital LLC
Mills, Charles−Lincolnshire Management Inc
Mills, Daniel−Northwater Capital Management Inc
Mills, Gordon−PTV Healthcare Capital
Mills, Jeffrey−Probitas Partners Inc
Mills, Jeffrey−Weston Presidio Capital
Mills, Jim−Vantagepoint Management Inc
Mills, Paul−Atlantic Canada Opportunities Agency
Mills, Peter−@Ventures
Mills, Steven−DCA Capital Partners LP
Mills, Timothy−Sanderling Ventures
Millstein, Lee−Cerberus Capital Management LP
Milne, David−SV Health Investors LLP
Milne, George−Radius Ventures LLC
Milne, Heidi−ArcLight Capital Holdings LLC
Milne, Neil−Abris Capital Partners Sp zoo
Milner, Gordon−Morrison & Foerster LLP
Milone, Kristin−Perseus LLC
Milroy, Thomas−BMO Capital Corp
Milstein, Alan−Blackstone Group LP
Miltenberger, William−Independent Bankers Capital Funds
Milukaite, Indre−StartupHighway
Mims, Cory−ICV Partners LLC
Min, Hur−Wonder Angels
Min, Hyeon Gi−SkyLake Investment & Co
Min, James−Montgomery & Co LLC
Min, Kyung-Min−Neoplux Co Ltd
Min, Peter−CLSA Capital Partners HK Ltd
Min, So-June−406 Ventures LLC
Mina, Alessandro−Sverica International Boston LLC
Mineiro, Duarte−Armilar Venture Partners Sociedade de Capital de Risco SA
Minella, David−Minella Capital Management LLC
Minello, Henry−Permira Advisers LLP
Miner, Jack−COGR Inc
Miner, John−Altien Ventures LLC
Miner, John−Pivotal Investments LLC
Ming, Cui−China Capital Management Ltd
Ming, Yeh−Silicon Valley Bancventures LP
Mingyan, Li−Bohai Sea Region Venture Capital Management Co Ltd
Minick, Scott−Arch Venture Partners LLC
Minihan, Kenneth−Paladin Capital Management LLC
Mink, Jennifer−Morrison & Foerster LLP
Minnehan, Brian−Natural Gas Partners
Minner, John−Pouschine Cook Capital Management LLC
Minner, John−Springboard Venture Fund LLC
Minnich, Kathy Ann−Ben Franklin Technology Partners Of Northeastern PA
Minnick, Mary−Lion Capital LLP
Minocherhomjee, Arda−Chicago Growth Partners LLC
Minor, Jonathan−Investcorp Technology Investments Group
Minor, Stephen−Torch Hill Investment Partners LLC
Minshall, Cathy−Emergence Capital Partners
Mintah, Nathan−8 Miles LLP
Minter, Alison−North Castle Partners LLC
Minton, Greg−Archer Capital Pty Ltd
Mintz, Daniel−Olympus Capital Holdings Asia Hong Kong Ltd
Mintz, Louis−JFLehman & Co
Mir, Abrar−Quadria Capital Investment Advisors Pvt Ltd
Mirabelli, Christopher−Healthcare Ventures LLC
Mirage, Jim−Hawk Capital Partners LP
Miran Khan, Aman−Bpe Unternehmensbeteiligungen GmbH
Miranda, Antonio−LJ2 & Co LLC
Miranda, Gonzalo−Austral Capital
Miranda, Luis Fernando−Salkantay Partners SAC
Miranda, Stan−Partners Capital Investment Group Holdings LLC
Mirani, Hemal−Baml Capital Access Funds Management LLC
Mirani, Hemal−CVC Asia Pacific Ltd
Mirante, Giuseppe−Bayside Capital Inc
Mirchandani, Sasha−Kae Capital
Mirheydar, Amir−Trivest Partners LP
Mirmira, Srinivas−Redshift Ventures Management Inc
Mirra, Anthony−Court Square Capital Partners LP
Mischianti, Louis−Olympus Partners
Misfeldt, Dayton−Bay City Capital LLC
Mishima, Tetsuya−Watervein Partners KK
Mishkin, Maxwell−Water Street Healthcare Partners LLC
Mishra, Anupam−Hellman & Friedman LLC
Mishra, Deep−Everstone Capital Management, Ltd.
Mishra, Dev−SV Health Investors LLP
Mishra, Sunil−New Mountain Capital I LLC
Misir, Mahendra−Palisade Capital Management LLC
Miskovsky, Jan−janom sro
Misra, Divya−Carlyle Group LP
Misra, Harsha−New Silk Route Partners, LLC
Misra, Kabir−SoftBank China & India Holdings Ltd
Misra, Kabir−Softbank Capital Partners L P
Misra, Keshav−Baring Private Equity Asia Ltd
Mistry, Sanjay−Quaker Partners Management LP
Miszerak, Martin−DVR Capital SpA
Mital, Neeraj−Evercore Inc
Mitchell, Andrew−Ironbridge Equity Partners Management Ltd
Mitchell, Andrew−NF Holdings Ltd
Mitchell, Andrew−ZIG Capital
Mitchell, Christopher−Spectrum Equity Investors LP
Mitchell, Clay−Fall Line Capital GP LLC
Mitchell, Daniel−Sequel Venture Partners
Mitchell, David−Transportation Resource Partners LP
Mitchell, Heather−Carlyle Group LP
Mitchell, Ivar−Andlinger & Co Inc
Mitchell, John−Audax Group, Inc.
Mitchell, Katherine−Scale Venture Partners
Mitchell, Kevin−Lariat Partners LP
Mitchell, Langdon−Siguler Guff & Company LP
Mitchell, Lee−Thoma Bravo LLC
Mitchell, Mark−Emerald Development Managers LP
Mitchell, Steven−Argonaut Private Equity LLC
Mitchell, Stuart−Ironbridge Capital Pty Ltd
Mitchell, Timothy−Ziff Brothers Investments LLC
Mitchell, Tom−TDR Capital LLP
Mitjavile, Regis−Ife Mezzanine SARL
Mitnik-Gankin, Luba−GEN3 Partners, Inc.
Mitomi, Fuyuo−Morrison & Foerster LLP
Mitra, Sanjeet−Sumeru Equity Partners, L.P.
Mitra, Subrata−Accel India Venture Fund
Mitrofanov, Sergei−Pulsar Ecosystem LLC
Mitsui, Maki−Carlyle Group LP
Mitsushima, Takahiro−NTT Finance Corp
Mittal, Prapti−Terawatt Ventures LLC
Mittendorff, Robert−Norwest Venture Partners
Mittman, Lawrence−Haynes and Boone LLC
Mitzschke, Jonas−Oaktree Capital Management LP
Miura-Ko, Ann−Floodgate Fund, L.P.
Mix, Harald−Altor Equity Partners AB
Mixer, David−Point Judith Capital
Mixon, Malachi−Resilience Capital Partners LLC
Miyake, Suguru−Japan Private Equity Co Ltd
Miyama, Kazuhiko−Global Brain Corp
Miyasaki, Alan−Blackstone Group LP
Miyasaki, Clarke−Kickstart Seed Fund LP
Miyata, Takuya−Scrum Ventures LLC
Miyazato, Shigeo−OGI Venture Capital Co Ltd
Miyazawa, Yusuke−Global Brain Corp
Mizandjian, Bernard−Natixis Private Equity SA
Mizeur, Mike−CCM Investment Advisers LLC
Mizoguchi, Naoto−Active Investment Partners
Mizrachi, Orit−Carlyle Group LP
Mizrahi, Gabriel−Northgate Capital LLC
Mizrahi, Jake−Golden Gate Capital Inc
Mizrahi, Jake−Oval Partners
Mizrahi, Jeffrey−Sand Oak Capital Partners LLC
Mizukami, Kei−CVC Asia Pacific Ltd
Mizukami, Kei−CVC Capital Partners Ltd
Mizukawa, Atsuhiko−Sumitomo Mitsui Trust Investment Co Ltd
Mizuno, Hiromichi−Coller Capital Ltd
Mizuno, Hiroyuki−Innovation Engine Inc
Mizutani, Kensaku−Integral Corp
Mkhari, Ipeleng−Motseng Investment Holdings (Pty) Ltd
Mkwanazi, Nhlanganiso−Medu Capital(Pty)Ltd
Mlavsky, Ed−GEMINI CAPITAL FUND MGMT LTD

Mo, Monita—Ascend Capital Partners
Moalemzadeh, Shary—Carlyle Group LP
Moalla, Nejib—Avenir SICAR
Moatti, Olivier—Abenex Capital SAS
Moatti, SC—Mighty Capital Management LLC
Mochizuki, Keisuke—Morrison & Foerster LLP
Mochizuki, Tomohiro—MBK Partners Inc
Mock, David—Gmg Capital Partners LP
Mock, Lawrence—Navigation Capital Partners Inc
Modahl, Joachim—Hitecvision AS
Modak, Kaushik—Rabo India Finance Ltd
Modena, Astorre—Terra Venture Partners
Modersitzki, Blake—Pelion Venture Partners
Modig, Charlotta—Volvo Group Venture Capital Corp
Mody, Minesh—Michigan Economic Development Corp
Moe, Benjamin—Osceola Capital Management LLC
Moe, Bryce—Skypoint Ventures LLC
Moelchert, Louis—Private Advisors LLC
Moeller, Thomas—BioMedPartners AG
Moens, Marc—Pentech Ventures LLP
Moerel, Wouter—AlpInvest Partners BV
Moerschel, Gregory—Beecken Petty O'Keefe & Company LLC
Moessner, Juergen—Global Capital Finance
Moffat, Kim—Sterling Partners GP LLC
Moffat, Mark—Blackstone Group LP
Moffat, Rob—Balderton Capital LLP
Mogford, John—First Reserve Corp
Mogge, Christian—BC Partners LLP
Mogoba, Mokgome—Vantage Venture Partners
Mogoroase, Cristina—Axxess Capital Partners SA
Mohammadioun, Said—TechOperators LLC
Mohammed, Idris—Development Partners International LLP
Mohammed, Osama—Khatif Holding Company KSC
Mohammed, Riyadh—Auldbrass Partners LP
Mohammed, Sadiq—ARM Capital Partners
Mohan, Ravi—Shasta Ventures LP
Mohanty, Prayag—IvyCap Ventures Advisors Pvt Ltd
Mohaupt, Verena—Findos Investor GmbH
Mohd Ali, Nur Baidzurah—Malaysia Venture Capital Management Bhd
Mohd Yunos, Shahril Anwar—Kumpulan Modal Perdana Sdn Bhd
Mohnot, Sheel—500 Startups, L.P.
Mohr, Doug—Sutter Hill Ventures
Mohr, Lawrence—RETRO VENTURE PARTNERS L P
Mohra, Vivek—First Abu Dhabi Bank PJSC
Mohri, Robert—Hypoid Partners
Mohta, Asheesh—Blackstone Group LP
Mohta, Nikhil—Carlyle Group LP
Moilanen, Mikko—Access Capital Partners SA
Moinet, Edouard—Cathay Capital Private Equity SAS
Moitra, Shamik—Aditya Birla Capital Advisors Pvt Ltd
Moje, Anja—Beaufort Capital GmbH
Mok, Ku Kay—Gobi Partners
Mok, Martin—EQT Funds Management Ltd
Mok, Weng Sun—Affinity Equity Partners HK Ltd
Molcho, Avi—Forbion Capital Partners
Moldavsky, Diana—500 Startups, L.P.
Moldow, Charles—Foundation Capital LLC
Moldt, Peter—Novo Holdings A/S
Molenaar, Boudewijn—Gilde Buy Out Partners BV
Molenaar, Boudewijn—Gilde Investment Management BV
Moley, Andrew—Lightspeed Management Company LLC
Molin, Marit—Frontier Equities VC LLC
Molina, Jose Luis—Altamar Private Equity SGIIC SAU
Molinari, Luca—Warburg Pincus LLC
Molinaro, Samuel—Progress Investment Management Co
Molke, Laurence—ArcLight Capital Holdings LLC
Moll, C. David—Infield Capital LLC
Moller, Christian—SE Blue Holding A/S
Moller, Christopher—Devon Park Bioventures LP
Moller, Mads—Nes Partner Holding ApS
Moller, Peter—FSN Capital Partners AS
Molloy, Richard—Gordon River Capital
Molner, John—Brown Brothers Harriman & Co
Molner, Phillip—Primus Capital
Moloto, Merafe—Motseng Investment Holdings (Pty) Ltd
Momin, Samad—Global Infrastructure Holdings
Momsen, Jon-Paul—Harbert Management Corp
Momsen, Robert—Medventure Associates
Monach, Andrew—Morrison & Foerster LLP
Monaco, Peter—Raptor Capital Management LP
Monaghan, Arthur—Granite Equity Partners LLC
Monagle, William—Z Capital HF Adviser LLC
Monahan, David—Colony Capital LLC
Monahan, Lee—Harren Equity Partners
Monat, Jeffrey—Merida Capital Partners LLC
Moncada, Morgan—DoubleRock LLC
Moncrief, L. Ray—Meritus Ventures LP
Mondre, Gregory—Silver Lake Partners LP
Money, Aaron—Friedman Fleischer & Lowe Cap Ptnrs L P
Money-Kyrle, Nicholas—Steadfast Capital GmbH
Monfrini, Julia—Monitor Clipper Partners LLC
Monfront, Regis—Credit Agricole Corporate and Investment Bank SA
Monga, Rajat—Yes Bank Ltd
Mongiardo, Eve—Irving Place Capital LLC
Monis, Marco—21 Centrale Partners SA
Moniz, Michael—Paladin Capital Management LLC
Monmousseau, Stephane—Pragma Capital SA
Monnier, Edward—Corridor Capital LLC
Monnot, Philippe—Gemmes Venture SA
Monribot, Mathias—Petit Poucet SAS
Monroe, Garth—Capital Royalty LP
Monroe, Mike—Blackeagle Partners Fund L P
Monroe, Richard—Pt Capital LLC
Monsalve, Sergio—Norwest Venture Partners
Monsour, Trey—Haynes and Boone LLC
Montagne, Paul—BrightVentures
Montana, Joe—Liquid 2 Ventures LP
Monteiro Chibante, Fernando Marcondes—Vinci Equities Gestora de Recursos Ltda
Montemurro, Jason—ACM Ltd
Montgomery, H. DuBose—Menlo Ventures
Montgomery, H. Dubose—Menlo Ventures
Montgomery, Jamie—March Capital Partners GP LLC
Montgomery, John—Westfield Capital Management Company LP
Montgomery, Michael—Montgomery & Co LLC
Montgomery, Richard—Enhanced Capital Partners LLC
Montoya, Mario—Windforce Ventures LLC
Mony, Vijay—Atar Capital LLC
Moock, Hans—HQ Equita GmbH
Moody, Brian—Solace Capital Partners LLC
Moody, Chris—Foundry Group LLC
Moody, Steve—Calvert Social Venture Partners, L.P.
Moomjy, Alex—Blackstone Group LP
Moon, Bernard—SparkLabs
Moon, Greg—Softbank Ventures Korea Inc
Moon, Michael—Calera Capital Management Inc
Mooney, Kyle—Morrison & Foerster LLP
Mooney, Sean—SFW Capital Partners LLC
Moons, Raf—BNP Paribas Fortis Private Equity Growth NV
Moor, Markus—Emerald Technology Ventures AG
Moore Baker, Kathryn—Reiten & Co AS
Moore, Brendan—Eos Partners LP
Moore, Bud—Valesco Industries Inc
Moore, Charles—Jacobson Partners
Moore, Charles—Trilantic Capital Management LP
Moore, Charles—Trilantic Capital Management LP
Moore, Chris—Redpoint Ventures
Moore, Church—Kelso & Company LP
Moore, Craig—Acas LLC
Moore, Crystal—Freeman Group LLC
Moore, Darla—Goff Capital Partners, L.P.
Moore, Dennis—Odyssey Investment Partners LLC
Moore, Doug—Pavilion Alternatives Group Ltd
Moore, Duncan—East West Capital Partners Pte Ltd
Moore, Geoffrey—Mohr Davidow Ventures
Moore, Geoffrey—Wildcat Venture Partners LLC
Moore, Greg—Bain Capital Inc
Moore, James—Platte River Ventures LLC
Moore, Jeff—Federal Economic Development Agency for Southern Ontario
Moore, Jeffrey—MP Healthcare Venture Management Inc
Moore, John—Marshall Ventures
Moore, John—Morrison & Foerster LLP
Moore, Katie—Hamilton Lane Advisors LLC
Moore, Kenneth—First Reserve Corp
Moore, Mark—Bain Capital Inc
Moore, Mark—Horsley Bridge Partners LLC
Moore, Michael—Maverick Capital Ltd
Moore, Nicholas—Macquarie Capital Alliance Management Pty Ltd
Moore, Nicholas—Macquarie Group Ltd
Moore, Nicholas—Macquarie Investment Management Ltd
Moore, Ovetta—Maryland Department of Business and Economic Development
Moore, Patrick—Trust Company of the West
Moore, Richard—WGL Holdings Inc
Moore, Robert Jay—Milbank Tweed Hadley & Mccloy LLP
Moore, Ryan—Accomplice LLC
Moore, Scott—Morrison & Foerster LLP
Moore, Simon—Carlyle Group LP
Moore, Stephen—Thayer Ventures
Moore, Steven—Brentwood Associates, L.P.
Moore, Steven—Brentwood Venture Capital
Moore, Taylor—Norwest Equity Partners
Moore, Vernon Francis—Asia Mezzanine Capital Advisers Ltd
Moores, Robert—Bridgepoint Advisers Ltd
Moorhead, Alex—Tandem Expansion Fund I LP

Moorhead, John—Eight Roads Ventures Europe
Moorin, Jay—ProQuest Investments
Moorjani, Dinesh—Comcast Ventures
Moorman, Lew—Scaleworks Inc
Moorse, Dan—HCI Equity LLC
Moose, Lisa—Third Security LLC
Moosholzer, Josef—TVM Capital GmbH
Mora, Frank—Huntington Capital I
Moragne, John—Trident Capital
Moral, Mauricio—Northgate Capital LLC
Morales, Jeff—Newstone Capital Partners LLC
Morali, Olivier—Bregal Capital LLP
Morali, Olivier—Bregal Investments LLP
Morali-Efinowicz, Monika—Advent International Corp
Moraly, Dana—Clearstone Venture Management Services LLC
Moraly, Dana—March Capital Partners GP LLC
Moran, Garrett—Blackstone Group LP
Moran, John—Overseas Private Investment Corp
Moran, John—Passport Capital LLC
Moran, Matt—Wind Point Advisors LLC
Moran, Michael—Brockway Moran & Partners Inc
Moran, Michael—Linsalata Capital Partners Inc
Moran, Peter—Doll Capital Management Inc
Moran, Richard—Trivest Partners LP
Morana, Stephen—Octopus Ventures Ltd
Morand, Pat—Open Prairie Ventures
Morandi, Nik—Pantheon Ventures (UK) LLP
Morathi, Raisibe—Identity Capital Partners (Pty) Ltd
Morck, Anders—Investment Latour AB
Mordehachvili, Paulo—Axxon Group Servicos De Consultoria E Assessoria Ltda
More, Anand—Bain Capital Inc
More, Avery—Menlo Ventures
More, Avery—Menlo Ventures
More, Robert—Alta Partners
Moreau, Bernard—Eurefi SA
Moreau, Olivier—Orium SAS
Moreau, Richard—Verus Investment Partners
Moredock, Jeffrey—CenterOak Partners LLC
Moreira Assad, Nelson—Bozano Agente Autonomo de Investimentos Ltda
Moreland, Ira—ICV Partners LLC
Moren, Arne—Ackra Invest AB
Moreno Trevino, Luis—Haynes and Boone LLC
Moreno, Michelle—Dresner Capital Resources Inc
Morenstein, Scott—Valence Life Sciences LLC
Moret, Didier—Sofimac Innovation SAS
Morff, Robert—Hatteras Venture Partners
Morfitt, Brian—Frazier Management LLC
Morgan, Bob—Northern Trust Corp
Morgan, David—JC Flowers & Co LLC
Morgan, Eric—National City Equity Partners Inc
Morgan, Evan—Revolution
Morgan, Frank—Coller Capital Ltd
Morgan, George—Ridgemont Partners Management LLC
Morgan, Howard—First Round Capital
Morgan, James—Jacobson Partners
Morgan, Jay—StepStone Group LP
Morgan, Joe—Montgomery & Co LLC
Morgan, John—Pantheon Ventures (UK) LLP
Morgan, Kelsey—Nex Cubed LLC
Morgan, Kyle—W Capital Management LLC

Morgan, Michael—Caltius Equity Partners
Morgan, Neil—Global Mining Capital Corp
Morgan, Raymond—Actua Corp
Morgan, Ryan—New World Angels, Inc.
Morgan, Steve—EXMARQ Capital Partners Inc
Morgan, Thomas—New Mountain Capital I LLC
Morgan, Tony—Onex Corp
Morgan, Tyson—Northport Investments
Morgan, Wanda—MSouth Equity Partners LLC
Morgenstein, Morris—Capital Resource Company of Connecticut
Morgenthal, Lawrence—Bank of America Capital Advisors (BACA)
Morgenthaler, Gary—Morgenthaler Ventures
Morgon, Virginie—Eurazeo SA
Morgunov, Max—Oceanic Partners Inc
Mori, Takeshi—Zenshin Capital Management
Morimoto, Bruce—Allon Therapeutics Inc
Morimoto, Taro—Coller Capital Ltd
Morin, Genevieve—Fondaction Csn
Morin, Kirsten—FLAG Capital Management LLC
Morita, Norberto—Southern Cross Capital Management SA
Moritz, J. Kenneth—Stonewood Capital Management Inc
Moritz, Jens—EQT Funds Management Ltd
Moriuchi, Takashi—Estancia Capital Management LLC
Moriya, Mitsuo—Toho Bank Ltd
Morkel, William—GroFin Capital (Pty) Ltd
Morkva, Oleg—IK Ineko PAT
Morland, Miles—Development Partners International LLP
Morley, Andrew—Montis Capital LLC
Morley, David—Actis LLP
Morndal, Staffan—Verdane Capital Advisors AS
Morningstar, John—Wellspring Capital Management LLC
Mornington, Arthur—Oakley Capital Ltd
Moro, Gary—Horizon Technology Finance Management LLC
Morokoff, Bill—Axioma Ventures LLC
Morphis, Rock—Heritage Group LLC
Morrell, Steven—Teknoinvest AS
Morrill, Nicholas—Rutland Partners LLP
Morris, Ben—Wesley Clover International Corporation
Morris, Bobby—Boxwood Capital Partners LLC
Morris, Brett—Techaccel LLC
Morris, Charles—Integral Capital Partners
Morris, Charlotte—Pantheon Ventures (UK) LLP
Morris, Daniel—Crossroads Liquidating Trust
Morris, David—Oracle Capital Partners LLC
Morris, David—Pine Street Capital Partners LP
Morris, Dylan—Charles River Ventures LLC
Morris, Edna—Axum Capital Partners LLC
Morris, Erik—Roark Capital Group Inc
Morris, Frederic—Brook Venture Partners LLC
Morris, Ian—Blackstone Group LP
Morris, J. Timothy—Proprium Capital Partners LP
Morris, John—Baml Capital Access Funds Management LLC
Morris, Jonathan—Wolfensohn & Company LLC
Morris, Mark—Blue Point Capital Partners LP
Morris, Mark—Morgan Creek Capital Management LLC

Morris, Michael—CREATION CAPITAL L L C
Morris, Paul—F&C Equity Partners PLC
Morris, Robert—Olympus Partners
Morris, Robert—Y Combinator Inc
Morris, Scott—First Capital Ventures LLC
Morris, Tim—BC General Partners LLC
Morris, Tim—Morris Capital Management LLC
Morrisett, Mike—Wearable World Inc
Morrison, Alastair—Standard Chartered Private Equity Ltd
Morrison, Andrew—Morrison & Foerster LLP
Morrison, Bill—Haynes and Boone LLC
Morrison, Briggs—MPM Capital LLC
Morrison, D. Neal—Pamlico Capital Management LP
Morrison, David—Canaccord Genuity Group Inc
Morrison, David—Lee Equity Partners LLC
Morrison, Helane—Hall Capital Partners LLC
Morrison, John—Goldner Hawn Johnson & Morrison Inc
Morrison, John—Goldner Hawn Johnson & Morrison Inc
Morrison, Thomas—Blackstone Group LP
Morrison, Tucker—Headwaters BD LLC
Morriss, Nicholas—EMAlternatives LLC
Morrissette, Mark—North Atlantic Capital
Morrissey, Peter—W R Hambrecht & Co L L C
Morrone, Jonathan—Wall Street Venture Capital Ltd
Morrow, Bradley—CAMBRIDGE CAPITAL PARTNERS L L C
Morse, David—Neuberger Berman LLC
Morse, Kelly—Greenline Ventures LLC
Morse, Robert—Oak Hill Capital Management Inc
Morse, Thomas—Liberty Ventures Inc
Morser, Christopher—Morgan Stanley Alternative Investment Partners LP
Morteani, Arne—ETF Partners LLP
Mortensen, Mikael—Scandinavian Life Science Venture
Mortimer, Michael—GHO Capital Partners LLP
Morton, Jenny—AG BD LLC
Morton, John—Overseas Private Investment Corp
Morton, William—WL Ross & Co LLC
Mosca, Franco—Idea Capital Funds Societa di Gestione del Risparmio SpA
Mosca, Guido—TRG Management LP
Moscardelli, Justin—Westfield Capital Management Company LP
Moscarella, John Paul—Emerging Energy & Environment LLC
Moscatelli, Lino—Como Venture Srl
Moscovitch, Lee—Zouk Capital LLP
Moseley, Allen—NMP Management Corp
Moser, M. Randy—Aurora Capital Group Ltd
Moses, Joshua—First Analysis Corp
Moses, Oliver—MTS Health Partners LP
Moskowitz, Lara—Cove Hill Partners LLC
Mosley, Emmett—JZ Capital Partners Ltd
Mosley, I. Sigmund—Imlay Investments
Mosoiu, Razvan—Mackenzie Capital, Srl.
Moss, Adam—Carlyle Group LP
Moss, Alex—Doughty Hanson and Co.
Moss, Amy Christine—Haynes and Boone LLC
Moss, Ben—Greenridge Investment Partners
Moss, Dan—Avante Mezzanine Inc

Moss, Dan–Updata Partners
Moss, Edwin–Hilltop Private Capital LLC
Moss, Edwin–Lincolnshire Management Inc
Moss, Malcolm–Beringea LLC
Moss, Nigel–Lloyds Development Capital (Holdings) Ltd
Moss, Rick–Better Ventures LLC
Moss, Rick–Hub Ventures
Mossler, Fred–VegasTechFund
Mosteller, Bob–Silver Creek Ventures Corp
Mostrom, Ryan–Redwood Capital Investments LLC
Motamedi, Amir–Onex Corp
Motechin, Brian–ZMC
Mothersele, Laura–Lightyear Capital LLC
Motiwala, Quaeed–Draper Nexus Venture Partners LLC
Motley, Joel–Delany Capital Management Corp
Motschmann, Cecil–MIG Verwaltungs AG
Motschmann, Michael–Alfred Wieder AG
Motschmann, Michael–MIG Verwaltungs AG
Mott, David–New Enterprise Associates Inc
Mott, Edward–Oxford Capital Partners Holdings Ltd
Motte, Adrien–Hellman & Friedman LLC
Motte, Alexandre–Ardian France SA
Motte, Olivier–Nord Capital Partenaires SAS
Motzfeldt, Christian–VAEKSTFONDEN
Moua, Chong–Boathouse Capital
Mougenot, Gilles–Argos Soditic SA
Moulton, Eben–Seacoast Capital
Moulton, Jonathan–Anglo Scientific Ltd
Mounce, Melissa–Baird Capital
Mount, David–Kleiner Perkins Caufield & Byers LLC
Mountjoy, Catherine–Pavilion Alternatives Group Ltd
Moura, Leonidas–I5 Empresas Consultoria e Participacoes Ltda
Mouradian, Rudolf–Qualium Investissement SAS
Moustafa, Yaser–NBK Capital Partners Ltd
Mouterde, Patrick–PAI Partners SAS
Movassate, Mojan–500 Startups, L.P.
Mowinckel, John–Investindustrial Services Ltd
Mowlem, Michael–LGV Capital Ltd
Moya, Josep Maria–Delta Partners FZ LLC
Moya-Angeler, Antonio–Advent International Corp
Moye, Andrew–AAC CAPITAL PARTNERS
Moynihan, Cheryl–Axum Capital Partners LLC
Moynihan, Chester–Allegro Funds Pty Ltd
Moyo, Nkosana–Batanai Capital Finance Pvt Ltd
Moyrand, Jacques–Eurekap SAS
Mozingo, Jason–Centerbridge Partners LP
Mpofu, Ndaba–Batanai Capital Finance Pvt Ltd
Mrozek, Therese–Weston Presidio Capital
Mruck, Christian–Advent International Corp
Muckel, Kent–Perella Weinberg Partners LP
Mudge, Jeffrey–Shoreview Industries
Mudryy, Kieran–4BIO Ventures Management Ltd
Muecke, Will–CoreCo Holdings LLC
Muehlenbeck, Frank–Calibrium Ltd
Muelder, Philip–Permira Advisers LLP
Mueller, Andreas–Leonardo Venture GmbH & Co KGaA
Mueller, Anneliese–GEF Management Corp
Mueller, Christoph–Shaw Kwei & Partners
Mueller, Florian–Online Solutions Ventures GmbH
Mueller, Frank–DPE Deutsche Private Equity GmbH
Mueller, Guenther–Milestone Venture Capital GmbH
Mueller, Hans-Ulrich–Partners Group Holding AG
Mueller, Herbert–S Kap Unternehmensbeteiligungs GmbH & Co KG
Mueller, Jason–Saw Mill Capital LLC
Mueller, John–CapitalWorks LLC
Mueller, Kurt–Target Partners GmbH
Mufuruki, Ali–East Africa Capital Partners
Mugford, Kristin–Bain Capital Inc
Muggia, William–Westfield Capital Management Company LP
Mugnai, Andrea–PM & Partners SpA
Muhammad, Muhsin–Axum Capital Partners LLC
Muhammedi, Zeshan–Fundrx Inc
Muhback, Andrew David–Morrison & Foerster LLP
Muhl, Dirk–CVC Capital Partners Ltd
Muhlbeier, Jack–Jasper Ridge Partners LP
Muhtadie, Fayez–Stone Point Capital LLC
Muijrers, Joep–Life Sciences Partners BV
Muijser, Floris–Egeria BV
Muilwijk, Rik–Navis Management Sdn Bhd
Muir, Craig–Third Rock Ventures LLC
Muir, Jeffrey–Fulcrum Equity Partners
Muizers, Tom–Gilde Buy Out Partners BV
Mukherjee, Amit–New Enterprise Associates Inc
Mukherjee, Anjan–Blackstone Group LP
Mukherjee, Debneel–Tholons Capital
Mukherjee, Debneel–WaveMaker Labs Pte Ltd
Mukherjee, S. Brian–Periscope Equity LLC
Mukherjee, Shomik–Actis LLP
Mukim, Rahul–Olympus Capital Holdings Asia Hong Kong Ltd
Mukohira, Tak–MP Healthcare Venture Management Inc
Mulani, Sunil–Jasper Ridge Partners LP
Mulas, Alessandro–CDP Equity SpA
Mulcahey, Brennan–Brook Venture Partners LLC
Mulcahy, Marcos–Southern Cross Capital Management SA
Mulcare, Robert–New Mountain Capital I LLC
Mulchandani, Nikhil–IXORA Ventures Pvt Ltd
Mulchandani, Sunder–IXORA Ventures Pvt Ltd
Mulder, Geert-Jan–Forbion Capital Partners
Mulder, Nikole–Bluestem Capital Partners
Muldoon, Kacey–NXT Ventures Fund 1 LLC
Mulgan, Geoff–National Endowment for Science Technology and the Arts
Mulherin, Harbert–West Oak Capital LLC
Mulherin, Steve–Polar Capital Investments
Mulla-Hussein, Nawal–Global Investment House KSCC
Mullany, Michael–Jafco Ventures
Mullen, Dave–Graycliff Partners LP
Mullen, David–Highland West Capital Ltd
Mullen, Fergal–Highland Capital Partners LLC
Mullen, Geoffrey–Morgan Stanley Alternative Investment Partners LP
Mullen, James–Morrison & Foerster LLP
Mullen, Jim–LIGHTHOUSE VENTURES L L C
Mullen, Justin–Merida Capital Partners LLC
Mullen, Kurt–G8 Capital LLC
Mullen, Mark–Double M Partners LP
Mullen, Terrence–Arsenal Capital Management LLC
Mullen, Terrence–Arsenal Capital Partners LP
Mullen, Terrence–Arsenal Capital Partners LP
Muller, Ken–Morrison & Foerster LLP
Muller, Paul–Hall Capital Partners LLC
Mullett, Conor–Lightview Capital
Mulliez, Jerome–Creadev SAS
Mulligan, Gregory–Bay Capital Investment Partners LLC
Mulligan, William–Primus Capital
Mullin, M. Hadley–TSG Consumer Partners, L.P.
Mullin, Mark–Haynes and Boone LLC
Mullins, Giny–Linx Partners LLC
Mullins, Jacob–Shasta Ventures LP
Mullins, Paul–Canada Pension Plan Investment Board
Mullis, Karen–RiverVest Venture Partners LLC
Mulloy, Corey–Highland Capital Partners LLC
Mulloy, Corey–Highland Capital Partners LLC
Mulloy, Jennifer–TA Associates Management LP
Mulrow, William–Blackstone Group LP
Mulshine, Christopher–Lazard Australia Private Equity
Multani, Arneek–Trident Capital
Mulvaney, Brian–Headwaters BD LLC
Mulvee, Conner–Welsh Carson Anderson & Stowe
Mulvey, Brian–Investor Growth Capital AB
Mulvey, Brian–PeakSpan Capital LLC
Mumford, Hugh–Electra Private Equity Plc
Mumford, John–Crosspoint Venture Partners 2001 LP
Mumford, Kevin–Elcano Capital LP
Muminoglu, Rana–Elevar Equity Advisors Pvt Ltd
Mumma, Mitchell–Intersouth Partners
Munafo, Christian–Thomas Weisel Partners Group Inc
Munce, Claudia–International Business Machines Corp
Mundassery, Appu–Bayside Capital Inc
Mundheim, Peter–Stone Point Capital LLC
Mundie, Don–Delta Capital Management LLC
Mundkur, Yatin–Artiman Management LLC
Mundt, Jason–Siguler Guff & Company LP
Mundt, Kevin–Vestar Capital Partners Inc
Munfa, Marc–Silversmith Capital Partners LLC
Muniz, Stephen–Puretech Ventures
Munjal, Salil–Yaletown Venture Partners
Munk, Anthony–Onex Corp
Munk, Rune–Coller Capital Ltd
Munn, Paul–Par Equity Llp
Munn, Richard–Oak Hill Advisors LP
Munne, Lluis - Maria–Phi Industrial Acquisitions SL
Munoz, Alain–Idinvest Partners SA
Munoz, Eduardo–Alantra
Munoz, Jose Maria–MCH Private Equity Asesores SL
Munoz, Rafael–MCH Private Equity Asesores SL
Munro, Scott–iNovia Capital Inc
Munson, Peter–Cardinal Equity Partners LLC
Munster, Gene–Loup Ventures
Munsters, Roderick–RobeCo Private Equity
Munthe, Gert–Herkules Capital AS
Munz, Michael–Clover Venture GmbH
Munzig, Peter–General Atlantic LLC
Murad, Alexander–Firm Factory Network AB
Murad, Hassan–Venture Capital Bank BSCC
Muraguchi, Kazutaka–Nippon Technology Venture Partners Ltd
Murali, Vinod–Innoven Capital India Pvt Ltd
Murata, Yusuke–Incubate Fund No1 Investment LPS
Murawski, Jacek–MCI Capital SA

Murcia, Michelle–West Capital Advisors LLC
Murdoch, Simon–Episode 1 Ventures LLP
Murdock, Jerry–Insight Venture Partners LLC
Murer, Robin–Apax Partners LLP
Murkley, Nevin–LBC Credit Partners Inc
Murnane, William–Wayzata Investment Partners LLC
Murphree, Dennis–Murphree Venture Partners
Murphy, Alice Jane–Goldman Sachs & Co LLC
Murphy, Andrew–Loup Ventures
Murphy, Ann–Tribal Ventures LLC
Murphy, Barbara–Carlyle Group LP
Murphy, Brian–Newspring Capital
Murphy, Brian–Portfolio Advisors, LLC
Murphy, Christopher–Valor Equity Parters L P
Murphy, David–Morrison & Foerster LLP
Murphy, Erin–Wynnchurch Capital Ltd
Murphy, Gerry–Blackstone Group LP
Murphy, Jeffrey–Ironbridge Equity Partners Management Ltd
Murphy, John–Investec Wentworth Private Equity Pty Ltd
Murphy, John–Probitas Partners Inc
Murphy, Jonathan–Francisco Partners LP
Murphy, Jonathan–Portfolio Advisors, LLC
Murphy, Kevin–Brentwood Capital Advisors LLC
Murphy, Kevin–Encore Consumer Capital Fund L P
Murphy, Kevin–Indigo Capital LLP
Murphy, Kevin–Pacific Alliance Capital Group Ltd
Murphy, Leslie–Belle Michigan Fund LP
Murphy, Mark–OMERS Infrastructure
Murphy, Martin–MVM Partners LLP
Murphy, Matt–Menlo Ventures
Murphy, Matt–Texas Next Capital LP
Murphy, Michael–Investec Ventures Ireland Ltd
Murphy, Paul–Sentinel Capital Partners LLC
Murphy, Ross–ArcLight Capital Holdings LLC
Murphy, Sharon–WP Global Partners Inc
Murphy, Shaun–Hovde Private Equity Advisors LLC
Murphy, Sue–Haynes and Boone LLC
Murphy, Susan–New York Times Co
Murphy, Thomas–Crestview Advisors, LLC
Murphy, William–Undisclosed Firm
Murray, Aaron–G8 Capital LLC
Murray, Campbell–Novartis Venture Funds
Murray, Dave–Southern Capitol Ventures LLC
Murray, James–Bridgepoint Advisers Ltd
Murray, James–Court Square Ventures LLC
Murray, Jim–Vector Capital Management LP
Murray, John–Technology Venture Partners Pty., Ltd.
Murray, Jonathan–Draper Triangle Ventures LP
Murray, Jonathan–Early Stage Partners LP
Murray, Justin–Murray Capital Ltd
Murray, Michael–Ontario Teachers' Pension Plan
Murray, Mike–Unitus Impact Partners LLC
Murray, Robert–Stonetree Capital Management LLC
Murray, Steve–Revolution
Murray, Steve–Softbank Capital Partners L P
Murray, Tim–Blackstone Group LP
Murray, Timothy–Chicago Growth Partners LLC
Murria, Vinodka–Elderstreet Investments Ltd
Murtagh, Kathryn–Harvard Management Company Inc
Murtaza, Narman–Oaktree Capital Management LP
Murthy, Mahesh–Seedfund
Murthy, Sandeep–Sherpalo Ventures

Murthy, Sundip–3i
Murthy, Sundip–3i Group PLC
Murugappan, Alagappan–CDC Group PLC
Musalem, Jose Miguel–Aurus Gestion de Inversiones SPA
Muscarello, Charles–Focal Point Ventures LLC
Muscat, Joe–Ernst & Young LLP
Muse, Rodney–Navis Management Sdn Bhd
Musech, Cary–Tonka Bay Equity Partners LLC
Musgrove, C. Kyle–Haynes and Boone LLC
Musicant, David–Ascribe Capital, LLC
Musicco, Nicole–Ontario Teachers' Pension Plan
Musindo, Melisa–Kleoss Capital (Pty) Ltd
Musits, Bela–Primary Venture Partners
Musoke, Ezra–InReturn Capital (K) Ltd
Musoke, Ezra–Jacana Partners
Mussafer, David–Advent International Corp
Mussellwhite, Jonathan–Motion Equity Partners LLP
Mustacchi, Alan–Dresner Capital Resources Inc
Musters, Reinier–Finch Capital Partners BV
Musumeci, Steven–HealthCor Partners Management LP
Musuraca, Mike–Blue Wolf Capital Partners LLC
Mutafchieva, Mina–Palamon Capital Partners LP
Muth, Peter–Stonewood Capital Management Inc
Muto, Frederick–Cooley LLP
Muto, Jun–Duet Capital Ltd
Mutschler, Sylvie–Ananda Ventures GmbH
Muuls, Francis–Meridia Capital Partners SL
Muzumdar, Abhijeet–Bessemer Venture Partners
Muzyczyszyn, Leszek–Innova Capital Sp z o o
Mworia, James–Centum Investment Company Plc
Myeroff, Randall–Glengary LLC
Myers, Anthony–Blackstone Group LP
Myers, Charles–Evercore Inc
Myers, Curtis–Red Rock Ventures
Myers, Daniel–Crosslink Capital Inc
Myers, David–Sovereign Capital Ltd
Myers, Glenn–Sippl Macdonald Ventures
Myers, Greg–Mason Wells Inc
Myers, Gregg–Global Infrastructure Holdings
Myers, Gregory–Metalmark Capital Holdings LLC
Myers, Herbert–Investcorp Bank BSC
Myers, Nina–Quad-C Management Inc
Myers, Robert–Equistone Partners Europe Ltd
Myers, Robert–MGI Holdings Inc
Myers, Sam–Balderton Capital LLP
Myhrvold, Cameron–Ignition Ventures Management LLC
Mylavarapu, Swati–Kleiner Perkins Caufield & Byers LLC
Mysyrowicz, Lance–Boost&Co SAS
Mytels, Dan–Salt Creek Capital Management LLC
Mytnik, Daniel–Palamon Capital Partners LP
NAGUMO, TOSHITADA–Fenox Venture Capital Inc
Naccarato, Clay–Grand Crossing Capital LLC
Nachyla, Monika–Abris Capital Partners Sp zoo
Nada, Hany–GGV Capital
Nada, Hany–GGV Capital
Nadal, Jack–Liberty Hall Capital Partners LP
Nadal, Miles–Peerage Capital Inc
Nadan, Eric–Diamond Castle Holdings LLC
Nadash, Dan–Potomac Energy Fund LP
Nadauld, James–Genstar Capital LLC
Nadkarni, Girish–IDFC Alternatives Ltd

Nadkarni, Kiran–Jumpstartup Fund Advisors Pvt Ltd
Nadon, Andre–Cfi Capital
Naegler, Karl–Gimv Investeringsmaatschappij Voor Vlanderen NV
Naether, Christian–Emeram Capital Partners GmbH
Naftulin, Ryan–Cooley LLP
Nagano, Thomas–Floor 13 GmbH
Nagaoka, Hirokazu–Tokio Marine Capital Co Ltd
Nagar, Sonia Sahney–Pritzker Group Venture Capital
Nagaraj, Sunil–Bessemer Venture Partners
Nagata, Takao–Mezzanine Corp
Nagatsuma, Yumiko–University of Tokyo Edge Capital Co Ltd
Nagel, Christian–Earlybird Venture Capital GmbH & Co KG
Nagel, Rick–Acorn Growth Companies
Nagel, Rolf–MVP Management GmbH
Nagim, Ryan–Acas LLC
Nagioff, Roger–JRJ Ventures LLP
Nagle, Arthur–Vestar Capital Partners Inc
Nagle, Rick–VectorPoint Ventures
Nagy, Daniel–MDB Capital Group LLC
Nagy, Tamas–Advent International Corp
Nahama, David–Vitruvian Partners LLP
Nahas, Mounir–Bayou Steel Corp
Nahass, Michael–NMS Capital Partners
Nahirny, James–Bain Capital Inc
Nahm, John–Strong Ventures LLC
Nahm, Tae Hea–Storm Ventures Inc
Nahmias, Vivian–Glynn Capital Management LLC
Nahum, Agnes–Access Capital Partners SA
Nahumi, Dror–Norwest Venture Partners
Naidoo, Jayendra–First South Investment Managers (Pty) Ltd
Naik, Sandeep–Apax Partners LLP
Naik, Sandeep–General Atlantic LLC
Naik, Ullas–Streamlined Ventures
Nailor, Brian–Global Infrastructure Holdings
Naini, Nader–Frazier Management LLC
Nair, Rahul–Everstone Capital Management, Ltd.
Nairn, Brian–Education Growth Partners LLC
Naito, Shinji–Sparx Capital Partners Co Ltd
Najjar, Michael–COGR Inc
Nakache, Patricia–Trinity Ventures LLP
Nakae, Gosuke–Mitsubishi International Corp
Nakagaki, Tetsujiro–Draper Nexus Venture Partners LLC
Nakagawa, Shunichiro–Tokio Marine Capital Co Ltd
Nakagawa, Taisuke–Global Brain Corp
Nakagawa, Takashi–SBI Investment Co Ltd
Nakamura, Charlie–A1 Investments & Resources Ltd
Nakamura, Hajime–New Horizon Capital Co Ltd
Nakamura, Hiroshi–Oaktree Capital Management LP
Nakamura, Koji–Beenos Inc
Nakamura, Saori–Morrison & Foerster LLP
Nakamura, Tadashi–Challenge Japan Invest Co Ltd
Nakano, Hironobu–CITIC Capital Partners Ltd
Nakazato, Takayuki–Olympus Capital Holdings Asia Hong Kong Ltd
Nakhapetyan, Gor–Troika Capital Partners Ltd
Nalamasu, Omkaram–Applied Ventures LLC
Nalavadi, Shantanu–New Silk Route Partners, LLC
Nally, Robert–CVF Technologies Corp
Nam, Gi Mun–Smilegate Investment Inc
Nam, Hodong–Altos Ventures

Nam, Injun–Next Venture Investment Corp
Nam, Jinwoo–Alpine Technology Investment Co Ltd
Nambiar, Anthony–Arcapita Inc
Namkung, David–Kinzie Capital Partners LLC
Nan, Cun–Shanghai Zhengsailian Venture Capital Management Co Ltd
Nance, Allen–Tech Square Labs LLC
Nand, Rahul–Lee Equity Partners LLC
Nanda, Tobias–Palladin Capital Group Inc
Nandi, Sanjay–Trilantic Capital Management LP
Nangle, David–Vostok Emerging Finance Ltd
Nankervis, Craig–First Analysis Corp
Nankivell, Natasha–Carlyle Group LP
Nankoin, Masayuki–Shinsei Bank Ltd
Nanto, David–Longworth Venture Partners, L.P.
Nanula, Richard–Colony Capital LLC
Naples, Aldo–Orizzonte SGR SpA
Napoleone, Gregorio–Stirling Square Capital Partners Lp
Napper II, Redell Vincent–FII Capital Partners LLC
Naqvi, Arif–Cupola Group
Naqvi, Asad–Wolfensohn & Company LLC
Narain, Sailendra–SIDBI Venture Capital Ltd
Narain, Vish–Tpg Growth LLC
Narang, Divjot–Nystar
Narang, Sameer–Hellman & Friedman LLC
Narang, Sumeet–Samara Capital Management Ltd
Narasin, Ben–Canvas Venture Fund
Narasin, Ben–New Enterprise Associates Inc
Narayan, Gautam–Apax Partners LLP
Narayan, Sridhar–GEF Management Corp
Narayan, T.K.–Oak Hill Advisors LP
Narayanan, Shankar–Carlyle Group LP
Narciso, Vincenzo–Union Bancaire Privee Private Equity
Nardari, Jason–Wellington Financial Lp
Nardecchia, Joseph–Balance Point Capital Partners, L.P.
Nardone, Gregg–Summit Partners LP
Nardone, Gregg–Summit Partners LP
Nardone, Randal–Fortress Investment Group LLC
Nardy, Vince–Rockwood Equity Partners LLC
Nark, Ted–KRG Capital Management LP
Naru, Sarath–Ventureast
Narukage, Yoshio–Daiwa Corporate Investment Co Ltd
Narula, Sameer–August Capital Partners
Narula, Yuki–Altpoint Capital Partners LLC
Narula, Yuki–Altpoint Ventures LP
Nasalroad, Eric–San Joaquin Capital LLC
Nasaw, David–Metropolitan Real Estate Equity Management LLC
Naschitz, Anat–OrbiMed Advisors LLC
Nasella, Henry–LNK Partners LLC
Nash, Irvin–New York Business Development Corp
Nash, Michael–Blackstone Group LP
Nash, Steve–Consigliere Brand Capital LLC
Nash, William–Haynes and Boone LLC
Nashat, Amir–Polaris Venture Partners
Nashif, Nina–Sandbox Industries LLC
Nasimi, Jamshir–Esterad Investment Co BSC
Nasir, Firas–Carlyle Group LP
Nasir, Mohammad Jamal–Pak Oman Investment Company Ltd
Nasky, Molly–Vista Ventures

Naslund, Fredrik–Nordic Capital
Nasurutia, Aaron–Global Partnerships
Nataf, Roberta–TCR Capital SAS
Natale, Anthony–Prism Ventureworks
Natali, Stephen–Edgewater Funds
Nataraj, Naveen–Evercore Inc
Natarajan, Venky–Lok Capital
Nath, Larry–Blackstone Group LP
Nath, Sanjay–Blume Venture Advisors
Nathan, Arthur–Haynes and Boone LLC
Nathan, Brad–Lynx Equity Ltd
Nathan, Jeffrey–Atlas Holdings FRM LLC
Nathan, Richard–Kensington Capital Partners Ltd
Nathanson, Thomas–Acas LLC
Nathoo, Raffiq–Blackstone Group LP
Nathoo, Salim–Apax Partners LLP
Nativi, Michael–Madison Capital Funding LLC
Natraj, Deepak–Aarin Asset Advisors LLP
Natrajan, Ajay–Karpreilly LLC
Naughton, Ray–4Th Level Ventures
Naughton, Thomas–New Energy Capital Corp
Nauiokas, Amy–Anthemis Group SA
Nault, David–iNovia Capital Inc
Navaratnam, Eeswaran–01 Ventures LLP
Navarrete, Minette–Kickstart Ventures Inc
Navarro, Eduardo–Tandem Capital Gestion
Navasota, Hiro–Navasota Group
Nave, Christopher–Brandon Capital Partners Pty Ltd
Naveh, Dan–Agate Medical Investments LP
Navin, Ashwin–i/o ventures
Navins, David–Glouston Capital Partners LLC
Nayar, Nitin–Warburg Pincus LLC
Nayden, Denis–Oak Hill Capital Management Inc
Nayeem, Sara–New Enterprise Associates Inc
Nayot, Ron–Diversis Capital LLC
Nayyar, Anmol–Ic2 Capital
Nayyerhabibi, Amir–Benhamou Global Ventures LLC
Nazarathy, Moshe–Giza Venture Capital
Nazari, Nersi–Pacific General Ventures LLC
Ndiaye, Papa Madiaw–Advanced Finance and Investment Group LLC
Neal, Jason–Landmark Partners Inc
Neal, Jeffrey–Horizon Capital Management
Neal, John–Linden LLC
Neal, Michelle–Bank of New York Mellon Corp
Neale, Joe–m8 Capital
Neale, Thomas–Patriot Capital Funding Inc
Neary, James–Warburg Pincus LLC
Neath, Martin–Adams Capital Management, Inc.
Nebel, Simon–Aravis SA
Nebesar, Adam–Bain Capital Inc
Nedeau, Nicholas–Lincolnshire Management Inc
Nedelec, Jean-Paul–Oaktree Capital Management LP
Nedjar, Manil–Emerging Capital Partners
Nedungalil, Ajit–TA Associates Management LP
Nee, Anthony–WGL Holdings Inc
Nee, Kevin–Wilshire Private Markets
Needham, Robert–Raptor Capital Management LP
Needley, Michael–Sovereign Capital Ltd
Neely, Matthew–Skytree Capital Partners LP
Neeman, Ofer–Evergreen Venture Partners
Neeman, Yuval–Trilogy Equity Partners Llc
Neermann, Joerg–Life Sciences Partners BV
Neerukonda, Naveen–LaSalle Capital

Neethling, Carl–Acorn Private Equity
Neff, P. Sherrill–Quaker Partners Management LP
Neff, P. Sherrill–Quaker Partners Management LP
Negi, Vik–HandsOn3 LLC
Negre, Louis–Pera Capital Partners Advisory Ltd
Negrea, Dan–Mtn Capital Partners LLC
Negroni, Hector–Fundamental Advisors LP
Negus, Kevin–CampVentures
Neighbours, David–Waud Capital Partners LLC
Neild, W. Carter–OrbiMed Advisors LLC
Neiman, Seth–Crosspoint Venture Partners 2001 LP
Neimark, Jason–New Water Capital LP
Neis, John–Venture Investors LLC
Nell, Oliver–Findos Investor GmbH
Nelles, Robert–EntwicklungsUnd Beteiligungs-gesellschaft Ostbelgiens AG
Nelsen, Brian–Carlyle Group LP
Nelsen, Robert–Arch Venture Partners LLC
Nelson, Adam–Social+Capital Partnership
Nelson, Andrea–Spell Capital Partners LLC
Nelson, Andrew–RCP Advisors LLC
Nelson, Anna Spangler–Wakefield Group
Nelson, Betsey–European Bank for Reconstruction and Development
Nelson, Carl–Clean Energy Venture Group
Nelson, Carl–HCI Equity LLC
Nelson, Curtis–Iowa Seed Fund II LLC
Nelson, Dean–Sageview Capital LP
Nelson, Frances–Oaktree Capital Management LP
Nelson, Hunter–Sterling Group LP
Nelson, Jessica–Algonquin Advisors LLC
Nelson, John–Brown Brothers Harriman & Co
Nelson, John–Shepherd Ventures LP
Nelson, Jonathan–Providence Equity Partners LLC
Nelson, Joshua–Thomas H Lee Partners LP
Nelson, Karen–Haynes and Boone LLC
Nelson, Lucas–Gotham Ventures LLC
Nelson, Lucas–Gotham Ventures LLC
Nelson, Matthew–Providence Equity Partners LLC
Nelson, Michael–Jabodon PT Co
Nelson, Mitchell–Asia Pacific Ventures
Nelson, Ralph–HealthEdge Investment Partners LLC
Nelson, Steve–Wakefield Group
Nelson, Timothy–Saw Mill Capital LLC
Nelson, Tom–Wakefield Group
Nelson, Travis–Pacific Partners
Nelson, Travis–Towerbrook Capital Partners LP
Nelson, Trevor–Alliance Consumer Growth LLC
Nelson, William–Haynes and Boone LLC
Nemchek, Lee–Oaktree Capital Management LP
Nemcova, Marie–Media Development Investment Fund Inc
Nemeskal, David–Intervale Capital LLC
Nemetz, Stacie–Oaktree Capital Management LP
Nemirovsky, Gady–Inspiration Ventures LLC
Nemo, Jon–AeroEquity Partners LLC
Nemsguern, Olivier–Activa Capital SAS
Nentchev, Nentcho–Blackstone Group LP
Neophytou, Savvas–Deepbridge Capital LLP
Neporent, Mark–Cerberus Capital Management LP
Nero, Leonard–MissionPoint Capital Partners LLC
Nesbeda, Eugene–COGR Inc
Nesbitt, Chris–Focus Acquisition Partners
Nesgos, Peter–Milbank Tweed Hadley & Mccloy LLP
Nessi, Claudio–Neomed Management As

Nesterovsky, Paul–Sinclair Ventures Inc
Nethercott, Brian–Lincolnshire Management Inc
Neto, David Travesso–FIR Capital Partners Gestao de Investimentos SA
Netravali, Arun–Omni Capital Group LLC
Nettles, Cory–Generation Growth Capital Inc
Neubauer, Markus–BERENBERG-BALKAN-BALTIKUM-UNIVERSAL-FONDS
Neubeck, Peter–TVM Capital GmbH
Neuenschwander, Rhett–HGGC LLC
Neuenschwander, Rhett–Tower Arch Capital LLC
Neuharth, Hugh–Fjord Ventures LLC
Neuhaus, Gottfried–Neuhaus Partners GmbH
Neuhauser, Horst–Schilling Unternehmensbeteiligung GmbH
Neumann, Ben–Brown Brothers Harriman & Co
Neumann, Ingeborg–Peppermint VenturePartners GmbH
Neumann, Jan-Daniel–Brockhaus Private Equity GmbH
Neumann, Martin–Creathor Venture Management GmbH
Neumann, Michael–Stone Canyon Industries LLC
Neumann, Steven–KRG Capital Management LP
Neumann, Thomas–Doughty Hanson and Co.
Neuplanche, Eric–Capital Croissance SAS
Neustaetter, Thomas–JK&B Capital LLC
Neustat, Todd–Charterhouse Group Inc
Neuville, Gerald–Remora Partners SA
Neuweiler, Hans–S Kap Unternehmensbeteiligungs GmbH & Co KG
Neuwirth, Daniel–Quad Ventures LLC
Nevas, David–Edison Partners
Nevas, David–Edison Partners
Nevatia, Vishal–True North
Nevin, John–Argosy Capital Group Inc
Nevin, Mike–Nova Capital Management, Ltd.
New, Jason–Blackstone Group LP
Newberry, Tom–CVC Capital Partners Ltd
Newbold, Gregory–Torch Hill Investment Partners LLC
Newborough, Philip–Bridges Fund Management Ltd
Newburger, Martin–KSL Capital Partners LLC
Newby, Tom–Lexington Partners Inc
Newell, Carol–Renewal Partners
Newell, James–Voyager Capital LLC
Newell, Jim–Houston Ventures
Newell, William–Kodiak Capital Group LLC
Newhall, Adair–Greenspring Associates Inc
Newhall, Ashton–Greenspring Associates Inc
Newhall, Kristin–High Road Capital Partners LLC
Newhall, Kristin–Riverside Co
Newhouse, Douglas–Sterling Investment Partners II LP
Newman, Ben–Blue Point Capital Partners LP
Newman, Brett–Blackstone Group LP
Newman, Bruce–Entrepreneur Partners LP
Newman, David–Ridgelift Ventures
Newman, Denis–Midmark Capital LP
Newman, Denis–Midmark Capital LP
Newman, Harold–Neuberger Berman LLC
Newman, Harris–TZP Group LLC
Newman, Henry–Solstice Capital
Newman, John–Wynnchurch Capital Ltd
Newman, Kenneth–Vexiom Equity Partners, L.P.
Newman, William–Northwest Technology Ventures
Newmark, Mitchell–Morrison & Foerster LLP
Newmark, Tammy–EcoEnterprises Fund
Newsome, Bruce–Haynes and Boone LLC
Newsome, Michael–Zachary Scott & Co
Newton, Anthony–Haynes and Boone LLC
Newton, Jeffrey–Gemini Investors Inc
Newton, Paul–Mosaic Private Equity Ltd
Newton, Tyler–Catalyst Investors LLC
Ng Ah Bah, Jeffrey–Venstar Capital Management Pte Ltd
Ng, Ben–SAIF Partners
Ng, Calvin–Disruptive Capital Pty Ltd
Ng, Carey–Mesa Verde Venture Partners LP
Ng, Chee We–Arsenal Capital Partners LP
Ng, Doris–Aif Capital Asia Iii LP
Ng, Edmond Chi-Man–Axiom Asia Private Capital Pte Ltd
Ng, Ellen–Warburg Pincus LLC
Ng, Jeffrey–Crosbie & Co Inc
Ng, Jit Meng–CLSA Capital Partners HK Ltd
Ng, Joyce–iGlobe Partners Ltd
Ng, Judith–Ingenious Haus Group
Ng, Khailee–500 Startups, L.P.
Ng, Kimberly–Thomas Weisel Partners Group Inc
Ng, Koon Siong–Zana Capital Pte Ltd
Ng, Philip–Feo Ventures Pte Ltd
Ng, Tee Khiang–Evia Capital Partners Pte Ltd
Ng, Vincent–Atlantic-Pacific Capital Inc
Ngo, Agnes–Startup Capital Ventures LP
Ngon, Ferdinand–Emerging Capital Partners
Ngoyi, Marlene–Catalyst Principal Partners LLC
Nguyen, Anthony–Yellowstone Capital, Inc.
Nguyen, Baochi–IDG Ventures USA
Nguyen, Cuong–Vinacapital Investment Management Ltd
Nguyen, Daniel–Ares Capital Corp
Nguyen, David–Court Square Capital Partners LP
Nguyen, Dennis–New Asia Partners LLC
Nguyen, Ken–Blackstone Group LP
Nguyen, Kim–Blu Venture Investors LLC
Nguyen, Lani–Accelerate-IT Ventures Management LLC
Nguyen, Philippe–Investors In Private Equity
Nguyen, Trung Ha–Vietnam Pioneer Partners
Nhlumayo, Siyabonga–Medu Capital(Pty)Ltd
Ni, Jing–Bright Stone Investment Management (Hong Kong) Ltd
Nibarger, Michael–Evergreen Pacific Partners GP LLC
Nice, Cole–Chart Venture Partners LP
Nicewicz, Rob–ABRY Partners LLC
Nicholas, Andrea–Colony Capital LLC
Nicholls, Janine–GHO Capital Partners LLP
Nicholls, Janine–Hermes Gpe Llp
Nichols, Alan–Blue Horizon Equity LLC
Nichols, Carl–Outlook Ventures
Nichols, Carol–TWV Capital Management LLC
Nichols, Curt–Intel Capital Corp
Nichols, Jeff–Haynes and Boone LLC
Nichols, Rob–Tasman Capital Investments Australia Pty Ltd
Nichols, Scott–Platform Partners Investment Company LLC
Nicholson, Chris–ACP Inc
Nicholson, Chris–Compass Capital Services Inc
Nicholson, Christopher–Evercore Inc
Nicholson, Donald–Small Enterprise Assistance Funds
Nicholson, Elliott–Sea Equity Ltd
Nicholson, Peter–Rcf Management LLC
Nickel, Andrea–Beringer Capital Inc
Nickel, Timothy–ABRY Partners LLC
Nickelberry, Kevin–Investcorp Bank BSC
Nicklas, Brent–Lexington Partners Inc
Nicklas, Michael–Valor Capital Group LLC
Nicklin, Matthew–First Analysis Corp
Nicklin, Oliver–First Analysis Corp
Nicod, Alain–VI Partners AG
Nicolais, Michael–Highlander Partners LP
Nicolaou, Christopher–Blackstone Group LP
Nicolay, Jason–MVP Capital LLC
Nicolson, Mark–Sl Capital Partners Llp
Nieda, Nobuhito–Blackstone Group LP
Niedel, James–New Leaf Venture Partners LLC
Niederhauser, Peter–Redalpine Venture Partners AG
Niederhofer, Max–Sunstone Capital A/S
Nieh, Midas L.G.–Grace Assets Management LLP
Nieh, Peter–Lightspeed Management Company LLC
Niehaus, Joseph–Accretia Capital LLC
Niehaus, Joseph–Housatonic Partners Management Co Inc
Niehenke, Alexander–Scale Venture Partners
Nielsen, Davide–NextEnergy Capital Ltd
Nielsen, Jack–Novo Holdings A/S
Nielsen, Jakob–Symbion Capital I A/S
Nielsen, Jesper Wadum–Odin Equity Partners K/S
Nielsen, Jimmy–Sunstone Capital A/S
Nielsen, Kirk–Versant Venture Management, LLC
Nielsen, Soren–Northcap Partners ApS
Nielson, William–Wall Street Venture Capital Ltd
Niemann, Darren–Focal Point Ventures LLC
Niemi, Christer–Sentica Partners Oy
Niers, Edwin–Bregal Investments LLP
Niers, Edwin–Good Energies AG
Nieto, Luis–Akoya Capital Partners LLC
Nieuwenburg, Jim–ACM Ltd
Niewiadomski, Karol–Silver Lake Partners LP
Night, Scott–Haynes and Boone LLC
Nigro, Melissa–Hamilton Lane Advisors LLC
Nii, Brad–Comvest Partners
Niiva, Eero–MB Rahastot Oy
Nijhawan, Preetish–Cervin Ventures
Nijjar, Harpreet–Darien Business Development Corp
Nijjar, Karamdeep–iNovia Capital Inc
Nikcevic, Vuk–Oaktree Capital Management LP
Nikodem, Gregory–Carlyle Group LP
Nikolay, Joern–General Atlantic LLC
Nikoloch, Karoly–Pivotal BioVenture Partners LLC
Nikolsky, Vladimir–Mail.Ru Group Ltd
Nikou, Andrew–AKN Holdings LLC
Nikou, Cyrus–Revolution Capital Group LLC
Nikrandt, Brieanne–Saybrook Capital LLC
Nikula, Jukka-Pekka–Midinvest Management Oy
Niles, Dana–Ampersand Capital Partners
Niles, Kimberley–North Atlantic Capital
Nilsen, Jorgen Andre–Televenture Management As
Nilsson, Jessica–Northzone Ventures
Nilsson, Jonas–Cinven Group Ltd
Nilsson, Keith–Tpg Growth LLC
Nilsson, Lina–Connecting Capital Sweden AB

Nilsson, Ludvig–Jade Investment Consulting (Shanghai) Co Ltd
Nilsson, Thomas–Alder
Nilsson, Veronica–NovAx AB
Nimmer, Andrew–Carlyle Group LP
Nims, Melissa–Linx Partners LLC
Ning, Jun–IDG Capital Partners Inc
Nir, Ronen–Carmel Ventures IV Principals Fund LP
Niroumand, Ramin–Finleap GmbH
Nirula, Vikram–True North
Nisenholtz, Martin–FirstMark Capital LLC
Nishimura, Youlee–Carlyle Group LP
Nitschke, Hendrik–Swift Capital Partners GmbH
Niu, Justin–IDG Capital Partners Inc
Niv, Eyal–Giza Venture Capital
Nivelle, Alex–A&M Capital Advisors LLC
Niwa, Norimitsu–CVC Asia Pacific Ltd
Niwa, Norimitsu–CVC Capital Partners Ltd
Nixon, John–Beacon Partners Inc
Nixon, William–Maven Capital Partners UK LLP
Nixon, William–Maven Capital Partners UK LLP
Niznik, Mark–Linx Partners LLC
Nkontchou, Alain–Enko Capital Management LLP
Nkontchou, Cyrille–Enko Capital Management LLP
Nkonyeni, Vuyisa–Kagiso Ventures
Nkosi, Prosper–Motseng Investment Holdings (Pty) Ltd
Noakes, David–Prostar Investments Pte Ltd
Noble, Diana–CDC Group PLC
Noble, Eric–Peterson Partners LP
Nobre, Lise–Butler Capital Partners SA
Nocen, Piotr–Resource Partners Sp z o o
Noe, Christopher–Dublin Capital Partners LP
Noe, Stephen–Charter Oak Equity, L.P.
Noe-Nordberg, Markus–Pamplona Capital Management LLP
Noel, Georges–BNP Paribas Fortis Private Equity Growth NV
Noel, Michael–Acorn Innovestments LLC
Noel, Rick–Varde Partners Inc
Noel, Stuart–Advantage Capital Partners
Noel, Yves–EntwicklungsUnd Beteiligungsgesellschaft Ostbelgiens AG
Noelcke, Christopher–New Mountain Capital I LLC
Noell, Charlie–JMI Management Inc
Nofsinger, Chrismon–Voyager Capital LLC
Nogales Gomiz, Laura–Inversion y Gestion de Capital de Riesgo de Andalucia SAU
Noh, Jisoo–Hamilton Lane Advisors LLC
Nohra, Guy–Alta Partners
Noiret, Franck–Innovation Capital SAS
Nokes, Humphrey–Gatx European Technology Ventures
Nolan, Joseph–Beverly Capital LLC
Nolan, Joseph–GTCR Golder Rauner LLC
Nolan, Leo–Rizk Ventures LLC
Nolan, Leo–Wall Street Venture Capital Ltd
Nolan, Michael–Milbank Tweed Hadley & Mccloy LLP
Nolan, Peter–Antares Capital Corp
Nolan, Robert–Halyard Capital
Nolan, Ron–KC Venture Group LLC
Nolan, Scott–Founders Fund, The
Nolan, William–HIG Capital LLC
Noland, Tom–Medcare Investment Fund Ltd

Nolen, George–Madison Capital Partners Corp
Nolen, Paul–Inverness Graham Investments
Nollet, Pierre–Arcis Finance SA
Nollmann, Walter–Alumni Capital Network Management Co LLC
Nolte, Lutz–Commission for Technology and Innovation CTI
Nomeir, Emily–Hamilton Lane Advisors LLC
Nomicos, Laki–Bain Capital Inc
Nomme, Jerome–Sun Capital Partners Inc
Noon, James–Hamilton Lane Advisors LLC
Noon, Michelle–Riverside Partners LLC
Noonan, Gareth–Cohen & Company Financial Ltd
Noonan, Ken–Advanced Technology Ventures
Noonan, Leslie–Summit Partners LP
Noonan, Tighe–4D Global Energy Advisors SAS
Noorani, Mehrdad–Global Infrastructure Holdings
Noorani, Zach–Foundation Capital LLC
Noordin, Eliza–Teak Capital Sdn Bhd
Nooruddin, Abdulla–Venture Capital Bank BSCC
Nord, Asgeir–Incitia Ventures AS
Nordan, Cary–Triangle Capital Partners L L C
Nordan, Doug–Beedie Capital Partners
Nordberg, Per–Fouriertransform AB
Nordemann, Gerhard–Gilde Equity Management GEM Benelux Partners BV
Nordenfalk, Johan–Catella AB
Nordhaus, Jeffrey–Oaktree Capital Management LP
Nordlander, Per–Verdane Capital Advisors AS
Nordquist, Ola–Permira Advisers LLP
Nordstrom, Mark–Summit Partners LP
Norfleet, Eric–Wafra Partners LLC
Norlander, Rebecca–Illuminate Ventures
Norman, Catherine–Shasta Ventures LP
Norman, Chad–Hercules Capital Inc
Norman, Geoff–Stafford Timberland Ltd
Normandeau, Robert–SeaFort Capital Inc
Norris, David–Forward Partners Ltd
Norris, Jack–Sk Capital Partners LP
Norris, Matt–Edgewater Funds
Norris, Nickie–New Heritage Capital LLC
Norris, Norman–Vital Venture Capital LLC
Norris, Patrick–Notion Capital Partners LLP
North, Chris–Permira Advisers LLP
Northrup, Charlie–10X Venture Partners LLC
Nortman, Benjamin–Hilco Consumer Capital Corp
Nortman, Kara–Upfront Ventures
Norton, Donald–Lexington Partners Inc
Norton, James–Pfingsten Partners LLC
Norton, Larry–Berwind Private Equity
Norton, Matthew–Cinven Group Ltd
Norton, Petre–Bergen Asset Management LLC
Nortrup, Peter–Comvest Partners
Nortrup, Peter–Turnspire Capital Partners LLC
Norum, Jim–ABP Capital LLC
Nosal, Miroslav–Ppf Investments Ltd
Nosek, Luke–Founders Fund, The
Nosek, Petr–Bain Capital Inc
Noser, Christopher–TVC Capital LLC
Nosseir, Amr–Perella Weinberg Partners LP
Notar, Richie–Raptor Capital Management LP
Noth, Pascal–Palamon Capital Partners LP
Notheis, Dirk–Rantum Capital Management GmbH
Nothias, Jean-Yves–Vesalius Biocapital Partners SARL

Notz, Peter–Ocean Avenue Capital Partners LP
Nouchi, Yuzo–Mitsubishi International Corp
Noudari, Anouar–Private Equity Investments II BV
Noumi, Kimikazu–Innovation Network Corporation of Japan
Nourse, Richard–Greencoat Capital LLP
Nouvellet, Dominique–Siparex Group
Nova, Daniel–Highland Capital Partners LLC
Nova, Daniel–Highland Capital Partners LLC
Novak, Ben–Impact Opportunities Fund LP
Novak, David–Clayton Dubilier & Rice LLC
Novak, E. Rogers–Novak Biddle Venture Partners LP
Novak, Paul–Capital for Business Inc
Novelli, Michele–Earlybird Venture Capital GmbH & Co KG
Novick, Andrew–Condor Capital Management Corp
Novick, Steven–Crescent Capital Group LP
Novik, Gilad–Horizons Ventures Ltd
Novitsky, Andrei–Essedel Oy
Novogratz, Amy–Aqua Spark BV
Novotny, Carl–Venture Capital Fund of New England
Nowaczyk, John–Milestone Partners LP
Nowinski-Chenoweth, Caralynn–Arch Development Partners LLC
Noyelle, Donatien–Azulis Capital SA
Noyes, Kurt–Huntington Capital I
Nozad, Pejman–Pear Ventures
Nozawa, Ryoko–Cayuga Venture Fund
Nsouli, Nadim–Providence Equity Partners LLC
Ntini, Themba–Median Fund PTY Ltd
Ntsoana, William–Akayi Capital Partners LLC
Nuber, Toby–Headwaters BD LLC
Nucci, Gino–Trust Company of the West
Nucci, Richard–FirstMark Capital LLC
Nueno, Pedro–Finaves I SA
Nugent, Brian–Accelerate-IT Ventures Management LLC
Nugent, Desmond–Gores Group LLC
Nugent, John–Argosy Capital Group Inc
Nugent, Mike–Vestigo Ventures LLC
Nuger, Jon–Berkshire Partners LLC
Null, Liz–Dw Healthcare Partners
Nunes, Brian–Gramercy Inc
Nunes, Celso–Dgf Investimentos Gestao De Fundos Ltda
Nunez, Ramon–MCH Private Equity Asesores SL
Nunlist, Aleksander–Private Equity Invest AG
Nunn, Bob–Intel Capital Corp
Nunn, Jake–New Enterprise Associates Inc
Nunn, Richard–Actinver Securities Inc
Nunnelley, Todd–Harbert Management Corp
Nurkin, Matthew–HealthCap Partners LLC
Nusbaum, Larry–Vertex Capital LLC
Nussbaum, Peter–Milbank Tweed Hadley & Mccloy LLP
Nussenbaum, Antoine–Felix Capital Partners LLP
Nussrallah, Steve–Value Plus Ventures LLC
Nutter, William–Tenth Street Capital Partners LLC
Nutting, Mike–Gores Group LLC
Nuzzo, David–J B Poindexter & Co Inc
Nwogugu, Obi–African Capital Alliance
Nyamayi, G. Tafadzwa–Takura Capital
Nyberg, Fredrik–Bioveda Capital Pte Ltd
Nye, Benjamin–Bain Capital Inc
Nye, Bob–JMI Management Inc

Nye, J. Benjamin–Bain Capital Venture Partners LLC
Nyholm, Nikolaj–Sunstone Capital A/S
Nyirjesy, Francis–Modern Africa Fund Managers, LLC
Nykin, Ilya–Prolog Ventures
Nykodym, Patricia–Friedman Fleischer & Lowe Cap Ptnrs L P
Nylander, Jan–Inlandsinnovation AB
Nystrom, Cody–SJF Ventures
O Donnell, Michael–Morrison & Foerster LLP
O Brian, Martin–Icc Venture Capital
O Brien, Andy–Blackstone Group LP
O Brien, Brien–Piper Jaffray Ventures Inc
O Brien, Carolyn–Oaktree Capital Management LP
O Brien, Christopher–Wynnchurch Capital Ltd
O Brien, Dennis–Gryphon Investors Inc
O Brien, Dennis–Gryphon Investors Inc
O Brien, Dennis–West Partners LLC
O Brien, Eric–Fall Line Capital GP LLC
O Brien, Eric–Lightspeed Management Company LLC
O Brien, Graham–Investec Ventures Ireland Ltd
O Brien, Kara–Edwards Capital LLC
O Brien, Kevin–CCMP Capital Advisors LP
O Brien, Kevin–Twin Haven Capital Partners LLC
O Brien, Michael–Investcorp Bank BSC
O Brien, Michael–Oxer Capital Inc
O Brien, Robert–CID Capital Inc
O Brien, Robert–Global Infrastructure Holdings
O Brien, Timothy–Five Crowns Capital Inc
O Bryan, Michael–Morrison & Foerster LLP
O Connell, Alan–Seroba Kernel Life Sciences Ltd
O Connell, Daniel–NeuroVentures Capital LLC
O Connell, Frank–Wall Street Venture Capital Ltd
O Connell, Jamie–Blackstone Group LP
O Connell, Michael–Accretia Capital LLC
O Connell, Michael-Kevin–Accretia Capital LLC
O Connor, Brian–Vestar Capital Partners Inc
O Connor, Christopher–Perella Weinberg Partners LP
O Connor, Conor–Enterprise Equity Venture Capital Group
O Connor, Diane–Headwaters BD LLC
O Connor, Donald–Tully and Holland Inc
O Connor, Henry–Multiplier Capital LP
O Connor, James–MVC Capital Inc
O Connor, John–Fort Washington Capital
O Connor, John–Lincolnshire Management Inc
O Connor, Karin–Serra Ventures LLC
O Connor, Patrick–Auven Therapeutics Management LLLP
O Connor, Rory–Lion Capital LLP
O Connor, Sean–New York Business Development Corp
O Connor, William–Morrison & Foerster LLP
O Dell, Bradley–Prospect Partners LLC
O Dell, David–Haynes and Boone LLC
O Donnell, Charles–Brooklyn Bridge Ventures
O Donnell, Christopher–Trillium Group LLC
O Donnell, James–Eagle Private Capital LLC
O Donnell, Jeffrey–Biostar Ventures II LLC
O Donnell, Laura–Haynes and Boone LLC
O Donnell, Michael–Morrison & Foerster LLP
O Donnell, Michael–Pepperwood Partners LLC
O Donnell, Niall–RiverVest Venture Partners LLC
O Donnell, Peter–Allied Growth Strategies & Management LLC
O Donnell, R. Timothy–Jefferson Capital Partners Ltd
O Donnell, Scott–Harbert Management Corp
O Donnell, Susan–Brown Brothers Harriman & Co
O Donnell, Thomas–TT Capital Partners LLC
O Donoghue, J. Clark–Brown Brothers Harriman & Co
O Driscoll, Hugh–Leaf Investments Ltd
O Driscoll, Rory–Scale Venture Partners
O Flaherty, Kevin–Pamplona Capital Management LLP
O Gorman, Kieran–Deepbridge Capital LLP
O Grady, Crevan–3i
O Grady, Crevan–3i Group PLC
O Grady, Standish–Granite Ventures LLC
O Grady, Standish–Granite Ventures LLC
O Hara, James–TSG Consumer Partners, L.P.
O Hara, Michael–Blackstone Group LP
O Hara, Patrick–Brazos Private Equity Partners LLC
O Hara, Seamus–Kernel Capital Partners
O Hara, Walter–Allen & Company of Florida, Inc.
O Hare, John–Saybrook Capital LLC
O Keefe, Kenneth–Beecken Petty O'Keefe & Company LLC
O Keefe, Linda–Elevate Ventures Inc
O Keefe, Mary Beth–Antares Capital Corp
O Keefe, Patrick–Excellere Capital Management LLC
O Keeffe, Geraldine–Life Sciences Partners BV
O Kelly, Conor–Investec Ventures Ireland Ltd
O Leary, Brendan–Prism Ventureworks
O Leary, Ciaran–Earlybird Venture Capital GmbH & Co KG
O Leary, Dennis–GMH Ventures
O Leary, Rich–Lacuna LLC
O Leary, Robert–Oaktree Capital Management LP
O Mahony, Daniel–Kernel Capital Partners
O Mahony, Daniel–Seroba Kernel Life Sciences Ltd
O Malley, Brian–Battery Ventures LP
O Malley, Devin–Summit Partners LP
O Malley, Michael–Inflection Point Ventures
O Malley, Patty–Global Catalyst Partners
O Mara, Joseph–Vitruvian Partners LLP
O Meara, Kevin–CVC Capital Partners Ltd
O Meara, S. Charles–Ziegler Alternative Investments
O Molony, Kearnon–Blackstone Group LP
O Neal, Roddy–Quadrant Mezzanine Partners LLC
O Neil, Stephen–HealthpointCapital LLC
O Neill, John–Graphite Capital Management LLP
O Neill, John–Levine Leichtman Capital Partners Inc
O Neill, Molly–Riverside Co
O Neill, Rory–Castlelake LP
O Neill, Stephen–57 Stars LLC
O Neill, Stephen–PCGI LLC
O Neill, Tara–Warburg Pincus LLC
O Reilly, Brian–Medley Capital LLC
O Reilly, Devin–Bain Capital Inc
O Reilly, Philip–Draper Esprit PLC
O Reilly, Robert–Acorn Innovestments LLC
O Riordain, Fearghal–Scottish Equity Partners LLP
O Rourke, James–Advantage Capital Partners
O Rourke, Robert–PPM America Capital Partners LLC
O Rourke, Tiarnan–Evercore Inc
O Shea, Greg–TWV Capital Management LLC
O Sullivan, Colm–PAI Partners SAS
O Sullivan, John–Delta Partners Ltd
O Sullivan, Robert–Comvest Partners
O Sullivan, Scarlett–SoftBank China & India Holdings Ltd
O Sullivan, Scarlett–Softbank Capital Partners L P
O Toole, Pauline Irwin–First Step Ltd
OBrien, Darren–Origami Capital Partners, LLC
OBrien, James M.–Napier Park Global Capital (US) LP
OBrien, Shaun–Spiral Sun Ventures LLC
ONeill, Patrick–Accelerate-IT Ventures Management LLC
Oakford, Scott–Hamilton Robinson LLC
Oakley, Julian–Evercore Inc
Oatey, Gary–Glengary LLC
Obayomi, Olumide–African Capital Alliance
Ober, Kevin–Divergent Venture Partners Affiliates I LP
Oberfield, Eric–Capvent AG
Oberg, Soren–Thomas H Lee Partners LP
Oberholtzer, Gregory–WP Global Partners Inc
Oberman, Micha–Kinrot Technology Ventures
Obermeyer, Wolfgang–Risikokapital Fonds Allgaeu GmbH & Co KG
Obermiller, Gary–Mill City Capital LP
Obershaw, Elizabeth–Horsley Bridge Partners LLC
Oblak, Geoffrey–Ascent Venture Management Inc
Obletz, Justin–Advantage Capital Partners
Obligen, Jeff–ZS Fund LP
Obluk, Karel–Credo Ventures as
Oboh, Anthony–Unique Venture Capital Management Company Ltd
Obregon, Andres–Carlyle Group LP
Obring, Kai–Emeram Capital Partners GmbH
Obuch, Bob–Palomar Ventures
Ocasek, Petr–Startup Yard Ltd
Occelli, Olivier–Kerala Ventures
Occhiogrosso, Neill–Investor Growth Capital AB
Occhipinti, John–Relay Ventures
Occhipinti, John–Woodside Fund
Occhipinti, Vincent–Woodside Fund
Ochoa, Carlos–Chilango Ventures LLC
Ochsenfeld, Frank–Coller Capital Ltd
Ocko, Matt–Data Collective LLC
Oconnor, Philip–Blackhorn Ventures Capital Management LLC
Octoman, Michael–Navis Management Sdn Bhd
Oddi, David–Goode Partners LLC
Oddo, Vincent–Birch Equity Partners LLC
Odefey, Andreas M.–Bpe Unternehmensbeteiligungen GmbH
Odeh, Emad–Capital Trust Ltd
Odell, Patrick–Brixey & Meyer Capital LLC
Oden, David–Haynes and Boone LLC
Oder, Troy–Golub Capital Master Funding LLC
Odibeli, Nkem–African Capital Alliance
Odigie, Felix–Valde Capital Investment Co
Odlander, Bjorn–Odlander Fredrikson & Co AB
Odom, David–Arsenal
Odom, David–OnPoint Technologies
Odugbesan, Lekan–Zephyr Management LP
Odunsi, Bolaji–Stirling Square Capital Partners Lp
Odutola, Wale–ARM Capital Partners
Oehmig, William–Sterling Group LP
Oelschig, Trevor–Bessemer Venture Partners

Oettmeier, Bret–Quadrangle Group LLC
Ofer, Abraham–Oaktree Capital Management LP
Ofer, Erez–Greylock Israel Global Management Ltd
Offenberg, Alan–Anholt (USA) LLC
Offenhauser, Peter–Stone Arch Capital LLC
Offermann, Daniel–Team Europe Management GmbH
Offermann, Peter–Ht Capital Advisors LLC
Ofori, Curtis–Greenhall Capital Partners LLC
Ofori, Otis–Greenhall Capital Partners LLC
Ofosu-Amaah, Nii Amaah–Berkshire Partners LLC
Ogden, Matt–Building Industry Partners LLC
Ogden, Mehmet–Valentis Capital LLC
Ogden, Thomas–Comerica Venture Capital Group
Oger, Dominique–Capatria SASU
Ogi, Takato–Ant Capital Partners Co Ltd
Ogince, Michael–Windforce Ventures LLC
Ogino, Akihiko–Daiwa Corporate Investment Co Ltd
Oglesby, William–Blackstone Group LP
Ogundare, Jumoke–ARM Capital Partners
Ogura, Jumpei–Carlyle Group LP
Oguri, Toshihiro–kk bhp
Oh, James–Transom Capital Group LLC
Oh, Kwang Lyul–Bokwang Investment Corp
Oh, Mitchell–Safanad Inc
Oh, Sammy–Palisade Capital Management LLC
Oh, Tai-Seung–Premier Partners LLC
Ohana, Bella–Israel Infinity Venture Capital Fund Israel LP
Ohayon, Ouriel–Isai Gestion SAS
Ohgishi, Takayuki–Tokio Marine Capital Co Ltd
Ohldin, Gabriella–Innovationskapital Nordic Advisors AB
Ohnesorge, Rudolf–Siemens Venture Capital GmbH
Ojanpera, Tero–Visionplus Oyj
Ok, Simon–Lexington Partners Inc
Oka, Jonathan–Edwards Capital LLC
Okada, Akihiko–NTT Finance Corp
Okada, Mark–Highland Capital Management LP
Okamoto, Akihiko–Recruit Strategic Partners Inc
Oken, Marc–Falfurrias Capital Partners LP
Okigbo, Chioma–ARM Capital Partners
Okonow, Dale–Watermill Group LLC
Oksanen, Petri–Francisco Partners LP
Okun, Robert–Synergy Partners International
Okupniarek, Gregory–Striker Partners
Oladele, Afolabi–African Capital Alliance
Olafsson, Sigfus–Castlelake LP
Olaguibel, Inigo–Qualitas Equity Partners Sgecr SA
Olale, Felix–LeapFrog Investments
Olan, Robert–Deerfield Management Company LP
Olanrewaju, Jide–Satya Capital Ltd
Olascoaga, Javier–Trilantic Capital Management LP
Olaso, Mariano–Altamar Private Equity SGIIC SAU
Olbort, Martin–Pinova Capital GmbH
Olbrechts, Cedric–Vendis Capital NV
Old, Robert–Loxbridge Research Llp
Olden, Niall–Kernel Capital Partners
Oldroyd, Graham–Bridgepoint Advisers Ltd
Olear, Greg–Updata Partners
Oleksik, Jacob–Dakota Venture Group Inc
Olesnavage, Mark–Hopen Life Science Ventures
Olexy, Mark–Atlantic-Pacific Capital Inc
Olfert, Chris–Lex Capital Management Inc
Olhoeft, Mark–Seabury Venture Partners LLC

Olieman, Harry–Pavilion Alternatives Group Ltd
Olifirova, Tatiana–RT-Invest OOO
Olinick, Andrew–3i
Olinick, Andrew–3i Group PLC
Oliva, Adele–1315 Capital LLC
Oliva, Adele–Quaker Partners Management LP
Oliva, Adele–Quaker Partners Management LP
Olivares, Will–Corigin Private Equity Group
Oliveira, Eduardo–Stratus Investimentos Ltda
Oliveira, Fernando–HIG Capital LLC
Oliveira, Joaquim–Rising Ventures SA
Oliveira, Rolando–Rising Ventures SA
Oliver, Alejandro–Nexxus Capital SA de CV
Oliver, Andrew–One Equity Partners LLC
Oliver, James–Evercore Inc
Oliver, Leigh–Carlyle Group LP
Oliver, Scott–Morrison & Foerster LLP
Olivier, Edmund–Oxford Bioscience Partners
Olivier, Maurice–BlueOcean Ventures SA
Olivier, Serge–Acces Capital Quebec
Oliw, Martin–Cevian Capital AB
Olkkola, Edward–Teakwood Capital LP
Olle, Bernat–Puretech Ventures
Ollier, Michele–Index Ventures
Ollila, David–Skypoint Ventures LLC
Ollila, Harri–Vnt Management Oy
Ollwerther, Robert–Avenue Capital Group LLC
Olmanson, Carleton–Lakeside Capital Management LLC
Olmedillo, Hector–Small Business Guarantee and Finance Corporation
Olmstead, Vinny–Vocap Investment Partners LLC
Olofsson, Gunnar–Inlandsinnovation AB
Olsen, Chris–Drive Capital LLC
Olsen, Dale–EXMARQ Capital Partners Inc
Olsen, Erik–Ferd Capital Partners AS
Olsen, Henrik–ETF Partners LLP
Olsen, Jamie–CMB Advisory Pty Ltd
Olsen, Per-Oluf–Birk Venture AS
Olsen, Wes–EXMARQ Capital Partners Inc
Olshansky, Joshua–Golden Gate Capital Inc
Olson, Bradley–Haynes and Boone LLC
Olson, Erik–Morrison & Foerster LLP
Olson, Max–Morrison & Foerster LLP
Olson, Mike–Trust Company of the West
Olson, Patrick–BlackRock Inc
Olson, Richard–Origami Capital Partners, LLC
Olson, Thiago–Tech Square Ventures
Olsoni, Karl–Capital Dynamics Sdn Bhd
Olsson, Morgan–Nordic Capital
Olsson, Robin–Kainos Capital LLC
Oltmans, Geoffrey–Silver Lake Partners LP
Olympia, Darwin–Breakout Capital LLC
Oma, Toshiyuki–MOVIDA JAPAN Inc
Omame, Eloho–General Atlantic LLC
Omari, Iyad–Frog Capital Ltd
Omidyar, Pam–Omidyar Network Commons LLC
Omidyar, Pierre–Omidyar Network Commons LLC
Omotoso, Deji–ARM Capital Partners
Onan, Christopher–Appian Ventures, Inc.
Onda, Jay–DOCOMO Innovations Inc
Ondish, Sean–Morgan Stanley Alternative Investment Partners LP
Ong, Geokyeow–Daiwa Securities SMBC Principal Investments Co., Ltd.

Ong, Gilbert–L Catterton Asia
Ong, Oliver–Rift Valley Equity Partners LLC
Ong, Peng–Monk's Hill Ventures Pte Ltd
Ong, Richard–RRJ Capital Fund
Ong, Shew Sze–OSK Ventures International Bhd
Oniovosa, Sam–African Capital Alliance
Ono, Hirofumi–e.ventures
Ono, Hirofumi–eVenture Capital Partners GmbH
Onovakpuri, Ulili–Kapor Capital
Onstott, Heather–LaunchCapital LLC
Opdendyk, Terry–ONSET Ventures
Oppenheimer, John–Beechtree Capital Ltd
Oppenheimer, Stephan–Moelis Capital Partners LLC
Oran, Stuart–Liberty Hall Capital Partners LP
Orange, Simon–Corpacq Ltd
Oravec, Brian–Everstone Capital Management, Ltd.
Oravkin, Jozef–Penta Investments Ltd
Orban, Krisztian–Oriens IM Hungary Szolgaltato Kft
Orban, M. Michel–RRE Ventures LLC
Orchard, Jason–Spring Mountain Capital LP
Orchowski, Markus–Clarus Ventures LLC
Orfao, David–General Catalyst Partners LLC
Organek, Jacob–Rosser Capital Partners
Orida, Deborah–Canada Pension Plan Investment Board
Orkin, David–Oaktree Capital Management LP
Orlando, Jim–OMERS Private Equity Inc
Orley, Gregg–O2 Investment Partners LLC
Orley, Rob–O2 Investment Partners LLC
Orlik, Tomas–Credo Ventures as
Ormond, Chase–Olympus Partners
Orn, Scott–Lighthouse Capital Partners LP
Oron, Yifat–Vertex Israel II Management Ltd
Oronsky, Arnie–InterWest Partners LLC
Oros, Daniel–Kleiner Perkins Caufield & Byers LLC
Oros, John–JC Flowers & Co LLC
Orr, Dennis–Morrison & Foerster LLP
Orr, Lawrence–Trinity Ventures LLP
Orr, R. Wilson–SSM Partners LP
Orsak, Michael–Worldview Technology Partners, Inc.
Orsatti, Paolo–Agire Invest SA
Orsen, Melissa–New Jersey Economic Development Authority
Orsi, Giovanni–Coller Capital Ltd
Orsten, Rod–AXIAL Group of Companies
Ortega, Christopher–TPG Capital Management LP
Ortega, Raul–Emerging Energy & Environment LLC
Ortenzio, Robert–Select Capital Ventures
Ortenzio, Rocco–Select Capital Ventures
Orthwein, Peter–Spring Capital Partners
Ortiz Portero, Gloria–Bankinter Capital Riesgo SGECR SA
Ortiz, Rafael–MoonSail Partners LP
Ortiz, Rafael–Palladium Equity Partners LLC
Ortiz-Vaamonde, Fernando–ProA Capital de Inversiones SGEIC SA
Orum, Nicholas–Gryphon Investors Inc
Osako, Yoshihiro–Tokio Marine Capital Co Ltd
Osawa, Koji–Global Catalyst Partners
Osborn, David–Align Capital LLC
Osborn, Warren–Stoneway Capital LC
Osborne, Richard–Madison Capital Partners Corp
Osborne, Stanley de–Kelso & Company LP
Osburn, Todd–Greyrock Capital Group

2544

Oshman, Andrew—Southwest Middle Market M&A
Oshman, Ilya—Pfizer Venture Investments
Osing, Tobias—Adiuva Capital GmbH
Osler, Andrew—G3W Ventures LLC
Osler, Andrew—Oaktree Capital Management LP
Osman, Ali—IECP Fund Management LLC
Osman, Bart—Lexington Partners Inc
Osman, Tariq—Castle Harlan Inc
Osmundson, Aaron—Headwaters BD LLC
Osnabrugge, Hans—Brooklyn Ventures BV
Osnoss, Joe—Silver Lake Partners LP
Osnoss, Raphael—General Atlantic LLC
Osofsky, Max—Riverside Partners LLC
Osorio, Abel—Battery Ventures LP
Osorio, Abel—Turnspire Capital Partners LLC
Ospalik, Rob—Baird Capital
Ossipow, Vincent—Omega Fund Management LLC
Ossmark, Andreas—Scope Capital Advisory AB
Ostawal, Narendra—Warburg Pincus LLC
Oster, Keith—Empeiria Capital Partners LLC
Ostheimer, Jason—Advancit Capital LLC
Ostin, Olav—Draper Esprit Secondaries LLP
Ostrander, Todd—Oneaccord Capital LLC
Ostro, Marc—Devon Park Bioventures LP
Ostrover, Douglas—Blackstone Group LP
Osumi, Ichiro—LJ2 & Co LLC
Oswald, Alexandra—Eureka Growth Capital
Oswald, Brian—Prospect Street Ventures
Otalora, Nhora—HarbourVest Partners LLC
Otani, Toshi—Translink Capital LLC
Otani, Toshi—Translink Capital LLC
Otawa, Mitsuru—Mizuho Capital Partners Co Ltd
Oteri, Silvia—Permira Advisers LLP
Otis, Meghan—Waveland Investments LLC
Otley, Victor—Gores Group LLC
Otsuka, Hiroyuki—Carlyle Group LP
Ott, Alexander—JVP Jerusalem Venture Partners Israel Management, Ltd.
Ott, Cecilia—Blackstone Group LP
Ott, Nathan—ABRY Partners LLC
Ottaviano, Andrea—L Catterton Europe SAS
Otten, Luc—Vinci Capital Switzerland SA
Otterling, Hans—Northzone Ventures
Otterson, John—Silicon Valley Bancventures LP
Otterstatter, Jonathan—Vilicus Ventures LLC
Otterstatter, Matt—Vilicus Ventures LLC
Otto, Allen—Blackstone Group LP
Otto, Steven—Jacana Partners
Ouaknine, Eric—Inerjys Ventures Inc
Ouaknine, Stephan—Inerjys Ventures Inc
Ouedraogo, Eric—Amethis Advisory SAS
Oulie, Andreas—Hitecvision AS
Oura, Yoshimitsu—Jafco Co Ltd
Ousseimi, Mimo—Gefinor Ventures
Oustinow, Pierre—Evercore Inc
Outcalt, David—Lexington Partners Inc
Outland, James—New Capital Partners
Ouyang, Xiangyu—Legend Capital Co Ltd
Ovel, Chad—Mekong Capital Ltd
Overbay, John—Broad Sky Partners LLC
Overbay, John—Court Square Capital Partners LP
Overbergen, Todd—Stellus Capital Management LLC
Overley, Kurt—White Oak Equity Partners LLC
Overli, Haakon—Dawn Capital LLP
Overmyer, Craig—Hopewell Ventures

Overson, Wesley—Morrison & Foerster LLP
Overton, David—Newbury Partners LLC
Overvelde, Michael—Crown Capital Partners Inc
Owen, Brett—Safanad Inc
Owen, Brian—Masthead Venture Partners
Owen, Douglas—Petra Capital Partners LLC
Owen, Dustin—Northern Plains Capital Ltd
Owen, Judy—Calumet Venture Fund
Owen, Matthew—Sovereign Capital Ltd
Owen, Stephen—Mustang Group LLC
Owen, Wes—Cyprium Investment Partners LLC
Owens, Alan—Morrison & Foerster LLP
Owens, Jennifer—SWMF Life Science Venture Fund, L.P.
Owens, Richard—Charlesbank Capital Partners LLC
Owens, Stephen—Staple Street Capital LLC
Owens, Todd—Broadhaven Capital Partners LLC
Oweson, Frederik—Scope Capital Advisory AB
Owsley, Henry—Bacchus Capital Management LLC
Owsley, Jonathan—Catterton Capital Corp
Owudunni, Seyi—Zephyr Management LP
Oxaal, John—Sevin Rosen Funds
Oxenham, Marivonne—Mcb Equity Fund Ltd
Oxley, Ian—Silverfleet Capital Partners LLP
Oyer, Philip—Medventure Associates
Oza, Rohan—CAVU Venture Partners, LLC
Ozaki, Kazunori—Translink Capital LLC
Ozaki, Kazunori—Vangoo Capital Ltd Co Ltd
Ozawa, Clare—Versant Venture Management, LLC
Ozbolt, Sean—Aurora Capital Group Ltd
Ozbolt, Sean—Bayside Capital Inc
Ozcan, Judith—Capital for Enterprise Ltd
Ozdalga, Yusuf—NCB Capital DIFC Ltd
Ozdogru, Huseyin—Esas Holding AS
Ozgen, A. Murat—Is Girisim Sermayesi Yatirim Ortakligi AS
Ozin, Stephen—Electra Private Equity Plc
Ozturk, Tayfun—Duet Capital Ltd
PRESS, ELLIOT—Deerfield Management Company LP
Paananen, Jokke—Intera Equity Partners Oy
Paardenkooper, Patrick—NIBC Principal Investments BV
Paasche, Michael—Providence Equity Partners LLC
Paaso, Marja-Reetta—Veturi Growth Partners Oy
Pabari, Mitesh—Hamilton Lane Advisors LLC
Pabari, Tushar—Headway Capital Partners LLP
Pace, Chris—Vintage Capital Partners, L.P.
Pace, Lars—Hamilton Lane Advisors LLC
Pace, Linda—Carlyle Group LP
Pacella, Maria—Beedie Capital Partners
Pacha, Robert—Evercore Inc
Pacifici, Jonathan—Wadi Ventures SCA
Pacitti, Christopher—Austin Ventures
Pack, Nicole—Venrock Inc
Packard, Chad—Pelion Venture Partners
Packard, Warren—DFJ Athena
Pade, James—Clearlake Capital Group LP
Pade, William—Oak Hill Capital Management Inc
Padovano, Carlo—One Equity Partners LLC
Padval, Umesh—Bessemer Venture Partners
Paff, Andrew—Headwaters BD LLC
Page Nelson, Liza—Investor Growth Capital AB
Page, Andrew—Foresight Group LLP
Page, Joseph—Gores Group LLC
Page, Marcia—Varde Partners Inc

Page, Matthew—Evercore Inc
Page, Michael—Eneas Capital SL
Page, Neil—RMB Corvest (Pty) Limited
Pagenkopf, Ulf—Silver Lake Partners LP
Paglia, Giovanni—LBO Italia Investimenti Srl
Pagliuca, Stephen—Bain Capital Inc
Pagnutti, Lou—Ernst & Young LLP
Pagowski, Piotr—Black Pearls VC SA
Pahlow, Marc—Rantum Capital Management GmbH
Pai, Christina—Able Capital Management LLC
Pai, Pranav—Elevate Innovation Partners LLC
Pai, Raj—GEF Management Corp
Paige, Robert—Brown Brothers Harriman & Co
Paillat, Mathieu—PAI Partners SAS
Paillier, Francois—Bridgepoint Portfolio Services SAS
Painter, Lucianne—Spring Mountain Capital LP
Painter, Michael—Plexus Capital LLC
Paisley, Thomas—Industrial Opportunity Partners LLC
Paiva, William—Sevin Rosen Funds
Pajarillo, Karen—Riverside Co
Pajarin, Elena—Diana Capital SGECR SA
Pajarola, Sandra—Partners Group Holding AG
Pak-Poy, Fiona—Innovation Capital Associates Pty, Ltd.
Pakianathan, Deepika—Delphi Ventures
Pakman, David—Venrock Inc
Pala, Gina—British Columbia Investment Management Corp
Paladino, Pam—Leading Ridge Capital Partners LLC
Palamara, Kevin—Provident Healthcare Partners
Palastanga, Tina—Global Leisure Partners Llc
Palexas, Zaharias—Parthenon Trust SA
Paley, Eric—Founder Collective LP
Palin, Adam—Global Private Equity PLC
Palkar, A. Vijay—GoldPoint Partners LLC
Palleschi, Nancy—Carlyle Group LP
Pallota, Joseph—Comvest Partners
Palm, Gunnar—Richmond Park Partners LLP
Palm, Michael—Sun Capital Partners Inc
Palmer, Adam—Carlyle Group LP
Palmer, Grant—Trilantic Capital Management LP
Palmer, Grant—Trilantic Capital Management LP
Palmer, Raquel—KPS Capital Partners LP
Palmer, Shirley—Synova Capital LLP
Palmer, Thomas—AH Ventures
Palmer, Tim—Charlesbank Capital Partners LLC
Palmeri, Stephanie—Uncork Capital
Palmese, Jeff—Sandbridge Capital LLC
Palmisano, Bob—SV Health Investors LLP
Palmisano, Robert—SV Health Investors LLP
Palmquist, Jonas—Scope Capital Advisory AB
Palmroth, Jussi—Vnt Management Oy
Palmunen, Marko—MB Rahastot Oy
Palod, Samir—3i Group PLC
Palod, Samir—3i Infrastructure PLC
Palsson, Johan—CapMan Oyj
Paluck, Robert—Centerpoint Venture Partners LP
Palumbo, Keith—Audax Group, Inc.
Palumbo, Robert—Accel-KKR
Pamias, Alberto—Delta Partners FZ LLC
Pan, Alex—Gsr Ventures Management Llc
Pan, Bob—ABRY Partners LLC
Pan, Chi—Noble (Beijing) Fund Management Inc
Pan, Chris—CID Group
Pan, Di—Greenwoods Asset Management Ltd

Pratt's Guide to Private Equity & Venture Capital Sources

Pan, Gordon—Baird Capital
Pan, Haifeng—Shenzhen Lihe Qingyuan Venture Capital Management Co., Ltd.
Pan, Jin—ShenZhen CDF-Capital Co Ltd
Pan, Qi—Broadline Capital LLC
Pan, Shijian—China King Link Corp
Pan, Shiming—Sunbridge Investment Management Co Ltd
Pan, Wenhui—Shanghai Sinohead Capital Co Ltd
Pan, Yulin—China King Link Corp
Panaccio, Michael—Starfish Ventures Pty Ltd
Panahy, Dara—Milbank Tweed Hadley & Mccloy LLP
Panandiker, Vibhav—KV Asia Capital Pte Ltd
Pancari, John—Evercore Inc
Panchal, Neel—Brown Brothers Harriman & Co
Pancrazi, Jacques—Qualium Investissement SAS
Panda, Brendan—Evercore Inc
Pandey, Abhay—Sequoia Capital India
Pandey, Alok—Vector Capital Management LP
Pandit, Kunal—Avista Capital Holdings LP
Pando, Alicia—Adams Street Partners LLC
Pandole, Darius—New Silk Route Partners, LLC
Pandullo, David—Frontier Capital LLC
Panem, Sandra—Cross Atlantic Partners
Pang, Adrian—CIT Group Inc
Pang, Chung Min—CLOVE CAPITAL PARTNERS LTD
Pang, Soh Har—Pavonis Group LLC
Paniccia, Anthony—Northleaf Capital Partners Ltd
Panoff, Brian—Granite Ventures LLC
Panos, Alexander—TSG Consumer Partners, L.P.
Pansing, Daniel—Merit Capital Partners IV LLC
Pantilione, Michael—LLR Partners Inc
Panton, David—Caribbean Equity Partners Ltd
Panton, David—Navigation Capital Partners Inc
Pantousis, John—Logo Ventures SA
Panturu, Sorin—Mackenzie Capital, Srl.
Pantuso, Lee—Presidio Ventures Inc
Panu, Stella—Maven Capital Partners UK LLP
Panu, Stella—Maven Capital Partners UK LLP
Panzier, Ron—Great Point Partners LLC
Panzo, Andrew—Newspring Capital
Pao, Ellen—Kapor Capital
Paolilo, Douglas—Blackstone Group LP
Papa, Mark—Riverstone Holdings LLC
Papa, Thomas—Ventana Capital Management LP
Papademetriou, Demetris—Middlemarch Partners LLC
Papadopoulos, Chris—Seven Mile Capital Partners LP
Papalas, Steve—Freeport Financial Partners LLC
Papanek, Julie—Canaan Partners
Papasan, Larry—MB VENTURE PARTNERS L L C
Papau, Todd—Northleaf Capital Partners Ltd
Papazian, Charles—Great Hill Equity Partners LLC
Pape, Florian—Orlando Management AG
Pape, Michael—Sigvion Capital
Papetti, Alessandro—Clessidra Societa di Gestione del Risparmio SpA
Papiernik, Antoine—Sofinnova Partners SAS
Pappageorge, Paul—Focus Acquisition Partners
Pappas, Arthur—Pappas Ventures
Pappas, Greg—Berkshire Partners LLC
Pappas, Jason—Antson Capital Partners LLC
Pappas, Nicholas—Mass Ventures
Pappas, Tracy—Synergy Life Science Partners LP
Pappendick, William—Bain Capital Inc

Paprocki, Ronald—Undisclosed Firm
Paquette, Jared—Bunker Hill Capital LP
Paquin, Jean-Pierre—Brown Brothers Harriman & Co
Paracchi, Pierluigi—Axon Partners Group Investment
Paranjpe, Ketki—L Catterton Asia
Parashar, Bharat—CLOVE CAPITAL PARTNERS LTD
Parasuram, Hemanth—Virgo Capital
Pardi, Robert—Evolvence Capital Ltd
Pardo, Chelly—First Israel Mezzanine Investors Ltd
Pardo, Geoff—Gilde Healthcare Partners BV
Pardoe, Richard—Chevron Technology Ventures L L C
Parekh, Deven—Insight Venture Partners LLC
Parekh, Grishma—Carlyle Group LP
Parekh, Jay—Blackstone Group LP
Parekh, Jayesh—Jungle Ventures Pte Ltd
Parekh, Rajesh—Advent Venture Partners LLP
Parella, Sharon—Morrison & Foerster LLP
Parfuss, Gero—Gruenderfonds GmbH Co KeG
Pargade, Jean-Pierre—Credit Agricole Aquitaine Expansion SAS
Parham, Iain—CVC Capital Partners Ltd
Pariat, Christell—Partech International
Parier, Christophe—Activa Capital SAS
Parikh, Krish—Lightspeed Management Company LLC
Parikh, Luv—Blackstone Group LP
Parikh, Shaunak—EW Healthcare Partners
Parikh, Tuhin—Blackstone Group LP
Parikh, Ursheet—Mayfield Fund
Paris, Laurent—Antares Capital Corp
Parise, George—Princeton Biopharma Capital Partners LLC
Parish, Brad—Levine Leichtman Capital Partners Inc
Parisot, Tristan—Acas LLC
Parisot, Tristan—European Capital
Parisot, Tristan—European Capital Financial Services Ltd
Parizek, William—Medley Capital LLC
Park, Anthony—Triangle Venture Capital Group
Park, Byung Moo—VOGO Fund Asset Management
Park, Chan-woo—IMM Private Equity Inc
Park, Chanho—Warburg Pincus LLC
Park, Chris—JC Asia Alpha Private Equity
Park, Christopher—Montgomery & Co LLC
Park, Chun Myung—LB Investment Inc
Park, Dan—Azure Capital Partners, L.P.
Park, David—Headlands Capital Management LLC
Park, David—Oaktree Capital Management LP
Park, Felix—Gryphon Investors Inc
Park, Howard—GI Partners
Park, Hui Wun—KTB Investment & Securities Co Ltd
Park, Hyeong-jun—Korea Investment Partners Co Ltd
Park, Hyung Gun—STIC Investment Inc
Park, Hyung Tae—Union Investment Partners
Park, JaeHyun—LB Investment Inc
Park, JeongGeun—LB Investment Inc
Park, Ji-woong—Korea Investment Partners Co Ltd
Park, Jin—Corstone Corp
Park, John—Blum Capital Partners LP
Park, Jong Hyeok—Smilegate Investment Inc
Park, JoungGun—LB Investment Inc
Park, Jun Tae—Hanwha Investment Corp
Park, Michele—Clarus Ventures LLC
Park, Minsik—STIC Investment Inc
Park, Moon Soo—Bokwang Investment Corp

Park, Sang Hyun—KTB Investment & Securities Co Ltd
Park, Sang-Ho—Korea Investment Partners Co Ltd
Park, Sang-joon—Korea Investment Partners Co Ltd
Park, Sung—Translink Capital LLC
Park, Sung—Translink Capital LLC
Park, Sungho—SV Investment Corp
Park, Tae Hyun—MBK Partners Inc
Park, Tae In—Kunyoung Investment Co Ltd
Park, Victoria—Oaktree Capital Management LP
Park, Young—First Capital Partners LLC
Park, Young-Taeg—Affinity Equity Partners HK Ltd
Parke, David—Burrill & Company
Parke, Marshall—Lexington Partners Inc
Parker, Andrew—Spark Capital
Parker, David—Ampersand Capital Partners
Parker, Douglas—Midmark Capital LP
Parker, Gary—Corporate Finance Associates Worldwide Inc
Parker, Jeffrey—Grandbanks Capital
Parker, John—Rho Capital Partners Inc
Parker, Kenneth—Haynes and Boone LLC
Parker, Matt—Greycroft Partners LLC
Parker, Paul—Landmark Partners Inc
Parker, Victor—Spectrum Equity Investors LP
Parkes, Jonny—Leaf Investments Ltd
Parkhill, Karen—Comerica Inc
Parkhoi, Henrik—Ld Equity
Parkin, David—HGGC LLC
Parkin, David—Tower Arch Capital LLC
Parkins, Lenard—Haynes and Boone LLC
Parkinson, Jeff—KEC Ventures Inc
Parkinson, Thomas—Adena Ventures
Parkinson, Thomas—Hopewell Ventures
Parks, Jeffrey—Riverwood Capital Group LLC
Parks, Kris—Tengram Capital Partners LLC
Parks, Lisa—Envest Ventures
Parks, Michael—Crescent Capital Group LP
Parks, Stephen—Topspin Partners LP
Parma, Leon—Genesis Financial Services Fund LLC
Parmanand, Jagdish—Symphony Asia Holdings Pte Ltd
Parmar, Kush—5AM Ventures LLC
Parnafes, Itzik—Battery Ventures LP
Parnafes, Itzik—Battery Ventures LP
Parnell, Mark—Patron Capital Advisers LLP
Parquet, Laurent—Butler Capital Partners SA
Parr, Jeffrey—Clairvest Group Inc
Parr, Shane—TGP Investments LLC
Parris, Brandon—Morrison & Foerster LLP
Parrish, William—Torch Hill Investment Partners LLC
Parrott, Glen—Rcf Management LLC
Parry, George—Atlantic Street Capital Management LLC
Parry, Rick—Deepbridge Capital LLP
Parry, Steve—NGEN Partners LLC
Parshall, David—PEI Funds LLC
Parshall, David—PEI Funds LLC
Parsky, Gerald—Aurora Resurgence Management Partners LLC
Parsley, Rod—Perella Weinberg Partners LP
Parson, Par-Jorgen—Northzone Ventures
Parsons, David—Focus Acquisition Partners
Parsons, Donald—Appian Ventures, Inc.
Parsons, James—RFE Investment Partners

2546

Parsons, Livingston–Accion International
Parsons, Maury–Pact Research Fund
Parsons, Steve–Z Capital HF Adviser LLC
Parthasarathy, Raja–IDFC Alternatives Ltd
Parthoens, Alain–Vesalius Biocapital Partners SARL
Parulo, Jennifer–Adams Capital Management, Inc.
Parziale, Paolo–Abbott Capital Management LLC
Parzick, Joseph–Cypress Advisors, L.P.
Parzick, Joseph–Torque Capital Group LLC
Pasanen, Jari–Suomen itsenaisyyden juhlarahasto
Pascal, Larry–Haynes and Boone LLC
Pascalizi, Francesco–Permira Advisers LLP
Pasko, Chris–Blackstone Group LP
Paslack, Ralf–nwk nordwest Kapitalbeteiligungs-gesellschaft der Sparkasse
Pasquale, Sandra–HarbourVest Partners LLC
Pasquesi, John–Otter Capital LLC
Passini, Mauro–Nova Gestao de Recursos Ltda
Passos, Sergio–Vinci Equities Gestora de Recursos Ltda
Paster, Anne-Mari–Omega Fund Management LLC
Paster, Kyle–Silver Lake Partners LP
Pasteur, Alexander–F-Prime Capital Partners
Pasteur, Alexander–MVM Partners LLP
Pastor, Frederico–Alantra
Pastoriza, James–Telecommunications Development Fund
Pastour, Benoit–Nord Capital Partenaires SAS
Pastre, Oliver–INTERNATIONAL MAGHREB MERCHANT
Patault, Didier–Sodero Participations SAS
Patch, William–Western States Investment Group
Patek, Kristina–Scope Capital Advisory AB
Patel, Aakash–Blue Wolf Capital Partners LLC
Patel, Aakash–Eos Partners LP
Patel, Amit–Owl Ventures LP
Patel, Anilkumar–Clearstone Venture Management Services LLC
Patel, Ash–Morado Venture Management LLC
Patel, Dinesh–Signal Peak Ventures
Patel, Dipan–Permira Advisers LLP
Patel, Hasmukh–Noverra Consulting and Capital Partners
Patel, Heidi–Rethink Impact Management LLC
Patel, Hetal–Trimaran Capital LLC
Patel, Janish–CVC Capital Partners Ltd
Patel, Kal–Vantagepoint Management Inc
Patel, Kavita–New Enterprise Associates Inc
Patel, Ketan–F-Prime Capital Partners
Patel, Keval–HIG Capital LLC
Patel, Keyur–Fuse Capital
Patel, Manish–Highland Capital Partners LLC
Patel, Minal–Foresight Group LLP
Patel, Neil–Healthbox LLC
Patel, Nim–iSherpa Capital
Patel, Prakesh–Angeleno Group Investors LLC
Patel, Purvi–Haynes and Boone LLC
Patel, Raj–Winton Ventures Ltd
Patel, Rajul–Proprium Capital Partners LP
Patel, Rishi–Plus Eight Capital Management LLC
Patel, Sameer–Angeles Equity Partners LLC
Patel, Sanjay–Gaja Capital Partners
Patel, Satya–Homebrew LLC
Patel, Shalin–Carlyle Group LP
Patel, Shamik–Tpg Growth LLC

Patel, Siddharth–CVC Capital Partners Ltd
Patel, Vimal–Bertram Capital Management LLC
Patel, Vipanj–iSherpa Capital
Patel, Viral–Blackstone Group LP
Paternot, Xavier–Vinci Capital Switzerland SA
Paterson, Calum–Scottish Equity Partners LLP
Paterson, John–Venture Corporation of Australia Pty Ltd
Paterson, Stuart–Scottish Equity Partners LLP
Pathak, Mangesh–Ambit Pragma Ventures Pvt Ltd
Pathak, Roy–TUFAN Venture Partners, Inc.
Pathria, Anu–Correlation Ventures LP
Pati, Buno–Centerview Partners LLC
Patil, Kunal–ICICI Venture Funds Management Company Ltd
Patinkin, Robin–Cedar Hill Associates LLC
Patkie, Arun–Everstone Capital Management, Ltd.
Paton, Colin–Next World Capital LLC
Paton, Jamie–First Reserve Corp
Patou, Gary–MPM Capital LLC
Patouillaud, Jean-Marc–Partech International
Patricio, Gabriel–Torch Hill Investment Partners LLC
Patrick, Chris–AnaCap Financial Partners Llp
Patrick, Grant–Beecken Petty O'Keefe & Company LLC
Patrick, Jim–Morgan Creek Capital Management LLC
Patrick, Liam–Fireman Capital Partners LLC
Patrick, Scott–Evercore Inc
Patrick, Steve–Blue Ridge Capital LLC
Patrick, Tricia–Advent International Corp
Patrick, Tricia–Bain Capital Inc
Patrickakos, Jennifer–CVC Capital Partners Ltd
Patricof, Alan–Greycroft Partners LLC
Patricola, Peter–First Atlantic Capital, Ltd.
Patron, Edward–Hall Capital Partners LLC
Patschkowski, Philipp–Coller Capital Ltd
Patsey, Kenneth–First Analysis Corp
Pattar, John–CLSA Capital Partners HK Ltd
Patterson, Arthur–Accel Partners & Co Inc
Patterson, Bob–Peninsula Ventures
Patterson, Cam–Excelerate Health Ventures LLC
Patterson, Dale–Genome Canada
Patterson, G. Douglas–Glencoe Capital LLC
Patterson, Jeffrey–Columbia Capital LP
Patterson, Michael–Vedanta Capital LP
Patterson, Paul–Integrated Partners
Patterson, Richard–Spire Capital Partners LP
Patterson, Simon–Silver Lake Partners LP
Patterson, Thomas–Madrone Capital Partners
Patterson, Tim–OMERS Private Equity Inc
Patterson, Tory–Catamount Ventures LP
Patterson, Tory–Owl Ventures LP
Pattison, Steven–National City Equity Partners Inc
Patton, Daniel–Savvis Inc
Patton, David–Cambridge Companies Spg LLC
Patton, Michael–Oakfield Capital Partners LLP
Patton, Michael–Provident Healthcare Partners
Patton, Ted–Hastings Equity Partners LLC
Paturle Guesnerot, Sophie–Demeter SAS
Patwardhan, Gopal–Duke Equity Partners Inc
Patwari, Naresh–ICICI Venture Funds Management Company Ltd
Paugam, Saik–Sagard SAS
Pauker, Armando–Apex Venture Partners LLC
Paul, Andrew–Enhanced Equity Fund, L.P.

Paul, Brian–Tenaya Capital, Inc.
Paul, Christian–Permira Advisers LLP
Paul, David–DWP Investments LLC
Paul, Jeremy–Argan Capital
Paul, Thaddeus–Carlyle Group LP
Paul, William–Bridgepoint Advisers Ltd
Pauley, Jay–Summit Partners LP
Pauley, Jay–Summit Partners LP
Pauli, Peter–BayBG Bayerische Beteiligungs-gesellschaft mbH
Paulke, Andreas–Deutsche Beteiligungs AG
Paull, Robert–LUX CAPITAL GROUP L L C
Paulmann, Joerg–Syfrex GmbH
Paulmier, Nicolas–Cinven Group Ltd
Paulo Teixeira, Pedro–TMG Partners LLC
Paulson, Greg–Duff Ackerman & Goodrich LLC
Paulus, Francois–Breega Capital SARL
Pauly, Lothar–Mobility Ventures LLC
Paumelle, Jean-Francois–Alto Invest SA
Pavey, Kent–Small World Group Incubator Pte Ltd
Pavkov, Pamela–Jasper Ridge Partners LP
Pavlik, James–Baird Capital
Pavloff, Dorothy–California Technology Ventures LLC
Pavlov, George–Tallwood Venture Capital
Pawlowicz, Romek–Orthogonal Partners LLP
Pawlowski, Anne-Sophie Aude–Carlyle Group LP
Paxia, Salvatore–Blackstone Group LP
Pay, Mark–CDC Group PLC
Payme, O. Bradley–Kurt Salmon Capital Advisors Inc
Payne, Alan–Bridgepoint Advisers II Ltd
Payne, Alan–Bridgepoint Advisers Ltd
Payne, Glenn–Derwent London PLC
Payne, Graham–Capstone Financial Group
Payne, Marni–Berkshire Partners LLC
Payot, Anthony–Unigestion Holding SC
Payro, Rafael–Alta Growth Capital SC
Peabody, Bo–Greycroft Partners LLC
Peacock, Bruce–SV Health Investors LLP
Peake, Tripp–Long River Ventures, Inc.
Pearce, Anne–Capital Dynamics Sdn Bhd
Pearce, Dave–Draper Nexus Venture Partners LLC
Pearce, David–ACM Ltd
Pearce, Douglas–British Columbia Investment Management Corp
Pearce, Dylan–Greycroft Partners LLC
Pearce, John–AssembleVC Fund I LP
Pearce, Jonathan–Blue Sage Capital LP
Pearce, Jonathon–Quadrant Private Equity
Pearce, Richard–Mosaic Capital Corp
Pearl, Jonathan–Golub Capital Master Funding LLC
Pearlman, Bret–Elevation Partners LP
Pearson, David–Carlyle Group LP
Pearson, Drew–General Atlantic LLC
Pearson, Michael–Alpina Capital Partners LLP
Pearson, Seth–Wellspring Capital Management LLC
Peate, Dan–Peate Ventures LLC
Pecanha, Claudio–BPE Investimentos
Peck, Aaron–Monroe Capital LLC
Peck, Adrian–Arcapita Inc
Peck, David–KPS Capital Partners LP
Peck, Donald–Lok Capital
Peck, Ian–Haynes and Boone LLC
Peck, Michael–Open Prairie Ventures
Pedersen, Allan Bach–Polaris Management A/S
Pedersen, Debra–Carlyle Group LP

Pedersen, Jacob–Northcap Partners ApS
Pederson, Steven–Sherpa Partners LLC
Pedley, Matt–Blackstone Group LP
Pedlow, Joseph–Blackstone Group LP
Pedragosa, Lluis–Marker Financial Advisors LLC
Pedretti, Mara–GP Investimentos Ltda
Pedroni, Emilio–First Atlantic Capital, Ltd.
Peechu, Sundeep–Felicis Ventures
Peek, Diane–GKM Newport Generation Funds
Peel, Doug–Kilmer Capital Partners Ltd
Peel, Joshua–Blackstone Group LP
Peel, Stephen–TPG Capital Management LP
Peele, Ron–Time Warner Investments
Peeler, D. Randolph–Berkshire Partners LLC
Peer, Jordan–Blackstone Group LP
Peet, Greg–Yaletown Venture Partners
Peet, Miles–Metropolitan Equity Partners LLC
Peeters, Jos–Capricorn Venture Partners NV
Pegg, David–Enhanced Equity Fund, L.P.
Pegler, Michael–Blackstone Group LP
Peiffer, Serge–Poincare Gestion SAS
Peinado, Arnold–Milbank Tweed Hadley & Mccloy LLP
Peiser, Brian–Edgewater Funds
Peix, Andrew–Serent Capital LLC
Peix, Andrew–Susquehanna Private Capital LLC
Pekala, Andrea–Carlyle Group LP
Pekkinen, Kaarina–Nordic Option Oy
Peleg, Oren–Oaktree Capital Management LP
Pelkonen, Arno–Taito Capital Partners Oy
Pell, Chris–Permira Advisers LLP
Pellegrini, Alex–Apax Partners LLP
Pellegrini, Lorenzo–Care Capital LLC
Pelletier, Jessica–Highland Capital Partners LLC
Pelletier, Mark–Acas LLC
Pelletier, Ricky–Openview Venture Partners LP
Pellicone, Evelyn–Crestview Advisors, LLC
Pellini, Matthew–Hamilton Lane Advisors LLC
Pelly, Chris–Castlelake LP
Pelly, Richard–European Investment Fund
Pelowski, Kenneth–Pinnacle Ventures
Peltier, P–Auriga Partners SA
Peltola, Juha–Vaaka Partners Oy
Peluso, Michelle–Technology Crossover Ventures LP
Pelzer, Joern–Pinova Capital GmbH
Pemberton, Gerard–Caribbean Development Capital Ltd
Pena, Isabel–MBF Healthcare Partners LP
Penarrocha, Luis–Portobello Capital Advisors SL
Pence, Jerry–Pivotal Group Inc
Pendergast, James–Albion Investors LLC
Pendergast, Mary-F-Prime Capital Partners
Penfold, Robert–Prudential Capital Group LP
Peng, Qingyun–Beijing Oriental-Focus Investment Management Co Ltd
Peng, Sean–WI Harper Group Inc
Peng, William–Warburg Pincus LLC
Peng, Xin–Shenzhen QF Capital Management Co Ltd
Peng, Yang–Qiming Venture Partners Ii LP
Peng, Yue–Boxin Capital
Peng, Zhen–Shanghai Tronfund Management Co Ltd
Peng, Zhiyuan–Beijing Oriental-Focus Investment Management Co Ltd
Penington, Michael–Longwall Venture Partners LLP
Peninon, Dominique–Access Capital Partners SA

Penman, Gordon–Venture Capital Fund of New England
Penman, James–Donnelly Penman & Partners Inc
Penmetsa, Arun–Storm Ventures Inc
Penn, Daniel–Mid-Ocean Partners LP
Penn, John–Haynes and Boone LLC
Penn, Kevin–Ascribe Capital, LLC
Penn, Mark–Stagwell Group LLC
Penn, Ronda–Plexus Capital LLC
Penn, Thomas–Meridian Venture Partners
Penn, Thomas–Penn Venture Partners, L.P.
Pennay, Lori–Cantor Ventures
Pennell, Keith–Dfw Capital Partners LP
Penner, Greg–DT Capital Partners
Penner, Greg–Madrone Capital Partners
Pennycard, Matthew–DTI Capital LLC
Pennycook, Carol–Davies Ward Phillips & Vineber
Penske, Roger–Transportation Resource Partners LP
Pentecost, Edward–National City Equity Partners Inc
Pentikainen, Ilkka–Vaaka Partners Oy
Pentimonti, E. Kenneth–Paladin Capital Management LLC
Pentimonti, E. Kenneth–Paladin Capital Management LLC
Pentland, Jeffrey–Northleaf Capital Partners Ltd
Penttila, Jarkko–Conor Venture Partners Oy
Pepe, Stefan–LaunchCapital LLC
Peperstraete, Bernard–NGN Capital LLC
Peponis, Arthur–AG BD LLC
Pepper, Andrew–Valco Capital Partners Partnership Ltd
Pepper, Douglas–Shasta Ventures LP
Percival, Philip–Syntegra Capital Investors Ltd
Percival, Sean–500 Startups, L.P.
Perdew, Kelly–Moonshots Capital
Pereira Lopes, Octavio–GP Investimentos Ltda
Pereira Pinto, Mario–Change Partners
Pereira, Bruno–Leblon Equities Gestao de Recursos Ltda
Pereira, Carlton–Tano Capital LLC
Pereira, Carol–ACP Inc
Pereira, Osvaldo–Park Square Capital LLP
Pereira, Paulo–Perella Weinberg Partners LP
Pereira, Thomas–Dubai International Capital LLC
Perekhojev, Alexei–Svarog Capital Advisors LTD
Perella, Joseph–Perella Weinberg Partners LP
Perelmuter, Guy–Vinci Equities Gestora de Recursos Ltda
Perelson, Robert–Oaktree Capital Management LP
Peres, Chemi–Pitango Venture Capital Management Israel, Ltd.
Peretie, Michel–RiverRock European Capital Partners LLP
Perez Barnes, Cesar–Southern Cross Capital Management SA
Perez de Jauregui, Carlos–Nazca Capital SGEIC SA
Perez, David–Palladium Equity Partners LLC
Perez, Francisco–Inseed Investimentos Ltda
Perez, Jeffrey–Third Security LLC
Perez, Mark–Virgo Investment Group LLC
Perez, Patrick–BNP Paribas Capital Partners SAS
Perez, Raul–Oakwood Medical Investors
Perez, Sergio–Qualitas Equity Partners Sgecr SA
Perez-Beato, Celia–Nazca Capital SGEIC SA
Perez-Montes, Antonio–ECM-Bulgarian Post-Privatisation Fund

Perez-Seoane, Carlos Prado–Espiga Capital Gestion SGCR SA
Perille, Robert–Frontier Venture Capital
Perille, Robert–Shamrock Capital Advisors LLC
Perkal, Richard–Irving Place Capital LLC
Perkins, Clark–Mercury Capital Investments
Perkins, Clark–Mercury Capital Investments
Perkins, David–Nations Funds Inc
Perkins, Gretchen–Huron Capital Partners LLC
Perkins, John–Crosslink Capital Inc
Perkins, Phillippa–Northleaf Capital Partners Ltd
Perkins, Sonja–Menlo Ventures
Perkins, Tracy–Greyrock Capital Group
Perkins, William–Small Ventures Usa LP
Perkins, Woodie–J B Poindexter & Co Inc
Perkovic, Angelina–Blackstone Group LP
Perks, Dominic–Hambro Perks Ltd
Perl, Jonathan–Boulder Ventures Ltd
Perlis, Michael–Softbank Capital Partners L P
Perlman, Andrew–GREATPOINT VENTURES
Perlman, Andy–CMEA Development Company LLC
Perlman, Jeffrey–LNK Partners LLC
Perlman, Jeffrey–Warburg Pincus LLC
Perlman, Matthew–Fenway Summer Ventures LP
Perlmutter, Aaron–Levine Leichtman Capital Partners Inc
Perlmutter, Roger–Column Group

Perlmutter, Tom–Behrman Capital
Perlyn, Eric–Blackstone Group LP
Pernick, Marc–Morrison & Foerster LLP
Pernisie, Dean–Gemini Investors Inc
Peroncini, Stefano–Axon Partners Group Investment
Peroncini, Stefano–Quantica Sgr SpA
Perony, Gilles–Azulis Capital SA
Perper, Scott–Pamlico Capital Management LP
Perpich, David–New York Times Co
Perrachon, John–Lincolnshire Management Inc
Perrault, Frederick–Investissements Novacap Inc
Perreault, Justin–Commonwealth Capital Ventures
Perreault, Justin–Pamplona Capital Management LLP
Perrelli, Jonathon–Fortify Ventures LLC
Perret, Laurent–Omnes Capital SAS
Perret, Marc–Gilde Healthcare Partners BV
Perricelli, Scott–LLR Partners Inc
Perriello, Christopher–AlpInvest Partners BV
Perrin, Elvire–Pavilion Alternatives Group Ltd
Perriquet, Stephane–21 Centrale Partners SA
Perris, Richard–CVC Capital Partners Ltd
Perry, C. Scott–Sentinel Capital Partners LLC
Perry, Christopher–CIVC Partners LP
Perry, Daniel–Milbank Tweed Hadley & Mccloy LLP
Perry, Harrison–EDG Partners LLC
Perry, James–Madison Dearborn Partners LLC
Perry, Lloyd–Argan Capital
Perry, Mark–Centinela Capital Partners LLC
Perry, Nathan–Greenline Ventures LLC
Perry, Stan–Haynes and Boone LLC
Perry, Xander–Anthem Capital Management Inc
Perskie, David–A&M Capital Advisors LLC
Persky, Michael–Alerion Partners LLC
Persons, Patrick–Impetus Capital LLC
Persson, Finn–Spintop Private Partners AB

Pratt's Guide to Private Equity & Venture Capital Sources

Pertsel, Anton—Altpoint Ventures LP
Pertuz, Brett—Altpoint Capital Partners LLC
Pertuz, Brett—Altpoint Ventures LP
Perutz, Mark—DBL Investors
Pescatello, Bill—Antares Capital Corp
Pescatori, Frederic—Bridgepoint Advisers Ltd
Pesce, Joseph—Great Point Partners LLC
Peshkatari, Tomas—Carlyle Group LP
Pesikoff, David—Triangle Peak Partners LP
Pestritto, Vanessa—Lattice Ventures LLC
Peter, Markus—Bellevue Asset Management AG
Petering, Andrew—Wolseley Private Equity
Peters, Audrey—Impact Capital Inc
Peters, Corey—Yukon Partners Management LLC
Peters, Marc David—Morrison & Foerster LLP
Peters, Nicholas—Parallel49 Equity
Peters, Richard—Transportation Resource Partners LP
Peters, Thomas—Impact Capital Inc
Peters, W. Fran—HarbourVest Partners LLC
Peterschmidt, David—280 Capital Partners LLC
Peterschmitt, Jean-Marc—European Bank for Reconstruction and Development
Petersen, Allan—Nautic Partners LLC
Petersen, Bernd—Odin Equity Partners K/S
Petersen, Christian—Catagonia Capital GmbH
Petersen, Gabriel—Blackstone Group LP
Petersen, Klaus—Park Square Capital LLP
Petersen, Michael—Cross Equity Partners AG
Petersen, Mike—Southbridge Capital Inc
Petersen, Timothy—Arboretum Ventures Inc
Petersen, Torsten—Saentis Capital Investment AG
Peterson, Barry—Northcreek Mezzanine
Peterson, Brian—Silversmith Capital Partners LLC
Peterson, Bryce—Comvest Partners
Peterson, Chad—Victory Park Capital Advisors LLC
Peterson, Clark—Lexington Partners Inc
Peterson, Clint—Peterson Partners LP
Peterson, Dan—Accretia Capital LLC
Peterson, Dan—Peterson Ventures LLC
Peterson, Danford—Fundamental Advisors LP
Peterson, Hunter—Riverside Co
Peterson, Hunter—Trinity Hunt Partners
Peterson, Joel—Peterson Partners LP
Peterson, Joel—Peterson Ventures LLC
Peterson, Matthew—Utah Fund of Funds LLC
Peterson, Paul—Wind Point Advisors LLC
Peterson, Pete—Saints Ventures
Peterson, Thomas—El Dorado Ventures
Peterson, Thomas—Social Leverage LLC
Peterson, Timothy—Milbank Tweed Hadley & Mccloy LLP
Peterson, Timothy—Sunbridge Capital Management LLC
Peterson, Trent—Catalyst Investment Managers Pty, Ltd.
Peterson, Trevor—Compass Partners International Llp
Petersson, Anders—IK Investment Partners Ltd
Petit Bon, Maurizio—Kreos Capital Managers Ltd
Petit, Francois—Cm Cic Mezzanine Sas
Petit, Hugo—MedCap AB (publ)
Petiy, Igor—GEN3 Partners, Inc.
Peto, Andre—COREST GmbH Corporate Restructuring
Petras, Jim—Early Stage Partners LP
Petrescu, Philipp—HOF Capital Inc

Petri, Michael—Summer Street Capital Partners LLC
Petrick, Mitch—Carlyle Group LP
Petrillo, Enrico—Excel Venture Management
Petrillo, Peter—Wafra Partners LLC
Petrini, Robert—Blackstone Group LP
Petrocelli, Philip—Gryphon Investors Inc
Petrocelli, Richard—Saratoga Partners LP
Petroff, Victor—Riverlake Partners LLC
Petrone, Carmine—Advent International Corp
Petrosino, Rodolfo—Ardian France SA
Petrossi, Louis—Single Oak Ventures LP
Petrossian, Stephane—OLMA Capital Management Ltd
Petrov, Andrei—Inbio Ventures DC Ltd
Petrov, Konstantin—New Europe Venture Equity
Petrov, Valeri—Bancroft Group Ltd
Petrow, Steven—Change Capital Partners LLP
Petruccioli, Stefania—Progressio SGR SpA
Petrucco, David—Kayne Anderson Capital Advisors LP
Petryk, Andrew—Brown Gibbons Lang & Company LLC
Petrzela, Michal—Lightyear Capital LLC
Petterle, Laura—Fontinalis Partners LLC
Petterson, Par—Stirling Square Capital Partners Lp
Pettersson, Anders—Arle Heritage LLP
Pettersson, Pontus—Cinven Group Ltd
Pettipas, Brian—Tricor Pacific Founders Capital Inc
Pettit, Justin—Dw Healthcare Partners
Pettit, Peter—MSouth Equity Partners LLC
Petty, Cathrin—CVC Capital Partners Ltd
Petty, Mark—9th Street Investments
Petty, Robert—Clearwater Capital Partners Cyprus Ltd
Petty, Scott—Signal Peak Ventures
Petty, Thomas—Adams Street Partners LLC
Petty, William—Beecken Petty O'Keefe & Company LLC
Petukhov, Sergei—CLS Capital Ltd
Petukhov, Sergei—Enso Ventures Ltd
Petzold, Kent—Arris Ventures LLC
Peyrat, Alan—Riverside Co
Peyret, Patrice—Nexit Ventures Oy
Peyser, Jim—NewSchools Venture Fund
Pezanosky, Stephen—Haynes and Boone LLC
Pezeshki, Niki—Felicis Ventures
Pezley, Daniel—Jordan Company LP
Pfahlert, Volker—SHS Gesellschaft fuer Beteiligungsmanagement mbH
Pfannmoller, Stefan—Venture Stars GmbH
Pfeffer, Cary—Third Rock Ventures LLC
Pfeffer, Michael—Post Capital Partners LLC
Pfeifer, Boris—Slovenski Podjetniski Sklad
Pfeiffer, Joachim—Kreissparkasse Reutlingen
Pfennings, Edo—Mentha Capital BV
Pfister, Peter—Morrison & Foerster LLP
Pfohl, Edgar—Montauk TriGuard Management Inc
Pfost, Dale—Advent Venture Partners LLP
Pham Vu, Giang—Mekong Capital Ltd
Pham, Traci—Capital Dynamics Sdn Bhd
Pharr-Lee, Cynthia—TWV Capital Management LLC
Phelan, John—MSD Capital LP
Phelan, Robin—Haynes and Boone LLC
Phelps, Daniel—Salt Creek Capital Management LLC
Phelps, Dennis—Institutional Venture Partners
Phelps, Gus—Summit Partners LP

Phelps, James—Kendall Capital Associates LLC
Phelps, Kevin—Trillium Group LLC
Pheng, Chia—VF Capital Sdn Bhd
Phenicie, Luke—Hammond Kennedy Whitney & Company Inc
Philbin, Phillip—Haynes and Boone LLC
Philbrick, P. Hunter—Hellman & Friedman LLC
Philbrick-Wheaton, Christie—Metropolitan Real Estate Equity Management LLC
Philip, Anand—Castle Harlan Inc
Philip, Ted—Highland Capital Partners LLC
Philippart, Nancy—Belle Michigan Fund LP
Philippon, Olivier—Ouest Croissance SAS
Philips, Marc—Arafura Ventures Inc
Phillipps, Andrew—PROfounders Capital Ltd
Phillips, Charles—Probitas Partners Inc
Phillips, David—Yellow Point Equity Partners LP
Phillips, Donna—Morgan Stanley Alternative Investment Partners LP
Phillips, Greg—Broadhaven Capital Partners LLC
Phillips, Jackson—Atairos Management LP
Phillips, Jackson—Avista Capital Holdings LP
Phillips, Jerry—Harbert Management Corp
Phillips, Jim—Pharos Capital Group LLC
Phillips, Joshua—Aurora Resurgence Management Partners LLC
Phillips, Joshua—Catalyst Health And Technology Partners LLC
Phillips, Joshua—Peninsula Pacific Strategic Partners LLC
Phillips, M. Troy—Beecken Petty O'Keefe & Company LLC
Phillips, Mark—Penta Capital Llp
Phillips, Michael—Apax Partners LLP
Phillips, Michael—FRANK RUSSELL CAPITAL CO
Phillips, Michael—Oaktree Capital Management LP
Phillips, Rick—Actis LLP
Phillips, Ryan—WP Global Partners Inc
Phillips, Stuart—Bay Partners
Phillips, Stuart—Ridgelift Ventures
Phillips, Susan—Omidyar Network Commons LLC
Philosophos, John—Great Oaks Venture Capital LLC
Philp, John—Fulcrum Capital Partners Inc
Phing, Meranee—Riverside Co
Phipps, Charles—Sevin Rosen Funds
Phipps, George—Jasper Ridge Partners LP
Phipps, Ogden—Snow Phipps Group LLC
Pho, Frank—Business Development Bank of Canada
Pho, Soon—Canyon Capital Advisors LLC
Phoenix, William—Mistral Equity Partners LP
Phua, Jimmy—Canada Pension Plan Investment Board
Phuong, Tan—PHI Capital Holdings Inc
Piana, Marco—VAM Investments SpA
Pianim, Nicholas—Duff Ackerman & Goodrich LLC
Pianko, Daniel—University Ventures
Piard, Montes—General Atlantic LLC
Piasecki, Mark—Silverfleet Capital Partners LLP
Pica, Vincent—Safanad Inc
Picchi, Bernard—Palisade Capital Management LLC
Piccinini, Giulio—Vision Capital LLP
Piccino, Didier—Seventure Partners SA
Pichler, Markus—Alps Venture Capital GmbH
Pickard, Paul—Stewart Capital Management LLC
Pickersgill, Michael—Torys LLP

2549

Pratt's Guide to Private Equity & Venture Capital Sources

Pickett, Brett–Evercore Inc
Picotte, Christopher–ArcLight Capital Holdings LLC
Picozza, Enrico–HLM Management Co LLC
Picozza, Enrico–HLM Management Co LLC
Pidwell, David–Alloy Ventures Inc
Piedrahita, Vicente–Thomas H Lee Partners LP
Piekarz, Guido–Salzburger Unternehmensbeteiligungs-gesellschaft mbH in Liqu
Pieken, Wolfgang–Inveni Capital Oy
Pierandri, Harry–Portfolio Advisors, LLC
Pierce, Chris–Nautic Partners LLC
Pierce, David–QVentures Management GmbH
Pierce, Kristina–Mesirow Financial Private Equity Inc
Piermarini, Charlie–BMO Capital Corp
Pierre, Jean-Claude–China Materialia LLC
Pierrepont, Seth–Sycamore Ventures Inc
Pierrin-Lepinard, Sophie–Banexi Ventures Partners SA
Pierson, Matt–10X Venture Partners LLC
Pierson, Steven–Lovell Minnick Partners LLC
Piesner, Eric–Morrison & Foerster LLP
Pietersen, Christopher–First Reserve Corp
Pietkiewicz, Paulina–Abris Capital Partners Sp zoo
Pietrantonio, Frank–Cooley LLP
Pietrasik, Cezary–Warburg Pincus LLC
Pietri, Todd–Activate Venture Partners
Pietruska, Alexander–Carlyle Group LP
Pietruszkiewicz, Adam–Icentis Capital Sp z o o
Pietruszkiewicz, Adam–Riverside Co
Pietrzak, John–Castle Creek Capital LLC
Piette, Josly–Meusinvest SA
Pignard, Jerome–Oryx Partner SARL
Pignato, Joseph–Allied Minds LLC
Pignatti-Morano, Vittorio–Trilantic Capital Management LP
Pignatti-Morano, Vittorio–Trilantic Capital Management LP
Pihlava, Sakari–Vendep Capital Oy
Pijl, Nico K.G.–Netherlands Development Finance Company NV
Pijl, Nico–Netherlands Development Finance Company NV
Pike, Chad–Blackstone Group LP
Pike, Christopher–Advent International Corp
Pike, Jason–Charlesbank Capital Partners LLC
Pilecki, Kurt–Bison Capital Asset Management LLC
Pillai, Nethan–iCapital M Sdn Bhd
Pillapakkam, Badri–Omidyar Network Commons LLC
Pillar, Simon–Pacific Equity Partners Pty Ltd
Pillay, Keshan–Makalani Holdings Ltd
Pilloux, Alain–European Bank for Reconstruction and Development
Pillsbury, Leland–Thayer Ventures
Pilson, John–Atlantic-Pacific Capital Inc
Pilson, Michael–Atlantic-Pacific Capital Inc
Pim, Roger–Sl Capital Partners Llp
Pimenta, Leonardo–Nova Gestao de Recursos Ltda
Pimkin, Dmitry–Rossiiskaia Korporatsiia Nanotekhnologii GK
Pimstein, David–Molash Group
Pin, Richard–Mbo Partenaires SAS
Pinard, Debbie–Wesley Clover International Corporation
Pinchev, Alex–Abundance Partners LLC
Pinciroli, Marco–Innogest Sgr SpA
Pindur, Daniel–CVC Capital Partners Ltd
Pinedo, Anna–Morrison & Foerster LLP
Pineiro, Ricardo–Foresight Group LLP
Ping, Ping–Chengwei Ventures
Pinkas, Robert–Brantley Venture Partners L P
Pinker, Juergen–Blackstone Group LP
Pinkerton, David–AIG Capital Partners Inc
Pinnell, John–Fordahl Capital SA
Pinsky, Seth–New York City Economic Development Corp
Pinto Peyronel, Sarah–Great Hill Equity Partners LLC
Pinto, Daniel–Stanhope Capital LLP
Pinto, Fernando–Carlyle Group LP
Pinto, Jaime–Pitt Capital Partners Ltd
Pinto, Jason–Amadeus Capital Partners Ltd
Pinto, Sarah–Great Hill Equity Partners LLC
Pinya, Oriol–Abac Capital SL
Pinya, Oriol–Apax Partners LLP
Piol, Alessandro–Vedanta Capital LP
Piorkowski, Christine–Snowbird Capital Inc
Piotrowski, AnnMarie–Batterson Venture Capital
Piper, Danny–Newcap Partners Inc
Piper, Jeffrey–Svoboda Capital Partners LLC
Piper, Joseph–Point B Capital LLC
Piper, Mike–Catapult Venture Managers Ltd
Pique Pijuan, Roger–Inveready Seed Capital SCR SA
Piquet, Bernardo–3G Capital Inc
Piree, John–RAF Industries, Inc.
Pires, Elezabeth–Investcorp Technology Investments Group
Pirkul, Neset–Cedar Springs Capital LLC
Piros, Elemer–Burrill & Company
Pirsch, Megan–Encore Consumer Capital Fund L P
Pisa, Albert–Milbank Tweed Hadley & Mccloy LLP
Pisani, Craig–Arrowhead Mezzanine LLC
Pishevar, Shervin–Menlo Ventures
Pisker, Andrew–Richmond Park Partners LLP
Pistilli, Jonathan–Morgan Stanley Alternative Investment Partners LP
Pistilli, Robert–Peak Rock Capital LLC
Pistillo, Bernie–Morrison & Foerster LLP
Pit, Jeroen–Bencis Capital Partners BV
Pitarra, George–Emergence Venture Partners LLC
Pitchford, Mark–Cooley LLP
Pitman, David–Oakfield Capital Partners LLP
Pitout, Simon–DP World Ltd
Pitroda, Salil–Symphony Technology Group LLC
Pitt, James–Lexington Partners Inc
Pitta de Gouveia Bodra, Ana Marta–Vinci Equities Gestora de Recursos Ltda
Pittaway, David–Castle Harlan Inc
Pitteloud, Dominique–Endeavour Vision SA
Pittman, Robert–Pilot Group LP
Piurko, Jonathan–Northwater Capital Management Inc
Pizarro, Peter–Small Business Guarantee and Finance Corporation
Pizzani, Paul–Cartesian Capital Group LLC
Pla, Agustin–3i Group PLC
Place, Jonathan–Odyssey Investment Partners LLC
Placek, Robert–Stonetree Capital Management LLC
Plaga, John–Canyon Capital Advisors LLC
Plain, Hank–Lightstone Ventures LP
Plamondon, Jean–Idinvest Partners SA
Planas, Miguel–Isis Venture Capital SL
Plantevin, Michel–Bain Capital Inc
Planting-Bergloo, Marcus–Segulah Advisor AB
Plassard, Aymeric–Weinberg Capital Partners SAS
Plastina, Ren–Varagon Capital Partners LP
Platek, Robert–MSD Capital LP
Platnick, Joseph–Iglobe Treasury Management Ltd
Platshon, Mark–Birchmere Ventures
Platt, Michael–Potomac Equity Partners LLC
Plattfaut, Eberhard–Wellington Partners GmbH
Plattner, Hasso–Hasso Plattner Ventures Management GmbH
Plauche, Charlie–S3 Ventures LLC
Plavin, Stephen–CT Investment Management Co LLC
Playfair, John–Macquarie Private Wealth Inc
Pleaner, Raymond–Sabvest Ltd
Plenge, Charles–Haynes and Boone LLC
Pless, John–Snow Phipps Group LLC
Pless, Paul–New Capital Partners
Pliam, Nick–Decheng Capital LLC
Pline, Jennifer–Harvard Management Company Inc
Pliner, Michael–Jerusalem Global Ventures
Plisson, Delphine–Neo Investment Partners LLP
Ploegmakers, Hein–Gilde Buy Out Partners BV
Plompen, Ronald–KPN Ventures BV
Plooster, Matt–Bridgepoint Investment Partners I LLLP
Plosker, Todd–Sun Capital Partners Inc
Plotkin, Adam–ff Venture Capital
Plotkin, Serge–Opus Capital
Plouffe, Justin–Carlyle Group LP
Pludwinski, Marvin–Lynx Equity Ltd
Plume, Stephen–Entrepreneurs Fund LP
Plume, Stephen–RB Webber and Comapny Inc
Plumley, Kent–Genesys Capital Partners Inc
Plummer, Charlie–Proterra Investment Partners LP
Plumridge, David–Hawkesbridge Capital
Plumridge, Scott–Halifax Group LLC
Plunkett, Stuart–Morrison & Foerster LLP
Pluvinet, Gerard–21 Centrale Partners SA
Poch, Gerald–FirstMark Capital LLC
Poddar, Abhishek–Banyantree Finance Pvt Ltd
Poddar, Anoop–Energy Ventures AS
Podlesak, Dennis–Domain Associates LLC
Poff, Mark–Swander Pace Capital LLC
Poffenberger, James–Mcm Capital Partners L P
Poggiali, Barbara–Earlybird Venture Capital GmbH & Co KG
Poggioli, Philippe–Access Capital Partners SA
Pogodin, Pavel–Haynes and Boone LLC
Pohl, Detlef–Siemens Venture Capital GmbH
Pohl, Susan–KC Venture Group LLC
Pohlen, Mike–North Sky Capital LLC
Pohren, Gene–57 Stars LLC
Pohren, Gene–PCGI LLC
Poiares Baptista, Joao Paulo–Burrill & Company
Poignonnec, Sacha–Rocket Internet AG
Poile, Joanne–Passport Capital LLC
Poindexter, Obrea–Morrison & Foerster LLP
Pointer, Tom–TOM Capital Associates Inc
Pokorney, Joel–Tecum Capital Partners
Pokorny i, Brian–SV Angel
Polack, Axel–TVM Capital GmbH
Polak, Keith–Versa Capital Management Inc
Polak, Patrick–Newion Investments BV

Polanco, Rafael—Evercore Inc
Poland, Jared—C3 Capital LLC
Polaneczky, Joseph—Merit Capital Partners IV LLC
Polano, Robert—Carduso Capital BV
Polato, N.—Veneto Sviluppo SpA
Polazzi, Anthony—Sun Capital Partners Inc
Polemitis, Antonis—Ledra Capital LLC
Poler, Dwight—Bain Capital Inc
Poletti, Philippe—Ardian France SA
Poletti, Robert—Levine Leichtman Capital Partners Inc
Polewik, Tamara—J.H. Whitney & Co LLC
Polidore, Clare—Trust Company of the West
Polikarpov, Sergey—Rossiiskaia Korporatsiia Nanotekhnologii GK
Polimino, Peter—Altus Capital Partners Inc
Poliner, Randall—Antares Capital Corporation
Polischuk, Trevor—OrbiMed Advisors LLC
Politi, Ricardo—Mindset Ventures
Politi, Santo—Spark Capital
Polizzi, Catherine—Morrison & Foerster LLP
Polk, Benjamin—Veritas Capital Fund Management LLC
Polke, Heinrich—L Eigenkapitalagentur
Pollack, Bruce—Centre Partners Management LLC
Pollack, Gina—Gores Group LLC
Pollack, Kenneth—Acas LLC
Pollack, Kimberly—Levine Leichtman Capital Partners Inc
Pollack, Lawrence—Grano Retail Investments Inc
Pollack, Lester—Centre Partners Management LLC
Pollak, Robert—SV Angel
Pollard, Stuart—Sanofi-Sunrise
Polli, Rolando—Ambienta SGR SpA
Pollman, Matthew—Tautona Group Lp
Pollock, Adam—Stellus Capital Management LLC
Pollock, Scott—B4 Ventures LLC
Pollock, Tristan—500 Startups, L.P.
Polmann, Berry—Adveq Management AG
Polo, David—Diana Capital SGECR SA
Polodna, Duane—World Investments Inc
Polovets, Leo—Susa Ventures LP
Pols, Mark—GGV Capital
Polydor, Peter—SAIL Capital Partners LLC
Pommen, Wayne—TorQuest Partners Inc
Pommerening, Christopher—Active Capital Partners SA
Pompa, Philip—Cielo Management LLC
Pompidou, Thomas—Crescent Point Group
Pompidou, Thomas—Marker Financial Advisors LLC
Ponazecki, Jay—Morrison & Foerster LLP
Ponce Romay, Roberto—CoreCo Holdings LLC
Ponce, Alejandro—Nexxus Group SAC
Pongweni, Cynthia—Mineworkers Investment Co
Ponikvar, Dale—Milbank Tweed Hadley & Mccloy LLP
Ponnert, Niklas—Origo Partners PLC
Ponnuru, Satya—Larsen Maccoll Partners LP
Ponti, Andrea—GHO Capital Partners LLP
Pontillo, Franco—Plataforma Capital Partners Gestao de Investimentos Ltda
Pool, Philip—Willis Stein & Partners LP
Poole, Scott—Ridgemont Partners Management LLC
Poole, Walker—Ridgemont Partners Management LLC
Poolman, Hans Roeland—1&12 Ventures BV

Poonawala, Akbar—Pivot Investment Partners LLC
Poonpol, Krating—500 Startups, L.P.
Poorman, John Kevin—PSP Capital Partners LLC
Popa-Radu, Emma—Advent International Corp
Popatia, Tawfiq—Onex Corp
Pope, Rory—Advent International Corp
Pope, Rory—Apposite Capital LLP
Pope, William—H2o Venture Partners Pe Ltd
Pople, Nick—Ludgate Investments Ltd
Popovich, Alexander—Versa Capital Management Inc
Popowich, Wendy—Palisade Capital Management LLC
Popp, Richard—Advanced Technology Ventures
Popp, Richard—Lightstone Ventures LP
Poppe, John—MidCap Equity Partners
Poppel, Ariel—Israel Infinity Venture Capital Fund Israel LP
Popusoi, Victor—NCH Capital Inc
Porbo, Shierly—Atlantic-Pacific Capital Inc
Porell, Robert—Gefinor Ventures
Porko, Lars—Evolver Investment Group Ltd
Porndhithi, Artapong—Lombard Investments Inc
Porras, Luis—Monterrey Capital Partners
Porreca, Carlo—Comvest Partners
Porte, Thierry—JC Flowers & Co LLC
Porten, Joe—Battery Ventures LP
Porteous, William—RRE Ventures LLC
Porter, Brook—Kleiner Perkins Caufield & Byers LLC
Porter, Claire—Champlain Capital Partners LP
Porter, David—Apposite Capital LLP
Porter, Gilbert—Haynes and Boone LLC
Porter, Mukya—Oaktree Capital Management LP
Porter, Stewart—Oakley Capital Ltd
Porter, Tim—MadroNA Venture Group
Porter, Timothy—Audax Group, Inc.
Portillo, Dan—Greylock Partners LLC
Portman, Anit—Investments in ATI Ltd
Portner, Mark—Shorenstein Co LLC
Portnoy, Jason—Subtraction Capital
Portwich, Anne—Life Sciences Partners BV
Porzio, Claudio—Vertis SGR SpA
Posada, Johanna—Elevar Equity Advisors Pvt Ltd
Posluns, David—Wifleur, Inc.
Posner, David—First Reserve Corp
Posner, Henry—Hawthorne Group
Posner, Ross—Ridge Capital Partners LLC
Posnick, David—Blackstone Group LP
Posselt, Wolfgang—Aurelia Private Equity GmbH
Possick, Jeffrey—MissionPoint Capital Partners LLC
Posthuma, Marcel—XSML Management BV
Potanin, Vladimir—KhK Interros ZAO
Potarazu, Krishna—JMI Management Inc
Pothier, Robert—Epic Ventures Inc
Potochny, James—Leaf Clean Energy USA LLC
Potocsnak, Lisa—Asset Management Co
Potocsnak, Lisa—Asset Management Co
Potokar, Robert—Resilience Capital Partners LLC
Potokin, Jon—Darby Overseas Investments, Ltd.
Potter, Allen—Allied Growth Strategies & Management LLC
Potter, Cheryl—Permira Advisers LLP
Potter, Douglas—Helmsman Funds Management, Ltd.
Potter, Garrett—Steelpoint Capital Partners LP
Potter, Rick—Northill Capital LLP

Potter, William—Palisade Capital Management LLC
Potters, Doug—CIVC Partners LP
Potthof, Ingo—Unternehmertum GmbH
Pottow, V. Frank—Greenhill Capital Partners LP
Pouletty, Philippe—Truffle Capital SAS
Poulsen, Stig—VAEKSTFONDEN
Poulson, Shauntel—NewSchools Venture Fund
Pouschine, John—Pouschine Cook Capital Management LLC
Poushanchi, Babak—Cota Capital Inc
Povstyanoy, Konstantin—Baring Vostok Capital Partners Ltd
Powar, Sonia—Boost&Co SAS
Powell, Earl—Trivest Partners LP
Powell, Earl—Westshore Capital Partners LP
Powell, John—Integral Capital Partners
Powell, Michael—Haynes and Boone LLC
Powell, Michael—Sofinnova Ventures Inc
Powell, Samuel—Silver Lake Partners LP
Power, Keith—Cove Hill Partners LLC
Powers, Brian—Hellman & Friedman LLC
Powers, Dennis—VectorPoint Ventures
Powers, Timothy—Haynes and Boone LLC
Powers, Werner—Haynes and Boone LLC
Powers, William—Kairos Venture Investments LLC
Pozatek, Andrew—Trailcreek Capital Group LLC
Pozos-Villarreal, Rolando—Cappello Capital Corp
Pradier, Arnaud—Sodica SASU
Prado, Antonio Henrique—Plataforma Capital Partners Gestao de Investimentos Ltda
Prado, Carlos—Espiga Capital Gestion SGCR SA
Prado, Dennis—Main Street Capital Holdings LLC
Prado, Ricardo—Sterling Partners GP LLC
Prado, Steven—Oaktree Capital Management LP
Prager, Brett—Dfw Capital Partners LP
Prahl, Peder—Triton Beteiligungsberatung GmbH
Prakash, Abhimanyu—Blackstone Group LP
Prakash, Arun—Virgo Capital
Prakash, Prashanth—Accel India Venture Fund
Prakash, Shalini—500 Startups, L.P.
Prakke, Frits—Alchemy Partners LLP
Prasad, N.K.—PATHFINDER INVESTMENT CO
Prasad, S.Vishwanatha—Caspian Advisors Pvt Ltd
Prasad, Satya—Morgan Stanley Alternative Investment Partners LP
Prasetya, Sigit—CVC Asia Pacific Ltd
Prasetya, Sigit—CVC Capital Partners Ltd
Prata, Gregory—Gotham Private Equity Partners LP
Pratt, Jamie—Atlantic Asset Management LLC
Pratt, Michael—Select Venture Partners LLC
Pratt, Stanley—Abbott Capital Management LLC
Praznuik, Ken—Manitoba Capital Fund
Preaux, Joelle—G Square Healthcare Private Equity Fund LLP
Precella, Karen—Haynes and Boone LLC
Predayna, Steve—New Capital Management Inc
Prehn, Guido—DPE Deutsche Private Equity GmbH
Preiner, Megan—Thomas H Lee Partners LP
Preissier, Jim—Panthera Capital Group
Preminger, Dana—Tene Kibbutz Investment Management Ltd
Premji, Najib—Mckenna Gale Capital Inc
Prencipe, Michele—Three Hills Capital Partners LLP
Prend, David—Rockport Capital Partners
Prendergast, Daniel—Blackstone Group LP

Prendergast, Will–Investec Ventures Ireland Ltd
Prentice, Geoffrey–Atomico Ventures
Prentice, Jeff–Arc Financial Corp.
Prentiss, Michael–Argenta Partners, L.P.
Prenzlow, Andre–Alpha Founders
Preovolos, Penelope–Morrison & Foerster LLP
Press, Anthony–Morrison & Foerster LLP
Presser, Stephen–Monomoy Capital Partners LLC
Pressler, Paul–Clayton Dubilier & Rice LLC
Pressler, Townes–Lime Rock Partners LLC
Pressman, Jason–Shasta Ventures LP
Pressnell, Jonathan–Greenbriar Equity Group LLC
Prestegaard, Richard–High Road Capital Partners LLC
Prestia, Giuseppe–Charterhouse Capital Partners LLP
Preston, Carr–Akoya Capital Partners LLC
Preston, Fraser–HIG Capital LLC
Preston, Robert–Epi-V LLP
Pretolani, Mauro–TLcom Capital LLP
Pretorius, Pieter–Treacle Venture Partners
Preve, Eugenio–Cinven Group Ltd
Prey, Scott–iSelect Fund LLC
Pribyl, Jeffrey–Blackstone Group LP
Pricco, Jennifer–Antares Capital Corp
Price, Bonnie–HCI Equity LLC
Price, Chris–Oak HC/FT Partners LP
Price, Harrison–NRD Capital Management LLC
Price, Joe–Bank of America Capital Advisors (BACA)
Price, Matt–Business Development Bank of Canada
Price, Michael–CEO Ventures
Price, Michael–Evercore Inc
Price, Paul–Prudential Capital Group LP
Price, Philip–Arle Heritage LLP
Price, Philip–PHD Equity Partners LLP
Price, Quintin–BlackRock Inc
Price, Roger–Innovation Capital Associates Pty, Ltd.
Price, Steven–Centerbridge Partners LP
Priddy, Robert–Comvest Partners
Priester, Wilbur–Blue Water Capital LLC
Priestley, William–LGV Capital Ltd
Prieto, Dave–Headwaters BD LLC
Prihti, Aki–Inveni Capital Oy
Prince, Gingee–Enhanced Capital Partners LLC
Princi, Anthony–Morrison & Foerster LLP
Princiotta, Joseph–Medley Capital LLC
Prins, Ewout–Holland Venture BV
Prins, Marius–Participatiemaatschappij Oost Nederland NV
Priston, Duncan–Bayside Capital Inc
Pritchard, Brad–Hercules Capital Inc
Pritchard, Gary–Palamon Capital Partners LP
Pritchett, J. Travis–Harbert Management Corp
Pritzker, J.B.–Pritzker Group Venture Capital
Pritzker, Penny–PSP Capital Partners LLC
Pritzker, Tony–Pritzker Group Venture Capital
Probst, Thomas–ADCURAM Group AG
Probstel, Isabelle–Apax Partners LLP
Procheus, Lars–Firm Factory Network AB
Prockl, Juergen–Myonic Holding GmbH
Procter, Benjamin–Watermill Group LLC
Proctor, David–Milestone Partners LP
Proctor, Kim–ACM Ltd
Proctor, Robert–Blu Venture Investors LLC
Profancik, Brian–ABP Capital LLC

Prokofiev, Andrey–GEN3 Partners, Inc.
Prokop, Kevin–Rockbridge Growth Equity LLC
Prokopich, Lori–Cassels Brock & Blackwell LLP
Pronczuk, Dariusz–Enterprise Investors Sp z o o
Pronk, Nikolai–Gilde Buy Out Partners BV
Proske, Daniela–BASF Venture Capital GmbH
Prosperi, Joe–Beringer Capital Inc
Prosser, Ena–Undisclosed Firm
Prosser, Sean–Morrison & Foerster LLP
Prost, Jacques–Credit Agricole Corporate and Investment Bank SA
Prostko, E. Richard–Vantagepoint Management Inc
Prostko, Rick–Comcast Ventures
Protasewich, Chris–Highland Capital Partners LLC
Protash, Eugene–Allen & Company of Florida, Inc.
Proto, Joseph–Windham Venture Partners
Prough, Stephen–Salem Partners LLC
Proujansky, Philip–Cayuga Venture Fund
Prout, Matthew–Falcon Investment Advisors LLC
Proven, John–Growth Works Capital Ltd
Provera, Nino–Ambienta SGR SpA
Provow, Travis Lee–Value Plus Ventures LLC
Prudhomme, Maurice–Solidarity Fund QFL
Pruett, Shelby–Gryffindor Capital Partners LLC
Pruitt, Jeffrey–Tallwave LLC
Pruss, Lenny–Amplify Partners LP
Pruss, Lenny–Redpoint Ventures
Pruthi, Vineet–Lincolnshire Management Inc
Pruzan, Robert–Centerview Partners LLC
Pruzansky, Mark–Apple Tree Partners
Pryce, Tim–Terra Firma Capital Partners Ltd
Pryma, Thomas–AEA Investors LLC
Pryor, Brian–MVP Capital LLC
Pryor, John–Calibrate Management Ltd
Pryor, John–Overseas Private Investment Corp
Psaros, Michael–KPS Capital Partners LP
Pucci, Giorgio–Arcadia SGR SpA
Puchniak, Robert–Richardson Capital Ltd
Pudhukottai, Sampathkumar–Kalaari Capital Partners LLC
Pudner, Rick–Nbd Sana Capital Ltd
Puelinckx, Kristoff–Delta Partners FZ LLC
Puertas, Juan–Ged Group
Puhakka, Hannu–MB Rahastot Oy
Puijpe, Edwin–Gebruder Heller Dinklage
Pujol, Jerome–Keensight Capital SAS
Pujol, Juan Eusebio–Miura Private Equity SGEIC SA
Pujol, Juan–JHP Enterprises LLC
Puliti, Riccardo–European Bank for Reconstruction and Development
Puljic, Goran–Oak Hill Advisors LP
Pullara, Sam–Sutter Hill Ventures
Pulley, Thomas–Fortress Investment Group LLC
Pulte, William–Pulte Capital Partners LLC
Pulte, William–Pulte Capital Partners LLC
Pummill, Christopher–Mason Wells Inc
Pundak-Mintz, Adi–GEMINI CAPITAL FUND MGMT LTD
Pungiluppi, Juan Antonio–Teka Capital SAS
Punhong, Duke–Graycliff Partners LP
Puntereri, Bailey–Atlantic-Pacific Capital Inc
Pupin, Antoine–Compass Partners International LLC
Pupo, Alex Luis–Aztec Equity Partners LLC
Purcell, Gregory–Arbor Private Investment Co LLC
Purcell, Jack–Ridgemont Partners Management LLC

Purcell, Michael–Sentinel Capital Partners LLC
Purcell, Tim–Linzor Capital Partners LP
Purker, Prashant–ICICI Venture Funds Management Company Ltd
Purkert, Gert–Aurelius AG
Purse, Charles–Blackstone Group LP
Purushothaman, Roopa–Everstone Capital Management, Ltd.
Purushothaman, Sudar–Fundamental Advisors LP
Purvis, Michael–Blackstone Group LP
Purwohardono, Andy Nugroho–CVC Capital Partners Ltd
Puscasiu, Chris–EQT Funds Management Ltd
Pusey, Christopher–KRG Capital Management LP
Puskoor, Dayakar–Naya Ventures LLC
Putnam, Mitch–32 Degrees Capital
Pyne, George–Bruin Sports Capital LLC
Pyne, Samuel–Haddington Ventures LLC
Qadir, Kamran–Jahangir Siddiqui Group Associates
Qassem, Abdullah–Nbd Sana Capital Ltd
Qi, Jue–Pride Investments Group Ltd
Qi, Li–TeChina Investment Management Ltd
Qi, Pei–Brain Robotics Capital LLC
Qi, Shen–Fortune Venture Capital Co Ltd
Qi, Shen–Fortune Venture Capital Corp
Qi, Yuwei–Shanghai NCE Venture Capital Management Co Ltd
Qian, Dianna–Fidelity Growth Partners Asia
Qian, Jack–New Mountain Capital I LLC
Qian, Meng–State Development & Investment Corp Ltd
Qian, Qiao–China Canada Angels Alliance Ltd
Qian, Xiaohua–SAIF Partners
Qiao, Jiangtao–Hollyhigh Intl Capital Co Ltd
Qiao, Jichang–Beijing Lebang Lecheng Venture Investment Managemet Co Ltd
Qiao, Qi–Richlink International Capital Co Ltd
Qiiu, Hongguang–Shanghai Realeader Investment Fund Management Co Ltd
Qin, Bin–Shanghai Realeader Investment Fund Management Co Ltd
Qin, Harry–Shanghai Peeli Investment Management Co Ltd
Qin, Ming–State Development & Investment Corp Ltd
Qin, Yangwen–Shenzhen Cornerstone of Entrepreneurial Cci Capital Ltd
Qing Ye, Judy–YiMei Capital Management
Qishta, Shadi–National Net Ventures
Qiu, Cynthia–Fang Group Co Ltd
Qiu, Dan–Shenzhen Green Pine Capital Partners Co Ltd
Qiu, John–Sinovation Ventures Ltd
Qiu, Liping–Milestone Capital Management Ltd
Qiu, Sinian–Hollyhigh Intl Capital Co Ltd
Qiu, Vicky–Ascribe Capital, LLC
Qiu, Zheng–BOCGI Zheshang Investment Fund Management Zhejiang Co Ltd
Qiu, Zhongwei–Hony Capital Beijing Co Ltd
Qu, Chengguo–Sunbridge Investment Management Co Ltd
Qu, Guoyu–CRP-Fanya Investment Consultants Beijing Co Ltd
Qu, Weidong–Zero2IPO Ventures
Qu, Xiang Jun–Changan Capital

Qu, Xiang Jun—XiAn Prutention Investment & Development Co Ltd
Qua-Enoo, Emmanuel—Southern Africa Enterprise Development Fund
Quackenbush, Kip—Nex Cubed LLC
Quadrio-Curzio, Stefano—BC Partners LLP
Quagliaroli, James—Spectrum Equity Investors LP
Quagliaroli, Jim—Silversmith Capital Partners LLC
Quake, Jeffrey—First Reserve Corp
Quandt, Rob—Bain Capital Inc
Quant, Shawn—Piper Jaffray Ventures Inc
Quarles, Randal—Carlyle Group LP
Quarls, Harry—Global Infrastructure Holdings
Quarta, Roberto—Clayton Dubilier & Rice LLC
Quasha, Alan—Vanterra Capital Ltd
Queally, Doyle—Blackstone Group LP
Quella, James—Blackstone Group LP
Quemada, Jorge—Cinven Group Ltd
Quesada, Guillermo Miro—Salkantay Partners SAC
Queveau, Philippe—CITA Gestion SA
Quigley, Jarrod—Morgan Stanley Alternative Investment Partners LP
Quigley, John—YL Ventures GP Ltd
Quigley, Matthew—Blackstone Group LP
Quigley, William—Clearstone Venture Management Services LLC
Quimby, Tom—Medley Capital LLC
Quinlan, Rory—Capital Dynamics Sdn Bhd
Quinlivan, David—Saints Ventures
Quinn, George—BlackRock Private Equity Partners AG
Quinn, Larry—Atlantic Bridge
Quinn, Michael—Innovation Capital Associates Pty, Ltd.
Quinn, Terrence—Kayne Anderson Capital Advisors LP
Quinn, Thomas—Jordan Company LP
Quinn, William—Versa Capital Management Inc
Quintella, Pedro—Vinci Equities Gestora de Recursos Ltda
Quintini, Renata—LUX CAPITAL GROUP L L C
Quirici, Alexandre—IDG Capital Partners Inc
Quisenberry, Chandler—Avista Capital Holdings LP
Quist, William—Industry Ventures LLC
Quist, William—Industry Ventures LLC
Quon, David—Orchard First Source Inc
Qureshi, Osman—Mubadala Infrastructure Partners Ltd
Quy, Roger—Technology Partners
R. Jones, Boyd—Fitch Crown Venture Capital Management (Shenzhen) Co Ltd
RMS Alseddiqi Alansaari, Jassim Mohammed—Abu Dhabi Capital Management LLC
Raabe, Richard—Venture Management LLC
Raaby Bronden, Christian—ATP Private Equity Partners
Rabb, Kee—Private Advisors LLC
Rabbat, Marcelo—Vinci Equities Gestora de Recursos Ltda
Rabe, Joachim—Corvus Capital GmbH
Rabenou, Darren—Terrapin Partners LLC
Rabil, Albert—Kayne Anderson Capital Advisors LP
Rabini, Johannes—Sobera Capital GmbH
Rabinovich, Eyal—Octopus Ventures Ltd
Rabinovici, Gabriel—Willow Impact

Rabinowitz, Ben—Amiti Ventures LLC
Rachal, Brian—Gridiron Capital LLC
Rachman, Marc—CVC Capital Partners Ltd
Rachwalski, John—Oak Hill Capital Management Inc
Racicot, Erika—Business Instincts Group
Raciti, Philip—CVC Capital Partners Ltd
Raciti, Robert—Silverfern Group Inc
Ract-Madoux, Wandrille—Weinberg Capital Partners SAS
Racusin, Robert—Virgo Investment Group LLC
Radchenko, Andrew—NCH Capital Inc
Radebe, Polo—Identity Capital Partners (Pty) Ltd
Radecki, Joseph—Headwaters BD LLC
Rader, Stacie—Flagship Pioneering
Radermacher, Brian—Panorama Point Partners LLC
Radhakrishnan, Anand—Investcorp Bank BSC
Radhakrishnan, Gayathri—Velocity Venture Capital Inc
Radhakrishnan, Ram—East West Capital Partners Pte Ltd
Radhakrishnan, Ramesh—Artiman Management LLC
Radic, Brian—LLR Partners Inc
Radis, Craig—PPM America Capital Partners LLC
Radosevich, H.Raymond—Verge Fund
Radzik, Mark—Granite Creek Partners LLC
Radziwilski, Jacek—Pekao Investment Banking SA
Rae, Amy—Vanedge Capital Inc
Rae, Katie—Techstars Central LLC
Raethorne, David—Causeway Capital Partners I LP
Rafanelli, Paolo—Fidi Toscana SpA
Rafart, Marcel—Nauta Capital SL
Rafferty, John—Morrison & Foerster LLP
Raffin, Thomas—Telegraph Hill Partners
Raffle, Tim—ECI Partners LLP
Rafii, Houtan—Beedie Capital Partners
Rafter, Robert—Morgan Stanley Alternative Investment Partners LP
Ragatz, Erik—Hellman & Friedman LLC
Raghavan, Nadathur—Nadathur Estates Pvt Ltd
Raghavan, Nikhil—Bain Capital Inc
Raghavan, Sesh—Evercore Inc
Raghavan, Varoon—Princeton Growth Ventures LLC
Ragins, David—Clarion Capital Partners LLC
Ragnesjo, Hans—EQT Funds Management Ltd
Raguraman, Ashwin—India Innovation Fund
Rahal, Najib—Investcorp Bank BSC
Rahe, Eric—Clayton Dubilier & Rice LLC
Rahe, Eric—JC Flowers & Co LLC
Rahebi, Bita—Morrison & Foerster LLP
Rahman, Rashad—Bruckmann Rosser Sherrill & Co LP
Rahmatollahi, Alexandre—Palamon Capital Partners LP
Rahmn, Jonas—KTH-Chalmers Capital KB
Rai, Rajesh—India Innovation Fund
Rai, Raul—FIL Capital Advisors (India) Pvt Ltd
Rai, Rohan—EagleTree Capital, LP
Raibley, Lewis—Castle Harlan Inc
Raich, Steven—LJ2 & Co LLC
Railhac, Thomas—Cinven Group Ltd
Raimondi, Jill—Housatonic Partners Management Co Inc
Raina, Vikrant—Boston Ventures
Raincock, Toby—Shard Capital Partners LLP
Rainer, Richard—Olimpia Partners Gestao de Recursos SA

Rainey, Don—Grotech Ventures
Rainone, Riccardo—PM & Partners SpA
Rains, Darryl—Morrison & Foerster LLP
Rainville, Pierre—First Stone Venture Partners Inc
Rainville, Todd—JMC Capital Partners LP
Raisson, Christian—Otium Capital SARL
Raisurana, Rahul—Standard Chartered Private Equity Ltd
Raj, Prem—NorthEdge Capital LLP
Raja, Anuradha—L Catterton Asia
Rajab, Mufeed—Investcorp Bank BSC
Rajab, Mufeed—Investcorp Technology Investments Group
Rajadhyaksha, Sunil—HandsOn3 LLC
Rajagopalan, Sreevatsan—Investcorp Technology Investments Group
Rajagopalan, Supraj—Cinven Group Ltd
Rajakumar, Bharani—DreamIt Ventures
Rajan, Hari—Corsair Capital LLC
Rajan, Sunil—Axioma Ventures LLC
Rajanathan, Gajan—Highland Capital Partners LLC
Rajaram, Vishesh—Ventureast
Rajaraman, Anand—Cambrian Ventures Inc
Rajcan, Martin—Blue Bear Capital LLC
Rajee, R—Canbank Venture Capital Fund Ltd
Rajendran, Sendil—Court Square Capital Partners LP
Rajesh, C—Nereus Capital
Rajkumar, Raj—Symphony Asia Holdings Pte Ltd
Rajput, Amit—Wellington Financial Lp
Raju, Champ—PPM America Capital Partners LLC
Raju, Rajesh—Kalaari Capital Partners LLC
Raju, Srini—Peepul Capital Llc
Raju, Vikram—IDFC Capital (Singapore) Pte Ltd
Rajwani, Suraj—DoubleRock LLC
Rakavy, Yuval—BRM Capital LLC
Raker, Geoffrey—Tailwind Capital Partners LP
Raker, Geoffrey—Thomas Weisel Partners Group Inc
Raker, Jill—Greenbriar Equity Group LLC
Raketic, Peter—Oaktree Capital Management LP
Rakhlin, Max—Lightyear Capital LLC
Rakin, Kevin—Highcape Partners LP
Rakishev, Kenges—Genesis Angels
Rakishev, Kenges—Singulariteam Ltd
Rallet, Jean-Michel—Mbo Partenaires SAS
Rallo, Eduardo—Pacific Community Ventures LLC
Ralph, Randal—Northwestern Mutual Capital LLC
Ralston, Geoff—Imagine K12 LLC
Ralston, Geoff—Y Combinator Inc
Ramachandran, Deepak—InvesteCo Capital Corp
Ramachandran, Kyle—Solaris Energy Capital LLC
Ramadori, Sam—Dundee Sarea LP
Ramakrishna, P.—Utthishta Management Advisors LLP
Ramamoorthy, Arun—Pinnacle Ventures
Raman, Sunil—Menlo Ventures
Ramanan, NV—Ananta Capital
Ramanathan, Krishna—Fulcrum Venture India
Ramani, Kamini—Mayfield Fund
Ramasamy, Dinesh—Pantheon Ventures (UK) LLP
Rambaud, Bertrand—Siparex Group
Ramdeen, Gerald—MILLENNIUM EQUITY TRADING L L C
Ramesh, A.—Ventureast
Ramesh, Rengarajan—EagleTree Capital, LP

Rametra, Surinder–HandsOn3 LLC
Ramich, J. Michael–Frontier Capital LLC
Ramich, Michael–Frontier Capital LLC
Ramineni, Anvesh–NSI Ventures
Ramirez, Alexandra–Wilshire Private Markets
Ramirez, Alvaro–Trimaran Capital LLC
Ramirez, Juan–Portobello Capital Advisors SL
Ramirez, Kathleen–Antares Capital LLC
Ramirez, Kurt–Moderne Ventures Fund I LP
Ramirez, Mike–Blackstone Group LP
Ramirez, Roberto–Boston Ventures
Ramirez, Roberto–Converge
Ramirez-Carr, Suzette–Oaktree Capital Management LP
Ramki, Kaushik–Northleaf Capital Partners Ltd
Rammer, Christian–Providence Equity Partners LLC
Ramnath, Renuka–Multiples Alternate Asset Management Pvt Ltd
Ramoisy, Christophe–Pragma Capital SA
Ramos, Ariel–Haynes and Boone LLC
Ramos, Hugo–Change Partners
Ramos, Vicente Miguel–Constitution Capital Partners LLC
Ramos-Fuentenebro, Miguel–Blackstone Group LP
Rampalli, Sridhar–Parampara Capital & Management Consultants LLP
Ramsauer, Robert–Blackstone Group LP
Ramsay, Brian–LJ2 & Co LLC
Ramsay, David–Care Capital LLC
Ramsay, Eric–Jasper Ridge Partners LP
Ramsay, Mike–Pentech Ventures LLP
Ramsey, Richard–Elysian Capital LLP
Ramus, Tristan–Spire Ventures, Ltd.
Ran, Lizhi–Beijing Extensive and Profound Information Technology Co Ltd
Rana, Bhavani–Amadeus Capital Partners Ltd
Ranadive, Vivek–Bow Capital Management LLC
Rand, Christopher–TriStar Technology Ventures LLC
Rand, Lee–Sun Mountain Capital Advisors LLC
Rand, Peter–Blackstone Group LP
Rand, Tom–ArcTern Ventures
Randall, A. Bradley–Nexo Capital Partners
Randall, Bill–Pacific Agri Capital Ltd
Randall, Larry–Alta Partners
Randall, Leigh–Topspin Partners LP
Randazzo, Chris–Main Line Equity Partners LLC
Randel, Johnny–StepStone Group LP
Randhawa, Harpal–Global Emerging Markets
Randolph, Laura–Oaktree Capital Management LP
Raney, Scott–Redpoint Ventures
Ranganathan, Natarajan–Helion Venture Partners LLC
Ranganathan, S.–Edelweiss Financial Services Ltd
Rangasami, Kevin–Mcb Equity Fund Ltd
Rangaswami, M.R.–Sand Hill Group LLC
Ranger, Joanne–Westerkirk Capital Inc
Ranger, Michael–Diamond Castle Holdings LLC
Rangitsch, Jeff–Castlelake LP
Rannala, Erik–MuckerLab LLC
Ransenberg, Scott–Riverwood Capital Group LLC
Ransford, Mark–Zephyr Management LP
Ransick, Kristi–NewSchools Venture Fund
Ranson, Michael–Blue Wolf Capital Partners LLC
Rantanen, Ilkka–Metric Capital Partners LLP
Rantanen, Jacqueline–Hamilton Lane Advisors LLC

Ranum, Anders–Sapphire Ventures LLC
Ranum, Anders–Sapphire Ventures LLC
Ranzetta, Theresia–Accel Partners & Co Inc
Rao, Amir–Crescent Capital Group LP
Rao, Bharat–Capital Square Partners Pte Ltd
Rao, Ganesh–Thomas H Lee Partners LP
Rao, N.P.–Indian Steps and Business Incubators Association
Rao, Raj–Global Infrastructure Holdings
Rao, Sri–Silversmith Capital Partners LLC
Rao, T. Sesha–Jacob Ballas Capital India Pvt Ltd
Rao, Zeena–ICV Partners LLC
Raoul, Andre–Pole Capital SAS
Rapaport, Alec–Commonfund Capital Inc
Rapisarda, Senia–Business Development Bank of Canada
Rapisarda, Senia–HarbourVest Partners LLC
Rapoport, Boris–Lightyear Capital LLC
Raposo, Gracinda–Ecs Capital SA
Rapp, Eric-Alan–Sunstone Capital A/S
Rappaport, Andrew–August Capital Management LLC
Rappaport, Stacey–Milbank Tweed Hadley & Mccloy LLP
Rapport, Michael–Behrman Capital
Rasche, Thom–Earlybird Venture Capital GmbH & Co KG
Raschle, Bruno–Adveq Management AG
Rasheed, Adel–Venture Capital Bank BSCC
Rashid, Saqib–Abraaj Capital Ltd
Rashotte, Tom–TD Capital Group Ltd
Rashtchy, Safa–Think Ventures LP
Rasmussen, Jesper–Axcel Industriinvestor A/S
Rasmussen, Michael–Carlyle Group LP
Rassin, Ryan–LBC Credit Partners Inc
Rastogi, Anupam–NGP Capital
Rastogi, Shantanu–Apax Partners LLP
Rastogi, Shantanu–General Atlantic LLC
Rastrick, John–NorthEdge Capital LLP
Rastrick, John–Phoenix Equity Partners Ltd
Ratanadaros, Na Chanok–Food Capitals PCL
Ratcliffe, Liam–New Leaf Venture Partners LLC
Raterman, Mark–LNC Partners
Rather, Jonathan–Welsh Carson Anderson & Stowe
Rathi, Parag–River Cities Capital Fund LP
Rathi, Preeti–Ignition Ventures Management LLC
Rathie, Sagar–UNC Kenan-Flagler Private Equity Fund
Rathinam, G–Actis LLP
Rathman, Lincoln–Vistech Corp
Rathod, Sanjay–Oaktree Capital Management LP
Ratliff, William–Haynes and Boone LLC
Ratnam, Dilip–Vista Ridge Capital Partners LLC
Ratnam, Kapila–Newspring Capital
Ratner, Albert–Glengary LLC
Ratoff, Steven–ProQuest Investments
Rattle, Philip–August Equity Llp
Ratzan, Brian–Pamplona Capital Management LLP
Ratzloff, Joe–Torch Hill Investment Partners LLC
Rauch, Max–Fronteris Consulting AG
Rauch, Robert–Gramercy Inc
Rauh, Jim–Golden Gate Capital Inc
Raulin, Nate–Excellere Capital Management LLC
Rauschenbusch, Erich–Grazia Equity GmbH
Rautter, Joachim–Peppermint VenturePartners GmbH
Rauvola, Bridget–Frazier Management LLC
Raval, Abhilash–Milbank Tweed Hadley & Mccloy LLP
Ravel, Yash–Proprium Capital Partners LP
Ravenna, Andrew–New Water Capital LP
Ravi, T.–Hive LLC
Ravi, T.M.–Clearstone Venture Management Services LLC
Ravich, Jess–Trust Company of the West
Ravindran, Sanuj–Asia Pacific Healthcare Advisors Pvt Ltd
Ravishankar, G.V.–Sequoia Capital India
Ravishankar, GV–Sequoia Capital India
Ravitch, Joseph–Raine Group LLC, The
Ravner, Flynn–Oaktree Capital Management LP
Rawald, Ronald–Cerberus Capital Management LP
Rawat, Mayank–Blackstone Group LP
Rawie, Damon–Advantage Capital Partners
Rawji, Irfhan–Relay Ventures
Rawlingson, James–Arix Bioscience PLC
Ray, Christopher–Natural Gas Partners
Ray, JW–Backlog Capital LLC
Ray, Matthew–Victory Park Capital Advisors LLC
Ray, Maxime–Saphir Capital Partners SA
Ray, Nilanjan–First Abu Dhabi Bank PJSC
Ray, Russell–HLM Management Co LLC
Raygorodetsky, Philip–Bayou Steel Corp
Raynard, Robert–Walden Venture Capital
Raynes, Michael–Waha Capital PJSC
Raynor, Daniel–Argentum Group LLC
Rays, Cedric–Motion Equity Partners LLP
Razi, Babak Cyrus–Third Wave Ventures
Razzano, Dante–Investindustrial Services Ltd
Razzini, Mario–Francisco Partners LP
Razzouk, Assaad–Sindicatum Carbon Capital Ltd
Rea, Peter–Glengary LLC
Rea, Steven–ATEL Ventures Inc
Read, Ian–Pfizer Venture Investments
Read, J. Leighton–Alloy Ventures Inc
Read, James–MML Capital Partners LLP
Read, Russell–Gulf Investment Corporation SAG
Read, William–Lakeview Equity Partners LLC
Reading, Jason–Aries Capital Partners LLC
Reagh, John–WRF Capital
Reals, Jeff–Performance Equity Management LLC
Reardon, John–Trident Capital
Reardon, Thomas–Westview Capital Partners LP
Reardon, Tighe–TVC Capital LLC
Reaves, Paul–Eastside Partners
Rebar, Thomas–SCP Private Equity Partners
Rebello, James–Southwest Middle Market M&A
Reber, Matthew–I315 Capital LLC
Rebetez, Jean-Claude–aventic partners AG
Reboucas, Marcelo–Casaforte Investimentos SA
Recanati, Leon–NGN Capital LLC
Recchia, Luiz–Stratus Investimentos Ltda
Reckhow, Grant–Hastings Equity Partners LLC
Reddon, Philip–Covington Capital Corp
Reddon, Philip–Market Square Equity Partners
Reddy, B. V. R. Mohan–August Capital Partners
Reddy, Karthik–Blume Venture Advisors
Reddy, Kiran–Clarus Ventures LLC
Reddy, Prabhakar–Naya Ventures LLC
Reddy, Sandeep–Peepul Capital Llc

Pratt's Guide to Private Equity & Venture Capital Sources

Reddy, Shashidhar–Kotak Investment Advisors Ltd
Redett, John–Carlyle Group LP
Redfield, Lindsay–Greenspring Associates Inc
Redlitz, Chris–Transmedia Capital Llc
Redman, Mark–OMERS Private Equity Inc
Redmer, Joachim–Triangle Venture Capital Group
Redmond, Ben–Risk Capital Partners Ltd
Redmond, Nate–Rustic Partners LP
Redmond, Steve–Northwater Capital Management Inc
Redpath, Tony–Ontario Centres of Excellence
Redstone, Shari–Advancit Capital LLC
Reed Saouaf, Jessica–Hall Capital Partners LLC
Reed, Amanda–Palomar Ventures
Reed, Brad–Solidus Company, L.P.
Reed, Creighton–W R Hambrecht & Co L L C
Reed, David–Capital Dynamics Sdn Bhd
Reed, David–Clearlight Partners LLC
Reed, Dominic–UNITED FINANCIAL GROUP ASSET MANAGEMENT
Reed, Douglas–Hatteras Venture Partners
Reed, Eric–Enterprise Equity Venture Capital Group
Reed, Jason–Wingate Partners LP
Reed, Jeffrey–Pantheon Ventures (UK) LLP
Reed, Marty–Roda Group, The
Reed, Matthew–Business Growth Fund PLC
Reed, Mitchell–Prudential Capital Group LP
Reed, Pal–Hitecvision AS
Reed, Pamela–Morrison & Foerster LLP
Reed, Phil–Highway 12 Ventures
Reed, Phillip–Highway 12 Ventures
Reed, Rusty–Persistence Partners, L.P.
Reed, Scott–Bankcap Partners Fund I LP
Reed, Scott–FLAG Capital Management LLC
Reed, Steven–Bankcap Partners Fund I LP
Reed, Steven–Inter-American Investment Corp
Reeders, Stephen–MVM Partners LLP
Reedy, Chandler–Warburg Pincus LLC
Reedy, Steve–CIT Group Inc
Rees, Julian–Castlelake LP
Rees, Robert–Startup Capital Ventures LP
Reese, Corby–Swander Pace Capital LLC
Reese, Luke–WinoNA Capital Management LLC
Reeser, Timothy–Aravaipa Ventures LLC
Reesing, Kyle–Strattam Capital LLC
Reetz, Robert–Haynes and Boone LLC
Reeve Uher, Paige–Blum Capital Partners LP
Reeve, Patrick–Albion Capital Group LLP
Reeves, Adam–Shoreview Industries
Reeves, Lisa–Vista Ventures
Regal, Mark–JPB Partners LLC
Regan, Brian–Welsh Carson Anderson & Stowe
Regan, Kathleen–Radius Ventures LLC
Regan, Kathryn–Landmark Partners Inc
Regan, Tom–Antares Capital Corp
Regante, Mark–Milbank Tweed Hadley & Mccloy LLP
Regazzi, John–Akoya Capital Partners LLC
Reger, Justin–LLR Partners Inc
Regev, Guy–Shaked Global Group
Regev, Omer–GEMINI CAPITAL FUND MGMT LTD
Regnery, George–Bedford Funding Capital Management LLC
Regueira, Marcus–FIR Capital Partners Gestao de Investimentos SA
Regulla, Suneel–Indo-nordic Private Equity AS

Reher, John–Brain Trust Accelerator Fund LP
Rehm, George–Calibrium Ltd
Rehm, Rudolph–Doll Capital Management Inc
Rehman, Aamir–Fajr Capital Ltd
Reibel, Andres–Pantheon Ventures (UK) LLP
Reich, Marc–Ironwood Investment Management LLC
Reich, Markus–Cross Equity Partners AG
Reichenbach, Horst–European Bank for Reconstruction and Development
Reichenberger, Wolfgang–inventages venture capital GmbH
Reichert, Bill–Garage Technology Ventures LLC
Reid, Alden–Grandbanks Capital
Reid, Georg–Bayern Kapital GmbH
Reid, Jason–Stagwell Group LLC
Reid, Mike–Frog Capital Ltd
Reid, Nicholas–Centerview Partners LLC
Reid, Robert–Blackstone Group LP
Reid, Ronan–4Th Level Ventures
Reid, Sean–Acas LLC
Reidel, Arthur–Horizon Ventures
Reigersman, Remmelt–Morrison & Foerster LLP
Reiland, Kathleen–Evercore Inc
Reilly, Cameron–Corridor Capital LLC
Reilly, Christopher–Karpreilly LLC
Reilly, John–Inverness Graham Investments
Reilly, Michael–Trust Company of the West
Reilly, Philip–Third Rock Ventures LLC
Reilly, Scott–Superior Capital Partners LLC
Reilly, Sean–Hudson Clean Energy Partners
Reimers, Megan–Revelry Brands LLC
Rein, Harry–Foundation Medical Partners LP
Reinaud, Florian–Innovation Capital SAS
Reinemo, Rikke–Herkules Capital AS
Reinert, Gordon–Pearl Street Capital Group
Reinhardt, Carl–Dev Equity LLC
Reinholdt, Steen–Internet Ventures Scandinavia
Reinisch, Peter–Global Life Science Ventures GmbH
Reinisch, William–Paladin Capital Management LLC
Reinke, Armin–Saarlaendische Wagnisfinanzierungsgesellschaft Mbh (Aka Swg)
Reinke, Gwen–Blum Capital Partners LP
Reinmann, Adam–Onex Corp
Reinseth, Bjorn–Ferd Capital Partners AS
Reinson, Martin–BPM Capital OU
Reisenberg, Jeffrey–Evercore Inc
Reiser, William–Bonaventure Capital LLC
Reiser, William–Fidelis Capital LLC
Reisner, Frederic–Andrew W Byrd & Co LLC
Reisner, Hunter–Citigroup Private Equity LP
Reisner, Rick–LFM Capital LLC
Reiss, David–Riverside Co
Reiss, Stan–Matrix Partners, L.P.
Reistetter, Rob–Quad-C Management Inc
Reitberger, Christian–Wellington Partners GmbH
Reiten, Narve–Reiten & Co AS
Reiter, Eric–Brentwood Associates, L.P.
Reiter, Eric–Brentwood Venture Capital
Reiter, R. Peter–RFE Investment Partners
Reithinger, Holger–Forbion Capital Partners
Rekhi, Kanwal–Inventus Capital Partners Fund I L P
Rekhi, Manu–Inventus Capital Partners Fund I L P
Rekusz, Zbigniew–Mid Europa Partners LLP
Relyea, Richard–3i
Relyea, Richard–3i Group PLC

Remala, Rao–Cronus Ventures
Remplbauer, Konrad–Oberoesterreichische Unternehmensbeteiligungs GmbH
Remsha, Victor–FINAM Global
Remtula, Aleem–Developing World Markets Inc
Remy, Philippe–NIVELINVEST SA
Remy, Pierre–Keensight Capital SAS
Ren, David–Cybernaut (China) Venture Capital Management Co Ltd
Ren, David–Providence Equity Partners LLC
Ren, Zack–Crimson Capital China
Renaud, Philippe–Fondations Capital SA
Renaudin, Louis–Ardens & Associes SAS
Rencurel, Dominique–Orkos Capital SAS
Renert, Doug–Tandem Entrepreneurs LLC
Rengaswamy, Ganesh–Lok Capital
Rengaswamy, Ganesh–Quona Capital Management Ltd
Renie, Philippe–Pechel Industries SAS
Renliang, Zhang–Bohai Sea Region Venture Capital Management Co Ltd
Renne, Marc–Gebruder Heller Dinklage
Renner, Rick–Econergy International Corp
Renoux, Etienne–Xange Private Equity SA
Renvoize, Jaime–Ascension Ventures Ltd
Renzi, Ned–Birchmere Ventures
Requadt, Scott–Clarus Ventures LLC
Rerisi, Meredith–Abbott Capital Management LLC
Rescho, Douglas–Lake Capital
Rescigno, Fabrizio–ILP III SARL
Resnick, Brad–Riverside Co
Resnick, Charles–Inflexion Partners
Resnick, Eric–KSL Capital Partners LLC
Resnick, Joshua–SV Health Investors LLP
Resnick, Kallan–Blackstone Group LP
Resnikoff, Alan–Shamrock Capital Advisors LLC
Resta, Massimo–Zouk Capital LLP
Retcher, Ryan–Solomon Global Holdings Inc
Rettie, Andrew–Elcano Capital LP
Retzer, Karin–Morrison & Foerster LLP
Retzloff, Mark–Greenmont Capital Partners
Reuter, David–LLR Partners Inc
Reuter, Hans–General Atlantic LLC
Reuter, Rich–Karpreilly LLC
Reutter, Andrew–Stone Point Capital LLC
Revers, Daniel–ArcLight Capital Holdings LLC
Revillon, Benjamin–Bex Capital SAS
Revoltella, Giovanni–Argan Capital
Revord, Michael–Aldine Capital Partners Inc
Revuelta, Jose Diaz-Rato–Torreal SA
Revzin, Bruce–Flybridge Capital Partners
Rey, David–Swicorp Capital Partners SA
Rey, Eric–Omnes Capital SAS
Rey, Florent–Abenex Capital SAS
Reycroft, Emily–Blackstone Group LP
Reymond, Kevin–Palladium Equity Partners LLC
Reynders, Robbie–Gores Group LLC
Reynolds, Barry–Accretia Capital LLC
Reynolds, Barry–Housatonic Partners Management Co Inc
Reynolds, Brian–Chatham Capital
Reynolds, David–Huron Capital Partners LLC
Reynolds, Douglas–Headwaters BD LLC
Reynolds, Greg–Comvest Partners
Reynolds, Ian Andrew–Bain Capital Inc

Reynolds, Ian—Avalt LLC
Reynolds, Jake—Technology Crossover Ventures LP
Reynolds, John—Lime Rock Partners LLC
Reynolds, Kevin—Bridgepoint Advisers II Ltd
Reynolds, Kevin—Bridgepoint Advisers Ltd
Reynolds, Marlene—Bain Capital Inc
Reynolds, Philip—KPMG Corporate Finance Inc
Reynolds, Roland—Industry Ventures LLC
Reynolds, Roland—Industry Ventures LLC
Reynoldson, Michael—InvestAmerica Venture Group, Inc.
Reyser, Horacio—Southern Cross Capital Management SA
Rezab, Ray—Zachary Scott & Co
Rezek, Colin—Vantage Venture Partners
Rhea, Michael—Antares Capital Corp
Rhee, Ceron—Jabodon PT Co
Rhee, In Sik—Rembrandt Venture Management LLC
Rhee, James—GB Credit Partners LLC
Rhim, Chang Sup—Hana Daetoo Securities Co Ltd
Rhim, Yuchul—H&Q Asia Pacific, Ltd.
Rhoades, Chris—SAIL Capital Partners LLC
Rhoades, David—Aether Investment Partners LLC
Rhoades, John—Acas LLC
Rhoads, Lisa—Easton Hunt Capital Partners LP
Rhodes, Jason—Atlas Venture Advisors Inc
Rhodes, Michael—Cooley LLP
Rhodes-Kropf, Matthew—Tectonic Ventures LP
Riabtsov, Sergei—Gruppa Sputnik OOO
Riak, Michael—Pantheon Ventures (UK) LLP
Ribar, Brandon—Fillmore Capital Partners LLC
Ribbink, Alexander—Prime Technology Ventures NV
Ribed, Luis—MCH Private Equity Asesores SL
Ribeiro Santos, Pedro—Armilar Venture Partners Sociedade de Capital de Risco SA
Ribeiro, Leonardo—Ocroma Investimentos E Gestao Ltda
Ribon, Denis—3i Group PLC
Ribon, Denis—Archimed SA
Ricatti, Matteo—Clessidra Societa di Gestione del Risparmio SpA
Ricci, Elisabetta—Towerbrook Capital Partners LP
Ricci, Kenneth—Directional Aviation Capital
Ricciardelli, Michael—Boston Ventures
Ricciotti, Walter—Virtus Capital Partners Srl
Rice, Amy—Oaktree Capital Management LP
Rice, Andre—Muller & Monroe Asset Management LC
Rice, Brian—Highland Capital Management LP
Rice, Darrel—Haynes and Boone LLC
Rice, Don—Capricorn Holdings LLC
Rice, Evan—Spinnaker Growth Partners (Pty) Ltd
Rice, Garrick—Sterling Partners GP LLC
Rice, John—Triathlon Medical Ventures LLC
Rice, Joseph—Clayton Dubilier & Rice LLC
Rice, Matt—Ballast Point Venture Partners LLC
Rice, Stephen—Riverside Co
Rice, Zeb—Angeleno Group Investors LLC
Riceman, Charles—Golub Capital Master Funding LLC
Rich, Brian—Catalyst Investors LLC
Rich, James—Gemini Investors Inc
Rich, Jason—Palisade Capital Management LLC
Rich, Matthew—Arlington Capital Partners
Richard, Bruce—Spell Capital Partners LLC

Richard, George—Maven Venture Partners
Richard, Olivier—Siparex Group
Richards, Amy—BC Partners LLP
Richards, Andrew—Barclays Capital Inc
Richards, Andrew—Swander Pace Capital LLC
Richards, Bradley—Haynes and Boone LLC
Richards, Dave—Capria Ventures LLC
Richards, Hugh—Exponent Private Equity LLP
Richards, Jamie—Foresight Group LLP
Richards, Jeff—GGV Capital
Richards, Jeff—GGV Capital
Richards, Jordan—Sverica International Boston LLC
Richards, Kristin—Greylock Partners LLC
Richards, Mark—Actis LLP
Richards, Oliver—Blue Bear Capital LLC
Richards, Robert—Plaza Ventures Ltd
Richards, Rod—Graphite Capital Management LLP
Richards, Ryan—Riverside Co
Richardson Knox, Ann—Haynes and Boone LLC
Richardson, Anders—Palisades Ventures
Richardson, Andrew—Investec Asset Management (Pty) Ltd
Richardson, Blair—Bow River Capital Partners LLC
Richardson, Christy—Thomas Weisel Partners Group Inc
Richardson, Craig—PHD Equity Partners LLP
Richardson, David—Impax Asset Management Ltd
Richardson, Hartley—Richardson Capital Ltd
Richardson, James—Torch Hill Investment Partners LLC
Richardson, John—Navigation Capital Partners Inc
Richardson, Josh—Longitude Capital Management Co LLC
Richardson, Josh—Longitude Capital Management Co LLC
Richardson, Julie—Providence Equity Partners LLC
Richardson, Mark—Wolseley Private Equity
Richardson, Neil—Wellington Partners GmbH
Richardson, Nick—Boost&Co SAS
Richardson, Paul—Renewal Partners
Richardson, Tarrus—IMB Development Corp
Richardson, William—Constitution Capital Partners LLC
Richey, Mark—West Capital Advisors LLC
Richey, Nathan—Bestige Holdings LLC
Richey, Nathan—Centre Lane Partners LLC
Richier, Jean-Manuel—Blackstone Group LP
Richings, Paul—Bridges Fund Management Ltd
Richman, Darren—Blackstone Group LP
Richmond, Aaron—Endeavour Capital Inc
Richmond, Melvin—New Magellan Venture Partners LLC
Richter, William—Cerberus Capital Management LP
Richter, William—MadroNA Venture Group
Ricketts, Thomas—Sands Capital Management LLC
Rickman, Robert—Rockley Group
Ricks, Michael—Formative Ventures
Ricks, Michael—Investor Growth Capital Inc
Rico, Jorge—MBF Healthcare Partners LP
Ricotta, Enrico—Mandarin Capital Partners SCA SICAR
Ricotta, Enrico—R&D Advisory Srl
Ricros, Alain—Aquitaine Creation Investissement SAS
Riddell, David—Blackstone Group LP

Riddle, John—Brown Gibbons Lang & Company LLC
Ridge, Alison—Access Capital Partners SA
Ridge, Charlie—Impax Asset Management Ltd
Riechert, Rodolfo—Brasil Plural Gestao de Recursos Ltda
Rieck, Lewis—Water Tower Capital LLC
Riedel, Chad—Source Capital LLC
Rieder, Urs—Capital Dynamics Sdn Bhd
Riediker, Martin—Commission for Technology and Innovation CTI
Riedlinger, William—Atlantic-Pacific Capital Inc
Riedmiller, Lisa—Palomar Ventures
Riedmiller, Lisa—Wavemaker Partners
Riefe, Benjamin—Benford Capital Partners LLC
Rieger, Glenn—Newspring Capital
Rieger, Norbert—Milbank Tweed Hadley & Mccloy LLP
Riehemann, Andreas—BASF New Business GmbH
Riehl, Heinrich—Trust Company of the West
Riehl, Peter—Bain Capital Inc
Rieke, Kurt—Hall Capital Partners LLC
Rieke, Matthew—Quaker Partners Management LP
Riepe, James—Relativity Capital LLC
Ries, Gerhard—BioMedPartners AG
Rietzler, Manfred—Sandpiper Digital Payments AG
Rifkin, Ben—Royal Street Investment and Innovation Center LLC
Rifkin, Daniel—North River Capital LLC
Rifkin, Martin—North River Capital LLC
Rifkin, Richard—North River Capital LLC
Rigas, Mathios—Capital Connect Venture Partners AKES
Rigau, Javier—Abac Capital SL
Rigau, Javier—Apax Partners LLP
Rigaud, Guy—RAC I SA
Righetto, Paolo—Aliante Partners Srl
Rightmire, Matt—Borealis Ventures
Rignell, Patrik—K III Sweden AB
Rigo, Lucia—General Atlantic LLC
Rigonatti, Edson—Astella Investimentos
Rigoni, Alan—Vila Rica Capital Gestora de Recursos Ltda
Riismaa, Hanno—Litcapital Asset Management UAB
Rijo, John—Stairway Capital Management
Rikert, Tom—Next World Capital LLC
Rikkers, James—Spell Capital Partners LLC
Rikkers, Laing—HealthpointCapital LLC
Riley, Daniel—New Mountain Capital I LLC
Riley, Ian—Vitruvian Partners LLP
Riley, Margaret—Vedanta Capital LP
Riley, Pat—Akoya Capital Partners LLC
Riley, Ren—Oak Investment Partners
Riley, Sandy—Richardson Capital Ltd
Rillo, Troy—Yorkville Advisors Management LLC
Rim, Charles—DFJ Athena
Rimas, Tony—Fraser McCombs Capital
Rimer, David—Index Ventures
Rimer, Neil—Index Ventures
Rimland, Edward—Silverfern Group Inc
Rinehart, Heidi—Antares Capital Corp
Riney, James—500 Startups, L.P.
Ring, Doug—Bedford Funding Capital Management LLC
Ringdahl, Jeffrey—American Beacon Advisors Inc
Ringer, Simon—Bridges Fund Management Ltd

Ringle, Brett—Remeditex Ventures LLC
Ringo, Cynthia—DBL Investors
Ringo, William—InCube Ventures LLC
Rini, Thomas—Cielo Management LLC
Rinnan, Rune—Televenture Management As
Rinne, Alexander—Milbank Tweed Hadley & Mccloy LLP
Rinner, Erick—Milestone Capital Partners Ltd
Riog Aldasoro, Jose Maria—Sociedad de Desarrollo de Navarra SL
Riopel, Patricia—Associes Magnum Capital Partners
Riordan, Aidan—Calvert Street Capital Partners Inc
Riordan, Brian—Wynnchurch Capital Ltd
Riordan, Richard—Freeman Spogli & Co LLC
Riordan, Richard—Riordan Lewis & Haden
Ripley, Alexander—Bain Capital Inc
Ripley, Richard—Haynes and Boone LLC
Ripley, Rosemary—NGEN Partners LLC
Ripley, Stacy—Oaktree Capital Management LP
Ripoll, Jacques—Banco Santander SA
Rippy, Laura—Fa Technology Ventures Corp
Risch, Martin—FIDES Business Partner AG
Rise, Arne—Hitecvision AS
Rishi, Raju—Sigma Prime Ventures LLC
Risk, Gerald—Accretia Capital LLC
Risley, Eric—Rutberg and Co LLC
Risman, Michael—Vitruvian Partners LLP
Rispoli, Pierre—Ixen Partners SA
Ristvedt, Pal—Lexington Partners Inc
Ritchie, E. Blair—Blackstone Group LP
Ritchie, Ian—Pentech Ventures LLP
Ritchie, Linda—Lotus Innovations LLC
Ritchie, Thomas—CI Capital Partners LLC
Ritrievi, Christopher—Indiana University
Ritter, Gordon—Emergence Capital Partners
Ritter, John—Balance Point Capital Partners, L.P.
Ritter, Markus—Private Equity Invest AG
Ritterbush, Stephen—Merida Capital Partners LLC
Rivard, Scott—Saw Mill Capital LLC
Rivelle, Tad—Trust Company of the West
Rivera, Gustavo—Ecus Administradora General de Fondos SA
Rivera, Miriam—Ulu Ventures
Rivera, Peter—Shamrock Capital Advisors LLC
Rivera, Sylvia—Morrison & Foerster LLP
Rivers, Jamie—BC Partners LLP
Rivers, Rufus—RLJ Equity Partners LLC
Rives, Alex—Arch Venture Partners LLC
Rivet, Bruno—Seventure Partners SA
Rivett, Paul—Fairfax Financial Holdings Ltd
Rivetti, Alessandro—R301 Capital
Riviere, Partick—Siparex Proximite Innovation SAS
Rivoire, Laurent—PAI Partners SAS
Rizk, Geoffrey—Rizk Ventures LLC
Rizk, Linda—Rizk Ventures LLC
Rizos, Andreas—Golding Capital Partners GmbH
Rizvi, Abbas—Investcorp Bank BSC
Rizvi, Abbas—Investcorp Technology Investments Group
Rizvi, Shabih—Kleiner Perkins Caufield & Byers LLC
Rizvi, Suhail—Rizvi Traverse Management LLC
Rizzi, Matteo—SBT Venture Capital
Rizzo, Matthew—OrbiMed Advisors LLC
Rizzuto, Carlo—Versant Venture Management, LLC
Rob, Robert—Stone-Goff Partners LLC

Robaina, Alberto—Trimaran Capital LLC
Robalinho, Frederico—Nova Gestao de Recursos Ltda
Robalinho, Pedro—Nova Gestao de Recursos Ltda
Robard, Yann—Whitehorse Liquidity Partners Inc
Robb, Russell—Tully and Holland Inc
Robb, William—Novaquest Infosystems Inc
Robb, William—Platte River Ventures LLC
Robbins, Arion—Revelstoke Capital Partners LLC
Robbins, David—Bayside Capital Inc
Robbins, David—Monomoy Capital Partners LLC
Robbins, David—Trevi Health Ventures LP
Robbins, David—Trust Company of the West
Robbins, Gregory—Golub Capital Master Funding LLC
Robbins, Joseph—Bain Capital Inc
Robbins, Kevin—Blue Delta Capital Partners LLC
Robert, Bertrand—Siparex Group
Robert, Philippe—Oceanbridge Partners LLC
Robert, Xavier—Bridgepoint Advisers Ltd
Roberto, Antonio—Connecticut Innovations Inc
Roberts, Bert—Sorenson Capital Partners LP
Roberts, Beverly—Wolfensohn & Company LLC
Roberts, Brad—Riverside Co
Roberts, Bryan—Venrock Inc
Roberts, Bryce—O'Reilly Alphatech Ventures LLC
Roberts, Charles—Loxbridge Research Llp
Roberts, Curt—Kickstart Seed Fund LP
Roberts, David—AG BD LLC
Roberts, Ellery—Rw Capital Partners LLC
Roberts, Eric—Valence Life Sciences LLC
Roberts, George—Openview Venture Partners LP
Roberts, Janice—Benhamou Global Ventures LLC
Roberts, Jean—Kohlberg & Co LLC
Roberts, Jonathan—Ignition Ventures Management LLC
Roberts, Jonathan—Ignition Ventures Management LLC
Roberts, Justin—Cove Hill Partners LLC
Roberts, Justin—Thomas H Lee Partners LP
Roberts, Kevin—Morrison & Foerster LLP
Roberts, Olivia—Palamon Capital Partners LP
Roberts, Paul—GoldPoint Partners LLC
Roberts, Peter—Longworth Venture Partners, L.P.
Roberts, R. Gregory—Morrison & Foerster LLP
Roberts, Sean—Huron Capital Partners LLC
Roberts, Simon—Diamond Castle Holdings LLC
Roberts, Simon—Harvest Partners LP
Roberts, Stephen—River Street Management LLC
Roberts, Thomas—Blackstone Group LP
Roberts, Thomas—Harbert Management Corp
Roberts, Thomas—Summit Partners LP
Roberts, Thomas—Summit Partners LP
Robertson, Alfred—Seneca Partners Inc
Robertson, Bruce—Hudson Ferry Capital LLC
Robertson, David—FrontRange Capital Partners LLC
Robertson, Elihu—Milbank Tweed Hadley & Mccloy LLP
Robertson, John—Cooley LLP
Robertson, John—Integrated Partners
Robertson, Julian—Tiger Management Corp
Robertson, Randy—Global Infrastructure Holdings
Robertson, Rebecca—Versant Venture Management, LLC
Robertson, Stefano—Golub Capital Master Funding

LLC
Robertson, Stephen—TDR Capital LLP
Robich, Jeff—Blue Point Capital Partners LP
Robichaud, Jennifer—Innovacorp
Robin, David—TCR Capital SAS
Robin, Henry—Invesco Private Capital Inc
Robine, Paul—TR Advisors Ltd
Robins, Gary—Rockpool Investments LLP
Robins, Paula—Angeleno Group Investors LLC
Robinson, Andrew—Oaktree Capital Management LP
Robinson, Anthony—Investcorp Bank BSC
Robinson, Art—32 Degrees Capital
Robinson, Barry—Phoenix Equity Partners Ltd
Robinson, Bill—Milestone Capital Partners Ltd
Robinson, Charlie—CRITICAL CAPITAL GROWTH FUND L P
Robinson, Dan—Oaktree Capital Management LP
Robinson, David—Admiral Capital Group
Robinson, Greg—RLG Capital LLC
Robinson, Gregory—Peninsula Ventures
Robinson, Gregory—Peninsula Ventures
Robinson, Hugo—Kings Park Capital LLP
Robinson, James—RRE Ventures LLC
Robinson, James—RRE Ventures LLC
Robinson, Jeffrey—Bain Capital Inc
Robinson, Joseph—Midmark Capital LP
Robinson, Lauren—Next Frontier Capital LLC
Robinson, Marc—Golub Capital Master Funding LLC
Robinson, Mark—Centerview Partners LLC
Robinson, Mark—Wave Equity Partners LLC
Robinson, Matt—Ascend Global Investments LLC
Robinson, Nathaniel—Virgo Capital
Robinson, Samuel—Portag3 Ventures Inc GP
Robinson, Stephen—Pittsburgh Equity Partners LP
Robinson, Steven—Antares Capital Corp
Robinson, Stuart—Levine Leichtman Capital Partners Inc
Robinson, Taylor—Lexington Partners Inc
Robison, John—NGEN Partners LLC
Robkin, David—Liberty Ventures Inc
Robles, Frank—Oakstone Venture Partners LLC
Robson, Colin—Robson Capital Partners Corp
Robson, Tim—Doughty Hanson and Co.
Rocca, Curtis—DCA Capital Partners LP
Rocchio, John—Newstone Capital Partners LLC
Rocco, Cynthia—Oaktree Capital Management LP
Rocha, Nelson—Vinci Equities Gestora de Recursos Ltda
Rochat, Christian—Clayton Dubilier & Rice LLC
Rochat, Frederic—Banque Lombard Odier & Cie SA
Roche, Ciara—Siris Capital Group LLC
Roche, Collin—GTCR Golder Rauner LLC
Roche, James—Blackstone Group LP
Roche, Maurice—Delta Partners Ltd
Roche, Pat—Glengary LLC
Roche, Roger—Ironwood Investment Management LLC
Roche, Sara—Atlantic Asset Management LLC
Roche, Terence—Cornerstone Advisors Inc
Rochelli, Elena—Providence Equity Partners LLC
Rochford, Richard—Haynes and Boone LLC
Rochkind, Brett—General Atlantic LLC
Rock, Terence—Centerpoint Venture Partners LP
Rockecharlie, David—KKR & Co LP
Rockefeller, Justin—Richmond Global

Pratt's Guide to Private Equity & Venture Capital Sources

Rockenhauser, Jorg–Permira Advisers LLP
Rockett, Elizabeth–Kaiser Permanente Ventures LLC
Rocklage, Scott–5AM Ventures LLC
Rockley, Whitney–McRock Capital Corp
Rockwell, John–DFJ Athena
Rodd, F. Morgan–Activate Venture Partners
Rodd, F. Morgan–Arrowpath Venture Capital
Rode, Nils–Adveq Management AG
Roden, Christopher–C3 Capital LLC
Roden, Christopher–MR Investment Partners
Rodgers, Anthony–Antson Capital Partners LLC
Rodgers, Helenmarie–KKR & Co LP
Rodgers, Joe–Monroe Capital LLC
Rodgers, Paul–Wilshire Private Markets
Rodin, Robert–Riordan Lewis & Haden
Rodionov, Dimitri–Apax Partners LLP
Rodrigue, Sylvie–Torys LLP
Rodrigues, Ross–Odyssey Investment Partners LLC
Rodrigues, Roy–Oak Investment Partners
Rodrigues, Thiago–GP Investimentos Ltda
Rodriguez Arregui, Alvaro–IGNIA Partners LLC
Rodriguez Pegas, Fabio–Vinci Equities Gestora de Recursos Ltda
Rodriguez, Antonio–Matrix Partners, L.P.
Rodriguez, Cecilio–Comvest Partners
Rodriguez, Cecilio–Comvest Partners
Rodriguez, Cristobal–Alantra
Rodriguez, D. Anthony–Morrison & Foerster LLP
Rodriguez, Daniel–Lee Equity Partners LLC
Rodriguez, Dave–Saybrook Capital LLC
Rodriguez, Frank–JLL Partners Inc
Rodriguez, Marco–Hastings Equity Partners LLC
Rodriguez, Marcos–Palladium Equity Partners LLC
Rodriguez, Rene–Medina Capital Partners Inc
Rodriguez, Ricardo–Southern Cross Capital Management SA
Rodriguez, Yamandu–Chilango Ventures LLC
Rodriguez-Pastor, Carlos–Nexuss Group SAC
Rodsky, Seth–Strand Equity Partners LLC
Rodzevik, Paul–Jordan Company LP
Roe, Jason–Kenda Capital BV
Roe, Wayne–InCube Ventures LLC
Roeder, Douglas–Delphi Ventures
Roeder, Richard–Vance Street Capital LLC
Roediger, John–Montgomery & Co LLC
Roehr, Jens–DMB Deutsche Mittelstandsbeteiligungs GmbH
Roehrs-Guenther, Pamela–Bm H Beteiligungs Managementgesellschaft Hessen mbH
Roell, Monika–Ananda Ventures GmbH
Roemer, Max W.–Suma Verwaltungs GmbH
Roenick, Russ–Transom Capital Group LLC
Roeper, Robert–Wave Equity Partners LLC
Roepers, Jack–New Enterprise East Investments
Roesing, Dirk–b to v Partners AG
Roever, Moritz–Medicis Capital GmbH
Rofe, Andy–Invesco Real Estate, Ltd.
Roffler, Roland–Partners Group Holding AG
Rogan, Manus–Undisclosed Firm
Rogan, Mike–Mosaic Private Equity Ltd
Rogero, David–Cressey and Company LP
Rogers, Alex–First Reserve Corp
Rogers, Alex–Performance Equity Management LLC
Rogers, Bill–Hudson Clean Energy Partners
Rogers, Bruce–KRG Capital Management LP

Rogers, Bruce–Mountaingate Capital Management LP
Rogers, Cynthia–Antares Capital Corp
Rogers, Jef–Gryphon Investors Inc
Rogers, Jesse–ACP Inc
Rogers, John–Bridges Fund Management Ltd
Rogers, John–Gryphon Investors Inc
Rogers, Joseph–Audax Group, Inc.
Rogers, Kenneth–Haynes and Boone LLC
Rogers, Paul–Next Coast Ventures LLC
Rogers, Robert–Vista Equity Partners LLC
Rogers, William–Halifax Group LLC
Rogoff, Eric–Falcon Investment Advisors LLC
Rogowski, Olaf–Findos Investor GmbH
Roh, Kyung Oh–AK Gangwon Investment Co Ltd
Rohac, Susan–Business Development Bank of Canada
Rohan, Daniel–KSL Capital Partners LLC
Rohatyn, Nicholas–TRG Management LP
Rohde, A.J.–Thoma Bravo LLC
Rohlen, Duke–Tautona Group Lp
Rohmann, Sven–Burrill & Company
Rohr, Alex–Merion Investment Partners LP
Rohr, Gary–iSherpa Capital
Rohr, George–NCH Capital Inc
Rohrich, Rod–PTV Healthcare Capital
Rohrs, Gary–North River Capital LLC
Rohwedder, Frank–Astorius Capital GmbH
Roiter, Warren–Trevi Health Ventures LP
Rojas, Javier–Kennet Partners Ltd
Rokosh, Norm–Triwest Capital Mgmt Corp
Roland, Kjell–Norfund
Rolfe, Alex–ACP Inc
Rolfe, Andrew–Towerbrook Capital Partners LP
Roll, Penelope–Ares Capital Corp
Rolland, Michael–Chartwell Investments, Inc.
Rollinger, Serge–Chameleon Invest SCA
Rollins, Andrew–Sigma Prime Ventures LLC
Romaglino, Christian–Brown Brothers Harriman & Co
Romain, Robert–Pera Capital Partners Advisory Ltd
Romaneiro, Marcos–3G Capital Inc
Romani, Enrique Lucas–Nordkapp Gestion SGIIC SA
Romaniello, Steve–Roark Capital Group Inc
Romankevich, Luba–Medley Capital LLC
Romano, Michael–Lightspeed Management Company LLC
Romano, Nicholas–Audax Group, Inc.
Romano, Philip–Scientific Health Development
Romans, Andrew–Founders Club LP
Romans, Andrew–Georgetown Venture Partners
Rome, Brett–North Hill Ventures LP
Romero, Hernan–Linzor Capital Partners LP
Romero, Russ–Oaktree Capital Management LP
Romic, Joseph–Acas LLC
Romney, John–Levine Leichtman Capital Partners Inc
Rompon, John–McNally Capital LLC
Ron, Aran–Fundrx Inc
Ron, Yosef–Mofet B-Yehuda Technological and Business Incubator
Ron, Yosef–Trendlines Group Ltd
Rona, Miguel–Altamar Private Equity SGIIC SAU
Ronc, Michel–Demeter SAS
Roncaglia, Mario–Vegagest Azionari Asia A

Rond, Patrick–Cyprium Investment Partners LLC
Ronel, Tara–Topanga Partners LP
Ronen, Osnat–Viola Private Equity I LP
Ronfeldt, Carsten–Danske Private Equity A/S
Rooders, Duncan–Matcorp Holding BV
Rooke, Jenny–F-Prime Capital Partners
Rooney, Joseph–Arsenal Capital Management LLC
Rooney, Joseph–Arsenal Capital Partners LP
Rooney, Joseph–Arsenal Capital Partners LP
Rooney, Kevin–Cooley LLP
Rooney, Peter–Carlyle Group LP
Rooney, Philip–Actua Corp
Rooney, Tory–Bruckmann Rosser Sherrill & Co LP
Roos, Christo–Ethos Private Equity (Proprietary) Ltd
Roose, Eric–Morrison & Foerster LLP
Rooseboom, Laura–Start Green Fund BV
Roosevelt, Jonathan–Industry Ventures LLC
Root, Anthony–Milbank Tweed Hadley & Mccloy LLP
Root, Cheryl–Trimaran Capital LLC
Root, Jonathan–U.S. Venture Partners
Root, Jonathan–U.S. Venture Partners
Root, Lisa–Blue Point Capital Partners LP
Roper, Chris–Canada Pension Plan Investment Board
Roques, Bernard-Louis–Truffle Capital SAS
Rorem, Carrie–Compass Capital Services Inc
Roriston, Robert–Lindsay Goldberg & Bessemer LP
Rosa, Katherine–JP Morgan Investment Management Inc
Rosa, Nick–Sandbox Industries LLC
Rosarius, Stephan–Orlando Management AG
Rosati, John–Triangle Venture Capital Group
Rosberg, Jenny–Skandia Innovation AB
Rosborough, Bradley–Headwaters BD LLC
Rosch, Joachim–BASF New Business GmbH
Rose, Alex–Crestview Advisors, LLC
Rose, David–Rose Tech Ventures LLC
Rose, Jay–Spectrum Healthcare Fund LLC
Rose, Jay–StepStone Group LP
Rose, John–Alpha Capital Partners, Ltd.
Rose, John–Capgen Financial Group LP
Rose, Kim–Valencia Capital LLC
Rose, Laurence–Cantor Ventures
Rose, Nicolas–Xange Private Equity SA
Rose, Odette–Oaktree Capital Management LP
Rose, Peter–Blackstone Group LP
Rose, Stuart–Tully and Holland Inc
Rose, T.J.–ABRY Partners LLC
Rose, William–Valencia Capital LLC
Roseberry, Edwin–Evercore Inc
Roselle, Arthur–Pamlico Capital Management LP
Roseman, Gavin–Stellus Capital Management LLC
Rosemond, Palmer–Comvest Partners
Rosen, Alexander–IDG Ventures USA
Rosen, Andrew–Kainos Capital LLC
Rosen, Daniel–Commerce Ventures Management LLC
Rosen, Daniel–Highland Capital Partners LLC
Rosen, David–Jabodon PT Co
Rosen, Eric–MSD Capital LP
Rosen, Jessica–Blackstone Group LP
Rosen, Jonathan–TDR Capital LLP
Rosen, Mark–Charlesbank Capital Partners LLC
Rosen, Michael–Pamplona Capital Management LLP
Rosen, Modi–MAGNUM COMMUNICATIONS FUND

L P
Rosen, Rick—HIG Capital LLC
Rosen, Rob—Boulder Brook Partners LLC
Rosen, Stephen—Cooley LLP
Rosen, Sue—Equity Partners
Rosenbaum, Jonathan—Simon Equity Partners LLC
Rosenbaum, Mark—Aurora Capital Group Ltd
Rosenbaum, Norman—Morrison & Foerster LLP
Rosenberg, Cheryl—Haynes and Boone LLC
Rosenberg, Daniel—Sterling Partners GP LLC
Rosenberg, David—Oaktree Capital Management LP
Rosenberg, Eric—Blackstone Group LP
Rosenberg, Jason—Sterling Partners GP LLC
Rosenberg, John—Technology Crossover Ventures LP
Rosenberg, Jonathan—Bio-Investigations Ltd
Rosenberg, Peter—Merida Capital Partners LLC
Rosenberg, Ralph—KKR & Co LP
Rosenberg, Robert—FFR Capital Partners
Rosenberg, William—Bio-Investigations Ltd
Rosenberry, Kenton—Enhanced Equity Fund, L.P.
Rosenberry, Kenton—Varsity Healthcare Partners
Rosenbloom, Micah—Founder Collective LP
Rosenblum, Bruce—Carlyle Group LP
Rosenfeld, Eric—Frontier Venture Capital
Rosengren, Albin—East Capital Private Equity AB
Rosenstein, Douglas—Gridiron Capital LLC
Rosenthal, David—MadroNA Venture Group
Rosenthal, Eyal—FINISTERE VENTURES L L C
Rosenthal, Gary—Sterling Group LP
Rosenthal, Gregg—University Ventures
Rosenthal, Jeffrey—Imperial Capital Corp
Rosenzweig, Arthur—Research Partners Ltd
Rosenzweig, Eric—Stone Point Capital LLC
Rosenzweig, Mayer—Ingleside Investors LLC
Rosenzweig, William—Physic Ventures LLC
Roshko, Peter—Boulder Ventures Ltd
Rosich, Mitchell—Athenian Fund Management Inc
Rosken, Iris—Atlantic Street Capital Management LLC
Roslyn, Marshall—Learn Capital Venture Partners LP
Rosmus, Roger—Aberdeen Gould Capital Markets Ltd
Ross, Antony—Bridges Fund Management Ltd
Ross, Avidan—Root Ventures
Ross, Cathy—Oasis Capital Partners LLC
Ross, Cecile—Pantheon Ventures (UK) LLP
Ross, Dallas—Kinetic Capital Partners
Ross, Edward—Fidus Capital LLC
Ross, Howard—LLR Partners Inc
Ross, Ian—Concentric Equity Partners, L.P.
Ross, John—Fidus Capital LLC
Ross, Matthew—Onex Corp
Ross, Michael—SV Health Investors LLP
Ross, Steven—Mcm Capital Partners L P
Ross, Steven—Mtn Capital Partners LLC
Ross, Stuart—Pinnacle Capital
Ross, Timothy—Bennett Jones Verchere
Ross, Timothy—Hudson Ferry Capital LLC
Ross, Wayne—Waveland Capital Group LLC
Rossbach, Michael—Triangle Venture Capital Group
Rossbach, Peter—Impax Asset Management Ltd
Rosselli, Michael—Yorkville Advisors Management LLC
Rossen, Jamie—Ascribe Capital, LLC
Rosser, Harold—Rosser Capital Partners
Rosser, Luke—Rosser Capital Partners

Rossetter, Stephen—Centripetal Capital Partners LLC
Rossetti, Paul—Ascribe Capital, LLC
Rossi, Alexander—Latin Idea Ventures LLC
Rossi, Mario—Swisscom AG
Rossi, Mauro—Perella Weinberg Partners LP
Rossi, Michael—Directional Aviation Capital
Rossi, Stephen—CounterPoint Capital Partners LLC
Rossignol, Charles-Henri—Cavipar SASU
Rossignol, Jacques—21 Centrale Partners SA
Rossow, Alfred—Tully and Holland Inc
Roszak, Matthew—Silkroad Equity LLC
Rotaeche, Roque—Harbert Management Corp
Rotberg, Joseph—Lee Equity Partners LLC
Roth, Anna—Fenway Summer Ventures LP
Roth, Bob—Cornerstone Advisors Inc
Roth, Byron—Roth Capital Partners LLC
Roth, David—Blackstone Group LP
Roth, Jim—LeapFrog Investments
Roth, Marsha—AG BD LLC
Roth, Millard—Corporate Growth Assistance Ltd
Roth, Peter—KBW Capital Partners I L P
Roth, Sarah—Riverside Co
Roth, Ted—Roth Capital Partners LLC
Roth, Werner—Edelweiss & Berge UG haftungsbeschraenkt & Co KG
Rothberg, Jim—Route 66 Ventures LLC
Rothe, Joachim—Life Sciences Partners BV
Rothenbusch, Holger—CDC Group PLC
Rothenfuber, Christoph—Milbank Tweed Hadley & Mccloy LLP
Rother, Ken—Cayuga Venture Fund
Rotheram, Sarah—Neo Investment Partners LLP
Rothfield, Elizabeth—Explorer Investments Sociedade de Capital de Risco SA
Rothfus, Eric—Alara Capital Partners LLC
Rothman, Matt—Hemisphere Capital
Rothschild, Mark—Graue Mill Partners LLC
Rothschild, Peter—Tamarix Capital Corp
Rothschild, Randall—Blackstone Group LP
Rothstein, Charles—Beringea LLC
Rotman, Kenneth—Clairvest Group Inc
Rotondo, Sam—Oaktree Capital Management LP
Rottele, Christoph—CVC Capital Partners Ltd
Rottenberg, Jason—Arsenal
Rottenberg, Jason—OnPoint Technologies
Rottier, Peter—Summit Partners LP
Rottner, Thomas—Platina Finance, Ltd.
Rouchon, Christian—Caisse Regionale de Credit Agricole Mutuel Sud Rhone Alpes
Rougon, Alain—21 Centrale Partners SA
Rous, Dave—Antares Capital Corp
Rouse, Mike—Tenth Street Capital Partners LLC
Rousseau, Anne—Arcis Finance SA
Roussel, Quinn—Rcf Management LLC
Rousset, Bruno—Eurekap SAS
Roussilhe, Stephane—PAI Partners SAS
Rousso, Alan—European Bank for Reconstruction and Development
Rouveyre, Nicolas—Ambrian Resources AG
Rouvinez, Christophe—Mueller Moehl Group
Roux de Bezieux, Geoffroy—Isai Gestion SAS
Roux, Bertrand—Auxitex SA
Roux, David—Silver Lake Partners LP
Rouzier, Eric—Clayton Dubilier & Rice LLC
Rovere, Silvia—Virtus Capital Partners Srl

Rovero, Maria—Finpiemonte Partecipazioni SpA
Roversi, Mauro—Ambienta SGR SpA
Rovine, Joshua—Blackstone Group LP
Rovinski, Benjamin—LCC Legacy Holdings Inc
Rovira, German—Eneas Capital SL
Rovner, Jeffrey—O'Melveny & Myers LLP
Rowan, John—Warburg Pincus LLC
Rowan, Marc—Apollo Global Management LLC
Rowan, Michel—Azulis Capital SA
Rowden, Kevin—Green Park & Golf Ventures LLC
Rowe, Brian—Frontenac Company LLC
Rowe, Joshua—Hawkesbridge Capital
Rowe, Kevin—Lake Capital
Rowe, Lee—Sorenson Capital Partners LP
Rowe, Mark—Partners Group Holding AG
Rowe, Paul—Fulcrum Capital Partners Inc
Rowe, Simon—Swicorp Capital Partners SA
Rowe, Timothy—NAV.VC
Rowghani, Mood—Kleiner Perkins Caufield & Byers LLC
Rowland, Barry—Canada Pension Plan Investment Board
Rowland, John—Alchemy Partners LLP
Rowland, Max—Diversified Trust Company Inc
Rowland-Jones, Toby—Impact Capital Inc
Rowles, Steve—Morrison & Foerster LLP
Rowntree, David—Highland West Capital Ltd
Rowntree, David—Parallel49 Equity
Roy, Devraj—Irving Place Capital LLC
Roy, Jack—Summit Partners LP
Roy, Luis—Telegraph Hill Group LLC
Roy, Noah—Greenbriar Equity Group LLC
Royan, Ajay—Mithril Capital Management LLC
Royan, William—Ontario Teachers' Pension Plan
Royce, Elliot—Allianz Capital Partners GmbH
Royer, Stephen—Shamrock Capital Advisors LLC
Royston, Chris—Patriot Capital Funding Inc
Royston, Ivor—Forward Ventures
Rozelle, Kacy—St Cloud Capital LLC
Rozengarten, Kobi—JVP Jerusalem Venture Partners Israel Management, Ltd.
Rozenstraten, Bert-Jan—AAC CAPITAL PARTNERS
Rozkin, Leonid—Francisco Partners LP
Rozman, Gabriel—Aconcagua Ventures
Rua, Daniel—Inflexion Partners
Ruane, James—Apax Partners LLP
Ruano, Rudy—Western Technology Investment
Ruatti, Jean Louis—Agro Invest SAS
Rubalcava, Alex—Stage Venture Partners LLC
Rubel, Michael—RFE Investment Partners
Rubenstein, Barry—Wheatley Partners
Rubenstein, Brian—BDS Capital Management LLC
Rubenstein, Eric—Intuitive Venture Partners LLC
Rubenstein, Gordon—Pacific Partners
Rubenstein, Samuel—Panacea Capital Advisors Inc
Rubin, Andy—Redpoint Ventures
Rubin, Ben—DreamIt Ventures
Rubin, Daniel—Alloy Ventures Inc
Rubin, Geoffrey—Canada Pension Plan Investment Board
Rubin, James—Wexford Capital LP
Rubin, Kenneth—Wexford Capital LP
Rubin, Paul—Olympus Partners
Rubino, Dean—Terrapin Partners LLC
Rubino, Scott—High Road Capital Partners LLC

Pratt's Guide to Private Equity & Venture Capital Sources

Rubinoff, Gary—Summerhill Venture Partners Management Inc
Rubinov, Leon—Incline Management Corp
Rubinov, Leon—PNC Equity Management Corp
Rubinstein, Kenneth—Haynes and Boone LLC
Rubinstein, Steven—Antares Capital Corp
Rubio, Javier—Nauta Capital SL
Ruby, Dale—Oaktree Capital Management LP
Ruby, Lucien—PEI Funds LLC
Ruby, Lucien—Thayer Ventures
Ruch, Joshua—Rho Capital Partners Inc
Ruckstuhl, Roland—Nextech Invest Ltd
Rudakov, Evgeny—Svarog Capital Advisors LTD
Rudat, William—Acas LLC
Rudberg, Aaron—Baird Capital
Rudd, Frank—Compass Partners International LLC
Rudd, Franklin J.—Compass Partners International Llp
Rudder, Christian—Corazon Capital LLC
Rudella, John—Silver Lake Partners LP
Ruder, Brian—Permira Advisers LLP
Ruder, Christopher—Portfolio Advisors, LLC
Rudge, John—Lexington Partners Inc
Rudge, Pedro—Leblon Equities Gestao de Recursos Ltda
Rudin, Murray—Riordan Lewis & Haden
Rudnick, Matthew—Audax Group, Inc.
Rudolph, Barry—Presidio Investors LLC
Rudolph, Richard—Bradford Equities Management LLC
Rudy, Thomas—Elevate Innovation Partners LLC
Rue, Travis—Headwaters BD LLC
Rueckel, Wallace—Questor Partners Holdings Inc
Rued, Scott—HCI Equity LLC
Rueda, Percy—Elm Equity Partners LLC
Ruediger, Manfred—Life Sciences Partners BV
Ruehne, Klaus—ATP Private Equity Partners
Ruffolo, John—OMERS Ventures
Rufini, Rossano—Synergo SGR SpA
Ruger, Jared—Bertram Capital Management LLC
Rughwani, Ashish—Dominus Capital LP
Ruh, William—Castle Creek Capital LLC
Ruhama, Yuval—SIDER ISRA'EL IYE`UTS KALKALI BE`AM
Ruhl, Dan—Oval Partners
Ruhlen, George—Carlyle Group LP
Ruigrok, Niels—NIBC Principal Investments BV
Ruijs, Maarten—CVC Asia Pacific Ltd
Ruiz, Fernando—Acas LLC
Ruiz, Gregory—ACP Inc
Ruiz, Gregory—Friedman Fleischer & Lowe Cap Ptnrs L P
Ruiz, Yolanda—Pacific Community Ventures LLC
Rumilly, Matt—Clearview Capital LLC
Runco, Jason—Blackeagle Partners Fund L P
Runkle, Matthew—ArcLight Capital Holdings LLC
Runnells, John—Vertical Group Inc
Runnquist, Kristofer—AAC CAPITAL PARTNERS
Ruof, Hansjorg—Draper Esprit Secondaries LLP
Ruosch-Conrad, Deborah—Milbank Tweed Hadley & Mccloy LLP
Rupe, Robert—Bacchus Capital Management LLC
Rupf, Immo—Cinven Group Ltd
Ruping, Karl—IncTANK Ventures
Ruppel, Philip—Advantage Capital Partners
Ruppert, R. Todd—Greenspring Associates Inc
Ruppli, Frederic—Ardens & Associes SAS
Rush, Andrew—Diamond Castle Holdings LLC
Rushing, Don—Morrison & Foerster LLP
Rushing, Dru—Bowside Capital LLC
Rusiecki, Michal—Enterprise Investors Sp z o o
Rusoff, S. Lawrence—Performance Equity Management LLC
Russ, Alexander—Evercore Inc
Russel, Jim—Andlinger & Co Inc
Russell, Christopher—Veronis Suhler Stevenson LLC
Russell, Douglas—MassMutual Ventures LLC
Russell, Erin—Vestar Capital Partners Inc
Russell, John—Ironbridge Capital Pty Ltd
Russell, Joseph—Blackstone Group LP
Russell, Nicholas—Tuckerman Capital
Russell, Richard—Small Enterprise Assistance Funds
Russell, Steven—INETWORKS LLC
Russell, Steven—Madison Dearborn Partners LLC
Russell, William—Sterling Investment Partners II LP
Russello, Gianni—Z Capital HF Adviser LLC
Russmeyer, Philip—Vitruvian Partners LLP
Russo, Guy—Canaan Partners
Russo, Jesus—Stratus Investimentos Ltda
Russo, Michele—Terra Firma Capital Partners Ltd
Rust, Anthony—GKM Newport Generation Funds
Rust, Christopher—Clear Venture Management LLC
Rustgi, Atul—Accolade Capital Management LLC
Rustgi, Atul—Accolade Capital Management LLC
Rutberg, Bryan—Rutberg and Co LLC
Rutherford, Jan—Scottish Equity Partners LLP
Rutherford, John—Parthenon Capital LLC
Rutherfurd, James—Pine Brook Road Partners LLC
Rutherfurd, Jim—3i
Rutherfurd, Jim—3i Group PLC
Rutili, Franco—Innogest Sgr SpA
Rutland, Peter—CVC Capital Partners Ltd
Rutledge, Rob—Genstar Capital LLC
Rutledge, Robyn Lawrie—TSG Consumer Partners, L.P.
Rutlin, Alexander—Mill City Capital LP
Ruttenberg, Eric—Tinicum Capital Partners
Rutter, Kent—Haynes and Boone LLC
Ruxton, Peter—Tembo Capital LLP
Ryabov, Boris—Bright Capital OOO
Ryan, Charles—Almaz Capital Partners
Ryan, Christopher—Riverside Capital Partners LLC
Ryan, Colin—Cycle Capital Management (CCM) Inc
Ryan, Cornelius—Oxford Bioscience Partners
Ryan, Daniel—Milestone Partners LP
Ryan, Daniel—Spring Bay Companies
Ryan, David—Mission Ventures Inc
Ryan, Dennis—Foresite Capital Management LLC
Ryan, Garrett—AG BD LLC
Ryan, John—ONSET Ventures
Ryan, Justin—Quadrant Private Equity
Ryan, Kenneth—Riverstone Holdings LLC
Ryan, M. Cliff—Riverstone Holdings LLC
Ryan, Michael—Hamilton Lane Advisors LLC
Ryan, Michael—Jacobson Partners
Ryan, Michael—Raptor Capital Management LP
Ryan, Neil—Tullis Health Investors
Ryan, Patrick—SV Health Investors LLP
Ryan, Renee—Johnson & Johnson Innovation-JJDC Inc
Ryan, Rhonda—Pavilion Alternatives Group Ltd
Ryan, Tobin—Seidler Equity Partners
Ryan, William—Glengary LLC
Rydbeck, Carl—Crosslink Capital Inc
Rygh, Tom—Nordic Capital
Ryland, Kyle—Sumeru Equity Partners, L.P.
Rytkonen, Kari—MB Rahastot Oy
Rytomaa, Marjatta—Sentica Partners Oy
Ryttergaard, Peter—Catacap Management A/S
Ryu, Deok-soo—Korea Investment Partners Co Ltd
Ryu, John—Scout Ventures LLC
Ryu, John—Scout Ventures LLC
S.V., Subramanya—Bessemer Venture Partners
STEELMAN, PETER—Deerfield Management Company LP
STEVENS, Mark A.—S Cubed Capital LLC
Saacks, Jonathan—Genesis Partners Ltd
Saad, Abdul Rahim—Investcorp Bank BSC
Saade, Javier—Fenway Summer Ventures LP
Saade, Javier—Global Emerging Markets
Saadeh, Salam—Active-M
Saah, Faris—Blackstone Group LP
Saba, Aladdin—BPE Partners
Sabarwal, Jaspal—Everstone Capital Management, Ltd.
Sabassier, Dominique—Natixis Private Equity SA
Sabater, Juan—Valor Equity Partners L P
Sabbaghian, Nader—R301 Capital
Sabben-Clare, Matthew—Cinven Group Ltd
Saberi, Nina—Castile Ventures
Sabet, Bijan—Spark Capital
Sabet, Joseph—Catalyst Investments LP
Sabet, Lori—Carlyle Group LP
Sabeti, Faris—BlueOcean Ventures SA
Sabin, John—Revolution
Sablinski, Tomasz—Auven Therapeutics Management LLLP
Sabo, Elias—Anholt (USA) LLC
Sabo, Marla—Fireman Capital Partners LLC
Sacha, Brent—Stonehenge Growth Capital LLC
Sachar, Laura—StarVest Partners LP
Sachdeva, Shivani—India Alternatives Investment Advisors Pvt Ltd
Sacher, William—Oaktree Capital Management LP
Sachidanand, Anil—ArthVeda Fund Management Pvt Ltd
Sachs, Barton—PTV Healthcare Capital
Sachs, Bruce—Charles River Ventures LLC
Sachs, Lewis—Gallatin Point Capital LLC
Sachse, Klaus—CBG Commerz Beteiligungskapital GmbH & Co KG
Sachse, Peter—VR Equitypartner GmbH
Sachwitz, Kirsten—Csi
Sack, Andy—Founders Co op
Sack, Ernst—Blue Bear Capital LLC
Sack, Ernst—Riverstone Holdings LLC
Sackett, Larry—Aequitos Capital Management LLC
Sackman, Donald—Independence Equity Management LLC
Sacks, Ian—Towerbrook Capital Partners LP
Sacks, Marc—Mesirow Financial Private Equity Inc
Sacks, Matt—New Enterprise Associates Inc
Sacks, Robert—Acas LLC
Sadaranganey, Neil—DOCOMO Innovations Inc
Sadden, Jack—Valesco Industries Inc

Saddi, Karim–Towerbrook Capital Partners LP
Sadeghi, Mani–Equifin Capital Partners
Sadeharju, Vesa–Vnt Management Oy
Sadek, Karim–Qalaa Holdings SAE
Sadek, Zachary–Parthenon Capital LLC
Sadeq, Karim–Qalaa Holdings SAE
Sadrian, Justin–Warburg Pincus LLC
Saemundsson, Alfheidur–Quadrangle Group LLC
Saer, John–GI Partners
Saetre, Ola–Hitecvision AS
Safady, Randa–University of Texas System
Safaii, David–Windspeed Ventures
Safaii, Matthew–Actua Corp
Safars, Michel–IT-Translation SA
Safer, Pennina–Medica Venture Partners, Ltd.
Safran, Peter–New Europe Venture Equity
Sagar, Akanksha–3 Degrees Asset Management Pte Ltd
Sagarriga, Javier Cebrian–Bonsai Venture Capital SCR de Regimen Comun SA
Sagoo, Reena–OMERS Infrastructure
Sah, Rohit–Trust Company of the West
Saha, Saurabh–Atlas Venture Advisors Inc
Sahay, Praveen–Wave Equity Partners LLC
Sahib, El Houssine–Almamed
Sahin, Burak Emin–Fiba Kapital Holding AS
Sahlman, Stephen–Candescent Partners LLC
Sahni, Varun–Global Impact Investors
Sahy, Jean-Mathieu–Capital Export SAS
Said, Rafic–Blackstone Group LP
Saifee, Moiz–Correlation Ventures LP
Saigal, Suvrat–First Abu Dhabi Bank PJSC
Saikia, Rohan–Great Point Partners LLC
Sailer, John–HealthCor Partners Management LP
Sailer, Michael–MVP Management GmbH
Saillant, Nicolas–Thefamily SAS
Sailors, Daniel–Riverstone Holdings LLC
Saiontz, Marc–Ascribe Capital, LLC
Saipe, Joshua–Spectrum Healthcare Fund LLC
Saito, Genta–Carlyle Group LP
Saito, Naotsugu–CLSA Capital Partners HK Ltd
Saiz, Alejandro–Nexxus Capital SA de CV
Sakai, Hiroshi–Active Investment Partners
Sakai, Stan–Defta Partners
Sakaji, Masayuki–Toho Bank Ltd
Sakakibara, Kentaro–Samurai Incubate Inc
Sakamoto, Atsuhiko–Bain Capital Inc
Sakauchi, Katsuyuki–Rising Japan Equity Inc
Saki, Lunga–Akayi Capital Partners LLC
Saklecha, Akhil–Artiman Management LLC
Sakoda, Jon–New Enterprise Associates Inc
Saks, Justin–Gryphon Investors Inc
Saks, Peeter–BaltCap Management Estonia OU
Sakurai, Hideaki–J-STAR Co Ltd
Salaber, Konrad–Wind Point Advisors LLC
Salamon, Michael–Birch Hill Equity Partners Management Inc
Salamon, Robert–BHMS Investments, L.P.
Salata, Jean Eric–Baring Private Equity Asia Ltd
Salaverria, Julia–Ysios Capital Partners SGECR SAU
Salazar Rojo, Pablo–IGNIA Partners LLC
Salazar, Raul–Macrocapitales SAFI SA
Saldutti, Joseph–Gridiron Capital LLC
Saleem, Junaid–Goldenmount Capital International Inc

Salehizadeh, Bijan–Highland Capital Partners LLC
Salehizadeh, Bijan–NaviMed Capital Advisors LLC
Salem, Enrique–Bain Capital Venture Partners LLC
Salem, Luis Fernando–BPE Investimentos
Salem, Paul–Providence Equity Partners LLC
Salembier, Andrew–Accolade Capital Management LLC
Salerno, Robert–Morrison & Foerster LLP
Sales, Chris–Cabot Square Capital Advisors Ltd
Sales, Whitney–Acceleprise LLC
Salewski, Anthony–Genstar Capital LLC
Salgar, Mauricio–Advent International Corp
Salhab, George–Saned Equity Partners Ltd
Saliba, Joseph–Ascent Equity Group LLC
Salice, Thomas–SFW Capital Partners LLC
Salim, David–Spice Private Equity AG
Salim, Michael–Brazos Private Equity Partners LLC
Salinger, Jeff–Stuart Mill Capital, Inc.
Salis, Miguel–Alantra
Salisbury, Ellen–Start Smart Labs
Salisbury, William–Mainsail Partners LP
Salkind, Gene–Steel Pier Capital Advisors LLC
Salkind, Louis–D E Shaw & Co LP
Sallaberry, Paul–Jafco Ventures
Salley, Christopher–Auldbrass Partners LP
Sallin, Kelly–NanoDimension Management Ltd
Sallitt, Henry–Fpe Capital LLP
Sallmard, Julien–Invus Group LLC
Salmon, Nicolas–OLMA Capital Management Ltd
Salmon, Stephen–Latterell Venture Partners LP
Salonoja, Pekka–Nexit Ventures Oy
Salsberg, Eric–Fairfax Financial Holdings Ltd
Salsbury, Matthew–Brown Brothers Harriman & Co
Saltarelli, Gerald–Edgewater Funds
Salter, Geoff–First Stone Venture Partners Inc
Salty, Samer–Zouk Capital LLP
Saltzman, Jonathan–Cypress Advisors, L.P.
Saltzman, Jonathan–Torque Capital Group LLC
Saltzman, Richard–Colony Capital LLC
Salvagno, Rob–Cisco Investments Inc
Salvato, Luca–Coller Capital Ltd
Salvatore, Louis–Blackstone Group LP
Salvo, Giuliano–Militello Capital LLC
Salyer, Stephen–Probitas Partners Inc
Salyers, Kyle–CHV Capital Inc
Salzstein, Inbal–AKN Holdings LLC
Samaha, Salim–Global Infrastructure Holdings
Samara, Eduardo–General Atlantic LLC
Samberg, Arthur–Twin Haven Capital Partners LLC
Samboursky, Kobi–Glilot Capital Investments GP Ltd
Samek, Edward–Carlyle Group LP
Samie, Kaveh–KKR & Co LP
Samios, Nikolas–German Startups Group Berlin GmbH & Co KGaA
Sammakia, Mohammed–Investcorp Bank BSC
Sammann, Todd–Colony Capital LLC
Sammell, Seymour–ZMC
Sammons, Jay–Carlyle Group LP
Sammut, Stephen–Burrill & Company
Samoladas, George–Blackstone Group LP
Sampat, Ravi–IEP Fund Advisors Pvt Ltd
Sampat, Ravi–Sealink Capital Partners
Sampath, Dilip–Panasonic Venture Group
Sampson, Mark–Vintage Capital Partners, L.P.
Sampson, Nicholas–Vexiom Equity Partners, L.P.

Sampson, Rodney–Tech Square Labs LLC
Samson, Louis–Platinum Equity LLC
Samson, Peter–Ironbridge Equity Partners Management Ltd
Samuel, Craig–Turnstone Capital Management LLC
Samuel, Dave–Freestyle Capital
Samuel, David–Birch Hill Equity Partners Management Inc
Samuel, David–Mosaic Venture Partners
Samuel, Jeremy–Anacacia Capital Pty Ltd
Samuels, Aliza–FLAG Capital Management LLC
Samuels, Ami–Gatewood Capital Partners LLC
Samuels, Ami–Poalim Cap Mark Tech, Ltd.
Samuels, Camille–Venrock Inc
Samuels, Judson–New Heritage Capital LLC
Samuelsson, Per–Odlander Fredrikson & Co AB
Samura, Reijiro–Ant Capital Partners Co Ltd
Samwer, Alexander–Global Founders Capital Management GmbH
Samwer, Marc–Global Founders Capital Management GmbH
Samwer, Oliver–Global Founders Capital Management GmbH
San Jose, Diego–Blackstone Group LP
Sanami, Takenori–Jafco Ventures
Sanan, Puneet–MVC Capital Inc
Sanchez, Daniel–Nauta Capital SL
Sanchez, Francisco–Pt Capital LLC
Sanchez, Regina Longo–Itau Unibanco Holding SA
Sanchez, Sergio–Evercore Inc
Sanchez-Asiain, Inigo–Portobello Capital Advisors SL
Sand, Christopher–Centre Partners Management LLC
Sand, Michael–Ascribe Capital, LLC
Sand, Ole–GEF Management Corp
Sandach, Limor–7 Health Ventures
Sandberg, Darren–Actua Corp
Sandejas, Paco–Narra Venture Capital
Sandell, Scott–New Enterprise Associates Inc
Sander, Thies–Project A Ventures GmbH & Co KG
Sanders, Howard–Auldbrass Partners LP
Sanders, Jason–Entangled Ventures LLC
Sanders, Nathan–Technology Crossover Ventures LP
Sanders, Richard–Permira Advisers LLP
Sanders, Ricky–Morris Capital Management LLC
Sanders, Robert–Nittany Lion Venture Capital
Sanders, Ronald–Colony Capital LLC
Sandersen, Erik–Incitia Ventures AS
Sanderson, Daniel–Colville Capital LLC
Sanderson, Philip–IDG Ventures USA
Sandford, John–Maui Capital Ltd
Sandifer, Michael–Open Field Capital LLC
Sandler, Ian–Carlyle Group LP
Sandler, Ian–Insight Venture Partners LLC
Sandler, Julie–MadroNA Venture Group
Sando, Tue–Gemcorp Capital LLP
Sandoski, Aaron–Norwich Ventures
Sandoval, Daniel–Diana Capital SGECR SA
Sandroshvili, Dato–Evercore Inc
Sandstrom, Jon–Morgan Stanley Alternative Investment Partners LP
Sandstrom, Sarah–Atlantic-Pacific Capital Inc
Sandu, Neculai–Axxess Capital Partners SA
Sandusky, Jason–Nittany Lion Venture Capital
Sandys, Peter–Seroba Kernel Life Sciences Ltd

Pratt's Guide to Private Equity & Venture Capital Sources

Sanfeliu, Josep–Ysios Capital Partners SGECR SAU
Sanford, P. Craig–Westshore Capital Partners LP
Sang, Rachel–CID Group
Sang, Xiaohong–JC Flowers & Co LLC
Sangal, Siddharth–Proprium Capital Partners LP
Sangalis, Stephen–Progress Equity Partners Ltd
Sangameswaran, Manikkan–ICICI Venture Funds Management Company Ltd
Sanger, Jim–Second Alpha Partners LLC
Sanger, Joshua–Riverstone Holdings LLC
Sanger, Philip–TEXO Ventures
Sanghai, Jiten–JLL Partners Inc
Sanghavi, Apurva–START Group LLC
Sanghavi, Rahul–Sealink Capital Partners
Sangster, Ray–Mti Partners Ltd
Sangudi, Genevieve–Carlyle Group LP
Sankey, N Darius–Zone Ventures
Sanner, Dan–Alpine Investors LP
Sano, Takashi–Global Brain Corp
Sanroma, Josep Ramon–ICF Capital SGEIC SAU
Sansom, Ron–Riverside Co
Sansone, Nicole–Ferrer Freeman & Co LLC
Sansone, Nicole–Peloton Equity LLC
Santangelo, Bill–Oaktree Capital Management LP
Santillana, Humberto–Foresight Group LLP
Santinelli, Paul–Guidepost Growth Equity
Santino, Jo–Indufin SA
Santinon, Francesco–Spirit Capital Partners Llp
Santisteban, Cipriano–Linzor Capital Partners LP
Santodomingo Martell, Angel–Banco Santander Brasil SA
Santoli, Barbara–LBO Italia Investimenti Srl
Santomassimo, Michael–Bank of New York Mellon Corp
Santoni, Mike–Harbour Group Ltd
Santoro, Charles–Sterling Investment Partners II LP
Santos Laureano, Aldo–Vinci Equities Gestora de Recursos Ltda
Santos, B. Paul–Tholons Capital
Santos, B. Paul–Wavemaker Partners
Santos, Diogo Chalbert–Ecs Capital SA
Santos, Fabio–Nova Gestao de Recursos Ltda
Santos, John–Brown Brothers Harriman & Co
Santos, Lamberto–AB Capital and Investment Corp
Santos, Paul–WaveMaker Labs Pte Ltd
Santospirito, Anthony–Cinven Group Ltd
Santulin, Alberto–Blackstone Group LP
Sanz, Sara–Inveready Seed Capital SCR SA
Saper, Jake–Emergence Capital Partners
Saporito, Alex–Edwards Capital LLC
Saraceni, Diana–360 Capital Management SA
Saraf, Anish–Warburg Pincus LLC
Saraf, Binit–ICICI Venture Funds Management Company Ltd
Saraf, Shirish–Samena Capital Management LLP
Sarasa, Jose Angel–Baring Private Equity Asia Ltd
Sarchet, M. Mark–Dresner Capital Resources Inc
Sargeant, Mark–Phoenix Equity Partners Ltd
Sargent, Chris–San Francisco Equity Partners LP
Sargent, Joseph–TENNANT CAPITAL PARTNERS L L C
Sargent, Robert–TENNANT CAPITAL PARTNERS L L C
Sargent, Thomas–TENNANT CAPITAL PARTNERS L L C
Sargent, William–Framestore Ventures
Saricoglu, Eren–Carlyle Group LP

Sarie, Alban–Naxicap Partners SA
Sarkar, Neel–Centennial Ventures Vii L P
Sarkhou, Faisal–KAMCO Investment Co KSCP
Sarkis, Walid–Bain Capital Inc
Sarkisyan, Yervand–Granatus Ventures CJSC
Sarkozy, P. Olivier–Carlyle Group LP
Sarlo, George–Walden Venture Capital
Sarma, Adarsh–Warburg Pincus LLC
Sarner, Michael–Acas LLC
Sarnoff, Stuart–Avenue Capital Group LLC
Sarocka, Arvydas–Litcapital Asset Management UAB
Sarracino, Steven–Activant Capital Group LLC
Sarraut, Jean-Philippe–iGlobe Partners Ltd
Sarsama, Juha–Panostaja Oyj
Saruggia, Federico–Permira Advisers LLP
Sarver, Ryan–Redpoint Ventures
Sarwar, Omair–SFW Capital Partners LLC
Sasaki, Daniel–Lloyds Development Capital (Holdings) Ltd
Sasaki, David–Omidyar Network Commons LLC
Sasaki, Koji–Tokio Marine Capital Co Ltd
Sasaki, Yusuke–Blackstone Group LP
Sasayama, Koji–Mezzanine Corp
Sasidharan, Anjana–Sequoia Capital India
Sasnauskas, Kestutis–East Capital Private Equity AB
Sasongko, Mark–Fluxus Ventures LLP
Sasson, Eric–Carlyle Group LP
Sasson, Ori–Primera Capital
Sasson, Sharam–Primera Capital
Satchcroft, Alex–Apax Partners LLP
Satchu, Reza–NEXT Canada
Sathaye, Shirish–Khosla Ventures LLC
Sathe, Rajeev–ArthVeda Fund Management Pvt Ltd
Sathe, Shrikant–Vedanta Capital LP
Satish, Peruvemba–Allstate Private Equity
Sato, Masaaki–Mezzanine Corp
Sato, Takanori–Mitsui & Co Global Investment Ltd
Sato, Taro–Innovation Network Corporation of Japan
Satrustegui, Enrique Centelles–Ged Group
Satterfield, Mike–Yaletown Venture Partners
Satterly, Annabelle–Medu Capital(Pty)Ltd
Satyavolu, Schwark–Trinity Ventures LLP
Sauerteig, B. Lance–Balance Point Capital Partners, L.P.
Saul, N. Grant–Hamilton Lane Advisors LLC
Saul, Shai–AL Capital Holdings 2016 Ltd
Saunders, Glen–Triodos International Fund Management BV
Saunders, Ingelise–Scandinavian Life Science Venture
Saunders, Matthew–Ryerson Futures Inc
Saunders, Robert–OCA Ventures
Saunders, Robin–Clearbrook Capital Partners LLP
Saunte, Adam–ATP Private Equity Partners
Saurel, Zita–Hellman & Friedman LLC
Sautter, Thilo–Cinven Group Ltd
Sauve, Thomas–T Squared Capital LLC
Sava, Guy–Heidrick & Struggles International Inc
Savage, Bob–Plymouth Venture Partners
Savage, James–HPEF Capital Partners Ltd
Savage, James–Longworth Venture Partners, L.P.
Savage, Jim–Longworth Venture Partners, L.P.
Savage, Tige–Revolution
Savage, Tige–Revolution Ventures LLC
Saval Perez, Arturo–Nexxus Capital SA de CV

Savar, Avi–DreamIt Ventures
Saverin, Alexandre–Kawa Capital Management Inc
Saviane, Roberto–Wise Venture SGR SpA
Savickas, Donatas–Siauliu Bankas AB
Savig, Joe–Accel-KKR
Savignol, Robert–M/C Venture Partners LLC
Saville, B. Hagen–Washington Equity Partners LLC
Savin, Alexander–Elbrus Kapital OOO
Savin, Allyson–Hovde Private Equity Advisors LLC
Savitz, Scott–Data Point Capital I LP
Savkov, Bojidar–Gemcorp Capital LLP
Savoie, Robert–Pinnacle Ventures
Savov, Sava–Oaktree Capital Management LP
Savul, Kim–TSG Consumer Partners, L.P.
Savvides, Savvas–Apax Partners LLP
Sawaf, Omar–Yellowstone Capital, Inc.
Sawhney, Ashwini–Z Capital HF Adviser LLC
Sawhney, Rahul–Z Capital HF Adviser LLC
Sawhney, Vikrant–Blackstone Group LP
Sawhney, Viraj–Warburg Pincus LLC
Sawiris, Onsi–HOF Capital Inc
Sawlani, Mukesh–Gennx360 Capital Partners LP
Sawwaf, Mu taz–Saned Equity Partners Ltd
Sawyer, Kenneth–Saints Ventures
Sawyer, Philip–Helix Ventures
Sawyer, William–OrbiMed Advisors LLC
Saxena, Daniel–Ventizz Capital Partners Advisory AG
Saxena, Himanshu–Starwood Capital Group I LP
Saxena, Manoj–Entrepreneurs Fund LP
Saxena, Parag–Vedanta Capital LP
Saxton, James–White Deer Energy LP
Saxton, Tracy–Pivotal BioVenture Partners LLC
Say, Mustafa–Ilab Holding AS
Sayama, Nobuo–Integral Corp
Sayao de Silva, Gilberto–Vinci Equities Gestora de Recursos Ltda
Sayarath, Justin–Kleiner Perkins Caufield & Byers LLC
Sayed, Tanzil–Dunamis Ventures
Sayers, Nicholas–Concentric Equity Partners, L.P.
Sayle, Robert–Thoma Bravo LLC
Sazej, Shahin–KJM Capital LLC
Scaife, Matthew–Causeway Capital Partners I LP
Scali, Anthony–Evercore Inc
Scanlan, David–Silverhawk Capital Partners LLC
Scanlon, Richard–Marker Financial Advisors LLC
Scannapieco, Dario–European Investment Bank
Scarampi, Galeazzo–V&A Capital
Scarborough, Michelle–Business Development Bank of Canada
Scarinci, Richard–Blackstone Group LP
Scarinci, Richard–Partners Capital Investment Group Holdings LLC
Scarlat, Cezar–Abris Capital Partners Sp zoo
Scarpa, Carmen–Tudor Ventures
Scarpis, Stefano–Alto Partners SRL
Scarsi, Mark–Milbank Tweed Hadley & Mccloy LLP
Scaturro, Philip–Allen & Company of Florida, Inc.
Scavazza, Ricardo–PII Investimentos Imobiliarios Ltda
Scaysbrook, David–Capital Dynamics Sdn Bhd
Scerbo, John–Catterton Partners Corp
Schaaff, Tom–Edison Partners
Schaafsma, Gerry–Anthem Capital Management Inc

Schaar, Werner–V+Beteiligungs 2 GmbH
Schaar, William–Horizon Partners, Ltd.
Schaberger, Peter–Riverside Co
Schacht, Henry–Warburg Pincus LLC
Schachter, Charlene–Greenhouse Capital Partners
Schade, Irmgard–Finatem Fonds Management Verwaltungs GmbH
Schade, Karl–Presidio Investors LLC
Schaefer, Cary–Fidus Capital LLC
Schaefer, Curt–TPH Partners LLC
Schaefer, Florian–Blackstone Group LP
Schaefer, Neil–Gennx360 Capital Partners LP
Schaefer, Stephen–Riverstone Holdings LLC
Schaefer, Steven–Graycliff Partners LP
Schaen, Scott–Pine Brook Road Partners LLC
Schaepe, Christopher–Lightspeed Management Company LLC
Schaeppi, Urs–Swisscom AG
Schafer, J. Michael–New Mexico Community Capital
Schafer, Lee–BlueFire Partners Capital Markets Group
Schafler, R. Scott–COGR Inc
Schaible, David–Spire Capital Partners LP
Schaible, Stephen–Evercore Inc
Schaller, Curt–Focus Healthcare Partners LLC
Schaller, Timothy–New Enterprise Associates Inc
Schaltenbrand, Nicole–Gladstone Investment Corp
Schannep, Cullen–Lexington Partners Inc
Schapira, Paul–CIG Securities Inc
Schapiro, Benjamin–Questmark Partners LP
Schapiro, Ian–G3W Ventures LLC
Schapiro, Ian–Oaktree Capital Management LP
Schapiro, Kenneth–Condor Capital Management Corp
Schardt, Andrew–Hamilton Lane Advisors LLC
Scharf, Dennis–Hamilton Lane Advisors LLC
Scharfenberger, Joseph–CCMP Capital Advisors LP
Scharfman, Scott–Mill Road Capital Management LLC
Schattner, Michael–Onondaga Venture Capital Fund LLC
Schaub, Dan–iSelect Fund LLC
Schauerman, Thomas–Norwest Equity Partners
Schechter, Jonathan–Indigo Group LLC
Schechter, Marc–Anderson Group LLC, The
Schechtmann, Patrick–SP Ventures Gestora de Recursos SA
Schecter, Adam–Wanxiang America Capital LLC
Schecter, Sam–Rosemont Investment Partners LLC
Scheerer, Andrea–Steadfast Capital GmbH
Scheetz, Ned–Aphelion Capital LLC
Scheffler, Wolfgang–Freudenberg Venture Capital GmbH
Scheichenost, Max–Alps Venture Capital GmbH
Schein, Jeremy–Corsair Capital LLC
Scheiner, Jonathan–Solaris Energy Capital LLC
Scheinfeld, Larry–Zelkova Ventures
Scheinrock, Jeff–GKM Newport Generation Funds
Schell, Richard–ONSET Ventures
Schell, Tony–ESCALATE CAPITAL I L P
Schell, Troy–Aether Investment Partners LLC
Schellenberg, David–Highland West Capital Ltd
Schellenberg, Duane–Arc Financial Corp.
Scheman, Ann–International Business Machines Corp

Schena, Graham–Sentinel Capital Partners LLC
Schenk, Leo–Synergia Capital Partners BV
Schenk, Philippe–J.W.Childs Associates LP
Schepis, Michelle–Morgan Stanley Alternative Investment Partners LP
Scher, Jennifer–Round Hill Music Royalty Fund LP
Scherer, Joshua–Perella Weinberg Partners LP
Scherer, Mirko–MPM Capital LLC
Scherr, Andrew–Southport Lane Management LLC
Scherrer, Bruno–Lone Star Fund Ltd
Scherrer, Doug–Clearlight Partners LLC
Schestag, Shawn–Sixpoint Partners LLC
Scheurl, David–Metric Capital Partners LLP
Schiavo, Chris–Battery Ventures LP
Schibl, Alain–Duet Capital Ltd
Schiciano, Kenneth–TA Associates Management LP
Schick, Barrett–First Reserve Corp
Schick, Bruno–Cinven Group Ltd
Schick, Florian–Bregal Capital LLP
Schick, Florian–Bregal Investments LLP
Schick, Louis–NewWorld Capital Group LLC
Schickedanz, Sean–Clean Pacific Ventures Management LLC
Schields, Luke–Dakota Venture Group Inc
Schieman, Susan–Blue Chip Venture Co
Schiess, Anya–Healthy Ventures Management LLC
Schiff, Andrew–Aisling Capital LLC
Schiff, David–Perella Weinberg Partners LP
Schiff, Frank–Mid-Ocean Partners LP
Schiff, James–Northwood Ventures
Schiff, Peter–Northwood Ventures
Schiffman, Cara–Advantage Capital Partners
Schifter, Trudi–iGlobe Partners Ltd
Schilberg, Barbara–BioAdvance
Schilcher, Hans–Raiffeisenlandesbank Oberoesterreich AG
Schildkraut, Jonathan–Evercore Inc
Schiller, Anke–V+Beteiligungs 2 GmbH
Schiller, Eric–Partnership Capital Growth LLC
Schiller, Nancy–Bulgarian-American Enterprise Fund
Schiller, Rolf–Sparkassenbeteiligungs Heilbronn Franken GmbH & Co KG
Schilling, Debra–Acero Capital, L.P.
Schilling, Mathias–Redpoint Eventures Consultoria Empresarial Ltda
Schilling, Mathias–e.ventures
Schilling, Mathias–eVenture Capital Partners GmbH
Schillinger, Doug–Dw Healthcare Partners
Schilpp, Paul–RFE Investment Partners
Schimmel, Robert–Noble Four Partners LLC
Schimmelpfennig, Joe–Roth Capital Partners LLC
Schindler, Chris–Ontario Teachers' Pension Plan
Schindler, Walter–SAIL Capital Partners LLC
Schioldager, Amy–BlackRock Inc
Schirmer, Mathias–Baird Capital
Schirmers, Bernhard–SHS Gesellschaft fuer Beteiligungsmanagement mbH
Schlachet, Loren–Riverside Co
Schlaepfer, Alexander–Aster Capital Partners SAS
Schlafman, Steve–Lerer Ventures II LP
Schlanger, Richard–Palm Beach Capital Management LLC
Schlegell, John–Endeavour Capital Inc
Schlein, Phil–HALO FUND L P

Schlein, Philip–U.S. Venture Partners
Schlein, Ted–Kleiner Perkins Caufield & Byers LLC
Schlenker, Andreas–Partech International
Schlenker, Steven–DN Capital Global Venture Capital Ii LP
Schlesinger, Thomas–Beecken Petty O'Keefe & Company LLC
Schley, Daniel–Dolphin Capital Group LLC
Schlick, Erich–Wellington Partners GmbH
Schliebs, Charles–INETWORKS LLC
Schlitzer, Guido–High Tech Grunderfonds Management GmbH Unspecified Fund
Schloop, Matthew–Pfingsten Partners LLC
Schloss, Craig–Morrison & Foerster LLP
Schlossareck, Steve–Quicksilver Ventures
Schlossberg, David–Fulton Capital LLC
Schlosser, Roderik–Providence Equity Partners LLC
Schmaltz, Dana–Yellow Wood Partners LLC
Schmalz, Darin–Maranon Capital LP
Schmeding, Carsten–WP Global Partners Inc
Schmeichel, Ron–Windsor Private Capital
Schmeisse, Daniel–Merida Capital Partners LLC
Schmelig, Karlheinz–Creathor Venture Management GmbH
Schmelter, Jay–RiverVest Venture Partners LLC
Schmickle, Michael–Palm Beach Capital Management LLC
Schmid, Bernhard–Xange Private Equity SA
Schmid, Edward–Ascent Venture Management Inc
Schmid, Peter–Actis LLP
Schmidly, Jason–Carousel Capital Partners
Schmidt, Bob–Fletcher Spaght Ventures LP
Schmidt, Brian–Varde Partners Inc
Schmidt, Eric–Innovation Endeavors LLC
Schmidt, Guilherme–Black River Asset Management LLC
Schmidt, Kim–Elmcore Group Inc
Schmidt, Lisa–Kinderhook Industries LLC
Schmidt, Randy–Lemhi Ventures, Inc.
Schmidt, Sven–Accel Partners & Co Inc
Schmidt, Tashi–Tola Capital LLC
Schmidt, Thomas–Lantern Asset Management LP
Schmidt, Volker–Emeram Capital Partners GmbH
Schmidt, Will–Advent International Corp
Schmidt-Chiari, Stani–Sea Equity Ltd
Schmidt-Fischer, Peter-Paul–Premium Equity Partners GmbH
Schmidt-Forger, Berthold–Afinum Management GmbH
Schmidt-Holtz, Rolf–Hanse Ventures BSJ GmbH
Schmieta, Stefan–Axioma Ventures LLC
Schmit, Georges–Eurefi SA
Schmitt, Dalton–CRP Companhia de Participacoes
Schmitt, George–TeleSoft Partners
Schmitt, Jean-Jolt Capital SAS
Schmitt, Paul–Novitas Capital LP
Schmitz, Frank–Blackstone Group LP
Schmitz, Hans-Jurgen–Mangrove Capital Partners SA
Schmitz, Mark–Springstar GmbH
Schmitz, Michael–JZ Capital Partners Ltd
Schmitz-Riol, Christine–Mountain Partners AG
Schmuck, David–Antares Capital Corp
Schmuckler, Joseph–Medley Capital LLC
Schnabel, Hansjorg–HQ Equita GmbH

Schnabel, John–Falcon Investment Advisors LLC
Schnabel, Michael–Centre Partners Management LLC
Schnadig, David–COGR Inc
Schnakenberg, Ben–High Road Capital Partners LLC
Schnall, Richard–Clayton Dubilier & Rice LLC
Schneble, Jeff–Wing Venture Capital
Schneer, George–Horizon Ventures
Schneider, Anton–Pecuniano GmbH
Schneider, Brian–Northstar Capital LLC
Schneider, Chanan–Agate Medical Investments LP
Schneider, Christian–Vesalius Biocapital Partners SARL
Schneider, Christoph–WKBG Wiener Kreditbuergschafts und Beteiligungsbank AG
Schneider, Christopher–Florescence Capital Co Ltd
Schneider, Christopher–Florescence Huamao Equity Capital Management Co Ltd
Schneider, Conradin–AIG Capital Partners Inc
Schneider, Geoff–Cava Capital
Schneider, Geoff–Cava Capital
Schneider, Geoff–Emerge Venture Capital
Schneirig, Jeffrey–Victory Park Capital Advisors LLC
Schneider, Richard–Easton Hunt Capital Partners LP
Schneider, Stefan–Floor 13 GmbH
Schneider, Todd–CHS Capital LLC
Schneider, Todd–Shorehill Capital LLC
Schneider, Toni–True Ventures LLC
Schneider-Guenther, Rolf–Baytech Venture Capital GmbH & Co KG
Schneiderman, Arthur–Global Catalyst Partners
Schneiorr, John–Allen & Company of Florida, Inc.
Schnell, David–Prospect Venture Partners
Schnell, Ralf–Siemens Venture Capital GmbH
Schneller, Cas–Friedman Fleischer & Lowe Cap Ptnrs L P
Schneur, Avner–Kormeli LLC
Schnitzler, Ralph–iVentureCapital GmbH
Schnorf, Werner–Zurmont Madison Management AG
Schober, Andreas–Hannover Finanz GmbH
Schocken, Joseph–Jesup & Lamont Securities Corp
Schocken, Joseph–Jesup & Lamont Securities Corp
Schockert, Alain–Banque Degroof Petercam SA
Schoemaker-Vazquez, Anne–Newspring Capital
Schoen, Andrew–New Enterprise Associates Inc
Schoen, Pieter–VOC Capital Partners BV
Schoendorf, Joseph–Accel Partners & Co Inc
Schoendorf, Nancy–Mohr Davidow Ventures
Schoenfeld, Jeffrey–Brown Brothers Harriman & Co
Schoenfeld, Mark–Carlyle Group LP
Schoenthal, Andrew–Harvest Partners LP
Schoenwetter, Lewis–CenterGate Capital LP
Schoernig, Michael–Fronteris Consulting AG
Schoff, Robert–Scorpion Capital Partners LP
Schofield, Jon–PHD Equity Partners LLP
Schokking, Ronald–Fairfax Financial Holdings Ltd
Scholl, David–Athenian Fund Management Inc
Scholl, Martin–Zuercher Kantonalbank
Scholl, Thomas–Novak Biddle Venture Partners LP
Scholnick, Daniel–Trinity Ventures LLP
Scholtz, David–Ariadne Capital Ltd
Schonberg, Joseph–Falfurrias Capital Partners LP
Schonberger, Stuart–CDH China Management Co., Ltd.

Schonenberger, Helmut–Unternehmertum GmbH
Schopp, David–Stonebridge Partners LP
Schorr, Chip–One Equity Partners LLC
Schorr, Dan–AEA Investors LLC
Schorr, Jonathan–NewSchools Venture Fund
Schottler, Jeffrey–Headwaters BD LLC
Schotz, Jon–Kayne Anderson Capital Advisors LP
Schou, Carsten–Pre-Seed Innovation A/S
Schou, Carsten–SEED Capital Management I/S
Schou-Petersen, Poul Erik–Nes Partner Holding ApS
Schoultz, Mikael–Platina Finance, Ltd.
Schouten, Rutger–Brooklyn Ventures BV
Schrager, Alan–Oak Hill Advisors LP
Schragmann, Holger–Capcellence Mittelstandspartner GmbH
Schraith, Jim–Frontier Venture Capital
Schreck, Hans–TVM Capital GmbH
Schreiber, Alain–ProQuest Investments
Schreiber, Detlef–CEE Management GmbH
Schreiber, Douglas–Lee Equity Partners LLC
Schreiber, Elisa–Greylock Partners LLC
Schreiber, Richard–Cavipar SASU
Schreiber, Ron–Softbank Capital Partners L P
Schremper, Ralf–Oakley Capital Ltd
Schreurs, Martijn–Gilde Buy Out Partners BV
Schricke, Herve–Xange Private Equity SA
Schrier, Douglas–Rembrandt Venture Management LLC
Schrimpff, Robert–Greencoat Capital LLP
Schrock, Jeff–Columbia Pacific Advisors LLC
Schroder, David–InvestAmerica Venture Group, Inc.
Schroder, Paul–Silverfern Group Inc
Schroeck, Maximilian–Cipio Partners GmbH
Schroeder, Bill–Rock Creek Capital LLC
Schroeder, Charles–Northstar Capital LLC
Schroeder, Christoph–Omos Equitypartners GmbH
Schroeder, Jon–Medley Capital LLC
Schroeder, Luke–Gryphon Investors Inc
Schroeder, Philipp–Active Capital Partners SA
Schroll, Josef–Schilling Unternehmensbeteiligung GmbH
Schruefer, Bernd–Astutia Ventures GmbH
Schubauer, James–Westbury Partners
Schubert, Felix von–Zouk Capital LLP
Schuck, Wolfgang–Maple Partners Finanl Group
Schuele, Alan–Sevin Rosen Funds
Schuele, John–Waitt Co
Schuemperli, Alexander–Sandpiper Digital Payments AG
Schuenke, Scott–MVC Capital Inc
Schueppert, Stenning–CenterGate Capital LP
Schuetz, Christian–b to v Partners AG
Schuh, Michael–Foundation Capital LLC
Schule, Lisa–GEF Management Corp
Schuler, Armin–BWK GmbH Unternehmensbeteiligungsgesellschaft
Schuler, Barry–Draper Fisher Jurvetson
Schuler, Ryan–Ahv Holding Company LLC
Schulhof, Jonathan–Global Technology Investment
Schulhof, Michael–Global Technology Investment
Schull, Phil–J B Poindexter & Co Inc
Schulman, Janie–Morrison & Foerster LLP
Schult, Reyke–Auden AG
Schult, Robert–VMG Partners, L.P.

Schulte, Daniel–B12 Capital Partners LLC
Schulte, Peter–CM Equity Partners LP
Schultz, Daniel–Gotham Ventures LLC
Schultz, Daniel–Gotham Ventures LLC
Schultz, Eric–Ascent Venture Management Inc
Schultz, Eric–Braemar Energy Ventures LP
Schultz, Grant–North River Capital LLC
Schultz, Howard–Maveron LLC
Schultz, Randall–Versa Capital Management Inc
Schultz, Scott–Brown Brothers Harriman & Co
Schultze, Jan-Gisbert–Acton Capital Partners GmbH
Schulz, Mark–Fontinalis Partners LLC
Schulz, Robert–Health Enterprise Partners LP
Schulze, Dennis–Carlyle Group LP
Schulze, Elias–Africa Group LLC
Schumacher, David–Ellipse Capital LLC
Schumacher, David–Svoboda Capital Partners LLC
Schumacher, Greg–Granite Equity Partners LLC
Schumacher, Patrick–Blackstone Group LP
Schuman, Gary–MDB Capital Group LLC
Schumann, Oliver–Capital Dynamics Sdn Bhd
Schunk, Markus–Holtzbrinck Ventures GmbH
Schupp, Heiko–Pantheon Ventures (UK) LLP
Schuppan, David–Cressey and Company LP
Schurink, Titus–Holland Private Equity BV
Schurz, James–Morrison & Foerster LLP
Schuster, Harry–Small Enterprise Assistance Funds
Schuster, Nathan–MavenHill Capital
Schut, Hans–Triodos International Fund Management BV
Schutte, Arjan–Core Innovation Capital I LP
Schutte, Rene–Sanlam Private Equity
Schutz, Jeffrey–Centennial Ventures Vii L P
Schuurbiers, Nico–VOC Capital Partners BV
Schwab, David–Sierra Ventures
Schwab, Martin–Pamplona Capital Management LLP
Schwab, Michael–Big Sky Partners
Schwab, Michael–Greenhouse Capital Partners
Schwab, Nelson–Carousel Capital Partners
Schwab, Wolf-Dieter–Mittelstaendische Beteiligungsgesellschaft Sachsen mbH
Schwab, Wolf-Dieter–Mittelstaendische Beteiligungsgesellschaft Sachsen-Anhalt
Schwabe, Robert–Forum Capital Partner
Schwaber, Glen–Israel Cleantech Ventures
Schwager, Gary–Griffon Venture Partners
Schwartz, Adam–AG BD LLC
Schwartz, Alan–First Reserve Corp
Schwartz, Andre–Brasil Plural Gestao de Recursos Ltda
Schwartz, Andrew–Blue Wolf Capital Partners LLC
Schwartz, Bela–Riverside Co
Schwartz, Brian–Blackstone Group LP
Schwartz, Brian–HIG Capital LLC
Schwartz, Brian–Huron Capital Partners LLC
Schwartz, Brian–Vestar Capital Partners Inc
Schwartz, Daniel–3G Capital Inc
Schwartz, David–Harvest Partners LP
Schwartz, Hagi–Western Technology Investment
Schwartz, Hilton–Focus Acquisition Partners
Schwartz, Jeffrey–Bain Capital Inc
Schwartz, Jeffrey–Gores Group LLC
Schwartz, Jennifer–Northwater Capital Management Inc

Schwartz, Keoni–ACP Inc
Schwartz, Kevin–Paine Schwartz Partners LLC
Schwartz, Mark–Launchpad Digital Health LLC
Schwartz, Mark–MissionPoint Capital Partners LLC
Schwartz, Mark–Palladin Capital Group Inc
Schwartz, Michael–JLL Partners Inc
Schwartz, Peter–Milbank Tweed Hadley & Mccloy LLP
Schwartz, Rodney–Catalyst Fund Management and Research Ltd
Schwartz, Ron–UBS Capital Markets LP
Schwartz, Scott–CIVC Partners LP
Schwartz, Sheryl–Natixis Private Equity SA
Schwartz, Tessa–Morrison & Foerster LLP
Schwartz, Theodore–Strand Equity Partners LLC
Schwartz, Todd–Strand Equity Partners LLC
Schwartz, William–Morrison & Foerster LLP
Schwartzman, Eric–Cooley LLP
Schwarz, Helfried–Milbank Tweed Hadley & Mccloy LLP
Schwarz, Ryan–NaviMed Capital Advisors LLC
Schwarzschild, Sarah–Metropolitan Real Estate Equity Management LLC
Schwed, Gustavo–Providence Equity Partners LLC
Schwegler, Georg–Deutsche Telekom Strategic Investments
Schweibold, Andrew–Vision Capital LLP
Schweiger, Frederic–Crossroads Liquidating Trust
Schweitzer, Barry–Elm Street Ventures LP
Schweitzer, Florian–b to v Partners AG
Schwen, Steve–Split Rock Partners LLC
Schwen, Steve–Split Rock Partners LLC
Schwen, Steve–St Paul Venture Capital Inc
Schwendimann, Werner–Aralon AG
Schwenk, Brian–1315 Capital LLC
Schwenk, Brian–Quaker Partners Management LP
Schwenk, Paul–Blade LLC
Schwenk, Richard–Argosy Capital Group Inc
Schwenke, J.–Business Partners Ltd
Schwenker, Adam–Qualcomm Ventures
Schwerin, Samuel–Millennium TVP Management Co LLC
Schwiep, Frances–Comcast Ventures
Schwimmer, Durant–Carlyle Group LP
Schwimmer, Jeremy–Sand Oak Capital Partners LLC
Schwinger, Steven–Snow Phipps Group LLC
Schwitzer, Jamie–Westcap Management Ltd
Schwyn, Andreas–Panda Capital Asia Ltd
Sciarretta, Louis–FLAG Capital Management LLC
Scibelli, Christopher–Trust Company of the West
Scifres, Donald–Sdl Ventures LLC
Sciorillo, Dean–Enertech Capital
Scofield, Jeffrey–Lime Rock Partners LLC
Scoggins, Christopher–Sequel Venture Partners
Scola, James–ABRY Partners LLC
Scollans, Brendan–Avista Capital Holdings LP
Scopa, James–MPM Capital LLC
Scott, Alexander–Pantheon Ventures (UK) LLP
Scott, Benjamin–LiveOak Venture Partners
Scott, Bruce–NBC Capital Pty Ltd
Scott, Buchan–Duke Street Capital Ltd
Scott, David–Oak Hill Capital Management Inc
Scott, Donald–Blackstone Group LP
Scott, Erik–Palladium Equity Partners LLC
Scott, Fredrick–Fredrick D Scott LLC
Scott, Hugh–Commonfund Realty
Scott, Jeffrey–Brown Brothers Harriman & Co
Scott, John–Harbert Management Corp
Scott, K. Dunlop–Columbia Partners Private Capital
Scott, Martin–Riverside Co
Scott, Mike–Platinum Equity LLC
Scott, Paul–Biostar Ventures II LLC
Scott, Pereklis–Bregal Investments LLP
Scott, Randy–Cross Valley Capital
Scott, Randy–HealthQuest Capital
Scott, Randy–HeathQuest Capital
Scott, Regan–Oaktree Capital Management LP
Scott, Sandy–Tandem Expansion Fund I LP
Scott, Steven–Penta Capital Llp
Scott, Thomas–Triton Pacific Capital LLC
Scott, Valerie–Swander Pace Capital LLC
Scotto, Anthony–Roark Capital Group Inc
Scowcroft, Brent–Torch Hill Investment Partners LLC
Scown, Michael–Intel Capital Corp
Screwvala, Ronnie–Unilazer Ventures Pvt Ltd
Scriven, James–International Finance Corp
Scrivens, Andrei–Z Capital HF Adviser LLC
Scronce, Timothy–Scronce and Associates LLC
Scrudato, Frank–Arsenal Capital Management LLC
Scrudato, Frank–Arsenal Capital Partners LP
Scull, John–Southern Cross Venture Partners Pty Ltd
Scully, Martin–Oyster Capital Partners
Scully, Thomas–Welsh Carson Anderson & Stowe
Seabrooke, Christopher–Sabvest Ltd
Seaburg, David–Cowen Capital Partners LLC
Seach, Steven–Sante Ventures
Seacrest, Cayman–Jasper Ridge Partners LP
Seagraves, Sarah–i2E, Inc
Seah, Choon Tong–ESW Manage Pte Ltd
Seah, Kian Wee–UOB Bioventures Management Pte Ltd
Seah, Kian Wee–UOB Venture Management Pte Ltd
Seal, Jonathan–Nova Capital Management, Ltd.
Seaman, Bradley–Parallel49 Equity
Seaman, Patrick–Pepperwood Partners LLC
Seaman, Scott–Gramercy Inc
Sears, Lowell–Sears Capital Management, Inc.
Sears, Michael–Siemens Venture Capital GmbH
Seats, Jason–Techstars Central LLC
Seaver, Christopher–CLSA Capital Partners HK Ltd
Seaver, Christopher–TRG Management LP
Seawell, Brooke–Formative Ventures
Sebag-Montefiore, Charles–Ludgate Investments Ltd
Sebastian, Roberto–Marsman-Drysdale Corp
Sebastian, Sean–Birchmere Ventures
Sebba, Yoav–Ofer Hi Tech Ltd
Sebek, Gary–2X CONSUMER PRODUCTS GROWTH PARTNERS L P
Sebel, Benjamin–Castle Harlan Aus Mezzanine
Sebold, Jordan–Newstone Capital Partners LLC
Sebotsa, Sonja–Identity Capital Partners (Pty) Ltd
Sebusch, Erick–CMEA Development Company LLC
Secco, Rudy–M Capital Partners SAS
Sechovec, Scott–TEL Venture Capital Inc
Sedgwick, David–Balmoral Wood Litigation Finance
Seeber, Jon–Updata Partners
Seegopaul, Josh–WL Ross & Co LLC
Seegopaul, Purnesh–Pangaea Ventures Ltd
Seehaus, Frank–Acton Capital Partners GmbH
Seehaus, Frank–Burda Digital Ventures GmbH
Seelenberger, Alexander–Aurus Gestion de Inversiones SPA
Seely, Charles–Real Ventures
Seese, Patrick–Headwaters BD LLC
Sefolo, Tshegofatso–zico capital
Sefrioui, Rachid–Finaventures
Segal, Aaron–Intuitive Venture Partners LLC
Segal, Barr–Trust Company of the West
Segal, Lloyd–Persistence Capital Partners Lp
Segal, Richard–Seavest Capital Partners LLC
Segal, Rick–Rethink Education LP
Segel, Robert–Park Street Capital LLC
Seger, Johan–Adelis Equity Partners AB
Segev-Gal, Rona–Pitango Venture Capital Management Israel, Ltd.
Seggerros, Andreas–Sunstone Capital A/S
Seggewiss, Herbert–Aheim Capital GmbH
Seghezzi, Graziano–Sofinnova Partners SAS
Seghin, Bruno–Navis Management Sdn Bhd
Segovia, Javier–Trust Company of the West
Segrest, Michael–Silver Creek Ventures Corp
Segrest, Michael–Silver Creek Ventures Corp
Sehgal, Sanjay–East West Capital Partners Pte Ltd
Seibert, Michael–Stone Canyon Venture Partners
Seibold, Peter–Evercore Inc
Seibold, Wolfgang–Earlybird Venture Capital GmbH & Co KG
Seidel, Carla–BASF New Business GmbH
Seidenberg, Beth–Kleiner Perkins Caufield & Byers LLC
Seidl, Robert–Motus Ventures
Seidler, Matt–Seidler Equity Partners
Seidler, Peter–Seidler Equity Partners
Seidler, Robert–Seidler Equity Partners
Seidman, Brian–Oaktree Capital Management LP
Seidman, Jeffrey–Harbert Management Corp
Seigler, J. Morgan–TA Associates Management LP
Seil, Beau–Unitus Impact Partners LLC
Seitz, Tasha–JK&B Capital LLC
Sekhar, Rama–Norwest Venture Partners
Sekine, Kanako–European Bank for Reconstruction and Development
Sekine, Takeshi–Innovation Network Corporation of Japan
Sekino, Hamilton–Nauta Capital SL
Sekino, Masaaki–It-Farm Corp
Sekula, Christopher–Accretia Capital LLC
Sela, Limor–Capital Point Ltd
Sela, Yossi–GEMINI CAPITAL FUND MGMT LTD
Selassie, Sengal–Brightwood Capital Advisors LLC
Selati, Robin–Madison Dearborn Partners LLC
Selbherr, Guy–MBG Baden-Wuerttemberg GmbH
Selby, Candice–TOM Capital Associates Inc
Selby, John–Valar Ventures Management LLC
Selby, Sunil–Trellis Capital Corp
Selden, William–Sterling Investment Partners II LP
Self, Holly–Frost Data Capital
Self, Robert–Oaktree Capital Management LP
Seligman, Joel–Undisclosed Firm
Selin, Mikael–Priveq Partners AB
Selke, Wesley–Better Ventures LLC
Selke, Wesley–Hub Ventures
Selkirk, Rod–Bridgepoint Advisers II Ltd
Selkirk, Rod–Bridgepoint Advisers Ltd
Sell, Charles–Andrew W Byrd & Co LLC

2565

Sellers, Patrick—Lloyds Development Capital (Holdings) Ltd
Sellers, Scott—Encore Consumer Capital Fund L P
Selman, Sanford—Asia West LLC
Selness, Chris—PFM Capital Inc
Selot, Vivek—Flatworld Capital LLC
Seltzer, Robert—Care Capital LLC
Seltzer, Stacey—Aisling Capital LLC
Seltzer, Theodore—Morrison & Foerster LLP
Selwood, Ryan—Canada Pension Plan Investment Board
Selzer, Kenneth—FINISTERE VENTURES L L C
Sem, Richard—Pantheon Ventures (UK) LLP
Semelmacher, Paula—Goode Partners LLC
Semenov, Igor—TA Venture
Semenzato, Michele—Wise Venture SGR SpA
Seminerio, John—Yaletown Venture Partners
Semmelbauer, Thilo—Insight Venture Partners LLC
Semmens, Guy—Argos Soditic SA
Semmler, Marcos—Demeter SAS
Semon, Dominique—Merlin Nexus
Sen, Hondo—LJ2 & Co LLC
Sen, Ines—Xange Private Equity SA
Sen, Kaustuv—Bain Capital Inc
Sena, Ken—Evercore Inc
Senan, Amar—Saints Ventures
Seneker, Todd—Columbia Pacific Advisors LLC
Senequier, Dominique—Ardian France SA
Senft, Derek—Tricor Pacific Founders Capital Inc
Senft, Roderick—Parallel49 Equity
Senft, Roderick—Tricor Pacific Founders Capital Inc
Senior, Enrique—Allen & Company of Florida, Inc.
Senkler, Robert—Advantus Capital Management Inc
Senkut, Aydin—Felicis Ventures
Sennequier, Marie—Proparco SA
Senni, Aziz—IMPACT Partenaires SAS
Senyei, Andrew—Enterprise Partners Management LLC
Seo, Byeong Wun—Hana Daetoo Securities Co Ltd
Seo, Jinho—Colony Capital LLC
Seok-kyu, Hong—Bokwang Investment Corp
Seppala, James—Blackstone Group LP
Seppanen, Petteri—Dasos Capital Oy
Sequeira, Neil—General Catalyst Partners LLC
Serebrisky, Diego—Advent International Corp
Serena di Lapigio, Ottavio—Lincolnshire Management Inc
Seretan, Wendy—Stone Canyon Venture Partners
Serfati, Fabrice—IGNIA Partners LLC
Sergeev, Andrey—Bright Capital OOO
Serkes, Jeffrey—Palisade Capital Management LLC
Serko, Richard—Wharton Equity Partners LLC
Sermon, Charles—Phase4 Ventures Ltd
Sernovitz, Gary—Lime Rock Partners LLC
Seroussi, Roy—Arsenal Capital Management LLC
Seroussi, Roy—Arsenal Capital Partners LP
Serra, Raquel—Angola Capital Partners
Serrano, Jason—Oak Hill Advisors LP
Serrato, Ruben—TEL Venture Capital Inc
Serrure, Piet—NIBC Principal Investments BV
Sert, Turan—Fiba Kapital Holding AS
Sertoglu, Cem—Earlybird Venture Capital GmbH & Co KG
Servais, Gaetan—Meusinvest SA
Serventi, Jesse—Renovus Capital Partners LP

Servitje, Rodrigo—B37 Ventures LLC
Seseri, Rudina—Fairhaven Capital Partners, L.P.
Seshadri, Hemachandra—JGI Ventures India Pvt Ltd
Seshadri, Sriranjan—Gaja Capital Partners
Sessa, Ivano—Bain Capital Inc
Sessions, Andrew—Thomas Weisel Partners Group Inc
Sessions, Benjamin—GEF Management Corp
Sessions, Lee—Intel Capital Corp
Seth, Rohit—Duchossois Technology Partners LLC
Sethi, Arjun—Social+Capital Partnership
Sethi, Rahul—Alpha Founders
Sethom, Mehdi—Swicorp Capital Partners SA
Sethuram, Jay—Crestlight Venture Productions LLC
Seto, Lysun—Attractor Investment Management Inc
Seton-Rogers, Sean—PROfounders Capital Ltd
Sett, Vivek—New Silk Route Partners, LLC
Settembrino, Jeff—Pine Tree Equity Management LP
Setterberg, Alison—Metropolitan Real Estate Equity Management LLC
Settle, Dana—Greycroft Partners LLC
Settle, Peter—Goldner Hawn Johnson & Morrison Inc
Settman, Peter—Firm Factory Network AB
Setubal, Roberto—Itau Unibanco Holding SA
Seu, David—Sumitomo Mitsui Trust Investment Co Ltd
Seubert, Florian—Maxburg Capital Partners
Sevdalian, Silva—Morgan Stanley Alternative Investment Partners LP
Severin, Oscar—Vitruvian Partners LLP
Severson, Patrick—Warburg Pincus LLC
Sevin, Philippe—Syntegra Capital Investors Ltd
Sevinga, Ieko—Van Lanschot Participaties BV
Sexton, Theresa—Claritas Capital LLC
Seybold, William—Farallon Capital Management LLC
Seymour, Scott—Evercore Inc
Seynhaeve, Denis—Blu Venture Investors LLC
Sezak, Sam—Blue Heron Capital LLC
Sha, Ye—Chengwei Ventures
Shaari, Mohammad Zainal—Khazanah Nasional Bhd
Shabashevich, Felix—Oaktree Capital Management LP
Shabecoff, Peter—Atlantic Street Capital Management LLC
Shachar, Erez—Evergreen Venture Partners
Shachar, Erez—Qumra Capital Israel I Ltd
Shachar, Yuval—Marker Financial Advisors LLC
Shackelford, Andrew—LaSalle Capital
Shackelton, Sarah—Abingworth Management Ltd
Shackleton, Anthony—Oaktree Capital Management LP
Shackleton, Sarah—Development Partners International LLP
Shadman, Ali—JK&B Capital LLC
Shafer, Matt—Vision Capital LLP
Shaffer, Christy—Hatteras Venture Partners
Shafir, Robert—Credit Suisse Asset Management LLC
Shagrin, Lawrence—Brockway Moran & Partners Inc
Shagrin, Lawrence—Millpond Equity Partners LLC
Shah, Agha Ahmed—Pak Oman Investment Company Ltd
Shah, Ajay—Altos Capital Partners LLC
Shah, Akshay—Blackstone Group LP
Shah, Alap—Oaktree Capital Management LP
Shah, Alkesh—Evercore Inc

Shah, Amit—Artiman Management LLC
Shah, Amit—Foundation Medical Partners LP
Shah, Arpan—Altimeter Capital Management LP
Shah, Ed—E I Capital LLP
Shah, Gaurav—Lok Capital
Shah, Hemen—8 Miles LLP
Shah, Hitesh—Enhanced Capital Partners LLC
Shah, Jehangir—Pak Oman Investment Company Ltd
Shah, Jigar—Inerjys Ventures Inc
Shah, Jigar—Wellington Partners GmbH
Shah, Kamlesh—Linden LLC
Shah, Khushboo—DreamIt Ventures
Shah, Kumar—GEF Management Corp
Shah, Mahendra—Vivo Capital LLC
Shah, Namita—Emerging Capital Partners
Shah, Neel—Oaktree Capital Management LP
Shah, Nimish—Venrock Inc
Shah, Nirav—Kainos Capital LLC
Shah, Prashant—Monta Vista Capital LP
Shah, Prashant—TiE LaunchPad
Shah, Pratik—Thomas Mcnerney and Partners LLC
Shah, Raj—Kotak Investment Advisors Ltd
Shah, Rajeev—RA Capital Management LLC
Shah, Rajesh—E I Capital LLP
Shah, Ranjit—Gaja Capital Partners
Shah, Ravi—McNally Capital LLC
Shah, Ron—Stripes Group LLC
Shah, Sanjiv—Baml Capital Access Funds Management LLC
Shah, Saurabh—3i Group PLC
Shah, Savan—Oaktree Capital Management LP
Shah, Shardul—Index Ventures
Shah, Snehal—Reliance Capital Ventures Ltd
Shah, Vivek—Stellus Capital Management LLC
Shahbaz, Shahzad—QInvest Ltd
Shahory, Lior—Incentive II Management Ltd
Shai Levy, Moshe—ProSeed Venture Capital Fund, Ltd.
Shaia, John—Saw Mill Capital LLC
Shaikh, Abdul Hafeez—New Silk Route Partners, LLC
Shaikh, Taimur—Clearpoint Investment Partners LLC
Shaiman, Lee—Blackstone Group LP
Shainski, Rina—Carmel Ventures IV Principals Fund LP
Shaked, Ohad—Shaked Global Group
Shakibnia, Alexander—Gemspring Capital LLC
Shalaby, Sameer—Select Venture Partners LLC
Shalev, Eddy—Genesis Partners Ltd
Shalev, Shiran—Battery Ventures LP
Shamapant, Venu—LiveOak Venture Partners
Shan, Helen—Mercer LLC
Shan, Shengyuan—Beijing Macro Vision Venture Capital Management Consultancy
Shan, Shuangxiang—China Science & Merchants Investment Management Group Co Ltd
Shan, Weijian—Pacific Alliance Group Ltd
Shanafelt, Armen—Lilly Ventures Management Company LLC
Shanahan, Kearney—Solamere Group LLC
Shanahan, Keven—Argosy Capital Group Inc
Shanahan, Michael—Egan Managed Capital LP
Shanahan, Michael—Egan Managed Capital LP
Shanahan, Timothy—Water Tower Capital LLC
Shanahan, William—Veritas Capital Fund Management LLC

Shanfield, Robert—Landmark Partners Inc
Shang, Conrad—Norwest Venture Partners
Shang, Jin—Beijing Jike Menggongchang Venture Capital Center (L.P.)
Shang, Mark—Serent Capital LLC
Shang, Xuanyu—Cybernaut (China) Venture Capital Management Co Ltd
Shanmugam, Sivaprakash Siva—Headwaters BD LLC
Shannon, Glenn—Shorenstein Co LLC
Shannon, James—Private Advisors LLC
Shannon, Jeffrey—COGR Inc
Shannon, Mary—Masthead Venture Partners
Shannon, Michael—KSL Capital Partners LLC
Shannon, Peter—Firelake Capital Management LLC
Shannon, Rick—CORE Partners LLC
Shannon, Timothy—Canaan Partners
Shao, Hongxia—Fortune Venture Capital Co Ltd
Shao, Jun—CAS Investment Management Co Ltd
Shao, Jun—Shenzhen Cornerstone of Entrepreneurial Cci Capital Ltd
Shao, Margaret—Fortune Venture Capital Corp
Shao, Nicholas—Carlyle Group LP
Shaoul, Edward—Headwaters BD LLC
Shaper, Peter—Genesis Park, L.P.
Shapero, Rich—Crosspoint Venture Partners 2001 LP
Shapira, Guy—Trevi Health Ventures LP
Shapiro, Barry—Anderson Group LLC, The
Shapiro, Bob—Sandbox Industries LLC
Shapiro, Brett—Varagon Capital Partners LP
Shapiro, David—KPS Capital Partners LP
Shapiro, David—Marquette Capital Partners Inc
Shapiro, James—Kearny Venture Partners LP
Shapiro, James—Thomas Weisel Partners Group Inc
Shapiro, Neil—GF Capital Management & Advisors LLC
Shapiro, Philip—Synova Capital LLP
Shapiro, Stephen—Advanced Technology Ventures
Shapiro, Stephen—Clayton Dubilier & Rice LLC
Shapiro, Stephen—Lightstone Ventures LP
Shapiro, Steve—Galen Associates Inc
Shapiro-Rothchild, Jaclyn—MVC Capital Inc
Shaposhnick, Lisa—Morgan Stanley Alternative Investment Partners LP
Shappy, Russell—Berwind Private Equity
Sharda, Mukesh—Capital Square Partners Pte Ltd
Share, Gregory—Ambina Partners LLC
Share, Gregory—Moelis Capital Partners LLC
Shareef, Dara—Glenmont Partners, LLC
Sharer, Kevin—Foundation Medical Partners LP
Sharif, Mohamed—Arcapita Inc
Shariff, Viq—Rizvi Traverse Management LLC
Sharifi, Amir—Ardian France SA
Sharko, Emily—Blackstone Group LP
Sharma, Aakanksha—IvyCap Ventures Advisors Pvt Ltd
Sharma, Ajay—Mill Road Capital Management LLC
Sharma, Alipt—GEF Management Corp
Sharma, Anshoo—Lightspeed Management Company LLC
Sharma, Anshu—Storm Ventures Inc
Sharma, Anupendra—Siemens Venture Capital GmbH
Sharma, Ashutosh—Norwest Venture Partners
Sharma, Ekta—Fireman Capital Partners LLC
Sharma, Lindsay—Industry Ventures LLC
Sharma, Mukesh—Menterra Venture Advisors Pvt Ltd
Sharma, Rajiv—Reliance Capital Ventures Ltd
Sharma, Ray—Extreme Venture Partners Inc
Sharma, Rohit—True Ventures LLC
Sharma, Sumit—New Silk Route Partners, LLC
Sharma, Sunny—OrbiMed Advisors LLC
Sharman, Abhishek—IEP Fund Advisors Pvt Ltd
Sharp, Alfred—Muller & Monroe Asset Management LLC
Sharp, Richard—Milbank Tweed Hadley & Mccloy LLP
Sharp, Richard—V-Ten Capital Partners LLC
Sharpe, J. Louis—AEA Investors LLC
Shasha, Tsachy—Docor International BV
Shata, Ammar—Al Khabeer Capital Co
Shaver, Mike—Real Ventures
Shaw, Benjamin—Marwyn Investment Management LLP
Shaw, David—D E Shaw & Co LP
Shaw, Gordon—Baring Private Equity Asia Ltd
Shaw, Hal—KSL Capital Partners LLC
Shaw, Ira—Landmark Partners Inc
Shaw, Jeph—New Energy Capital Corp
Shaw, Kyle—Shaw Kwei & Partners
Shaw, Matthew—Sunrock Ventures Management LLC
Shaw, Philip—Invesco Private Capital Inc
Shaw, Ralph—Shaw Venture Partners
Shaw, Rob—Frog Capital Ltd
Shaw, Robert—Arete Corp
Shaw, Roman—DT Capital Partners
Shaw, Soo Wei—Gobi Partners
Shaw-Thomas, Amy—University of Texas System
Shay, Izhar—Canaan Partners
Shaya, Dennis—Abundance Partners LLC
Shayne, Gary—Coast2Coast Investments Pty Ltd
Shea, Joanne—Perseus LLC
Shea, Paul—Beechbrook Capital LLP
Shea, Sebastian—G Square Healthcare Private Equity Fund LLP
Shea, W. Andrew—Gennx360 Capital Partners LP
Shea, W. Andrew—Hilltop Private Capital LLC
Sheahan, Bernie—International Finance Corp
Shearburn, John—Warburg Pincus LLC
Shebik, Steve—Allstate Private Equity
Shebitz, Adam—Palladium Equity Partners LLC
Shechter, Haim—Giza Venture Capital
Shectman, Art—Elephant Ventures LLC
Sheehan, Andrew—Sutter Hill Ventures
Sheehan, Gerald—Snow Phipps Group LLC
Sheehan, Kevin—Multiplier Capital LP
Sheehan, Kevin—Orix Venture Finance
Sheehan, Patrick—ETF Partners LLP
Sheehan, Timothy—Beecken Petty O'Keefe & Company LLC
Sheehy, Matthew—Silverhawk Capital Partners LLC
Sheehy, Robert—Inverness Management LLC
Sheeren, Christopher—Huron Capital Partners LLC
Sheffert, Christopher—Inoca Capital Partners LLC
Sheffery, Michael—OrbiMed Advisors LLC
Sheft, Peter—Zephyr Management LP
Sheft, Robert—Roark Capital Group Inc
Sheftel, Bradley—Valor Equity Partners L P
Shehab, Thomas—Arboretum Ventures Inc
Shehade, George—Amwal QSCC
Sheikh, Ahmad—SFW Capital Partners LLC
Sheikh, Mubasher—Permira Advisers LLP
Shein, Michael—Chartwell Investments, Inc.
Sheinbein, Rachel—CMEA Development Company LLC
Sheiner, Andrew—Altas Partners LP
Sheinerman, Kira—Burrill & Company
Shek, Shuk Fan—Blackstone Group LP
Shelby, Brian—Blackstone Group LP
Shelby, David—Northport Investments
Shelby, Josh—Northport Investments
Sheldon, Behshad—Apple Tree Partners
Sheldon, Ronald—Advent International Corp
Shell, Lori—Frontier Capital LLC
Shelley, Ian—KPMG Corporate Finance Inc
Shelton, Charles—Nancy Creek Capital
Shelton, Hal—Blu Venture Investors LLC
Shelton, Ryan—Pharos Capital Group LLC
Shemetov, Maxim—UK SGKM OOO
Shen, Bill—Encore Consumer Capital Fund L P
Shen, David—Olympus Capital Holdings Asia Hong Kong Ltd
Shen, Frank—Cnstar Capital Pte Ltd
Shen, Han—Northern Light Venture Capital Development Ltd
Shen, Howard—H&Q Asia Pacific, Ltd.
Shen, James—Qualcomm Ventures
Shen, Robert—H&Q Asia Pacific, Ltd.
Shen, Ronnie—Lexington Partners Inc
Shen, Shawn—Mingly Capital
Shen, Yuzhi—ZEVC Management Co Ltd
Shen, Zhongmin—Hudson Clean Energy Partners
Shenderovich, Edward—7Vizhn OOO
Sheng, Christy—Mingly Capital
Sheng, Gang—Suzhou Oriza Holdings Co Ltd
Sheng, Lei—GGV Capital
Sheng, Sherman—SAIF Partners
Shenoi, Sailesh—Aditya Birla Capital Advisors Pvt Ltd
Shenthar, Shyam—O3 Capital Advisors Pvt Ltd
Shepard, James—Gennx360 Capital Partners LP
Shepard, Michael—Heron Capital LLC
Shepard, Sharon—Boston Community Capital Inc
Shepard, William—Provident Healthcare Ventures LLC
Shepherd, Jay—Clearlight Partners LLC
Shepherd, Pam—Greenmont Capital Partners
Shepherd, Sydney—Kinetic Ventures LLC
Shepler, Robert—Telegraph Hill Partners
Sheppard, Nicholas—Bruckmann Rosser Sherrill & Co LP
Sher, Dani—Anchorage Capital Partners Ltd
Sherer, Paul—Matrix Partners, L.P.
Sheridan, Charles—Huron Capital Partners LLC
Sheridan, Ian—Vestigo Ventures LLC
Sheridan, Philip—Raven Capital Pty Ltd
Sheridan, Trey—Ridgemont Partners Management LLC
Sherlund, Richard—Perella Weinberg Partners LP
Sherman, Darren—Orchestra Medical Ventures LLC
Sherman, J. Todd—Camden Partners Holdings LLC
Sherman, Michael—Chrysalix Energy
Sherman, Richard—SCP Private Equity Partners
Sherman, Robert—Boston Millennia Partners LP
Sherriff, Andrew—Pantheon Ventures (UK) LLP
Sherrill, Stephen—Bruckmann Rosser Sherrill & Co LP

Sherwin, Elton–Ridgewood Capital Management LLC
Sherwin, Stephen–Third Rock Ventures LLC
Sherwood, David–Century Capital Management / Massachusetts Inc
Sherwood, Ned–LionRock Capital Ltd
Sherwood, Ned–ZS Fund LP
Sheth, Anish–Altpoint Capital Partners LLC
Sheth, Manish–Jm Finl Invest Managers Ltd
Shettigar, Shivanand–Yes Bank Ltd
Shettle, Robert–Barings Corporate Investors
Shevlin, James–Acas LLC
Shevlin, Jeremy–Crestone Capital LLC
Shevrin, Phil–Softbank Capital Partners L P
Shevtsova, Maria–Digital Media Partners Pte Ltd
Shey, Chauncey–Sbcvc Fund Ii L P
Shi, Anping–Shenzhen Capital Group Co Ltd
Shi, Curt–Follow Seed Australia Pty Ltd
Shi, Hong–Greenwoods Asset Management Ltd
Shi, Hongxiang–State Development & Investment Corp Ltd
Shi, Lan–Cybernaut (China) Venture Capital Management Co Ltd
Shi, Minjian–Guangdong Jinri Investment Ltd
Shi, Yunzhong–Jiangsu Addor Equity Investment Fund Management Co Ltd
Shia, William–Gramercy Inc
Shiachy, Heidi–Gatewood Capital Partners LLC
Shiang, Willian–Carlyle Group LP
Shibad, Salil–Jumpstart Foundry
Shibata, Hidetoshi–Innovation Network Corporation of Japan
Shibusawa, Yoshiyuki–Jafco Co Ltd
Shibuya, Seiji–Yamaguchi Capital Co Ltd
Shideler, Jason–Madison Dearborn Partners LLC
Shields, Jack–Acas LLC
Shields, John–Abingworth Management Ltd
Shields, John–Blackstone Group LP
Shields, John–Boston Capital Ventures LP
Shields, John–Greenmont Capital Partners
Shiffman, Adir–Disruptive Capital Pty Ltd
Shifron, Dalit–ProSeed Venture Capital Fund, Ltd.
Shigemura, Barton–Alcatel-Lucent Ventures
Shih, Ben–Jafco Ventures
Shikata, Osamu–Shikata Venture Fund
Shiland, Jay–MTS Health Partners LP
Shillito, James–Broad Sky Partners LLC
Shim, Jaewoo–Clearwater Capital Partners Cyprus Ltd
Shim, Mike–Cava Capital
Shimamura, Yoshihide–Daiwa Corporate Investment Co Ltd
Shimer, Daniel–Teakwood Capital LP
Shimmin, Jonathan–AlpInvest Partners BV
Shimoko, Michael–Enerdigm Ventures LLC
Shimp, John–Ridgemont Partners Management LLC
Shin, Albert–Strategic Value Partners LLC
Shin, Changhoon–VOGO Fund Asset Management
Shin, Jae Ha–VOGO Fund Asset Management
Shin, Jee–ProQuest Investments
Shin, Kicheon–Atinum Investment Co Ltd
Shin, Michael–Acas LLC
Shin, Peter–KTB Ventures, Inc.
Shin, Steven–Morgan Stanley Alternative Investment Partners LP

Shinar, Eyal–Battery Ventures LP
Shinder, Richard–Perella Weinberg Partners LP
Shinderman, Mark–Milbank Tweed Hadley & Mccloy LLP
Shine, Timothy–Commonfund Realty
Shinichi, Saijo–WiL Inc
Shinkwin, Tom–Enterprise Equity Venture Capital Group
Shinoura, Yuichi–Iyogin Capital Co Ltd
Shinoyama, Ayu–Global Brain Corp
Shiosaki, Kazumi–MPM Capital LLC
Shipelov, Andrey–RT-Invest OOO
Shipley, Richard–Shiprock Capital LLC
Shipman, Christopher–Catalyst Investors LLC
Shipp, Terrance–Merit Capital Partners IV LLC
Shirai, Takehiro–It-Farm Corp
Shiralagi, Kumar–Kalaari Capital Partners LLC
Shiraliyev, Gadir–Pulsar Ecosystem LLC
Shiram, Ram–Sherpalo Ventures
Shirazi, Desmund–Oaktree Capital Management LP
Shirreffs, David–WL Ross & Co LLC
Shishkin, Tim–Ruvento Ventures Pte Ltd
Shitrit, Moshe–Investments in ATI Ltd
Shiu, Elaine–Northleaf Capital Partners Ltd
Shivani, Girish–YourNest Capital Advisors Pvt Ltd
Shlasky, Gady–Impact Capital Inc
Shles, Julian–JP Morgan Investment Management Inc
Shlesinger, Joseph–Clearspring Capital Partners
Shmelev, Alexander–United Capital Partners Advisory OOO
Shobe, Brett–Tritium Partners LLC
Shoch, John–Alloy Ventures Inc
Shochat, Eden–Genesis Partners Ltd
Shockley, Dan–LFM Capital LLC
Shoemaker, John–Milestone Partners LP
Shoemaker, Peter–Wedbush Capital Partners LP
Shoemaker, Raleigh–Berkshire Partners LLC
Shofet, Jonathan–NB Private Equity Partners Ltd
Shoff, C. Christopher–Cooley LLP
Shoham, Amnon–SIDER ISRA'EL IYE`UTS KALKALI BE`AM
Shohet, David–MergerTech Advisors
Shokina, Vera–Runa Capital
Sholem, Barry–MSD Capital LP
Shome, Surojit–Rabo India Finance Ltd
Shonekan, Chief Ernest–African Capital Alliance
Shong, Hugo–IDG Capital Partners Inc
Shonk, Christopher–ATX Seed Ventures
Shor, Glenn–JFLehman & Co
Shorenstein, Brandon–Shorenstein Co LLC
Shorin, James–Horizon Holdings LLC
Shorrock, Mark–Low Carbon Accelerator Ltd
Short, Don–CORE Partners LLC
Short, Martin–Lion's Head Global Partners LLP
Shortill, Tim–OPTrust Private Markets Group
Shortsleeve, Brian–General Catalyst Partners LLC
Shostak, Linda–Morrison & Foerster LLP
Shottes, Mark–Carlyle Group LP
Shourie, Rajath–Oaktree Capital Management LP
Shove, Greg–Kohlberg Ventures LLC
Showalter, Carl–Opus Capital
Shperling, Ohad–Carmel Ventures IV Principals Fund LP
Shpichok, Olga–Rossiiskaia Korporatsiia Nanotekhnologii GK

Shrestha, Abhaya–Corinthian Capital Group LLC
Shriner, Rick–Woodside Fund
Shrivastava, Samir–Madison India Capital Management Co
Shroff, Zubeen–Galen Associates Inc
Shroyer, Christopher–InDecatur Ventures LLC
Shryock, David–Shorebank Capital Corp
Shtereva, Parvoleta–Gemcorp Capital LLP
Shu, David–Quadrille Capital SAS
Shu, Frank–Proprium Capital Partners LP
Shu, Ray–Antares Capital Corp
Shuart, Rick–Caltius Mezzanine
Shuchman, Daniel–MSD Capital LP
Shuchman, Salem–Entrepreneur Partners LP
Shuey, Eric–Revelstoke Capital Partners LLC
Shufro, Mark–Greyrock Capital Group
Shujaie, Hassan–Arcapita Inc
Shukhman, Anat–GEMINI CAPITAL FUND MGMT LTD
Shukla, Prakash–HandsOn3 LLC
Shukla, Venktesh–Monta Vista Capital LP
Shuler, Robert–All-American Holdings LLC
Shulman, John–Juggernaut Partners LP
Shulman, Zachary–Cayuga Venture Fund
Shumadine, Anne–Signature Financial Management Inc
Shuman, Stanley–Allen & Company of Florida, Inc.
Shumway, Clay–Highland Capital Management LP
Shurtleff, Robert–Divergent Venture Partners Affiliates I LP
Shusan, David–Partners Capital Investment Group Holdings LLC
Shuster, Alexander–Inbio Ventures DC Ltd
Shute, William–University of Texas System
Shuttleworth, Patrick–First Avenue Partners, L.P.
Shuttleworth, Philip–ECI Partners LLP
Shutzer, William–Evercore Inc
Shyu, David–Newbury Partners LLC
Siadat, Barry–Sk Capital Partners LP
Siber, Richard–Coral Ventures Inc
Sica, Frank–Tailwind Capital Partners LP
Sicard, Gilles–Cerea Partenaire SAS
Sicard, Jean-Pierre–CDC Climat SA
Sichel, Olivier–Sofinnova Partners SAS
Sicoli, Richard–Westbury Partners
Sicupira, Carlos–3G Capital Inc
Sidberry, Demetrius–Hamilton Lane Advisors LLC
Siddiqi, Naveed–Phase4 Ventures Ltd
Siddiqui, Asim–Crosbie & Co Inc
Siddiqui, Mustafa–Blackstone Group LP
Sidhu, Beth–Stagwell Group LLC
Sidhu, Gurmit–Abundance Venture Capital Sdn Bhd
Sidler, Michael–Redalpine Venture Partners AG
Sidwa, James–Capital Partners, Inc.
Siebecker, Ann–Carlyle Group LP
Siebert, Christopher–Pfingsten Partners LLC
Sieczkiewicz, Gregory–MPM Capital LLC
Siefke, Michael–Bain Capital Inc
Sieg, Wilson–Tmfox Venture Partners Co Ltd
Siegal, Jeffrey–Metalmark Capital Holdings LLC
Siegel, Bernard–KSL Capital Partners LLC
Siegel, Brian–H Katz Capital Group Inc
Siegel, John–Columbia Capital LP
Siegel, Jonathan–Accel Partners & Co Inc
Siegel, Kenneth–Morrison & Foerster LLP

Siegel, Mark–Menlo Ventures
Siegel, Philip–Tritium Partners LLC
Siegel, Phillip–Austin Ventures
Siegel, Robert–X/Seed Capital Management
Siegel, Robert–X/Seed Capital Management
Siegel, Steven–KSL Capital Partners LLC
Siegel, Tom–Shepherd Ventures LP
Siegel, Tom–Shepherd Ventures LP
Siegwart, Pascal–Aster Capital Partners SAS
Siek, Michael–Spencer Trask Ventures Inc
Sieler, Miguel–Truffle Capital SAS
Siemer, David–WaveMaker Labs Pte Ltd
Siemer, David–Wavemaker Partners
Siemerink, Hein–Peak Capital BV
Siemers, Hans-Heinrich–Technologie und Gruenderzentrum Walldorf Stiftung GmbH
Siemplenski, Michael–First Analysis Corp
Sienkiewicz, Piotr–Hardgamma Ventures Sp z o o
Sienna, Lee–Ontario Teachers' Pension Plan
Sierra, Juan–Blackstone Group LP
Sievers, Jorn–HTG Ventures AG
Sievert, Christian–Segulah Advisor AB
Siew, Ling Low–LionRock Capital Ltd
Siewert, Patrick–Carlyle Group LP
Sifry, David–Entrepreneurs Fund LP
Sifton, Mike–Beringer Capital Inc
Sigal, Zack–LLR Partners Inc
Sigalovsky, Irina–GEN3 Partners, Inc.
Sigalow, Ian–Greycroft Partners LLC
Sigel, Anthony–Kilmer Capital Partners Ltd
Sigg, Rudolf–Zuercher Kantonalbank
Sigler, Mary–Platinum Equity LLC
Signoret, Carlos–Hispania Capital Partners LLC
Signori, Marco–Finanziaria Regionale Friuli Venezia Giulia SpA
Siguler, George–Siguler Guff & Company LP
Sikes, Toni–Calumet Venture Fund
Sikkens, Han–Summit Partners LP
Sikora, Ian–NSI Ventures
Silber, A.–Brookfield Asset Management Inc
Silber, Paul–Blu Venture Investors LLC
Silberberg, Paul–CMS Mezzanine Fund
Silberman, Joe–Listen LLC
Siletto, Joseph–Bio Equity Risk Management LLC
Siletto, Joseph–Sweetwater Capital Partners LP
Sill, Igor–Geneva Venture Group Inc
Sillitoe, Andrew–Apax Partners LLP
Sills, Anthony–Langholm Capital LLP
Silton, Michael–Act One Ventures LP
Silva Ricciardi, Antonio–Haitong Capital SCR SA
Silva, Catherine–Main Street Capital Corp
Silva, Christopher–Allied Minds LLC
Silva, Oscar–Global Banking Corporation BSCC
Silveira, Dee–Westfield Capital Management Company LP
Silver, Boris–FundersClub Inc
Silver, David–Bennett Jones Verchere
Silver, Joel–Trilogy Growth LP
Silver, Mark–York Plains Investment Corp
Silver, Samuel–American Beacon Advisors Inc
Silvera, David–Rosemont Investment Partners LLC
Silverberg, Brad–Ignition Ventures Management LLC
Silverio, Matthew–Hamilton Lane Advisors LLC
Silverman, Andrew–Capital Resource Partners
Silverman, Ari–Lion Equity Partners LLC

Silverman, David–Crosslink Capital Inc
Silverman, Eric–Milbank Tweed Hadley & Mccloy LLP
Silverman, Ian–Siris Capital Group LLC
Silverman, Jeffrey–Perella Weinberg Partners LP
Silverman, Jeremy–Frontenac Company LLC
Silverman, Lauren–Novartis Venture Funds
Silverman, Mark–Catamount Ventures LP
Silvershatz, Avishai–Israel Infinity Venture Capital Fund Israel LP
Silverstein, Jonathan–OrbiMed Advisors LLC
Silvestre, Manuel–Altamar Private Equity SGIIC SAU
Silvestri, Glen–Ontario Teachers' Pension Plan
Silvestri, Joseph–Court Square Capital Partners LP
Sim, Pik Sian–Arcapita Inc
Sim, Rodney–Macquarie Capital Markets Canada Ltd
Simao, Raymond–Sanlam Private Equity
Simard, Pierre–Champlain Capital Partners LP
Simard, Pierre–Corporation Financiere Champlain Canada Inc
Simas, Matt–SilverStream Capital LLC
Simatos, Michael–Investcorp Technology Investments Group
Simkhovitch, Ira–Industry Ventures LLC
Simko, Susan–Prairiegold Venture Partners
Simm, Ian–Impax Asset Management Ltd
Simm, Jonathan–Altitude Partners LLP
Simmons Mendoza, Mary–Haynes and Boone LLC
Simmons, Andrew–High Street Capital
Simmons, Brian–CHS Capital LLC
Simmons, Brian–Shorehill Capital LLC
Simmons, David–Carlyle Group LP
Simmons, John–JC Simmons & Associates
Simmons, L. E.–SCF Partners LP
Simmons, Walker–Pamlico Capital Management LP
Simo, Gyorgy–Day One Capital Kockazati Tokealap Kezelo Zrt
Simon, Andreas–Capvis Equity Partners AG
Simon, Anne–Blackstone Group LP
Simon, Caitlin–Shorenstein Co LLC
Simon, Christophe–Idinvest Partners SA
Simon, Daniel–Wedbush Capital Partners LP
Simon, David–LJ2 & Co LLC
Simon, Gary–Velocity Venture Capital Inc
Simon, Ivelisse Rodriguez–Avante Mezzanine Inc
Simon, John–General Catalyst Partners LLC
Simon, John–Sigma Prime Ventures LLC
Simon, Lawrence–Clearview Capital LLC
Simon, Nicholas–Clarus Ventures LLC
Simon, Rafael–Vantagepoint Management Inc
Simon, Robert–Bradford Equities Management LLC
Simon, Robert–Business Development Bank of Canada
Simon, Robert–Saints Ventures
Simon, Scott–Blackstone Group LP
Simon, Stephen–Simon Equity Partners LLC
Simones Lopes, Luiz Ildefonso–Brookfield Asset Management Inc
Simoni, Catherine–Carlyle Group LP
Simoni, Richard–Asset Management Co
Simonian, Hrach–Canaan Partners
Simonian, Steve–AllegisCyber
Simonneau, Emmanuel–Sigma Gestion SA
Simonov, Roman–Siguler Guff & Company LP

Simonova, Lyubov–Almaz Capital Partners
Simonowicz, Joanna–Innova Capital Sp z o o
Simons, Jim–Split Rock Partners LLC
Simons, John–Resonetics LLC
Simonson, Ray–VERDEXUS
Simpkins, Neil–Blackstone Group LP
Simpson, Bryan–Gideon Hixon Fund LP
Simpson, John–Broadhaven Capital Partners LLC
Simpson, John–Canyon Capital Advisors LLC
Simpson, Kate–Truebridge Capital Partners LLC
Simpson, Steven–Wheelhouse Capital Partners LLC
Simpson, Todd–iNovia Capital Inc
Sims, Edgar–Nancy Creek Capital
Sims, Laura–Sageview Capital LP
Sims, Marla–Brown Brothers Harriman & Co
Sims, Tim–Pacific Equity Partners Pty Ltd
Sinai, Nick–Insight Venture Partners LLC
Sincich, David–StoneCreek Capital
Sinclair, David–LUX CAPITAL GROUP L L C
Sinclair, Peter–Leapfrog Ventures L P
Sindecuse, Judy–Capital Innovators LLC
Sindwani, Deepak–Bain Capital Inc
Sine, Jeffrey–Raine Group LLC, The
Sinensky, Arthur–Alumni Capital Network Management Co LLC
Sinfield-Hain, Craig–Investcorp Technology Investments Group
Sing-Wood Yeh, Woody–Amkey Ventures LLC
Singappuli, Waruna–N D B Capital Holdings PLC
Singbartl, Lars–Warburg Pincus LLC
Singer, Carl–Fundamental Management Corp
Singer, Carlyle–Acumen Fund Inc
Singer, David–Foundation Capital LLC
Singer, David–Maverick Capital Ltd
Singer, John–Advent International Corp
Singer, Marc–BEV Capital
Singer, Marc–Osage Venture Partners
Singer, Maria–Blackstone Group LP
Singer, Mortimer–Marvin TRAUB LLC
Singerman, Brian–Founders Fund, The
Singh, Ajit–Artiman Management LLC
Singh, Alok–New Mountain Capital I LLC
Singh, Anjuli–Rezon8 Capital & Advisory Group LLC
Singh, Bharat–Sequoia Capital India
Singh, Devinjit–Carlyle Group LP
Singh, K. Paul–Rezon8 Capital & Advisory Group LLC
Singh, Kanwaljit–Helion Venture Partners LLC
Singh, Kuljeev–iGan Partners Inc
Singh, Mallika–Omidyar Network Commons LLC
Singh, Paul–Disruption Corporation
Singh, Pavninder–Bain Capital Inc
Singh, Praneet–Siguler Guff & Company LP
Singh, Rahul–Cross Atlantic Capital Partners LLC
Singh, Raj–Redwood Venture Partners
Singh, Rajan–New Silk Route Partners, LLC
Singh, Ravi–Sycamore Ventures Inc
Singh, Shailendra Jit–Sequoia Capital India
Singh, Shailendra–Sequoia Capital India
Singh, Shailesh–2I Capital Asset Management Co Ltd
Singh, Shashank–Apax Partners LLP
Singh, Tom–Zouk Capital LLP
Singh, Vic–Eniac Ventures LP
Singha, Aman–Waveland Capital Group LLC
Singhal, Neeraj–HOF Capital Inc

Pratt's Guide to Private Equity & Venture Capital Sources

Singhal, Nitin–EagleTree Capital, LP
Singhal, Rajesh–Milestone Religare Investment Advisors Pvt Ltd
Singhal, Sandeep–Nexus Venture Partners
Singhal, Sandeep–Westbridge Capital Advisors (India) Pvt Ltd
Singhal, Sanjiv–Banyantree Finance Pvt Ltd
Singhania, Ayush–Aurora Capital Group Ltd
Singleton, Lincoln–Evercore Inc
Singleton, Steven–Mountain Group Capital LLC
Sinha, Bipul–Lightspeed Management Company LLC
Sinha, Jayant–Omidyar Network Commons LLC
Sinha, Jit–JMI Management Inc
Sinha, Nikhil–Adams Capital Management, Inc.
Sinha, Sandeep–Lumis Partners
Sinik, John–Metric Capital Partners LLP
Sinius, Vytautas–Siauliu Bankas AB
Sinnett, Jeffrey–Kamylon Capital LLC
Sinyor, Joe–Actis LLP
Siperstein, Boris–Lighthouse Fund LLC
Sipp, Vesna–Hamilton Lane Advisors LLC
Sippl, Roger–Sippl Macdonald Ventures
Sippl, Sam–Marwit Capital Corp
Sipple, Harald–ECM Equity Capital Management GmbH
Sipple, James–Auven Therapeutics Management LLLP
Sirinakis, Kyparissia–Epidarex Capital
Sirlin, Cliff–LaunchCapital LLC
Sirnio, Craig–HALO FUND L P
Sirois, Charles–Tandem Expansion Fund I LP
Sirois, Denis–ID Capital
Sirois, Denis–Propulsion Ventures Inc
Sirois, Francois-Charles–ID Capital
Sirois, Luc–Hacking Health Accelerator Inc
Sirwalla, Naozad–Kotak Investment Advisors Ltd
Siscovick, Ben–IA Ventures
Sisko, Brian–Safeguard Scientifics Inc
Sisodraker, Divesh–Vanedge Capital Inc
Sissel, Gregory–Platte River Ventures LLC
Sissman, Patrick–Redwood Capital Investments LLC
Sisteron, Yves–Upfront Ventures
Sisto, Al–Nauta Capital SL
Sites, John–Wexford Capital LP
Sitko, Bradley–MTS Health Partners LP
Sitton, Liesl–Bayboston Managers LLC
Sivakumar, Ramamurthy–Intel Capital Corp
Sivanithy, Dushy–Pantheon Ventures (UK) LLP
Siveyer, Paul–Tembo Capital LLP
Sivri, Baris–Adm Capital
Siwale, Sulanji–GEF Management Corp
Siwinski, Steven–High Road Capital Partners LLC
Sjarbaini, Chatib–1&12 Ventures BV
Sjodin, Fredrik–Sageview Capital LP
Sjogren, Marta–Northzone Ventures
Skaanild, Christian–Capital International Inc
Skaarberg, Rolf–Kistefos Venture Capital As
Skaff, Dan–Radicle Impact
Skaff, Michael–Seneca Partners Inc
Skagseth, Erlend–Sarsia Seed Management AS
Skala-Pozniak, Agnieszka–Innovation Nest Sp z o o
Skapinker, Mark–Brightspark Ventures
Skare, Leif Andre–Energy Ventures AS
Skegro, Borislav–Quaestus Private Equity doo
Skero, Kathleen–Blackstone Group LP

Skidmore, Alyse–North Castle Partners LLC
Skie, Scott–Baird Capital
Skillen, Lynn–Sun Capital Partners Inc
Skillins, Eric–Cfi Capital
Skinner, Henry–Novartis Venture Funds
Skinner, Spencer–Active Private Equity
Skinner, Stuart–Bounds Equity Partners, LLC
Skinner, William–Phoenix Equity Partners Ltd
Skjervold, Herbjorn–Proventure Management AS
Sklar, Jason–Shamrock Capital Advisors LLC
Sklarin, Chris–Edison Partners
Sklarin, Chris–Edison Partners
Sklodowski, Jacek–IQ Partners SA
Skok, David–Matrix Partners, L.P.
Skok, Michael–AssembleVC Fund I LP
Skok, Natasha–Tallwood Venture Capital
Skoler, Steven–Friend Skoler & Co. LLC
Skrenta, Stephen–Blackstone Group LP
Skryabin, Konstantin–Burrill & Company
Skrzynski, Joseph–Castle Harlan Aus Mezzanine
Skurbe, Matthew–Blackstone Group LP
Skutelis, Janis–FlyCap AIFP SIA
Skvortsov, Dima–Morgan Stanley Alternative Investment Partners LP
Skvortsov, Serguei–Troika Capital Partners Ltd
Slade, Dominic–Alchemy Partners LLP
Slade, Ed–Quest Capital Inc
Slade, Georgiana–Milbank Tweed Hadley & Mccloy LLP
Slade, Michael–Second Avenue Partners
Slade, Stephen–PTV Healthcare Capital
Sladnick, Clifford–Brown Gibbons Lang & Company LLC
Slagel, Dean–Esperante BV
Slamm, Joseph–Hudson Clean Energy Partners
Slapansky, Edward–Blackstone Group LP
Slater, Aaron–Value Investments Peru SAFI
Slater, Ben–Highlander Partners LP
Slater, Iain–CBPE Capital LLP
Slatford, Karen–Pentech Ventures LLP
Slatoff, Karl–ZMC
Slaton, Kevin–Insight Equity Holdings LLC
Slatter, Ben–Rutland Partners LLP
Slavet, James–Greylock Partners LLC
Slavin, William–Arc Financial Corp.
Sledzik, Jim–Energy Ventures AS
Sleeper, Nathan–Clayton Dubilier & Rice LLC
Slessman, George–GBT Capital LLC
Slessman, William–GBT Capital LLC
Slettengren, Anders–NovAx AB
Sligar, James–Milbank Tweed Hadley & Mccloy LLP
Slighton, Eric–Aktis Capital Group
Slinkard, Robert–Atairos Management LP
Slipper, James–Gresham Llp
Sloan, Bradley–Questa Capital Management LLC
Sloan, H. Bradley–Parthenon Capital LLC
Sloan, James–Carlyle Group LP
Sloan, Meg–Foundation Capital LLC
Sloan, William–Morrison & Foerster LLP
Sloane, Eric–Southfield Capital Advisors LLC
Sloboda, E.J.–Sidereal Capital Group LLC
Sloboda, E.J.–Wicks Group of Companies LLC
Slodowitz, Mitch–Accretive LLC
Slominski, Shane–Tonka Bay Equity Partners LLC
Slonecker, Derron–Perella Weinberg Partners LP

Sloop, Andrew–Nexo Capital Partners
Slootweg, Sander–Forbion Capital Partners
Slotkin, David–Morrison & Foerster LLP
Sloutski, Niklas–Accent Equity Partners AB
Slovik, Adam–Select Venture Partners LLC
Slusar, Mark–Enhanced Capital Partners LLC
Slusky, Alexander–Vector Capital Management LP
Slutzkin, Craig–New Leaf Venture Partners LLC
Slutzky, Daniel–Qumra Capital Israel I Ltd
Slye, Jack–LLR Partners Inc
Smach, Thomas–Riverwood Capital Group LLC
Small, Daniel–Star Mountain Capital LLC
Small, Nick–CIT Group Inc
Small, Robert–Berkshire Partners LLC
Smallbone, Tim–Inflexion PLC
Smaller, Daniel–Algebra Capital Ltd
Smalley, Clive–Duet Capital Ltd
Smallridge, James–Core Capital Partners LLP
Smallwood, Ivan–Morrison & Foerster LLP
Smardon, Dave–Nibiru Capital Management Ltd
Smart, Alexander–WestBridge Fund Managers Ltd
Smart, Chad–Capitalworks Investment Partners (Pty) Ltd
Smart, Gregg–Fenway Partners LLC
Smart, Shawn–HealthRight Partners
Smeets, Gerd–KeBeK Management NV
Smelt, Philip–Lexington Partners Inc
Smeltzer, James–Cardinal Equity Partners LLC
Smereczynski, Daniel–First Analysis Corp
Smerklo, Mike–Next Coast Ventures LLC
Smets, Julien–BNP Paribas Fortis Private Equity Growth NV
Smidt, Joergen–Sunstone Capital A/S
Smiga, Jonathan–Keen Growth Capital Advisors LLC
Smikle, Basil–Akayi Capital Partners LLC
Smildzins, Troy–Seidler Equity Partners
Smiley, Ryan–Riordan Lewis & Haden
Smirnov, Konstantin–Baring Vostok Capital Partners Ltd
Smit, Andries–Motseng Investment Holdings (Pty) Ltd
Smith, Adam–Medina Capital Partners Inc
Smith, Adrian–Ignition Ventures Management LLC
Smith, Adrian–Ignition Ventures Management LLC
Smith, Amanda–Waterman Capital Ltd
Smith, Andrew–Morrison & Foerster LLP
Smith, Ben–InReach Ventures LLP
Smith, Benjamin–Accelerator Ventures
Smith, Bob–JMI Management Inc
Smith, Brian–PCM Companies LLC
Smith, Brian–Partnership Capital Growth LLC
Smith, Brian–Peninsula Ventures
Smith, Brian–S3 Ventures LLC
Smith, Brien–NB Private Equity Partners Ltd
Smith, Brigitte–GBS Venture Partners
Smith, Brook–Ancor Capital Partners
Smith, Bryan–Montauk TriGuard Management Inc
Smith, Byron–Mountain Group Capital LLC
Smith, C. Neil–Crescent Point Energy Corp
Smith, Cameron–CHS Capital LLC
Smith, Christopher–Coral Ventures Inc
Smith, Clifford–RAIN Source Capital, Inc.
Smith, Dabney–Mosaic Capital Partners LLC
Smith, Daniel–Blackstone Group LP
Smith, Daniel–F&C Equity Partners PLC

2570

Smith, David—Bay Hills Capital Partners II LP
Smith, David—Capital Dynamics Sdn Bhd
Smith, Deborah—Investcorp Bank BSC
Smith, Derek—Oaktree Capital Management LP
Smith, Doug—Symphony Technology Group LLC
Smith, Douglas—Collaborative Fund
Smith, Dustin—Acas LLC
Smith, Dwight—Morrison & Foerster LLP
Smith, Elizabeth—CCMP Capital Advisors LP
Smith, Evereth—NewWorld Capital Group LLC
Smith, Frederick—Sinclair Ventures Inc
Smith, Gary Mitchel—Morrison & Foerster LLP
Smith, Gary—Encore Consumer Capital Fund L P
Smith, Geoffrey—Ascent Biomedical Ventures
Smith, Greg—IP Group PLC
Smith, Gregg—Evolution Corporate Advisors LLC
Smith, Harry—Oaktree Capital Management LP
Smith, Howard—First Analysis Corp
Smith, Hudson—HGGC LLC
Smith, Hudson—Thoma Bravo LLC
Smith, Ian—Aquiline Capital Partners LLC
Smith, Ian—Cooley LLP
Smith, James—Sinclair Ventures Inc
Smith, Jason—Lime Rock Partners LLC
Smith, Jed—Catamount Ventures LP
Smith, Jed—Owl Ventures LP
Smith, Jeffrey—BlackRock Inc
Smith, Jill—Bow River Capital Partners LLC
Smith, Jim—Mohr Davidow Ventures
Smith, John—AEA Investors LLC
Smith, John—Vexiom Equity Partners, L.P.
Smith, Jose Miguel—Evercore Inc
Smith, Juan Carlos—Eneas Capital SL
Smith, Justin—Ark Applications LLC
Smith, Karl—FRANK RUSSELL CAPITAL CO
Smith, Kathleen—Jabodon PT Co
Smith, Keith—Capital Point Partners LLC
Smith, Kenneth—Park Street Capital LLC
Smith, Kevin—Clayton Dubilier & Rice LLC
Smith, Laurence—Sixpoint Partners LLC
Smith, Louise—Private Advisors LLC
Smith, M. Daniel—Capstone Financial Group
Smith, Marcus—Third Security LLC
Smith, Mark—Savvis Inc
Smith, Martin Alderson—Blackstone Group LP
Smith, Matt—Foresight Group LLP
Smith, Matthew—Abbott Capital Management LLC
Smith, Matthew—Odeon Capital Partners LP
Smith, Melissa—Acas LLC
Smith, Nancy—Arc Financial Corp.
Smith, Nicholas—Milbank Tweed Hadley & Mccloy LLP
Smith, Nick Gordon—Pamplona Capital Management LLP
Smith, Nicole—Morrison & Foerster LLP
Smith, Paul—Rural American Fund LP
Smith, Pelham—Prophet Equity LLC
Smith, Peter—Akkadian Ventures LLC
Smith, Peter—Fortress Investment Group LLC
Smith, Peter—Starboard Capital Partners LLC
Smith, Philip—Stone Canyon Venture Partners
Smith, R. Adam—Circle Peak Capital LLC
Smith, R. Bob—Ark Applications LLC
Smith, Raymond—Potomac Equity Partners LLC
Smith, Renny—Staley Capital Management LLC

Smith, Richard—European Capital Financial Services Ltd
Smith, Rick—CrossCut Ventures Management LLC
Smith, Robert—C3 Capital LLC
Smith, Robert—Castanea Partners Inc
Smith, Robert—Petra Capital Partners LLC
Smith, Roger—Smart Ventures Inc
Smith, Sarah—Advent International Corp
Smith, Scott—Celgene Corp
Smith, Scott—Palo Alto Investors LLC
Smith, Simon—Nova Capital Management, Ltd.
Smith, Stanley—Syncom Management Co Inc
Smith, Stephen—Banyan Capital Advisors LLC
Smith, Stephen—Masthead Venture Partners
Smith, Steven—Aurora Capital Group Ltd
Smith, Steven—Aurora Resurgence Management Partners LLC
Smith, Steven—HGGC LLC
Smith, T. Otey—RLJ Equity Partners LLC
Smith, Teresa—Walden International
Smith, Terry—SFW Capital Partners LLC
Smith, Thomas—Lombard Investments Inc
Smith, Thomas—Mason Wells Inc
Smith, Thomas—Piper Jaffray Ventures Inc
Smith, Todd—Willis Stein & Partners LP
Smith, Tom—Baird Capital
Smith, Tony—Amicus Partners
Smith, Travis—ACM Ltd
Smith, W. Stephen—Morrison & Foerster LLP
Smith, W. Thomas—TTV Capital LLC
Smith, Wesley—CIT Group Inc
Smith, Wilson—Patriot Financial Partners LP
Smither, Helen—Blackstone Group LP
Smitshoek, Roy—Moneta Capital Partners Ltd
Smoragiewicz, Christine—Intervale Capital LLC
Smotherman, Zack—Battery Ventures LP
Smulders, Patrick—Towerbrook Capital Partners LP
Smyrski, Tyler—Yellow Point Equity Partners LP
Smyth, Derek—OMERS Ventures
Smyth, Peter—Broadlake Capital Ltd
Smyth, Shayne—Perle Ventures Pty Ltd
Smythe, James—Single Oak Ventures LP
Sneck, Seppo—SmartCap AS
Sneddon, David—Scottish Equity Partners LLP
Snell, Scott—Oak Hill Advisors LP
Sng, Joel—Formation 8 Partners LP
Snider, Bill—Broadoak Capital Partners LLC
Snider, John—Trust Company of the West
Snipes, Kellie—Blue Ridge Capital LLC
Snir, Yoram—Greylock Israel Global Management Ltd
Snoek, Jasper—Doen Participaties BV
Snow, Ian—Snow Phipps Group LLC
Snow, John—Quabbin Capital Inc
Snow, Scott—Bb&T Capital Partners LLC
Snowden, Murray—Parallax Capital Partners LLC
Snyder, Brett—Nicolet Capital Partners LLC
Snyder, Christopher—Verus Investment Partners
Snyder, Darren—Prairie Capital, L.P.
Snyder, James—Hammond Kennedy Whitney & Company Inc
So, Jason—SAIF Partners
So, John—Metropolitan Real Estate Equity Management LLC
Soane, David—Phoenix Venture Partners LLC
Soane, Mark—Appian Ventures, Inc.

Soanes, Darren—OMERS Infrastructure
Soares, Joseph—Blackstone Group LP
Sobczak, Iliana—Blackstone Group LP
Sobeck, Joshua—747 Capital LLC
Sobecki, Christopher—Invus Group LLC
Sobel, Robert—Brahman Management LLC
Sobel, Scott—Valor Capital Group LLC
Soberg, Jon—Blumberg International Partners LLC
Sobieski, Ian—Band of Angels Venture Fund LP
Sobiloff, Peter—Insight Venture Partners LLC
Sobol, Edward—Welsh Carson Anderson & Stowe
Sobol, Jason—Evercore Inc
Sobti, Amit—Warburg Pincus LLC
Socks, David—Frazier Management LLC
Socolof, Stephen—New Venture Partners LLC
Soderberg, Bo—Nordic Capital
Soderberg, Ricard—Active Capital Partners SA
Soderling, Steve—Tonka Bay Equity Partners LLC
Soderlund, Patrik—Mountain Cleantech AG
Soderstrom, Carl—Green Park & Golf Ventures LLC
Soderstrom, Carl—Health Wildcatters
Soeda, Shigeyuki—DBJ Capital Co., Ltd
Soendgerath, Bjoern—Ventizz Capital Partners Advisory AG
Soeryadjaya, Michael William P.—Saratoga Investama Sedaya Tbk PT
Soffe, Alex—Kickstart Seed Fund LP
Soh, Susan—Perella Weinberg Partners LP
Sohail, Faysal—CMEA Development Company LLC
Sohoni, Reshma—Seedcamp Investments LLP
Soignet, Steven—Arcus Ventures
Soignet, Steven—Cross Atlantic Partners
Sokol, Marc—JK&B Capital LLC
Sokolic, David—Battery Ventures LP
Sokoloff, Jonathan—Leonard Green & Partners LP
Solaiman, Mohamed—Kingdom Holding Co
Solak, Hakan—Fischer Buchschacher Gruppe AG
Solari, Joseph—Saugatuck Capital Co
Soldano, James—Sterling Investment Partners II LP
Sollberger, Simon—Innovate Partners LLC
Solmssen, Christopher—Evercore Inc
Solomon, Christopher—Welsh Carson Anderson & Stowe
Solomon, Curt—New York Business Development Corp
Solomon, David—Meritage Funds
Solomon, Glenn—GGV Capital
Solomon, Glenn—GGV Capital
Solomon, Katie—Genstar Capital LLC
Solomon, Michael—Leonard Green & Partners LP
Solomons, Alton—Sanlam Private Equity
Solon, Mark—Highway 12 Ventures
Solonitsyn, Slava—Ruvento Ventures Pte Ltd
Solorzano, Luis—Advent International Corp
Solotar, Joan—Blackstone Group LP
Solovy, Mark—Monroe Capital LLC
Solow, Todd—Norwest Equity Partners
Solvik, Peter—Sigma Partners
Soman, Tanya—500 Startups, L.P.
Somani, Ashutosh—Warburg Pincus LLC
Somasegar, Soma—MadroNA Venture Group
Somers, Louise—Blackstone Group LP
Somerville, Hunter—Greenspring Associates Inc
Somerville, Lorne—CVC Capital Partners Ltd
Sommerschield, Bill—Lake Capital

2571

Somoza, Rafael—Accretia Capital LLC
Son, In Ho—Stonebridge Capital Inc
Soncini, Ivan—Unipol Merchant Banca per le Imprese SpA
Sondell, Jason—Norwest Equity Partners
Sondker, Edward—Genesis Financial Services Fund LLC
Sone, Todd—Signet Healthcare Partners
Soneya, Fred—Haatch Ltd
Song, Alan—Sbcvc Fund Ii L P
Song, Dong-hyun—Korea Investment Partners Co Ltd
Song, Hong—Hony Capital Beijing Co Ltd
Song, Injun—IMM Private Equity Inc
Song, Jaehwan—Next Venture Investment Corp
Song, Jay—Premier Partners LLC
Song, Jerry—China Science & Merchants Investment Management Group Co Ltd
Song, Ki Han—Shinwon Venture Capital Co Ltd
Song, Madeline—Siemens Venture Capital GmbH
Song, Michael—Providence Equity Partners LLC
Song, Shaohuan—Shanghai Leading Capital Co Ltd
Song, Shirlene—Carlyle Group LP
Song, Steven—Altpoint Capital Partners LLC
Song, Winston—Vestar Capital Partners Inc
Song, Xiaoming—CDH China Management Co., Ltd.
Song, Yeong Hwan—Q Capital Partners Co Ltd
Song, Yuming—Millennium Ark Investment Co Ltd
Soni, Amit—General Atlantic LLC
Soni, Bobby—Novo Holdings A/S
Soni, Vipul—Brynwood Partners L.P.
Sonntag, Rich—Pivotal Group Inc
Sonshine, Daniel—TorQuest Partners Inc
Sonsini, Peter—New Enterprise Associates Inc
Sontag, Frederick—Spring Bay Companies
Sontum, Christian—Norvestor Equity AS
Soo Boon, Koh—Iglobe Treasury Management Ltd
Sood, Kunal—Pantheon Ventures (UK) LLP
Sood, Rajat—General Atlantic LLC
Sood, Varun—Capvent AG
Soong, Jacky—Pacific Alliance Capital Group Ltd
Soong, Tai-Sen—CDIB BioScience Venture Management
Sopp, David—Kamylon Capital LLC
Sopuch, Jaroslav—Benson Oak Capital Ltd
Soraparu, Steven—Waller Capital Partners LLC
Soravia, Erwin—Wing Equity Management
Soravia, Hanno—Wing Equity Management
Sorbara, Nicole—Macquarie Group Ltd
Soref, Ezer—Giza Venture Capital
Sorel, Pierre—Access Capital Partners SA
Sorensen, E. Per—Vistech Corp
Sorensen, Jan H—Ld Equity
Sorenson, Luke—Sorenson Capital Partners LP
Soria, Ramon—Peninsula Capital Advisors LLP
Soriano, Ferran—Nauta Capital SL
Soriano, Howard—GEN3 Partners, Inc.
Soriene, Daiva—Siauliu Bankas AB
Sormani, Marco—Varenne Capital Partners SAS
Soros, George—Soros Strategic Partners LP
Sorrel, Lawrence—Tailwind Capital Partners LP
Sorrel, Lawrence—Thomas Weisel Partners Group Inc
Sorum, Christian—Oderc AS
Sorum, Rune—Televentre Management As
Sorzon, Eli—Xenia Venture Capital Ltd
Sosa del Valle, Jose—Lexington Partners Inc

Sosa, Bertrand—MPower Ventures, L.P.
Sosin, Tyler—Menlo Ventures
Soso, Tito—L-Gam Advisers LLP
Sotiriou, Evan—OrbiMed Advisors LLC
Soto, Jaime—MCH Private Equity Asesores SL
Soto, Tom—Craton Equity Partners LLC
Sotoloff, Peter—Blackstone Group LP
Sotomayor, Raul—Southern Cross Capital Management SA
Soubra, Ahmad—I2Bf Global Ventures
Souder, Andrew—RAF Industries, Inc.
Souillard, Yann—Lloyds Development Capital (Holdings) Ltd
Soukarieh, Rabih—United Gulf Bank Securities Co. B.S.C
Soule, Edgar—Audax Group, Inc.
Soule, Erin—Acas LLC
Souleles, Thomas—Madison Dearborn Partners LLC
Soumare, Idriss—BC Partners LLP
Sousa Bittencourt, Felipe—Vinci Equities Gestora de Recursos Ltda
Sousa, Laura—Algonquin Advisors LLC
Sousa, Paulo—European Bank for Reconstruction and Development
Soussa, Scott—Blackstone Group LP
South, Jeremy—SouthPac Partners Inc
South, W. Spencer—Lazarus Capital Partners
Southall, Joanne—Capital Dynamics Sdn Bhd
Southwell, Paul—AAC CAPITAL PARTNERS
Souto, Flavio—Vila Rica Capital Gestora de Recursos Ltda
Souvignier, Chad—Research Corporation Technologies
Souviron, Laurent—m8 Capital
Souweine, Isaac—Real Ventures
Souza, Antonio—Evercore Inc
Souza, Marcio—Baring Private Equity Asia Ltd
Sovak, W. Sean—Lighthouse Fund LLC
Sovik, Atle—Verdane Capital Advisors AS
Sowelem, Mostafa—Qalaa Holdings SAE
Sowers, Jason—WinoNA Capital Management LLC
Sowton, Tim—Detroit Renaissance
Sowul, Christian—Vista Equity Partners LLC
Soyoye, Babatunde—Helios Investment Partners LLP
Spaeth, Jason—Varde Partners Inc
Spaght, Pearson—Fletcher Spaght Ventures LP
Spahn, Stephen—Quad Ventures LL
Spahr, Christopher—Partnership Capital Growth LLC
Spaht, Holden—Thoma Bravo LLC
Spain, Kevin—Emergence Capital Partners
Spalding, Richard—Kearny Venture Partners LP
Spalding, Richard—Thomas Weisel Partners Group Inc
Spalter, Jonathan—Pantheon Ventures (UK) LLP
Spangler, Stuart—Oaktree Capital Management LP
Spann, Stephen—PTV Healthcare Capital
Spanos, Gus—Spanos Barber Jesse & Co LLC
Sparacino, Frank—First Analysis Corp
Sparkman, Thorne—Slater Technology Fund Inc
Sparrow, Richard—Scottish Equity Partners LLP
Spasov, Peter—Marlin Equity Partners LLC
Spassov, Mirtcho—GEF Management Corp
Spatscheck, Reinhilde—SHS Gesellschaft fuer Beteiligungsmanagement mbH
Spear, Daniel—Morgan Stanley Alternative Investment Partners LP
Spearing, Nicholas—Milbank Tweed Hadley & Mccloy LLP
Spears, Robert—Shoreline Venture Management, LLC
Speer, Eric—Wellington Financial Lp
Speer, Nicholas—Riverside Co
Speer, Robert—CM Equity Partners LP
Speicher, Eric—Oaktree Capital Management LP
Speiser, Mike—Sutter Hill Ventures
Spell, William—Spell Capital Partners LLC
Spellman, Andrew—Fireman Capital Partners LLC
Spellman, Andrew—Raptor Capital Management LP
Spence, Adam—Acas LLC
Spence, B. Andrew—Palladian Capital Partners LLC
Spence, Gene—COLLABORATIVE CAPITAL L L C
Spence, Keith—Global Mining Capital Corp
Spence, Tim—Graphite Capital Management LLP
Spencer, David—Emerald Hill Capital Partners Ltd
Spencer, David—Texas Intrepid Ventures LLC
Spencer, Donald—Siguler Guff & Company LP
Spencer, Jamey—Able Capital Management LLC
Spencer, Jeb—TVC Capital LLC
Spencer, Lofton—Antares Capital Corp
Spencer, Raymond—RSVP Capital
Spencer, Robert—Baker & McKenzie LLP
Spencer, Tiffany—Bessemer Venture Partners
Spencer, Timothy—Archer Capital Pty Ltd
Spener, Todd—FTL Capital LLC
Sperans, James—Morgan Stanley Alternative Investment Partners LP
Sperling, Joerg—Alpina Capital Partners LLP
Spero, Benjamin—Spectrum Equity Investors LP
Spero, Donald—New Markets Venture Partners
Spero, Kurt—Galtere Ltd
Sperry, Robert—Kainos Capital LLC
Sperzel, George—GTCR Golder Rauner LLC
Spetzler, Matt—Francisco Partners LP
Speziali, Giuseppe—Fincalabra SpA
Spiegel, Leo—Mission Ventures Inc
Spiegel, William—Pine Brook Road Partners LLC
Spielvogel, Scott—One Rock Capital Partners LLC
Spierin, Brendan—Icc Venture Capital
Spies, Robert—Thomas H Lee Partners LP
Spievak, Jason—Persistence Partners, L.P.
Spigelman, Melvin—Wellington Partners GmbH
Spiliotes, Nicholas—Morrison & Foerster LLP
Spilizewski, Karen—RiverVest Venture Partners LLC
Spillane, Brian—Warburg Pincus LLC
Spillane, Geoffrey—Gridiron Capital LLC
Spilman, John—Union Grove Venture Partners 2014 LLC
Spinale, Paul—Islington Capital Partners LLC
Spindler, Rob—Canada Pension Plan Investment Board
Spinner, Bob—Sigma Partners
Spinrad, Yaakov—Cane Investment Partners LLC
Spira, Christopher—True Capital Partners LLP
Spiri, Dominic—Terra Firma Capital Partners Ltd
Spirn, Samuel—Berkshire Partners LLC
Spiteri, Steven—Riverside Co
Spitz, Rick—Pepperwood Partners LLC
Spitz, William—Diversified Trust Company Inc
Spitzer, Erika—Leonard Green & Partners LP
Spitzer, Silda—NewWorld Capital Group LLC

Spiva, Ed–Anthem Capital Management Inc
Spivak, Fred–KPS Capital Partners LP
Spliet, Eric–BNP Paribas Fortis Private Equity Growth NV
Splinter, Michael–WISC Partners LP
Splinter, Pat–Vantagepoint Management Inc
Spoerri, Joshua–OpCapita LLP
Spofford, Christopher–Broadhaven Capital Partners LLC
Spong, Stephanie–Royal Street Investment and Innovation Center LLC
Spoon, Alan–Polaris Venture Partners
Spoon, Ryan–Polaris Venture Partners
Spork, Ulrik–Novo Holdings A/S
Spors, Christoph–Capiton AG
Spoto, Thomas–AlpInvest Partners BV
Spragins, Alan–Columbia Pacific Advisors LLC
Sprecher, Harry–Panda Capital Asia Ltd
Spreng, David–Crescendo Venture Management LLC
Spriggs, Meg–Shorenstein Co LLC
Spring, Hank–Karpreilly LLC
Spring, Peter–Bain Capital Inc
Spring, Thomas–Syntaxis Capital Unternehmens und Finanzierungsberatung GmbH
Spring, Tyler–NMS Capital Partners
Sprogis, Karen–Blackstone Group LP
Sprole, Jared–Arcady Capital Company
Sprott, Ryan–Great Range Capital
Spruijtenburg, Ger–ICOS Capital Management BV
Sprung, Lloyd–Evercore Inc
Spungen, Aliana–AG BD LLC
Spurny, Stanislav–Benson Oak Capital Ltd
Sridhar, P.–Peepul Capital Llc
Srikrishnan, Bharath–Pine Brook Road Partners LLC
Srinivas, K–EQ India Advisors
Srinivas, T.R.–O3 Capital Advisors Pvt Ltd
Srinivasan, Balaji–Andreessen Horowitz LLC
Srinivasan, K. A.–Ventureast
Srinivasan, Krishna–LiveOak Venture Partners
Srinivasan, P.R.–Exponentia Capital Partners LLP
Srinivasan, Ram–Wellington Partners GmbH
Srinivasan, Savitha–International Business Machines Corp
Sriniwasan, S.–Kotak Investment Advisors Ltd
Srivasta, Anurag–Jungle Ventures Pte Ltd
Srivastava, Anupam–Intel Capital Corp
Srivastava, Manish–Onex Corp
Srivastava, Nagarjun–Alpha Founders
Srivastava, Sajal–TriplePoint Capital LLC
Srivastava, Vishesh–Bluegem Capital Partners LLP
Srivathsa, Rajesh–Ojas Venture Partners
Srivorakul, John–Ardent Capital Ltd
Srivorakul, Tom–Ardent Capital Ltd
Sroka, Roy–Wynnchurch Capital Ltd
St John, Marc–CVC Capital Partners Ltd
St. John, Morgan–Morpheus Capital Advisors LLC
St. Amand, Tara–Broadoak Capital Partners LLC
St. Jean, Brian–ABRY Partners LLC
St. Jean, David–Centerview Partners LLC
St. John, Charles–Motion Equity Partners LLP
St. Pierre, Tina–Landmark Partners Inc
Staal, Marc–AAC CAPITAL PARTNERS
Stabile, Robert–CCMP Capital Advisors LP
Stacey, Edward–IQ Capital Partners LLP
Stacey, Julie–Sterling Partners GP LLC

Stack, David–MPM Capital LLC
Stack, Richard–Synergy Life Science Partners LP
Stader, Dirk–Media Ventures GmbH
Stadler, Beda–Commission for Technology and Innovation CTI
Stadler, Dave–Paean Advisors Pty Ltd
Staffieri, Brett–Riverstone Holdings LLC
Stafford, Mark–Panorama Point Partners LLC
Stahl, Christian–Apax Partners LLP
Stahl, Richard–Elm Street Ventures LP
Stahr, Clancey–Zenshin Capital Management
Stait, Julian–Milbank Tweed Hadley & Mccloy LLP
Stalder, Dana–Matrix Partners, L.P.
Stalfort, Sean–PBM Capital Group LLC
Stalker, Anthony–Adm Capital
Staller, Bradley–Sterling Group LP
Stallings, James–PS 27 Ventures LLC
Stamas, Paul–General Atlantic LLC
Stammes, Arjo–Avedon Capital Partners BV
Stamp, Mark–Milbank Tweed Hadley & Mccloy LLP
Stampacchia, Otello–Omega Fund Management LLC
Stamps, E. Roe–Summit Partners LP
Stan, Iulian–Societatea de Investitii Financiare Transilvania SA
Stanbro, Kyle–Brook Venture Partners LLC
Stanca, Lorenzo–Mandarin Capital Partners SCA SICAR
Stanczuk, Matthew–Carlyle Group LP
Standbridge, Michael–Iglobe Treasury Management Ltd
Standing, Amy–Summer Street Capital Partners LLC
Stanfield, Cordis–IECP Fund Management LLC
Stanford, Dan–Newcap Partners Inc
Stanford, Henry–Albion Capital Group LLP
Stang, Steven–Growth Works Capital Ltd
Stankiewicz, Malgorzata–Bachleda Grupa Inwestycyjna Sp z o o
Stanley, Jocelyn–CHS Capital LLC
Stanley, Michael–Goode Partners LLC
Stanley, Scott–Global Infrastructure Holdings
Stanley, Theodore–UpStart Ventures Management LLC
Stansky, Brian–Integral Capital Partners
Stanton, Carl–Wellspring Capital Management LLC
Stanton, John–Trilogy Equity Partners Llc
Stanton, Luke–Skytree Capital Partners LP
Stanton, Scott–Morrison & Foerster LLP
Stapleton, Paul–Kayne Anderson Capital Advisors LP
Stapleton, Paul–MVP Capital LLC
Stapp, Jerry–Siris Capital Group LLC
Stapp, Terry–Blue Equity LLC
Starcevich, John–Pfingsten Partners LLC
Stares, John–Terra Firma Capital Partners Ltd
Staresinic, Michael–Sprott Resource Corp
Stark, Diego–Southern Cross Capital Management SA
Stark, F. John–Water Tower Capital LLC
Stark, Gary–Alpha Capital Partners, Ltd.
Stark, Justin–EDG Partners LLC
Stark, Melissa–Water Tower Capital LLC
Stark, Michael–Blackstone Group LP
Stark, Michael–Crosslink Capital Inc
Starkand, Javier–Consonance Capital Partners LP
Starke, Richard–Banyan Capital Advisors LLC
Starkel, Murray–Tillridge Global Agribusiness Partners

Starkey, Judith–Galen Associates Inc
Starkweather, Brad–Grey Mountain Partners LLC
Starling, William–Synergy Life Science Partners LP
Starodubova, Iryna–Horizon Capital Management
Starr, Ira–Long Point Capital
Starr, Jason–WinoNA Capital Management LLC
Starr, Kevin–Third Rock Ventures LLC
Starr-Frederick, Katrina–Hastings Equity Partners LLC
Stasik, Jared–Detroit Venture Partners LLC
Stassen, Dave–Split Rock Partners LLC
Stassi, Zachary–Blackstone Group LP
Stata, Raymie–Start Smart Labs
Stata, Raymond–Stata Venture Partners
Stathopoulos, Nikos–BC Partners LLP
Staton, Daniel–Walnut Group
Staub, Mark–PPM America Capital Partners LLC
Staub, Martin–Invision AG
Staubli, Thomas–Partners Group Holding AG
Staudinger, John–Riverstone Holdings LLC
Stav, Yigal–Israel Cleantech Ventures
Stavis, Robert–Bessemer Venture Partners
Stavropoulos, Andreas–Draper Fisher Jurvetson
Stay, Tim–Unitus Impact Partners LLC
Steains, Anthony–Blackstone Group LP
Steans, Jennifer–Concentric Equity Partners, L.P.
Steed, Christopher–Paladin Capital Management LLC
Steedman, Olivia–Ontario Teachers' Pension Plan
Steeg, Bryce–Valar Ventures Management LLC
Steel, Damien–OMERS Ventures
Steel, David–Core Capital Partners LLP
Steel, Michael Jacob–Morrison & Foerster LLP
Steele, Jeremy–Harbert Management Corp
Steele, Richard–Longmeadow Capital Partners LLC
Steele, Rob–Thomas Weisel Partners Group Inc
Steele, Thomas–Morrison & Foerster LLP
Steelhammer, Bob–Sun Capital Partners Inc
Steen Rasmussen, Soeren–VAEKSTFONDEN
Steen, Marten–Odlander Fredrikson & Co AB
Steenberg, Russ–BlackRock Inc
Steene, Paul–Litorina Capital Advisors AB
Steenkiste, David–Eos Partners LP
Steenrod, Wright–Chrysalis Ventures Inc
Steers, Helen–FRANK RUSSELL CAPITAL CO
Steers, Helen–Pantheon Ventures (UK) LLP
Stefanel, Matteo–Apis Partners LLP
Stefani, Pascal–Advent International Corp
Stefanovic, Milos–Mittelstaendische Beteiligungsgesellschaft
Stefanovic, Nikola–Small Enterprise Assistance Funds
Steffen, Gunter–ZFHN Zukunftsfonds Heilbronn GmbH & Co KG
Steffens, John–HealthpointCapital LLC
Steffens, John–Spring Mountain Capital LP
Steffens, Jorge–DLM Invista Gestao de Recursos Ltda
Steffy, David–CHL Medical Partners LP
Steg, Jean-Michel–Blackstone Group LP
Stegelmann, Murry–True North
Steggall, James–ArcLight Capital Holdings LLC
Stegmann, Jurgen–RobeCo Private Equity
Steibl, Michael–Alpha Founders

2573

Pratt's Guide to Private Equity & Venture Capital Sources

Steidle, Jack—Antares Capital Corp
Steier, Gregory—Brown Brothers Harriman & Co
Steig, Joseph—Long River Ventures, Inc.
Steiker, Joel—Murex Investments, Inc.
Steiker, Joel—Murex Investments, Inc.
Steil, Justin—Evercore Inc
Stein, Andrew—Cowen Capital Partners LLC
Stein, Andrew—Florescence Capital Co Ltd
Stein, Andrew—Florescence Huamao Equity Capital Management Co Ltd
Stein, David—Leaders Funds
Stein, Derek—BlackRock Inc
Stein, Hayley—Blackstone Group LP
Stein, Jason—Windforce Ventures LLC
Stein, John—Fidelis Capital LLC
Stein, Jonathan—COGR Inc
Stein, Josh—Draper Fisher Jurvetson
Stein, Martin—Blackford Capital LLC
Stein, Michael—iGan Partners Inc
Stein, Peter—Trinity Hunt Partners
Stein, Raoul—Kreos Capital Managers Ltd
Stein, Sarah—Hall Capital Partners LLC
Stein, William—Blackstone Group LP
Steinbacher, Uwe—SHS Gesellschaft fuer Beteiligungsmanagement mbH
Steinback, Michael—Stonebridge Partners LP
Steinberg, Bernard—TRG Management LP
Steinberg, Beth—MTS Health Partners LP
Steinberg, David—Puretech Ventures
Steinberg, Jordan—Blackstone Group LP
Steinberg, Julian—Alliance Consumer Growth LLC
Steinbrueck, Brian—Wingate Partners LP
Steindorf, Michael—Trinity Hunt Partners
Steiner, Eugen—Odlander Fredrikson & Co AB
Steiner, Manfred—Brown Gibbons Lang & Company LLC
Steiner, Perry—Arlington Capital Partners
Steiner, Perry—Arlington Capital Partners
Steiner, Rene—FIDES Business Partner AG
Steinlin, Walter—Commission for Technology and Innovation CTI
Steinour, Stephen—Crossharbor Capital Partners
Stelin, Carlos—Duet Capital Ltd
Stella, Jose—Accretia Capital LLC
Stelling, George—Marginxl Capital Partners LLC
Stelling, Krista—Marginxl Capital Partners LLC
Stemberg, Thomas—Highland Capital Partners LLC
Stenbaek, Claus—Keyhaven Capital Partners Ltd
Stenberg, Olle—Chalmers Innovation
Stenberg, Scott—Innoventures Capital Partners
Stencel, Daniel—Pegasus Capital Advisors LP
Stengel, Brian—Waller Capital Partners LLC
Stenlund, Henrik—Vostok Emerging Finance Ltd
Stento, Gregory—Baml Capital Access Funds Management LLC
Stenton, Raymond—NorthEdge Capital LLP
Stephan, Scholl—S Kap Unternehmensbeteiligungs GmbH & Co KG
Stephens, Emily—Oaktree Capital Management LP
Stephens, John—EMAlternatives LLC
Stephens, P. Bart—Blockchain Capital
Stephens, W. Bradford—Blockchain Capital
Stephenson, Charles—Southwest Middle Market M&A
Stephenson, Gabe—Gryphon Investors Inc
Stephenson, Napoleon—Hamilton Lane Advisors LLC
Stephenson, Thomas—Verge Fund
Sterenberg, Daniel—Carlyle Group LP
Stern, Adam—Acas LLC
Stern, Adam—Crescent Capital Group LP
Stern, Adam—Spencer Trask Ventures Inc
Stern, Craig—Riverside Partners LLC
Stern, Daniel—Reservoir Capital Group LLC
Stern, David—Clearstone Venture Management Services LLC
Stern, Ernest—TRG Management LP
Stern, Howard—Northwestern Mutual Capital LLC
Stern, Jeffrey—Forum Capital Partner
Stern, Jonathan—Fundamental Advisors LP
Stern, Lee—Levine Leichtman Capital Partners Inc
Stern, Mitchell—Dresner Capital Resources Inc
Stern, Paul—Golub Capital Master Funding LLC
Stern, Paul—Wharton Equity Partners LLC
Stern, Peter—Morrison & Foerster LLP
Stern, Phil—Fairbridge Venture Partners
Stern, Robert—Morrison & Foerster LLP
Stern, Ronald—Stern Partners Inc
Stern, Ross—Summit Partners LP
Stern, Todd—Capital Point Partners LLC
Stern, William—Morrison & Foerster LLP
Sternberg, Menachem—Eagle Trading Systems Inc
Sternheimer, Philip—Hellman & Friedman LLC
Stetson, Chuck—PEI Funds LLC
Steuart, John—Prolog Ventures
Steve, Matt—Tecum Capital Partners
Stevenin, Frederic—PAI Partners SAS
Stevens, Blake—180 Degree Capital Corp
Stevens, C. Scotland—OrbiMed Advisors LLC
Stevens, Jeff—Accretia Capital LLC
Stevens, Jeff—Anacapa Partners, L.P.
Stevens, Jeff—Anacapa Partners, L.P.
Stevens, Richard—Mill Creek Capital Advisors LLC
Stevens, Scott—Pamlico Capital Management LP
Stevens, Sean—Norwest Mezzanine Partners
Stevens, Taylor—Morrison & Foerster LLP
Stevens, William—Westerkirk Capital Inc
Stevenson, Gary—MB VENTURE PARTNERS L L C
Stevenson, James—ABS Capital Partners, Inc.
Stevenson, Jeffrey—Veronis Suhler Stevenson LLC
Stevenson, Lawrence—Clearspring Capital Partners
Stevenson, Sharon—Okapi Venture Capital LLC
Stewart, Alistair—Allon Therapeutics Inc
Stewart, Andrew—Arrowhead Mezzanine LLC
Stewart, Brian—Levine Leichtman Capital Partners Inc
Stewart, Donald—Spire Capital Partners LP
Stewart, E. Jack—Venture Capital Fund of New England
Stewart, Eric—Method Advisors LLC
Stewart, Hugh—Shackleton Ventures Ltd
Stewart, James—HPEF Capital Partners Ltd
Stewart, James—True Ventures LLC
Stewart, John—AllegisCyber
Stewart, John—Arc Financial Corp.
Stewart, John—Monomoy Capital Partners LLC
Stewart, Michael—Carlyle Group LP
Stewart, Michael—Stellex Capital Management LP
Stewart, Richard—Bramdean Asset Management LLP
Stewart, Robert—Spring Capital Partners
Stewart, Stephen—Mckenna Gale Capital Inc
Stewart, Victoria—Abingworth Management Ltd
Stewart, Will—Asia Pacific Ventures
Steyer, Thomas—Hellman & Friedman LLC
Steyn, David—AllianceBernstein LP
Steyn, Howard—Catterton Partners Corp
Stickney, Andrew—Vermont Center for Emerging Technologies
Stiefel, Elliot—Palisade Capital Management LLC
Stienes, David—LLR Partners Inc
Stier, Ronald—Arcady Capital Company
Stiff, Jamie—Genesys Capital Partners Inc
Stiff, Jamie—Genesys Capital Partners Inc
Stigge, Mary—Treetop Ventures Inc
Still, George—Norwest Venture Partners
Stillman, Matthew—PROfounders Capital Ltd
Stilman, Randy—Hamilton Lane Advisors LLC
Stimson, Keith—Gryphon Investors Inc
Stinton, Dale—Second Century Ventures LLC
Stirling, Colin—Spirit Capital Partners Llp
Stirnberg, Tobias—Milbank Tweed Hadley & Mccloy LLP
Stirton, Bryce—Responder Ventures LLC
Stitch, Katie—W Capital Management LLC
Stitou, Abdeltif—Silk Invest Ltd
Stitt, William—MTS Health Partners LP
Stjernfeldt, Carl—Castile Ventures
Stobo, John—ABS Capital Partners, Inc.
Stock, Justin Michael—Morrison & Foerster LLP
Stockner, Werner—S Partner Kapital AG
Stockton, John—Autotech Management LLC
Stockton, Robert—White Oak Equity Partners LLC
Stockwell, Geoffrey—Blackstone Group LP
Stoddard, Thomas—Blackstone Group LP
Stoddart, James—Undisclosed Firm
Stoebe, Konrad—Warburg Pincus LLC
Stoeckemann, Klaus—Peppermint VenturePartners GmbH
Stoeckle, Greg—WL Ross & Co LLC
Stoek, Thomas—Premium Equity Partners GmbH
Stoessel, Francois—GMT Communications Partners LLP
Stoesser, Nils—Arle Heritage LLP
Stoesser, Nils—Candover Investments PLC
Stoffer, Jason—Maveron LLC
Stojkovich, Mio—Matthew Pritzker Company LLC
Stok, Kees—KPN Ventures BV
Stokes, Iain—Terra Firma Capital Partners Ltd
Stokes, John—Real Ventures
Stokes, Richard—HIG Capital LLC
Stolar, Frederic—Sagard SAS
Stolbach, Ben—Insight Equity Holdings LLC
Stoll, Peter—Blackstone Group LP
Stolle, Bryan—Mohr Davidow Ventures
Stolpman, Aaron—CMBIgroup
Stoltz, Joseph—Median Fund PTY Ltd
Stonberg, David—Neuberger Berman LLC
Stone, Brent—ABRY Partners LLC
Stone, Jeffery—Wakabayashi Fund LLC
Stone, Jeffrey—Speyside Equity LLC
Stone, Jeremy—Sun Capital Partners Inc
Stone, Lorra—IDG Ventures USA
Stone, Mark—Gores Group LLC
Stone, Matthew—Monitor Clipper Partners LLC
Stone, Max—D E Shaw & Co LP
Stone, Nicholas—Cyprium Investment Partners LLC

2574

Stone, Paul—5AM Ventures LLC
Stone, Sheldon—Oaktree Capital Management LP
Stoneberg, David—NB Private Equity Partners Ltd
Stonecipher, Charles—Trilogy Equity Partners Llc
Stonehill, David—Carlyle Group LP
Stoner, Chelsea—Battery Ventures LP
Stoner, Chelsea—Battery Ventures LP
Stoner, Elizabeth—MPM Capital LLC
Stoner, Mark—Bayou City Energy LP
Stoner, Thomas—Econergy International Corp
Storch, Christian—Clayton Dubilier & Rice LLC
Storch, Eric—Blackstone Group LP
Storch, Eric—Oak Hill Advisors LP
Storchak, Anton—RT-Invest OOO
Storey, Jeffrey—CenturyLink Inc
Storey, Mark—Alcuin Capital Partners LLP
Stork, Ryan—BlackRock Inc
Storrow, Jamie—Northleaf Capital Partners Ltd
Story, Jason—Hangar Ventures LLC
Story, John—Catalyst Investment Managers Pty, Ltd.
Stott, Allen—JPB Partners LLC
Stott, David—Wind Point Advisors LLC
Stott, Janet—TL Ventures Inc
Stott, Tony—Midven Ltd
Stoupe, Louise—Morrison & Foerster LLP
Stout, C. Morris—Swander Pace Capital LLC
Stowater, Tyler—Bluestem Capital Partners
Stowe, Richard—Health Enterprise Partners LP
Stowell, Jeff—Royal Street Investment and Innovation Center LLC
Stowell, Mike—Arris Ventures LLC
Stracke, Tim—Target Partners GmbH
Straface, Nancy—Bessemer Venture Partners
Straface, Samuel—Pittsburgh Life Sciences Greenhouse
Strafehl, Richard—Meridius Capital
Strain, Christian—Summit Partners LP
Strain, Hilary—Wing Venture Capital
Strait, Richard—Northwestern Mutual Capital LLC
Strand-Nielsen, Frode—FSN Capital Partners AS
Strandberg, Goran—Verdane Capital Advisors AS
Strandberg, Steven—Westbridge Ventures LLC
Strandt, Randy—Beedie Capital Partners
Strang, Jim—Hamilton Lane Advisors LLC
Stranz, Michael—ARAX Capital Partners GmbH
Strasberg, Jeffrey—Ridgewood Capital Management LLC
Strascheg, Falk F.—Extorel GmbH
Strashna, Oksana—Horizon Capital Management
Strassberg, Matthew—Mid Europa Partners LLP
Strasser, Scott—GB Credit Partners LLC
Stratenwerth, Georg—Advent International Corp
Stratton, Oliver—Candover Investments PLC
Stratton, Ryan—HGGC LLC
Stratton, Ryan—Tower Arch Capital LLC
Strauch, Mark—Alpine Investors LP
Straus, Joan—Mill Creek Capital Advisors LLC
Straus, John—Jordan Company LP
Strauss, Noel—SF Holding Corp
Straut, Radu—Societatea de Investitii Financiare Banat Crisana SA
Strawbridge, James—Cooley LLP
Strawbridge, James—Worldview Technology Partners, Inc.
Stray, Bjorn—Northzone Ventures

Streator, James—Thomas Weisel Partners Group Inc
Street, David—Tembo Capital LLP
Street, Kevin—Darwin Private Equity LLP
Street, Paul—True North
Streeter, Jackson—Florida Institute for Commercialization of Public Research
Streetman, Ben—PTV Healthcare Capital
Streisfeld, Matthew—Oak HC/FT Partners LP
Streit Quintini, Renata—Felicis Ventures
Streit, Tim—Huron River Venture Partners LLC
Stresing, Christoph—MicroMountains Venture AG
Stringer, Christopher—Private Advisors LLC
Stringfellow, Martin—Indigo Capital LLP
Stringham, Tom—University Venture Fund
Stroebel, Birgit—newten Ventures GmbH
Stroeve, Jan—Varova BV
Stroh, John—Five Crowns Capital Inc
Strohm, David—Greylock Partners LLC
Strohmenger, Rainer—Wellington Partners GmbH
Strom, David—Whitecastle Investments Ltd
Strom, John—Haddington Ventures LLC
Stromberg, Per—ICA Gruppen AB
Strombom, Jon—Stewart Capital Management LLC
Stromholm, Fredrik—Altor Equity Partners AB
Stronach, Andrew—Sprott Resource Corp
Strong, David—Morrison & Foerster LLP
Strong, Frank—Trillium Group LLC
Strong, Geoffrey—Blackstone Group LP
Strong, Raymond—Evercore Inc
Strother, Mary—Athenian Fund Management Inc
Strothman, Peter—Water Street Healthcare Partners LLC
Stroub, Ryan—Thomas Weisel Partners Group Inc
Stroupe, T. Richard—Blu Venture Investors LLC
Struble, Robert—Blu Venture Investors LLC
Strug, Lowell—Evercore Inc
Strum, Derek—Clayton Dubilier & Rice LLC
Strycharz, Joseph—Mosaic Capital Partners LLC
Stuart, Bryan—Abundant Venture Partners LLC
Stuart, Lawrence—Quantum Capital
Stuart, Scott—Sageview Capital LP
Stubblefield, Richard—Lighthouse Capital Partners LP
Stubbs, Timothy—Sun Capital Partners Inc
Stubitz, Steven—Acas LLC
Stubler, Michael—Draper Triangle Ventures LP
Stuck, Bart—Signal Lake Management LLC
Stuck, Barton—Signal Lake Management LLC
Stuckert, Ryan—Siguler Guff & Company LP
Stuckey, Robert—Carlyle Group LP
Studd, Thomas—Vitruvian Partners LLP
Studdard, Jay—MavenHill Capital
Studdard, John—Linsalata Capital Partners Inc
Studzinski, John—Blackstone Group LP
Stukalo, Mikhail—Svarog Capital Advisors LTD
Stulberger, Adam—Tailwind Capital Partners LP
Stulberger, Adam—Thomas Weisel Partners Group Inc
Stull, Steven—Advantage Capital Partners
Stultz, Elliot—Allstate Private Equity
Stummer, Raimund—Fronteris Consulting AG
Stump, Jeffrey—Andreessen Horowitz LLC
Stump, Jeremy—Merit Capital Partners IV LLC
Stunkel, Michael—Springstar GmbH

Stuntz, Mayo—Pilot Group LP
Sturek, David—BelHealth Investment Partners LLC
Sturgeon, Peter—Sorenson Capital Partners LP
Sturgill, Jerry—Headwaters BD LLC
Sturgis, Fred—Resurgens Technology Partners LLC
Sturiale, Nick—Ignition Ventures Management LLC
Sturiale, Nick—Ignition Ventures Management LLC
Sturm, Timothy—Harwood Capital LLP
Sturmer, Andre—Trivest Trium Investments (Pty) Ltd
Styles, Arden—Business Instincts Group
Su, Alan—Carlyle Group LP
Su, David—Norwest Venture Partners
Su, Jane—Blum Capital Partners LP
Su, Jeffrey—Mingly Capital
Su, Jiang—Beijing Holch Investment Management, Ltd.
Su, Paul—3i Group PLC
Su, Weichou—StepStone Group LP
Su, Yingqi—Cybernaut (China) Venture Capital Management Co Ltd
Su, Zhao Frank—Bain Capital Inc
Suan, Lim Lek—Aif Capital Asia Iii LP
Suarez, Inoki—Varagon Capital Partners LP
Suarez, Jose—Investor Growth Capital AB
Suarez, Jose—Investor Growth Capital Inc
Subhedar, Sanjay—Storm Ventures Inc
Subotousky, Santiago—Emergence Capital Partners
Subramaniam, N.—Baring Private Equity Asia Ltd
Subramaniam, Somasundaram—New Science Ventures LLC
Subramanian, Anand—Macquarie Capital Alliance Management Pty Ltd
Subramanian, Anand—Macquarie Capital Markets Canada Ltd
Subramanian, Bharath—Capital Z Partners Ltd
Subramanian, Bharti—Teakwood Capital LP
Subramanian, Biswajit—Providence Equity Partners LLC
Subramanian, Ishwar—Axon Partners Group Investment
Subramanian, K. G.—Nexus Venture Partners
Subramanian, K. Ganapathy—Jumpstartup Fund Advisors Pvt Ltd
Such, Craig—Stratim Capital LLC
Suchodolski, Sergio—Arlon Group LLC
Suckling, Mark—Digital Media Partners Pte Ltd
Sud, Atul—EFG Wealth Management India Pvt Ltd
Sudeck, William—Solomon Global Holdings Inc
Sudo, Robert—Providence Equity Partners LLC
Suel, Jay—Sorenson Capital Partners LP
Suel, Patrick—Panasonic Venture Group
Suen, Jacquelyn—Farallon Capital Management LLC
Suffredini, Peter—Jordan Company LP
Sufrin, Zachary—Atlas Holdings FRM LLC
Sugar, Daniel—Veritas Capital Fund Management LLC
Sugarman, Mark—MHS Capital Management LLC
Sugden, Chris—Edison Partners
Sugden, Christopher—Edison Partners
Sugimoto, Tomoya—Longreach Group Ltd
Sugimoto, Yuji—Bain Capital Inc
Suh, Alexander—California Technology Ventures LLC
Suh, Alexander—Jacobs Capital Group LLC
Suh, Don—SkyLake Investment & Co
Suhk, Ho Cheol—KDB Capital Corp

2575

Suit, Dickson—Ironwood Investment Management LLC
Sujan, Suvir—Nexus Venture Partners
Sujitno, Jeff—Mckenna Gale Capital Inc
Sukhatme, Mayukh—Apple Tree Partners
Sulger, Justin—AnaCap Financial Partners Llp
Suliman, Fawzia—First South Investment Managers (Pty) Ltd
Sullens, Stephens—Blackstone Group LP
Sullivan, Carol—Jolimont Capital Pty Ltd
Sullivan, Chris—Blackstone Group LP
Sullivan, Christopher—MVC Capital Inc
Sullivan, David—Castle Island Partners LLC
Sullivan, Donald—Greylock Partners LLC
Sullivan, Graham—American Industrial Partners
Sullivan, Gregory—Friend Skoler & Co. LLC
Sullivan, Jeanne—StarVest Partners LP
Sullivan, John—Capgen Financial Group LP
Sullivan, John—Foundation Medical Partners LP
Sullivan, Kevin—Riverside Partners LLC
Sullivan, Mark—Linden LLC
Sullivan, Mel—Framestore Ventures
Sullivan, Michael—Forest Hill Partners LLC
Sullivan, Michael—Prophet Equity LLC
Sullivan, Michael—Westshore Capital Partners LP
Sullivan, Rick—Gainline Capital Partners, L.P.
Sullivan, Rick—Lincolnshire Management Inc
Sullivan, Robert—Oaktree Capital Management LP
Sullivan, Sean—Antares Capital Corp
Sullivan, Susan—Fulham & Co Inc
Sullivan, Thomas—Glengary LLC
Sullivan, Tim—Oceanic Partners Inc
Sullivan, Timothy—Madison Dearborn Partners LLC
Sullivan, William—Torch Hill Investment Partners LLC
Sumers, Gary—Blackstone Group LP
Summe, Gregory—Carlyle Group LP
Summe, Marc—Hadley Capital
Summerhayes, Mark—RMB Investment Advisory Pty Ltd
Summers, William—Glengary LLC
Sumner, Martin—Carlyle Group LP
Sun, Anthony—Aisling Capital LLC
Sun, Bing—Boxin Capital
Sun, Chen—Shenzhen Green Pine Capital Partners Co Ltd
Sun, Dayi—Jade Investment Consulting (Shanghai) Co Ltd
Sun, Dongsheng—Shenzhen Capital Group Co Ltd
Sun, Elaine—Evercore Inc
Sun, Guoxiang—DT Capital Partners
Sun, Henry—Pacific Enterprise Capital LLC
Sun, Hui—Shenzhen Ruiying Zhuoyue Capital Management Partnership (LP)
Sun, Jeffrey—MDB Capital Group LLC
Sun, Jianjun—Asia Mezzanine Capital Advisers Ltd
Sun, Jing—Sparkland Capital
Sun, Jiping—CAC Capital Management Co Ltd
Sun, Jiping—China Venture Capital Co Ltd
Sun, Jiyuan—Carlyle Group LP
Sun, Jungeng—Shenzhen Hongshisan Capital Co Ltd
Sun, Liqing—Shenzhen Green Pine Capital Partners Co Ltd
Sun, Paul—Gridiron Capital LLC
Sun, Qiang Chang—Warburg Pincus LLC
Sun, Ruikun—Qiming Venture Partners Ii LP

Sun, Tao—Providence Equity Partners LLC
Sun, Xidong—Shanghai Zhengsailian Venture Capital Management Co Ltd
Sun, Yi—Horsley Bridge Partners LLC
Sun, Yingzhe—Richlink International Capital Co Ltd
Sun, Yizheng—China Merchants Securities Co Ltd
Sun, Yonghong—Hony Capital Beijing Co Ltd
Sun, Zhenwu—Shanghai Beyond Binghong Equity Investment Management Co Ltd
Sundar, S. G. Shyam—IDFC Alternatives Ltd
Sunday, James—Landmark Partners Inc
Sunde, Peter—Ferd Capital Partners AS
Sunderland, Neil—Adinvest AG
Sundstrom, Mirja—MB Rahastot Oy
Sundstrom, Tove—Nord Kapitalforvaltning AS
Sundstrom, Vilhelm—Axcel Industriinvestor A/S
Sung, Jeffrey—Method Advisors LLC
Sunho, Choi—Corstone Corp
Sunol, Rafael—Alta Partners Capital
Sunstein, Steven—Waveland Capital Group LLC
Suonenlahti, Mikko—Draper Esprit PLC
Superina, Nick—Questmark Partners LP
Surer, Thibault—Astorg Partners SAS
Suri, Monish—Prime Technology Ventures NV
Suriya, Abdul—ICICI Venture Funds Management Company Ltd
Surma, Karl E.—Schilling Unternehmensbeteiligung GmbH
Suruta, Kazuhiko—Daiwa Corporate Investment Co Ltd
Survis, Gary—Insight Venture Partners LLC
Susan, Lior—Formation 8 Partners LP
Suse, Philip—Baker & McKenzie LLP
Suslak, Neil—Braemar Energy Ventures LP
Sussebach, Karl—CtechBA Pty Ltd
Sussman, Philip—Channel Group LLC, The
Sussman, Robert—Highlander Partners LP
Sussner, Heiner—Miramar Venture Partners L P
Suster, Mark—Launchpad LA Inc
Suster, Mark—Upfront Ventures
Suter, Joachim—Pavilion Alternatives Group Ltd
Suter, Johannes—SVC-AG fuer KMU Risikokapital
Sutherland, David—Middleburg Capital Development Ltd
Sutherland, Jason—Brazos Private Equity Partners LLC
Sutherland, Nikola—Duke Street Capital Ltd
Sutherland, William—Kensington Capital Partners Ltd
Sutka, Joe—BlackRock Inc
Sutphin, Paul—Waud Capital Partners LLC
Sutter, Martin—EW Healthcare Partners
Sutter, William—Hopewell Ventures
Suttin, Adam—J.W.Childs Associates LP
Sutton, Brett—Affinity Equity Partners HK Ltd
Sutton, Douglas—Huron Capital Partners LLC
Suurmunne, Vesa—Nordic Mezzanine Ltd
Suzuki, Aisaku—Integral Corp
Suzuki, Hiroshi—Mizuho Capital Co Ltd
Suzuki, Kenji—Works Capital Inc
Suzuki, Masahiro—Autotech Management LLC
Suzuki, Nobutake—Global Brain Corp
Svardstrom, Jakob—KTH-Chalmers Capital KB
Svensson, Anders—ICA Gruppen AB
Svider, Raymond—BC Partners LLP

Svihovsky, Jaromir—Rockaway Capital SE
Svoboda, John—Svoboda Capital Partners LLC
Svrluga, Bradley—Primary Venture Partners
Swackhamer, Michael—Princeton Ventures Management LLC
Swagar, Ryan—venture51 Capital Fund LLP
Swail, Glen—TOM Capital Associates Inc
Swain, Cassandra—Morrison & Foerster LLP
Swaminathan, Guhan—Virgo Capital
Swamy, Jaganath—Ananta Capital
Swan, Cheryl—Canada Pension Plan Investment Board
Swan, Jed—Drydock Ventures LP
Swan, Kevin—Water Street Healthcare Partners LLC
Swan, Kevin—iNovia Capital Inc
Swani, Sanjay—Welsh Carson Anderson & Stowe
Swann, Richard—Inflexion PLC
Swann, Thomas—First Analysis Corp
Swanson, Brad—Developing World Markets Inc
Swanson, Chuck—SAIL Capital Partners LLC
Swanson, David—Anholt (USA) LLC
Swanson, David—Antares Capital Corp
Swanson, Mark—Lane Five Ventures LLC
Swanson, Matthew—Ridgewood Capital Management LLC
Swanson, Paul—LEGEND PARTNERS I L P
Swart, Gregory—Farallon Capital Management LLC
Swartling, Karl—Sixth Swedish National Pension
Swartz, James—Accel Partners & Co Inc
Swartz, Robert—Hicks Equity Partners LLC
Swartzman, Steven—C3 Capital LLC
Sweedler, William—Tengram Capital Partners LLC
Sweeney, Christopher—Water Street Healthcare Partners LLC
Sweeney, Kevin—Carlyle Group LP
Sweeney, Ryan—Accel Partners & Co Inc
Sweeney, Thecla—Birch Hill Equity Partners Management Inc
Sweet, Andrew—Rhone Capital LLC
Sweet, Tony—Derwent London PLC
Sweet-Escott, Tom—Exponent Private Equity LLP
Sweeting, James—Investcorp Bank BSC
Swenberg, Scot—CID Capital Inc
Swenson, David—SSM Partners LP
Swenson, Ingrid—Bertram Capital Management LLC
Swenson, Jeff—Thomas H Lee Partners LP
Swenson, Ron—Western Technology Investment
Swift, Jack—Crestone Capital LLC
Swift, Jack—Northern Lights Capital Group LLC
Swift, Robert—Stirling Square Capital Partners Lp
Swildens, Hans—Industry Ventures LLC
Swildens, Hans—Industry Ventures LLC
Swimmer, Ted—Fidus Capital LLC

Swinand, Andrew—Abundant Venture Partners LLC
Swindell, James—Evercore Inc
Swirski, George—Abris Capital Partners Sp zoo
Sy, Alice—Small Business Guarantee and Finance Corporation
Syburg, John—Blackthorne Partners, Ltd.
Sydow, Jason—Questmark Partners LP
Syed, Tanzeen—Great Hill Equity Partners LLC
Sykes, Howard—Global Infrastructure Holdings
Sykes, Paul—Capitau Advisory Ltd
Sykes, Toby—EW Healthcare Partners

Sykora, Ben–Bow River Capital Partners LLC
Sylvester, Mark–Invenshure LLC
Sylvester, Robert–Speyside Equity LLC
Sym-Smith, C. Ian–Ventana Capital Management LP
Sym-Smith, David–Mobility Ventures LLC
Syme, Kirk–Weston Presidio Capital
Symington, Timothy–Invent Ventures Inc
Symon, Warren–Newbury Partners LLC
Symondson, David–Electra Private Equity Plc
Symons, Richard–Uniseed Management Pty Ltd
Synnergren, Jonas–Cevian Capital AB
Syron, Brendan–Scout Ventures LLC
Sysoyev, Yevgen–AVentures Capital TOV
Sywolski, Bob–JMI Management Inc
Syz, Christoph–Zurmont Madison Management AG
Szalai, Tamas–Bancroft Group Ltd
Szalony, Johann–WKBG Wiener Kreditbuergschafts und Beteiligungsbank AG
Szasz, Margit–COVENT Toke Befekteto Zartkoruen Mukodo Rt
Szczepanski, Przemek–Syntaxis Capital Unternehmens und Finanzierungsberatung GmbH
Szczolek, Hubert–Black Pearls VC SA
Sze, David–Greylock Partners LLC
Sze, Eddy–Csfb Private Equity Advisers
Szekasy, Nicolas–Kaszek Ventures I LP
Szekely, David–Whitestar Capital Ltd
Szekely, Les–Equity Venture Partners Pty Ltd
Szigethy, Andrea–Morgan Creek Capital Management LLC
Szigeti, Mihaly–Crosslink Capital Inc
Szoke, Istvan–CVC Capital Partners Ltd
Szonyi, Andrew–First Nations Equity Inc
Szu, Candice–Carlyle Group LP
Szymanski, Maciej–Waterland Private Equity Investments BV
Szymanski, Pawel–Icentis Capital Sp z o o
Ta-Ngoc, Luc–Invus Group LLC
Tabacinic, Moris–NCH Capital Inc
Tabbara, Marwan–Stratum WLL
Tabbiner, Louise–Providence Equity Partners LLC
Taber, Gregory–Linsalata Capital Partners Inc
Taber, Mark–Great Hill Equity Partners LLC
Taber, Mark–Great Hill Equity Partners LLC
Tabet, Karim–Providence Equity Partners LLC
Tabet, Sylvio–Colony Capital LLC
Tabib, Hamid–Siguler Guff & Company LP
Tablis, Eugene–Bergen Asset Management LLC
Tabors, David–Battery Ventures LP
Tabu, Jay–HGGC LLC
Tabu, Soichiro–Oaktree Capital Management LP
Tabus, Valentin–Axxess Capital Partners SA
Tacke, Kelly–Capital Southwest Corp
Tadewaldt, Millie–Sandbox Industries LLC
Tadler, Richard–TA Associates Management LP
Taetle, Alan–NMP Management Corp
Taeyub, Kim–Standard Chartered Private Equity Ltd
Tafintsev, Denis–Horizon Capital Management
Tagaya, Osamu–ANGEL CAPITAL NETWORK INC
Taggar, Harj–Y Combinator Inc
Tagliaferri, Mark–GI Partners
Taha, Emad–Infra Capital Investments PJSC
Tahta, Richard–Episode 1 Ventures LLP
Tai, Augustus–Trinity Ventures LLP
Tai, David–China Export & Credit Insurance Corp

Tai, David–ChinaRun Capital Partners Chongqing Ltd
Tai, William–Charles River Ventures LLC
Taillefer, Alexandre–XPND Capital
Tait, Michael–Newstone Capital Partners LLC
Takahashi, Hideya–Oaktree Capital Management LP
Takahashi, Shinichi–Innovation Network Corporation of Japan
Takahashi, Yoshimi–SBI Investment Korea Co Ltd
Takamatsu, Takehisa–Lone Star Fund Ltd
Takamiya, Shinichi–Globis Capital Partners & Co
Takano, Makoto–Genuine Startups KK
Takao, Kentaro–Oaktree Capital Management LP
Takashi, Yoshida–Okasan Venture Capital Co Ltd
Takashina, Tadashi–Ant Capital Partners Co Ltd
Takasu, Narutake–Morrison & Foerster LLP
Takasugi, Tadashi–Mitsubishi International Corp
Takeda, Goro–Sofinnova Ventures Inc
Takei, Mayumi–Active Investment Partners
Takeuchi, Seiji–Toho Bank Ltd
Takian, Randy–Avenue Capital Group LLC
Takita, John–Itochu Technology Inc
Takke, Christina–Forbion Capital Partners
Talalla, Dominic–Trellis Capital Corp
Talbot, Jean-Sebastien–GMT Communications Partners LLP
Talbot, Kevin–Rbc Capital Partners
Talbot, Kevin–Relay Ventures
Talbott, Devin–Enlightenment Capital
Taliaferro, S.S.–Private Advisors LLC
Tall, Spencer–AllegisCyber
Tallering, Kenneth–Industrial Opportunity Partners LLC
Talley, Timothy–Columbia Partners Private Capital
Tallur, Inder–BelHealth Investment Partners LLC
Talone, Joao–Magnum Industrial Partners
Talone, Joao–Magnum Industrial Partners SL
Talwatte, Gehan–Lyceum Capital
Tam, Bing Chung–Fidelity Growth Partners Asia
Tamagnini, Maurizio–CDP Equity SpA
Tamashunas, Bob–Seaport Capital LLC
Tamashunas, Bob–Seaport Capital LLC
Tambellini, Matthew–Blackstone Group LP
Tambourin, Pierre–Sem Genopole SAEM
Tamburi, David–Health Enterprise Partners LP
Taminian, Hagop–Silicon Badia
Tamir, Ron–Kaedan Capital LLC
Tamke, George–Clayton Dubilier & Rice LLC
Tammineed, Anil–Angeleno Group Investors LLC
Tamoiunas, Rokas–StartupHighway
Tamura, Hiro–Atomico Ventures
Tan Climaco, Gloria–Argosy Partners, Inc.
Tan, Albert–Haynes and Boone LLC
Tan, Angela–Crest Capital Partners
Tan, Bien Chuan–OWW Capital Partners Pte Ltd
Tan, Binxian–Shenzhen Green Pine Capital Partners Co Ltd
Tan, Boon Wah–Sembawang Capital Pte Ltd
Tan, Chow Boon–Credence Partners Pte Ltd
Tan, Christopher–Financial Technology Ventures
Tan, Collwyn–Hamilton Lane Advisors LLC
Tan, Daren–Golden Equator Capital Pte Ltd
Tan, David–Crest Capital Partners
Tan, Edmund–Zana Capital Pte Ltd
Tan, Edwin–Capital Partners, Inc.

Tan, Eric–CID Group
Tan, Frankie–iGlobe Partners Ltd
Tan, Glendon–Crest Capital Partners
Tan, Gregory–Morrison & Foerster LLP
Tan, Huidong–Shanghai Fortune United Investment Group Co Ltd
Tan, James–L Catterton Asia
Tan, Joan–Sixpoint Partners LLC
Tan, Jui–Bluerun Ventures LP
Tan, Keith–Dymon Asia Equity Pte Ltd
Tan, Kenneth–Southern Capital Group Pte Ltd
Tan, Khai–Bridgepoint Advisers Ltd
Tan, Kim Seng–Tembusu Partners Pte Ltd
Tan, Kim Song–Frontier Investment & Capital Advisors Pte Ltd
Tan, Kit Jong–Natixis Private Equity SA
Tan, Kurt–Artesian Capital Management Australia Pty Ltd
Tan, Nang Yong–Pama Ventura Indonesia PT
Tan, Peter–Skyven Asset Management Pte Ltd
Tan, Peter–Stone Canyon Industries LLC
Tan, Poh Heng–Blackstone Group LP
Tan, Ron–First Alverstone Partners Pte Ltd
Tan, Terence–Infotech Ventures Co Ltd
Tan, Thomas–CLSA Capital Partners HK Ltd
Tan, Tommy–Tc Capital Pte Ltd
Tan, Venantius–Morrison & Foerster LLP
Tan, Wan That–Aventures Capital Management Pte Ltd
Tan, Wenqing–Shenzhen Oriental Fortune Capital Co Ltd
Tan, Yinglan–Sequoia Capital India
Tan, Zhengjun–Beijing Tianxing Chuanglian Investment Management Co., Ltd.
Tan, Zhi–Northern Light Venture Capital Development Ltd
Tan, Zhihu–New Access Capital
Tanaka, Akio–e.ventures
Tanaka, Akio–eVenture Capital Partners GmbH
Tanaka, H. Jumbo–Strategic Value Partners LLC
Tanaka, Josue–European Bank for Reconstruction and Development
Tanaka, Ryan–Diversis Capital LLC
Tanaka, Susumu–Worldview Technology Partners, Inc.
Tanamli, Sharif–Ht Capital Advisors LLC
Tanczos, Peter–Euroventures Capital Tanacsado Kft
Tandon, Manas–Tpg Growth LLC
Tandon, Nikhilesh–Jasper Ridge Partners LP
Tandon, Rajat–Proprium Capital Partners LP
Tandon, Shailendra–Asia Pacific Healthcare Advisors Pvt Ltd
Tandy, Joshua–Nexo Capital Partners
Taneja, Hemant–General Catalyst Partners LLC
Tanenbaum, James–Morrison & Foerster LLP
Tang, Bin–Shanghai Fosun Capital Investment Management Co Ltd
Tang, BoBo–Pride Investments Group Ltd
Tang, Chi Chun–China Everbright Ltd
Tang, Chong–Phoenix Asset Management Co Ltd
Tang, Dansong–Shenzhen Weixi Investment Partnership Co Ltd
Tang, Hamilton–CDIB Capital International Corp
Tang, Hamilton–Shanghai SMC Capital Co Ltd
Tang, Helen–Siguler Guff & Company LP

Pratt's Guide to Private Equity & Venture Capital Sources

Tang, Hongwei–Shenzhen Richland Investment Co Ltd
Tang, Jennifer–Avenue Capital Group LLC
Tang, Joe–Ventech SA
Tang, Kainan–Elevation China Capital
Tang, Kay Hua–Centurion Investment Management Pte Ltd
Tang, Lei–Spring Capital Asia Ltd
Tang, Miranda–CLSA Capital Partners HK Ltd
Tang, Samuel–Montauk TriGuard Management Inc
Tang, Tin Lok–Lunar Capital Management Ltd
Tang, Xueqing–Purple Horse Fund
Tang, Zhimin–Shenzhen Tiantu Capital Management Center LP
Tang, Zhongcheng–Shenzhen Co-Win Venture Capital Investments Ltd
Tang, Zurong–Ivy Capital Ltd
Tange, Masaru–Draper Nexus Venture Partners LLC
Tangen, Darren–Colony Capital LLC
Tango, Jo–Kepha Partners
Tanguy, Patrick–Wendel SE
Taniguchi, Koshiro–Daiwa Corporate Investment Co Ltd
Tanimoto, Toru–Ant Capital Partners Co Ltd
Taniya, Mamoru–Genuine Startups KK
Taniyama, Koichiro–Innovation Network Corporation of Japan
Tanna, Akshay–Tpg Growth LLC
Tanne, Michael–Akkadian Ventures LLC
Tannenbaum, Jeff–Bluerun Ventures LP
Tanner, David–Arlon Group LLC
Tanner, David–Oaktree Capital Management LP
Tanner, Douglas–Milbank Tweed Hadley & Mccloy LLP
Tanner, William–Athenian Fund Management Inc
Tanner, William–Reservoir Venture Partners 2 LP
Tanno, Shinsuke–Toho Bank Ltd
Tanriover, Inan–Esas Holding AS
Tansey, Casey–U.S. Venture Partners
Tansey, Casey–U.S. Venture Partners
Tansey, Greg–Riverlake Partners LLC
Tanzer, David–Blackstone Group LP
Tanzi, Stefano–21 Centrale Partners SA
Tao, James–Houston Health Ventures LLC
Tao, Tang–Eastern Bell Venture Capital Co Ltd
Tao, Tao–Shenzhen Cornerstone of Entrepreneurial Cci Capital Ltd
Tao, Tina–Sinovation Ventures Ltd
Tao, Ye–Keytone Ventures
Tapp, James–KT Capital Management LLC
Tara, Matt–General Catalyst Partners LLC
Taragin, Bruce–Blumberg International Partners LLC
Tarantino, William–Morrison & Foerster LLP
Tarasov, Mikhail–UNITED FINANCIAL GROUP ASSET MANAGEMENT
Tarasov, Vadim–Altpoint Ventures LP
Tardif, Jean Paul–ID Capital
Tardif, Jean-Paul–Propulsion Ventures Inc
Tarini, Mark–ArcLight Capital Holdings LLC
Tarjanne, Artturi–Nexit Ventures Oy
Tarlowe, Jeff–Pharma Capital Ventures
Tarlton, Rosemary–Morrison & Foerster LLP
Tarnowski, Thomas–Summit Partners LP
Tarr, Bernard–Kinetic Ventures LLC
Tarr, Dick–MB VENTURE PARTNERS L L C

Tashev, Todor–Omidyar Network Commons LLC
Tashev, Todor–Omidyar Technology Ventures LLC
Tasker, Tim–Ernst & Young LLP
Tasso, Justin–Oak Hill Advisors LP
Tatarchevskiy, Bogdan–Developing World Markets Inc
Tate, David–Draper Esprit Secondaries LLP
Tate, Eric Akira–Morrison & Foerster LLP
Tate, Jordan–Montage Partners Inc
Tateno, Koichi–Unison Capital, Inc.
Tatsuoka, Keisuke–Global Brain Corp
Tatum, Alexander–Constitution Capital Partners LLC
Taub, Andrew–Catterton Partners Corp
Taube, Seth–Medley Capital LLC
Taubenfeld, David–Haynes and Boone LLC
Tauber, Jan–Genesis Capital sro
Taubman, Mark–Undisclosed Firm
Taufner, Michael–Alps Venture Capital GmbH
Taunt, Nigel–Impax Asset Management Ltd
Taura, Kyle–Kian Capital Partners LLC
Taussig, Alex–Highland Capital Partners LLC
Taussig, James–GF Capital Management & Advisors LLC
Tavel, Sarah–Greylock Partners LLC
Tavridis, Efstathios–Incubation for Growth SA
Tavridis, Stathis–Incubation for Growth SA
Taweel, Kevin–Accretia Capital LLC
Tawfik, Raouf–Qalaa Holdings SAE
Taxin, Julia–Grotech Ventures
Tay, Choon Chong–Vertex Venture Holdings Ltd.
Tayeh, David–Investcorp Bank BSC
Taylor, Allison–Invico Capital Corp
Taylor, Brain–Rizk Ventures LLC
Taylor, Brandon–Carlyle Group LP
Taylor, Brook–Vinacapital Investment Management Ltd
Taylor, Colin–Dlj Merchant Banking Partners
Taylor, Craig–Alloy Ventures Inc
Taylor, Diana–Wolfensohn & Company LLC
Taylor, Drew–Digitalis Ventures LLC
Taylor, Errol–Milbank Tweed Hadley & Mccloy LLP
Taylor, Gary–Knight s Bridge Capital Corp
Taylor, J.E.–Metropolitan Real Estate Equity Management LLC
Taylor, James–Gramercy Inc
Taylor, Jennifer Lee–Morrison & Foerster LLP
Taylor, Jo–Ontario Teachers' Pension Plan
Taylor, Jonathan–European Investment Bank
Taylor, Lawrence–Pfingsten Partners LLC
Taylor, Lucius–ArcLight Capital Holdings LLC
Taylor, Mark–Beringea LLC
Taylor, Martin–Vista Equity Partners LLC
Taylor, Matthew–Lombard Investments Inc
Taylor, Matthew–Rockpool Investments LLP
Taylor, Michael–Adams Street Partners LLC
Taylor, Mike–Teakwood Capital LP
Taylor, Paulette–Sanderling Ventures
Taylor, Peter–Duke Street Capital Ltd
Taylor, R. Keith–Carlyle Group LP
Taylor, Robert–Advent International Corp
Taylor, Robert–Centinela Capital Partners LLC
Taylor, Thomas–JLL Partners Inc
Taylor, Todd–Falfurrias Capital Partners LP
Taylor, William–Mountaineer Capital, L.P.
Taylor-Smith, Ralph–Battelle Ventures LP

Tayo-Aboaba, Yemisi–First Funds Ltd
Tchenguiz, Robert–Aletheia Partners Ltd
Tcherdakoff, Nicholas–Auriga Partners SA
Tcherdakoff, Nicholas–Telecom Technologies Transfert 3T SAS
Tchibanda, Mariam–Emerging Capital Partners
Teachout, Sarah–Haynes and Boone LLC
Teagle, Scott–Headwaters BD LLC
Teague, Jane–Florida Institute for Commercialization of Public Research
Tebbutt, Jerry–European Capital Financial Services Ltd
Teboul, Nicolas–Weinberg Capital Partners SAS
Tecce, Frederick–Cross Atlantic Capital Partners LLC
Tech, Mercedes–Hypatia Capital Group LLC
Tedeschi, Colin–Connecticut Innovations Inc
Tedesco, Greg–Abacus Private Equity Ltd
Tedesco, Peter–Olympus Partners
Tedesko, Jennifer–Atlantic-Pacific Capital Inc
Tedford, Alastair–Albion Investors LLC
Teeger, John–Founders Equity, Inc.
Teele, Brett–Mohr Davidow Ventures
Teele, Brett–Wildcat Venture Partners LLC
Teen, Timothy–Chart Venture Partners LP
Tefft, E. Lyndon–Commonfund Capital Inc
Tegan, Jennifer–Cayuga Venture Fund
Tegan, Jennifer–Cayuga Venture Fund
Tegenmark, Christian–Segulah Advisor AB
Tehi, Marlene–Evolution Capital Partners LLC
Tehranian, Terrence–Pioneer Point Partners LLP
Teich, Thomas–ArcLight Capital Holdings LLC
Teichert, Christian–Venista Ventures GmbH & Co KG
Teillon, Geoffrey–Pouschine Cook Capital Management LLC
Teillon, Marc–Vista Equity Partners LLC
Teitelbaum, David–Cerberus Capital Management LP
Teixeira Favaro, Felipe–Performa Investimentos Ltda
Tejani, Shams–Abacus Private Equity Ltd
Tejera, Carlos–Gala Capital Partners SL
Tekkora, Baran–Riverstone Holdings LLC
Teklu, Jonathan–Springstar GmbH
Tekten, Turker–Stratejik Yonetim Hizmetleri AS
Televantos, John–Arsenal Capital Management LLC
Televantos, John–Arsenal Capital Partners LP
Televantos, John–Arsenal Capital Partners LP
Teli, Sitar–Connect Ventures LLP
Tellegen, Nina–Doen Participaties BV
Teller, Sam–Launchpad LA Inc
Telles, Marcel–3G Capital Inc
Teltschik, Justin–Carlyle Group LP
Temam, Franck–PAI Partners SAS
Temperton, Ian–Climate Change Capital Ltd
Temple, Jeffrey–Morrison & Foerster LLP
Temple, Stephen–Asia Mezzanine Capital Advisers Ltd
Templeton, Chuck–S2G Ventures LLC
Templeton, Dougal–E3 Media Ltd
Templeton, Troy–Trivest Partners LP
Ten Have, Hendrik Jan–Standard Investment BV
Ten, Alexey–Kazyna Kapital Management AO
Tenbroek, James–Wind Point Advisors LLC
Teng, Nelson–Charter Life Sciences II L P
Tengku Hamzah, Mohd Fahmi–FirstFloor Capital Sdn Bhd

Tenhunen, Torsti–KoppiCatch Oy
Tennison, Glen–Dane Creek Capital Corp
Tensen, Olaf–AAC CAPITAL PARTNERS
Teo, Jonathan–General Catalyst Partners LLC
Teo, ShanMae–Providence Equity Partners LLC
Teplitsky, Michael–Wynnchurch Capital Ltd
Tepner, Harvey–WL Ross & Co LLC
Tepper, Robert–Third Rock Ventures LLC
Tepper, Yaniv–Angeleno Group Investors LLC
Teramoto, Wendy–WL Ross & Co LLC
Terazawa, Yukihiro–Morrison & Foerster LLP
Terbeek, Mark–Greycroft Partners LLC
Terekhov, Eugene–Pepperwood Partners LLC
Terhardt, Peter–S Refit AG
Terje Rian, Dag–Televenture Management As
Terkowitz, Ralph–ABS Capital Partners, Inc.
Terney, Lars–Nordic Capital
Terraneo, Sonja–Clayton Dubilier & Rice LLC
Terrasi, Kevin–Plymouth Venture Partners
Terrazas de la Cerda, Roberto–Nexxus Capital SA de CV
Terrentine, Tim–SWMF Life Science Venture Fund, L.P.
Terry, Barnaby–Elderstreet Investments Ltd
Terry, Clarence–Sun Capital Partners Inc
Terry, Eric–Haynes and Boone LLC
Terry, Josh–Highland Capital Management LP
Terry, Kenneth–Anholt (USA) LLC
Terry, Kenneth–Elysian Capital LLP
Terry, Sandie–Center For Innovative Technology
Tertzakian, Peter–Arc Financial Corp.
Terzic, Vjenceslav–Quaestus Private Equity doo
Teschke, Jeffrey–J.W.Childs Associates LP
Tesconi, Lee–Lexington Partners Inc
Teslia, Ken–Extreme Venture Partners Inc
Tesone, Emmanuel–354 Partners LLC
Tesseyman, Nick–European Bank for Reconstruction and Development
Tessitore, Tony–Gramercy Inc
Tessler, Daniel–Argentum Group LLC
Tessler, Lenard–Cerberus Capital Management LP
Teten, David–HOF Capital Inc
Teten, David–ff Venture Capital
Tetteroo, Ronald–Georgetown Venture Partners
Tetzlaff, Dirk–DMB Deutsche Mittelstandsbeteiligungs GmbH
Teufel, Mark–Resource Financial Corp
Tevanian, Avadis–Elevation Partners LP
Tewari, Gaurav–Highland Capital Partners LLC
Tewari, Gaurav–Sapphire Ventures LLC
Thacker, David–Greylock Partners LLC
Thaker, Sailesh–Sustainable Development Technology Canada
Thakker, Dharmesh–Battery Ventures LP
Thakker, Paresh–Evolvence Capital Ltd
Thakran, Ravi–L Catterton Asia
Thakur, Devindra–Investcorp Bank BSC
Thakur, Preet–Asia Pacific Healthcare Advisors Pvt Ltd
Thaler-Wolski, Christian–Wellington Partners GmbH
Thalmann, Oliver–Aravis SA
Thanapisitkul, Win–Taurus Ventures GP LLC
Thangaraj, Immanuel–EW Healthcare Partners
Thapar, Pankaj–Everstone Capital Management, Ltd.
Tharrington, Owen–Gridiron Capital LLC

Thathachari, Arun–Signal Hill Equity Partners
Thau, Stephen–Morrison & Foerster LLP
Thees, Anderson–Redpoint Eventures Consultoria Empresarial Ltda
Thees, Anderson–e.ventures
Thees, Anderson–eVenture Capital Partners GmbH
Theile-Ochel, Hubertus–Golding Capital Partners GmbH
Theiler, Gerwin–Capiton AG
Thek, Ray–Wasabi Ventures LLC
Thelin, Jean-Noel–LYRIQUE Srrl
Theodore, Terry–Wynnchurch Capital Ltd
Theorell Christofferson, Monalotte–Scope Capital Advisory AB
Theriault, Annie–Northwater Capital Management Inc
Thermond, Jeff–X/Seed Capital Management
Thesseling, Joost–CI Capital Partners LLC
Thet, Zaw–CrossCut Ventures Management LLC
Thexton, Kent–OMERS Ventures
Thibault, Chantal–OMERS Private Equity Inc
Thibault, De Saint Priest–Acofi Gestion SA
Thiel, Fred–Ventana Capital Management LP
Thiel, Peter–Founders Fund, The
Thiel, Peter–Valar Ventures Management LLC
Thiele-Sardina, Roy–HighBAR Ventures
Thielen, Rob–Elbrus Kapital OOO
Thiery, Marc–DPE Deutsche Private Equity GmbH
Thies, Mark–New Canaan Funding
Thimmaya, Arjun–Warburg Pincus LLC
Thiruvadi, S.–Canbank Venture Capital Fund Ltd
Thivessen, Manfred–Kapitalbeteiligungsgesellschaft NRW GmbH
Thlabanelo, Boitumelo–Bopa Moruo
Thodupunoori, Sridhar–JDRF International
Thoene, Max–Accel-KKR
Thole, Robert–Gilde Investment Management BV
Thoma, Carl–Thoma Bravo LLC
Thomann, Mark–Spiral Sun Ventures LLC
Thomann, Thierry–Ciclad Participations SAS
Thomas, Andrew–Stonebridge Partners LP
Thomas, Brett–CAVU Venture Partners, LLC
Thomas, Brian–Prudential Capital Group LP
Thomas, Chris–Fontinalis Partners LLC
Thomas, Christopher–Aterian Investment Management LP
Thomas, David–Court Square Capital Partners LP
Thomas, David–Intel Capital Corp
Thomas, David–Seneca Partners Ltd
Thomas, Ed–Karpreilly LLC
Thomas, Fritz–Oak Hill Advisors LP
Thomas, George–CapAleph Advisors India Pvt Ltd
Thomas, Greg–Westview Capital Partners LP
Thomas, J. Mikesell–Castle Creek Capital LLC
Thomas, James–Phoenix Equity Partners Ltd
Thomas, James–Thomas Mcnerney and Partners LLC
Thomas, Jason–Carlyle Group LP
Thomas, Joji–Baring Private Capital Asia Ltd
Thomas, Jonathan–Saybrook Capital LLC
Thomas, Joseph–Hovde Private Equity Advisors LLC
Thomas, Joseph–Svoboda Capital Partners LLC
Thomas, Katie–Mill Creek Capital Advisors LLC
Thomas, Lindsay–Morrison & Foerster LLP
Thomas, Mark–Monitor Clipper Partners LLC
Thomas, Milford–Syncom Management Co Inc

Thomas, Nigel Donald–Alpha Founders
Thomas, Oliver–Grafton Capital Ltd
Thomas, Paul–Gresham Llp
Thomas, Paul–Seraphim Capital (General Partner) LLP
Thomas, Robert–Osceola Capital Management LLC
Thomas, Roger–Rizk Ventures LLC
Thomas, Stephen–Bain Capital Inc
Thomas, T. Peter–Ata Ventures
Thomas, Tim–Bridgepoint Advisers II Ltd
Thomas, Timothy–Bridgepoint Advisers Ltd
Thomas, William–TGP Investments LLC
Thomassen, Lars–Axcel Industriinvestor A/S
Thomazi, Charles–Ontario Teachers' Pension Plan
Thomison, David–i2E, Inc
Thompson Motta, Roberto Moses–3G Capital Inc
Thompson, Andrew–Wafra Partners LLC
Thompson, Bennett–KRG Capital Management LP
Thompson, Bennett–Mountaingate Capital Management LP
Thompson, Blair–TDR Capital LLP
Thompson, David–Morgan Stanley Private Equity
Thompson, Donald–Sinclair Ventures Inc
Thompson, Eric–Greenspring Associates Inc
Thompson, Gerlinde–Oaktree Capital Management LP
Thompson, Hamlen–Westfield Capital Management Company LP
Thompson, Jeremy–ONCAP INVESTMENT PARTNERS L P
Thompson, Joseph–Alara Capital Partners LLC
Thompson, Kip–Portland Private Equity LP
Thompson, Marcus–Evercore Inc
Thompson, Matt–Skyview Capital LLC
Thompson, Matthew–Enhanced Equity Fund, L.P.
Thompson, Paul–Pamplona Capital Management LLP
Thompson, Paul–Transition Capital Partners
Thompson, Peter–OrbiMed Advisors LLC
Thompson, Philip–Alta Communications Inc
Thompson, Randy–Argon Venture Partners
Thompson, Rick–Four Rivers Partners LP
Thompson, Ryan–Lex Capital Management Inc
Thompson, Stephen–Brandon Capital Partners Pty Ltd
Thompson, Tom–Stratim Capital LLC
Thompson, Tom–WP Global Partners Inc
Thompson, Trey–Perella Weinberg Partners LP
Thomsen, Georgia–Capital Factory Properties LLC
Thomsen, Joanne–Ontario Centres of Excellence
Thomsen, Mikal–Trilogy Equity Partners Llc
Thomsic, Michael–Headwaters BD LLC
Thomson, Bryan–British Columbia Investment Management Corp
Thomson, John–Pulse Equity Partners LLC
Thomson, Robert–Pentech Ventures LLP
Thongchua, Pongpaichayont–Alpha Founders
Thonis, Michael–Charlesbank Capital Partners LLC
Thor, Chuan–Highland Capital Partners LLC
Thor, Chuan–Highland Capital Partners LLC
Thorarinsson, Smari–Nyskopunarsjodur
Thorburn, David–Clydesdale Bank PLC
Thoresen, Lars–Verdane Capital Advisors AS
Thorleifsson, Tellef–Northzone Ventures
Thorlund Haahr, Peter–VIA equity A/S

Pratt's Guide to Private Equity & Venture Capital Sources

Thorndike, Lanny–Century Capital Management / Massachusetts Inc
Thorndike, William–Accretia Capital LLC
Thorndike, William–Housatonic Partners Management Co Inc
Thorne, Christopher–Broadline Capital LLC
Thorne, Heather–Swander Pace Capital LLC
Thornell, Erik–Segulah Advisor AB
Thornton, Andrew–LBC Credit Partners Inc
Thornton, John–Austin Ventures
Thornton, John–San Shan Capital Partners Ltd
Thornton, John–Tregaron Capital Co LLC
Thornton, Matthew–Sixpoint Partners LLC
Thornton, Scott–Trust Company of the West
Thorp, Clay–Hatteras Venture Partners
Thorp, James–Aavin Equity Advisors LLC
Thorpe, Allen–Hellman & Friedman LLC
Thorpe, Andrew–Morrison & Foerster LLP
Thorsen, Jamie–BMO Capital Corp
Thorsen, Morten–Union Bancaire Privee Private Equity
Thorsen, Peter–Kirk & Thorsen Invest A/S
Thorsheim, Christopher–Falcon Investment Advisors LLC
Thrush, Allison–Fortress Investment Group LLC
Thuemmler, Andreas–Corporate Finance Partners CFP Beratungs GmbH
Thuet, Lawrence–Blackstone Group LP
Thukral, Nikhil–Catterton Partners Corp
Thum, Oliver–Elvaston Capital Management GmbH
Thum, Oliver–H2 Equity Partners BV
Thunelius, Gerald–Atlantic Asset Management LLC
Thurk, Paul–Arch Venture Partners LLC
Thurow, Ethan–Calera Capital Management Inc
Thurston, Julian–Morrison & Foerster LLP
Thuve, Anders–Verdane Capital Advisors AS
Thygesen, Jacob–Axcel Industriinvestor A/S
Thyssen, Erik–AlpInvest Partners BV
Tian, Esther–Broadhaven Capital Partners LLC
Tian, Jie–DragonVenture, Inc.
Tian, Joe–DT Capital Partners
Tian, Suning–Tianyun Ruihai Venture Capital Inc
Tian, Terry–GGV Capital
Tian, Yue–GEF Management Corp
Tibelius, Karl–Genome Canada
Tibshrany, Allen–City Capital Ventures LLC
Tichenor, Andrew–Blue Heron Capital LLC
Tichenor, Timothy–Barnard Associates, Inc.
Tichio, Robert–Riverstone Holdings LLC
Ticknor, Carolyn–Inflexion Partners
Tidwell, Brandon–Signal Peak Ventures
Tidwell, Ken–Carlyle Group LP
Tidwell, Kevin–GEF Management Corp
Tidwell, Mark–Haynes and Boone LLP
Tiemann, M. Shane–Kelso & Company LP
Tiemann, Shane–Veritas Capital Fund Management LLC
Tien-Hurter, Wen Sin–Grace Assets Management LLP
Tiernan, Declan–Oak Hill Advisors LP
Tierney, James–Trimaran Capital LLC
Tierney, Matthew–Aperture Venture Partners LLC
Tieu, Joana–Walden International
Tighe, Kenneth–India Venture Partners
Tigipko, Viktoriya–TA Venture

Tijerina, Teofilo–Cielo Management LLC
Tijerina, Teofilo–EDCO Ventures
Tikkanen, Klas–Nordic Capital
Tikker, Blair–KRG Capital Management LP
Tiktik, Ahmet–Islamic Development Bank
Tilander, Fredrik–Backstage Invest AB
Tilenius, Eric–Tilenius Investments
Tili, Marco–Garanzia Partecipazioni e Finanziamenti SpA
Till, David–Oakley Capital Ltd
Till, Michael–Actis LLP
Tillen, Alistair–Bridges Fund Management Ltd
Tilley, Brian–Dfw Capital Partners LP
Tilley, Josh–Morgan Creek Capital Management LLC
Tilly, Anne–Odyssee Venture SAS
Tilson, John–Brown Gibbons Lang & Company LLC
Timlin, James–Archipel Capital LLC
Timlin, Joe–Growth Works Capital Ltd
Timm, Spencer–XPV Capital Corp
Timmerman, William–Graham Partners Inc
Timmermans, Willem–Magellan Capital Partners Ltd
Timmis, Gerald–Valstone Partners LLC
Timoll, Garth–Top Tier Capital Partners LLC
Timor, Emanuel–Vertex Israel II Management Ltd
Timsit, Thierry–Astorg Partners SAS
Tindle, Glenn–Jog Capital Inc
Ting, Gary–Cnstar Capital Pte Ltd
Ting, Lindsay–Castanea Partners Inc
Ting, Simon–BOC International Holdings Ltd
Tingaud, Alain–Sofinnova Partners SAS
Tinholt, Peter–Oriens Capital
Tinker, John–Sandler Capital Management
Tinney, Paul–Wellrock Capital Partners LLC
Tipping, Stephen–Condor Capital Management Corp
Tippins, John–Stonewood Capital Management Inc
Tirabassi, Salvatore–M/C Venture Partners LLC
Tirbeni, Andrew–TPG Capital Management LP
Tirbeni, Andrew–Tpg Growth LLC
Tiringer, Christian–ARAX Capital Partners GmbH
Tirjan, Paul–Spindletop Capital Management LLC
Tirkkonen, Timo–Inventure Oy
Tirosh, Gadi–JVP Jerusalem Venture Partners Israel Management, Ltd.
Tirumala, Sudershan–EQ India Advisors
Tiscali, Sergio–Unipol Merchant Banca per le Imprese SpA
Tisch, David–Techstars Central LLC
Tischendorf, Jens–Cevian Capital AB
Tisdale, Andrew–Providence Equity Partners LLC
Tisdell, Stephen–Resonetics LLC
Tison, Francois–360 Capital Management SA
Tissot, Bertrand–Omnes Capital SAS
Tittiger, Gottfried–Industrial Growth Partners
Titus, M. David–Windward Ventures
Tiveron, Maurizio–Alcedo Societa di Gestione del Risparmio SpA
Tiwari, Amit–Invesco Private Capital Inc
Tjahjono, Bagus–BT Venture Fund Management LLC
Tjan, Anthony–Cue Ball Group LP
Tjia, Ming Tze–Southern Capital Group Pte Ltd
To, Kilin–Sycamore Ventures Inc
Toader, Daniela–Axxess Capital Partners SA
Tobelem, Simon–Arie Capital Ltd
Tobias, Andrea–Brandon Capital Partners Pty Ltd
Tobias, Martin–Yaletown Venture Partners

Tobieson, Karl–MedCap AB (publ)
Tobin, Edward–1847 Holdings LLC
Tobin, Jeffry–Millpond Equity Partners LLC
Tobin, Scott–Battery Ventures LP
Tobin, Scott–Battery Ventures LP
Todd Jealous, Benjamin–Kapor Capital
Todd, James–Industrial Opportunity Partners LLC
Todd, James–Wolseley Private Equity
Todd, Robert–Red Rock Ventures
Todorov, Tzvetomir–Bulgarian-American Enterprise Fund
Toenes, Michael–BC Brandenburg Capital GmbH
Toennesen, Erik–Skagerak Venture Capital AS
Toews, Steven–Crescent Point Energy Corp
Tofil, Glenn–England Capital Partners LLC
Toft, Niels–Ld Equity
Tofte Hansen, Thomas–Nordic Venture Partners Aps
Togut, David–Evercore Inc
Toh, James–Novo Tellus Capital Partners Pte Ltd
Toh, Wong Chin–Southern Capital Group Pte Ltd
Tokumo, Yuichi–Carlyle Group LP
Toliver, Stephanie–HealthCap Partners LLC
Tolk, Jeffrey–3 Degrees Asset Management Pte Ltd
Tolkoff, M. Joshua–Ironwood Investment Management Inc
Tolles, Bryan–Blackeagle Partners Fund L P
Tolmie, David–Edgewater Funds
Tolzmann, Erik–Westward Partners LLC
Tom, Kevin–St Cloud Capital LLC
Tom, Kevin–Wedbush Capital Partners LP
Tomai, William–Centre Lane Partners LLC
Tomasello, Anthony–INETWORKS LLC
Tomasevic, Ned–Toma Capital Management LLC
Tomashek, Andrew–Goldner Hawn Johnson & Morrison Inc
Tomassini, Mark–Noble Four Partners LLC
Tomazela, Paulo–Inseed Investimentos Ltda
Tombas, Enrique–Suma Capital SGECR SA
Tome, Fernando–Trilantic Capital Management LP
Tome, Fernando–Trilantic Capital Management LP
Tomei, Joseph–Equifin Capital Partners
Tomes, John–Hilco Equity Management LLC
Tominaga, Yoshinobu–Nomura Co Ltd
Tomioka, Takaomi–Carlyle Group LP
Tomlin, Stephen–Avalon Ventures, LLC
Tomlinson, Audrey–New York Business Development Corp
Tommila, Tapio–Panostaja Oyj
Tomova, Guergana–Felicis Ventures
Tompkins, Ben–Eden Ventures Ltd
Tompkins, Craig–Pfingsten Partners LLC
Tompkins, Graves–General Atlantic LLC
Toms, Robert–Smedvig Capital Ltd
Toncheva, Dafina–U.S. Venture Partners
Toncheva, Dafina–U.S. Venture Partners
Tonelli, Dabney–Helios Investment Partners LLP
Tong, Aaron–Sierra Ventures
Tong, Bryant–Nth Power LLC
Tong, James–Gobi Partners
Tong, Jeffrey–Third Rock Ventures LLC
Tong, Rich–Qiming Venture Partners Ii LP
Tong, Richard–Ignition Capital Partners
Tong, Shihao–Qiming Venture Partners Ii LP
Tong, Tony–Mingly Capital
Tong, Victor–Decheng Capital LLC

Tong, William–Gobi Partners
Tong, Yu–Beijing Holch Investment Management, Ltd.
Tong, Yuenong–Conduit Ventures Ltd
Tong, Zhaoping–Shenzhen Green Pine Capital Partners Co Ltd
Tongkrabin, Sayarm–Food Capitals PCL
Tongzi, Ping–Shenzhen Co-Win Venture Capital Investments Ltd
Tonning, Arne–Alliance Venture AS
Tonsfeldt, Steve–Cooley LLP
Tonussi, Domenico–Finint Partners Srl
Tony, Sumit–Gennx360 Capital Partners LP
Tookey, Tim–Old Mutual PLC
Toomey, John–Baml Capital Access Funds Management LLC
Toomey, Richard–Bayboston Managers LLC
Toone, Curtis–Sorenson Capital Partners LP
Tooth, Matthew–Blackstone Group LP
Topbas, Meric–Crescent Capital Group LP
Topche, Brett–MentorTech Ventures LLC
Topfer, Alan–Castletop Capital
Topfer, Morton–Castletop Capital
Topfer, Richard–Castletop Capital
Topham, David–HGGC LLC
Topham, David–Tower Arch Capital LLC
Topham, Lynn–Cerberus Capital Management LP
Topley, Joe–StepStone Group LP
Toporek, Michael–Brookstone Partners LLP
Toporek, Michael–Brookstone Partners LLP
Topper, James–Frazier Management LLC
Toppino, J-P–Pacific Alliance Group Ltd
Torazzi, Roberto–Alto Partners SRL
Tordjman, Rafaele–Sofinnova Partners SAS
Torgeby, Johan–Skandinaviska Enskilda Banken AB
Toro, Christian–Acas LLC
Toro, Svein-Olav–Kongsberg Innovasjon AS
Torralba, David–Doughty Hanson and Co.
Torrence, Kathy–Calvert Fund
Torres de Oliveira, Bruno Esmeraldo–MHFT Investimentos SA
Torres, Edward–Lilly Ventures Management Company LLC
Torres, Jason–Mansa Capital Management LLC
Torres, Juan–Advent International Corp
Torsen, Hans–Proventure Management AS
Torstensen, Peter–SEED Capital Management I/S
Torti, Frank–New Enterprise Associates Inc
Toscanini, Arthur–GEN3 Partners, Inc.
Totah, Sami–Viola Private Equity I LP
Totaro, Patty–Chatham Capital
Toth, Donna–Atlantic-Pacific Capital Inc
Toth, Louis–Comcast Ventures
Toth, Robert–CCMP Capital Advisors LP
Totia, Sever–Edison Partners
Tottman, Chris–Notion Capital Partners LLP
Totty, Matthew–Redwood Capital, Inc.
Toups, Rebecca–Longuevue Capital
Touraine, Agnes–JVP Jerusalem Venture Partners Israel Management, Ltd.
Touran, Bobby–Wasabi Ventures LLC
Tournier, Marc–Tocqueville Finance SA
Toussaint, John–Bain Capital Inc
Touvelle, Steven–Northcreek Mezzanine
Tower, Frank–Gold Hill Capital Management LLC

Towers, Lois–Pantheon Ventures (UK) LLP
Townley, Adam–CtechBA Pty Ltd
Townsend, Dan–Top Tier Capital Partners LLC
Townsend, David–Bb&T Capital Partners LLC
Townsend, Jason–Resonant Venture Partners
Townsend, John–Tiger Management Corp
Townsend, Mark–Tricor Pacific Founders Capital Inc
Townsend, Robert–Morrison & Foerster LLP
Townsend, Tracy–WGL Holdings Inc
Townshend, Peter–Monterey Venture Partners LLC
Townson, Michael–Brown Brothers Harriman & Co
Toy, Charles–57 Stars LLC
Toy, Charles–PCGI LLC
Toy, Stephen–WL Ross & Co LLC
Toy, Thomas–SmartForest Ventures
Toyonaga, Barry–Ventana Capital Management LP
Toyoshima, Kazukiyo–Global Venture Capital Inc
Toyota, Tetsuro–Innovation Network Corporation of Japan
Trachsler, Silvan–Golding Capital Partners GmbH
Trachtenberg, Mark–Haynes and Boone LLC
Tracy, Alex–Perella Weinberg Partners LP
Tracy, Philip–Intersouth Partners
Trader, Andrew–Maveron LLC
Traenkle, Kevin–Colony Capital LLC
Trainor, Katherine–Halifax Group LLC
Trainor, William–Mutual Capital Partners
Trala, Anna May–GTCR Golder Rauner LLC
Trammell, Joel–Lone Rock Technology Group LLC
Tramon, Cyril–Phillimore Investissement SAS
Tran, Benjamin–PHI Capital Holdings Inc
Tran, Philo–GEF Management Corp
Tran, Tuan–Intervale Capital LLC
Tran-Viet, Hai–Signal Hill Equity Partners
Trang, John–Persistence Capital Partners Lp
Tranie, Charles-Henry–Jaina Capital SASU
Tranie, Francois–21 Centrale Partners SA
Trank, Albert–Prudential Capital Group LP
Trauttmansdorff, Thomas–Gruenwald Equity Management GmbH
Travers, David–Rustic Partners LP
Traversone, Andrea–Amadeus Capital Partners Ltd
Traylor, Chris–Flywheel Ventures
Traylor, David–Headwaters BD LLC
Traynor, Sean–Welsh Carson Anderson & Stowe
Trbovich, John–Arsenal
Trbovich, John–OnPoint Technologies
Treacy, Michael–GEN3 Partners, Inc.
Treadwell, J.T.–Symphony Technology Group LLC
Treadwell, John–Symphony Technology Group LLC
Treadwell, Mead–Pt Capital LLC
Tredwell, Daniel–CoveView Capital Partners LLC
Treitz, Ewa–Black Pearls VC SA
Treleaven, Carl–New World Angels, Inc.
Treliving, Jim–T & M Management Services Ltd
Trelles, Vicente–Med Opportunity Partners LLC
Trelstad, Brian–Bridges Fund Management Ltd
Tremblay, Stephane–Investissements Novacap Inc
Trenchard, Bill–First Round Capital
Trentelman, Ton–Berggruen Holdings Inc
Trentini, Matthew–Farallon Capital Management LLC
Trentos, John–Fifth Street Capital LLC
Treppoz, Stephane–Isai Gestion SAS
Treskow, Michael–Eight Roads Ventures Europe
Treu, Jesse–Domain Associates LLC

Treurnicht, Ilse–Ontario Centres of Excellence
Trevino, Luis–Beamonte Capital Partners LLC
Trevisan, Jason–Polaris Venture Partners
Trevisani, Robert–ArcLight Capital Holdings LLC
Trevor, Stephen–Avenue Capital Group LLC
Trezza, Nikki-Ann–CCMP Capital Advisors LP
Triantos, Nick–Ignition Ventures Management LLC
Tribe, Matthew–Equity Venture Partners Pty Ltd
Tribell, W. Todd–Digital Capital AG
Trick, Chris–Jabodon PT Co
Tricolli, Mark–Enhanced Equity Fund, L.P.
Triebsch, Brad–CVF Capital Partners LLC
Triedman, J. Russell–Lindsay Goldberg & Bessemer LP
Trigg, Andrew–Graycliff Partners LP
Trijbels, Frank–AAC CAPITAL PARTNERS
Triki, Nabil–Swicorp Capital Partners SA
Trincano, Louis–Access Capital Partners SA
Trinkaus, Michael–Portfolio Advisors, LLC
Triolet, Nathalie–Naxicap Partners SA
Triplett, Michael–Insight Venture Partners LLC
Tripp, Eric–BMO Capital Corp
Tristao, Ronaldo–Triscorp Investimentos Ltda
Trivedi, J M–Actis LLP
Trivedi, Nikhil–Shasta Ventures LP
Trofimov, Mikhail–United Capital Partners Advisory OOO
Troiano, Michael–G20 Associates LLC
Tromiczak, Tina–Pfingsten Partners LLC
Trommels, Willem–ICOS Capital Management BV
Trotter, Donald–Atlantic Asset Management LLC
Trotter, Lloyd–Gennx360 Capital Partners LP
Trotter, Owen–Key Capital Partners
Troup, Charlie–Duke Street Capital Ltd
Trouten, Alex–MavenHill Capital
Trouveroy, Olivier–Mtn Capital Partners LLC
Trouveroy, Yves–E Capital Management Scrl
Trovato, Peter–Copley Equity Partners LLC
Troxell, Garth–Summer Street Capital Partners LLC
Troxler, Erwin–HBM Healthcare Investments AG
Troy, Alex–Brookside International
Troy, John–Prostar Investments Pte Ltd
Troy, Robert–Geneva Venture Group Inc
Troyer, Beth–Antares Capital Corp
Truant, Edward–Balmoral Wood Litigation Finance
Truant, Edward–Imperial Capital Corp
Trucharte, Pedro–Inveready Seed Capital SCR SA
Trudeau, Robert–Technology Crossover Ventures LP
Trueb, Eric–Capvis Equity Partners AG
Truelle, Nicholas–Weinberg Capital Partners SAS
Truetzel, David–Augury Capital Partners
Truitt, Craig–Private Advisors LLC
Trujill, David–TPG Capital Management LP
Truman, Matthew–True Capital Partners LLP
Truslow, Ned–RFE Investment Partners
Trussler, Douglas–Bison Capital Asset Management LLC
Truwit, Mitch–Apax Partners LLP
Tsai, Andy–StepStone Group LP
Tsai, Christine–500 Startups, L.P.
Tsai, Jack–CID Group
Tsai, Mei-Ying–MSD Capital LP
Tsai, Robin–VMG Partners, L.P.
Tsai, Tenno–HIG Capital LLC
Tsang, Christina–HPEF Capital Partners Ltd

2581

Tsang, David–Acorn Campus Ventures
Tsang, Hon Nam–Guangdong Investment Ltd
Tsang, Jarlon–H&Q Asia Pacific, Ltd.
Tsang, Peter–Riverside Co
Tsang, Sidney–HAO Capital
Tsao, Ray–Probitas Partners Inc
Tsao, Robert–Fortune Venture Capital Corp
Tsao, Thomas–Gobi Partners
Tsarkov, Oleg–Svarog Capital Advisors LTD
Tsay, Ching-Yen–CDIB Capital Group
Tsay, Y–PTI Ventures
Tse, Andy–Aif Capital Asia Iii LP
Tse, Andy–Baird Capital
Tse, Kai–Structural Capital GP LLC
Tse, Kai–TriplePoint Capital LLC
Tse, Lawrence–Gobi Partners
Tseitlin, Ariel–Scale Venture Partners
Tselentis, Paul–24Haymarket Ltd
Tseng, Philip–Tennenbaum Capital Partners LLC
Tseng, Steven–Golden Equator Capital Pte Ltd
Tseung, Kar Keung–LionRock Capital Ltd
Tsitsiragos, Dimitris–International Finance Corp
Tsomik, Leonard–Carlyle Group LP
Tsoromocos, Chris–Stern Partners Inc
Tsou, Wayne Wen-Tsui–Carlyle Group LP
Tsuchida, Ryoma–DBJ Capital Co., Ltd
Tsui, Doug–Horizon Ventures
Tsui, Sung Lam–Shaw Kwei & Partners
Tsuji, Hideki–University of Tokyo Edge Capital Co Ltd
Tsuji, Satoshi–J-STAR Co Ltd
Tsuji, Toshihiko–Sumitomo Mitsui Trust Investment Co Ltd
Tsukada, Kiyohiko–Oaktree Capital Management LP
Tsukagoshi, Masanobu–IncTANK Ventures
Tsuria, Yossi–Jerusalem Global Ventures
Tsuyoshi, Akio–Navasota Group
Tucher, Alison–Morrison & Foerster LLP
Tuchscherer, Robert–Golub Capital Master Funding LLC
Tucker, Andrew–Brown Brothers Harriman & Co
Tucker, Garland–Triangle Capital Partners L L C
Tucker, James–COGR Inc
Tucker, James–Clearview Capital LLC
Tucker, James–Cyrus Capital Partners LLC
Tucker, Justin–Oaktree Capital Management LP
Tucker, Ken–SAIF Partners
Tucker, Robert–Capital Partners, Inc.
Tucker, Scott–JMC Capital Partners LP
Tuckerman, David–CMEA Development Company LLC
Tuckley, Steven–Beringea LLC
Tudge, Steven–ECI Partners LLP
Tudor, John–Friedman Fleischer & Lowe Cap Ptnrs L P
Tudor, Richard–24Haymarket Ltd
Tuer, Kevin–Communitech Ltd
Tufariello, Anthony–Fortress Investment Group LLC
Tuff, Timothy–Ampersand Capital Partners
Tufts, Linda–Fletcher Spaght Ventures LP
Tufts, Robert–Ventana Capital Management LP
Tugnait, Kamaljit–Barings (UK) Ltd
Tukiainen, Juha–MB Rahasto Oy
Tuli, Gaurav–Eight Roads Ventures Europe
Tuli, Gaurav–F-Prime Capital Partners
Tullis, James–Tullis Health Investors
Tullis, John–Tullis Health Investors

Tullman, Howard–G2T3V LLC
Tullo, Thomas–Compass Partners International LLC
Tulloch, Shane–Meakem Becker Venture Capital LLC
Tully, Daniel–Altaris Capital Partners LLC
Tully, Michael–Sandler Capital Management
Tully, Patrick–Liberty Mutual Innovation
Tully, Timothy–Tully and Holland Inc
Tulonen, Marko–Visionplus Oyj
Tulp, Alfred–NIBC Principal Investments BV
Tumanov, Oleg–Frontier Ventures
Tuncel, Mete–Carlyle Group LP
Tune, Kathleen–Thomas Mcnerney and Partners LLC
Tung, Cheng-Cheng–Cathay Financial Holding Co Ltd
Tung, David–Carlyle Group LP
Tung, Eric–Mobeus Equity Partners LLP
Tung, Hans–GGV Capital
Tung, Jeffrey–Timberline Venture Partners
Tunguz, Tomasz–Redpoint Ventures
Tunnell, David–Hellman & Friedman LLC
Tunney, Michael–Lioncourt Investments Ltd
Tunnicliffe, Jonathan–Novaquest Infosystems Inc
Tuominen, Tanu-Matti–Visionplus Oyj
Tuovinen, Jari–Visionplus Oyj
Tur, Moshe–SIDER ISRA'EL IYE`UTS KALKALI BE`AM
Turchin, Judy–Blackstone Group LP
Turck, Matt–FirstMark Capital LLC
Turdukulov, Nurbek–Kain Capital LLC
Turevsky, Igor–Ecomachines Ventures Ltd
Turfus, Ralph–Yaletown Venture Partners
Turillo, Michael–Spencer Trask Ventures Inc
Turitz, Drew–Sandbox Industries LLC
Turkanis, Barry–NXT Ventures Fund 1 LLC
Turkewilz, Jordan–ZMC
Turkmen, Kerim–Mid Europa Partners LLP
Turley, Garret–Bridges Fund Management Ltd
Turner, Amherst–Amherst Fund LLC
Turner, Andrew–Northern Lights Capital Group LLC
Turner, Court–Avalon Ventures, LLC
Turner, Daniel–Montreux Equity Partners
Turner, Guy–Hyde Park Venture Partners
Turner, James–Oaktree Capital Management LP
Turner, Jamie–Accretia Capital LLC
Turner, Jeffrey–Hillcrest Capital Partners LP
Turner, John–Haynes and Boone LLC
Turner, John–Westview Capital Partners LP
Turner, Lynne–MergerTech Advisors
Turner, Mark–F&C Equity Partners PLC
Turner, Matthew–Irving Place Capital LLC
Turner, Maura–Charlesbank Capital Partners LLC
Turner, Michael–Wesley Clover International Corporation
Turner, Patrick–Crescent Capital Group LP
Turner, Patrick–Veronis Suhler Stevenson LLC
Turner, Roger–Steelhouse Ventures Ltd
Turner, Ryan–Lighthouse Capital Partners LP
Turner, Stephen–Entrepreneurs Fund LP
Turner, William–Signature Capital LLC
Turowsky, Jason–Falconhead Capital LLC
Turowsky, Jason–Intervale Capital LLC
Turpin, Karen–Tavistock Group Inc
Turza, Ivica–Riverside Co
Tuten, Henderson–Rcf Management LLC
Tutrone, Anthony–NB Private Equity Partners Ltd
Tuttle, Richard–Prospect Partners LLC

Tuttle, Thomas–Kinderhook Industries LLC
Tuttman, Benjamin–Castanea Partners Inc
Tuulimo, Paivi–Midinvest Management Oy
Tuunala, Pentti–Sentica Partners Oy
Tveit, Helge–Energy Ventures AS
Tveitane, Tor–Harbert Management Corp
Twiford, J. Rainer–Camp One Ventures LLC
Tybur, James–Performance Equity Management LLC
Tyburski, Jonathan–Versa Capital Management Inc
Tye, Anna–Carlyle Group LP
Tye, Steve–Croft & Bender LLC
Tylee, Gregory–Second City Capital Partners
Tyler, Aaron–Lighthouse Capital Partners LP
Tynan, Peter–GEF Management Corp
Tyndall, Mark–Artemis Investment Management LLP
Tyra, Vincent–Southfield Capital Advisors LLC
Tyree, Michael–Edwards Capital LLC
Tyree, William–Brown Brothers Harriman & Co
Tyrrell, Gary–Woodside Fund
Tyrrell, Mike–Venrock Inc
Tyrrell, Thomas–Glengary LLC
Tysdal, Tyler–Impact Opportunities Fund LP
Tysoe, Ronald–LEGEND PARTNERS I L P
Tyson, Blair–Milbank Tweed Hadley & Mccloy LLP
Tzakis, Tom–Pylon Capital
Tzeng, John–Harbinger Venture Management
Tzililis, Dimitri–E I Capital LLP
Tzivelis, Dimitrios–BC Partners LLP
Tzruya, Yoav–JVP Jerusalem Venture Partners Israel Management, Ltd.
Uahwatanasakul, Kalaya–Lombard Investments Inc
Uberla, Jorg–ETF Partners LLP
Uchida, Mitsutoshi–Morrison & Foerster LLP
Uchikata, Junitsu–JAFCO Investment (Asia Pacific) Ltd
Uchiyama, Hirotaka–CLSA Capital Partners HK Ltd
Ucok, Evren–Earlybird Venture Capital GmbH & Co KG
Uddin, Zia–Monroe Capital LLC
Udelhofen, John–Madison Capital Partners Corp
Udow-Phillips, Marianne–Belle Michigan Fund LP
Uebe, Victor–Leblon Equities Gestao de Recursos Ltda
Ueda, Kenichi–Ant Capital Partners Co Ltd
Ueda, Teruaki–Daiwa Corporate Investment Co Ltd
Ufer, Evan–Plymouth Venture Partners
Ugolini, Enzo–Valentis Capital LLC
Ugras, N. George–Adams Capital Management, Inc.
Uhari, Tommi–Karma Ventures OU
Uhl, Jessica–Royal Dutch Shell PLC
Uhlemann, Jurgen–J C M B Beteiligungs GmbH
Uhlemann, Marcel–J C M B Beteiligungs GmbH
Uhlman, Thomas–New Venture Partners LLC
Ukeles, Meir–Israel Cleantech Ventures
Ukropina, Rob–Black Diamond Ventures Inc
Ulbak, Rune–ATP Private Equity Partners
Ulecia, Javier–Bullnet Capital Sc R SA
Ulevitch, Richard–5AM Ventures LLC
Ulevitch, Richard–Aravis SA
Ullah, Salman–Merus Capital Investment
Ullman, Christopher–Carlyle Group LP
Ullman, Mark–Charter Oak Equity, L.P.
Ullom, Lance–Blu Venture Investors LLC
Ulman, Doug–Spindletop Capital Management LLC
Ulmansky, Reuven–Wadi Ventures SCA

Ulrich, Catherine—FirstMark Capital LLC
Ulrich, Nicholas—Stonehenge Partners Inc
Umedaly, Mossadiq—Wellington Partners GmbH
Umholtz, Tony—Osceola Capital Management LLC
Underdown, Brian—LCC Legacy Holdings Inc
Underwood, John—Pfingsten Partners LLC
Unell, Troy—Antares Capital Corp
Unertl, Justin—Excellere Capital Management LLC
Unger, Howard—Saw Mill Capital LLC
Ungerer, Scott—Enertech Capital
Ungerman, Mark—Morrison & Foerster LLP
Unneland, Trond—Chevron Technology Ventures L L C
Unrein, Lawrence—JP Morgan Investment Management Inc
Unruh, Paul—TeleSoft Partners
Unsworth, David—Rbc Capital Partners
Unterberger, Steve—Carrick Capital Management Company LLC
Unterman, Thomas—Rustic Partners LP
Uotila, Mika—Sentica Partners Oy
Upadhyay, Tarun—Blu Venture Investors LLC
Upadhyaya, Rajal—Catalyst Principal Partners LLC
Upton, Richard—Harbor Light Capital Partners LLC
Uranga Lamadrid, Raul A.—Gerbera Capital Asesores SC
Urban, George—Harren Equity Partners
Urban, Ward—Starboard Capital Partners LLC
Urband, Jason—Lariat Partners LP
Urbanek, Brian—Sun Capital Partners Inc
Urbina, Daniel—Cielo Management LLC
Urekew, Timothy—Brown Brothers Harriman & Co
Uribe, Angel—Southern Cross Capital Management SA
Uring, Thierry—Rhone Dauphine Developpement SA
Urquhart, James—Pond Venture Partners Ltd
Urquhart, Richard—Investors Management Corp
Urquidi, Pedro—Oaktree Capital Management LP
Urrea, Cesar—Zephyr Management LP
Ursini, Silvio—Neo Investment Partners LLP
Ursprung, Tobias—Capvis Equity Partners AG
Ury, Daniel—Equifin Capital Partners
Usher, Mark—Wellington Financial Lp
Ushio, Misti—180 Degree Capital Corp
Usifer, Doug—Headwaters BD LLC
Usman, Nassim—Lightstone Ventures LP
Usry, Horace—Gemini Partners, Inc.
Utay, Marc—Clarion Capital Partners LLC
Utgard, Thomas—Stonehenge Partners Inc
Uudam, Margus—Karma Ventures OU
Uzumeri, Erol—Searchlight Capital Partners LLC
Uzzaman, Anis—Fenox Venture Capital Inc
Uzzi, Gerard—Milbank Tweed Hadley & Mccloy LLP
Vachelard, Jacques—Naxicap Partners SA
Vachet, Claude—Cycle Capital Management (CCM) Inc
Vacura, Rick—Morrison & Foerster LLP
Vadapalas, Joseph—Nexos Capital Partners
Vading, Marten—Kreos Capital Managers Ltd
Vaessen, Maarten—Varova BV
Vagliano, Justin—Greenwoods Capital Partners
Vahaly, Brian—NextGen Venture Partners LLC
Vahey, Patrick—Greenline Ventures LLC
Vahia, Ojas—Topspin Partners LP
Vaidya, Ash—Wellington Financial Lp

Vaillant, Gerard—Idinvest Partners SA
Vainio, Petri—EW Healthcare Partners
Vaish, Paresh—SFW Capital Partners LLC
Vaissie, Baptiste—Oaktree Capital Management LP
Vakil, Suken—JMI Management Inc
Valdenaire, Olivier—Endeavour Vision SA
Valdes, Antoine—Alto Invest SA
Valdes, Mirna—Ridgewood Capital Management LLC
Valdez, Mark—Playground Ventures GP LLC
Valdmanis, Warren—Bain Capital Inc
Vale, Brad—Johnson & Johnson Innovation-JJDC Inc
Vale, Christopher—Rexiter Capital Management Ltd
Valencia, Anthony—Trust Company of the West
Valencony, Francois—Merieux Developpement SAS
Valentin-Pereira, Ludovic—Omnes Capital SAS
Valentine, Donald—Sequoia Capital Operations LLC
Valentiny, Marc—Bain Capital Inc
Valenty, Jeffrey—Flatworld Capital LLC
Valenzuela, Miguel—Belmert Capital SA
Valenzuela, Miguel—Carlyle Group LP
Valeri, Andrea—Blackstone Group LP
Valerio, Domenico—Aescap Venture I BV
Valerio, Luca—H-Farm SpA
Valfells, Helga—Nyskopunarsjodur
Valiente, Nancy—Evercore Inc
Valimaa, Kalle—Miraimon Oy
Valis, Tomas—Celtic House Venture Partners Inc
Valkin, Adam—General Catalyst Partners LLC
Vallabhaneni, Venkat—Parampara Capital & Management Consultants LLP
Vallejo, Juan Carlos—Nexuss Group SAC
Valler, Yaron—Hasso Plattner Ventures Management GmbH
Valliappan, Kumar—Metalmark Capital Holdings LLC
Valtos, William—ICCP Venture Partners Inc
Valvano, Ralph—JC Flowers & Co LLC
Valvasori, Franco—Alcedo Societa di Gestione del Risparmio SpA
Vamvakas, Nick—Investcorp Bank BSC
Van Aelten, Willem—Vendis Capital NV
Van Alkemade, Floris—Solid Ventures BV
Van Apeldoorn, Keith—Stern Partners Inc
Van Barneveld, Jaap—Newion Investments BV
Van Beaver, Stephen—Pilot House Ventures Group, LLC
Van Beneden, Patrick—Gimv Investeringsmaatschappij Voor Vlaanderen NV
Van Beuningen, Fred—Chrysalix Energy
Van Bladel, Sigrid—Aberdare Ventures
Van Der Burg, E.J.—NIBC Principal Investments BV
Van Der Mersbrugghe, Guy—Orium SAS
Van Der Velden, Peter—LCC Legacy Holdings Inc
Van Deventer, John—Cabot Square Capital Advisors Ltd
Van Dijk, Ed—Gebruder Heller Dinklage
Van Droogenbroeck, Eric—Sofindev Management NV
Van Duinen, Scott—Halifax Group LLC
Van Dussen, Jason—Golub Capital Master Funding LLC
Van Dyck, Carlo—QiFund Partners NV
Van Eesteren, William—Wilshire Private Markets
Van Efferink, Fred—ICOS Capital Management BV
Van Es, Judith—Blum Capital Partners LP
Van Es, P.F.C.—Antea Participates Management BV
Van Fleet, Todd—First Analysis Corp

Van Goethem, Robert—3i Group PLC
Van Griethuysen, Hans—Fiera Capital (UK) Ltd
Van Harten, Kenton—Hancock Park Associates A California LP
Van Hecke, Michel—SBI - BMI
Van Heusden, Jim—Gimv Investeringsmaatschappij Voor Vlaanderen NV
Van Horn, Todd—Linden LLC
Van Houten, Scott—Audax Group, Inc.
Van Huffel, Gert—KeBeK Management NV
Van Kippersluis, Idgar—Standard Investment BV
Van Loan, Nicholas—Stratim Capital LLC
Van Mil, Johan—Peak Capital BV
Van Nouhuys, Karen—Investcorp Bank BSC
Van Nouhuys, Karen—Investcorp Technology Investments Group
Van Olphen, Jurgen—Transequity Network BV
Van Olst, Marc—Spinnaker Growth Partners (Pty) Ltd
Van Ommeren, Dirk J.—Wendel SE
Van Oord, Heleen—Peak Capital BV
Van Oppen, Peter—Trilogy Equity Partners Llc
Van Pelt, Trina—Intel Capital Corp
Van Quaquebeke, Dirk—Alps Venture Capital GmbH
Van Rappard, Rolly—CVC Capital Partners Ltd
Van Rossum, Patrick—Varova BV
Van Sante, Yves—QAT Investments SA
Van Sickle, John—Sentinel Capital Partners LLC
Van Staden, Dewald—Motseng Investment Holdings (Pty) Ltd
Van Steenkiste, Jim—Oaktree Capital Management LP
Van Steijn, Paul—AAC CAPITAL PARTNERS
Van Swaay, Hans—LYRIQUE Srrl
Van Tuin, Jon—Clearview Capital LLC
Van Uchelen, Kees-Jan—Silverfern Group Inc
Van Veen, Rein—PointBreak Private Equity
Van Vloten, Tatjana—Pantheon Ventures (UK) LLP
Van Voorhis, Kimberly—Morrison & Foerster LLP
Van Vuren, Erik—Antares Capital Corp
Van Wijk, Marcel—Premium Equity Partners GmbH
Van Zant, Jason—Keystone Capital Inc
Van Zujilen, Eric—E Capital Management Scrl
Van de Grampel, Paul-Jeroen—Capital International Inc
Van de Laar, Tonn—H2 Equity Partners BV
Van de Water, Sasha—Keyhaven Capital Partners Ltd
Van den Berg, Willem—Value Creation Capital BV
Van den Bosch, H.J.—Antea Participates Management BV
Van den Brande, Barend—Big Bang Ventures CVA
Van den Heuvel, Remco—5Square BV
Van der Berg, Wouter—Brooklyn Ventures BV
Van der Chijs, Marc—CrossPacific Capital Partners
Van der Hoeven, Gert Jan—H2 Equity Partners BV
Van der Linden, Ruud—Capital-E NV
Van der Meer, Roland—Fuse Capital
Van der Merwe, Warren—Vantage Venture Partners
Van der Sluys, Gerry—Business Creation Investments AG
Van der Tuin, Patrick—Brooklyn Ventures BV
Van der Veen, Erwin—Capital Mills Invest BV
Van t Hoenderdaal, Lars—Main Capital Partners BV
VanCleef, Kim—Altus Capital Partners Inc
VanDegrift, Douglass—Linden LLC
VanDerMeid, Jeremy—Monroe Capital LLC

2583

Pratt's Guide to Private Equity & Venture Capital Sources

VanHoy, Scott—Leeds Equity Advisors Inc
Vance, Pamela—Axioma Ventures LLC
Vancini, Roberto—Leonardoweb Group Srl
Vande Capelle, Kristof—Gimv Investeringsmaatschappij Voor Vlaanderen NV
Vandekerckhove, Andrew—Centre Partners Management LLC
Vanden Beukel, Christine—Crescent Capital Group LP
Vandenberg, Chip—Trivest Partners LP
Vandenbulcke, Manu—Gimv Investeringsmaatschappij Voor Vlaanderen NV
Vander Ark, Tom—Learn Capital Venture Partners LP
Vander Meeren, Steven—Yukon NV
Vander Schaaff, Tom—Edison Partners
Vander Vort, John—Charlesbank Capital Partners LLC
Vander Vort, John—MPM Capital LLC
Vander Weele, Ken—Creation Investments Capital Management LLC
VanderBruggen, Peter—Leeward Ventures Management SA
Vanderbeck, Sunny—Satori Capital LLC
Vandermyde, Lee—Stone Pointe LLC
Vandervelden, James—Pleasant Bay Capital Partners LLC
Vandervoorde, Patrick—CDC Infra Management SAS
Vandevenne, Rurik—River Cities Capital Fund LP
Vang Hansen, Martin—VAEKSTFONDEN
Vanggaard, Joachim—Finance Zealand Management ApS
Vangstrup, Torben—ATP Private Equity Partners
Vanhaerents, Koen—Baker & McKenzie LLP
Vanhamme, Heidi—Broad Sky Partners LLC
Vanhooren, Stefaan—Gevaert SA
Vanhoutte, Tom—Capricorn Venture Partners NV
Vanluchene, Pascal—E NV
Vannarsdall, Adrienne—River Cities Capital Fund LP
Vanquaethem, Stefaan—Vectis Participations NV
Vansina, Floris—KeBeK Management NV
Vanzyl, Adrian—Wavemaker Partners
Vardell, Thomas—Northgate Capital LLC
Vardy, Peter—Vardy Property Group
Varelas, Chris—Riverwood Capital Group LLC
Vargas, Fidel—Centinela Capital Partners LLC
Varghese, Shaji—EQ India Advisors
Varma, Amar—Extreme Venture Partners Inc
Varma, Amit—Quadria Capital Investment Advisors Pvt Ltd
Varma, Samit—Anthem Venture Partners
Varma, Somit—Warburg Pincus LLC
Varma, Vaneeta—Mayfield Fund
Varnell, John—Fairfax Financial Holdings Ltd
Varoli, Corrado—Evercore Inc
Varshney, Hari—Varshney Capital Corp
Varshney, Peeyush—Varshney Capital Corp
Varshney, Praveen—Varshney Capital Corp
Varshneya, Rajeev—Blade Partners
Vartiainen, Pekka—Sunstone Capital A/S
Varughese, John—Perella Weinberg Partners LP
Vasan, Robin—Mayfield Fund
Vasanji, Nadim—Northleaf Capital Partners Ltd
Vashi, Anant—Headwaters BD LLC
Vashistha, Ankita—Tholons Capital
Vasiliadis, Peter—Morgan Stanley Alternative Investment Partners LP
Vasiliev, Mikhail—NCH Capital Inc

Vasilyev, Tatiana—Brown Brothers Harriman & Co
Vasishth, Vishal—Obvious Ventures Management LLC
Vaslet, Charles—Emerald Technology Ventures AG
Vassallo, Mark—Lightyear Capital LLC
Vassallo, Steven—Foundation Capital LLC
Vassallo, Trae—Kleiner Perkins Caufield & Byers LLC
Vassel, Robert—Swander Pace Capital LLC
Vassileva, Albena—Advent International Corp
Vasudevan, Sunil—True North
Vaters, Robert—Med Opportunity Partners LLC
Vauchy, Benoit—Permira Advisers LLP
Vaughan, Richard—Polar Capital Investments
Vaughn, Douglas—Triangle Capital Partners L L C
Vaughn, Jennifer—Acas LLC
Vaury, Jean-Francois—Ciclad Participations SAS
Vaury, Jean-Jacques—U I Gestion SA
Vavrichek, David—Deerpath Capital Management LP
Vazirani, Pravin—Menlo Ventures
Vazquez, Ed—Oaktree Capital Management LP
Vazquez, Leonardo—Leblon Equities Gestao de Recursos Ltda
Veale, Geoffrey—Milestone Partners LP
Veale, Stuart—Beringea LLC
Veatch, Bill—Morrison & Foerster LLP
Vecchio, Gerard—Century Capital Management / Massachusetts Inc
Vedaprakash, Medha—Rho Capital Partners Inc
Vedra, Robert—Industrial Opportunity Partners LLC
Vedrines, Michel—Butler Capital Partners SA
Vedro, John—Susquehanna Private Capital LLC
Veeck, Alan—Meakem Becker Venture Capital LLC
Veering, Pritt—BPM Capital OU
Vega, Nathalia—Global Partnerships
Veijalainen, Sami—Dasos Capital Oy
Veilleux, Francois—GTI Capital, Inc.
Veitch, Brian James—Steadfast Capital GmbH
Veith, Anthony—Clearview Capital LLC
Veitinger, Klaus—OrbiMed Advisors LLC
Vejlsgaard, Nikolaj—Axcel Industriinvestor A/S
Vejseli, Karen—Carlyle Group LP
Velasco, Eduardo—L Catterton Europe SAS
Velez, Maroa—Brown Brothers Harriman & Co
Velez, Pablo—Oaktree Capital Management LP
Vellanki, Mahesh—Redpoint Ventures
Velu, Rengasamy—Oaktree Capital Management LP
Vendetti, Dino—Formative Ventures
Venerable, Mike—CincyTech
Venezia, John—Evercore Inc
Venkatachalam, Kapil—Technology Crossover Ventures LP
Venkatachalam, Lakshmi—Asian Development Bank
Venkatachalam, Sandhya—Social+Capital Partnership
Venkatadari, Bobba—Ventureast
Venkataraman, Rajamani—IIFL Holdings Ltd
Venkataraman, Sriram—Avista Capital Holdings LP
Vennettilli, David—Strand Equity Partners LLC
Ventosa, Alejandro—Palladium Equity Partners LLC
Ver Hulst, Nicolas—Alpha Group
Verardo, Dino—Sageview Capital LP
Verba, Alex—Stairway Capital Management
Verbeek, Hubert—Holland Venture BV
Verbeek, Joost—Rabo Participaties BV
Verbica, Peter—Firestarter Partners LLC
Verbiest, Ast—KeBeK Management NV

Verdi, Mark—Avalt LLC
Verdier, Philippe—Siparex Proximite Innovation SAS
Verdood, Stephane—Vesalius Biocapital Partners SARL
Vergani, Nicolo—Lincolnshire Management Inc
Vergara Madrigal, Jorge—MPower Ventures, L.P.
Verge, W. Michael—PineBridge Investments LLC
Verges, Philip—Undisclosed Firm
Verhagen, Thomas—NV Industriebank Liof
Verhalen, Andrew—Matrix Partners, L.P.
Verheijen, Danladi—Verod Capital Management Ltd
Verhoeff, Otto—Castlelake LP
Verlaine, Jean-Pierre—ILP III SARL
Verland, Sten—Sunstone Capital A/S
Verma, A.—SBI Capital Ventures
Verma, Rishi—Gennx360 Capital Partners LP
Vermette, Chris—Oaktree Capital Management LP
Vermeulen, C.M.—NIBC Principal Investments BV
Vermeulen, J.H.—NIBC Principal Investments BV
Vernal, Mike—Sequoia Capital Operations LLC
Verneholt, Lars—Litorina Capital Advisors AB
Vernet, Beatrice—Turenne Capital Partenaires SASU
Vernhes, Paul—Cohen & Company Financial Ltd
Vernick, Shoshana—Sterling Partners GP LLC
Vernigora, Alexey—Runa Capital
Verplanke, Cilian Jansen—Karmijn Kapitaal Management BV
Verri, Marcio—Kinea Investimentos Ltda
Verrier, Patrice—Abenex Capital SAS
Versaw, Jennifer—Relativity Capital LLC
Vervoort, Maarten—AlpInvest Partners BV
Vesanen, Jari—Guida Invest Oy
Veschi, Christine—Blackstone Group LP
Vescio, Joe—Portland Private Equity LP
Vescovo, Victor—Insight Equity Holdings LLC
Vestergaard-Poulsen, Soren—CVC Capital Partners Ltd
Vettel, Matthew—Great Hill Equity Partners LLC
Veyssiere, Frederic—Innovacom Gestion SAS
Viakara, Anil—SoftBank China & India Holdings Ltd
Viard, Etienne—Proparco SA
Vicar, Ondrej—Genesis Capital sro
Vicary, Scott—GEF Management Corp
Vickery, Rob—Stage Venture Partners LLC
Victor, Jonathan—Balmoral Advisors LLC
Victor, Joseph—5AM Ventures LLC
Vidal, Dominique—Index Ventures
Vidal, Fabrice—Cerea Partenaire SAS
Vidal, Francisco—Brown Brothers Harriman & Co
Vidal, Philippe—Credit Industriel et Commercial SA
Viders, Zachary—Kohlberg & Co LLC
Videt, Pote—Lombard Investments Inc
Vieira Tortelli, Olavo—Vinci Equities Gestora de Recursos Ltda
Vieira, Tiago—Capital Criativo SCR SA
Vieira-Ribeiro, Simon—Gsr Ventures Management Llc
Viergutz, Philip—AlpInvest Partners BV
Vietor, Richard—PEI Funds LLC
Vig, Rajneesh—Tennenbaum Capital Partners LLC
Vigano, Paul-J.H. Whitney & Co LLC
Vignola, Eric—Beacon Partners Inc
Vignola, Leonard—Beacon Partners Inc
Vigoda, Robert—Catalyst Health And Technology Partners LLC

Vigouroux, John–Accelerate-IT Ventures Management LLC
Vijayakar, Sameer–Churchill Equity Inc
Vijayavargiya, Sonali–Augment Ventures Fund I LP
Vijums, Judith–HCI Equity LLC
Vik, Jostein–Viking Venture As
Vila Gonzalez, Felipe–Fondo de Fondos
Vila, Fernando–Prax Capital Management Co
Vilain, Jean-Christophe–Aravis SA
Vilain, Serege–Srib
Viles, Peter–Trust Company of the West
Villa, James–AEA Investors LLC
Villa, Sebastian–Southern Cross Capital Management SA
Villabroza, Allan–Overseas Private Investment Corp
Villalobos Baldioceda, Eugenia–EcoEnterprises Fund
Villalobos, Julio–Axon Partners Group Investment
Villalonga, Juan–Hermes Growth Partners Ltd
Villanueva, Jim–Global Partnerships
Villanueva, Marcus–Eaglehill Advisors LLC
Villar, Rodrigo–Adobe Capital
Villecroze, Stephane–Demeter SAS
Villers, Ned–Water Street Healthcare Partners LLC
Villhard, Peter–Thompson Street Capital Partners LP
Villinger, Thomas–ZFHN Zukunftsfonds Heilbronn GmbH & Co KG
Vilosius, Kristjan–UP Invest OU
Vinas, Jordi–Nauta Capital SL
Vincent, George–UNC Kenan-Flagler Private Equity Fund
Vincent, Jeff–Grey Mountain Partners LLC
Vincent, John–Revel Partners LLC
Vinci, Justin–Fundamental Advisors LP
Vinciquerra, Michael–Brown Gibbons Lang & Company LLC
Vinck, Andre–Interuniversitair Micro-Electronica Centrum
Vineberg, S.Neil–Wearable World Inc
Vineburg, Stephen–CVC Capital Partners Ltd
Viner, Les–Torys LLP
Vinet, Anne-Sophie–Phillimore Investissement SAS
Vinish, Lorne–Saskatchewan Opportunities Corp
Vira, Paras–Oaktree Capital Management LP
Virani, Aleem–KV Private Equity Inc
Virk, Kanad–Standard Chartered Private Equity Ltd
Virnig, Chip–Thoma Bravo LLC
Virtue, Ted–Mid-Ocean Partners LP
Visbal, Ricardo–Global Partnerships
Viscogliosi, Anthony–Viscogliosi Brothers LLC
Viscogliosi, John–Viscogliosi Brothers LLC
Viscogliosi, Marc–Viscogliosi Brothers LLC
Vishvanathan, S.–SBI Capital Ventures
Visioni, Mario–Alto Partners SRL
Viso, Nemesio–Stonehenge Growth Capital LLC
Visontay, Garry–Right Click Capital
Visontay, Garry–Sydney Seed Fund Management Pty Ltd
Visser, Peter–Egeria BV
Visuri, Mauri–Nordic Option Oy
Viswanadham, Krishna–Skyview Capital LLC
Viswanathan, Ravi–New Enterprise Associates Inc
Vitale, Marco–Fondo Italiano d'Investimento SGR SpA
Vitale, Raffaele–PAI Partners SAS

Vitangcol, Alvin–Capital Midwest Fund LP
Viton, Richard–IA Capital Group Inc
Vitrat, Robert–Midi Pyrenees Croissance SA
Vitullo, Nicole–Domain Associates LLC
Vitus, Andy–Scale Venture Partners
Vlaar, Radboud–Finch Capital Partners BV
Vlasic, Paul–RSVP Capital
Vliebergh, Vincent–Korys Management NV
Voeks, Robert–Private Advisors LLC
Voelker, Martin–VR Equitypartner GmbH
Vogel, Andrew–ZMC
Vogel, Bernard–Endeavour Vision SA
Vogel, Christian–CFH Beteiligungsgesellschaft mbH
Vogel, Christian–Myonic Holding GmbH
Vogel, Dale–Montlake Capital LLC
Vogel, James–Digitech Venture Capital Fund Inc
Vogel, Jeffrey–Court Square Capital Partners LP
Vogel, Michael–V+Beteiligungs 2 GmbH
Vogel, Neil–FirstMark Capital LLC
Vogel, Richard–Loeb Enterprises LLC
Vogelbaum, Martin–Rho Capital Partners Inc
Vogelhut, Joshua–Atlantic-Pacific Capital Inc
Vogelstein, John–Warburg Pincus LLC
Vogt, Christine–Albion Investors LLC
Vogt, Torsten–Permira Advisers LLP
Vohlmuth, Ivan–Royalton Partners
Voillet, Pierre–Bamboo SAS
Vojnits, Tamas–Oriens IM Hungary Szolgtato Kft
Vold, Henning–Norvestor Equity AS
Voli, Emilio–Apax Partners LLP
Volio, Jorge–Volio Capital SA
Vollebregt, Erik–Kenda Capital BV
Vollum, Don–Vista Ridge Capital Partners LLC
Volpe, Louis–Kodiak Venture Partners LP
Volpi, Nic–Permira Advisers LLP
Volpi, Nicola–Permira Advisers LLP
Voltolina, Giovanna–Motion Equity Partners LLP
Volz, Gabriele–Wealthcap Initiatoren GmbH
Von Deylen, Jeffrey–Savvis Inc
Von Fischer, P.Scott–Prudential Capital Group LP
Von Frankenberg, Alexander–High Tech Grunderfonds Management GmbH Unspecified Fund
Von Gueltlingen, Susanne–Siemens Venture Capital GmbH
Von Haacke, Ulf–3i Group PLC
Von Hase, Niels–Trivest Trium Investments (Pty) Ltd
Von Kreuter, James–Headwaters BD LLC
Von Rohr, Johannes–Alpha Founders
Von Scharfenberg, Harald–Bvt Holding GmbH & Co KG
Von Stein, Scott–Medley Capital LLC
Von Stroh, Eric–Long Point Capital
Von Wiedebach-Nostitz, Tibor–Bvt Holding GmbH & Co KG
Von Zuben, Max–Wicks Group of Companies LLC
Von dem Knesebeck, Gregor–K5 Advisors GmbH & Co KG
Von dem Knesebeck, Julia–K5 Advisors GmbH & Co KG
Von dem Knesebeck, Philipp–K5 Advisors GmbH & Co KG
Vonnahme, Ludger–CMP Capital Management Partners GmbH
Voo, Correy–01 Ventures LLP
Vora, Rupa–IDFC Alternatives Ltd

Vorbrich, Peter Alan–CarVal Investors LLC
Vorhoff, Robbert–General Atlantic LLC
Vorobeychik, Philip–Insight Venture Partners LLC
Vorona, Nancy–Center For Innovative Technology
Voskamp, Gijs–Ludgate Investments Ltd
Voskarides, Christiana–Blackstone Group LP
Vosper, Paul–Morgan Stanley Alternative Investment Partners LP
Voss, Annette–Unigestion Holding SA
Voss, Sherwin–Denovo Health Partners LLC
Vosseller, Troy–gener8tor
Vossen, Michael–Lakeside Capital Management LLC
Vostrizansky, Michael–Edwards Capital LLC
Votron, Jean-Paul–BNP Paribas Fortis Private Equity Growth NV
Voytov, Ilya–Vector Capital Management LP
Vrionis, John–Lightspeed Management Company LLC
Vu, Clara–Horsley Bridge Partners LLC
Vuitton, Laetitia–Idinvest Partners SA
Vukovic, Srdjan–Soros Strategic Partners LP
Vuorela, Panu–Vaaka Partners Oy
Vuotto, Julie–Glencoe Capital LLC
Vyas, Anand–Ask Pravi Capital Advisors Pvt Ltd
Vyas, Vinnie–Crossover Advisors Pvt Ltd
Vyas, Vivek–Apax Partners LLP
WANG, ELISE–Deerfield Management Company LP
WHEELER, CAMERON–Deerfield Management Company LP
Wacaster, Steven–Warren Equity Partners LLC
Wachen, Mark–DreamIt Ventures
Wachsman, David–Thomas H Lee Partners LP
Wachsmuth, Marc–Capital-E NV
Wachter, David–W Capital Management LLC
Wachtman, Jim–SV Health Investors LLP
Wack, Patrick–Rho Capital Partners Inc
Wada, Keisuke–Incubate Fund No1 Investment LPS
Wada, Kengo–Mezzanine Corp
Waddell, John–Archangel Informal Investment Ltd
Waddell, Kristin–Spell Capital Partners LLC
Waddington, Ryan–Huron River Venture Partners LLC
Wade, Brian–Atlantic-Pacific Capital Inc
Wade, Gary–Mckenna Gale Capital Inc
Wade, Hugh–Madison Capital Funding LLC
Wade, James–M/C Venture Partners LLC
Wadhwani, Ashish–IvyCap Ventures Advisors Pvt Ltd
Wadhwani, Dan–Velocity Venture Capital Inc
Wadhwani, Romesh–Altos Capital Partners LLC
Wadih, Anibal–GEF Management Corp
Wadlington, Claire–Fa Technology Ventures Corp
Wadsworth, Chris–Ceyuan Ventures Management LLC
Wadsworth, Eliot–Housatonic Partners Management Co Inc
Wadsworth, Jordan–Sun Capital Partners Inc
Wadsworth, Robert–Baml Capital Access Funds Management LLC
Wagatsuma, Yukako–Morrison & Foerster LLP
Wagenberg, Alex–Carlyle Group LP
Wagenberg, Lawrence–Wheatley Partners
Wagle, Sameer–Asia Pacific Healthcare Advisors Pvt Ltd
Wagner, Alyse–Leonard Green & Partners LP
Wagner, Bradaigh–Endeavour Capital Inc

Wagner, Bryan—Creation Investments Capital Management LLC
Wagner, Christina—Inveni Capital Oy
Wagner, Dennis—Cyprium Investment Partners LLC
Wagner, Elliot—Carlyle Group LP
Wagner, Eran—GEMINI CAPITAL FUND MGMT LTD
Wagner, Eric—Montgomery & Co LLC
Wagner, Ira—European Capital
Wagner, Ira—European Capital Financial Services Ltd
Wagner, J. Peter—Accel Partners & Co Inc
Wagner, Jim—Evergreen Group Ventures LLC
Wagner, John—Granite Hall Partners Inc
Wagner, Karen—Ysios Capital Partners SGECR SAU
Wagner, Markus—i5invest Beratungs GmbH
Wagner, Rachael—Atairos Management LP
Wagner, Rachael—Lindsay Goldberg & Bessemer LP
Wagonfeld, Alison—Emergence Capital Partners
Wahi, Pradeep—Blu Venture Investors LLC
Wahla, Ahmed—Kohlberg & Co LLC
Wahlen, Edwin—Cgw Southeast Partners
Wahlsten, Ralf—Open Ocean Capital Oy
Wahrhaftig, David—Kelso & Company LP
Wai, Patrick Yee Chee—OSK Ventures International Bhd
Wainer, Danielle—Elevar Equity Advisors Pvt Ltd
Waite, Andrew—SCF Partners LP
Waite, Chad—Greylock Partners LLC
Waitz, Laura—Blackstone Group LP
Waizer, Yoav—Medica Venture Partners, Ltd.
Wakasa, Tetsuo—JVIC Venture Capital Co Ltd
Wakashita, Hiro—Riverside Co
Wakeman, Fred—Advent International Corp
Walch-Watson, Patrice—Canada Pension Plan Investment Board
Walcott, Jesse—Torch Hill Investment Partners LLC
Wald, Hiroshi—Austral Capital
Wald, Ryan—Gores Group LLC
Walden, Michael—Rethink Education LP
Walden, Michael—Seavest Capital Partners LLC
Waldman, David—Quark Ventures LLC
Waldman, Thomas—Gores Group LLC
Waldorf, Gregory—Accel Partners & Co Inc
Waldron, Jared—Northleaf Capital Partners Ltd
Waldstreicher, Jonathan—Apple Tree Partners
Waldvogel, Christian—Vinci Capital Switzerland SA
Walecka, John—Redpoint Ventures
Walendowski, Dawid—Highlander Partners LP
Walfish, Marc—Merit Capital Partners IV LLC
Walgenbach, Ewald—BC Partners LLP
Walinsky, Marc—Jwi Capital LLC
Walji, Zenobia—Oaktree Capital Management LP
Walk, Hunter—Homebrew LLC
Walker, Andrew—Milbank Tweed Hadley & Mccloy LLP
Walker, Breaux—New Access Capital
Walker, C. Thayer—Algonquin Advisors LLC
Walker, Chet—Forsyth Capital Investors LLC
Walker, Colin—Crosbie & Co Inc
Walker, Courtdale—Developing World Markets Inc
Walker, Dan—Fpe Capital LLP
Walker, Ian—Northgate Capital LLC
Walker, Jack—Quad-C Management Inc
Walker, James—Clearspring Capital Partners
Walker, Joe—Freeport Financial Partners LLC
Walker, John—Kensington Capital Partners Ltd
Walker, Kathy—OPENAIR Equity Partners
Walker, Lee—Owner Resource Group LLC
Walker, Mark—Millstein & Co LP
Walker, Mark—New Magellan Venture Partners LLC
Walker, Mike—Mobeus Equity Partners LLP
Walker, Nicole—Baird Capital
Wall, Doug—Volcano Capital LLC
Wall, Kevin—Craton Equity Partners LLC
Wall, Thomas—Kelso & Company LP
Wallace, Ben—Azalea Capital LLC
Wallace, Brian—Access Venture Partners
Wallace, George—SV Health Investors LLP
Wallace, Jason—Blackstone Group LP
Wallace, Jonathan—Wwc Capital Fund L P
Wallace, Ken—Industry Ventures LLC
Wallace, Ken—Industry Ventures LLC
Wallace, Laurie—Yaletown Venture Partners
Wallace, Neil—Primary Capital Ltd
Wallace, Peter—Blackstone Group LP
Wallace, Reymond—Sterling Group LP
Wallace, Robert—Tallwave LLC
Wallace, Wayne—Mutual Capital Partners
Wallach, Israel—WL Ross & Co LLC
Wallander, Ray—Wayzata Investment Partners LLC
Waller, Paul—Hamilton Lane Advisors LLC
Walley, Noah—Investor Growth Capital AB
Walley, Noah—Investor Growth Capital Inc
Wallis, Darren—Alara Capital Partners LLC
Wallis, Ian—MML Capital Partners LLP
Wallis, James—Lime Rock Partners LLC
Wallis, James—Natural Gas Partners
Walls, Garrett—AG BD LLC
Walls, Stephen—Next Wave Partners LLP
Wallsten, Erik—Adobe Capital
Walouke, Douglas—Fund Evaluation Group LLC
Walrod, David—Bridgescale Partners LP
Walsh, Colin—Crescent Capital NI Ltd
Walsh, David—Kayne Anderson Capital Advisors LP
Walsh, Dennis—AeroEquity Partners LLC
Walsh, Dennis—Blackstone Group LP
Walsh, Frank—Enterprise Equity Venture Capital Group
Walsh, Kevin—Horizon Technology Finance Management LLC
Walsh, Mark—Versa Capital Management Inc
Walsh, Meggan—CIT Group Inc
Walsh, Michael—Ardenton Capital Corp
Walsh, Michael—Structure Capital LP
Walsh, Paul—Calera Capital Management Inc
Walsh, Robert—Evercore Inc
Walsh, Timothy—CCMP Capital Advisors LP
Walsh, Tom—Vector Capital Management LP
Walsh, William—Portfolio Advisors, LLC
Walter, Jochen—Baytech Venture Capital GmbH & Co KG
Walters, Eric—Morrison & Foerster LLP
Walters, Frank—Silver Lake Partners LP
Walters, Greg—Baker & McKenzie LLP
Walters, Jeff—Capstone Financial Partners LLC
Walters, Jeffrey—LaSalle Capital
Walton, Alan—Oxford Bioscience Partners
Walton, Andrew—Ironbridge Equity Partners Management Ltd
Walton, Andrew—Signal Hill Equity Partners
Walton, Derek—Acas LLC
Walton, Frances—Nystar
Walton, Roger—Castile Ventures
Walton, Sarah—Gemcorp Capital LLP
Walton, Wyche—New MainStream Capital
Walvoord, Andy—Greenline Ventures LLC
Walzer, Oliver—Incuray AG
Wan, Joseph—Cinven Group Ltd
Wan, Mark—Three Arch Partners LP
Wand, Michael—Carlyle Group LP
Wanek, David—Western Technology Investment
Wang, Alfredo—Antares Capital Corp
Wang, Amy—MDB Capital Group LLC
Wang, Andy—Innovation Camp Investment Consulting (Shanghai) Co Ltd
Wang, Baohua—Milestone Capital Management Ltd
Wang, Bei—Richlink International Capital Co Ltd
Wang, Bill—Morgan Stanley Private Equity
Wang, Bingshi—Southern Raytai Fund Management Co Ltd
Wang, Bruce—Hony Capital Beijing Co Ltd
Wang, Changzhen—Shenzhen QF Capital Management Co Ltd
Wang, Dajun—Ample Luck International Capital Group Ltd
Wang, David—OrbiMed Advisors LLC
Wang, Dennis—MBK Partners Inc
Wang, Dong—Will Capital
Wang, Dongxiang—Avantage Ventures Capital LLC
Wang, Enpei—Shenzhen Rongchuang Venture Capital Co Ltd
Wang, Fanglu—CITIC Capital Partners Ltd
Wang, Feng—Beijing Jike Menggongchang Venture Capital Center (L.P.)
Wang, Frances—China Renaissance Capital Investment Ltd
Wang, Frank—Medley Capital LLC
Wang, Fred—Adams Street Partners LLC
Wang, Fred—Trinity Ventures LLP
Wang, Gang—Shanghai Cheng Feng Investment Co Ltd
Wang, Gigi—iGlobe Partners Ltd
Wang, Gregory Feihong—Morrison & Foerster LLP
Wang, Guangyu—China King Link Corp
Wang, Hai—Zhongrong International Trust Co Ltd
Wang, Hang—Beijing Hosen Capital Management Center LP
Wang, Hans—CVC Asia Pacific Ltd
Wang, Hao—Greenwoods Asset Management Ltd
Wang, Hui—Hanfor (Beijing) Investment Co Ltd
Wang, Hui—HighLight Capital
Wang, Irene—Falcon Investment Advisors LLC
Wang, Janet—Oaktree Capital Management LP
Wang, Jennifer—Phoenix Venture Partners LLC
Wang, Jia—Shenzhen Jin sheng Shuo Industry Asset Management Co., Ltd.
Wang, Jiaming—Shenzhen Gold Match Silver Fund Management Co Ltd
Wang, Jian—Shenzhen Dongfang Shengfu Venture Capital Management Co Ltd
Wang, Jianbo—Prime Value Capital Management Ltd
Wang, Jianping—Guangdong Xiyu Investment Management Co Ltd
Wang, Jianqing—Legend Capital Co Ltd
Wang, Jiansheng—Actis LLP
Wang, Jimmy—Cmia Capital Partners Pte Ltd

Wang, Jimmy–HPEF Capital Partners Ltd
Wang, Jingbo–IDG Capital Partners Inc
Wang, Joan–Pacific Venture Partners Co Ltd
Wang, John–China Science & Merchants Investment Management Group Co Ltd
Wang, Jonas–Sycamore Ventures Inc
Wang, Jonathan–Legend Capital Co Ltd
Wang, Jonathan–OrbiMed Advisors LLC
Wang, Joseph–Jade Investment Consulting (Shanghai) Co Ltd
Wang, Jun–Beijing Tianxing Chuanglian Investment Management Co., Ltd.
Wang, Jun–L Catterton Asia
Wang, Junfeng–Legend Capital Co Ltd
Wang, Keddy–Ascend Capital Partners
Wang, Kevin–Altimeter Capital Management LP
Wang, Laure–Asia Alternatives Management LLC
Wang, Le-Chun–PAC-LINK Management Corp
Wang, Lei–Boxin Capital
Wang, Liang–Rongxin Capital Fund Management Ltd
Wang, Libo–Shanghai Fortune United Investment Group Co Ltd
Wang, Lie–Shanghai Lianxin Investment Management Co Ltd
Wang, Lihong–Bain Capital Inc
Wang, Lin–CDH China Management Co., Ltd.
Wang, Lin–Chatham Capital
Wang, Linda–Hony Capital Beijing Co Ltd
Wang, Liqun–LYRIQUE Srrl
Wang, Lynn–Centenium-Pinetree China Private Equity
Wang, May–Gobi Partners
Wang, Mingyao–Legend Star Venture Incubator
Wang, Nengguang–Legend Capital Co Ltd
Wang, Patrick–Evercore Inc
Wang, Paul–Pacific Venture Partners Co Ltd
Wang, Ping–Korea Investment Partners Co Ltd
Wang, Ping–Luxin Venture Capital Group Co Ltd
Wang, Qi–Qiming Venture Partners Ii LP
Wang, Qian–Warburg Pincus LLC
Wang, Qiuhu–Kaiwu Capital Co Ltd
Wang, Qiwen–Shenzhen Cornerstone of Entrepreneurial Cci Capital Ltd
Wang, Sha–Cybernaut (China) Venture Capital Management Co Ltd
Wang, Shangjun–Greenwoods Asset Management Ltd
Wang, Shaodong–Bright Stone Investment Management (Hong Kong) Ltd
Wang, Shaojun–Beijing Capital Investment Co Ltd
Wang, Sheffield–Agile Venture Capital LLC
Wang, Shuhe–Grace Assets Management LLP
Wang, Shunlong–Hony Capital Beijing Co Ltd
Wang, Sing–Tpg Growth LLC
Wang, Stanley–SAIF Partners
Wang, T. Chester–Acorn Campus Ventures
Wang, Tao–Bright Stone Investment Management (Hong Kong) Ltd
Wang, Tianyang–Shenzhen Green Pine Capital Partners Co Ltd
Wang, Tim–Blackstone Group LP
Wang, Tom–PTI Ventures
Wang, Tony–Centenium-Pinetree China Private Equity

Wang, Victor–HOF Capital Inc
Wang, Wei–Shenzhen Co-Win Venture Capital Investments Ltd
Wang, Wenyong–Burrill & Company
Wang, William–Avantage Ventures Capital LLC
Wang, Xiaodong–Greenwoods Asset Management Ltd
Wang, Xiaoju–ZEVC Management Co Ltd
Wang, Xiaoli–ZEVC Management Co Ltd
Wang, Xiaoyong–Sharewin Equity Fund Management Co Ltd
Wang, Xin–Investor Growth Capital AB
Wang, Xin–Investor Growth Capital Inc
Wang, Xin–New Horizon Capital
Wang, Xinwei–CRP-Fanya Investment Consultants Beijing Co Ltd
Wang, Xuemei–Tianjin Gobi-Hitech Investment Management Co Ltd
Wang, Yan–BOC International Holdings Ltd
Wang, Yantao–CAC Capital Management Co Ltd
Wang, Ye–Liuhe Capital LLC
Wang, Ye–Sinovation Ventures Ltd
Wang, Yi–Beijing Tianxing Chuanglian Investment Management Co., Ltd.
Wang, Yi–Ceyuan Ventures Management LLC
Wang, Yigong–WI Harper Group Inc
Wang, Yijun–China Venture Capital Co Ltd
Wang, Ying–Northern Light Venture Capital Development Ltd
Wang, Yong–Innovation Camp Investment Consulting (Shanghai) Co Ltd
Wang, Yong–Shenzhen Green Pine Capital Partners Co Ltd
Wang, Yunlin–Hunan Xiangtou Holdings Group Co Ltd
Wang, Zhen–hanghai SmallVille Financial Advisor Co Ltd
Wang, Zheng–Silver Lake Partners LP
Wang, Zhenmu–Fujian Red Bridge Capital Management Co Ltd
Wang, Zhenmu–Prax Capital Management Co
Wang, Zhenyu–CDH China Management Co., Ltd.
Wang, Zhenzhong–Tianjin Binhai Haisheng Equity Investment Fund Mgmt Co.
Wang, Zhiping–Beijing Tianxing Chuanglian Investment Management Co., Ltd.
Wang, Zhonghui–Zero2IPO Ventures
Wanger, Anthony–GBT Capital LLC
Wangli, Sherry–MW Capital Inc
Wanske, Bruno–Pricoa Capital Group Ltd
Waravanitcha, Naravadee–Food Capitals PCL
Warbey, James–Milbank Tweed Hadley & Mccloy LLP
Warburg, Richard–Auven Therapeutics Management LLLP
Ward, Andrew–Riverstone Holdings LLC
Ward, Carter–ArcLight Capital Holdings LLC
Ward, Charles–Perella Weinberg Partners LP
Ward, Collins–Lee Equity Partners LLC
Ward, David–Mti Partners Ll
Ward, David–Salix Ventures LP
Ward, Greg–Macquarie Group Ltd
Ward, Greg–Macquarie Investment Management Ltd
Ward, Jim–Alsop Louie Partners
Ward, John–Key Venture Partners
Ward, Julia–Algebra Capital Ltd

Ward, Michael–Morrison & Foerster LLP
Ward, Mike–Questmark Partners LP
Ward, Nathan–Palm Beach Capital Management LLC
Ward, Paul–Pantheon Ventures (UK) LLP
Ward, Peter–Rcapital Ltd
Ward, Scott–Sightline Partners LLC
Ward, Sean–Blue Point Capital Partners LP
Ward, Shannon–Oaktree Capital Management LP
Ward, Tracy–Strand Equity Partners LLC
Warden, Robert–Pamplona Capital Management LLP
Warden, Steven–Varagon Capital Partners LP
Warden, Todd–Harbor Light Capital Partners LLC
Wardi, Teddie–Insight Venture Partners LLC
Wardlaw, William–Freeman Spogli & Co LLC
Wardman-Browne, Stuart–Amwin Management Pty Ltd
Wardrop, Brian–Arx Equity Partners Sp z o o
Ware, Zach–VegasTechFund
Waring, David–Evercore Inc
Warland, Shannon–Muller & Monroe Asset Management LLC
Warland, Shannon–Muller & Monroe Asset Management LLC
Warner, Eric–Pavilion Alternatives Group Ltd
Warner, Greg–Ingleside Investors LLC
Warner, Ileen–Jefferson Education Accelerator LLC
Warner, John–CCMP Capital Advisors LP
Warner, Louis–Founders Factory Ltd
Warnholtz, Christian–Wamex Private Equity Management
Warnken-Brill, John–Vista Equity Partners LLC
Warnock, Greg–Mercato Management LLC
Warnock, Todd–Roundtable Healthcare Partners LP
Waroquier, David–Mangrove Capital Partners SA
Warrell, Geoffrey–Julip Run Capital LLC
Warren, Chris–ECI Partners LLP
Warren, Gus–FirstMark Capital LLC
Warren, Jermaine–ICV Partners LLC
Warren, Kenneth–LJ2 & Co LLC
Warren, Laura–Hamilton Lane Advisors LLC
Warren, Lisa–Research Partners Ltd
Warren, Michael–Oak Hill Capital Management Inc
Warren, Todd–Divergent Venture Partners Affiliates I LP
Warren, Tracy–Battelle Ventures LP
Warren, Wilson–Lexington Partners Inc
Warrick, Vincent–Thompson Street Capital Partners LP
Warriner, Don–Headwaters BD LLC
Warwick, Ian–Deepbridge Capital LLP
Waserstein, David–I2Bf Global Ventures
Washburn, Alexander–Columbia Pacific Advisors LLC
Washing, Thomas–Sequel Venture Partners
Washington, Alex–Wind Point Advisors LLC
Washington, Keysha–Breakout Capital LLC
Washington, Kirk–Yaletown Venture Partners
Washington, Vivian–Grace Assets Management LLP
Wasilisin, John–Maryland Technology Development Corp
Wasim, Tarim–Hellman & Friedman LLC
Waskovich, James–Princeton Ventures Management LLC
Wassenaar, Olivia–Riverstone Holdings LLC

2587

Pratt's Guide to Private Equity & Venture Capital Sources

Wasserman, David—Clayton Dubilier & Rice LLC
Wasserman, Thomas—HPS Investment Partners LLC
Wassink, Kuif—Baker & McKenzie LLP
Wasso-Jonikas, Louise—AG BD LLC
Wasti, Ali—Azure Capital Partners, L.P.
Watanabe, August—Twilight Venture Partners
Watanabe, Gwen—Saratoga Ventures, L.P.
Watanabe, Hiroshi—Gogin Capital Co Ltd
Watanabe, Kyoko—Defta Partners
Watanabe, Ryuji—Mitsubishi International Corp
Watanabe, Yasuharu—Worldview Technology Partners, Inc.
Watanabe, Yusuke—Carlyle Group LP
Waterfield, J. Randall—Cappello Capital Corp
Waterfield, Richard—Cappello Capital Corp
Waterhouse, Daniel—Balderton Capital LLP
Waterhouse, Daniel—Wellington Partners GmbH
Waterhouse, Frank—Highland Capital Management LP
Waterman, David—DeltaPoint Capital Management LLC
Waterman, Nash—Morgan Stanley Alternative Investment Partners LP
Waters, James—Compass Partners International LLC
Waters, Steve—Compass Partners International Llp
Waters, Thomas—Sinclair Ventures Inc
Waterson, Tim—Gold Hill Capital Management LLC
Waterstreet, Jack—Insight Equity Holdings LLC
Watkins, Dan—Mercury Fund
Watkins, John—M/C Venture Partners LLC
Watkins, Timothy—Valor Equity Parters L P
Watler, Kenneth—Hancock Park Associates A California LP
Watson, Christopher—Aquiline Capital Partners LLC
Watson, David—Redwood Capital Investments LLC
Watson, Gordon—Victory Park Capital Advisors LLC
Watson, Harry—Blackeagle Partners Fund L P
Watson, J. Derek—Windjammer Capital Investors LLC
Watson, James—CMEA Development Company LLC
Watson, Jesse—Virgo Investment Group LLC
Watson, Paul—Digitech Venture Capital Fund Inc
Watson, Tom—JPB Partners LLC
Watt, Chris—ECI Partners LLP
Watt, Fred—CVC Capital Partners Ltd
Watt, Hamet—Upfront Ventures
Watt, Peter—Helmsman Funds Management, Ltd.
Watt, Trevor—Hellman & Friedman LLC
Watts, Andrew—Oaktree Capital Management LP
Watts, Claudius—Carlyle Group LP
Watts, J. C.—Oakcrest Capital Partners LLC
Watts, Jeff—FRANK RUSSELL CAPITAL CO
Watts, Mark—Marwyn Investment Management LLP
Watts, Mark—PHD Equity Partners LLP
Watts, Michael—Linden LLC
Watts, Nigel—Asclepios Bioresearch (UK) Ltd
Watts, Todd—Strathspey Crown LLC
Watts, William—J.W.Childs Associates LP
Waugh, Stuart—Northleaf Capital Partners Ltd
Waugh, Stuart—TD Capital Group Ltd
Wautier, Jean-Baptiste—BC Partners LLP
Wax, David—WL Ross & Co LLC
Waxman, Albert—Psilos Group Managers LLC
Waxman, David—Equip Ventures LLC
Waxman, David—TenOneTen Ventures LP
Wayne, Steven—Oak Hill Advisors LP

Weatherston, Kevin—CORE Partners LLC
Weaver, Allen—Prudential Capital Group LP
Weaver, Graham—Alpine Investors LP
Weaver, Kent—Accretia Capital LLC
Weavers-Wright, Elaine—Haatch Ltd
Weavers-Wright, Scott—Haatch Ltd
Weavers-Wright, Sophie—Haatch Ltd
Webb, Brad—Claremont Creek Ventures LP
Webb, C.A.—AssembleVC Fund I LP
Webb, David—SFW Capital Partners LLC
Webb, David—SunTx Capital Partners LP
Webb, Jeffrey—Industrial Growth Partners
Webb, Jeffrey—Ridge Capital Partners LLC
Webb, Lincoln—British Columbia Investment Management Corp
Webb, Winifred—Tennenbaum Capital Partners LLC
Webber, Brian—American Discovery Capital LLC
Webber, David—Stonehenge Growth Capital LLC
Webber, Graham—Future Capital Partners Ltd
Webber, Jeffrey—Entrepreneurs Fund LP
Webber, Jeffrey—RB Webber and Comapny Inc
Weber, Barbara—Third Rock Ventures LLC
Weber, Eckard—Domain Associates LLC
Weber, Jameson—Oaktree Capital Management LP
Weber, Jeffrey—DC Capital Partners LLC
Weber, Johannes—Ananda Ventures GmbH
Weber, John—Court Square Capital Partners LP
Weber, John—Laurel Capital Partners
Weber, John—Roth Capital Partners LLC
Weber, Michael—Riverside Co
Weber, Patrick—EQT Funds Management Ltd
Weber, Rochus—Risikokapital Fonds Allgaeu GmbH & Co KG
Weber, Sarik—Hanse Ventures BSJ GmbH
Weber, Sonnfried—BayBG Bayerische Beteiligungsgesellschaft mbH
Weber, Sven—SharesPost Financial Corp
Weber, Sven—Silicon Valley Bancventures LP
Weber, Tony—Natural Gas Partners
Webering, Jan—BTH Berlin Technologie Holding GmbH
Webster, Andrew—Boost&Co SAS
Webster, David—Fusion Capital
Webster, Ian—Axioma Ventures LLC
Webster, Robert—Twin Haven Capital Partners LLC
Webster, Thomas—Vintage Capital Partners, L.P.
Wecken, Gerlach—Next Wave Funds
Wedbush, Eric—Wedbush Capital Partners LP
Wedel, Michael—B12 Capital Partners LLC
Wedner, Marcus—CIVC Partners LP
Wee, Caroline—Baring Private Equity Asia Ltd
Wee, Ericson—AB Capital and Investment Corp
Wee, Ronnie—Incuvest Pte Ltd
Weed, Alan—Arbor Private Investment Co LLC
Weekes, Jeffrey—Palisade Capital Management LLC
Weene, Adam—Saban Capital Group Inc
Wegman, Ewout—5Square BV
Wegner, Patricia—MergerTech Advisors
Wegter, Mark—Life Sciences Partners BV
Weheba, Sami—Itqan Capital Co
Wehrfritz, Jim—Antares Capital Corp
Wehrle, John—DTI Capital LLC
Wehrle, Neil—Betaworks Studio LLC
Wei, Boh Sang—Southern Capital Group Pte Ltd
Wei, David—Amino Capital Management Company LLC

Wei, Eric—Advent International Corp
Wei, Frank—Warburg Pincus LLC
Wei, James—Worldview Technology Partners, Inc.
Wei, Jianping—ABC Capital Management Co Ltd
Wei, Ke—General Atlantic LLC
Wei, Lidong—Beijing Huinong Capital Management Co Ltd
Wei, Tina—FLAG Capital Management LLC
Wei, Xiaoshuang—Shenzhen Team-top Investment Management Co Ltd
Wei, Zhou—Jade Investment Consulting (Shanghai) Co Ltd
Wei, Zhu—Standard Chartered Private Equity Ltd
Weiblen, Martin—Heidelbergcapital Asset Management GmbH
Weichert, Rudolf—Indus Holding AG
Weidemoyer, Matthew—Blackstone Group LP
Weiden, David—Khosla Ventures LLC
Weidenhammer, Chris—Tillery Capital LLC
Weidner, James—Atlantic-Pacific Capital Inc
Weidner, Jan—Blackstone Group LP
Weigand, Johnathan—Steel Pier Capital Advisors LLC
Weigand, Nestor—Siguler Guff & Company LP
Weiguo, Zhao—Ceyuan Ventures Management LLC
Weikart, Eric—Cornerstone Advisors Inc
Weil, Burton—Venture Associates Partners LLC
Weiland, Armin—Partners Group Holding AG
Weilby Knudsen, Thomas—Internet Ventures Scandinavia
Weiler, Melissa—Crescent Capital Group LP
Weilgus, Joseph—Syno Capital LLC
Weimer, Carolyn—Carlyle Group LP
Weinberg, Andrew—Lindsay Goldberg & Bessemer LP
Weinberg, Michael—Levine Leichtman Capital Partners Inc
Weinberg, Peter—Perella Weinberg Partners LP
Weinberg, Ronald—Weinberg Capital Group
Weinberg, Ronald—Weinberg Capital Group
Weinberger, Paul—Gcp Gamma Capital Partners Beratungs & Beteiligungs AG
Weinberger, Paul—i5invest Beratungs GmbH
Weiner, Dennis—Responder Ventures LLC
Weiner, Glenn—Barings LLC
Weiner, Jonathan—Oak HC/FT Partners LP
Weiner, Joshua—First Reserve Corp
Weiner, Marc—Tandem Expansion Fund I LP
Weiner, Michael—Ares Capital Corp
Weiner, Scott—Pappas Ventures
Weinfeld, Alan—Gatewood Capital Partners LLC
Weingeist, Daniel—Kayne Anderson Capital Advisors LP
Weinhoff, Gregory—CHL Medical Partners LP
Weinman, Barry—AllegisCyber
Weinmann, Mike—Capital Royalty LP
Weinmann, Thomas—Astorius Capital GmbH
Weinryb, Merav—Pitango Venture Capital Management Israel, Ltd.
Weinstein, Allan—Gainline Capital Partners, L.P.
Weinstein, Evan—CI Capital Partners LLC
Weinstein, Paul—Azure Capital Partners, L.P.
Weinstein, Steve—Novartis Venture Funds
Weintraub, Josh—Cerberus Capital Management LP
Weir, Christopher—Potomac Energy Fund LP

Weir, Jeremy—Galena Asset Management Ltd
Weirich, Jochen—Partners Group Holding AG
Weisel, Rebecca—Lexington Partners Inc
Weisenfeld, Andrew—MTS Health Partners LP
Weiser, Marc—RPM Ventures Management LLC
Weiskam, Andreas—Sapphire Ventures LLC
Weiskam, Andreas—Sapphire Ventures LLC
Weisker, Jeffrey—Fund Evaluation Group LLC
Weisman, Wayne—SCP Private Equity Partners
Weiss, Bill—Acas LLC
Weiss, Christian—Project A Ventures GmbH & Co KG
Weiss, Daniel—Angeleno Group Investors LLC
Weiss, Eli—Genstar Capital LLC
Weiss, Ira—Hyde Park Venture Partners
Weiss, Joel—Jerusalem Global Ventures
Weiss, Marc—Partners Group Holding AG
Weiss, Paul—Venture Investors LLC
Weiss, Randy—Triathlon Medical Ventures LLC
Weiss, Robert—Bain Capital Inc
Weiss, Robyn—Wilshire Private Markets
Weiss, Russell—Morrison & Foerster LLP
Weiss, Shai—Virgin Green Fund
Weiss, Warren—Foundation Capital LLC
Weisschaedel, Gerhard—Invision AG
Weisskoff, Robert—F-Prime Capital Partners
Weissman, Andrew—Union Square Ventures LLC
Weissmann, Richard—KSL Capital Partners LLC
Weithman, Tom—Center For Innovative Technology
Weitzberg, Toni—Nordic Capital
Weitzman, Patty—Antares Capital Corp
Weklar, Edward—Arlington Capital Partners
Wekselblatt, Joseph—AG BD LLC
Welborn, Kyle—Cultivation Capital
Welborn, Stephen—Wynnchurch Capital Ltd
Welch, Alan—Carousel Capital Partners
Welch, Andrew—Revelstoke Capital Partners LLC
Welch, Christopher—Method Advisors LLC
Welch, Colin—TSG Consumer Partners, L.P.
Welch, Richard—Colony Capital LLC
Welch, Thomas—Victory Park Capital Advisors LLC
Weld, Daniel—MadroNA Venture Group
Weld, Timothy—StepStone Group LP
Welde, Joar—Viking Venture As
Weldon, Guy—Bridgepoint Advisers Ltd
Weldon, Kent—Thomas H Lee Partners LP
Weldon, Norman—Partisan Management Group Inc
Weldon, Raymond—Brookside International
Welge, Peter—DMB Deutsche Mittelstandsbeteiligungs GmbH
Wellauer, Thomas—BlackRock Private Equity Partners AG
Weller, Andrew—Industrial Opportunity Partners LLC
Weller, Harry—New Enterprise Associates Inc
Weller, R. Jason—Willis Stein & Partners LP
Welles, Timothy—Pine Street Capital Partners LP
Wellford, Brandon—Innova Memphis Inc
Wellman, Daniel—Crestview Advisors, LLC
Wells, Calvin—Ascend Global Investments LLC
Wells, Michael—Princeton Biopharma Capital Partners LLC
Wells, Norman—SFW Capital Partners LLC
Welo, Morten—FSN Capital Partners AS
Welsch, Todd—AEA Investors LLC
Welsh, Patrick—Vocap Investment Partners LLC
Welsh, Patrick—Welsh Carson Anderson & Stowe

Weltman, Robert—Genstar Capital LLC
Welton, Stephen—Business Growth Fund PLC
Welzel, Michael—Cbr Management GmbH
Wen, Aaron—Orchid Asia Group Management Ltd
Wen, Baoma—Capital Today China Growth HK Ltd
Wen, Chenhui—Prime Value Capital Management Ltd
Wen, David—Carlyle Group LP
Wen, Dustin—Allshare Capital
Wen, Lei—Beijing Tianxing Chuanglian Investment Management Co., Ltd.
Wen, Sidney—Steamboat Ventures
Wen, Zhijun—Greenwoods Asset Management Ltd
Wen, Zhimin—San Shan Capital Partners Ltd
Wendelken, Hans-Juergen—Freudenberg Venture Capital GmbH
Wendell, Michel—Nexit Ventures Oy
Wendell, Peter—Sierra Ventures
Wendell, Rob—Marwit Capital Corp
Weng, Jingjing—Xiamen Aceon Venture Investment Co Ltd
Weng, Jiyi—Ivy Capital Ltd
Weng, Yinuo—Shanghai Hongzhang Investment Management Co Ltd
Wenger, Albert—Union Square Ventures LLC
Wenick, Eric—glendonTodd Capital LLC
Wenn, Bruno—DEG Deutsche Investitions- und Entwicklungsgesellschaft mbH
Wenngren, Erik—Spintop Private Partners AB
Wennmachers, Margit—Andreessen Horowitz LLC
Wentink, Timothy—Madison Capital Funding LLC
Wentworth, Carol—Draper Fisher Jurvetson
Wentzel, Johan—Sentica Partners Oy
Wepsic, Eric—D E Shaw & Co LP
Werdegar, Maurice—Western Technology Investment
Werndl, Manfred—Salzburger Unternehmensbeteiligungs-gesellschaft mbH in Liqu
Werner, Harold—Healthcare Ventures LLC
Werner, Lionel—Euro Capital SAS
Wernicke, Carl—Oak Hill Advisors LP
Werry, Scott—Altas Partners LP
Wertheim, Harvey—Harvest Partners LP
Wertheimer, Stephen—W Capital Management LLC
Wertlieb, Neil—Milbank Tweed Hadley & Mccloy LLP
Wertz, Boris—Acton Capital Partners GmbH
Wertz, Boris—GrowLab Ventures Inc
Werwaiss, John—Lindsay Goldberg & Bessemer LP
Wesner, Blaine—Austin Ventures
Wessan, Neil—CIT Group Inc
Wessel, Paul—Milbank Tweed Hadley & Mccloy LLP
Wessel, Tadd—OrbiMed Advisors LLC
Wessel-Aas, Stein—Anchor Capital Management Ltd
Wessel-As, Stein—Anchor Capital Management Ltd
Wesselink, Pieter—Export Venture Capital Corporation (Pty) Ltd
Wessels, Manie—Spinnaker Growth Partners (Pty) Ltd
Wesson, Bruce—Galen Associates Inc
West, Alan—Pittsburgh Life Sciences Greenhouse
West, Bob—Aurora Resurgence Management Partners LLC
West, Brad—Pritzker Group Venture Capital
West, Casey—SSM Partners LP
West, Collin—Correlation Ventures LP
West, Dick—Midwest Venture Alliance

West, Dobson—Spell Capital Partners LLC
West, Gary—West Partners LLC
West, Jenny—Probitas Partners Inc
West, John—Cottonwood Capital Partners LLC
West, John—Cottonwood Capital Partners LLC
West, Kurt—Nexo Capital Partners
West, Robert—Aurora Capital Group Ltd
West, Steven—Wexford Capital LP
West, Thomas—Brown Gibbons Lang & Company LLC
West, William—Investure LLC
Westberg, Jonathan—Lake Capital
Westbrook, Thomas—Bb&T Capital Partners LLC
Westby, Mike—Loxbridge Research Llp
Westcott, James—Blackstone Group LP
Westdyk, Tom—CIT Group Inc
Wester, Forest—Trivest Partners LP
Westergaard, Emile—Perella Weinberg Partners LP
Westerkamp, George—AlpInvest Partners BV
Westermann, Philipp—Proprium Capital Partners LP
Westervelt, William—Ashby Point Capital
Westley, Peter—Blum Capital Partners LP
Westly, Steven—Westly Group LLC
Westman, Daniel—Morrison & Foerster LLP
Weston, Denny—Fluke Venture Partners II LP
Weston, Graham—Geekdom LC
Weston, Jamie—Spring Mountain Capital LP
Weston, R. Patrick—Azalea Capital LLC
Westphal, Christoph—Longwood Founders Management LLC
Westphal, Rouven—Hasso Plattner Ventures Management GmbH
Westra, James—Advent International Corp
Westwater, John—Phase4 Ventures Ltd
Westwood, Dallin—Southwest Middle Market M&A
Wetherbee, Jeffrey—Glenmont Partners, LLC
Wetherell, David—Biomark Capital
Wetherell, David—Burrill & Company
Wetreich, Jonathan—Brown Brothers Harriman & Co
Wetzel, Robert—Augury Capital Partners
Wetzels, Mark—Egeria BV
Wever, Sean—5Square BV
Wewege, Anton—GroFin Capital (Pty) Ltd
Wexlberger, Christian—Inovis Capital GmbH
Weymouth, Elizabeth—Riverstone Holdings LLC
Whalen, Bryan—Trust Company of the West
Whalen, Christopher—Harvest Partners LP
Whalen, Kristian—Platte River Ventures LLC
Whaley, John—Norwest Equity Partners
Whaley, John—Norwest Mezzanine Partners
Whang, Derek—Carlyle Group LP
Whang, Tae Cheol—Capstone Partners LLC
Whatley, Mark—Evercore Inc
Wheat, Jason—Diversified Trust Company Inc
Wheatley, Michael—Blackeagle Partners Fund L P
Wheaton, Calbraith—ABS Capital Partners, Inc.
Wheelahan, Richard—CapitalSouth Partners LLC
Wheeler, Brian—Bertram Capital Management LLC
Wheeler, Carrie—TPG Capital Management LP
Wheeler, Ellie—Greycroft Partners LLC
Wheeler, Jonathan Edward—Morrison & Foerster LLP
Wheeler, Kurt—Clarus Ventures LLC
Wheeler, Thomas—Core Capital Partners Ii L P
Whelan, Edward—Berkshire Partners LLC
Whelan, J.P.—Kern Whelan Capital LLC
Whelan, Lori—Silversmith Capital Partners LLC

2589

Whelan, Matthew–Brentwood Associates, L.P.
Whelan, Matthew–Brentwood Venture Capital
Whelan, Sean–ECI Partners LLP
Whelan, Tim–AEA Investors LLC
Whileman, David–3i Group PLC
Whiley, Gareth–Silverfleet Capital Partners LLP
Whims, Jim–Alsop Louie Partners
Whims, Jim–Techfund Capital Europe
Whipple, Robert–Apax Partners LLP
Whipple, Robert–COGR Inc
Whisner, Corey–Rotunda Capital Partners LLC
Whisner, Corey–Thoma Bravo LLC
Whitaker, Jim–VentureLink Funds
Whitaker, Steven–Equistone Partners Europe Ltd
Whitby-Smith, Robert–Albion Capital Group LLP
Whitcomb, Aber–i/o ventures
Whitcomb, Daniel–Siguler Guff & Company LP
White, Andy–VegasTechFund
White, Anna Erickson–Morrison & Foerster LLP
White, Ben–Notion Capital Partners LLP
White, Brandon–Charlesbank Capital Partners LLC
White, Gregory–Thomas H Lee Partners LP
White, Gregory–Thomas Weisel Partners Group Inc
White, James–Pacific Advantage Capital Ltd
White, James–Sutter Hill Ventures
White, Jason–Jog Capital Inc
White, Jeanette–Northleaf Capital Partners Ltd
White, Jeff–Trestle Ventures
White, Jeffrey–Skyview Capital LLC
White, John–Calibrate Management Ltd
White, John–Founders Equity, Inc.
White, John–Murphree Venture Partners
White, John–Rivers Capital Partners Ltd
White, Jos–Notion Capital Partners LLP
White, Kevin–Court Square Capital Partners LP
White, Marshall–Acas LLC
White, Marshall–Bb&T Capital Partners LLC
White, Matthew–Falcon Investment Advisors LLC
White, Michael–Enercap Capital Partners
White, Michael–Harbert Management Corp
White, Morty–Wynnchurch Capital Ltd
White, Neil–HGGC LLC
White, Patrick–Hercules Capital Inc
White, Patrick–Monroe Capital LLC
White, Phil–3i Infrastructure PLC
White, Ronald–Morrison & Foerster LLP
White, Sean–Spire Capital Partners LP
White, Simon–Altitude Partners LLP
White, Steve–Skywood Ventures LLC
White, T. Scott–Private Advisors LLC
White, Timothy–Blackstone Group LP
White, W. Spalding–Salem Capital Partners, LP (FKA: Venture Capital Solutions)
Whitehead, George–Octopus Ventures Ltd
Whitehouse, David–Tennenbaum Capital Partners LLC
Whitehouse, Jonathan–Southern Cross Venture Partners Pty Ltd
Whitehouse, Jonathan–Talu Ventures Pty Ltd
Whitelaw, Robert–Graue Mill Partners LLC
Whitelaw, Sarah–Hall Capital Partners LLC
Whiteley, Jeremiah–Fund Evaluation Group LLC
Whiteley, Phyllis–Mohr Davidow Ventures
Whiteman, Raymond–Carlyle Group LP
Whiteman, Raymond–Stellex Capital Management LP
Whitestone, Randall–Carlyle Group LP
Whiting, Gordon–AG BD LLC
Whitley, Samuel–Digitech Venture Capital Fund Inc
Whitlock, Peter–Century Capital Management / Massachusetts Inc
Whitlock, Steve–PTV Healthcare Capital
Whitman, Andrew–2X CONSUMER PRODUCTS GROWTH PARTNERS L P
Whitman, Anne–Long Road Investment Counsel LLC
Whitcom, Brad–Renovus Capital Partners LP
Whitman, John–Sycamore Ventures Inc
Whitman, Keith–O'Melveny & Myers LLP
Whitman, Michael–Blackstone Group LP
Whitman, Michael–Citigroup Private Equity LP
Whitmire, Jason–Earlybird Venture Capital GmbH & Co KG
Whitney, Benson–Gideon Hixon Fund LP
Whitney, Griffin–Mistral Equity Partners LP
Whitney, Joseph–Treehouse Health LLC
Whitney, Kenneth–Blackstone Group LP
Whitney, Marcus–Jumpstart Foundry
Whitt, Jason–Vantagepoint Management Inc
Whittaker, Curt–New Energy Capital Corp
Whittel, Robert–Asssurance Mezzanine Fund
Whittemore, Alexander–Summit Partners LP
Whittemore, Alexander–Summit Partners LP
Whittemore, Nathaniel–Learn Capital Venture Partners LP
Whitticom, Mike–Truebridge Capital Partners LLC
Whittingham, Steven–Blue Equity LLC
Whittington, Todd–Loud Capital LLC
Whittle, Jonathan–Quona Capital Management Ltd
Whittle, Kevin–Sovereign Capital Ltd
Whorton, David–Tugboat Ventures LP
Whorton, David–Tugboat Ventures LP
Wiacek, Walter–Fenway Partners LLC
Wiberg, William–Advanced Technology Ventures
Wiberg, William–G20 Associates LLC
Wick, Chad–Maywic Select Investments
Wick, Tyler–ABRY Partners LLC
Wicker, Alain–Siparex Proximite Innovation SAS
Wicker, Mark–Morrison & Foerster LLP
Wickersheim, Micah–Pfingsten Partners LLC
Wickham, Bob–Rotunda Capital Partners LLC
Wicki, Andreas–HBM Healthcare Investments AG
Wickwire, Thomas–Carlyle Group LP
Widder, Ken–Latterell Venture Partners LP
Widdoes, L. Curtis–Skywood Ventures LLC
Widenhaupt, Jan–Advisum GmbH
Widmann, Mike–Silver Lake Partners LP
Widmann, Thomas–Wellington Partners GmbH
Widner, Melissa–Seapoint Ventures
Widroe, Greg–MVP Capital LLC
Wieclawski, Robert–Avallon Sp z o o
Wieczorek, John–Axiom Venture Partners LP
Wieder, Alfred–Alfred Wieder AG
Wiedman, Bill–Ascribe Capital, LLC
Wiedmer, Alexander–Iris Capital Management SAS
Wieduwilt, Marcel–Partners Group Holding AG
Wiegand, Andrew–Superior Capital Partners LLC
Wiegman, Albert–Langholm Capital LLP
Wien, Jared–Sun Capital Partners Inc
Wien, Per–Reiten & Co AS
Wienbar, Sharon–Scale Venture Partners
Wiencken, Kim–Northcap Partners ApS
Wiener, Bret–Gemspring Capital LLC
Wiener, Harold–Terra Venture Partners
Wiener, Klaus–Generali Private Equity Investments GmbH
Wierck, Ryan–Wafra Partners LLC
Wiersinga, Aldebert–Value Creation Capital BV
Wiese, Hanns-Peter–Global Life Science Ventures GmbH
Wiesen, Eric–Bullpen Capital LP
Wiesen, Eric–RRE Ventures LLC
Wiesenthal, Mark–Platinum Equity LLC
Wiesinger, Christian–Siemens Technology Accelerator GmbH
Wietrzyk, Robert–Lead Equities GmbH
Wigand, Jim–Millstein & Co LP
Wiggins, Steve–EW Healthcare Partners
Wigginton, Jim–True North Equity LLC
Wiggs, Peter–Archer Capital Pty Ltd
Wigle, Jeff–Banyan Capital Partners LP
Wigmore, Gary–Milbank Tweed Hadley & Mccloy LLP
Wignall, Mark–Mobeus Equity Partners LLP
Wijaya, Joyo–Tandem Entrepreneurs LLC
Wijnen, Marcel–Rabo Participaties BV
Wijono, Rizal–Shk Fund Management Ltd
Wikenheiser, Dean–Stone Arch Capital LLC
Wikse, Hans–Procuritas Partners Kb
Wikstrom, Tommy–AAC CAPITAL PARTNERS
Wilam, Piotr–Innovation Nest Sp z o o
Wilbert, Randy–CLSA Capital Partners HK Ltd
Wilcove, Brian–Artiman Management LLC
Wilcox, Kenneth–Silicon Valley Bancventures LP
Wilcox, Kevin–SF Holding Corp
Wilcox, Mike–Blackstone Group LP
Wilcox, Russ–Pillar Companies Management LLC
Wilde, Peter–Providence Equity Partners LLC
Wildeman, Rob–Parallel49 Equity
Wilder, Hugh–Carlyle Group LP
Wilds, David–First Avenue Partners, L.P.
Wildstein, Amy–Springboard Venture Fund LLC
Wildstein, Evan–Kohlberg & Co LLC
Wiley, Ben–Sixpoint Partners LLC
Wiley, James–Rizk Ventures LLC
Wiley, Nicole–Morgan Stanley Alternative Investment Partners LP
Wilford, Don–First Stone Venture Partners Inc
Wilford, M. Brad–Jordan Company LP
Wilhelm, Bernd–Hanseatische VC GmbH
Wilhelm, David–Adena Ventures
Wilhelm, Klemens–Fulcrum Capital Partners Inc
Wilhelm, Marcel–Brockhaus Private Equity GmbH
Wilhelm, Robert–Solid Ventures BV
Wilhelm, Robert–Van Den Ende & Deitmers BV
Wilhelmsen, Jens A.–Anchor Capital Management Ltd
Wilhem, Cack–Scale Venture Partners
Wilhjelm, Anne Cathrine–SEED Capital Management I/S
Wilke, Tiffany–Phenomenelle Angels Management LLC
Wilken, Dirk–CD Venture GmbH
Wilkerson, Darryl–Acorn Growth Companies
Wilkerson, Kathleen–Next Frontier Capital LLC
Wilkerson, L. John–Galen Associates Inc

Wilkey, Brent–Aqua Alta SA
Wilkins, Andrew–Atlantic Street Capital Management LLC
Wilkins, Andy–Atlantic Street Capital Management LLC
Wilkins, Eric–Pamlico Capital Management LP
Wilkins, Herb–Syncom Management Co Inc
Wilkins, Jay–Harvest Partners LP
Wilkinson, Alan–AEA Investors LLC
Wilkinson, Benjamin–Draper Esprit PLC
Wilkinson, Craig–Lloyds Development Capital (Holdings) Ltd
Wilkinson, Leslie–Martin Companies LLC
Wilkosz, Leon–DaneVest Tech Fund Advisors
Willard, Dustin–HarbourVest Partners LLC
Willard, Paul–Subtraction Capital
Willems, Ron–Participatiemaatschappij Oost Nederland NV
Willemse, Jurie–GroFin Capital (Pty) Ltd
Willemstein, Willem–Velocity Capital BV
Willer, Kevin–Chicago Ventures
Willer, Kevin–Pritzker Group Venture Capital
Willert, John–Capital Partners, Inc.
Willetts, Adrian–Bridgepoint Advisers II Ltd
Willetts, Adrian–Bridgepoint Advisers Ltd
Willey, Teri–Arch Development Partners LLC
Willhite, William–Thompson Street Capital Partners LP
Willhite, William–WILsquare Capital LLC
Williams, Alex–Terra Firma Capital Partners Ltd
Williams, Alexander–First Reserve Corp
Williams, Andrew–Gramercy Inc
Williams, Andrew–Michigan Accelerator Fund I Management LLC
Williams, Bill–Galen Associates Inc
Williams, Bradford–Crestview Advisors, LLC
Williams, Brent–Halifax Group LLC
Williams, Brian–Hopewell Ventures
Williams, Carl–Riverstone Holdings LLC
Williams, Christopher–AG BD LLC
Williams, Christopher–Madison Capital Funding LLC
Williams, Christopher–Oak Hill Capital Management Inc
Williams, Daniel–Ascent Equity Group LLC
Williams, Daniel–Bay Capital Investment Partners LLC
Williams, Daniel–Jordan Company LP
Williams, David–Alacon Ventures LLC
Williams, David–Dunedin Capital Partners Ltd
Williams, Edward–Brook Venture Partners LLC
Williams, Evan–Obvious Ventures Management LLC
Williams, Forrest–Transition Capital Partners
Williams, Glynn–Epi-V LLP
Williams, Greg–Accel-KKR
Williams, Greg–Duff Ackerman & Goodrich LLC
Williams, Hugh–Pitt Capital Partners Ltd
Williams, Ian–Lyceum Capital
Williams, James–Carlyle Group LP
Williams, James–Yuuwa Capital LP
Williams, Jeff–Covera Ventures LP
Williams, Jeff–Hangar Ventures LLC
Williams, Jeffrey–AllegisCyber
Williams, Jeffrey–Tudor Ventures
Williams, John–Yankee Equity Solution
Williams, Jr., Richard–Columbia Capital Group, Inc.

Williams, Michael–Tenex Capital Management LP
Williams, Mike–Star Capital Partners Ltd
Williams, Nigel–Royalton Partners
Williams, Paul–First Capital Group Management Company LLC
Williams, Ralph–Single Oak Ventures LP
Williams, Rhys–Columbia Partners Private Capital
Williams, Rhys–New World Angels, Inc.
Williams, Richard–Westview Capital Partners LP
Williams, Robert–J.H. Whitney & Co LLC
Williams, Robert–Milbank Tweed Hadley & Mccloy LLP
Williams, Steve–Cornerstone Advisors Inc
Williams, Steven–Sierra Ventures
Williams, Terry–Nextstage Capital LP
Williams, Tim–Calumet Venture Fund
Williams, Tom–West Cirque Resources Ltd
Williams, Vincent–Silicon Valley Bancventures LP
Williamson, Andrew–Physic Ventures LLC
Williamson, Carlos–Axis Capital Management
Williamson, Craig–SI Capital Partners Llp
Williamson, Elizabeth–Frontenac Company LLC
Williamson, Julie–Terra Firma Capital Partners Ltd
Williamson, Kristin–Hamilton Lane Advisors LLC
Williamson, Mark–Calera Capital Management Inc
Williamson, Mark–Evercore Inc
Williamson, W.A–Southwest Middle Market M&A
Willich, Barrett–Beverly Capital LLC
Willingham, Mike–Pepperwood Partners LLC
Willis, Christopher–Industrial Opportunity Partners LLC
Willis, Eric–CounterPoint Capital Partners LLC
Willis, Michael–Virgin Green Fund
Willmoth, John–Chrysalis Ventures Inc
Wills, Jack–Probitas Partners Inc
Wills, Stace–Emedici Capital Inc
Willson, Stephen–Unilever Ventures Ltd
Wilmerding, Alexander–Pantheon Ventures (UK) LLP
Wilmot, Richard–Partners Innovation Fund LLC
Wilms, Olav–BC Brandenburg Capital GmbH
Wilmsen, James–WILsquare Capital LLC
Wilner, Steven–Westfield Capital Management Company LP
Wilska, Kari-Pekka–Bluerun Ventures LP
Wilson, Adrian–Square 1 Ventures
Wilson, Andrew–Barings (UK) Ltd
Wilson, Barry–Huntington Capital I
Wilson, Benjamin–PEI Funds LLC
Wilson, Bryan–Morrison & Foerster LLP
Wilson, D. Kyle–Broadoak Capital Partners LLC
Wilson, David–Growth Works Capital Ltd
Wilson, David–Panoramic Growth Equity (Fund Management) LLP
Wilson, Dennis–Gramercy Inc
Wilson, Fred–Union Square Ventures LLC
Wilson, Garry–Endless LLP
Wilson, Gregory–Maxim Partners LLC
Wilson, Henry–Northwood Ventures
Wilson, James–New MainStream Capital
Wilson, James–Rock Hill Capital Group LLC
Wilson, Jason–Prospect Street Ventures
Wilson, Jeffrey–Kayne Anderson Capital Advisors LP
Wilson, Jennifer–North River Capital LLC
Wilson, Jeremy–Newroad Capital Partners LLC
Wilson, Jonathan–Siguler Guff & Company LP

Wilson, Joseph–Golub Capital Master Funding LLC
Wilson, Karen–InterWest Partners LLC
Wilson, Keith–Cranberry Capital LLC
Wilson, Kevin–Cloud Equity Group LLC
Wilson, L–Primus Capital
Wilson, Larry–FirstMark Capital LLC
Wilson, Lindsay–Fulcrum Capital Partners Inc
Wilson, Marcus–Breakaway
Wilson, Matthew–Lion Capital LLP
Wilson, Matthew–Oaktree Capital Management LP
Wilson, Matthew–True Wind Capital Management LLC
Wilson, Michael–TA Associates Management LP
Wilson, Pamela–WL Ross & Co LLC
Wilson, Pat–Quona Capital Management Ltd
Wilson, Paul–Bailador Investment Management Pty Ltd
Wilson, Peter–Baml Capital Access Funds Management LLC
Wilson, Peter–Warburg Pincus LLC
Wilson, Phil–Intervale Capital LLC
Wilson, Richard–Apax Partners LLP
Wilson, Richard–F&C Asset Management PLC
Wilson, Russ–Trivest Partners LP
Wilson, Scott–Swiftsure Capital LLC
Wilson, Seth–HeadHaul Capital Partners LLC
Wilson, Steve–Connection Capital LLP
Wilson, Stoddard–Rockport Capital Partners
Wilson, Stuart–OCP Asia Hong Kong Ltd
Wilson, Ted–Pinnacle Ventures
Wilson, Tim–Artiman Management LLC
Wilson, Timothy–Blue Sky Private Equity
Wilson, Timothy–Partech International
Wilson, Tom–Morrison & Foerster LLP
Wilton, Mark–Barings (UK) Ltd
Wiltse, Jeannette–Relay Ventures
Wiltshire, Andrew–Harvard Management Company Inc
Wimmeroth, Oliver–Venista Ventures GmbH & Co KG
Winarsky, Norman–SRI International
Winblad, Ann–Hummer Winblad Venture Partner
Winbladh, Hjalmar–Creandum AB
Wincek, Roseanne–Institutional Venture Partners
Winden, Andrew William–Morrison & Foerster LLP
Winder, Caleb–Biotechonomy Ventures LLC
Winemiller, Bert–JMI Management Inc
Wingard, Bowman–Thomas Weisel Partners Group Inc
Wingard, Daniel–Tecum Capital Partners
Wingard, Michael–Rw Capital Partners LLC
Winges, Brad–Piper Jaffray Ventures Inc
Wingfield, David–Rutland Partners LLP
Winkler, Frank-Markus–Capiton AG
Winkler, Torsten–Vitruvian Partners LLP
Winn, Christopher–Miralta Capital Inc
Winneg, Robert–New England Capital Partners
Winokur, Herbert–Capricorn Holdings LLC
Winshall, Walter–Collaborative Seed and Growth Partners LLC
Winship, Christopher–Financial Technology Ventures
Winslow, Frank–Quad-C Management Inc
Winslow, Poul–Canada Pension Plan Investment Board
Winston, Ashley–Millstein & Co LP

Pratt's Guide to Private Equity & Venture Capital Sources

Winterer, William–Parthenon Capital LLC
Winterling, Stefan–Paragon Partners GmbH
Winters, Ana–MMF Capital Management LLC
Winters, Robert–Zesiger Capital Group LLC
Winters, Terence–Valley Ventures
Wintersberger, Karlheinz–Proregio Mittelstandsfinanzierungs AG
Wincher, Angus–Evercore Inc
Winton, Patricia–ArcLight Capital Holdings LLC
Wipfli, Cyrill–Partners Group Holding AG
Wipiejewski, Torsten–Vnt Management Oy
Wippman, Tom–Sterling Partners GP LLC
Wirtz, Peter–3i Group PLC
Wisch, Steven–IEP Fund Advisors Pvt Ltd
Wisdom, Kenneth–Portfolio Advisors, LLC
Wise, James–Balderton Capital LLP
Wise, Jim–Haddington Ventures LLC
Wise, Stephen–Carlyle Group LP
Wish, Nathanial–Responder Ventures LLC
Wishart, Michael–Tyche Partners LP
Wissink, Ronald–Value Creation Capital BV
Wit, Alexander–Phi Industrial Acquisitions SL
Wit, Harold–Allen & Company of Florida, Inc.
Witchey, Curtis–Brantley Venture Partners L P
Witchey, Curtis–Brantley Venture Partners L P
Witczak, Tomasz–Pekao Investment Banking SA
Witham, Gibb–Paladin Capital Management LLC
Witheiler, Matthew–Flybridge Capital Partners
Witherington, Hunter–SSM Partners LP
Witherington, Jim–SSM Partners LP
Witmer, Richard–Brown Brothers Harriman & Co
Witt, Andrew–Colony Capital LLC
Witt, Laura–ABS Capital Partners, Inc.
Witte, Matthew–Marwit Capital Corp
Wittels, David–Diamond Castle Holdings LLC
Wittelsberger, Stacey–Patriot Capital Funding Inc
Wittenbrink, Kelly–Thompson Street Capital Partners LP
Witthohn, Joseph–FTFD Fund Distributor Inc
Wittman, Marlene–Aquitaine Investment Advisors Ltd
Wittrup, Kevin–RSVP Capital
Wizel, Neil–First Reserve Corp
Wodlinger, David–Arlington Capital Partners
Wodlinger, David–Arlington Capital Partners
Woelfel, Sarah–Jmk Consumer Growth Partners LLC
Woergaard, Henrik–Cohen & Company Financial Ltd
Wohlstadter, Justin–BOLDstart Ventures II LP
Woida, Christopher–Axioma Ventures LLC
Woiwode, Thomas–Versant Venture Management, LLC
Wojcik, Maciej–TDJ SA
Wojtal, Dedee–Phenomenelle Angels Management LLC
Wojtkowski, Ryszard–Resource Partners Sp z o o
Wojtowicz, Zbigniew–Investors Towarzystwo Funduszy Inwestycyjnych SA
Wolak, John–Morgan Stanley Alternative Investment Partners LP
Wolf, Alexis–Beekman Group LLC
Wolf, Amy–River Hollow Partners LLC
Wolf, Bryan–Intel Capital Corp
Wolf, Christopher–Sverica International Boston LLC
Wolf, Daniel–Cerberus Capital Management LP
Wolf, Eric–Bow River Capital Partners LLC

Wolf, Jeffrey–Sunrock Ventures Management LLC
Wolf, Jochen–BWK GmbH Unternehmensbeteiligungsgesellschaft
Wolf, Larry–Quark Ventures LLC
Wolf, Neil–Vantagepoint Management Inc
Wolf, Waltraud–Mittelstaendische Beteiligungsgesellschaft
Wolfe, Aaron–Sun Capital Partners Inc
Wolfe, Chris–Capital Z Partners Ltd
Wolfe, Daniel–180 Degree Capital Corp
Wolfe, David–Envest Ventures
Wolfe, Jason–Cohen & Company Financial Ltd
Wolfe, Jeremy–Jasper Ridge Partners LP
Wolfe, Josh–LUX CAPITAL GROUP L L C
Wolfe, Kirk–MK Capital
Wolfe, Stephen–Growth Street Management LLC
Wolfe, Stephen–Mainsail Partners LP
Wolfe, Stephen–Vector Capital Management LP
Wolfensohn, Adam–Wolfensohn & Company LLC
Wolfensohn, Naomi–Wolfensohn & Company LLC
Wolfers, Shannon–Pacific Equity Partners Pty Ltd
Wolff, Peter–enjoyventure Management GmbH
Wolff, Scott–Ascribe Capital, LLC
Wolfington, J. Eustace–Liberty Capital Management Corp
Wolfman, Alexander–Avenue Capital Group LLC
Wolfman, Robert–Montage Partners Inc
Wolfram, Tyler–Oak Hill Capital Management Inc
Wolfsheimer, Ronald–Calvert Fund
Wolfson, David–Milbank Tweed Hadley & Mccloy LLP
Wolfson, Gene–Catalyst Investors LLC
Wolfson, Rob–HIG Capital LLC
Wollaeger, Timothy–Sanderling Ventures
Wollak, Nick–Axxon Group Servicos De Consultoria E Assessoria Ltda
Wollenhaupt, Tobias–Adiuva Capital GmbH
Woloson, Brad–JMI Management Inc
Woloson, Todd–Greenmont Capital Partners
Wolpert, Richard–Amplify.LA
Wolsdorf, Marcus–HW Capital GmbH
Wolstenholme, Iain–Gresham Llp
Wolstenholme, Iain–Primary Capital Ltd
Wolter, Jan–Target Partners GmbH
Woltery, HJ–Strategic Value Partners LLC
Woltron, Klaus–MINAS Beteiligungs- u. Management GmbH
Womack, Carol–Diversified Trust Company Inc
Womsley, Robert–Citigroup Private Equity LP
Womsley, Robert–Water Street Healthcare Partners LLC
Won, Emily–Longview Asset Management Ltd
Wong, Alexander–D E Shaw & Co LP
Wong, Bing–Pantheon Ventures (UK) LLP
Wong, Bruce–Abacus Private Equity Ltd
Wong, Christine–Shk Fund Management Ltd
Wong, Daniel–Anchorage Capital Partners Ltd
Wong, Darren–Ceyuan Ventures Management LLC
Wong, David–Audax Group, Inc.
Wong, Edward–TSG Consumer Partners, L.P.
Wong, Elaine–HAO Capital
Wong, Erik–Pantheon Ventures (UK) LLP
Wong, Eugene–On Capital Ltd
Wong, Eugene–Sirius Venture Consulting Pte Ltd
Wong, Felix–Florida Capital Partners Inc

Wong, Gilbert–Bull Capital Partners Ltd
Wong, Helen–Qed Global
Wong, Henry–Diamond TechVentures
Wong, Henry–Garage Technology Ventures LLC
Wong, Hing–Walden International
Wong, Jason–Horizons Ventures Ltd
Wong, Jason–Medley Capital LLC
Wong, Karen–Milbank Tweed Hadley & Mccloy LLP
Wong, Ken–Shk Fund Management Ltd
Wong, Lyon–Lightspeed Management Company LLC
Wong, Michael–GI Partners
Wong, Raymond–HPEF Capital Partners Ltd
Wong, Raymond–Spring Mountain Capital LP
Wong, Rebecca–Global Private Equity PLC
Wong, Richard–Accel Partners & Co Inc
Wong, Shirley–TNF Ventures Pte Ltd
Wong, Simon–Samena Capital Management LLP
Wong, Steve–Tpg Growth LLC
Wong, Thomas–Oak Hill Advisors LP
Wong, Thomas–Proprium Capital Partners LP
Wong, Timothy–Trilogy Equity Partners Llc
Wong, Tze Kai–Banyan Ventures Sdn Bhd
Wong, Wing–Longreach Group Ltd
Wonnacott, Larry–Symmetry Investment Advisors Inc
Woo, Jacqueline–Acumen Fund Inc
Woo, Warren–Monroe Capital LLC
Wood, Al–Comvest Partners
Wood, Andrew–Advent Venture Partners LLP
Wood, Andrew–Change Capital Partners LLP
Wood, C. Timothy–Modern Africa Fund Managers, LLC
Wood, Daniel–Mesa Verde Venture Partners LP
Wood, Donald–Draper Fisher Jurvetson
Wood, Ian–Greenhill Capital Partners LP
Wood, Jon–PROfounders Capital Ltd
Wood, Pam–Parallax Capital Partners LLC
Wood, Steve–Cowboy Technologies LLC
Wood, Steven–Inverness Graham Investments
Wood, Susan–Sindicatum Carbon Capital Ltd
Woodall, Mark–Wellington Partners GmbH
Woodburn, William–Global Infrastructure Holdings
Woodcock, Timothy–Oakfield Capital Partners LLP
Woodeson, Matthew–Northleaf Capital Partners Ltd
Woodley, Ryan–Polaris Venture Partners
Woodman, Rob–Sofinnova Partners SAS
Woodmansee, M. Andrew–Morrison & Foerster LLP
Woodroffe, Shane–Enercap Capital Partners
Woodruff, John–Waller Capital Partners LLC
Woods, Chris–Shard Capital Partners LLP
Woods, Jim–OMERS Infrastructure
Woods, Joseph–Fort Washington Capital
Woods, Mark–Chartwell Investments, Inc.
Woods, Willie–ICV Partners LLC
Woodson, Wade–Sigma Partners
Woodsum, Stephen–Summit Partners LP
Woodward, Alexander–Bridge City Management LLC
Woodward, David–Socius Capital Group LLC
Woodward, Laura–Tekla Capital Management LLC
Woodward, Patricia–Camden Partners Holdings LLC
Woodward, Tim–Nth Power LLC
Woodward, Tim–Prelude Ventures LLC
Woodward, William–Anthem Venture Partners
Woodworth, Alfred–Echelon Ventures LLC
Woody, Jason–Palm Ventures LLC

Woody, Jim–Latterell Venture Partners LP
Woody, Ken–Innova Memphis Inc
Woolbert, Jeffrey–Bain Capital Inc
Wooldridge, Ronald–Turnstone Capital Management LLC
Wooldridge, Zach–Elm Creek Partners
Woolfenden, Rupert–Canaccord Genuity Group Inc
Woolgar, Mark–Rift Valley Equity Partners LLC
Woolley, Geoffrey–Epic Ventures Inc
Woolsey, R. James–LUX CAPITAL GROUP L L C
Woolsey, R. James–Vantagepoint Management Inc
Wooten, Ronald–Novaquest Infosystems Inc
Work, Chris–Solaris Energy Capital LLC
Working, Mark–Zachary Scott & Co
Workman, Adam–CT Investment Partners LLP
Worley, Eric–Platinum Equity LLC
Wormley, Paul–Hadley Capital
Worning, Niels–Polaris Management A/S
Worrell, David–Monterey Venture Partners LLC
Wort, Wouter–Atomico Ventures
Worth, Stephen–Evercore Inc
Worth, W. Andrew–Fidus Capital LLC
Worthington, Robert–Nations Funds Inc
Worthy, Ford–Pappas Ventures
Wortman, Dave–Spring Mill Venture Partners
Woseth, Rob–Water Tower Capital LLC
Wossagk, Sebastian–Acton Capital Partners GmbH
Wotiz, Matthew–OrbiMed Advisors LLC
Wozniak, Jacek–Enterprise Investors Sp z o o
Wozniak, Tomasz–Black Pearls VC SA
Wrenn, Tom–ECI Partners LLP
Wriedt, Oliver–Providence Equity Partners LLC
Wright, Amie–Acas LLC
Wright, Christopher–Crescent Capital Group LP
Wright, Christopher–Pilgrim Capital Partners LLC
Wright, Dalton–Kickstart Seed Fund LP
Wright, Dan–NorthEdge Capital LLP
Wright, Daniel–HBM Holdings Co
Wright, J.D.–CIVC Partners LP
Wright, Jason–Apax Partners LLP
Wright, Lee–Diamond Castle Holdings LLC
Wright, Nick–Catapult Venture Managers Ltd
Wright, Nigel–Onex Corp
Wright, Rob–Grey Mountain Partners LLC
Wright, Roger–Nibiru Capital Management Ltd
Wright, Thomas–Hawthorne Group
Wright, Tim–Compass Partners International Llp
Wright, Tim–Grandbanks Capital
Wrone, Jason–Open Prairie Ventures
Wrubel, Lee–Foundation Medical Partners LP
Wu, Benjamin–Huntsman Family Investments LLC
Wu, Blake–New Enterprise Associates Inc
Wu, Charles–Carlyle Group LP
Wu, Charles–WI Harper Group Inc
Wu, Ching–Canvas Venture Fund
Wu, Ching–Morgenthaler Ventures
Wu, Damon–Morgan Stanley Alternative Investment Partners LP
Wu, David–Maveron LLC
Wu, Fengzhi–Qiming Venture Partners Ii LP
Wu, Fengzhi–Shenzhen Green Pine Capital Partners Co Ltd
Wu, Gaopan–Shenzhen Weixi Investment Partnership Co Ltd
Wu, Gaoyuan–Shenzhen Weixi Investment Partnership Co Ltd
Wu, Guangyu–Shanghai Broadview Capital Management Co Ltd
Wu, Haiqing–Will Capital
Wu, Hajie–Lunar Capital Management Ltd
Wu, Huating–Vision Knight Capital
Wu, Hui–Burrill & Company
Wu, Jeffrey–Behrman Capital
Wu, Jiajia–Shenjin Investment Management Co Ltd
Wu, Jianfeng–ZEVC Management Co Ltd
Wu, John–Northern Light Venture Capital Development Ltd
Wu, Joshua–GGV Capital
Wu, Jun–Amino Capital Management Company LLC
Wu, Jun–Johnson & Johnson Innovation-JJDC Inc
Wu, Kai–RA Capital Management LLC
Wu, Kelvin–AID Partners Capital Ltd
Wu, Lisa–Norwest Venture Partners
Wu, Neil–PAC-LINK Management Corp
Wu, Ping–Principle Capital Ltd
Wu, Ping–SummitView Capital
Wu, Qiaofeng–Zhongrong International Trust Co Ltd
Wu, Robert–Flexis Capital LLC
Wu, Rongguo–Shanghai Realeader Investment Fund Management Co Ltd
Wu, Rosita–Sirius Venture Consulting Pte Ltd
Wu, Ruizhong–Elevation China Capital
Wu, Sam–Carlyle Group LP
Wu, Scott–Blue Horizon Equity LLC
Wu, Shaohong–Shenzhen Jiupai Capital Management Co Ltd
Wu, Shiyong–Junsan Capital
Wu, Sonny–Gsr Ventures Management Llc
Wu, Tao–Changan Capital
Wu, Tao–Noah Private Wealth Management Centre Co Ltd
Wu, Tao–Suzhou Shengshang United Investment Center Partnership Ltd
Wu, Tony–Northern Light Venture Capital Development Ltd
Wu, Tony–Redpoint Ventures
Wu, Tony–Sparkland Capital
Wu, Victor–Lexington Partners Inc
Wu, Wayne–VMG Partners, L.P.
Wu, Wei–ShenZhen CDF-Capital Co Ltd
Wu, Wilson–Cybernaut (China) Venture Capital Management Co Ltd
Wu, Xinghua–CCBT Private Equity Fund
Wu, Xiongzhi–Sino-Can Harvest Capital Co Ltd
Wu, Yibing–Citic Private Equity Funds Management Co Ltd
Wu, Ying–IDG Capital Partners Inc
Wu, Zonghe–Shanghai Lianxin Investment Management Co Ltd
Wuellner, Sarah–Promus Equity Partners
Wuellner, Tom–Wanxiang America Capital LLC
Wuestling, John–Greenspring Associates Inc
Wugmeister, Miriam–Morrison & Foerster LLP
Wulf, Karsten–newten Ventures GmbH
Wulf, Valerie–Phenomenelle Angels Management LLC
Wulff, Marco–Montana Capital Partners AG
Wulfing, Klaus–Perella Weinberg Partners LP
Wunderlich, Hans-Dieter–Dipl.-Kfm. Wunderlich & Partner
Wuoristo, Jussi–Vitruvian Partners LLP
Wuppermann, Conny–palero capital GmbH
Wyard, Brett–Carlyle Group LP
Wyard, Brett–Solace Capital Partners LLC
Wyatt, Gordon–Accuitive Medical Ventures LLC
Wyatt, Jamie–Bridgepoint Advisers Ltd
Wyatt, Tully–CenterOak Partners LLC
Wyck, Arnaud–Accelerate-IT Ventures Management LLC
Wycoff, W. Kirk–Patriot Financial Partners LP
Wygaerts, Guy–Indufin SA
Wygas, Martin–Lyceum Capital
Wyke, Andrew–Hambro Perks Ltd
Wyles, Toby–Vitruvian Partners LLP
Wylie, Cay–Ridgemont Partners Management LLC
Wylie, John–Lazard Australia Private Equity
Wyly, Christiana–Satori Capital LLC
Wyly, Evan–Maverick Capital Ltd
Wymbs, Robert–Platinum Equity LLC
Wyncoll, Oliver–Bridges Fund Management Ltd
Wynne, Joseph–BelHealth Investment Partners LLC
Wynne, Joseph–BelHealth Investment Partners LLC
Wynperle, William–Shamrock Capital Advisors LLC
Wynter, Lindsay–Gores Group LLC
Wyse, Roger–Burrill & Company
Wyse, Roger–Spruce Capital Partners LLC
Wyss, Ralph–Gilde Buy Out Partners BV
Wyss, Ralph–Gilde Investment Management BV
Wyszynski, Wojciech–Bachleda Grupa Inwestycyjna Sp z o o
Xavier, Asish–Johnson & Johnson Innovation-JJDC Inc
Xavier, Bernard–Formative Ventures
Xavier, Bernard–SummitView Capital
Xi, Xuanhua–BOCOM International Holdings Co Ltd
Xia, Chaoyang–Ivy Capital Ltd
Xia, Fatima–Grace Assets Management LLP
Xia, Mingchen–Hamilton Lane Advisors LLC
Xia, Yaofeng–Boxin Capital
Xian, Feng–Ivy Capital Ltd
Xiang, Jianbiao–Hangzhou Incapital Management Co., Ltd
Xiang, Justin–Syno Capital LLC
Xiao, Bing–Fortune Venture Capital Corp
Xiao, Changbo–Rongxin Capital Fund Management Ltd
Xiao, Feng–Carlyle Group LP
Xiao, Hua–Shenzhen Green Pine Capital Partners Co Ltd
Xiao, Janet–Morrison & Foerster LLP
Xiao, Yangyu–New Enterprise Investment Co Ltd
Xie, Dahong–Zana Capital Pte Ltd
Xie, Jianping–IDG Capital Partners Inc
Xie, Li–Changan Capital
Xie, Li–Hangzhou Haibang Investment Management Co Ltd
Xie, Yijing–CRP-Fanya Investment Consultants Beijing Co Ltd
Xie, Ying–Milestone Capital Management Ltd
Xie, Yinghai–Milestone Capital Management Ltd
Xie, Zhigang–Beijing Huinong Capital Management Co Ltd
Xin, Eric–CITIC Capital Partners Ltd
Xin, Jie–China International Capital Corp Ltd
Xin, Sinan–Carlyle Group LP

Xin, Yaozhou–CRP-Fanya Investment Consultants Beijing Co Ltd
Xing, Alexandre–Shanghai SMC Capital Co Ltd
Xing, Fay–Decheng Capital LLC
Xiong, Donghong–Noble (Beijing) Fund Management Inc
Xiong, Fen–PreIPO Capital Partners Ltd
Xiong, Jeff–Seven Seas Partners
Xiong, Jiantao–China Merchants Securities Co Ltd
Xiong, Renjie–Fortune Venture Capital Co Ltd
Xiong, Renjie–Fortune Venture Capital Corp
Xiong, Xiangdong–Meridian Growth Fund Management Co Ltd
Xitian, Wang–Jilin Huizheng Investment Co Ltd
Xu, Albert–3i Group PLC
Xu, Baiqi–Zhejiang Sinowisdom Capital Co Ltd
Xu, David–Ascribe Capital, LLC
Xu, David–Mingly Capital
Xu, Dawei–Sino-Can Harvest Capital Co Ltd
Xu, Eric–GGV Capital
Xu, Eric–Mingly Capital
Xu, Forest–WI Harper Group Inc
Xu, Grace–Sinovation Ventures Ltd
Xu, Hai–Shanghai Lianxin Investment Management Co Ltd
Xu, Han–Shanghai Broadview Capital Management Co Ltd
Xu, Hang–SAIF Partners
Xu, Hanjie–Shanghai NewMargin Ventures Co Ltd
Xu, Hanjie–ZheShang Venture Capital Co Ltd
Xu, Jack–Seven Seas Partners
Xu, Jackie–Kleiner Perkins Caufield & Byers LLC
Xu, Jinshang–VcWiLL Capital
Xu, Katherine–Mingly Capital
Xu, Ken–Gobi Partners
Xu, Lei–Prax Capital Management Co
Xu, Liang–SummitView Capital
Xu, Lixin–Shenzhen Green Pine Capital Partners Co Ltd
Xu, Mason–Hony Capital Beijing Co Ltd
Xu, Qiang–Decheng Capital LLC
Xu, Rebecca–Asia Alternatives Management LLC
Xu, Sue–Amino Capital Management Company LLC
Xu, Weibin–Shenzhen Cornerstone of Entrepreneurial Cci Capital Ltd
Xu, Weizheng–Tririver Capital Corp
Xu, Wenrong–Prax Capital Management Co
Xu, Xin–Capital Today China Growth HK Ltd
Xu, Yang–Beijing Flourish Libra Venture Capital Co Ltd
Xu, Yong Hong–SAIF Partners
Xu, Yuedong–Will Capital
Xu, Zhiming–CBC Capital
Xu, Zhixian–Elevation China Capital
Xue, Cun–Invimed Europejskie Centrum Macierzynstwa Sp z o o
Xue, Mengjun–Shanghai Fortune United Investment Group Co Ltd
Xue, Minghui–Mandarin Capital Partners SCA SICAR
YE, JIA JIA–OXEON Partners
Yaakub, Encick Nor Idzam–Musharaka Venture Management Sdn Bhd
Yabe, Nobuhiro–Marubeni Corp
Yablunsky, Robert–SCP Private Equity Partners

Yacos, Mark–Visium Asset Management LP
Yacoub, Fady–HOF Capital Inc
Yadergardjam, Farsin–Co Investor AG
Yaffe, Achi–GI Partners
Yagan, Sam–Corazon Capital LLC
Yagan, Sam–Hyde Park Venture Partners
Yager, Steven–Gores Group LLC
Yaghoobzadeh, Hootan–Staple Street Capital LLC
Yago, Noah–JVP Jerusalem Venture Partners Israel Management, Ltd.
Yahav, Oren–Gatewood Capital Partners LLC
Yahav, Oren–Poalim Cap Mark Tech, Ltd.
Yahia, Laurance–Liberty Mutual Innovation
Yakobovich, Elisheva–Vertex Israel II Management Ltd
Yakura, Chie–Morrison & Foerster LLP
Yakushev, Vladimir–UK SGKM OOO
Yalman, Kerim–Pera Capital Partners Advisory Ltd
Yam, Chunqi–First Eastern Investment Group
Yama, Arthur–Aquitaine Investment Advisors Ltd
Yamada, Hiroshi–Jafco Co Ltd
Yamada, Kazuhiro–Carlyle Group LP
Yamada, Keith–CIVC Partners LP
Yamaguchi, Hitoshi–Unison Capital, Inc.
Yamaguchi, Masahiro–SMBC Venture Capital Co Ltd
Yamaguchi, Yasuhisa–DBJ Capital Co., Ltd
Yamakawa, Hiroshi–Mitsubishi UFJ Capital Co Ltd
Yamakawa, Takayoshi–Dream Incubator Inc
Yamamoto, Hiroshi–Mizuho Capital Co Ltd
Yamamoto, Osamu–Unison Capital, Inc.
Yamamoto, Reijiro–Integral Corp
Yamamoto, Tetsuya–University of Tokyo Edge Capital Co Ltd
Yamashita, Go–Blackstone Group LP
Yamashita, Kevin–Bertram Capital Management LLC
Yamazaki, Tsuyoshi–Integral Corp
Yan, Andrew–SAIF Partners
Yan, Guijun–Everbright Jinkong Shanghai Investment Management Co Ltd
Yan, Jeacy–IDG Capital Partners Inc
Yan, Jingran–HighLight Capital
Yan, Kenneth–HAO Capital
Yan, Tangfeng–Prime Value Capital Management Ltd
Yan, Yong–Beijing Tianxing Chuanglian Investment Management Co., Ltd.
Yanagi, Eric–Mill Road Capital Management LLC
Yanagi, Tad–Yellow Wood Partners LLC
Yanci, Alberto–ProA Capital de Inversiones SGEIC SA
Yanez, Maggie–Marquette Capital Partners Inc
Yang, Alan–Blackstone Group LP
Yang, Alan–China Canada Angels Alliance Ltd
Yang, Angela–Siguler Guff & Company LP
Yang, Bedy–500 Startups, L.P.
Yang, Bing–Shanghai Beyond Binghong Equity Investment Management Co Ltd
Yang, Caiqin–Shenzhen Ruiying Zhuoyue Capital Management Partnership (LP)
Yang, Charles–Tririver Capital Corp
Yang, Chih-Yuan–AME Cloud Ventures LLC
Yang, Daniel–SAIF Partners
Yang, David–CID Group
Yang, David–CID Group
Yang, Du Seung–KTB Investment & Securities Co Ltd

Yang, Ed–Acer Technology Ventures Asia Pacific
Yang, Edward–Baring Private Equity Asia Ltd
Yang, Eileen–Crimson Capital China
Yang, Fei–Guangdong Pacific Technology Venture Co Ltd
Yang, Fei–IDG Capital Partners Inc
Yang, Geoffrey–Redpoint Ventures
Yang, Guang–China Merchants Kunlun Equity Invest Management Co Ltd
Yang, Helen–Acas LLC
Yang, Hongtao–Sino Resources Investment Co Ltd
Yang, Jackie–Translink Capital LLC
Yang, Jackie–Translink Capital LLC
Yang, Janet–Novak Biddle Venture Partners LP
Yang, Jianbo–Mingly Capital
Yang, Joseph–Saints Ventures
Yang, Junping–Shenzhen Hongshisan Capital Co Ltd
Yang, Justin–Ferrer Freeman & Co LLC
Yang, Justin–Peloton Equity LLC
Yang, Lei–WestSummit Capital Management Ltd
Yang, Lin–Legend Capital Co Ltd
Yang, Ling–Beijing Tianxing Chuanglian Investment Management Co., Ltd.
Yang, Ling–Carlyle Group LP
Yang, Mei Ni–Hamilton Lane Advisors LLC
Yang, Michael–Comcast Ventures
Yang, Michael–Digital Entertainment Ventures LLC
Yang, Pang-yien–Pacific Venture Partners Co Ltd
Yang, Paul–CDIB Capital Group
Yang, Ran–CAC Capital Management Co Ltd
Yang, Ray–Northern Light Venture Capital Development Ltd
Yang, Rene–Vista Equity Partners LLC
Yang, Robert–Blackstone Group LP
Yang, Rui–Tianjin Binhai Haisheng Equity Investment Fund Mgmt Co.
Yang, Steve–CID Group
Yang, Steven–Adveq Management AG
Yang, Wei–Zhongrong International Trust Co Ltd
Yang, Wolfgang–Vcchina Ltd
Yang, Xiang-dong–Carlyle Group LP
Yang, Xiaohua–Shanghai Dingjia Ventures Co Ltd
Yang, Yoonmo–Arsenal Capital Partners LP
Yang, Yue–Guangxin Investment Management Beijing Co Ltd
Yang, Zhenyu–Feima Fund
Yang, Zhilong–ZheShang Venture Capital Co Ltd
Yang, Zhiwei–Gsr Ventures Management Llc
Yankowitz, Bennett–Single Oak Ventures LP
Yanni, Anthony–Asssurance Mezzanine Fund
Yanowitch, Lawrence–Morrison & Foerster LLP
Yansong, Cao–Israel Infinity Venture Capital Fund Israel LP
Yao Wei Min, Henry–SEAVI Advent Corporation Ltd
Yao, Bo–Ping An Life Insurance Co of China Ltd
Yao, Chengjie–Rico Harvest (Shanghai) Private Equity Management Ltd.
Yao, Guohua–Boxin Capital
Yao, Jack–Seven Seas Partners
Yao, Jianming–Kaiwu Capital Co Ltd
Yao, Jiping–Prax Capital Management Co
Yao, Yaping–Highland Capital Partners LLC
Yap Ho, Paulina–Oaktree Capital Management LP
Yap Kean Chong, Kenny–Rico Harvest (Shanghai) Private Equity Management Ltd.

Yap, Daryl—American Industrial Partners
Yap, Daryl—Bregal Investments LLP
Yap, Greg—Menlo Ventures
Yap, Kelvin—HarbourVest Partners LLC
Yap, Kian Woon—Cmia Capital Partners Pte Ltd
Yap, Tony—Catalyst Investment Managers Pty, Ltd.
Yaphe, Scott—Schooner Capital LLC
Yarbrough, Benjamin—Merit Capital Partners IV LLC
Yardley, Daniel—Patriot Capital Funding Inc
Yarel, Adi—MAGNUM COMMUNICATIONS FUND L P
Yarmon, Joel—Draper Associates Inc
Yarnell, David—BEV Capital
Yarovoy, Bogdan—SmartHub OOO
Yashiro, Masamoto—Ripplewood Holdings LLC
Yassin, Akram—First Abu Dhabi Bank PJSC
Yasuda, Akihiko—Asia Alternatives Management LLC
Yasuda, Isao—Global Brain Corp
Yates, James—IK Investment Partners Ltd
Yates, Philip—Bregal Investments LLP
Yates, Philip—Perella Weinberg Partners LP
Yates, Tim—Commonfund Capital Inc
Yau, Jane—Oaktree Capital Management LP
Yau, Philip—GI Partners
Yau, Shane—HPEF Capital Partners Ltd
Yavonditte, Michael—ff Venture Capital
Yazdani, Bobby—Cota Capital Inc
Ybarra, Paloma—Altamar Private Equity SGIIC SAU
Ye, Ayden—Sierra Ventures
Ye, Bin—Zero2IPO Ventures
Ye, Greg—Suzhou Datai Venture Capital Investment Management Co Ltd
Ye, Jim—Shanghai Broadview Capital Management Co Ltd
Ye, Jun—SAIF Partners
Ye, Yuming—Guangxin Investment Management Beijing Co Ltd
Yee, Chee Wai—OSK Ventures International Bhd
Yee, Clara—Rembrandt Venture Management LLC
Yee, Danny—Aktis Capital Group
Yee, David—Oaktree Capital Management LP
Yee, Doris—Iglobe Treasury Management Ltd
Yee, Yale—Montgomery & Co LLC
Yegeubayev, Aidar—Kazyna Kapital Management AO
Yeh, Ching Ju—CITIC Capital Partners Ltd
Yeh, Chris—Wasabi Ventures LLC
Yeh, Huoy-Ming—SmartForest Ventures
Yeh, Kuantai—Highland Capital Partners LLC
Yeh, Lung—Enspire Capital Pte Ltd
Yeh, Richard—Brown Brothers Harriman & Co
Yek Meng, Wong—Tembusu Ventures Pte Ltd
Yellurkar, Devdutt—Charles River Ventures LLC
Yen, Richard—Saban Capital Group Inc
Yen, Tuff—Seraph Group
Yeo, Andrew—Novo Tellus Capital Partners Pte Ltd
Yeo, Keat Chuan—EDB Investments Pte Ltd
Yeo, Marvin—Frontier Investment & Capital Advisors Pte Ltd
Yeo, Yongdong—Darwin Venture Capital Co Ltd
Yeoham, Paul—Progress Equity Partners Ltd
Yeow, David—Incuvest Pte Ltd
Yepes, Rafael—Promotora de Proyectos SA
Yepez, J. Alberto—Trident Capital
Yepez, J. Alberto—Trident Capital Cybersecurity Fund I LP
Yeremyan, Toros—Brentwood Associates, L.P.

Yeremyan, Toros—Brentwood Venture Capital
Yerramilli-Rao, Bobby—Hermes Growth Partners Ltd
Yesayan, Mourad—Paladin Capital Management LLC
Yett, Paul—Hamilton Lane Advisors LLC
Yeung, Edith—500 Startups, L.P.
Yeung, Yeung Heung—SAIF Partners
Yi, Hee-Jin—Valstone Partners LLC
Yi, Jin—Keytone Ventures
Yi, Marc—Intel Capital Corp
Yi, Myung—Acas LLC
Yi, Peter—Jafco Ventures
Yi-Dar, Teo—SEAVI Advent Corporation Ltd
Yianni, John—Earlybird Venture Capital GmbH & Co KG
Yie, Charles—Ampersand Capital Partners
Yih, Dieter—Milbank Tweed Hadley & Mccloy LLP
Yilmaz, Cem—Private Equity Invest AG
Yim, Charles—eVenture Capital Partners GmbH
Yim, Jae Wu—True Global Partners
Yim, Peter—Morrison & Foerster LLP
Yim, Sang Hyeon—Industrial Bank Of Korea
Yin, Donghai—Ivy Capital Ltd
Yin, Elizabeth—500 Startups, L.P.
Yin, Feng—Principle Capital Ltd
Yin, Kevin-Gsr Ventures Management Llc
Yin, Sherry—Morrison & Foerster LLP
Ying, Alex—Carlyle Group LP
Ying, David—Evercore Inc
Ying, Sheng—Guangzhou Anjianxin Investment Management Co Ltd
Ying, Song—Noah Private Wealth Management Centre Co Ltd
Ying, Wei—CDH China Management Co., Ltd.
Ying, Wenlu—Jiangsu High-tech Investment Group Co Ltd
Yinghai, Xie—CDIB Capital International Corp
Yinheng, Wen—Guangdong Investment Ltd
Yip, Edward—Norwest Venture Partners
Yip, Eric—Ichigo Inc
Yip, Kevin—Shanghai NewMargin Ventures Co Ltd
Yip, Stephen W.G.—GreenView Associates LLC
Yip, Tommy Y.—Emerald Hill Capital Partners Ltd
Yirilli, Michael—ABRY Partners LLC
Yli-Tainio, Risto—Nexit Ventures Oy
Yoanidis, Bob—Southbridge Capital Inc
Yoda, Hajime—FGI Capital Partners Inc
Yoder, Jay—Pavilion Alternatives Group Ltd
Yoffe, Amir—CIC Partners, L.P.
Yogev, Rinat—Capital Dynamics Sdn Bhd
Yohannan Moore, Kristin—Morrison & Foerster LLP
Yohannes, Biniam—Catalyst Principal Partners LLC
Yokell, Abe—Rockport Capital Partners
Yokoyama, Atsushi—Bain Capital Inc
Yokoyama, Tadashi—Femto Startup LLP
Yonce, Clifford—Siguler Guff & Company LP
Yonce, Donald—Mobility Ventures LLC
Yoneyama, Tomoko—J-Seed Ventures Inc
Yong, Markus—Incuvest Pte Ltd
Yong, Soo—Walden International
Yong, Yaw-Nam—Qleap Accelerators Ltd
Yongo, Eddie—Goeast Ventures Ltd
Yontef, Barry—Penfund Partners Inc
Yoo, Christopher—Glencoe Capital LLC
Yoo, Joon Tae—CAMBRIDGE CAPITAL PARTNERS L L C
Yoo, Paul—500 Startups, L.P.

Yoo, Seok Jin—SBI Investment Korea Co Ltd
Yoo, Sung-wook—Korea Investment Partners Co Ltd
Yoo, Yong Hwan—KTB Investment & Securities Co Ltd
Yook, Jay—AKN Holdings LLC
Yoon, Byeong Chun—Hi Investment & Securities Co Ltd
Yoon, Charles—Monitor Clipper Partners LLC
Yoon, David—Blackstone Group LP
Yoon, Gene—Bregal Investments LLP
Yoon, John—Leonard Green & Partners LP
Yoon, Jong Yeon—Kiwoom Investment Co Ltd
Yoon, Jong-Ha James—MBK Partners Inc
Yoon, Kwan—Bluerun Ventures LP
Yoon, Sang Gyeong—Intellectual Discovery Ventures
Yoon, Seung Yong—KTB Investment & Securities Co Ltd
Yoon, Sung—KTB Ventures, Inc.
Yoon, Suzanne—Versa Capital Management Inc
Yoong, Sim—Kaizen Private Equity
Yordan, Peter—JC Flowers & Co LLC
York, David—Top Tier Capital Partners LLC
York, Gwill—Lighthouse Capital Partners LP
Yort, Monty—Gennx360 Capital Partners LP
Yosef-Or, Tomer—ABRY Partners LLC
Yoshimoto, Kiyoshi—Nomura Co Ltd
Yoshimura, Ryugo—Morrison & Foerster LLP
Yoshizawa, Masamichi—Longreach Group Ltd
You, Jinbai—Jiangsu Addor Equity Investment Fund Management Co Ltd
Youlden, Mike—Doughty Hanson and Co.
Young, Alan—Prostar Investments Pte Ltd
Young, Andrew—Permira Advisers LLP
Young, Arthur—Blum Capital Partners LP
Young, Benjamin—Strategic Value Partners LLC
Young, Bradford—Pavilion Alternatives Group Ltd
Young, Brian—Eos Partners LP
Young, Caroline—Hammond Kennedy Whitney & Company Inc
Young, Chris—Revel Partners LLC
Young, Cristian—Smedvig Capital Ltd
Young, David—Bluerun Ventures LP
Young, David—Cooley LLP
Young, David—Small World Group Incubator Pte Ltd
Young, Dendy—Blu Venture Investors LLC
Young, Douglas—Microvest Capital Management LLC
Young, Eric—Canaan Partners
Young, Frank—Apple Tree Partners
Young, Frank—EW Healthcare Partners
Young, Frank—Sverica International Boston LLC
Young, Greg—Burrill & Company
Young, Greg—Spruce Capital Partners LLC
Young, Hugh—Aberdeen Asset Management PLC
Young, J. Robert—Gramercy Inc
Young, J. Steven—HGGC LLC
Young, James—5AM Ventures LLC
Young, Jason—RedBird Capital Partners Platform LP
Young, Jason—Vanterra Capital Ltd
Young, Jeff—Origami Capital Partners, LLC
Young, Jeremy—Warburg Pincus LLC
Young, Ken—CVC Capital Partners Ltd
Young, Marc—Morrison & Foerster LLP
Young, Mark—Canaccord Genuity Group Inc
Young, Matt—Platinum Equity LLC
Young, Matthew—Triangle Capital Partners L L C
Young, Michael—Quadrant Mezzanine Partners LLC

2595

Pratt's Guide to Private Equity & Venture Capital Sources

Young, Paul Anthony–CtechBA Pty Ltd
Young, Philip–Samena Capital Management LLP
Young, Philip–U.S. Venture Partners
Young, Robert–Mirador Capital
Young, Stan–Calvert Fund
Young, T. Michael–Capstreet Group LLC
Young, Tim–Eniac Ventures LP
Young, Will–VegasTechFund
Young, William–Clarus Ventures LLC
Young, William–Monitor Clipper Partners LLC
Young, Woody–Perella Weinberg Partners LP
Young, Zeynep–Next Coast Ventures LLC
Youngblood, Kneeland–Pharos Capital Group LLC
Younger, William–Sutter Hill Ventures
Youngkin, Glenn–Carlyle Group LP
Youngren, Bryce–Polaris Venture Partners
Younis, Zafer–500 Startups, L.P.
Younus, Fawad–National ICT R&D Fund
Youssefmir, Jacques–Ocean Avenue Capital Partners LP
Youstra, Bill–Kohlberg Ventures LLC
Yrigoyen, Juan–Chilango Ventures LLC
Yu, Andy–Centenium-Pinetree China Private Equity
Yu, Ben–Sierra Ventures
Yu, Bo-Kunwu Jiuding Capital Holdings Co Ltd
Yu, Bruce–GGV Capital
Yu, Bruce–GGV Capital
Yu, Chen–Vivo Capital LLC
Yu, Dongseung–Shinhan Venture Capital Co Ltd
Yu, Drake–IDG Capital Partners Inc
Yu, Erica–GGV Capital
Yu, Feng–Shanghai Atlas Capital Ltd
Yu, Huang–ShenZhen GTJA Investment Group Co Ltd
Yu, Intack–Asia Culture Technology Investment
Yu, Jia–Qiming Venture Partners Ii LP
Yu, Jianming–New Horizon Capital
Yu, Jie–Rongxin Capital Fund Management Ltd
Yu, John–WestSummit Capital Management Ltd
Yu, Jonathan–iGlobe Partners Ltd
Yu, Laetitia–HPEF Capital Partners Ltd
Yu, Li–Fair Value Capital
Yu, Minhong–Feima Fund
Yu, Peter–Cartesian Capital Group LLC
Yu, Qian–Fidelity Growth Partners Asia
Yu, Sungwoon–Softbank Ventures Korea Inc
Yu, Tiecheng–Dojane Capital
Yu, Weibin–Shenzhen Cornerstone of Entrepreneurial Cci Capital Ltd
Yu, William–Cansbridge Capital Corp
Yu, Xinhua–IDG Capital Partners Inc
Yu, Yanxin–Shenzhen Jiupai Capital Management Co Ltd
Yu, Zhihong–Fortune Venture Capital Co Ltd
Yu, Zhihong–Fortune Venture Capital Corp
Yuan, Aiyu–StepStone Group LP
Yuan, Bing–Hony Capital Beijing Co Ltd
Yuan, Brian–Unisun Beijing Investment Co Ltd
Yuan, David–Redpoint Ventures
Yuan, David–Technology Crossover Ventures LP
Yuan, Huaizhong–ChangAn Blue Oak Venture Capital Co Ltd
Yuan, James–Masi Ltd
Yuan, Ruihua–Shanghai Cenova Ventures Management Co Ltd
Yuan, Runbing–Zero2IPO Ventures

Yuan, Weigang–Heaven-Sent Capital Management Group Co Ltd
Yuan, Ye–Ceyuan Ventures Management LLC
Yudkoff, Royce–ABRY Partners LLC
Yue, Jingfei–Shenzhen Green Pine Capital Partners Co Ltd
Yue, Stan–Genesis Capital Consulting & Management Ltd
Yue, Zhiming–Warburg Pincus LLC
Yuen, Todd–Beedie Capital Partners
Yukevich, Stanley–Morrison & Foerster LLP
Yumoto, Tatsuya–J-STAR Co Ltd
Yun, Joon–Palo Alto Investors LLC
Yun, Kay–Spectrum Healthcare Fund LLC
Yun, Ted–Moelis Capital Partners LLC
Yun, Ted–NexPhase Capital LLC
Yun, Wejie–Tyche Partners LP
Yurkwich, Adrian–Silverfleet Capital Partners LLP
Yusko, Mark–Morgan Creek Capital Management LLC
Yusoff, Tairuddin–Pembangunan Ekuiti Sdn Bhd
Yuwono, Jennivine–Southern Capital Group Pte Ltd
Yuzpe, Steve–Sprott Resource Corp
Yvonne, Chen–WI Harper Group Inc
Zaballos, Peter–Formative Ventures
Zabbal, Christian–Black Coral Capital LLC
Zabel, Juergen–Bm H Beteiligungs Managementgesellschaft Hessen mbH
Zabik, Joseph–Broadhaven Capital Partners LLC
Zabik, Michael–RedBird Capital Partners Platform LP
Zable, Robert–Blackstone Group LP
Zabriskie, John–Puretech Ventures
Zabrzycki, Pawel–BPM Capital OU
Zachary, George–Charles River Ventures LLC
Zachem, Tyler–Broad Sky Partners LLC
Zaczepinski, Guy–Century Park Capital Partners LLC
Zadno, Reza–InterWest Partners LLC
Zadourian, Keith–Irving Place Capital LLC
Zafar, Asad–Fajr Capital Ltd
Zafar, Shahan–Riverside Partners LLC
Zagnoev, Shaun–Ethos Private Equity (Proprietary) Ltd
Zagorski, Marcin–Black Pearls VC SA
Zagula, John–Ignition Capital Partners
Zagula, John–Qiming Venture Partners Ii LP
Zagunis, Harold–TriplePoint Capital LLC
Zahedi, Sebastian–Glynn Capital Management LLC
Zahler, Eric–Sagamore Capital Group LLC
Zahn, Larry–Silicon Valley Bancventures LP
Zahran, Moamen–Al Aman Investment Company KPSC
Zahringer, George–NexPhase Capital LLC
Zahrobsky, Tim–ABS Capital Partners, Inc.
Zaic, Gregory–Nexus Medical Partners
Zaidman, Amir–7 Health Ventures
Zainal, Ali–Investcorp Bank BSC
Zainal, Essa–Arcapita Inc
Zainal, Mahmood–Venture Capital Bank BSCC
Zajaczkowska-Ejsymont, Magdalena–TDJ SA
Zajicek, Hubert–Health Wildcatters
Zak, John–Portal Capital LLC
Zak, Michael–Charles River Ventures LLC
Zakem, George–Northleaf Capital Partners Ltd
Zalatimo, Zade–Carlyle Group LP

Zaldivar, Luis–Palladium Equity Partners LLC
Zalenski, Erik–Croft & Bender LLC
Zales, Matthew–Pine Brook Road Partners LLC
Zaleski, Mark–PROfounders Capital Ltd
Zaman, Abdul Samad–Esterad Investment Co BSC
Zaman, Kazi Arif Uz–Everstone Capital Management, Ltd.
Zamarriego, Alfredo–CVC Capital Partners Ltd
Zambelli, Anthony–Seneca Partners Inc
Zambito, Steve–Long Road Investment Counsel LLC
Zameli, Ayman–Pivotal Group Inc
Zamlong, Daniel–Warburg Pincus LLC
Zanarini, Jeff–HIG Capital LLC
Zand, Mark–Wexford Capital LP
Zandbergen, Bart–Greenfield Capital Partners BV
Zanios, Thomas–Gemspring Capital LLC
Zanios, Thomas–Odyssey Investment Partners LLC
Zannino, Richard–CCMP Capital Advisors LP
Zanone, Joseph–Bay Hills Capital Partners II LP
Zanone, Joseph–Duff Ackerman & Goodrich LLC
Zaplatynsky, John–Pender West Capital Partners, Inc.
Zapotocky, Stefan–LPC Capital Partners GmbH
Zappa, James–ANGEL CAPITAL NETWORK INC
Zappala, Timothy–Arsenal Capital Management LLC
Zappala, Timothy–Arsenal Capital Partners LP
Zappala, Timothy–Arsenal Capital Partners LP
Zapparoli, Paolo–Synergo SGR SpA
Zara, Chester–Antares Capital Corp
Zaremba, Bruno–Vinci Equities Gestora de Recursos Ltda
Zaro, Andrew–Cavalry Investments LLC
Zarou, Sam–Marker Financial Advisors LLC
Zartler, William–Solaris Energy Capital LLC
Zarur, Andrey–Kodiak Venture Partners LP
Zarzhevsky, Alexander–Blackstone Group LP
Zaslavsky, Dennis–Waveland Investments LLC
Zastawny, Tomasz–Quark Ventures LLC
Zaumeyer, Brian–Odyssey Investment Partners LLC
Zauqi, Muhammad–FirstFloor Capital Sdn Bhd
Zavala Resendiz, Israel–Gerbera Capital Asesores SC
Zavala, Alfredo–Realza Capital SGECR SA
Zavala, Santiago–500 Startups, L.P.
Zaveri, Darshana–Catalyst Health And Technology Partners LLC
Zaveri, Jay–Social+Capital Partnership
Zaveri, Muzzammil–Kleiner Perkins Caufield & Byers LLC
Zaveri, Nakul–GEF Management Corp
Zawadzki, Michael–Blackstone Group LP
Zawisza, Michal–Avallon Sp z o o
Zaytsev, Evgeny–Helix Ventures
Zazulak, Michael–Parallax Capital Partners LLC
Zbar, Brett–Aisling Capital LLC
Zebidi, Hichem–Evercore Inc
Zebro, David–Strategic Investments, L.P.
Zebrowski, Mark–Morrison & Foerster LLP
Zech, Rodney–Kinzie Capital Partners LLC
Zeev, Oren–Primera Capital
Zeevi, Avi–Carmel Ventures IV Principals Fund LP
Zeevi, Benny–AL Capital Holdings 2016 Ltd
Zehavi, Zeev–Johnson & Johnson Innovation-JJDC Inc
Zeidel, Robert–Corporation Financiere Champlain

Canada Inc
Zeidler, Susanne—Deutsche Beteiligungs AG
Zeiger, Martin—Signet Healthcare Partners
Zeiler, Daniel—S Kap Unternehmensbeteiligungs GmbH & Co KG
Zein, Ian—Vitulum Ventures BV
Zeine, Fawzi—GFH Capital Ltd
Zeitlin, Gregg—Reservoir Capital Group LLC
Zeitz, Sascha—Mercer Private Markets AG
Zekkos, Michail—Permira Advisers LLP
Zekveld, Paul—NIBC Principal Investments BV
Zelin, Steve—Blackstone Group LP
Zell, Joseph—Grotech Ventures
Zeller, Marco—IBB Beteiligungs GmbH
Zellner, Claus—Allianz Capital Partners GmbH
Zelman, Helen—Lemnos Labs
Zelnick, Strauss—ZMC
Zeltner, David—Milbank Tweed Hadley & Mccloy LLP
Zeluck, Gregory—Carlyle Group LP
Zemah, Yigal—Berggruen Holdings Inc
Zemans, David—Milbank Tweed Hadley & Mccloy LLP
Zemke, Ingo—ICS Partners GmbH
Zeng, Edward—SILK Ventures Ltd
Zeng, Hua—Shenzhen Hongshisan Capital Co Ltd
Zeng, Jenny—Jade Investment Consulting (Shanghai) Co Ltd
Zeng, Jenny—Maple Valley Investments Co Ltd
Zeng, Ming—ShenZhen CDF-Capital Co Ltd
Zeng, Ramon—Doll Capital Management Inc
Zeng, Xiaoyu—Shenzhen Green Pine Capital Partners Co Ltd
Zeng, Zheng—Shenzhen QF Capital Management Co Ltd
Zeng, Zhijie—CITIC Capital Partners Ltd
Zenger, Bradley—Pivotal Investments LLC
Zenni, James—Bayou Steel Corp
Zent, Charles—First Analysis Corp
Zenuk, Mark—Tillridge Global Agribusiness Partners
Zeprun, Howard—Trident Capital Cybersecurity Fund I LP
Zerauschek, Pietro—Foresight Group LLP
Zesati, Humberto—Latin Idea Ventures LLC
Zesiger, Albert—Zesiger Capital Group LLC
Zesiger, Barrie—Zesiger Capital Group LLC
Zeuner, Brandon—venture51 Capital Fund LLP
Zezza, David—Pacific Advantage Capital Ltd
Zha, Li—Invimed Europejskie Centrum Macierzynstwa Sp z o o
Zhan, Chuan—CAC Capital Management Co Ltd
Zhang, Alex—Redpoint Ventures
Zhang, Alexa—Wilshire Private Markets
Zhang, Ally—Siguler Guff & Company LP
Zhang, Baoguo—Shanghai Tongjiang Investment Management Co Ltd
Zhang, Boxiao—Shenzhen Co-Win Venture Capital Investments Ltd
Zhang, Chaoming—Prime Value Capital Management Ltd
Zhang, Charles—DT Capital Partners
Zhang, Dachun—Shanghai Fosun Capital Investment Management Co Ltd
Zhang, Dong—Zhongrong International Trust Co Ltd
Zhang, E.—InnoSpring Inc
Zhang, Eric—Carlyle Group LP
Zhang, Eric—General Atlantic LLC

Zhang, Eric—HAO Capital
Zhang, Felix—Artesian Capital Management Australia Pty Ltd
Zhang, Feng—Ginkgo Group Co Ltd
Zhang, Gavin—Maple Valley Investments Co Ltd
Zhang, George—Small Enterprise Assistance Funds
Zhang, Hai Tao—Rongzhong Capital Investment Group Co Ltd
Zhang, Haitao—Wuhan Proton Venture Capital Fund Management Co Ltd
Zhang, Haiyan—Shenzhen Tiantu Capital Management Center LP
Zhang, Hua—State Development & Investment Corp Ltd
Zhang, Hui—Beijing Tianxing Chuanglian Investment Management Co., Ltd.
Zhang, James Ju—Suzhou Datai Venture Capital Investment Management Co Ltd
Zhang, Jason—CDH China Management Co., Ltd.
Zhang, Jason—Morgan Creek Capital Management LLC
Zhang, Jerry—CITIC Capital Partners Ltd
Zhang, Jianbin—IDG Capital Partners Inc
Zhang, Jianbing—Sharewin Equity Fund Management Co Ltd
Zhang, Jiantao—Shanghai Broadview Capital Management Co Ltd
Zhang, Jing—ChinaEquity Group Inc
Zhang, Joan—ABC Capital Management Co Ltd
Zhang, Ju—China Merchants Kunlun Equity Invest Management Co Ltd
Zhang, Ju—Lightspeed Management Company LLC
Zhang, Jun—Chongqing Zhengyin Guanghui Equity Investment Mgmt Co., Ltd.
Zhang, Jun—Guangdong Infore Capital Management Co Ltd
Zhang, Junxi—Shenzhen Jidi Xintian Venture Investment Co Ltd
Zhang, Kai—Beijing Macro Vision Venture Capital Management Consultancy
Zhang, Ke—Shanghai Tronfund Management Co Ltd
Zhang, Kevin—Upfront Ventures
Zhang, Kun—Prax Capital Management Co
Zhang, Lawrence—Allshare Capital
Zhang, Lei—Guangzhou Sinvo Spring Investment Management Co Ltd
Zhang, Lei—Ivy Capital Ltd
Zhang, Li—Trilantic Capital Management LP
Zhang, Li—Trilantic Capital Management LP
Zhang, Lin—Legend Star Venture Incubator
Zhang, Lingjia—Cinda Capital Management Co Ltd
Zhang, Luanduo—Golden Bridge Venture Capital, L.P.
Zhang, Min—Jiangsu Jinmao Venture Capital Management Co Ltd
Zhang, Nan—Shanghai Lianxin Investment Management Co Ltd
Zhang, Pei—Shanghai Broad Resources Investment Management Co Ltd
Zhang, Peter—IDG Capital Partners Inc
Zhang, Pu—Genesis Capital Consulting & Management Ltd
Zhang, Qiangyun—Bright Stone Investment Management (Hong Kong) Ltd
Zhang, Ray—PPM America Capital Partners LLC

Zhang, Reggie—Redpoint Ventures
Zhang, Richard—Apax Partners LLP
Zhang, Rui—CITIC SECURITIES INTERNATIONAL PRTNS LTD
Zhang, Sengui—Industrial Technology Investment Corp
Zhang, Sharon—Shanghai Peeli Investment Management Co Ltd
Zhang, Suyang—IDG Capital Partners Inc
Zhang, Tianli—Beijing Hosen Capital Management Center LP
Zhang, Wei—New Access Capital
Zhang, Wei—Safeguard Scientifics Inc
Zhang, Wen—LYRIQUE Srrl
Zhang, Xiao—Shenzhen Co-Win Venture Capital Investments Ltd
Zhang, Xiaowan—China Media Capital Co Ltd
Zhang, Xiaoyu—Shenzhen Jidi Xintian Venture Investment Co Ltd
Zhang, Xin—Bioveda China Fund
Zhang, Xunjun—Shenzhen Cornerstone of Entrepreneurial Cci Capital Ltd
Zhang, Xuwei—Zhejiang Sinowisdom Capital Co Ltd
Zhang, Yanhua—Noble (Beijing) Fund Management Inc
Zhang, Yi—Shanghai Trustbridge Partners Investment Management Co Ltd
Zhang, Yichen—CITIC Capital Partners Ltd
Zhang, Ying—CBC Capital
Zhang, Yong—China King Link Corp
Zhang, Yong—Qiming Venture Partners Ii LP
Zhang, Yonghan—HGI Finaves China Fund
Zhang, Yunhe—Bright Stone Investment Management (Hong Kong) Ltd
Zhang, Yuqing—Shenzhen Hongshisan Capital Co Ltd
Zhanghong, Hu—CCB International Group Holdings Ltd
Zhao, Anyu—Hunan Everassion Equity Investment Management Co Ltd
Zhao, Byron—CLSA Capital Partners HK Ltd
Zhao, Changgui—Will Capital
Zhao, Chao—LB Investment Inc
Zhao, Chenning—FountainVest Partners Asia Ltd
Zhao, Chunlin—Ample Luck International Capital Group Ltd
Zhao, Flora—SAIF Partners
Zhao, Gang—HighLight Capital
Zhao, Helen—Beijing Macro Vision Venture Capital Management Consultancy
Zhao, Hui—Shenzhen Oriental Fortune Capital Co Ltd
Zhao, James—Vivo Capital LLC
Zhao, Jason—Cybernaut (China) Venture Capital Management Co Ltd
Zhao, Jing—Shanghai GMALL Venture Capital Management Co Ltd
Zhao, Jun—DT Capital Partners
Zhao, Junfeng—Shenzhen Rongchuang Venture Capital Co Ltd
Zhao, Limei—Israel Infinity Venture Capital Fund Israel LP
Zhao, Luping—Beijing Huinong Capital Management Co Ltd

Zhao, Rachel−MBK Partners Inc
Zhao, Su−ZheShang Venture Capital Co Ltd
Zhao, Tian−PreIPO Capital Partners Ltd
Zhao, Wayne−Vcchina Ltd
Zhao, Weiguo−Beijing N5 Capital Consulting Co Ltd
Zhao, Xifeng−Boxin Capital
Zhao, Yachao−Bioveda China Fund
Zhao, Zhongqiu−Beijing Huinong Capital Management Co Ltd
Zhao, Zhongyi−Kunwu Jiuding Capital Holdings Co Ltd
Zheng, Chungang−Shenzhen Hongshisan Capital Co Ltd
Zheng, Hairuo−Prime Mont Venture Capital Co Ltd
Zheng, Haitao−Amino Capital Management Company LLC
Zheng, HongHong−Canton Venture Capital Co Ltd
Zheng, Jie−WL Ross & Co LLC
Zheng, Linda−Conduit Ventures Ltd
Zheng, Michael−Mandarin Capital Partners SCA SICAR
Zheng, Scott−PreIPO Capital Partners Ltd
Zheng, William−LB Investment Inc
Zheng, Yu−Shanghai Divine Investment Management Co Ltd
Zhilinsky, Evgeny−Fenox Venture Capital Inc
Zhong, Dong−Actis LLP
Zhong, Donglin−Shanghai Huitong Tianxia Equity Investment Co Ltd
Zhong, Forrest−Venture TDF Pte Ltd
Zhong, Fu−Panthera Capital Group
Zhong, Lian−Shenzhen Capital Group Co Ltd
Zhou, Chengjian−Feima Fund
Zhou, Chunfang−Jiangsu Addor Equity Investment Fund Management Co Ltd
Zhou, Dan−Shanghai Sova Capital Co Ltd
Zhou, Daniel−OrbiMed Advisors LLC
Zhou, Donglei−Shanghai Trustbridge Partners Investment Management Co Ltd
Zhou, Heng−Meridian Growth Fund Management Co Ltd
Zhou, Hong−Richlink International Capital Co Ltd
Zhou, Jian−Shanghai Lianxin Investment Management Co Ltd
Zhou, Jie−Morrison & Foerster LLP
Zhou, Jun−Shanghai Beyond Binghong Equity Investment Management Co Ltd
Zhou, Ke−Shenzhen Weixi Investment Partnership Co Ltd
Zhou, Lei−HGI Finaves China Fund
Zhou, Liang−Sino Resources Investment Co Ltd
Zhou, Lili−Cornerstone Capital Holdings LLC
Zhou, Lin Lin−Broadline Capital LLC
Zhou, Lin Lin−Principle Capital Ltd
Zhou, Min−Beijing Hualin Hechuang Investment Management Co Ltd
Zhou, Min−China Materialia LLC
Zhou, Mingchen−Uni-Quantum Fund Management Co Ltd
Zhou, Ning−Infotech Ventures Co Ltd
Zhou, Quan−IDG Capital Partners Inc
Zhou, Shengli−Shenzhen Hongshisan Capital Co Ltd
Zhou, Shuhua−Kaiwu Capital Co Ltd
Zhou, Shuiwen−Shanghai NewMargin Ventures Co Ltd
Zhou, Tony−Shanghai Amara Equity Investment Management Co Ltd
Zhou, Wei−Jade Investment Consulting (Shanghai) Co Ltd
Zhou, Xiaochuan−Sunbridge Investment Management Co Ltd
Zhou, Xiaopeng−Beijing Tianxing Chuanglian Investment Management Co., Ltd.
Zhou, Xin−Shenzhen Weixi Investment Partnership Co Ltd
Zhou, Xing−Beijing Said Wise Fund Co Ltd
Zhou, Yan−Shanghai Divine Investment Management Co Ltd
Zhou, Yongkai−Shanghai NewMargin Ventures Co Ltd
Zhou, Yongqing−Noble (Beijing) Fund Management Inc
Zhou, Yun−CBC Capital
Zhou, Yun−Shanghai Beyond Binghong Equity Investment Management Co Ltd
Zhou, Zhibo−Shenzhen Weixi Investment Partnership Co Ltd
Zhou, Zhixiong−Keytone Ventures
Zhu, Alex−CID Group
Zhu, Daming−DT Capital Partners
Zhu, Dezhen−Shanghai Guohe Capital
Zhu, Guoying−Zhejiang University Venture Capital Co Ltd
Zhu, Hailong−Vision Knight Capital
Zhu, Haitong−ABC Capital Management Co Ltd
Zhu, Huican−Amino Capital Management Company LLC
Zhu, Jack−Bain Capital Inc
Zhu, Jianhua−Beijing Holch Investment Management, Ltd.
Zhu, Jianhuan−IDG Capital Partners Inc
Zhu, Jonathan Jia−Bain Capital Inc
Zhu, Linan−Legend Capital Co Ltd
Zhu, Liyu−Beijing Tianxing Chuanglian Investment Management Co., Ltd.
Zhu, Mark−Silver Lake Partners LP
Zhu, Michael−Gobi Partners
Zhu, Peifeng−Fair Value Capital
Zhu, Qing−Shenzhen Co-Win Venture Capital Investments Ltd
Zhu, Qinqi−Feima Fund
Zhu, Wan Li−Fairhaven Capital Partners, L.P.
Zhu, Wei−Beijing Hexin Dongli Investment Management Co Ltd
Zhu, Wei−Standard Chartered Private Equity Ltd
Zhu, Wendy−AlpInvest Partners BV
Zhu, Xiao ou−Shanghai Beyond Binghong Equity Investment Management Co Ltd
Zhu, Xiaohu−Gsr Ventures Management Llc
Zhu, Xiaoou−Shanghai Beyond Binghong Equity Investment Management Co Ltd
Zhu, Yanfeng−Shenzhen Rongchuang Venture Capital Co Ltd
Zhu, Yin−Shanghai Lianxin Investment Management Co Ltd
Zhu, Zhongyuan−Greenwoods Asset Management Ltd
Zhu, Zhongyuan−HighLight Capital
Zhuang, Tao−Citic Private Equity Funds Management Co Ltd
Zhukovsky, Jonathan−Select Venture Partners LLC
Zhuo, Bing−Bioveda China Fund
Zhuo, Fumin−GGV Capital
Zhuo, Fumin−GGV Capital
Zhuo, TX−Karlin Ventures
Zicari, Michael−Eaglehill Advisors LLC
Zide, Stephen−Bain Capital Inc
Ziebelman, Peter−Palo Alto Venture Partners
Ziebelman, Peter−Palo Alto Venture Partners
Zief, Yaniv−Acas LLC
Ziegler, Ryan−Edison Partners
Ziegler, Ryan−Edison Partners
Ziegler, Wolfgang−Findos Investor GmbH
Zielinski, Robert−Riordan Lewis & Haden
Ziff, Stephen−Coller Capital Ltd
Zihal, Michael−New York Business Development Corp
Zikatanov, Nikola−NCH Capital Inc
Zilber, Leon−Siguler Guff & Company LP
Zilberman, Daniel−Warburg Pincus LLC
Zilberman, David−Comcast Ventures
Zilka, Yahal−MAGNUM COMMUNICATIONS FUND L P
Zimbalist, Jonathan−Eureka Growth Capital
Zimits, Eric−Granite Ventures LLC
Zimits, Eric−Granite Ventures LLC
Zimmer, David−Ecolutions Management GmbH
Zimmer, Erik−Thomas H Lee Partners LP
Zimmerer, Yimin−Walden International
Zimmermann, Andre−SHS Gesellschaft fuer Beteiligungsmanagement mbH
Zimmerman, Caldwell−Kian Capital Partners LLC
Zimmerman, Carl−Spectrum Healthcare Fund LLC
Zimmerman, Harry−Spindletop Capital Management LLC
Zimmerman, Joshua−Milbank Tweed Hadley & Mccloy LLP
Zimmerman, Moshe−Teuza a Fairchild Technology Venture Ltd
Zimmerman, Peter−Shoreview Industries
Zimmerman, Rosanne−Warburg Pincus LLC
Zimmerman, Trevor−Blackhorn Ventures Capital Management LLC
Zimmermann, Jens Yahya−New Silk Route Partners, LLC
Zimmermann, Jens Yahya−New Silk Route Partners, LLC
Zindel, Shani−F&C Equity Partners PLC
Zink, Jeppe−Northzone Ventures
Zinkernagel, Rolf−Aravis SA
Zinkula, Jerry−Allstate Private Equity
Zinterhofer, Eric−Searchlight Capital Partners LLC
Ziobehr, Christopher−Caldera Venture Partners LLC
Ziolkowski, Andrew−Cultivian Ventures LLC
Zipp, Bob−Amicus Capital LLC
Zirener, Joerg−One Equity Partners LLC
Zissis, Peter−Birch Hill Equity Partners Management Inc
Zisson, Alex−Thomas Mcnerney and Partners LLC
Zito, Matt−Travel Startups Incubator LLC
Zivin, James−Mill Road Capital Management LLC
Zlateva, Roumi−Lovell Minnick Partners LLC
Zlotchenko, Sol−Select Venture Partners LLC
Zmijeski, Casey−Fifth Street Capital LLC
Zocco, Giuseppe−Index Ventures
Zoch, Michael−Kinderhook Industries LLC
Zochling, Stephan−Lead Equities GmbH
Zoellner, Scott−AEA Investors LLC
Zoetemeijer, Rop−ICOS Capital Management BV
Zoghbi, Jean-Philippe−Sofimac Innovation SAS

Zoghbi, Seifallah Sami–Abraaj Capital Ltd
Zohar, Daphne–Puretech Ventures
Zolfaghari, Paul–Carrick Capital Management Company LLC
Zoll, Joe–Liberty Capital Management Corp
Zoller, Eric–Sixpoint Partners LLC
Zollo, Steve–Platinum Equity LLC
Zolman, Jeffrey–RFE Investment Partners
Zomback, Russell–Brightwood Capital Advisors LLC
Zone, Guy–NIVELINVEST SA
Zoralioglu, Selahattin–Pamplona Capital Management LLP
Zorc, Olga–Roundtable Healthcare Partners LP
Zorner, Paul–FINISTERE VENTURES L L C
Zornig, Julien–Astorius Capital GmbH
Zou, Hong–Korea Investment Partners Co Ltd
Zouber, Danny–North Sky Capital LLC
Zrebiec, J. L.–Clayton Dubilier & Rice LLC
Zuaiter, Abbas–Soros Strategic Partners LP
Zube, Marc–Callista Holdings GmbH & Co KG
Zuberi, Bilal–General Catalyst Partners LLC
Zuberi, Bilal–LUX CAPITAL GROUP L L C
Zubko, Mark–Apax Partners LLP
Zucchini, Juan Pablo–Advent International Corp
Zucker, Jeffrey–Green Lion Partners LLC
Zucker, Mitchell–Pegasus Capital Advisors LP
Zuckerberg, Arielle–Kleiner Perkins Caufield & Byers LLC
Zug, David–HarbourVest Partners LLC
Zuga, Matt–Highcape Partners LP
Zullow, Frederick–Milbank Tweed Hadley & Mccloy LLP
Zupan, Tom–Riverlake Partners LLC
Zur Muhlen, Adriaan–Glouston Capital Partners LLC
Zur, Ari–Brockway Moran & Partners Inc
Zurawski, Philippe–Omnes Capital SAS
Zurita, Miguel–Altamar Private Equity SGIIC SAU
Zurita, Miguel–Mercapital SL
Zurita, Miguel–Mercapital SL
Zuschke, Stefan–BC Partners LLP
Zwemstra, Charly–Main Capital Partners BV
Zwemstra, Charly–NIBC Principal Investments BV
Zwicker, Ian–W R Hambrecht & Co L L C
Zyer, David–OCA Ventures
Zyla, Patrick–Castle Harlan Inc
Zyngier, Charles–Carlyle Group LP
bin Abdul Razak, Mohamed Nazir–Cimb Private Equity Sdn Bhd
d Agrain, Corinne–ACE Management SA
d Argoubet, Christian–Apax Partners Development SA
d Engremont, Gaelle–PAI Partners SAS
d Incelli, Stephen–Sk Capital Partners LP
de Abreu, Luiz Eduardo Franco–MHFT Investimentos SA
de Araujo, Beatriz–Baker & McKenzie LLP
de Baubigny, Juliet–Kleiner Perkins Caufield & Byers LLC
de Bie, Bart–Prospect Street Ventures
de Bodinat, Henri–Time for Growth SA
de Boer, Klaas–Entrepreneurs Fund Management LLP
de Bonneville, Pierre–Trust Company of the West
de Bruyn, Ben–ENR Russia Invest SA
de Carvalho, Jose Augusto–Axxon Group Servicos De Consultoria E Assessoria Ltda
de Cremoux, Isabelle–Seventure Partners SA

de Fouquet, Pierre–Iris Capital Management SAS
de Graaf, Edwin–Gilde Healthcare Partners BV
de Groot, Han–VOC Capital Partners BV
de Haan, Michiel–Aescap Venture I BV
de Jager, Piet-Hein–Private Equity Investments II BV
de Jong, Rob–AlpInvest Partners BV
de Klerk, Paul–AlpInvest Partners BV
de Klerk, Paul–NIBC Principal Investments BV
de Koning, John–Life Sciences Partners BV
de Lacerda, Guilherme Narciso–Banco Nacional de Desenvolvimento Economico e Social BNDES
de Leusse, Paul–Credit Agricole Corporate and Investment Bank SA
de Leyva, Enrique–Magnum Industrial Partners
de Leyva, Enrique–Magnum Industrial Partners SL
de Lint, Christiaan–Headway Capital Partners LLP
de Longuemar, Thierry–Asian Development Bank
de Luna, Leo–Split Rock Partners LLC
de Marchis, Ranieri–UniCredit SpA
de Marcos, Saul–Abac Capital SL
de Meester, Joris–NIBC Principal Investments BV
de Mevius, Frederic–Verlinvest SA
de Mojana, Francesco–Permira Advisers LLP
de Neergaard, Claes–Industrifonden
de Nor, Edward–G Square Healthcare Private Equity Fund LLP
de Panafieu, Thierry–Hera Capital Partners Pte Ltd
de Peloux, Dominique–Chequers Capital Partners SA
de Pencier, Michael–InvesteCo Capital Corp
de Perignon, Henri–Quadrille Capital SAS
de Planta, Renaud–Banque Pictet & Cie SA
de Posson, Lionel–Sun Capital Partners Inc
de Puybaudet, Jean–Capital Export SAS
de Rubertis, Francesco–Index Ventures
de Run, Hamish–Hermes Gpe Llp
de San Pablo, Carlos–IG Expansion Business Development SL
de Serdio, Ricardo–PAI Partners SAS
de Tissot, Benedicte–Atalante SAS
de Tonnac, Remy–Vertex Israel II Management Ltd
de Turenne, Noel–Montlake Capital LLC
de Vregille, Olivier–PAI Partners SAS
de Walque, Xavier–Compagnie Benelux Participations SA
de la Chapelle, Justin–AEA Investors LLC
de la Rosa, Borja–Abac Capital SL
de la Rosa, Juan Manuel–Baker & McKenzie LLP
de la Serna, Nora–Corinthian Capital Group LLC
de la Sota, Igor–Valco Capital Partners Partnership Ltd
deGoa, Damian–PBM Capital Group LLC
deKlerk, Jon–Performance Equity Management LLC
deLaar, Mark–Summit Partners LP
deLaar, Mark–Summit Partners LP
del Canizo, Miguel–Bullnet Capital Sc R SA
di Benedetto, Jean-Pierre–Argos Soditic SA
di Gresy, Emanuele–Virtus Capital Partners Srl
di Lorenzo, Marcelo–3i Group PLC
du Pont, Benjamin–Chartline Capital Partners
du Toit, Hendrik–Investec Asset Management (Pty) Ltd
el-Effendi, Wicky–Matador Capital Partners LLC
van Ballekom, Pim–European Investment Bank
van Barlingen, Harrold–Thuja Capital BV
van Beurden, Ben–Royal Dutch Shell PLC
van Boxtel, Desiree–Karmijn Kapitaal Management BV

van Cuylenberg, Peter–Crescendo Venture Management LLC
van Deventer, Sander–Forbion Capital Partners
van Doesburg, Stef–Greenfield Capital Partners BV
van Gessel, Zoran–Bencis Capital Partners BV
van Golstein Brouwers, Marilou–Triodos International Fund Management BV
van Hoevell, Haroun–Riverstone Holdings LLC
van Horne, Charles–Abbott Capital Management LLC
van Kuijk, Rob–Finles NV
van Maanen, Sander–AlpInvest Partners BV
van Oost, John–Fluxus Ventures LLP
van Os, Alexander–Yellow&Blue Investment Management BV
van Oudvorst, Jan–Finles NV
van Slingelandt, Barthout–XSML Management BV
van Someren, Alex–Amadeus Capital Partners Ltd
van Steenbergen, D. Jeff–ACM Ltd
van Thiel, Gijs–747 Capital LLC
van Trigt, Frank–Egeria BV
van Tuyll, Julia–Lion Capital LLP
van Wezel, Edward–Biogeneration Ventures BV
van Wyk, John–Actis LLP
van Zutphen, Lesley–Bencis Capital Partners BV
van den Berg, Marc–Vantagepoint Management Inc
van der Beek, Wim–Aavishkaar Venture Management Services Pvt Ltd
van der Laan, Carien–Karmijn Kapitaal Management BV
van der Meer, Pieter–Gilde Healthcare Partners BV
van der Zwan, Mark–Morgan Stanley Alternative Investment Partners LP
von Bauer, Eric–Capital Strategy Management Co
von Bohlen, Friedrich–Dievini Hopp Biotech Holding GmbH & Co KG
von Diest, Friedrich–Sirius Venture Partners GmbH
von Dohlen, Gerard–Broadhaven Capital Partners LLC
von Emster, Kurt–Abingworth Management Ltd
von Emster, Kurt–Venbio Partners LLC
von Engelhardt, Nicolai–Co Investor AG
von Frenckell, Mikael–Sponsor Capital Oy
von Freyberg, Berthold–Target Partners GmbH
von Friedeburg, Stephanie–International Finance Corp
von Hutten, Alexander–Mountain Cleantech AG
von Kalckreuth, Goetz–inventages venture capital GmbH
von Meibom, Hans-Dieter–Palladion Partners Gesellschaft fuer Private Equity mbH
von Moeller, Krischan–Paragon Partners GmbH
von Peter, Johann-Melchior–One Equity Partners LLC
von Preyss, Daniel–Impax Asset Management Ltd
von Rothenburg, Daniel–Oaktree Capital Management LP
von Schroeter, Carlo–Westview Capital Partners LP
von der Goltz, Alex–Boston Capital Ventures LP
von der Goltz, Alex–CoreCo Holdings LLC
von der Goltz, Johan–Boston Capital Ventures LP
von der Goltz, Johan–Brooke Private Equity Associates Management LLC
von der Osten, Dinnies–Goodvent Beteiligungsmanagement GmbH & Co KG
von der Ropp, Malte–Corporate Finance Partners CFP Beratungs GmbH